PRONUNCIATION KEY

ă	pat
ā	aid, fey, pay
â	air, care, wear
ä	father
b	bib
ch	church
d	deed
ĕ	pet, pleasure
ē	be, bee, easy, leisure
f	fast, fife, off, phase, rough
g	gag
h	hat
hw	which
ĭ	pit
ī	by, guy, pie
î	dear, deer, fierce, mere
j	judge
k	cat, kick, pique
l	lid, needle
m	am, man, mum
n	no, sudden
ng	thing
ŏ	horrible, pot
ō	go, hoarse, row, toe
ô	alter, caught, for, paw
oi	boy, noise, oil
ou	cow, out
o͝o	took
o͞o	boot, fruit
p	pop
r	roar
s	miss, sauce, see
sh	dish, ship
t	tight
th	path, thin
th	bathe, this
ŭ	cut, rough
û	circle, firm, heard, term, turn, urge, word
v	cave, valve, vine
w	with
y	yes
yo͞o	abuse, use
z	rose, size, xylophone, zebra
zh	garage, pleasure, vision
ə	about, silent, pencil, lemon, circus
ər	butter

FOREIGN

œ	*French* feu
ü	*French* tu
KH	*Scottish* loch
N	*French* bon

STRESS

Primary stress ′

bi·ol′o·gy |bī ŏl′ə jē|

Secondary stress ′

bi′o·log′i·cal |bī′ə lŏj′ĭ kəl|

The American Heritage

STUDENT'S DICTIONARY

Houghton Mifflin Company

Boston • New York

Cover Photograph: *Statue of Liberty*, Eric Meola, The Image Bank

Words that are believed to be registered trademarks have been checked with authoritative sources. No investigation has been made of common-law trademark rights in any word, because such investigation is impracticable. Words that are known to have current registrations are shown with an initial capital and are also identified as trademarks. The inclusion of any word in this Dictionary is not, however, an expression of the publishers' opinion as to whether or not it is subject to proprietary rights. Indeed, no definition in this Dictionary is to be regarded as affecting the validity of any trademark.

Library of Congress Cataloging-in-Publication Data

The American heritage student's dictionary.

Summary: A dictionary for use in grades six through nine with an entry list derived from printed materials used in schools. Includes a section on how to use the dictionary.

1. English language—Dictionaries, Juvenile.
[1. English language—Dictionaries] I. Houghton Mifflin Company.
PE1628.5.A46 1986 423 86–7337
ISBN 0-395-40417-7

Manufactured in the United States of America

Contents

Staff

Picture Credits

The following list of credits includes the names of many of the organizations and individuals who helped secure illustrations for this Dictionary. The editors wish to thank all of them—as well as others not specifically mentioned—for their assistance. We are grateful to Matthew Kalmenoff for his pen-and-ink drawings of plants and animals, to Cal Sacks for his fine diagrams, and to Ron Schick for specially commissioned photographs. All human anatomy drawings were supplied by Neil Hardy. The credits are arranged alphabetically by entry word, which is printed in boldface type. The abbreviations NAS and NYPL stand for, respectively, the National Audubon Society and The New York Public Library.

aardvark Ernest Walker from NAS; **Aberdeen Angus** American Angus Assoc.; **acanthus** (Corinthian capital) Epidaurus Museum; **accolade** Pictorial Parade; **accordion** M. Hohner, Inc.; **ace** U.S. Playing Card Co.; **acorn** John H. Gerard from NAS; **acrobat** Pictorial Parade; **adjacent angle** Cal Sacks; **admiral** The American Museum of Natural History; **adz, aerosol bomb** Jean Erdoes; **Afghan** Columbia Minerva Co.; **Afghan hound** Evelyn M. Shafer; **African violet** Roche; **agave** Matthew Kalmenoff; **aircraft carrier** U.S. Navy; **Airedale** Evelyn M. Shafer; **airship** Nebraska State Historical Society; **akimbo** Ron Schick; **albatross** Annan Photo Features; **alfalfa, algae, alligator** Matthew Kalmenoff; **alternator, altitude** Cal Sacks; **amaryllis** Burpee Seeds; **ameba** Matthew Kalmenoff; **amplitude** Cal Sacks; **anaconda** Dade W. Thornton from NAS; **anchor** Baldt Anchor, Chain & Forge Div. of Universal Marion Corp.; **angle[2]** Cal Sacks; **animated cartoon** Don Duga; **annual ring** Cal Sacks; **ant** Bernard Gluck from NAS; **anteater** R. Van Nostrand from NAS; **anther** Robert H. Wright from NAS; **anticline** From *Principles of Geology*, 2nd Edition, by James Gilluly, A.C. Waters, and A.O. Woodford, W.H. Freeman and Co., Copyright © 1951; **antler** Art by Enid Kotschning from "Horns and Antlers" by Walter Modell, Copyright © April, 1969, by Scientific American, Inc., all rights reserved; **apogee** Cal Sacks; **appaloosa** Toy A. Hemontolor; **appliqué** Shelburne Museum, Inc., Photographer Einars J. Mengis; **arcade** The Metropolitan Museum of Art, The Cloisters Collection; **armadillo** Leonard Lee Rue from NAS; **armor** The Metropolitan Museum of Art, Rogers Fund, 1904; **arrowhead** Museum of the American Indian, Heye Foundation; **artesian well** Cal Sacks; **artichoke** Treat Davidson from NAS; **asparagus** U.S. Dept. of Agriculture; **assagai** South African Tourist Corp.; **aster** A.W. Ambler from NAS; **astronaut** NASA; **atoll** Cal Sacks; **auk** The New-York Historical Society; **autograph** From *Collecting Autographs and Manuscripts* by Charles Hamilton, Copyright © 1961 by the University of Oklahoma Press; **awl** Stanley Tools; **axolotl** A.W. Ambler from NAS.

baboon Annan Photo Features; **backhand** Russ Adams, Courtesy USLTA; **badger** Matthew Kalmenoff; **balalaika** The Metropolitan Museum of Art, Gift of Mr. Ustin Smolensky, 1948; **bald eagle** Library of Congress—Philip Gendreau from NAS; **bamboo** Prints Division, NYPL; **banana** Ghana Info Service, Accra; **banyan** Robert C. Hermes from NAS; **bark[2]** Jane Latta—Jane Latta—John H. Gerard from NAS; **barometer** Cal Sacks; **barracuda** Matthew Kalmenoff; **bassoon** Ron Schick; **bat[2]** Matthew Kalmenoff; **bathysphere** New York Zoological Society; **battlement** Philip Gendreau; **beagle** Evelyn M. Shafer; **bear[2]** Leonard Lee Rue from NAS; **bearskin** The British Travel Assoc.; **beaver[1]** A.A. Francesconi from NAS; **bedbug** U.S. Dept. of Agriculture; **bee[1]** Annan Photo Features; **beetle[1]** John H. Gerard from NAS; **begonia** A.W. Ambler from NAS; **belfry** Culver Pictures, Inc.; **belladonna** Matthew Kalmenoff; **bellows** Ronald Bowen; **benzene ring** John Keaveny; **Bernoulli's law** Cal Sacks; **bicycle** Bicycle Institute of America, Inc.; **bighorn** Annan Photo Features; **binary numeration system** Cal Sacks; **biplane** National Archives; **bird of paradise** Matthew Kalmenoff; **bison** Allan D. Cruickshank from NAS; **bit[2]** Stanley Tools; **blackberry** Sweeney, Krist, & Dimm; **black-eyed Susan** A.W. Ambler from NAS; **black widow** Alfred Renfro from NAS; **blast furnace** United States Steel Corp.; **bleeding-heart** Roche; **blindman's buff** Ron Schick; **block** Cal Sacks; **blockhouse** John Keaveny; **bloodhound** Evelyn M. Shafer; **bloomers** *The Illustrated London News*, 1851; **blue jay** Karl H. Maslowski from NAS; **boar** Azaria Alon from NAS; **bobwhite** Jackson Abbott; **bola** *Centaurs of Many Lands* by Edward L. Tinker, Humanities Research Center, University of Texas, drawing by Albert Guiraldez; **boll weevil** Lewis S. Maxwell from NAS; **bolt** Russell, Burdsall & Ward Bolt and Nut Co.; **bongo drums** Charles Perry Weimer; **bonnet** National Gallery of Art, Index of American Design; **borzoi** Tamboer Borzoi Kennels; **boxer[2]** Evelyn M. Shafer; **Brazil nut** Library of the New York Botanical Gardens; **breadfruit** *Tropical Trees of Hawaii* by Dorothy and Bob Hargreaves; **breeches buoy** U.S. Coast Guard; **bridle** *The Western Horseman;* **brontosaur** Matthew Kalmenoff; **Brownie** Girl Scouts of the U.S.A.; **Brussels sprouts** Matthew Kalmenoff; **buffalo** P.W. Hay from NAS; **bulldog** Evelyn M. Shafer; **bullroarer** Charles C. Colley, Arizona Pioneers' Historical Society; **burnoose** Brassai, Rapho Guillumette; **bustle[2]** The Metropolitan Museum of Art, Harris Brisbane Dick Fund, 1932; **buzzard** Allan D. Cruickshank from NAS.

cacomistle Woodrow Goodpaster from NAS; **caftan** Marc and Evelyn Bernheim, Rapho Guillumette; **caliper** L.S. Starrett Co.; **calla lily** Matthew Kalmenoff; **calumet** Library of Congress; **camel** R. Van Nostrand from NAS—San Diego Zoo; **Canada goose** Annan Photo Features; **candlestick** The Metropolitan Museum of Art, Bequest of A.T. Clearwater, 1933; **canoe** Great Canadian; **cantilever** Cal Sacks; **canvasback** The New-York Historical Society; **capsule** Roche—NASA; **caravel** The Mariners Museum, Newport News, Va.; **caribou** Cesco Ciapanna from NAS; **caricature** Brown Brothers—Culver Pictures, Inc.; **carrot** Burpee Seeds; **cartwheel** Gus Peterson; **casement** *Stagecraft and Scene Design* by H.P. Philippi, Houghton Mifflin Co.; **cashew** Matthew Kalmenoff; **catamaran** Duncan Sutphen, Inc.; **catapult** Cal Sacks; **cat's cradle** Gabriel Gély, Ottawa; **cecropia moth** Gaston LePage from NAS; **cell** Matthew Kalmenoff; **chalice** The Metropolitan Museum of Art, The Cloisters Collection, Purchase, 1947; **chamois** The American Museum of Natural History; **chandelier** Henry Francis du Pont Winterthur Museum; **chassis** Cal Sacks; **cheetah** *Drawing at the Zoo* by Raymond Sheppard, Studio Publications, 1949; **chestnut** Henry Mayer from NAS; **chevron** U.S. Navy; **chignon** Culver Pictures, Inc.; **Chimera** Museum of Archaeology, Florence; **chimpanzee** San Diego Zoo; **chin** Ron Schick; **chipmunk** Allan D. Cruickshank from NAS; **chord[2]** Cal Sacks; **chromosome** Oak Ridge National Laboratory; **chrysalis** Matthew Kalmenoff; **cicada** Dade W. Thornton from NAS; **circle** Carl Bass; **circumscribed** Cal Sacks; **civet** Matthew Kalmenoff; **clam** The American Museum of Natural History; **clapboard** Jane Latta; **clarinet** Ron Schick; **clavichord** Worcester Art Museum; **cleaver** Clyde Cutlery Corp.; **clef** Cal Sacks; **clipper** Peabody Museum of Salem; **closed curve** Cal Sacks; **clover** Robert H. Wright from NAS; **cloverleaf** Philip Gendreau; **club** U.S. Playing Card Co.; **club moss** Hugh Spencer from NAS; **cobra** Eric Hosking from NAS; **cockatoo** Alfred Baily from NAS; **cockleshell** John H. Gerard from NAS; **coconut palm** H.W. Kitchen from NAS; **coelacanth** The American Museum of Natural History; **coffer** Monkmeyer Press Photo Service; **collar** Frank Ltd., Mombasa, Kenya; **collie** Annan Photo Features; **columbine** Hugh Spencer from NAS; **comb** The Metropolitan Museum of Art, Gift of Emily Crane Chadbourne, 1952—A.W. Ambler from NAS; **comet** Yerkes Observatory; **commode** The Metropolitan Museum of Art, The Sylmaris Collection, Gift of George Coe Graves, 1931; **commutator, compass** Cal Sacks; **composite** Matthew Kalmenoff; **compound eye** Stephen Dalton from NAS; **computer** Courtesy, Digital Equipment Corp.; **concave** Carl Bass; **concertina** Annan Photo Features; **conch** The American Museum of Natural History; **condor** Carl B. Koford from NAS; **cone** Carl Bass; **conger** Matthew Kalmenoff; **conic section** Carl Bass; **contact lens** Cal Sacks; **convex** Carl Bass; **conveyer** Annan Photo Features; **coot** Allan D. Cruickshank from NAS; **copperhead** John H. Gerard from NAS; **corn** Grant Heilman Photography; **coronet** By permission of Ede and Ravenscroft Ltd., London; **corselet** The Metropolitan Museum of Art, Gift of William H. Riggs, 1913; **cotter pin** Cal Sacks; **cotton** Watson from Monkmeyer Press Photo Service; **cotyledon** Matthew Kalmenoff; **cowry, coyote** The American Museum of Natural History; **crab[1]** Matthew Kalmenoff; **craft** Elizabeth Barry/The Picture Cube; **crane** A.W. Ambler from NAS—Bucyrus-Erie Co.; **crater** California Institute of Technology; **crazy quilt** Shelburne Museum, Inc., Photographer Einars J. Mengis; **crescent** R.C. Dickinson; **cricket[1]** Annan Photo Features; **crocodile** Matthew Kalmenoff; **crochet** Graphic Enterprises, Inc.; **crosier** Stiftsammlungen, Klosternenberg; **crossbow** The Trustees of the British Museum; **crown** British Travel Assoc.; **crow's-nest** Philip Gendreau; **cruet** Anchor Hocking Corp.; **crystal** The American Museum of Natural History; **cucumber** Roche; **cuneiform** Louvre; **cutlass** Collection of Hamilton Cochran; **cuttlefish** Matthew Kalmenoff; **cylinder** Carl Bass; **cymbals** Ron Schick.

dachshund Evelyn M. Shafer; **daffodil** Roche; **Dalmatian** Evelyn M. Shafer; **dance** Allen Smith; **dapple-gray** Walter Chandoha; **davit** U.S. Navy; **death's-head** Library of Congress; **decagon, decahedron** Cal Sacks; **décolleté** Courtesy, Museum of Fine Arts, Boston, Elizabeth Day McCormick Collection; **decoy** The Museum of Fine Arts, Boston, M. and M. Karolik Collection; **deer** Hugh M. Halliday from NAS; **delphinium** Roche; **delta wing** U.S. Air Force; **derby** Culver Pictures, Inc.; **desperado** © The Leader Co.; **dewlap** Grant Heilman Photography; **diamond** U.S. Playing Card Co.; **diamondback** William Allen, Jr., from NAS; **differential gear, diffraction, dihedral angle** Richard Glassman; **dingo** Australian News & Information Bureau; **dipper** (constellation) George Lindbloom; **dirigible** University of Georgia Library; **dirndl** Austrian Trade Bureau; **disc jockey** Allen Smith; **dish antenna** Richard Glassman; **disk brake** General Motors; **distaff** Old Sturbridge Village; **divider** Stanley Tools; **Doberman pinscher** Evelyn M. Shafer; **dolphin** Charles Meyer from NAS—*Fishes of the Bahamas and Adjacent Tropical Waters* by James E. Böhlke and Charles C.G. Chaplin, illustrated by Steven P. Gigliotti and Fritz Janschka, published for the Academy of Natural Sciences of Philadelphia by Livingston Publishing Co., Wynnewood, Pa., 1968; **domino[1]** Prints Division, NYPL; **domino[2]** Janice Fullman/The Picture Cube; **dormouse** Annan Photo Features; **doublet** Bodleian Library, Oxford, England; **dragon** Prints Division, NYPL; **dragonfly** Hugh Spencer from NAS; **drawknife** Stanley Tools; **dredge[1]** Great Lakes Dredge & Dock Co.; **dribble** Chris Stafford; **drill press** Egyptian State Tourist Administration; **drogue parachute** U.S. Air Force; **duck** Allan D. Cruickshank from NAS—Pierre Berger from NAS; **dugong** Matthew Kalmenoff; **Dutchman's-breeches** Roche.

earring David S. Strickler/The Picture Cube; **easel** Ron Schick; **eaves** *The Gingerbread Age* by John Maass, Copyright © 1957 by John Maass, Reproduced by permission of Holt, Rinehart and Winston, Inc.; **echelon** U.S. Air Force; **eclipse** John G. Kirk, Kitt Peak National Observatory; **edelweiss** Swiss National Tourist Office; **eel** *Ichthyology* by Lagler, Bardach, and Miller, John Wiley & Sons, 1962; **egg[1]** Jack Dermid from NAS—Gordon Smith from NAS; **eland** Dade W. Thornton from NAS; **elderberry** Roche; **electrician** Paula Rhodes/The Picture Cube; **electromagnet** Ohio Magnetics Div., Howell International, Inc.; **elephant** Annan Photo Features—Cy La Tour; **elk** Allan D.Cruickshank from NAS; **ellipse** Carl Bass; **elm** Roche; **embroidery** The Metropolitan Museum of Art, Gift of Mrs. Robert W. de Forest, 1933; **emu** A.W. Ambler from NAS; **endive** U.S. Dept. of Agriculture; **engineer** Julie O'Neil/The Picture Cube, 1984; **English horn** Ron Schick; **ensemble** Arnold J. Saxe, 1982; **eohippus** The American Museum of Natural History; **equestrian statue** Mrs. Pedro Beltran, Lima, Peru; **eraser** Ron Schick; **ermine** Annan Photo Features—Colonial Williamsburg; **Eton collar** Hills & Saunders of Eton Ltd.; **ewer** Museum of the City of New York; **excavate** Frank Siteman, 1980; **experiment** J. Dunn; **exterior angle** Cal Sacks; **eyestalk** Annan Photo Features.

fairy ring U.S. Dept. of Agriculture; **falcon** Allan D. Cruickshank from NAS; **fallow deer** Annan Photo Features; **fang** John H. Gerard from NAS; **fasteners** Talon Educ. Service—Scovill Manuf. Co.—NYPL, Gift of J. Walter Thompson Co.; **faucet** "Handbook of Building Terms and Definitions" by Herbert Waugh and Nelson Burbank, Simmons-Boardman Publishing Corp.; **fault, feather** Cal Sacks; **feelers** N.E. Beck, Jr., from NAS—Mary E. Browning from NAS; **Ferris wheel** Culver Pictures, Inc.; **ferryboat** Southern Pacific Railroad; **fez** Brian Brake; Rapho Guillumette; **fiddler** Frank Siteman, 1980; **fiddler crab** John H. Gerard from NAS; **field glasses** Frank Siteman, 1980; **fife** Louvre, Photo Giraudon; **fig[1]** Roche—Annan Photo Features; **figurehead** National Gallery of Art, Index of American Design; **file[2]** Cal Sacks; **filigree** Vestlandske Kunstindustri Museum, Bergen, Norway; **fin[1]** Francis & Shaw, Inc.; **fire engine** NYC Fire Dept.; **fire escape** Photo Berenice Abbott, Museum of the City of New York; **fisher** San Diego Zoo; **flatboat** Princeton University Library, Sinclair Hamilton Collection; **fleur-de-lis** Detail of Border Design of Constantine Tapestries, designed by Peter Paul Rubens, Collection of the Philadelphia Museum of Art; **flintlock** The Metropolitan Museum of Art, Gift of Wilfred Wood, 1956; **flipper** Annan Photo Features; **flounce[1]** Photo Collection Georges Sirot, Paris; **flower, fluke** Matthew Kalmenoff; **flutist** Ron Schick; **flying fish** H.E. Edgerton from NAS; **foil** Bruce Repko, 1978; **font[1]** Copyright Poul Pedersen; **fore-and-aft** *Sailing and Small Crafts Down the Ages* by Edgar L. Bloomster, U.S. Naval Institute, 1940; **forehand** Russ Adams, Courtesy USLTA; **foreshorten** Brera, Milan; **forge**[1] Culver Pictures, Inc.; **forget-me-not** Roche; **fossil** Annan Photo Features—The American Museum of Natural History; **foundry** Robert V. Echert, Jr/The Picture Cube, 1982; **four-poster** John E. Thierman; **fox** Karl H. Maslowski from NAS; **freesia** Roche; **French curve** Cal Sacks; **frigate bird** H.I. Fisher from NAS; **frog** George Porter from NAS—Talon Educ. Service; **frond** John H. Gerard from NAS; **fuchsia** Roche; **fulcrum** Frances Davies; **furrow** UPI.

gable Wayne Andrews; **galaxy** California Institute of Technology, Mt. Wilson and Palomar Observatories; **gannet** Gaston LePage from NAS; **gargoyle** French Government Tourist Office; **garter** *The Illustrated London News,* 1953; **gavial** Matthew Kalmenoff; **gecko** Gordon S. Smith from NAS; **gerbil** The American Museum of Natural History; **German shepherd** Evelyn M. Shafer; **geyser** Union Pacific Railroad; **Gila monster** Annan Photo Features; **ginkgo** Hugh Spencer from NAS; **giraffe** Arthur Markowitz from NAS; **gladiolus** Roche; **glass blower** Steuben Glass; **glider** Charles Rotkin, P.F.I.; **glockenspiel** American Music Conference; **gnu** A.W. Ambler from NAS; **goat** Jeanne White from NAS; **goatee** Cal Sacks, Courtesy Eduardo Lopez-Castillo; **goldfish** Annan Photo Features; **gondola** Italian Government Tourist Office; **goose** Roche from NAS; **gopher** Matthew Kalmenoff; **gorilla** A.W. Ambler from NAS; **gourd** John H. Gerard from NAS; **grackle** Allan D. Cruickshank from NAS; **grampus** Matthew Kalmenoff; **grape** U.S. Dept. of Agriculture; **grapeshot** West Point Museum Collection; **grasshopper** Leonard Lee Rue from NAS; **grease paint** Jane Latta; **Great Dane** Evelyn M. Shafer; **grebe** Annan Photo Features; **greyhound** Evelyn M. Shafer; **grind** Ewing Galloway; **grizzly bear** Annan Photo Features; **grosbeak** G. Ronald Austing from NAS; **ground squirrel** Keith D. Henley from NAS; **grouse**[1] Annan Photo Features; **grunt** Kitchen-Kinne from NAS; **guillotine** Carnavalet Museum, Photo Bulloz; **guinea fowl** A.W. Ambler from NAS; **guinea pig** John H. Gerard from NAS; **gull** Robert Meyerriecks from NAS; **guppy** The American Museum of Natural History.

hackle A.W. Ambler from NAS; **hacksaw** Stanley Tools; **halibut** Bureau of Commercial Fisheries; **halo** Museo Diocesano, Cortona, Photo Alinari; **halter** NASCO, Ft. Atkinson, Wisc.; **handcuff** Brown Brothers; **handlebar mustache** Amateur Bicycle League of America; **handstand** Ron Schick; **hansom** Brown Brothers; **hare** P.W. Hay from NAS; **harlequin** Dance Collection, NYPL; **harp** Ron Schick; **hasp** Cal Sacks; **hatchet** Stanley Tools; **hawk**[1] Karl H. Maslowski from NAS; **headboard** Theodore Roosevelt Birthplace; **headstand** Ron Schick; **heart** (playing card) U.S. Playing Card Co.; **hedgehog** A.W. Ambler from NAS; **helicon** *The History of Musical Instruments* by Curt Sachs, Copyright 1940 by W.W. Norton, renewed 1968 by Irene Sachs; **helix** Carl Bass; **hemlock** Roche; **hemstitch** The Cooper-Hewitt Museum of Design, Smithsonian Institution; **hepatica** Roche; **hermit crab** Matthew Kalmenoff; **heron** Annan Photo Features; **herringbone, hexagon** Cal Sacks; **hibachi** Portland Stove Foundry; **hieroglyphic** The Brooklyn Museum; **highjump** UPI; **hippopotamus** Marc and Evelyn Bernheim, Rapho Guillumette; **hive** Annan Photo Features; **hockey** Beardsley Ruml, II, Harvard Sports News Bureau, 1980; **holly, hollyhock** Roche; **Holstein** Grant Heilman Photography; **honeysuckle** William J. Jahoda from NAS; **hoop** Robert C. Hermes from NAS; **horn** Art by Enid Kotschning from "Horns and Antlers" by Walter Modell, Copyright © April, 1969, by Scientific American, Inc., all rights reserved; **horse chestnut** Roche—Lynwood Chase from NAS; **horseshoe crab** Hugh Spencer from NAS; **hourglass** The American Museum of Natural History; **houseboat** Annan Photo Features; **howdah** Frank Siteman, 1980; **hull** Cal Sacks—Annan Photo Features; **hummingbird** Jackson Abbott; **hurdle** UPI; **hyacinth** Roche; **hydrofoil** The Boeing Co.; **hyena** Annan Photo Features; **hypotenuse** Carl Bass; **hyrax** A.W. Ambler from NAS.

ibis Allan D. Cruickshank from NAS; **ichthyosaur** Matthew Kalmenoff; **ideogram** Ta-tsun Chen; **igloo** Steve and Dolores McCutcheon, Alaska Pictorial Service; **iguana** Dade W. Thornton from NAS; **illumination** Biblioteca Laurengiana, Florence, Photo Scala; **impala** J.D. Ovington from NAS; **impression** Annan Photo Features; **incandescent lamp** General Electric; **inclined plane** Cal Sacks; **incubator** Air-Shields; **Indian paintbrush, ingest** Matthew Kalmenoff; **inkstand** Philadelphia Museum of Art; **inlay** Photo Alinari; **insect** (ant) Bernard Gluck from NAS—(grasshopper) Leonard Lee Rue from NAS—(hornet) Annan Photo Features; **instruments** *The History of Musical Instruments* by Curt Sachs, Copyright © 1940 by W.W. Norton, renewed 1968 by Irene Sachs *Stedman's Medical Dictionary,* 21st Edition, © 1966, The Williams & Wilkins Co., Baltimore, Md.; **interior angle** Cal Sacks; **iris** (plant) F.S. Westeake from NAS; **ironwork** Photo Trends; **irrigation** Grant Heilman Photography; **isosceles triangle** Cal Sacks; **ivy** Roche.

jackhammer Read D. Brugger/The Picture Cube; **jack rabbit** Karl H. Maslowski from NAS; **jaguar** R. Van Nostrand from NAS; **jeep** U.S. Army; **jellyfish** Annan Photo Features; **jog** Allen Smith; **John Bull** The Bettmann Archives; **joker** U.S. Playing Card Co.; **joust** Universitätsbibliothek, Heidelberg; **juggler** *Circus* by Bertha B. Burlieth, Putnam, 1930; **jumping jack** Museum of the City of New York; **junk**[2] The Science Museum, London.

kangaroo A.W. Ambler from NAS; **katydid** Alvin E. Staffan from NAS; **kelp** Matthew Kalmenoff; **kettledrum** Ron Schick; **key**[1] Annan Photo Features; **killdeer** Jerry Focht from NAS; **kilt** Ewing Galloway; **kimono** *Japanese Costumes* by H. Minnich, Charles E. Tuttle, 1963; **kingfisher** Annan Photo Features; **kinkajou** Robert H. Hermes from NAS; **kite** Rohn Engh Photography; **knight** The Pierpont Morgan Library, New York; **knitting** Bernhard Ulmann Co.; **knot** Phoebe McGuire—Culver Pictures, Inc.; **koala** Pat Witherspoon from NAS; **kudu** P.W. Hay from NAS.

ladle Annan Photo Features; **ladybug** Richard Parker from NAS; **lantern** Brown Brothers; **larva** Lynnwood Chase from NAS; **latch** Cal Sacks; **leaf** Matthew Kalmenoff; **leapfrog** Ron Schick; **lectern** Florene Maine Antiques; **lei**[1] Matson Lines; **lemming** John H. Gerard from NAS; **lemur** San Diego Zoo; **leopard** Eric Hosking from NAS; **leotard** Danskin, Inc.; **levee** Ewing Galloway; **lever** Frances Davies; **lily** Roche; **lily of the valley** A.W. Ambler from NAS; **limpet** Annan Photo Features; **line segment** Richard Glassman; **lion** Jeanne White from NAS; **litchi** Kit and Max Hunn; **llama** A.W. Ambler from NAS; **lobe** Matthew Kalmenoff; **lock**[1] Eaton, Yale & Towne—Panama Canal Co.; **locomotive** Association of American Railroads; **locust**[1] J.M. Conrader from NAS; **longhorn** U.S. Dept. of Agriculture; **loom**[2] Brown Brothers; **loon**[1] H. Charles Laun from NAS; **lotus** A.W. Ambler from NAS; **louver** Cal Sacks; **lynx** San Diego Zoo; **lyrebird** Matthew Kalmenoff.

macaw New York Zoological Society; **magnification** From *Needlepoint* by Hope Hanley, used by permission of Charles Scribner's Sons and Mrs. Roman V. Mrozinski, Copyright © 1964 Hope Hanley; **magpie** Philip Strowbridge from NAS; **majorette** Frank Armstrong, News and Information Service University of Texas at Austin; **mallard** Gordon Smith from NAS; **mammoth** Matthew Kalmenoff; **manatee** Reprinted from *Natural History,* Jan., 1930; **mandrill** R. Van Nostrand from NAS; **manual alphabet** Gallaudet College, Washington, D.C.; **Manx cat** Walter Chandoha; **marionette** Ron Schick, Courtesy of Bil Baird Marionettes; **marmoset** Annan Photo Features; **mask** Annan Photo Features—The Museum of Primitive Art—U.S. Army; **Maypole** Radio Times Hulton Picture Library, London; **medal** U.S. Air Force—Fernando de Mello Vianna; **medallion** Bad. Landesmuseum, Karlsruhe, Bild Archive; **medicine man** The American Museum of Natural History; **megalith** Charles Woolf, M.P.S., Newquay; **Menorah** Murray Belsky; **meridian** Francis & Shaw, Inc.; **mesa** Josef Muench; **metamorphosis** (eggs) Walter Dawn—(larva, pupa, emerging adult) Annan Photo Features—(adults) Hal H. Harrison from NAS; **mezuzah** Jewish Theological Seminary of America, New York; **microphone** Arnold J. Saxe, 1982; **microscope** Cal Sacks; **midrib** Matthew Kalmenoff; **milestone** Brown Brothers; **milk** Frank Siteman, 1980; **millipede** N.E. Beck, Jr., from NAS; **mime** City Center, New York; **minaret** Donald Ferguson from Monkmeyer Press Photo Service; **mink** Ed Cesar from NAS; **mistletoe** Field Museum of Natural History; **mitt** Spalding & Bros., Inc.; **moccasin** The Museum of the American Indian, Heye Foundation; **mole**[2] Matthew Kalmenoff; **monarch** Hal H. Harrison from NAS; **mongoose** Lewis Wayne Walker from NAS; **monocle** Culver Pictures, Inc.; **monogram** Prints Division, NYPL; **moose** Annan Photo Features; **morel** Hugh Spencer from NAS; **morning-glory** John H. Gerard from NAS; **mosaic** Vatican Museum, Museum of Roman Civilization; **mosquito** John H. Gerard from NAS; **motion picture** Stock Shots to Order, Inc.; **mountain goat** Annan Photo Features; **muff**[2] Culver Pictures, Inc.; **mule**[1] Annan Photo Features; **mummy**[1] The Granger Collection; **muzzle** Kendra K. Ho, Courtesy of Lenny Ross School for Dogs, Inc.

nail *Popular Mechanics;* **narcissus** Roche; **narwhal** Matthew Kalmenoff; **nautilus** Annan Photo Features; **Neanderthal man** The American Museum of Natural History; **nebula** Yerkes Observatory; **nectarine** The Keith Thomas Co.; **needlepoint** From *Needlepoint* by Hope Hanley, used by permission of Charles Scribner's Sons and Mrs. Roman V. Mrozinski, Copyright © 1964 Hope Hanley; **nest** Allan D. Cruickshank from NAS—Annan Photo Features—Karl H. Maslowski from NAS; **Newfoundland**[2] Evelyn M. Shafer; **newt** Jack Dermid from NAS; **nightshade** Matthew Kalmenoff; **nimbus** The Minneapolis Institute of Arts; **nonagon** Richard Glassman; **noose** Phoebe McGuire; **note** Cal Sacks; **nucleus** Matthew Kalmenoff; **nun** Allen Smith.

obelisk Hirmer Verlag, Munich; **obi** Allen Smith; **observatory** Mt. Wilson and Palomar Observatories; **octagon, octahedron** Carl Bass; **officer** Arnold J. Saxe, 1983; **okapi** New York Zoological Society; **okra** Roche; **olive** Theodore R. Sills, Inc.; **onion** Matthew Kalmenoff; **openwork** Photo Trends; **operator** Reproduced by permission, A.T.&T. Corporate Archive; **opossum** Hal H. Harrison, NAS; **orange** T.H. Everett; **orang-utan** Matthew Kalmenoff; **orchid** Roche; **organ** Aeolian-Skinner Organ Co.; **oriole** Henry C. Johnson, NAS; **ostrich** A.W. Ambler from NAS; **outboard motor** The Fisher-Pierce Co., Inc.; **outrigger** Annan Photo Features; **oval** Frank Siteman, 1980; **overalls** Jane Latta; **overpass** Port of New York Authority; **overshot** Bruce Roberts, Rapho Guillumette; **owl** (below) Hal H. Harrison, NAS.

paddle wheel Standard Oil Co.; **paisley** The Cooper-Hewitt Museum of Design, Smithsonian Institution; **panda** Gordon Smith from NAS; **pansy** Roche; **panther** A.W. Ambler from NAS; **papyrus** John H. Gerard from NAS; **parabola** Carl Bass; **parakeet** Walter Chandoha; **paramecium** Walter Dawn; **parasol** *Le Théâtre,* Courtesy Agnes De Mille; **parka** Steve and Dolores McCutcheon, Alaska Pictorial Service; **parrot** Walter Chandoha; **passenger pigeon** Culver Pictures, Inc.; **passionflower** Karl Weidmann from NAS; **patchwork** The Metropolitan Museum of Art, Gift of Mr. and Mrs. Sidney Hosmer, 1948; **peach** Grant Heilman Photography; **peacock** A.W. Ambler from NAS; **peccary** Woodrow Goodpaster from NAS; **pelican** Jeanne White from NAS; **penguin** Zoological Society of London; **pentagon** Richard Glassman; **peony** Roche; **perch**[2] U.S. Fish & Wildlife Service; **peregrine falcon** G. Ronald Austing from NAS; **periscope** Cal Sacks; **periwinkle**[1] John H. Gerard from NAS; **Persian cat** Walter Chandoha; **persimmon** Matthew Kalmenoff; **perspective** Cal Sacks; **petrel** The New York Historical Society; **petunia** John H. Gerard from NAS; **pheasant** Annan Photo Features; **philodendron** Roche; **phlox** Library of the New York Botanical Gardens; **pig** Grant Heilman Photography; **pika** Leonard Lee Rue from NAS; **pillory** The Mansell Collection, London; **pipette** Corning Glass Works; **pistil** Matthew Kalmenoff; **pitcher**[2] The Metropolitan Museum of Art, Rogers Fund, Purchase, 1955; **pitcher plant** T.H. Everett; **plaid** Sara Krizmanich; **plane**[3] *Pacific Coast Trees* by Howard E. McMinn and Evelyn Maino, University of California Press, 1963; **platypus** Matthew Kalmenoff; **playground** Frank Siteman, 1979; **plow** Grant Heilman Photography; **pocketknife** Culver Pictures, Inc.; **pod** Grant Heilman Photography; **pogo stick** Peter Vandermark; **poison ivy** Grant Haist from NAS; **polar bear** Annan Photo Features; **pole vault** Pictorial Parade; **pomegranate** John H. Gerard from NAS; **poncho** Tim Kantor, Rapho Guillumette; **poodle** Walter Chandoha; **porcupine** Allan D. Cruickshank from NAS; **porpoise** Painting by Else Bostelmann, © National Geographic Society; **Portuguese man-of-war** The American Museum of Natural History; **potato** Matthew Kalmenoff; **potter's wheel** Bruce Roberts, Rapho Guillumette; **powder horn** John E. Theirman; **prairie dog** M. Kalmenoff; **pressure suit** NASA; **prickly pear** Grant Heilman Photography; **primrose** Roche; **prism** Cal Sacks; **profile** Ron Schick; **prominence** Mt. Wilson and Palomar Observatories; **pronghorn** Allan D. Cruickshank, NAS; **propeller** Cessna Aircraft Co.—Bethlehem Steel Corp.; **protractor** Keuffel & Esser Co.; **pseudopod** M. Kalmenoff; **pterodactyl** The American Museum of Natural History; **pueblo** Paolo Koch, Rapho Guillumette; **puffball** Annan Photo Features; **puffin** Prentice K. Stout, NAS; **puppet** Children's Television Workshop; **pushup** Ron Schick; **pussy willow** Roche; **pyramid** Pictorial Parade—Jane Latta.

quartet Allen J. Smith; **quartz** The American Museum of Natural History; **Queen Anne's lace** Roche; **quetzal** Robert C. Hermes from NAS; **quill** Matthew Kalmenoff.

raccoon Betty Barford from NAS; **radish** Roche; **ragweed** A.W. Ambler from NAS; **rake**[1] Grant Heilman Photography; **ram** Harry Engels from NAS; **rapier** The Metropolitan Museum of Art, Gift of William H. Riggs, 1913; **rat** "Rats" by S.A. Barnett, Copyright © January, 1967, by Scientific American, Inc., all rights reserved; **rattlesnake** Annan Photo Features; **raven** The New-York Historical Society; **ray**[2] Annan Photo Features; **reaper** Grant Heilman Photography; **rebus** Collection of Mr. and Mrs. Sherman Post Haight; **recorder** Murray Belsky; **redwood** Lola B. Graham from NAS; **reel**[1] Pflueger Corp.; **register** NCR Corporation; **reindeer** Matthew Kalmenoff; **relief** Museo Nazionàle, Naples, Photo Anderson; **remora** Matthew Kalmenoff; **respirator** Walter S. Silver; **retriever** Evelyn M. Shafer; **revolver** Smith & Wesson, Inc., **rhinoceros** Jane Latta; **rhododendron** Roche; **rifle** West Point Museum Collection; **roadrunner** Matthew Kalmenoff; **robin** M.F. Soper from NAS—Allan D. Cruickshank from NAS; **roller coaster** Philip Gendreau; **rose**[1] A.W. Ambler from NAS—Jack Dermid from NAS; **rosette** Roche—R. Van Nostrand from NAS; **rotisserie** International Appliance Corp.; **rudder** New York State Historical Assoc., Cooperstown; **rune** Alice Koeth; **rye** Grant Heilman Photography.

saber-toothed tiger The American Museum of Natural History; **saguaro** Grant Heilman Photography; **salute** Boy Scouts of America; **samovar** Murray Belsky; **sampan** Annan Photo Features; **sand dollar** Walter Dawn; **sandpiper** Allan D. Cruickshank from NAS; **sari** Annan Photo Features; **Saturn**[1] Yerkes Observatory; **saxophone** Ron Schick; **scaffolding** Arnold J. Saxe, 1983; **scallop** (collar) Simplicity Pattern Co., Inc.; **scepter** Louvre, Photo Alinari-Giraudon; **schnauzer** Evelyn M. Shafer; **scorpion** Dade W. Thornton from NAS; **Scottish terrier** Walter Chandoha; **scrimshaw** Seamen's Bank for Savings, New York; **sculpture** Frank Siteman, 1980; **scythe** George

Eastman House Collection; **sea anemone** Paul Unger, Photo Library, Inc.; **sea horse** A.W. Ambler from NAS; **sea lion** P. Berger from NAS; **sea otter** Matthew Kalmenoff; **seat belt** Davis Aircraft Products Co., Inc.; **secretary bird** *Introducing Birds,* by V.J. Stanek, Golden Pleasure Books, London, 1963; **sector** Richard Glassman; **seesaw** Monkmeyer Press Photo Service; **semaphore** General Railway Signal Co.; **sentry** British Travel Assoc.; **sepal** Matthew Kalmenoff; **serape** Ewing Galloway; **sewing machine** Pfaff; **sextant** Victory Museum, Portsmouth; **shagbark** John H. Gerard from NAS; **shako** Smithsonian Institution; **shamrock** Frances Davies; **shark** Matthew Kalmenoff; **shawl** Murray Belsky; **shield** Hofkirche, Innsbruck; **shofar** The Jewish Theological Seminary of America, New York; **shovel** Grant Heilman Photography—Annan Photo Features; **shrimp** Matthew Kalmenoff; **shuffleboard** Cunard Line; **Siamese cat** Jeanne White from NAS; **sideburns** The National Archives; **silhouette** The Metropolitan Museum of Art, Bequest of Mary Martin, 1938; **silkworm** New York Zoological Society; **similar triangles** Richard Glassman; **siphon** John Keaveny; **sitar** Marilyn Silverstone, Magnum; **ski** Annan Photo Features; **skimmer** The New-York Historical Society; **skullcap** Israeli Government Tourist Office; **skunk** Ed Cesar from NAS; **skyscraper** Chicago Architectural Photo Co.; **sled** Steve and Dolores McCutcheon, Alaska Pictorial Service—Walter Chandoha; **sleigh** Culver Pictures, Inc.; **slide** Allen Moore; **sloop** Stanley Rosenfeld; **sloth bear** San Diego Zoo; **slug** Alvin E. Staffan from NAS; **snail** Annan Photo Features; **snapdragon** Library of the New York Botanical Gardens; **snipe** Joe Van Wormer from NAS; **snow leopard** R. Van Nostrand from NAS; **snowshoe** Public Archives of Canada; **soccer** UPI; **sofa** The Metropolitan Museum of Art, Gift of L.E. Katzenbach Fund, 1966; **Solomon's seal** Matthew Kalmenoff; **sombrero** Brown Brothers; **sorghum** Grant Heilman Photography; **sousaphone** Philip Gendreau; **southwester** Culver Pictures, Inc.; **spade** U.S. Playing Card Co.; **Spanish moss** John H. Gerard from NAS; **spathe, sperm whale** Matthew Kalmenoff; **sphinx** John Ross; **spider** Jerome Wexler from NAS; **spinning wheel** Culver Pictures, Inc.; **spinnaker** Philip Gendreau; **spirogyra, sponge** Matthew Kalmenoff; **spoonbill** Allan D. Cruickshank from NAS; **sporran** Philip Gendreau; **spur** Hugh Spencer from NAS, Douglas Gorsline; **squid** Robert Hermes from NAS; **squirrel** Allan D. Cruickshank from NAS; **stag** Hugh M. Halliday from NAS; **stalactite, stalagmite** National Park Service; **stamen** Robert H. Wright from NAS; **starfish** G. Clifford Carl from NAS; **station wagon** General Motors; **St. Bernard** Evelyn M. Shafer; **steam roller** Owen Franken, Stock, Boston, 1978; **steeple** Samuel Chamberlain; **stegosaur** The American Museum of Natural History; **stethoscope** Bernard Cole; **Stetson** Standard Oil Co.; **stickball** Will Faller; Monkmeyer Press Photo Service; **stilt** (child on stilts) Brown Brothers; **stirrup** Grant Heilman Photography; **stoat** Zoological Society of London; **stoop**[2] Museum of the City of New York; **stork** Eric Hosking from NAS; **straight angle** Richard Glassman; **strawberry** Grant Heilman Photography; **streetcar** Frank Rawsome, Jr.; **string bean** Matthew Kalmenoff; **stroller** Janice Fullman/The Picture Cube, 1981; **sturgeon** Matthew Kalmenoff; **submarine** U.S. Navy; **subway** NYC Transit Authority; **sugar beet** Grant Heilman Photography; **sugar cane** Matthew Kalmenoff; **sumac** Hugh Spencer from NAS; **sundial** Parke-Bernet Galleries; **sunflower** Roche—Annan Photo Features; **surcoat** The Pierpont Morgan Library, New York; **surfboard** Annan Photo Features; **surrey** George Eastman House Collection; **surveyor** Margaret Thompson/The Picture Cube, 1984; **suspenders** Walter Chandoha; **suspension bridge** Californians, Inc.; **swallow**[2] Allan D. Cruickshank from NAS; **swallowtail** Stephen Dalton from NAS; **swan** Annan Photo Features; **sweep** Jane Latta—Princeton University Library, Sinclair Hamilton Collection; **sweet pea, sweet William** Roche; **swing** Allen Moore; **sword** The Metropolitan Museum of Art, Bequest of A.T. Clearwater, 1933; **swordfish** Matthew Kalmenoff; **syncline** From *Principles of Geology,* 2nd Edition, by James Gilluly, A.C. Waters, and A.O. Woodford, W.H. Freeman and Co., Copyright © 1951.

tadpole Matthew Kalmenoff; **tallith** The Jewish Theological Seminary of America, New York; **tambourine** Hugh Rogers, Monkmeyer Press Photo Service; **tam-o'-shanter** Allen D. Moore; **tangent** Carl Bass—Richard Glassman; **tapir** A.W. Ambler from NAS; **tarantula** Princeton University Library, Sinclair Hamilton Collection; **tarsier** A.W. Ambler from NAS; **tassel** Frank Siteman, 1980; **tattoo**[2] Philip Gendreau; **teal** Allan D. Cruickshank from NAS; **teddy bear** Theodore Roosevelt Assoc.; **tektite** The American Museum of Natural History; **tendril** Matthew Kalmenoff; **ten-gallon hat** Library of Congress; **tern**[1] The New-York Historical Society; **terrapin** Jack Dermid from NAS; **terrarium** Gottscho-Schleisner, Inc.; **tetrahedron** Carl Bass; **thatched roof** The British Tourist Authority; **thistle** Roche; **thole pin** The Marine Historical Association, Mystic, Conn.; **thrasher** Allan D. Cruickshank from NAS; **throne** Pictorial Parade; **tiara** Rapho Guillumette © Ottawa Karsh; **tiger** Bucky Reeves from NAS; **tiger lily** Roche; **time clock** Walter S. Silver; **tiptoe** Ron Schick; **titmouse** The New-York Historical Society; **toad** George Porter from NAS; **toga** Museo Archeologico, Florence, Photo Alinari; **tomahawk** Museum of the American Indian, Heye Foundation; **tomato** Roche; **tom-tom** Marc and Evelyn Bernheim, Rapho Guillumette; **topiary** Paul Genereux; **tortoiseshell** Museum of the City of New York; **totem pole** The American Museum of Natural History; **towhee** The New-York Historical Society; **tractor** Don Breneman, United States Department of Agriculture, 1975; **traffic light** Philip Gendreau; **trap** Brown Brothers; **treadmill** Library of Congress; **tree frog** George Porter from NAS; **trefoil** Jean Roubier; **triangle** Carl Bass—Ron Schick; **triceratops** Matthew Kalmenoff; **tricycle** F.A.O. Schwarz; **trilobite** The American Museum of Natural History; **trivet** Henry Francis du Pont Winterthur Museum; **trombone** Ron Schick; **truss** *The Illustrated London News;* **T-square** J.L. Hammett Co.; **tuatara** Alfred M. Bailey from NAS; **tugboat** Moran Towing; **tulip** Roche; **tuning fork** Kitching Co.; **turkey** The New-York Historical Society, John H. Gerard from NAS; **turtle** P. Berger from NAS; **turtleneck** Cal Sacks; **typewriter** SCM Corp.; **tyrannosaur** Matthew Kalmenoff.

umbra Cal Sacks; **umbrella** Bruce Roberts, Rapho Guillumette; **undershot** Jane Latta; **unicorn** The Metropolitan Museum of Art, The Cloisters Collection, Gift of John D. Rockefeller, Jr., 1937; **upright** Steinway & Sons.

valance Window Shade Manufacturers Assoc.; **vane** The New-York Historical Society; **vector** Richard Glassman; **veil** Philip Gendreau; **vendor** Frank Siteman, 1980; **Venn diagram** Richard Glassman; **Venus's-flytrap** Hugh Spencer from NAS; **vernier caliper** Brown & Sharpe Mfg., Co.; **viceroy** Gaston LePage from NAS; **vicuña** A.W. Ambler from NAS; **viola**[1] Ron Schick; **violet** Roche; **violin** Ron Schick; **Virginia creeper** Jane Latta; **visor** Roger-Viollet; **volcano** Western Ways, Tad Nichols; **vole** Annan Photo Features; **volvox, vorticella** Matthew Kalmenoff; **vulture** Allan D. Cruickshank from NAS.

wagon Bruce Roberts, Rapho Guillumette; **wallaby** Zoological Society of London; **walrus** Annan Photo Features; **wapiti** Willis Peterson; **wart hog, wasp** Jeanne White from NAS; **water buffalo** Georg Gerster, Rapho Guillumette; **water lily** Roche; **water-ski** Monkmeyer Press Photo Service; **wattle** Annan Photo Features; **wavelength** Richard Glassman; **weasel** Karl H. Maslowski from NAS; **weave** Cal Sacks—Ewing Galloway; **weight** Ohaus Scale Corp.; **whalebone, whale** Matthew Kalmenoff; **wheat** Grant Heilman Photography; **wheelbarrow** Cal Sacks; **whelk** John H. Gerard from NAS; **whip** From The Charles M. Russell Book by Harold McCracken; **whistle** Field Manufacturing Co.; **whorl** Roche; **wicket** Van De Poll, Monkmeyer Press; **wickiup** Smithsonian Institution, American Ethnology Collection; **wing** (bird) Cal Sacks; **wisteria** Roche; **witch hazel** Gottscho-Schleisner; **wolf** A.W. Ambler, NAS; **wolverine** Annan Photo Features; **wombat** Australian News & Information Bureau; **worm** (earthworm), **wren** John H. Gerard, NAS; **wrench** New Britain Machine—Rigid Tool.

xylophone Ron Schick.

yeast *Botany,* 3rd Edition, by Carl L. Wilson and Walter E. Loomis, Copyright 1952, © 1957, 1962 by Holt, Rinehart and Winston, Inc.; Reprinted by permission; **yew** Roche; **yoke** (oxen) Grant Heilman Photography; **yucca** Joseph Muench.

zebra Annan Photo Features; **zebu** Matthew Kalmenoff; **zinnia** Roche; **zone** Francis & Shaw, Inc.

Introduction

The American Heritage Student's Dictionary is a newly revised work in the Houghton Mifflin series of dictionaries. It updates a product of years of planning and computerized research, as well as two full years of intensive writing and editing by a large and experienced staff of lexicographers. It embodies the many innovations in lexicography introduced by *The American Heritage Dictionary of the English Language,* principally in the areas of design and illustrations and guidance on matters of usage.

The American Heritage Student's Dictionary is intended for use in American schools in grades 6 through 9. Accordingly, we tried to find out in an objective way which words are actually encountered by the people in these grades. The language that is **spoken** by students and their teachers could in theory be examined through an immense program of tape recordings, but a project of such complexity and magnitude must be left to the future. We concentrated on getting really good evidence from the **printed** language used by the educational system itself, as carried in the huge bulk of school materials.

The entry list of *The American Heritage Student's Dictionary* should be especially useful because it was based, mostly, on textbooks, magazines, encyclopedias, workbooks, and other printed materials that are used in schools. We know, because our computerized research told us, that the words we chose appear often. In some cases they appear in important specialized ways—in science or mathematics, for example—rather than simply often. We also think that our selection should be useful because the computer gave us thousands of examples of how the words occurred in sentences. (When you look up definitions in *The American Heritage Student's Dictionary,* you will find many of these examples of word use right after the definition.)

The definitions have been carefully written with simplicity, clarity, and accuracy according to modern principles of lexicography and linguistics, many of which have never before been embodied in any dictionary. There are more than 2,000 pictorial illustrations, many of them especially commissioned photographs depicting children of various ages in the pursuit of different activities. There are many useful tables (as of the Roman numerals and the Morse code) and a special section on Weights and Measures and the Metric System with appropriate conversion charts. Hundreds of geographical and biographical entries are also included alphabetically in the main body of the Dictionary for greater convenience of the user. Etymologies, usage notes, a short pronunciation key, and much useful additional information are attractively presented interspersed with the illustrations in the wide margins of the Dictionary. A section on how to use the Dictionary starts on page ix and was especially designed to explain the basic editorial policies of the Dictionary in terms of definitions, typographical presentation of the entries, pronunciation system, and all other features of the Dictionary.

How to Use Your Dictionary

The word or phrase you look up in the Dictionary is called a *main entry* or an *entry word* or simply an *entry*. *The American Heritage Student's Dictionary* contains about 35,000 main entries, which amount to about 55,000 different words if inflected forms are counted, and about 70,000 separately defined meanings and uses. To furnish the spellings, pronunciations, meanings, and histories of so many words requires a systematic way of presenting information.

English words are not evenly distributed among the twenty-six letters of the alphabet. Notice, for example, that words beginning with the letters **C** and **S** occupy much more space than words beginning with the letters **U, V, W, X, Y,** and **Z.**

If you examine the A–Z list in your Dictionary, you will notice that it is made up of three parts. The first part contains all the entries that begin with the letters **A** through **G**; the second part, all that begin with the letters **H** through **Q**; and the third part, all that begin with the letters **R** through **Z.** Thinking of the alphabet as being divided into these three main parts yields a pattern like this:

A B C D E F G / H I J K L M N O P Q / R S T U V W X Y Z

Being familiar with this pattern helps you to locate words more quickly in the Dictionary. Suppose you are looking up the words **precious, quaint,** and **refined.** If you open your Dictionary toward the end of the second part (about two-thirds of the way through), you will be very close to the words you want.

Guide Words

To help you find the right page, dictionary makers, or *lexicographers,* put *guide words,* together with the page number, at the top of each page. The guide words are printed in boldface type:

783 **sea gull** | **seasonal**

The guide word to the left of the vertical bar tells you the first entry on the page. The one to the right of the vertical bar tells you the last entry on the page. Thus, the guide words on page 783 tell you that **sea gull** and **seasonal** and all entries that fall between them are listed on that page.

Finding the Entry

To help you find a word quickly, lexicographers have arranged all entries in alphabetical order; the entry words are printed in boldface type a little to the left of the rest of the column. On page 233 you will find the first entries in the letter **D** listed thus:

d, D |dē| *n., pl.* **d's** or **D's. 1.** The fourth letter of the English alphabet. **2. D** The lowest passing grade given to a student. **3. D** The Roman numeral for the number 500. **4. D** In music, the second tone in the scale of C major. [SEE NOTE]
D The symbol for deuterium.
d. 1. died. **2.** In British currency, penny; pence.
D.A. district attorney.
dab[1] |dăb| *v.* **dabbed, dab•bing. 1.** To apply with short, light strokes: *dab grease on a burn.* **2.** To pat quickly and lightly: *dab the face with cold cream.* —*n.* **1.** A small amount, lump, or mass. **2.** A light, poking stroke or pat. [SEE NOTE]
dab[2] |dăb| *n.* A flatfish related to the flounders. [SEE NOTE]
dab•ble |dăb'əl| *v.* **dab•bled, dab•bling. 1.** To splash or spatter: *Raindrops dabbled her dress with spots.* **2.** To splash in and out of water

A brief examination of the left-hand column will tell you the following:

1. There is one entry for both the lower-case and upper-case letter **d, D,** one entry for the capital letter **D,** and one entry for the lower-case letter **d.** The first entry at each letter of the alphabet (always in the form **d, D**) contains information that applies only to that particular letter of the alphabet, for example, how it can be used as a school grade, as a Roman numeral, or as a representation of a musical tone. The entry **D** tells you that the capital letter **D** without a period is the chemical symbol for the element deuterium. The entry **d.** tells you that when the lower-case letter **d** is followed by a period, it is the abbreviation for *died* and the abbreviation for the former British unit of money *penny* and its plural *pence*.

2. An entry word is syllabicated by means of centered dots: **dab•ble.**

3. In order to arrange words alphabetically, lexicographers have to consider the first three, four, five, or more letters of a word (many words begin, for example, with the letter combination **da-**), as they did when they arranged **dab**[1], **dab**[2], **dabble, da capo, Dacca, dace,** and **dachshund** in sequence.

4. Some entries consist of more than one word. These may be written as phrases (**water buffalo, water color**) or as hyphenated compounds (**baby-sit, heavy-duty**). Such phrases and hyphenated compounds are alphabetized as if they were written solid.

5. Abbreviations are alphabetized in the same sequence as words.

Superscript Numbers

In English it is not unusual to find two or more completely different words whose spelling is identical but whose meanings and histories have little, if anything, in common. Such words are called *homographs*. To distinguish homographs lexicographers arrange them as separate entries and give each of them a number called a *superscript number*. These superscript numbers are printed after the entry word and above the line:

helm[1] |hĕlm| *n.* **1.** The steering gear of a ship, especially the tiller or wheel. **2.** A position of leadership or control. [SEE NOTE]
helm[2] |hĕlm| *n. Archaic.* A helmet. [SEE NOTE]

Most pairs or larger sets of homographs are given brief notes with their histories, or *etymological notes,* through which you can find out why the homographs are different words.

When you see a superscript number to the right of an entry word, be sure to check the other entries that are spelled the same and are marked with superscripts. You cannot be sure that you have found the word you are looking for until you have checked all other words that are spelled the same.

Anatomy of an Entry

Lexicographers want to give as much information as possible about each entry word; they also want to enter as many words as possible within a certain level of vocabulary. To solve this problem, lexicographers, since they are restricted by limitations of space, have developed a highly systematic way of presenting information within each entry. Take the time now to learn some important features of your Dictionary. By doing so, you will save yourself time and effort later, and you will be able to get all the help you need from your Dictionary each time you consult it.

The major features found in an entry are:

The Entry Word

The entry word, syllabicated, is printed in boldface type a little to the left of the column. The boldface entry word gives you the correct spelling of the entry. Some words, however, can be spelled correctly in more than one way. If more than one spelling is in common use, the Dictionary will give all the acceptable spellings. Variant spellings are combined at the main entry only if they are pronounced alike and if they occur next to each other in alphabetical order. Variant spellings are most frequently entered separately.

Pronunciation

The pronunciation, enclosed in vertical bars, appears immediately after the boldface entry word; differing pronunciations within an entry are given wherever necessary, as in shifts of part of speech and in other special cases. Within the vertical bars appear letters and various other symbols, in lightface and boldface type, that seem to be respellings of the entry word. To use the pronunciation system of this Dictionary effectively, you should learn the meaning of the symbols that represent sounds, shown on page xviii.

Part-of-Speech Labels

1. The following italicized labels, which follow the pronunciation of the entry words, are used to indicate parts of speech:

n.	(noun)	*conj.*	(conjunction)
adj.	(adjective)	*prep.*	(preposition)
adv.	(adverb)	*v.*	(verb)
pron.	(pronoun)	*interj.*	(interjection)

The additional italicized labels below are used as needed to indicate inflected forms:

pl.	(plural)
sing.	(singular)

We also use the label *pl.n.* for words such as **clothes** and **cattle,** that are used only in the plural.

2. Many words can function as more than one part of speech. For example, **paint** can be both a verb (as in *a man painting a wall*) and a noun (as in *a gallon of paint*). In such cases, the different parts of speech are defined in a single entry called a *combined entry*. In an entry of this kind, each part of speech receives its own part-of-speech label; this label comes before all elements that apply to that part of speech, and may be followed by any elements (pronunciation, other labels, etc.) that can appear after the entry word itself:

> **ad-lib** |ăd **lĭb'**| *Informal. v.* **ad-libbed, ad-lib•bing.** To make up (lines, music, movements, etc.) while performing: *ad-lib a joke. The actor forgot his lines and ad-libbed.* —*n.* A line, speech, action,

If, however, a language label or another label applies to the entire entry, that label precedes all part-of-speech labels, and the pronunciation is followed by a period:

> **nix** |nĭks|. *Slang. n.* Nothing. —*adv.* No: *Nix on that idea.* —*interj.* Stop! Watch out! —*v.* To say no to; reject; deny; veto: *The boss nixed my*

The following do *not* receive part-of-speech labels:

Phrasal entries, such as **ad hoc, good night, mountain lion,** etc.

Biographical and geographic terms.

Abbreviations, symbols, and acronyms.

In addition to the part-of-speech labels listed above, the label *definite article* is used in this Dictionary for the entry **the,** and the label *indefinite article* is used for the entries **a** and **an.** Three additional labels that are not readily identifiable as belonging to any of the parts of speech listed above are also used. These labels are *modifier, phrasal verb,* and *Idiom*.

Modifiers

Any English noun can be used to modify another noun in the manner of an adjective. Nouns so used, called *modifiers* in this Dictionary, can be distinguished from regular adjectives by testing them in the following constructions:

1. Modifiers make sense in the first of the constructions below and not in the second:

the (a, an) ________ noun

The (a, an) noun seems ________.

For example,

the blue wall (adjective + noun),

an apple tree (modifier + noun),

The wall seems blue (adjective + noun)

are all acceptable. However,

The tree seems apple (modifier + noun)

does not make sense.

2. Nouns used as modifiers cannot themselves

be modified by a word such as *very, extremely,* or *highly,* nor can they be compared.

There are, of course, exceptions to these rules. For example, certain adjectives, such as **unique,** cannot be compared.

In this Dictionary, when a noun is often used as a modifier and when the use is natural and common, one or more examples of this use, labeled ***modifier,*** are given immediately after the noun definition. A large body of citations from actual school materials was used extensively as a source for such examples.

> **check-out** |chĕk'out'| *n.* **1.** The act or process of checking out, as at a supermarket, library, or hotel. **2.** A place where something, such as merchandise, may be paid for, taken out, etc. **3.** A test or inspection, as of a machine, for working condition, accuracy, etc. —***modifier:*** *a check-out counter; the check-out line.*

Phrasal Verbs

A *phrasal verb* is a verb phrase in which the first word is the main-entry word used as a verb. The second element of the phrase is usually a preposition but may also be a conjunction or an adverb.

In this Dictionary, the label ***phrasal verb*** introduces such verb phrases, which follow all verb definitions.

Note that only idiomatic, nonliteral senses of such combinations are entered and defined. A verb combination consisting of the entry word plus **on, off, away, in,** etc., used in any of its generally recognized adverbial senses is not included. Thus, **back out,** meaning "to retire or withdraw from something," is defined in that sense only (not in the sense "leaving a parking space in reverse").

> *majority of voters backed him.* —***phrasal verbs.*** **back down.** To withdraw from a stand that one has taken: *There was a fight because neither side was willing to back down.* **back off.** To retreat or retire, as from an untenable or dangerous position: *games in which the winner is the one who backs off last.* **back out.** To retire or withdraw from something: *He accepted the invitation but backed out at the last minute.* **back up. 1.** To move

Idioms

An *idiom* is a group of words whose meaning as a group cannot be deduced from the meanings of the individual words in the group. Such phrases are usually defined at the entry for the key word in the phrase. For example, **bone of contention** is defined at **bone.**

In this Dictionary, idioms are placed at the very end of the definition in alphabetical order. Each idiom is shown in boldface type; only the first one is preceded by the introductory label ***Idiom.*** Note also that alphabetical order alone, not part-of-speech status, determines the order in which these idioms appear.

> ***Idioms.*** **bone of contention.** The subject of a dispute. **feel in (one's) bones.** To have an intuition of. **have a bone to pick with.** To have reason

Inflected Forms

Inflected forms are forms of the entry word that differ from the main-entry form. Inflected forms of nouns tell you whether the noun is singular or plural; inflected forms of adjectives and adverbs tell you if these words have comparative and superlative degrees formed with *-er* and *-est;* and inflected forms of verbs tell you if a verb has an irregular past tense, past participle, and present participle, or any other irregular form, such as an irregular third person singular present tense.

In this Dictionary, when a noun, verb, adjective, or adverb undergoes an irregular change in form, the irregular form is given in boldface type, usually written out in full and fully syllabicated, immediately following the part-of-speech label or the numbered sense of the definition to which it applies. In addition, inflected forms offering possible spelling problems are entered. Inflected forms are pronounced when necessary.

> **fly²** |flī| *n., pl.* **flies. 1.** Any of a large number of winged insects, especially one of a group that
>
> **high** |hī| *adj.* **high•er, high•est. 1. a.** Having a relatively great elevation; extending far upward:
>
> **fly¹** |flī| *v.* **flew** |flo͞o|, **flown** |flōn|, **fly•ing, flies. 1.** To move through the air with the aid of wings or winglike parts: *Birds fly.* **2.** To travel through

Regular inflections are normally not entered. For the purposes of this Dictionary, regular inflections include:

1. Plurals formed by the addition of *-s* or *-es*. The regular plural is shown, however, when there is an irregular variant plural or when the spelling of the regular plural might present difficulties, as with words ending in *-o*.

> **ra•di•o** |rā′dē ō′| *n., pl.* **ra•di•os.** 1. The use of electromagnetic waves lying between about 10
>
> **to•ma•to** |tə mā′tō| *or* |-mä′-| *n., pl.* **to•ma•toes.** 1. The fleshy, usually reddish fruit of a widely

2. Past tenses and past participles formed by the addition of *-ed* with no other change in the verb form, as **marked, parked,** etc.

3. Present participles formed by the addition of *-ing* with no other change in the verb form, as **marking, parking,** etc.

4. Present-tense forms, with the exception of such highly irregular forms as **is, has,** etc.

For every adjective whose comparative and superlative degrees are formed by adding *-er* and *-est,* we show the comparative and superlative forms immediately following the label *adj.* regardless of whether the forms are regular or irregular. These inflected forms are written out in full, fully syllabicated, and pronounced where necessary.

> **fast**[1] |făst| *or* |fäst| *adj.* **fast•er, fast•est.** 1. Moving quickly; swift; rapid: *a fast runner; a fast*
>
> **flat**[1] |flăt| *adj.* **flat•ter, flat•test.** 1. Having a smooth, even surface; level: *flat land.* 2. Not
>
> **good** |go͝od| *adj.* **bet•ter** |bĕt′ər|, **best** |bĕst|. 1. Having positive or desirable qualities; not bad

The inflected forms of verbs are listed in the following order: past tense, past participle (if it differs from the past tense), present participle, and sometimes third person singular present tense.

Separate Entries for Inflected Forms

1. Verbs such as **have, be, can, do,** etc., have several frequently recorded archaic inflected forms such as **hath, art, doth, dost,** etc., involving change of the stem form. These forms are entered separately.

> **hast** |hăst|. *Archaic.* A form of the present tense of **have,** used with *thou.*
>
> **hath** |hăth|. *Archaic.* A form of **has.**

2. Inflected forms of verbs having only one syllable in which vowel changes signal tense changes are entered separately if there are any intervening entries. Thus **flew,** the past tense of **fly,** is a separate entry.

3. Inflected forms of irregular verbs separated by intervening entries are not entered when the irregularity consists of a readily recognizable change, such as the change from a final *-y* to *-ies* or *-ied*. Therefore, **carried** and **carries** are not entered separately, even though the entries **carrier** through **carrousel** intervene.

4. Irregular plurals are entered separately wherever there is an intervening entry and the change in the ending is not a regular one (as in the change from *-y* to *-ies*). Thus we show

> **child** |chīld| *n., pl.* **chil•dren** |chĭl′drən|. 1. A person from the time of birth to the stage of physical maturity; a young boy or girl. 2. A
>
> **chil•dren** |chĭl′drən| *n.* Plural of **child.**

At the entry **filly** we show the irregular plural **fillies,** but we do not enter **fillies** (the change is regular) separately in spite of the intervening entries **filling, filling station, fillip,** and **Fillmore.**

5. Irregular comparative and superlative forms are separately entered when there are any intervening entries. This rule applies, however, only to those cases where the spelling change occurs in the root of the word, not in the suffixes only. That is, **airier** and **airiest** are not separately entered as inflected forms of **airy** because the spelling change from **airy** affects only the suffix. But in the case of

> **dry** |drī| *adj.* **dri•er** or **dry•er, dri•est** or **dry•est.** 1. Free from liquid or moisture; not wet or

we show

> **dri•er**[2] |drī′ər| *adj.* A comparative of **dry.**
>
> **dri•est** |drī′ĭst| *adj.* A superlative of **dry.**
>
> **drift** |drĭft| *v.* 1. To be or cause to be carried

because these changes affect the root of the word.

The Definition: *Order of Definitions*

Meanings within a complex entry are arranged on the same principle as those in *The American Heritage Dictionary of the English Language*. With the use of our citations from school materials, it would have been possible for the first time to arrange the meanings in order of frequency, with the most familiar meanings first and the least familiar last. This arrangement has been attempted, with inadequate data, in some dictionaries. But despite this opportunity, we believe that while the order of frequency is extremely interesting in various ways, it serves no practical purpose in a general dictionary.

The "analytical" order used in *The American Heritage Dictionary of the English Language* is an effort to arrange a complex word in a psychologically meaningful order, with one subgroup leading into another, so that the word can to some extent be perceived as a structured unit rather than as a string of unrelated senses. This system is also used in *The American Heritage Student's Dictionary*.

Since most English words have more than one sense, the typical dictionary entry contains not just one but several definitions.

The Definition: *Numbers and Letters*

When an entry has more than one definition, these are numbered in sequence. In a combined entry, the definitions are numbered in separate sequences beginning with **1.** after each part of speech. When one numbered definition has two or more closely related senses, these are indicated by the letters **a.**, **b.**, **c.**, etc., as in the definition numbered **2.** in this example:

> **big** |bĭg| *adj.* **big•ger, big•gest. 1.** Of great size; large: *a big house; a big city; a big appetite.* **2. a.** Grown-up: *You're a big boy now.* **b.** Older: *my big sister.* **3.** Prominent; influential: *a big industrialist.* **4.** Of great significance; momentous: *a big day in my life; practice for the big game.* **5.** Full of self-importance; boastful: *a big talker.* **6.** Outstanding or extreme in some respect: *a big fake.* —*adv.* **1.** With an air of

Boldface Subentries

If a noun has a sense or senses in which it often appears in the plural, this fact is indicated at those senses:

> **ground**[1] |ground| *n.* **1.** The solid surface of the earth; land; soil. **2.** Often **grounds.** An area or plot of land set aside or designated for a special

The same style is used for any change in the form of a word as it shifts from one sense to another:

> **con•sti•tu•tion** |kŏn′stĭ to͞o′shən| *or* |-tyo͞o′-| *n.* **1.** The basic law of a politically organized body, such as a nation or state. **2. the Constitution.** The written constitution of the United States, adopted in 1787 and put into effect in 1789. **3.** The way in which something or someone is made up, especially the physical make-up of a person: *a boy with a strong constitution.* **4.** The act of setting up. [SEE NOTE on p. 200]

The same style is used for *boldface phrasal alternates,* which are common phrasal combinations equivalent to, or often more specifically applicable to, the word or numbered sense being defined. They consist of the entry word plus another term entered elsewhere in the Dictionary and always take the form of separate words, as distinguished from compounds or hyphenated forms.

> **hock•ey** |hŏk′ē| *n.* **1.** Also **ice hockey.** A game played on ice, in which two opposing teams of skaters, using curved sticks, try to drive a flat disk, or puck, into the goal of the opponents' team. **2.** Also **field hockey.** A similar game

The definition of some entries may also contain the definition of a subentry that is a closely related term. The subentry being defined appears in boldface type and has a pronunciation if necessary. We use this style when the word or phrase that is the subentry would occur next or nearly next to the main entry and when the meaning of the subentry is closely and smoothly tied to the meaning of the entry word.

> **dia•mond•back** |dī′mənd băk′| *or* |dī′ə-| *n.* **1.** Also **diamondback rattlesnake.** A large rattlesnake of the southern United States and Mexico, with diamond-shaped markings on the back. **2.** Also **diamondback terrapin.** A turtle of the southeastern coast of the United States, with knobby or ridged markings on the upper shell.

In the case of certain military ranks, such as **lieutenant,** the full definition appears only at the main entry **lieutenant,** where **first lieutenant** and **second lieutenant** are fully defined:

> **lieu•ten•ant** |lo͞o tĕn'ənt| *n.* **1.** An officer in the Army, Air Force, or Marine Corps ranking below a captain. A **first lieutenant** ranks above a **second lieutenant. 2.** An officer in the Navy

Examples in Definitions

In addition to giving clear definitions for words, this Dictionary provides thousands of examples to show how a word is actually used in context. Examples are especially useful for illustrating figurative senses of a word, transitive and intransitive verbs, and multiple senses of very common words that have a wide general use, as adverbs and prepositions such as **up, down, on,** and **off** and verbs such as **go, get, be,** etc. Notice how the illustrative examples provided at the entry help you understand the definitions themselves.

> **a•round** |ə round'| *prep.* **1.** Near in time to; close to: *around the year 1450.* **2.** All about; all over in: *The reporter looked around the room.* Also used adverbially: *Come up to the shop and I'll take you around.* **3.** In a circle surrounding: *Soon they were whirling around the tree trunk.* Also used adverbially: *The workmen gathered around to get paid off.* **4.** In a group or groups surrounding: *the Indian tribes around the Great*
>
> **flaw** |flô| *n.* A blemish, crack, or other defect; an imperfection: *a flaw in a diamond; a flaw in an argument; a flaw in his character.* —*v.* To make or become defective.

Definition by Example

A certain category of words usually functions both adjectivally and adverbially with no difference in meaning except for the shift in function, for example, most words ending in *-ward* (**homeward, earthward**), words such as **uptown, upstream,** etc. In such cases we define the adverb fully, and the adjectival sense is defined only by an example consisting typically of a noun phrase.

> **home•ward** |hōm'wərd| *adv.* Also **home•wards** |hōm'wərdz|. Toward home: *They turned their canoe and paddled homeward.* —*adj.: the homeward journey.*

Main-Entry Words Having Meaning Only in a Phrase

A certain small class of words has current meaning only in phrasal combinations. Other dictionaries give the archaic or obsolete senses of such words in order to be able to include the phrase, but in this Dictionary we have discarded these senses and kept only those senses that invariably occur in phrasal combinations. These are handled as idiomatic phrases except that the key word is the main entry with pronunciation, with inflected forms where necessary, and with the part-of-speech label.

> **a•back** |ə băk'| *adv.* **—taken aback.** Surprised or stopped by something startling or disagreeable.

In these cases no attempt is made to define the word except in its phrasal context.

We also define by example, as subentries, past participles and present participles used adjectivally. They appear in boldface type at the end of the corresponding verb definition and are fully syllabicated.

> **flat•ter** |flăt'ər| *v.* **1.** To compliment (someone) excessively and often insincerely, especially in order to win favor. **2.** To please or gratify: *Receiving the award flattered me.* **3.** To make more attractive than is actually the case: *The photograph flatters her.* **—flat'ter•ing** *adj.: flattering remarks; a flattering hat.* **—flat'ter•er** *n.*
>
> **grate**[1] |grāt| *v.* **grat•ed, grat•ing. 1.** To fragment, shred, or powder by rubbing against an abrasive surface: *Grate the nutmegs into a fine powder.* **2.** To make or cause to make a harsh grinding or rasping sound by rubbing: *You grate like a jay and squeak like a mouse. He grated the two rocks together.* **3.** To irritate; annoy: *That sound grates on my nerves.* **—grat'ed** *adj.: grated cheese.* ¶*These*

Run-on Entries

Additional words formed from the main-entry word by the addition of a suffix will be found at the end of many entries. These *run-on entries* are obviously related to the main-entry word and have the same essential meaning, but they have a different grammatical function, as indicated by the part-of-speech label. The use of run-on entries saves valuable space that would otherwise be used for definitions that would merely be repetitions of previous definitions or for a word formula that would give no more information than the part-of-speech label does. Run-on entries appear in boldface type, followed by a part-of-speech label. All run-ons are syllabicated; stress is indicated for all such undefined forms that have more than one syllable, and pronunciation is indicated as needed.

> **help•ful** |hĕlp′fəl| *adj.* Providing help; useful: *a helpful person; helpful methods.* —**help′ful•ly** *adv.* —**help′ful•ness** *n.*

When different run-on forms have the same grammatical function, they are separated by a comma and have a single part-of-speech label.

> **lu•cid** |lo͞o′sĭd| *adj.* **1.** Easily understood; clear: *a lucid explanation.* **2.** Mentally sound; sane; rational: *The senile man has his lucid hours.* —**lu•cid′i•ty, lu′cid•ness** *n.* —**lu′cid•ly** *adv.*

Variants

For the purposes of this Dictionary, a *variant* is a differently spelled but obviously closely related form of an entry word. In *The American Heritage Student's Dictionary* variant spellings may be combined in a main entry, before pronunciation, only if:

They occur in unbroken alphabetical sequence.

They are pronounced alike.

There are no major differences in inflections, as an alternative set of principal parts for a verb, to be shown.

No additional designation, such as the labels *British, Slang,* etc., needs to be shown.

1. In the case of *primary variants,* forms that occur with the same degree of frequency, the following style is used:

> **cat•a•log** or **cat•a•logue** |kăt′l ôg′| *or* |-ŏg′| *n.* **1.** A list of items, usually in alphabetical order, with a description of each: *a library catalog.* **2.** A book or pamphlet containing such a

2. Where one form is distinctly preferred but the second (the *secondary variant*) is sufficiently common and valid to merit entry, the following style is used:

> **lunch•room,** also **lunch-room** |lŭnch′ro͝om′| *or* |-ro͞om′| *n.* The cafeteria or room in a building, such as a school, where lunch is eaten.

3. Variants with the alternate endings *-ic* and *-ical* are shown in a combined entry, regardless of the difference in pronunciation and the possibility of intervening entries:

> **bi•o•graph•i•cal** |bī′ə grăf′ĭ kəl| or **bi•o•graph•ic** |bī′ə grăf′ĭk| *adj.* Of or based on a person's life: *biographical information.*

Variants as Separate Entries

Most variant forms are separately entered. They always appear as separate entries when:

There are any intervening entries.

There is a difference in pronunciation, regardless of whether or not there are intervening entries.

There is a radical difference in inflected forms.

The form for the main entry and the separate entry for the variant form are as follows:

> **a•me•ba** |ə mē′bə| *n., pl.* **a•me•bas.** A very small, one-celled organism that has an indefinite, changeable form. [SEE PICTURE]
>
> **a•moe•ba** |ə mē′bə| *n., pl.* **a•moe•bas** or **a•moe•bae** |ə mē′bē|. A form of the word **ameba.**

Note that the variant form is not shown at all at the main entry.

When a word that has a variant occurs in compounds, the variant is not repeated at the compound; for example, the variant **colour** is entered separately as "A British form of the word **color,**" but **colour** is not repeated at **colorblind** and other compounds.

Alternate Terms

Alternate terms are words or terms in which the variation involves more than simple spelling; that is, the words have more than one form, which can vary considerably, sometimes consisting of a form having some resemblance to the primary main entry but more often being a word or phrasal entry entirely different in form but having the same meaning as the primary entry.

When the alternate term is a main entry, the preferred form is given in the definition:

darning needle. **1.** A long needle with a big eye, using in darning. **2.** A dragonfly.

Hol•land |**hŏl′**ənd|. A country, the Netherlands.

bicarbonate of soda. **Sodium bicarbonate.**

In the last case, the definition is set in boldface type because the main entry is a phrasal compound; this indicates that the entry for the preferred form is to be found in its proper alphabetical order in the letter **S**.

When two forms are applicable and one, though perhaps more strictly correct, is technical and likely to be less familiar than a commoner, simpler term, they are treated thus:

clav•i•cle |**klăv′**ĭ kəl| *n.* A bone that connects the sternum and the scapula; the collarbone.

col•lar•bone |**kŏl′**ər bōn′| *n.* A bone that connects the breastbone and the shoulder blade; the clavicle.

In a few instances, alternate terms are both so firmly established as to be interchangeable. In such cases, they are treated as follows:

Neth•er•lands, the |**nĕ*th*′**ər ləndz|. A country in northwestern Europe, north of Belgium, on the North Sea. Population, 13,592,000. Constitutional capital, Amsterdam; de facto capital, The Hague. Also called *Holland.* **—Neth′er•land′er** *n.*

Pronunciation

Pronunciation is given for all main entries and for other forms as needed. It is indicated in vertical bars following the form to which it applies.

The set of symbols used is designed to enable the reader to reproduce a satisfactory pronunciation with no more than quick reference to the key. All pronunciations given are acceptable in all circumstances. When more than one is given, the first is assumed to be the most common, but the difference in frequency may be insignificant.

Americans do not all speak alike; nevertheless, they can understand one another, at least on the level of speech sounds. For most words a single set of symbols can represent the pronunciation found in each regional variety of American English, provided the symbols are planned for the purpose stated above: to enable the reader to reproduce a satisfactory pronunciation. When a single pronunciation is offered in this Dictionary, the reader will supply those features of his own regional speech that are called forth by his reading of the key. Apart from regional variations in pronunciation, there are variations among social groups. The pronunciations recorded in this Dictionary are exclusively those of educated speech. In every community, educated speech is accepted and understood by everyone, including those who do not themselves use it.

Pronunciation Key

A shorter form of this key appears at the bottom of each left-hand page.

Explanatory Notes

ə: This nonalphabetical symbol is called a *schwa.* The symbol is used in the Dictionary to represent a reduced vowel, that is, a vowel that receives the weakest level of stress (which can be thought of as no stress) within a word and that therefore nearly always has a different quality than it would if it were stressed, as in **telegraph** |**tĕl′**ə grăf′| and **telegraphy** |tə**lĕg′**rə fē|. Vowels are never reduced to a single exact vowel; the schwa sound varies, sometimes according to the "full" vowel it is representing and often according to the sounds surrounding it.

â: These symbols represent vowels that have
î been altered by a following *r.* This situation
û can be understood by considering the words
ər **Mary, merry,** and **marry.** In some regional varieties of American English, all three words are pronounced alike: |**mĕr′**ē|. However, in many individual American speech patterns, the three words are distinguished. It is this pattern that the Dictionary represents, thus: **Mary**

ă	pat	m	am, man, mum	v	cave, valve, vine
ā	aid, fey, pay	n	no, sudden	w	with
â	air, care, wear	ng	thing	y	yes
ä	father	ŏ	horrible, pot	yo͞o	abuse, use
b	bib	ō	go, hoarse, row, toe	z	rose, size, xylophone, zebra
ch	church	ô	alter, caught, for, paw	zh	garage, pleasure, vision
d	deed	oi	boy, noise, oil	ə	about, silent, pencil, lemon, circus
ĕ	pet, pleasure	ou	cow, out	ər	butter
ē	be, bee, easy, leisure	o͝o	took		**FOREIGN**
f	fast, fife, off, phase, rough	o͞o	boot, fruit	œ	*French* feu
g	gag	p	pop	ü	*French* tu
h	hat	r	roar	KH	*Scottish* loch
hw	which	s	miss, sauce, see	N	*French* bon
ĭ	pit	sh	dish, ship		**STRESS**
ī	by, guy, pie	t	tight		Primary stress ′
î	dear, deer, fierce, mere	th	path, thin		**bi·ol′o·gy** |bī ŏl′ə jē|
j	judge	*th*	bathe, this		Secondary stress ′
k	cat, kick, pique	ŭ	cut, rough		**bi′o·log′i·cal** |bī′ə lŏj′ĭ kəl|
l	lid, needle	û	circle, firm, heard, term, turn, urge, word		

|mâr′ē|, **merry** |mĕr′ē|, **marry** |măr′ē|. Some words are heard in all three pronunciations, indistinctly grading one into another. For these words the Dictionary represents only (â), for example, **care** |kâr|, **dairy** |dâr′ē|.

In words such as **hear, beer,** and **dear,** the vowel could be represented by (ē) were it not for the effect of the following *r*, which makes it approach (ĭ) in sound. In this Dictionary a special symbol (î) is used for this combination, as in **beer** |bîr|.

The symbol (û), used in **her** |hûr|, **fur** |fûr|, etc., has a regular regional variant that is not separately recorded. In one pattern the effect of the *r* is heard simultaneously with the vowel; in the other some, but not all, such syllables are heard with a vowel like (ŭ) or (ə) before the onset of the *r*.

ô: There are regional differences in the distinc-
ō tions among various pronunciations of the syllable *-or*. In pairs such as **for, four; horse, hoarse;** and **morning, mourning,** the vowel varies between (ô) and (ō). In this Dictionary these vowels are represented as follows: **for** |fôr|, **four** |fôr| *or* |fōr|; **horse** |hôrs|, **hoarse** |hôrs| *or* |hōrs|. Other words for which both forms are shown include those such as **more** |môr| *or* |mōr| and **glory** |glôr′ē| *or* |glōr′ē|.

ô: Another group of words with variation in the
ŏ pronunciation of the *-or* syllable includes words such as **forest** and **horrid,** in which the pronunciation of *o* before *r* varies between (ô) and (ŏ). In these words the |ôr| pronunciation is given first: **forest** |fôr′ĭst| *or* |fŏr′-|.

Syllabic Consonants

Two consonants are often represented as complete syllables. These are *l* and *n* (called *syllabics*) when they occur after stressed syllables ending in or followed by *d* or *t* in such words as **cradle** |krād′l|, **rattle** |răt′l|, **redden** |rĕd′n|, and **cotton** |kŏt′n|. Both syllabic *l* and syllabic *n* also occur following *-rt* and *-rd* in such words as **myrtle** |mûr′tl|, **hurdle** |hûr′dl|, **certain** |sûr′tn|, and **ardent** |är′dnt|. Syllabic *n* is not shown following *-nd* or *-nt,* as in **abandon** |ə băn′dən| and **mountain** |moun′tən|; but syllabic *l* is shown in that position: **candle** |kăn′dl|, **mantle** |măn′tl|.

Stress

In this Dictionary, stress, the relative degree of loudness with which the syllables of a word (or phrase) are spoken, is indicated in three different ways. An unmarked syllable has the weakest stress in the word. The strongest, or *primary,* stress is marked with a bold mark (′). The syllable that receives the primary stress is set in boldface type. An intermediate level of stress, here called *secondary,* is marked with a similar but lighter mark (′).

Words of one syllable show no stress mark, since there is no other stress level to which the syllable is compared.

Syllabication

The pronunciations are syllabicated for clarity. Syllabication of the pronunciation does not necessarily match the syllabication of the entry word being pronounced. The former follows strict, though not obvious, phonological rules; the latter represents the established practice of printers and editors.

Homophones

Homophones, words that are different in spelling but identical in pronunciation, are entered in this Dictionary as an aid to readers who know a word by sound but are not sure of the spelling. Homophones are listed in alphabetical order, the main-entry form preceding the others, at the end of the definition before all run-ons, preceded by the phrase *These sound alike;* they are entered only when the first pronunciations at the main entries are identical.

Homophones are not shown for regular inflected forms. Thus at **rode** we have

rode |rōd| . . . *These sound alike* **rode, road.**

But we do not include **rowed** in the list of homophones.

Proper nouns and foreign words are not entered as homophones.

Pictures

The pictures are set in the outside margin of each page. Each entry that is accompanied by a picture carries the reference [SEE PICTURE]. Many of the pictures are selected or adapted from *The*

American Heritage Dictionary of the English Language. About 1,000 were newly created or selected for this Dictionary. The individual picture credits are listed on pages v–vii.

Geographic and Biographical Entries

Geographic and biographical entries are included in the alphabetical listing of this Dictionary. These entries follow a special set of rules regarding style of presentation.

1. Identically spelled names of persons are combined, and subentries are arranged in chronological order:

> **Ad•ams** |ăd'əmz|. **1. Samuel.** 1722–1803. American Revolutionary patriot. **2. John.** 1735–1826. Second President of the United States (1797–1801). **3. John Quincy.** 1767–1848. Sixth President of the United States (1825–29); son of John Adams.

2. Names of persons and names of places that are spelled identically are never combined in a single entry:

> **Lin•coln** |lĭng'kən|. The capital of Nebraska. Population, 148,000.
> **Lin•coln** |lĭng'kən|, **Abraham.** 1809–1865. Sixteenth President of the United States (1861–65); assassinated.

3. Place names that are spelled identically are usually combined in a single entry. However, some of the rivers and states of the United States that would normally be combined are entered separately in order to show a boldface undefined word, called a *run-on,* that applies to the state only:

> **Ar•kan•sas¹** |är'kən sô'|. A Southern state of the United States. Population, 2,285,513. Capital, Little Rock. —**Ar•kan'san** |är kăn'zən| *adj.*
> **Ar•kan•sas²** |är'kən sô'| *or* |är kăn'zəs|. A river rising in Colorado and flowing generally southeast into the Mississippi River.

Notes

Interspersed with the pictures, and often filling what would otherwise be blank pages, is a variety of notes. Through these notes the lexicographer can address the reader directly on a great range of topics that are not strictly "lexical" and so do not fit into the format of dictionary entries.

Usage Notes

Two main resources are used for disputed topics: the American Heritage Usage Panel, consisting of over 100 writers and others known for their ability in using the English language (their names are listed in the front of *The American Heritage Dictionary of the English Language*), and the citations from school materials. These resources supply evidence about the state of educated opinion and educational practice on disputed questions of usage. Sometimes they confirm each other, sometimes they are at variance. Etymology is also often invoked to explain the origin of the trouble.

Style Guide

Punctuation

Apostrophe

1. Indicates the possessive case of nouns, proper nouns, and indefinite pronouns:

   her aunt's house
   Keats's "Ode to Psyche"
   someone's bright idea
   the workers' union

2. Indicates the plurals of figures, letters, or words used as such:

   42's and *53*'s — *x*'s, *y*'s, and *z*'s
   in the 1700's — too many *however*'s

3. Indicates the omission of letters in contractions:

   isn't — o'clock

4. Indicates the omission of figures:

   the class of '42

Brackets

1. Enclose words or passages in quotations to indicate the insertion of material written by someone else:

   And summer's lease [allotted time] hath all too short a date [duration]; . . .

2. Enclose material inserted within matter already in parentheses:

   (Washington [,D.C.], January, 1986)

Colon

1. Introduces words, phrases, or clauses that explain, amplify, exemplify, or summarize what has gone before:

   Suddenly I knew where we were: Paris.

   The lasting influence of Greece's dramatic tradition is indicated by words still in our vocabulary: *chorus, comedy,* and *drama.*

2. Introduces a long quotation:

   In his Gettysburg Address, Lincoln said: "Fourscore and seven years ago our fathers brought forth on this continent a new nation, conceived in liberty, and dedicated to the proposition that all men are created equal. . . ."

3. Introduces lists:

   Among the conjunctive adverbs are the following: *so, therefore, hence,* and *however.*

4. Separates chapter and verse numbers in references to Biblical quotations:

   Esther 2:17

5. Separates hour and minute in time:

   1:30 p.m.
   a 9:15 class

6. Follows the salutation in a formal letter:

   Dear Sir or Madam:
   Gentlemen:

Comma

1. Separates the clauses of a compound sentence connected by a coordinating conjunction:

   There is a difference between the musical works of Mozart and Haydn, and it is a difference worth discovering.

The comma may be omitted in short compound sentences in which the connection between the clauses is close:

I got in the car and I drove and drove.

2. Separates *and* or *or* from the final item in a series of three or more:

   Lights of red, green, and blue wavelengths may be mixed to produce all colors.

3. Separates two or more adjectives modifying the same noun if *and* could be used between them without changing the meaning:

   a stolid, heavy gait
   a polished mahogany desk

4. Sets off a nonrestrictive clause or phrase (one that if eliminated would not change the meaning of the sentence):

   The thief, who had entered through the window, went straight to the safe.

   The comma should not be used when the clause or phrase is restrictive (essential to the meaning of the sentence):

   The thief who had entered through the window went straight to the safe.

5. Sets off words or phrases in apposition to a noun or noun phrase:

   Plato, the Greek philosopher, was a pupil of Socrates'.

   The comma should not be used if such words or phrases further specify the noun that goes before:

   The Greek philosopher Plato was a pupil of Socrates'.

6. Sets off transitional words and short expressions that require a pause in reading:

   Did he, after all, look American?
   I live with my family, of course.
   Indeed, the sight of you gave me quite a jolt.

7. Sets off words used to introduce a sentence:

   Well, why don't you do as I ask?

8. Sets off a subordinate clause or a long phrase that precedes the principal clause:

   By the time they finally found the restaurant, they were no longer hungry.

9. Sets off short quotations, sayings, and the like:

   The candidate said, "Actions speak louder than words."

   "I don't know if I can," Lee said, "but maybe I will."

10. Indicates the omission of a word or words:

    To err is human; to forgive, divine.

11. Sets off the year from the month in dates:

    January 1, 1986, was New Year's Day.

12. Sets off the state from the city in geographic names:

    Boston, Massachusetts, is a big city.

13. Separates series of four or more figures into thousands, millions, etc.:

    57,395 12,364,903

    The comma is not used in dates or page numbers:

    the year 1986 page 1617

14. Sets off words used in direct address:

    The meeting is open to questions, ladies and gentlemen.

15. Separates a phrase that transforms a statement into a question:

    You did say you had the book, didn't you?

16. Sets off any sentence elements that might be misread if the comma were not used:

    Some time after, the actual date was set.
    Whenever possible, friends provide help.

17. Follows the salutation and complimentary close of informal letters and the complimentary close of formal letters:

    Dear Patsy,
    Sincerely,

Dash

1. Indicates a sudden break or abrupt change in continuity:

   Well, you see—I—I've—I'm just not sure.

   And then the problem—if it is a problem—can be solved.

2. Sets apart an explanatory or defining phrase:

   Foods high in protein—meat, fish, eggs, and cheese—should be part of the daily diet.

3. Sets apart parenthetical material:

   The pianist stares soulfully heavenward—to the great delight of the audience—while playing Chopin.

4. Marks an unfinished sentence:

   "But if the plane is late—" I began.

5. Sets off a summary phrase or clause:

   Noam Chomsky, Morris Halle, Roman Jakobson—these are among America's most prominent linguists.

6. Sets off the name of an author or a source, as at the end of a quotation:

   There never was a good war, or a bad peace.
   —*Benjamin Franklin*

Ellipses

1. Indicate the omission of words or sentences in quoted material:

   "Nor have we been wanting in Attentions to our British Brethren. . . . They too have been deaf to the Voice of Justice. . . ."

2. Indicate a pause in speech:

   "Yes . . . I mean . . . what have I done?" she stammered.

3. Indicate the omission of a line or lines of poetry:

   Come away, O human child!

   . . . .

   For the world's more full of weeping than
   you can understand.
   —*William Butler Yeats*

Exclamation Point

Indicates a command, strong emotion, or an emphatic phrase or sentence:

Go home immediately!
What a soccer game that was!
You can't be serious!
Bravo!
No!

Hyphen

1. At the end of a line, indicates that part of a word of more than one syllable has been carried over to the following line:

   Mark Twain, the very famous American author, wrote *Huckleberry Finn*.

2. Joins the elements of some compounds:

   great-grandparent   ne'er-do-well

3. Joins the elements of compound modifiers preceding a noun:

   built-in bookcases
   a happy-go-lucky fellow
   ten high-school students
   a two-thirds share

4. Indicates that two or more compounds share a single base:

   three- and four-volume sets of books

5. Separates the prefix and root in some combinations:

   anti-Communism, pro-American (prefix + proper noun or adjective)

   re-election, co-author (prefix ending with a vowel + root beginning with a vowel)

   re-form, reform; re-creation, recreation (to distinguish between similar words of different meanings)

6. Substitutes for the word *to* between two figures or words:

   pages 6-20
   the Boston-New York shuttle

Parentheses

1. Enclose material that is not an essential part of the sentence and that if not included would not alter its meaning:

   In an hour's time (some say less) the firefighters had extinguished the flames.

2. Often enclose letters or numerals to indicate subdivisions of a series:

   A movement in sonata form consists of the following sections: (a) the exposition; (b) the development; and (c) the recapitulation, which is often followed by a coda.

Period

1. Indicates the end of a complete declarative or mild imperative sentence:

   We attend a large school.
   Come home when you can.

2. Follows the abbreviation of a word or words:

Jan.	pp.
Jr.	Co.

Question Mark

1. Indicates the end of a direct question:

   What kind of work would you like to do?

   but

   I wonder who said "Speak softly and carry a big stick."
   I asked when they would leave.

2. Indicates uncertainty:

   Ferdinand Magellan (1480?–1521)

Quotation Marks

Double Quotation Marks

1. Enclose direct quotations:

   "What was Berlin like during the war?" she asked.

   "Gentlemen," the store manager said to the salespeople, "our first customer has arrived."

   According to one critic, the conductor was "readier to persuade than to dictate."

2. Enclose words or phrases to clarify their meaning or use, or to indicate that they are being used in a special way:

   "Dey" is a title that was formerly given to governors of Algiers.
   "The Big Apple," a name for New York City, is a phrase that was originated by jazz musicians.

3. Set off the translation of a foreign word or phrase:

   déjà vu, "already seen"

4. Set off the titles of series of books; of articles or chapters in publications; of essays; of short poems; of individual radio and television programs; and of songs and short musical pieces:

   "The Horizon Concise History" series
   "Some Notes on Case Grammar in English"
   Chapter 9, "Four in Freedom"
   Shelley's "Ode to the West Wind"
   "60 Minutes"
   Schubert's "Death and the Maiden"

Single Quotation Marks

Enclose quoted material within a quotation:

Mary said, "I heard the thief yell, 'Quick! Let's get out of here!' "

Use with Other Punctuation Marks

Put commas and periods *inside* closing quotation marks; put semicolons and colons *outside*. Other punctuation (question marks and exclamation points) should be put *inside* the closing quotation marks only when it is actually part of the matter being quoted.

Semicolon

1. Separates the clauses of a compound sentence having no coordinating conjunction:

   The questions are provided by the analyst; the answers come from the data.

2. Separates the clauses of a compound sentence in which the clauses contain internal punctuation, even when the clauses are joined by a conjunction:

   Picnic baskets in hand, we walked to the beach, chose a sunny spot, and spread out the blankets; and the rest of the group followed us in a station wagon.

3. Separates elements of a series in which items already contain commas:

   Among the guests were Katherine Ericson; her daughter, Alice; Henry Faulkner, formerly of the Redding Institute; and two couples whom I could not identify.

4. Separates clauses of a compound sentence joined by a conjunctive adverb (*nonetheless, therefore, hence,* etc.):

   We demanded a refund; otherwise we said we would get in touch with the Better Business Bureau.

Virgule (also called *slant* or *slash*)

1. Separates the numerator of a fraction from the denominator:

   4/5 9/10 2/3

2. Represents the word *per:*

   55 miles/hour

3. Means "or" between the words *and* and *or:*

   Take skates and/or skis when you visit the Adirondacks.

4. Separates two or more lines of poetry quoted in text:

   The actor had a memory lapse when he came to the lines "Why? all delights are vain, but that most vain / Which, with pain purchas'd, doth inherit pain," and had to improvise.

Capitalization

The following should be capitalized:

1. The first word of a sentence:

   Some diseases are acute; others are chronic.
   Aren't you my new neighbor?
   Great! Let's go!

2. The first word of each line in a poem:

   Poets that lasting marble seek
   Must carve in Latin or in Greek.
   —*Edmund Waller*

3. The first word of a direct quotation unless it is closely woven into the sentence:

   Helen asked, "Do you think Satie was a serious composer?"

   "For me," I answered, "he was simply amusing."

   G.B. Shaw said that "assassination is the extreme form of censorship."

4. The first word of the salutation and of the complimentary close of a letter:

   My dear Joyce,
   Sincerely yours,

5. All words except articles, prepositions, and conjunctions in the titles of books, articles, poems, plays, etc.:

   All Quiet on the Western Front
   "The Finiteness of Natural Language"
   "When the Lamp Is Shattered"
   Cat on a Hot Tin Roof

6. Proper nouns and adjectives:

   Bruno Walter Hegel, Hegelian

   Do not capitalize words derived from proper nouns and adjectives and having distinct special meanings:

   chinese red

7. The standard names of geographic divisions, districts, regions, and localities:

   the North Western Hemisphere
   the Midwest Manhattan

   Do not capitalize points of the compass unless referring to specific regions:

   Holyoke, Massachusetts, is eight miles north of Springfield. Turn east on Route 91.

8. The popular names of districts, regions, and localities:

   the Windy City the East Side

9. The names of rivers, lakes, mountains, oceans, etc.:

   Connecticut River Rocky Mountains

10. Names for a supreme or sacred being, and for the Bible and other sacred books:

    God the Messiah
    the Virgin Mary the Bible
    Allah the Koran
    Jehovah the Talmud

11. The names of religious denominations:

    Catholicism
    Judaism
    Buddhism
    the Roman Catholic Church
    Islam
    Protestantism

12. The names of historical periods, events, documents, etc.:

    the Middle Ages
    the Reformation
    the American Revolution
    World War II
    the Battle of Shiloh
    the Magna Carta

13. The names of political entities, divisions, parties, etc.:

the Byzantine Empire
Democrat
the Democratic Party
Republican
the Republican Party
the Populist movement

14. The names of legislative and judicial bodies:

the Senate
the House of Representatives
the United States Supreme Court
Parliament
Diet
Knesset

15. The names of departments, bureaus, etc., of the Federal government:

the Department of Agriculture

16. The names of treaties, acts, laws, etc.:

the Versailles Treaty
the Sherman Antitrust Law

17. Titles—civil, military, noble, honorable, etc.—when they precede a name:

Justice Frankfurter	Queen Elizabeth II
General MacArthur	Pope John Paul II
Mayor Neal	Professor Kittredge

But all references to the President and Vice President of the United States should be capitalized:

President Reagan	the President
Vice President Bush	the Vice President

18. Descriptive titles that accompany or are used instead of a person's name:

Ivan the Terrible   the Iron Chancellor

19. The names of peoples:

Portuguese   Spanish

20. The names of languages and of periods in the history of languages:

German   Old High German

21. The names of geological eras, periods, etc.:

the Paleozoic era   the Bronze Age

22. The names of the constellations, planets, and stars:

the Milky Way   Mars

23. Genus—but not species—names in binomial nomenclature:

Chrysanthemum leucanthemum

24. The names of holidays, holy days, months of the year, and days of the month:

Independence Day	Passover
January	Monday

25. Personifications:

I met Murder in the way— / He had a mask like Castlereagh.

—*Percy Bysshe Shelley*

26. Trademarks:

Xerox

27. The names of buildings, streets, parks, organizations, etc.:

the White House
Independence Avenue
National Education Association

Italics

1. Indicate titles of books, plays, and poems of book length:

For Whom the Bell Tolls
The Little Foxes
Paradise Lost

2. Indicate words, letters, or numbers used as such:

The word *buzz* sounds like what it stands for.
Can't often means *won't*.
She formed her *n*'s like *u*'s.
A *6* looks like an upside-down *9*.

3. Emphasize a word or phrase. This device should be used sparingly:

When you're quoted on the evening news, you have *arrived*.

4. Indicate foreign words and phrases that have not been assimilated into English:

his *Sturm und Drang* period

5. Indicate the names of the plaintiff and defendant in legal citations:

   Marbury v. *Madison*

6. Indicate the titles of long musical compositions:

   The Messiah
   Die Götterdämmerung
   Bartok's *Concerto for Orchestra*
   Elgar's *Enigma Variations*

7. Indicate the titles of magazines and newspapers:

   The New Yorker
   the New York *Daily News*
   The New York Times

8. Set off the titles of motion pictures and television series:

   Gone with the Wind   *Masterpiece Theater*

9. Distinguish the names of genera and species in scientific names:

   Homo sapiens

10. Set off the names of ships, planes, trains, and often spacecraft:

    U.S.S. *Kitty Hawk*
    The Spirit of St. Louis
    Voyager II or Voyager II

11. Set off the names of paintings and sculpture:

    Mona Lisa

Guide to the Parts of an Entry

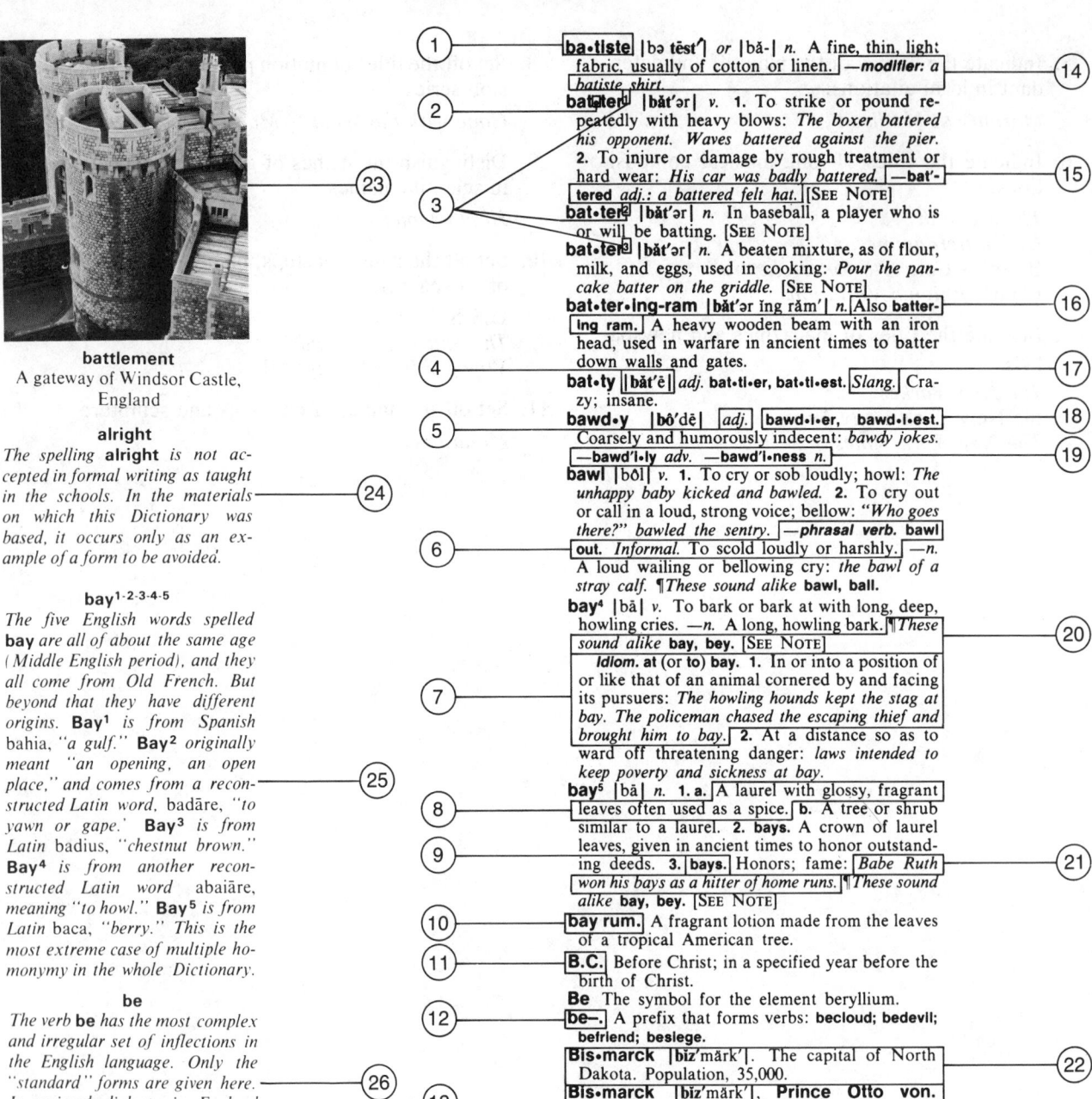

battlement
A gateway of Windsor Castle, England

alright
The spelling **alright** *is not accepted in formal writing as taught in the schools. In the materials on which this Dictionary was based, it occurs only as an example of a form to be avoided.*

bay[1-2-3-4-5]
The five English words spelled **bay** *are all of about the same age (Middle English period), and they all come from Old French. But beyond that they have different origins.* **Bay¹** *is from Spanish* bahía, *"a gulf."* **Bay²** *originally meant "an opening, an open place," and comes from a reconstructed Latin word,* badāre, *"to yawn or gape."* **Bay³** *is from Latin* badius, *"chestnut brown."* **Bay⁴** *is from another reconstructed Latin word* abaiāre, *meaning "to howl."* **Bay⁵** *is from Latin* baca, *"berry." This is the most extreme case of multiple homonymy in the whole Dictionary.*

be
The verb **be** *has the most complex and irregular set of inflections in the English language. Only the "standard" forms are given here. In regional dialects in England and America, there are many variants, such as* I been, you was, he be, *etc.*

ba•tiste |bə tēst′| *or* |bă-| *n.* A fine, thin, light fabric, usually of cotton or linen. *—**modifier:** a batiste shirt.*

bat•ter¹ |băt′ər| *v.* **1.** To strike or pound repeatedly with heavy blows: *The boxer battered his opponent. Waves battered against the pier.* **2.** To injure or damage by rough treatment or hard wear: *His car was badly battered.* —**bat′tered** *adj.: a battered felt hat.* [SEE NOTE]

bat•ter² |băt′ər| *n.* In baseball, a player who is or will be batting. [SEE NOTE]

bat•ter³ |băt′ər| *n.* A beaten mixture, as of flour, milk, and eggs, used in cooking: *Pour the pancake batter on the griddle.* [SEE NOTE]

bat•ter•ing-ram |băt′ər ĭng răm′| *n.* Also **battering ram.** A heavy wooden beam with an iron head, used in warfare in ancient times to batter down walls and gates.

bat•ty |băt′ē| *adj.* **bat•ti•er, bat•ti•est.** *Slang.* Crazy; insane.

bawd•y |bô′dē| *adj.* **bawd•i•er, bawd•i•est.** Coarsely and humorously indecent: *bawdy jokes.* —**bawd′i•ly** *adv.* —**bawd′i•ness** *n.*

bawl |bôl| *v.* **1.** To cry or sob loudly; howl: *The unhappy baby kicked and bawled.* **2.** To cry out or call in a loud, strong voice; bellow: *"Who goes there?" bawled the sentry.* —***phrasal verb.* bawl out.** *Informal.* To scold loudly or harshly. *—n.* A loud wailing or bellowing cry: *the bawl of a stray calf.* ¶*These sound alike* **bawl, ball.**

bay⁴ |bā| *v.* To bark or bark at with long, deep, howling cries. *—n.* A long, howling bark. ¶*These sound alike* **bay, bey.** [SEE NOTE]

***Idiom.* at** (or **to**) **bay. 1.** In or into a position of or like that of an animal cornered by and facing its pursuers: *The howling hounds kept the stag at bay. The policeman chased the escaping thief and brought him to bay.* **2.** At a distance so as to ward off threatening danger: *laws intended to keep poverty and sickness at bay.*

bay⁵ |bā| *n.* **1. a.** A laurel with glossy, fragrant leaves often used as a spice. **b.** A tree or shrub similar to a laurel. **2. bays.** A crown of laurel leaves, given in ancient times to honor outstanding deeds. **3. bays.** Honors; fame: *Babe Ruth won his bays as a hitter of home runs.* ¶*These sound alike* **bay, bey.** [SEE NOTE]

bay rum. A fragrant lotion made from the leaves of a tropical American tree.

B.C. Before Christ; in a specified year before the birth of Christ.

Be The symbol for the element beryllium.

be–. A prefix that forms verbs: **becloud; bedevil; befriend; besiege.**

Bis•marck |bĭz′märk′|. The capital of North Dakota. Population, 35,000.

Bis•marck |bĭz′märk′|, **Prince Otto von.** 1815–1898. German statesman.

1. Main entry
2. Syllable division
3. Homographs
4. Pronunciation
5. Part-of-speech label
6. Phrasal verb
7. Idiom
8. Definition
9. Boldface subentry
10. Compound entry
11. Abbreviation
12. Prefix
13. Biographical entry
14. Modifier
15. Definition by example
16. Variant
17. Usage label
18. Inflected forms
19. Run-on entries
20. Homophones
21. Example
22. Geographic entry
23. Picture
24. Usage note
25. Etymology
26. Additional information note

Aa

a, A |ā| *n., pl.* **a's** or **A's.** **1.** The first letter of the English alphabet. **2. A** The best or highest grade, as in school. **3. A** In music, the sixth tone in the scale of C major. [SEE NOTE]

a |ə| *or* |ā *when stressed*| *indefinite article.* Also before a vowel **an** |ăn| *or* |ən|. **1.** —Used as a determiner before a noun to make it stand for any individual in the class named by the word: *a dog; an apple.* It works in the same way with plural forms modified by *few, good many,* or *great many: a few dogs; a good many apples; a great many rules.* It is also placed before number collectives like *dozen, hundred,* etc.: *a dozen eggs; a hundred dollars.* **2.** —Used as an equivalent of other determiners: **a.** One: *I didn't say a word.* **b.** The same: *Birds of a feather flock together.* **c.** Any; each: *A mad dog must be destroyed.* **d.** A particular example of a (named class): *He's just a baby.* **e.** A kind of: *Root beer is a soft drink.* **3.** —Used as a preposition meaning "in each" or "per": *once a month.* [SEE NOTE]

a–[1]. A prefix meaning "not" or "without": **atypical.**

a–[2]. A prefix meaning "on," "in," or "to": **aboard, astern.** When it means "in the act of" or "on the way to," it is written with a hyphen: *a-fishing, a-singing.*

aard•vark |**ärd**'värk'| *n.* A burrowing African animal with large ears and a long snout. [SEE PICTURE]

Aar•on |âr'ən| *or* |ăr'-|. In the Bible, the first high priest of the Hebrews.

A.B. Bachelor of Arts (Latin *Artium Baccalaureus*).

ab•a•ci |ăb'ə sī| *n.* A plural of **abacus.**

a•back |ə **băk'**| *adv.* —**taken aback.** Surprised or stopped by something startling or disagreeable.

ab•a•cus |ăb'ə kəs| *n., pl.* **ab•a•cus•es** or **ab•a•ci** |ăb'ə sī|. A counting and computing device consisting of a frame holding parallel rods with sliding beads.

a•baft |ə **băft'**| *or* |ə **bäft'**| *adv.* At a ship's stern or from astern: *It was fast sailing with the wind abaft.* —*prep.* Toward the stern from: *The deck was rotten abaft the mainmast.*

ab•a•lo•ne |ăb'ə **lō'**nē| *n.* A soft-bodied, edible sea animal having a large, shallow shell with a brightly colored, iridescent lining.

a•ban•don |ə **băn'**dən| *v.* **1.** To leave and stop looking after (someone); desert: *abandon one's family.* **2.** To cease to use or occupy and leave behind: *abandon ship; abandon a disabled car; abandon one's farm and move to the city.* **3.** To give up; cease work on; stop trying to accomplish: *abandon an attempt; abandon a project.* **4.** To give up completely: *abandon all hope.* **5.** To yield (oneself) to an impulse or emotion: *abandon oneself to despair.* —*n.* An action, condition, or manner of relaxed or reckless carelessness: *played his mouth organ with gay abandon. The soldier rode with the skillful abandon of a cowboy.* —**a•ban'don•ment** *n.*

a•ban•doned |ə **băn'**dənd| *adj.* **1.** Deserted or given up; derelict: *an abandoned house; abandoned cars along the road.* **2.** Recklessly unrestrained: *an abandoned life of luxury.*

a•base |ə **bās'**| *v.* **a•based, a•bas•ing.** To lower in rank, dignity, or reputation; humble. —**a•base'ment** *n.*

a•bash |ə **băsh'**| *v.* To make ashamed or uneasy; embarrass; disconcert.

a•bate |ə **bāt'**| *v.* **a•bat•ed, a•bat•ing.** To make or become less in amount or intensity: *The horse turned the curve without abating his speed. The storm has abated.* —**a•bate'ment** *n.*

ab•at•toir |ăb'ə twär'| *n.* A slaughterhouse.

ab•bess |ăb'ĭs| *n.* A nun who is the head of a convent.

ab•bey |ăb'ē| *n., pl.* **ab•beys.** **1.** A monastery or convent. **2.** A church that once belonged to a monastery.

ab•bot |ăb'ət| *n.* A monk who is the head of a monastery.

ab•bre•vi•ate |ə **brē'**vē āt'| *v.* **ab•bre•vi•at•ed, ab•bre•vi•at•ing.** **1.** To reduce (a word or group of words) to a shorter form by leaving out some of the letters. **2.** To shorten: *abbreviate a novel.* [SEE NOTE at **abridge**]

ab•bre•vi•a•tion |ə brē'vē **ā'**shən| *n.* **1.** The act or process of abbreviating. **2.** A shortened form of a word or group of words, for example, *Mr.* for *Mister* and *U.S.A.* for *United States of America.*

ABC |ā'bē'**sē'**| *n., pl.* **ABC's.** **1.** Often **ABC's.** The alphabet: *learn one's ABC's.* **2.** The basic facts of a subject: *the ABC of chemistry.*

ab•di•cate |ăb'dĭ kāt'| *v.* **ab•di•cat•ed, ab•di•cat•ing.** To give up (power or responsibility) formally: *abdicate the throne. Queen Wilhelmina abdicated in 1948.* —**ab'di•ca'tion** *n.*

ab•do•men |ăb'də mən| *or* |ăb **dō'**-| *n.* **1.** In human beings and other mammals, the front part of the body from below the chest to about where the legs join, containing the stomach, intestines, and other organs of digestion. **2.** The hindmost division of the body of an insect.

ab•dom•i•nal |ăb **dŏm'**ə nəl| *adj.* Of the abdomen. —**ab•dom'i•nal•ly** *adv.*

ab•duct |ăb **dŭkt'**| *v.* To carry away by force; kidnap. —**ab•duc'tion** *n.*

1 2 3

The letter **A** *comes originally from the Phoenician* 'aleph *(1), which meant "ox." It was borrowed by the Greeks as* alpha *(2) and was given its present shape by the Romans (3).*

a

The indefinite article **a, an** *occurs about one third as often as the definite article* **the.** *In the five million words from which this Dictionary was made, there were about 125,000 occurrences of* **a** *and about 15,000 of* **an.**

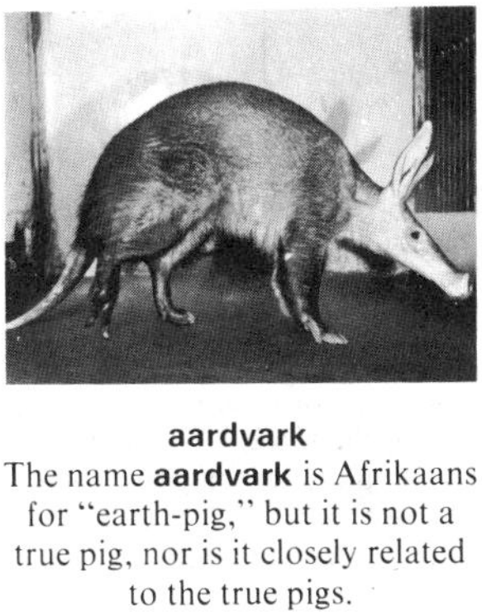

aardvark

The name **aardvark** is Afrikaans for "earth-pig," but it is not a true pig, nor is it closely related to the true pigs.

Aberdeen Angus bull

able/-able
The suffix **-able** *is not identical with the adjective* **able,** *although they both come from Latin and have come to have virtually the same meaning. The suffix is from the Latin verb-suffix* -ābilis, *meaning "capable of," while the adjective is from the Latin adjective* habilis, *meaning "manageable, apt, clever."*

abominable snowman
Even if the **abominable snowman** *exists, which has never been proved, his name is a mistake; it is based on a misunderstanding of the Tibetan for "man-bear." The alleged descriptions of him are outlandish but hardly "abominable."*

ab•duc•tor |ăb dŭk′tər| *n.* Someone who abducts; a kidnaper.

a•beam |ə bēm′| *adv.* Directly abreast of a ship's position: *The lifeboat was nearly abeam of us before we sighted it.*

a•bed |ə bĕd′| *adv.* In bed: *He lay abed.*

A•bel |ā′bəl|. In the Bible, the second son of Adam, murdered by his brother Cain.

Ab•er•deen An•gus |ăb′ər dēn′; ăng′gəs|. One of a breed of black, hornless cattle originally developed in Scotland and raised chiefly as a source of beef. [SEE PICTURE]

ab•er•rant |ăb ĕr′ənt| *or* |ə bĕr′-| *adj.* Differing from what is normal or typical: *aberrant behavior.*

ab•er•ra•tion |ăb′ə rā′shən| *n.* **1.** An act or condition of differing from what is normal or typical. **2.** A mental lapse or quirk. **3. a.** A fault or defect in an optical instrument, such as a mirror, lens, or telescope, that causes images formed by it to be blurred or distorted. **b.** The distortion or blurring of images resulting from this. See **chromatic aberration, spherical aberration. 4.** An apparent change in the position of a celestial object as the motion of the earth changes the position of the observer and the distance that the light from the object must travel to reach him.

a•bet |ə bĕt′| *v.* **a•bet•ted, a•bet•ting.** To encourage or aid, especially in doing something wrong: *The assassin was abetted by several accomplices.* **—a•bet′ment** *n.*

a•bet•tor |ə bĕt′ər| *n.* A person who encourages or aids someone else.

a•bey•ance |ə bā′əns| *n.* A postponement or temporary suspension: *hold a matter in abeyance until a later date.*

ab•hor |ăb hôr′| *v.* **ab•horred, ab•hor•ring.** To regard with horror or loathing: *abhor violence in all forms.*

ab•hor•rence |ăb hôr′əns| *or* |-hŏr′-| *n.* A feeling of horror or loathing: *an abhorrence of war.*

ab•hor•rent |ăb hôr′ənt| *or* |-hŏr′-| *adj.* Hateful; horrible: *abhorrent crimes.*

a•bide |ə bīd′| *v.* **a•bode** |ə bōd′| or **a•bid•ed, a•bid•ing. 1.** To remain; stay. **2.** To live; reside. **3.** To wait patiently for; await. **4.** To put up with; bear. **5. —abide by. a.** To live up to; fulfill: *abide by an agreement.* **b.** To agree to; submit to: *abide by a decision.*

a•bid•ing |ə bī′dĭng| *adj.* Long-lasting; permanent: *abiding love; abiding faith.*

Ab•i•djan |ăb′ĭ jän′|. The capital of the Ivory Coast. Population, 282,000.

a•bil•i•ty |ə bĭl′ĭ tē| *n., pl.* **a•bil•i•ties. 1.** The power to do something: *the ability to speak.* **2.** Talent; skill: *a person of great musical ability.*

ab•ject |ăb′jĕkt′| *or* |ăb jĕkt′| *adj.* **1.** Lacking all self-respect or resolve: *an abject coward; abject surrender.* **2.** Deeply hopeless and miserable: *abject poverty.* **—ab′ject′ly** *adv.*

ab•jure |ăb jo͝or′| *v.* **ab•jured, ab•jur•ing.** To vow to give up; repudiate: *abjure one's beliefs.*

a•blaze |ə blāz′| *adj.* **1.** On fire; in flames; blazing: *The tent was ablaze.* **2.** Radiant with bright color.

a•ble |ā′bəl| *adj.* **a•bler, a•blest. 1.** Having the power, ability, or means to do something: *He is able to work part-time.* **2.** Capable; talented: *He is an extremely able worker.* **—a′bly** *adv.* [SEE NOTE]

-able. A suffix used to form adjectives meaning: **1.** Capable or worthy of: *eatable; lovable.* **2.** Tending toward: *sizable.* [SEE NOTE]

a•ble-bod•ied |ā′bəl bŏd′ēd| *adj.* Physically strong and healthy.

able-bodied seaman. A merchant seaman certified for all seaman's duties.

a•bloom |ə blo͞om′| *adj.* In bloom; flowering.

ab•lu•tion |ə blo͞o′shən| *n.* A washing of the body, especially as part of a religious ceremony.

Ab•na•ki |ăb nä′kē| *n., pl.* **Ab•na•ki** or **Ab•na•kis. 1.** A North American Indian tribe of the northeastern United States and southern Quebec, Canada. **2.** A member of this tribe. **3.** The Algonquian language of this tribe.

ab•ne•ga•tion |ăb′nĭ gā′shən| *n.* Self-denial.

ab•nor•mal |ăb nôr′məl| *adj.* Not normal; unusual. **—ab•nor′mal•ly** *adv.*

ab•nor•mal•i•ty |ăb′nôr măl′ĭ tē| *n., pl.* **ab•nor•mal•i•ties. 1.** The condition of not being normal. **2.** Something that is not normal.

a•board |ə bôrd′| *or* |ə bōrd′| *adv.* On, onto, or inside a ship, train, etc.: *All aboard!* *—prep.* On, onto, or inside: *life aboard ship.*

a•bode¹ |ə bōd′|. A past tense and past participle of **abide.**

a•bode² |ə bōd′| *n.* The place where one lives; a home: *Mt. Olympus was the abode of the gods.*

a•bol•ish |ə bŏl′ĭsh| *v.* To put an end to: *The Thirteenth Amendment abolished slavery.*

ab•o•li•tion |ăb′ə lĭsh′ən| *n.* **1.** The act of abolishing. **2.** Often **Abolition.** The prohibition of slavery in the United States.

ab•o•li•tion•ist |ăb′ə lĭsh′ə nĭst| *n.* A person who favored the abolition of slavery in the United States.

A-bomb |ā′bŏm′| *n.* An **atomic bomb.**

a•bom•i•na•ble |ə bŏm′ə nə bəl| *adj.* **1.** Outrageously bad; atrocious: *an abominable crime.* **2.** Bad in general: *abominable weather; abominable handwriting.* **—a•bom′i•na•bly** *adv.*

abominable snowman. A large, hairy, manlike or apelike creature that supposedly lives on the snow-covered heights of the Himalaya Mountains. [SEE NOTE]

a•bom•i•nate |ə bŏm′ə nāt′| *v.* **a•bom•i•nat•ed, a•bom•i•nat•ing.** To regard as outrageously bad; detest.

a•bom•i•na•tion |ə bŏm′ə nā′shən| *n.* **1.** A feeling of outrage and disgust. **2.** Something that produces outrage and disgust.

ab•o•rig•i•nal |ăb′ə rĭj′ə nəl| *adj.* **1.** Of an aborigine or aborigines: *aboriginal customs.* **2.** Native; indigenous: *aboriginal peoples.*

ab•o•rig•i•ne |ăb′ə rĭj′ə nē| *n.* Any member of a group of people who are the first known to have lived in a given region.

a•bort |ə bôrt′| *v.* **1.** To give birth to offspring not developed enough to survive. **2.** To be born at a stage of development too early to allow survival: *The embryo aborted.* **3.** To end before completion: *The mission aborted. The pilot aborted the landing.*

a•bor•tion |ə bôr′shən| *n.* **1.** The birth of an embryo or fetus before it is developed enough to survive, especially when caused intentionally. **2.** Any abnormal end to growth or development,

ă pat/ā pay/â care/ä father/ĕ pet/ ē be/ĭ pit/ī pie/î fierce/ŏ pot/ ō go/ô paw, for/oi oil/o͝o book/ o͞o boot/ou out/ŭ cut/û fur/ *th* the/th thin/hw which/zh vision/ ə ago, item, pencil, atom, circus

as of an embryo or an organ. **3.** Anything that is incompletely or badly formed.

a•bor•tive |ə **bôr'**tĭv| *adj.* Not reaching full or complete development: *an abortive case of the flu; an abortive revolution.* —**a•bor'tive•ly** *adv.*

a•bound |ə **bound'**| *v.* **1.** To be rich (in); teem: *The area abounds in wildlife of every description.* **2.** To be abundant or plentiful: *Wildlife abounds in the region.*

a•bout |ə **bout'**| *prep.* **1.** Concerning: *stories about animals.* **2.** In the nature of: *something odd about his accent.* **3.** In connection with or in reference to: *what Indian rituals really were about.* **4.** In the matter of: *careful about handling broken glass.* **5.** Over or for: *crazy about cowboys.* **6. a.** On the point of. Followed by the infinitive with *to: about to go.* **b.** *Informal.* Anywhere near intending: *I'm not about to do anything he asks.* **7.** Near in time; close to: *about noon.* Also used adverbially: *about ready to start.* **8.** All around: *Look about you before dark for a good campsite.* Also used adverbially: *looking about for a hiding place.* **9.** Around in: *a bear prowling about the woods.* —*adv.* **1.** Approximately; roughly: *The hummingbird's egg is about the size of a pea.* **2.** To and fro: *Great waves tossed the ship about.* **3.** Around so as to face in the reverse direction: *Instantly the shark whipped about.* —*adj.* In circulation; astir: *School's closed, and there's no one about.*

Idiom. up and about. Out of bed and moving around.

a•bout-face |ə **bout'**fās'| *or* |ə **bout'fās'**| *n.* **1.** The act of pivoting the body to face in the opposite direction from the original in military marching drills. **2.** A change of attitude or standpoint to the opposite of an original one: *The candidate did an about-face in regard to that issue.*

a•bove |ə **bŭv'**| *adv.* **1.** In or to a higher place or position. **2.** In an earlier part of a text: *figures quoted above.* —*prep.* **1.** Over or higher than: *seagulls hovering just above the waves.* **2.** Upstream or uphill from: *The road is snowed in above this point.* **3.** Superior to in rank or quality: *The President is above all military officers.* **4.** In excess of; over: *Last week's spending was above normal.* —*adj.* Appearing or stated earlier: *the above figures.*

a•bove•board |ə **bŭv'**bôrd'| *or* |-bōrd'| *adv.* & *adj.* Without deceit or trickery; open; straightforward. [SEE NOTE]

ab•ra•ca•dab•ra |ăb'rə kə **dăb'**rə| *n.* A word once thought to have magical powers of healing.

a•brade |ə **brād'**| *v.* **a•brad•ed, a•brad•ing.** To rub off or wear away by friction.

A•bra•ham |ā'brə hăm'|. In the Bible, the first patriarch of the Hebrews.

a•bra•sion |ə **brā'**zhən| *n.* **1.** The act or process of abrading or rubbing away. **2.** An injury in which part of the skin has been scraped or rubbed away.

a•bra•sive |ə **brā'**sĭv| *or* |-zĭv| *adj.* **1.** Hard enough to be used in rubbing away or polishing other materials. **2.** Causing friction or resentment in people: *an abrasive personality.* —*n.* An abrasive substance used in rubbing or polishing.

a•breast |ə **brĕst'**| *adv.* & *adj.* **1.** Standing or advancing side by side: *They lined up four abreast.* **2.** On a par with; up to date with: *keeping abreast of the latest fashions.*

a•bridge |ə **brĭj'**| *v.* **a•bridged, a•bridg•ing.** **1.** To reduce the length of; condense: *abridge a novel.* **2.** To limit; curtail: *"The right of citizens of the United States to vote shall not be denied or abridged...on account of sex."* (U.S. Constitution, 19th Amendment). —**a•bridged'** *adj.*: *an abridged version of a novel.* [SEE NOTE]

a•bridg•ment, also **a•bridge•ment** |ə **brĭj'**mənt| *n.* **1.** The act of abridging or the condition of being abridged. **2.** An abridged version of a book, article, etc.

a•broad |ə **brôd'**| *adv.* & *adj.* **1.** In or to foreign places: *going abroad.* **2.** Broadly or widely: *scattering seeds abroad.* **3.** Outdoors and about: *There were people abroad in spite of the downpour.* **4.** In circulation: *There's a nasty rumor abroad.*

ab•ro•gate |**ăb'**rə gāt'| *v.* **ab•ro•gat•ed, ab•ro•gat•ing.** To annul (a law, privileges, etc.); abolish: *abrogate a treaty.* —**ab'ro•ga'tion** *n.*

a•brupt |ə **brŭpt'**| *adj.* **1.** Unexpected; sudden: *an abrupt change.* **2.** Very steep: *an abrupt cliff.* **3.** Short and brief so as to suggest rudeness, displeasure, etc.; brusque: *an abrupt answer.* —**a•brupt'ly** *adv.* —**a•brupt'ness** *n.*

ab•scess |**ăb'**sĕs'| *n.* A mass of pus that forms and collects at one place in the body. —*v.* To form an abscess. —**ab'scessed'** *adj.*: *an abscessed tooth.*

ab•scis•sa |ăb **sĭs'**ə| *n., pl.* **ab•scis•sas** or **ab•scis•sae** |-**sĭs'**ē'|. In a system of plane Cartesian coordinates, the first coordinate, that is, the number that is the measure of the distance, measured parallel to the *x*-axis between a point and the *y*-axis.

ab•scond |ăb **skŏnd'**| *v.* To leave quickly and secretly and hide oneself, especially to avoid arrest: *The cashier had absconded with the money.*

ab•sence |**ăb'**səns| *n.* **1.** The state of being away: *take over the troop in the officer's absence.* **2.** The period during which one is away: *an absence of four days.* **3.** A lack: *an absence of reliable information.*

ab•sent |**ăb'**sənt| *adj.* **1.** Not present; not on hand: *Two pupils are absent today.* **2.** Lacking; missing: *Scales are absent in eels.* **3.** Not paying attention; absorbed in thought: *an absent look on his face.* —*v.* |ăb **sĕnt'**|. To keep (oneself) away: *absent oneself from work.*

ab•sen•tee |ăb'sən **tē'**| *n.* A person who is absent, as from work. —***modifier:*** *an absentee landlord; an absentee ballot.*

ab•sen•tee•ism |ăb'sən **tē'**ĭz'əm| *n.* Habitual failure to appear, especially for work or other regular duty.

ab•sent•ly |**ăb'**sənt lē| *adv.* As if lost in thought: *stared absently at the wall.*

ab•sent-mind•ed |**ăb'**sənt **mīn'**dĭd| *adj.* Tending to be lost in thought and to forget what one is doing. —**ab'sent-mind'ed•ly** *adv.* —**ab'sent-mind'ed•ness** *n.*

ab•sinthe |**ăb'**sĭnth| *n.* A strong green alcoholic liquor flavored with wormwood.

ab•so•lute |**ăb'**sə lo͞ot'| *adj.* **1.** Complete; total: *absolute silence.* **2.** Not limited in any way: *absolute monarchy; absolute freedom.* **3.** Without reservation; unqualified: *He has my absolute confidence.*

aboveboard

Dr. Johnson in his Dictionary *(1755) has a useful note at this word: "A figurative expression, borrowed from gamesters [gamblers], who, when they put their hands under the table, are changing their cards."*

abridge

Abridge *is not connected with bridges. It comes from Old French* abregier, *which is from Latin* abbreviāre, *"to shorten":* ad, *"toward,"* + brevis, *"short."* Abbreviāre *was later separately borrowed directly into English as* **abbreviate,** *which is thus a doublet of* **abridge.**

absolute pitch

Absolute pitch, *the ability to remember the pitches of musical tones for very long periods, is fairly rare. It is found most often among people who have some musical ability, but it is not necessarily a sign of talent. While it appears to be inborn in some individuals, there is evidence that it can be acquired through training. It is valuable to a musician, but it can be a nuisance, as it is, for example, when a piano or organ tuned to a nonstandard pitch must be used.*

abstemious

Abstemious *is a remarkable word in that it contains all of the five vowels in their correct alphabetical order.*

ă pat/ā pay/â care/ä father/ĕ pet/ ē be/ĭ pit/ī pie/î fierce/ŏ pot/ ō go/ô paw, for/oi oil/ŏŏ book/ ōō boot/ou out/ŭ cut/û fur/ *th* the/th thin/hw which/zh vision/ ə ago, item, pencil, atom, circus

absolute ceiling. The greatest altitude at which an aircraft or missile can normally maintain level flight.

absolute humidity. The weight of water vapor contained in a unit volume of air.

ab•so•lute•ly |ăb′sə **lōōt′**lē | *or* |**ăb′**sə lōōt′- | *adv.* **1.** Completely; perfectly: *absolutely essential; absolutely certain; stand absolutely still.* **2.** Without reservation or qualification; positively: *do absolutely nothing; get absolutely nowhere; absolutely refuse to answer.*

absolute magnitude. The magnitude that a given star would have if it were seen from a distance of 10 parsecs or 32.6 light-years.

absolute music. Instrumental music that has no express connection or association with ideas outside of music. See **program music.**

absolute pitch. 1. The precise pitch of a tone as established by its frequency. **2.** The ability to remember the pitches of tones precisely and reliably. [SEE NOTE]

absolute temperature. Temperature measured with absolute zero used as the reference.

absolute value. A number or its opposite, whichever is not negative. For example, | + 3 | = +3 and | -3 | = +3, | 0 | = 0.

absolute zero. The temperature at which any material substance contains the least possible amount of heat energy. This temperature is -273.15°C or -459.67°F.

ab•so•lu•tion |ăb′sə **lōō′**shən | *n.* A formal release from sin; forgiveness.

ab•so•lu•tism |**ăb′**sə lōō tĭz′əm | *n.* A form of government in which the monarch rules with unlimited power.

ab•so•lu•tist |**ăb′**sə lōō′tĭst | *n.* Someone who advocates absolutism. —*adj.* Founded on absolutism: *absolutist governments.*

ab•solve |ăb **zŏlv′** | *or* |**-sŏlv′** | *v.* **ab•solved, ab•solv•ing. 1.** To clear of blame of guilt. **2.** To grant formal forgiveness to for sins committed. **3.** To release, as from a promise or an obligation. —**ab•solv′a•ble** *adj.* —**ab•solv′er** *n.*

ab•sorb |ăb **sôrb′** | *or* |**-zôrb′** | *v.* **1.** To take in; soak up: *A sponge absorbs moisture.* **2.** To take in and assimilate: *Plants absorb energy from the sun.* **3.** To take in or receive (a pulse or flow of energy) with little or none of it being transmitted or reflected: *Thick rugs absorb sound.* **4.** To receive or withstand with little effect or reaction: *able to absorb great punishment.* **5.** To occupy the full attention of: *completely absorbed by his work.* **6.** To occupy completely; take up entirely: *The work absorbs all of my time.* **7.** To assume the burden of: *absorb the extra costs.*

ab•sorb•ent |ăb **sôr′**bənt | *or* |**-zôr′-** | *adj.* Capable of absorbing: *absorbent cotton.* —*n.* A substance that is capable of absorbing.

ab•sorb•ing |ăb **sôr′**bĭng | *or* |**-zôr′-** | *adj.* Holding one's interest or attention; engrossing: *an absorbing novel; an absorbing game.*

ab•sorp•tion |ăb **sôrp′**shən | *or* |**-zôrp′-** | *n.* **1.** The act or process of absorbing. **2.** Mental concentration.

absorption spectrum. A spectrum consisting of a series of dark lines and bands, produced when light or other radiation passes through a medium that absorbs part of it and lets the rest pass.

ab•stain |ăb **stān′** | *v.* To keep from doing something voluntarily; refrain: *He abstains from eating candy.* —**ab•stain′er** *n.*

ab•ste•mi•ous |ăb **stē′**mē əs | *adj.* Sparing, especially in the use of alcohol or food. —**ab•ste′mi•ous•ly** *adv.* [SEE NOTE]

ab•sten•tion |ăb **stĕn′**shən | *n.* **1.** The practice of abstaining. **2.** An act of abstaining, especially the withholding of a vote at an election: *one vote for, two against, and four abstentions.*

ab•sti•nence |**ăb′**stə nəns | *n.* A refraining from drinking alcoholic beverages, from eating certain foods, etc. —**ab′sti•nent** *adj.*

ab•stract |**ăb′**străkt′ | *or* |ăb **străkt′** | *adj.* **1.** Theoretical rather than practical: *an abstract approach to the problem.* **2.** Difficult to understand: *Your explanation is too abstract for me.* **3.** Expressing a general quality or property thought of separately from the person or thing possessing it: *abstract words like "truth" and "justice."* **4.** In art, concerned with designs or shapes that do not represent any recognizable person or thing: *an abstract painting; an abstract sculpture.* —*n.* |**ăb′**străkt′|. A brief summary of the main points of a text: *an abstract of a speech.* —*v.* |ăb **străkt′**|. **1.** To make a summary of: *It was not easy to abstract his article.* **2.** To separate; remove: *processes to abstract metal from ore.* —**ab•stract′ly** *adv.* —**ab•stract′ness** *n.*

ab•stract•ed |ăb **străk′**tĭd | *adj.* Lost or deep in thought; absent-minded: *an abstracted look on her face.* —**ab•stract′ed•ly** *adv.*

ab•strac•tion |ăb **străk′**shən | *n.* **1.** The act or process of separating or removing: *the abstraction of metal from ore.* **2.** An abstract idea: *abstractions hard to understand.* **3.** Absent-mindedness: *In his abstraction, he didn't say hello.*

ab•strac•tion•ism |ăb **străk′**shə nĭz′əm | *n.* A style in modern art that is primarily concerned with designs and shapes that do not represent any recognizable person or thing.

ab•struse |ăb **strōōs′** | *adj.* Difficult to understand: *abstruse works of philosophy.* —**ab•struse′ly** *adv.* —**ab•struse′ness** *n.*

ab•surd |ăb **sûrd′** | *or* |**-zûrd′** | *adj.* Contrary to common sense; ridiculous: *an absurd suggestion.* —**ab•surd′ly** *adv.*

ab•surd•i•ty |ăb **sûr′**dĭ tē | *or* |**-zûr′-** | *n., pl.* **ab•surd•i•ties. 1.** The state of being absurd; foolishness. **2.** An absurd action, thing, or idea.

A•bu Dha•bi |ä′bōō **dä′**bē|. The capital of the United Arab Emirates. Population, 347,000.

a•bun•dance |ə **bŭn′**dəns | *n.* A great amount or quantity; a plentiful supply: *an abundance of natural resources.*

a•bun•dant |ə **bŭn′**dənt | *adj.* **1.** Existing in great supply; very plentiful: *abundant rainfall.* **2.** Rich; abounding: *a forest abundant in trees.* —**a•bun′dant•ly** *adv.*

a•buse |ə **byōōz′** | *v.* **a•bused, a•bus•ing. 1.** To use improperly; misuse: *The barons abused their privileges.* **2.** To hurt or injure by treating badly; mistreat: *Dickens abused his eyesight by reading in poor light.* **3.** To attack or injure with words; revile. —*n.* |ə **byōōs′**|. **1.** Improper use; misuse: *the abuse of power.* **2.** Mistreatment. **3.** A corrupt practice or custom: *an attempt to correct governmental abuses.* **4.** Insulting language: *take a lot of abuse.*

a•bu•sive |ə byōō'sĭv| *adj.* Containing coarse and insulting language: *abusive remarks.* —**a•bu'sive•ly** *adv.* —**a•bu'sive•ness** *n.*

a•but |ə bŭt'| *v.* **a•but•ted, a•but•ting.** To touch at one end or side; border: *My house abuts on his property.*

a•but•ment |ə bŭt'mənt| *n.* **1.** A structure that supports the end of a bridge, arch, beam, or other similar span. **2.** A structure that anchors the cables of a suspension bridge.

a•bys•mal |ə bĭz'məl| *adj.* Very low in level or quality; deeply inferior: *abysmal ignorance.*

a•byss |ə bĭs'| *n.* **1.** A very deep and large hole: *into the abyss of the volcano.* **2.** A huge emptiness: *through the abyss of outer space.*

ac, a.c., AC, A.C. alternating current.

Ac The symbol for the element actinium.

a•ca•cia |ə kā'shə| *n.* Any of several mostly tropical trees with feathery leaves and clusters of small, usually yellow flowers.

ac•a•dem•ic |ăk'ə dĕm'ĭk| *adj.* **1.** Of a school or college: *an academic degree.* **2.** Relating to studies that are liberal or classical rather than technical or vocational. **3.** Valid in theory but irrelevant in practice: *That is an academic point.* —**ac'a•dem'i•cal•ly** *adv.*

a•cad•e•mi•cian |ə kăd'ə mĭsh'ən| *or* |ăk'ə də-| *n.* A member of an academy or society of learned men, artists, etc.

a•cad•e•my |ə kăd'ə mē| *n., pl.* **a•cad•e•mies.** **1.** A school for a special field of study: *a naval academy.* **2.** A private secondary school. **3.** A society of learned men formed to promote high standards in art, literature, or science.

A•ca•di•a |ə kā'dē ə|. A former French colony of eastern Canada. —**A•ca'di•an** *adj. & n.*

a•can•thus |ə kăn'thəs| *n., pl.* **a•can•thus•es.** **1.** A plant of the Mediterranean region with large, thistlelike leaves. **2.** Decoration in the form of such leaves, as the carving on the capital of a Corinthian column. [SEE PICTURE]

a cap•pel•la |ä'kə pĕl'ə|. In music, without instrumental accompaniment: *an a cappella chorus. The duet was sung a cappella.*

A•ca•pul•co |ăk'ə pōōl'kō|. A resort city of Mexico, on the Pacific. Population, 50,000.

ac•cede |ăk sēd'| *v.* **ac•ced•ed, ac•ced•ing.** **1.** To consent; agree; yield: *I acceded to her request.* **2.** To come or succeed to a public office or position: *He acceded to the presidency.*

ac•cel•er•an•do |ăk sĕl'ə răn'dō|. In music: *adj.* Gradually becoming faster. —*adv.* So as to become faster. —*n., pl.* **ac•cel•er•an•dos.** A gradual speeding up.

ac•cel•er•ate |ăk sĕl'ə rāt'| *v.* **ac•cel•er•at•ed, ac•cel•er•at•ing.** **1.** To increase in speed; speed up; quicken. **2.** In physics, to undergo or cause to undergo a change in velocity. **3.** To cause to happen earlier; hasten: *measures to accelerate a tax reform.*

ac•cel•er•a•tion |ăk sĕl'ə rā'shən| *n.* **1.** The act or process of accelerating; an increase in speed. **2.** The rate at which velocity changes per unit of time. [SEE NOTE]

ac•cel•er•a•tor |ăk sĕl'ə rā'tər| *n.* **1.** A control that increases the speed of a machine when it is applied, especially the pedal that increases the flow of fuel to an automotive engine. **2.** A substance that speeds up a chemical reaction. **3.** Any of various devices that accelerate atomic particles or nuclei to high energies for use in research in nuclear physics.

ac•cel•er•om•e•ter |ăk sĕl'ə rŏm'ĭ tər| *n.* An instrument that measures and indicates acceleration, often used in aircraft and spacecraft.

ac•cent |ăk'sĕnt'| *n.* **1.** The stress placed on a particular syllable of a word. **2.** An **accent mark.** **3.** A style of speech or pronunciation that is typical of a certain region or country: *She speaks with a French accent.* **4. a.** A special stress given to a musical note within a measure or phrase. **b.** A mark indicating that this is to be done. —*v.* **1.** To stress in speech or in music: *accent the first syllable of a word; accent every third note.* **2.** To place an accent mark over. **3.** To give emphasis or prominence to.

accent mark. **1.** A mark used to indicate which syllable of a word is stressed in pronunciation. **2.** In certain foreign languages, and in English words borrowed from such languages, a mark placed over a letter to indicate a certain feature of pronunciation. For example, in the word "exposé" the final "e" is pronounced /ā/.

ac•cen•tu•ate |ăk sĕn'chōō āt'| *v.* **ac•cen•tu•at•ed, ac•cen•tu•at•ing.** **1.** To mark or pronounce with an accent. **2.** To give prominence to; emphasize; point up.

ac•cept |ăk sĕpt'| *v.* **1.** To take (something offered): *going to Sweden to accept the award.* **2.** To say yes to: *I accept your invitation.* **3.** To agree to: *accept a proposal.* **4.** To regard as true; believe in: *Einstein's friends hotly refused to accept his theory.* **5.** To reconcile oneself to; tolerate: *Win or lose, accept the outcome graciously.* **6.** To receive with favor into a place or group: *They've begun to accept him at school.* **7.** To take up; assume: *You must accept the responsibility of obeying traffic laws.*

ac•cept•a•ble |ăk sĕp'tə bəl| *adj.* **1.** Fitting; suitable: *an acceptable man for the job.* **2.** Proper; correct: *an acceptable pronunciation.* **3.** Welcome; agreeable: *acceptable working conditions; an acceptable meal.* —**ac•cept'a•bil'i•ty** *n.* —**ac•cept'a•bly** *adv.*

ac•cept•ance |ăk sĕp'təns| *n.* **1.** The act of taking something offered: *the acceptance of a bribe.* **2.** The condition of being accepted: *Many prejudiced peole feel insecure about their acceptance by others.* **3.** Favorable reception; approval: *Despite its critics, the theory slowly gained acceptance.*

ac•cess |ăk'sĕs'| *n.* **1.** The act of entering; entrance: *gain access through the basement.* **2.** Means or permission to enter, reach, or use: *have access to secret information.* **3.** Way of approaching or reaching: *a city with easy access to the sea.* **4.** A sudden outburst; a fit: *an access of rage.*

access code A special code that allows access to information or data that has been stored in a computer.

ac•ces•si•ble |ăk sĕs'ə bəl| *adj.* Easy to reach, approach, or obtain: *The lake is easily accessible from the highway. These documents are accessible to all staff members.* —**ac•ces'si•bil'i•ty** *n.* —**ac•ces'si•bly** *adv.*

ac•ces•sion |ăk sĕsh'ən| *n.* The act of coming to power or high office: *the king's accession to the throne.*

acanthus
Above: Leaf and flowers of the plant
Below: Capital of a Corinthian column with acanthus-leaf decoration

acceleration

As velocity is defined in units of distance per unit of time (velocity = distance / time), and acceleration is defined in units of velocity per unit of time (acceleration = velocity / time), we can say that acceleration = distance / time / time, or distance / time². Therefore acceleration is expressed as "miles per hour per second" (mi./hr./sec.), or "feet per second per second" (ft./sec.²), or in some similar form.

ac•ces•so•ry |ăk sĕs′ə rē| *n., pl.* **ac•ces•so•ries.** **1.** An extra that goes with and adds to the overall effect of something, as a scarf, hat, or pin worn with a dress. **2.** Someone who aids a lawbreaker but who is not present at the time of the crime. Someone who aids a criminal before a crime is committed is called an **accessory before the fact,** and someone who aids him after a crime is committed is an **accessory after the fact.** —*adj.* Supplementing something more important.

ac•ci•dent |ăk′sĭ dənt| *n.* **1.** Something that happens without being planned in advance: *Our meeting was an accident.* **2.** An unexpected and undesirable event; mishap: *a traffic accident.* **3.** Chance or coincidence: *I met him by accident.*

ac•ci•den•tal |ăk′sĭ dĕn′tl| *adj.* Happening without being expected or intended: *the accidental discovery of diamonds in South Africa.* —*n.* In music, a sharp, flat, or natural that is not in the key signature. —**ac′ci•den′tal•ly** *adv.*

ac•ci•dent-prone |ăk′sĭ dənt prōn′| *adj.* Tending to have accidents.

ac•claim |ə klām′| *v.* To greet with loud approval; praise; applaud: *His new novel has been acclaimed by all the critics.* —*n.* Loud or enthusiastic praise, applause, or approval.

ac•cla•ma•tion |ăk′lə mā′shən| *n.* **1.** Enthusiastic praise or applause; acclaim. **2.** An enthusiastic oral vote of approval taken without making an actual count: *The motion was approved by acclamation.* ¶ *These sound alike* **acclamation, acclimation.**

ac•cli•mate |ə klī′mĭt| *or* |ăk′lə māt′| *v.* **ac•cli•mat•ed, ac•cli•mat•ing.** To adapt or become adapted to new conditions: *Certain animals acclimate quickly to city life. The keepers acclimated the animals to the zoo.*

ac•cli•ma•tion |ăk′lə mā′shən| *n.* The process of acclimating or condition of being acclimated. ¶ *These sound alike* **acclimation, acclamation.**

ac•cli•ma•tize |ə klī′mə tīz′| *v.* **ac•cli•ma•tized, ac•cli•ma•tiz•ing.** To acclimate. —**ac•cli′ma•ti•za′tion** *n.*

ac•co•lade |ăk′ə lād′| *or* |ăk′ə läd′| *n.* **1.** Praise; acclaim: *the accolades of the critics.* **2.** A ceremonial tap on the shoulder with the flat of a sword, given when knighthood is granted. [SEE PICTURE]

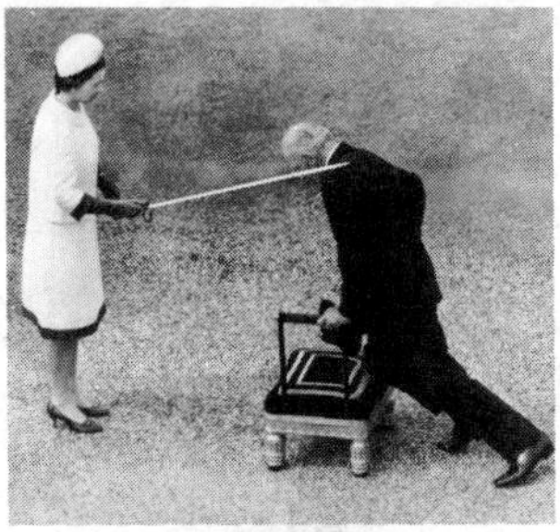

accolade
Queen Elizabeth II giving the accolade to Francis Chichester in 1967, in honor of his single-handed circumnavigation of the globe

ac•com•mo•date |ə kŏm′ə dāt′| *v.* **ac•com•mo•dat•ed, ac•com•mo•dat•ing.** **1.** To do (someone) a favor; oblige; help: *I shall try to accommodate you in this matter.* **2.** To provide with lodging or living space. **3.** To have room for; hold: *an airport built to accommodate the largest planes.* **4.** To become adjusted, as the eyes do in focusing on objects at differing distances.

ac•com•mo•dat•ing |ə kŏm′ə dā′tĭng| *adj.* Helpful and obliging.

ac•com•mo•da•tion |ə kŏm′ə dā′shən| *n.* **1.** The act of accommodating. **2.** A favor: *He did it for me as an accommodation.* **3.** An agreement or compromise: *reach a satisfactory accommodation.* **4.** Often **accommodations. a.** Room and board; lodging: *We requested accommodations for two nights.* **b.** Seats on a train, airplane, etc. **5.** Adaptation or adjustment by an organism or organ, as by the eyes in focusing on objects at differing distances.

ac•com•pa•ni•ment |ə kŭm′pə nĭ mənt| *or* |ə kŭmp′nĭ-| *n.* **1.** Anything that goes along with or supplements something else: *Crisp croutons are a good accompaniment to soups.* **2.** Music played along with a solo part or a number of principal parts as support or embellishment. **3.** Music to be performed along with another presentation, such as a dance.

ac•com•pa•nist |ə kŭm′pə nĭst| *or* |ə kŭmp′nĭst| *n.* A musician who performs an accompaniment.

ac•com•pa•ny |ə kŭm′pə nē| *v.* **ac•com•pa•nied, ac•com•pa•ny•ing, ac•com•pa•nies.** **1.** To go along with: *I accompanied Mother when she went shopping.* **2.** To occur or happen with: *Thunder accompanies lightning.* **3.** To supplement: *The teacher accompanied the lesson with slides.* **4.** To support (a singer, musician, etc.) by playing an accompaniment: *Can you accompany this song? Janet sang, and Paul accompanied.*

ac•com•plice |ə kŏm′plĭs| *n.* Someone who aids a lawbreaker in a crime but is not necessarily present at the time of the crime.

ac•com•plish |ə kŏm′plĭsh| *v.* To carry out; achieve; complete: *accomplish an assignment.*

ac•com•plished |ə kŏm′plĭsht| *adj.* **1.** Completed; finished: *an accomplished mission.* **2.** Skilled; expert: *an accomplished musician; an accomplished hostess.*

ac•com•plish•ment |ə kŏm′plĭsh mənt| *n.* **1.** The act of carrying out; completion: *the accomplishment of a task.* **2.** Something accomplished; an achievement: *He is proud of his accomplishments.* **3.** An acquired skill: *Singing is one of her many accomplishments.*

ac•cord |ə kôrd′| *v.* **1.** To give; grant: *Citizens are accorded certain rights.* **2.** To be in agreement or harmony: *His ideas accord with mine.* —*n.* **1.** Agreement; harmony: *His ideas are in accord with mine.* **2.** A settlement, as between conflicting wishes: *The strikers and the employers reached an accord.*

Idiom. **of (one's) own accord.** By oneself; without assistance or outside influence: *She made this decision of her own accord. The balloon came down of its own accord.*

ac•cor•dance |ə kôr′dns| *n.* —**in accordance with.** In agreement with; in keeping with: *act in accordance with the rules.*

ac•cord•ing•ly |ə kôr′dĭng lē| *adv.* **1.** In keeping with what is known, stated, or expected: *Learn the rules and act accordingly.* **2.** Therefore; consequently.

according to. **1.** As stated or indicated by; on the authority of: *according to historians; according to statistics.* **2.** In keeping with; in agreement with: *Proceed according to instructions.* **3.** As determined by: *a list arranged according to the first letter of each word.* **4.** In proportion to: *Clothing is sized according to body measurements.*

ac•cor•di•on |ə kôr′dē ən| *n.* A musical instrument consisting of a hand-held reed organ in which the player creates a supply of air by operating a pleated bellows contained in the instrument itself.

ac•cost |ə kôst′| *or* |ə kŏst′| *v.* To come up to and speak to: *A stranger accosted me in the street.*

ac•count |ə kount′| *n.* **1.** A written or spoken description of events; a narrative: *an exciting account of his adventures.* **2.** A set of reasons;

ă pat/ā pay/â care/ä father/ĕ pet/ ē be/ĭ pit/ī pie/î fierce/ŏ pot/ ō go/ô paw, for/oi oil/ŏŏ book/ ōō boot/ou out/ŭ cut/û fur/ *th* the/th thin/hw which/zh vision/ ə ago, item, pencil, atom, circus

explanation: *Give an account for your strange behavior.* **3.** Often **accounts.** A record or written statement, especially of business dealings or money received or spent. **4.** A business arrangement, as with a bank or store, in which money is kept, exchanged, or owed: *a savings account; a charge account.* **5.** Importance; standing; worth: *a man of little account.* —*v.* To consider; regard: *I account myself well paid for my trouble.* —***phrasal verb.* account for.** **1.** To give the reason for; explain: *We cannot account for these strange happenings.* **2.** To take into consideration; note: *Account for all the facts in giving your answer.* **3.** To be responsible for: *Carelessness accounts for many accidents.*

***Idioms.* call to account.** To demand an explanation from: *He was called to account for being late so often.* **give an account of (oneself).** To behave in a certain way; be noted for one's actions: *The firemen gave a fine account of themselves in action.* **on account of** or **on (someone's) account.** Because of: *We were late on account of traffic. Don't worry on her account.* **on no account.** Under no circumstances; never: *On no account should the live wires be touched.* **on that (this,** or **any) account.** For that (this, or any) reason: *He was very strong, and was chosen as a guard on that account.* **take account of** or **take into account.** To take note of; consider: *In solving a problem, take everything into account. Take account of the weather in choosing your clothes.* **turn to good account.** To make good use of; convert to an advantage: *turn one's losses to good account.*

ac•count•a•ble |ə **koun'**tə bəl| *adj.* Obliged to answer for one's actions; responsible: *Congressmen are accountable to the people who elect them.* —**ac•count'a•bil'i•ty** *n.*

ac•count•ant |ə **koun'**tənt| *n.* A person who keeps or inspects the financial records of business concerns or individuals.

ac•count•ing |ə **koun'**tĭng| *n.* The occupation, process, or methods of keeping the financial records of a business.

ac•cou•ter |ə **ko͞o'**tər| *v.* To outfit with clothing and equipment, especially for a particular purpose: *The explorers were accoutered for outdoor living.*

ac•cou•ter•ments |ə **ko͞o'**tər mənts| *pl.n.* **1.** Articles of clothing or equipment; trappings. **2.** A soldier's equipment apart from his clothing and weapons.

ac•cou•tre |ə **ko͞o'**tər| *v.* **ac•cou•tred, ac•cou•tring.** British form of the word **accouter.**

ac•cou•tre•ments |ə **ko͞o'**tər mənts| *pl.n.* British form of the word **accouterments.**

Ac•cra |**ăk'**rə| *or* |ə **krä'**|. The capital of Ghana. Population, 615,000.

ac•cred•it |ə **krĕd'**ĭt| *v.* **1.** To approve or record as having met certain standards: *This college has been accredited by the state.* **2.** To send or appoint (an ambassador, envoy, etc.) with official standing. —**ac•cred'it•ed** *adj.: an accredited college.*

ac•cre•tion |ə **krē'**shən| *n.* **1.** The process of increasing in size as a result of being added to or growing. **2.** Something added that produces such an increase: *an accretion of rust in the water pipes.*

ac•cru•al |ə **kro͞o'**əl| *n.* **1.** The process of accruing; increase. **2.** Something that has accrued.

ac•crue |ə **kro͞o'**| *v.* **ac•crued, ac•cru•ing.** **1.** To increase or accumulate by a natural or usual process: *Interest accrues in a savings account.* **2.** To come or result as an addition or gain: *the various benefits that accrue from scientific research.*

ac•cu•mu•late |ə **kyo͞o'**myə lāt'| *v.* **ac•cu•mu•lat•ed, ac•cu•mu•lat•ing.** To gather together; pile up; collect: *He accumulated a great deal of money in a short period of time. Snow has begun to accumulate on the sidewalk.*

ac•cu•mu•la•tion |ə kyo͞o'myə **lā'**shən| *n.* **1.** The collection or amassing of something: *the accumulation of knowledge.* **2.** An accumulated amount or mass of something: *an accumulation of rubbish.*

ac•cu•ra•cy |**ăk'**yər ə sē| *n.* **1.** Freedom from error; correctness: *check the results for accuracy.* **2.** Exactness; precision: *the accuracy of his aim.* **3.** *pl.* **ac•cu•ra•cies.** A degree of exactness, as in the size of machine parts.

ac•cu•rate |**ăk'**yər ĭt| *adj.* **1.** Free from errors or mistakes; correct: *accurate answers.* **2.** Exact; precise: *an accurate description; an accurate method of measurement.* —**ac'cu•rate•ly** *adv.* —**ac'cu•rate•ness** *n.* [SEE NOTE]

accurate

Accurate *is from Latin* accūrātus, *"done with care, exact," which is from* accūrāre, *"to give care to, to do carefully":* ad-, *"toward,"* + cūra, *"care."*

ac•curs•ed |ə **kûr'**sĭd| *or* |ə **kûrst'**| *adj.* **1.** Under a curse; damned: *"Gentlemen...now abed will think themselves accursed they were not here."* (Shakespeare). **2.** Hateful or very unfortunate: *"Accursed, unhappy...day!"* (Shakespeare). —**ac•curs'ed•ly** *adv.*

ac•cu•sa•tion |ăk'yo͞o **zā'**shən| *n.* A statement or formal declaration that a person has been guilty of wrongdoing: *He vigorously denied the accusation.*

ac•cuse |ə **kyo͞oz'**| *v.* **ac•cused, ac•cus•ing.** To blame (someone) for wrongdoing in a statement or formal declaration: *He was accused of the crime.* —**ac•cus'er** *n.*

ac•cused |ə **kyo͞ozd'**| *n.* —**the accused.** The defendant or defendants in a criminal case.

ac•cus•tom |ə **kŭs'**təm| *v.* To make familiar with; get (someone) used to: *Astronauts must accustom themselves to unusual conditions during their long space flights.*

ac•cus•tomed |ə **kŭs'**təmd| *adj.* Usual; habitual; familiar: *The frogs were making their accustomed noises.* —**accustomed to.** Used to; familiar with; in the habit of: *Eskimos are accustomed to cold. He is accustomed to doing things his own way.*

ace |ās| *n.* **1.** A playing card with one figure of its suit in the center. **2.** In tennis, a point scored when one's opponent fails to return a serve. **3.** A fighter pilot who has destroyed a number of enemy planes. **4.** A person who is outstanding or an expert in his field: *our team's pitching ace.* —***modifier:*** *an ace reporter; the team's ace quarterback.* [SEE PICTURE]

ace

***Idiom.* within an ace of.** On the verge of; very near to: *within an ace of calling for help.*

ac•e•tate |**ăs'**ĭ tāt'| *n.* **1.** Any salt or ester of acetic acid: *lead acetate.* **2.** Cellulose acetate or a product, such as a fabric, derived from it.

a•ce•tic acid |ə **sē'**tĭk| *or* |ə **sĕt'**ĭk|. An acid composed of carbon, hydrogen, and oxygen and having the formula $C_2H_4O_2$. It occurs naturally in

acid

All acids are chemical compounds that have hydrogen bound into them in a way that allows it to split off in solution and become a hydrogen ion or ions. It is the presence of more hydrogen ions than hydroxyl ions in a solution that makes it acid. Certain salts, such as ammonium chloride, give an acid reaction in solution. While a true acid contributes hydrogen ions to the solution, a salt of this kind removes hydroxyl ions to produce a similar effect.

acorn

acquaintance

"**Acquaintance**, n. *A person whom we know well enough to borrow from, but not well enough to lend to." —Ambrose Bierce,* The Devil's Dictionary *(1911).*

ă pat/ā pay/â care/ä father/ĕ pet/ ē be/ĭ pit/ī pie/î fierce/ŏ pot/ ō go/ô paw, for/oi oil/o͝o book/ o͞o boot/ou out/ŭ cut/û fur/ *th* the/th thin/hw which/zh vision/ ə ago, item, pencil, atom, circus

vinegar and is also produced commercially from ethyl alcohol and from wood. It is used as a solvent, in making rubber and plastics, and in photographic chemicals.

ac•e•tone |**ăs'**ĭ tōn'| *n.* A compound composed of carbon, hydrogen, and oxygen and having the formula C_3H_6O. It is a colorless, strong-smelling, volatile liquid that burns very readily. It is widely used as a solvent.

a•cet•y•lene |ə **sĕt'**l ēn'| *or* |-ĭn| *n.* A colorless, very flammable gas composed of carbon and hydrogen and having the formula C_2H_2. It is used as a fuel in welding and is also burned to produce light.

a•ce•tyl•sal•i•cyl•ic acid |ə sēt'l săl'ĭ **sĭl'**ĭk|. A chemical name for aspirin.

ache |āk| *v.* **ached, ach•ing. 1.** To hurt with or feel a steady pain: *My tooth aches. I ache all over.* **2.** To be unhappy or distressed: *The sight of it makes my heart ache.* **3.** To want very much; long; yearn: *I am aching to see her again.* —*n.* **1.** A steady pain: *the ache in her tired feet.* **2.** A feeling of sadness or longing: *the ache in my heart.*

a•chieve |ə **chēv'**| *v.* **a•chieved, a•chiev•ing. 1.** To succeed in accomplishing, producing, or gaining: *achieve the desired effect; achieve recognition.* **2.** To get to; reach; attain: *achieve a height of six feet; achieve a goal.*

a•chieve•ment |ə **chēv'**mənt| *n.* **1.** The act or process of attaining or accomplishing something: *their efforts in the achievement of their goals.* **2.** Progress toward or success in reaching a goal: *limited achievements in securing world peace.* **3.** An outstanding act or accomplishment: *his great achievements in science.*

A•chil•les |ə **kĭl'**ēz|. In Greek mythology, a Greek hero of the Trojan War. He was killed by an arrow shot into his heel, the only part of his body that could be wounded.

ach•ro•mat•ic |ăk'rə **măt'**ĭk| *adj.* Of or indicating a color, such as black, white, or gray, that can be described in terms of its brightness alone. —**ach'ro•mat'i•cal•ly** *adv.*

achromatic lens. A lens or system of lenses designed to form an image without adding colored fringes to its outlines.

ac•id |**ăs'**ĭd| *n.* **1.** Any of many substances that when dissolved in water are capable of reacting with a base to form water and a salt. Acids can be identified by the fact that they turn blue litmus to red and have a characteristic sour taste. **2.** *Slang.* A drug, L.S.D. —*adj.* **1.** Of or containing an acid or acids. **2.** Sour; tart: *Lemons have an acid taste.* —**ac'id•ly** *adv.* —**ac'id•ness** *n.* [SEE NOTE]

a•cid•ic |ə **sĭd'**ĭk| *adj.* Of, containing, or tending to form an acid.

a•cid•i•fy |ə **sĭd'**ə fī'| *v.* **a•cid•i•fied, a•cid•i•fy•ing, a•cid•i•fies.** To make or become acid: *Vinegar acidifies water. Milk becomes sour when it acidifies.*

a•cid•i•ty |ə **sĭd'**ĭ tē| *n.* The condition or quality of being acid.

ac•i•do•sis |ăs'ĭ **dō'**sĭs| *n.* A diseased condition in which the blood is more acidic or less alkaline than normal.

acid test. A situation that provides a completely decisive test.

a•cid•u•lous |ə **sĭj'**ə ləs| *or* |ə **sĭd'**yə-| *adj.* Sharp or sour in feeling or manner: *acidulous criticism.*

ac•knowl•edge |ăk **nŏl'**ĭj| *v.* **ac•knowl•edged, ac•knowl•edg•ing. 1.** To admit the existence or truth of: *acknowledge one's mistakes.* **2.** To recognize the standing or authority of: *He was acknowledged as supreme ruler.* **3.** To express thanks for: *acknowledge a favor.* **4.** To recognize and reply to: *acknowledge the cheers of the crowd.* **5.** To state that one has received: *acknowledge a letter.*

ac•knowl•edg•ment, also **ac•knowl•edge•ment** |ăk **nŏl'**ĭj mənt| *n.* **1.** The act of acknowledging; recognition: *bowed his head in acknowledgment of guilt.* **2.** Something done or sent in answer to or recognition of another's action: *send an acknowledgment of an invitation.*

ac•me |**ăk'**mē| *n.* The highest point; greatest degree; peak: *the acme of perfection.*

ac•ne |**ăk'**nē| *n.* A condition in which the oil glands of the skin become infected and form pimples.

ac•o•lyte |**ăk'**ə līt'| *n.* A person who assists a priest in the celebration of Mass.

a•corn |**ā'**kôrn'| *or* |**ā'**kərn| *n.* The nut of an oak tree, having a hard shell set in a woody, cuplike base. [SEE PICTURE]

a•cous•tic |ə **ko͞o'**stĭk| or **a•cous•ti•cal** |ə**ko͞o'**stĭ kəl| *adj.* **1.** Of sound, the sense of hearing, or acoustics. **2.** Having a desired effect on sound or the sense of hearing: *acoustic tile; acoustical aids.* —**a•cous'ti•cal•ly** *adv.*

a•cous•tics |ə **ko͞o'**stĭks| *n.* **1.** *(used with a singular verb).* The scientific study of sound and its effects: *Acoustics is taught to engineers.* **2.** *(used with a plural verb).* The overall effect of sound produced and heard in a particular place, especially an enclosed space: *The acoustics of a concert hall are poor for speech.*

ac•quaint |ə **kwānt'**| *v.* To make familiar or informed: *acquaint oneself with the facts of the situation.*

ac•quaint•ance |ə **kwān'**təns| *n.* **1.** Knowledge of or familiarity with something: *acquaintance with the facts.* **2.** A relationship resulting from being acquainted with someone: *cultivate his acquaintance.* **3.** A person whom one knows. [SEE NOTE]

***Idiom.* make (someone's) acquaintance** or **make acquaintance with.** To get to know; become familiar with.

ac•quaint•ance•ship |ə **kwān'**təns shĭp'| *n.* The condition of being acquainted; acquaintance.

ac•quaint•ed |ə **kwān'**tĭd| *adj.* **1.** Familiar; informed: *I am well acquainted with the neighborhood.* **2.** Known to each other: *They became acquainted at school.*

ac•qui•esce |ăk'wē **ĕs'**| *v.* **ac•qui•esced, ac•qui•esc•ing.** To agree or yield without protest: *acquiesce to a demand; acquiesce in a decision.*

ac•qui•es•cent |ăk'wē **ĕs'**ənt| *adj.* Agreeing or submitting without protest. —**ac'qui•es'cence** *n.* —**ac'qui•es'cent•ly** *adv.*

ac•quire |ə **kwīr'**| *v.* **ac•quired, ac•quir•ing.** To get to have; gain; obtain: *acquire knowledge; acquire new skills.* —**ac•quired'** *adj.: an acquired skill.* —**ac•quir'a•ble** *adj.*

ac•quire•ment |ə kwīr′mənt| *n.* **1.** The act or process of acquiring. **2.** A skill or ability gained by effort or experience: *a talented man of many acquirements.*

ac•qui•si•tion |ăk′wĭ zĭsh′ən| *n.* **1.** The act or process of acquiring. **2.** Something acquired, especially as an addition to a collection or one's possessions: *the museum's newest acquisitions.*

ac•quis•i•tive |ə kwĭz′ĭ tĭv| *adj.* Eager to acquire possessions, information, etc.: *an acquisitive collector of odds and ends; an acquisitive mind.* —**ac•quis′i•tive•ly** *adv.* —**ac•quis′i•tive•ness** *n.*

ac•quit |ə kwĭt′| *v.* **ac•quit•ted, ac•quit•ting. 1.** To free or clear from a formal accusation of wrongdoing: *The jury acquitted him of the crime.* **2.** —**acquit oneself.** To conduct oneself; behave: *The warriors acquitted themselves bravely.*

ac•quit•tal |ə kwĭt′l| *n.* The freeing of a person from an accusation of wrongdoing by the judgment of a court.

a•cre |ā′kər| *n.* A unit of area equal to 43,560 square feet or 4,840 square yards, used in measuring land. [SEE NOTE]

a•cre•age |ā′kər ĭj| *n.* Land area as measured or expressed in acres.

a•cre-foot |ā′kər fo͝ot′| *n., pl.* **-feet** |-fēt′|. The volume of water that will cover an area of one acre to a depth of one foot; 43,560 cubic feet of water.

ac•rid |ăk′rĭd| *adj.* **1.** Harsh or bitter to the sense of taste or smell: *acrid smoke.* **2.** Sharp or biting in tone or manner: *acrid comments.* —**ac′rid•ly** *adv.* —**ac′rid•ness** *n.*

Ac•ri•lan |ăk′rə lăn′| *n.* A trademark for a soft, strong synthetic fiber used in making carpets and various fabrics.

ac•ri•mo•ni•ous |ăk′rə mō′nē əs| *adj.* Bitter and ill-natured: *acrimonious bickering.* —**ac′ri•mo′ni•ous•ly** *adv.*

ac•ri•mo•ny |ăk′rə mō′nē| *n.* Bitterness or ill-natured sharpness of feeling or tone.

ac•ro•bat |ăk′rə băt′| *n.* Someone skilled in actions or stunts requiring great agility and balance, such as performing on a trapeze or tightrope. [SEE PICTURE]

ac•ro•bat•ic |ăk′rə băt′ĭk| *adj.* **1.** Of an acrobat: *an acrobatic act in a circus.* **2.** Suggesting the skill of an acrobat: *an acrobatic leap from a burning building.* —**ac′ro•bat′i•cal•ly** *adv.*

ac•ro•bat•ics |ăk′rə băt′ĭks| *n. (used with a plural verb).* **1.** The art or actions of an acrobat: *Acrobatics require long training.* **2.** Behavior that suggests the skill of an acrobat: *the monkey's amusing acrobatics.*

ac•ro•nym |ăk′rə nĭm′| *n.* A word or name formed by combining the first letters in a group of words. *Radar* is an acronym from *ra*dio *d*etection *a*nd *r*anging. [SEE NOTE]

A•crop•o•lis |ə krŏp′ə lĭs| *n.* The hill in Athens on which the Parthenon stands.

a•cross |ə krôs′| *or* |ə krŏs′| *prep.* **1. a.** To or from the other side of: *driving across the continent.* **b.** On the other side of: *a hill across the valley.* **2.** At right angles to the direction indicated by *along:* **a.** Crosswise over: *A frog leaped across our path.* **b.** Crosswise upon: *The horse had one dark stripe along his spine and another across his withers.* —*adv.* **1. a.** From one side to the other: *He called across to us.* **b.** In breadth: *A tornado may be only 100 feet across.* **2.** Over: *I want to get my point across.*

a•crost |ə krôst′| *or* |ə krŏst′| *prep.* & *adv.* A dialectal form of the word **across.**

a•cros•tic |ə krô′stĭk| *or* |ə krŏs′tĭk| *n.* An arrangement of lines, as in a poem or puzzle, in which the first letters of each line spell out a name, quotation, or message.

a•cryl•ic |ə krĭl′ĭk| *adj.* Of any synthetic fiber or resin derived from **acrylic acid,** $C_3H_4O_2$, or some related organic chemical compound.

act |ăkt| *v.* **1.** To do something; perform an action: *saved many lives by acting quickly.* **2.** To serve; function: *Sally acted as chairman. The heart acts like a pump.* **3.** To behave; conduct oneself: *act like a grown-up; act as you always do.* **4. a.** Perform in or as if in a dramatic presentation: *act in a play; act a part.* **b.** Play the part of; perform as: *acted Juliet in the senior play.* **c.** Be performed: *This play has been acted in many cities.* **5.** To pretend; put on a false show: *He tried to look brave, but he was only acting.* **6.** To have an effect: *the force of gravity acting on the earth.* —**phrasal verbs. act on** (or **upon**). To do something as a result of: *He acted on my advice.* **act out.** Perform in or as if in a play; dramatize: *act out a story.* **act up.** To behave in an unusual or undesirable way; misbehave: *Our old jalopy is acting up again.* —*n.* **1.** A kind of movement or behavior; action: *such acts as running, writing, or breathing.* **2.** A thing done; a deed: *an act of bravery; unlawful acts.* **3.** The process of doing something: *caught in the act of stealing.* **4. a.** A performance for an audience, often forming part of a longer show: *a magician's act.* **b.** One of the main divisions of a play or other dramatic work: *an opera in five acts.* **5.** An insincere pretense; false show: *His boasting is just an act.* **6.** A law, especially one enacted by a legislative body: *an act of Congress.*

ACTH A hormone that is secreted by the pituitary gland and that stimulates the adrenal glands to produce cortisone and related hormones.

act•ing |ăk′tĭng| *adj.* Serving temporarily or in place of another person: *the acting principal.* —*n.* The occupation or performance of an actor.

ac•tin•ic ray |ăk tĭn′ĭk|. Any form of radiation, such as, for example, ultraviolet rays or x-rays, that can cause chemical changes in an object that it strikes.

ac•tin•i•um |ăk tĭn′ē əm| *n.* Symbol **Ac** One of the elements, a highly radioactive metal found in uranium ores. Its longest-lived isotope is Ac 227, having a half-life of 21.7 years. Atomic number 89; melting point 1,050°C; boiling point 3,200°C.

ac•tion |ăk′shən| *n.* **1. a.** A thing done; deed: *take responsibility for one's actions. Actions speak louder than words.* **b.** Often **actions.** Behavior; conduct: *a small child's amusing actions.* **2.** The activity, process, or fact of doing something: *Verbs show action.* **3.** Motion; movement: *the constant action of a pendulum.* **4.** Energetic or effective activity: *firemen springing into action; an emergency requiring immediate action.* **5.** The activities or events of a play, story, etc.: *The action of "Macbeth" takes place in Scotland.* **6.** Any physical change, as in position, size, mass, energy, velocity, etc., that an object or system

acre

The word **acre** *is one of the oldest technical words we have. It descends directly from the prehistoric Indo-European word* agros, *"a field, a pasture for cattle." This changed to* akraz *in Germanic and then to* æcer *in Old English. The Indo-European word also appears (via Latin) in* **agriculture.**

acrobat

acronym

Acronyms *are a fairly new and very convenient way of forming new words and names. They are especially popular in official and political circles, where very long titles for institutions and systems are common. Thus* UNESCO *(*United Nations Educational, Scientific, and Cultural Organization*) and* MIRV *(*Multiple Independently Targeted Re-entry Vehicle*).*

undergoes: *the action of a sail in the wind.* **7. a.** The way in which something works or exerts its influence, often within a larger system: *the action of a computer; the action of the liver in digestion.* **b.** The effect of this: *the corrosive action of acid on metal.* **8.** The operating parts of a mechanism: *the action of a piano.* **9.** Battle; combat: *send the troops into action.* **10.** A lawsuit. —**modifier:** *Verbs are action words. Make quick action sketches.*

***Idiom.* take action.** To do something as a result of something else that has taken place: *The colonists took action against the tax laws.*

ac•ti•vate |ăk′tə vāt′| *v.* **ac•ti•vat•ed, ac•ti•vat•ing. 1.** To make active; set in operation or motion. **2.** To start or accelerate a chemical reaction in, as by heating. —**ac′ti•va′tion** *n.*

ac•tive |ăk′tĭv| *adj.* **1.** Moving or tending to move about; engaged in physical action: *Athletes are more active than office workers.* **2.** Performing or capable of performing an action or process; functioning; working: *active cells in living plants and animals; an active volcano.* **3.** Taking part or requiring participation in activities: *an active member of the club; soldiers in active service.* **4.** Full of energy; busy: *an active and useful life; an active mind.* **5.** Causing action or change; effective: *active efforts for improvement.* **6.** In grammar, showing or expressing action: *an active verb.* See **active voice. 7.** Tending to form chemical compounds easily: *an active element.* **8.** In music, suggesting that something follows: *active tones.* —*n.* The active voice in grammar. —**ac′tive•ly** *adv.* —**ac′tive•ness** *n.*

active voice. In grammar, a form of a transitive verb or phrasal verb that shows that the subject of the sentence is performing or causing the action expressed by the verb. In the sentence *John bought the book, bought* is in the active voice. See **passive voice.**

ac•tiv•ist |ăk′tə vĭst| *n.* A person who believes in or takes part in direct effective action to bring about changes in government, social conditions, etc. —***modifier:*** *an activist point of view.* —**ac′tiv•ism′** *n.*

ac•tiv•i•ty |ăk tĭv′ĭ tē| *n., pl.* **ac•tiv•i•ties. 1.** The condition or process of being active; action. **2.** A particular kind of action or behavior: *the nesting activities of birds.* **3.** A planned or organized thing to do, as in a school subject or social group. **4.** Energetic movement or action; busyness: *The department store was a scene of great activity.*

ac•tor |ăk′tər| *n.* A performer, especially a person who acts a part in a play, motion picture, or other dramatic performance.

ac•tress |ăk′trĭs| *n.* A female actor.

ac•tu•al |ăk′cho͞o əl| *adj.* Existing or happening in fact; real.

ac•tu•al•i•ty |ăk′cho͞o ăl′ĭ tē| *n., pl.* **ac•tu•al•i•ties.** Real existence or circumstance; reality; fact.

ac•tu•al•ly |ăk′cho͞o ə lē| *adv.* In fact; really.

ac•tu•ar•y |ăk′cho͞o ĕr′ē| *n., pl.* **ac•tu•ar•ies.** A person who computes insurance risks and premiums.

ac•tu•ate |ăk′cho͞o āt′| *v.* **ac•tu•at•ed, ac•tu•at•ing. 1.** To put into action or motion: *a lever that actuates the brake.* **2.** To cause or inspire to act; motivate: *explorers actuated by a spirit of adventure.* —**ac′tu•a′tion** *n.* —**ac′tu•a′tor** *n.*

a•cu•men |ə kyo͞o′mən| *or* |ăk′yə-| *n.* Quickness and wisdom in making judgments.

a•cute |ə kyo͞ot′| *adj.* **1.** Keen; perceptive: *an acute sense of hearing; an acute awareness of one's surroundings.* **2.** Sharp and intense: *an acute pain in one's chest.* **3.** Developing suddenly and reaching a crisis quickly: *an acute disease; acute appendicitis.* **4.** Very serious; critical: *an acute need for funds.* **5.** Of less than 90 degrees: *an acute angle.* —**a•cute′ly** *adv.* —**a•cute′ness** *n.*

acute accent. In certain foreign languages, and in English words borrowed from such languages, a mark (á) used over a vowel to indicate how it is sounded. For example, in the word "cliché" the final "e" is pronounced /ā/.

acute angle. An angle that is smaller than a right angle; an angle whose measure in degrees is between 0° and 90°.

ad |ăd| *n.* An advertisement. ¶*These sound alike* **ad, add.**

ad–. A prefix borrowed from Latin *ad,* meaning "toward, to"; **adhere** is from Latin *adhaerere,* to stick to. When *ad-* is followed by *c, f, g, l, n, r, s,* or *t,* it becomes *ac-, af-, ag-, al-, an-, ar-, as-,* or *at-,* respectively.

A.D. In a specified year after the birth of Christ. *A.D.* stands for Latin *anno Domini,* "in the year of the Lord."

ad•age |ăd′ĭj| *n.* A short proverb or saying generally considered to be wise and true; for example, "Haste makes waste" is an adage.

a•da•gio |ə dä′jō| *or* |-jē ō|. In music: *adj.* Slow. —*adv.* Slowly. —*n., pl.* **a•da•gios.** A slow section of a composition.

Ad•am |ăd′əm|. In the Bible, the first man, husband of Eve. [SEE NOTE]

ad•a•mant |ăd′ə mənt| *or* |-mănt′| *adj.* Firm and unyielding: *She was adamant in her decision.* —**ad′a•mant•ly** *adv.* [SEE NOTE]

ad•a•man•tine |ăd′ə măn′tĭn| *or* |-tēn′| *or* |- tīn′| *adj.* **1.** Having a hardness like that of a diamond: *an adamantine rock.* **2.** Unyielding; hard: *the tyrant's adamantine will.*

Ad•ams |ăd′əmz|. **1. Samuel.** 1722–1803. American Revolutionary patriot. **2. John.** 1735–1826. Second President of the United States (1797–1801). **3. John Quincy.** 1767–1848. Sixth President of the United States (1825–29); son of John Adams.

Adam's apple. The lump at the front of the throat where a part of the larynx projects forward, most noticeable in men. [SEE NOTE]

a•dapt |ə dăpt′| *v.* **1.** To change or adjust for a certain purpose: *adapt our methods to meet the new situation.* **2.** To make or become fitted for a particular environment, condition, use, etc., as through a process of natural development: *Gills and fins adapt a fish for living in water. Camels have adapted to desert conditions.* —**a•dap′ted** *adj.*: *claws well adapted for digging.* [SEE NOTE at **adopt**]

a•dapt•a•ble |ə dăp′tə bəl| *adj.* Able to change or be adjusted so as to fit in with new or different situations, uses, etc. —**a•dapt′a•bil′i•ty** *n.*

ad•ap•ta•tion |ăd′ăp tā′shən| *n.* **1.** The act or process of adapting; change or adjustment to meet new conditions. **2.** Something that is pro-

Adam/Adam's apple

The name **Adam** *comes from Hebrew* Ādām, *"man." (This comes from* adāmā, *"earth," and literally means "the one made from earth"; in the book of Genesis, God made man—Adam—out of earth.)* **Adam's apple** *arises from the Hebrew phrase* tappuach hā-ādām, *"swelling of the man (on the throat)":* tappuach, *"lump, swelling,"* + hā-ādām, *"the man." Because* tappuach *also means "apple," the phrase was misunderstood as "Adam's apple." It was then mythologically explained that a piece of the forbidden apple had stuck in Adam's throat and that the lump was named from this.*

adamant

Adamant *comes from Greek* adamas, *the name of a hard metal, probably steel. It was later also used to mean "diamond" and "magnet" and as a poetic word for anything extremely hard. The meaning "firm and unyielding" is the only one now in common use.*

ă pat/ā pay/â care/ä father/ĕ pet/ ē be/ĭ pit/ī pie/î fierce/ŏ pot/ ō go/ô paw, for/oi oil/o͝o book/ o͞o boot/ou out/ŭ cut/û fur/ *th* the/th thin/hw which/zh vision/ ə ago, item, pencil, atom, circus

duced by being adapted: *The movie was an adaptation of a story.* **3.** A part, development, or type of behavior that fits an animal or plant for a particular way of living.

a•dapt•er |ə dăp′tər| *n.* A device whose purpose is to allow two or more pieces of equipment to operate together where they would not otherwise do so.

a•dap•tive |ə dăp′tĭv| *adj.* **1.** Of or related to adaptation. **2.** Tending to adapt easily.

a•daz•zle |ə dăz′əl| *adj.* Dazzling; brilliant; shining.

add |ăd| *v.* **1.** To find the sum of (two or more numbers): *Add 8 and 5. Add 6 to 8.* **2.** To carry out the steps necessary to find a sum: *Doris can add in her head.* **3.** To put on as a new part; connect, join, or unite: *add a suffix to a word; add an annex to a building.* **4.** To put in as something extra: *add salt to a mixture; add stamps to a collection.* **5.** To take on as an addition: *Many nouns form the plural by adding "s."* **6.** To say as something extra; say further: *"Be careful," she added.* **7.** To contribute (something extra): *Each sentence adds information. He adds to his savings each week.* —**add′ed** *adj.: an added advantage.* —***phrasal verb.*** **add up to. 1.** To result in: *A daily measurement of rainfall adds up to a valuable yearly record.* **2.** To mean; indicate: *Those warning signs add up to trouble.* ¶*These sound alike* **add, ad.**

ad•dax |ăd′ăks′| *n.* An African antelope with long, spirally twisted horns. [SEE PICTURE]

ad•dend |ăd′ĕnd| *or* |ə dĕnd′| *n.* Any one of a set of numbers that are to be added. For example, in 9 + 2 = 11, the numbers 9 and 2 are addends.

ad•der[1] |ăd′ər| *n.* **1.** Any of several poisonous Old World snakes, especially the common viper of northern Europe and Asia. **2.** Any of several nonpoisonous snakes popularly believed to be harmful. [SEE NOTE]

add•er[2] |ăd′ər| *n.* A device that performs addition, as in a digital computer. [SEE NOTE]

ad•der's-tongue |ăd′ərz tŭng′| *n.* A plant, the **dogtooth violet.**

ad•dict |ăd′ĭkt| *n.* **1.** A person who has an uncontrollable craving for a harmful, habit-forming substance, especially a narcotic drug. **2.** A devoted fan: *a science-fiction addict.*

ad•dict•ed |ə dĭk′tĭd| *adj.* **1.** Slavishly dependent on a harmful, habit-forming substance, especially a narcotic drug: *addicted to drugs; an addicted person.* **2.** Given to, as a habit: *addicted to lying.* **3.** Devoted to, as a hobby or interest: *addicted to poetry.*

ad•dict•ing |ə dĭk′tĭng| *adj.* Causing addiction; habit-forming: *an addicting drug.*

ad•dic•tion |ə dĭk′shən| *n.* The condition of being addicted, especially slavish dependence on harmful, habit-forming drugs.

ad•dic•tive |ə dĭk′tĭv| *adj.* Causing addiction; habit-forming: *a physically addictive drug.*

adding machine. A portable machine, operated from a keyboard, that is capable of finding sums and sometimes differences, products, and quotients as well.

Ad•dis Ab•a•ba |ăd′ĭs ăb′ə bə|. The capital of Ethiopia. Population, 1,011,565.

Ad•di•son's disease |ăd′ĭ sənz|. A disease in which the adrenal cortex does not function properly, resulting in weakness, anemia, and abnormal coloration of the skin. It is usually fatal unless treated with hormones.

ad•di•tion |ə dĭsh′ən| *n.* **1. a.** A binary operation that assigns to a pair of numbers, the addends, a unique number, the sum. **b.** The process of finding the sum of two or more numbers. **c.** A problem involving the finding of sums: *Do these additions in our new arithmetic.* **2.** The act of adding something extra to a thing: *the addition of seasoning to food.* **3.** An added thing, part, or person: *an addition to the family.* —***modifier:*** *solve addition problems.*

Idioms. **in addition.** Also; besides: *His life story was written, and in addition legends sprang up.* **in addition to.** Along with; besides: *In addition to textile mills, there are clothing factories.*

ad•di•tion•al |ə dĭsh′ə nəl| *adj.* Added; extra: *What additional information must you have?* —**ad•di′tion•al•ly** *adv.*

ad•di•tive |ăd′ĭ tĭv| *adj.* Of addition: *work subtraction problems by the additive method.* —*n.* A substance added to something else in small amounts in order to improve it in some way.

additive inverse. Either one of a pair of numbers, as *a* and *-a,* whose sum is zero (0).

ad•dle |ăd′l| *v.* **ad•dled, ad•dling. 1.** To mix up, confuse, or muddle: *Drink addled his head.* **2.** To spoil: *Heat addled the eggs. The eggs addled.*

ad•dress |ə drĕs′| *n.* **1.** |*also* ăd′rĕs′|. **a.** The place where someone lives, works, or receives mail or where a business is located: *your home address.* **b.** A direction on a piece of mail, giving the name and location of the receiver or sender: *a return address.* **2.** A formal speech: *the President's inaugural address.* **3.** Spoken or written communication. A **form of address** is a title or set of words used when speaking or writing formally to someone, such as an official. **4.** A way of speaking or behaving: *a man of blunt address.* —***modifier:*** *an address book.* —*v.* **1.** To speak to: *The man addressed him respectfully.* **2.** To give a speech to: *The mayor will address our club.* **3.** To refer to directly; call; greet: *Address the judge as "Your Honor."* **4.** To put a direction on (a piece of mail) to show where it should go: *address an envelope.* **5.** To direct to a particular person, group, or place: *She addressed her remarks to the newcomers.* —***phrasal verb.*** **address (oneself) to. 1.** To speak to. **2.** To direct (one's) efforts or attention toward: *You must address yourself to the homework assignment.*

ad•dress•ee |ăd′rĕs ē′| *or* |ə drĕs′ē′| *n.* The person to whom a letter or package is addressed.

ad•duce |ə do͞os′| *or* |ə dyo͞os′| *v.* **ad•duced, ad•duc•ing.** To give or offer as an example or means of proof: *He adduced no evidence to support his conclusions.*

A•den |äd′n| *or* |ăd′n|. The capital of Southern Yemen. Population, 240,000.

ad•e•noids |ăd′n oidz′| *pl.n.* Growths of glandular tissue, similar to that of lymph nodes, that occur in the nose above the throat. When swollen they may obstruct breathing and make speech difficult. [SEE PICTURE]

a•dept |ə dĕpt′| *adj.* Skillful and effective; proficient: *adept at sewing; an adept mechanic.* —**a•dept′ly** *adv.* —**a•dept′ness** *n.*

addax

adder[1·2]

Adder[2], *obviously, comes from* **add,** *while* **adder**[1] *has a surprising origin. It was originally* nadder, *but the phrase* a nadder *gradually turned into* an adder. *This has happened with a number of other English words, such as* **apron** *and* **orange.**

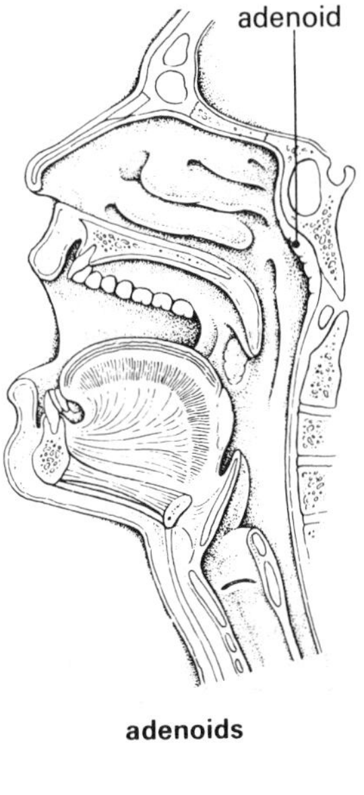

adenoids

adieu/adios/good-by
Adieu *is the French for "to God," short for "I commend you to God."* **Adios** *is the same in Spanish. English* **good-by** *is similar; it is originally from "God be with you," gradually shortened to "God be wi' you," then to "Godbuy," then finally to "good-by."*

ad infinitum
"Big fleas have little fleas
Upon their backs to bite 'em;
Little fleas have smaller fleas,
And so ad infinitum." (An old anonymous rhyme.)

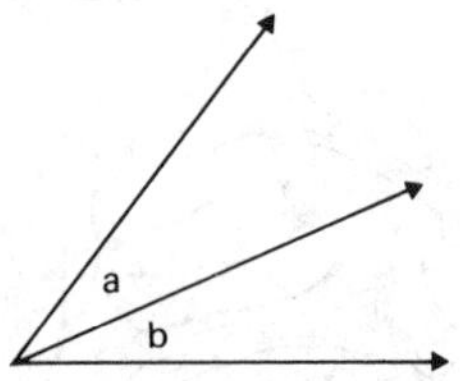

adjacent angles

ă pat/ā pay/â care/ä father/ĕ pet/ ē be/ĭ pit/ī pie/î fierce/ŏ pot/ ō go/ô paw, for/oi oil/ŏŏ book/ ōō boot/ou out/ŭ cut/û fur/ *th* the/th thin/hw which/zh vision/ ə ago, item, pencil, atom, circus

ad•e•qua•cy |ăd′ĭ kwə sē| *n.* The condition of being sufficient to meet needs; sufficiency or suitability.

ad•e•quate |ăd′ĭ kwĭt| *adj.* **1.** Sufficient; enough: *adequate supplies.* **2.** Good, large, rich, or full enough: *an adequate diet.* **3.** Passable, but not really good: *an adequate but uninspired performance.* **4.** Suitable: *adequate to their needs.* —**ad′e•quate•ly** *adv.*

ad•here |ăd hîr′| *v.* **ad•hered, ad•her•ing. 1.** To stick or hold fast: *The wallpaper adheres to the wall.* **2.** To remain loyal; give continuing support: *adhere to one's religious beliefs.* **3.** To follow closely, without changes: *They adhered to the original plan.*

ad•her•ence |ăd hîr′əns| *n.* **1.** The process or condition of adhering or sticking fast. **2.** Faithful attachment; loyalty; devotion: *adherence to one's principles.*

ad•her•ent |ăd hîr′ənt| *n.* A loyal supporter or follower. —*adj.* Sticking or holding fast.

ad•he•sion |ăd hē′zhən| *n.* **1.** The process or condition of sticking fast or adhering. **2.** Loyal attachment or devotion. **3.** A condition in which body tissues that are normally separate are joined together: *an adhesion of the intestinal walls.*

ad•he•sive |ăd hē′sĭv| *adj.* Tending to hold fast to another material; sticky. —*n.* An adhesive substance, such as paste or glue.

adhesive tape. A white tape coated with a sticky substance on one side and often used to hold bandages in place.

ad hoc |ăd hŏk′|. For a specific purpose, case, etc.: *an ad hoc commission.* This expression was originally a Latin phrase.

ad•i•a•bat•ic |ăd′ē ə băt′ĭk| *or* |ā′dī ə-| *n.* Occurring without gain or loss of heat: *The passage of sound through air is essentially adiabatic.* —**ad′i•a•bat′i•cal•ly** *adv.*

a•dieu |ə dōō′| *or* |ə dyōō′| *interj.* Good-by; farewell. —*n., pl.* **a•dieus** or **a•dieux** |ə dōōz′| *or* |ə dyōōz′|. A farewell. ¶ *These sound alike* **adieu, ado.** [SEE NOTE]

ad in•fi•ni•tum |ăd ĭn′fə nī′təm|. Endlessly. This expression was originally a Latin phrase. [SEE NOTE]

a•di•os |ä′dē ōs′| *or* |ăd′ē-| *interj. Spanish.* Good-by; farewell. [SEE NOTE]

ad•i•pose |ăd′ə pōs′| *adj.* Of or containing animal fat; fatty: *adipose tissue.*

Ad•i•ron•dack Mountains |ăd′ə rŏn′dăk′|. Also **Ad•i•ron•dacks.** A section of the Appalachian Mountains in northern New York State.

adj. adjective.

ad•ja•cent |ə jā′sənt| *adj.* **1.** Next to; adjoining: *the room adjacent to mine.* **2.** Nearby; neighboring: *the city and adjacent farm lands.* **3.** Situated side by side: *adjacent pages in a book.* —**ad•ja′cent•ly** *adv.*

adjacent angles. A pair of angles that have a vertex and a ray in common and that are located on opposite sides of the common ray. [SEE PICTURE]

ad•jec•ti•val |ăj′ĭk tī′vəl| *adj.* Of or acting as an adjective: *an adjectival phrase.* —**ad′jec•ti′val•ly** *adv.*

ad•jec•tive |ăj′ĭk tĭv| *n.* In grammar, a word used to describe a noun or to limit its meaning. For example, in the sentence *The young boy is very tall, young* and *tall* are adjectives. Most adjectives can be modified by words such as "very," "highly," and "extremely" and can be compared either by the addition of the *-er* and *-est* endings or by the placement of the words "more" and "most" in front of them; for example, *the younger boy, the youngest boy; the more intelligent girl, the most intelligent girl.*

ad•join |ə join′| *v.* **1.** To be next to or share a boundary with: *The bath adjoins the bedroom.* **2.** To lie side by side: *The rooms adjoin.*

ad•join•ing |ə joi′nĭng| *adj.* **1.** Connected or touching along one side or edge: *a bedroom and adjoining bath.* **2.** Next: *the adjoining room.* **3.** Next to; beside: *the rooms adjoining the courtyard.* **4.** Next to one another: *adjoining houses.*

ad•journ |ə jûrn′| *v.* **1.** To bring (a meeting or session) to an official close, putting off further business until later: *I move that the meeting be adjourned. There is a motion to adjourn.* **2.** To come to an official close; break up: *The legislature adjourned in July.* **3.** *Informal.* To move from one place to another: *We adjourned to the living room.* —**ad•journ′ment** *n.*

ad•judge |ə jŭj′| *v.* **ad•judged, ad•judg•ing. 1.** To determine, rule, or declare by law: *The accused murderer was adjudged insane.* **2.** To award by law: *He was adjudged $5,000 in damages.*

ad•junct |ăj′ŭngkt′| *n.* A separate, less important thing added to something: *The card shop is an adjunct of the bookstore.*

ad•jure |ə jŏŏr′| *v.* **ad•jured, ad•jur•ing.** To command solemnly; ask or urge earnestly: *I adjure you to confess the truth.*

ad•just |ə jŭst′| *v.* **1.** To change, set, or regulate in order to achieve a desired result: *adjust the volume control on a radio.* **2.** To move into the proper position; arrange: *He adjusted his spectacles.* **3.** To be capable of being moved, set, or regulated: *The cutting blade adjusts.* **4.** To change so as to fit: *adjust roller skates to the size of the foot.* **5.** To change or adapt to suit existing conditions or new requirements: *Animals adjust themselves to their environment. That camera adjusts automatically.* **6.** To become accustomed; adapt oneself: *adjust to life in the big city.* **7.** To change by adding or subtracting something: *adjust an estimated price.* **8.** To settle (a claim, complaint, dispute, etc.). **9.** To correct: *Can this buzzing noise be adjusted?* —**ad•just′ed** *adj.*: *a well-adjusted, self-confident child.* —**ad•just′er** *n.*

ad•just•a•ble |ə jŭs′tə bəl| *adj.* Capable of being adjusted: *an adjustable lens.*

ad•just•ment |ə jŭst′mənt| *n.* **1. a.** The act of adjusting: *adjustment to low pressure.* **b.** A particular act of adjusting; a change or alteration: *Only minor adjustments were needed.* **2.** The condition of being adjusted: *machinery in proper adjustment.* **3.** A means by which a device can be adjusted. **4.** A way of adjusting or being adjusted; a setting: *Find the best adjustment of the tool for your purposes.* **5.** The ability to be adjusted: *The car has more seat adjustment than we could use.* **6.** Settlement, as of a claim, complaint, or dispute. **7.** A change or correction, such as a refund or exchange: *The store made an adjustment on the faulty merchandise.*

ad•ju•tant |ăj′ə tənt| *n.* Any army officer who

acts as an assistant to the commanding officer.

ad-lib |ăd **lĭb'**| *Informal.* v. **ad-libbed, ad-lib•bing.** To make up (lines, music, movements, etc.) while performing: *ad-lib a joke. The actor forgot his lines and ad-libbed.* —*n.* A line, speech, action, etc., made up on the spot: *a good ad-lib.* —***modifier:*** *an ad-lib remark.*

ad•man |**ăd'**măn'| *n., pl.* **-men** |-mĕn'|. *Informal.* A man who works in the advertising business.

ad•min•is•ter |ăd **mĭn'**ĭ stər| *v.* **1.** To govern: *administer a colony.* **2.** To direct or manage: *The government administers the affairs of the people.* **3.** To put into effect; carry out: *authority to administer laws.* **4.** To give formally or officially: *administer the sacraments; administer an oath.* **5.** To give and supervise: *administer a test.* **6.** To give as a remedy or treatment: *administer artificial respiration.* **7.** To give or deal out; dispense: *administer justice.* **8.** To cause or convey: *Static electricity administers shocks.*

ad•min•is•tra•tion |ăd mĭn'ĭ **strā'**shən| *n.* **1.** The act of administering: *the administration of justice.* **2.** Management: *business administration.* **3.** The officials who manage an institution or organization: *the school administration.* **4.** Government: *the results of colonial administration.* **5. a.** Often **Administration.** The group of officials in charge of running a local, state, or national government. **b. the Administration.** The President of the United States along with his cabinet officers and the departments that they head. **6.** The time that a chief executive is in office or that a government is in power: *during the Truman administration.* **7. Administration.** A government agency: *the Federal Housing Administration.* —***modifier:*** *the administration building.*

ad•min•is•tra•tive |ăd **mĭn'**ĭ strā'tĭv| *or* |- strə-| *adj.* Of, for, or relating to government or management: *an administrative officer.*

ad•min•is•tra•tor |ăd **mĭn'**ĭ strā'tər| *n.* **1.** A person in charge of directing or managing affairs; an executive or official. **2.** A person whom a court appoints to manage the property left by a dead person.

ad•mi•ra•ble |**ăd'**mər ə bəl| *adj.* Worthy of admiration; excellent: *admirable qualities.* —**ad'•mi•ra•bly** *adv.*

ad•mi•ral |**ăd'**mər əl| *n.* **1.** The commander in chief of a navy or fleet. **2.** Any of several high-ranking officers in the U.S. Navy ranking above a captain, including, in descending order of rank, **admiral, vice admiral,** and **rear admiral.** **3.** Any of several brightly colored butterflies. [SEE NOTE & PICTURE]

Admiral of the Fleet. An officer having the highest rank in the U.S. Navy.

ad•mi•ral•ty |**ăd'**mər əl tē| *n., pl.* **ad•mi•ral•ties.** **1.** A court that tries cases involving ships and shipping. **2. Admiralty.** The British navy department.

ad•mi•ra•tion |ăd'mə **rā'**shən| *n.* **1.** Pleasure, wonder, and delight in someone or something: *They gazed at the statue in admiration.* **2.** A high opinion; respect; esteem: *the admiration of a son for his father.* **3.** Praise and approval: *The child wanted attention and admiration.* **4.** An object of wonder or respect: *The ballerina was the admiration of younger dancers.*

ad•mire |ăd **mīr'**| *v.* **ad•mired, ad•mir•ing.** **1.** To look at or regard with wonder, pleasure, etc.: *admire a mountain view.* **2.** To have a high opinion of; feel respect for: *They admired her courage.* —**ad•mir'er** *n.* [SEE NOTE]

ad•mir•ing |ăd **mīr'**ĭng| *adj.* Showing or expressing admiration: *an admiring glance.* —**ad•mir'ing•ly** *adv.*

ad•mis•si•ble |ăd **mĭs'**ə bəl| *adj.* Accepted or permitted; allowable: *Hearsay evidence is not admissible in court.*

ad•mis•sion |ăd **mĭsh'**ən| *n.* **1.** The act of allowing to enter or join: *the admission of new states to the Union.* **2.** The right to enter: *They applied for admission.* **3.** A price charged or paid to enter a place: *The spectators paid admission.* **4.** Acceptance and entry of an applicant into an institution, profession, club, etc.: *gain admission to medical school.* **5.** An acknowledgment or confession: *He did it by his own admission.* **6.** A fact that is admitted or confessed: *a dangerous admission.* —***modifier:*** *an admission fee.*

ad•mit |ăd **mĭt'**| *v.* **ad•mit•ted, ad•mit•ting.** **1.** To acknowledge or confess as a fact: *I must admit that you are right. Never admit defeat.* **2.** To allow or permit to enter: *This pass will admit one person free.* **3.** To accept and take in as a new member, student, patient, etc.: *The hospital admitted the accident victim.* **4.** To give opportunity for; allow; permit: *That problem admits of no solution.*

ad•mit•tance |ăd **mĭt'**ns| *n.* Permission or right to enter: *The sign said "no admittance."*

ad•mit•ted•ly |ăd **mĭt'**ĭd lē| *adv.* By general admission; without denial: *They are, admittedly, scared.*

ad•mix•ture |ăd **mĭks'**chər| *n.* **1.** The act of mixing. **2.** A combination, mixture, or blend. **3.** Anything added in mixing.

ad•mon•ish |ăd **mŏn'**ĭsh| *v.* **1.** To criticize for a fault in a kind but serious way: *He admonished them for their lateness.* **2.** To advise, warn, urge, or caution: *She admonished us to be careful.*

ad•mo•ni•tion |ăd'mə **nĭsh'**ən| *n.* A gentle criticism or friendly warning: *Heed his admonition.*

ad•mon•i•to•ry |ăd **mŏn'**ĭ tôr'ē| *or* |-tōr'ē| *adj.* Giving or expressing a warning; urging caution: *an admonitory word of advice.*

a•do |ə **dōō'**| *n.* Fuss; bother: *He set off without further ado.* ¶*These sound alike* **ado, adieu.**

a•do•be |ə **dō'**bē| *n.* **1. a.** Brick made of clay and straw that is dried in the sun. **b.** One such brick. **2.** Clay or soil from which such bricks are made. **3.** A structure built with such bricks. —***modifier:*** *an adobe house; adobe bricks.*

ad•o•les•cence |ăd'l **ĕs'**əns| *n.* **1.** The period of physical and psychological development that leads from childhood to adulthood. **2.** Any transitional period of development between youth and maturity: *the adolescence of a nation.*

ad•o•les•cent |ăd'l **ĕs'**ənt| *n.* A boy or girl, especially a teen-ager, in the stage of development between childhood and adulthood. —*adj.* Of or going through adolescence: *an adolescent youngster.* [SEE NOTE]

A•don•is |ə **dŏn'**ĭs| *or* |ə **dō'**nĭs|. **1.** In Greek mythology, a youth whom the goddess Aphrodite loved for his beauty. **2.** Any very handsome man.

red admiral

admiral/admire

Admiral *is not connected to* **admire,** *although it seems to have been influenced by it. It comes ultimately from Arabic* 'amir-al-mā, *"commander of the sea."* **Admire** *is from Latin* admīrārī, *"to look at with wonder."*

adolescent/adult

Adolescent *comes from Latin* adolescens, *"growing up." This is basically formed from* ad, *"toward," and a root* al-, ol-, *or* ul-, *"to grow." The* -esc- *is an element that gives the meaning "beginning to" or "tending to."* **Adult** *is from Latin* adultus, *"grown up," from the same basic elements but without the* -esc-. *See also* **adultery.**

adopt/adapt
Adapt *is related to* **apt**, *and* **adopt** *is related to* **opt**. **Adapt** *is from Latin* adaptāre, *"to make fit, to adjust":* ad-, *"toward,"* + aptus, *"fit, apt."* **Adopt** *is from Latin* adoptāre, *"to choose for oneself, to select, to adopt":* ad-, *"toward,"* + optāre, *"to choose, desire, opt."*

adult/adultery
adult *and* **adultery** *are not related, although both come from Latin. For the origin of* **adult**, *see* **adolescent**. **Adultery** *comes from Latin* adulterāre, *"to approach unlawfully, to corrupt, to commit adultery with"; this is formed from* ad, *"toward," and* alter- *or* ulter-, *"other, different, wrong."*

ă pat/ā pay/â care/ä father/ĕ pet/ē be/ĭ pit/ī pie/î fierce/ŏ pot/ō go/ô paw, for/oi oil/ŏŏ book/ōō boot/ou out/ŭ cut/û fur/*th* the/th thin/hw which/zh vision/ə ago, item, pencil, atom, circus

a•dopt |ə **dŏpt'**| *v.* **1.** To take (a new member) into one's family, tribe, or nation and treat as one's own: *adopt a child; a captive adopted by the Indians.* **2.** To take and make one's own: *Samuel Clemens adopted the name Mark Twain.* **3.** To accept and use or follow: *adopt a suggestion; adopt new methods.* **4.** To pass by vote or approve officially: *adopt a new state constitution.* **5.** To put on; assume: *He adopted a confident air to hide his uneasiness.* **6.** To take on; acquire: *The foreign word "concerto" has adopted an English plural.* —**a•dopt'ed** *adj.: an adopted child; his adopted country.* [SEE NOTE]

a•dop•tion |ə **dŏp'**shən| *n.* **1.** The act of adopting or the condition of being adopted: *the adoption of a child; the boy's adoption by the Indians.* **2.** Acceptance and use: *the adoption of new methods.* **3.** Official approval; passage: *the adoption of the Bill of Rights.* —***modifier:*** *The adoption agency found them a child.*

a•dop•tive |ə **dŏp'**tĭv| *adj.* Acquired or related by adoption: *the boy's adoptive parents.*

a•dor•a•ble |ə **dôr'**ə bəl| *or* |ə **dōr'**-| *adj.* **1.** *Informal.* Delightful; lovable; charming: *an adorable child.* **2.** *Archaic.* Worthy of worship or adoration; divine. —**a•dor'a•bly** *adv.*

ad•o•ra•tion |ăd'ə **rā'**shən| *n.* **1.** Worship of God or of any divine being. **2.** Great and devoted love.

a•dore |ə **dôr'**| *or* |ə **dōr'**| *v.* **a•dored, a•dor•ing. 1.** To worship: *"O, come let us adore Him."* **2.** To love deeply and devotedly; idolize: *He adored his sweetheart.* **3.** *Informal.* To like very much: *They adore skiing.* —**a•dored'** *adj.: her adored cousin.* —**a•dor'ing** *adj.: an adoring audience.*

a•dorn |ə **dôrn'**| *v.* **1.** To decorate with something beautiful or ornamental: *adorn fingers with rings.* **2.** To be an ornament to: *Colored birds adorned the golden cages.*

a•dorn•ment |ə **dôrn'**mənt| *n.* **1.** The act of adorning; decoration: *jewelry worn for personal adornment.* **2.** Something that adorns or beautifies; an ornament or decoration: *They wore no jewels or other adornments.*

ad•re•nal |ə **drē'**nəl| *adj.* **1.** Of adrenalin or the glands that produce it. **2.** Close to the kidneys. —*n.* One of the **adrenal glands.**

adrenal glands. Either of two endocrine glands, located one above each kidney, that produce adrenalin and certain other hormones.

a•dren•a•lin or **a•dren•a•line** |ə **drĕn'**ə lĭn| *n.* A hormone produced by the adrenal glands. It acts to quicken the pulse, raise blood pressure, and, in general, to prepare the body for vigorous action, as in response to danger. It is sometimes used to treat asthma.

A•dri•at•ic Sea |ā'drē **ăt'**ĭk| *or* |ăd'rē-|. A part of the Mediterranean Sea lying between Italy on the west and Yugoslavia and Albania on the east.

a•drift |ə **drĭft'**| *adv. & adj.* Drifting or floating without direction: *a fleet of fishing boats set adrift by the hurricane.*

a•droit |ə **droit'**| *adj.* Skillful or clever at doing or handling something difficult: *an adroit answer to a tricky question.* —**a•droit'ly** *adv.* —**a•droit'ness** *n.*

ad•sorb |ăd **sôrb'**| *or* |**-zôrb'**| *v.* To attract and hold (a substance) on a surface: *Platinum adsorbs hydrogen.*

ad•sorp•tion |ăd **sôrp'**shən| *or* |**-zôrp'**-| *n.* The process of adsorbing or the condition of being adsorbed.

ADST, A.D.S.T. Atlantic Daylight-Saving Time.

ad•u•la•tion |ăj'ōō **lā'**shən| *n.* **1.** Excessive praise or flattery arising from hero-worship: *The leader sought respect, not adulation.* **2.** Uncritical admiration; hero worship: *the boy's adulation of the athlete.*

ad•u•la•to•ry |**ăj'**ōō lə tôr'ē| *or* |-tōr'ē| *adj.* Praising or flattering excessively; uncritically admiring: *an adulatory biographer.*

a•dult |ə **dŭlt'**| *or* |**ăd'**ŭlt'| *n.* **1.** An organism that is fully grown and usually capable of carrying on reproduction. **2.** A person who is legally of age; a grown-up: *Ask an adult to help you.* **3.** A mature person who is responsible for what he does: *He treated the boy as an adult.* —***modifier:*** *an adult adviser.* —*adj.* **1.** Fully developed and mature. **2.** Of or for mature persons: *adult entertainment.* **3.** Involving grown-up responsibility: *The young people did adult work.* [SEE NOTE]

a•dul•ter•ate |ə **dŭl'**tə rāt'| *v.* **a•dul•ter•at•ed, a•dul•ter•at•ing.** To make inferior or impure by the addition of unnecessary, improper, or otherwise undesirable ingredients: *adulterate wine with water.* —**a•dul'ter•at'ed** *adj.: adulterated foods.* —**a•dul'ter•a'tion** *n.*

a•dul•ter•er |ə **dŭl'**tər ər| *n.* A man who commits adultery.

a•dul•ter•ess |ə **dŭl'**tər ĭs| *or* |-trĭs| *n.* A woman who commits adultery.

a•dul•ter•ous |ə **dŭl'**tər əs| *adj.* Of or guilty of adultery: *an adulterous relationship; an adulterous husband.*

a•dul•ter•y |ə **dŭl'**tə rē| *or* |-trē| *n., pl.* **a•dul•ter•ies.** The act of being unfaithful to one's husband or wife by having sexual relations with another. [SEE NOTE]

a•dult•hood |ə **dŭlt'**hŏŏd'| *n.* The time or condition of being fully grown or developed; maturity.

adv. adverb.

ad•vance |ăd **văns'**| *or* |**-väns'**| *v.* **ad•vanced, ad•vanc•ing. 1.** To move forward, onward, or ahead: *He advanced the ball ten yards. Did the army advance or retreat?* **2.** To make progress; improve or grow: *We are advancing in our studies.* **3.** To aid the growth or progress of; promote: *Scientific research advances knowledge.* **4.** To raise or rise in rank or position: *advance a man from private to sergeant. He advanced to the rank of captain.* **5.** To put forward; propose or offer: *advance a theory.* **6.** To move ahead to a later time: *Advance your watch one hour. As spring advanced, the ice thawed.* **7.** To move from a later to an earlier time: *advance a deadline from June to May.* **8.** To increase in amount or value: *Costs were advancing.* **9.** To lend or pay (money) ahead of time: *The company advanced him a week's pay.* **10.** To seem to stand out to the eye, as warm colors do. —**ad•vanc'ing** *adj.: an advancing army; advancing technology.* —***phrasal verb.*** **advance on** (or **upon**). To move against, as when attacking: *Troops advanced on the enemy fort.* —*n.* **1.** A forward step; improvement: *re-*

cent advances in science. **2.** Progress; development: *medical advance; the advance of technology.* **3. a.** Forward or onward movement: *the advance of the fire through the grass.* **b.** An attack: *an enemy advance on the fort.* **4.** A loan or payment made ahead of time: *Can you get an advance on your allowance?* **5.** A rise or increase in amount or value: *a price advance.* **6. advances.** Approaches or efforts made to win someone's friendship or favor: *She spurned his advances.* **7.** A gain made by moving forward: *a ten-yard advance.* **8.** A route or line of forward movement: *The waves rolled shoreward, rearing high all along their advance.* **9.** A **spark advance.** *—adj.* **1.** Made or given ahead of time: *no advance warning.* **2.** Going before: *the advance guard.* **3.** Farthest ahead: *an army's advance post.*

Idioms. **in advance.** **1.** Ahead of time: *Make your arrangements in advance.* **2.** In front: *He stood a little distance in advance.* **in advance of.** Ahead of: *Her ideas were in advance of her time.*

ad•vanced |ăd **vănst′**| *or* |**-vänst′**| *adj.* **1.** Highly developed or complex: *an advanced civilization.* **2.** At a higher level than others: *an advanced student; advanced courses.* **3.** Ahead of the times; progressive: *advanced ideas.* **4. a.** Far along in course: *illness in its advanced stages.* **b.** Very old: *a man of advanced age.*

ad•vance•ment |ăd **văns′**mənt| *or* |**-väns′-**| *n.* **1.** The act of advancing. **2.** A forward step; improvement: *new advancements in science.* **3.** Development; progress: *the advancement of knowledge.* **4.** Getting ahead; promotion: *opportunity for advancement.*

ad•van•tage |ăd **văn′**tĭj| *or* |**-vän′-**| *n.* **1.** A good point or favorable feature: *the advantages of city life.* **2.** A benefit that puts one in a favorable position: *They gave the children many advantages.* **3.** Benefit or profit: *She turned the handicap to her advantage.* **4.** A favorable or preferred position: *His early start gave him the advantage.*

Idioms. **take advantage of.** **1.** To put to good use; benefit by: *take advantage of an opportunity.* **2.** To treat unfairly for selfish reasons: *Don't take advantage of smaller children.* **to advantage.** To good effect; favorably: *The hat shows off her face to advantage.*

ad•van•ta•geous |ăd′văn **tā′**jəs| *or* |ăd′vən-| *adj.* Profitable; favorable; useful; beneficial: *an advantageous location.* **—ad′van•ta′geous•ly** *adv.*

ad•vent |**ăd′**vĕnt′| *n.* **1.** The coming of a new person or thing: *before the advent of the airplane.* **2. Advent.** The birth or coming of Christ. **3. Advent.** The church season including the four Sundays before Christmas. [See Note]

ad•ven•ture |ăd **vĕn′**chər| *n.* **1.** A bold, dangerous, or risky undertaking: *They set out on a daring space adventure.* **2.** An unusual, exciting, or memorable experience: *the adventures of Marco Polo.* **3.** Excitement, danger, or discovery arising from bold action or new experience: *in search of adventure.* ***—modifier:*** *an adventure story.* *—v.* **ad•ven•tured, ad•ven•tur•ing.** To go in search of new or exciting experiences: *Where shall we adventure?* [See Note]

ad•ven•tur•er |ăd **vĕn′**chər ər| *n.* **1.** A person who seeks or has adventures. **2.** A person who seeks wealth in dangerous undertakings or by less than honest means.

ad•ven•ture•some |ăd **vĕn′**chər səm| *adj.* Bold; daring; adventurous.

ad•ven•tur•ous |ăd **vĕn′**chər əs| *adj.* **1.** Fond of adventure; seeking new experience; willing to take risks: *adventurous youths.* **2.** Full of adventure or risk: *their adventurous journey.* **3.** Of or like adventure: *an adventurous feeling.* **—ad•ven′tur•ous•ly** *adv.*

ad•verb |**ăd′**vûrb′| *n.* In grammar, a word used to modify a verb, an adjective, or another adverb. For example, in the sentences *Bob left early, Ann is very pretty,* and *The dog ran very fast,* the words *early, very,* and *fast* are adverbs. Adverbs usually answer questions beginning with "when," "where," and "how" and modify other words with respect to time, place, manner, or degree: *Bob left early* (time), *She went upstairs* (place), *Dick reads well* (manner), *Ann is very pretty* (degree). Many adverbs can be compared: *Dick reads well, but Joe reads better. Bob left early but should have left earlier.*

ad•ver•bi•al |ăd **vûr′**bē əl| *adj.* **1.** Used as an adverb: *an adverbial phrase.* **2.** Of an adverb: *an adverbial form.* *—n.* A phrase or clause used as an adverb. An **adverbial of place** tells where. In the sentence *She was in the yard,* the phrase *in the yard* is an adverbial of place. An **adverbial of manner** tells how. In the sentence *He ran very fast,* the phrase *very fast* is an adverbial of manner. **—ad•ver′bi•al•ly** *adv.*

ad•ver•sar•y |**ăd′**vər sĕr′ē| *n., pl.* **ad•ver•sar•ies.** An opponent or enemy: *He is an adversary worthy of my sword.*

ad•verse |ăd **vûrs′**| *or* |**ăd′**vûrs′| *adj.* **1.** Not favorable; hostile: *adverse criticism; an adverse decision.* **2.** In an opposite direction: *adverse currents.* **—ad•verse′ly** *adv.*

ad•ver•si•ty |ăd **vûr′**sĭ tē| *n., pl.* **ad•ver•si•ties.** Great misfortune; hardship.

ad•ver•tise |**ăd′**vər tīz′| *v.* **ad•ver•tised, ad•ver•tis•ing.** **1.** To make known; call attention to: *The girl advertised her marital status by wearing a ring.* **2.** To call public attention to (a product), as by announcing on the radio, placing a notice in a newspaper, etc.: *Manufacturers advertise their products.* **3.** To give public notice of something, as of something wanted or offered for sale: *We advertised in the lost and found section of the paper.* **—ad′ver•tis′er** *n.*

ad•ver•tise•ment |ăd′vər **tīz′**mənt| *or* |ăd **vûr′**-tĭs mənt| *or* |-tĭz-| *n.* A public notice, as in a newspaper or on the radio, to call attention to a product, a meeting, etc.

ad•ver•tis•ing |**ăd′**vər tī′zĭng| *n.* **1.** The act of calling public attention to a product. **2.** The business of preparing and distributing advertisements. **3.** Advertisements in general. ***—modifier:*** *the advertising business.*

ad•vice |ăd **vīs′**| *n.* Opinion about how to solve a problem; guidance. [See Note]

ad•vis•a•ble |ăd **vī′**zə bəl| *adj.* Worth recommending or suggesting; wise; sensible: *Indiscriminate use of drugs is not advisable.* **—ad•vis′a•bil′i•ty** *n.* **—ad•vis′a•bly** *adv.*

ad•vise |ăd **vīz′**| *v.* **ad•vised, ad•vis•ing.** **1.** To give advice to or offer advice; recommend: *I advise you to call in an expert. Economists advise on the financial state of the nation.* **2.** To seek advice; consult: *Mr. Lorry advised with Lucie*

advent/adventure

Latin advenīre, *"to come to, to arrive, to happen," was formed from* ad-, *"toward,"* + venīre, *"to come."* Advenīre *formed the noun* adventus, *"a coming, an arrival," which was borrowed into English as* **advent.** *The future participle of* advenīre *was* adventūrus, *"about to happen, yet to come"; in Late Latin this formed the noun* adventūra, *"the thing that will happen, future events, chance." This became* aventure *in Old French, and was borrowed into English as* **adventure,** *first meaning "chance or fortune," later also meaning "risk, dangerous action."*

advice

"I have lived thirty years on this planet; and I have yet to hear the first syllable of valuable or even earnest advice from my seniors."
—Henry David Thoreau, Walden.

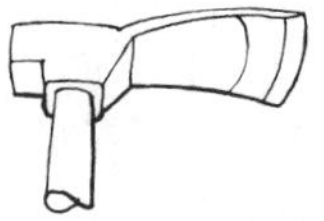

adz

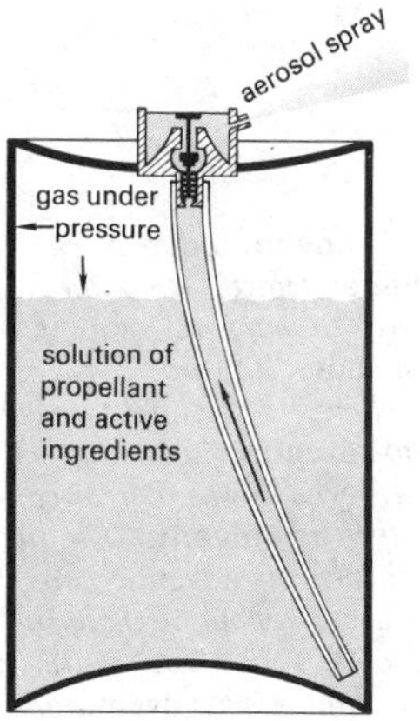

aerosol bomb

affect[1-2]

Affect[1] *and* **affect**[2] *are closely but complexly related.* **Affect**[1] *is from Latin* affectāre, *"to strive after, aim at," which is a special derivative of* afficere, *"to have an effect on, to apply (oneself) to."* **Affect**[2] *is directly from* afficere.

ă pat/ā pay/â care/ä father/ĕ pet/ē be/ĭ pit/ī pie/î fierce/ŏ pot/ō go/ô paw, for/oi oil/ŏŏ book/ōō boot/ou out/ŭ cut/û fur/*th* the/th thin/hw which/zh vision/ə ago, item, pencil, atom, circus

about the doctor. **3.** To inform; notify: *The paper advised us of the ship's arrival.*

ad•vised |ăd **vīzd'**| *adj.* **1.** Thought out; considered: *a poorly advised decision.* **2.** Informed; notified: *He is kept advised of all new developments in his field.*

ad•vis•ed•ly |ăd **vī'**zĭd lē| *adv.* With careful consideration; deliberately.

ad•vis•er, also **ad•vi•sor** |ăd **vī'**zər| *n.* **1.** A person who offers advice, especially officially or professionally. **2.** A teacher who advises students in selecting courses and planning careers.

ad•vi•so•ry |ăd **vī'**zə rē| *adj.* Advising or having the power to advise: *an advisory committee.*

ad•vo•ca•cy |**ăd'**və kə sē| *n.* Active support, as of an idea, cause, or policy.

ad•vo•cate |**ăd'**və kāt'| *v.* **ad•vo•cat•ed, ad•vo•cat•ing.** To be or speak in favor of; recommend; urge: *advocate repeal of a law.* —*n.* |**ăd'**və kĭt| *or* |-kāt'|. **1.** A person who supports or speaks in favor of a cause: *an advocate of gun control.* **2.** *British.* A courtroom lawyer.

adz or **adze** |ădz| *n.* An axlike tool used for dressing wood. [SEE PICTURE]

Ae•ge•an Sea |ĭ **jē'**ən|. A part of the Mediterranean Sea lying between Greece and Turkey.

Ae•ne•as |ĭ **nē'**əs|. In Greek and Roman legend, the Trojan warrior, son of Aphrodite, who is the hero of the *Aeneid.*

Ae•ne•id |ĭ **nē'**ĭd|. The Latin epic poem by Virgil relating the adventures of Aeneas and his followers after the fall of Troy.

ae•on |**ē'**ŏn'| *or* |**ē'**ən| *n.* A form of the word **eon.**

aer•ate |**âr'**āt'| *v.* **aer•at•ed, aer•at•ing. 1.** To supply or charge (a substance) with air or another gas, such as carbon dioxide. **2.** To supply with oxygen and purge of carbon dioxide: *The lungs aerate the blood.* —**aer•a'tion** *n.*

aer•i•al |**âr'**ē əl| *or* |ā **îr'**ē əl| *adj.* **1.** Of, in, or caused by the air. **2.** Of, for, or by aircraft. **3.** High; lofty. **4.** Growing in air without underground support: *aerial roots; aerial plants.* —*n.* An antenna, as for a radio.

aer•i•al•ist |**âr'**ē ə lĭst| *n.* An acrobat who performs on a tightrope or trapeze.

aer•ie |**âr'**ē| *or* |**îr'**ē| *n.* A form of the word **eyrie.** ¶*These sound alike* **aerie, airy, eyrie, eyry.**

aer•obe |**âr'**ōb'| *n.* An aerobic organism.

aer•o•bic |â **rō'**bĭk| *adj.* Needing or using oxygen in the form that appears in air: *aerobic organisms.*

aer•o•drome |**âr'**ə drōm'| *n.* *British.* An airport.

aer•o•dy•nam•ics |âr'ō dī **năm'**ĭks| *n.* *(used with a singular verb).* The scientific study of the motions of and forces associated with air and other gases, especially as they interact with solid objects.

aer•ol•o•gy |â **rŏl'**ə jē| *n.* Meteorology that is based on the study of the entire atmosphere rather than just the part that is close to the earth's surface.

aer•o•nau•tic |âr'ə **nô'**tĭk| or **aer•o•nau•ti•cal** |âr'ə **nô'**tĭ kəl| *adj.* Of or relating to aeronautics or aircraft.

aer•o•nau•tics |âr'ə **nô'**tĭks| *n.* *(used with a singular verb).* **1.** The science and engineering involved in flight in the air and in the design, construction, and operation of aircraft: *Aeronautics is quite complex.* **2.** The theory and practice of aerial navigation.

aer•o•pause |**âr'**ə pôz'| *n.* The level of the atmosphere above which aircraft cannot fly.

aer•o•plane |**âr'**ə plān'| *n.* British form of the word **airplane.**

aer•o•sol |**âr'**ə sôl'| *or* |-sŏl'| *or* |-sōl'| *n.* **1.** A system composed of a large number of tiny particles of a liquid or solid suspended in a gas. **2.** A substance, such as a paint or insecticide, packaged under pressure for use in this form. **3.** Also **aerosol bomb.** A container or package used in this way and small enough to be held in the hand. [SEE PICTURE]

aer•o•space |**âr'**ə spās'| *n.* **1.** The region consisting of the earth's atmosphere and outer space. **2.** The science and technology of flight both in the earth's atmosphere and in outer space. —*modifier: the aerospace industry.*

Ae•sir |**ē'**sĭr| *pl.n.* The gods of Norse mythology.

Ae•sop |**ē'**sŏp'| *or* |**ē'**səp|. Greek writer of animal fables in the sixth century B.C.

aes•thete |**ĕs'**thēt'| *n.* A form of the word **esthete.**

aes•thet•ic |ĕs **thĕt'**ĭk| *adj.* A form of the word **esthetic.**

aes•thet•ics |ĕs **thĕt'**ĭks| *n.* A form of the word **esthetics.**

AF, A.F. air force.

a•far |ə **fär'**| *adv.* Far away; far off: *The mountain is visible from afar.*

a•feard, also **a•feared** |ə **fîrd'**| *adj.* An archaic and dialectal form of the word **afraid.**

af•fa•ble |**ăf'**ə bəl| *adj.* Mild-mannered and pleasant; gentle; friendly. —**af'fa•bly** *adv.*

af•fair |ə **fâr'**| *n.* **1.** A matter or concern: *a private affair; a scandalous affair involving two companies.* **2.** An occurrence, action, event, or procedure: *I have heard several versions of this affair. Setting one's hair is a 20-minute affair.* **3. affairs.** Matters of business interest or public concern: *world affairs; affairs of state.* **4.** A social gathering: *The ball was a glittering affair.* **5.** A thing or object: *The new boat is not a very large affair.* **6.** A romance: *They had a short love affair.*

af•fect[1] |ə **fĕkt'**| *v.* **1.** To have an influence on; bring about a change in: *Geography affects people's ways of living.* **2.** To touch or move the emotions of: *How does rudeness affect you?* **3.** To attack or infect: *Anthrax affects cattle and sheep.* —**af•fect'ing** *adj.: an affecting tale of woe.* [SEE NOTE]

af•fect[2] |ə **fĕkt'**| *v.* **1.** To imitate in order to make a desired impression; pretend to have; assume: *He affected an English accent because he thought it sounded better.* **2.** To like; prefer: *He affects striped shirts.* —**af•fect'ed** *adj.: an affected voice.* [SEE NOTE]

af•fec•ta•tion |ăf'ĕk **tā'**shən| *n.* Artificial behavior designed to impress others; pretense.

af•fec•tion |ə **fĕk'**shən| *n.* **1.** A fond or tender feeling toward someone or something; fondness. **2.** A disease or diseased condition. **3.** Often **affections.** Feeling or emotion.

af•fec•tion•ate |ə **fĕk'**shə nĭt| *adj.* Having or showing affection; tender; loving. —**af•fec'tion•ate•ly** *adv.*

af•fer•ent |ăf′ər ənt| *adj.* Directed or leading toward a central organ or part of an organism: *an afferent nerve.*

af•fi•ance |ə fī′əns| *v.* **af•fi•anced, af•fi•anc•ing.** To promise in marriage: *He affianced his daughter to a young minister.* —**af•fi′anced** *adj.*: *the affianced couple.*

af•fi•da•vit |ăf′ĭ dā′vĭt| *n.* A written declaration made under oath before a notary public or other authorized officer.

af•fil•i•ate |ə fĭl′ē āt′| *v.* **af•fil•i•at•ed, af•fil•i•at•ing.** To associate or join, as with a larger or more important body: *The local affiliated with the national union.* —*n.* |ə fĭl′ē ĭt| *or* |-āt′|. A person or company associated or joined with another: *We have affiliates abroad as well as here.* —**af•fil′i•a′tion** *n.*

af•fin•i•ty |ə fĭn′ĭ tē| *n., pl.* **af•fin•i•ties. 1.** A natural attraction; liking: *Our dog has an affinity for people.* **2.** A similarity based on relationship: *The two cousins have a closer affinity to their ancestors than most members of their family.* **3.** A chemical or physical attraction.

af•firm |ə fûrm′| *v.* **1.** To declare positively; say firmly. **2.** To give approval or validity to; confirm.

af•firm•a•tion |ăf′ər mā′shən| *n.* **1.** The act of affirming. **2.** Something affirmed.

af•firm•a•tive |ə fûr′mə tĭv| *adj.* Giving assent; responding positively, as with the word *yes.* —*n.* **1.** A positive answer or response. **2. the affirmative.** The side in a debate that supports the question being debated. —**af•firm′a•tive•ly** *adv.*

af•fix |ə fĭks′| *v.* To add on; attach: *He affixed the seal to the document.* —*n.* |ăf′ĭks′|. Something added on or attached, especially a prefix or suffix.

af•flict |ə flĭkt′| *v.* To cause distress to; cause to suffer; trouble greatly: *Mankind is afflicted with many ills.*

af•flic•tion |ə flĭk′shən| *n.* **1.** A condition of pain or distress. **2.** A cause of pain or suffering: *Scurvy used to be a common affliction among sailors.*

af•flu•ence |ăf′lo͞o əns| *n.* **1.** Wealth; riches. **2.** A plentiful supply; abundance.

af•flu•ent |ăf′lo͞o ənt| *adj.* Having plenty of money; fairly rich. —**af′flu•ent•ly** *adv.*

af•ford |ə fôrd′| *or* |ə fōrd′| *v.* **1.** To be able to pay for or spare: *We can't afford a new TV set. I can't afford the time.* **2.** To be able to do or be without: *more than we can afford to spend right now. This is one game we can't afford to lose.* **3.** To give or furnish; provide: *The shelter afforded protection from the rain.* **4.** To be able to do without harming oneself: *He can afford to be kind.*

af•fright |ə frīt′| *v. Archaic.* To frighten; terrify.

af•front |ə frŭnt′| *v.* **1.** To insult intentionally. **2.** To offend strongly. —*n.* **1.** An intentional insult. **2.** A strong offense.

Af•ghan |ăf′găn′| *or* |-gən| *n.* **1.** A native or inhabitant of Afghanistan. **2. afghan.** A colorful wool blanket or shawl made of knitted or crocheted squares, circles, diamonds, etc. **3.** Also **Afghan hound.** A large, slender dog with long, thick hair, a pointed snout, and drooping ears. —*adj.* Of Afghanistan or the Afghans. [SEE PICTURES]

af•ghan•i |ăf găn′ē| *n.* The basic unit of money of Afghanistan.

Af•ghan•i•stan |ăf găn′ĭ stăn′|. A country in southwestern Asia, between Iran and Pakistan. Population, 15,540,000. Capital, Kabul.

a•fi•ci•o•na•do |ə fĭsh′ə nä′dō| *n., pl.* **a•fi•ci•o•na•dos.** An enthusiastic admirer; devotee.

a•field |ə fēld′| *adv.* **1.** Often **far (or farther) afield. a.** Away from one's usual environment; to or at a distance: *He wandered far afield in search of his brother.* **b.** Off or away from the subject: *His accusations went farther afield.* **2.** In or on the field: *Afield, a knife is a tool.*

a•fire |ə fīr′| *adj. & adv.* On fire or as if on fire; burning: *The room was afire. His ideas set them afire.*

AFL, A.F.L., A.F. of L. The American Federation of Labor.

a•flame |ə flām′| *adj.* In flames or as if in flames; flaming: *The house is aflame.*

AFL-CIO, A.F.L.-C.I.O. The American Federation of Labor and Congress of Industrial Organizations.

a•float |ə flōt′| *adj.* **1.** Floating: *The raft was afloat on the lake.* **2.** On a boat or ship; at sea. **3.** In circulation: *Talk of a storm is afloat.* **4.** Flooded: *The basement was afloat.*

a•flut•ter |ə flŭt′ər| *adj.* In a flutter; excited; agitated.

a•foot |ə fo͝ot′| *adj. & adv.* **1.** On foot; walking. **2.** In the process of happening; astir: *Something strange is afoot.*

a•fore |ə fôr′| *or* |ə fōr′| *prep. & adv.* An archaic and dialectal form of the word **before.**

a•fore•men•tioned |ə fôr′mĕn′shənd| *or* |ə fōr′-| *adj.* Mentioned before.

a•fore•said |ə fôr′sĕd′| *or* |ə fōr′-| *adj.* Spoken of before.

a•fore•thought |ə fôr′thôt′| *or* |ə fōr′-| *adj.* Planned beforehand; premeditated: *malice aforethought.*

a•foul |ə foul′| *adj.* In a snarl; tangled.
Idiom. **run (or fall) afoul of.** To have trouble with: *the criminal ran afoul of the authorities.*

a•fraid |ə frād′| *adj.* **1.** Filled with fear; fearful. **2.** Reluctant; hesitant: *not afraid of work.* **3.** Regretful: *I'm afraid you don't understand.*

a•fresh |ə frĕsh′| *adv.* Anew; again: *We must start afresh.*

Af•ri•ca |ăf′rĭ kə|. A continent located south of Europe between the Atlantic and Indian oceans. —**Af′ri•can** *adj. & n.*

African violet. A popular house plant, originally from Africa, with violetlike, usually purplish flowers. [SEE PICTURE]

Af•ri•kaans |ăf′rĭ käns′| *or* |-känz′| *n.* The chief language of South Africa, developed from 17th-century Dutch.

Af•ri•kan•er |ăf′rĭ kä′nər| *n.* An Afrikaans-speaking descendant of the Dutch settlers of South Africa.

Af•ro |ăf′rō′| *n., pl.* **Af•ros.** A hair style in which dense frizzy hair is worn naturally. —*adj.* Directly or indirectly African in style.

Af•ro-A•mer•i•can |ăf′rō ə mĕr′ĭ kən| *n.* An American of African descent. —**Af′ro-A•mer′i•can** *adj.*

aft |ăft| *or* |äft| *adv. & adj.* Toward or near a ship's stern: *going aft; the aft cabin.*

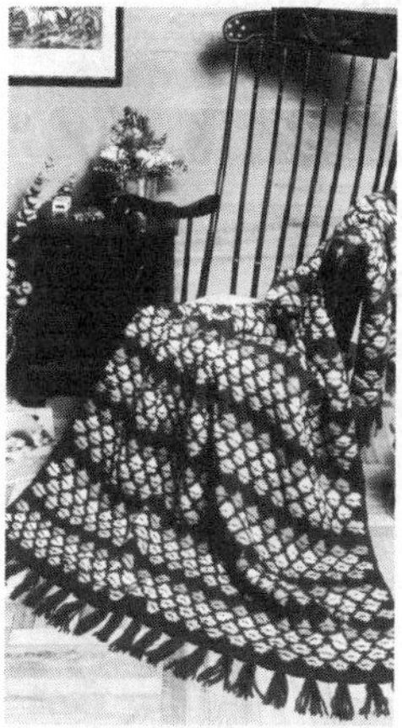

Afghan coverlet

Afghan hound

African violet
The African violet is not related to the true violets, although the flowers of both kinds of plants look somewhat alike.

afterward/afterwards
In the materials from which this Dictionary was made, **afterward** *appeared 69 times and* **afterwards** *134 times.*

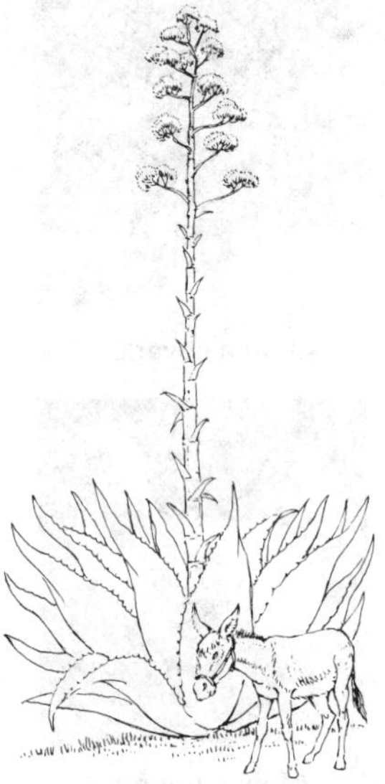
agave

Ag
The symbol **Ag** *is taken from* **argentum,** *the Latin word for silver.*

ă pat/ā pay/â care/ä father/ĕ pet/ ē be/ĭ pit/ī pie/î fierce/ŏ pot/ ō go/ô paw, for/oi oil/o͝o book/ o͞o boot/ou out/ŭ cut/û fur/ *th* the/th thin/hw which/zh vision/ ə ago, item, pencil, atom, circus

af•ter |ăf′tər| *or* |äf′-| *prep.* **1.** In a place or order following: *The caboose comes after the freight cars.* **2. a.** In pursuit of: *running after the fire engine.* **b.** Out to get: *They're after me.* **3.** About; concerning: *I asked after you.* **4.** At a later time than: *after the war.* **5.** Past the hour of: *five minutes after three.* **6.** With the same name as: *named after her mother.* *—conj.* As soon as or following the time that: *We can eat after we get home.* *—adv.* **1.** Afterward: *forever after.* **2.** Behind: *And Jill came tumbling after.* *—adj.* **1.** Later: *in after years.* **2.** Nearer a ship's stern: *the after quarter.*

after all. In spite of everything; nevertheless: *We'll win the game after all.*

af•ter•birth |ăf′tər bûrth′| *or* |äf′-| *n.* The material expelled from the uterus after a human being or other mammal is born. It consists of the placenta and fetal membranes.

af•ter•burn•er |ăf′tər bûr′nər| *or* |äf′-| *n.* A device that increases the power of a jet engine by injecting extra fuel into the stream of hot exhaust gases where the extra fuel burns.

af•ter•deck |ăf′tər dĕk′| *or* |äf′-| *n.* The part of a ship's deck past amidships toward the stern.

af•ter•ef•fect |ăf′tər ĭ fĕkt′| *or* |äf′-| *n.* An effect that follows its cause after a delay, especially a delayed bodily or mental response to something: *His nervousness was an aftereffect of the accident.*

af•ter•glow |ăf′tər glō′| *or* |äf′-| *n.* **1.** Light that remains after the removal of the source of illumination, as the atmospheric glow after sunset. **2.** A comfortable feeling after a pleasant experience.

af•ter•im•age |ăf′tər ĭm′ĭj| *or* |äf′-| *n.* An image that continues to be seen when the original cause of its being seen is no longer there.

af•ter•life |ăf′tər līf′| *or* |äf′-| *n.* Life or existence after death.

af•ter•math |ăf′tər măth′| *or* |äf′-| *n.* A consequence or result, especially of a disaster or misfortune: *the aftermath of a hurricane.*

af•ter•noon |ăf′tər no͞on′| *or* |äf′-| *n.* The part of the day from noon until sunset. ***—modifier:*** *an afternoon nap; afternoon tea.*

af•ter•taste |ăf′tər tāst′| *or* |äf′-| *n.* A taste that remains in the mouth after the substance that caused it is no longer there.

af•ter•thought |ăf′tər thôt′| *or* |äf′-| *n.* An idea that occurs to a person after an event, decision, etc.

af•ter•ward |ăf′tər wərd| *or* |äf′-| *adv.* At a later time; subsequently. [SEE NOTE]

af•ter•wards |ăf′tər wərdz| *or* |äf′-| *adv.* Afterward. [SEE NOTE]

Ag The symbol for the element silver. [SEE NOTE]

a•gain |ə gĕn′| *adv.* **1.** Once more; anew. **2.** To a previous place or position. **3.** Furthermore. **4.** On the other hand: *He might go, and then again he might not.*

a•gainst |ə gĕnst′| *prep.* **1.** In a direction or course opposite to: *sailing against the wind.* **2.** So as to come into contact with: *waves dashing against the shore.* **3.** In hostile opposition or resistance to: *struggling against change.* **4.** Contrary to: *against my better judgment.* **5.** In contrast to: *dark colors against a light background.* **6.** As a defense or safeguard from: *wearing gloves against the chill.* **7.** To the account or debt of: *drew a check against my bank balance.*

A•ga•na |ə gä′nyə|. The capital of Guam. Population, 881.

a•gar |ā′gär| *or* |ä′gär| *n.* A jellylike material that is prepared from algae that live in the sea and is used as the base of media on which bacteria are grown.

ag•ate |ăg′ĭt| *n.* **1.** A type of quartz that is cloudy in appearance and streaked with color. **2.** A child's marble made of this or a similar material.

a•ga•ve |ə gä′vē| *or* |ə gä′-| *n.* Any of several tropical American plants with large, thick leaves that are often the source of a fiber used for making rope or sacks. [SEE PICTURE]

age |āj| *n.* **1.** The period or length of time during which someone or something has existed. **2.** A lifetime or lifespan. **3.** A specific moment in life: *the age of five.* **4.** The time in life when a person assumes adult rights and responsibilities: *He is under age. He became of age yesterday.* **5.** The latter part of life; the condition of being old. **6.** Often **Age.** any distinctive period of history or geology: *the space age; the age of the dinosaurs.* **7. a.** A long span of time or history: *The earth changed as the ages passed.* **b.** A long time: *She worked for an age on the dress.* *—v.* **aged, ag•ing. 1.** To cause to grow old: *Trouble aged the man.* **2.** To become old: *He aged quickly.* **3.** To allow time for alcoholic beverages, cheese, or meat to mature or become flavorful.

-age. A suffix that forms nouns and means: **1.** Collectively; in general: **leafage; mileage. 2.** Condition; state: **bondage; marriage. 3.** Charge or fee: **postage. 4.** Residence or place: **orphanage. 5.** Act or result: **spoilage.**

aged[1] |ājd| *adj.* **1.** Of the age of: *a girl aged five.* **2.** Mature: *an aged cheese.*

ag•ed[2] |ā′jĭd| *adj.* Old; elderly. *—n.* **the aged.** Very old people: *Some of the aged receive pensions.*

age•less |āj′lĭs| *adj.* **1.** Seeming never to grow old. **2.** Existing forever; eternal.

age-long |āj′lông′| *or* |-lŏng′| *adj.* Lasting for a long time: *the age-long evolution of mammals.*

a•gen•cy |ā′jən sē| *n., pl.* **a•gen•cies. 1.** Someone or something that helps achieve an end; a means. **2.** A business or service authorized to act for others: *a real estate agency; a detective agency.* **3.** A governmental department of administration or regulation.

a•gen•da |ə jĕn′də| *pl.n. (used with a singular verb).* The less frequently used singular is **a•gen•dum** |ə jĕn′dəm|. A list of things to be done, as a program of business at a meeting.

a•gent |ā′jənt| *n.* **1.** Someone with the power or authority to act for another: *a railroad agent; a publicity agent.* **2.** A representative of a government or a governmental department: *an FBI agent.* **3.** A means by which something is done or caused: *agents of erosion.*

age-old |āj′ōld′| *adj.* Very old; ancient: *an age-old enemy; age-old rocks.*

ag•glom•er•ate |ə glŏm′ə rāt′| *v.* **ag•glom•er•at•ed, ag•glom•er•at•ing.** To make or form into a rounded mass. *—adj.* |ə glŏm′ər ĭt| *or* |-ə rāt′|. Gathered or shaped into a rounded mass. *—n.*

|ə glŏm′ər ĭt| *or* |-ə rāt′|. **1.** A jumbled mass of things heaped together. **2.** A volcanic rock consisting of rounded and angular fragments fused together in a disordered way.

ag•glom•er•a•tion |ə glŏm′ə rā′shən| *n.* **1.** The act of making a confused or jumbled mass of things heaped together. **2.** A jumbled mass; agglomerate.

ag•glu•ti•nate |ə glo͞ot′n āt′| *v.* **ag•glu•ti•nat•ed, ag•glu•ti•nat•ing. 1.** To join together, as with glue. **2.** To undergo or cause to undergo agglutination.

ag•glu•ti•na•tion |ə glo͞ot′n ā′shən| *n.* **1.** The adhesion of distinct parts. **2.** A process in which a group of microorganisms, blood cells, etc., clump together or are caused to clump together into a mass. **3.** The mass formed in this way.

ag•gran•dize |ə grăn′dīz′| *or* |ăg′rən dīz′| *v.* **ag•gran•dized, ag•gran•diz•ing. 1.** To increase the scope of; enlarge; extend. **2.** To make greater in power, influence, etc. —**ag•grand′dize•ment** |ə-grăn′dĭz mənt| *or* |-dīz′-| *n.*

ag•gra•vate |ăg′rə vāt′| *v.* **ag•gra•vat•ed, ag•gra•vat•ing. 1.** To make worse: *aggravate an injury.* **2.** To irritate; provoke. [SEE NOTE]

ag•gra•va•tion |ăg′rə vā′shən| *n.* **1.** The act or process of aggravating. **2.** Irritation; annoyance.

ag•gre•gate |ăg′rə gĭt| *or* |-gāt′| *adj.* Gathered into or considered together as a mass, sum, or whole; total or combined. —*n.* **1.** Any total or whole; a gross amount. **2.** The materials, such as sand and stone, used to give body to concrete. —*v.* |ăg′rə gāt′| **ag•gre•gat•ed, ag•gre•gat•ing. 1.** To gather into a mass, sum, or whole. **2.** To total up to; amount to. —**ag′gre•ga′tion** *n.*

ag•gres•sion |ə grĕsh′ən| *n.* **1.** The action of a country in launching an unprovoked attack on another country: *An act of aggression often starts a war.* **2.** Hostile action or behavior.

ag•gres•sive |ə grĕs′ĭv| *adj.* **1.** Quick to attack or start a fight: *an aggressive youngster.* **2.** Vigorous; energetic: *an aggressive salesman.* —**ag•gres′sive•ly** *adv.* —**ag•gres′sive•ness** *n.*

ag•gres•sor |ə grĕs′ər| *n.* A person or country that attacks another without cause or justification.

ag•grieve |ə grēv′| *v.* **ag•grieved, ag•griev•ing. 1.** To distress or afflict. **2.** To injure or treat unjustly; wrong. —**ag•grieved′** *adj.*: *an aggrieved prisoner; an aggrieved orphan.*

a•ghast |ə găst′| *or* |ə gäst′| *adj.* Shocked or horrified, as by something terrible.

ag•ile |ăj′əl| *or* |ăj′īl′| *adj.* **1.** Able to move quickly and easily; nimble. **2.** Mentally alert. —**ag′ile•ly** *adv.*

a•gil•i•ty |ə jĭl′ĭ tē| *n.* The quality or condition of being agile; nimbleness.

a•gin |ə gĭn′| *adv. & prep.* A dialectal form of the words **again** and **against.** [SEE NOTE]

ag•i•tate |ăj′ĭ tāt′| *v.* **ag•i•tat•ed, ag•i•tat•ing. 1.** To shake or stir up violently: *The storm agitated the sea.* **2.** To disturb; upset. **3.** To stir up public interest in a cause: *agitate for passage of a new law.*

ag•i•ta•tion |ăj′ĭ tā′shən| *n.* **1.** The act of violently shaking or stirring up. **2.** Great emotional disturbance or excitement. **3.** Energetic action to arouse public interest in a cause.

ag•i•ta•tor |ăj′ĭ tā′tər| *n.* **1.** A mechanism that stirs or shakes, as in a washing machine. **2.** A person active in stirring up interest in a cause.

a•gleam |ə glēm′| *adj.* Brightly shining.

a•glit•ter |ə glĭt′ər| *adj.* Glittering; sparkling.

a•glow |ə glō′| *adj.* Glowing brightly.

ag•nos•tic |ăg nŏs′tĭk| *n.* Someone who disclaims any knowledge of God but does not deny the possibility of his existence.

ag•nos•ti•cism |ăg nŏs′tĭ sĭz′əm| *n.* The theory or practices of agnostics.

a•go |ə gō′| *adj.* Gone by; past: *two years ago.* —*adv.* In the past: *They lived there long ago.*

a•gog |ə gŏg′| *adj.* Full of eager anticipation; greatly excited.

a•gon•ic line |ā gŏn′ĭk|. A line connecting points on the earth's surface where the magnetic declination is zero.

ag•o•nize |ăg′ə nīz′| *v.* **ag•o•nized, ag•o•niz•ing.** To suffer great distress: *agonize over a decision.*

ag•o•niz•ing |ăg′ə nī′zĭng| *adj.* Causing great pain or anguish: *an agonizing decision.* —**ag′o•niz′ing•ly** *adv.*

ag•o•ny |ăg′ə nē| *n., pl.* **ag•o•nies.** Intense and prolonged pain or suffering.

ag•o•ra |ăg′ər ə| *n., pl.* **ag•o•rae** |ăg′ə rē| or **ag•o•ras.** The marketplace of an ancient Greek city, used as a meeting place.

a•gou•ti |ə go͞o′tē| *n., pl.* **a•gou•tis.** A tropical American rodent with a rabbitlike body and short ears. [SEE PICTURE]

a•grar•i•an |ə grâr′ē ən| *adj.* Of or concerning farm land or its ownership: *agrarian reform; agrarian countries.*

a•gree |ə grē′| *v.* **a•greed, a•gree•ing. 1.** To have or share the same opinion; concur: *I agree with you.* **2.** To consent; say "yes": *Her parents would never agree to the marriage.* **3.** To be in harmony or accord: *The two versions of the story do not agree.* **4.** To arrive at a settlement: *agree on a price. The jury could not agree on a verdict.* **5.** To be easily digested or good for one's health: *Onions do not agree with me. The climate here does not agree with him.* **6.** In grammar, to correspond in number, gender, case, or person: *In this sentence the verb agrees with the subject.*

a•gree•a•ble |ə grē′ə bəl| *adj.* **1.** Pleasing; pleasant: *an agreeable odor.* **2.** Willing to agree or consent: *He was agreeable to the suggestion.* —**a•gree′a•ble•ness** *n.* —**a•gree′a•bly** *adv.*

a•greed |ə grēd′| *adj.* Determined by common consent: *the agreed price; the agreed meeting place.*

a•gree•ment |ə grē′mənt| *n.* **1.** Harmony of opinion: *complete agreement on the subjects discussed.* **2.** An arrangement or understanding between two parties: *a gentleman's agreement.* **3.** In grammar, correspondence between words in gender, number, case, or person.

ag•ri•cul•ture |ăg′rĭ kŭl′chər| *n.* The science, art, and business of cultivating the soil in order to produce useful crops and livestock; farming. —**ag′ri•cul′tur•al** *adj.* [SEE NOTE]

a•gron•o•my |ə grŏn′ə mē| *n.* The use of scientific knowledge and methods in farming; scientific farming. —**a•gron′o•mist** *n.*

a•ground |ə ground′| *adv. & adj.* Stranded in shallow water or on a reef or shoal: *The ship ran aground during the storm.*

aggravate

Many writers and teachers have for years disapproved of the use of **aggravate** *to mean "irritate." But their efforts to stamp it out have completely failed, since this sense has been in continuous use since about 1600, and is now probably the commonest use of the word.*

agin

In standard usage, **agin** *occurs as a mostly humorous substitute for* **against** *when the person who is "against" something is felt to be especially stubborn or unreasonable. When* **agin** *is used in this way in writing, it is usually put in quotation marks: "They attended every meeting and were always 'agin' something."*

agouti

agriculture

Agriculture *comes from Latin* agrī cultūra, *"the care or cultivation of land."* Agrī *is the possessive case of* ager, *"land, a field." This is descended from the prehistoric Indo-European word* agros, *"a field, a pasture," which is also represented in the English word* **acre.**

ain't
The contracted form **ain't** *developed at about the time of the settlement of America. It has never been accepted in formal English.*

aircraft carrier

Airedale

ă pat/ā pay/â care/ä father/ĕ pet/ ē be/ĭ pit/ī pie/î fierce/ŏ pot/ ō go/ô paw, for/oi oil/o͝o book/ o͞o boot/ou out/ŭ cut/û fur/ *th* the/th thin/hw which/zh vision/ ə ago, item, pencil, atom, circus

a•gue |ā'gyo͞o| *n.* **1.** A fever, like that of malaria, in which there are periods of chills, fever, and sweating. **2.** A chill.
ah |ä| *interj.* A word used to express surprise, delight, pity, and other emotions.
a•ha |ä hä'| *interj.* A word used to express satisfaction, pleasure, or triumph: *Aha! I've got you now!*
a•head |ə hĕd'| *adv.* **1.** At or to the front: *moving ahead.* **2.** In advance: *To get tickets you have to phone ahead.* **3.** Forward or onward. *—adj.* Which leads or is located further forward: *the road ahead.*
Idiom. **get ahead.** To near or attain success.
ahead of. In front of: *the road ahead of us.*
a•hem |ə hĕm'| *interj.* An exclamation made by clearing the throat, used to attract attention or to express doubt or warning.
a•hoy |ə hoi'| *interj.* A word used by sailors to hail a ship or person or to attract attention.
aid |ād| *v.* To help or assist: *aid a friend in distress.* *—n.* **1.** Help; assistance: *foreign aid.* **2.** Something or someone that helps or is helpful: *a hearing aid; visual aids used in teaching.* ¶*These sound alike* **aid, aide.**
aide |ād| *n.* **1.** An assistant or helper: *a Presidential aide.* **2.** An aide-de-camp. ¶*These sound alike* **aide, aid.**
aide-de-camp |ād'də kămp'| *n., pl.* **aides-de-camp.** A military officer acting as secretary and assistant to a general.
ai•grette |ā grĕt'| *or* |ā'grĕt'| *n.* **1.** A tuft of upright plumes or feathers, especially those from an egret's tail. **2.** A plumelike spray of jewels worn on the head.
ail |āl| *v.* **1.** To be ill: *My mother is ailing.* **2.** To cause pain; make ill: *What's ailing you?* ¶*These sound alike* **ail, ale.**
ai•lan•thus |ā lăn'thəs| *n., pl.* **ai•lan•thus•es.** A tree that has pointed leaflets in a featherlike arrangement and is very common in cities.
ai•ler•on |ā'lə rŏn'| *n.* Either of a pair of movable flaps on the wings of an airplane that can be used to make the airplane turn on the axis between its nose and tail.
ail•ment |āl'mənt| *n.* A mild illness or disease that is usually long-lasting and sometimes permanent: *a heart ailment.*
aim |ām| *v.* **1.** To direct (a weapon, blow, remark, etc.) at someone or something: *aim a gun at a target. He aimed and fired.* **2.** To have as a goal: *We aim to please.* *—n.* **1. a.** The pointing of a weapon at a target: *take careful aim.* **b.** The ability of a person to hit a target: *His aim is deadly.* **2.** Purpose; goal: *one's aim in life.*
aim•less |ām'lĭs| *adj.* Without direction or purpose. **—aim'less•ly** *adv.* **—aim'less•ness** *n.*
ain't |ānt|. Dialectal contracted form of the phrases *am not, is not, are not, have not,* and *has not.* [SEE NOTE]
air |âr| *n.* **1.** The colorless, odorless, tasteless mixture of gases that surrounds the earth. It contains about 78 per cent nitrogen and 21 per cent oxygen, with the remaining part being made up of argon, carbon dioxide, neon, helium, and other gases. Air also contains varying amounts of water vapor, dust particles, and assorted pollutants. **2.** The open space above the earth: *a photograph taken from the air. The batter hit the ball high into the air. Music filled the air.* **3.** Transportation by aircraft: *travel by air; ship goods by air.* **4.** The general look or appearance of a person or thing: *He has a very dignified air.* **5. airs.** An affected, unnatural way of acting, intended to impress people: *put on airs; give oneself airs.* **6.** A melody or tune. **—*modifier:*** *an air bubble; air travel; air power; air currents.* *—v.* **1. a.** To expose to the air so as to dry, cool, or freshen; ventilate: *air a blanket.* **b.** To become fresh or cool by exposure to the air: *give the room a chance to air out.* **2.** To express publicly: *air one's grievances.* ¶*These sound alike* **air, are[2], e'er, ere, heir.**
Idioms. **clear the air.** To clear up tension or misunderstanding through frank and open discussion. **on the air.** Being broadcast. **up in the air.** Not settled; undecided. **walk on air.** To feel very happy or elated.
air base. A base for military aircraft.
air•borne |âr'bôrn'| *or* |-bōrn'| *adj.* **1.** Carried or transported by air: *airborne troops.* **2.** In flight; flying: *He unfastened his seat belt as soon as the plane was airborne.*
air brake. A type of brake, often used on trains or large trucks, that is operated by the power of compressed air.
air•brush |âr'brŭsh'| *n.* A small spray gun used to apply paints, inks, or dyes to a surface, as in painting or drawing.
air coach. Accommodations on a passenger plane that are lower in price and less luxurious than those in first class.
air-con•di•tion |âr'kən dĭsh'ən| *v.* **1.** To ventilate (an enclosed space) by means of an air conditioner or air conditioners. **2.** To provide with air conditioning. **—air'-con•di'tioned** *adj.: an air-conditioned room; an air-conditioned theater.*
air conditioner. A device, especially a cooling device, that regulates the temperature and humidity of the air in an enclosure.
air conditioning. A system of air conditioners or the condition that it produces.
air-cool |âr'ko͞ol'| *v.* To cool by a flow of air. **—air'-cooled'** *adj.: an air-cooled engine.*
air•craft |âr'krăft'| *or* |-kräft'| *n., pl.* **air•craft.** Any machine or device, such as an airplane, helicopter, glider, or dirigible, that is capable of flying.
aircraft carrier. A naval ship designed to serve as a seagoing air base, having a long flat deck on which aircraft can take off and land. [SEE PICTURE]
air•drome |âr'drōm'| *n.* **1.** An airport or landing field. **2.** A hangar.
Aire•dale |âr'dāl'| *n.* A large terrier with a wiry tan and black coat. [SEE PICTURE]
air•field |âr'fēld'| *n.* A place, usually with paved runways, where aircraft can take off and land.
air•flow |âr'flō'| *n.* A flow of air, especially when caused by the motion of an aircraft, automobile, or similar object.
air•foil |âr'foil'| *n.* A surface, such as an aircraft wing or propeller blade, designed to interact with a flow of air and produce a desired force or set of forces.
air force. Often **Air Force.** The branch of a country's armed forces equipped with planes.
air•glow |âr'glō'| *n.* A glow seen in the night

sky, resulting from chemical changes produced by radiation from the sun when it strikes the upper atmosphere.

air gun. A gun that is discharged by compressed air.

air hole. **1.** A hole through which air can pass, as in the frozen surface of a body of water. **2.** A hole or bubble filled with air.

air•i•ly |âr′ə lē| *adv.* In a light or airy manner; gaily; jauntily.

air•ing |âr′ĭng| *n.* **1.** Exposure to the air for drying, cooling, freshening, etc. **2.** Public expression or discussion. **3.** Exercise out of doors: *I took my dog for an airing.*

air lane. A regular route of travel for aircraft.

air•less |âr′lĭs| *adj.* **1.** Without air. **2.** Lacking fresh air; stuffy.

air letter. A sheet of paper, with an imprinted airmail stamp, on which a letter may be written. The paper is folded to form an envelope.

air•lift |âr′lĭft′| *n.* A system of transporting troops or supplies by air when surface routes are blocked. —*v.* To transport by air when ground routes are blocked.

air•line |âr′līn′| *n.* A company that transports passengers and freight by air.

air•lin•er |âr′lī′nər| *n.* A large commercial passenger plane.

air lock. An airtight chamber, usually between regions of different pressure, into which it is capable of being opened. It allows passage between the regions with a minimum escape of air.

air•mail |âr′māl′| *adj.* Of or for use with air mail: *an airmail letter; an airmail stamp.*

air mail. **1.** Mail transported by air. **2.** The system of transporting mail by air.

air•man |âr′mən| *n., pl.* **-men** |-mən|. An enlisted man of the lowest rank in the U.S. Air Force.

air mass. A large body of air that has approximately the same temperature and humidity throughout.

air•plane |âr′plān′| *n.* Any of various vehicles that are heavier than air but that are capable of flying through it. Airplanes are held aloft by lift produced by airfoils such as wings and driven by rotating propellers or jet engines.

air pocket. A downward current of air that makes an aircraft lose altitude suddenly.

air•port |âr′pôrt′| *or* |-pōrt′| *n.* A permanent facility that provides space for aircraft to take off and land and that is equipped with a control tower, hangars, refueling equipment, and accommodations for passengers and cargo.

air pressure. The force that air exerts on each unit of a surface that it touches.

air pump. A pump used to compress air or to cause it to flow.

air raid. An attack by hostile military aircraft armed with bombs.

air rifle. A rifle, usually of low power, from which pellets are propelled by compressed air.

air sac. An air-filled space in the body, especially an alveolus of a lung or one of the spaces in a bird's body that connect the lungs and bone cavities.

air•ship |âr′shĭp′| *n.* A self-propelled, steerable aircraft that is lighter than air; a dirigible. [SEE PICTURE]

air•sick |âr′sĭk′| *adj.* Suffering from airsickness: *an airsick passenger.*

air•sick•ness |âr′sĭk′nĭs| *n.* Nausea and discomfort experienced when riding in an aircraft, as a result of nervousness, the motions of the aircraft, or changes in pressure.

air speed. The speed with which the air moves past an object, especially when the air is relatively stationary and the object is in motion, as in the case of a moving aircraft. [SEE NOTE]

air•stream |âr′strēm′| *n.* A flow of air, especially one such as that which passes by an aircraft because of the action of its propellers.

air•strip |âr′strĭp′| *n.* A flat, clear area that can serve as an airfield, usually only temporarily or in emergencies.

air•tight |âr′tīt′| *adj.* **1.** Allowing no air or other gas to pass in or out: *an airtight seal.* **2.** Having no weak points; sound: *an airtight excuse.*

air•waves |âr′wāvz′| *pl.n.* The means by which radio and television programs are broadcast.

air•way |âr′wā′| *n.* **1.** A passage through which air circulates, as in ventilating a mine. **2.** A route for aircraft; an air lane.

air•wor•thy |âr′wûr′*thē*| *adj.* Ready for and capable of flight: *an airworthy airplane.*

air•y |âr′ē| *adj.* **air•i•er, air•i•est.** **1.** With air freely circulating: *The house was light and airy.* **2.** Light-hearted; gay: *airy songs.* **3.** Light as air; delicate: *airy silk.* **4.** Unreal or impractical; without substance: *airy schemes.* ¶*These sound alike* **airy, aerie, eyrie, eyry.**

aisle |īl| *n.* **1.** A passageway between rows of seats, as in a church or theater. **2.** Any passageway, as between counters in a department store. ¶*These sound alike* **aisle, I'll, isle.**

a•jar |ə jär′| *adj. & adv.* Partially open: *leave the door ajar.*

a•kim•bo |ə kĭm′bō| *adj. & adv.* With the hands on the hips and the elbows bent outward. [SEE PICTURE]

a•kin |ə kĭn′| *adj.* **1.** Related by blood. **2.** Derived from the same origin: *The word "maternal" is akin to the word "mother."*

Al The symbol for the element aluminum.

-al[1]. A suffix that forms adjectives from some nouns: **adjectival; postal.**

-al[2]. A suffix that forms nouns from some verbs: **denial; arrival.**

Ala. Alabama.

Al•a•bam•a |ăl′ə **băm′**ə|. A Southern state of the United States. Population, 3,475,000. Capital, Montgomery. —**Al′a•bam′an** *adj. & n.*

al•a•bas•ter |ăl′ə băs′tər| *or* |-bä′stər| *n.* Any of various hard, translucent, often tinted or banded minerals that consist mainly of salts of calcium.

à la carte |ä′ lə **kärt′**| *or* |ăl′ə|. With a separate price for each item on the menu.

a•lack |ə **lăk′**| *interj. Archaic.* A word used to express sorrow, regret, or alarm.

a•lac•ri•ty |ə **lăk′**rĭ tē| *n.* Speed and willingness in acting or responding: *He carried out the assignment with alacrity.*

A•lad•din |ə **lăd′**n|. In the *Arabian Nights,* a boy who acquired a magic lamp with which he could summon a genie to fulfill any desire.

Al•a•mo, the |**ăl′**ə mō′|. A mission building in San Antonio, Texas, besieged and captured by

airship

air speed

It is often convenient to measure the progress of an aircraft by its **air speed,** *but when there is a wind the air speed may not be the true speed.*

akimbo

al-
A number of English words that begin with al- *are borrowed from Arabic. The element* al- *in them is the Arabic word for "the." Thus* **alchemy** *is from* al-khimīya, *"the art of transmutation,"* **alcove** *is from* al-qubbah, *"the vault,"* **algebra** *is from* al-jebr, *"the science of reuniting,"* **alkali** *is from* al-qalīy, *"the ashes."*

albatross

albedo
Albedo *is most often used in describing a planet or other body that shines by reflected light. The albedo of the moon is about seven per cent; that of Venus is about 59 per cent.*

ă pat/ā pay/â care/ä father/ĕ pet/ ē be/ĭ pit/ī pie/î fierce/ŏ pot/ ō go/ô paw, for/oi oil/o͝o book/ o͞o boot/ou out/ŭ cut/û fur/ *th* the/th thin/hw which/zh vision/ ə ago, item, pencil, atom, circus

Mexican forces in 1836. Its entire garrison was killed.

à la mode |ä′ lə **mōd′**| *or* |ăl′ə|. Served with ice cream: *apple pie à la mode.*

a•larm |ə **lärm′**| *n.* **1.** Sudden fear caused by a sense of danger: *There is no cause for alarm.* **2.** A warning of approaching danger: *a false alarm.* **3.** A device sounded to warn people of danger: *a fire alarm; a burglar alarm.* **4.** An **alarm clock.** ***—modifier:*** *an alarm system.* *—v.* To fill with alarm; frighten.

alarm clock. A clock that can be set to sound a bell or buzzer at a certain hour in order to wake a person up.

a•larmed |ə **lärmd′**| *adj.* **1.** Frightened: *alarmed by the sudden explosion.* **2.** Gravely concerned: *become alarmed over recent events.*

a•larm•ing |ə **lär′**mĭng| *adj.* Causing great fear or anxiety: *Crime is increasing at an alarming rate.* —**a•larm′ing•ly** *adv.*

a•larm•ist |ə **lär′**mĭst| *n.* A person who spreads false rumors of impending danger.

a•las |ə **lăs′**| *or* |ə **läs′**| *interj.* A word used to express sorrow, regret, or grief.

A•las•ka |ə **lăs′**kə|. The largest state of the United States, located in extreme northwestern North America. Population, 400,481. Capital, Juneau. —**A•las′kan** *adj. & n.*

alb |ălb| *n.* A long, white linen robe with tapered sleeves that fit closely at the wrist, worn by a priest as he celebrates Mass.

al•ba•core |**ăl′**bə kôr′| *or* |-kōr′| *n.* A large ocean fish that is one of the main sources of canned tuna.

Al•ba•ni•a |ăl **bā′**nē ə| *or* |**-bān′**yə|. A country in southeastern Europe, on the Adriatic Sea between Yugoslavia and Greece. Population, 2,591,000. Capital Tiranë.

Al•ba•ni•an |ăl **bā′**nē ən| *or* |**-bān′**yən| *n.* **1.** A native or inhabitant of Albania. **2.** The Indo-European language of Albania. *—adj.* Of Albania, the Albanians, or their language.

Al•ba•ny |**ôl′**bə nē|. The capital of New York State. Population, 101,727.

al•ba•tross |**ăl′**bə trôs′| *or* |-trŏs′| *n.* A large, web-footed sea bird with a hooked beak and very long wings. [See Picture]

al•be•do |ăl **bē′**dō| *n., pl.* **al•be•dos.** The fraction of the light or other electromagnetic radiation that is reflected from a surface that it strikes. [See Note]

al•be•it |ôl **bē′**ĭt| *conj.* Even though; although: *They proposed an imaginative, albeit somewhat impractical, idea.*

Al•ber•ta |ăl **bûr′**tə|. A province of western Canada. Population, 2,207,856. Capital, Edmonton.

al•bin•ism |**ăl′**bə nĭz′əm| *n.* Absence of normal skin, hair, and eye coloring; the condition of being an albino.

al•bi•no |ăl **bī′**nō| *n., pl.* **al•bi•nos.** A person who has abnormally pale skin and very light hair and lacks normal eye coloring, or an animal with white fur or feathers and red eyes.

Al•bi•on |**ăl′**bē ən|. An literary name for Britain.

al•bum |**ăl′**bəm| *n.* **1.** A book with blank pages on which photographs, stamps, etc., can be mounted. **2.** A set of phonograph records sold together in one binding.

al•bu•men |ăl **byo͞o′**mən| *n.* A nourishing substance, such as the white of a chicken's egg, that surrounds a developing embryo.

al•bu•min |ăl **byo͞o′**mən| *n.* Any of several simple proteins that dissolve in water and are coagulated by heat. They are found in egg white, blood serum, milk, and various plant and animal tissues.

Al•bu•quer•que |**ăl′**bə kûr′kē|. The largest city of New Mexico. Population, 294,000.

al•che•mist |**ăl′**kə mĭst| *n.* A person who practices alchemy.

al•che•my |**ăl′**kə mē| *n.* An early system of beliefs and practices, somewhat akin to modern chemistry, that had among its aims the changing of common metals into gold and the preparation of a potion that gives eternal youth.

al•co•hol |**ăl′**kə hôl′| *or* |-hŏl′| *n.* **1.** Any of a large number of chemically related organic compounds that contain the radical -OH, especially the form that occurs in wines and liquors. **2.** Beer, wine, and liquor in general.

al•co•hol•ic |ăl′kə **hô′**lĭk| *or* |**-hŏl′**ĭk| *adj.* **1.** Of, containing, or resulting from alcohol, especially ethanol. **2.** Of or suffering from alcoholism. *—n.* A person who overindulges in or is addicted to liquor or other drinks that contain alcohol; a habitual drunkard.

al•co•hol•ism |**ăl′**kə hô lĭz′əm| *n.* **1.** Excessive drinking of or addiction to liquor or other drinks that contain alcohol. **2.** The diseased conditions, mainly of the nervous and digestive systems, that result from this.

Al•cott |**ôl′**kət| *or* |-kŏt′|, **Louisa May.** 1832–1888. American author of popular novels for young people.

al•cove |**ăl′**kōv′| *n.* A small room opening on a larger one without being separated from it by a wall.

al•der |**ôl′**dər| *n.* Any of several trees or shrubs that grow in cool, damp places.

al•der•man |**ôl′**dər mən| *n., pl.* **-men** |-mən|. A member of the lawmaking body of a city or town.

Al•der•ney |**ôl′**dər nē| *n., pl.* **Al•der•neys.** One of a breed of cattle raised for milk and milk products.

ale |āl| *n.* A fermented, bitter alcoholic beverage similar to, but heavier than beer. ¶*These sound alike* **ale, ail.**

a•lee |ə **lē′**| *adv.* Away from the wind; to leeward.

ale•house |**āl′**hous′| *n.* A place where ale is sold and drunk.

a•lert |ə **lûrt′**| *adj.* **1.** Mentally quick; perceptive; intelligent: *an alert child.* **2.** Watchful; attentive; vigilant: *A good driver must remain constantly alert.* *—v.* **1.** To warn of approaching danger. **2.** To make aware of: *alert the public to the need for pollution control.* *—n.* **1.** A warning signal against danger or attack. **2.** The period during which one must obey this signal. —**a•lert′ly** *adv.* —**a•lert′ness** *n.*

Idiom. **on the alert.** Watchful and ready; on guard.

A•leut |ə **lo͞ot′**| *or* |**ăl′**ē o͞ot′| *n., pl.* **A•leut** or **A•leuts.** **1.** A native of the Aleutian Islands. **2.** Either of two languages, related to Eskimo, spoken by the Aleuts. —**A•leu′tian** |ə **lo͞o′**shən| *adj.*

A•leu•tian Islands |ə lo͞o′shən|. A chain of islands extending southwest from Alaska.

ale•wife |āl′wīf′| *n., pl.* **-wives** |-wīvz′|. A herringlike fish that is common off the Atlantic coast of North America.

Al•ex•an•der the Great |ăl′ĭg **zăn′**dər| *or* |- **zăn′**-|. 356–323 B.C. King of Macedonia, conqueror of an empire that extended from Asia Minor and Egypt to India.

Al•ex•an•dri•a |ăl′ĭg **zăn′**drē ə| *or* |**-zăn′**-|. A city and seaport on the Mediterranean coast of Egypt. Population, 2,032,000.

al•fal•fa |ăl **făl′**fə| *n.* A plant with cloverlike leaves and purple flowers, grown as feed for cattle and other livestock. [SEE PICTURE]

Al•fred the Great |**ăl′**frĭd|. A.D. 849–899. King of Wessex; united southern England by defeating the Danes.

al•gae |**ăl′**jē| *pl.n.* The less frequently used singular is **al•ga** |**ăl′**gə|. Members of a large group of plants that lack true roots, stems, and leaves but often have green coloring and grow mostly in water. Algae have a wide variety of shapes and forms, ranging from single cells to large, spreading seaweeds. [SEE PICTURE]

al•ge•bra |**ăl′**jə brə| *n.* A mathematical generalization of a set of numbers, a set of sets, a set of statements, etc., and the operations that can be performed on them.

al•ge•bra•ic |ăl′jə **brā′**ĭk| *adj.* Of or used in algebra. —**al′ge•bra′i•cal•ly** *adv.*

al•ge•bra•ist |**ăl′**jə brā′ĭst| *n.* A person who studies or is skilled in algebra.

Al•ge•ri•a |ăl **jîr′**ē ə|. A country in northwestern Africa, on the Mediterranean Sea. Population, 16,275,000. Capital, Algiers. —**Al•ge′ri•an** *adj. & n.*

al•gid |**ăl′**jĭd| *adj.* Cool or cold; chilly. —**al•gid′i•ty** *n.*

Al•giers |ăl **jîrz′**|. The capital and largest city of Algeria, on the Mediterranean Sea. Population, 1,648,000.

Al•gon•qui•an |ăl **gŏng′**kwē ən| *or* |-kē ən| *n.* A large family of Indian languages spoken over a large area of North America. Some important Algonquian languages are Ojibwa, Cree, and Blackfoot. —**Al•gon′qui•an** *adj.*

Al•gon•quin |ăl **gŏng′**kwĭn| *or* |-kĭn| *n., pl.* **Al•gon•quin** or **Al•gon•quins. 1.** A North American Indian tribe of southeastern Canada. **2.** A member of this tribe. **3.** The Algonquian language of this tribe.

al•go•rithm |**ăl′**gə rĭth′əm| *n.* A mathematical rule or process for computing a desired result: *an algorithm for division.*

a•li•as |**ā′**lē əs| *n.* An assumed name used by a person wishing to conceal his identity. *—adv.* Otherwise named: *William Blake alias James Flynn.*

A•li Ba•ba |**ä′**lē **bä′**bə|. In the *Arabian Nights,* a woodcutter who gains entrance to the treasure cave of the forty thieves by saying the magic words "Open, Sesame!"

al•i•bi |**ăl′**ə bī′| *n., pl.* **al•i•bis. 1.** A legal defense whereby a defendant attempts to prove he was not present at the time a crime was committed. **2.** *Informal.* An excuse: *No more of your alibis!*

a•li•en |**ā′**lē ən| *or* |**āl′**yən| *adj.* **1.** Of or coming from another country; foreign. **2.** Not natural; not characteristic: *The experiment produced an alien result.* **3.** Inconsistent or opposed; contradictory: *an idea wholly alien to one's philosophy.* *—n.* **1.** A person living in one country though a citizen of another; a foreigner. **2.** In science fiction, an intelligent being from anywhere other than Earth.

al•ien•ate |**āl′**yə nāt′| *or* |**ā′**lē ə-| *v.* **al•ien•at•ed, al•ien•at•ing.** To lose the friendship or support of; estrange: *He alienated everyone with his crude behavior.* —**al′ien•a′tion** *n.*

al•ien•ist |**āl′**yə nĭst| *or* |**ā′**lē ə-| *n.* A psychiatrist, especially one accepted by a court of law as an expert.

a•light[1] |ə **līt′**| *adj.* **1.** Lighted; lit up: *His eyes became suddenly alight.* **2.** On fire; burning: *The house was completely alight before the firemen arrived.* [SEE NOTE]

a•light[2] |ə **līt′**| *v.* **a•light•ed** or **a•lit** |ə **lĭt′**|, **a•light•ing. 1.** To come down and settle gently: *A bird alighted on the windowsill.* **2.** To get off; dismount: *alight from a train.* [SEE NOTE]

a•lign |ə **līn′**| *v.* **1.** To arrange in a straight line: *The chairs were aligned in two rows.* **2.** To ally (oneself) with one side of an argument, cause, etc.: *France considers that the British are always inclined to align themselves behind American positions.* **3.** To adjust (a device, mechanism, or some of its parts) in order to produce a proper relationship or condition: *Please align the wheels of my car.*

a•lign•ment |ə **līn′**mənt| *n.* **1.** The act of arranging in a straight line. **2.** Arrangement or position in a straight line: *poor alignment of the teeth.* **3.** The policy of allying with a certain bloc: *The government pursued a policy of alignment with the West.* **4.** The process of aligning a device or mechanism or the condition of being aligned: *perform an alignment on a car. The car is out of alignment.*

a•like |ə **līk′**| *adj.* **1.** Having close resemblance; similar: *Alice and her mother are very much alike.* **2.** Exactly or nearly exactly the same: *No two people are alike.* *—adv.* In the same way or manner or to the same degree: *We must try to treat everyone alike.*

al•i•men•ta•ry |ăl′ə **mĕn′**tə rē| *or* |**-mĕn′**trē| *adj.* Of food or nutrition.

alimentary canal. The tube that extends from the mouth to the anus and forms the digestive system, consisting, in human beings, of the pharynx, esophagus, stomach, and intestines.

al•i•mo•ny |**ăl′**ə mō′nē| *n., pl.* **al•i•mo•nies.** An allowance for support made under court order and usually given by a man to his former wife.

al•i•phat•ic |ăl′ĭ **făt′**ĭk| *adj.* Containing carbon atoms that are linked together in chains rather than in rings: *an aliphatic hydrocarbon.*

a•lit |ə **lĭt′**|. A past tense and past participle of **alight.**

a•live |ə **līv′**| *adj.* **1.** Having life; living: *This man is wanted dead or alive.* **2.** In existence or operation; not extinct or inactive: *The Red Sox kept their pennant hopes alive by winning a double-header.* **3.** Full of life; animated; alert: *The audience came alive when she began to sing.* **4.** —Used in certain exclamations: *Man alive! Sakes alive!*

Idioms. **alive to.** Sensitive to; aware of: *He was*

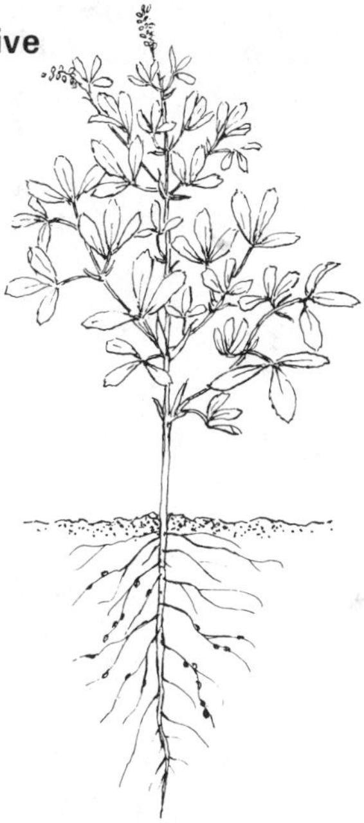

alfalfa

Alfalfa is one of a group of plants whose roots develop knoblike clusters of bacteria that enrich the soil by producing nitrogen compounds. For this reason, it is widely planted in alternation with other crops.

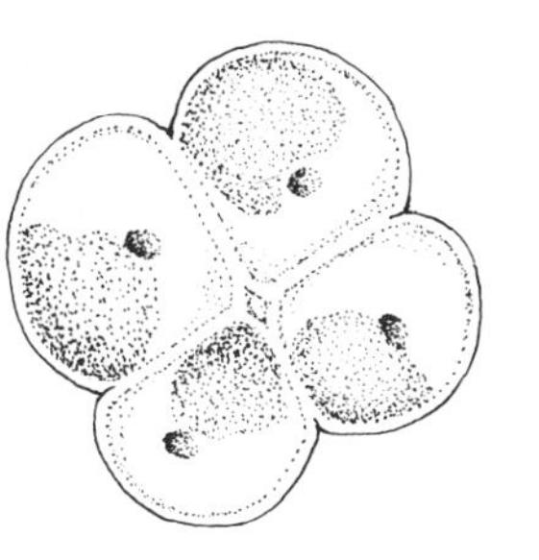

algae

Colony of single-celled algae, much enlarged

alight[1-2]

Alight[1] *and* **alight**[2] *are, neatly enough, connected to* **light**[1] *(brightness) and* **light**[2] *(not heavy), respectively.* **Alight**[1] *is simply an Old English compound of* on light *(like* afire *from* on fire*).* **Alight**[2] *comes from an Old English verb* ālīhtan, *"to lighten, to take the weight off something," hence "to dismount from a horse, to get down at a particular spot."*

all
All *is probably the commonest adjective in the English language. In the materials on which this Dictionary is based,* **all** *is estimated to occur nearly 3,300 times per one million words, or once every 300 words.*

alley¹·²
Alley¹ *is from Old French* alee, *"a walk, a passage," from* aller, *"to walk."* **Alley²** *is an eighteenth-century slang word from* alabaster, *of which these superior marbles were then made.*

ă pat/ā pay/â care/ä father/ĕ pet/ē be/ĭ pit/ī pie/î fierce/ŏ pot/ō go/ô paw, for/oi oil/ŏŏ book/ōō boot/ou out/ŭ cut/û fur/*th* the/th thin/hw which/zh vision/ə ago, item, pencil, atom, circus

alive to the moods of others. **alive with.** Swarming with: *The pond was alive with fish.*

al•ka•li |ăl′kə lī′| *n., pl.* **al•ka•lis. 1.** Sodium hydroxide, potassium hydroxide, or any similar compound formed from a related metal. All compounds of this kind are very strong bases. **2.** Sodium carbonate, potassium carbonate, or any similar salt formed from a related metal. All salts of this kind are strong bases. **3.** Any of various basic mineral salts found in natural water and in arid soils.

al•ka•line |ăl′kə lĭn| *or* |-līn′| *adj.* **1.** Of or like an alkali or alkalis. **2.** Capable of neutralizing an acid; basic.

al•ka•lin•i•ty |ăl′kə **lĭn′**ĭ tē| *n.* The alkali concentration or alkaline quality of a substance.

al•ka•loid |ăl′kə loid′| *n.* Any one of a class of organic compounds that contain nitrogen and have powerful effects on living organisms. Many of them are derived from plants. Nicotine, quinine, and morphine are examples of alkaloids.

al•ka•lo•sis |ăl′kə **lō′**sĭs| *n.* A diseased condition in which the blood is more alkaline or less acidic than normal.

all |ôl| *adj.* **1.** The total extent or number of: *All five boys are good students. He has lived all his life in Boston.* **2.** The whole of: *He spent all day in court.* **3.** The utmost possible: *in all truth.* **4.** Every: *all manner of men.* **5.** Any: *proven beyond all doubt.* **6.** Nothing but; only: *all skin and bones.* —*pron.* Each and every one: *All aboard the ship were drowned.* —*n.* Everything one has: *He gave all.* —*adv.* **1.** Wholly; entirely: *she's all wrong.* **2.** Each; apiece: *a score of five all.* **3.** Exclusively: *The cake is all for him.* —*Note: All* is often used with certain function words to form prepositional and adverbial groups. Some of the most frequent groups are: **above all.** Before everything else; most of all: *truth above all.* **after all.** Nevertheless: *The girls decided to go shopping after all.* **all but.** Very nearly: *She all but fainted.* **all in all.** Everything being taken into account: *All in all he's a good athlete.* **all the same.** Nevertheless: *She's a nice person, all the same.* ¶ *These sound alike* **all, awl.** [SEE NOTE]

Idioms. **all in.** *Informal.* Tired or exhausted. **all of.** Not less than: *It's all of ten miles to town.* **all out.** With every effort possible: *The team went all out to win.* **all over. 1.** Finished. **2.** Everywhere: *books scattered all over.* **3.** *Informal.* Thoroughly or typically: *That's me all over.*

al•la bre•ve |ä′lə **brĕv′**ā|. A musical direction indicating that the half note is the unit of measure, as when a measure containing four quarter notes is to be read as being in 2/2 time.

Al•lah |ăl′ə| *or* |ä′lə| *n.* The Moslem name for God.

all-A•mer•i•can |ôl′ə **mĕr′**ĭ kən| *adj.* **1.** Typical of the best in the United States: *an all-American boy.* **2.** In sports, chosen as the best in the United States at a particular position: *an all-American fullback.* **3.** Composed entirely of American elements or materials: *The orchestra played an all-American program.* —*n.* In amateur team sports, a player who is chosen as the best in the United States at a particular position.

al•lan•to•is |ə **lăn′**tō ĭs| *n., pl.* **al•lan•to•i•des** |ăl′ən**tō′**ĭ dēz|. A membranous sac that develops from the lower end of the alimentary canal of the embryos of reptiles, birds, and mammals. In mammals it takes part in forming the placenta and umbilical cord.

all-a-round |ôl′ə round′| *adj.* All-round.

al•lay |ə **lā′**| *v.* **1.** To lessen; reduce; relieve: *allay pain.* **2.** To set to rest; calm: *allay one's fears.*

all clear. A signal, usually by siren, that an air raid or air-raid drill is over.

al•le•ga•tion |ăl′ĭ **gā′**shən| *n.* A statement made without proof.

al•lege |ə **lĕj′**| *v.* **al•leged, al•leg•ing. 1.** To declare to be true, usually without offering proof. **2.** To cite as an excuse: *He refused to contribute, alleging his poverty.*

al•leged |ə **lĕjd′**| *adj.* Stated to be as described but not so proved: *the alleged kidnaper of the child.* —**al•leg′ed•ly** |ə **lĕj′**ĭd lē| *adv.*

Al•le•ghe•ny Mountains |ăl′ə **gā′**nē|. Also **Al•le•ghe•nies.** A section of the Appalachian Mountains extending from Pennsylvania to Virginia.

al•le•giance |ə **lē′**jəns| *n.* Loyalty or devotion to one's country, to a king, or to a cause: *pledge allegiance to the United States.*

al•le•go•ry |ăl′ə gôr′ē| *or* |-gōr′-| *n., pl.* **al•le•go•ries.** A story, play, or picture that conveys a symbolic meaning within its literal meaning. —**al′le•gor′i•cal** *adj.* —**al′le•gor′i•cal•ly** *adv.*

al•le•gret•to |ăl′ĭ **grĕt′**ō|. In music: *adj.* Slightly slower than allegro. —*adv.* Slightly less quickly than allegro. —*n., pl.* **al•le•gret•tos.** An allegretto section of a composition.

al•le•gro |ə **lĕg′**rō| *or* |ə **lā′**grō|. In music: *adj.* Quick. —*adv.* Quickly. —*n., pl.* **al•le•gros.** A quick section of a composition.

al•lele |ə **lēl′**| *n.* Any of the possible forms in which a single gene can occur.

al•le•lu•ia |ăl′ə **lōō′**yə| *interj.* Hallelujah.

al•le•mande |ăl′ə mănd′| *or* |-mänd′| *or* |ăl′ə**mănd′**| *or* |**-mänd′**| *n.* **1. a.** A stately dance that originated in about the 16th century. **b.** A musical composition written to accompany or as if to accompany this dance, often used as the first movement of a suite. **2.** A lively dance of the 18th century, similar to a waltz.

al•ler•gen |ăl′ər jən| *n.* A substance that causes an allergy.

al•ler•gic |ə **lûr′**jĭk| *adj.* **1.** Resulting from allergy. **2.** Having an allergy or allergies.

al•ler•gist |ăl′ər jĭst| *n.* A physician who specializes in the treatment of allergies.

al•ler•gy |ăl′ər jē| *n., pl.* **al•ler•gies.** A disorder in which exposure to a small amount of a substance, generally a protein, fat, or carbohydrate, or to an environmental influence, such as heat or cold, causes an abnormal and often violent reaction that may include difficulty in breathing, sneezing, watering of the eyes, and shock.

al•le•vi•ate |ə **lē′**vē āt′| *v.* **al•le•vi•at•ed, al•le•vi•at•ing.** To make more bearable; relieve; lessen: *alleviate pain.* —**al•le′vi•a′tion** *n.*

al•ley¹ |ăl′ē| *n., pl.* **al•leys. 1.** A narrow street or passageway between or behind buildings. **2.** A **bowling alley.** [SEE NOTE]

Idiom. **up (one's) alley.** *Slang.* Suited to one's abilities or interests.

al•ley² |ăl′ē| *n., pl.* **al•leys.** A large playing marble, often used as a shooter. [SEE NOTE]

alley cat. A homeless cat that wanders through city streets and alleys.

al•ley•way |ăl′ē wā′| *n.* A narrow passage between buildings.

All Fools' Day. **April Fools' Day.**

al•li•ance |ə lī′əns| *n.* **1.** A formal agreement or union between nations, organizations, or individuals: *Britain and France sealed their alliance with a treaty.* **2.** Any union or relationship by family ties, marriage, friendship, etc.: *Marriage is an alliance between two people.*

al•lied |ə līd′| *or* |ăl′īd′| *adj.* **1.** Joined together in an alliance. **2.** Similar; related: *Biochemistry and biophysics are allied sciences.* **3. Allied.** Of allied countries, especially the countries that fought against Germany and her allies in World Wars I and II.

Al•lies |ăl′īz′| *or* |ə līz′| *pl.n.* A group of allied countries, especially the United States, Great Britain, France, Russia, and other countries that fought together in World Wars I and II.

al•li•ga•tor |ăl′ĭ gā′tər| *n.* **1.** A large reptile with sharp teeth and powerful jaws. Its snout is blunter than that of the closely related crocodiles. **2.** Leather made from the hide of an alligator. [SEE NOTE & PICTURE]

alligator pear. An avocado.

all-im•por•tant |ôl′ĭm pôr′tnt| *adj.* Very important; vital; crucial.

al•lit•er•a•tion |ə lĭt′ə rā′shən| *n.* The repetition of consonants for poetic or rhetorical effect. [SEE NOTE]

al•lit•er•a•tive |ə lĭt′ə rā′tĭv| *or* |-ər ə tĭv| *adj.* Showing alliteration: *an alliterative phrase.*

al•lo•cate |ăl′ə kāt′| *v.* **al•lo•cat•ed, al•lo•cat•ing.** To set aside for a particular purpose; allot: *allocate funds for research and development.* —**al′lo•ca′tion** *n.*

al•lo•saur |ăl′ə sôr′| *n.* A meat-eating dinosaur with a large head, sharp teeth, and sharp claws.

al•lo•saur•us |ăl′ə sôr′əs| *n.* An allosaur.

al•lot |ə lŏt′| *v.* **al•lot•ted, al•lot•ting.** **1.** To distribute or parcel out: *allot portions of land.* **2.** To assign a portion for a particular purpose; allocate: *allot sufficient time for study; allot money for home construction.*

al•lot•ment |ə lŏt′mənt| *n.* **1.** The act of allotting. **2.** Something allotted.

al•lo•trope |ăl′ə trōp′| *n.* Any of the different forms in which certain elements, such as sulfur and phosphorus, can appear under the same conditions. Red phosphorus and white phosphorus are allotropes.

al•lo•trop•ic |ăl′ə trŏp′ĭk| *adj.* Of or having allotropes.

all-out |ôl′out′| *adj.* Using all one's resources; vigorous: *an all-out effort.*

all-o•ver |ôl′ō′vər| *adj.* Covering an entire surface: *an all-over pattern.*

al•low |ə lou′| *v.* **1.** To let do or happen; permit: *No dancing allowed! Please allow me to finish.* **2.** To let have; permit to have: *allow oneself five dollars a day.* **3.** To let in; permit the presence of: *No dogs allowed!* **4.** To provide; allot: *allow time for discussion.* **5.** To make provision: *allow for bad weather.* **6.** To admit; concede; grant: *I'll allow that some mistakes have been made.* **7.** To give as a discount or in exchange: *He allowed me $20 on my old typewriter.*

al•low•a•ble |ə lou′ə bəl| *adj.* Capable of being allowed; permissible.

al•low•ance |ə lou′əns| *n.* **1.** The act of allowing. **2.** An amount of money, food, etc., given at regular intervals or for a specific purpose: *a 25¢ weekly allowance; a travel allowance.* **3.** A price reduction given in exchange for used merchandise: *an allowance of $500 on one's old car.*
Idiom. **make allowance** (or **allowances**) **for.** To take into account; allow for: *make allowance for his inexperience.*

al•loy |ăl′oi′| *or* |ə loi′| *n.* **1.** A solid metal in which the atoms of a metallic element and those of one or more other elements, metallic or nonmetallic, are intermingled: *Pewter is an alloy of copper, antimony, and lead.* **2.** Anything added that lowers quality or value: *contentment without the alloy of regret.* —*v.* |ə loi′|. **1.** To combine (metal and sometimes other substances) to form an alloy. **2.** To lessen the quality or value of; mar: *My excitement was alloyed with doubts.*

all right. **1.** Satisfactory; average: *His work is all right, but it could be better.* **2.** Correct: *These figures are perfectly all right.* **3.** Not sick or injured; safe: *Are you all right? He came out of the crash all right.* **4.** Very well; yes: *All right, I'll go.* **5.** Without a doubt: *That's him all right!*

all-round |ôl′round′| *adj.* **1.** Able to do many or all things well: *an all-round athlete.* **2.** Comprehensive in extent: *an all-round education.*

All Saints' Day. A Christian festival celebrated on November 1 in honor of all the saints.

All Souls' Day. November 2, observed by the Roman Catholic Church as a day of prayer for the souls in purgatory.

all•spice |ôl′spīs′| *n.* The fragrant, strong-flavored berries of a tropical American tree, dried and used as a spice.

all-star |ôl′stär′| *adj.* Made up entirely of star performers: *an all-star cast; an all-star baseball team.*

all-time |ôl′tīm′| *adj.* Unsurpassed until now; of all time: *set an all-time attendance record. He is one of the all-time great players of the game.*

al•lude |ə lo͞od′| *v.* **al•lud•ed, al•lud•ing.** To refer to indirectly; mention casually or in passing.

al•lure |ə lo͝or′| *v.* **al•lured, al•lur•ing.** To attract; entice; tempt: *I was allured to the movie by the ads.* —**al•lur′ing** *adj.*: *an alluring description; an alluring possibility.* —*n.* Strong attraction; fascination: *the allure of the sea.*

al•lu•sion |ə lo͞o′zhən| *n.* Indirect mention; passing or casual reference to something.

al•lu•vi•a |ə lo͞o′vē ə| *n.* A plural of **alluvium.**

al•lu•vi•al |ə lo͞o′vē əl| *adj.* Of or composed of alluvium.

alluvial fan. A fan-shaped mass of alluvium deposited by a river at a place where its flow becomes less swift.

al•lu•vi•um |ə lo͞o′vē əm| *n., pl.* **al•lu•vi•ums** or **al•lu•vi•a** |ə lo͞o′vē ə|. Any sediment, such as mud, sand, or gravel, carried and deposited by a flow of water.

al•ly |ə lī′| *v.* **al•lied, al•ly•ing, al•lies.** To join or unite for a specific purpose: *The United States allied itself with Russia during World War II.* —*n.* |ăl′ī′| *or* |ə lī′|, *pl.* **al•lies.** A person or country that is allied to another.

al•ma ma•ter, also **Al•ma Ma•ter** |ăl′mə mä′-

alligator
American alligator
True alligators live only in rivers, lakes, and swamps of the southeastern United States and in China; but crocodiles and similar large reptiles are often mistakenly called alligators.

alliteration
An example of **alliteration** *carried to extremes is the anonymous poem* The Siege of Belgrade, *which begins:*
"An Austrian army,
awfully arrayed,
Boldly, by battery,
besieged Belgrade;
Cossack commanders
cannonading come,
Dealing destruction's
devastating doom."
It goes all the way through to z, *and then back to* a.

alma mater
Alma mater *is Latin for "fostering mother." It was originally a title of various Roman goddesses, but was taken over as a fond and respectful name for one's school.*

alpaca

alright
The spelling **alright** *is not accepted in formal writing as taught in the schools. In the materials on which this Dictionary was based, it occurs only as an example of a form to be avoided.*

ă pat/ā pay/â care/ä father/ĕ pet/ ē be/ĭ pit/ī pie/î fierce/ŏ pot/ ō go/ô paw, for/oi oil/o͝o book/ o͞o boot/ou out/ŭ cut/û fur/ *th* the/th thin/hw which/zh vision/ ə ago, item, pencil, atom, circus

tər | *or* |äl′mə|. **1.** The school, college, or university that a person has attended. **2.** The song or anthem of a school, college, or university. [SEE NOTE]

al•ma•nac |ôl′mə năk′| *or* |ăl′-| *n.* A book published once a year containing calendars, statistics, and other information in many different fields.

Al Ma•nam•ah |ăl′ mə **năm′**ə|. The capital of Bahrain. Population, 89,000.

al•might•y |ôl **mī′**tē| *adj.* All-powerful; omnipotent: *almighty God.* —*n.* **the Almighty.** God.

al•mond |ä′mənd| *or* |**ăm′**ənd| *n.* **1.** An oval, edible nut with a soft, light-brown shell. **2.** A tree that bears such nuts.

al•most |**ôl′**mōst| *or* |ôl **mōst′**| *adv.* Slightly short of; nearly: *almost done but not quite.*

alms |ämz| *pl.n.* Money or goods given to the poor as charity.

alms•house |**ämz′**hous′| *n.* A public home for the poor; a poorhouse.

al•ni•co |**ăl′**nĭ kō′| *n., pl.* **al•ni•cos.** Any of several alloys of aluminum, cobalt, copper, iron, nickel, and often other metals, used in making strong permanent magnets.

al•oe |**ăl′**ō| *n.* **1.** Any of several tropical plants with thick, spiny-toothed leaves and red or yellow flowers. **2. aloes** *(used with a singular verb).* A bitter medicinal drug made from the dried juice of these plants, used as a laxative.

a•loft |ə **lôft′**| *or* |ə **lŏft′**| *adv.* **1.** In or into a high place. **2.** In or toward a ship's upper rigging.

a•lo•ha |ä **lō′**hä′| *interj.* A word used as a greeting or farewell. It is the Hawaiian word for "love."

a•lone |ə **lōn′**| *adj.* **1.** Without the company of anyone or anything else: *she lives alone.* **2.** Only; solely: *God alone knows.* **3.** With nothing else added: *New York City alone has over eight million people.* —*adv.* Without aid or help: *I can do it alone.*

Idioms. **leave alone.** To leave in peace; not bother or interrupt. **let alone. 1.** To leave alone. **2.** Not to speak of: *I can't even do arithmetic, let alone algebra.* **stand alone.** To be without equal.

a•long |ə **lông′**| *or* |ə **lŏng′**| *adv.* **1.** In a line with something or following the length or path of it: *trees growing along by the river.* Also used prepositionally: *a parade moving along the main street.* **2.** Forward: *moving along.* **3.** In association; together: *one thing along with another.* **4.** As company; as a companion: *Bring your parents along.* **5.** Somewhat advanced: *The evening was well along.* **6.** Approaching: *Along about midnight we went home.*

Idioms. **all along.** Always or all the time: *I was right all along.* **get along. 1.** To go onward. **2.** To manage successfully or survive: *I'll get along somehow.* **3.** To be compatible; agree.

a•long•side |ə **lông′**sīd| *or* |**-lŏng′-**| *prep.* By the side of; side by side with: *The boat pulled up alongside the dock.* Also used adverbially: *The boat pulled up alongside.*

alongside of. Alongside: *Country and city kids were sitting alongside of one another.*

a•loof |ə **lo͞of′**| *adj.* Distant, reserved, or indifferent in manner: *an aloof personality. He remained aloof during the discussion.* —**a•loof′ly** *adv.*

a•loud |ə **loud′**| *adv.* **1.** Louder than a whisper: *She is afraid to say it aloud.* **2.** With the voice: *Read the story aloud.*

al•pac•a |ăl **păk′**ə| *n.* **1.** A South American animal related to the llama, having long, silky wool. **2.** Cloth made from the wool of this animal. **3.** A stiff, glossy fabric woven from wool and other fibers. [SEE PICTURE]

al•pen•stock |**ăl′**pən stŏk′| *n.* A long staff with an iron point, used by mountain climbers.

al•pha |**ăl′**fə| *n.* **1.** The first letter of the Greek alphabet, written Α, α. In English it is represented as *A, a.* **2.** The first of anything; beginning.

al•pha•bet |**ăl′**fə bĕt′| *n.* The letters used to represent the different sounds of a language, arranged in a set order.

al•pha•bet•i•cal |ăl′fə **bĕt′**ĭ kəl| or **al•pha•bet•ic** |ăl′fə **bĕt′**ĭk| *adj.* **1.** Arranged in the order of the alphabet: *In a dictionary the words are listed in alphabetical order.* **2.** Based on or using an alphabet: *an alphabetic system of writing.* —**al′pha•bet′i•cal•ly** *adv.*

al•pha•bet•ize |**ăl′**fə bĭ tīz′| *v.* **al•pha•bet•ized, al•pha•bet•iz•ing.** To arrange in alphabetical order.

alpha particle. A positively charged particle that consists of two protons and two neutrons bound together. It is identical with the nucleus of a helium atom.

alpha ray. A stream of alpha particles.

al•pine |**ăl′**pīn′| *or* |-pĭn| *adj.* **1.** Of, on, or growing in high mountains. **2. Alpine.** Of or having to do with the Alps.

Alps |ălps|. A mountain system of Europe, extending through France, Switzerland, Italy, Austria, and Yugoslavia.

al•read•y |ôl **rĕd′**ē| *adv.* By this time.

al•right |ôl **rīt′**| *adv.* A form of the phrase **all right.** [SEE NOTE]

Al•sace |**ăl′**săs′| *or* |ăl **săs′**|. A former province of northeastern France.

Al•sace-Lor•raine |**ăl′**săs′lô **rān′**| *or* |ăl **săs′**-|. A region of northeastern France, a part of Germany between 1871 and 1919.

Al•sa•tian |ăl **sā′**shən| *n.* A native or inhabitant of Alsace. —*adj.* Of Alsace or the Alsatians.

al•so |**ôl′**sō| *adv.* **1.** Likewise: *Much equipment is needed to launch a spacecraft; much is also needed to bring it back.* **2.** In addition; besides: *Labels not only tell the size but also give other valuable information.* —*conj.* And in addition: *He studied French and math, also music and drawing.*

al•tar |**ôl′**tər| *n.* A table or similar structure, often in a church or temple, used in religious ceremonies. ¶ *These sound alike* **altar, alter.**

al•ter |**ôl′**tər| *v.* **1.** To change in some respect; make or become different: *alter one's appearance. The situation has altered dramatically in recent weeks.* **2.** To adjust (a garment) for a better fit: *You will have to have this jacket altered.* **3.** *Informal.* To castrate or spay (a cat, dog, etc.). ¶ *These sound alike* **alter, altar.**

al•ter•a•tion |ôl′tə **rā′**shən| *n.* **1.** The act or process of changing or altering: *minerals formed by chemical alteration of igneous rocks.* **2.** A change: *many alterations to a dress.*

al•ter•ca•tion |ôl′tər **kā′**shən| *or* |ăl′-| *n.* A noisy, angry quarrel.

al•ter•nate |ôl′tər nāt′| *or* |ăl′-| *v.* **al•ter•nat•ed, al•ter•nat•ing. 1.** To do, perform, use, or occur in turn by changing back and forth: *alternate one's clothes. Day alternates with night. We alternated driving the car.* **2.** To pass back and forth between conditions, activities, etc.: *alternate between hope and despair.* —*adj.* |ôl′tər nĭt| *or* |ăl′-|. **1.** Occurring in turns; succeeding each other: *alternate periods of rain and drought.* **2.** Every other; every second: *work on alternate days of the week.* **3.** In place of another: *an alternate route.* —*n.* |ôl′tər nĭt| *or* |ăl′-|. A person acting in place of another.

alternate interior angles. The pair of angles that lie on opposite sides of a transversal that cuts a pair of lines, and that are also included between the pair of lines, especially when the pair of lines is parallel.

al•ter•nate•ly |ôl′tər nĭt lē| *or* |ăl′-| *adv.* In alternate order; in turn: *The crowd alternately booed and cheered the players.*

alternating current. An electric current that reverses its direction of flow at regular intervals.

al•ter•na•tion |ôl′tər **nā′**shən| *or* |ăl′-|. Regular and repeated change between two or more things: *the alternation of the seasons.*

al•ter•na•tive |ôl **tûr′**nə tĭv| *or* |ăl-| *n.* **1.** One of two or more possibilities from which to choose: *Raising taxes may be unpopular, but the alternatives are even worse.* **2.** A choice between two or more possibilities: *The alternative is between increased taxes or a budget deficit.* **3.** A remaining choice or additional option: *You leave me no alternative.* —*adj.* Allowing a choice between two or more possibilities: *I can suggest two alternative plans.* —**al•ter′na•tive•ly** *adv.*

al•ter•na•tor |ôl′tər nā′tər| *or* |ăl′-| *n.* An electric generator that makes alternating current. [SEE PICTURE]

al•though |ôl *thō′*| *conj.* Even though.

al•tim•e•ter |ăl **tĭm′**ĭ tər| *n.* An instrument that measures and indicates the height at which an object, such as an aircraft, is located.

al•ti•tude |ăl′tĭ to͞od′| *or* |-tyo͞od′| *n.* **1.** A height measured in relation to a reference level such as sea level or the earth's surface. **2.** In astronomy, the angle between a line aimed at the horizon and a line aimed at a celestial object: *a star at an altitude of 18°.* **3.** In geometry: **a.** A line segment perpendicular to the base of a figure and extending from the base to the opposite vertex, side, or surface. **b.** The measure of the segment. [SEE PICTURE]

al•to |ăl′tō| *n., pl.* **al•tos. 1.** A low singing voice of a woman or boy or, sometimes, a high singing voice of a man, lower than a soprano and higher than a tenor. **2.** A person having such a voice. **3.** A part written in the range of this voice. **4.** An instrument having about the same range as this voice. —***modifier:*** *an alto flute.*

al•to•cu•mu•lus |ăl′tō **kyo͞o′**myə ləs| *n.* A rounded, fleecy white or gray cloud formation, found typically at a height of 2½ miles.

al•to•geth•er |ôl′tə **gĕth′**ər| *or* |**ôl′**tə gĕth′ər| *adv.* **1.** Completely: *Soon the noise faded away altogether.* **2.** With all included or counted: *Altogether there are 36 teachers in the school.* **3.** As a whole: *Altogether the iceberg of average size may be about the height of a skyscraper.*

al•to•stra•tus |ăl′tō **strā′**təs| *or* |**-străt′**əs| *n.* A cloud formation that extends in bluish or gray sheets or layers, typically at a height of 3½ miles.

al•tru•ism |**ăl′**tro͞o ĭz′əm| *n.* Concern for the welfare of others. —**al′tru•ist** *n.*

al•tru•is•tic |ăl′tro͞o **ĭs′**tĭk| *adj.* Showing concern for the welfare of others.

al•um |**ăl′**əm| *n.* **1.** Any of various sulfates in which a trivalent metal, such as aluminum, chromium, or iron, is combined with a univalent metal, such as potassium or sodium. **2.** Aluminum potassium sulfate, $AlK(SO_4)_2$, a compound of this type.

a•lu•mi•na |ə **lo͞o′**mə nə| *n.* Any one of several forms of aluminum oxide, Al_2O_3, such as bauxite or corundum, that occur naturally.

al•u•min•i•um |ăl′yə **mĭn′**ē əm| *n.* British form of the word **aluminum.**

a•lu•min•ize |ə **lo͞o′**mə nīz′| *v.* **a•lu•min•ized, a•lu•min•iz•ing.** To cover, coat, or treat with aluminum or aluminum paint.

a•lu•mi•num |ə **lo͞o′**mə nəm| *n.* Symbol **Al** One of the elements, a lightweight, silvery-white metal. Atomic number 13; atomic weight 26.98; valence +3; melting point 660.2°C; boiling point 2,467°C. [SEE NOTE]

a•lum•na |ə **lŭm′**nə| *n., pl.* **a•lum•nae** |ə **lŭm′**nē′|. A woman who has graduated from a certain school, college, or university.

a•lum•nus |ə **lŭm′**nəs| *n., pl.* **a•lum•ni** |ə **lŭm′**nī′|. A man who has graduated from a certain school, college, or university.

al•ve•o•lar |ăl **vē′**ə lər| *adj.* Of alveoli or an alveolus.

al•ve•o•lus |ăl **vē′**ə ləs| *n., pl.* **al•ve•o•li** |ăl **vē′**ə lī′|. **1.** Any of the tiny air-filled sacs in the lungs from which oxygen passes into the blood and which, in turn, receive carbon dioxide; an air sac. **2.** Any small bodily pit or cavity, such as a tooth socket.

al•ways |**ôl′**wāz| *or* |-wēz| *adv.* **1.** On every occasion; without exception: *He always leaves at six o'clock.* **2.** Continuously; forever: *They will always be friends.*

am |ăm|. First person singular present tense of **be.**

am, AM amplitude modulation.

Am The symbol for the element americium.

a.m., A.M. before noon.

a•mal•gam |ə **măl′**gəm| *n.* An alloy consisting of mercury and another metal or metals.

a•mal•ga•mate |ə **măl′**gə māt′| *v.* **a•mal•ga•mat•ed, a•mal•ga•mat•ing. 1.** To alloy (a metal) with mercury. **2.** To unite, combine, or merge; consolidate: *amalgamate three companies. The conquered nations never amalgamated with their conquerors.*

a•mal•ga•ma•tion |ə măl′gə **mā′**shən| *n.* **1.** The process of amalgamating. **2.** A combination or consolidation, as of classes, business companies, etc.; a union.

am•a•ni•ta |ăm′ə **nī′**tə| *or* |**-nē′**tə| *n.* Any of several related mushrooms, many of which are very poisonous.

am•a•ryl•lis |ăm′ə **rĭl′**ĭs| *n.* A plant that grows from a bulb and produces large, lilylike, reddish or white flowers. [SEE PICTURE]

a•mass |ə **măs′**| *v.* To gather; accumulate: *amass wealth; amass knowledge.*

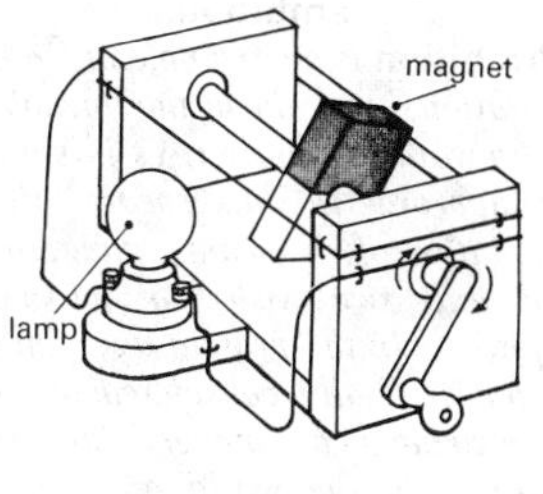

alternator

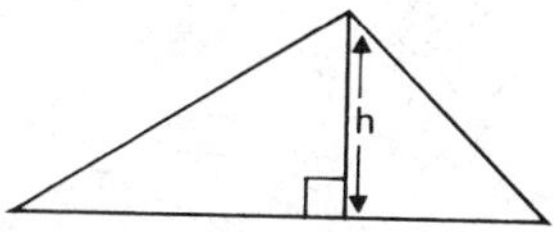

altitude of a triangle

aluminum

Aluminum *is the most abundant metal in the earth's crust, and is obtained chiefly from bauxite. It is very widely used to make strong, lightweight, corrosion-resistant alloys, especially for tools and construction materials.*

amaryllis

ambition

Ambition *is an example of "melioration," in which the meaning of a word gradually rises in status or approval. In Shakespeare's time ambition often meant "dangerous or excessive wish for personal power." In the present age, ambition is usually considered one of the virtues—a commendable urge to rise in the world or perform creative tasks.*

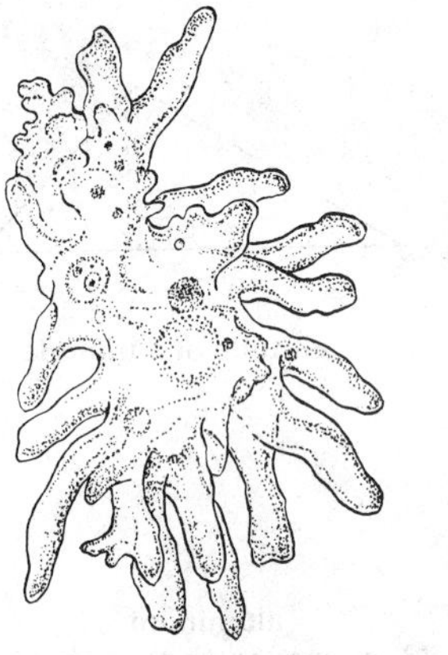

ameba

The scientific name of this organism is *Amoeba,* but the simplified spelling **ameba** is often used as its "common name." In the materials on which this Dictionary was based, **ameba** occurred four times as often as **amoeba**.

amends

Amends *has a plural form because it comes from an Old French plural,* amendes, *meaning "penalties, reparations."*

ă pat/ā pay/â care/ä father/ĕ pet/ ē be/ĭ pit/ī pie/î fierce/ŏ pot/ ō go/ô paw, for/oi oil/o͝o book/ o͞o boot/ou out/ŭ cut/û fur/ *th* the/th thin/hw which/zh vision/ ə ago, item, pencil, atom, circus

am•a•teur |**ăm′**ə cho͝or′| *or* |-chər| *or* |-tyo͝or′| *n.* **1.** A person who engages in an art, science, or sport for enjoyment rather than for money. **2.** A person who does something without professional skill. ***—modifier:*** *an amateur boxer; an amateur orchestra; amateur sports.*

am•a•teur•ish |ăm′ə **cho͝or′**ĭsh| *or* |**-tûr′-**| *or* |**-tyo͝or′-**| *adj.* **1.** Done or performed as one would expect of an amateur rather than a professional: *an amateurish performance.* **2.** Lacking professional skill: *an amateurish performer.* **—am′a•teur′ish•ly** *adv.*

a•maze |ə **māz′**| *v.* **a•mazed, a•maz•ing.** To fill with surprise or wonder; astonish: *The idea of a torrent of water carving a mile-deep canyon out of solid rock amazes me.* **—a•mazed′** *adj.: He stood there with an amazed look on his face.*

a•maze•ment |ə **māz′**mənt| *n.* Great surprise; astonishment.

a•maz•ing |ə **mā′**zĭng| *adj.* Causing great surprise or amazement; astonishing: *The game resulted in an amazing upset.* **—a•maz′ing•ly** *adv.*

Am•a•zon[1] |**ăm′**ə zŏn′| *or* |-zən|. **1.** In Greek mythology, a member of a race of female warriors. **2.** A tall, athletic woman.

Am•a•zon[2] |**ăm′**ə zŏn′| *or* |-zən|. The longest river in South America, rising in the Peruvian Andes and flowing about 4,000 miles through Brazil into the Atlantic Ocean.

am•bas•sa•dor |ăm **băs′**ə dər| *n.* **1.** A diplomatic official of the highest rank who represents his government in another country. **2.** Any messenger or representative: *a good-will ambassador.*

am•ber |**ăm′**bər| *n.* **1.** A light or brownish-yellow fossil resin used for making jewelry and ornaments. **2.** A brownish yellow. ***—modifier:*** *an amber necklace.* —*adj.* Brownish yellow.

am•ber•gris |**ăm′**bər grĭs′| *or* |-grēs′| *n.* A grayish, waxy material formed in the intestines of sperm whales, often found floating at sea or washed ashore. It is used in making perfumes.

am•bi•dex•trous |ăm′bĭ **dĕk′**strəs| *adj.* Able to use both hands equally well; neither right-handed nor left-handed.

am•bi•gu•i•ty |ăm′bĭ **gyo͞o′**ĭ tē| *n., pl.* **am•bi•gu•i•ties. 1.** The condition of being ambiguous. **2.** Something that is ambiguous: *There were numerous ambiguities in his statement.*

am•big•u•ous |ăm **bĭg′**yo͞o əs| *adj.* Having two or more possible meanings or interpretations; unclear; vague: *an ambiguous statement by the Governor.*

am•bi•tion |ăm **bĭsh′**ən| *n.* **1. a.** A strong desire to get or become something: *His ambition was to become a fearless detective.* **b.** The thing desired: *He spent a lot of money to achieve his one great ambition.* **2.** Initiative; drive: *people of great energy and ambition.* [SEE NOTE]

am•bi•tious |ăm **bĭsh′**əs| *adj.* **1.** Eager to succeed: *The ambitious lad learned very quickly.* **2.** Eager to succeed in doing some specified thing: *The more she thought about it, the more ambitious she felt to learn public speaking.* **3.** Eager for power and glory: *As his power grew, this ambitious ruler took the title of emperor.* **4.** Aiming high; extensive and far-reaching: *ambitious goals; an ambitious schedule.* **—am•bi′tious•ly** *adv.*

am•biv•a•lence |ăm **bĭv′**ə ləns| *n.* The existence, at the same time, of two conflicting feelings, such as love and hate.

am•biv•a•lent |ăm **bĭv′**ə lənt| *adj.* Showing or marked by ambivalence: *ambivalent feelings; an ambivalent attitude.*

am•ble |**ăm′**bəl| *v.* **am•bled, am•bling.** To walk or move along at a slow, leisurely pace: *The horses ambled out of the corral. We ambled aimlessly down the street.* —*n.* An ambling gait, as of a horse.

am•bro•sia |ăm **brō′**zhə| *n.* **1.** In Greek mythology, the food of the gods. **2.** Anything highly pleasing to one's taste or smell. **—am•bro′sial** *adj.*

am•bu•lance |**ăm′**byə ləns| *n.* A large automobile especially equipped to rush sick and injured people to a hospital.

am•bu•la•to•ry |**ăm′**byə lə tôr′ē| *or* |-tōr′ē| *adj.* Able to walk; not confined to one's bed: *an ambulatory patient.*

am•bus•cade |ăm′bə **skād′**| *n.* An ambush: *the terrible shambles of a successful Indian ambuscade.*

am•bush |**ăm′**bo͝osh′| *n.* **1.** A surprise attack made from a concealed position: *The Frankish ranks at the rear fell victims of an ambush.* **2.** The concealment from which such an attack is made: *The tiger trembles as he crouches in ambush.* —*v.* To attack from a concealed position: *Rommel ambushed and destroyed much of the British tank forces.*

a•me•ba |ə **mē′**bə| *n., pl.* **a•me•bas.** A very small, one-celled organism that has an indefinite, changeable form. [SEE PICTURE]

a•me•bic dysentery |ə **mē′**bĭk|. A disease of human beings, caused by a parasitic ameba. Its symptoms are diarrhea, abdominal cramps, and fever.

a•me•lio•rate |ə **mēl′**yə rāt′| *v.* **a•me•lio•rat•ed, a•me•lio•rat•ing.** To make or become better; improve. **—a•me′lio•ra′tion** *n.*

a•men |**ā′mĕn′**| *or* |**ä′mĕn′**| *interj.* So be it; truly. A word used at the end of a prayer.

a•me•na•ble |ə **mē′**nə bəl| *or* |ə **mĕn′**ə-| *adj.* **1.** Willing to yield or cooperate; agreeable: *I am amenable to your suggestion.* **2.** Responsible; answerable; accountable: *We are all amenable to the law.*

a•mend |ə **mĕnd′**| *v.* **1.** To change or add to (a parliamentary motion, law, or constitution). **2.** To state or restate (something) with improved wording. **3.** To mend or repair: *What's done cannot be amended.*

a•mend•ment |ə **mĕnd′**mənt| *n.* **1.** A legally adopted change added to a law or body of laws: *the 1956 amendment to the Social Security Act; an amendment to the Constitution.* **2.** Formal revision: *Some treaties embody clauses providing for amendment.*

a•mends |ə **mĕndz′**| *pl.n.* **—make amends.** To make up (to someone) for insult or injury: *He sent her roses to make amends for not having called.* [SEE NOTE]

a•men•i•ties |ə **mĕn′**ĭ tēz| *pl.n.* **1.** The courteous acts of polite social behavior: *observe the social amenities.* **2.** Anything that provides or increases comfort; a convenience: *an apartment with all the amenities.*

A•mer•i•ca |ə **mĕr′**ĭ kə|. **1.** The **United States of**

America. 2. North America. 3. the Americas. North America, Central America, and South America.

A•mer•i•can |ə mĕr′ĭ kən| *n.* A native or inhabitant of the United States or the Americas. *—adj.* Of America, the Americas, the Americans, or their languages and cultures.

A•mer•i•ca•na |ə mĕr′ĭ kä′nə| *or* |-kăn′ə| *or* |-kā′nə| *pl.n.* A collection of things relating to American history, folklore, etc.

American English. English as spoken in the United States.

American Indian. A member of any of the earliest known peoples, except the Eskimos, to have lived in North America, South America, and the West Indies.

A•mer•i•can•ism |ə mĕr′ĭ kə nĭz′əm| *n.* A word or phrase originating in or peculiar to American English. [SEE NOTE]

A•mer•i•can•ize |ə mĕr′ĭ kə nīz′| *v.* **A•mer•i•can•ized, A•mer•i•can•iz•ing.** To make American in manner, customs, or speech. —**A•mer′i•can•i•za′tion** *n.*

American plan. A system of hotel management whereby the amount charged a guest per day includes meals as well as room and service. See **European plan.**

American Revolution. The war fought from 1775 to 1783 between Great Britain and the 13 American colonies by which the colonies won independence. Also called *Revolutionary War* and *War of Independence.*

American Samoa. A group of islands in the South Pacific Ocean, a territory of the United States. Population, 32,395. Capital, Pago Pago.

American Spanish. Spanish as spoken in the Western Hemisphere.

am•er•ic•i•um |ăm′ə rĭsh′ē əm| *n.* Symbol **Am** One of the elements, a white metal. It has isotopes with mass numbers ranging from 237 to 246 and half-lives ranging from 25 minutes to 7,950 years. Atomic number 95; valences +3, +4, +5, +6.

am•e•thyst |ăm′ə thĭst| *n.* A purple or violet form of transparent quartz used as a gemstone.

a•mi•a•ble |ā′mē ə bəl| *adj.* Friendly; good-natured. —**a′mi•a•bil′i•ty** *n.* —**a′mi•a•bly** *adv.*

am•i•ca•ble |ăm′ĭ kə bəl| *adj.* Friendly in tone: *an amicable discussion.* —**am′i•ca•bly** *adv.*

a•mid |ə mĭd′| *prep.* **1.** In the middle of: *Her bobbing head appeared amid the breakers.* **2.** With the accompaniment of: *Thus, amid blood and agony, the Alamo fell.* [SEE NOTE]

a•mid•ships |ə mĭd′shĭps′| *adv.* In or toward the middle part of a ship. *—prep.* In the middle part of: *a fore-and-aft plank amidships a boat.*

a•midst |ə mĭdst| *prep.* **1.** In the middle of: *a house amidst the trees.* **2.** With the accompaniment of: *a swirl of bizarre costumes amidst a cacophony of drums and bells.* [SEE NOTE]

a•mi•no acid |ə mē′nō| *or* |ăm′ə nō′|. Any of a class of organic compounds that contain the groups NH_2CH– and COOH– and that are essential components of proteins.

A•mish |ä′mĭsh| *or* |ăm′ĭsh| *pl.n.* Mennonites of a sect that settled in the United States.

a•miss |ə mĭs′| *adj.* Wrong; faulty; improper: *Something is amiss. I can find nothing amiss.*

***Idiom.* take amiss.** To feel offended by: *I hope you won't take my remark amiss.*

am•i•ty |ăm′ĭ tē| *n.* Peaceful relations, as between nations; friendship.

Am•man |ä′män′|. The capital of Jordan. Population, 711,850.

am•me•ter |ăm′mē′tər| *n.* An instrument that measures an electric current and indicates its value, usually in amperes.

am•mo•nia |ə mōn′yə| *or* |ə mō′nē ə| *n.* **1.** A colorless gas, with a strongly irritating odor, that is composed of nitrogen and hydrogen and has the formula NH_3. It is used to manufacture fertilizers and a wide variety of other nitrogen-containing compounds. **2.** A solution of ammonia in water; ammonium hydroxide.

ammonia water. Ammonium hydroxide.

am•mo•nite |ăm′ə nīt′| *n.* One of the flat, coiled shells of various extinct mollusks, found as fossils.

am•mo•ni•um |ə mō′nē əm| *n.* An ion, NH_4^+, that consists of four hydrogen atoms bound to a single nitrogen atom and that has a single positive charge.

ammonium chloride. A white crystalline salt, NH_4Cl, that consists of an ammonium ion and a chloride ion bound together. It has an acid reaction in a water solution, and is used in dry cells, as a soldering flux, and in other industrial applications.

ammonium hydroxide. A solution of ammonia in water. It gives a basic reaction in solution, and is often used as a general cleanser.

ammonium nitrate. A colorless crystalline salt, NH_4NO_3, composed of ammonium ions and nitrate ions bound together. It is used in fertilizers, explosives, and solid rocket propellants.

am•mo•noid |ăm′ə noid′| *n.* An ammonite.

am•mu•ni•tion |ăm′yə nĭsh′ən| *n.* **1.** Anything that can be discharged from a firearm. **2.** Anything that helps to support one's argument or point of view.

am•ne•sia |ăm nē′zhə| *n.* A partial or total loss of memory, especially when caused by shock, brain injury, or some form of mental or physical illness. [SEE NOTE]

am•nes•ty |ăm′nĭ stē| *n., pl.* **am•nes•ties.** A governmental pardon, especially for political offenses. [SEE NOTE]

am•ni•on |ăm′nē ən| *or* |-ŏn′| *n., pl.* **am•ni•ons** or **am•ni•a** |ăm′nē ə|. A sac made of a thin, tough membrane and containing a watery liquid in which the embryo of a reptile, bird, or mammal floats.

a•moe•ba |ə mē′bə| *n., pl.* **a•moe•bas** or **a•moe•bae** |ə mē′bē|. A form of the word **ameba.**

a•mok |ə mŭk′| *or* |ə mŏk′| *adv.* A form of the word **amuck.**

a•mong |ə mŭng′| *prep.* **1.** In or through the midst of. **2.** In the company of: *among friends.* **3.** With portions to each of: *The soda was shared out among them.* **4.** Between one another: *fighting among themselves.* [SEE NOTE]

a•mongst |ə mŭngst′| *prep.* A form of the word **among.** [SEE NOTE]

a•mor•al |ā môr′əl| *or* |ā mŏr′-| *adj.* **1.** Not admitting of moral distinctions or judgments; neither moral nor immoral. **2.** Lacking moral judgment or sensibility; not caring about right or wrong.

am•o•rous |ăm′ər əs| *adj.* Feeling or expressing

Americanism

One kind of **Americanism** *consists of words or expressions used only in American English, and not in British or any other variety of English. Some of these are* Chicano, hero sandwich, get to first base. *The other kind are words that originated in American English and have spread to other branches of English. Examples are* muskrat, gooey, typewriter, escalate.

amid/amidst

Amid *and* **amidst** *are variant forms of the same word. In the materials on which this Dictionary was based,* **amid** *occurred 36 times and* **amidst** *only 16 times.*

amnesty/amnesia

Amnesia *and* **amnesty** *come from two closely related Greek words, both meaning "forgetfulness." The words,* amnēsia *and* amnēstia, *are both formed from the prefix* a-, *"not," and the root* mnē-, mnā-, *"remember."*

among/amongst

The variant form **amongst** *occurred 25 times in the materials on which this Dictionary was based, as against more than 1300 occurrences of* **among.** *There was no difference in their meanings or levels of usage.*

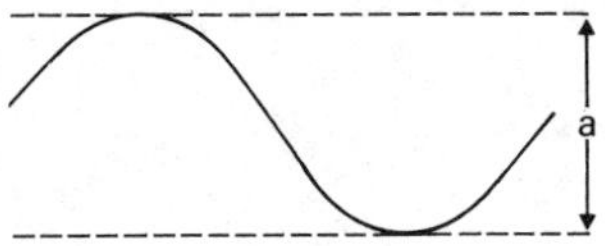

amplitude

love: *an amorous young man; an amorous look.* **—am'or•ous•ly** *adv.* **—am'or•ous•ness** *n.*

a•mor•phous |ə môr'fəs| *adj.* **1.** Lacking definite form or shape: *an amorphous mass.* **2.** Having no definite crystal structure: *Glass is an amorphous substance.*

A•mos |ā'məs|. A Hebrew prophet of the eighth century B.C.

a•mount |ə mount'| *n.* **1.** The total of two or more quantities; sum: *The amount of your bill is $8.72.* **2.** Quantity: *a meager amount of rainfall.* —*v.* **1.** To add up in number or quantity: *His sales amounted to $655.* **2.** To add up in quality or effect: *He didn't amount to anything. Some promises don't amount to much.* **3.** To be equivalent in effect: *In some cases, disobeying orders amounts to treason.*

a•mour |ə mo͝or'| *n.* A love affair, especially an illicit one.

am•per•age |ăm'pər ĭj| *or* |ăm'pîr'ĭj| *n.* The strength of an electric current as measured or expressed in amperes.

am•pere |ăm'pîr'| *n.* A unit of electric current, equal to a flow of one coulomb per second.

am•per•sand |ăm'pər sănd'| *n.* The character or sign (&) representing *and.*

am•phet•a•mine |ăm fĕt'ə mēn'| *or* |-mĭn| *n.* **1.** A colorless liquid composed of carbon, hydrogen, and nitrogen and having the formula $C_9H_{13}N$. From it are derived a number of drugs that act to stimulate the central nervous system. **2.** A drug derived from amphetamine.

am•phib•i•an |ăm fĭb'ē ən| *n.* **1.** An animal, such as a frog, toad, or salamander, that lives in water and breathes with gills during its early life stage and that develops lungs and breathes air as an adult. **2.** A vehicle that is capable of traveling both on land and in water. **3.** An aircraft that is capable of taking off from and landing on either land or water. —*adj.* **1.** Of or belonging to the group of animals that includes the amphibians. **2.** Built as an amphibian.

am•phib•i•ous |ăm fĭb'ē əs| *adj.* **1.** Able to live both on land and in water. **2.** Capable of traveling both on land and in water: *an amphibious vehicle.* **3.** Launched from the sea with navy, air, and land forces against an enemy on land: *an amphibious operation.*

am•phi•bole |ăm'fə bōl'| *n.* Any one of a large number of rocks that are composed of silicate minerals and are similar in structure.

am•phi•the•a•ter, also **am•phi•the•a•tre** |ăm'fə thē'ə tər| *n.* **1.** An oval or round structure having tiers of seats rising gradually outward from an open space, or arena, at the center. **2.** A level area surrounded by ground that slopes upward.

am•ple |ăm'pəl| *adj.* **am•pler, am•plest.** **1.** Generously sufficient; abundant: *ample rainfall; ample funds.* **2.** Extensive or more than adequate in size: *the ample spaces of public halls.* **3.** Portly; full: *His girth is a bit more ample than before.* **4.** Exhaustive or voluminous: *ample explanations; ample evidence.* **5.** Sufficient: *The pool of single men was no longer ample to fill the monthly draft quotas.*

am•pli•fi•ca•tion |ăm'plə fĭ kā'shən| *n.* **1. a.** A process by which a flow of energy, especially one that changes with time, is multiplied while all of its other characteristics remain the same. **b.** The result of this process. **2.** An expansion of any statement or idea.

am•pli•fi•er |ăm'plə fī'ər| *n.* A device, especially an electronic device, that produces or is capable of producing amplification.

am•pli•fy |ăm'plə fī'| *v.* **am•pli•fied, am•pli•fy•ing, am•pli•fies.** **1.** To act as an amplifier: *A transistor can be used to amplify.* **2.** To produce amplification of: *A public-address system amplifies a speaker's voice.* **3.** To add to (something spoken or written); expand; make complete: *amplified his earlier remarks.*

am•pli•tude |ăm'plĭ to͞od'| *or* |-tyo͞od'| *n.* **1.** Greatness of size; extent. **2.** Abundance; fullness. **3. a.** The largest value taken on by a quantity whose measure changes, especially when the changes occur with time. **b.** The largest amount by which the measure of such a quantity varies from its average value. [SEE PICTURE]

amplitude modulation. A system of radio transmission in which the amplitude of the carrier wave is adjusted so that it is proportional to the measure of the sound or other information that is to be transmitted.

am•ply |ăm'plē| *adv.* More than sufficiently; generously; liberally: *Edison's ambitions were amply realized.*

am•pu•tate |ăm'pyo͞o tāt'| *v.* **am•pu•tat•ed, am•pu•tat•ing.** To cut off (a part of the body), especially by surgery. **—am'pu•ta'tion** *n.*

am•pu•tee |ăm'pyo͞o tē'| *n.* A person who has had one or more limbs removed by amputation.

Am•ster•dam |ăm'stər dăm'|. The constitutional capital of the Netherlands, on the Zuider Zee. Population, 850,000.

a•muck |ə mŭk'| *adv.* **1.** In a wild manner, with intent to do violence or kill: *He ran amuck.* **2.** In a jumbled manner; all over: *When father carves a duck, potatoes fly amuck, and the squash and cabbage leap in space.* [SEE NOTE]

am•u•let |ăm'yə lĭt| *n.* A charm worn to ward off evil or injury, especially one worn around the neck.

a•muse |ə myo͞oz'| *v.* **a•mused, a•mus•ing.** **1.** To entertain agreeably; divert: *He amused me with adventure stories.* **2.** To cause to laugh or smile by giving pleasure.

a•mused |ə myo͞ozd'| *adj.* **1.** Expressing amusement: *an amused smile.* **2.** Agreeably diverted: *an amused and interested young man.* **—a•mus'ed•ly** |ə myo͞o'zĭd lē| *adv.*

a•muse•ment |ə myo͞oz'mənt| *n.* **1.** A feeling or condition of being pleasantly entertained: *He was too overcome with amusement to say a word.* **2.** Entertainment; diversion: *They performed music for their own edification and amusement.* **3.** A means of entertaining or of being entertained: *The fiesta provides amusement for everyone.*

amusement park. A commercially operated park having stands for the sale of refreshments and offering various forms of entertainment.

a•mus•ing |ə myo͞o'zĭng| *adj.* Pleasantly entertaining or comical; diverting: *an amusing trick.* **—a•mus'ing•ly** *adv.*

am•y•lase |ăm'ə lās'| *n.* Any of various enzymes that convert starches to sugars, as in digestion.

am•y•lop•sin |ăm'ə lŏp'sĭn| *n.* The starch-

amuck

Amuck *is one of the few English words borrowed from Malay. Malays used occasionally to go into a peculiar rage in which they would run wild and kill people at random. A man in this state was called* amoq, *"fighting mad."*

ă pat/ā pay/â care/ä father/ĕ pet/ ē be/ĭ pit/ī pie/î fierce/ŏ pot/ ō go/ô paw, for/oi oil/o͝o book/ o͞o boot/ou out/ŭ cut/û fur/ *th* the/th thin/hw which/zh vision/ ə ago, item, pencil, atom, circus

digesting enzyme produced by the pancreas.

an |ən| *or* |ăn *when stressed*| *indefinite article.* A form of *a* used before words beginning with a vowel or with an unpronounced *h: an elephant; an hour.*

-an. A suffix that forms nouns and adjectives: **American; Mexican.**

a•nab•o•lism |ə năb′ə lĭz′əm| *n.* The phase of metabolism in which simple substances are combined to form the complex materials found in living tissue. —**an′a•bol′ic** |ăn′ə bŏl′ĭk| *adj.*

a•nach•ro•nism |ə năk′rə nĭz′əm| *n.* **1.** The placing of something as existing or happening at other than its proper or historical time. **2.** Anything out of its proper time: *Cavalry is an anachronism in modern warfare.*

a•nach•ro•nis•tic |ə năk′rə nĭs′tĭk| *adj.* Out of proper time; misplaced chronologically: *One anachronistic detail in the play is having General Washington get a message by telegraph.* —**a•nach′ro•nis′ti•cal•ly** *adv.*

an•a•con•da |ăn′ə kŏn′də| *n.* A large, nonpoisonous tropical American snake that coils around and crushes its prey. [SEE PICTURE]

a•nae•mi•a |ə nē′mē ə| *n.* A form of the word **anemia.**

a•nae•mic |ə nē′mĭk| *adj.* A form of the word **anemic.**

an•aer•obe |ăn′ə rōb′| *or* |ăn âr′ōb′| *n.* An anaerobic organism.

an•aer•o•bic |ăn′ə rō′bĭk| *or* |ăn′â rō′-| *adj.* Living or functioning in an environment that lacks oxygen in the form that appears in air: *anaerobic bacteria.*

an•aes•the•sia |ăn′ĭs thē′zhə| *n.* A form of the word **anesthesia.**

an•aes•the•si•ol•o•gist |ăn′ĭs thē′zē ŏl′ə jĭst| *n.* A form of the word **anesthesiologist.**

an•aes•the•si•ol•o•gy |ăn′ĭs thē′zē ŏl′ə jē| *n.* A form of the word **anesthesiology.**

an•aes•thet•ic |ăn′ĭs thĕt′ĭk| *adj. & n.* A form of the word **anesthetic.**

an•aes•the•tist |ə nĕs′thĭ tĭst| *n.* A form of the word **anesthetist.**

an•aes•the•tize |ə nĕs′thĭ tīz′| *v.* **an•aes•the•tized, an•aes•the•tiz•ing.** A form of the word **anesthetize.**

an•a•gram |ăn′ə grăm′| *n.* **1.** A word or phrase formed by changing the order of the letters of another word or phrase. **2. anagrams.** A game in which players form words from a collection of letters by arranging, rearranging, or adding to them. [SEE NOTE]

a•nal |ā′nəl| *adj.* Of, near, or having to do with the anus.

an•al•ge•si•a |ăn′əl jē′zē ə| *or* |-jē′zhə| *n.* A condition, most often produced by a drug or drugs, in which a person remains conscious but has reduced sensitivity to pain.

an•al•ge•sic |ăn′əl jē′zĭk| *or* |-sĭk| *n.* A drug that produces analgesia; a painkiller. —*adj.* Of or causing analgesia.

an•a•log computer |ăn′ə lôg′| *or* |-lŏg′|. A computer in which numbers are represented by measurable quantities such as lengths, electric currents, or voltages. A slide rule is a simple analog computer.

a•nal•o•gous |ə năl′ə gəs| *adj.* Similar or parallel in certain ways: *The relation between addition and subtraction is analogous to that between multiplication and division.*

analogue computer. A form of the phrase **analog computer.**

a•nal•o•gy |ə năl′ə jē| *n., pl.* **a•nal•o•gies. 1.** An inference that if two unrelated things are alike in some ways they are probably alike in others: *Mosaic Law became a large collection of cases from which judges could draw analogies.* **2.** A parallel: *The beehive finds its human analogy in the city.*

an•a•lyse |ăn′ə līz′| *v.* **an•a•lysed, an•a•lys•ing.** British form of the word **analyze.**

a•nal•y•sis |ə năl′ĭ sĭs| *n., pl.* **a•nal•y•ses** |ə-năl′ĭ sēz′|. **1. a.** The breaking up of a substance into its component parts, usually by chemical means, and the identification of each component. **b.** A written report of the information obtained in this way. **2.** The process of separating a subject into its parts and studying them so as to determine its nature: *an analysis of the Presidential election.* **3.** Psychoanalysis.

an•a•lyst |ăn′ə lĭst| *n.* **1.** A person who performs an analysis. **2.** A psychoanalyst.

an•a•lyt•ic |ăn′ə lĭt′ĭk| or **an•a•lyt•i•cal** |ăn′-ə lĭt′ĭ kəl| *adj.* Of or concerned with analysis: *analytical chemistry.* —**an′a•lyt′i•cal•ly** *adv.*

analytical balance. A very sensitive balance used in chemical analysis for weighing.

analytic geometry. A mathematical technique in which geometric figures are identified in terms of numbers and variables that represent the coordinates of their points, and their properties are studied by means of algebra.

an•a•lyze |ăn′ə līz′| *v.* **an•a•lyzed, an•a•lyz•ing. 1.** To perform or prepare an analysis of: *They analyzed the ore and found iron in it.* **2.** To examine in detail. **3.** To psychoanalyze.

an•a•pest, also **an•a•paest** |ăn′ə pĕst′| *n.* **1.** In poetry or verse, a metrical foot composed of two short syllables followed by one long one. **2.** A line of verse using this meter: *"Twas the night before Christmas and all through the house"* (Clement Moore).

an•a•phase |ăn′ə fāz′| *n.* The stage of mitosis in which the chromosomes, at this point doubled in number, move to separate into identical groups which move to opposite parts of the cell.

an•ar•chic |ăn är′kĭk| or **an•ar•chi•cal** |ăn-är′kĭ kəl| *adj.* **1.** Of or promoting anarchy. **2.** Lacking order or control; lawless.

an•ar•chism |ăn′ər kĭz′əm| *n.* **1.** The theory that all forms of government are bad and should be abolished. **2.** Rejection of all forms of organization or authority.

an•ar•chist |ăn′ər kĭst| *n.* A person who favors or engages in anarchism. —**an′ar•chis′tic** *adj.*

an•ar•chy |ăn′ər kē| *n., pl.* **an•ar•chies. 1.** Absence of any governmental authority: *a time when there was no government on earth, and when men lived in a condition of anarchy.* **2.** Disorder and confusion resulting from lack of authority: *the violence that will surely take our schools down the road to anarchy.*

an•as•tig•mat•ic |ăn ăs′tĭg măt′ĭk| *adj.* Capable of forming an accurate image of a point; not astigmatic: *an anastigmatic lens.*

a•nath•e•ma |ə năth′ə mə| *n.* **1.** A formal ban, curse, or excommunication imposed by a church.

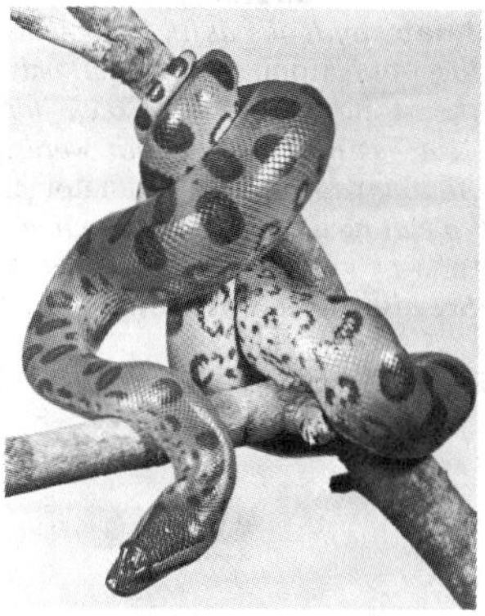

anaconda

anagram

swine / wines / sinew
trifle / filter
supersonic / percussion

anatomy
Anatomy *looks as if it contains the word* atom, *but in fact only the* -tom-, *which is Greek for "cut," is the same in both words. Anatomy is from Greek* anatomē, *"a cutting up, medical dissection"* (ana-, *"up,"* and tom-, *"cut"*). *See also the note at* **atom**.

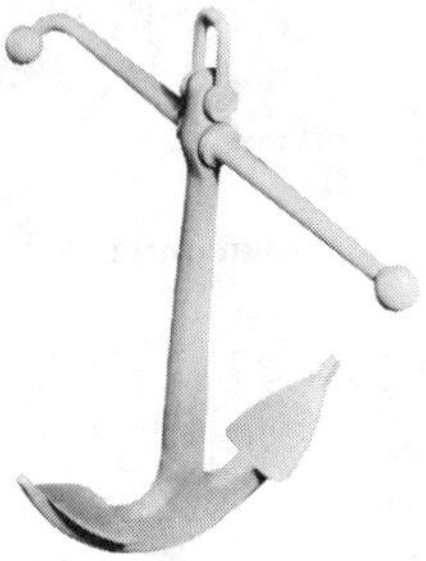

anchor
Anchor *is from Greek* ankura, *"a hook, an anchor." This word is formed on the Indo-European root* ank-, *meaning "to bend" or "something bent." The root occurs very clearly in several other English words, notably* **angle** *and* **ankle**.

and
And *is probably the third commonest word in English* (**the** *and* **of** *are first and second*). *In the five million words on which this Dictionary was based,* **and** *occurs over 133,000 times—more than two and one-half* **and's** *in every 100 words.*

ă pat/ā pay/â care/ä father/ĕ pet/ē be/ĭ pit/ī pie/î fierce/ŏ pot/ō go/ô paw, for/oi oil/ŏŏ book/ōō boot/ou out/ŭ cut/û fur/*th* the/th thin/hw which/zh vision/ə ago, item, pencil, atom, circus

2. A strong denunciation or condemnation. 3. Someone or something intensely disliked.

a•nath•e•ma•tize |ə năth'ə mə tīz'| *v.* **a•nath•e•ma•tized, a•nath•e•ma•tiz•ing.** To proclaim an anathema on; denounce; curse.

an•a•tom•i•cal |ăn'ə tŏm'ĭ kəl| or **an•a•tom•ic** |ăn'ə tŏm'ĭk| *adj.* 1. Of or concerned with anatomy or dissection. 2. Of the structure of an organism as opposed to its functioning: *an anatomical abnormality.* —**an'a•tom'i•cal•ly** *adv.*

a•nat•o•mist |ə năt'ə mĭst| *n.* A person who specializes in anatomy.

a•nat•o•mize |ə năt'ə mīz'| *v.* **a•nat•o•mized, a•nat•o•miz•ing.** 1. To cut apart or dissect in order to study the structure: *The biologist anatomized the fish.* 2. To perform a detailed analysis of.

a•nat•o•my |ə năt'ə mē| *n., pl.* **a•nat•o•mies.** 1. The structure of a plant or an animal or of any of its parts. 2. The scientific study of the shape and structure of living things. 3. The dissection or cutting apart of a plant or animal in order to study its structure. 4. The human body: *the rugged anatomy of an athlete.* [SEE NOTE]

-ance. A suffix that forms nouns from verbs: **compliance; resemblance.**

an•ces•tor |ăn'sĕs'tər| *n.* 1. Any person from whom one is descended, especially if of a generation earlier than a grandparent. 2. An organism or type of organism, either known or supposed to exist, from which later organisms have evolved. 3. A forerunner; prototype: *The harpsichord is an ancestor of the piano.*

an•ces•tral |ăn sĕs'trəl| *adj.* 1. Of ancestors: *ancestral spirits.* 2. Coming from ancestors: *ancestral wealth.* 3. Being an ancestor: *the ancestral Indo-European language, from which English and Greek are descended.* —**an•ces'tral•ly** *adv.*

an•ces•try |ăn'sĕs'trē| *n., pl.* **an•ces•tries.** 1. A line of descent through a collection of ancestors; lineage. 2. Ancestors taken as a group. 3. A process of development; history: *The ancestry of automobiles goes back nearly 200 years.*

an•chor |ăng'kər| *n.* 1. A heavy iron or steel object attached to a ship by a cable and dropped overboard to keep the ship in place, either by its weight or by catching on the sea bottom. 2. Any of various devices used to provide a rigid point of support, as for securing a rope or cable. 3. Something that helps one feel secure. 4. In radio and television, an anchorman or anchorwoman. —*v.* 1. To hold fast or secure by or as if by an anchor. 2. To drop anchor or be held by an anchor, as a ship. 3. To act as anchorman or anchorwoman. [SEE NOTE & PICTURE]

an•chor•age |ăng'kər ĭj| *n.* 1. A place where ships can anchor. 2. The action of anchoring or the condition of being held by an anchor.

An•chor•age |ăng'kər ĭj|. The largest city in Alaska, on the southern coast. Population, 173,992.

an•cho•rite |ăng'kə rīt'| *n.* A person who for religious reasons has withdrawn from society to live alone; a hermit.

an•chor•man |ăng'kər măn'| *n., pl.* **-men** |-mĕn'|. 1. In radio and television, the narrator of a news broadcast in which several correspondents give reports. 2. A member of a relay team, usually the strongest, who runs last.

an•chor•wom•an |ăng'kər wŏŏm'ən| *n., pl.* **-wom•en** |-wĭm'ĭn|. In radio and television, a woman who narrates a news broadcast in which several correspondents give reports.

an•cho•vy |ăn'chō vē| *or* |ăn chō'vē| *n., pl.* **an•cho•vies.** A small, herringlike sea fish, often salted and canned.

an•cient |ān'shənt| *adj.* 1. Very old; aged. 2. Of times long past, especially belonging to the historical period before the fall of Rome in A.D. 476. —*n.* 1. A very old person. 2. **the ancients.** The Greeks or Romans of ancient times. —**an'cient•ly** *adv.* —**an'cient•ness** *n.*

an•cil•lar•y |ăn'sə lĕr'ē| *adj.* Serving as help or support but not of first importance; subordinate; subsidiary: *an ancillary road.*

-ancy. A suffix that forms nouns from verbs: *compliancy; expectancy.*

and |ənd| *or* |ən| *or* |ănd *when stressed*| *conj.* 1. Together with or along with; as well as. 2. Added to; plus: *Two and two makes four.* 3. As a result: *Seek, and ye shall find.* 4. To. Used between finite verbs in the infinitive or imperative: *Try and find it.* [SEE NOTE]

an•dan•te |ān dän'tā| *or* |ăn dăn'tē|. In music: *adj.* Moderately slow. —*adv.* Moderately slowly. —*n.* A moderately slow section of a composition.

an•dan•ti•no |än'dän tē'nō| *or* |ăn'dăn-|. In music: *adj.* Slightly faster than andante. —*adv.* Slightly more quickly than andante. —*n., pl.* **an•dan•ti•nos.** An andantino section of a composition.

An•der•sen |ăn'dər sən|, **Hans Christian.** 1805–1870. Danish author of fairy tales.

An•der•son |ăn'dər sən|, **Marian.** Born 1902. American concert and opera contralto.

An•des |ăn'dēz|. A mountain chain extending the length of western South America.

and•i•ron |ănd'ī'ərn| *n.* One of a pair of metal supports for holding up logs in a fireplace.

and/or. Used to indicate that either *and* or *or* may be used to connect words, phrases, or clauses depending upon what meaning is intended, as in the sentence *Thin the paint with turpentine and/or linseed oil.*

An•dor•ra |ăn dôr'ə| *or* |-dŏr'ə|. A principality in the Pyrenees between France and Spain. Population 20,000. Capital, Andorra la Vella.

An•drew |ăn'drōō|. In the New Testament, one of the Twelve Apostles.

an•dro•gen |ăn'drə jən| *n.* Any of various hormones that act in the development and maintenance of masculine physical characteristics. —**an'dro•gen'ic** |ăn'drə jĕn'ĭk| *adj.*

an•droid |ăn'droid'| *n.* In science fiction, an artificially created man.

an•ec•dote |ăn'ĭk dōt'| *n.* A short account of an interesting or humorous occurrence or event. —**an'ec•do'tal** *adj.*

a•ne•mi•a |ə nē'mē ə| *n.* A diseased condition in which the blood, because of a lack of hemoglobin, too few red blood cells, or poorly formed red blood cells, cannot carry enough oxygen to the body tissues.

a•ne•mic |ə nē'mĭk| *adj.* 1. Of anemia. 2. Suffering from anemia.

an•e•mom•e•ter |ăn'ə mŏm'ĭ tər| *n.* An instrument that measures and indicates the strength of the wind, usually in terms of its speed.

a•nem•o•ne |ə nĕm′ə nē| *n.* **1.** Any of several plants with cup-shaped white, purple, or red flowers. **2.** See **sea anemone.**

a•nent |ə nĕnt′| *prep.* Regarding; concerning; about.

an•er•oid barometer |ăn′ə roid′|. A barometer that measures atmospheric pressure by means of the changes in shape of an elastic disk that covers a chamber in which there is a partial vacuum.

an•es•the•sia |ăn′ĭs thē′zhə| *n.* A condition in which some or all of the senses, especially the sense of touch, stop operating, either completely or in part. This condition can be produced by disease or intentionally by the administration of drugs.

an•es•the•si•ol•o•gist |ăn′ĭs thē′zē ŏl′ə jĭst| *n.* A physician whose specialty is anesthesiology.

an•es•the•si•ol•o•gy |ăn′ĭs thē′zē ŏl′ə jē| *n.* The medical study of anesthetics, their effects, and their use.

an•es•thet•ic |ăn′ĭs thĕt′ĭk| *adj.* **1.** Of, resembling, or causing anesthesia. **2.** Without sensation or feeling; insensitive. —*n.* A drug that causes anesthesia.

an•es•the•tist |ə nĕs′thĭ tĭst| *n.* A physician having special training in the administration of anesthetics.

an•es•the•tize |ə nĕs′thĭ tīz′| *v.* **an•es•the•tized, an•es•the•tiz•ing.** To put into a condition of anesthesia, especially by means of a drug: *They anesthetized her in preparation for surgery.*

a•new |ə nōō′| *or* |ə nyōō| *adv.* Over again: *ready to start anew.*

an•gel |ān′jəl| *n.* **1.** One of the immortal beings serving as attendants or messengers of God. **2.** A dear person: *Every one of the little angels is sound asleep.* **3.** A familiar spirit: *the bright angel of his genius; the dark angel of his disease.* **4.** *Informal.* A person who provides financial support for something.

an•gel•fish |an′jəl fĭsh′| *n., pl.* **an•gel•fish** or **an•gel•fish•es.** Any of several tropical fishes with a flattened body and bright coloring or showy markings. [SEE PICTURE]

angel food cake. A light, white, spongy cake made with stiffly beaten egg whites, sugar, and flour.

an•gel•ic |ăn jĕl′ĭk| *adj.* Of or like angels: *the angelic host; angelic voices.* —**an•gel′i•cal•ly** *adv.*

An•ge•le•no |ăn′jə lē′nō| *n., pl.* **An•ge•le•nos.** A native or inhabitant of Los Angeles.

An•ge•lus, also **an•ge•lus** |ăn′jə ləs| *n.* **1.** In the Roman Catholic Church, a devotional prayer at morning, noon, and sunset in celebration of Annunciation. **2.** A bell rung as a call to recite this prayer.

an•ger |ăng′gər| *n.* A feeling of great displeasure or hostility toward someone or something, caused by a sense of injury or wrong; rage; wrath. —*v.* To make or become angry: *Her laughter angered him, but he angers much too easily.*

an•gi•na |ăn jī′nə| *n.* **1.** Painful, choking spasms or a disease that causes such spasms. **2. Angina pectoris.**

angina pec•to•ris |pĕk′tə rĭs|. A severe tightening and pain in the chest, often extending into the left shoulder and arm. It generally results from an insufficient supply of blood to the heart muscle, usually because of coronary disease.

an•gi•o•sperm |ăn′jē ə spûrm′| *n.* Any of a large group of plants that have flowers and produce seeds enclosed in an ovary, or fruit; a flowering plant.

an•gle¹ |ăng′gəl| *v.* **an•gled, an•gling. 1.** To fish with a hook and line. **2.** To try to get something by using schemes or tricks: *He angled for a promotion.* [SEE NOTE]

an•gle² |ăng′gəl| *n.* **1.** A flat geometric figure formed by a pair of rays that begin at a common point. **2.** A projecting corner, as of a building. **3.** The place, position, or direction from which an object is presented to view; point of view: *a handsome building, from any angle.* **4.** A particular part or phase, as of a problem; an aspect: *studying every angle of the question.* —***modifier:*** *an angle bracket.* —*v.* **an•gled, an•gling. 1.** To move or hit at an angle: *angling the camera for a closer view; angled his approach shot beyond the green.* **2.** To turn or proceed at an angle: *He angled sharply to the left. The road angles through marshy land.* [SEE NOTE & PICTURE]

angle iron. A length of iron or steel bent into a right angle along its length and used as a structural support.

angle of incidence. The angle formed by the path of radiation or the path of a body striking a surface and a line drawn perpendicular to the surface at the point of impact.

angle of reflection. The angle formed by the path of radiation or the path of a body reflected from a surface and a line drawn perpendicular to the surface at the point of impact.

angle of refraction. The angle formed by the path of refracted radiation and a line drawn perpendicular to the refracting surface at the point where the refraction occurred.

an•gler |ăng′glər| *n.* **1.** One who fishes with a hook and line. **2.** An anglerfish.

an•gler•fish |ăng′glər fĭsh′| *n., pl.* **an•gler•fish** or **an•gler•fish•es.** A deep-sea fish with a flap of skin hanging from a stalklike projection over its large mouth. The flap acts as bait to attract smaller fish.

An•gles |ăng′gəlz| *pl.n.* A Germanic people who settled in Britain in the 5th century A.D. and together with the Jutes and Saxons formed the Anglo-Saxon peoples.

an•gle•worm |ăng′gəl wûrm′| *n.* An earthworm, especially when used as fishing bait.

An•gli•can |ăng′glĭ kən| *adj.* Of or characteristic of the Anglican Church. —*n.* A member of the Anglican Church.

Anglican Church. The Church of England and those churches in other nations that are in complete agreement with it.

An•gli•can•ism |ăng′glĭ kə nĭz′əm| *n.* The beliefs, practices, and form of organization of the Anglican Church.

An•gli•cize, also **an•gli•cize** |ăng′glĭ sīz′| *v.* **An•gli•cized, An•gli•ciz•ing.** To make English or similar to English in form, style, or character: *The name Odysseus, or Ulixes in Latin, was Anglicized as Ulysses.*

an•gling |ăng′glĭng| *n.* The act or sport of fishing with a hook and line.

An•glo-Sax•on |ăng′glō săk′sən| *n.* **1.** A mem-

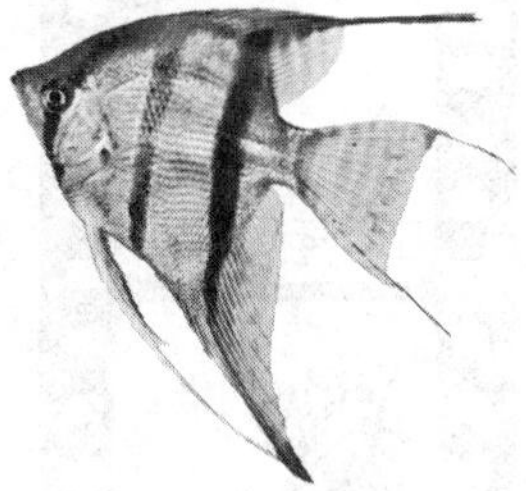

angelfish
This kind of freshwater angelfish is often kept in home aquariums

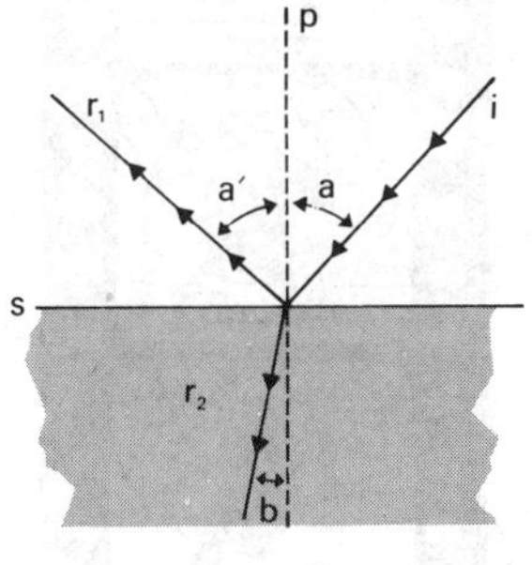

angle²
Angles of incidence, reflection, and refraction

angle¹·²
Angle¹ *and* ***angle²*** *have separate histories, but they ultimately go back to the same prehistoric Indo-European root,* ank-, *meaning "something bent or crooked." This root forms, on the one hand, Old English* ang-ul-, *"a hook, a fishhook," hence* **angle¹**, *and, on the other hand, Latin* ang-ulus, *"a corner, an angle," which via French produced* **angle²**.

animated cartoon

ber of one of the Germanic peoples who settled in Britain in the 5th and 6th centuries A.D. These people were the Angles, the Saxons, and the Jutes. **2.** Any of the descendants of these people. **3.** **Old English.** —**An'glo-Sax'on** *adj.*

An•go•la |ăng gō'lə|. A country on the west coast of southern Africa. Population, 5,798,000. Capital, Luanda.

An•go•ra |ăng gôr'ə| *or* |-gōr'ə| *n.* **1.** Also **Angora goat.** A goat with long, silky hair. **2.** Also **Angora cat.** A cat with long, soft hair, popular as a pet. **3.** Also **Angora rabbit.** One of a breed of rabbits with long, soft hair. **4. angora.** Yarn or cloth made from the hair of an Angora goat or rabbit.

an•gry |ăng'grē| *adj.* **an•gri•er, an•gri•est. 1.** Feeling or showing anger: *an angry customer; an angry expression; angry at her; angry about his behavior; angry with himself; angry over his error.* **2.** Seeming to threaten: *angry dark clouds.* **3.** Inflamed: *an angry wound.* —**an'gri•ly** *adv.* —**an'gri•ness** *n.*

ang•strom, also **Ang•strom, Ång•strom** |ăng'strəm| *n.* A unit of length equal to one hundred-millionth (10^{-8}) of a centimeter. It is used mainly in expressing wavelengths of light and shorter electromagnetic radiation.

an•guish |ăng'gwĭsh| *n.* A pain of the body or mind that causes one agony; torment; torture.

an•guished |ăng'gwĭsht| *adj.* Feeling, expressing, or caused by anguish: *anguished souls clinging to a sinking ship; a wounded elephant's anguished trumpeting.*

an•gu•lar |ăng'gyə lər| *adj.* **1.** Of, having, forming, or consisting of an angle or angles. **2.** Measured in terms of an angle: *angular distance.* **3.** Bony and lean: *a nervous, angular lady.* **4.** Sharp-cornered: *bulky or angular packages.* **5.** Lacking grace or smoothness: *an angular gait; angular melodies.*

an•gu•lar•i•ty |ăng'gyə lăr'ĭ tē| *n., pl.* **an•gu•lar•i•ties.** The condition or quality of being angular.

an•hy•dride |ăn hī'drīd'| *n.* **1.** A chemical compound formed from another by the removal of water. **2.** A metallic oxide that reacts with water to form a base or a nonmetallic oxide that reacts with water to form an acid.

an•hy•drous |ăn hī'drəs| *adj.* Without water, especially water of crystallization.

an•i•line |ăn'ə lĭn| *n.* A colorless, oily, poisonous liquid composed of carbon, hydrogen, and nitrogen and having the formula C_6H_7N. It is derived from benzene and is used in making dyes, rubber, drugs, and varnishes.

aniline dye. Any of various dyes that are made from aniline.

an•i•mad•ver•sion |ăn'ə măd vûr'zhən| *or* |- shən| *n.* Hostile criticism or a remark that directs criticism or blame.

an•i•mal |ăn'ə məl| *n.* **1.** A living being that generally differs from a plant by being able to move from place to place, by growing to a definite, limited size and shape, and by eating food rather than manufacturing it by a special process. **2. a.** Any such living being other than a human being. **b.** A mammal as distinguished from a bird, reptile, fish, insect, etc. **3.** A person whose bearing or behavior suggests an animal as distinguished from a human being; a brutish person. —*adj.* **1.** Of animals. **2.** Relating to the physical or sensual nature of man rather than to his mind or soul: *animal vitality; men's crude, animal tastes.*

an•i•mal•cule |ăn'ə măl'kyōōl| *n.* An animal of very small or microscopic size, such as an ameba or a paramecium.

animal husbandry. The care and breeding of domestic animals such as cattle and horses.

an•i•mate |ăn'ə mĭt| *adj.* **1.** Living: *animate things.* **2.** Belonging to the class of nouns that stand for living things: *The word "dog" is animate, the word "car" inanimate.* —*v.* |ăn'ə māt'| **an•i•mat•ed, an•i•mat•ing. 1.** To give life to or make to come alive. **2.** To inspire or motivate: *She was animated by the noblest patriotism.* **3.** To produce as an animated cartoon: *Walt Disney animated stories such as Snow White.*

an•i•mat•ed |ăn'ə mā'tĭd| *adj.* **1.** Lively: *Her personality was energetic and animated.* **2.** Designed so as to appear alive and move in a lifelike manner: *animated puppets.* —**an'i•mat'ed•ly** *adv.*

animated cartoon. A motion picture in which the series of images on the film is made from hand-drawn originals. [SEE PICTURE]

an•i•mat•er |ăn'ə mā'tər| *n.* A form of the word **animator.**

an•i•ma•tion |ăn'ə mā'shən| *n.* **1.** The condition or quality of being alive; liveliness; vitality. **2.** The process or processes by which an animated cartoon is prepared. **3.** An animated cartoon.

a•ni•ma•to |ā'nə mä'tō| *or* |ăn'ə-|. In music: *adj.* Animated; lively. —*adv.* In a lively, animated way.

an•i•ma•tor |ăn'ə mā'tər| *n.* An artist or technician who works at making animated cartoons.

an•i•mism |ăn'ə mĭz'əm| *n.* A belief among primitive tribes that natural objects and forces have souls.

an•i•mos•i•ty |ăn'ə mŏs'ĭ tē| *n., pl.* **an•i•mos•i•ties.** Hatred, enmity, or hostility that is shown openly.

an•i•mus |ăn'ə məs| *n.* **1.** An intention or purpose; a motive behind an action. **2.** A feeling of animosity; hatred.

an•i•on |ăn'ī'ən| *n.* An ion that has a negative charge and that is therefore attracted by a positively charged electrode, or anode.

an•ise |ăn'ĭs| *n.* **1.** A plant with small, licorice-flavored seeds. **2.** The seeds of this plant, used for flavoring.

an•i•seed |ăn'ĭ sēd'| *n.* The seed of the anise plant.

An•ka•ra |ăng'kər ə| *or* |äng'-|. The capital of Turkey, in the central part of the country. Population, 1,209,000.

an•kle |ăng'kəl| *n.* **1.** The joint between the foot and leg. **2.** The slender part of the leg just above this joint.

an•klet |ăng'klĭt| *n.* **1.** A bracelet or chain worn around the ankle. **2.** A short sock reaching to just above the ankle.

an•nals |ăn'əlz| *pl.n.* **1.** A record of events written in the order of their occurrence, year by year. **2.** Any descriptive account or record; a history.

An•nap•o•lis |ə năp'ə lĭs|. The capital of Mary-

ă pat/ā pay/â care/ä father/ĕ pet/ ē be/ĭ pit/ī pie/î fierce/ŏ pot/ ō go/ô paw, for/oi oil/ŏŏ book/ ōō boot/ou out/ŭ cut/û fur/ *th* the/th thin/hw which/zh vision/ ə ago, item, pencil, atom, circus

land and site of the U.S. Naval Academy. Population, 28,000.

an•neal |ə nēl'| *v.* **1.** To treat (glass or a metal) by heating and slow cooling in order to toughen and reduce brittleness. **2.** To temper.

an•ne•lid |ăn'ə lĭd| *n.* A worm, such as an earthworm or leech, with a body divided into ringlike segments.

an•nex |ə nĕks'| *v.* **1.** To add or join to, especially to a larger or more significant thing: *Put a decimal point after the number before you annex zeros.* **2.** To add (territory) to an existing country or other area: *The city is trying to annex two of the suburbs.* —*n.* |ăn'ĕks'|. An extra building that is added to another, bigger building and used for some related purpose: *the library annex.*

an•nex•a•tion |ăn'ĭk sā'shən| *n.* The act of annexing: *Germany's annexation of Czechoslovakian territory.*

an•ni•hi•late |ə nī'ə lāt'| *v.* **an•ni•hi•lat•ed, an•ni•hi•lat•ing.** To destroy completely; wipe out. —**an•ni'hi•la'tion** *n.*

an•ni•ver•sa•ry |ăn'ə vûr'sə rē| *n., pl.* **an•ni•ver•sa•ries. 1.** The yearly returning of the date of an event that happened in an earlier year: *a wedding anniversary.* **2.** A celebration on this date. —***modifier:*** *an anniversary party.*

an•no Dom•i•ni |ăn'ō dŏm'ə nī'| *or* |dŏm'ə-nē'|. In the year of the Lord. A Latin phrase, almost always abbreviated to A.D., used to indicate dates since the birth of Christ: *The Emperor Nero committed suicide* A.D. *64* (or *in 64* A.D. or *in the year 64* A.D.).

an•no•tate |ăn'ō tāt'| *v.* **an•no•tat•ed, an•no•tat•ing.** To furnish (a literary work) with explanatory notes.

an•no•ta•tion |ăn'ō tā'shən| *n.* **1.** The act or process of annotating. **2.** An explanatory note.

an•nounce |ə nouns'| *v.* **an•nounced, an•nounc•ing. 1.** To bring to public notice; give formal notice of: *The principal announced a change in our schedule.* **2.** To make known the presence or arrival of: *The doorman announced us by telephone.* **3.** To serve as an announcer of: *announced hockey games on television.*

an•nounce•ment |ə nouns'mənt| *n.* **1.** The act of announcing. **2.** A public declaration to make known something that has happened or that will happen; an official statement: *An announcement will be made soon.* **3.** A printed or published notice: *Read this announcement.*

an•nounc•er |ə noun'sər| *n.* A person who announces, as on television or over a public-address system.

an•noy |ə noi'| *v.* To bother or irritate: *Crocodiles are in trouble when they annoy elephants.*

an•noy•ance |ə noi'əns| *n.* **1.** Irritation or displeasure: *He won, much to his rival's surprise and annoyance.* **2.** Something causing trouble or irritation; a nuisance: *Heartburn is a relatively minor annoyance.* **3.** The action of bothering or injuring: *bold tactics of annoyance.*

an•noyed |ə noid'| *adj.* Displeased, angry, or offended: *Jim never stayed annoyed too long.* —**an•noy'ed•ly** |ə noi'ĭd lē| *adv.*

an•noy•ing |ə noi'ĭng| *adj.* Troublesome or irritating: *an annoying habit.* —**an•noy'ing•ly** *adv.*

an•nu•al |ăn'yo͞o əl| *adj.* **1.** Occurring or done every year; yearly: *an annual medical examination.* **2.** Of a year; determined by a year's time: *an annual income; the annual turnover of merchandise.* **3.** Living and growing for only one year or season: *annual plants.* —*n.* **1.** A periodical published yearly; a yearbook. **2.** A plant that grows, flowers, produces seeds, and dies in a single year or season. —**an'nu•al•ly** *adv.* [SEE NOTE]

annual ring. One of the layers of wood formed each year in a tree trunk or other woody stem, showing as a ring-shaped band in cross section. [SEE PICTURE]

an•nu•i•ty |ə no͞o'ĭ tē| *or* |ə nyo͞o'-| *n., pl.* **an•nu•i•ties. 1. a.** An amount of money paid at regular intervals. **b.** A sequence of such payments. **2.** An investment on which a person receives fixed payments during his lifetime or for a certain number of years.

an•nul |ə nŭl'| *v.* **an•nulled, an•nul•ling.** To make or declare void; nullify; cancel: *The court annulled his marriage.*

an•nu•lar |ăn'yə lər| *adj.* Forming or shaped like a ring. —**an'nu•lar•ly** *adv.*

annular eclipse. A type of solar eclipse in which the moon blocks all but a bright ring around the edge of the sun.

an•nul•ment |ə nŭl'mənt| *n.* **1.** The act of annulling. **2.** A legal declaration stating that a marriage was never valid.

An•nun•ci•a•tion |ə nŭn'sē ā'shən| *n.* **1.** The angel Gabriel's announcement to Mary that she was to become the mother of Jesus. **2.** The festival, on March 25, celebrating this.

an•nun•ci•a•tor |ə nŭn'sē ā'tər| *n.* An electrical signaling device, used in hotels and manually controlled elevators, that indicates on a switchboard the source of each call.

an•ode |ăn'ōd'| *n.* **1.** A **positive electrode. 2.** In a battery or other device that is supplying current, the negative electrode.

an•o•dyne |ăn'ə dīn'| *n.* A medicine that relieves pain.

a•noint |ə noint'| *v.* **1.** To apply oil, ointment, or a similar substance to. **2.** To apply oil to in a religious ceremony as a means of making pure or holy: *"My head with oil thou dost anoint."* (Psalms 23:5). —**a•noint'ment** *n.*

a•nom•a•lous |ə nŏm'ə ləs| *adj.* Differing from what is normal or common; abnormal.

a•nom•a•ly |ə nŏm'ə lē| *n., pl.* **a•nom•a•lies. 1.** Deviation or departure from what is normal or common; abnormality. **2.** Something that is unusual, irregular, or abnormal: *He was a bachelor, in itself an anomaly in that part of the country.*

a•non |ə nŏn'| *adv.* **1.** Again; then. Used chiefly in the phrases *ever and anon* and *now and anon.* **2.** *Archaic.* Soon; presently: *"Of this discourse we more will hear anon."* (Shakespeare).

anon. Anonymous.

an•o•nym•i•ty |ăn'ə nĭm'ĭ tē| *n.* The condition of being anonymous: *The Swiss have a taste for anonymity.*

a•non•y•mous |ə nŏn'ə məs| *adj.* **1.** Nameless or unnamed: *a panel of medical experts and anonymous young addicts.* **2.** Not having a well-known name: *a handful of anonymous colonial explorers.* **3.** Of unknown source: *an anonymous letter.* —**a•non'y•mous•ly** *adv.*

a•noph•e•les |ə nŏf'ə lēz'| *n.* A mosquito that

annual, etc.

Annual *comes from Latin* annuālis, *"yearly," which is from* annus, *"a year."* **Anniversary** *is from Latin* anniversārius, *"yearly returning, coming once a year":* annus + vers-, *"turn."* **Annuity** *is from Medieval Latin* annuitās, *"yearly payment," also from* annus.

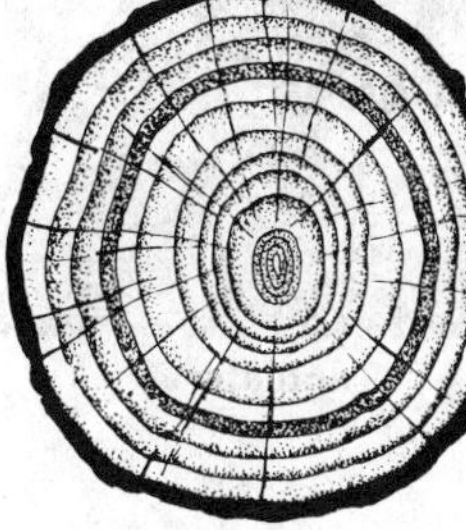

annual ring

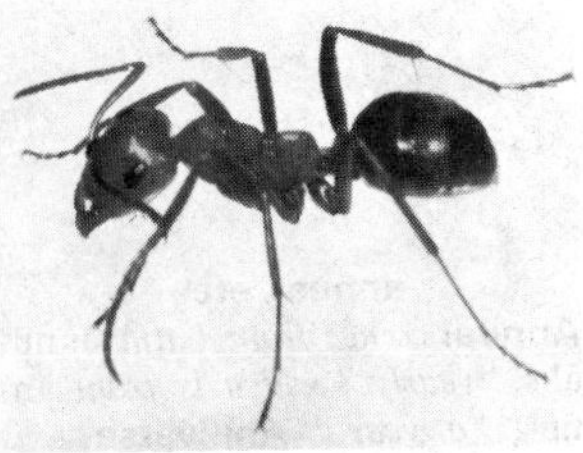

ant

anteater

anther
Anthers of tiger lily

ă pat/ā pay/â care/ä father/ĕ pet/ ē be/ĭ pit/ī pie/î fierce/ŏ pot/ ō go/ô paw, fôr/oi oil/o͝o book/ o͞o boot/ou out/ŭ cut/û fur/ *th* the/th thin/hw which/zh vision/ ə ago, item, pencil, atom, circus

carries malaria parasites and transmits the disease to human beings.

an•oth•er |ə nŭ*th*′ər| *adj.* **1.** Different: *another way of doing things.* **2.** Changed: *He's been another person since he got that job.* **3. a.** Some other and later: *We'll discuss this at another time.* **b.** Some other and former: *She belongs to another era.* **4.** Additional; one more: *having another cup of coffee.* **5.** New: *He thinks he's another Babe Ruth.* —*pron.* **1.** An additional or different one. **2.** Something or someone different from or in contrast to the first one named: *A baby is one thing to baby-sit, a 6-year-old another.* **3.** One of a group of things: *one thing and another.*

an•o•rex•i•a |ăn′ə **rĕk**′sē ə| *n.* Loss of appetite, especially as a result of disease or psychological disorder.

an•swer |**ăn**′sər| *or* |**än**′-| *n.* **1.** A spoken or written reply, as to a question, statement, request, or letter. **2.** An act that serves as a reply or response. **3. a.** A solution or result, as to a problem. **b.** The correct solution or response. **4.** In music, a statement of a theme in response to another statement of the same or a different theme, especially in a fugue. —*v.* **1.** To reply to or respond in words or action: *She answered him curtly. Answer to your name when it is called.* **2.** To be liable or accountable for: *You will have to answer for this waste.* **3.** To serve the purpose; do: *If a pen is not available, a hard pencil may answer.* **4.** To match or correspond: *a car answering to this description.*

an•swer•a•ble |**ăn**′sər ə bəl| *or* |**än**′-| *adj.* **1.** Responsible; accountable; liable: *You are answerable to your conscience and answerable for any bad conduct.* **2.** Able to be answered: *scientific questions not wholly answerable.*

ant |ănt| *n.* Any of various insects that live in complexly organized colonies, often digging and tunneling in the ground or wood. Most ants are wingless; only the males and queens have wings. ¶*These sound alike* **ant, aunt.** [SEE PICTURE]

-ant. A suffix that forms nouns and adjectives: **deodorant; resultant.**

ant•ac•id |ănt **ăs**′ĭd| *adj.* Capable of neutralizing an acid; basic. —*n.* An antacid substance, especially one used medically to neutralize excess stomach acid.

an•tag•o•nism |ăn **tăg**′ə nĭz′əm| *n.* **1.** Unfriendly feeling; hostility. **2.** Mutual resistance; opposition.

an•tag•o•nist |ăn **tăg**′ə nĭst| *n.* **1.** A person who opposes and actively competes with another; an adversary; opponent. **2.** Either of a pair of drugs or other substances that neutralize each other in the body: *An antitoxin is the antagonist of a toxin.* **3.** Either of a pair of muscles that produce opposite motions.

an•tag•o•nis•tic |ăn tăg′ə **nĭs**′tĭk| *adj.* **1.** Opposed; contending: *antagonistic points of view.* **2.** Unfriendly; hostile: *an antagonistic attitude.* —**an•tag′o•nis′ti•cal•ly** *adv.*

an•tag•o•nize |ăn **tăg**′ə nīz′| *v.* **an•tag•o•nized, an•tag•o•niz•ing.** To earn the dislike of: *He antagonized his father by acting bored.*

An•ta•na•na•ri•vo |ăn′tə năn′ə **rē**′vō|. The capital of Madagascar. Population, 452,000.

Ant•arc•tic |ănt **ärk**′tĭk| *or* |-**är**′tĭk| *adj.* Of or in the regions surrounding the South Pole: *the Antarctic climate.* —*n.* **the Antarctic.** Antarctica and its surrounding waters.

Ant•arc•ti•ca |ănt **ärk**′tĭ kə| *or* |-**är**′tĭ kə|. The continent surrounding the South Pole, almost entirely covered by a sheet of ice.

Antarctic Circle. The parallel of latitude 66 degrees 33 minutes south, forming the boundary between the South Temperate Zone and the South Frigid Zone.

an•te |**ăn**′tē| *n.* In poker, a bet that each player must make to begin or stay in the game.

ante-. A prefix meaning "in front of" or "before": **antechamber; antecedent.**

ant•eat•er |**ănt**′ē′tər| *n.* **1.** Any of several long-snouted tropical American animals that feed on ants and other insects, which they catch with a long, sticky tongue. **2.** Any of several similar animals. [SEE PICTURE]

an•te-bel•lum |ăn′tē **bĕl**′əm| *adj.* Belonging to the period prior to the Civil War: *an ante-bellum mansion.*

an•te•ce•dent |ăn′tĭ **sēd**′nt| *adj.* Going before; preceding; prior. —*n.* **1.** Someone or something that goes before or precedes. **2.** An occurrence or event prior to another. **3. antecedents.** A person's ancestors, ancestry, or past life. **4.** The word, phrase, or clause to which a pronoun refers, especially a relative pronoun. In the phrase *the book that you gave him, book* is the antecedent of *that.*

an•te•cham•ber |**ăn**′tē chām′bər| *n.* A waiting room at the entrance to a larger and more important room.

an•te•date |**ăn**′tĭ dāt′| *v.* **an•te•dat•ed, an•te•dat•ing. 1.** To be of an earlier date than: *This novel antedates his more mature works.* **2.** To give a date earlier than the actual date; date back.

an•te•di•lu•vi•an |ăn′tĭ də **lo͞o**′vē ən| *adj.* **1.** Of the period before the Flood. **2.** Very old; antiquated: *The dragon, a happy Bohemian, told antediluvian anecdotes to the boy.*

an•te•lope |**ăn**′tə lōp′| *n., pl.* **an•te•lope** or **an•te•lopes. 1.** Any of various swift-running, often slender, long-horned animals of Africa and Asia. **2.** An animal similar to a true antelope, especially the pronghorn of western North America.

an•ten•na |ăn **tĕn**′ə| *n.* **1.** *pl.* **an•ten•nae** |ăn**tĕn**′ē|. One of the pair of long, slender feelers growing on the head of an insect or a crustacean such as a lobster or shrimp. **2.** *pl.* **an•ten•nas.** Any of various metallic devices that are capable of projecting radio waves from a transmitter into space or intercepting radio waves and delivering them to a receiver.

an•te•ri•or |ăn **tîr**′ē ər| *adj.* **1.** Placed in front; located forward. **2.** Prior in time; earlier. **3.** In lower animals, near the head. **4.** In human beings and higher animals, on, near, or toward the surface of the body on which the abdomen is found.

an•te•room |**ăn**′tē ro͞om′| *or* |-ro͝om′| *n.* An antechamber.

an•them |**ăn**′thəm| *n.* **1.** A song of praise or loyalty: *a national anthem.* **2.** A choral composition, usually of moderate length, with a sacred text.

an•ther |**ăn**′thər| *n.* The pollen-bearing part at the upper end of the stamen of a flower. [SEE PICTURE]

ant•hill |ănt′hĭl′| *n.* A mound of earth formed by ants in digging or building a nest.

an•thol•o•gy |ăn thŏl′ə jē| *n., pl.* **an•thol•o•gies.** A collection of writings, such as poems or stories, by various authors.

an•thra•cite |ăn′thrə sīt′| *n.* A form of coal that is hard and consists mainly of pure carbon. It makes relatively little smoke when it burns.

an•thrax |ăn′thrăks′| *n.* An infectious disease of mammals, mainly cattle and sheep, that can also be transmitted to human beings. It is caused by bacteria and is usually fatal.

an•thro•poid |ăn′thrə poid′| *adj.* Resembling a human being; manlike: *Gorillas and chimpanzees are anthropoid apes.* —*n.* An anthropoid ape.

an•thro•po•log•i•cal |ăn′thrə pə lŏj′ĭ kəl| *adj.* Of anthropology. —**an′thro•po•log′i•cal•ly** *adv.*

an•thro•pol•o•gist |ăn thrə pŏl′ə jĭst| *n.* A scientist who specializes in anthropology.

an•thro•pol•o•gy |ăn′thrə pŏl′ə jē| *n.* The scientific study of the origins and physical, social, and cultural development and behavior of human beings.

anti–. A prefix meaning "opposed," "against," or "counteracting": **antisocial; antifreeze.** When *anti-* is followed by a capital letter or the letter *i,* it appears with a hyphen: *anti-American; anti-intellectual.* [SEE NOTE]

an•ti•air•craft |ăn′tē âr′krăft′| *or* |-kräft′| *adj.* Used, especially from a position on the ground, for defense against attack by aircraft: *antiaircraft weapons.*

an•ti•bi•ot•ic |ăn′tē bī ŏt′ĭk| *n.* Any of a group of substances such as penicillin and streptomycin, produced by certain fungi, bacteria, and other organisms, that are capable of destroying microorganisms or stopping their growth. They are widely used in the treatment and prevention of diseases. —*adj.* Of, using, or acting as an antibiotic or antibiotics: *antibiotic therapy; an antibiotic drug.*

an•ti•bod•y |ăn′tĭ bŏd′ē| *n., pl.* **an•ti•bod•ies.** Any of various proteins that are found in the blood and that are generated in reaction to foreign proteins or carbohydrates. They are capable of acting against these foreign substances and so give immunity against certain microorganisms and toxins.

an•tic |ăn′tĭk| *adj.* Odd; ludicrous. —*n.* Often **antics.** An odd or extravagant act or gesture; a caper; prank.

An•ti•christ |ăn′tĭ krīst′| *n.* **1.** In early Christian prophecy, a great enemy who would set himself up against Christ at the end of the world. **2. antichrist.** Any enemy of Christ.

an•tic•i•pate |ăn tĭs′ə pāt′| *v.* **an•tic•i•pat•ed, an•tic•i•pat•ing. 1.** To foresee, expect, or consider in advance: *We hadn't anticipated so many guests.* **2.** To act upon before an expected time: *Most Americans responded to the ban on cyclamates by anticipating it.* **3.** To project as part of the future: *In his book he anticipates a Utopia ruled by an elite.* **4.** To deal with in advance: *I try to anticipate trouble.*

an•tic•i•pa•tion |ăn tĭs′ə pā′shən| *n.* **1.** Expectation, especially happy or eager expectation: *Her mind was bright with memories and anticipation.* **2.** Foreknowledge or apprehension: *His face was pinched in anticipation of the pain.*

an•ti•cli•mac•tic |ăn′tē klī măk′tĭk| *adj.* Of or accompanied by an anticlimax. —**an′ti•cli•mac′ti•cal•ly** *adv.*

an•ti•cli•max |ăn′tē klī′măks′| *n.* **1.** A decline or letdown viewed as a disappointing contrast to what has gone before. **2.** Something that represents such a decline, as a less important or trivial event following one or more significant ones: *The business of nominating a vice-presidential candidate is usually an anticlimax.*

an•ti•cline |ăn′tĭ klīn′| *n.* A formation in which several strata of rock are folded so that they slope down on both sides of a crest. [SEE PICTURE]

an•ti•cy•clone |ăn′tē sī′klōn′| *n.* A system of winds that spiral outward around a region of high barometric pressure, moving clockwise in the Northern Hemisphere and counterclockwise in the Southern Hemisphere.

an•ti•dote |ăn′tĭ dōt′| *n.* **1.** A substance that counteracts the effects of poison. **2.** Anything that counteracts something injurious.

an•ti•freeze |ăn′tĭ frēz′| *n.* A liquid added to another liquid, such as water, to lower its freezing point.

an•ti•gen |ăn′tĭ jən| *n.* Anything that stimulates the production of an antibody when introduced into the body.

an•ti•gene |ăn′tĭ jēn′| *n.* A form of the word **antigen.**

an•ti•grav•i•ty |ăn′tē grăv′ĭ tē| *n.* In science fiction, a force that counteracts gravity, making possible levitation, interstellar travel, etc.

An•ti•gua and Bar•bu•da |ăn tē′gwə; bär bōō′-də|. An island country in the northern Leeward Islands in the West Indies. Population, 72,000. Capital, St. John's.

an•ti•his•ta•mine |ăn′tē hĭs′tə mēn′| *or* |-mĭn| *n.* Any of various drugs designed to relieve symptoms of allergies or colds by interfering with the production or action of histamine.

An•til•les |ăn tĭl′ēz|. The islands of the West Indies, divided into the Greater Antilles (Cuba, Hispaniola, and Puerto Rico) and the **Lesser Antilles** (Leeward Islands, Windward Islands, Barbados, and Trinidad and Tobago).

an•ti•log |ăn′tĭ lôg′| *or* |-lŏg′| *n.* A shortened form of the word **antilogarithm,** generally used in writing mathematical expressions.

an•ti•log•a•rithm |ăn′tē lô′gə rĭth′əm| *or* |-lŏg′ə-| *n.* The number that corresponds to a given logarithm. For example, if $y = \log x$, then $x = \text{antilog } y$.

an•ti•ma•cas•sar |ăn′tĭ mə kăs′ər| *n.* A small cover placed on the backs or arms of chairs or sofas to keep them from getting dirty.

an•ti•mat•ter |ăn′tĭ măt′ər| *n.* A theoretically possible form of matter in which every atomic particle is replaced by its corresponding antiparticle.

an•ti•mo•ny |ăn′tə mō′nē| *n.* Symbol **Sb** One of the elements, the most common form of which is a hard, extremely brittle, blue-white metal. Atomic number 51; atomic weight 121.75; valences −3, +3, +5; melting point 630.5°C; boiling point 1,380°C. [SEE NOTE]

an•ti•neu•tri•no |ăn′tē nōō trē′nō| *or* |-nyōō-| *n.* The antiparticle corresponding to the neutrino.

anti-

Anti- *is a popular prefix at the moment. Many of the new* anti- *words are not included in this or any other dictionary, partly because their meanings are obvious and partly because we don't yet know if they will last. Examples:* anticrime *(bill),* antidrug *(program),* antihijack *(precautions),* anti-inflation *(campaign),* antipollution *(laws),* antipoverty *(legislation),* antiriot *(laws). The words people make up can tell you a lot about what kind of people they are (or think they are).*

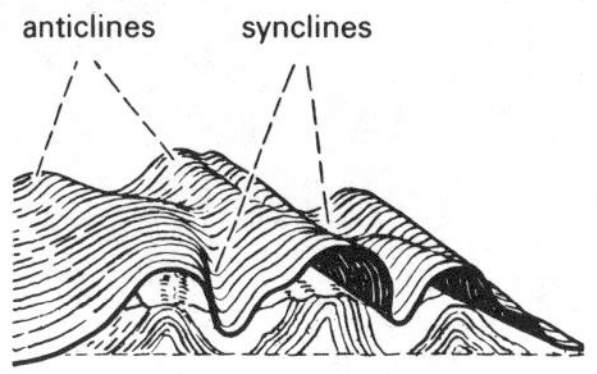

anticline
Sketch of a bed of limestone

antimony

Antimony *has four allotropic forms and occurs principally as a sulfide in minerals. It is used to make flameproofing compounds, paints, semiconductor devices, and ceramics. The symbol for antimony, Sb, is taken from Latin* stibium, *"antimony."*

antler
Antlers of caribou

Antlers should not be confused with the horns of cattle, goats, and related animals, which are not shed and grown again.

ă pat/ā pay/â care/ä father/ĕ pet/ ē be/ĭ pit/ī pie/î fierce/ŏ pot/ ō go/ô paw, for/oi oil/ŏŏ book/ ōō boot/ou out/ŭ cut/û fur/ *th* the/th thin/hw which/zh vision/ ə ago, item, pencil, atom, circus

an•ti•neu•tron |ăn'tē **nōō**'trŏn'| *or* |-**nyōō**'-| *n.* The antiparticle that corresponds to the neutron.

an•ti•par•ti•cle |ăn'tē **pär**'tĭ kəl| *n.* Either of a pair of atomic particles, such as a positron and electron, that are identical in mass but exactly opposite in electric charge, magnetic properties, and spin.

an•ti•pas•to |ăn'tē **pä**'stō| *or* |-**păs**'tō| *n.* An Italian dish of assorted appetizers.

an•tip•a•thy |ăn **tĭp**'ə thē| *n., pl.* **an•tip•a•thies. 1.** A feeling of dislike or opposition: *his antipathy to new ideas.* **2.** A person or thing that causes such dislike.

an•ti•per•spi•rant |ăn'tē **pûr**'spər ənt| *n.* A preparation applied to the skin to reduce or prevent perspiration.

an•tiph•o•nal |ăn **tĭf**'ə nəl| *adj.* Of or using antiphony. —**an•tiph'o•nal•ly** *adv.*

an•tiph•o•ny |ăn **tĭf**'ə nē| *n.* An arrangement in which the performers of a musical composition are divided into two or more groups that play, or sing, alternately.

an•tip•o•dal |ăn **tĭp**'ə dəl| *adj.* **1.** Of antipodes. **2.** Located at opposite ends of a diameter, especially a diameter of the earth. **3.** Exactly opposite; diametrically opposed: *antipodal theories.*

an•tip•o•des |ăn **tĭp**'ə dēz'| *pl.n.* **1. a.** A pair of points that are located at opposite ends of a diameter, especially a diameter of the earth. **b.** A place at an antipodal point of the earth. **2.** Two things that are exact opposites.

an•ti•pro•ton |ăn'tē **prō**'tŏn'| *n.* The antiparticle that corresponds to the proton.

an•ti•quar•i•an |ăn'tĭ **kwâr**'ē ən| *adj.* Of antiquaries or the study of antiquities. —*n.* An antiquary.

an•ti•quar•y |**ăn**'tĭ kwĕr'ē| *n., pl.* **an•ti•quar•ies.** A student or collector of antiquities.

an•ti•quat•ed |**ăn**'tĭ kwā'tĭd| *adj.* Old-fashioned; outmoded: *antiquated elegance.*

an•tique |ăn **tēk**'| *adj.* **1.** Being an antique: *antique firearms; antique furniture.* **2.** Archaic or former: *Music in the antique sense included the study of mathematics.* **3.** Of or belonging to antiquity: *an antique land.* **4.** Very old: *An antique woman hobbled after him.* —*n.* **1.** Something made at a period much earlier than the present: *The car was old enough to be an antique.* **2.** Something having special value because of its age, especially a work of art or handicraft that is over 100 years old: *treasured antiques such as the Windsor chair.*

an•tiq•ui•ty |ăn **tĭk**'wĭ tē| *n., pl.* **an•tiq•ui•ties. 1.** Ancient times: *Great engineering projects were carried out far back in antiquity.* **2.** Greek and Roman times: *The idea of selling one's soul to the Devil dates from late antiquity.* **3.** Considerable age: *a village of great antiquity.* **4.** The quality of being old: *Tinted varnishes were used to simulate antiquity.* **5. antiquities.** Relics and monuments of former times: *I can show you many antiquities if you're interested.*

an•ti-Sem•i•tism |ăn'tē **sĕm**'ĭ tĭz'əm| *n.* Prejudice against or hostility toward Jews. —**an'ti-Se•mit'ic** |ăn'tē sə **mĭt**'ĭk| *adj.*

an•ti•sep•tic |ăn'tĭ **sĕp**'tĭk| *adj.* **1.** Capable of destroying microorganisms, especially those that produce disease, fermentation, or rot. **2.** Free of microorganisms: *Surgery is done under antiseptic conditions.* —*n.* An antiseptic substance or agent.

an•ti•slav•er•y |ăn'tē **slā**'və rē| *or* |-**slāv**'rē| *adj.* Opposed to or against slavery.

an•ti•so•cial |ăn'tē **sō**'shəl| *adj.* **1.** Avoiding the society or company of others; not sociable. **2.** Opposed to or interfering with society: *drugs that cause crime or aggressive antisocial behavior.* —**an'ti•so'cial•ly** *adv.*

an•ti•sub•ma•rine |ăn'tē **sŭb**'mə rēn'| *or* |- sŭb'mə **rēn**'| *adj.* Involving or used in the detection and destruction of submarines.

an•ti•tank |ăn'tē **tăngk**'| *adj.* Designed for use against tanks or other armored vehicles: *an antitank weapon.*

an•tith•e•sis |ăn **tĭth**'ĭ sĭs| *n., pl.* **an•tith•e•ses** |ăn **tĭth**'ĭ sēz'|. **1.** Direct contrast; opposition: *Between our good intentions and our vices there is always antithesis.* **2.** The direct or exact opposite: *Vice is the antithesis of virtue.* **3.** In speech or writing, a contrast of strongly opposed ideas placed side by side; for example, "Millions for defense but not a cent for tribute" (Robert Goodloe Harper) contains an antithesis.

an•ti•tox•in |ăn'tē **tŏk**'sĭn| *n.* **1.** An antibody formed in response to and to act against a biological toxin, such as one produced by bacteria. **2.** An animal serum containing antibodies of this type.

an•ti•trades |**ăn**'tĭ trādz'| *pl.n.* The westerly winds that move above the trade winds of the tropics and become the westerly winds of the middle latitudes.

an•ti•trust |ăn'tē **trŭst**'| *adj.* Opposing or regulating trusts or similar business monopolies considered not in the best interests of the public: *an antitrust suit; antitrust laws.*

an•ti•ven•in |ăn'tē **vĕn**'ĭn| *n.* **1.** An antitoxin that counteracts a venom. **2.** A human or animal serum containing such an antitoxin.

an•ti•war |ăn'tē **wôr**'| *adj.* Opposing war: *an antiwar demonstration by college students.*

ant•ler |**ănt**'lər| *n.* One of a pair of bony, often branched growths on the head of a deer or related animal. Antlers are usually borne only by males, and are shed and grown again from year to year. [SEE PICTURE]

ant lion. An insect whose larva digs holes to trap ants and other insects for food. The adult insect resembles a dragonfly.

an•to•nym |**ăn**'tə nĭm'| *n.* A word having a sense opposite to a sense of another word; for example, *fat* is an antonym of *skinny.*

Ant•werp |**ăn**'twərp|. A city in northern Belgium. Population, 671,000.

a•nus |**ā**'nəs| *n., pl.* **a•nus•es.** The opening at the lower end of the alimentary canal from which the wastes that remain after food is digested are excreted.

an•vil |**ăn**'vĭl| *n.* A heavy block of iron or steel, with a smooth, flat top on which metals are shaped by hammering.

anx•i•e•ty |ăng **zī**'ĭ tē| *n., pl.* **anx•i•e•ties. 1.** A feeling of uneasiness and distress about something in the future; worry: *He was filled with anxiety about his mother's return.* **2.** Eagerness or earnestness, often marked by uneasiness: *her anxiety to do well.*

anx•ious |**ăngk**'shəs| *or* |**ăng**'-| *adj.* **1.** Having a feeling of uneasiness; worried: *The mother was anxious about her child.* **2.** Marked by uneasiness or worry: *anxious moments.* **3.** Eagerly earnest or desirous: *anxious to begin.* —**anx'ious•ly** *adv.* —**anx'ious•ness** *n.*

an•y |ĕn'ē| *adj.* **1.** One or some, no matter which, out of three or more: *Take any book you want.* **2.** Every: *Any kid in my gang would do the same.* **3.** Some: *Is there any soda?* **4.** Much: *He doesn't need any strength to chop kindling.* —*pron.* Any person or thing or any persons or things; anybody or anything. —*adv.* At all: *He doesn't feel any better.*

an•y•bod•y |ĕn'ē bŏd'ē| *or* |-bŭd'ē| *pron.* Any person; anyone. —*n.* A person of any importance: *everybody who is anybody.*

an•y•how |ĕn'ē hou'| *adj.* **1.** In any case; at any rate; anyway: *The twins were sick, but they were too little to play anyhow.* **2.** Just the same; nevertheless; anyway: *You may know these words, but study them anyhow.*

an•y•more |ĕn'ē môr'| *or* |-mōr'| *adv.* Now. Used only in negative or interrogative constructions: *We mustn't talk anymore.*

an•y•one |ĕn'ē wŭn'| *or* |-wən| *pron.* Any person; anybody. [SEE NOTE]

an•y•place |ĕn'ē plās'| *adv.* Anywhere: *I can go anyplace I like.*

an•y•thing |ĕn'ē thĭng'| *pron.* Any object, occurrence, or matter whatever.

an•y•time |ĕn'ē tīm'| *adv.* **1.** At any time: *Anytime we see plant leaves turning brown we should cut them.* **2.** At any time whatsoever: *It was as tricky a job of roping as they'd ever see anytime.*

an•y•way |ĕn'ē wā'| *adv.* **1.** In any case; at any rate; anyhow: *Both girls would wear, or anyway carry, white gloves.* **2.** Just the same; nevertheless; anyhow: *The ball was slippery, but Henry caught it anyway.* [SEE NOTE]

an•y•ways |ĕn'ē wāz'| *adv.* A form of the word **anyway.** [SEE NOTE]

an•y•where |ĕn'ē hwâr'| *or* |-wâr'| *adv.* **1.** To, in, or at any place: *They travel anywhere they want to.* **2.** At all: *Before my hand was anywhere near him he was gone.*

anywhere from. Any quantity or amount within specified bounds: *Brushing should eliminate anywhere from 45 to 95 percent of dental cavities.*

A-one |ā'wŭn'| *adj. Informal.* First-class; excellent.

a•or•ta |ā ôr'tə| *n.* The largest artery of the body, starting at the left ventricle of the heart and branching to carry blood to all the organs of the body except the lungs. [SEE PICTURE]

a•pace |ə pās'| *adv.* At a rapid pace; swiftly: *Inflation grew apace.*

A•pach•e |ə păch'ē| *n., pl.* **A•pach•e** or **A•pach•es.** **1.** A tribe of Plains Indians of the southwestern United States. **2.** A member of this tribe. **3.** The Athapascan language of this tribe. —**A•pach'e** *adj.*

a•part |ə pärt'| *adv.* **1.** At a distance in time or position from each other: *two trees about ten feet apart.* Also used adjectivally: *They were seldom apart in the daytime.* **2.** To either side or in opposite directions from each other: *The negatively charged foil strips swing apart.* **3. a.** In or into separate pieces: *A fault is a place where rock has broken and moved apart.* **b.** To pieces.

apart from. Other than; aside from: *Apart from her temper, she's all right.*

a•part•heid |ə pärt'hīt'| *or* |-hāt'| *n.* An official policy of the Republic of South Africa enforcing racial segregation and white supremacy.

a•part•ment |ə pärt'mənt| *n.* A room or suite of rooms used by one household in a building occupied by more than one household.

apartment house. A building divided into apartments; an apartment building.

ap•a•thet•ic |ăp'ə thĕt'ĭk| *adj.* Lacking or not showing strong feeling; uninterested; indifferent: *apathetic about school.* —**ap'a•thet'i•cal•ly** *adv.*

ap•a•thy |ăp'ə thē| *n.* Lack of feeling or interest; indifference: *the public's apathy on many urgent problems.*

ape |āp| *n.* **1.** One of the larger animals belonging to the same group as monkeys and human beings, such as a gorilla, chimpanzee, or orang-utan. **2.** Any monkey. **3.** One who imitates or mimics. —*v.* **aped, ap•ing.** To imitate the actions of; mimic.

a•peak |ə pēk'| *adv.* In a vertical position: *holding their oars apeak.* —*adj.* **1.** With the ship directly overhead just before sailing: *Anchor's apeak.* **2.** In a vertical position: *The oars are apeak.*

a•pé•ri•tif |ä pĕr'ĭ tēf'| *n.* A drink, usually of a fortified wine, taken before a meal to stimulate the appetite.

ap•er•ture |ăp'ər chər| *n.* **1.** A hole or opening: *an aperture in the wall.* **2.** An opening or entrance through which light or other electromagnetic radiation can pass into a camera, telescope, or other instrument.

a•pex |ā'pĕks'| *n., pl.* **a•pex•es** or **a•pi•ces** |ā'pĭ-sēz'| *or* |ăp'ĭ-|. **1.** The peak or highest point of something: *The apex of his career.* **2.** The highest point of a geometric figure; a vertex.

a•pha•sia |ə fā'zhə| *n.* The loss of some or all of the ability to express and understand ideas, generally as a result of damage to the brain. —**a•pha'sic** *adj. & n.*

a•phe•li•on |ə fē'lē ən| *or* |ə fēl'yən| *n., pl.* **a•phe•li•a** |ə fē'lē ə| *or* |ə fēl'yə|. The point in the orbit of a planet or other celestial body that travels around the sun at which it is farthest from the sun.

a•phid |ā'fĭd| *or* |ăf'ĭd| *n.* A small, soft-bodied insect that sucks sap from plants.

aph•o•rism |ăf'ə rĭz'əm| *n.* A short, ingenious saying expressing a general truth; for example, "The only way to have a friend is to be one" is an aphorism.

aph•ro•dis•i•ac |ăf'rə dĭz'ē ăk'| *n.* A drug or food that stimulates sexuality. —*adj.* Sexually stimulating.

Aph•ro•di•te |ăf'rə dī'tē|. The Greek goddess of love, identified with the Roman goddess Venus.

A•pi•a |ə pē'ə|. The capital of Western Samoa. Population, 32,000.

a•pi•ar•y |ā'pē ĕr'ē| *n., pl.* **a•pi•ar•ies.** A place where bees and beehives are kept as a source of honey.

a•pi•ces |ā'pĭ sēz'| *or* |ăp'ĭ-| *n.* A plural of **apex.**

a•piece |ə pēs'| *adv.* To or for each one; each: *Give them an apple apiece.*

anyone

In the materials on which this Dictionary was based, **anyone** *occurred more than twice as often as* **anybody.**

anyway

In the materials on which this Dictionary was based, **anyhow** *and* **anyway** *are used exactly alike in both meanings, with* **anyway** *occurring about five times more often than* **anyhow.** *Both words are used mostly in speech and in storytelling. The expressions* in any case, at any rate, *and* nevertheless *are more usual than* **anyway** *in formal writing.*

anyways

In the materials on which this Dictionary was based, the form **anyways** *occurred only twice, once in a representation of dialectal speech and once in a grammar book where it was given as an example of incorrect English.*

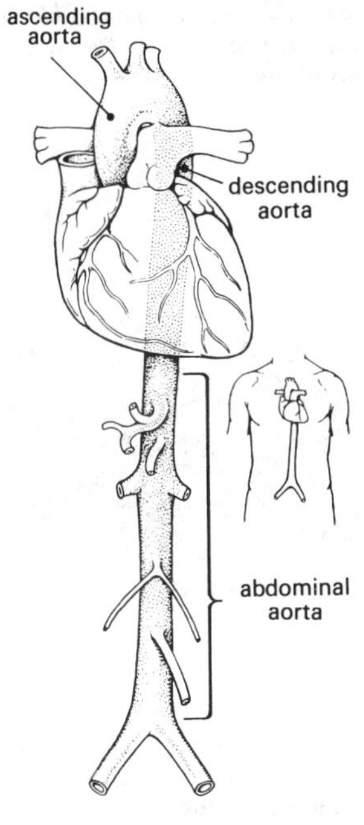

aorta

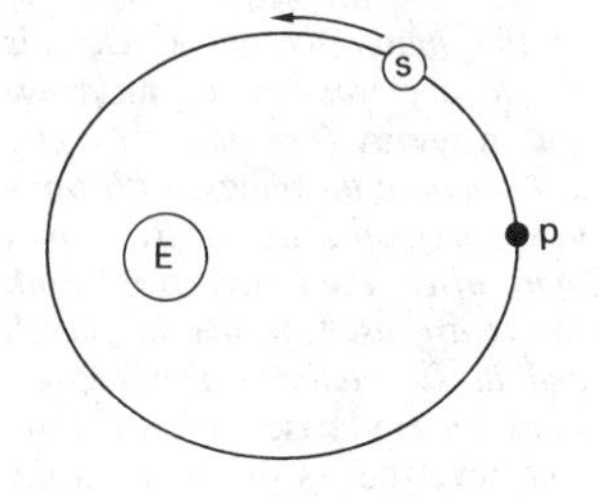

apogee
E earth, s satellite, p point of apogee.

apothecary
An **apothecary** *is a man who keeps a store of drugs, and the the word comes ultimately from Greek* apothēkē, *"a storehouse." As often happens in English, we have another word from the same source, but in so different a form that it would be impossible to guess the connection. The word is* **boutique**.

appaloosa

ă pat/ā pay/â care/ä father/ĕ pet/ ē be/ĭ pit/ī pie/î fierce/ŏ pot/ ō go/ô paw, for/oi oil/o͝o book/ o͞o boot/ou out/ŭ cut/û fur/ *th* the/th thin/hw which/zh vision/ ə ago, item, pencil, atom, circus

a•plomb |ə **plŏm′**| *or* |ə **plŭm′**| *n.* Self-confidence; poise; assurance: *She handles difficult situations with aplomb.*

A•poc•a•lypse |ə **pŏk′**ə lĭps′| *n.* The last book of the New Testament, Revelation.

a•poc•a•lyp•tic |ə pŏk′ə **lĭp′**tĭk| *adj.* Prophetic, especially of the destiny of mankind: *Revolution became the apocalyptic program for instant social transformation and rebirth.*

A•poc•ry•pha |ə **pŏk′**rə fə| *n.* **1.** The fourteen Biblical books not included in the Old Testament by Protestants as being of doubtful authorship and authority. Eleven of these books are accepted by the Roman Catholic Church. **2.** Various early Christian writings excluded from the New Testament.

a•poc•ry•phal |ə **pŏk′**rə fəl| *adj.* Of doubtful origin; false: *There are widespread tales, some apocryphal no doubt, but some surely true, of titanic battles between lions and leopards.*

ap•o•gee |**ăp′**ə jē′| *n.* **1.** The point in the orbit of a natural or artificial satellite of the earth at which the satellite is farthest from the earth. **2.** The highest point; apex. [SEE PICTURE]

A•pol•lo |ə **pŏl′**ō|. The Greek god of the sun, prophecy, music, medicine, and poetry.

a•pol•o•get•ic |ə pŏl′ə **jĕt′**ĭk| *adj.* Expressing or making an apology: *"My watch has stopped," he said with an apologetic smile.* —**a•pol′o•get′i•cal•ly** *adv.*

a•pol•o•gist |ə **pŏl′**ə jĭst| *n.* A person who argues in defense or justification of an idea, cause, etc.: *an apologist for conservation.*

a•pol•o•gize |ə **pŏl′**ə jīz′| *v.* **a•pol•o•gized, a•pol•o•giz•ing.** To make an apology; say one is sorry.

a•pol•o•gy |ə **pŏl′**ə jē| *n., pl.* **a•pol•o•gies. 1.** A statement expressing regret for an offense or fault: *make an apology for being late.* **2.** A defense or justification, as of an idea, cause, etc.: *an apology for capital punishment.*

ap•o•plec•tic |ăp′ə **plĕk′**tĭk| *adj.* Of, like, causing, or suffering from apoplexy.

ap•o•plex•y |**ăp′**ə plĕk′sē| *n.* A condition in which a blood vessel in the brain breaks or becomes blocked and causes tissue damage that may result in loss of muscular control, paralysis, unconsciousness, and, often, death.

a•pos•ta•sy |ə **pŏs′**tə sē| *n.* An abandonment of one's religious faith, political party, creed, loyalty, etc.

a•pos•tate |ə **pŏs′**tāt′| *or* |-tĭt| *n.* A person who abandons or forsakes his faith, political principles, beliefs, etc.

a•pos•tle |ə **pŏs′**əl| *n.* **1.** Often **Apostle.** One of the twelve original disciples of Christ. **2.** A missionary of the early Christian Church: *St. Patrick, the apostle of Ireland.* **3.** A person who leads or strongly supports a cause or movement: *an apostle of conservation.*

Apostles' Creed. A Christian creed traditionally thought to have been written by the Twelve Apostles. It begins, "I believe in God the Father Almighty."

ap•os•tol•ic |ăp′ə **stŏl′**ĭk| *adj.* **1.** Of the Apostles or the times when they lived. **2.** Of the pope as successor to Saint Peter.

a•pos•tro•phe |ə **pŏs′**trə fē′| *n.* A mark (') used to indicate the omission of a letter or letters from a word (*aren't*), the possessive case (*Tom's hat*), and certain plurals, especially those of numbers and letters.

apothecaries' measure. A system of liquid volume measure used in pharmacy.

apothecaries' weight. A system of weights used in pharmacy.

a•poth•e•car•y |ə **pŏth′**ĭ kĕr′ē| *n., pl.* **a•poth•e•car•ies.** A person who has been trained in the preparation of drugs and medicines; a pharmacist; druggist. [SEE NOTE]

a•poth•e•o•sis |ə pŏth′ē **ō′**sĭs| *or* |ăp′ə **thē′**ə-sĭs| *n., pl.* **a•poth•e•o•ses** |ə pŏth′ē **ō′**sēz′| *or* |ăp′ə **thē′**ə sēz′|. **1.** The elevation to divine rank or status; deification: *the apotheosis of a Roman emperor.* **2.** A glorified ideal.

Ap•pa•la•chi•a |ăp′ə **lā′**chē ə| *or* |-chə| *or* |- **lăch′**ē ə| *or* |-**lăch′**ə|. A region of the southern Appalachian Mountains, including parts of Maryland, Virginia, West Virginia, Kentucky, Tennessee, and North Carolina.

Ap•pa•la•chi•an Mountains |ăp′ə **lā′**chē ən| *or* |-chən| *or* |-**lăch′**ē ən| *or* |-**lăch′**ən|. Also **Ap•pa•la•chi•ans.** The major mountain chain of eastern North America, extending from Canada to Alabama.

ap•pall |ə **pôl′**| *v.* To fill with horror and amazement; shock: *The poor living conditions appalled me.* —**ap•pall′ing** *adj.: an appalling amount of drug addiction.*

ap•pa•loo•sa |ăp′ə **lo͞o′**sə| *n.* A horse with a spotted rump, originally bred in northwestern North America. [SEE PICTURE]

ap•pa•ra•tus |ăp′ə **rā′**təs| *or* |-**răt′**əs| *n., pl.* **ap•pa•ra•tus** or **ap•pa•ra•tus•es. 1.** The means by which a specified function or task is performed: *Modern music draws on an immense new technical apparatus.* **2.** Equipment, especially laboratory equipment: *a fine lab and a wealth of apparatus.* **3.** A device or mechanism formed by a group of parts working together, as in a machine or in the body: *The dolphin possesses a built-in sonar apparatus.* **4.** A system: *a growing economic apparatus.*

ap•par•el |ə **păr′**əl| *n.* Clothing; attire: *children's apparel.* —*v.* **ap•par•eled** or **ap•par•elled, ap•par•el•ing** or **ap•par•el•ling.** To dress or clothe: *The queen was richly appareled.*

ap•par•ent |ə **păr′**ənt| *or* |ə **pâr′**-| *adj.* **1.** Readily understood or seen; obvious: *for no apparent reason.* **2.** Appearing as such but not necessarily so; seeming: *an apparent advantage.* —**ap•par′ent•ly** *adv.*

ap•pa•ri•tion |ăp′ə **rĭsh′**ən| *n.* **1.** A ghost; specter. **2.** An eerie sight.

ap•peal |ə **pēl′**| *n.* **1.** An urgent or earnest request; *an appeal for help.* **2.** The power of attracting or of arousing interest: *The countryside has appeal.* **3. a.** The transfer or request for transfer of a case from a lower court to a higher court for a new hearing. **b.** A case so transferred. —*v.* **1.** To make an urgent or earnest request: *I appeal to you to help him.* **2.** To be attractive or interesting: *That dress appeals to her.* **3.** In law, to make or apply for an appeal. —**ap•peal′ing** *adj.: appealing clothes.*

ap•pear |ə **pîr′**| *v.* **1.** To come into view: *A ship appeared on the horizon.* **2.** To come before the public: *She has appeared in two plays.* **3.** To seem or look: *The coat appears to be navy blue.* **4.** To present oneself formally before a court of law.

ap•pear•ance |ə pîr′əns| *n.* **1.** The act of appearing; a coming into sight: *the sudden appearance of enemy ships on the horizon.* **2.** The act of coming into public view: *nine years since his last personal appearance.* **3.** The way something or someone looks or appears; outward aspect: *A good appearance makes other people wish to know you better.* **4.** A pretense or semblance; false show: *keeping up an appearance of diligence.* **5.** **appearances.** Outward indications; circumstances: *They are poor, yet to all appearances, very cheerful despite their poverty.*

Idiom. **put in an appearance.** To attend; appear briefly: *only putting in an appearance at the party to please his sister.*

ap•pease |ə pēz′| *v.* **ap•peased, ap•peas•ing.** **1.** To calm or pacify, especially by giving what is demanded: *He appeased the child with an ice-cream cone.* **2.** To satisfy; relieve: *A glass of water appeased his thirst.*

ap•pease•ment |ə pēz′mənt| *n.* **1.** An act of appeasing or a condition of being appeased. **2.** A policy of attempting to avoid war by meeting the demands of a threatening nation.

ap•pel•late |ə pĕl′ĭt| *adj.* Having the power to hear appeals and to reverse previous court decisions: *an appellate court.*

ap•pel•la•tion |ăp′ə lā′shən| *n.* A name or title: *He is known by the appellation "Big Bill."*

ap•pend |ə pĕnd′| *v.* To attach; add: *The committee appended a list of errors to the report.*

ap•pend•age |ə pĕn′dĭj| *n.* **1.** Something appended or attached: *The handle on a coffee cup is a useful appendage.* **2.** Any part or organ of the body that hangs or projects from another part: *A finger is an appendage of the hand.*

ap•pen•dec•to•my |ăp′ən dĕk′tə mē| *n., pl.* **ap•pen•dec•to•mies.** The removal of the vermiform appendix by means of surgery.

ap•pen•di•ces |ə pĕn′dĭ sēz′| *n.* A plural of **appendix.**

ap•pen•di•ci•tis |ə pĕn′dĭ sī′tĭs| *n.* Inflammation of the vermiform appendix.

ap•pen•dix |ə pĕn′dĭks| *n., pl.* **ap•pen•dix•es** or **ap•pen•di•ces** |ə pĕn′dĭ sēz′|. **1.** A section at the end of a book containing additional information, tables, etc. **2.** A slender, closed tube attached to the large intestine near the point at which it joins the small intestine; the vermiform appendix.

ap•per•tain |ăp′ər tān′| *v.* To belong as a function or part; have relation: *the problems that appertain to social and economic reform.*

ap•pe•tite |ăp′ĭ tīt′| *n.* **1.** The desire for food. **2.** A strong desire for something: *an appetite for work.* [SEE NOTE]

ap•pe•tiz•er |ăp′ĭ tī′zər| *n.* A food or drink taken before a meal to arouse the appetite.

ap•pe•tiz•ing |ăp′ĭ tī′zĭng| *adj.* Stimulating or appealing to the appetite; tasty: *an appetizing meal.*

ap•plaud |ə plôd′| *v.* **1.** To express praise of or approval by clapping the hands, etc.: *applaud the actors. The audience applauded for ten minutes.* **2.** To express approval publicly: *The newspapers applauded the President's stand.*

ap•plause |ə plôz′| *n.* **1.** Praise or approval expressed by the clapping of hands. **2.** Public approval.

ap•ple |ăp′əl| *n.* **1.** A firm, rounded, often red-skinned edible fruit. **2.** A tree that bears such fruit. —***modifier:*** *an apple pie.*

Idiom. **apple of (one's) eye.** Something or someone especially liked or loved: *Bob was the apple of the teacher's eye.*

ap•ple•jack |ăp′əl jăk′| *n.* Brandy distilled from hard cider.

ap•ple-pie order |ăp′əl pī′|. *Informal.* With everything in the right place; in very good condition.

ap•ple•sauce |ăp′əl sôs′| *n.* Apples stewed to a pulp and sweetened.

ap•pli•ance |ə plī′əns| *n.* A machine, such as a toaster or electric stove, used to perform a household task. —***modifier:*** *an appliance dealer; the appliance industry.*

ap•pli•ca•ble |ăp′lĭ kə bəl| *or* |ə plĭk′ə-| *adj.* Capable of being applied; appropriate. —**ap′pli•ca•bly** *adv.*

ap•pli•cant |ăp′lĭ kənt| *n.* A person who applies for something: *an applicant for a job.*

ap•pli•ca•tion |ăp′lĭ kā′shən| *n.* **1.** The act of applying. **2.** Something that is applied, such as a medicine or a cosmetic. **3.** A method of applying or using; a specific use: *the application of science to industry.* **4.** The capacity of being usable; relevance: *Geometry has practical applications.* **5.** Careful work and attention; diligence. **6. a.** A request, as for a job or admittance to a school. **b.** The form or document upon which such a request is made.

ap•pli•ca•tor |ăp′lĭ kā′tər| *n.* An instrument for applying something, such as medicine or glue.

ap•plied |ə plīd′| *adj.* Put into practice; used: *applied science.*

ap•pli•qué |ăp′lĭ kā′| *n.* A decoration, design, or trimming made by sewing or attaching pieces of one material to the surface of another. —*v.* **ap•pli•quéd, ap•pli•qué•ing.** To put on or apply as appliqué: *appliqué a monogram on a jacket.* [SEE PICTURE]

ap•ply |ə plī′| *v.* **ap•plied, ap•ply•ing, ap•plies.** **1.** To put on, upon, or to: *apply glue sparingly to the edges.* **2.** To put to or adapt for a special use: *Soon the government started to apply all its money to the war debt.* **3.** To put into action: *apply brakes.* **4.** To use (a special word or phrase) in referring to someone or something: *"Underground Railroad" was the name applied to the system used to aid in the escape of fugitive slaves.* **5.** To devote (oneself or one's efforts) to something: *He applied himself to books.* **6.** To be pertinent or relevant; concern: *This rule does not apply to you; however, it applies in all other cases.* **7.** To request employment, acceptance, or admission: *He applied for a job. She applied to a college.*

ap•point |ə point′| *v.* **1.** To select or designate for an office, position, or duty. **2.** To decide on or set by authority: *He appointed three o'clock for the meeting.* **3.** To furnish; equip: *The room was appointed with fine silver.*

ap•point•ee |ə poin′tē′| *or* |ăp′oin-| *n.* A person who is appointed to an office or position.

ap•point•ment |ə point′mənt| *n.* **1. a.** The act

appetite

Appetite *comes from Latin* appetitus, *"a longing for, a desire, an appetite." This is from* appetere, *"to strive after, to long for, to desire":* ad-, *"toward,"* + petere, *"to seek."*

appliqué
Floral design appliquéd to a quilted coverlet

apprehend/apprentice
Apprehend *is from Latin* ap-prehendere, *"to take hold of"* (ad-, *"toward,"* + prehendere, *"to grasp"*). Apprehendere *developed the two separate meanings "to arrest" and "to grasp with the mind, understand," from which senses 1 and 2 of* **apprehend** *are taken. (Sense 3 is a later English development.) In Old French,* apprehendere *became* aprendre *and came to mean "to learn." From* aprendre *was formed the word* aprentis, *"one who learns." This was borrowed into English as* **apprentice**.

apprenticeship
Noah Webster, in his American Dictionary *of 1828, has the following entry at* apprenticeship: *"The term for which an apprentice is bound to serve his master. This term in England is by statute seven years." Children as young as six years old used to be bound as apprentices.*

ă pat/ā pay/â care/ä father/ĕ pet/ē be/ĭ pit/ī pie/î fierce/ŏ pot/ō go/ô paw, for/oi oil/ŏŏ book/ōō boot/ou out/ŭ cut/û fur/*th* the/th thin/hw which/zh vision/ə ago, item, pencil, atom, circus

of appointing to an office or position: *The appointment of a Chief Justice is an important decision.* **b.** The office or position to which a person has been appointed: *Wagner accepted the appointment as conductor to the King of Saxony.* **2.** An arrangement for a meeting at a particular time or place: *Dr. Jones cannot change the time of our appointment.* **3. appointments.** Furnishings, fittings, or equipment: *table appointments; room appointments.* —*modifier: an appointment book.*

ap•por•tion |ə **pôr**′shən| *or* |ə **pōr**′-| *v.* To divide and assign according to some plan or proportion; allot.

ap•por•tion•ment |ə **pôr**′shən mənt| *or* |ə-**pōr**′-| *n.* The act of apportioning or the condition of being apportioned: *The apportionment of direct taxes on the basis of state population.*

ap•po•site |**ăp**′ə zĭt| *adj.* Appropriate or pertinent.

ap•po•si•tion |ăp′ə **zĭsh**′ən| *n.* **1.** The act of placing side by side or next to each other. **2. a.** In grammar, a construction in which a noun or noun phrase is placed with another noun as a further explanation or description. In the sentence *Helen, the sister of Allen, is very pretty, Helen* and *the sister of Allen* are in apposition. **b.** The relationship between such nouns or noun phrases.

ap•pos•i•tive |ə **pŏz**′ĭ tĭv| *adj.* In or concerning apposition: *an appositive phrase.* —*n.* A noun or phrase that is placed in apposition with another noun. In the sentence *Helen, the sister of Allen, is very pretty,* the appositive is *the sister of Allen.*

ap•prais•al |ə **prā**′zəl| *n.* **1. a.** The act of setting a value or price: *making appraisals of local housing markets.* **b.** The result of such an act; a valuation: *an unrealistic appraisal of his estate.* **2.** An official or expert estimate of the quality, worth, etc., of: *The expansion of business education created the need for a national appraisal of this kind of education.*

ap•praise |ə **prāz**′| *v.* **ap•praised, ap•prais•ing.** **1.** To set a value on; fix a price for: *Homer appraised the house and the outbuildings with one glance.* **2.** To estimate or judge critically the quality, amount, size, etc., of: *Executives appraised him as a valuable worker in the plant.*

ap•pre•cia•ble |ə **prē**′shə bəl| *adj.* Capable of being noticed or measured; noticeable. —**ap•pre′cia•bly** *adv.*

ap•pre•ci•ate |ə **prē**′shē āt′| *v.* **ap•pre•ci•at•ed, ap•pre•ci•at•ing.** **1.** To recognize the worth, quality, importance, etc., of; value highly: *He appreciated the freedoms he had.* **2.** To be aware of the artistic values of; enjoy and understand critically or emotionally: *He appreciates literature and music.* **3.** To be thankful for: *The boys appreciated your help.* **4.** To be aware of or sensitive to; realize: *She appreciates their problems.* **5.** To raise or rise in price or value.

ap•pre•ci•a•tion |ə prē′shē **ā**′shən| *n.* **1.** The recognition of the worth, quality, importance, etc., of: *an appreciation of the accomplishments of mankind.* **2.** Awareness of artistic values; understanding and enjoyment: *showing a great appreciation of music and sculpture.* **3.** Gratitude; gratefulness: *They expressed their appreciation with a gift.* **4.** A rise in value or price.

ap•pre•cia•tive |ə **prē**′shə tĭv| *or* |-shē ā′-| *adj.* Showing or feeling appreciation: *an appreciative audience.* —**ap•pre′cia•tive•ly** *adv.*

ap•pre•hend |ăp′rĭ **hĕnd**′| *v.* **1.** To take into custody; arrest. **2.** To grasp mentally; understand: *He can apprehend the theories of Einstein.* **3.** To look forward to fearfully; anticipate with anxiety. [SEE NOTE]

ap•pre•hen•sion |ăp′rĭ **hĕn**′shən| *n.* **1.** Fear or dread of what may happen; anxiety about the future. **2.** The ability to understand; understanding. **3.** The act of capturing; an arrest.

ap•pre•hen•sive |ăp′rĭ **hĕn**′sĭv| *adj.* Anxious or fearful; uneasy: *an apprehensive glance; apprehensive about the future.* —**ap′pre•hen′sive•ly** *adv.*

ap•pren•tice |ə **prĕn**′tĭs| *n.* **1.** A person who works for another without pay in return for instruction in a craft or trade. **2.** One, usually a member of a labor union, who is learning a trade. **3.** Any beginner. —*modifier: an apprentice carpenter.* —*v.* **ap•pren•ticed, ap•pren•tic•ing.** To place as an apprentice: *His father apprenticed him to a silversmith.* [SEE NOTE]

ap•pren•tice•ship |ə **prĕn**′tĭs shĭp′| *n.* **1.** The condition of being an apprentice: *His apprenticeship prevented him from marrying.* **2.** The period during which one is an apprentice: *another duty in his long apprenticeship as a future king.* [SEE NOTE]

ap•prise |ə **prīz**′| *v.* **ap•prised, ap•pris•ing.** To cause to know; inform: *He apprised her of the principal's message.*

ap•proach |ə **prōch**′| *v.* **1.** To come or go near or nearer (someone or something) in place or time: *People could approach the king only while crawling on their knees. As spring approached, our work neared completion.* **2.** To come close to in quality, appearance, etc.; approximate: *What approaches the joy of singing?* **3.** To begin to deal with or work on: *approach the science lesson; approach a task.* **4.** To make a proposal to; make overtures to: *He approached the president for a job.* —*n.* **1.** The act of approaching: *The howling of dogs announced the approach of the stranger. Flocks fly southward at the approach of winter.* **2.** A way or method of dealing or working with someone or something: *a new approach to the problem; the scientific approach.* **3.** A way of reaching a place; an access: *the approach to the bridge.*

ap•proach•a•ble |ə **prō**′chə bəl| *adj.* **1.** Capable of being reached; accessible. **2.** Easily approached; friendly: *an approachable person.* —**ap•proach′a•bil′i•ty** *n.*

ap•pro•ba•tion |ăp′rə **bā**′shən| *n.* **1.** The act of approving, especially officially; approval: *A bill was passed that received the approbation of all the branches of the Government.* **2.** Praise; commendation: *not a murmur of approbation or blame.*

ap•pro•pri•ate |ə **prō**′prē ĭt| *adj.* Suitable for a particular person, condition, occasion, or place; proper: *appropriate clothes; an appropriate blend of music and text.* —*v.* |ə **prō**′prē āt′| **ap•pro•pri•at•ed, ap•pro•pri•at•ing.** **1.** To set apart for a particular use: *Congress appropriated money for education.* **2.** To take possession of exclusively for oneself, often without permission. —**ap•pro′pri•ate•ly** *adv.* —**ap•pro′pri•ate•ness** *n.*

ap•pro•pri•a•tion |ə prō′prē **ā**′shən| *n.* **1.** The act of appropriating to oneself or to a specific use. **2.** Public funds set aside for a specific purpose.

ap•prov•al |ə **proo͞**′vəl| *n.* **1.** Favorable regard: *The voters will express their approval by voting for him again.* **2.** An official sanction: *"The Authorized Version" was published with the approval of King James I by English Bible scholars.*
Idiom. on approval. For examination or trial by a potential customer without the obligation to buy.

ap•prove |ə **proo͞v**′| *v.* **ap•proved, ap•prov•ing. 1.** To think of favorably; consider right or good: *The Puritans did not approve of card playing or other pleasures on Sunday.* **2.** To confirm or consent to officially; sanction; ratify: *The Senate approved the treaty.*

ap•prov•ing•ly |ə **proo͞**′vĭng lē| *adv.* In a manner that expresses approval: *He nodded approvingly.*

approx. approximate; approximately.

ap•prox•i•mate |ə **prŏk**′sə mĭt| *adj.* Almost exact or accurate: *the approximate height of a building.* —*v.* |ə **prŏk**′sə māt′| **ap•prox•i•mat•ed, ap•prox•i•mat•ing.** To come close to; be nearly the same as: *The temperatures of the Mediterranean Sea approximate those of Caribbean waters.* —**ap•prox′i•mate•ly** *adv.*

ap•prox•i•ma•tion |ə prŏk′sə **mā**′shən| *n.* Something that is almost, but not quite, exact, correct, or true: *The table contains decimal approximations of square roots.*

ap•pur•te•nance |ə **pûr**′tn əns| *n.* **1.** Something added to another, more important thing; an appendage; accessory. **2. appurtenances.** Any equipment, such as clothing or tools, used for a specific purpose; gear. **3.** In law, a right, privilege, or property that belongs with a principal property and goes along with it in case of sale, inheritance, etc.

Apr. April.

ap•ri•cot |**ăp**′rĭ kŏt′| *or* |**ā**′prĭ-| *n.* **1.** A juicy, yellow-orange fruit similar to a peach. **2.** A tree that bears such fruit. **3.** A yellowish orange. —*adj.* Yellowish orange. [See Picture]

A•pril |**ā**′prəl| *n.* The fourth month of the year, after March and before May. It has 30 days. —***modifier:*** *April showers.* [See Note]

April Fools' Day. A traditional day for playing practical jokes, occurring on April 1.

a•pron |**ā**′prən| *n.* **1.** A garment tied around the waist to protect the clothes in front, sometimes having a bib that covers the upper part of the body. **2.** The paved strip in front of an airport hangar. **3.** The part of the stage in a theater that is in front of the curtain. [See Note]

ap•ro•pos |ăp′rə **pō**′| *adj.* Relevant or fitting: *He said non-fiction was more apropos for our time than fiction.* —*adv.* By the way; incidentally: *Apropos, where were you last night?* —*prep.* Concerning; regarding: *Apropos our date, I'm afraid I can't make it. I remember a funny story apropos of politics.*

apse |ăps| *n.* A semicircular, usually domed, projection of a building, especially the end of a church in which the altar is located.

apt |ăpt| *adj.* **1.** Exactly suitable; appropriate: *an apt reply.* **2.** Likely: *Where are barnacles most apt to be found? People are apt to be impressed by the latest jet planes.* **3.** Having a tendency; inclined: *I would be apt to accept his statement.* **4.** Quick to learn: *an apt student.* —**apt′ly** *adv.* —**apt′ness** *n.*

ap•ti•tude |**ăp**′tĭ to͞od′| *or* |-tyo͞od′| *n.* **1.** A natural ability or talent: *She has a singular aptitude for dealing with everyday problems.* **2.** Quickness in learning and understanding.

aptitude test. A test used to measure a person's ability to learn some particular skill or acquire information.

aq•ua |**ăk**′wə| *or* |**ä**′kwə| *n.* **1.** Water. **2.** A light bluish green. —*adj.* Light bluish green.

Aq•ua-lung |**ăk**′wə lŭng′| *or* |**ä**′kwə-| *n.* A trademark for a scuba, a device used for underwater breathing.

aq•ua•ma•rine |ăk′wə mə **rēn**′| *or* |ä′kwə-| *n.* **1.** A transparent blue-green variety of beryl, used as a gemstone. **2.** A light greenish blue. —*adj.* Light greenish blue.

aq•ua•naut |**ăk**′wə nôt′| *or* |**ä**′kwə-| *n.* A person trained to work or assist in scientific research conducted in underwater installations, especially those deep in the sea.

aq•ua•plane |**ăk**′wə plān′| *or* |**ä**′kwə-| *n.* A board on which a person stands and rides while it is towed over the water by a motorboat. —*v.* **aq•ua•planed, aq•ua•plan•ing.** To ride on an aquaplane.

aqua re•gi•a |**rē**′jē ə|. A fuming, corrosive mixture of nitric acid and hydrochloric acid that is able to dissolve gold and platinum. It is often used for testing metals.

a•quar•i•um |ə **kwâr**′ē əm| *n., pl.* **a•quar•i•ums** or **a•quar•i•a** |ə **kwâr**′ē ə|. **1.** A water-filled tank or other container for keeping and displaying fish or other water animals, and often water plants. **2.** A place where such animals and plants are displayed to the public.

A•quar•i•us |ə **kwâr**′ē əs|. The eleventh sign of the zodiac.

a•quat•ic |ə **kwăt**′ĭk| *or* |ə **kwŏt**′-| *adj.* **1.** Of or in water: *an aquatic environment.* **2.** Living or growing in or on the water: *aquatic mammals; aquatic plants.* **3.** Taking place in or on the water: *aquatic sports.*

aq•ua•tint |**ăk**′wə tĭnt′| *or* |**ä**′kwə-| *n.* **1.** A printing process in which shadings are produced by etching a copper plate, from which the imprint is made, to different depths. **2.** A print made by this process. —*v.* To produce prints or etchings by this process.

aq•ue•duct |**ăk**′wĭ dŭkt′| *n.* **1.** A large pipe or channel made to carry water from a distant source. **2.** A bridgelike structure designed to carry such a pipe or channel across low ground or a river.

a•que•ous |**ā**′kwē əs| *or* |**ăk**′wē-| *adj.* Of, like, containing, or dissolved in water.

aqueous humor. A clear fluid that fills the space between the cornea and lens of the eye.

aq•ui•fer |**ăk**′wĭ fər| *or* |**ä**′kwĭ-| *n.* A layer of underground sand, gravel, or spongy rock in which water collects.

aq•ui•line |**ăk**′wə līn′| *or* |-lĭn| *adj.* Curved or hooked like an eagle's beak: *an aquiline nose.*

A•qui•nas |ə **kwī**′nəs|, **Thomas.** 1225?–1274. Italian Dominican monk, philosopher, and theologian.

apricot

April

April *is from Latin* Aprīlis, *and like some of the other Latin month names it comes from Etruscan; the form* apru *is probably an Etruscan shortening of Greek* Aphroditē. *So April is "the month of Aphrodite (or Venus)."*

apron

"An apron" *was originally* "a napron." *The change occurred in the sixteenth century.* Napron *is from Old French, and is related to* **napkin.**

arcade

arch[1-2]

Arch[1] *comes (via French) from Latin* arcus, *"a bow, a bend, an arc."* **Arch[2]** *is a special development of the prefix* **arch-**, *"chief." In the sixteenth and seventeenth centuries, this was used as an adjective in phrases like* an arch hypocrite *and* an arch liar, *meaning originally "an extreme hypocrite," "an extreme liar." From this use a new meaning gradually arose: "sly, cunning, roguish."*

ar |âr| *or* |är| *n.* A form of the word **are** (unit of area).

Ar The symbol for the element argon.

-ar. A suffix that forms adjectives from nouns: **angular; linear.**

Ar•ab |**ăr'**əb| *n.* **1.** A native of Arabia. **2.** A member of a Semitic people of the Middle East and North Africa. —**Ar'ab** *adj.*

ar•a•besque |ăr'ə **bĕsk'**| *n.* **1.** An ornamental pattern of interwoven flowers, leaves, or geometric forms. **2.** A ballet position in which the dancer stands on one leg with the other leg extending straight back.

A•ra•bi•a |ə **rā'**bē ə|. A peninsula in the Middle East, lying between the Red Sea and the Persian Gulf and including the countries of Saudi Arabia, Yemen, and Southern Yemen. —**A•ra'bi•an** *adj. & n.*

Arabian Nights. A collection, originally written in Arabic, of ancient folk tales, partly from Persian and Indian sources and dating from the 10th century A.D.

Ar•a•bic |**ăr'**ə bĭk| *n.* The Semitic language of the Arabs. —*adj.* **1.** Of the Arabs or their language. **2.** Of the script used in writing Arabic, Persian, and some other languages.

Arabic numerals. Numerals formed with the symbols 1, 2, 3, 4, 5, 6, 7, 8, 9, and 0 in a place-value notation.

a•rach•nid |ə **răk'**nĭd| *n.* One of a group of animals that resemble insects but have eight rather than six legs, and a body divided into two rather than three parts. Spiders and scorpions are arachnids.

a•rag•o•nite |ə **răg'**ə nīt'| *or* |**ăr'**ə gə-| *n.* A mineral form of crystalline calcium carbonate.

A•rap•a•ho |ə **răp'**ə hō'| *n., pl.* **A•rap•a•ho** or **A•rap•a•hos. 1.** A North American Indian tribe formerly living in Colorado and Wyoming. **2.** A member of this tribe. **3.** The Algonquian language of this tribe.

Ar•au•ca•ni•an |ăr'ô **kā'**nē ən| *n.* A family of South American Indian languages of Chile and Argentina. —**Ar'au•ca'ni•an** *adj.*

Ar•a•wak |**ăr'**ə wäk'| *or* |-wăk'| *n., pl.* **Ar•a•wak** or **Ar•a•waks. 1.** A South American Indian people of certain areas of the Guianas. **2.** A member of this people. **3.** The Arawakan language of this people.

Ar•a•wak•an |ăr'ə **wä'**kən| *or* |-**wăk'**ən| *n.* A family of South American Indian languages of a wide region of the Amazon basin. —**Ar'a•wak'an** *adj.*

ar•bi•ter |**är'**bĭ tər| *n.* **1.** Someone chosen to judge a dispute; an arbitrator. **2.** Something or someone having the power to ordain or judge at will: *living in a world where science is the final arbiter; the arbiter of the fashion world.*

ar•bi•trar•y |**är'**bĭ trĕr'ē| *adj.* **1.** Based on whim or impulse, not on reason or law: *arbitrary trade regulations imposed by the authorities.* **2.** Using or based on absolute or dictatorial powers: *an arbitrary government; an arbitrary decree.* —**ar'bi•trar'i•ly** *adv.* —**ar'bi•trar'i•ness** *n.*

ar•bi•trate |**är'**bĭ trāt'| *v.* **ar•bi•trat•ed, ar•bi•trat•ing. 1.** To decide as an arbitrator: *arbitrate the navigation rights between Israel and Egypt.* **2.** To submit to judgment by arbitration: *The various factions agreed to arbitrate their quarrels.* **3.** To serve as an arbitrator: *The strong nations were in perpetual rivalry, with no one to arbitrate between them.*

ar•bi•tra•tion |är'bĭ **trā'**shən| *n.* The process of referring the issues in a dispute to an impartial person or group for judgment or settlement.

ar•bi•tra•tor |**är'**bĭ trā'tər| *n.* A person chosen to settle a dispute or controversy.

ar•bor |**är'**bər| *n.* A shaded bower, often made of latticework on which vines or other climbing plants grow: *a grape arbor; a rose arbor.*

Arbor Day. A day observed in many areas by planting trees, often in the spring.

ar•bo•re•al |är **bôr'**ē əl| *or* |-**bōr'**-| *adj.* **1.** Of or resembling a tree. **2.** Living in trees: *arboreal animals.*

ar•bo•re•tum |är'bə **rē'**təm| *n., pl.* **ar•bo•re•tums** or **ar•bo•re•ta** |är'bə **rē'**tə|. A place for the study and exhibition of growing trees, especially rare trees.

ar•bor•vi•tae |är'bər **vī'**tē| *n.* An evergreen tree with small, scalelike leaves, often planted in gardens.

ar•bu•tus |är **byōō'**təs| *n., pl.* **ar•bu•tus•es.** A trailing plant with evergreen leaves and pink or white flowers that bloom in early spring.

arc |ärk| *n.* **1.** A portion of a curve, especially of a circle. **2.** A bright streak produced when an electric current jumps across the gap between two electrodes separated by a gas. —*v.* To form an arc. ¶*These sound alike* **arc, ark.**

ar•cade |är **kād'**| *n.* **1.** A row of arches supported by columns or pillars. **2.** A roofed passageway between buildings, with shops on either side. [SEE PICTURE]

Ar•ca•di•a |är **kā'**dē ə|. **1.** A mountainous region of ancient Greece, regarded as an ideal of rural simplicity and peacefulness. **2.** Any similar region.

arch[1] |ärch| *n.* **1. a.** A curved structure that spans an open space and supports a roadway, ceiling, or similar load. The downward thrust of the load over the open space is transferred to the sides. **b.** A monument built in this form. **2.** Something curved like an arch: *the arch of the rainbow.* **3.** Any of various arch-shaped structures of the body, especially in the foot. —***modifier:*** *an old arch bridge.* —*v.* **1.** To cause to form an arch or similar curve: *The cat arched his back.* **2.** To extend in an arch: *The bridge arched across the river.* [SEE NOTE]

arch[2] |ärch| *adj.* Mischievous; roguish: *an arch reply.* —**arch'ly** *adv.* [SEE NOTE]

arch–. A prefix meaning "principal" or "chief": **archduke; archenemy.**

ar•chae•o•log•i•cal |är'kē ə **lŏj'**ĭ kəl| *adj.* Of or concerned with archaeology.

ar•chae•ol•o•gist |är'kē **ŏl'**ə jĭst| *n.* A person who practices archaeology.

ar•chae•ol•o•gy |är'kē **ŏl'**ə jē| *n.* The scientific study of the remains of past human activities, such as burials, buildings, tools, and pottery.

ar•chae•op•ter•yx |är'kē **ŏp'**tər ĭks| *n.* An extinct bird found as a fossil and having certain of the characteristics of a reptile.

ar•cha•ic |är **kā'**ĭk| *adj.* **1.** Of a very early, often primitive, period: *archaic fish.* **2.** Not current; antiquated: *archaic laws.* **3.** In language, designating a term that was once common and continues to have a limited general use, but is now used only when it is intended to suggest an earlier style.

ar•cha•ism |är′kē ĭz′əm| *or* |-kā-| *n.* An archaic word or expression.

arch•an•gel |ärk′ān′jəl| *n.* A member of the higher order of angels.

arch•bish•op |ärch′bĭsh′əp| *n.* A bishop of the highest rank, heading an archdiocese or church province.

arch•dea•con |ärch′dē′kən| *n.* A church official, chiefly of the Anglican Church, in charge of temporal and other affairs in a diocese.

arch•di•o•cese |ärch′dī′ə sĭs| *or* |-sēs′| *n.* The area under an archbishop's jurisdiction.

arch•duch•ess |ärch′dŭch′ĭs| *n.* **1.** The wife of an archduke. **2.** A former royal princess of Austria.

arch•duke |ärch′do͞ok′| *or* |-dyo͞ok′| *n.* A former royal prince of Austria.

arch•en•e•my |ärch′ĕn′ə mē| *n., pl.* **arch•en•e•mies.** A chief or most important enemy.

ar•che•o•log•i•cal |är′kē ə lŏj′ĭ kəl| *adj.* A form of the word **archaeological.**

ar•che•ol•o•gist |är′kē ŏl′ə jĭst| *n.* A form of the word **archaeologist.**

ar•che•ol•o•gy |är′kē ŏl′ə jē| *n.* A form of the word **archaeology.**

arch•er |är′chər| *n.* A person who engages in archery.

arch•er•y |är′chə rē| *n.* The sport or skill of shooting with a bow and arrows.

ar•che•type |är′kĭ tīp′| *n.* An original model or form after which other, similar things are patterned.

Ar•chi•me•des |är′kə mē′dēz|. 287?–212 B.C. Greek mathematician and inventor.

ar•chi•pel•a•go |är′kə pĕl′ə gō′| *n., pl.* **ar•chi•pel•a•goes** or **ar•chi•pel•a•gos. 1.** A large group of islands. **2.** A sea in which there is a large group of islands.

ar•chi•tect |är′kĭ tĕkt′| *n.* **1.** A person who designs and directs the construction of buildings and other large structures. **2.** Anyone who plans or designs a project, especially one that requires long, hard work: *the architects of the Constitution.*

ar•chi•tec•tur•al |är′kĭ tĕk′chər əl| *adj.* Of architecture. —**ar′chi•tec′tur•al•ly** *adv.*

ar•chi•tec•ture |är′kĭ tĕk′chər| *n.* **1.** The art and occupation of designing and directing the construction of buildings and other large structures. **2.** A style of building: *Greek architecture.* **3.** A structure or structures in general: *strange architecture reaching up into the dark sky.* **4.** Any orderly construction: *the architecture of a story.*

ar•chi•trave |är′kĭ trāv′| *n.* A horizontal piece supported by the columns of a building in classical architecture.

ar•chives |är′kīvz′| *pl.n.* **1.** The records or documents of an organization, institution, or nation. **2.** The place where such records are kept.

arch•way |ärch′wā′| *n.* **1.** A passageway under an arch. **2.** An arch that covers or encloses an entrance or passageway.

-archy. A word element meaning "a kind of rule or government": **matriarchy.**

arc lamp. A lamp in which light is produced by an electric arc that crosses between electrodes separated by a gas.

arc•tic |ärk′tĭk| *or* |är′tĭk| *adj.* **1.** Extremely cold; frigid: *arctic weather.* **2. Arctic.** Of the region lying north of the Arctic Circle: *the long Arctic day.* —*n.* **the Arctic.** The region lying north of the Arctic Circle.

Arctic Circle. The parallel of latitude 66 degrees 33 minutes north; the boundary between the North Temperate and North Frigid zones.

Arctic Ocean. The ocean surrounding the North Pole, north of the Arctic Circle.

ar•dent |är′dnt| *adj.* **1.** Expressing or full of warmth of passion, emotion, desire, etc.; passionate: *an ardent lover. With grandeur and ardent intensity the melody soars above the chords.* **2.** Strongly enthusiastic; extremely devoted; eager: *an ardent defender of his cause.* —**ar′dent•ly** *adv.*

ar•dor |är′dər| *n.* **1.** Great warmth or intensity of passion, emotion, desire, etc.: *eyes blazing with savage ardor. The melody soars above the chords with increasing ardor and brilliance.* **2.** Intense enthusiasm or devotion; zeal: *The priests became worried about the ardor he sets off in his followers.*

ar•du•ous |är′jo͞o əs| *adj.* Demanding great effort; difficult: *arduous training; an arduous task.* —**ar′du•ous•ly** *adv.* —**ar′du•ous•ness** *n.*

are¹ |är|. **1.** Second person singular present tense of **be. 2.** First, second, and third person plural present tense of **be.**

are² |âr| *or* |är| *n.* A unit of area equal to 100 square meters. ¶*These sound alike* **are², air, e'er, ere, heir.** [SEE NOTE]

ar•e•a |âr′ē ə| *n.* **1.** A section or region, as of land: *a farming area; the New York area.* **2.** A surface, especially a part of the earth's surface: *a landing area.* **3.** The measure of a region of a surface, either flat or curved or of a closed surface, such as a sphere, usually expressed in units such as square feet, square meters, square miles, etc. **4.** A range, as of activity, study, etc.

Area code, also **area code.** A three-digit number assigned to a telephone area and used when calling from one such area to another.

a•re•na |ə rē′nə| *n.* **1.** The space in the center of an ancient Roman amphitheater where athletic contests and other spectacles were held. **2.** A modern auditorium for sports events. **3.** An area of conflict or activity: *the political arena.*

aren't |ärnt| *or* |är′ənt|. **1.** Are not: *They aren't there.* **2.** Am not. Used in questions: *I'm properly dressed for school, aren't I?* [SEE NOTE]

Ar•es |âr′ēz|. The Greek god of war.

Ar•gen•ti•na |är′jən tē′nə|. A country in southern South America, between Chile and the Atlantic. Population, 27,862,771. Capital, Buenos Aires. —**Ar′gen•tine′** |är′jən tēn′| *or* |-tīn′|, **Ar′gen•tin′e•an** |är′jən tĭn′ē ən| *adj. & n.*

Ar•go |är′gō′|. In Greek mythology, Jason's ship in his search of the Golden Fleece.

ar•gon |är′gŏn′| *n.* Symbol **Ar** One of the elements, a colorless, odorless, chemically inert gas. Atomic number 18; atomic weight 39.95; melting point −189.2°C; boiling point −185.7°C. [SEE NOTE]

Ar•go•naut |är′gə nôt′| *n.* In Greek mythology, any of the men who sailed with Jason in search of the Golden Fleece.

ar•go•sy |är′gə sē| *n., pl.* **ar•go•sies. 1.** A big sailing merchant ship. **2.** A fleet of such ships. [SEE NOTE]

are²

Are², *like the rest of the terms in the metric system, was coined by the French Academy of Sciences after the French Revolution. It was taken from Latin* ārea, *"area." Although it was intended to be the basic unit of area, it is now little used, even in France, except in its compound* **hectare** *(100 ares).*

aren't

Aren't *standing for* are not *is just as acceptable as* **isn't** *for* is not. **Aren't** *standing for* am not *(in the phrase* aren't I*) is originally a British variant of* **ain't.** *Unlike* **ain't,** *it is now fairly acceptable, especially when used in speech or informal writing.*

argon

Argon *makes up about one per cent of the atmosphere. It is used in welding and in electric lamps and electron tubes.*

argosy

Ragusa *(now Dubrovnik, Yugoslavia) on the Adriatic Sea used to be a great trading port belonging to Venice. Richly laden ships from Ragusa were familiar as far away as England in Shakespeare's time; the English called them* Ragusees *or* Argosies.

arithmetic mean
If the set A *contains just 4, 18, 2, and 8, then the* **arithmetic mean** *of* A *is (4 + 18 + 2 + 8) ÷ 4 = 8.*

arm¹·²
Arm¹, *like most of the words for basic parts of the body, is part of the native Old English vocabulary and has hardly changed in 1200 years.* **Arm²** *is a borrowed word; it was taken, in the plural, from French* armes, *which is from Latin* arma, *"arms, weapons." The Old English word and the Latin word are themselves from the same prehistoric Indo-European word,* armo-. *The original meaning was that of* **arm¹**; *the meaning "weapon" is a secondary and fairly obvious development.*

ă pat/ā pay/â care/ä father/ĕ pet/ē be/ĭ pit/ī pie/î fierce/ŏ pot/ō go/ô paw, for/oi oil/ŏŏ book/ōō boot/ou out/ŭ cut/û fur/*th* the/th thin/hw which/zh vision/ə ago, item, pencil, atom, circus

ar•gue |är′gyōō| *v.* **ar•gued, ar•gu•ing. 1.** To give reasons for or against (an opinion, proposal, etc.); debate: *The lawyer argued the case in court. The senator argued in favor of the law.* **2.** To engage in a quarrel; dispute: *Tom often argued with his friends.*

ar•gu•ment |är′gyə mənt| *n.* **1.** A quarrel or dispute. **2.** A discussion of differing points of view; a debate. **3.** A statement in support of a position; a reason.

ar•gu•men•ta•tive |är′gyə mĕn′tə tĭv| *adj.* **1.** Given to or liking to argue: *an argumentative person.* **2.** Containing or full of arguments: *an argumentative paper.* —**ar′gu•men′ta•tive•ly** *adv.*

Ar•gus |är′gəs|. In Greek mythology, a giant with a hundred eyes.

ar•gyle or **ar•gyll,** also **Ar•gyle** or **Ar•gyll** |är′gīl′| *n.* **1.** A knitting pattern made up of diamond shapes in contrasting colors. **2.** A sock knit in such a pattern. —***modifier:*** *argyle socks.*

a•ri•a |är′ē ə| *n.* A piece written for a solo singer accompanied by instruments, as in an opera, cantata, or oratorio.

Ar•i•ad•ne |ăr′ē ăd′nē|. In Greek mythology, the daughter of King Minos who helped Theseus escape from the Labyrinth.

ar•id |ăr′ĭd| *adj.* **1.** Having little or no rainfall; dry; parched: *an arid desert; an arid wasteland.* **2.** Lifeless; dull: *a long, arid book.* —**a•rid′i•ty** |ə rĭd′ĭ tē| *n.*

Ar•ies |âr′ēz| *or* |-ē ēz′|. The first sign of the zodiac.

a•right |ə rīt′| *adv.* Properly; correctly.

A•ri•ka•ra |ə rē′kə rə| *n., pl.* **A•ri•ka•ra** or **A•ri•ka•ras. 1.** A tribe of Plains Indians of North and South Dakota. **2.** A member of this tribe. **3.** The Caddoan language of this tribe.

a•rise |ə rīz′| *v.* **a•rose** |ə rōz′|, **a•ris•en** |ə rĭz′ən|, **a•ris•ing. 1.** To get up: *He arose from his chair.* **2.** To come into being; appear: *Take advantage of opportunities that arise. Myths arose as an attempt to explain natural occurrences.* **3.** To ascend; move upward: *A mist rose from the lake.* **4.** To result; proceed: *The situation arose from some temporary defect.*

ar•is•toc•ra•cy |ăr′ĭ stŏk′rə sē| *n., pl.* **ar•is•toc•ra•cies. 1. a.** A social class based on inherited wealth, status, and sometimes titles. **b.** A government controlled by such a class. **2.** An entrenched superior group: *the aristocracy of Wall Street bankers.*

a•ris•to•crat |ə rĭs′tə krăt′| *or* |ăr′ĭ stə-| *n.* **1.** A member of the aristocracy or nobility. **2.** Someone or something with the tastes, preferences, or other characteristics of the aristocracy or the upper class. **3.** A person who favors government by the aristocracy.

a•ris•to•crat•ic |ə rĭs′tə **krăt′**ĭk| *or* |ăr′ĭs tə-| *adj.* **1.** Of or like the aristocracy; noble: *aristocratic manners.* **2.** Having an aristocracy as a form of government: *aristocratic city-states.* —**a•ris′to•crat′i•cal•ly** *adv.*

Ar•is•tot•le |ăr′ĭ stŏt′l|. 384–322 B.C. Greek philosopher, a pupil of Plato.

a•rith•me•tic |ə rĭth′mə tĭk| *n.* **1.** The study of the properties of and relations between numbers on which the operations of addition, subtraction, multiplication, division, raising to powers, and extracting roots are performed, and also the study of the properties of the operations themselves. **2.** Computation using these operations: *Bookkeeping can require a lot of arithmetic.* —*adj.* **ar•ith•met•ic** |ăr′ĭth **mĕt′**ĭk| or **ar•ith•met•i•cal** |ăr′ĭth **mĕt′**ĭ kəl|. Of arithmetic: *arithmetic procedures; arithmetic computations.*

ar•ith•met•ic mean |ăr′ĭth **mĕt′**ĭk|. An average of a set of quantities or numbers obtained by adding all the members of the set and dividing the result by the number of members in the set. [SEE NOTE]

ar•ith•met•ic progression |ăr′ĭth **mĕt′**ĭk|. A sequence of numbers such as 1, 3, 5, 7, 9, . . . , or 3, 7, 11, 15, . . . , in which the difference between any successive pair of numbers is the same.

Ariz. Arizona.

Ar•i•zo•na |ăr′ĭ zō′nə|. A Southwestern state of the United States. Population, 2,717,866. Capital, Phoenix. —**Ar′i•zo′nan** *adj. & n.*

ark |ärk| *n.* **1.** In the Bible, the ship built by Noah for survival during the Flood. **2.** Also **Ark of the Covenant.** In the Bible, the chest containing the Ten Commandments on stone tablets, carried by the Hebrews during their wanderings. **3. Holy Ark.** A cabinet in a synagogue in which the scrolls of the Torah are kept. ¶ *These sound alike* **ark, arc.**

Ark. Arkansas.

Ar•kan•sas¹ |är′kən sô′|. A Southern state of the United States. Population, 2,285,513. Capital, Little Rock. —**Ar•kan′san** |är **kăn′**zən| *adj.*

Ar•kan•sas² |är′kən sô′| *or* |är **kăn′**zəs|. A river rising in Colorado and flowing generally southeast into the Mississippi River.

arm¹ |ärm| *n.* **1. a.** Either of the upper limbs of the human body, connecting the hand and wrist to the shoulder. **b.** The similar forelimb of an animal, as of an ape or a bear. **2.** A part that branches or seems to branch from a main body as an arm does: *an arm of the sea; the arm of a starfish.* **3.** A part on which the arm rests: *the arm of a chair.* **4.** Authority or effect that extends or seems to extend from a main source: *the arm of the law.* [SEE NOTE]

Idioms. **arm in arm.** With the arm of one person linked in the arm of another. **at arm's length. 1.** With the arm extended straight out from the body: *He held the picture at arm's length and looked at it.* **2.** At a distance; not on friendly or intimate terms: *Roberts keeps all his fellow workers at arm's length.* **twist (someone's) arm.** To force or press (someone) to do as one wishes. **with open arms.** In a very friendly manner: *welcomed them with open arms.*

arm² |ärm| *n.* **1. arms.** Weapons, especially those used in warfare or defense. **2.** A weapon. Used mainly in combination with another word: *a firearm such as a pistol or rifle.* **3. arms.** Warfare or military power: *The besieged city could not be taken by force of arms.* **4. arms.** A design or emblem used as an identifying mark by a family, nation, etc. —*v.* **1.** To equip with weapons or other means of defense: *The brothers armed themselves with sticks and faced the intruders. Porcupines are armed with sharp quills.* **2.** To prepare for war, as by amassing weapons and training soldiers: *Italy was arming, and Benito Mussolini was boasting of his nation's power.* **3.** To equip or provide with something necessary or useful: *Jonathan armed himself with a letter* *of recommendation before going to be interviewed for a new job.* —**armed'** *adj.: an armed police escort.* [SEE NOTE on p. 46]

***Idiom.* up in arms.** Stirred up and ready to fight.

ar•ma•da |är **mä'**də| *or* |**-mā'-**| *n.* A big fleet of warships. [SEE NOTE]

ar•ma•dil•lo |är'mə **dĭl'**ō| *n., pl.* **ar•ma•dil•los.** A burrowing mammal of southern North America and South America, having a covering of jointed, armorlike, bony plates. [SEE NOTE at **armada** & PICTURE]

Ar•ma•ged•don |är'mə **gĕd'**n|. **1.** In the Bible, the site of the final battle between good and evil, to occur at the end of the world. **2.** Any decisive conflict.

ar•ma•ment |**är'**mə mənt| *n.* **1.** The weapons with which a warship, warplane, etc., is equipped. **2.** Often **armaments.** All the military forces and war equipment of a country.

ar•ma•ture |**är'**mə chər| *n.* **1.** The principal moving part of an electric machine or device, as the rotating part of a motor or generator or the vibrating part of a buzzer. **2.** A framework, especially one used as a support for clay sculpture.

arm•band |**ärm'**bănd'| *n.* A piece of cloth worn around the upper arm, often as a sign of mourning or of membership in a group.

arm•chair |**ärm'**châr'| *n.* A chair with supports on the sides for one's arms. —*adj.* Not involved; remote from the field or action: *an armchair quarterback.*

armed forces. The military forces of a country.

Ar•me•ni•a |är **mē'**nē ə| *or* |**-mēn'**yə|. A former country southeast of the Black Sea, now divided between the Soviet Union and Turkey.

Ar•me•ni•an |är **mē'**nē ən| *or* |**-mēn'**yən| *n.* **1.** A person of Armenian descent. **2.** The Indo-European language of Armenia. —*adj.* Of Armenia, the Armenians, or their language.

arm•ful |**ärm'**fŏŏl'| *n., pl.* **arm•fuls.** As much as one or both arms can hold.

arm•hole |**ärm'**hōl'| *n.* An opening for the arm in a garment or the place where a sleeve is attached.

ar•mi•stice |**är'**mĭ stĭs| *n.* A suspension of fighting between two armies by agreement; a truce.

Armistice Day. The former name for **Veterans Day.**

ar•mor |**är'**mər| *n.* **1.** A heavy covering worn to protect the body in battle, especially a suit of metal worn in olden times by knights or warriors. **2.** Any protective covering, such as the bony plates covering an armadillo or the metal plates on tanks or warships. **3.** The armored vehicles of an army. —*v.* To cover or protect with armor: *armor a warship.* [SEE PICTURE]

ar•mored |**är'**mərd| *adj.* **1.** Covered with or having armor: *ten armored vehicles.* **2.** Equipped with armored vehicles: *an armored division.*

ar•mor•er |**är'**mər ər| *n.* A person who makes or repairs weapons.

armor plate. A specially made hard steel plate designed to withstand enemy fire and protect warships, military aircraft, etc.

ar•mor•y |**är'**mə rē| *n., pl.* **ar•mor•ies.** **1.** A storehouse for military weapons; an arsenal. **2.** The headquarters of a military reserve force. **3.** A weapons factory.

ar•mour |**är'**mər| *n.* & *v.* British form of the word **armor.**

arm•pit |**ärm'**pĭt'| *n.* The hollow under the arm at the shoulder.

ar•my |**är'**mē| *n., pl.* **ar•mies.** **1.** A large body of men organized and trained for warfare on land. **2.** Often **Army.** The entire military land forces of a country. **3.** Often **Army.** The largest unit in a country's army: *the Ninth Army of the U.S. Army.* **4.** A large group of people organized for a cause. **5.** Any large group, as of people or animals: *An army of shoppers appeared for the sale.* —**modifier:** *an army officer.*

ar•ni•ca |**är'**nĭ kə| *n.* **1.** A plant with yellow, daisylike flowers. **2.** A medical preparation made from these flowers, used to treat sprains and bruises.

Ar•nold |**är'**nəld|, **Benedict.** 1741–1801. American army officer in the Revolutionary War; tried to surrender West Point to the British.

a•ro•ma |ə **rō'**mə| *n.* A pleasant, characteristic smell; fragrance.

ar•o•mat•ic |ăr'ə **măt'**ĭk| *adj.* **1.** Having an aroma; fragrant. **2.** Of or containing the ring of six linked carbon atoms characteristic of benzene and related organic compounds.

a•rose |ə **rōz'**|. Past tense of **arise.**

a•round |ə **round'**| *prep.* **1.** Near in time to; close to: *around the year 1450.* **2.** All about; all over in: *The reporter looked around the room.* Also used adverbially: *Come up to the shop and I'll take you around.* **3.** In a circle surrounding: *Soon they were whirling around the tree trunk.* Also used adverbially: *The workmen gathered around to get paid off.* **4.** In a group or groups surrounding: *the Indian tribes around the Great Lakes.* **5.** Round about so as to enclose: *Vines had grown up around the lower branches.* **6.** On or to the farther side of: *just around the corner.* Also used adverbially: *After a month off Cape Horn, they finally got around.* —*adv.* About so as to face in the reverse direction: *The horses were turned around double-quick.* —*adj.* Available: *I'll be around when you need me.*

a•rouse |ə **rouz'**| *v.* **a•roused, a•rous•ing.** **1.** To awaken from or as if from sleep. **2.** To stir up; stimulate; excite.

ar•peg•gi•o |är **pĕj'**ē ō'| *or* |**-pĕj'**ō| *n.* **1.** The playing of a chord so that its tones begin in succession rather than all at once. **2.** A chord executed in this way.

ar•raign |ə **rān'**| *v.* **1.** To summon before a court of law to answer a charge or indictment. **2.** To accuse; charge. —**ar•raign'ment** *n.*

ar•range |ə **rānj'**| *v.* **ar•ranged, ar•rang•ing.** **1.** To put in a deliberate order or relation: *Arrange these words alphabetically.* **2.** To plan; prepare: *The government arranges transportation for tourists. We arranged for them to meet.* **3.** To come to an agreement about: *The dealers arranged prices for the items.* **4.** To prepare an arrangement of (music): *He arranged the piano piece for orchestra.* —**ar•rang'er** *n.*

ar•range•ment |ə **rānj'**mənt| *n.* **1.** The act of arranging: *Arrangement of flowers is an intricate art.* **2.** The order in which things are arranged: *an alphabetical arrangement of words.* **3.** A col-

armada

An **armada** *and an* **armadillo** *have much in common. The Spanish word for "armed" or "armored" is* armado, *which comes from Latin* arma, *"weapons." In Spanish,* armada *is "an armed fleet," and* armadillo *is "a little armored animal" (*-illo *is a diminutive ending).*

armadillo

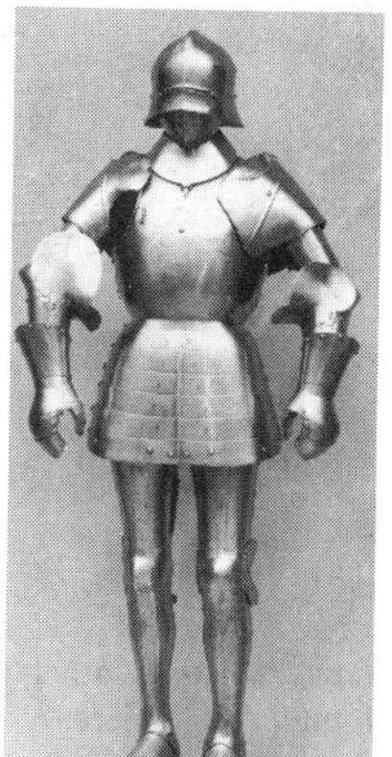

armor
Fifteenth-century Italian

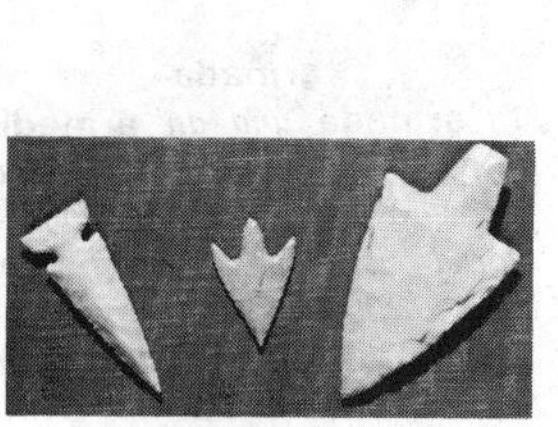

arrowhead
Indian flint arrowheads from Texas *(left, center)* and Florida *(right)*

arsenic
Arsenic *has three allotropic forms, and is obtained from minerals. It is used in insect poisons, weed killers, and semiconductor devices.*

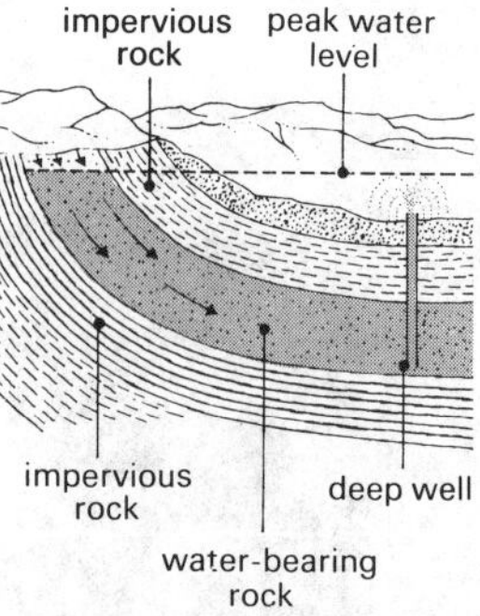

artesian well

ă pat/ā pay/â care/ä father/ĕ pet/ ē be/ĭ pit/ī pie/î fierce/ŏ pot/ ō go/ô paw, for/oi oil/ŏŏ book/ ōō boot/ou out/ŭ cut/û fur/ *th* the/th thin/hw which/zh vision/ ə ago, item, pencil, atom, circus

lection or set of things that have been arranged *a flower arrangement.* **4.** An agreement. **5. arrangements.** Plans or preparations: *Make arrangements for a vacation.* **6.** A version of a musical composition that differs from the original in style, difficulty, or use of performers: *a jazz arrangement of a Bach fugue.*

ar•rant |ăr′ənt| *adj.* Thoroughgoing; out-and-out: *an arrant coward.*

ar•ras |ăr′əs| *n.* **1.** A tapestry woven with rich designs. **2.** A wall hanging, especially of tapestry.

ar•ray |ə rā′| *n.* **1.** An orderly arrangement: *an array of data.* **2.** An impressive display or collection: *a formidable array of talent.* **3.** Clothing or finery: *The princess was clad in rich array.* **4. a.** A set of numbers written in some particular pattern, especially in a rectangular pattern with the numbers aligned in vertical columns and horizontal rows. **b.** A set of objects, usually identical objects, printed on a page to represent some number. —*v.* **1.** To arrange or draw up, as troops. **2.** To dress up, especially in fine clothes; adorn: *She was splendidly arrayed in red velvet.*

ar•rears |ə rîrz′| *pl.n.* **1.** Unpaid or overdue debts: *You have arrears of $23.00.* **2.** The state of being behind in fulfilling payments or an obligation: *in arrears.*

ar•rest |ə rĕst′| *v.* **1.** To seize and hold under authority of law. **2.** To stop the progress of; check: *arresting the growth of the tree.* **3.** To capture and hold; engage: *The chapter arrested the reader's attention.* —*n.* The act of arresting.
***Idiom.* under arrest.** Held in legal custody.

ar•rest•ing |ə rĕs′tĭng| *adj.* Capturing and holding the attention; striking: *an arresting display of courage.*

ar•ri•val |ə rī′vəl| *n.* **1.** The act of arriving: *the arrival of the general at the airport.* **2.** The attainment of a goal or objective: *His arrival at the decision came after much thought.* **3.** Someone or something that has arrived: *many new arrivals at the resort hotel.*

ar•rive |ə rīv′| *v.* **ar•rived, ar•riv•ing. 1.** To reach a destination; come to a place: *They arrived in the city on time.* **2.** To reach a goal or objective: *They arrived at an understanding.* **3.** To come: *When the great day arrived, the children drove with their parents to the palace gates.*

ar•ro•gance |ăr′ə gəns| *n.* The quality or condition of being arrogant.

ar•ro•gant |ăr′ə gənt| *adj.* Excessively and unpleasantly self-important, as in disregarding all other opinions but one's own. —**ar′ro•gant•ly** *adv.*

ar•ro•gate |ăr′ə gāt′| *v.* **ar•ro•gat•ed, ar•ro•gat•ing.** To take, claim, or assume without right: *The governor arrogated for himself the right to say he knew what was good for the colony.*

ar•row |ăr′ō| *n.* **1.** A straight, thin shaft, shot from a bow and made of wood, with a pointed head at one end and feathers at the other. **2.** Anything similar in shape, as a sign or mark used to indicate direction.

ar•row•head |ăr′ō hĕd′| *n.* The pointed tip of an arrow. [SEE PICTURE]

ar•row•root |ăr′ō rōōt′| *or* |-rŏŏt′| *n.* An edible, easily digested starch made from the root of a tropical American plant.

ar•roy•o |ə roi′ō| *n., pl.* **ar•roy•os. 1.** A small stream. **2.** A dry gulch cut out by a stream.

ar•se•nal |är′sə nəl| *n.* **1.** A building for the storage, manufacture, or repair of arms and ammunition. **2.** A stock of weapons.

ar•se•nate of lead |är′sə nĭt| *or* |-nāt′|. **Lead arsenate.**

ar•se•nic |är′sə nĭk| *n.* Symbol **As** One of the elements, the most common form of which is a brittle, gray, highly poisonous metal. Atomic number 33; atomic weight 74.92; valences +3 and +5. Gray arsenic melts when heated under pressure at 817°C and sublimes at 613°C. [SEE NOTE]

ar•son |är′sən| *n.* The crime of intentionally setting fire to buildings or other property.

art[1] |ärt| *n.* **1.** The work of man in imitating, changing, or counteracting nature: *The beauty of this park owes more to art than to nature.* **2. a.** Painting, sculpture, poetry, music, or other activities involving the creation of what is considered beautiful: *the fine arts; a work of art.* **b.** The study of these activities: *I took art in school.* **c.** A work or works resulting from these activities, as a painting or a piece of sculpture: *His art is unusual in both color and form.* **3.** A practical skill; craft; knack: *the art of sewing.* **4.** The body of knowledge of a particular field: *the art of medicine; the industrial arts.* **5. arts.** The liberal arts; the humanities: *college of arts and sciences.* —***modifier:*** *art forms; an art dealer.*

art[2] |ärt|. *Archaic.* A form of the present tense of **be**, used with *thou.*

Ar•te•mis |är′tə mĭs|. The Greek goddess of the moon and the hunt.

ar•te•ri•al |är tîr′ē əl| *adj.* **1.** Of an artery or arteries. **2.** Bright red and charged with oxygen; not venous: *arterial blood.*

ar•te•ri•ole |är tîr′ē ōl′| *n.* Any of the small branches in which an artery ends, especially one that connects to capillaries.

ar•te•ri•o•scle•ro•sis |är tîr′ē ō sklə rō′sĭs| *n.* A diseased condition in which the walls of the arteries become thickened and hard and interfere with the circulation of the blood.

ar•ter•y |är′tə rē| *n., pl.* **ar•ter•ies. 1.** Any of the blood vessels that carry blood from the heart to the capillaries. **2.** A major transportation route from which other routes branch.

ar•te•sian well |är tē′zhən|. A deep well that passes through hard, impermeable rock and reaches water that is under enough pressure to rise to the surface without being pumped. [SEE PICTURE]

art•ful |ärt′fəl| *adj.* **1.** Showing art or skill; skillful: *an artful cook.* **2.** Crafty; cunning: *an artful lawyer.* —**art′ful•ly** *adv.* —**art′ful•ness** *n.*

ar•thrit•ic |är thrĭt′ĭk| *adj.* Of or suffering from arthritis. —*n.* A person affected with arthritis.

ar•thri•tis |är thrī′tĭs| *n.* Inflammation and stiffness of a joint or joints in the body.

ar•thro•pod |är′thrə pŏd′| *n.* Any of a large group of animals with a segmented body and jointed legs. Insects, spiders, and crustaceans such as lobsters and crabs are arthropods.

Ar•thur |är′thər|. A legendary king of ancient Britain who gathered his knights at the Round Table. —**Ar•thu′ri•an** |är thŏŏr′ē ən| *adj.*

Ar•thur |är′thər|, **Chester Alan.** 1830–1886.

Twenty-first President of the United States (1881–85).

ar•ti•choke |är′tĭ chōk′| *n.* **1.** The unopened flower head of a thistlelike plant, covered with thick, leaflike scales and eaten as a vegetable. **2.** The plant itself. [SEE PICTURE]

ar•ti•cle |är′tĭ kəl| *n.* **1.** A written piece that forms an independent part of a publication; a report; essay. **2.** A section or item of a written document: *an article of the Constitution.* **3.** An individual thing; item: *A bed is an article of furniture.* **4.** In grammar, any of a class of words that function as determiners and are used to introduce nouns and to specify their application. In English the articles are *a, an,* and *some* (indefinite articles) and *the* (definite article).

Articles of Confederation. The first Constitution of the United States adopted by the original 13 states in 1781 and lasting until 1788.

ar•tic•u•late |är **tĭk′**yə lĭt| *adj.* **1.** Spoken clearly and distinctly: *articulate speech.* **2.** Capable of speaking clearly and expressively: *articulate people.* **3.** Endowed with the power of speech. **4.** Having joints or segments. *—v.* |är **tĭk′**yə lāt′| **ar•tic•u•lat•ed, ar•tic•u•lat•ing. 1.** To utter (a speech sound or sounds) distinctly; enunciate: *Articulate the following words. He articulates well.* **2.** To express verbally: *He articulated the sentiments of the group.* **3.** To join or hold together in such a way as to permit movement: *The elbow articulates the arm. The hand and arm articulate at the wrist.* **—ar•tic′u•late•ly** *adv.* **—ar•tic′u•late•ness** *n.*

ar•tic•u•la•tion |är tĭk′yə **lā′**shən| *n.* **1.** The act or process of speaking clearly; enunciation. **2.** A point at which things articulate or a thing is articulated; a joint.

ar•ti•fact |är′tə făkt′| *n.* An object produced by human workmanship, especially an item of primitive art.

ar•ti•fice |är′tə fĭs| *n.* A clever device or stratagem; a ruse.

ar•ti•fi•cial |är′tə **fĭsh′** əl| *adj.* **1.** Made by man rather than occurring in nature: *an artificial sweetener; artificial flowers.* **2.** Not genuine or natural; affected: *an artificial display of affection.* **—ar′ti•fi′ci•al′i•ty** |är′tə fĭsh′ē **ăl′**ĭ tē| *n.* **—ar′ti•fi′cial•ly** *adv.*

artificial respiration. Any of several methods by which a living person who has stopped breathing may be revived. These methods usually involve forcing air rhythmically in and out of the lungs.

ar•til•ler•y |är **tĭl′**ə rē| *n.* **1.** Large mounted guns that are too heavy to carry and are served by crews. **2.** The branch of an army that specializes in the use of such guns.

ar•til•ler•y•man |är **tĭl′**ə rē mən| *n., pl.* **-men** |-mən|. A soldier in the artillery.

ar•ti•san |är′tĭ zən| *n.* One manually skilled in making a certain product; a craftsman.

art•ist |är′tĭst| *n.* **1.** A person who practices any of the fine arts, especially painting, sculpture, or music. **2.** A person who works in one of the performing arts. **3.** A person who shows skill and creativity in his work.

ar•tis•tic |är **tĭs′**tĭk| *adj.* **1.** Of art or artists: *acclaimed by all European artistic circles.* **2.** Sensitive to beauty: *an artistic temperament.* **3.** Showing skill and good taste: *an artistic flower arrangement.* **—ar•tis′ti•cal•ly** *adv.*

art•ist•ry |är′tĭ strē| *n.* **1.** Artistic quality or workmanship: *the artistry of a performance; Indian headdresses and vessels that are an example of pure native American artistry.* **2.** Artistic ability and talent: *the artistry of the performers.*

art•less |ärt′lĭs| *adj.* **1.** Free from deceit; guileless: *an artless child.* **2.** Not artificial; natural: *artless beauty.* **—art′less•ly** *adv.* **—art′less•ness** *n.*

art nou•veau |är′ no͝o **vō′**| *or* |ärt′|. A style of decoration and architecture first popular in the 1890's, using curved lines and flower shapes.

art song. A song, generally an expressive setting of a poem, intended for use in a recital or concert.

art•work |ärt′wûrk′| *n.* **1. a.** The hand-making of decorative or artistic objects: *The Navaho Indians are famous for their artwork.* **b.** The decorations or objects so made: *They wanted to save the artwork on the walls of the building.* **2.** The illustrations and decorative elements of a book as distinct from the text.

art•y |är′tē| *adj.* **art•i•er, art•i•est.** Pretentiously artistic in manner or style: *an arty movie.*

-ary. A suffix that forms adjectives from nouns: **budgetary; parliamentary.**

Ar•y•an |âr′ē ən| *or* |ăr′-| *n.* **1.** A former name for Indo-European. **2.** In Nazi ideology, a Caucasian Gentile. **—Ar′y•an** *adj.* [SEE NOTE]

as |ăz| *or* |əz *when unstressed*| *adv.* **1.** Equally: *You'll have to go a long way to find someone as nice.* **2.** For instance: *large carnivores, as tigers.* *—Note: As* is used with certain words to form the following adverbial groups: **as good as.** Practically: *When he got home he was as good as dead.* **as much as.** Virtually: *She as much as admitted having lied.* **as well.** Also; too: *People were there from out of town as well.* **as yet.** So far; up until now: *I haven't heard from him as yet.* *—conj.* **1.** To the same degree or quantity that; equally with: *sweet as sugar.* **2.** In the same way that: *When in Rome, do as the Romans do.* **3.** At the same time that; while: *She winked as our eyes met.* **4.** Since; because: *He stayed home, as he was ill.* **5.** Though: *Nice as it is, I don't want it.* **6.** *Informal.* That: *I don't know as I can.* *—Note: As* is used with certain words to form the following conjunctional groups: **as far as.** To the extent that: *She is home as far as I know.* **as if** (or **though**). In the same way that it would be if: *She acted as if she wanted to leave.* **as long as.** Since: *As long as you're writing them, please say hello for me.* **as soon as.** Immediately after: *We'll get to work as soon as we're told what to do.* *—pron.* **1.** That; who; which. Preceded by *same* or *such* as antecedent: *I got the same grade as you.* Used in some dialects (and formerly in standard English) with a noun or pronoun as antecedent: *Those as want to can come with me.* **2.** A fact that: *Roses are red, as we all know.* *—Note: As* is used with *much* to form a pronominal group: **as much.** All that; the same: *I might have guessed as much.* *—prep.* **1.** The same as; like: *He stared as a man possessed.* **2.** In the role or function of: *acting as a peacemaker.* *—Note: As* is used with certain words to form the following prepositional groups: **as for.** With regard to; concerning: *As for me, I'll stay.* **as of.** At or on (a specified time or

artichoke
Above: Opened flower head
Below: Unopened flower head

Aryan

Aryan *comes from Sanskrit* ārya *and Old Persian* ariya, *the name of the easternmost branch of the* **Indo-Europeans,** *who invaded Iran and India around 1500* B.C. *The term has been misleadingly used to mean a blond, blue-eyed type supposed to be the basic ancestral German. This racial type is properly called* **Nordic.**

date): *This assignment is due as of Monday.* **as to.** **1.** Concerning; about: *different views as to the best way to start.* **2.** According to; by: *The stones were classified as to hardness.* **as well as.** Besides: *a brilliant student as well as a good athlete.*

Idioms. as is. *Informal.* Just the way it is, without changes. **as it were.** In a manner of speaking: *He was a Robin Hood, as it were, until the cops caught up with him.*

As The symbol for the element arsenic.

as•a•fet•i•da |ăs'ə fĕt'ĭ də| *n.* A plant substance with a very unpleasant odor, formerly used in medicine.

as•bes•tos, also **as•bes•tus** |ăs bĕs'təs| *or* |ăz-| *n.* Either of two similar fibrous minerals that are resistant to heat, flames, and chemical action. Asbestos is used in making insulation, fireproofing material, and brake linings.

as•cend |ə sĕnd'| *v.* **1.** To go or move upward; rise: *The balloon ascended rapidly.* **2.** To climb to or toward the top of: *The climbers ascended the mountain.* **3.** To come to occupy: *Few kings have ascended their thrones under more inauspicious circumstances.*

as•cend•an•cy |ə sĕn'dən sē| *n.* Dominance in position or power: *America has gained ascendancy in the Western world.*

as•cend•ant |ə sĕn'dənt| *adj.* Coming into a position of power or influence: *Repressive Communism may once again be ascendant in Czechoslovakia.* —*n.* —**in the ascendant.** Rising in power or influence.

as•cend•ing |ə sĕn'dĭng| *adj.* Moving, going, or growing upward: *in ascending order of importance; a tree with ascending branches.* —**as•cend'ing•ly** *adv.*

as•cen•sion |ə sĕn'shən| *n.* **1.** The act or process of ascending. **2. the Ascension.** The ascent of Christ into heaven after his death and resurrection.

as•cent |ə sĕnt'| *n.* **1.** The act of ascending or moving upward: *the first stages of ascent of a rocket through the atmosphere.* **2.** The act of climbing up: *their ascent of Mont Blanc.* **3.** An upward slope: *The boy climbed the steep ascent to the palace.* **4.** The act or process of rising from a lower level, degree, status, etc.; development: *man in his slow ascent from earliest savagery to modern civilization.* —**modifier:** *the ascent stage of the lunar module.* ¶*These sound alike* **ascent, assent.**

as•cer•tain |ăs'ər tān'| *v.* To find out: *ascertain the truth.* —**as'cer•tain'a•ble** *adj.*

as•cet•ic |ə sĕt'ĭk| *n.* A person who renounces comforts and pleasures in order to practice rigid self-denial, often as an act of religious devotion. —*adj.* Of an ascetic; self-denying; austere: *an ascetic man; an ascetic life.*

as•cet•i•cism |ə sĕt'ĭ sĭz'əm| *n.* Ascetic practice or discipline.

a•scor•bic acid |ə skôr'bĭk|. A compound composed of carbon, hydrogen, and oxygen and having the formula $C_6H_8O_6$; vitamin C. It is found in citrus fruits, tomatoes, potatoes, and leafy vegetables. A person who takes too little of this vitamin may develop scurvy.

as•cot |ăs'kət| *or* |-kŏt'| *n.* A wide necktie or scarf tied so that the broad ends are laid flat, one on top of the other.

as•cribe |ə skrīb'| *v.* **as•cribed, as•crib•ing.** To attribute to a specific cause, origin, or source: *He ascribed his victory to superior strategy.*

as•crip•tion |ə skrĭp'shən| *n.* The act of ascribing.

a•sep•tic |ə sĕp'tĭk| *or* |ā sĕp'-| *adj.* Free of microorganisms that are capable of causing disease: *aseptic surgical instruments.*

a•sex•u•al |ā sĕk'shōō əl| *adj.* **1.** Neither male nor female; sexless: *an asexual organism.* **2.** Not involving sex organs or the union of sex cells: *asexual reproduction.*

As•gard |ăs'gärd'| *or* |ăz'-|. In Norse mythology, the abode of the gods.

ash¹ |ăsh| *n.* **1.** The solid material that remains after something has been burned completely. **2.** The fine particles of solid matter thrown out in a volcanic eruption. **3. ashes.** Human remains, especially after cremation. [SEE NOTE]

ash² |ăsh| *n.* **1.** A tree with leaflets in a feather-like arrangement and strong, tough wood. **2.** The wood of such a tree, used for making baseball bats and other sports equipment. —**modifier:** *ash leaves.* [SEE NOTE]

a•shamed |ə shāmd'| *adj.* **1.** Feeling shame or guilt: *He was very much ashamed of his fear of drowning.* **2.** Reluctant through fear of shame or embarrassment: *ashamed to tell anyone that a little girl had kicked him in the face.*

ash can. A large metal receptacle for ashes or trash.

ash•en |ăsh'ən| *adj.* Like the color of ashes; pale: *ashen gray. Paul turned ashen with fear.*

a•shore |ə shôr'| *or* |ə shōr'| *adv.* On or to the shore: *stepped ashore on an island; go ashore.*

ash•tray |ăsh'trā'| *n.* A small receptacle for tobacco ashes.

Ash Wednesday. The first day of Lent.

A•sia |ā'zhə| *or* |ā'shə|. The largest of the continents, extending from Europe and Africa on the west to the Pacific Ocean on the east.

Asia Minor. A peninsula lying between the Black and Mediterranean seas, including most of modern Turkey.

A•sian |ā'zhən| *or* |ā'shən| *n.* A native or inhabitant of Asia. —*adj.* Of Asia or the Asians. [SEE NOTE]

A•si•at•ic |ā'zhē ăt'ĭk| *or* |ā'shē-| *or* |ā'zē-| *adj.* Asian. —*n.* An Asian. [SEE NOTE]

a•side |ə sīd'| *adv.* **1.** To one side: *step aside; draw the curtain aside.* **2.** Apart: *a day set aside for rejoicing.* **3.** In reserve: *money put aside for Christmas presents.* **4.** Out of one's thoughts or mind: *put one's fears aside.* —*n.* A line spoken by a character in a play that the other actors on stage are not supposed to hear.

aside from. Apart from; except for: *Aside from a miracle, nothing can save our team from losing.*

as•i•nine |ăs'ə nīn'| *adj.* Stupid or silly: *That's an asinine remark.*

ask |ăsk| *or* |äsk| *v.* **1.** To put a question to: *Her mother asked her why she was crying.* **2.** To seek an answer to: *You learn to ask the right questions of the world in which you live.* **3. a.** To request or beg: *In this dedication of a nation, we humbly ask the blessing of God.* **b.** To make a request: *The American Government took the lead in asking for the withdrawal of Israeli troops.* **4. a.** To seek information about; inquire about:

ash¹·²

ash¹ *and* **ash²** *have always meant what they mean now. The first was* asce *in Old English and* asg- *in Indo-European, even then meaning "burnt residue." The tree was* æsc *in Old English and* osk- *in Indo-European.*

Asian/Asiatic

Asiatic *is used interchangeably with* **Asian** *in referring to places, plants, animals, etc.:* the Asiatic part of Turkey; the Asiatic python. *However, in referring to people and their doings,* **Asiatic** *is felt to be slightly offensive in an old-fashioned way*

ă pat/ā pay/â care/ä father/ĕ pet/ ē be/ĭ pit/ī pie/î fierce/ŏ pot/ ō go/ô paw, for/oi oil/ŏŏ book/ ōō boot/ou out/ŭ cut/û fur/ *th* the/th thin/hw which/zh vision/ ə ago, item, pencil, atom, circus

If you are in doubt ask the way. Mary asked his whereabouts. **b.** To make inquiries: *Ask at the desk. Some asked for information about boat trips. Don't ask after her mother's health. She refused to ask about her assignment.* **5.** To invite: *Why don't we ask them to our house tonight?* **6. a.** To charge: *ask a reasonable price.* **b.** To expect or demand: *This is asking too much of a child.*

a•skance |ə skăns′| *adv.* **1.** With a sidelong glance. **2.** With distrust or disapproval: *He looked askance at such rumors.*

a•skew |ə skyo͞o′| *adv. & adj.* Out of line; crooked; awry: *She always wears her hat askew. The picture is askew.*

a•slant |ə slănt′| *or* |ə slänt′| *adj.* Slanting: *We saw a crack of moonlight aslant on the floor.* —*adv.* At a slant: *The front of the wreck was knocked aslant from the rear end.* —*prep.* Obliquely over or across: *a shaft of sunlight moving aslant the wall.*

a•sleep |ə slēp′| *adj.* **1.** Sleeping: *You must have been asleep when the phone rang.* **2.** Numb: *My foot is asleep.* —*adv.* Into a sleep: *He fell asleep quickly after his long hike.*

asp |ăsp| *n.* Any of several poisonous Old World snakes, especially a small cobra of northern Africa and southwestern Asia.

as•par•a•gus |ə spăr′ə gəs| *n.* **1.** The young, tender stalks of a cultivated plant, cooked and eaten as a vegetable. **2.** The plant itself. [SEE PICTURE]

as•pect |ăs′pĕkt′| *n.* **1.** The appearance of an idea, situation, plan, etc., as viewed by the mind; an element or facet: *scholarly research that explores every aspect of music; all aspects of a case.* **2.** Appearance; look: *a shaggy-haired man of almost barbarian aspect.*

as•pen |ăs′pən| *n.* A poplar tree with leaves that flutter in even the lightest of breezes.

as•per•i•ty |ă spĕr′ĭ tē| *n.* Sharpness of temper; irritability: *a note of asperity in one's voice.*

as•per•sion |ə spûr′zhən| *or* |-shən| *n.* A damaging or slanderous report or remark: *His speech cast aspersions on my motives.*

as•phalt |ăs′fôlt′| *n.* **1.** A thick, sticky, brownish-black mixture of petroleum tars used in paving, roofing, and waterproofing. **2.** A paving material composed of sand, small stones, gravel, and asphalt. —*v.* To pave or coat with asphalt. —*modifier:* *asphalt sidewalks; asphalt highways.*

as•pho•del |ăs′fə dĕl′| *n.* A plant of the Mediterranean region with white or yellow flowers.

as•phyx•i•a |ăs fĭk′sē ə| *n.* Death or loss of consciousness caused by a lack of oxygen.

as•phyx•i•ate |ăs fĭk′sē āt′| *v.* **as•phyx•i•at•ed, as•phyx•i•at•ing.** To undergo or cause to undergo asphyxia; smother; suffocate: *Without air they will asphyxiate. The smoke nearly asphyxiated us.* —**as•phyx′i•a′tion** *n.*

as•pic |ăs′pĭk| *n.* A jelly made from chilled meat juices or vegetable juices and served as a garnish or as a molded dish.

as•pir•ant |ə spīr′ənt| *or* |ăs′pər-| *n.* A person who desires or strives for a particular position or honor: *an aspirant for fame.*

as•pi•rate |ăs′pə rāt′| *v.* **as•pi•rat•ed, as•pi•rat•ing.** **1.** To remove (a liquid or gas) from a body cavity by suction, as by using an aspirator. **2.** To pronounce the sound of the letter "h" as in *help.* —*n.* |ăs′pər ĭt|. The sound of the letter "h" as in *help.*

as•pi•ra•tion |ăs′pə rā′shən| *n.* **1.** A strong desire, as for the realization of an ambition, an ideal, etc.: *unsympathetic with the students' aspirations for involvement in determining the role of their schools.* **2.** The process of removing a liquid or gas from a body cavity by suction. **3.** The pronunciation of the sound of the letter "h," especially when it occurs at the beginning of a word.

as•pi•ra•tor |ăs′pə rā′tər| *n.* A suction pump, especially a small one used to draw fluids from body cavities.

as•pire |ə spīr′| *v.* **as•pired, as•pir•ing.** To have a great ambition; desire strongly: *aspire to become a good player; aspire to great knowledge.*

as•pi•rin |ăs′pə rĭn| *or* |-prĭn| *n.* **1.** A white, crystalline compound of carbon, hydrogen, and oxygen in the proportions $C_9H_8O_4$, commonly used as a drug to relieve fever and pain; acetylsalicylic acid. **2.** A tablet of aspirin: *An aspirin may relieve your headache.*

ass |ăs| *n.* **1.** A donkey or similar hoofed animal related to the horse. **2.** A silly or stupid person.

as•sa•gai |ăs′ə gī′| *n.* A light spear, often with an iron tip, used by southern African tribesmen. [SEE PICTURE]

as•sail |ə sāl′| *v.* **1.** To attack physically or with words: *He assailed his opponents and their policies with bitter invective.* **2.** To set upon from or as if from all sides; beset: *Darker suspicions assailed him now.*

as•sail•ant |ə sā′lənt| *n.* A person who assails; an attacker.

as•sas•sin |ə săs′ĭn| *n.* A murderer, especially one who kills a public official or other prominent figure for political reasons.

as•sas•si•nate |ə săs′ə nāt′| *v.* **as•sas•si•nat•ed, as•sas•si•nat•ing.** To murder (a public figure), usually for political reasons. —**as•sas′si•na′tion** *n.* [SEE NOTE]

as•sault |ə sôlt′| *n.* **1.** A violent physical or verbal attack: *a large-scale assault upon the enemy walls. In his press conference the senator launched an assault upon the corrupt local politicians.* **2.** The way of beginning an activity: *Edison's greatest invention was his organized assault on every aspect of a problem.* —*v.* To attack violently: *The Vikings assaulted England.*

assault and battery. An illegal act in which a threat of attack on another person is carried out.

as•say |ăs′ā′| *or* |ă sā′| *n.* **1.** A chemical analysis of something, especially an ore or drug. **2.** A specimen or sample subjected to an assay. —*v.* |ă sā′| *or* |ăs′ā′|. **1.** To analyze (a substance) chemically. **2.** To be shown by an assay to contain some ingredient: *The ore assayed at 1 per cent uranium.* **3.** To test and evaluate the worth, status, etc., of: *assaying the strategic balance in the Middle East.* **4.** To attempt; try: *In spite of the heavy chains on her legs, she still assayed to go.* —**as•say′er** *n.*

as•se•gai |ăs′ə gī′| *n.* A form of the word **assagai.**

as•sem•blage |ə sĕm′blĭj| *n.* **1.** A collection of persons or things: *speaking before a large assemblage in the palace; family groups and the more*

asparagus

assagai

assassination
"Assassination has never changed the history of the world." —Benjamin Disraeli (1865).

complex assemblages represented by mammalian societies. **2.** The act of gathering or fitting together.

as•sem•ble |ə sĕm′bəl| *v.* **as•sem•bled, as•sem•bling. 1.** To bring or come together as a group: *The teachers assembled their classes in the auditorium. Three policemen had assembled in the hall.* **2.** To perform the assembly of; put together: *The mechanic assembled the engine. These parts are assembled into a unit.* **3.** To fit together: *The unit assembles quite easily.* —**as•sem′bler** *n.*

as•sem•bly |ə sĕm′blē| *n., pl.* **as•sem•blies. 1.** A group of persons gathered together for a common purpose. **2. Assembly.** A legislative body: *the State Assembly.* **3. a.** The process of putting together a number of parts to make up a complete unit. **b.** A number of parts that work together as a unit; apparatus: *the steering assembly of a truck.*

assembly line. An arrangement in which articles are assembled in successive stages, passing from worker to worker or machine to machine, generally on some kind of conveyor.

as•sem•bly•man |ə sĕm′blē mən| *n., pl.* **-men** |-mən|. A member of a legislative assembly.

as•sent |ə sĕnt′| *n.* Agreement, as to a proposal, especially in a formal or impersonal manner: *The prime minister desired the king's assent.* —*v.* To express agreement: *Matt assented to the trip readily.* ¶*These sound alike* **assent, ascent.**

as•sert |ə sûrt′| *v.* **1.** To state or declare positively; claim: *reluctant to assert that his story is true.* **2.** To insist upon recognition of: *a tacit desire of the jury to assert its independence.* **3.** To compel obedience of; enforce: *a land where life is tough and nature asserts her own laws.*

Idiom. **assert (oneself).** To express oneself boldly or forcefully.

as•ser•tion |ə sûr′shən| *n.* **1.** The act of asserting. **2.** A positive statement or claim, especially one for which no proof is offered: *From both sections of the nation there issued bold assertions of cultural superiority.*

as•ser•tive |ə sûr′tĭv| *adj.* Bold and self-confident, especially in putting forward one's opinions; positive: *an assertive and sometimes abrasive newspaperman.* —**as•ser′tive•ly** *adv.* —**as•ser′tive•ness** *n.*

as•sess |ə sĕs′| *v.* **1.** To estimate the value of (property) for taxation: *Mr. Graham's house was assessed at $9,000.* **2. a.** To set the amount of (a tax, fine, etc.). **b.** To charge (a person) with a tax, fine, or other special payment: *Each member will be assessed fifty cents.* **3.** To analyze and determine the significance, importance, etc., of; estimate; evaluate: *special skills in assessing personality weaknesses; soberly assessing each man as future leader of the group.* —**as•sess′a•ble** *adj.*

as•sess•ment |ə sĕs′mənt| *n.* **1.** The act of assessing. **2.** An amount assessed: *Expenses of the Board of Governors are paid out of assessments upon the other member banks.*

as•ses•sor |ə sĕs′ər| *n.* An official whose job it is to assess the tax value of property.

as•set |ăs′ĕt′| *n.* **1.** A valuable quality or possession: *Her smile is a real asset. The water birds of the continent remain the island's most spectacular asset.* **2. assets.** All the property owned by a person, business, etc., that has money value and may be applied directly or indirectly to the payment of debts. [SEE NOTE]

asset

After the Normans conquered England (1066), they introduced many of their own laws and legal expressions, written in the Norman dialect of Old French. One such expression was aver asetz, *"to have enough"; this was used of a man who* had enough *property to pay his debts. The word* asetz, *actually meaning "enough," was taken by the English to be a plural noun meaning "items of property." It was borrowed into English as* **assets.** *Eventually, in the nineteenth century, the new singular form* **asset** *was invented. This is an example of back-formation. Note that in modern French the word became* assez, *and it still simply means "enough."*

as•sid•u•ous |ə sĭj′o͞o əs| *adj.* Diligent; industrious: *an assiduous worker.* —**as•sid′u•ous•ly** *adv.* —**as•sid′u•ous•ness** *n.*

as•sign |ə sīn′| *v.* **1.** To set apart for a particular purpose; designate: *assign a day for the trial.* **2.** To appoint, as to a duty: *The commander assigned the fighter group to the Mediterranean area.* **3.** To give out; allot: *assign rooms to the boarders; assigning the task of retrieving the space capsule to the recovery force.* **4.** To regard as belonging to; ascribe; attribute: *Each time you assign a living thing to the set to which it belongs, you are making a classification.* —**as•sign′er** *n.*

as•sign•ment |ə sīn′mənt| *n.* **1.** The act of assigning. **2.** Something assigned, especially a task or job: *What's the chemistry assignment for tomorrow?* **3.** A post of duty to which one is assigned: *The embassy in Paris will be his first assignment outside the United States.*

as•sim•i•late |ə sĭm′ə lāt′| *v.* **as•sim•i•lat•ed, as•sim•i•lat•ing. 1. a.** To take in, digest, and convert (nutrients) into living tissue: *The body assimilates protein.* **b.** To be assimilated, as a nutrient. **2.** To take in or be taken in; incorporate; absorb: *rich merchants striving to assimilate the culture and ideals of the French court; technological changes that are difficult to assimilate.* **3.** To take in or be taken into the cultural or social tradition of a group: *The United States assimilated immigrants of many nationalities. Many ethnic groups assimilated rapidly.*

as•sim•i•la•tion |ə sĭm′ə lā′shən| *n.* **1.** The act or process of assimilating: *assimilation of food; assimilation of new immigrants.* **2.** In linguistics, the process by which a sound is modified to resemble a nearby sound. For example, the prefix *in-* in *intolerable* becomes *im-* in *impossible* by assimilation.

As•sin•i•boin |ə sĭn′ə boin′| *n., pl.* **As•sin•i•boin** or **As•sin•i•boins. 1.** A North American Indian tribe of northeastern Montana and the adjacent area of Canada. **2.** A member of this tribe. **3.** The Siouan language of this tribe.

as•sist |ə sĭst′| *v.* To help; aid: *The whole community labored to assist a family in distress. Vocabulary drills will follow the lesson to assist in the choice of appropriate answers.* —*n.* **1.** An act of giving aid; help: *give someone a quick assist.* **2. a.** A handling of the ball that enables a runner to be put out in baseball. **b.** A pass that enables a teammate to score, as in basketball or hockey.

as•sis•tance |ə sĭs′təns| *n.* Help; aid: *financial assistance to farmers.*

as•sis•tant |ə sĭs′tənt| *n.* One who assists; a helper: *the President's special assistant.* —*adj.* Acting under the authority of another person: *an assistant coach.*

as•siz•es |ə sī′zĭz| *pl.n.* A court session held periodically in each of the counties of England and Wales.

assn. association.

assoc. associate; association.

as•so•ci•ate |ə sō′shē āt′| *or* |-sē-| *v.* **as•so•ci•at•ed, as•so•ci•at•ing. 1.** To bring together in one's mind or imagination; connect: *We associate automobiles with Detroit.* **2.** To join in a relationship as a worker, member, partner, etc.:

He learned that Mr. Elkins was associated with the firm of Harper and Brothers. **3.** To connect (oneself) with a cause, group, etc.: *He associated himself with the fund drive. She always refused to associate with the older girls.* —*n.* |ə sō′shē ĭt| *or* |-āt′| *or* |-sē-|. **1.** A partner; colleague: *my business associate.* **2.** A member without full status: *an associate of the museum society.* —*adj.* |ə sō′shē ĭt| *or* |-āt′| *or* |-sē-|. **1.** Joined with another and having equal or nearly equal status; sharing in responsibility or authority: *an associate judge.* **2.** Having only partial status: *an associate member of a club.*

as•so•ci•a•tion |ə sō′sē ā′shən| *or* |-shē-| *n.* **1.** The act of associating: *Skillful readers make associations of ideas.* **2.** A partnership or friendship: *his close association with the president.* **3.** A group of people joined together for a common purpose; a society: *a trade association.* **4.** An idea or train of ideas triggered by another idea or by a stimulus: *What associations does the word "geography" bring to your mind?*

as•so•ci•a•tive |ə sō′shē ā′tĭv| *or* |-sē-| *or* |- shə tĭv| *adj.* Of the associative property or an operation that has the associative property.

associative property. The property of a binary mathematical operation that when applied in succession to a set of elements produces the same result regardless of the way the numbers are grouped. Suppose that *a, b,* and *c* are numbers and ♦ is a binary mathematical operation. If (*a* ♦ *b*) ♦ *c* = *a* ♦ (*b* ♦ *c*), the operation ♦ has the associative property. [SEE NOTE]

as•so•nance |ăs′ə nəns| *n.* **1.** Similarity in sound, especially the repetition in poetry of the same vowel sounds. **2.** A partial rhyme in which the stressed vowel sounds are the same but the consonants are different, as in *tent* and *sense.*

as•sort |ə sôrt′| *v.* To separate into groups according to kinds; sort; classify.

as•sort•ed |ə sôr′tĭd| *adj.* Of various kinds; different: *boys of assorted sizes; assorted cakes.*

as•sort•ment |ə sôrt′mənt| *n.* A collection of various kinds; variety: *an unusual assortment of people; an assortment of vegetables.*

asst. assistant.

as•suage |ə swāj′| *v.* **as•suaged, as•suag•ing. 1.** To make less burdensome or painful: *kind words to assuage his sorrow.* **2.** To satisfy; appease: *assuage one's thirst.* **3.** To pacify; calm: *apologies to assuage his anger.*

as•sume |ə so͞om′| *v.* **as•sumed, as•sum•ing. 1.** To take for granted; suppose: *Let's assume that all units of measure used are equal.* **2.** To take upon oneself; undertake: *assuming responsibilities for himself and his family.* **3.** To invest oneself with: *The Count of Provence did not hesitate to assume the title Louis XVIII in 1795.* **4.** To take on; adopt: *An apparently inert virus will assume the properties of life when it invades fresh cells.* **5.** To take for oneself or as one's right: *nations that assume authority to impose fishing limits in their offshore waters.* **6.** To feign; pretend: *always assuming an air of indifference.*

as•sumed |ə so͞omd′| *adj.* **1.** Fictitious; adopted: *an assumed name.* **2.** Taken for granted: *an assumed fact.*

as•sump•tion |ə sŭmp′shən| *n.* **1.** The act of assuming. **2.** An idea or statement accepted as true without any proof: *acting on the assumption that Russia was also interested in world peace.* **3. the Assumption. a.** In theology, the bodily taking up of the Virgin Mary into heaven. **b.** The church festival on August 15 commemorating this.

as•sur•ance |ə sho͝or′əns| *n.* **1.** A positive statement intended to inspire confidence; a guarantee: *He gave us his solemn assurance that he would pay.* **2.** Confidence; certainty: *The question could be answered with assurance.* **3.** Self-confidence: *playing with complete assurance.*

as•sure |ə sho͝or′| *v.* **as•sured, as•sur•ing. 1.** To declare confidently: *I can assure you that we shall take appropriate action.* **2.** To make certain; guarantee; ensure: *They helped the Republican campaign of 1800 and helped assure Jefferson's election.* **3.** To give confidence to; reassure: *The doctor assured her that she would recover.*

as•sured |ə sho͝ord′| *adj.* **1.** Confident: *an assured manner.* **2.** Certain; guaranteed: *an assured success.* —**as•sur′ed•ly** |ə sho͝or′ĭd lē| *adv.*

As•syr•i•a |ə sîr′ē ə|. An ancient empire extending, at the height of its power, from the Persian Gulf to the Mediterranean Sea and into Egypt. —**As•syr′i•an** *adj.* & *n.*

AST, A.S.T. Atlantic Standard Time.

As•tar•te |ə stär′tē|. The goddess of love and fertility of ancient Phoenicia.

as•ta•tine |ăs′tə tēn′| *or* |-tĭn| *n.* *Symbol* **At** One of the elements, an unstable, radioactive substance that resembles iodine in some of its properties. Its longest-lived isotope is At 210, having a half-life of 8.3 hours. Atomic number 85; valences –1, +1, +3, +5, +7.

as•ter |ăs′tər| *n.* Any of several plants with white, purplish, or pink daisylike flowers. [SEE NOTE & PICTURE]

as•ter•isk |ăs′tə rĭsk′| *n.* A symbol (*) used in printed and written matter to indicate an omission or a reference to a footnote.

a•stern |ə stûrn′| *adv.* **1.** Behind a ship. **2.** At or toward the rear of a ship.

as•ter•oid |ăs′tə roid′| *n.* Any of numerous objects that orbit the sun, chiefly in the region between Mars and Jupiter. They range in size from about one to several hundred miles in diameter and are often irregular in shape.

asth•ma |ăz′mə| *or* |ăs′-| *n.* A chronic disease that is often allergic in origin. Its chief symptom is tightness of the chest with coughing and difficulty in breathing.

asth•mat•ic |ăz măt′ĭk| *or* |ăs-| *adj.* **1.** Of asthma. **2.** Having asthma: *an asthmatic child.* —*n.* A person with asthma.

a•stig•ma•tism |ə stĭg′mə tĭz′əm| *n.* A defect in a lens, especially in the lens of the eye, that causes the image of a point or small dot to be distorted. —**as′tig•mat′ic** |ăs′tĭg măt′ĭk| *adj.*

a•stir |ə stûr′| *adj.* **1.** In a condition of motion, activity, or excitement; moving about: *The miners' camp was astir after the news of the gold discovery.* **2.** Out of bed; up: *The farmer was astir before dawn.*

as•ton•ish |ə stŏn′ĭsh| *v.* To fill with wonder; amaze; surprise: *The apple astonished the king, and he called everyone over to see it.* —**as•ton′ished** *adj.: an astonished silence; her brother's astonished face.* [SEE NOTE]

associative property

It is not hard to see that the equation shown is correct when ♦ is + or ×, and incorrect when ♦ is ÷ or −. Therefore addition and multiplication have the **associative property,** *and division and subtraction do not have it.*

aster

The **aster** *looks quite like an* **asterisk,** *which is reasonable when you know their etymologies.* **Aster** *is from Greek* astēr, *"star," and* **asterisk** *is from its diminutive* asteriskos, *"little star, asterisk." And* astro- *in words like* **astronaut** *and* **astronomy** *is from Greek* astron, *a variant of* astēr.

astonish/astound

Astonish *was earlier* astone *(the* -ish *is a verb ending, as in* finish, vanish*).* **Astound** *was originally* astoned, *meaning "amazed," from this same verb* astone. *So* **astonish** *and* **astound** *are virtually the same word. Still more astonishing: the word* astone *itself is from the same source as the word* **stun**; *see the note at* **stun.**

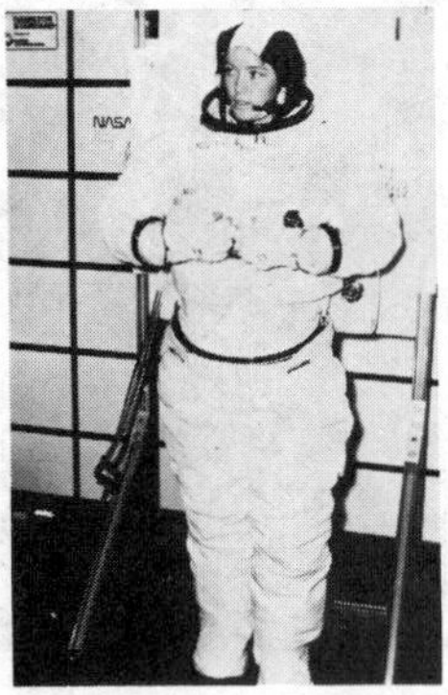

astronaut
***Astronaut** is an example of a word coming before the thing it refers to. It was used in science fiction for years before there were any real astronauts. The same thing seems to be happening with* **robot.**

asunder
In the materials on which this Dictionary was based, **asunder** *occurred only in poetry and very formal writing.*

ă **pat**/ā **pay**/â **care**/ä **father**/ĕ **pet**/ē **be**/ĭ **pit**/ī **pie**/î **fierce**/ŏ **pot**/ō **go**/ô **paw**, **for**/oi **oil**/ŏŏ **book**/ōō **boot**/ou **out**/ŭ **cut**/û **fur**/*th* **the**/th **thin**/hw **which**/**zh** vision/ə **ago**, item, pencil, atom, circus

as•ton•ish•ing |ə **stŏn**'ĭ shĭng| *adj.* Greatly surprising; amazing: *an astonishing victory; an astonishing discovery.* —**as•ton'ish•ing•ly** *adv.*

as•ton•ish•ment |ə **stŏn**'ĭsh mənt| *n.* Great surprise; amazement: *The old lady stood petrified with astonishment, peering over her glasses.*

a•stound |ə **stound'**| *v.* To strike with sudden wonder; astonish: *Our victory completely astounded him.* —**a•stound'ing** *adj.*: *an astounding color combination.* [SEE NOTE on p. 53]

a•strad•dle |ə **străd'**l| *prep.* Astride; astride of: *astraddle a horse.*

as•tra•khan |**ăs'**trə kăn'| *or* |-kən| *n.* Curly fur made from the skins of young lambs from Astrakhan, in the U.S.S.R.

a•stray |ə **strā'**| *adv.* Away from the correct goal or path: *being led astray by bad advice.*

a•stride |ə **strīd'**| *prep.* **1.** With a leg on each side of; bestriding: *He jumped astride his back.* Also used adverbially: *riding astride.* **2.** On both sides of or spanning: *a safe position astride the bridge.*

astride of. Astride: *He stood astride of the fallen enemy.*

as•trin•gent |ə **strĭn'**jənt| *adj.* Tending to draw together or tighten living tissue. —*n.* An astringent substance or drug, such as alum. —**as•trin'gen•cy** *n.*

as•tro•dome |**ăs'**trə dōm'| *n.* An enclosed stadium with a translucent dome, in which sports events, such as football games, can be held under all weather conditions.

as•tro•gate |**ăs'**trə gāt'| *v.* **as•tro•gat•ed, as•tro•gat•ing.** To navigate a spacecraft in space. —**as'tro•ga'tion** *n.*

as•tro•ga•tor |**ăs'**trə gā'tər| *n.* A person trained to navigate a spacecraft.

as•tro•labe |**ăs'**trə lāb'| *n.* An instrument formerly used by mariners to determine the altitude of the sun and other celestial bodies.

as•tro•log•i•cal |ăs'trə **lŏj'**ĭ kəl| *adj.* Of astrology.

as•trol•o•gy |ə **strŏl'**ə jē| *n.* The art of predicting the course of human events through the study of the positions of the stars and planets, which are believed to have a supernatural influence. —**as•trol'o•ger** *n.*

as•tro•naut |**ăs'**trə nôt'| *n.* A person trained to serve as a member of the crew of a spacecraft. [SEE NOTE & PICTURE]

as•tro•nau•tics |ăs'trə **nô'**tĭks| *n.* *(used with a singular verb).* The science and engineering involved in space flight and in the design, construction, and operation of spacecraft.

as•tron•o•mer |ə **strŏn'**ə mər| *n.* A scientist who specializes in astronomy.

as•tro•nom•i•cal |ăs'trə **nŏm'**ĭ kəl| or **as•tro•nom•ic** |ăs'trə **nŏm'**ĭk| *adj.* **1.** Of astronomy. **2.** Too large to be easily imagined; immense: *The national budget is astronomical.* —**as'tro•nom'i•cal•ly** *adv.*

astronomical unit. A unit of distance equal to the average distance between the earth and the sun, about 93 million miles. This unit is used in measuring the distances that separate bodies located in outer space.

as•tron•o•my |ə **strŏn'**ə mē| *n.* The scientific study of the part of the universe that lies beyond the earth, especially the observation of stars, planets, comets, galaxies, etc.

as•tro•phys•ics |ăs'trō **fĭz'**ĭks| *n.* *(used with a singular verb).* The study of physical phenomena that occur in stars and in outer space.

As•tro•turf |**ăs'**trō tûrf'| *n.* A trademark for an artificial grasslike ground covering.

as•tute |ə **stōōt**| *or* |ə **styōōt'**| *adj.* Keen in judgment; shrewd: *an astute politician of the old school; an astute appraisal.* —**as•tute'ly** *adv.* —**as•tute'ness** *n.*

A•sun•ción |ä'sōōn **syôn'**|. The capital of Paraguay. Population, 387,000.

a•sun•der |ə **sŭn'**dər| *adj.* **1.** Into separate parts or groups: *The crowd parted asunder.* **2.** Apart in position or direction. [SEE NOTE]

a•sy•lum |ə **sī'**ləm| *n.* **1.** A hospital or shelter for the helpless or insane. **2.** A place of refuge. **3.** Protection and immunity from extradition granted to a political offender from another country: *The hijacker requested asylum.*

at |ăt| *or* |ət *when unstressed*| *prep.* **1.** —Used to indicate position, location, or state: *at home; at rest.* **2.** —Used to indicate a direction or goal: *look at us; jump at the chance.* **3.** —Used to indicate location in time: *at noon.* **4.** —Used to indicate manner, means, or cause: *getting there at top speed.* **5.** —Used informally as an intensive with *where: trying to figure out where things are really at.* —*Note: At* is used with certain words to form the following adverbial groups: **at all.** In any way whatsoever: *no good at all.* **at once. 1.** At one time; simultaneously: *everything happening at once.* **2.** Immediately: *Leave the room at once.* **at one.** In harmony: *feeling at one with the world.*

At The symbol for the element astatine.

at•a•vism |**ăt'**ə vĭz'əm| *n.* The reappearance in a strain of organisms of a hereditary trait that has been absent for several generations.

at•a•vis•tic |ăt'ə **vĭs'**tĭk| *adj.* Reappearing after an absence of several generations; being an atavism.

a•tax•i•a |ə **tăk'**sē ə| *n.* Loss or lack of muscular coordination.

a•tax•y |ə **tăk'**sē| *n.* A form of the word **ataxia.**

ate |āt|. Past tense of **eat.** ¶*These sound alike* **ate, eight.**

-ate[1]. A suffix that forms adjectives: **affectionate; inanimate.**

-ate[2]. A suffix that forms verbs: **laminate; pollinate.**

at•el•ier |ăt'l **yā'**| *n.* An artist's studio.

a tem•po |ä **tĕm'**pō|. In music, returning to the original tempo.

Ath•a•pas•can |ăth'ə **păs'**kən| *n.* A family of Indian languages of the western United States and Canada and parts of Alaska. Apache and Navaho are two important Athapascan languages. —**Ath'a•pas'can** *adj.*

a•the•ism |**ā'**thē ĭz'əm| *n.* Denial of the existence of God.

a•the•ist |**ā'**thē ĭst| *n.* A person who denies the existence of God. —**a'the•is'tic** *adj.*

Ath•ens |**ăth'**ənz|. The capital of Greece and the leading city of ancient Greece. Population, 2,540,000. —**A•the'ni•an** |ə **thē'**nē ən| *adj.* & *n.*

ath•lete |**ăth'**lēt'| *n.* **1.** A person who takes part in competitive sports. **2.** A person possessing a natural aptitude for physical exercises and sports.

athlete's foot. A contagious skin disease caused

by parasitic fungi. It generally attacks the feet where it causes the skin to itch, blister, and crack.

ath•let•ic |ăth lĕt′ĭk| *adj.* **1.** Of or for athletics: *athletic ability.* **2.** Of or for athletes: *a good athletic build; an athletic club.* **3.** Physically strong; muscular. —**ath•let′i•cal•ly** *adv.*

ath•let•ics |ăth lĕt′ĭks| *n. (used with a plural verb).* Athletic activities; sports.

athletic supporter. An elastic support for the male genitals, worn during sports.

a•thwart |ə thwôrt′| *adv.* **1.** From side to side across: *The sector held by the Second Division lies athwart the path of the enemy.* **2.** At right angles to the center line of a ship or boat. —*prep.* **1.** Across. **2.** Across the center line or course of: *a cruiser standing athwart the course of the destroyer.* **3.** Against: *spending habits quite athwart their austere background.*

-ation. A suffix that forms nouns from verbs: **civilization; negotiation.**

-ative. A suffix that forms adjectives: **authoritative; formative.**

At•lan•ta |ăt lăn′tə|. The capital and largest city of Georgia. Population, 487,000.

At•lan•tic Daylight-Saving Time |ăt lăn′tĭk|. Daylight-saving time as reckoned in the region between the meridians 52.5° and 67.5° west of Greenwich, England. The eastern edge of Canada is in this region. See **time zone.**

Atlantic Ocean. The second largest of the oceans, extending from the Arctic to the Antarctic between the Americas on the west and Europe and Africa on the east.

Atlantic Standard Time. Standard time as reckoned in the region between the meridians at 52.5° and 67.5° west of Greenwich, England. The eastern edge of Canada is in this region. See **time zone.**

At•lan•tis |ăt lăn′tĭs|. A fabled island or continent of ancient times, said to have sunk beneath the sea during an earthquake.

at•las |ăt′ləs| *n.* A book or bound collection of maps.

at•mos•phere |ăt′mə sfîr′| *n.* **1.** The gas that surrounds a body in space, especially the air that surrounds the earth, and is held by the body's gravitational field. **2.** A unit of pressure equal to the pressure of the atmosphere at sea level, about 14.7 pounds per square inch. **3.** The air or climate of a place: *the dry atmosphere of the desert.* **4.** Environment or surroundings regarded as having a psychological, physical, or other influence: *A hospital should have a quiet atmosphere.* **5.** A general feeling or mood: *the atmosphere of a story.*

at•mos•pher•ic |ăt′mə sfĕr′ĭk| or **at•mos•pher•i•cal** |ăt′mə sfĕr′ĭ kəl| *adj.* Of, in, or from the atmosphere: *atmospheric pressure; atmospheric flight.* —**at′mos•pher′i•cal•ly** *adv.*

at•mos•pher•ics |ăt′mə sfĕr′ĭks| *n. (used with a singular verb).* Electromagnetic radiation produced by natural phenomena such as lightning.

at•oll |ăt′ôl′| *or* |-ŏl′| *or* |ā′tôl′| *or* |ā′tŏl′| *n.* A coral island or a string of coral islands and reefs forming a ring that encloses a lagoon wholly or in part. [SEE PICTURE]

at•om |ăt′əm| *n.* **1. a.** The smallest unit of an element, consisting of a dense positively charged nucleus surrounded by a system of electrons equal in number to the protons in the nucleus. The entire structure is electrically neutral and remains intact in chemical reactions, except for the removal, transfer, or exchange of certain electrons. **b.** A unit of this kind regarded as a source of nuclear energy. **2.** A bit or jot: *There is not an atom of sense in what he says.* [SEE NOTE]

a•tom•ic |ə tŏm′ĭk| *adj.* **1.** Of an atom or atoms. **2.** Of or using nuclear energy; nuclear: *an atomic power plant.*

atomic age. The present age; the time in which nuclear energy was discovered and used.

atomic bomb. A bomb that derives its explosive force from nuclear energy, especially energy produced by the fission of heavy atomic nuclei, as those of uranium 235.

atomic clock. A device that keeps time extremely precisely by, essentially, counting the occurrences of something that happens in an atomic system at regular intervals.

atomic energy. Energy that is released as a result of reactions that involve atomic nuclei.

atomic fission. **Nuclear fission.**

atomic fusion. **Nuclear fusion.**

atomic mass. The mass of an atom or of a part of an atom, usually expressed as a number of atomic mass units.

atomic mass unit. A unit of mass equal to 1/12 the mass of a carbon atom that has the mass number 12; approximately 1.6604×10^{-24} gram.

atomic number. The number of protons in an atomic nucleus.

atomic pile. A **nuclear reactor.**

atomic power. **Atomic energy.**

atomic reactor. A **nuclear reactor.**

atomic weight. The average weight of an atom of an element, usually expressed in relation to the isotope of carbon taken to have a weight of 12.

at•om•ize |ăt′ə mīz′| *v.* **at•om•ized, at•om•iz•ing. 1.** To break apart or separate into atoms. **2.** To break (a liquid) up into a fine mist.

at•om•iz•er |ăt′ə mī′zər| *n.* A device for producing a fine spray, especially of a perfume or medicine.

a•ton•al |ā tō′nəl| *adj.* In music, having no apparent key or tonality.

a•to•nal•i•ty |ā′tō năl′ĭ tē| *n.* **1.** A style of musical composition in which the use of a tonal center is avoided. **2.** The condition of being atonal.

a•tone |ə tōn′| *v.* **a•toned, a•ton•ing.** To make amends for a sin, fault, etc.: *atone for tardiness by doing extra work.* [SEE NOTE]

a•tone•ment |ə tōn′mənt| *n.* **1.** Th act of atoning; expiation. **2. the Atonement.** The sacrifice and death of Christ to redeem mankind.

a•top |ə tŏp′| *prep.* On top of: *The Supreme Court stands atop the judicial pyramid.*

ATP A compound of carbon, hydrogen, nitrogen, oxygen, and phosphorus, in the proportions $C_{10}H_{16}N_5O_{13}P_3$, that acts as an energy source in metabolism, especially where muscular activity is involved.

a•tri•a |ā′trē ə| *n.* A plural of **atrium.**

a•trip |ə trĭp′| *adj.* Just clear of the bottom; aweigh: *with sails unfurled and anchor atrip.*

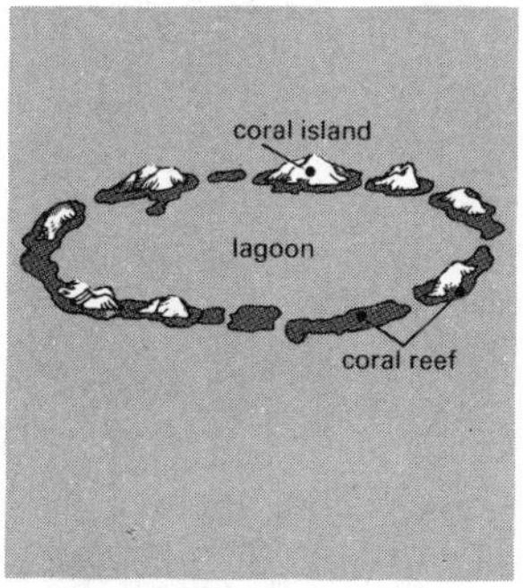

atoll

atom

Atom *comes from Greek* atomos, *"uncuttable, indivisible"* (a-, *"not,"* + tom-, *"cut"*). *This word was used to describe the basic particles of matter that some Greek scientists believed must exist, although they had no means of testing it. In modern times, of course, it has been found that the "indivisible" atom is made up of subatomic particles.*

atone

Atone *is one of the few English words directly formed from a phrase. Its basic meaning was "to bring into agreement, to harmonize," and it comes from the phrase* at one, *"in agreement or harmony." Later the verb came to mean "to make up for."*

a•tri•um |ā′trē əm| *n., pl.* **a•tri•a** |ā′trē ə| or **a•tri•ums.** **1.** The open entrance court of an ancient Roman house. **2.** A cavity or chamber of the body, especially one of the chambers of the heart that receive blood from the veins.

a•tro•cious |ə trō′shəs| *adj.* **1.** Extremely evil or cruel; wicked: *an atrocious crime.* **2.** Very bad; abominable: *atrocious weather.* —**a•tro′cious•ly** *adv.* —**a•tro′cious•ness** *n.*

a•troc•i•ty |ə trŏs′ĭ tē| *n., pl.* **a•troc•i•ties.** Something atrocious, especially an extremely evil or cruel act: *wartime atrocities.*

at•ro•phy |ăt′rə fē| *n.* The wasting away of the body or of any of its organs or tissues. —*v.* **at•ro•phied, at•ro•phy•ing, at•ro•phies.** To waste away or cause to waste away: *The muscle atrophied from disuse. Illness had atrophied the patient's body.*

at•ro•pin |ăt′rə pĭn| *n.* A form of the word **atropine.**

at•ro•pine |ăt′rə pēn′| *or* |-pĭn| *n.* A very poisonous, bitter alkaloid composed of carbon, hydrogen, nitrogen, and oxygen in the proportions $C_{17}H_{23}NO_3$. It is obtained from belladonna and related plants and has a variety of medical uses.

at•tach |ə tăch′| *v.* **1.** To fasten on or join; connect: *attach the wires. The wires attach here.* **2.** To bind by ties of affection or loyalty: *He is very attached to his mother.* **3.** To think of as belonging to; consider to have: *I attach no importance to his objections.* **4.** To add (something) at the end; append: *He attached his signature to the document.* **5.** To assign (military personnel) to a unit on a temporary basis. **6.** To take or seize (property) by court order: *The bank attached his salary.* **7.** To go with; fasten itself: *the present stigma that attaches to their political views.*

at•ta•ché |ăt′ə shā′| *n.* A person assigned to the staff of a diplomatic mission to serve in some particular capacity: *a cultural attaché.*

attaché case. A briefcase resembling a small suitcase, with hinges and flat sides.

at•tach•ment |ə tăch′mənt| *n.* **1.** The act of attaching or condition of being attached. **2.** Something that attaches as a supplementary part; an accessory: *The vacuum cleaner has several attachments.* **3.** A bond of affection or loyalty: *a strong attachment to a friend.*

at•tack |ə tăk′| *v.* **1. a.** To set upon with violent force: *Even large animals were usually afraid to attack a buffalo herd. Germany attacked the Soviet Union in 1941.* **b.** To launch an assault: *The troops attacked at dawn.* **2.** To criticize strongly or in a hostile manner: *The candidates attacked each other in the debate.* **3.** To affect harmfully; afflict: *Flu attacked thousands of people.* **4.** To start work on with purpose and vigor: *The government attacked the farm surplus problem with federal funds.* —*n.* **1.** The act of attacking; an assault. **2.** An occurrence or onset of a disease, especially when sudden: *a heart attack.* **3.** The manner in which a musical tone, phrase, or passage is begun: *a hard, cutting attack.* —**at•tack′er** *n.*

ă pat/ā pay/â care/ä father/ĕ pet/ ē be/ĭ pit/ī pie/î fierce/ŏ pot/ ō go/ô paw, for/oi oil/ŏŏ book/ ōō boot/ou out/ŭ cut/û fur/ *th* the/th thin/hw which/zh vision/ ə ago, item, pencil, atom, circus

at•tain |ə tān′| *v.* **1.** To gain, accomplish, or achieve by effort: *Correct grammar is a magic tool for attaining confidence in writing and speaking.* **2.** To arrive at or reach through time, growth, movement, etc.: *He attained the age of 80.* —**at•tain′a•ble** *adj.*

at•tain•der |ə tān′dər| *n.* In law, the loss of all civil rights by a person who has been sentenced for a serious crime.

at•tain•ment |ə tān′mənt| *n.* **1.** The act of attaining: *Despite its attainment of independence, Cuba remained in a semicolonial situation.* **2.** Often **attainments.** Something attained; an acquirement, as of a skill, ability, etc.: *a man well-known for his scientific attainments.*

at•taint |ə tānt′| *v.* In law, to condemn by sentence of attainder.

at•tar |ăt′ər| *n.* A fragrant oil obtained from the petals of flowers, especially roses, and used in making perfume.

at•tempt |ə tĕmpt′| *v.* To make an effort; try: *They will fight if anyone attempts to steal their cargo.* —*n.* **1.** An effort or try: *the first of many attempts to win back the Holy Land.* **2.** An attack; assault: *an attempt on the king's life.* —**at•tempt′a•ble** *adj.*

at•tend |ə tĕnd′| *v.* **1.** To be present at; go to: *Some pupils attend school in the morning only.* **2.** To follow as a result or accompany as a circumstance: *an undertaking attended by many risks. Bad luck attended the team.* **3.** To wait upon or be in waiting; serve: *two servants attending him; many courtiers attending upon the king.* **4.** To take care of: *nurses attending the victims of the fire.* **5.** To apply oneself; give care and thought: *attend to one's business. Please attend to the matter at hand.* **6.** To pay attention; heed: *If there are any rules, nobody attends to them.*

at•ten•dance |ə tĕn′dəns| *n.* **1. a.** The act or practice of being present: *His attendance at school is regular.* **b.** The act or state of waiting upon someone or something, as at a hospital: *a physician in attendance; three ladies in attendance upon the duchess.* **2.** The persons or number of persons present: *an attendance of 50,000 at the football game.*

at•ten•dant |ə tĕn′dənt| *n.* A person who attends or waits on another: *one of the queen's attendants; a parking-lot attendant.* —*adj.* Accompanying or consequent: *attendant circumstances; the sun and its own attendant family of faithfully circling planets.*

at•ten•tion |ə tĕn′shən| *n.* **1.** Concentration of the mental powers upon something or someone: *Read the article carefully and pay attention to the details about forests. The speaker held the listeners' attention for more than an hour.* **2.** Observant consideration; notice: *Your suggestion has come to our attention.* **3. attentions.** Acts of courtesy or consideration, especially in trying to win a person's love: *The girl seemed to return his attentions.* **4.** The posture taken by a soldier, with the body erect, eyes to the front, arms at the sides, and heels together. Often used as a command.

at•ten•tive |ə tĕn′tĭv| *adj.* **1.** Giving attention to something; alert: *He was attentive during class.* **2.** Considerate; thoughtful: *an attentive husband.* —**at•ten′tive•ly** *adv.* —**at•ten′tive•ness** *n.*

at•ten•u•ate |ə tĕn′yōō āt′| *v.* **at•ten•u•at•ed, at•ten•u•at•ing.** **1.** To make or become slender. **2.** To reduce in strength, force, power, etc.; weaken. —**at•ten′u•a′tion** *n.*

at•test |ə tĕst′| *v.* **1.** To declare or state to be true, correct, or genuine, especially by signing one's name as a witness: *attest a will.* **2.** To give evidence or proof of; prove: *Their rounded shapes attest the great age of the mountains.* **3.** To bear witness: *The second pyramid of Giza attests to the mathematical skill of Egyptian engineers.*

at•test•ed |ə tĕs′tĭd| *adj.* Recorded in written form: *The word "chestnut," meaning "an old or stale story or joke," is first attested in 1883.*

at•tic |ăt′ĭk| *n.* The space in a house just under the roof; a garret. [SEE NOTE]

at•tire |ə tīr′| *v.* **at•tired, at•tir•ing.** To dress, especially in fine or formal clothing: *an emperor attired in ceremonial robes.* —*n.* Clothing, costume, or apparel: *white tennis attire.*

at•ti•tude |ăt′ĭ to͞od′| *or* |-tyo͞od′| *n.* **1.** A state of mind with regard to someone or something; a point of view: *What is the speaker's attitude toward the kind of life he is describing?* **2.** A position of the body indicative of a mood or condition: *The boy was sprawled on the couch in a relaxed attitude.* **3.** The position of a vehicle, such as an automobile, aircraft, or spacecraft, in relation to its direction of motion or some other reference line.

at•tor•ney |ə tûr′nē| *n., pl.* **at•tor•neys.** A person, especially a lawyer, legally appointed to act as agent for another.

attorney at law. A lawyer.

attorney general *pl.* **attorneys general.** The chief law officer of a state or of the United States.

at•tract |ə trăkt′| *v.* To draw or direct to oneself or itself by some quality or action: *A magnet attracts nails. Their beaches attract many tourists.*

at•trac•tion |ə trăk′shən| *n.* **1.** The act or power of attracting: *the attraction of a magnet.* **2.** Something that attracts: *The Sphinx and the Pyramids are some of Egypt's greatest attractions.*

at•trac•tive |ə trăk′tĭv| *adj.* **1.** Capable of attracting: *the attractive force of magnetism.* **2.** Pleasing to the eye or mind; appealing: *an attractive girl; an attractive offer.* —**at•trac′tive•ly** *adv.* —**at•trac′tive•ness** *n.*

at•trib•ute |ə trĭb′yo͞ot| *v.* **at•trib•ut•ed, at•trib•ut•ing.** To regard or consider as belonging to or resulting from someone or something; ascribe: *They were naive in attributing the powers of the magician to his disguise. Air pollution has been partly attributed to cars.* —*n.* |ăt′rə byo͞ot′|. A quality or characteristic belonging to a person or thing; a distinctive feature: *Jim's attributes are intelligence and honesty.* —**at•trib′ut•a•ble** *adj.* —**at′tri•bu′tion** |ăt′rə byo͞o′shən| *n.*

at•tri•tion |ə trĭsh′ən| *n.* **1.** A gradual loss of number or strength due to constant stress: *a war of attrition.* **2.** A wearing away or rubbing down by friction. **3.** A gradual, natural reduction in membership or personnel, as through retirement, resignation, or death.

at•tune |ə to͞on′| *or* |ə tyo͞on′| *v.* **at•tuned, at•tun•ing.** To bring into harmony; adjust: *a person attuned to the times.*

atty. attorney.

a•typ•i•cal |ā tĭp′ĭ kəl| *adj.* Not typical; abnormal: *atypical behavior.* —**a•typ′i•cal•ly** *adv.*

au•burn |ô′bərn| *n.* A reddish brown. —*adj.* Reddish brown: *auburn hair.*

Auck•land |ôk′lənd|. A city and seaport of New Zealand, on North Island. Population, 742,786.

auc•tion |ôk′shən| *n.* A public sale in which goods or property is sold to the highest bidder. —***modifier:*** *an auction block; auction rooms.* —*v.* To sell at an auction: *auction a house; auction off a diamond ring.*

auc•tion•eer |ôk′shə nîr′| *n.* A person who conducts an auction.

au•da•cious |ô dā′shəs| *adj.* **1.** Fearlessly daring: *an audacious explorer.* **2.** Arrogant; impudent. —**au•da′cious•ly** *adv.*

au•dac•i•ty |ô dăs′ĭ tē| *n., pl.* **au•dac•i•ties. 1.** Courage and resolution; boldness: *The audacity of a few navigators led to the discovery of the New World.* **2.** Insolence; impudence.

au•di•ble |ô′də bəl| *adj.* Capable of being heard: *an audible whisper.* —**au′di•bil′i•ty, au′di•ble•ness** *n.* —**au′di•bly** *adv.* [SEE NOTE]

au•di•ence |ô′dē əns| *n.* **1.** The people gathered to see and hear a play, movie, concert, etc. **2.** The readers, hearers, or viewers reached by a book, radio broadcast, or television program. **3.** A formal hearing or conference: *an audience with the pope.*

au•di•o |ô′dē ō′| *adj.* **1.** Of or having to do with sound or hearing. **2.** Of or for reproduction or broadcasting of sound. —*n.* Sound or an electrical signal that corresponds to sound.

audio frequency. A wave frequency between 20 hertz and 20,000 hertz. [SEE NOTE]

au•di•om•e•ter |ô′dē ŏm′ĭ tər| *n.* An instrument used to measure how well a person can hear.

au•di•o-vis•u•al |ô′dē ō vĭzh′o͞o əl| *adj.* Of or pertaining to educational materials, such as filmstrips or recordings, that make use of electrical devices to present information in both visible and audible form.

au•di•o•vis•u•als |ô′dē ō vĭzh′o͞o əlz| *n.* *(used with a plural verb).* Educational materials that present information in audible and visible form.

au•dit |ô′dĭt| *n.* An official and thorough examination of financial records or accounts. —*v.* **1.** To examine and verify (financial records or accounts). **2.** To attend (a college course) without receiving academic credit.

au•di•tion |ô dĭsh′ən| *n.* A test or trial performance, as of a musician who is applying for employment. —*v.* **1.** To perform in an audition: *He auditioned for a part in the play.* **2.** To give (a performer) an audition.

au•di•tor |ô′dĭ tər| *n.* **1.** A hearer or listener: *the auditors of a concert.* **2.** A person who examines financial records or accounts in order to check their accuracy. **3.** A person who audits courses.

au•di•to•ri•um |ô′dĭ tôr′ē əm| *or* |-tōr′-| *n., pl.* **au•di•to•ri•ums** or **au•di•to•ri•a** |ô′dĭ tôr′ē ə| *or* |-tōr′-|. **1.** A large room or building designed for a big audience. **2.** The part of a church or theater in which the audience is seated.

au•di•to•ry |ô′dĭ tôr′ē| *or* |-tōr′ē| *adj.* Of hearing or the organs of hearing.

auditory nerve. The nerve that carries impulses associated with hearing and balance from the inner ear to the brain.

Aug. August.

au•ger |ô′gər| *n.* A tool for boring holes. ¶ *These sound alike* **auger, augur.**

aught |ôt| *pron. Archaic.* Anything at all. Used

attic
An **attic** *was originally a small decorative gable at the top and front of a house. It was so called because it was often designed in the* Attic *style of architecture, which comes from* Attica, *the region in Greece of which Athens was the capital.*

audible
All the words from **audible** *to* **auditory** *come from the Latin verb* audīre, *"to hear."* **Audacious** *comes from the very similar (but unrelated) Latin verb* audēre, *"to dare."*

audio frequency
These frequencies are called **audio frequencies** *because sound waves whose frequencies lie in this range are the only ones that can be heard by normal human ears.*

august/August
The adjective **august** *comes from Latin* augustus, *which originally meant "consecrated," or "blessed with signs of divine favor." When Octavian Caesar took supreme power at Rome in 27* B.C., *he adopted the title* Augustus *to indicate that he was divinely set apart from other men. The title was used by all the later emperors, and the word came to mean "royal, majestic." Also in honor of Augustus, the eighth month was renamed* mensis Augustus, *from which we have* **August.**

especially in phrases like *for aught I care ("for all I care"), for aught I know* ("for all I know"), etc. *—adv.* At all. ¶*These sound alike* **aught, ought.**

aug•ment |ôg **mĕnt'**| *v.* To make larger; increase: *The library has been augmented by 5,000 new books.* **—aug'men•ta'tion** *n.*

au gra•tin |ō grät'n| *or* |grăt'n|. Topped with bread crumbs and often grated cheese and browned in an oven.

au•gur |**ô'**gər| *v.* To give promise of: *Early returns augured victory for him. —n.* A religious official of ancient Rome who foretold events by omens from the entrails of birds, thunder, etc. ¶*These sound alike* **augur, auger.**

***Idiom.* augur well** (or **ill**). To indicate or promise a favorable or unfavorable outcome: *A cloudless sky augurs well for the picnic.*

au•gu•ry |**ô'**gyə rē| *n., pl.* **au•gu•ries. 1.** The art or practice of auguring. **2.** A sign or omen.

au•gust |ô **gŭst'**| *adj.* Inspiring awe or reverence; majestic: *the august bearing of the king.* **—au•gust'ly** *adv.* [SEE NOTE]

Au•gust |**ô'** gəst| *n.* The eighth month of the year, after July and before September. It has 31 days. ***—modifier:*** *an August heat wave; an August vacation.* [SEE NOTE]

Au•gus•ta |ô **gŭs'**tə|. The capital of Maine. Population, 21,819.

Au•gus•tine |**ô'**gə stēn'| *or* |ô **gŭs'**tĭn|, **Saint.** A.D. 354–430. Early Christian church father and philosopher.

Au•gus•tus[1] |ô **gŭs'**təs| *n.* A title of the Roman emperors after the reign of Augustus.

Au•gus•tus[2] |ô **gŭs'**təs|. Original name, Gaius Octavius. Known as Octavian. 63 B.C.–A.D. 14. Founder of the imperial Roman government.

auk |ôk| *n.* Any of several black and white northern sea birds with a chunky body and short wings. [SEE PICTURE]

auld |ôld| *adj. Scottish.* Old.

auld lang syne |**ôld'** lăng **zīn'**| *or* |**sīn'**|. The good old days long past.

aunt |ănt| *or* |änt| *n.* **1.** The sister of one's father or mother. **2.** The wife of one's uncle. ¶*These sound alike* **aunt, ant.**

au•ra |**ôr'**ə| *n.* A distinctive air or quality that characterizes a person or thing: *an aura of mystery about him.*

au•ral |**ôr'**əl| *adj.* Of or received by the ear: *aural stimulation.* ¶*These sound alike* **aural, oral.**

au•re•ole |**ôr'**ē ōl'| *n.* **1.** In art, a circle of light around the head of a sacred figure. **2.** A glow that surrounds a luminous celestial object, such as the sun, especially when it is seen through a fog or haze.

Au•re•o•my•cin |ôr'ē ō **mī'**sĭn| *n.* A trademark for a powerful antibiotic drug obtained from soil bacteria.

au re•voir |ō' rə **vwär'**|. *French.* Until we meet again; good-by.

au•ri•cle |**ôr'**ĭ kəl| *n.* **1.** The external part of the ear. **2.** A chamber of the heart that receives blood from a vein; an atrium. ¶*These sound alike* **auricle, oracle.**

au•ric•u•lar |ô **rĭk'**yə lər| *adj.* **1.** Of hearing or the ears. **2.** Of an auricle of the heart.

au•rochs |**ôr'**ŏks'| *n., pl.* **au•rochs.** An extinct horned animal of the Old World, believed to be the ancestor of domestic cattle.

au•ro•ra |ô **rôr'**ə| *or* |ô **rōr'**ə| *or* |ə **rôr'**ə| *or* |ə **rōr'**ə| *n.* A brilliant display of flashing and moving lights visible in the night sky, chiefly in the polar regions. It is thought to result from electrically charged particles, especially those from the sun, that are drawn into the atmosphere by the earth's magnetic field.

aurora aus•tra•lis |ô **strā'**lĭs|. The aurora of the Southern Hemisphere; the southern lights.

aurora bo•re•al•is |bôr'ē **ăl'**ĭs| *or* |bōr'-|. The aurora of the Northern Hemisphere; the northern lights.

aus•pic•es |**ô'**spĭ sĭz| *or* |-sēz'| *pl.n.* Protection and support; patronage: *The contest was run under the auspices of our organization.*

aus•pi•cious |ô **spĭsh'** əs| *adj.* Showing signs of a successful outcome or result; favorable: *an auspicious beginning for a business venture.* **—aus•pi'cious•ly** *adv.* **—aus•pi'cious•ness** *n.*

aus•tere |ô **stîr'**| *adj.* **1.** Having a stern personality or appearance; somber: *an unsmiling, austere man.* **2.** Severely simple, as in living habits. **3.** Harsh or barren: *an austere land to live in.* **4.** Without decoration; plain: *austere living quarters.* **—aus•tere'ly** *adv.*

aus•ter•i•ty |ô **stĕr'**ĭ tē| *n., pl.* **aus•ter•i•ties. 1.** The condition of being austere. **2.** Lack of luxury; extreme restraint in spending: *wartime austerity.* ***—modifier:*** *austerity financial measures.*

Aus•tin |**ô'**stən|. The capital of Texas. Population, 345,496.

Aus•tra•lia |ô **strāl'**yə|. **1.** A continent lying southeast of Asia between the Pacific and Indian oceans. **2.** A country comprising this continent and the nearby island of Tasmania. Population, 13,417,000. Capital, Canberra.

Aus•tra•lian |ô **strāl'**yən| *n.* **1.** A native or citizen of Australia. **2.** An aborigine of Australia. *—adj.* Of Australia or the Australians.

Aus•tri•a |**ô'**strē ə|. A country in central Europe. Population, 7,500,000. Capital, Vienna. **—Aus'tri•an** *adj. & n.*

au•then•tic |ô **thĕn'**tĭk| *adj.* **1.** Worthy of belief; true; credible: *In the plot characters were authentic, situations realistic.* **2.** Not counterfeit or copied; genuine: *an authentic Gutenberg Bible.*

au•then•ti•cate |ô **thĕn'**tĭ kāt'| *v.* **au•then•ti•cat•ed, au•then•ti•cat•ing. 1.** To establish as being true; prove: *Can you authenticate this story?* **2.** To establish (a painting, antique, etc.) as being genuine. **—au•then'ti•cat'ed** *adj.: an authenticated painting.* **—au•then'ti•ca'tion** *n.*

au•then•tic•i•ty |ô'thĕn **tĭs'**ĭ tē| *n.* The condition or quality of being authentic.

au•thor |**ô'**thər| *n.* **1.** A person who writes a book, story, article, etc. **2.** The beginner or originator of something: *the author of an idea. —v.* To be the author of: *He has authored several books.*

au•thor•i•tar•i•an |ə thôr'ĭ **târ'**ē ən| *or* |ə thŏr'-| *adj.* Characterized by or favoring absolute obedience to authority. *—n.* A person who believes in or practices authoritarian behavior.

au•thor•i•ta•tive |ə **thôr'**ĭ tā'tĭv| *or* |ə **thŏr'**-| *adj.* **1.** Having or arising from proper authority; official: *the general's authoritative manner.* **2.** Having or showing expert knowledge: *authoritative sources.* **—au•thor'i•ta'tive•ly** *adv.* **—au•thor'i•ta'tive•ness** *n.*

auk
The **great auk,** which was unable to fly, was once common on northern Atlantic coasts, but has been extinct for over 100 years.

ă pat/ā pay/â care/ä father/ĕ pet/ ē be/ĭ pit/ī pie/î fierce/ŏ pot/ ō go/ô paw, for/oi oil/ŏŏ book/ ōō boot/ou out/ŭ cut/û fur/ *th* the/th thin/hw which/zh vision/ ə ago, item, pencil, atom, circus

au•thor•i•ty |ə thôr′ĭ tē| *or* |ə thŏr′-| *n. pl.* **au•thor•i•ties. 1. a.** The right and power to command, determine, enforce laws, etc.: *The principal had the authority to close the school.* **b.** A person or organization having this right and power: *school authorities; the Transit Authority.* **2.** An accepted source of expert information, as a book or person: *an authority on history.* **3.** Power to influence or affect resulting from knowledge or experience: *write with authority.*

au•thor•i•za•tion |ô′thər ĭ zā′shən| *n.* **1.** The act of authorizing. **2.** Permission or right granted by someone with authority.

au•thor•ize |ô′thə rīz′| *v.* **au•thor•ized, au•thor•iz•ing. 1.** To grant authority or power to: *The President authorized him to form a commission.* **2.** To approve or give permission for: *authorize a highway project.*

au•thor•ship |ô′thər shĭp′| *n.* The origin, as of a book: *a book of unknown authorship.*

au•to |ô′tō| *n., pl.* **au•tos.** *Informal.* An automobile.

auto–[1]. A word element meaning "self" or "self-caused": **autobiography; autoharp.**

auto–[2]. A word element meaning "self-propelling": **autogiro.**

au•to•bi•o•graph•i•cal |ô′tō bī′ə grăf′ĭ kəl| or **au•to•bi•o•graph•ic** |ô′tō bī′ə grăf′ĭk| *adj.* Of or based on a person's own life. —**au′to•bi′o•graph′i•cal•ly** *adv.*

au•to•bi•og•ra•phy |ô′tō bī ŏg′rə fē or |-bē-| *n., pl.* **au•to•bi•og•ra•phies.** The story of a person's life written by himself.

au•toc•ra•cy |ô tŏk′rə sē| *n., pl.* **au•toc•ra•cies. 1.** Government by a person having absolute power. **2.** A country having this form of government.

au•to•crat |ô′tə krăt′| *n.* A ruler having absolute power.

au•to•crat•ic |ô′tə krăt′ĭk| *adj.* **1.** Of the nature of an autocracy: *an autocratic government.* **2.** Like an autocrat; arrogant: *He has a very autocratic manner.* —**au′to•crat′i•cal•ly** *adv.*

au•to•gi•ro |ô′tō jī′rō| *n., pl.* **au•to•gi•ros.** An aircraft that is somewhat like a helicopter except that the overhead rotor that supports it is driven by wind rather than by an engine. The aircraft is powered by a propeller, and while it can take off and land at steep angles, it must maintain forward motion to stay aloft.

au•to•graph |ô′tə grăf′| *or* |-gräf′| *n.* **1.** A signature, usually of a famous person, that is saved by an admirer or collector. **2.** A manuscript in the author's own handwriting. —***modifier:*** *an autograph collection.* —*v.* To write one's name or signature on. [SEE PICTURE]

au•to•gy•ro |ô′tō jī′rō| *n., pl.* **au•to•gy•ros.** A form of the word **autogiro.**

au•to•harp |ô′tō härp′| *n.* A musical instrument that is somewhat like a zither and that is equipped with a device that damps all of its strings except those that form a desired chord.

au•to•mat |ô′tə măt′| *n.* A restaurant in which the customers obtain food from coin-operated machines.

au•tom•a•ta |ô tŏm′ə tə| *n.* A plural of **automaton.**

au•to•mate |ô′tə māt′| *v.* **au•to•mat•ed, au•to•mat•ing. 1.** To enable (a process, factory, machine, etc.) to operate with little or no human supervision; make automatic. **2.** To make use of automatic machinery and processes: *Costs forced the factory to automate.*

au•to•mat•ic |ô′tə măt′ĭk| *adj.* **1.** Capable of operating correctly without the control of a human being; self-operating or self-regulating: *an automatic elevator; an automatic process.* **2.** Done or produced by the body without conscious control or awareness: *The heartbeat is automatic.* **3.** Capable of firing continuously until out of ammunition: *an automatic rifle.* —*n.* A device or machine, especially a firearm, that is wholly or partially automatic.

au•to•ma•tion |ô′tə mā′shən| *n.* **1.** The automatic operation or control of a process, machine, or system. **2.** The engineering techniques and equipment needed to accomplish this.

au•tom•a•ton |ô tŏm′ə tŏn′| *or* |-tən| *n., pl.* **au•tom•a•tons** or **au•tom•a•ta** |ô tŏm′ə tə|. An automatic machine, especially a robot.

au•to•mo•bile |ô′tə mə bēl′| *or* |-mō′bēl′| *or* |ô′tə-mə bēl′| *n.* A land vehicle equipped to carry a driver and several passengers, generally moving on four wheels and propelled by an engine that burns gasoline. —***modifier:*** *an automobile engine; an automobile accident.*

au•to•mo•tive |ô′tə mō′tĭv| *or* |ô′tə mō′tĭv| *adj.* **1.** Capable of propelling itself. **2.** Of automobiles, trucks, buses, or other land vehicles that can propel themselves.

au•to•nom•ic |ô′tə nŏm′ĭk| *adj.* Of the autonomic nervous system.

autonomic nervous system. The part of the nervous system of a vertebrate that regulates involuntary action, as of the intestines, heart, or glands.

au•ton•o•mous |ô tŏn′ə məs| *adj.* Self-governing; independent: *an autonomous organization; autonomous regions.* —**au•ton′o•mous•ly** *adv.*

au•ton•o•my |ô tŏn′ə mē| *n.* Self-government.

au•top•sy |ô′tŏp′sē| *or* |ô′təp-| *n., pl.* **au•top•sies.** A medical examination of a dead human body, especially to determine the cause of death.

au•tumn |ô′təm| *n.* The season of the year between summer and winter, lasting from the autumnal equinox in late September to the winter solstice in late December. —***modifier:*** *autumn colors.* [SEE NOTE]

au•tum•nal |ô tŭm′nəl| *adj.* Of autumn.

autumnal equinox. The equinox, occurring on about September 22 or 23, in which the sun is moving from north to south, marking the beginning of autumn in the Northern Hemisphere.

aux•il•ia•ry |ôg zĭl′yə rē| *or* |-zĭl′ə-| *adj.* **1.** Giving assistance or support: *Conflict is auxiliary to drama.* **2.** Held in or used as a reserve: *an auxiliary engine.* —*n., pl.* **aux•il•ia•ries. 1.** One that helps; an assistant. **2.** An **auxiliary verb. 3.** An organization that is subsidiary to a larger one: *a women's auxiliary.* **4. auxiliaries.** Foreign troops serving a country in war.

auxiliary verb. A verb that comes first in a verb phrase and helps form the tense, mood, or voice of the main verb. *Have, may, can, must,* and *will* are some auxiliary verbs.

aux•in |ôk′sĭn| *n.* Any of various hormones or similar synthetic substances that affect the growth of plants.

autograph
Daniel Boone
Thomas Jefferson
Napoleon

autumn/fall
The original Old English word for the season after summer was **harvest.** *In the sixteenth century two new expressions began to be used:* **autumn,** *borrowed from Latin* autumnus, *and "fall of the leaf," later shortened to* **fall. Autumn** *became the standard British term, and* **fall** *became standard in American English.*

a•vail |ə vāl'| *v.* To be of use or advantage to: *Nothing can avail him now.* —*n.* Use, benefit, or advantage: *His efforts were to no avail.*

Idiom. **avail (oneself) of.** To make use of; take advantage of.

a•vail•a•ble |ə vā'lə bəl| *adj.* **1.** Capable of being obtained: *Tickets are available at the box office.* **2.** Capable of being reached; at hand and ready to serve: *All available volunteers were pressed into service.* —**a•vail'a•bil'i•ty** *n.*

av•a•lanche |ăv'ə lănch'| *or* |-länch'| *n.* A large mass of material such as snow, ice, or earth that falls or slides down the side of a mountain. [SEE NOTE]

avalanche
Avalanche, *appropriately enough, is one of the few English words that comes from Switzerland. In Swiss French it is* avalantse, *and in the dialect of Savoy (the French Alps) it is* lavantse.

Av•a•lon |ăv'ə lŏn'|. In medieval legend, an island paradise in the western seas where King Arthur and other heroes went at death.

a•vant•garde |ä'vänt gärd'| *n.* The people who are the leaders in promoting new or unconventional styles, especially in the arts. —*adj.* Exhibiting new or advanced ideas; ultramodern: *an avant-garde magazine.*

av•a•rice |ăv'ər ĭs| *n.* Extreme fondness for hoarding money.

av•a•ri•cious |ăv'ə rĭsh'əs| *adj.* Extremely fond of getting money and not spending it; miserly.

a•vast |ə văst'| *or* |ə väst'| *interj.* Hold on! Stop! Used as a command aboard ship.

ave., Ave. avenue.

A•ve Ma•ri•a |ä'vā mə rē'ə|. A Latin prayer to the Virgin Mary. [SEE NOTE]

Ave Maria
Ave Maria *is Latin for "Hail, Mary!" The prayer is based on Gabriel's greeting to Mary, described in Luke 1:28. It came into use as a prayer in the late Middle Ages.*

a•venge |ə vĕnj'| *v.* **a•venged, a•veng•ing.** To take revenge for: *taking up arms to avenge an insult.* —**a•veng'er** *n.*

av•e•nue |ăv'ə no͞o'| *or* |-nyo͞o'| *n.* **1.** A wide street or thoroughfare. **2.** A means of reaching or achieving something: *We must seek new avenues of trade.*

a•ver |ə vûr'| *v.* **a•verred, a•ver•ring.** To state positively and firmly; assert; affirm: *The defendant continued to aver his innocence.*

av•er•age |ăv'ər ĭj| *or* |ăv'rĭj| *n.* A number, especially the arithmetic mean, that is derived from and considered typical or representative of a set of numbers. —*v.* **av•er•aged, av•er•ag•ing. 1.** To compute the average of (a set of numbers). **2.** To have or attain as an average: *The temperature averages 75 degrees.* —*adj.* **1.** Computed or determined as an average: *an average velocity. Europe has an average population density of 155 persons per square mile.* **2.** Numerically typical: *Before Henry Ford's time, the average factory worker received less than $2 a day.* **3.** Normal or ordinary: *an average American.* **4.** Not exceptional; undistinguished: *He is just an average student.*

Idiom. **on the average.** Using the average as a basis of judgment.

a•verse |ə vûrs'| *adj.* Opposed; reluctant: *Cats are usually extremely averse to getting wet.*

a•ver•sion |ə vûr'zhən| *or* |-shən| *n.* A strong dislike: *He has an aversion to work.*

a•vert |ə vûrt'| *v.* **1.** To turn away or aside: *avert one's eyes.* **2.** To keep from happening; prevent: *The successful handling of the crisis helped us avert an international incident.*

a•vi•an |ā'vē ən| *adj.* Of or relating to birds.

a•vi•ar•y |ā'vē ĕr'ē| *n., pl.* **a•vi•ar•ies.** A large cage or enclosure for birds, as in a zoo.

a•vi•a•tion |ā'vē ā'shən| *or* |ăv'ē-| *n.* The operation of aircraft. —***modifier:*** *an aviation cadet.*

a•vi•a•tor |ā'vē ā'tər| *or* |ăv'ē-| *n.* A person who flies or is capable of flying aircraft; a pilot.

a•vi•a•trix |ā'vē ā'trĭks| *or* |ăv'ē-| *n.* A female aviator.

av•id |ăv'ĭd| *adj.* **1.** Eager: *avid for power.* **2.** Ardent; enthusiastic: *an avid reader; an avid hunter.* —**a•vid'i•ty** |ə vĭd'ĭ tē| *n.* —**av'id•ly** *adv.*

a•vi•on•ics |ā'vē ŏn'ĭks| *or* |ăv'ē-| *n.* *(used with a singular verb).* Electronics as it is applied to aircraft and spacecraft.

av•o•ca•do |ăv'ə kä'dō| *or* |ä'və-| *n. pl.* **av•o•ca•dos. 1.** A tropical American fruit with leathery green or blackish skin and bland-tasting yellow-green pulp. **2.** A tree that bears such fruit. —***modifier:*** *an avocado salad.*

av•o•ca•tion |ăv'ə kā'shən| *n.* An activity engaged in, usually for pleasure, in addition to one's regular work.

a•void |ə void'| *v.* **1.** To keep away from; stay clear of; shun: *avoid crowds; avoid rich foods.* **2.** To evade, dodge: *quick enough to avoid the blow.* **3.** To prevent; keep from happening: *a clumsy attempt to avoid getting wet.* **4.** To refrain from: *Burma has avoided taking sides in the cold war.* —**a•void'a•ble** *adj.* —**a•void'ance** *n.*

av•oir•du•pois weight |ăv'ər də poiz'|. A system of weighing in which a pound, equal to 453.59 grams, is divided into 16 equal parts called ounces.

a•vow |ə vou'| *v.* To acknowledge openly; admit freely: *avow one's guilt.*

a•vow•al |ə vou'əl| *n.* An open admission or acknowledgment.

a•vowed |ə voud'| *adj.* Openly acknowledged: *Even dictators had the avowed purpose of making men free.* —**a•vow'ed•ly** |ə vou'ĭd lē| *adv.*

aw |ô| *interj.* A word used to express doubt, disgust, etc. ¶ *These sound alike* **aw, awe.**

a•wait |ə wāt'| *v.* **1.** To wait for: *Everyone awaited news of his loved ones.* **2.** To be in store for: *No one knows what awaits him in life.*

a•wake |ə wāk'| *v.* **a•woke** |ə wōk'|, **a•waked, a•wak•ing. 1.** To rouse or emerge from sleep; wake up: *The alarm clock awoke me at seven. He awoke at dawn.* **2.** To become aware of: *Americans are awaking to the importance of drug control.* **3.** To produce (a feeling, memory, etc.): *Her beauty awoke a feeling of love in him.* —*adj.* Not asleep: *He was awake all night.*

a•wak•en |ə wā'kən| *v.* **1.** To wake up: *The clatter of a passing truck awakened me. I awakened early because of the noise.* **2.** To stir up or produce (a feeling, thoughts, etc.): *Her feigned sweetness awakened a strong suspicion in his mind.*

a•wak•en•ing |ə wā'kə nĭng| *n.* **1.** The act of waking up. **2.** The act or process of rousing from inactivity or indifference; a stirring up: *a great awakening of interest in ecology.*

a•ward |ə wôrd'| *v.* **1.** To give or bestow (a prize, medal, etc.) for outstanding performance or quality: *The committee awarded him the Pulitzer Prize for Drama.* **2.** To give or grant by legal or governmental decision: *award damages to a plaintiff; award a contract to the lowest bidder.* —*n.* **1.** Something, such as a prize, medal, etc., awarded for outstanding performance or quality. **2.** Something judged as due by legal decision.

ă pat/ā pay/â care/ä father/ĕ pet/ ē be/ĭ pit/ī pie/î fierce/ŏ pot/ ō go/ô paw, for/oi oil/o͝o book/ o͞o boot/ou out/ŭ cut/û fur/ *th* the/th thin/hw which/zh vision/ ə ago, item, pencil, atom, circus

a•ware |ə wâr′| *adj.* Being mindful or conscious of; knowing; cognizant: *be aware of one's shortcomings.* —**a•ware′ness** *n.*

a•way |ə wā′| *adv.* **1.** At or to a distance: *a house two miles away.* **2.** In or to a different place or direction: *Don't look away now.* **3.** From one's presence or possession: *Take these things away. Her old bicycle was given away by the janitor.* **4.** Out of existence: *fading away.* **5.** Continuously: *working away.* **6.** Immediately: *Fire away!* —*adj.* **1.** Absent: *He's away from home.* **2.** At a distance: *He's miles away.* **3.** Played on the opposing team's home grounds: *home games and away games.* **4.** In baseball, out: *Count is three and two with two away in the ninth.* ¶*These sound alike* **away, aweigh.**

Idiom. **do** (or **make**) **away with. 1.** To get rid of: *doing away with outmoded laws.* **2.** To murder.

awe |ô| *n.* A feeling of wonder, fear, and respect inspired by something mighty or majestic: *gazing in awe at the mountains.* —*v.* **awed, aw•ing.** To fill with awe: *The size of the plane awed everyone.* ¶*These sound alike* **awe, aw.**

a•weigh |ə wā′| *adj.* Just clear of the bottom, as the anchor of a ship at the moment of sailing. ¶*These sound alike* **aweigh, away.**

awe•some |ô′səm| *adj.* Inspiring awe: *awesome power; an awesome sight.* —**awe′some•ly** *adv.* —**awe′some•ness** *n.*

aw•ful |ô′fəl| *adj.* **1.** Inspiring awe or fear; fearsome: *the awful stillness before the tornado.* **2.** *Informal.* Very bad or unpleasant; horrible: *awful weather; an awful book.* **3.** *Informal.* Great; considerable: *an awful lot of homework.* ¶*These sound alike* **awful, offal.**

aw•ful•ly |ô′fə lē| *or* |ô′flē| *adv.* **1.** In a manner that inspires awe; terribly. **2.** *Informal.* Very: *He did seem awfully confused.* **3.** *Informal.* Very badly: *She behaved awfully.* **4.** *Informal.* Very much. Used as an intensive: *Thanks awfully.*

a•while |ə **hwīl′**| *or* |ə **wīl′**| *adv.* For a short time: *We waited awhile.* [SEE NOTE]

awk•ward |ôk′wərd| *adj.* **1.** Not moving gracefully; clumsy: *an awkward dancer.* **2.** Unnatural or clumsy, as in speech, behavior, etc.: *Jill became shy and awkward whenever Bob was around.* **3.** Causing embarrassment; trying: *an awkward silence.* **4.** Difficult to handle or manage; cumbersome: *an awkward bundle to carry.* —**awk′ward•ly** *adv.* —**awk′ward•ness** *n.*

awl |ôl| *n.* A pointed tool for making holes, as in wood or leather. ¶*These sound alike* **awl, all.** [SEE PICTURE]

awn•ing |ô′nĭng| *n.* A protective rooflike canvas screen set up over a window, door, etc.

a•woke |ə wōk′|. Past tense of **awake.**

A.W.O.L., a.w.o.l., AWOL, awol |ā′wôl′|. In the armed forces, absent (or absence) without leave.

a•wry |ə **rī′**| *adv.* **1.** Turned or twisted to one side or out of shape; askew: *The knife weighted his pocket and stretched his jacket awry.* **2.** Wrong; amiss: *Our plans went awry.* —*adj.* To one side; crooked: *His tie is all awry.*

ax or **axe** |ăks| *n., pl.* **ax•es** |ăk′sĭz|. A chopping or cutting tool consisting of a head with a sharp blade, mounted on a long handle.

ax•es. *n.* **1.** |ăk′sēz′|. Plural of **axis. 2.** |ăk′sĭz|. Plural of **ax.**

ax•i•al |ăk′sē əl| *adj.* Of, on, around, or forming an axis.

ax•i•om |ăk′sē əm| *n.* **1.** An established rule, principle, or law. **2.** In mathematics and logic, a statement that is assumed to be true without proof. [SEE NOTE]

ax•i•o•mat•ic |ăk′sē ə **măt′ĭk**| or **ax•i•o•mat•i•cal** |ăk′sē ə **măt′ĭ** kəl| *adj.* Of or like an axiom; self-evident. —**ax′i•o•mat′i•cal•ly** *adv.*

ax•is |ăk′sĭs| *n., pl.* **ax•es** |ăk′sēz′|. **1.** A straight line around which an object or geometric figure rotates or can be imagined to rotate: *The axis of the earth passes through both of its poles.* **2.** A line, ray, or line segment with respect to which a figure or object is symmetrical. **3.** A reference line from which or along which distances or angles are measured in a system of coordinates: *the x-axis.* **4. the Axis.** The alliance of Germany, Italy, Japan, and other nations that opposed the Allies in World War II.

ax•le |ăk′səl| *n.* **1.** A supporting shaft or spindle on which one or more wheels revolve. **2.** An axletree.

ax•le•tree |ăk′səl trē′| *n.* A bar or rod on which the weight of a vehicle rests, having at each end a spindle on which a wheel turns.

ax•o•lotl |ăk′sə lŏt′l| *n.* Any of several salamanders of Mexico and western North America that, unlike most amphibians, keep and continue to breathe with external gills when mature. [SEE PICTURE]

ax•on |ăk′sŏn′| *n.* The core of a nerve fiber that usually carries impulses away from the body of a nerve cell.

ay[1] |ā| *interj.* **1.** Alas; ah. **2.** —**ay me.** *Archaic.* Alas; ah, me.

ay[2] |ā| *adv.* **1.** *Archaic.* Always. **2.** —**for ay.** *Archaic.* Forever. **3.** —**forever and ay.** Forever and ever.

aye, also **ay** |ī| *interj.* **1.** Yes. **2.** —Used to affirm a previous statement and introduce further amplification: *a flying ship, aye, a ship with wings that could sail through the sky.* —*n., pl.* **ayes. 1.** A vote of "yes." **2. the ayes.** Those who vote yes: *The ayes have it; the motion is carried.* ¶*These sound alike* **aye, eye, I.**

Ay•ma•ra |ī′mä **rä′**| *n.* **1.** An Indian people of Bolivia and Peru. **2.** A member of this people. **3.** The language of this people.

Ayr•shire |âr′shîr| *or* |-shər| *n.* One of a breed of brown and white dairy cattle originally raised in Scotland.

a•zal•ea |ə **zāl′**yə| *n.* Any of several shrubs often cultivated for their variously colored flowers.

az•i•muth |ăz′ə məth| *n.* The direction directly toward some particular object, usually measured as an angle from some direction that has been chosen as a reference.

A•zores |ā′zôrz′| *or* |ā′zōrz′| *or* |ə **zôrz′**| *or* |ə **zōrz′**|. A group of Portuguese islands in the North Atlantic. Population, 335,000.

Az•tec |ăz′tĕk′| *n.* **1.** A member of an Indian people of central Mexico, noted for their civilization, destroyed by Cortés in 1519. **2.** The language of this people; Nahuatl.

az•ure |ăzh′ər| *n.* A light to medium blue, like that of the sky on a clear day. —*adj.* Light to medium blue.

awhile

The spelling **awhile** *is often used for* a while, *as in the phrases* after awhile, for awhile, *and* awhile ago. *Although spelling books generally prohibit this form, it is coming into common use. In the materials on which this Dictionary was based, roughly one third of the occurrences of* **awhile** *reflect this trend in spelling, with sentences like* He dived and splashed for awhile.

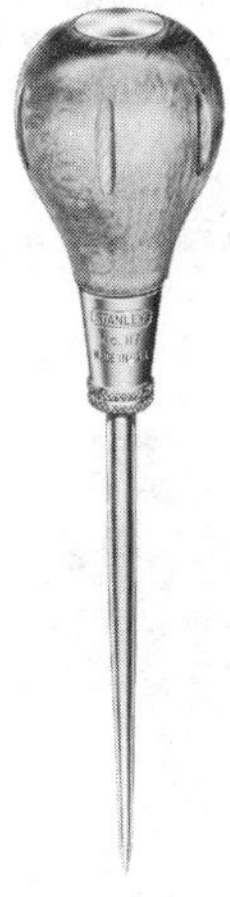

awl

axiom

A familiar idea that is often stated as an **axiom** *in geometry is the following: Any figure can be moved in space with no change in its size or shape.*

axolotl

Bb

1 2 3

The letter **B** *comes originally from the Phoenician letter* bēth *(1), which meant "house." It was borrowed by the Greeks in a changed form as* bēta *(2). This was taken over by the Romans and given the rounded shape (3) that it still has.*

baboon
Mother and baby

back
The prepositional phrases **back of** *and* **in back of** *arose in American English, and are not used in British and other branches of English. Even in American usage, many people still feel that these phrases are informal and prefer to use* **behind** *in formal writing.*

ă pat/ā pay/â care/ä father/ĕ pet/ ē be/ĭ pit/ī pie/î fierce/ŏ pot/ ō go/ô paw, for/oi oil/ŏŏ book/ ōō boot/ou out/ŭ cut/û fur/ *th* the/th thin/hw which/zh vision/ ə ago, item, pencil, atom, circus

b, B |bē| *n., pl.* **b's** or **B's. 1.** The second letter of the English alphabet. **2. B** In music, the seventh tone in the scale of C major. [SEE NOTE]

B The symbol for the element boron.

Ba The symbol for the element barium.

B.A. Bachelor of Arts.

baa |bă| *or* |bä| *n.* The bleating sound made by a sheep. *—v.* **baaed, baa•ing.** To bleat, as a sheep does.

Bab•bitt metal |**băb'**ĭt|. Any of several soft alloys of tin, copper, and antimony used to provide lubrication of moving mechanical parts.

bab•ble |**băb'**əl| *v.* **bab•bled, bab•bling. 1.** To utter indistinct or meaningless words or sounds. **2.** To talk idly or foolishly; chatter. **3.** To make a continuous low murmuring sound, like a brook. *—n.* **1.** Indistinct or meaningless words or sounds: *a babble of voices as the merchants called out their wares.* **2.** Idle or foolish talk; chatter. **3.** A continuous low murmuring sound, as of a brook.

babe |bāb| *n.* A baby; an infant.
Idiom. **babe in the woods.** An innocent or naive person in an unfamiliar or dangerous situation.

Ba•bel |**bā'**bəl| *or* |**băb'**əl| *n.* **1.** In the Bible, the site of a tower that was being built to reach the heavens. God halted its construction by suddenly causing everyone to speak different languages. **2. babel.** A confusion of sounds, voices, or languages.

ba•boon |bă **bōōn'**| *n.* A large African monkey with a long, doglike face. [SEE PICTURE]

ba•bush•ka |bə **bōōsh'**kə| *n.* A woman's head scarf worn tied under the chin.

ba•by |**bā'**bē| *n., pl.* **ba•bies. 1.** A very young child; an infant. **2.** The youngest member of a family. **3.** A person who acts like a baby. *—modifier: a baby bird; my baby sister; baby talk; a baby carriage.* *—v.* **ba•bied, ba•by•ing, ba•bies.** To treat like a baby; coddle.

ba•by•ish |**bā'**bē ĭsh| *adj.* **1.** Like a baby; childlike. **2.** Childish; immature.

Bab•y•lon |**băb'**ə lən| *or* |-lŏn'| *n.* The capital of ancient Babylonia.

Bab•y•lo•ni•a |băb'ə **lō'**nē ə|. A powerful empire of ancient times, located in the area of present-day Iraq. Capital, Babylon.

Bab•y•lo•ni•an |băb'ə **lō'**nē ən| *n.* **1.** A native of Babylonia or Babylon. **2.** The Semitic language of the Babylonians. *—adj.* Of Babylonia, Babylon, the Babylonians, or their language and culture.

ba•by's-breath |**bā'**bēz brĕth'| *n.* A plant with branching clusters of small white flowers.

ba•by-sit |**bā'**bē sĭt'| *v.* **-sat** |-săt'|, **-sit•ting.** To care for a child or children when the parents are not at home.

baby sitter. A person hired to baby-sit.

baby tooth. A **milk tooth.**

bac•ca•lau•re•ate |băk'ə **lôr'**ē ĭt| *n.* **1.** The academic degree held by a bachelor. **2.** An address delivered to a graduating class at commencement. *—modifier: a baccalaureate degree; a baccalaureate sermon.*

Bach |bäKH|, **Johann Sebastian.** 1685–1750. German composer.

bach•e•lor |**băch'**ə lər| *or* |**băch'**lər| *n.* **1.** A man who has not married. **2. a.** A person who has received a college or university degree after completing his undergraduate studies. **b. Bachelor.** The title of a person with this degree: *Bachelor of Arts; Bachelor of Science.*

bach•e•lor's-but•ton |**băch'**ə lərz bŭt'n| *or* |**băch'**lərz-| *n.* The cornflower.

ba•cil•lus |bə **sĭl'**əs| *n., pl.* **ba•cil•li** |bə **sĭl'**ī'|. Any of various rod-shaped bacteria.

back |băk| *n.* **1.** In human beings and other vertebrates, the region of the body that is closest to the spine; the region from the base of the neck to the pelvis. **2.** The spine; backbone. **3.** The rear or reverse side of something. **4.** In football, any of the players in a team's backfield. *—adv.* **1.** To or toward the rear: *Move back, please.* **2.** To or toward a former place, time, or condition: *They went back to their old home.* **3.** In a delayed condition: *The rains set the construction job back many days.* **4.** In reserve or concealment: *He held part of the candy back.* **5.** In return: *If he hits you, hit him back.* *—Note: Back, sometimes preceded by in, is often used with of to form the prepositional group* **back** (or **in back**) **of.** Behind: *a tool shed back of the barn.* *—adj.* **1.** At the back or rear: *the back porch.* **2.** Remote or off the main roads: *back country; a back road.* **3.** Overdue: *trying to pay the back rent.* *—v.* **1.** To move or cause to move backward, especially by way of retreating: *As she talked, she kept on backing slowly toward the door. The police backed the crowd into a corner.* **2.** To drive or proceed backward or in reverse: *The driver backed the heavy truck onto the ferry. The train backed into the tunnel.* **3.** To shift in a counterclockwise direction: *During the night the wind backed around to the northeast.* **4.** To support: *A majority of voters backed him.* *—phrasal verbs.* **back down.** To withdraw from a stand that one has taken: *There was a fight because neither side was willing to back down.* **back off.** To retreat or retire, as from an untenable or dangerous position: *games in which the winner is the one who* *backs off last.* **back out.** To retire or withdraw from something: *He accepted the invitation but backed out at the last minute.* **back up. 1.** To move in a reverse direction: *The ship backed up and turned around.* **2.** To retreat: *The boxer was giving ground, backing up.* **3.** To rise and flow backward: *Gas was backing up and leaking into the room.* **4.** To support: *He backs up law and order all the way.* **5.** To assist, especially as an auxiliary: *Scouts backed up municipal lifeguards in the emergency.* [SEE NOTE on p. 62]

***Idioms.* back and fill. 1.** To maneuver a sailing vessel in a narrow channel by adjusting the sails so as to let the wind in and out of them in alternation. **2.** To keep taking different sides. **behind (one's) back.** When one is not present: *I hear she's saying nasty things about me behind my back.* **break the back of.** To destroy: *The army broke the back of the resistance.*

back•ache |**băk**′āk′| *n.* A pain or discomfort in the region of the spine or back.

back•board |**băk**′bôrd′| *or* |-bōrd′| *n.* In basketball, an elevated, vertical sheet of wood or other material to which the basket is attached.

back•bone |**băk**′bōn′| *n.* **1.** The system of bones that forms the main support of a vertebrate; the spinal column; spine. **2.** Strength of character; courage; fortitude: *Attacking the senators required plenty of backbone on the part of the reporter.* **3.** A principal support; mainstay: *Agriculture is the backbone of the economy.*

back•break•ing |**băk**′brā′kĭng| *adj.* Requiring great physical exertion; exhausting.

back•drop |**băk**′drŏp′| *n.* A curtain, often painted to show a scene in the background, hung at the back of a stage.

back•er |**băk**′ər| *n.* A person who supports or gives aid to a person, group, or enterprise.

back•field |**băk**′fēld′| *n.* In football, the group of a team's players stationed behind the linemen.

back•fire |**băk**′fīr′| *n.* **1.** A controlled fire started in the path of an oncoming uncontrolled fire in order to deprive it of fuel and so extinguish it. **2.** In a gasoline engine, an explosion of fuel that ignites too soon or an explosion of unburned fuel in the exhaust system. —*v.* **back•fired, back•fir•ing. 1.** To have a backfire, as an engine might. **2.** To burn in an engine at the wrong time. **3.** To lead to a result opposite to that intended: *His elaborate plan backfired.*

back-for•ma•tion |**băk**′fôr mā′shən| *n.* **1.** A word formed by the subtraction of a part assumed to be separable from the original word. **2.** The formation of words in such a manner. [SEE NOTE]

back•gam•mon |**băk**′găm′ən| *n.* A game for two persons played on a specially marked board with pieces whose moves are determined by throws of dice.

back•ground |**băk**′ground′| *n.* **1. a.** The part of a picture, scene, view, etc., that appears as if in the distance: *a river painted in the background.* **b.** The general scene or surface upon which designs, figures, etc., are seen or represented: *a white background covered with blue stars.* **2.** An inconspicuous position: *remaining in the background during the wedding.* **3.** Soft music played to accompany the dialogue or action in a play, motion picture, etc. **4.** The circumstances or events surrounding or leading up to something: *filling her in on the background of the case.* **5.** A person's experience, training, and education: *a perfect background for the job.* **6.** A person's national, racial, or family origin: *people of different backgrounds.*

back•hand |**băk**′hănd′| *n.* **1.** In sports, a stroke, as of a racket, made with the back of the hand facing forward. **2.** Handwriting with letters that slant to the left. —***modifier:*** *a backhand stroke.* —*adv.* With a backhand stroke or motion: *hit the ball backhand.* [SEE PICTURE]

back•hand•ed |**băk**′hăn′dĭd| *adj.* **1.** With the motion or direction of a backhand: *a backhanded stroke in tennis.* **2.** Containing a disguised insult or rebuke: *a backhanded compliment.* —*adv.* Backhand: *hit the ball backhanded.*

back•ing |**băk**′ĭng| *n.* **1.** Material that forms or strengthens the back of something: *a tablecloth with a felt backing.* **2. a.** Support or aid: *financial backing.* **b.** Approval; endorsement: *a request with official backing from the mayor.* **3.** Persons who provide aid or support: *a candidate with a large backing in the Catholic neighborhoods.*

back•lash |**băk**′lăsh′| *n.* **1.** A sudden or violent backward whipping motion. **2.** Strong and hostile reaction on the part of one social group to the demands made by another.

back•log |**băk**′lôg′| *or* |-lŏg′| *n.* An accumulation, especially of unfinished work or unfilled orders.

back•pack |**băk**′păk′| *n.* **1.** A knapsack, often mounted on a lightweight frame, that is worn on the back to carry camping supplies. **2.** A piece of equipment made to be used while being carried on the back. —*v.* **1.** To hike while carrying supplies in a backpack: *The girls and their guide backpacked to the lake.* **2.** To carry in a backpack: *backpacking canned foods and fishing gear.*

back•rest |**băk**′rĕst′| *n.* A rest for the back.

back-seat driver |**băk**′sēt′|. **1.** A passenger in a car who frequently advises, corrects, or nags the driver. **2.** Any person who persists in giving unsolicited advice.

back•side |**băk**′sīd′| *n.* **1.** The back or rear part of something. **2.** *Informal.* A person's rump.

back•slide |**băk**′slīd′| *v.* **-slid** |-slĭd′|, **-slid** or **-slid•den** |-slĭd′n|, **-slid•ing.** To lapse into sin or improper habits, especially in religious matters. —**back′slid′er** *n.*

back•spin |**băk**′spĭn′| *n.* In sports, a spin on a ball that tends to make it reverse the direction in which it is traveling.

back•stage |**băk**′stāj′| *adv.* **1.** In or toward the area of a theater that is behind where the performers appear. **2.** In or toward a place closed to public view: *backstage at a political convention.* —***modifier:*** *a backstage orchestra; backstage political maneuverings.*

back•stop |**băk**′stŏp′| *n.* A screen or fence in back of the playing area, as in tennis or baseball, used to stop a ball's movement.

back•stroke |**băk**′strōk′| *n.* A swimming stroke executed with the swimmer on his back and moving the arms alternately upward and backward.

back•track |**băk**′trăk′| *v.* **1.** To return over the route by which one has come. **2.** To reverse one's position or policy.

back-formation

One might think that the noun automation *was formed from the verb* automate. *In fact it was the other way around. The word* automation *came into existence first (it was formed from* automatic*), and after a while it seemed to need a verb to go with it;* automate *was thus formed by* **back-formation.** *This process is rather rare in English. Other examples are* edit *from* editor *and* laze *from* lazy.

backhand

badger

back-up |băk′ŭp′| *n.* **1.** A reserve, as of provisions. **2.** A person standing by and ready to serve as a substitute. **3.** An accumulation or overflow caused by the blockage or clogging of something. —***modifier:*** *a back-up pilot.*

back•ward |băk′wərd| *adv.* Also **back•wards** |băk′wərdz|. **1.** In a direction opposite to forward: *He jumped backward to get out of the way.* **2.** Rear end first: *With its hind legs a toad can dig its way into the ground backward.* **3.** In reverse order or direction: *Palindromes are words or sentences that are the same when read backward or forward.* **4.** To a worse condition: *The country is drifting steadily backward.* **5.** Into the past: *Japan's industrial era extends backward only a little over a hundred years.* —*adj.* **1. a.** Behind others, as in economic or social progress: *backward peoples; backward areas of the world.* **b.** Unprogressive; reactionary: *lapsing into the old, backward ways.* **2.** Directed or moving toward the rear: *a backward glance; a backward tumble.*

Idiom. **bend over backward.** To do one's utmost: *He bent over backward to be fair.*

back•ward•ness |băk′wərd nĭs| *n.* The condition of being backward, as in economic or social progress.

back•wash |băk′wŏsh′| *or* |-wôsh′| *n.* **1.** The backward flow of water produced by the oars or propeller of a boat. **2.** The backward flow of air from a propeller of an aircraft. **3.** The result of some disturbing or irregular event or condition: *Burned-down plantations were the backwash of the infantry's advance.*

back•wa•ter |băk′wô′tər| *or* |-wŏt′ər| *n.* **1.** Water held back by a dam, especially a body of stagnant water thus formed. **2.** A place or situation regarded as stagnant or backward. —***modifier:*** *a backwater town.*

back•woods |băk′wo͝odz′| *or* |**-wo͝odz′**| *pl.n.* Heavily wooded areas, usually isolated from populated areas. —***modifier:*** *a backwoods region.*

back•woods•man |**băk′**wo͝odz′mən| *or* |**-wo͝odz′-**| *n., pl.* **-men** |-mən|. A person who lives in the backwoods.

back•yard |**băk′yärd′**| *n.* A form of the phrase **back yard.**

back yard. A yard at the back of a house.

ba•con |**bā′**kən| *n.* The salted and smoked meat from the back and sides of a pig.

bac•te•ri•a |băk **tîr′**ē ə| *pl.n.* The less frequently used singular is **bac•te•ri•um** |băk **tîr′**ē əm|. Very small one-celled organisms often considered to be plants, although they usually lack green coloring.

bac•te•ri•al |băk **tîr′**ē əl| *adj.* Of or caused by bacteria: *bacterial diseases.*

bac•te•ri•ol•o•gist |băk tîr′ē **ŏl′**ə jĭst| *n.* A scientist who specializes in bacteriology.

bac•te•ri•ol•o•gy |băk tîr′ē **ŏl′**ə jē| *n.* The scientific study of bacteria.

bac•te•ri•um |băk **tîr′**ē əm| *n.* Singular of **bacteria.**

Bac•tri•an camel |**băk′**trē ən|. A two-humped camel of central and southwestern Asia. [SEE PICTURE on p.131]

bad |băd| *adj.* **worse** |wûrs|, **worst** |wûrst|. **1.** Not good; inferior; poor: *a bad book; a bad painter.* **2.** Unfavorable: *bad luck; bad weather; get a bad impression.* **3.** Disagreeable; unpleasant: *a bad odor; be in a bad mood.* **4.** Disagreeable; disturbing: *bad news; a bad dream.* **5.** Faulty; incorrect; improper: *bad grammar; use bad judgment; bad manners.* **6.** Not working properly; defective: *The car's brakes are bad.* **7.** Disobedient; naughty: *Johnny was a bad boy today.* **8.** Harmful in effect; detrimental: *Candy is bad for your teeth.* **9.** In poor health; ill; diseased: *I feel bad today. He has a bad knee.* **10.** Severe; violent; intense: *a bad cold; a bad snowstorm.* **11.** Sorry; regretful: *I feel very bad about what happened.* **12.** Rotten; spoiled: *a bad apple.* —*n.* Something bad: *You must learn to accept the bad with the good.* ¶*These sound alike* **bad, bade.** —**bad′ness** *n.*

Idioms. **be in bad.** *Informal.* To be in trouble or disfavor. **not half** (or **so**) **bad.** Reasonably good. **too bad.** Regrettable; unfortunate: *It's too bad you didn't think of it sooner.*

bade |băd| *or* |bād|. A past tense of **bid.** ¶*These sound alike* **bade, bad.**

badge |băj| *n.* An emblem worn to show rank, office, or membership, or as an award or honor.

badg•er |**băj′**ər| *n.* **1.** A burrowing animal with short legs and thick, grayish fur. **2.** The fur of a badger. —*v.* To trouble with many questions or protests; pester: *The speaker was badgered by the angry audience.* [SEE PICTURE]

bad•ly |**băd′**lē| *adv.* **1.** Not well; poorly: *a job badly done.* **2.** Very much; greatly: *passengers badly injured in the accident.* [SEE NOTE]

bad•man |**băd′**măn′| *n., pl.* **-men** |-mĕn′|. A bandit or outlaw.

bad•min•ton |**băd′**mĭn′tən| *n.* A game in which players use a light, long-handled racket to hit a shuttlecock back and forth over a high net.

bad•mouth |**băd′**mouth′| *or* |-mouth′| *v. Slang.* To criticize, often unfairly or spitefully.

Baf•fin Island |**băf′**ĭn|. A large Canadian island lying between Greenland and the mainland of Canada.

baf•fle |**băf′**əl| *v.* **baf•fled, baf•fling. 1.** To cause uncertainty in; puzzle: *Use the dictionary for any word that baffles you.* **2.** To provide with or enclose with a structure that stops or regulates the movement of a gas, of sound, or of a liquid: *baffle a loudspeaker.* —**baf′fled** *adj.: a baffled look.* —**baf′fling** *adj.: a baffling problem.* —*n.* A structure or enclosure designed to stop or regulate the movement of a gas, of sound, or of a liquid. —**baf′fle•ment** *n.*

bag |băg| *n.* **1.** A container made of paper, cloth, leather, etc., used for carrying various articles. **2. a.** A bag with something in it: *buy a bag of onions.* **b.** The amount that a bag holds: *eat a bag of peanuts.* **3.** Any of various other containers such as a purse or a suitcase. **4.** The amount of game caught or killed in a hunting expedition. **5.** Something hanging loosely like a bag: *bags under one's eyes.* **6.** In baseball, a base. **7.** *Slang.* An area of interest, skill, etc.: *Cooking is not her bag.* —*v.* **bagged, bag•ging. 1.** To put into a bag. **2.** To capture or kill, as game. **3.** To hang loosely like a bag.

ba•gel |**bā′**gəl| *n.* A ring-shaped roll with a tough, chewy texture.

bag•gage |**băg′**ĭj| *n.* **1.** The trunks, bags, suitcases, or boxes in which a person carries his belongings while traveling; luggage. **2.** The

badly

Many people feel that the expression He felt badly *is illogical. After all, we say* He felt happy, *not* He felt happily. *Nevertheless, the expression* He felt badly *is widely used to mean "He felt sick," and even more widely to mean "He felt regretful."*

ă pat/ā pay/â care/ä father/ĕ pet/ ē be/ĭ pit/ī pie/î fierce/ŏ pot/ ō go/ô paw, for/oi oil/o͝o book/ o͞o boot/ou out/ŭ cut/û fur/ *th* the/th thin/hw which/zh vision/ ə ago, item, pencil, atom, circus

movable equipment and supplies of an army. —**modifier:** *a baggage compartment.*

bag•gy |băg'ē| *adj.* **bag•gi•er, bag•gi•est.** Loose-fitting: *baggy trousers.* —**bag'gi•ness** *n.*

Bagh•dad |băg'dăd'|. The capital and largest city of Iraq. Population, 1,850,000.

bag•pipe |băg'pīp'| *n.* Often **bagpipes.** A musical instrument that consists, usually, of a double reed pipe for playing melodies and several other pipes that play drones, with all the pipes supplied with air from a large bag into which the player blows. —**bag'pip'er** *n.*

bah |bä| *or* |bă| *interj.* A word used to express contempt or disgust.

Ba•ha•ma Islands |bə hä'mə| *or* |-hā'-|. Also **Ba•ha•mas.** A group of islands in the Atlantic Ocean east and southeast of Florida, constituting an independent country. Population, 197,000. Capital, Nassau. —**Ba•ha'mi•an** |bə hā'mē ən| *or* |-hä'-| *adj. & n.*

Bah•rain or **Bah•rein** |bä rān'|. A group of islands in the Persian Gulf, constituting an independent country. Population, 359,000. Capital, Al Manamah.

baht |bät| *n., pl.* **bahts** or **baht.** The basic unit of money of Thailand.

Bai•kal |bī käl'|. The world's deepest freshwater lake, located in southern Siberia.

bail[1] |bāl| *n.* **1.** Money supplied for the temporary release of an arrested person and guaranteeing his appearance for trial. **2.** The release so obtained. **3.** Someone who supplies the money for such a release. —*v.* **1.** To secure the release of (an arrested person) by providing bail: *He bailed his brother out of jail.* **2.** —**bail out. a.** To release or deliver (someone or something) from a difficult situation: *It took an American loan to bail out their economy.* **b.** To parachute from an airplane in distress. ¶ *These sound alike* **bail, bale.** [SEE NOTE]

bail[2] |bāl| *v.* **1.** To remove (water) from a boat by repeatedly filling a container and emptying it: *bail with a coffee can.* **2.** To empty (a boat) of water by this means: *bail out the boat.* ¶ *These sound alike* **bail, bale.** [SEE NOTE]

bail•iff |bā'lĭf| *n.* An official who guards prisoners and maintains order in a courtroom.

bail•i•wick |bā'lə wĭk'| *n.* **1.** The office or district of a bailiff. **2.** A person's specific area of interest, skill, or authority.

bait |bāt| *n.* **1.** Food placed on a hook or in a trap to lure fish, birds, or other animals. **2.** Anything used to lure or entice. —*v.* **1.** To put bait on: *bait a fishhook.* **2.** To set dogs upon (a chained animal) for sport. **3.** To torment with repeated verbal attacks, insults, or ridicule.

baize |bāz| *n.* A thick, often green, woolen or cotton cloth that looks like felt, used chiefly on billiard tables.

bake |bāk| *v.* **baked, bak•ing. 1.** To cook in an oven with steady, dry heat: *She baked bread. The muffins baked very quickly.* **2.** To harden or dry by heating in or as if in an oven: *Man learned to bake clay containers to make them stronger. The ground baked in the hot sun.* —**baked'** *adj.: baked potatoes; baked beans.*

bak•er |bā'kər| *n.* A person who bakes and sells bread, cakes, etc.

baker's dozen. A group of thirteen; one dozen plus one.

bak•e•ry |bā'kə rē| *n., pl.* **bak•e•ries.** A place where products such as bread, cake, and pastries are baked or sold.

bak•ing |bā'kĭng| *n.* **1.** The act or process of baking. **2.** The amount baked at one time.

baking powder. Any of several powdered mixtures of baking soda, starch, and an acidic compound such as cream of tartar, that are used as leavening.

baking soda. Sodium bicarbonate, especially when used as leavening.

bal•a•lai•ka |băl'ə lī'kə| *n.* A musical instrument that is somewhat like a guitar but has a triangular body and three strings. It is often used in Russian folk music. [SEE PICTURE]

bal•ance |băl'əns| *n.* **1.** A device in which the weight of an object is measured by putting it at one end of a rod that swings on a pivot at its center and adding known weights to the other side until the rod is level and motionless. **2.** A condition in which all forces or influences are cancelled by equal and opposite forces or influences: *Reach a balance on both sides of the scale before removing the object. Man has upset the balance in nature by killing off certain species.* **3.** A condition in which an equation represents a correct statement in mathematics or chemistry. **4. a.** An equality between the debit and credit sides of an account: *A bookkeeper must achieve a balance at the end of the month.* **b.** A difference between two such sides: *There is a balance due of $50.00.* **5.** Something left over; a remainder: *The balance of the evidence goes against him.* **6.** A satisfying proportion or arrangement achieved between parts or elements; harmony: *a balance of color in the room.* **7.** A state of bodily stability, as when standing erect: *I was thrown off balance by the gust of wind.* **8.** Emotional stability; sanity: *He seemed off balance after his long illness.* **9.** An action or influence that results in even, suitable, or fair distribution, as of power among branches of a government: *the U.S. system of checks and balances.* **10.** A **balance wheel.** —*v.* **bal•anced, bal•anc•ing. 1.** To be in, bring into, or come into a condition of balance: *balance the nation's budget. Balance the weights on both sides of the scale.* **2.** To hold in a condition of stability or balance: *She could not balance a clam shell on her big toe.* **3.** To weigh or measure in or as if in a balance.
Idioms. **in the balance.** With the result or outcome still uncertain. **strike a balance.** To reach a condition between extremes.

balance of trade. The difference in value between the total exports and the total imports of a nation.

balance wheel. A wheel that regulates the speed of a machine, as in a clock or watch.

bal•bo•a |băl bō'ə| *n.* The basic unit of money of Panama.

Bal•bo•a |băl bō'ə|, **Vasco de.** 1475–1517. Spanish explorer; discovered the Pacific Ocean (1513).

bal•brig•gan |băl brĭg'ən| *n.* A knitted cotton material used for underwear, hose, etc.

bal•co•ny |băl'kə nē| *n., pl.* **bal•co•nies. 1.** A platform projecting from the wall of a building and surrounded by a railing. **2.** An upper section of seats in a theater or auditorium.

bail[1-2]

Bail[1] *and* **bail**[2] *may possibly be related.* **Bail**[1] *basically meant "custody," and it comes from Old French* baillier, *"to take into one's custody, to take in charge."* Baillier *is from Latin* bāiulus, *"a porter, a carrier."* **Bail**[2] *originally meant "a bucket" and is from Old French* bail, *"a bucket."* Bail *may also be from Latin* bāiulus; *if so, the meaning must have changed from "a carrier" to "a container, a bucket." But this is only a possibility.*

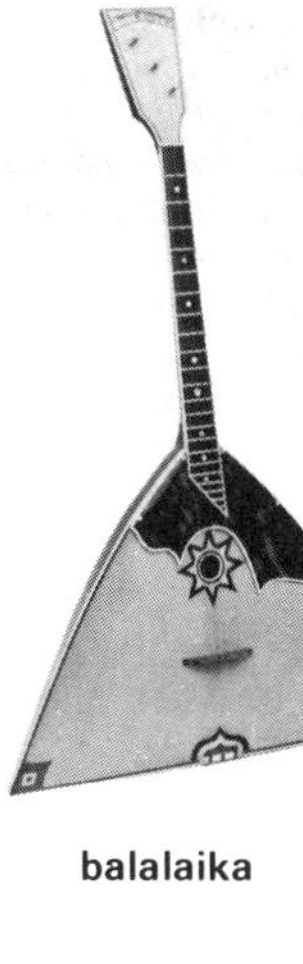

balalaika

bald eagle
The **bald eagle** is often called the American eagle, and is used as an emblem of the United States, as on the Great Seal.

ball[1-2]
Ball[1] *is from Old Norse* bölr, *and is distantly related to such words as* **boll, boulder,** *and* **balloon. Ball[2]** *comes (via Old French and Latin) from Greek* ballizein, *"to dance," and is related to* **ballad** *and* **ballet.**

bald |bôld| *adj.* **bald•er, bald•est. 1.** Lacking hair on the top of the head. **2.** Lacking natural or usual covering: *a bald spot in the lawn.* **3.** Having a white head: *the bald eagle.* **4.** Plain; blunt: *a bald statement.* —**bald'ness** *n.*

bald eagle. A North American eagle with a dark body and wings and a white head and tail. [SEE PICTURE]

bal•der•dash |**bôl'**dər dăsh'| *n.* Words without sense; nonsense.

bald•head•ed |**bôld'**hĕd'ĭd| *adj.* Having no hair on one's head.

bald•pate |**bôld'**pāt'| *n.* A baldheaded person.

bal•dric |**bôl'**drĭk| *n.* A belt worn over one shoulder across the chest to the opposite hip, used to support a sword or bugle.

bale |bāl| *n.* A large bound package or bundle of raw or finished material: *a bale of hay.* —*v.* **baled, bal•ing.** To wrap in bales. ¶*These sound alike* **bale, bail.** —**bal'er** *n.*

Bal•e•ar•ic Islands |băl'ē **ăr'**ĭk|. A group of Spanish islands, including Majorca and Minorca, in the Mediterranean Sea east of Spain; a province of Spain.

ba•leen |bə **lēn'**| *n.* Whalebone.

bale•ful |**bāl'**fəl| *adj.* **1.** Threatening; menacing: *a baleful look on his face.* **2.** Producing evil or harm; harmful: *a baleful influence.* —**bale'ful•ly** *adv.* —**bale'ful•ness** *n.*

Ba•li |**bä'**lē|. An island and province of Indonesia, lying off the eastern end of Java. Population, 2,195,000. —**Ba'li•nese'** |bä'lə **nēz'**| *or* |**-nēs'**| *adj.* & *n.*

balk |bôk| *v.* **1.** To stop short and refuse to go on: *His pony jumped across a deep ravine, and all the others balked.* **2.** To refuse; recoil; shrink: *They balked at the terms of the settlement.* **3.** To check or thwart: *The police balked their escape plans.* **4.** In baseball, to make an illegal motion before pitching, allowing a runner to advance a base. —*n.* In baseball, the act of balking.

Bal•kan |**bôl'**kən| *adj.* Of the Balkans or their inhabitants. —*n.* **the Balkans** or **the Balkan States.** The states of the Balkan Peninsula.

Balkan Peninsula. A peninsula in southeastern Europe, comprising Yugoslavia, Rumania, Albania, Bulgaria, and Greece.

balk•y |**bô'**kē| *adj.* **balk•i•er, balk•i•est.** Frequently stopping short and refusing to go on; stubborn; obstinate: *a balky mule.*

ball[1] |bôl| *n.* **1. a.** Something that is spherical or nearly spherical; a round object: *The earth is a great round ball.* **b.** Such an object used in various sports and games: *a tennis ball; a beach ball.* **c.** A game, especially baseball, played with such an object. **2.** A ball moving, thrown, hit, or kicked in a certain way: *a fly ball; a curve ball.* **3.** In baseball, a pitch not swung at by the batter and judged by the umpire to have passed outside the strike zone. **4.** Anything shaped like or resembling a ball: *a ball of yarn. The kitten curled up into a ball in front of the fireplace.* **5.** Any rounded part that projects, as from a bone or a part of the body: *the ball of the foot.* **6.** A solid projectile or shot for a firearm: *a cannon ball.* —**modifier:** *a ball game; a ball team.* —*v.* —**ball up.** *Slang.* To confuse or bungle. ¶*These sound alike* **ball, bawl.** [SEE NOTE]

Idioms. **on the ball.** *Slang.* Alert, competent, or efficient. **play ball. 1.** To play in a game using a ball. **2.** *Informal.* To cooperate.

ball[2] |bôl| *n.* **1.** A formal social dance. **2.** *Slang.* A wonderful time: *had a ball at the beach.* ¶*These sound alike* **ball, bawl.** [SEE NOTE]

bal•lad |**băl'**əd| *n.* **1.** A poem, often intended to be sung, that tells a story in a simple manner. **2.** Music to which a ballad could be sung. **3.** A popular love song.

ball and chain. A heavy iron ball fastened by a chain to a prisoner's leg.

ball-and-sock•et joint |**bôl'**ən **sŏk'**ĭt|. A type of joint in which a ball attached to one of the pieces to be joined fits closely into a socket in the other piece, allowing some motion in practically every direction. Joints of this kind often occur between bones.

bal•last |**băl'**əst| *n.* **1.** Any heavy material carried in a vehicle mainly to provide weight: *Submarines use water as ballast.* **2.** Gravel or small stones used to form a foundation for a roadway or for railroad tracks. —*v.* To provide with or fill in with ballast.

ball bearing. 1. A bearing, as for a turning shaft, in which the moving and stationary parts are held apart by a number of small, hard balls that turn between them and reduce friction. **2.** A small, hard ball used in such a bearing.

bal•le•ri•na |băl'ə **rē'**nə| *n.* A principal female dancer in a ballet company.

bal•let |bă **lā'**| *or* |**băl'**ā'| *n.* **1.** A form of artistic dancing based on a technique composed of jumps, turns, poses, etc., all requiring great precision and grace of movement: *a school offering classes in ballet.* **2. a.** A theatrical dance form that is performed in costume and combines the arts of ballet dancing, music, painting, and drama to convey a story, a theme, or an atmosphere: *Modern ballet dates from the end of the 19th century.* **b.** A theatrical performance of this dance form: *Are you going to the ballet tonight?* **3.** Music written or used for ballet. **4.** A company or group that performs ballet. —**modifier:** *a ballet school; a ballet company.*

bal•lis•tic |bə **lĭs'**tĭk| *adj.* Of ballistics or projectiles.

ballistic missile. A projectile that is guided during the time that it is propelled and allowed to assume a free-falling path or to coast toward its target thereafter.

bal•lis•tics |bə **lĭs'**tĭks| *n. (used with a singular verb).* **1.** The scientific study of the characteristics of projectiles and the way they move in flight. **2.** The study of firearms and ammunition.

bal•loon |bə **lo͞on'**| *n.* **1.** A large, flexible bag filled with helium, hot air, or some other gas that is lighter than normal air, used to lift loads, such as instruments or passengers, into the air. **2.** A small, brightly colored rubber bag that floats through the air when inflated, used as a child's toy. —*v.* To swell out like a balloon: *The baby took his first breath and the air sacs ballooned out. His enormous body had ballooned even more with the years.*

bal•loon•ist |bə **lo͞o'**nĭst| *n.* A person who flies in a balloon.

bal•lot |**băl'**ət| *n.* **1.** A piece of paper on which a voter marks his choice or choices, especially in

ă pat/ā pay/â care/ä father/ĕ pet/ē be/ĭ pit/ī pie/î fierce/ŏ pot/ō go/ô paw, for/oi oil/o͝o book/o͞o boot/ou out/ŭ cut/û fur/*th* the/th thin/hw which/zh vision/ə ago, item, pencil, atom, circus

barn |bärn| *n.* A large farm building used for storing grain, hay, and other farm products and for sheltering cattle and other livestock. —***modifier:*** *the barn door.*

bar•na•cle |**bär'**nə kəl| *n.* A small, hard-shelled sea animal that attaches itself to underwater rocks, pilings, the bottoms of ships, etc.

barn•storm |**bärn'**stôrm'| *v.* To travel about the countryside appearing in shows or making political speeches. —**barn'storm'er** *n.*

barn•yard |**bärn'**yärd'| *n.* The yard or area of ground around a barn. —***modifier:*** *the barnyard fence.*

bar•o•graph |**băr'**ə grăf'| *or* |-gräf'| *n.* An instrument that produces a graph of atmospheric pressure.

ba•rom•e•ter |bə **rŏm'**ĭ tər| *n.* **1.** An instrument that measures and indicates atmospheric pressure and is widely used in the study and forecasting of weather. **2.** Something that shows shifts and changes like those of the weather; an indicator: *Wealth is sometimes considered a barometer of success.* [SEE PICTURE]

bar•o•met•ric |băr'ə **mĕt'**rĭk| *adj.* Of or measured by a barometer.

barometric pressure. The pressure of the atmosphere as measured by a barometer.

bar•on |**băr'**ən| *n.* **1. a.** A member of the British peerage holding a title and rank below that of a viscount. **b.** A nobleman of similar rank in certain other countries. **2.** In feudal times, a man with rights, lands, and a title received directly from a king. **3.** A businessman of great wealth and influence: *a railroad baron.* **4. baron of beef.** A cut of beef consisting of a double sirloin. ¶*These sound alike* **baron, barren.**

bar•on•ess |**băr'**ə nĭs| *n.* **1.** The wife of a baron. **2.** A woman holding a rank equal to that of a baron in her own right.

bar•on•et |**băr'**ə nĭt| *or* |băr'ə **nĕt'**| *n.* In Great Britain, a person holding a hereditary title of honor and ranking below a baron.

ba•ro•ni•al |bə **rō'**nē əl| *adj.* **1.** Of a baron. **2.** Suitable for a baron; stately or splendid.

bar•o•ny |**băr'**ə nē| *n., pl.* **bar•o•nies.** The rank or domain of a baron.

ba•roque |bə **rōk'**| *adj.* **1.** Often **Baroque.** Of or in a style of art and architecture developed in Europe from about 1550 to 1700 and having extremely elaborate and ornate forms. **2.** Often **Baroque.** Of or in a style of musical composition that flourished in Europe from about 1600 to 1750 and was notable for strictness of form and elaborateness of ornamentation. **3.** Irregular in shape: *a baroque pearl.* **4.** Elaborate and fantastic; outlandish: *a strange, baroque novel.* —*n.* The baroque style or period in art, architecture, and music.

ba•rouche |bə **rōōsh'**| *n.* A horse-drawn carriage with a folding top, passenger seats facing one another, and a driver's seat outside.

barque |bärk| *n.* A form of the word **bark** (ship). ¶*These sound alike* **barque, bark.**

bar•racks |**băr'**əks| *n. (used with a singular or plural verb).* A building or group of buildings used to house soldiers, workers, etc.: *This barracks was built during the Civil War. The barracks were crowded.*

bar•ra•cu•da |băr'ə **kōō'**də| *n., pl.* **bar•ra•cu•das** or **bar•ra•cu•da.** A sea fish with a long, narrow body and very sharp teeth, found mostly in tropical waters. [SEE PICTURE]

bar•rage |bə **räzh'**| *n.* **1.** A concentrated firing of guns or missiles, often as a screen or protection for military troops. **2.** An overwhelming attack or outpouring, as of blows or words: *a barrage of fists; a barrage of questions.* —*v.* **bar•raged, bar•rag•ing.** To direct a barrage at: *barrage the speaker with questions.*

bar•rel |**băr'**əl| *n.* **1.** A large wooden container with round, flat ends of equal size and sides that bulge out slightly. **2. a.** A barrel with something in it: *a barrel of oil.* **b.** The amount held by a barrel: *peel a barrel of potatoes.* **3.** Any of various measures of volume or capacity ranging from 31 to 42 gallons, especially a quantity of petroleum equal to 31.5 gallons. **4. a.** The long tube of a gun, through which the bullet travels. **b.** A cylindrical machine part. **5.** *Informal.* A great amount: *a barrel of fun.* **6.** The barrellike body of an animal, such as a horse. —*v.* **bar•reled** or **bar•relled, bar•rel•ing** or **bar•rel•ling. 1.** To put or pack in a barrel or barrels. **2.** *Slang.* To move at breakneck speed: *He barreled along the highway at 80 miles an hour.*

bar•rel-chest•ed |**băr'**əl chĕs'tĭd| *adj.* Having a broad, bulging chest: *a strong, barrel-chested young man.*

bar•rel•house |**băr'**əl hous'| *n.* An early style of jazz with an accented two-beat rhythm.

barrel organ. A portable musical instrument, similar to a small organ, in which the airflow to the pipes is controlled by valves that are operated by turning a barrel with a hand crank.

bar•ren |**băr'**ən| *adj.* **1.** Lacking or unable to produce growing plants or crops: *a barren desert; barren soil.* **2.** Unable to bear offspring or fruit. **3.** Not useful or productive: *barren efforts.* **4.** Empty; bare: *a life barren of pleasure; the room's barren simplicity.* —*n.* Often **barrens.** A tract of land that is barren or covered only with scrubby growth. ¶*These sound alike* **barren, baron.** —**bar'ren•ness** *n.*

bar•rette |bə **rĕt'**| *or* |bä-| *n.* A bar-shaped or oval clip used to hold the hair in place.

bar•ri•cade |**băr'**ĭ kād'| *or* |băr'ĭ **kād'**| *n.* An often hastily built or placed fencelike or wall-like structure set up to close off a passageway, to keep back attackers or crowds, etc. —*v.* **bar•ri•cad•ed, bar•ri•cad•ing.** To close off, block, or protect with a barricade.

bar•ri•er |**băr'**ē ər| *n.* **1.** A fence, wall, or other structure built to hold back or obstruct movement or passage. **2.** A geographical or natural feature, such as a mountain range or body of water, that acts as a barrier: *The English Channel was a barrier against Nazi ground forces.* **3.** Anything that obstructs; an obstacle: *Lack of education can be a barrier to success.*

barrier reef. A long narrow ridge of coral or rock near and parallel to a coastline.

bar•ring |**bär'**ĭng| *prep.* **1.** Apart from the possibility of; excepting: *Barring a last-minute change, we'll be the first to arrive.* **2.** Except for: *This is their first public performance, barring a preview in Boston.*

bar•ri•o |**bär'**ryō| *n., pl.* **bar•ri•os. 1.** A neighborhood or community in a U.S. city where

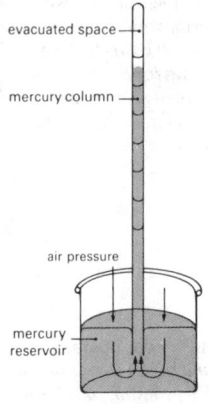

barometer
The height of the mercury in the tube depends on and is a measure of the atmospheric pressure.

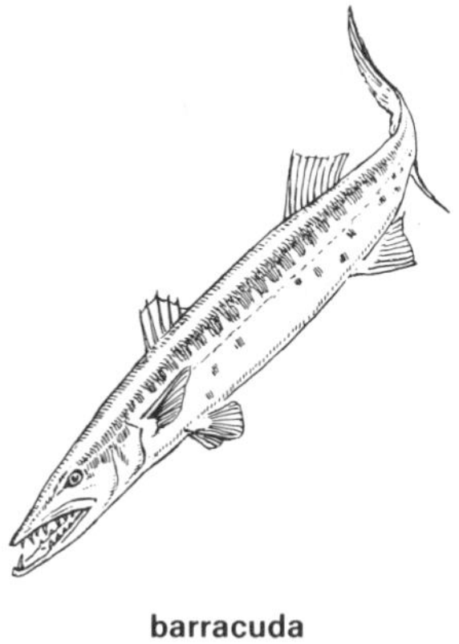

barracuda
The **barracuda** has a reputation for being very ferocious, but has rarely been known to attack human beings.

barrow[1-2]

Barrow[1] *and* **barrow**[2] *are both Old English words. The first is from Old English* bearwe, *"basket, wheelbarrow," and is closely related to the verb* **bear,** *"to carry."* **Barrow**[2] *is from Old English* beorg, *"mound, hill," and is related to* **burg** *and* **borough.**

base[1-2]**/basis/bass**[1-2]

Base[1] *and* **basis** *are from Greek* basis, *"a pedestal, a platform."* **Base**[2] *and* **bass**[2] *are originally variant spellings of a Middle English word spelled* bas, *meaning "low," and coming from Latin* bassus, *"low."* **Bass**[1] *(the fish) is an Old English word, originally* baers; *it meant "prickly fish, fish with a spiny back," and is distantly related to* **bristle.**

base

All **bases** *are chemical compounds that have hydroxyl groups bound into them in a way that allows them to split off in solution and become hydroxyl ions. It is the presence of more hydroxyl ions than hydrogen ions in a solution that makes it* **basic.** *Certain salts, such as sodium carbonate, give a* **basic** *reaction in solution. While a true* **base** *contributes hydroxyl ions to the solution, a salt of this kind removes hydrogen ions to produce a similar effect.*

ă pat/ā pay/â care/ä father/ĕ pet/ē be/ĭ pit/ī pie/î fierce/ŏ pot/ō go/ô paw, for/oi oil/ŏŏ book/ōō boot/ou out/ŭ cut/û fur/*th* the/th thin/hw which/zh vision/ə ago, item, pencil, atom, circus

Spanish is spoken. **2.** A village or back-country community in the Philippines.

bar•ris•ter |băr'ĭ stər| *n. Chiefly British.* A lawyer who argues cases in a law court.

bar•row[1] |băr'ō| *n.* **1.** A wheelbarrow. **2.** A traylike frame with handles at each end, used for carrying loads. [SEE NOTE]

bar•row[2] |băr'ō| *n.* A large mound of earth or stones placed over a grave in ancient times. [SEE NOTE]

Bart. baronet.

bar•tend•er |bär'tĕn'dər| *n.* A person who mixes and serves alcoholic drinks at a bar.

bar•ter |bär'tər| *v.* To trade in exchange for something else, without using money: *barter home-grown vegetables for clothing. The settlers bartered with the Indians for furs.* —*n.* The act or practice of bartering.

ba•sal |bā'səl| *or* |-zəl| *adj.* **1.** Of, at, or forming a base: *a plant with a tuft of basal leaves.* **2.** Basic; fundamental; primary.

basal metabolism. The least amount of energy an organism can use to maintain its life processes when at complete rest.

ba•salt |bə sôlt'| *or* |bā'sôlt'| *n.* A hard, dense, dark rock formed by volcanic action.

base[1] |bās| *n.* **1.** The lowest or bottom part: *the base of the cliff.* **2.** A part or layer on which something rests or is placed for support; foundation: *Soft ground makes a poor base for buildings.* **3.** The chief ingredient or element of something; basis: *a paint with an oil base.* **4.** A starting point or central place; headquarters: *The explorers established a base at the foot of the mountain.* **5.** A center of supplies or operations for a military or naval force. **6.** A starting point, safety area, or goal in certain sports, especially, in baseball, one of the four corners of the infield that must be touched by a runner to score a run. **7. a.** The side or face that is considered to be the bottom of a geometric figure. **b.** The measure of such a face or side. **8. a.** In a system of numeration, the factor by which a number is multiplied when its numeral is shifted one place to the left. For example, if ten is the base, 42 is ten times as great as 4.2. **b.** The number to which an exponent or logarithm is applied. For example, if $6^2 = 6 \times 6 = 36$, six is the base. **c.** The number to which the per cent is applied in a percentage problem. For example, if 40 is the base, 20 per cent of 40 is 8. **9.** A word or word part to which other parts may be added. For example, in *filled, refill,* and *filling, fill* is the base. **10.** Any of a large class of substances, typically the hydroxides of metals, that when dissolved in water are capable of reacting with an acid to form a salt, are capable of turning blue litmus red, and have a characteristic slippery feel and bitter taste. **11.** The terminal of a transistor that acts somewhat like the grid of a vacuum tube. —***modifier:*** *the base runners; a base word.* —*v.* **based, bas•ing. 1.** To support; found: *base an opinion on facts; base a judgment on available evidence.* **2.** To use or have as a starting point or base: *The composer based this song on an old folk melody. We base part of our fleet in the Pacific.* ¶*These sound alike* **base, bass**[2]. [SEE NOTE]

base[2] |bās| *adj.* **bas•er, bas•est. 1.** Morally bad or wrong; mean; detestable: *base instincts; a base act.* **2.** Lowly; menial: *forced into base slavery.* **3.** Not rare or of great value: *base metals such as iron and lead.* ¶*These sound alike* **base, bass**[2]. [SEE NOTE] —**base'ly** *adv.* —**base'ness** *n.*

base•ball |bās'bôl'| *n.* **1.** A game played with a bat and ball on a field with four bases laid out in a diamond pattern. Two teams of nine players take turns at bat and in the field, the members of the team at bat trying to score runs by touching all the bases. **2.** The ball used in this game. —***modifier:*** *baseball players; a baseball bat.*

base•board |bās'bôrd'| *or* |-bōrd'| *n.* A molding along the lower edge of a wall, where it meets the floor of a room.

base•less |bās'lĭs| *adj.* Having no basis or foundation in fact; unfounded: *baseless claims.*

base•man |bās'mən| *n., pl.* **-men** |-mən|. In baseball, one of three players, the **first baseman,** the **second baseman,** or the **third baseman,** who play defensively at or near one of the bases.

base•ment |bās'mənt| *n.* The lowest story of a building, often below ground level.

ba•ses[1] |bā'sēz'| *n.* Plural of **basis.**

bas•es[2] |bā'sĭz| *n.* Plural of **base.**

bash |băsh| *v. Informal.* To strike with a heavy, crushing blow: *collided with a tree and bashed in the fender of the car.* —*n.* **1.** *Informal.* A heavy, crushing blow. **2.** *Slang.* A party.

bash•ful |băsh'fəl| *adj.* Timid and embarrassed with other people; shy. —**bash'ful•ly** *adv.* —**bash'ful•ness** *n.*

ba•sic |bā'sĭk| *adj.* **1.** Forming a base, foundation, or basis; fundamental; underlying: *the basic framework of the English language.* **2.** Main; essential; primary: *the basic ingredients of a mixture.* **3.** First and necessary before doing or undertaking something else: *the basic training of a soldier.* **4.** In chemistry: **a.** Producing an excess of hydroxyl ions in solution. **b.** Of, producing, or resulting from a base. —*n.* Often **basics.** Something basic or fundamental: *learning the basics of an art technique.*

ba•si•cal•ly |bā'sĭk lē| *adv.* In a basic way; fundamentally; essentially.

bas•il |băz'əl| *or* |bā'zəl| *n.* A plant with spicy, pleasant-smelling leaves used to flavor cooked foods and salads.

ba•sil•i•ca |bə sĭl'ĭ kə| *n.* **1.** A type of ancient Roman building having two rows of columns dividing the interior into a central hall with two side aisles, and an arched, semicircular part at one end. **2.** A building of this type used as a Christian church.

bas•i•lisk |băs'ə lĭsk| *or* |băz'-| *n.* In myths and legends, a lizardlike creature said to have the power of killing by its breath.

ba•sin |bā'sən| *n.* **1.** A round, open, shallow container often used for holding water to wash in. **2. a.** A basin with something in it: *a basin of water.* **b.** The amount that a basin holds: *drenched by a basin of water.* **3.** A natural or man-made hollow or enclosed place filled with water: *a deep basin at the foot of the falls; a basin for large boats dug along the canal.* **4.** The entire region from which a river and its tributaries collect water: *the Amazon basin.*

ba•sis |bā'sĭs| *n., pl.* **ba•ses** |bā'sēz'|. **1.** Something that serves as a foundation; an underlying cause, idea, fact, etc.: *On what basis did you make* *this decision?* **2.** The main part or basic ingredient. **3.** A standard by which something is rated or compared: *a project on an experimental basis.* **4.** Terms of social relationship; footing: *on a first-name basis.* [SEE NOTE]

bask |băsk| *or* |bäsk| *v.* **1.** To lie or rest and enjoy a pleasant warmth: *turtles basking on a log in the sun.* **2.** To take pleasure; live happily: *She was content to bask in the glory of her husband's fame.*

bas•ket |băs′kĭt| *or* |bä′skĭt| *n.* **1.** A container made of interwoven twigs, strips of wood, rushes, etc. **2. a.** A basket with something in it: *a basket of flowers.* **b.** The amount that a basket holds: *eat a basket of peaches.* **3.** In basketball: **a.** A metal hoop with an open-ended net suspended from it, placed at a height of ten feet above the court. **b.** A goal scored by throwing the ball through this hoop.

bas•ket•ball |băs′kĭt bôl′| *or* |bä′skĭt-| *n.* **1.** A game played by two teams of five players on a court with a raised basket at each end. Players pass and dribble a ball and score by throwing the ball through the basket defended by the other team. **2.** The large, round ball used in this game. *—**modifier:** a basketball game.*

bas•ket•ry |băs′kĭ trē| *or* |bä′skĭ-| *n.* **1.** The craft or process of making baskets. **2.** Baskets in general.

basket weave. A method or pattern of weaving in which double threads are interwoven to produce a plain latticework effect.

bas mitz•vah |bäs mĭts′və|. A form of the phrase **bat mitzvah.**

Basque |băsk| *n.* **1.** A member of a people who live in the western Pyrenees of France and Spain. **2.** The language of this people. The Basque language is unrelated to any other language so far as is now known. —**Basque** *adj.*

bas-re•lief |bä′rĭ lēf′| *or* |bä′rĭ lēf′| *n.* A sculpture or kind of sculpture in which figures are raised slightly from a flat background.

bass¹ |băs| *n., pl.* **bass** or **bass•es.** Any of several freshwater or saltwater fishes caught for food or sport. [SEE NOTE]

bass² |bās| *n.* **1.** The lowest range of musical tones: *The acoustics here bring out the bass.* **2.** The lowest man's singing voice. **3.** A man having such a voice. **4.** A part written in the range of this voice. **5.** An instrument, especially a double bass, having about the same range as this voice. *—**modifier:** a bass voice; a bass aria.* ¶ *These sound alike* **bass, base.** [SEE NOTE]

bass clef |bās|. A symbol used in writing music. It indicates that the note written on the fourth line from the bottom of the staff is the F below middle C.

bass drum |bās|. A large, cylindrical drum that makes a deep, booming sound when struck.

bas•set |băs′ĭt| *n.* Also **basset hound.** A dog with a long, heavily built body, short legs, and long, drooping ears.

Basse•terre |bäs târ′| *or* |bäs-|. The capital of St. Kitts-Nevis. Population, 15,000.

bas•set horn |băs′ĭt|. An alto clarinet that is pitched a fourth below an ordinary clarinet.

bas•si•net |băs′ə nĕt′| *or* |băs′ə nĕt′| *n.* A basket resting on legs, usually with a hood at one end, used as a crib for a small baby.

bas•so |băs′ō| *or* |bä′sō| *n., pl.* **bas•sos.** The lowest man's singing voice or a singer having such a voice; a bass.

basso con•tin•u•o |kən tĭn′yo͞o ō′|. A **figured bass.**

bas•soon |bə so͞on′| *or* |bă-| *n.* A low-pitched woodwind instrument having a long wooden body connected to a double reed by a bent metal tube. —**bas•soon′ist** *n.* [SEE PICTURE]

bass viol |bās|. A **double bass.**

bass•wood |băs′wo͝od′| *n.* **1.** A linden tree of North America. **2.** The soft, light wood of such a tree.

bast |băst| *n.* The strong, fibrous part of certain plant stems, used for making rope, cord, etc.

bas•tard |băs′tərd| *n.* **1.** A child born of parents who are not married to each other; an illegitimate child. **2.** *Slang.* **a.** A mean person. **b.** A fellow; guy. *—**modifier:** the Duke's bastard son. —adj.* Of mixed or uncertain origin, and considered inferior: *The proud natives regarded English as a bastard language.*

baste¹ |bāst| *v.* **bast•ed, bast•ing.** To sew with long loose stitches meant to be taken out when the final sewing is done. [SEE NOTE]

baste² |bāst| *v.* **bast•ed, bast•ing.** To moisten (meat) with melted fat or other liquid while roasting. [SEE NOTE]

Bas•tille |bă stēl′|. A fortress in Paris used as a prison until captured on July 14, 1789, at the beginning of the French Revolution.

Bastille Day. A national holiday in France, celebrated on July 14 in memory of the capture of the Bastille in 1789.

bast•ing |bā′stĭng| *n.* Often **bastings.** Large, loose stitches used to baste material.

bas•tion |băs′chən| *or* |-tē ən| *n.* **1.** A part built out from the main body of a fort or rampart. **2.** Any strongly protected or well-defended position; a stronghold.

bat¹ |băt| *n.* A wooden stick or club used for hitting a ball, as in baseball. *—v.* **bat•ted, bat•ting. 1.** To hit with or as if with a bat: *He batted the ball out of the ball park. The waves batted her back and forth.* **2.** To be the hitting team or hitter in baseball: *Our team batted first.* **3.** In baseball, to have (a certain percentage) as a batting average: *He is batting .276 this season.* [SEE NOTE]

Idioms. **at bat.** Having a turn as a hitter in baseball: *Mike was at bat in the third inning.* **go to bat for.** To support or defend: *a father who goes to bat for his son.* **right off the bat.** Without hesitation; immediately.

bat² |băt| *n.* A mammal with a mouselike body and thin, leathery wings that extend from long, thin, fingerlike bones of the forelimbs to the hind legs and tail. [SEE NOTE & PICTURE]

Idiom. **have bats in (one's) belfry.** *Slang.* To have strange or foolish ideas; be crazy.

bat³ |băt| *v.* **bat•ted, bat•ting.** To move with a flapping motion; blink: *She batted her eyelashes at him flirtatiously.* [SEE NOTE]

Idiom. **bat an eye.** To show surprise: *Jim didn't bat an eye at her answer.*

bat•boy |băt′boi′| *n.* A boy who takes care of a baseball team's bats and equipment.

batch |băch| *n.* **1.** An amount prepared at one time: *bake a batch of cookies; mix a batch of*

bassoon

baste¹·²

Baste¹ *is from Old French and originally meant "to sew with bast (fiber)."* **Baste²** *is of unknown origin; various theories about its history have been suggested, but none of them is convincing. All that can be said is that it does not seem to be related to* **baste¹**. *There are still several thousand words in English whose origins are unknown and many more that can only be traced a short way.*

bat¹·²·³

Bat¹ *is an Old English word, originally spelled* batt, *meaning "a club." It may be related to* **batter¹**. **Bat²** *was earlier* bakke, *and was borrowed from a Scandinavian name for the animal; it is ultimately a shortened and altered form of Old Norse* ledhr-blakka, *"the leather-flapper, the bat."* **Bat³** *is probably a variant of* **abate**, *"to lower."*

bat²

bathysphere
Famous ocean explorer William Beebe (1877–1962) seated on the bathysphere in which he made many deep-sea diving expeditions.

batten[1-2]
Batten[1] *is a respelling of French* baton, *"stick, bit of wood, baton."* **Batten[2]** *comes from Old Norse* batna, *"to improve," hence "to grow fat."*

batter[1-2-3]
Batter[1] *is from Old French* battre, *from Latin* battuere, *"to beat."* **Bat[1]**, **battle**, *and* **combat**, *all containing the idea "to strike or beat," also come from* battuere. **Batter[2]**, *obviously, is from* **bat[1]**. **Batter[3]**, *perhaps meaning "stuff that is beaten," is probably related to* **batter[1]**.

ă pat/ā pay/â care/ä father/ĕ pet/ ē be/ĭ pit/ī pie/î fierce/ŏ pot/ ō go/ô paw, for/oi oil/o͝o book/ o͞o boot/ou out/ŭ cut/û fur/ *th* the/th thin/hw which/zh vision/ ə ago, item, pencil, atom, circus

cement. **2.** A group or number of similar things: *threw away a batch of old papers.*

ba•teau |bă tō′| *n., pl.* **ba•teaux** |bă tōz′|. A light, flat-bottomed boat, used in Canada and Louisiana. *—adj.* Cut at the neck in a wide, boat-shaped opening: *a bateau neckline.*

bat•ed |bā′tĭd| *adj.* **—with bated breath.** With one's breath held in, as in excitement or awe.

bath |băth| *or* |bäth| *n., pl.* **baths** |bă*thz*| *or* |bä*thz*| *or* |băths| *or* |bäths|. **1. a.** The act of washing or soaking the body in water. **b.** The water used for a bath. **2.** A soaking in or exposure to a liquid or something similar to a liquid: *a steam bath; a sun bath.* **3.** A bathtub or bathroom: *an apartment with three rooms and a bath.* **4. baths.** A building equipped for bathing: *the ruins of Roman public baths.* **5.** A liquid, or a liquid and its container, in which an object is dipped or soaked in order to process it in some way: *a bath of dye.* ***—modifier:*** *a bath towel.*

bathe |bā*th*| *v.* **bathed, bath•ing. 1.** To clean or refresh by washing or soaking the body in water; give a bath to or take a bath: *bathe the baby; bathe before breakfast.* **2.** To soak in a liquid: *Florence bathed her swollen leg.* **3.** To make wet; moisten: *Tears bathed her cheeks.* **4.** To seem to wash or pour over; flood: *Moonlight bathed the porch.* **5.** To go into the water for swimming or recreation. **—bath′er** *n.*

ba•thet•ic |bə thĕt′ĭk| *adj.* Marked by bathos: *a bathetic passage in a novel.*

bath•house |băth′hous′| *or* |bäth′-| *n., pl.* **-hous•es** |-hou′zĭz|. **1.** A building equipped for bathing. **2.** A building, as at a beach, used by swimmers for changing clothes.

bathing cap. A tight rubber cap worn to keep the hair dry while swimming.

bathing suit. A garment worn to swim in.

bath•o•lith |băth′ə lĭth′| *n.* Igneous rock that has melted and flowed into surrounding strata at great depths.

ba•thos |bā′thŏs′| *n.* A sudden and incongruous change from a lofty or serious style to one that is very commonplace

bath•robe |băth′rōb′| *or* |bäth′-| *n.* A loose robe worn before and after bathing and for lounging.

bath•room |băth′ro͞om′| *or* |-ro͝om′| *or* |bäth′-| *n.* A room for taking a bath or shower, usually also containing a sink and toilet.

bath•tub |băth′tŭb′| *or* |bäth′-| *n.* A tub to bathe in, usually having faucets and a drain, and permanently installed in a bathroom.

bath•y•scaph |băth′ĭ skăf′| *n.* A form of the word **bathyscaphe.**

bath•y•scaphe |băth′ĭ skăf′| *or* |-skāf′| *n.* A deep-sea research vessel consisting essentially of a large buoyant chamber filled with gasoline and having a manned observation capsule secured to its bottom. The vessel is able to move freely over the ocean bottom.

bath•y•sphere |băth′ĭ sfîr′| *n.* A strong, spherical chamber in which a crew can be lowered by cable deep into the ocean to make underwater observations. [SEE PICTURE]

ba•tik |bə tēk′| *or* |băt′ĭk| *n.* **1.** A method of dyeing a design on cloth by putting wax over the parts of the cloth not meant to be dyed. **2.** Cloth so dyed. ***—modifier:*** *a batik scarf.*

ba•tiste |bə tēst′| *or* |bă-| *n.* A fine, thin, light fabric, usually of cotton or linen. ***—modifier:*** *a batiste shirt.*

bat mitz•vah |bät mĭts′və|. A Jewish religious ceremony for girls, similar to the more commonly held bar mitzvah for boys.

ba•ton |bə tŏn′| *or* |băt′n| *n.* **1.** A thin, tapered stick often used by the conductor in leading a band, chorus, or orchestra. **2.** A stick or staff such as that twirled by a drum major or majorette, passed in a relay race, or carried as a symbol of office.

Bat•on Rouge |băt′n ro͞ozh′|. The capital of Louisiana. Population, 219,486.

bats |băts| *adj. Slang.* Crazy; insane.

bats•man |băts′mən| *n., pl.* **-men** |-mən|. A batter in baseball or cricket.

bat•tal•ion |bə tăl′yən| *n.* A large group of soldiers organized as a unit, usually consisting of two or more companies. **2.** A large group of people: *a battalion of firemen.*

bat•ten[1] |băt′n| *n.* A narrow strip of wood, such as one used on a boat or ship to fasten a covering over a hatch or to stiffen the edge of a sail. *—v.* **—batten down.** To fasten or hold down with or as if with such strips: *batten down the hatches in preparation for a storm.* [SEE NOTE]

bat•ten[2] |băt′n| *v.* To feed or thrive and grow fat. [SEE NOTE]

bat•ter[1] |băt′ər| *v.* **1.** To strike or pound repeatedly with heavy blows: *The boxer battered his opponent. Waves battered against the pier.* **2.** To injure or damage by rough treatment or hard wear: *His car was badly battered.* **—bat′tered** *adj.: a battered felt hat.* [SEE NOTE]

bat•ter[2] |băt′ər| *n.* In baseball, a player who is or will be batting. [SEE NOTE]

bat•ter[3] |băt′ər| *n.* A beaten mixture, as of flour, milk, and eggs, used in cooking: *Pour the pancake batter on the griddle.* [SEE NOTE]

bat•ter•ing-ram |băt′ər ĭng răm′| *n.* Also **battering ram.** A heavy wooden beam with an iron head, used in warfare in ancient times to batter down walls and gates.

bat•ter•y |băt′ə rē| *n., pl.* **bat•ter•ies. 1. a.** A number of electric cells connected together to supply more current or voltage than any one of them can alone. **b.** A small dry cell designed to power a flashlight or other portable electric device. **2. a.** A group or set of large guns, as of artillery. **b.** A place where such guns are set up. **c.** A unit of soldiers in the artillery, equivalent to a company in the infantry. **3.** A group of things or people used or doing something together: *The celebrity faced a battery of flashbulbs and reporters as he stepped from the plane.* **4.** In baseball, the combination of a team's pitcher and catcher. **5.** An unlawful beating of another person. See **assault and battery.**

bat•ting |băt′ĭng| *n.* Cotton or wool fibers wadded into rolls or sheets, used to stuff mattresses, line quilts, etc.

batting average. The ratio of the number of a baseball player's hits to the number of times he has been at bat. If a player has had 25 hits in 100 times at bat, his batting average is .250.

bat•tle |băt′l| *n.* **1.** A fight between two armed groups or contestants, usually on a large scale. **2.** Any hard struggle or sharp conflict: *a political* *battle; a battle of wits.* —*v.* **bat•tled, bat•tling. 1.** To fight in or as if in battle; struggle: *The troops battled bravely.* **2.** To fight against: *We battled the storm for hours.* —**bat'tler** *n.*

bat•tle-ax or **bat•tle-axe** |**băt'**l ăks'| *n.* **1.** A heavy ax with a broad head, used as a weapon in ancient and medieval times. **2.** *Slang.* A quarrelsome, overbearing woman.

battle cry. 1. A shout to spur on fighting, uttered by troops in battle. **2.** A slogan used by the supporters of a cause.

bat•tle•dore |**băt'**l dôr'| *or* |-dōr'| *n.* A wooden paddle similar to that used in table tennis, used in an early form of the game of badminton to strike the shuttlecock back and forth.

bat•tle•field |**băt'**l fēld'| *n.* **1.** A field or area where a battle is fought. **2.** Any area of conflict: *the battlefield of the war against poverty.*

bat•tle•front |**băt'**l frŭnt'| *n.* The area where opponents meet or clash in battle: *a contest fought on military and political battlefronts.*

bat•tle•ground |**băt'**l ground'| *n.* A place of fighting or conflict; a battlefield.

bat•tle•ment |**băt'**l mənt| *n.* Often **battlements.** A wall with indented openings, built along the top edge of a tower, castle, fort, etc., and formerly used as protection and concealment for soldiers in warfare. [SEE PICTURE]

battle royal. 1. A battle or confused fight in which many people take part. **2.** A bitter, intense quarrel.

bat•tle•ship |**băt'**l shĭp'| *n.* A warship of the largest size and having the heaviest guns and armor.

bat•ty |**băt'**ē| *adj.* **bat•ti•er, bat•ti•est.** *Slang.* Crazy; insane.

bau•ble |**bô'**bəl| *n.* **1.** A showy ornament or trinket of little value. **2.** A stick topped by a grotesquely carved head, carried by a court jester in former times.

baux•ite |**bôk'**sīt'| *n.* Any of a class of natural materials that contain aluminum and that constitute its most important ore.

Ba•var•i•a |bə **vâr'**ē ə|. A state in the southern part of West Germany. Capital, Munich. —**Ba•var'i•an** *adj.* & *n.*

bawd•y |**bô'**dē| *adj.* **bawd•i•er, bawd•i•est.** Coarsely and humorously indecent: *bawdy jokes.* —**bawd'i•ly** *adv.* —**bawd'i•ness** *n.*

bawl |bôl| *v.* **1.** To cry or sob loudly; howl: *The unhappy baby kicked and bawled.* **2.** To cry out or call in a loud, strong voice; bellow: *"Who goes there?" bawled the sentry.* —***phrasal verb.* bawl out.** *Informal.* To scold loudly or harshly. —*n.* A loud wailing or bellowing cry: *the bawl of a stray calf.* ¶*These sound alike* **bawl, ball.**

bay[1] |bā| *n.* A body of water partly surrounded by land but having a wide outlet to the sea. ¶*These sound alike* **bay, bey.** [SEE NOTE]

bay[2] |bā| *n.* **1.** A part of a room or building that projects beyond the main outside wall and is often surrounded by windows on three sides. **2.** A similar alcove or compartment: *a bomb bay in an aircraft.* **3.** Often **sick bay.** A room or compartment that is used as a hospital on a ship. ¶*These sound alike* **bay, bey.** [SEE NOTE]

bay[3] |bā| *adj.* Reddish brown: *a bay horse.* —*n.* **1.** A reddish brown. **2.** A reddish-brown horse. ¶*These sound alike* **bay, bey.** [SEE NOTE]

bay[4] |bā| *v.* To bark or bark at with long, deep, howling cries. —*n.* A long, howling bark. ¶*These sound alike* **bay, bey.** [SEE NOTE]

***Idiom.* at** (or **to**) **bay. 1.** In or into a position of or like that of an animal cornered by and facing its pursuers: *The howling hounds kept the stag at bay. The policeman chased the escaping thief and brought him to bay.* **2.** At a distance so as to ward off threatening danger: *laws intended to keep poverty and sickness at bay.*

bay[5] |bā| *n.* **1. a.** A laurel with glossy, fragrant leaves often used as a spice. **b.** A tree or shrub similar to a laurel. **2. bays.** A crown of laurel leaves, given in ancient times to honor outstanding deeds. **3. bays.** Honors; fame: *Babe Ruth won his bays as a hitter of home runs.* ¶*These sound alike* **bay, bey.** [SEE NOTE]

bay•ber•ry |**bā'**bĕr'ē| *n., pl.* **-ber•ries. 1.** A shrub with gray, waxy, pleasant-smelling berries used to make candles. **2.** A berry of such a shrub.

bay leaf. The spicy leaf of a laurel, used as flavoring in cooking.

bay•o•net |**bā'**ə nĭt| *or* |-nĕt'| *or* |bā'ə **nĕt'**| *n.* A knife attached to the muzzle end of a rifle for use in close combat. —*v.* **bay•o•net•ed** or **bay•o•net•ted, bay•o•net•ing** or **bay•o•net•ting.** To stab with a bayonet.

bay•ou |**bī'**o͞o| *or* |**bī'**ō| *n., pl.* **bay•ous.** A sluggish, marshy body of water connected with a river, lake, etc., and common in the southern United States.

bay rum. A fragrant lotion made from the leaves of a tropical American tree.

bay window. A window or group of windows projecting from the outer wall of a building and forming an alcove in the room or part within.

ba•zaar |bə **zär'**| *n.* **1.** An Oriental market, usually consisting of a street lined with shops and stalls. **2.** A store where various kinds of things are sold. **3.** A fair or sale, usually to raise money for a charity: *a church bazaar.*

ba•zoo•ka |bə **zo͞o'**kə| *n.* A portable military weapon consisting of a tube from which antitank rockets are launched.

BB |**bē'**bē'| *n.* A size of lead shot that is 0.18 inch in diameter and is fired from a **BB gun,** a rifle or pistol usually operated by compressed air or carbon dioxide.

B.C. Before Christ; in a specified year before the birth of Christ.

Be The symbol for the element beryllium.

be–. A prefix that forms verbs: **becloud; bedevil; befriend; besiege.**

be |bē| *v.*

	1st person	2nd person	3rd person
Present Tense			
singular	**am** (ăm)	**are** (är)†	**is** (ĭz)
plural	**are**	**are**	**are**

†*Archaic 2nd person singular* **art** (ärt)

Present Participle: **being** (**bē'**ĭng)

Present Subjunctive: **be**

Past Participle: **been** (bĭn)

Past Subjunctive: **were**

Past Tense			
singular	**was** (wŭz, wŏz)	**were** (wûr)‡	**was**
plural	**were**	**were**	**were**

‡*Archaic 2nd person singular* **wast** (wŏst) or **wert** (wûrt)

battlement
A gateway of Windsor Castle, England

bay[1-2-3-4-5]
The five English words spelled **bay** *are all of about the same age (Middle English period), and they all come from Old French. But beyond that they have different origins.* **Bay**[1] *is from Spanish* bahia, *"a gulf."* **Bay**[2] *originally meant "an opening, an open place," and comes from a reconstructed Latin word,* badāre, *"to yawn or gape."* **Bay**[3] *is from Latin* badius, *"chestnut brown."* **Bay**[4] *is from another reconstructed Latin word,* abaiāre, *meaning "to howl."* **Bay**[5] *is from Latin* baca, *"berry." This is the most extreme case of multiple homonymy in the whole Dictionary.*

be
The verb **be** *has the most complex and irregular set of inflections in the English language. Only the "standard" forms are given here. In regional dialects in England and America, there are many variants, such as* I been, you was, he be, *etc.*

beagle

1. To exist: *I think, therefore I am.* Often used with *there: There once was a poor woodcutter.* **2.** To occupy a position. Often used with a specifying prepositional phrase: *The groceries are on the table.* **3.** To take place; occur: *Where is the show?* **4.** To come or go. Used mainly in the perfect tense: *Have you ever been to town?* **5.** *Archaic.* To belong; befall. Used in the subjunctive, and now only in a few set phrases: *Peace be unto you.* **6.** —Used as a copula in such senses as: **a.** To equal in identity or meaning: *That book is mine.* **b.** To signify or stand for: *A is excellent; C is passing.* **c.** To belong to a specified class or group: *Man is a primate.* **d.** To have or show a specified quality or characteristic: *She is lovely. All men are mortal.* **7.** —Used as an auxiliary verb in certain constructions, as: **a.** With the past participle of a class of verbs to form the passive voice: *Elections are held once a year.* **b.** With the present participle of a verb to express a continuing action: *We are working to improve housing conditions.* **c.** With the past participle of certain verbs of motion to form the perfect tense: *"Where be those roses gone which sweetened so our eyes?"* (Sir Philip Sidney). **d.** With *to* and the infinitive of another verb to indicate: (1) duty or necessity: *I am to inform you that the package has arrived.* (2) supposition: *How am I to know the answer?* (3) the future: *She was to become the first woman aviator. They are to be married Monday.* ¶*These sound alike* **be, bee.** [SEE NOTE]

Idiom. **let be.** *Informal.* To let (someone) alone: *Go away and let me be.*

beach |bēch| *n.* The usually sandy or pebbly shore of a body of water. —***modifier:*** *a beach towel.* —*v.* To haul or drive (a boat) ashore. ¶*These sound alike* **beach, beech.**

beach•head |**bēch**′hĕd′| *n.* A military position on an enemy shoreline captured by advance troops of an invading force.

bea•con |**bē**′kən| *n.* **1.** A fire, light, radio signal, or any other signaling device used to guide ships, airplanes, etc. **2.** A tower or other installation bearing such a device. **3.** Any force that warns or guides: *She is a beacon of hope.*

bead |bēd| *n.* **1.** A small, often round, piece of glass, metal, wood, etc., having a hole in it through which a string can be drawn. **2. beads.** A necklace of beads on a string. **3. beads.** A rosary. **4.** Any small, round object, such as a drop of moisture: *a bead of sweat.* **5.** A small knob of metal located at the muzzle of a rifle or pistol and used in taking aim. —*v.* To decorate with beads or beading: *bead a dress.* —**bead′ed** *adj.: beaded moccasins.*

bead•ing |**bē**′dĭng| *n.* **1.** A trimming, decoration, or design made out of beads. **2.** Any narrow trimming, such as a piece of lace with openings through which ribbon may be run.

bead•work |**bēd**′wûrk′| *n.* Decorative work in beads.

bead•y |**bē**′dē| *adj.* **bead•i•er, bead•i•est.** Small, round, and shining, often with suspicion, greed, etc.: *The mink saw the bass and waited, his beady eyes gleaming.*

bea•gle |**bē**′gəl| *n.* A small hound with a smooth coat and drooping ears, often used as a hunting dog. [SEE PICTURE]

beak |bēk| *n.* **1.** The hard, horny projecting mouth parts of a bird; a bill. **2.** A projecting part that resembles a bird's beak.

beak•er |**bē**′kər| *n.* **1.** A laboratory container consisting of a cylinder that is open at one end and has a pouring lip. **2.** A large drinking cup with a wide mouth.

beam |bēm| *n.* **1.** A long, rigid piece of wood or metal used to support or reinforce a structure or a part of a structure. **2.** The widest part of a ship. **3.** In a balance, the bar from which the weights are hung. **4.** A group of particles or waves traveling close together in parallel paths. **5.** Light projected into space, as by a flashlight or searchlight. **6.** A **radio beam. 7.** A faint indication; a glimpse; gleam: *a beam of hope.* —*v.* **1.** To emit or transmit (radiant energy or a radio signal) in a beam. **2.** To send off light; shine: *the sun beaming in the sky.* **3.** To smile broadly: *His face beamed with delight.*

bean |bēn| *n.* **1. a.** Any of several plants having seeds in pods that are usually long and narrow. **b.** The seed or pod of such a plant, often used as food. **2.** A seed or pod similar to a bean: *a coffee bean; a vanilla bean.* **3.** *Slang.* The head. —***modifier:*** *a bean plant; bean soup.* —*v. Slang.* To hit on the head.

Idiom. **spill the beans.** To tell something that was meant to be kept secret.

bean•bag |**bēn**′băg′| *n.* A small cloth bag filled with dried beans and used as a toy.

bean curd. A soft, cheeselike food made from puréed soybeans, shaped into small cakes, and used in Oriental cooking.

bean•ie |**bē**′nē| *n.* A small, round cap without a brim, worn on the top part of the head.

bean•pole |**bēn**′pōl′| *n.* **1.** A thin pole around which a bean vine twines as it grows. **2.** *Slang.* A tall, thin person.

bean sprout. The young, tender shoot of certain beans, such as the soybean, used in Oriental cooking.

bean•stalk |**bēn**′stôk′| *n.* The stem of a bean plant.

bear[1] |bâr| *v.* **bore** |bôr| *or* |bōr|, **borne** |bôrn| *or* |bōrn|, **bear•ing. 1.** To hold up; support: *a vine strong enough to bear the weight of a grown man; men bearing the burden of national leadership in wartime.* **2. a.** To move while supporting; carry: *a train bearing the remains of the 34th President of the United States to his beloved Kansas.* **b.** To hold above or aloft; carry: *Delightful scents are borne on soft breezes.* **c.** To carry so as to tell; transmit: *bear good tidings.* **3.** To carry on one's person: *the right to bear arms.* **4.** To assume; accept: *bearing the blame for his actions.* **5.** To carry (oneself) in a specified way: *The poor lady bore herself with much dignity.* **6.** To have in the heart or mind: *bear a grudge.* **7.** To have as a visible characteristic; show: *buildings bearing the scars of military occupation; a document bearing the king's seal; sisters bearing a strong resemblance to their mother.* **8.** To give or offer; provide: *bear false witness. A hoarse voice shouted, "Bear a hand, my hearties."* **9.** To put up with; endure: *They bore their hardships well. He couldn't bear the pain any longer. How could she bear to see him torn apart by a tiger?* **10.** To stand up under; permit of: *This case will not bear investigation.* **11.** To give birth to: *She has borne five children.*

See **born.** **12.** To produce; yield: *fruit trees that bear well; a bond bearing 5% interest. Some trees bear fruit early in the spring.* **13. a.** To exert pressure: *an old man bearing heavily on his cane.* **b.** To exert influence: *bringing pressure to bear to settle the dispute.* **14.** To have relevance; apply: *problems that do not bear upon the life of the islanders.* **15.** To proceed or turn in a given direction: *At the corner, bear right.* —***phrasal verbs.*** **bear down on.** To move rapidly: *The engineer released the brakes and bore down on the track to keep on schedule.* **bear out.** To prove right; confirm: *The cloudy sky bore out the promise of snow that had been in the wind.* **bear up.** To find strength to resist; keep up one's spirits: *She bore up well during her long illness.* ¶ *These sound alike* **bear, bare.** [SEE NOTE]

Idioms. **bear in mind.** To be careful; take heed or watch out for: *Bear in mind that we're reporting, not taking sides.* **bear with.** To be patient or indulgent with; tolerate: *Please bear with me a little longer.*

bear[2] |bâr| *n.* **1.** A large animal with a shaggy coat, a very short tail, and a flat-footed walk. **2.** A rough, clumsy person. —***modifier:*** *bear meat.* ¶ *These sound alike* **bear, bare.** [SEE NOTE & PICTURE]

bear•a•ble |bâr′ə bəl| *adj.* Capable of being borne; tolerable.

beard |bîrd| *n.* **1.** The hair on the chin and cheeks of a man. **2.** A hairy or hairlike tuft or growth, as on an animal's face or throat or on an ear of grain. —*v.* To face or defy boldly: *The hunters bearded the lion in his lair.*

beard•ed |bîr′dĭd| *adj.* Having a beard or beardlike part: *Abraham Lincoln's bearded face; a bearded ear of wheat.*

bear•er |bâr′ər| *n.* **1.** A person who carries or supports something: *a flag bearer.* **2.** A person who presents a check or other money order for payment.

bear•ing |bâr′ĭng| *n.* **1.** The manner or way in which a person carries himself: *She has the air and bearing of a full-grown woman.* **2.** Relevance or relationship: *He is firmly convinced that poetry is simply nonsense that has no bearing on our lives today.* **3.** A supporting part of a structure. **4.** A mechanical part that supports a moving part, especially a turning shaft, and allows it to move with little friction. **5.** Direction, especially angular direction as used in navigation: *The ship took a bearing on the lighthouse.* **6. bearings.** The knowledge of one's position in relation to his surroundings: *The explorers lost their bearings in the dark.*

bear•ish |bâr′ĭsh| *adj.* Like a bear; rough, clumsy, or rude.

bear•skin |bâr′skĭn′| *n.* **1.** A rug made from the skin of a bear. **2.** A tall, black fur cap worn with a uniform. [SEE PICTURE]

beast |bēst| *n.* **1.** An animal other than a human being, especially a large, four-footed animal. **2.** A brutal person.

beast•ly |bēst′lē| *adj.* **beast•li•er, beast•li•est. 1.** Like a beast; savage; cruel: *a beastly person.* **2.** Unpleasant; disagreeable: *a beastly story.* —**beast′li•ness** *n.*

beast of burden. An animal, such as a horse or donkey, used to carry loads or pull vehicles.

beat |bēt| *v.,* **beat, beat•en** |bēt′n| or **beat, beat•ing. 1. a.** To hit or strike repeatedly so as to inflict pain or injury: *The gang beat the boy black and blue. They beat him soundly with fists and clubs.* **b.** To shake or strike repeatedly: *beat the rugs; beat a ball back and forth.* **2. a.** To pound forcefully and repeatedly; dash: *The angry storm waves beat against the coast.* **b.** To fall in torrents: *The rain beat down hard.* **c.** To shine or glare intensely: *The noonday sun beat down on my aching body.* **3. a.** To produce sound by striking, hitting, or tapping (something) repeatedly: *beat a drum.* **b.** To mark or count (a rhythm or pulse) by tapping, moving, or striking, as with a part of the body: *Beat the meter lightly with your foot. A car's windshield wiper beats a steady rhythm.* **4.** To grow louder and softer at a regular rate, as do two tones that are close in pitch when they are played together. **5. a.** To shape or flatten by pounding: *The Eskimos beat the copper into spearheads.* **b.** To break up by pounding: *Beat rock into smaller pieces.* **6.** To throb; pulsate: *A newborn baby's heart beats about 140 times a minute. His heart was beating with excitement.* **7.** To flap repeatedly: *Hummingbirds beat their wings very fast.* **8.** To mix rapidly in order to blend or make frothy: *beat the egg whites.* **9. a.** To prove superior to, conquer, or defeat, as in a contest or battle: *Tortoises can beat hares sometimes. Germany was finally beaten.* **b.** To surpass or be superior to: *He beat my record. Riding beats walking.* **10.** To forge or make by treading over: *The Pilgrims beat a path across the wilderness.* —***phrasal verbs.*** **beat back.** To force to retreat: *Conservationists beat back powerful mining interests.* **beat off.** To repel: *John, holding a raised stick, stood prepared to beat off an attack.* **beat up.** To give a beating to; thrash: *He beat up an old man.* —*n.* **1.** A sound, stroke, or blow, when made repeatedly: *the beat of galloping hoofs.* **2.** A periodic pulsation or throb: *the beat of your heart.* **3. a.** One of the succession of units that make up meter in music: *There are four beats in this measure.* **b.** A gesture that marks one of these units. **4.** The manner in which a conductor beats: *He has a clear beat.* **5.** A change in strength or loudness, as in two tones that are close in pitch when they are played together. **6.** The area generally covered by a policeman, guard, newspaper reporter, etc. —*adj. Informal.* Tired; worn-out: *I'm really beat after a full day's work in the broiling sun.* ¶ *These sound alike* **beat, beet.**

Idioms. **beat it.** *Informal.* To go away; get going: *You better beat it before he gets back.* **beat (one's) brains out.** *Informal.* To try energetically: *I beat my brains out helping him.*

beat•en |bēt′n|. A past participle of **beat.** —*adj.* **1.** Thinned or formed by hammering: *beaten tin.* **2.** Much traveled: *beaten paths.*

Idiom. **off the beaten track** (or **path**). Not well-known or familiar; unusual.

beat•er |bē′tər| *n.* **1.** Someone or something that beats, especially an instrument for beating: *a carpet beater.* **2.** A person who drives wild game from under cover for a hunter or a hunting party.

be•a•tif•ic |bē′ə tĭf′ĭk| *adj.* Showing extreme joy or bliss: *a beatific smile.*

be•at•i•fy |bē ăt′ə fī′| *v.* **be•at•i•fied, be•at•i•fy•**

bear[2]
Alaskan brown bear

bear[1-2]
Bear[1] *is a very basic word that has kept the same basic meaning for over five thousand years. In Old English it was* beran; *this descends from the prehistoric Indo-European root* bher-, *which meant both "to carry" and "to bear a child," just as* **bear[1]** *still does.* **Bear[2]** *was* bera *in Old English and comes from a separate but identical Indo-European root,* bher-, *meaning "brown." See also* **bruin.**

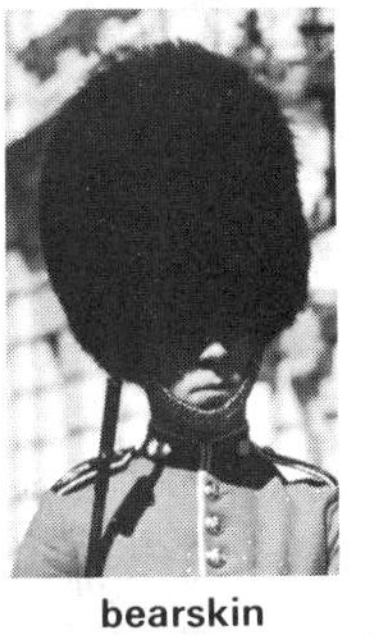

bearskin
A private of the Grenadier Guards

beauty
"Beauty in things exists in the mind which contemplates them." —*David Hume (1711–1776).*
"Beauty is truth, truth beauty" —*John Keats (1795–1821).*

beaver[1]

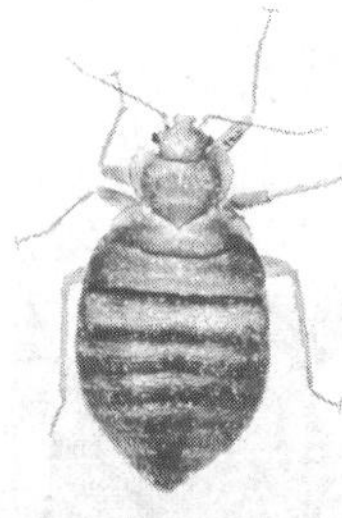

bedbug

ă pat/ā pay/â care/ä father/ĕ pet/ ē be/ĭ pit/ī pie/î fierce/ŏ pot/ ō go/ô paw, for/oi oil/o͝o book/ o͞o boot/ou out/ŭ cut/û fur/ *th* the/th thin/hw which/zh vision/ ə ago, item, pencil, atom, circus

ing, be•at•i•fies. **1.** To make extremely happy. **2.** In the Roman Catholic Church, to honor (a deceased person) by declaring him blessed and thus worthy of public veneration.

beat•ing |**bē'**tĭng| *n.* **1.** Punishment by hitting or whipping: *He has done no wrong, yet they were preparing to give him a beating.* **2.** A defeat: *The boys from Mexico took a beating from the team from Bridgeport.* **3.** The regular variation in strength that occurs when waves of different frequencies come together.

be•at•i•tude |bē **ăt'**ĭ to͞od'| *or* |-tyo͞od'| *n.* **1.** Supreme blessedness. **2. the Beatitudes.** Nine declarations made by Christ in the Sermon on the Mount, beginning "Blessed are . . ."

beau |bō| *n., pl.* **beaus** or **beaux** |bōz|. **1.** The sweetheart of a woman or girl. **2.** A dandy; a dude. ¶*These sound alike* **beau, bow[1].**

Beau•fort scale |**bō'**fərt|. A system in which wind velocities are put into numbered categories ranging from 0 to 12 or 0 to 17, with 0 corresponding to *calm* and 12 or 17 corresponding to *hurricane.*

beaut |byo͞ot| *n. Slang.* Something outstanding or unusual of its kind: *Her mistake was a real beaut.* ¶*These sound alike* **beaut, butte.**

beau•te•ous |**byo͞o'**tē əs| *or* |-tyəs| *adj.* Beautiful.

beau•ti•cian |byo͞o **tĭsh'**ən| *n.* Someone who is skilled in the various services offered by beauty parlors.

beau•ti•ful |**byo͞o'**tə fəl| *adj.* Showing or having beauty in any of its forms: *a beautiful girl; beautiful scenery.* —**beau'ti•ful•ly** *adv.*

beau•ti•fy |**byo͞o'**tə fī'| *v.* **beau•ti•fied, beau•ti•fy•ing, beau•ti•fies.** To make beautiful: *Green parks and wide boulevards beautify the newer parts of the city.* —**beau'ti•fi•ca'tion** *n.*

beau•ty |**byo͞o'**tē| *n., pl.* **beau•ties. 1.** A pleasing quality or a combination of such qualities that delights the senses and raises the spirit or appeals to the mind: *the beauty of the singer's voice; glaciers adding beauty to the natural scenery; seeing more beauty and passion in his poetry than ever before.* **2.** A person or thing that is beautiful: *She had been a beauty in her day. Emerson appreciated the beauties of the countryside.* **3.** A feature that is most gratifying or effective: *The beauty of his writing was its simplicity.* **4.** *Informal.* An outstanding example: *His black eye is a real beauty.* [SEE NOTE]

beauty parlor. A shop in which women have their hair styled, nails manicured, etc.

beauty salon. A **beauty parlor.**

beaux |bōz| *n.* A plural of **beau.**

beaux-arts |bō **zär'**| *pl.n. French.* The fine arts.

bea•ver[1] |**bē'**vər| *n.* **1. a.** An animal with thick fur, a flat, paddlelike tail, and large, strong front teeth. Beavers live in and near lakes and streams and gnaw down trees to build dams and lodges in the water. **b.** The fur of a beaver. **2.** Often **beaver hat.** A man's tall hat, formerly made of beaver fur; a top hat. —***modifier:*** *a beaver dam; beaver skins.* [SEE PICTURE]

bea•ver[2] |**bē'**vər| *n.* A movable piece of metal armor worn on the front of a knight's helmet to protect his mouth and chin.

be•calmed |bĭ **kämd'**| *adj.* Motionless because of a lack of wind.

be•came |bĭ **kām'**|. Past tense of **become.**

be•cause |bĭ **kôz'**| *or* |**-kŭz'**| *conj.* **1.** For the reason that: *He left because he was sick.* **2.** *Informal.* That: *The reason why he was late was because he was sick.* **3.** On account of being: *The room was uncomfortable because too hot.*

because of. On account of: *He stayed home because of illness.*

beck |bĕk| *n.* A gesture of beckoning.
Idiom. **at (one's) beck and call.** Willingly obedient; at one's service.

beck•on |**bĕk'**ən| *v.* **1.** To signal (someone) to come, as by nodding or waving: *The captain beckoned us over to watch him. He beckoned to the ferryman to take him across.* **2.** To seem attractive to or to seem to attract: *A garden beckons the weary. On the Pacific Coast, promised lands beckoned.*

be•cloud |bĭ **kloud'**| *v.* To darken with or as if with clouds; obscure: *This recent development beclouds the real political issues.*

be•come |bĭ **kŭm'**| *v.* **be•came** |bĭ **kām'**|, **be•come, be•com•ing. 1.** To grow or come to be: *The town became a city.* **2.** To be appropriate or suitable to: *Such talk ill becomes a man of his rank.* **3.** To look good on or cause to look good on; adorn: *The new dress becomes her.* **4. —become of.** To happen to or be the subsequent condition of: *I wonder what has become of all my old schoolmates. What will become of her?*

be•com•ing |bĭ **kŭm'**ĭng| *adj.* **1.** Appropriate; suitable: *with the wisdom becoming to an old philosopher.* **2.** Well suited to the appearance of the wearer: *a becoming hat.*

bed |bĕd| *n.* **1.** A piece of furniture for resting and sleeping, consisting mainly of a flat rectangular frame and a mattress, with or without bedclothes, resting on springs. **2.** A mattress: *I've seen the women fill a mattress tick with feathers to make feather beds.* **3.** A mattress and bedclothes: *According to an old Japanese custom the mother made up the beds on the floor.* **4.** Any place or surface upon which one may sleep: *The children sleep on bamboo beds that fasten in the tree branches.* **5. a.** A small plot for cultivating or growing things: *a bed of flowers.* **b.** A similar plot on the bottom of the sea: *an oyster bed; rocks surrounded by deep kelp beds.* **6.** Anything that forms a bottom or supporting part: *the bed of a stream; lobster on a bed of rice.* **7.** A mass of rock, ore, etc., that extends under a large area and is bounded, especially from above, by different material. —***modifier:*** *bed sheets; a bed lamp.* —*v.* **bed•ded, bed•ding. 1.** To provide with a bed or sleeping quarters: *unable to bed all their guests.* **2.** To make a bed for (an animal): *He bedded his horses down before suppertime.* **3.** To set or plant in a bed of soil: *We're lucky if we can bed the potatoes by noon tomorrow.*

be•daub |bĭ **dôb'**| *v.* To smear; soil.

be•daz•zle |bĭ **dăz'**əl| *v.* **be•daz•zled, be•daz•zling.** To dazzle completely; confuse; bewilder. —**be•daz'zle•ment** *n.*

bed•bug |**bĕd'**bŭg'| *n.* A small, wingless, biting insect that has a flat reddish body and is often a pest in houses, especially in bedding. [SEE PICTURE]

bed•cham•ber |**bĕd'**chām'bər| *n.* A bedroom.

bed•clothes |**bĕd'**klōz'| *or* |-klōthz'| *pl.n.* Coverings, such as sheets and blankets, used on a bed.

bed·ding |bĕd′ĭng| *n.* **1.** Sheets, blankets, and mattresses for beds. **2.** Straw, hay, etc., for animals to sleep on; litter. **3.** The way in which layers of sedimentary rock are arranged.

be·deck |bĭ **dĕk′**| *v.* To cover with decorations; adorn.

be·dev·il |bĭ **dĕv′**əl| *v.* **1.** To plague; trouble; harass: *European history was bedeviled by rivalry between France and Germany.* **2.** To possess as with a devil; bewitch. —**be·dev′il·ment** *n.*

be·dew |bĭ **dōō′**| *or* |**-dyōō′**| *v.* To wet with or as if with dew: *Poor Jo bedewed the pincushion with bitter tears.*

bed·fel·low |**bĕd′**fĕl′ō| *n.* **1.** A person with whom one shares a bed. **2.** An associate or ally.

be·di·zen |bĭ **dī′**zən| *or* |**-dĭz′**ən| *v.* To dress or ornament in a gaudy manner.

bed·lam |**bĕd′**ləm| *n.* **1.** A place or situation of confusion, disorder, or noisy uproar: *After breakfast the happy bedlam of unwrapping Christmas presents began.* **2.** *Archaic.* An insane asylum.

Bed·ou·in |**bĕd′**ōō ĭn| *or* |**bĕd′**wĭn| *n.* An Arab who is a member of a nomadic tribe of North Africa, Arabia, and Syria.

bed·pan |**bĕd′**păn′| *n.* A container designed to be used instead of a toilet by a bedridden person.

be·drag·gled |bĭ **drăg′**əld| *adj.* Wet, drenched, messy, etc.: *bedraggled clothes; the bedraggled officers of a sinking ship.*

bed·rid·den |**bĕd′**rĭd′n| *adj.* Confined to bed because of sickness or weakness.

bed·rock |**bĕd′**rŏk′| *n.* The solid rock that lies beneath the soil and all other loose material on the surface of the earth.

bed·roll |**bĕd′**rōl′| *n.* Blankets or a sleeping bag rolled up to be carried by a camper or by anyone who sleeps outdoors.

bed·room |**bĕd′**rōōm′| *or* |-rŏŏm′| *n.* A room for sleeping in. —***modifier:*** *a bedroom door.*

bed·side |**bĕd′**sīd′| *n.* The space alongside a bed. —***modifier:*** *a bedside table.*

bed·sore |**bĕd′**sôr′| *or* |-sōr′| *n.* An often serious ulcer of the skin caused by pressure, occurring in persons who are bedridden for long periods.

bed·spread |**bĕd′**sprĕd′| *n.* An outer covering for a bed, spread over the sheets or blankets to conceal them.

bed·stead |**bĕd′**stĕd′| *or* |-stĭd| *n.* The frame supporting the springs and mattress of a bed.

bed·time |**bĕd′**tīm′| *n.* The time when a person usually goes to bed.

bee[1] |bē| *n.* Any of several winged, often stinging insects that gather pollen and nectar from flowers. Some bees, such as the honeybee, live together in colonies. ¶*These sound alike* **bee, be.** [SEE NOTE & PICTURE]

***Idiom.* a bee in (one's) bonnet.** An idea that fills most of one's thoughts.

bee[2] |bē| *n.* A gathering where people work together or compete against one another: *a quilting bee; a spelling bee.* ¶*These sound alike* **bee, be.** [SEE NOTE]

bee·bread |**bē′**brĕd′| *n.* A brownish substance made by bees from pollen and nectar and fed to their young.

beech |bēch| *n.* **1.** A tree with smooth, light-colored bark, small, edible nuts, and strong, heavy wood. **2.** The wood of such a tree. —***modifier:*** *dense beech woods.* ¶*These sound alike* **beech, beach.**

beech·nut |**bēch′**nŭt′| *n.* The nut of a beech tree, encased in a prickly husk.

beef |bēf| *n.* **1. a.** The flesh of a full-grown steer, bull, ox, or cow, used as meat. **b.** *pl.* **beeves** |bēvz|. Such an animal raised for meat. **2.** Human strength or muscle; brawn. **3.** *pl.* **beefs.** *Slang.* A complaint. —***modifier:*** *beef stew.*

beef·steak |**bēf′**stāk′| *n.* A slice of beef suitable for broiling or frying.

beef·y |**bē′**fē| *adj.* **beef·i·er, beef·i·est.** Heavy, strong, and muscular; brawny: *a beefy wrestler.*

bee·hive |**bē′**hīv′| *n.* **1.** A natural or man-made shelter for a swarm of bees. **2.** A very busy place.

bee·line |**bē′**līn′| *n.* The fastest and most direct course, as one that might be taken by a bee going to its hive.

Be·el·ze·bub |bē **ĕl′**zə bŭb′|. The Devil.

been |bĭn|. Past participle of **be.** ¶*These sound alike* **been, bin.**

beep |bēp| *n.* A short sound, such as that made by an automobile's horn or a radio transmitter. —*v.* **1.** To make such sounds: *The transmitter beeped steadily.* **2.** To sound the horn of an automobile: *The cars beeped and beeped, but no one moved.*

beer |bîr| *n.* **1.** An alcoholic beverage brewed from malt and hops. **2.** Any of various soft drinks, such as root beer. —***modifier:*** *a beer can.* ¶*These sound alike* **beer, bier.**

bees·wax |**bēz′**wăks′| *n.* **1.** The yellowish or brownish wax produced by honeybees for making their honeycombs. **2.** A processed and purified form of this wax used for commercial purposes, as in making candles, crayons, and polishes.

beet |bēt| *n.* **1. a.** A plant with a thick, rounded, dark-red root eaten as a vegetable. **b.** Also **sugar beet.** A form of this plant with a large, whitish root from which sugar is made. **2.** The root of either of these plants. ¶*These sound alike* **beet, beat.**

bee·tle[1] |**bēt′**l| *n.* Any of various insects that have the hind wings folded and hidden under the horny or leathery front wings when not flying. ¶*These sound alike* **beetle, betel.** [SEE NOTE & PICTURE]

bee·tle[2] |**bēt′**l| *n.* A kind of wooden mallet. ¶*These sound alike* **beetle, betel.** [SEE NOTE]

bee·tle-browed |**bēt′**l broud′| *adj.* Having large, overhanging brows: *the beetle-browed skull of a Neanderthal man.*

bee·tling |**bēt′**l ĭng| *adj.* Prominent or overhanging: *beetling brows; beetling cliffs.*

beeves |bēvz| *n.* A plural of **beef.**

be·fall |bĭ **fôl′**| *v.* **be·fell** |bĭ **fĕl′**|, **be·fall·en** |bĭ-**fôl′**ən|, **be·fall·ing.** To happen to: *Great misfortunes befell the Arctic explorers.*

be·fit |bĭ **fĭt′**| *v.* **be·fit·ted, be·fit·ting.** To be suitable to or appropriate for: *The Senate, as befits a democratic legislative body, accurately represents the nation.*

be·fore |bĭ **fôr′**| *or* |**-fōr′**| *adv.* **1.** Earlier; previously: *I told you about her before.* **2.** *Archaic.* In front; ahead: *"With the cross of Jesus going on*

bee[1]
honeybee

bee[1-2]
We inherit the name of the **bee**[1] *in unbroken descent from the earliest times, with little change; it was* beo *in Old English,* bīon- *in prehistoric Germanic, and* bhei- *in Indo-European.* **Bee**[2] *is an Americanism and first appeared in the eighteenth century. It has been suggested that it derives from* bean days, *an old expression used in the north of England and meaning a kind of gathering in which neighbors got together to work on large jobs.*

beetle[1]
stag beetle

beetle[1-2]
A **beetle**[1] *bites, a* **beetle**[2] *beats. In Old English, the insect was* bitela, *from* bītan, *"to bite"; the mallet was* bīetel, *related to* bēatan, *"to beat."* **Beetling** *and* **beetle-browed** *are of unknown origin.*

begonia

ă pat/ā pay/â care/ä father/ĕ pet/ ē be/ĭ pit/ī pie/î fierce/ŏ pot/ ō go/ô paw, for/oi oil/ŏŏ book/ ōō boot/ou out/ŭ cut/û fur/ *th* the/th thin/hw which/zh vision/ ə ago, item, pencil, atom, circus

before." (Sabine Baring-Gould). *—prep.* **1.** Ahead of; earlier than: *He got there before me.* **2.** Prior to: *the old days before the war.* **3.** In front of: *Eat what's set before you.* **4. a.** Under the consideration of: *the case now before the court.* **b.** In the presence of: *He was brought before the judge.* **5.** In preference to or in higher esteem than: *I'd take the Rolling Stones before Bob Dylan any day.* *—conj.* **1.** In advance of the time when: *before he went.* **2.** Sooner than: *He would die before he would give in.*

be•fore•hand |bĭ **fôr'**hănd'| *or* |**-fōr'-**| *adv.* In advance; ahead of time: *The class starts on the hour, but I always get there beforehand.*

Idiom. **be beforehand with.** To anticipate or be ready for: *If you are beforehand with your enemies, you stand a better chance of winning.*

be•foul |bĭ **foul'**| *v.* To make dirty; soil: *smokestacks befouling the air.*

be•friend |bĭ **frĕnd'**| *v.* To act as a friend to; assist.

be•fud•dle |bĭ **fŭd'**l| *v.* **be•fud•dled, be•fud•dling.** To confuse; perplex: *The fox used many wiles to befuddle the hunters.*

beg |bĕg| *v.* **begged, beg•ging. 1.** To ask or ask for humbly or earnestly; plead or plead for: *I beg your pardon. I beg of you not to leave the baby alone.* **2.** To ask or ask for as charity: *He begs for a living. He was so poor that he had to beg his meals from door to door.* **3. —beg off.** To ask to be excused from: *She begged off the invitation to the party.*

Idiom. **go begging.** To go or remain unclaimed or unwanted: *His paintings went begging for many years.*

be•gan |bĭ **găn'**|. Past tense of **begin.**

be•gat |bĭ **găt'**|. *Archaic.* A past tense of **beget.**

be•get |bĭ **gĕt'**| *v.* **be•got** |bĭ **gŏt'**|, **be•got•ten** |bĭ-**gŏt'**n| or **be•got, be•get•ting. 1.** To father; sire. **2.** To cause to exist; produce: *Knowledge begets knowledge.* **—be•get'ter** *n.*

beg•gar |**bĕg'**ər| *n.* **1.** A person who begs as a means of living. **2.** Any very poor person; a pauper. *—v.* **1.** To make very poor; ruin. **2. —beggar description.** To be impossible to describe: *Her beauty beggars description.*

beg•gar•ly |**bĕg'**ər lē| *adj.* **1.** Of or like a beggar; poor: *beggarly clothes; a beggarly appearance.* **2.** Mean; contemptible: *a beggarly king.*

beg•gar-ticks |**bĕg'**ər tĭks'| *n.* **1.** *(used with a singular or plural verb).* A plant with seeds that cling to clothing or the fur of animals by means of tiny, hooked bristles: *Beggar-ticks is a common weed. Beggar-ticks grow in swampy places.* **2.** *(used with a plural verb).* The seeds of this plant: *Beggar-ticks were clinging to our socks.*

be•gin |bĭ **gĭn'**| *v.* **be•gan** |bĭ **găn'**|, **be•gun** |bĭ-**gŭn'**|, **be•gin•ning. 1.** To start to do (something); commence: *George began his schooling at five years of age. The plant began to grow. The play begins at 8:00.* **2.** To come or cause to come into being; originate: *Charity begins at home. The men began the newspaper as a political weapon.* **3.** To have as a starting point: *A proper noun always begins with a capital letter.*

be•gin•ner |bĭ **gĭn'**ər| *n.* Someone who is just starting to learn or do something; a novice.

be•gin•ning |bĭ **gĭn'**ĭng| *n.* **1.** The act or process of bringing or being brought into existence; a start: *assuming responsibility for the beginning of the strike.* **2.** The time or point when something begins or is begun: *the beginning of the world. No one likes to wear glasses in the beginning.* **3.** The place where something begins or is begun; an initial section, division, etc.; first part: *at the beginning of the play. A good beginning helps get the reader interested.* **4.** A source or origin: *Near these diggings a shantytown grew, the beginning of the city of Kimberley.* **5.** Often **beginnings.** The early phase; an initial or rudimentary period: *the beginnings of a volcano. Last year you learned about the beginnings of our nation.*

be•gone |bĭ **gôn'**| *or* |**-gŏn'**| *interj.* A word used to express dismissal.

be•go•nia |bĭ **gōn'**yə| *n.* Any of several plants often grown for their showy flowers or colorfully marked leaves. [SEE PICTURE]

be•got |bĭ **gŏt'**|. The past tense and a past participle of **beget.**

be•got•ten |bĭ **gŏt'**n|. A past participle of **beget.**

be•grime |bĭ **grīm'**| *v.* **be•grimed, be•grim•ing.** To soil with dirt or grime.

be•grudge |bĭ **grŭj'**| *v.* **be•grudged, be•grudg•ing. 1.** To envy (someone) the possession or enjoyment of something: *She begrudged him his youth. She begrudged his youth.* **2.** To give with reluctance: *He begrudged every penny he gave us.*

be•guile |bĭ **gīl'**| *v.* **be•guiled, be•guil•ing. 1.** To deceive; trick: *He beguiled me into lending him the money.* **2.** To amuse; delight: *They beguiled us with song.* **3.** To pass pleasantly: *stories written to beguile the time during a journey.*

be•guine |bĭ **gēn'**| *n.* **1.** A lively dance that originated in the West Indies. **2.** The music for this dance.

be•gum |**bē'**gəm| *n.* A Moslem princess or lady of rank.

be•gun |bĭ **gŭn'**|. Past participle of **begin.**

be•half |bĭ **hăf'**| *or* |**-häf'**| *n.* Interest; benefit.

Idioms. **in behalf of.** In the interest of; for the benefit of: *The farmers were acting in behalf of their neighbors.* **on behalf of.** On the part of: *I'll thank you now, on behalf of Mrs. Jones.*

be•have |bĭ **hāv'**| *v.* **be•haved, be•hav•ing. 1.** To act, react, perform, or function in a certain way: *The car behaves well at high speed.* **2. a.** To conduct oneself in a specified way: *He behaved badly.* **b.** To conduct oneself properly: *If you behave, you may stay up late.* **3. —behave oneself.** To act properly; do what is right.

be•hav•ior |bĭ **hāv'**yər| *n.* **1.** The way in which a person behaves; conduct: *on his best behavior.* **2.** The actions or reactions of persons or things under specified circumstances: *studying the behavior of matter at extremely low temperatures.*

be•hav•ior•al |bĭ **hāv'**yər əl| *adj.* Of behavior: *behavioral changes that promoted the survival of a species of insects.* **—be•hav'ior•al•ly** *adv.*

be•hav•iour |bĭ **hāv'**yər| *n.* British form of the word **behavior.**

be•head |bĭ **hĕd'**| *v.* To remove the head from: *The people rebelled and beheaded their king and queen.*

be•held |bĭ **hĕld'**|. Past tense and past participle of **behold.**

be•he•moth |bĭ **hē'**məth| *or* |**bē'**ə məth| *n.* **1.** A huge animal, perhaps the hippopotamus, mentioned in the Old Testament. **2.** Anything huge in size.

be•hest |bĭ **hĕst′**| *n.* A command or strong request; an urgent prompting: *At the behest of the general, I made the journey.*

be•hind |bĭ **hīnd′**| *prep.* **1.** At the back or in the rear of: *the shed behind the barn.* Often used with a reflexive object: *He glanced quickly behind him.* Also used adverbially: *He sneaked up on us from behind.* **2.** On the farther side of or on the other side of (something intervening): *He had a secret cabinet behind the painting.* **3.** Underlying; in the background of: *Behind his every thought and action the ideal of peace was present.* **4.** In support of: *Although many opposed him, most of the army was behind De Gaulle.* **5. a.** Following: *A bulletproof security car drove close behind the President's car.* **b.** In pursuit of: *His heart beat faster as he heard the sound of horses' hoofs behind him.* —*adv.* **1.** In the place or situation that is left: *With good-bys for the friends who stayed behind, the traders departed.* **2.** Falling back or backward. Often used adjectivally: *He was always behind in his homework.* —*n. Informal.* The buttocks or backside.

be•hind•hand |bĭ **hīnd′**hănd′| *adj.* Late; remiss or slow: *He is always behindhand with the rent.*

be•hold |bĭ **hōld′**| *v.* **be•held** |bĭ **hĕld′**|, **be•hold•ing.** To gaze upon; look at; see: *In the distance Lewis and Clark beheld the shining mountains reflecting the snowfields that crown their heights.* —**be•hold′er** *n.*

be•hold•en |bĭ **hōl′**dən| *adj.* Indebted: *Electricity has made man beholden to the machine.*

be•hoove |bĭ **hōōv′**| *v.* **be•hooved, be•hoov•ing.** To be necessary, right, or proper for: *It behooves you to study this in depth.*

beige |bāzh| *n.* A light grayish or yellowish brown. —*adj.* Light grayish or yellowish brown.

Bei•jing |**bā′jĭng′**|. The capital of China. Population, 8,500,000.

be•ing |**bē′**ĭng| *n.* **1.** The state of existing; existence: *That style came into being in the thirties.* **2.** Someone or something that is alive: *a human being. Dainty elves and other little beings danced around in his dream.* **3.** One's basic or essential nature: *Such conflict strikes at our very being.* **4. the Supreme Being.** God.

Bei•rut |bā **rōōt′**| *or* |**bā′**rōōt′|. The capital of Lebanon. Population, 700,000.

be•jew•el |bĭ **jōō′**əl| *v.* **be•jew•eled** or **be•jew•elled, be•jew•el•ing** or **be•jew•el•ling.** To ornament with jewels.

be•la•bor |bĭ **lā′**bər| *v.* **1.** To attack with blows; beat. **2.** To attack verbally; assail. **3.** To go over repeatedly; harp on: *Let's not belabor the point of this explanation.*

be•lat•ed |bĭ **lā′**tĭd| *adj.* Tardy; too late: *belated greetings.* —**be•lat′ed•ly** *adv.*

be•lay |bĭ **lā′**| *v.* **1.** To secure (a rope) around a belaying pin. **2.** To secure (a mountain climber) with a rope. **3.** To stop. Used chiefly in the imperative: *Belay there!*

belaying pin. A pin on the rail of a ship used for securing ropes.

belch |bĕlch| *v.* **1.** To expel gas noisily from the stomach through the mouth. **2.** To send out or eject (smoke, flames, etc.) violently: *The house belched smoke from its windows.* —*n.* An act or instance of belching.

bel•dam, also **bel•dame** |**bĕl′**dəm| *n.* An old woman, especially an unpleasant or ugly one.

be•lea•guer |bĭ **lē′**gər| *v.* **1.** To surround with troops; besiege: *beleaguer a city.* **2.** To persecute constantly, as by threats, demands, etc.; harass. —**be•lea′guered** *adj.*: *a beleaguered fort.*

Bel•fast |**bĕl′**făst′| *or* |-făst′| *or* |bĕl **făst′**| *or* |**-făst′**|. The capital and largest city of Northern Ireland. Population, 390,000.

bel•fry |**bĕl′**frē| *n., pl.* **bel•fries.** **1.** A tower or steeple in which one or more bells are hung. **2.** The part of a steeple in which the bells are hung.

Bel•gium |**bĕl′**jəm|. A country in northwestern Europe. Population, 10,000,000. Capital, Brussels. —**Bel′gian** |**bĕl′**jən| *adj. & n.*

Bel•grade |**bĕl′**grād′| *or* |bĕl **grād′**|. The capital of Yugoslavia. Population, 772,000.

Be•li•al |**bē′**lē əl| *or* |**bēl′**yəl|. In the Bible, the Devil.

be•lie |bĭ **lī′**| *v.* **be•lied, be•ly•ing, be•lies.** **1.** To give a wrong or false idea of: *His cheerful tone belied his feelings of anger and frustration.* **2.** To be inconsistent with; contradict: *Nineteenth-century America went on a pleasure-seeking binge that belied its puritanical past.*

be•lief |bĭ **lēf′**| *n.* **1.** Acceptance or conviction of the truth and existence of something; confidence; trust: *the colonists' belief in government under a written law; always prepared to defend his belief in justice for all.* **2.** The mental habit or condition of placing trust and confidence in a person or thing; faith: *We have one belief, belief in Christ.* **3.** Something believed or accepted as true: *He stated his belief, which is that the sun, not the earth, was the center around which the planets revolved.* **4.** Something taught or accepted by a group of persons as forming part of a religion: *old heathen beliefs.* **5.** An opinion: *It is my belief that we will win the game.*

be•lieve |bĭ **lēv′**| *v.* **be•lieved, be•liev•ing.** **1.** To accept as true or real: *Everyone in the club believed that Dinky had seen a monster.* **2.** To have confidence or faith: *I believe her. I don't believe in her.* **3.** To have faith, especially religious faith: *believe in God.* **4.** To have confidence in the value, worth, existence, etc., of: *He believes in getting plenty of sleep.* **5.** To expect; think or suppose: *I believe it will snow tomorrow.* —**be•liev′a•ble** *adj.* —**be•liev′er** *n.*

***Idiom.* make believe.** To pretend.

be•lit•tle |bĭ **lĭt′**l| *v.* **be•lit•tled, be•lit•tling.** To cause to seem small or unimportant; disparage.

Be•lize |bə **lēz′**|. A country of northeastern Central America on the Caribbean Sea. Population, 145,000. Capital, Belmopan.

bell |bĕl| *n.* **1.** A hollow metal instrument, usually cup-shaped with a flared opening. It makes a metallic tone when struck. **2.** Something having a flared opening like that of a bell: *the bell of a trumpet.* **3. bells.** A musical instrument consisting of a set of metal tubes tuned to a chromatic scale and struck with a small hammer to produce clear, silvery tunes. **4.** A **diving bell.** —***modifier:*** *a bell tower.* —*v.* **1.** To put a bell on. **2.** To flare like a bell: *His pants bell nicely below the knee.* ¶*These sound alike* **bell, belle.**

Bell |bĕl|, **Alexander Graham.** 1847–1922.

belfry
On the old church at Sleepy Hollow, painted in 1882.

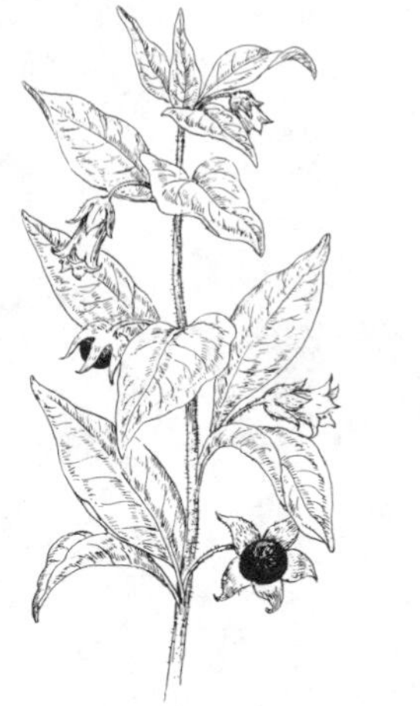

belladonna

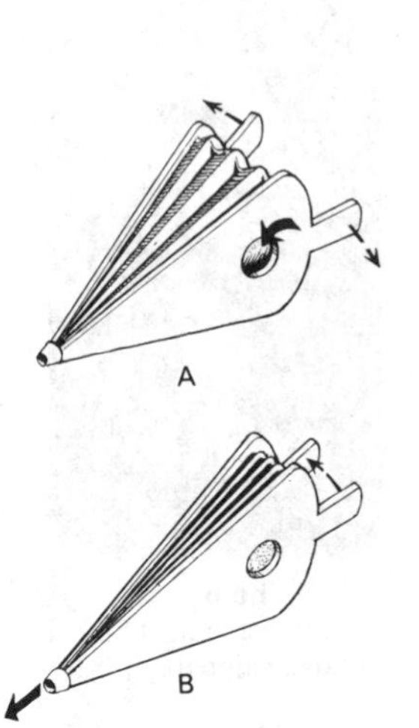

bellows
A. Air is admitted through open valve *(large arrow)* as bellows is expanded
B. Valve closes and air is expelled through nozzle *(large arrow)* as bellows is compressed

ă pat/ā pay/â care/ä father/ĕ pet/ ē be/ĭ pit/ī pie/î fierce/ŏ pot/ ō go/ô paw, for/oi oil/ŏŏ book/ ōō boot/ou out/ŭ cut/û fur/ *th* the/th thin/hw which/zh vision/ ə ago, item, pencil, atom, circus

Scottish-born American scientist; inventor of the telephone.

bel•la•don•na |bĕl'ə **dŏn**'ə| *n.* **1.** A poisonous plant with purplish flowers and small black berries. **2.** A medicinal substance containing the drug atropine, which is derived from this plant. [SEE PICTURE]

bell•bot•tom |**bĕl**'bŏt'əm| *adj.* Having legs that flare out at the bottom: *bellbottom trousers.*

bell•bot•toms, also **bell-bot•toms** |**bĕl**'bŏt'əmz| *n. (used with a plural verb).* Trousers with legs that flare out at the bottom.

bell•boy |**bĕl**'boi'| *n.* A boy or man employed by a hotel to carry luggage, run errands, etc.

belle |bĕl| *n.* **1.** A very attractive girl or woman. **2.** The most popular or attractive girl or woman at a specified place: *the belle of the ball.* ¶*These sound alike* **belle, bell.**

belles-let•tres |bĕl **lĕt**'rə| *n. (used with a singular verb).* Literature viewed in terms of artistic rather than informative or teaching content.

bell•flow•er |**bĕl**'flou'ər| *n.* Any of several plants with bell-shaped, usually purplish-blue flowers.

bell•hop |**bĕl**'hŏp'| *n. Informal.* A bellboy.

bel•li•cose |**bĕl**'ĭ kōs'| *adj.* Warlike, as in manner or disposition: *a bellicose nation.*

bel•lig•er•ence |bə **lĭj**'ər əns| *n.* A warlike or hostile attitude, nature, or disposition.

bel•lig•er•ent |bə **lĭj**'ər ənt| *adj.* **1.** Inclined to fight; hostile; quarrelsome: *a belligerent, loose-tongued bully.* **2.** Of or engaged in warfare: *a belligerent nation.* —*n.* A person or nation engaged in war. —**bel•lig'er•ent•ly** *adv.*

bell jar. A large, bell-shaped glass container with an open bottom, used to protect delicate instruments and used in experiments to provide a space that is sealed off from the atmosphere.

bel•low |**bĕl**'ō| *n.* **1.** The loud, roaring sound made by a bull or certain other large animals. **2.** A loud, deep shout or cry. —*v.* **1.** To roar as a bull does. **2.** To shout in a deep, loud voice: *"Kill the umpire!" bellowed the angry spectator.*

bel•lows |**bĕl**'ōz| *or* |-əz| *n. (used with a singular or plural verb).* A device for pumping air, consisting of a chamber with openings controlled by valves so that air can enter only at one and leave only at another as the chamber is forced to expand and contract. [SEE PICTURE]

bell•weth•er |**bĕl**'wĕ*th*'ər| *n.* A male sheep that wears a bell and leads a flock.

bel•ly |**bĕl**'ē| *n., pl.* **bel•lies. 1.** In human beings and other mammals, the front part of the body below the chest; the abdomen. **2.** The stomach. **3.** The underside of the body. **4.** The deep, hollow interior of something: *out of the belly of Hell; a ship's belly.* —*v.* **bel•lied, bel•ly•ing, bel•lies.** To swell; bulge: *A puff of air bellied the sails out. The sails bellied in the breeze.*

bel•ly•ache |**bĕl**'ē āk'| *n.* Any pain or discomfort in the stomach or abdomen. —*v.* **-ached, -ach•ing.** *Slang.* To grumble or complain in a whining way.

bel•ly•but•ton |**bĕl**'ē bŭt'n| *n. Informal.* The navel.

be•long |bĭ **lông**'| *or* |**-lŏng**'| *v.* **1.** To have a proper or suitable place: *The suit belongs in the closet.* **2.** —**belong to. a.** To be the property of; be owned by: *This watch once belonged to my grandmother.* **b.** To be a member of: *He belongs to a labor union.*

be•long•ings |bĭ **lông**'ĭngz| *or* |**-lŏng'-**| *pl.n.* The things that belong to someone; possessions: *She lost all her personal belongings.*

be•lov•ed |bĭ **lŭv**'ĭd| *or* |**-lŭvd**'| *adj.* Dearly loved. —*n.* A person who is dearly loved.

be•low |bĭ **lō**'| *adv.* **1.** Following or farther down on a page: *Below is a list of good fiction for boys.* **2.** In or to a lower place or level: *They paused on the bridge to admire the rapids below.* Also used prepositionally: *We stood at the window and watched the people in the street below us.* **3.** On or to a lower floor or deck: *The trunks were stowed in a compartment below.* **4.** Further down, as along a slope or valley: *From below, the thousands of toiling men looked like ants at work.* Also used prepositionally: *an old mine a hundred feet down the hill below our hut.* **5.** On earth: *all creatures here below.* —*prep.* **1.** Underneath; under; beneath: *Below the earth there was a race of wicked gnomes.* **2.** Lower than, as on a graduated scale: *We use negative numbers to show temperatures below zero.* Also used adverbially: *temperatures of zero and below.*

belt |bĕlt| *n.* **1.** A band of leather, cloth, plastic, etc., worn around the waist for decoration or to hold up trousers, weapons, etc. **2.** A **seat belt. 3.** A band that forms a closed loop and passes over two or more wheels or pulleys, serving to transmit motion from one to another or to carry objects. **4.** A geographical region that is distinctive in some specific way: *the corn belt; the Bible belt.* —**modifier:** *a belt buckle.* —*v.* **1.** To encircle with or as if with a belt: *The equator belts the earth.* **2.** To fasten with a belt: *The officer belted on his canteen.* **3.** *Informal.* To strike; hit: *belting him on the nose. He belted three homers in one game.* **4.** To sing loudly: *She belted out a song.*

***Idioms.* hit below the belt.** To fight in an unfair manner. **tighten (one's) belt.** To become thrifty and frugal.

belt•ing |**bĕl**'tĭng| *n.* **1.** Material used to make belts. **2.** Belts in general.

be•lu•ga |bə **lōō**'gə| *n.* **1.** A sturgeon of the Black and Caspian seas, whose roe is used for caviar. **2.** A small white or grayish whale of northern waters.

be•ma |**bē**'mə| *n., pl.* **be•ma•ta** |**bē**'mə tə|. **1.** The enclosed area around the altar of an Eastern Orthodox church. **2.** A bimah.

be•moan |bĭ **mōn**'| *v.* To moan about; lament; bewail: *bemoan one's fate.*

be•mused |bĭ **myōōzd**'| *adj.* **1.** Confused; stupefied. **2.** Lost in thought; preoccupied.

bench |bĕnch| *n.* **1.** A long seat for two or more persons, with or without a back. **2.** A sturdy table on which a carpenter, shoemaker, or other craftsman works. **3.** The seat for judges in a courtroom. **4.** The office or position of a judge. **5. a.** The place where the members of an athletic team sit when they are not playing. **b.** The reserve players on an athletic team. —*v.* To remove (a player) from a team's line-up.

bench mark. A surveyor's mark made on some stationary object, used as a reference point in reckoning differences in level, as in tidal observations and in surveying.

bend |bĕnd| *v.* **bent** |bĕnt|, **bend•ing. 1. a.** To make or become curved, crooked, or angular: *He bent his elbow. Press with the knife to bend the wire. The willows bent in the breeze.* **b.** To incline the body or part of the body; stoop: *bending over to pick up the ball; with the head bent over the book.* **c.** To be capable of being bent: *Green wood will bend easily.* **2.** To take or cause to take a new direction: *Light does not bend around you as it passes by. The lenses of a telescope bend the rays of light that go through them.* **3.** To turn or direct (one's eyes, attention, etc.): *Celester bent a lively glance at Ronald.* **4.** To decide; resolve: *nations whose rulers are bent on conquest. Why was he so bent on following them?* **5.** To yield or force to yield: *Hanoi will not bend to U.S. desires. The barons bent the king to their will.* **6.** To change deceptively; distort: *bending the facts to fit a conclusion.* —*n.* **1.** A turn, curve, or bent part: *I can see a ship coming around the river bend.* **2. the bends.** **Caisson disease.**

be•neath |bĭ **nēth'**| *prep.* **1. a.** Directly underneath: *The cat is sleeping beneath the stove.* Also used adverbially: *The diagram is explained in the legend printed beneath.* **b.** Underneath in relation to something that screens or shelters: *Beneath the tall date trees they planted figs and olives.* Also used adverbially: *The branches parted, and a patch of sunlight reached the mossy ground beneath.* **c.** Underneath or on the other side of an intervening surface: *The water stored in rock and soil beneath the ground is called groundwater.* Also used adverbially: *Certain delineations enable us to see the body structures beneath.* **2.** At a level lower than or further down from: *We found a spring just beneath the summit.* Also used adverbially: *At the top of the hill he turned and looked down into the plain beneath.* **3.** Far below or unworthy of: *beneath contempt.*

ben•e•dic•tion |bĕn'ĭ **dĭk'**shən| *n.* **1.** A blessing. **2.** A request for God's blessing, usually recited at the close of a religious service.

ben•e•fac•tor |**bĕn'**ə făk'tər| *n.* A person who gives financial or other aid to another.

be•nef•i•cence |bə **nĕf'**ĭ səns| *n.* **1.** The action of doing good; kindness; charity. **2.** A charitable act or gift.

be•nef•i•cent |bə **nĕf'**ĭ sənt| *adj.* Doing or bringing about good: *a beneficient king.*

ben•e•fi•cial |bĕn'ə **fĭsh'**əl| *adj.* Bringing benefit; advantageous: *Many bacteria are beneficial to man.*

ben•e•fi•ci•ar•y |bĕn'ə **fĭsh'**ē ĕr'ē| *or* |-**fĭsh'**ə rē| *n., pl.* **ben•e•fi•ci•ar•ies. 1.** Anyone who derives benefit from something: *Low-income families will be the major beneficiaries of the new housing plan.* **2.** A person who is designated to receive funds from an insurance policy or will upon the death of another.

ben•e•fit |**bĕn'**ə fĭt| *n.* **1.** Something that is of help; an advantage: *The field trip was of great benefit to the students.* **2.** Often **benefits.** Payments made in accordance with a wage agreement, insurance contract, or public assistance program: *unemployment benefits.* **3.** A theatrical performance or social event held to raise money for a worthy cause. —***modifier:*** *a benefit performance at the opera house.* —*v.* **1.** To be helpful or beneficial to: *a program designed to benefit the greatest number of people.* **2.** To receive help; profit: *benefit from his example.*

benefit of the doubt. A favorable judgment made in the absence of more complete information.

be•nev•o•lence |bə **nĕv'**ə ləns| *n.* An inclination to do good; kindliness; good will.

be•nev•o•lent |bə **nĕv'**ə lənt| *adj.* **1.** Desiring or inclined to do good; kindly: *a benevolent king; a benevolent attitude.* **2.** Designed for charitable purposes: *a benevolent fund.*

be•night•ed |bĭ **nī'**tĭd| *adj.* In a state of moral or intellectual backwardness; unenlightened.

be•nign |bĭ **nīn'**| *adj.* **1.** Kind; gentle: *His face was fatherly and benign.* **2.** Mild; favorable: *a benign climate.* **3.** Not seriously harmful or malignant: *a benign illness; a benign tumor.* —**be•nig'ni•ty** |bĭ**nĭg'**nĭ tē| *n.*

Be•nin |bə **nĭn'**| *or* |-**nēn'**|. A country on the southern coast of West Africa. Population, 3,338,000. Capital, Porto-Novo.

ben•ny |**bĕn'**ē| *n., pl.* **ben•nies.** *Slang.* A Benzedrine pill.

bent |bĕnt|. Past tense and past participle of **bend.** —*adj.* **1.** Curved or crooked: *a bent nail.* **2.** Resolved; determined: *a man bent on traveling around the world.* —*n.* A tendency or inclination: *a strong bent for change.*

ben•thos |**bĕn'**thŏs'| *n.* **1.** The bottom of a sea or lake. **2.** The organisms living on sea or lake bottoms.

be•numb |bĭ **nŭm'**| *v.* To make numb; deprive of feeling: *The cold benumbed our fingers.*

Ben•ze•drine |**bĕn'**zĭ drēn'| *n.* A trademark for a brand of amphetamine.

ben•zene |**bĕn'**zēn'| *or* |bĕn **zēn'**| *n.* A clear, colorless liquid that burns very easily. It is composed of carbon and hydrogen and has the formula C_6H_6. It is derived from petroleum and is used to make detergents, insect poisons, motor fuels, and other chemicals. [SEE NOTE]

ben•zine |**bĕn'**zēn'| *or* |bĕn **zēn'**| *n.* A mixture of liquid hydrocarbons that is distilled from petroleum and used as a solvent.

ben•zo•ate of soda |**bĕn'**zō āt'| *or* |-ĭt|. **Sodium benzoate.**

ben•zo•ic acid |bĕn **zō'**ĭk|. An organic acid composed of carbon, hydrogen, and oxygen and having the formula $C_7H_6O_2$. It is used to season tobacco and in perfumes and germicides.

ben•zo•in |**bĕn'**zō ĭn| *or* |-zoin'| *n.* Any of various resins that contain benzoic acid and that are obtained from certain trees of Southeast Asia. They are used in making perfumes, ointments, and medicines.

ben•zol |**bĕn'**zôl'| *or* |-zōl'| *n.* Benzene.

Be•o•wulf |**bā'**ə wo͝olf'|. The hero of the Old English epic poem of the same name.

be•queath |bĭ **kwēth'**| *or* |-**kwēth'**| *v.* **1.** To leave (property) in a will. **2.** To pass on or hand down.

be•quest |bĭ **kwĕst'**| *n.* **1.** The act of bequeathing. **2.** Something that is bequeathed in a will.

be•rate |bĭ **rāt'**| *v.* **be•rat•ed, be•rat•ing.** To scold severely; upbraid.

be•reave |bĭ **rēv'**| *v.* **be•reaved** or **be•reft** |bĭ **rĕft'**|, **be•reav•ing.** To deprive of (a loved person) by death.

be•reft |bĕ **rĕft'**|. A past tense and past parti-

benzene

One of the interesting properties of **benzene** *is that the six carbon atoms it contains are arranged in a ring called the* **benzene ring.** *A very large number of organic compounds are related to benzene in that they preserve its ring structure.*

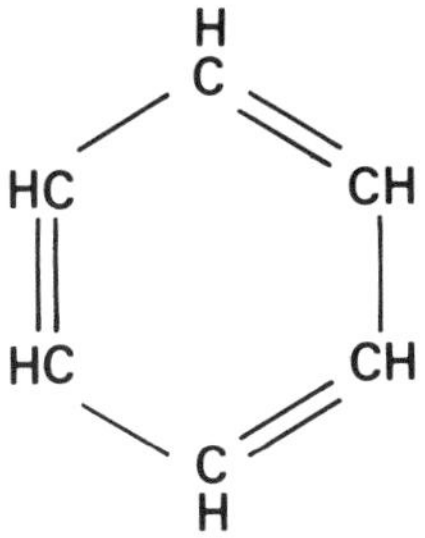

benzene ring

Each C represents a carbon atom, each H a hydrogen atom, and the straight lines are chemical bonds

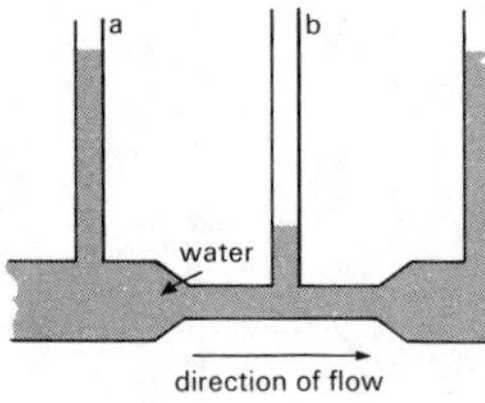

Bernoulli's law
The lower height of the water in the tube b shows that the pressure in the narrow section of the pipe is less than that in the wide sections.

This law was discovered by and is named after Daniel Bernoulli *(1700–1782), a Swiss mathematician.*

berry
The **blueberry** *and the* **strawberry** *are among the fruits that are best known as berries. To a botanist, however, a* **berry** *is any fleshy, many-seeded fruit that develops from a single ovary, such as a grape, tomato, or eggplant.*

ciple of **bereave.** —*adj.* Deprived; denied: *bereft of all hope.*

be•ret |bə **rā′**| *or* |**bĕr′**ā′| *n.* A soft, round, flat cap of wool or felt.

ber•ga•mot |**bûr′**gə mŏt′| *n.* A plant with a strong, pleasant odor and clusters of red or purplish flowers.

ber•i•ber•i |**bĕr′**ē **bĕr′**ē| *n.* A disease of the nervous system, caused by a lack of vitamin B_1. Its symptoms include partial paralysis of the hands and feet and weakness.

Ber•ing Sea |**bîr′**ĭng| *or* |**bĕr′**-| *or* |**bâr′**-|. A part of the Pacific Ocean between Alaska and Siberia.

Bering Strait. A narrow waterway between Alaska and Siberia, connecting the Bering Sea and the Arctic Ocean.

ber•ke•li•um |bər **kē′**lē əm| *or* |**bûrk′**lē əm| *n.* Symbol **Bk** One of the elements, a metal first produced by bombarding an americium isotope with helium ions. It has nine isotopes with mass numbers ranging from 243 to 250 and half-lives ranging from 3 hours to 1,380 years. Atomic number 97; valences +3, +4.

Ber•lin |bər **lĭn′**|. A city in northeastern East Germany, formerly the capital of Germany but divided since 1945 into East Berlin, the capital of East Germany, and West Berlin, a part of West Germany.

Ber•mu•da |bər **myōō′**də|. A group of British islands in the Atlantic Ocean, about 600 miles east of the coast of the United States. Population, 60,000. Capital, Hamilton.

Bermuda shorts. Shorts that end slightly above the knees.

Bern, also **Berne** |bûrn|. The capital of Switzerland. Population, 170,000.

Ber•noul•li's law |bər **nōō′**lēz|. Also **Bernoulli's principle.** The law of physics that states that a fluid in motion exerts less pressure on a surface parallel to the direction of flow than does a stationary fluid. The pressure decreases as the velocity of the fluid increases. [SEE NOTE & PICTURE]

ber•ry |**bĕr′**ē| *n., pl.* **ber•ries. 1.** A usually small, juicy fruit with many seeds rather than a single stone. **2.** A seed or dried kernel, as of coffee. ¶ *These sound alike* **berry, bury.** [SEE NOTE]

ber•serk |bər **sûrk′**| *or* |-**zûrk′**| *adj.* In or into a crazed or violent frenzy: *He went berserk and started firing at everyone in sight.*

berth |bûrth| *n.* **1.** A built-in bed or bunk in a ship or a railroad sleeping car. **2.** A space at a wharf for a ship to dock or anchor. **3.** A position of employment; a job. ¶ *These sound alike* **berth, birth.**

ber•yl |**bĕr′**əl| *n.* A mineral composed chiefly of beryllium, aluminum, silicon, and oxygen in the proportions $Be_3Al_2Si_6O_{18}$. It is the chief source of beryllium and is also used as a gem.

be•ryl•li•um |bə **rĭl′**ē əm| *n.* Symbol **Be** One of the elements, a lightweight, rigid, steel-gray metal. Atomic number 4; atomic weight 9.01; valence +2; melting point 1,278°C; boiling point 2,970°C.

be•seech |bĭ **sēch′**| *v.* **be•sought** |bĭ **sôt′**| or **be•seeched, be•seech•ing.** To ask earnestly; entreat; implore: *Spare me, I beseech you!*

be•seem |bĭ **sēm′**| *v.* To be suitable or becoming to; befit: *Such scandalous behavior hardly beseems you.*

be•set |bĭ **sĕt′**| *v.* **be•set, be•set•ting. 1.** To trouble persistently; afflict; distress: *all the ills that beset mankind.* **2.** To attack from all sides: *Along the garden path he was beset by dogs.*

be•side |bĭ **sīd′**| *prep.* **1.** At the side of: *She sat down beside her boyfriend.* **2.** In comparison with: *He is quite short beside his brother.* **3.** Apart from; wide of: *His remark was entirely beside the point.*

***Idiom.* beside (oneself).** Out of one's wits with excitement, anger, etc.: *The winners were beside themselves with joy.*

be•sides |bĭ **sīdz′**| *adv.* **1.** In addition: *He saw to it that every warrior was mounted and had a spare horse besides.* **2.** Moreover; furthermore: *He was uneasy at having to talk to such a big crowd, and besides it was getting late.* —*prep.* **1.** In addition to: *The Congress of Vienna did other things besides remaking Europe.* **2.** Other than; except for: *There's nothing to eat here besides a little roast pork.*

be•siege |bĭ **sēj′**| *v.* **be•sieged, be•sieg•ing. 1.** To surround and blockade in order to capture; lay siege to: *a tale of an Assyrian king who besieged Jerusalem three thousand years ago.* **2.** To crowd around and hem in: *Any newly emerged ant is soon besieged by other returning ants.* **3.** To harass; importune: *Reporters, society people, and artists besieged the press secretary with requests for an invitation.*

be•smirch |bĭ **smûrch′**| *v.* **1.** To soil; stain. **2.** To dim the purity of; tarnish; dishonor: *besmirch someone's good name.*

be•sought |bĭ **sôt′**|. A past tense and past participle of **beseech.**

be•spat•ter |bĭ **spăt′**ər| *v.* To soil by splashing with mud, paint, etc.

be•speak |bĭ **spēk′**| *v.* **be•spoke** |bĭ **spōk′**|, **be•spok•en** |bĭ **spō′**kən| or **be•spoke, be•speak•ing.** To be or give a sign of; indicate: *a haggard look on her face that bespoke years of suffering.*

be•spec•ta•cled |bĭ **spĕk′**tə kəld| *adj.* Wearing eyeglasses.

be•spoke |bĭ **spōk′**|. Past tense and a past participle of **bespeak.**

be•spok•en |bĭ **spō′**kən|. A past participle of **bespeak.**

be•sprin•kle |bĭ **sprĭng′**kəl| *v.* **be•sprin•kled, be•sprin•kling.** To sprinkle over: *besprinkle the meat with salt.*

Bes•se•mer converter |**bĕs′**ə mər|. A large pear-shaped container in which the Bessemer process is performed on molten iron.

Bessemer process. A process in which molten iron is converted to steel by forcing compressed air through it and burning out excess carbon and other impurities.

best |bĕst| *adj.* Superlative of **good. 1.** —Used to indicate the highest degree of excellence, quality, achievement, etc.: *the best craftsmen in the world; the hockey team's best score.* **2.** —Used to indicate the highest degree of appropriateness or suitability: *the best place to dig a well.* **3.** —Used to indicate highest social standing or respectability: *The "best" people often have community spirit.* **4.** —Used to indicate the largest portion of something specified: *the best part of a long journey.*

ă pat/ā pay/â care/ä father/ĕ pet/ ē be/ĭ pit/ī pie/î fierce/ŏ pot/ ō go/ô paw, for/oi oil/ŏŏ book/ ōō boot/ou out/ŭ cut/û fur/ *th* the/th thin/hw which/zh vision/ ə ago, item, pencil, atom, circus

5. —Used to indicate the highest degree of closeness: *his best friend.* —*adv.* Superlative of **well. 1.** In the most excellent way; most properly or successfully: *Which of the two pictures best fits your description?* **2.** Most: *What does he like to eat best?* —*n.* Someone or something that is best, as: **1.** The best person or persons: *Misfortune can come to the best of us.* **2.** One's best effort or appearance: *do your best; look your best.* **3.** One's best wishes or regards: *Give them my best.* —*v.* To get the better of; defeat: *besting their rivals in every game.* [SEE NOTE]

***Idioms.* as best (one) can.** As well as one can: *Try to remedy the situation as best you can.* **at best. 1.** Interpreted most favorably; at most: *His remark was at best a well-meaning blunder.* **2.** Under the most favorable conditions: *This car does 120 at best.* **for the best.** For the ultimate good: *His departure, though regrettable, was for the best.* **get the best of.** To defeat or outwit: *Nobody's ever gotten the best of me.* **had best.** Should; ought to: *You had best get out of here.* **make the best of it.** To do as well as possible under unfavorable conditions: *It's cold and wet, but we'll just have to make the best of it.* **Sunday best.** One's best clothes.

bes•tial |bĕs′chəl| *or* |bĕst′yəl| *adj.* Like a horrible beast; savage; cruel. —**bes′tial•ly** *adv.*

be•stir |bĭ stûr′| *v.* **be•stirred, be•stir•ring.** To stir to action; rouse: *The Indians of America are now beginning to bestir themselves.*

best man. The chief attendant of the bridegroom at a wedding.

be•stow |bĭ stō′| *v.* To give or present, especially as a gift or honor; confer: *an award bestowed on the nine best defensive players each season.* —**be•stow′al** *n.*

be•strew |bĭ strōō′| *v.* **be•strewed, be•strewn** |bĭ strōōn′| or **be•strewed, be•strew•ing. 1.** To scatter (a surface) with things so as to cover it: *children bestrewing the table with toys.* **2.** To lie or be scattered over: *Bones and bodies of the dead bestrewed the stone floors of the vault.*

be•stride |bĭ strīd′| *v.* **be•strode** |bĭ strōd′|, **be•strid•den** |bĭ strĭd′n|, **be•strid•ing.** To sit or stand on with one leg on each side; straddle: *bestride a horse.*

best seller. A book whose sales are among the highest at a given time.

best-sell•ing |bĕst′sĕl′ĭng| *adj.* Selling in the largest numbers at a given time: *a best-selling novel.*

bet |bĕt| *n.* **1.** An agreement between two parties taking opposing points of view or opposite sides in a game or contest that the party proved correct or victorious will collect something from the other. **2.** Something, as an object or amount, risked in a wager; the stake: *His bet on the race was $50.* **3.** Something, as a person, animal, event, etc., on which a wager is made: *The football team seemed a safe bet this season.* **4.** Something that is preferable or best above others: *The short route is probably your best bet.* —*v.* **bet, bet•ting. 1.** To risk or wager (something) in a bet; make a bet: *betting $10 on a race; bet on a football game. The administration has urged unions and employers not to bet on continuous inflation.* **2.** To state with confidence, as in a bet: *I bet he doesn't answer!*

be•ta |bā′tə| *or* |bē′-| *n.* **1.** The second letter of the Greek alphabet, written Β, β. In English it is represented as *B, b.* **2.** The second item in any series.

be•take |bĭ tāk′| *v.* **be•took** |bĭ tŏŏk′|, **be•tak•en** |bĭ tā′kən|, **be•tak•ing.** To take (oneself); go: *I decided to betake myself to a movie.*

beta particle. An electron or positron traveling at a very high speed, generally emitted by an atomic nucleus undergoing radioactive decay.

be•ta•tron |bā′tə trŏn′| *or* |bē′-| *n.* A machine that accelerates electrons to very high velocities and therefore to very high energies by means of magnetic fields that change with time.

be•tel |bēt′l| *n.* An Asian plant whose leaves are chewed together with the **betel nut,** the seed of a palm tree, by people of southeastern Asia for the stimulating effect thus produced. ¶*These sound alike* **betel, beetle.**

Be•tel•geuse |bēt′l jōōz′| *or* |bĕt′l jœz′| *n.* A bright-red variable star located near the celestial equator and about 527 light-years from Earth. [SEE NOTE]

be•think |bĭ thĭngk′| *v.* **be•thought** |bĭ thôt′|, **be•think•ing.** To remind (oneself); remember: *bethink oneself of an idea.*

Beth•le•hem |bĕth′lĭ hĕm′| *or* |-lē əm|. The birthplace of Christ, a town five miles south of Jerusalem.

be•thought |bĭ thôt′|. Past tense and past participle of **bethink.**

be•tide |bĭ tīd′| *v.* **be•tid•ed, be•tid•ing.** To happen to: *Woe betide anyone who disobeys!*

be•times |bĭ tīmz′| *adv.* In good time; early: *He awoke betimes.*

be•to•ken |bĭ tō′kən| *v.* To give a sign of; point to; indicate: *His speech betokens a new attitude on the subject.*

be•took |bĭ tŏŏk′|. Past tense of **betake.**

be•tray |bĭ trā′| *v.* **1.** To commit treason against; be a traitor to: *betray one's country.* **2.** To be disloyal to: *betray a friend; betraying the confidence of the voters.* **3.** To allow to become known, either by accident or intentionally; give away: *betray a secret.* **4.** To give evidence of; indicate: *The slight redness of his cheeks betrayed confusion.* —**be•tray′er** *n.*

be•tray•al |bĭ trā′əl| *n.* The act of betraying, especially through disloyalty and deception.

be•troth |bĭ trōth′| *or* |-trôth′| *v.* **1.** To promise to give in marriage. **2.** To promise to marry.

be•troth•al |bĭ trō′thəl| *or* |-trô′thəl| *n.* A promise to marry; an engagement.

be•trothed |bĭ trōthd′| *or* |-trôtht′| *n.* A person engaged to be married.

bet•ter[1] |bĕt′ər| *adj.* Comparative of **good. 1.** —Used to indicate a higher degree of excellence or quality: *Jim is better at reading than John. Which of the twins is the better skater? This is a better book than most.* Also used adverbially (as the comparative of **well**): *Jim reads better than John.* **2.** —Used to indicate a higher degree of appropriateness or suitability: *Some of these greetings would be better for friendly letters, and some would be better for business letters.* **3.** —Used to indicate higher social standing or respectability: *In politics, the "better" element constituted his ultimate strength.* **4.** —Used to indicate an improved condition: *Better roads*

Betelgeuse

The name **Betelgeuse** *comes, via French, from Arabic* bit al-jauza, *"shoulder of the giant" (the "giant" is the constellation Orion). The star is much used in navigation. Sailors and airmen have subjected the awkward-seeming name to a humorous folk etymology, pronouncing it* Beetle juice.

better/best

Better *and* **best** *were* betera *and* betest *in Old English. They are both descended from a root* bat-, *meaning "good" but unrelated to the word* **good.** *A similar situation exists in German, Latin, Italian, French, Spanish, Portuguese, and Greek; in all of these languages the basic word for "good" has a completely irregular comparative and superlative. The same is true for the words meaning "bad."*

helped transportation to move forward. Many days passed before he began to feel better. **5.** —Used to indicate the greater portion of something specified: *I knew it might be the better part of an hour before she woke up.* —*adv.* Comparative of **well. 1.** More: *I averaged a shade better than 20 miles per gallon on the road test. The play was first performed better than 20 years ago.* **2.** In a superior manner: *With a larger brain, you are better able to think and to do things.* **3.** More commonly: *Thomas Jackson, better known as "Stonewall" Jackson.* **4.** To a larger degree: *The pine trees are better adapted to this environment.* **5.** More fully: *Better than any other businessman of his time, he saw the future of railroads.* **6.** —Used as an auxiliary in informal speech: *You better stay here.* —*v.* **1.** To surpass or exceed: *His record stood until 1965, when another athlete bettered it.* **2.** To improve (oneself): *teaching the poor to better themselves.* —*n.* **1.** The superior of two: *Both of you are good at this, but which is the better?* **2. betters.** One's superiors: *Don't interrupt your betters.* ¶*These sound alike* **better, bettor.** [SEE NOTE on p. 85]

Idioms. **better off. 1.** Comparative of **well off:** *The Poles are better off today than they were betweeen the two world wars.* **2.** Better advised: *Although she is married, she would be better off filing a separate tax raturn.* **had better.** Ought to: *We had better be leaving now.* **know better than.** To know well enough not to: *He knew better than to waste time looking over his shoulder.*

bet•ter² |bĕt′ər| *n.* A form of the word **bettor.**

bet•ter•ment |bĕt′ər mənt| *n.* The act of improving or a condition of being improved: *work for the betterment of housing conditions.*

bet•tor |bĕt′ər| *n.* A person who bets. ¶*These sound alike* **bettor, better.**

be•tween |bĭ twēn′| *prep.* **1.** —Used to indicate: **a.** Spatial separation: *He felt queer to be outside his fence, with nothing between him and the big world.* **b.** Intermediate state or interval: *When I was neither man nor boy, but between both, I wanted to see the world.* **c.** Position or motion of something enclosed by specified things on either side: *The flood waters were flowing very fast between the banks.* **2.** —Used to indicate: **a.** Reciprocal actions of two or more persons or groups: *I can't buy skates for both of you, so decide between you which stands the better chance of winning the race.* **b.** Spatial connection: *a canal between Chicago and La Salle.* **3.** —Used to indicate: **a.** Relation of difference or comparison: *not much to choose between the two cars.* **b.** Relation of quantity or degree: *There are between thirteen and fourteen hundred minerals in the earth's crust.* —*adv.* In an intermediate space, position, or time: *New York, Albany, and several stations between.* —*Note: Between is often used preceded by in to form the adverbial group* **in between.** In an intermediate space, position, or time.

Idiom. **between you and me.** Confidentially: *Between you and me, I think she failed the test.*

be•twixt |bĭ twĭkst′| *prep. & adv. Archaic.* Between.

betwixt and between. In the middle; in an indecisive state; neither the one nor the other.

Bev•a•tron, also **bev•a•tron** |bĕv′ə trŏn′| *n.* An accelerator capable of raising protons to energies of about one billion electron volts.

bev•el |bĕv′əl| *n.* **1.** A surface formed when two planes meet at an angle other than 90° and form an edge. **2.** The angle at which these planes meet. **3.** Also **bevel square.** A tool used to measure or mark such angles. —***modifier:*** *a bevel edge.* —*v.* **bev•eled** or **bev•elled, bev•el•ing** or **bev•el•ling.** To cut a bevel (on something): *Why not bevel the edge of the shelf?*

bev•er•age |bĕv′ər ĭj| *or* |bĕv′rĭj| *n.* Any of various drinks, such as milk, tea, juice, beer, etc., usually excluding water.

bev•y |bĕv′ē| *n., pl.* **bev•ies. 1.** A flock of quail or similar birds. **2.** A group, especially of girls or young women.

be•wail |bĭ wāl′| *v.* To express sorrow or regret over; bemoan: *bewail one's fate.*

be•ware |bĭ wâr′| *v.* To watch out for; be on guard against. Used chiefly in the imperative and infinitive: *Beware of pickpockets! We were warned to beware of suspicious-looking people.*

be•wil•der |bĭ wĭl′dər| *v.* To confuse greatly; puzzle: *Their questions bewildered him.* —**be•wil′dered** *adj.: a bewildered look.* —**be•wil′der•ing** *adj.: a bewildering statement.* —**be•wil′dered•ly** *adv.* —**be•wil′der•ment** *n.*

be•witch |bĭ wĭch′| *v.* **1.** To cast a spell over: *What will the fairies do to me? Will they bewitch me?* **2.** To captivate completely; fascinate; charm: *The pianist bewitched his listeners with his incredible technique.* —**be•witch′ing** *adj.: a bewitching smile.*

bey |bā| *n.* **1.** A governor of a province in the Ottoman Empire. **2.** A ruler of the former kingdom of Tunis. ¶*These sound alike* **bey, bay.**

be•yond |bē ŏnd′| *or* |bĭ yŏnd′| *prep.* **1.** On the far side of: *A bird called sadly in the forest beyond the hut.* Also used adverbially: *We drove through an archway of trees into the bright sunlight beyond.* **2.** Farther than the limit of: *Place a ruler on the top edge of a desk so that half of it sticks out beyond the desk.* **3.** After (a specified time): *No papers will be accepted beyond this deadline.* **4.** Outside the reach or scope of: *beyond hope; beyond recall.*

Idiom. **beyond (one).** Outside one's comprehension: *It's beyond me how he could have done this.*

bez•el |bĕz′əl| *n.* **1.** A bevel or slant on the edge of a cutting tool. **2.** The part of a gem on which facets have been cut. **3.** A groove or flange designed to hold something, such as a gem or the crystal of a watch.

Bhu•tan |bo͞o tăn′| *or* |-tän′|. A country in the Himalaya Mountains between India and Tibet. Population, 1,298,000. Capital, Thimbu. —**Bhu′tan•ese′** |bo͞o′tə nēz′| *or* |-nēs′| *adj. & n.*

bi–. A prefix meaning "two" or "twice": **bimonthly; bisect.** [SEE NOTE]

Bi The symbol for the element bismuth.

bi•a•ly |bē ä′lē| *n., pl.* **bi•a•lys.** A flat roll topped with onions.

bi•as |bī′əs| *n.* **1.** A line crossing the weave of cloth at a slant: *cut cloth on the bias.* **2.** An inclination for or against someone or something that inhibits impartial judgment; prejudice: *a strong bias against youth; a reader influenced by his bias in favor of dogs; a newspaper with a strong conservative bias.* —***modifier:*** *a neckline with bias*

bi-

Bi- *is from Latin* bi-, *a form of the adverb* bis, *"twice."* Bis *and* **twice** *are doublets; they are both descended from the prehistoric Indo-European adverb* dwi- *or* dwis, *"two times."*

edges; bias seams. —*v.* **bi•ased** or **bi•assed, bi•as•ing** or **bi•ass•ing.** To cause to have a prejudiced view; influence unfairly: *The prosecutor's statement was disallowed for fear it would bias the jury.* —**bi'ased** *adj.: a biased report.*

bib |bĭb| *n.* **1.** A kind of cloth napkin tied under a child's chin to keep him from spilling food on his clothes. **2.** The part of an apron or pair of overalls worn over the chest.

Bi•ble |**bī'**bəl| *n.* **1.** The sacred book of Christianity, a collection of ancient writings including the books of both the Old Testament and the New Testament. **2.** The Old Testament, the sacred book of Judaism; Hebrew Scriptures. **3.** The sacred writings of any religion. **4. bible.** A book considered authoritative in its field. [SEE NOTE]

Bib•li•cal, also **bib•li•cal** |**bĭb'**lĭ kəl| *adj.* Of, derived from, or in keeping with the Bible.

bib•li•o•graph•i•cal |bĭb'lē ə **grăf'**ĭ kəl| or **bib•li•o•graph•ic** |bĭb'lē ə **grăf'**ĭk| *adj.* Of bibliography.

bib•li•og•ra•phy |bĭb'lē **ŏg'**rə fē| *n., pl.* **bib•li•og•ra•phies. 1.** A list of the works of a specific author or publisher. **2.** A list of the books and other writings on a specific subject consulted by an author. [SEE NOTE]

bi•cam•er•al |bī **kăm'**ər əl| *adj.* Composed of two houses or chambers: *The United States Congress is a bicameral legislature.*

bi•car•bo•nate |bī **kär'**bə nĭt| *or* |-nāt'| *n.* **1.** The ion or radical $-HCO_3-$. **2.** A chemical compound containing this ion.

bicarbonate of soda. **Sodium bicarbonate.**

bi•cen•ten•ni•al |bī'sĕn **tĕn'**ē əl| *adj.* **1.** Of or in honor of a 200th anniversary: *a bicentennial celebration.* **2.** Occurring once every 200 years. —*n.* A 200th anniversary or its celebration: *the bicentennial of American independence.*

bi•ceps |**bī'**sĕps'| *n., pl.* **bi•ceps.** Any muscle that has two points of attachment at one end, especially: **a.** The large muscle at the front of the upper arm that bends the elbow. **b.** The large muscle at the back of the thigh that bends the knee.

bi•chlo•ride |bī **klôr'**īd'| *or* |**-klōr'-**| *n.* A chemical compound that contains two atoms of chlorine per molecule.

bichloride of mercury. **Mercuric chloride.**

bick•er |**bĭk'**ər| *v.* To argue over an unimportant matter; squabble: *The girls bickered over whose turn it was to wash dishes.*

bi•con•cave |bī'kŏn **kāv'**| *or* |bī **kŏn'**kāv'| *adj.* Concave on both sides or surfaces: *a biconcave lens.*

bi•con•vex |bī'kŏn **vĕks'**| *or* |bī **kŏn'**vĕks'| *adj.* Convex on both sides or surfaces: *a biconvex lens.*

bi•cus•pid |bī **kŭs'**pĭd| *adj.* Having two points, as has the crescent moon. —*n.* A bicuspid tooth, especially a premolar.

bi•cy•cle |**bī'**sĭ kəl| *or* |-sĭk'əl| *n.* A light vehicle consisting of a metal frame on which two wheels are mounted, one behind the other. It has a seat for the rider, who steers the front wheel by means of handlebars and drives the rear wheel by means of pedals. —***modifier:*** *a bicycle shop.* —*v.* **bi•cy•cled, bi•cy•cling.** To ride on a bicycle. —**bi'cy•clist'** *n.* [SEE PICTURE]

bid |bĭd| *v.* **1. bid** or **bade** |băd| *or* |bād|, **bid•den** |**bĭd'**n| or **bid, bid•ding. a.** To order; command; direct: *My mother bade me look in the mirror. The children did as they were bidden.* **b.** To ask for insistently: *A weeping child bids me pluck the full moon from the sky. He bid me come.* **c.** To request to come; invite: *Mr. Lorry was the only one bidden to the marriage.* **d.** To say or express (a greeting, a wish, or farewell): *Do not hasten to bid me adieu.* **2. bid, bid•ding. a.** To offer (an amount of money) as a price for something: *I once bid a quarter on a huge moose head. How much am I bid for this?* **b.** To contract for (a certain number of tricks) in card games, as in bridge: *I bid three clubs.* —*n.* **1. a.** An offer to pay or accept a certain amount of money for something: *The auctioneer was looking for a higher bid. Only sealed bids will be accepted.* **b.** An amount bid: *He bid $10.00.* **2.** A declaration of the number of tricks one expects to win in certain card games such as bridge: *My bid is three hearts.* **3.** An announced intention or effort to achieve something: *a bid for the Presidency.*

***Idiom.* bid fair.** To appear likely; seem.

bid•der |**bĭd'**ər| *n.* A person who makes a bid at an auction, in seeking a contract, or in a card game.

bid•ding |**bĭd'**ĭng| *n.* **1.** The making of bids, as at an auction or in a card game. **2.** An order or command: *I went there at his bidding.* **3.** An invitation; request: *At her bidding, I accepted.*

bid•dy |**bĭd'**ē| *n., pl.* **bid•dies. 1.** A hen or young chick. **2.** A talkative old woman.

bide |bīd| *v.* **bid•ed** or **bode** |bōd|, **bid•ed, bid•ing.**

***Idiom.* bide (one's) time.** To wait patiently for the right moment.

bi•en•ni•al |bī **ĕn'**ē əl| *adj.* **1.** Lasting or living for two years: *biennial plants.* **2.** Occurring every second year. —*n.* A plant that grows and produces leaves in its first year and that flowers, produces seeds, and dies in its second year.

bier |bîr| *n.* A stand on which a dead person or a coffin is placed while lying in state or when being carried to the grave. ¶*These sound alike* **bier, beer.**

bi•fo•cal |bī **fō'**kəl| *or* |**bī'**fō'-| *adj.* **1.** Focusing light rays at two different points: *a bifocal lens.* **2.** Designed to correct both near and distant vision: *bifocal eyeglasses.* —*n.* **1.** A lens ground so that it has two focal lengths; a bifocal lens. **2. bifocals.** A pair of eyeglasses having bifocal lenses to correct both near and distant vision.

big |bĭg| *adj.* **big•ger, big•gest. 1.** Of great size; large: *a big house; a big city; a big appetite.* **2. a.** Grown-up: *You're a big boy now.* **b.** Older: *my big sister.* **3.** Prominent; influential: *a big industrialist.* **4.** Of great significance; momentous: *a big day in my life; practice for the big game.* **5.** Full of self-importance; boastful: *a big talker.* **6.** Outstanding or extreme in some respect: *a big fake.* —*adv.* **1.** With an air of self-importance; boastfully: *"Toad talked big about all he was going to do in the days to come."* (Kenneth Grahame). **2.** *Slang.* With great success: *Your act went over big.* —**big'ness** *n.*

big•a•mist |**bĭg'**ə mĭst| *n.* A person who commits bigamy.

Bible/bibliography

Bible *and* **bibliography** *come from Greek* biblos, *"a book, a scroll of papyrus." This came from* Biblos, *the name of a Phoenician city from which the Greeks imported supplies of Egyptian papyrus.*

bicycle

bighorn

big•a•mous |bĭg′ə məs| *adj.* Guilty of bigamy.
big•a•my |bĭg′ə mē| *n.* The crime of marrying one person while still legally married to another.
Big Dipper. A group of stars in the constellation Ursa Major, consisting of seven stars, four forming the bowl and three the handle of a dipper-shaped arrangement.
big-heart•ed |bĭg′här′tĭd| *adj.* Generous; kind. —**big′-heart′ed•ly** *adv.* —**big′-heart′ed•ness** *n.*
big•horn |bĭg′hôrn′| *n.* A wild mountain sheep of western North America, with large, curving horns in the male. [SEE PICTURE]
bight |bīt| *n.* **1. a.** A loop in a rope. **b.** The middle or slack part of an extended rope. **2. a.** A curve in a shoreline. **b.** A wide bay formed by such a curve.
big•ot |bĭg′ət| *n.* A person who is intolerant of a creed, belief, etc., that differs from his own and is often prejudiced against people holding them.
big•ot•ed |bĭg′ə tĭd| *adj.* Intolerant of other creeds or beliefs; prejudiced.
big•ot•ry |bĭg′ə trē| *n.* Intolerance of other creeds or beliefs; prejudice.
big shot. *Slang.* A very important person.
big tree. The giant sequoia of the mountains of southern California.
big•wig |bĭg′wĭg′| *n. Informal.* An important person; a dignitary.
bike |bīk|. *Informal. n.* A bicycle. —*v.* **biked, bik•ing.** To ride a bicycle.
bi•ki•ni |bĭ kē′nē| *n.* A very brief two-piece bathing suit worn by women. [SEE NOTE]

bikini
The **bikini** *was named after* Bikini Atoll *in the Marshall Islands, Western Pacific, where the United States tested atomic bombs in 1946. Newspapers claimed that the first bikini bathing suits had an "atomic" impact.*

bi•lat•er•al |bī lăt′ər əl| *adj.* **1.** Of two sides that correspond point for point. **2.** Affecting or undertaken by two sides: *a bilateral agreement.* —**bi•lat′er•al•ly** *adv.*
bilateral symmetry. A form or arrangement with similar parts arranged on two opposite sides, as in the body of many animals, including those that have a backbone.
bile |bīl| *n.* **1.** A bitter, alkaline, greenish liquid that is produced by the liver, stored in the gallbladder, and aids in the digestion of fats. **2.** Bitterness of temper; ill humor.
bilge |bĭlj| *n.* **1. a.** The lowest inner part of a ship's hull, up to where the sides become vertical. **b.** Also **bilge water.** The foul water that collects in this part. **2.** The bulging part of a barrel. **3.** *Slang.* Stupid talk; nonsense. —*v.* **bilged, bilg•ing. 1.** To spring a leak in the bilge: *The ship struck a rock and immediately started bilging.* **2.** To bulge.
bi•lin•gual |bī lĭng′gwəl| *adj.* **1.** Able to speak two languages equally well. **2.** Written or expressed in two languages.
bil•ious |bĭl′yəs| *adj.* **1.** Of, like, or containing bile. **2.** Of or suffering distress caused by malfunction of the liver or gallbladder. **3.** Reminding one or suggestive of bilious distress or bile, especially in color: *a bilious complexion.* **4.** Of a peevish disposition; bad-tempered.
bilk |bĭlk| *v.* To cheat, defraud, or swindle: *He bilked unsuspecting clients out of thousands of dollars.*
bill[1] |bĭl| *n.* **1.** A statement of charges for goods supplied or work performed: *a telephone bill.* **2.** A piece of paper money worth a certain amount: *a ten-dollar bill.* **3.** The entertainment offered by a theater: *an interesting bill at the Paramount.* **4.** An advertising poster: *"Post no bills!"* **5.** A draft of a law presented for approval to a legislature: *a conservation bill.* **6.** A document presented to a court and containing a formal statement of a case or complaint. —*v.* **1. a.** To send a statement of charges to: *Bill me for the balance.* **b.** To enter on a statement of charges; prepare a bill of: *Will you please bill these purchases to my brother's account.* **2.** To advertise or list on a bill or program: *I see that the play is billed as a family comedy.* [SEE NOTE]
Idiom. **fill the bill.** To be satisfactory; meet all requirements.
bill[2] |bĭl| *n.* **1.** The hard, horny, projecting mouth parts of a bird; a beak. **2.** A beaklike part or projection. —*v.* To touch beaks together. [SEE NOTE]
Idiom. **bill and coo.** To kiss and murmur lovingly.

bill[1-2]
Bill[1] *is from Medieval Latin* billa *or* bulla, *"a seal," also "a sealed document." (See* **bull**[2]*.)* **Bill**[2] *is an Old English word that has always meant "a bird's beak."*

bill•board |bĭl′bôrd′| *or* |-bōrd′| *n.* A large upright board for the display of advertisements in public places or alongside highways.
bil•let |bĭl′ĭt| *n.* A lodging for soldiers in a nonmilitary building. —*v.* To house (soldiers), especially in nonmilitary buildings: *The army billeted the soldiers in the village. The soldiers billeted in an old farmhouse.*
bill•fold |bĭl′fōld′| *n.* A small case that folds flat, used for carrying paper money in a pocket or handbag; a wallet.
bil•liard |bĭl′yərd| *adj.* Of the game of billiards: *a billiard table.*
bil•liards |bĭl′yərdz| *n.* (*used with a singular verb*). A game, played on a cloth-covered table with raised, cushioned edges, in which a cue is used to hit three balls against one another or the side cushions of the table.
bill•ing |bĭl′ĭng| *n.* The order in which performers' names are listed in programs and advertisements and on theater marquees: *The two actors share top billing.*
bil•lion |bĭl′yən| *n.* **1.** In the United States, one thousand million; 1,000,000,000 or 10^9. **2.** In Great Britain and some other countries, one million million; 1,000,000,000,000 or 10^{12}.
bil•lion•aire |bĭl′yə nâr′| *n.* A person whose wealth amounts to at least a billion dollars, pounds, or other monetary unit.
bil•lionth |bĭl′yənth| *n.* **1.** In a set of items arranged to match the natural numbers in a one-to-one correspondence, the item that matches the number one billion. **2.** One of one billion equal parts of a unit. —**bil′lionth** *adj.*
bill of exchange. A written order to pay a specified sum of money to a particular person.
bill of fare. A menu.
bill of lading. A receipt issued to a shipper by a railroad or other carrier, promising delivery of the merchandise to the addressee.
Bill of Rights. The first ten amendments to the Constitution of the United States, guaranteeing certain rights and privileges to the people, as freedom of speech.
bill of sale. A document certifying that an item of personal property has been formally transferred to a new owner.
bil•low |bĭl′ō| *n.* **1.** A great wave or surge of the sea. **2.** A great rising mass of something: *billows of smoke.* —*v.* **1.** To rise or surge in or as if in

ă pat/ā pay/â care/ä father/ĕ pet/ ē be/ĭ pit/ī pie/î fierce/ŏ pot/ ō go/ô paw, for/oi oil/ŏŏ book/ ōō boot/ou out/ŭ cut/û fur/ *th* the/th thin/hw which/zh vision/ ə ago, item, pencil, atom, circus

billows: *Flames and smoke billowed over the wild bushland.* **2.** To swell or cause to swell out; bulge: *The Bedouins galloped toward the enemy with their robes billowing in the wind. The wind billowed their robes.*

bil•low•y |bĭl'ō ē| *adj.* Surging or swelling like a great wave; full of or marked by billows: *billowy sails; billowy clouds.*

bil•ly |bĭl'ē| *n., pl.* **bil•lies.** Also **billy club.** A short wooden club, especially one carried by a policeman.

billy goat. A male goat.

bi•mah |bē'mə| *n.* The platform from which services are conducted in a synagogue; a bema.

bi•man•u•al |bī măn'yo͞o əl| *adj.* Using or requiring the use of both hands.

bi•met•al |bī mĕt'l| *adj.* Bimetallic. *—n.* A bimetallic strip or similar device.

bi•me•tal•lic |bī mə tăl'ĭk| *adj.* **1.** Consisting of two metals: *a bimetallic strip.* **2.** Of or based on the system of bimetallism.

bimetallic strip. A strip made of two different metals bonded firmly together so that, as a result of the different rates of expansion of the two metals, it changes in shape as the temperature changes. It is used in thermometers, thermostats, and similar devices.

bi•met•al•lism |bī mĕt'l ĭz'əm| *n.* The use of both gold and silver as a standard of value in a monetary system.

bi•month•ly |bī mŭnth'lē| *adj.* Occurring once every two months. *—adv.* Once every two months. *—n., pl.* **bi•month•lies.** A publication issued bimonthly.

bin |bĭn| *n.* An enclosed space for storing food, coal, etc. ¶*These sound alike* **bin, been.**

bi•na•ry |bī'nə rē| *adj.* **1.** Of or based on the number 2 or the binary numeration system. **2. a.** Consisting of just two chemical elements: *a binary compound.* **b.** Containing just two different kinds of atoms: *a binary molecule.* **3.** Of two different parts or components. *—n., pl.* **bi•na•ries.** Something that is binary, especially a binary star.

binary digit. Either of the digits 0 or 1, used in representing numbers in the binary numeration system; a bit.

binary numeral. A numeral in the binary numeration system. An expanded binary numeral has the general form $a_n2^n + a_{n-1}2^{n-1} + \ldots + a_02^0$, where each a can have only the value 0 or 1. Place values are used, as they are with decimal numerals, when the numeral is not in expanded form.

binary numeration system. A system of numeration, based on 2, in which the numerals are represented as sums of powers of 2 and in which all numerals can be written using just the symbols 0 and 1. [SEE PICTURE]

binary operation. An operation, such as addition, that is applied to two elements of a set to produce a single element of the set.

binary star. A system made up of two stars that move together and rotate about a point located between them. These stars are so close together that for many astronomical observations they seem to be a single object.

bin•au•ral |bī nôr'əl| *or* |bĭn ôr'-| *adj.* **1.** Of, having, or hearing with two ears. **2.** Of a system of sound reproduction in which a different sound can be directed to each of the listener's ears. [SEE NOTE]

bind |bīnd| *v.* **bound** |bound|, **bind•ing. 1. a.** To fasten, tie, or make secure by tying: *Bind the sheaves of grain together.* **b.** To make or hold prisoner by or as if by tying: *The soldiers bound him to the tree. He was gagged and bound by the soldiers.* **2. a.** To bandage: *He bound up the squirrel's wound.* **b.** To fasten around; wrap: *The gypsy was bound up in paper streamers by the dancers.* **3.** To hold together or cause to hold together; unite: *If you remain bound together in peace, you will be strong. Strong family ties bind generation with generation.* **4.** To hamper the movement of (someone or something) by being tight and uncomfortable: *tight-fitting pants that bind the rider; fabrics that stretch with the body movements and do not bind.* **5.** To hold or restrain with or as if with bonds: *centuries of tradition that bind people to their land.* **6.** To place under legal obligation: *The terms of the contract bind him for a year.* **7.** To hold or employ as an apprentice, servant, etc.; indenture: *The young man was bound out to work for seven years.* **8.** To cover with a border or edging for added protection or decoration: *bind a seam with tape.* **9.** To enclose and fasten between covers: *bind a book in leather.* **10.** To constipate. *—n. Informal.* A difficult or confining situation: *caught in a legal bind.*

bind•er |bīn'dər| *n.* **1.** A person who binds books. **2.** A notebook cover with rings for holding sheets of paper. **3.** Something used to tie or fasten, as cord, rope, etc. **4.** A material added to something to make it hold together. **5.** A machine that reaps and ties grain.

bind•er•y |bīn'də rē| *n., pl.* **bind•er•ies.** A place where books are bound.

bind•ing |bīn'dĭng| *n.* **1.** The cover that holds together the pages of a book. **2.** A strip of tape or fabric sewn over an edge or seam to protect or decorate it. *—adj.* Imposing a firm obligation; obligatory: *a binding agreement.*

binding energy. 1. The energy released when a group of particles join to form a single atom or when a group of atoms join to form a molecule. **2.** The energy required to move an electron infinitely far from its position in an atom.

bind•weed |bīnd'wēd'| *n.* A plant with twining stems and pink or white trumpet-shaped flowers.

binge |bĭnj| *n. Informal.* **1.** A drunken spree. **2.** A period of uncontrolled self-indulgence: *go on a shopping binge.*

bin•go |bĭng'gō| *n.* A game of chance played by covering numbers on a printed card as they are called out. The winner is the player who covers the first five numbers in a row in any direction. *—**modifier:** a bingo card; a bingo player.*

bin•na•cle |bĭn'ə kəl| *n.* The stand on which a ship's compass case is supported.

bin•oc•u•lar |bə nŏk'yə lər| *or* |bī-| *adj.* Of or involving both eyes at once: *binocular vision.* *—n.* Often **binoculars.** Any optical device, such as a microscope or a pair of field glasses, used by both eyes at once.

bi•no•mi•al |bī nō'mē əl| *adj.* Of or having two names or terms. *—n.* **1.** A mathematical expression that is written as a sum or difference of

Binary	Decimal
0	0
1	1
10	2
11	3
100	4
101	5
110	6
111	7
1000	8
1001	9
1010	10
1011	11
1100	12
1101	13
1110	14
1111	15

binary numeration system
The table shows conversions of binary numerals to decimal numerals.

binaural
Binaural *and* **stereophonic** *are sometimes used as synonyms, but they are slightly different. In a* **binaural** *system the sounds are sent directly to the listener's ear without being allowed to mix in the air. This is not true of a* **stereophonic** *system.*

two terms, as, for example, $3a + 2b$. **2.** A scientific plant or animal name consisting of two parts. *Passer domesticus,* the scientific name of the common house sparrow, is a binomial.

bio–. A word element meaning "life" or "living organisms": **biology; biodegradable.**

bi•o•cell |bī′ō sĕl′| *n.* A device in which living bacteria generate electricity directly from a substance that acts as a fuel.

bi•o•chem•i•cal |bī′ō **kĕm′**ĭ kəl| *adj.* Of biochemistry. **—bi′o•chem′i•cal•ly** *adv.*

bi•o•chem•ist |bī′ō **kĕm′**ĭst| *n.* A scientist who specializes in biochemistry.

bi•o•chem•is•try |bī′ō **kĕm′**ĭ strē| *n.* The study of the chemical composition of the substances that form living matter and of the chemical processes that go on in living matter.

bi•o•de•grad•a•ble |bī′ō dĭ **grā′**də bəl| *adj.* Capable of being decomposed by natural biological processes: *a biodegradable detergent.*

bi•o•e•lec•tric•i•ty |bī′ō ĭ lĕk **trĭs′**ĭ tē| *n.* Electricity produced by or in living cells or organisms.

bi•o•gen•e•sis |bī′ō **jĕn′**ĭ sĭs| *n.* **1.** The generation of living things from other living things. **2.** The theory that holds that this is the only way in which living things are produced.

bi•og•raph•er |bī **ŏg′**rə fər| *or* |bē-| *n.* A person who writes a biography.

bi•o•graph•i•cal |bī′ə **grăf′**ĭ kəl| or **bi•o•graph•ic** |bī′ə **grăf′**ĭk| *adj.* Of or based on a person's life: *biographical information.*

bi•og•ra•phy |bī **ŏg′**rə fē| *or* |bē-| *n., pl.* **bi•og•ra•phies.** A written account of a person's life.

bi•o•log•i•cal |bī′ə **lŏj′**ĭ kəl| *adj.* **1.** Of biology: *the biological sciences.* **2.** Of or affecting living things: *biological processes such as growth and digestion.* **—bi′o•log′i•cal•ly** *adv.*

biological warfare. The use in war of disease-producing organisms, destructive insects, specialized poisons, etc., to destroy crops, livestock, or human life.

bi•ol•o•gist |bī **ŏl′**ə jĭst| *n.* A scientist who specializes in biology.

bi•ol•o•gy |bī **ŏl′**ə jē| *n.* The scientific study of living things and life processes, including growth, structure, and reproduction. Among the branches of biology are the sciences of botany, zoology, and ecology.

bi•o•lu•mi•nes•cence |bī′ō lo͞o′mə **nĕs′**əns| *n.* The giving off of light by living organisms such as fireflies or certain fish or fungi. **—bi′o•lu′mi•nes′cent** *adj.*

bi•ome |**bī′**ōm′| *n.* The combination of plant and animal life typical of a region having a particular kind of climate: *an arctic biome.*

bi•o•met•rics |bī′ō **mĕt′**rĭks| *n.* *(used with a singular verb).* The statistical study of biological data.

bi•on•ics |bī **ŏn′**ĭks| *n.* *(used with a singular verb).* The study of living things for the purpose of learning principles from their structure and organization that can be applied to engineering and other areas.

bi•o•phys•i•cist |bī′ō **fĭz′**ĭ sĭst| *n.* A scientist who specializes in biophysics.

bi•o•phys•ics |bī′ō **fĭz′**ĭks| *n.* *(used with a singular verb).* The physics of life processes.

bi•op•sy |**bī′**ŏp′sē| *n., pl.* **bi•op•sies.** The study of tissues taken from a living person or organism, especially in an examination for the presence of a disease.

bi•o•sphere |**bī′**ə sfîr′| *n.* The part of the earth and its surroundings in which living organisms exist, consisting of a band or envelope extending from the earth's crust to the outer atmosphere.

bi•ot•ic |bī **ŏt′**ĭk| *adj.* Of living organisms: *plants and animals forming a biotic community.*

bi•o•tin |**bī′**ə tĭn| *n.* A colorless crystalline vitamin composed of carbon, hydrogen, nitrogen, oxygen, and sulfur in the proportions $C_{10}H_{16}N_2O_3S$. It is often considered part of the vitamin B complex and is found in liver, egg yolk, milk, and yeast.

bi•par•ti•san |bī **pär′**tĭ zən| *adj.* Composed of or supported by two political parties, especially the Republican and Democratic parties: *a bipartisan bill.*

bi•par•tite |bī **pär′**tīt′| *adj.* **1.** Having two parts. **2.** Drawn up in two corresponding parts, one for each party: *a bipartite treaty.*

bi•ped |**bī′**pĕd′| *n.* An animal with two feet. Birds and human beings are bipeds.

bi•plane |**bī′**plān′| *n.* An early type of airplane having two sets of wings attached to it at different levels. [SEE PICTURE]

biplane
Wright Brothers' airplane over Fort Myer, Virginia, in 1908

bi•ra•cial |bī **rā′**shəl| *adj.* Of, for, or consisting of members of two ethnic groups: *a biracial committee.*

birch |bûrch| *n.* **1.** Any of several trees with papery, easily peeled bark. **2.** The hard wood of such a tree. **3.** A rod of a birch tree, used for whipping. *—modifier: birch bark; a birch forest.* *—v.* To whip (someone) with a birch rod.

bird |bûrd| *n.* **1.** Any of a group of warm-blooded animals that lay eggs and have feathers and wings. **2.** A light, feather-tipped object hit in the game of badminton. **3.** *Slang.* A person, especially one who is odd or unusual: *a queer bird.* *—modifier: bird life; a bird sanctuary; bird feathers.*

Idioms. **birds of a feather.** People of the same character, personality, tastes, etc. **kill two birds with one stone.** To accomplish two things with one effort.

bird•bath |**bûrd′**băth′| *or* |-bäth′| *n., pl.* **-baths** |-bă*th*z′| *or* |-bä*th*z′| *or* |-băths′| *or* |-bäths′|. A wide, shallow basin filled with water for birds to bathe in or drink.

bird•call |**bûrd′**kôl′| *n.* **1.** The song of a bird. **2.** A small device that produces sounds that imitate the song of a bird.

bird dog. A dog trained to help hunt game birds.

bird•house |**bûrd′**hous′| *n., pl.* **-hous•es** |-hou′zĭz|. A man-made shelter for birds, often designed to look like a house.

bird•ie |**bûr′**dē| *n.* **1.** *Informal.* A small bird. **2.** In golf, a score of one stroke under par for a hole.

bird•lime |**bûrd′**līm′| *n.* A sticky substance smeared on twigs to catch small birds.

bird of paradise. Any of several birds of New Guinea and Australia, usually having brightly colored, showy feathers. [SEE PICTURE]

bird of paradise

bird of passage. **1.** A bird that migrates. **2.** A person who wanders from place to place.

bird of prey. A bird, such as a hawk, eagle, or owl, that hunts and kills other animals for food.

ă pat/ā pay/â care/ä father/ĕ pet/ ē be/ĭ pit/ī pie/î fierce/ŏ pot/ ō go/ô paw, for/oi oil/o͝o book/ o͞o boot/ou out/ŭ cut/û fur/ *th* the/th thin/hw which/zh vision/ ə ago, item, pencil, atom, circus

bird•seed |bûrd′sēd′| *n.* A mixture of different kinds of seeds, used for feeding birds.

bird's-eye |bûrdz′ī′| *adj.* **1.** Marked with small, rounded spots: *furniture made of bird's-eye maple; cotton cloth with a bird's-eye weave.* **2.** Seen from high above: *a bird's-eye view of the countryside.*

bi•ret•ta |bə rĕt′ə| *n.* A stiff, square cap worn by members of the Roman Catholic clergy in black, purple, or red, according to rank.

Bir•ming•ham. 1. |bûr′mĭng hăm′|. The largest city in Alabama. Population, 284,413. **2.** |bûr′-mĭng əm|. The second-largest city in England. Population, 1,100,000.

birth |bûrth| *n.* **1.** The act of being born; the beginning of a person's existence: *The baby weighed more than eight pounds at birth.* **2.** A beginning or origin: *the birth of an idea.* **3.** Family background; ancestry: *a man of noble birth.* ¶ *These sound alike* **birth, berth.**

Idiom. **give birth to.** To bring into being: *Electricity has given birth to many appliances.*

birth certificate. An official document listing a person's parents and the date, place, and time of his birth.

birth•day |bûrth′dā′| *n.* **1.** The day of a person's birth. **2.** The anniversary of that day. —*modifier:* *a birthday party; a birthday cake.*

birth•mark |bûrth′märk′| *n.* A mark or blemish present on the body from birth.

birth•place |bûrth′plās′| *n.* The place where someone is born or where something originates.

birth•rate |bûrth′rāt′| *n.* The number of births per thousand of a given population in a given interval of time, usually one year.

birth•right |bûrth′rīt′| *n.* A right to which a person is entitled because of his birth or origin: *Freedom of speech is an American birthright.*

Bis•cay, Bay of |bĭs′kā|. A large inlet of the Atlantic Ocean, west of France and north of Spain.

bis•cuit |bĭs′kĭt| *n.* **1.** A small, flaky cake of bread leavened with baking powder or soda. **2.** *British.* A cracker.

bi•sect |bī sĕkt′| *or* |bī′sĕkt′| *v.* To cut or divide into two equal parts.

bi•sec•tor |bī sĕk′tər| *or* |bī′sĕk′-| *n.* Something that bisects, especially a straight line, ray, or line segment that bisects an angle or a line segment.

bi•sex•u•al |bī sĕk′shōō əl| *adj.* **1.** Of or involving both sexes: *bisexual reproduction.* **2.** Having male and female reproductive organs in a single individual: *Earthworms are bisexual.*

bish•op |bĭsh′əp| *n.* **1.** A high-ranking Christian clergyman, in modern churches usually in charge of a diocese. **2.** A chessman that can move diagonally across any number of unoccupied spaces of the same color.

bish•op•ric |bĭsh′əp rĭk| *n.* The officer, rank, or diocese of a bishop.

Bis•marck |bĭz′märk′|. The capital of North Dakota. Population, 44,485.

Bis•marck |bĭz′märk′|, **Prince Otto von.** 1815–1898. German statesman.

bis•muth |bĭz′məth| *n.* Symbol **Bi** One of the elements, a white, brittle metal. Atomic number 83; atomic weight 208.98; valences +3, +5; melting point 271.3°C; boiling point 1,560°C.

bi•son |bī′sən| *or* |-zən| *n., pl.* **bi•son. 1.** An oxlike animal of western North America, having a shaggy, dark-brown mane and short, curved horns. Also called *buffalo.* **2.** A similar European animal.

bisque |bĭsk| *n.* A thick cream soup: *lobster bisque.*

Bis•sau |bĭ sou′|. The capital of Guinea-Bissau. Population, 109,000.

bit[1] |bĭt| *n.* **1.** A small piece or amount: *a bit of driftwood that the tide has left. It didn't help a bit.* **2.** A brief amount of time; a moment: *wait a bit.* **3.** A small role, as in a play or movie. **4.** *Informal.* An amount equal to 1/8 of a dollar. Used only in even multiples: *two bits; four bits.* —*modifier:* *a bit part in a play.* [SEE NOTE]

Idioms. **a bit of.** To some extent; somewhat: *She is a bit of a flirt.* **bit by bit.** Little by little; gradually: *His work improved bit by bit.* **do (one's) bit.** To make one's contribution; carry one's share. **not a bit.** Not at all: *not a bit damp.* **quite a bit.** A large amount: *Quite a bit of snow fell.*

bit[2] |bĭt| *n.* **1.** A tool for drilling that fits into a brace or electric drill. **2.** The metal mouthpiece of a bridle, used to control the horse. **3.** The part of a key that enters the lock and works the mechanism. [SEE NOTE & PICTURE]

bit[3] |bĭt| *n.* **1. a.** Either of the binary digits 0 or 1. **b.** Either of any pair of characters that are equivalent to 0 and 1. **2.** A unit of information equivalent to the choice between two equally likely alternatives. [SEE NOTE]

bit[4] |bĭt|. Past tense and a past participle of **bite.**

bitch |bĭch| *n.* A female dog or related animal, such as a coyote.

bite |bīt| *v.* **bit** |bĭt|, **bit•ten** |bĭt′n| or **bit, bit•ing. 1.** To cut or tear with or as if with the teeth: *The dog bit the cat. A tortoise cannot bite because it has no teeth. The woodcutter's ax bit into the tree with regular strokes.* **2.** To pierce the skin of (a person or animal) with the fangs, stinger, etc.: *A mosquito bit him in the leg. At nightfall clouds of mosquitoes would rise to bite.* **3.** To cause to sting or smart: *The cold wind was biting his face.* **4.** To take strong hold of; grip or seize: *The wheels bit the gravel and the car departed. The wheels have difficulty in biting when the road is icy.* **5.** To take or swallow bait: *Fish seem to bite more just before it starts to rain.* —*n.* **1.** A wound or injury resulting from biting: *a mosquito bite.* **2.** An amount of food taken into the mouth at one time; a mouthful: *Let me have a bite of your sandwich.* **3.** *Informal.* A light meal or snack: *a bite of lunch.* ¶ *These sound alike* **bite, byte.**

bit•ing |bī′tĭng| *adj.* **1.** Tending to bite; sharp; cutting: *a biting wind; biting criticism.* **2.** Causing a stinging sensation; caustic: *fumes with a biting odor.* —**bit′ing•ly** *adv.*

bit•ten |bĭt′n|. A past participle of **bite.**

bit•ter |bĭt′ər| *adj.* **bit•ter•er, bit•ter•est. 1.** Having or being a taste that is sharp or unpleasant: *a bitter drink.* **2.** Causing sharp pain to the body or discomfort to the mind; harsh: *a bitter wind; bitter memories.* **3.** Hard to accept, admit, or bear: *the bitter truth; settlers returning to face the bitter task of rebuilding their farms.* **4.** Showing or proceeding from strong dislike or animosity: *bitter foes; a bitter fight.* **5.** Resulting from severe grief, anguish, etc.: *cry bitter tears.* **6.** Having or

bison
American bison

bit[1-2-3]

Bit[1] *is from Old English* bita, *"a piece bitten off."* **Bit**[2] *is from Old English* bite, *"a sting or bite," later used to mean "a bit for a horse." Both are ultimately related to* **bite. Bit**[3] *is a very modern word, coined in imitation of* **bit**[1] *but actually coming from the phrase* binary digit.

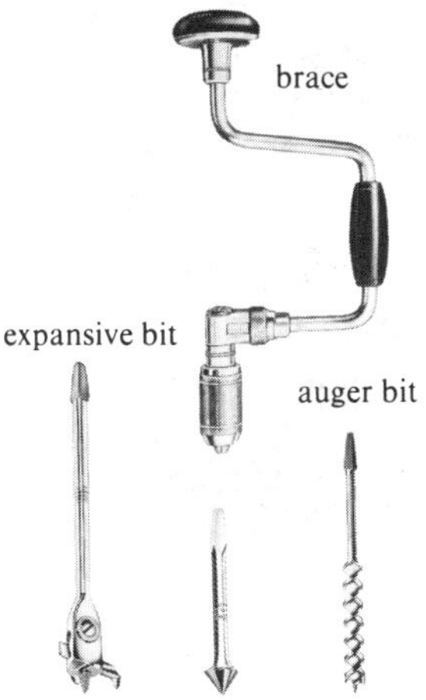

bit[2]
Bits with a brace

blackberry

blackbody

A perfect **blackbody** *cannot be made, but for many purposes a large hollow chamber with a single small hole in it is good enough. The hole is actually the* **blackbody**, *for any radiation that enters it bounces around inside the chamber and does not come out again.*

black-eyed Susan

ă **pat**/ā **pay**/â **care**/ä **father**/ĕ **pet**/ ē **be**/ĭ **pit**/ī **pie**/î **fierce**/ŏ **pot**/ ō **go**/ô **paw**, **for**/oi **oil**/o͝o **book**/ o͞o **boot**/ou **out**/ŭ **cut**/û **fur**/ *th* **the**/th **thin**/hw **which**/**zh** vision/ ə **ago**, item, pencil, atom, circus

showing a resentful feeling of disappointment: *He was bitter about not being accepted.* —**bit'ter•ly** *adv.* —**bit'ter•ness** *n.*

bit•tern |bĭt'ərn| *n.* A long-necked, brownish wading bird that hides among reeds with its beak pointing upward.

bit•ter•root |bĭt'ər ro͞ot'| *or* |-ro͝ot'| *n.* A plant of western North America with showy, short-stemmed pink or white flowers.

bit•ters |bĭt'ərz| *pl.n.* A bitter, usually alcoholic, liquid used in cocktails or as a tonic.

bit•ter•sweet |bĭt'ər swēt'| *n.* **1.** A woody vine with yellowish fruits that split open and expose seeds with fleshy red coverings. **2.** A kind of nightshade with purple flowers and poisonous red berries. *—adj.* |bĭt'ər **swēt'**|. Sweet or pleasant and bitter or unpleasant at the same time: *bittersweet memories.*

bi•tu•men |bĭ **to͞o'**mən| *or* |**-tyo͞o'**-| *n.* Any of various mixtures of hydrocarbons and other substances found in asphalt and tar. They occur naturally or are produced from petroleum and coal.

bi•tu•mi•nous |bĭ **to͞o'**mə nəs| *or* |**-tyo͞o'**-| *adj.* **1.** Like or containing bitumen. **2.** Of bituminous coal.

bituminous coal. A grade of coal that contains a high percentage of bituminous material and burns with a smoky flame.

bi•va•lent |bī **vā'**lənt| *adj.* In chemistry, having a valence of +2 or −2.

bi•valve |**bī'**vălv'| *n.* A mollusk, such as a clam or oyster, having a shell consisting of two hinged parts. *—adj.* **1.** Having a hinged shell: *a bivalve mollusk.* **2.** Consisting of two similar parts: *a bivalve shell.*

biv•ou•ac |**bĭv'**o͞o ăk'| *or* |**bĭv'**wăk'| *n.* A temporary camp made by soldiers in the field. *—v.* **biv•ou•acked, biv•ou•ack•ing, biv•ou•acks** or **biv•ou•acs.** To camp in a bivouac.

bi•week•ly |bī **wēk'**lē| *adj.* Occurring every two weeks. *—adv.* Once every two weeks. *—n., pl.* **bi•week•lies.** A publication issued biweekly.

bi•zarre |bĭ **zär'**| *adj.* Very strange or odd; grotesque: *a bizarre hat; a bizarre idea.*

Bk The symbol for the element berkelium.

blab |blăb| *v.* **blabbed, blab•bing. 1.** To tell (a secret), especially through careless talk. **2.** To chatter indiscreetly.

blab•ber•mouth |**blăb'**ər mouth'| *n., pl.* **-mouths** |-mou*th*z'|. *Slang.* A person who talks carelessly and at length.

black |blăk| *n.* **1. a.** The darkest or least bright of the series of colors that runs through all the shades of gray to white; the opposite of white; the darkest of all colors. **b.** Clothing of this color, especially for mourning: *a man dressed in black.* **2.** Any member of a Negroid people; a Negro. *—adj.* **black•er, black•est. 1.** Of or nearly of the color black. **2.** Without light: *a black, moonless night.* **3.** Belonging to an ethnic group having dark skin, especially Negroid. **4.** Gloomy; depressing: *a black day; black thoughts.* **5.** Often **Black.** Marked by disaster: *The stock market crashed on Black Friday.* **6.** Deserving of or indicating censure or dishonor: *the industry's blackest record as a polluter of the rivers.* **7.** Evil; wicked: *black deeds.* **8.** Angry; sullen: *a black look on his face.* **9.** Served without cream or milk: *black coffee.* *—v.* To make black, as with polish: *black a shoe.* ***—phrasal verb.*** **black out. 1.** To put out or conceal all lights that might help enemy aircraft find a target during an air raid at night. **2.** To lose consciousness temporarily. **3.** To produce or undergo a blackout: *The city was blacked out by the power failure. The government blacked out the news issuing from the rebel provinces.* **4.** To forbid the transmission of (a television program): *The commissioner blacked out the football game in New York City. New Haven had not been blacked out for the football game.* —**black'ness** *n.*

Idiom. **in the black.** On the credit side of a ledger; prosperous.

black-and-blue |**blăk'**ən **blo͞o'**| *adj.* Discolored as a result of blood that has escaped from broken blood vessels and clotted under the skin; bruised: *black-and-blue marks.*

black•ball |**blăk'**bôl'| *v.* To vote against and prevent (someone) from being admitted to an organization, as by placing a black ball in a ballot box. *—n.* A negative vote.

black belt. The rank of expert in a system of self-defense such as judo or karate.

black•ber•ry |**blăk'**bĕr'ē| *n., pl.* **-ber•ries. 1.** The blackish, glossy, edible berry of a thorny plant. **2.** A plant that bears such berries. [SEE PICTURE]

black•bird |**blăk'**bûrd'| *n.* Any of several birds with black or mostly black feathers.

black•board |**blăk'**bôrd'| *or* |-bōrd'| *n.* A panel, once black, now often colored, for writing on with chalk; a chalkboard.

black•bod•y |**blăk'**bŏd'ē| *n., pl.* **-bod•ies.** A theoretical object that absorbs completely any radiant energy that strikes it. [SEE NOTE]

black•damp |**blăk'**dămp'| *n.* A gas, mostly a mixture of carbon dioxide and nitrogen, found in mines after fires and explosions.

Black Death. An extremely deadly form of plague that was widespread throughout Europe and much of Asia in the 14th century.

black•en |**blăk'**ən| *v.* **1.** To make or become black or dark: *Smoke blackened the sky. The sky blackened before the storm.* **2.** To speak evil of; defame: *blacken an officer's reputation.*

black eye. A black-and-blue discoloration of the skin around the eye, resulting from a blow.

black-eyed Su•san |**blăk'**īd' **so͞o'**zən|. A plant with hairy stems and flowers with orange-yellow rays surrounding a dark-brown center. [SEE PICTURE]

Black•foot |**blăk'**fo͝ot'| *n., pl.* **Black•foot** or **Black•feet** |**blăk'**fēt'|. **1.** A North American Indian tribe of Montana, Alberta, and Saskatchewan. **2.** A member of this tribe. **3.** The Algonquian language of this tribe.

black•guard |**blăg'**ərd| *or* |-ärd'| *n.* A low, unprincipled person; a scoundrel.

black•head |**blăk'**hĕd'| *n.* A mass of fatty material and dirt that collects in and blocks one of the pores of the skin.

black•ing |**blăk'**ĭng| *n.* A black paste or liquid used as shoe polish.

black•ish |**blăk'**ĭsh| *adj.* Somewhat black.

black•jack |**blăk'**jăk'| *n.* **1.** A small, leather-covered club with a flexible handle. **2.** A card game, twenty-one. *—v.* To strike with a blackjack.

black light. Any invisible form of light such as infrared or, especially, ultraviolet light.

black•list |**blăk**'lĭst'| *n.* A list of persons or organizations to be disapproved, boycotted, or suspected of disloyalty. *—v.* To place (a name) on a blacklist.

black magic. Magic practiced for evil purposes, especially in league with the Devil.

black•mail |**blăk**'māl'| *n.* **1.** The extortion of money or something of value from a person by the threat of exposure of something criminal or discreditable about him. **2.** Money or something of value paid or demanded as blackmail. *—v.* To subject (someone) to blackmail. **—black'-mail'er** *n.* [SEE NOTE]

black market. **1.** The illegal business of buying or selling goods in violation of price controls, rationing, etc. **2.** The place where this trading is carried on.

black•out |**blăk**'out'| *n.* **1.** The act of putting out or concealing all lights that might help enemy aircraft find a target during a night raid. **2.** A temporary loss of consciousness. **3.** A suppression or stoppage: *a news blackout; an electric-power blackout.* **4.** The act of prohibiting the transmission of a television program in the area adjacent to its place of origin.

Black Power. A cultural and political movement among black Americans that emphasizes racial pride and tries to achieve social equality by creating black political and cultural institutions rather than seeking integration into the white community.

Black Sea. A large inland sea, between Europe and Asia Minor.

black sheep. A person considered undesirable or disgraceful by his family or group.

black•smith |**blăk**'smĭth'| *n.* A person who forges and shapes iron into horseshoes and other objects.

black•snake |**blăk**'snāk'| *n.* **1.** Any of several dark-colored, nonpoisonous snakes. **2.** A long, tapering whip of braided leather.

black tea. A dark tea made from fermented leaves.

black•thorn |**blăk**'thôrn'| *n.* A thorny shrub with white flowers and bluish-black, plumlike fruit.

black tie. **1.** A black bow tie worn with a dinner jacket or tuxedo as part of men's semiformal evening clothes. **2.** Semiformal evening clothes for men: *He was dressed in black tie.* **—*modifier:* (black-tie):** *a black-tie occasion.*

black•top |**blăk**'tŏp'| *n.* A bituminous material, such as asphalt, used to pave roads. *—v.* **black•topped, black•top•ping.** To pave with blacktop.

black widow. A spider of which the poisonous female is black with a red mark on the underside. [SEE PICTURE]

blad•der |**blăd**'ər| *n.* **1.** Any of various sacs found in most animals and made of elastic membrane, especially the sac in which urine is held until it is eliminated. **2. a.** A hollow structure or sac, such as a blister or an air sac in certain seaweeds. **b.** Anything resembling such a sac: *the bladder of a football.*

blade |blād| *n.* **1.** The flat, sharp-edged part of a cutting instrument, such as a knife, saw, razor, or sword. **2.** The thin, flat part of something, such as an oar, bone, etc.: *a shoulder blade.* **3.** A thin, narrow leaf of a grass or similar plant. **4.** The broad, flattened part of a leaf, extending from the stalk. **5.** The metal part of an ice skate. **6.** A dashing young man: *a gay blade.*

blame |blām| *v.* **blamed, blam•ing.** **1.** To hold (someone or something) at fault; to think of as guilty or responsible: *Farmers often blame coyotes for much more harm than they really do.* **2.** To find fault with; censure: *We cannot blame them for wanting to play outdoors.* *—n.* **1.** Responsibility or guilt for a fault: *His problem now is to find out where to put the blame for the accident.* **2.** Condemnation or censure, as for a fault: *not a murmur of approbation or blame, nor the least applause.*

***Idiom.* be to blame.** To deserve censure; be at fault: *People are to blame for many forest fires.*

blamed |blāmd| *adj. Slang.* Used as an intensive: *a blamed fool.*

blame•less |**blām**'lĭs| *adj.* Free from blame or guilt; innocent. **—blame'less•ly** *adv.* **—blame'-less•ness** *n.*

blame•wor•thy |**blām**'wûr'*thē*| *adj.* Deserving blame. **—blame'wor'thi•ness** *n.*

blanch |blănch| *or* |blänch| *v.* **1.** To make lighter in color; bleach or whiten. **2.** To turn pale: *She blanched when she heard the news.* **3.** To place (almonds, tomatoes, etc.) briefly in boiling water in order to remove the skins. **4.** To precook (vegetables) by plunging into boiling water, as before freezing.

blanc•mange |blə **mänj**'| *or* |**-mänzh**'| *n.* A milk pudding, thickened with cornstarch.

bland |blănd| *adj.* **bland•er, bland•est.** **1.** Pleasant or soothing in manner; gentle: *a bland smile.* **2.** Having a moderate, soft, or soothing quality; not irritating or stimulating: *a bland diet; bland foods; a bland climate.* **3.** Lacking distinctive character; dull; flat: *a bland speech.* **—bland'ly** *adj.* **—bland'ness** *n.*

blan•dish•ment |**blăn**'dĭsh mənt| *n.* Often **blandishments.** A word or act meant to coax or flatter: *His blandishments didn't persuade her.*

blank |blăngk| *adj.* **blank•er, blank•est.** **1.** Containing or covered with nothing; free of decoration, writing, etc.: *a blank wall; a blank piece of paper.* **2.** Vacant of ideas or expression: *a blank mind; a blank stare.* *—n.* **1.** The condition of being empty: *Her mind was a complete blank on the subject.* **2. a.** An empty space, such as a line to be filled in with an answer or comment. **b.** A document or form with empty spaces to be filled in: *a pad of order blanks.* **3.** A mark, such as a dash, used in place of a letter or word. **4.** A cartridge, as for a firearm, having a charge of powder but no bullet or other projectile. *—v.* To prevent from scoring in a game: *Our team blanked theirs 4-0.* **—blank'ly** *adv.*

***Idiom.* go blank.** To become suddenly empty or void: *The movie screen goes blank. His mind went blank.*

blan•ket |**blăng**'kĭt| *n.* **1.** A warm covering of soft, thick cloth, as one used on a bed. **2.** Any thick covering: *a blanket of snow.* *—v.* To cover with or as if with a blanket: *The lumberjacks blanketed themselves from chin to toe. Great white snowflakes blanketed the suburbs of the city.* *—adj.* Covering a wide range of conditions or

blackmail

The mail *of* blackmail *is an old word meaning "tax money" and is not related to either of the modern words* **mail**[1] *and* **mail**[2]*. In the sixteenth century and before, the border country between England and Scotland was not controlled by either government. Independent robber chiefs collected protection money, called* black mail, *"the black tax," from the people; if the people refused to pay, they were plundered.*

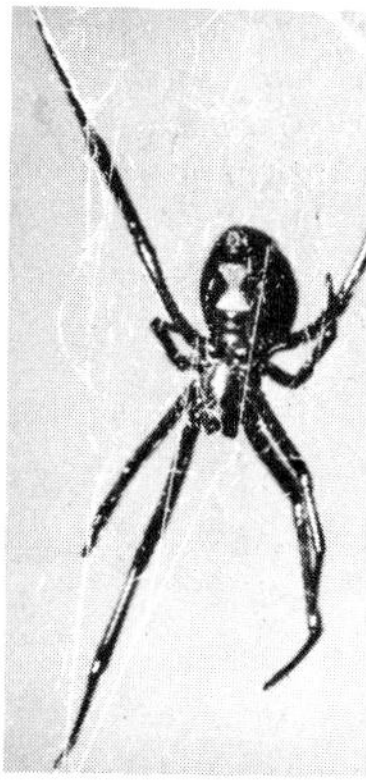

black widow
Only the female black widow (shown here) has a dangerous bite. The male is small and harmless.

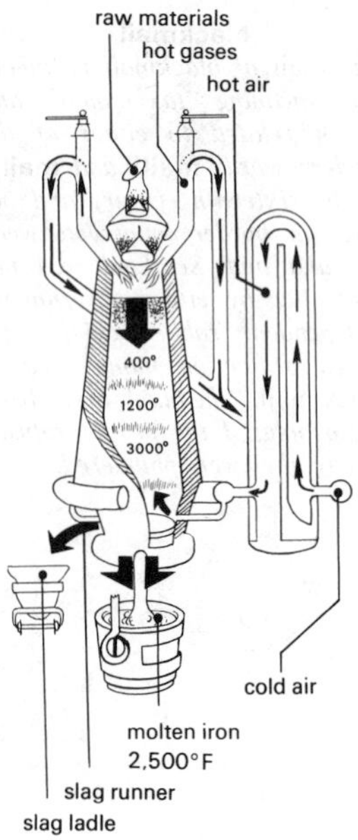

blast furnace

blaze[1-2]
Blaze[1] *is from Old English* blæse, *"torch, bright fire."* **Blaze[2]** *is from Low German* bles, *"white mark." Ultimately, the Old English word and the Low German word are both descended from a prehistoric Germanic word,* blas-, *meaning "bright or white object."*

ă pat/ā pay/â care/ä father/ĕ pet/ ē be/ĭ pit/ī pie/î fierce/ŏ pot/ ō go/ô paw, for/oi oil/ŏŏ book/ ōō boot/ou out/ŭ cut/û fur/ *th* the/th thin/hw which/zh vision/ ə ago, item, pencil, atom, circus

requirements: *a blanket insurance policy.*

blank verse. Verse written in unrhymed lines, usually of iambic pentameter.

blare |blâr| *n.* A loud, strident noise, as of a trumpet or horn: *a blare of bugles.* —*v.* **blared, blar•ing. 1.** To make a blare: *The Jeep came into the village with its horn blaring.* **2.** To produce with a blare or blares: *A brass band blared the national anthem and the game started. The sergeant blared out a command.*

blar•ney |**blär'**nē| *n.* Smooth, flattering talk.

Blar•ney Stone |**blär'**nē|. A famous stone located in the ruins of Blarney Castle, Ireland, supposed to impart great powers of eloquence and persuasion to anyone kissing it.

bla•sé |blä **zā'**| *or* |**blä'**zā| *adj.* Uninterested, unexcited, or bored because of constant exposure or indulgence: *New Yorkers tend to be blasé about tall buildings.*

blas•pheme |blăs **fēm'**| *or* |**blăs'**fēm'| *v.* **blas•phemed, blas•phem•ing.** To speak of (God or something sacred) in a disrespectful way.

blas•phe•mous |**blăs'**fə məs| *adj.* Disrespectful and impious. —**blas'phe•mous•ly** *adv.*

blas•phe•my |**blăs'**fə mē| *n., pl.* **blas•phe•mies.** Any word or action that is disrespectful of God or something sacred.

blast |blăst| *or* |bläst| *n.* **1.** A strong gust of wind. **2.** Any strong rush or stream of air, gas, steam, etc., from an opening. **3. a.** The act of blowing a whistle, trumpet, etc. **b.** The noise made by this. **4. a.** An explosion: *an atomic blast; a blast of dynamite.* **b.** The quantity of explosive used at one time. **c.** The sound of or a sound like an explosion. **5.** A violent verbal attack or outburst. —*v.* **1. a.** To blow up or tear apart with or as if with an explosive: *blasting rocks in the quarry.* **b.** To make, open, or dislodge (something) by or as if by an explosion: *blast a road through the mountain. He blasted his way into the hearts of the people.* **2.** To destroy or shatter as if by an explosion: *Defeat blasted our hopes.* **3.** To wither before flowering or bearing fruit or seeds. **4. a.** To make sudden loud sounds: *The buglers blasted their horns* **b.** To blare continuously: *The radio blasted out the top ten hits.* **5. a.** To attack or bombard, as with explosive weapons: *The planes blasted London.* **b.** To criticize severely: *The reviewer blasted the movie.* **6.** To spray abrasive particles against in order to clean or test: *They blasted the wall with sand.* —***phrasal verb.*** **blast off.** To begin flight: *The spacecraft will blast off at three o'clock.* —*interj. Slang.* A word used to express anger or disgust.

Idiom. **(at) full blast.** At the highest speed or capacity.

blast furnace. A furnace in which combustion is made more intense by a forced draft of air, especially when used in extracting metals from ores. [SEE PICTURE]

blast•off, also **blast-off** |**blăst'**ôf'| *or* |-ŏf'| *or* |**bläst'**-| *n.* The launching of a rocket or spacecraft.

blas•tu•la |**blăs'**chōō lə| *n., pl.* **blas•tu•las** or **blas•tu•lae** |**blăs'**chōō lē'|. An early stage in the development of an embryo. In this stage it consists of a hollow sphere bounded by a single layer of cells.

bla•tant |**blāt'**nt| *adj.* **1.** Unpleasantly loud. **2.** Offensively conspicuous; obvious: *a blatant lie.* —**bla'tan•cy** |**blāt'**n sē| *n.* —**bla'tant•ly** *adv.*

blaze[1] |blāz| *n.* **1. a.** A brightly burning fire: *He assembled a pile of twigs and kindling to make a blaze.* **b.** A destructive fire: *People stood watching the blaze destroy the building.* **2.** Any bright or direct light: *the blaze of day.* **3.** A brilliant or striking display: *The flowers were a blaze of color.* **4.** A sudden outburst, as of activity, emotion, etc.: *The horse went down the track in a blaze of speed. Art culminated in the glorious blaze of the Renaissance.* **5. blazes.** Used as an oath: *How in blazes did it get in the paper?* —*v.* **blazed, blaz•ing. 1.** To burn brightly: *a fire blazing on the broad hearth.* **2.** To shine or shimmer brightly, as with light, heat, etc.: *The cloudless sky blazed with stars. The hot noonday sun blazed down upon the grain fields.* **3.** To be resplendent: *The garden blazed with colorful flowers.* **4.** To flare up suddenly: *His temper blazed up again.* **5.** To shoot rapidly and steadily: *The fighter planes blazed away at the targets.* —**blaz'ing** *adj.*: *a blazing fire; the blazing sun.* [SEE NOTE]

blaze[2] |blāz| *n.* **1.** A white spot on the face of a horse or other animal. **2.** A mark cut on a tree to indicate a trail. —*v.* **blazed, blaz•ing.** To indicate (a trail) by marking trees with cuts. [SEE NOTE]

blaz•er |**blā'**zər| *n.* A lightweight informal sport jacket, often striped or brightly colored.

bla•zon |**blā'**zən| *n.* A **coat of arms.** —*v.* To decorate or adorn with or as if with blazons.

bldg. building.

bleach |blēch| *v.* **1.** To remove the color from (fibers, fabrics, etc.) by means of sunlight, chemicals, etc.; whiten: *bleach a denim shirt; bones bleaching in the blazing desert sun.* **2.** To lighten the color of (hair). —*n.* Any chemical agent used for bleaching.

bleach•ers |**blē'**chərz| *pl.n.* Tiered wooden planks for seating spectators at a public event, especially an outdoor event, such as a baseball game.

bleaching powder. A powder, such as chlorinated lime, used in solution as a bleach.

bleak |blēk| *adj.* **bleak•er, bleak•est. 1.** Exposed to the winds; barren and windswept: *bleak moors.* **2.** Cold and harsh: *a damp, bleak wind.* **3.** Gloomy; somber; dreary: *bleak thoughts.* —**bleak'ly** *adv.* —**bleak'ness** *n.*

blear |blîr| *v.* **1.** To blur (the eyes) with or as if with tears. **2.** To blur; dim.

blear•y |**blîr'**ē| *adj.* **blear•i•er, blear•i•est. 1.** Blurred by or as if by tears: *bleary eyes.* **2.** Vague or indistinct; blurred: *a bleary photograph.*

bleat |blēt| *n.* **1.** The hoarse, broken cry of a goat, sheep, or calf. **2.** A sound resembling this. —*v.* **1.** To utter the cry of a goat, sheep, or calf. **2.** To make a similar sound.

bleed |blēd| *v.* **bled** |blĕd|, **bleed•ing. 1.** To lose blood. **2.** To take blood from: *Doctors long ago bled patients as a supposed cure.* **3.** To feel sympathetic grief: *My heart bleeds for you.* **4. a.** To draw off (a liquid or gas) from a container, pipe, etc.: *He bled the air from the car's brakes.* **b.** To draw liquid or gas from; drain. **5.** To become mixed and run, as dyes in wet cloth.

bleed•er |**blē'**dər| *n.* A person who bleeds excessively from even small cuts; a hemophiliac.

bleed•ing-heart |**blē′**dĭng härt′| *n.* A garden plant with nodding, pink flowers and finely divided leaves. [SEE PICTURE]

blem•ish |**blĕm′**ĭsh| *n.* A disfiguring mark; flaw: *skin blemishes; a blemish on one's reputation.* —*v.* To impair or spoil by a flaw; disfigure; mar: *Scratches blemished the table.*

blench |blĕnch| *v.* To draw back or shy away, as from fear; flinch.

blend |blĕnd| *v.* **1.** To combine completely so that the parts or ingredients are not distinct or set apart; mix thoroughly: *The cook blended milk and flour. Sugar blends easily.* **2.** To mingle or shade in as a part of: *The sofa blends well with the colors of the room.* —*n.* Something blended; a harmonious mixture or combination: *a blend of colors; a blend of tea.*

blend•er |**blĕn′**dər| *n.* An electrical appliance with whirling blades, used to blend or purée foods.

bless |blĕs| *v.* **blessed** or **blest** |blĕst|, **bless•ing. 1.** To make holy; consecrate: *"The Lord blessed the sabbath day"* (Exodus 20:11). **2.** To make the sign of the cross over. **3.** To call divine favor upon: *"God Bless America."* **4.** To praise as holy; glorify: *"Bless the Lord, O my soul"* (Psalm 103:1). **5.** To endow, favor, or enrich: *The land was blessed with natural resources. He is blessed with a good memory.* **6.** Used as an intensive: *Bless her heart, she gave me a dime.*

bless•ed |**blĕs′**ĭd| *adj.* **1.** Worthy of worship; holy: *The second person of the Blessed Trinity.* **2.** Very fortunate: *"Blessed are the meek"* (Matthew 5:5). **3.** Used as an intensive: *not a blessed dime.* —**bless′ed•ly** *adv.* —**bless′ed•ness** *n.*

Blessed Virgin. The Virgin Mary.

bless•ing |**blĕs′**ĭng| *n.* **1.** A prayer calling for divine favor. **2.** A short prayer given at mealtime. **3.** Approval; sanction: *With the Pope's blessing the Portuguese invaded the islands.* **4.** Often **blessings.** Anything that brings happiness or well-being: *the blessings of liberty.*

blest |blĕst|. A past tense and past participle of **bless.**

blew |blo͞o|. Past tense of **blow.** ¶*These sound alike* **blew, blue.**

blight |blīt| *n.* **1.** A disease that withers or destroys plants. **2.** Anything that is harmful or destructive. —*v.* To ruin; destroy: *A mishap blighted his hopes.*

blimp |blĭmp| *n.* A small airship that is not rigid.

blind |blīnd| *adj.* **blind•er, blind•est. 1.** Without the sense of sight; sightless. **2.** Performed without the use of sight: *blind navigation.* **3.** Unwilling or unable to perceive or understand: *She was blind to his faults.* **4.** Not based on reason or evidence: *blind faith.* **5.** Without forethought or reason: *in a blind rage.* **6.** Hidden or screened from sight: *a blind intersection.* **7.** Closed at one end: *a blind alley.* —*n.* **1.** Something that shuts out light or hinders vision: *windows protected by solid wood blinds.* **2.** A shelter for concealing hunters. **3.** Something that conceals the true nature of an activity, especially of an illegal or improper one; a subterfuge: *a candy store that was a blind for drug peddling.* —*v.* **1.** To deprive of sight. **2.** To deprive (a person) of judgment or reason: *Greed blinded him to the danger.* **3.** To dazzle. —**blind′ing** *adj.: a blinding flash; blinding speed.* —**blind′ly** *adv.* —**blind′ness** *n.*

blind•ers |**blīn′**dərz| *pl.n.* A pair of leather flaps attached to a horse's bridle to keep him looking forward rather than to the side.

blind•fold |**blīnd′**fōld′| *v.* To cover the eyes of with a cloth: *blindfold a prisoner.* —**blind′fold′ed** *adj.: a blindfolded captive.* —*n.* A piece of cloth put over the eyes and tied around the head to keep someone from seeing. —*adj.* With eyes covered: *a blindfold captive.*

blind•man's buff |**blīnd′**mănz′|. A game in which one person, blindfolded, tries to catch and identify one of the other players. [SEE PICTURE]

blind spot. 1. The small area, insensitive to light, where the optic nerve enters the retina of the eye. **2.** A place that has poorer radio reception than the region surrounding it. **3.** Any part of an area that cannot be observed directly. **4.** A subject about which a person is noticeably ignorant or prejudiced.

blink |blĭngk| *v.* **1.** To close and open (the eye or eyes) rapidly; wink: *He blinked his eyes. He blinked because of the sunshine.* **2.** To flash off and on: *lights blinking on the horizon.* **3.** To close the eyes to; ignore: *He blinked at their dishonest practices.* —*n.* **1.** A very brief closing of the eye or eyes. **2.** A brief flash of light. ***Idiom.* on the blink.** *Slang.* Out of order.

blink•er |**blĭng′**kər| *n.* **1.** A light that blinks as a means of sending a message or warning. **2. blinkers.** Blinders.

blintz |blĭnts| or **blin•tze** |**blĭnt′**sə| *n.* A thin, rolled pancake with a filling such as cream cheese or fruit.

blip |blĭp| *n.* Anything seen on a radar screen that may indicate that an object has been detected.

bliss |blĭs| *n.* Extreme happiness; joy.

bliss•ful |**blĭs′**fəl| *adj.* Full of or causing bliss: *a blissful silence; blissful ignorance of imminent danger.* —**bliss′ful•ly** *adv.* —**bliss′ful•ness** *n.*

blis•ter |**blĭs′**tər| *n.* **1.** A thin, fluid-filled sac that forms on the skin as a result of a burn or an irritation. **2.** Any bulge like this, as on a painted surface. **3.** A rounded, often transparent, structure that projects from an aircraft, used for observation or as a gun position. —*v.* To form or cause to form blisters: *Her skin blistered from poison ivy. Tight shoes blistered his feet.*

blis•ter•ing |**blĭs′**tər ĭng| *adj.* **1.** Extremely hot: *a blistering sun.* **2.** Very strong; intense: *blistering criticism.* **3.** Extremely rapid: *a blistering pace.*

blithe |blī*th*| *or* |blīth| *adj.* **blith•er, blith•est.** Filled with gaiety; cheerful; carefree. —**blithe′ly** *adv.* —**blithe′ness** *n.*

blitz |blĭts| *n.* **1.** A blitzkrieg. **2.** An intense air raid or series of air raids. **3.** Any intense, swift attack. —*v.* To subject to a blitz.

blitz•krieg |**blĭts′**krēg′| *n.* A swift, sudden military attack, usually by air and land forces. [SEE NOTE]

bliz•zard |**blĭz′**ərd| *n.* A very heavy snowstorm with strong winds.

bloat |blōt| *v.* To swell or cause to swell or puff up, as with liquid or gas: *ripped open the dead bull's belly so it wouldn't bloat; mosquitoes and midges that bloated our faces.*

bleeding-heart

blindman's buff

blitzkrieg

Blitzkrieg *is German for "lightning war":* blitz, *"lightning,"* + krieg, *"war."*

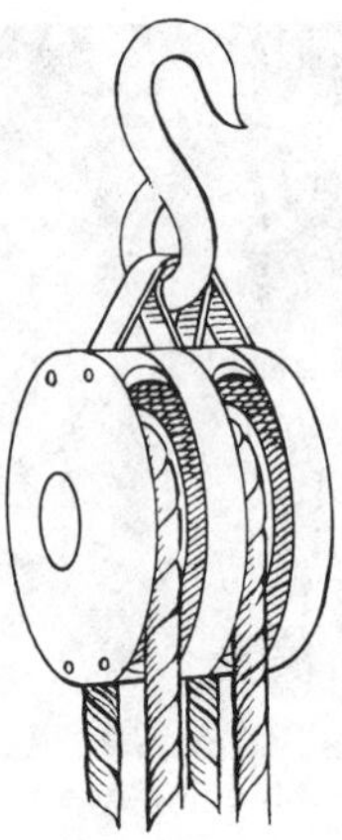

block

blockhouse
Blockhouse at the site of the Battle of Saratoga, showing slits for rifles and openings for downward fire

bloodhound

blob |blŏb| *n.* **1.** A soft, formless mass: *a blob of wax.* **2.** A shapeless splotch of color.

bloc |blŏk| *n.* A group of persons, states, or nations, united geographically or by common interests or political aims: *the Communist bloc; the farm bloc in Congress.* ¶*These sound alike* **bloc, block.**

block |blŏk| *n.* **1.** A solid piece of wood or other hard substance having one or more flat sides. **2.** Such a piece on which chopping or cutting is done. **3.** A stand from which articles are displayed at an auction. **4.** A mold or form upon which something is shaped or displayed: *a hat block.* **5.** A pulley or set of pulleys set in a casing. **6.** The metal casing that contains the cylinders of an engine. **7.** A set of like items sold or handled as a unit: *a block of stock; blocks of tickets.* **8.** An obstacle or hindrance. **9. a.** A section of a city or town enclosed by four intersecting streets. **b.** That part of a street which lies between two successive cross streets. **10.** A large building divided into separate units, such as apartments. **11.** A length of railroad track controlled by one set of signals. **12.** In sports, an act of obstructing an opponent, especially, in football, a legal act of using one's body to obstruct an opponent and thus protect the teammate who has the ball. *—v.* **1.** To shape or form with or on a block: *block a hat.* **2.** To stop or hinder the passage or progress of or movement through: *They blocked his entry. Fallen trees blocked the road.* **3.** In football, to stop or hinder the movement of (an opponent or the ball) by means of physical interference. ¶*These sound alike* **block, bloc.** [SEE PICTURE]

block•ade |blŏ **kād′**| *n.* The closing off of a city or harbor by troops or warships to prevent people and supplies from going in and out. *—v.* **block•ad•ed, block•ad•ing.** To set up a blockade against.

block•ade-run•ner |blŏ **kād′**rŭn′ər| *n.* A ship or person that attempts to go through or past an enemy blockade.

block and tackle. An arrangement of pulleys and ropes used for lifting heavy objects.

block•bust•er |**blŏk′**bŭs′tər| *n. Informal.* **1.** A bomb capable of destroying a city block. **2.** Anything extremely impressive or startling.

block•head |**blŏk′**hĕd′| *n.* A stupid person.

block•house |**blŏk′**hous′| *n., pl.* **-hous•es** |-hou′zĭz|. **1.** A fort made of heavy timbers, with a projecting upper story. **2.** A fortification made of concrete, with loopholes for firing. **3.** A heavily reinforced building from which the launching of rockets or space vehicles is observed and controlled. [SEE PICTURE]

block system. A system that provides for the safe, orderly movement of railroad trains by dividing the track into sections or blocks, each of which is controlled by a **block signal** that indicates whether or not a train may enter.

bloke |blōk| *n. British Slang.* A fellow; man.

blond |blŏnd| *adj.* **blond•er, blond•est.** **1.** Having fair hair and skin: *a blond boy.* **2.** Light-colored: *blond hair; blond furniture.* *—n.* A blond person, especially a man or boy. ¶*These sound alike* **blond, blonde.** **—blond′ness** *n.*

blonde |blŏnd| *adj.* **blond•er, blond•est.** Having fair hair and skin: *a blonde girl.* *—n.* A woman or girl with fair hair and skin. ¶*These sound alike* **blonde, blond.**

blood |blŭd| *n.* **1.** The red fluid circulated through the body by the action of the heart, distributing oxygen, nutrients, hormones, etc., and carrying waste to the excretory organs. **2.** Temperament; temper; disposition: *his hot blood; a drop of sporting blood.* **3.** Descent from a common ancestor; family relationship; kinship: *They are related by blood.* **4.** Racial or national ancestry: *Japanese blood.* **5.** Members considered as a class; personnel: *the best young blood of the nation.* **6.** A dashing young man; rake. *—modifier: a blood transfusion; a blood relative.* *—adj.* Purebred: *a blood mare.*

Idioms. **bad blood.** Enmity; hatred: *bad blood between them.* **in cold blood.** Without emotion; deliberately; coldly. **make (one's) blood boil.** To make very angry. **make (one's) blood run cold.** To terrify.

blood bank. **1.** A supply of blood plasma or of whole blood classified according to blood groups for use in transfusions. **2.** A place where a supply of this kind is stored.

blood bath. An act of savage and widespread killing; a massacre.

blood count. A medical test in which the cells in a given volume of a person's blood are classified and counted.

blood•cur•dling |**blŭd′**kûrd′lĭng| *adj.* Causing great horror; terrifying.

blood•ed |**blŭd′**ĭd| *adj.* **1.** Having blood or a temperament of a specified kind: *a cold-blooded reptile; hot-blooded warriors.* **2.** Thoroughbred: *blooded horses.*

blood group. Any of the four main types, A, B, AB, and O, into which human blood is divided on the basis of the presence or absence of certain proteins and antibodies; blood type.

blood•hound |**blŭd′**hound′| *n.* A hound with a smooth coat, drooping ears, loose folds of skin around the face, and a keen sense of smell. [SEE PICTURE]

blood•less |**blŭd′**lĭs| *adj.* **1.** Having no blood. **2.** Pale and anemic in color. **3.** Accomplished without killing: *a bloodless revolution.* **4.** Lacking spirit: *a dull, bloodless tale.* **—blood′less•ly** *adv.* **—blood′less•ness** *n.*

blood•line |**blŭd′**līn′| *n.* A direct line of descent.

blood•mo•bile |**blŭd′**mə bēl′| *n.* A motor vehicle equipped for collecting blood from donors.

blood poisoning. **1.** A disease in which the blood contains poisons; toxemia. **2.** A disease in which the blood contains bacteria or poisons produced by them; septicemia.

blood pressure. The pressure that the blood exerts on the walls of the arteries or other blood vessels.

blood pudding. A sausage made from cooked pig's blood and suet.

blood•root |**blŭd′**rōōt′| *or* |-rŏŏt′| *n.* A woodland plant with a fleshy root, red juice, and a single white flower.

blood•shed |**blŭd′**shĕd′| *n.* The shedding of blood, especially the injuring or killing of human beings.

blood•shot |**blŭd′**shŏt′| *adj.* Inflamed and overfilled with blood, often with the small blood vessels enlarged: *bloodshot eyes.*

ă pat/ā pay/â care/ä father/ĕ pet/ ē be/ĭ pit/ī pie/î fierce/ŏ pot/ ō go/ô paw, for/oi oil/ŏŏ book/ ōō boot/ou out/ŭ cut/û fur/ *th* the/th thin/hw which/zh vision/ ə ago, item, pencil, atom, circus

blood•stone |**blŭd**'stōn'| *n.* A deep-green, cloudy form of quartz that is flecked with red. It is often used as a gem.

blood•stream |**blŭd**'strēm'| *n.* Also **blood stream.** The blood flowing through the circulatory system of a living body.

blood•suck•er |**blŭd**'sŭk'ər| *n.* A leech or any other animal that sucks blood. —**blood'suck'ing** *adj.* & *n.*

blood test. A medical examination of a sample of blood.

blood•thirst•y |**blŭd**'thûr'stē| *adj.* Eager to cause or see the shedding of blood; cruel. —**blood'thirst'i•ly** *adv.* —**blood'thirst'i•ness** *n.*

blood type. A **blood group.**

blood vessel. Any elastic tube or passage in the body through which blood circulates; an artery, vein, or capillary.

blood•y |**blŭd**'ē| *adj.* **blood•i•er, blood•i•est. 1.** Bleeding: *a bloody nose.* **2.** Stained with blood: *bloody bandages.* **3.** Of or containing blood: *a bloody froth on his mouth.* **4.** Causing or marked by bloodshed: *a bloody fight; a bloody dictatorship.* —*v.* **blood•ied, blood•y•ing, blood•ies.** To make bloody. —**blood'i•ly** *adv.* —**blood'i•ness** *n.*

bloom |bloo͞m| *n.* **1.** The flower or blossoms of a plant. **2.** The condition or time of flowering: *a rose in bloom.* **3.** A condition or time of great development, vigor, or beauty: *Humanism reached full bloom in the Renaissance.* **4.** A thin powdery coating on some fruits, leaves, or stems: *the bloom on a plum.* —*v.* **1.** To bear flowers; blossom. **2.** To flourish: *New playgrounds are blooming across the country.*

bloom•er |**bloo͞**'mər| *n.* **1.** An outfit designed for women in the 19th century, consisting of baggy trousers gathered at the ankles and worn under a shorter skirt. **2. bloomers.** Baggy trousers gathered at the knee, once worn by women and girls for sports, riding bicycles, etc. **3. bloomers.** Similar pants worn as underwear. [SEE NOTE & PICTURE]

bloom•ing |**bloo͞**'mĭng| *adj.* **1.** Flowering; blossoming. **2.** Flourishing, as with health, beauty, or vigor. **3.** *Slang.* Used as an intensive: *He tried to beat the whole blooming team.*

blos•som |**blŏs**'əm| *n.* **1.** A flower or flowers, especially of a tree that bears fruit: *apple blossoms.* **2.** The condition or time of flowering: *peach trees in blossom.* —*v.* **1.** To come into flower; bloom. **2.** To flourish: *Literary societies blossomed during the 19th century.*

blot |blŏt| *n.* **1.** A stain or spot: *an ink blot.* **2.** Any patch that resembles a stain or spot: *a blot of dense green in the forest.* **3.** Something that takes away from beauty or excellence: *a blot on his character; a blot on the nation's history.* —*v.* **blot•ted, blot•ting. 1.** To spot or stain: *Ink spots blotted the page. Ink often blots permanently.* **2.** To dry or soak up with absorbent material. —***phrasal verb.* blot out. 1.** To hide from view; obscure: *Storm clouds blotted out the sunlight.* **2.** To destroy completely; annihilate: *The tidal wave blotted out the island's population.*

blotch |blŏch| *n.* **1.** A spot or blot; a splotch. **2.** A discoloration on the skin; a blemish. —*v.* To mark or become marked with blotches.

blot•ter |**blŏt**'ər| *n.* A piece or pad of thick, absorbent paper used to dry a surface by soaking up a liquid, such as excess ink from something written or a fluid that has been spilled.

blouse |blous| *or* |blouz| *n.* **1.** An outer garment, especially a loosely fitting shirt, worn on the upper part of the body by women and children. **2.** A loose garment like a smock, worn by some workmen and peasants in Europe. **3.** The jacket of a U.S. Army uniform.

blow[1] |blō| *v.* **blew** |bloo͞|, **blown** |blōn|, **blow•ing. 1.** To be in motion, as air: *The wind blew all night. It was blowing hard.* **2.** To be moved or cause to move by means of a current of air: *His hat blew off. The gale blew the ship off course.* **3.** To send out a current of air, as from the mouth or from a bellows: *blow on your soup to cool it.* **4. a.** To cause (a musical wind instrument) to sound by forcing breath through it: *blow a trumpet.* **b.** To sound: *The trumpets blew a fanfare. The whistle blows at noon.* **5.** To clear by forcing air through: *blowing his nose noisily.* **6.** To shape (a pliable material, such as molten glass) by forcing air into it. **7.** To cause (an electrical fuse) to melt and open a circuit. **8.** To spout water and air, as a whale does. —***phrasal verbs.* blow off.** To allow (a gas under pressure, as steam or air) to escape. **blow out. 1.** To extinguish or be extinguished by blowing: *blow out a candle.* **2.** To fail suddenly and violently, as a tire. **3.** To melt and open an electric circuit: *The fuse blew out.* **blow over. 1.** To reach a lower level: *The storm will blow over soon.* **2.** To be forgotten: *The scandal blew over quickly.* **blow up. 1.** To come into being: *A storm blew up.* **2.** To explode. **3.** To fill with air; inflate. **4.** To enlarge (a photographic image or print). **5.** *Informal.* To lose one's temper. —*n.* A blast of air or wind. [SEE NOTE]

***Idioms.* blow hot and cold.** To change one's opinion often on a given matter; vacillate. **blow off steam.** *Informal.* To give release to one's anger or other feeling in words.

blow[2] |blō| *n.* **1.** A sudden hard stroke or hit, as with the fist or a weapon. **2.** A sudden, unexpected shock or great misfortune: *Her illness was quite a blow to him.* [SEE NOTE]

***Idiom.* come to blows.** To begin to fight.

blow[3] |blō| *v.* **blew** |bloo͞|, **blown** |blōn|, **blow•ing.** To bloom; blossom. [SEE NOTE]

blow•er |**blō**'ər| *n.* A device that produces a flow of air or other gas through a duct or an enclosed space.

blow•gun |**blō**'gŭn'| *n.* A long, narrow pipe through which pellets or poison darts can be blown.

blow•hole |**blō**'hōl'| *n.* **1.** A nostril at the top of the head of a whale or related animal. **2.** A hole in the ice through which seals, whales, and other water animals come up for air. **3.** A vent that allows air or other gas to escape. **4.** In a metal casting or a piece of glass, a defect that consists of a trapped bubble of air.

blown |blōn|. Past participle of **blow.**

blow•out |**blō**'out'| *n.* A sudden and violent loss of air pressure, as by or from an automobile tire.

blow•pipe |**blō**'pīp'| *n.* **1.** A narrow tube through which a controlled flow of air is blown into a flame in order to concentrate and direct the heat. **2.** A long, narrow iron pipe used to gather, work, and blow molten glass. **3.** A blowgun.

bloomers

Amelia Jenks *Bloomer* (1818–1894), editor and feminist, shown above in 1851, hoped to popularize a "rational costume" for women as an alternative to the huge hooped crinoline dress of the period. Her costume had Turkish-style trousers, which became known as **bloomers,** worn under a midi-length skirt. It was a serious contribution to the "woman's rights" movement and a direct forerunner of the modern pantsuit. But at the time most people treated the idea of trousers for women as shocking and ridiculous. Mrs. Bloomer eventually gave up the costume, but her name has remained in the language.

blow[1-2-3]

Blow[1] *is from Old English* blāwan, *"to blow," and is related to* **blast** *and* **bladder**. **Blow**[2] *is originally a northern English word, spelled* blaw, *of uncertain origin.* **Blow**[3] *is from Old English* blōwen, *"to bloom," and is related to* **bloom** *and* **blossom**.

blubber[1-2]

Blubber[1] *originally meant "to foam or bubble"; it comes from the Middle English noun* blober, *"foam, bubbles." This word also later came to mean "fish entrails, whale oil"; hence* **blubber[2]**.

blue jay

bluff[1-2]

Bluff[1] *is from Dutch* bluffen, *which originally meant "to swell up," hence "to boast."* **Bluff[2]** *may also be from Dutch; there is an obsolete Dutch word* blaf, *meaning "broad or flat"; but this connection is not very convincing, and must be regarded as uncertain, which is often the case in etymology.*

blunderbuss

ă pat/ā pay/â care/ä father/ĕ pet/ ē be/ĭ pit/ī pie/î fierce/ŏ pot/ ō go/ô paw, for/oi oil/o͝o book/ o͞o boot/ou out/ŭ cut/û fur/ *th* the/th thin/hw which/zh vision/ ə ago, item, pencil, atom, circus

blow•sy |blou'zē| *adj.* **blow•si•er, blow•si•est.** A form of the word **blowzy.**

blow•torch |blō'tôrch'| *n.* A device in which gasoline or some other fuel is mixed with air and burned to produce a flame hot enough to melt solder and other soft metals.

blow•up |blō'ŭp'| *n.* **1.** An explosion. **2.** A photographic enlargement. **3.** A violent outburst of temper.

blow•zy |blou'zē| *adj.* **blow•zi•er, blow•zi•est. 1.** Ruddy and bloated in appearance. **2.** Not tidy; disheveled; messy.

blub•ber[1] |blŭb'ər| *v.* **1.** To cry or sob in a noisy manner. **2.** To say while crying and sobbing: *The child blubbered his name.* [SEE NOTE]

blub•ber[2] |blŭb'ər| *n.* The thick layer of fat under the skin of whales, seals, and certain other sea animals. [SEE NOTE]

bludg•eon |blŭj'ən| *n.* A short, heavy club with one end loaded or thicker than the other. —*v.* To beat or strike with a bludgeon.

blue |blo͞o| *n.* **1.** The color of the sky on a clear day or of a sapphire. **2.** Often **Blue. a.** A Union soldier in the Civil War. **b.** The Union Army. **3. the blue. a.** The sea. **b.** The sky. —*adj.* **blu•er, blu•est. 1.** Of the color blue. **2.** Having gray or purplish color, as from cold or a bruise. **3.** Gloomy; depressed. ¶*These sound alike* **blue, blew.** —**blue'ly** *adv.* —**blue'ness** *n.*

Idioms. **once in a blue moon.** Very rarely; seldom. **out of the blue. 1.** From an unexpected or unknown source. **2.** At a completely unexpected time.

blue baby. A newborn baby who, because of a heart or lung defect, has too little oxygen in its blood and a bluish tint to its skin.

blue•bell |blo͞o'bĕl'| *n.* Any of several plants with blue, bell-shaped flowers.

blue•ber•ry |blo͞o'bĕr'ē| *n., pl.* **-ber•ries. 1.** A round, juicy, edible blue or purplish berry. **2.** A shrub that bears such berries.

blue•bird |blo͞o'bûrd'| *n.* A North American bird with blue feathers and, usually, a rust-colored breast.

blue blood. 1. Noble or aristocratic descent. **2.** A member of the aristocracy or other high social group.

blue•bon•net |blo͞o'bŏn'ĭt| *n.* A plant of western North America, with clusters of blue flowers.

blue•bot•tle |blo͞o'bŏt'l| *n.* A fly with a bright metallic-blue body.

blue cheese. A tangy cheese streaked with bluish mold.

blue•fish |blo͞o'fĭsh'| *n., pl.* **blue•fish** or **blue•fish•es.** A bluish or greenish ocean fish caught for food or sport.

blue•grass |blo͞o'grăs'| *or* |-gräs'| *n.* A lawn and pasture grass with bluish or grayish leaves and stems.

blue•ing |blo͞o'ĭng| *n.* A form of the word **bluing.**

blue•ish |blo͞o'ĭsh| *adj.* A form of the word **bluish.**

blue jay. A North American bird with a crested head and blue feathers with white and black markings. [SEE PICTURE]

blue jeans. Boys' or girls' trousers of blue denim or similar cloth.

blue law. 1. A law passed in colonial New England to govern personal behavior and particularly to state which activities are prohibited on Sunday. **2.** Any law restricting Sunday activities.

blue•print |blo͞o'prĭnt'| *n.* **1.** A photographic copy of architectural plans, technical drawings, etc., usually appearing as white lines on a blue background. **2.** A carefully worked-out plan. —*v.* To make a blueprint of.

blue ribbon. The first prize or highest award.

blues |blo͞oz| *n.* **1.** *(used with a singular or plural verb).* A type of jazz that typically is slow in tempo, has twelve-measure phrases, and makes frequent use of flatted tones, especially the third and seventh tones of the scale. **2.** Lowness of spirit; melancholy. —***modifier:*** *a blues singer.*

blu•ets |blo͞o'ĭts| *n.* A low-growing plant with slender stem and small, light-blue flowers.

blue whale. A very large whale with a bluish-gray back and narrow grooves along the throat and belly.

bluff[1] |blŭf| *v.* To deceive or mislead, especially by a false display of strength or confidence: *He bluffed his captors into letting him go. He bluffed all night at the card table.* —*n.* **1.** The act or an example of deceiving or misleading by a false display of strength or confidence. **2.** Someone who bluffs. —**bluff'er** *n.* [SEE NOTE]

Idiom. **call (someone's) bluff.** To challenge or expose someone's bluff.

bluff[2] |blŭf| *n.* A steep headland, cliff, river bank, etc. —*adj.* **bluff•er, bluff•est. 1.** Gruff or blunt in manner but not unkind. **2.** Having a broad, steep front: *bluff river banks.* —**bluff'ly** *adv.* —**bluff'ness** *n.* [SEE NOTE]

blu•ing |blo͞o'ĭng| *n.* A blue substance added to rinse water to prevent white fabrics from turning yellow during laundering.

blu•ish |blo͞o'ĭsh| *adj.* Somewhat blue.

blun•der |blŭn'dər| *n.* **1.** A foolish or stupid mistake. —*v.* **1.** To make a stupid mistake. **2.** To move clumsily or blindly; stumble: *A small fly blundered into the spider's web.* —**blun'der•er** *n.*

blun•der•buss |blŭn'dər bŭs'| *n.* **1.** An old type of gun with a wide muzzle for scattering shot at close range. **2.** A stupid, clumsy person. [SEE PICTURE]

blunt |blŭnt| *adj.* **blunt•er, blunt•est. 1.** Having a thick, dull edge or end; not pointed. **2.** Abrupt and frank in manner. —*v.* **1.** To dull the edge of. **2.** To make less effective; weaken; deaden: *The army blunted the enemy onslaught.* —**blunt'ly** *adv.* —**blunt'ness** *n.*

blur |blûr| *v.* **blurred, blur•ring.** To make or become indistinct, vague, or hazy: *Clouds blurred the mountain. Her eyes blurred with tears.* —*n.* Something that is indistinct and hazy: *The distant crowd was a blur of faces.*

blurb |blûrb| *n.* A brief, favorable publicity notice, as on the jacket of a book.

blur•ry |blûr'ē| *adj.* **blur•ri•er, blur•ri•est.** Indistinct and hazy: *blurry sounds; a blurry picture.*

blurt |blûrt| *v.* To say suddenly and without thought: *ashamed of having blurted out my secret.*

blush |blŭsh| *v.* **1.** To become suddenly red in the face from modesty, embarrassment, or shame. **2.** To feel ashamed. —*n.* **1.** A sudden reddening of the face caused by modesty, embarrassment, or shame. **2.** A reddish or rosy color: *The sun's last* *blushes tinted the faraway hills.*

blus•ter |blŭs′tər| *v.* **1.** To blow in loud, violent gusts: *Winds blustered around the house.* **2.** To utter noisy boasts or threats. *—n.* **1.** A violent, gusty wind. **2.** Noisy confusion; commotion. **3.** Loud, boastful, or threatening talk. **—blus′ter•y, blus′ter•ous** *adj.*

blvd. boulevard.

bo•a |bō′ə| *n.* **1.** Any of several large, nonpoisonous snakes, such as the **boa constrictor** of tropical America, that coil around and crush their prey. **2.** A long, fluffy scarf of fur, feathers, etc.

boar |bôr| *or* |bōr| *n.* **1.** A male pig. **2.** Also **wild boar.** A wild pig with dark bristles. ¶ *These sound alike* **boar, bore.** [SEE PICTURE]

board |bôrd| *or* |bōrd| *n.* **1.** A flat length of sawed lumber; a plank. **2.** A flat piece of wood or similar material adapted for some special use. **3.** A table top or similar panel on which certain games are played. **4. a.** A table set for serving a meal: *a modest board.* **b.** Food served daily to paying guests: *room and board.* **5.** A group of persons organized to transact or administer some particular business: *board of trustees.* **6.** A bulletin board, blackboard, or the like. *—v.* **1.** To close with boards: *boarding up the windows.* **2. a.** To provide with food and lodging for a charge. **b.** To live as a paying guest. **3.** To go aboard (a ship, train, or plane).

Idioms. **go by the board.** To be lost beyond recall. **on board.** Aboard.

board•er |bôr′dər| *or* |bōr′-| *n.* A person who pays for and receives both meals and lodging at another person's home. ¶ *These sound alike* **boarder, border.**

board foot. *pl.* **board feet.** A unit of measure for lumber, equal to the volume of an unplaned board one foot long, one foot wide, and one inch thick; 144 cubic inches of wood.

boarding house. A private home that provides meals and lodging for paying guests.

board•ing•house |bôr′dĭng hous′| *or* |bōr′-| *n., pl.* **-hous•es** |-hou′zĭz|. A form of the phrase **boarding house.**

boarding school. A school where pupils are provided with meals and lodging.

board•walk |bôrd′wôk′| *or* |bōrd′-| *n.* A public walk or promenade along a beach, usually constructed of wooden planks.

boast |bōst| *v.* **1.** To brag vainly or proudly about something relating to oneself. **2.** To take pride in the possession of: *The area boasted great vineyards and gardens.* **3.** To speak with pride: *He boasted of the wonderful things he had brought from the store.* *—n.* **1.** A bragging or boastful statement. **2.** A source of pride: *The city's only boast is an avenue of palm trees.* **—boast′er** *n.*

boast•ful |bōst′fəl| *adj.* Tending to boast or brag. **—boast′ful•ly** *adv.* **—boast′ful•ness** *n.*

boat |bōt| *n.* **1.** A small open craft. **2.** A ship. **3.** A dish shaped like a boat: *a gravy boat.* ***—modifier:*** *a boat race.* *—v.* To travel by boat; row or sail: *boat across the lake.*

Idiom. **in the same boat.** In the same predicament.

boat•house |bōt′hous′| *n., pl.* **-hous•es** |-hou′zĭz|. A house in which boats are kept.

boat•man |bōt′mən| *n., pl.* **-men** |-mən|. A person who works on, deals with, or operates boats.

boat•swain |bō′sən| *n.* A warrant officer or petty officer in charge of a ship's deck crew, rigging, and anchors.

bob¹ |bŏb| *n.* **1.** A thick, jerking movement of the head or body. **2.** A small knoblike weight that hangs: *a plumb bob.* **3.** A fishing float or cork. **4.** A short haircut on a woman or child. *—v.* **bobbed, bob•bing. 1. a.** To move or jerk up and down: *kites bobbing on the breeze; a boxer bobbing his head.* **b.** To emerge or appear suddenly: *The cork bobbed up to the top of the water.* **2.** To grab at floating or hanging objects with the teeth: *bob for apples.* **3.** To cut short: *She has bobbed her hair.* [SEE NOTE]

bob² |bŏb| *n., pl.* **bob.** *British Slang.* A shilling. [SEE NOTE]

bob•bin |bŏb′ĭn| *n.* A spool or reel that holds thread or yarn in place for spinning, weaving, knitting, sewing, or the making of lace.

bob•ble |bŏb′əl| *v.* **bob•bled, bob•bling. 1.** To bob up and down. **2.** In baseball or football, to fumble: *He bobbled a ground ball.* *—n.* A fumble or miss; an error.

bob•by |bŏb′ē| *n., pl.* **bob•bies.** *British Slang.* A policeman.

bob•by pin |bŏb′ē|. A small metal hair clip having springy ends pressed tightly together to hold the hair in place.

bobby socks. Short, thick socks, typically worn by teen-age girls.

bob•by•sox•er |bŏb′ē sŏk′sər| *n.* Also **bobby soxer.** A teen-age girl of the 1940's who followed current fads.

bob•cat |bŏb′kăt′| *n.* A North American wild cat with spotted, reddish-brown fur and a short tail.

bob•o•link |bŏb′ə lĭngk′| *n.* A black, white, and tan American songbird.

bob•sled |bŏb′slĕd′| *n.* **1.** A long racing sled whose front runners are controlled by a steering wheel. **2. a.** A long sled made of two shorter sleds joined one behind the other. **b.** Either of these two smaller sleds. *—v.* **bob•sled•ded, bob•sled•ding.** To ride or race in a bobsled.

bob•tail |bŏb′tāl′| *n.* **1.** A short tail or a tail that has been cut short. **2.** An animal, especially a horse, with such a tail. *—adj.* Having a short tail: *a bobtail nag.*

bob•white |bŏb hwīt′| *or* |-wīt′| *n.* A brown and white North American quail with a call that sounds like its name. [SEE PICTURE]

bode¹ |bōd| *v.* **bod•ed, bod•ing.** To be a sign or omen of (something to come): *A heavy sea boded trouble for the passengers on board.*

bode² |bōd|. A past tense of **bide.**

bod•ice |bŏd′ĭs| *n.* **1.** The fitted upper part of a dress. **2.** A woman's vest that laces in front, worn over a blouse.

bod•i•less |bŏd′ē lĭs| *adj.* Having no body, form, or substance.

bod•i•ly |bŏd′l ē| *adj.* Of the body: *bodily ailments; bodily needs.* *—adv.* **1.** In the flesh; in person: *always with us in spirit, if not bodily.* **2.** As a complete body; as a whole: *an animal lifted bodily by the eagle.*

bod•kin |bŏd′kĭn| *n.* **1.** A small, pointed instrument for making holes in cloth or leather.

boar
A wild boar

bob¹⁻²
Bob¹ *in various senses first appears in the Middle English period; beyond that its history is unknown.* **Bob²** *first appears in a slang dictionary of the early nineteenth century. Its origin too is unknown, and since the British shilling is being abolished, the word itself is presumably destined to disappear.*

bobwhite

Bohemian

Bohemia *is the name of a medieval Slavic kingdom that is now a part of Czechoslovakia. In the late Middle Ages, the Gypsies came to Europe from India and Persia, and some of them passed through Bohemia. Later they claimed that Bohemia was their native country, and thus* **Bohemian** *came to mean "Gypsy" or any Gypsylike wandering person or hobo. In the mid-nineteenth century, the name was applied to those artists, writers, and others who cultivated a defiantly unconventional life-style. (Their successors have called themselves* beatniks *and* hippies.*)*

boil[1-2]

Boil[1] *is from Old French* bouillir, *which is from Latin* bullīre, *"to bubble."* **Boil[2]** *is from Old English* byle, *"a boil or pustule." The two words are probably ultimately related; if so, the underlying meaning was "to swell."*

bola
Argentine Gaucho preparing to release bola

ă pat/ā pay/â care/ä father/ĕ pet/ ē be/ĭ pit/ī pie/î fierce/ŏ pot/ ō go/ô paw, for/oi oil/ŏŏ book/ ōō boot/ou out/ŭ cut/û fur/ *th* the/th thin/hw which/zh vision/ ə ago, item, pencil, atom, circus

2. A blunt needle for pulling tape or ribbon through loops or a hem. 3. *Archaic.* A small dagger or stiletto.

bod•y |bŏd'ē| *n., pl.* **bod•ies.** 1. The entire physical structure and substance of a living thing, especially a human being or animal. 2. The part of this structure that is left after death; a corpse; carcass. 3. The main part of this structure excluding the head and limbs; a trunk; torso. 4. Any well-defined object or collection of matter: *a celestial body; a body of water.* 5. A group of persons considered or acting together: *the student body; a governing body.* 6. A collection of related things: *a body of information.* 7. The main or central part of something: *the body of a ship; the great body of literature.* 8. Consistency of substance; density; strength: *a wine with fine body.* 9. *Informal.* A person: *the oddest things a body ever saw.* 10. In a violin, guitar, or other stringed instrument, a hollow chamber whose resonance reinforces the tone; a sound box. —*modifier: body heat; body cells.*

bod•y•guard |bŏd'ē gärd'| *n.* A person or group of persons who escort and are responsible for protecting one or more specific persons against possible attack.

body politic. The whole people of a nation or state, regarded as a political unit.

Boer |bōr| *or* |bôr| *n.* A South African of Dutch descent. —**Boer** *adj.*

bog |bôg| *or* |bŏg| *n.* Soft, water-soaked ground; a marsh; swamp. —*v.* **bogged, bog•ging.** 1. To cause to sink in or as if in a bog: *Rain had bogged the village in a sea of mud.* 2. To hinder or slow: *Storms bogged down the troops.*

bo•gey |bō'gē| *n., pl.* **bo•geys.** 1. A bogy; hobgoblin. 2. In golf, a score of one stroke over par on a hole.

bog•gle |bŏg'əl| *v.* **bog•gled, bog•gling.** To hesitate or evade, as if in fear or doubt: *He boggled at the thought of opening someone else's letter.*

bog•gy |bô'gē| *or* |bŏg'ē| *adj.* **bog•gi•er, bog•gi•est.** Like a bog or full of bogs; swampy. —**bog'gi•ness** *n.*

bo•gie |bō'gē| *n.* A form of the word **bogy** (hobgoblin).

Bo•go•tá |bō'gə tä'|. The capital and largest city of Colombia. Population, 2,800,000.

bo•gus |bō'gəs| *adj.* Counterfeit; fake: *a gang that is passing bogus bills to storekeepers.*

bo•gy |bō'gē| *n., pl.* **bo•gies.** 1. An evil or mischievous spirit; hobgoblin. 2. Something that causes one worry, trouble, or annoyance.

Bo•he•mi•an |bō hē'mē ən| *n.* Often **bohemian.** A person, especially an artist, who does not follow conventional standards of behavior. —*modifier: bohemian habits.* [SEE NOTE]

boil[1] |boil| *v.* 1. To heat (a liquid) to a temperature at which it vaporizes, with bubbles of vapor breaking through the liquid's surface. 2. To change from a liquid to a vapor with bubbles breaking through the surface: *Water boils at 212°F.* 3. a. To put into boiling water, as in cooking. b. To undergo the action of boiling, as in being cooked: *boil an egg.* 4. To seethe, as with anger. 5. To rush or churn: *The water boiled through the rapids.* —**boiled'** *adj.: a boiled potato.* —*phrasal verbs.* **boil away.** To evaporate by boiling. **boil down.** 1. To reduce in volume or amount by boiling. 2. To reduce or be reduced to a simpler form: *boil the problem down to its basic elements. The whole problem boils down to two basic elements.* **boil over.** 1. To overflow while boiling. 2. To explode in rage; lose one's temper. —*n.* The boiling point or the condition of being boiled: *First you should bring the soup to a rapid boil.* [SEE NOTE]

boil[2] |boil| *n.* A painful, pus-filled swelling of the skin and the tissue beneath it, caused by a local bacteria infection. [SEE NOTE]

boil•er |boi'lər| *n.* 1. A vessel in which a liquid, usually water, is heated and often vaporized for use in an engine, turbine, or heating system. 2. A container, such as a kettle, for boiling liquids. 3. A storage tank for hot water.

boil•ing |boi'lĭng| *adj.* 1. Heated to the boiling point: *boiling water.* 2. Intensely angry. —*adv.: boiling hot; boiling mad.*

boiling point. 1. The temperature at which a liquid boils, especially under standard atmospheric conditions. 2. *Informal.* The point at which a person loses his temper.

Boi•se |boi'zē| *or* |-sē|. The capital and largest city of Idaho. Population, 102,451.

bois•ter•ous |boi'stər əs| *or* |-strəs| *adj.* 1. Rough and stormy; violent: *boisterous winds.* 2. Noisy and lacking restraint or discipline: *boisterous cheers; a boisterous mob.* —**bois'ter•ous•ly** *adv.* —**bois'ter•ous•ness** *n.*

bo•la |bō'lə| *n.* A rope with weights attached, used in South America to catch cattle or game by entangling their legs. [SEE PICTURE]

bo•las |bō'ləz| *n.* A form of the word **bola.**

bold |bōld| *adj.* **bold•er, bold•est.** 1. Without fear; brave; courageous: *bold explorers.* 2. Showing or requiring courage; daring; audacious: *a bold proposal.* 3. Taking undue liberties; impudent; forward: *a bold glance; a bold reply.* 4. Clear and distinct to the eye; vivid; clear: *bold colors; in bold relief; a bold handwriting.* 5. Abrupt; steep: *a bold cliff.* 6. Designating boldface type. —**bold'ly** *adv.* —**bold'ness** *n.*
Idiom. **make bold.** To take the liberty; dare.

bold•face |bōld'fās'| *n.* Type that has thick heavy lines to make it immediately noticeable. All entry words in this Dictionary are printed in boldface. —*modifier: a boldface entry in a dictionary.*

bold-faced |bōld'fāst'| *adj.* Printed or marked for printing in boldface.

bole |bōl| *n.* The trunk of a tree. ¶*These sound alike* **bole, boll, bowl.**

bo•le•ro |bō lâr'ō| *or* |bə-| *n., pl.* **bo•le•ros.** 1. A very short jacket of Spanish origin, worn open in the front. 2. a. A Spanish dance. b. The music for this dance.

bol•i•var |bŏl'ə vər| *n.* The basic unit of money of Venezuela.

Bo•lí•var |bō lē'vär|, **Simón.** 1783–1830. Venezuelan leader who helped liberate a large area of western and northern South America from Spanish rule.

Bo•liv•i•a |bō lĭv'ē ə| *or* |bə-|. An inland country in western South America. Population, 5,470,-000. Capitals, La Paz and Sucre. —**Bo•liv'i•an** *adj. & n.*

boll |bōl| *n.* A rounded seed pod, especially of the cotton plant. ¶*These sound alike* **boll, bole, bowl.**

boll weevil. A long-snouted beetle that lays its eggs in the buds and bolls of the cotton plant, where the larvae hatch and cause great damage. [SEE PICTURE]

bo•lo•gna |bə lō′nē| *or* |-nə| *or* |-nyə| *n.* A seasoned smoked sausage made of mixed meats.

Bol•she•vik |**bōl′**shə vĭk′| *or* |**bŏl′**-| *n.* **1.** A Communist, especially a Russian Communist of Lenin's time. **2.** Often **bolshevik.** *Informal.* Any radical. —***modifier:*** *the Bolshevik revolution.*

Bol•she•vism |**bōl′**shə vĭz′əm| *or* |**bŏl′**-| *n.* **1.** The theories and practices developed by the Bolsheviks between 1903 and 1917 with a view to seizing governmental power and establishing the world's first Communist state. **2.** Soviet Communism, especially during the first generation following the Russian Revolution.

bol•ster |**bōl′**stər| *n.* A long, narrow pillow or cushion. —*v.* To strengthen or reinforce.

bolt |bōlt| *n.* **1.** A threaded rod or pin onto which a nut is screwed, used to hold two parts together. **2.** A sliding bar for fastening a door or gate. **3.** A metal bar or rod in a lock that is pushed out or withdrawn at a turn of the key. **4.** A sliding bar that positions the cartridge in a rifle and closes the breech. **5.** A large roll of cloth, especially as it comes from the loom. **6.** A flash of lightning or a thunderbolt. **7.** A sudden dash or dart toward or away from something: *made a bolt for freedom.* —*v.* **1.** To attach or fasten with a bolt or bolts: *bolted the rack to the wall.* **2.** To lock with a bolt: *Bolt the door. This door bolts with difficulty.* **3.** To make off suddenly: *bolting from the room; a horse that shied and bolted.* **4.** To eat quickly and with little chewing; gulp. **5.** To break away from (a political party): *The candidate bolted the Democratic ticket. Several members rejected the motion and bolted on the spot.* [SEE PICTURE]

Idioms. **bolt from the blue.** A sudden, usually shocking, surprise. **shoot (one's) bolt.** To do one's utmost; exhaust every resource.

bomb |bŏm| *n.* **1.** An explosive weapon constructed to go off upon striking a given object, area, or other target, or by another means, such as a timing mechanism. **2.** Any of various weapons exploded to release smoke, gas, or other destructive materials. **3.** A container for holding a substance under pressure, as a preparation for killing insects, that can be released as a spray or gas. —***modifier:*** *a bomb shelter.* —*v.* To attack, damage, or destroy with a bomb or bombs.

bom•bard |bŏm **bärd′**| *v.* **1.** To attack with bombs, explosive shells, etc. **2.** To assail or shower (a person), as with questions, insults, etc. **3.** To act on (a target, such as an element, atom, etc.) with high-energy radiation or particles: *Physicists bombard atoms to study them.* —**bom•bard′ment** *n.*

bom•bar•dier |bŏm′bər **dîr′**| *n.* The member of a bomber crew who operates the bombing equipment.

bom•bast |**bŏm′**băst′| *n.* Speech or writing having an extravagant, pompous style; wordy, high-flown language. —**bom•bas′tic** *adj.*

Bom•bay |bŏm **bā′**|. A city in western India, a port on the Arabian Sea. Population, 5,971,000.

bomb bay. The compartment in a bomber from which the bombs are dropped.

bomb•er |**bŏm′**ər| *n.* **1.** A military airplane that carries and drops bombs. **2.** A person who attacks with bombs. —***modifier:*** *a bomber squadron.*

bomb•shell |**bŏm′**shĕl′| *n.* **1.** A bomb. **2.** A great surprise or shock.

bomb•sight |**bŏm′**sīt′| *n.* A device in a military aircraft for aiming bombs.

bo•na fide |**bō′**nə fīd′| *or* |**fī′**dē| *or* |**bŏn′**ə|. **1.** Done or made in good faith; sincere: *a bona fide offer.* **2.** Genuine; authentic: *a bona fide discovery.*

bo•nan•za |bə **năn′**zə| *n.* **1.** A rich mine or vein of ore. **2.** Something that provides a large profit or great wealth: *conservation programs that promise a bonanza to fishermen.*

bon•bon |**bŏn′**bŏn′| *n.* A candy with a creamy center and, often, a chocolate coating.

bond |bŏnd| *n.* **1.** Anything that binds, ties, or fastens together, as a cord or rope. **2.** Often **bonds.** A force that unites; a tie; link: *a strong bond between the newspaper and its readers.* **3.** An attraction or link that holds a pair of atoms together in a molecule or chemical compound, produced in general by a transfer or sharing of one or more electrons. **4. a.** Money paid as bail. **b.** A person who provides bail; bondsman. **5.** A certificate of debt issued by a government or corporation that guarantees repayment with interest, on a specified date, of money borrowed from the purchaser of the certificate. **6.** An insurance contract that guarantees payment to an employer in the event of financial loss caused by the actions of an employee. —*v.* To place (an employee) under bond so as to insure his employer against loss.

bond•age |**bŏn′**dĭj| *n.* The condition of a slave or serf; servitude.

bond•hold•er |**bŏnd′**hōl′dər| *n.* The owner of a bond or bonds.

bond•serv•ant |**bŏnd′**sûr′vənt| *n.* A person obligated to work for another without wages; a slave or serf.

bonds•man |**bŏndz′**mən| *n., pl.* **-men** |-mən|. **1.** A male bondservant. **2.** A person who provides bail for another.

bone |bōn| *n.* **1. a.** The hard, dense, calcified tissue that forms the skeleton of most vertebrates. **b.** One of the many distinct structures making up such a skeleton: *the bones of the foot.* **c.** A fragment of such a structure. **d. bones.** The skeleton. **2. bones.** Mortal remains: *God rest his bones.* —***modifier:*** *bone structure; bone tissue.* —*v.* **boned, bon•ing.** In cooking, to remove the bones from. —***phrasal verb.*** **bone up on.** *Informal.* To study (a subject) intensively, usually at the last minute; review; cram.

Idioms. **bone of contention.** The subject of a dispute. **feel in (one's) bones.** To have an intuition of. **have a bone to pick with.** To have reason to quarrel with. **make no bones about.** To be completely frank about. **to the bone.** Thoroughly; completely: *cutting expenses to the bone.*

bone•black |**bōn′**blăk′| *n.* A black material made by roasting bones in an airtight container. It contains about 10 per cent charcoal, and is used as a pigment, as a filtering agent, and in whitening sugar.

bone•head |**bōn′**hĕd′| *n.* *Slang.* A dunce.

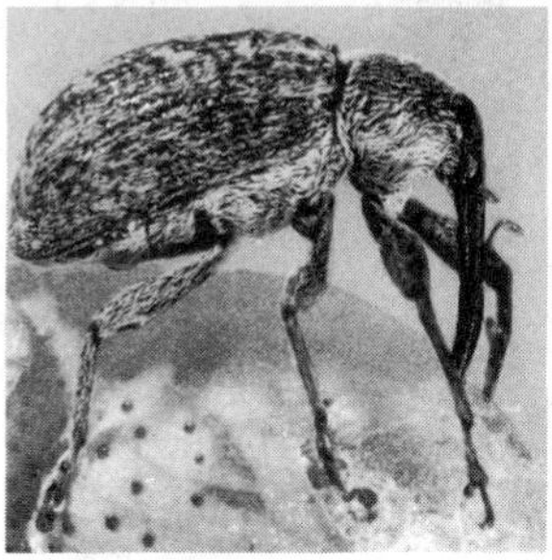

boll weevil

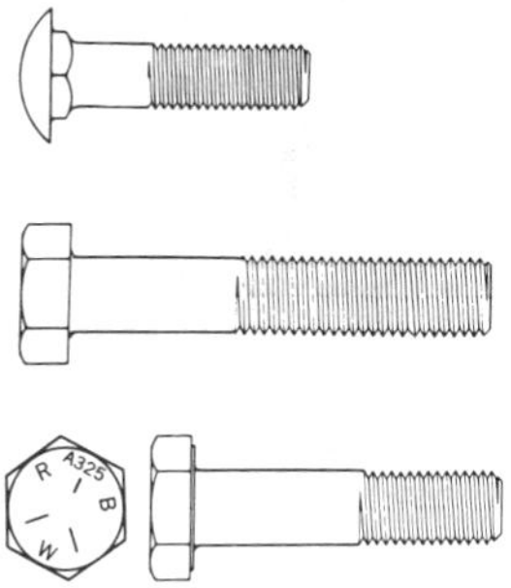

bolt

bongo drums

bone meal. Bones crushed and ground to a coarse powder, used as fertilizer and animal feed.

bon•er |bō′nər| *n. Slang.* A blunder.

bon•fire |**bŏn′**fīr′| *n.* A large outdoor fire.

bong |bŏng| *or* |bông| *n.* A deep ringing sound, as of a bell. —*v.* To ring; sound: *Dirk heard the clock in the tower bong out the hour.*

bon•go drums |**bŏng′**gō| *or* |**bông′**-|. A pair of small drums, usually tuned to different pitches, that are held between the knees and beaten with the hands. [SEE PICTURE]

bon•gos or **bon•goes** |**bŏng′**gōz| *or* |**bông′**-| *pl.n.* **Bongo drums.**

bo•ni•to |bə **nē′**tō| *n., pl.* **bo•ni•to** or **bo•ni•tos.** An ocean fish related to the tuna, caught for food and sport.

Bonn |bŏn|. The capital of West Germany, on the Rhine River. Population, 300,000.

bon•net |**bŏn′**ĭt| *n.* **1.** A hat for a woman or child, tied with ribbons under the chin and often having a wide brim in front that shades the face. **2.** A cap without a brim, worn by men in Scotland. **3.** A headdress of feathers worn by some American Indians. **4.** *British.* The hood of an automobile. **5.** A removable metal cover for part or all of a machine. [SEE PICTURE]

bon•ny, also **bon•nie** |**bŏn′**ē| *adj.* **bon•ni•er, bon•ni•est. 1.** Pleasing to the eye; pretty: *his bonny bride.* **2.** Vigorous; spirited: *Eleanor Roosevelt was a bonny fighter, at her best in the arena.*

bon•sai |**bōn′**sī| *or* |**bŏn′**-| *n., pl.* **bon•sai. 1.** The art of growing trees in small flowerpots or dishes, and keeping them to a very small size. **2.** A tree grown in this way.

bo•nus |**bō′**nəs| *n., pl.* **bo•nus•es.** Something given or paid in addition to what is usual or expected.

bon voy•age |bŏn′ voi **äzh′**|. *French.* A phrase used to wish a departing traveler a pleasant journey.

bon•y |**bō′**nē| *adj.* **bon•i•er, bon•i•est. 1.** Of or resembling bone. **2.** Full of bones: *a bony piece of meat.* **3.** Having bones that stick out or show through; thin; gaunt: *bony elbows.* **4.** Having a skeleton of bones rather than cartilage: *bony fishes as distinguished from sharks and rays.*

bonnet

boo |bo͞o| *n.* A vocal sound uttered to show dislike or disapproval. —*interj.* **1.** Used to express dislike or disapproval. **2.** Used to frighten or surprise. —*v.* **booed, boo•ing. 1.** To make such sounds: *The fans booed angrily.* **2.** To say "boo" to; jeer: *They booed both the referee and the visiting players.*

boob |bo͝ob| *n. Slang.* A stupid or foolish person; dunce.

boo•by |**bo͞o′**bē| *n., pl.* **boo•bies. 1.** A stupid person; dunce. **2.** A large, tropical sea bird with white or brown and white feathers and a long, pointed bill.

booby prize. An award given for the lowest score in a game or contest.

booby trap. 1. A hidden bomb or mine set to go off when some harmless-looking object attached to it is moved or touched. **2.** Any trap or device for catching a person off guard.

boog•ie-woog•ie |**bo͝og′**ē **wo͝og′**ē| *or* |**bo͞o′**gē-**wo͞o′**gē| *n.* A style of jazz piano playing in which, typically, a figure having a distinctive rhythmic and melodic pattern is repeated over and over in the bass.

boo•hoo |bo͞o′**ho͞o′**| *v.* **boo•hooed, boo•hoo•ing.** To weep loudly; sob.

book |bo͝ok| *n.* **1.** A set of printed or written pages fastened together along one edge and enclosed between covers. **2.** A long written work or a collection of writings or pictures that may be published between covers: *read a book; write a book.* **3.** A main division of a larger written or printed work: *a book of the Bible.* **4. the Book** or **the Good Book.** The Bible. **5.** A bound volume of blank pages in which to write, record, or paste things: *an address book.* **6. a.** A volume in which records are kept of money received, owed, and paid. **b. books.** Financial records: *A bookkeeper keeps books.* **7.** A small packet of similar things bound together: *a book of matches.* **8.** The words or script of a play, musical, or opera. —***modifier:*** *a book report; a play in book form.* —*v.* **1.** To arrange for in advance; reserve or schedule: *He was asked to book tickets to all hit shows.* **2.** To write down charges against (a person) in a police record: *book a suspect.*

Idioms. **an open** (or **closed**) **book.** Something easy (or hard) to learn about or understand. **by the book.** According to the established rules. **in (one's) book.** In one's opinion, knowledge, or experience: *In my book he was one of the all-time greats.* **throw the book at.** *Slang.* **1.** To make all possible charges against (an offender). **2.** To scold or punish severely.

book•bind•er |**bo͝ok′**bīn′dər| *n.* A person whose business is binding books.

book•case |**bo͝ok′**kās′| *n.* A piece of furniture with shelves for holding books.

book•end |**bo͝ok′**ĕnd′| *n.* A prop placed at the end of a row of books to keep them upright.

book•ish |**bo͝ok′**ĭsh| *adj.* **1.** Fond of books and study; studious. **2.** Depending too much on books rather than experience. **3.** Showing off one's learning in a dull, dry, or conceited way.

book•keep•ing |**bo͝ok′**kē′pĭng| *n.* The work or skill of keeping records of money received, owed, etc., by a business. —**book′keep′er** *n.*

book learning. Knowledge gained from books rather than from experience.

book•let |**bo͝ok′**lĭt| *n.* A small book or pamphlet, usually with paper covers.

book•mak•er |**bo͝ok′**mā′kər| *n.* Someone who accepts and pays off bets, as on a horse race. —**book′mak′ing** *n.*

book•mark |**bo͝ok′**märk′| *n.* An object, such as a ribbon or a strip of leather, placed between the pages of a book to mark one's place.

book•mo•bile |**bo͝ok′**mə bēl′| *n.* A truck with shelves of books in it, used as a traveling library.

Book of Common Prayer. The book of services and prayers used in the Anglican churches.

Book of Mormon. The sacred text of the Mormon Church. See **Mormon.**

book•plate |**bo͝ok′**plāt′| *n.* A label pasted inside a book and bearing the owner's name.

book•rack |**bo͝ok′**răk′| *n.* **1.** A small rack or shelf for books. **2.** A frame or rack for holding an open book; bookstand.

book•shelf |**bo͝ok′**shĕlf′| *n., pl.* **-shelves** |-shĕlvz′|. A shelf on which books are kept.

ă pat/ā pay/â care/ä father/ĕ pet/ ē be/ĭ pit/ī pie/î fierce/ŏ pot/ ō go/ô paw, for/oi oil/o͝o book/ o͞o boot/ou out/ŭ cut/û fur/ *th* the/th thin/hw which/zh vision/ ə ago, item, pencil, atom, circus

book•stand |bo͝ok′stănd′| *n.* **1.** A small counter where books are sold. **2.** A frame or rack for holding an open book; bookrack.

book•store |bo͝ok′stôr′| *or* |-stōr′| *n.* A store where books are sold.

book•worm |bo͝ok′wûrm′| *n.* A person who spends much time reading or studying.

Bool•e•an algebra |bo͞o′lē ən|. A form of algebra that generalizes the operations of logic and allows their properties to be learned. Boolean algebra has been important in the development of modern computers.

boom[1] |bo͞om| *n.* **1.** A deep, hollow sound, as from an explosion. **2.** A sudden increase, as in growth or production. **3. a.** A time of sudden, rapid growth or expansion. **b.** A time of prosperity. —***modifier:*** *boom times.* —*v.* **1. a.** To make a deep, hollow sound: *The cannon boomed.* **b.** To say or speak with such a sound: *"No!" boomed the giant. A deep voice boomed out.* **2.** To grow or develop rapidly; thrive; flourish: *Business is booming.* —**boom′ing** *adj.: a booming voice; a booming industry.* [SEE NOTE]

boom[2] |bo͞om| *n.* **1.** A long pole extending from the mast of a boat to hold or stretch out the bottom of a sail. **2. a.** A long pole or similar structure that extends upward and outward from the mast of a derrick and supports the object being lifted. **b.** A similar support that holds a microphone. [SEE NOTE]

boo•mer•ang |bo͞o′mə răng′| *n.* A flat, curved piece of wood that can be thrown so that it returns to the thrower. It was originally used by the native people of Australia. —*v.* To have the opposite effect of that intended, harming the originator instead of the target: *Unjust accusations often boomerang, making people dislike the attacker and sympathize with the person attacked.* [SEE PICTURE]

boom town. A town that experiences sudden growth and prosperity, as after a discovery of gold, silver, or oil.

boon[1] |bo͞on| *n.* **1.** A help or blessing: *Delay would be a blow to us and a boon to our competitors.* **2.** A favor, request, or service: *"Sire, I have a boon to ask of you."* [SEE NOTE]

boon[2] |bo͞on| *adj.* Friendly and jolly; sociable: *a boon companion.* [SEE NOTE]

boon•docks |bo͞on′dŏks′| *pl.n. Slang.* —**the boondocks. 1.** Rough, uncleared country. **2.** Rural country far from cities; the backwoods.

Boone |bo͞on|, **Daniel.** 1734–1820. American frontiersman who explored and settled Kentucky.

boor |bo͝or| *n.* A crude person with rude or clumsy manners.

boor•ish |bo͝or′ĭsh| *adj.* Crude, rude, and offensive: *boorish behavior.* —**boor′ish•ly** *adv.* —**boor′ish•ness** *n.*

boost |bo͞ost| *v.* **1.** To lift by pushing up from below: *He boosted her into the saddle.* **2.** To increase; raise: *boost sales; boost morale.* **3.** To stir up enthusiasm for; promote: *boost one's home town.* **4.** To encourage; aid: *boost one's career.* —*n.* **1.** A push upward or ahead: *Give her a boost.* **2.** An increase: *a boost in salary.*

boost•er |bo͞o′stər| *n.* **1.** Something that increases the power or effectiveness of a system or device: *a battery booster.* **2.** An amplifier for radio signals: *a television booster.* **3.** Also **booster rocket.** A rocket used to launch a missile or space vehicle. **4.** Also **booster shot.** A dose of a vaccine or serum given to a person who is already immune in order to prolong or strengthen his immunity. **5.** Anything that boosts something: *The holiday was a morale booster.* **6.** An enthusiastic promoter, as of civic pride.

boot[1] |bo͞ot| *n.* **1.** A kind of shoe that covers the foot and ankle and usually part of the leg, generally made of leather or rubber. **2.** Something shaped like a boot, as a peninsula: *the Italian boot.* **3.** A kick. **4.** *British.* The trunk of an automobile. —*v.* **1.** To kick: *He booted the football forty yards.* **2.** To put boots on. —**boot′ed** *adj.: The cowboys were booted and spurred.* [SEE NOTE]

***Idioms.* lick (someone's) boots.** To flatter and obey the way a slave would. **the boot.** *Slang.* Dismissal, as from a job.

boot[2] |bo͞ot| *v. Archaic.* To benefit, help, or avail: *It boots you little to worry.* —**to boot.** In addition; besides: *He offered them a salary and free food to boot.* [SEE NOTE]

boot•black |bo͞ot′blăk′| *n.* A person who cleans and polishes shoes for a living.

boot camp. A training camp for soldiers who have just joined the Army.

boot•ee |bo͞o′tē| *n.* A soft baby shoe, usually knitted. ¶*These sound alike* **bootee, booty.**

Bo•ö•tes |bō ō′tēz| *n.* A kite-shaped constellation in the Northern Hemisphere near the handle of the Big Dipper.

booth |bo͞oth| *n., pl.* **booths** |bo͞o*thz*| *or* |bo͞oths|. **1.** A small enclosed compartment: *a telephone booth.* **2.** A small stall or stand where things are sold or entertainment is provided. **3.** A seating compartment consisting of a table enclosed by two facing benches with high backs.

Booth |bo͞oth|, **John Wilkes.** 1838–1865. American actor who assassinated Abraham Lincoln.

boot•jack |bo͞ot′jăk′| *n.* A forked device that holds a boot while a person pulls his foot out of it.

boot•leg |bo͞ot′lĕg′| *v.* **boot•legged, boot•leg•ging.** To make, sell, or transport (liquor) illegally. —*adj.* Made, sold, or transported illegally: *bootleg whiskey.* —**boot′leg′ger** *n.*

boot•less |bo͞ot′lĭs| *adj.* Useless; fruitless: *a bootless effort.*

boot•lick•er |bo͞ot′lĭk′ər| *n.* Someone who attempts to gain favor through slavish obedience or flattery.

boo•ty |bo͞o′tē| *n., pl.* **boo•ties. 1.** Loot taken from an enemy in war. **2.** Any seized or stolen goods: *pirates' booty.* **3.** Treasure: *Divers brought up booty from a sunken ship.* ¶*These sound alike* **booty, bootee.**

booze |bo͞oz| *n. Informal.* Alcoholic drink.

bop |bŏp| *v.* **bopped, bop•ping.** *Informal.* To hit or strike. —*n.* A blow or punch.

bo•rate |bôr′āt′| *or* |bōr′-| *n.* A salt of boric acid.

bo•rax |bôr′ăks′| *or* |-əks| *or* |bōr′-| *n.* Sodium borate, either in hydrated or anhydrous form.

Bor•deaux[1] |bôr dō′|. A seaport in southwestern France. Population, 265,000.

Bor•deaux[2] |bôr dō′| *n., pl.* **Bor•deaux** |bôr-

boom[1-2]

Boom[1] *originated in Middle English as* bummen, *which seems to be an onomatopoeic word, formed to imitate the sound it describes.* **Boom[2]** *is from Dutch and originally meant "tree" or "pole."*

boomerang
Australian aborigine with boomerang

boon[1-2]

Boon[1] *is from Old Norse* bōn, *"prayer, request."* **Boon[2]** *is an example of a word that was once in general use but is now restricted to one single phrase, "boon companion." It originally meant simply "good or gracious," and comes from Old French* bone, *which came from Latin* bonus, *"good." The Old French word survives in modern French as* bon, *"good," which is one of the commonest words in the language.*

boot[1-2]

Boot[1] *is from Old French* bote, *but its further origin is unknown.* **Boot[2]** *is from Old English* bōt, *"advantage or reward." It is related to* **better.**

bore[1-2-3]
Bore[1] *is from Old English* borian, *"to drill."* **Bore[2]** *is of completely unknown origin.* **Bore[3]** *is from Old Norse* bara, *"wave."*

born/borne
The phrase **be born** *was originally simply the passive of* **bear,** *but it has become a fully independent verb with its own spelling. When the physical action of the mother in bearing the child is directly referred to with* by *and the true passive, the spelling* **borne** *is still used:* Three children were borne by this woman. *Much more often it is simply the fact of a birth that is spoken of, without reference to physical childbearing:* Three children were born in the village that spring. I was born to poor but honest parents.

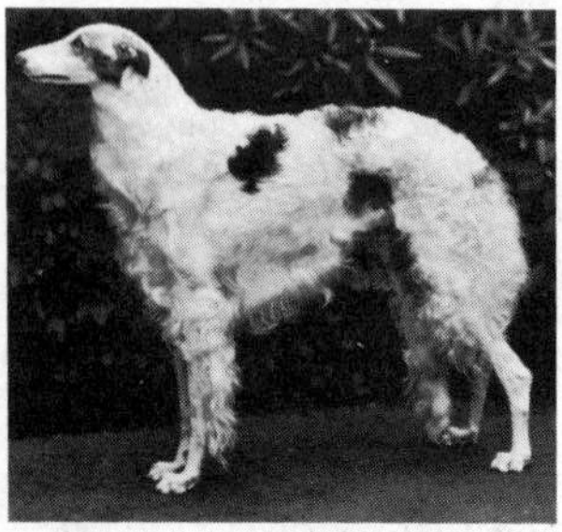
borzoi

ă pat/ā pay/â care/ä father/ĕ pet/ ē be/ĭ pit/ī pie/î fierce/ŏ pot/ ō go/ô paw, for/oi oil/ŏŏ book/ ōō boot/ou out/ŭ cut/û fur/ *th* the/th thin/hw which/zh vision/ ə ago, item, pencil, atom, circus

dō′|. A red or white wine made near the city of Bordeaux, France.

bor•der |bôr′dər| *n.* **1.** The line where one country, state, or region ends and another begins; a boundary: *across the Canadian border.* **2.** An edge, margin, or rim: *They picnicked on the border of the pond.* **3.** A strip that outlines an edge: *a border of herbs around a flower bed.* —***modifier:*** *border guards.* —*v.* **1.** To share a boundary with; be next to: *What countries border Italy?* **2.** To form an edge or boundary for: *Mountains border this lowland region.* **3.** To put a border or edging on: *border a collar with lace.* —***phrasal verb.*** **border on** (or **upon**). **1.** To be next to; touch: *What oceans and seas border on Africa?* **2.** To come close to; approach: *This weather borders on the ideal.* ¶*These sound alike* **border, boarder.**

Idiom. **south of the border.** In or to Latin America, especially Mexico.

bor•der•land |bôr′dər lănd′| *n.* **1.** Land on or near a border or frontier. **2.** An indefinite area or condition in which two different things seem to overlap: *the borderland between dreams and reality.*

bor•der•line |bôr′dər līn′|. **1.** A dividing line; border; boundary. **2.** An indefinite line between two different conditions: *on the borderline between passing and failing.* —*adj.* Not clearly within a certain class or limit; uncertain; doubtful: *a borderline case.*

Border States. The former slave states of Delaware, Maryland, Kentucky, and Missouri, adjacent to the northern free states. None of them joined the Confederacy during the Civil War.

bore[1] |bôr| *or* |bōr| *v.* **bored, bor•ing. 1.** To make (a hole, tunnel, well, etc.) by drilling or digging. **2.** To make a hole in or through (something), as with a drill or auger. **3.** To seem to penetrate like a drill: *deep-set eyes boring into his.* —*n.* **1.** The inside diameter of a hole, tube, cylinder, etc. **2.** A bored hole, as in a pipe or the barrel of a firearm. ¶*These sound alike* **bore, boar.** [SEE NOTE]

bore[2] |bôr| *or* |bōr| *v.* **bored, bor•ing.** To make weary by failing to interest or by seeming dull: *The speaker bored the audience.* —**bor′ing** *adj.: a boring speech.* —*n.* An uninteresting or tiresome person or thing. ¶*These sound alike* **bore, boar.** [SEE NOTE]

bore[3] |bôr| *or* |bōr| *n.* A large, often destructive wave caused by a flood tide that rushes upstream into a narrowing estuary. ¶*These sound alike* **bore, boar.** [SEE NOTE]

bore[4] |bôr| *or* |bōr|. Past tense of **bear.** ¶*These sound alike* **bore, boar.**

bore•dom |bôr′dəm| *or* |bōr′-| *n.* Weariness of mind or spirit caused by lack or loss of interest.

bor•er |bôr′ər| *or* |bōr′-| *n.* **1.** A tool used for boring or drilling. **2.** An insect or insect larva that bores into plants or wood.

bo•ric acid |bôr′ĭk| *or* |bōr′-|. A white or colorless crystalline material composed of hydrogen, boron, and oxygen and having the formula H_3BO_3. It is used as an antiseptic, as a preservative, and in industrial chemicals.

born |bôrn| *or* |bōrn|. A past participle of **bear** (to give birth to). —*v.* —**be born. 1.** To begin one's life: *She was born in Denver in 1947.* **2.** To come into existence; originate: *The Republican Party was born in 1854.* —*adj.* **1.** By birth or natural talent: *a born artist.* **2.** Destined from birth: *born to sing.* **3.** Coming or resulting from: *wisdom born of experience.* [SEE NOTE]

born-a•gain |bôrn′ə gĕn′| *adj.* Of or being a person who has made a conversion to Jesus Christ as personal savior: *a born-again Christian.*

borne |bôrn| *or* |bōrn|. A past participle of **bear.** [SEE NOTE]

Bor•ne•o |bôr′nē ō′|. A large island of the Indonesian Archipelago, divided among Indonesia, Malaysia, and Brunei.

bo•ron |bôr′ŏn′| *or* |bōr′-| *n.* Symbol **B** One of the elements, a soft, brown solid. Atomic number 5; atomic weight 10.81; valences -3, +3; melting point 2,300°C. Boron sublimes at 2,550°C.

bor•ough |bûr′ō| *or* |bŭr′ō| *n.* **1.** A self-governing incorporated town, as in certain U.S. states. **2.** One of the five administrative units of New York City. **3.** A governmental district in Alaska, corresponding to a county. ¶*These sound alike* **borough, burro, burrow.**

bor•row |bŏr′ō| *or* |bôr′ō| *v.* **1.** To get (something) to use for a time with the promise of returning or replacing it later: *borrow a library book; borrow money.* **2.** To obtain money on loan: *He borrowed from the bank.* **3.** To take (a word, idea, method, etc.) from another source and use it as one's own: *We borrowed the word "kindergarten" from German in the 19th century.* **4.** In subtraction, to add 10 to the value of a digit while subtracting 1 from the digit in the place to the left; to perform the inverse of carrying in addition. —**bor′row•er** *n.*

bor•row•ing |bŏr′ō ĭng| *or* |bôr′-| *n.* **1.** The act of asking for and accepting loans: *Borrowing sometimes loses friends.* **2.** The act of taking words, ideas, etc., from another source: *Latin was a source of borrowing for English.* **3.** A word taken from another language: *English borrowings from French.* **4.** A sum of money borrowed and owed: *large borrowings from a bank.*

borscht |bôrsht| *n.* A Russian beet soup served hot or cold, often with sour cream.

bor•zoi |bôr′zoi′| *n.* A large, slender dog with a narrow, pointed head and a silky coat. [SEE PICTURE]

bosh |bŏsh| *n. Informal.* Nonsense.

bos•ky |bŏs′kē| *adj.* Covered with or shaded by bushes and trees: *a bosky dell.*

bo's'n or **bos'n** |bō′sən| *n.* Forms of the word **boatswain.**

bos•om |bŏŏz′əm| *or* |bōō′zəm| *n.* **1.** The human chest or breast. **2.** The part of a garment that covers the chest: *Darts are used to shape the bosom of a dress.* **3.** A person's heart regarded as the center of feelings and convictions: *Empty your bosom of its sorrows.* **4.** The heart or center of anything: *a spy in the bosom of the republic.* **5.** A small, intimate circle: *in the bosom of his family.* —*adj.* Close; intimate: *bosom friends.*

Bos•po•rus |bŏs′pər əs|. A narrow strait near Istanbul separating the European part of Turkey from the Asian part.

boss[1] |bôs| *or* |bŏs| *n.* **1.** The person in charge, who makes decisions: *You're the boss.* **2.** The employer or supervisor of one or more workers.

3. A powerful politician who controls many votes and who can influence public policy behind the scenes. **4.** The leader of any group: *The bull was the boss of the herd.* —*v.* **1.** To give orders to; order around: *He tried to bully and boss them, but they refused to be bossed around.* **2.** To be in charge of; supervise: *take over and boss things.* —*adj. Slang.* First-rate; great: *Pop music is boss.* [SEE NOTE]

boss² |bôs| *or* |bŏs| *n.* A raised, knoblike ornament projecting from a flat surface. [SEE NOTE]

boss•ism |**bô'**sĭz'əm| *or* |**bŏs'**ĭz'əm| *n.* The control of a political organization by a political boss.

boss•y |**bô'**sē| *or* |**bŏs'**ē| *adj.* **boss•i•er, boss•i•est.** Fond of ordering others around; domineering.

Bos•ton |**bô'**stən| *or* |**bŏs'**tən|. The capital and largest city of Massachusetts. Population, 641,000. —**Bos•to'ni•an** |bô **stō'**nē ən| *or* |bŏs-**tō'**-| *adj.* & *n.*

bo•sun |**bō'**sən| *n.* A form of the word **boatswain.**

bo•tan•i•cal |bə **tăn'**ĭ kəl| or **bo•tan•ic** |bə-**tăn'**ĭk| *adj.* Of plants or botany: *a collection of botanical specimens.* —**bo•tan'i•cal•ly** *adv.*

botanical garden, also **botanic garden.** A place for the study and exhibition of growing plants.

bot•a•nist |**bŏt'**n ĭst| *n.* A scientist who specializes in botany.

bot•a•ny |**bŏt'**n ē| *n.* The scientific study of plants.

botch |bŏch| *v.* To ruin through careless or clumsy work; bungle: *botch a repair job.* —*n.* A bad job or poor piece of work; a mess.

bot•fly |**bŏt'**flī'| *n., pl.* **-flies.** Also **bot fly.** A fly that lays its eggs on or under the skin of horses, sheep, and other animals. The parasitic larvae develop inside the animal's body, often causing great harm.

both |bōth| *pron.* The one as well as the other; the two alike. **a.** —Used alone: *If one is guilty, both are.* **b.** —Used with *of* and a pronoun: *both of them.* **c.** —Used in apposition with a pronoun: *You both skate well. They were both crazy.* —*adj.* The two; the one as well as the other. **a.** —Used before an unmodified noun: *both sides of the valley.* **b.** —Used before a noun modified with a demonstrative: *Instead of a plain green or brown skirt, she chose a tweed that emphasized both these colors.* **c.** —Used before a noun modified with a possessive: *Both my parents are gone.* —*conj.* —Used as a correlative conjunction in the construction *both . . . and* to indicate and emphasize a grouping by two: *Both the United States and Great Britain claimed the Oregon Country.*

both•er |**bŏth'**ər| *v.* **1. a.** To disturb: *Don't bother her while she's studying.* **b.** To annoy, irritate, or pester: *The flies bothered the horse.* **2. a.** To concern, worry, or trouble: *He was bothered by their silence.* **b.** To puzzle: *A problem had been bothering them.* **3.** To take the trouble: *Don't bother to get up.* **4.** To trouble or concern oneself: *You don't have to bother with that.* **5.** To cause trouble to: *Traffic jams don't bother a helicopter.* —*n.* **1.** An annoying thing; a nuisance: *Having to wait was a bother.* **2.** Trouble: *a lot of bother for nothing.* —*interj.* A word used to express annoyance or irritation.

both•er•some |**bŏth'**ər səm| *adj.* Causing trouble; annoying; troublesome.

Bot•swa•na |bŏt **swä'**nə|. A country in southern Africa. Population, 661,000. Capital, Gaborone.

bot•tle |**bŏt'**l| *n.* **1.** A container, usually made of glass, having a narrow neck and a mouth that can be corked or capped. **2. a.** A bottle with something in it: *buy a bottle of soda.* **b.** The amount that a bottle holds: *drink a bottle of milk.* **3.** A bottle of milk with a nipple on it: *Give the baby his bottle.* **4.** A bottle of alcoholic liquor. —*modifier: bottle caps.* —*v.* **bot•tled, bot•tling.** To put in a bottle or bottles: *This machine bottles soda.* —**bot'tled** *adj.: bottled drinks.* —*phrasal verb.* **bottle up. 1.** To hold in; restrain: *bottle up one's emotions.* **2.** To seal up; block: *Union navies bottled up southern ports.*

bot•tle•neck |**bŏt'**l nĕk'| *n.* **1.** A narrow route or passage where movement is slowed down. **2.** Any condition that slows or hinders progress.

bot•tom |**bŏt'**əm| *n.* **1.** The lowest part or edge of anything: *the bottom of a page.* **2.** The lowest inside or outside surface: *oars in the bottom of a boat; barnacles on the bottom of a boat.* **3.** The lowest part of something deep or high: *the bottom of the hill.* **4.** The solid surface under a body of water: *The diver went to the bottom.* **5.** The underlying truth or cause; basis; heart: *get to the bottom of the matter.* **6.** Often **bottoms.** The low, alluvial land that adjoins a river. **7.** The seat of a chair: *a cane bottom.* **8.** *Informal.* The buttocks. —*modifier: the bottom drawer.*

Idioms. **at bottom.** Basically: *At bottom he was a kindly man.* **from top to bottom.** Thoroughly: *They searched the house from top to bottom but found nothing.*

bot•tom•land |**bŏt'**əm lănd'| *n.* Often **bottomlands.** Low-lying land along a river: *Mississippi River bottomlands.* —*modifier: bottomland grass.*

bot•tom•less |**bŏt'**əm lĭs| *adj.* **1.** Having no bottom. **2.** Too deep to be measured: *a bottomless pool.*

bot•u•lism |**bŏch'**ə lĭz'əm| *n.* A serious, often fatal form of food poisoning whose symptoms are vomiting, stomach pains, coughing, weakness, and disturbance of vision. It is caused by bacteria that grow in improperly canned foods and that produce several poisons that act on the nervous system.

bou•doir |**bōō'**dwär'| *or* |-dwôr'| *n.* A woman's private sitting room, dressing room, or bedroom.

bouf•fant |bōō **fänt'**| *adj.* Full and puffed-out, as a hairdo, skirt, or sleeve.

bou•gain•vil•le•a |bōō'gən **vĭl'**ē ə| *or* |-**vĭl'**yə| *n.* A tropical vine with small flowers surrounded by red, purple, or orange leaves that look like petals.

bough |bou| *n.* A large branch of a tree. ¶*These sound alike* **bough, bow², bow³.**

bought |bôt|. Past tense and past participle of **buy.**

bouil•la•baisse |bōō'yə **bās'**| *n.* A highly seasoned thick soup made with several kinds of fish and shellfish.

bouil•lon |**bōōl'**yŏn'| *or* |-yən| *n.* A clear, thin soup of liquid in which meat has been boiled:

boss¹⁻²

Boss¹ *is an Americanism that has passed into general use in worldwide English. It is one of the few words borrowed from the Dutch during the period in which they had the colony of New Netherland (in parts of New Jersey and New York). The Dutch word was* bass, *meaning "master," a word used by workers when speaking to an employer or overseer.* **Boss²** *is from Old French* boce, *from a reconstructed Latin word,* bottia, *"a lump or swelling."*

boulevard/bulwark
The Middle High German word bolwerc *meant "timber-work, palisade, rampart"* (bole, *"timber,"* + werc, *"work"). This was borrowed into English as* **bulwark**. *Separately,* bolwerc *was borrowed into Old French as* boloart, *later becoming* boulevard, *"city wall." In the eighteenth century, many European cities had expanded outside their old fortifications, which they no longer needed anyway. Some cities, notably Paris, pulled down their ramparts and built wide walks or promenades in the space. Thus* boulevard *came to mean "a spacious promenade," and was borrowed into English as* **boulevard**.

bound[1-2-3-4]
Bound[1] *is from Old French* bondir, *"to bounce."* **Bound**[2] *is from Old French* bunde, *"a boundary."* **Bound**[3] *is from* **bind**. **Bound**[4] *was originally* boun, *meaning "prepared, ready to go," from Old Norse* būinn, *"prepared."*

boutique
Boutique *comes from the French word for "small shop," which in turn comes from Provençal* botica, *which is an altered form of Greek* apothēkē, *"a storehouse." The Greek word is a compound of* apo, *"away," and* thē-, *"put": "a place where one puts things away." The English word* **apothecary** *also comes from* apothēkē.

ă pat/ā pay/â care/ä father/ĕ pet/ ē be/ĭ pit/ī pie/î fierce/ŏ pot/ ō go/ô paw, for/oi oil/ŏŏ book/ ōō boot/ou out/ŭ cut/û fur/ *th* the/th thin/hw which/zh vision/ ə ago, item, pencil, atom, circus

beef bouillon. —**modifier:** *bouillon cubes.* ¶*These sound alike* **bouillon, bullion.**

boul•der |**bōl'**dər| *n.* A large, rounded mass of rock lying on the ground or imbedded in the soil, and usually different in composition from other nearby rocks.

boul•e•vard |**bŏŏl'**ə värd'| *or* |**bōō'**lə-| *n.* A broad city street, often lined with trees. [SEE NOTE]

bounce |bouns| *v.* **bounced, bounc•ing. 1. a.** To hit a surface and be turned back from it, sometimes several times in succession: *The ball bounced up and down.* **b.** To move as a result of this; rebound: *How high did the ball bounce?* **2.** To move with a bobbing, jolting, or vibrating motion: *Cars bounced down the dirt road.* **3.** To jump, spring, or bound in a lively way: *She bounced out of bed.* **4.** To be reflected: *The sound waves hit an obstacle and bounced back as an echo.* **5.** To cause to bounce: *He bounced a ball.* **6.** *Informal.* To be sent back by a bank as worthless: *The check bounced.* **7.** *Slang.* To throw (someone) out forcefully. —*n.* **1.** An act of bouncing or a bouncing movement; a bound or rebound. **2.** A reflection. **3.** Capacity to bounce; springiness: *a ball with bounce.* **4.** Liveliness: *There is a lilt and bounce to her voice.*

bounc•er |**boun'**sər| *n. Slang.* A person employed to throw disorderly persons out of a nightclub, bar, etc.

bounc•ing |**boun'**sĭng| *adj.* Large; healthy; thriving: *a bouncing baby; a series of bouncing crops.*

bouncing Bet |bĕt|. A plant with rounded clusters of fragrant pink or white flowers.

bounc•y |**boun'**sē| *adj.* **bounc•i•er, bounc•i•est. 1.** Tending to bounce: *a bouncy ball.* **2.** Springy; elastic: *bouncy, spongelike material.* **3.** Lively; energetic: *bouncy tunes.*

bound[1] |bound| *v.* **1.** To leap, jump, or spring: *He bounded over the gate.* **2.** To move by leaping: *The deer bounded away.* **3.** To bounce or rebound: *pebbles bounding down the path.* **4.** To beat or throb violently: *Her heart bounded with excitement.* —*n.* **1.** A leap, jump, or spring: *He cleared the steps with a bound.* **2.** A bounce. **3.** A violent beat or throb: *Her heart gave a bound.* [SEE NOTE]

bound[2] |bound| *n.* **1.** Often **bounds. a.** A limit: *Her joy knew no bounds.* **b.** A boundary: *within the bounds of the state.* **2.** In mathematics, an **upper bound** or **lower bound.** —*v.* **1.** To be the boundary of: *Water bounds the city on three sides.* **2.** To contain within limits; enclose: *the surface bounded by a trapezoid.* **3.** To tell what countries, states, or areas surround: *Can you bound California?* [SEE NOTE]

Idiom. **out of bounds. 1.** Beyond the boundaries of a playing field: *The ball went out of bounds.* **2.** Beyond the usual, legal, or safe limits: *His enthusiasm gets out of bounds.*

bound[3] |bound|. Past tense and past participle of **bind.** —*adj.* **1.** Certain: *We are bound to be late.* **2.** Under obligation; obliged: *bound by a promise; duty bound.* **3.** Restricted; governed: *Is a representative bound by every impulse of the voters?* **4.** Confined or held by or as if by bonds; tied: *bound and gagged; molecules bound into a crystal.* **5.** Enclosed in a cover or binding: *a bound book.* **6.** Resolved: *She is bound and determined to go.* **7.** Occurring only in combination: *The ending "-ness" in "kindness" is a bound form.* [SEE NOTE]

Idiom. **bound up with.** Closely associated or connected with: *The migration of birds is bound up with food supplies.*

bound[4] |bound| *adj.* Ready to start; on the way; going: *An American ship bound for America is a homeward bound ship.* [SEE NOTE]

bound•a•ry |**boun'**də rē| *or* |-drē| *n., pl.* **bound•a•ries. 1.** An edge, limit, or dividing line marking the place where a country, state, or other region ends: *The Gulf of Mexico forms the southern boundary of Louisiana.* **2.** Something that divides a set of points into three subsets, one that coincides with itself and two others. For example, the circumference of a circle divides the points in a plane into three sets, those that are inside, those that are on the circumference, and those that are outside.

bound•en |**boun'**dən| *adj.* Being an obligation; required: *your bounden duty.*

bound•less |**bound'**lĭs| *adj.* Without any known limits; infinite: *the boundless universe.*

boun•te•ous |**boun'**tē əs| *adj.* **1.** Generous: *bounteous kindness.* **2.** Plentiful: *bounteous blessings.* —**boun'te•ous•ly** *adv.*

boun•ti•ful |**boun'**tə fəl| *adj.* **1.** Plentiful; abundant: *bountiful crops.* **2.** Giving generously and kindly: *a bountiful gentleman. The bountiful river irrigates the entire valley.* —**boun'ti•ful•ly** *adv.* —**boun'ti•ful•ness** *n.*

boun•ty |**boun'**tē| *n., pl.* **boun•ties. 1.** Generosity in giving: *dependent on a patron's bounty.* **2.** Plentiful gifts or provisions: *the bounty of the earth.* **3.** A reward for performing a service for the government, as capturing an outlaw or killing a destructive animal.

bou•quet. *n.* **1.** |bō **kā'**| *or* |bōō-|. A bunch of flowers. **2.** |bōō **kā'**|. A pleasant odor, especially of a wine.

bour•bon |**bûr'**bən| *n.* A whiskey distilled from fermented corn mash.

bour•geois |bŏŏr **zhwä'**| *or* |**bŏŏr'**zhwä'| *n., pl.* **bour•geois.** A member of the middle class or bourgeoisie. —*adj.* **1.** Of or like the middle class. **2.** Caring too much about respectability and possessions.

bour•geoi•sie |bŏŏr'zhwä **zē'**| *n.* The middle class as opposed to the aristocracy or the laboring class.

bourn or **bourne** |bôrn| *or* |bōrn| *or* |bŏŏrn| *n. Archaic.* **1.** A boundary, limit, or frontier: *"the undiscovered country from whose bourn no traveler returns"* (Shakespeare). **2.** A goal or destination. **3.** A realm; domain: *"from out our bourne of Time and Place"* (Alfred Tennyson).

bour•rée |bōō **rā'**| *or* |bōō-| *n.* **1.** A quick, lively French dance of the 17th century. **2.** Music written to accompany or as if to accompany this dance.

bout |bout| *n.* **1.** A contest: *a boxing bout.* **2.** A period or spell: *severe bouts of fever.*

bou•tique |bōō **tēk'**| *n.* A small retail shop that sells gifts, fashionable clothes, etc. [SEE NOTE]

bou•ton•niere or **bou•ton•nière** |bōōt'n **îr'**| *or* |bōōt'n **yâr'**| *n.* A flower worn in a buttonhole, usually on a lapel.

bo•vine |bō′vīn′| *or* |-vēn′| *adj.* **1.** Of, related to, or resembling a cow or cattle. **2.** Dull and placid: *a bovine stare.* —*n.* A cow, ox, or related animal.

bow[1] |bō| *n.* **1.** A weapon used to shoot arrows, consisting of a curved strip of wood, metal, etc., with a string stretched tightly from end to end. **2.** A slender, springy rod having horsehair stretched between two raised ends, used in playing the violin, viola, and related stringed instruments. **3. a.** A knot tied with a loop or loops at either end. **b.** A ribbon decoration made up of a cluster of loops. **4.** A curve or arch, as of lips or eyebrows. **5.** A rainbow. —*v.* **1.** To play using a bow: *He bowed a fiddle. That cellist bows beautifully.* **2.** To bend into a curved shape: *His legs bow awkwardly.* ¶*These sound alike* **bow[1], beau.** [SEE NOTE]

bow[2] |bou| *v.* **1.** To bend (the body, head, or knee) in greeting, agreement, respect, etc.: *bow politely from the waist; bow the head in prayer.* **2.** To express by bowing: *They bowed their thanks.* **3.** To bend downward: *Age bowed her back. He bowed beneath the heavy load.* **4.** To give in; yield: *They refused to bow to pressure.* —**bowed′** *adj.: bowed heads.* —***phrasal verbs.*** **bow down to** (or **before**). **1.** To yield or submit to. **2.** To worship. **bow out.** To withdraw or resign. —*n.* **1.** A bending of the body or head, as when showing respect or accepting applause. **2.** Any sign of respect, recognition, etc.: *The President's trip was a bow to Europe.* ¶*These sound alike* **bow[2], bough, bow[3].** [SEE NOTE]

Idioms. **bow and scrape.** To behave in a slavish, fawning way. **make (one's) bow.** To make one's first appearance or debut. **take a bow.** To acknowledge and accept applause, as by standing up or coming out on stage.

bow[3] |bou| *n.* The front section of a ship or boat. ¶*These sound alike* **bow[3], bough, bow[2].** [SEE NOTE]

bow•el |bou′əl| *or* |boul| *n.* **1.** An intestine, especially of a human being. **2.** Often **bowels.** The part of the digestive tract below the stomach. **3. bowels.** The inmost depths of anything: *in the bowels of the earth.*

bow•er |bou′ər| *n.* **1.** A leafy, shaded nook or shelter; an arbor. **2.** A lady's private chamber.

bow•head |bō′hĕd′| *n.* Also **bowhead whale.** A whale of northern seas, having a large head with a curved top.

bow•ie knife |bō′ē| *or* |bo͞o′ē|. A long hunting knife with a single-edged blade.

bowl[1] |bōl| *n.* **1.** A rounded, hollow container or dish that can hold liquid, food, etc. **2. a.** A bowl with something in it: *a bowl of goldfish.* **b.** The amount that a bowl holds: *eat a bowl of soup.* **3.** The curved, hollow part of a spoon, pipe, etc. **4.** Anything shaped like a curved dish or dome: *the blue bowl of the sky.* **5.** A region characterized by a product, crop, or feature: *the rice bowl of Asia.* **6. a.** A bowl-shaped stadium or outdoor theater. **b.** One of several special football games played after the usual season ends: *the Rose Bowl.* ¶*These sound alike* **bowl, bole, boll.** [SEE NOTE]

bowl[2] |bōl| *v.* **1.** To play the game of bowling: *Do you like to bowl?* **2.** To play (a game) of bowling: *He bowls six games a day.* **3.** To roll a ball or take a turn in bowling: *You bowl first.* **4.** To make (a score) in bowling: *Her brother bowled 137.* **5.** To move smoothly and rapidly: *The bus bowled along the road.* —***phrasal verb.*** **bowl over.** **1.** To knock over. **2.** To surprise greatly; stun: *The announcement bowled them over.* ¶*These sound alike* **bowl, bole, boll.** [SEE NOTE]

bow•leg•ged |bō′lĕg′ĭd| *or* |-lĕgd′| *adj.* Having bowlegs.

bow•legs |bō′lĕgz′| *pl.n.* Legs that curve outward at or below the knee.

bowl•er[1] |bō′lər| *n.* A person who bowls.

bowl•er[2] |bō′lər| *n. British.* A man's derby hat.

bowl•ing |bō′lĭng| *n.* **1.** A game played by rolling a heavy ball down a wooden alley in an attempt to knock down ten wooden pins at the opposite end; tenpins. **2.** A similar game, such as ninepins or skittles. **3.** Also **lawn bowling.** A game played on a level lawn, or **bowling green,** by rolling a wooden ball as close as possible to a target ball. —***modifier:*** *a bowling ball; a bowling tournament.*

bowling alley. **1.** A building where people go to bowl, containing bowling lanes. **2.** One of the long, smooth, narrow wooden lanes in such a building.

bow•man |bō′mən| *n., pl.* **-men** |-mən|. A person who shoots with a bow and arrow; an archer.

bow•sprit |bou′sprĭt′| *or* |bō′-| *n.* A long pole sticking out at the front of a sailing ship, holding ropes or wires that run to the front mast and sails.

bow•string |bō′strĭng′| *n.* The string of a bow, used to shoot an arrow.

bow tie |bō|. A small necktie tied in a bow.

bow-wow |bou′wou′| *or* |-wou′| *n.* **1.** The bark of a dog. **2.** A child's word for a dog.

box[1] |bŏks| *n.* **1.** A stiff container made of cardboard, wood, metal, etc., usually having four sides and a top or lid. **2. a.** A box with something in it: *buy a box of crayons.* **b.** The amount that a box holds: *eat a box of cereal.* **3.** A rectangle: *Draw a box around the correct answer.* **4.** Anything shaped or enclosed like a box, as a separate seating compartment in a theater or courtroom, a sentry's shelter, or the marked-off space in which a baseball batter stands. **5.** An outer case with a mechanism inside: *a fire-alarm box.* **6.** A pigeonhole for mail: *a post-office box.* **7.** A chest or trunk: *The seaman unpacked his box.* —***modifier:*** *a box top.* —*v.* **1.** To put or pack in a box: *box a gift.* **2.** To enclose in a rectangle: *box the title of the story.* —**boxed′** *adj.: a boxed gift; a boxed illustration on a page.* —***phrasal verb.*** **box in** (or **up**). To enclose, surround, or hem in: *The enemy troops boxed them in.* [SEE NOTE]

box[2] |bŏks| *v.* **1.** To fight with the fists in a boxing match: *Boxers box in a ring.* **2.** To hit or slap with the hand: *She boxed him on the ear.* —*n.* A blow or slap with the hand: *a box on the ear.* [SEE NOTE]

box[3] |bŏks| *n.* **1.** A shrub or tree with small, evergreen leaves and hard, yellowish wood. **2.** The wood of this shrub. [SEE NOTE]

box•car |bŏks′kär′| *n.* An enclosed railway car used to carry freight.

bow[1-2-3]

Bow[1] *is from Low German* boog, *"shoulder," also "bow of a ship."* **Bow[2]** *is an Old English verb,* būgan, *basically meaning "to bend."* **Bow[3]** *is an Old English noun,* boga, *basically meaning "something bent" and related to* **bow[2]**.

bowl[1-2]

Bowl[1] *is from Old English* bolla, *"a pot or bowl."* **Bowl[2]** *is from Old French* boule, *"a ball," which is from Latin* bulla, *"a bubble, a ball," also "a seal";* bulla *is the source of several other English words, including* **bill[1]** *and* **bull[2]**.

box[1-2-3]

Box[1] *and* **box[3]** *have always been spelled* box, *even in Old English, and they come from the same source. They were borrowed (separately) from Greek* puxis, *"box tree," a tree that has very hard, fine wood that must have been used for making boxes.* **Box[2]** *first appears in Middle English, but its history before that is unknown.*

boxer[2]

boy/girl

In the school materials on which this Dictionary was based, **boy** *and* **boys** *occurred more than twice as often as* **girl** *and* **girls**. *This was generally true in every grade from 3 to 9 and in every subject except Home Economics. The total number of occurrences were:* **boy/boys**: *4,700*
girl/girls: *2,200*

Boyle's law

This principle was formulated by and is named for Robert Boyle *(1627–1691), an English scientist.*

ă pat/ā pay/â care/ä father/ĕ pet/ ē be/ĭ pit/ī pie/î fierce/ŏ pot/ ō go/ô paw, for/oi oil/ŏŏ book/ ōō boot/ou out/ŭ cut/û fur/ *th* the/th thin/hw which/zh vision/ ə ago, item, pencil, atom, circus

box•er[1] |bŏk'sər| *n.* A person who fights with his fists, especially to earn money.

box•er[2] |bŏk'sər| *n.* A dog with a short, smooth, brownish coat and a short, square-jawed face. [SEE PICTURE]

boxer shorts. Loose-fitting shorts worn by men as underwear.

box•ing |bŏk'sĭng| *n.* The sport of fighting with the fists, especially when padded gloves are worn and special rules are followed. —***modifier:*** *a boxing match.*

boxing glove. One of two heavily padded leather mittens worn by a boxer to protect his fists while fighting.

box office. The place where tickets are sold in a theater, auditorium, or stadium.

box seat. A seat in a box at a theater or stadium.

box stall. An enclosed stall for a single animal.

box•wood |bŏks'wŏŏd'| *n.* The hard, light-yellow, fine-grained wood of the box shrub, used to make rulers, musical instruments, etc.

box•y |bŏk'sē| *adj.* **box•i•er, box•i•est.** Rather square in shape: *a boxy station wagon.*

boy |boi| *n.* **1.** A male child or a youth who has not yet reached manhood. **2. a.** A son: *my own sister's boy.* **b.** A brother: *the Jones boys.* **3.** A youth who does some special work: *a shepherd boy.* **4.** *Informal.* A fellow; guy: *a night out with the boys.* —*interj.* A word used to express mild astonishment, elation, etc.: *Oh boy! That's a car for you.* [SEE NOTE]

boy•cott |boi'kŏt'| *n.* An organized group refusal to use a product or service or to buy from or deal with a business, nation, etc., as a means of protest or pressure. —*v.* To take part in an organized group refusal to use, buy from, deal with, attend, etc.: *boycott a store; boycott a meeting.*

boy•friend |boi'frĕnd'| *n.* Also **boy friend. 1.** *Informal.* A sweetheart or frequent date of a woman or girl. **2.** A male friend.

boy•hood |boi'hŏŏd'| *n.* The time of being a boy.

boy•ish |boi'ĭsh| *adj.* Of, like, or suitable for a boy: *a boyish smile.* —**boy'ish•ly** *adv.* —**boy'ish•ness** *n.*

Boyle's law |boilz|. The principle of physics that if a confined gas is kept at a fixed temperature the product of its pressure and volume is a constant. [SEE NOTE]

Boy Scout. A member of the **Boy Scouts,** an organization for boys that helps to develop self-reliance, good citizenship, and outdoor skills.

boy•sen•ber•ry |boi'zən bĕr'ē| *n., pl.* **-ber•ries.** A large, dark-red berry related to the loganberry, blackberry, and raspberry.

Br The symbol for the element bromine.

bra |brä| *n.* A brassiere.

brace |brās| *n.* **1. a.** A device that holds two or more parts together or in place. **b.** A support, as a beam in a building. **2.** A medical device used to support a part of the body. **3.** Often **braces.** An arrangement of wires and bands fixed to crooked teeth in order to straighten them. **4.** Either of the symbols { }, used in printing and writing to connect several lines of text and in mathematics to enclose the listing of the elements of a set. **5.** The symbol {, used in music to connect several staves. **6.** A rotating handle that holds a drill or bit, used for boring holes. **7.** A pair: *a brace of partridges.* **8. braces.** *British.* Suspenders. —*v.* **braced, brac•ing. 1.** To support; strengthen; reinforce: *brace a sloping shed with timbers.* **2.** To prepare for a blow, shock, struggle, etc.: *Brace yourselves for the coming test.* **3.** To prop or hold firmly in place: *She braced her feet against the floorboard.* **4.** To fill with energy; refresh; stimulate: *The cold, clear air of the slopes braced the skiers.* —**brac'ing** *adj.: a cool, bracing breeze.* —***phrasal verb.*** **brace up. 1.** To summon up lost strength or courage: *Brace up and make a man of yourself.* **2.** To straighten up one's body: *He braced up and threw back his shoulders.*

brace•let |brās'lĭt| *n.* A band or chain worn around the wrist or arm as an ornament.

brach•i•o•pod |brăk'ē ə pŏd'| *or* |brä'kē-| *n.* A sea animal with paired upper and lower shells attached to a stalk.

brack•en |brăk'ən| *n.* **1.** A large fern with branching fronds. **2.** A place overgrown with such ferns.

brack•et |brăk'ĭt| *n.* **1.** A support or fixture fastened to a surface and sticking out to hold something, such as a shelf, candle, etc. **2.** A shelf supported by brackets. **3.** Either of the pair of symbols [ ], used to enclose printed or written material or to enclose a set of mathematical symbols that are to be considered a single expression. **4.** A group, class, or range within a numbered or graded series: *the 9-to-12 age bracket; a high tax bracket.* —*v.* **1.** To put brackets around: *bracket words inserted in a quotation.* **2.** To classify or group together: *bracket taxpayers according to their earnings.* **3.** To support with a bracket or brackets.

brack•ish |brăk'ĭsh| *adj.* **1.** Slightly salty and not fit to drink: *brackish lake water.* **2.** Bad-tasting.

bract |brăkt| *n.* A leaflike plant part below a flower or flower cluster. Most bracts are thin and inconspicuous, but some are showy or brightly colored and resemble petals.

brad |brăd| *n.* A thin nail with a small head. —*v.* **brad•ded, brad•ding.** To fasten with brads.

brag |brăg| *v.* **bragged, brag•ging. 1.** To praise oneself or one's deeds, possessions, family, etc., in an attempt to show off and impress others; boast. **2.** To talk boastfully: *He bragged about how brave he was.* —*n.* **1.** Boastful or conceited talk: *full of brag.* **2.** Something boasted about.

brag•gart |brăg'ərt| *n.* A person who brags a lot.

Brah•ma |brä'mə|. In the Hindu religion, the god who created the world.

Brah•man |brä'mən| *n.* **1.** A member of the highest Hindu caste, originally composed of priests. **2.** One of a breed of cattle with a hump between the shoulders and a fold of loose skin hanging below the neck.

Brah•man•ism |brä'mə nĭz'əm| *n.* **1.** The religion of ancient India. **2.** The caste system of the Brahmans of India.

Brah•min |brä'mĭn| *n.* A form of the word **Brahman.**

Brahms |brämz|, **Johannes.** 1833–1897. German composer.

braid |brăd| *v.* **1.** To weave or twist together

three or more strands of (hair, fiber, fabric, etc.); plait. **2.** To make by weaving strands together: *braid a straw rug.* —*n.* **1.** A ropelike piece of plaited hair. **2.** A strip of braided material, such as cloth, cord, yarn, or straw, used for trimming clothes, making mats, etc.

braid•ed |brā′dĭd| *adj.* **1.** Woven into ropelike strands: *braided hair.* **2.** Wearing the hair in braids: *braided maidens.* **3.** Made by braiding: *braided rugs.* **4.** Moving in channels that crisscross: *braided streams.*

braid•ing |brā′dĭng| *n.* Braided material; braid.

Braille, also **braille** |brāl| *n.* A system of writing and printing used by blind people, in which raised dots representing letters, numbers, and punctuation are read by feeling them with the fingertips.

brain |brān| *n.* **1. a.** The large mass of gray nerve tissue enclosed in the skull of a vertebrate. It interprets sensory impulses, coordinates and controls bodily activities and functions, and is the center of thought and feeling. **b. brains.** The nerve tissue that makes up the brain. **2. brains.** The brains of an animal used as food. **3.** The mind: *The plan took shape in his brain.* **4. brains.** Intelligence: *She has brains and courage.* —***modifier:*** *brain cells.* —*v. Slang.* To hit hard on the head. [SEE PICTURE]

***Idiom.* rack (or beat) (one's) brains.** To try very hard to think of, figure out, or solve something.

brain child. *Informal.* An original plan, idea, or invention.

brain•less |brān′lĭs| *adj.* Having no brains; stupid. —**brain′less•ly** *adv.* —**brain′less•ness** *n.*

brain•storm |brān′stôrm′| *n. Informal.* A sudden inspiration or clever idea.

brain•wash |brān′wŏsh′| *or* |-wôsh′| *v.* To indoctrinate (someone) until he is willing to give up his own basic convictions and passively accept an opposing set of beliefs.

brain wave. Any of various small, rhythmically fluctuating voltages that arise from electrical activity in the brain and that can be measured between points on the scalp.

brain•work |brān′wûrk′| *n.* Mental work, such as thought, planning, organization, or calculation. —**brain′work′er** *n.*

brain•y |brā′nē| *adj.* **brain•i•er, brain•i•est.** *Informal.* Intelligent; smart.

braise |brāz| *v.* **braised, brais•ing.** To brown (meat or vegetables) in fat and then simmer in a little liquid in a covered container.

brake[1] |brāk| *n.* **1.** Often **brakes.** A device for slowing or stopping motion, as of a vehicle or machine. **2.** Often **brakes.** A restraint that slows or stops an ongoing action or process: *put a brake on rising prices.* **3.** A machine for bending and folding sheet metal. —***modifier:*** *press the brake pedal.* —*v.* **braked, brak•ing. 1.** To slow or stop with a brake or brakes: *brake a train.* **2.** To operate or apply a brake or brakes: *Slow down and brake before turning.* ¶*These sound alike* **brake, break.** [SEE NOTE]

brake[2] |brāk| *n.* **1.** Bracken or a similar fern. **2.** An area overgrown with dense bushes, briers, etc.; a thicket. ¶*These sound alike* **brake, break.** [SEE NOTE]

brake[3] |brāk|. *Archaic.* A past tense of **break.** ¶*These sound alike* **brake, break.**

brake•man |brāk′mən| *n., pl.* **-men** |-mən|. A railroad employee who assists the conductor and checks on the operation of the train's brakes.

bram•ble |brăm′bəl| *n.* A prickly plant or shrub such as the blackberry or raspberry.

bram•bly |brăm′blē| *adj.* **bram•bli•er, bram•bli•est.** Full of brambles: *a brambly thicket.*

bran |brăn| *n.* The outer husks of wheat, rye, and other grain, sifted out from the flour after grinding.

branch |brănch| *or* |bränch| *n.* **1.** One of the woody stem parts dividing out from the trunk, limb, or main stem of a tree or shrub. **2.** Any part going out from a main part like a tree branch: *the branches of an antler.* **3.** A part or division of a larger whole: *Biology is a branch of science.* **4.** A division of government: *the executive branch.* **5.** A local unit or office of a business, institution, etc.: *a bank branch.* **6. a.** A division of a family or tribe. **b.** A subdivision of a family of languages. **7. a.** An arm or offshoot of a larger river or stream. **b.** Any small stream, creek, etc. —***modifier:*** *a branch line of a railroad; branch water.* —*v.* To divide or spread out in branches or branchlike parts: *The road branches into two forks. Small roots branch out from the big root.* —**branched′** *adj.: a deer's branched horns.* —**branch′ing** *adj.: branching antlers.* —***phrasal verbs.* branch off.** To go off from the central part in a different direction: *A path branched off from the road.* **branch out.** To expand one's business, activities, etc., into a new area: *The seamstress branched out into dress design.*

brand |brănd| *n.* **1. a.** A name or symbol that identifies a product; a trademark. **b.** The make of a product marked in this way: *a brand of soap.* **2.** A distinctive style or type: *his novel brand of crooning.* **3. a.** A mark burned into flesh with a hot iron, put on cattle as a symbol of ownership and once put on criminals as a symbol of shame. **b.** An iron used to make such a mark. **4.** Any mark of disgrace. **5.** A piece of burning or charred wood. —***modifier:*** *a brand name.* —*v.* **1.** To mark with a brand: *Cowboys branded the calves.* **2.** To mark with a label of shame and disgrace; stigmatize: *The tribunal branded them as traitors.*

bran•dish |brăn′dĭsh| *v.* To wave or exhibit in a dramatic or threatening way: *The cave man brandished a club.*

brand-new |brănd′no͞o′| *or* |-nyo͞o′| *adj.* Completely new; not used.

bran•dy |brăn′dē| *n., pl.* **bran•dies.** An alcoholic liquor distilled from wine or fermented fruit juice.

brant |brănt| *n.* A small wild goose with dark feathers.

brash[1] |brăsh| *adj.* **1.** Hasty and unthinking; rash. **2.** Shamelessly bold; impudent; saucy. —**brash′ly** *adv.* —**brash′ness** *n.*

brash[2] |brăsh| *n.* A mass of fragments, as of ice floating in the sea.

Bra•sí•lia |brä zēl′yə|. The capital of Brazil. Population, 710,900.

brass |brăs| *or* |bräs| *n.* **1.** Any of various alloys that contain chiefly copper and zinc. **2.** Ornaments, objects, or utensils made of such metal: *Polish the brass.* **3.** Often **brasses.** In music: **a.** Any brass instrument. **b.** The brass

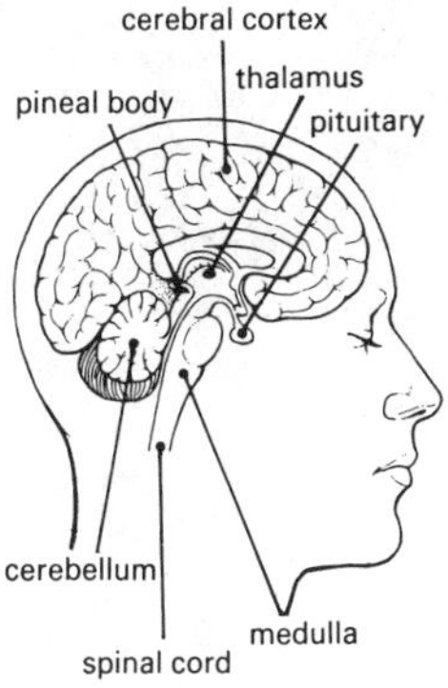

brain

brake[1-2]

Brake[1] *is borrowed from Dutch* braeke, *"machine for crushing flax."* Braeke *was also used as the designation for various other devices, hence its modern English meaning. It is ultimately related to* **break. Brake[2]** *is from Old English* fern-braca, *"clump of ferns"; the* -braca, *meaning "clump or thicket," is related to* **bracken.**

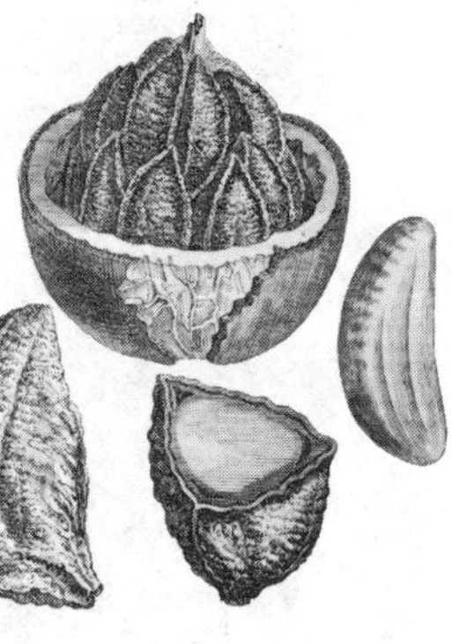

Brazil nut
Nuts and open pod

breadfruit

instruments of an orchestra or band. **4.** *Informal.* Shameless boldness; impudence; nerve. **5.** *Slang.* High-ranking officers or officials. —***modifier:*** *brass buttons; the brass players.*

bras•siere or **bras•sière** |brə zîr′| *n.* A woman's undergarment worn to support the breasts.

brass instrument. Any of the group of musical instruments that includes the trumpet, trombone, French horn, and tuba. These are typically made of brass or a similar metal and are sounded by pressing the lips and blowing into a cup-shaped or funnel-shaped mouthpiece.

brass tacks. *Informal.* Essential facts: *Let's get down to brass tacks.*

brass•y |brăs′ē| *or* |brä′sē| *adj.* **brass•i•er, brass•i•est. 1.** Of, decorated with, or having the yellowish color of brass. **2.** Of, like, or featuring the tone of a brass instrument or instruments. **3.** *Informal.* Shamelessly bold; impudent; brazen. —**brass′i•ly** *adv.* —**brass′i•ness** *n.*

brat |brăt| *n.* A nasty or spoiled child.

bra•va•do |brə vä′dō| *n., pl.* **bra•va•does** or **bra•va•dos.** A show of pretended or defiant courage; false bravery.

brave |brāv| *adj.* **brav•er, brav•est.** Having or showing courage. —*n.* A North American Indian warrior. —*v.* **braved, brav•ing.** To undergo or face with courage: *FBI agents brave many dangers.* —**brave′ly** *adv.* —**brave′ness** *n.*

brav•er•y |brā′və rē| *or* |brāv′rē| *n., pl.* **brav•er•ies.** The condition or quality of being brave; courage.

bra•vo |brä′vō| *or* |brä vō′| *interj.* Excellent; well done. —*n., pl.* **bra•vos.** A shout of approval or praise.

bra•vu•ra |brə vyŏŏr′ə| *n.* **1.** Brilliant technique or style in performance, as in music, dance, etc. **2.** A showy display.

brawl |brôl| *n.* A noisy fight or quarrel. —*v.* To quarrel noisily.

brawn |brôn| *n.* Muscular strength and power: *Lumberjacks need brawn.*

brawn•y |brô′nē| *adj.* **brawn•i•er, brawn•i•est.** Strong and muscular.

bray |brā| *n.* **1.** The loud, harsh cry of a donkey. **2.** A loud, harsh sound resembling this: *the bray of trumpets.* —*v.* **1.** To utter the loud, harsh cry of a donkey. **2.** To make a sound resembling this: *The foghorn brayed all night.*

bray•er |brā′ər| *n.* In printing, a small hand roller used to spread ink evenly over type.

braze |brāz| *v.* **brazed, braz•ing.** To join (pieces of metal) together using a hard solder with a high melting point.

bra•zen |brā′zən| *adj.* **1.** Rudely bold; impudent; insolent: *a brazen remark.* **2.** Made of or resembling brass: *the sound of a brazen bell.* —*v.* To face or undergo with bold self-assurance: *Danger was upon him, but he brazened it out.* —**bra′zen•ly** *adv.* —**bra′zen•ness** *n.*

bra•zier |brā′zhər| *n.* A metal pan for holding burning coals or charcoal.

Bra•zil |brə zĭl′|. The largest country in South America, occupying nearly half the entire continent. Population, 104,642,000. Capital, Brasília. —**Bra•zil′ian** *adj.* & *n.*

Brazil nut. The edible nut of a tropical American tree, having a hard, three-sided, dark-brown shell. [SEE PICTURE]

Braz•za•ville |brăz′ə vĭl′|. The capital of the Congo. Population, 160,000.

breach |brēch| *n.* **1.** A violation or infraction, as of a law, legal obligation, or promise: *a breach of contract.* **2.** A gap or hole, especially in a solid structure: *Water poured through a breach in the dike.* **3.** A disruption of friendly relations; an estrangement: *An argument caused a breach between them.* —*v.* To make a hole or gap in; break through: *Soldiers breached the enemy's line.* ¶ *These sound alike* **breach, breech.**

breach of promise. The failure to keep a promise, especially a promise to marry someone.

bread |brĕd| *n.* **1.** A staple food made from moistened, usually leavened, flour or meal kneaded and baked. **2.** Food in general, regarded as necessary to sustain life: *"Give us this day our daily bread."* (The Bible, Matthew 6:11). **3.** The necessities of life; livelihood: *earn one's bread.* **4.** *Slang.* Money. —***modifier:*** *a bread plate; bread mold.* —*v.* To coat (food) with bread crumbs before cooking. —**bread′ed** *adj.: a breaded cutlet.* ¶ *These sound alike* **bread, bred.**

Idiom. **break bread.** To eat or share a meal: *Let us break bread together.*

bread-and-but•ter |brĕd′n bŭt′ər| *adj.* **1.** Having to do with or connected with earning a livelihood or making money: *a bread-and-butter job.* **2.** Expressive of thanks for hospitality: *a bread-and-butter letter.*

bread•bas•ket |brĕd′băs′kĭt| *n.* **1.** A region serving as a principal source of grain. **2.** *Slang.* The stomach.

bread•fruit |brĕd′fro͞ot′| *n.* The large, round, edible fruit of a tropical tree, having a rough skin and starchy flesh that resembles bread when roasted. [SEE PICTURE]

breadth |brĕdth| *n.* **1.** The distance from side to side of something, as distinguished from length or thickness; width. **2.** Freedom from narrowness, as of interests, attitudes, etc.: *breadth of mind.* **3.** Wide extent or scope: *Leonardo da Vinci's mind was remarkable for the breadth and quality of his intellectual curiosity.*

bread•win•ner |brĕd′wĭn′ər| *n.* A person who earns money to support a household.

break |brāk| *v.* **broke** |brōk|, **bro•ken** |brō′kən|, **break•ing. 1. a.** To crack or split into two or more fragments as the result of force, a blow, or strain: *break a mirror. Glass breaks easily. The chain broke.* **b.** To burst or cause to burst: *A heated balloon will break. He broke the balloon.* **2.** To detach or become detached by or as if by force; pull apart: *He broke a branch from the tree. Don't break off branches from these trees. At a certain speed, space vehicles can break free of the earth's gravity.* **3.** To fracture a bone of: *break an arm.* **4.** To make or become unusable; ruin: *Dad broke my electric trains. My watch broke.* **5.** To force or make one's way; penetrate: *The pushmi-pullyu tried to break through the ring of monkeys. The armies broke through at the border.* **6.** To move away; escape or escape from: *He had the chance to break out of the ghetto. Few molecules break away from the liquid.* **7.** To run or dash suddenly: *The runner broke for home plate.* **8.** To emerge suddenly, as above the surface of water: *The swimmers broke the surface near the raft.* **9. a.** To violate by failing to follow, conform, observe, etc.; fail to keep: *break a law; break a promise.* **b.** To call off: *break a date; break an engagement.* **10. a.** To disrupt or destroy the regularity, order, continuity, or completeness of: *break a circuit; break ranks; break the silence; break a set of books.* **b.** To put an end to, as by force, opposition, etc.: *The police broke the wildcat strike. His vote broke the tie.* **c.** To interrupt or end abruptly: *break off a conversation; break off relations with another country.* **11.** To scatter or disperse: *The Romans broke in panic before the war elephants of Pyrrhus.* **12.** To change suddenly in pitch: *His voice broke with emotion.* **13.** To come into being; appear, especially suddenly: *Daylight broke at six. A smile broke upon his lips.* **14. a.** To begin suddenly to produce something: *break out into a cold sweat; break out in tears; plants breaking into bloom.* **b.** To begin to be uttered suddenly; burst out: *A general cry broke forth from the crowd.* **15.** To surpass or outdo: *break a record.* **16.** To collapse or crash into surf and foam: *Follow the white foam line of the wave as it breaks on the beach.* **17. a.** To cause to give up a habit: *Try to break him of smoking.* **b.** To give up; discontinue: *break a habit.* **18.** To make or become known: *She broke the news of his father's death to him gently. The story of the scandal broke on Friday.* **19.** To train to obey; tame: *break a wild mustang.* **20. a.** To weaken or destroy; crush; subdue: *break an enemy's resistance; break his proud spirit.* **b.** To overwhelm or be overwhelmed with sorrow: *His indifference broke her heart. His heart broke when she died.* **21.** To lessen or diminish in force or effect: *His fever broke. The storm broke suddenly. He broke the fall with his hands.* **22.** To reduce in rank; demote: *At the court martial, they broke the sergeant to private.* **23.** *Informal.* To reduce to or exchange for smaller monetary units: *Break a dollar for our bus fare.* **24.** *Informal.* To cause to be without money; bankrupt: *These medical bills will break me yet.* **25.** In baseball, to curve suddenly at or near the plate: *The pitch broke away from the batter.* —***phrasal verbs.*** **break down. 1.** To shatter or collapse by or as if by breaking: *Don't break down the door. Class barriers break down completely during military service.* **2.** To fail to function: *The truck broke down on the highway.* **3. a.** To decompose chemically. **b.** To analyze or consider in parts: *Break the exercise down into several steps.* **4.** To undergo electrical breakdown. **5.** To become distressed: *She broke down and cried.* **6.** To have a mental or physical collapse: *Some people break down in emergencies.* **break in. 1.** To enter forcibly or illegally: *The burglars broke in and stole our television.* **2.** To interrupt a conversation: *He broke in with some irrelevant statement.* **3. a.** To train or instruct in order to accustom to new work: *break in a new secretary.* **b.** To overcome the stiffness of: *break in new shoes.* **break in on.** To interrupt or intrude: *break in on a conversation.* **break into. 1.** To enter forcibly and illegally: *The burglars broke into the house.* **2.** To start or begin suddenly: *The horse broke into a wild gallop. The girl broke into tears.* **break off.** To stop speaking or doing something abruptly: *He broke off in the middle of a sentence.* **break out. 1.** To be affected with a skin irritation, such as acne or a rash: *Chocolate makes me break out.* **2.** To begin suddenly: *Rioting broke out during the night. A war broke out in the Middle East.* **break up. 1. a.** To break into pieces or fragments: *Rain breaks up rock over centuries.* **b.** To separate into smaller parts: *break up a word into syllables.* **2.** To bring or come to an end: *break up a fight; break up a family. The marriage broke up.* **3.** *Informal.* To burst or cause to burst into laughter: *The comedienne broke up the crowd. The crowd broke up.* **break with.** To give up or stop following: *He broke with the conservatism of his father.* —*n.* **1.** A result of breaking; a fracture or crack: *a break in a bone.* **2. a.** A gap or opening: *a break in the clouds.* **b.** A beginning: *the break of day.* **3.** An interruption or disruption of regularity, continuity, etc.: *a break in a conversation; a break in an electrical circuit.* **4.** A pause or interval, as from work: *Take a break.* **5.** A sudden run; dash: *The soldier made a break for cover.* **6.** An attempt to escape: *a jail break.* **7.** A departure from: *a break with tradition.* **8.** A sudden or marked change: *a break in the weather.* **9.** An unexpected occurrence or chance: *a lucky break.* ¶*These sound alike* **break, brake.**

break•a•ble |brā'kə bəl| *adj.* Capable of being broken; fragile.

break•age |brā'kĭj| *n.* **1.** The act of breaking. **2.** A quantity broken. **3.** Loss or damage as a result of breaking. **4.** Compensation, as in money, for such loss or damage.

break•down |brāk'doun'| *n.* **1.** The process of breaking down or the condition resulting from this. **2.** The passage of an electric current through an insulator or a material that does not normally allow current to pass, usually as a result of a failure or an excessively high voltage. **3.** A collapse of physical or mental health. **4.** Decomposition or disintegration into parts, elements, etc. **5.** An analysis or summary consisting of itemized data: *a breakdown on the price of a new car.*

break•er |brā'kər| *n.* Someone or something that breaks, especially: **a.** A wave that breaks into foam on a shore. **b.** A **circuit breaker.**

break•fast |brĕk'fəst| *n.* The first meal of the day. —***modifier:*** *a breakfast table.* —*v.* To eat breakfast. [SEE NOTE]

break•neck |brāk'nĕk'| *adj.* Reckless; dangerous: *breakneck speed.*

break•through |brāk'thro͞o'| *n.* A major achievement or success that permits further progress, as in technology.

break•up |brāk'ŭp'| *n.* The act of breaking up; a separation or dispersal: *the breakup of rock at the earth's surface; the breakup of a marriage.*

break•wa•ter |brāk'wô'tər| *or* |-wŏt'ər| *n.* A barrier that protects a harbor or shore from the full impact of waves; a jetty.

bream |brēm| *n., pl.* **bream** or **breams.** A European freshwater fish with a flattened body and silvery scales.

breast |brĕst| *n.* **1.** In mammals, especially human beings, one of the glands in which a female produces milk to feed her young offspring. **2.** The upper part of the front surface of the body, extending from the neck to the abdomen. **3.** This part of the body regarded as the seat of affection or emotion. —*v.* To face or advance

breakfast

The spelling (but not the pronunciation) of **breakfast** *reveals the origin of the word. It arose in the fifteenth century from the phrase* to break one's fast, *"to end one's fast after a night of not eating." See* **fast²**.

breastplate
Sixteenth century

breeches buoy

ă pat/ā pay/â care/ä father/ĕ pet/
ē be/ĭ pit/ī pie/î fierce/ŏ pot/
ō go/ô paw, for/oi oil/ŏŏ book/
ōō boot/ou out/ŭ cut/û fur/
th the/th thin/hw which/zh vision/
ə ago, item, pencil, atom, circus

against boldly: *He breasted every hurdle in his path.*

***Idiom.* make a clean breast of.** To make a full confession of.

breast•bone |**brĕst'**bōn'| *n.* The bone to which the collarbones and ribs are joined; the sternum.

breast•plate |**brĕst'**plāt'| *n.* A piece of metal armor worn over the chest to protect it in battle. [SEE PICTURE]

breast stroke. A swimming stroke in which one lies face down and extends the arms in front of the head, then sweeps them back laterally while performing a frog kick.

breast•work |**brĕst'**wûrk'| *n.* A temporary, hastily constructed fortification, usually breast-high.

breath |brĕth| *n.* **1.** The air inhaled into and exhaled from the lungs. **2.** The ability to breathe, especially with ease: *He became short of breath as he ran up the hill.* **3.** The act or process of breathing. **4.** A single cycle of breathing, especially an inhalation: *The singer took a deep breath.* **5.** A slight breeze: *not a breath of air.* **6.** A trace or suggestion: *Bears come out of hibernation at the first breath of spring.*

***Idioms.* hold (one's) breath 1.** To stop inhaling and exhaling for a short time. **2.** To wait anxiously or excitedly. **in the same breath.** At the same time: *saying "yes" and "no" to their offer in the same breath.* **out of breath.** Breathing hard; panting, as from exertion. **save** (or **waste) (one's) breath.** To refrain from (or engage in) futile talking, especially when asking or persuading: *Save your breath—he won't do what you asked.* **take (one's) breath away.** To awe, excite, or surprise greatly. **under (one's) breath.** In a whisper: *He stood with his arms crossed, whistling softly under his breath.*

breathe |brē*th*| *v.* **breathed, breath•ing. 1.** To inhale and exhale: *All mammals breathe air. Quiet! Don't even breathe.* **2.** To pause to rest or to regain breath, as after action: *Give me a moment to breathe.* **3.** To communicate or impart (a quality) as if by breathing: *The artist breathed life into the portrait of his children.* **4.** To utter, especially quietly; whisper: *Don't breathe a word of this.*

***Idiom.* breathe (one's) last.** To die.

breath•er |**brē'***th*ər| *n. Informal.* A short rest period.

breath•less |**brĕth'**lĭs| *adj.* **1.** Out of breath; panting: *He was breathless after running.* **2.** Holding the breath from excitement or suspense: *a breathless audience.* **3.** Inspiring or marked by excitement that makes one hold the breath: *a breathless silence.* **4.** Having no breeze; still: *a breathless day.* **—breath'less•ly** *adv.* **—breath'less•ness** *n.*

breath•tak•ing |**brĕth'**tā'kĭng| *adj.* Inspiring awe; very exciting: *a breathtaking view of the canyon; a breathtaking performance.*

breath•y |**brĕth'**ē| *adj.* **breath•i•er, breath•i•est.** Marked by noisy breathing: *a breathy voice.*

bred |brĕd|. Past tense and past participle of **breed.** ¶*These sound alike* **bred, bread.**

breech |brēch| *n.* **1.** The lower rear part of the human trunk; the buttocks. **2.** The part of a firearm to the rear of the barrel. ¶*These sound alike* **breech, breach.**

breech•cloth |**brēch'**klôth'| *or* |-klŏth'| *n., pl.* **-cloths** |-klô*thz*'| *or* |-klŏ*thz*'| *or* |-klôths'| *or* |-klŏths'|. A cloth worn to cover the loins.

breech•clout |**brēch'**klout'| *n.* A form of the word **breechcloth.**

breech•es |**brĭch'**ĭz| *pl.n.* **1.** Short, fitted trousers ending at or just below the knees. **2.** *Informal.* Any trousers.

breeches buoy. A device used for rescue at sea, made up of canvas breeches attached to a life preserver that is suspended to a pulley running along a line from ship to ship or ship to shore. [SEE PICTURE]

breech•load•er |**brēch'**lō'dər| *n.* A gun or firearm that is loaded at the breech. **—breech'load'ing** *adj.*

breed |brēd| *v.* **bred** |brĕd|, **breed•ing. 1.** To produce or reproduce by giving birth, hatching, etc.; produce (offspring): *Mosquitoes breed rapidly. This mare has bred champions.* **2. a.** To raise (animals or plants), often to produce new or improved types. **b.** To mate so as to produce offspring: *bred his fine mare to a noble stallion.* **3.** To bring about; give rise to: *clouds called thunderheads because they breed storms.* **4.** To rear or train; bring up: *bred to behave like gentlemen.* **5.** To originate and thrive: *Fads breed in empty heads and full purses.* *—n.* **1.** A particular type or variety of animal, or sometimes a plant, often produced by mating selected parents to produce certain wanted characteristics: *a hardy breed of cattle; a breed of hybrid corn.* **2.** A type or kind of person or thing: *a new breed of politicians.*

breed•er |**brē'**dər| *n.* **1.** A person who breeds animals or plants: *a cattle breeder; a poultry breeder.* **2.** Anything that causes, creates, or gives birth to something; a source: *War has always been a great machine breeder.*

breeder reactor. A nuclear reactor that in addition to producing energy produces more fissionable material than it uses up.

breed•ing |**brē'**dĭng| *n.* **1.** A line of descent; ancestry. **2.** The training of persons in the proper forms of conduct. **3.** The producing of offspring or young. **4.** The raising of animals or plants, especially so as to produce new or improved varieties. ***—modifier:*** *breeding grounds.*

breeze |brēz| *n.* A light air current; gentle wind. *—v.* **breezed, breez•ing.** *Informal.* To move rapidly and without effort: *She breezed down the street. The girls breezed into the room.*

breeze•way |**brēz'**wā'| *n.* A roofed, open-sided passageway connecting two buildings, such as a house and a garage.

breez•y |**brē'**zē| *adj.* **breez•i•er, breez•i•est. 1.** Exposed to breezes; windy. **2.** Lively; sprightly: *a writer's breezy style.* **—breez'i•ly** *adv.*

breth•ren |**brĕ*th*'**rən| *n. Archaic.* Plural of **brother.**

breve |brĕv| *or* |brēv| *n.* **1.** A mark (˘) placed over a vowel to show that it has a short sound, as the (ă) in *bat.* **2.** A similar mark used to indicate that a syllable is unstressed in a foot of verse.

bre•vet |brə **vĕt'**| *n.* A commission, often granted as an honor, promoting a military officer in rank without an increase in pay or authority.

bre•vi•ar•y |**brē'**vē ĕr'ē| *or* |**brĕv'**ē-| *n., pl.* **bre•**

vi•ar•ies. In the Roman Catholic and Anglican churches, a book containing the daily prayers, hymns, and other readings of priests.

brev•i•ty |brĕv′ĭ tē| *n.* Briefness, as of expression; shortness: *Good syntax helps you to achieve clarity and brevity. "Brevity is the soul of wit"* (Shakespeare).

brew |bro͞o| *v.* **1.** To make (beer or ale) from malt and hops. **2.** To make (a beverage) by boiling, steeping, or mixing ingredients. **3.** To devise or plan; concoct: *brewed a scheme for gaining revenge.* **4.** To be imminent; threaten to occur: *Trouble brewed throughout much of Latin America.* —*n.* **1.** A beverage made by brewing. **2.** The quantity brewed at one time.

brew•er |bro͞o′ər| *n.* A person whose business is brewing beer, ale, etc.

brew•er•y |bro͞o′ə rē| *or* |bro͝or′ē| *n., pl.* **brew•er•ies.** A place where malt liquors, such as beer, are manufactured.

brew•ing |bro͞o′ĭng| *n.* The act, process, or business of making malt liquors, such as beer.

bri•ar[1] |brī′ər| *n.* **1.** A shrub with a hard, woody root used to make tobacco pipes. **2.** A pipe made from this root. [SEE NOTE]

bri•ar[2] |brī′ər| *n.* A form of the word **brier** (thorny shrub). [SEE NOTE]

bribe |brīb| *n.* **1.** Anything, such as money, property, etc., offered or given to someone to make him act dishonestly: *The judge was dismissed for accepting bribes.* **2.** Something offered or serving to influence or persuade: *There were tidbits or other bribes awaiting the children after the rehearsal.* —*v.* **bribed, brib•ing.** To give or offer a bribe to.

brib•er•y |brī′bə rē| *n., pl.* **brib•er•ies.** The act of giving, offering, or taking a bribe.

bric-a-brac |brĭk′ə brăk′| *n.* Small objects displayed in a room as ornaments.

brick |brĭk| *n.* **1.** An oblong block of clay, baked by the sun or in a kiln until hard and used as building and paving material. **2.** These blocks considered as a group or as a kind of material: *houses of red brick; when the Romans learned the use of brick.* **3.** Any object shaped like such a block: *a brick of cheese.* —***modifier:*** *a brick house; a brick oven.* —*v.* **1.** To build, line, or pave with bricks. **2.** To close, wall, or fill with bricks: *He bricked up the well.*

brick•bat |brĭk′băt′| *n.* A piece of brick thrown as a weapon.

brick•lay•er |brĭk′lā′ər| *n.* A person who builds walls, chimneys, or other structures by laying bricks. —**brick′lay′ing** *n.*

bri•dal |brīd′l| *adj.* Of a bride or a marriage ceremony: *a bridal veil; the bridal party.* ¶*These sound alike* **bridal, bridle.**

bride |brīd| *n.* A woman recently married or about to be married.

bride•groom |brīd′gro͞om′| *or* |-gro͝om′| *n.* A man recently married or about to be married.

brides•maid |brīdz′mād′| *n.* A young woman who attends the bride at a wedding.

bridge[1] |brĭj| *n.* **1.** A structure providing a way across a waterway, railroad, or other obstacle. **2.** The upper bony ridge of the human nose. **3.** The part of a pair of eyeglasses that rests against this ridge. **4.** A thin piece of wood that supports the strings above the sounding board in some stringed instruments. **5.** A structure that replaces one or more missing natural teeth, usually anchored to natural teeth at both ends. **6.** A platform above the main deck of a ship from which the ship is controlled. **7.** A short musical passage that connects two sections of a composition. —***modifier:*** *pay your bridge tolls; a bridge tower.* —*v.* **bridged, bridg•ing. 1.** To build a bridge over: *bridge Long Island Sound.* **2. a.** To cross by or as if by a bridge: *His life spanned three generations and bridged a whole era in American politics.* **b.** To overcome: *bridge difficulties.* [SEE NOTE]

Idiom. **burn (one's) bridges (behind one).** To eliminate the possibility of retreat.

bridge[2] |brĭj| *n.* Any of several card games for four, derived from whist. [SEE NOTE]

bridge•head |brĭj′hĕd′| *n.* A military position established by advance troops on the enemy's side of a river or pass.

Bridge•town |brĭj′toun′|. The capital of Barbados. Population, 105,000.

bridge•work |brĭj′wûrk′| *n.* One or more bridges used to replace missing teeth.

bridg•ing |brĭj′ĭng| *n.* Wooden braces between beams in a floor or roof, used to reinforce the beams and keep them apart.

bri•dle |brīd′l| *n.* The straps, bit, and reins fitted about a horse's head, used to control the animal. —*v.* **bri•dled, bri•dling. 1.** To put a bridle on: *bridle a horse.* **2.** To control with or as if with a bridle: *Bridle your temper!* **3.** To lift the head and draw in the chin as an expression of scorn, resentment, etc.: *bridle with anger.* ¶*These sound alike* **bridle, bridal.** [SEE PICTURE]

bridle path. A path for horseback riding.

brief |brēf| *adj.* **brief•er, brief•est. 1.** Short in time or duration: *a brief period; a brief description.* **2.** Short in length: *a brief report.* —*n.* **1.** A lawyer's summary of the facts relating to a case or argument. **2. briefs.** Short, tight-fitting underpants. —*v.* To give detailed instructions, information, or advice to: *The squadron commander briefed the pilots before the raid. The staff briefed the President inadequately for the conference.* —**brief′ly** *adv.* —**brief′ness** *n.*

Idiom. **in brief.** In summary; in a few words.

brief•case |brēf′kās′| *n.* A portable case of leather or similar material, used for carrying books, papers, etc.

brief•ing |brē′fĭng| *n.* **1.** The act or procedure of giving or receiving detailed instructions, information, or advice: *He arrives in the morning to give the President an intelligence briefing.* **2.** The instructions, information, or advice conveyed during a briefing.

bri•er[1] |brī′ər| *n.* A thorny shrub, especially a prickly-stemmed rosebush. [SEE NOTE]

bri•er[2] |brī′ər| *n.* A form of the word **briar** (shrub with woody root). [SEE NOTE]

brig[1] |brĭg| *n.* A two-masted square-rigged sailing ship carrying two or more headsails and a spanker. [SEE NOTE]

brig[2] |brĭg| *n.* **1.** A ship's prison. **2.** In military slang, any guardhouse. [SEE NOTE]

bri•gade |brĭ gād′| *n.* **1.** A large army unit. **2.** A unit of the U.S. Army composed of two or more regiments. **3.** Any large group organized for a specific purpose: *a fire brigade.*

briar/brier

The words **briar** *and* **brier** *are often confused because they sound alike and are both the names of shrubs. But neither the shrubs nor their names are related in any way.* **Briar** *comes from French* bruyère, *and* **brier** *from Old English* brēr. *It is just an unfortunate coincidence.*

bridge[1-2]

Bridge[1] *is an Old English word, originally* brycg. *The game of* **bridge**[2] *first developed in the late nineteenth century in eastern Europe. The word was originally* biritch *and probably comes from Russian* birich, *"caller, official announcer."*

bridle

brig[1-2], **etc.**

All of the words beginning with brig- *(except* **bright***) are related. The medieval Italian word* brigare, *"to fight," had two derivatives: (1)* brigata, *"a troop of soldiers," and (2)* brigante, *"a lightly armed soldier," also "an armed robber, a bandit."* Brigata *was borrowed into Old French as* brigade *and thence into English as* **brigade** *(hence* **brigadier***).* Brigante *was borrowed into Old French as* brigand *and thence into English as* **brigand**. *From* brigante *also was formed the Italian word* brigantino, *"light and fast sailing ship," also "pirate ship." This was borrowed into Old French as* brigandin, brigantine *and thence into English as* **brigantine**. **Brig**[1] *is a shortening of* **brigantine**. **Brig**[2] *is probably from* **brig**[1].

brig•a•dier |brĭg'ə dîr'| *n.* Also **brigadier general.** A general of the lowest rank.

brig•and |brĭg'ənd| *n.* A member of a roving band of robbers.

brig•an•tine |brĭg'ən tēn'| *n.* A kind of two-masted sailing ship similar to a brig.

bright |brīt| *adj.* **bright•er, bright•est. 1.** Emitting or reflecting light readily or in large amounts; shining: *the bright sun shining through the branches; bright brass knobs; bright, sparkling jewels; bright black eyes.* **2.** Containing little or no black, white, or gray; vivid or intense: *a bright green; bright colors.* **3.** Bathed in or exposed to a brilliant, steady light: *a very cold, bright day.* **4.** Quick-witted; smart: *a bright, attractive little boy; a bright idea.* **5.** Happy; cheerful: *a bright, smiling face; a bright tune.* **6.** Promising: *a bright future.* **—bright'ly** *adv.*

bright•en |brīt'n| *v.* **1.** To make or become bright or brighter: *Sunlight brightened the room. Some stars brighten and dim regularly.* **2.** To make or become happy or more cheerful: *Praise usually brightens a person's day. The four young faces brightened at her approach.*

bright•ness |brīt'nĭs| *n.* **1.** The condition or quality of being bright. **2.** The measure of how bright an object or color is.

Bright's disease |brīts|. A prolonged inflammation of the kidneys; chronic nephritis. [SEE NOTE]

Bright's disease
This disease was first described by Richard Bright *(1789–1858), British physician.*

bril•liant |brĭl'yənt| *adj.* **1. a.** Shining brightly; glittering: *A brilliant sun blazed in the sky.* **b.** Bathed in light; luminous: *The day will be cold but brilliant.* **2.** Very vivid in color: *The sky was a brilliant blue.* **3.** Extremely intelligent or inventive: *a brilliant man; a brilliant political campaign.* **4.** Splendid; magnificent: *the brilliant court life of Versailles.* **5.** Excellent; wonderful: *a brilliant article; a brilliant performance.* **6. a.** Clear and penetrating, as a musical sound: *The trumpet has a firm, brilliant tone.* **b.** Very rich in quality; sparkling: *Romantic composers created a world of brilliant orchestral color.* —*n.* A diamond or other precious gem cut so that it catches the light and sparkles. **—bril'liance, bril'lian•cy** *n.* **—bril'liant•ly** *adv.*

brim |brĭm| *n.* **1.** The rim or uppermost edge of a cup, glass, etc. **2.** A rim on a hat that stands out around the crown. —*v.* **brimmed, brim•ming.** To be full to or as if to the brim; to be full almost to the point of overflowing: *In Imperial Rome fountains brimmed with free water for Rome's inhabitants. Her eyes were brimming with mischief.*

brim•ful |brĭm'fo͝ol'| *adj.* Full to or as if to the brim; completely full: *a glass brimful of milk; a boy brimful of bright ideas.*

brim•stone |brĭm'stōn'| *n.* Sulfur. Used in modern speech and writing only in the phrase **fire and brimstone,** used to suggest the atmosphere of hell.

brin•dle |brĭn'dl| *adj.* Tan, brown, or gray with darker streaks or spots: *a brindle cow; a bulldog with a brindle coat.* —*n.* A combination of tan, brown, or gray with darker streaks or spots.

brin•dled |brĭn'dld| *adj.* Brindle.

brine |brīn| *n.* **1.** Water that contains a large amount of dissolved salt, especially sodium chloride. **2.** The ocean or sea. **3.** Salt water used for preserving or pickling foods.

bring |brĭng| *v.* **brought** |brôt|, **bring•ing. 1.** To take with oneself to a place; carry along or escort: *Bring the books upstairs. Bring me a glass of water. Soldiers were sent to bring the prisoner back for questioning.* **2. a.** To cause to appear: *His account brought into view the details of the accident.* **b.** To be accompanied by: *A cool wind brings cooler weather.* **c.** To cause to occur or happen; result in: *an accident that may bring injury. The flood brought death to thousands. A weak ruler can bring disaster for a nation.* **3.** To sell for: *Diamonds always bring high prices.* **4.** To succeed in persuading; convince: *He could not bring himself to tell her the sad news.* **5.** To call to mind; recall: *bring back memories; bring the past vividly to life.* **6.** To act upon or treat in such a way as to put into a specified situation, location, or condition: *a fox brought to bay by hounds. Something had to be done to bring the West closer to the rest of the nation. Cover and bring the solution to a boil.* **7.** To put forward (a legal action, charges, etc.) against someone in court: *bring suit.* **—phrasal verbs. bring about.** To cause to happen: *Cotton helped bring about the success of Virginia and other Southern colonies.* **bring around. 1.** To cause to adopt an opinion or course of action: *Many threats finally brought him around.* **2.** To cause to recover consciousness. **bring down. 1. a.** To lower: *The merchants had to bring their prices down.* **b.** To cause to fall or collapse: *The revolution brought down the monarchy.* **2.** To kill: *He could bring down a bear with one shot.* **3.** To cause (anger, punishment, etc.) to fall: *The rebellion brought down the king's wrath upon their heads.* **bring forth.** To bear (fruit or young). **bring forward.** To produce; present: *Can you bring forward any proof of your statement?* **bring in. 1.** To give or submit (a verdict): *The jury brought in a verdict of not guilty.* **2.** To produce or yield (profits or income): *Their annual sales bring in ten million dollars.* **bring off.** To accomplish successfully: *The composer brought off a great success with his new opera.* **bring on.** To result in; cause: *The abuse heaped upon him during the trial brought on a stroke of paralysis.* **bring out. 1.** To reveal or expose: *Notice the different ideas one word can bring out.* **2.** To produce or publish: *The company is bringing out new items.* **bring up. 1.** To take care of and educate (a child); rear: *The nurse was careful to bring them up as befitted their royal rank.* **2.** To introduce into discussion; mention: *bring up a subject.* [SEE NOTE]

bring/brought
The past tense of **bring,** *like many "irregular" features in any language, is a survival of what was once a regular system in an earlier stage of the language. In Old English,* **bring, brought** *were* bringan, brohte, *and in the prehistoric Germanic language they were* brengan, brankhta. *The internal change of the vowel from* e *to* a *was a normal system of verb inflection in Germanic and other Indo-European languages. In modern English, the system has been entirely replaced, and the past tense of a verb is regularly formed by adding* -ed *to the present stem, except in old native verbs like* **bring, sing,** *etc.*

brink |brĭngk| *n.* **1.** The upper edge of a steep place: *the brink of the crater.* **2.** The verge of something: *on the brink of extinction; at the brink of war.*

brin•y |brī'nē| *adj.* **brin•i•er, brin•i•est.** Of or like brine; salty.

bri•quette or **bri•quet** |brĭ kĕt'| *n.* A block of compressed coal dust or charcoal, used for fuel.

brisk |brĭsk| *adj.* **brisk•er, brisk•est. 1.** Moving or acting quickly; lively; energetic: *a brisk walk; his wife, brisk despite her years.* **2.** Very active; not sluggish: *a brisk demand for books. Business is brisk.* **3.** Fresh and invigorating: *a brisk morning.* **—brisk'ly** *adv.* **—brisk'ness** *n.*

bris•ket |brĭs'kĭt| *n.* **1.** The chest of an animal. **2.** Meat from this part.

bris•ling |brĭs'lĭng| *n.* A small sardine.

bris•tle |brĭs'əl| *n.* A short, coarse, stiff hair or

ă pat/ā pay/â care/ä father/ĕ pet/ ē be/ĭ pit/ī pie/î fierce/ŏ pot/ ō go/ô paw, for/oi oil/o͝o book/ o͞o boot/ou out/ŭ cut/û fur/ *th* the/th thin/hw which/zh vision/ ə ago, item, pencil, atom, circus

hairlike part. —*v.* **bris•tled, bris•tling. 1.** To raise the bristles stiffly: *The dog bristled and showed his teeth.* **2.** To stand out stiffly like bristles: *His short hair bristled.* **3.** To show sudden anger or annoyance: *The boy bristled at being called a name.* **4.** To be thick with or as if with bristles or bristlelike projections: *a notebook that bristles with information. The path bristled with thorns.*

brist•ly |brĭs′lē| *adj.* **brist•li•er, brist•li•est. 1.** Of, like, or having bristles. **2.** Easily angered or irritated: *a bristly disposition.*

Brit. Britain; British.

Brit•ain |brĭt′n|. **Great Britain.** [SEE NOTE]

Bri•tan•nia |brĭ tăn′yə| *or* |-tăn′ē ə|. **1.** A poetic name for Great Britain. **2.** A female personification of Great Britain.

britch•es |brĭch′ĭz| *pl.n. Informal.* Breeches. ***Idiom.* too big for (one's) britches.** *Informal.* Overconfident; cocky; arrogant.

Brit•i•cism |brĭt′ĭ sĭz′əm| *n.* A word, phrase, or idiom characteristic of or peculiar to British English.

Brit•ish |brĭt′ĭsh| *n.* **1. the British** *(used with a plural verb).* The people of Great Britain. **2.** The Celtic language of the ancient Britons. —*adj.* Of Great Britain, the British, or their language.

British Co•lum•bi•a |kə lŭm′bē ə|. The westernmost province of Canada, bordering in the west on the Pacific Ocean and Alaska. Population, 2,466,608. Capital, Victoria.

British English. English as spoken in Great Britain.

British Isles. Great Britain, Ireland, and adjacent smaller islands.

British thermal unit. The amount of heat that is needed to raise the temperature of one pound of water by one degree Fahrenheit. This unit is used mainly to measure heat, but it can be applied to any form of energy. [SEE NOTE]

British Virgin Islands. See **Virgin Islands.**

Brit•on |brĭt′n| *n.* **1.** A native or inhabitant of Great Britain. **2.** A member of the Celtic people of ancient Britain.

Brit•ta•ny |brĭt′n ē|. A region of northwestern France.

brit•tle |brĭt′l| *adj.* Likely to break because of inelasticity and hardness; easily snapped: *brittle bones.* —*n.* A hard candy made of browned sugar and nuts. —**brit′tle•ness** *n.*

broach |brōch| *v.* **1.** To talk or write about for the first time; begin to discuss: *He did not know how to broach the subject tactfully.* **2.** To pierce in order to draw off liquid: *He broached the keg.* —*n.* **1.** A tool used to shape or enlarge a hole. **2.** A spit for roasting meat. ¶*These sound alike* **broach, brooch.**

broad |brôd| *adj.* **broad•er, broad•est. 1.** Wide from side to side. **2.** Large in expanse; spacious. **3.** Clear; bright: *broad daylight; the broad gold wake of the afternoon.* **4.** Covering a wide scope; general: *a broad vocabulary; a broad topic.* **5.** Main or essential: *the broad sense of a word.* **6.** Plain and obvious: *a broad hint.* **7.** Liberal; tolerant: *a man of broad views.* **8.** Coarse; vulgar: *a broad joke.* **9.** Indicating the sound of *a* as it is pronounced when the *a* in *bath* or *ask* is pronounced like the *a* in *father.* —*n.* The broad part of something. —**broad′ness** *n.*

broad•ax, broad•axe |brôd′ăks′| *n.* An ax with a wide, flat head and a short handle, used as a weapon or for cutting timber.

broad•band |brôd′bănd′| *adj.* Of, having, or relating to a wide band of electromagnetic frequencies.

broad•cast |brôd′kăst′| *or* |-käst′| *v.* **broad•cast** or **broad•cast•ed, broad•cast•ing. 1.** To transmit over a wide area by radio or television: *The station broadcasts from noon to midnight. All the networks will broadcast his speech.* **2.** To make known over a wide area: *broadcast everything he overheard; broadcast emotional states by facial expressions.* **3.** To sow (seed) over a wide area; scatter. —*n.* **1.** A radio or television program or transmission. **2.** The act of scattering seed. —*adj.* **1.** Of transmission by radio or television: *Broadcast time is limited.* **2.** Scattered over a wide area. —*adv.* In a scattered manner; far and wide. —**broad′cast′er** *n.*

broad•cast•ing |brôd′kăs′tĭng| *or* |-kä′stĭng| *n.* The transmitting of programs by radio or television. —***modifier:*** *a broadcasting system.*

broad•cloth |brôd′klôth′| *or* |-klŏth′| *n.* **1.** A fine woolen cloth with a smooth, glossy texture. **2.** A closely woven silk, cotton, or synthetic cloth with a narrow rib, resembling poplin. —***modifier:*** *a broadcloth dress.*

broad•en |brôd′n| *v.* **1.** To make or become broad or broader: *broaden a street. The thruway broadens at the toll gates.* **2.** To extend the limits of: *broaden the scope of your reading.*

broad jump. 1. A jump made for distance rather than height, either from a standing position or a moving start. **2.** A contest in which participants perform such a jump.

broad-leaf |brôd′lēf′| *adj.* Broad-leaved.

broad-leafed |brôd′lēft′| *adj.* Broad-leaved.

broad-leaved |brôd′lēvd′| *adj.* Having comparatively broad leaves rather than narrow, needlelike leaves like those of the pines and related trees: *broad-leaved evergreens such as holly and rhododendron.*

broad•loom |brôd′lo͞om′| *adj.* Woven on a wide loom, as a rug or carpet. —*n.* A carpet woven on a wide loom.

broad•ly |brôd′lē| *adv.* In a general way: *broadly speaking.*

broad-mind•ed |brôd′mīn′dĭd| *adj.* Having liberal and tolerant views and opinions.

broad•side |brôd′sīd′| *n.* **1.** A ship's side above the water line. **2.** A firing of all the guns on one side of a ship. **3.** An explosive verbal attack. —*adv.* **1.** With the side turned toward a specified object: *The tugs were broadside to the big ocean liner.* **2.** On or along the side facing: *The wave caught them broadside and filled the canoe.*

broad•sword |brôd′sôrd′| *or* |-sōrd′| *n.* A sword with a broad blade for cutting rather than thrusting. [SEE PICTURE]

broad•tail |brôd′tāl′| *n.* The flat, glossy, rippled fur made from the pelt of a prematurely born Asian lamb. —***modifier:*** *a broadtail coat.*

Broad•way |brôd′wā′| *n.* **1.** A street in New York City, extending the entire length of Manhattan Island, noted for the theatrical district located at or near its midtown section. **2.** This theater district. **3.** The American theater industry: *He's been in movies and on Broadway.* —***modifier:*** *a Broadway musical.*

Britain

Britain *is the ancient and geographic name of the largest island of the British Isles. It is the only correct name (except for the poetic name* **Albion***) to use for the land before 800* A.D. *It is also the usual short name for* **Great Britain** *as a nation. See also note at* **England.**

British thermal unit

Since it was found to be difficult to measure the **British thermal unit** *in experiments and to relate it to other units, it was redefined in terms of electrical units. One British thermal unit equals about 1/3 watt-hour.*

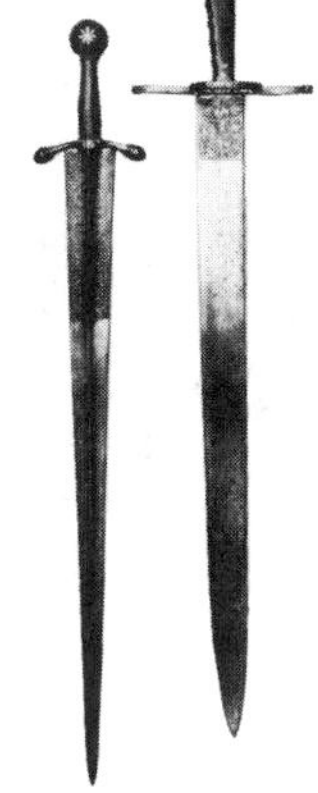

broadsword
Sixteenth-century German

brogue[1·2]
A **brogue[2]** *was formerly a crude rawhide shoe worn by country people in Ireland. The word comes from Gaelic* brōg. **Brogue[1]** *is probably the same word. Compare the American word* leatherstocking, *used in the early nineteenth century as a name for hunters and backwoodsmen who wore deerskin leggings.*

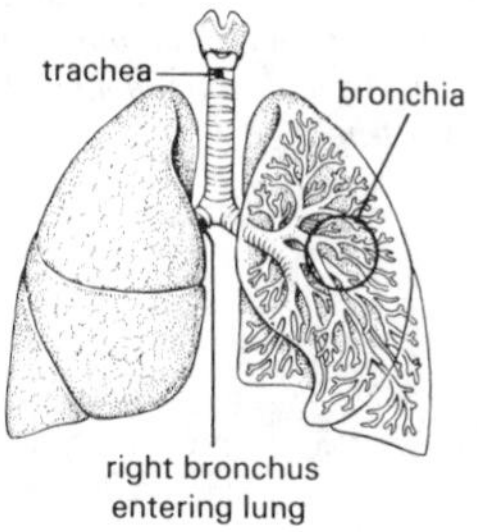

bronchus

brontosaur

ă pat/ā pay/â care/ä father/ĕ pet/ ē be/ĭ pit/ī pie/î fierce/ŏ pot/ ō go/ô paw, for/oi oil/o͝o book/ o͞o boot/ou out/ŭ cut/û fur/ *th* the/th thin/hw which/zh vision/ ə ago, item, pencil, atom, circus

bro·cade |brō kād′| *n.* A heavy cloth with a rich, raised design woven into it, often with threads of silver, gold, or colored silk. —*modifier: a brocade dress.* —*v.* **bro·cad·ed, bro·cad·ing.** To weave with a raised design. —**bro·cad′ed** *adj.: brocaded draperies.*

broc·co·li |brŏk′ə lē| *n.* A plant closely related to the cauliflower and cabbage, having green, densely clustered flower buds and stalks eaten as a vegetable.

bro·chure |brō sho͝or′| *n.* A small pamphlet or booklet.

bro·gan |brō′gən| *n.* A heavy work shoe coming to the ankle.

brogue[1] |brōg| *n.* A strong dialectal accent, especially an Irish accent. [See Note]

brogue[2] |brōg| *n.* A heavy oxford shoe with rows of tiny holes on top for decoration. [See Note]

broil |broil| *v.* **1.** To cook close to direct heat: *She broiled the fish. The fish broiled for ten minutes.* **2.** To expose or become exposed to great heat: *The desert sun broiled the men in the caravan. The tourists broiled under the tropical sun.* —**broiled′** *adj.: a broiled chicken.* —**broil′ing** *adj.: a broiling sun.*

broil·er |broi′lər| *n.* **1.** A pan or grill for broiling. **2.** The part of a stove used for broiling. **3.** A young chicken suitable for broiling.

broke |brōk|. Past tense of **break.** —*adj. Informal.* Lacking money.

bro·ken |brō′kən|. Past participle of **break.** —*adj.* **1.** Shattered or fractured: *broken pieces; a broken leg.* **2.** Out of order; not functioning: *a broken watch.* **3.** Not kept; violated: *a broken promise.* **4.** Spoken imperfectly: *broken English.* **5.** Overwhelmed, as by sadness, hardship, etc.: *a broken heart; a broken spirit.* **6.** Divided and disrupted by change: *a broken home.* **7.** Stopping and starting at intervals; having gaps; not continuous: *a broken line on a highway.* **8.** Lacking parts; not complete: *a broken set of books.* **9.** Rough; uneven: *patches of broken ground.*

bro·ken-down |brō′kən doun′| *adj.* **1.** In poor condition, as from old age: *a broken-down horse.* **2.** Out of working order: *a broken-down car.*

bro·ken·heart·ed |brō′kən här′tĭd| *adj.* Overwhelmed with grief or dispair.

bro·ker |brō′kər| *n.* A person who buys or sells stocks, real estate, etc., for another, receiving a fee or commission in return.

bro·ker·age |brō′kər ĭj| *n.* **1.** The business of a broker. **2.** The fee paid to a broker.

bro·me·li·ad |brō mē′lē ăd′| *n.* One of several related plants, such as the pineapple or Spanish moss, that often grow on trees, rocks, etc., with their roots exposed to the air.

bro·mide |brō′mīd′| *n.* **1.** A chemical compound of bromine and another element or a radical. **2.** A compound of this kind containing bromine and a metal such as potassium or sodium, used as a sedative.

bro·mine |brō′mēn′| *n.* Symbol **Br** One of the elements, a heavy, reddish-brown liquid with irritating fumes. Atomic number 35; atomic weight 79.91; valences -1, $+1$, $+3$, $+5$, $+7$; melting point -7.2°C; boiling point 58.78°C.

bron·chi |brŏng′kī′| *or* |-kē′| *n.* Plural of **bronchus.**

bron·chi·a |brŏng′kē ə| *pl.n.* The less frequently used singular is **bron·chi·um** |brŏng′kē əm|. Bronchial tubes that are smaller than the bronchi and larger than bronchioles.

bron·chi·al |brŏng′kē əl| *adj.* Of the bronchi, the bronchia, or the bronchioles.

bronchial tube. A bronchus or any of its branches.

bron·chi·ole |brŏng′kē ōl′| *n.* Any of the fine, thin-walled tubes into which the bronchi divide.

bron·chi·tis |brŏng kī′tĭs| *n.* Inflammation of the mucous membrane of the bronchial tubes. —**bron·chit′ic** |-kĭt′ĭk| *adj.*

bron·chi·um |brŏng′kē əm| *n.* Singular of **bronchia.**

bron·cho·scope |brŏng′kə skōp′| *n.* A slender tube with a small light on the end, used to examine the inside of the bronchi.

bron·chus |brŏng′kəs| *n., pl.* **bron·chi** |brŏng′kī′| *or* |-kē′|. Either of the tubes into which the trachea divides, leading directly to the lungs. [See Picture]

bron·co |brŏng′kō| *n., pl.* **bron·cos.** A small wild or half-wild horse of western North America.

bron·co·bust·er |brŏng′kō bŭs′tər| *n.* A cowboy who breaks wild horses to the saddle.

bron·to·saur |brŏn′tə sôr′| *n.* A very large dinosaur that lived in swamps and streams and fed on plants. [See Picture]

bron·to·sau·rus |brŏn′tə sôr′əs| *n.* A brontosaur.

bronze |brŏnz| *n.* **1.** Any of various alloys of copper that usually contain tin, sometimes with small amounts of other elements such as antimony and phosphorus. **2.** A work of art made of bronze. **3.** A yellowish or olive brown. —*modifier: bronze tools; a bronze statue.* —*adj.* Yellowish or olive brown. —*v.* **bronzed, bronz·ing.** To make or become like bronze: *Do they still bronze baby shoes? The sun bronzed their faces. Her skin bronzes easily.* —**bronzed′** *adj.: a bronzed skin.* —**bronz′y** *adj.*

Bronze Age. The period in human history between the Stone Age and the Iron Age, marked by the use of bronze implements and weapons. In Europe, it extended roughly from 3500 B.C. to 1000 B.C.

brooch |brōch| *or* |bro͞och| *n.* A large pin worn as an ornament, fastened to the clothing with a clasp. ¶ *These sound alike* **brooch, broach.**

brood |bro͞od| *n.* **1.** A group, as of young birds, hatched from eggs laid at the same time by the same mother. **2.** The children in one family: *The little house was too small for the Bensons' active brood.* —*v.* **1.** To sit on and hatch (eggs). **2.** To think at length and unhappily; worry anxiously: *She brooded about her failure.*

brood·er |bro͞o′dər| *n.* **1.** Someone or something that broods. **2.** A heated enclosure in which young chickens are raised.

brood·ing |bro͞o′dĭng| *adj.* Gloomy; depressing: *the old, dark castle with its brooding shadows.* —**brood′ing·ly** *adv.*

brood·y |bro͞o′dē| *adj.* **brood·i·er, brood·i·est.** **1.** Sad and thoughtful; moody. **2.** Inclined to sit on eggs to hatch them: *a broody hen.*

brook[1] |bro͝ok| *n.* A small, natural stream of fresh water. —*modifier: brook water; a brook trout.* [See Note on p. 117]

brook[2] |bro͝ok| *v.* To tolerate: *scarcely in the mood to brook delay.* [SEE NOTE]

broom |bro͞om| *or* |bro͝om| *n.* **1.** A device for sweeping, usually consisting of strands of straw bound together and attached to a long stick. **2.** A shrub with yellow flowers, small leaves, and many straight, slender branches. *—**modifier:** a broom closet; a broom handle.* ¶ *These sound alike* **broom, brougham.**

broom•corn |**bro͞om′**kôrn′| *or* |**bro͝om′**-| *n.* A grass with stiff, branching stalks that are used to make brooms and brushes.

broom•stick |**bro͞om′**stĭk′| *or* |**bro͝om′**-| *n.* The long handle of a broom.

broth |brôth| *or* |brŏth| *n.* **1.** The water in which meat, fish, or vegetables have been boiled; stock. **2.** A clear soup made from this stock.

broth•er |**brŭ*th*′**ər| *n.* **1.** A boy or man having the same mother and father as another person. **2. a.** A kindred human being; a fellow man. **b.** A fellow member of a group, such as a profession or fraternity. **3.** A member of a men's Christian religious order who is not a priest.

broth•er•hood |**brŭ*th*′**ər ho͝od′| *n.* **1.** The relationship of being a brother or brothers. **2.** Brotherly feelings or friendship toward other human beings; fellowship: *Martin Luther King, Jr., was awarded the Nobel Peace Prize because of his contribution to the cause of human brotherhood.* **3.** A group of men united for a common purpose; a fraternity, labor union, etc.

broth•er-in-law |**brŭ*th*′**ər ĭn lô′| *n., pl.* **broth•ers-in-law. 1.** The brother of one's husband or wife. **2.** The husband of one's sister. **3.** The husband of the sister of one's husband or wife.

broth•er•ly |**brŭ*th*′**ər lē| *adj.* Of or appropriate to brothers; affectionate. —**broth′er•li•ness** *n.*

brougham |bro͞om| *or* |**bro͞o′**əm| *or* |**brō′**əm| *n.* A closed automobile or a four-wheeled carriage with an open driver's seat. ¶ *These sound alike* **brougham, broom.**

brought |brôt|. Past tense and past participle of **bring.** [SEE NOTE on p. 114]

brow |brou| *n.* **1.** The forehead. **2.** Either of the lines of hair growing above the eyes; an eyebrow. **3.** An expression of the face: *a puzzled brow.* **4.** The upper edge of a steep place: *the brow of a precipice.*

brow•beat |**brou′**bēt′| *v.* **brow•beat, brow•beat•en** |**brou′**bēt′n|, **brow•beat•ing.** To bully or intimidate, as with a domineering manner.

brown |broun| *n.* The color of chocolate, coffee, or most kinds of soil. *—adj.* **brown•er, brown•est. 1.** Of the color brown. **2.** Suntanned. *—v.* **1.** To make or become brown: *Mud browned the river. The river browned after the rain.* **2.** To cook until brown on the outside: *He browned the meat. Meat browns quickly.*

brown Bet•ty |**bĕt′**ē|. Also **brown betty.** A baked pudding of apples, bread crumbs, brown sugar, butter, and spices.

brown coal. Lignite.

Brown•i•an motion |**brou′**nē ən|. The rapid, irregular movements made by tiny particles suspended in a liquid or gas, caused by collisions with molecules of the surrounding liquid or gas. [SEE NOTE]

brown•ie |**brou′**nē| *n.* **1.** In folklore, a small, elflike creature, said to perform household chores while people are asleep. **2.** A rich, chewy chocolate cooky with nuts.

Brown•ie |**brou′**nē| *n.* A junior Girl Scout. *—**modifier:** a Brownie troop.* [SEE PICTURE]

brown•ish |**brou′**nĭsh| *adj.* Somewhat brown.

brown•out |**broun′**out′| *n.* **1.** A dimming or partial concealment of the lights in a city, especially as a defense against air raids. **2.** A partial stoppage or loss: *an electric power brownout.*

brown•stone |**broun′**stōn′| *n.* **1.** A brownish-red sandstone once widely used as a building material. **2.** A house built or faced with such stone.

brown study. A state of deep thought or melancholy.

brown sugar. Unrefined or partially refined sugar with a flavor similar to that of molasses.

browse |brouz| *v.* **browsed, brows•ing. 1. a.** To inspect in a leisurely and casual way: *browse through a book.* **b.** To look over goods in a store casually without seriously intending to buy them: *browse around in a department store.* **2.** To feed on leaves, young shoots, twigs, and other plants. *—n.* Vegetation, such as leaves, young shoots, and twigs, eaten by animals: *Very little browse is available during blizzards.* —**brows′er** *n.*

bru•in |**bro͞o′**ĭn| *n.* A name or nickname for a bear. [SEE NOTE]

bruise |bro͞oz| *n.* **1.** An injury in which small blood vessels in the skin are broken by pressure or a blow, producing discoloration but leaving the skin itself unbroken. **2.** A similar injury to a fruit, plant, or vegetable. *—v.* **bruised, bruis•ing. 1.** To make a bruise or bruises on. **2.** To become discolored as a result of a bruise: *Her skin bruises easily.* **3.** To hurt psychologically; offend: *bruise someone's feelings.*

bruis•er |**bro͞o′**zər| *n. Slang.* A large, beefy man.

bruit |bro͞ot| *v.* To spread news of; repeat: *The rumor was bruited about all over town.* ¶ *These sound alike* **bruit, brute.**

brunch |brŭnch| *n.* A meal eaten late in the morning as breakfast and lunch.

Bru•nei |**bro͞o′**nī′|. A country of southeastern Asia, occupying part of northwest Borneo. Population, 213,000. Capital, Bandar Seri Begawan.

bru•net |bro͞o **nĕt′**| *adj.* Dark or brown in color: *brunet hair.* *—n.* A person, especially a man or boy, with dark or brown hair.

bru•nette |bro͞o **nĕt′**| *adj.* Having dark or brown hair: *Is she blonde or brunette?* *—n.* A girl or woman with dark or brown hair.

brunt |brŭnt| *n.* The main impact, force, or burden: *They bore the brunt of the attack.*

brush[1] |brŭsh| *n.* **1.** An implement consisting of bristles, hairs, or wire fastened to a handle, for use in scrubbing, applying paint, or grooming the hair. **2.** An application of a brush. **3.** Something that resembles a brush, as the bushy tail of a fox. **4.** A brief, sharp fight; a skirmish: *frequent brushes with the law.* **5.** A light touch in passing; a graze. **6.** An electrically conductive part, generally of graphite, that makes rubbing or sliding contact with another part, such as a commutator, and completes a circuit, as in a motor or generator. *—**modifier:** brush strokes; a brush handle.* *—v.* **1. a.** To clean, polish, sweep, or groom with a brush. **b.** To be capable of being brushed: *The caked mud brushed off the mat easily.*

brook[1-2]

Brook[1] *and* **brook[2]** *are both native Old English words. The stream was* brōc, *and the verb was* brūcan, *which originally meant "to enjoy."*

Brownian motion

Brownian motion *was first described by Robert* Brown *(1773–1858), a Scottish botanist.*

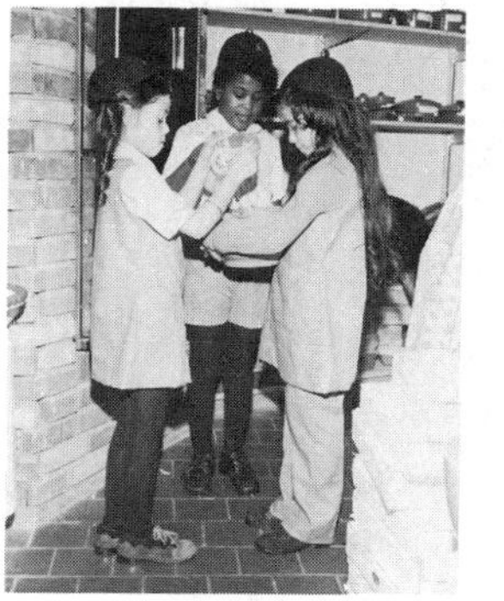

Brownie

bruin

Bruin *is the Dutch word for "brown," and the word* **bear[2]** *itself originally meant "the brown one." These are both examples of a kind of taboo in which people avoided saying the "real" name of an animal by using a substitute. The taboo is connected with ancient hunting magic: If the hunter mentions the animal's true name, the animal spirit can hear him.*

brush[1-2]

Brush[2] *is from Old French* broce, *"twigs, brushwood."* **Brush[1]** *is from Old French* brosse, *"a broom or brush," which is probably a variant of the same* broce, *since brooms and brushes have often been made of twigs.*

Brussels sprouts

buck[1-2-3-4]

Buck[1] *is from Old English* buc, *"stag";* **buck[2]**, **buck[3]**, *and* **buck[4]** *are Americanisms derived indirectly from* **buck[1]**. *In early pioneering days, deerskins were used as a unit of barter among Indians and traders, and they were often called* bucks, *for* buckskins; *this seems to have produced the later slang expression* **buck[2]**, *meaning "a dollar."* **Buck[3]** *is probably from sense 3 of* **buck[1]**. **Buck[4]** *comes from the poker games of the old West, where a* buckhorn knife *was customarily moved around the table to indicate who was to be the next dealer.*

ă pat/ā pay/â care/ä father/ĕ pet/ ē be/ĭ pit/ī pie/î fierce/ŏ pot/ ō go/ô paw, for/oi oil/o͝o book/ o͞o boot/ou out/ŭ cut/û fur/ *th* the/th thin/hw which/zh vision/ ə ago, item, pencil, atom, circus

2. To apply with a brush. **3.** To remove with or as if with a brush: *brush the dirt off one's jacket.* **4.** To pay little or no attention to; dismiss abruptly: *brush the matter aside. He impatiently brushed away the news of the war.* **5.** To touch lightly in passing: *His arm brushed hers in the hall. A heavy body brushed against him.* —***phrasal verb.*** **brush up.** To refresh one's knowledge of a certain subject. [SEE NOTE]

brush[2] |brŭsh| *n.* **1. a.** A dense growth of shrubs or small trees. **b.** Land covered with such growth. **2.** Broken-off branches; brushwood. —***modifier:*** *a brush fire.* [SEE NOTE]

brush•land |**brŭsh'**lănd'| *n.* Land with a dense growth of shrubs or small trees.

brush-off |**brŭsh'**ôf'| *or* |-ŏf'| *n. Slang.* An abrupt dismissal.

brush•wood |**brŭsh'**wo͝od'| *n.* **1.** Cut or broken-off branches. **2.** A dense growth of shrubs or small trees; a brush.

brush•work |**brŭsh'**wûrk'| *n.* **1.** Work done with a brush. **2.** The way in which a painter applies paint with a brush.

brusque |brŭsk| *adj.* Rudely abrupt in manner or speech; curt; blunt. —**brusque'ly** *adv.* —**brusque'ness** *n.*

Brus•sels |**brŭs'**əlz|. The capital and largest city of Belgium. Population, 1,075,000.

Brussels sprouts. **1.** A type of cabbage that has small, budlike heads growing from a thick stalk. **2.** The heads of this plant, eaten as a vegetable. [SEE PICTURE]

bru•tal |**bro͞ot'**l| *adj.* Like a brute; cruel; harsh. —**bru'tal•ly** *adv.*

bru•tal•i•ty |bro͞o **tăl'**ĭ tē| *n., pl.* **bru•tal•i•ties.** **1.** The condition or quality of being brutal. **2.** A brutal act.

bru•tal•ize |**bro͞ot'**l īz'| *v.* **bru•tal•ized, bru•tal•iz•ing.** **1.** To make brutal: *Hardships and fatigue brutalized the soldiers.* **2.** To treat brutally.

brute |bro͞ot| *n.* **1.** An animal as distinct from a man; a beast. **2.** A cruel person; one who lacks humanity. —*adj.* Not involving mental effort; entirely physical: *brute force.* ¶*These sound alike* **brute, bruit.**

brut•ish |**bro͞o'**tĭsh| *adj.* Resembling a brute; coarse: *rough fellows with dirty, brutish faces.* —**brut'ish•ly** *adv.* —**brut'ish•ness** *n.*

Bru•tus |**bro͞o'**təs|, **Marcus Junius.** 85?–42 B.C. Roman political and military leader; participated in the assassination of Julius Caesar.

Bry•an |**brī'**ən|, **William Jennings.** 1860–1925. American lawyer; three times Presidential candidate (1896, 1900, and 1908).

bry•o•phyte |**brī'**ə fīt'| *n.* Any member of a large group of plants that includes the mosses and liverworts.

B.S.A. Boy Scouts of America.

B.Sc. Bachelor of Science.

Btu British thermal unit.

bu, bu. bushel.

bub•ble |**bŭb'**əl| *n.* **1.** A rounded, more or less spherical object composed of a thin, often transparent wall of liquid or plastic material enclosing a pocket of gas. **2.** A small, rounded pocket of gas that rises to the surface of a liquid or remains trapped in a solid or plastic material. **3.** A glass or plastic dome. **4.** Something, such as an idea or plan, that gives early promise of success but suddenly collapses: *In 1929 the bubble burst for investors in stocks.* —*v.* **bub•bled, bub•bling.** **1.** To form, cause to form, or rise in bubbles: *The water bubbled and churned. Gases bubbled from the vat.* **2.** To move or flow with a gurgling sound. **3.** To show activity or emotion in a lively way: *bubbled with energy; bubbling over with fun.*

bubble chamber. A device for detecting the paths of charged atomic particles by observation of the trails of bubbles that they leave in a superheated liquid.

bubble gum. Chewing gum that can be blown into bubbles.

bu•bo |**bo͞o'**bō| *or* |**byo͞o'**-| *n., pl.* **bu•boes.** An inflamed swelling of a lymph node, especially in the armpit or groin.

bu•bon•ic plague |byo͞o **bŏn'**ĭk| *or* |bo͞o-|. A very contagious, usually fatal disease caused by bacteria that are often transmitted to human beings by fleas that have fed on infected rats or other rodents. Its symptoms include chills, fever, vomiting, diarrhea, and inflamed lymph nodes.

buc•ca•neer |bŭk'ə **nîr'**| *n.* A pirate.

Bu•chan•an |byo͞o **kăn'**ən| *or* |bə-|, **James.** 1791–1868. Fifteenth President of the United States (1857–61).

Bu•cha•rest |**bo͞o'**kə rĕst'| *or* |**byo͞o'**-|. The capital and largest city of Rumania. Population, 1,507,000.

buck[1] |bŭk| *n.* **1.** The full-grown male of the deer or of certain other animals, such as the rabbit. **2.** A sudden leap forward and upward, as by a horse or mule. **3.** *Informal.* A high-spirited young man. —*v.* **1.** To leap upward with the head down, especially to throw off a rider: *The bronco bucked and kicked.* **2.** To throw off (a rider) by bucking. **3.** To charge into: *The fullback bucked the opponents' line.* **4.** To contend with or struggle against; oppose: *bucking a 20-knot head wind. Every evening they had to buck heavy traffic to return home.* —***phrasal verb.*** **buck up.** *Informal.* To gather one's courage or raise one's spirits. [SEE NOTE]

buck[2] |bŭk| *n. Slang.* A dollar. [SEE NOTE]

buck[3] |bŭk| *adj.* In military slang, the lowest rank in a specified category: *a buck private.* [SEE NOTE]

buck[4] |bŭk| *n.* A marker formerly placed before a poker player to indicate that he is to be the next dealer. [SEE NOTE]

Idiom. **pass the buck.** To shift responsibility or blame to someone else.

buck•a•roo |bŭk'ə **ro͞o'**| *n.* A cowboy.

buck•board |**bŭk'**bôrd'| *or* |-bōrd'| *n.* An open four-wheeled carriage with the seat attached to a flexible board.

buck•et |**bŭk'**ĭt| *n.* **1.** A round, open container with a curved handle, used for carrying water, coal, sand, etc. **2. a.** A bucket with something in it: *a bucket of water.* **b.** The amount that a bucket holds: *pour a bucket of sand.* **c. buckets.** An unexpectedly great amount or quantity: *The rain came down in buckets.* **3.** Something resembling a bucket, such as the scoop on a steam shovel.

Idiom. **kick the bucket.** *Slang.* To die.

bucket seat. A seat with a rounded, padded back, as in sports cars and airplanes.

buck•eye |**bŭk'**ī'| *n.* **1.** A tree, such as the horse chestnut, with upright reddish or white flower clusters and glossy brown nuts. **2.** The nut of such a tree.

buck•le |bŭk′əl| *n.* **1.** A clasp, usually having a frame and catch, used to fasten one end of a strap or belt to the other. **2.** An ornament that looks like such a clasp, as one on top of a shoe. **3.** A bend, bulge, warp, or other distortion. —*v.* **buck•led, buck•ling. 1.** To fasten with a buckle: *Buckle my sandal. Does your belt buckle or tie?* **2.** To bend, warp, or crumple under pressure or heat: *the ever-changing crust of the earth buckling in some places, rising in others, and sinking in still others. Changing stresses buckled great rock masses along a fault.* **3.** To collapse: *I tried to stand up, but my legs buckled under me.* —***phrasal verb.* buckle down.** To begin working hard and with determination.

buck•ler |bŭk′lər| *n.* A small round shield that is either carried or worn on the arm.

buck•ram |bŭk′rəm| *n.* A coarse cotton cloth stiffened with glue, used for binding books, lining garments, etc.

buck•saw |bŭk′sô′| *n.* A saw usually set in an H-shaped frame, used for cutting wood.

buck•shot |bŭk′shŏt′| *n.* A large lead shot, used in shotgun shells for hunting game.

buck•skin |bŭk′skĭn′| *n.* **1.** A soft, strong leather, grayish yellow in color, made from the skins of deer or sheep. **2. buckskins.** Breeches or shoes made of this leather. —***modifier:*** *buckskin pants.*

buck•tooth |bŭk′tōōth′| *n.* A prominent, projecting upper front tooth.

buck•wheat |bŭk′hwēt′| *or* |-wēt′| *n.* **1.** A plant with small, triangular seeds that are often ground into flour. **2.** The seeds of this plant. —***modifier:*** *buckwheat pancakes; buckwheat crop.*

bu•col•ic |byōō kŏl′ĭk| *adj.* **1.** Of shepherds; pastoral: *bucolic poetry.* **2.** Of country life; rustic: *a bucolic scene.*

bud |bŭd| *n.* **1. a.** A small swelling on a branch or stem, containing an undeveloped flower, shoot, or leaves. **b.** The stage of being a bud or having buds: *roses in bud.* **2.** A small outgrowth on an organism, such as a yeast or hydra, that grows to become a complete new organism. **3.** A stage of early or incomplete development: *That boy is a scientist in the bud.* —*v.* **bud•ded, bud•ding. 1.** To form or produce a bud or buds. **2.** To be in an early stage; begin to develop. —**bud′ding** *adj.: a budding scientist.*

Bu•da•pest |bōō′də pĕst′|. The capital and largest city of Hungary, on the Danube River. Population, 2,000,000.

Bud•dha |bōō′də| *or* |bŏŏd′ə|. Title of Guatama Siddhartha. 563?–483? B.C. Indian philosopher and the founder of Buddhism.

Bud•dhism |bōō′dĭz′əm| *or* |bŏŏd′ĭz′-| *n.* **1.** The doctrine, attributed to Buddha, that suffering is inseparable from existence but that one can escape it by entering into a state of perfect bliss called nirvana, achieved by self-purification of the mind and senses. **2.** The religion of parts of Asia represented by the many sects that follow this doctrine. —**Bud′dhist** *n. & adj.*

bud•dy |bŭd′ē| *n., pl.* **bud•dies.** *Informal.* A close friend; comrade.

budge |bŭj| *v.* **budged, budg•ing. 1.** To move or cause to move slightly: *The boulder did not budge. They cannot budge the boulder.* **2.** To alter or cause to alter a position or attitude: *They won't budge on certain points relating to the new contract. After the prime minister had made up his mind, no one could budge him.*

budg•er•i•gar |bŭj′ə rē gär′| *n.* A small green, blue, or yellow parakeet often kept as a pet.

bud•get |bŭj′ĭt| *n.* **1.** An itemized list of probable expenditures and income for a given period, usually showing how the money available is going to be divided up and spent. **2.** The sum of money allotted for a certain purpose or time. —*v.* To plan in advance for the allocation of: *Try to budget your allowance. Make a chart to budget your time more wisely.* —***modifier:*** *a budget book.* —**bud′get•ar′y** |bŭj′ĭ tĕr′ē| *adj.*

budg•ie |bŭj′ē| *n. Informal.* A budgerigar.

Bue•nos Ai•res |bwā′nəs âr′ēz| *or* |īr′ēz| *or* |bō′nəs|. The capital and largest city of Argentina. Population, 6,735,000.

buff¹ |bŭf| *n.* **1.** A soft, thick, yellowish leather made from the skins of buffalo, elk, or oxen. **2.** The color of this leather; a yellowish tan. **3.** An implement covered with soft material and used for polishing. —***modifier:*** *a buff jerkin.* —*adj.* Yellowish tan. —*v.* To polish or shine with a buff. [SEE NOTE]

buff² |bŭf| *n. Informal.* A person who has great interest in, and some knowledge of, a subject: *an opera buff; a railroad buff.* [SEE NOTE]

buf•fa•lo |bŭf′ə lō′| *n., pl.* **buf•fa•loes** or **buf•fa•los** or **buf•fa•lo. 1.** Any of several oxlike African or Asian animals with large, outward-curving horns. **2.** The North American bison. [SEE PICTURE]

Buf•fa•lo |bŭf′ə lō′|. A city of western New York State. Population, 357,870.

buff•er¹ |bŭf′ər| *n.* A tool used to shine or polish. [SEE NOTE]

buff•er² |bŭf′ər| *n.* **1.** Something that lessens or absorbs the shock of a blow or collision: *Use a block of paneling as a buffer for hammering in each piece.* **2.** A substance capable of stabilizing the acidity or alkalinity of a solution, practically neutralizing, within limits, any acid or base that is added. **3.** Something located between two rival powers, lessening the danger of conflict. —***modifier:*** *a buffer state.* —*v.* To treat (a solution) with a buffer. [SEE NOTE]

buf•fet¹ |bə fā′| *or* |bōō-| *n.* **1.** A large sideboard with drawers and cupboards for storing china, silverware, and table linens. **2. a.** A counter from which food is served. **b.** A restaurant with such a counter. **3.** A meal at which guests serve themselves from dishes arranged on a table or sideboard. —***modifier:*** *a buffet supper; a buffet table.* [SEE NOTE]

buf•fet² |bŭf′ĭt| *v.* To strike against forcefully; batter: *The rough sea buffeted the small boat as it passed the reefs.* —*n.* A blow or cuff made with or as if with the hand. [SEE NOTE]

buf•foon |bə fōōn′| *n.* **1.** A clown or jester. **2.** A person who makes coarse jokes. —**buf•foon′er•y** *n.*

bug |bŭg| *n.* **1.** Any of a group of wingless or four-winged insects with sucking mouth parts. **2.** Any insect, spider, or similar creature. **3.** *Informal.* A microorganism that causes disease; a germ. **4.** A fault or defect in a system or device.

buff¹⁻²

Buff¹ *is a shortening of* **buffalo.** *In the early nineteenth century, the unpaid volunteer firemen of New York City, who wore buff coats, became known as* the fire buffs. **Buff²** *is a general extension of this to all other kinds of amateur enthusiasm.*

buffalo

buffer¹⁻²

Buffer¹ *is from the verb* **buff¹** *(to polish).* **Buffer²** *is from an obsolete verb* buff, *meaning "to cushion, to soften the shock of," from the same French source as* **buffet²**.

buffet¹⁻²

Buffet¹ *is from French* buffet, *"a sideboard," of unknown origin.* **Buffet²** *is from the homonymous French word* buffet, *from* buffe, *"a soft blow," which is an onomatopoeic word.*

bugle

5. A hidden electronic device that allows private conversations to be overheard. **6.** *Slang.* An enthusiast; a buff. —*v.* **bugged, bug•ging. 1.** To jut; protrude: *His eyes almost bugged out of his head.* **2.** *Slang.* To annoy; trouble; pester: *Father was bugging me about my poor grades.* **3.** To equip (a room, telephone circuit, etc.) with a concealed electronic listening device.

bug•a•boo |bŭg′ə bo͞o′| *n.* An imaginary or real object of fear.

bug•bear |bŭg′bâr′| *n.* An object of excessive concern or fear.

bug-eyed |bŭg′īd′| *adj. Slang.* Having large, protruding eyes: *bug-eyed monsters.*

bug•gy |bŭg′ē| *n., pl.* **bug•gies. 1.** A small, light carriage drawn by a horse. **2.** A baby carriage.

bu•gle |byo͞o′gəl| *n.* A brass instrument that is similar to a trumpet but mellower in tone and that usually has no valves. —***modifier:*** *a bugle corps.* —*v.* **bu•gled, bu•gling.** To play a bugle. —**bu′gler** *n.* [SEE PICTURE]

build |bĭld| *v.* **built** |bĭlt|, **build•ing. 1.** To make or form by fitting together materials or parts; construct; erect: *build a house. You can build a new word by using a suffix or a prefix with a root word. The architects all built in a different style.* **2.** To be responsible for the building of: *The forests of Sweden and Norway built the prosperity of modern Scandinavia.* **3.** To bring into being or create according to a definite plan, process, etc.: *Iron is used to build hemoglobin. To build strong muscles, you need plenty of exercise.* **4.** To make steadily and gradually; create and add to: *Reading helps you build a richer vocabulary.* **5.** To establish a basis for; found: *You can build your knowledge of their behavior upon the information received. Don't build too many hopes on his promises.* **6.** To develop an idea, theory, etc.: *Discoveries in science are made because scientists build on the work done by other scientists.* **7.** To progress toward a maximum, as of intensity, emotion, etc.: *A good mystery novel builds from the first chapters toward its final climax.* —***phrasal verbs.* build in.** To construct as a permanent part of. **build up. 1.** To construct in stages or by degrees: *When corals die, their skeletons add to others and build up reefs from the bottom of the sea.* **2.** To develop or make steadily and gradually; create and add to: *build up a business. You can build up your vocabulary rapidly if you read a lot.* **3.** To increase, as in size, value, etc.: *an actress noted for building up small roles.* **4.** To cover with buildings: *This area is getting built up.* **5.** To give excessively favorable publicity or praise to: *The press built him up with a series of editorials.* —*n.* The physical make-up of a person or thing: *He was short and broad in build.*

build•ed |bĭl′dĭd|. *Archaic.* A past tense and past participle of **build.**

build•er |bĭl′dər| *n.* **1.** Someone or something that builds: *the builder of a house. A river is a great builder of new land by depositing mud and sand along its lower shores.* **2.** A person who creates or develops something: *a remarkable ruler and empire builder.*

build•ing |bĭl′dĭng| *n.* **1.** Something that is built; any structure such as a house, store, school, etc. **2.** The act, process, or occupation of constructing. —***modifier:*** *a building block.*

build-up, also **build•up** |bĭld′ŭp′| *n.* **1.** The act or process of building up: *the build-up of ashes and lava; the build-up of hate.* **2.** Extravagant praise; widely favorable publicity: *She gave the fund-raising committee a nice build-up.*

built |bĭlt|. Past tense and past participle of **build.**

built-in |bĭlt′ĭn′| *adj.* **1.** Constructed as a nondetachable part of a larger unit: *a built-in cupboard; a built-in safety device.* **2.** Natural; inherent: *a built-in skill; a built-in sense of danger.*

built-up |bĭlt′ŭp′| *adj.* **1.** Made by fastening layers or sections one on top of the other. **2.** Occupied by several buildings: *a built-up urban section.*

Bu•jum•bu•ra |bo͞o′jəm **bo͝or′**ə| *or* |bo͞o **jo͞om′**-bo͝or′ə|. The capital of Burundi. Population, 101,000.

bulb |bŭlb| *n.* **1.** A rounded plant part that develops underground and contains the undeveloped shoots of a new plant that will grow from it. **2.** A rounded part of something: *the bulb of a thermometer; the bulb of a syringe.* **3.** An incandescent lamp or its glass housing. **4.** Any of various rounded structures in the body, especially the medulla oblongata.

bul•bar |bŭl′bər| *or* |-bär′| *adj.* Of, like, or affecting one of the rounded structures of the body, especially the medulla oblongata: *bulbar poliomyelitis.*

bul•bous |bŭl′bəs| *adj.* **1.** Growing from or producing a bulb: *The tulip is a bulbous plant.* **2.** Bulb-shaped: *a bulbous nose.*

Bul•gar•i•a |bŭl **gâr′**ē ə| *or* |bo͝ol-|. A country in southeastern Europe, on the Black Sea. Population, 8,679,000. Capital, Sofia.

Bul•gar•i•an |bŭl **gâr′**ē ən| *or* |bo͝ol-| *n.* **1.** A native or inhabitant of Bulgaria. **2.** The Slavic language of Bulgaria. —*adj.* Of Bulgaria, the Bulgarians, or their language.

bulge |bŭlj| *n.* A protruding part; an outward curve or a swelling: *bulges under their coats indicating pistols; the western bulge of Africa.* —*v.* **bulged, bulg•ing.** To swell or cause to swell beyond the usual size: *His little eyes bulged with surprise. The pair of pistols bulged his coat.* —**bulg′ing** *adj.*: *bulging muscles.*

bulg•y |bŭl′jē| *adj.* **bulg•i•er, bulg•i•est.** Protruding or swelling outward; protuberant. —**bulg′i•ness** *n.*

bulk |bŭlk| *n.* **1.** Great size, mass, or volume: *the whale's monstrous bulk.* **2.** The major portion of something; greater part: *The bulk of the margarine now sold is colored.* —*v.* To be or appear to be great in size or importance; loom: *Sightseeing bulked large in our vacation plans.*

***Idiom.* in bulk.** In a mass; loose: *seeds shipped in bulk.*

bulk•head |bŭlk′hĕd′| *n.* **1.** One of the vertical walls that divide the inside of a ship into compartments. **2.** A wall or embankment, as in a mine or tunnel, built to protect against earth slides, fire, water, or gas.

bulk•y |bŭl′kē| *adj.* **bulk•i•er, bulk•i•est. 1.** Extremely large; massive: *Most of the early reptiles were bulky, slow-moving creatures.* **2.** Taking up much space; clumsy; unwieldy: *a bulky package; bulky clothing.* —**bulk′i•ly** *adv.* —**bulk′i•ness** *n.*

bull[1] |bo͝ol| *n.* **1. a.** The full-grown male of cat-

ă pat/ā pay/â care/ä father/ĕ pet/ ē be/ĭ pit/ī pie/î fierce/ŏ pot/ ō go/ô paw, for/oi oil/o͝o book/ o͞o boot/ou out/ŭ cut/û fur/ *th* the/th thin/hw which/zh vision/ ə ago, item, pencil, atom, circus

tle. **b.** The male of certain other large mammals, such as the elephant or moose. **2.** The uncastrated adult male of domestic cattle. **3.** *Slang.* Foolish talk. —*v.* To push; force: *The halfback bulled through the line. I bulled my way through the traffic.* [SEE NOTE]

***Idioms.* shoot the bull.** *Slang.* **1.** To spend time talking. **2.** To talk foolishly. **take the bull by the horns.** To take prompt and bold action.

bull[2] |bo͝ol| *n.* An official document issued by the pope. [SEE NOTE]

bull•dog |bo͝ol′dôg′| *or* |-dŏg′| *n.* A stocky, short-haired dog with a large head and strong, square jaws. —*v.* **bull•dogged, bull•dog•ging.** To throw (a steer) down by wrestling it to the ground. —**bull′dog′ger** *n.* [SEE PICTURE]

bull•doze |bo͝ol′dōz′| *v.* **bull•dozed, bull•doz•ing. 1.** To clear, dig up, or move with a bulldozer. **2.** *Slang.* To bully.

bull•doz•er |bo͝ol′dō′zər| *n.* A large, powerful tractor having a metal blade in front for moving earth, rocks, and small trees.

bul•let |bo͝ol′ĭt| *n.* A metal projectile made to be fired from a pistol or other small firearm.

bul•le•tin |bo͝ol′ĭ tn| *or* |-tĭn| *n.* **1.** A statement on a matter of public interest, as in a newspaper, on television, or on radio: *a weather bulletin.* **2.** A publication, such as a periodical or pamphlet, issued by an organization.

bul•let•proof |bo͝ol′ĭt pro͞of′| *adj.* Designed to stop or repel bullets: *bulletproof glass.*

bull•fight |bo͝ol′fīt′| *n.* A spectacle, especially in Spain and Mexico, in which a bull is fought and killed with a sword by a matador. —**bull′fight′er** *n.* —**bull′fight′ing** *n.*

bull•finch |bo͝ol′fĭnch′| *n.* A European bird with a short, thick bill and a red breast.

bull•frog |bo͝ol′frôg′| *or* |-frŏg′| *n.* A large frog with a deep, hollow croak.

bull•head |bo͝ol′hĕd′| *n.* **1.** A North American freshwater catfish with a large head. **2.** Any of several other large-headed fish.

bull•head•ed |bo͝ol′hĕd′ĭd| *adj.* Very stubborn; headstrong. —**bull′head′ed•ness** *n.*

bul•lion |bo͝ol′yən| *n.* Gold or silver bars or ingots, especially when used for minting coins. ¶ *These sound alike* **bullion, bouillon.**

bull•ock |bo͝ol′ək| *n.* A young ox or bull.

bull•pen |bo͝ol′pĕn′| *n.* An area in a baseball stadium for pitchers to warm up before or during a game.

bull•ring |bo͝ol′rĭng′| *n.* A circular arena for bullfighting.

bull•roar•er |bo͝ol′rôr′ər| *or* |-rōr′-| *n.* A wooden slat, attached to a string, that makes a roaring noise when whirled. [SEE PICTURE]

bull session. *Informal.* A rambling, informal group discussion.

bull's eye. 1. a. The small central circle on a target. **b.** A shot that hits this circle. **2. a.** A more or less hemispherical lens used to concentrate light. **b.** A lantern or lamp having such a lens.

bull's-eye |bo͝olz′ī′| *n.* A form of the phrase **bull's eye.**

bull terrier. A short-haired dog with a long muzzle and large jaws.

bull•whip |bo͝ol′hwĭp′| *or* |-wĭp′| *n.* A long whip of braided rawhide with a knotted end.

bul•ly |bo͝ol′ē| *n., pl.* **bul•lies.** A tough, belligerent person who habitually picks on or beats up smaller or weaker people. —*v.* **bul•lied, bul•ly•ing, bul•lies.** To pick on or browbeat as a bully does. —*adj. Informal.* Excellent; spendid.

bul•rush |bo͝ol′rŭsh′| *n.* Any of several tall, grasslike plants that grow in wet places.

bul•wark |bo͝ol′wərk| *or* |bŭl′-| *n.* **1.** A wall or barrier serving as a fortification. **2.** Any protection or defense: *calling on all friends of the Union to form a bulwark around the Constitution that cannot be shaken.* **3.** A breakwater. **4. bulwarks.** The part of a ship's side that is above the upper deck. [SEE NOTE on p. 106]

bum |bŭm| *n.* **1.** A tramp; hobo. **2.** A person who avoids work; a loafer. —*v.* **bummed, bumming.** *Informal.* **1.** To wander about like a tramp; loaf: *He bummed around the streets instead of working.* **2.** To obtain by begging; mooch: *bum cigarettes.* —*adj. Slang.* **1.** Worthless: *a bum tip.* **2.** Disabled: *a bum knee.*

bum•ble•bee |bŭm′bəl bē′| *n.* A large, hairy bee that flies with a humming sound.

bum•bling |bŭm′blĭng| *adj.* Clumsy; inept: *a bumbling idiot.*

bump |bŭmp| *v.* **1.** To come up or knock against (someone or something) with a forceful jolt, thud, etc.: *Jerry fell down as he bumped the skater in front of him. Don't bump against the wall. A handsome young fellow bumped into her.* **2.** To knock together jarringly or heavily: *The boys didn't look where they were going and bumped heads.* **3.** To proceed with jerks and jolts: *an old car bumping down the road.* —*n.* **1.** A light blow, collision, or jolt. **2.** A small swelling, as that which results from a blow, an insect sting, etc. **3.** A small place that rises above the level of the surface surrounding it. [SEE NOTE]

bump•er[1] |bŭm′pər| *n.* Something, especially a horizontal metal bar attached to the front or rear of an automobile, that serves to absorb shock in the event of a collision. [SEE NOTE]

bump•er[2] |bŭm′pər| *n.* A drinking vessel filled to the top. —*adj.* Abundant: *a bumper crop.* [SEE NOTE]

bump•kin |bŭmp′kĭn| *n.* An awkward or unsophisticated person: *a country bumpkin.*

bump•y |bŭm′pē| *adj.* **bump•i•er, bump•i•est. 1.** Full of bumps or lumps: *a bumpy cushion.* **2.** Causing jerks and jolts: *a bumpy road.* —**bump′i•ly** *adv.* —**bump′i•ness** *n.*

bun |bŭn| *n.* **1.** A small bread roll, often sweetened. **2.** A roll or coil of hair worn at the back of the head.

bunch |bŭnch| *n.* **1.** A group of like things that are growing, fastened, or placed together: *a bunch of fresh celery; a bunch of keys.* **2.** *Informal.* A small group of people: *a good bunch of girls.* —*v.* **1.** To gather into or form a cluster or tuft: *She was bunching her parsley for sale. His jacket seemed to bunch under his shoulder.* **2.** To swell or protrude: *His muscles bunched out.*

bun•dle |bŭn′dl| *n.* **1.** A number of objects bound or wrapped together: *a bundle of sticks.* **2.** Anything tied up for carrying; a package. —*v.* **bun•dled, bun•dling. 1.** To tie, wrap, or otherwise secure together. **2.** To send quickly; hustle: *The boy was bundled off to school.* **3.** To dress warmly: *We bundled up in fur coats.*

bull[1-2]

Bull[1] *is from Old English* bula, *which is an early borrowing from Old Norse* boli, *"bull."* **Bull[2]** *is from Latin* bulla, *which originally meant "a bubble," hence "a blob of sealing wax, a seal," hence "a sealed document."*

bulldog

bullroarer
Hopi medicine man using bullroarer in ceremonial dance

bump/bumper[1-2]

Bump *is an imitative word that first appeared in the sixteenth century.* **Bumper[1]**, *obviously, is directly from* **bump.** *The verb* **bump** *used also to mean "to swell, to be big" (from senses 2 and 3 of the noun). Thus in the seventeenth century* **bumper[2]**, *meaning "a full glass of drink," arose.*

bunk¹⁻²
Bunk¹ *is of unknown origin.* **Bunk²** *is shortened from* **bunkum,** *which was originally* buncombe, *coming from* Buncombe *County, North Carolina. In about 1820, Felix Walker, a Congressman whose constituency included this county, made an exceptionally boring and irrelevant speech in the House of Representatives; he afterward explained that his supporters demanded this kind of thing—"I was speaking to* Buncombe.*" By 1828 the word was Washington slang for "pretentious nonsense," and by 1900 it had been shortened to* **bunk².**

bunting¹⁻²⁻³
Bunting¹ *first appears in the eighteenth century and is of unknown origin.* **Bunting²** *goes back to the thirteenth century but is also of unknown origin.* **Bunting³** *is supposed to have come from an old nursery rhyme that starts: "Bye, Baby Bunting." But this is not very helpful since the meaning and origin of the name in the nursery rhyme are also entirely unknown.*

burden¹⁻²
Burden¹, *which has an archaic variant* burthen, *is from Old English* byrthen *and is related to* **bear¹. Burden²** *is from French* bourdon, *"bass drone of a bagpipe," hence "repetitive accompaniment."*

ă pat/ā pay/â care/ä father/ĕ pet/ē be/ĭ pit/ī pie/î fierce/ŏ pot/ō go/ô paw, for/oi oil/ŏŏ book/ōō boot/ou out/ŭ cut/û fur/*th* the/th thin/hw which/zh vision/ə ago, item, pencil, atom, circus

bung |bŭng| *n.* **1.** A stopper for the hole in a cask. **2.** The hole itself; a bunghole.

bun•ga•low |**bŭng'**gə lō'| *n.* A small one-story house.

bung•hole |**bŭng'**hōl'| *n.* The hole in a cask through which the liquid is poured in or drained out.

bun•gle |**bŭng'**gəl| *v.* **bun•gled, bun•gling.** To manage or handle badly; botch: *They never bungled anything. The pitcher bungled throughout the game.* —**bun'gler** *n.*

bun•ion |**bŭn'**yən| *n.* A painful, inflamed swelling at the bursa of the big toe.

bunk¹ |bŭngk| *n.* **1.** A narrow bed built like a shelf against a wall. **2.** A narrow bed. —*v.* To occupy makeshift sleeping quarters: *bunk on the sofa tonight.* [SEE NOTE]

bunk² |bŭngk| *n. Slang.* Empty talk; nonsense. [SEE NOTE]

bun•ker |**bŭng'**kər| *n.* **1.** A bin for coal on a ship. **2.** An obstacle, usually sand in a shallow depression, on a golf course. **3.** A fortification or earthwork, as a deep trench or tunnel.

bunk•house |**bŭngk'**hous'| *n., pl.* **-hous•es** |-hou'zĭz|. Sleeping quarters, usually with bunks, on a ranch or in a camp.

bun•ny |**bŭn'**ē| *n., pl.* **bun•nies.** *Informal.* A rabbit.

Bun•sen burner |**bŭn'**sən|. A device consisting usually of a vertical tube attached to a source of fuel gas that is burned to provide a hot flame for laboratory purposes.

bunt |bŭnt| *v.* To bat (a baseball) with a half swing so that the ball falls in front of the infielders. —*n.* **1.** An instance of bunting. **2.** A ball that is bunted.

bun•ting¹ |**bŭn'**tĭng| *n.* **1.** A light cotton or woolen cloth used for making flags. **2.** Flags in general. **3.** Long strips of cloth with flaglike stripes or colors, used for holiday decoration. [SEE NOTE]

bun•ting² |**bŭn'**tĭng| *n.* Any of several birds with a short, cone-shaped bill. [SEE NOTE]

bun•ting³ |**bŭn'**tĭng| *n.* A baby blanket like a small sleeping bag with a hood, used to hold a baby and keep him warm. [SEE NOTE]

buoy |**bōō'**ē| *or* |boi| *n.* **1.** A float used as a channel or anchorage marker. **2.** A **life preserver.** —*v.* **1.** To keep afloat. **2.** To cheer; hearten: *The news buoyed his spirits.*

buoy•an•cy |**boi'**ən sē| *or* |**bōō'**yən-| *n.* **1.** The tendency or capacity to float in a liquid or to rise in air or other gas. **2.** The upward force that a fluid exerts on an object less dense than itself. **3.** The ability to recover quickly from setbacks. **4.** Lightness of spirit; cheerfulness.

buoy•ant |**boi'**ənt| *or* |**bōō'**yənt| *adj.* **1.** Capable of floating or of keeping things afloat. **2.** Animated; sprightly: *He was a compact, buoyant mass of energy and high spirits.* **3.** Resilient; elastic: *a buoyant step.* —**buoy'ant•ly** *adv.*

bur¹ |bûr| *n.* A seed, fruit, nut, or flower head enclosed in a rough, prickly covering.

bur² |bûr| *n.* & *v.* A form of the word **burr** (sound).

bur•ble |**bûr'**bəl| *v.* **bur•bled, bur•bling.** To bubble; gurgle: *The stream burbled between mossy banks.*

bur•den¹ |**bûr'**dn| *n.* **1.** Something that is carried; a load: *carrying a heavy burden uphill.* **2.** Something endured or assumed as a duty, responsibility, etc., often with difficulty: *the burden of taxation; the major burdens of war; carrying an enormous burden of administrative routine.* **3.** Something that oppresses, depresses, or encumbers: *finding out the origin of his complexes to rid him of their burden; carrying through life the heavy burden of illiteracy.* —*v.* To load with or as if with something difficult to bear: *heavy ornaments burdening the branches of the Christmas tree. Don't burden your memory with useless information.* [SEE NOTE]

Idiom. **of burden.** Used for carrying heavy loads: *a beast of burden.*

bur•den² |**bûr'**dn| *n.* **1.** The chorus or refrain of a song or other musical composition. **2.** A bass accompaniment for a song. **3.** A main or recurring idea or theme: *the burden of the argument.* [SEE NOTE]

burden of proof. The responsibility of proving a charge or allegation.

bur•den•some |**bûr'**dn səm| *adj.* Hard to bear; heavy; arduous: *a burdensome task.*

bur•dock |**bûr'**dŏk'| *n.* A coarse, weedy plant with large leaves and purplish flowers surrounded by hooked bristles.

bu•reau |**byŏŏr'**ō| *n., pl.* **bu•reaus** or **bu•reaux** |**byŏŏr'**ōz|. **1.** A chest of drawers. **2.** An office for a specific kind of business: *a travel bureau.* **3.** A department of a government: *the Bureau of Indian Affairs.*

bu•reauc•ra•cy |byŏŏ **rŏk'**rə sē| *n., pl.* **bu•reauc•ra•cies. 1.** Government that is administered through bureaus and departments. **2.** The departments and their officials as a group. **3.** Any administration, as of a business, in which the need to follow rules and regulations impairs effective action.

bu•reau•crat |**byŏŏr'**ə krăt'| *n.* **1.** An official of a bureaucracy. **2.** Someone who insists on rigid adherence to rules and routines. —**bu'reau•crat'ic** *adj.*

bur•geon |**bûr'**jən| *v.* **1.** To put forth new buds, leaves, or shoots; begin to sprout or grow. **2.** To develop as if by sprouting or growing; flourish.

bur•ger |**bûr'**gər| *n. Informal.* A hamburger.

bur•gess |**bûr'**jĭs| *n.* **1.** A citizen of an English borough. **2.** A member of the lower house of the colonial legislature of either Virginia or Maryland.

burgh•er |**bûr'**gər| *n.* In medieval times, an inhabitant of a borough or town, especially a merchant or tradesman.

bur•glar |**bûr'**glər| *n.* A person who commits burglary; a housebreaker.

bur•glar•ize |**bûr'**glə rīz'| *v.* **bur•glar•ized, bur•glar•iz•ing.** To commit burglary in; rob.

bur•gla•ry |**bûr'**glə rē| *n., pl.* **bur•gla•ries.** The crime of breaking into a building or house with the intention of stealing.

bur•go•mas•ter |**bûr'**gə măs'tər| *or* |-mä'stər| *n.* The mayor of a town in Austria, Belgium, the Netherlands, or Germany.

Bur•gun•dy¹ |**bûr'**gən dē|. A region in eastern France, at one time a kingdom.

Bur•gun•dy² |**bûr'**gən dē| *n., pl.* **Bur•gun•dies. 1.** A red or white wine made in Burgundy. **2.** A similar wine made in another place.

bur•i•al |bĕr′ē əl| *n.* The act of placing a dead body in a grave, a tomb, or in the sea. —***modifier:*** *a burial chamber; burial rites.*

burl |bûrl| *n.* **1.** A large, rounded outgrowth on a tree trunk or branch. **2.** Wood from such a growth, usually with a marked grain.

bur•lap |**bûr**′lăp′| *n.* A coarse cloth made of hemp, jute, or flax, used to make bags, sacks, curtains, coverings, etc. —***modifier:*** *a burlap bag.*

bur•lesque |bər **lĕsk**′| *n.* **1.** A ludicrous or mocking imitation; a parody. **2.** Vaudeville entertainment with singing, dancing, and vulgar comedy. —*adj.* **1.** Of burlesque entertainment: *a burlesque theater.* **2.** Mockingly imitative. —*v.* **bur•lesqued, bur•les•quing.** To imitate mockingly.

bur•ly |**bûr**′lē| *adj.* **bur•li•er, bur•li•est.** Heavy and strong; muscular: *burly members of the college football team.* —**bur′li•ness** *n.*

Bur•ma |**bûr**′mə|. A country in Southeast Asia. Population, 29,560,000. Capital, Rangoon.

Bur•mese |bər **mēz**′| *or* |-**mēs**′| *n., pl.* **Bur•mese. 1.** A native or inhabitant of Burma. **2.** The language of Burma, related to Tibetan. —*adj.* Of Burma, the Burmese, or their language.

burn¹ |bûrn| *v.* **burned** or **burnt** |bûrnt|, **burn•ing. 1.** To undergo or cause to undergo combination with oxygen or a similar chemical agent, especially with the production of flames and heat. **2.** To undergo or cause to undergo damage, destruction, or injury by fire, heat, or a chemical agent, such as an acid or alkali: *The house burned to the ground. Don't burn the roast. He burned his fingers with a match.* **3.** To use as fuel: *This car burns a lot of gasoline.* **4.** To produce by fire or heat: *The sparks burned holes in the rug.* **5.** To make or become sunburned: *The sun burned his skin to a bright red color. Fair skin burns easily.* **6.** To produce light and heat by or as if by fire: *Wood burns easily. The sun burned bright in the sky.* **7.** To feel or be consumed with strong emotion: *burn with anger.* **8.** To cause to feel or feel a burning sensation: *The air burned his lungs. Iodine burns a lot.* —**burn′ing** *adj.: a burning house; a burning desire.* —***phrasal verbs.*** **burn out. 1.** To stop burning from lack of fuel. **2.** To wear out or fail, especially because of heat. **burn up. 1.** To consume or be consumed by fire. **2.** *Slang.* To make or become very angry. —*n.* **1.** An injury produced by fire, heat, or a chemical agent. **2.** Damage that results from burning: *a burn in the tablecloth.* **3.** In aerospace, one firing of a rocket: *The rocket made a good burn.* **4.** A sunburn. [SEE NOTE]

burn² |bûrn| *n.* A stream or brook in Scotland. [SEE NOTE]

burn•er |**bûr**′nər| *n.* **1.** A furnace or other device in which something is burned. **2.** The part of a stove, furnace, lamp, etc., in which a flame is produced.

bur•nish |**bûr**′nĭsh| *v.* To make smooth and glossy by or as if by rubbing; polish: *burnish a brass doorknob.* —**bur′nished** *adj.: a burnished shield; panels inlaid with burnished gold.*

bur•noose, also **bur•nous** |bər **no͞os**′| *n.* A long, loose, flowing cloak with a hood, worn by Arabs. [SEE PICTURE]

burn•out |**bûrn**′out′| *n.* **1.** A failure of a device because of burning, heat, or friction. **2.** The end of a burn in a rocket engine, especially when the fuel has been exhausted or shut off.

burnt |bûrnt|. A past tense and past participle of **burn.** —*adj.* **1.** Affected by or as if by fire; scorched: *burnt grass; acres of burnt land.* **2.** Burned on an altar as a religious sacrifice: *"My son, God will provide himself a lamb for a burnt offering."* (The Bible, Genesis 22:8).

burnt sienna. 1. A reddish-brown pigment. **2.** A reddish brown.

burp |bûrp| *v.* To belch or cause to belch: *He burped. She burped the baby after feeding.* —*n.* A belch.

burp gun. A portable, lightweight submachine gun.

burr¹ |bûr| *n.* **1. a.** A rough sound, as the trilled "r" of Scottish pronunciation. **b.** A whirring sound. **2.** A bit, as on a dentist's drill. —*v.* To pronounce with a burr.

burr² |bûr| *n.* A form of the word **bur** (prickly seed).

Burr |bûr|, **Aaron.** 1756–1836. Vice President of the United States under Thomas Jefferson (1801–05); killed Alexander Hamilton in a duel.

bur•ro |**bûr**′ō| *or* |**bo͝or**′ō| *or* |**bŭr**′ō| *n., pl.* **bur•ros.** A small donkey, usually used for riding or for carrying loads. ¶*These sound alike* **burro, borough, burrow.**

bur•row |**bûr**′ō| *or* |**bŭr**′ō| *n.* A hole or tunnel dug in the ground by a small animal, such as a rabbit or mole. —*v.* **1.** To make (a tunnel, hole, shelter, etc.) by or as if by digging or tunneling: *burrow a long tunnel in a river bank. She burrowed her way in among the big shrubs. They saw gophers burrowing in the fields.* **2.** To move or pass through something by or as if by digging or tunneling: *Moles burrow through the soil in search of earthworms. Bridges cross rivers, and tunnels burrow underneath them.* **3.** To live or hide in or as if in a burrow: *Some animals burrow under the ground during the heat of the day.* —**bur′row•ing** *adj.: a burrowing animal.* ¶*These sound alike* **burrow, borough, burro.** —**bur′row•er** *n.*

bur•sa |**bûr**′sə| *n., pl.* **bur•sae** |**bûr**′sē| or **bur•sas.** A saclike body cavity, especially one that is between the parts of a joint or at some other point where there is friction.

bur•sar |**bûr**′sər| *or* |-sär′| *n.* A treasurer, as at a college or university.

bur•si•tis |bər **sī**′tĭs| *n.* Inflammation of a bursa, especially in the shoulder, elbow, or knee.

burst |bûrst| *v.* **burst, burst•ing. 1.** To break open or cause to break open suddenly and violently: *The balloon may burst. Water passing through the cells of the fruit bursts them.* **2.** To come forth, emerge, or arrive suddenly and in full force: *She burst into the room. Lava burst forth from the volcano.* **3.** To be or seem to be full to the point of breaking open; swell: *He burst with pride.* **4.** To give sudden utterance or expression: *He burst out laughing. She burst into tears.* —*n.* **1.** A sudden outbreak or outburst; an explosion: *a burst of gunfire; a burst of laughter.* **2.** A sudden and intense increase; a rush: *a burst of speed.*

Bu•run•di |bo͝o **ro͞on**′dē|. A small country in east-central Africa, south of Rwanda. Population, 3,680,000. Capital, Bujumbura.

bur•y |**bĕr**′ē| *v.* **bur•ied, bur•y•ing, bur•ies. 1.** To

burn¹

Burns *of the skin are classified according to their seriousness. A first-degree burn reddens the skin; a second-degree burn produces blisters; and a third-degree burn destroys and chars the skin.*

burn¹·²

Burn¹ *is from Old English* byrnan, *and* **burn²** *is from Old English* burna; *both words have retained their original meanings. Ultimately they descend from the same prehistoric Indo-European root, which meant "to boil," hence on the one hand "to burn" (***burn¹***), and on the other hand "to bubble" (***burn²***).*

burnoose

bust[1-2]
Bust[1] *is from Italian* busto, *"piece of sculpture."* **Bust[2]** *is a variant of* **burst**.

bustle[1-2]
Bustle[1] *was earlier* buskle, *and comes from an Old Norse word meaning "to prepare oneself."* **Bustle[2]** *comes from German* Buschel, *"a bunch or pad."*

bustle[2]
From a nineteenth-century French fashion plate

ă pat/ā pay/â care/ä father/ĕ pet/ ē be/ĭ pit/ī pie/î fierce/ŏ pot/ ō go/ô paw, for/oi oil/o͝o book/ o͞o boot/ou out/ŭ cut/û fur/ *th* the/th thin/hw which/zh vision/ ə ago, item, pencil, atom, circus

place (a dead body) in a grave, a tomb, or in the sea. **2.** To place in the ground and cover with earth: *The dog buried his bone in the garden.* **3.** To conceal by or as if by covering with earth: *Frogs and toads bury themselves in the ground for their winter sleep.* **4.** To cover from view; hide: *Christine buried her face in the pillow.* **5.** To embed; sink: *He was found dead with a knife buried in his heart.* **6.** To occupy (oneself) with deep concentration; absorb: *He buried himself in his books.* **7.** To put an end to; abandon: *Help me bury the old quarrel.* ¶*These sound alike* **bury, berry.**

bus |bŭs| *n., pl.* **bus•es** or **bus•ses. 1.** A long motor vehicle equipped to carry a large number of passengers. **2.** An electrical conductor, often large and carrying heavy currents, that supplies several circuits. ***—modifier:*** *a bus stop; a bus driver.* *—v.* **bused** or **bussed, bus•ing** or **bus•sing, bus•es** or **bus•ses.** To transport in a bus. ¶*These sound alike* **bus, buss.**

bus•boy |**bŭs'**boi'| *n.* A waiter's helper who clears the table, pours water, etc., in a restaurant.

bush |bo͝osh| *n.* **1.** A low, branching, woody plant; a shrub. **2.** Land covered with dense, shrubby growth, especially such land with few or no settlers. ***—modifier:*** *bush country.*

Idiom. **beat around the bush.** To delay in getting to the point in speaking or writing.

Bush |bo͝osh|, **George Herbert Walker.** Born 1924. Forty-first President of the United States (1989–1993).

bushed |**bo͝osht**| *adj. Informal.* Extremely tired.

bush•el |**bo͝osh'**əl| *n.* **1.** A unit of volume or capacity used in dry measure in the United States and equal to 4 pecks or 2,150.42 cubic inches. **2.** A container with approximately this capacity.

bush•ing |**bo͝osh'**ĭng| *n.* **1.** A metal tube that acts as a guide or bearing for a moving part. **2.** A lining of insulation for a hole through which an electrical conductor passes.

bush•mas•ter |**bo͝osh'**măs'tər| *or* |-măs'stər| *n.* A large, poisonous tropical American snake.

bush•whack |**bo͝osh'**hwăk'| *or* |-wăk'| *v. Informal.* To ambush.

bush•y |**bo͝osh'**ē| *adj.* **bush•i•er, bush•i•est. 1.** Overgrown with bushes. **2.** Thick and shaggy: *a squirrel's bushy tail.* **—bush'i•ness** *n.*

bus•i•ly |**bĭz'**ə lē| *adv.* In a busy manner.

busi•ness |**bĭz'**nĭs| *n.* **1.** A person's occupation, trade, or work: *He went into the detective business.* **2.** Commercial, industrial, and professional dealings in general: *New systems are now being used in business and industry.* **3.** A commercial establishment, such as a store or factory. **4.** The volume or amount of trade: *Business is bad this year.* **5.** One's rightful or proper concern: *That is none of his business.* **6.** An affair; matter: *He went about the business at hand.* ***—modifier:*** *business administration; a business suit.*

busi•ness•like |**bĭz'**nĭs līk'| *adj.* Systematic; efficient; orderly.

busi•ness•man |**bĭz'**nĭs măn'| *n., pl.* **-men** |-mĕn'|. A man engaged in business.

busi•ness•wom•an |**bĭz'**nĭs wo͝om'ən| *n., pl.* **-wom•en** |-wĭm'ĭn|. A woman engaged in business.

bus•ing, also **bus•sing** |**bŭs'**ĭng| *n.* The transportation of children by bus to schools outside their neighborhoods, especially as a means of achieving racial integration.

bus•kin |**bŭs'**kĭn| *n.* **1.** A laced boot reaching halfway to the knee, especially one with a thick sole worn in ancient times by actors in Greek and Roman tragedies. **2.** Tragedy.

buss |bŭs|. *Archaic. n.* A loud smacking kiss. *—v.* To kiss with a loud smacking sound. ¶*These sound alike* **buss, bus.**

bus•ses |**bŭs'**ĭz|. **1.** A plural of the noun **bus. 2.** A third person singular present tense of the verb **bus.**

bust[1] |bŭst| *n.* **1.** A woman's bosom; breast. **2.** A sculpture of a person's head, shoulders, and upper chest. [SEE NOTE]

bust[2] |bŭst|. *Slang. v.* **1.** To break or burst: *I busted the rope. That dress will bust apart at the seams.* **2.** To cause to become or become bankrupt: *The strike busted several industries.* **3.** To reduce the rank of; demote: *bust a sergeant to corporal.* **4.** To hit; punch: *I'm going to bust him in the jaw.* **5.** To place under arrest. *—n.* **1.** A failure; a flop. **2.** A financial depression. **3.** A state of bankruptcy. **4.** A punch or blow. **5.** An arrest. [SEE NOTE]

bus•tard |**bŭs'**tərd| *n.* A large brownish or grayish bird of open, grassy regions of Africa and other parts of the Eastern Hemisphere.

bus•tle[1] |**bŭs'**əl| *v.* **bus•tled, bus•tling.** To hurry or cause to hurry busily and excitedly: *The mechanics bustled about the airfield. He bustled the man out of the room.* **—bus'tling** *adj.: a bustling crowd.* *—n.* A stir of activity; commotion. [SEE NOTE]

bus•tle[2] |**bŭs'**əl| *n.* A pad or frame worn by women in earlier times to puff out the back of a long skirt. [SEE NOTE & PICTURE]

bus•y |**bĭz'**ē| *adj.* **bus•i•er, bus•i•est. 1.** Occupied with work; active: *He was as busy as a bee.* **2.** Crowded with activity: *a busy morning.* **3.** In use, as a telephone line: *His phone is busy.* **4.** Cluttered with detail: *a busy bulletin board.* *—v.* **bus•ied, bus•y•ing, bus•ies.** To make (oneself) busy; occupy (oneself): *I busied myself with my chores.* **—bus'y•ness** *n.*

bus•y•bod•y |**bĭz'**ē bŏd'ē| *n., pl.* **bus•y•bod•ies.** A nosy or meddling person.

but |bŭt| *conj.* **1.** Contrary to expectation: *Usually the night was cold, but this night the air was hot and sticky.* **2.** On the contrary. Used to connect coordinate elements: *We offer not a pledge but a request.* **3.** Nevertheless: *He felt something bad was going to happen, but he tried to tell himself he was being silly.* **4.** However: *We know he's crazy, but why would he want to burn his own house down?* Often used with strong emphasis to introduce a new step of an argument: *When something vibrates it may make a sound. But, can you always hear a sound when something vibrates?* **5.** Still: *We don't have anything much to say. But maybe we can think of something among us.* **6.** Yet: *It is probable but not certain that the moon is without life.* **7.** Except for the fact. Used with *that: I would never have heard of him but that my grandmother once knew him.* **8.** —Used with interjectional expressions: *Wow! But that little one in the red jacket skates well!* *—adv.* **1. a.** Only; merely: *This is but one case in many.*

b. No more than: *They had skated but a few moments when the church bell rang.* **2.** More than: *He never did hear her name but once again.* **3.** *Informal.* Really; very: *I want that job finished but pronto.* —*prep.* **1.** Except; barring: *The new plan worked in all but a few places.* **2.** Other than: *the whole truth and nothing but the truth.* —*n.* An objection to what one is saying: *no ifs, ands, or buts. "Yes, but . . ." she began. "No buts!" he shouted.* —*Note: But* is often used followed by *for* to form the prepositional group **but for. 1.** Were it not for: *But for me all would have been lost.* **2.** Except for: *The words "big" and "pig" are spelled alike but for one letter.* ¶*These sound alike* **but, butt.**

bu•ta•di•ene |byo͞o′tə **dī′**ēn′| *or* |-dī **ēn′**| *n.* A colorless, flammable gas composed of carbon and hydrogen in the proportions C_4H_6. It is obtained from petroleum and is used in making synthetic rubber.

bu•tane |**byo͞o′**tān′| *n.* A gas composed of carbon and hydrogen and having the formula C_4H_{10}. It is produced from petroleum and is used as a fuel and in the manufacture of synthetic rubber.

butch•er |**bo͝och′**ər| *n.* **1.** A person who kills animals and prepares their meat for food. **2.** A person who sells meat. **3.** A person who cruelly kills without reason. —*v.* **1.** To slaughter or prepare (animals) for market. **2.** To kill (people) in large numbers and without reason. **3.** To botch up; bungle. —***modifier:*** *butcher shop.*

butch•er•y |**bo͝och′**ə rē| *n., pl.* **butch•er•ies.** Cruel or savage killing.

but•ler |**bŭt′**lər| *n.* The chief male servant of a household.

butt[1] |bŭt| *n.* Someone who is a target of ridicule or scorn: *The bully made Joe the butt of his jokes.* ¶*These sound alike* **butt, but.** [SEE NOTE]

butt[2] |bŭt| *v.* To hit or push with the head or horns: *The angry goat butted the intruder.* —*n.* A push or blow with the head or horns. —***phrasal verb.*** **butt in** (or **into**). *Informal.* To meddle; intrude; interfere. ¶*These sound alike* **butt, but.** [SEE NOTE]

butt[3] |bŭt| *n.* **1.** The thicker end of something: *the butt of a rifle.* **2.** An unused or unburned end: *a cigarette butt.* ¶*These sound alike* **butt, but.** [SEE NOTE]

butte |byo͞ot| *n.* A hill that rises sharply from the surrounding area and has a flat top.

but•ter |**bŭt′**ər| *n.* **1.** A soft, yellowish, fatty food churned from milk or cream. **2.** A similar substance, such as certain food spreads. —***modifier:*** *a butter dish.* —*v.* **1.** To spread with butter. **2.** To flatter: *She buttered him up.*

but•ter-and-eggs |**bŭt′**ər ən **ĕgz′**| *n.* *(used with a singular or plural verb).* A plant with a long cluster of pale-yellow and orange flowers.

but•ter•cup |**bŭt′**ər kŭp′| *n.* **1.** A plant with glossy yellow, cup-shaped flowers. **2.** A flower of this plant.

but•ter•fat |**bŭt′**ər făt′| *n.* The fat that is contained in milk and from which butter is made.

but•ter•fin•gers |**bŭt′**ər fĭng′gərz| *n.* *(used with a singular verb).* A clumsy person who is always dropping things.

but•ter•fish |**bŭt′**ər fĭsh′| *n., pl.* **but•ter•fish** or **but•ter•fish•es.** An ocean fish with a flattened body, often used for food.

but•ter•fly |**bŭt′**ər flī′| *n., pl.* **but•ter•flies. 1.** One of many insects with four broad, often colorful wings, a narrow body, and slender antennae with knobs at the tips. **2.** A swimming stroke in which both arms are drawn upward out of the water and forward while the legs perform an up-and-down kick. —***modifier:*** *a butterfly net.*

but•ter•milk |**bŭt′**ər mĭlk′| *n.* The thick, sour liquid that remains after butter has been churned from milk. —***modifier:*** *buttermilk sherbet.*

but•ter•nut |**bŭt′**ər nŭt′| *n.* **1.** The oily, edible nut of a North American tree related to the walnuts. **2.** A tree that bears such nuts. [SEE NOTE]

but•ter•scotch |**bŭt′**ər skŏch′| *n.* A candy or a flavoring made from brown sugar and butter. —***modifier:*** *butterscotch ice cream; butterscotch syrup.*

but•tock |**bŭt′**ək| *n.* **1.** Either of the rounded, fleshy parts of the rump. **2. buttocks.** The rump.

but•ton |**bŭt′**n| *n.* **1.** A disk or knob of plastic, metal, etc., sewn to cloth, usually fitting through a slit or loop to fasten separate edges together, but sometimes used only for decoration. **2.** A part that is pushed to work a switch, as to ring a bell, turn on a light, or start a machine. **3.** A round, flat pin with words or a design on it: *a candidate's campaign button.* —*v.* To fasten with a button or buttons: *button a shirt. Does her dress button or zip?*

but•ton-down |**bŭt′**n doun′| *adj.* **1.** Buttoning to the body of a shirt: *a button-down collar.* **2.** Having a button-down collar: *a button-down shirt.*

but•ton•hole |**bŭt′**n hōl′| *n.* A slit in a garment or in cloth used to hold and fasten a button. —*v.* **but•ton•holed, but•ton•hol•ing.** To stop (a person) and make him listen, as if grabbing him by the buttonhole in his coat lapel.

but•ton•wood |**bŭt′**n wo͝od′| *n.* The sycamore tree of North America.

but•tress |**bŭt′**rĭs| *n.* **1.** A structure, often of brick or stone, built against a wall for support. **2.** Anything that serves to support or reinforce. —*v.* **1.** To brace or reinforce with a buttress. **2.** To sustain or bolster: *buttress an argument with evidence.*

bux•om |**bŭk′**səm| *adj.* Healthily plump: *a buxom woman.* —**bux′om•ness** *n.*

buy |bī| *v.* **bought** |bôt|, **bought, buy•ing. 1.** To acquire (goods) in exchange for money or something of equal value: *He bought jewels for her. We usually buy on the installment plan.* **2.** To be capable of purchasing: *Money buys less and less every day.* **3.** *Informal.* To bribe. —*n. Informal.* Something cheaper than usual; a bargain: *His car was a good buy.* ¶*These sound alike* **buy, by.**

buy•er |**bī′**ər| *n.* **1.** A person who buys goods; a customer. **2.** A person who buys merchandise for a retail store.

buzz |bŭz| *v.* **1.** To make a low, droning sound like that of a bee: *The alarm clock buzzed.* **2.** To move making this sound: *The bees buzzed about from flower to flower.* **3.** To signal, as with a buzzer: *She buzzed the maid.* **4.** To be alive with activity and talk: *The girls buzzed about as their mother cooked.* **5.** *Informal.* To fly a plane low over. —**buzz′ing** *adj.:* *a buzzing noise.* —*n.* A low, droning sound, such as the one made by

butt[1-2-3]

Butt[1] *originally meant "a target used in archery practice," and it comes from Old French.* **Butt**[2] *comes from Norman French* buter, *"to push or strike."* **Butt**[3] *probably comes from Old Norse* būtr, *"a block of wood."*

butternut

The bark of the **butternut** *tree yields a brownish coloring that was used to dye the uniforms of Confederate soldiers during the Civil War. The uniforms, and then the soldiers themselves, came to be known as* butternuts.

buzzard
Turkey buzzard

bees: *the buzz of a mosquito.*

buz•zard |bŭz′ərd| *n.* **1.** Any of several North American vultures. See **turkey buzzard.** **2.** *Chiefly British.* Any of several broad-winged hawks. [SEE PICTURE]

buz•zer |bŭz′ər| *n.* An electrical device that makes a buzzing noise when switched on, used to give a signal or warning.

buzz saw. A power-driven circular saw.

by |bī| *prep.* **1.** Through the action or authorship **of:** *work assigned by the teacher; a novel by Cervantes.* **2.** With the help or use of: *typesetting by computer; crossing by ferry.* **3. a.** In accordance with: *playing by the rules.* **b.** According to: *by his own account.* **4.** Through the method of: *He succeeded by working hard.* **5.** Through the route of; via: *got home by a shortcut.* **6.** During: *sleeping by day.* **7.** In the amount of: *letters by the thousands.* **8.** Past: *A car drove by us.* Also used adverbially: *The jeep raced by.* **9.** After: *day by day.* **10.** Along: *jogging by the river.* **11.** Next to: *the chair by the window.* **12.** In the presence or name of: *I swear by the book.* **13.** In or at (someone's place): *Come by when you feel like it.* **14.** Not later than: *finish by noon.* **15.** With the difference of or to the extent of: *shorter by three inches.* —*adv.* **1.** On hand; nearby: *stand by.* **2.** Aside: *putting some money by for later.* ¶*These sound alike* **by, buy.**

Idioms. **by and by.** Before long; later. **by and large.** On the whole; mostly. **by the way.** Incidentally.

by–. A prefix meaning: **1.** Near; at hand: **bystander.** **2.** Out of the way; aside: *byroad.* **3.** Secondary: **by-product.**

by-and-by |bī′ən bī′| *n.* Some future time; the future.

bye-bye |bī′bī′| *interj. Informal.* Good-by.

by•gone |bī′gôn′| *or* |-gŏn′| *adj.* Gone by; past: *bygone days.* —*n.* A past occurrence.

Idiom. **let bygones be bygones.** To forget past differences; be reconciled.

by•law |bī′lô′| *n.* A law governing the internal affairs of an organization.

by-line, also **by•line** |bī′līn′| *n.* A line at the head of a newspaper or magazine article giving the writer's name.

by-pass, also **by•pass** |bī′păs′| *or* |-päs′| *n.* **1.** A road that passes around a city or other congested area. **2.** A path that leads around some component of a system, as in an electric circuit, system of pipes, etc. —*v.* To go or send around by or as if by means of a by-pass.

by-play |bī′plā′| *n.* Secondary action taking place while the main action is going on, as on a theater stage.

by-pro•duct |bī′prŏd′əkt| *n.* **1.** Something produced in the making of something else. **2.** A secondary result; side effect.

byre |bīr| *n.* A cow stable; barn.

By•ron |bī′rən|, **George Gordon,** Lord. 1788–1824. English poet.

by•stand•er |bī′stăn′dər| *n.* A person who is present at an event but does not take part.

byte |bīt| *n.* A sequence of adjacent binary digits that is operated on as a unit by a computer and is usually shorter than a word. ¶*These sound alike* **byte, bite.**

by•way |bī′wā′| *n.* A road not often used; a side road.

by•word |bī′wûrd′| *n.* **1.** A well-known saying; a proverb. **2.** An object of scorn.

Byz•an•tine |bĭz′ən tēn′| *or* |-tīn′| *or* |bĭ zăn′tĭn| *adj.* Of Byzantium, its inhabitants, or their culture. —*n.* An inhabitant of Byzantium.

Byzantine Empire. The empire established in A.D. 330, when Constantine transferred the capital of the Roman Empire from Rome to Constantinople (now Istanbul). It lasted until 1453, when Constantinople fell to the Turks.

By•zan•ti•um |bĭ zăn′shē əm| *or* |-tē əm|. **1.** A Greek city on the site of which the city of Constantinople (now Istanbul) was built in A.D. 330. **2.** The Byzantine Empire and culture.

Cc

c, C |sē| *n., pl.* **c's** or **C's.** **1.** The third letter of the English alphabet. **2.** **C** In music, the first tone in the scale of C major. [SEE NOTE]

C **1.** Celsius. **2.** centigrade. **3.** The symbol for the element carbon.

Ca The symbol for the element calcium.

cab |kăb| *n.* **1.** A taxicab. **2.** A one-horse carriage for public hire. **3.** A compartment for the operator or driver of a train, locomotive, etc. —**modifier:** *a cab driver; cab fare.*

ca•bal |kə băl′| *n.* **1.** A small group of people organized to carry out a secret plot or conspiracy **2.** A plot organized by such a group.

ca•ban•a |kə băn′ə| *n.* A shelter on a beach, used as a bathhouse.

ca•ba•ña |kə băn′yə| *n.* A form of the word **cabana.**

cab•a•ret |kăb′ə rā′| *n.* **1.** A restaurant where there are short programs of live entertainment. **2.** The floor show in such a place.

cab•bage |kăb′ĭj| *n.* A plant with a large, rounded head of tightly overlapping leaves eaten as a vegetable. —**modifier:** *cabbage soup.*

cab•by |kăb′ē| *n., pl.* **cab•bies.** *Informal.* A cab driver.

cab•in |kăb′ĭn| *n.* **1.** A small, simply built house; a cottage or hut. **2.** A room that serves as living quarters for a passenger or officer on a ship. **3.** The part of an airplane in which the passengers ride.

cabin boy. A boy who serves the officers and passengers on board a ship.

cabin class. A class of accommodations on some passenger ships, lower than first class and higher than tourist class.

cabin cruiser. A powerboat with a cabin.

cab•i•net |kăb′ə nĭt| *n.* **1.** A case or cupboard with drawers, shelves, or compartments for storing or displaying objects: *a kitchen cabinet; a filing cabinet; a curio cabinet.* **2.** Often **Cabinet.** A group of people appointed by a head of state or prime minister to act as official advisers and to head the various departments of state. —**modifier:** *a cabinet door; a cabinet member.*

cab•i•net•mak•er |kăb′ə nĭt mā′kər| *n.* A person who makes fine articles of wooden furniture.

cab•i•net•work |kăb′ə nĭt wûrk′| *n.* Fine wooden furniture made by a cabinetmaker.

ca•ble |kā′bəl| *n.* **1.** A strong, thick rope made of hemp or other fiber. **2.** A rope made of strands of steel wire. **3.** A group of insulated electrical conductors that are bound together as a unit. **4.** A unit of length used in nautical measurement, equal to 720 feet in the United States and 608 feet in Great Britain. **5.** A cablegram. —*v.* **ca•bled, ca•bling.** To send a cablegram to (a person or place): *She cabled her husband, and he cabled back.*

cable car. A vehicle pulled by a cable that moves in an endless loop.

ca•ble•gram |kā′bəl grăm′| *n.* A telegraph message sent by means of a submarine cable.

cable television. A commercial television system in which the signals that transmit the visual images and sound are delivered to subscribers' receivers by means of a cable.

ca•boose |kə bo͞os′| *n.* A small car, usually at the end of a freight train, that has kitchen and sleeping facilities for the crew.

Cab•ot |kăb′ət|, **John.** 1450–1498. Italian explorer in the service of England; discovered the mainland of North America (1497).

ca•ca•o |kə kä′ō| *or* |-kā′ō| *n.* **1.** The seeds from the pods of a tropical American tree, used to make chocolate and cocoa. **2.** A tree that bears such seeds. [SEE NOTE at **chocolate**]

cach•a•lot |kăsh′ə lŏt′| *or* |-lō′| *n.* The **sperm whale.**

cache |kăsh| *n.* **1.** A hiding place for a supply of provisions, weapons, etc. **2.** A supply of something hidden in such a place. —*v.* **cached, cach•ing.** To hide or store away in a cache. ¶*These sound alike* **cache, cash.**

cack•le |kăk′əl| *v.* **cack•led, cack•ling.** **1.** To make the shrill, broken sound of a hen that has just laid an egg. **2.** To laugh or speak with a sound that resembles this. —*n.* **1.** The cry of a hen that has just laid an egg. **2.** A similar sound.

cac•o•mis•tle |kăk′ə mĭs′əl| *n.* A raccoonlike animal of southwestern North America, having a long, black-banded tail. [SEE PICTURE]

ca•coph•o•nous |kə kŏf′ə nəs| *adj.* Harsh and unpleasant in sound; dissonant.

ca•coph•o•ny |kə kŏf′ə nē| *n., pl.* **ca•coph•o•nies.** Harsh, unpleasant sound; dissonance.

cac•tus |kăk′təs| *n., pl.* **cac•ti** |kăk′tī′| or **cac•tus•es.** One of many kinds of plants that have thick, leafless, often spiny stems and that grow in hot, dry places.

cad |kăd| *n.* An ungentlemanly man.

ca•dav•er |kə dăv′ər| *n.* A dead body, especially a human body that is to be dissected and studied.

ca•dav•er•ous |kə dăv′ər əs| *adj.* Resembling a corpse; pale and gaunt.

cad•die |kăd′ē| *n.* A person hired by a golfer to carry his clubs. —*v.* **cad•died, cad•dy•ing.** To serve as a caddie.

cad•dis fly |kăd′ĭs|. An insect that lives near lakes and streams. Its larva, the **caddis worm,** is

1 *2* *3*

The letter **C** *comes from the same source as the letter G—the Greek letter* gamma, *which had two shapes (1, 2). When the Romans borrowed this letter (3), they at first used it both for the sound* g *and for the sound* k. *Later they invented a new letter for* g *and kept the old one, (3), for* k *(and also for soft* c, *or* s*). Our letter* C *comes straight from theirs.*

cacomistle

cadmium

Cadmium *is obtained mainly from zinc, copper, and lead ores. It is used in storage batteries, pigments, and many kinds of solder.*

caftan
Moroccan storyteller

ă pat/ā pay/â care/ä father/ĕ pet/ ē be/ĭ pit/ī pie/î fierce/ŏ pot/ ō go/ô paw, for/oi oil/o͝o book/ o͞o boot/ou out/ŭ cut/û fur/ *th* the/th thin/hw which/zh vision/ ə ago, item, pencil, atom, circus

enclosed in a tubelike case covered with grains of sand or tiny pieces of wood or shell.

Cad•do |**kăd'**ō| *n., pl.* **Cad•do** or **Cad•dos.** An Indian who speaks a Caddoan language.

Cad•do•an |**kăd'**ō ən| *n.* A family of North American Indian languages spoken in some states just west of the Mississippi River. —**Cad'do•an** *adj.*

cad•dy |**kăd'**ē| *n., pl.* **cad•dies.** A small box or other container, especially for holding tea.

ca•dence |**kād'**ns| *n.* **1.** The beat or pulsation of music, marching, dancing, etc. **2.** A progression of chords that brings a phrase or other division of a musical composition to a close. **3.** The general rise and fall of the voice in speaking.

ca•den•za |kə **dĕn'**zə| *n.* A section of a concerto, aria, or other solo musical composition in which the soloist shows off his technique by performing music that is very elaborate and free in style.

ca•det |kə **dĕt'**| *n.* A student at a military or naval academy who is training to be an officer.

cad•mi•um |**kăd'**mē əm| *n.* Symbol **Cd** One of the elements, a soft, bluish-white metal. Atomic number 48; atomic weight 112.40; valence +2; melting point 320.9°C; boiling point 765°C. [SEE NOTE]

cad•re |**kăd'**rē| *n.* A group of trained persons around which a larger organization can be built.

ca•du•ce•us |kə **do͞o'**sē əs| *or* |**-dyo͞o'-**| *n.* In Greek mythology, the winged, snake-entwined staff of Hermes.

Cae•sar |**sē'**zər| *n.* A title of Roman emperors after the reign of Augustus.

Cae•sar |**sē'**zər|, **Gaius Julius.** 100–44 B.C. Roman statesman and general.

Cae•sar•e•an section, also **cae•sar•e•an section** |sĭ **zâr'**ē ən|. A surgical operation in which an incision is made through the abdominal wall and uterus in order to remove a fetus.

cae•su•ra |sĭ **zho͝or'**ə| *or* |**-zo͝or'**ə| *or* |sĭz**yo͝or'**ə| *n.* A short pause at the end of a phrase of music or verse.

ca•fé |kă **fā'**| *or* |kə-| *n.* A coffee house, restaurant, or bar.

caf•e•te•ri•a |kăf'ĭ **tîr'**ē ə| *n.* A restaurant in which the customers are served at a counter and carry their meals to tables on trays.

caf•feine, also **caf•fein** |kă **fēn'**| *or* |**kăf'**ēn'| *n.* A bitter, white alkaloid composed of carbon, hydrogen, nitrogen, and oxygen in the proportions $C_8H_{10}N_4O_2$. It acts as a stimulant, and is found in coffee, tea, and cola beverages.

caf•tan |**kăf'**tən| *or* |kăf **tăn'**| *n.* A coatlike robe having long sleeves and sometimes tied with a sash, worn in the Near East. [SEE PICTURE]

cage |kāj| *n.* **1.** An enclosure for confining birds or animals, having a grating of wires or bars to let in air or light. **2.** Anything similar to a cage: *a cashier's cage.* **3.** A backstop used for baseball batting practice. —*v.* **caged, cag•ing.** To put in a cage: *cage a wild animal.*

cag•ey, also **cag•y** |**kā'**jē| *adj.* **cag•i•er, cag•i•est.** Wary; shrewd: *a cagey lawyer.* —**cag'i•ly** *adv.* —**cag'i•ness** *n.*

ca•hoots |kə **ho͞ots'**| *pl.n. Informal.* —**in cahoots.** Working secretly together: *The policeman was suspected of being in cahoots with a racketeer.*

cai•man |**kā'**mən| *n., pl.* **cai•mans.** A large tropical American reptile related to and resembling the alligators.

Cain |kān|. In the Bible, the eldest son of Adam and Eve, who killed his brother Abel out of jealousy.

Idiom. **raise Cain.** *Slang.* To create an uproar; make trouble.

cairn |kârn| *n.* A mound of stones serving as a landmark or memorial.

Cai•ro |**kī'**rō|. The capital of Egypt and the largest city in Africa, on the Nile River. Population, 4,961,000.

cais•son |**kā'**sŏn'| *or* |-sən| *n.* **1.** A watertight structure inside of which underwater construction work is done, as in the building of tunnels, bridges, dams, etc. **2.** A watertight float, a camel. **3.** A floating structure used to close the entrance of a dock or canal lock. **4. a.** A large container for military ammunition. **b.** A horse-drawn vehicle once used to carry military ammunition.

caisson disease. A painful and often fatal disorder found in divers and persons who work in caissons filled with compressed air. It occurs when such persons return to normal atmospheric pressure too quickly, thus allowing bubbles of nitrogen to accumulate in their blood vessels and tissues. Also called *the bends.*

ca•jole |kə **jōl'**| *v.* **ca•joled, ca•jol•ing.** To persuade by flattery or insincere talk; coax: *He cajoled me into joining their club.*

ca•jol•er•y |kə **jō'**lə rē| *n.* Persuasion by means of flattery or insincere talk.

Ca•jun |**kā'**jən| *n.* A native of Louisiana descended from French-speaking exiles from a colony in eastern Canada.

cake |kāk| *n.* **1.** A baked, sweetened mixture of flour, liquid, eggs, and other ingredients, often round in shape and with icing on top: *a wedding cake.* **2.** A thin mixture of dough or batter, baked or fried, and usually round and flat in shape: *a wheat cake.* **3.** A fried or baked mixture of minced food: *a fish cake.* **4.** A shaped or molded solid mass of something, such as soap or ice. —*modifier: a cake knife; a cake mix.* —*v.* **caked, cak•ing.** To form a compact mass or layer upon: *His shoes were caked with mud.*

cake•walk |**kāk'**wôk'| *n.* **1.** Formerly, a walk to music in which the couples performing the most original steps won cakes as prizes. **2. a.** A strutting dance based on this. **b.** Music for this dance.

cal, Cal calorie.

Cal. California (unofficial).

cal•a•bash |**kăl'**ə băsh'| *n.* **1. a.** A large gourd with a tough, shell-like rind. **b.** The similar fruit of a tropical American tree. **2.** A bowl, ladle, pipe, etc., made from the hollowed-out shell of such a gourd or fruit.

cal•a•mine |**kăl'**ə mīn'| *or* |-mĭn| *n.* A pink powder used in skin lotions and composed of zinc oxide, ZnO, with a small amount of ferric oxide, Fe_2O_3.

ca•lam•i•tous |kə **lăm'**ĭ təs| *adj.* Causing or resulting in a calamity; disastrous.

ca•lam•i•ty |kə **lăm'**ĭ tē| *n., pl.* **ca•lam•i•ties.** Something that causes great distress and suffering; a disaster.

cal•car•e•ous |kăl kâr'ē əs| *adj.* Of, like, or containing calcium carbonate or limestone; chalky.

cal•ci•fi•ca•tion |kăl'sə fĭ kā'shən| *n.* **1.** A process in which something becomes hard and stony by filling up with salts of calcium. **2.** The hardening of living tissues as a result of this process. **3.** A hard deposit of calcium salts, as in living tissue.

cal•ci•fy |kăl'sə fī'| *v.* **cal•ci•fied, cal•ci•fy•ing, cal•ci•fies.** To undergo or cause to undergo calcification.

cal•ci•mine |kăl'sə mīn'| *n.* A mixture of zinc oxide, water, glue, and, often, coloring, used to coat walls and ceilings. —*v.* **cal•ci•mined, cal•ci•min•ing.** To coat or wash (a surface) with calcimine.

cal•cine |kăl'sīn'| *v.* **cal•cined, cal•cin•ing.** To treat (a substance) by heating it to a high temperature without causing it to melt. —**cal'ci•na'tion** *n.*

cal•cite |kăl'sīt'| *n.* A crystalline substance that is the main component of minerals such as chalk, limestone, and marble. It is composed of calcium, carbon, and oxygen and has the formula $CaCO_3$.

cal•ci•um |kăl'sē əm| *n.* Symbol **Ca** One of the elements, a silvery, moderately hard metal. Atomic number 20; atomic weight 40.08; valence +2; melting point 842 to 848°C; boiling point 1,487°C. [SEE NOTE]

calcium carbide. A crystalline, grayish-black compound of carbon and calcium that has the formula CaC_2. It generates acetylene when placed in contact with water.

calcium carbonate. A white or colorless crystalline compound of calcium, carbon, and oxygen that has the formula $CaCO_3$. It occurs naturally as chalk, limestone, and marble, and is used in a wide variety of products.

calcium chloride. A white, crystalline salt composed of calcium and chlorine and having the formula $CaCl_2$. It attracts water very strongly, and is used mainly as a drying agent and preservative.

calcium hydroxide. A soft, white powder, $Ca(OH)_2$, composed of calcium, hydrogen, and oxygen, used in making mortar, cement, and a variety of industrial products; slaked lime.

calcium oxide. A white, lumpy powder, CaO, used in making steel, glass, and insecticides and as an industrial alkali; quicklime.

cal•cu•late |kăl'kyə lāt'| *v.* **cal•cu•lat•ed, cal•cu•lat•ing. 1.** To find or determine (an answer or result) by using mathematics: *calculate complex engineering problems. Today's astronomers can calculate easily and with good accuracy the positions of various heavenly bodies.* **2.** To make an estimate of: *Can you calculate the cost of the electricity you use?*

cal•cu•lat•ed |kăl'kyə lā'tĭd| *adj.* **1.** Carefully estimated in advance: *a calculated risk.* **2.** Determined by mathematical calculation.

cal•cu•lat•ing |kăl'kyə lā'tĭng| *adj.* **1.** Used in or for performing calculation: *a calculating machine.* **2.** Shrewd; crafty; scheming: *a calculating businessman.*

cal•cu•la•tion |kăl'kyə lā'shən| *n.* The act, process, or result of calculating: *All the calculations in the ledger turned out to be correct.*

cal•cu•la•tor |kăl'kyə lā'tər| *n.* **1.** A person who calculates. **2.** A machine, operated by keyboard, that automatically performs the operations of arithmetic.

cal•cu•lus |kăl'kyə ləs| *n., pl.* **cal•cu•li** |kăl'kyə lī'| or **cal•cu•lus•es. 1.** An abnormal hard mass, usually of mineral salts, that forms in the body; a stone, as in the urinary bladder, gallbladder, or kidney. **2.** A branch of mathematics, an extended form of algebra, that is capable of dealing with problems that involve rates of change.

Cal•cut•ta |kăl kŭt'ə|. A city in eastern India. Population, 3,149,000.

cal•dron |kôl'drən| *n.* A large kettle for boiling. [SEE NOTE]

Cal•e•do•ni•a |kăl'ĭ dō'nē ə|. Scotland. Used chiefly in poetry.

cal•en•dar |kăl'ən dər| *n.* **1.** A man-made system for measuring and showing divisions of time by days, weeks, months, and years. **2.** A chart showing the months, weeks, and days of a certain year. **3.** A list of dates, as of events or things to be done; arranged in order of time of occurrence: *a social calendar; a business calendar.* —***modifier:*** *a calendar month.* ¶ *These sound alike* **calendar, calender.**

cal•en•der |kăl'ən dər| *n.* A machine in which paper or cloth is given a smooth, glossy finish by being pressed between rollers. —*v.* To treat (paper or cloth) with a calender. ¶ *These sound alike* **calender, calendar.**

calf[1] |kăf| *or* |käf| *n., pl.* **calves** |kăvs| *or* |kävs|. **1.** The young of cattle; a young cow or bull. **2.** The young of certain other animals, such as the elephant or whale. **3.** A type of leather made from the hide of a calf; calfskin. [SEE NOTE]

calf[2] |kăf| *or* |käf| *n., pl.* **calves** |kăvz| *or* |kävz|. The muscular back part of the human leg between the knee and ankle. [SEE NOTE]

calf•skin |kăf'skĭn'| *or* |käf'-| *n.* The hide of a calf or leather made from it. —***modifier:*** *a calfskin bag.*

cal•i•ber |kăl'ə bər| *n.* **1.** The diameter of the inside of a tube, especially the bore of a firearm. **2.** The diameter of a bullet or other projectile intended for a firearm: *a .45-caliber bullet.* **3.** Degree of worth or distinction: *a man of high caliber.* [SEE NOTE]

cal•i•brate |kăl'ə brāt'| *v.* **cal•i•brat•ed, cal•i•brat•ing. 1.** To mark the scale of (a measuring instrument) with graduations: *Tom built and calibrated an ammeter.* **2.** To check (a measuring instrument) against a standard and adjust it for accuracy. **3.** To determine the caliber of (a tube). —**cal'i•bra'tion** *n.*

cal•i•co |kăl'ĭ kō| *n., pl.* **cal•i•coes** or **cal•i•cos. 1.** A cotton cloth with a figured pattern printed on it in color. **2.** *British.* Plain white cotton cloth. —***modifier:*** *a calico apron.* —*adj.* Covered with spots of a different color: *a calico cat.*

ca•lif |kā'lĭf| *or* |kăl'ĭf| *n.* A form of the word **caliph.**

Calif. California.

Cal•i•for•nia |kăl'ə fôr'nyə| *or* |-fôr'nē ə|. A Pacific Coast state of the United States. Population, 23,668,562. Capital, Sacramento. —**Cal'i•for'nian** *adj. & n.*

cal•i•for•ni•um |kăl'ə fôr'nē əm| *n.* Symbol **Cf**

calcium

Calcium *compounds occur in bone, shells, leaves, and minerals such as limestone and gypsum. They are used in making plaster, Portland cement, and quicklime. The word* **calcium** *comes from Latin* calx, *"limestone," from which we have also the word* **chalk.**

caldron

The word **caldron** *comes from Old North French* caudron, *which is from Late Latin* caldāria, *"kettle, caldron," from Latin* calidus, *"hot." It would be quite appropriate to cook* **chowder** *in a* **caldron.** *For the reason, see note at* **chowder.**

calf[1-2]

Calf[1] *was* cealf *in Old English, and it descends from a prehistoric Germanic word,* kalbam; *its meaning has never changed.* **Calf**[2] *is from Old Norse* kalfi, *but the further history of this word is unknown.*

caliber

The **calibers** *of rifles, pistols, and machine guns are usually expressed in decimal fractions of an inch:* a .30-caliber rifle; a .50-caliber machine gun. *Calibers of larger guns are expressed in millimeters.*

One of the elements, a metal first produced by bombarding a curium isotope with helium ions. It has isotopes with mass numbers ranging from 244 to 254 with half-lives ranging from 25 minutes to 800 years. Atomic number 98.

cal•i•per |kăl'ə pər| *n.* **1.** Often **calipers** *(used with a plural verb).* An instrument having two points or surfaces that can be adjusted so that they just enclose or just fit inside an object that is to be measured, the distance between the points being determined from a rule or a scale on the instrument. **2.** A **vernier caliper.** [SEE PICTURE]

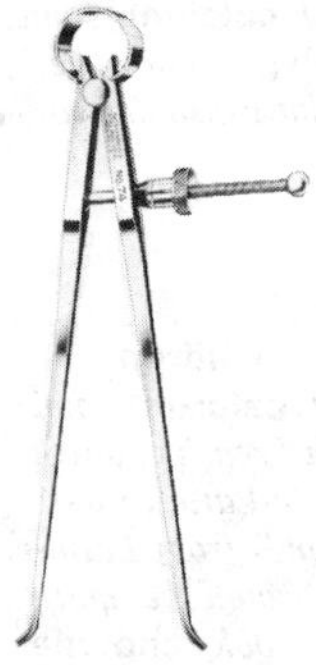

caliper
Glass blower's calipers

ca•liph |kā'lĭf| *or* |kăl'ĭf| *n.* The political and religious head of a Moslem state.

cal•iph•ate |kăl'ə fāt'| *or* |-fĭt| *or* |kā'lə-| *n.* The office or reign of a caliph or the land under his rule.

cal•is•then•ics |kăl'ĭs thĕn'ĭks| *pl.n.* **1.** Exercises done to develop physical fitness. **2.** *(used with a singular verb).* The practice of such exercises.

calk[1] |kôk| *n.* **1.** A pointed piece of metal on the bottom of a horse's shoe, designed to prevent slipping. **2.** A similar piece on a shoe or boot. —*v.* **1.** To fasten calks on. **2.** To cut or injure with a calk.

calk[2] |kôk| *v.* A form of the word **caulk.**

calk•ing |kô'kĭng| *n.* A form of the word **caulking.**

call |kôl| *v.* **1. a.** To speak or utter in a loud voice; cry; shout: *call out a number from a list. They swam for some time, calling for help.* **b.** To read out loudly: *call the roll; call off a list of names.* **2.** To send for; summon: *call the fire department; call the doctor.* **3. a.** To refer to or address by a specified name: *Call me Bill for short. He calls the president of the company by his first name.* **b.** To give a name to; name: *What an Englishman calls the "boot" of a car, an American calls the "trunk."* **c.** To describe as; designate: *call someone a liar.* **4.** To estimate as being; regard as; consider: *a home he could call his own. That's what I call nerve! The moon's revolution in its orbit is equal to what we would call seven hours.* **5.** To telephone: *Call me on Thursday. I'll call when I'm in town.* **6.** To awaken: *Call me just before eight.* **7.** To make a brief stop at: *The boys called at every house.* **8.** To command or invite to assemble; convoke: *call a meeting.* **9.** To bring into being, effect, action, etc., as by giving an order: *call a strike. Either country could call an end to the trade agreements.* **10.** To halt or postpone; suspend: *call a game on account of rain.* **11.** To predict accurately: *He called the outcome of the election.* **12.** To demand payment of: *call a loan.* **13.** In baseball, to indicate a decision in regard to (a pitch, ball, player, etc.): *The umpire called him safe.* **14.** In poker, to demand to see the hand of (an opponent) by matching his bet. —***phrasal verbs.*** **call back.** To telephone in return. **call for. 1.** To go and get or pick up: *I'll call for you at eight.* **2.** To require; demand: *a job that calls for patience.* **3.** To provide for; prescribe: *The recipe calls for half a cup of sugar.* **4.** To give an order for; appeal: *He called for a revolution against Spain.* **call in. 1.** To summon for help or consultation: *call in a specialist.* **2.** To take out of circulation: *call in silver dollars.* **call off.** To cancel: *call off a game; call off a trip.* **call on. 1.** To ask (someone) to speak: *The teacher called on me first.* **2.** To appeal to (someone) to do something: *I call on everyone here to contribute something.* **call up. 1.** To call on the telephone **2.** To summon into military service. —*n.* **1.** A shout or loud cry: *a call for help.* **2. a.** The typical cry of an animal, especially a bird: *the deep braying call of the cow moose; the call of the screech owl.* **b.** An instrument or sound made to imitate such a sound, used as a lure: *a hunter's moose call; a boy playing a whip-poorwill call on the whistle.* **c.** A word habitually used by a person in the performance of his duties: *"Mark Twain" was the call that Sam Clemens often heard when he was a river pilot on the Mississippi. Can you follow the calls in square dancing?* **3.** A signal, as made by a horn, bell, etc.: *a bugle call.* **4. a.** The act of calling on the telephone: *Keep your calls brief and to the point.* **b.** An instance of this: *Were there any calls for me?* **5.** A short visit: *a social call on the local Chamber of Commerce.* **6. a.** An appeal or summons for a certain course of action: *people responding to the call for liberty, equality, and fraternity.* **b.** An appeal or command to assemble, come, etc.: *a draft call; volunteers answering the fire call.* **c.** Attraction or appeal; fascination: *the call of the wild.* **7.** Need or reason; justification: *There was no call for that remark.* **8. a.** Demand, as for a certain product: *There isn't much call for inkstands today.* **b.** A claim of any kind: *Many calls are made on his time. The automobile industry has first call on steel production.* **9.** In sports, the decision of an official.

Idioms. **call into question.** To raise doubt about. **call to mind.** To remind of. **close call.** A narrow escape: *After his close call with the police, he was very careful to avoid trouble for over a week.* **on call.** Available when summoned; ready: *a nurse on call.*

cal•la |kăl'ə| *n.* Also **calla lily.** A plant with a showy, usually white, petallike leaf enclosing a clublike flower stalk. [SEE PICTURE]

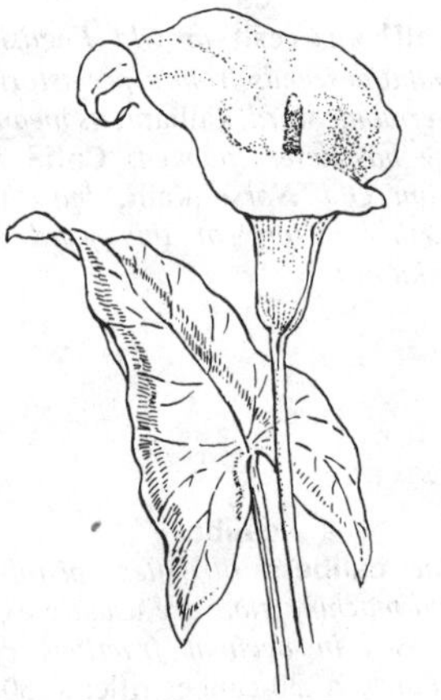

calla lily

call•er |kô'lər| *n.* **1.** A person who calls, especially one who calls out the steps in square dancing. **2.** A person paying a short visit.

cal•lig•ra•phy |kə lĭg'rə fē| *n.* Beautiful handwriting; fine penmanship. —**cal•lig'ra•pher** *n.*

call•ing |kô'lĭng| *n.* **1.** An inner urge, especially one that seems to come from a divine source. **2.** An occupation, profession, or career.

calling card. A card bearing one's name and often one's address and telephone number, used for social or business purposes.

cal•li•o•pe |kə lī'ə pē'| *or* |kăl'ē ōp'| *n.* A musical instrument consisting of a set of steam whistles that are controlled from a keyboard. It is used mostly at carnivals and circuses.

cal•li•per |kăl'ə pər| *n.* A form of the word **caliper.**

call letters. The series of letters or letters and numbers that identifies a radio or television transmitting station.

call number. A number used in libraries to classify a book and indicate its location.

cal•los•i•ty |kə lŏs'ĭ tē| *n., pl.* **cal•los•i•ties. 1. a.** A hard growth or mass, such as a callus. **b.** The condition of having calluses. **2.** Lack of feeling; hardheartedness.

cal•lous |kăl′əs| *adj.* **1.** Having calluses. **2.** Unfeeling; unsympathetic. —*v.* To make or become callous. ¶*These sound alike* **callous, callus.** —**cal′lous•ly** *adv.* —**cal′lous•ness** *n.*

cal•low |kăl′ō| *adj.* Immature; inexperienced: *a callow youth.* —**cal′low•ly** *adv.* —**cal′low•ness** *n.*

call-up |kôl′ŭp′| *n.* An order to report for military service.

cal•lus |kăl′əs| *n., pl.* **cal•lus•es. 1.** A small area of the skin that has become hardened and thick, usually because of prolonged pressure or rubbing. **2.** The hard, bony material that forms around and between the broken ends of a bone. ¶*These sound alike* **callus, callous.**

calm |käm| *adj.* **calm•er, calm•est. 1.** Peacefully quiet; not excited; composed: *She spoke in a calm voice.* **2.** Nearly motionless; undisturbed; serene: *the calm, placid lake; a calm summer evening.* —*n.* **1.** A condition of tranquillity or peace; quiet: *She sat down with deceptive calm. Her scream blasted the calm of the dining room.* **2. a.** Lack of motion; stillness: *the calm of the sea.* **b.** Lack of turbulent winds: *The eye of the hurricane is an area of calm in the middle of the storm.* —*v.* To make or become calm: *Mother was trying to calm father. The wild horse calmed down.* —**calm′ly** *adv.* —**calm′ness** *n.*

cal•o•mel |kăl′ə mĕl′| *or* |-məl| *n.* Mercurous chloride, especially when used as a purgative.

ca•lor•ic |kə lôr′ĭk| *or* |-lŏr′-| *adj.* Of heat or calories.

cal•o•rie |kăl′ə rē| *n.* **1.** A unit of heat used in physics, chemistry, and related sciences, equal to the amount of heat needed to raise one gram of water one degree Celsius (centigrade). **2.** Often **Calorie.** A unit of heat used in biology and related sciences, equal to the amount of heat needed to raise 1,000 grams of water one degree Celsius (centigrade).

cal•o•rif•ic |kăl′ə rĭf′ĭk| *adj.* Of or generating heat.

cal•o•rim•e•ter |kăl′ə rĭm′ĭ tər| *n.* An instrument that measures and indicates heat. Its scale usually indicates calories, multiples of calories, or fractions of calories.

cal•u•met |kăl′yə mĕt′| *or* |kăl′yə mĕt′| *n.* A pipe smoked by North American Indians as a token of peace. [SEE PICTURE]

ca•lum•ni•ate |kə lŭm′nē āt′| *v.* **ca•lum•ni•at•ed, ca•lum•ni•at•ing.** To make false statements about; slander.

ca•lum•ni•ous |kə lŭm′nē əs| *adj.* Containing or implying calumny; slanderous.

cal•um•ny |kăl′əm nē| *n., pl.* **cal•um•nies. 1.** A false statement made to injure another person's reputation. **2.** The making of such a statement; slander.

Cal•va•ry |kăl′və rē|. The hill outside the ancient city of Jerusalem where Christ was crucified.

calve |kăv| *or* |käv| *v.* **calved, calv•ing. 1.** To give birth to a calf. **2.** To break and drop off a large mass of ice: *Glaciers calve.*

calves |kăvz| *or* |kävz| *n.* Plural of **calf.**

Cal•vin |kăl′vĭn|, **John.** 1509–1564. French religious reformer who lived in Switzerland.

ca•ly•ces |kā′lĭ sēz′| *or* |kăl′ĭ-| *n.* A plural of **calyx.**

ca•lyp•so |kə lĭp′sō| *n.* A type of folk music that originated in the West Indies, characterized by improvised lyrics about humorous or timely subjects.

ca•lyx |kā′lĭks| *or* |kăl′ĭks| *n., pl.* **ca•lyx•es** or **ca•ly•ces** |kā′lĭ sēz′| *or* |kăl′ĭ-|. The outer protective covering of a flower, consisting of leaflike, usually green parts called sepals.

cam |kăm| *n.* A wheel, either mounted off center or not circular in shape, that as it turns transmits back-and-forth motion to another part.

ca•ma•ra•de•rie |kä′mə rä′də rē| *n.* Good will and warm feeling between or among friends; comradeship.

cam•ber |kăm′bər| *n.* **1. a.** A slightly arched surface, as of a road or a ship's deck. **b.** The condition of being slightly arched. **c.** The degree to which a surface is arched in this way: *a road with a sharp camber.* **2.** The adjustment of automobile wheels, usually the front pair, so that they are closer together at the bottom than at the top. —*v.* To make or be slightly arched.

cam•bi•um |kăm′bē əm| *n.* A layer of tissue in the stems and roots of many seed-bearing plants. It consists of cells that divide rapidly and give rise to other tissues necessary for growth, support, and protection.

Cam•bo•di•a |kăm bō′dē ə|. A country in Southeast Asia. Population, 7,890,000. Capital, Phnom Penh. —**Cam•bo′di•an** *adj.* & *n.*

Cam•bri•an |kăm′brē ən| *n.* Also **Cambrian period.** A geologic period that began about 600 million years ago and ended about 500 million years ago, characterized by warm seas and desert land areas. —***modifier:*** *Cambrian rock strata.*

cam•bric |kăm′brĭk| *n.* A fine white linen or cotton cloth.

cambric tea. A hot drink made from milk, sugar, water, and sometimes tea.

Cam•bridge |kăm′brĭj|. **1.** A city in eastern England, the site of Cambridge University. Population, 100,000. **2.** A city in eastern Massachusetts, opposite Boston, the site of Harvard University and the Massachusetts Institute of Technology. Population, 99,000.

came |kām|. Past tense of **come.**

cam•el |kăm′əl| *n.* **1.** A long-necked, humped animal of northern Africa and western Asia, used in desert regions for riding and carrying loads. **2.** A type of float used to raise a sunken ship; a caisson. [SEE PICTURE]

ca•mel•lia |kə mĕl′yə| *or* |-mē′lē ə| *n.* **1.** A shrub with glossy, evergreen leaves and showy, many-petaled flowers. **2.** The flower of such a shrub.

Cam•e•lot |kăm′ə lŏt′|. The legendary town where King Arthur had his court.

camel's hair. 1. The soft, fine hair of a camel or a substitute for it, as hair from a squirrel's tail. **2.** A soft, heavy cloth, usually light tan, made chiefly of camel's hair. —***modifier:*** **(camel's-hair):** *a camel's-hair coat.*

cam•e•o |kăm′ē ō′| *n., pl.* **cam•e•os.** A gem or medallion with a carved, raised design, especially one having layers of different colors that are cut so that the design is of one color and the background of another.

cam•er•a |kăm′ər ə| *or* |kăm′rə| *n.* **1.** A lightproof enclosure, used in making photographs, that is equipped with a lens that focuses the light

calumet

camel
The Arabian camel, or dromedary *(above)*, has a single hump. The Bactrian camel *(below)*, of more northern regions, has two humps

camp¹⁻²
Camp¹ *is from Old North French* camp, *which is from Latin* campus, *"open field, sports field, battlefield."* **Camp²** *appeared in the early 1960's; like many slang words, it is difficult to track down, and so far no convincing origin has been suggested for it.*

can¹⁻²
The verbal auxiliary **can¹** *has two negative forms:* cannot *(formal or emphatic) and* can't *(mostly informal). It is often used informally for* may *(as in the sentence* Can I go now?*).* **Can¹** *comes from Old English* can, *"he knows how," which is from* cunnan, *"to know"; it is related to the word* **know**. **Can²** *was* canne, *"a cup," in Old English; it descends from a prehistoric Germanic word,* kannon-.

Canada goose

ă pat/ā pay/â care/ä father/ĕ pet/ē be/ĭ pit/ī pie/î fierce/ŏ pot/ō go/ô paw, for/oi oil/ŏŏ book/ōō boot/ou out/ŭ cut/û fur/*th* the/th thin/hw which/zh vision/ə ago, item, pencil, atom, circus

from an image on a photographic film that is briefly exposed by a shutter. **2.** The unit of a television system that receives an image and changes it into electrical signals.

cam•er•a•man |kăm'ər ə măn'| *or* |kăm'rə-| *n., pl.* **-men** |-mĕn'|. A person who is skilled at operating a motion-picture or television camera. —**cam'er•a•wom'an** *n.*

Cam•e•roon, also **Cam•e•roun** |kăm'ə rōōn'|. A country on the west coast of central Africa. Population, 6,280,000. Capital, Yaoundé.

cam•i•sole |kăm'ĭ sōl'| *n.* A short, sleeveless undergarment worn by a woman or girl under a sheer blouse or dress.

cam•o•mile |kăm'ə mīl'| *n.* A strong-smelling plant with daisylike flowers and feathery leaves. The dried flowers can be steeped in hot water to make **camomile tea,** used as a tonic.

cam•ou•flage |kăm'ə fläzh'| *n.* The concealment or disguise of people, animals, or things through the use of colors or patterns that make them appear to be part of the natural surroundings. —*v.* **cam•ou•flaged, cam•ou•flag•ing.** To conceal or disguise by camouflage: *camouflage a bunker. Insects are camouflaged to resemble their natural surroundings.*

camp¹ |kămp| *n.* **1.** A place where a group of people, such as vacationers, miners, soldiers, or prisoners, live temporarily in tents, cabins, huts, or other informal shelters. **2.** A group of people who have the same ideas or beliefs; a faction: *people in different political camps.* —*v.* **1.** To live in or as if in a camp: *He and his friends camped for a month in the Rocky Mountains. The families camped in the basement of the old house.* **2.** To sleep outdoors, especially in a tent: *They camped out under the stars.* [SEE NOTE]

camp² |kămp| *n.* Artificiality of manner or style, appreciated for its outlandish or humorous qualities: *Some fine examples of camp are the extravagant Hollywood movies of the 20's and 30's.* —*adj.* Having or done in such manner or style: *a camp movie.* [SEE NOTE]

cam•paign |kăm pān'| *n.* **1.** A series of military operations undertaken to achieve a specific purpose in a certain area. **2.** Organized activity to attain some political, social, or commercial goal. —***modifier:*** *a campaign speech.* —*v.* To engage in a campaign. —**cam•paign'er** *n.*

cam•pa•ni•le |kăm'pə nē'lē| *n.* A bell tower, especially one near but not attached to a church.

camp•er |kăm'pər| *n.* **1.** A person who camps outdoors. **2.** A boy or girl who attends a summer camp. **3.** A vehicle, often resembling an automobile-and-trailer combination, designed to serve as a dwelling place and used for camping or on long motor trips.

camp•fire |kămp'fīr'| *n.* An outdoor fire in a camp, used for warmth, cooking, or as a site for social gatherings.

Camp Fire Girl. A member of an organization for girls that provides recreation and develops practical skills.

cam•phor |kăm'fər| *n.* A white, crystalline compound of carbon, hydrogen, and oxygen in the proportions $C_{10}H_{16}O$, obtained from the wood of the **camphor tree** of eastern Asia. It vaporizes easily and is used as an insect repellent, in industry in making films, plastics, and explosives, and in medicine as a stimulant.

cam•phor•ate |kăm'fə rāt'| *v.* **cam•phor•at•ed, cam•phor•at•ing.** To treat with camphor.

camp•ing |kăm'pĭng| *n.* The act or practice of sleeping out in tents or other informal shelters, often while traveling or vacationing. —***modifier:*** *camping equipment; a camping trip.*

camp•site |kămp'sīt'| *n.* An area used for camping.

cam•pus |kăm'pəs| *n., pl.* **cam•pus•es. 1.** The grounds of a school, especially of a college or university. **2.** A school, such as a college, university, or boarding school, considered as an entity. —***modifier:*** *a campus protest.*

cam•shaft |kăm'shăft'| *or* |-shäft'| *n.* A turning shaft fitted with one or more cams, as in a gasoline engine.

can¹ |kăn| *or* |kən *when unstressed*| *v. aux.* Past tense **could** |kŏŏd| *or* |kəd *when unstressed*|. —Used with verbs to indicate that the subject: **1.** Knows how to: *She can skate well.* **2. a.** Is able or enabled to: *a place where people can put their ideas to work.* **b.** Will be able to: *I'll take you where you can find out about him.* **c.** Is inherently able or designed to: *Green plants can make their own food.* **3.** Feels free to: *We cannot accept this money.* **4.** Is logically or by rules enabled to: *You cannot punch or kick your opponent in judo.* **5.** Has permission to: *If you eat your vegetables, you can have dessert.* **6.** Is asked or invited to: *If you want to come, you can meet us there.* **7.** Has to or will have to: *If you don't behave, you can leave the room.* **8.** May possibly: *What can he have to say to me? Can you have the wrong address?* **9.** May sometimes: *Guessing at someone else's thoughts can prove disastrous.* [SEE NOTE]

can² |kăn| *n.* **1.** A small, cylindrical, airtight container, usually made of tin, in which food and beverages are preserved. **2. a.** A can with something in it: *a can of peaches.* **b.** The amount that a can holds: *drink a can of beer.* **3.** A much larger container of similar shape: *a garbage can.* —*v.* **canned, can•ning.** To preserve (food) in a sealed container. [SEE NOTE]

Can. Canada; Canadian.

Ca•naan |kā'nən|. In Biblical times, the part of Palestine between the Jordan River and the Mediterranean Sea, regarded by the Hebrews as the Promised Land.

Can•a•da |kăn'ə də|. A country in North America, lying north of the United States and extending from the Atlantic to the Pacific Ocean. Population, 22,992,604. Capital, Ottawa.

Canada goose. A North American wild goose with gray, black, and white feathers. [SEE PICTURE]

Ca•na•di•an |kə nā'dē ən| *n.* A native or inhabitant of Canada. —*adj.* Of or relating to Canada or the people of Canada.

Canadian French. French as spoken in Canada.

ca•nal |kə năl'| *n.* **1.** A waterway that is wholly or partly artificial, used for irrigation, drainage, or navigation. **2.** A tube or duct, as in the body: *the alimentary canal.* **3.** One of the faint lines seen on the surface of Mars, now thought to be geological features.

ca•nal•ize |kə năl'īz'| *or* |kăn'l īz'| *v.* **ca•nal•ized, ca•nal•iz•ing.** To furnish with or make into a canal or canals: *canalize an area. The engineers canalized the stream to make a waterway.*

Canal Zone. A strip of territory extending five miles on either side of the Panama Canal, formerly administered by the United States for the operation of the canal.

can•a•pé |**kăn'**ə pā'| *or* |-pē'| *n.* A cracker or a small piece of bread topped with a spread or tasty pieces of meat, fish, etc.

ca•nar•y |kə **nâr'**ē| *n., pl.* **ca•nar•ies. 1.** A usually yellow songbird that is popular as a pet. **2.** Also **canary yellow.** A light, bright yellow. *—adj.* Light, bright yellow. [SEE NOTE]

Ca•nar•y Islands |kə **nâr'**ē|. A group of Spanish islands off the northwest coast of Africa. Population, 1,017,000.

ca•nas•ta |kə **năs'**tə| *n.* A card game related to rummy and played with two decks of cards.

Can•ber•ra |**kăn'**bĕr'ə| *or* |-bər ə|. The capital of Australia. Population, 168,000.

can•can |**kăn'**kăn'| *n.* A lively acrobatic dance, performed by women entertainers, in which the legs are kicked very high.

can•cel |**kăn'**səl| *v.* **can•celed** or **can•celled, can•cel•ing** or **can•cel•ling. 1. a.** To abandon or give up (an idea, activity, etc.); call off: *cancel plans for a movie; cancel an appointment.* **b.** To declare without effectiveness, validity, etc.; annul: *cancel a magazine subscription.* **2.** To make marks or perforations in (a postage stamp, check, etc.) to indicate that it may not be used again. **3.** To make up for; offset; balance: *Two opposing votes cancel each other out.* **4. a.** To divide both the numerator and denominator of a fraction by a common factor by or as if by crossing it out in both places. **b.** To divide in the same way both of the expressions that are connected by an equal sign, =, or by either of the inequality signs, $<$ or $>$, by a common factor. **c.** To similarly remove a quantity, *a,* and its additive inverse, *-a,* from an expression.

can•cel•la•tion |kăn'sə **lā'**shən| *n.* **1.** The act of canceling. **2.** A mark made on a stamp, check, etc., to indicate that it has been canceled.

can•cer |**kăn'**sər| *n.* **1.** Any of various serious and often fatal diseases in which cells of the body grow in an abnormal and unchecked way, often spreading throughout the body. **2.** A mass of cells that grows and spreads in this manner; a malignant tumor. *—**modifier:** a cancer cell.*

Can•cer |**kăn'**sər|. The fourth sign of the zodiac.

can•cer•ous |**kăn'**sər əs| *adj.* Of or like a cancer: *a cancerous growth.*

can•del•a |kăn **dĕl'**ə| *n.* A unit used to express the brightness or intensity of a source of light, equal to $\frac{1}{60}$ of the intensity of the light emitted per square centimeter by a blackbody heated to a temperature of 1,773°C.

can•de•la•brum |kăn'dl **ä'**brəm| *or* |-**ăb'**rəm| *or* |-**ā'**brəm| *n., pl.* **can•de•la•bra** |kăn'dl **ä'**brə| *or* |-**ăb'**rə| *or* |-**ā'**brə| or **can•de•la•brums.** A large decorative candlestick with several arms or branches for holding candles.

can•did |**kăn'**dĭd| *adj.* **1.** Direct and frank; straightforward; open: *a candid opinion.* **2.** Not posed or rehearsed: *a candid photograph.* *—***can'did•ly** *adv.* *—***can'did•ness** *n.*

can•di•da•cy |**kăn'**dĭ də sē| *n., pl.* **can•di•da•cies.** The fact or condition of being a candidate.

can•di•date |**kăn'**dĭ dāt'| *or* |-dĭt| *n.* A person who seeks or is nominated for an office, prize, honor, etc.

can•died |**kăn'**dēd| *adj.* Cooked in or coated with a glaze of sugar: *candied sweet potatoes.*

can•dle |**kăn'**dl| *n.* **1.** A solid stick of wax, tallow, or other fatty substance with a wick inside that is lit and burned to provide light. **2.** In physics, a candela. *—**modifier:** candle wax.*

***Idiom.* not hold a candle to.** To be not nearly as good as: *He can't hold a candle to any of his colleagues.*

can•dle•light |**kăn'**dl līt'| *n.* The light given off by a candle.

can•dle•pow•er |**kăn'**dl pou'ər| *n.* The brightness or intensity of a source of light as expressed in candelas.

can•dle•stick |**kăn'**dl stĭk'| *n.* A holder with a cup or spike for a candle or candles. [SEE PICTURE]

can•dor |**kăn'**dər| *n.* The quality of saying freely what one thinks; openness; frankness.

can•dy |**kăn'**dē| *n., pl.* **can•dies.** A sweet food made from sugar or syrup that is mixed with various ingredients, such as fruit, nuts, butter, or chocolate. *—v.* **can•died, can•dy•ing, can•dies. 1.** To cook, preserve, or coat with sugar or syrup: *candy apples.* **2.** To turn to sugar: *The molasses candied along the edges of the barrel.*

cane |kān| *n.* **1.** A stick used as an aid in walking. **2.** Anything similar in shape to such a stick: *a candy cane.* **3. a.** A slender, woody, easily bent plant stem. **b.** A plant having such stems. **c.** Strips of such stems woven together to make chair seats or other objects. *—v.* **caned, can•ing. 1.** To beat with a walking stick. **2.** To make or repair (furniture) with cane.

cane•brake |**kān'**brāk'| *n.* A dense growth of canes.

cane sugar. A sugar obtained from the juice of sugar cane; sucrose.

ca•nine |**kā'**nīn'| *adj.* Of or typical of dogs or related animals. *—n.* **1.** A dog or related animal, such as a wolf or coyote. **2.** Also **canine tooth.** One of the teeth between the incisors and the first bicuspids; an eyetooth.

can•is•ter |**kăn'**ĭ stər| *n.* **1.** A container, usually of metal, for holding coffee, tea, flour, spices, etc. **2.** A metallic cylinder, filled with shot or tear gas, that bursts and scatters its contents when fired from a gun.

can•ker |**kăng'**kər| *n.* An ulcerlike sore on the lips or in the mouth.

can•ker•ous |**kăng'**kər əs| *adj.* **1.** Of, like, or affected with a canker; ulcerous. **2.** Tending to cause a canker.

can•ker•worm |**kăng'**kər wûrm'| *n.* A moth caterpillar that damages fruit trees and shade trees by feeding on their leaves.

can•na |**kăn'**ə| *n.* A garden plant native to the tropics, with large leaves and showy red or yellow flowers.

can•na•bis |**kăn'**ə bĭs| *n.* The hemp plant; marijuana.

canned |kănd| *adj.* **1.** Preserved and sealed in an airtight can or jar: *canned vegetables.* **2.** *Informal.* Recorded or taped: *canned music.*

can•nel |**kăn'**l| *n.* Also **cannel coal.** A form of

canary

In its original wild state in the Canary Islands, *the* **canary** *is a dull yellowish-green. The bright, clear yellow of the familiar caged birds is the result of many generations of breeding in captivity.*

candlestick

canoe

canon[1-2]

Canon[1] *and* **canon**[2] *are both ultimately from Greek* kanōn, *"a rule." The meaning of* **canon**[2] *was originally "one who is bound by the rule of the church."*

cant[1-2]

Cant[1] *used to mean "an edge" and later came to mean "a corner, an angle." It comes from Latin* canthus, *"rim of a wheel."* **Cant**[2] *is from Latin* cantāre, *"to sing." It is related to* **chant.**

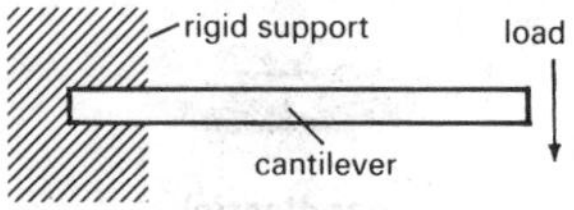

cantilever

bituminous coal that burns with a bright, smoky flame.

can•ner•y |**kăn′**ə rē| *n., pl.* **can•ner•ies.** A factory where meat, vegetables, etc., are canned.

can•ni•bal |**kăn′**ə bəl| *n.* **1.** A person who eats the flesh of human beings. **2.** Any animal that feeds on others of its own kind.

can•ni•bal•ism |**kăn′**ə bə lĭz′əm| *n.* The practices of a cannibal. —**can′ni•bal•is′tic** *adj.*

can•ni•bal•ize |**kăn′**ə bə līz′| *v.* **can•ni•bal•ized, can•ni•bal•iz•ing.** To remove useful parts from (damaged or worn-out equipment) for use in the repair of other equipment.

can•ning |**kăn′**ĭng| *n.* The process of preserving foods in airtight cans or jars.

can•non |**kăn′**ən| *n., pl.* **can•nons** or **can•non. 1.** A large gun mounted on wheels or on a fixed base. **2.** A firearm whose caliber is .60 or larger. ¶*These sound alike* **cannon, canon.**

can•non•ade |kăn′ə **nād′**| *v.* **can•non•ad•ed, can•non•ad•ing.** To assault or bombard with heavy cannon fire. —*n.* A long, heavy artillery assault or bombardment.

can•non•ball |**kăn′**ən bôl′| *n.* Also **cannon ball.** A round projectile fired or to be fired from a cannon.

can•non•eer |kăn′ə **nîr′**| *n.* A gunner or artilleryman.

can•not |**kăn′**ŏt′| *or* |kă **nŏt′**| *or* |kə-|. The negative form of **can.**

can•ny |**kăn′**ē| *adj.* **can•ni•er, can•ni•est.** Careful and shrewd in one's actions and dealings. —**can′ni•ly** *adv.* —**can′ni•ness** *n.*

ca•noe |kə **nōō′**| *n.* A light, slender boat with pointed ends that is moved by paddles. —*v.* **ca•noed, ca•noe•ing.** To paddle or travel in a canoe. —**ca•noe′ist** *n.* [SEE PICTURE]

can•on[1] |**kăn′**ən| *n.* **1.** A law or code of laws enacted by a church. **2.** A basic principle or general standard: *the canons of good behavior.* **3.** The books of the Bible officially recognized by a Christian church. **4.** Often **Canon.** The most important part of the Mass. **5.** A musical composition or passage in which a melody is introduced by one part and restated by a second part before the first part has finished its statement. Often additional parts are introduced in the same manner. ¶*These sound alike* **canon, cannon.** [SEE NOTE]

can•on[2] |**kăn′**ən| *n.* A clergyman serving in a cathedral or collegiate church. ¶*These sound alike* **canon, cannon.** [SEE NOTE]

ca•non•i•cal |kə **nŏn′**ĭ kəl| or **ca•non•ic** |kə-**nŏn′**ĭk| *adj.* **1.** Of or prescribed by canon law. **2.** Officially approved; authoritative. **3.** Of or like a musical canon.

can•on•ize |**kăn′**ə nīz′| *v.* **can•on•ized, can•on•iz•ing.** To declare (a dead person) to be a saint. —**can′on•i•za′tion** *n.*

canon law. The official body of laws governing a Christian church.

can•o•py |**kăn′**ə pē| *n., pl.* **can•o•pies. 1.** A kind of tentlike roof, usually held up on posts or poles, covering a bed, entrance, sacred object, or important person. **2.** Any similar covering: *a canopy of leafy branches.* **3.** The transparent sliding enclosure over an aircraft's cockpit. —*v.* **can•o•pied, can•o•py•ing, can•o•pies.** To spread over with a canopy.

canst |kănst|. *Archaic.* A form of the present tense of **can,** used with *thou.*

cant[1] |kănt| *n.* **1.** Slant or slope: *the cant of a roof.* **2. a.** A forceful push that causes something to tilt to one side. **b.** The tilt resulting from such a push. —**modifier:** *The carpenter beveled the corners and gave them a cant edge.* —*v.* **1.** To give a slanting edge to; bevel. **2.** To tilt or cause to tilt to one side. **3.** To swing around: *The gunboat came just abeam of us and then canted off to southward.* ¶*These sound alike* **cant, can't.** [SEE NOTE]

cant[2] |kănt| *n.* **1.** Whining or singsong speech, as used by beggars. **2.** Insincere talk. **3.** The special vocabulary used by a certain group or class of people: *thieves' cant.* ¶*These sound alike* **cant, can't.** [SEE NOTE]

can't |kănt| *or* |känt|. Can not. ¶*These sound alike* **can't, cant.**

can•ta•bi•le |kän **tä′**bē lā′| *or* |-bĭ-| *or* |kən-|. In music: *adj.* Smooth and lyrical; songlike. —*adv.* Smoothly and lyrically. —*n.* A cantabile passage or movement.

can•ta•loupe, also **can•ta•loup** |**kăn′**tl ōp′| *n.* A melon with a ribbed, rough rind and sweet-smelling orange flesh.

can•tank•er•ous |kăn **tăng′**kər əs| *adj.* Ill-tempered and quarrelsome; disagreeable; contrary. —**can•tank′er•ous•ly** *adv.*

can•ta•ta |kən **tä′**tə| *n.* A musical composition, shorter than an opera or an oratorio, that consists of a number of short pieces for voices and instruments.

can•teen |kăn **tēn′**| *n.* **1.** A container for carrying drinking water. **2.** A store on or near a military base, where supplies and refreshments are provided for servicemen.

can•ter |**kăn′**tər| *n.* A slow, easy gallop. —*v.* To ride or run at a canter: *He cantered the horse across the field. The horse cantered down the road.* ¶*These sound alike* **canter, cantor.**

can•ti•cle |**kăn′**tĭ kəl| *n.* A song or chant, especially a hymn whose words are taken directly from the Bible.

can•ti•le•ver |**kăn′**tl ē′vər| *or* |-ĕv′ər| *n.* A beam or other projecting structure that is supported at one end only. —*v.* To build or extend outward as a cantilever. [SEE PICTURE]

cantilever bridge. A bridge formed by a pair of spans that are supported on piers at each end and counterbalanced and that extend toward each other and are joined by a connecting span in the center.

can•tle |**kăn′**tl| *n.* The raised part at the back of a saddle.

can•to |**kăn′**tō| *n., pl.* **can•tos.** A major division of a long poem.

can•ton |**kăn′**tən| *or* |-tŏn′| *n.* In Switzerland, the main political unit. The Swiss Confederation has 22 cantons.

Can•ton |**kăn′**tŏn′| *or* |kăn **tŏn′**|. A port city in southeastern China. Population, 3,000,000.

Can•ton•ese |kăn′tə **nēz′**| *or* |-**nēs′**| *n., pl.* **Can•ton•ese. 1.** The dialect of Chinese spoken in and around Canton. **2.** A native or inhabitant of Canton. —*adj.* Of Canton, the Cantonese, or their dialect.

can•ton•ment |kăn **tōn′**mənt| *or* |-**tŏn′**-| *n.* Temporary quarters for a body of soldiers.

ă pat/ā pay/â care/ä father/ĕ pet/ ē be/ĭ pit/ī pie/î fierce/ŏ pot/ ō go/ô paw, for/oi oil/ŏŏ book/ ōō boot/ou out/ŭ cut/û fur/ *th* the/th thin/hw which/zh vision/ ə ago, item, pencil, atom, circus

can•tor |kăn′tər| *n.* **1.** The official who leads the congregation in prayer and sings the music used in a Jewish religious service. **2.** The person who leads a church choir or congregation in singing. ¶*These sound alike* **cantor, canter.**

can•vas |kăn′vəs| *n.* **1.** A heavy, coarse cloth of cotton, hemp, or flax, used for making tents, sails, etc. **2.** An oil painting on canvas or a piece of canvas used to paint on. **3.** The floor of a ring for boxing or wrestling. —***modifier:*** *a canvas hat.* ¶*These sound alike* **canvas, canvass.**

can•vas•back |kăn′vəs băk′| *n.* A North American duck with a reddish head and neck and a whitish back. [SEE PICTURE]

can•vass |kăn′vəs| *v.* **1.** To visit (a person or region) to get votes, hear opinions, make sales, etc. **2.** To examine or discuss. —*n.* **1.** The act of canvassing; a poll or survey: *a house-to-house canvass to find out how people intend to vote in the election.* **2.** A thorough examination or detailed discussion. ¶*These sound alike* **canvass, canvas.** —**can′vass•er** *n.*

can•yon |kăn′yən| *n.* A deep, narrow cleft in the earth with steep cliff walls on both sides, formed by running water; a gorge.

caou•tchouc |kou′cho͝ok′| *or* |kou **cho͝ok′**| *n.* Natural rubber.

cap |kăp| *n.* **1. a.** A covering that fits closely on the head, usually soft and having no brim but sometimes having a visor. **b.** A graduate's mortarboard. **2.** A small, circular, tight-fitting cover: *a bottle cap; a radiator cap.* **3.** A circular, overhanging top attached to a stem: *a mushroom cap.* **4. a.** A **percussion cap. b.** A small explosive charge enclosed in paper for use in a toy gun. **5.** *Informal.* A **capital letter.** —*v.* **capped, cap•ping. 1.** To put a cap or top on; cover the top of: *cap a bottle; a region composed of sea and rock and forest, where the mountains are capped by eternal snows.* **2.** To outdo; excel: *Each joke capped the one before.*

cap. **1.** capacity. **2.** capital (city). **3.** capital letter.

ca•pa•bil•i•ty |kā′pə **bĭl′**ĭ tē| *n., pl.* **ca•pa•bil•i•ties. 1.** The quality of being capable; ability; capacity: *prove one's capability for a job.* **2.** Often **capabilities.** Potential ability: *Good composers know the capabilities of each instrument.* **3.** Estimated maximum power to be used or developed for a specific purpose: *America's nuclear capability.*

ca•pa•ble |kā′pə bəl| *adj.* **1.** Able; skilled; competent: *a capable teacher.* **2.** —**capable of. a.** Having the ability or capacity for: *a boy capable of being a great athlete; a jar capable of holding more than a quart.* **b.** Open to; subject to: *a statement capable of several interpretations.* —**ca′pa•bly** *adv.*

ca•pa•cious |kə **pā′**shəs| *adj.* Able to contain a large quantity; roomy; large: *a capacious suitcase.* —**ca•pa′cious•ly** *adv.* —**ca•pa′cious•ness** *n.*

ca•pac•i•tance |kə **păs′**ĭ təns| *n.* The ability of an object to collect and store electric charge. The measure of capacitance is the quotient of the amount of stored charge divided by the electrical potential of the object.

ca•pac•i•tive |kə **păs′**ĭ tĭv| *adj.* Of or resulting from capacitance.

capacitive reactance. The opposition to an electric current caused by the presence of capacitance in a circuit.

ca•pac•i•tor |kə **păs′**ĭ tər| *n.* A device with two terminals that when connected into an electric circuit increases the capacitance between the two points at which it is connected.

ca•pac•i•ty |kə **păs′**ĭ tē| *n., pl.* **ca•pac•i•ties. 1.** The ability to hold, receive, or contain: *a can with a capacity of three quarts; a theater with a small seating capacity.* **2.** Ability; capability: *a person's capacity for learning.* **3. a.** The maximum amount that can be contained: *a trunk filled to capacity.* **b.** The maximum or most efficient level of production: *a machine operating at full capacity.* **4.** Position: *act in one's capacity as chairman.* **5.** *Archaic.* Capacitance.

ca•par•i•son |kə **păr′**ĭ sən| *n.* **1.** A covering, as of cloth, put over a horse or harness for decoration. **2.** Rich or fancy clothing; finery. —*v.* **1.** To put a caparison on: *caparison a horse.* **2.** To dress in splendid clothes.

cape¹ |kāp| *n.* A sleeveless outer garment fastened at the throat and worn hanging loose over the shoulders. [SEE NOTE]

cape² |kāp| *n.* A point or head of land projecting into a sea or other body of water; a promontory. [SEE NOTE]

ca•per¹ |kā′pər| *v.* To jump about playfully; gambol: *The lambs capered about the meadow.* —*n.* **1.** A playful leap or hop: *the capers of a frisky pony.* **2. a.** An antic; prank. **b.** *Slang.* A criminal escapade. [SEE NOTE]

ca•per² |kā′pər| *n.* A pickled flower bud of a Mediterranean shrub, used to season food or eaten as a relish. [SEE NOTE]

Cape Town, also **Cape•town** |kāp′toun′|. The legislative capital of South Africa. Population, 698,000.

Cape Verde |vûrd|. A group of islands in the Atlantic Ocean off the northwest coast of Africa, constituting an independent country. Population, 324,000. Capital, Praia.

cap•il•lar•i•ty |kăp′ə **lăr′**ĭ tē| *n.* The attraction or repulsion between touching surfaces of a liquid and a solid that prevents the surface of the liquid from being flat.

cap•il•lar•y |**kăp′**ə lĕr′ē| *n., pl.* **cap•il•lar•ies. 1.** Any of the tiny blood vessels that connect the smallest arteries to the smallest veins. **2.** A tube that has a very small inside diameter. —*adj.* **1.** Of or like a capillary or capillaries. **2.** Having a very small inside diameter. **3.** Of capillarity: *capillary attraction; capillary repulsion.* **4.** Of or like a hair; fine; slender.

cap•i•tal |**kăp′**ĭ tl| *n.* **1.** A city that is the seat of a state or national government. **2.** Wealth or property that is invested to produce more wealth. **3.** A **capital letter. 4.** The top part, or head, of a pillar or column. —***modifier:*** *capital investments; capital gains.* —*adj.* **1.** First and foremost; principal. **2.** Excellent: *a capital fellow.* **3.** Punishable by or involving death: *a capital offense; capital punishment.* ¶*These sound alike* **capital, capitol.** [SEE NOTE at **chattel**]

cap•i•tal•ism |**kăp′**ĭ tl ĭz′əm| *n.* An economic system, marked by a free market and open competition, in which goods are produced for profit, labor is performed for wages, and the means of production and distribution are privately owned.

canvasback

cape¹·²

Cape¹ *and* **cape²** *both come into English through French and Provençal, and both ultimately come from Latin* caput, *"head," but with quite different meanings.* **Cape²** *is straightforward: "head," hence "a head of land, a headland." In the case of* **cape¹**, *Latin* caput *developed a late derivative,* cappa, *meaning "hat" and later also "cloak."*

caper¹·²

Caper¹ *is from French* capriole, *which is from Italian* capriola, *"a goat's leap," from Latin* caper, *"goat."* **Caper²** *is ultimately from Greek* kapparis, *"caper plant."*

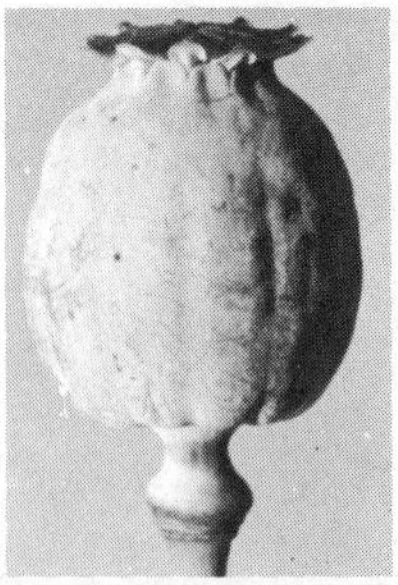

capsule
Above: Capsule of poppy
Below: Capsule of *Apollo 9*

car
The history of the word **car** *is full of history. The ancient Celts had a kind of wagon called a* karros, *which they used to transport armies and whole migrating tribes. The Romans, who did not originally make much use of vehicles, adopted both the wagon and its name, changed to* carrus. *The word passed into Norman French as* carre *and then into Middle English as* **car**. *It was by this time only a poetic word, used of the chariots of classical gods and heroes, until in the 1820's it was applied in America to railroad vehicles. Finally, in the 1890's, the term* **motor car** *was coined for what had been called a "horseless carriage."*

ă **pat**/ā **pay**/â **care**/ä **father**/ĕ **pet**/ ē **be**/ĭ **pit**/ī **pie**/î **fierce**/ŏ **pot**/ ō **go**/ô **paw**, **for**/oi **oil**/ŏŏ **book**/ ōō **boot**/ou **out**/ŭ **cut**/û **fur**/ *th* **the**/th **thin**/hw **which**/zh **vision**/ ə **ago**, item, pencil, atom, circus

cap•i•tal•ist |kăp′ĭ tl ĭst| *n.* **1. a.** A person who invests capital in business, especially a large investor in an important business. **b.** Any person of great wealth. **2.** A person who supports capitalism. *—**modifier:** a capitalist system; a capitalist point of view.* —**cap′i•tal•is′tic** *adj.* —**cap′i•tal•is′ti•cal•ly** *adv.*

cap•i•tal•ize |kăp′ĭ tl īz′| *v.* **cap•i•tal•ized, cap•i•tal•iz•ing. 1. a.** To begin a word with a capital letter: *Capitalize the first word in every sentence.* **b.** To write or print in capital letters: *You should capitalize the title of a book report.* **2.** To turn to advantage; profit by: *capitalize on an opponent's errors.* —**cap′i•tal•i•za′tion** *n.*

capital letter. A letter, such as A or B, written or printed in a size larger than its corresponding small letter.

Cap•i•tals |kăp′ĭ tlz|. The National Hockey League team from Washington.

cap•i•tol |kăp′ĭ tl| *n.* **1. Capitol.** The temple of Jupiter in ancient Rome. **2. Capitol.** The building in Washington, D.C., occupied by the Congress of the United States. **3.** The building in which a state legislature assembles. ¶*These sound alike* **capitol, capital.**

ca•pit•u•late |kə **pĭch′**ə lāt′| *v.* **ca•pit•u•lat•ed, ca•pit•u•lat•ing.** To surrender under stated conditions; give in; yield: *capitulate to the enemy.*

ca•pit•u•la•tion |kə pĭch′ə **lā′**shən| *n.* **1.** The act of capitulating. **2.** A statement of the main points of a topic; an outline.

ca•pon |kā′pŏn′| *or* |-pən| *n.* A male chicken that has been castrated and specially raised for use as food.

ca•pric•cio |kə **prē′**chō| *or* |-chē ō| *n., pl.* **ca•pric•cios.** An instrumental musical composition written in a free, fanciful style.

ca•price |kə **prēs′**| *n.* **1.** An impulsive change of mind; a whim: *the caprices of a woman.* **2.** In music, a capriccio.

ca•pri•cious |kə **prĭsh′**əs| *or* |-**prē′**shəs| *adj.* **1.** Subject to sudden, unpredictable changes; impulsive; fickle: *a capricious child.* **2.** Often changing; unreliable; irregular: *treacherous reefs and capricious currents; capricious weather.* —**ca•pri′cious•ly** *adv.* —**ca•pri′cious•ness** *n.*

Cap•ri•corn |kăp′rĭ kôrn′|. The tenth sign of the zodiac.

cap•size |kăp′sīz′| *or* |kăp **sīz′**| *v.* **cap•sized, cap•siz•ing.** To overturn: *A huge wave capsized our boat. The ship capsized in the storm.*

cap•stan |kăp′stən| *n.* **1.** A vertical cylinder used to wind in the anchor cable of a ship. **2.** A small rotating cylinder that drives the magnetic tape past the heads of a tape recorder.

cap•su•lar |kăp′sə lər| *or* |-syōō-| *adj.* Of, like, or enclosed in a capsule.

cap•sule |kăp′səl| *or* |-syōōl| *n.* **1.** A small container, usually of gelatin or another soluble material, that contains a dose of a medicine to be taken by mouth. **2.** A sac or similar structure that encloses an organ or a part of the body. **3.** A compartment that can be separated from the rest of a spacecraft, especially one designed to accommodate a crew. **4.** A seed case that dries and splits open. [SEE PICTURE]

Capt. captain.

cap•tain |kăp′tən| *n.* **1.** The leader of a group; chief: *the captain of the football team.* **2.** The person in command of a ship. **3.** An officer in the Army, Air Force, or Marine Corps ranking above a first lieutenant and below a major. **4.** An officer in the Navy ranking above a commander and below a rear admiral.

cap•tain•cy |kăp′tən sē| *n., pl.* **cap•tain•cies.** The rank, authority, or skill of a captain.

cap•tain•ship |kăp′tən shĭp′| *n.* Captaincy.

cap•tion |kăp′shən| *n.* **1.** A title or explanation accompanying an illustration or photograph. **2.** A heading, as of a legal document or a chapter of a book. —*v.* To furnish a caption for.

cap•tious |kăp′shəs| *adj.* **1.** Inclined to criticize trivial defects; faultfinding: *a captious book reviewer.* **2.** Designed to confuse or ensnare, especially in an argument: *a captious question.* —**cap′tious•ness** *n.*

cap•ti•vate |kăp′tə vāt′| *v.* **cap•ti•vat•ed, cap•ti•vat•ing.** To fascinate or charm with wit, beauty, intelligence, etc. —**cap′ti•vat′ing** *adj.: a captivating woman; a captivating story.* —**cap′ti•va′tion** *n.*

cap•tive |kăp′tĭv| *adj.* **1. a.** Held prisoner: *a captive bear.* **b.** Under restraint or control; not free: *a captive nation; captive peoples.* **2.** Obliged to be present: *a captive audience.* —*n.* A person or animal held captive; a prisoner.

cap•tiv•i•ty |kăp **tĭv′**ĭ tē| *n., pl.* **cap•tiv•i•ties.** A period or the condition of being captive: *Few aardvarks have lived long in captivity.*

cap•tor |kăp′tər| *n.* Someone who takes or holds another as a captive.

cap•ture |kăp′chər| *v.* **cap•tured, cap•tur•ing. 1. a.** To get hold of, as by skill, force, etc.: *capture a city. He captured the horse with a lasso.* **b.** To get or hold the interest of: *capture the imagination.* **c.** To hold or preserve in permanent form: *capture a likeness in a photo.* **2.** To get possession of, as in a contest; win: *The Dodgers captured the pennant.* **3.** To incorporate into a whole; absorb: *The hydrogen nucleus captured a neutron.* —*n.* **1.** The act of capturing or process of being captured. **2.** Someone or something that has been captured.

cap•u•chin |kăp′yōō chĭn| *or* |-shĭn| *n.* A long-tailed South American monkey with hoodlike tufts of hair on the head.

cap•y•ba•ra |kăp′ə **bä′**rə| *or* |-**băr′**ə| *n.* A large, short-tailed South American rodent that lives in or near water and may grow to a length of four feet.

car |kär| *n.* **1.** An automobile. **2.** A passenger vehicle with wheels that moves on rails or tracks, as a railroad car. **3.** The part of an elevator in which passengers ride. *—**modifier:** a car dealer; car prices.* [SEE NOTE]

car•a•bao |kăr′ə **bou′**| *or* |kä′rə **bä′**ō| *n., pl.* **car•a•baos.** An animal, the **water buffalo,** so called especially in the Philippine Islands.

car•a•cal |kăr′ə kăl′| *n.* A wild cat of Africa and southern Asia, having short tan fur and long, tufted ears.

Ca•ra•cas |kə **rä′**kəs| *or* |-**răk′**əs|. The capital and largest city of Venezuela. Population, 1,959,000.

car•a•cul |kăr′ə kəl| *n.* The loosely curled fur of a lamb of the karakul sheep of central Asia.

ca•rafe |kə **răf′**| *or* |-**räf′**| *n.* A glass bottle for serving water or wine at the table.

car•a•mel |kăr′ə məl| *or* |-mĕl′| *or* |kär′məl| *n.* **1.** A smooth, chewy candy. **2.** Sugar heated to a brown syrup and used for coloring and sweetening foods.

car•a•pace |kăr′ə pās′| *n.* A hard outer covering, such as the upper shell of a turtle or the armorlike covering of a lobster.

car•at |kăr′ət| *n.* **1.** A unit of weight for precious stones, equal to 200 milligrams or about 1/140 of an ounce. **2.** A form of the word **karat.** ¶ *These sound alike* **carat, carrot.**

car•a•van |kăr′ə văn′| *n.* **1.** An expedition of merchants, pilgrims, etc., traveling together, especially through desert regions. **2.** Any file of vehicles or pack animals. **3.** *British.* A home on wheels, as a trailer, a gypsy wagon, etc.

car•a•van•sa•ry |kăr′ə **văn′**sə rē| *n., pl.* **car•a•van•sa•ries.** In Eastern countries, an inn with a large courtyard for the accommodation of caravans.

car•a•vel |kăr′ə vĕl′| *n.* A small, light three-masted sailing ship of the type used by Columbus. [SEE PICTURE]

car•a•way |kăr′ə wā′| *n.* **1.** A plant with strong-tasting crescent-shaped seeds, used as flavoring in baking and cooking. **2.** The seeds of this plant.

car•bide |kär′bīd′| *n.* A chemical compound, especially calcium carbide, consisting of carbon and a metal.

car•bine |kär′bīn′| *or* |-bēn′| *n.* A light rifle with a short barrel, originally designed for cavalry use.

car•bo•hy•drate |kär′bō **hī′**drāt′| *or* |-bə-| *n.* Any of a group of chemical compounds, including sugars, starches, and cellulose, that are composed of carbon, hydrogen, and oxygen. Most often these compounds contain two hydrogen atoms for every oxygen atom, and they can be broken down into carbon and water.

car•bo•lat•ed |kär′bə lā′tĭd| *adj.* Containing or treated with phenol.

car•bol•ic acid |kär **bŏl′**ĭk|. Phenol.

car•bon |kär′bən| *n.* **1.** Symbol **C** A nonmetallic element, occurring as a powdery, crystalline solid, such as graphite or diamond. Atomic number 6; atomic weight 12.01; valences -4, +2, +4; sublimes above 3,500°C; boiling point 4,827°C. **2. a.** A sheet of carbon paper. **b.** A copy made by using carbon paper; a carbon copy. [SEE NOTE]

carbon 14. An isotope of carbon that contains two more neutrons in its nucleus than ordinary carbon does and that therefore has an atomic weight of 14. It is radioactive and has a half-life of 5,700 years. [SEE NOTE]

car•bo•na•ceous |kär′bə **nā′**shəs| *adj.* Of, containing, or yielding carbon.

car•bon•ate |kär′bə nāt′| *v.* **car•bon•at•ed, car•bon•at•ing.** To charge with carbon dioxide gas, as a beverage. —*n.* |kär′bə nāt′| *or* |-nĭt|. A salt or ester of carbonic acid. —**car′bon•a′tion** *n.* —**car′bon•a′tor** *n.*

carbonated water. **Soda water.**

carbon copy. A duplicate of anything written or typed, made by inserting a sheet of carbon paper between the original and the copy.

carbon cycle. **1.** The series of natural processes in which carbon dioxide from the air is changed to carbohydrates by plants in photosynthesis and these carbohydrates are eaten by animals that return the carbon dioxide to the air as a waste product of metabolism. **2.** The **carbon-nitrogen cycle.**

carbon dioxide. A colorless, odorless gas that does not burn. It is composed of carbon and oxygen and has the formula CO_2. It is produced in any process, such as combustion, respiration, or organic decomposition, in which carbon combines completely with oxygen. It is used in refrigeration, in fire extinguishers, and in carbonated drinks.

car•bon•ic acid |kär **bŏn′**ĭk|. A weak acid composed of hydrogen, carbon, and oxygen and having the formula H_2CO_3. It exists only in solution and decomposes readily into carbon dioxide and water.

car•bon•if•er•ous |kär′bə **nĭf′**ər əs| *adj.* Of, producing, or containing carbon or coal.

Car•bon•if•er•ous |kär′bə **nĭf′**ər əs| *n.* Also **Carboniferous period.** A geologic period that began about 345 million years ago and ended about 280 million years ago. During this period much of the earth was covered with dense plant growth that eventually sank into swamps and finally hardened into coal. —***modifier:*** *a Carboniferous forest.*

car•bon•ize |kär′bə nīz′| *v.* **car•bon•ized, car•bon•iz•ing.** **1.** To change (a substance that contains carbon) to carbon alone, as by applying heat. **2.** To treat, coat, or combine with carbon. —**car′bon•i•za′tion** *n.*

carbon monoxide. A colorless, odorless gas that is extremely poisonous. It is composed of carbon and oxygen and has the formula CO. Carbon monoxide is formed when carbon or any substance that contains carbon burns incompletely. [SEE NOTE]

car•bon-ni•tro•gen cycle |kär′bən **nī′**trə jən|. A thermonuclear process in which four hydrogen nuclei fuse to form a helium nucleus. In this reaction, which provides the energy of certain types of stars, carbon nuclei act as a catalyst, and certain isotopes of nitrogen are formed in intermediate stages.

carbon paper. A lightweight paper coated on one side with a dark coloring matter, used between sheets of writing paper for making copies.

carbon tetrachloride. A colorless liquid that does not burn. It vaporizes easily, is quite poisonous, is composed of carbon and chlorine, and has the formula CCl_4. Carbon tetrachloride is used in fire extinguishers and as a solvent.

Car•bo•run•dum |kär′bə **rŭn′**dəm| *n.* A trademark for an abrasive made of silicon carbide.

car•boy |kär′boi′| *n.* A large bottle, usually protected by a crate or basket, in which dangerous liquids, such as acids, are shipped.

car•bun•cle |kär′bŭng′kəl| *n.* A painful, pus-producing inflammation that normally affects a small area of the skin and the tissue beneath it. It has a serious effect on the entire system and can be fatal.

car•bu•re•tor |kär′bə rā′tər| *or* |-byə-| *n.* A part of a gasoline engine that vaporizes or atomizes the gasoline and mixes it with air in such a way that it will burn properly.

car•cass |kär′kəs| *n.* **1.** The dead body of an animal. **2.** Anything likened to a carcass: *the*

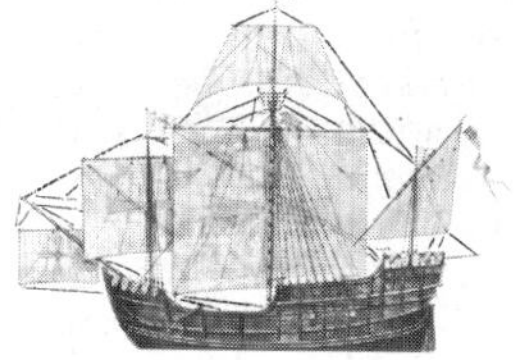

caravel

carbon

Carbon *is an abundant element in the universe and an important constituent of all living things. Its allotropic forms range from the extremely soft, black graphite to the extemely hard, translucent diamond. Carbon atoms can form chemical bonds with each other as well as with atoms of different elements. Because of this, there is an enormous number of carbon compounds. The separate branch of chemistry called* organic chemistry *is the study of carbon compounds.*

carbon 14

Carbon 14 *occurs naturally in all objects that contain carbon. Because it decays radioactively at a known rate, it is used to determine the age of ancient objects.*

carbon monoxide

The engines used in cars and trucks (and also in power lawn mowers and similar machines) are practically never able to burn their fuel completely. Their exhausts, therefore, contain dangerous amounts of **carbon monoxide.**

card[1-2]

Card[1] *comes from Old French* carte, *from Latin* charta, *from Greek* khartēs, *"sheet of papyrus," which is from Egyptian (the Egyptians invented papyrus). The word* **chart** *comes from the same source.* **Card[2]**, *an old technical word, comes from Latin* cārere, *which is descended from* kars-, *the prehistoric Indo-European word meaning "to card wool."*

cardinal

ă **pat**/ā **pay**/â **care**/ä **father**/ĕ **pet**/ ē **be**/ĭ **pit**/ī **pie**/î **fierce**/ŏ **pot**/ ō **go**/ô **paw**, **for**/oi **oil**/ŏŏ **book**/ ōō **boot**/ou **out**/ŭ **cut**/û **fur**/ *th* **the**/th **thin**/hw **which**/**zh** **vision**/ ə **ago**, **item**, **pencil**, **atom**, **circus**

carcasses of old cars in a junkyard. **3.** *Informal.* A person's living or dead body.

car•cin•o•gen |kär sĭn'ə jən| *or* |kär'sə nə jĕn'| *n.* A substance that tends to cause cancer. —**car'cin•o•gen'ic** |kär'sə nə **jĕn'**ĭk| *adj.*

car•ci•no•ma |kär'sə **nō'**mə| *n., pl.* **car•ci•no•mas** or **car•ci•no•ma•ta** |kär'sə **nō'**mə tə|. A malignant tumor derived from skin, mucous membrane, or other tissue that serves as a covering for an organ or structure; a type of cancer.

card[1] |kärd| *n.* A small, rectangular piece of stiff paper, thin plastic, or pasteboard, used for a variety of purposes: **1.** One of a set of 52 cards bearing numbers, figures, etc., and divided into four suits, spades, hearts, diamonds, and clubs, used for various games and for telling fortunes. **2.** One used to send messages or greetings: *a post card; a Christmas card.* **3.** One bearing a person's name, a book's title, or other information, used for identification, classification, etc.: *a calling card; a draft card; a file card.* —***modifier:*** *a card table; card games.* [SEE NOTE]

Idioms. **have a card up (one's) sleeve.** To have a secret resource held in reserve. **in the cards.** Likely or destined to happen.

card[2] |kärd| *n.* A brush with teeth of wire, used to comb out fibers of wool, flax, or cotton before spinning. —*v.* To comb out with a tool like this: *card wool.* [SEE NOTE]

card•board |**kärd'**bôrd'| *or* |-bōrd'| *n.* A thin, stiff pasteboard made of paper pulp.

car•di•ac |**kär'**dē ăk'| *adj.* Of, near, or having to do with the heart: *a cardiac disorder; a cardiac patient.*

Car•diff |**kär'**dĭf|. The capital of Wales. Population, 281,000.

car•di•gan |**kär'**dĭ gən| *n.* A sweater or knitted jacket without a collar, opening down the front and usually buttoning.

car•di•nal |**kär'**dn əl| *adj.* Of primary importance; chief; foremost: *the cardinal element of a plan.* —*n.* **1.** An official of the Roman Catholic Church whose rank is just below that of the pope. **2.** A North American bird with a crested head and bright red feathers. **3.** A **cardinal number.** [SEE PICTURE]

cardinal number. A number that indicates how many elements are in a set, without indicating their relative order.

cardinal point. One of the four principal directions on a compass; north, south, east, or west.

car•di•o•gram |**kär'**dē ə grăm'| *n.* **1.** The curve traced by a cardiograph. **2.** *Informal.* An electrocardiogram.

car•di•o•graph |**kär'**dē ə grăf'| *or* |-gräf'| *n.* An instrument used to record graphically the movements of the heart.

car•di•ol•o•gist |kär'dē **ŏl'**ə jĭst| *n.* A physician who specializes in cardiology.

car•di•ol•o•gy |kär'dē **ŏl'**ə jē| *n.* The scientific study of the heart, its diseases, and their treatment.

car•di•o•pul•mo•nar•y |kär'dē ō **pŏŏl'**mə-nĕr'ē| *adj.* Of or relating to the heart and lungs.

cardiopulmonary resuscitation. A procedure used after cardiac arrest in which cardiac massage, mouth-to-mouth resuscitation, and drugs are used to restore breathing.

car•di•o•vas•cu•lar |kär'dē ō **văs'**kyə lər| *adj.* Of the heart and blood vessels.

cards |kärdz| *n. (used with a singular verb).* **1.** Any card game played with cards, as canasta or poker. **2.** The playing of such games: *Are you good at cards?*

care |kâr| *n.* **1. a.** Mental distress, caused by fear, doubt, anxiety, etc.; trouble; worry: *free from care.* **b.** A cause of such a state of mind: *troubled by the cares involved in raising a large family.* **2. a.** Serious attention or effort; painstaking application: *You should devote more care to your work.* **b.** Caution in avoiding harm, damage, etc.: *Glass, handle with care.* **3.** Supervision; charge; keeping: *in the care of a nurse.* —*v.* **cared, car•ing. 1.** To be worried or concerned: *I don't care what happens. I don't care about going. Who cares?* **2.** To be willing or desirous; want: *I don't care to be on the football team. Would you care to go for a walk?* **3.** To like: *Does John really care for that girl?* **4.** To take charge of; look after: *Who will care for the baby?*

Idioms. **take care.** To be careful. **take care of. 1.** To look after: *take care of a child.* **2.** To attend to: *take care of our flight reservations.*

CARE |kâr|. A nonprofit organization that sends packages of food and clothing to needy people overseas.

ca•reen |kə **rēn'**| *v.* **1.** To tilt (a ship) onto its side, on the shore, in order to clean or repair its bottom. **2.** To lurch or swerve while in motion: *The car careened on the icy road.*

ca•reer |kə **rîr'**| *n.* **1.** A profession; occupation: *a medical career.* **2.** The general progress or course of one's life, especially in one's profession: *an officer with a distinguished career.* —***modifier:*** *a career girl; a career officer.* —*v.* To move or run at full speed: *The startled horse went careering off through the meadow.*

Idiom. **in full career.** At full speed.

care•free |**kâr'**frē'| *adj.* Without worries or responsibilities: *a carefree life.*

care•ful |**kâr'**fəl| *adj.* **1.** Taking care; cautious; prudent: *Be careful about signing legal papers.* **2.** Done with care; thorough; conscientious: *a careful job on one's homework.* **3.** Showing care; mindful; solicitous: *Being polite means being careful of other people's feelings.* —**care'ful•ly** *adv.* —**care'ful•ness** *n.*

care•less |**kâr'**lĭs| *adj.* **1.** Not taking care; inattentive; negligent: *a careless worker; careless about one's appearance.* **2.** Done or made without care; slipshod: *a careless job.* **3.** Resulting from negligence: *a careless mistake.* **4.** Said or done without thought; inconsiderate: *a careless remark.* —**care'less•ly** *adv.* —**care'less•ness** *n.*

ca•ress |kə **rĕs'**| *n.* A gentle touch or gesture of fondness, tenderness, or love. —*v.* To touch or stroke affectionately.

car•et |**kăr'**ĭt| *n.* A proofreading symbol used to indicate where something is to be inserted in a line of printed or written matter.

care•tak•er |**kâr'**tā'kər| *n.* A person employed to look after and take care of a house, an estate, etc.

care•worn |**kâr'**wôrn'| *or* |-wōrn'| *adj.* Showing signs of worry; haggard: *the soldiers' gaunt, careworn faces.*

car•fare |**kär'**fâr'| *n.* The amount charged for a ride on a streetcar, bus, etc.

car•go |kär′gō| *n., pl.* **car•goes** or **car•gos.** The freight carried by a ship, airplane, etc. *—modifier: a cargo ship; a cargo plane.*

car•hop |kär′hŏp′| *n.* A person employed by a drive-in restaurant to wait on customers in their cars.

Car•ib |kăr′ĭb| *n., pl.* **Car•ib** or **Car•ibs.** **1.** A group of Indian peoples of northern South America and the Lesser Antilles. **2.** A member of one of these peoples. **3.** Any language of the Cariban family. —**Car′ib** *adj.*

Car•i•ban |kăr′ə bən| *or* |kə rē′bən| *n.* **1.** A family of Indian languages spoken by the Caribs. **2.** A Carib. —**Car′i•ban** *adj.*

Car•ib•be•an |kăr′ə bē′ən| *or* |kə rĭb′ē-| *n.* **1.** A Carib Indian. **2.** **the Caribbean.** The Caribbean Sea and its islands. *—adj.* **1.** Of the Caribbean Sea and its islands. **2.** Of the Carib or their language.

Caribbean Sea. A part of the Atlantic Ocean bounded by the West Indies, Central America, and South America.

car•i•bou |kăr′ə bo͞o′| *n., pl.* **car•i•bou** or **car•i•bous.** A deer of arctic regions of North America, with large, spreading antlers in both the males and females. [SEE PICTURE]

car•i•ca•ture |kăr′ĭ kə cho͝or′| *or* |-chər| *n.* **1.** A picture or description of a person or thing in which certain distinctive features are greatly exaggerated or distorted to produce a comic effect. **2.** The art of creating such pictures or descriptions: *He is a master of caricature.* *—v.* **car•i•ca•tured, car•i•ca•tur•ing.** To represent in caricature. —**car′i•ca•tur′ist** *n.* [SEE PICTURE]

car•ies |kâr′ēz′| *n., pl.* **car•ies.** **1.** Decay of a bone or tooth. **2.** A cavity formed by decay in a tooth.

car•il•lon |kăr′ə lŏn′| *or* |-lən| *n.* A set of bells hung in a tower and played from a keyboard.

car•mine |kär′mĭn| *or* |-mīn′| *n.* A deep or purplish red. *—adj.* Deep or purplish red.

car•nage |kär′nĭj| *n.* Great slaughter, especially in war; massacre.

car•nal |kär′nəl| *adj.* Of the flesh; sensual: *carnal desires.*

car•na•tion |kär nā′shən| *n.* **1.** A plant cultivated for its fragrant, many-petaled white, pink, or red flowers. **2.** A flower of this plant.

car•nel•ian |kär nēl′yən| *n.* A pale to deep red type of clear quartz used as a gem.

car•ni•val |kär′nə vəl| *n.* **1.** The season just before Lent, marked by celebrating and feasting. **2.** Any time of merrymaking; a festival. **3.** An outdoor show, usually having a Ferris wheel, entertainment booths, side shows, etc.

car•ni•vore |kär′nə vôr′| *or* |-vōr′| *n.* **1.** An animal that feeds on the flesh of other animals, especially any such animal belonging to a group that includes the dogs, cats, bears, and weasels. **2.** A carnivorous plant.

car•niv•o•rous |kär nĭv′ər əs| *adj.* **1.** Feeding on the flesh of other animals. **2.** Having leaves or other parts that are able to trap insects and absorb nourishment from them: *The pitcher plant and Venus's-flytrap are carnivorous.*

car•no•tite |kär′nə tīt′| *n.* A yellow mineral that is used mainly as an ore of uranium and vanadium.

car•ol |kăr′əl| *n.* A song of joy, especially for Christmas. *—v.* **car•oled** or **car•olled, car•ol•ing** or **car•ol•ling.** To celebrate with carols. ¶*These sound alike* **carol, carrel.** —**ca′rol•er** *n.*

car•om |kăr′əm| *n.* **1. a.** In billiards, a shot in which the cue ball strikes two other balls, one after the other. **b.** In pool, a shot in which a ball is bounced off a cushion in order to strike another ball or reach a pocket. **2.** Any collision followed by a rebound, as of a ball bouncing off a wall. *—v.* To strike and rebound: *The ball caromed off the wall.*

car•o•tene |kăr′ə tēn′| *n.* An orange to red hydrocarbon that has the formula $C_{40}H_{56}$. It has three forms, occurs in many plants as a pigment, and is converted to vitamin A by the liver of an animal.

ca•rot•id |kə rŏt′ĭd| *n.* Either of the two large arteries in the neck that carries blood to the head. *—adj.* Of either or both of these arteries.

ca•rous•al |kə rou′zəl| *n.* A noisy, riotous drinking party.

ca•rouse |kə rouz′| *v.* **ca•roused, ca•rous•ing.** To drink a great deal of liquor, usually while having a noisy and merry time.

car•ou•sel |kăr′ə sĕl′| *or* |-zĕl′| *n.* A merry-go-round.

carp¹ |kärp| *v.* To find fault and complain constantly; nag or fuss: *She is always carping at her husband.* [SEE NOTE]

carp² |kärp| *n., pl.* **carp** or **carps.** A freshwater fish often bred in ponds and lakes and used as food. [SEE NOTE]

car•pal |kär′pəl| *adj.* Of or near the carpus. *—n.* Any bone of the carpus. ¶*These sound alike* **carpal, carpel.**

car•pel |kär′pəl| *n.* A part of the pistil of a seed-bearing plant in which the seeds develop. ¶*These sound alike* **carpel, carpal.**

car•pen•ter |kär′pən tər| *n.* A person who builds or repairs wooden objects and structures.

car•pen•try |kär′pən trē| *n.* The work or trade of a carpenter.

car•pet |kär′pĭt| *n.* **1.** A thick, heavy covering for a floor or the woven fabric of which it is made. **2.** Anything that covers a surface like a carpet: *a carpet of leaves and grass.* *—v.* To cover with or as if with a carpet.

***Idiom.* on the carpet.** Being scolded by someone in authority.

car•pet•bag |kär′pĭt băg′| *n.* A kind of traveling bag originally made of carpet fabric.

car•pet•bag•ger |kär′pĭt băg′ər| *n.* A Northerner who went to the South after the Civil War to make money by exploiting the unsettled conditions there.

car•pet•ing |kär′pĭ tĭng| *n.* **1.** Material or fabric used for carpets. **2.** A carpet or carpets: *a room with wall-to-wall carpeting.*

carpet sweeper. A hand-operated device on small wheels that picks up dirt from rugs and carpets with a revolving brush.

car•pi |kär′pī′| *n.* Plural of **carpus.**

car pool. An arrangement among a number of car owners who agree to take turns driving each other or their children to a regular destination, such as work, school, etc.

car•port |kär′pôrt′| *or* |-pōrt′| *n.* A shelter for a car under a roof projecting from the side of a house.

caribou
The **caribou** is considered by naturalists to be identical to the reindeer of the Old World, but unlike the reindeer it has never been domesticated.

caricature
Above: Theodore Roosevelt
Below: Caricature of Roosevelt as a bull moose (in 1912 he founded the Progressive Party, which was familiarly known as the "Bull Moose Party")

carp¹·²
Carp¹ *is from Old Norse* karpa, *"to boast."* **Carp²** *comes (via French) from Late Latin* carpa, *the name of a fish found in the Danube.*

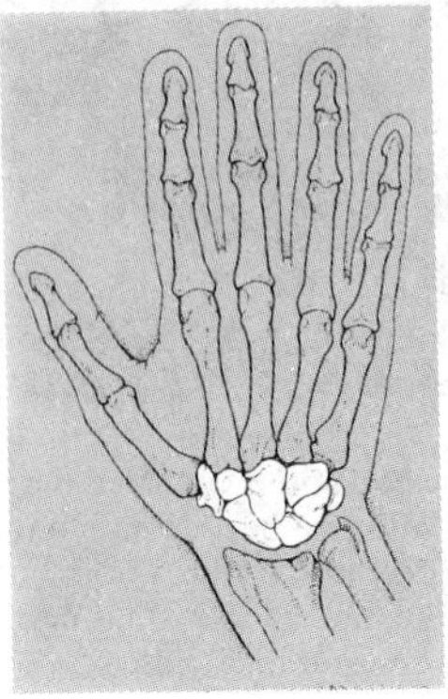

carpus

carrot

ă pat/ā pay/â care/ä father/ĕ pet/ ē be/ĭ pit/ī pie/î fierce/ŏ pot/ ō go/ô paw, for/oi oil/ŏŏ book/ ōō boot/ou out/ŭ cut/û fur/ *th* the/th thin/hw which/zh vision/ ə ago, item, pencil, atom, circus

car•pus |kär′pəs| *n., pl.* **car•pi** |kär′pī′|. **1.** The wrist. **2.** The bones that make up the wrist. [SEE PICTURE]

car•rel |kăr′əl| *n.* A nook near the stacks in a library, used for private study. ¶*These sound alike* **carrel, carol.**

car•riage |kăr′ĭj| *n.* **1.** A four-wheeled passenger vehicle, usually drawn by horses. **2.** A small vehicle for a baby or a doll that is pushed along and often can be folded. **3.** A structure with wheels on which a heavy object, such as a cannon, is moved. **4.** A moving or movable machine part that holds or shifts another part. **5.** The manner in which the body is held; posture. **6.** *British.* A railroad passenger car.

car•ri•er |kăr′ē ər| *n.* **1.** A device or mechanism that moves or guides something. **2.** A person or animal that can pass a disease on to others while himself showing, at least for a while, none of the symptoms of the disease. **3.** A flow of energy, especially electrical energy, that can be varied in some way to make it correspond to speech, music, images, etc., that are to be transmitted. **4.** An **aircraft carrier.**

carrier pigeon. A **homing pigeon.**

carrier wave. An electromagnetic wave that can be modulated in frequency and is used as a carrier, as in radio broadcasting.

car•ri•on |kăr′ē ən| *n.* The decaying flesh of dead animals: *Vultures feed on carrion.*

Car•roll |kăr′əl|, **Lewis.** 1832–1898. English author, creator of *Alice in Wonderland.*

car•rot |kăr′ət| *n.* **1.** A plant with feathery leaves and a long, tapering, yellow-orange root. **2.** The root of this plant, eaten as a vegetable. ¶*These sound alike* **carrot, carat, karat.** [SEE PICTURE]

car•rou•sel |kăr′ə sĕl′| *or* |-zĕl′| *n.* A form of the word **carousel.**

car•ry |kăr′ē| *v.* **car•ried, car•ry•ing, car•ries. 1.** To bear in one's hands or arms, on one's shoulders or back, etc., while moving: *carry the groceries into the house; teach a dog to fetch and carry.* **2.** To transport or convey: *Railroads carry coal.* **3. a.** To sustain the weight of; bear: *These columns were designed to carry the roof.* **b.** To maintain through personal effort, talent, etc.: *This production established the fact that a few performers could carry a Broadway show.* **4.** To keep, wear, or hold on one's person: *carry a gun. I never carry much money with me.* **5.** To act as the means by which (a person or thing) moves or is moved from one place to another: *A pipe carries water. That road carries a lot of traffic.* **6.** To hold and move (the body or a part of the body) in a certain way: *She carries herself very gracefully.* **7.** To transmit (a disease): *Mosquitoes carry malaria.* **8.** To be capable of being transmitted: *Her voice carries very well.* **9.** To have in stock; have for sale: *Drugstores carry a great variety of products.* **10.** To sing (a tune, melody, etc.) on key. **11.** To put (a digit) into the next column to the left, as in performing addition. **12.** To have as a usual or necessary attribute, accompaniment, consequence, etc.; involve: *a crime that carries a heavy penalty. The offer carries a money-back guarantee.* **13.** To contain: *The report carried a grim warning.* **14.** To win the sympathy, agreement, etc., of: *He carried his audience with him.* **15. a.** To win a majority of the votes in: *In 1936 President Roosevelt carried 46 states. The bill carried the state legislature.* **b.** To be approved: *The motion is carried. The motion carried by a wide margin.* **16.** To prolong, extend, or continue in space, time, or degree: *carry a fence around a field; an unbending will that carried him to the point where he became the conqueror of most of Europe; carry demands too far.* **17.** To print or broadcast: *All the papers carried the story. All the major networks carried the speech.* **18.** In football, to run with (the ball). —***phrasal verbs.*** **carry away.** To arouse great emotion or enthusiasm in: *I was carried away by the music.* **carry off. 1.** To win: *He carried off first prize.* **2.** To cause the death of; kill: *The epidemic carried off thousands.* **carry on. 1.** To engage in; conduct: *carry on a conversation; carry on a correspondence.* **2.** To continue despite difficulties or setbacks. **3.** *Informal.* To act hysterically or childishly: *What is he carrying on about?* **carry out.** To fulfill; execute; accomplish: *carry out a plan; carry out orders.* —*n., pl.* **car•ries. 1.** In baseball and golf, the lift of a ball that makes it travel a considerable distance: *The ball had plenty of carry.* **2.** In football, a run with the ball: *He averaged four yards per carry.* **3.** A portage, as between two bodies of water: *a short overland carry from one lake to the next.* **4.** The operation of placing a digit in the next column to the left, as in addition.

car•ry•all |kăr′ē ôl′| *n.* A large bag, basket, or pocketbook.

car•ry•ings-on |kăr′ē ĭngz ŏn′| *or* |-ôn′| *pl.n.* *Informal.* Wild, foolish, or improper behavior.

Car•son |kär′sən|, **Christopher ("Kit").** 1809–1868. American frontiersman.

Car•son City |kär′sən|. The capital of Nevada. Population, 32,022.

cart |kärt| *n.* **1.** A two-wheeled wooden vehicle pulled by a horse or other animal and used to transport goods or people. **2.** Any small, light vehicle, such as a grocery cart or golf cart, moved by hand. —*v.* To transport in or as if in a cart: *Trucks cart goods across the country.*

carte blanche |kärt′ blänch′| *or* |blănch′|. Complete freedom of action.

car•tel |kär tĕl′| *n.* An association of business firms, usually from different countries, organized to control prices, production, etc.

Car•ter |kär′tər|, **James Earl (Jimmy), Jr.** Born 1924. Thirty-ninth President of the United States (1977–81).

Car•te•sian coordinates |kär tē′zhən|. The numbers locating a point in a Cartesian coordinate system, as the abscissa and the ordinate in a plane system.

Cartesian coordinate system. 1. A system for locating any point in a plane by giving its distances from each of a pair of lines that intersect, often at right angles, measured along a parallel to the other line. **2.** A similar system for locating any point in space, using three planes that intersect, often at right angles.

Cartesian product of sets. The set of all ordered pairs that can be formed with the first element of each pair chosen from one set and the second element chosen from a second set; cross product.

Car•thage |kär′thĭj|. An ancient city and empire on the north coast of Africa that dominated the western Mediterranean until its defeat by Rome in the second century B.C. —**Car'tha·gin'i·an** |kär'thə **jĭn'**ē ən| *adj.* & *n.*

Car·tier |kär **tyā'**|, **Jacques.** 1491–1557. French navigator and explorer of Canada; discovered the St. Lawrence River.

car·ti·lage |**kär'**tl ĭj| *n.* A tough, white connective tissue that is attached to the surfaces of bones in regions near joints. It forms a fairly large part of the skeleton of young vertebrates, but is mostly converted to bone as maturity approaches.

car·ti·lag·i·nous |kär'tl **ăj'**ə nəs| *adj.* **1.** Of or like cartilage. **2.** Having a skeleton that consists mainly of cartilage: *a cartilaginous fish.*

car·tog·ra·phy |kär **tŏg'**rə fē| *n.* The art of making maps or charts. —**car·tog'ra·pher** *n.*

car·ton |**kär'**tn| *n.* **1.** A cardboard box made in various sizes and used to hold goods, liquids, etc. **2. a.** A carton with something in it: *buy a carton of cigarettes; buy a carton of milk.* **b.** The amount that a carton holds: *smoke a carton of cigarettes; drink a carton of milk.*

car·toon |kär **to͞on'**| *n.* **1.** A drawing, as in a newspaper or magazine, usually having a caption, showing a humorous situation or illustrating an opinion on a public issue. **2.** An **animated cartoon. 3.** A **comic strip.**

car·toon·ist |kär **to͞o'**nĭst| *n.* A person who draws cartoons, as for a newspaper.

car·tridge |**kär'**trĭj| *n.* **1. a.** A tubular container of metal or metal and cardboard that holds the powder that propels the bullet or shot from a small firearm. **b.** Such a case fitted with a bullet or loaded with shot; a round. **2.** Any small, readily removable unit such as the pickup of a phonograph or a case of photographic film that is loaded directly into a camera.

cart·wheel |**kärt'**hwēl'| *or* |-wēl'| *n.* **1.** The wheel of a cart. **2.** A handspring in which the body turns over sideways with the arms and legs spread like the spokes of a wheel.

carve |kärv| *v.* **carved, carv·ing. 1.** To form or shape (an object, design, etc.) by cutting a material such as wood, stone, etc.: *Indians carved totem poles out of logs.* **2.** To shape or decorate (a material) by cutting: *carve ivory to make ornaments.* **3.** To inscribe or write by cutting: *He carved his initials on the tree.* **4. a.** To cut (roast meat or poultry) in pieces for people to eat: *carve a turkey. This roast carves easily.* **b.** To cut from a roast: *carve off a slice of white meat.* —**phrasal verbs. carve out. 1.** To form by or as if by carving: *Rushing water carved out gullies in the hill.* **2.** To achieve by great effort or ability: *England carved out an empire in the New World.* **carve up.** To divide into smaller sections: *carve up a Congressional district.* —**carv'er** *n.*

carv·ing |**kär'**vĭng| *n.* **1.** The act or process of carving, especially of cutting wood, stone, etc., to form an object or design. **2.** An object or design formed by cutting: *an ivory carving.*

car·y·at·id |kăr'ē **ăt'**ĭd| *n., pl.* **car·y·at·ids** or **car·y·at·i·des** |kăr'ē **ăt'**ĭ dēz'|. A supporting column sculptured in the shape of a woman, as used by the ancient Greeks, Romans, etc.

ca·sa·ba |kə **sä'**bə| *n.* A melon with a yellow rind and sweet, whitish flesh.

Cas·a·blan·ca |kăs'ə **blăng'**kə| *or* |kä'sə-**bläng'**kə|. The largest city in Morocco. Population, 1,371,000.

cas·cade |kăs **kād'**| *n.* **1.** A small waterfall, usually one of many, that flows over steep rocks. **2.** Anything resembling a cascade: *a cascade of sparks.* **3.** Any succession of processes, operations, or units: *a cascade of amplifier stages.* —*v.* **cas·cad·ed, cas·cad·ing.** To fall in or like a cascade: *The river cascades over a shelf of granite rock. The cards cascaded to the floor.*

case[1] |kās| *n.* **1.** An instance or example of the existence or occurrence of something: *Explain your answer in each case. It was a case of mistaken identity.* **2.** A situation or state of affairs: *In that case there is nothing to be done.* **3.** A matter under investigation: *the case of the missing heiress.* **4.** An occurrence of disease or disorder: *a case of tuberculosis.* **5.** A legal action; lawsuit: *The Supreme Court declined to hear the case.* **6.** A set of reasons or arguments offered in support of something: *state one's case; the case for socialized medicine.* **7.** In grammar, the set of forms of a noun, pronoun, or adjective that shows relationships among words in a sentence. In some languages, such as Latin, these relationships are indicated by special endings of the nouns, pronouns, or adjectives or by special forms of these words. In English these relationships are usually indicated by the position of words within the sentence. Adjectives have no case endings. Nouns show a special form only for the possessive case; for example, in the phrase *John's coat, John's* is in the possessive case. Personal pronouns have three cases: the *subjective case,* the *objective case,* and the *possessive case.* For example, in the sentence *She gave John a book, she* is in the subjective case; in *John thanked her for the gift, her* is in the objective case; and in *John gave Jane his pen, his* is in the possessive case. [SEE NOTE]

***Idioms.* in any case.** No matter what happens; in any event. **in case.** If it happens that; if: *in case the need arises.* **in case of.** If there should happen to be; in the event of.

case[2] |kās| *n.* **1.** A large box for shipping something: *a packing case.* **2. a.** A case with something in it: *ship a case of beer bottles.* **b.** The amount that a case holds: *drink a case of beer.* **3.** A container or protective cover for holding or carrying jewelry, eyeglasses, etc. **4.** In printing, a tray for storing type. See **upper case, lower case.** —*v.* **cased, cas·ing.** To put into or cover with a case. [SEE NOTE]

case·hard·en |**kās'**här'dn| *v.* To harden the surface of iron, steel, etc., usually by some form of treatment with heat.

case history. In fields such as medicine, psychology, and sociology, an organized set of facts about how a condition under treatment or study developed in an individual or group.

ca·sein |**kā'**sēn'| *or* |-sē ĭn| *n.* A white, tasteless, odorless protein derived from milk and cheese, used in making foods, plastics, adhesives, and paints.

case·ment |**kās'**mənt| *n.* **1.** A window sash that opens outward on hinges. **2.** A window fitted with such sashes. [SEE PICTURE]

cash |kăsh| *n.* **1.** Money in the form of cur-

case[1·2]

Case[1] *is borrowed from Old French* cas, *which is from Latin* cāsus, *"a falling, an event." This is a noun formed from the verb* cadere, *"to fall, to happen."* **Case**[2] *is borrowed from Old North French* casse, *which descends from Latin* capsa, *"a container, a box." This noun is formed from the verb* capere, *"to take, to hold, to contain."*

casement

rency; coins or bills: *five dollars in cash.* **2.** Money or payment in the form of currency or a check as opposed to credit or delayed payment: *He paid cash for his new car.* —**modifier:** *a cash box.* —*v.* To exchange for or convert into ready money: *cash a check.* ¶*These sound alike* **cash, cache.**

***Idiom.* cash in on.** To take advantage of.

cash crop. A crop grown especially for sale and providing an important source of income.

cash•ew |**kăsh**′o͞o| *or* |kə **sho͞o**′| *n.* **1.** The kidney-shaped, edible nut of a tropical American tree. **2.** A tree that bears such nuts. [SEE PICTURE]

cash•ier¹ |kă **shîr**′| *n.* A person employed to receive and pay out money, as in a store, restaurant, hotel, or bank.

cash•ier² |kă **shîr**′| *v.* To dismiss in disgrace from a position of command or responsibility.

cashier's check. A check drawn by a bank on its own funds and signed by the bank's cashier.

cash•mere |**kăzh**′mîr′| *or* |**kăsh**′-| *n.* **1.** Fine, soft wool growing beneath the outer hair of the **Cashmere goat** of the mountains of India and Tibet. **2.** Yarn or cloth made from this wool. —**modifier:** *a cashmere sweater.*

cash register. A machine that records the amount of each cash sale and also contains a drawer for holding the money.

cas•ing |**kā**′sĭng| *n.* **1.** A protective case or covering, as for an automobile tire, rocket, etc. **2.** The cleaned intestines of cattle, sheep, or hogs, used for wrapping sausage meat. **3.** The frame or framework for a door or window.

ca•si•no |kə **sē**′nō| *n., pl.* **ca•si•nos. 1.** An establishment for gambling and other entertainment. **2.** A form of the word **cassino.**

cask |kăsk| *or* |käsk| *n.* **1.** A barrel of any size for holding liquids. **2. a.** A cask with something in it: *store a cask of wine.* **b.** The amount that a cask holds: *spill a cask of Burgundy.*

cas•ket |**kăs**′kĭt| *or* |**kä**′skĭt| *n.* **1.** A small case or chest for jewels or other valuables. **2.** A coffin.

Cas•pi•an Sea |**kăs**′pē ən|. The largest inland body of water in the world, surrounded by the Soviet Union and Iran.

cas•sa•va |kə **sä**′və| *n.* **1.** A tropical American plant with a large, starchy root. **2.** Starch from this root, used to make tapioca and as food in tropical regions.

cas•se•role |**kăs**′ə rōl′| *n.* **1.** A dish, usually of pottery or glass, in which food is both baked and served. **2.** Food baked in such a dish.

cas•sette |kə **sĕt**′| *or* |kă-| *n.* **1.** A lightproof case containing a roll of film that can be inserted directly into a camera. **2.** A small case containing magnetic tape for use in a tape recorder, in certain electric typewriters, etc.

cas•sia |**kăsh**′ə| *or* |**kăs**′ē ə| *n.* **1. a.** An Asian tree with bark resembling cinnamon. **b.** The bark of this tree, used as a spice. **2.** Any of several related trees and plants, some of which yield the medicine senna.

cas•si•no |kə **sē**′nō| *n.* A card game in which players match cards on the table with cards in the hand.

Cas•si•o•pe•ia |kăs′ē ə **pē**′ə| *n.* A constellation in the sky of the Northern Hemisphere.

cas•sock |**kăs**′ək| *n.* A robe reaching to the feet, usually black in color, worn by the clergymen of certain churches.

cas•so•wa•ry |**kăs**′ə wĕr′ē| *n., pl.* **cas•so•wa•ries.** A large bird of New Guinea and northern Australia. It is unable to fly and has a bony, crownlike projection on the top of its head. [SEE PICTURE]

cast |kăst| *or* |käst| *v.* **cast, cast•ing. 1.** To throw: *cast dice. The fishermen cast their nets at dawn.* **2.** To throw off; shed: *The snake cast its skin.* **3.** To cause to fall upon something: *cast a shadow; cast a spell; cast doubt upon something.* **4.** To turn or direct: *cast a glance in someone's direction. Try to cast your mind back several years.* **5.** To deposit (a ballot); give (a vote): *The chairman cast his vote and broke the tie.* **6. a.** To assign a certain role to: *The director cast him as Romeo.* **b.** To choose actors for: *cast a new play.* **7. a.** To form (an object) by pouring a molten or soft material into a mold and allowing it to harden: *The artist cast the sculpture in bronze.* **b.** To pour (a material) in forming an object in this way. **8.** To be capable of being shaped in a mold: *Some metals cast easily.* —***phrasal verbs.*** **cast about for.** To search or look for: *cast about for a method of escape.* **cast aside.** To discard or abandon. **cast down.** To turn downward: *cast down one's eyes.* **cast off.** To release a ship from a dock. **cast on.** To make the first row of stitches in knitting. —*n.* **1.** The act of throwing or casting: *a cast of the dice.* **2.** The actors in a play, movie, etc.: *There were only four people in the cast.* **3.** A hard, stiff bandage, usually of gauze and plaster, used to keep a broken or damaged bone or joint from moving. **4. a.** An object cast in or as if in a mold. **b.** An impression formed in a mold: *a cast in plaster of a face.* **5.** A hue or shade: *The cloth has a slightly reddish cast.* **6.** Outward form, quality, or appearance: *This puts a different cast on the matter.* **7.** A slight squint or strabismus: *a cast in her left eye.* ¶*These sound alike* **cast, caste.**

***Idioms.* cast down.** Low in spirit; depressed. **cast lots.** To draw lots in order to determine something by chance. **cast (one's) lot with.** To join or side with for better or for worse.

cas•ta•nets |kăs′tə **nĕts**′| *pl.n.* A pair of hollowed-out shells of wood or ivory, used as a percussion instrument and struck together with the fingers to make a sharp click. Castanets are used typically by performers of Spanish dances. [SEE PICTURE]

cast•a•way |**kăst**′ə wā′| *or* |**käst**′-| *n.* **1.** A shipwrecked person. **2.** A person or thing that has been discarded.

caste |kăst| *or* |käst| *n.* **1.** In India, one of the hereditary social classes of the Hindus. **2.** Any social class distinguished by rank, profession, etc. ¶*These sound alike* **caste, cast.**

cas•tel•lat•ed |**kăs**′tə lā′tĭd| *adj.* Having turrets and battlements like a castle.

cast•er |**kăs**′tər| *or* |**kä**′stər| *n.* **1.** A worker who shapes molten metal. **2.** A small roller or wheel attached under a piece of furniture or other heavy object to make it easier to move.

cas•ti•gate |**kăs**′tĭ gāt′| *v.* **cas•ti•gat•ed, cas•ti•gat•ing.** To criticize severely; berate. —**cas′ti•ga′tion** *n.*

cashew
Leaves and nuts

cassowary

castanets

ă **pat**/ā **pay**/â **care**/ä **father**/ĕ **pet**/ ē **be**/ĭ **pit**/ī **pie**/î **fierce**/ŏ **pot**/ ō **go**/ô **paw**, **for**/oi **oil**/o͝o **book**/ o͞o **boot**/ou **out**/ŭ **cut**/û **fur**/ *th* **the**/th **thin**/hw **which**/zh **vision**/ ə **ago**, **item**, **pencil**, **atom**, **circus**

cast•ing |kăs′tĭng| *or* |kä′stĭng| *n.* **1.** The act or process of making casts or molds. **2.** An object that has been formed in a mold from a molten or soft material.

cast iron. A hard, brittle alloy of iron that contains from 2.0 to 4.5 per cent carbon and smaller percentages of silicon, sulfur, manganese, and phosphorus. —***modifier:* (cast-iron):** *a cast-iron frying pan.*

cas•tle |kăs′əl| *or* |kä′səl| *n.* **1.** A fort or fortified group of buildings dominating the surrounding country, especially one built in medieval times. **2.** Any building that looks like a castle. **3.** A place of privacy and safety: *A man's home is his castle.* **4.** A chess piece, rook. —***modifier:*** *a castle wall.* —*v.* **cas•tled, cas•tling.** In chess, to move the king two or three spaces toward a rook and place the rook on the other side. [SEE NOTE at **chateau**]

castoff |kăst′ôf′| *or* |-ŏf′| *or* |käst′-| *n.* Someone or something that has been discarded or thrown away.

cas•tor¹ |kăs′tər| *or* |kä′stər| *n.* An oily, brown substance with a strong odor, obtained from glands in the skin of beavers and used in making various medicines and perfumes.

cas•tor² |kăs′tər| *or* |kä′stər| *n.* A form of the word **caster.**

castor oil. An oil pressed from the beanlike seeds of a tropical plant, used as a light lubricant and in medicine to promote movement of the bowels.

cas•trate |kăs′trāt′| *v.* **cas•trat•ed, cas•trat•ing.** To remove the sex glands, especially the testes, of; geld or spay. —**cas•tra′tion** *n.*

Cas•tries |käs′trēz′| *or* |-trēs′|. The capital of St. Lucia. Population, 43,000.

cas•u•al |kăzh′o͞o əl| *adj.* **1.** Happening by chance; not planned; accidental: *a casual meeting.* **2. a.** Showing little interest; unconcerned; nonchalant: *a casual manner.* **b.** Offhand; passing: *a casual remark.* **3. a.** Without ceremony or formality: *addressing his friends in a casual way.* **b.** Suited for everyday wear or use; informal: *casual dress.* **4.** Not serious or thorough; superficial: *a casual inspection; a casual reader of a newspaper.* **5.** Not close or intimate: *a casual friendship.* —**cas′u•al•ly** *adv.* —**cas′u•al•ness** *n.*

cas•u•al•ty |kăzh′o͞o əl tē| *n., pl.* **cas•u•al•ties. 1. a.** A person who is killed or injured in an accident. **b.** A person who is killed, wounded, captured, or missing during a military action. **2.** A serious accident, especially one in which someone is killed.

cat |kăt| *n.* **1.** An animal with soft fur and claws that can be drawn in, kept as a pet or for catching mice and rats. **2.** Any of several animals related to the domestic cat, such as a lion, tiger, leopard, or lynx. [SEE NOTE]

***Idiom.* let the cat out of the bag.** To give away a secret; let a secret be known.

ca•tab•o•lism |kə tăb′ə lĭz′əm| *n.* The phase of metabolism in which tissues are broken down and the complex molecules of protoplasm are changed into simpler ones. —**cat′a•bol′ic** |kăt′ə-bŏl′ĭk| *adj.*

cat•a•clysm |kăt′ə klĭz′əm| *n.* **1.** A sudden and violent change in the earth's crust. **2.** A great upheaval or disaster, such as a flood, earthquake, revolution, or war. —**cat′a•clys•mic** |kăt′ə klĭz′-mĭk| *adj.*

cat•a•combs |kăt′ə kōmz′| *pl.n.* A series of underground passages containing small compartments for coffins and graves.

cat•a•lep•sy |kăt′l ĕp′sē| *n.* A condition, often associated with epilepsy or certain mental disorders, in which a person becomes rigid and unaware of his surroundings and does not respond to external stimuli. —**cat′a•lep′tic** |kăt′l ĕp′tĭk| *adj.*

cat•a•log or **cat•a•logue** |kăt′l ôg′| *or* |-ŏg′| *n.* **1.** A list of items, usually in alphabetical order, with a description of each: *a library catalog.* **2.** A book or pamphlet containing such a list: *a mail-order catalog.* —*v.* **cat•a•loged** or **cat•a•logued, cat•a•log•ing** or **cat•a•logu•ing.** To list in a catalog; make a catalog of.

ca•tal•pa |kə tăl′pə| *n.* A tree with large, heart-shaped leaves, showy flower clusters, and long, slender, beanlike pods.

ca•tal•y•sis |kə tăl′ĭ sĭs| *n.* The action of a catalyst, especially in a chemical reaction.

cat•a•lyst |kăt′l ĭst| *n.* A substance that alters the rate at which a physical or, especially, a chemical reaction takes place, usually by making it go faster.

cat•a•lyt•ic |kăt′l ĭt′ĭk| *adj.* Of or using a catalyst.

cat•a•lyze |kăt′l īz′| *v.* **cat•a•lyzed, cat•a•lyz•ing.** To act as a catalyst in or for.

cat•a•ma•ran |kăt′ə mə răn′| *n.* **1.** A boat with two parallel hulls. **2.** A long raft made of logs tied together. [SEE PICTURE]

cat•a•mount |kăt′ə mount′| *n.* A mountain lion or wildcat.

cat•a•pult |kăt′ə pŭlt′| *or* |-po͝olt′| *n.* **1.** An ancient military device for hurling stones, spears, arrows, or other missiles. **2.** A mechanism for launching aircraft from the deck of a ship. —*v.* **1.** To hurl or launch from or as if from a catapult: *The volcano catapults boulders the size of small houses. The success of his movie catapulted him into stardom.* **2.** To move suddenly as if propelled from a catapult: *When he heard the fire alarm, he catapulted out of bed.* [SEE PICTURE]

cat•a•ract |kăt′ə răkt′| *n.* **1.** A very large waterfall. **2.** A condition in which the lens of an eye or the membrane that covers it turns cloudy, causing total or partial blindness.

ca•tarrh |kə tär′| *n.* Inflammation of mucous membranes, especially of the nose and throat.

ca•tas•tro•phe |kə tăs′trə fē| *n.* A great and sudden calamity, such as an earthquake or flood.

cat•a•stroph•ic |kăt′ə strŏf′ĭk| *adj.* Like or resulting in a catastrophe: *a catastrophic fire; a catastrophic failure.* —**cat′a•stroph′i•cal•ly** *adv.*

cat•a•to•ni•a |kăt′ə tō′nē ə| *n.* A condition, associated with schizophrenia, in which a patient remains quiet, immobile, and dazed and responds to few stimuli.

cat•a•ton•ic |kăt′ə tŏn′ĭk| *adj.* Of or in a state of catatonia. —*n.* A catatonic person.

Ca•taw•ba |kə tô′bə| *n., pl.* **Ca•taw•ba** or **Ca•taw•bas. 1.** A North American Indian tribe of North and South Carolina. **2.** A member of this tribe. **3.** The Siouan language of this tribe.

cat•bird |kăt′bûrd′| *n.* A dark-gray North

cat

The domestic **cat** *seems to have been introduced into Europe during the late Roman Empire, probably from North Africa. In the fourth century* A.D., *the word* cattus *was introduced into Latin; the animal was then apparently a newcomer. The word, following the animal, made its way into all the languages of Europe. The Anglo-Saxons already had it when they invaded Britain. In German it is* katze, *in French* chat, *in Spanish* gato, *in Italian* gatto, *and in Russian* kot.

catamaran

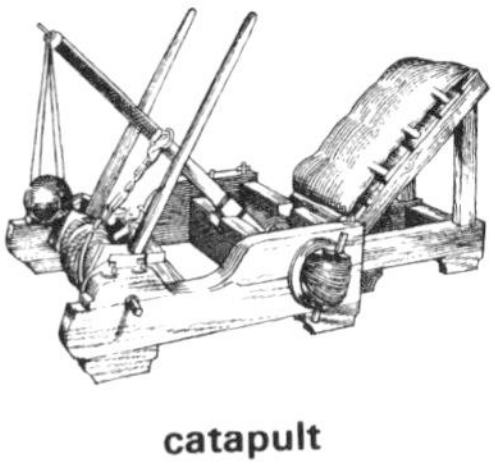

catapult

Catholic
The word **Catholic** *comes from Greek* katholikos, *meaning "universal, general." To the early Christians, "the catholic church" meant "the whole worldwide church." After the separation of the Eastern and Western churches (1054), the Eastern Church called itself "Orthodox," while the Western Church called itself "Catholic." Since the Protestant Reformation, in the sixteenth century, it is chiefly the Roman Church that has been called Catholic. Some of the Protestant churches, such as the Church of England, still also consider themselves Catholic, although none of the churches is truly universal. Used with a small* c, *the word still has its original meaning.*

ă pat/ā pay/â care/ä father/ĕ pet/ ē be/ĭ pit/ī pie/î fierce/ŏ pot/ ō go/ô paw, for/oi oil/ŏŏ book/ ōō boot/ou out/ŭ cut/û fur/ *th* the/th thin/hw which/zh vision/ ə ago, item, pencil, atom, circus

American songbird with a call like the mewing of a cat.

cat•boat |**kăt'**bōt'| *n.* A small sailboat with a single sail on a mast set far forward in the bow.

cat•call |**kăt'**kôl'| *n.* A loud, shrill call or whistle of disapproval or derision, usually directed from an audience toward a speaker or performer.

catch |kăch| *v.* **caught** |kôt|, **catch•ing. 1.** To get hold of or grasp (something moving): *catch a ball.* **2.** To trap or ensnare: *catch mice; catch fish.* **3.** To capture or seize, especially after a chase: *catch a thief.* **4.** To come upon suddenly; take by surprise: *catch someone unawares. We caught the enemy napping.* **5.** To become stuck or lodged: *The bone caught in my throat.* **6.** To be in time for; reach in time to board: *Can we still catch the 3:00 train?* **7.** To become infected with; contract: *catch a cold.* **8.** To hook or snag: *I caught my dress on a nail. My skirt caught on the rosebush.* **9.** To cause to become or become held or fastened: *I caught my finger in the door. This lock will not catch.* **10.** To hit; strike: *The blow caught him on the head.* **11.** To attract: *I tried to catch your attention, but you were too busy to notice.* **12.** To take or get momentarily: *catch sight of someone. We were only able to catch a glimpse of him.* **13.** To begin to burn, operate, work, etc.: *The house caught fire. The fire caught. The plane will take off as soon as the motor catches.* **14.** To hear: *I didn't catch what you said.* **15.** To see (a play, motion picture, etc.): *Let's try to catch a movie.* **16.** To check or stop (oneself) in some sort of action: *I was about to criticize him but I caught myself in time.* **17.** In baseball, to play as the catcher. ***—phrasal verbs.*** **catch on.** *Informal.* **1.** To understand; get the idea: *The girls caught on to the new dance steps quickly.* **2.** To become fashionable or popular. **catch up. 1.** To come up from behind; overtake: *Give us a chance to catch up. We've almost caught up with them.* **2.** To become involved with, often against one's wish: *caught up in the scandal.* **3.** To bring up to date: *I have to catch up on my correspondence.* **4.** To absorb completely: *He is always caught up in his work.* —*n.* **1.** The act or an instance of grabbing and holding a ball: *The center fielder made a diving catch.* **2.** The amount of something caught, especially fish. **3.** A device, such as a hook or latch, for fastening or closing something. **4.** A simple game in which two people throw a ball back and forth to each other. **5.** *Informal.* A hidden or tricky condition; a pitfall: *The offer is so generous that I'm sure there's a catch to it.*

Idiom. **catch (one's) breath.** To rest so as to be able to continue.

catch•all |**kăch'**ôl'| *n.* **1.** A box, closet, etc., for storing odds and ends. **2.** Something, such as a phrase, word, law, etc., that covers many different situations.

catch•er |**kăch'**ər| *n.* **1.** A person or thing that catches. **2.** In baseball, the player stationed behind home plate who catches pitches.

catch•ing |**kăch'**ĭng| *adj.* Easily transmitted from one person to another; contagious.

catch•up |**kăch'**əp| *or* |**kĕch'**-| *n.* A form of the word **ketchup.**

catch•word |**kăch'**wûrd'| *n.* A word, phrase, etc. that is often repeated; a slogan.

catch•y |**kăch'**ē| *adj.* **catch•i•er, catch•i•est. 1.** Easily remembered: *a catchy tune.* **2.** Tricky; deceptive: *a catchy question.*

cat•e•chism |**kăt'**ə kĭz'əm| *n.* A short book giving a brief summary of the basic principles of a religion in the form of questions and answers.

cat•e•gor•i•cal |kăt'ə **gôr'**ĭ kəl| *or* |**-gŏr'**-| *adj.* Without exception or qualification; absolute: *a categorical rejection of an offer.* —**cat'e•gor'i•cal•ly** *adv.* —**cat'e•gor'i•cal•ness** *n.*

cat•e•go•ry |**kăt'**ə gôr'ē| *or* |-gōr'ē| *n., pl.* **cat•e•go•ries.** A class or division in a system of classification.

ca•ter |**kā'**tər| *v.* **1. a.** To provide with what is needed or wanted, as services, food, drinks, etc.: *The inn caters to tourists and businessmen. The little grocery store caters to the whole neighborhood.* **b.** To supply and serve food and drinks for: *cater a wedding.* **2.** To act with special consideration: *The governor was accused of catering to big business.*

cat•er-cor•nered |**kăt'**ər kôr'nərd| *adv.* A form of the word **catty-cornered.**

ca•ter•er |**kā'**tər ər| *n.* A person who provides and serves food, drinks, etc., for weddings, banquets, and other festive occasions.

cat•er•pil•lar |**kăt'**ər pĭl'ər| *or* |**kăt'**ə-| *n.* The wormlike, often hairy larva of a butterfly or moth.

cat•er•waul |**kăt'**ər wôl'| *v.* To utter a shrill cry or screech like that of a cat. —*n.* A cat's shrill or howling cry.

cat•fish |**kăt'**fĭsh'| *n., pl.* **cat•fish** or **cat•fish•es.** Any of several scaleless, mostly freshwater fishes with whiskerlike feelers near the mouth.

cat•gut |**kăt'**gŭt'| *n.* A tough, thin cord made from the dried intestines of certain animals, used in making strings for musical instruments and tennis rackets, and in sewing closed surgical wounds.

ca•thar•tic |kə **thär'**tĭk| *adj.* Tending to bring on one or more bowel movements; purgative; laxative. —*n.* A cathartic drug or medicine.

Ca•thay |kă **thā'**|. *Archaic.* China.

ca•the•dral |kə **thē'**drəl| *n.* **1.** The principal church of a bishop's see. **2.** Any large or important church. ***—modifier:*** *a cathedral square.*

cath•e•ter |**kăth'**ĭ tər| *n.* A thin, flexible tube made to be inserted into a duct of the body for any of a number of medical purposes, such as the removal of a blockage.

cath•ode |**kăth'**ōd'| *n.* **1.** A **negative electrode. 2.** In a battery or other device that is supplying current, the positive electrode.

cath•ode-ray tube |**kăth'**ōd rā'|. A vacuum tube in which a stream of electrons is directed against a phosphor screen where, under the influence of electric or magnetic fields, it traces a picture or display. The picture tube of a television set is a cathode-ray tube.

cath•o•lic |**kăth'**ə lĭk| *or* |**kăth'**lĭk| *adj.* Open or sympathetic to many styles, types, or varieties: *a man with catholic tastes and interests.*

Cath•o•lic |**kăth'**ə lĭk| *or* |**kăth'**lĭk| *adj.* **1.** Of or belonging to the whole body of Christians or the universal Christian church. **2. a.** Of or belonging to the ancient, undivided Christian church. **b.** Of or belonging to any of the Christian churches, especially the Roman Catholic

Church, that claim origin in it. —*n.* A Roman Catholic. [SEE NOTE on p. 144]

Ca•thol•i•cism |kə thŏl'ĭ sĭz'əm| *n.* The faith, doctrine, practice, and organization of the Roman Catholic Church.

cat•i•on |kăt'ī'ən| *n.* An ion that has a positive charge and is, therefore, attracted by a negatively charged electrode, or cathode.

cat•kin |kăt'kĭn| *n.* A dense, often drooping cluster of small, scalelike flowers, as those of a birch or willow.

cat•nap |kăt'năp'| *n.* A short nap. —*v.* **cat•napped, cat•nap•ping.** To take a short nap.

cat•nip |kăt'nĭp| *n.* A plant with a strong, spicy smell that is very attractive to cats.

cat-o'-nine-tails |kăt'ə nīn'tālz'| *n., pl.* **cat-o'-nine-tails.** A whip consisting of nine knotted cords fastened to a handle, formerly used for flogging.

cat's cradle. A child's game in which an intricately looped string is transferred from the hands of one player to the hands of the next, resulting in a succession of different loop patterns and designs. [SEE PICTURE]

Cats•kill Mountains |kăt'skĭl'|. Also **Catskills.** A mountain range in southeastern New York State.

cat•sup |kăt'səp| *or* |kăch'əp| *or* |kĕch'-| *n.* A form of the word **ketchup.**

cat•tail |kăt'tāl'| *n.* A tall marsh plant with long, straplike leaves and a tube-shaped cluster of tiny, brown flowers.

cat•tle |kăt'l| *pl.n.* Horned, hoofed animals of the kind bred and raised for beef and dairy products; cows, bulls, or oxen. —***modifier:*** *a cattle ranch.* [SEE NOTE]

cat•tle•man |kăt'l mən| *or* |-măn'| *n., pl.* **-men** |-mən| *or* |-mĕn'|. A man who raises cattle. —**cat'tle•wom'an** *n.*

cat•ty |kăt'ē| *adj.* **cat•ti•er, cat•ti•est.** Spiteful; mean; malicious: *catty remarks.* —**cat'ti•ly** *adv.* —**cat'ti•ness** *n.*

cat•ty-cor•ner |kăt'ē kôr'nər| *adv.* A form of the word **catty-cornered.**

cat•ty-cor•nered |kăt'ē kôr'nərd| *adv.* Diagonally: *Place the table catty-cornered.*

cat•walk |kăt'wôk'| *n.* A narrow elevated pathway, as on the sides of a bridge.

Cau•ca•sian |kô kā'zhən| *n.* **1.** A native or inhabitant of the Caucasus. **2.** A Caucasoid person. —*adj.* **1.** Of the Caucasus or its inhabitants. **2.** Caucasoid.

Cau•ca•soid |kô'kə soid'| *adj.* Of the major division of the human species whose members characteristically have skin color ranging from very light to brown, eye color ranging from light blue to brown, and hair ranging from straight to wavy or curly. This division is considered to include the native inhabitants of Europe, northern Africa, southwestern Asia, and the Indian subcontinent and their descendants in other parts of the world. —*n.* A Caucasoid person.

Cau•ca•sus |kô'kə səs|. A mountain range in the Soviet Union, between the Black and Caspian seas.

cau•cus |kô'kəs| *n.* **cau•cus•es** or **cau•cus•ses.** A meeting of members of a political party to decide on a question of policy or to choose a candidate for office. —*v.* **cau•cused** or **cau•cussed, cau•cus•ing** or **cau•cus•sing, cau•cus•es** or **cau•cus•ses.** To gather in or hold a caucus.

cau•dal |kôd'l| *adj.* Of, at, or near the tail or hind parts.

caught |kôt|. Past tense and past participle of **catch.**

caul•dron |kôl'drən| *n.* A form of the word **caldron.**

cau•li•flow•er |kô'lĭ flou'ər| *or* |kŏl'ĭ-| *n.* A plant closely related to the cabbage and broccoli, having a rounded head of densely clustered whitish flowers, eaten as a vegetable.

caulk |kôk| *v.* **1.** To make (a boat) watertight by packing the seams with caulking. **2.** To make (joints of a pipe, seams, cracks, etc.) watertight or airtight by filling in with caulking.

caulk•ing |kô'kĭng| *n.* A material, such as oakum or tar, used to caulk the seams of a boat or joints and cracks in pipes.

caus•al |kô'zəl| *adj.* Being or constituting a cause: *causal connection between the tides and the action of the sun and the moon.*

cause |kôz| *n.* **1.** A person or thing that makes something happen: *He was the cause of all her troubles. Scientists are seeking the cause of cancer.* **2.** A good or sufficient reason for a certain feeling, action, etc.: *There is no cause for alarm.* **3.** An idea or goal to which many people are dedicated: *the cause of peace. He died for a noble cause.* —*v.* **caused, caus•ing.** To be the cause of; make happen; bring about: *Germs cause disease. Please don't cause me any trouble. What caused him to act like that?*

cause•way |kôz'wā'| *n.* A raised roadway, as across marshland or water.

caus•tic |kô'stĭk| *adj.* **1.** Able to burn, corrode, or eat things away by chemical action. **2.** Sarcastic; biting; cutting: *caustic remarks.* —*n.* A caustic material or substance.

caustic soda. **Sodium hydroxide.**

cau•ter•ize |kô'tə rīz'| *v.* **cau•ter•ized, cau•ter•iz•ing.** To burn or sear (a wound, dead tissue, etc.) with a caustic or a hot instrument in order to stop bleeding or prevent infection. —**cau'ter•i•za'tion** *n.*

cau•tion |kô'shən| *n.* **1.** Care so as to avoid possible danger or trouble: *He climbed the icy steps with caution.* **2.** A warning: *a word of caution. Some hair sprays carry the caution "Keep away from the eyes."* —*v.* To warn against possible trouble or danger: *He cautioned them not to go near that dog.*

Idiom. **throw caution to the winds.** To be reckless.

cau•tious |kô'shəs| *adj.* Showing or having caution; careful: *a cautious driver.* —**cau'tious•ly** *adv.* —**cau'tious•ness** *n.*

cav•al•cade |kăv'əl kād'| *or* |kăv'əl kād'| *n.* A ceremonial procession of people on horseback or in horse-drawn carriages.

cav•a•lier |kăv'ə lîr'| *n.* **1.** An armed horseman; a knight. **2.** A gallant or chivalrous gentleman. **3. Cavalier.** A supporter of King Charles I during the English civil war (1642–52). —*adj.* Casual and indifferent and often arrogant, high-handed, or haughty: *The men were very upset by the captain's cavalier answer to their complaints.* —**cav'a•lier'ly** *adv.* [SEE NOTE]

cav•al•ry |kăv'əl rē| *n., pl.* **cav•al•ries.** Troops

cat's cradle
Eskimo woman displaying the loop position often used in cat's cradle

cattle
In many societies where money and industry are not highly developed, **cattle** *are a basic form of personal wealth. The Medieval Latin word* capitāle *meant "wealth, property, capital." In northern Old French this word became* catel, *which was borrowed into Middle English as* **cattle,** *first meaning "wealth, property" and later coming to mean "livestock, domestic beasts." The original meaning is separately preserved in the word* **chattel.**

cavalier/chevalier
Latin caballus, *"horse," had a derivative,* caballārius, *"horseman, knight." This became* chevalier *in Old French, and was borrowed into English as* **chevalier.** *Separately the Latin word passed into Italian as* cavaliere, *which was later borrowed into French as* cavalier *and from French into English as* **cavalier. Cavalier** *is thus a doublet of* **chevalier.**

cecropia moth

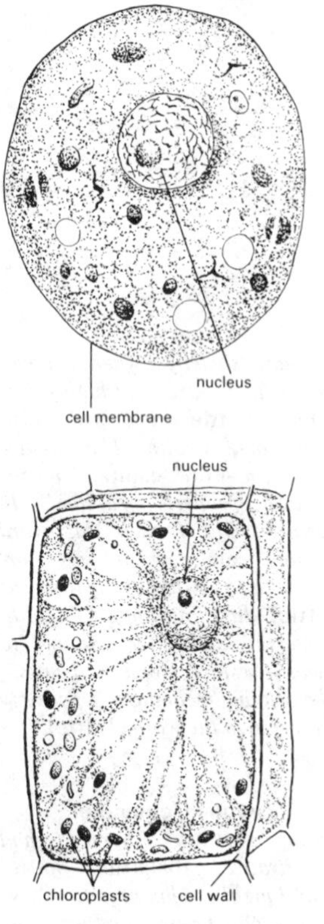

cell
Above: Animal cell
Below: Plant cell

ă pat/ā pay/â care/ä father/ĕ pet/ ē be/ĭ pit/ī pie/î fierce/ŏ pot/ ō go/ô paw, for/oi oil/ŏŏ book/ ōō boot/ou out/ŭ cut/û fur/ *th* the/th thin/hw which/zh vision/ ə ago, item, pencil, atom, circus

trained to fight on horseback or, more recently, in armored vehicles. [SEE NOTE at **chivalry**]

cav•al•ry•man |kăv′əl rē mən| *n., pl.* **-men** |-mən|. A soldier in the cavalry.

cave |kāv| *n.* A hollow beneath the earth's surface with an opening to the outside. —*v.* **caved, cav•ing.** —**cave in.** To fall in or cause to fall in; collapse: *The ground above the cesspool caved in. The flood caved in the banks of the river destroying many new homes.*

cave man. A human being of prehistoric times who lived in caves.

cav•ern |kăv′ərn| *n.* A large cave.

cav•ern•ous |kăv′ər nəs| *adj.* Resembling a cavern; huge, deep, and hollow.

cav•i•ar, also **cav•i•are** |kăv′ē är′| *n.* The eggs of a sturgeon or other large fish, prepared with salt and eaten as an appetizer.

cav•il |kăv′əl| *v.* **cav•iled** or **cav•illed, cav•il•ing** or **cav•il•ling.** To find fault unnecessarily; raise unimportant objections.

cav•i•tate |kăv′ĭ tāt′| *v.* **cav•i•tat•ed, cav•i•tat•ing.** To undergo cavitation.

cav•i•ta•tion |kăv′ĭ tā′shən| *n.* The sudden formation and collapse of bubbles in a liquid as a result of low pressures caused by ultrasonic waves or mechanical forces, as those of a rotating screw propeller.

cav•i•ty |kăv′ĭ tē| *n., pl.* **cav•i•ties. 1.** A hollow or hole. **2.** A hollow area within the body: *the abdominal cavity.* **3.** A hollow area in a tooth, caused by decay.

ca•vort |kə vôrt′| *v.* To leap about playfully; romp; frolic.

caw |kô| *n.* The hoarse, harsh call of a crow or similar bird. —*v.* To make this sound.

Cay•enne |kī ĕn′| *or* |kā′-|. The capital of French Guiana. Population, 30,461.

cayenne pepper. A very strong, sharp-tasting seasoning made from the ground pods of a kind of red pepper. See **pepper.**

cay•man |kā′mən| *n., pl.* **cay•mans.** A form of the word **caiman.**

Ca•yu•ga |kā yōō′gə| *or* |kī-| *n., pl.* **Ca•yu•ga** or **Ca•yu•gas. 1.** A North American Indian tribe of central New York State. **2.** A member of this tribe. **3.** The Iroquoian language of this tribe. —**Ca•yu′ga** *adj.*

cay•use |kī yōōs′| *n.* A horse, especially an Indian pony, of the southwestern United States.

Cay•use |kī yōōs′| *n., pl.* **Cay•use** or **Cay•us•es. 1.** A North American Indian tribe of Oregon. **2.** A member of this tribe. **3.** The Sahaptin language of this tribe.

Cb The symbol for the element columbium.

cc cubic centimeter.

C clef. A sign used to indicate which line of a musical staff represents middle C (261.7 cycles per second), used in forming the soprano clef, the alto clef, and the tenor clef.

Cd The symbol for the element cadmium.

CDST, C.D.S.T. Central Daylight-Saving Time.

Ce The symbol for the element cerium.

cease |sēs| *v.* **ceased, ceas•ing.** To come or bring to an end; stop: *The noise ceased. The factory ceased production.* —*n.* —**without cease.** Without stopping; incessantly: *She talked without cease.*

cease-fire |sēs′fīr′| *n.* A suspension of fighting in a war; a truce.

cease•less |sēs′lĭs| *adj.* Without stop; endless: *a ceaseless war between the two parties; ceaseless noise.* —**cease′less•ly** *adv.*

ce•cro•pi•a moth |sĭ krō′pē ə|. A large North American moth having wings with red, white, and black markings. [SEE PICTURE]

ce•dar |sē′dər| *n.* **1.** Any of several evergreen trees related to the pines and firs, having reddish, pleasant-smelling wood. **2.** The wood of such a tree. —***modifier:*** *a cedar chest; cedar forests.*

cede |sēd| *v.* **ced•ed, ced•ing.** To surrender possession of, usually by treaty; yield formally. ¶*These sound alike* **cede, seed.**

ce•di |sē′dē′| *n.* The basic unit of money of Ghana.

ce•dil•la |sĭ dĭl′ə| *n.* A mark beneath the letter *c* in French and Portuguese and in certain words borrowed into English, indicating that the letter is to be pronounced (s), as in *façade.*

ceil•ing |sē′lĭng| *n.* **1.** The inside upper surface of a room. **2.** An upper boundary, such as the maximum altitude at which an airplane can fly or the limit of upward visibility. **3.** A maximum limit: *price and wage ceilings.*

cel•e•brate |sĕl′ə brāt′| *v.* **cel•e•brat•ed, cel•e•brat•ing. 1.** To mark (a special occasion) with festive activity: *celebrate one's birthday. They celebrated by having a big party.* **2.** To perform (a religious ceremony): *The priest celebrated Mass.* **3.** To praise; honor; extol: *Let us celebrate the memory of this great man.* —**cel′e•bra′tion** *n.*

cel•e•brat•ed |sĕl′ə brā′tĭd| *adj.* Famous: *a celebrated musician.*

ce•leb•ri•ty |sə lĕb′rĭ tē| *n., pl.* **ce•leb•ri•ties. 1.** A famous person. **2.** Fame; renown: *He achieved celebrity as a football player.*

ce•ler•i•ty |sə lĕr′ĭ tē| *n.* Quickness; speed.

cel•er•y |sĕl′ə rē| *n.* A plant with crisp, juicy stems eaten raw or cooked and small, greenish seeds used as seasoning. —***modifier:*** *celery salt.*

ce•les•ta |sə lĕs′tə| *n.* A musical instrument consisting of a set of metal bars that produce bell-like tones when struck by hammers that are controlled from a keyboard.

ce•leste |sə lĕst′| *n.* A form of the word **celesta.**

ce•les•tial |sə lĕs′chəl| *adj.* **1.** Of or related to the sky: *Stars and planets are celestial bodies.* **2.** Of heaven; divine: *Angels are celestial beings.*

celestial equator. A great circle on the celestial sphere in the plane of the earth's equator.

celestial pole. Either of the points at which the extensions of the earth's axis intersect the celestial sphere.

celestial sphere. An imaginary sphere, having the earth at its center, on whose surface the sun, moon, stars, etc., appear to move.

cel•i•ba•cy |sĕl′ə bə sē| *n.* The condition of being unmarried, especially for religious reasons.

cel•i•bate |sĕl′ə bĭt| *n.* A person who, especially for religious reasons, remains unmarried.

cell |sĕl| *n.* **1.** A small, confining room, as in a prison, asylum, or convent. **2.** The smallest unit of living substance, consisting in general of a tiny mass of cytoplasm enclosed by a membrane and containing a nucleus and various other structures. While many organisms consist of single cells, larger organisms consist of vast numbers of cells acting in coordination. **3.** A single unit that is capable of changing some form of energy, such as chemical energy, radiant energy, or heat, into electricity. ¶ *These sound alike* **cell, sell.** [SEE PICTURE]

cel•lar |sĕl′ər| *n.* **1.** A storage room beneath a house. **2.** A dark, cool room for storing wines. ¶ *These sound alike* **cellar, seller.**

cel•list, also **'cel•list** |chĕl′ĭst| *n.* A person who plays the cello.

cel•lo, also **'cel•lo** |chĕl′ō| *n., pl.* **cel•los.** A musical instrument of the violin family, having four strings and a pitch an octave below that of the viola.

cel•lo•phane |sĕl′ə fān′| *n.* A thin, flexible, transparent material made from cellulose that is obtained from wood pulp and used as a moisture-proof wrapping.

cel•lu•lar |sĕl′yə lər| *adj.* Of, like, or containing a cell or cells.

cel•lu•lite |sĕl′yə līt′| *n.* A fatty deposit, as under the skin around the thighs.

Cel•lu•loid |sĕl′yə loid′| *n.* A trademark for a colorless, flammable material made from cellulose. It is used in making photographic film and a large number of other items.

cel•lu•lose |sĕl′yə lōs′| *n.* A carbohydrate that is insoluble in water and that is the main component of plant tissues. It is used in making a variety of products including paper, cellophane, textiles, and explosives. [SEE NOTE]

cellulose acetate. A synthetic resin used in making lacquers, photographic film, and magnetic tape.

Cel•si•us |sĕl′sē əs| *or* |-shəs| *adj.* Of the Celsius scale.

Celsius scale. A temperature scale on which the freezing point of water is 0° and the boiling point of water is 100° under normal atmospheric pressure. [SEE NOTE]

Celt |kĕlt| *or* |sĕlt| *n.* **1.** A member of an ancient European people, including the Britons and the Gauls. **2.** Someone who speaks or a descendant of someone who speaks a Celtic language. [SEE NOTE]

Celt•ic |kĕl′tĭk| *or* |sĕl′-| *adj.* Of the Celts or their languages. —*n.* A group of Indo-European languages including Welsh and Gaelic.

ce•ment |sĭ mĕnt′| *n.* **1.** A material, such as Portland cement, that with water forms a paste that can be molded or poured and that hardens into a solid mass capable of holding other solids together. **2.** A substance, such as glue, that hardens to hold things together. —***modifier:*** *a cement floor.* —*v.* **1.** To join or cover with or as if with cement. **2.** To make binding; strengthen.

cem•e•ter•y |sĕm′ĭ tĕr′ē| *n., pl.* **cem•e•ter•ies.** A place for burying the dead; a graveyard.

Ce•no•zo•ic |sē′nə zō′ĭk| *or* |sĕn′ə-| *n.* Also **Cenozoic era.** A geologic era that began about 63 million years ago and extends to the present, characterized by the development of birds and mammals and the continents in their present form. —***modifier:*** *a Cenozoic fossil.*

cen•ser |sĕn′sər| *n.* A vessel in which incense is burned, especially one swung on chains in a religious ceremony. ¶ *These sound alike* **censer, censor.**

cen•sor |sĕn′sər| *n.* A person who has the power to remove or suppress material considered harmful in literature, news, letters, etc. —*v.* To remove material from or prevent the publication of: *censor a news story.* ¶ *These sound alike* **censor, censer.**

cen•so•ri•ous |sĕn sôr′ē əs| *or* |-sōr′-| *adj.* Very critical. —**cen•so′ri•ous•ly** *adv.*

cen•sor•ship |sĕn′sər shĭp′| *n.* The act or practice of censoring.

cen•sure |sĕn′shər| *n.* The expression of strong disapproval or criticism. —*v.* **cen•sured, cen•sur•ing.** To express strong disapproval of; criticize: *The press censured the mayor severely.*

cen•sus |sĕn′səs| *n., pl.* **cen•sus•es.** An official count of population, often including statistics on age, sex, etc., and other factual information about people.

cent |sĕnt| *n.* **1.** A subdivision of the dollar of the U.S. **2.** A subdivision of the dollar of Australia, Canada, Ethiopia, Guyana, Jamaica, Liberia, Malaysia, New Zealand, Trinidad and Tobago, Western Samoa, Hong Kong, and Singapore. **3.** A subdivision of the guilder of the Netherlands, Surinam, and the Netherland Antilles, the leone of Sierra Leone, the piaster of South Vietnam, the rand of the Republic of South Africa, the rupee of Ceylon and Mauritius, and the yuan of the Republic of China. **4.** A subdivision of the shilling of Kenya, Tanzania, Uganda, and the Somali Republic. **5.** A small sum of money: *I haven't a cent to my name.* ¶ *These sound alike* **cent, scent, sent.**

cen•taur |sĕn′tôr′| *n.* In Greek mythology, a creature having the head, arms, and trunk of a man and the body and legs of a horse.

cen•ta•vo |sĕn tä′vō| *n., pl.* **cen•ta•vos.** A unit of money equal to 1/100 of the colon of El Salvador, the cordoba of Nicaragua, the escudo of Portugal, the lempira of Honduras, the cruzeiro of Brazil, the peso of Argentina, Bolivia, Colombia, Cuba, the Dominican Republic, Mexico, and the Philippines, the quetzal of Guatemala, the sol of Peru, and the sucre of Ecuador.

cen•ten•ar•y |sĕn tĕn′ə rē| *or* |sĕn′tə nĕr′ē| *n., pl.* **cen•ten•ar•ies.** **1.** A period of 100 years. **2.** A centennial. —*adj.* Centennial.

cen•ten•ni•al |sĕn tĕn′ē əl| *n.* A 100th anniversary or a celebration of it. —*adj.* **1.** Of a period of 100 years. **2.** Happening once every 100 years: *a centennial celebration.*

cen•ter |sĕn′tər| *n.* **1. a.** A point that is equally distant from every point of a circle or a sphere. **b.** A point that is equally distant from each vertex of a regular polygon. **2.** The middle position, part, or place of something: *the center of a table; the center of the earth.* **3.** A place of concentrated activity: *a shopping center.* **4.** A person or thing that is the chief object of attention, interest, etc. **5.** A player on a team stationed in or near the middle of a playing area or forward line. —***modifier:*** *a center point; a center section.* —*v.* **1.** To place in or at the center: *center a picture on a page.* **2.** To concentrate or be concentrated in a person or place: *Executive power is centered in the President. Industry centered in the cities during the Industrial Revolution.* **3.** To have as a main theme, interest, or concern; focus: *Attention centered on the baby. The conversation centered on air pollution.* **4.** To pass (a football) from the line of scrimmage to a back.

cellulose

The basic chemical component of **cellulose** *has the formula* $C_6H_{10}O_5$*, but cellulose is a polymer consisting of a vast number of these units joined together. Its formula, therefore, is given as* $(C_6H_{10}O_5)_x$*, that is, as* x *of the basic units joined together.*

Celsius scale

The **Celsius scale** *was invented by Anders* Celsius *(1701–1744), Swedish astronomer.*

Celt

In English, a c *followed by an* e *is almost always pronounced* s. *To pronounce* **Celt** *as /sĕlt/ is therefore perfectly regular. Nonetheless, it is more correct historically to pronounce it /kĕlt/, because the earliest known form of the name, in Greek, was* Keltoi. *Before the expansion of Rome, the Celts dominated most of western and central Europe, but now their languages are confined to the British Isles and Brittany. There are fewer than three million Celtic-speakers, and their number is dwindling.*

centipede
Centipedes, together with the insects, spiders, lobsters, and crabs, belong to a large group of organisms called arthropods.

cen•ter•board |sĕn′tər bôrd′| *or* |-bōrd′| *n.* A flat board or metal plate that can be lowered through the bottom of a sailboat to stabilize it and prevent it from drifting.

center of gravity. A point in a material body through which the force equal to the sum of all the gravitational forces acting on the body acts. In a uniform gravitational field, this point coincides with the center of mass.

center of mass. A point in a material body or system of material bodies that behaves as if all of the mass of the body or system were concentrated at that point and all external forces acted on that point only.

center of symmetry. A point *O* in a figure having the property that for any point *A* in the figure there can be found a point *A′* where *O* is the midpoint of the line segment connecting *A* and *A′*. For example, the center of a circle is its center of symmetry.

cen•ter•piece |sĕn′tər pēs′| *n.* An ornamental object or bowl of flowers placed at the center of a dining table.

centi–. A word element meaning: **1.** A hundred: **centipede. 2.** A hundredth: **centigram.**

cen•ti•grade |sĕn′tĭ grād′| *adj.* Of or relating to a temperature scale that divides the interval between the boiling and freezing points of water into 100°; Celsius.

cen•ti•gram |sĕn′tĭ grăm′| *n.* A unit of mass or weight; 1/100 gram. See **metric system.**

cen•time |sän′tēm′| *n.* **1.** A subdivision of the franc of France, Belgium, Burundi, Cameroun, Central African Republic, Chad, Congo (Brazzaville), Dahomey, Gabon, Guinea, Ivory Coast, Luxembourg, Malagasy Republic, Mali, Mauritania, Niger, Rwanda, Senegal, Switzerland, Togo, Upper Volta, and of various overseas departments and territories of France. **2. a.** A subdivision of the dinar of Algeria. **b.** A subdivision of the gourde of Haiti.

cen•ti•me•ter |sĕn′tə mē′tər| *n.* A unit of length; 1/100 meter. See **metric system.**

cen•ti•pede |sĕn′tə pēd′| *n.* Any of a group of animals with a wormlike body divided into many segments, each with a pair of legs. The front pair have venom glands and are used as jaws that can give a painful bite. [SEE PICTURE]

century
Century, *and other words such as* **cent** *that are connected with "hundred," comes from Latin* centum, *"hundred," which is descended from the prehistoric Indo-European word for "hundred,"* kəmtom. *The Indo-Europeans, living in the early Bronze Age, had a fully developed decimal system of counting, which we have directly inherited.*

cen•tral |sĕn′trəl| *adj.* **1.** At, near, or being the center: *the central part of a state.* **2.** Having the dominant or controlling power: *a central authority uniting people under one government.* **3.** Main, principal, or chief: *the central character of a story.* —**cen′tral•ly** *adv.*

Central African Republic. A country in central Africa, south of Chad. Population, 2,370,000. Capital, Bangui.

Central America. The part of North America between Mexico and South America, consisting of Guatemala, Belize, El Salvador, Honduras, Nicaragua, Costa Rica, and Panama.

central angle. An angle formed by two rays from the center of a circle.

Central Daylight-Saving Time. Daylight-saving time as reckoned in the region between the meridians at 82.5° and 97.5° west of Greenwich, England. The midwestern United States is in this region. See **time zone.**

central heating. A system of heating a building from a single source with steam or hot water circulating through pipes.

cen•tral•ize |sĕn′trə līz′| *v.* **cen•tral•ized, cen•tral•iz•ing.** To bring or come under a central, controlling authority: *centralize political power in the federal government.* —**cen′tral•i•za′tion** *n.*

central nervous system. In a vertebrate animal, the brain and spinal cord.

Central Standard Time. Standard time as reckoned in the region between the meridians at 82.5° and 97.5° west of Greenwich, England. The midwestern United States is in this region. See **time zone.**

cen•tre |sĕn′tər| *n.* Chiefly British form of the word **center.**

cen•trif•u•gal |sĕn trĭf′yə gəl| *or* |-trĭf′ə gəl| *adj.* Moving or directed away from a center or axis.

centrifugal force. The apparent force, as observed from a body that is moving in a curve or rotating, that acts outward from the center of the curve or the axis of rotation.

cen•tri•fuge |sĕn′trə fyo͞oj′| *n.* Any device that consists essentially of a chamber whirled about a central axis in such a way that centrifugal force propels its contents toward its outer wall.

cen•tri•ole |sĕn′trē ōl′| *n.* A tiny structure found in the centrosome of a cell that plays a part in the division of the cell.

cen•trip•e•tal |sĕn trĭp′ĭ tl| *adj.* Directed or moving toward a center or axis.

centripetal force. The force acting on a body that moves in a curve or rotates about an axis that acts toward the center of the curve or the axis of rotation.

cen•trist |sĕn′trĭst| *n.* Someone who avoids both left-wing and right-wing extremes in politics.

cen•tro•some |sĕn′trə sōm′| *n.* A small mass that is contained in, but different from, the cytoplasm of a cell.

cen•tu•ri•on |sĕn to͝or′ē ən| *or* |-tyo͝or′-| *n.* An officer commanding a unit of a hundred men in the army of ancient Rome.

cen•tu•ry |sĕn′chə rē| *n., pl.* **cen•tu•ries. 1.** A period of 100 years. **2.** Each of the 100-year periods counted forward or backward since the time of Christ's birth: *the 20th century.* [SEE NOTE]

century plant. A tropical American plant with long, thick, stiff leaves and greenish flowers that may not bloom until after the plant has been growing for 10, 20, or more years.

ce•phal•ic |sə făl′ĭk| *adj.* Of, on, in, or near the head or skull.

Ce•phe•id |sē′fē ĭd| *n.* Also **Cepheid variable.** A type of star whose brightness varies in a regular, periodic way.

ce•ram•ic |sə răm′ĭk| *n.* **1.** A hard, brittle, heat-resistant and corrosion-resistant material made by treating clay or some other mineral with extreme heat and used in making pottery, electrical insulators, and other products. **2.** Often **ceramics.** Objects made of this material. **3. ceramics** *(used with a singular verb).* The art or technique of making things from this material: *Ceramics is his hobby.* —***modifier:*** *a ceramic dish; ceramic techniques.*

ce•re•al |sîr′ē əl| *n.* **1.** The seeds of certain grasses, such as wheat, oats, or corn, used as

ă **pat**/ā **pay**/â **care**/ä **father**/ĕ **pet**/ ē **be**/ĭ **pit**/ī **pie**/î **fierce**/ŏ **pot**/ ō **go**/ô **paw**, **for**/oi **oil**/o͝o **book**/ o͞o **boot**/ou **out**/ŭ **cut**/û **fur**/ *th* **the**/th **thin**/hw **which**/zh **vision**/ ə **ago**, **item**, **pencil**, **atom**, **circus**

food. **2.** A grass bearing such grain. **3.** A food, such as a breakfast food, made from such grain. ¶*These sound alike* **cereal, serial.**

cer•e•bel•lum |sĕr'ə **bĕl'**əm| *n., pl.* **cer•e•bel•lums** or **cer•e•bel•la** |sĕr'ə **bĕl'**ə|. A part of the brain, located at the rear of the skull, that regulates and coordinates complex muscular movements. [SEE PICTURE]

ce•re•bra |**sĕr'**ə brə| *or* |sə **rē'**brə| *n.* A plural of **cerebrum.**

cer•e•bral |**sĕr'**ə brəl| *or* |sə **rē'**-| *adj.* Of the brain or cerebrum.

cerebral cortex. The outer layer of gray tissue that covers the two parts of the cerebrum, responsible for most of the higher functions of the nervous system.

cerebral hemorrhage. A condition in which a blood vessel in the cerebrum breaks and releases blood into the nearby tissue; a stroke. The damage caused to the nervous system by the pressure of the escaped blood and by starvation of the cells often results in paralysis or death.

cerebral palsy. Weakness and lack of coordination of the muscles, resulting from damage to the brain, usually at or before birth.

cer•e•bro•spi•nal |sĕr'ə brō **spī'**nəl| *or* |sə-rē'-| *adj.* Of the brain and spinal cord.

cer•e•brum |**sĕr'**ə brəm| *or* |sə **rē'**-| *n., pl.* **ce•re•brums** or **ce•re•bra** |**sĕr'**ə brə| *or* |sə **rē'**brə|. The large, rounded structure of the brain that fills most of the skull, divided by a deep groove into two parts that are joined at the bottom.

cere•ment |**sîr'**mənt| *or* |**sĕr'**ə mənt| *n.* A shroud used to wrap a dead body.

cer•e•mo•ni•al |sĕr'ə **mō'**nē əl| *adj.* Of a ceremony: *ceremonial dances.* —*n.* **1.** A ceremony: *Indians used many songs and dances in their tribal ceremonials.* **2.** The formal rules of ceremony observed in social life, religious worship, etc.: *The sporting element in American political life is as deep-rooted as the ceremonial that surrounds and dignifies it.* —**cer'e•mo'ni•al•ly** *adv.*

cer•e•mo•ni•ous |sĕr'ə **mō'**nē əs| *adj.* **1.** Fond of ceremony and formality; formally polite: *The Japanese are a ceremonious people.* **2.** In accordance with a set of prescribed forms or rites; formal: *The temple was crowded for the ceremonious offerings to the gods.* —**cer'e•mo'ni•ous•ly** *adv.* —**cer'e•mo'ni•ous•ness** *n.*

cer•e•mo•ny |**sĕr'**ə mō'nē| *n., pl.* **cer•e•mo•nies. 1.** A formal act or set of acts performed in honor or celebration of an occasion, such as a wedding, funeral, etc.: *a wedding ceremony; the ceremony of hoisting the flag.* **2.** Formality: *He was welcomed with great ceremony.*

***Idiom.* stand on ceremony.** To insist on or behave with great formality: *In private life, the Prince doesn't like to stand on ceremony.*

Če•ren•kov effect |chə **rĕng'**kôf| *or* |sə-|. The emission of light when a particle passes through a transparent nonconducting solid faster than light can travel in that particular solid. [SEE NOTE]

Ce•res[1] |**sîr'**ēz|. The Roman goddess of agriculture.

Ce•res[2] |**sîr'**ēz| *n.* The first asteroid discovered, having an orbit between Mars and Saturn.

ce•rise |sə **rēs'**| *or* |**-rēz'**| *n.* A deep red. —*adj.* Deep red.

ce•ri•um |**sîr'**ē əm| *n.* Symbol **Ce** One of the elements, a lustrous, gray rare-earth metal. Atomic number 58; atomic weight 140.12; valences +3, +4; melting point 795°C; boiling point 3,468°C.

cer•met |**sûr'**mĕt'| *n.* A material consisting of a mixture of ceramic and metallic particles bonded together, usually by heat.

cer•tain |**sûr'**tn| *adj.* **1.** Having no doubt; positive: *Are you certain that you left the book here?* **2.** Established beyond doubt or question; definite: *Whether he will do it is not certain.* **3.** Sure to come or happen; inevitable: *certain death.* **4.** Not named or specified but assumed to be known: *There are certain laws for automobile safety.* **5.** Named but not familiar or well-known: *a certain Mr. Smith.* **6.** Some but not much; limited: *to a certain degree.* [SEE NOTE]

***Idiom.* for certain.** Surely; without doubt: *It will happen for certain.*

cer•tain•ly |**sûr'**tn lē| *adv.* Surely; definitely: *He is certainly the best player on the team.*

cer•tain•ty |**sûr'**tn tē| *n., pl.* **cer•tain•ties. 1.** The condition or quality of being certain; freedom from doubt; sureness: *She can speak with poise and certainty in front of a group. There is no certainty that he will arrive tonight.* **2.** A clearly established fact: *It is not a certainty that cancer is caused by a virus.*

cer•tif•i•cate |sər **tĭf'**ĭ kĭt| *n.* **1.** An official document giving information, such as date and place of birth, about a person. **2.** A document certifying or stating that a person may practice certain professions, such as teaching. **3.** A document or piece of paper that serves as a substitute for something of monetary value: *a stock certificate.*

cer•ti•fi•ca•tion |sûr'tə fĭ **kā'**shən| *n.* **1. a.** The act of certifying. **b.** The condition of being certified. **2.** A certified document or statement; certificate.

certified check. A check guaranteed by a bank to be covered by sufficient funds on deposit.

certified mail. Mail whose delivery is recorded by the return of a receipt to the sender.

certified public accountant. A public accountant who has received a certificate stating that he has met the state's legal requirements in his profession.

cer•ti•fy |**sûr'**tə fī'| *v.* **cer•ti•fied, cer•ti•fy•ing, cer•ti•fies. 1.** To confirm or guarantee as being true, meeting a standard, etc.: *certify a copy of a document; certify a check. The Federal Aviation Administration certifies aircraft.* **2.** To give a certificate to (someone) stating that all requirements have been met for engaging in certain studies, professions, etc.: *certify a teacher. The new plan began training and certifying 14- and 15-year-olds to take farm jobs.* **3.** To declare with certainty: *The doctor certified that the operation was essential.*

cer•ti•tude |**sûr'**tĭ to͞od'| *or* |-tyo͞od'| *n.* The condition of being certain; freedom from all doubt; complete assurance: *The certitude of the astronauts amazes all of us.*

ce•ru•le•an |sə **ro͞o'**lē ən| *adj.* Sky blue.

Cer•van•tes |sər **văn'**tēz|, **Miguel de.** 1547–1616. Spanish author who wrote *Don Quixote.*

cer•vi•cal |**sûr'**vĭ kəl| *adj.* Of a neck or cervix.

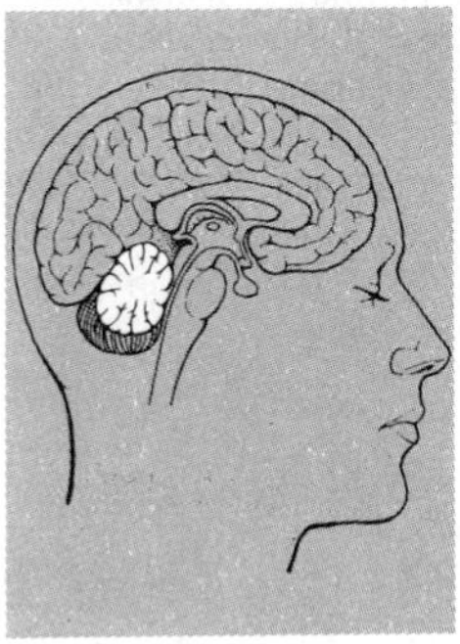

cerebellum

Čerenkov effect

The **Čerenkov effect** *was discovered by P. A. Čerenkov, a Soviet physicist born in 1904.*

certain

"But in this world nothing can be said to be certain, except death and taxes." — *Benjamin Franklin.*

cf.

Cf. *is short for the Latin word* confer, *meaning "compare." From the Middle Ages up until the nineteenth century, many scientific and scholarly books were written in Latin, and we have thus inherited several Latin abbreviations. The other most common ones are* **e.g., i.e., n.b.,** *and* **etc.**

chaff¹·²

Chaff¹ *goes back to Old English. It was originally spelled* ceaf. **Chaff²** *first occurs in the nineteenth century as a slang word. It has been suggested that it is related to* **chafe** *(in the sense "to scold") or to* **chaff¹** *(in the extended sense "trivial nonsense"). Neither suggestion is very convincing.*

chalice

ă pat/ā pay/â care/ä father/ĕ pet/ ē be/ĭ pit/ī pie/î fierce/ŏ pot/ ō go/ô paw, for/oi oil/ŏŏ book/ ōō boot/ou out/ŭ cut/û fur/ *th* the/th thin/hw which/zh vision/ ə ago, item, pencil, atom, circus

cer•vix |sûr′vĭks| *n., pl.* **cer•vix•es** or **cer•vi•ces** |sûr′vĭ sēz′| *or* |sər vī′sēz|. **1.** The neck. **2.** A neck-shaped part of the body, as the outer end of the uterus.

ce•si•um |sē′zē əm| *n.* Symbol **Cs** One of the elements, a soft, silvery metal. Atomic number 55; atomic weight 132.91; valence +1; melting point 28.5°C; boiling point 690°C.

ces•sa•tion |sĕ sā′shən| *n.* The act of ceasing or stopping; a halt: *a cessation of activity.*

ces•sion |sĕsh′ən| *n.* An act of ceding; the act of giving up territory to another country by treaty.

cess•pool |sĕs′po͞ol′| *n.* A covered hole or pit in the ground for receiving drained sewage.

ce•ta•cean |sĭ tā′shən| *n.* A whale, porpoise, or related fishlike mammal. *—adj.* Of or belonging to the group of mammals that includes the whales and porpoises.

Cey•lon |sĭ lŏn′|. The former name for **Sri Lanka.**

Cf The symbol for the element californium.

cf. compare. [SEE NOTE]

C.G. 1. coast guard. **2.** commanding general. **3.** consul general.

ch. chapter.

cha-cha |chä′chä′| *n.* A rhythmic ballroom dance that originated in Latin America.

cha•conne |shä kôn′| *n.* A musical form consisting of a set of variations on a repeated series of chords or a repeated bass.

Chad |chăd|. A country in north-central Africa, south of Libya. Population, 4,309,000. Capital, Ndjamena.

chafe |chāf| *v.* **chafed, chaf•ing. 1.** To irritate by rubbing: *The starched collar chafed his neck. Her skin chafes easily.* **2.** To feel prolonged irritation; be impatient: *chafe at the delay.*

chaff¹ |chăf| *n.* Grain husks that have been separated from the seeds by threshing. [SEE NOTE]

chaff² |chăf| *v.* **chaffed, chaff•ing.** To make fun of good-naturedly; tease: *His classmates chaffed him about his clothes.* [SEE NOTE]

chaf•finch |chăf′ĭnch| *n.* A small European songbird with reddish-brown feathers.

chafing dish. A pan set above a heating device, used to cook food or keep it warm at the table.

cha•grin |shə grĭn′| *n.* A strong feeling of annoyance accompanied by embarrassment or humiliation. *—v.* To cause to feel chagrin; annoy greatly: *I was greatly chagrined at receiving dozens of letters of complaint.*

chain |chān| *n.* **1.** A series of connected links, usually of metal, used to bind or hold, transmit motion, or serve as an ornament. **2. chains.** Something that restrains or confines: *break the chains of captivity.* **3.** A series of connected or related things: *a chain of events.* **4.** A number of stores, restaurants, theaters, etc., under common ownership or management. **5.** A unit of length used in land surveying, equal to 66 feet. **6.** A mountain range. *—v.* To bind or confine with or as if with a chain or chains.

chain gang. A group of convicts chained together when doing heavy labor outside their prison.

chain mail. Armor that will bend, made of metal rings that are connected like links in a chain.

chain reaction. 1. A series of events each of which causes or influences the next. **2.** A reaction of this kind involving atomic nuclei, especially one in which the neutrons produced when one nucleus fissions cause other nuclei to fission in such a way that the reaction keeps itself going.

chain saw. A power saw with teeth set on a circular chain.

chain store. Any of a number of retail stores under the same ownership or management.

chair |châr| *n.* **1.** A piece of furniture on which one person may sit, consisting of a seat, back, and usually four legs. **2.** A position of authority, as that of a chairman or professor: *the chair of ancient history.* **3.** The chairman of a meeting: *address a question to the chair. —v.* **1.** To install in office. **2.** To preside over (a meeting).

chair•man |châr′mən| *n., pl.* **-men** |-mən|. **1.** A person in charge of a meeting. **2.** A person who directs the work of a committee, assembly, board, or similar group.

chair•man•ship |châr′mən shĭp′| *n.* The office of a chairman or the period during which a chairman is in office.

chaise |shāz| *n.* A light, usually two-wheeled carriage with a folding top, drawn by one horse.

chaise longue |shāz′ lông′| *pl.* **chaise longues** or **chaises longues** |shāz′ lông′|. A long chair on which one can sit and stretch out one's legs.

cha•lah |KHä′lə| *n.* A form of the word **challah.**

chal•ced•o•ny |kăl sĕd′n ē| *n., pl.* **chal•ced•o•nies.** A type of quartz that has a milky appearance and varies from transparent to translucent. It is used as a gemstone.

cha•let |shă lā′| *n.* **1. a.** A house with a gently sloping overhanging roof, common in Switzerland. **b.** A house built in this style. **2.** The hut of a herdsman in the Alps.

chal•ice |chăl′ĭs| *n.* **1.** A cup or goblet. **2.** A cup for the consecrated wine of the Eucharist. [SEE PICTURE]

chalk |chôk| *n.* **1.** A soft mineral composed mainly of calcium carbonate, formed chiefly from fossil seashells. **2.** A piece of this material or a similar substance, used for various purposes, especially for making marks on a blackboard or other surface. *—modifier: chalk cliffs; chalk deposits; a chalk drawing; a chalk mark. —v.* **1.** To mark, draw, or write with chalk. **2.** To treat or cover with chalk. *—phrasal verb.* **chalk up. 1.** To earn or score: *a team that chalks up victories; chalk up a record number of points.* **2.** To credit: *Any success or failure of your group will be chalked up for or against you.*

chalk•board |chôk′bôrd′| *or* |-bōrd′| *n.* A panel, usually green or black, for writing on with chalk; a blackboard.

chalk•y |chô′kē| *adj.* **chalk•i•er, chalk•i•est.** Of or like chalk. *—***chalk′i•ness** *n.*

chal•lah |KHä′lə| *n.* A white bread, made with eggs and usually baked in the shape of a braid. Jews traditionally serve this bread on the Sabbath.

chal•lenge |chăl′ənj| *n.* **1.** An invitation or call to take part in a contest or fight to see who is better, stronger, etc.: *a challenge to a race. The Black Knight accepted the challenge of his enemies and attacked.* **2.** A sentry's call for identification: *"Who goes there?" was the challenge of the* *soldier.* **3. a.** A special quality naturally belonging to something and requiring full use of one's abilities, energy, or resources: *a student fascinated by the beauties of language and the challenge of mathematics.* **b.** Something having this quality: *The universe is a great challenge to men. Writing an essay is a challenge under any circumstances.* —*v.* **chal•lenged, chal•leng•ing. 1.** To call to engage in a contest or fight: *We challenged them to a game of basketball.* **2.** To order to halt and be identified: *The sentries challenged everybody who walked by.* **3.** To summon to action, effort, or use; stimulate: *a problem that challenges the imagination.* **4.** To question or dispute the truth or rightness of: *challenge a statement.* —**chal'leng•ing** *adj.: a challenging job.* —**chal'leng•er** *n.*

chal•lis, also **chal•lie** |**shăl'**ē| *n.* A lightweight fabric of wool, cotton, or rayon, usually having a printed pattern. —***modifier:*** *a challis tie.*

cham•ber |**chām'**bər| *n.* **1.** A private room in a house, especially a bedroom. **2.** A room in which a person of high rank receives visitors. **3. chambers.** A judge's office in a courthouse. **4.** A room reserved for some special purpose: *a torture chamber.* **5.** The hall used by a group of lawmakers or the group itself: *Inside the Capitol are the two chambers where the laws are made, the Senate and the House of Representatives. The Senate is called the upper chamber of the legislature.* **6.** An enclosed space or compartment, especially in a machine: *a bullet in the chamber of a rifle.*

cham•ber•lain |**chām'**bər lĭn| *n.* An official who manages the household of a king or nobleman.

cham•ber•maid |**chām'**bər mād'| *n.* A woman who cleans and takes care of bedrooms, as in a hotel.

chamber music. Music written for a small group of instruments and suitable for performance in a private home or small concert hall.

chamber of commerce. An association of businessmen and merchants for the promotion of business interests in its community.

cham•bray |**shăm'**brā'| *n.* A fine, lightweight gingham cloth, woven with white threads crossing colored ones to give a frosted look. —***modifier:*** *a chambray dress.*

cha•me•leon |kə **mēl'**yən| *or* |**-mē'**lē ən| *n.* Any of several lizards that can change color rapidly. [See Note]

cham•fer |**chăm'**fər| *v.* **1.** To cut off the edge or corner of (a board); bevel. **2.** To cut a groove in; flute. —*n.* **1.** A beveled edge or corner. **2.** A furrow or groove in a piece of wood.

cham•ois |**shăm'**ē| *n.* **1.** A goatlike animal of mountainous regions of Europe. **2.** Soft, yellowish leather originally made from the skin of this animal, used for washing and polishing. [See Picture]

cham•o•mile |**kăm'**ə mīl'| *n.* A form of the word **camomile.**

champ[1] |chămp| *v.* To chew or bite (food, a bit, etc.) noisily: *a horse champing his bit; a horse chewing and champing with great vigor.*

Idiom. **champ at the bit.** To be impatient: *The boys were champing at the bit to start the game.*

champ[2] |chămp| *n. Informal.* A champion.

cham•pagne |shăm **pān'**| *n.* **1.** A sparkling white wine produced in Champagne, a region of France. **2.** A similar wine made in another area. —***modifier:*** *a champagne glass; champagne bottles.* ¶*These sound alike* **champagne, champaign.**

cham•paign |shăm **pān'**| *n.* Level and open country; a plain. ¶*These sound alike* **champaign, champagne.**

cham•pi•on |**chăm'**pē ən| *n.* **1.** Someone or something acknowledged as the best of all, having defeated others in competition. **2.** A person who fights for or defends a cause, movement, etc.: *a champion of freedom.* —***modifier:*** *a champion boxer; the champion team.* —*v.* To fight for or defend (a cause, movement, etc.): *He championed the rights of poor people.*

cham•pi•on•ship |**chăm'**pē ən shĭp'| *n.* **1. a.** The position or title of a champion. **b.** A contest held to determine a champion. **2.** Defense or support: *He was well known for his championship of human rights.* —***modifier:*** *the championship team.*

chance |chăns| *or* |chăns| *n.* **1.** The force that controls the happening of events without any causes that can be seen or understood; the way things happen; luck: *Poker is a game in which chance plays an important part. Let's leave our next meeting to chance.* **2.** The likelihood that something will happen; probability; possibility: *She has little chance of winning the tournament.* **3.** An opportunity: *He never misses a chance to play basketball. She will not give him a chance to talk.* **4.** A risk or gamble: *You're taking a chance by disobeying instructions.* **5.** A raffle or lottery ticket. —***modifier:*** *a chance meeting with a friend.* —*v.* **chanced, chanc•ing. 1.** To happen by accident: *It chanced that she was there, too.* **2.** To take a chance with; risk: *I'll chance another throw of the dice.* **3.** —**chance on** or **upon.** To come upon or meet accidentally: *I chanced upon an old friend today.*

chan•cel |**chăn'**səl| *or* |**chăn'-**| *n.* The space around the altar of a church for the clergy and choir.

chan•cel•lor |**chăn'**sə lər| *or* |-slər| *or* |**chăn'-**| *n.* **1.** The chief minister of state in some European countries. **2.** In some universities, the president or another officer of high rank. **3.** The presiding judge of a court of equity in the United States. See **equity.**

chan•cer•y |**chăn'**sə rē| *or* |**chăn'-**| *n., pl.* **chan•cer•ies. 1.** A court dealing with cases that are not covered by common law and that have to be tried according to a special body of laws; a court of equity. See **equity. 2.** An office for the collection and safekeeping of official documents: *a papal chancery.* **3.** An office in which the business of a diocese is conducted. **4.** The office of an embassy or consulate.

chan•cre |**shăng'**kər| *n.* A hard, dull-red, insensitive sore, usually an early sign of syphilis, that forms on the skin.

chanc•y |**chăn'**sē| *or* |**chăn'-**| *adj.* **chanc•i•er, chanc•i•est.** Uncertain as to outcome; risky: *a chancy undertaking.*

chan•de•lier |shăn'də **lîr'**| *n.* A fixture that holds a number of light bulbs or candles and is suspended from a ceiling. [See Picture]

chan•dler |**chănd'**lər| *or* |**chănd'-**| *n.* **1.** A person who makes or sells candles. **2.** A person

chameleon

The lizards considered to be true **chameleons** *live only in warm regions of the Old World, but the name is widely used for a small New World lizard that can also change color.*

chamois

chandelier

chanticleer
Chanticleer, *from the French words* chanter, *"to sing," and* cler, *"clear," was the name of the cock in the medieval tale* Reynard the Fox.

chap[1-2]/chaparral/chaps
Chap[1] *first appeared in the fourteenth century, and is possibly borrowed from Low German.* **Chap[2]** *is a sixteenth-century slang shortening of* chapman, *an old word meaning "dealer, peddler." It is rather similar to the word "customer" used in such modern slang expressions as "He's a queer customer."* **Chaps** *is from Mexican Spanish* chaparreras, *"chaps," which originally meant "leggings for riding through a* **chaparral.** *And Spanish* chaparral *is from* chaparro, *"oak bush," which is from Basque.*

ă pat/ā pay/â care/ä father/ĕ pet/ ē be/ĭ pit/ī pie/î fierce/ŏ pot/ ō go/ô paw, for/oi oil/ŏŏ book/ ōō boot/ou out/ŭ cut/û fur/ *th* the/th thin/hw which/zh vision/ ə ago, item, pencil, atom, circus

who sells goods or equipment of a specified kind, especially for ships.

change |chānj| *v.* **changed, chang•ing. 1.** To make or become different; alter: *change the spelling of a word; change the colors of a picture. Some insects change as they grow up. Their lives are changing fast.* **2.** To take, put, or use (something) in place of another, usually of the same kind: *change one's clothes. It will take me five minutes to change. He changed into his diving suit. The company changed its name and address.* **3. a.** To give and receive (one thing for another); exchange; switch: *"Would you change places with me?" I asked.* **b.** To exchange (a unit of money) for smaller units: *change a dollar.* **4.** To put fresh clothes or coverings on: *change a baby; change a bed.* **5.** To become deeper in tone: *As the vocal cords thicken, the boys' voices change.* —*n.* **1.** The act, process, or result of changing: *make a change in the schedule. A change in word order may cause a change in meaning.* **2. a.** The money of smaller denomination exchanged for a unit of higher denomination: *Will you give me change for a dollar?* **b.** The money returned when the amount given in paying for something is more than what is due. **c.** A number of coins: *change jingling in one's pocket.* **3.** Something different that can be used, done, etc., for variety; a break in one's routine: *This Sunday we will breakfast early for a change.* **4.** A fresh set of clothing. —**change'a•ble** *adj.*

Idiom. **change hands.** To pass from one owner to another: *The company changed hands this year.*

change•less |chānj'lĭs| *adj.* Never changing; constant. —**change'less•ness** *n.*

change•ling |chānj'lĭng| *n.* **1.** In folklore, an ugly or stupid fairy child secretly exchanged for a human child by the fairies or elves. **2.** Any child secretly exchanged for another.

change•o•ver |chānj'ō'vər| *n.* A change from one activity, way of doing something, etc., to another.

change purse. A small pouch with a clasp or drawstring, used to carry coins.

chan•nel |chăn'əl| *n.* **1.** The depression or cut in the earth through which a river or stream passes. **2.** A part of a river or harbor deep enough to form a passage for ships. **3.** A broad strait: *the English Channel.* **4.** A passage for liquids. **5.** Any course or way through which news, ideas, etc., may travel: *opening new channels of information.* **6.** A band of radio-wave frequencies reserved for broadcasting or communication: *a television channel.* **7. channels.** Official routes of communication: *go through channels to get what one wants.* —*v.* **chan•neled** or **chan•nelled, chan•nel•ing** or **chan•nel•ling. 1.** To form a channel in or through. **2.** To direct or guide along a desired route.

Channel Islands. A group of British islands in the English Channel off the coast of France. Population, 123,000.

chant |chănt| *or* |chänt| *n.* **1.** A vocal melody, often with many words or syllables sung on the same note, in which the rhythm is controlled largely by the words. **2.** A melody of this kind, traditionally used with a religious text: *a Gregorian chant.* **3.** A sustained, rhythmic call or shout. —*v.* **1.** To sing (words) to a chant. **2.** To sing, especially in the manner of a chant. **3.** To call out in a sustained, rhythmic way.

chan•tey |shăn'tē| *or* |chăn'-| *n., pl.* **chan•teys.** A work song sung by sailors in earlier times to the rhythm of their motions while working. ¶ *These sound alike* **chantey, shanty.**

chan•ti•cleer |chăn'tĭ klîr'| *or* |shăn'-| *n.* A nickname for a rooster. [SEE NOTE]

Cha•nu•kah |KHä'nŏŏ kä'| *or* |-nə kə| *or* |hä'-| *n.* A Jewish festival, usually in December, lasting eight days. It is in memory of the rededication of the Temple at Jerusalem after a Jewish victory over the Syrians in 165 B.C.

cha•os |kā'ŏs'| *n.* **1.** Great disorder or confusion. **2.** Often **Chaos.** The shapeless and disordered state of unformed matter and infinite space supposed to have existed before the creation of the universe.

cha•ot•ic |kā ŏt'ĭk| *adj.* In a state of chaos; in great disorder or confusion. —**cha•ot'i•cal•ly** *adv.*

chap[1] |chăp| *v.* **chapped, chap•ping.** To make or become dry, scaly, and cracked: *His lips chapped from the cold. Harsh soaps will chap the hands. Her lips chap easily.* —*n.* A soreness and roughness of the skin, as that caused by cold. [SEE NOTE]

chap[2] |chăp| *n. Informal.* A man or boy; fellow. [SEE NOTE]

chap. chapter.

chap•ar•ral |shăp'ə răl'| *or* |chăp'-| *n.* A dense growth of tangled, often thorny shrubs, especially in the southwestern United States and Mexico. [SEE NOTE]

cha•peau |shă pō'| *n., pl.* **cha•peaux** |shă pōz'| or **cha•peaus** |shă pōz'|. *French.* A hat.

chap•el |chăp'əl| *n.* **1. a.** A small church. **b.** A small place, with its own altar, within a church, reserved for special services. **2.** A place for religious services in a school, hospital, etc. **3.** Religious services held at a chapel: *Students were required to attend chapel.*

chap•er•on, also **chap•er•one** |shăp'ə rōn'| *n.* **1.** An older person who attends a dance or party for young, unmarried people to see that they behave properly. **2.** An older or married woman who accompanies a young, unmarried woman in public. —*v.* To act as a chaperon: *chaperon a party; chaperon a girl.*

chap•lain |chăp'lən| *n.* **1.** A clergyman attached to a chapel. **2.** A person, as a clergyman, who conducts religious services for a legislative body, a military unit, etc.

chap•let |chăp'lĭt| *n.* **1.** A wreath for the head. **2.** A short rosary. **3.** Any string of beads.

chaps |chăps| *or* |shăps| *pl.n.* Heavy leather trousers without a seat, worn over trousers by cowboys to protect their legs. [SEE NOTE]

chap•ter |chăp'tər| *n.* **1.** Any of the main divisions of a book, usually numbered or titled. **2.** A local branch of a club, fraternity, etc.

char |chär| *v.* **charred, char•ring.** To reduce or become reduced to charcoal, as by incomplete burning.

char•ac•ter |kăr'ĭk tər| *n.* **1.** The combination of qualities or features that makes one person, group, or thing different from another: *The character of the town is calm and peaceful.* **2.** A person's moral nature: *a man of bad character.* **3.** Moral strength; integrity; honesty: *a person of* *character.* **4.** A person portrayed in a novel, play, movie, etc. **5.** *Informal.* A person who is appealingly odd or humorous. **6.** A person; individual: *He's a tough character.* **7.** Status; role; capacity: *in his character as father.* **8.** A symbol, such as a letter or number, used in representing information, as in printing or writing. **9.** Any physical trait of a living thing that is controlled by one or more genes.

***Idiom.* in (or out of) character.** Consistent (or not consistent) with someone's general character or behavior.

char•ac•ter•is•tic |kăr'ĭk tə **rĭs'**tĭk| *adj.* Indicating a special feature of or showing the character of a person or thing: *the zebra's characteristic stripes; the characteristic quiet of the countryside.* —*n.* **1.** Something characteristic of a person or thing; a feature or quality: *Noise is a characteristic of most cities.* **2.** The integral part of a logarithm. For example, if 2.713 is a logarithm, 2 is the characteristic. —**char'ac•ter•is'ti•cal•ly** *adv.*

char•ac•ter•ize |**kăr'**ĭk tə rīz'| *v.* **char•ac•ter•ized, char•ac•ter•iz•ing. 1.** To describe the character or qualities of; portray: *He characterized her as lively and kind.* **2.** To be a characteristic or quality of: *Hardness and strength characterize steel.* —**char'ac•ter•i•za'tion** *n.*

cha•rade |shə **rād'**| *n.* **1. a. charades** *(used with a singular or plural verb).* A game in which words or phrases are acted out in pantomime, often syllable by syllable, until guessed by the other players. **b.** An instance of acting out a word, syllable, etc., in this way. **2.** Something thought to resemble a charade, as a pretense.

char•coal |**chär'**kōl'| *n.* **1.** A black, porous material composed chiefly of carbon, produced by heating wood or sometimes bone until the lighter materials in it are driven off as smoke. It is used as a fuel, a filtering material, and for drawing. **2.** A stick of this material, used for drawing. —***modifier:*** *a charcoal fire; a charcoal drawing.*

chard |chärd| *n.* Also **Swiss chard.** A plant closely related to the common beet, having leaves resembling and eaten like those of spinach.

charge |chärj| *v.* **charged, charg•ing. 1.** To ask as payment: *The grocer charged 50 cents for a dozen eggs. A toll is charged on some roads. How much will you charge me for repairing my car?* **2.** To postpone payment on by recording the amount owed: *Charge the groceries to my account.* **3.** To rush or rush at in or as if in a forceful attack: *The bullfighter stepped aside as the bull charged. The soldiers charged the fort. Joe charged angrily through the hall.* **4. a.** To accuse; blame: *They charged him with the crime.* **b.** To make an accusation: *The senator charged that factories were polluting the river.* **5.** To command; order: *The sentry charged the intruder to halt.* **6.** To entrust with a duty, task, or responsibility: *The Bureau of Indian Affairs is charged with the job of helping thousands of Indians.* **7.** To fill; load: *charge a gun. The coach charged his team with reckless spirit.* **8. a.** To make (something) electrically positive or negative. **b.** To pass or receive electrical energy into (a device, such as a storage battery or capacitor, that is capable of storing it): *charge the battery of a car. Is that battery charging?* —*n.* **1.** An amount asked or made as payment: *There is no charge for this service.* **2.** Care; supervision; control: *the scientist in charge of the experiment; take charge of the meeting.* **3.** Someone or something for which one is responsible: *The counselors at the play group took their young charges for a ride on the roller coaster.* **4.** A duty, responsibility, or obligation: *regarded his errand as a solemn charge.* **5.** An order or command: *a judge's charge to the jury; a charge in writing to be present.* **6.** An accusation, especially one made formally, as in a legal case: *arrested on a false charge.* **7.** A rushing, forceful attack: *the charge of an angry bull; a cavalry charge.* **8. a.** The property of matter that accounts for all electrical effects and by which objects not in contact can exert forces on each other independent of gravity. It occurs in two forms, positive charge and negative charge, with like charges repelling each other and unlike charges attracting each other. **b.** A measure of this property. **c.** The amount of this property possessed by an object or particle or enclosed within a region of space. **d.** The amount of electricity, as measured by this property, that can be drawn from a storage battery or the like. **9.** The maximum quantity that an apparatus or container can hold at one time. **10.** An amount of explosive to be set off at one time. **11.** *Informal.* A feeling of pleasant excitement; a thrill.

charge account. A business arrangement of credit, as with a store, in which a customer receives goods, purchases, or services and pays for them at a later time.

char•gé d'af•faires |shär **zhā'** də **fâr'**|. *pl.* **char•gés d'af•faires. 1.** A government official who temporarily takes over the duties of an absent ambassador or minister. **2.** A diplomatic representative of the lowest rank.

charg•er[1] |**chär'**jər| *n.* **1.** A horse ridden in battle; a war-horse. **2.** A device used to charge electric storage batteries. [SEE NOTE]

charg•er[2] |**chär'**jər| *n. Archaic.* A large, shallow dish; a platter. [SEE NOTE]

char•i•ot |**chăr'**ē ət| *n.* A horse-drawn two-wheeled vehicle used in ancient times in battle, races, processions, etc. —***modifier:*** *chariot wheels; a chariot race.* [SEE PICTURE]

char•i•o•teer |chăr'ē ə **tîr'**| *n.* A person who drives a chariot.

cha•ris•ma |kə **rĭz'**mə| *n.* A special quality of individuals who show an exceptional ability to lead and win the devotion of large numbers of people.

char•is•mat•ic |kăr'ĭz **măt'**ĭk| *adj.* Having the quality of charisma: *a charismatic president.*

char•i•ta•ble |**chăr'**ĭ tə bəl| *adj.* **1.** Showing love or good will; full of kindness: *her warm, charitable spirit.* **2.** Generous in giving help to the needy. **3.** Tolerant or lenient in judging others. **4.** Of or for helping the needy: *charitable institutions.* —**char'i•ta•bly** *adv.*

char•i•ty |**chăr'**ĭ tē| *n., pl.* **char•i•ties. 1. a.** God's love for mankind. **b.** Good will or brotherly love toward others: *"With malice toward none; with charity for all"* (Abraham Lincoln). **2.** Tolerance and leniency in judging others. **3.** A kind or generous act. **4.** Help or relief to the needy: *raising money for charity.* **5.** An institution or fund established to help the needy: *a ten-dollar donation to a charity.*

charger[1·2]

Charger[1] *is of course from* **charge. Charger**[2] *first appears in the fourteenth century; some dictionaries claim that it too is from* **charge** *and that it therefore originally meant "a dish for* charging *or loading up." But there is no proof of this. In any case, the word is only in the Dictionary at all because it appears in the Bible some 20 times—the most notable occasion being when Salome is given the head of John the Baptist on a* **charger** *(Matthew 14:8).*

chariot

Charles's law
This law was formulated by Jacques Charles *(1746–1823), French physicist.*

chase[1-2]
Chase[1] *is from Old French* chasser, *"to hunt," which is from Latin* captiāre *or* captāre, *"to seize or take."* **Chase**[2] *originally meant "a groove cut in metal" and is from Old French* chas, *"enclosure," from Latin* capsa, *"container, box."*

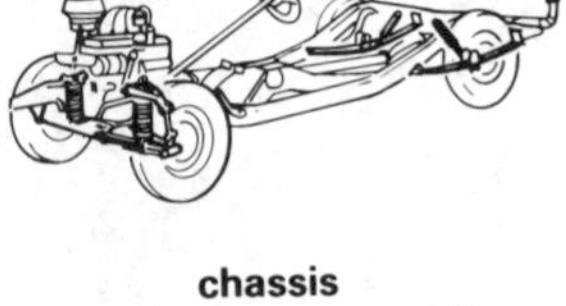

chassis
Chassis of an automobile

ă pat/ā pay/â care/ä father/ĕ pet/ ē be/ĭ pit/ī pie/î fierce/ŏ pot/ ō go/ô paw, for/oi oil/o͝o book/ o͞o boot/ou out/ŭ cut/û fur/ *th* the/th thin/hw which/zh vision/ ə ago, item, pencil, atom, circus

char•la•tan |shär′lə tən| *n.* A person who deceives others by falsely claiming to have expert knowledge or skill in a special subject or field of activity.

Char•le•magne |shär′lə mān′|. A.D. 742–814. King of the Franks; founder and first ruler of what became the Holy Roman Empire.

Charles's law |chärl′zĭz|. The law stating that the volume of a fixed mass of a gas whose pressure is kept constant varies directly with the absolute temperature. [SEE NOTE]

Charles•ton[1] |chärl′stən|. **1.** The capital of West Virginia. Population, 63,968. **2.** A city in southeastern South Carolina. Population, 69,510.

Charles•ton[2] |chärl′stən| *n.* A quick, lively dance of the 1920's.

char•ley horse |chär′lē|. *Informal.* A muscle cramp or stiffness, especially in the arm or leg.

char•lotte |shär′lət| *n.* A dessert made in a mold lined with ladyfingers or sponge cake and filled with a creamy custard, fruit, etc.

Char•lotte |shär′lət|. The largest city in North Carolina. Population, 314,447.

Charlotte A•ma•lie |ə mäl′yə|. The capital of the Virgin Islands of the United States. Population, 11,670.

Char•lotte•town |shär′lət toun′|. The capital of Prince Edward Island Province, Canada. Population, 17,063.

charm |chärm| *n.* **1.** The power or ability to please or delight; appeal: *the charm of the peaceful countryside.* **2.** A personal quality or manner that attracts or wins over others: *What others try to accomplish with force or threats, Roland does with charm.* **3.** A saying, action, etc., supposed to have magical power; a magic spell. **4.** An object kept or worn for its supposed magical effect, as in warding off evil; an amulet. **5.** A trinket or small ornament worn hanging on a bracelet, chain, etc. —*v.* **1.** To please; delight. **2.** To win over; beguile: *He charmed his opponents into letting him have his way.* **3.** To affect by or as if by magic; bewitch. —**charm′er** *n.*
Idiom. **like a charm.** Exceedingly well.

charm•ing |chär′mĭng| *adj.* Delightful; attractive; very pleasing: *a charming girl; charming manners.* —**charm′ing•ly** *adv.*

char•nel |chär′nəl| *n.* Often **charnel house.** A building, room, or vault in which the bodies or bones of the dead are placed.

chart |chärt| *n.* **1.** Something written or drawn, as a table or graph, that presents information in an organized, easily viewed form. **2.** A map showing coastlines, water depths, or other information of use to navigators. —*v.* **1.** To show or record on a chart; make a chart of: *chart the daily changes in temperature.* **2.** To plan by or as if by means of a chart: *chart a course.*

char•ter |chär′tər| *n.* **1.** A written grant or document from a ruler, government, etc., giving certain rights to the people, a group or organization, or an individual: *The Magna Charta is a famous charter granted by King John of England in 1215. A charter was given by the government to build the Baltimore and Ohio Railroad.* **2.** A document, such as a constitution, stating the principles, function, and form of a governing body or organization: *The United Nations is governed by a charter.* **3.** The hiring or renting of a bus, aircraft, boat, etc., for a special use. —***modifier:*** *a charter flight; charter states.* —*v.* **1.** To grant a charter to; establish by charter: *Congress chartered the bank for twenty years.* **2.** To hire or rent by charter: *The travel club chartered a plane.* —**char′ter•er** *n.*

char•treuse |shär tro͞oz′ *or* -tro͞os′| *n.* **1.** A light-green or yellow liqueur. **2.** A light yellowish green. —*adj.* Light yellowish green.

char•wom•an |chär′wo͝om′ən| *n., pl.* **-wom•en** |-wĭm′ĭn|. *British.* A woman employed to do cleaning in an office building or a household.

char•y |châr′ē| *adj.* **char•i•er, char•i•est. 1.** Not too trustful; cautious; wary: *chary of walking on thin ice.* **2.** Not free or wasteful; sparing: *a thrifty man, chary even of pennies.* —**char′i•ly** *adv.* —**char′i•ness** *n.*

Cha•ryb•dis |kə rĭb′dĭs|. See **Scylla.**

chase[1] |chās| *v.* **chased, chas•ing. 1.** To go quickly after and try to catch or overtake; pursue: *Our dog chased the thief.* **2.** To drive away: *chased the invading army from their country; sunlight chasing the gloom of night.* **3.** *Informal.* To hurry; rush: *chasing aimlessly about the city.* —*n.* **1.** The act of chasing; rapid pursuit: *a wild chase to catch up with the runaways.* **2. the chase.** The sport of hunting game. [SEE NOTE]
Idiom. **give chase.** To chase; pursue.

chase[2] |chās| *v.* **chased, chas•ing.** To decorate (metal) with engraved or embossed designs. —**chased′** *adj.: a box with a chased silver cover.* [SEE NOTE]

chas•er |chā′sər| *n.* **1.** Someone or something that chases or pursues. **2.** A drink of water, beer, etc., taken after a drink of undiluted liquor.

chasm |kăz′əm| *n.* **1.** A deep crack or opening in the surface of the earth; a narrow gorge. **2.** A gap, such as that caused by a difference of opinion or attitude: *chasms in communication.*

Chas•si•dim |KHä sē′dĭm| *pl.n.* The less frequently used singular is **Chas•sid** |KHä′sĭd|. An Orthodox Jewish group, founded in Poland in about 1750, emphasizing joyous and intense devotion to God.

chas•sis |shăs′ē| *or* |chăs′ē| *n., pl.* **chas•sis. 1.** The metal frame of an automobile or similar vehicle, including the engine, wheels, axles, gears, brakes, and steering system but excluding the body. **2.** The landing gear of an aircraft. **3.** The structure that holds and supports the parts of a radio, phonograph, or other piece of electronic equipment. [SEE PICTURE]

chaste |chāst| *adj.* **1.** Not having experienced sexual intercourse or not having engaged in sexual intercourse with a person to whom one is not married. **2.** Virtuous; pure. **3.** Not ornate or extreme; simple. —**chaste′ly** *adv.*

chas•ten |chā′sən| *v.* **1.** To punish in order to discipline or correct. **2.** To cause to become subdued or meek; restrain; temper: *a spirit chastened by hard experience.*

chas•tise |chăs tīz′| *v.* **chas•tised, chas•tis•ing.** To punish for misbehavior or wrongdoing: *the firm manner of a strict mother chastising a bad boy.* —**chas•tise′ment** *n.*

chas•ti•ty |chăs′tĭ tē| *n.* The condition or quality of being chaste; moral purity or virginity.

chat |chăt| *v.* **chat•ted, chat•ting.** To converse in a relaxed, friendly, informal manner. —*n.* **1.** A relaxed, friendly, informal conversation. **2.** A North American songbird with a yellow breast.

cha•teau, also **châ•teau** |shă **tō**| *n., pl.* **cha•teaux** or **châ•teaux** |shă **tōz'**|. A French castle or big, impressive country house or estate. [SEE NOTE]

chat•e•laine |**shăt'**l ān'| *n.* **1.** The mistress of a castle. **2.** A clasp or chain worn by a woman at the waist for holding keys, a watch, etc.

chat•tel |**chăt'**l| *n.* An article of personal property that can be moved or transferred from place to place, as distinguished from a house or land. [SEE NOTE]

chat•ter |**chăt'**ər| *v.* **1.** To make rapid, wordless sounds that resemble speech, as some animals and birds do. **2.** To talk rapidly and at length about something unimportant; jabber. **3.** To make a rapid series of rattling or clicking noises: *His teeth chattered with cold. The machine gun chattered.* —*n.* **1.** Aimless talk about unimportant matters. **2.** The sharp, rapid sounds made by some birds or animals. **3.** Any series of quick rattling or clicking sounds: *the chatter of machines.* —**chat'ter•er** *n.*

chat•ter•box |**chăt'**ər bŏks'| *n.* A person who seems to talk all the time.

chatter mark. 1. A mark on the surface of a rock where a glacier has rubbed another rock against it. **2.** A mark, as on wood, metal, or plastic, caused by vibration of a cutting tool.

chat•ty |**chăt'**ē| *adj.* **chat•ti•er, chat•ti•est. 1.** Fond of or full of informal conversation. **2.** Having the tone or effect of informal conversation: *a chatty book about life in the White House.* —**chat'ti•ly** *adv.* —**chat'ti•ness** *n.*

Chau•cer |**chô'**sər|, **Geoffrey.** 1340?–1400. English poet, author of *The Canterbury Tales.*

chauf•feur |**shō'**fər| *or* |shō **fûr'**| *n.* A person who is hired to drive an automobile or who works in a similar capacity. —*v.* To serve as a chauffeur for: *chauffeuring visiting relatives.*

chau•vin•ism |**shō'**və nĭz'əm| *n.* **1.** Unthinking and boastful devotion to one's country or a cause; fanatical patriotism. **2.** Prejudiced belief in the superiority of one's own group: *male chauvinism.* —**chau'vin•ist** *n.* [SEE NOTE]

chau•vin•is•tic |shō'və **nĭs'**tĭk| *adj.* Of chauvinism or chauvinists. —**chau'vin•is'ti•cal•ly** *adv.*

cheap |chēp| *adj.* **cheap•er, cheap•est. 1.** Low in price; inexpensive or comparatively inexpensive: *Tomatoes are cheap this week.* **2.** Charging low prices: *a cheap restaurant.* **3.** Requiring little effort: *a cheap victory.* **4.** Of or considered of little value: *The country was wild and lawless, and life was very cheap.* **5.** Of poor quality or standards; inferior: *cheap, badly made shoes that wear out quickly.* **6.** In low or unpleasant taste; vulgar: *cheap humor.* **7.** Not spending or giving money generously; stingy. —*adv.* At a low price: *an old house that he bought cheap.* ¶*These sound alike* **cheap, cheep.** —**cheap'ly** *adv.* —**cheap'ness** *n.*

cheap•en |**chē'**pən| *v.* To make or become cheap or cheaper.

cheap•skate |**chēp'**skāt'| *n. Slang.* A stingy person.

cheat |chēt| *v.* **1.** To deprive of something dishonestly or unfairly; defraud or swindle: *They cheated the Indians of their land. If you don't eat healthful foods you may be cheating yourself.* **2.** To act dishonestly: *cheat on an exam; cheat at cards.* **3.** To elude or escape as if by trickery or deception: *The daring mountain climbers cheated death.* —*n.* **1.** A person who cheats. **2.** The action of someone who cheats; a fraud or swindle. —**cheat'er** *n.*

check |chĕk| *v.* **1.** To stop, restrain, or control: *The driver checked the horses in front of the barn. They checked erosion by building terraces across the slopes. She checked a sudden impulse to giggle.* **2.** To test, examine, or make sure of, as for correctness or good condition: *Check your answers after doing the arithmetic problems. He checked the number in the telephone directory. The pilot checked his plane before taking off.* **3.** —**check on** or **check up on.** To investigate; look into; keep track of: *The policeman drove by to check on the old house. The school authorities did not check up on him.* **4.** To note or consult for information, permission, etc.: *He checked the temperature each morning. Check with your teacher before leaving class.* **5.** To correspond item for item; agree: *His list checked with hers.* **6.** To mark with a sign to show that something has been noted or chosen or is correct: *Read the sentences below, and check the statements that are true. Check each item on the list.* **7.** To place for temporary safekeeping: *They checked their baggage at the airport.* **8.** To mark with a pattern of squares: *Her apron is checked in white and blue.* **9.** In chess, to move so as to place (the opponent's king) under direct attack. —**checked'** *adj.: a checked shirt; a checked pattern.* —***phrasal verbs.*** **check in.** To register, as at a hotel. **check out. 1.** To leave after going through a required procedure, as after paying a hotel bill. **2.** To take after having counted or recorded and, often, after paying: *check out groceries at a supermarket; check out books from the library.* —*n.* **1.** A stop; halt: *The strike caused a check in production.* **2.** A restraint or control: *keeping a check on one's impulses.* **3.** Careful examination or investigation to determine accuracy, efficiency, etc., or to control or regulate: *a check of the addition and subtraction; keeping close check on his lands and possessions.* **4.** A standard for testing or comparing. **5.** A mark made to show that something has been noted, selected, or is accurate. **6.** A written order to a bank to pay a certain amount from funds on deposit. **7.** A ticket or slip for identifying and claiming something: *a baggage check.* **8.** A bill at a restaurant. **9. a.** A pattern of squares resembling a checkerboard. **b.** A single square in such a pattern. **c.** A fabric printed or woven with such a pattern. **10.** In chess, the situation of the king when under threat of direct attack by an opponent's piece. —***modifier:*** *a check mark; a check list.* —*interj.* In chess, a warning that the king is under threat of direct attack.

check•book |**chĕk'**bo͝ok'| *n.* A book or booklet containing blank checks, given by a bank to a depositor who has a checking account.

check•er |**chĕk'**ər| *n.* **1. a. checkers** *(used with a singular verb).* A game played on a checkerboard by two players, each using 12 round, flat pieces of a different color from those of his opponent. Each player tries to capture all of his opponent's

chateau/castle

A **chateau** *is a French* **castle***; both words come from Latin* castellum, *"fort." This word passed into the northern dialect of Old French as* castel, *which was borrowed into Middle English as* **castle**. *In the Parisian dialect of Old French, on the other hand, it became* chastel *(a Latin hard c- regularly became a ch- in central Old French). In modern French,* chastel *became* château *(a circumflex accent often indicates that an old* s *has been dropped). And* **chateau** *was then separately borrowed into English.*

chattel/cattle/capital

Cattle *and* **chattel** *are indirectly variants of Medieval Latin* capitāle, *"wealth, property, capital." In the northern dialect of Old French, this word became* catel*—see* **cattle**. *In the Parisian dialect of Old French, it became* chatel, *which was borrowed into English as* **chattel**. *Later, the same Latin word,* capitāle, *was borrowed directly into English to produce the financial sense of the word* **capital**.

chauvinism

Chauvinism *is from French* chauvinisme, *which first appeared in 1843, and was formed from the name of Nicolas* Chauvin, *an old soldier who had served under Napoleon and was famous for his outbursts of extreme patriotism.*

pieces. **b.** One of the round, flat pieces used in this game. **2.** One of the squares in a pattern of many squares. **3.** Someone or something that checks, as for accuracy or making a count or for measurement. **—modifier:** *a checker game; the checker players.* —*v.* To mark with a pattern of squares.

check•er•board |**chĕk′**ər bôrd′| *or* |-bōrd′| *n.* A game board divided into 64 squares of alternating colors, on which the game of checkers or chess may be played. **—modifier:** *a checkerboard pattern.*

check•ered |**chĕk′**ərd| *adj.* **1.** Marked with or divided into squares. **2.** Having light and dark patches, as a pattern of sunlight and shadows. **3.** Full of many changes; varied: *his checkered career.*

checking account. A bank account from which money may be withdrawn or payments made from the amount deposited by writing checks.

check•mate |**chĕk′**māt′| *v.* **check•mat•ed, check•mat•ing. 1.** In chess, to move so as to place (an opponent's king) under an attack from which there is no escape. **2.** To defeat or foil by or as if by making such a move. —*n.* **1.** A chess move or position that places an opponent's king under direct and inescapable attack. **2.** A situation in which one is completely foiled or defeated.

check-out |**chĕk′**out′| *n.* **1.** The act or process of checking out, as at a supermarket, library, or hotel. **2.** A place where something, such as merchandise, may be paid for, taken out, etc. **3.** A test or inspection, as of a machine, for working condition, accuracy, etc. **—modifier:** *a check-out counter; the check-out line.*

check•room |**chĕk′**ro͞om′| *or* |-ro͝om′| *n.* A room where coats, packages, baggage, etc., may be left temporarily.

check•up |**chĕk′**ŭp′| *n.* A thorough examination or inspection, as for health or general working condition: *regular medical checkups; an engine checkup.*

Ched•dar, also **ched•dar** |**chĕd′**ər| *n.* A firm, usually yellowish cheese first made in Cheddar, a village in England.

cheek |chēk| *n.* **1.** The part of the face below the eye and between the nose and ear on either side. **2.** *Informal.* Impudence; sauciness.

Idiom. **cheek by jowl.** In close contact or intimate association.

cheek•bone |**chēk′**bōn′| *n.* A small, four-cornered bone on the side of the face just below the eye, forming the outermost point of the cheek.

cheek•y |**chē′**kē| *adj.* **cheek•i•er, cheek•i•est.** Saucy; impudent; impertinent. **—cheek′i•ly** *adv.* **—cheek′i•ness** *n.*

cheep |chēp| *n.* A high-pitched chirp, like that of a young bird. —*v.* To make such a sound. ¶*These sound alike* **cheep, cheap.**

cheer |chîr| *v.* **1.** To shout in praise, approval, encouragement, etc.: *The audience cheered and clapped.* **2.** To praise, encourage, or urge by shouting: *Crowds gathered to cheer the President. The fans cheered the runner on.* **3.** To give encouragement or support to; hearten: *Although tired and hungry, the brave men cheered one another as they marched.* **4.** To make or become happier or more cheerful: *His songs and good spirits cheered us. In spite of my disappointment, I soon cheered up.* —*n.* **1.** A shout of praise, approval, encouragement, etc.: *The crowd gave a loud cheer for the winning team.* **2.** A rhyme, chant, etc., shouted in encouragement or approval, as for a school's team at a game. **3.** Gaiety; happiness; good spirits: *Grandfather was always full of cheer and good stories.*

Idiom. **be of good cheer.** *Archaic.* To be full of joy, courage, or hope.

cheer•ful |**chîr′**fəl| *adj.* **1.** In good spirits; happy; gay: *He was cheerful at breakfast.* **2.** Producing a feeling of cheer; pleasant and bright: *a cozy, cheerful room.* **3.** Willing; good-humored: *his cheerful acceptance of responsibility.* **—cheer′ful•ly** *adv.* **—cheer′ful•ness** *n.*

cheer•lead•er |**chîr′**lē′dər| *n.* A person, often one of a group of students, who starts and leads the cheering of spectators at a game.

cheer•less |**chîr′**lĭs| *adj.* Lacking cheer; gloomy and depressing. **—cheer′less•ly** *adv.* **—cheer′less•ness** *n.*

cheer•y |**chîr′**ē| *adj.* **cheer•i•er, cheer•i•est.** Bright and cheerful: *a cheery smile; a cheery fire.* **—cheer′i•ly** *adv.* **—cheer′i•ness** *n.*

cheese |chēz| *n.* **1.** A food, soft to firm in texture, made from pressed curds of milk, often seasoned and aged. **2.** A shaped or molded mass of this food. **—modifier:** *cheese crackers.*

cheese•burg•er |**chēz′**bûr′gər| *n.* A hamburger topped with melted cheese.

cheese•cake |**chēz′**kāk′| *n.* Also **cheese cake.** A creamy cake made with sweetened cream cheese, cottage cheese, etc.

cheese•cloth |**chēz′**klôth′| *or* |-klŏth′| *n.* A thin, loosely woven cotton cloth like gauze, originally used for wrapping cheese.

chee•tah |**chē′**tə| *n.* A spotted, long-legged, swift-running wild cat of Africa and southwestern Asia. [SEE PICTURE]

cheetah
The **cheetah** can run faster than any other animal, but only for comparatively short distances. In former times, cheetahs were trained in India and Persia to hunt antelope.

chef |shĕf| *n.* A cook, especially the chief cook of a large kitchen staff, as in a restaurant.

chem. chemical; chemist; chemistry.

chem•i•cal |**kĕm′**ĭ kəl| *adj.* **1.** Of or involving chemistry: *a chemical discovery.* **2.** Used in or produced by means of chemistry: *a chemical symbol; a chemical change.* —*n.* Any of the substances classed as elements or the compounds formed from them. **—chem′i•cal•ly** *adv.*

chemical engineering. Engineering that is concerned with the industrial production of chemicals and chemical products.

Chemical Mace |mās|. A trademark for a mixture of organic chemicals used in aerosol form as a weapon that disables by intense irritation of the eyes, respiratory tract, and skin.

chemical warfare. Warfare involving the use of chemicals such as poisons and irritants that act directly against human beings and crops and other plants.

che•mise |shə **mēz′**| *n.* **1.** A woman's undergarment like a short, loose slip. **2.** A dress that hangs straight from the shoulders.

chem•ist |**kĕm′**ĭst| *n.* **1.** A scientist who specializes in chemistry. **2.** *British.* A pharmacist.

chem•is•try |**kĕm′**ĭ strē| *n.* **1.** The scientific study of the composition, structure, properties, and reactions of matter, especially at the level of atoms and molecules. **2.** The structure, proper-

ă pat/ā pay/â care/ä father/ĕ pet/ ē be/ĭ pit/ī pie/î fierce/ŏ pot/ ō go/ô paw, for/oi oil/o͝o book/ o͞o boot/ou out/ŭ cut/û fur/ *th* the/th thin/hw which/zh vision/ ə ago, item, pencil, atom, circus

ties, and reactions of a substance or a system of substances: *the chemistry of the blood.*

chemistry set. A collection of chemical materials and apparatus designed for use by young persons of school age in performing educational experiments.

chem•o•syn•the•sis |kĕm′ə **sĭn′**thĭ sĭs| *or* |kē′-mə-| *n.* A process, as carried on by some living things, in which nutrients or other organic substances are manufactured using the energy of chemical reactions.

chem•o•syn•thet•ic |kĕm′ə sĭn **thĕt′**ĭk| *or* |kē′-mə-| *adj.* Of or carrying on chemosynthesis.

chem•o•ther•a•py |kĕm′ə **thĕr′**ə pē| *or* |kē′-mə-| *n.* The use of chemicals in treating diseases. —**che′mo•ther′a•peu′tic** *adj.*

che•nille |shə **nēl′**| *n.* **1.** Cord or yarn with a fuzzy, velvety pile, used for making fringes, tassels, etc. **2.** Fabric made with this cord, used for bedspreads, rugs, and curtains.

cheque |chĕk| *n.* Chiefly British form of the word **check** (written order to a bank).

cher•ish |**chĕr′**ĭsh| *v.* **1.** To care for tenderly and affectionately; love: *The old man cherished the little foundling as if she were his own child.* **2.** To keep or regard fondly; value highly; hold dear: *Americans cherish personal rights and freedom.* —**cher′ished** *adj.: cherished possessions.*

Cher•o•kee |**chĕr′**ə kē′| *or* |chĕr′ə **kē′**| *n., pl.* **Cher•o•kee** or **Cher•o•kees. 1.** A North American Indian tribe that formerly lived in North Carolina and Georgia and now lives in Oklahoma. **2.** A member of this tribe. **3.** The Iroquoian language of this tribe.

che•root |shə **rōōt′**| *n.* A cigar with square-cut ends.

cher•ry |**chĕr′**ē| *n., pl.* **cher•ries. 1.** A small, rounded, fleshy, usually red fruit with a hard stone. **2.** A tree that bears such fruit. **3.** The wood of such a tree. **4.** A deep or purplish red. —***modifier:*** *a cherry pie; cherry blossoms.* —*adj.* Deep or purplish red.

cher•ub |**chĕr′**əb| *n.* **1.** *pl.* **cher•u•bim** |**chĕr′**ə bĭm| *or* |-yə bĭm| or **cher•ubs.** An angel, usually shown in pictures as a beautiful, winged child with a chubby face. **2.** A sweet, pretty, or innocent-looking child.

che•ru•bic |chə **rōō′**bĭk| *adj.* Of, resembling, or suggestive of a cherub: *a cherubic child; a cherubic smile.*

cher•u•bim |**chĕr′**ə bĭm| *or* |-yə bĭm| *n.* A plural of **cherub** (angel).

Ches•a•peake Bay |**chĕs′**ə pēk′|. An inlet of the Atlantic Ocean in Virginia and Maryland.

chess |chĕs| *n.* A game played on a chessboard between two players, each starting with 16 pieces that are moved in various ways. The object of the game is to put the opponent's king out of action. —***modifier:*** *a chess tournament.*

chess•board |**chĕs′**bôrd′| *or* |-bōrd′| *n.* A board with 64 squares in alternating colors, used in playing chess.

chess•man |**chĕs′**măn′| *or* |-mən| *n., pl.* **-men** |-mĕn′| *or* |-mən|. One of the pieces, a king, queen, bishop, knight, rook, or pawn, used in the game of chess.

chest |chĕst| *n.* **1.** The part of the body between the neck and the abdomen, enclosed by the ribs and breastbone. **2.** A sturdy box with a lid, used for holding or storing things, for shipping goods, etc.: *a tool chest; a treasure chest.* **3.** Also **chest of drawers.** A piece of furniture with several drawers, used chiefly for keeping clothes; a bureau or dresser. —***modifier:*** *the chest cavity.*

chest•nut |**chĕs′**nŭt′| *or* |-nət| *n.* **1.** A smooth, reddish-brown, edible nut enclosed in a prickly bur that splits open. **2.** A tree that bears such nuts. **3.** The wood of such a tree. **4.** A reddish brown. **5.** A reddish-brown horse. **6.** An old, stale joke or story. —*adj.* Reddish brown. [SEE NOTE & PICTURE]

chev•a•lier |shĕv′ə **lîr′**| *n.* **1.** A knight or nobleman. **2.** A member of certain honorary groups or orders. [SEE NOTE on p. 145]

chev•i•ot |**shĕv′**ē ət| *n.* A rough wool cloth used for suits, coast, etc.

chev•ron |**shĕv′**rən| *n.* A badge made up of stripes meeting at an angle, worn on the sleeve of a military, naval, or police uniform to show rank, merit, etc. [SEE PICTURE]

chew |chōō| *v.* **1.** To grind, crush, or gnaw with the teeth or jaws: *To help digestion, chew your food thoroughly. Grasshoppers chew with a sideways motion.* **2.** To think about; ponder: *chewed the idea over in his mind for a long time.* —***phrasal verb.* chew out.** *Slang.* To scold. —*n.* **1.** The act of chewing. **2.** Something held in the mouth and chewed: *a chew of tobacco.* —**chew′er** *n.*

***Idiom.* chew the fat** (or **rag**). *Slang.* To talk casually or idly; chat.

chewing gum. A sweet, flavored preparation for chewing, usually made from chicle.

che•wink |chĭ **wĭngk′**| *n.* A bird, the towhee.

chew•y |**chōō′**ē| *adj.* **chew•i•er, chew•i•est.** Needing much chewing: *chewy candy.*

Chey•enne[1] |shī **ăn′**| *or* |**-ĕn′**|. The capital of Wyoming. Population, 47,283.

Chey•enne[2] |shī **ăn′**| *or* |**-ĕn′**| *n., pl.* **Chey•enne** or **Chey•ennes. 1.** A North American Indian tribe of Montana and Oklahoma that formerly lived in Minnesota and the Dakotas. **2.** A member of this tribe. **3.** The Algonquian language of this tribe. —**Chey•enne′** *adj.*

chi |kī| *n.* The 22nd letter of the Greek alphabet, written X, χ. In English, it is represented as *kh* or *ch.*

Chiang Kai-shek |**chyăng′ kī′**shĕk′| *or* |**chăng′**|. 1887–1975. Chinese statesman.

Chib•cha |**chĭb′**chə| *n., pl.* **Chib•cha** or **Chib•chas. 1.** An extinct South American Indian tribe once living in Colombia. **2.** A member of this tribe. **3.** The language of this tribe.

chic |shēk| *adj.* Stylish; fashionable. —*n.* Style and elegance in dress or manner. ¶*These sound alike* **chic, sheik.**

Chi•ca•go |shĭ **kä′**gō| *or* |**-kô′**-|. The second-largest city in the United States, located in northeastern Illinois on Lake Michigan. Population, 3,005,072. —**Chi•ca′go•an** *n.*

chi•can•er•y |shĭ **kā′**nə rē| *n.* Deception or trickery used to outwit others or to gain an advantage.

Chi•ca•no |chĭ **kä′**nō| *or* |shĭ-| *n.* A Mexican-American.

chick |chĭk| *n.* **1.** A young chicken. **2.** The young of any bird. **3.** A child. **4.** *Slang.* A girl; young woman.

chick•a•dee |**chĭk′**ə dē′| *n.* A small, plump bird

chestnut

Chestnut trees were once plentiful in the eastern United States, but the American chestnut has been almost completely wiped out by the *chestnut blight,* a disease caused by a fungus.

chestnut

Sense **6** *of the word* **chestnut** *is an Americanism, and a good example of a word that many people would like to track down and explain. But the* Dictionary of Americanisms *(1951) concludes: "The numerous accounts of the origin of this use are all incapable of proof. A writer in* Notes & Queries *(1889) VII.52 stated: 'I first heard the word in 1882, in a theatrical chop-house (Brown's) in New York.'"*

chevron

chickpea

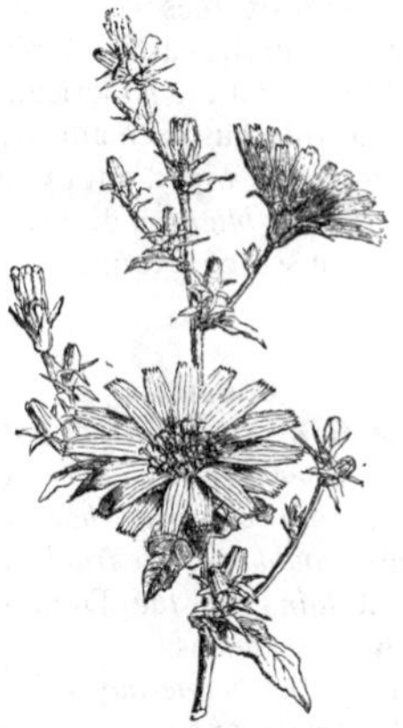

chicory

chignon

ă pat/ā pay/â care/ä father/ĕ pet/ ē be/ĭ pit/ī pie/î fierce/ŏ pot/ ō go/ô paw, for/oi oil/ŏŏ book/ ōō boot/ou out/ŭ cut/û fur/ *th* the/th thin/hw which/zh vision/ ə ago, item, pencil, atom, circus

that is mostly gray with a darker, caplike marking on the head.

chick•a•ree |chĭk′ə rē′| *n.* A small, reddish-gray squirrel of northwestern North America.

Chick•a•saw |chĭk′ə sô′| *n., pl.* **Chick•a•saw** or **Chick•a•saws.** **1.** A North American Indian tribe of Oklahoma that formerly lived in Mississippi. **2.** A member of this tribe. **3.** The Muskhogean language of this tribe.

chick•en |chĭk′ən| *or* |-ĭn| *n.* **1.** The common fowl raised for eggs or food; a hen or rooster. **2.** The meat of this fowl. *—adj. Slang.* Afraid; cowardly. ***—modifier:*** *a chicken coop.*

chick•en-heart•ed |chĭk′ən här′tĭd| *or* |chĭk′-ĭn-| *adj.* Cowardly; timid.

chicken pox. A contagious virus disease, mainly of young children, in which the skin breaks out in spots and mild fever occurs.

chicken wire. A wire mesh usually made with six-sided openings, used as fencing where chickens are kept and in or around similar areas.

chick•pea |chĭk′pē′| *n.* The round, pealike, edible seed of a bushy plant. [SEE PICTURE]

chick•weed |chĭk′wēd′| *n.* A low-growing, weedy plant with small white flowers.

chic•le |chĭk′əl| *n.* The thickened, milky juice of a tropical American tree, used as the main ingredient of chewing gum.

chic•o•ry |chĭk′ə rē| *n.* **1.** A plant with blue, daisylike flowers, and leaves used as salad. **2.** The root of this plant, dried, roasted, and ground and added to or used as a substitute for coffee. [SEE PICTURE]

chide |chīd| *v.* **chid•ed** or **chid** |chĭd|, **chid•ed** or **chid** or **chid•den** |chĭd′n|, **chid•ing.** To scold; reprove.

chief |chēf| *n.* A person with the highest rank or authority; a leader: *the chief of the tribe; the chief of the fire department.* *—adj.* **1.** Highest in rank or authority: *the chief engineer.* **2.** Most important; main; principal: *the country's chief crop.* ***Idiom.*** **in chief.** With the highest rank or greatest authority: *editor in chief.*

chief justice. Also **Chief Justice.** A judge who presides over a court of several judges, as the United States Supreme Court.

chief•ly |chēf′lē| *adv.* Mainly; mostly; especially: *grassy land used chiefly for grazing.* *—adj.* Of or like a chief: *his chiefly duties.*

chief of state. Often **Chief of State.** Someone who serves as the formal head of a nation.

chief•tain |chēf′tən| *n.* The leader of a tribe, clan, or similar group.

chif•fon |shĭ fŏn′| *or* |shĭf′ŏn′| *n.* A soft, sheer, airy fabric of silk or rayon, used for scarfs, veils, dresses, etc. ***—modifier:*** *a chiffon scarf.* *—adj.* In cooking, light and fluffy in consistency: *lemon chiffon pie.*

chif•fo•nier |shĭf′ə nîr′| *n.* A narrow chest of drawers, often with a mirror attached.

chif•fo•robe |shĭf′ə rōb′| *n.* A piece of furniture that has drawers and a wardrobe for hanging clothes.

chig•ger |chĭg′ər| *n.* A tiny mite that in its immature stage clings to the skin of a human being or animal and causes intense itching.

chi•gnon |shēn′yŏn′| *or* |shēn yŏn′| *n.* A roll of hair worn by a woman at the back of the head or nape of the neck. [SEE PICTURE]

Chi•hua•hua |chĭ wä′wä| *or* |-wə| *n.* A very small dog of a breed that originated in Mexico.

chil•blain |chĭl′blān′| *n.* Redness and soreness of the hands, feet, or ears, resulting from exposure to damp cold.

child |chīld| *n., pl.* **chil•dren** |chĭl′drən|. **1.** A person from the time of birth to the stage of physical maturity; a young boy or girl. **2.** A son or daughter; offspring. **3.** An older person who behaves like a child; an immature person. **4.** Often **children.** A descendant: *children of Abraham.* ***—modifier:*** *child care; child psychology.* ***Idiom.*** **with child.** Pregnant.

child•bear•ing |chīld′bâr′ĭng| *n.* Pregnancy and childbirth.

child•bed fever |chīld′bĕd′|. Infection of the lining of the uterus and the bloodstream after childbirth.

child•birth |chīld′bûrth′| *n.* The act or process of giving birth to a child.

childe |chīld| *n. Archaic.* A youth of noble birth.

child•hood |chīld′ho͝od′| *n.* The time or condition of being a child: *Indians were taught from childhood to be brave.* ***—modifier:*** *her childhood years; a childhood friend.*

child•ish |chīl′dĭsh| *adj.* **1.** Of, typical of, or for a child: *a high, childish voice; childish games.* **2.** Thoughtless or foolish in a manner not suitable for a mature person: *childish, sulking behavior.* *—***child′ish•ly** *adv.* *—***child′ish•ness** *n.*

child•less |chīld′lĭs| *adj.* Having no children.

child•like |chīld′līk′| *adj.* Having a natural, lovable, or spontaneous quality often associated with children: *childlike faith and simplicity.*

chil•dren |chĭl′drən| *n.* Plural of **child.**

child's play. Something very easy to do; anything ridiculously simple.

Chil•e |chĭl′ē|. A country on the Pacific coast of South America, extending from Peru to the south. Population, 10,405,000. Capital, Santiago. *—***Chil′e•an** *adj.* & *n.*

chil•e con car•ne |chĭl′ē kŏn kär′nē|. Also **chili con carne.** A spicy dish made with chili, meat, and often beans.

chil•i |chĭl′ē| *n., pl.* **chil•ies.** **1. a.** The very sharp-tasting pod of a kind of red pepper. **b.** A seasoning made from the dried or ground pods of this pepper. **2. Chile con carne.** ¶*These sound alike* **chili, chilly.**

chili sauce. A thick, spicy sauce made with tomatoes, onions, and chili.

chill |chĭl| *n.* **1.** Moderate to penetrating coldness: *a chill in the air; the bleak chill of the Antarctic region.* **2.** A feeling of coldness, as from illness or fear: *Chills and sneezing are signs of a cold. The mysterious sounds sent icy chills down my back.* **3.** A dampening of enthusiasm or spirit: *The bad news put a chill into the merrymakers.* *—adj.* **chill•er, chill•est.** **1.** Cold; chilly: *a chill north wind.* **2.** Discouraging or unfriendly: *His suggestions were met with a chill response.* *—v.* **1.** To make or become cold: *The icy wind chilled his face. Put the dessert in the refrigerator to chill.* **2.** To produce a feeling of cold, fear, or dismay in: *The eerie story chilled all who heard it.* **3.** To dampen; subdue: *Bad luck has chilled his enthusiasm.* *—***chill′er** *n.*

chill•y |chĭl′ē| *adj.* **chill•i•er, chill•i•est.** **1.** Fairly cold; cold enough to cause or feel discomfort:

Damp, chilly weather is common in London. We grew chilly when the campfire went out. **2.** Not enthusiastic or warm in feeling; unfriendly: *a chilly reaction to the new plan.* **3.** Producing a feeling of fear or dismay: *the chilly horrors of unknown dangers.* ¶ *These sound alike* **chilly, chill.** —**chill'i•ness** *n.*

chime |chīm| *n.* **1.** Often **chimes.** A set of bells tuned to different pitches and rung to make musical sounds. **2.** Often **chimes.** An orchestral instrument consisting of a set of metal tubes tuned to a musical scale and struck to make bell-like sounds. **3.** A musical sound produced by or as if by bells or chimes. —*v.* **chimed, chim•ing. 1.** To ring, as a bell or set of chimes. **2.** To sound together in harmony or agreement: *Spring peepers chimed in the marsh.* **3.** To announce (the time of day) by ringing bells: *The clock chimed three o'clock.* —***phrasal verb.*** **chime in.** To join in, as in a song, conversation, etc.

chi•me•ra |kə mîr'ə| *or* |kī-| *n.* **1. Chimera.** In Greek mythology, a fire-breathing monster with the head of a lion, the body of a goat, and the tail of a serpent. **2.** Any fantastic or impossible idea or fancy. [SEE PICTURE]

chi•mer•i•cal |kə mĕr'ĭ kəl| *or* |-mîr'-| *or* |kī-| *adj.* Unrealistic; fantastic: *chimerical theories about the end of the world.*

chim•ney |chĭm'nē| *n., pl.* **chim•neys. 1.** A hollow, usually vertical structure for the passage of smoke and gases rising from a fireplace, stove, furnace, etc., often projecting above the roof of a house. **2.** The glass tube, often wide at the center and narrow at the top, placed around the flame of a lamp. **3.** Something resembling a chimney, such as a narrow cleft in a cliff. —***modifier:*** *a chimney flue.*

chimney sweep. Also **chimney sweeper.** A person, often a young boy, employed to clean soot from chimneys.

chimp |chĭmp| *n. Informal.* A chimpanzee.

chim•pan•zee |chĭm'păn zē'| *or* |chĭm păn'zē| *n.* A dark-haired African ape with a high degree of intelligence.

chin |chĭn| *n.* The lowest part of the face, formed by the center part of the front of the lower jaw. —***modifier:*** *chin whiskers; a helmet with a chin strap.* —*v.* **chinned, chin•ning.** To pull (oneself) up with the arms while grasping an overhead horizontal bar so that the chin clears the bar. [SEE PICTURE]

chi•na |chī'nə| *n.* **1.** Fine, hard porcelain, originally made in China from a type of white clay, often decorated with bright colors. **2.** Articles, such as dishes or decorative figures, made from this porcelain or similar pottery. —***modifier:*** *a china teacup; the china cupboard.*

Chi•na |chī'nə|. **1.** Officially, People's Republic of China. The most populous country in the world, occupying the eastern and central part of the Asian mainland. Population, 958,090,000. Capital, Peking. **2.** Officially, Republic of China. See **Taiwan.**

chi•na•ber•ry |chī'nə bĕr'ē| *n., pl.* **-ber•ries.** A tree with feathery leaves, purplish flowers, and round, yellow fruit, common in the southern United States.

Chi•na•man |chī'nə mən| *n., pl.* **-men** |-mən|. A Chinese man or person. The word "Chinaman" is often considered offensive.

Chi•na•town |chī'nə toun'| *n.* A part of a city, such as San Francisco or New York, inhabited chiefly by Chinese people or people of Chinese descent.

chi•na•ware |chī'nə wâr'| *n.* Dishes and other articles made of china or similar pottery.

chinch |chĭnch| *n.* A bedbug.

chinch bug. A small, black-and-white insect that feeds on and damages wheat and other grains and grasses.

chin•chil•la |chĭn chĭl'ə| *n.* **1.** A squirrellike South American animal with soft, pale gray fur. **2.** The fur of this animal. **3.** A heavy woolen cloth with a nubby surface, often used for overcoats. —***modifier:*** *a chinchilla wrap.*

chine |chīn| *n.* **1.** The backbone; spine. **2.** A cut of meat containing part of the backbone.

Chi•nese |chī nēz'| *or* |-nēs'| *n., pl.* **Chi•nese. 1.** A native or inhabitant of China. **2.** A person of Chinese descent. **3.** Any of a group of languages and dialects, especially Mandarin, spoken in China. —*adj.* Of China, the Chinese, or their languages and culture.

Chinese checkers. A game for two to six players in which marbles are moved from hole to hole on a star-shaped board.

Chinese lantern. A decorative lantern made of thin, brightly colored paper.

chink[1] |chĭngk| *n.* A narrow crack or opening. —*v.* To seal or close narrow cracks or openings by filling: *They chinked the spaces between the logs of the cabin wall with mud.*

chink[2] |chĭngk| *n.* A short, clinking sound, as of metal striking together: *the chink of coins.* —*v.* To make such a sound.

chi•no |chē'nō| *n., pl.* **chi•nos. 1.** A strong cotton cloth used for uniforms and sport clothes. **2. chinos.** Trousers made of this material.

chi•nook |shĭ no͝ok'| *or* |chĭ-| *n.* **1.** A moist, warm wind that blows from the ocean onto the coasts of Washington and Oregon. **2.** A warm, dry wind that comes down from the eastern slopes of the Rocky Mountains.

Chi•nook |shĭ no͝ok'| *or* |chĭ-| *n., pl.* **Chi•nook** or **Chi•nooks. 1.** A North American Indian tribe formerly living in Oregon. **2.** A member of this tribe. **3.** The Chinookan language of this tribe.

Chi•nook•an |shĭ no͝ok'ən| *or* |chĭ-| *n.* A family of North American Indian languages spoken in Washington and Oregon. —*adj.* Of Chinookan or the Chinook.

Chinook jargon. A blend of English, French, Chinookan, and other North American Indian dialects used by traders in the Pacific Northwest.

chin•qua•pin |chĭng'kə pĭn'| *n.* **1.** A tree that is related to the chestnut and that bears similar nuts. **2.** The edible nut of such a tree.

chintz |chĭnts| *n.* A cotton cloth usually glazed and glossy on the surface and printed in brightly colored patterns. —***modifier:*** *chintz curtains.*

chin-up |chĭn'ŭp'| *n.* The act or exercise of chinning oneself on an overhead bar.

chip |chĭp| *n.* **1.** A fragment or small piece cut or broken off: *a chip of wood.* **2.** A mark left when a small piece is broken off: *a chip in the marble.* **3.** A small disk that is used in poker and other games to represent money. **4.** A thin slice of

Chimera
Etruscan bronze of the fifth century B.C.

chinning

chipmunk

chivalry/cavalry
The Italian word cavaliere, *"horseman, knight," formed a derivative,* cavalleria, *"troop of horsemen or knights." This was borrowed into French as* cavallerie *and from French into English as* **cavalry**. *Meanwhile, the Old French word* chevalier, *"knight" (a doublet of Italian* cavaliere*), formed a similar derivative,* chevalerie, *meaning either "troop of horsemen" or "the quality of being a knight, knightliness." This was borrowed into English as* **chivalry**. *We thus have two matched sets of doublets:* **cavalier/chevalier** *and* **cavalry/chivalry**.

chlorine
Chlorine *is obtained chiefly from sodium chloride (common salt). It forms compounds with nearly all other elements, and is used widely to purify water. It is also used to produce a wide variety of consumer goods, including antiseptics, insecticides, solvents, plastics, and paints.*

ă pat/ā pay/â care/ä father/ĕ pet/ ē be/ĭ pit/ī pie/î fierce/ŏ pot/ ō go/ô paw, for/oi oil/ŏŏ book/ ōō boot/ou out/ŭ cut/û fur/ *th* the/th thin/hw which/zh vision/ ə ago, item, pencil, atom, circus

food: *a potato chip.* **5. chips.** French-fried potatoes: *fish and chips.* —*v.* **chipped, chip•ping.** To break off a fragment or fragments from (something), as by hitting, jarring, scraping, etc.: *chip the edge of the glass. Women don't like their nails to chip. These glasses chip if you are not careful.* —*phrasal verb.* **chip in.** *Informal.* To contribute money: *How many people chipped in for the present?*

Idioms. **a chip off the old block.** A child that resembles either of its parents. **chip on (one's) shoulder.** A persistent feeling of resentment or bitterness: *He has had a chip on his shoulder ever since the argument with his friends.*

chip•munk |chĭp′mŭngk′| *n.* A small animal resembling a squirrel but smaller and having a striped back. [SEE PICTURE]

chipped beef. Dried beef, thinly sliced.

chip•per |chĭp′ər| *adj. Informal.* Active; cheerful; sprightly.

Chip•pe•wa |chĭp′ə wô′| *or* |-wä′| *or* |-wā′| *n., pl.* **Chip•pe•wa** or **Chip•pe•was.** A North American Indian tribe, the Ojibwa, or one of its members.

chi•rop•o•dy |kə rŏp′ə dē| *or* |shə-| *n.* Podiatry. —**chi•rop′o•dist** *n.*

chi•ro•prac•tic |kī′rə prăk′tĭk| *n.* A method of treating diseases by manipulating the spine and certain other structures of the body, usually without the use of drugs or surgery.

chi•ro•prac•tor |kī′rə prăk′tər| *n.* A person who practices chiropractic.

chirp |chûrp| *n.* A short, high-pitched sound, such as that made by a small bird or a cricket. —*v.* To make or say with such a sound: *The crickets chirped noisily. "We were waiting for you," chirped Miss Folgil cheerily.*

chirr |chûr| *n.* A harsh, trilling sound, such as that made by a cricket. —*v.* To make such a sound. ¶*These sound alike* **chirr, churr.**

chir•rup |chûr′əp| *or* |chĭr′-| *n.* The sound of repeated chirping; a series of chirps. —*v.* To make such a sound.

chis•el |chĭz′əl| *n.* A metal tool with a sharp, beveled edge, used in cutting and shaping stone, wood, or metal. —*v.* **chis•eled** or **chis•elled, chis•el•ing** or **chis•el•ling. 1.** To shape with or use a chisel: *The sculptor chiseled the statue out of stone. He chisels in his workroom.* **2.** *Slang.* To cheat or obtain by deception. —**chi′sel•er** *n.*

chit-chat |chĭt′chăt′| *n.* Small talk; gossip. —*v.* **chit-chat•ted, chit-chat•ting.** To make small talk; gossip.

chi•tin |kī′tĭn| *n.* A horny substance that is the main component of the shells of crustaceans and of the outer coverings of insects.

chit•lings or **chit•lins** |chĭt′lĭnz| *pl.n.* Forms of the word **chitterlings.**

chi•ton |kīt′n| *or* |kī′tŏn′| *n.* **1.** A loosely draped gown or tunic, the usual garment worn by men and women in ancient Greece. **2.** A mollusk with a single shell consisting of narrow, overlapping plates.

chit•ter |chĭt′ər| *v.* To chatter like a bird, monkey, etc.: *wide-eyed monkeys chittering in the trees. A covey of little birds chittered and flurried with their wings.*

chit•ter-chat•ter |chĭt′ər chăt′ər| *n.* Trivial and incessant chatter.

chit•ter•lings |chĭt′lĭnz| *pl.n.* The fried small intestines of a pig, used as food.

chiv•al•rous |shĭv′əl rəs| *adj.* **1.** Of or as of the age of chivalry: *in the chivalrous days of King Arthur.* **2. a.** Having the qualities of the ideal knight; brave; honorable: *the story of Roland, the chivalrous nephew of Charlemagne.* **b.** Gallant and courteous; considerate: *He was always extremely chivalrous toward the fair sex.*

chiv•al•ry |shĭv′əl rē| *n.* **1.** The medieval institution of knighthood and its customs: *the code of chivalry.* **2.** The qualities of the ideal knight, as gallantry, bravery, courtesy, honor, devotion to the weak, etc.: *The defeated general set an example of chivalry that has never been surpassed.* [SEE NOTE]

chive |chīv| *n.* **1.** A plant related to the onion, with narrow, grasslike leaves. **2. chives.** The onion-flavored leaves of this plant, used as seasoning.

chlo•ral |klôr′əl| *or* |klōr′-| *n.* A colorless, oily liquid composed of carbon, chlorine, hydrogen, and oxygen and having the formula C_2Cl_3HO. It is used in making chloral hydrate and DDT.

chloral hydrate. A colorless, crystalline compound of carbon, chlorine, hydrogen, and oxygen. It has the formula $C_2Cl_3H_3O_2$ and is used as a powerful sedative.

chlo•rate |klôr′āt′| *or* |klōr′-| *n.* The radical or ion $-ClO_3$ or a salt or ester that contains it.

chlor•dane |klôr′dān′| *or* |klōr′-| *n.* A thick, colorless, odorless liquid composed of carbon, hydrogen, and chlorine and having the formula $C_{10}H_6Cl_8$. It is very poisonous and is mainly used to kill insects.

chlo•ride |klôr′īd′| *or* |klōr′-| *n.* A chemical compound formed of chlorine and another element or radical.

chloride of lime. Chlorinated lime.

chlo•rin•ate |klôr′ə nāt′| *or* |klōr′-| *v.* **chlo•rin•at•ed, chlo•rin•at•ing.** To treat or combine with chlorine or one of its compounds. —**chlo′ri•na′tion** *n.*

chlorinated lime. A white powder made by treating slaked lime with chlorine and used as a bleach and disinfectant.

chlo•rine |klôr′ēn′| *or* |-ĭn| *or* |klōr′-| *n.* Symbol **Cl** One of the elements, a very irritating, greenish-yellow gas. Atomic number 17; atomic weight 35.45; valences –1, +1, +3, +5, +7; melting point –100.98°C; boiling point –34.6°C. [SEE NOTE]

chlor•o•form |klôr′ə fôrm′| *or* |klōr′-| *n.* A clear, colorless, heavy liquid composed of carbon, hydrogen, and chlorine and having the formula $CHCl_3$. It is used in refrigeration, in industrial chemicals, and sometimes as an anesthetic.

Chlo•ro•my•ce•tin |klôr′ō mī sēt′n| *or* |klōr′-| *n.* A trademark for an antibiotic obtained from certain soil bacteria.

chlo•ro•phyll, also **chlo•ro•phyl** |klôr′ə fĭl| *or* |klōr′-| *n.* Any one of several green pigments composed of carbon, hydrogen, magnesium, nitrogen, and oxygen, found in green plants and other living things that carry on photosynthesis. Chlorophyll is very complex in structure. It appears to absorb light and so provide the energy used in photosynthesis.

chlor•o•plast |**klôr′**ə plăst′| *or* |**klōr′**-| *n.* A very small, green structure within a plant cell and containing chlorophyll.

chock |chŏk| *n.* A block or wedge placed under something, such as a boat, barrel, or wheel, to keep it from moving. *—v.* To hold in place with a chock or chocks.

chock-full |**chŏk′fo͝ol′**| *adj.* Completely filled; stuffed: *a bus chock-full of people.*

choc•o•late |**chô′**kə lĭt| *or* |**chŏk′**ə-| *or* |**chôk′**-lĭt| *or* |**chŏk′**-| *n.* **1.** Husked, roasted, and ground cacao seeds. Chocolate for cooking is sold in powdered or block form. **2.** A sweet drink or candy made with chocolate. ***—modifier:*** *a chocolate cake.* [SEE NOTE]

Choc•taw |**chŏk′**tô′| *n., pl.* **Choc•taw** or **Choc•taws.** **1.** A North American Indian tribe of Oklahoma, formerly living in Mississippi and Alabama. **2.** A member of this tribe. **3.** The Muskhogean language of this tribe.

choice |chois| *n.* **1.** The act of choosing; selection: *Did price influence your choice?* **2.** The power, right, or possibility to choose; option: *You leave me no choice in this matter.* **3.** Someone or something chosen: *His choices were roast beef, mashed potatoes, and gravy.* **4.** A variety from which to choose: *a wide choice of schools.* *—adj.* **choic•er, choic•est.** **1.** Of fine quality; very good; select: *choice tidbits; choice vegetables.* **2.** Graded by U.S. government standards as higher than good and lower than prime: *choice cuts of beef.*

choir |kwīr| *n.* **1.** An organized group of singers, especially one that performs regularly in a church. **2.** Any musical group or band: *A brass choir was suggested to accompany the group of singers.* ¶*These sound alike* **choir, quire.**

choir•boy |**kwīr′**boi′| *n.* A boy who is a member of a choir.

choke |chōk| *v.* **choked, chok•ing.** **1.** To stop or interfere with the breathing of (a person or animal), especially by squeezing, blocking, or damaging the windpipe or by poisoning the air. **2.** To reduce the amount of air supplied to (an engine) so that it will start and warm up more easily. **3.** To be unable to breathe, swallow, or speak normally, as when the throat is blocked. **4.** To stop or suppress by or as if by strangling: *choke back tears. Sobs choked her words.* **5.** To clog up; congest: *At times, there were so many silver salmon that they almost choked the coastal rivers.* ***—phrasal verb.*** **choke up.** To be unable to speak because of strong emotion. *—n.* **1.** The act or sound of choking. **2.** A device that controls the amount of air taken in by an engine.

choke•cher•ry |**chōk′**chĕr′ē| *n., pl.* **choke•cher•ries.** **1.** A shrub or tree with narrow clusters of small, white flowers and bitter-tasting dark-red or blackish fruit. **2.** The fruit of such a shrub.

choke•damp |**chōk′**dămp′| *n.* Blackdamp.

chok•er |**chō′**kər| *n.* **1.** Someone or something that chokes. **2.** A short necklace that fits closely around the throat.

chol•er |**kŏl′**ər| *n.* Anger; irritability. ¶*These sound alike* **choler, collar.**

chol•er•a |**kŏl′**ər ə| *n.* A serious, often fatal disease that is infectious and often epidemic. It is caused by microorganisms, and its symptoms include diarrhea, vomiting, and cramps.

chol•er•ic |**kŏl′**ər ĭk| *or* |kə **lĕr′**ĭk| *adj.* Easily made angry; bad-tempered.

cho•les•ter•ol |kə **lĕs′**tə rôl′| *or* |-rōl′| *or* |-rŏl′| *n.* A white, soapy compound of carbon, hydrogen, and oxygen ($C_{27}H_{46}O$) that occurs in many animal and plant tissues and substances, especially in bile, gallstones, the brain, the blood, egg yolk, and seeds. It sometimes collects on the inner walls of the arteries and causes them to harden.

chol•la |**choi′**ə| *n.* A very spiny cactus with thick, branching stems.

chomp |chŏmp| *v.* A form of the word **champ** (bite).

choose |cho͞oz| *v.* **chose** |chōz|, **cho•sen** |**chō′**zən|, **choos•ing.** **1.** To select (someone or something) from a greater number; pick out: *He chose red. She had to choose between iced tea and a soda.* **2.** To see fit; decide: *Nature chose to make the whale a large creature. He chose to stay. You can do as you choose.*

choos•y |**cho͞o′**zē| *adj.* **choos•i•er, choos•i•est.** Hard to please; fussy.

chop |chŏp| *v.* **chopped, chop•ping.** **1.** To cut by striking with a heavy, sharp tool, such as an ax: *chop wood; chop a trail through the jungle; chop down a tree.* **2.** To strike repeatedly with or as if with an ax: *chop away at a block of ice.* **3.** To cut up into small pieces; mince: *chop onions; chop up a steak.* **4.** To cut short: *She chopped off her sentence in the middle of a word.* *—***chopped′** *adj.: chopped onions.* *—n.* **1.** A quick, short cutting stroke or blow. **2.** A small cut of meat that usually contains a bone. **3.** A short, irregular movement of waves.

Cho•pin |**shō′**păn′|, **Frédéric.** 1810–1849. Polish composer and pianist.

chop•per |**chŏp′**ər| *n.* **1.** *Slang.* A helicopter. **2.** Someone or something that chops.

chop•py |**chŏp′**ē| *adj.* **chop•pi•er, chop•pi•est.** **1.** Full of short, irregular waves: *choppy seas.* **2.** Shifting quickly; not smooth; jerky: *a choppy sentence style.*

chops |chŏps| *pl.n.* Jaws, cheeks, or jowls.

chop•sticks |**chŏp′**stĭks| *pl.n.* A pair of slender, tapering sticks made of wood or ivory, used as eating utensils in China, Japan, and some other Asian countries.

chop su•ey |**chŏp′ so͞o′**ē|. A Chinese-American dish made with bits of meat, bean sprouts, and other vegetables and served with rice.

cho•ral |**kôr′**əl| *or* |**kōr′**-| *adj.* Of, for, or sung by a chorus or choir.

cho•rale |kə **răl′**| *or* |-**räl′**| *or* |kō-| *n.* A Protestant hymn tune or a harmonized version of such a hymn tune. ¶*These sound alike* **chorale, corral.**

chorale prelude. An instrumental composition, especially for organ, based on a chorale.

chord[1] |kôrd| *n.* A combination of three or more musical tones sounded at the same time. *—v.* To play chords, as on a piano. ¶*These sound alike* **chord, cord.** *—***chord′al** *adj.* [SEE NOTE]

chord[2] |kôrd| *n.* A straight line segment that connects two points of a curve. ¶*These sound alike* **chord, cord.** [SEE NOTE & PICTURE]

chor•date |**kôr′**dāt′| *n.* A member of a large group of animals with a spinal column or a cordlike strip of cartilage along the back. To this

chocolate, etc.

The words **cacao, cocoa,** *and* **coconut** *have for years been confused. Two entirely different trees are involved: (1) The* **cacao** *tree of tropical America produces both* **cocoa** *and* **chocolate.** *The name* **cacao** *comes from Nahuatl (Aztec)* cacahuatl, *and* **chocolate** *comes from* xocolatl *in the same language. The word* **cocoa** *is simply a variant of* **cacao.** *(2) The* **coconut** *or* **coco palm** *originally grew in the East Indies, but is now widespread. Its name is not a native name like* **cacao,** *but comes from Portuguese* coco, *"goblin," referring to the "face" formed by the three holes at the base of the coconut. The variant spelling* **cocoanut** *is based on a mistake made by, of all people, Samuel Johnson, who in his* Dictionary *of 1751 confused* **coconut** *with* **cacao.**

chord[1-2]/cord

Cord *is from Latin* chorda, *"catgut, string, string of a musical instrument."* **Chord[2],** *"straight line," results from an old respelling of* **cord** *(after its Latin original,* chorda*).* **Chord[1]** *is a shortening of* **accord,** *and it originally meant "harmony." The* h *in* **chord[1]** *results from confusion with Latin* chorda, *as if a musical chord could only be produced by a stringed instrument.*

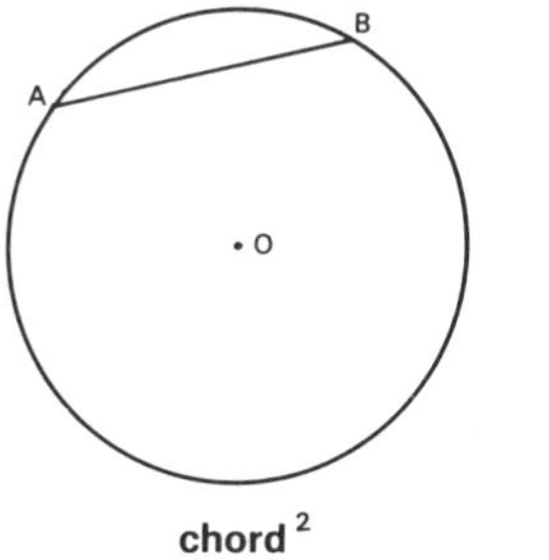

chord[2]

The line segment AB is a chord of circle O

chow[1-2]/chow mein
Chow[1] *and* **chow[2]** *are both from the Pidgin English of the Far East. It has been suggested that they are related, since some Far Eastern people eat dogs as a delicacy; but more probably they are separate words.* **Chow[1]** *seems to be from Chinese* kou, *"dog," and* **chow[2]** *from Chinese* ch'ao, *"to stir, fry, cook."* **Chow mein** *is from Chinese* ch'ao mien, *"fried noodles" (this* ch'ao *is the same as that in* **chow[2]***).*

chowder
Chowder *was apparently brought to North America in the eighteenth century by French fishermen or settlers in eastern Canada; from there it spread to New England. The French word for it was* chaudière, *"caldron, cooking pot," hence "fish stew." This goes back to Old French, and then to Latin* caldāria, *"caldron."*

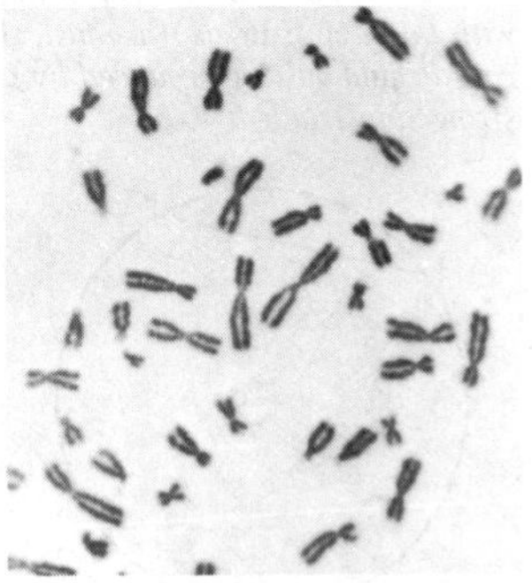

chromosome
Chromosomes from a white blood cell of a normal man

ă pat/ā pay/â care/ä father/ĕ pet/ ē be/ĭ pit/ī pie/î fierce/ŏ pot/ ō go/ô paw, for/oi oil/ŏŏ book/ ōō boot/ou out/ŭ cut/û fur/ *th* the/th thin/hw which/zh vision/ ə ago, item, pencil, atom, circus

group belong wormlike animals such as the lancelets as well as all vertebrates, including man.

chore |chôr| *or* |chōr| *n.* **1.** A routine or minor task. **2.** An unpleasant task.

cho•re•a |kô rē'ə| *or* |kō-| *n.* A disorder of the nervous system that causes the arms, legs, and face to twitch and move uncontrollably. Chorea is found mostly in children.

cho•re•o•graph |kôr'ē ə grăf'| *or* |-gräf'| *or* |kōr'-| *v.* To create the choreography of (a ballet or other stage work).

cho•re•og•ra•pher |kôr'ē ŏg'rə fər| *or* |kōr'-| *n.* Someone who creates, arranges, and directs ballets or dances.

cho•re•og•ra•phy |kôr'ē ŏg'rə fē| *or* |kōr'-| *n.* The art of creating and arranging ballets or dances.

cho•ri•on |kôr'ē ŏn'| *or* |kōr'-| *n.* The outer membrane that encloses the embryo of a reptile, bird, or mammal.

chor•is•ter |kôr'ĭ stər| *or* |kōr'-| *or* |kŏr'-| *n.* **1.** Someone, especially a choirboy, who sings in a choir. **2.** A choir leader.

chor•tle |chôr'tl| *v.* **chor•tled, chor•tling.** To chuckle throatily. *—n.* A snorting chuckle.

cho•rus |kôr'əs| *or* |kōr'-| *n., pl.* **cho•rus•es.** **1.** An organized group of singers who perform together. **2.** A musical composition or a part of a musical composition written for such a group. **3.** A group of singers and dancers who play a supporting role in an opera, musical comedy, etc. **4.** A section of music that is repeated after each verse of a song; a refrain. **5.** Something said by many people at one time: *a chorus of criticism.* *—**modifier:** a chorus singer.* *—v.* **cho•rused** or **cho•russed, cho•rus•ing** or **cho•rus•sing.** To sing or utter at the same time.

chose |chōz|. Past tense of **choose.**

chos•en |chō'zən|. Past participle of **choose.**

chow[1] |chou| *n.* A dog with a long, thick, reddish-brown or black coat and a blackish tongue. [SEE NOTE]

chow[2] |chou| *n. Slang.* Food. [SEE NOTE]

chow•der |chou'dər| *n.* A thick soup of seafood, especially clams, or vegetables, often in a milk base. [SEE NOTE]

chow mein |chou' mān'|. A Chinese-American dish of bits of meat and cooked vegetables, served over fried noodles. [SEE NOTE]

Christ |krīst| *n.* Jesus, the son of Mary, regarded by Christians as being the Son of God and the Messiah foretold by the prophets of the Old Testament.

chris•ten |krĭs'ən| *v.* **1.** To baptize into a Christian church. **2.** To give a name to at baptism. **3.** To name, especially at a ceremony: *christen a ship.* **4.** *Informal.* To use for the first time.

Chris•ten•dom |krĭs'ən dəm| *n.* **1.** Christians in general. **2.** The Christian world.

chris•ten•ing |krĭs'ə nĭng| *n.* The Christian ceremony of baptism, in which a child is named.

Chris•tian |krĭs'chən| *n.* Someone who believes in Christ or follows a religion based on his teachings. *—adj.* **1.** Believing in Christ or in a religion based on his teachings. **2.** Of Christ, Christianity, or Christians. **3.** Following the example of Christ; showing qualities such as gentleness, humility, etc.

Chris•ti•an•i•ty |krĭs'chē ăn'ĭ tē| *n.* **1.** The Christian religion. **2.** Christians in general. **3.** The condition or fact of being a Christian.

Christian name. A name given at birth or baptism.

Christian Science. The religious system founded by Mary Baker Eddy that emphasizes healing through spiritual means. —**Christian Scientist.**

Christ•mas |krĭs'məs| *n.* **1.** A holiday occurring on December 25 and celebrating the birth of Jesus. **2.** The Christian festival from December 24 (Christmas Eve) through January 6 (Epiphany). *—**modifier:** Christmas decorations; a Christmas party.*

Christ•mas•tide |krĭs'məs tīd'| *n.* The festival and season of Christmas.

Christmas tree. An evergreen or artificial tree decorated with ornaments or lights at Christmas time.

chro•mate |krō'māt'| *n.* A salt or ester of chromic acid.

chro•mat•ic |krō măt'ĭk| *adj.* **1.** Of or using color or colors. **2.** Of or based on the chromatic scale, as a melody or chord. —**chro•mat'i•cal•ly** *adv.*

chromatic aberration. A distortion of the color of an image that is caused by different degrees to which a lens bends light of different wavelengths.

chromatic scale. A musical scale in which an octave is made up of twelve notes, each separated from the next by a semitone.

chro•ma•tin |krō'mə tĭn| *n.* The substance in the nucleus of a cell that absorbs dyes very easily.

chro•ma•tog•ra•phy |krō'mə tŏg'rə fē| *n.* A method of separating a complex liquid or gaseous mixture by allowing it to pass through or over a material that absorbs each component at a different rate. The components appear in distinct bands, often of different colors.

chrome |krōm| *n.* **1.** Chromium. **2.** A material plated with chromium or one of its alloys. *—**modifier:** a chrome mirror.*

chro•mic |krō'mĭk| *adj.* Of or containing chromium, especially with a valence of +3.

chromic acid. An unstable acid composed of hydrogen, chromium, and oxygen and having the formula H_2CrO_4. It is a powerful oxidizing agent and exists only in solution.

chro•mi•um |krō'mē əm| *n.* Symbol **Cr** One of the elements, a hard, gray metal capable of being highly polished. Atomic number 24; atomic weight 52.00; valences +2, +3, +6; melting point 1,890°C; boiling point 2,482°C.

chro•mo•some |krō'mə sōm'| *n.* Any of the elongated structures that make up the chromatin in the nucleus of a cell. These structures are composed mainly of DNA, and control the characteristics passed to the daughter cells that are formed when the cell divides. —**chro'mo•so'mal** *adj.* [SEE PICTURE]

chro•mo•sphere |krō'mə sfîr'| *n.* **1.** A glowing, transparent layer of gas surrounding the photosphere of the sun. It is several thousand miles thick and is rich in hydrogen, helium, and calcium. **2.** A similar layer in the atmosphere of a star.

chron•ic |krŏn'ĭk| *adj.* **1.** Lasting for a long time; continuing: *a chronic disease.* **2.** Subject to a disease or habit for a long time: *a chronic alcoholic; a chronic liar.* —**chron'i•cal•ly** *adv.*

chron•i•cle |krŏn'ĭ kəl| *n.* A record of historical events arranged in order of occurrence. —*v.* **chron•i•cled, chron•i•cling.** To record, as in a chronicle: *Several almanacs are published that chronicle the events and developments of the year.* —**chron'i•cler** *n.*

chron•o•log•i•cal |krŏn'ə lŏj'ĭ kəl| *adj.* Arranged in order of time of occurrence: *keep all historical facts in chronological order.* —**chron'o•log'i•cal•ly** *adv.*

chro•nol•o•gy |krə nŏl'ə jē| *n., pl.* **chro•nol•o•gies.** **1.** The science that deals with determining the dates and order of events. **2.** A chronological list or table: *a true chronology of ice-age history.* **3.** The arrangements of events in time: *His chronology of the war is full of errors.*

chro•nom•e•ter |krə nŏm'ĭ tər| *n.* A very accurate clock or other timepiece, especially as used in scientific experiments, navigation, or astronomical observations.

chrys•a•lid |krĭs'ə lĭd| *n.* A chrysalis.

chrys•a•lis |krĭs'ə lĭs| *n. pl.* **chrys•a•lis•es** or **chry•sal•i•des** |krĭ săl'ĭ dēz'|. The inactive, or pupal, stage in the development of butterflies and certain moths, enclosed in a tough case from which the fully developed adult eventually emerges. [SEE PICTURE]

chry•san•the•mum |krĭ săn'thə məm| *n.* **1.** A plant having many cultivated forms with showy, variously colored flowers. **2.** The flower of such a plant.

chub |chŭb| *n., pl.* **chub** or **chubs.** A small freshwater fish related to the carp.

chub•by |chŭb'ē| *adj.* **chub•bi•er, chub•bi•est.** Round and plump: *a chubby face.*

chuck[1] |chŭk| *v.* **1.** To pat affectionately, especially under the chin. **2.** To throw out; discard: *chuck an old suit; chuck a ball out the window.* —*n.* An affectionate pat, especially under the chin. [SEE NOTE]

chuck[2] |chŭk| *n.* **1.** A cut of beef extending from the neck to the ribs. **2.** In a machine such as a drill or lathe, a rotating clamp that holds either a tool or the work. [SEE NOTE]

chuck•le |chŭk'əl| *v.* **chuck•led, chuck•ling.** To laugh quietly or to oneself. —*n.* A quiet laugh of amusement.

chuck•le•head |chŭk'əl hĕd'| *n. Informal.* A stupid person; a blockhead.

chuck wagon. A wagon equipped with food and cooking utensils for a team of workers on the move, as on a cattle drive.

chuck•wal•la |chŭk'wä'lə| *n.* A lizard of desert regions of the southwestern United States.

chug |chŭg| *n.* A dull, explosive sound made by or as if by an engine running slowly. —*v.* **chugged, chug•ging. 1.** To make such sounds: *The little train chugs on its trip up the mountain.* **2.** To move making such sounds: *The little train chugged along.*

chum[1] |chŭm|. *Informal.* —*n.* A close friend or companion; a pal. —*v.* **chummed, chum•ming.** To be on terms of close friendship; keep company: *He chums around with a lot of his old classmates.* [SEE NOTE]

chum[2] |chŭm| *n.* Bait consisting of cut-up fish scattered on the water. —*v.* **chummed, chum•ming.** To fish with chum. [SEE NOTE]

chum•my |chŭm'ē| *adj.* **chum•mi•er, chum•mi•est.** *Informal.* Friendly; intimate.

chunk |chŭngk| *n.* **1.** A thick piece of something: *a chunk of ice.* **2.** A large portion or amount: *He spent a big chunk of his life in jail.*

chunk•y |chŭng'kē| *adj.* **chunk•i•er, chunk•i•est. 1.** Short, strong, and somewhat fat; stocky: *a chunky horse.* **2.** Thick: *a chunky piece of cake.* —**chunk'i•ness** *n.*

church |chûrch| *n.* **1.** A building for worship, especially Christian worship. **2.** A Christian congregation. **3.** Religious services in a church: *going to church.* **4.** Often **Church.** A specified Christian denomination: *the Baptist Church.* **5. the Church. a.** All Christians regarded as a single spiritual body. **b.** The **Roman Catholic Church. 6.** The clerical profession; clergy: *One of his sons entered the church, and the others joined the army.* **7.** Ecclesiastical power as distinguished from secular power: *separation of church and state.* —***modifier:*** *a church bell.*

church•go•er |chûrch'gō'ər| *n.* A person who attends church services regularly.

Church•ill |chûr'chĭl|, **Sir Winston.** 1874–1965. British statesman and prime minister.

church•man |chûrch'mən| *n., pl.* **-men** |-mən|. **1.** A clergyman. **2.** A member of an established church.

Church of Christ, Scientist. The official name of the Christian Science Church. See **Christian Science.**

Church of England. The national church of England, established in the 16th century when it stopped recognizing the pope as its head.

Church of Jesus Christ of Latter-day Saints. The official name of the Mormon Church.

church•war•den |chûrch'wôr'dn| *n.* A lay officer in the Anglican or Episcopal Church who helps manage parish business or legal affairs.

church•yard |chûrch'yärd'| *n.* A yard adjacent to a church, often used as a cemetery.

churl |chûrl| *n.* A rude, surly person; a boor.

churl•ish |chûr'lĭsh| *adj.* Rude; boorish. —**churl'ish•ly** *adv.*

churn |chûrn| *n.* A container in which milk or cream is beaten vigorously in order to make butter. —*v.* **1.** To beat (milk or cream) in a churn to make butter. **2.** To move or swirl about violently.

churr |chûr| *n.* A whirring or trilling sound made by some insects and birds. —*v.* To make this sound. ¶*These sound alike* **churr, chirr.**

chute |sho͞ot| *n.* **1.** A vertical or slanting passage down which things can be dropped or slid: *a laundry shute.* **2.** A waterfall or rapid. **3.** *Informal.* A parachute. ¶*These sound alike* **chute, shoot.**

chut•ney |chŭt'nē| *n., pl.* **chut•neys.** A relish made of fruits, spices, and herbs.

chyle |kīl| *n.* A thick, whitish liquid, consisting of lymph and tiny fat globules, absorbed from the intestine during digestion.

chyme |kīm| *n.* The thick, soft mass of partly digested food that is passed from the stomach to the small intestine.

ci•ca•da |sĭ kā'də| *or* |-kä'-| *n.* An insect with a broad head and transparent wings. The males have specialized organs that produce a high-pitched, droning sound. [SEE PICTURE]

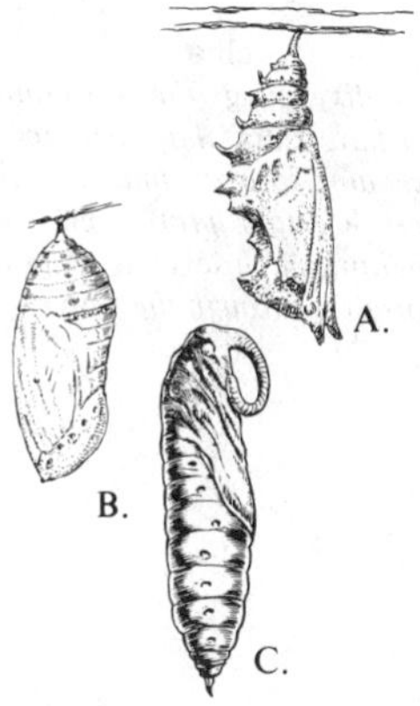

chrysalis
A. Chrysalis of the mourning cloak butterfly
B. Chrysalis of the monarch butterfly
C. Chrysalis of a hawk moth

chuck[1-2]
Chuck[1] *may possibly come from Old French* choquer, *"to strike," which is the source of the word* **shock[1]**. **Chuck[2]** *is probably a variant of* **chock,** *"wedge."*

chum[1-2]
Chum[1] *comes from the slang of Oxford University, England. The word first appeared in the seventeenth century with the meaning "roommate," and it probably comes from* chamber-mate. *(The word* **crony** *has an amazingly parallel history.)* **Chum[2]** *is an American word of unknown origin, first appearing in the mid-nineteenth century.*

cicada

cilia
The cells lining the respiratory tract have **cilia** *that help to remove any foreign material that enters. Certain protozoans, such as paramecia, use cilia to propel themselves through the water.*

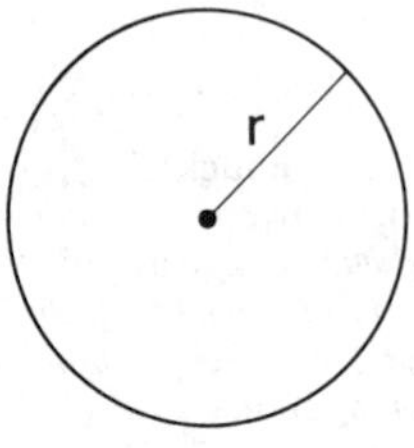

circle
Circle of radius r

circuit breaker
A **circuit breaker** *is used as a safety device. It insures that the current flowing in a circuit does not become strong enough to damage equipment or cause a fire.*

ă pat/ā pay/â care/ä father/ĕ pet/ ē be/ĭ pit/ī pie/î fierce/ŏ pot/ ō go/ô paw, for/oi oil/ŏŏ book/ ōō boot/ou out/ŭ cut/û fur/ *th* the/th thin/hw which/zh vision/ ə ago, item, pencil, atom, circus

Cic•e•ro |sĭs′ə rō′|, **Marcus Tullius.** 106–43 B.C. Roman statesman and orator.

-cide. A word element meaning: **1.** A killer of: **insecticide. 2.** An act of killing: **suicide.**

ci•der |sī′dər| *n.* The juice pressed from apples, used as a beverage or to produce vinegar. The fermented drink is **hard cider.** The unfermented drink is **soft cider.**

ci•gar |sĭ gär′| *n.* A small roll of tobacco leaves used for smoking. ***—modifier:*** *a cigar box.*

cig•a•rette |sĭg′ə **rĕt′**| *or* |**sĭg′**ə rĕt′| *n.* A small roll of finely cut tobacco for smoking, enclosed in a wrapper of thin paper. ***—modifier:*** *a cigarette holder.*

cil•i•a |**sĭl′**ē ə| *pl.n.* The less frequently used singular is **cil•i•um** |**sĭl′**ē əm|. **1.** The tiny hairlike structures that project from the surface of certain cells and that are often capable of a sweeping, rhythmic motion. **2.** The eyelashes. [SEE NOTE]

cil•i•ate |**sĭl′**ē ĭt| *or* |-āt′| *adj.* Having cilia. *—n.* A microorganism, such as a paramecium, having cilia.

cil•i•at•ed |**sĭl′**ē ā′tĭd| *adj.* Having cilia; ciliate.

cinch |sĭnch| *n.* **1.** A strap encircling a horse's body and used for holding the saddle or pack. **2.** *Slang.* Something easy; a sure thing. *—v.* **1.** To tighten the cinch on (a horse). **2.** *Slang.* To make certain of: *cinch a victory.*

cin•cho•na |sĭn **kō′**nə| *or* |**-chō′-**| *or* |sĭng-| *n.* A South American tree whose bark is the source of quinine.

Cin•cin•nat•i |sĭn′sə **năt′**ē|. A city in southwestern Ohio. Population, 385,457.

cin•der |**sĭn′**dər| *n.* **1.** A piece of partly burned material, such as coal or wood, that cannot be burned further. **2. cinders.** Pieces of ash.

cinder block. A hollow concrete block made with coal cinders and used in building.

Cin•der•el•la |sĭn′də **rĕl′**ə|. The fairy-tale girl who, with the help of a fairy godmother, escapes from a life of toil and marries a prince.

cin•e•ma |**sĭn′**ə mə| *n.* **1.** A motion-picture theater. **2. the cinema. a.** The motion-picture industry. **b.** The art of making motion pictures. —**cin′e•mat′ic** |sĭn′ə **măt′**ĭk| *adj.*

cin•e•ma•tog•ra•pher |sĭn′ə mə **tŏg′**rə fər| *n.* A motion-picture cameraman or projectionist.

cin•na•bar |**sĭn′**ə bär′| *n.* **1.** A heavy, reddish mineral form of mercuric sulfide that is the most important ore of mercury. **2.** Red mercuric sulfide used as a pigment.

cin•na•mon |**sĭn′**ə mən| *n.* **1.** A spice made from the dried and often ground reddish brown bark of a tropical Asian tree. **2.** A tree from which this bark is obtained. **3.** A reddish brown. *—adj.* Reddish brown.

cinque•foil |**sĭngk′**foil′| *n.* Any of several plants usually having leaves divided into five leaflets and small, yellow flowers.

CIO, C.I.O. Congress of Industrial Organizations.

ci•on |**sī′**ən| *n.* A form of the word **scion** (twig or shoot).

ci•pher |**sī′**fər| *n.* **1. a.** The numeral 0. **b.** The number zero. **2.** A form of secret code in which letters of the alphabet are interchanged according to some plan. *—v.* **1.** To put (a message) into a cipher. **2.** To do arithmetic.

cir•ca |**sûr′**kə| *prep.* About: *antiques made circa 1790.*

cir•cle |**sûr′**kəl| *n.* **1.** A closed plane curve that has all of its points at the same distance from a particular fixed point called its center. **2.** A region of a plane having such a curve as its outer boundary. **3.** Anything having the general shape of this curve. **4.** A group of people sharing common interests, activities, etc.: *a circle of friends; a sewing circle. He is well known in scientific circles.* *—v.* **cir•cled, cir•cling. 1.** To draw or form a circle around. **2. a.** To move or travel in a circle around: *The helicopter circled the landing strip. Magellan circled the globe.* **b.** To move in a circle: *The airplane circled in the sky.* [SEE PICTURE]

cir•clet |**sûr′**klĭt| *n.* **1.** A small circle. **2.** An ornament shaped like a circle, as a ring, bracelet, or headband.

cir•cuit |**sûr′**kĭt| *n.* **1. a.** A closed curve, such as a circle or an ellipse. **b.** Any path that forms such a curve. **c.** A region having such a curve as its outer boundary. **2.** A closed path through which an electric current flows or may flow. **3.** A connection of electrical or electronic parts or devices intended to accomplish some purpose: *a radio circuit.* **4. a.** A regular route followed by a judge from town to town for the purpose of trying cases in each one of them. **b.** The district or area visited by such a judge. **c.** A similar route, such as that of a salesman. **5.** An association of theaters in which plays, acts, or films move from theater to theater for presentation. **6.** An association of teams, clubs, or arenas of competition: *the tennis circuit.*

circuit breaker. A switch that automatically interrupts the flow of an electric current if the current becomes larger than a certain value. [SEE NOTE]

circuit court. In some states, a court holding sessions in various places in the area over which it has jurisdiction.

cir•cu•i•tous |sər **kyōō′**ĭ təs| *adj.* Going a long way around; indirect: *a circuitous route home.* —**cir•cu′i•tous•ly** *adv.*

circuit rider. A preacher who went from church to church in a district.

cir•cuit•ry |**sûr′**kĭ trē| *n.* **1.** The plan for an electric or electronic circuit. **2.** Electric or electronic circuits in general: *the circuitry of a television set.*

cir•cu•lar |**sûr′**kyə lər| *adj.* **1.** Of, shaped like, or shaped nearly like a circle. **2.** Forming or moving in a circle: *circular motion.* *—n.* A printed advertisement, notice, etc., intended for public distribution. —**cir′cu•lar•ly** *adv.*

circular saw. A power saw whose blade is a toothed metal disk that cuts as the blade rotates at a high speed.

cir•cu•late |**sûr′**kyə lāt′| *v.* **cir•cu•lat•ed, cir•cu•lat•ing. 1.** To move or flow or cause to move or flow in a closed path: *Blood circulates through the body. The heart circulates the blood.* **2.** To move or flow freely: *The fan helps the air circulate.* **3.** To spread or distribute widely: *Rumors tend to circulate quickly.*

circulating library. A library from which books may be borrowed.

cir•cu•la•tion |sûr′kyə **lā′**shən| *n.* **1.** The act or process of circulating. **2.** The movement of blood through the blood vessels of the body: *a person with poor circulation.* **3.** The passage of something, such as money or news, from person to person or from place to place: *There aren't many two dollar bills in circulation.* **4. a.** The distribution of printed matter, such as newspapers and magazines: *This magazine has wide circulation.* **b.** The number of copies of a newspaper, magazine, etc., sold or distributed to the public: *a daily circulation of 400,000.*

cir•cu•la•to•ry |**sûr'**kyə lə tôr'ē| *or* |-tōr'ē| *adj.* **1.** Of or involving circulation. **2.** Of the circulatory system.

circulatory system. The heart, blood vessels, and lymphatic system of the body.

circum–. A prefix meaning "around, on all sides": **circumnavigate.**

cir•cum•cen•ter of a triangle |**sûr'**kəm sĕn'tər|. The center of the circle that passes through all the vertices of a triangle.

cir•cum•cise |**sûr'**kəm sīz'| *v.* **cir•cum•cised, cir•cum•cis•ing.** To remove the foreskin of (a boy or man) by surgery.

cir•cum•ci•sion |sûr'kəm **sĭzh'**ən| *n.* The act or process of removing the foreskin by surgery.

cir•cum•fer•ence |sər **kŭm'**fər əns| *n.* **1.** The length of a circle. **2.** The boundary of a circle.

cir•cum•flex |**sûr'**kəm flĕks'| *n.* A mark (â) used over a vowel in certain languages or in a pronunciation key to indicate how the vowel is pronounced.

cir•cum•lo•cu•tion |sûr'kəm lō **kyōō'**shən| *n.* A wordy or roundabout expression; for example, *the husband of my mother's sister* is a circumlocution for *my uncle.*

cir•cum•nav•i•gate |sûr'kəm **năv'**ĭ gāt'| *v.* **cir•cum•nav•i•gat•ed, cir•cum•nav•i•gat•ing.** To sail completely around: *circumnavigate the earth.* —**cir'cum•nav'i•ga'tion** *n.*

cir•cum•po•lar |sûr'kəm **pō'**lər| *adj.* **1.** In or near one of the polar regions of the earth. **2.** Seen to move in a circle about one of the celestial poles: *a circumpolar star.*

cir•cum•scribe |**sûr'**kəm skrīb'| *or* |sûr'kəm-**skrīb'**| *v.* **cir•cum•scribed, cir•cum•scrib•ing.** **1.** To enclose (a polygon) with a plane curve so that the curve passes through every vertex of the polygon. **2.** To enclose (a plane curve) with a polygon so that each side of the polygon is tangent to the curve. **3.** To be a geometric figure that encloses another in one of these ways: *The circle circumscribes the triangle.* **4.** To confine within or as if within bounds; limit: *Old age circumscribes one's activities.* [SEE PICTURE]

cir•cum•spect |**sûr'**kəm spĕkt'| *adj.* Careful; cautious: *He was circumspect in shopping for a used car.* —**cir'cum•spec'tion** *n.* —**cir'cum•spect'ly** *adv.*

cir•cum•stance |**sûr'**kəm stăns'| *n.* **1. a.** Often **circumstances.** One of the conditions, facts, or events connected with and usually affecting another event, a person, or a course of action: *Write a few lines giving the circumstances of why the car stopped. Do circumstances determine when you will eat away from home?* **b.** The sum of all these conditions, facts, or events that are beyond one's control: *a victim of circumstance. The hermit was a touchy, sensitive person who had been conditioned by circumstance to suspect everyone.* **2.** **circumstances.** Financial condition: *a man in comfortable circumstances.* **3.** Formal display; ceremony: *pomp and circumstance.*

Idioms. **under no circumstances.** In no case; never: *Under no circumstances should you use the laboratory without supervision.* **under** (or **in**) **the circumstances.** Given these conditions; such being the case: *Under the circumstances, that was the best solution I could find.*

cir•cum•stan•tial |sûr'kəm **stăn'**shəl| *adj.* **1.** Of or dependent upon circumstances: *a circumstantial solution to the plot of the mystery novel.* **2.** Not of primary importance; incidental: *circumstantial matters.* **3.** Full of facts or details; complete: *a circumstantial account.*

circumstantial evidence. Evidence not directly relevant to the facts in a legal dispute.

cir•cum•vent |sûr'kəm **vĕnt'**| *or* |**sûr'**kəm vĕnt'| *v.* **1.** To get the better of or overcome by ingenuity: *circumvent an enemy army.* **2.** To avoid by or as if by passing around: *circumvent a problem.* —**cir'cum•ven'tion** *n.*

cir•cus |**sûr'**kəs| *n., pl.* **cir•cus•es.** **1.** A big show put on by acrobats, clowns, and trained animals. **2.** The traveling company that puts on the circus. **3.** A circular arena, surrounded by tiers of seats and often covered by a tent, in which the circus is performed. **4.** An open-air arena used by the ancient Romans for athletic contests and public spectacles. **5.** *Informal.* A place or activity in which there is wild confusion or disorder. —***modifier:*** *circus animals.*

cir•rho•sis |sĭ **rō'**sĭs| *n.* A chronic disease in which the tissue of the liver is gradually destroyed and replaced by scar tissue, the entire organ shrinking and hardening in the process.

cir•ri |**sĭr'**ī'| *n.* Plural of **cirrus.**

cir•ro•cu•mu•lus |sĭr'ō **kyōō'**myə ləs| *n.* A cloud composed of a series of small, regularly arranged parts, found typically about five miles above the earth.

cir•ro•stra•tus |sĭr'ō **strā'**təs| *or* |**-străt'**əs| *n.* A thin, hazy cloud, often covering the sky and producing a halo effect, found typically about six miles above the earth.

cir•rus |**sĭr'**əs| *n., pl.* **cir•ri** |**sĭr'**ī'|. A type of cloud composed of white, fleecy patches or bands, found at heights of about seven miles above the earth.

cis•tern |**sĭs'**tərn| *n.* A large tank or reservoir for holding water, especially rainwater.

cit•a•del |**sĭt'**ə dl| *or* |-dĕl'| *n.* **1.** A fortress overlooking a city. **2.** Any stronghold.

ci•ta•tion |sī **tā'**shən| *n.* **1.** A reference or quotation. **2.** A summons to appear in court. **3.** An official recommendation for bravery.

cite |sīt| *v.* **cit•ed, cit•ing.** **1.** To quote or mention as an authority or example: *Let me cite two cases of what I have in mind.* **2.** To summon to appear in court. **3.** To mention and commend for meritorious action: *The policeman was cited for bravery beyond the call of duty.* ¶ *These sound alike* **cite, sight, site.**

cit•i•zen |**sĭt'**ĭ zən| *n.* **1.** A person owing loyalty to and entitled to the protection of a given country. **2.** A resident of a city or town, especially one entitled to vote and enjoy other privileges there. [SEE NOTE]

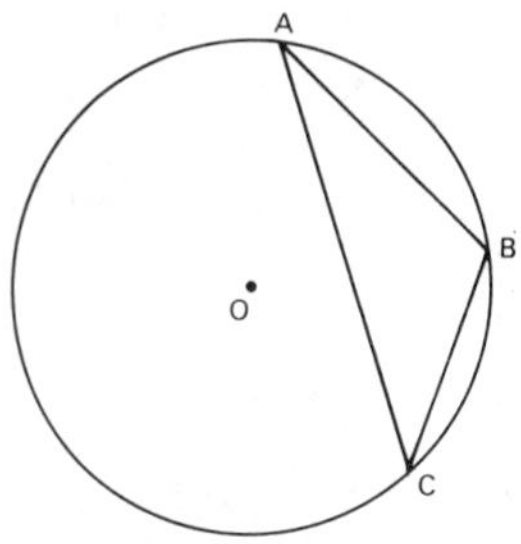

circumscribed
Circle O is circumscribed about triangle ABC

citizen
"If a man be gracious and courteous to strangers, it shows he is a citizen of the world." —*Francis Bacon (1561–1626).*

cit•i•zen•ry |sĭt′ĭ zən rē| *n.* Citizens in general.

cit•i•zen•ship |sĭt′ĭ zən shĭp′| *n.* The status of a citizen with its duties, rights, and privileges.

cit•rate |sĭt′rāt′| *or* |sĭ′trāt′| *n.* A salt or ester of citric acid.

cit•ric |sĭt′rĭk| *adj.* Of or obtained from citrus fruits.

citric acid. An acid that is composed of carbon, hydrogen, and oxygen and has the formula $C_6H_8O_7$. It is found in oranges, grapefruit, lemons, and other fruit.

cit•ron |sĭt′rən| *n.* **1. a.** A thick-skinned fruit similar to a lemon but larger. **b.** A tree that bears such fruit. **2.** Also **citron melon.** A melon with a thick, hard rind. **3.** The candied rind of either of these fruits, used especially in baking.

cit•ron•el•la |sĭt′rə nĕl′ə| *n.* An aromatic oil obtained from a tropical grass and used in insect repellents and perfumes.

cit•rus |sĭt′rəs| *adj.* Also **cit•rous.** Of or belonging to a group of related trees or fruits that includes the orange, lemon, lime, and grapefruit. *—n., pl.* **cit•rus•es** or **cit•rus.** A tree belonging to this group.

civet

cit•y |sĭt′ē| *n., pl.* **cit•ies. 1.** A center of population, commerce, and culture; a large and important town. **2.** All the people living in a city. *—**modifier:** city life; city government.*

city hall. 1. The building in which the offices of a city government are located. **2.** A city government, especially its officials considered as a group.

cit•y-state |sĭt′ē stāt′| *n.* An independent state consisting of a city and its surrounding territory: *a city-state of ancient Greece.*

civ•et |sĭv′ĭt| *n.* **1.** Also **civet cat.** A catlike African or Asian animal having scent glands that produce a fluid with a strong, musky odor. **2.** This fluid, used in making perfumes. [SEE PICTURE]

civ•ic |sĭv′ĭk| *adj.* **1.** Of a city or community: *a civic event.* **2.** Of a citizen or citizens: *civic duties.*

civ•ics |sĭv′ĭks| *n. (used with a singular verb).* The study of how local and national government works and of the rights and duties of citizens.

civ•il |sĭv′əl| *adj.* **1.** Of a citizen or citizens: *civil rights.* **2.** Of a branch of government other than the legislative, judicial, or military: *civil service.* **3. a.** Within a country or community: *civil war.* **b.** Of the internal affairs of a country or community and its citizens: *civil disorder.* **4.** Of the general public and its affairs as distinguished from military or church affairs: *a civil marriage; civil authorities.* **5.** Polite; courteous: *a civil reply.* —**civ′il•ly** *adv.*

civil defense. The measures to be taken by an organized body of civilian volunteers for the protection of life and property in the case of a natural disaster or an attack by an enemy.

civil disobedience. The refusal to obey laws that are regarded as unjust.

civil engineer. An engineer trained in the design and construction of projects such as bridges, roads, dams, etc.

ci•vil•ian |sĭ vĭl′yən| *n.* A person not serving in the armed forces. *—**modifier:** a civilian government; civilian clothes.*

ci•vil•i•ty |sĭ vĭl′ĭ tē| *n., pl.* **ci•vil•i•ties. 1.** Courtesy. **2.** An act or expression of courtesy.

civ•i•li•za•tion |sĭv′ə lĭ zā′shən| *n.* **1.** A condition of human society marked by an advanced stage of development in the arts, sciences, religion, government, etc.: *man's progression from barbarism to civilization.* **2.** A culture and society developed by a particular nation, region, or period: *the civilization of ancient Rome; modern civilization.* **3.** *Informal.* Modern society with its conveniences: *return to civilization after two weeks of camping.*

civ•i•lize |sĭv′ə līz′| *v.* **civ•i•lized, civ•i•liz•ing.** To bring from a primitive to a highly developed state of society and culture; educate.

civ•i•lized |sĭv′ə līzd′| *adj.* **1.** Having or indicating a highly developed society and culture; not primitive: *civilized life; a civilized country.* **2.** Polite or cultured; refined: *a civilized person.*

civil law. The body of law dealing with the rights of private citizens, as distinguished from military law and criminal law.

civil liberty. The legal guarantee of individual rights such as freedom of speech, thought, and action.

civil marriage. A marriage performed by a civil official, such as a justice of the peace.

civil rights. Rights belonging to an individual by virtue of his status as a citizen.

civil servant. A person employed in the civil service.

civil service. 1. All branches of public service that are not legislative, judicial, or military. **2.** In general, the persons employed by the civil branch of the government.

civil war. 1. A war between factions or regions of one country. **2. Civil War.** In the United States, the war between the Union (the North) and the Confederacy (the South), lasting from 1861 to 1865. Also called *War Between the States.*

Cl The symbol for the element chlorine.

clab•ber |klăb′ər| *n.* Sour, curdled milk. *—v.* To curdle.

clack |klăk| *v.* To make the sudden, sharp sound of objects struck together: *Typewriters clacked in every office of the newspaper.* *—n.* A sudden, sharp sound: *the clack of a bat hitting a baseball.* *¶These sound alike* **clack, claque.**

clad¹ |klăd| *v.* **clad, clad•ding.** To coat or cover the surface of (a metal) with another metal.

clad² |klăd|. A past tense and past participle of **clothe.**

clad•ding |klăd′ĭng| *n.* A metal coating bonded to the surface of another metal.

claim |klām| *v.* **1.** To demand or ask for (something) as one's own or one's due: *claim luggage; claim a reward.* **2.** To declare to be true; assert: *Some students claim that they can study better with the radio turned on.* **3.** To deserve or call for; require: *political matters that claim all his attention.* *—n.* **1.** A demand or request for something as one's rightful due: *file a claim for losses.* **2.** A basis for demanding something; right to ask for: *Columbus gave Spain a claim to all land he discovered.* **3.** A statement of something as fact; assertion: *an advertisement that makes false claims concerning certain foods.* **4.** Something claimed, especially a tract of land claimed by a miner or homesteader.

***Idiom.* lay claim to.** To assert one's right to or ownership of.

ă pat/ā pay/â care/ä father/ĕ pet/ ē be/ĭ pit/ī pie/î fierce/ŏ pot/ ō go/ô paw, for/oi oil/ŏŏ book/ ōō boot/ou out/ŭ cut/û fur/ *th* the/th thin/hw which/zh vision/ ə ago, item, pencil, atom, circus

claim•ant |klā′mənt| *n.* A person making a claim.

clair•voy•ance |klâr **voi′**əns| *n.* The supposed power to perceive things that are out of the range of human senses.

clair•voy•ant |klâr **voi′**ənt| *n.* A person said to have powers of clairvoyance.

clam |klăm| *n.* A soft-bodied water animal that has a double, hinged shell and that burrows into sand or mud. Many kinds of clams are used as food. —***modifier:*** *a clam shell; clam juice.* —*v.* **clammed, clam•ming.** To dig or hunt for clams. —***phrasal verb.* clam up.** To refuse to talk. [SEE PICTURE]

clam•bake |**klăm′**bāk′| *n.* A picnic at which clams and other foods are baked.

clam•ber |**klăm′**bər| *v.* To climb with difficulty, especially on all fours: *clamber up a slope.*

clam•my |**klăm′**ē| *adj.* **clam•mi•er, clam•mi•est.** Unpleasantly damp, sticky, and usually cold: *clammy clothes; clammy hands.* —**clam′mi•ness** *n.*

clam•or |**klăm′**ər| *n.* **1.** A loud, continuous, and usually confused noise: *the clamor of a crowd.* **2.** A strong or loud demand: *a clamor for less pollution.* —*v.* To make a clamor: *The children clamored for ice cream.*

clam•or•ous |**klăm′**ər əs| *adj.* Making or full of clamor: *a clamorous party.* —**clam′or•ous•ly** *adv.*

clamp |klămp| *n.* A device for gripping or fastening things together, generally consisting of two parts that can be brought together by turning a screw. —*v.* To grip or fasten with or as if with a clamp. —***phrasal verb.* clamp down.** *Informal.* To become more strict.

clan |klăn| *n.* **1.** A group of families, as in the Scottish Highlands, claiming a common ancestor. **2.** Any group of relatives, friends, etc.

clan•des•tine |klăn **dĕs′**tĭn| *adj.* Done secretly or kept secret, usually for some unlawful purpose: *a clandestine meeting.* —**clan•des′tine•ly** *adv.*

clang |klăng| *v.* To make a loud, ringing, metallic sound or sounds: *clang a bell. The bells clanged to announce the victory.* —*n.* A clanging sound.

clank |klăngk| *n.* A loud, ringing, metallic sound: *The gate closed with a clank.* —*v.* To make a clank.

clan•nish |**klăn′**ĭsh| *adj.* Inclined to cling together and exclude outsiders: *a clannish people.* —**clan′nish•ly** *adv.*

clans•man |**klănz′**mən| *n., pl.* **-men** |-mən|. A person belonging to a clan.

clap |klăp| *v.* **clapped, clap•ping. 1.** To strike (the hands) together with a brisk movement and an abrupt, loud sound: *The audience clapped with enthusiasm. The teacher clapped his hands to get the class's attention.* **2.** To come together suddenly with a sharp noise: *The door clapped shut.* **3.** To tap with the open hand, as in hearty greeting: *clap him on the shoulder.* **4.** To put, move, or send suddenly: *clapped him in jail.* —*n.* **1.** A loud, sharp, or explosive noise: *a clap of thunder.* **2.** A slap.

clap•board |**klăb′**ərd| *or* |**klăp′**bôrd′| *or* |-bōrd′| *n.* A long, narrow board with one edge thicker than the other, overlapped to cover the outside walls of a frame house. —***modifier:*** *a clapboard house.* [SEE PICTURE]

clap•per |**klăp′**ər| *n.* **1.** The hammerlike object, hung inside a bell, that strikes the bell to make it sound. **2. clappers.** A percussion instrument consisting of two flat pieces of wood held between the fingers and struck together.

clap•trap |**klăp′**trăp′| *n.* Insincere, worthless speech or writing, calculated to win applause.

claque |klăk| *n.* A group of persons hired to applaud at a performance. ¶*These sound alike* **claque, clack.**

clar•et |**klăr′**ĭt| *n.* A dry red wine.

clar•i•fy |**klăr′**ə fī′| *v.* **clar•i•fied, clar•i•fy•ing, clar•i•fies. 1.** To make or become clear or easier to understand. **2.** To make (a liquid, butter, etc.) clear or pure by removing unwanted solid matter, as by heating: *clarify butter.* —**clar′i•fi•ca′tion** *n.*

clar•i•net |klăr′ə **nĕt′**| *n.* A woodwind instrument with a single-reed mouthpiece, a cylindrical body, and a flaring bell. It has a hollow, reedy tone, and is played by covering holes in its body with the finger and by means of keys. —**clar′i•net′ist** *n.* [SEE PICTURE]

clar•i•on |**klăr′**ē ən| *n.* **1.** An old type of valveless trumpet with a clear, shrill tone. **2.** The sound made by by this trumpet or a similar sound. —*adj.* Shrill and clear.

clar•i•ty |**klăr′**ĭ tē| *n.* **1.** Distinctness, as of shape, outline, sound, etc.: *an actor renowned for the clarity of his speech; a photograph remarkable for its clarity.* **2.** Great precision and terseness: *a young writer striving to achieve clarity and unity of style.*

clash |klăsh| *v.* **1.** To strike together or collide with a loud harsh noise: *The knights clashed their swords swiftly. The cymbals clashed loudly.* **2.** To strike or meet violently: *where the warm air of the Gulf Stream clashes against the winds of the Arctic. The armies clashed in battle.* **3.** To be strongly out of harmony; come into conflict: *Orange and purple clash. The candidates clashed on that issue.* —*n.* **1.** A conflict, opposition, or disagreement: *a clash of cultures; a clash between political parties.* **2.** A loud, harsh metallic sound: *a clash of cymbals; a clash of weapons.*

clasp |klăsp| *or* |kläsp| *n.* **1.** A fastener, such as a hook or buckle, used to hold two objects or parts together. **2.** A firm grasp or embrace. —*v.* **1.** To fasten with a clasp: *clasp a necklace.* **2.** To grasp or embrace tightly.

class |klăs| *or* |kläs| *n.* **1.** A set or collection. **2.** A group of persons having approximately the same economic and social standing: *the middle class; the working class.* **3.** A group of animals or plants having certain similar characteristics, ranking between an order and a phylum. All mammals belong to the same class of animals. All mosses belong to the same class of plants. **4. a.** A group of students or alumni graduated in the same year: *the class of 1961.* **b.** A group of students meeting together for instruction. **c.** The period during which such a group meets: *before class; during class.* **5. a.** A grade of mail: *a letter sent first class.* **b.** The quality of accommodations on a public vehicle: *travel first class.* **6.** *Slang.* Great style or quality: *This new restaurant has class.* —***modifier:*** *meeting old friends at a class reunion; minimizing the dangers of class conflicts in some cities of the nation.* —*v.* To assign to a

clam
The quahog, a hard-shelled clam often used as food

clapboard

clarinet
Clarinets are made in a number of sizes that cover the range from contrabass to soprano.

class/classic/classical
Class *is from Latin* classis, *"division of the Roman people." This word had an adjective,* classicus, *first meaning simply "belonging to a class" but later meaning "of the first or highest class";* **classic** *and* **classical** *come from this. Beginning in the sixteenth century, the best of the Greek and Roman authors were called* **classic** *or* **classical**. *Later both words were applied to anything Greek or Roman regardless of excellence.*

clavichord
Sixteenth-century Flemish painting

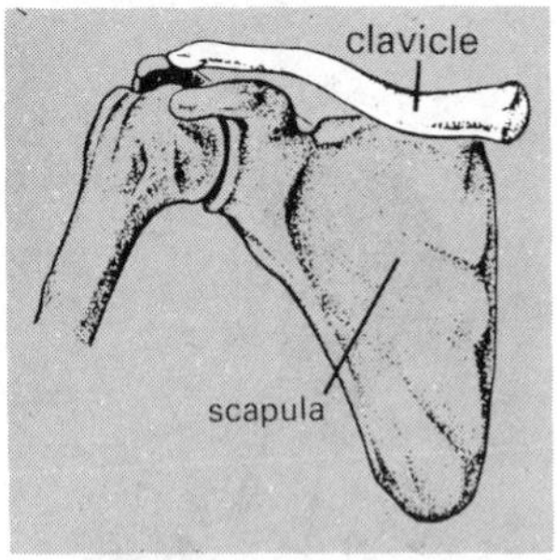

clavicle

ă pat/ā pay/â care/ä father/ĕ pet/ ē be/ĭ pit/ī pie/î fierce/ŏ pot/ ō go/ô paw, for/oi oil/ŏŏ book/ ōō boot/ou out/ŭ cut/û fur/ *th* the/th thin/hw which/zh vision/ ə ago, item, pencil, atom, circus

class; classify: *class insects; class a book as a mystery novel.* [SEE NOTE]

clas•sic |klăs′ĭk| *adj.* **1. a.** Long regarded as or serving as an outstanding example of its kind; model: *a classic case of neglect. The Derby is a classic horse race.* **b.** Well-known and typical: *the classic situation of boy meets girl.* **2.** Of ancient Greece and Rome or their literature or art: *classic times; classic styles of architecture.* —*n.* **1.** An artist, author, or work traditionally considered to be of the highest rank: *Shakespeare is a classic. "Gulliver's Travels" is a classic.* **2. the classics.** The literature of ancient Greece and Rome. **3.** A traditional, famous event, as in sports: *The World Series is baseball's fall classic.* [SEE NOTE]

clas•si•cal |klăs′ĭ kəl| *adj.* **1. a.** Of or pertaining to the culture of ancient Greece and Rome: *classical architecture; a classical scholar.* **b.** In the style of ancient Greek and Roman art, literature, etc.: *a building having classical elements well integrated with modern designs.* **2. a.** Of the musical style that prevailed in Europe in the late part of the 18th century. Haydn and Mozart are considered the most important composers who used this style. **b.** Of concert music or all music other than popular music and folk music. **3.** Standard or traditional rather than new or experimental: *classical methods of navigation.* **4.** Of physics in which the theory of relativity and quantum theory are not applied: *the classical theory of light.* [SEE NOTE]

clas•si•cism |klăs′ĭ sĭz′əm| *n.* **1.** The rules and ideals, as of form, simplicity, and proportion, that are the basis of the art and literature of ancient Greece and Rome. **2.** The use of such rules or principles in artistic creation.

clas•si•cist |klăs′ĭ sĭst| *n.* **1.** A follower of classicism. **2.** A student of or an authority on ancient Greece and Rome.

clas•si•fi•ca•tion |klăs′ə fĭ kā′shən| *n.* **1.** The act or result of classifying; arrangement: *the classification of books according to subject.* **2.** A category, name, or rating: *Nouns have four classifications: common, proper, collective, and abstract.*

clas•si•fied |klăs′ə fīd′| *adj.* Available only to authorized persons; secret: *classified information.*

classified advertisement. An advertisement, usually brief and in small type, printed in a newspaper; a want ad.

clas•si•fy |klăs′ə fī′| *v.* **clas•si•fied, clas•si•fy•ing, clas•si•fies. 1.** To arrange in classes or assign to a class; sort; categorize: *A librarian classifies books.* **2.** To designate (information) as secret and available only to authorized persons. —**clas′si•fi′er** *n.*

class•mate |klăs′māt′| *or* |kläs′-| *n.* A member of the same class in a school, college, etc.

class•room |klăs′rōōm′| *or* |-rŏŏm′| *or* |kläs′-| *n.* A room in which classes are held in a school, college, etc.

class•y |klăs′ē| *adj.* **class•i•er, class•i•est.** *Slang.* Stylish; elegant: *a classy hat.*

clat•ter |klăt′ər| *v.* To make or move with a rattling sound: *clatter along on roller skates.* —*n.* A rattling sound: *the clatter of dishes.*

clause |klôz| *n.* **1.** In grammar, a sentence or part of a sentence containing its own subject and a verb or verb phrase. **2.** A distinct part of a document.

claus•tro•pho•bi•a |klô′strə fō′bē ə| *n.* An abnormal fear of being enclosed in small spaces.

clav•i•chord |klăv′ĭ kôrd′| *n.* An early type of keyboard musical instrument sounded by small metal hammers that strike the strings as keys are pushed. [SEE PICTURE]

clav•i•cle |klăv′ĭ kəl| *n.* A bone that connects the sternum and the scapula; the collarbone. [SEE PICTURE]

cla•vier |klə vîr′| *or* |klā′vē ər| *or* |klăv′ē ər| *n.* **1.** A keyboard of a musical instrument such as a piano. **2.** Any stringed keyboard musical instrument, such as a harpsichord.

claw |klô| *n.* **1.** A sharp, often curved nail on the toe of an animal or bird. **2.** A pincerlike part, as of a lobster or crab, used for grasping. —*v.* To scratch or dig with or as if with claws.

claw hammer. A hammer having a head with one end forked for removing nails.

clay |klā| *n.* A firm, fine-grained earth that is soft and pliable when wet and that consists mainly of various silicates of aluminum. When fired at high temperatures, it becomes a hard, stony material. It is used in making bricks, pottery, and tiles. —***modifier:*** *a clay pot; a clay pipe.*

clay pigeon. A disk-shaped target of brittle, claylike material hurled by a trap in skeet and trapshooting.

clean |klēn| *adj.* **clean•er, clean•est. 1.** Free from dirt, stain, or impurities; unsoiled: *clean clothing; a clean glass; clean water.* **2.** Free from guilt or wrongdoing: *a clean life; a clean record.* **3.** Having a smooth edge or surface; even; regular: *a clean break in a bone; a clean line.* **4.** Entire; thorough; complete: *a clean escape.* **5.** Blank: *a clean page.* **6.** Free from clumsiness; skillful; adroit: *a clean throw.* **7.** Obeying the rules; sportsmanlike; fair: *a clean fighter.* **8.** Producing little radioactive fallout or contamination: *a clean nuclear bomb.* —*adv.* **1. a.** So as to be clean: *wash dishes clean.* **b.** In a clean manner: *play the game clean.* **2.** *Informal.* Entirely; completely: *He clean forgot he ever had a trouble in the world.* —*v.* **1.** To rid of dirt, stain, etc.: *clean a room.* **2.** To prepare (fowl, fish, etc.) for cooking. —***phrasal verbs.*** **clean out. 1.** To rid of dirt, trash, etc.: *clean out the garage.* **2.** *Informal.* To deprive completely, as of money; remove everything from: *A bad year for sales cleaned out the company's treasury. The gamblers cleaned him out at poker.* **clean up. 1.** To rid of dirt or disorder: *clean up one's room.* **2.** *Informal.* To make a large sum of money in a short period of time. —**clean′ness** *n.*

Idioms. **a clean bill of health. 1.** A diagnosis that one is in very good health. **2.** A statement of the soundness of: *The company got a clean bill of health from the government.* **come clean.** To confess the truth; confess: *The suspect finally came clean.*

clean-cut |klēn′kŭt′| *adj.* **1.** Having a distinct, sharp outline: *a car with clean-cut lines.* **2.** Neat and trim in appearance: *a clean-cut boy.*

clean•er |klē′nər| *n.* **1.** A person whose job it is to clean. **2.** A machine or substance used in cleaning.

clean•ly |klĕn′lē| *adj.* **clean•li•er, clean•li•est.**

Habitually and carefully neat and clean: *A cat is a very cleanly animal.* —*adv.* **|klĕn′lē|**. In a clean manner: *The fruit stems had been severed cleanly by a knife.* —**clean′li•ness** *n.*

cleanse |klĕnz| *v.* **cleansed, cleans•ing.** To make clean or pure: *cleanse a wound; cleanse a person of sin.*

cleans•er **|klĕn′zər|** *n.* A substance used for cleaning: *a tooth cleanser.*

clean•up **|klēn′ŭp′|** *n.* The act or process of cleaning up. —*adj.* Fourth in a baseball batting order: *the cleanup batter.*

clear |klîr| *adj.* **clear•er, clear•est. 1.** Free from clouds, mist, or haze: *a clear day.* **2.** Free from anything that dims, darkens, or obscures; transparent: *clear water.* **3.** Free from obstruction or hindrance; open: *a clear view. The road was clear.* **4.** Easily perceived by the eye or ear; distinct: *a clear picture; a clear sound; a clear voice.* **5.** Plain or evident to the mind; easily understood: *Make it clear what you mean.* **6.** Obvious; unmistakable: *a clear case of cheating.* **7.** Free from doubt or confusion; certain: *Are you clear about what has to be done?* **8.** Free from guilt; untroubled: *a clear conscience.* **9.** Having no blemishes: *a clear skin.* **10.** Freed from contact or connection; disengaged: *We are now clear of danger.* **11.** Without charges or deductions; net: *He earned a clear $15,000.* —*adv.* **1.** Out of the way: *He jumped clear of the oncoming car.* **2.** Distinctly; clearly: *Speak loud and clear before an audience.* **3.** *Informal.* All the way; entirely: *She cried clear through the night.* —*v.* **1.** To make or become clear, light, or bright: *clear the windshield of mist. The day cleared.* **2.** To make free of obstruction: *clear the way; clear land of trees.* **3.** To remove or get rid of: *clear snow from the road.* **4.** To pass by, under, or over without contact: *The runner cleared every hurdle.* **5.** To free from a legal charge; acquit: *The jury cleared him of the murder charge.* **6.** To free (the throat) of phlegm by coughing. **7. a.** To gain official approval in: *The bill cleared the Senate.* **b.** To get (a ship or its cargo) free by fulfilling customs and harbor requirements. **8.** To pass (a check, bill of exchange, etc.) through a clearinghouse: *clear a check. All checks cleared yesterday.* **9.** To earn (an amount of money) as net profit or earnings. —***phrasal verbs.*** **clear away.** To take away; remove: *clear away the dishes.* **clear off.** To remove something from in order to make clear: *clear off a table.* **clear out.** *Informal.* To leave a place, often quickly: *The thieves cleared out before the police arrived.* **clear up.** To make or become free, as of confusion, blemishes, clouds, etc.: *clear up a mystery. His skin cleared up. The sky cleared up.* —**clear′ness** *n.*

Idioms. **clear the air.** To dispel emotional tensions or differences: *His joke cleared the air.* **in the clear.** Free from burdens or dangers: *Once that is done, we will be in the clear.*

clear•ance **|klîr′əns|** *n.* **1.** The act of clearing. **2.** A sale to dispose of old merchandise at reduced prices. **3.** An intervening distance or space, as between a road and the ceiling of a tunnel: *no clearance for trucks passing under this bridge.* **4.** Permission for an airplane, ship, or other vehicle to proceed, as after an inspection of cargo or during certain traffic conditions. **5.** Official certification that a person is free from suspicion, guilt, etc.: *You need clearance to handle classified material.*

clear-cut **|klîr′kŭt′|** *adj.* **1.** Not vague or confused: *a clear-cut statement.* **2.** Plain; evident: *a clear-cut victory.*

clear•ing **|klîr′ĭng|** *n.* An area of land from which trees and other obstructions have been removed: *a clearing in a forest.*

clear•ing•house **|klîr′ĭng hous′|** *n., pl.* **-hous•es** |-hou′zĭz|. An office where banks exchange checks, drafts, and other notes and settle accounts.

clear•ly **|klîr′lē|** *adv.* **1.** Distinctly; plainly: *speak clearly.* **2.** Without or beyond a doubt: *Clearly, we need more money. Was he wrong? Clearly.*

cleat |klēt| *n.* **1.** A piece of iron, rubber, or leather attached to the sole of a shoe to keep it from slipping. **2.** A piece of metal or wood with projecting arms or ends on which a rope can be wound.

cleav•age **|klē′vĭj|** *n.* **1. a.** The act of splitting. **b.** A split. **2.** The tendency of rocks, minerals, and crystals to split along definite planes and have smooth surfaces where such splitting has taken place. **3. a.** The series of cell divisions by which a fertilized egg becomes a blastula. **b.** Any stage in this series of divisions.

cleave[1] |klēv| *v.* **cleft** |klĕft| or **cleaved** or **clove** |klōv|, **cleft** or **cleaved** or **clo•ven** **|klō′vən|**, **cleav•ing. 1. a.** To split, as by a sudden blow: *The ax cleft the piece of wood.* **b.** To be capable of being split: *Certain woods cleave easily.* **2.** To make or proceed through by or as if by cutting: *cleave a path in the woods; a ship cleaving the waves.* [SEE NOTE]

cleave[2] |klēv| *v.* **cleaved** or **clove** |klōv|, **cleaved, cleav•ing.** To cling: *cleave to a belief. Barnacles cleave to a hull.* [SEE NOTE]

cleav•er **|klē′vər|** *n.* A tool used by butchers for cutting meat, consisting of a broad, heavy blade and a short handle. [SEE PICTURE]

clef |klĕf| *n.* A symbol placed on a musical staff to tell which pitch each of the various lines and spaces represents. [SEE PICTURE]

cleft |klĕft|. A past tense and past participle of **cleave** (to split). —*adj.* Split or partially split: *a cleft chin.* —*n.* A separation, split, or hollow: *a cleft in a rock; a cleft in a chin.*

cleft palate. A split in the roof of the mouth, occurring as a birth defect.

clem•a•tis **|klĕm′ə tĭs|** *n.* Any of several climbing vines with white or purplish flowers and plumelike seeds. [SEE PICTURE]

clem•en•cy **|klĕm′ən sē|** *n.* **1.** Leniency; mercy: *The judge showed clemency in sentencing the defendant.* **2.** Mildness, especially of weather.

clem•ent **|klĕm′ənt|** *adj.* **1.** Lenient or merciful: *a clement ruler.* **2.** Pleasant; mild: *clement weather.* —**clem′ent•ly** *adv.*

clench |klĕnch| *v.* **1.** To close (a hand or the teeth) tightly: *clench one's fist.* **2.** To grasp or grip tightly: *A halfback clenches a football.*

Cle•o•pat•ra |klē′ə **păt′**rə| *or* **|-pä′**trə| *or* **|-pä′**trə|. 69–30 B.C. Queen of Egypt (51–49 B.C. and 48–30 B.C.).

cler•gy **|klûr′**jē| *n., pl.* **cler•gies.** Ministers, priests, and rabbis in general.

cleave[1·2]
Cleave[1] *and* **cleave[2]** *go back to similar Old English words,* clēofan *and* cleofian, *respectively. Both* **cleave[1]** *and, especially,* **cleave[2]** *are becoming rather rare.*

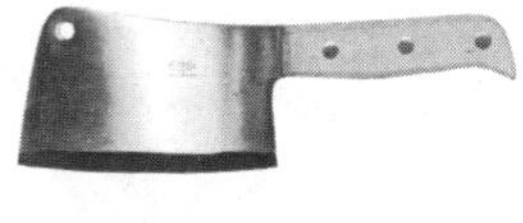
cleaver

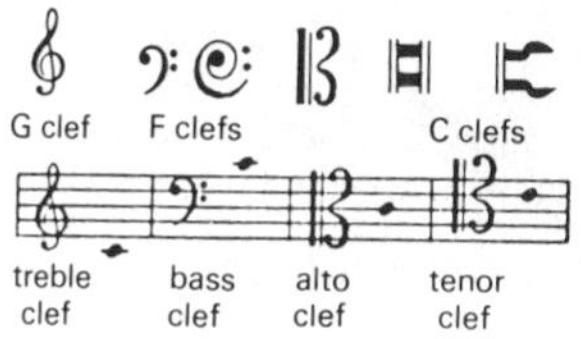

clef

clematis

climax
An example of a **climax community** *is a forest of maple and beech trees that has gone through a succession of changes beginning with small lichens growing on bare rocks, through growths of mosses, ferns, and other kinds of trees.*

clip[1-2]/clipper
Clip[1] *is from Old Norse* klippa, *"to cut short." The meaning "fast pace" arises from "to cut short," hence "to go fast," whence* **clipper,** *the fast sailing ship.* **Clip[2]** *goes back to Old English* clyppan, *"to embrace or fasten."*

ă **pat**/ā **pay**/â **care**/ä **father**/ĕ **pet**/ē **be**/ĭ **pit**/ī **pie**/î **fierce**/ŏ **pot**/ō **go**/ô **paw**, **for**/oi **oil**/ŏŏ **book**/ōō **boot**/ou **out**/ŭ **cut**/û **fur**/*th* **the**/th **thin**/hw **which**/**zh** vision/ə **ago**, item, pencil, atom, circus

cler•gy•man |klûr′jē mən| *n., pl.* **-men** |-mən|. A member of the clergy.

cler•ic |klĕr′ĭk| *n.* A member of the clergy.

cler•i•cal |klĕr′ĭ kəl| *adj.* **1.** Of clerks or office workers: *clerical work.* **2.** Of the clergy or a clergyman: *clerical garb.*

clerk |klûrk| *n.* **1.** An office worker who keeps records, does filing, etc. **2.** A person who keeps the records of a court or legislative body and performs other routine duties. **3.** A person who sells merchandise in a store.

Cleve•land |klēv′lənd|. The largest city in Ohio, on Lake Erie. Population, 573,822.

Cleve•land |klēv′lənd|, **(Stephen) Grover.** 1837–1908. Twenty-second and twenty-fourth President of the United States (1885–89 and 1893–97).

clev•er |klĕv′ər| *adj.* **clev•er•er, clev•er•est. 1.** Bright; intelligent; quick-witted. **2.** Showing skill, wit, or ingenuity: *a clever plan; a clever trick.* —**clev′er•ly** *adv.* —**clev′er•ness** *n.*

cli•ché |klē shā′| *or* |klĭ-| *n.* A trite or overused expression or idea; "quiet as a mouse" is a cliché.

click |klĭk| *n.* A short, sharp sound. —*v.* **1.** To make or cause to make such a sound: *click one's heels. The dial clicks into place.* **2.** *Informal.* To be completely successful.

cli•ent |klī′ənt| *n.* **1.** A person consulting a professional man, such as a lawyer, accountant, etc. **2.** A customer or patron.

cli•en•tele |klī′ən tĕl′| *n.* All the regular clients or customers of a store, a doctor, etc.

cliff |klĭf| *n.* A high, steep, or overhanging face of rock.

cliff dweller. A member of certain prehistoric Indian tribes of the southwestern United States who lived in caves in the sides of cliffs.

cliff•hang•er |klĭf′hăng′ər| *n.* **1.** A melodrama presented in episodes and in which each episode ends in suspense. **2.** Any contest whose outcome is uncertain until the end.

cli•mac•tic |klī măk′tĭk| *adj.* Of or forming a climax: *the climactic events that led to the invasion of the island.*

cli•mate |klī′mĭt| *n.* **1.** The general or average weather conditions of a certain region, including temperature, rainfall, and wind. **2.** A region having certain weather conditions: *a polar climate.* **3.** A general atmosphere or attitude: *A climate of fear prevailed over much of the country.*

cli•mat•ic |klī măt′ĭk| *adj.* Of climate.

cli•ma•tol•o•gy |klī′mə tŏl′ə jē| *n.* The scientific study of climate.

cli•max |klī′măks′| *n.* **1.** That point in a series of events marked by greatest intensity or effect, usually occurring at or near the end. **2.** Often **climax community.** The stage at which a community of plants and animals reaches its full development and tends to change no further. —*v.* To bring or come to a climax: *His brilliant portrayal of Hamlet climaxed a long and distinguished career. The movie climaxed in the realistic scenes of the invasion.* [SEE NOTE]

climb |klīm| *v.* **1. a.** To go up, over, or through (something) by using the hands and feet; ascend: *climb a ladder; climb over a fence; climb up a tree. Monkeys climb well.* **b.** To move downward, especially by means of the hands and feet: *climb down a ladder.* **2.** To go higher; rise: *The sun climbed in the sky. The rocket climbed steadily. His fever began to climb.* **3.** To get in or out of: *climb into a cab; climb aboard a train; climb out of bed; climb out of a wet suit.* **4.** To grow upward by clinging to or twining around something, as a vine does. —*n.* **1.** The act of climbing: *a hard climb up the mountain; Hitler's climb to power.* **2.** A place to be climbed: *That hill was a good climb.* ¶*These sound alike* **climb, clime.**

climb•er |klī′mər| *n.* **1.** Someone or something that climbs: *a mountain climber.* **2.** *Informal.* A person trying to gain a higher social position. **3.** A plant, such as a vine, that climbs.

clime |klīm| *n.* Climate. Used chiefly in poetry. ¶*These sound alike* **clime, climb.**

clinch |klĭnch| *v.* **1.** To fasten securely, as with a nail or bolt. **2.** To settle definitely: *clinch a deal; clinch a championship.* **3.** In boxing, to hold the opponent's body with one or both arms to prevent or hinder his punches. —*n.* In boxing, the act or an example of clinching.

clinch•er |klĭn′chər| *n. Informal.* A final point, fact, or remark, as in an argument.

cling |klĭng| *v.* **clung** |klŭng|, **cling•ing. 1.** To hold tight or adhere to something: *cling to a rope. Dirt clings to a surface.* **2.** To stay near; remain close: *The children cling to their mother.* **3.** To remain attached; refuse to abandon: *cling to old beliefs; cling to a hope.* —*n.* A clingstone peach. —***modifier:*** *canned cling peaches.*

cling•stone |klĭng′stōn′| *n.* A fruit, especially a peach with pulp that does not separate easily from the stone. —***modifier:*** *a clingstone peach.*

clin•ic |klĭn′ĭk| *n.* **1.** A training session for medical students in which they observe while patients are examined and treated. **2.** An institution associated with a hospital or medical school that deals mainly with outpatients. **3.** A medical institution run by several specialists working in cooperation. **4.** An institution that provides special counseling or training: *a language clinic.*

clin•i•cal |klĭn′ĭ kəl| *adj.* **1.** Of or connected with a clinic. **2.** Of or related to direct examination and treatment of patients. **3.** Very objective; not emotional; analytical: *a clinical attitude.*

clink[1] |klĭngk| *v.* To make or cause to make a light, sharp, ringing sound: *clink glasses after a toast. The ice clinked in the glass.* —*n.* A light, sharp, ringing sound.

clink[2] |klĭngk| *n. Slang.* A prison; jail.

clink•er |klĭng′kər| *n.* **1.** A lump of incombustible matter left over after coal has burned. **2.** *Slang.* A mistake or error, especially in a musical performance.

Clin•ton |klĭn′tən|, **William Jefferson ("Bill").** Born 1946. Forty-second President of the United States (since 1993).

clip[1] |klĭp| *v.* **clipped, clip•ping. 1.** To cut with scissors or shears: *clip an ad out of the newspaper; clip a hedge.* **2.** To cut short; trim: *clip his beard.* **3.** To fail to pronounce or write fully: *He clipped his words when speaking.* **4.** *Informal.* To strike with a quick, sharp blow. **5.** *Slang.* To cheat, overcharge, or swindle. —*n.* **1.** The act of clipping. **2.** The wool clipped from sheep at one shearing. **3.** Something clipped off, as a sequence clipped from a movie film. **4.** *Informal.* A quick, sharp blow. **5.** *Informal.* A brisk pace: *move along at a good clip.* [SEE NOTE]

clip[2] |klĭp| *n.* **1.** A device for gripping something or for holding things together: *a paper clip.* **2.** A piece of jewelry that fastens with a clasp or clip. —*v.* **clipped, clip•ping.** To fasten with a clip: *clip on an earring; clip the papers together.* [SEE NOTE on p. 170]

clip•board |**klĭp**'bôrd'| *or* |-bōrd'| *n.* A portable writing board with a spring clip at the top for holding papers or a writing pad.

clip•per |**klĭp**'ər| *n.* **1.** A person who clips, cuts, or shears. **2. clippers.** An instrument or tool for clipping, cutting, or shearing: *nail clippers; a barber's clippers.* **3.** A sailing vessel built for great speed, having tall masts and sharp lines. [SEE PICTURE; SEE NOTE on p. 170]

clip•ping |**klĭp**'ĭng| *n.* **1.** Something cut or trimmed off: *fingernail clippings.* **2.** An article, advertisement, or photograph clipped from a newspaper or other publication.

clique |klēk| *or* |klĭk| *n.* A small group of people who stick together and remain aloof from others.

cli•tel•lum |klĭ **tĕl**'əm| *or* |klī-| *n., pl.* **cli•tel•la** |klĭ **tĕl**'ə| *or* |klī-|. A thickened, bandlike section around the body of an earthworm.

clit•o•ris |**klĭt**'ər ĭs| *or* |**klī**'tər-| *n.* A small cylindrical organ that forms part of the external female reproductive system. It is somewhat like the penis in males, but the urethra does not pass through it.

clo•a•ca |klō **ā**'kə| *n., pl.* **clo•a•cae** |klō **ā**'sē|. A tubelike or saclike part at the lower end of the digestive tract of a bird, reptile, frog, etc. It serves as an outlet for body wastes and eggs or sperms.

cloak |klōk| *n.* **1.** A loose outer garment or wrap, usually having no sleeves. **2.** Something that covers or conceals. —*v.* To cover up; hide.

cloak•room |**klōk**'ro͞om'| *or* |-ro͝om'| *n.* A room, as in a school, theater, or other public building, in which coats and other outdoor clothing may be left temporarily.

clob•ber |**klŏb**'ər| *v. Slang.* **1.** To hit or pound with great force. **2.** To defeat completely.

cloche |klōsh| *n.* A woman's close-fitting bell-shaped hat. [SEE NOTE]

clock[1] |klŏk| *n.* An instrument for indicating time, consisting of a numbered dial with moving hands or pointers. —***modifier:*** *a clock hand; a clock tower.* —*v.* To record the time or speed of. [SEE NOTE]

clock[2] |klŏk| *n.* A design embroidered or woven on the side of a sock or stocking, at and above the ankle. [SEE NOTE]

clock•wise |**klŏk**'wīz'| *adv.* In the same direction as the rotating hands of a clock: *turn clockwise.* —*adj.: a clockwise movement.*

clock•work |**klŏk**'wûrk'| *n.* The mechanism of a clock.

Idiom. **like clockwork.** With perfect regularity and precision.

clod |klŏd| *n.* **1.** A lump of earth or clay. **2.** A dull, ignorant, or stupid person; a dolt.

clod•hop•per |**klŏd**'hŏp'ər| *n.* **1.** A clumsy country fellow; a lout. **2. clodhoppers.** Big, heavy shoes.

clog |klŏg| *n.* A heavy shoe, usually having a wooden sole. —*v.* **clogged, clog•ging.** To become or cause to become obstructed or blocked up: *The pipes clogged with rust. Heavy traffic clogged the highway.*

clois•ter |**kloi**'stər| *n.* **1.** A monastery or convent. **2.** A covered walk along the side of a building, such as a convent, church, etc., with open arches facing into a courtyard. —*v.* To confine in or as if in a cloister; seclude.

clomp |klŏmp| *v.* To walk heavily and noisily.

clop |klŏp| *n.* The drumming sound of a horse's hoofs as they strike a pavement. —*v.* **clopped, clop•ping.** To make or move with such a sound.

close |klōs| *adj.* **clos•er, clos•est. 1.** Near in space or time: *The airport is close to town. My birthday is close to yours.* **2.** Near in relationship; intimate: *a close friend. They worked together in close harmony.* **3.** With little or no space in between; tight; compact: *a close fit; a close weave.* **4.** Rigorous; strict: *keeping a close watch on the prisoner.* **5.** Confining; narrow; crowded: *close quarters.* **6.** Very short or near to the surface: *a close haircut; a close shave.* **7.** Lacking fresh air; stuffy: *It's very close in this room.* **8.** Almost even: *a close race; a close election.* **9.** Thorough; careful: *Pay close attention.* **10.** Stingy; miserly: *He is very close with his money.* **11.** Secretive: *She is very close about her personal life.* —*adv.* Near: *stick close together. She stood close by.* —*v.* |klōz| **closed, clos•ing. 1.** To shut: *close one's eyes; close the doors.* **2.** To declare or be declared not open to the public: *The store closes at six o'clock. The mayor closed all streets for snow removal.* **3.** To fill or stop up: *closing the cracks in the wall with plaster; closing the gap between rich and poor countries.* **4.** To bring or come to an end; conclude: *close a letter. The play closed after ten performances.* **5.** To draw or come together: *It took eight stitches to close the wound. His arms closed about her.* —***phrasal verbs.*** **close down.** To stop operating: *close down a factory.* **close in.** To surround and advance upon: *The enemy is closing in on us.* **close out.** To sell at a reduced price in order to dispose of quickly. —*n.* |klōz|. A conclusion; end: *the close of day. The meeting came to a close.* ¶*These sound alike* **close** (*v.* & *n.*), **clothes.** —**close'ly** *adv.* —**close'ness** *n.*

Idiom. **a close call.** A narrow escape.

closed circuit. An electric circuit providing an uninterrupted path through which current can flow.

closed-cir•cuit television |**klōzd'sûr**'kĭt|. Television that is transmitted by cable rather than by being broadcast and that is available only to receivers connected directly to the cable, often used in education, industry, etc.

closed curve. A curve that can be thought of as having its beginning and end at any one of its points. The circle and ellipse are familiar closed curves. [SEE PICTURE]

closed shop. A company or business in which only union members or people who agree to join the union within a certain time may be hired.

close-fist•ed |**klōs'fĭs**'tĭd| *adj.* Stingy; miserly.

close-mouthed |**klōs'mouthd**'| *or* |**-moutht**'| *adj.* Not talking much; giving away very little information; discreet.

close-out |**klōz**'out'| *n.* A sale in which goods are offered at greatly reduced prices in order to dispose of them.

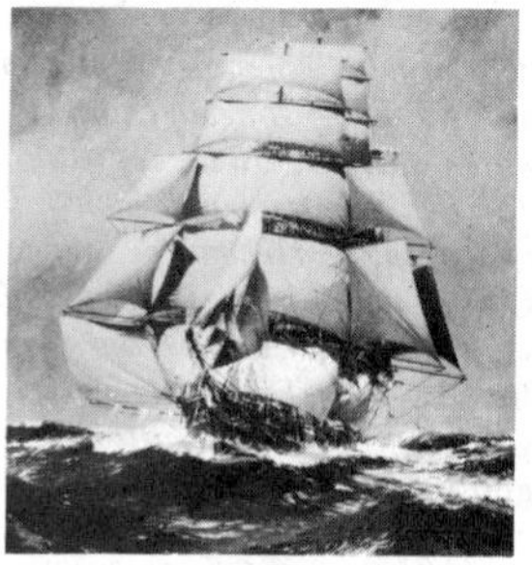

clipper

clock[1-2]/cloche

Clock[1] *originally meant specifically a chiming clock, a clock with a bell. The instrument was introduced into England in the fourteenth century from the Netherlands; the word is from Dutch* clocke, *"bell, chiming clock," which is from Old French* cloche, *"bell." Much later, the French word was borrowed again as* **cloche,** *the name for the bell-shaped hat popular in the 1920's.* **Clock**[2] *may originally have been a bell-shaped ornament and may also come from Dutch* clocke.

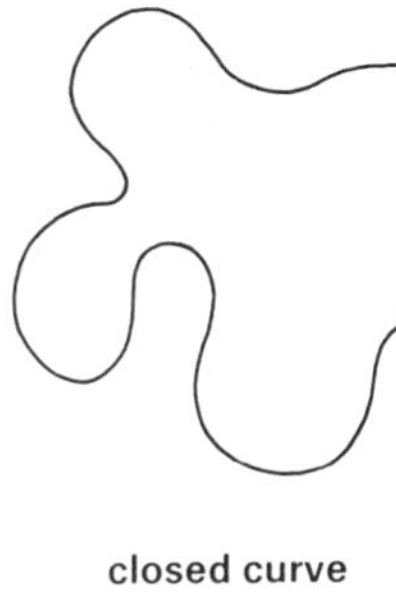

closed curve

clove[1-2]
It is strange but somehow typical of the English language that two words spelled **clove,** *of utterly different origin, should both refer to strong kitchen seasonings.* **Clove**[1] *was originally the nail-shaped bud itself, not the plant. In Middle English it was* cloue of gilofre, *from Old French* clou de gilofre; clou *meant "nail," and* gilofre *was the original name of the plant.* **Clove**[2] *basically meant "split-off part," and goes back to Old English* clufu, *which is related to* **cleave**[1].

clover

cloverleaf

club

ă pat/ā pay/â care/ä father/ĕ pet/ ē be/ĭ pit/ī pie/î fierce/ŏ pot/ ō go/ô paw, for/oi oil/o͝o book/ o͞o boot/ou out/ŭ cut/û fur/ *th* the/th thin/hw which/zh vision/ ə ago, item, pencil, atom, circus

clos•et |**klŏz'ĭt**| *n.* **1.** A small room or cabinet for hanging clothes, storing linens or supplies, etc. **2.** A small private room for study or prayer. —*v.* To enclose in a private room, as for discussion: *He closeted himself with an adviser. They were closeted together for hours.*

close-up |**klōs'ŭp'**| *n.* **1.** A picture taken at close range. **2.** A close or intimate look or view. —***modifier:*** *a close-up picture.*

clo•sure |**klō'**zhər| *n.* **1.** The act of closing. **2.** Something that closes or shuts. **3.** A form of the word **cloture. 4.** The property of a set of numbers in which when a given mathematical operation is performed on any pair of them, the result is also a member of the set. Suppose that *a* and *b* are any numbers belonging to the set *S* and ♦ is a mathematical operation; if *a*♦*b* is always a member of *S,* then *S* is said to have closure under ♦.

clot |klŏt| *n.* A thickened or solid mass formed from a liquid: *a blood clot.* —*v.* **clot•ted, clot•ting.** To form or cause to form into clots.

cloth |klôth| *or* |klŏth| *n., pl.* **cloths** |klô*thz*| *or* |klŏ*thz*| *or* |klôths| *or* |klŏths|. **1.** Material produced by joining natural or man-made fibers, as by weaving, knitting, or matting them together. Cloth may be made of cotton, wool, silk, flax, nylon, etc. **2.** A piece of cloth used for a special purpose, as a tablecloth, washcloth, or dishcloth. **3. the cloth.** The clergy. —***modifier:*** *a cloth cap.*

clothe |klō*th*| *v.* **clothed** or **clad** |klăd|, **cloth•ing. 1.** To put clothes on or provide clothes for; dress: *feed and clothe a family.* **2.** To cover, as if with clothing: *trees clad in leafy splendor.*

clothes |klōz| *or* |klō*thz*| *pl.n.* **1.** Coverings worn on the body; garments, such as shirts, trousers, dresses, etc. **2.** Bedclothes. ¶*These sound alike* **clothes, close** (*v.* & *n.*).

clothes•horse |**klōz'**hôrs'| *or* |**klō***thz***'-**| *n.* **1.** A frame on which clothes are hung to dry or air. **2.** A person who has an excessive interest in clothes and is frequently displaying new outfits.

clothes•line |**klōz'**līn'| *or* |**klō***thz***'-**| *n.* A rope or wire on which clothes are hung to dry.

clothes•pin |**klōz'**pĭn'| *or* |**klō***thz***'-**| *n.* A clip of wood or plastic for fastening clothes to a clothesline.

cloth•ier |**klōth'**yər| *or* |-ē ər| *n.* A person who makes or sells clothing or cloth.

cloth•ing |**klō'***th*ĭng| *n.* Clothes or garments in general. —***modifier:*** *a clothing store.*

clo•ture |**klō'**chər| *n.* A rule in a legislative body that cuts off debate so that a vote may be taken.

cloud |kloud| *n.* **1. a.** A visible object of fairly indefinite shape formed of a collection of water droplets or ice particles suspended in the air. **b.** Any similar object formed of suspended particles or droplets, as of dust, steam, or smoke. **2.** A moving mass of things on the ground or in the air that is so large and dense that it appears to resemble a cloud: *a cloud of locusts.* **3.** Something that depresses or makes gloomy: *The bad news cast a cloud over the proceedings.* —***modifier:*** *cloud formations.* —*v.* **1.** To cover or become covered with or as if with clouds: *Heavy mist clouded the hills. Exhaust fumes clouded the air. The sky clouded over.* **2.** To make gloomy, obscure, or confused: *Superstition clouded their thinking.* **3.** To taint; tarnish; sully: *The incident clouded his reputation.*

cloud chamber. A device in which the paths of charged subatomic particles are made visible as trails of droplets. It contains a supersaturated vapor that condenses on the ions formed along the path of the charged particle.

cloud•less |**kloud'**lĭs| *adj.* Free from clouds.

cloud seeding. A method of making a cloud give up its moisture as rain, usually by releasing into the cloud a quantity of silver iodide or particles of solid carbon dioxide.

cloud•y |**klou'**dē| *adj.* **cloud•i•er, cloud•i•est. 1.** Full of or covered with clouds; overcast: *a cloudy sky; a cloudy day.* **2.** Not clear; murky: *cloudy water.* —**cloud'i•ly** *adv.* —**cloud'i•ness** *n.*

clout |klout| *n.* **1.** A heavy blow, especially with the fist. **2.** In baseball, a long, powerful hit. **3.** *Informal.* Power, prestige, or influence: *political clout.* —*v.* To hit hard.

clove[1] |klōv| *n.* The dried, aromatic flower bud of a tropical Asian plant, used whole or ground as a spice. [SEE NOTE]

clove[2] |klōv| *n.* One of the sections of a garlic bulb or similar plant bulb. [SEE NOTE]

clove[3] |klōv|. **1.** A past tense of **cleave** (to split). **2.** A past tense of **cleave** (to cling).

clove hitch. A knot, commonly used to tie up a small boat by hitching it to a post, consisting of two turns, the second being held under the first.

clo•ven |**klō'**vən|. A past participle of **cleave** (to split). —*adj.* Split or divided into two parts: *the cloven hoofs of deer or cattle.*

clo•ver |**klō'**vər| *n.* Any of several plants with leaves divided into three leaflets and tightly clustered heads of small, often fragrant flowers. [SEE PICTURE]

***Idiom.* in clover.** Living a life of ease, comfort, and prosperity.

clo•ver•leaf |**klō'**vər lēf'| *n., pl.* **-leaves** |-lēvz'|. An interchange at which two highways crossing each other on different levels have curving entrance and exit ramps, enabling vehicles to go in any of four directions. [SEE PICTURE]

clown |kloun| *n.* **1.** A comic entertainer, especially a performer in a circus who tells jokes and does tricks or humorous stunts; a buffoon or jester. **2.** A person who is always making jokes or acting foolishly: *the office clown.* —*v.* **1.** To perform as a clown in a circus or other show. **2.** To behave like a clown; act foolishly.

cloy |kloi| *v.* To displease or make weary by giving too much of something good, especially of something too rich or sweet.

cloy•ing |**kloi'**ĭng| *adj.* Excessive to the point of being distasteful: *cloying praise.* —**cloy'ing•ly** *adv.*

club |klŭb| *n.* **1.** A heavy stick, usually thicker at one end than at the other, used as a weapon. **2.** A stick designed to drive a ball in certain games, especially golf. **3. a.** A black figure, shaped like a trefoil or clover leaf, on a playing card. **b.** A card bearing this figure. **c. clubs.** The suit in a deck of cards having this figure as its symbol. **4. a.** A group of people organized for a common purpose: *a tennis club.* **b.** The room, building, or other facilities used by such a group. **5.** A professional baseball team. —***modifier:*** *club members; club rules.* —*v.* **clubbed, club•bing. 1.** To strike or beat with or as if with a club. **2.** To join together for a common purpose: *All the girls clubbed together to work on the new tutoring plan.* [SEE PICTURE on p. 172]

club•foot |klŭb′fo͝ot′| *n., pl.* **-feet** |-fēt′|. **1.** Any one of many deformities of the foot that arise as birth defects. **2.** A foot having such a deformity. —**club′foot′ed** *adj.*

club•house |klŭb′hous′| *n., pl.* **-hous•es** |-hou′zĭz|. **1.** A building occupied by a club. **2.** A locker room used by an athletic team.

club moss. Any of a group of low-growing evergreen plants that have small, scalelike leaves and do not bear flowers. [SEE PICTURE]

club sandwich. A sandwich, usually of three slices of toast, with a filling of meat, tomato, lettuce, and mayonnaise.

club soda. A sparkling, unflavored water used in making various drinks.

cluck |klŭk| *n.* The low, short, throaty sound made by a hen sitting on eggs or caring for young chicks. —*v.* To make such a sound.

clue |klo͞o| *n.* Something, such as a footprint, fingerprint, or odd piece of information, that helps to solve a problem or mystery.

clump |klŭmp| *n.* **1.** A thick group or cluster of trees, bushes, etc. **2.** A thick mass of dirt, sod, etc. **3.** A heavy, dull sound, as of footsteps. —*v.* To walk with a heavy, dull sound.

clum•sy |klŭm′zē| *adj.* **clum•si•er, clum•si•est. 1.** Lacking grace or deftness; awkward: *a clumsy walk; clumsy animals.* **2.** Difficult to handle or maneuver: *clumsy wooden shoes.* **3.** Done without skill; inept: *a clumsy attempt to gain votes.* —**clum′si•ly** *adv.* —**clum′si•ness** *n.*

clung |klŭng|. Past tense and past participle of **cling.**

clunk |klŭngk| *n.* A dull thumping sound made by one thing striking another.

clus•ter |klŭs′tər| *n.* A group of similar things growing or grouped close together: *a cluster of flowers; a star cluster.* —*v.* To gather or grow in clusters: *Everyone clustered around the fire.*

clutch[1] |klŭch| *v.* To hold or grasp tightly: *She was clutching a baby in her arms.* —*n.* **1.** A tight hold or grip. **2. a.** A device used to connect and disconnect two sections of a rotating shaft, usually with one section of the shaft connected to a source of power and the other end connected to something being driven. **b.** The lever, pedal, or other control that operates such a device, as in an automobile, truck, etc. **3. clutches.** Control or power; possession: *fall into the clutches of the enemy.* **4.** *Informal.* A critical situation: *our best hitter in the clutch.* [SEE NOTE]

clutch[2] |klŭch| *n.* **1.** The eggs produced at a single laying. **2.** A brood of chicks hatched from such eggs. [SEE NOTE]

clut•ter |klŭt′ər| *n.* A collection of things scattered about in a disorderly fashion; a jumble. —*v.* To fill in such a way as to block movement or action: *clutter up a room with newspapers.*

cm centimeter.

Cm The symbol for the element curium.

CNS, C.N.S. central nervous system.

co–. A prefix meaning "jointly, together, or mutually": **co-author; coexist.**

Co The symbol for the element cobalt.

co. 1. company. **2.** county.

c/o care of.

coach |kōch| *n.* **1.** A large, closed four-wheeled carriage pulled by horses. **2.** A railroad passenger car. **3.** A low-priced class of passenger accommodations on a train, airplane, or bus. **4.** In sports: **a.** A person in charge of a football, basketball, or other athletic team. **b.** In baseball, a nonplaying member of the team at bat who stands near first or third base and directs the base runners. **c.** A person who provides individual instruction in a certain sport: *a tennis coach.* **5.** A person who gives private instruction, as in singing or acting. —*v.* **1.** To teach or train: *coach a football team; coach actors for an audition; coach for the State University.* **2.** To prompt or help in answering a difficult question: *No coaching!* [SEE NOTE]

coach•man |kōch′mən| *n., pl.* **-men** |-mən|. A man who drives a coach.

co•ad•ju•tor |kō ăj′ə tər| *or* |kō′ə jo͞o′tər| *n.* An assistant or helper.

co•ag•u•lant |kō ăg′yə lənt| *n.* A substance that causes coagulation. —***modifier:*** *a coagulant drug.*

co•ag•u•late |kō ăg′yə lāt′| *v.* **co•ag•u•lat•ed, co•ag•u•lat•ing. 1.** To change (a liquid) into a solid or nearly solid mass; clot. **2.** To undergo such a change: *Egg white coagulates when heated.*

co•ag•u•la•tion |kō ăg′yə lā′shən| *n.* The act or process of coagulating.

coal |kōl| *n.* **1. a.** A dark-brown to black natural solid substance formed from fossilized plants. It consists mainly of carbon, and is widely used as a fuel and raw material. **b.** A piece of this substance. **2.** A glowing or charred piece of wood, coal, or other solid fuel; ember. —***modifier:*** *a coal bin.* —*v.* To supply with or take on a supply of coal: *coal a ship. The tanker docked to coal.* ¶*These sound alike* **coal, kohl.**

coal•er |kō′lər| *n.* A ship, train, or other vehicle that carries or supplies coal.

co•a•lesce |kō′ə lĕs′| *v.* **co•a•lesced, co•a•lesc•ing.** To grow or blend into one; fuse.

coal forest. A growth of the large, treelike plants that existed millions of years ago, and whose fossil remains are found today in the form of coal.

coal gas. 1. The mixture of gases, used commercially as a fuel, driven off when bituminous coal is heated without air. **2.** The poisonous mixture of gases released when coal burns, especially when there is not enough air.

co•a•li•tion |kō′ə lĭsh′ən| *n.* A temporary alliance of political parties or factions. —***modifier:*** *a coalition government; a coalition party.*

coal oil. Kerosene.

coal tar. A thick, sticky black liquid obtained by heating coal in the absence of air. It is used as a raw material for many dyes, drugs, organic chemicals, and industrial materials.

coarse |kôrs| *or* |kōrs| *adj.* **coars•er, coars•est. 1.** Not smooth; rough: *coarse skin; coarse material.* **2.** Consisting of large particles: *coarse sand.* **3.** Not refined; crude; rude: *coarse language.* ¶*These sound alike* **coarse, course.** —**coarse′ly** *adv.* —**coarse′ness** *n.*

coars•en |kôr′sən| *or* |kōr′-| *v.* To make or become coarse.

coast |kōst| *n.* **1.** The edge of the land facing the sea. **2.** A region next to or near the sea. —*v.*

club moss

The **club mosses** of today are small, often mosslike plants, but millions of years ago some kinds grew to the size of very tall trees.

clutch[1-2]

Clutch[1] *goes back to Old English* clyccan, *"to clench."* **Clutch**[2] *is from Middle English* clecken, *"to hatch eggs," which was borrowed from Old Norse* klekja.

coach

Coach *is one of the very few words we have from Hungarian. In the late fifteenth century, the Hungarians began to use a kind of large four-wheeled carriage called a* kocsi, *from the small town of* Kocs. *The* kocsi *soon spread all over Europe, and its name followed it. In German it became* kutsche, *which was borrowed into French as* coche *and from French into English as* **coach**.

cobra
Indian cobra

cock$^{1\text{-}2}$

Cock[1] *goes back to Old English* cocc, *which was borrowed from Latin* coccus, *"rooster," from* coco, *an onomatopoeic word for crowing or clucking.* **Cock**[2] *is probably related to an Old English word meaning "hill" that survives only in a few English place names.*

cockatoo

ă pat/ā pay/â care/ä father/ĕ pet/ ē be/ĭ pit/ī pie/î fierce/ŏ pot/ ō go/ô paw, for/oi oil/ŏŏ book/ ōō boot/ou out/ŭ cut/û fur/ *th* the/th thin/hw which/zh vision/ ə ago, item, pencil, atom, circus

1. To move or continue to move down a slope or without the use of power: *Let's coast down the hill on a sled! The car coasted to a stop.* **2.** To sail along or near a coast.

coast•al |kō'stəl| *adj.* On, along, or near a coast.

coast•er |kō'stər| *n.* A small, round tray placed under a bottle or glass to protect a table top or other surface.

coast guard, also **Coast Guard.** A military organization whose job is to patrol the coast of a nation, carry out rescue operations of ships in trouble, and enforce immigration, navigation, and customs laws.

coast•line |kōst'līn'| *n.* The shape or outline of a seacoast.

coat |kōt| *n.* **1.** An outer garment with sleeves, usually worn for warmth or protection. **2.** A jacket worn as the top part of a suit. **3.** The hair or fur of an animal. **4.** A layer of something spread over a surface: *a coat of paint.* —*v.* To cover with a layer: *Dust coated the table.*

co•a•ti |kō ä'tē| *n., pl.* **co•a•tis.** An animal of the southwestern United States and tropical America, related to and resembling the raccoon but with a longer tail and snout.

co•a•ti•mun•di |kō ä'tē mŭn'dē| *n., pl.* **co•a•ti•mun•dis.** The coati.

coat•ing |kō'tĭng| *n.* A layer of a substance spread over a surface, as for protection or decoration.

coat of arms. *pl.* **coats of arms.** An emblem on a shield, that serves as the insignia of a nation, family, institution, etc.

coat of mail. *pl.* **coats of mail.** An armored coat made of chain mail or overlapping metal plates, worn in the Middle Ages.

coat•room |kōt'rōōm'| *or* |-rŏŏm'| *n.* A cloakroom.

coat•tail |kōt'tāl'| *n.* Often **coattails.** The loose rear flap of a coat, especially the lower back part of a man's cutaway or swallow-tailed coat.

co-au•thor |kō ô'thər| *or* |kō'ô'-| *n.* One of two or more people who work together in writing a book.

coax |kōks| *v.* **1.** To persuade or try to persuade by gentle urging: *He coaxed the monkey into the cage.* **2.** To obtain by such persuasion: *coax a smile from a girl.*

co•ax•i•al cable |kō ăk'sē əl|. A cable composed of two electrical conductors one of which surrounds the other, the two being separated by an insulator. Cables of this type are used to carry telephone, telegraph, and television signals.

cob |kŏb| *n.* **1.** The long, hard central part of an ear of corn; a corncob. **2.** A male swan. **3.** A stocky, short-legged horse.

co•balt |kō'bôlt'| *n.* Symbol **Co** One of the elements, a hard, brittle metal that resembles nickel and iron in appearance. Atomic number 27; atomic weight 58.93; valences +2, +3; melting point 1,495°C; boiling point 2,900°C.

cobalt 60. A radioactive isotope of cobalt having a mass number of 60. It is an intense source of gamma rays and is used in medicine and industry.

cobalt blue. A blue to green pigment consisting of a mixture of cobalt oxide and aluminum oxide.

cob•ble |kŏb'əl| *n.* A cobblestone. —*v.* **cob•bled, cob•bling.** To pave with cobblestones. —**cob'bled** *adj.*: *narrow cobbled streets.*

cob•bler[1] |kŏb'lər| *n.* A shoemaker.

cob•bler[2] |kŏb'lər| *n.* A fruit pie topped with a biscuit crust and baked in a deep dish.

cob•ble•stone |kŏb'əl stōn'| *n.* A naturally rounded stone formerly much used for paving streets.

co•bra |kō'brə| *n.* **1.** A poisonous Asian or African snake that can spread out the skin of its neck to form a flattened hood. **2.** Leather made from the skin of a cobra. [SEE PICTURE]

cob•web |kŏb'wĕb'| *n.* A web spun by a spider or a strand of such a web.

co•ca |kō'kə| *n.* A South American tree or shrub whose leaves contain cocaine and similar substances.

co•caine, also **co•cain** |kō kān'| *or* |kō'kān'| *n.* An alkaloid extracted from the leaves of the coca plant. It is composed of carbon, hydrogen, nitrogen, and oxygen in the proportions $C_{17}H_{21}NO_4$. It is a powerful, habit-forming narcotic, and is sometimes used as a local anesthetic.

coc•cus |kŏk'əs| *n., pl.* **coc•ci** |kŏk'sī'|. Any of various bacteria with a spherical shape.

coc•cyx |kŏk'sĭks| *n., pl.* **coc•cy•ges** |kŏk sī'jēz| *or* |kŏk'sə jēz'|. A small bone found, in human beings, at the base of the spinal column.

coch•i•neal |kŏch'ə nēl'| *or* |kŏch'ə nēl'| *n.* A bright-red dye made from the dried bodies of a tropical American insect.

coch•le•a |kŏk'lē ə| *n., pl.* **coch•le•ae** |kŏk'lē-ē'|. A spiral tube of the inner ear that resembles a snail shell. It contains the nerve endings necessary for hearing.

cock[1] |kŏk| *n.* **1.** A full-grown male chicken; a rooster. **2.** Any male bird. **3.** A faucet or valve for regulating the flow of a liquid or gas. **4. a.** The hammer of a gun. **b.** Its position when drawn back for firing. —*v.* **1.** To set the hammer of (a gun) in firing position. **2.** To draw back into a taut position in order to release suddenly: *cock the shutter on a camera. The pitcher cocked his arm back and fired the ball.* **3.** To tilt or turn up to one side: *cock one's hat.* [SEE NOTE]

cock[2] |kŏk| *n.* A cone-shaped pile of straw or hay. [SEE NOTE]

cock•ade |kŏ kād'| *n.* A rosette or knot of ribbon usually worn on the hat as a badge.

cock-a-doo•dle-doo |kŏk'ə dōōd'l dōō'| *interj.* A word used to imitate the loud, shrill cry of a crowing rooster.

cock-and-bull story |kŏk'ən bŏŏl'|. An absurd or highly improbable tale.

cock•a•too |kŏk'ə tōō'| *or* |kŏk'ə tōō'| *n.* An Australian parrot with a crested head. [SEE PICTURE]

cock•a•trice |kŏk'ə trĭs| *n.* A mythical serpent supposed to have the power of killing by its glance.

cocked hat. A three-cornered hat with the brim turned up.

cock•er•el |kŏk'ər əl| *n.* A young rooster.

cock•er spaniel |kŏk'ər|. A dog with long, drooping ears and a silky coat.

cock-eyed |kŏk'īd'| *adj.* **1.** Cross-eyed. **2.**

Slang. Crooked; askew. **3.** *Slang.* Ridiculous; absurd.

cock•fight |**kŏk'**fīt'| *n.* A fight, on the outcome of which bets are placed, between two cocks with metal spurs attached to their legs.

cock•le |**kŏk'**əl| *n.* A soft-bodied sea animal having a pair of heart-shaped shells with narrow, riblike markings.

cock•le•bur |**kŏk'**əl bûr'| *n.* **1.** A coarse, weedy plant with prickly burs. **2.** The bur of such a plant.

cock•le•shell |**kŏk'**əl shĕl'| *n.* **1.** A shell of a cockle. **2.** A small, light, fragile boat. [SEE PICTURE]

cock•ney |**kŏk'**nē| *n., pl.* **cock•neys.** Often **Cockney.** The distinctive dialect or accent of the cockneys, people who are natives or inhabitants of a certain section of London. —*adj.* Of cockney or the cockneys.

cock•pit |**kŏk'**pĭt'| *n.* The part of an airplane where the pilot and copilot sit.

cock•roach |**kŏk'**rōch'| *n.* A flat-bodied brownish insect that is often a pest in homes.

cocks•comb |**kŏks'**kōm'| *n.* **1.** The fleshy comb on the head of a rooster. **2.** A jester's cap, topped with a strip of red cloth notched like a rooster's crest. **3.** A garden plant with dense, featherlike clusters of flowers.

cock•sure |**kŏk'**shŏŏr'| *adj.* Completely sure, especially too sure of oneself. —**cock'sure'ly** *adv.*

cock•tail |**kŏk'**tāl'| *n.* **1.** A mixed alcoholic drink containing whisky, gin, vodka, etc., combined with other liquors and sometimes fruit juices. **2.** An appetizer of seafood or fruit: *a shrimp cocktail.* —**modifier:** *a cocktail glass.*

cock•y |**kŏk'**ē| *adj.* **cock•i•er, cock•i•est.** Too sure of oneself; arrogant; conceited. —**cock'i•ly** *adv.* —**cock'i•ness** *n.*

co•coa |**kō'**kō'| *n.* **1.** A powder made from roasted ground cacao seeds from which much of the fat has been removed. **2.** A sweet drink made with cocoa and milk or water. [SEE NOTE on p. 161]

cocoa butter. A yellowish, waxy solid obtained from cacao seeds and used in making soap, cosmetics, and confections.

co•co•nut, also **co•coa•nut** |**kō'**kə nŭt'| *or* |-nət| *n.* The large, hard-shelled nut of a tropical palm tree, the **coconut palm,** having sweet white meat and a hollow center filled with a cloudy liquid called **coconut milk.** [SEE PICTURE; SEE NOTE on p.161]

co•coon |kə **kōōn'**| *n.* A caselike covering of silky strands spun by the larva of a moth or other insect as protection during its pupal, or inactive, stage.

co•co palm |**kō'**kō|. The coconut palm. See **coconut.**

cod |kŏd| *n., pl.* **cod** or **cods.** An ocean fish caught in large numbers as food.

C.O.D. cash on delivery.

Cod, Cape |kŏd|. A peninsula of southeastern Massachusetts extending into the Atlantic.

co•da |**kō'**də| *n.* A passage that ends a musical movement or composition.

cod•dle |**kŏd'**l| *v.* **cod•dled, cod•dling. 1.** To cook in water just below the boiling point. **2.** To treat tenderly; pamper; baby.

code |kōd| *n.* **1.** A system of signals used to represent the letters and numerals in a message that is to be transmitted: *a telegraphic code.* **2.** A system of words, symbols, or letters given arbitrary meanings, usually used to keep messages secret. **3.** Any system of numbers used to represent a geographic area, as a Zip Code. **4.** A systematically arranged collection of laws or rules and regulations: *a building code; a military code.* —*v.* **cod•ed, cod•ing.** To put (a text, numbers, etc.) into a code.

co•deine |**kō'**dēn'| *n.* An alkaloid derived from opium or morphine and composed of carbon, hydrogen, nitrogen, and oxygen in the proportions $C_{18}H_{21}NO_3$. It is used to promote sleep and to relieve coughing and pain.

cod•fish |**kŏd'**fĭsh'| *n., pl.* **cod•fish** or **cod•fish•es. 1.** A cod. **2.** The flesh of a cod, used as food. —**modifier:** *codfish cakes.*

codg•er |**kŏj'**ər| *n. Informal.* An odd or somewhat eccentric old man.

cod•i•cil |**kŏd'**ĭ səl| *n.* A supplement or appendix to a will.

cod•i•fy |**kŏd'**ə fī'| *or* |**kō'**də-| *v.* **cod•i•fied, cod•i•fy•ing, cod•i•fies.** To arrange (laws) into a code. —**cod'i•fi•ca'tion** *n.* —**cod'i•fi'er** *n.*

cod•ling moth |**kŏd'**lĭng|. A small moth whose caterpillars feed on and damage apples and other fruits.

cod-liv•er oil |**kŏd'**lĭv'ər|. An oil rich in vitamins A and D, obtained from the livers of cod.

Co•dy |**kō'**dē|, **William Frederick.** Known as "Buffalo Bill." 1846–1917. American frontiersman, scout, and showman.

co-ed or **co•ed** |**kō'**ĕd'| *n. Informal.* A girl student at a co-educational college. —*adj.* Coeducational: *a co-ed school.*

co-ed•u•ca•tion or **co•ed•u•ca•tion** |kō'ĕj-ōō **kā'**shən| *n.* The system whereby boys and girls attend the same school and the same classes. —**co'-ed•u•ca'tion•al** or **co'ed•u•ca'tion•al** *adj.*

co•ef•fi•cient |kō'ə **fĭsh'**ənt| *n.* A number by which another number or an algebraic term is multiplied; a factor.

coefficient of expansion. A number that indicates the amount that a unit of a substance expands for a given change in temperature. For example, a substance that has a coefficient of linear expansion of 0.01 per degree C would become 1 per cent longer when raised to a temperature 1°C above some temperature that is chosen as a reference.

coe•la•canth |**sē'**lə kănth'| *n.* A fish believed to have been extinct for millions of years, and known only from fossil remains until a living specimen was caught off the coast of southern Africa in 1938. [SEE PICTURE]

coe•len•ter•ate |sĭ **lĕn'**tə rāt'| *or* |-tər ĭt| *n.* Any of a large group of simple animals with a hollow cuplike or tubelike body, as a hydra, jellyfish, sea anemone, or coral.

co•erce |kō **ûrs'**| *v.* **co•erced, co•erc•ing.** To force or compel into doing something by pressure, threats, or intimidation. —**co•er'cion** |kō-**ûr'**shən| *n.*

co•er•cive |kō **ûr'**sĭv| *adj.* Tending to coerce: *coercive measures.*

co•ex•ist |kō'ĭg **zĭst'**| *v.* To live or exist together, at the same time, or in the same place.

cockleshell
Eastern North America

coconut palm

coelacanth

co•ex•ist•ence |kō′ĭg **zĭs′**təns| *n.* **1.** The state of existing together. **2.** The state of living together in peace despite conflicting political systems or ideologies.

co•ex•ten•sive |kō′ĭk **stĕn′**sĭv| *adj.* Occupying the same space; having the same limits or boundaries: *Washington D.C. is coextensive with the District of Columbia.*

cof•fee |**kô**′fē| *or* |**kŏf′**ē| *n.* **1.** A brown drink prepared from the ground, beanlike seeds of a tropical tree. **2.** The whole or ground seeds of this tree. **3.** Often **coffee tree.** A tree that bears such seeds. **4.** A dark or yellowish brown. —*modifier: a coffee cup.* —*adj.* Dark or yellowish brown. [SEE PICTURE]

coffee

coffee cake. A cake to be eaten with coffee, often containing nuts and raisins and covered with sugar or icing.

coffee house. A restaurant where coffee and other refreshments are served.

cof•fee•pot |**kô**′fē pŏt′| *or* |**kŏf′**ē-| *n.* A covered pot with a handle and spout, for making and pouring coffee.

coffee shop. A small restaurant in which light meals are served.

coffee table. A long, low table, often placed in front of a sofa.

cof•fer |**kô′**fər| *or* |**kŏf′**ər| *n.* **1.** A strongbox for holding money. **2. coffers.** A treasury, as of a nation; financial resources: *The king's coffers were exhausted.* [SEE PICTURE]

coffer
Coffer of the type used to carry gold bullion and other valuables by stagecoach in the American West

cof•fer•dam |**kô′**fər dăm′| *or* |**kŏf′**ər-| *n.* **1.** A temporary enclosure built in the water and pumped dry to allow construction work on the bottom of a river, harbor, etc. **2.** A watertight chamber attached to the side of a ship for making repairs below the water line.

cof•fin |**kô′**fĭn| *or* |**kŏf′**ĭn| *n.* A box in which a dead person is buried.

cog |kŏg| *n.* **1.** Any one of a series of teeth or notches on the rim of a wheel that can mesh with similar notches on another wheel and allow motion to be transmitted from one wheel to the other. **2.** A cogwheel.

co•gent |**kō′**jənt| *adj.* Forceful and convincing: *a cogent presentation of the facts.* —**co′gen•cy** |**kō′**jən sē| *n.* —**co′gent•ly** *adv.*

cog•i•tate |**kŏj′**ĭ tāt′| *v.* **cog•i•tat•ed, cog•i•tat•ing.** To think carefully; reflect; ponder. —**cog′i•ta′tion** *n.*

co•gnac |**kōn′**yăk′| *or* |**kŏn′**-| *n.* A fine brandy originally made in the region of Cognac, a town in western France. —*modifier: a cognac bottle.*

cog•nate |**kŏg′**nāt′| *adj.* Descended from a common source: *French and Spanish are cognate languages.* —*n.* A thing, especially a word, related to another: *The English word "hound" and the German word "Hund" are cognates.*

cog•ni•tion |kŏg **nĭsh′**ən| *n.* The mental process or faculty by which knowledge is acquired.

cog•ni•zance |**kŏg′**nĭ zəns| *n.* **1.** Knowledge or awareness: *He had no cognizance of the situation.* **2.** Ability to understand: *facts that are beyond the cognizance of most children.*

cog•ni•zant |**kŏg′**nĭ zənt| *adj.* Aware; conscious: *I am cognizant of the problem.*

cog•wheel |**kŏg′**hwēl′| *or* |-wēl′| *n.* A wheel with cogs or teeth in its rim that mesh with those of another wheel to transmit or receive motion.

co•hab•it |kō **hăb′**ĭt| *v.* To live together as man and wife. —**co•hab′i•ta′tion** *n.*

co•here |kō **hîr′**| *v.* **co•hered, co•her•ing.** To stick or hold together in a mass, as mud or wet sand does.

co•her•ent |kō **hîr′**ənt| *adj.* **1.** Sticking together: *coherent particles.* **2.** Logically connected; easy to understand: *coherent speech.* **3.** Composed of waves that oscillate in a fixed, orderly way: *the coherent light of a laser.* —**co•her′ence, co•her′en•cy** *n.* —**co•her′ent•ly** *adv.*

co•he•sion |kō **hē′**zhən| *n.* **1.** The force of attraction that holds the parts of a body together. **2.** The condition of cohering; a tendency to stick together; unity: *Repeated wars strengthen the remarkable cohesion of the German nation.*

co•he•sive |kō **hē′**sĭv| *adj.* **1.** Tending to cohere; sticking together: *the cohesive nature of water.* **2.** Producing cohesion: *cohesive forces.* —**co•he′sive•ly** *adv.* —**co•he′sive•ness** *n.*

co•hort |**kō′**hôrt′| *n.* **1.** In ancient Rome, one of the divisions of a legion. **2.** A companion or associate.

coif |koif| *n.* **1.** A hoodlike cap that fits closely on the head, as one worn under a nun's veil. **2.** A skullcap, such as one worn under a knight's helmet or an English lawyer's wig.

coif•fure |kwä **fyo͝or′**| *n.* A woman's hair style; hairdo.

coil |koil| *n.* **1.** Anything made by winding something long and flexible around a center or an axis a number of times: *a coil of rope.* **2.** One of such a series of windings or turns. **3.** An electrical device consisting of a number of such turns of insulated wire, used as an electromagnet or to store energy in the form of a magnetic field. —*v.* To wind into a coil or a shape like that of a coil.

coin |koin| *n.* A piece of metal, usually flat and round, issued by a government for use as money. —*v.* **1.** To make (coins) from metal; mint; strike: *coin silver dollars.* **2.** To make coins from (metal): *coin gold.* **3.** To invent (a word or phrase). ¶*These sound alike* **coin, quoin.**

coin•age |**koi′**nĭj| *n.* **1.** The process of making coins: *the coinage of silver.* **2.** Metal coins in general. **3. a.** A coined word or phrase: *The word "seabed" is a new coinage.* **b.** The invention of new words: *"Seabed" is of recent coinage.*

co•in•cide |kō′ĭn **sīd′**| *v.* **co•in•cid•ed, co•in•cid•ing. 1.** To be in the same position in space at the same time: *Points A and B coincide.* **2.** To correspond exactly; be identical. **3.** To occur at the same time or during the same period of time: *Our birthdays coincide.*

co•in•ci•dence |kō **ĭn′**sĭ dəns| *n.* **1.** A combination of events or circumstances that, though accidental, is so remarkable that it seems to have been planned or arranged: *By a strange coincidence, John Adams and Thomas Jefferson both died on the 50th anniversary of the signing of the Declaration of Independence.* **2.** The condition of occupying the same point in space or time: *a curious coincidence of events.*

co•in•ci•dent |kō **ĭn′**sĭ dənt| *adj.* Matching point for point; coinciding: *coincident circles.*

co•in•ci•den•tal |kō ĭn′sĭ **dĕn′**tl| *adj.* Occurring as or resulting from coincidence. —**co•in′ci•den′tal•ly** *adv.*

ă pat/ā pay/â care/ä father/ĕ pet/ ē be/ĭ pit/ī pie/î fierce/ŏ pot/ ō go/ô paw, for/oi oil/o͝o book/ o͞o boot/ou out/ŭ cut/û fur/ *th* the/th thin/hw which/zh vision/ ə ago, item, pencil, atom, circus

coke |kōk| *n.* The solid material, chiefly carbon, that remains after the coal gas and coal tar have been removed from bituminous coal by heat. It is used as a fuel and in making steel.

cok•ing coal |**kō′**kĭng|. Any bituminous coal that is suitable for conversion into coke.

Col. **1.** colonel. **2.** Colorado (unofficial).

co•la[1] |**kō′**lə| *n.* A carbonated drink made with an extract from the nuts of a tropical tree.

co•la[2] |**kō′**lə| *n.* A plural of **colon** (intestine).

col•an•der |**kŭl′**ən dər| *or* |**kŏl′**-| *n.* A bowl-shaped kitchen utensil with holes in the bottom, used for draining off liquids from foods. [SEE PICTURE]

cold |kōld| *adj.* **cold•er, cold•est.** **1.** Having a low temperature: *cold air; cold water; a cold day.* **2. a.** At a lower temperature than normal or desirable: *cold hands and feet.* **b.** Feeling no warmth; chilled: *I am cold.* **3.** Not cordial or friendly: *a cold person; a cold reception.* **4.** *Informal.* In games, still far from an object being sought. **5.** *Informal.* Unconscious: *The blow knocked him cold.* —*adv. Informal.* **1.** Completely; thoroughly; absolutely: *cold sober. He turned me down cold. He was stopped cold on the 40-yard line.* **2.** Without preparation or prior notice: *He entered the game cold.* —*n.* **1. a.** A relative lack of heat. **b.** The feeling caused by this. **2.** A common virus infection in which the respiratory tract becomes inflamed, often with accompanying fever, chills, coughing, and sneezing. —**cold′ly** *adv.* —**cold′ness** *n.*

Idioms. **get** (or **have**) **cold feet.** To lack courage; be or become timid or fearful. **in cold blood.** Without feeling or regret. **out in the cold.** Neglected; abandoned; ignored. **throw cold water on.** To dampen enthusiasm for.

cold-blood•ed |**kōld′blŭd′**ĭd| *adj.* **1.** Having a body temperature that changes according to the temperature of the surroundings. Fish, frogs, and reptiles are cold-blooded. **2. a.** Having no feeling or emotion: *a cold-blooded killer.* **b.** Done without feeling or emotion: *a cold-blooded murder.* —**cold′-blood′ed•ly** *adv.*

cold cream. A creamy cosmetic for cleansing and softening the skin.

cold cuts. Slices of assorted cold meats.

cold front. The forward edge of a mass of cold atmospheric air that moves toward and finally replaces a mass of warm air.

cold-heart•ed |**kōld′här′**tĭd| *adj.* Lacking sympathy or feeling; callous. —**cold′-heart′ed•ly** *adv.* —**cold′-heart′ed•ness** *n.*

cold shoulder. *Informal.* Deliberate coldness or disregard; a snub.

cold sore. A small sore on the lips that often accompanies a fever or cold.

cold storage. The storage of food, furs, etc., in a refrigerated place.

cold war. Intense and hostile rivalry between nations, stopping just short of direct military conflict, especially as it existed between the Communist and non-Communist blocs after World War II.

cold wave. A time during which the weather is unusually cold.

cole•slaw |**kōl′**slô′| *n.* Also **cole slaw.** A salad of shredded raw cabbage with a dressing. [SEE NOTE]

co•le•us |**kō′**lē əs| *n., pl.* **co•le•us•es.** A plant grown for its colorful leaves, which are often marked with red, purple, or yellow.

col•ic |**kŏl′**ĭk| *n.* A sharp, severe pain or cramp in the abdomen.

col•i•se•um |kŏl′ĭ **sē′**əm| *n.* A large stadium or hall for sports events, exhibitions, etc.

co•li•tis |kō **lī′**tĭs| *or* |kə-| *n.* An inflammation of the mucous membrane that lines the colon.

col•lab•o•rate |kə **lăb′**ə rāt′| *v.* **col•lab•o•rat•ed, col•lab•o•rat•ing.** **1.** To work together on a project: *The two friends collaborated on the final script for the show.* **2.** To cooperate with an enemy that has invaded one's country. —**col•lab′o•ra′tion** *n.*

col•lab•o•ra•tor |kə **lăb′**ə rā′tər| *n.* **1.** A person who collaborates on a project. **2.** A person who collaborates with enemy invaders.

col•lage |kō **läzh′**| *or* |kə-| *n.* An artistic composition made by pasting various materials or objects onto a surface in a seemingly random or haphazard manner.

col•la•gen |**kŏl′**ə jən| *n.* A tough, fibrous protein found in bone, cartilage, and connective tissue.

col•lapse |kə **lăps′**| *v.* **col•lapsed, col•laps•ing.** **1.** To fall down or inward suddenly; cave in: *Part of the roof collapsed under the weight of the snow.* **2.** To break down or fail suddenly and completely: *collapse from overwork. The Russian monarchy collapsed in 1917.* **3.** To fold together compactly: *This chair collapses very easily.* **4.** To reduce to the main points; present briefly: *His résumé can be collapsed into a few sentences.* —*n.* **1.** The act of or an example of collapsing: *the collapse of the building; the collapse of negotiations.* **2.** A sudden and complete loss of strength or stamina; a breakdown: *He was in a state of collapse.*

col•laps•i•ble |kə **lăp′**sə bəl| *adj.* Capable of being collapsed or folded compactly: *a collapsible tent.*

col•lar |**kŏl′**ər| *n.* **1.** The part of a shirt, coat, or dress that stands up or folds down around the neck. **2.** A separate band for the neck, as one of lace, linen, or jewels. **3.** A leather or metal band put around the neck of an animal, such as a dog. **4.** The part of a harness that fits around a horse's neck and over its shoulders. **5.** A band or marking resembling a collar. **6.** Any one of many ringlike machine parts. —*v. Informal.* To catch and hold as if by the collar; capture; arrest. ¶*These sound alike* **collar, choler.** —**col′lar•less** *adj.* [SEE PICTURE]

col•lar•bone |**kŏl′**ər bōn′| *n.* A bone that connects the breastbone and the shoulder blade; the clavicle.

col•lard |**kŏl′**ərd| *n.* Often **collards.** A leafy cabbagelike vegetable. ¶*These sound alike* **collard, collared.**

col•lared |**kŏl′**ərd| *adj.* Having a collarlike part or marking: *a collared lizard.* ¶*These sound alike* **collared, collard.**

col•late |kə **lāt′**| *or* |kō-| *or* |**kŏl′**āt′| *v.* **col•lat•ed, col•lat•ing.** To examine and compare carefully (copies of texts, books, etc.) in order to discover differences between them: *collate a guest list; collate a revised edition with the original manuscript.* —**col•la′tion** *n.*

col•lat•er•al |kə **lăt′**ər əl| *adj.* **1.** Situated or

colander

coleslaw

Coleslaw *is from Dutch* koolsla, *"cabbage salad":* kool, *"cabbage,"* + sla, *"salad." In English, it is often pronounced* cold slaw, *since it is after all a cold dish. This kind of alteration is a classic example of "folk etymology."*

collar
Masai woman

running side by side; parallel. **2.** Additional; secondary; supporting: *collateral evidence; a collateral purpose of the expedition.* **3.** Guaranteed by something pledged: *a collateral loan.* —*n.* Something pledged as security for a loan.

col•league |kŏl′ēg′| *n.* A fellow member of a profession, staff, or organization; an associate.

col•lect |kə lĕkt′| *v.* **1.** To bring or come together in a group; gather; accumulate: *He collected firewood. Sharks often collect in blood-stained water.* **2.** To pick up and take away: *collect garbage.* **3.** To accumulate as a hobby or for study: *collect stamps; collect information.* **4.** To obtain payment of: *came to collect five dollars.* **5.** To recover control of: *trying to collect herself after the accident. He collected his senses.* —*adj.* With payment to be made by the receiver: *a collect call.* —*adv.* So that the receiver is charged: *He called his parents collect.* —**col•lect′i•ble, col•lect′a•ble** *adj.*

col•lect•ed |kə lĕk′tĭd| *adj.* **1.** In full control of oneself; composed; calm. **2.** Gathered together: *the collected works of Shakespeare.* —**col•lect′ed•ly** *adv.* —**col•lect′ed•ness** *n.*

col•lec•tion |kə lĕk′shən| *n.* **1.** The act or process of collecting. **2.** A group of things brought or kept together for study or use or as a hobby: *a collection of paintings; a collection of folk songs; a coin collection.* **3.** An accumulation; deposit: *the collection of grime in the motor.* **4. a.** The act of seeking and taking up money: *the collection in a church service.* **b.** The amount taken.

col•lec•tive |kə lĕk′tĭv| *adj.* **1.** Formed by collecting; assembled or accumulated into a whole: *the collective accomplishments of the past.* **2.** Of a number of persons or nations considered or acting as one: *the collective opinion of the committee; our collective security.* —*n.* **1.** A business or undertaking set up on the principle of ownership and control of the means of production and distribution by the workers involved, usually under the supervision of a government. **2.** A **collective noun.** —**col•lec′tive•ly** *adv.*

collective bargaining. Negotiation between an employer or group of employers and workers organized and acting as a body.

collective farm. A farm or a group of farms managed and worked by a group of laborers under the supervision of a government.

collective noun. A noun that names a collection of persons or things regarded as a unit. [SEE NOTE]

collective noun

A **collective noun** *takes a singular verb when it refers to the collection as a whole and a plural verb when it refers to the members of the collection as separate persons or things:* The orchestra was playing. The orchestra have all gone home. *A collective noun should not be treated as both singular and plural in the same construction:* The family is determined to press its (*not* their) claim.

col•lec•tiv•ism |kə lĕk′tə vĭz′əm| *n.* A system under which the ownership and control of the means of producing and distributing goods is in the hands of the people as a group or whole. —**col•lec′tiv•ist** *adj. & n.*

col•lec•tiv•ize |kə lĕk′tə vīz′| *v.* **col•lec•tiv•ized, col•lec•tiv•iz•ing.** To organize (an economy, industry, or business) on the basis of collectivism. —**col•lec′tiv•i•za′tion** *n.*

col•lec•tor |kə lĕk′tər| *n.* **1.** Someone or something that collects: *a garbage collector; a coin collector; a tax collector; a lint collector in a machine.* **2.** The terminal of a transistor that corresponds to the plate of a vacuum tube.

col•leen |kŏl′ēn′| *or* |kŏ lēn′| *n.* An Irish girl.

col•lege |kŏl′ĭj| *n.* **1.** A school of higher learning, entered after high school, that grants a bachelor's degree. **2.** A division within a university. **3.** A school for special study, often connected with a university: *teachers college.* **4.** A body of persons having a common purpose, duties, or profession: *a college of surgeons; the electoral college.* —**modifier:** *a college professor; college education.*

col•le•gian |kə lē′jən| *or* |-jē ən| *n.* A college student.

col•le•giate |kə lē′jĭt| *or* |-jē ĭt| *adj.* Of or suited to a college or college students: *collegiate activities; his collegiate days.*

collegiate church. **1.** A church other than a cathedral having a chapter of canons. **2.** A church associated with other churches under a common body of pastors.

col•lide |kə līd′| *v.* **col•lid•ed, col•lid•ing.** **1.** To strike or bump together with violent, direct impact: *The planes collided in midair.* **2.** To disagree strongly; clash: *Many Presidents have collided with the Senate over foreign policy.*

col•lie |kŏl′ē| *n.* A large dog with long hair and a narrow snout, originally used in Scotland to herd sheep. [SEE PICTURE]

collie

col•lier |kŏl′yər| *n. British.* **1.** A coal miner. **2.** A coal ship.

col•lier•y |kŏl′yə rē| *n., pl.* **col•lier•ies.** *British.* A coal mine.

col•li•sion |kə lĭzh′ən| *n.* **1.** The act or process of colliding; a bumping together; a crash. **2.** A clash of ideas or interests; a conflict.

col•lo•cate |kŏl′ə kāt′| *v.* **col•lo•cat•ed, col•lo•cat•ing.** To place together or in proper order; arrange. —**col′lo•ca′tion** *n.*

col•lo•di•on |kə lō′dē ən| *n.* A very flammable solution of nitrocellulose in alcohol and ether used to hold surgical dressings, as a coating for the skin, and in making photographic plates.

col•lo•di•um |kə lō′dē əm| *n.* A form of the word **collodion.**

col•loid |kŏl′oid′| *n.* A system composed of a large number of tiny particles suspended in a gas, liquid, or solid, usually remaining suspended for long periods of time. Paints, gelatins, and fogs are systems of this kind. —*adj.* Of a colloid.

col•loi•dal |kə loid′l| *adj.* Of a colloid.

col•lo•qui•al |kə lō′kwē əl| *adj.* Used in or suitable to spoken language or to writing that seeks the effect of speech; not formal. —**col•lo′qui•al•ly** *adv.*

col•lo•qui•al•ism |kə lō′kwē ə lĭz′əm| *n.* **1.** Colloquial style or quality. **2.** A colloquial expression; for example, *I'm still in there pitching* is a colloquialism.

col•lo•quy |kŏl′ə kwē| *n., pl.* **col•lo•quies.** A conversation, especially a formal one.

col•lu•sion |kə lo͞o′zhən| *n.* Secret agreement between two or more persons seeking to deceive or cheat another or others. —**col•lu′sive** |kə-lo͞o′sĭv| *adj.*

Colo. Colorado.

co•logne |kə lōn′| *n.* A scented liquid made of alcohol and fragrant oils.

Co•logne |kə lōn′|. A city in West Germany, on the Rhine River. Population, 850,000.

Co•lom•bi•a |kə lŭm′bē ə|. A country on the northwestern coast of South America. Population, 23,952,000. Capital, Bogotá. —**Co•lom′bi•an** *adj. & n.*

ă **pat**/ā **pay**/â **care**/ä **father**/ĕ **pet**/ ē **be**/ĭ **pit**/ī **pie**/î **fierce**/ŏ **pot**/ ō **go**/ô **paw**, **for**/oi **oil**/o͝o **book**/ o͞o **boot**/ou **out**/ŭ **cut**/û **fur**/ *th* **the**/th **thin**/hw **which**/zh **vision**/ ə **ago**, **item**, **pencil**, **atom**, **circus**

Co•lom•bo |kə lŭm′bō|. The capital and largest city of Sri Lanka. Population, 852,000.

co•lon¹ |kō′lən| *n.* **1.** A punctuation mark (:) used after a word introducing a quotation, explanation, example, or series. **2.** The sign (:) used between numbers or groups of numbers in expressions of time (2:30 a.m.) and ratios (1:2). [SEE NOTE]

co•lon² |kō′lən| *n.* The main part of the large intestine. [SEE NOTE]

co•lon³ |kō lōn′| *n.* **1.** The basic unit of money of Costa Rica. **2.** The basic unit of money of El Salvador. [SEE NOTE]

colo•nel |kûr′nəl| *n.* An officer in the U.S. Army, Air Force, or Marine Corps ranking below a brigadier general. A **lieutenant colonel** ranks below a colonel. ¶*These sound alike* **colonel, kernel.** [SEE NOTE]

co•lo•ni•al |kə lō′nē əl| *adj.* **1.** Of or possessing colonies: *colonial rule. France and England were colonial powers.* **2.** Often **Colonial.** Of the 13 original American colonies: *the colonial period; in colonial times.* **3.** Often **Colonial.** Of the style of architecture often found in the American colonies. **4.** Living in, forming, or consisting of a colony: *colonial organisms.* —*n.* A person who lives in a colony. —**co•lo′ni•al•ly** *adv.*

co•lo•ni•al•ism |kə lō′nē ə lĭz′əm| *n.* A governmental policy of acquiring or maintaining foreign territory as colonies.

co•lo•ni•al•ist |kə lō′nē ə lĭst| *n.* A person who advocates colonialism. —***modifier:*** *a colonialist policy.*

col•o•nist |kŏl′ə nĭst| *n.* **1.** An original settler or founder of a colony. **2.** A person who lives in a colony.

col•o•nize |kŏl′ə nīz′| *v.* **col•o•nized, col•o•niz•ing.** To establish or establish in a colony: *Norwegian Vikings originally colonized Iceland.* —**col′o•ni•za′tion** *n.* —**col′o•niz′er** *n.*

col•on•nade |kŏl′ə nād′| *n.* A series of columns placed at regular intervals.

col•o•ny |kŏl′ə nē| *n., pl.* **col•o•nies. 1.** A group of people who settle in a distant land but remain subject to their native country: *The English Pilgrims founded the Plymouth Colony.* **2.** A territory ruled by a distant power. **3.** A group of people of the same nationality, religion, interests, etc., living together in one area: *the American colony in Paris.* **4.** A group of the same kind of animals, plants, or one-celled organisms living or growing together in close association: *a colony of ants; a colony of bacteria.* **5. the Colonies.** The 13 British colonies that became the original United States of America and that included Connecticut, Delaware, Georgia, Maryland, Massachusetts, New Hampshire, New Jersey, New York, North Carolina, Pennsylvania, Rhode Island, South Carolina, and Virginia.

col•or |kŭl′ər| *n.* **1.** The property by which the sense of vision can distinguish things, such as a red rose and a yellow rose, that are alike in size, shape, and texture. The color of a thing depends mainly on the wavelengths of the light that it emits, reflects, or transmits. **2.** A dye, pigment, paint, or other coloring substance. **3.** The general appearance of the skin; complexion: *Ill health made her color poor.* **4.** The complexion of a person not classed as a Caucasoid, especially that of a Negro: *discrimination based on color.* **5. colors.** A flag or banner, as of a country or military unit. **6.** Vivid and interesting detail, as of a scene or its description in writing: *the abundant color of a bullfighting ring.* **7.** Traits of personality or behavior that appeal to the eye or mind: *a political figure with a great deal of color.* **8.** Musical tone color; timbre. —***modifier:*** *color photography; color television.* —*v.* **1.** To give color to or change the color of. **2.** To take on or change color. **3.** To become red in the face; blush. **4.** To give a distinctive character or quality to. **5.** To influence, especially by distortion or misrepresentation: *Self-interest colored his judgment.*

Idioms. **show (one's) true colors.** To reveal one's actual nature or character. **with flying colors.** With great success.

Col•o•ra•do |kŏl′ə ră′dō| *or* |-răd′ō|. A Rocky Mountain state of the west-central United States. Population, 2,888,834. Capital, Denver. —**Col′o•ra′dan** *adj. & n.*

Colorado River. A river rising in Colorado and flowing through Utah and Arizona into the Pacific between Lower California and Mexico.

col•or•a•tion |kŭl′ə rā′shən| *n.* **1.** Arrangement of colors: *Protective coloration helps some animals to hide from their enemies.* **2.** The sum of the beliefs or principles of a person, group, etc.: *Spain's political coloration caused her to be isolated.*

col•or•a•tu•ra |kŭl′ər ə to͝or′ə| *or* |-tyo͝or′ə| *n.* **1. a.** Complicated ornaments and rapid figures in vocal music. **b.** Music having such ornamentation. **2.** A singer who specializes in the performance of coloratura, especially a high-pitched soprano.

col•or•blind |kŭl′ər blīnd′| *adj.* Partly or completely unable to see differences in color. —**col′or•blind′ness** *n.*

col•or•cast |kŭl′ər kăst′| *or* |-käst′| *v.* **col•or•cast** or **col•or•cast•ed, col•or•cast•ing.** To broadcast (a television program) in color. —*n.* A television program broadcast in color.

col•ored |kŭl′ərd| *adj.* **1.** Having color. **2.** Often **Colored.** Negro or of any ethnic group other than Caucasoid; dark-skinned. The word "colored" is often considered offensive. **3.** Not strictly factual or objective; distorted by prejudice or self-interest.

col•or•ful |kŭl′ər fəl| *adj.* **1.** Full of color or colors: *insects that fly on colorful wings.* **2.** Rich in variety or vivid detail: *a colorful language; a colorful narrative.* **3.** Exciting the senses or the imagination: *colorful ballets; a colorful political style.* —**col′or•ful•ly** *adv.* —**col′or•ful•ness** *n.*

col•or•ing |kŭl′ər ĭng| *n.* **1.** The manner or process of applying color: *laws regulating the coloring of margarine.* **2.** Any substance used to color something: *a food coloring; a hair coloring.* **3.** Appearance with respect to color: *animals protected by their coloring.* —***modifier:*** coloring *matter; a coloring agent.*

col•or•less |kŭl′ər lĭs| *adj.* **1.** Without color: *Most bacteria are colorless.* **2.** Weak in color; pallid: *a frail, colorless invalid.* **3.** Lacking variety or interest; dull: *A story with no description would be colorless.* **4.** Lacking individuality or distinction: *a colorless candidate.* —**col′or•less•ly** *adv.* —**col′or•less•ness** *n.*

colon¹·²·³

Colon¹ *is from Latin* cōlon, *which is from Greek* kōlon, *"limb, piece," hence "clause of a sentence."* **Colon²** *is from Latin* colon, *which is from Greek* kolon, *"large intestine."* **Colon³** *is from Spanish* colón, *after Cristobal* Colón, *the Spanish version of Christopher* Columbus.

colonel

Colonel *comes from French* colonel, *which comes from Italian* colonello, *"commander of a column," from* colonna, *"column (of troops)." The utterly irregular English pronunciation results from the fact that in French the form* colonel /kō lō **nĕl**′/ *had a variant,* coronel /kō rō **nĕl**′/; *and even though this variant died out, it remained the basis of the English pronunciation, in spite of the spelling difference.*

columbine
The name **columbine** comes from Medieval Latin *herba columbina*, "dovelike plant," from *columba*, "dove." The illustration shows how the hanging flower can in fact look like a cluster of doves or pigeons.

comb
Above: Tortoiseshell comb
Below: Comb of a rooster

ă pat/ā pay/â care/ä father/ĕ pet/ ē be/ĭ pit/ī pie/î fierce/ŏ pot/ ō go/ô paw, for/oi oil/o͝o book/ o͞o boot/ou out/ŭ cut/û fur/ *th* the/th thin/hw which/zh vision/ ə ago, item, pencil, atom, circus

color line. A barrier, created by custom, law, or economic differences, that separates nonwhite persons from whites.

co•los•sal |kə lŏs′əl| *adj.* Very great in size, extent, or degree; enormous; gigantic: *colossal statues, many times life-size; a risk requiring colossal self-confidence.* —**co•los′sal•ly** *adv.*

co•los•sus |kə lŏs′əs| *n., pl.* **co•los•si** |kə lŏs′ī′| or **co•los•sus•es.** **1.** A huge statue. **2.** Anything of enormous size or importance.

col•our |kŭl′ər| *n.* & *v.* British form of the word **color.**

colt |kōlt| *n.* A young horse or related animal such as a zebra, especially a male.

colt•ish |kōl′tĭsh| *adj.* **1.** Of a colt. **2.** Like a colt; lively; playful. —**colt′ish•ly** *adv.*

Co•lum•bi•a |kə lŭm′bē ə|. **1.** The capital of South Carolina. Population, 99,296. **2.** A river rising in British Columbia, Canada, and flowing into the Pacific Ocean.

col•um•bine |kŏl′əm bīn′| *n.* Any of several plants with colorful flowers that have five narrow, projecting parts. [SEE PICTURE]

co•lum•bi•um |kə lŭm′bē əm|. Symbol **Cb** Niobium, one of the elements.

Co•lum•bus |kə lŭm′bəs|. The capital of Ohio. Population, 564,871.

Co•lum•bus |kə lŭm′bəs|, **Christopher.** 1451–1506. Italian navigator and explorer; opened the New World to exploration.

Columbus Day. October 12, a holiday celebrated officially on the second Monday in October in honor of Christopher Columbus.

col•umn |kŏl′əm| *n.* **1.** A pillar or upright structure, usually shaped like a cylinder, used in a building as a support or as a decoration. **2.** Anything that resembles a pillar in shape or use: *a column of mercury in a thermometer; the spinal column.* **3.** One of two or more vertical sections of a page, lying side by side but separated from each other, in which lines of print are arranged. **4.** A feature article that appears regularly in a newspaper or magazine. **5.** A formation, as of soldiers or trucks, in which members or rows follow one behind the other.

co•lum•nar |kə lŭm′nər| *adj.* **1.** Having the shape of a column. **2.** Having or constructed with columns.

col•umned |kŏl′əmd| *adj.* Built with or having columns: *a columned porch.*

co•lum•ni•a•tion |kə lŭm′nē ā′shən| *n.* The use or arrangement of columns in a building.

col•um•nist |kŏl′əm nĭst| *or* |-ə mĭst| *n.* A person who writes a column for a newspaper or magazine.

com-. A prefix borrowed from Latin *com-*, meaning "together, with"; **compete** is from Latin *competere,* "to strive together." Before *l* or *r, com-* becomes *col-* or *cor-*. Before vowels, *h,* or *gn,* it is reduced to *co-*. Before all other consonants, except *p, b,* or *m,* it becomes *con-*.

co•ma[1] |kō′mə| *n., pl.* **co•mas.** A state of deep unconsciousness resulting from disease, injury, or poisoning of the brain.

co•ma[2] |kō′mə| *n., pl.* **co•mae** |kō′mē|. The shining cloud that makes up most of the head of a comet.

Co•man•che |kə măn′chē| *n., pl.* **Co•man•che** or **Co•man•ches.** **1.** A North American tribe of Plains Indians now of Oklahoma. **2.** A member of this tribe. **3.** The Uto-Aztecan language of this tribe. —**Co•man′che** *adj.*

co•ma•tose |kō′mə tōs′| *or* |kŏm′ə-| *adj.* **1.** In a state of coma; deeply unconscious. **2.** Of or like a coma: *a comatose trance.*

comb |kōm| *n.* **1.** A thin strip of plastic, bone, or hard rubber, having teeth and used to arrange or fasten the hair. **2.** Something resembling a comb in shape or use, as a card for arranging and cleansing wool. **3.** The brightly colored ridge of flesh on the top of the head of a rooster, hen, or certain other birds. **4.** A honeycomb. —*v.* **1.** To dress or arrange with a comb. **2.** To search thoroughly: *combed many books for information.* [SEE PICTURE]

com•bat |kəm băt′| *or* |kŏm′băt′| *v.* **com•bat•ed** or **com•bat•ted, com•bat•ing** or **com•bat•ting.** To fight or struggle against: *new drugs that combat infection; combat the enemy.* —*n.* |kŏm′băt′|. Armed conflict: *He was killed in combat.* —***modifier:*** *combat boots; a combat unit; combat deaths.*

com•bat•ant |kəm băt′nt| *or* |kŏm′bə tnt| *n.* A person engaged in fighting or combat.

combat fatigue. A usually temporary mental disorder caused by the exhaustion and pressure of combat or similar situations. Its symptoms include anxiety, depression, and irritability.

com•bat•ive |kəm băt′ĭv| *adj.* **1.** Ready or disposed to fight; belligerent. **2.** Requiring or developing physical strength, endurance, etc: *a combative sport.*

comb•er |kō′mər| *n.* **1.** A person or instrument that combs. **2.** A long wave of the sea that has reached its peak or broken into foam.

com•bi•na•tion |kŏm′bə nā′shən| *n.* **1. a.** The act or process of combining. **b.** The condition of being combined. **2.** Something that results from combining two or more things: *An alloy is a combination of metals.* **3.** Any of the subsets that can be selected from a set when the order in which the elements are taken is ignored. **4.** The sequence of numbers or letters that opens a combination lock.

combination lock. A lock that can be opened only by turning the dial with which it is equipped to a particular sequence of positions.

com•bine |kəm bīn′| *v.* **com•bined, com•bin•ing.** **1.** To bring or come together; make or become united; join: *The novel combines an interesting story and a message. Plot and theme combine to form an excellent work.* **2.** To join or cause to join (two or more substances) to make a single substance, such as a chemical compound or an alloy. —*n.* |kŏm′bīn′|. **1.** A power-operated machine that cuts, threshes, and cleans grain. **2.** A group of persons or companies acting together in a business transaction.

combining form. A word element that combines with other word forms to create new words: *under-*, as in *undersell.*

com•bo |kŏm′bō| *n., pl.* **com•bos.** *Informal.* A small group of musicians: *a jazz combo.*

com•bus•ti•bil•i•ty |kəm bŭs′tə bĭl′ĭ tē| *n.* The tendency of a substance to catch fire and burn.

com•bus•ti•ble |kəm bŭs′tə bəl| *adj.* **1.** Capable of catching fire and burning. **2.** Easily aroused or stirred to action; explosive: *his combustible nature; a combustible situation.*

com•bus•tion |kəm bŭs′chən| *n.* **1.** The process of burning. **2.** A chemical reaction, especially a combination with oxygen, that goes on rapidly and produces light and heat.

combustion chamber. An enclosed space, as in an engine, in which a fuel undergoes controlled burning.

Comdr. commander.

Comdt. commandant.

come |kŭm| *v.* **came** |kām|, **come, com•ing. 1.** To advance toward the speaker or toward a place that is indicated; approach. **2.** To reach a particular point; arrive. **3.** To arrive at a particular result or end: *came to an agreement; plans that came to nothing.* **4.** To move toward or arrive at a particular condition: *a job coming along well; came to her wits' end.* **5.** To move or be brought to a particular position: *came to a sudden stop.* **6.** To extend; reach: *water that came to my waist.* **7. a.** To exist at a particular point or place: *The date of birth comes after the name in this listing.* **b.** To rank; have priority: *Your work should come first.* **8.** To happen: *How did she come to be asked?* **9.** To happen as a result; derive; proceed: *This comes of your stubbornness. Success comes from hard work.* **10.** To occur in the mind: *The thought came to her.* **11.** To issue from; descend: *She comes from a good family.* **12.** To be a native or have been a resident of: *Joe comes from Chicago.* **13.** To become: *The catch came open.* **14.** To be available or obtainable: *shoes that come in many styles.* **15.** To prove or turn out to be: *a dream that came true.* —***phrasal verbs.*** **come about.** To occur; take place; happen. **come across. 1.** To meet by chance. **2.** *Slang.* To do or give what is wanted: *came across with my money.* **come around. 1.** To recover; revive. **2.** To change one's opinion or position: *She came around after she heard the whole story.* **come back.** To return to past success after a period of misfortune. **come by.** To acquire; get. **come down. 1.** To lose wealth or position. **2.** To be descended from or handed down by: *a custom that comes down from colonial times.* **3.** To become ill: *came down with a cold.* **come in for.** *Informal.* To receive; get: *His work came in for criticism.* **come into.** To inherit: *Ann came into a small fortune.* **come off. 1.** To happen; occur: *The trip came off on schedule.* **2.** To be found to be; turn out: *a party that came off successfully.* **come out. 1.** To become known: *The whole story came out in the trial.* **2.** To be issued or brought out: *His new book just came out.* **3.** To declare publicly: *He has come out for the tax proposal.* **4.** To make a formal social debut. **5.** To result; end up; turn out. **come to. 1.** To regain consciousness: *He came to in the hospital.* **2.** To amount to: *The bill came to $11.50.* **come up.** To manifest itself; arise: *The question didn't come up.* **come up to.** To equal: *This book doesn't come up to yours.* **come up with.** *Informal.* To propose; produce: *Come up with some new ideas.*

Idiom. **how come?** *Informal.* Why?

come•back |kŭm′băk′| *n.* **1.** A return to former prosperity or high rank. **2.** A reply, especially a quick, witty one; a retort.

co•me•di•an |kə mē′dē ən| *n.* **1.** A professional entertainer who tells jokes or does other things intended to make audiences laugh. **2.** Any person who amuses or tries to be amusing. **3.** An actor in comedy.

co•me•di•enne |kə mē′dē ĕn′| *n.* A female comedian.

come•down |kŭm′doun′| *n.* A decline or drop in status, position, or self-esteem: *Having to accept help from his younger brother was a comedown for him.*

com•e•dy |kŏm′ĭ dē| *n., pl.* **com•e•dies. 1.** A play, motion picture, or other work in which the story and characters are humorous and that ends happily. **2.** The branch of drama made up of such plays. **3.** Anything, such as an occurrence in real life, that resembles a dramatic work of this kind.

comedy of manners. A comedy that ridicules the ways of fashionable society.

come-hith•er |kŭm′hĭ*th*′ər| *adj.* Seductive; alluring; beguiling: *a come-hither look.* —*n.* A seductive or alluring invitation.

come•ly |kŭm′lē| *adj.* **come•li•er, come•li•est.** Having a pleasing appearance; attractive. —**come′li•ness** *n.*

com•er |kŭm′ər| *n.* **1.** Someone or something that arrives or comes. **2.** *Informal.* Someone or something that shows promise of reaching success.

co•mes•ti•ble |kə mĕs′tə bəl| *adj.* Fit to be eaten; edible. —*n.* Anything that can be eaten as a food.

com•et |kŏm′ĭt| *n.* A mass of material that travels around the sun in an immense elongated orbit. When close enough to the sun to be visible, a comet appears characteristically as an object with a glowing head attached to a long, vaporous tail that always points away from the sun. [SEE NOTE & PICTURE]

comet

Comet Alcock, September 1, 1959

Comets *are thought to be composed of frozen water, ammonia, methane, and carbon dioxide, mixed with solid meteoric material. When the comet is close to the sun, a part of the frozen material vaporizes, forming the coma that surrounds the solid material and streaming off into space under the influence of the solar wind to form the tail.*

come•up•pance |kŭm′ŭp′əns| *n. Informal.* Punishment or retribution that one deserves.

com•fort |kŭm′fərt| *v.* To soothe in time of grief or fear; console. —**com′fort•ing** *adj.*: *a comforting thought.* —*n.* **1.** A condition of ease or well-being: *For comfort indoors the temperature should be about 70°.* **2.** Relief in time of grief or fear: *The frightened child held the toy bear for comfort.* **3.** A person that gives relief from grief or worry: *The child was a comfort to me.* **4.** A thing that gives ease or well-being: *comforts such as air conditioning.* **5.** The capacity or ability to give physical ease and well-being: *The comfort of a chair depends on the purpose for which it is intended.*

com•fort•a•ble |kŭmf′tə bəl| *or* |kŭm′fər tə bəl| *adj.* **1.** Giving comfort: *a comfortable home; giving up a comfortable position to become a monk.* **2.** In a state of comfort; at ease in body or mind: *comfortable despite the storm; not comfortable in his company.* —**com′fort•a•ble•ness** *n.* —**com′fort•a•bly** *adv.*

com•fort•er |kŭm′fər tər| *n.* **1.** A person who soothes or consoles. **2.** A thick, warm quilt used as a bed cover.

comfort station. A public toilet or restroom.

com•fy |kŭm′fē| *adj.* **com•fi•er, com•fi•est.** *Informal.* Comfortable.

com•ic |kŏm′ĭk| *adj.* **1.** Of comedy. **2.** Funny; humorous; amusing. —*n.* **1.** A person who is funny or amusing, especially an entertainer. **2.** **comics.** *Informal.* Comic strips.

comic book. A book of comic strips.

comic strip

commensal

Commensal *originally meant "eating at the same table": Latin* com-, *"together,"* + mensa, *"table." A barnacle attached to a whale benefits from the commensal relationship by getting transportation that may help in obtaining food; Spanish moss, a rootless epiphyte, depends on the tree it grows on for secure anchorage.*

ă **pat**/ā **pay**/â **care**/ä **father**/ĕ **pet**/ ē **be**/ĭ **pit**/ī **pie**/î **fierce**/ŏ **pot**/ ō **go**/ô **paw**, **for**/oi **oil**/ŏŏ **book**/ ōō **boot**/ou **out**/ŭ **cut**/û **fur**/ *th* **the**/th **thin**/hw **which**/**zh** vision/ ə **ago**, item, pencil, atom, circus

com•i•cal |kŏm′ĭ kəl| *adj.* Causing amusement or laughter; funny. —**com′i•cal•ly** *adv.* —**com′i•cal•ness** *n.*

comic book. A booklet of comic strips.

comic opera. An opera or operetta with a humorous story, some spoken dialogue, and, usually, a happy ending.

comic strip. A series of cartoons that tells a joke or a story. [SEE PICTURE]

com•ing |kŭm′ĭng| *adj.* **1.** Approaching: *during the coming season.* **2.** *Informal.* Showing promise of fame or success: *a coming man in politics.* —*n.* Arrival: *With the coming of spring, days become longer.*

com•ing-out |kŭm′ĭng out′| *n. Informal.* A social debut. —***modifier:*** *a coming-out party; the coming-out season.*

com•ma |kŏm′ə| *n.* A punctuation mark (,) used to indicate a separation of elements within a sentence.

com•mand |kə mănd′| *or* |-mänd′| *v.* **1.** To direct with authority; give orders to: *Beggars are in no position to command. He commanded me to leave.* **2.** To have control or authority over; rule: *Pershing commanded our overseas army.* **3.** To deserve and receive as due: *large type that commands attention; a statement that commands respect.* **4.** To dominate by position; overlook: *a hill that commands the approach to the city.* —*n.* **1.** An order or direction: *commands that were always clear.* **2.** The possession or exercise of authority to command: *all the strength at his command. The admiral was in command.* **3.** Ability to control or use; mastery: *command of the seas; a command of four languages.* **4. a.** The extent or range of authority of one in command. **b.** The forces and areas under the control of one officer. **c.** A group of officers or officials with authority to command: *the German high command at Stalingrad.* —***modifier:*** *a command performance; the command post; command headquarters; a command ship.*

com•man•dant |kŏm′ən dănt′| *or* |-dänt′| *n.* A commanding officer of a military organization.

com•man•deer |kŏm′ən dîr′| *v.* To seize (property) for public use, especially for military use; confiscate.

com•mand•er |kə măn′dər| *or* |-män′-| *n.* **1.** An officer in the Navy ranking below a captain. A **lieutenant commander** ranks below a commander. **2.** An officer of any rank in command of a military unit.

commander in chief. *pl.* **commanders in chief.** **1.** The supreme commander of all the armed forces of a nation. **2.** The officer commanding a major armed force.

com•mand•ing |kə măn′dĭng| *or* |-män′-| *adj.* **1.** Having command; in charge: *the commanding general.* **2.** Having the air of command; impressive: *a clear, commanding voice.* **3.** Dominating by reason of position: *from a commanding height; a commanding lead.*

com•mand•ment |kə mănd′mənt| *or* |-mänd′-| *n.* **1.** A command; order. **2.** Often **Commandment.** Any of the Ten Commandments.

com•man•do |kə măn′dō| *or* |-män′-| *n., pl.* **com•man•dos** or **com•man•does.** A member of a small fighting force trained for making quick raids into enemy territory.

com•mem•o•rate |kə mĕm′ə rāt′| *v.* **com•mem•o•rat•ed, com•mem•o•rat•ing.** **1.** To honor the memory of: *A large crowd gathered at the park to commemorate the victory.* **2.** To be a memorial to, as a holiday, ceremony, or statue: *a day that commemorates the end of World War II.* —**com•mem′o•ra′tion** *n.*

com•mem•o•ra•tive |kə mĕm′ə rā′tĭv| *or* |-ər-ə tĭv| *adj.* Serving to commemorate.

com•mence |kə mĕns′| *v.* **com•menced, com•menc•ing.** To begin; start: *The festivities commenced with the singing of the national anthem.*

com•mence•ment |kə mĕns′mənt| *n.* **1.** A beginning; start. **2.** A graduation ceremony in which students receive their diplomas. —***modifier:*** *a commencement day.*

com•mend |kə mĕnd′| *v.* **1.** To speak highly of; praise: *The mayor commended the commission for its painstaking report.* **2.** To recommend: *commend someone for employment.* **3.** To put in the care of someone: *commend him to his mother's care.*

com•mend•a•ble |kə mĕn′də bəl| *adj.* Praiseworthy: *a commendable performance.* —**com•mend′a•bly** *adv.*

com•men•da•tion |kŏm′ən dā′shən| *n.* **1.** Recommendation or praise. **2.** An official award or citation.

com•men•sal |kə mĕn′səl| *adj.* Describing or living in a relationship in which two different kinds of organisms live in close attachment or partnership, and in which one usually benefits from the association and the other is not harmed. —*n.* A plant or animal living in such a relationship. [SEE NOTE]

com•men•sal•ism |kə mĕn′sə lĭz′əm| *n.* A commensal relationship.

com•men•su•ra•ble |kə mĕn′sər ə bəl| *or* |-shər-| *adj.* **1.** Able to be measured by a common unit. **2.** Properly proportioned; fitting; suitable: *Congress invoked harsh measures commensurable to the danger of the situation.* —**com•men′su•ra•bly** *adv.*

com•men•su•rate |kə mĕn′sər ĭt| *or* |-shər-| *adj.* **1.** Of the same size, extent, or length of time. **2.** Corresponding in size or degree; proportionate: *a large salary commensurate with his long service.*

com•ment |kŏm′ĕnt′| *n.* **1.** A written note or a remark that explains, interprets, or gives an opinion on something: *a critic's comment on a play; the mayor's comment on the governor's speech.* **2.** Talk; gossip: *Her divorce caused much comment in the town.* —*v.* To make a comment; remark.

com•men•tar•y |kŏm′ən tĕr′ē| *n., pl.* **com•men•tar•ies.** **1.** An explanation or interpretation; a series of comments: *a news commentary.* **2.** Anything that illustrates or reflects on something else: *The scandal is a sad commentary on our city government.*

com•men•ta•tor |kŏm′ən tā′tər| *n.* **1.** A person who writes commentaries. **2.** A writer or broadcaster who explains or gives his opinion of events in the news.

com•merce |kŏm′ərs| *n.* The buying and selling of goods, especially on a large scale, as between nations; trade; business.

com•mer•cial |kə mûr′shəl| *adj.* **1.** Of or engaged in commerce: *commercial capitals; a commercial airport.* **2. a.** Having profit as its chief aim: *too scholarly to be a good commercial book.* **b.** Intended to be self-supporting; not having a subsidy: *the commercial theaters of Europe, distinguished from state theaters.* **3.** Sponsored by an advertiser or supported by advertising: *a commercial message; commercial television.* —*n.* An advertisement on radio or television. —**com•mer'cial•ly** *adv.*

com•mer•cial•ism |kə **mûr'**shə lĭz'əm| *n.* The practices of commerce or business, especially those that give chief importance to the making of profit. —**com•mer'cial•is'tic** *adj.*

com•mer•cial•ize |kə **mûr'**shə līz'| *v.* **com•mer•cial•ized, com•mer•cial•iz•ing. 1.** To make commercial; apply methods of business to: *commercialize agriculture.* **2.** To do, make, exploit, etc., mainly for profit: *Many of the island's tourist attractions have been commercialized.* —**com•mer'cial•i•za'tion** *n.*

com•min•gle |kə **mĭng'**gəl| *v.* **com•min•gled, com•min•gling.** To blend or mix together; combine: *cities where people of many nationalities commingle; a story that commingles tragedy and comedy.*

com•mis•er•ate |kə **mĭz'**ə rāt'| *v.* **com•mis•er•at•ed, com•mis•er•at•ing.** To feel or express sorrow or pity for; sympathize: *One defeated candidate commiserates with another.*

com•mis•er•a•tion |kə mĭz'ə **rā'**shən| *n.* A feeling or expression of sorrow or sympathy for the misfortune of another; compassion.

com•mis•sar |**kŏm'**ĭ săr'| *n.* A former title of a Soviet government official now known as a minister.

com•mis•sar•i•at |kŏm'ĭ **sâr'**ē ət| *n.* **1. a.** A department of an army in charge of providing food and other supplies for the troops. **b.** The officers in charge of this department. **2.** A food supply. **3.** A former name for a major government department in the Soviet Union.

com•mis•sar•y |**kŏm'**ĭ sĕr'ē| *n., pl.* **com•mis•sar•ies. 1.** A store maintained by a company or an army post for the sale of food and supplies to its employees or personnel. **2.** A lunchroom or cafeteria that serves the employees of a company or the personnel of an institution, such as a university. **3.** A person to whom a special duty is given by a superior; a representative; deputy.

com•mis•sion |kə **mĭsh'**ən| *n.* **1. a.** The act of granting authority to someone to carry out a certain job or duty. **b.** The job or duty assigned by such a grant: *Investigating charges of fraud in the last election was their commission.* **2.** Often **Commission.** A group of people who have been given authority by law to perform certain duties: *The Federal Trade Commission investigates false and misleading advertising.* **3.** The act of committing or perpetrating something: *statistics on the commission of crime; the commission of a blunder.* **4.** Money in the form of a fee or a percentage of a sale price paid to a salesman or agent for his services: *His 10 per cent commission on the $500 sale was $50.* **5.** Appointment to one of several ranks in the armed forces. See **commissioned officer.** —*v.* **1.** To grant a commission to: *The king commissioned Magellan to find a western route. The composer was commissioned to write an opera. He was commissioned a second lieutenant.* **2.** To place an order for: *commissioned a portrait of himself by a leading artist.* **3.** To put (a ship) into active service.
***Idioms.* in commission. 1.** In active service, as a ship. **2.** In use or in usable condition. **out of commission. 1.** Not in active service. **2.** Not in use or not in working condition.

commissioned officer. An officer appointed to one of several ranks in the armed forces. The lowest rank held by commissioned officers in the U.S. Army, Air Force, and Marine Corps is second lieutenant, and in the Navy ensign.

com•mis•sion•er |kə **mĭsh'**ə nər| *n.* **1.** A member of a commission. **2.** An official in charge of a governmental department: *a police commissioner.* **3.** An official chosen as administrative head of an organized professional sport: *a baseball commissioner.*

com•mit |kə **mĭt'**| *v.* **com•mit•ted, com•mit•ting. 1.** To do, perform, or perpetrate: *commit perjury; commit suicide.* **2.** To place in the charge or keeping of another; entrust: *commit all administrative functions to one person.* **3.** To place in confinement or custody, as by an official act: *He was convicted and committed to prison.* **4.** To put in a certain condition or form, as for future use or preservation: *committed the secret code to memory; seldom committed anything to writing.* **5. a.** To pledge (oneself) to a position: *The decision must be ethical if we are to commit ourselves to it.* **b.** To bind or obligate: *He was committed to follow the terms of the will.*

com•mit•ment |kə **mĭt'**mənt| *n.* **1.** The act of giving in charge or entrusting; consignment: *commitment of children to foster homes; the commitment of criminals to labor camps.* **2.** A pledge or obligation, as to follow a certain course of action: *our treaty commitments to protect small nations; a commitment to work for peaceful change.*

com•mit•tee |kə **mĭt'**ē| *n.* A group of people chosen to do a particular job or to fulfill specified duties: *the membership committee of our club.*

com•mit•tee•man |kə **mĭt'**ē mən| *or* |-măn'| *n., pl.* **-men** |-mən| *or* |-mĕn'|. A member of a committee.

com•mode |kə **mōd'**| *n.* **1.** A low cabinet or chest of drawers. **2.** A movable stand with a washbowl or a container to be used as a toilet. [SEE PICTURE]

com•mo•di•ous |kə **mō'**dē əs| *adj.* Having plenty of room; spacious. —**com•mo'di•ous•ly** *adv.* —**com•mo'di•ous•ness** *n.*

com•mod•i•ty |kə **mŏd'**ĭ tē| *n., pl.* **com•mod•i•ties. 1.** Anything that is useful or that can be turned to profit. **2.** An article of trade or commerce, as an agricultural or mining product.

com•mo•dore |**kŏm'**ə dôr'| *or* |-dōr'| *n.* An officer in the U.S. Navy ranking above a captain and below a rear admiral. This rank was last used in World War II.

com•mon |**kŏm'**ən| *adj.* **com•mon•er, com•mon•est. 1. a.** Belonging to or shared equally by two or more: *common interests; angles with a common side.* **b.** Of the community as a whole; public: *the common good; common knowledge.* **2.** Found or occurring often and in many places; usual; widespread: *when filling stations became common;*

commode
Early nineteenth-century American

road surfaces in common use. **3.** Most widely known of its kind; without distinction; average; ordinary: *a common gray spider; a common soldier; the common man.* **4.** Of no special quality; standard; plain: *a matter of common courtesy.* **5.** Of mediocre or inferior quality; not costly or rare: *common cloth.* **6.** Vulgar; unrefined or coarse in manner: *behavior that branded her as common.* —*n.* Often **commons.** A tract of land belonging to or used by a community as a whole. —**com'mon•ness** *n.*

***Idiom.* in common.** Equally with another or others; jointly: *qualities they have in common.*

common denominator. A number that contains the denominator of each of a set of fractions as a factor. For example, since 1/4 = 25/100, 1/25 = 4/100, 3/10 = 30/100, and 4/5 = 80/100, the fractions 1/4, 1/25, 3/10, and 4/5 can be expressed with the common denominator 100. [SEE NOTE]

common denominator
When each of a set of fractions is expressed in terms of a **common denominator,** *the sum of the set can be expressed as a fraction whose numerator is the sum of all the numerators and whose denominator is the common denominator.*

common divisor. A **common factor.**

com•mon•er |kŏm'ə nər| *n.* A person without noble rank or title.

common factor. A number that is a factor of two or more other numbers, especially when all of the numbers are integers. For example, 3 is a common factor of 9 and 15.

common fraction. A fraction whose numerator and denominator are both integers.

common law. The system of law based on court decisions and on customs and usages rather than on an organized body of written laws or statutes. —***modifier:* (common-law):** *a common-law right.*

common logarithm. A logarithm for which the number ten is used as the base.

com•mon•ly |kŏm'ən lē| *adv.* Generally; ordinarily: *words not commonly used today.*

Common Market. An economic union of European countries, including Belgium, Denmark, France, West Germany, Greece, Ireland, Italy, Luxembourg, the Netherlands, and the United Kingdom, organized to reduce tariff barriers and stimulate trade and cooperation in other areas.

common multiple. A number that contains each of a set of given numbers as a factor, especially when all of the numbers are integers. For example, the integers 2 and 3 have 12 as a common multiple. The set of all integers having 12 as a common multiple contains 1, 2, 3, 4, 6, 12, and no other numbers.

common noun. A noun that represents one or more members of a class and that can be used immediately following the word "the." Common nouns include all nouns that do not name a particular person, place, or thing. In the example *John owned the car that hit a pedestrian, car* and *pedestrian* are common nouns.

com•mon•place |kŏm'ən plās'| *adj.* Ordinary; common; uninteresting: *reporting a commonplace occurrence in an exciting way; whether one's vocabularly is commonplace or elegant.* —*n.* **1.** A statement or remark that is dull or worn out through use: *Today's slang expressions often become the commonplaces of tomorrow.* **2.** Something ordinary or common: *Air conditioning has come to be regarded as a commonplace.*

com•mons |kŏm'ənz| *n.* **1.** *(used with a plural verb).* The common people as distinguished from the aristocracy or nobility. **2.** *(used with a singular or plural verb).* Food provided at meals for a large group, especially at a college. **3.** *(used with a singular verb).* Daily fare; food. **4.** *(used with a singular verb).* A place for dining. **5. Commons** *(used with a singular or plural verb).* The **House of Commons.**

common school. A public elementary school.

common sense. Native good judgment as distinguished from special knowledge gained through school or study; sound ordinary sense. —***modifier:* (common-sense):** *common-sense behavior; a common-sense view.* [SEE NOTE]

common sense
Common sense *was originally a technical term in early psychological theory. It referred to a supposed "inner sense," a kind of brain center that was supposed to organize the impressions received from the five physical senses (sight, hearing, taste, touch, and smell). This idea dropped out of use in the seventeenth century, but the phrase* **common sense** *then took on approximately its present meaning.*

common time. In music, a meter in which each measure contains four quarter notes.

com•mon•weal |kŏm'ən wēl'| *n.* **1.** The public good or welfare. **2.** *Archaic.* A commonwealth.

com•mon•wealth |kŏm'ən wĕlth'| *n.* **1.** The people of a nation or state. **2.** A nation or state governed by the people; a republic. **3. Commonwealth. a.** The official title of some U.S. states, including Kentucky, Massachusetts, Pennsylvania, and Virginia. **b.** The official title of Puerto Rico. **c.** The official title of some democratic countries, such as Australia. **4. the Commonwealth.** The **Commonwealth of Nations.**

Commonwealth of Nations. The political community consisting of the United Kingdom, its dependencies, and certain independent countries that were formerly British colonies.

com•mo•tion |kə mō'shən| *n.* **1.** Violent motion; agitation; tumult. **2.** Political or social unrest or disturbance.

com•mu•nal |kə myo͞o'nəl| *or* |kŏm'yə nəl| *adj.* **1.** Of or relating to a commune or a community: *the new generation's communal living, away from the cities.* **2.** Belonging to or serving the people of a community; public: *the communal dining room.* —**com•mu'nal•ly** *adv.*

com•mune¹ |kə myo͞on'| *v.* **com•muned, com•mun•ing. 1.** To exchange thoughts and feelings; talk intimately: *commune with friends.* **2.** To be in close touch or have a relationship with: *commune with nature.* **3.** To receive Communion.

com•mune² |kŏm'yo͞on'| *n.* **1.** In some European countries, such as France and Italy, the smallest division of local government. **2.** A community organized with a government for promoting local interests. **3.** In some Communist countries, such as China, a unit of the state, organized on a local or community level. **4.** A small community whose members have common interests and in which property is often shared or owned jointly. **5. the Commune.** The revolutionary committee that governed Paris from 1789 to 1795.

com•mu•ni•ca•ble |kə myo͞o'nĭ kə bəl| *adj.* Able to be communicated or transmitted from person to person: *communicable diseases.* —**com•mu'ni•ca•ble•ness** *n.* —**com•mu'ni•ca•bly** *adv.*

com•mu•ni•cant |kə myo͞o'nĭ kənt| *n.* **1.** A person who receives, or is entitled to receive, Communion. **2.** A person who communicates.

com•mu•ni•cate |kə myo͞o'nĭ kāt'| *v.* **com•mu•ni•cat•ed, com•mu•ni•cat•ing. 1.** To make known; impart: *A good speaker communicates his thoughts clearly.* **2.** To have an exchange, as of thoughts, ideas, or information: *The telephone makes it possible to communicate over vast distances. Difference in age often makes it very difficult for* *persons to communicate.* **3.** To transmit, as a disease; pass on. **4.** To be connected: *a hallway that communicates with the servants' quarters.*

com•mu•ni•ca•tion |kə myōō′nĭ **kā′**shən| *n.* **1.** The act of communicating; transmission. **2.** The exchange of thoughts, information, or messages, as by speech, signals, or writing. **3.** Something communicated; a message. **4. communications.** A system for sending and receiving messages, as by mail, telephone, radio, etc.

com•mu•ni•ca•tive |kə **myōō′**nĭ kā′tĭv| *or* |-kə-tĭv| *adj.* Communicating thoughts or information readily; not secretive.

com•mun•ion |kə **myōōn′**yən| *n.* **1.** The act or condition of sharing, as of thoughts, feelings, or interests. **2.** Spiritual or religious fellowship. **3.** A body of Christians with the same religious faith; a denomination. **4. Communion. a.** The Christian sacrament commemorating Christ's Last Supper; the Eucharist. **b.** The consecrated bread and wine used in this sacrament. **c.** The part of the Mass in which this sacrament is received.

com•mu•ni•qué |kə myōō′nĭ **kā′**| *or* |kə **myōō′**-nĭ-kā′| *n.* An official announcement, such as one issued to the press.

com•mu•nism |**kŏm′**yə nĭz′əm| *n.* **1.** Any social system characterized by the absence of classes and by common ownership of the means of production and common sharing of labor and products. **2. Communism. a.** The international movement aimed at the eventual establishment of this society. **b.** The doctrines of this movement; Marxism-Leninism. **c.** The political and economic system of any country governed by a Communist party.

Com•mu•nist |**kŏm′**yə nĭst| *n.* **1.** A member of a Communist Party. **2.** Often **communist.** A person who believes in or advocates communism. *—adj.* **1.** Of a Communist Party or its membership. **2.** Often **communist.** Of communism in general.

com•mu•nis•tic |kŏm′yə **nĭs′**tĭk| *adj.* Based on or favoring the principles of communism. —**com′mu•nis′ti•cal•ly** *adv.*

Communist Party. A political party having or claiming to have a Marxist-Leninist program.

com•mu•ni•ty |kə **myōō′**nĭ tē| *n., pl.* **com•mu•ni•ties. 1. a.** A group of people living in the same locality and under the same government. **b.** The district or locality in which they live. **2.** A group of people who have close ties, as through common nationality or interests: *New York's Puerto Rican community; the intellectual community.* **3.** Similarity or identity; closeness: *A community of interests helped to unite them.* **4.** A group of plants and animals that live together in the same surroundings and that are often dependent on one another for existence.

community chest. A fund raised by contributions from residents and businesses of an area and used for charity.

community college. A junior college established to serve a certain community.

community property. Property owned jointly by a husband and wife.

com•mu•ta•tion |kŏm′yə **tā′**shən| *n.* **1.** The act of lessening or making something less severe, as a death penalty or prison sentence. **2.** The travel of a commuter.

com•mu•ta•tive |kə **myōō′**tə tĭv| *or* |**kŏm′**yə tā′-tĭv| *adj.* Of the commutative property or an operation that has this property.

commutative property. The property of a mathematical operation that when applied to a pair of numbers gives the same result regardless of the order in which the numbers are taken. Suppose that a and b are numbers and ♦ is a mathematical operation. If $a ♦ b = b ♦ a$, the operation ♦ has the commutative property.

com•mu•ta•tor |**kŏm′**yə tā′tər| *n.* A switching device used in electric motors and generators to make a current flow in a desired direction through a desired path. [SEE PICTURE]

com•mute |kə **myōōt′**| *v.* **com•mut•ed, com•mut•ing. 1.** To reduce (a legal sentence) to a less severe one: *commute the death penalty to life imprisonment.* **2.** To travel as a commuter. *—n. Informal.* The distance traveled by a commuter: *a 22-mile commute.*

com•mut•er |kə **myōō′**tər| *n.* A person who travels regularly between a home in one community and work in another.

Com•o•ros |**kŏm′**ə rōz′|. A group of islands off the southeastern coast of Africa, constituting an independent nation. Population, 292,000. Capital, Moroni.

com•pact¹ |kəm **păkt′**| *or* |kŏm-| *or* |**kŏm′**păkt′| *adj.* **1.** Closely and firmly united or packed together; solid; dense: *flowers growing in compact clusters.* **2.** Packed into or arranged within a small space: *a compact package; compact living quarters.* **3.** Brief and to the point; concise: *written in a compact style.* **4.** Expressed in mathematical notation that is brief; not expanded: *a compact numeral.* *—v.* |kəm **păkt′**|. To press or join firmly together. *—n.* |**kŏm′**păkt′|. **1.** A small case containing face powder, a powder puff, usually a mirror, and sometimes rouge. **2.** A relatively small automobile. —**com•pact′ly** *adv.* —**com•pact′ness** *n.* [SEE NOTE]

com•pact² |**kŏm′**păkt′| *n.* An agreement or covenant; a contract. [SEE NOTE]

com•pac•tor |kəm **păk′**tər| *or* |kŏm-| *n.* A machine that compresses refuse into relatively small packs for handy disposal.

com•pan•ion |kəm **păn′**yən| *n.* **1.** A person who accompanies or associates with another; a comrade. **2.** A person hired to assist, live with, or travel with another: *working as a companion to an elderly woman.* **3.** One of a pair or set of things. [SEE NOTE]

com•pan•ion•a•ble |kəm **păn′**yə nə bəl| *adj.* Suited to be a good companion; friendly. —**com•pan′ion•a•bly** *adv.*

com•pan•ion•ship |kəm **păn′**yən shĭp′| *n.* The relationship of companions; friendly feeling; fellowship.

com•pan•ion•way |kəm **păn′**yən wā′| *n.* A staircase leading from a ship's deck to the area below.

com•pa•ny |**kŭm′**pə nē| *n., pl.* **com•pa•nies. 1.** A group of people; a gathering. **2.** A guest or guests: *broth good enough for company.* **3. a.** A companion or companions: *finding them not very lively company.* **b.** Companionship: *grateful for her company.* **4.** Society in general; one's associates: *the company they keep; competing in fast*

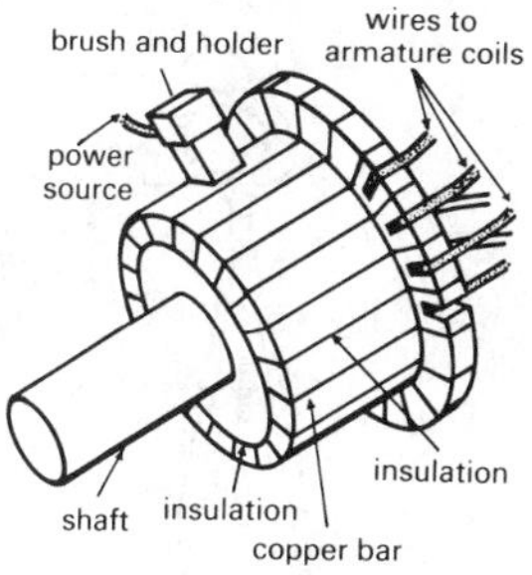

commutator

compact¹·²

Compact¹ *is from Latin* compactus, *"thickset" firmly joined together."* **Compact²** *is from Latin* compactum, *"an agreement," from* compactus, *a homonym of the other word, meaning "agreed together." In both words,* com- *means "together." The* pac- *in each case is ultimately from one Indo-European root,* pag-, *which meant "to join."*

companion

After the decline of the Roman Empire, when "barbarian" peoples invaded all the western provinces, there was a long period of contact and exchange between the Germanic and the Roman cultures. This contact is vividly reflected in language. For instance, the Germanic word ga-khlaibaz *meant "he who shares one's bread, a sworn friend," from* ga-, *"together,"* + khlaibaz, *"loaf." This word was taken into Latin not by borrowing but by translation; a new word was made up from the equivalent Latin elements. The word was* compāniō, *from* com-, *"together,"* + pānis, *"bread." It became* compaignon *in Old French, and was borrowed into English as* **companion**.

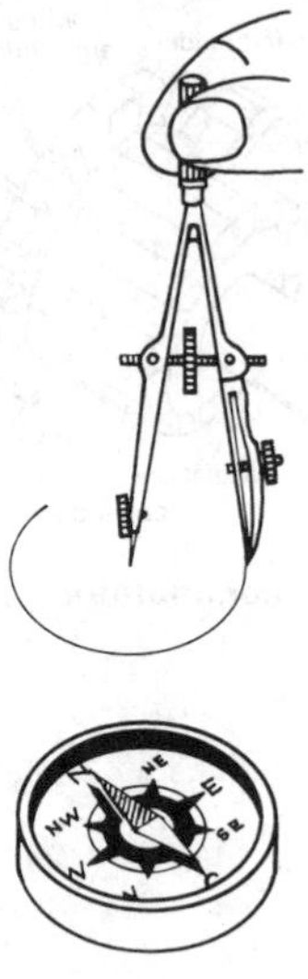

compass

company. **5.** A business enterprise; a firm. **6.** A body of performers organized to present stage works, such as plays, operas, and ballets, or to produce motion pictures. **7.** A unit of soldiers, especially one consisting of two or more platoons. **8.** The officers and crew of a ship: *the ship's company.* —***modifier:*** *the company manager; the company commander.*

Idioms. **in company with.** Together with: *went in company with her brother.* **keep company. 1.** To carry on courtship. **2.** To accompany or serve as a companion: *asked me to keep her company tonight.* **part company.** To end an association or friendship.

company union. 1. A labor union whose membership includes only employees of a single business or corporation. **2.** Such a union controlled by the employer rather than by the union membership.

com•pa•ra•ble |**kŏm′**pər ə bəl| *adj.* **1.** Capable of being compared; having like traits; similar or equivalent: *two errors comparable in magnitude.* **2.** Worthy of being compared: *a day comparable only to the one when the baby was born.* —**com′pa•ra•bly** *adv.*

com•par•a•tive |kəm **păr′**ə tĭv| *adj.* **1.** Based on or making a comparison: *the comparative study of customs and mores.* **2.** Estimated by comparison; measured in relation to something else; relative: *the comparative sizes of the earth and other bodies; having comparative freedom from government regulation.* —*n.* In grammar, the form of an adjective or adverb that indicates an increase in quality, quantity, or some other relation expressed by the adjective or adverb, as in the sentences *My house is bigger than yours, I have fewer books than John,* and *She left earlier than Louise.* Comparatives are usually formed by the addition of the ending *-er* to the adjective or adverb, as in "fewer" and "earlier." In some cases, as in "bigger," the last consonant is doubled. Some comparatives are completely different from the original adjective or adverb. For example, the comparatives of the adjectives "good" and "bad" are "better" and "worse," and the comparative of the adverb "well" is "better." Many adjectives do not have a true comparative; the comparatives of such adjectives are formed by the placement of the word "more" before the adjective, as in the sentence *This plane is more comfortable than the train.* The comparative of most adverbs is also formed in the same way. For example, in the sentence *My car seats five more comfortably than yours,* the adverb "comfortably" shows a degree of comparison. —**com•par′a•tive•ly** *adv.*

com•pare |kəm **pâr′**| *v.* **com•pared, com•par•ing. 1.** To represent as similar; liken: *compare a lawn to a large emerald.* **2.** To examine so as to note the similarities and differences of: *compare the skills of an astronaut with those of an airplane pilot.* **3.** To be worthy of comparison: *words that do not compare with deeds; bargains that compare with those offered anywhere.* **4.** In grammar, to form the positive, comparative, or superlative of (an adjective or adverb). —*n.* Comparison: *a view so striking it was beyond compare.*

com•par•i•son |kəm **păr′**ĭ sən| *n.* **1.** The act of comparing: *A scientist measures and makes comparisons.* **2.** The result of comparing; a statement or estimate of similarities and differences: *a comparison of your work and mine.* **3.** The condition of being capable or worthy of being compared; close similarity: *no comparison between hand-made shoes and cheap ones.* **4.** In grammar, the changing of the form of an adjective or adverb to indicate the three degrees of positive, comparative, and superlative.

com•part•ment |kəm **pärt′**mənt| *n.* **1.** One of the parts or spaces into which an area is subdivided. **2.** A separate room, section, or chamber: *a storage compartment.*

com•pass |**kŭm′**pəs| *or* |**kŏm′-**| *n.* **1. a.** An instrument used to determine geographical direction, usually consisting of a magnetic needle mounted so that it can turn and align itself with the earth's magnetic field. **b.** Any of several other instruments used for this purpose, especially a gyrocompass or a radio compass. **2.** A device used for drawing circles or arcs of circles, usually consisting of a pair of rigid arms hinged together in a V shape, one of the arms holding a sharp point that serves as an anchor and the other holding a pencil or other drawing tool. **3. a.** A range or scope; extent: *not within the compass of your authority.* **b.** The range of a voice or musical instrument. —***modifier:*** *a compass bearing; a compass needle.* —*v.* To go around or surround. [SEE PICTURE]

compass card. A disk marked with the 32 points of the compass and the 360 degrees of a circle. It is mounted so as to turn with the magnetic needle of a compass.

com•pas•sion |kəm **păsh′**ən| *n.* The feeling of sharing the suffering of another, together with a desire to give aid or show mercy.

com•pas•sion•ate |kəm **păsh′**ə nĭt| *adj.* Feeling or showing compassion. —**com•pas′sion•ate•ly** *adv.*

com•pat•i•ble |kəm **păt′**ə bəl| *adj.* Able to live or perform in agreement or harmony with another or others. —**com•pat′i•bil′i•ty** *n.* —**com•pat′i•bly** *adv.*

com•pa•tri•ot |kəm **pā′**trē ət| *or* |-ŏt′| *n.* A person from one's own country; a fellow countryman.

com•peer |kəm **pîr′**| *or* |**kŏm′**pîr′| *n.* **1.** A person of equal status or rank. **2.** A comrade or associate.

com•pel |kəm **pĕl′**| *v.* **com•pelled, com•pel•ling. 1.** To make (someone) do something, as by force, necessity, or powerful influence: *Young men are compelled to serve in the armed forces in times of national emergency. The sudden storm compelled us to return indoors. I felt compelled to read to the end of the story.* **2.** To make necessary; demand; exact: *His bravery compels our admiration.*

com•pel•ling |kəm **pĕl′**ĭng| *adj.* Having a very strong influence or effect; powerful; forceful: *a compelling argument; the countryside's quiet, compelling charm.* —**com•pel′ling•ly** *adv.*

com•pen•di•ous |kəm **pĕn′**dē əs| *adj.* Giving facts or information about a subject in brief but complete form.

com•pen•di•um |kəm **pĕn′**dē əm| *n.* An organized, detailed summary of facts, information, etc.

com•pen•sate |**kŏm′**pən sāt′| *v.* **com•pen•sat•**

ed, com•pen•sat•ing. **1.** To act as or provide a balancing effect; make up: *On the day we return to standard time we gain an hour to compensate for the hour lost when we went on daylight-saving time. A baseball player who is not a speedy runner can compensate by powerful hitting.* **2.** To make payment or amends to or for; repay: *You will be compensated for the work you have done.* —**com•pen'sa•to'ry** |kəm **pĕn'**sə tôr'ē| *or* |-tōr'ē| *adj.*

com•pen•sa•tion |kŏm'pən **sā'**shən| *n.* **1.** Something given as payment or amends, as for work, loss, or injury: *honest labor with just compensation; unemployment compensation; a pension granted as compensation for bodily injury.* **2.** Something used, needed, or done to balance or make up for something else: *heat used as compensation for a fall in temperature.* **3.** The act or process of compensating.

com•pen•sa•tor |**kŏm'**pən sā'tər| *n.* Something that compensates, especially a control device that corrects for changes or errors in the operation of a system: *a temperature compensator.*

com•pete |kəm **pēt'**| *v.* **com•pet•ed, com•pet•ing.** **1.** To strive against another or others to win something; take part in or as if in a contest; be a rival: *compete in a race; compete for a girl's affection.* **2.** To strive successfully; be compared favorably: *Many countries produce fine wines, but none can compete with France in quality and variety.*

com•pe•tence |**kŏm'**pĭ tns| *n.* Ability to do what is required; skill: *Alice steered with competence through the heavy traffic. I do not doubt his competence as a mechanic.*

com•pe•tent |**kŏm'**pĭ tnt| *adj.* **1.** Able to do what is required; capable: *a competent worker.* **2.** Satisfactory; adequate: *a competent job.* **3.** Having official or legal standing; fully qualified: *medical treatment given by a competent registered physician.* —**com'pe•tent•ly** *adv.*

com•pe•ti•tion |kŏm'pĭ **tĭsh'**ən| *n.* **1.** The act of competing in or as if in a contest: *won the race in competition with ten contestants.* **2.** A contest or similar test of skill or ability: *a skating competition; a baking competition.* **3.** Rivalry or struggle to win an advantage, success, profit, etc., from another or others: *keen competition between the two teams; laws intended to protect a nation's business against foreign competition; the competition between plants for nutrients in the soil.* **4.** The one or ones against whom one competes: *Is the competition as good as our team?*

com•pet•i•tive |kəm **pĕt'**ĭ tĭv| *adj.* **1.** Of, in, or decided by competition: *competitive games; a product priced so as to be competitive with others.* **2.** Liking or inclined to compete: *a competitive person.* —**com•pet'i•tive•ly** *adv.* —**com•pet'i•tive•ness** *n.*

com•pet•i•tor |kəm **pĕt'**ĭ tər| *n.* A person, team, business organization, etc., that competes with another or others; a contestant; an opponent or rival.

com•pi•la•tion |kŏm'pə **lā'**shən| *n.* **1.** The act of compiling. **2.** Something that has been compiled, such as a collection of written works, a report, or a similar body of information.

com•pile |kəm **pīl'**| *v.* **com•piled, com•pil•ing.** **1.** To put together (facts, information, statistics, etc.) into a single collection, set, or record: *compile the results of a series of experiments for a science report.* **2.** To write or compose (a book) using material gathered from various sources: *compile a dictionary.* —**com•pil'er** *n.*

com•pla•cence |kəm **plā'**səns| *n.* A form of the word **complacency.**

com•pla•cen•cy |kəm **plā'**sən sē| *n.* A feeling of untroubled or overconfident satisfaction with oneself; smugness.

com•pla•cent |kəm **plā'**sənt| *adj.* **1.** Pleased or contented with oneself in an untroubled or uncritical manner; self-satisfied; smug: *The coach was worried because his team had won so often they had become complacent.* **2.** Showing such contentment or self-satisfaction: *plump, smiling, complacent faces.* ¶*These sound alike* **complacent, complaisant.** —**com•pla'cent•ly** *adv.*

com•plain |kəm **plān'**| *v.* **1.** To express feelings of annoyance, pain, unhappiness, etc.: *Sally worked hard all day and never complained. Grandfather complained of a pain in his back.* **2.** To say in an unhappy or dissatisfied way. **3.** To make a report or accusation about something one considers wrong or troublesome: *complain to the telephone company about a mistake in one's bill.*

com•plain•ant |kəm **plā'**nənt| *n.* Someone who makes a formal complaint, as in a court of law.

com•plaint |kəm **plānt'**| *n.* **1.** A statement, sound, etc., expressing annoyance, unhappiness, or pain: *the farmer's complaint that his cottage was damp enough to give rheumatism to a wild duck; the hungry complaint of the gulls.* **2.** A cause or reason for complaining; a grievance: *The tenants made a list of their complaints to send to the landlord.* **3.** A formal statement or accusation about something causing trouble or dissatisfaction: *The storekeeper signed a complaint accusing the man of robbery.* **4.** Something, such as an illness, that causes pain or discomfort: *Colds are a common winter complaint.*

com•plai•sant |kəm **plā'**sənt| *or* |-zənt| *adj.* Showing a desire or willingness to please; cheerfully obliging or agreeable. ¶*These sound alike* **complaisant, complacent.** —**com•plai'sance** *n.* —**com•plai'sant•ly** *adv.*

com•ple•ment |**kŏm'** plə mənt| *n.* **1.** Something that completes, makes up a whole, or brings to perfection: *An attractive table setting is a complement to a well-prepared meal.* **2.** The number or amount needed to make something complete: *library shelves with a full complement of books; hire enough teachers to bring the staff up to complement.* **3.** In grammar, a word or group of words that follows a transitive or linking verb and completes a predicate or sentence. A complement may be the direct object, as "worm" in *The robin ate the worm,* an indirect object, as "rabbi" in *Mother passed the rabbi the mashed potatoes,* a noun or noun phrase, as "time of the year" in *Spring is my favorite time of the year,* or an adjective, as "cold" in *The water feels cold.* **4.** Either of a pair of angles whose measures add up to 90 degrees. **5.** Either of a pair of complementary colors. —*v.* |**kŏm'**plə mĕnt'|. To make complete; add to the effect of; be a complement to: *That hat complements your dress perfectly.* ¶*These sound alike* **complement, compliment.** [SEE NOTE]

com•ple•men•ta•ry |kŏm'plə **mĕn'**tə rē| *or*

complement/compliment

Complement *and* **compliment** *are doublets (separate descendants of one original word);* **complement** *has both the original spelling and the original meaning. Latin* complēre, *"to fill up, to complete," has the derivative noun* complēmentum, *"something that fills up or completes, a complement"; this was borrowed directly into English as* **complement.** *Separately, when Latin* complēre *passed into the Romance languages, it developed a new range of meanings: "to fill up, to fulfill" and especially "to fulfill social obligations, to comply, to be courteous"; and the noun* complēmentum, *becoming* cumplimiento *in Spanish,* complimento *in Italian, and* compliment *in French, took on the meanings "fulfillment of obligations" and "politeness, a piece of courtesy, a polite phrase." French* compliment *was borrowed into English as* **compliment.**

|-trē| *adj.* Serving as a complement; completing something or supplying what is lacking or needed: *The economies of two countries are complementary when each manufactures what the other needs.* ¶*These sound alike* **complementary, complimentary.**

complementary angles. A pair of angles whose measures add up to 90 degrees.

complementary color. One of a pair of contrasting colors that form gray or white when mixed in the proper proportions, as blue-green and red. [SEE NOTE]

com•plete |kəm **plēt'**| *adj.* **1.** Having all necessary, usual, or wanted parts; not lacking anything: *a complete skeleton of a dinosaur; a complete meal; a holiday that did not seem complete because of rain.* **2.** Thorough; full; entire: *turn a complete somersault; have complete control over one's emotions.* **3.** Ended; finished. **4.** Fully or additionally equipped or supplied: *an auditorium complete with public address system.* —*v.* **com•plet•ed, com•plet•ing. 1.** To add what is missing or needed to (something) so as to form a finished or correct whole: *Complete the sentences in the exercise by filling in the blanks.* **2.** To finish work, progress, etc., on: *The farmers completed the framework of the barn. Magellan never completed the voyage around the world because he was killed in the Philippine Islands.* **3.** To succeed in finishing; accomplish: *complete a forward pass; complete one's education.* —**com•plete'ness** *n.*

com•plete•ly |kəm **plēt'**lē| *adv.* Entirely; totally; altogether: *Her hat is trimmed with completely useless flowers. The ice is completely melted.*

com•ple•tion |kəm **plē'**shən| *n.* **1.** The act or process of completing something: *his successful completion of the task.* **2.** The condition of being completed: *carry plans through to completion.*

com•plex |kəm **plěks'**| *or* |**kŏm'**plěks'| *adj.* **1.** Consisting of many connected or interrelated parts, constituents, factors, etc.; intricately formed or organized: *a complex system of roads and highways; the complex sound of a great orchestra; the complex relationship between living things and their environment.* **2.** Difficult to understand or figure out; complicated: *complex problems; complex ideas.* —*n.* |**kŏm'**plěks'|. **1.** A system or unit consisting of a large number of parts that are related in a complicated way: *a radar complex; a complex of cities and suburbs.* **2.** A connected group of ideas, wishes, feelings, etc., which influence a person's behavior and personality without his being aware of them. —**com•plex'ly** *adv.*

complex fraction. A fraction in which the numerator or the denominator is or is expressed as a fraction. [SEE NOTE]

com•plex•ion |kəm **plěk'**shən| *n.* **1.** The natural color, texture, and appearance of the skin, especially of the face. **2.** General character, aspect, or nature: *the complexion of a situation.*

com•plex•i•ty |kəm **plěk'**sĭ tē| *n., pl.* **com•plex•i•ties. 1.** The condition of being complex: *the complexity of modern civilization.* **2.** Something complex: *Most people encounter complexities in their lives.*

complex number. A number that can be expressed as $a + bi$, where a and b are real numbers and $i^2 = -1$.

complex sentence. A sentence containing an independent clause and one or more dependent clauses. In the complex sentence *My cabin never leaks when it rains although there are many small holes in the roof,* the independent clause is *My cabin never leaks,* and *when it rains* and *although there are many small holes in the roof* are dependent clauses.

com•pli•ance |kəm **plī'**əns| *n.* The act of complying; action or obedience in accordance with a rule, request, command, etc.; conformity: *Compliance with a country's laws is expected of all citizens. In compliance with your request, I am sending you my autographed picture.*

com•pli•an•cy |kəm **plī'**ən sē| *n.* A form of the word **compliance.**

com•pli•ant |kəm **plī'**ənt| *adj.* Yielding readily to the wishes or requests of others: *He has a compliant nature.*

com•pli•cate |**kŏm'**plĭ kāt'| *v.* **com•pli•cat•ed, com•pli•cat•ing. 1.** To make hard to understand, solve, or deal with; make confusing or perplexing: *The extra information only complicates the problem. Inventions such as automobiles and television have often complicated our lives.* **2.** To make complex or intricate: *The added parts complicate the machinery.*

com•pli•ca•ted |**kŏm'**plĭ kā'tĭd| *adj.* **1.** Containing or consisting of intricately combined or tangled parts: *a box with a complicated lock fastening the lid; yarn snarled into a complicated tangle.* **2.** Not easy to understand, deal with, or make one's way through; perplexing: *a game with complicated rules; a long, complicated explanation.*

com•pli•ca•tion |kŏm'plĭ **kā'**shən| *n.* **1.** Something that complicates: *Try not to add complications to an already difficult procedure.* **2.** An intricate or confused relationship of parts: *the complications of the diving equipment limit its use to experts.* **3.** A condition that arises during the course of a disease or ailment and makes it worse.

com•plic•i•ty |kəm **plĭs'**ĭ tē | *n.* Involvement as an accomplice in a crime or wrongdoing; the condition of being an accomplice.

com•pli•ment |**kŏm'**plə mənt| *n.* **1.** An expression of praise or admiration: *Miss Coe hands out compliments and criticism in a fair, impartial manner. Tony paid Maria many compliments on her excellent cooking.* **2.** A mark or gesture of honor or courtesy: *The troops fired a salute as a compliment to the visiting general.* **3. compliments.** Good wishes; regards: *Please extend my compliments to your wife.* —*v.* To praise with a compliment or compliments; pay a compliment to: *The coach complimented Clyde on his great pitching.* ¶*These sound alike* **compliment, complement.** [SEE NOTE on p. 187]

com•pli•men•ta•ry |kŏm'plə **měn'**tə rē| *or* |-trē| *adj.* **1.** Containing or resembling a compliment or compliments; giving or expressing praise: *The critic was not very complimentary in his review of the movie. Paul's comments about my apple pie were highly complimentary.* **2.** Given free: *complimentary tickets to the ball game; a complimentary copy of a new book.* **3.** Containing a formal expression of regards, courtesy, etc.: *"Yours truly" is a commonly used complimentary*

complementary color

The behavior of **complementary colors** *varies somewhat depending on whether they are the colors of light or the colors of pigments. Mixtures of complementary colors that are colors of light can be made to give white light, not surprisingly, as there is no such thing as gray light. Since, however, no pigment is perfectly reflective, mixtures of complementary pigment pairs always contain some black and thus appear gray. Also, since the primary colors of pigments and light are different, so are the complementary pairs.*

complex fraction

A fraction of this kind can always be written as a simple fraction; if a, b, c, *and* d *are all integers (whole numbers), then it can be shown that* (a/b)/(c/d) = (a × d) / (b × c). *The closure property of the integers under multiplication assures that* a × d *and* b × c *are both integers.*

ă **pat**/ā **pay**/â **care**/ä **father**/ĕ **pet**/ ē **be**/ĭ **pit**/ī **pie**/î **fierce**/ŏ **pot**/ ō **go**/ô **paw**, **for**/oi **oil**/ŏŏ **book**/ ōō **boot**/ou **out**/ŭ **cut**/û **fur**/ *th* **the**/th **thin**/hw **which**/zh **vision**/ ə **ago**, **item**, **pencil**, **atom**, **circus**

closing of a letter. ¶*These sound alike* **complimentary, complementary.**

com•ply |kəm **plī**| *v.* **com•plied, com•ply•ing, com•plies.** To act in accordance with a request, rule, order, etc.: *The audience begged for more, and the singer complied by giving several encores.*

com•po•nent |kəm **pō**′nənt| *n.* **1.** Any of the parts that together make up a whole: *A large computer consists of thousands of components.* **2.** Either of the numbers *x* or *y* that make up an ordered pair (*x*, *y*). *—adj.* Of, being, or acting as a component: *Resistors, transistors, and diodes are component parts of a computer.*

com•port |kəm **pôrt**′| *or* |**-pōrt**′| *v.* **—comport oneself.** To act in a certain way; behave: *She comported herself very well as hostess.*

com•port•ment |kəm **pôrt**′mənt| *or* |**-pōrt′-**| *n.* Behavior; conduct; manner: *the solemn comportment of a judge in court.*

com•pose |kəm **pōz**′| *v.* **com•posed, com•pos•ing. 1.** To make up; form: *Our lungs are composed of air tubes with many branches. The sentences that compose a paragraph should all relate to the same topic.* **2.** To make or create by putting parts or elements together: *An artist composes a picture by arranging forms and colors that seem to belong together.* **3.** To create (poetry, music, etc.): *The poet Robert Frost composed a poem in honor of President John F. Kennedy. Mozart began composing music when he was a small boy. Chopin composed mostly for the piano.* **4.** To make calm, controlled, or orderly: *compose one's mind before making a speech. Stop giggling and compose yourself.* **5.** To settle or adjust, as a point of disagreement: *The two nations composed their differences and agreed on the terms of a peace treaty.* **6.** To arrange or set (type or matter to be printed).

com•posed |kəm **pōzd**′| *adj.* In control of one's emotions; calm; serene. **—com•pos′ed•ly** |kəm**pō**′zĭd lē| *adv.*

com•pos•er |kəm **pō**′zər| *n.* A person who composes, especially a creator of musical works.

com•pos•ite |kəm **pŏz**′ĭt| *adj.* **1.** Made up of distinctly different parts: *A composite face is made by putting together the eyes, mouth, nose, etc., from different pictures.* **2.** Of or belonging to a plant family with flower heads made up of many small, densely clustered flowers that give the impression of a single bloom. These small flowers may be of two kinds, as in the daisy, or of a single kind, as in the dandelion. *—n.* **1.** Something made by combining different parts: *The crossbow was a composite of wood, horn, and sinew designed for maximum spring and strength.* **2.** A composite plant, such as the daisy or dandelion. [SEE PICTURE]

composite number. A natural number that has at least one positive integral factor other than itself and 1; a natural number that is not a prime number.

com•po•si•tion |kŏm′pə **zĭsh**′ən| *n.* **1.** The putting together of parts or elements to form a whole; the act, process, or art of composing. **2.** A work created by such a process, especially a musical work. **3.** A short essay, story, etc., written as a school exercise. **4.** The parts or constituents forming a whole, and the way in which they are combined; make-up: *the composition of a mineral.* **5.** The arrangement of parts or elements forming a whole, as in an artistic work: *the composition of a painting.* **6.** A material consisting of a mixture of substances. **7.** The setting of type for printing.

com•po•si•tion•al |kŏm′pə **zĭsh**′ə nəl| *adj.* Of, relating to, or used in composition, as in music or art.

com•pos•i•tor |kəm **pŏz**′ĭ tər| *n.* A person who arranges or sets type for printing; a typesetter.

com•post |**kŏm**′pōst′| *n.* A mixture of decaying plant or animal substances such as leaves or manure, used to enrich the soil.

com•po•sure |kəm **pō**′zhər| *n.* Control over one's emotions; calm, steady manner or spirit: *Phil felt a shiver of fear run down his spine, but quickly regained his composure.*

com•pote |**kŏm**′pōt′| *n.* **1.** Sweetened stewed fruit, served as a dessert. **2.** A long-stemmed dish for holding fruit, candy, or nuts.

com•pound¹ |**kŏm**′pound′| *n.* **1.** Something consisting of a combination of two or more parts, ingredients, etc.: *The fragrance filling the bakery shop was a compound of fresh bread, apple pie, and chocolate.* **2.** Also **compound word.** A word consisting of a combination of two or more other words and forming a single unit with its own meaning. A compound word may be written without a space or hyphen, as *everybody* or *loudspeaker,* or with a hyphen or hyphens, as *baby-sitter* or *heart-to-heart.* A combination such as *ice cream,* written as separate words but having its own special meaning, is often considered a compound. **3.** An unmixed substance that consists of atoms of at least two different elements combined in definite proportions, usually having properties different from any of the elements it contains. *—v.* |kŏm **pound**′| *or* |kəm-|. **1.** To make up or put together by combining parts, ingredients, qualities, etc.: *The pharmacist compounded the medicine the doctor ordered. The room's stuffy atmosphere was compounded of dark walls, heavy draperies, and old fringed lamps.* **2.** To compute (interest) on the principal plus all the interest earned to that time. **3.** To add to; increase: *The world's scientific knowledge is compounded year after year and century after century by the discoveries of individual scientists.* *—adj.* |**kŏm**′pound′| *or* |kəm **pound**′|. Consisting of two or more parts, ingredients, elements, substances, etc., forming a single unit or whole. [SEE NOTE]

com•pound² |**kŏm**′pound′| *n.* A group of houses enclosed by a wall, fence, or other barrier. [SEE NOTE]

compound eye. An eye, as of an insect or crustacean, consisting of many small, light-sensitive parts, each of which forms part of an image. [SEE PICTURE]

compound fraction. A **complex fraction.**

compound fracture. A bone fracture in which a sharp piece of bone cuts through nearby soft tissue and makes an open wound.

compound interest. Interest computed on an amount of money constituting the principal plus all the unpaid interest already earned.

compound leaf. A leaf, as of a clover or sumac, composed of several leaflets attached to a single stalk.

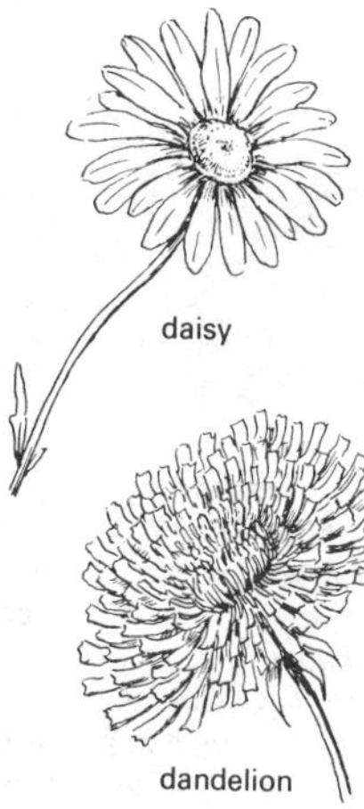

composite
Flowers of composite plants

compound¹⁻²

Compound¹ *is from Old French* compondre, *which is from Latin* compōnere, *"to put together":* com-, *"together,"* + pōnere, *"to put."* **Compound²** *is a good example of "folk etymology," the process by which an unfamiliar foreign word is reshaped to resemble a familiar but unrelated word. The Malay word* kampong, *"village," was borrowed by the colonial Dutch as* kampoeng; *they used the word to mean "a part of an oriental city set apart for foreigners."* Kampoeng *was then borrowed by the British in India as* **compound²**, *reshaped by the influence of* **compound¹**.

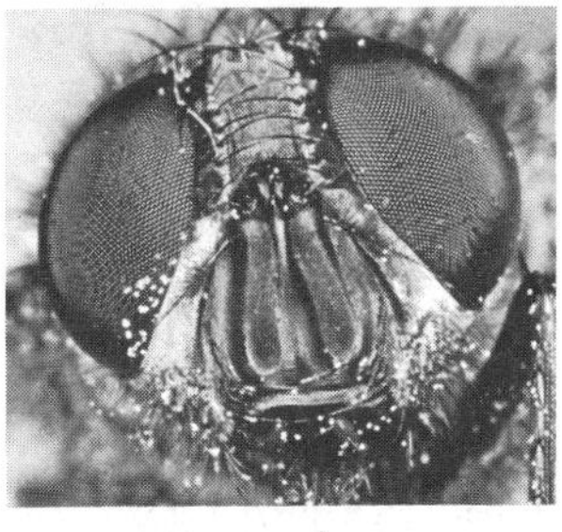

compound eye
Bluebottle fly

compound sentence. A sentence of two or more independent clauses, usually joined by a conjunction such as *and, but,* or *or;* for example, *The problem was difficult, but I finally found the answer* is a compound sentence.

com•pre•hend |kŏm′prĭ **hĕnd′**| *v.* **1.** To grasp mentally; understand: *You are unusually well informed if you comprehend the idea of nuclear fission.* **2.** To take in; include: *The metropolitan area of a city comprehends the surrounding suburbs.*

com•pre•hen•si•ble |kŏm′prĭ **hĕn′**sə bəl| *adj.* Capable of being understood; understandable: *Reading the introduction will help make the book more comprehensible.*

com•pre•hen•sion |kŏm′prĭ **hĕn′**shən| *n.* **1.** The act or fact of understanding: *Reading depends on the comprehension of the ideas expressed by the words used.* **2.** The ability to understand: *a prejudiced, narrow-minded man of limited comprehension; unsolved problems about life and the universe that are still beyond our comprehension.*

com•pre•hen•sive |kŏm′prĭ **hĕn′**sĭv| *adj.* Including much; broad in scope; thorough: *This chapter ends with a comprehensive explanation of punctuation.* —**com′pre•hen′sive•ly** *adv.* —**com′pre•hen′sive•ness** *n.*

com•press |kəm **prĕs′**| *v.* **1.** To put pressure on (a substance) so as to reduce the space it takes up. **2.** To squeeze or press together: *Lawrence narrowed his eyes and compressed his lips into a thin, tight line.* **3.** To shorten or condense as if by squeezing or pressing: *A proverb often compresses the wisdom of centuries of experience into a single sentence.* —**com•pressed′** *adj.: compressed gases; compressed food tablets.* —*n.* |**kŏm′**prĕs′|. A soft pad of gauze, cotton, or other material, often moistened or medicated, applied to some part of the body, especially to a wound or injury.

compressed air. Air that has been put under pressure greater than the pressure of the atmosphere, often used to operate machinery or provide a source of oxygen.

com•press•i•ble |kəm **prĕs′**ə bəl| *adj.* Capable of being compressed. —**com•press′i•bil′i•ty** *n.*

com•pres•sion |kəm **prĕsh′**ən| *n.* **1.** The act or process of compressing. **2.** The condition of being compressed. —***modifier:*** *the compression stroke of a piston; a compression bandage.*

com•pres•sive |kəm **prĕs′**ĭv| *adj.* Compressing or capable of compressing.

com•pres•sor |kəm **prĕs′**ər| *n.* Something that compresses, especially a device used to compress a gas, as in a refrigerator.

com•prise |kəm **prīz′**| *v.* **com•prised, com•pris•ing.** **1.** To consist of; be composed of; include: *The Union comprises fifty states.* **2.** To make up; form; constitute: *Native tribes comprise the bulk of the island's population.* [SEE NOTE]

comprise

The traditional view of this verb is that only sense 1 is correct and that for sense 2 the word **compose** *should be used. This is the view of more than half of the American Heritage Panel on English Usage. But the use of* **comprise** *in sense 2 is undeniably gaining ground. In the school materials on which this Dictionary was based, one third of the occurrences of* **comprise,** *all in formal writing, were in sense 2, as in "temperate forests, which comprise only 7 per cent of the world's land."*

com•pro•mise |**kŏm′**prə mīz′| *n.* **1.** A settlement of differences between opposing sides in which each side gives up some of its claims and agrees to some of the demands of the other. **2.** An adjustment, agreement, or choice reached by yielding on certain details or matters of principle, or by combining qualities of different things: *He chose a medium-sized car as a compromise between the comfort of a large, expensive one and the economy of a small one. Idealistic young people are often angry at their parents' compromises with The System.* —***modifier:*** *a compromise agreement.* —*v.* **com•pro•mised, com•pro•mis•ing.** **1.** To yield or make adjustments in certain demands, principles, details, etc.; settle by taking the middle way between extremes: *Laura refused to put on an extra sweater but compromised by wearing her winter overcoat.* **2.** To expose to dishonor or suspicion: *Fred was unwilling to tell all he knew about the accident for fear of compromising his best friend.*

comp•trol•ler |kən **trō′**lər| *n.* A business executive or government official who supervises financial affairs; controller.

com•pul•sion |kəm **pŭl′**shən| *n.* **1.** Force or influence that compels or makes it necessary for someone to do something: *The prisoner confessed under compulsion. Following a vote, the minority yielded to the wishes of the majority without compulsion.* **2. a.** An often unreasonable urge or impulse that is practically impossible to control: *a compulsion to overeat.* **b.** An action done in response to such an urge: *Overeating is a compulsion with her.*

com•pul•sive |kəm **pŭl′**sĭv| *adj.* Of, having, or resulting from a strong, irresistible impulse: *a compulsive eater. When she is nervous she has a compulsive desire to talk.* —**com•pul′sive•ly** *adv.* —**com•pul′sive•ness** *n.*

com•pul•so•ry |kəm **pŭl′**sə rē| *adj.* **1.** Required by law, regulations, etc.: *Education is compulsory for children in most countries.* **2.** Of or by force or compulsion: *compulsory powers of the law. He was held in prison as a compulsory guest of the authorities.*

com•punc•tion |kəm **pŭngk′**shən| *n.* A feeling that one has done something one shouldn't; a guilty feeling: *He had no compunctions about eating all the cookies.*

com•pu•ta•tion |kŏm′pyo͞o **tā′**shən| *n.* The act, process, method, or result of computing; mathematical calculation.

com•pute |kəm **pyo͞ot′**| *v.* **com•put•ed, com•put•ing.** **1.** To work out (a result, answer, solution, etc.) by mathematics; calculate: *The bank computed the interest correctly.* **2.** To solve problems by mathematics.

com•put•er |kəm **pyo͞o′**tər| *n.* A device that computes, especially one of many complex electronic devices that are capable of doing arithmetic at high speeds, of making certain decisions, of storing and analyzing data, and, often, of controlling machinery. See **analog computer, digital computer.** [SEE PICTURE]

computer

com•put•er•ize |kəm **pyo͞o′**tə rīz′| *v.* **com•put•er•ized, com•put•er•iz•ing.** **1.** To process or store (information) by means of an electronic computer. **2.** To convert (a process, operation, or device) so that it can make use of or be controlled by an electronic computer or a system of electronic computers.

com•rade |**kŏm′**răd′| *n.* **1.** A companion, especially one who shares one's activities. **2.** Often **Comrade.** A word meaning fellow citizen or fellow member, often used before a person's name, especially in Communist countries or among members of the Communist Party.

com•rade•ship |**kŏm′**răd shĭp′| *n.* Association as comrades; companionship.

ă pat/ā pay/â care/ä father/ĕ pet/ ē be/ĭ pit/ī pie/î fierce/ŏ pot/ ō go/ô paw, for/oi oil/o͝o book/ o͞o boot/ou out/ŭ cut/û fur/ *th* the/th thin/hw which/zh vision/ ə ago, item, pencil, atom, circus

con¹ |kŏn| *n.* An argument, opinion, etc., against something: *discussing the pros and cons of the subject.* —*adv.* Against: *arguing pro and con.* —*adj.: the arguments pro and con.*

con² |kŏn| *v.* **conned, con•ning.** To study or examine carefully, especially to learn or memorize something.

con³ |kŏn| *v.* **conned, con•ning.** *Slang.* To trick or coax (someone) into doing something by first winning his confidence.

con–. See **com–.**

Con•a•kry |**kän'**ə krē|. The capital of Guinea. Population, 526,000.

con•cave |kŏn **kāv'**| *or* |**kŏn'**kāv'| *adj.* Curved inward like the inner surface of a sphere. —*n.* A concave surface, line, etc. [SEE PICTURE]

con•cav•i•ty |kŏn **kăv'**ĭ tē| *n., pl.* **con•cav•i•ties. 1.** The condition of being concave. **2.** A concave surface or structure.

con•ceal |kən **sēl'**| *v.* To keep from being seen, noticed, or known; hide: *A bank of clouds concealed the setting sun. Jill smiled and joked to conceal her hurt feelings.*

con•ceal•ment |kən **sēl'**mənt| *n.* **1.** The act of concealing or hiding something: *his concealment of the treasure in a hollow tree.* **2.** A means of concealing or a condition of being concealed: *markings on an insect's wings that serve as concealment; come out of concealment; a place of concealment.*

con•cede |kən **sēd'**| *v.* **con•ced•ed, con•ced•ing. 1.** To admit as true or real, often unwillingly or hesitantly; acknowledge: *Jenny conceded that the new house might be pleasant to live in. Frank was about to concede defeat when suddenly his opponent faltered.* **2. a.** To give; yield; grant: *After many years, the government conceded the right to vote to all citizens.* **b.** To give up on (something in which one has had a strong claim or interest), often before results have been fully established: *The candidate conceded the election before all the votes had been counted.*

con•ceit |kən **sēt'**| *n.* **1.** Too high an opinion of one's abilities, worth, etc.; vanity. **2.** An unusual or witty idea or expression.

con•ceit•ed |kən **sē'**tĭd| *adj.* Too proud of oneself or one's accomplishments; vain. —**con•ceit'•ed•ly** *adv.*

con•ceiv•a•ble |kən **sē'**və bəl| *adj.* Capable of being thought of; imaginable; possible: *It is conceivable that life exists on other planets besides Earth.* —**con•ceiv'a•bly** *adv.*

con•ceive |kən **sēv'**| *v.* **con•ceived, con•ceiv•ing. 1.** To form or develop in the mind: *James Watt conceived the idea of the steam engine from watching a boiling kettle when he was a boy.* **2. a.** To have an idea or concept; think: *People in ancient times conceived of the earth as flat.* **b.** To imagine; consider: *We could not conceive that such a strange and beautiful place really existed.* **3.** To become pregnant or become pregnant with: *conceive after many years of marriage; conceive a child.*

con•cen•trate |**kŏn'**sən trāt'| *v.* **con•cen•trat•ed, con•cen•trat•ing. 1.** To keep or direct one's thoughts, attention, or efforts: *In Centerburg the children concentrate on arithmetic and basketball, and the grown-ups tend to business and running the town. The audience concentrated sharply in an effort to understand the speaker.* **2.** To draw or gather together in or toward one place or point: *The population of the country is concentrated in large cities. The clouds concentrated over the western horizon.* **3.** To increase the concentration of (a solution or mixture). —**con'cen•trat'ed** *adj.: a concentrated effort; a concentrated solution.* —*n.* A product made by increasing the proportion of a substance in a solution or mixture: *orange juice concentrate.*

con•cen•tra•tion |kŏn'sən **trā'**shən| *n.* **1.** Close, undivided attention: *The secret of doing your homework in less time is complete concentration.* **2.** A close gathering or dense grouping: *the concentration of population in larger cities.* **3.** The act or process of concentrating or the result of being concentrated. **4.** The amount of a particular substance contained in a given amount of a solution or mixture: *the concentration of salt in sea water.*

concentration camp. A large, fenced-in prison area for prisoners of war or those regarded as undesirable by a government, as in Nazi Germany and Nazi-dominated countries before and during World War II.

con•cen•tric |kən **sĕn'**trĭk| *adj.* Having a center in common: *a set of concentric circles.* —**con•cen'•tri•cal•ly** *adv.*

con•cept |**kŏn'**sĕpt'| *n.* A general idea or understanding, especially one based on known facts or observation: *the concept that all matter is made up of elements.*

con•cep•tion |kən **sĕp'**shən| *n.* **1.** A mental picture or understanding; idea: *The study of astronomy gives us some conception of the huge extent of the universe.* **2.** A beginning or formation of an idea: *a history of art from its earliest conception in the mind of primitive man to the most complex recent works.* **3.** The fusing of a sperm and egg to form a cell that is capable of developing into a new organism.

con•cep•tu•al |kən **sĕp'**cho͞o əl| *adj.* Of, involving, or based on a concept or concepts. —**con•cep'tu•al•ly** *adv.*

con•cern |kən **sûrn'**| *v.* **1.** To be about; have to do with: *The story concerns a queen who has been changed into a swan by an evil magician.* **2.** To have an effect on; be of importance or interest to: *The work of the President concerns both the government and the people.* **3.** To take up the attention of; interest; involve: *A good host concerns himself with making his guests feel comfortable.* **4.** To fill with care or anxiety; worry; trouble: *Her poor eating habits concern me greatly.* —*n.* **1.** A matter that relates to or affects someone or something; a thing of interest or importance: *If you are in a burning building, your chief concern is to warn the other occupants and get out as quickly as possible.* **2. a.** Serious care or interest: *The doctor's gentle concern helped the anxious patient get over her troubles.* **b.** Worry; anxiety: *He made his speech without the slightest trace of concern or nervousness.* **3.** A business establishment or organization; firm: *Repair shops and barber shops are concerns that deal in services rather than goods.*

con•cerned |kən **sûrnd'**| *adj.* **1.** Interested or affected; involved: *The adventure was a perilous one for all concerned. As far as I'm concerned, the*

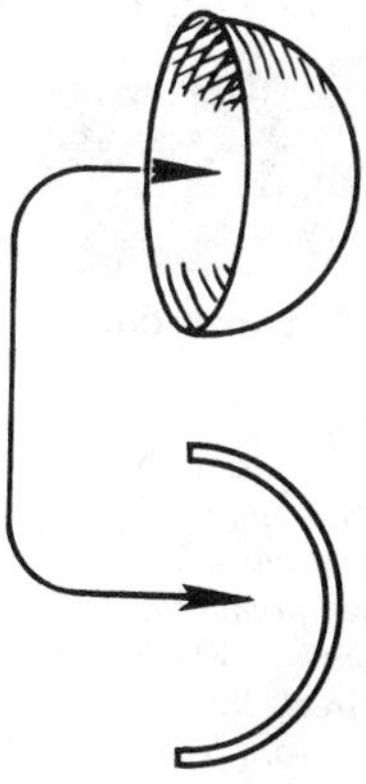

concave

concertina

conch
Conch *comes from Greek* konkhē, *"mussel, shellfish." The preferred pronunciation in English is /kŏngk/, which reflects the hard Greek* kh. *But every other English word ending in* -nch *is pronounced with a soft* ch, *as in* bench, inch, *and* lunch. *As a result, many people cannot bring themselves to pronounce this word /kŏngk/ and so use the more "logical" secondary pronunciation, /kŏnch/.*

conch

ă pat/ā pay/â care/ä father/ĕ pet/ ē be/ĭ pit/ī pie/î fierce/ŏ pot/ ō go/ô paw, for/oi oil/ŏŏ book/ ōō boot/ou out/ŭ cut/û fur/ *th* the/th thin/hw which/zh vision/ ə ago, item, pencil, atom, circus

whole club can parade around in mink sweatshirts. **2.** Worried; anxious; troubled: *a concerned expression on his face.*

con•cern•ing |kən **sûr**′nĭng| *prep.* About; in regard to: *weird stories concerning visitors from outer space.*

con•cert |**kŏn**′sûrt′| *or* |-sərt| *n.* A musical performance given by a number of singers or instrumentalists or a combination of both. —***modifier:*** *a concert violinist; a concert hall.*
***Idiom.* in concert.** As a single unit or group; together: *working in concert.*

concert band. A large band, usually containing a variety of woodwind, brass, and percussion instruments and giving public performances for an audience.

con•cert•ed |kən **sûr**′tĭd| *adj.* Planned or accomplished together with others; combined: *a concerted fund-raising drive.*

con•cer•ti |kən **chĕr**′tē| *n.* A plural of **concerto.**

con•cer•ti•na |kŏn′sər **tē**′nə| *n.* A type of small accordion. [SEE PICTURE]

con•cer•ti•no |kŏn′chər **tē**′nō| *n., pl.* **con•cer•ti•nos. 1.** A short concerto. **2.** The group of solo instruments used in a concerto grosso.

con•cer•tize |**kŏn**′sər tīz′| *v.* **con•cer•tized, con•cer•tiz•ing.** To perform in concerts.

con•cert•mas•ter |**kŏn**′sərt măs′tər| *or* |-mä′stər| *n.* The principal first violinist of an orchestra, who may sometimes act as an assistant conductor.

con•cer•to |kən **chĕr**′tō| *n., pl.* **con•cer•tos** or **con•cer•ti** |kən **chĕr**′tē|. A musical composition written for one or more solo instruments and an orchestra.

concerto gros•so |**grō**′sō|. A concerto in which there are two or more solo instruments.

concert pitch. The system of musical pitch in which the A above middle C has a frequency of 440 hertz (cycles per second).

con•ces•sion |kən **sĕsh**′ən| *n.* **1.** An act of yielding or conceding: *settle a dispute by mutual concession.* **2.** Something yielded or conceded: *His promise to take them fishing was a concession to their demands.* **3. a.** A right to operate a business in a certain place: *an oil concession in the Middle East.* **b.** The place where such a business operates: *the food concession at the ball park.*

con•ces•sion•aire |kən sĕsh′ə **nâr**′| *n.* A person who holds or operates a business concession.

conch |kŏngk| *or* |kŏnch| *n., pl.* **conchs** |kŏngks| or **conch•es** |**kŏn**′chĭz|. **1.** A tropical sea animal related to the snails, having a large, often brightly colored spiral shell. **2.** The shell of such an animal. ¶*These sound alike* **conch, conk.** [SEE NOTE & PICTURE]

con•cil•i•ate |kən **sĭl**′ē āt′| *v.* **con•cil•i•at•ed, con•cil•i•at•ing.** To overcome the anger or distrust of; win over: *She tried to conciliate her angry husband by serving his favorite dessert.*

con•cil•i•a•tion |kən sĭl′ē **ā**′shən| *n.* The act of winning over an unfriendly person, group, etc., as by giving in on certain points: *He found he could make more friends by conciliation than by holding a grudge.*

con•cil•i•a•to•ry |kən **sĭl**′ē ə tôr′ē| *or* |-tōr′ē| *adj.* Intending to conciliate or having the effect of conciliating: *a conciliatory attitude.*

con•cise |kən **sīs**′| *adj.* Expressing much in a few words; brief and clear: *a concise paragraph; the author's concise treatment of the subject.* —**con•cise′ly** *adv.* —**con•cise′ness** *n.*

con•clave |**kŏn**′klāv′| *or* |**kŏng**′-| *n.* A private or secret meeting or meeting place.

con•clude |kən **klōōd**′| *v.* **con•clud•ed, con•clud•ing. 1.** To bring or come to an end; close; finish: *The speaker concluded his speech by urging the audience to vote for his candidate. The concert concluded with a loud chord.* **2.** To arrange or settle finally: *conclude a peace treaty.* **3.** To form an opinion or judgment; decide: *The scientist examined the fossil bones and concluded that they had belonged to a dinosaur.*

con•clu•sion |kən **klōō**′zhən| *n.* **1.** The close or closing part of something; end: *the conclusion of a story.* **2.** A judgment or decision based on one's experience, one's examination of facts or results, etc.: *Scientists check each other's observations and results in order to arrive at accurate conclusions.* **3.** A final arrangement or settlement, as of a treaty.
***Idiom.* in conclusion.** As a last statement; finally.

con•clu•sive |kən **klōō**′sĭv| *adj.* Putting an end to doubt, question, or uncertainty; decisive: *a conclusive argument.* —**con•clu′sive•ly** *adv.*

con•coct |kən **kŏkt**′| *v.* **1.** To make by mixing or combining ingredients or parts: *concoct a stew from leftover meat and vegetables; concoct a magic potion; concoct a motor bike from parts found in the junkyard.* **2.** To make up; invent: *concoct an excuse.*

con•coc•tion |kən **kŏk**′shən| *n.* **1.** Something concocted, especially a mixture of ingredients: *a concoction of mashed bananas, strawberries, and whipped cream.* **2.** The act or process of concocting something: *the concoction of a new recipe.*

con•com•i•tant |kən **kŏm**′ĭ tənt| *adj.* Happening or existing along with something else; accompanying: *concomitant circumstances.* —*n.* Something that happens or is found along with something else: *Poor health is often a concomitant of poverty.* —**con•com′i•tant•ly** *adv.*

con•cord |**kŏn**′kôrd′| *or* |**kŏng**′-| *n.* **1.** A friendly or harmonious relationship: *The two tribes lived in peace and concord.* **2.** An agreement establishing such a relationship.

Con•cord |**kŏng**′kərd|. **1.** The capital of New Hampshire. Population, 29,500. **2.** A town near Boston, Massachusetts, the site of an early battle in the Revolutionary War.

con•cor•dance |kən **kôr**′dns| *n.* **1.** A state of agreement or harmony; concord. **2.** An alphabetical index of the words in a written work or collection of works, showing where they occur: *a concordance to the Bible.*

con•course |**kŏn**′kôrs′| *or* |-kōrs′| *or* |**kŏng**′-| *n.* **1.** A large crowd gathered or moving together. **2.** A large open space in which crowds gather or pass through, as in a railroad station. **3.** A wide road or avenue.

con•crete |**kŏn**′krēt′| *or* |kŏn **krēt**′| *n.* A building or paving material made of sand, pebbles, crushed stone, etc., held together by a mass of cement or mortar. —***modifier:*** *concrete walls; a concrete walk.* —*adj.* |kŏn **krēt**′| *or* |**kŏn**′krēt′|. **1.** Existing as or shown by the existence of something material or real; actual: *concrete ob-*

jects such as trees or shoes; concrete evidence that dinosaurs once roamed the earth. **2.** Not indefinite, abstract, or general; specific: *concrete ideas; describing a scene in familiar, concrete terms.* —**con•crete'ly** *adv.* —**con•crete'ness** *n.*

con•cre•tion |kən **krē'**shən| *n.* **1.** A hard, solid mass of material that forms in a tissue or cavity of the body; calculus. **2.** A rounded mass of rock included in a sedimentary rock of another kind. **3.** The process of accumulating to form a mass.

con•cu•bine |**kŏng'**kyə bīn'| *or* |**kŏn'**-| *n.* A woman who lives with and has a sexual relationship with a man but is not married to him.

con•cur |kən **kûr'**| *v.* **con•curred, con•cur•ring.** **1.** To have the same opinion; agree: *I concur with many people on the need to stop pollution.* **2.** To occur at the same time: *Happiness and success do not always concur.*

con•cur•rence |kən **kûr'**əns| *or* |-**kŭr'**-| *n.* **1.** Agreement of opinion: *the concurrence of all four umpires that the runner was out.* **2.** An occurrence of events, action, efforts, etc., at the same time.

con•cur•rent |kən **kûr'**ənt| *or* |-**kŭr'**-| *adj.* **1.** Happening at the same time: *concurrent events.* **2.** Having one and only one point in common: *a set of concurrent lines.* —**con•cur'rent•ly** *adv.*

con•cus•sion |kən **kŭsh'**ən| *n.* **1.** A violent jarring; a shock: *A concussion resulted from the blast.* **2.** An injury to a soft tissue of the body, especially the brain, resulting from a hard blow.

con•demn |kən **dĕm'**| *v.* **1.** To express strong disapproval of; denounce: *The treaty condemned the use of war to solve international problems and called for peaceful settlement of disputes.* **2. a.** To judge to be guilty and state the punishment for: *The suspect was arrested, tried, and condemned in a single day.* **b.** To sentence to a particular kind of punishment: *The prisoner was condemned to death.* **3.** To cause or compel to undergo an unhappy fate; doom: *The shipwrecked sailor felt himself condemned to a lonely, silent life.* **4.** To declare unfit for use: *The city condemned the old jail on Water Street.* **5.** To take over (private property) for public use: *The state condemned the Carter farm for the construction of a much-needed expressway.*

con•dem•na•tion |kŏn'dĕm **nā'**shən| *or* |-dəm-| *n.* **1. a.** The act of condemning. **b.** The condition or fact of being condemned. **2.** An expression of strong disapproval.

con•den•sa•tion |kŏn'dĕn **sā'**shən| *or* |-dən-| *n.* **1.** The process by which part or all of a gas or a mixture of gases becomes liquid or, sometimes, solid: *the condensation of steam to water.* **2.** A liquid or solid, especially water or ice, formed by this process: *the condensation on the bathroom mirror.* **3.** A brief or shortened form or presentation of something: *a one-hour condensation of the event on television.* **4.** The act or process of thus shortening something: *the condensation of a long story.* [SEE NOTE]

con•dense |kən **dĕns'**| *v.* **con•densed, con•dens•ing.** **1.** To change from a gas to a liquid or sometimes solid form: *Water vapor in the air often condenses on grass as dew. A sudden temperature drop may condense water vapor to ice.* **2.** To become or cause to become more concentrated, compact, or dense: *condense milk into a thick, syrupy substance. Evaporation condenses the mixture.* **3.** To put into brief or shortened form: *condense the history of a country into a single chapter.*

condensed milk. Sweetened cow's milk that has been made very thick by evaporation.

con•dens•er |kən **dĕn'**sər| *n.* **1.** A device used to cause a gas or vapor to condense. **2.** A capacitor, an electrical device.

con•de•scend |kŏn'dĭ **sĕnd'**| *v.* **1.** To agree to do something one regards as being beneath one's social rank or dignity: *The king condescended to join the peasants' party. My brother condescended to take out the garbage.* **2.** To act in a manner that shows one considers oneself superior to others: *Rich, snobbish Mrs. Newleigh condescends to all her neighbors.*

con•de•scend•ing |kŏn'dĭ **sĕn'**dĭng| *adj.* Showing that one considers oneself superior to others; patronizing: *gave a condescending nod as his only greeting.* —**con'de•scend'ing•ly** *adv.*

con•de•scen•sion |kŏn'dĭ **sĕn'**shən| *n.* An attitude or action that shows one considers oneself superior to others.

con•di•ment |**kŏn'**də mənt| *n.* A sauce, relish, spice, etc., used as a seasoning for food.

con•di•tion |kən **dĭsh'**ən| *n.* **1.** A state of being or existence; the way something or someone is: *They worked hard to restore the old house to its original condition. Astronauts must become accustomed to the condition known as weightlessness. As the tyrant gained more power, the condition of the people became worse.* **2. a.** A state of general health or fitness: *Exercise every day to keep yourself in good condition.* **b.** Readiness for use; working order: *The brakes of the car are in poor condition.* **3.** A disease, ailment, etc.: *Some young people are troubled by a skin condition called acne.* **4.** Often **conditions.** A situation that affects or influences an activity, event, etc.; circumstances: *The committee gathered facts about living and working conditions. Under normal conditions the human heart beats about 72 times every minute.* **5.** Something stated as necessary or desirable; a requirement; provision: *The ambassador insisted that the commercial treaty must meet certain conditions.* **6.** Social rank or position: *A congressman must be able to deal with people of all conditions and see every point of view.* —*v.* **1.** To put into good or proper condition; make fit: *Carl exercised regularly to condition himself for the football season.* **2.** To have a strong influence on; affect: *Water has conditioned the development and way of life of fishes.* **3.** To adapt; accustom; train: *Our ears have been conditioned to melody, harmony, and rhythm in music.* **4.** To cause (a living organism) to develop a conditioned response.

***Idiom.* on (the) condition that.** If; provided: *Connie will cook dinner on condition that she doesn't have to wash the dishes.*

con•di•tion•al |kən **dĭsh'**ə nəl| *adj.* **1.** Depending on a circumstance, outcome, etc.; not absolute or complete: *conditional approval.* **2.** In grammar, expressing a condition on which an outcome or possibility depends. In the sentence *We'll go swimming if it's sunny tomorrow, if it's sunny tomorrow* is a conditional clause. —*n.* A

condensation

Condensation *of water vapor from the atmosphere occurs when moist air comes into contact with a surface whose temperature is below the dew point, a temperature that is determined by the absolute humidity of the atmosphere. Under these circumstances, the water vapor changes to dew, which is a liquid, or, if the surface is cold enough, to frost, which is a solid.*

condor

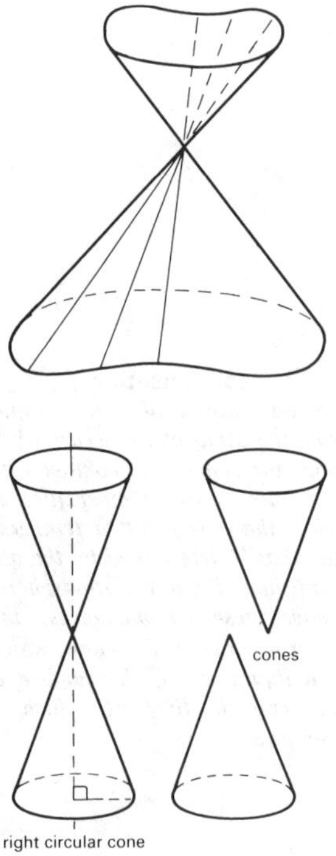

cone

statement that can be expressed in the form *If* A, *then* B; for example, *If a pair of lines intersect, then the vertical angles formed are equal* is a conditional. —**con•di′tion•al•ly** *adv.*

conditioned response. A new or changed response that an organism produces as a result of a particular stimulus after it has been given training of a certain type.

con•di•tion•er |kən **dĭsh′**ə nər| *n.* A device or substance used to improve something in some way: *an air conditioner; a bottle of hair conditioner.*

con•dole |kən **dōl′**| *v.* **con•doled, con•dol•ing.** To express sympathy, especially for a person who has experienced sorrow or misfortune: *I condoled with him over the death of his grandmother.*

con•do•lence |kən **dō′**ləns| *n.* Sympathy or an expression of sympathy for a person who has experienced sorrow or misfortune: *send a letter of condolence to the family of a person who has died.*

con•do•min•i•um |kŏn′də **mĭn′**ē əm| *n.* An apartment building in which the individual apartments are owned by the tenants.

con•done |kən **dōn′**| *v.* **con•doned, con•don•ing.** To forgive, overlook, or ignore (wrongdoing or offensive behavior) without protest or punishment: *Their pranks are too troublesome to condone.*

con•dor |**kŏn′**dôr′| *or* |-dər| *n.* A very large vulture of the mountains of California or South America. [SEE PICTURE]

con•du•cive |kən **dōō′**sĭv| *or* |**-dyōō′-**| *adj.* Tending to cause, promote, or help bring about: *The noisy atmosphere in the study hall is not conducive to work.*

con•duct |kən **dŭkt′**| *v.* **1.** To lead; guide: *conduct a tour.* **2.** To direct the course of; manage: *conduct a religious service; conduct an experiment; conduct negotiations; conduct a business.* **3.** To lead or direct (musicians or a musical work): *conduct a chamber orchestra. He conducts very well. He conducted Beethoven's Ninth Symphony.* **4.** To act as a path for (electricity or some other flow of energy): *Most metals conduct heat well.* **5. conduct oneself.** To act properly; do what is right. —*n.* |**kŏn′**dŭkt′|. **1.** The way a person acts; behavior: *disorderly conduct.* **2.** The act of directing or controlling; management; administration: *The President is responsible for the conduct of foreign affairs.*

con•duc•tance |kən **dŭk′**təns| *n.* The measure of the ability of a body to conduct electricity, expressed in mhos.

con•duc•tion |kən **dŭk′**shən| *n.* The transmission or passage of something through a medium or along a path, especially when what passes is a flow of energy, such as electricity or heat, and the medium does not appear to move.

con•duc•tive |kən **dŭk′**tĭv| *adj.* Having the property of conductivity; capable of conducting.

con•duc•tiv•i•ty |kŏn′dŭk **tĭv′**ĭ tē| *n.* The ability of something to act as a path for a flow of energy, especially electricity.

con•duc•tor |kən **dŭk′**tər| *n.* **1. a.** A person who conducts; the leader, guide, or director of a group or organization. **b.** The person who conducts an orchestra, band, or other group of musical performers. **2.** The person in charge of a railroad train, bus, or streetcar. **3.** A substance or material that provides an easy path for a flow of energy in the form of heat, light, sound, or, especially, electricity.

con•duit |**kŏn′**dĭt| *or* |-dōō ĭt| *n.* **1.** A channel or pipe for carrying water, gas, or other fluid. **2.** A tube or pipe through which electric wires or cables pass.

cone |kōn| *n.* **1. a.** A **conical surface.** **b.** Any similar surface, such as one formed by all the rays that begin at a given point and pass through a curve not in the same plane as the point, or by all the line segments connecting such a point and such a curve. **c.** Any surface of this kind in which the given curve is a circle, especially one in which the line connecting the given point and the center of the circle is perpendicular to the plane of the circle; a right circular cone. **2. a.** Any figure having such a surface as its outer boundary; a solid cone. **b.** Anything having the shape of such a figure: *an ice-cream cone.* **3.** A rounded or long cluster of woody scales containing the seeds of a pine, fir, hemlock, or related tree. **4.** A tropical sea animal related to the snails, having a tapering, often colorfully marked shell. **5.** Any of the structures in the retina of the eye that are sensitive to light and that perceive differences between colors. [SEE PICTURE]

Con•el•rad |**kŏn′**l răd′| *n.* A system designed to prevent enemy aircraft attacking the United States from using radio broadcasts as aids to navigation. Under the system all broadcasting is stopped except for that done by emergency stations operating on 640 and 1,240 kilohertz (kilocycles per second).

Con•es•to•ga wagon |kŏn′ĭ **stō′**gə|. A heavy covered wagon, first built at Conestoga, Pennsylvania, used by American pioneers in their westward travel.

co•ney |**kō′**nē| *or* |**kŭn′**ē| *n., pl.* **co•neys.** A form of the word **cony.**

con•fec•tion |kən **fĕk′**shən| *n.* A sweet preparation, such as candy or preserves.

con•fec•tion•er |kən **fĕk′**shə nər| *n.* A person who makes or sells candy, preserves, and other confections.

confectioner's sugar. A fine, powdery sugar with some cornstarch added, used in making candy, icing, etc.

con•fec•tion•er•y |kən **fĕk′**shə nĕr′ē| *n., pl.* **con•fec•tion•er•ies.** **1.** Candies and other confections. **2.** A confectioner's shop.

con•fed•er•a•cy |kən **fĕd′**ər ə sē| *n., pl.* **con•fed•er•a•cies.** **1.** A political union of several peoples or states: *A powerful confederacy of Creek Indians. Several Greek cities formed a confederacy.* **2. the Confederacy.** The **Confederate States of America.**

con•fed•er•ate |kən **fĕd′**ər ĭt| *adj.* **1.** Belonging to a confederacy. **2. Confederate.** Of the Confederate States of America: *the Confederate ironclad "Merrimac."* —*n.* **1.** An associate in a plot or crime; an accomplice. **2.** A member of a confederacy. **3. Confederate.** A supporter of the Confederate States of America. —*v.* |kən **fĕd′**ə-rāt′| **con•fed•er•at•ed, con•fed•er•at•ing.** To join together in a confederation; form into or become part of a confederacy.

ă pat/ā pay/â care/ä father/ĕ pet/
ē be/ĭ pit/ī pie/î fierce/ŏ pot/
ō go/ô paw, for/oi oil/ŏŏ book/
ōō boot/ou out/ŭ cut/û fur/
th the/th thin/hw which/zh vision/
ə ago, item, pencil, atom, circus

Confederate States of America. The confederacy of 11 Southern states that seceded from the United States in 1860 and 1861. They were Alabama, Arkansas, Florida, Georgia, Louisiana, Mississippi, North Carolina, South Carolina, Tennessee, Texas, and Virginia. [SEE PICTURE]

con•fed•er•a•tion |kən fĕd′ə **rā′**shən| *n.* A confederacy: *The weaknesses of a loose confederation became increasingly apparent.*

con•fer |kən **fûr′**| *v.* **con•ferred, con•fer•ring. 1.** To hold a conference; consult together: *The President conferred with his advisers.* **2.** To bestow or award: *The general conferred a medal on the two marines.*

con•fer•ence |**kŏn′**fər əns| *or* |-frəns| *n.* **1.** A meeting to discuss a subject or a number of subjects: *a news conference; a peace conference; a summit conference.* **2.** A regional association of athletic teams. —*modifier: a conference room.*

con•fess |kən **fĕs′**| *v.* **1. a.** To make known (one's sins) to a priest or to God. **b.** To hear the confession of: *A priest confessed them.* **2.** To state openly that one has committed a crime or done something bad: *The suspect confessed to the crime. He confessed that he had broken the window.* **3.** To admit (a fault): *He confessed his mistake.* **4.** To admit conversationally: *I must confess I was surprised.*

con•fes•sion |kən **fĕsh′**ən| *n.* **1.** The act of telling one's sins to a priest or to God. **2.** The act of confessing or admitting; acknowledgment. **3.** Something confessed.

con•fes•sion•al |kən **fĕsh′**ə nəl| *n.* A small booth in which a priest hears confessions.

con•fes•sor |kən **fĕs′**ər| *n.* **1.** A priest who hears confessions. **2.** Someone who accepts intimate confidences and consoles: *She acted as counselor and confessor to the whole group.*

con•fet•ti |kən **fĕt′**ē| *n.* *(used with a singular verb).* Small pieces of colored paper scattered about on festive occasions.

con•fi•dant |kŏn′fĭ **dănt′**| *or* |**-dänt′**| *or* |**kŏn′**fĭ dănt′| *or* |-dänt′| *n.* A person to whom one confides personal matters or secrets.

con•fide |kən **fīd′**| *v.* **con•fid•ed, con•fid•ing. 1.** To tell confidentially: *confide a secret to a friend.* **2. confide in.** To tell or share one's secrets with: *I know I can confide in you.*

con•fi•dence |**kŏn′**fĭ dəns| *n.* **1.** A feeling of assurance, especially of self-assurance: *states his case with confidence. He lacks confidence in himself.* **2.** Trust or reliance: *won my confidence. I am placing my confidence in you.* **3.** A trusting relationship: *I have decided to take you into my confidence.* **4.** The assurance that someone will keep a secret: *I am telling you this in strict confidence.* **5.** Something confided; a secret.

con•fi•dent |**kŏn′**fĭ dənt| *adj.* Feeling or showing confidence; sure of oneself; certain: *The team is confident of victory on Sunday. Mr. Jones approached the lectern with a confident air.* —**con′fi•dent•ly** *adv.*

con•fi•den•tial |kŏn′fĭ **dĕn′**shəl| *adj.* **1.** Told in confidence; secret: *confidential information.* **2.** Entrusted with private matters: *a confidential secretary.* **3.** Showing confidence or intimacy: *a confidential tone of voice.* —**con′fi•den′tial•ly** *adv.*

con•fig•u•ra•tion |kən fĭg′yə **rā′**shən| *n.* The figure formed by the arrangements of the parts of something; outline; contour.

con•fine |kən **fīn′**| *v.* **con•fined, con•fin•ing. 1.** To limit in area or extent: *Nineteenth-century New York was confined to Manhattan.* **2.** To restrict in movement: *Foreign merchants were confined to a small enclave. He was confined to bed for a week.* **3.** To imprison: *The Nazis confined many people to concentration camps.* **4.** To restrict (speech, activity, etc.): *Confine your answers to the questions asked.*

con•fine•ment |kən **fīn′**mənt| *n.* **1.** A condition of being confined: *The Indians were doomed to confinement on reservations.* **2.** The time during which a pregnant woman is engaged in the process of childbirth and needs care in bed afterward.

con•fines |**kŏn′**fīnz′| *pl.n.* The limits of a space or area; borders: *within the confines of one county.*

con•firm |kən **fûrm′**| *v.* **1.** To give moral strength to: *"confirm thy soul in self-control, thy liberty in law"* ("America the Beautiful"). **2.** To support or establish the validity of: *The news confirmed the rumors. Experiments confirmed the theory.* **3.** To give or get definite evidence: *We have confirmed that man can live on the moon.* **4.** To make (an appointment or action) binding: *confirmed the governor in office; confirm your plane reservations.* **5.** To admit to full membership in a church.

con•fir•ma•tion |kŏn′fər **mā′**shən| *n.* **1.** The act of confirming: *senatorial confirmation of an ambassador.* **2.** Something that confirms; proof: *This was confirmation of his suspicions.* **3.** A Christian ceremony in which a young person is made a full member of a church. **4.** In Judaism, a ceremony marking the completion of a young person's religious training.

con•firmed |kən **fûrmd′**| *adj.* Firmly settled in a habit or condition: *a confirmed bachelor.*

con•fis•cate |**kŏn′**fĭ skāt′| *v.* **con•fis•cat•ed, con•fis•cat•ing.** To seize (private property) from someone in order that it may be withheld, redistributed, or destroyed. —**con′fis•ca′tion** *n.*

con•flict |**kŏn′**flĭkt′| *n.* **1.** Prolonged fighting; warfare: *Armed conflict could erupt at any time.* **2.** A clash of opposing ideas, interests, etc.: *a personality conflict.* —*v.* |kən **flĭkt′**|. To be in opposition; differ; clash: *State regulations may not conflict with federal laws.* —**con•flict′ing** *adj.: conflicting evidence; a conflicting interpretation; conflicting dates.*

con•flu•ence |**kŏn′**flo͞o əns| *n.* **1.** The flowing together of two or more streams. **2.** The point where such streams come together.

con•form |kən **fôrm′**| *v.* To follow an established pattern: *The wise person generally conforms to the rules and customs of his society. You are conforming when you obey your parents and teachers. The plans must conform to the recently approved building code.*

con•for•ma•tion |kŏn′fər **mā′**shən| *n.* **1.** The way something is formed; shape or structure. **2.** The act or condition of conforming.

con•form•ist |kən **fôr′**mĭst| *n.* Someone who conforms to current attitudes or practices; a person who always does what he thinks other people expect him to do.

con•form•i•ty |kən **fôr′**mĭ tē| *n.* **1.** Agreement;

Confederate battle flag

harmony: *act in conformity with established custom.* **2.** Action or behavior that is in agreement with current rules, customs, principles, etc.: *an advertising campaign that appeals to one's sense of conformity.* **3.** The condition of being in agreement with accepted or established rules, customs, etc.: *brief remarks that should help you in observing the rules of good grammar when conformity is advisable.*

con•found |kən **found'**| *or* |kŏn-| *v.* **1.** To bewilder, puzzle, or perplex: *The pitcher confounded the batters with his knuckle ball.* **2.** To mix up; mistake (one thing) for another: *confound good and evil; confound fiction and fact.* —*interj.* A word used to express anger or annoyance: *Confound it! Confound you!*

con•found•ed |kən **found'**dĭd| *or* |kŏn-| *v.* **1.** Bewildered; puzzled. **2.** Used as an intensive: *that confounded brother of mine!* —**con•found'ed•ly** *adv.* —**con•found'ed•ness** *n.*

con•front |kən **frŭnt'**| *v.* **1.** To come face to face with; stand before: *allow the defendant to confront his accuser. The problems that confront us seem overwhelming.* **2.** To meet or face boldly or defiantly: *A couple of hoodlums confronted him on the street.* **3.** To bring face to face; challenge to accept or deny: *When confronted with all the evidence, the suspect confessed.*

con•fron•ta•tion |kŏn'frən **tā'**shən| *n.* **1.** The act of confronting: *An accused person has the right of confrontation with regard to his accuser.* **2.** A direct encounter; a clash, as of rivals, opponents, or opposite political points of view: *the Arab-Israeli confrontation. Conflicts and confrontation caused the cancellation of classes.*

Con•fu•cian |kən **fyōō'**shən| *adj.* Of or relating to Confucius, his teachings, or his followers. —*n.* A person who follows the teachings of Confucius; a Confucianist.

Con•fu•cian•ism |kən **fyōō'**shə nĭz'əm| *n.* The principles of conduct based on the teachings of Confucius and stressing personal virtue, devotion to family and ancestors, and social harmony and justice. —**Con•fu'cian•ist** *n.*

Con•fu•cius |kən **fyōō'**shəs|. 551–479 B.C. Chinese philosopher and teacher.

con•fuse |kən **fyōōz'**| *v.* **con•fused, con•fus•ing. 1.** To mislead; mix up; throw off: *The purpose of camouflage is to confuse the enemy.* **2.** To fail to distinguish between; mistake for something else: *Don't confuse the words "principal" and "principle."* **3.** To make unclear; blur: *Such statements merely confuse the issue.* —**con•fused'** *adj.*: *a confused look; a confused situation.* —**con•fus'ing** *adj.*: *confusing instructions.*

con•fu•sion |kən **fyōō'**zhən| *n.* **1.** The act of confusing or mixing up: *Commas often help to prevent confusion.* **2.** The condition of being confused; bewilderment: *The news threw us all into confusion.* **3.** Disorder or chaos: *The enemy retreated in confusion.*

con•fute |kən **fyōōt'**| *v.* **con•fut•ed, con•fut•ing.** To prove to be wrong or false; refute.

con•ga |**kŏng'**gə| *n.* **1. a.** A dance of Latin-American origin in which the dancers form a long, winding line. **b.** Music for this dance. **2.** A type of tall, narrow drum that is beaten with the hands.

con•geal |kən **jēl'**| *v.* **1.** To change or cause to change from a liquid to a solid, as by freezing. **2.** To thicken or coagulate.

con•ge•ner |**kŏn'**jə nər| *n.* A member of the same class, group, or genus.

con•gen•ial |kən **jēn'**yəl| *adj.* **1.** Having the same tastes, habits, etc.: *two congenial persons.* **2.** Of a pleasant disposition; friendly; amiable: *a congenial host.* **3.** Suited to one's nature; pleasant; agreeable: *congenial work; congenial surroundings.* —**con•ge'ni•al'i•ty** |kən jē'nē **ăl'**ĭ tē| *n.* —**con•gen'ial•ly** *adv.*

con•gen•i•tal |kən **jĕn'**ĭ tl| *adj.* **1.** Existing from the time of birth but not hereditary: *a congenital defect.* **2.** Being such as if by nature: *A congenital thief.* —**con•gen'i•tal•ly** *adv.*

con•ger |**kŏng'**gər| *n.* Also **conger eel.** A large ocean eel. [SEE PICTURE]

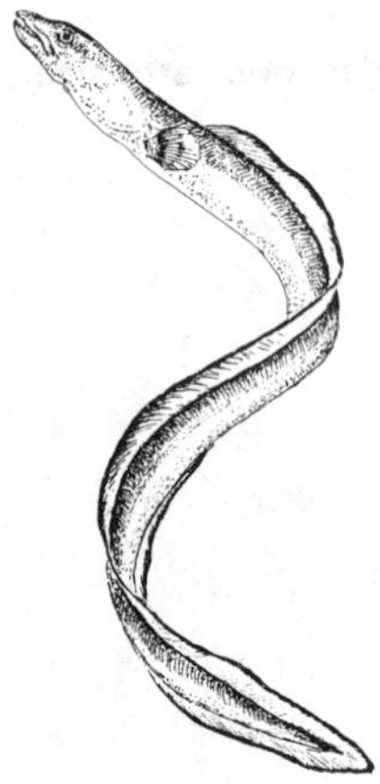

conger

con•gest |kən **jĕst'**| *v.* **1.** To overfill; overcrowd. **2. a.** To cause an abnormally large amount of blood to collect in (a vessel or organ of the body). **b.** To become filled with an abnormally large amount of blood. —**con•gest'ed** *adj.*: *a congested street; congested cities.*

con•ges•tion |kən **jĕs'**chən| *n.* **1.** A condition of overcrowding: *traffic congestion.* **2.** A condition in which too much blood collects in an organ or tissue of the body.

con•ges•tive |kən **jĕs'**tĭv| *adj.* Of or involving congestion: *congestive heart failure.*

con•glom•er•ate |kən **glŏm'**ər ĭt| *n.* **1.** A mass of material that clings together. **2.** A rock that consists of pebbles, gravel, etc., cemented together by hardened clay or a similar material. **3.** A business corporation that operates in numerous widely diversified fields. —*adj.* Formed together into a mass.

con•glom•er•a•tion |kən glŏm'ə **rā'**shən| *n.* A collection or accumulation of many different things.

Con•go[1] |**kŏng'**gō|. A country in west-central Africa west of Zaire, with a short coastline on the Atlantic Ocean. Population, 1,537,000. Capital, Brazzaville.

Congo[2]. A river in Africa, flowing through Zaire into the Atlantic Ocean.

Con•go•lese |kŏng'gə **lēz'**| *or* |-**lēs'**| *n., pl.* **Con•go•lese.** A native or inhabitant of the Congo. —*adj.* Of the Congo or the Congolese.

con•grat•u•late |kən **grăch'**ə lāt'| *v.* **con•grat•u•lat•ed, con•grat•u•lat•ing. 1.** To speak to (someone) with praise for an achievement or any good event. **2.** —**congratulate oneself.** To take pleasure in something one has successfully done, performed, etc.

con•grat•u•la•tion |kən grăch'ə **lā'**shən| *n.* **1.** The act of congratulating: *a few quiet words of congratulation.* **2. congratulations.** An expression used in congratulating someone.

con•grat•u•la•to•ry |kən **grăch'**ə lə tôr'ē| *or* |-tōr'ē| *adj.* Expressing congratulation: *a congratulatory message.*

con•gre•gate |**kŏng'**grə gāt'| *v.* **con•gre•gat•ed, con•gre•gat•ing.** To gather together; assemble: *Salmon congregate here in huge numbers.* —**con'gre•ga'tor** *n.*

con•gre•ga•tion |kŏng'grə **gā'**shən| *n.* **1.** A gathering of people or things. **2.** A group of people gathered for religious worship.

con•gre•ga•tion•al |kŏng'grə **gā'**shə nəl| *adj.*

ă pat/ā pay/â care/ä father/ĕ pet/ ē be/ĭ pit/ī pie/î fierce/ŏ pot/ ō go/ô paw, for/oi oil/ŏŏ book/ ōō boot/ou out/ŭ cut/û fur/ *th* the/th thin/hw which/zh vision/ ə ago, item, pencil, atom, circus

1. Of a congregation. 2. **Congregational.** Of Congregationalism or Congregationalists.

con•gre•ga•tion•al•ism |kŏng′grə gā′shə nə lĭz′əm| *n.* 1. Church government in which each local congregation governs itself. 2. **Congregationalism.** The system of government and religious beliefs of a Protestant denomination in which each member church is self-governing. —**con′gre•ga′tion•al•ist, Con′gre•ga′tion•al•ist** *adj. & n.*

con•gress |kŏng′grĭs| *n.* 1. A formal meeting of persons representing various nations, organizations, or professions to discuss problems. 2. The lawmaking body of a republic. 3. **Congress.** In the United States, the Senate and House of Representatives, the two assemblies whose members are elected to make the laws of the nation.

con•gres•sion•al |kən grĕsh′ə nəl| *adj.* 1. Of a congress. 2. **Congressional.** Of the Congress of the United States.

Congressional Record. A daily publication containing a word-for-word report of the speeches and proceedings of the United States Congress.

con•gress•man, also **Con•gress•man** |kŏng′grĭs mən| *n., pl.* **-men** |-mən|. A member of the United States Congress, especially of the House of Representatives.

con•gru•ence |kŏng′gro͞o əns| *or* |kən gro͞o′əns| *n.* 1. The condition of being congruent. 2. A mathematical statement that two things are congruent.

con•gru•en•cy |kŏng′gro͞o ən sē| *or* |kən gro͞o′ən-sē| *n.* A form of the word **congruence.**

con•gru•ent |kŏng′gro͞o ənt| *or* |kən gro͞o′ənt| *adj.* In geometry, matching exactly; having the same size and shape: *congruent triangles.* —**con′gru•ent•ly** *adv.*

con•gru•i•ty |kən gro͞o′ĭ tē| *or* |kŏn-| *n., pl.* **con•gru•i•ties.** 1. Agreement; harmony. 2. Congruence, as of geometric figures.

con•ic |kŏn′ĭk| *adj.* Of or shaped like a cone. —*n.* A **conic section.**

con•i•cal |kŏn′ĭ kəl| *adj.* A form of the word **conic.**

conical surface. A geometric surface formed by the set of all lines that pass through both a given plane curve and a point not in the plane curve.

conic section. Any one of a group of plane curves, including the circle, ellipse, hyperbola, and parabola, that can be formed by the intersection of a plane and a right circular conical surface. [SEE PICTURE]

con•i•fer |kŏn′ə fər| *or* |kō′nə-| *n.* A tree, such as a pine, fir, or hemlock, that bears cones.

co•nif•er•ous |kō nĭf′ər əs| *or* |kə-| *adj.* 1. Bearing cones: *coniferous trees such as pines and hemlocks.* 2. Of cone-bearing trees: *a coniferous forest.*

conj. In grammar, conjunction.

con•jec•tur•al |kən jĕk′chər əl| *adj.* Based on or inclined to conjecture.

con•jec•ture |kən jĕk′chər| *n.* 1. The formation of an opinion or conclusion from incomplete or insufficient evidence; guesswork: *The origin of language is a matter of pure conjecture.* 2. A statement, opinion, or conclusion based on guesswork; a guess: *Make a conjecture about the outcome of the election.* —*v.* **con•jec•tured, con•jec•tur•ing.** To make a conjecture; guess.

con•joint |kən joint′| *adj.* Joined together; combined; associated. —**con•joint′ly** *adv.*

con•ju•gal |kŏn′jə gəl| *adj.* Having to do with marriage or the relationship between husband and wife. —**con′ju•gal•ly** *adv.*

con•ju•gate |kŏn′jə gāt′| *v.* **con•ju•gat•ed, con•ju•gat•ing.** 1. To give the various inflected forms of (a verb). For example, the verb "to have" is conjugated *I have, you have, he has, we have, you have, they have.* 2. To undergo conjugation, as in the process of reproduction. —*adj.* |kŏn′jə gĭt| *or* |-gāt′|. Joined together, especially in pairs; coupled.

con•ju•ga•tion |kŏn′jə gā′shən| *n.* 1. a. The inflection of a particular verb. b. A presentation of the complete set of inflected forms of a verb. 2. A type of sexual reproduction in which single-celled organisms of the same species join together and exchange nuclear material before undergoing fission. 3. The union of sex cells.

con•junc•tion |kən jŭngk′shən| *n.* 1. A combination or association: *The local police acted in conjunction with the FBI.* 2. The occurrence together of two events, conditions, etc. 3. A word, such as *and, but, or,* etc., that connects other words in a sentence. 4. The relative position of two planets or other celestial bodies when they are located along the same meridian on the celestial sphere. [SEE NOTE].

con•junc•ti•va |kŏn′jŭngk tī′və| *n., pl.* **con•junc•ti•vas** or **con•junc•ti•vae** |kŏn′jŭngk tī′vē|. The mucous membrane that lines the inside of the eyelid and covers the surface of the eyeball.

con•junc•tive |kən jŭngk′tĭv| *adj.* Joined or serving to join together.

conjunctive adverb. An adverb used as a conjunction. For example, the word "however" is a conjunctive adverb.

con•junc•ti•vi•tis |kən jŭngk′tə vī′tĭs| *n.* Inflammation, often very contagious, of the conjunctiva.

con•jure |kŏn′jər| *or* |kən jo͝or′| *v.* **con•jured, con•jur•ing.** 1. To summon (a devil or spirit) by oath or magic spell. 2. To produce as if by magic: *conjure a miracle.* 3. To practice magic; perform magic tricks. 4. —**conjure up.** To call to mind: *The mention of Africa conjures up images of jungles and wild animals.*

con•jur•er, also **con•ju•ror** |kŏn′jər ər| *n.* A magician, especially one who claims to be able to summon spirits by oath or spell.

conk |kŏngk| *or* |kôngk|. *Slang.* *v.* To hit, especially on the head. —***phrasal verb.*** **conk out.** 1. To fail suddenly: *The engine conked out.* 2. To tire after exertion. ¶ *These sound alike* **conk, conch.**

Conn. Connecticut.

con•nect |kə nĕkt′| *v.* 1. To join or come together; link: *A new road connects the two towns. Capillaries connect the arteries and veins. Route 11 connects with Route 20 near Syracuse.* 2. To think of as related; associate: *There would appear to be no reason to connect the two events.* 3. To plug into an electrical circuit: *connect a television set.* 4. To link by telephone: *I'll connect you with the switchboard.* 5. *Informal.* In baseball, to hit the ball solidly: *The batter connected for a home*

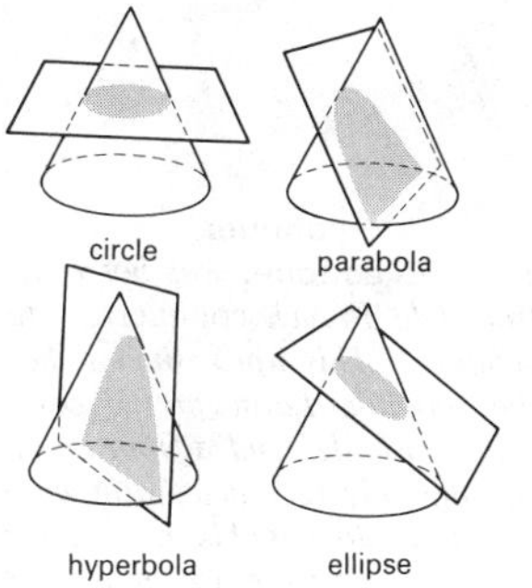

conic section
circle
parabola
hyperbola
ellipse

conjunction

Conjunction *comes from Latin* coniunctiō, *"a joining together," from* coniungere, *"to join together": com-, "together," +* iungere, *"to join." See note at* **join.**

run. —**con•nect'ing** *adj: a connecting highway; connecting rooms.*

Con•nect•i•cut |kə nĕt'ĭ kət|. A New England state of the United States. Population, 3,105,576. Capital, Hartford.

con•nec•tion |kə nĕk'shən| *n.* **1.** The act of connecting or condition of being connected. **2.** Something that connects or joins; a link: *a bad telephone connection. There are excellent road and rail connections between the two cities.* **3.** A relationship: *the connection between the sun and the seasons.* **4.** An association in the mind: *I knew I had met him somewhere, but I couldn't make the connection.* **5.** Context: *In this connection I might mention the following incidents.* **6.** Often **connections.** An associate or acquaintance with whom one has a mutually beneficial relationship. **7.** A transfer from one plane, train, or bus to another: *I missed my connection in Chicago.*

***Idiom.* in connection with.** With reference to: *He is here in connection with his work.*

con•nec•tive |kə nĕk'tĭv| *adj.* Connecting or serving to connect. —*n.* **1.** Anything that connects. **2.** In grammar, a word, such as a conjunction, that connects other words or clauses.

connective tissue. Any of the various tissues that form the framework and support of the animal body, including such tissues as bone, cartilage, mucous membrane, and fat.

con•ning tower |kŏn'ĭng|. **1.** A raised, enclosed structure on the deck of a submarine, used for observation and as a means of entrance and exit. **2.** The armored pilothouse of a warship.

con•nip•tion |kə nĭp'shən| *n. Informal.* A fit of anger or other violent emotion; a tantrum.

con•nive |kə nīv'| *v.* **con•nived, con•niv•ing. 1.** To pretend not to notice something that should be reported or condemned: *The chief connived at wrongdoing in the police department.* **2.** To cooperate secretly or underhandedly: *The detective was accused of conniving with racketeers.* —**con•niv'ance** *n.*

con•nois•seur |kŏn'ə sûr'| *n.* A person with a thorough knowledge of or appreciation for a certain subject in which good taste is needed: *a connoisseur of art.*

con•no•ta•tion |kŏn'ə tā'shən| *n.* A secondary meaning suggested by a certain word in addition to its literal meaning.

con•no•ta•tive |kŏn'ə tā'tĭv| *adj.* Connoting something; having a connotation: *Words like "white" and "light" could have highly connotative meanings in certain contexts.*

con•note |kə nōt'| *v.* **con•not•ed, con•not•ing.** To suggest or imply in addition to literal meaning: *The word "orient" often connotes mystery, ornate temples, and faraway places.*

con•nu•bi•al |kə nōō'bē əl| *or* |-nyōō'-| *adj.* Having to do with marriage or the relationship between husband and wife; conjugal.

con•quer |kŏng'kər| *v.* **1.** To win mastery over by war: *In 1066 the Norman French conquered England.* **2.** To gain control over (a hostile environment, challenge, etc.): *Scientists have always battled to conquer disease. But Laura, in true pioneer spirit, conquered homesickness.* **3.** To gain great recognition from (a group): *In 1839 he went to Paris to conquer the operatic world.* **4.** To gain the favor of (someone): *Zeus came down to conquer Danae.* **5.** To be victorious; win: *Then conquer we must, for our cause it is just.* —**con'quered** *adj.: a conquered nation.* —**con'quer•ing** *adj.: a conquering army.* [SEE NOTE]

conquer

The word **conquer** *was borrowed from Old French* conquerre, *"to conquer." This word, since it has the common Latin prefix* con-, *is obviously descended from Latin. But the only recorded Latin word that it could possibly have come from is* conquīrere, *which (a) does not have quite the right shape to produce* conquerre *in Old French, and (b) did not mean "to conquer"; it meant "to search for, to try to get." It is therefore assumed that after the fall of the Roman Empire, when writing was little used,* conquīrere *must have changed to* conquērere *and acquired the new meaning "to get by force, to conquer."*

con•quer•or |kŏng'kər ər| *n.* **1.** Someone who conquers: *the conqueror of Wales.* **2. the Conqueror.** William I of England.

con•quest |kŏn'kwĕst'| *or* |kŏng'-| *n.* **1.** An act of conquering. **2.** Something conquered. **3.** Someone whose favor is won. **4. the Conquest.** The Norman Conquest of England.

con•quis•ta•dor |kŏn kwĭs'tə dôr'| *n.* One of the Spanish conquerors of Mexico and Peru in the 16th century.

con•san•guin•i•ty |kŏn'săng gwĭn'ĭ tē| *n.* Relationship by descent from the same ancestor.

con•science |kŏn'shəns| *n.* An inner sense in a person that distinguishes right from wrong: *My conscience is clear.*

***Idiom.* on (one's) conscience.** Causing one to feel guilty.

con•sci•en•tious |kŏn'shē ĕn'shəs| *or* |kŏn'sē-| *adj.* Showing or done with care and seriousness of purpose: *a conscientious worker; a conscientious job.* —**con'sci•en'tious•ly** *adv.* —**con'sci•en'tious•ness** *n.*

conscientious objector. A person who refuses to serve in the armed forces on the basis of moral or religious beliefs.

con•scious |kŏn'shəs| *adj.* **1.** Using one's mental powers; capable of thought, will, or perception: *Man is a conscious being.* **2.** Able to perceive and understand what is happening: *He is badly injured but still conscious.* **3.** Having or showing self-consciousness; aware: *He is conscious of his shortcomings.* **4.** Done with awareness; intentional; deliberate: *a conscious insult; make a conscious effort to speak more distinctly.* —**con'scious•ly** *adv.*

con•scious•ness |kŏn'shəs nĭs| *n.* **1.** The condition of being conscious: *lose consciousness; regain consciousness.* **2.** Awareness: *The Puritans had a mighty consciousness of sin and found themselves forever punishing somebody.* **3.** All the ideas, opinions, feelings, etc., held or thought to be held by a person or group: *Lengthy conflicts were not a part of the American consciousness.*

con•script |kən skrĭpt'| *v.* To draft for service in the armed forces. —*n.* |kŏn'skrĭpt'|. A person who is drafted into the armed forces. —*adj.* |kŏn'skrĭpt|. Conscripted; drafted. —**con•scrip'tion** *n.*

con•se•crate |kŏn'sĭ krāt'| *v.* **con•se•crat•ed, con•se•crat•ing. 1.** To declare or set apart as sacred: *consecrate a church.* **2.** To dedicate to some worthy purpose: *consecrate one's life toward improving the lot of the poor.* —**con'se•cra'tion** *n.*

con•sec•u•tive |kən sĕk'yə tĭv| *adj.* Following in order, without a break or interruption; successive: *It rained for five consecutive days. Once he hit four home runs in four consecutive times at bat.* —**con•sec'u•tive•ly** *adv.* —**con•sec'u•tive•ness** *n.*

con•sen•sus |kən sĕn'səs| *n.* Collective opinion; general agreement: *The consensus among voters is that the new program is a good one.*

con•sent |kən sĕnt'| *v.* To give permission; agree: *She gave him no peace until he consented. They finally consented to help me. They would not*

ă **pat**/ā **pay**/â **care**/ä **father**/ĕ **pet**/ ē **be**/ĭ **pit**/ī **pie**/î **fierce**/ŏ **pot**/ ō **go**/ô **paw**, **for**/oi **oil**/ŏŏ **book**/ ōō **boot**/ou **out**/ŭ **cut**/û **fur**/ *th* **the**/th **thin**/hw **which**/**zh** vision/ ə **ago**, **item**, **pencil**, **atom**, **circus** *consent to any recognition of civil rights.* —*n.* Agreement and acceptance: *"Governments . . . deriving their just powers from the consent of the governed"* (Declaration of Independence). *Powhatan gave his consent to his daughter's marriage to John Rolfe.*

con•se•quence |kŏn'sĭ kwĕns'| *or* |-kwəns| *n.* **1.** Something that follows from an action or condition; an effect; result: *Have you considered the consequences of your decision?* **2.** Importance; significance: *a matter of no consequence.*

con•se•quent |kŏn'sĭ kwĕnt'| *or* |-kwənt| *adj.* Following as an effect or result: *heavy rains and the consequent flooding of the farmlands.*

con•se•quen•tial |kŏn'sĭ kwĕn'shəl| *adj.* **1.** Consequent. **2.** Important; significant.

con•se•quent•ly |kŏn'sĭ kwĕnt'lē| *or* |-kwənt-| *adv.* As a result; therefore.

con•ser•va•tion |kŏn'sər vā'shən| *n.* **1.** The act or process of conserving; a saving: *a conservation of time and human effort.* **2.** The controlled use and systematic protection of natural resources: *It has been said that conservation is everybody's business.* —**modifier:** *a conservation problem; a conservation department.*

con•ser•va•tion•ist |kŏn'sər vā'shə nĭst| *n.* **1.** A trained conservation worker. **2.** An active supporter of conservation.

conservation of energy. A principle of physics that the total energy of a self-contained system remains constant regardless of what changes occur inside the system. [SEE NOTE]

conservation of mass. A principle of physics that the mass of a self-contained system remains constant regardless of the interaction of its parts. [SEE NOTE]

conservation of mass-en•er•gy |măs'ĕn'ər-jē|. A principle of physics that mass can be converted to energy and vice versa and that with this fact taken into account the total amount of mass and energy in a self-contained system remains constant regardless of changes in the system. The relation between mass and energy is given by Einstein's equation $E = mc^2$, where E is energy, m mass, and c the speed of light.

con•serv•a•tism |kən sûr'və tĭz'əm| *n.* **1.** In politics, the tendency to maintain the existing order and to resist or oppose change. **2.** The principles and practices of persons or groups that have such a tendency.

con•serv•a•tive |kən sûr'və tĭv| *adj.* **1.** Tending to oppose change; favoring traditional values. **2.** Not showy: *a conservative dark suit.* **3.** Moderate; cautious; restrained: *a conservative estimate.* **4.** Belonging to a conservative party or political group. **5. Conservative.** Belonging to that branch of Judaism standing midway between Orthodox and Reform in its willingness to accept changes in traditional ritual and custom. —*n.* **1.** Someone who is conservative. **2.** Often **Conservative.** A member of a conservative party. —**con•serv'a•tive•ly** *adv.*

con•serv•a•to•ry |kən sûr'və tôr'ē| *or* |-tōr'ē| *n., pl.* **con•ser•va•to•ries. 1.** A glass-enclosed room or small greenhouse in which plants are grown. **2.** A school of music or dramatic art.

con•serve |kən sûrv'| *v.* **con•served, con•serv•ing. 1.** To use (a supply) carefully, without waste: *conserve one's energy; conserve groceries during a food shortage.* **2.** To take systematic measures to keep (a resource) in good condition: *Science and common sense teach us to conserve our forests.* **3.** To preserve (fruits) by cooking with sugar. —*n.* |kŏn'sûrv'|. Often **conserves.** A jam made of fruits stewed in sugar.

con•sid•er |kən sĭd'ər| *v.* **1.** To deliberate upon; examine: *The committee met to consider the question of taking in new members.* **2.** To think over; reflect on; contemplate: *consider an offer; an important question for you to consider.* **3.** To regard as; look upon: *I consider it an honor. Greenland is considered part of North America.* **4.** To take into account; bear in mind: *He plays very well if you consider the fact that he has only just begun taking lessons.* **5.** To be thoughtful of; show consideration for: *consider the feelings of other people.*

con•sid•er•a•ble |kən sĭd'ər ə bəl| *adj.* Fairly large or great in amount, extent, or degree: *a considerable income. I have given considerable thought to the matter.* —**con•sid'er•a•bly** *adv.*

con•sid•er•ate |kən sĭd'ər ĭt| *adj.* Taking into account other people's feelings; thoughtful. —**con•sid'er•ate•ly** *adv.* —**con•sid'er•ate•ness** *n.*

con•sid•er•a•tion |kən sĭd'ə rā'shən| *n.* **1.** Careful thought; deliberation: *The matter is under consideration. We shall give your proposal careful consideration.* **2.** A factor to be considered in making a decision: *The health of the community is the most important consideration.* **3.** Thoughtful concern for others: *He shows no consideration for people's feelings.* **4.** A payment for a service rendered: *He agreed to do it for a small consideration.*

***Idiom.* take into consideration.** To take into account; allow for.

con•sid•ered |kən sĭd'ərd| *adj.* Reached after careful thought: *This is my considered opinion.*

con•sid•er•ing |kən sĭd'ər ĭng| *prep.* In view of: *Considering the mistakes that were made, it was a wonder that the job got done at all.* —*conj.* Inasmuch as; because: *Considering there's more than enough to eat, he's welcome to join us for supper.*

con•sign |kən sīn'| *v.* **1.** To give over to the care of another; entrust: *consign an orphan to a guardian.* **2.** To deliver (merchandise) for sale. **3.** To assign to a lower or less important position; relegate: *The pitcher was consigned to the bullpen.*

con•sign•ment |kən sīn'mənt| *n.* **1.** The delivery of something for sale or safekeeping. **2.** Something that is consigned, as for sale: *receive a consignment of umbrellas.*

***Idiom.* on consignment.** Sent to a retailer with the understanding that he is expected to pay after selling.

con•sist |kən sĭst'| *v.* **1.** To be made up or composed: *New York City consists of five boroughs.* **2.** To have a basis; lie; rest: *The beauty of his style consists in its simplicity.*

con•sis•ten•cy |kən sĭs'tən sē| *n.* **1.** Adherence or conformity to the same principles or course of action: *His statements lack consistency.* **2.** The degree of firmness, stiffness, or thickness: *mix water and clay to the consistency of thick cream.*

con•sist•ent |kən sĭs'tənt| *adj.* **1.** Continually

conservation of energy

This principle is sometimes stated in the simplified form "Energy can neither be created nor destroyed." This, however, does not account for nuclear energy, and reflects the assumption that the universe is self-contained, which has not been proved.

conservation of mass

This principle has been stated in the form "Matter can neither be created nor destroyed." In this form, it has the same defects as the simplified statement of conservation of energy. See **conservation of mass-energy**.

adhering to the same principles or course of action: *a consistent advocate of reform; follow a consistent policy.* **2.** In agreement; not contradictory: *a statement consistent with those he has previously made.* —**con•sist'ent•ly** *adv.*

con•sis•to•ry |kən sĭs'tə rē| *n., pl.* **con•sis•to•ries. 1. a.** A session of the cardinals of the Roman Catholic Church, presided over by the pope. **b.** The governing assembly of certain Protestant churches. **2.** A place in which such an assembly meets.

con•so•la•tion |kŏn'sə lā'shən| *n.* **1.** Comfort during a time of disappointment or sorrow. **2.** Something that consoles: *The one consolation is that he will not be gone for long.*

consolation prize. A prize given to someone who participates in but does not win a contest.

con•sole[1] |kən sōl'| *v.* **con•soled, con•sol•ing.** To comfort in time of disappointment or sorrow.

con•sole[2] |kŏn'sōl'| *n.* **1.** A cabinet for a radio or television set, designed to stand on the floor. **2.** The part of an organ facing the player, containing the keyboard, stops, and pedals. **3.** A panel housing the controls for electrical or mechanical equipment. **4.** A decorative bracket for supporting a cornice, shelf, or other object.

con•sol•i•date |kən sŏl'ĭ dāt'| *v.* **con•sol•i•dat•ed, con•sol•i•dat•ing. 1.** To merge into fewer or into one: *De Gaulle planned to consolidate France's 95 departments into 21 regions. Several small businesses consolidated into one large corporation.* **2.** To make or become secure and strong: *consolidated his political base. His power consolidated during the struggle.* —**con•sol'i•dat'ed** *adj.: a consolidated company.* —**con•sol'i•da'tion** *n.*

con•som•mé |kŏn'sə mā'| *n.* A clear soup made of meat or vegetable broth.

con•so•nance |kŏn'sə nəns| *n.* **1.** Agreement; harmony; accord. **2.** A kind of rhyme formed between the final consonant sounds of words, for example, *rain* and *tone.* **3. a.** In music, a combination of tones that sounds as smooth as or smoother than the combinations that come before it and that need not be followed by a resolution. **b.** The quality or characteristic of being a consonance. [SEE NOTE]

con•so•nant |kŏn'sə nənt| *n.* **1.** A speech sound made by a partial or complete obstruction of the flow of air as it escapes through one's mouth. **2.** A letter of the alphabet representing such a sound, as *b, m, s, t,* etc. —***modifier:*** *a consonant sound.* —*adj.* **1.** In music: **a.** Of or having consonance or consonances. **b.** Consisting chiefly of consonances. **2.** In agreement; in keeping: *remarks consonant with his beliefs.*

con•so•nan•tal |kŏn'sə năn'tl| *adj.* Of or containing a consonant or consonants.

con•sort |kŏn'sôrt'| *n.* A husband or wife, especially of a monarch. —*v.* |kən sôrt'|. To keep company; associate: *consort with gangsters.*

con•spic•u•ous |kən spĭk'yo͞o əs| *adj.* Attracting attention; striking the eye: *a conspicuous error.* —**con•spic'u•ous•ly** *adv.* —**con•spic'u•ous•ness** *n.*

con•spir•a•cy |kən spîr'ə sē| *n., pl.* **con•spir•a•cies.** A secret plan to commit an unlawful act.

con•spir•a•tor |kən spîr'ə tər| *n.* A person who takes part in a conspiracy; a plotter.

con•spir•a•to•ri•al |kən spîr'ə tôr'ē əl| *or* |-tōr'-| *adj.* Of or relating to a conspiracy: *conspiratorial activity.*

con•spire |kən spīr'| *v.* **con•spired, con•spir•ing. 1.** To plan together secretly, especially to commit an illegal act: *conspire to kidnap a public official.* **2.** To work together; combine: *Many factors conspired to defeat him.*

con•sta•ble |kŏn'stə bəl| *n.* **1.** A public officer in a town or village with somewhat less authority than a sheriff. **2.** *British.* A policeman. [SEE NOTE]

con•stab•u•lar•y |kən stăb'yə lĕr'ē| *n., pl.* **con•stab•u•lar•ies. 1. a.** The constables of a certain district. **b.** The district itself. **2.** An armed police force organized like a military unit.

con•stan•cy |kŏn'stən sē| *n.* **1.** The quality of remaining constant; uniformity. **2.** Faithfulness; loyalty.

con•stant |kŏn'stənt| *adj.* **1.** Not changing; remaining the same: *maintain a constant speed.* **2.** Happening all the time; persistent: *constant interruptions; constant arguments; constant reminders.* **3.** Without interruption; continuous: *in constant use. The patient requires constant care.* **4.** Steadfast in loyalty, affection, etc.; faithful: *a constant friend.* —*n.* **1.** Something that never changes. **2. a.** A symbol whose value does not change during the course of a mathematical discussion, problem, or analysis. **b.** A number, such as π, that has a fixed value. —**con'stant•ly** *adv.*

Con•stan•ti•no•ple |kŏn'stăn tə nō'pəl|. The former name for Istanbul.

con•stel•la•tion |kŏn'stə lā'shən| *n.* **1. a.** Any of 88 groups of stars that are thought to resemble objects, animals, and mythological characters, and that have been named after them. **b.** The region of the sky or celestial sphere occupied by such a group of stars. **2.** A group or gathering of distinguished persons or things.

con•ster•na•tion |kŏn'stər nā'shən| *n.* Great alarm, shock, or amazement; dismay.

con•sti•pate |kŏn'stə pāt'| *v.* **con•sti•pat•ed, con•sti•pat•ing.** To cause constipation in.

con•sti•pa•tion |kŏn'stə pā'shən| *n.* Difficult or infrequent movement of the bowels.

con•stit•u•en•cy |kən stĭch'o͞o ən sē| *n., pl.* **con•stit•u•en•cies. 1.** A body of voters. **2.** A district represented by a delegate elected to a legislature.

con•stit•u•ent |kən stĭch'o͞o ənt| *adj.* **1.** Making up part of a whole: *An atom is a constituent element of a molecule.* **2.** Authorized to draw up or change a constitution: *a constituent assembly.* —*n.* **1.** A constituent part. **2.** Someone represented by an elected official; a voter.

con•sti•tute |kŏn'stĭ to͞ot'| *or* |-tyo͞ot'| *v.* **con•sti•tut•ed, con•sti•tut•ing. 1.** To make up; form: *Ten members constitute a quorum. This constitutes a new phase of the operation.* **2.** To set up; establish: *Governments are constituted by the people.* **3.** To appoint, as to an office; designate: *The assembly constituted them ambassadors to the King.* —**con'sti•tut'ed** *adj.: constituted authorities.*

con•sti•tu•tion |kŏn'stĭ to͞o'shən| *or* |-tyo͞o'-| *n.* **1.** The basic law of a politically organized body, such as a nation or state. **2. the Constitution.** The written constitution of the United States, adopt-

consonance
In traditional harmony the intervals considered to be **consonances** *are unisons, octaves, perfect fifths, and thirds. The perfect fourth is a consonance as long as it is not the lowest interval in a chord. Many modern composers use as consonances sounds that were once considered dissonances.*

constable
In the period when the Roman Empire was breaking up, an officer in charge of horses was called comes stabuli, *"count (or companion) of the stable" (see note at* **count***). This term passed into Old French as* conestable *and also moved up in the world; it was used as the title of the chief court official of the early French kings, and eventually for the commander in chief of the army. It was borrowed into English as* **constable,** *and shifted in level again, being used for various low-ranking peace officers, as it is in its modern uses in America (sense 1) and Britain (sense 2).*

constitution
"The [United States] Constitution . . . is unquestionably the wisest ever yet presented to men."
Thomas Jefferson (1789).
"We shall never make the constitution of England a strictly logical one, and I do not think that it is desirable that we should try."
—Benjamin Disraeli (1867).

ă **pat**/ā **pay**/â **care**/ä **father**/ĕ **pet**/ ē **be**/ĭ **pit**/ī **pie**/î **fierce**/ŏ **pot**/ ō **go**/ô **paw**, **for**/oi **oil**/o͝o **book**/ o͞o **boot**/ou **out**/ŭ **cut**/û **fur**/ *th* **the**/th **thin**/hw **which**/zh **vision**/ ə **ago**, **item**, **pencil**, **atom**, **circus**

ed in 1787 and put into effect in 1789. **3.** The way in which something or someone is made up, especially the physical make-up of a person: *a boy with a strong constitution.* **4.** The act of setting up. [SEE NOTE on p. 200]

con•sti•tu•tion•al |kŏn′stĭ **tōō′**shə nəl| *or* |**-tyōō′-**| *adj.* **1.** Of a constitution: *a constitutional convention; a constitutional amendment.* **2.** Consistent with or permissible according to a constitution: *The proposed law is not constitutional.* **3.** Established by or operating under a constitution: *a constitutional monarchy.* **4.** Basic or inherent in one's make-up: *a constitutional inability to say "yes."* —*n.* A walk taken for one's health. —**con′sti•tu′tion•al•ly** *adv.*

con•sti•tu•tion•al•i•ty |kŏn′stĭ tōō′shə **năl′**ĭ tē| *or* |-tyōō′-| *n.* Validity according to a constitution: *The Supreme Court upheld the constitutionality of the law.*

con•strain |kən **strān′**| *v.* To compel by physical or moral force; oblige: *I feel constrained to voice my objections.*

con•strained |kən **strānd′**| *adj.* Uneasy; unnatural: *a constrained facial expression.*

con•straint |kən **strānt′**| *n.* **1.** The threat or use of force to control the action of others: *acting under constraint.* **2.** Something that restricts or hampers. **3.** The condition of holding back one's natural feelings or behavior; lack of ease; a forced or unnatural manner: *The soldiers showed constraint in the general's presence.*

con•strict |kən **strĭkt′**| *v.* To make or become smaller or narrower, as by contracting: *constrict a blood vessel. His muscles constricted.*

con•stric•tion |kən **strĭk′**shən| *n.* **1.** The act or process of constricting. **2.** A feeling of pressure or tightness: *a constriction in one's throat.* **3.** Something that constricts.

con•stric•tor |kən **strĭk′**tər| *n.* **1.** A muscle that contracts or compresses a part or organ of the body. **2.** A snake that coils around and crushes its prey.

con•struct |kən **strŭkt′**| *v.* **1.** To build; erect: *construct new houses.* **2.** To compose; devise: *construct a sentence.* **3.** To draw (a required geometric figure), usually using no more than a straightedge and a compass as aids.

con•struc•tion |kən **strŭk′**shən| *n.* **1.** The act or process of constructing: *Two new hotels are under construction.* **2.** The business or work of building. **3.** The way in which something is put together; design: *A chisel is a tool of simple construction.* **4.** The interpretation or explanation given a certain statement. **5. a.** The arrangement of words to form a meaningful phrase, clause, or sentence. **b.** The group of words so arranged. —***modifier:*** *a construction company; a construction worker.*

con•struc•tive |kən **strŭk′**tĭv| *adj.* Serving a useful purpose or helping to improve something: *constructive suggestions.* —**con•struc′tive•ly** *adv.*

con•strue |kən **strōō′**| *v.* **con•strued, con•stru•ing.** To place a certain meaning on; interpret: *One can construe his statement in a number of ways.*

con•sul |**kŏn′**səl| *n.* **1.** An official appointed by a government to live in a foreign city, look after his country's commercial interests, and give assistance to its citizens who live or travel there. **2.** Either of the two chief magistrates of the ancient Roman republic, elected for a term of one year. —**con′su•lar** |**kŏn′**sə lər| *adj.*

con•su•late |**kŏn′**sə lĭt| *n.* **1.** The building or offices occupied by a consul. **2.** The office or term of office of a consul.

con•sult |kən **sŭlt′**| *v.* **1.** To go to for advice: *consult your doctor.* **2.** To have an advisory discussion: *The U.S. consulted with the Canadian government.* **3.** To refer to for information: *consult the instruction booklet.*

con•sult•ant |kən **sŭl′**tənt| *n.* Someone who gives expert or professional advice.

con•sul•ta•tion |kŏn′səl **tā′**shən| *n.* **1.** An act of consulting: *seek closer consultations between members of NATO.* **2.** A conference at which advice is given or views are exchanged.

con•sult•a•tive |kən **sŭl′**tə tĭv| *adj.* For consultation: *a consultative council.*

con•sult•ing |kən **sŭl′**tĭng| *adj.* Acting as a consultant: *a consulting engineer.*

con•sume |kən **sōōm′**| *v.* **con•sumed, con•sum•ing.** **1.** To eat or drink: *You probably consume Vitamin A in every meal you eat.* **2.** To use up: *The Saturn V launch vehicle consumes 1,000 tons of fuel per minute. Haggling over the details consumed precious weeks.* **3.** To buy and use: *Americans consume an enormous amount of cotton.* **4.** To destroy, as by fire: *A moth flutters into the fire and is consumed.*

con•sum•er |kən **sōō′**mər| *n.* Someone who buys and uses goods and services: *The manufacturers passed on the price increase to the consumers.* —***modifier:*** *consumer goods; the consumer price index.* [SEE NOTE]

con•sum•ing |kən **sōō′**mĭng| *adj.* **1.** Destroying as by fire: *the consuming flames of hell.* **2.** Overwhelming: *a consuming desire to see her again.*

con•sum•mate |**kŏn′**sə māt′| *v.* **con•sum•mat•ed, con•sum•mat•ing.** To bring to completion; conclude: *consummate a business deal.* —*adj.* |kən **sŭm′**ĭt|. **1.** Complete or perfect in every respect: *consummate happiness.* **2.** Highly skilled; polished: *a consummate artist.* —**con′sum•ma′tion** *n.*

con•sump•tion |kən **sŭmp′**shən| *n.* **1.** The act of consuming. **2.** A quantity consumed. **3.** A wasting away of body tissues. **4.** An old word for tuberculosis of the lungs.

con•sump•tive |kən **sŭmp′**tĭv| *adj.* Of or suffering from consumption. —**con•sump′tive•ly** *adv.*

cont. continued.

con•tact |**kŏn′**tăkt′| *n.* **1.** The condition of touching or coming together: *physical contact; body contact.* **2.** The condition of being in touch: *He put me in contact with the right people. The natives of New Guinea have no contact with the outside world.* **3.** *Informal.* An acquaintance who is in a position to be of help: *He has numerous contacts in the government.* **4. a.** A touching together of two conductors in a way that allows an electric current to flow; a connection. **b.** An electrical part that can be moved so as to touch or not touch a similar part and so open or close a circuit: *the contacts of a switch.* —*v.* |**kŏn′**tăkt′| *or* |kən **tăkt′**|. **1.** To come into contact with; touch. **2.** To get in touch with; communicate

consumer

Two new words relating to **consumers** *have emerged:* consumerism, *"the movement seeking to protect the rights of consumers by requiring such practices as the honest labeling of packages"; and* consumerist, *"an active member of this movement." These words first began to appear in early 1970 (or perhaps before). If they last a little longer, they will take their place in the Dictionary.*

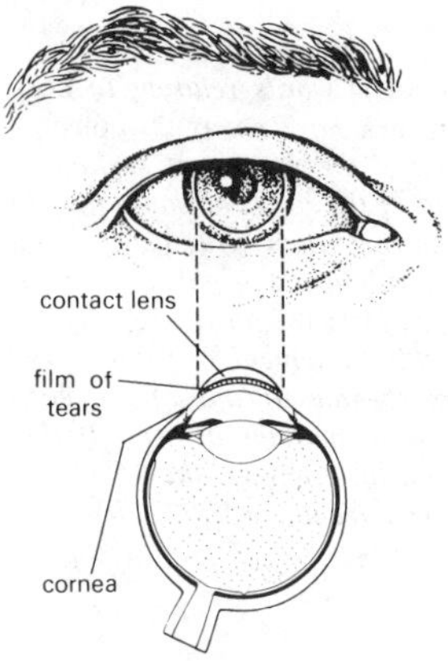

contact lens

contain

Contain *comes from Old French* contenir, *which is from Latin* continēre, *"to hold together":* com-, *"together,"* + tenēre, *"to hold."* Continēre *had other extended meanings that have affected English words in a rather complicated way. It also meant: (a) "to hold back, restrain"; (b) "to keep together, remain, continue"; and (c) "to contain, hold." See the notes at* **content** *and* **continent.**

content[1-2]

Content[1] *is from Medieval Latin* contentum, *"something contained," from* contentus, *the past participle of* continēre, *"to contain."* **Content[2]** *is from the same Latin word,* contentus, *but in the different sense "restrained" (*continēre *also meant "to restrain", see note at* **contain***).*

ă **pat**/ā **pay**/â **care**/ä **father**/ĕ **pet**/ ē **be**/ĭ **pit**/ī **pie**/î **fierce**/ŏ **pot**/ ō **go**/ô **paw**, **for**/oi **oil**/ŏŏ **book**/ ōō **boot**/ou **out**/ŭ **cut**/û **fur**/ *th* **the**/th **thin**/hw **which**/**zh** vision/ ə **ago**, item, pencil, atom, circus

with. **3.** To make an electrical connection with.

contact lens. A tiny lens designed to correct a defect in vision, worn directly on the cornea of the eye and practically invisible when in place. [SEE PICTURE]

con•ta•gion |kən **tā'**jən| *n.* **1.** The transmission of disease by direct or indirect contact. **2.** A disease that is or can be transmitted in this way.

con•ta•gious |kən **tā'**jəs| *adj.* **1.** Capable of being transmitted by direct or indirect contact: *a contagious disease.* **2.** Carrying or capable of carrying disease. **3.** Tending to spread from person to person: *contagious laughter.*

con•tain |kən **tān'**| *v.* **1.** To have within itself; hold: *Orange juice contains vitamin C. The document contains important information.* **2.** To consist of; comprise; include: *A gallon contains four quarts.* **3.** To hold back; restrain: *I could scarcely contain my laughter.* [SEE NOTE]

con•tain•er |kən **tā'**nər| *n.* Anything, such as a box, can, jar, barrel, etc., used to hold something.

con•tain•ment |kən **tān'**mənt| *n.* The policy of attempting to prevent the expansion of an opposing power or ideology.

con•tam•i•nate |kən **tăm'**ə nāt'| *v.* **con•tam•i•nat•ed, con•tam•i•nat•ing.** To make impure, bad, or less good by mixture or contact; pollute; foul.

con•tam•i•na•tion |kən tăm'ə **nā'**shən| *n.* **1. a.** The act or process of contaminating. **b.** The condition of being contaminated. **2.** Something that contaminates; an impurity.

contd. continued.

con•temn |kən **tĕm'**| *v.* To view or regard with contempt; despise.

con•tem•plate |**kŏn'**təm plāt'| *v.* **con•tem•plat•ed, con•tem•plat•ing. 1.** To look at, often quietly and solemnly: *The men contemplated the treasure in blissful silence.* **2.** To think about, especially in a detached way: *I contemplated my strange situation.* **3.** To think about doing (something): *The student contemplated a career in science.* **4.** To expect: *They contemplated various kinds of trouble.*

con•tem•pla•tion |kŏn'təm **plā'**shən| *n.* The act of contemplating; thoughtful observation or meditation.

con•tem•pla•tive |kən **tĕm'**plə tĭv| *adj.* Of or devoted to contemplation: *a contemplative look; the contemplative life.* **—con•tem'pla•tive•ly** *adv.*

con•tem•po•ra•ne•ous |kən tĕm'pə **rā'**nē əs| *adj.* Originating, existing, or occurring at the same time. **—con•tem'po•ra'ne•ous•ly** *adv.*

con•tem•po•rar•y |kən **tĕm'**pə rĕr'ē| *adj.* **1.** Living or occurring during the same period of time. **2.** Current; modern: *contemporary history; a contemporary composer.* **—***n., pl.* **con•tem•po•rar•ies. 1.** A person of the same age as another: *John and I are contemporaries.* **2.** A person living at the same time as another: *a composer much admired by his contemporaries.* **3.** A person of the present age.

con•tempt |kən **tĕmpt'**| *n.* **1. a.** A feeling that someone or something is inferior and undesirable: *The English used to regard foreigners with contempt.* **b.** The condition of being regarded in this way: *The League of Nations rapidly fell into contempt.* **2.** Open disobedience to a court of law or to Congress.

con•tempt•i•ble |kən **tĕmp'**tə bəl| *adj.* Deserving contempt: *a contemptible trick.* **—con•tempt'i•ble•ness** *n.* **—con•tempt'i•bly** *adv.*

con•temp•tu•ous |kən **tĕmp'**chōō əs| *adj.* Feeling or showing contempt: *A contemptuous refusal.* **—con•temp'tu•ous•ly** *adv.* **—con•temp'tu•ous•ness** *n.*

con•tend |kən **tĕnd'**| *v.* **1.** To fight, as in battle: *The Greek cities contended for supremacy.* **2.** To compete, as in a race: *I could not contend with him in speed.* **3.** To oppose or dispute: *He contended the court order.* **4.** To claim or maintain: *The police contend that they are not adequately protected.* **—con•tend'er** *n.*

con•tent[1] |**kŏn'**tĕnt'| *n.* **1.** Often **contents.** Something that is contained in a receptacle: *empty a jar of its contents.* **2.** Often **contents.** The subject matter of a document, book, etc.: *The contents of the letter were not revealed.* **3.** The amount of a substance contained in something: *the fat content of milk. Eggs have a high protein content.* [SEE NOTE]

con•tent[2] |kən **tĕnt'**| *adj.* Happy with what one has; satisfied: *I am content with my lot in life.* **—***n.* Contentment; satisfaction. **—***v.* To make content or satisfied: *Such things do not content me.* [SEE NOTE]

Idiom. **to (one's) heart's content.** As much as one wishes.

con•tent•ed |kən **tĕn'**tĭd| *adj.* **1.** Satisfied with things as they are; content. **2.** Showing contentment: *a contented look on one's face.* **—con•tent'ed•ly** *adv.*

con•ten•tion |kən **tĕn'**shən| *n.* **1.** A battle, competition, or dispute: *They played in fierce but friendly contention.* **2.** A claim or argument: *His contention was that the proceedings were invalid.*

Idiom. **in** (or **out of**) **contention.** In a position (or having no chance) to win: *Three teams are still in contention for the pennant.*

con•ten•tious |kən **tĕn'**shəs| *adj.* Inclined to argue; quarrelsome. **—con•ten'tious•ly** *adv.* **—con•ten'tious•ness** *n.*

con•tent•ment |kən **tĕnt'**mənt| *n.* The condition or quality of being contented; satisfaction.

con•test |**kŏn'**tĕst'| *n.* **1.** A struggle or fight in which two or more rivals compete for victory or superiority: *A contest developed for the position of majority leader in the Senate.* **2.** Any competition, usually between entrants who perform separately and are rated by a panel of judges: *a beauty contest; a skating contest.* **—***v.* |kən **tĕst'**| *or* |**kŏn'**tĕst'|. **1.** To compete for: *contest a prize.* **2.** To dispute; challenge: *The heirs bitterly contested the will.*

con•test•ant |kən **tĕs'**tənt| *n.* Someone who takes part in a contest.

con•text |**kŏn'**tĕkst'| *n.* **1.** The setting of words and ideas in which a particular word or statement appears: *In some contexts "mad" means "insane"; in other contexts it means "angry."* **2.** A general setting or set of circumstances in which a particular event occurs: *in the context of modern city life.*

con•tex•tu•al |kən **tĕks'**chōō əl| *adj.* Of or resulting from context: *a special contextual meaning.*

con•tig•u•ous |kən **tĭg'**yōō əs| *adj.* Having a common boundary; adjoining: *New Hampshire is the only state contiguous to Maine.*

con•ti•nence |kŏn′tə nəns| *n.* Self-restraint, especially with regard to passions and desires; moderation.

con•ti•nent¹ |kŏn′tə nənt| *adj.* Self-restrained; moderate. [SEE NOTE]

con•ti•nent² |kŏn′tə nənt| *n.* **1.** One of the main land masses of the earth, including Africa, Antarctica, Asia, Australia, Europe, North America, and South America. **2. the Continent.** The mainland of Europe. [SEE NOTE]

con•ti•nen•tal |kŏn′tə nĕn′tl| *adj.* **1.** Of or like a continent: *continental limits; a continental state.* **2.** Often **Continental.** Of the mainland of Europe: *Napoleon forbade Continental countries to import British goods.* **3. Continental.** Of the American colonies during and just after the Revolutionary War: *the Continental Congress.* —*n.* **1.** Often **Continental.** An inhabitant of the mainland of Europe. **2. Continental.** A soldier in the Continental Army during the Revolutionary War. **3.** A piece of paper money issued by the Continental Congress during the Revolutionary War: *The saying "not worth a continental" came about because this money was soon worthless.*

Continental Congress. Either of two legislative assemblies of the American colonies and then of the United States. The first met in 1774; the second was the legislative and executive body of the government from 1775 until the Constitution took effect in 1789.

continental divide. **1.** A region of high ground from each side of which the river systems of a continent flow in opposite directions. **2.** Often **Continental Divide.** In western North America, the stretch of high ground formed by the crests of the Rocky Mountains.

continental shelf. A portion of the edge of a continent covered to a generally shallow depth by the ocean and extending to a point where it slopes steeply downward into the deep part of the ocean.

con•tin•gen•cy |kən tĭn′jən sē| *n., pl.* **con•tin•gen•cies.** **1.** An event that may occur but is not likely or intended; a possibility. **2.** The condition of being contingent.

con•tin•gent |kən tĭn′jənt| *adj.* **1.** Liable but not likely to occur; possible. **2.** Dependent on circumstances not yet known: *The success of our picnic is contingent on the weather.* **3.** Happening by chance; accidental. —*n.* **1.** A representative group forming part of a gathering; a delegation: *the Maine contingent at the Democratic national convention.* **2.** A share contributed to a general effort: *The armored division included a contingent from New York.* —**con•tin′gent•ly.** *adv.*

con•tin•u•al |kən tĭn′yo͞o əl| *adj.* **1.** Repeated regularly and frequently: *the continual banging of the shutters.* **2. a.** Steady; not interrupted or broken: *a continual noise.* **b.** Continuing over a long period of time: *He hoped for a change from his continual diet of vegetables.* —**con•tin′u•al•ly** *adv.* [SEE NOTE]

con•tin•u•ance |kən tĭn′yo͞o əns| *n.* **1.** The act or an example of continuing or lasting: *the continuance of the circumstances that led to the fight.* **2.** Adjournment of legal proceedings to a future date.

con•tin•u•a•tion |kən tĭn′yo͞o ā′shən| *n.* **1. a.** The act or process of continuing: *The enormous profits of the slave trade became the most convincing argument for its continuation.* **b.** An example of this: *Today's fair weather is a continuation of yesterday's.* **2.** An extension to a further point: *The Mediterranean is a continuation of the Atlantic.* **3.** A sequel, as in a television series.

con•tin•ue |kən tĭn′yo͞o| *v.* **con•tin•ued, con•tin•u•ing.** **1.** To keep on or persist in: *The rain continued for days. The police continued their investigation.* **2.** To begin again after halting; resume: *Our program will continue after station identification.* **3.** To remain in a particular job, condition, place, etc.: *She will continue as our principal for another year. The weather continued stormy for weeks.*

con•ti•nu•i•ty |kŏn′tə no͞o′ĭ tē| *or* |-nyo͞o′-| *n., pl.* **con•ti•nu•i•ties.** **1.** An uninterrupted succession: *You broke the continuity of my thoughts.* **2.** The condition of being continuous.

con•tin•u•ous |kən tĭn′yo͞o əs| *adj.* Continuing without interruption; unbroken: *Living cells must have a continuous supply of oxygen. To him, life was a continuous experiment.* —**con•tin′u•ous•ly** *adv.* —**con•tin′u•ous•ness** *n.* [SEE NOTE]

continuous spectrum. A spectrum that covers a range of wavelengths without breaks or gaps.

con•tin•u•um |kən tĭn′yo͞o əm| *n., pl.* **con•tin•u•a** |kən tĭn′yo͞o ə| or **con•tin•u•ums.** Something that can be divided into parts as small as desired; something that extends in a smooth, unbroken manner.

con•tort |kən tôrt′| *v.* To twist or become twisted severely out of shape.

con•tor•tion |kən tôr′shən| *n.* **1.** The act or result of contorting; a twisted position or expression: *violent body contortions.* **2.** An unduly or unnecessarily complicated or awkward action: *going through all sorts of contortions to justify a wrong decision.*

con•tor•tion•ist |kən tôr′shə nĭst| *n.* A person who performs acrobatic feats involving contorted, grotesque postures.

con•tour |kŏn′to͝or′| *n.* **1.** The outline of a figure, body, or mass: *the contour of the American coast.* **2.** A **contour line.** **3.** Often **contours.** The surface of a curving form: *the contours of her body.* —*adj.* **1.** Following the contour lines of uneven terrain to limit erosion of topsoil: *contour plowing.* **2.** Shaped to fit the outline or form of something: *contour sheets; a contour chair.* —*v.* **1.** To give a curving surface or outline to. **2.** To build or construct (a road) to follow the contour of the land.

contour line. A line drawn on a map in such a way that each point on the line is at the same elevation above sea level.

contour map. A map that shows elevations above sea level and surface features of the land by means of contour lines.

contra–. A prefix meaning "against, contrary": **contradistinction.**

con•tra•band |kŏn′trə bănd′| *n.* **1.** Goods prohibited by law from being shipped, especially during time of war. **2.** Smuggling. **3.** Smuggled goods. —***modifier:*** *a contraband shipment.*

con•tra•bass |kŏn′trə bās′| *n.* A **double bass.** —*adj.* Pitched an octave below the normal bass range.

con•tra•bas•soon |kŏn′trə bə so͞on′| *n.* A

continent¹·²

Continent¹ *is from Latin* continēns, *"restraining oneself," from* continēre, *"to restrain."* Continēre *also meant "to continue," and in this sense* continēns *also meant "continuing, continuous," and was used to mean "continuous land, mainland, a continent." In this use* continēns *was separately borrowed into English as* **continent²**. *See note at* **contain.**

continual/continuous

The traditional idea is that **continuous** *should refer only to unbroken continuity, while* **continual** *can also be used of intermittent or repetitive effects. In the school materials from which this Dictionary was made, the distinction did not seem to be observed. Both words were almost always used to express unbroken continuity, and both were also occasionally used of repetitive effects. In the case of the adverbs derived from* **continuous** *and* **continual,** *the distinction seems to have more force; while* **continually** *was used about equally in both senses,* **continuously** *was used only to mean "without a break."*

large bassoon pitched about an octave below an ordinary bassoon and having a similar timbre.

con•tra•cep•tion |kŏn′trə **sĕp′**shən| *n.* The prevention of conception.

con•tra•cep•tive |kŏn′trə **sĕp′**tĭv| *adj.* Capable of preventing conception. —*n.* A contraceptive substance or device.

con•tract |**kŏn′**trăkt′| *n.* **1.** A formal agreement, enforceable by law, between two or more persons or groups. **2.** A document stating the terms of such an agreement. —*v.* |kən **trăkt′**|. **1.** To draw together; make or become smaller in length, width, etc.: *contract one's muscles. The pupils of his eyes contracted.* **2.** To arrange or make by a formal agreement: *contract a marriage; contract for garbage collection.* **3.** To get; acquire: *contract the mumps; contract a debt.*

con•trac•tile |kən **trăk′**təl| *adj.* Able to contract, be compressed, or cause contraction: *the contractile vacuole of a paramecium; contractile muscle fibers.*

con•trac•tion |kən **trăk′**shən| *n.* **1.** The act or process of contracting: *contraction of a disease.* **2.** A condensed form of a word or pair of words; for example, *isn't* is a contraction of *is not.* **3. a.** The process by which a muscle becomes shorter or more tense. **b.** An act of squeezing or tightening by a muscle or a muscular organ: *contractions of the stomach.*

con•trac•tor |**kŏn′**trăk′tər| *or* |kən **trăk′**-| *n.* A businessman who contracts to provide materials and labor for construction jobs.

con•trac•tu•al |kən **trăk′**cho͞o əl| *adj.* Of or provided for in a contract: *a contractual obligation.* —**con•trac′tu•al•ly** *adv.*

con•tra•dict |kŏn′trə **dĭkt′**| *v.* **1.** To assert or express the opposite of (a statement): *The witness seemed to contradict his previous testimony.* **2.** To declare to be untruthful or untrue: *She contradicted her father.* **3.** To be contrary to or inconsistent with: *magic tricks that contradict what the eye sees.*

con•tra•dic•tion |kŏn′trə **dĭk′**shən| *n.* **1.** The act of contradicting or the condition of being contradicted: *He can't stand contradiction.* **2.** An inconsistency; discrepancy: *There's a contradiction in what you're saying.* **3.** In mathematics and logic: **a.** A statement that contains or depends on two ideas that cannot both be true at once. **b.** A statement that contradicts something. [SEE NOTE]

contradiction
A simple example of a **contradiction** *is the statement that "the number x must be larger than 5 but smaller than 3." Often, it is possible to prove an idea by assuming that it is not true and showing that this assumption leads to a contradiction.*

con•tra•dic•to•ry |kŏn′trə **dĭk′**tə rē| *adj.* **1.** In opposition; opposing. **2.** Having elements or parts not in agreement: *In many ways he was a contradictory political figure.* **3.** In the habit of contradicting. —**con′tra•dic′to•ri•ly** *adv.*

con•tra•dis•tinc•tion |kŏn′trə dĭ **stĭngk′**shən| *n.* Distinction by contrasting or by opposing qualities: *science in contradistinction to art.*

con•tral•to |kən **trăl′**tō| *n., pl.* **con•tral•tos. 1.** The lowest woman's singing voice or voice part, lower than soprano and higher than tenor. **2.** A woman having such a voice. —***modifier:*** *a contralto voice; a contralto aria.*

con•trap•tion |kən **trăp′**shən| *n. Informal.* A mechanical device; gadget.

con•tra•pun•tal |kŏn′trə **pŭn′**tl| *adj.* Of, using, or involving musical counterpoint: *a contrapuntal passage; complex contrapuntal writing.*

con•tra•ri•wise |**kŏn′**trĕr′ē wīz′| *adv.* In a contrary manner or direction.

con•tra•ry |**kŏn′**trĕr′ē| *adj.* **1.** Completely different; opposed: *contrary points of view.* **2.** Opposite in direction or position: *In a dance of contrary motions dancers form lines that move in opposite directions.* **3.** Adverse; unfavorable: *a contrary wind.* **4.** |*also* kən **trâr′**ē|. Stubbornly opposed to others; willful: *He's just a contrary person.* —*n., pl.* **con•tra•ries.** The opposite: *I believe the contrary to be true.* —*adv.* In opposition; counter: *He acted contrary to all advice.* —**con′tra′ri•ly** *adv.* —**con′tra′ri•ness** *n.*

***Idiom.* on the contrary.** In opposition to the previous statement; conversely.

con•trast |kən **trăst′**| *v.* **1.** To compare in order to reveal differences: *The poem contrasts good and evil.* **2.** To show differences when compared: *Black contrasts with white.* —*n.* |**kŏn′**trăst′|. **1.** Comparison, especially in order to reveal differences: *In contrast to the dry lands of northern Africa, it rains almost every day in the central portion of Africa.* **2.** Striking difference between things compared: *the contrast between father and son.* **3.** Something that is strikingly different from something else: *What a contrast he is to his father!*

con•trib•ute |kən **trĭb′**yo͞ot| *v.* **con•trib•ut•ed, con•trib•ut•ing. 1.** To give or supply in common with others: *contribute time and money; contribute to the heart fund.* **2.** To aid in bringing about: *Exercise contributes to better health.* **3.** To submit (something written) for publication: *He contributes a poem every issue. He contributes regularly to several magazines.*

con•tri•bu•tion |kŏn′trĭ **byo͞o′**shən| *n.* **1.** The act of contributing. **2.** Something contributed: *He gave a small contribution to the fund.*

con•trib•u•tor |kən **trĭb′**yə tər| *n.* A person who donates or supplies something: *a contributor of funds; a contributor of magazine articles.*

con•trib•u•to•ry |kən **trĭb′**yə tôr′ē| *or* |-tōr′ē| *adj.* Contributing toward a result; helping to bring about a result: *a contributory factor.*

con•trite |kən **trīt′**| *or* |**kŏn′**trīt′| *adj.* Feeling or caused by guilt: *a contrite sinner; contrite tears.* —**con•trite′ly** *adv.* —**con•trite′ness** *n.*

con•tri•tion |kən **trĭsh′**ən| *n.* Sincere repentance: *Full of contrition and shame, he tried to make amends for his disloyalty.*

con•triv•ance |kən **trī′**vəns| *n.* Something that is contrived, as a mechanical device or a clever plan.

con•trive |kən **trīv′**| *v.* **con•trived, con•triv•ing. 1.** To devise cleverly: *contrive a new scheme.* **2.** To bring about through clever scheming: *contrive a victory; contrive to gain admission.* **3.** To make, especially by improvisation: *Scarlett contrived a dress out of an old curtain.*

con•trived |kən **trīvd′**| *adj.* Artificial; unnatural: *a movie with a contrived plot.*

con•trol |kən **trōl′**| *v.* **con•trolled, con•trol•ling. 1.** To exercise authority or influence over; direct: *The Romans controlled a huge empire that included people of many races in many parts of the world.* **2.** To regulate the operation of: *control a machine.* **3.** To hold in check; restrain: *control one's emotions; control a horse.* **4.** To check or regulate (a scientific experiment), as by carrying

ă pat/ā pay/â care/ä father/ĕ pet/ ē be/ĭ pit/ī pie/î fierce/ŏ pot/ ō go/ô paw, for/oi oil/o͝o book/ o͞o boot/ou out/ŭ cut/û fur/ *th* the/th thin/hw which/zh vision/ ə ago, item, pencil, atom, circus

out a similar experiment in which the factor whose effect is being studied is not present. —*n.* **1.** Authority or power to regulate, direct, or dominate: *the coach's control over the team.* **2.** A means of restraint: *a price control.* **3.** Something with which a scientific experiment can be compared in order to check its results. **4.** Usually **controls.** The knobs, levers, pedals, etc., that are used in setting and regulating the operating conditions of a machine. —**con•trol'la•ble** *adj.*

con•trol•ler |kən trō'lər| *n.* **1.** Someone or something that controls, especially an automatic device that regulates the operation of a machine. **2.** A person who regulates a flow of traffic, especially air traffic. **3.** A business executive or government official who supervises financial affairs; comptroller.

control stick. A lever used to control the elevators and ailerons of some airplanes.

control tower. A tower from which the landing, takeoff, and standby areas of an airport are easily visible and from which the movements of aircraft and other vehicles are controlled by radio and radar.

con•tro•ver•sial |kŏn'trə **vûr'**shəl| *adj.* Tending to cause argument or debate: *a controversial issue.* —**con'tro•ver'sial•ly** *adv.*

con•tro•ver•sy |**kŏn'**trə vûr'sē| *n., pl.* **con•tro•ver•sies. 1.** Argument; debate: *He is the subject of much controversy.* **2.** A public dispute between sides holding opposing views: *the controversy over state aid to private schools.*

con•tro•vert |**kŏn'**trə vûrt'| *v.* To contradict; dispute; deny: *The facts controvert his argument.* —**con'tro•vert'i•ble** *adj.*

con•tu•ma•cious |kŏn'tōō **mā'**shəs| *or* |-tyōō-| *adj.* Stubbornly rebellious or disobedient; insubordinate. —**con'tu•ma'cious•ly** *adv.*

con•tu•me•ly |**kŏn'**tōō mə lē| *or* |-tyōō-| *or* |-təm lē| *n., pl.* **con•tu•me•lies. 1.** Rudeness; scorn; insolence. **2.** An insulting remark or act.

con•tuse |kən **tōōz'**| *or* |-**tyōōz'**| *v.* **con•tused, con•tus•ing.** To injure without breaking the skin; bruise.

con•tu•sion |kən **tōō'**zhən| *or* |-**tyōō'**-| *n.* A bruise.

co•nun•drum |kə **nŭn'**drəm| *n.* **1.** A riddle in which a question is answered by a pun. **2.** A baffling problem.

con•va•lesce |kŏn'və **lĕs'**| *v.* **con•va•lesced, con•va•lesc•ing.** To regain health and strength after illness or injury; recuperate.

con•va•les•cence |kŏn'və **lĕs'**əns| *n.* **1.** Gradual return to health and strength after illness or injury. **2.** The time needed for this.

con•va•les•cent |kŏn'və **lĕs'**ənt| *adj.* **1.** Of or for convalescence: *a convalescent home.* **2.** Gradually returning to health and strength after illness or injury. —*n.* A convalescent patient.

con•vec•tion |kən **vĕk'**shən| *n.* The transfer of heat by actual movement of a heated liquid or gas. [SEE NOTE]

con•vec•tor |kən **vĕk'**tər| *n.* A device, somewhat like a radiator, that heats air and circulates it within a space by convection.

con•vene |kən **vēn'**| *v.* **con•vened, con•ven•ing.** To assemble or cause to assemble: *Congress will convene next month. The governor convened the legislature.*

con•ven•ience |kən **vēn'**yəns| *n.* **1.** The quality of being convenient; suitability: *the convenience of traveling by airplane.* **2.** Personal comfort or advantage: *A limousine was provided for his convenience.* **3.** Anything that saves time and effort, as a device, service, etc.: *Our kitchen has all the modern conveniences. Shopping by telephone is a great convenience.*

***Idiom.* at (one's) convenience.** When it is convenient for one.

con•ven•ient |kən **vēn'**yənt| *adj.* **1.** Easy to reach; within easy reach: *a convenient location; a home convenient to the shopping center.* **2.** Suited to one's comfort, needs, or purpose: *a convenient appliance.* —**con•ven'ient•ly** *adv.*

con•vent |**kŏn'**vənt| *or* |-vĕnt'| *n.* **1.** A community of nuns. **2.** A building occupied by nuns; a nunnery.

con•ven•tion |kən **vĕn'**shən| *n.* **1.** A formal assembly or meeting: *a teachers' convention; a constitutional convention.* **2.** A widely accepted practice; custom: *The use of commas is a convention of written English.* **3.** A formal agreement or compact, as between nations: *the Geneva Conventions on treatment of war prisoners.*

con•ven•tion•al |kən **vĕn'**shə nəl| *adj.* Following accepted practice, customs, or taste: *a conventional greeting; a conventional plan for a house.* —**con•ven'tion•al•ly** *adv.* —**con•ven'tion•al'i•ty** *n.*

con•verge |kən **vûrj'**| *v.* **con•verged, con•verg•ing. 1.** To come together in one place: *The three roads converged.* **2.** In mathematics, to have a limit, as an infinite sequence.

con•ver•gent |kən **vûr'**jənt| *adj.* Tending to converge; merging: *convergent forces; convergent paths.* —**con•ver'gence** *n.*

con•ver•sant |kən **vûr'**sənt| *or* |**kŏn'**vər-| *adj.* Familiar, as by study: *conversant with medieval history.* —**con•ver'sant•ly** *adv.*

con•ver•sa•tion |kŏn'vər **sā'**shən| *n.* An informal talk in which people exchange thoughts and feelings.

con•ver•sa•tion•al |kŏn'vər **sā'**shə nəl| *adj.* Of conversation: *in a normal conversational tone.* —**con'ver•sa'tion•al•ly** *adv.*

con•ver•sa•tion•al•ist |kŏn'vər **sā'**shə nə lĭst| *n.* A person who converses.

con•verse[1] |kən **vûrs'**| *v.* **con•versed, con•vers•ing.** To talk informally with others: *converse about family matters.* [SEE NOTE]

con•verse[2] |**kŏn'**vûrs'| *n.* **1.** The opposite or reverse of something: *Dark is the converse of light.* **2.** Either one of a pair of conditionals in which the hypothesis and conclusion of one are, respectively, the conclusion and hypothesis of the other. —*adj.* |kən **vûrs'**| *or* |**kŏn'**vûrs'|. Opposite; contrary: *a converse statement.* —**con•verse'ly** *adv.* [SEE NOTE]

con•ver•sion |kən **vûr'**zhən| *or* |-shən| *n.* **1.** The act or process of changing a thing into another form, substance, or product: *the conversion of electricity to heat.* **2.** A change from one use or purpose to another: *the conversion of an ocean liner into a museum.* **3.** A change in which a person adopts a new religion or new beliefs: *the boy's conversion to Catholicism.*

con•vert |kən **vûrt'**| *v.* **1.** To change into another form, substance, or condition: *convert carbon dioxide into sugar. Electricity converts easily*

convection

Typically, a fluid (a liquid or a gas) becomes less dense as it is heated. As a result, it is forced upward by the cooler fluid that falls to replace it. Under the proper conditions, this action causes a current in the body of fluid.

converse[1-2]

Converse[1] *and* **converse**[2] *are related but separate words.* **Converse**[2] *comes from Latin* conversus, *"turned around, opposite," from* convertere, *"to turn around, convert":* com-, *"together, completely,"* + vertere, *"to turn."* **Converse**[1] *is from Old French* converser, *which is from Latin* conversārī, *"to associate with, keep company with":* com-, *"together, with,"* + versārī, *"to live, move around" (related to* vertere, *"to turn").*

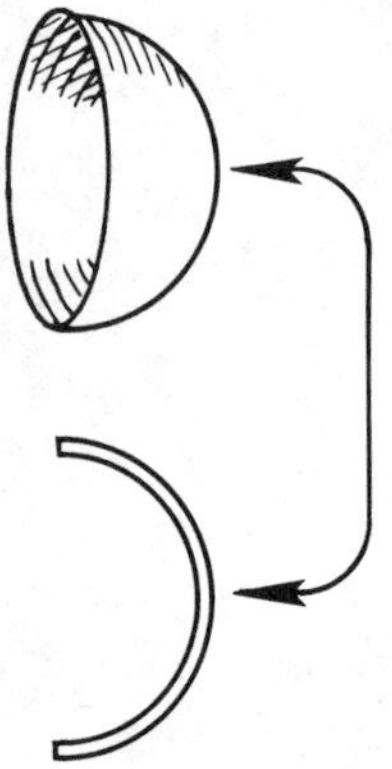

convex

conveyer
Belt for sorting chocolates

conviction
The two meanings of **conviction** *are so different that they might well be thought of as separate words, like* **converse¹** *and* **converse²**. *But the etymology of* **conviction** *shows clearly enough that it is, historically at least, a single unit. Latin* convincere *basically meant "to defeat," but it had two special applications: (a) "to defeat someone in argument, persuade," and (b) "to prove someone guilty of a crime."* Convincere *was borrowed into English as* **convince**, *taking on only sense (a); and its abstract noun* convictiō *was borrowed as* **conviction**, *taking on both senses.*

ă pat/ā pay/â care/ä father/ĕ pet/ ē be/ĭ pit/ī pie/î fierce/ŏ pot/ ō go/ô paw, for/oi oil/o͝o book/ o͞o boot/ou out/ŭ cut/û fur/ *th* the/th thin/hw which/zh vision/ ə ago, item, pencil, atom, circus

into other forms of energy. **2.** To change from one use to another; adapt to a new purpose: *convert a home into a library; an outfielder converted into a shortstop.* **3.** To persuade (a person) to adopt a particular religion or belief: *convert the Indians to Christianity.* **4.** To exchange for something of equal value: *converting dollars into French money. Bonds convert into cash.* **5.** To express (a quantity) in another way: *convert 100 yards into meters.* **6.** To score a point or points after a touchdown in football. *—n.* |**kŏn**'vûrt'|. A person who has adopted a new religion or belief.

con•vert•er |kən **vûr**'tər| *n.* **1.** A mechanical device that changes alternating current to direct current or vice versa. **2.** An electronic device that changes the frequency of a radio signal. **3.** A **Bessemer converter.**

con•vert•i•ble |kən **vûr**'tə bəl| *adj.* **1.** Capable of being converted. **2.** Having a top that can be folded back or removed, as an automobile. *—n.* A convertible automobile. **—con•vert'i•bil'i•ty** *n.* **—con•vert'i•bly** *adv.*

con•vex |kŏn **vĕks**'| *or* |**kŏn**'vĕks| *or* |kən-| *adj.* Curving outward like the outer boundary of a circle or sphere. [SEE PICTURE]

con•vex•i•ty |kən **vĕk**'sĭ tē| *n., pl.* **con•vex•i•ties. 1.** The condition of being convex. **2.** A convex surface, line, or body.

con•vey |kən **vā**'| *v.* **1.** To take or carry from one place to another: *A helicopter conveyed us to the city.* **2.** To serve as a means of transmission for: *Cables convey electrical power.* **3.** To make known; communicate: *Words convey meaning.*

con•vey•ance |kən **vā**'əns| *n.* **1.** The act of conveying. **2.** Something used to convey, especially a vehicle, such as an automobile or bus.

con•vey•er, also **con•vey•or** |kən **vā**'ər| *n.* **1.** Someone or something that conveys. **2.** A mechanical device, such as a continuous moving belt, that carries things from one place to another. [SEE PICTURE]

con•vict |kən **vĭkt**'| *v.* To find or prove guilty of an offense, especially in a court of law. *—n.* |**kŏn**'vĭkt'|. Someone who has been found guilty of a crime and sentenced to prison.

con•vic•tion |kən **vĭk**'shən| *n.* **1.** The act or process of finding or proving guilt. **2.** A strong opinion or belief: *act according to one's true convictions.* [SEE NOTE]

con•vince |kən **vĭns**'| *v.* **con•vinced, con•vinc•ing.** To cause (someone) to believe or feel certain; persuade: *Our actions finally convinced him of our sincerity.*

con•vinc•ing |kən **vĭn**'sĭng| *adj.* Serving to convince; persuasive: *a convincing argument.* **—con•vinc'ing•ly** *adv.*

con•viv•i•al |kən **vĭv**'ē əl| *adj.* **1.** Jolly; sociable: *a convivial man.* **2.** Festive: *a convivial gathering.* **—con•viv'i•al'i•ty** *n.*

con•vo•ca•tion |kŏn'və **kā**'shən| *n.* **1.** The act of convoking. **2.** A summoned assembly, as of clergymen and laymen.

con•voke |kən **vōk**'| *v.* **con•voked, con•vok•ing.** To call together; cause to assemble: *The President convoked the new Congress.*

con•vo•lute |**kŏn**'və lo͞ot'| *adj.* Rolled or folded together with one part over another; coiled: *the convolute shape of a conch shell.*

con•vo•lut•ed |**kŏn**'və lo͞o'tĭd| *adj.* **1.** Having convolutions; coiled; twisted: *a convoluted path.* **2.** Complicated; intricate: *a convoluted argument.*

con•vo•lu•tion |kŏn'və **lo͞o**'shən| *n.* **1.** A tortuous winding, folding, or interlacing. **2.** One of the folds of the surface of the brain.

con•voy |**kŏn**'voi'| *or* |kən **voi**'| *v.* To accompany as a protective escort: *The destroyers convoyed the aircraft carrier.* *—n.* |**kŏn**'voi'|. **1. a.** A group of ships or vehicles, protected on their way by an armed escort. **b.** The escort itself. **2.** A column of military trucks, tanks, etc.

con•vulse |kən **vŭls**'| *v.* **con•vulsed, con•vuls•ing. 1.** To disturb violently; rock: *The revolution convulsed all of society.* **2.** To cause to laugh uproariously: *His quips convulsed the classroom.* **3.** To cause (a person or animal) to have convulsions.

con•vul•sion |kən **vŭl**'shən| *n.* **1.** Often **convulsions.** A violent involuntary muscular contraction or an irregular series of such contractions; a fit; seizure. **2.** A violent turmoil or upheaval: *convulsions of the earth's crust.*

con•vul•sive |kən **vŭl**'sĭv| *adj.* **1.** Of or like a convulsion or convulsions. **2.** Having or causing convulsions. **—con•vul'sive•ly** *adv.*

co•ny |**kō**'nē| *or* |**kŭn**'ē| *n., pl.* **co•nies. 1.** A rabbit, especially the common European rabbit. **2.** The fur of a rabbit. **3.** A rabbitlike animal, such as the pika or the hyrax.

coo |ko͞o| *n., pl.* **coos. 1.** The low, murmuring sound made by a pigeon or dove. **2.** A sound similar to this. *—v.* **cooed, coo•ing. 1.** To make the murmuring sound of a pigeon or dove. **2.** To speak with a sound similar to this. ¶*These sound alike* **coo, coup.**

cook |ko͝ok| *v.* **1.** To prepare (food) for eating by using heat. **2.** To undergo cooking. ***—phrasal verb.*** **cook up.** *Informal.* To concoct; invent: *cook up an excuse.* *—n.* Someone who cooks.

cook•book |**ko͝ok**'bo͝ok'| *n.* A book containing recipes and other information about cooking.

cook•er |**ko͝ok**'ər| *n.* A utensil or appliance for cooking: *a pressure cooker.*

cook•er•y |**ko͝ok**'ə rē| *n.* The preparation of food.

cook•house |**ko͝ok**'hous'| *n., pl.* **-hous•es** |-hou'zĭz|. A building or shed for cooking, as in a lumber camp.

cook•out |**ko͝ok**'out'| *n.* A meal cooked and eaten outdoors.

cook•y or **cook•ie** |**ko͝ok**'ē| *n., pl.* **cook•ies.** Any small, usually flat cake made from sweetened dough.

cool |ko͞ol| *adj.* **cool•er, cool•est. 1.** Moderately cold; neither warm nor very cold: *cool weather.* **2.** Giving or allowing relief from heat: *a cool breeze; a cool blouse.* **3.** Calm; unexcited: *a cool head in a crisis.* **4.** Indifferent or disdainful; unenthusiastic: *a cool reception.* *—v.* **1.** To make or become less warm: *cool a room by opening a window; let the pie cool for a few minutes when you take it out of the oven.* **2.** To make or become less excited: *cool one's passion. Her anger cooled.* ***—phrasal verb.*** **cool off.** *Informal.* To become less heated or excited. *—n.* **1.** Anything that is cool or moderately cold: *the cool of the evening.* **2.** *Slang.* Calmness of mind: *lost his cool.* **—cool'ly** *adv.* **—cool'ness** *n.*

Idioms. **cool it.** *Slang.* To calm down; relax. **cool (one's) heels.** *Informal.* To be kept waiting.

cool•ant |**kōō'**lənt| *n.* Something that cools, especially a fluid that circulates through a machine or over some of its parts in order to draw off heat.

cool•er |**kōō'**lər| *n.* **1.** A device or container for cooling something: *a water cooler; a picnic cooler full of soda bottles.* **2.** *Slang.* Jail.

cool-head•ed |**kōōl'hĕd'**ĭd| *adj.* Not easily excited or flustered; calm. —**cool'-head'ed•ly** *adv.* —**cool'-head'ed•ness** *n.*

Coo•lidge |**kōō'**lĭj|, **(John) Calvin.** 1872–1933. Thirtieth President of the United States (1923–29).

coo•lie |**kōō'**lē| *n.* An unskilled Oriental laborer. ¶*These sound alike* **coolie, coulee.**

coon |kōōn| *n. Informal.* A raccoon.

coon•skin |**kōōn'**skĭn'| *n.* The pelt of the raccoon. —***modifier:*** *a coonskin cap.*

coop |kōōp| *n.* **1.** A cage for poultry or small animals. **2.** *Slang.* Any place of confinement. —*v.* To confine; shut in: *He has been cooped up in his room all day.* ¶*These sound alike* **coop, coupe.**

Idiom. **fly the coop.** *Slang.* To escape.

co-op |**kō'**ŏp'| *or* |kō **ŏp'**| *n.* A cooperative.

coop•er |**kōō'**pər| *n.* A person who makes or repairs barrels.

co•op•er•ate |kō **ŏp'**ə rāt'| *v.* **co•op•er•at•ed, co•op•er•at•ing.** To work or act with another or others for a common purpose: *Everyone cooperated in decorating the classroom.*

co•op•er•a•tion |kō ŏp'ə **rā'**shən| *n.* **1.** Joint action: *This treaty will promote international cooperation.* **2.** Assistance; support: *The principal sought the cooperation of the students.* **3.** Willingness to cooperate: *Please show more cooperation.*

co•op•er•a•tive |kō **ŏp'**ər ə tĭv| *or* |-ə rā'tĭv| *adj.* **1.** Done in cooperation with others: *a cooperative effort; cooperative farming.* **2.** Willing to help or cooperate: *a cooperative patient.* —*n.* An enterprise, building, etc., owned jointly by those who use its facilities or services: *a consumers' cooperative.* —***modifier:*** *a cooperative store; a cooperative apartment.* —**co•op'er•a•tive•ly** *adv.* —**co•op'er•a•tive•ness** *n.*

co-opt |kō **ŏpt'**| *v.* **1.** To elect as a fellow member of a group or body: *The school board co-opted Dr. Smith.* **2.** To appropriate or imitate for one's own purposes: *The administration co-opted the students' demands.* **3.** To win over through subtle bribery: *The students claimed that the administration was trying to co-opt them.*

co•or•di•nate |kō **ôr'**dn ĭt| *or* |-āt'| *n.* **1.** Someone or something that is equal in importance, rank, or degree. **2.** In mathematics, any one of an ordered set of numbers that give the location of a point, as in a system of Cartesian coordinates. —*adj.* **1.** Of equal importance, rank, or degree. **2.** Of or based on coordinates: *a coordinate system.* —*v.* |kō **ôr'**dn āt'| **co•or•di•nat•ed, co•or•di•nat•ing.** To work or cause to work together efficiently in a common cause or effort; harmonize: *When an acrobat's muscles no longer coordinate perfectly, he is through. The nervous system coordinates all the body's activities.*

coordinate conjunction. A conjunction that connects two grammatical elements having identical construction, for example, *and* in *books and pencils,* or in *out of sight or out of mind,* and *yet* in *a man who tried hard, yet failed completely.*

co•or•di•na•tion |kō ôr'dn **ā'**shən| *n.* **1.** An act of coordinating or a condition of being coordinated. **2.** The organized action of muscles or groups of muscles in the performance of complicated movements or tasks.

co•or•di•na•tor |kō **ôr'**dn ā'tər| *n.* **1.** Someone or something that coordinates. **2.** In grammar, a form, such as a coordinate conjunction, that connects a word or word group.

coot |kōōt| *n.* **1.** A water bird with dark-gray feathers and a short bill. **2.** *Informal.* A foolish old man. [SEE PICTURE]

coot•ie |**kōō'**tē| *n. Slang.* A louse that is a parasite on the skin of human beings.

cop¹ |kŏp| *n. Informal.* A police officer; a policeman. [SEE NOTE]

cop² |kŏp| *v.* **copped, cop•ping.** —**cop out.** *Slang.* To fail or refuse to commit oneself: *Don't cop out on the pollution issue.* [SEE NOTE]

co•pal |**kō'**pəl| *n.* A yellow to red resin obtained from certain tropical trees and used in varnishes.

cope¹ |kōp| *v.* **coped, cop•ing.** To contend or strive, especially successfully: *coped with heavy traffic.* [SEE NOTE]

cope² |kōp| *n.* **1.** A long cloak, cape, or mantle worn by priests or bishops during special ceremonies or processions. **2.** Something that provides covering in the form of an arch, vault, or canopy: *Over them vast and high extended the cope of a cedar.* **3.** The top, as of a flask or mold. [SEE NOTE]

Co•pen•ha•gen |**kō'**pən hā'gən| *or* |-hä'-|. The capital and largest city of Denmark. Population, 925,000.

co•pe•pod |**kō'**pə pŏd'| *n.* Any of several very small water animals related to the shrimps. Copepods exist in huge numbers in all the oceans and seas, and are a main source of food for many different kinds of water animals, including jellyfish, many kinds of fishes, and huge whales.

Co•per•ni•can |kō **pûr'**nĭ kən| *or* |kə-| *adj.* Of the theory, formulated by Nicolaus Copernicus, that the earth rotates on its axis and, with the other planets of the solar system, revolves around the sun.

Co•per•ni•cus |kō **pûr'**nĭ kəs| *or* |kə-|, **Nicolaus.** 1473–1543. Polish astronomer.

co•pi•lot |**kō'**pī'lət| *n.* The second or relief pilot of an airplane.

cop•ing |**kō'**pĭng| *n.* The top part of a wall or roof, usually slanted so as to shed rainwater.

coping saw. A saw with a narrow, short blade attached to an open frame, used for cutting designs in wood.

co•pi•ous |**kō'**pē əs| *adj.* Large in quantity; abundant: *Rainfall is copious in the tropics.* —**co'pi•ous•ly** *adv.* —**co'pi•ous•ness** *n.*

co•plan•ar |kō **plā'**nər| *adj.* In the same plane: *coplanar points.*

cop-out |**kŏp'**out'| *n. Slang.* Failure to commit oneself.

cop•per |**kŏp'**ər| *n.* **1.** Symbol **Cu** One of the elements, a reddish-brown metal that is an excellent conductor of heat and electricity. Atomic number 29; atomic weight 63.54; valences +1,

coot

cop¹·²

In British criminal slang, cop *has meant "to catch" in two almost opposite senses: (a) "to arrest" and (b) "to get, to take, to be subjected to," as in* He copped six months. *From sense (a), a policeman was called a* copper *(first known from the 1850's), and this was soon shortened to* **cop¹**. *From sense (b) developed various special phrases, all slang, such as* cop it, *"to get into trouble" or even "to die," and* cop a plea, *"to plead guilty" (i.e., fail to defend oneself). The modern slang verb* **cop out** *probably originates from this; but slang etymologies are often impossible to pin down exactly.*

cope¹·²

Cope¹ *originally meant "to strive with, fight against, hit," and was borrowed from Old French* couper, *"to hit," from* coup, *"a hit, a blow" (the same word as* **coup**). **Cope²** *was* cāp *in Old English, and was borrowed from Late Latin* cappa *or* cāpa, *"cloak" (the same word as* **cape¹**).

+2; melting point 1,083°C; boiling point 2,595°C. **2.** A small coin made of copper or an alloy of copper. **3.** A reddish brown. —***modifier:*** *copper wire; a copper pot.* —*v.* To coat or finish with a layer of copper. —*adj.* Reddish brown.

cop•per•as |**kŏp′**ər əs| *n.* A greenish, crystalline form of ferrous sulfate, $FeSO_4$, used in making fertilizers and in purifying water.

cop•per•head |**kŏp′**ər hĕd′| *n.* A poisonous reddish-brown snake of the eastern United States. [SEE PICTURE]

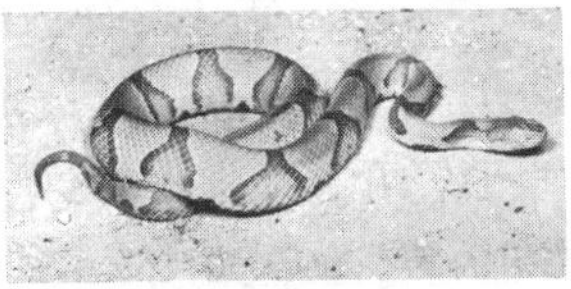

copperhead

cop•per•smith |**kŏp′**ər smĭth′| *n.* A worker or manufacturer of objects in copper.

copper sulfate. A poisonous blue salt of copper having the formula $CuSO_4$. It is used in agriculture and in a number of industrial processes.

cop•per•y |**kŏp′**ə rē| *adj.* Of or like copper.

cop•ra |**kŏp′**rə| *n.* Dried coconut meat, pressed to extract its oil.

copse |kŏps| *n.* A thicket of small trees or bushes.

Copt |kŏpt| *n.* **1.** A native of Egypt descended from the ancient Egyptians. **2.** A member of the Coptic Church.

cop•ter |**kŏp′**tər| *n. Informal.* A helicopter.

Cop•tic |**kŏp′**tĭk| *n.* The language of the Copts, related to the Semitic languages and now used only in the Coptic Church. —*adj.* **1.** Of the Copts or their language. **2.** Of the Coptic Church.

Coptic Church. The Christian church of Egypt that does not follow the belief in the Trinity.

cop•u•la |**kŏp′**yə lə| *n.* A verb, usually a form of *be,* that identifies the predicate of a sentence with the subject. In the sentence *The girls are beautiful,* the copula is *are.*

cop•u•late |**kŏp′**yə lāt′| *v.* **cop•u•lat•ed, cop•u•lat•ing.** To engage in sexual intercourse; mate. —**cop′u•la′tion** *n.*

cop•y |**kŏp′**ē| *n., pl.* **cop•ies. 1.** An imitation or reproduction of something original; a duplicate: *a copy of a letter; a copy of a famous painting.* **2.** One specimen or example of a printed text or picture: *a copy of the June issue of the magazine; autographed copies of her new book.* **3.** Written material to be set in type and printed. **4.** Someone or something that provides good material for a writer: *An underdog who surprises his opponent is always good copy.* —*v.* **cop•ied, cop•y•ing, cop•ies. 1.** To make something that is exactly like an original; reproduce: *He copied part of your letter.* **2.** To follow as a model or pattern; imitate: *Her admirers copied the way in which she wore her hair.*

cop•y•book |**kŏp′**ē bo͝ok′| *n.* A book with models of penmanship to imitate.

copy boy. A boy or young man in a newspaper office who carries copy and runs errands.

cop•y•ist |**kŏp′**ē ĭst| *n.* A person who makes written copies, as of a manuscript.

cop•y•right |**kŏp′**ē rīt′| *n.* The legal right to exclusive publication, production, sale, or distribution of a literary, musical, dramatic, or artistic work. —*v.* To secure a copyright for.

cop•y•writ•er |**kŏp′**ē rī′tər| *n.* A person who writes advertising copy.

co•quet•ry |**kō′**kĭ trē| *or* |kō **kĕt′**rē| *n., pl.* **co•quet•ries.** Flirtation.

co•quette |kō **kĕt′**| *n.* A woman who flirts with men.

co•qui•na |kō **kē′**nə| *n.* **1.** A small clam with a pair of thin, often brightly colored shells. **2.** A soft, porous limestone containing shells and coral, used for building.

cor•a•cle |**kôr′**ə kəl| *or* |**kŏr′**-| *n.* A small, rounded boat made like a wicker basket covered with hide, used by the ancient Britons and Irish and still sometimes by fishermen on the lakes of Wales and Ireland.

cor•al |**kôr′**əl| *or* |**kŏr′**-| *n.* **1.** A hard, stony substance formed by the skeletons of tiny sea animals massed together in great numbers. It is often white, pink, or reddish, and some kinds are used for making jewelry. **2. a.** One of the tiny animals that form this substance. **b.** A mass of this substance, often branched or rounded in shape. **3.** A yellowish pink or reddish orange. —***modifier:*** *a coral reef; a coral bracelet.* —*adj.* Yellowish pink or reddish orange.

coral snake. A poisonous American snake marked with red, black, and yellow bands.

cord |kôrd| *n.* **1.** A string or small rope of twisted strands. **2. a.** An insulated, flexible electric wire fitted with a plug or plugs. **b.** A type of electric wire used in this way: *20 feet of lamp cord.* **3.** A structure of the body that resembles a cord: *the spinal cord.* **4.** A unit of measure for cut firewood, equal to a stack that measures four feet by four feet by eight feet. **5.** A raised ridge or rib on the surface of cloth. **6.** Cloth, such as corduroy, having raised ridges or ribs. —*v.* To cut and stack (firewood) in cords. ¶*These sound alike* **cord, chord.** [SEE NOTE on p. 161]

cord•age |**kôr′**dĭj| *n.* **1. a.** Cords or ropes in general. **b.** The ropes in a ship's rigging. **2.** An amount of wood in a specified area, measured in cords.

cor•dial |**kôr′**jəl| *adj.* Hearty; sincere: *cordial relations.* —*n.* A liqueur. —**cor′dial•ly** *adv.*

cor•dial•i•ty |kôr **jăl′**ĭ tē| *or* |kôr′jē **ăl′**-| *n.* Heartiness; warmth; sincerity.

cor•dil•le•ra |kôr′dĭl **yâr′**ə| *or* |kôr **dĭl′**ər ə| *n.* A chain of mountains, especially the main mountain range of a large land mass.

cor•do•ba |**kôr′**də bə| *n.* The basic monetary unit of Nicaragua.

cor•don |**kôr′**dn| *n.* **1.** A line of people, military posts, ships, etc., stationed around an area to protect or enclose it. **2.** A ribbon or cord worn as a decoration or badge of honor or rank.

cor•do•van |**kôr′**də vən| *n.* Also **cordovan leather.** A soft, fine leather now generally made of split horsehide, used for shoes, boots, etc.

cor•du•roy |**kôr′**də roi′| *or* |kôr′də **roi′**| *n.* **1.** A thick, heavy cotton cloth with a velvety surface of raised ribs or ridges. **2. corduroys.** Trousers made of this fabric. —***modifier:*** *a corduroy coat.* —*adj.* Made of logs laid crosswise on the ground: *a corduroy road.*

cord•wood |**kôrd′**wo͝od′| *n.* **1.** Wood cut and piled in cords. **2.** Wood sold by the cord.

core |kôr| *or* |kōr| *n.* **1.** The hard or stringy central part of certain fruits, such as an apple or pear, containing the seeds. **2.** The innermost or most important part of anything; heart; essence: *the vital core of the work that the scientist does.* **3.** A piece of magnetic material, such as a rod of soft iron, placed inside an electrical coil or transformer to intensify and provide a path for the magnetic field produced by the windings. *—v.* **cored, cor•ing.** To remove the core of: *core apples.* ¶*These sound alike* **core, corps.**

CORE |kôr| *or* |kōr|. Congress of Racial Equality, an organization that works to promote equal rights for blacks.

co•ri•an•der |kôr′ē ăn′dər| *or* |kōr′-| *n.* A plant with spicy seeds used as seasoning.

Cor•inth |kôr′ĭnth| *or* |kŏr′-|. **1.** A region of ancient Greece, lying on an isthmus joining the Peloponnesian peninsula with the mainland. **2.** An ancient Greek city in this region.

Co•rin•thi•an |kə rĭn′thē ən| *adj.* **1.** Of ancient Corinth. **2.** Of or belonging to an order of ancient Greek and Roman architecture characterized by a slender column with an ornate, bell-shaped top, or capital, decorated with a design of acanthus leaves: *a Corinthian column; a Corinthian capital.* *—n.* A native of ancient Corinth.

cork |kôrk| *n.* **1.** The light, spongy outer bark of the **cork oak,** a tree of the Mediterranean region. It is used for bottle stoppers, insulation, life rafts, flooring, etc. **2. a.** A bottle stopper or other object made from this material. **b.** A bottle stopper made of rubber, plastic, etc. **3.** A tissue of dead cells that forms on the outer side of the cambium in the stems of woody plants. ***—modifier:*** *a cork floor.* *—v.* To close or stop up with a cork: *cork a bottle.*

cork•er |kôr′kər| *n. Slang.* Someone or something remarkable or astounding.

cork•screw |kôrk′skro͞o′| *n.* **1.** A device for drawing corks from bottles, consisting of a pointed metal spiral attached to a handle. **2.** A spiral. *—adj.* Spiral in shape; twisted. *—v.* To twist into or move in a spiral.

cork•y |kôr′kē| *adj.* **cork•i•er, cork•i•est.** Of or like cork. **—cork′i•ness** *n.*

corm |kôrm| *n.* A rounded underground plant stem similar to a bulb.

cor•mo•rant |kôr′mər ənt| *n.* A water bird with blackish feathers, webbed feet, and a hooked bill.

corn^{1} |kôrn| *n.* **1.** A tall plant grown for its large ears that bear kernels used as food. **2.** The ears or kernels of this plant. **3.** *British.* Any plant, such as wheat or rye, widely grown for its grain. **4.** Anything considered trite, outdated, or too melodramatic or sentimental. ***—modifier:*** *corn chowder.* *—v.* To preserve and season with salt or in brine: *corn beef.* **—corned′** *adj.: corned beef; corned pork.* [SEE NOTE & PICTURE]

corn^{2} |kôrn| *n.* A horny thickening of the skin, usually on or near a toe, resulting from pressure or rubbing. [SEE NOTE]

corn bread. A kind of bread made from cornmeal.

corn•bread |kôrn′brĕd′| *n.* A form of the phrase **corn bread.**

corn•cake |kôrn′kāk′| *n.* Also **corn cake.** A johnnycake.

corn•cob |kôrn′kŏb′| *n.* The long, hard central part of an ear of corn. ***—modifier:*** *a corncob pipe.*

corn•crib |kôrn′krĭb′| *n.* A bin or building for storing and drying ears of corn, with slatted sides for ventilation.

cor•ne•a |kôr′nē ə| *n.* A tough, transparent membrane that forms the forward portion of the outer coat of the eyeball. It covers the iris and lens.

cor•ner |kôr′nər| *n.* **1. a.** The point at which two lines or surfaces meet: *the upper left-hand corner of the page; the corner of a table.* **b.** The area formed by the intersection of two lines, edges, surfaces, etc.: *out of the corner of his eye. Sit in the corner of the room.* **2.** The place where two roads or streets meet: *Meet me at the corner of Oak and Pine.* **3.** Any region, especially a remote one: *from all corners of the world.* **4.** A threatening or difficult position: *He has me in a corner over the issue.* **5.** A monopoly, as of a stock or commodity, that enables the supplier to control the price: *a corner on the wheat market.* ***—modifier:*** *a corner drugstore.* *—v.* **1.** To drive into a threatening or difficult position from which it is almost impossible to escape: *The dog cornered the cat.* **2.** To gain control of: *He cornered the market on wheat in order to raise prices.*

Idiom. **cut corners.** *Informal.* To trim expenses; economize.

cor•ner•back |kôr′nər băk′| *n.* In football, either of two defensive backs stationed behind the linebackers and relatively near the sidelines.

cor•ner•stone |kôr′nər stōn′| *n.* **1.** A stone at one of the corners of a building's foundation, often inscribed and set in place with a special ceremony. **2.** The main basis or foundation of something.

cor•net |kôr nĕt′| *n.* A musical instrument that is very similar to the trumpet but that has a mellower tone.

cor•net•ist, also **cor•net•tist** |kôr nĕt′ĭst| *n.* A person who plays a cornet.

corn•field |kôrn′fēld′| *n.* A field where corn is grown.

corn•flow•er |kôrn′flou′ər| *n.* A garden plant with flowers that are usually deep blue, but sometimes white or pink.

corn•husk |kôrn′hŭsk′| *n.* The leafy covering surrounding an ear of corn.

cor•nice |kôr′nĭs| *n.* **1.** The uppermost projection of stone or molding at the top of a wall or column. **2.** The molding at the top of the walls of a room, just below the ceiling. **3.** An overhanging mass of snow, ice, or rock. **4.** A horizontal frame used to conceal curtain rods.

corn•meal |kôrn′mēl′| *n.* Also **corn meal.** Coarse meal made from ground corn kernels. ***—modifier:*** *cornmeal mush.*

corn pone. Corn bread that is made without milk or eggs, baked in rounded patties.

corn•stalk |kôrn′stôk′| *n.* The stem of the corn plant.

corn•starch |kôrn′stärch′| *n.* A starchy flour made from corn, used as a thickener in cooking.

cor•nu•co•pi•a |kôr′nə kō′pē ə| *n.* **1.** A cone-shaped container overflowing with fruit, flowers, etc., symbolizing prosperity. Also called *horn of plenty.* **2.** A cone-shaped ornament or container.

corn•y |kôr′nē| *adj.* **corn•i•er, corn•i•est.** *Slang.* Trite, dated, melodramatic, or too sentimental.

co•rol•la |kə rŏl′ə| *n.* The part of a flower consisting of separate petals or petals joined together in a tubelike or trumpetlike form.

cor•ol•lar•y |kôr′ə lĕr′ē| *or* |kŏr′-| *n., pl.* **cor•ol•lar•ies.** **1.** A statement that follows with little

corn^{1}
Above: Corn plant
Below: Ear of corn

corn$^{1-2}$

Corn^{1} *originally meant any kind of edible grain, as it still does in British (sense 3). The word goes back to Old English and before that to the prehistoric Indo-European word for "grain,"* grəno-. *Sense 4 of* **corn^{1}** *originated in musicians' slang in the 1930's;* corn-fed *was used sarcastically by jive or jazz musicians to refer to country or "hillbilly" music; hence the word* **corny.** **Corn^{2}** *is from Old French* corne, *"horn," hence "horny skin on the foot," from Latin* cornu, *"horn."*

coronet
English duke's coronet, with stylized strawberry leaves
The word **coronet** is from Old French *coronette*, "little crown, crownlet," diminutive of *corone*, "crown."

corporal[1-2]
Corporal[2] *is from Old French* corporel, *which is from Latin* corporālis, *"of the body," from* corpus, *"body."* **Corporal[1]** *originates in Italian* caporale, *"head or chief soldier," from* capo, *"head, chief," from Latin* caput, *"head."* Caporale *was borrowed into French as* caporal. *In French the variant* corporal *arose, presumably because of the idea that it was the same word as* **corporal[1]**, *meaning "man in charge of a body of troops." The variant disappeared in French, but was borrowed into English as* **corporal[1]**.

corpus
Corpus *is the Latin word for "body." It has long been used to mean "a particular body of literature." This Dictionary is based on a corpus of five million words taken from one thousand books used in American schools in grades 3 through 9.*

or no proof from a statement already proven. **2.** A natural consequence or effect; a result: *We settled our routes and as a corollary the rough date of departure.*

co•ro•na |kə rō′nə| *n., pl.* **co•ro•nas** or **co•ro•nae** |kə rō′nē|. **1.** The mass of ionized gas that surrounds the chromosphere of the sun. During an eclipse of the sun the corona is visible as a shining, irregularly shaped ring around the sun. **2.** A faintly colored shining ring seen around a celestial body, especially the moon or sun, when it is looked at through a cloud or haze.

co•ro•na•graph |kə rō′nə grăf′| *or* |-gräf′| *n.* An instrument that allows visual or photographic study of the sun's corona in the absence of an eclipse.

cor•o•nar•y |kôr′ə nĕr′ē| *or* |kŏr′-| *adj.* **1.** Of either of the arteries that branch from the aorta and supply blood directly to the heart. **2.** Of the heart. *—n., pl.* **cor•o•nar•ies.** *Informal.* A **coronary thrombosis.**

coronary thrombosis. The blockage of a coronary artery by a blood clot, often leading to destruction of heart muscle and sometimes to death.

cor•o•na•tion |kôr′ə nā′shən| *or* |kŏr′-| *n.* The act or ceremony of crowning a king, queen, or other monarch.

cor•o•ner |kôr′ə nər| *or* |kŏr′-| *n.* A public official who investigates any death not clearly due to natural causes.

cor•o•net |kôr′ə nĕt′| *or* |kŏr′-| *n.* **1.** A crown for princes and nobles, smaller than a king's or queen's crown. **2.** A band for the head, as one of gold, jewels, etc. [SEE PICTURE]

corp. corporation.

cor•po•ra |kôr′pər ə| *n.* Plural of **corpus.**

cor•po•ral[1] |kôr′pər əl| *or* |-prəl| *n.* A noncommissioned officer in the U.S. Army, Air Force, or Marine Corps ranking below a sergeant. A **lance corporal** in the Marine Corps ranks below a corporal. [SEE NOTE]

cor•po•ral[2] |kôr′pər əl| *or* |-prəl| *adj.* Of the body; bodily: *corporal needs.* [SEE NOTE]

corporal punishment. Physical punishment applied to a convicted offender and including the death penalty.

cor•po•rate |kôr′pər ĭt| *or* |-prĭt| *adj.* **1.** Of a corporation: *There is widespread corporate abuse in matters of ecology.* **2.** Shared by the members of a group; collective: *corporate effort; corporate responsibility.* **3.** Formed into a corporation: *The University became a body corporate.*

cor•po•ra•tion |kôr′pə rā′shən| *n.* A group of persons acting under a legal charter as a separate organization with privileges and liabilities distinct from those of its members. *—**modifier:** a corporation president.*

cor•po•re•al |kôr pôr′ē əl| *or* |-pōr′-| *adj.* **1.** Of the body. **2.** Of a material nature; tangible.

corps |kôr| *or* |kōr| *n., pl.* **corps** |kôrz| *or* |kōrz|. **1.** Often **Corps.** A section or branch of the armed forces having a special function: *The Marine Corps is trained to make landings from the sea.* **2.** A large army unit composed of two or more divisions. **3.** Any group of people acting together: *the White House press corps; a drum and bugle corps.* ¶*These sound alike* **corps, core.**

corps de bal•let |kôr′ də bă lā′|. The dancers in a ballet troupe who perform as a group with no solo parts.

corpse |kôrps| *n.* A dead body, especially of a human being.

corps•man |kôr′mən| *or* |kōr′-| *n., pl.* **-men** |-mən|. In the U.S. Navy, an enlisted man trained as a medical assistant.

cor•pu•lent |kôr′pyə lənt| *adj.* Having a large, overweight body; fat. **—cor′pu•lence** *n.*

cor•pus |kôr′pəs| *n., pl.* **cor•po•ra** |kôr′pər ə|. A large collection of writings of a specific kind or on a specific subject. [SEE NOTE]

cor•pus•cle |kôr′pə səl| *or* |-pŭs′əl| *n.* **1.** A body cell, such as a red or white blood cell, that is capable of moving or being moved about freely. **2.** A particle such as an electron or photon.

cor•ral |kə răl′| *n.* **1.** A fenced-in area for keeping cattle or horses. **2.** An enclosed area within a circle of wagons for defense against attack: *The wagons formed a corral for protection.* *—v.* **cor•ralled, cor•ral•ling. 1.** To drive (livestock) into and hold in a corral. **2.** To arrange (wagons) in a corral. **3.** *Informal.* To round up; seize: *corralling all the books on this subject.* ¶*These sound alike* **corral, chorale.**

cor•rect |kə rĕkt′| *v.* **1. a.** To remove the mistakes from: *Correct your paper before you hand it in.* **b.** To indicate or mark the errors in: *The teacher corrected the tests.* **2.** To make or set right, as by adjusting, changing, etc.: *correct a wrong impression. The carpenter corrected the curvature in the wood.* **3.** To rebuke or punish for the purpose of improving: *correct a child for being rude.* *—adj.* **1.** Free from error; accurate: *Your paper is absolutely correct.* **2.** Conforming to approved standards; proper: *the correct method; correct behavior.* **—cor•rect′ly** *adv.* **—cor•rect′ness** *n.*

cor•rec•tion |kə rĕk′shən| *n.* **1.** The act or process of correcting: *The correction of term papers is an important task for a teacher.* **2.** Something that is offered or substituted for a mistake or fault; an improvement: *a paper full of corrections in red pencil.*

cor•rec•tive |kə rĕk′tĭv| *adj.* Intended or tending to correct: *a corrective measure.* *—n.* Something that corrects: *Glasses are a corrective for faulty vision.*

cor•re•late |kôr′ə lāt′| *or* |kŏr′-| *v.* **cor•re•lat•ed, cor•re•lat•ing. 1.** To put into or establish in a relationship with each other: *correlating your new garments with those in your present wardrobe; an attempt to correlate art and religious thought.* **2.** To have systematic connection; be related: *statistics indicating that divorce and alcoholism definitely correlate.*

cor•re•la•tion |kôr′ə lā′shən| *or* |kŏr′-| *n.* **1.** A relationship; systematic connection; correspondence. **2.** An act of correlating or a condition of being correlated.

cor•rel•a•tive |kə rĕl′ə tĭv| *adj.* Related; corresponding. *—n.* Either of two related or corresponding things. **—cor•rel′a•tive•ly** *adv.*

correlative conjunction. A conjunction that regularly occurs as part of a pair of conjunctions and that indicates a reciprocal or complementary relation. Among the most common correlative conjunctions are *both* and *and,* as in *feeling both*

ă **pat**/ā **pay**/â **care**/ä **father**/ĕ **pet**/ ē **be**/ĭ **pit**/ī **pie**/î **fierce**/ŏ **pot**/ ō **go**/ô **paw**, **for**/oi **oil**/o͝o **book**/ o͞o **boot**/ou **out**/ŭ **cut**/û **fur**/ *th* **the**/th **thin**/hw **which**/zh **vision**/ ə **ago**, **item**, **pencil**, **atom**, **circus**

tired and discouraged; either and *or,* as in *either sulking or crying;* and *neither* and *nor,* as in *heeding neither advice nor good sense.*

cor•re•spond |kôr′ĭ **spŏnd′**| *or* |kŏr′-| *v.* **1.** To be in agreement; match or compare closely: *Her selfish actions do not correspond with her unselfish words.* **2.** To be similar, equal, or equivalent: *The eyelids correspond to the shutter of a camera.* **3.** To communicate by letter, especially on a regular basis.

cor•re•spond•ence |kôr′ĭ **spŏn′**dəns| *or* |kŏr′-| *n.* **1.** Agreement; conformity; similarity: *a correspondence between spelling and pronunciation.* **2. a.** Communication by the exchange of letters: *He remained in correspondence with all his school friends.* **b.** The letters exchanged: *funds to publish all the late President's private correspondence.* —***modifier:*** *a correspondence course; a correspondence school.*

cor•re•spond•ent |kôr′ĭ **spŏn′**dənt| *or* |kŏr′-| *n.* **1.** Someone who communicates by letter, especially on a regular basis. **2.** Someone hired by a newspaper, radio station, etc., to report on news from faraway places.

cor•re•spond•ing |kôr′ĭ **spŏn′**dĭng| *or* |kŏr′-| *adj.* Matching closely; analogous: *The teacher said that all plural noun forms in the list had corresponding singular forms.* —**cor′re•spond′ing•ly** *adv.*

cor•ri•dor |**kôr′**ĭ dər| *or* |-dôr′| *or* |**kŏr′-**| *n.* **1.** A narrow hallway or passageway with rooms opening onto it. **2.** A narrow strip of land, especially one that is a means of reaching something, such as the sea.

cor•rob•o•rate |kə **rŏb′**ə rāt′| *v.* **cor•rob•o•rat•ed, cor•rob•o•rat•ing.** To support or confirm by new evidence; attest the truth or accuracy of: *Two witnesses corroborated his statement.* —**cor•rob′o•ra′tion** *n.* —**cor•rob′o•ra′tive** *adj.*

cor•rode |kə **rōd′**| *v.* **cor•rod•ed, cor•rod•ing. 1.** To dissolve or wear away (a material, structure, etc.), especially by chemical action. **2.** To be dissolved or worn away.

cor•ro•sion |kə **rō′**zhən| *n.* **1.** The act or process of corroding, especially of a metal. **2.** The condition of being corroded. **3.** A substance, such as rust, produced by corroding.

cor•ro•sive |kə **rō′**sĭv| *adj.* **1.** Capable of producing or tending to produce corrosion. **2.** Destructive to the feelings; harsh: *corrosive criticism.* —*n.* A corrosive substance. —**cor•ro′sive•ly** *adv.* —**cor•ro′sive•ness** *n.*

corrosive sublimate. **Mercuric chloride.**

cor•ru•gate |**kôr′**ə gāt′| *or* |**kŏr′-**| *v.* **cor•ru•gat•ed, cor•ru•gat•ing.** To shape or fold into alternating and parallel ridges and grooves.

corrugated iron. A kind of sheet iron used in construction, shaped in parallel ridges and grooves for rigidity.

cor•ru•ga•tion |kôr′ə **gā′**shən| *or* |kŏr′-| *n.* **1.** The act or process of corrugating. **2.** The condition of being corrugated. **3.** A groove or ridge in a corrugated surface.

cor•rupt |kə **rŭpt′**| *adj.* **1.** Lacking in moral restraint; depraved: *the corrupt court of an aging Roman emperor.* **2.** Marked by or open to bribery, the selling of political favors, etc.; dishonest: *a corrupt government; a corrupt judge.* **3.** Decaying; putrid. **4.** Containing errors or alterations, as a text: *a corrupt translation.* —*v.* **1.** To ruin morally; cause to behave wickedly. **2.** To destroy the honesty or integrity of, as by bribing. **3.** To taint; infect; spoil. **4.** To change the original form of (a text, language, etc.). —**cor•rupt′ly** *adv.* —**cor•rupt′ness** *n.*

cor•rupt•i•ble |kə **rŭp′**tə bəl| *adj.* Capable of being corrupted, as by bribery.

cor•rup•tion |kə **rŭp′**shən| *n.* **1.** The act or process of corrupting. **2.** Dishonesty or improper behavior, as by a person in a position of authority. **3.** Decay; rottenness. **4.** A change in the form of language: *The word "automation" is a corruption of "automatic operation."*

cor•sage |kôr **säzh′**| *n.* A small bouquet of flowers worn by a woman at the shoulder or waist or on the wrist.

cor•sair |**kôr′**sâr′| *n.* **1.** A pirate, especially along the Mediterranean coast of North Africa. **2.** A pirate ship.

corse•let *n.* **1.** |**kôrs′**lĭt|. Metal armor worn to protect the body, especially the upper body or torso. **2.** |kôr′sə **lĕt′**|. A light corset. [See Picture]

cor•set |**kôr′**sĭt| *n.* A close-fitting undergarment, stiffer than a girdle and sometimes tightened by lacing, worn mainly by women to support or shape the waist and hips.

Cor•si•ca |**kôr′**sĭ kə|. An island, a part of France, in the Mediterranean Sea. Population, 275,000. —**Cor′si•can** *adj.* & *n.*

cor•tege |kôr **tĕzh′**| *or* |**-tāzh′**| *n.* **1.** A train of attendants; a retinue. **2.** A ceremonial procession, especially a funeral procession.

Cor•tés |kôr **tĕz′**|, **Hernando.** 1485–1547. Spanish explorer, conqueror of Mexico.

cor•tex |**kôr′**tĕks′| *n., pl.* **cor•ti•ces** |**kôr′**tĭ sēz′| or **cor•tex•es. 1.** The outer layer of an organ or part of the body, especially of the cerebrum or the adrenal glands. **2.** A layer of tissue under the outermost part of plant stems and roots.

cor•ti•cal |**kôr′**tĭ kəl| *adj.* **1.** Of, involving, or consisting of a cortex. **2.** Of, associated with, or depending on the cerebral cortex: *the cortical functions of the brain.*

cor•ti•sone |**kôr′**tĭ sōn′| *or* |-zōn′| *n.* A hormone produced by the adrenal cortex. It is active in carbohydrate metabolism, and is used in treating disorders such as rheumatoid arthritis, allergies, and gout.

co•run•dum |kə **rŭn′**dəm| *n.* An extremely hard mineral composed mainly of aluminum oxide. It occurs in gem varieties such as ruby and sapphire and in common forms that are used as abrasives.

cor•vette |kôr **vĕt′**| *n.* **1.** A gunboat used to protect a convoy from submarines. **2.** In former times, any of several types of small warships with one tier of guns.

cos cosine.

co•sine |**kō′**sīn′| *n.* In a right triangle, a function of an acute angle defined by the quotient of the measure of the side adjacent to it divided by the measure of the hypotenuse.

cos•met•ic |kŏz **mĕt′**ĭk| *n.* A preparation, such as face powder or skin cream, designed to beautify the body. —***modifier:*** *a cosmetic cream; a cosmetic case.*

cos•mic |**kŏz′**mĭk| *adj.* Of the universe, espe-

corselet
Sixteenth-century Italian

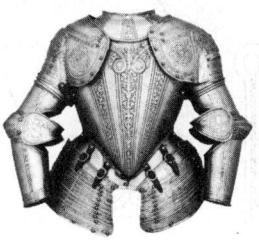

cosmonaut

Cosmonaut *is borrowed from Russian* kosmonavt, *which was made up from Greek* kosmos, *"universe,"* + nautēs, *"sailor." It is curious that while Americans usually use the Russian term when speaking of a Soviet astronaut, the Russians call both kinds* kosmonavt. *This is perhaps because the first actual spaceman was a Russian (1961), and western reporters were sufficiently impressed to borrow the Russian term rather than translate it, while the Russians continue to mark their priority by not using the American term. If so, the situation is a kind of monument to the "space race."*

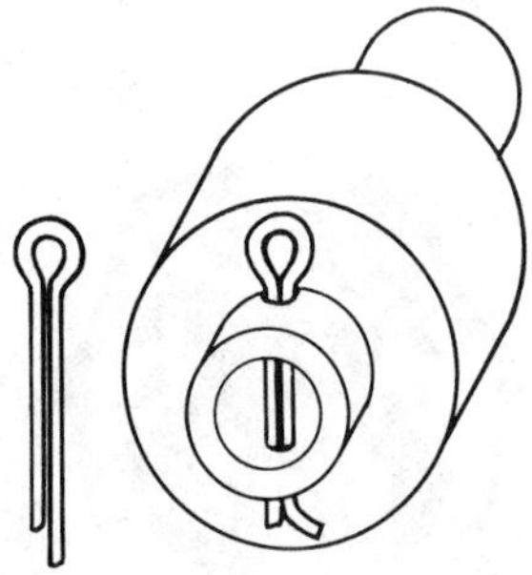

cotter pin

cotton

ă **pat**/ā **pay**/â **care**/ä **father**/ĕ **pet**/ ē **be**/ĭ **pit**/ī **pie**/î **fierce**/ŏ **pot**/ ō **go**/ô **paw**, **for**/oi **oil**/o͝o **book**/ o͞o **boot**/ou **out**/ŭ **cut**/û **fur**/ *th* **the**/th **thin**/hw **which**/**zh** vision/ ə **ago**, item, pencil, atom, circus

cially as distinct from the earth and, often, the solar system. —**cos'mi•cal•ly** *adv.*

cosmic dust. Fine, solid particles of matter in space.

cosmic ray. A stream of radiation, consisting of high-energy atomic nuclei, fragments, and particles and some electromagnetic waves, that enters the atmosphere from outer space.

cos•mog•o•ny |kŏz **mŏg'**ə nē| *n., pl.* **cos•mog•o•nies. 1.** The scientific study of the origin and development of the universe. **2.** A theory of the development of the universe: *the cosmogonies of ancient peoples.*

cos•mog•ra•phy |kŏz **mŏg'**rə fē| *n., pl.* **cos•mog•ra•phies. 1.** The scientific study of the general features of nature and the universe. **2.** A description of the universe.

cos•mol•o•gy |kŏz **mŏl'**ə jē| *n., pl.* **cos•mol•o•gies. 1.** The philosophical study of the origin and structure of the universe. **2. a.** The scientific study of the structure and workings of the universe. **b.** A theory of the structure and workings of the universe.

cos•mo•naut |**kŏz'**mə nôt'| *n.* A person trained to fly a spacecraft. [SEE NOTE]

cos•mo•pol•i•tan |kŏz'mə **pŏl'**ĭ tn| *adj.* **1.** Of the entire world or from many different parts of the world: *a cosmopolitan crowd of delegates to the United Nations.* **2.** Showing worldly experience, education, cultivation, etc.; at home in all parts of the world: *a cosmopolitan person.* **3.** Having a population composed of elements from all parts of the world, from all social levels, etc.; sophisticated; not provincial or narrow: *San Francisco is a very cosmopolitan city.* **4.** Living or growing in all parts of the world; widely distributed: *The house sparrow is a cosmopolitan bird.* —*n.* A person whose many interests and broad outlook enable him to feel at home everywhere.

cos•mos |**kŏz'**məs| *n.* **1.** The universe regarded as an orderly, harmonious whole. **2.** Any system regarded as orderly, harmonious, and whole. **3.** A garden plant with pink, white, or red daisylike flowers.

Cos•sack |**kŏs'**ăk'| *n.* A member of a people of southern Russia, noted as horsemen. —**Cos'sack'** *adj.*

cost |kôst| *n.* **1.** An amount paid or required in payment for a purchase. **2.** Something that is needed or given in order to obtain something else; a loss or penalty: *He took a firm stand at the cost of his job.* **3. costs.** The expenses of litigation in court. —*v.* **cost, cost•ing. 1.** To have or require as a price: *A year's subscription of six issues of the magazine costs five dollars. It costs so much to live in New York City!* **2.** To cause to lose: *The strike cost him his job.*

Idiom. **at all costs.** Whatever the cost may be: *At all costs I had to have that big apple at the top of the tree.*

cos•ta |**kŏs'**tə| *n., pl.* **cos•tae** |**kŏs'**tē|. A rib or a riblike part of an organism.

cos•tal |**kŏs'**təl| *adj.* Of, near, or involving the ribs.

Cos•ta Ri•ca |**kŏs'**tə **rē'**kə| *or* |**kô'**stə|. A country in Central America, between Nicaragua and Panama. Population, 2,000,000. Capital, San José. —**Costa Rican.**

cost•ly |**kôst'**lē| *adj.* **cost•li•er, cost•li•est. 1.** High-priced; expensive: *costly jewelry.* **2.** Involving great loss or sacrifice: *a costly war.* —**cost'li•ness** *n.*

cos•tume |**kôs'**to͞om'| *or* |-tyo͞om'| *n.* **1.** The clothes or style of dress typical of a certain time, place, or people: *peasants in native costume.* **2.** A set of clothes suitable for a certain occasion or season: *a skating costume.* **3.** Clothes worn by someone playing a part or dressing up in disguise: *an actor's costume; a Halloween costume.* —*v.* |kŏ **sto͞om'**| *or* |-**styo͞om'**| **cos•tumed, cos•tum•ing.** To dress in a costume: *She was costumed as Marie Antoinette.*

costume ball. A dance at which fancy masquerade costumes are worn.

costume jewelry. Jewelry made of inexpensive materials, such as base metals, enamels, imitation stones, etc.

cos•tum•er |kŏ **sto͞o'**mər| *or* |-**styo͞o'**-| *n.* A person who makes or supplies costumes, as for plays.

co•sy |**kō'**zē| *adj.* **co•si•er, co•si•est,** & *n., pl.* **co•sies.** A form of the word **cozy.**

cot |kŏt| *n.* A narrow bed usually made of canvas stretched over a folding frame.

cote |kōt| *n.* A shed or coop for small animals or birds. ¶*These sound alike* **cote, coat.**

co•te•rie |**kō'**tə rē| *n.* A group of people who share interests and associate frequently.

co•til•lion |kō **tĭl'**yən| *or* |kə-| *n.* **1.** A lively, intricate dance of the 18th century. **2.** A formal ball, especially one at which girls are presented to society.

cot•tage |**kŏt'**ĭj| *n.* **1.** A small country house. **2.** A summer residence at a seaside resort.

cottage cheese. A soft white cheese made of curds of skim milk.

cot•tag•er |**kŏt'**ĭ jər| *n.* A person who lives in a cottage.

cot•ter |**kŏt'**ər| *n.* **1.** A bolt, wedge, key, or pin that fits into a slot in order to hold mechanical parts together. **2.** A **cotter pin.**

cotter pin. A split pin that fits through two or more holes in order to fasten parts together, and that is secured in place by bending the ends of the split part. [SEE PICTURE]

cot•ton |**kŏt'**n| *n.* **1.** A plant grown in warm regions for the downy white fibers that surround its seeds. **2.** The soft, fine fibers of this plant. **3.** Thread or cloth made from this fiber. **4.** Often **cottons.** Clothing made from this cloth. —*modifier: a cotton fabric.* [SEE PICTURE]

cotton candy. **Spun sugar.**

cotton gin. A machine that frees cotton fibers of seeds, hulls, and other small objects.

cot•ton•mouth |**kŏt'**n mouth'| *n., pl.* **-mouths** |-mouths'| *or* |-mou*th*z'|. A snake, the **water moccasin.**

cot•ton•seed |**kŏt'**n sēd'| *n.* The seed or seeds of the cotton plant, pressed to obtain **cottonseed oil,** which is used in cooking and in making paints, soaps, etc.

cot•ton•tail |**kŏt'**n tāl'| *n.* An American rabbit with a short, fluffy white tail.

cot•ton•wood |**kŏt'**n wo͝od'| *n.* An American poplar tree having seeds with cottonlike tufts.

cot•ton•y |**kŏt'**n ē| *adj.* **1.** Of or like cotton: fluffy or downy. **2.** Covered with cottonlike down or fibers.

cot•y•le•don |kŏt′l ēd′n| *n.* A leaflike part of the embryo plant within a seed. It contains stored food for the newly developing plant and often appears above the ground as the seed begins to sprout. Cotyledons are often called *seed leaves.* [SEE PICTURE]

couch |kouch| *n.* A long piece of furniture, usually upholstered and often having a back, on which one may sit or recline; a lounge; sofa. *—v.* To word in a certain manner; phrase: *demands couched in the single word "submission."*

cou•gar |ko͞o′gər| *n.* The **mountain lion.**

cough |kôf| *or* |kŏf| *v.* **1. a.** To force air from the lungs in a sudden, noisy way, usually in an attempt to clear mucus or foreign material from the respiratory tract. **b.** To clear from the respiratory tract in this way: *He coughed up blood.* **2.** To make a sound like that of coughing: *The engine coughed and sputtered.* *—n.* **1.** The act or process of coughing. **2.** An illness marked by frequent and persistent coughing.

could |ko͝od| *or* |kəd *when unstressed*|. Past tense of **can** (to be able).

could•n't |**ko͝od′**nt|. Could not.

couldst |ko͝odst|. *Archaic.* A form of the present tense of **could,** used with *thou.*

cou•lee |**ko͞o′**lē| *n.* In the western United States, a deep gulch formed by rainwater or melting snow, often dry in summer. ¶*These sound alike* **coulee, coolie.**

cou•lomb |**ko͞o′**lŏm′| *or* |-lōm′| *n.* A unit of electric charge equal to the quantity of charge transferred in one second by a steady current of one ampere, equal to about the charge carried by 6.25×10^{18} electrons. [SEE NOTE]

coun•cil |**koun′**səl| *n.* **1.** A gathering of persons called together to discuss or settle a problem or question. **2.** A group of people chosen to make laws or rules governing something: *a city council; student council.* **3.** The discussion or deliberation of such a gathering or group: *The Sioux were in council to give the vote of life and death to the unsuspecting settlers.* ¶*These sound alike* **council, counsel.**

coun•cil•man |**koun′**səl mən| *n., pl.* **-men** |-mən|. A member of a council, especially of the group that makes the laws of a city.

coun•cil•or, also **coun•cil•lor** |**koun′**sə lər| *or* |-slər| *n.* A member of a council. ¶*These sound alike* **councilor, counselor.**

coun•sel |**koun′**səl| *n.* **1.** Advice; guidance: *I will marry no one without your counsel.* **2.** *pl.* **counsel.** A lawyer or group of lawyers giving legal advice. *—v.* **coun•seled** or **coun•selled, coun•sel•ing** or **coun•sel•ling.** To give advice: *counseled parents.* ¶*These sound alike* **counsel, council.**

coun•sel•or, also **coun•sel•lor** |**koun′**sə lər| *or* |-slər| *n.* **1.** Someone who advises or guides; an adviser: *a school counselor.* **2.** A lawyer. **3.** Someone who supervises children at a summer camp. ¶*These sound alike* **counselor, councilor.**

count[1] |kount| *v.* **1. a.** To list (the members of a set) and match them in order with the natural numbers (1, 2, 3, . . .), often using the last number reached as the measure of the set. **b.** To determine the measure of (such a set) in this way. **2.** To total; add up: *Count your change before leaving the store.* **3. a.** To recite the natural numbers in order up to and including (a particular number): *Count three and jump.* **b.** To recite natural numbers in order: *count from 1 to 10.* **4.** To keep time in music by counting. **5.** To take account of; include: *There are seven in my family, counting me.* **6.** To have importance; be of value: *It is not how often you read but how you read that counts.* **7.** To regard; consider: *You can count the income yielded by the new properties as a long-term gain.* **8. —count on.** To rely on; depend on: *You can count on her help.* **—phrasal verbs. count in.** To include: *If there's a game today, count me in.* **count off. 1.** To separate into groups by counting: *We counted off four groups of students to help with the job.* **2.** To call out numbers so as to divide into groups, maintain the order of a line, etc.: *Count off by twos.* **count out.** To exclude: *If there's going to be any roughness, you can count me out.* *—n.* **1.** The act of counting or calculating. **2.** A number reached by counting. **3.** In law, any of the separate charges listed in an indictment: *He was tried on five counts of larceny.* [SEE NOTE]

count[2] |kount| *n.* **1.** In some European countries, a title of nobility corresponding to that of an English earl. **2.** A man holding such a title. [SEE NOTE]

count•a•ble |**koun′**tə bəl| *adj.* **1.** Capable of being counted. **2.** Capable of being matched with the positive integers in a one-to-one correspondence.

count•down |**kount′**doun′| *n.* The act or process of counting intervals of time backward from some optionally chosen point to indicate the time remaining until a scheduled event, such as the firing of a rocket, is to take place.

coun•te•nance |**koun′**tə nəns| *n.* **1.** Appearance, especially the expression of the face: *a grave countenance.* **2.** The face: *the human countenance.* **3.** Composure; self-control: *Meg tried to keep her countenance in front of her accusers.* **4.** Approval; encouragement: *He refused to give countenance to her plans.* *—v.* **coun•te•nanced, coun•te•nanc•ing.** To give approval to; condone: *legislators refusing to countenance fiscal irresponsibility.*

count•er[1] |**koun′**tər| *n.* **1.** A narrow table on which goods are sold, food is served, etc. **2.** A small object, such as a stone or bead, that represents a number or digit when in a certain position, as on an abacus. [SEE NOTE]

count•er[2] |**koun′**tər| *n.* Someone or something that counts, especially an electrical or electronic device that automatically counts things or occurrences of events. [SEE NOTE]

coun•ter[3] |**koun′**tər| *adj.* Contrary; opposing: *His views appeared to be counter to the views of the great scientists of the day.* *—v.* **1.** To move or act in opposition to; oppose: *He is trying to counter that impression.* **2.** To return (a blow) with another blow. *—n.* Someone or something that counters; an opposite. *—adv.* In a contrary manner or direction. [SEE NOTE]

counter–. A prefix meaning: **1.** Contrary; opposite: **counteract; counterclockwise. 2.** Retaliatory; in return: **counterattack. 3.** Complementary; corresponding: **countersign.**

coun•ter•act |koun′tər **ăkt′**| *v.* To lessen and oppose the effects of by contrary action; check.

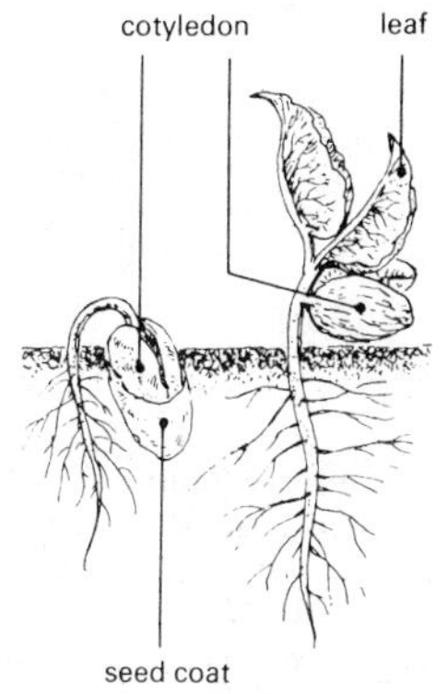

cotyledon
Bean seedling with two cotyledons

coulomb

This unit is named after Charles A. Coulomb *(1736–1806), French physicist.*

count[1-2]

Count[1] *is from Old French* conter *or* compter, *which is from Latin* computāre, *"to add up":* com-, *"together,"* + putāre, *"to think, reckon."* **Compute** *is directly from this word and is thus a doublet of* **count**[1]. **Count**[2] *is from Old French* comte, *which is from Latin* comes, *"companion." During the late Roman Empire* comes *came first to mean "courtier" and then "state official." This was taken over into the early medieval kingdoms, until it became a hereditary title of nobility.*

counter[1-2-3]

Counter[1] *is from Old French* conteoir, *which is from Medieval Latin* computātōrium, *"counting place," from* computāre, *"to count, to compute."* **Counter**[2] *is directly from* **count**[1]; *since* **count**[1] *and* **compute** *are doublets,* **counter**[2] *and* **computer** *are also doublets, and* **counter**[1] *(above) is very closely related.* **Counter**[3] *is from Old French* contre, *from Latin* contrā, *"against."*

coun•ter•at•tack |**koun**′tər ə tăk′| *n.* An attack made to oppose, return, or halt an enemy attack. —*v.* |koun′tər ə **tăk′**|. To attack in return.

coun•ter•bal•ance |**koun**′tər băl′əns| *n.* A force or weight that acts as a balance for another force or weight. —*v.* |koun′tər **băl′**əns| **coun•ter•bal•anced, coun•ter•bal•anc•ing.** To act as a counterbalance to.

coun•ter•clock•wise |koun′tər **klŏk′**wīz′| *adv.* In a direction opposite to that of the movement of the hands of a clock. —*adj.: counterclockwise motion.*

coun•ter•es•pi•o•nage |koun′tər **ĕs′**pē ə-näzh′| *or* |-nĭj| *n.* Espionage undertaken to uncover and counteract enemy espionage.

coun•ter•feit |**koun**′tər fĭt| *v.* **1.** To make in imitation of what is genuine in order to deceive: *He was found guilty of counterfeiting money.* **2.** To pretend: *counterfeit remorse.* —*adj.* **1.** Made in imitation of what is genuine in order to deceive: *a counterfeit dollar bill.* **2.** Pretended; simulated: *counterfeit repentance.* —*n.* Something counterfeited. —**coun′ter•feit′er** *n.*

coun•ter•in•tel•li•gence |koun′tər ĭn **tĕl′**ĭ-jəns| *n.* The work of keeping valuable information from an enemy, preventing subversion and sabotage, and gathering political and military information.

coun•ter•mand |koun′tər **mănd′**| *or* |**-mänd′**| *v.* To cancel or reverse (a command or order).

coun•ter•meas•ure |**koun**′tər mĕzh′ər| *n.* A measure or action taken to oppose or offset another.

coun•ter•of•fen•sive |koun′tər ə **fĕn′**sĭv| *n.* A large-scale attack by an army, designed to stop the offensive of an enemy force.

coun•ter•pane |**koun**′tər pān′| *n.* A bedspread or quilt.

coun•ter•part |**koun**′tər pärt′| *n.* A person or thing exactly or very much like another, as in function, relation, etc.: *The modern counterpart of a horse and buggy is a car.*

coun•ter•point |**koun**′tər point′| *n.* **1.** A musical technique in which two or more distinct melodies are combined so that they can be performed at the same time as a single whole. **2.** A secondary melody designed to go along with a principal melody.

coun•ter•poise |**koun**′tər poiz′| *n.* A weight or force that balances or equally counteracts another. —*v.* **coun•ter•poised, coun•ter•pois•ing.** To equal in weight or force; counterbalance.

Counter Reformation. A reform movement within the Roman Catholic Church during the 16th century and the first half of the 17th century in response to the Protestant Reformation.

coun•ter•rev•o•lu•tion |koun′tər rĕv′ə **lōō′**-shən| *n.* A movement arising in opposition to a revolution.

coun•ter•sign |**koun**′tər sīn′| *v.* To sign (a previously signed document), as to guarantee authenticity. —*n.* A secret sign or signal, especially one given in response to a military sentry to obtain permission to pass.

coun•ter•sink |**koun**′tər sĭngk′| *v.* **coun•ter•sunk** |**koun**′tər sŭngk′|, **coun•ter•sink•ing.** **1.** To enlarge the top part of (a hole) so that a screw or bolthead will lie flush with or below the surface. **2.** To drive a screw or bolt into (such a hole). —*n.* **1.** A tool for making such a hole. **2.** A hole made in this way.

coun•ter•ten•or |**koun**′tər tĕn′ər| *n.* **1.** A man's voice higher than a tenor; alto. **2.** A person having such a voice.

coun•ter•weight |**koun**′tər wāt′| *n.* A weight that acts as a counterbalance.

count•ess |**koun**′tĭs| *n.* **1.** The wife or widow of a count or earl. **2.** A woman holding a rank equal to that of a count in her own right.

counting number. A whole number greater than zero; a natural number; a positive integer.

count•less |**kount′**lĭs| *adj.* Too many to be counted; very numerous.

coun•try |**kŭn′**trē| *n., pl.* **coun•tries.** **1. a.** A nation or state: *all the countries of the world.* **b.** The territory of a nation or state: *the country of France.* **2.** The land of one's birth or citizenship: *He returned to his country at the end of the war.* **3.** The people of a nation or state: *The country does not want war.* **4.** A large area of land having certain physical, geographic, or other distinguishing features: *mountain country; sheep country.* **5.** The region outside of cities or heavily populated districts; rural area: *go to the country for a vacation.* —**modifier:** *a country boy; country life.* [SEE NOTE]

country club. A suburban club with facilities for golf, other outdoor sports, and social activities.

coun•try•man |**kŭn′**trē mən| *n., pl.* **-men** |-mən|. A person from one's own country.

coun•ty |**koun′**tē| *n., pl.* **coun•ties.** **1.** In the United States, an administrative subdivision of a state. **2.** A major territorial division in Great Britain and Ireland. —**modifier:** *a county fair; the county sheriff.* [SEE NOTE]

county seat. A town or city that is the center of government in its county.

coup |kōō| *n., pl.* **coups** |kōōz|. A brilliantly executed move or action that obtains the desired results: *The ambassador pulled off quite a coup with the signing of the new agreement.* ¶*These sound alike* **coup, coo.** [SEE NOTE]

coup d'é•tat |kōō′ dā **tä′**|. *pl.* **coups d'é•tat** |kōō′ dā **tä′**|. The sudden overthrow of a government, bringing a new group into power.

coupe |kōōp| *n.* A former model of closed, two-door automobile. ¶*These sound alike* **coupe, coop.** [SEE NOTE]

cou•pé |kōō **pā′**| *n.* **1.** A form of the word **coupe.** **2.** A closed four-wheel carriage with two seats inside and one outside. [SEE NOTE]

cou•ple |**kŭp′**əl| *n.* **1.** Two things of the same kind; a pair. **2.** A man and woman united in some way, as by marriage. **3.** *Informal.* A small but indefinite number; a few; several: *a couple of days.* —*v.* **cou•pled, cou•pling.** **1.** To link together; attach; join: *couple cars of a train. Intelligence coupled with hard work accounted for her success.* **2.** To link (physical systems, especially electric circuits) so that energy is transferred from one to the other.

cou•pler |**kŭp′**lər| *n.* **1.** Something that links or connects, especially a device that holds two railroad cars together. **2.** On certain keyboard instruments, such as the organ and harpsichord, a device that allows each key to sound two or more notes, either on the same or different keyboards.

cou•plet |**kŭp′**lĭt| *n.* A unit of two successive

country/county

These two quite similar words are entirely unrelated. **Country** *was* cuntree *in Middle English, and was borrowed from Old French* contree; *this is from the rather surprising Medieval Latin phrase* (terra) contrāta, *"(land) lying opposite or facing one," that is, "landscape, countryside." A* **county** *was originally the territory governed by a* **count²**.

coup/coupe/coupé

Coup *is from French* coup, *"a stroke, a hit, a move, an action"; this descends from Late Latin* colpus, *"a punch, a hit, a cut."* **Coup d'état** *is from the French for "stroke of state."* **Coupe,** *the automobile, is a recent American alteration of* **coupé,** *the carriage.* **Coupé** *is from French* (carosse) coupé, *"cut-off or shortened (carriage)," from* couper, *"to cut"; and* couper *in turn is from Late Latin* colpāre, *"to cut," from* colpus, *"a punch, a cut" (see above). All these words are thus related, but note that there is also an unrelated French word* coupe, *"cup," that sometimes appears on menus as the name of a kind of dessert made with fruit, ice cream, etc.*

ă **pat**/ā **pay**/â **care**/ä **father**/ĕ **pet**/ ē **be**/ĭ **pit**/ī **pie**/î **fierce**/ŏ **pot**/ ō **go**/ô **paw**, **for**/oi **oil**/ŏŏ **book**/ ōō **boot**/ou **out**/ŭ **cut**/û **fur**/ *th* **the**/th **thin**/hw **which**/zh **vision**/ ə **ago**, **item**, **pencil**, **atom**, **circus**

lines of verse that rhyme and have the same meter.

cou•pling |kŭp′lĭng| *n.* Something that links or connects, especially a device that holds railroad cars together; a coupler.

cou•pon |ko͞o′pŏn| *or* |kyo͞o′-| *n.* **1.** One of a number of small certificates attached to a bond that represent sums of interest that can be collected at certain specified dates. **2. a.** A detachable part of a ticket, advertisement, etc., that entitles the bearer to certain benefits, such as a cash refund or a gift. **b.** A printed form, as in an advertisement, on which to write one's name and address when sending away for something.

cour•age |kûr′ĭj| *or* |kŭr′-| *n.* The quality of mind or spirit that enables one to face danger or hardship with confidence, resolution, and firm control of oneself; bravery. [SEE NOTE]

cou•ra•geous |kə rā′jəs| *adj.* Having or displaying courage. —**cou•ra′geous•ly** *adv.* —**cou•ra′geous•ness** *n.*

cour•i•er |kûr′ē ər| *or* |ko͝or′-| *n.* A messenger, especially one on urgent or official diplomatic business.

course |kôrs| *or* |kōrs| *n.* **1. a.** Onward movement in a particular direction; progress; advance: *the course of events.* **b.** Onward movement in time; duration: *in the course of a week.* **2.** The route or direction taken by something or someone: *the course of a stream. Our course was due south.* **3.** An area of land or water on which a race is held or a sport is played: *a golf course.* **4.** A way of behaving or acting: *Your best course is to do it now.* **5.** A typical manner of proceeding; regular development: *The law took its course. He performs his duty as a matter of course.* **6.** An orderly sequence: *a course of medical treatments.* **7. a.** A series of classes, as in school, on a certain subject: *an algebra course.* **b.** A complete body of studies in a school: *a four-year course in engineering.* **8.** A part of a meal served as a unit at one time: *Soup was our first course.* —*v.* **coursed, cours•ing.** To flow or move swiftly: *Blood coursed through his veins. Copious tears coursed down his cheeks.* ¶*These sound alike* **course, coarse.**

***Idioms.* in due course.** In proper order; at the right time. **of course.** Without a doubt; certainly; naturally: *Of course we will do it.*

cours•er |kôr′sər| *or* |kōr′-| *n.* A swift horse. Used chiefly in poetry.

court |kôrt| *or* |kōrt| *n.* **1.** A courtyard. **2.** A short street, especially an alley enclosed by buildings on three sides. **3.** An area marked and fitted for tennis, handball, basketball, etc. **4.** A royal mansion or palace. **5.** The people who attend a monarch. **6. a.** A sovereign's governing body, including ministers and state advisers. **b.** An official meeting of this body, presided over by the sovereign. **7. a.** A judge or body of officials who hear and make decisions on legal cases. **b.** The room or building in which such cases are heard; a courthouse or courtroom. **8.** A regular session of a judicial assembly. —***modifier:*** *court life; a court jester; a court decision favoring the defendant; court procedures.* —*v.* **1.** To treat with flattery and attention; seek the favor of: *Some parents court their children by acting like friends.* **2.** To woo and seek to marry: *Bill courted Anne for a long time. Bob and Jane courted in secret for many years.* **3.** To try to win or obtain: *The senator proclaimed himself a liberal, courted popularity, and tried to get the nomination of his party.* **4.** To invite (something bad), often foolishly or unwittingly: *court disaster.*

***Idiom.* out of court.** Without a trial: *The case was settled out of court.*

cour•te•ous |kûr′tē əs| *adj.* Considerate toward others; gracious; polite. —**cour′te•ous•ly** *adv.* —**cour′te•ous•ness** *n.*

cour•te•san |kôr′tĭ zən| *or* |kōr′-| *n.* A prostitute, especially one who sold her favors only to men of high rank or great wealth.

cour•te•sy |kûr′tĭ sē| *n., pl.* **cour•te•sies. 1.** Polite behavior or a gracious manner. **2.** An act or gesture showing politeness: *He saluted, and the Confederate general returned the courtesy.* **3.** Consent or favor; indulgence: *received a wool blanket by courtesy of the airline.*

court•house |kôrt′hous′| *or* |kōrt′-| *n., pl.* **-hous•es** |-hou′zĭz|. A building in which courts of law are held.

cour•ti•er |kôr′tē ər| *or* |kōr′-| *n.* An attendant at the court of a king or other ruler.

court•ly |kôrt′lē| *or* |kōrt′-| *adj.* **court•li•er, court•li•est. 1.** Of a royal court: *musical life then confined to courtly circles.* **2.** Suitable for a royal court; dignified, polite, etc.: *a courtly ceremony; courtly manners.* —**court′li•ness** *n.*

court-mar•tial |kôrt′mär′shəl| *or* |kōrt′-| *n., pl.* **courts-mar•tial. 1.** A military court of officers appointed to try persons for offenses under military law. **2.** A trial by such a court. —*v.* **court-mar•tialed** or **court-mar•tialled, court-mar•tial•ing** or **court-mar•tial•ling.** To try (someone) by court-martial.

Court of St. James's |jāmz′ĭz|. The British royal court.

court•room |kôrt′ro͞om′| *or* |-ro͝om′| *or* |kōrt′-| *n.* A room in which court proceedings are carried on.

court•ship |kôrt′shĭp′| *or* |kōrt′-| *n.* The act or period of courting a woman.

court•yard |kôrt′yärd′| *or* |kōrt′-| *n.* An open space surrounded by walls or buildings.

cous•in |kŭz′ən| *n.* **1.** A child of one's aunt or uncle. **2.** A less close relative. ¶*These sound alike* **cousin, cozen.**

co•va•lent bond |kō vā′lənt|. A chemical bond formed by the sharing of one or more electrons, especially pairs of electrons, between atoms.

cove |kōv| *n.* A small, sheltered bay or inlet.

cov•e•nant |kŭv′ə nənt| *n.* A formal binding agreement made by two or more persons or parties; a contract. —*v.* To promise or pledge by a formal agreement: *The club covenanted to accept no new members.*

cov•er |kŭv′ər| *v.* **1.** To place (something) upon, over, or in front of, so as to protect, conceal, etc.: *cover a table. She covered her ears.* **2.** To occupy the surface of; spread over: *Dust covered the table. A rug covered the floor.* **3.** To have an extent of: *an assignment covering a period of weeks; a farm covering 100 acres.* **4.** To travel or journey over: *We covered 200 miles a day this summer. We also covered ten states.* **5.** To report the details of (an event or situation), as for a newspaper. **6.** To be enough money for: *Will*

courage

"Courage is a quality so necessary for maintaining virtue that it is always respected, even when it is associated with vice." —Samuel Johnson (1784).

"Courage is resistance to fear, mastery of fear—not absence of fear."—Mark Twain.

cow^1-2

Cow¹ *was* cū *in Old English,* kōuz *in prehistoric Germanic, and* gwōus *in Indo-European. Note that the sound changes are not random but regular; Indo-European* gw- *always changed to* k- *or* kw- *in Germanic.* **Cow²** *is more obscure; it may possibly be from Old Norse* kūga, *"to oppress."*

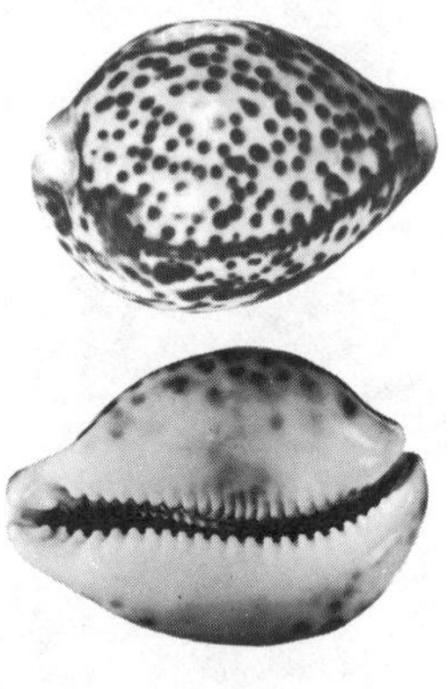

cowry

coyote

ă pat/ā pay/â care/ä father/ĕ pet/ ē be/ĭ pit/ī pie/î fierce/ŏ pot/ ō go/ô paw, for/oi oil/ŏŏ book/ ōō boot/ou out/ŭ cut/û fur/ *th* the/th thin/hw which/zh vision/ ə ago, item, pencil, atom, circus

five dollars cover the cost of it? **7.** To protect, as from loss: *Is your house covered by fire insurance?* **8. a.** To keep a gun aimed at: *The policeman covered the suspect.* **b.** To protect (a person) by firing a gun at an enemy: *The detective covered his partner, who moved closer to the house.* **9.** In sports, to guard the play of (an opponent) or defend (an area or position): *The pitcher usually covers first base on a bunt.* **10.** To conceal or hide: *cover up one's ignorance. She covered her embarrassment by laughing.* **11.** *Informal.* To act as a substitute for someone absent: *He is covering for the ailing star of the play.* **12.** To hide something in order to save someone from punishment, embarrassment, etc.: *cover up for a colleague.* —*n.* **1.** Something placed on or attached to something else, as for protection: *the cover on a bed; book covers.* **2.** Vegetation covering an area. **3. a.** Shelter of any kind: *seek cover during a storm.* **b.** Natural or artificial protection by other armed units: *under a cover of mortar fire.* **4.** Something that conceals or disguises: *That business is a cover for illegal activity.* **5.** A table setting for one person.

***Idioms.* under cover.** Secretly: *Spies work under cover.* **under separate cover.** Within a separate envelope.

cov•er•age |kŭv′ər ĭj| *n.* **1.** The extent to or way in which something is reported, as by a newspaper or a television station. **2.** The extent of protection given by an insurance policy.

cov•er•alls |kŭv′ər ôlz′| *pl.n.* A one-piece garment of trousers and shirt, worn over other clothes to protect them.

cover crop. A crop planted to prevent soil erosion in winter and to enrich the soil when plowed into the ground in the spring.

covered wagon. A large wagon covered with an arched canvas top, used by American pioneers for travel across the prairie.

cov•er•ing |kŭv′ər ĭng| *n.* Something that covers, protects, or hides: *a brightly colored cloth covering for a bed.*

cov•er•let |kŭv′ər lĭt| *n.* A bedspread.

cov•ert |kŭv′ərt| *or* |kō′vərt| *adj.* **1.** Covered; sheltered. **2.** Concealed; secret: *a covert look; reasons often obscure and covert.* —*n.* **1.** A covered or sheltered place; a hiding place. **2.** Underbrush that offers cover for game animals or birds. —**cov′ert•ly** *adv.*

cov•er-up, also **cov•er•up** |kŭv′ər ŭp′| *n.* **1.** An effort or strategy designed to conceal something, as a crime or scandal, that could be harmful or embarrassing if known. **2.** An enveloping garment.

cov•et |kŭv′ĭt| *v.* **1.** To desire (something belonging to another). **2.** To wish for strongly; crave. —**cov′et•ed** *adj.*: *a coveted award.*

cov•et•ous |kŭv′ĭ təs| *adj.* Very desirous, often of something belonging to another; greedy. —**cov′et•ous•ly** *adv.* —**cov′et•ous•ness** *n.*

cov•ey |kŭv′ē| *n., pl.* **cov•eys.** A group or small flock of partridges, grouse, or other birds.

cow¹ |kou| *n.* **1.** The full-grown female of cattle. **2.** The female of certain other large mammals, such as the elephant or moose. —***modifier:*** *a cow pasture.* [SEE NOTE]

cow² |kou| *v.* To frighten or subdue with threats or a show of force. [SEE NOTE]

cow•ard |kou′ərd| *n.* A person who lacks courage to face danger, pain, or hardship, or who shows fear in a shameful way.

cow•ard•ice |kou′ər dĭs| *n.* Lack of courage or a shameful show of fear when facing danger, pain, or a conflict.

cow•ard•ly |kou′ərd lē| *adj.* Lacking courage or showing fear in a shameful way. —*adv.* In the manner of a coward; basely. —**cow′ard•li•ness** *n.*

cow•bell |kou′bĕl′| *n.* A bell hung from a collar around a cow's neck to make her easy to find.

cow•bird |kou′bûrd′| *n.* An American blackbird that lays its eggs in the nests of other kinds of birds.

cow•boy |kou′boi′| *n.* In the western United States, a hired man, usually working on horseback, who tends cattle.

cow•catch•er |kou′kăch′ər| *n.* An iron grille or frame on the front of a locomotive to clear away obstacles from the track.

cow•er |kou′ər| *v.* To crouch or draw back, as from fear or pain; cringe.

cow•hand |kou′hănd′| *n.* A cowboy.

cow•herd |kou′hûrd′| *n.* A person who herds or tends cattle.

cow•hide |kou′hīd′| *n.* **1. a.** The skin or hide of a cow. **b.** Leather made from this hide. **2.** A strong, heavy, flexible whip, usually made of braided leather. —***modifier:*** *a cowhide belt.*

cowl |koul| *n.* **1.** A monk's hood, usually attached to a robe. **2.** A robe or cloak having such a hood. **3.** The part of the front of an automobile body that supports the windshield and dashboard. **4.** A cowling.

cow•lick |kou′lĭk′| *n.* A tuft of hair that stands up from the head and will not lie flat.

cowl•ing |kou′lĭng| *n.* A removable metal cover for an engine, especially an engine of an aircraft.

co•work•er |kō′wûr′kər| *n.* A fellow worker.

cow•poke |kou′pōk′| *n.* *Informal.* A cowboy.

cow•pox |kou′pŏks′| *n.* A contagious skin disease of cattle. It is caused by a virus that is used to vaccinate human beings against smallpox.

cow•punch•er |kou′pŭn′chər| *n.* *Informal.* A cowboy.

cow•ry or **cow•rie** |kou′rē| *n., pl.* **cow•ries.** A tropical sea mollusk with a glossy, often brightly marked shell. [SEE PICTURE]

cow•slip |kou′slĭp′| *n.* **1.** An Old World primrose with fragrant yellow flowers. **2.** The **marsh marigold.**

cox•swain |kŏk′sən| *or* |-swān′| *n.* **1.** A person who steers a boat or racing shell or has charge of its crew. **2.** The sailor in charge of a ship's boat.

coy |koi| *adj.* **coy•er, coy•est. 1.** Retiring in manner; shy. **2.** Pretending to be shy or modest so as to attract the interest of others. —**coy′ly** *adv.* —**coy′ness** *n.*

coy•dog |kī′dôg′, -dŏg′, koi′-| *n.* A predatory animal, probably a cross between a wolf and a coyote, that now ranges widely throughout the United States.

coy•o•te |kī ō′tē| *or* |kī′ōt′| *n.* A wolflike animal common in western North America. [SEE PICTURE]

coz•en |kŭz′ən| *v.* To deceive by means of a petty trick. ¶ *These sound alike* **cozen, cousin.** —**coz′en•er** *n.*

co•zy |kō′zē| *adj.* **co•zi•er, co•zi•est.** Snug and

comfortable: *a cozy room; a cozy fire.* —*n.* A padded or knitted covering placed over a teapot to keep the tea hot. —**co'zi•ly** *adv.* —**co'zi•ness** *n.*

cp. compare.

C.P.A. certified public accountant.

Cpl. corporal.

CPR |sē'pē är'| *n.* Cardiopulmonary resuscitation.

cps cycles per second.

Cr The symbol for the element chromium.

crab[1] |krăb| *n.* An animal related to the lobsters and shrimps, having a broad flattened body and five pairs of legs, of which the front pair are large and pincerlike. —*v.* **crabbed, crab•bing.** To hunt or catch crabs. [SEE NOTE & PICTURE]

crab[2] |krăb| *n.* **1.** A **crab apple. 2.** *Informal.* A bad-tempered, complaining person; a grouch. —*v.* **crabbed, crab•bing.** *Informal.* To complain irritably. [SEE NOTE]

crab apple. 1. A small, sour, applelike fruit. **2.** A tree that bears such fruit.

crab•bed |krăb'ĭd| *adj.* **1.** Crabby. **2.** Difficult to read: *crabbed handwriting.* [SEE NOTE]

crab•by |krăb'ē| *adj.* **crab•bi•er, crab•bi•est.** Grouchy; ill-tempered. —**crab'bi•ly** *adv.* —**crab'bi•ness** *n.* [SEE NOTE]

crab•grass |krăb'grăs'| *or* |-gräs'| *n.* A coarse grass that spreads rapidly and is often considered a nuisance by gardeners.

crack |krăk| *v.* **1.** To break with a sharp sound: *The tree limb cracked. She cracked the tiles.* **2.** To make or cause to make a sharp, snapping sound: *The rifle cracked. He cracked a whip.* **3.** To break or cause to break without dividing into parts; split: *The cup cracked. The hot tea cracked the china.* **4.** To break open or into: *Thieves cracked the safe.* **5.** To break down; give out: *He cracked under the strain.* **6.** To strike with a sudden sharp sound: *I cracked my head on the railing.* **7.** To change sharply in pitch or timbre; break: *Her voice cracked.* **8.** To solve: *We cracked the spies' code.* **9.** *Informal.* To tell or say (a joke or something witty). **10.** To decompose (a complex substance, especially petroleum) into simpler chemical compounds. —***phrasal verbs.*** **crack down.** *Informal.* To become more severe or strict: *He cracked down on tardiness.* **crack up.** *Informal.* **1.** To crash; collide. **2.** To have a mental or physical breakdown. **3.** To break up; disintegrate. —*n.* **1.** A sharp, snapping sound. **2.** A partial split or break; a flaw. **3.** A narrow space: *The door was opened just a crack.* **4.** A sharp blow. **5.** A cracking tone or sound: *a crack in her voice.* **6.** *Slang.* An attempt: *Take a crack at the job.* **7.** *Informal.* A flippant or sarcastic remark. **8.** An instant; moment: *the crack of dawn; the crack of doom.* —*adj.* Excelling in skill; first-rate: *a crack shot.*

Idiom. **cracked up to be.** *Slang.* Believed to be.

crack•down |krăk'doun'| *n.* An action taken to stop an illegal or disapproved activity: *a crackdown on gambling.*

cracked |krăkt| *adj.* **1.** Having a crack or cracks: *a cracked dish.* **2.** Broken into pieces: *cracked ice.* **3.** *Slang.* Crazy; insane.

crack•er |krăk'ər| *n.* **1.** A thin, crisp wafer or biscuit. **2.** A firecracker.

crack•er•jack |krăk'ər jăk'| *n.* *Slang.* Something or someone of excellent quality or ability.

crack•ing |krăk'ĭng| *n.* The process of decomposing a complex substance, especially petroleum, into simpler compounds, usually by means of heat and, often, various catalysts.

crack•le |krăk'əl| *v.* **crack•led, crack•ling. 1.** To make slight sharp, snapping sounds, as a small fire does. **2.** To crush (paper, cellophane, etc.) with such sounds. —*n.* **1.** The act or sound of crackling. **2.** A network of fine cracks on the surface of glazed pottery, china, or glassware.

crack•ling |krăk'lĭng| *n.* **1.** Sharp, snapping sounds like those produced by a fire or by the crushing of paper. **2.** The crisp brown rind of roasted pork. **3.** Often **cracklings.** Crisp bits of connective tissue remaining after pork fat has been melted down, as in making lard.

crack•pot |krăk'pŏt'| *n.* *Slang.* A person having very strange ideas. —***modifier:*** *a crackpot scientific theory.*

crack•up |krăk'ŭp'| *n.* **1.** *Informal.* A collision, as of an airplane or an automobile. **2.** *Slang.* A mental or physical breakdown.

-cracy. A word element meaning "government, rule": **democracy.**

cra•dle |krād'l| *n.* **1.** A small bed for a baby, usually mounted on rockers. **2.** A place of origin; birthplace: *Greece, the cradle of Western civilization.* **3.** Infancy: *showed an interest in music almost from the cradle.* **4.** A framework of wood or metal used to support something being built or repaired, as a ship. **5.** A frame attached to a scythe, used to catch grain as it is cut so that it can be laid flat. —*v.* **cra•dled, cra•dling. 1.** To place in or as if in a cradle: *cradle a baby.* **2.** To hold closely; support: *cradled the trophy in his arms; my rifle cradled on my knees.*

craft |krăft| *or* |kräft| *n.* **1.** Skill or ability in something, especially in work done with the hands or in the arts. **2.** Skill in deception or evasion; cunning: *She kept her eyes down and with craft hid her tears from sight.* **3.** An occupation or trade: *masterpieces of the jeweler's craft; learning my craft.* **4.** *pl.* **craft.** A boat, ship, aircraft, or spacecraft. —*v.* To make by hand. —**craft'ed** *adj.: crafted furniture.* [SEE PICTURE]

crafts•man |krăfts'mən| *or* |kräfts'-| *n., pl.* **-men** |-mən|. A skilled worker, especially one who practices a craft.

crafts•man•ship |krăfts'mən shĭp'| *or* |kräfts'-| *n.* Skill in a craft, as shown in a piece of work.

craft union. A labor union limited in membership to workers in the same craft.

craft•y |krăf'tē| *or* |kräf'-| *adj.* **craft•i•er, craft•i•est.** Skilled in underhanded dealing and deceit; cunning. —**craft'i•ly** *adv.* —**craft'i•ness** *n.*

crag |krăg| *n.* A steep projection of rock forming part of a cliff, mountain, etc.

crag•gy |krăg'ē| *adj.* **crag•gi•er, crag•gi•est. 1.** Having crags: *a craggy mountain.* **2.** Rugged in appearance: *a craggy face.* —**crag'gi•ness** *n.*

cram |krăm| *v.* **crammed, cram•ming. 1.** To force, press, or squeeze (persons or things) into too small a space. **2.** To fill (something) too tightly. **3.** To stuff oneself with food; eat greedily. **4.** *Informal.* To study intensely, especially just before an examination.

cramp[1] |krămp| *n.* **1.** A painful involuntary contraction of a muscle, usually resulting from strain or a chill. **2.** A temporary partial paralysis

crab[1-2]/crabbed/crabby

Crab[1] *was* crabba *in Old English and originally meant "scratching animal."* **Crab[2]** *was probably* scrab *originally, coming from a Scandinavian word for the fruit. Sense* **2** *of* **crab[2]** *is from the idea of sourness.* **Crabbed** *and* **crabby** *probably arise equally from the sourness of* **crab[2]** *and from the scratching, pinching, sideways-walking* **crab[1]**.

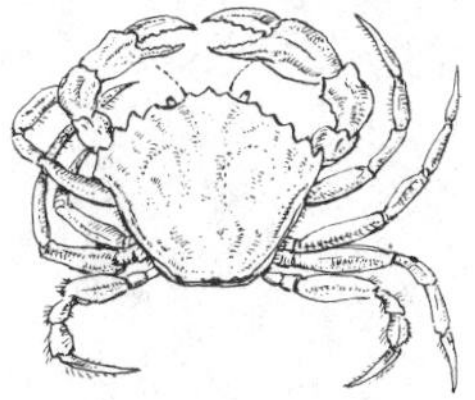

crab[1]

craft

cramp[1-2]

Cramp[1] *probably comes from Old High German* krampho, *"cramp," and* **cramp[2]** *comes from Middle Dutch* crampe, *"hook." The two Germanic words are probably related; the underlying sense might have been "bend, something bent," hence "doubled over with pain,* **cramp[1]**," *and "hook,* **cramp[2]**."

crane
The similarity between the bird *(above)* and the mechanical device *(below)* can readily be seen in these pictures

crater
A crater on the surface of the moon.

ă **pat**/ā **pay**/â **care**/ä **father**/ĕ **pet**/ ē **be**/ĭ **pit**/ī **pie**/î **fierce**/ŏ **pot**/ ō **go**/ô **paw**, **for**/oi **oil**/ŏŏ **book**/ ōō **boot**/ou **out**/ŭ **cut**/û **fur**/ *th* **the**/th **thin**/hw **which**/**zh** vision/ ə **ago**, item, pencil, atom, circus

of muscles that are used to excess: *a leg cramp.* **3. cramps.** Sharp, persistent pains in the abdomen. *—v.* To have or cause to have a cramp or cramps. [SEE NOTE on p. 217]

cramp[2] |**krămp**| *n.* **1.** An iron bar bent at both ends, used to hold together blocks of stone or timber in building. **2.** A frame with an adjustable part to hold pieces together; a clamp. **3.** Anything that restrains: *put a cramp in his style.* *—v.* **1.** To hold together with a cramp. **2.** To confine or restrain: *cramped his style.* **3.** To jam (the wheels of a car) hard to the right or left: *cramping the wheels into the curb when parking.* **—cramped'** *adj.: a cramped apartment.* [SEE NOTE on p. 217]

cram•pon |**krăm'**pən| *n.* **1.** A hinged pair of curved iron bars used for raising weights. **2.** A spiked iron plate attached to the shoe to prevent slipping when climbing or walking on ice.

cran•ber•ry |**krăn'**bĕr'ē| *n., pl.* **-ber•ries. 1.** The tart, shiny, red berry of a slender vine that grows in damp places. **2.** A plant that bears such berries. *—**modifier:** cranberry sauce.*

crane |krān| *n.* **1.** A large wading bird with a long neck, long legs, and a long bill. **2.** A machine for lifting heavy objects by means of cables attached to a movable boom. **3.** Any one of many devices in which a swinging arm or rod is used to support a load. *—v.* **craned, cran•ing.** To stretch or strain for a better view: *Jo craned forward to watch. We craned our necks.* [SEE PICTURE]

cra•ni•al |**krā'**nē əl| *adj.* Of the skull.

cra•ni•um |**krā'**nē əm| *n., pl.* **cra•ni•ums** or **cra•ni•a** |**krā'**nē ə|. **1.** The skull of a vertebrate animal. **2.** The part of the skull that encloses the brain.

crank |krăngk| *n.* **1.** A device for converting motion in a straight line into rotary motion, consisting of a rod or handle attached at right angles to a shaft that is free to turn. **2. a.** An irritable person; a grouch. **b.** A person with odd or eccentric ideas. *—v.* **1.** To start or operate (a device) by means of a crank. **2.** To start or operate (an engine) by means of a crank or an auxiliary motor.

crank•case |**krăngk'**kās'| *n.* The case that encloses the crankshaft and associated parts in engines that operate by means of pistons that move back and forth. It also acts as a reservoir for oil in some engines.

crank•shaft |**krăngk'**shăft'| *or* |-shäft'| *n.* A shaft turned by a crank, especially in an engine driven by pistons, the shaft that is made to turn as the pistons move back and forth.

crank•y |**krăng'**kē| *adj.* **crank•i•er, crank•i•est. 1.** Ill-tempered; irritable; peevish. **2.** Eccentric; odd. **—crank'i•ly** *adv.* **—crank'i•ness** *n.*

cran•ny |**krăn'**ē| *n., pl.* **cran•nies.** A small opening, as in a wall or rock face; a crevice.

crape |krāp| *n.* A form of the word **crepe,** used especially for black crepe that is used as a sign or band of mourning.

crap•pie |**krăp'**ē| *n.* A North American freshwater fish related to the sunfishes.

craps |krăps| *n. (used with a singular verb).* A gambling game played with a pair of dice.

crash |krăsh| *v.* **1.** To fall, strike, or collide suddenly, violently, and noisily: *The dishes slid from the shelf and crashed to the floor. A tree crashed down on a man, killing him. Splinters crashed into the side of his head. The car crashed against a tree. Georgia's forwards crashed over North Carolina's defense.* **2.** To break through (something) violently: *The elephants made the forest shudder as they crashed through the trees. The scream of the horned owl crashed through the stillness of the night.* **3.** To fail suddenly: *The stock market crashed in 1929.* **4.** To make a sudden loud noise: *Can you hear the cymbals crash?* **5.** To cause to crash: *The great whale began to crash its tail again and again into the water. With anger he crashed a left hand into Lindy's face.* **6.** To dash to pieces; smash: *The girl crashed all her pots and jars.* **7.** *Informal.* To join or enter without being invited: *crash a party.* **—crash'ing** *adj.: a crashing sound.* *—n.* **1.** A loud noise, as of a sudden impact, collapse, etc.: *a crash of thunder.* **2.** A violent collision: *He was killed in a car crash.* **3.** A sudden, severe decline in business: *The Depression started with the crash of 1929.* *—**modifier:** no survivors among the crash victims.* *—adj.* Marked by an intense effort to produce or accomplish something: *a crash program to finish the building; a crash diet.*

crash dive. A rapid dive by a submarine, especially in an emergency.

crash helmet. A padded helmet, as one worn by a racing-car driver, to protect the head.

crash-land |**krăsh'lănd'**| *v.* To land and damage (an aircraft) under emergency conditions.

crass |krăs| *adj.* **crass•er, crass•est.** Stupid or unfeeling; coarse: *a crass person; crass ignorance.* **—crass'ly** *adv.* **—crass'ness** *n.*

-crat. A word element meaning "participant in or supporter of a type of government or class": **autocrat; bureaucrat.**

crate |krāt| *n.* A large packing case made of slats of wood. *—v.* **crat•ed, crat•ing.** To pack into a crate.

cra•ter |**krā'**tər| *n.* **1.** A bowl-shaped depression at the mouth of a volcano or geyser. **2.** A pit that resembles this, as one made by an explosion. **3.** Any of a large number of circular depressions surrounded by high, jagged ridges, found on the surface of the moon, possibly resulting from meteor impacts. [SEE PICTURE]

cra•vat |krə **văt'**| *n.* A necktie or a scarf worn as a tie.

crave |krāv| *v.* **craved, crav•ing.** To have a very strong desire for: *crave an ice-cream soda.*

cra•ven |**krā'**vən| *adj.* Very cowardly. **—cra'ven•ly** *adv.* **—cra'ven•ness** *n.*

crav•ing |**krā'**vĭng| *n.* A very strong desire; yearning: *a craving for peanuts.*

craw |krô| *n.* **1.** The crop of a bird's digestive system. **2.** The stomach, especially of an animal.

craw•fish |**krô'**fĭsh'| *n., pl.* **-fish** or **-fish•es.** A crayfish.

crawl |krôl| *v.* **1.** To move slowly on the hands and knees or by dragging oneself; creep: *The baby crawled across the room.* **2.** To move or advance slowly or with great effort: *crawl home in the heavy traffic.* **3. a.** To be covered with crawling things: *The sidewalk crawled with ants.* **b.** To shiver as if covered with crawling things: *His skin crawled in horror.* *—n.* **1.** A very slow pace: *They proceeded at a crawl.* **2.** A rapid swimming stroke performed face down and consisting of alternating overarm strokes and a flutter kick. —**crawl'er** *n.*

cray•fish |krā'fĭsh'| *n., pl.* **-fish** or **-fish•es.** A freshwater animal that resembles a lobster but is much smaller. [SEE NOTE]

cray•on |krā'ŏn'| *or* |-ən| *n.* A stick of colored wax used for drawing. —*v.* To draw, color, or decorate with crayons.

craze |krāz| *n.* Something very popular for a brief time; a fad: *This new toy should be the craze this year.* —*v.* **crazed, craz•ing.** To make insane or seemingly insane: *He was crazed by long exposure to extreme cold.*

cra•zy |krā'zē| *adj.* **cra•zi•er, cra•zi•est. 1.** Mentally ill; insane: *Was the murderer crazy?* **2.** *Informal.* Not sensible; impractical: *a crazy idea; a crazy hat. You're crazy to go swimming in this weather.* **3.** *Informal.* Full of enthusiasm: *I'm crazy about pet shows.* —**cra'zi•ly** *adv.* —**cra'zi•ness** *n.*

***Idiom.* like crazy.** *Informal.* Very much: *hurts like crazy.*

crazy quilt. A patchwork quilt made of oddly shaped pieces of cloth that are not arranged in an orderly pattern. [SEE PICTURE]

creak |krēk| *v.* **1.** To give off a grating or squeaking sound, as from friction, movement, etc.: *The rusty gate creaked when I swung it open.* **2.** To move with a squeaking sound: *The wagon creaked down the road.* —**creak'ing** *adj.: a creaking door.* —*n.* A grating or squeaking sound, as one produced by friction, movement, etc. ¶*These sound alike* **creak, creek.**

creak•y |krē'kē| *adj.* **creak•i•er, creak•i•est.** Giving off a creak or creaks: *a creaky door.* —**creak'•i•ly** *adv.* —**creak'i•ness** *n.*

cream |krēm| *n.* **1.** The yellow, fatty part of milk that tends to separate and rise to the surface when milk stands. **2.** The color of cream; a yellowish white. **3.** Any of various foods containing cream: *ice cream.* **4.** A cosmetic or other preparation that is soft and creamy: *a skin cream; shaving cream.* **5.** The best part: *the cream of the crop.* —**modifier:** *a cream pitcher.* —*v.* **1.** To beat (butter) until it is creamy. **2.** To prepare (vegetables, meat, etc.) in a creamy sauce. **3.** *Slang.* To defeat or beat overwhelmingly: *Our team creamed theirs.* —*adj.* Yellowish white.

cream cheese. A soft white cheese made of cream and milk.

cream•er |krē'mər| *n.* A small pitcher for cream.

cream•e•ry |krē'mə rē| *n., pl.* **cream•e•ries.** A place where dairy products are prepared or sold.

cream of tartar. Potassium bitartrate.

cream•y |krē'mē| *adj.* **cream•i•er, cream•i•est. 1.** Rich in cream. **2.** Resembling cream, as in richness, texture, or color. —**cream'i•ly** *adv.* —**cream'i•ness** *n.*

crease |krēs| *n.* **1.** A fold, wrinkle, or line, usually formed by pressure: *a pants crease.* **2.** A rectangular area marked off in front of the goal in hockey and lacrosse. —*v.* **creased, creas•ing.** To make or become creased, folded, or wrinkled: *crease a piece of paper. His face creased with age.*

cre•ate |krē āt'| *v.* **cre•at•ed, cre•at•ing. 1.** To bring into existence; originate: *create a musical composition.* **2.** To give rise to; produce: *The story created feelings of terror.*

cre•a•tion |krē ā'shən| *n.* **1.** The act or process of creating: *the creation of an empire; the creation of a canyon by erosion; the creation of a national bank.* **2.** Something produced by invention and imagination: *an artist's creation.* **3.** The universe, the world, and all created beings and things. **4. the Creation.** The story of the earth's origin as told in Genesis. **5.** *Informal.* Everywhere: *He wandered all over creation.*

cre•a•tive |krē ā'tĭv| *adj.* Having the ability or power to create things; original and expressive: *a creative writer; creative work.* —**cre•a'tive•ly** *adv.* —**cre•a'tive•ness** *n.*

cre•a•tiv•i•ty |krē'ā tĭv'ĭ tē| *n.* The quality of being creative; originality and inventiveness.

cre•a•tor |krē ā'tər| *n.* **1.** Someone who creates: *creators of sculpture.* **2. Creator.** God: *"endowed by their Creator with certain unalienable Rights"* (Declaration of Independence).

crea•ture |krē'chər| *n.* **1.** A living being, especially an animal. **2.** A human being; a person: *The chief's daughter was a lovely creature. The poor creature begged at the city gate.* **3.** Any being that appears strange, alien, or frightening: *a book about creatures from another galaxy.*

crèche |krĕsh| *n.* A representation of the Nativity, usually consisting of figures of the infant Jesus, Mary, Joseph, shepherds, the Magi, and animals such as sheep and camels.

cre•dence |krēd'ns| *n.* Acceptance as true; belief.

cre•den•tial |krĭ dĕn'shəl| *n.* **1.** Something that entitles a person to confidence, credit, or authority. **2.** Often **credentials.** A letter or other written evidence of a person's qualifications or status.

cred•i•bil•i•ty |krĕd'ə bĭl'ĭ tē| *n.* The condition or quality of being credible.

cred•i•ble |krĕd'ə bəl| *adj.* **1.** Believable; plausible: *a credible news report.* **2.** Worthy of confidence; reliable: *a credible witness.* —**cred'i•bly** *adv.*

cred•it |krĕd'ĭt| *n.* **1.** Belief or confidence; trust: *I placed full credit in the truthfulness of the state records.* **2.** Reputation or standing: *It is to his credit that he worked without complaining.* **3.** A source of honor or distinction: *a credit to his team.* **4.** Approval, honor, or acclaim for some act or quality; praise: *They shared the credit for the book's success.* **5.** Certification that a student has fulfilled a requirement by completing a course of study. **6.** An acknowledgment of work done, as in the production of a book, motion picture, or play. **7.** A reputation for repaying debts and being financially honest: *He has good credit at all stores.* **8. a.** A system of buying goods or services by charging the amount, with payment due at a later time: *buy on credit.* **b.** Confidence in a buyer's ability and intention to pay at some future time: *The store extended credit to him.* **c.** The period of time allowed before a debt must be paid. **9.** The amount of money in the account of a person or group, as at a bank. **10.** In accounting: **a.** The amount paid on a debt. **b.** The right-hand side of an account, on which such payments are

crayfish

A **crayfish** *is not in fact a fish, and the word "fish" does not properly belong in its name. It was originally* crevis, *but was changed to* **crayfish** *by folk etymology.* Crevis *was borrowed from Old French* crevise, *which in turn came from a Germanic word,* krabitja, *related to* **crab**[1].

crazy quilt

creek

Noah Webster, in his American Dictionary *of 1828, gives the British sense of* **creek** *first and says that the meaning "small river" is only used "in some of the American states." He adds: "This sense is not justified by etymology [since the word originally meant "notch or crack"], but as streams often enter into creeks and small bays . . . the name has been extended to small streams in general." The transition is now complete; the old sense is never used in America, and the American sense is never used in England.*

crescent

ă pat/ā pay/â care/ä father/ĕ pet/ ē be/ĭ pit/ī pie/î fierce/ŏ pot/ ō go/ô paw, for/oi oil/o͝o book/ o͞o boot/ou out/ŭ cut/û fur/ *th* the/th thin/hw which/zh vision/ ə ago, item, pencil, atom, circus

entered. —*modifier:* *a credit risk; a credit rating.* —*v.* **1.** To believe; trust: *He credited her explanation for the delay.* **2.** To give honor to (a person) for something: *They credit him with founding modern biology.* **3.** To attribute (something) to a person: *Some credit the song to Haydn.* **4.** To give academic credits to (a student). **5.** In accounting: **a.** To give credit for (a payment). **b.** To give credit to (a payer).

cred•it•a•ble |**krĕd'**ĭ tə bəl| *adj.* Deserving commendation: *a creditable attempt to solve the problem.* —**cred'it•a•bil'i•ty** *n.* —**cred'it•a•bly** *adv.*

credit card. A card issued by a business concern authorizing the holder to buy on credit.

cred•i•tor |**krĕd'**ĭ tər| *n.* A person or firm to whom money is owed.

cre•do |**krē'**dō| *or* |**krā'**-| *n., pl.* **cre•dos. 1.** A statement of belief; a creed: *The senator's credo of male superiority has become a myth in Italy's social history.* **2.** Often **Credo.** The Apostles' Creed or the Nicene Creed.

cre•du•li•ty |krĭ **do͞o'**lĭ tē| *or* |**-dyo͞o'**-| *n.* The tendency to believe too readily; gullibility.

cred•u•lous |**krĕj'**ə ləs| *adj.* Tending to believe too readily; gullible.

Cree |krē| *n., pl.* **Cree** or **Crees. 1.** A North American Indian tribe formerly living in Ontario, Manitoba, and Saskatchewan. **2.** A member of this tribe. **3.** The Algonquian language of this tribe.

creed |krēd| *n.* **1.** A formal statement of religious belief. **2.** Any statement or system of belief or principles that guides a person's actions.

creek |krēk| *or* |krĭk| *n.* **1.** A small stream, often a shallow tributary to a river. **2.** *British.* A small inlet in a shoreline. ¶*These sound alike* **creek, creak.** [SEE NOTE]

Idiom. **up the** (or **a**) **creek.** *Informal.* In a difficult position or situation.

Creek |krēk| *n., pl.* **Creek** or **Creeks. 1.** A confederation of North American Indian tribes formerly living in Georgia, Alabama, and northern Florida. **2.** A member of any of these tribes. **3.** Their Muskhogean language.

creel |krēl| *n.* A wicker basket used for carrying fish.

creep |krēp| *v.* **crept** |krĕpt|, **creep•ing. 1.** To move slowly or cautiously with the body close to the ground: *A cat crept cautiously toward a mouse.* **2.** To advance or spread slowly: *A reddish glow crept into his cheeks.* **3.** To have a tingling sensation, as if covered with crawling things: *His flesh crept in horror.* **4.** To grow along the ground or by clinging to a surface, as some vines do. —*n.* **1.** *Slang.* An undesirable person. **2. the creeps.** *Informal.* A sensation of fear and repugnance, as if things were crawling on one's skin: *This place gives me the creeps.*

creep•er |**krē'**pər| *n.* **1.** Someone or something that creeps. **2.** A plant with stems that grow along the ground or cling to a surface for support. **3. creepers.** A one-piece suit for a baby.

creep•y |**krē'**pē| *adj.* **creep•i•er, creep•i•est.** Producing or having a tingling sensation, as if things were creeping on one's skin: *a creepy dark night. The deserted house made her feel creepy.*

cre•mate |**krē'**māt'| *or* |krĭ **māt'**| *v.* **cre•mat•ed, cre•mat•ing.** To burn (a corpse) to ashes. —**cre•ma'tion** *n.*

cre•ma•to•ri•um |krē'mə **tôr'**ē əm| *or* |**-tōr'**-| *n., pl.* **cre•ma•to•ri•ums** or **cre•ma•to•ri•a** |krē'mə **tôr'**ē ə| *or* |**-tōr'**-|. A crematory.

cre•ma•to•ry |**krē'**mə tôr'ē| *or* |-tōr'ē| *n., pl.* **cre•ma•to•ries. 1.** A furnace for burning the bodies of the dead. **2.** A building in which such a furnace is housed.

Cre•ole |**krē'**ōl'| *n.* **1.** Any person of European descent born in the West Indies or Spanish America. **2.** Any person of mixed European and Negro ancestry. **3.** A descendant of the original French settlers of the southern United States, especially of Louisiana. **4.** The regional dialect of French spoken by these people of Louisiana. **5.** Any language formed when two or more groups of people speaking different languages have prolonged contact with one another: *Haitian Creole is a mixture of French and the native tongue of Haiti.* —*adj.* **1.** Of the Creoles or their languages and cultures. **2. creole.** Cooked with a sauce containing tomatoes, green peppers, and onions.

cre•o•sol |**krē'**ə sōl'| *or* |-sôl'| *n.* An aromatic liquid compound of carbon, hydrogen, and oxygen in the proportions $C_8H_{10}O_2$, obtained from tar from the wood of beech trees and used in making creosote.

cre•o•sote |**krē'**ə sōt'| *n.* A yellow to brown oily liquid obtained from coal tar and wood tar, used mainly as a wood preservative and disinfectant. —*v.* **cre•o•sot•ed, cre•o•sot•ing.** To treat with creosote.

crepe or **crêpe** |krāp| *n.* **1.** A light, soft, thin cloth with a crinkled surface, made of silk, cotton, wool, or rayon. **2.** A piece or band of black crepe, worn or hung as a sign of mourning. **3. Crepe rubber.** —*modifier:* *a crepe dress.*

crepe paper. Paper like crepe with crinkles or puckers in it, made in various colors.

crepe rubber. Rubber with a crinkled texture, used for shoe soles.

crept |krĕpt|. Past tense and past participle of **creep.**

cres•cen•do |krə **shĕn'**dō| *or* |**-sĕn'**-|. In music: *n., pl.* **cres•cen•dos. 1.** A gradual increase in loudness. **2.** A musical passage performed in a crescendo. —*adj.* Gradually increasing in loudness. —*adv.* With a crescendo.

cres•cent |**krĕs'**ənt| *n.* **1.** The figure of the moon as it appears in its first quarter, with concave and convex edges ending in points. **2.** Anything shaped like this. —*adj.* **1.** Shaped like a crescent. **2.** Increasing; waxing: *the crescent phase of the moon.* [SEE PICTURE]

cre•sol |**krē'**sōl'| *or* |-sôl'| *n.* Any one of three compounds of carbon, hydrogen, and oxygen that are related to phenol and have the formula C_7H_8O. They are used in resins and as disinfectants.

cress |krĕs| *n.* Any of several plants, such as watercress, with sharp-tasting leaves used in salads.

cres•set |**krĕs'**ĭt| *n.* A torch consisting of a metal cup containing burning oil or pitch and mounted on the top of a pole or building.

crest |krĕst| *n.* **1.** A projecting tuft or outgrowth on the head, especially a tuft of feathers on a bird's head. **2.** A plume of feathers or a fanlike ornament worn on top of a warrior's helmet. **3.** The top of something, such as a mountain or wave. **4.** A design placed above the shield on a coat of arms and also used by itself on silverware, stationery, etc. —*v.* **1.** To reach the top of: *The climbers crested the mountain on the third day.* **2.** To form into or rise to a crest.

crest•ed |krĕs′tĭd| *adj.* Having a crest or a certain kind of crest: *the crested head of the blue jay; a white-crested wave.*

crest•fall•en |krĕst′fô′lən| *adj.* Dejected; depressed. —**crest′fall′en•ly** *adv.*

Cre•ta•ceous |krĭ tā′shəs| *n.* Also **Cretaceous period.** A geologic period that began 135 million years ago and ended 63 million years ago, characterized by the development of flowering plants and the disappearance of dinosaurs. —***modifier:*** *a Cretaceous rock.* —*adj.* **cretaceous.** Of, like, or containing chalk.

Crete |krēt|. A Greek island in the Mediterranean Sea. Population, 500,000. —**Cre′tan** *adj. & n.*

cre•tin |krē′tĭn| *or* |krēt′n| *n.* A person afflicted with cretinism.

cre•tin•ism |krē′tĭ nĭz′əm| *or* |krēt′n ĭz′əm| *n.* A stoppage of mental and physical development in early childhood, resulting from a lack of thyroid hormone.

cre•tonne |krĭ tŏn′| *or* |krē′tŏn′| *n.* A heavy cotton, linen, or rayon cloth with colorful printed patterns, used for curtains and for chair or sofa covers. —***modifier:*** *cretonne curtains.*

cre•vasse |krə văs′| *n.* **1.** A deep crack, as in a glacier; a chasm. **2.** A crack in a dike or levee.

crev•ice |krĕv′ĭs| *n.* A narrow crack or opening; a fissure; cleft.

crew[1] |kro͞o| *n.* **1. a.** The persons manning a ship, aircraft, etc. **b.** All the persons manning a ship or aircraft except the officers. **2.** A team of oarsmen. **3.** Any group of people who work together: *the stage crew for the new play.*

crew[2] |kro͞o|. A past tense of **crow.**

crew cut. A man's close-cropped haircut.

crew•el |kro͞o′əl| *n.* A loosely twisted worsted yarn used for a kind of embroidery called **crewel work** or **crewel embroidery,** done in a variety of stitches and colorful designs.

crew•man |kro͞o′mən| *n., pl.* **-men** |-mən|. A member of a crew.

crib |krĭb| *n.* **1.** A small bed for a baby, with high sides. **2.** A small building for storing grain. **3.** A rack or trough from which cattle or horses eat. **4.** *Informal.* A list of answers or information consulted dishonestly during an examination. —*v.* **cribbed, crib•bing.** *Informal.* **1.** To use a crib in examinations; cheat. **2.** To copy dishonestly; plagiarize.

crib•bage |krĭb′ĭj| *n.* A card game in which the score is kept by inserting small pegs into holes arranged in rows on a small board.

crick[1] |krĭk| *n.* A painful cramp or muscular spasm, especially in the back or the neck. —*v.* To cause a crick in, as by turning or wrenching. [SEE NOTE]

crick[2] |krĭk| *v.* To make a sharp, crackling sound: *The frying bacon cricked and rustled in the pan.* [SEE NOTE]

crick•et[1] |krĭk′ĭt| *n.* A leaping insect. The male produces a chirping sound by rubbing the front wings together. [SEE NOTE & PICTURE]

crick•et[2] |krĭk′ĭt| *n.* **1.** An outdoor game, popular in Great Britain, played with bats, a ball, and wickets by two teams of 11 players each. **2.** Fair play. [SEE NOTE]

cri•er |krī′ər| *n.* **1.** A person who cries. **2.** A person who shouts out public announcements: *a town crier.*

crime |krīm| *n.* **1.** A serious violation of the law. A person may commit a crime either by acting in a way the law forbids or by failing to act as the law requires. **2.** Unlawful activity in general. **3.** *Informal.* A shame; a pity: *It's a crime to waste this glass of milk.* —***modifier:*** *crime prevention; crime literature.*

Cri•me•a |krī mē′ə|. A peninsula of the Soviet Union, extending into the Black Sea. —**Cri•me′an** *adj.*

crim•i•nal |krĭm′ə nəl| *n.* A person who has committed or been convicted of a crime. —*adj.* **1.** Having the nature of crime: *criminal acts.* **2.** Guilty of crime. —**crim′i•nal•ly** *adv.*

criminal law. Law involving crime and its punishment.

crim•i•nol•o•gist |krĭm′ə nŏl′ə jĭst| *n.* A person who specializes in criminology.

crim•i•nol•o•gy |krĭm′ə nŏl′ə jē| *n.* The scientific study of crime, criminals, and criminal behavior.

crimp |krĭmp| *v.* **1.** To press or bend into small, regular folds or ridges; corrugate. **2.** To form (hair) into tight curls or waves. —*n.* Something produced by crimping, as a curl or fold.

crimp•y |krĭm′pē| *adj.* **crimp•i•er, crimp•i•est. 1.** Having crimps; wavy. **2.** Unpleasantly cold and damp: *the crimpy air of late fall.*

crim•son |krĭm′zən| *or* |-sən| *n.* A vivid purplish red. —*adj.* Vivid purplish red. —*v.* To make or become crimson: *The fire crimsoned the sky. The sky crimsoned and then paled.*

cringe |krĭnj| *v.* **cringed, cring•ing. 1.** To shrink back, as in fear; cower: *He cringed whenever the bully came near him.* **2.** To be filled with disgust: *Dutchmen cringe at the popular image of the Low Countries as quaintly photogenic lands.*

crin•kle |krĭng′kəl| *v.* **crin•kled, crin•kling. 1.** To make or become wrinkled or creased: *crinkle paper. His eyes crinkled merrily at the corners.* **2.** To make a soft, crackling sound; rustle. —*n.* A wrinkle or crease: *He had crinkles of good humor around his eyes.*

cri•noid |krī′noid′| *n.* Any of several sea animals belonging to the same group as the starfishes and sea urchins, having featherlike or petallike arms radiating from a stalk by which they are attached to a surface.

crin•o•line |krĭn′ə lĭn| *n.* **1.** A stiff cloth used for linings, hats, and puffed-out petticoats. **2.** A stiff petticoat of this cloth, worn to make a skirt stand out. **3.** A **hoop skirt.**

crip•ple |krĭp′əl| *n.* A person with a bodily defect that hinders normal functioning or movement. —*v.* **crip•pled, crip•pling. 1.** To make into a cripple: *Polio crippled many children.* **2.** To disable; damage: *The storm crippled the ship.* —**crip′pled** *adj.: a crippled old man.*

cri•sis |krī′sĭs| *n., pl.* **cri•ses** |krī′sēz′|. **1.** An unstable condition in political, international, or economic affairs; a time of danger: *the crisis in the Middle East.* **2.** A decisive, crucial point or

crick[1-2]

Crick[1] *first appeared in the fifteenth century; its origin is unknown.* **Crick**[2] *is probably from French* criquer, *which is an onomatopoeic word formed in Old French, representing various sharp sounds. It is also the source of* **cricket**[1] *and (possibly) of* **cricket**[2].

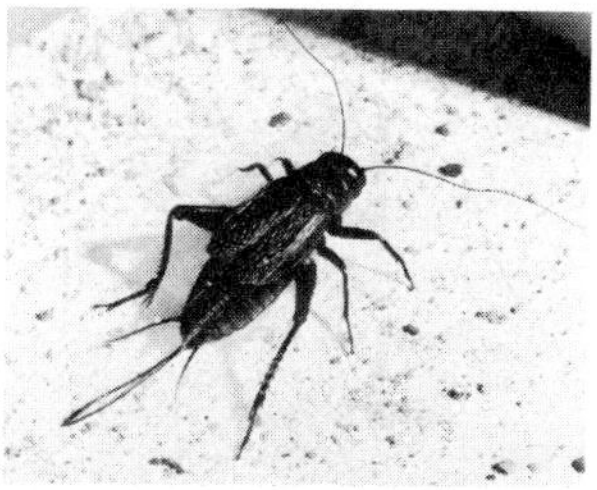

cricket[1]

Cricket[1] *is from Old French* criquet, *"grasshopper, cricket," from* criquer, *"to chirp, crackle, make a sharp sound." The game of* **cricket**[2] *goes back to the sixteenth century at least. The word may possibly be from a similar but separate Old French word* criquet; *this meant "a kind of bat used in a ball game," and is also from* criquer, *referring to the sound of the bat hitting the ball. See also note at* **crick.**

critter
The word **critter** *was originally used in farming or ranch areas of the United States for a horse or other animal kept as livestock, but is now used informally and somewhat humorously for any animal.*

crochet

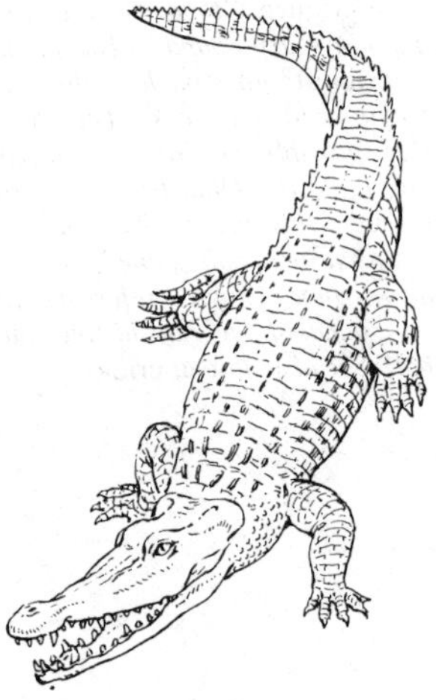

crocodile

ă **pat**/ā **pay**/â **care**/ä **father**/ĕ **pet**/ ē **be**/ĭ **pit**/ī **pie**/î **fierce**/ŏ **pot**/ ō **go**/ô **paw**, **for**/oi **oil**/o͝o **book**/ o͞o **boot**/ou **out**/ŭ **cut**/û **fur**/ *th* **the**/th **thin**/hw **which**/zh **vision**/ ə **ago**, **item**, **pencil**, **atom**, **circus**

situation in the course of anything; a turning point: *an environmental crisis.* **3.** A sudden change, for better or worse, in the course of a serious illness.

crisp |krĭsp| *adj.* **crisp•er, crisp•est.** **1.** Having a pleasing dryness or crustiness from cooking: *crisp fried chicken.* **2.** Fresh and firm; not wilted: *crisp lettuce.* **3.** Freshly processed; not wrinkled: *a crisp shirt; a crisp dollar bill.* **4.** Refreshingly cold, dry, and bracing: *crisp autumn air.* **5.** Sharp, clear, and concise: *crisp sentences.* —*v.* To make or become crisp, as by heating or cooking. —**crisp'ly** *adv.* —**crisp'ness** *n.*
Idiom. **burned to a crisp.** Badly or completely burned.

crisp•er |**krĭs**'pər| *n.* A compartment in a refrigerator used for storing vegetables to keep them fresh.

crisp•y |**krĭs**'pē| *adj.* **crisp•i•er, crisp•i•est.** Crisp. —**crisp'i•ness** *n.*

criss•cross |**krĭs**'krôs'| *or* |-krŏs'| *v.* **1.** To mark with or form a pattern of crossing lines: *Animal trails crisscross the woods. Trails crisscross through the underbrush.* **2.** To move crosswise over or through: *Ships crisscrossed the sea.* —**criss'crossed'** *adj.*: *crisscrossed cables; crisscrossed threads.* —*n.* A mark or pattern made of crossing lines. —*adj.* Crossing one another: *crisscross lines.* —*adv.* In crossing directions: *Her stockings were lying crisscross across the chair.*

cri•te•ri•on |krī **tîr**'ē ən| *n., pl.* **cri•te•ri•a** |krī-**tîr**'ē ə| or **cri•te•ri•ons.** A rule or standard on which a judgment can be based: *What are your criteria for judging the quality of his work?*

crit•ic |**krĭt**'ĭk| *n.* **1.** A person who forms and expresses judgments of the good and bad qualities of anything. **2.** A person whose job is judging and reporting on the worth of something intended as an artistic work or on its performance: *a book critic; a music critic.* **3.** A person who finds fault.

crit•i•cal |**krĭt**'ĭ kəl| *adj.* **1.** Of a critic or critics: *critical writings on art.* **2.** Inclined to judge severely; likely to find fault. **3.** Marked by or exercising careful evaluation and judgment: *critical reading; a critical thinker.* **4.** Crucial or decisive: *the critical moment; a critical need for land.* **5. a.** Of or involving the crisis stage of a disease. **b.** Extremely serious or dangerous: *a critical injury; in critical condition.* **6.** Necessary; essential: *Determination is a critical element in such a venture.* —**crit'i•cal•ly** *adv.*

critical angle. The smallest angle of incidence at which a ray of light can strike the boundary between two media and be totally reflected.

critical mass. The smallest mass of fissionable material, such as plutonium 239 or uranium 235, that will sustain a nuclear chain reaction.

critical point. The conditions of temperature and pressure in which the liquid and gaseous forms of a pure, stable substance have the same density.

critical pressure. The smallest amount of pressure that can liquefy a gas that is at its critical temperature.

critical temperature. The temperature above which a gas cannot be liquefied, regardless of the pressure applied.

crit•i•cism |**krĭt**'ĭ sĭz'əm| *n.* **1.** The act of forming and expressing judgments about the worth of something. **2.** Unfavorable judgment; censure; disapproval. **3.** The art or practice of passing judgment on something intended as an artistic work, as writing or sculpture. **4.** A review or report giving an opinion or opinions of the worth of something.

crit•i•cize |**krĭt**'ĭ sīz'| *v.* **crit•i•cized, crit•i•ciz•ing.** **1.** To judge the merits and faults of; evaluate: *The painter stepped back to note the effect, added a touch of color, and criticized the effect again.* **2.** To judge severely; find fault with: *newspapers criticizing the mayor.* **3.** To express or utter criticism: *He seldom criticizes or praises.*

cri•tique |krĭ **tēk**'| *n.* A critical review or commentary, such as an evaluation of an artistic work.

crit•ter |**krĭt**'ər| *n. Informal.* A creature, especially an animal. [SEE NOTE]

croak |krōk| *n.* A low, hoarse sound, such as that made by a frog or crow. —*v.* **1.** To make such a sound: *Bullfrogs croaked in the pond.* **2.** To speak with a low, hoarse voice: *"I've a terrible cold," he croaked.*

Croat |krōt| *or* |**krō**'ăt'| *n.* A native or inhabitant of Croatia.

Cro•a•tia |krō' **ā**'shə|. A republic of Yugoslavia.

Cro•a•tian |krō **ā**'shən| *adj.* Of Croatia, the Croats, or their language. —*n.* **1.** A Croat. **2.** The language of the Croats; Serbo-Croatian.

croc |krŏk| *n. Informal.* A crocodile.

cro•chet |krō **shā**'| *v.* **cro•cheted** |krō **shād**'|, **cro•chet•ing** |krō **shā**'ĭng|. To make (a piece of needlework) by looping thread or yarn into connected links with a hooked needle called a **crochet hook:** *She crocheted a sweater. Can you crochet?* —*n.* This type of needlework: *She is expert at crochet.* [SEE PICTURE]

cro•ci |**krō**'sī'| *n.* A plural of **crocus.**

crock |krŏk| *n.* An earthenware vessel.

crock•er•y |**krŏk**'ə rē| *n.* Pots, plates, jars, etc., made of earthenware.

Crock•ett |**krŏk**'ĭt|, **David ("Davy").** 1786–1836. American frontiersman, later a member of the U.S. House of Representatives. He died at the Alamo.

croc•o•dile |**krŏk**'ə dīl'| *n.* **1.** A large tropical water reptile with thick, armorlike skin, sharp teeth, and long, narrow jaws. **2.** Leather made from the hide of a crocodile. —***modifier:*** *a crocodile belt.* [SEE PICTURE]

crocodile tears. An insincere display of grief.

croc•o•dil•i•an |krŏk'ə **dĭl**'ē ən| *or* |-**dĭl**'yən| *n.* A crocodile or related reptile, such as an alligator or caiman. —*adj.* Of or related to crocodiles.

cro•cus |**krō**'kəs| *n., pl.* **cro•cus•es** or **cro•ci** |**krō**'sī'|. **1.** A low-growing garden plant with purple, yellow, or white flowers that bloom early in spring. **2.** A red variety of iron oxide, Fe_2O_3, used for rubbing and polishing.

Croe•sus |**krē**'səs|. Died 546 B.C. A king of fabled wealth in Asia Minor.

croft |krôft| *or* |krŏft| *n. British & Scottish.* **1.** A small enclosed field or pasture near a house. **2.** A small tenant farm.

croft•er |**krôf**'tər| *or* |**krŏf**'-| *n. British & Scottish.* A person who rents and cultivates a croft.

crois•sant |krwä säɴ′| *n.* A rich, buttery crescent-shaped roll.

Cro-Mag•non man |krō măg′nən| *or* |-măn′yən|. An early form of modern man known from skeletal remains found in southern France.

crom•lech |krŏm′lĕk′| *n.* A dolmen.

Crom•well |krŏm′wĕl′| *or* |-wəl| *or* |krŭm′-|, **Oliver.** 1599–1658. English statesman and general, ruler of England (1653–58).

crone |krōn| *n.* A witchlike old woman.

cro•ny |krō′nē| *n., pl.* **cro•nies.** A friend or companion: *He enjoyed chatting with his old cronies.* [SEE NOTE]

crook |kro͝ok| *n.* **1.** Something bent or curved: *holding a bag of groceries in the crook of her arm.* **2.** An implement or tool with a bent or curved part: *a shepherd's crook.* **3.** *Informal.* A person who makes his living dishonestly; a thief. —*v.* To bend or curve: *He crooked his arm around the package. The road crooks to the right.*

Idiom. **by hook or by crook.** By any means possible: *We'll get there in time for the banquet by hook or by crook.*

crook•ed |kro͝ok′ĭd| *adj.* **1. a.** Having an irregular shape: *crooked fingers.* **b.** Following an irregular course: *a crooked street.* **c.** At an irregular angle: *a crooked picture on the wall.* **2.** *Informal.* Dishonest: *a crooked merchant.* —**crook′ed•ly** *adv.* —**crook′ed•ness** *n.*

croon |kro͞on| *v.* **1. a.** To sing or hum softly: *She crooned as she knitted.* **b.** To produce an effect on (someone) by so doing: *a mother crooning her baby to sleep.* **2.** To sing (popular songs) in a sentimental manner: *croon a hit song. He crooned into a closely held microphone.* **3.** To say tenderly: *the man and woman crooning words of love to each other.* —*n.* A soft singing, humming, or murmuring.

croon•er |kro͞o′nər| *n.* A person who croons, especially a singer of popular songs who uses a soft, sentimental style of singing.

crop |krŏp| *n.* **1. a.** Cultivated plants or plant products such as grain, fruit, and vegetables: *Wheat is a widely grown crop.* **b.** The amount of such a product grown or gathered in a single season or place: *a corn crop.* **2.** A group or quantity appearing at one time: *a crop of new ideas.* **3.** A short whip used in horseback riding, with a loop serving as a lash. **4. a.** A pouchlike part below the esophagus in the digestive tract of a bird, where food is stored and partially digested. **b.** A similar part in the digestive tract of an insect, earthworm, etc. —*v.* **cropped, crop•ping. 1.** To cut or bite off the stems or top of (a plant): *Horses cropped the grass.* **2.** To cut (hair) short. **3.** To appear: *When did that word first crop up in English writings?*

crop•land |krŏp′lănd′| *n.* Land for or suitable for growing crops.

crop•per[1] |krŏp′ər| *n.* A sharecropper.

crop•per[2] |krŏp′ər| *n.* **1.** A heavy fall. **2.** A disastrous failure.

Idiom. **come a cropper. 1.** To fall heavily; tumble. **2.** To fail suddenly or disastrously.

cro•quet |krō kā′| *n.* A lawn game in which each player uses a mallet to hit a wooden ball through a course of wickets. —***modifier:*** *a croquet mallet.* —*v.* **cro•queted** |krō kād′|, **cro•quet•ing** |krō-kā′ĭng|. To drive away (an opponent's ball) by hitting it with another ball.

cro•quette |krō kĕt′| *n.* A small cake of minced food, often coated with bread crumbs and fried in deep fat: *salmon croquettes.*

cro•sier |krō′zhər| *n.* A staff with a crook or cross at the end, carried by or before an abbot, bishop, or archbishop as a symbol of office. [SEE PICTURE]

cross |krôs| *or* |krŏs| *n.* **1.** An upright post with a horizontal piece near the top, used in former times as an instrument of execution for certain types of criminals. **2.** Any trial or affliction: *Everyone has his own cross to bear.* **3. a. the Cross.** The cross upon which Christ was crucified. **b.** A symbolic representation of this cross. **4.** A crucifix. **5.** Any of various medals or emblems in this shape. **6. a.** Any mark or pattern formed by the intersection of two lines. **b.** Such a mark (X) used as a signature by a person who cannot read or write. **7. a.** The process of crossbreeding. **b.** An animal or plant produced by crossbreeding; a hybrid. **8.** A combination of two different things. —*v.* **1.** To go or extend across: *The boy crossed the road. The bridge crosses the river.* **2.** To intersect: *at the corner where Elm crosses Main Street.* **3.** To place crosswise: *cross one's legs.* **4.** *Informal.* To thwart or contradict: *She doesn't like to be crossed.* **5.** To crossbreed. **6.** To draw a line across: *Cross your T's.* **7.** To make the sign of the cross on (oneself): *She crossed herself and entered the chapel.* **8.** To delete or eliminate by or as if by drawing a line through: *cross out lines of a poem; cross the names off the dean's list.* **9.** To meet and pass: *We crossed each other on the way to the market. Our letters crossed in the mail.* —*adj.* **1.** Lying crosswise: *a cross street.* **2.** Showing ill humor; irritable or annoyed.

cross•bar |krôs′bär′| *or* |krŏs′-| *n.* A horizontal bar, line, or stripe.

cross•beam |krôs′bēm′| *or* |krŏs′-| *n.* A horizontal beam or girder.

cross•bones |krôs′bōnz′| *or* |krŏs′-| *n.* A representation of two bones placed crosswise, usually under a skull, used as a symbol of death or a warning of danger.

cross•bow |krôs′bō′| *or* |krŏs′-| *n.* A medieval weapon consisting of a bow fixed across a wooden stock, with grooves on the stock to direct the projectile. [SEE PICTURE]

cross•breed |krôs′brēd′| *or* |krŏs′-| *v.* **cross•bred** |krôs′brĕd′| *or* |krŏs′-|, **cross•breed•ing. 1.** To produce (a hybrid animal or plant) by mating individuals of different breeds or varieties. **2.** To mate so as to produce hybrid offspring. —*n.* An animal or plant produced by crossbreeding; a hybrid.

cross-coun•try |krôs′kŭn′trē| *or* |krŏs′-| *adj.* **1.** Cutting across open countryside: *a cross-country race.* **2.** From one side of a country to the other: *a cross-country trip.* —*adv.: ride cross-country; travel cross-country.*

cross•cut saw |krôs′kŭt′| *or* |krŏs′-|. **1.** A hand saw for cutting wood across the grain. **2.** A large saw designed for two men.

cross-ex•am•ine |krôs′ĭg zăm′ĭn| *or* |krŏs′-| *v.* **cross-ex•am•ined, cross-ex•am•in•ing. 1.** To question in court (a witness already examined by the opposing side). **2.** To question (someone) very closely, especially in order to check the answers

crony

Oxford and Cambridge, the two oldest English universities, have always had rich vocabularies of slang, some of which has made its way into general English. In the late seventeenth century at Cambridge, the student slang word for "friend" was chrony, *later* **crony**. *This is supposed to be from Greek* khronios, *"lasting a long time," here used to mean "of the same time, a contemporary or classmate." Compare note at* **chum**.

crosier
Thirteenth-century German

crossbow
The bow is so powerful that it must be cranked into firing position with a winding gear.

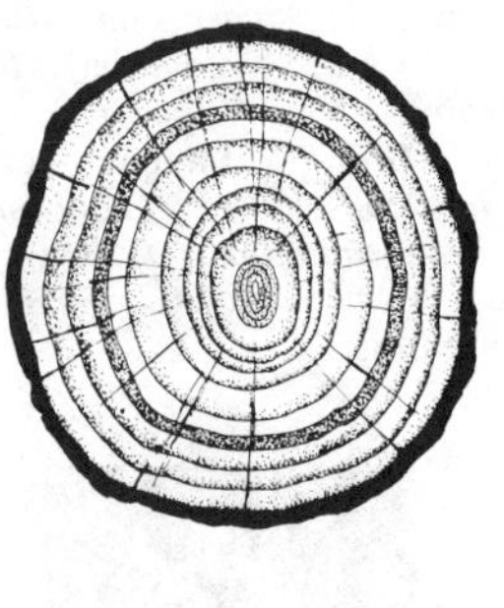

cross section
Cross section of a tree trunk

against other answers given before. **—cross-ex•am'i•na'tion** *n.* **—cross'-ex•am'in•er** *n.*

cross-eye |krôs'ī'| *or* |krŏs'ī'| *n.* A condition in which one or both of the eyes turn inward toward the nose. **—cross'-eyed'** *adj.*

cross-fer•ti•li•za•tion |krôs'fûr'tl ĭ zā'shən| *or* |krŏs'-| *n.* Fertilization in which the sex cells that unite are from different individuals, often of different varieties or species.

cross-fer•ti•lize |krôs'fûr'tl īz'| *or* |krŏs'-| *v.* **cross-fer•ti•lized, cross-fer•ti•liz•ing.** To fertilize or be fertilized by means of cross-fertilization.

cross•fire |krôs'fīr'| *or* |krŏs'-| *n.* In armed conflict, lines of fire from two or more positions, crossing each other and directed at a single target.

cross-grained |krôs'grānd'| *or* |krŏs'-| *adj.* Having an irregular, transverse, or diagonal grain: *a piece of cross-grained wood.*

cross-hatch |krôs'hăch'| *or* |krŏs'-| *v.* To shade (part of a drawing) with two or more sets of intersecting parallel lines.

cross•ing |krô'sĭng| *or* |krŏs'ĭng| *n.* **1.** A place at which a street, railroad, river, etc., may be crossed. **2.** The place where two or more things cross; an intersection. **3.** A voyage across an ocean: *The liner had made hundreds of crossings from America to Europe.*

cross-leg•ged |krôs'lĕg'ĭd| *or* |krŏs'-| *adj.* With ankles crossed and knees spread wide, as when sitting on the ground: *a cross-legged position.* —*adv.*: *sitting cross-legged.*

cross•o•ver |krôs'ō'vər| *or* |krŏs'-| *n.* A short stretch of connecting railroad track by which trains can be switched from one line to another.

cross•piece |krôs'pēs'| *or* |krŏs'-| *n.* A horizontal bar, beam, etc., used as a crossbar or crossbeam.

cross-pol•li•nate |krôs'pŏl'ə nāt'| *or* |krŏs'-| *v.* **cross-pol•li•nat•ed, cross-pol•li•nat•ing.** To fertilize (a plant or flower) with pollen from another. **—cross'-pol'li•na'tion** *n.*

cross product. A set of ordered pairs formed from two sets by matching each member of one set with each member of the other set; Cartesian product. Suppose that $A = \{a, b, c\}$, and $B = \{i, j, k\}$, then $A \times B = (a, i), (a, j), (a, k), (b, i), (b, j), (b, k), (c, i), (c, j), (c, k)$.

cross-ref•er•ence |krôs'rĕf'ər əns| *or* |krŏs'-| *n.* A note directing the reader from one part of a book, catalogue, etc., to another part containing related information.

cross•road |krôs'rōd'| *or* |krŏs'-| *n.* **1.** A road that crosses another road. **2. crossroads. a.** A place, usually in the countryside, where two or more roads meet. **b.** *(used with a singular verb).* A crucial point or place.

cross section. 1. a. A cut in a three-dimensional object formed as though a plane had passed through it, usually at right angles to one of its axes. **b.** A piece cut in this way or a picture or drawing of such a piece. **2.** A representative sample of something meant to be typical of the whole: *Dickens's novels present a cross section of life.* [SEE PICTURE]

cross-stitch |krôs'stĭch'| *or* |krŏs'-| *n.* A stitch shaped like an X, used in sewing and embroidery.

cross•walk |krôs'wôk'| *or* |krŏs'-| *n.* A path marked off for pedestrians crossing a street.

cross•way |krôs'wā'| *or* |krŏs'-| *n.* A crossroad.

cross•ways |krôs'wāz'| *or* |krŏs'-| *adv.* Crosswise.

cross•wise |krôs'wīz'| *or* |krŏs'-| *adv.* **1.** So as to cross something: *a wind blowing crosswise.* **2.** One crossing another: *logs laid crosswise on the fire.* —*adj.* Crossing: *a crosswise direction.*

cross•word puzzle |krôs'wûrd'| *or* |krŏs'-|. A printed square divided into small boxes, many of them numbered, and a list of numbered clues. A numbered box is the first letter of a word suggested by the clue. Words cross through each other as the boxes are filled in.

crotch |krŏch| *n.* **1.** A point where a branch separates from a tree; a fork: *the crotch of a tree.* **2. a.** The angle, or region of the angle, formed by the branching out of the legs from the trunk. **b.** The region of a garment where the leg seams meet.

crotch•et |krŏch'ĭt| *n.* **1.** An odd notion; whim; peculiarity: *an old man full of crotchets.* **2.** A small hook or hooked instrument.

crotch•et•y |krŏch'ĭ tē| *adj.* Given to whims; stubborn and eccentric: *a crotchety old man.* **—crotch'et•i•ness** *n.*

crouch |krouch| *v.* To lower the body by bending or squatting: *The tall man crouched to get into the small car.* —*n.* The act or posture of crouching: *skiing in a crouch.*

croup |kro͞op| *n.* A diseased condition that affects the larynx in children, producing difficult and noisy breathing and a hoarse cough.

crou•pi•er |kro͞o'pē ər| *or* |-pē ā'| *n.* A person employed by a gambling casino to collect and pay bets at a gaming table.

crou•ton |kro͞o'tŏn'| *or* |kro͞o tŏn'| *n.* A small piece of toasted or fried bread, used as a garnish in soups, salads, etc.

crow[1] |krō| *n.* A large, glossy black bird with a harsh, hoarse call.

***Idioms.* as the crow flies.** In a straight line: *From here to New York it is 50 miles as the crow flies.* **eat crow.** To be put into a humiliating position, as by having to admit an error.

crow[2] |krō| *n.* **1.** The loud, high-pitched cry of a rooster. **2.** A loud, wordless sound of pleasure. —*v.* **1.** *Past tense* **crowed** or **crew** |kro͞o|. To utter the loud, high-pitched cry of a rooster. **2.** To make a loud, wordless sound of pleasure: *The baby kicked and crowed.* **3.** To boast: *He crowed about his fast new car.*

Crow |krō| *n., pl.* **Crow** or **Crows. 1.** A North American Indian tribe now settled in Montana. **2.** A member of this tribe. **3.** The Siouan language of this tribe.

crow•bar |krō'bär'| *n.* A straight bar of iron or steel, slightly bent at one end, used as a lever for lifting or prying.

crowd |kroud| *n.* **1.** A large number of persons gathered together; a throng: *a crowd waiting for a train. The circus drew quite a crowd.* **2. the crowd.** People in general; the populace: *He does what he wants to do; he doesn't follow the crowd.* **3.** A particular social group; a clique: *the college crowd; associate with a bad crowd.* —*v.* **1.** To fill by massing together in: *Shoppers crowded the store.* **2.** To press tightly or cram: *The guests*

ă pat/ā pay/â care/ä father/ĕ pet/ē be/ĭ pit/ī pie/î fierce/ŏ pot/ō go/ô paw, for/oi oil/o͝o book/o͞o boot/ou out/ŭ cut/û fur/*th* the/th thin/hw which/zh vision/ə ago, item, pencil, atom, circus

crowded into the dining room. He crowded more books onto the shelf. —**crowd'ed** *adj.: crowded streets; a crowded bus.*

crown |kroun| *n.* **1.** A head covering, often made of gold set with jewels, worn by a king or queen as a symbol of ruling power. **2.** The person, authority, or government of a king or queen: *a servant of the crown; the heir to the crown.* **3.** A wreath worn on the head as a mark of victory, honor, or position: *a crown of laurel.* **4.** The top part of something: *the crown of a person's head.* **5.** The part of a hat fitting over the top of the head. **6. a.** The part of a tooth that projects beyond the gum. **b.** Any artificial substitute for the natural crown of a tooth. **7.** A former British coin. **8.** A championship title: *He won the heavyweight boxing crown.* **9. the Crown.** The constitutional government of a monarchy, especially of the United Kingdom of Great Britain and Northern Ireland. —*v.* **1.** To place a crown upon the head of, thus investing with royal power: *crown a new king.* **2.** To place a wreath upon the head of, as a mark of victory, honor, or position: *crown the victor with laurel.* **3.** To form the topmost part of; cover the top of: *Snow crowned the mountain peaks.* **4.** To be the highest achievement of: *The Nobel Prize crowned his career.* **5.** To put a crown on (a tooth). **6.** *Informal.* To hit on the head: *Be quiet or I'll crown you.* [SEE NOTE & PICTURE]

crown colony. A British colony governed by a crown-appointed governor.

crown prince. The male heir to a throne.

crown princess. **1.** The wife of a crown prince. **2.** A female who is heir to a throne.

crow's-nest |krōz'nĕst'| *n.* A small lookout platform located near the top of a ship's mast. [SEE PICTURE]

cro•zier |krō'zhər| *n.* A form of the word **crosier.**

cru•cial |kro͞o'shəl| *adj.* Of the utmost importance; decisive: *a crucial decision.* —**cru'cial•ly** *adv.*

cru•ci•ble |kro͞o'sə bəl| *n.* A container made of a material, such as graphite or porcelain, with a very high melting point, used in processing substances at very high temperatures.

cru•ci•fix |kro͞o'sə fĭks'| *n.* An image of Christ on the cross.

cru•ci•fix•ion |kro͞o'sə **fĭk'**shən| *n.* **1.** The act of crucifying or condition of being crucified. **2. the Crucifixion.** The execution of Christ on the cross.

cru•ci•form |kro͞o'sə fôrm'| *adj.* Cross-shaped.

cru•ci•fy |kro͞o'sə fī'| *v.* **cru•ci•fied, cru•ci•fy•ing, cru•ci•fies. 1.** To put (a person) to death by nailing or binding to a cross. **2.** To persecute; torment, as by devastating criticism: *The press crucified the senator for his ill-timed statements.*

crud |krŭd| *n. Slang.* **1.** An encrustation of filth, refuse, grease, etc. **2.** A worthless person.

crude |kro͞od| *adj.* **crud•er, crud•est. 1.** In an unrefined or natural state; raw: *crude oil.* **2.** Lacking tact or refinement: *a crude person; a crude expression.* **3.** Not skillfully made or done; rough: *a crude sketch; a crude attempt.* —**crude'ly** *adv.* —**crude'ness** *n.*

cru•di•ty |kro͞o'dĭ tē| *n., pl.* **cru•di•ties. 1.** The condition or quality of being crude; crudeness: *the crudity of the drawing.* **2.** A rude or vulgar remark or action.

cru•el |kro͞o'əl| *adj.* **cru•el•er, cru•el•est. 1.** Liking to cause pain or suffering; unkind; merciless: *a cruel man.* **2.** Causing suffering; painful: *a cruel wind.* —**cru'el•ly** *adv.* —**cru'el•ness** *n.*

cru•el•ty |kro͞o'əl tē| *n., pl.* **cru•el•ties. 1.** The condition or quality of being cruel: *cruelty to animals. The czars held the Russian people down for centuries, often with great cruelty.* **2.** A cruel act, remark, etc.: *She suffered many cruelties at the hands of her enemies.*

cru•et |kro͞o'ĭt| *n.* A small glass bottle for holding vinegar, oil, or other condiments at the table. [SEE PICTURE]

cruise |kro͞oz| *v.* **cruised, cruis•ing. 1.** To sail or travel about in an unhurried way, as for pleasure, to patrol an area, etc.: *A boat was cruising near the coast. A police car cruised the streets.* **2.** To run an automobile, aircraft, ship, etc., at a speed that is somewhat less than its maximum but at which it is most efficient. —*n.* A sea voyage for pleasure: *He enjoyed his cruise to Bermuda.* —***modifier:*** *a cruise ship.* ¶*These sound alike* **cruise, cruse.**

cruis•er |kro͞o'zər| *n.* **1.** A medium-sized warship of high speed and a large cruising range, with less armor and less firepower than a battleship. **2.** A large motorboat whose cabin is equipped with living facilities. **3.** A **squad car.**

crul•ler |krŭl'ər| *n.* A small, sweet cake of twisted dough fried in deep fat.

crumb |krŭm| *n.* **1.** A tiny piece or particle of food. **2.** A fragment; scrap: *crumbs of knowledge.* **3.** *Slang.* A worthless person.

crum•ble |krŭm'bəl| *v.* **crum•bled, crum•bling.** To break or fall into small pieces or crumbs: *He crumbled crackers into his soup. The lump of dirt crumbled easily.*

crum•my |krŭm'ē| *adj.* **crum•mi•er, crum•mi•est.** *Slang.* **1.** Of poor quality; worthless: *a crummy movie.* **2.** Miserable; wretched: *feeling crummy all afternoon.*

crum•pet |krŭm'pĭt| *n.* A light, soft bread similar to a muffin, baked on a griddle and often toasted.

crum•ple |krŭm'pəl| *v.* **crum•pled, crum•pling. 1.** To crush out of shape or so as to form creases or wrinkles: *Take care not to crumple your dress. Tinfoil crumples easily.* **2.** To fall down: *A shot rang out, and he crumpled to the floor.*

crunch |krŭnch| *v.* **1.** To grind or crush with a noisy or cracking sound; chew noisily: *crunch peanuts.* **2.** To move with a crushing or cracking sound: *The ship crunched through the ice.* **3.** To make a crushing or cracking sound: *The snow crunched under my boots.* —*n.* **1.** The act of crunching. **2.** A crushing or cracking sound: *the crunch of one's boots in the snow.*

crunch•y |krŭn'chē| *adj.* **crunch•i•er, crunch•i•est.** Crisp; brittle: *crunchy potato chips.*

cru•sade |kro͞o **sād'**| *n.* **1.** Often **Crusade.** Any of a series of military expeditions undertaken by European Christians from the 11th through the 13th century with the proclaimed goal of recovering the Holy Land from the Moslems. **2.** A campaign or movement for a reform, cause, or ideal: *a crusade against crime; a crusade for civil rights.* —*v.* **cru•sad•ed, cru•sad•ing.** To take part

crown

Crown *is from Old French* corone, *which is from Latin* corōna, *"garland, wreath."*

crow's-nest

On the former British liner *Queen Mary*

cruet

in a crusade: *He crusaded for better schools.*

cru•sad•er |kro͞o sā′dər| *n.* **1.** Often **Crusader.** A person who takes part in a crusade. **2.** A person who advocates or works for a reform, cause, or ideal: *a crusader for civil rights.* [SEE PICTURE]

cruse |kro͞oz| *or* |kro͞os| *n.* A small jar or pot for holding oil, wine, etc. ¶*These sound alike* **cruse, cruise.**

crush |krŭsh| *v.* **1.** To press, squeeze, or bear down on with great force so as to break or injure: *The big, burly man crushed Chad's hand with a friendly handshake. The telegraph pole smashed down through the driver's seat and crushed the front wheels of the car.* **2.** To break, grind, or pound into very fine particles: *crush rocks.* **3.** To crumple; wrinkle: *Try not to crush your suit. Cotton fabrics crush easily.* **4.** To shove; crowd: *The dogs in their excitement crushed the boy against the wall.* **5.** To put down; subdue: *crush a rebellion.* **6.** To overwhelm; destroy: *Ten years in prison could not crush his spirit.* —**crushed′** *adj.: crushed ice; crushed pineapple.* —**crush′ing** *adj.: a crushing victory; a crushing blow.* —*n.* **1.** A dense crowd of people that generates uncomfortable pressure: *I was caught in the crush and nearly fainted.* **2.** A substance prepared by or as if by crushing: *raspberry crush.* **3.** *Informal.* A strong, often foolish and brief, liking for someone.

crystal
Topaz crystal

crust |krŭst| *n.* **1. a.** The hard outer layer of bread. **b.** A piece of bread consisting mostly of this part. **2.** A pastry shell, as of a pie. **3.** Any hard outer layer or covering: *the earth's crust.* —*v.* **1.** To cover or become covered with a crust: *Mother crusted the pie. The gravy crusted over.* **2.** To cover with a crustlike layer; encrust: *Jewels crusted the sword hilt.*

crus•ta•cean |krŭ stā′shən| *n.* Any of a group of animals, such as a lobster, crab, or shrimp, that live mostly in water and have a body with a hard outer covering.

crust•y |krŭs′tē| *adj.* **crust•i•er, crust•i•est. 1.** Of or having a crust: *crusty bread.* **2.** Surly; curt; rude: *He's a crusty individual.* —**crust′i•ly** *adv.* —**crust′i•ness** *n.*

crutch |krŭch| *n.* **1.** A staff or support used by lame or injured persons as an aid in walking and usually having a padded crosspiece at the top that fits under the armpit. **2.** Anything that one depends on for support: *Religion has often served as a spiritual crutch for living through the rigors of hard times.*

crux |krŭks| *n.* A basic or essential point: *the crux of a problem.*

cru•zei•ro |kro͞o zâr′ō| *n., pl.* **cru•zei•ros.** The basic unit of money of Brazil.

cry |krī| *v.* **cried, cry•ing, cries. 1.** To shed tears and make sobbing sounds expressive of grief, sorrow, pain, etc.; weep: *She cried when she heard the news of his death. She cried for joy.* **2.** To call loudly; shout: *He cried to his pals across the street to join him.* **3.** To make loud sounds expressive of fear, distress, or other strong emotion: *cry out in pain. The baby cried all night.* **4.** To utter a characteristic sound or call, as an animal does. **5.** To announce for sale; hawk: *A peddler cries his wares.* —*n., pl.* **cries. 1.** A loud call; shout: *a cry for help.* **2.** Any loud sound expressive of fear, distress, pain, etc.: *a cry of anger.* **3.** A fit of weeping: *She needs to have a good cry.* **4.** The characteristic sound or call of certain kinds of animals or birds: *the cry of a wolf; the cry of a peacock.* **5.** A public or general demand or complaint; a clamor; outcry: *a public cry for vengeance.* **6.** A call to action; slogan: *a battle cry.*
Idioms. **a far cry.** A greatly different thing; a long way: *This movie is a far cry from the usual Hollywood production.* **in full cry.** In hot pursuit, as hounds hunting.

ă pat/ā pay/â care/ä father/ĕ pet/
ē be/ĭ pit/ī pie/î fierce/ŏ pot/
ō go/ô paw, for/oi oil/o͝o book/
o͞o boot/ou out/ŭ cut/û fur/
th the/th thin/hw which/zh vision/
ə ago, item, pencil, atom, circus

cry•ba•by |krī′bā′bē| *n., pl.* **cry•ba•bies.** A person who cries, whines, or complains with little cause.

cry•ing |krī′ĭng| *adj.* Demanding immediate action or remedy: *a crying shame; a crying need.*

cry•o•gen•ics |krī′ō jĕn′ĭks| *n. (used with a singular verb).* The scientific study of phenomena that occur at very low temperatures.

cry•o•sur•ger•y |krī′ō sûr′jə rē| *n.* Surgery in which instruments that are cooled to very low temperatures, as by means of liquid nitrogen, are used.

crypt |krĭpt| *n.* An underground vault or chamber, especially one that is used as a tomb beneath a church.

cryp•tic |krĭp′tĭk| *adj.* Mysterious; puzzling; ambiguous: *a cryptic message.* —**cryp′ti•cal•ly** *adv.*

cryp•to•gram |krĭp′tə grăm′| *n.* Something written in a secret code or cipher.

cryp•to•graph |krĭp′tə grăf′| *or* |-gräf′| *n.* **1.** A cryptogram. **2.** A device used to encode and decode messages and documents.

cryp•tog•ra•pher |krĭp tŏg′rə fər| *n.* A person who specializes in cryptography.

cryp•tog•ra•phy |krĭp tŏg′rə fē| *n.* The study and use of secret codes and ciphers.

crys•tal |krĭs′təl| *n.* **1. a.** A three-dimensional structure composed of atoms, molecules, or ions arranged in basic units that are repeated throughout the structure. **b.** The basic unit of such a structure. **c.** A body, such as a piece of quartz, having such a structure, often having characteristic visible plane faces. **d.** Any body having such a structure and used in an electronic circuit because it has some special desired property. **2 a.** A clear, colorless glass of high quality. **b.** An object made of this glass. **3.** A transparent cover that protects the face of a watch or clock. —***modifier:*** *a crystal vase.* —*adj.* Clear; transparent. [SEE PICTURE]

crystal ball. A glass globe used in crystal gazing.

crystal gazing. The practice of peering into a crystal ball, believed to impart a knowledge of the future.

crys•tal•line |krĭs′tə lĭn| *or* |-līn′| *adj.* Of or like crystal.

crystalline lens. The lens of the vertebrate eye.

crys•tal•li•za•tion |krĭs′tə lĭ zā′shən| *n.* The process of crystallizing.

crys•tal•lize |krĭs′tə līz′| *v.* **crys•tal•lized, crys•tal•liz•ing. 1.** To cause to form crystals or take on crystalline structure. **2.** To take on crystalline form. **3.** To give or take on a definite and permanent form: *The scientist finally crystallized his ideas. During the revolution, new parties and factions crystallized.*

crys•tal•log•ra•phy |krĭs′tə lŏg′rə fē| *n.* The scientific study of crystals and their structure.

Cs The symbol for the element cesium.
C.S.A. Confederate States of America.
CST, C.S.T. Central Standard Time.
Ct. Connecticut (unofficial).
ct. cent.
C.T. Central Time.
Cu The symbol for the element copper.
cu. cubic.
cub |kŭb| *n.* **1.** The young of certain animals, such as the bear, wolf, or lion. **2.** A beginner, especially in newspaper reporting. **3. Cub.** A **Cub Scout.**
Cu•ba |kyo͞o′bə|. An island nation in the Caribbean Sea, south of Florida. Population, 9,090,000. Capital, Havana. —**Cu′ban** *adj. & n.*
cub•by•hole |kŭb′ē hōl′| *n.* A snug or cramped space or room: *She put the house keys in a cubbyhole. He has a cubbyhole for an office.*
cube |kyo͞ob| *n.* **1.** A geometric solid having six congruent square faces. **2.** Anything having this shape or almost this shape: *a sugar cube.* **3.** The product that results when the same number is used three times as a factor. For example, the cube of x (written x^3) is equal to $x \times x \times x$. —*v.* **cubed, cub•ing. 1.** To form the cube of (a number). **2.** To express or determine the volume of (a container or space) in cubic units. **3.** To cut or form into a cube or cubes.
cube root. A number that when taken three times as a factor gives a result equal to a given number. If a is a cube root of b (written $a = \sqrt[3]{b}$), then $a \times a \times a = b$. This is true, for example, when $a = 2$ and $b = 8$ or when $a = 3$ and $b = 27$.
cu•bic |kyo͞o′bĭk| *adj.* **1.** Shaped like or nearly like a cube. **2.** Being a unit of volume equal to a cube having a specified unit of linear measure as its edge: *a cubic inch; a cubic foot.* **3.** Of or involving a number or a variable that has been raised to the third power: *a cubic equation.* —*n.* A cubic equation or curve.
cu•bi•cal |kyo͞o′bĭ kəl| *adj.* **1.** Cubic. **2.** Of or involving volume: *cubical dimensions.* ¶*These sound alike* **cubical, cubicle.**
cu•bi•cle |kyo͞o′bĭ kəl| *n.* A very small room or compartment. ¶*These sound alike* **cubicle, cubical.**
cubic measure. 1. A unit, such as a cubic inch or a cubic foot, used to measure volume. **2.** A system of such units.
cub•ism |kyo͞o′bĭz′əm| *n.* A style of 20th-century painting that portrays the subject matter in geometric forms, without realistic detail. —**cub′ist** *adj. & n.*
cu•bit |kyo͞o′bĭt| *n.* An ancient unit of linear measure ranging from about 17 to 22 inches. It was originally equal to the distance from the tip of the middle finger to the elbow.
Cub Scout. A member of the junior division of the Boy Scouts.
cuck•oo |ko͞o′ko͞o| *or* |ko͝ok′o͞o| *n.* **1.** A European bird with grayish feathers and a call that sounds like its name. **2.** A related American bird. —*adj. Informal.* Crazy; foolish.
cuckoo clock. A wall clock with a small mechanical cuckoo that pops out at regular intervals to announce the time.
cu•cum•ber |kyo͞o′kŭm′bər| *n.* **1.** A long vegetable with a green rind and white, watery flesh, eaten in salads and used for pickling. **2.** The vine on which it grows. [SEE PICTURE]
cud |kŭd| *n.* Food that has been swallowed and brought up to the mouth again for further chewing by animals such as cattle, sheep, etc.
cud•dle |kŭd′l| *v.* **cud•dled, cud•dling. 1.** To hold tenderly and close; fondle: *cuddle a baby in one's arms.* **2.** To nestle; snuggle: *cuddle up in bed.* —*n.* A hug or embrace.
cud•dle•some |kŭd′l səm| *adj.* Lovable; inviting cuddling: *a cuddlesome baby.*
cud•dly |kŭd′lē| *adj.* **cud•dli•er, cud•dli•est.** Cuddlesome.
cudg•el |kŭj′əl| *n.* A short, heavy club. —*v.* **cudg•eled** or **cudg•elled, cudg•el•ing** or **cudg•el•ling.** To strike or beat with a cudgel.
***Idiom.* cudgel (one's) brains.** To think hard.
cue¹ |kyo͞o| *n.* **1.** A word or signal given to remind an actor or singer to speak, sing, or move in a prescribed way during a performance. **2.** Any hint or reminder as a signal for action. —*v.* **cued, cu•ing.** To give (a person) a cue. ¶*These sound alike* **cue, queue.** [SEE NOTE]
cue² |kyo͞o| *n.* A long, tapered stick used to strike a ball in billiards and pool. ¶*These sound alike* **cue, queue.** [SEE NOTE]
cuff¹ |kŭf| *n.* **1.** A band or fold of cloth at the bottom of a sleeve. **2.** The part of a sleeve or glove, or a separate band, worn over the wrist. **3.** The turned-up fold at the bottom of a trouser leg. **4.** A handcuff. [SEE NOTE]
cuff² |kŭf| *v.* To strike with the open hand; slap: *The two children cuffed each other.* —*n.* A blow or slap with the open hand: *a cuff on the ear.* [SEE NOTE]
cuff link. One of a pair of buttonlike fasteners for shirt cuffs, usually ending in a rod that passes through a buttonhole, with a movable bar that snaps back to hold it in place.
cui•rass |kwĭ răs′| *n.* **1.** A piece of armor protecting both the breast and the back. **2.** The breastplate alone. [SEE PICTURE]
cui•sine |kwĭ zēn′| *n.* A style of cooking: *French cuisine; a restaurant with an excellent cuisine.*
cul-de-sac |kŭl′dĭ săk′| *or* |ko͝ol′-| *n., pl.* **cul-de-sacs.** A blind alley or dead-end street.
cu•li•nar•y |kyo͞o′lə nĕr′ē| *or* |kŭl′ə-| *adj.* Of a kitchen or cookery: *culinary ware; culinary skill.*
cull |kŭl| *v.* **1.** To pick out from others; gather selectively: *cull the prettiest flowers; cull passages from a poet's work.* **2.** To search through; comb: *cull the forests for firewood.*
cul•mi•nate |kŭl′mə nāt′| *v.* **cul•mi•nat•ed, cul•mi•nat•ing.** To reach the highest point or degree; climax: *With the approach of the crest of the tidal wave, the water level rises, culminating in high water or high tide. A series of minor demonstrations culminated in open rebellion.* —**cul′mi•na′tion** *n.*
cu•lottes |ko͞o lŏts′| *or* |kyo͞o-| *pl.n.* The less often used singular is **cu•lotte** |ko͞o lŏt′| *or* |kyo͞o-|. A garment for women, consisting of or ending in full, skirtlike trousers.
cul•pa•ble |kŭl′pə bəl| *adj.* Deserving censure; blameworthy: *culpable behavior.* —**cul′pa•bil′i•ty** *n.* —**cul′pa•bly** *adv.*
cul•prit |kŭl′prĭt| *n.* A person guilty or believed to be guilty of a crime or offense.
cult |kŭlt| *n.* **1.** A system of religious worship,

cucumber
Vine and fruit

cue¹·²
Cue¹ *first appeared in the sixteenth century; its origin is unknown.* **Cue²** *is from French* queue, *"tail" (referring to the tapering shape of a billiard cue). See note at* **queue.**

cuff¹·²
Cuff¹ *goes back to the fourteenth century and originally meant "glove, mitten."* **Cuff²** *goes back to the sixteenth century. Both are of unknown origin.*

cuirass
Sixteenth-century Italian

cuneiform

especially one centering on a single deity or spirit: *Hindu cults.* **2.** A great or excessive attachment or devotion to a person, principle, etc.: *Nazism is a cult that developed in Germany after World War I.* **3.** A group of persons sharing a certain interest: *a member of a fashionable political cult.*

cul•ti•vate |kŭl′tə vāt′| *v.* **cul•ti•vat•ed, cul•ti•vat•ing. 1.** To prepare and care for (land) on which plants are grown, as by plowing, loosening the soil, or adding fertilizer. **2.** To grow and tend (plants or crops). **3.** To develop by study or teaching: *cultivate one's mind; cultivate a love of music in one's children.* **4.** To seek the acquaintance or good will of (a person). —**cul′ti•vat′ed** *adj.: cultivated land; a cultivated person.*

cul•ti•va•tion |kŭl′tə vā′shən| *n.* **1.** The process of tilling or growing: *the cultivation of tobacco; bring land under cultivation.* **2.** Development: *cultivation of one's mind.* **3.** Culture; refinement: *a man of great cultivation.*

cul•ti•va•tor |kŭl′tə vā′tər| *n.* **1.** A person who cultivates. **2.** A tool or machine for loosening the earth and destroying weeds around growing plants.

cul•tur•al |kŭl′chər əl| *adj.* Of culture: *Paris is the cultural center of Europe.* —**cul′tur•al•ly** *adv.*

cul•ture |kŭl′chər| *n.* **1.** The result of intellectual development, as evidenced by a high degree of taste, refinement, appreciation of the arts, etc.: *a man of great culture and charm.* **2.** Intellectual and artistic activity and the works produced by this: *Our libraries and museums bring culture to the people.* **3.** The arts, beliefs, customs, institutions, and all other products of human work and thought created by a people or group at a particular time: *The culture of western Europe owes much to Greece.* **4.** Development of the mind or body through special training: *He believes in physical culture.* **5.** The raising of animals or growing of plants, especially for use or improved development: *bee culture; African violet culture.* **6. a.** The growing of microorganisms or tissues in a specially prepared nutrient substance. **b.** Such a growth, as of bacteria or tissue. —*v.* **cul•tured, cul•tur•ing.** To grow (microorganisms, tissues, etc.) in a specially prepared nutrient substance.

cul•tured |kŭl′chərd| *adj.* **1.** Well-educated; refined: *The professor is a cultured man.* **2.** Grown or produced under artificial and controlled conditions: *cultured pearls.*

cul•ver•in |kŭl′vər ĭn| *n.* **1.** A type of early musket. **2.** A heavy cannon used in the 16th and 17th centuries.

cul•vert |kŭl′vərt| *n.* A drain crossing under a road or embankment.

cum |ko͝om| *or* |kŭm| *prep.* Combined with; together with: *an attic-cum-studio.*

cum•ber |kŭm′bər| *v.* To burden or trouble: *cumber a person with worries.*

cum•ber•some |kŭm′bər səm| *adj.* **1.** Heavy and awkward to carry, wear, etc.; burdensome: *cumbersome baggage; cumbersome garments.* **2.** Clumsy and inefficient: *a cumbersome method of plowing.*

cum•brance |kŭm′brəns| *n.* A burden; bother: *Her chores became a cumbrance to her.*

cum•brous |kŭm′brəs| *adj.* Cumbersome.

cum•in |kŭm′ən| *n.* **1.** A plant with spicy seeds used as seasoning. **2.** The seeds of this plant.

cum lau•de |ko͝om lou′də| *or* |-dē| *or* |kŭm lô′dē|. With honor: *He was graduated cum laude from Harvard.* This expression was originally a Latin phrase.

cum•mer•bund |kŭm′ər bŭnd′| *n.* A broad sash worn around the waist, especially as part of a man's evening clothes.

cu•mu•la•tive |kyo͞o′myə lā′tĭv| *or* |-lə tĭv| *adj.* Increasing or growing steadily or in stages: *the cumulative bad effects of cigarette smoking.* —**cu′mu•la′tive•ly** *adv.* —**cu′mu•la′tive•ness** *n.*

cu•mu•lo•nim•bus |kyo͞o′myə lō nĭm′bəs| *n., pl.* **cu•mu•lo•nim•bus•es** or **cu•mu•lo•nim•bi** |kyo͞o′myə lō nĭm′bī′|. A very dense cloud with massive projections that billow upward. It occurs at an average height of about 4 miles and usually produces heavy rains, thunderstorms, or hailstorms.

cu•mu•lus |kyo͞o′myə ləs| *n., pl.* **cu•mu•li** |kyo͞o′myə lī′|. A dense, white, fluffy cloud that billows upward from a flat base and occurs at an average height of about 2 miles.

cu•ne•i•form |kyo͞o′nē ə fôrm′| *or* |kyo͞o nē′-| *adj.* **1.** Of or designating the wedge-shaped characters used in writing by the Babylonians, Asyrians, and other peoples of ancient Mesopotamia. **2.** Of or designating documents or inscriptions written in such characters. —*n.* Cuneiform writing. [SEE PICTURE]

cun•ning |kŭn′ĭng| *adj.* **1.** Sly; crafty; clever: *a cunning scheme. The weasel is a small but cunning animal.* **2.** *Informal.* Charming; cute: *a cunning little child.* —*n.* Slyness; craftiness: *The fox is an animal of great cunning.* —**cun′ning•ly** *adv.*

cup |kŭp| *n.* **1.** A small, open container, usually with a handle, from which to drink coffee, soup, etc. **2. a.** A cup with something in it: *pour a cup of tea.* **b.** The amount that a cup holds: *drink a cup of coffee.* **3.** In cooking, a measure equal to 8 ounces or 16 tablespoons. **4.** Something similar in shape to a cup: *the cup of a flower.* **5.** A cup-shaped vessel awarded as a prize or trophy. **6.** In golf, a hole or the metal container inside a hole. —*v.* **cupped, cup•ping.** To form in such a way as to resemble a cup: *cup one's hands.*

cup•board |kŭb′ərd| *n.* A closet or cabinet, usually with shelves for storing food, dishes, etc.

cup•cake |kŭp′kāk′| *n.* A small cake baked in a cup-shaped container.

cup•ful |kŭp′fo͝ol′| *n., pl.* **cup•fuls.** The amount a cup will hold.

Cu•pid |kyo͞o′pĭd|. The Roman god of love.

cu•pid•i•ty |kyo͞o pĭd′ĭ tē| *n.* Excessive desire for wealth; greed.

cu•po•la |kyo͞o′pə lə| *n.* **1.** A small dome on top of a roof. **2.** Also **cupola furnace.** A type of blast furnace in which a metal, especially iron, is melted for casting.

cu•pric |kyo͞o′prĭk| *adj.* Of or containing copper, especially with a valence of +2.

cu•prous |kyo͞o′prəs| *adj.* Of or containing copper, especially with a valence of +1.

cur |kûr| *n.* **1.** A dog of mixed breed; a mongrel, especially one that is unwanted or considered worthless. **2.** A hateful or cowardly person.

cur•a•ble |kyo͝or′ə bəl| *adj.* Capable of being healed or cured: *a curable illness.*

ă pat/ā pay/â care/ä father/ĕ pet/ ē be/ĭ pit/ī pie/î fierce/ŏ pot/ ō go/ô paw, for/oi oil/o͝o book/ o͞o boot/ou out/ŭ cut/û fur/ *th* the/th thin/hw which/zh vision/ ə ago, item, pencil, atom, circus

Cu•ra•çao |kyo͝or'ə **sou'**| *or* |-**sō'**|. The largest island of the Netherlands Antilles, off the northern coast of Venezuela. Population, 196,000.

cu•ra•re |kyo͞o **rä'**rē| *n.* Any one of a number of extracts obtained from certain trees of South America, used in medicine as muscle-relaxing agents and by some Indian tribes as poisons.

cu•rate |**kyo͝or'**ĭt| *n.* **1.** A clergyman who assists a rector or vicar. **2.** A clergyman who has charge of a parish.

cur•a•tive |**kyo͝or'**ə tĭv| *adj.* Serving or tending to cure: *curative medicine.* —*n.* Something that cures; a remedy.

cu•ra•tor |kyo͞o **rā'**tər| *or* |**kyo͝or'**ā'-| *n.* A person in charge of a museum, library, etc.

curb |kûrb| *n.* **1.** A concrete or stone rim along the edge of a sidewalk. **2.** Something that checks or restrains: *a curb on spending.* **3.** A chain or strap used together with a bit to restrain a horse. —*v.* **1.** To check, restrain, or control: *curb one's temper; curb inflation.* **2.** To walk (a dog) in the gutter so as not to soil the sidewalk.

curb•stone |**kûrb'**stōn'| *n.* A stone or row of stones that make up a curb.

curd |kûrd| *n.* **1.** Often **curds.** The thick part of milk that separates from the whey and is used to make cheese. **2.** A food, such as bean curd, that resembles curd.

cur•dle |**kûr'**dl| *v.* **cur•dled, cur•dling. 1.** To form or cause to form into curds: *Add vinegar until the milk starts to curdle. Be careful not to curdle the milk.* **2.** To seem to thicken and stop running, as because of fear, shock, etc.: *My blood curdled at the sight of the accident.*

cure |kyo͝or| *n.* **1.** A medical treatment or a series of such treatments designed to restore health. **2.** Restoration of health; recovery from disease. **3.** A drug or some similar agent that restores health. —*v.* **cured, cur•ing. 1.** To restore to good health. **2.** To do away with (a harmful condition or influence): *She tried to cure the confusion with name tags.* **3.** To use a chemical, physical, or other process in preparing, preserving, or finishing (a substance or material): *cure fish by salting and drying; cure ham. This adhesive cures easily.*

cure-all |**kyo͝or'**ôl'| *n.* Something that cures all diseases or evils; a panacea.

cu•rette |kyo͞o **rĕt'**| *n.* A scooplike surgical instrument used to remove dead tissue or growths from cavities of the body.

cur•few |**kûr'**fyo͞o| *n.* **1.** An order requiring certain groups of people to retire from the streets at a certain hour. **2.** The time during which such an order is in effect. [SEE NOTE]

cu•rie |**kyo͝or'**ē| *or* |kyo͞o **rē'**| *n.* A unit of radioactivity that is equal to the radioactivity of a sample of an element in which 37 billion (3.7×10^{10}) nuclear disintegrations occur each second. [SEE NOTE]

cu•ri•o |**kyo͝or'**ē ō'| *n., pl.* **cu•ri•os.** A rare or unusual object of art.

cu•ri•os•i•ty |kyo͝or'ē **ŏs'**ĭ tē| *n., pl.* **cu•ri•os•i•ties. 1.** A desire to know or learn: *He burned with curiosity over what was in the box.* **2.** Something unusual or extraordinary: *Many of today's curiosities, such as trolley cars, were commonplace sights not long ago.*

cu•ri•ous |**kyo͝or'**ē əs| *adj.* **1.** Eager to acquire information or knowledge: *A scientist is always curious to learn more.* **2.** Interesting because unusual or extraordinary: *a curious fact.* **3.** Excessively inquisitive; prying; nosy. —**cu'ri•ous•ly** *adv.* —**cu'ri•ous•ness** *n.*

cu•ri•um |**kyo͝or'**ē əm| *n.* Symbol **Cm** One of the elements, a metal first produced by bombarding plutonium with helium ions. It has 13 isotopes with mass numbers ranging from 238 to 250 and half-lives ranging from 64 minutes to 16.4 million years. Atomic number 96.

curl |kûrl| *v.* **1.** To twist into or form coils or ringlets: *curl one's hair. Her hair curls naturally.* **2.** To make or become curved or twisted: *Heat curls paper. Her lips curled into a smile.* **3.** To wind: *curl the paper around the pencil.* **4.** To move in a curve or spiral: *Smoke curled from the chimney.* —***phrasal verb.*** **curl up.** To sit or lie cozily with the legs drawn up. —*n.* **1.** A coil or ringlet of hair. **2.** Something with a spiral or coiled shape: *a curl of smoke.*

curl•er |**kûr'**lər| *n.* A device, such as a roller, on which a strand of hair is wound for curling.

cur•lew |**kûr'**lo͞o| *or* |-lyo͞o| *n.* A shore bird with brownish feathers and a long, downward-curving bill.

curl•i•cue |**kûr'**lĭ kyo͞o'| *n.* A fancy twist or curl, such as a flourish made with a pen.

curl•ing |**kûr'**lĭng| *n.* A Scottish game played on ice, in which two four-player teams slide heavy, rounded stones toward a mark in the center of a circle at either end. [SEE PICTURE]

curl•y |**kûr'**lē| *adj.* **curl•i•er, curl•i•est. 1.** Having curls or tending to curl: *curly hair.* **2.** Having a wavy grain or markings, as wood: *curly maple.* —**curl'i•ness** *n.*

cur•rant |**kûr'**ənt| *or* |**kŭr'**-| *n.* **1 a.** The small, sour, usually red or blackish fruit of a prickly shrub, used for making jelly. **b.** A shrub that bears such fruit. **2.** A seedless raisin, used chiefly in baking. —***modifier:*** *currant preserve.* ¶ *These sound alike* **currant, current.** [SEE NOTE]

cur•ren•cy |**kûr'**ən sē| *or* |**kŭr'**-| *n., pl.* **cur•ren•cies. 1.** Any form of money in actual use in a country: *Switzerland's currency is one of the world's most dependable.* **2.** A general or common acceptance; widespread use or circulation: *Many newly formed words and expressions have short currency.*

cur•rent |**kûr'**ənt| *or* |**kŭr'**-| *adj.* **1.** Belonging to the present time; present-day: *current events.* **2.** Passing from one to another; circulating, as money. **3.** Commonly accepted; in general or widespread use: *a word that is no longer current.* —*n.* **1.** A mass of liquid or gas that is in motion: *a current of air.* **2. a.** A flow of electric charge. **b.** The amount of electric charge that passes a point in a unit of time, usually expressed in amperes. **3.** A general tendency or movement, as of events, opinions, etc. ¶ *These sound alike* **current, currant.** [SEE NOTE]

cur•rent•ly |**kûr'**ənt lē| *or* |**kŭr'**-| *adv.* At the time now passing; at present: *a movie currently showing at the local theater.*

cur•ric•u•lum |kə **rĭk'**yə ləm| *n., pl.* **cur•ric•u•la** |kə **rĭk'**yə lə| or **cur•ric•u•lums.** All the courses of study offered at a particular educational institution.

cur•ry[1] |**kûr'**ē| *or* |**kŭr'**ē| *v.* **cur•ried, cur•ry•ing,**

curfew

Curfew *was* curfeu *or* coeverfu *in Middle English; it was borrowed from Old French* cuevrefeu, *"cover the fire" (i.e., "put your lights out"):* couvrir, *"to cover,"* + feu, *"fire."*

curie

This unit is named in honor of Marie Curie *(1867–1934), Polish-born French chemist.*

curling

currant/current

Currant *comes from Middle English* raysons of Coraunte, *"raisins of Corinth";* Coraunte *is from the Norman French spelling of* Corinth, *a city that exported dried grapes in the Middle Ages.* **Current** *is from Latin* currere, *"running," the present participle of* currere, *"to run."*

cur•ries. To groom (a horse) with a currycomb. [SEE NOTE]

***Idiom.* curry favor.** To seek or gain favor by flattery.

cur•ry² |kûr'ē| *or* |kŭr'ē| *n., pl.* **cur•ries. 1.** Also **curry powder.** A sharp-flavored mixture of powdered spices. **2.** A pungent sauce or dish seasoned with curry. ***—modifier:*** *a curry sauce. —v.* **cur•ried, cur•ry•ing.** To season with curry. [SEE NOTE]

cur•ry•comb |kûr'ē kōm'| *or* |kŭr'-| *n.* A comb with metal teeth, used for grooming horses.

curse |kûrs| *n.* **1. a.** An appeal to a supernatural power to bring down evil or harm upon someone or something. **b.** The evil thus invoked. **2.** A word or group of words expressing great hatred or anger; an oath: *shout curses at someone.* **3.** Something that causes great evil or harm; a scourge: *Mankind's greatest curse is poverty. —v.* **cursed** or **curst** |kûrst|, **curs•ing. 1.** To wish harm on; place a curse on: *The old gypsy cursed the soldiers as they led her to the stake.* **2.** To bring great harm to; afflict: *We are cursed with bad luck.* **3.** To swear at: *He cursed the day he was born.* **4.** To use bad language; swear: *He cursed like a trooper.*

curs•ed |kûr'sĭd| *or* |kûrst| *adj.* **1.** Under a curse; damned. **2.** Deserving to be cursed; detestable: *He keeps blowing that cursed bugle.* **—curs'ed•ly** *adv.*

cur•sive |kûr'sĭv| *adj.* Of or designating writing or printing in which the letters are joined together; flowing: *cursive writing. —n.* A cursive character or letter.

cur•so•ry |kûr'sə rē| *adj.* Hasty and superficial; not thorough. **—cur'so•ri•ly** *adv.*

curt |kûrt| *adj.* **curt•er, curt•est.** Rudely brief and abrupt in speech or manner; brusque: *a curt reply.* **—curt'ly** *adv.* **—curt'ness** *n.*

cur•tail |kər tāl'| *v.* To cut short; reduce: *We must curtail our spending.*

cur•tain |kûr'tn| *n.* **1.** A piece of cloth or similar material hanging in a window or other opening as a decoration, shade, or screen: *a curtain in the doorway; the curtain in a theater that hides the stage from view.* **2.** Something that acts as a screen or cover: *hidden by a curtain of black smoke; a curtain of secrecy.* ***—modifier:*** *a curtain rod. —v.* To provide or shut off with or as if with a curtain: *curtain the windows. A spy's work is always curtained with mystery.*

curt•sey |kûrt'sē| *n. & v.* A form of the word **curtsy.**

curt•sy |kûrt'sē| *n., pl.* **curt•sies.** A gesture of respect made by women by bending the knees and lowering the body while keeping one foot forward. *—v.* **curt•sied, curt•sy•ing, curt•sies.** To make a curtsy.

cur•va•ture |kûr'və chər| *n.* **1. a.** The act of curving or the condition of being curved. **b.** The degree to which something is curved: *a slight curvature in a board.* **2.** A curving or bending of a body part, especially when abnormal.

curve |kûrv| *n.* **1. a.** A line that departs from straightness in a smooth, continuous way. **b.** A surface that departs from flatness in a similar way. **2.** Anything that has the general shape of a curve: *a curve in the road; the curve of a person's chin.* **3.** A line or trace drawn on a surface, especially the graph of a continuous function or relation on a coordinate plane. **4.** Also **curve ball.** In baseball, a ball that veers to one side as it nears the batter. *—v.* **curved, curv•ing. 1.** To move in or take the shape of a curve: *The road curves sharply just ahead.* **2.** To cause to curve: *curve a metal band.* **—curv'ing** *adj.: curving horns; curving branches.*

cur•vet |kûr'vĭt| *n.* A light leap of a horse, in which the forelegs come down as the hind legs are raised. *—v.* |kər vĕt'| *or* |kûr'vĭt| **cur•vet•ted** or **cur•vet•ed, cur•vet•ting** or **cur•vet•ing.** To leap in this manner.

cur•vi•lin•e•ar |kûr'və lĭn'ē ər| *adj.* Of, formed by, or bounded by curved lines. **—cur'vi•lin'e•ar•ly** *adv.*

cush•ion |ko͝osh'ən| *n.* **1.** A pad or pillow with a soft filling, used to sit, lie, or rest on. **2.** Anything used to absorb or soften the impact of something: *Rubber stripping was nailed around the opening to form a cushion against which the door could be closed.* **3.** The rim bordering a billiard table. *—v.* **1.** To furnish with a cushion or cushions. **2.** To lessen or soften the impact of: *cushion a blow.*

cusp |kŭsp| *n.* A point or pointed end, as on the new moon or on a part of the body.

cus•pid |kŭs'pĭd| *n.* A tooth having a single point; a canine.

cus•pi•dor |kŭs'pĭ dôr'| *n.* A bowl-shaped receptacle for spitting into; a spittoon.

cuss |kŭs|. *Informal. v.* To curse. *—n.* **1.** A curse. **2.** An odd person: *He's a silly old cuss.*

cuss•ed |kŭs'ĭd| *adj. Informal.* **1.** Cursed. **2.** Perverse; stubborn: *a cussed old man.*

cus•tard |kŭs'tərd| *n.* A puddinglike dessert of milk, sugar, eggs, and flavoring.

cus•to•di•an |kŭ stō'dē ən| *n.* **1.** A person who has charge of something; a caretaker. **2.** A person who takes care of a building; a janitor.

cus•to•dy |kŭs'tə dē| *n., pl.* **cus•to•dies. 1.** The act or right of caring for or guarding, especially when granted by a court: *The mother was given custody of the children.* **2.** The condition of being kept or guarded: *Leave your valuables in custody at the bank.* **3.** The condition of being detained or held under guard, especially by the police: *a criminal in protective custody.*

cus•tom |kŭs'təm| *n.* **1.** An accepted practice or convention followed by tradition: *tribal customs. Shaking hands when meeting someone is an ancient custom.* **2.** A habitual practice of an individual: *His custom was to think a moment before he spoke. —adj.* **1.** Made to order: *He liked expensive cars that were beautiful, sleek custom jobs.* **2.** Making or selling made-to-order goods: *a custom tailor; a custom shop.*

cus•tom•ar•y |kŭs'tə mĕr'ē| *adj.* Established by custom; usual; habitual: *sit in one's customary place.* **—cus'tom•ar'i•ly** *adv.*

cus•tom-built |kŭs'təm bĭlt'| *adj.* Built according to the specifications of the buyer: *a custom-built car.*

cus•tom•er |kŭs'tə mər| *n.* **1.** A person who buys goods or services, especially on a regular basis. **2.** *Informal.* A person with whom one must deal: *a real tough customer.*

cus•tom•house |kŭs'təm hous'| *n., pl.* **-hous•es** |-hou'zĭz|. A government building where customs duties are levied and collected.

curry¹·²

Curry¹ *comes from Old French* coreer, *"to prepare or equip, to groom a horse." The expression* **curry favor** *is a corruption of* to curry Favel; Favel *was the name of a fictional chestnut horse proverbial for his cunning, so that* to curry Favel *meant "to polish up one's cunning" and especially "to flatter."* **Curry²,** *which was introduced from India, is from Tamil* kari, *"sauce."*

ă pat/ā pay/â care/ä father/ĕ pet/ ē be/ĭ pit/ī pie/î fierce/ŏ pot/ ō go/ô paw, for/oi oil/o͝o book/ o͞o boot/ou out/ŭ cut/û fur/ *th* the/th thin/hw which/zh vision/ ə ago, item, pencil, atom, circus

cus•tom-made |kŭs′təm **mād′**| *adj.* Made according to the specifications of the buyer: *custom-made draperies.*

cus•toms |**kŭs′**təmz| *n. (used with a singular verb).* **1. a.** A duty or tax imposed on goods imported from another country. **b.** The government agency that collects such taxes. **2.** The inspection of goods and baggage entering a country. **—modifier:** *a customs inspector.*

cut |kŭt| *v.* **cut, cut•ting. 1.** To penetrate with or as if with a sharp edge or instrument; make a narrow opening in: *He held the coins so tightly that they cut his hands. The cold cut right through me.* **2.** To form, shape, or divide by penetrating or separating: *Cut the cake in half. Cut out the paper doll. Rivers and streams can cut through rocks.* **3. a.** To allow penetration or separation, as with a sharp instrument: *Butter cuts easily.* **b.** To perform the action of penetrating or separating: *This knife does not cut well.* **4.** To separate from the main body of something; detach: *Cut off his head. Cut the meat away from the legs of the chicken.* **5.** To shorten; trim: *cut hair; cut the lawn.* **6.** To reap; harvest: *cut wheat.* **7.** To cause to fall by sawing: *Each year lumberjacks cut millions of trees.* **8.** To grow (teeth) through the gums: *The baby cut two new teeth.* **9.** To interrupt: *cut electric power for two hours. Plans were cut short by his death.* **10.** To reduce the size or amount of: *cut taxes; cut down noise; cut back on sales.* **11.** To lessen the strength of; dilute: *He cut the drink with water.* **12.** To eliminate; remove: *He cut the third act from the play.* **13.** To edit (film or audio tape). **14.** To hurt: *His remark cut me deeply.* **15.** *Informal.* To be absent from purposely: *I cut my first class today.* **16.** To change direction abruptly: *He cut the wheels to the right.* **17.** To divide (a deck of cards) in two, as before dealing. **—cut′** *adj.: cut flowers.* **—phrasal verbs. cut in. 1.** To interrupt. **2.** To interrupt a dancing couple in order to dance with one of them. **cut off. 1.** To separate: *The aborigines were cut off from contact with more advanced cultures.* **2.** To stop; discontinue: *He cut off the ignition.* **cut out. 1.** To be suited: *He is not cut out for city life.* **2.** *Informal.* To stop; cease: *Cut that out right now!* **3.** *Informal.* To depart. **cut up.** *Informal.* To misbehave. *—n.* **1.** The result of cutting; an opening; a slit, wound, etc.: *a cut in the material; a cut on his hand.* **2.** A piece of meat that has been cut from the animal: *cuts of fresh pork.* **3.** A reduction: *a pay cut.* **4.** The style in which something is cut, as clothes or gems. **5.** A wounding remark; an insult: *That was an unkind cut directed at her.* **6. a.** The act of cutting out a part, especially in order to shorten or improve: *Who will make the cuts in the new movie?* **b.** The part that is cut out.

cut-and-dried |**kŭt′**n **drīd′**| *adj.* **1.** In accordance with a formula; prearranged: *There are no cut-and-dried rules for writing.* **2.** Lacking freshness or imagination; ordinary; routine: *Stay away from the cut-and-dried sort of advertising.*

cu•ta•ne•ous |kyōō **tā′**nē əs| *adj.* Of, involving, or affecting the skin.

cut•a•way |**kŭt′**ə wā′| *n.* Also **cutaway coat.** A man's formal daytime coat, cut so that the front edges slope away from the waist to form tails at the back.

cut•back |**kŭt′**băk′| *n.* A decrease; curtailment: *a cutback in government spending.*

cute |kyōōt| *adj.* **cut•er, cut•est. 1.** Delightfully pretty or dainty: *a cute girl; a cute hat; a cute little dog.* **2.** Obviously designed to charm; affected; precious: *a cute remark.* **—cute′ness** *n.*

cu•ti•cle |**kyōō′**tĭ kəl| *n.* **1.** The outer layer of skin; the epidermis. **2.** The hardened strip of skin at the base of a fingernail or toenail.

cut•lass |**kŭt′**ləs| *n.* A heavy sword with a curved single-edged blade. [SEE PICTURE]

cut•ler•y |**kŭt′**lə rē| *n.* Cutting implements, such as knives and scissors.

cut•let |**kŭt′**lĭt| *n.* **1.** A thin slice of meat, as of veal, from the leg or ribs. **2.** A flat croquette of chopped meat or fish.

cut•off |**kŭt′**ôf′| *or* |-ŏf′| *n.* **1.** An indicated limit or stopping point. **2.** A cutting off of something, as a flow of steam, water, etc. **3.** A device used to stop a flow, as of a liquid or gas. **4.** A short cut or by-pass.

cut•out |**kŭt′**out′| *n.* **1.** Something cut out or intended to be cut out. **2.** A device that acts as a by-pass or cutoff, especially in an electric circuit.

cut•ter |**kŭt′**ər| *n.* **1.** A worker whose job involves cutting some material, such as cloth, glass, or stone. **2.** A cutting device or machine: *a cooky cutter.* **3.** A Coast Guard vessel of more than 65 feet in length. **4.** A ship's boat, powered by a motor or pulled with oars, used for transporting stores or passengers. **5.** A kind of fast single-masted sailing vessel.

cut•throat |**kŭt′**thrōt′| *n.* Someone who cuts throats; a murderer. *—adj.* Ruthless; merciless: *cutthroat competition.*

cut•ting |**kŭt′**ĭng| *n.* **1.** A part cut off from a main body: *cuttings and scrapings.* **2.** A stem, twig, leaf, etc., removed from a plant and placed in soil, sand, or water to form roots and develop into a new plant. *—adj.* **1.** Capable of or designed for cutting: *a cutting blade.* **2.** Sarcastic and insulting: *a cutting remark.*

cut•tle•bone |**kŭt′**l bōn′| *n.* The chalky shell inside the body of the cuttlefish, used to supply calcium to caged birds.

cut•tle•fish |**kŭt′**l fĭsh′| *n., pl.* **-fish** or **-fish•es.** A soft-bodied sea animal related to the squids and octopuses. It has ten armlike tentacles, a chalky shell inside its body, and can squirt a dark, inky liquid. [SEE PICTURE]

cut•worm |**kŭt′**wûrm′| *n.* A moth caterpillar that often destroys plants by eating through the stems at ground level.

cwt. hundredweight.

–cy. A suffix that forms nouns: **bankruptcy; piracy.**

cy•a•nide |**sī′**ə nīd′| *n.* Any one of a large group of salts and esters containing the radical CN, especially the very poisonous salts sodium cyanide and potassium cyanide. *—v.* **cy•a•nid•ed, cy•a•nid•ing.** To treat (a substance or material) with a cyanide.

cy•an•o•gen |sī **ăn′**ə jən| *n.* A colorless gas that is poisonous and burns easily. It is composed of carbon and nitrogen and has the formula C_2N_2. It is sometimes used as a rocket fuel.

cy•a•no•sis |sī′ə **nō′**sĭs| *n.* A condition in which the skin appears blue as a result of too little oxygen in the blood.

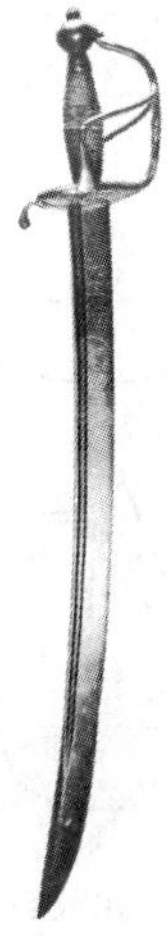

cutlass

The **cutlass** is an obsolete weapon, and in general English the word is only used historically. But it has survived in the English-speaking parts of the Caribbean, such as Jamaica and Guyana, where **cutlass** is the usual word for a machete.

cuttlefish

cy•ber•net•ics |sī′bər nĕt′ĭks| *n.* *(used with a singular verb).* The scientific study of the control processes of electronic, mechanical, and biological systems, especially the mathematical study of the way in which the information essential to these processes is transmitted.

cy•cad |sī′kăd′| *n.* A large tropical plant that resembles a palm tree with fernlike leaves.

cyc•la•mate |sĭk′lə māt′| *or* |sī′klə-| *n.* A salt of cyclamic acid, especially the sodium and calcium salts, used as sweetening agents that do not supply calories.

cyc•la•men |sĭk′lə mən| *or* |sī′klə-|. A plant having showy pink, red, or white flowers with petals that are turned back.

cyc•la•mic acid |sĭk′lə mĭk| *or* |sī′klə-|. An organic chemical compound of carbon, hydrogen, oxygen, nitrogen, and sulfur, having the formula $C_6H_{13}NO_3S$.

cy•cle |sī′kəl| *n.* **1. a.** A single occurrence of an event or series of events that is regularly repeated. **b.** The time during which this event or series of events occurs. **c.** A regularly repeated series of events. **2.** A series of poems, songs, etc., that deal with a single theme or hero. **3.** A bicycle or motorcycle. —*v.* **cy•cled, cy•cling. 1.** To occur in or pass through a cycle. **2.** To ride a bicycle or motorcycle.

cy•clic |sī′klĭk| *or* |sĭk′lĭk| or **cy•cli•cal** |sī′klĭ-kəl| *or* |sĭk′lĭ-| *adj.* **1.** Of or occurring in cycles. **2.** Of chemical compounds having atoms arranged in a ring. —**cy′cli•cal•ly** *adv.*

cy•clist |sī′klĭst| *n.* Someone who rides a motorcycle, bicycle, or similar vehicle.

cy•clone |sī′klōn′| *n.* **1.** An atmospheric disturbance consisting of a mass or rapidly rotating air. In the Southern Hemisphere the direction of rotation is clockwise, while in the Northern Hemisphere the rotation is counterclockwise. **2.** Any violent rotating windstorm, such as a tornado. —**cy•clon′ic** |sī klŏn′ĭk| *adj.*

cyclone cellar. An underground shelter in or near a house, used for protection from violent windstorms such as tornadoes.

cy•clo•tron |sī′klə trŏn′| *n.* An accelerator capable of giving atomic particles energies of up to several tens of millions of electron volts. It accelerates the particles in a spiral path by means of a fixed magnetic field and an electric field whose strength varies with time.

cyg•net |sĭg′nĭt| *n.* A young swan. ¶*These sound alike* **cygnet, signet.**

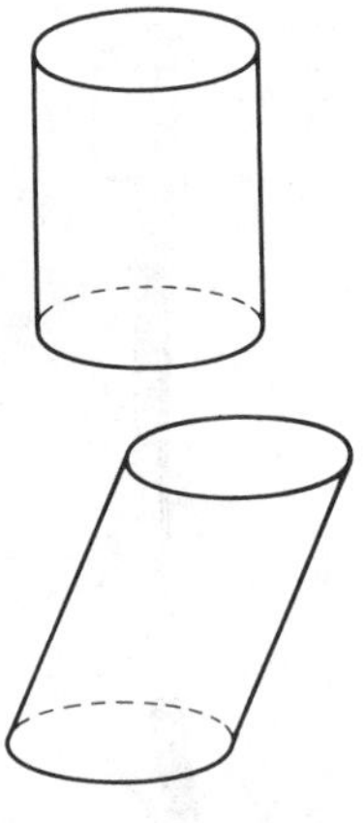

cylinder
right circular cylinder
oblique circular cylinder

cyl•in•der |sĭl′ən dər| *n.* **1. a.** A **cylindrical surface. b.** A figure bounded by a surface of this kind and by two parallel planes that intersect the surface, especially when the given curve used to generate the surface is a circle and the given line is perpendicular to the plane of the circle; a right circular cylinder. **2.** Any object or container having such a shape. **3.** The chamber in which a piston moves back and forth, as in an engine or pump. **4.** The chamber of a revolver that holds the cartridges. **5.** A roller, as one used in a printing press. [SEE PICTURE]

cy•lin•dri•cal |sə lĭn′drĭ kəl| *adj.* Of or shaped like a cylinder. —**cy•lin′dri•cal•ly** *adv.*

cylindrical surface. A surface that contains all the lines that intersect a given plane curve and that are parallel to a given line.

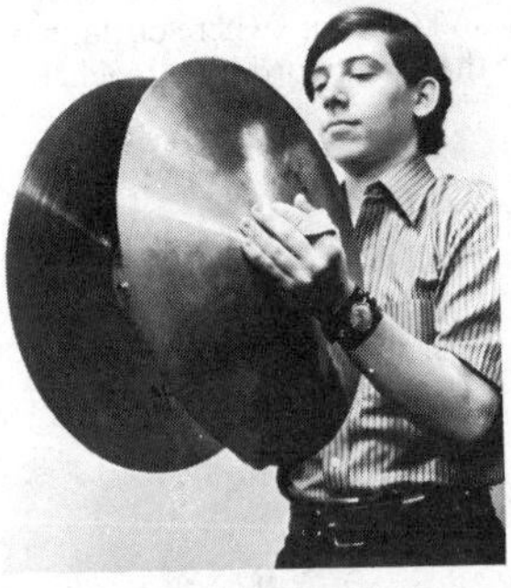

cymbals

cym•bal |sĭm′bəl| *n.* One of a pair of musical percussion instruments consisting of a dish-shaped sheet of brass that is sounded either by being struck with a drumstick or by being struck against another identical sheet of brass. ¶*These sound alike* **cymbal, symbol.** [SEE PICTURE]

cyn•ic |sĭn′ĭk| *n.* A person who believes that all men act entirely out of selfish interests and shows this by being contemptuous and sarcastic.

cyn•i•cal |sĭn′ĭ kəl| *adj.* Contemptuous of the motives or virtues of others; mocking and sneering: *a cynical remark.* —**cyn′i•cal•ly** *adv.*

cyn•i•cism |sĭn′ĭ sĭz′əm| *n.* **1.** A cynical attitude. **2.** A cynical comment or act.

cy•no•sure |sī′nə shŏŏr′| *or* |sĭn′ə-| *n.* A center of attention or interest.

cy•pher |sī′fər| *n.* A form of the word **cipher.**

cy•press |sī′prəs| *n.* **1.** An evergreen tree of warm regions, with small, scalelike needles. **2.** Often **bald cypress.** A related tree that grows in swamps and sheds its needles each year. **3.** The wood of any of these trees.

Cy•prus |sī′prəs|. An island nation in the Mediterranean Sea, south of Turkey. Population, 650,000. Capital, Nicosia.

Cy•ril•lic |sĭ rĭl′ĭk| *adj.* Of the Cyrillic Alphabet.

Cyrillic Alphabet. An old Slavic alphabet used in a modified form for Russian, Bulgarian, and several other Slavic languages.

cyst |sĭst| *n.* **1.** Any sac or bladder in the body, especially an abnormal one composed of a membrane containing a gas, liquid, or soft solid material. **2.** A protective capsulelike structure in which certain organisms enclose themselves during inactive periods.

cys•tic |sĭs′tĭk| *adj.* **1.** Of or like a cyst. **2.** Having, containing, or enclosed in a cyst. **3.** Of the gallbladder or urinary bladder.

cystic fi•bro•sis |fī brō′sĭs|. A congenital disease of mucous glands throughout the body, usually developing in childhood and resulting in disorders of the lungs and pancreas.

cys•ti•tis |sĭ stī′tĭs| *n.* Inflammation of the urinary bladder.

cy•tol•o•gist |sī tŏl′ə jĭst| *n.* A scientist who specializes in cytology.

cy•tol•o•gy |sī tŏl′ə jē| *n.* The scientific study of the formation, structure, and function of cells.

cy•to•plasm |sī′tə plăz′əm| *n.* The protoplasm outside a cell nucleus. —**cy′to•plas′mic** *adj.*

czar |zär| *n.* A former emperor of Russia.

czar•e•vitch |zär′ə vĭch| *n.* The eldest son of a Russian czar.

cza•rev•na |zä rĕv′nə| *n.* **1.** The daughter of a Russian czar. **2.** The wife of a czarevitch.

cza•ri•na |zä rē′nə| *n.* The wife of a Russian czar.

czar•ism |zär′ĭz′əm| *n.* The system of government in Russia under the czars; autocracy.

Czech |chĕk| *n.* **1.** Any native or inhabitant of Czechoslovakia. **2.** A member of one of the two peoples of Czechoslovakia. The other people are the Slovaks. **3.** The Slavic language of Czechoslovakia. —*adj.* Of Czechoslovakia, the Czechs, or their language.

Czech•o•slo•va•ki•a |chĕk′ə slō vä′kē ə| *or* |-văk′ē ə|. A country in central Europe. Population, 15,000,000. Capital, Prague. —**Czech′o•slo′vak, Czech′o•slo•vak′i•an** *adj. & n.*

ă pat/ā pay/â care/ä father/ĕ pet/ ē be/ĭ pit/ī pie/î fierce/ŏ pot/ ō go/ô paw, for/oi oil/ŏŏ book/ ōō boot/ou out/ŭ cut/û fur/ *th* the/th thin/hw which/zh vision/ ə ago, item, pencil, atom, circus

Dd

d, D |dē| *n., pl.* **d's** or **D's. 1.** The fourth letter of the English alphabet. **2. D** The lowest passing grade given to a student. **3. D** The Roman numeral for the number 500. **4. D** In music, the second tone in the scale of C major. [SEE NOTE]
D The symbol for deuterium.
d. 1. died. **2.** In British currency, penny; pence.
D.A. district attorney.
dab¹ |dăb| *v.* **dabbed, dab•bing. 1.** To apply with short, light strokes: *dab grease on a burn.* **2.** To pat quickly and lightly: *dab the face with cold cream.* —*n.* **1.** A small amount, lump, or mass. **2.** A light, poking stroke or pat. [SEE NOTE]
dab² |dăb| *n.* A flatfish related to the flounders. [SEE NOTE]
dab•ble |**dăb'**əl| *v.* **dab•bled, dab•bling. 1.** To splash or spatter: *Raindrops dabbled her dress with spots.* **2.** To splash in and out of water playfully: *She dabbled her feet in the pond.* **3.** To go head down, tail up in shallow water, as some ducks diving for food. **4.** To do or work on something casually, not seriously: *He dabbled in magic.* —**dab'bler** *n.*
da ca•po |dä **kä'**pō|. In music, from the beginning. An Italian phrase used as a direction to repeat the opening section of a composition.
Dac•ca |**dăk'**ə| *or* |**dä'**kə|. The capital of Bangladesh. Population, 1,680,000.
dace |dās| *n., pl.* **dace** or **dac•es.** A small freshwater fish related to the minnows.
dachs•hund |**däks'**ho͝ont'| *or* |**däks'**ho͝ond'| *n.* A small dog with a long body, drooping ears, and very short legs. [SEE PICTURE]
Da•cron |**dā'**krŏn'| *or* |**dăk'**rŏn'| *n.* A trademark for a synthetic textile fiber or fabric that resists stretching and wrinkling.
dad |dăd| *n. Informal.* Father.
dad•dy |**dăd'**ē| *n., pl.* **dad•dies.** *Informal.* Father.
daddy long•legs |**lông'**lĕgz'| *or* |**lŏng'**-| *pl.* **daddy long•legs.** A spiderlike animal with a small, rounded body and long, slender legs.
da•do |**dā'**dō| *n., pl.* **da•does. 1.** A rectangular channel, as one cut in a piece of wood. **2.** A tool, such as a special plane or power-saw blade, used to cut such channels.
daf•fo•dil |**dăf'**ə dĭl| *n.* A garden plant having showy, usually yellow flowers with a trumpet-shaped central part. [SEE PICTURE]
daf•fy |**dăf'**ē| *adj.* **daf•fi•er, daf•fi•est.** *Informal.* **1.** Silly; zany. **2.** Crazy.
daft |dăft| *or* |däft| *adj.* **1.** Crazy; mad. **2.** Foolish; stupid.
da Ga•ma |də **găm'**ə|, **Vasco.** 1469?–1524. Portuguese navigator; sailed around Africa to India.
dag•ger |**dăg'**ər| *n.* **1.** A short, pointed weapon with sharp edges, used for stabbing. **2.** Something that looks or stabs like a dagger, such as a bee's sting. **3.** A dagger-shaped symbol (†) used as a reference mark in printing.
da•guerre•o•type |də **gâr'**ə tīp'| *n.* **1.** An early photographic process in which an image was formed on a silver-coated metal plate that had been treated to make it sensitive to light. **2.** A photograph made by this process.
dahl•ia |**dăl'**yə| *or* |**däl'**-| *n.* A garden plant with showy flowers of various colors.
Da•ho•mey |də **hō'**mē|. Benin.
dai•ly |**dā'**lē| *adj.* **1.** Done, happening, or appearing every day or weekday: *a daily walk.* **2.** For each day: *a daily record.* **3.** Day-to-day; everyday: *daily living; for daily use.* —*adv.* **1.** Every day: *the average amount of food eaten daily.* **2.** Once a day: *Wind the clock daily.* —*n., pl.* **dai•lies.** A newspaper published every day or every weekday.
dain•ty |**dān'**tē| *adj.* **dain•ti•er, dain•ti•est. 1.** Lovely in a fine, delicate way: *dainty embroidery.* **2.** Light, graceful, and carefully precise: *dainty little steps.* **3.** Small and delicate or fancy: *dainty sandwiches.* **4.** Very careful in choosing; fussy; finicky: *a dainty eater.* **5.** Delicious; choice; tasty: *dainty appetizers.* —*n., pl.* **dain•ties.** A choice, delicious food; a delicacy. —**dain'ti•ly** *adv.* —**dain'ti•ness** *n.*
dair•y |**dâr'**ē| *n., pl.* **dair•ies. 1.** A room or building where milk and cream are stored, prepared for use, or made into butter and cheese. **2.** A company or store that prepares or sells milk and milk products. —***modifier:*** *dairy products.* [SEE NOTE at **diary**]
dair•y•ing |**dâr'**ē ĭng| *n.* The business of running a company or store that prepares or sells milk and milk products.
dair•y•maid |**dâr'**ē mād'| *n.* A girl or woman who works in a dairy or on a dairy farm.
dair•y•man |**dâr'**ē mən| *n., pl.* **-men** |-mən|. A man who owns, manages, or works in a dairy.
da•is |**dā'**ĭs| *or* |**dās**| *n.* A raised platform for a throne, a speaker, or a group of honored guests.
dai•sy |**dā'**zē| *n., pl.* **dai•sies.** Any of several plants having flowers with many narrow, petallike rays surrounding a buttonlike center.
Da•kar |dä **kär'**|. The capital and largest city of Senegal. Population, 581,000.
Da•ko•ta |də **kō'**tə| *n., pl.* **Da•ko•ta** or **Da•ko•tas. 1.** A large group of North American Indian tribes commonly called Sioux. **2.** A member of one of these tribes. **3.** The Siouan language of these Indians.

(1) (2) (3) (4)

The letter **D** *comes originally from the Phoenician letter* dāleth *(1), which meant "door." The Greeks borrowed it as* delta *(2); they also turned it on end and gave it a semicircular shape (3). This shape was borrowed by the Romans (4), and it is still the basic shape of our modern capital D.*

dab¹·²

Dab¹ *is probably from Middle Dutch* dabben, *"to touch, tap."* (**Dabble** *comes from a related Dutch word,* dabbelen.) **Dab²** *is of obscure origin.*

dachshund

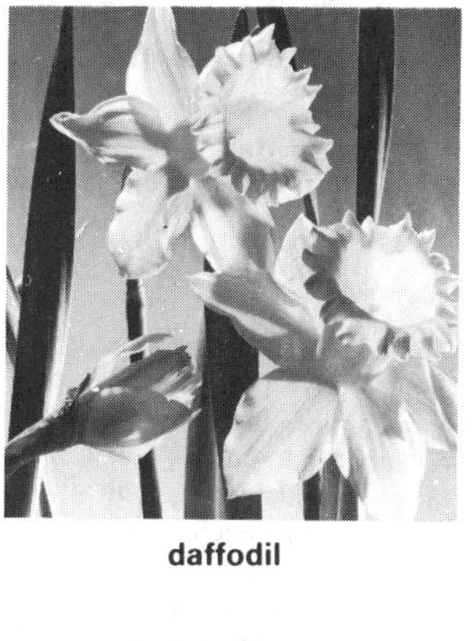

daffodil

Dalmatian

dam[1-2]

Dam[1] *is probably from Low German* dam. **Dam[2]** *is a Middle English variant of* **dame**, *"lady, mother."*

dance

ă pat/ā pay/â care/ä father/ĕ pet/ ē be/ĭ pit/ī pie/î fierce/ŏ pot/ ō go/ô paw, for/oi oil/o͝o book/ o͞o boot/ou out/ŭ cut/û fur/ *th* the/th thin/hw which/zh vision/ ə ago, item, pencil, atom, circus

Da•lai La•ma |dä′lī lä′mə|. The highest priest of Buddhism in Tibet and traditional ruler of Tibet.

dale |dāl| *n.* A valley.

Dal•las |dăl′əs|. A city in northeastern Texas. Population, 904,078.

dal•li•ance |dăl′ē əns| *or* |dăl′yəns| *n.* **1.** Playful flirting. **2.** Dawdling and wasting of time.

dal•ly |dăl′ē| *v.* **dal•lied, dal•ly•ing, dal•lies. 1.** To flirt playfully; toy; trifle: *Don't dally with temptation.* **2.** To waste time; dawdle.

Dal•ma•tian |dăl mā′shən| *n.* A dog having a short, smooth white coat with many small black spots. [SEE PICTURE]

dam[1] |dăm| *n.* **1.** A barrier built across a waterway to control the flow or raise the level of the water. **2.** A body of water controlled by such a barrier. *—v.* **dammed, dam•ming. 1.** To build a dam across (a waterway): *Engineers dammed the river.* **2.** To hold back; restrain; check: *dam back tears; dam up emotions.* **—dammed′** *adj.: a dammed creek.* ¶*These sound alike* **dam, damn.** [SEE NOTE]

dam[2] |dăm| *n.* A female parent of a four-footed animal. ¶*These sound alike* **dam, damn.** [SEE NOTE]

dam•age |dăm′ĭj| *n.* **1. a.** Harm or injury that causes loss or makes a thing less valuable or useful: *damage done to a car in an accident.* **b.** The loss caused or the cost of repair: *Did the damage amount to $100?* **2. damages. a.** In law, money to be paid to make up for an injury or loss: *sue for damages.* **b.** Individual injuries to property or persons: *repair all damages.* *—v.* **dam•aged, dam•ag•ing.** To harm, hurt, or injure: *Some insects damage plants.* **—dam′aged** *adj.: a damaged building.* **—dam′ag•ing** *adj.: Damaging gossip harmed her reputation.*

dam•as•cene |dăm′ə sēn′| *or* |dăm′ə sēn′| *v.* **dam•as•cened, dam•as•cen•ing.** To decorate (metal) with wavy patterns of inlay or etching. *—n.* Etched or inlaid work in metal.

Da•mas•cus |də măs′kəs|. The capital and largest city of Syria. Population, 837,000.

Damascus steel. An early form of steel having wavy markings, developed in the Near East and used mainly for making sword blades.

dam•ask |dăm′əsk| *n.* **1.** A rich, glossy fabric woven with patterns that show on both sides, as a silk used for draperies or a linen used for tablecloths. **2. Damascus steel.** ***—modifier:*** *a damask curtain.*

dame |dām| *n.* **1. Dame.** A title, used somewhat like Mrs., formerly given to the mistress of a household or to a schoolmistress who ran a **dame school,** in which she taught children in her home. **2. Dame.** In Great Britain: **a.** A title of honor corresponding to a knight's title of *Sir.* **b.** The legal title of a knight's or baronet's wife. **3.** Any lady or wife. **4.** *Slang.* A woman.

damn |dăm| *v.* **1.** To condemn as being very bad: *Reviewers damned the show.* **2.** To condemn to everlasting punishment: *Faust's pact with the devil damned him.* **3.** To forget, ignore, or disregard: *Damn the expense.* **4.** To swear at or curse by saying "damn." *—interj.* A word used to express anger, irritation, or disappointment. *—adj. & adv. Informal.* Used as an intensive: *a damn fool. You're damn right.* *—n. Informal.* The least bit; jot: *not worth a damn.* ¶*These sound alike* **damn, dam.**

***Idiom.* give a damn.** *Informal.* To care: *They don't give a damn.*

dam•na•ble |dăm′nə bəl| *adj.* Deserving to be strongly condemned; hateful: *a damnable traitor.* **—dam′na•bly** *adv.*

dam•na•tion |dăm nā′shən| *n.* The condition of being damned to everlasting punishment.

damnd•est or **damned•est** |dăm′dĭst| *adj.* Superlative of **damned.**

***Idiom.* do (one's) damndest.** To do one's very best.

damned |dămd| *adj.* **damned•er, damned•est. 1.** Condemned or doomed: *damned souls.* **2.** *Informal.* **a.** Dreadful; awful: *this damned weather.* **b.** Used as an intensive: *a damned fool; none of your damned business.* *—adv. Informal.* Used as an intensive: *a damned good idea.*

damn•ing |dăm′ĭng| *adj.* Causing someone to be condemned: *damning testimony.*

damp |dămp| *adj.* **damp•er, damp•est. 1.** Slightly wet; moist: *damp ground; a damp sponge.* **2.** Humid: *damp air.* *—n.* **1.** Moisture in the air, on the surface of, or throughout something; humidity: *Don't go out in the damp.* **2.** Fog; mist: *forest dews and damps.* **3.** Any foul or poisonous gas that pollutes the air in a mine. *—v.* **1.** To make damp; moisten: *Perspiration damped his palm.* **2.** To put out (a fire) by cutting off its air supply. **3.** To discourage; cool; lessen: *A peacemaker tries to damp resentments.* **4.** To reduce the strength of (a wave or vibration). **—damp′ly** *adv.* **—damp′ness** *n.*

damp•en |dăm′pən| *v.* **1.** To moisten or become moist: *dampen a sponge. The air dampened.* **2.** To lower, diminish, or depress: *The delay dampened their excitement.*

damp•er |dăm′pər| *n.* **1.** A movable plate in the flue of a furnace or stove for controlling the draft. **2.** Any device that weakens or eliminates waves or vibrations. **3.** One of a set of pads that can be made to press against the strings of a keyboard musical instrument to stop them from sounding. **4.** A depressing or restraining influence: *His disapproval of the wedding put a damper on the party.*

dam•sel |dăm′zəl| *n.* A young girl; maiden.

dam•sel•fly |dăm′zəl flī′| *n., pl.* **-flies.** An insect related to the dragonflies, but smaller and with a slender body and wings that are folded together when at rest.

dam•son |dăm′zən| *n.* **1.** A small, egg-shaped, dark-purple plum. **2.** A tree that bears such plums.

dance |dăns| *or* |däns| *v.* **danced, danc•ing. 1.** To move with rhythmic steps and motions, as when keeping time to music: *They dance gracefully.* **2.** To perform (a special set of steps and motions): *dance the minuet; dance a solo.* **3.** To leap, skip, or prance about: *He was dancing up and down.* **4.** To bob up and down: *daffodils dancing in the breeze.* **5.** To move by dancing: *She danced into the room.* **—danc′ing** *adj.: dancing shadows on the wall.* *—n.* **1.** A set of rhythmic steps and motions, usually performed to music: *a folk dance.* **2.** A party at which people dance: *an informal dance.* **3.** One round or turn of dancing: *May I have this dance?* **4.** Often **the dance.** The art of dancing: *She studied dance.* **5.** A piece of music designed as an accompaniment for dancing. [SEE PICTURE]

danc•er |dăn'sər| *or* |dän'-| *n.* **1.** A person who dances, is dancing, or can dance. **2.** A performer who dances in front of an audience.

dan•de•li•on |dăn'dl ī'ən| *n.* A common, weedy plant with many-rayed yellow flowers and with toothed leaves that are sometimes eaten in salads. After the flowers have bloomed, the ripe seeds form a fluffy, rounded mass. [SEE PICTURE & NOTE]

dan•der[1] |dăn'dər| *n. Informal.* Temper: *His dander is up.*

***Idiom.* get (one's) dander up.** *Informal.* To become angry.

dan•der[2] |dăn'dər| *n.* Tiny particles from the hair or fur of dogs, cats, or other animals, sometimes a cause of allergy in human beings.

dan•dle |dăn'dl| *v.* **dan•dled, dan•dling.** To move (a small child) up and down on the knee or in the arms: *He was dandled on his grandmother's knee.*

dan•druff |dăn'drəf| *n.* Small white scales of skin that are formed on and shed from the scalp.

dan•dy |dăn'dē| *n., pl.* **dan•dies. 1.** A man who prides himself on his elegant clothes and fine appearance. **2.** *Informal.* Something very good of its kind: *This horse is a dandy.* —*adj.* **dan•di•er, dan•di•est.** *Informal.* Very good; fine; first-rate: *That's a dandy idea!*

Dane |dān| *n.* A native of Denmark.

dan•ger |dān'jər| *n.* **1.** The chance, threat, or risk of harm or destruction; peril: *The settlers faced danger with courage.* **2.** The condition of being exposed to harm or loss: *He was in danger of falling.* **3.** A possible cause or chance of harm; a threat or hazard: *Fog is a danger to pilots.* —***modifier:*** *a danger signal.*

dan•ger•ous |dān'jər əs| *adj.* **1.** Full of risk or threat of harm; hazardous: *a dangerous job.* **2.** Able or likely to cause harm: *a dangerous animal.* —**dan'ger•ous•ly** *adv.* —**dan'ger•ous•ness** *n.*

dan•gle |dăng'gəl| *v.* **dan•gled, dan•gling. 1.** To hang loosely and swing or sway: *A key dangled from the chain.* **2.** To cause to swing loosely: *He sat dangling his feet in the water.* **3.** To hang uncertainly or insecurely: *That issue dangles in the balance.*

dangling participle. A participle that is not clearly connected with the word it modifies, so that it seems to modify the wrong word. For example, in the sentence "Sitting at my desk, a loud noise startled me," *sitting* is a dangling participle. (The *noise* doesn't sit.)

Dan•iel |dăn'yəl|. In the Bible, a Hebrew prophet who was thrown into the lions' den and came out unharmed.

Dan•ish |dā'nĭsh| *n.* The Germanic language of Denmark. —*adj.* Of Denmark, the Danes, or their language.

dank |dăngk| *adj.* **dank•er, dank•est.** Uncomfortably damp; chilly and wet: *the dankest of medieval dungeons.* —**dank'ness** *n.*

Dan•te A•li•ghie•ri |dän'tā ä'lē gyâr'ē|. 1265–1321. Italian poet, author of the *Divine Comedy.*

Dan•ube |dăn'yo͞ob|. A river rising in southern Germany and flowing through Austria, Hungary, Yugoslavia, and Rumania into the Black Sea.

daph•ni•a |dăf'nē ə| *n.* A small sea animal related to the shrimps and lobsters. Some kinds are used as food for tropical fish in aquariums.

dap•per |dăp'ər| *adj.* **1.** Neatly dressed; trim; spruce: *a dapper bridegroom.* **2.** Small and active: *a dapper bellboy.*

dap•ple |dăp'əl| *v.* **dap•pled, dap•pling.** To mark with spots, streaks, or patches of a different color or shade: *Sunlight filtering through the leaves dappled the ground.* —*adj.* Dappled: *dapple horses.*

dap•pled |dăp'əld| *adj.* **1.** Marked with spots, streaks, or patches of a different color or shade: *a dappled fawn; dappled gray.* **2.** Full of swiftly changing forms and patterns: *dappled dreams.*

dap•ple-gray |dăp'əl grā'| *adj.* Gray with darker gray markings. [SEE PICTURE]

Dar•da•nelles |där'dn ĕlz'|. A strait in Turkey that, together with the Sea of Marmara and the Bosporus, connects the Mediterranean Sea and the Black Sea.

dare |dâr| *v.* **dared, dar•ing. 1.** To have enough boldness to; be brave enough to: *He did not dare to speak to her. I wonder how he dares to speak up.* Often used without *to* in negative or interrogative sentences or in sentences that indicate doubt: *He dare not speak to her. He wondered whether he dared speak to her. Dare he speak up?* **2.** To have the strength or courage to face or risk: *daring the inclement weather of the steppes. When the situation called for bold measures, he always dared.* **3.** To challenge: *He dared me to climb over the fence. She always dares him to play the champion.* **4. dare say** or **dare•say** |dâr'sā'|. To think (it) very likely: *"I can do better than that," he said. "I dare say you can," replied the old lady.* —*n.* A challenge. [SEE NOTE]

dare•dev•il |dâr'dĕv'əl| *n.* A person who takes risks with reckless boldness. —***modifier:*** *a daredevil stunt pilot; daredevil feats.*

Dar es Sa•laam |där' ĕs sə läm'|. The capital of Tanzania. Population, 757,000.

dar•ing |dâr'ĭng| *adj.* **1.** Willing to take risks; fearless; adventurous: *a daring test pilot.* **2.** Performed or undertaken despite risk; bold; audacious: *a daring plan of escape.* **3.** Going somewhat beyond accepted custom: *a daring outfit.* —*n.* Active bravery; boldness; courage. —**dar'ing•ly** *adv.*

Da•ri•us I |də rī'əs|. 558?–486 B.C. King of Persia, defeated in battle at Marathon.

dark |därk| *adj.* **dark•er, dark•est. 1.** Without light or with very little light: *a dark tunnel.* **2.** Dusky or dim enough to make outlines indistinct or shadowy: *It's getting dark.* **3.** Having no lights on: *go home to a dark house.* **4.** Dim, gray, or cloudy rather than bright: *a dark winter day.* **5.** Reflecting little of the light that strikes it: *a dark color.* **6.** Of a deep shade closer to black or brown than to white: *dark gray; dark skin; a dark cloud.* **7.** Having a deep, low sound: *a dark, velvety tone.* **8.** Tinted to reduce glare: *dark glasses.* **9.** Hopeless; gloomy; dismal; despairing: *He takes a dark view of things.* **10.** Sullen; threatening: *a dark scowl.* **11.** Evil; ominous: *dark deeds.* **12.** Unexplored; mysterious; unknown: *in darkest Africa.* **13.** Secret; hidden: *Keep our plans dark.* **14.** Without knowledge or learning; ignorant: *living in the dark ages.* —*n.* **1.** Absence

dandelion
The name **dandelion** comes from Old French *dent de lion,* "lion's tooth"; its leaves are sharply indented and resemble rows of teeth. See note at **indent.**

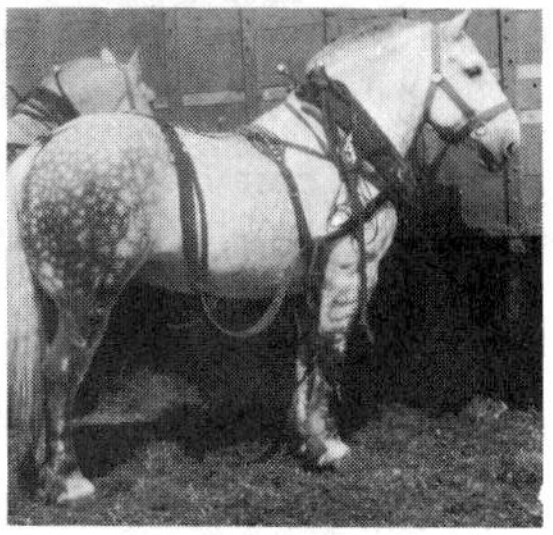

dapple-gray
Dapple-gray horse

dare
Dare, *like* **need,** *is sometimes used as an ordinary verb and sometimes as a modal auxiliary. For example, it is possible to say either* He does not dare to speak *(ordinary verb) or* He dare not speak *(modal auxiliary); in the materials on which this Dictionary was based, these two alternatives were used roughly the same number of times.*

darn[1, 2]

Darn[1] *is probably from Norman French* darne, *"a piece of cloth."* **Darn[2]** *is an example of euphemism, or, as it is sometimes called, "taboo deformation." The word* **damn** *used to be marked by a strong social taboo, so that it could not be spoken at all in polite society. But in the deformed variant* **darn[2]**, *the taboo was softened or avoided entirely.*

data

Datum *is Latin for "something given, a given fact," and* **data** *is its plural, meaning "given facts." But the word* **data** *is increasingly understood as "information" rather than "facts," so that it is often treated as a singular noun. This usage was considered acceptable by 50 per cent of the American Heritage Usage Panel. However, in the school materials on which this Dictionary was based, the traditional plural construction was used far more often than the newer singular. Examples: (plural)* Numerical data are obtained by counting and measuring; *(singular)* This data shows the test scores of six students.

ă pat/ā pay/â care/ä father/ĕ pet/ ē be/ĭ pit/ī pie/î fierce/ŏ pot/ ō go/ô paw, for/oi oil/o͝o book/ o͞o boot/ou out/ŭ cut/û fur/ *th* the/th thin/hw which/zh vision/ ə ago, item, pencil, atom, circus

of light; darkness: *groping around in the dark.* **2.** Night or nightfall: *Come home before dark. Wait until dark.* **3.** A dark shade or color: *the darks and lights in a painting.*

***Idiom.* in the dark.** **1.** In secret. **2.** In ignorance; uninformed: *Don't keep us in the dark about your intentions.*

Dark Ages. The early part of the Middle Ages from about A.D. 500 to about A.D. 1000, thought of as a time when learning was neglected and knowledge hidden away.

dark•en |där′kən| *v.* **1.** To make or become dark or darker: *Clouds darkened the sky. The sky darkened. Twilight darkens into night.* **2.** To grow clouded, sad, or somber: *Her face darkened at the news.* **—dark′ened** *adj.: a darkened room.* **—dark′en•ing** *adj.: the darkening sky.*

dark•ly |därk′lē| *adv.* **1.** With a dark color or shade: *Clouds spread darkly across the sky.* **2.** Mysteriously: *He hinted darkly.* **3.** Threateningly; sullenly: *Her eyes glowered darkly.* **4.** With obscured vision; dimly; faintly: *"For now we see through a glass, darkly"* (The Bible, I Corinthians 13:12).

dark•ness |därk′nĭs| *n.* **1.** Absence of light; partial or total blackness: *the darkness before dawn.* **2.** Night: *Darkness fell quickly.* **3.** Dark quality, shade, or color: *the darkness of her eyes.* **4.** Despair, ignorance, or hopelessness. **5.** Evil: *the forces of darkness.*

dark•room |därk′ro͞om′| *or* |-ro͝om′| *n.* A room in which photographic materials are processed, either in total darkness or under light to which they are not sensitive.

dar•ling |där′lĭng| *n.* **1.** A dearly loved person; beloved: *my darling.* Often used as a term of address: *Hello, darling.* **2.** A favorite: *She's her mother's darling.* **3.** A lovable person: *He's such a darling.* *—adj.* **1.** Dearest; beloved: *my darling girl.* **2.** *Informal.* Charming; adorable: *What darling ducklings!*

darn[1] |därn| *v.* To mend (cloth) by weaving new thread across a hole: *Darn the socks. She darns skillfully.* *—n.* A place repaired by darning. **—darn′er** *n.* [SEE NOTE]

darn[2] |därn| *v.* To swear at or curse by saying "darn." *—interj.* A word used to express anger, irritation, or disappointment. *—adj. & adv. Informal.* Used as an intensive: *a darn fool; a darn good thing.* *—n. Informal.* The least bit; jot: *not worth a darn.* [SEE NOTE]

***Idiom.* give a darn.** *Informal.* To care.

darned |därnd| *adj. & adv. Informal.* Used as an intensive: *a darned liar; a darned good car.*

darning needle. **1.** A long needle with a big eye, using in darning. **2.** A dragonfly.

dart |därt| *v.* **1.** To move suddenly and swiftly: *A squirrel darted across the path.* **2.** To shoot out or send forth with a swift, sudden movement: *They darted furious glances behind them.* *—n.* **1.** A small, arrowlike missile with a sharp point, either thrown at a target by hand or shot from a blowgun, crossbow, etc. **2. darts** *(used with a singular verb).* A game in which darts are thrown at a board or other target. **3.** Anything shaped or shot like a dart: *darts of flame.* **4.** A quick, rapid movement: *A sudden dart downward ended the flight.* **5.** A tapered tuck taken in a garment to make it fit better. ***—modifier:*** *a dart board.*

dar•tle |där′tl| *v.* **dar•tled, dar•tling.** To shoot out repeatedly: *a bright star that dartles red and blue sparks.*

Dar•win |där′wĭn|, **Charles Robert.** 1809–1882. English naturalist who set forth the theory of evolution.

dash |dăsh| *v.* **1.** To race or rush with sudden speed: *He dashed down the stairs. They dashed her to the hospital.* **2.** To strike, knock, or hurl with violent force: *Salt spray dashed against the deck. The storm dashed the ship against the rocks.* **3.** To break or smash by striking violently: *He dashed the glass to the ground.* **4.** To write hurriedly: *dash off a letter.* **5.** To splash: *They dashed water on her to revive her.* **6.** To destroy; wreck; ruin: *He dashed her most cherished hopes.* *—n.* **1.** A quick run or rush: *a dash for shelter.* **2.** A short, fast race: *the 100-yard dash.* **3.** A small amount; a bit: *a dash of spice.* **4.** Lively spirit or style: *entertainers full of dash.* **5.** A swift, short, forceful stroke: *an artist's dashes of color; the dash of oars.* **6.** A punctuation mark (—) used to show a pause, break, or omission or to set off part of a sentence from the rest. **7.** In Morse code, a long sound or signal used in combination with the dot, a shorter sound, to represent letters, numbers, and punctuation.

dash•board |dăsh′bôrd′| *or* |-bōrd′| *n.* The panel beneath the windshield in an automobile, containing instruments, dials, and controls.

dash•ing |dăsh′ĭng| *adj.* **1.** Brave, bold, and daring: *a dashing hero.* **2.** Showy or stylish: *a dashing sport jacket.*

das•tard•ly |dăs′tərd lē| *adj.* **1.** Cowardly, low, and mean: *a dastardly deed.* **2.** Dangerous and disgusting; vile: *a dastardly experiment.*

da•ta |dā′tə| *or* |dăt′ə| *or* |dä′tə| *pl.n.* The less frequently used singular is **da•tum** |dā′təm| *or* |dăt′əm| *or* |dä′təm|. **1.** Information, especially when it is to be analyzed or used as the basis for a decision. **2.** Numerical information suitable for processing by computer. [SEE NOTE]

data processing. Sorting, classification, analysis, and other similar operations performed on numerical information to make it available for further use, especially when done by machines. ***—modifier:*** **(data-processing):** *a data-processing device.*

date[1] |dāt| *n.* **1. a.** Time stated in terms of the month, day, and year or any of these: *The date was May 13, 1851.* **b.** A statement of calendar time: *Put a comma between the day of the month and the year in dates.* **2.** The day of the month: *The date changes at midnight. On what date was the wedding?* **3.** The time when something happened or is to happen: *dates in history; the date set for the picnic.* **4.** The time when something started, existed, or was made or published: *the date of a tree; the date of a book.* **5.** A time or period in history: *Egyptian tombs of an early date.* **6.** *Informal.* A social engagement: *a date for lunch with a client.* **7.** *Informal.* **a.** An appointment to go out socially with a member of the opposite sex: *Tom asked Ann for a date.* **b.** One's partner on a date or dates: *He danced with his date.* *—v.* **dat•ed, dat•ing.** **1.** To mark with a date: *a letter dated May 1; a deed dated 1865.* **2.** To determine the age, time, or origin of: *They dated the rock by studying the fossils in it.* **3.**

Informal. To go on a date or dates with: *Ann dates several boys.* **4.** *Informal.* To go on dates with a partner or as a couple: *Ann dates a lot. Do Ann and Jim date?* —***phrasal verb.*** **date back** (or **back to** or **from**). To have a particular point of origin in the past: *The stone tools dated back thousands of years.*

Idioms. **out of date.** No longer current, valid, or useful: *That information is out of date.* **to date.** Up to the present time: *conclusions based on our experience to date.* **up to date.** In line with current knowledge, modern methods, or recent styles: *bring farming methods up to date.*

date[2] |dāt| *n.* The sweet, one-seeded, oval or oblong fruit of a tropical palm tree, the **date palm.** —***modifier:*** *date groves.*

dat•ed |dā'tĭd| *adj.* **1.** Marked with a date: *a dated receipt.* **2.** Old-fashioned or out of fashion: *a dated style.*

date line. The International Date Line.

date•line |dāt'līn'| *n.* A phrase at the beginning of a news story or report that gives its date and place of origin.

da•tum |dā'təm| *or* |dăt'əm| *or* |dä'təm| *n.* **1.** *pl.* **da•ta** |dā'tə| *or* |dăt'ə| *or* |dä'tə|. An item of information; a unit of data. **2.** *pl.* **da•ta** or **da•tums.** A point, line, or surface used as a reference, as in mapping or geology.

daub |dôb| *v.* **1.** To cover or smear with a soft, sticky substance such as plaster or mud: *The muskrat daubed the walls of his house with mud.* **2.** To paint hastily or crudely: *The children daubed their faces with paint.* —*n.* **1.** An act of daubing. **2.** Something daubed on: *a daub of grease.* **3.** Any soft, sticky coating material: *a house of wattle and daub.* **4.** A crude painting.

daugh•ter |dô'tər| *n.* **1.** One's female child; a female offspring. **2.** Any female descendant: *all the daughters of Eve.*

daughter cell. Any of the offspring cells formed when a cell undergoes division.

daugh•ter-in-law |dô'tər ĭn lô'| *n., pl.* **daugh•ters-in-law.** The wife of one's son.

daunt |dônt| *or* |dänt| *v.* To discourage or dishearten: *The difficulty did not daunt her.*

daunt•less |dônt'lĭs| *or* |dänt'-| *adj.* Not easily discouraged; brave; fearless: *a man of dauntless spirit.* —**daunt'less•ly** *adv.* — **daunt'less•ness** *n.*

dau•phin |dô'fĭn| *n.* The eldest son of a king of France. Used as a title from 1349 to 1830.

dav•en•port |dăv'ən pôrt'| *or* |-pōrt'| *n.* A large sofa, often convertible into a bed.

Da•vid |dā'vĭd|. In the Bible, the second king of Israel, successor to Saul, father of Solomon, and author of many Psalms.

da Vin•ci |də vĭn'chē|, **Leonardo.** 1452–1519. Italian painter, sculptor, architect, scientist, and engineer.

Da•vis |dā'vĭs|, **Jefferson.** 1808–1889. President of the Confederate States of America (1861–65).

dav•it |dăv'ĭt| *or* |dā'vĭt| *n.* A small crane attached to the side of a ship, used for lowering and hoisting small boats. [SEE PICTURE]

Da•vy Jones |dā'vē jōnz'|. The spirit of the sea.

Davy Jones's locker. The bottom of the sea, regarded as the grave of persons drowned or buried at sea.

daw |dô| *n.* The jackdaw.

daw•dle |dôd'l| *v.* **daw•dled, daw•dling. 1.** To take more time than necessary; linger: *No one dawdled over lunch.* **2.** To move slowly and aimlessly; loiter: *She saw him dawdling along the other side of the street.* —**daw'dler** *n.*

dawn |dôn| *n.* **1.** The first appearance of daylight in the morning: *They get up at dawn.* **2.** Early morning when daylight first appears: *the first faint light of dawn. He woke in the gray dawn.* **3.** The first appearance of anything; beginning: *the dawn of another day; before the dawn of recorded history.* —*v.* **1.** To begin to grow light in the morning: *We rose when the day dawned.* **2.** To come into existence; begin; start: *A new age is dawning.* —***phrasal verb.*** **dawn on.** To come as a realization to: *Eventually it dawned on us that he was serious.*

day |dā| *n.* **1.** The time of light between sunrise and sunset. **2. a.** The 24-hour period during which the earth makes one complete rotation on its axis. **b.** The period during which any celestial body makes a similar rotation. **3. a.** One of the numbered 24-hour periods into which a month or year is divided: *nine days before Christmas.* **b.** One of the seven named divisions of a week: *What day was May 21?* **4.** The part of the day devoted to work or study: *the eight-hour day; the school day.* **5.** Often **Day.** A day devoted to some special purpose, event, or observance: *graduation day; New Year's Day.* **6. days.** A period filled with a certain activity: *Your ranching days are over.* **7.** A time: *A day will come when you'll be grown up.* **8.** Often **days.** A particular period of time; age; era: *the present day; these days; in medieval days.* **9. a.** Often **days.** A period of existence: *before the days of automobiles.* **b.** The period of someone's youth, career, achievement, or success: *Both sisters were great belles in their day.* **10. days.** Life; lifetime: *They lived happily for the rest of their days.* **11.** The amount of distance covered in an ordinary day of travel: *The outlaws had a full day's start on the sheriff.* —***modifier:*** *day camp; a day school.*

Idioms. **day after day.** For many days in succession or for an indefinite series of days: *Day after day they worked in the field.* **day in, day out.** Every day without a change or break.

day•break |dā'brāk'| *n.* The time each morning when light first appears; dawn: *They got up before daybreak.*

day-by-day |dā'bī dā'| *adj.* Daily: *the day-by-day work of the ranch.*

day care. The providing of daytime supervision, training, medical services, etc., for children of preschool age or for the elderly. —***modifier:*** **(day-care):** *a day-care center.*

day•dream |dā'drēm'| *n.* A waking dream of the imagination, especially one in which hopes and wishes come true. —*v.* **day•dreamed** or **day•dreamt** |dā'drĕmt'|, **day•dream•ing. 1.** To have daydreams: *daydreaming about space flight.* **2.** To imagine in a daydream or daydreams: *She loves to daydream exciting adventures.* —**day'-dream'er** *n.*

day•light |dā'līt'| *n.* **1.** The light of day; direct light of the sun. **2.** Dawn: *at work before daylight.* **3.** Daytime. —***modifier:*** *daylight hours.*

day•lights |dā'līts'| *pl.n. Slang.* Life; sense; wits: *scare the daylights out of him.*

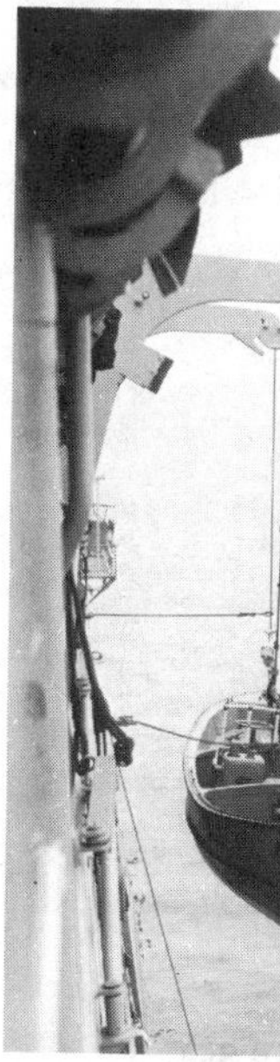

davit

day•light-sav•ing time |dā'līt'sā'vĭng|. Time during which clocks are set one hour ahead of standard time, used in late spring, summer, and early fall to provide extra daylight.

Day of Atonement. **Yom Kippur.**

day•star |dā'stär'| *n.* **1.** The **morning star.** **2.** *Archaic.* The sun.

day•time |dā'tīm'| *n.* The time between dawn and dark; day. —***modifier:*** *the daytime sky.*

day-to-day |dā'tə dā'| *adj.* **1.** Of, done, or happening every day; daily: *day-to-day routine work.* **2.** Limited to one day at a time: *running the company on a day-to-day basis.*

daze |dāz| *v.* **dazed, daz•ing.** To stun or confuse, as with a blow, shock, or surprise: *The noise dazed and deafened them.* —**dazed'** *adj.*: *a dazed look.* —*n.* A stunned or confused condition: *He fell flat and lay there in a daze.*

daz•zle |dăz'əl| *v.* **daz•zled, daz•zling.** **1.** To make nearly or momentarily blind with too much bright light: *The sunlight dazzled her, and she shielded her eyes.* **2.** To amaze, impress, or astonish with a spectacular display: *The pianist dazzled us with his incredible technique. That opera singer never fails to dazzle.* —**daz'zled** *adj.*: *dazzled eyes; dazzled admirers.* —*n.* **1.** Something that dazzles: *The moon was a dazzle of silver in the leaves.* **2.** Blinding brightness; glare: *the dazzle of oncoming headlights.*

daz•zling |dăz'lĭng| *adj.* **1.** So bright as to be blinding: *dazzling sunlight.* **2.** Blazing with light or color: *dazzling jewels.* **3.** Extremely impressive; spectacular: *a dazzling burst of speed.* **4.** Radiantly beautiful: *a dazzling smile.* —**daz'zling•ly** *adv.*

dB decibel.

dc, d.c., DC, D.C. direct current.

D.C. District of Columbia.

D.D.S. Doctor of Dental Surgery.

DDT A powerful insecticide that is also poisonous to human beings and animals. It remains active in the environment for many years.

de–. A prefix meaning: **1.** Reversal: **decode. 2.** Removal: **defrost. 3.** Reduction: **demote.**

dea•con |dē'kən| *n.* **1.** A church officer who assists the minister by performing duties that a layman can perform. **2.** In certain churches, a clergyman ranking below a priest.

dead |dĕd| *adj.* Sometimes **dead•er, dead•est. 1.** No longer alive or living: *dead animals; a dead tree.* **2.** Having lost life: *dead of typhoid fever.* **3.** Marked for certain death; doomed: *A solitary baboon is a dead baboon.* **4.** Lacking live or living things; inanimate; lifeless: *the dead, cold moon; as dead as a stone.* **5.** Insensible; numb: *His frostbitten toes felt dead.* **6.** Not moving or circulating; motionless: *dull dead heat.* **7.** No longer used or needed for use: *a dead language; dead files.* **8.** Out of operation, especially because of a fault or breakdown: *The radio went dead.* **9. a.** Not connected to a source of electric power: *a dead circuit.* **b.** Drained of electricity; discharged: *a dead battery.* **10.** Without activity, interest, or excitement: *This town is dead after 9:00 P.M.* **11.** No longer active: *a dead volcano.* **12.** Having little or no bounce: *a dead ball.* **13. a.** Complete; total; absolute: *dead silence.* **b.** Abrupt: *a dead stop.* **14. a.** Exact: *dead center.* **b.** Sure; certain: *a dead shot.* —*n.* **1.** Those who have died; dead people: *mourn the dead; bury our dead.* **2.** The darkest, coldest, or most silent part: *the dead of night; the dead of winter.* —*adv.* **1. a.** Completely; absolutely: *Surface winds were nearly dead calm.* **b.** Abruptly: *She stopped dead in her tracks.* **2.** Straight; directly: *dead ahead.*

Idiom. **play dead.** To lie motionless on one's back as if dead: *The dog played dead.*

dead•beat |dĕd'bēt'| *n. Slang.* A loafer who sponges on others.

dead•en |dĕd'n| *v.* **1.** To make less intense, keen, or strong: *anesthetics to deaden pain; mufflers to deaden engine noise.* **2.** To take away feeling or sensation from: *deaden a tooth before drilling.* **3.** To discourage and depress: *Dull, repetitious work deadens the spirit.*

dead end. A street, alley, or other passage that is closed or blocked off at one end. —***modifier:*** **(dead-end):** *a dead-end street.*

dead heat. A race in which two or more contestants finish at the same time; a tie.

dead letter. A letter that is not delivered or claimed, usually because the address is wrong or impossible to read.

dead•line |dĕd'līn'| *n.* A set time by which something must be done, finished, or settled; a time limit.

dead•lock |dĕd'lŏk'| *n.* A standstill that occurs when opposing forces are equally strong and neither will give way. —*v.* To bring or come to a deadlock: *The wage dispute deadlocked the labor negotiations. The peace talks deadlocked over treaty terms.*

dead•ly |dĕd'lē| *adj.* **dead•li•er, dead•li•est. 1.** Causing or capable of causing death: *deadly diseases; a deadly weapon.* **2.** Dangerous or violent enough to kill: *a deadly enemy.* **3.** Suggesting death; deathlike: *deadly silence.* **4.** Absolute; utter: *deadly earnestness.* **5.** Extreme; terrible: *deadly strain.* **6.** Extremely accurate or effective: *He sank a deadly hook shot.* **7.** *Informal.* Terribly dull and boring: *a deadly party.* —*adv.* **1.** Completely; utterly: *I'm deadly serious.* **2.** So as to resemble death: *It was deadly cold.*

dead•pan |dĕd'păn'| *adj. Informal.* Characterized by a blank face that betrays no emotion or amusement: *a deadpan expression.*

dead reckoning. A method of navigation in which the position of a ship or aircraft is estimated from its course and speed, the time it was traveled, and whatever is known of winds and currents. The estimated position is not checked by astronomical observations or other navigational aids.

Dead Sea. A salt lake between Israel and Jordan. 1,292 feet below sea level. [SEE NOTE]

deaf |dĕf| *adj.* **deaf•er, deaf•est. 1.** Lacking the ability to hear, either completely or in part. **2.** Unwilling to listen: *He was deaf to their protests.* —**deaf'ness** *n.*

deaf•en |dĕf'ən| *v.* To make deaf, especially temporarily, as by a loud noise: *The explosion deafened him.*

deaf-mute |dĕf'myōōt'| *or* |-myōōt'| *n.* Also **deaf mute.** A person who can neither speak not hear. —***modifier:*** *a deaf-mute child.*

deal |dēl| *v.* **dealt** |dĕlt|, **deal•ing. 1.** To be concerned or involved: *Astronomy deals with the stars and planets.* **2.** To do business; trade or

Dead Sea

The **Dead Sea,** *called in the Bible the "Salt Sea" or the "Sea of the Plain," is intensely hot and still. It has no outlet, and its surface lies 1,292 feet below sea level. Fish cannot live in its waters, which are many times saltier than the ocean and about as salty as Great Salt Lake in Utah.*

The Dead Sea scrolls were discovered, beginning in 1947, in caves on the northwestern shore of the sea. These manuscripts, written about 2,000 years ago, are mostly copies of and commentaries on books of the Bible.

ă **pat**/ā **pay**/â **care**/ä **father**/ĕ **pet**/ ē **be**/ĭ **pit**/ī **pie**/î **fierce**/ŏ **pot**/ ō **go**/ô **paw**, **for**/oi **oil**/ŏŏ **book**/ ōō **boot**/ou **out**/ŭ **cut**/û **fur**/ *th* **the**/th **thin**/hw **which**/zh **vision**/ ə **ago**, **item**, **pencil**, **atom**, **circus**

bargain: *a merchant who deals in diamonds; a trader who deals with the Indians.* **3.** To give: *The judge dealt out harsh sentences. The champion dealt his opponent a mighty blow.* **4.** To hand out (cards) to players in a card game: *Deal the cards. It's your turn to deal.* —***phrasal verb.*** **deal with. 1.** To behave toward; treat: *He dealt with them as equals.* **2.** To handle or manage; take care of; cope with: *deal with an emergency.* —*n.* **1.** *Informal.* An agreement or bargain, as in business or politics: *It's a deal.* **2. a.** The distribution of playing cards. **b.** A player's turn to deal. **c.** A hand of cards dealt. —**deal'er** *n.*

Idiom. **a great** (or **good**) **deal. 1.** A considerable amount; a lot: *We learned a great deal.* **2.** Much; considerably: *a good deal thinner.*

deal•ing |dē'lĭng| *n.* **1. dealings.** Agreements or relations with others, especially when involving money or trade: *business dealings.* **2.** Treatment of others: *fair dealing.*

dealt |dĕlt|. Past tense and past participle of **deal.**

dean |dēn| *n.* **1.** An official of a college or university in charge of a certain school or faculty: *dean of the Faculty of Law.* **2.** An official of a college or high school who counsels students and enforces rules: *dean of women.* **3.** The head clergyman in charge of a cathedral: *the dean of St. Paul's.* **4.** The oldest or most respected member of a group or profession: *the dean of American medicine.*

dear |dîr| *adj.* **dear•er, dear•est. 1. a.** Loved and cherished: *his dear ones; my dearest friend.* **b.** Greatly valued; precious: *everything dear to them.* **2.** Highly esteemed or regarded. Often used as a term of address in speaking or writing letters: *my dear fellow; Dear Sir.* **3.** Close to the heart: *your dearest interests.* **4.** High in price; expensive; costly: *Steak is too dear to waste.* —*adv.* At a high cost: *You will pay dear for that mistake.* —*n.* **1.** A dearly loved person: *my own dear.* Often used as a term of address: *Yes, dear.* **2.** A person of whom one is fond: *the poor dear.* —*interj.* A word used to express distress or surprise: *Oh dear! Dear me!* ¶*These sound alike* **dear, deer.** —**dear'ly** *adv.* —**dear'ness** *n.* [SEE NOTE]

dearth |dûrth| *n.* **1.** Lack; scarcity: *a dearth of medical knowledge.* **2.** Famine.

death |dĕth| *n.* **1. a.** The act or fact of dying: *the hour of her death.* **b.** The end of life: *remain true until death.* **2.** The condition of being dead: *He lay still, pretending death.* **3.** A manner of dying: *a painless death.* **4.** A cause of dying: *Such a fall is certain death.* **5.** The destroyer of life, thought of as a person, skeleton, poison, etc.: *"Death, be not proud"* (John Donne). *"The valiant never taste of death but once"* (Shakespeare). **6.** The ending, destruction, or extinction of anything: *the death of a dream; the death of stars.* **7.** A dull, dreary existence without enjoyment or hope of change: *a living death.* **8.** Execution: *a crime punishable by death.* —***modifier:*** *the death penalty.*

Idioms. **put to death.** To kill or execute: *The condemned man was put to death.* **to death. 1.** So as to die: *He feared the explorers would freeze to death.* **2.** To an extreme degree; very much: *bored to death.* **to the death.** Until one kills, is killed, or dies: *a fight to the death.*

death•bed |dĕth'bĕd'| *n.* **1.** The bed on which a person dies. **2.** A dying person's last hours of life. —***modifier:*** *a deathbed conversion.*

death•blow |dĕth'blō'| *n.* A fatal blow, event, or occurrence: *An earthquake proved to be the deathblow to their plans.*

death cup. A poisonous white or whitish mushroom with a cuplike swelling at the base of the stalk.

death•less |dĕth'lĭs| *adj.* Enduring forever; undying; immortal: *deathless fame.*

death•like |dĕth'līk'| *adj.* Suggesting or resembling death; deathly: *a deathlike hush.*

death•ly |dĕth'lē| *adj.* **1.** Suggesting death; deathlike: *a deathly pallor.* **2.** Extreme; terrible: *a deathly fear of snakes.* **3.** Causing death; fatal. —*adv.* **1.** So as to resemble death: *She was deathly pale.* **2.** Very: *deathly ill.*

death rate. 1. The number of deaths in a given unit of population in a given period of time. **2.** The percentage of people who die after contracting a given disease; fatality rate.

death's-head |dĕths'hĕd'| *n.* The human skull as a symbol of death. [SEE PICTURE]

Death Valley. A desert valley in southeastern California and western Nevada, containing the lowest point in the Western Hemisphere (282 feet below sea level).

de•ba•cle |dā bä'kəl| *or* |-băk'əl| *or* |də-| *n.* A sudden, disastrous collapse, downfall, or defeat.

de•bar |dē bär'| *v.* **de•barred, de•bar•ring.** To forbid, prohibit, exclude, or bar: *He was debarred from exercising his profession.*

de•bark |dĭ bärk'| *v.* **1.** To unload, as from a ship: *debark passengers.* **2.** To disembark: *American tourists debarked at the port.* —**de'bar•ka'tion** |dē'bär kā'shən| *n.*

de•base |dĭ bās'| *v.* **de•based, de•bas•ing.** To lower in character, quality, dignity, or worth: *Don't debase the language by misusing it. Inflation debases the currency.* —**de•base'ment** *n.*

de•bat•a•ble |dĭ bā'tə bəl| *adj.* Open to question, argument, or dispute: *a debatable theory.*

de•bate |dĭ bāt'| *n.* **1. a.** A discussion or consideration of the arguments for and against something: *a dull Senate debate.* **b.** An argument or dispute between persons holding opposing views: *The proposal to raise taxes provoked violent debates.* **2.** A formal contest in which opponents argue for opposite sides of an issue. **3.** Discussion or argument: *She has a logical mind in debate.* —*v.* **de•bat•ed, de•bat•ing. 1.** To present or discuss arguments for and against (a question, theory, proposal, etc.): *We debated the motion before voting. Debate and vote seriously.* **2.** To consider and try to decide: *I was debating what to do.* **3.** To call into question; argue about; dispute: *The wisdom of that decision is still debated.* **4.** To engage in a formal public argument over an issue or issues: *Lincoln and Douglas debated. Lincoln debated Douglas.* —**de•bat'ing** *adj.:* *the debating team.* —**de•bat'er** *n.*

de•bauch |dĭ bôch'| *v.* To lead away from good toward evil; corrupt morally.

de•bauch•er•y |dĭ bô'chə rē| *n.* Too much indulgence in weakening or corrupting pleasures.

de•bil•i•tate |dĭ bĭl'ĭ tāt'| *v.* **de•bil•i•tat•ed, de•bil•i•tat•ing.** To make feeble; weaken: *The disease debilitated her body.*

dear

Sense 4, "expensive," of **dear** *is becoming rare and sounds quite strange to many people; but it is close to the original meaning of the word. It was* dēore *in Old English, and it descends from prehistoric Germanic* deuriaz, *which meant "valuable, beloved." The practice of beginning a letter, even to a stranger, with* Dear ---- *or* Dear Sir *originated with the elaborate politeness of the seventeenth century.*

death's-head

debt
The unpronounced b *in this word is due to pure perversity. Late Latin* dēbita, *"things owed, debt," passed into Old French as* dette *(a completely regular development), which was borrowed into Middle English as* det *or* dette. *The spelling* det *and the pronunciation* /dĕt/ *were now in complete agreement. But in the thirteenth century, the Old French word was respelled* debte *by people who knew its Latin origin and wanted to "restore" the lost* b; *the English followed suit and respelled* det *as* **debt**; *and thus we are left with one of the unique and pointless oddities for which English is remarkable. Note that the French thought better of it and have returned to the spelling* dette.

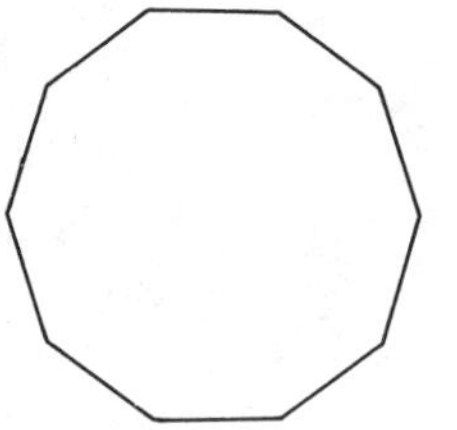

decagon

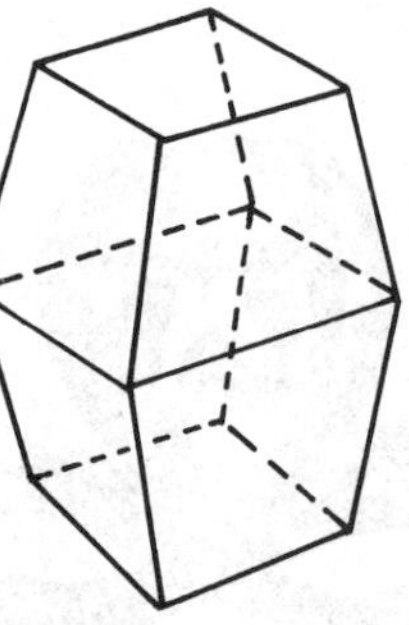

decahedron

ă pat/ā pay/â care/ä father/ĕ pet/ ē be/ĭ pit/ī pie/î fierce/ŏ pot/ ō go/ô paw, for/oi oil/ŏŏ book/ ōō boot/ou out/ŭ cut/û fur/ *th* the/th thin/hw which/zh vision/ ə ago, item, pencil, atom, circus

de•bil•i•ty |dĭ **bĭl'**ĭ tē| *n., pl.* **de•bil•i•ties.** Abnormal bodily weakness; feebleness.

deb•it |**dĕb'**ĭt| *n.* A debt charged to and recorded in an account. —*v.* To charge with or as a debt: *Debit my account with $10. Debit the purchase to my account.*

deb•o•nair, also **deb•o•naire** |dĕb'ə **nâr'**| *adj.* **1.** Having a cheerful, carefree, self-confident air; jaunty: *a debonair man about town.* **2.** Gracious and charming: *She was polite and debonair.*

de•brief |dē **brēf'**| *v.* **1.** To question in order to obtain knowledge gathered on a mission: *Astronauts are debriefed after returning from the moon.* **2.** To instruct (a government agent or similar employee) not to reveal classified or secret information after his employment has ceased.

de•bris, also **dé•bris** |də **brē'**| *or* |**dā'**brē'| *n.* The scattered remains of something broken, destroyed, or discarded; fragments; rubble.

debt |dĕt| *n.* **1.** Something, such as money, owed by one person to another: *a $200 debt. The people owed him an immense debt for his services to the country.* **2.** The condition of owing; indebtedness. [SEE NOTE]

debt•or |**dĕt'**ər| *n.* A person who owes something to another.

de•bunk |dē **bŭngk'**| *v. Informal.* To expose or ridicule the falseness or exaggerated claims of: *The writer debunked television commercials.*

De•bus•sy |də **byōō'**sē| *or* |dĕb'yōō **sē'**|, **Claude.** 1862–1918. French composer.

de•but, also **dé•but** |dā **byōō'**| *or* |dĭ-| *or* |**dā'**byōō'| *n.* **1.** A first public appearance, as of an actor on the stage. **2.** The formal presentation of a girl to society.

deb•u•tante, also **dé•bu•tante** |**dĕb'**yōō tänt'| *or* |**dā'**byōō-| *or* |dĕb'yōō **tänt'**| *n.* A young woman making a debut into society.

Dec. December.

deca–. A word element meaning "ten": **decagon; decathlon.**

dec•ade |**dĕk'**ād'| *n.* **1.** A group of ten. **2.** A period of ten years.

dec•a•dence |**dĕk'**ə dəns| *or* |dĭ **kād'**ns| *n.* A process, condition, or period of deterioration or decline, as in morals or art.

dec•a•dent |**dĕk'**ə dənt| *or* |dĭ **kād'**nt| *adj.* Marked by or in a condition of decadence: *a decadent empire; a decadent society.*

dec•a•gon |**dĕk'**ə gŏn'| *n.* A plane geometric figure having ten sides and ten angles. [SEE PICTURE]

dec•a•he•dron |dĕk'ə **hē'**drən| *n.* A solid geometric figure that is bounded by ten plane faces. [SEE PICTURE]

Dec•a•logue, also **Dec•a•log, dec•a•logue, dec•a•log** |**dĕk'**ə lôg'| *or* |-lŏg'| *n.* The **Ten Commandments.**

de•camp |dĭ **kămp'**| *v.* **1.** To pack up and leave a camping ground; break camp: *The battalion decamped at night.* **2.** To leave secretly or suddenly; run away: *The thief decamped when the police arrived.*

de•cant |dĭ **kănt'**| *v.* To pour (a liquid, especially wine) from one container into another.

de•cant•er |dĭ **kăn'**tər| *n.* A decorative glass bottle used for holding liquids, such as wine.

de•cap•i•tate |dĭ **kăp'**ĭ tāt'| *v.* **de•cap•i•tat•ed, de•cap•i•tat•ing.** To cut off the head of; behead.

de•cath•lon |dĭ **kăth'**lən| *or* |-lŏn'| *n.* An athletic contest in which each contestant participates in ten different track and field events.

de•cay |dĭ **kā'**| *v.* **1.** To rot or cause to become rotten; decompose: *Fungi decay wood. Dead trees gradually decay.* **2.** To lose radioactive atoms as a result of nuclear disintegrations. **3.** To decline in health or strength; waste away. —*n.* **1.** The breaking down or decomposition of plant or animal substances by the action of bacteria or fungi. **2. Radioactive decay. 3.** A gradual deterioration to an inferior state.

de•cease |dĭ **sēs'**| *n.* Death.

de•ceased |dĭ **sēst'**| *adj.* No longer living; dead: *my deceased father.* —*n.* **the deceased.** A dead person or persons.

de•ce•dent |dĭ **sēd'**nt| *n.* In law, the deceased.

de•ceit |dĭ **sēt'**| *n.* The act or practice of deceiving; dishonesty.

de•ceit•ful |dĭ **sēt'**fəl| *adj.* **1.** Practicing deceit; false; lying. **2.** Deliberately misleading; deceptive: *a deceitful advertisement.* —**de•ceit'ful•ly** *adv.* —**de•ceit'ful•ness** *n.*

de•ceive |dĭ **sēv'**| *v.* **de•ceived, de•ceiv•ing.** To make (a person) believe something that is not true; mislead. —**de•ceiv'er** *n.*

de•cel•er•ate |dē **sĕl'**ə rāt'| *v.* **de•cel•er•at•ed, de•cel•er•at•ing.** **1.** To decrease the speed of. **2.** To decrease in speed.

de•cel•er•a•tion |dē sĕl'ə **rā'**shən| *n.* **1.** The act or process of decelerating. **2.** The rate at which something decelerates.

De•cem•ber |dĭ **sĕm'**bər| *n.* The 12th month of the year, after November and before January. It has 31 days. —**modifier:** *December snow.*

de•cent |**dē'**sənt| *adj.* **1.** Conforming to the standards of propriety; proper: *decent behavior.* **2.** Kind; considerate: *It was decent of her to let you have it.* **3.** Adequate; passable: *a decent salary.* **4.** *Informal.* Properly or modestly dressed. —**de'cen•cy** *n.* —**de'cent•ly** *adv.*

de•cen•tral•ize |dē **sĕn'**trə līz'| *v.* **de•cen•tral•ized, de•cen•tral•iz•ing.** **1.** To distribute the functions or powers of (a government, central authority, etc.) among several local authorities: *decentralize a school system.* **2.** To cause to withdraw from an area of concentration: *decentralize an industry.* —**de•cen'tral•i•za'tion** *n.*

de•cep•tion |dĭ **sĕp'**shən| *n.* **1.** The act of deceiving: *practice deception.* **2.** Something that deceives, as a trick or lie.

de•cep•tive |dĭ **sĕp'**tĭv| *adj.* Intended or tending to deceive: *deceptive methods; the deceptive calm before the storm.* —**de•cep'tive•ly** *adv.*

deci–. A word element meaning "one-tenth": **deciliter.**

dec•i•bel |**dĕs'**ə bəl| *or* |-bĕl'| *n.* A unit used in expressing the loudness of sounds.

de•cide |dĭ **sīd'**| *v.* **de•cid•ed, de•cid•ing.** **1.** To reach or cause to make a decision: *Have you decided what you will do? What decided you to leave the company?* **2. a.** To determine or settle (a question, doubt, outcome, etc.): *The court decided the case.* **b.** To give a judgment: *The judge decided against the defendant.*

de•cid•ed |dĭ **sī'**dĭd| *adj.* **1.** Clear-cut; definite; unquestionable: *a decided advantage.* **2.** Resolute; unhesitating: *He has a decided manner of talking.* —**de•cid'ed•ly** *adv.*

de•cid•u•ous |dĭ sĭj′o͞o əs| *adj.* **1.** Falling off at the end of a season or growing period: *the deciduous leaves of the maple; deer with deciduous antlers.* **2.** Shedding leaves at the end of the growing season: *deciduous trees.*

dec•i•li•ter |**dĕs**′ə lē′tər| *n.* A unit of volume equal to one-tenth of a liter.

dec•i•mal |**dĕs**′ə məl| *n.* **1.** A numeral in the decimal system of numeration. **2.** A numeral based on 10, used with a decimal point in expressing a decimal fraction. —*adj.* **1.** Of or based on 10. **2.** Of, expressed as, or capable of being expressed as a decimal.

decimal fraction. A fraction in which the denominator is 10 or a power of 10. In the decimal system of numeration, 29/100 would be written .29, and 29/1000 would be written .029.

decimal place. The relative position of a digit to the right of a decimal point, the position immediately to the right of the point being the first, the next to the right the second, etc. For example, .079 has three decimal places.

decimal point. A period placed at the left of a decimal numeral that represents a decimal fraction to distinguish it from an integer, or between the fractional and integral parts of a decimal mixed numeral.

decimal system of numeration. A system of numeration, based on 10, in which the numbers are represented using the digits 0, 1, 2, 3, 4, 5, 6, 7, 8, 9.

dec•i•mate |**dĕs**′ə māt′| *v.* **dec•i•mat•ed, dec•i•mat•ing.** To destroy or kill a large part of: *The tidal wave decimated the population.* —**dec′i•ma′tion** *n.* [SEE NOTE]

dec•i•me•ter |**dĕs**′ə mē′tər| *n.* A unit of length equal to one-tenth of a meter.

de•ci•pher |dĭ **sī**′fər| *v.* **1.** To change (a message) from a code or cipher to ordinary language; decode. **2.** To read or interpret (something hard to understand or illegible).

de•ci•sion |dĭ **sĭzh**′ən| *n.* **1.** A final or definite conclusion; a judgment: *made a decision about what should be done; a jury's decision.* **2.** Firmness of character or action; determination: *a man of decision.*

de•ci•sive |dĭ **sī**′sĭv| *adj.* **1.** Having the power to settle something; conclusive: *a decisive argument; a decisive victory.* **2.** Characterized by decision and firmness; resolute: *a decisive person.* —**de•ci′sive•ly** *adv.* —**de•ci′sive•ness** *n.*

deck |dĕk| *n.* **1. a.** One of the horizontal partitions dividing a ship into different levels. **b.** Any of the levels aboard a ship. **2.** Any platform like the deck of a ship: *a sun deck.* **3.** A pack of playing cards. —*v.* To decorate or adorn: *She decked herself out for a party.*

***Idiom.* on deck.** *Slang.* On hand; standing by.

deck hand. A member of a ship's crew assigned to work on deck.

de•claim |dĭ **klām**′| *v.* **1.** To speak loudly, pompously, or in a theatrical manner. **2.** To recite formally: *declaim a poem.*

dec•la•ma•tion |dĕk′lə **mā**′shən| *n.* **1.** The act of declaiming. **2.** Something declaimed.

de•clam•a•to•ry |dĭ **klăm**′ə tôr′ē| *or* |-tōr′ē| *adj.* **1.** Of or suitable for declaiming: *a declamatory poem.* **2.** Pretentious and bombastic: *a long declamatory explanation.*

dec•la•ra•tion |dĕk′lə **rā**′shən| *n.* **1.** A formal statement or announcement. **2.** A document listing goods that are taxable or subject to duty.

Declaration of Independence. A proclamation, adopted on July 4, 1776, declaring the 13 American colonies independent of Great Britain.

de•clar•a•tive |dĭ **klăr**′ə tĭv| *adj.* Making a statement; not being a question or order: *a declarative sentence.*

de•clare |dĭ **klâr**′| *v.* **de•clared, de•clar•ing.** **1.** To state with emphasis; affirm: *He declared that he was right.* **2.** To state officially or formally: *Congress declared war.* **3.** To announce one's choice, opinion, etc.: *declare for a candidate.* **4.** To make a full statement of (dutiable goods) when entering a country at customs.

de•clen•sion |dĭ **klĕn**′shən| *n.* **1.** In certain languages, the inflection of nouns, pronouns, and adjectives in such categories as case, number, or gender. **2.** A class of words of one language with the same or a similar system of inflections.

dec•li•na•tion |dĕk′lə **nā**′shən| *n.* **1. Magnetic declination.** **2.** The angular distance to a point on the celestial sphere, measured north or south of the celestial equator along a great circle that passes through the point and both of the celestial poles.

de•cline |dĭ **klīn**′| *v.* **de•clined, de•clin•ing.** **1.** To refuse to accept or do: *decline an offer. I asked him to do it, but he declined.* **2.** To become less or decrease, as in strength, value, etc.: *A person's health declines in old age. Prices declined.* **3.** To slope downward. **4.** In certain languages, to give the inflected forms of (a noun, pronoun, or adjective). —*n.* **1.** The process or result of declining; deterioration: *The country was in a period of decline.* **2.** A change to a lower level or state: *a decline in prices.* **3.** A downward slope.

de•cliv•i•ty |dĭ **klĭv**′ĭ tē| *n., pl.* **de•cliv•i•ties.** A downward slope, as of a hill.

de•coct |dĭ **kŏkt**′| *v.* To extract (the flavor or active principle of) by boiling.

de•coc•tion |dĭ **kŏk**′shən| *n.* **1.** The act or process of decocting. **2.** A substance obtained by decocting.

de•code |dē **kōd**′| *v.* **de•cod•ed, de•cod•ing.** To change (information) from a form that is in code to a form suitable for use.

dé•colle•té |dā′kŏl **tā**′| *adj.* **1.** Having a low neckline, as an evening dress. **2.** Wearing a dress with a low neckline. [SEE PICTURE]

de•com•pose |dē′kəm **pōz**′| *v.* **de•com•posed, de•com•pos•ing.** **1.** To separate or break down into component parts or basic elements. **2.** To decay; rot. —**de•com′po•si′tion** *n.*

de•com•press |dē′kəm **prĕs**′| *v.* **1.** To release from pressure or compression. **2.** To return (a person who has been working in or breathing compressed air) to normal atmospheric pressure, especially at a rate that is slow enough to be safe. —**de′com•pres′sion** *n.*

decompression sickness. Caisson disease.

de•con•tam•i•nate |dē′kən **tăm**′ə nāt′| *v.* **de•con•tam•i•nat•ed, de•con•tam•i•nat•ing.** **1.** To free of contamination. **2.** To make safe by freeing of harmful substances, such as poisonous chemicals or radioactive materials. —**de′con•tam′i•na′tion** *n.*

decimate

Decimate *comes from Latin* decimāre, *"to kill every tenth man," from* decimus, *"tenth." This was the traditional Roman punishment for troops who mutinied or who allowed legionary standards to be captured by the enemy. One man in every ten, selected by lot, was executed. This was actually carried out on a number of historic occasions. The practice has occasionally been revived in modern times, as it was by the English in Ireland in the seventeenth century.*

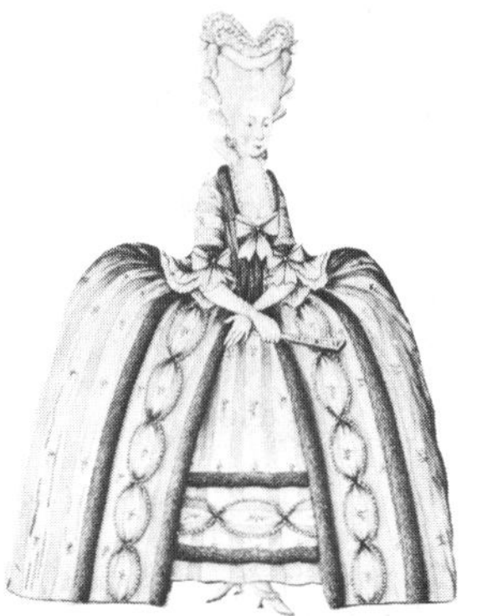

décolleté

decoy
Painted wooden decoy of a swan

deduce/deduct
Deduce *and* **deduct** *were both borrowed, in the early sixteenth century, from Latin* dēdūcere, *"to lead or bring away":* dē-, *"away,"* + dūcere, *"to lead." This word developed two specific senses:* **a.** *"to subtract" and* **b.** *(in Medieval Latin) "to derive a conclusion from, to infer."* **Deduce** *and* **deduct** *were at first used interchangeably (and confusingly), but gradually separated out into their present meanings.* **Deduction,** *however, still serves as the noun for both of them.*

deer

ă pat/ā pay/â care/ä father/ĕ pet/ ē be/ĭ pit/ī pie/î fierce/ŏ pot/ ō go/ô paw, for/oi oil/o͝o book/ o͞o boot/ou out/ŭ cut/û fur/ *th* the/th thin/hw which/zh vision/ ə ago, item, pencil, atom, circus

de•con•trol |dē'kən **trōl'**| *v.* **de•con•trolled, de•con•trol•ling.** To free from control, especially from government control: *decontrol prices.*

dé•cor, also **de•cor** |**dā'**kôr'| *or* |dā **kôr'**| *n.* **1.** The decorative style of a room, home, restaurant, etc. **2.** Stage scenery. **3.** Decoration; ornamentation.

dec•o•rate |**dĕk'**ə rāt'| *v.* **dec•o•rat•ed, dec•o•rat•ing. 1.** To furnish with something attractive, beautiful, or striking; adorn: *decorate a Christmas tree.* **2.** To paint, paper, and select and organize the furnishings of (a room, house, etc.): *decorate a new home.* **3.** To confer a medal or honor upon: *decorate a soldier for bravery.*

dec•o•ra•tion |dĕk'ə **rā'**shən| *n.* **1.** The act or process of decorating. **2.** Something that adorns or beautifies; an ornament. **3.** A medal awarded for bravery or heroism.

Decoration Day. Memorial Day.

dec•o•ra•tive |**dĕk'**ər ə tĭv| *or* |**dĕk'**ə rā'-| *adj.* Serving to decorate; ornamental: *a decorative design.* —**dec'o•ra•tive•ly** *adv.*

dec•o•ra•tor |**dĕk'**ə rā'tər| *n.* A person who decorates, especially an interior decorator.

dec•o•rous |**dĕk'**ər əs| *or* |dĭ **kôr'**əs| *or* |-**kōr'**-| *adj.* Showing decorum; proper: *decorous language; decorous behavior.* —**dec'o•rous•ness** *n.*

de•co•rum |dĭ **kôr'**əm| *or* |-**kōr'**-| *n.* Appropriateness of behavior or conduct; propriety.

de•coy |**dē'**koi'| *or* |dĭ **koi'**| *n.* **1.** A model of a duck or other bird, used by hunters to attract wild birds or animals. **2.** A person who leads another into danger or a trap. —*v.* |dĭ **koi'**|. To lure into danger or a trap. [SEE PICTURE]

de•crease |dĭ **krēs'**| *v.* **de•creased, de•creas•ing.** To make or become gradually less or smaller; diminish: *decrease one's speed. Our supply of food is rapidly decreasing.* —*n.* |**dē'**krēs'| *or* |dĭ-**krēs'**|. The act or process of decreasing; a decline: *a decrease in production.*

de•cree |dĭ **krē'**| *n.* **1.** An authoritative order; a law; edict. **2.** The judgment of a court. —*v.* **de•creed, de•cree•ing.** To establish or decide by decree.

dec•re•ment |**dĕk'**rə mənt| *n.* In mathematics, the amount by which a variable decreases or is decreased.

de•crep•it |dĭ **krĕp'**ĭt| *adj.* In poor condition because of old age or long use; worn-out; broken-down: *a decrepit old man; a decrepit car.* —**de•crep'it•ly** *adv.*

de•crep•i•tude |dĭ **krĕp'**ĭ to͞od'| *or* |-tyo͞od'| *n.* The condition of being decrepit; weakness.

de•cres•cen•do |dē'krə **shĕn'**dō| *or* |dā'-|. In music: *n., pl.* **de•cres•cen•dos. 1.** A gradual decrease in loudness; diminuendo. **2.** A musical passage performed with a decrescendo. —*adj.* Gradually decreasing in loudness. —*adv.* With a decrescendo.

de•cry |dĭ **krī'**| *v.* **de•cried, de•cry•ing, de•cries.** To condemn as being wrong or bad: *The senator decried the President's action.*

ded•i•cate |**dĕd'**ĭ kāt'| *v.* **ded•i•cat•ed, ded•i•cat•ing. 1.** To set apart for a special purpose: *dedicate a church.* **2.** To give or commit (oneself) fully to something, such as a course of action; devote: *The scientist dedicated himself to research.* **3.** To address (a book, performance, etc.) to someone as a mark of respect.

ded•i•ca•tion |dĕd'ĭ **kā'**shən| *n.* **1.** The act of dedicating: *the dedication of a building.* **2.** The condition of being dedicated: *dedication to duty.* **3.** A note in a book, musical composition, etc., dedicating it to someone.

de•duce |dĭ **do͞os'**| *or* |-**dyo͞os'**| *v.* **de•duced, de•duc•ing. 1.** To reach (a conclusion) by reasoning. **2.** To reach (a conclusion) that follows directly from one or more general principles; determine by logical deduction. [SEE NOTE]

de•duct |dĭ **dŭkt'**| *v.* To take away (a quantity from another); subtract: *A company deducts an amount from a person's salary to pay his income tax.* [SEE NOTE]

de•duct•i•ble |dĭ **dŭk'**tə bəl| *adj.* Capable of being deducted, especially exempt from inclusion in one's income in figuring the tax on it.

de•duc•tion |dĭ **dŭk'**shən| *n.* **1.** The act of deducting; subtraction. **2.** Something that is or may be deducted: *Certain business expenses are legitimate tax deductions.* **3. a.** The act or process of deducing. **b.** A method of logical reasoning in which each conclusion necessarily follows from the propositions stated. **c.** A conclusion reached by this method.

de•duc•tive |dĭ **dŭk'**tĭv| *adj.* Of or involving logical deduction. —**de•duc'tive•ly** *adv.*

deed |dēd| *n.* **1.** An act or thing done; action: *do a good deed.* **2.** A legal document showing ownership of property. —*v.* To transfer or give (property) by means of a deed.

deem |dēm| *v.* To judge; consider; think: *The mayor deemed it necessary to build a new school.*

deep |dēp| *adj.* **deep•er, deep•est. 1.** Extending to or located at an unspecified or specified distance below a surface: *a deep hole. The lake is 200 feet deep.* **2.** Extending from front to rear, or inward from the outside, for an unspecified or specified distance: *a deep closet. The lot is 100 feet deep.* **3.** Far distant down or in: *He was deep in the woods.* **4.** Extreme; profound; intense: *a deep silence; a deep sleep.* **5.** Very much absorbed or involved: *deep in thought.* **6.** Showing much thought or feeling; strongly felt: *a deep understanding; a deep love.* **7.** Difficult to understand; requiring great thought: *a deep mystery.* **8.** Containing little or no white, gray, or black; not pale; intense; vivid: *a deep red.* **9.** Low in pitch: *a deep voice.* —*adv.* **1.** Far down or into: *dig deep.* **2.** Well on in time; late: *work deep into the night.* —*n.* **1.** A deep place, especially one in the ocean and over 18,000 feet in depth. **2.** The most intense or extreme part: *the deep of night.* —**deep'ly** *adv.* —**deep'ness** *n.*

deep•en |**dē'**pən| *v.* To make or become deep or deeper.

deep-root•ed |**dēp'**ro͞o'tĭd| *or* |-**ro͝ot'**ĭd| *adj.* Firmly implanted; deep-seated.

deep-sea |**dēp'**sē'| *adj.* Of deep parts of the sea: *a deep-sea diver.*

deep-seat•ed |**dēp'**sē'tĭd| *adj.* Deeply rooted; strongly entrenched: *a deep-seated problem.*

deer |dîr| *n., pl.* **deer.** Any of several hoofed animals of which the males usually have antlers. ¶*These sound alike* **deer, dear.** [SEE PICTURE]

deer•skin |**dîr'**skĭn'| *n.* **1.** The skin of a deer. **2.** Leather made from this skin. **3.** A garment made from such leather. —**modifier:** *a deerskin jacket.*

def. definition.

de•face |dĭ fās′| *v.* **de•faced, de•fac•ing.** To mar or spoil the surface or appearance of; disfigure: *deface a poster with a crayon.*

de fac•to |dē făk′tō|. **1.** In existence; real: *de facto segregation.* **2.** Actually exercising power: *a de facto ruler.* [SEE NOTE on p. 245]

def•a•ma•tion |dĕf′ə mā′shən| *n.* Slander or libel; calumny.

de•fame |dĭ fām′| *v.* **de•famed, de•fam•ing.** To attack or damage the reputation of by slander or libel.

de•fault |dĭ fôlt′| *n.* **1.** A failure to do what is required, especially a failure to pay a debt: *guilty of default.* **2.** The failure of one or more competitors or teams to participate in or complete a contest: *win by default.* —*v.* **1.** To fail to do what is required, especially to fail to pay: *default a debt. He defaulted on his contract.* **2.** To lose a contest by failing to participate in or complete it. —**de•fault′er** *n.*

de•feat |dĭ fēt′| *v.* **1.** To win victory over; overcome: *defeat an enemy army. Our team defeated theirs.* **2.** To prevent the success of; thwart: *defeat one's purposes.* —*n.* **1.** The condition of being defeated; failure to win: *Napoleon's defeat at Waterloo; admit defeat.* **2.** The act of defeating: *the Jets' defeat of the Colts.*

de•feat•ism |dĭ fē′tĭz′əm| *n.* Acceptance of or resignation to defeat when it is not certain; lack of confidence in winning. —**de•feat′ist** *n.*

def•e•cate |dĕf′ĭ kāt′| *v.* **def•e•cat•ed, def•e•cat•ing.** To empty the bowels of waste matter. —**def′e•ca′tion** *n.*

de•fect |dē′fĕkt′| *or* |dĭ fĕkt′| *n.* A lack of something necessary or desirable for completion or perfection; a deficiency: *a physical defect; a speech defect; an engine defect; a defect in a piece of china.* —*v.* |dĭ fĕkt′|. To desert one's country, party, etc., in order to adopt or join another.

de•fec•tion |dĭ fĕk′shən| *n.* The act of deserting one's country, party, etc.

de•fec•tive |dĭ fĕk′tĭv| *adj.* **1.** Having a defect or flaw; faulty: *defective merchandise.* **2.** Lacking in normal mental or physical development. —*n.* A person whose mental or physical development is below normal. —**de•fec′tive•ly** *adv.*

de•fec•tor |dĭ fĕk′tər| *n.* A person who defects from a country, party, etc.

de•fence |dĭ fĕns′| *n.* Chiefly British form of the word **defense.**

de•fend |dĭ fĕnd′| *v.* **1.** To protect from attack, harm, or challenge; guard: *He defended himself by hitting back. The team will defend its title.* **2.** To support, as by argument; justify: *Defend your answer.* **3.** To argue the case of (a defendant) in a court of law. —**de•fend′er** *n.*

de•fend•ant |dĭ fĕn′dənt| *n.* The person against whom a legal action is brought.

de•fense |dĭ fĕns′| *n.* **1.** The act of defending against attack, harm, or challenge; protection: *soldiers fighting in defense of their country.* **2.** Anything that defends: *defenses built by an army.* **3.** In sports, the team or those players on the team attempting to stop the opposition from scoring. **4.** The reply of a defendant to the complaints against him. —**de•fense′less** *adj.*

de•fen•si•ble |dĭ fĕn′sə bəl| *adj.* Capable of being defended or justified: *a defensible position.*

de•fen•sive |dĭ fĕn′sĭv| *adj.* Of or for defense; protecting from attack: *defensive walls; a defensive player.* —*n.* A defensive position or attitude. —**de•fen′sive•ly** *adv.* —**de•fen′sive•ness** *n.*

Idiom. **on the defensive.** Expecting or being subjected to attack.

de•fer¹ |dĭ fûr′| *v.* **de•ferred, de•fer•ring.** To put off until a future time; postpone: *defer an action.* —**de•fer′ra•ble** *adj.* [SEE NOTE]

de•fer² |dĭ fûr′| *v.* **de•ferred, de•fer•ring.** To comply with or submit to the wishes, opinion, or decision of another; yield: *I deferred to him on that matter.* [SEE NOTE]

def•er•ence |dĕf′ər əns| *n.* Courteous respect, as for the wishes, opinions, or condition of another: *In deference to his age he was permitted to remain seated.*

def•er•en•tial |dĕf′ə rĕn′shəl| *adj.* Marked by courteous respect: *deferential behavior.* —**def′er•en′tial•ly** *adv.*

de•fer•ment |dĭ fûr′mənt| *n.* The act or an example of deferring; a postponement: *a draft deferment.*

de•fer•ral |dĭ fûr′əl| *n.* A deferment.

de•fi•ance |dĭ fī′əns| *n.* Open resistance to authority; refusal to obey: *a gesture of defiance.*

de•fi•ant |dĭ fī′ənt| *adj.* Full of defiance; openly resisting authority: *a defiant attitude.* —**de•fi′ant•ly** *adv.*

de•fi•cien•cy |dĭ fĭsh′ən sē| *n., pl.* **de•fi•cien•cies. 1.** A lack; shortage: *a vitamin deficiency.* **2.** A shortcoming; drawback; defect.

deficiency disease. A disease, such as pellagra, that results from a diet lacking in one or more vitamins or other essential nutrients.

de•fi•cient |dĭ fĭsh′ənt| *adj.* **1.** Lacking an important element or elements; inadequate: *a deficient diet; deficient in judgment.* **2.** Defective; imperfect: *a mentally deficient person.*

def•i•cit |dĕf′ĭ sĭt| *n.* The amount by which a sum of money falls short of the required or expected amount; a shortage: *a budget deficit.*

de•file¹ |dĭ fīl′| *v.* **de•filed, de•fil•ing. 1.** To make filthy or dirty; pollute. **2.** To spoil the sacredness or purity of: *defile a holy place.* —**de•file′ment** *n.* [SEE NOTE]

de•file² |dĭ fīl′| *n.* A narrow gorge or pass preventing the easy passage of a group, as of soldiers. [SEE NOTE]

de•fine |dĭ fīn′| *v.* **de•fined, de•fin•ing. 1.** To state the precise meaning or meanings of (a word, phrase, etc.). **2.** To describe; specify: *define one's duties.* **3.** To make distinct or clear in outline: *The building was clearly defined against the evening sky.* **4.** To fix the limits of: *defining the borders between the two countries.*

def•i•nite |dĕf′ə nĭt| *adj.* **1.** Clearly defined; precise; exact: *a definite plan; a definite time.* **2.** Known positively; beyond doubt; sure: *It's not definite that he'll go.* —**def′i•nite•ly** *adv.*

definite article. The word **the,** used to introduce an identified or immediately identifiable noun or noun phrase.

def•i•ni•tion |dĕf′ə nĭsh′ən| *n.* **1.** A statement of the precise meaning or meanings of a word, phrase, etc. **2.** The act of making clear and distinct: *a definition of one's purposes.* **3.** The clarity of an image, as in photography or television. [SEE NOTE]

defer¹·²/differ

Defer¹ *is etymologically the same word as* **differ.** *Both come from Latin* differre, *"to carry in various directions, to scatter, to separate"* (dis-, *"apart,"* + ferre, *"to carry"*). *This word had a wide range of meanings, including:* **a.** *"to put off, to delay," hence the meaning of* **defer¹**; *and* **b.** *"to be separate, to be different," hence* **differ. Defer²** *comes from another Latin verb,* dēferre, *"to carry away"* (dē-, *"away,"* + ferre, *"to carry"*). *This verb came to mean, among other things, "to report to someone, to refer something to someone's judgment"; from these meanings* **defer²** *in English eventually developed its present meaning, "to submit oneself, be deferential."*

defile¹·²

Defile¹ *was originally* defoulen *in Middle English, and was borrowed from Old French* defouler, *"to trample down, to injure":* de-, *"down,"* + fouler, *"to tread."* **Defile²** *is from French* defile, *an old technical military term meaning "a narrow place where only a thin column of troops can pass." This is from* defiler, *"to march in single file":* de-, *"off,"* + file, *"line of troops, file."*

definition

Definitions *in dictionaries cannot be truly precise. Meaning is still mysterious, and every word is unique. Most dictionaries, including this one, define a word by a phrase or by another word that seems to mean the same thing. But a phrase cannot have exactly the same meaning as a single word, and there are almost no words that are exactly synonymous. The best a definition can do is provide a clear and close approximation that enables the reader to recognize or reconstruct a meaning in his own mind.*

de·fin·i·tive |dĭ **fĭn**′ĭ tĭv| *adj.* **1.** Final; conclusive: *a definitive victory.* **2.** Being the most complete and true: *a definitive biography.*

de·flate |dĭ **flāt**′| *v.* **de·flat·ed, de·flat·ing.** **1.** To release contained air or gas from: *deflate a balloon. The balloon deflated.* **2.** To reduce the confidence, pride, happiness, etc., of: *My low mark on the test deflated me.*

de·fla·tion |dĭ **flā**′shən| *n.* **1.** The act of deflating or condition of being deflated. **2.** A reduction in the general price level of an economy, brought on by a decrease in the amount of money in circulation or by a decrease in the amount of spending.

de·flect |dĭ **flĕkt**′| *v.* To cause to turn aside or turn aside: *The tree deflected the car. The bullet glanced off the rock and deflected.*

de·flec·tion |dĭ **flĕk**′shən| *n.* **1. a.** The act or process of deflecting. **b.** The condition of being deflected. **2. a.** The movement of something, such as the pointer of a measuring instrument, from its normal or rest position. **b.** The amount of this movement.

de·fo·li·ant |dē **fō**′lē ənt| *n.* A chemical sprayed or dusted on plants to make their leaves fall off.

de·fo·li·ate |dē **fō**′lē āt′| *v.* **de·fo·li·at·ed, de·fo·li·at·ing.** To cause the leaves of (a tree or other plant) to fall off, especially by the use of a chemical spray. **—de·fo′li·a′tion** *n.*

de·for·est |dē **fôr**′ĭst| *or* |**-fŏr**′-| *v.* To cut down and clear away the trees or forests from. **—de·for′es·ta′tion** *n.*

de·form |dĭ **fôrm**′| *v.* **1.** To change the shape of or become changed in shape by pressure or stress. **2.** To mar the appearance of; make ugly; disfigure: *Anger deformed his face.* **—de·formed′** *adj.: a deformed leg.*

de·for·ma·tion |dē′fôr **mā**′shən| *or* |dĕf′ər-| *n.* **1.** A change of shape: *Some objects return to their original shapes after deformation.* **2.** An irregular or unpredictable change in the form of a word. [See Note]

deformation
Linguistic taboos are the major cause of **deformation** *in words. Individual words or concepts often come under a taboo, or social prohibition, so that people are reluctant to speak a particular word normally; thus abnormal variants are produced. Only taboo, for example, could account for the deformation of* goddamned *into* dad-burned, doggone, *and* goldarn.

de·form·i·ty |dĭ **fôr**′mĭ tē| *n., pl.* **de·form·i·ties.** **1.** A condition, such as clubfoot, in which a part of the body is abnormally formed. **2.** A part of the body that is deformed or misshapen.

de·fraud |dĭ **frôd**′| *v.* To take from or deprive of by trickery; cheat; swindle.

de·fray |dĭ **frā**′| *v.* To pay or provide for payment of (costs or expenses): *Contributions will defray the cost of a political campaign.*

de·frost |dē **frôst**′| *or* |**-frŏst**′| *v.* **1.** To free or become free of ice or frost: *defrost a windshield. This refrigerator defrosts quickly.* **2.** To thaw or cause to thaw: *defrost a steak from the freezer.* **—de·frost′er** *n.*

deft |dĕft| *adj.* Quick and skillful: *a deft motion; deft hands.* **—deft′ly** *adv.* **—deft′ness** *n.*

de·funct |dĭ **fŭngkt**′| *adj.* No longer in existence, operation, or use; dead: *a defunct law; a defunct organization.*

de·fy |dĭ **fī**′| *v.* **de·fied, de·fy·ing, de·fies.** **1.** To oppose or challenge openly or boldly: *defy the law; defy tradition; defy the elements.* **2.** To withstand; be beyond: *defy belief; defy description; defy solution.*

deg, deg. degree (temperature).

De Gaulle |də **gōl**′| *or* |**gôl**′|, **Charles.** 1890–1970. French general and statesman; president of France (1945–46 and 1959–69).

de·gen·er·a·cy |dĭ **jĕn**′ər ə sē| *n.* The condition of being degenerate.

de·gen·er·ate |dĭ **jĕn**′ər ĭt| *adj.* In a much worse or lower condition for having lost what is considered normal or desirable, as mental or moral qualities: *a degenerate person.* —*n.* A morally or psychologically abnormal person. —*v.* |dĭ **jĕn**′ə rāt′| **de·gen·er·at·ed, de·gen·er·at·ing.** To sink into a much worse or lower condition; deteriorate: *political debate that degenerated into partisan squabbling.*

de·gen·er·a·tion |dĭ jĕn′ə **rā**′shən| *n.* **1. a.** The process of degenerating. **b.** The condition of being degenerate. **2.** The deterioration, usually permanent, of specific cells or organs of the body, often as a result of disease or injury.

de·grade |dĭ **grād**′| *v.* **de·grad·ed, de·grad·ing.** **1.** To lower in rank, status, or dignity; abase. **2.** To bring shame, disgrace, or contempt upon; corrupt: *Stealing degrades a person.* **—deg′ra·da′tion** |dĕg′rə **dā**′shən| *n.*

de·gree |dĭ **grē**′| *n.* **1.** One of a series of steps or stages in a process, course of action, etc.: *proceed slowly and by degrees.* **2.** Relative intensity, amount, or extent, as of a quality, attribute, action, state of being, etc.: *a high degree of accuracy; various degrees of skill in reading.* **3.** Relative social or official rank, position, etc. **4.** One of the forms used in the comparison of an adjective or adverb; for example, the superlative degree of "new" is "newest." **5.** A classification according to seriousness, as of a burn. **6. a.** An academic title awarded by a college or university after completion of a required course of study. **b.** A similar title granted as an honor: *an honorary degree.* **7.** One of the units into which a temperature scale is divided: *10 degrees Fahrenheit.* **8.** A unit of arc or angular measure equal to $^1/_{360}$ of a complete revolution. **9. a.** The sum of all the exponents of the variables in an algebraic term. For example, if a and b are constants and x and y are variables, $abxy^2$ is of the third degree. **b.** In a polynomial in simple form, the degree of the term of the highest degree. For example, $x^3 + 2xy + x$ is of the third degree. **10. a.** One of the tones of a musical scale. **b.** A line or space of a musical staff.

de·gree-day |dĭ **grē**′dā′| *n.* A unit used in estimating the amount of fuel or power required for heating buildings. It is equal to the number of degrees by which the average temperature on a given day falls below some standard temperature, usually 65°F.

de·hu·man·ize |dē **hyōō**′mə nīz′| *v.* **de·hu·man·ized, de·hu·man·iz·ing.** To deprive of human qualities, especially to make mechanical or routine: *Some people think that computers dehumanize our life.* **—de·hu′man·i·za′tion** *n.*

de·hu·mid·i·fy |dē′hyōō **mĭd**′ə fī′| *v.* **de·hu·mid·i·fied, de·hu·mid·i·fy·ing, de·hu·mid·i·fies.** To decrease the humidity of: *An air conditioner dehumidifies the air.* **—de′hu·mid′i·fi′er** *n.*

de·hy·drate |dē **hī**′drāt′| *v.* **de·hy·drat·ed, de·hy·drat·ing.** To lose or cause to lose water or moisture; make or become dry.

de·hy·dra·tion |dē′hī **drā**′shən| *n.* **1.** The act or process of dehydrating. **2.** A diseased con-

ă pat/ā pay/â care/ä father/ĕ pet/ē be/ĭ pit/ī pie/î fierce/ŏ pot/ō go/ô paw, for/oi oil/ŏŏ book/ōō boot/ou out/ŭ cut/û fur/*th* the/th thin/hw which/zh vision/ə ago, item, pencil, atom, circus

dition in which the body or one of its organs or parts loses too much water.

de•ice |dē īs′| *v.* **de•iced, de•ic•ing.** To free or keep free of ice. —**de•ic′er** *n.*

de•i•fy |dē′ə fī′| *v.* **de•i•fied, de•i•fy•ing, de•i•fies.** To raise to divine rank; make a god of. —**de′i•fi•ca′tion** *n.*

deign |dān| *v.* To be kind or gracious enough to: *The speaker deigned to answer the hecklers' questions.*

de•i•ty |dē′ĭ tē| *n., pl.* **de•i•ties. 1.** A god or goddess. **2. the Deity.** God.

de•ject•ed |dĭ jĕk′tĭd| *adj.* Low in spirits; depressed: *The boy grew more and more melancholy and pale and dejected.* —**de•ject′ed•ly** *adv.*

de•jec•tion |dĭ jĕk′shən| *n.* The condition of being dejected; unhappiness; depression.

de ju•re |dē jo͝or′ē|. By right. [SEE NOTE]

deka–. A form of the word element **deca-.**

Del. Delaware.

Del•a•ware[1] |dĕl′ə wâr′| *n., pl.* **Del•a•ware** or **Del•a•wares. 1.** A North American Indian tribe of the Delaware River Valley. **2.** A member of this tribe. **3.** The Algonquian language of this tribe. Also called *Leni-Lenape* and *Lenape.* —**Del′a•war′e•an** |dĕl′ə **wâr′**ē ən| *adj.*

Del•a•ware[2] |**dĕl′**ə wâr′|. A Middle Atlantic state of the United States. Population, 595,225. Capital, Dover.

de•lay |dĭ **lā′**| *v.* **1.** To put off until a later time; postpone: *We will have to delay dinner an hour.* **2.** To cause to be late or behind schedule: *Urgent business delayed me in getting home.* —*n.* **1.** The act of delaying or condition of being delayed: *It will be done without delay.* **2.** A period of time during which someone or something is delayed: *a delay of 15 minutes.*

de•lec•ta•ble |dĭ **lĕk′**tə bəl| *adj.* Greatly pleasing; enjoyable: *a delectable piece of cake.*

del•e•gate |**dĕl′**ĭ gāt′| *or* |-gĭt| *n.* **1.** A person chosen to speak and act for another person or for a group to which he belongs; a representative; agent. **2.** A person who represents a Territory of the United States in the House of Representatives. **3.** A member of the lower house of the legislature of Maryland, Virginia, or West Virginia. —*v.* |**dĕl′**ĭ gāt′| **del•e•gat•ed, del•e•gat•ing. 1.** To select (a person) as a representative. **2.** To appoint (a person) as agent: *delegated him to study the problem.* **3.** To give or entrust to an agent or representative: *delegate power.*

del•e•ga•tion |dĕl′ĭ **gā′**shən| *n.* **1.** The act of delegating. **2.** The condition of being delegated; appointment. **3.** A person or persons chosen to represent another or others.

de•lete |dĭ **lēt′**| *v.* **de•let•ed, de•let•ing.** To strike out; remove; eliminate: *delete a name from a list; delete the last sentence of a paragraph.*

del•e•te•ri•ous |dĕl′ĭ **tîr′**ē əs| *adj.* Harmful; injurious: *the deleterious effects of smoking.*

de•le•tion |dĭ **lē′**shən| *n.* **1.** An act or instance of deleting. **2.** A word, sentence, paragraph, etc., that has been deleted.

del•i |**dĕl′**ē| *n., pl.* **del•is.** *Informal.* A delicatessen.

de•lib•er•ate |dĭ **lĭb′**ər ĭt| *adj.* **1.** Done or said on purpose; intentional: *a deliberate lie.* **2.** Not hasty or hurried; slow: *a deliberate person.* **3.** Careful; cautious: *a deliberate choice.* —*v.* |dĭ **lĭb′**ə rāt′| **de•lib•er•at•ed, de•lib•er•at•ing. 1.** To try to decide by careful thought or consideration; reflect: *He deliberated whether or not to buy it.* **2.** To talk over or discuss (something) carefully: *The council deliberated the new proposals. The Senate deliberated throughout the night.* —**de•lib′er•ate•ly** *adv.* —**de•lib′er•ate•ness** *n.*

de•lib•er•a•tion |dĭ lĭb′ə **rā′**shən| *n.* **1.** Careful thought or consideration: *He decided without much deliberation.* **2.** Slowness and care: *We must move with deliberation in this matter.* **3. deliberations.** Formal discussion or debate on all sides of an issue.

de•lib•er•a•tive |dĭ **lĭb′**ə rā′tĭv| *or* |-ər ə tĭv| *adj.* Assembled or organized for deliberation or debate: *A legislature is a deliberative body.*

del•i•ca•cy |**dĕl′**ĭ kə sē| *n., pl.* **del•i•ca•cies. 1.** The quality of being delicate. **2.** A choice food. **3.** Frailty of bodily constitution or health: *Teddy Roosevelt, despite childhood physical delicacy, became a vigorous man.* **4.** Fineness of quality or appearance; softness or daintiness: *embroidery with great delicacy of ornamentation.* **5.** A need for taste and tact in handling: *the delicacy of international negotiations.*

del•i•cate |**dĕl′**ĭ kĭt| *adj.* **1. a.** Very finely made, executed, etc.: *delicate lace.* **b.** Requiring skill: *delicate surgery.* **2.** Easily broken or damaged; fragile: *a delicate eggshell.* **3.** Frail in health: *She is delicate, so she must get plenty of rest.* **4.** Not vivid or strong in intensity; very subtle: *a delicate pink; a delicate flavor.* **5.** Keen in sensitivity, response, etc.: *a delicate musical instrument.* **6.** Requiring tactful treatment: *a delicate matter.* —**del′i•cate•ly** *adv.* —**del′i•cate•ness** *n.*

del•i•ca•tes•sen |dĕl′ĭ kə **tĕs′**ən| *n.* A store that sells cooked or prepared foods, such as cheeses, salads, relishes, smoked meats, etc.

de•li•cious |dĭ **lĭsh′**əs| *adj.* Very pleasing, especially to the taste and smell. —**de•li′cious•ly** *adv.* —**de•li′cious•ness** *n.*

de•light |dĭ **līt′**| *n.* **1.** Great pleasure; joy: *His face beamed with delight.* **2.** Something that gives great pleasure or enjoyment: *Such a scene is a delight to the eye.* —*v.* To please greatly: *a city that cannot fail to delight the visitor.*

de•light•ed |dĭ **lī′**tĭd| *adj.* Greatly pleased; very happy: *We were delighted to hear the news.* —**de•light′ed•ly** *adv.*

de•light•ful |dĭ **līt′**fəl| *adj.* Giving delight; very pleasing: *We had a delightful time at the party.* —**de•light′ful•ly** *adv.* —**de•light′ful•ness** *n.*

De•li•lah |dĭ **lī′**lə|. In the Bible, a Philistine woman who betrayed Samson to the Philistines by having his hair cut off as he slept, thus depriving him of his strength.

de•lim•it |dĭ **lĭm′**ĭt| *v.* To establish the limits or boundaries of.

de•lin•e•ate |dĭ **lĭn′**ē āt′| *v.* **de•lin•e•at•ed, de•lin•e•at•ing. 1.** To draw or trace the outline of: *delineate the state of California on a map.* **2.** To describe in detail: *delineate the numerous accomplishments of the organization.* **3.** To state or establish the exact limits or extent of: *delineate his duties carefully.* —**de•lin′e•a′tion** *n.*

de•lin•quen•cy |dĭ **lĭng′**kwən sē| *n., pl.* **de•lin•quen•cies. 1.** Negligence or failure in doing what is required. **2. Juvenile delinquency.**

de•lin•quent |dĭ **lĭng′**kwənt| *adj.* **1.** Failing or neglecting to do what is required by law or

de jure/de facto

***De facto** and **de jure** are lawyers' Latin for "in fact" and "in law." They are used as a contrasted pair in situations where it must be recognized that the effective reality is not the legal reality. Thus the Sinai Peninsula has been since 1967 under the **de facto** control of Israel, although it remains **de jure** part of the United Arab Republic.*

delphinium

delta wing

ă pat/ā pay/â care/ä father/ĕ pet/ ē be/ĭ pit/ī pie/î fierce/ŏ pot/ ō go/ô paw, for/oi oil/ŏŏ book/ ōō boot/ou out/ŭ cut/û fur/ *th* the/th thin/hw which/zh vision/ ə ago, item, pencil, atom, circus

obligation: *a delinquent parent.* **2.** Overdue in payment: *a delinquent account.* —*n.* **1.** A person who neglects or fails to do what is required by law or obligation. **2.** A **juvenile delinquent.** —**de•lin'quent•ly** *adv.*

del•i•quesce |dĕl'ĭ **kwĕs'**| *v.* **del•i•quesced, del•i•quesc•ing.** To dissolve and become liquid by absorbing moisture from the air, as certain chemical compounds do.

del•i•ques•cence |dĕl'ĭ **kwĕs'**əns| *n.* **1.** The act or process of deliquescing. **2.** The ability to deliquesce. —**del'i•ques'cent** *adj.*

de•lir•i•ous |dĭ **lîr'**ē əs| *adj.* **1.** In a state of delirium. **2.** Of or characteristic of delirium: *delirious ravings.* —**de•lir'i•ous•ly** *adv.*

de•lir•i•um |dĭ **lîr'**ē əm| *n., pl.* **de•lir•i•ums** or **de•lir•i•a** |dĭ **lîr'**ē ə|. **1.** A temporary state of mental confusion and clouded consciousness resulting from high fever, poisoning, or shock. **2.** Uncontrolled excitement or emotion.

delirium tre•mens |**trē'**mənz|. A violent delirium caused by alcohol poisoning.

de•liv•er |dĭ **lĭv'**ər| *v.* **1.** To take (letters, packages, etc.) to the persons to whom they are addressed or to one or more specific destinations: *deliver a package; deliver newspapers. The downtown stores do not deliver to the suburbs.* **2.** To send against; aim; strike: *deliver a blow.* **3.** To give or utter: *deliver a speech; deliver a lecture.* **4.** To liberate; set free: *deliver someone from bondage.* **5.** To rescue; save: *Deliver us from our enemies.* **6.** To surrender; hand over: *deliver a criminal to the authorities.* **7. a.** To assist in the birth of: *Dr. Adams delivered the baby.* **b.** To assist (a female) in giving birth: *deliver a woman of a child.* —**de•liv'er•er** *n.*

Idiom. **deliver (oneself) of.** To utter with force or feeling.

de•liv•er•ance |dĭ **lĭv'**ər əns| *n.* Rescue from danger or slavery.

de•liv•er•y |dĭ **lĭv'**ə rē| *n., pl.* **de•liv•er•ies. 1.** The act of delivering or conveying: *I have a number of deliveries to make.* **2.** Something that is delivered: *There is a delivery for you downstairs.* **3.** The act or process of giving birth: *Two doctors assisted in the delivery of the baby.* **4.** A person's manner of speaking, singing, etc., in public: *The content of his speech was excellent, but his delivery was poor.* **5.** The way of throwing or discharging a ball, as in baseball, tennis, etc.: *an overhand delivery.* —***modifier:*** *a delivery boy; a delivery truck; a hospital delivery room.*

dell |dĕl| *n.* A small, secluded valley.

del•phin•i•um |dĕl **fĭn'**ē əm| *n.* A tall garden plant with long clusters of flowers that are usually blue, but sometimes white or pink. [SEE PICTURE]

del•ta |**dĕl'**tə| *n.* **1.** The fourth letter of the Greek alphabet, written Δ, δ. In English it is represented as *D, d.* **2.** A usually triangular mass of sand, mud, and earth, as that accumulated at the mouth of a river. **3.** A notation for an increase or decrease in a mathematical variable; for example, a change in x may be denoted by Δx.

delta wing. An aircraft whose sharply swept-back wings make it look more or less triangular. —***modifier:*** **(delta-wing):** *a delta-wing plane.* [SEE PICTURE]

de•lude |dĭ **lōōd'**| *v.* **de•lud•ed, de•lud•ing.** To deceive the mind or judgment of; mislead.

del•uge |**dĕl'**yōōj| *n.* **1.** A great flood; heavy downpour. **2.** An overwhelming influx of something: *a deluge of mail.* **3. the Deluge.** The Flood mentioned in the Bible. —*v.* **del•uged, del•ug•ing. 1.** To overrun with water. **2.** To inundate in overwhelming numbers: *deluged with messages of congratulation.*

de•lu•sion |dĭ **lōō'**zhən| *n.* A false belief held in spite of evidence to the contrary.

de•lu•sive |dĭ **lōō'**sĭv| *adj.* Tending to deceive or mislead; deceptive. —**de•lu'sive•ly** *adv.*

de luxe |də **lŏŏks'**| *or* |**lŭks'**|. Of especially fine quality; elegant; luxurious.

de•luxe |də **lŏŏks'**| *or* |**-lŭks'**| *adj.* A form of the phrase **de luxe.**

delve |dĕlv| *v.* **delved, delv•ing.** To search deeply and laboriously in order to obtain information: *delve into the secrets of the universe.*

Dem. Democrat; Democratic.

de•mag•net•ize |dē **măg'**nĭ tīz'| *v.* **de•mag•net•ized, de•mag•net•iz•ing.** To deprive of magnetism.

dem•a•gog•ic |dĕm'ə **gŏj'**ĭk| *adj.* Of or like a demagogue: *a demagogic speech.*

dem•a•gogue |**dĕm'**ə gôg'| *or* |-gŏg'| *n.* A leader who wins people to his side by appealing to their emotions and prejudices.

dem•a•gogu•er•y |**dĕm'**ə gô'gə rē| *or* |-gŏg'ə-| *n.* The practices or emotional style of speech of a demagogue.

dem•a•go•gy |**dĕm'**ə gō'jē| *or* |-gô'jē| *or* |-gŏj'ē| *n.* The principles and practices of a demagogue.

de•mand |dĭ **mănd'**| *or* |**-mänd'**| *v.* **1.** To ask for insistently: *demand better working conditions.* **2.** To need or require: *This work demands great concentration.* —*n.* **1.** An insistent request: *wage demands.* **2.** A requirement, need, or claim: *the many demands on my time.* **3.** The condition of being sought after: *Silver is now in great demand.* **4.** A desire and readiness on the part of the public to purchase a certain commodity: *a great demand for cashmere sweaters.*

de•mand•ing |dĭ **măn'**dĭng| *or* |**-män'-**| *adj.* Requiring or expecting a great deal of others: *a very demanding task.*

de•mar•cate |dĭ **mär'**kāt'| *or* |**dē'**mär kāt'| *v.* **de•mar•cat•ed, de•mar•cat•ing. 1.** To set the boundaries of; delimit. **2.** To separate clearly as if by boundaries; distinguish.

de•mar•ca•tion |dē'mär **kā'**shən| *n.* **1.** The act of marking boundaries. **2.** A separation; distinction: *a line of demarcation.*

de•mean |dĭ **mēn'**| *v.* **1.** To lower in dignity or stature. **2.** To humble (oneself): *demean oneself by continually asking for favors.*

de•mean•or |dĭ **mē'**nər| *n.* The way in which a person behaves or conducts himself.

de•ment•ed |dĭ **mĕn'**tĭd| *adj.* Having a serious mental disorder; insane. —**de•ment'ed•ly** *adv.*

de•mer•it |dĭ **mĕr'**ĭt| *n.* **1.** A quality deserving blame; a fault. **2.** A mark entered against someone's record for bad conduct or poor work.

de•mesne |dĭ **mān'**| *or* |**-mēn'**| *n.* **1.** In medieval times, the lands retained by a feudal lord for his own use. **2.** An area under a person's control; domain.

De•me•ter |dĭ mē′tər|. The Greek goddess of agriculture and fertility.

demi-. A word element meaning "half": **demigod.** [SEE NOTE]

dem•i•god |dĕm′ē gŏd′| *n.* A mythological being, such as the son of a god and a mortal.

dem•i•john |dĕm′ĭ jŏn′| *n.* A large bottle with a narrow neck, usually encased in wickerwork.

de•mil•i•ta•rize |dē mĭl′ĭ tə rīz′| *v.* **de•mil•i•ta•rized, de•mil•i•ta•riz•ing.** To ban military forces in: *demilitarize an area.* —**de•mil′i•ta•rized′** *adj.*: *a demilitarized zone.*

de•mise |dĭ mīz′| *n.* **1.** The death of a person. **2.** The end, fall, collapse, or ruin of something: *the demise of a great newspaper.*

dem•i•tasse |dĕm′ē tăs′| *or* |-täs′| *n.* **1.** A small cup of black coffee, usually served after dinner. **2.** The cup itself.

de•mo•bi•lize |dē mō′bə līz′| *v.* **de•mo•bi•lized, de•mo•bi•liz•ing.** To discharge from military service or use. —**de•mo′bi•li•za′tion** *n.*

de•moc•ra•cy |dĭ mŏk′rə sē| *n., pl.* **de•moc•ra•cies. 1. a.** A form of government in which power belongs to the people, who express their will through elected representatives. **b.** A country with this form of government. **2.** Respect for the rights of every individual in a society.

dem•o•crat |dĕm′ə krăt′| *n.* **1.** A person who advocates democracy. **2. Democrat.** A member or a supporter of the Democratic Party.

dem•o•crat•ic |dĕm′ə krăt′ĭk| *adj.* **1.** Of, like, or advocating democracy. **2.** Based on the principle of equal rights for all. **3. Democratic.** Of or belonging to the Democratic Party. —**dem′o•crat′i•cal•ly** *adv.*

Democratic Party. One of the two major political parties of the United States, dating from 1828. [SEE PICTURE]

de•moc•ra•tize |dĭ mŏk′rə tīz′| *v.* **de•moc•ra•tized, de•moc•ra•tiz•ing.** To make democratic. —**de•moc′ra•ti•za′tion** *n.*

de•mod•u•late |dē mŏj′ə lāt′| *or* |-mŏd′yə-| *v.* **de•mod•u•lat•ed, de•mod•u•lat•ing.** To separate from (a carrier wave) the information that it carries as a result of being modulated. —**de•mod′u•la′tion** *n.*

de•mod•u•la•tor |dē mŏj′ə lā′tər| *or* |-mŏd′yə-| *n.* A device, especially an electronic circuit, that demodulates.

de•mol•ish |dĭ mŏl′ĭsh| *v.* **1.** To tear down completely; wreck; level: *The wrecking crew demolished the old building.* **2.** To do away with completely: *demolish an argument.*

dem•o•li•tion |dĕm′ə lĭsh′ən| *n.* The action or business of destroying buildings, installations, etc., especially by means of explosives. —*modifier: a demolition crew; a demolition bomb.*

de•mon |dē′mən| *n.* **1.** An evil spirit; devil. **2.** A person who is very enthusiastic or energetic in a given activity: *a demon for work.*

de•mo•ni•ac |dĭ mō′nē ăk′| *adj.* **1.** Of or like a demon. **2.** Seemingly caused by a demon; frenzied. —*n.* A person who is or seems to be possessed by a demon. —**de′mo•ni′a•cal•ly** |dē′mə nī′ə kə lē| *adv.*

de•mo•ni•a•cal |dē′mə nī′ə kəl| *adj.* A form of the word **demoniac.**

de•mon•stra•ble |dĭ mŏn′strə bəl| *adj.* Capable of being shown or proved.

dem•on•strate |dĕm′ən strāt′| *v.* **dem•on•strat•ed, dem•on•strat•ing. 1.** To prove; leave no doubt about: *demonstrate one's ability to do the job.* **2. a.** To describe or explain by experiment, reasoning, etc.: *demonstrate the harmful effects of tobacco.* **b.** To display, operate, or explain (a product): *demonstrate a new washing machine.* **3.** To show or reveal: *demonstrate great courage.* **4.** To participate in a demonstration.

dem•on•stra•tion |dĕm′ən strā′shən| *n.* **1.** A logical proof: *the demonstration of a theorem.* **2.** A display, operation, or description of a product: *a demonstration of a new car.* **3.** A display or outward show: *a demonstration of solidarity between the two groups.* **4.** A public display of group opinion, as by a rally or march: *an antiwar demonstration.* [SEE PICTURE]

de•mon•stra•tive |dĭ mŏn′strə tĭv| *adj.* **1.** Serving to show or prove. **2.** Openly expressing one's feelings, especially affection. **3.** In grammar, specifying or singling out the person or thing referred to; for example, *these* is a demonstrative pronoun. —*n.* A demonstrative pronoun or adjective.

dem•on•stra•tor |dĕm′ən strā′tər| *n.* **1.** A person who demonstrates something. **2.** A person who takes part in a public demonstration.

de•mor•al•ize |dĭ môr′ə līz′| *or* |-mŏr′-| *v.* **de•mor•al•ized, de•mor•al•iz•ing.** To weaken the confidence or morale of; dishearten; discourage: *His failure to make any progress demoralized him completely.* —**de•mor′al•i•za′tion** *n.*

De•mos•the•nes |dĭ mŏs′thə nēz′|. 384–322 B.C. Greek statesman and orator.

de•mote |dĭ mōt′| *v.* **de•mot•ed, de•mot•ing.** To lower in rank or position: *He was demoted from captain to lieutenant.* —**de•mo′tion** *n.*

de•mur |dĭ mûr′| *v.* **de•murred, de•mur•ring.** To raise objections; object: *demur at working late hours.* —*n.* An objection.

de•mure |dĭ myŏŏr′| *adj.* **de•mur•er, de•mur•est.** Shy or modest, sometimes falsely so. —**de•mure′ly** *adv.* —**de•mure′ness** *n.*

de•mur•ral |dĭ mûr′əl| *n.* A form of the word **demur.**

den |dĕn| *n.* **1.** The shelter or retreat of a wild animal; a lair. **2.** A small, secluded room for study or relaxation. **3.** A small, dimly lit place, usually used for an illegal activity: *an opium den.* **4.** A unit of about eight Cub Scouts.

de•nar•i•us |dĭ nâr′ē əs| *n., pl.* **de•nar•i•i** |dĭ nâr′ē ī′|. An ancient Roman coin.

de•na•ture |dē nā′chər| *v.* **de•na•tured, de•na•tur•ing.** To change (a substance) so as to remove certain properties while leaving others intact.

denatured alcohol. Ethanol that has had substances added to it to make it unfit for drinking and on which no liquor tax needs to be paid.

den•drite |dĕn′drīt′| *n.* **1. a.** A mineral that crystallizes in another mineral in a way that produces a branching or treelike mark. **b.** A mineral or rock marked in this way. **2.** A branching part of a nerve cell that transmits impulses toward the cell body.

den•gue |dĕng′gē| *or* |-gā| *n.* A severe infectious disease of tropical and subtropical regions, transmitted by mosquitoes. Its symptoms include fever, rash, and severe pains in the joints.

demi-/hemi-/semi-

*These three prefixes all mean "half"; **hemi-** and **semi-** are related, but **demi-** is separate. **Hemi-** and **semi-** are, respectively, borrowed from Greek* hēmi- *and Latin* sēmi-, *which are both descended from Indo-European* sēmi-, *"half." (Note that an Indo-European* s- *regularly becomes* h- *in Greek but remains* s- *in Latin; compare the note at **six.**) **Demi-**, on the other hand, comes from French* demi, *which is from Latin* dīmidius, *"divided down the middle, halved, half":* dī-, *"apart,"* + medius, *"middle."*

Democratic Party
Symbol of the party

dental, dentist, etc.
These words all come from Latin dēns, dent-, *"tooth." This descends from* dent-, *the Indo-European word for "tooth." (See note at* **tooth***; notice that an Indo-European* d- *regularly remains* d- *in Latin but changes to* t- *in Germanic.)*

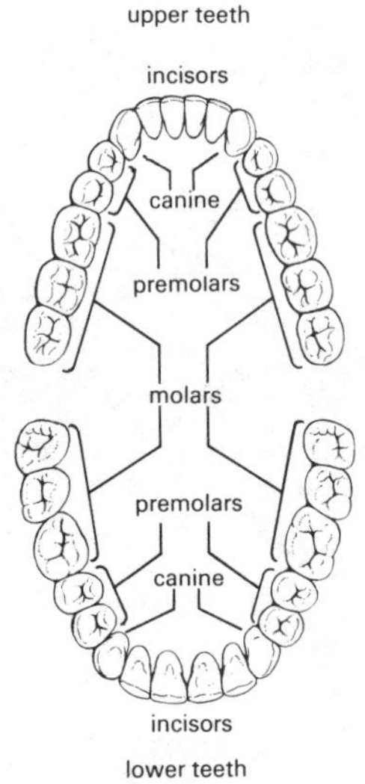

dentition
Dentition of a typical adult human being

ă pat/ā pay/â care/ä father/ĕ pet/ ē be/ĭ pit/ī pie/î fierce/ŏ pot/ ō go/ô paw, for/oi oil/o͝o book/ o͞o boot/ou out/ŭ cut/û fur/ *th* the/th thin/hw which/zh vision/ ə ago, item, pencil, atom, circus

de•ni•al |dĭ **nī**′əl| *n.* **1.** The act of denying: *He was very emphatic in his denial of the charges.* **2.** A statement that an accusation or allegation is false: *The charges prompted an immediate denial from the mayor.* **3.** A refusal to grant something: *the denial of a request; a denial of one's rights.*

den•ier |**dĕn**′yər| *n.* A unit of fineness for nylon, rayon, and silk yarns. A yarn rated at 1 denier weighs 50 milligrams per 450 meters of its length.

den•i•grate |**dĕn**′ĭ grāt′| *v.* **den•i•grat•ed, den•i•grat•ing.** To make false statements about the character of; defame. —**den′i•gra′tion** *n.*

den•im |**dĕn**′əm| *n.* **1.** A coarse, heavy cotton cloth used for work clothes and sport clothes, especially **blue denim,** used for overalls, blue jeans, and dungarees. **2. denims.** Overalls or trousers made of denim. —***modifier:*** *denim trousers; a denim jacket.*

den•i•zen |**dĕn**′ĭ zən| *n.* A person, plant, or animal that lives in a particular place: *The lion is a denizen of the jungle.*

Den•mark |**dĕn**′märk′|. A country in northern Europe, extending north from Germany between the North and Baltic seas. Population, 5,045,000. Capital, Copenhagen.

de•nom•i•na•tion |dĭ nŏm′ə **nā**′shən| *n.* **1.** A name; designation. **2.** An organized group of religious congregations: *people of all denominations.* **3.** A unit of money: *bills of small denomination.* —**de•nom′i•na′tion•al** *adj.*

de•nom•i•na•tor |dĭ **nŏm**′ə nā′tər| *n.* **1.** A number that tells how many equivalent subsets a whole set is to be divided into. For example, in the fraction $^2/_7$, 7, the denominator, indicates that the whole set is divided into 7 equivalent subsets; 2, the numerator, compares 2 of these subsets with the whole set. **2.** The numeral written below the line in a common fraction.

de•no•ta•tion |dē′nō **tā**′shən| *n.* **1.** The act of denoting. **2.** The exact meaning of a word, as opposed to its connotation.

de•note |dĭ **nōt**′| *v.* **de•not•ed, de•not•ing. 1.** To mean explicitly; signify: *The prefix "multi-" denotes "many" or "much."* **2.** To be a sign of; mark: *The blue areas on the map denote water.*

dé•noue•ment, also **de•noue•ment** |dā′no͞o-**mäN**′| *n.* **1.** The outcome or resolution of the plot of a drama or novel. **2.** Any outcome.

de•nounce |dĭ **nouns**′| *v.* **de•nounced, de•nounc•ing. 1.** To express very strong disapproval of; condemn openly: *denounce a proposed law.* **2.** To accuse formally; inform against: *denounce a traitor.*

dense |dĕns| *adj.* **dens•er, dens•est. 1.** Having relatively high density: *dense rock.* **2.** Thick; not easily penetrated: *a dense forest; a dense fog.* **3.** Thickheaded; dull. —**dense′ly** *adv.* —**dense′ness** *n.*

den•si•ty |**dĕn**′sĭ tē| *n., pl.* **den•si•ties. 1. a.** The mass per unit of volume of a substance under standard or given conditions of temperature and pressure. **b.** The amount of something per unit of measure, especially per unit of length, area, or volume: *a population density of five people per square mile.* **2.** The degree to which a medium or material, such as a photographic negative, blocks the passage of light. **3.** The condition of being dense; thickness of consistency; impenetrability: *the density of the forest.* **4.** Stupidity; dullness.

dent |dĕnt| *n.* A hollow place in a surface, usually caused by pressure or a blow: *a dent in a fender.* —*v.* To make a dent in or get dents in: *dent a fender. Some metals dent easily.*

den•tal |**dĕn**′tl| *adj.* **1.** Of or for the teeth: *a dental drill.* **2.** Of or involving dentistry: *a dental practice.* [SEE NOTE]

den•ti•frice |**dĕn**′tə frĭs| *n.* A substance, such as a powder or paste, used for cleaning the teeth.

den•tin |**dĕn**′tĭn| *n.* A form of the word **dentine.**

den•tine |**dĕn**′tēn′| *n.* The hard, calcium-containing part of a tooth that surrounds the pulp and root canals and lies beneath the enamel.

den•tist |**dĕn**′tĭst| *n.* A person whose profession is dentistry. [SEE NOTE]

den•tist•ry |**dĕn**′tĭ strē| *n.* The study, detection, treatment, and prevention of diseases of the teeth and related structures in the mouth, including the repair or replacement of defective teeth.

den•ti•tion |dĕn **tĭsh**′ən| *n.* **1.** The type, number, and arrangement of teeth, as in an animal. **2.** The process of cutting or growing teeth; teething. [SEE PICTURE]

den•ture |**dĕn**′chər| *n.* A set of artificial teeth designed to replace missing natural teeth.

de•nude |dĭ **no͞od**′| *or* |-**nyo͞od**′| *v.* **de•nud•ed, de•nud•ing.** To remove the covering from; lay bare: *Erosion of the soil denuded the rock.*

de•nun•ci•a•tion |dĭ nŭn′sē **ā**′shən| *or* |-shē-| *n.* The act of denouncing; open condemnation.

Den•ver |**dĕn**′vər|. The capital and largest city of Colorado. Population, 513,000.

de•ny |dĭ **nī**′| *v.* **de•nied, de•ny•ing, de•nies. 1.** To declare untrue; contradict: *deny an accusation.* **2.** To refuse to acknowledge; disavow: *deny one's guilt.* **3.** To refuse to grant; withhold: *deny a request.* **4.** To deprive: *I hate to deny you this pleasure.*

de•o•dor•ant |dē **ō**′dər ənt| *n.* A preparation used to prevent body odor.

de•o•dor•ize |dē **ō**′də rīz′| *v.* **de•o•dor•ized, de•o•dor•iz•ing.** To make free of odors, especially unpleasant odors.

de•ox•i•dize |dē **ŏk**′sĭ dīz′| *v.* **de•ox•i•dized, de•ox•i•diz•ing.** To remove oxygen, especially chemically combined oxygen, from.

de•ox•y•gen•ate |dē **ŏk**′sə jə nāt′| *v.* **de•ox•y•gen•at•ed, de•ox•y•gen•at•ing.** To remove oxygen from.

de•ox•y•ri•bo•nu•cle•ic acid |dē ŏk′sē rī′bō-no͞o **klē**′ĭk| *or* |-nyo͞o-|. DNA.

de•part |dĭ **pärt**′| *v.* **1.** To go away; leave: *depart from the house.* **2.** To vary, as from a regular course; deviate: *depart from custom.*

de•part•ed |dĭ **pär**′tĭd| *adj.* Dead; deceased. —*n.* One or more persons who have died.

de•part•ment |dĭ **pärt**′mənt| *n.* A separate division of an organization, such as a government, company, store, or college, having a specialized function: *the Defense Department; the fire department; the shoe department; the English department.*

de•part•men•tal |dē′pärt **mĕn**′tl| *adj.* Of a department: *departmental administration.*

department store. A large store, selling many kinds of goods, that is broken up into departments according to the kinds of goods sold.

de•par•ture |dĭ **pär**′chər| *n.* **1.** The act of going away or starting out. **2.** A deviation or diver-gence, as from an established rule, plan, or procedure.

de•pend |dĭ **pĕnd'**| *v.* **1.** To be determined; hinge or rest: *Much depends on what happens in the next few weeks.* **2.** To be certain about; place trust: *You can depend on me to be there on time.* **3.** To rely, as for support or help: *He depends on Social Security for income.*

de•pend•a•ble |dĭ **pĕn'**də bəl| *adj.* Reliable. —**de•pend'a•bil'i•ty** *n.* —**de•pend'a•bly** *adv.*

de•pend•ence |dĭ **pĕn'**dəns| *n.* **1.** The condition of being dependent on someone or something: *a child's dependence on his parents.* **2.** Reliance; trust: *I place little dependence in his statements.*

de•pend•en•cy |dĭ **pĕn'**dən sē| *n., pl.* **de•pend•en•cies. 1.** Dependence. **2.** A territory or state ruled by another country from which it is separated geographically.

de•pend•ent |dĭ **pĕn'**dənt| *adj.* **1.** Determined by someone or something else: *The outcome is dependent on a number of circumstances.* **2.** Needing the help of another to exist or function: *Every plant and animal is dependent in some way upon other living things.* **3.** Ruled by an outside power: *a dependent territory.* —*n.* A person who relies on another for support: *a tax allowance for each dependent.* —**de•pend'ent•ly** *adv.*

dependent clause. A clause that cannot stand alone as a full sentence and that functions as a noun, adjective, or adverb within a sentence. For example, in the sentence *When I saw him he was feeling fine, when I saw him* is a dependent clause.

dependent variable. A mathematical variable that takes a value for each value taken by an independent variable. For example, in $y = x^2 + 2x$, y is the dependent variable.

de•pict |dĭ **pĭkt'**| *v.* To represent in words, painting, etc.; describe or show: *a book depicting life in ancient Rome.* —**de•pic'tion** *n.*

de•pil•a•to•ry |dĭ **pĭl'**ə tôr'ē| *or* |-tōr'ē| *adj.* Able to remove hair: *a depilatory lotion.* —*n., pl.* **de•pil•a•to•ries.** A substance, such as a liquid or cream, used to remove unwanted body hair.

de•plete |dĭ **plēt'**| *v.* **de•plet•ed, de•plet•ing.** To reduce the amount of (something) until little or none remains; use up; exhaust: *Our oil supplies have been seriously depleted.* —**de•ple'tion** *n.*

de•plor•a•ble |dĭ **plôr'**ə bəl| *or* |-**plōr'**-| *adj.* **1.** Worthy of strong disapproval or reproach: *deplorable behavior.* **2.** Inspiring sorrow; grievous: *deplorable living conditions.* —**de•plor'a•bly** *adv.*

de•plore |dĭ **plôr'**| *or* |-**plōr'**| *v.* **de•plored, de•plor•ing. 1.** To regard with strong disapproval: *I deplore his cruelty.* **2.** To feel sorrow about: *We all deplore our leader's death.*

de•ploy |dĭ **ploi'**| *v.* To station or spread out in a systematic or strategic pattern: *deploy troops in preparation for a battle. The riflemen deployed on both sides of the narrow pass.* —**de•ploy'ment** *n.*

de•pop•u•late |dē **pŏp'**yə lāt'| *v.* **de•pop•u•lat•ed, de•pop•u•lat•ing.** To reduce sharply the population of: *The flood depopulated much of the region.*

de•port |dĭ **pôrt'**| *or* |-**pōrt'**| *v.* **1.** To behave (oneself) in a certain manner: *He deports himself like a king.* **2.** To expel (a foreigner) from a country. [SEE NOTE]

de•por•ta•tion |dē'pôr **tā'**shən| *or* |-pōr-| *n.* Banishment from a country, especially the expulsion of an undesirable foreigner.

de•port•ment |dĭ **pôrt'**mənt| *or* |-**pōrt'**-| *n.* Behavior; conduct.

de•pose |dĭ **pōz'**| *v.* **de•posed, de•pos•ing.** To remove from a position of power: *depose a king.*

de•pos•it |dĭ **pŏz'**ĭt| *v.* **1.** To lay or put down: *deposited his books on the table.* **2.** To place (an amount of money) in a bank account. **3.** To put down, place, or be placed by a natural process, especially in a layer or layers. —*n.* **1. a.** An amount of money for or in a bank account. **b.** The condition of being deposited in a bank account: *a thousand dollars on deposit.* **2.** An amount of money given as a guarantee that something will be returned, bought, etc. **3.** A mass of material that builds up by a natural process: **a.** Mineral or sandy material left by moving water. **b.** Solid or semisolid material that builds up in a space or cavity of the body.

dep•o•si•tion |dĕp'ə **zĭsh'**ən| *n.* **1.** The act of deposing, as from office. **2.** Testimony given under oath and usually in written form.

de•pos•i•tor |dĭ **pŏz'**ĭ tər| *n.* A person who deposits money in a bank.

de•pos•i•to•ry |dĭ **pŏz'**ĭ tôr'ē| *or* |-tōr'ē| *n., pl.* **de•pos•i•to•ries.** A place where something is deposited for safekeeping.

de•pot |**dē'**pō| *n.* **1.** A railroad or bus station. **2.** A warehouse or storehouse. **3.** A place where military equipment and supplies are stored. **4.** A station where military troops are assembled, classified, and assigned.

de•prave |dĭ **prāv'**| *v.* **de•praved, de•prav•ing.** To make morally bad; corrupt.

de•prav•i•ty |dĭ **prăv'**ĭ tē| *n., pl.* **de•prav•i•ties. 1.** A depraved condition; moral corruption. **2.** A wicked or perverse act.

dep•re•cate |**dĕp'**rĭ kāt'| *v.* **dep•re•cat•ed, dep•re•cat•ing. 1.** To express disapproval of: *Both parties deprecated war.* **2.** To speak of as having little value; belittle: *He modestly deprecated his own contribution.* —**dep're•ca'tion** *n.* [SEE NOTE]

de•pre•ci•ate |dĭ **prē'**shē āt'| *v.* **de•pre•ci•at•ed, de•pre•ci•at•ing. 1.** To lower the worth of or go down in value: *Farmers depreciate their harvesting equipment for tax purposes. A car depreciates in value each year.* **2.** To belittle: *We don't mean to depreciate the animal; the lion is splendid really.* [SEE NOTE]

de•pre•ci•a•tion |dĭ prē'shē **ā'**shən| *n.* **1.** A decrease or loss in value because of wear, age, or other cause. **2.** In accounting, an allowance made for this loss in one's financial records.

dep•re•da•tion |dĕp'rĭ **dā'**shən| *n.* The act or an example of destruction, plunder, or ravaging.

de•press |dĭ **prĕs'**| *v.* **1.** To make gloomy or dejected: *The sad news depressed everyone.* **2.** To press down: *depress the accelerator in a car.* **3.** To cause to decline in strength, activity, or value: *The decline in business has depressed the stock market.* —**de•press'ing** *adj.*: *depressing news; a depressing sight.*

de•pres•sant |dĭ **prĕs'**ənt| *adj.* Tending to slow vital body processes; opposite in effect to a stimulant. —*n.* A depressant drug.

de•pressed |dĭ **prĕst'**| *adj.* **1.** Gloomy; dejected: *The news left me depressed for several days.* **2.** Suffering economic hardship, as from poverty

deport

Deport *is a single word with a single origin, but its two quite separate meanings result from two stages of borrowing. In sense 1 the word was borrowed, in the sixteenth century, from Old French* deporter, *"to carry oneself, behave," which is from Latin* dēportāre, *"to carry off"* (dē-, *"away,"* + portāre, *"to carry").* Dēportāre *also meant "to send away, to exile, to deport," and in this sense it was reborrowed directly into English, in the seventeenth century, to provide sense 2 of* **deport**. *Note that* **deport** *has two nouns,* **deportation** *(for sense 2) and* **deportment** *(for sense 1).*

deprecate/depreciate

The basic meanings of these two similar verbs are very different, as can best be seen through their etymologies. **Deprecate** *is from Latin* dēprecārī, *"to pray against, to keep a misfortune away by prayer"* (dē-, *"away,"* + precārī, *"to pray"); hence in English* **deprecate** *means "to try to avoid, to disapprove of."* **Depreciate** *is from Latin* dēpretiāre, *"to reduce the price of," hence "to make light of"* (dē-, *"down,"* + pretium, *"price"). The extension of* **depreciate** *to its sense 2, "to belittle," is old and well established. But the extension of* **deprecate** *to virtually the same meaning is recent, and is still resisted (or deprecated) by nearly 50 per cent of the American Heritage Usage Panel.*

derby/Derby

Derby *or* Derbyshire *is the name of one of the counties of England. It is always pronounced* /**där**′bē/ *by the English (just as they pronounce* clerk /klärk/*). The Earls of* Derby *take their title from the name of the county. In 1780 the 12th Earl founded the famous horse race called the* Derby, *from which various American races are called* **Derby**. *But the Americans refused to accept the illogical pronunciation and pronounced it* /**dûr**′bē/. *The* **derby** *hat is so named because it was much worn by horse-racing people; but the English, who wear it mostly as a formal business hat, call it a* **bowler²**.

derby

derringer

The **derringer** was invented by Henry *Deringer* (1806–1868), American gunsmith.

ă pat/ā pay/â care/ä father/ĕ pet/ ē be/ĭ pit/ī pie/î fierce/ŏ pot/ ō go/ô paw, for/oi oil/o͝o book/ o͞o boot/ou out/ŭ cut/û fur/ *th* the/th thin/hw which/zh vision/ ə ago, item, pencil, atom, circus

and unemployment: *a program of aid to depressed areas.* **3.** Sunk below the surrounding region: *the depressed center of a crater.*

de•pres•sion |dĭ **prĕsh**′ən| *n.* **1.** A mental state of gloom, sadness, or melancholy. **2.** An area that is sunk below its surroundings; a hollow. **3.** A period of drastic decline in economic activity, marked by widespread unemployment and hardship. **4.** The act of pressing down.

de•pres•sive |dĭ **prĕs**′ĭv| *adj.* In or characterized by a state of mental depression. —*n.* A depressive person.

dep•ri•va•tion |dĕp′rə **vā**′shən| *n.* **1.** The act of depriving. **2.** The condition of being deprived.

de•prive |dĭ **prīv**′| *v.* **de•prived, de•priv•ing.** To take something away from; prevent from having; deny: *He was deprived of his rights.*

depth |dĕpth| *n.* **1. a.** The dimension of an object that is not thought of as its length or width, usually the distance from top to bottom or front to back. **b.** A distance downward or inward from a surface: *The diver descended to a depth of 100 feet.* **2.** Deep learning, thought, feeling, etc.: *a person of great depth. It is a novel of great depth.* **3.** Lowness of pitch, as of a voice or musical tone. **4. depths. a.** A deep part or place in something: *the ocean depths.* **b.** The greatest degree of something: *the depths of despair.*

***Idioms.* in depth.** Thorough and detailed: *a study in depth.* **out of (one's) depth.** Beyond the range of one's understanding.

depth charge. An explosive charge designed for use underwater, especially one launched from a ship's deck for use against submarines.

dep•u•ta•tion |dĕp′yə **tā**′shən| *n.* A person or group appointed to act for others; a delegation.

de•pute |dĭ **pyo͞ot**′| *v.* **de•put•ed, de•put•ing.** To appoint (someone) as an agent or representative.

dep•u•tize |**dĕp**′yə tīz′| *v.* **dep•u•tized, dep•u•tiz•ing.** To appoint as a deputy.

dep•u•ty |**dĕp**′yə tē| *n., pl.* **dep•u•ties. 1.** A person appointed to act in place of, or as an assistant to, another. **2.** In certain countries, such as France, a member of a legislative body.

de•rail |dē **rāl**′| *v.* To go off or cause to go off the tracks: *Fallen trees on the tracks derailed the express. The train derailed near Buffalo.* —**de•rail′ment** *n.*

de•range |dĭ **rānj**′| *v.* **de•ranged, de•rang•ing.** To unbalance mentally; make insane: *The shock of the disaster deranged him.* —**de•ranged′** *adj.*: *a deranged mind.* —**de•range′ment** *n.*

der•by |**dûr**′bē| *n., pl.* **der•bies.** A stiff felt hat with a round crown and a narrow, curved brim. [SEE NOTE & PICTURE]

Der•by |**dûr**′bē| *n.* A major race for three-year-old horses. [SEE NOTE]

der•e•lict |**dĕr**′ə lĭkt′| *n.* **1.** A homeless, jobless person abandoned by society. **2.** Abandoned property, especially a ship abandoned at sea. —*adj.* **1.** Neglectful; remiss: *derelict in one's duty.* **2.** Deserted by an owner; abandoned: *He bought the derelict mansion cheap.*

der•e•lic•tion |dĕr′ə **lĭk**′shən| *n.* Willful failure to do what is required; deliberate neglect.

de•ride |dĭ **rīd**′| *v.* **de•rid•ed, de•rid•ing.** To laugh at with contempt or scorn; scoff at; mock.

der•in•ger |**dĕr**′ĭn jər| *n.* A form of the word **derringer.**

de•ri•sion |dĭ **rĭzh**′ən| *n.* Scorn; ridicule.

de•ri•sive |dĭ **rī**′sĭv| *adj.* Expressing ridicule; mocking: *derisive laughter.* —**de•ri′sive•ly** *adv.* —**de•ri′sive•ness** *n.*

der•i•va•tion |dĕr′ə **vā**′shən| *n.* **1.** The act or process of deriving: *the derivation of a formula.* **2.** Something that is derived: *The word "vodka" is a derivation from Russian.* **3.** The source from which something, especially a word, is derived; origin: *The word "vodka" is of Russian derivation.* **4.** The historical origin and development of a word; etymology. **5.** In linguistics, the morphological process by which new words are formed from existing words, chiefly by the addition of affixes, such as prefixes or suffixes, to roots, stems, or words.

de•riv•a•tive |dĭ **rĭv**′ə tĭv| *adj.* Derived or obtained from another source: *a derivative word.* —*n.* **1.** A word formed from another by derivation: *The word "vocational" is a derivative from "vocation."* **2.** A substance obtained in some way from another substance, especially a chemical compound that is obtained from another by a well-defined process and that keeps some essential feature of the original compound: *a petroleum derivative; an acetate derivative.*

de•rive |dĭ **rīv**′| *v.* **de•rived, de•riv•ing. 1.** To obtain or receive from a source: *derive pleasure from music.* **2.** To originate from a certain source: *The word "algebra" derives from Arabic.* **3.** To trace the origin of (a word).

der•ma¹ |**dûr**′mə| *n.* The layer of skin, beneath the epidermis, that contains nerve endings, sweat glands, and blood and lymph vessels.

der•ma² |**dûr**′mə| *n.* Kishke.

der•mal |**dûr**′məl| *adj.* Of or involving the skin.

der•ma•tol•o•gist |dûr′mə **tŏl**′ə jĭst| *n.* A physician who specializes in dermatology.

der•ma•tol•o•gy |dûr′mə **tŏl**′ə jē| *n.* The medical study of the skin, its diseases, and their treatment.

der•mis |**dûr**′mĭs| *n.* The derma, a layer of the skin.

der•o•gate |**dĕr**′ə gāt′| *v.* **der•o•gat•ed, der•o•gat•ing. 1.** To detract; take away: *derogate from one's reputation.* **2.** To make seem inferior; belittle; disparage: *derogate the qualities of a book.* —**der′o•ga′tion** *n.*

de•rog•a•to•ry |dĭ **rŏg**′ə tôr′ē| *or* |-tōr′ē| *adj.* Tending to derogate; disparaging; harshly critical: *a derogatory remark.* —**de•rog′a•to′ri•ly** *adv.*

der•rick |**dĕr**′ĭk| *n.* **1.** A large crane for lifting and moving heavy objects. It consists of a movable boom equipped with pulleys and cables and connected to the base of a stationary vertical beam. **2.** A tall framework used to support the equipment used in drilling an oil well or some similar hole.

der•ring-do |**dĕr**′ĭng **do͞o**′| *n.* Daring spirit and action: *a man of derring-do.*

der•rin•ger |**dĕr**′ĭn jər| *n.* A small pistol with a short barrel and a large bore. [SEE PICTURE]

der•vish |**dûr**′vĭsh| *n.* A member of any of various Moslem religious orders, some of which engage in whirling dances.

des•cant |**dĕs**′kănt′| *n.* A secondary, ornamental melody played or sung above a main melody and its harmony and accompaniment, if any. —*v.* |dĕs **kănt**′|. To talk at length; expound.

Des•cartes |dā kärt′|, **René.** 1596–1650. French philosopher and mathematician.

de•scend |dĭ sĕnd′| *v.* **1.** To move from a higher to a lower place; go or come down: *descend the stairs. The airplane descended quickly.* **2.** To arrive in an overwhelming manner: *Our relatives descended upon us this weekend.* **3.** To slope or incline downward: *The narrow path descended gradually.* **4.** To come down from a source or origin; have as an ancestor or ancestry: *The Japanese people believed that their emperor was descended from the gods.* **5.** To pass by inheritance or transmission: *The estate descended to his three daughters.*

de•scend•ant |dĭ sĕn′dənt| *n.* A person or animal considered as descended from specified ancestors.

de•scent |dĭ sĕnt′| *n.* **1.** The act or an example of descending: *They began the descent from the top of the mountain.* **2.** A downward slope. **3.** Family origin; ancestry: *She is of French descent.* ¶ *These sound alike* **descent, dissent.**

de•scribe |dĭ skrīb′| *v.* **de•scribed, de•scrib•ing. 1.** To give a verbal account of; tell about in detail: *describe one's experiences.* **2.** To transmit an impression, image, etc., of with words; picture verbally: *describe a room.* **3.** To trace or draw: *Describe a circle with your compass.*

de•scrip•tion |dĭ skrĭp′shən| *n.* **1.** The act, process, or technique of describing; verbal representation: *He is not good at description.* **2.** An account in words describing something. **3.** A kind or variety; sort: *people of every description.*

de•scrip•tive |dĭ skrĭp′tĭv| *adj.* Serving to describe; making a description of something: *descriptive words; a descriptive passage.* —**de•scrip′tive•ly** *adv.* —**de•scrip′tive•ness** *n.*

de•scry |dĭ skrī′| *v.* **de•scried, de•scry•ing, de•scries.** To catch sight of (something distant or obscure): *descry a ship on the horizon.*

des•e•crate |dĕs′ĭ krāt′| *v.* **des•e•crat•ed, des•e•crat•ing.** To treat (something sacred) with little reverence or respect. —**des′e•cra′tion** *n.*

de•seg•re•gate |dē sĕg′rĭ gāt′| *v.* **de•seg•re•gat•ed, de•seg•re•gat•ing.** To abolish racial segregation in (public schools, public housing, etc.) —**de•seg′re•ga′tion** *n.*

des•ert¹ |dĕz′ərt| *n.* A dry, barren region, often covered with sand, having little or no vegetation. —***modifier:*** *desert life; a desert animal.* —*adj.* Uninhabited: *a desert island.* [SEE NOTE]

de•sert² |dĭ zûrt′| *v.* **1.** To forsake or leave; abandon: *He deserted his wife.* **2.** To leave (the army or an army post) illegally and with no intention of returning: *He deserted his post just before the attack. The corporal deserted yesterday.* —**de•sert′ed** *adj.: a deserted street.* ¶ *These sound alike* **desert, dessert.** —**de•sert′er** *n.* —**de•ser′tion** *n.* [SEE NOTE]

de•sert³ |dĭ zûrt′| *n.* Often **deserts.** That which is deserved or merited, especially a punishment: *He received his just deserts.* ¶ *These sound alike* **desert, dessert.** [SEE NOTE]

de•serve |dĭ zûrv′| *v.* **de•served, de•serv•ing.** To be worthy of; have a right to; merit: *He deserved better treatment than he got.* [SEE NOTE]

de•serv•ed•ly |dĭ zûr′vĭd lē| *adv.* As is right and fair; justly: *He received the award most deservedly.*

de•serv•ing |dĭ zûr′vĭng| *adj.* Worthy of reward or praise: *a deserving person.*

des•ha•bille |dĕs′ə bēl′| *n.* A form of the word **dishabille.**

des•ic•cate |dĕs′ĭ kāt′| *v.* **des•ic•cat•ed, des•ic•cat•ing.** To make thoroughly dry, as by the action of heat or chemicals.

de•sign |dĭ zīn′| *v.* **1.** To draw up plans for (something), especially by means of sketches, drawings, etc.: *design a building; design dresses.* **2.** To plan or intend for a specific purpose: *This dictionary is especially designed for students in school.* —*n.* **1.** A drawing or sketch giving the details of how something is to be made. **2.** An arrangement of lines, figures, or objects into a pattern: *a wallpaper design.* **3.** A purpose or intention: *He left early by design in order to help them.* **4.** Often **designs.** A plan or scheme intended to gain something.

des•ig•nate |dĕz′ĭg nāt′| *v.* **des•ig•nat•ed, des•ig•nat•ing. 1.** To indicate or specify; point out; show: *Markers designate the boundary.* **2.** To give a name or title to; characterize: *Our period of history has been designated by some as the Atomic Age.* **3.** To select for a particular duty, office, or purpose; appoint: *We designated him to represent us at the meeting.*

des•ig•na•tion |dĕz′ĭg nā′shən| *n.* **1.** The act of designating. **2.** An identifying name or title.

de•sign•ed•ly |dĭ zī′nĭd lē| *adv.* On purpose; intentionally.

de•sign•er |dĭ zī′nər| *n.* A person who creates the design of clothing, stage settings, etc.

de•sign•ing |dĭ zī′nĭng| *adj.* Having designs on someone or something; scheming; conniving.

de•sir•a•ble |dĭ zīr′ə bəl| *adj.* **1.** Of such quality as to be desired; pleasing; fine: *a desirable neighborhood.* **2.** Worth doing; advantageous; advisable: *desirable reform.* —**de•sir′a•bil′i•ty, de•sir′a•ble•ness** *n.* —**de•sir′a•bly** *adv.*

de•sire |dĭ zīr′| *v.* To wish or long for; want; crave: *anything your heart desires. Our country desires only peace.* —**de•sired′** *adj.: achieve the desired effect.* —*n.* **1.** A wish, longing, or craving: *man's endless desire to explore new horizons.* **2.** Something desired.

de•sir•ous |dĭ zīr′əs| *adj.* Wishing; desiring: *desirous of further information.*

de•sist |dĭ zĭst′| *or* |-sĭst′| *v.* To cease doing something: *desist from speaking out of turn.*

desk |dĕsk| *n.* **1.** A piece of furniture having a flat top on which to write and a number of drawers for papers, pencils, and other items. **2.** A table, counter, or booth at which a public service is generally offered: *an information desk.*

Des Moines |də moin′| *or* |moinz′|. The capital and largest city of Iowa. Population, 198,000.

des•o•late |dĕs′ə lĭt| *adj.* **1.** Having little or no vegetation; barren. **2.** Having few or no inhabitants; deserted: *a desolate wilderness.* **3.** Lonely and sad; wretched; forlorn: *a child with a desolate air.* —*v.* |dĕs′ə lāt′| **des•o•lat•ed, des•o•lat•ing. 1.** To make desolate, especially to lay waste to: *A fire desolated the forest.* **2.** To make lonely, wretched, etc. —**des′o•late•ly** *adv.*

des•o•la•tion |dĕs′ə lā′shən| *n.* **1.** The condition of being desolate: *desolation caused by a forest fire.* **2.** The act of making desolate. **3.** A wasteland. **4.** Loneliness or misery.

desert¹·²

These two words are related, but **desert³** *belongs, with* **deserve** *and* **dessert,** *to the* **serve** *group; see note at* **dessert. Desert²** *is from French* déserter, *"to abandon," which is from Latin* dēsertus, *"abandoned"; this is from* dēserere, *"to untie oneself from, to leave"* (dē-, *"away, un-,"* + serere, *"to tie, to connect").* **Desert¹** *is from Old French* deserte, *which is from Latin* dēsertum, *"wasteland," from* dēsertus, *"abandoned" (as above).*

dessert/deserve/desert³

*(***Desert¹** *and* **desert²** *form a separate group; see note at* **desert.***)* **Deserve** *is from Old French* deservir, *"to earn, to be entitled to reward in return for service"; this is from Latin* dēservīre, *"to serve well"* (dē-, *"down, completely,"* + servīre, *"to serve").* **Desert³** *is from Old French* desert, *"something earned," from* deservir, *"to earn" (as above).* **Dessert** *is from Old French* desserte, *"clearing of the table," hence "fruit eaten after the main meal is cleared away"; this is from* desservir, *"to un-serve, to clear the table"* (des-, *"away, un-,"* + servir, *"to serve"*; servir *is from* servīre, *the same Latin word as above).*

desperado

detail
Detail of the mechanism of a matchlock

ă pat/ā pay/â care/ä father/ĕ pet/ ē be/ĭ pit/ī pie/î fierce/ŏ pot/ ō go/ô paw, for/oi oil/ŏŏ book/ ōō boot/ou out/ŭ cut/û fur/ *th* the/th thin/hw which/zh vision/ ə ago, item, pencil, atom, circus

de So•to |dĭ sō′tō|, **Hernando.** 1500?–1542. Spanish explorer; discoverer of the Mississippi River.

de•spair |dĭ spâr′| *n.* **1.** Utter lack of hope: *She cried out in despair.* **2.** Someone or something that causes great grief or torment: *He was the despair of his family.* —*v.* To lose all hope: *The doctors despaired of being able to save him.*

de•spair•ing |dĭ spâr′ĭng| *adj.* **1.** Feeling a sense of despair: *despairing victims of the hurricane.* **2.** Indicating or expressing despair: *The prisoners exchanged despairing glances.* —**de•spair′ing•ly** *adv.*

des•patch |dĭ spăch′| *v.* & *n.* A form of the word **dispatch.**

des•per•a•do |dĕs′pə rä′dō| *n., pl.* **des•per•a•does** or **des•per•a•dos.** A desperate, dangerous criminal, especially one of the old western U.S. [SEE PICTURE]

des•per•ate |dĕs′pər ĭt| *or* |-prĭt| *adj.* **1.** In a critical or hopeless situation and thus ready to do anything: *a desperate criminal.* **2.** Having an urgent or overwhelming need for something: *desperate for food; desperate for money.* **3.** Nearly hopeless; critical; grave: *Things look desperate.* **4.** Undertaken in critical or nearly hopeless circumstances: *desperate measures; a last desperate attempt.* **5.** Indicating or expressing despair: *a desperate look on his face.* **6.** Extreme; very great: *in desperate need; a desperate urge.* —**des′per•ate•ly** *adv.*

des•per•a•tion |dĕs′pə rā′shən| *n.* Despair or extreme action resulting from it: *reach the point of desperation.*

des•pi•ca•ble |dĕs′pĭ kə bəl| *or* |dĭ spĭk′ə-| *adj.* Deserving contempt or disdain; vile: *a despicable person; a despicable act.* —**des′pi•ca•ble•ness** *n.* —**des′pi•ca•bly** *adv.*

de•spise |dĭ spīz′| *v.* **de•spised, de•spis•ing.** To regard with contempt or scorn.

de•spite |dĭ spīt′| *prep.* In spite of: *They won despite overwhelming odds.*

de•spoil |dĭ spoil′| *v.* To rob of possessions; plunder; ravage. —**de•spoil′er** *n.*

de•spon•dent |dĭ spŏn′dənt| *adj.* In low spirits; depressed; dejected. —**de•spon′den•cy** *n.* —**de•spon′dent•ly** *adv.*

des•pot |dĕs′pət| *n.* A ruler with absolute power over his subjects; a tyrant.

des•pot•ic |dĭ spŏt′ĭk| *adj.* Ruling with absolute power, often without regard for the wishes of one's subjects. —**des•pot′i•cal•ly** *adv.*

des•pot•ism |dĕs′pə tĭz′əm| *n.* A government in which a ruler holds absolute power over his subjects.

des•sert |dĭ zûrt′| *n.* The last course of a lunch or dinner, often consisting of fruit, ice cream, or pastry. —*modifier: a dessert dish.* ¶*These sound alike* **dessert, desert**[2]**, desert**[3]. [SEE NOTE on p. 251]

des•ti•na•tion |dĕs′tə nā′shən| *n.* The place to which someone or something is going or directed.

des•tine |dĕs′tĭn| *v.* **des•tined, des•tin•ing.** To determine beforehand, as if by some force or power over which one has no control: *a defeat that destined Theodore Roosevelt to political exile.*

des•ti•ny |dĕs′tə nē| *n., pl.* **des•ti•nies. 1.** The fortune, fate, or lot of a particular person or thing, considered as something determined or appointed in advance: *His destiny was a life spent at sea.* **2.** The power that is believed to determine events in advance of their occurrence.

des•ti•tute |dĕs′tĭ tōōt′| *or* |-tyōōt′| *adj.* Completely impoverished; penniless: *Many people were left destitute by the flood.*

des•ti•tu•tion |dĕs′tĭ tōō′shən| *or* |-tyōō′-| *n.* Extreme poverty.

de•stroy |dĭ stroi′| *v.* **1.** To ruin completely; wipe out; lay waste: *The explosion destroyed several homes.* **2.** To put to death; kill: *The injured racehorse had to be destroyed.* **3.** To put an end to; eliminate.

de•stroy•er |dĭ stroi′ər| *n.* **1.** Someone or something that destroys. **2.** A fast, highly maneuverable warship, carrying light armor and heavy guns, torpedoes, and depth charges.

de•struct |dĭ strŭkt′| *n.* The intentional destruction of a rocket, missile, etc., after launching.

de•struc•tion |dĭ strŭk′shən| *n.* **1.** The act of destroying. **2.** Heavy damage: *The tornado caused great destruction.* **3.** A means of destroying: *Heroin is the destruction of many people.*

de•struc•tive |dĭ strŭk′tĭv| *adj.* **1.** Causing destruction: *a destructive storm.* **2.** Condemning rather than offering helpful suggestions; not constructive: *destructive criticism.* —**de•struc′tive•ly** *adv.* —**de•struc′tive•ness** *n.*

destructive distillation. A process in which a substance such as wood or coal is decomposed by heat, producing solid, liquid, and gaseous materials that are collected for various uses.

des•ul•to•ry |dĕs′əl tôr′ē| *or* |-tōr′ē| *adj.* Moving from one thing to another; disconnected; rambling. —**des′ul•to′ri•ly** *adv.*

de•tach |dĭ tăch′| *v.* **1.** To separate; disconnect: *Detach the side panels from the chassis.* **2.** To send on a special mission; assign.

de•tached |dĭ tăcht′| *adj.* **1.** Standing apart; disconnected; separate: *detached houses.* **2.** Free from emotion or strong feeling: *a detached view of this problem.*

de•tach•ment |dĭ tăch′mənt| *n.* **1.** The act or process of separating or disconnecting. **2.** The condition of remaining apart from one's surroundings or the concerns of others; independence of thought or action. **3.** Absence of prejudice or bias. **4.** A body of troops or ships selected from a larger unit for a special duty.

de•tail |dĭ tāl′| *or* |dē′tāl′| *n.* **1.** An individual or specific item; a particular: *No two people have fingerprints that are exactly alike in every detail.* **2.** Such particulars in relation to a whole: *A small map usually includes less detail than a large map.* **3.** A small part of a work of art, such as a painting, considered separately and often enlarged: *Look at this detail of a Renaissance painting.* **4. a.** A small group of soldiers assigned to a specific duty. **b.** The duty assigned: *Our group has guard detail for this week.* —*v.* |dĭ tāl′|. **1.** To give the particulars of: *She detailed all the necessary information.* **2.** To assign (soldiers) to a specific duty. —**de•tailed′** *adj.: detailed information.* [SEE PICTURE]

de•tain |dĭ tān′| *v.* **1.** To delay; impede. **2.** To keep in custody; confine. —**de•tain′ment** *n.*

de•tect |dĭ tĕkt′| *v.* **1.** To discover or notice the existence, presence, or fact of: *He detected a symptom of the disease. I detected something strange in her silence.* **2.** To recover useful information from (a modulated carrier wave); demodulate. —**de•tect'a•ble, de•tect'i•ble** *adj.* —**de•tec'tion** *n.*

de•tec•tive |dĭ tĕk'tĭv| *n.* A person, usually a policeman, whose work is investigating and trying to solve crimes. —***modifier:*** *a detective story.*

de•tec•tor |dĭ tĕk'tər| *n.* **1.** Any device that indicates when some agent or influence, such as radioactivity, magnetism, heat, explosive vapor, or excessive moisture, is present. **2.** An electronic circuit, as in a radio or television receiver, that demodulates an incoming signal.

de•ten•tion |dĭ tĕn'shən| *n.* **1.** The act of detaining or keeping in custody; confinement. **2.** The condition of being kept in custody.

de•ter |dĭ tûr'| *v.* **de•terred, de•ter•ring.** To prevent or discourage, as by fear. —**de•ter'ment** *n.*

de•ter•gent |dĭ tûr'jənt| *n.* A cleaning agent, especially one that increases the ability of water to wet surfaces and helps to emusify oils and fats and that is made mainly of synthetic products. —***modifier:*** *a detergent soap.*

de•te•ri•o•rate |dĭ tîr'ē ə rāt'| *v.* **de•te•ri•o•rat•ed, de•te•ri•o•rat•ing.** To make or become inferior in quality, character, or value: *Moisture deteriorates powder. The railroads deteriorated as air travel grew.* —**de•te'ri•o•ra'tion** *n.*

de•ter•mi•na•tion |dĭ tûr'mə nā'shən| *n.* **1.** The act of arriving at a decision or the decision arrived at: *A determination of who would go was made at the meeting.* **2.** Firmness of purpose: *her determination to win.* **3.** The calculation or measurement of the qualities of something: *the determination of the age of the fossil.*

de•ter•mine |dĭ tûr'mĭn| *v.* **de•ter•mined, de•ter•min•ing.** **1.** To fix, settle, or decide: *Determine whether each of the following is true or false.* **2.** To be the cause of; influence: *Climate determines how men live in different parts of the world.* **3.** To cause (someone) to decide: *Her love of animals determined her to be a veterinarian.* **4.** To establish by investigation; find out: *Public opinion can be determined by plebiscites.* **5.** To identify or fix in a precise mathematical way: *determine the value of a variable.*

de•ter•mined |dĭ tûr'mĭnd| *adj.* Showing determination; firm: *a determined effort.* —**de•ter'mined•ly** *adv.*

de•ter•min•er |dĭ tûr'mə nər| *n.* A word belonging to a group of noun modifiers generally considered to include articles, demonstrative pronouns, demonstrative adjectives, possessive adjectives, and a few other words, such as the adjectives *any, both, hundred,* and *dozen,* that occupy either the first position in a noun phrase or the second or third position after another determiner. Determiners, unlike adjectives, cannot be compared, and they do not normally appear after a linking verb. Many determiners can stand in the place of the noun phrase that they introduce. For example, *an* in *an apple, the* in *the book, any* in *Any car will do,* and *hundred* in *There were a hundred books here and a hundred there* are determiners.

de•ter•rence |dĭ tûr'əns| *or* |-tŭr'-| *n.* The act or a means of deterring.

de•ter•rent |dĭ tûr'ənt| *or* |-tŭr'-| *n.* Someone or something that deters. —*adj.* Serving to deter or restrain.

de•test |dĭ tĕst'| *v.* To dislike strongly; abhor; loathe. —**de•test'ed** *adj.: my most detested duty.*

de•test•a•ble |dĭ tĕs'tə bəl| *adj.* Intensely disliked; abominable. —**de•test'a•bly** *adv.*

de•throne |dē thrōn'| *v.* **de•throned, de•thron•ing.** To remove from a throne or other position of power. —**de•throne'ment** *n.*

det•o•nate |dĕt'n āt'| *v.* **det•o•nat•ed, det•o•nat•ing.** To explode or cause to explode. —**det'o•na'tion** *n.*

det•o•na•tor |dĕt'n ā'tər| *n.* A device used to set off an explosive.

de•tour |dē'tŏŏr'| *or* |dĭ tŏŏr'| *n.* **1.** A road used temporarily instead of a main road. **2.** A deviation from a direct route or course. —*v.* To take or cause to take a detour.

de•tract |dĭ trăkt'| *v.* To take away or lessen the desirable nature of; diminish: *Bad manners can detract from one's attractiveness.* —**de•trac'tion** *n.*

de•trac•tor |dĭ trăk'tər| *n.* Someone who disparages or slanders another.

det•ri•ment |dĕt'rə mənt| *n.* **1.** Damage; harm: *causing pollution, to the detriment of society.* **2.** Something that causes damage, harm, etc.: *His behavior was a detriment to our cause.*

det•ri•men•tal |dĕt'rə mĕn'tl| *adj.* Causing damage, harm, or loss; injurious. —**det'ri•men'tal•ly** *adv.*

de•tri•tus |dĭ trī'təs| *n.* Loose fragments, particles, or grains, especially those formed by the disintegration of rocks.

De•troit |dĭ troit'|. The largest city in Michigan. Population, 1,203,339.

deuce[1] |dōōs| *or* |dyōōs| *n.* **1.** A playing card with two figures of its suit; a two. **2.** In tennis, a tie score when a game can be won by winning two successive points. [SEE NOTE]

deuce[2] |dōōs| *or* |dyōōs| *n. Informal.* The devil. [SEE NOTE]

deu•te•ri•um |dōō tîr'ē əm| *or* |dyōō-| *n.* An isotope of hydrogen that contains one more neutron in its nucleus than ordinary hydrogen does. Its atomic weight is about 2.014.

Deu•ter•on•o•my |dōō'tə rŏn'ə mē| *or* |dyōō'-| *n.* The fifth book of the Old Testament.

Deut•sche mark |doi'chə märk|. The basic unit of money of West Germany.

deut•sche•mark |doi'chə märk'| *n.* A form of the phrase **Deutsche mark.**

de•val•ue |dē văl'yōō| *v.* **de•val•ued, de•val•u•ing.** **1.** To lessen the value of. **2.** To lower the exchange value of (currency). —**de•val'u•a'tion** *n.*

dev•as•tate |dĕv'ə stāt'| *v.* **dev•as•tat•ed, dev•as•tat•ing.** To lay waste; ruin: *The storms devastated much of the country.* —**dev'as•tat'ing** *adj.: a devastating blow.*

dev•as•ta•tion |dĕv'ə stā'shən| *n.* **1.** The act of devastating. **2.** The condition of being devastated; ruin; destruction: *Dikes saved Holland from devastation by flooding.*

de•vel•op |dĭ vĕl'əp| *v.* **1.** To grow or cause to grow; realize or cause to realize the potentials of: *develop industry; develop a good vocabulary. Nations develop in a variety of ways.* **2.** To bring or come into being; generate: *develop a habit; develop a new engine. Rituals often develop over*

deuce[1·2]

Deuce[1] *is from Old French* deus, *"two," which is from Latin* duōs, duo, *"two."* **Deuce[2]** *is probably from Low German* duus!, *"two!," a gambler's shout of annoyance at throwing the lowest possible score at dice;* duus *in turn is ultimately from Latin* duōs, *"two," as above.*

develop

Develop *comes from French* développer, *which was* desveloper *in Old French; its basic meaning is "to unfold"* (des-, *"un-,"* + voloper, *"to wrap")*.

devil/evil

The **devil** *is* **evil**, *but the two words were not originally so similar to each other, and they are not connected in any way. In Old English,* **devil** *was* dēofol, *and* **evil** *was* yfel. Dēofol *was one of the first Christian terms to be introduced into the Germanic languages. It came from Greek* diabolos, *literally "the slanderer," a word used in the Bible to mean "Satan."* Yfel *is a native word, descended from prehistoric Germanic* ubilaz, *meaning "excessive, going too far," therefore "evil."*

dewlap
Brahman cow and calf

ă **pat**/ā **pay**/â **care**/ä **father**/ĕ **pet**/ ē **be**/ĭ **pit**/ī **pie**/î **fierce**/ŏ **pot**/ ō **go**/ô **paw**, **for**/oi **oil**/ŏŏ **book**/ ōō **boot**/ou **out**/ŭ **cut**/û **fur**/ *th* **the**/th **thin**/hw **which**/zh **vision**/ ə **ago**, item, pencil, atom, circus

centuries. **3. a.** To acquire or contract: *develop a disease.* **b.** To acquire gradually: *develop a taste.* **4.** To make or become visible or apparent gradually: *Early frost may prevent leaves from developing their best colors. If a problem develops, we can solve it.* **5.** To lay out, unfold, or reveal gradually: *develop a story; develop an idea.* **6.** To grow or progress from a primitive stage to a more mature stage. **7.** To treat (a photosensitive material) with chemicals in order to make visible the image recorded on it. **8.** To vary and elaborate on (a musical theme). **9.** To build new houses, schools, stores, etc., on (an otherwise undeveloped area). [SEE NOTE]

de•vel•op•er |dĭ **vĕl**′ə pər| *n.* **1.** Someone who develops something, especially someone who builds houses on formerly unused land. **2.** A chemical used in developing a photographic film or similar material.

de•vel•op•ment |dĭ **vĕl**′əp mənt| *n.* **1.** The act or process of developing: *the development of industry in Africa.* **2.** The result of developing; something developed: *industrial development.* **3.** An event; a happening: *a recent development in the talks.* **4.** A group of dwellings built by the same builder. —**de•vel′op•men′tal** *adj.*

de•vi•ant |**dē**′vē ənt| *adj.* Different from what is normal, standard, or accepted: *deviant behavior.* —*n.* A person whose attitude, character, or behavior is deviant.

de•vi•ate |**dē**′vē āt′| *v.* **de•vi•at•ed, de•vi•at•ing.** To vary or differ from an established norm or pattern. —*n.* |**dē**′vē ĭt|. A person whose attitude, character, or behavior is deviant.

de•vi•a•tion |dē′vē **ā**′shən| *n.* **1.** The act, process, or an example of deviating. **2.** The amount by which something has deviated: *a deviation of 20 per cent.*

de•vice |dĭ **vīs**′| *n.* **1.** Something that is made, designed, or used for a particular purpose, especially a machine that performs one or more tasks. **2.** Something used in a literary or artistic work to achieve a particular effect. **3.** A plan, scheme, or trick.

dev•il |**dĕv**′əl| *n.* **1.** Often **Devil.** In Christian tradition, the ruler of Hell and chief spirit of evil, often depicted as a man with horns, a tail, and cloven hoofs; Satan. **2.** A lesser spirit of evil, serving Satan; a demon. **3.** A person who is wicked or bad-tempered. **4.** An unfortunate person: *The poor devil had nothing to eat.* **5.** A person who is daring, clever, or full of mischief. **6.** *Informal.* Anything difficult or hard to manage: *He had the devil of a time. A devil of a wind was blowing.* **7. the devil.** *Informal.* Used as an oath. —*v.* **dev•iled** or **dev•illed, dev•il•ing** or **dev•il•ling. 1.** To prepare (food) with pungent seasoning or condiments, such as mustard: *devil eggs.* **2.** To annoy, torment, or harass. [SEE NOTE]

dev•il•fish |**dĕv**′əl fĭsh′| *n., pl.* **-fish** or **-fish•es. 1.** Also **devil ray.** A large ocean fish having a flattened body with winglike extensions at the sides. **2.** A large octopus.

dev•il•ish |**dĕv**′ə lĭsh| *adj.* **1.** Wicked; fiendish. **2.** Mischievous. —**dev′il•ish•ly** *adv.* —**dev′il•ish•ness** *n.*

dev•il-may-care |**dĕv**′əl mā **kâr**′| *adj.* Careless; reckless.

dev•il•ment |**dĕv**′əl mənt| *n.* Behavior marked by pranks; mischief.

dev•il•try |**dĕv**′əl trē| *n., pl.* **dev•il•tries. 1.** Reckless mischief. **2.** Wickedness.

de•vi•ous |**dē**′vē əs| *adj.* **1.** Straying from the straight or direct course; roundabout. **2.** Done in an underhand manner; tricky; shifty: *devious means.* —**de′vi•ous•ly** *adv.* —**de′vi•ous•ness** *n.*

de•vise |dĭ **vīz**′| *v.* **de•vised, de•vis•ing.** To form or arrange in the mind; plan; invent; contrive.

de•void |dĭ **void**′| *adj.* —**devoid of.** Completely lacking; without.

de•volve |dĭ **vŏlv**′| *v.* **de•volved, de•volv•ing.** To pass or be passed on to a successor or substitute: *During the President's illness his functions devolved upon the Vice President.*

De•vo•ni•an |dĭ **vō**′nē ən| *n.* Also **Devonian period.** A geologic period that began 405 million years ago and ended 345 million years ago, characterized by the appearance of forests and amphibians. —*modifier: a Devonian forest.*

de•vote |dĭ **vōt**′| *v.* **de•vot•ed, de•vot•ing. 1.** To give or apply (one's time, attention, or self) entirely to a specified activity, cause, person, etc.: *He devoted himself to lecturing, preaching, and writing.* **2.** To set apart for a specific purpose; dedicate: *He devoted 10 of his acres to sheep.* —**de•vot′ed** *adj.: a devoted friend.*

dev•o•tee |dĕv′ə **tē**′| *n.* Someone who is extremely devoted to something; a fan.

de•vo•tion |dĭ **vō**′shən| *n.* **1.** Strong attachment; loyalty; faithfulness: *his devotion to his mother; devotion to a cause.* **2.** Religious zeal; piety. **3. devotions.** An act of religious observance or prayer, especially when private.

de•vo•tion•al |dĭ **vō**′shə nəl| *adj.* Of or suited to devotion, especially religious devotion.

de•vour |dĭ **vour**′| *v.* **1.** To swallow or eat up greedily: *Hungry campers devoured all the food.* **2.** To destroy or consume: *white blood cells that devour germs.* **3.** To take in greedily with the senses or mind: *devouring every book on judo.*

de•vout |dĭ **vout**′| *adj.* **1.** Deeply religious; pious: *a devout man.* **2.** Sincere; earnest: *a devout wish for her success.* —**de•vout′ly** *adv.* —**de•vout′ness** *n.*

dew |dōō| *or* |dyōō| *n.* **1.** Water droplets that condense from the air, mostly at night, onto cool surfaces. **2.** Any moisture appearing in small drops, as tears. —*v.* To moisten with or as if with dew. ¶*These sound alike* **dew, do, due.**

dew•ber•ry |**dōō**′bĕr′ē| *or* |**dyōō**′-| *n., pl.* **-ber•ries.** A type of blackberry with trailing stems.

dew•drop |**dōō**′drŏp′| *or* |**dyōō**′-| *n.* A drop of dew.

Dew•ey decimal system |**dōō**′ē| *or* |**dyōō**′ē|. A system for classifying library books by subject through the use of three-digit categories, each category being further subdivided by the addition of decimals to the number.

dew•lap |**dōō**′lăp′| *or* |**dyōō**′-| *n.* A loose fold of skin hanging from the neck of certain animals, such as some dogs or cattle. [SEE PICTURE]

dew point. The temperature, which changes with relative humidity, at which dew condenses from the air.

dew•y |**dōō**′ē| *or* |**dyōō**′ē| *adj.* **dew•i•er, dew•i•est. 1.** Moist with or as if with dew: *dewy fields.* **2.** Resembling dew; refreshing; pure.

dex•ter•i•ty |dĕk stĕr′ĭ tē| *n.* **1.** Skill in the use of the hands or body. **2.** Mental skill or adroitness; cleverness.

dex•ter•ous |**dĕk′**strəs| *adj.* Having dexterity; skillful in the use of the hands, mind, or body. —**dex′ter•ous•ly** *adv.* [SEE NOTE]

dex•trin |**dĕk′**strĭn| *n.* A white or yellow powder made by decomposing starch with water. It forms a colloidal mixture with water, and is used as an adhesive.

dex•trose |**dĕk′**strōs′| *n.* A sugar found in plant and animal tissues and also made synthetically from starch. Its chemical formula is $C_6H_{12}O_6$.

Di The symbol for the element didymium.

di–. A word element meaning "two, twice, double": **dicotyledon.**

dia–. A prefix meaning "through, across": **diaphanous; diagonal.**

di•a•be•tes |dī′ə **bē′**tĭs| *or* |-tēz| *n.* **1.** Any of several disorders of metabolism that cause excessive passage of urine and persistent thirst. **2.** Diabetes mellitus.

diabetes mel•li•tus |mə **lī′**təs|. A form of diabetes in which too little insulin is produced by the pancreas, resulting in an inability of the body to use carbohydrates. Its symptoms include an abnormally high level of sugar in the blood and urine, and it is fatal unless treated.

di•a•bet•ic |dī′ə **bĕt′**ĭk| *adj.* Of, involving, or suffering from diabetes. —*n.* A diabetic person, especially one having diabetes mellitus.

di•a•bol•i•cal |dī′ə **bŏl′**ĭ kəl| or **di•a•bol•ic** |dī′ə **bŏl′**ĭk| *adj.* Of or like the devil; extremely wicked: *a diabolical murder.*

di•a•ce•tyl•mor•phine |dī′ə sēt′l **môr′**fēn′| *or* |dī ăs′ĭ tl-| *n.* The chemical word for heroin.

di•a•crit•i•cal mark |dī′ə **krĭt′**ĭ kəl|. Any of various marks added to a letter or letters and used to indicate a certain feature of pronunciation. The long mark over the *i* in the pronunciation of **bite** |bīt| is a diacritical mark.

di•a•dem |**dī′**ə dĕm′| *n.* A crown or ornamental band worn on the head as a sign of royalty.

di•ag•nose |**dī′**əg nōs′| *or* |-nōz′| *or* |dī′əg**nōs′**| *or* |-**nōz′**| *v.* **di•ag•nosed, di•ag•nos•ing.** **1.** To identify or distinguish (a disease). **2.** To make a careful examination of (someone or something), as in identifying a disease or difficulty.

di•ag•no•sis |dī′əg **nō′**sĭs| *n., pl.* **di•ag•no•ses** |dī′əg **nō′**sēz′|. **1. a.** The act or process of examining in order to identify or determine the nature of a disease or malfunction. **b.** The conclusion reached as a result of such an examination. **2. a.** Any close examination of something. **b.** The conclusion reached.

di•ag•nos•tic |dī′əg **nŏs′**tĭk| *adj.* Of, involving, or used in diagnosis. —**di′ag•nos′ti•cal•ly** *adv.*

di•ag•nos•ti•cian |dī′əg nŏ **stĭsh′**ən| *n.* A person, especially a physician, who specializes in or is skillful in making diagnoses.

di•ag•o•nal |dī **ăg′**ə nəl| *adj.* **1. a.** Joining two vertices of a polygon that are not adjacent. **b.** Joining two vertices of a polyhedron that are not adjacent. **2.** Slanting or oblique. —*n.* A diagonal line segment. —**di•ag′o•nal•ly** *adv.*

di•a•gram |**dī′**ə grăm′| *n.* A visual display, such as a drawing or sketch, that shows how something works or indicates the relationships between its parts. —*v.* **di•a•grammed** or **di•a•gramed, di•a•gram•ming** or **di•a•gram•ing.** To show or represent by or as if by a diagram.

di•al |**dī′**əl| *n.* **1.** A circular figure, such as the face of a clock, having a scale of measure arranged along its circumference and one or more movable pointers that indicate the measure that is to be read from the scale. **2.** Any similar indicating device, whether actually circular or not. **3.** A control whose position or setting is shown by such a device, especially: **a.** The control that selects the station to which a radio or television receiver is tuned. **b.** A movable wheel mounted over a circular scale of numbers and letters and used to signal the number to which a telephone call is made. —*v.* **di•aled** or **di•alled, di•al•ing** or **di•al•ling.** **1.** To control or select by means of a dial, as a radio or telephone. **2.** To use a dial, as on a telephone.

di•a•lect |**dī′**ə lĕkt′| *n.* A regional variety of a language, distinguished from other varieties by pronunciation, vocabulary, etc.: *Cockney is a dialect of English.* —**di′a•lect′al** *adj.*

di•a•logue, also **di•a•log** |**dī′**ə lôg′| *or* |-lŏg′| *n.* **1.** A conversation between two or more persons. **2.** The words spoken by the characters of a play or story. **3.** A literary work written in the form of a conversation. **4.** An exchange of ideas or opinions.

dial tone. A continuous, easily identified tone that sounds in a telephone receiver, telling the user that a call can be dialed.

di•am•e•ter |dī **ăm′**ĭ tər| *n.* **1.** A straight line segment that passes through the center of a circle or sphere with both of its ends on the boundary. **2.** The measure of such a line segment.

di•a•met•ri•cal |dī′ə **mĕt′**rĭ kəl| *adj.* Of or along a diameter.

di•a•met•ri•cal•ly |dī′ə **mĕt′**rĭ kə lē| *adv.* **1.** Directly across a circle or sphere; along a diameter. **2.** Absolutely; completely: *diametrically opposed points of view.*

dia•mond |**dī′**mənd| *or* |**dī′**ə-| *n.* **1.** A crystalline form of carbon that is the hardest of all known substances. It is used in some of its varieties as a gemstone. Varieties that are not of gem quality are used in cutting tools and as abrasives. **2.** A figure (♦) with four equal sides forming two inner obtuse angles and two inner acute angles. **3. a.** A red figure, shaped like a diamond, on a playing card. **b.** A card bearing this figure. **c. diamonds.** The suit in a deck of cards having this figure as its symbol. **4. a.** A baseball infield. **b.** The whole playing field. **c.** Baseball in general. —***modifier:*** *a diamond ring.* [SEE NOTE & PICTURE]

dia•mond•back |**dī′**mənd băk′| *or* |**dī′**ə-| *n.* **1.** Also **diamondback rattlesnake.** A large rattlesnake of the southern United States and Mexico, with diamond-shaped markings on the back. **2.** Also **diamondback terrapin.** A turtle of the southeastern coast of the United States, with knobby or ridged markings on the upper shell. [SEE PICTURE]

Di•an•a |dī **ăn′**ə|. The Roman goddess of the moon and of hunting.

di•a•pa•son |dī′ə **pā′**zən| *or* |-sən| *n.* Either of two types of stops on an organ that form the

dexterous/adroit
These words both associate skill with the right-hand side. **Adroit** *comes from the French phrase* à droit, *"to the right" or "rightly."* **Dexterous** *comes from Latin* dexter, *meaning "on the right side" or "skillful."*

diamond
Diamond *is from Medieval Latin* diamas, diamant-, *a corrupted form of Greek* adamas, adamant-, *meaning first "hard metal" and later "diamond," from which we have also the word* **adamant.**

diamondback
Diamondback rattlesnake

tonal basis for the entire scale of the instrument.

di•a•per |dī'ə pər| *or* |dī'pər| *n.* **1.** A piece of soft cloth or other material that absorbs wetness, folded and pinned around a baby to serve as underpants. **2. a.** A regularly repeated pattern of small diamonds, circles, squares, etc. **b.** Cloth with such a pattern woven in it. **—modifier:** *a diaper pin.* **—v.** To put a diaper on (a baby).

di•aph•a•nous |dī ăf'ə nəs| *adj.* Allowing light to show through; transparent. **—di•aph'a•nous•ly** *adv.* **—di•aph'a•nous•ness** *n.*

di•a•phragm |dī'ə frăm'| *n.* **1.** A muscular membrane that separates the organs of the chest from those of the abdomen and acts in forcing air into and out of the lungs. **2.** Any similar membrane that divides or separates. **3.** A thin disk, as in a microphone, earphone, or similar instrument, that vibrates by means of an electrical signal and makes sound waves or that vibrates by means of sound waves and helps to turn them into electrical signals. **4.** A disk having a fixed or variable opening that regulates the amount of light that passes through a lens or optical instrument.

di•ar•rhe•a, also **di•ar•rhoe•a** |dī'ə rē'ə| *n.* A condition in which bowel movements are excessively frequent and abnormally watery.

di•a•ry |dī'ə rē| *n., pl.* **di•a•ries. 1.** A daily record of personal experiences, events, observations, or opinions. **2.** A book for keeping such a record. [SEE NOTE]

di•as•to•le |dī ăs'tə lē| *n.* The normal, rhythmically occurring relaxation and expansion of the heart chambers, during which the chambers fill with blood.

di•a•stol•ic |dī'ə stŏl'ĭk| *adj.* Of, during, or involving a diastole: *diastolic blood pressure.*

di•as•tro•phism |dī ăs'trə fĭz'əm| *n.* The process or processes by which the main geological features of the earth, such as continents, mountains, and oceans, are formed.

di•a•tom |dī'ə tŏm'| *or* |-təm| *n.* Any of various tiny, one-celled water algae with hard, glasslike cell walls.

di•a•ton•ic scale |dī'ə tŏn'ĭk|. A type of musical scale in which an octave is made up of seven tones arranged so that adjacent tones are separated by half-steps and whole steps only. The eighth tone in such a scale is a repetition of the first at the interval of an octave. See **major scale, minor scale.**

di•a•tribe |dī'ə trīb'| *n.* A bitter and abusive criticism; a complete denunciation.

dice |dīs| *pl.n.* The less frequently used singular is **die** |dī|. **1.** A pair of small cubes that are tossed on a flat surface in playing certain games of chance. The six sides of each cube are numbered from one to six with small dots. **2.** Any game of chance in which dice are used. **—v. diced, dic•ing.** To cut into small cubes.

dick•ens |dĭk'ənz| *interj.* Devil; deuce: *What the dickens is going on here?*

Dick•ens |dĭk'ənz|, **Charles.** 1812–1870. English novelist.

dick•er |dĭk'ər| *v.* To bargain; haggle.

dick•ey |dĭk'ē| *n., pl.* **dick•eys. 1.** A separate shirt front like a bib, often including a collar, worn around the neck under a jacket, sweater, etc. **2.** A shirt collar. **3.** A bib.

Dick test |dĭk|. A test of a person's susceptibility to scarlet fever, made by injecting toxins of the disease just under the skin. [SEE NOTE]

di•cot |dī'kŏt'| *n.* A dicotyledon.

di•cot•y•le•don |dī kŏt'l ēd'n| *n.* A flowering plant with two cotyledons, or seed leaves.

di•cot•y•le•don•ous |dī kŏt'l ēd'n əs| *adj.* Having two cotyledons: *Beans and peas are dicotyledonous plants.*

dic•ta |dĭk'tə| *n.* A plural of **dictum.**

Dic•ta•phone |dĭk'tə fōn'| *n.* A trademark for a small machine that records and reproduces dictation for typing.

dic•tate |dĭk'tāt'| *or* |dĭk tāt'| *v.* **dic•tat•ed, dic•tat•ing. 1.** To say or read aloud so that another person may record or write down what is said: *The superintendent dictated the letter. He usually dictates just after the mail is opened.* **2.** To prescribe with authority; impose; require: *The buyers themselves dictate rising or falling price levels.* **3.** To give orders or commands. **—n.** |dĭk'tāt'|. An order; command; directive: *They followed the dictates of their consciences.*

dic•ta•tion |dĭk tā'shən| *n.* **1. a.** The act of dictating material to another to be written down. **b.** The material dictated. **2.** An order or command.

dic•ta•tor |dĭk'tā'tər| *or* |dĭk tā'tər| *n.* A ruler who has complete authority and unlimited power over the government of a country, especially a tyrant.

dic•ta•to•ri•al |dĭk'tə tôr'ē əl| *or* |-tōr'-| *adj.* **1.** Of a dictator: *dictatorial powers.* **2.** Suitable for a dictator; domineering; bossy: *his dictatorial manner.* **—dic'ta•to'ri•al•ly** *adv.*

dic•ta•tor•ship |dĭk tā'tər shĭp'| *or* |dĭk'tā'-| *n.* **1.** The position or rule of a dictator. **2. a.** A form of government in which one person or class has complete authority and unlimited power. **b.** A country having such a government.

dic•tion |dĭk'shən| *n.* **1.** The choice and use of words in speaking or writing. **2.** Quality of speech or singing judged by clarity and distinctness of pronunciation.

dic•tion•ar•y |dĭk'shə nĕr'ē| *n., pl.* **dic•tion•ar•ies. 1.** A book containing an alphabetical list of words with information given for each word. Such information includes meaning, pronunciation, etymology, usage, and synonyms. **2.** A similar book limited to one category of words: *a dictionary of music; a medical dictionary.* **3.** A book containing an alphabetical list of words translated into another language: *a Russian-English dictionary.* **—modifier:** *a dictionary entry.* [SEE NOTE]

dic•tum |dĭk'təm| *n., pl.* **dic•ta** |dĭk'tə| or **dic•tums. 1.** A dogmatic pronouncement. **2.** A popular saying; a maxim.

did |dĭd|. Past tense of **do.**

di•dac•tic |dī dăk'tĭk| *n.* **1.** Intended to instruct, guide, or teach: *a didactic paper.* **2.** Intended to instruct morally, especially moralizing excessively. **—di•dac'ti•cal•ly** *adv.* **—di•dac'ti•cism'** |dī dăk'tĭ sĭz'əm| *n.*

did•n't |dĭd'nt|. Did not.

Di•do |dī'dō|. In Roman mythology, the queen of Carthage.

didst |dĭdst|. *Archaic.* A form of the past tense of **do,** used with *thou.*

diary/dairy
Dairy *was* daierie *in Middle English; it comes from* daie, *which originally meant "a woman who makes bread" but later meant "a woman who makes butter and cheese."* **Diary** *comes from Latin* diārium, *"daily record," from* diēs, *"day."*

Dick test
This test was devised by George and Gladys Dick (both born in 1881), American physicians.

dictionary
Samuel Johnson, in his English Dictionary *(1755), defined the word* **dictionary** *as: "A book containing the words of a language arranged in alphabetical order, with explanations of their meanings; a lexicon." Noah Webster, in his* American Dictionary *(1828), paid Johnson the compliment of simply quoting Johnson's definition of* **dictionary**. *The compliment is hereby repeated.*

di•dym•i•um |dī dĭm′ē əm| *n.* Symbol **Di** A mixture of praseodymium and neodymium, once thought to be a separate element.

die[1] |dī| *v.* **died, dy•ing. 1.** To cease living; become dead: *Many people die of heart attacks.* **2.** To lose force or vitality; become weak: *The noise died down. The winds died away. The fire died out.* **3.** To cease existing; become extinct: *Old ideas die hard. The bill died in committee.* **4.** To experience extreme agony: *die of embarrassment.* **5.** *Informal.* To desire greatly: *I'm dying to go to the movies.* ¶*These sound alike* **die, dye.** [SEE NOTE]

die[2] |dī| *n.* **1.** *pl.* **dies.** Any one of several types of machine parts or devices that shape materials that are being worked, generally by stamping, cutting, punching, or some similar operation. **2.** *pl.* **dice** |dīs|. One of a pair of dice. ¶*These sound alike* **die, dye.** [SEE NOTE]

die-hard, also **die•hard** |dī′härd′| *n.* Someone who stubbornly refuses to abandon a position and resists change. *—modifier: a die-hard conservative.*

di•e•lec•tric |dī′ĭ lĕk′trĭk| *n.* A substance that hardly conducts electricity at all; a nonconductor or insulator. *—adj.* Of, like, or characteristic of a dielectric.

die•sel |dē′zəl| *n.* Something powered by a diesel engine, especially a locomotive. *—adj.* Powered by or intended for a diesel engine: *diesel locomotive; diesel fuel.*

diesel engine, also **Diesel engine.** An internal-combustion engine in which the fuel is sprayed directly into the cylinder and ignited by the heat of air that has been highly compressed by the piston.

di•et[1] |dī′ĭt| *n.* **1.** The usual food and drink consumed by a person or animal. **2.** A regulated selection of foods, often prescribed for medical reasons, especially for gaining or losing weight. *—modifier: diet soda.* *—v.* To eat and drink a prescribed selection of foods. **—di′et•er** *n.* [SEE NOTE]

di•et[2] |dī′ĭt| *n.* A deliberative assembly; legislature. [SEE NOTE]

di•e•tar•y |dī′ĭ tĕr′ē| *adj.* Of or involving diet. *—n., pl.* **di•e•tar•ies.** A system or set of rules for regulating a diet.

di•e•tet•ic |dī′ĭ tĕt′ĭk| *adj.* **1.** Of diet or the regulation of diet. **2.** Made or processed for use in special diets: *dietetic foods.*

di•e•tet•ics |dī′ĭ tĕt′ĭks| *n. (used with a singular verb).* The scientific study of diet and its relation to health and hygiene.

di•eth•yl ether |dī ĕth′əl|. Ether formed from ethanol.

di•e•ti•tian, also **di•e•ti•cian** |dī′ĭ tĭsh′ən| *n.* A person who specializes in dietetics.

dif•fer |dĭf′ər| *v.* **1.** To be unlike in form, quality, amount, or nature: *The climate often differs from one part of a state to another.* **2.** To be of a different opinion; disagree: *They differed over the amount to give their church. I beg to differ with you.* [SEE NOTE on p. 243]

dif•fer•ence |dĭf′ər əns| *or* |dĭf′rəns| *n.* **1.** The condition of being unlike or different; variation: *the difference between a man and a scarecrow.* **2.** A degree or amount of variation: *a difference of 3 feet.* **3.** A disagreement; quarrel: *a difference of opinion.* **4. a.** The amount by which one number or quantity is greater or less than another. **b.** The number that results when one number is subtracted from another.

dif•fer•ent |dĭf′ər ənt| *or* |dĭf′rənt| *adj.* **1.** Having differences; unlike: *The sea horse is different from any other fish.* **2.** Distinct; separate: *Different people like different things.* **3.** Unusual: *a really different hairdo.* **—dif′fer•ent•ly** *adv.*

dif•fer•en•tial |dĭf′ə rĕn′shəl| *adj.* Of or involving subtraction or differences. *—n.* A **differential gear.**

differential gear. An arrangement of gears that allows one turning shaft to drive two other shafts at any two different speeds as long as the sum of the speeds of the driven shafts is constant. [SEE PICTURE]

dif•fer•en•ti•ate |dĭf′ə rĕn′shē āt′| *v.* **dif•fer•en•ti•at•ed, dif•fer•en•ti•at•ing. 1.** To serve as a distinction between; be the difference in or between: *The qualities of colors differentiate them.* **2.** To understand or show the differences between: *Differentiate the various types of materials shown here.* **3.** To distinguish: *How do biologists differentiate between the plant and animal kingdoms?* **4.** To become different or distinct. **—dif′fer•en′ti•a′tion** *n.*

dif•fi•cult |dĭf′ĭ kŭlt′| *or* |-kəlt| *adj.* **1.** Hard to do, accomplish, or perform: *a difficult task; a difficult operation.* **2.** Hard to understand or solve: *a difficult word; a difficult problem.* **3.** Hard to please, manage, or satisfy: *a difficult person to get along with.* **4.** Rigorous; arduous: *a difficult climb.* **5.** Involving trouble, conflicts, worries, etc.: *difficult times.*

dif•fi•cul•ty |dĭf′ĭ kŭl′tē| *or* |-kəl tē| *n., pl.* **dif•fi•cul•ties. 1.** The condition or quality of being difficult: *the difficulty of the experiment.* **2.** Great effort and trouble: *He walked with difficulty.* **3.** A source of trouble or worry: *Alice's chief difficulty was in managing her flamingo.* **4. dif•ficulties. a.** A troublesome or embarrassing state of affairs: *He met financial difficulties and finally had to declare bankruptcy.* **b.** Problems or conflicts: *getting help for emotional difficulties.*

dif•fi•dent |dĭf′ĭ dənt| *adj.* Timid; shy. **—dif′fi•dence** *n.* **—dif′fi•dent•ly** *adv.*

dif•fract |dĭ frăkt′| *v.* To cause to undergo or undergo diffraction.

dif•frac•tion |dĭ frăk′shən| *n.* The bending or deflection of light or other radiation as it passes an obstacle such as the edge of a slit or aperture. [SEE PICTURE]

diffraction grating. A surface, usually of glass or polished metal, having a large number of fine parallel grooves cut into it, used to produce spectra of reflected or transmitted light.

dif•fuse |dĭ fyōōz′| *v.* **dif•fused, dif•fus•ing. 1.** To undergo or cause to undergo diffusion. **2.** To scatter; disseminate: *diffuse ideas; diffuse knowledge.* *—adj.* |dĭ fyōōs′|. **1.** Widely spread or scattered. **2.** Wordy; long-winded: *a diffuse description.*

dif•fu•sion |dĭ fyōō′zhən| *n.* **1.** The process of diffusing or the condition of being diffused: *the diffusion of knowledge.* **2.** The gradual mixing of two or more substances as a result of random motion of their molecules. **3.** The spreading out of light or other radiation through a space so

die[1-2]

Die[1] *was* diegan *in Old English; it was borrowed from Old Norse* deyja, *"to die." (***Dead** *and* **death** *are related to it.)* **Die**[2] *was* dee *in Middle English, and was borrowed from Old French* de, *which is from Latin* datum, *"playing piece." The form* **dice,** *originally a normal plural, has long been used to mean "a set of dice" or "the game of dice." The final -s of all English plurals that ended in -s was originally pronounced /s/, not /z/ as most of them now are;* **dice** *has preserved this pronunciation.*

diet[1-2]

Diet[1] *is from Greek* diaita, *"way of living, life-style, diet." Some of the ancient Greeks were very interested in diet and developed complete systems of life in which food, exercise, and even psychological activity were closely regulated.* **Diet**[2] *is from Medieval Latin* diēta, *"day's meeting," from* diēs, *"day."*

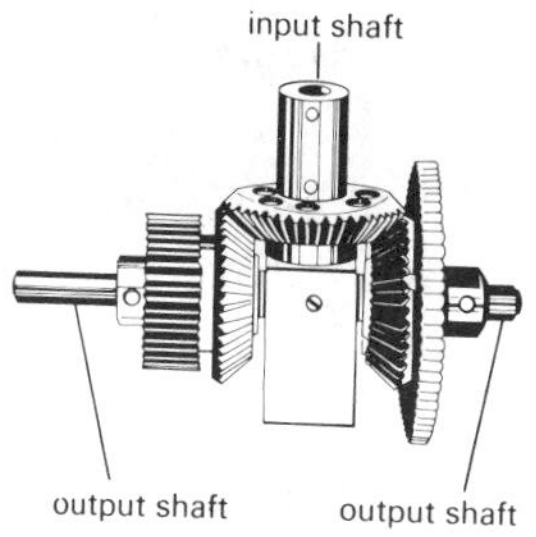

differential gear

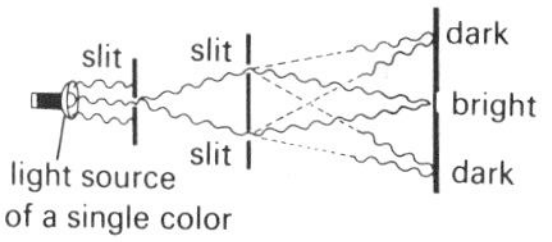

diffraction

The light waves alternately cancel and reinforce each other, producing a series of light and dark bands.

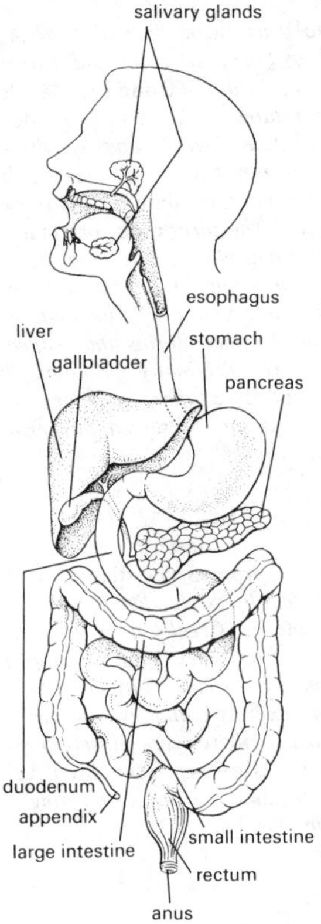

digestive system

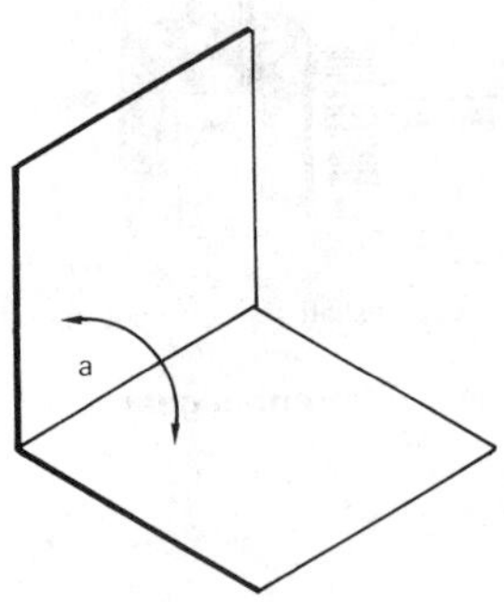

dihedral angle

ă pat/ā pay/â care/ä father/ĕ pet/ ē be/ĭ pit/ī pie/î fierce/ŏ pot/ ō go/ô paw, for/oi oil/ŏŏ book/ ōō boot/ou out/ŭ cut/û fur/ *th* the/th thin/hw which/zh vision/ ə ago, item, pencil, atom, circus

that its intensity becomes more or less uniform with direction.

dig |dĭg| *v.* **dug** |dŭg|, **dig•ging. 1.** To break, turn over, or remove (earth) with a tool, such as a spade, or with the hands. **2.** To make (an excavation) by digging: *They dug a mine shaft.* **3.** To obtain by digging: *Today we must dig potatoes.* **4.** To learn or discover by investigation or study: *dig up information.* **5.** To search for: *dig for gold; patiently digging for facts.* **6.** To force or thrust against: *dug a gun into his back; thorns that dug into his leg.* **7.** To make one's way by or as if by digging: *We dug through a pile of old newspapers to find our book.* **8.** *Slang.* To understand or appreciate: *students who don't dig classical music.* —*phrasal verb.* **dig in. 1.** To entrench oneself. **2.** *Informal.* To begin to work or eat in earnest. —*n.* **1.** A poke; a punch: *a dig in the ribs.* **2.** *Informal.* A sarcastic or cutting remark; a gibe. —**dig'ger** *n.*

di•gest |dĭ jĕst'| *or* |dī-| *v.* **1.** To change (food) or become changed into a form that is easily absorbed into the body, as by chemical and muscular action in the alimentary canal: *digest food. Some foods digest easily.* **2.** To absorb mentally; comprehend: *He digests whole books about history.* —*n.* |dī'jĕst'|. An arrangement of summarized written materials; a synopsis.

di•gest•i•ble |dĭ jĕs'tə bəl| *or* |dī-| *adj.* Capable of being digested. —**di•gest'i•bil'i•ty** *n.*

di•ges•tion |dĭ jĕs'chən| *or* |dī-| *n.* **1. a.** The processes by which food is changed into simple substances that the body can absorb. **b.** The ability to carry on these processes: *poor digestion.* **c.** The result of these processes. **2.** The decomposition of organic matter in sewage by bacteria.

di•ges•tive |dĭ jĕs'tĭv| *or* |dī-| *adj.* Of, aiding, or active in digestion. —**di•ges'tive•ly** *adv.*

digestive system. The alimentary canal together with the glands, such as the liver, salivary glands, and pancreas, that produce substances necessary for digestion. [SEE PICTURE]

dig•it |dĭj'ĭt| *n.* **1.** A finger or toe. **2. a.** A symbol, such as one of the Arabic numerals, 0, 1, 2, 3, 4, 5, 6, 7, 8, and 9, used in the decimal system of numeration. **b.** Such a symbol used in any system of numeration.

dig•i•tal |dĭj'ĭ tl| *adj.* **1.** Of, like, or involving a digit, especially a finger. **2.** Having digits. **3.** Expressed as a series of digits, as for use by a computer: *digital information.* **4.** Using or representing information as series of digits: *a digital clock.* —*n.* A key moved or struck by a finger, as on a piano. —**dig'i•tal•ly** *adv.*

digital computer. A computer that performs operations on data that are represented as series of digits, especially binary digits.

dig•i•tal•is |dĭj'ĭ tăl'ĭs| *n.* A drug prepared from the dried leaves and seeds of the foxglove, used as a powerful heart stimulant.

dig•ni•fied |dĭg'nə fīd'| *adj.* Having or expressing dignity; serious and stately; poised.

dig•ni•fy |dĭg'nə fī'| *v.* **dig•ni•fied, dig•ni•fy•ing, dig•ni•fies. 1.** To give dignity or honor to: *His presence dignified the office.* **2.** To add to the status of; make seem important: *He would not dignify gossip by replying to it.*

dig•ni•tar•y |dĭg'nĭ tĕr'ē| *n., pl.* **dig•ni•tar•ies.** A person of high rank or position.

dig•ni•ty |dĭg'nĭ tē| *n., pl.* **dig•ni•ties. 1.** The condition of being worthy or honorable: *a certain dignity in every human being.* **2.** The respect and honor that go with an important position or station: *the dignity of the Senate.* **3.** A high office or rank. **4.** A stately or poised manner.

di•gress |dĭ grĕs'| *or* |dī-| *v.* To stray from the main subject in writing or speaking. —**di•gres'sion** *n.*

di•he•dral |dī hē'drəl| *adj.* Formed by a pair of planes or sections of planes that intersect: *a dihedral angle.* —*n.* **1.** A dihedral angle. **2.** The upward or downward slope of an aircraft wing. [SEE PICTURE]

dik-dik |dĭk'dĭk'| *n.* A very small African antelope.

dike |dīk| *n.* **1.** A wall or embankment built to hold back water and prevent flooding. **2.** A long mass of igneous rock that cuts across the structure of adjoining rock. —*v.* **diked, dik•ing.** To protect or provide with a dike.

di•lap•i•dat•ed |dĭ lăp'ĭ dā'tĭd| *adj.* In a condition of partial ruin or disrepair: *a dilapidated farmhouse.*

di•lap•i•da•tion |dĭ lăp'ĭ dā'shən| *n.* A condition of partial ruin or disrepair: *The plantation house showed signs of dilapidation.*

di•late |dī lāt'| *or* |dĭ-| *or* |dī'lāt'| *v.* **di•lat•ed, di•lat•ing.** To make or become wider or larger: *The horse dilated its nostrils and whinnied. His eyes dilated with fear.* —**di•la'tion** *n.*

dil•a•to•ry |dĭl'ə tôr'ē| *or* |-tōr'ē| *adj.* Tending or intended to cause delay: *dilatory military maneuvers.*

di•lem•ma |dĭ lĕm'ə| *n.* A situation that requires a person to choose between courses of action that are equally difficult or unpleasant: *He faced the dilemma of giving in or losing his job.*

dil•et•tante |dĭl'ĭ tänt'| *or* |-tän'tē| *or* |-tănt'| *or* |-tăn'tē| *or* |dĭl'ĭ tănt'| *n.* A person with an amateurish or superficial interest in an art or branch of knowledge.

dil•i•gence |dĭl'ə jəns| *n.* **1.** Long, steady effort in one's job or studies. **2.** Careful attention.

dil•i•gent |dĭl'ə jənt| *adj.* **1.** Industrious; hardworking: *a diligent student.* **2.** Done with great care: *a diligent search.* —**dil'i•gent•ly** *adv.*

dill |dĭl| *n.* **1.** A plant with very fine, feathery leaves and spicy seeds. **2.** The leaves or seeds of this plant, used as seasoning.

dil•ly•dal•ly |dĭl'ē dăl'ē| *v.* **dil•ly•dal•lied, dil•ly•dal•ly•ing, dil•ly•dal•lies.** To waste time; dawdle.

di•lute |dĭ lōōt'| *or* |dī-| *v.* **di•lut•ed, di•lut•ing. 1.** To make (a solution) thinner or less concentrated, as by adding solvent. **2.** To make weaker or less potent, as by mixing or dispersing: *dilute wine with water.* —*adj.* Weak: *dilute acid.*

di•lu•tion |dĭ lōō'shən| *or* |dī-| *n.* **1. a.** The act or process of diluting. **b.** The condition of being diluted. **2.** A diluted substance: *a 50 per cent dilution of a saturated solution.*

dim |dĭm| *adj.* **dim•mer, dim•mest. 1.** Faintly lighted: *a dim corner of the big hall.* **2.** Shedding a small amount of light: *a dim lantern; a dim star.* **3.** Lacking brightness: *dim colors.* **4.** Faintly outlined, indistinct, or obscure: *a church steeple dim against the sky.* **5.** Lacking keenness; not sharp: *His eyesight is dim.* **6.** Negative; unfavorable: *taking a dim view of excuses.* —*v.*

dimmed, dim•ming. To make or become dim: *She dimmed the headlights. The auditorium lights dimmed.* —**dim'ly** *adv.* —**dim'ness** *n.*

dime |dīm| *n.* **1.** A U.S. or Canadian coin worth ten cents. **2.** A small sum of money; any money: *I haven't a dime to my name.*

Idiom. **on a dime.** Almost instantly and in a small space: *The car can stop on a dime.*

di•men•sion |dĭ mĕn'shən| *n.* **1.** The measure of how far something extends in space. **2.** Any of the physical properties, especially mass, length, and time, that are considered basic and from which other measures are derived: *Velocity has the dimensions of length divided by time.* **3.** The smallest number of independent coordinates that give the location of a unique point in a mathematical space: *a space of four dimensions.* **4.** Often **dimensions.** Extent; scope: *Wagner added new dimensions to opera.* —*v.* **1.** To cut or shape to specific dimensions: *Each part is dimensioned to fit any model.* **2.** To indicate the dimensions of, as on a drawing, blueprint, etc.

di•men•sion•al |dĭ mĕn'shə nəl| *adj.* **1.** Of a dimension or dimensions. **2.** Having a specified number of dimensions: *a two-dimensional geometric figure.*

di•min•ish |dĭ mĭn'ĭsh| *v.* To make or become smaller or less: *A drought diminished their food supply. The king's authority diminished steadily after the revolt.*

di•min•u•en•do |dĭ mĭn'yo͞o ĕn'dō|. In music: *n., pl.* **di•min•u•en•dos** or **di•min•u•en•does. 1.** A gradual decrease in loudness; a decrescendo. **2.** A musical passage played with a diminuendo. —*adj.* Gradually decreasing in loudness. —*adv.* With a diminuendo.

dim•i•nu•tion |dĭm'ə no͞o'shən| *or* |-nyo͞o'-| *n.* **1.** The act or process of diminishing. **2.** A reduction; decrease.

di•min•u•tive |dĭ mĭn'yə tĭv| *adj.* **1.** Of very small size; tiny. **2.** Expressing smallness or affection, as the diminutive suffixes *-let* in *booklet, -ette* in *dinette,* and *-kin* in *lambkin.* —*n.* A diminutive suffix, word, or name. —**di•min'u•tive•ly** *adv.* —**di•min'u•tive•ness** *n.*

dim•i•ty |dĭm'ĭ tē| *n., pl.* **dim•i•ties.** A thin, crisp cotton cloth with raised threads that form checks or stripes in the wave, used chiefly for curtains and dresses.

dim•mer |dĭm'ər| *n.* Any one of many devices used to reduce the brightness of electric lights.

di•morph |dī'môrf'| *n.* Either one of a pair of dimorphic forms.

di•mor•phic |dī môr'fĭk| *adj.* Occurring in two different forms, as the crystals of a mineral. —**di•mor'phism'** *n.*

dim•ple |dĭm'pəl| *n.* A small indentation in the flesh on a part of the human body, as on the cheek. —*v.* **dim•pled, dim•pling. 1.** To produce dimples in: *The rain dimpled the pool.* **2.** To form dimples: *Her face dimpled with delight.*

din |dĭn| *n.* Loud, confused, prolonged noise that is usually distracting and may also be very distressing: *the din of battle.* —*v.* **dinned, din•ning. 1.** To make a din. **2.** To impart by wearying repetition: *din an idea into her head.*

di•nar |dĭ när'| *n.* The basic unit of money of Iraq, Jordan, Kuwait, Southern Yemen, Algeria, Libya, Tunisia, and Yugoslavia.

dine |dīn| *v.* **dined, din•ing. 1.** To eat dinner: *We dined early. She dined on chicken and dumplings.* **2.** To entertain at dinner: *We dined the visiting mayors.* —**din'ing** *adj.: a dining hall; a dining table; a dining area.* ¶ *These sound alike* **dine, dyne.**

din•er |dī'nər| *n.* **1.** A person eating dinner. **2.** A railroad car in which meals are served. **3.** A restaurant that has a long counter and is shaped like a railroad car.

di•nette |dī nĕt'| *n.* **1.** A nook or alcove for informal meals. **2.** The table and chairs used in a dinette.

ding |dĭng| *n.* A ringing or clanging sound, as of a bell. —*v.* To ring or clang.

ding-dong |dĭng'dông'| *or* |-dŏng'| *n.* The peal of a bell or any series of similar repeated sounds.

din•ghy |dĭng'ē| *n., pl.* **din•ghies.** A small boat, especially a rowboat.

din•gle |dĭng'gəl| *n.* A small wooded valley; a dell.

din•go |dĭng'gō| *n., pl.* **din•goes.** A wild dog of Australia, with a yellowish-brown coat. [SEE PICTURE]

din•gy |dĭn'jē| *adj.* **din•gi•er, din•gi•est. 1.** Dirty; soiled; grimy: *a dingy coat.* **2.** Drab; squalid: *a dingy room.* —**din'gi•ly** *adv.* —**din'gi•ness** *n.*

dining room. A room in which meals are served.

dink•y |dĭng'kē| *adj.* **dink•i•er, dink•i•est.** *Informal.* Small; insignificant.

din•ner |dĭn'ər| *n.* **1.** The main meal of the day, served at noon or in the evening. **2.** A formal meal in honor of a person or an occasion. —***modifier:*** *a dinner plate; a dinner party.*

dinner jacket. A man's jacket, often part of a tuxedo, worn with a black bow tie on semiformal or formal occasions.

di•no•saur |dī'nə sôr'| *n.* Any of many kinds of often gigantic reptiles that lived millions of years ago and are now extinct. [SEE NOTE]

dint |dĭnt| *n.* —**by dint of.** By force, power, or exertion: *By dint of much research, he traced the manuscript back to 1840.*

di•o•cese |dī'ə sĭs| *or* |-sēs'| *n.* The district or churches under the leadership of a bishop.

di•ode |dī'ōd'| *n.* **1.** An electron tube that has two electrodes, especially a tube that allows current to flow in one direction only. **2.** A semiconductor or other solid-state electronic device that allows current to flow in one direction only.

di•o•ram•a |dī'ə răm'ə| *or* |-rä'mə| *n.* A three-dimensional miniature scene with painted modeled figures and background.

di•ox•ide |dī ŏk'sīd'| *n.* An oxide containing two atoms of oxygen per molecule.

dip |dĭp| *v.* **dipped, dip•ping. 1.** To plunge briefly in or into a liquid: *She dipped a piece of bread in her coffee. Six pairs of oars dipped rhythmically.* **2.** To reach into, so as to obtain something: *He dipped into the can for fresh bait.* **3.** To scoop up by plunging the hand or a container into and out of a liquid; bail: *dipping stagnant water out of the trough.* **4.** To color or dye by putting into a liquid: *dipped the curtains a bright color.* **5.** To make (a candle) by repeatedly putting a wick in melted wax or tallow. **6.** To lower and raise (a flag) in salute. **7.** To drop or sink suddenly: *The colt dipped its head. The plane dipped as it fought the wind.* **8.** To slope downward or appear to

dingo

dinosaur

Dinosaurs *are known to us from fossil remains of the Mesozoic era, from 230 million to 63 million years ago. Although the dinosaurs included the largest land animals ever known to exist, some kinds were no larger than dogs.*

sink: *The sun dipped toward the horizon.* **9.** To read or study here and there in: *She dipped into English history.* —*n.* **1.** A brief plunge: *a dip in the sea.* **2.** A liquid into which something is dipped. **3.** A creamy food mixture, as of softened cheese, into which crackers may be dipped. **4.** An amount taken up by dipping; a scoop: *a double dip of ice cream.* **5.** A downward slope; a decline or drop: *a dip in the road.*

diph•the•ri•a |dĭf thîr′ē ə| *or* |dĭp-| *n.* A serious contagious disease caused by infection with certain bacilli. Its symptoms include high fever, weakness, and the formation in the throat and other air passages of false membranes that cause difficulty in breathing.

diph•thong |dĭf′thông′| *or* |-thŏng′| *or* |dĭp′-| *n.* A speech sound beginning with one vowel sound and moving to another within the same syllable. For example, *oy* in the word *boy* is a diphthong.

di•plod•o•cus |dĭ plŏd′ə kəs| *n.* A very large plant-eating dinosaur.

dip•loid |dĭp′loid′| *adj.* Having chromosomes that, except for those that determine sex, exist in essentially identical pairs; having a pair of genes for each characteristic. —*n.* A diploid cell or individual.

di•plo•ma |dĭ plō′mə| *n.* A document or certificate showing that a person has earned a degree from or completed a course of study at a school, college, or university. [SEE NOTE]

di•plo•ma•cy |dĭ plō′mə sē| *n., pl.* **di•plo•ma•cies. 1.** The art or practice of managing relations between nations without use of warfare. It includes the arranging of treaties and other agreements. **2.** Skill in dealing with others; tact.

dip•lo•mat |dĭp′lə măt′| *n.* **1.** A person appointed to represent his government in its dealings with other governments. **2.** A person who has skill in dealing with others.

dip•lo•mat•ic |dĭp′lə măt′ĭk| *adj.* **1.** Of diplomacy or diplomats: *diplomatic means; diplomatic relations; the diplomatic corps.* **2.** Showing skill in dealing peacefully with others; tactful. —**dip′lo•mat′i•cal•ly** *adv.* [SEE NOTE]

dip•per |dĭp′ər| *n.* **1.** A person or thing that dips. **2.** A cup with a long handle for scooping up liquids. **3. Dipper.** Either of two constellations, the Big Dipper or the Little Dipper. **4.** A bird, the **water ouzel.** [SEE PICTURES]

dip•so•ma•ni•a |dĭp′sə mā′nē ə| *or* |-mān′yə| *n.* An uncontrollable craving for alcoholic liquors. —**dip′so•ma′ni•ac′** |dĭp′sə mā′nē ăk′| *n.*

dire |dīr| *adj.* **dir•er, dir•est. 1.** Warning of disaster or other terrible consequences: *dire predictions.* **2.** Having dreadful or terrible consequences; disastrous: *a dire catastrophe.* **3.** Urgent; grave: *in dire need.*

di•rect |dĭ rĕkt′| *or* |dī-| *v.* **1.** To conduct the affairs of; manage; regulate: *He directs a large business.* **2.** To determine; control: *Instinct directs much of an animal's behavior.* **3.** To conduct (a musical composition or a group of musicians): *The composer directed his own symphony. He directs with a baton.* **4.** To guide and supervise the dramatic presentation and acting of (a play, film, etc.): *He directed the film version of the book.* **5.** To instruct, order, or command: *The king directed them to free the prisoner. Fill out the form as your teacher directs.* **6.** To aim, point, or guide (someone or something) to or toward: *Please direct him to the post office.* —*adj.* **1.** Proceeding or lying in a straight course or line; not deviating: *moving in a direct line across the desert.* **2.** Straightforward; candid; frank: *plain, direct talk.* **3.** With nothing intervening or interfering; immediate: *direct sunlight.* **4.** Absolute; total: *direct opposites.* **5.** Of unbroken descent or lineage: *a direct descendant of King David.* —*adv.* In a straight line; directly: *He flew direct to New York.* —**di•rect′ness** *n.*

direct current. An electric current that does not change its direction of flow.

directed number. A positive or negative number.

di•rec•tion |dĭ rĕk′shən| *or* |dī-| *n.* **1.** Management, supervision, or guidance of a process, activity, performance, or production: *He is on a strict diet under the direction of the doctor. The movie's success is due chiefly to his expert direction.* **2. directions.** Instructions for doing something. **3.** An order or command: *He was forced to write the letter at the direction of the kidnappers.* **4. a.** The angle between a reference line drawn through a point and a straight line connecting that point with another point. **b.** A straight line leading from one point to another. **c.** The angle between such a line and true north as shown on a compass. **d.** The line or course along which a person or thing moves. **5.** Orientation or bearing in relation to surroundings: *She has no sense of direction.*

di•rec•tion•al |dĭ rĕk′shə nəl| *or* |dī-| *adj.* Of, involving, or indicating direction, especially a single specified direction. —*n.* One of the directional signals of an automobile or other motor vehicle. —**di•rec′tion•al•ly** *adv.*

directional antenna. A radio, television, or radar antenna that is most sensitive to signals arriving from a particular direction.

directional signal. Either one of two flashing lights mounted on an automobile or other motor vehicle, used to indicate the driver's intention to turn to the right or left.

direction finder. A device, consisting essentially of a radio receiver connected to a movable directional antenna, for determining the direction from which a radio signal comes.

di•rec•tive |dĭ rĕk′tĭv| *or* |dī-| *n.* An order or instruction, especially one issued by a governmental or military agency.

di•rect•ly |dĭ rĕkt′lē| *or* |dī-| *adv.* **1.** In a direct line; straight: *The bull headed directly toward her.* **2.** Exactly: *directly south of Alaska.* **3.** Without anything or anyone intervening: *The Senator spoke directly to the President.* **4.** Without delay; at once: *I'll meet you there directly.*

direct object. In English and some other languages, the word or words in a sentence designating the person or thing that receives the action of the verb. For example, in the sentence *The boy broke the dish,* the direct object is *the dish.*

di•rec•tor |dĭ rĕk′tər| *or* |dī-| *n.* **1.** A person who supervises, controls, or manages something. **2.** A member of a group of persons who control or govern the affairs of a corporation or institution, such as a university or hospital. **3.** A

diploma/diplomatic

Diploma *is from Greek* diplōma, *"something folded, an official document, a passport," from* diplos, *"double."* **Diplomatic** *originally meant "concerned with official documents"; in the early eighteenth century it took on the meaning "concerned with the documents of international relations."*

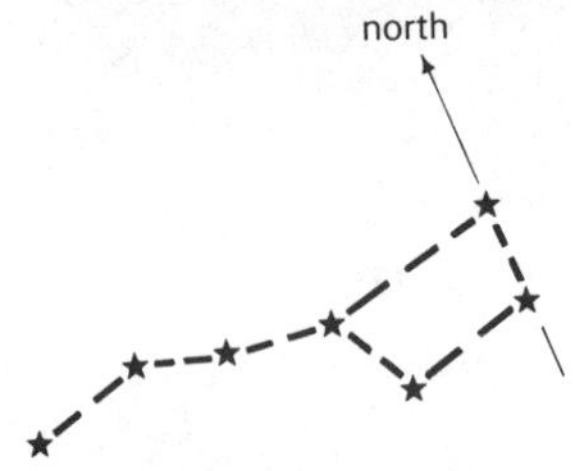

dipper
Above: Cowboy with dipper
Below: Big Dipper, a constellation

ă pat/ā pay/â care/ä father/ĕ pet/ē be/ĭ pit/ī pie/î fierce/ŏ pot/ō go/ô paw, for/oi oil/ŏŏ book/ōō boot/ou out/ŭ cut/û fur/*th* the/th thin/hw which/zh vision/ə ago, item, pencil, atom, circus

person who supervises or guides the performers in a play, motion picture, opera, television show, or other entertainment.

di•rec•tor•ate |dĭ rĕk′tər ĭt| *or* |dī-| *n.* **1.** The office or position of a director. **2.** A group or staff of directors of a corporation or institution.

di•rec•to•ry |dĭ rĕk′tə rē| *or* |dī-| *n., pl.* **di•rec•to•ries.** A list of names, addresses, or other facts: *a telephone directory.*

direct proportion. A relationship between a pair of variables in which a specified quotient of one divided by the other remains constant. For example, if x and y are variables and k is a constant, and if $y = kx$, then x and y are in direct proportion.

direct variation. In mathematics, a form of variation in which a pair of variables, say x and y, maintain a direct proportion, often written in the form $y = kx$, where k is a constant.

dire•ful |dīr′fəl| *adj.* Dreadful; frightful: *He had removed their direful scourge, the dragon.*

dirge |dûrj| *n.* A sad, solemn piece of music, such as a funeral hymn or lament.

dir•i•gi•ble |dîr′ə jə bəl| *or* |dĭ rĭj′ə-| *n.* An early type of lighter-than-air craft, usually made with a stiff framework, that could be steered. [SEE NOTE & PICTURE]

dirk |dûrk| *n.* A dagger.

dirn•dl |dûrn′dəl| *n.* **1.** A dress with a full, gathered skirt and a tight bodice. **2.** A full, gathered skirt of this type. —**modifier:** *a dirndl skirt.* [SEE PICTURE]

dirt |dûrt| *n.* **1.** Earth or soil: *Rock and dirt came tumbling down from the mountain.* **2.** A filthy or soiling substance, such as mud: *A detergent removes dirt from clothes.* **3.** Obscene language: *He yelled dirt at them as they departed.* **4.** Malicious or scandalous gossip: *This magazine publishes dirt about movie stars.* —**modifier:** *a dirt road; dirt spots.*

dirt•y |dûr′tē| *adj.* **dirt•i•er, dirt•i•est. 1.** Soiled; grimy; unclean: *dirty clothes; a dirty floor.* **2.** Contaminated; polluted: *Fish cannot live in dirty water.* **3.** Dark or threatening: *a dirty look.* **4.** Stormy and disagreeable; rough and unpleasant: *dirty weather.* **5.** Dishonorable; unfair: *a dirty deal that cheated many people; a dirty fighter.* **6.** Obscene or indecent: *dirty jokes.* —*v.* **dirt•ied, dirt•y•ing, dirt•ies.** To make or become soiled and grimy: *She dirtied her dress. White dresses dirty easily.* —*adv.* **1.** Unfairly: *play dirty.* **2.** Indecently.

dis–. A prefix meaning: **1.** Negation or lack: **disobey, distrust. 2.** Reversal: **disapprove. 3.** Removal or rejection: **discard.**

dis•a•bil•i•ty |dĭs′ə bĭl′ĭ tē| *n., pl.* **dis•a•bil•i•ties. 1.** The condition of lacking or losing a physical or mental capacity: *The old man feared disability more than death.* **2.** Something that disables; a handicap.

dis•a•ble |dĭs ā′bəl| *v.* **dis•a•bled, dis•a•bling.** To weaken or destroy the normal capacity or abilities of; cripple; incapacitate: *The wound disabled him. The storm disabled the steamer's engine.* —**dis•a′bled** *adj.: a disabled veteran.*

dis•a•buse |dĭs′ə byo͞oz′| *v.* **dis•a•bused, dis•a•bus•ing.** To free from a falsehood or misconception.

dis•ad•van•tage |dĭs′əd văn′tĭj| *or* |-vän′-| *n.* **1.** An unfavorable condition or circumstance; a handicap: *A disadvantage of river transportation is its slowness.* **2.** Damage; harm; loss: *The new ruling worked to our disadvantage.*

dis•ad•van•taged |dĭs′əd văn′tĭjd| *or* |-vän′-| *adj.* Suffering under severe economic and social disadvantage: *disadvantaged children.*

dis•af•fect |dĭs′ə fĕkt′| *v.* To cause to lose affection or loyalty; alienate. —**dis′af•fec′tion** *n.*

dis•a•gree |dĭs′ə grē′| *v.* **dis•a•greed, dis•a•gree•ing. 1.** To fail to correspond: *Your answer to the first problem disagrees with mine.* **2.** To have a different opinion; fail to agree: *Scientists disagree on the origin of craters on the moon.* **3.** To dispute; quarrel. **4.** To have bad effects: *Fried food disagrees with her.*

dis•a•gree•a•ble |dĭs′ə grē′ə bəl| *adj.* **1.** Unpleasant; distasteful: *a strong and disagreeable odor.* **2.** Quarrelsome; bad-tempered: *a vain, disagreeable boy.* —**dis′a•gree′a•ble•ness** *n.* —**dis′a•gree′a•bly** *adv.*

dis•a•gree•ment |dĭs′ə grē′mənt| *n.* **1.** A failure to agree; difference; inconsistency. **2.** A difference of opinion. **3.** A dispute or quarrel caused by a difference of opinion.

dis•ap•pear |dĭs′ə pîr′| *v.* **1.** To pass out of sight, hearing, etc., either gradually or suddenly; vanish: *The ship disappeared over the horizon. The sound of the siren finally disappeared as the fire engine got far away.* **2.** To leave or depart; go away: *She disappears every time the dishes need washing.* **3.** To cease to exist: *Whole countries disappeared as boundaries changed.*

dis•ap•pear•ance |dĭs′ə pîr′əns| *n.* The act or an example of disappearing: *The disappearance of the dinosaurs is often thought to be a mystery.*

dis•ap•point |dĭs′ə point′| *v.* **1.** To fail to satisfy the hope, desire, or expectation of: *The candidate's speech disappointed his younger followers.* **2.** To fail to keep an appointment with or a promise to: *He went only because he did not want to disappoint the children.* —**dis′ap•point′ing** *adj.: a disappointing performance.*

dis•ap•point•ed |dĭs′ə poin′tĭd| *adj.* **1.** Made unhappy by the failure of one's hopes or expectations: *a disappointed team.* **2.** Showing such unhappiness: *many disappointed faces; in a disappointed voice.* **3.** Unfulfilled; frustrated: *my disappointed ambitions.*

dis•ap•point•ment |dĭs′ə point′mənt| *n.* **1.** The act of disappointing. **2.** The feeling of being disappointed: *Disappointment was a sickness in him.* **3.** A person or thing that disappoints: *The picnic was a disappointment.*

dis•ap•prov•al |dĭs′ə pro͞o′vəl| *n.* Dislike or unfavorable judgment of something; condemnation: *John Brown's disapproval of slavery.*

dis•ap•prove |dĭs′ə pro͞ov′| *v.* **dis•ap•proved, dis•ap•prov•ing. 1.** To have an unfavorable opinion; condemn: *opponents whose ideas you disapprove of. He always disapproves of what I say.* **2.** To refuse to approve: *They disapproved his request.*

dis•arm |dĭs ärm′| *v.* **1.** To take weapons from; deprive of the means of attack or defense: *The policeman disarmed the robber.* **2.** To reduce one's armed forces or supply of weapons. **3.** To overcome the suspicion or unfriendliness of; win the confidence of: *His kind words disarmed her.*

dirigible

The word **dirigible** *is from French* dirigeable, *"steerable." Steerable powered balloons were not made practical until the end of the nineteenth century. In 1885 the* Oxford English Dictionary *commented as follows at the entry* balloon: *"to large balloons a car strong enough to carry human beings can be attached, and hence they are used for observing atmospheric phenomena, for military reconnoitering, and, though with little success at present, as a means of traveling through the air."*

dirndl

disaster

Disaster *is from Italian* disastro, *"unfavorable star, stroke of hostile fate, extremely bad luck":* dis-, *"bad,"* + astro, *"star" (stars being regarded as controlling human fortunes).* Astro *is from Latin* astrum, *which is from Greek* astron, *"star"; see* **aster**.

disc/disk

Greek diskos, *"a discus" or "something shaped like a discus," was borrowed into Latin as* discus *(the Romans did not use the letter* k, *so they always turned a Greek* k *into a* c*). When the word was borrowed into English, it was originally spelled* **disk**, *but because of the Latin spelling the variant* **disc** *also occurs.* **Disk** *is still the primary spelling. In the materials on which this Dictionary is based,* **disk** *occurs nearly twice as often as* **disc**, *except in reference to phonograph records or recordings, for which* **disc** *is preferred.*

disc jockey

ă **pat**/ā **pay**/â **care**/ä **father**/ĕ **pet**/ ē **be**/ĭ **pit**/ī **pie**/î **fierce**/ŏ **pot**/ ō **go**/ô **paw**, **for**/oi **oil**/ŏŏ **book**/ ōō **boot**/ou **out**/ŭ **cut**/û **fur**/ *th* **the**/th **thin**/hw **which**/**zh** vision/ ə **ago**, item, pencil, atom, circus

dis•ar•ma•ment |dĭs är′mə mənt| *n.* A reduction of a country's armed forces or weapons of war.

dis•arm•ing |dĭs är′mĭng| *adj.* Serving to remove suspicion or unfriendliness; endearing: *a disarming smile.* —**dis•arm′ing•ly** *adv.*

dis•ar•range |dĭs′ə rānj′| *v.* **dis•ar•ranged, dis•ar•rang•ing.** To upset the order or arrangement of: *The wind disarranged her hair.*

dis•ar•ray |dĭs′ə rā′| *n.* **1.** A state of disorder or confusion: *The mail lay in disarray on his desk.* **2.** Disordered or insufficient dress.

dis•as•sem•ble |dĭs′ə sĕm′bəl| *v.* **dis•as•sem•bled, dis•as•sem•bling.** To take or come apart: *He disassembled the engine so that he could repair it. The jigsaw puzzle disassembled when she bumped into the table.*

dis•as•ter |dĭ zăs′tər| *or* |-zä′stər| *n.* **1.** Great destruction, distress, or misfortune; grave calamity. **2.** A total failure: *a performance that was a disaster; a financial disaster.* —***modifier:*** *a disaster area.* [SEE NOTE]

dis•as•trous |dĭ zăs′trəs| *or* |-zä′strəs| *adj.* Causing disaster; ruinous: *disastrous floods.* —**dis•as′trous•ly** *adv.*

dis•a•vow |dĭs′ə vou′| *v.* To disclaim or deny knowledge of, responsibility for, or association with; disown: *He disavowed the deeds of his followers.*

dis•a•vow•al |dĭs′ə vou′əl| *n.* The act or an example of disavowing; a denial or repudiation.

dis•band |dĭs bănd′| *v.* To break up and separate: *disband an orchestra.*

dis•bar |dĭs bär′| *v.* **dis•barred, dis•bar•ring.** To expel (a lawyer) from the legal profession. —**dis•bar′ment** *n.*

dis•be•lief |dĭs′bĭ lēf′| *n.* The refusal or reluctance to believe.

dis•be•lieve |dĭs′bĭ lēv′| *v.* **dis•be•lieved, dis•be•liev•ing.** **1.** To refuse to believe in; reject: *He disbelieved their talk of wealth beyond the sea.* **2.** To withhold belief: *They disbelieved in the Pharaoh as a god.*

dis•burse |dĭs bûrs′| *v.* **dis•bursed, dis•burs•ing.** To pay out (money): *disburse large sums of money for an advertising campaign.*

dis•burse•ment |dĭs bûrs′mənt| *n.* **1.** The act of disbursing. **2.** Money paid out.

disc |dĭsk| *n.* **1.** *Informal.* A phonograph record: *His latest disc has a brand-new sound.* **2.** A form of the word **disk.** [SEE NOTE]

dis•card |dĭs kärd′| *v.* **1.** To throw away. **2.** In card games: **a.** To lay aside an undesired card or cards from one's hand. **b.** To play a card other than a trump and different in suit from the card led. —*n.* |**dĭs**′kärd′|. **1.** The act of discarding. **2.** A person or thing discarded.

dis•cern |dĭ sûrn′| *or* |-zûrn′| *v.* **1.** To detect or make out (something that is not clear or easily recognizable to the eye or mind): *We could discern only a heap of rocks. They tried to discern signs of a change in the leaders.* **2.** To make out the distinctions of or differences between; distinguish: *discern fact from rumor.*

dis•cern•i•ble |dĭ sûr′nə bəl| *or* |-zûr′-| *adj.* Capable of being recognized; perceptible: *no discernible progress.* —**dis•cern′i•bly** *adv.*

dis•cern•ing |dĭ sûr′nĭng| *or* |-zûr′-| *adj.* Showing keen observation and judgment; able to make distinctions: *a discerning literary critic; a discerning opinion.* —**dis•cern′ing•ly** *adv.*

dis•cern•ment |dĭ sûrn′mənt| *or* |-zûrn′-| *n.* Keenness in detecting, distinguishing, or selecting: *With great discernment, he chose the person best fitted for the job.*

dis•charge |dĭs chärj′| *v.* **dis•charged, dis•charg•ing.** **1.** To get rid of; unload or empty: *a ship discharging its cargo.* **2.** To release, as from confinement or duty: *He was discharged from prison. The Army discharged him in 1946.* **3.** To dismiss from employment: *His boss discharged him because he was always tardy.* **4.** To send or pour forth: *The Illinois River discharges into the Mississippi.* **5.** To shoot or fire: *discharge a volley of arrows.* **6.** To perform the obligations or requirements of (an office, duty, or task): *discharged his last official act as mayor.* **7.** To comply with the terms of (a debt or promise). **8. a.** To cause (a battery, capacitor, etc.) to give up its stored electric charge. **b.** To give up an electric charge. —*n.* |**dĭs**′chärj′| *or* |dĭs **chärj**′|. **1.** An act of unloading: *a discharge of freight.* **2. a.** Dismissal or release from employment, service, or confinement. **b.** A certificate showing such release. **3.** An act of pouring or flowing forth; emission: *a steady discharge of pus.* **4.** Something poured or flowing forth: *a gummy discharge from the tree trunk.* **5.** An act of firing a weapon or projectile. **6.** Performance or fulfillment: *honored for heroism in the discharge of his duties.* **7. a.** A release of stored electric charge, as from a battery or capacitor. **b.** A flow of electricity in a substance, especially a gas, that is normally a nonconductor, often with the production of light or other radiation.

dis•ci•ple |dĭ sī′pəl| *n.* A person who accepts the teachings of a master and often assists in spreading them.

dis•ci•pli•nar•i•an |dĭs′ə plə nâr′ē ən| *n.* A person who enforces or believes in strict discipline: *a stern disciplinarian.*

dis•ci•pli•nar•y |**dĭs**′ə plə nĕr′ē| *adj.* Of or used for discipline: *disciplinary problems.*

dis•ci•pline |**dĭs**′ə plĭn| *n.* **1. a.** Training that tends to mold a specific skill, behavior, etc.: *years of discipline to become a pianist.* **b.** Controlled behavior resulting from such training: *discipline and courage under fire.* **2.** Punishment intended to correct or train. **3.** A branch of knowledge or of teaching: *One of the oldest disciplines is mathematics.* —*v.* **dis•ci•plined, dis•ci•plin•ing.** **1.** To train by instruction and control: *The Spartans disciplined themselves by a life of self-denial.* **2.** To punish in order to reform or train: *discipline a child.*

disc jockey. A radio announcer who presents and comments on phonograph records. [SEE PICTURE]

dis•claim |dĭs klām′| *v.* To deny or give up any claim to or connection with; disown.

dis•claim•er |dĭs klā′mər| *n.* A denial, as of a claim, a connection, knowledge, or responsibility; a disavowal.

dis•close |dĭs klōz′| *v.* **dis•closed, dis•clos•ing.** **1.** To expose to view; uncover: *Their excavations disclosed part of an ancient town.* **2.** To make known; divulge: *The report disclosed many things not generally known before.*

dis•clo•sure |dĭs klō′zhər| *n.* **1.** The act of disclosing: *withheld disclosure of the new information.* **2.** Something disclosed or made known: *the disclosure that gold had been discovered.*

dis•col•or |dĭs kŭl′ər| *v.* To make or become different in color; spoil in color; stain: *when flood waters discolor paintings; metal that discolors upon contact with acid.*

dis•col•or•a•tion |dĭs kŭl′ə rā′shən| *n.* **1.** The act of discoloring. **2.** A condition of being discolored; stain.

dis•com•bob•u•late |dĭs′kəm bŏb′yə lāt′| *v.* **dis•com•bob•u•lat•ed, dis•com•bob•u•lat•ing.** *Slang.* To confuse; upset. [SEE NOTE]

dis•com•fit |dĭs kŭm′fĭt| *n.* **1.** To prevent the fulfillment of plans or purposes; frustrate. **2.** To make uneasy, uncertain, or confused.

dis•com•fi•ture |dĭs kŭm′fĭ chər| *n.* **1.** Frustration; disappointment. **2.** Discomfort; embarrassment.

dis•com•fort |dĭs kŭm′fərt| *n.* **1.** The condition of being uncomfortable in body or mind. **2.** Something that disturbs comfort.

dis•com•mode |dĭs′kə mōd′| *v.* **dis•com•mod•ed, dis•com•mod•ing.** To put to inconvenience; disturb.

dis•com•pose |dĭs′kəm pōz′| *v.* **dis•com•posed, dis•com•pos•ing.** To disturb the composure or calm of; agitate; perturb.

dis•com•po•sure |dĭs′kəm pō′zhər| *n.* The absence of composure; agitation.

dis•con•cert |dĭs′kən sûrt′| *v.* To upset the self-possession of; perturb. —**dis′con•cert′ing** *adj.: spoke in a disconcerting tone.*

dis•con•nect |dĭs′kə nĕkt′| *v.* **1.** To break or interrupt the connection of or between. **2.** To stop the flow of current in (an electrical device) by breaking its connection to its source of power. —**dis′con•nec′tion** *n.*

dis•con•nect•ed |dĭs′kə nĕk′tĭd| *adj.* Not connected; consisting of or marked by unrelated parts; not forming a clear or logical whole: *disconnected snatches of melody.* —**dis′con•nect′ed•ly** *adv.*

dis•con•so•late |dĭs kŏn′sə lĭt| *adj.* Very sad; gloomy; dismal. —**dis•con′so•late•ly** *adv.*

dis•con•tent |dĭs′kən tĕnt′| *n.* The absence of contentment; dissatisfaction.

dis•con•tent•ed |dĭs′kən tĕn′tĭd| *adj.* Restlessly unhappy; not satisfied. —**dis′con•tent′ed•ly** *adv.*

dis•con•tin•ue |dĭs′kən tĭn′yo͞o| *v.* **dis•con•tin•ued, dis•con•tin•u•ing.** To bring or come to an end; terminate: *discontinue making duplicate copies; a publication that will discontinue next week.*

dis•con•ti•nu•i•ty |dĭs kŏn′tə no͞o′ĭ tē| *or* |-nyo͞o′-| *n., pl.* **dis•con•ti•nu•i•ties. 1.** Lack of continuity; absence of logical or orderly succession. **2.** A break or gap.

dis•con•tin•u•ous |dĭs′kən tĭn′yo͞o əs| *adj.* Marked by breaks or interruptions. —**dis′con•tin′u•ous•ly** *adv.* —**dis′con•tin′u•ous•ness** *n.*

dis•cord |dĭs′kôrd′| *n.* **1.** Lack of agreement among persons, groups, or things; dissension: *strife and discord within the government.* **2.** A combination of musical tones that is considered to sound harsh or unpleasant; dissonance.

dis•cor•dant |dĭs kôr′dnt| *adj.* **1.** Not in agreement or accord; marked by conflict. **2.** Disagreeable in sound; harsh or dissonant. —**dis•cor′dance, dis•cor′dan•cy** *n.* —**dis•cor′dant•ly** *adv.*

dis•co•theque |dĭs′kə tĕk′| *or* |dĭs′kə tĕk′| *n.* A nightclub that offers dancing to amplified recorded music.

dis•count |dĭs′kount′| *or* |dĭs kount′| *v.* **1.** To deduct or subtract (a specified amount or percentage) from a cost or price. **2.** To disregard or doubt (something) as being an exaggeration or not trustworthy: *German agents discounted the chance of a Normandy invasion.* —*n.* |dĭs′kount′|. A reduction from the full or standard amount of a price or debt: *A 15 per cent discount on a car means that we pay 85 per cent of the price.* —*adj.* Selling at prices below those set by manufacturers: *a discount store; discount goods.*

dis•cour•age |dĭ skûr′ĭj| *or* |-skŭr′-| *v.* **dis•cour•aged, dis•cour•ag•ing. 1.** To make less hopeful or enthusiastic; depress: *The size of the problem discouraged me.* **2.** To make unwilling or unlikely to do something; dissuade: *His friends discouraged him from going.* **3.** To try to prevent, check, or hinder; inhibit: *They lit a fire to discourage mosquitoes.* —**dis•cour′ag•ing** *adj.: many discouraging failures.*

dis•cour•age•ment |dĭ skûr′ĭj mənt| *or* |-skŭr′-| *n.* **1.** A condition of being discouraged: *Weakened by discouragement and hardship, he fell sick and died.* **2.** Something that discourages: *the discouragements of pioneer farming.*

dis•course |dĭs′kôrs′| *or* |-kōrs′| *n.* **1.** Expression in the form of speech or writing. **2.** A formal discussion, either spoken or written, of a subject. —*v.* |dĭ skôrs′| *or* |-skōrs′| **dis•coursed, dis•cours•ing.** To speak or write formally and at length: *The mayor discoursed on the role of city government in public education.*

dis•cour•te•ous |dĭs kûr′tē əs| *adj.* Lacking courtesy; not polite; rude. —**dis•cour′te•ous•ly** *adv.* —**dis•cour′te•ous•ness** *n.*

dis•cour•te•sy |dĭs kûr′tĭ sē| *n., pl.* **dis•cour•te•sies. 1.** Lack of courtesy; rudeness. **2.** An act or statement that is rude.

dis•cov•er |dĭ skŭv′ər| *v.* **1.** To arrive at through observation or study; obtain knowledge of: *discover interesting chords by experimenting at a keyboard.* **2.** To be the first to find, learn of, or observe: *Vitus Bering discovered the strait that now bears his name.* —**dis•cov′er•er** *n.*

dis•cov•er•y |dĭ skŭv′ə rē| *n., pl.* **dis•cov•er•ies. 1.** The act or an example of discovering: *the day that honors Columbus and his discovery of the Americas.* **2.** Something discovered: *One of the greatest discoveries in science.* [SEE NOTE]

dis•cred•it |dĭs krĕd′ĭt| *v.* **1.** To damage in reputation; disgrace: *A report that seeks to discredit him.* **2.** To cast doubt on; cause to be distrusted: *new evidence that discredits your work.* **3.** To refuse to believe in: *discredit a story as mere rumor.* —**dis•cred′it•ed** *adj.: old and discredited theories; a discredited person.* —*n.* **1.** Loss or damage to one's reputation: *This does you no discredit.* **2.** Lack or loss of trust or belief; doubt: *bringing his medical findings into discredit.* **3.** Someone or something that brings disgrace or distrust: *He is a discredit to us all.*

dis•cred•it•a•ble |dĭs krĕd′ĭ tə bəl| *adj.* Deserving of or resulting in discredit. —**dis•cred′it•a•bly** *adv.*

discombobulate
This word is a humorous invention, of American origin, made up to sound like Latin but not actually coming from any Latin word. It has had a number of variant forms, such as discombobracate *and* discomboborate

discovery
"I do not much wish well to discoveries, for I am always afraid they will end in conquest and robbery." —Samuel Johnson (1773).

discriminate, etc.
It is remarkable that a word can stand for two such different meanings without one or the other meaning being driven out. From the original meaning "to judge sensitively between" arose the meaning "to judge unfairly against." Note that in the derivative noun **discrimination** *the two senses also coexist on equal terms. But the two adjectives are tending to be polarized;* **discriminating** *primarily keeps the earlier, good, meaning, while* **discriminatory** *almost always means "prejudicial."*

ă pat/ā pay/â care/ä father/ĕ pet/ ē be/ĭ pit/ī pie/î fierce/ŏ pot/ ō go/ô paw, for/oi oil/ŏŏ book/ ōō boot/ou out/ŭ cut/û fur/ *th* the/th thin/hw which/zh vision/ ə ago, item, pencil, atom, circus

dis•creet |dĭ skrēt'| *adj.* **1.** Having or showing caution or self-restraint in one's speech or behavior; showing good judgment; prudent: *a polite and discreet girl; keeping a discreet distance from a strange animal.* **2.** Not obtrusive or showy; modest: *make-up packaged in a discreet little tube.* ¶ *These sound alike* **discreet, discrete.** —**dis•creet'ly** *adv.* —**dis•creet'ness** *n.*

dis•crep•an•cy |dĭ skrĕp'ən sē| *n., pl.* **dis•crep•an•cies.** Lack of agreement; difference; inconsistency: *great discrepancies in statistics on the population of the two cities.*

dis•crep•ant |dĭ skrĕp'ənt| *adj.* Showing discrepancy; disagreeing.

dis•crete |dĭ skrēt'| *adj.* Being a separate thing; individual; distinct. ¶ *These sound alike* **discrete, discreet.** —**dis•crete'ly** *adv.*

dis•cre•tion |dĭ skrĕsh'ən| *n.* **1.** The quality of being discreet; the exercise of caution or good judgment in speech or behavior; prudence. **2.** Freedom of action or judgment: *leaving vast discretion to the government.*
Idiom. **at (one's) discretion.** In accordance with one's wishes or judgment.

dis•cre•tion•ar•y |dĭ skrĕsh'ə nĕr'ē| *adj.* Left to or regulated by one's own discretion or judgment: *discretionary powers.*

dis•crim•i•nate |dĭ skrĭm'ə nāt'| *v.* **dis•crim•i•nat•ed, dis•crim•i•nat•ing. 1.** To make a clear distinction between; distinguish: *discriminate good qualities from bad.* **2.** To act on the basis of prejudice; show unfairness: *employers who discriminated against workers for union activity.* [SEE NOTE]

dis•crim•i•nat•ing |dĭ skrĭm'ə nā'tĭng| *adj.* **1.** Able to recognize small differences or draw fine distinctions: *He became discriminating in his choice of fine food.* **2.** Serving to distinguish or set apart from others; distinctive: *decency, that discriminating quality of a gentleman.* **3.** Showing prejudice. —**dis•crim'i•nat'ing•ly** *adv.*

dis•crim•i•na•tion |dĭ skrĭm'ə nā'shən| *n.* **1.** The ability to distinguish, especially to recognize small differences or make fine distinctions: *Her choice of furnishings showed little artistic discrimination.* **2.** Acts or attitudes based on prejudice; unfairness or injustice toward a particular group of persons.

dis•crim•i•na•tor |dĭ skrĭm'ə nā'tər| *n.* **1.** Someone or something that discriminates. **2.** An electronic circuit that converts variations in the frequency or phrase of a signal into another signal whose amplitude varies with time. A discriminator is often used to demodulate FM signals.

dis•crim•i•na•to•ry |dĭ skrĭm'ə nə tôr'ē| *or* |-tōr'ē| *adj.* **1.** Showing prejudice; biased. **2.** Discriminating. —**dis•crim'i•na•to'ri•ly** *adv.*

dis•cur•sive |dĭ skûr'sĭv| *adj.* Covering a wide field of subjects; rambling; digressive. —**dis•cur'sive•ly** *adv.* —**dis•cur'sive•ness** *n.*

dis•cus |dĭs'kəs| *n.* A disk of wood and metal that is hurled for distance in athletic contests.

dis•cuss |dĭ skŭs'| *v.* **1.** To speak together about; debate: *The school board discussed the matter for hours but could agree on nothing.* **2.** To examine (a subject) by means of speech or writing; treat of: *the section of your book that discusses this point of grammar.*

dis•cus•sion |dĭ skŭsh'ən| *n.* **1.** The consideration of a subject by two or more persons; a conversation in which ideas and opinions are exchanged. **2.** An examination or presentation of a subject, as in a lecture or book.

dis•dain |dĭs dān'| *v.* **1.** To treat as inferior; show contempt for; *disdaining all her brother's friends.* **2.** To refuse aloofly: *She disdained to answer the letter.* —*n.* Mild contempt and aloofness.

dis•dain•ful |dĭs dān'fəl| *adj.* Showing disdain. —**dis•dain'ful•ly** *adv.*

dis•ease |dĭ zēz'| *n.* Any condition of an organism that makes it unable to function in the normal, proper way, especially a condition that results from infection, inherent weakness, or pressures of the environment.

dis•eased |dĭ zēzd'| *adj.* Affected with or suffering from disease.

dis•em•bark |dĭs'ĕm bärk'| *v.* To go or put ashore from a ship: *disembark in Boston; forbade the captain to disembark a single passenger.* —**dis•em'bar•ka'tion** *n.*

dis•em•bod•y |dĭs'ĕm bŏd'ē| *v.* **dis•em•bod•ied, dis•em•bod•y•ing, dis•em•bod•ies.** To free (the soul or spirit) from the body. —**dis'em•bod'i•ment** *n.*

dis•em•bow•el |dĭs'ĕm bou'əl| *v.* To remove the entrails from. —**dis'em•bow'el•ment** *n.*

dis•en•chant |dĭs'ĕn chănt'| *or* |-chänt'| *v.* To free from enchantment or false belief; disillusion: *One look at the surroundings was enough to disenchant her.* —**dis'en•chant'ment** *n.*

dis•en•cum•ber |dĭs'ĕn kŭm'bər| *v.* To free from something that hinders or burdens: *disencumbered himself of his overcoat.*

dis•en•fran•chise |dĭs'ĕn frăn'chīz'| *v.* **dis•en•fran•chised, dis•en•fran•chis•ing.** To disfranchise. —**dis'en•fran'chise'ment** *n.*

dis•en•gage |dĭs'ĕn gāj'| *v.* **dis•en•gaged, dis•en•gag•ing. 1.** To make or become free from something that holds fast, entangles, or connects: *tried to disengage her leg from the underbrush. The gears disengaged, and the car drifted downhill.* **2.** To free or release (oneself), as from a previous involvement or course of action. —**dis'en•gage'ment** *n.*

dis•en•tan•gle |dĭs'ĕn tăng'gəl| *v.* **dis•en•tan•gled, dis•en•tan•gling.** To free from entanglement or confusion. —**dis'en•tan'gle•ment** *n.*

dis•fa•vor |dĭs fā'vər| *n.* **1.** Lack of favor or approval; dislike or low regard: *He earned the disfavor of all by his dishonesty.* **2.** The condition of being disliked or disapproved of: *a book in disfavor with the clergy.*

dis•fig•ure |dĭs fĭg'yər| *v.* **dis•fig•ured, dis•fig•ur•ing.** To spoil the appearance or shape of; mar. —**dis•fig'ure•ment, dis•fig'u•ra'tion** *n.*

dis•fran•chise |dĭs frăn'chīz'| *v.* **dis•fran•chised, dis•fran•chis•ing.** To take a right to citizenship from, especially the right to vote. —**dis•fran'chise'ment** *n.*

dis•gorge |dĭs gôrj'| *v.* **dis•gorged, dis•gorg•ing. 1.** To bring up and discharge from the throat or stomach; vomit. **2.** To pour forth or throw up.

dis•grace |dĭs grās'| *n.* **1.** The condition of being strongly and generally disapproved: *She could not stand the disgrace of a divorce.* **2.** Something that brings shame, dishonor, or disfavor. —*v.* **dis•graced, dis•grac•ing. 1.** To be a cause of shame, dishonor, or disfavor to: *I felt that I had disgraced my family.* **2.** To put (someone) out of favor: *After the defeat, the generals were disgraced by the king.*

dis•grace•ful |dĭs grās′fəl| *adj.* Worthy of or causing shame, dishonor, or disfavor: *a disgraceful secret that was kept from the public.* —**dis•grace′ful•ly** *adv.*

dis•grun•tle |dĭs grŭn′tl| *v.* **dis•grun•tled, dis•grun•tling.** To make discontented: *The younger members of the club were disgruntled by all the changes in the rules of the game.* —**dis•grun′tled** *adj.*: *disgruntled employees.*

dis•guise |dĭs gīz′| *n.* **1.** Clothes or other personal effects, such as make-up, worn to conceal one's true identity: *He wore the disguise of a beggar.* **2.** Any form of concealment or camouflage: *Some animals have several disguises.* —*v.* **dis•guised, dis•guis•ing. 1.** To conceal the identity of, as with clothes or other effects: *He disguised himself.* **2.** To conceal: *He tried to disguise his impatience.*

dis•gust |dĭs gŭst′| *v.* To make (someone) feel sick, annoyed, offended, etc. —*n.* A feeling of sickness, extreme annoyance, etc.

dis•gust•ed |dĭs gŭs′tĭd| *adj.* Showing or affected by disgust: *a disgusted look.* —**dis•gust′ed•ly** *adv.*

dis•gust•ing |dĭs gŭs′tĭng| *adj.* Causing disgust: *disgusting food; a disgusting performance.* —**dis•gust′ing•ly** *adv.*

dish |dĭsh| *n.* **1. a.** A flat or shallow container for holding or serving food. **b.** The amount that a dish holds. **2.** A particular variety or preparation of food: *Lemon chiffon pie is his favorite dish.* **3.** Anything having the generally concave shape of a dish, especially the reflector of a radio, television, or radar antenna. —*v.* To serve (food) in a dish or dishes: *dish up the meat; dish out the vegetables.* [SEE PICTURE]

dis•ha•bille |dĭs′ə bēl′| *n.* The condition of being only partly dressed or dressed in a sloppy or informal way.

dis•heart•en |dĭs här′tn| *v.* To destroy the courage or spirit of; cause to lose hope: *Their lack of interest disheartened him.* —**dis•heart′en•ing** *adj.*: *disheartening news.*

di•shev•eled |dĭ shĕv′əld| *adj.* Untidy; not orderly; disarranged: *disheveled hair.*

dis•hon•est |dĭs ŏn′ĭst| *adj.* **1.** Inclined to lie, cheat, or deceive: *a dishonest girl.* **2.** Showing or resulting from falseness or fraud: *a dishonest answer; dishonest gains.* —**dis•hon′est•ly** *adv.*

dis•hon•es•ty |dĭs ŏn′ĭ stē| *n., pl.* **dis•hon•es•ties. 1.** Lack of honesty or integrity. **2.** A dishonest act or statement.

dis•hon•or |dĭs ŏn′ər| *n.* Loss of honor, respect, or reputation; disgrace; shame. —*v.* To deprive of honor; disgrace.

dis•hon•or•a•ble |dĭs ŏn′ər ə bəl| *adj.* Causing or deserving loss of respect or reputation; shameful; unworthy. —**dis•hon′or•a•ble•ness** *n.* —**dis•hon′or•a•bly** *adv.*

dish•tow•el |dĭsh′tou′əl| *n.* A towel for drying dishes.

dish•wash•er |dĭsh′wŏsh′ər| *or* |-wô′shər| *n.* **1.** A machine that washes dishes. **2.** A person hired to wash dishes, especially in a restaurant.

dis•il•lu•sion |dĭs′ĭ lo͞o′zhən| *v.* To free or deprive of an idea or belief that proves false or in error; disenchant: *Many newcomers to the country were disillusioned by their surroundings.* —*n.* The condition of being deprived of a false idea or belief; disenchantment. —**dis′il•lu′sion•ment** *n.* —**dis′il•lu′sive** *adj.*

dis•in•cli•na•tion |dĭs ĭn′klĭ nā′shən| *n.* Unwillingness; reluctance; aversion.

dis•in•clined |dĭs′ĭn klīnd′| *adj.* Unwilling; reluctant: *disinclined to pay such a big price.*

dis•in•fect |dĭs′ĭn fĕkt′| *v.* To rid of microorganisms that are capable of causing diseases. —**dis′in•fec′tion** *n.*

dis•in•fec•tant |dĭs′ĭn fĕk′tənt| *n.* A substance that halts the action of microorganisms that cause disease by killing them. —*adj.* Capable of acting as a disinfectant: *a disinfectant bath.*

dis•in•her•it |dĭs′ĭn hĕr′ĭt| *v.* To take from (a person) the right to inherit: *Father disinherited my younger brother.*

dis•in•te•grate |dĭs ĭn′tĭ grāt′| *v.* **dis•in•te•grat•ed, dis•in•te•grat•ing.** To break or cause to break into separate pieces.

dis•in•te•gra•tion |dĭs ĭn′tĭ grā′shən| *n.* **1. a.** The act or process of disintegrating. **b.** The condition of being disintegrated. **2.** A process in which an atomic nucleus is transformed as it throws off radiation or one or more of its component particles; radioactive decay.

dis•in•ter |dĭs′ĭn tûr′| *v.* **dis•in•terred, dis•in•ter•ring.** To dig up or remove from or as if from a grave. —**dis′in•ter′ment** *n.*

dis•in•ter•est•ed |dĭs ĭn′trĭ stĭd| *or* |-tə rĕs′tĭd| *adj.* Free of self-interest; without bias or hope of personal gain: *the disinterested warnings of a friend.* —**dis•in′ter•est•ed•ly** *adv.* [SEE NOTE]

dis•joint |dĭs joint′| *v.* To take apart at the joints. —*adj.* In mathematics, containing no elements in common; having the empty set as an intersection: *disjoint sets.*

dis•joint•ed |dĭs join′tĭd| *adj.* **1.** Separated at the joints. **2.** Out of joint; dislocated. **3.** Lacking order or coherence; disconnected: *a disjointed speech.* —**dis•joint′ed•ly** *adv.*

disk |dĭsk| *n.* **1.** Any thin, flat, circular plate. **2.** Anything that resembles such a plate, as a celestial body or a part of an organism. **3.** The central part of a composite flower such as the daisy or sunflower, containing many tiny, densely clustered flowers. **4.** A round flat plate coated with a magnetic substance on which data for a computer may be stored. **5.** A form of the word **disc** (phonograph record). [SEE NOTE on p. 262]

disk brake. A brake that acts to slow or stop a rotating part by clamping a disk that is attached to the rotating part. [SEE PICTURE]

disk•ette |dĭ skĕt′| *n.* A floppy disk.

disk jockey. A form of the phrase **disc jockey.**

dis•like |dĭs līk′| *v.* **dis•liked, dis•lik•ing.** To have a feeling of distaste for; feel aversion toward. —*n.* A feeling of distaste or aversion.

dis•lo•cate |dĭs′lō kāt′| *or* |dĭs lō′kāt′| *v.* **dis•lo•cat•ed, dis•lo•cat•ing. 1.** To move (an organ or part of the body) out of its normal position, especially to displace (a bone) from a socket or joint. **2.** To throw into disorder; upset: *The snowstorm dislocated traffic.*

dis•lodge |dĭs lŏj′| *v.* **dis•lodged, dis•lodg•ing.** To move or force out of position.

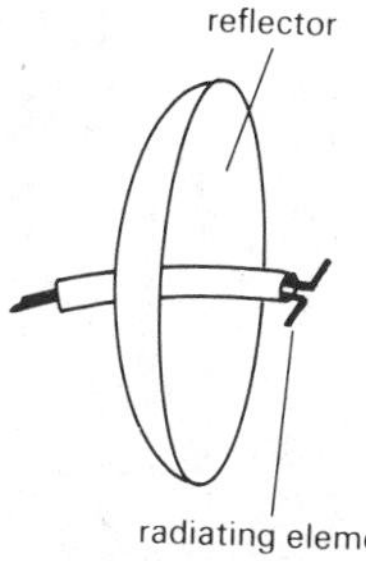

dish antenna

disinterested

Interest *means "curiosity," but it also means "personal advantage, self-interest."* **Disinterested** *gets its meaning from this second sense. Ninety-three per cent of the American Heritage Usage Panel considers it unacceptable to use* **disinterested** *as if it came from the first sense. The accepted word for "not interested" is* **uninterested.**

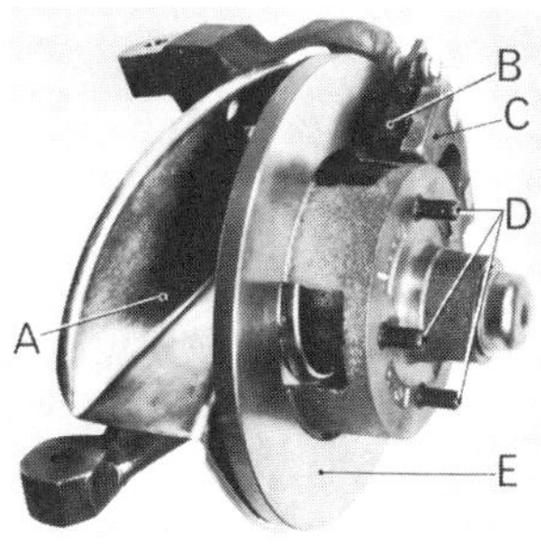

disk brake
A. Cooling duct
B. Pressure pad
C. Caliper
D. Wheel mounting bolts
E. Rotor

dis•loy•al |dĭs loi′əl| *adj.* Lacking in loyalty. —**dis•loy′al•ly** *adv.*

dis•loy•al•ty |dĭs loi′əl tē| *n., pl.* **dis•loy•al•ties.** **1.** Lack of loyalty to persons or things entitled to allegiance or support, as one's friends, superiors, or country. **2.** A disloyal act.

dis•mal |dĭz′məl| *adj.* **1.** Causing gloom or depression; dreary: *a dismal fog.* **2.** Feeling or showing gloom: *a face as dismal as three days of rainy weather.* **3.** Causing dread or dismay; dire: *Out of this dismal destruction a wildlife preserve was born.* —**dis′mal•ly** *adv.* [SEE NOTE]

dis•man•tle |dĭs măn′tl| *v.* **dis•man•tled, dis•man•tling.** **1.** To strip of furnishings or equipment: *dismantled an apartment; dismantle a factory.* **2.** To take apart: *dismantle a piano.*

dis•may |dĭs mā′| *v.* **1.** To fill with dread; make anxious or afraid. **2.** To discourage or trouble greatly. —*n.* A sudden loss of courage or confidence that prevents one from acting effectively.

dis•mem•ber |dĭs mĕm′bər| *v.* **1.** To cut, tear, or pull off the limbs of: *The mouth parts of wasps can dismember other insects.* **2.** To divide into pieces: *dismember a large company.* —**dis•mem′ber•ment** *n.*

dis•miss |dĭs mĭs′| *v.* **1.** To discharge, as from employment: *King Richard dismissed his advisers.* **2.** To direct or allow to leave: *The students were dismissed for the holidays.* **3.** To put out of one's mind; regard as unworthy of further consideration: *The tourists dismissed the Irish weather as simply wet and cold.* **4.** To refuse to accept or recognize; reject; repudiate: *dismiss one's obligations.* **5.** To put (a claim or action) out of court without further hearing: *The judge dismissed the case for lack of sufficient evidence.*

dis•miss•al |dĭs mĭs′əl| *n.* **1.** An act of dismissing: *early dismissal of students in hot weather.* **2.** An order or notice of discharge: *His dismissal was not made public.*

dis•mount |dĭs mount′| *v.* **1.** To get off or down, as from a horse. **2.** To remove (a thing) from its support or mounting: *dismounted the machine gun.* **3.** To take apart (a mechanism).

dis•o•be•di•ence |dĭs′ə bē′dē əns| *n.* Refusal or failure to follow orders or instructions.

dis•o•be•di•ent |dĭs′ə bē′dē ənt| *adj.* Not obedient. —**dis′o•be′di•ent•ly** *adv.*

dis•o•bey |dĭs′ə bā′| *v.* To refuse or fail to obey: *pedestrians who disobey traffic signals; a dog that seldom disobeyed.*

dis•or•der |dĭs ôr′dər| *n.* **1.** Lack of order or regular arrangement; confusion; untidiness: *soldiers fleeing in disorder; hair blowing in wild disorder.* **2.** A public disturbance; violation of the peace. **3.** Any disturbance of health or function in body or mind: *a nervous disorder.* —*v.* **1.** To throw into disorder; muddle. **2.** To upset the mental or physical health of.

dis•or•dered |dĭs ôr′dərd| *adj.* **1.** In a condition of disorder; disarranged. **2.** Abnormal or ill in body or mind; diseased.

dis•or•der•ly |dĭs ôr′dər lē| *adj.* **1.** Not neat or tidy: *a disorderly room.* **2.** Lacking discipline and self-control; disturbing the public peace: *a disorderly crowd; disorderly conduct.* —**dis•or′der•li•ness** *n.*

dis•or•gan•ize |dĭs ôr′gə nīz′| *v.* **dis•or•gan•ized, dis•or•gan•iz•ing.** To destroy the organization or orderly arrangement of; throw into confusion. —**dis•or′gan•ized′** *adj.: a disorganized person.*

dis•o•ri•ent |dĭs ôr′ē ĕnt′| *or* |-ōr′-| *v.* To cause (a person) to lose awareness of his relationship with his surroundings, as with respect to time or space. —**dis•o′ri•en•ta′tion** *n.*

dis•own |dĭs ōn′| *v.* To refuse to claim or accept as one's own; repudiate; reject: *disown one's son; disowned any connection with our group.*

dis•par•age |dĭ spăr′ĭj| *v.* **dis•par•aged, dis•par•ag•ing.** To represent or speak of as small, unimportant, or inferior; belittle: *disparaged his role in the expedition.* —**dis•par′age•ment** *n.*

dis•par•ag•ing |dĭ spăr′ə jĭng| *adj.* Expressing criticism or low opinion; slighting: *a disparaging remark.* —**dis•par′ag•ing•ly** *adv.*

dis•pa•rate |dĭs′pər ĭt| *or* |dĭ spăr′-| *adj.* Completely distinct or different in kind; entirely dissimilar: *disparate theories about the origin of man.* —**dis′pa•rate•ly** *adv.*

dis•par•i•ty |dĭ spăr′ĭ tē| *n., pl.* **dis•par•i•ties.** **1.** Inequality; difference: *the disparity in population figures.* **2.** Lack of similarity; unlikeness: *a marked disparity between their stories.*

dis•pas•sion•ate |dĭs păsh′ə nĭt| *adj.* Not influenced by strong personal feelings or emotions; not biased; impartial: *dispassionate criticism.* —**dis•pas′sion•ate•ly** *adv.*

dis•patch |dĭ spăch′| *v.* **1.** To send off to a specific destination or on specific business: *dispatch a letter; dispatch battleships to the scene of the invasion.* **2.** To complete or dispose of promptly: *dispatched his business and left.* **3.** To put to death quickly and without ceremony. —*n.* **1.** The act of sending off: *the dispatch of a representative to the peace talks.* **2.** Quickness and efficiency in performance: *the prey he killed with such dispatch.* **3.** A written message, especially an official communication, sent with speed: *a dispatch from the Allied high command.* **4.** A news report sent to a newspaper or broadcasting station.

dis•patch•er |dĭ spăch′ər| *n.* A person employed to control the departure and movements of trains, taxicabs, or delivery trucks or to route telegraph communications.

dis•pel |dĭ spĕl′| *v.* **dis•pelled, dis•pel•ling.** To make disappear by or as if by scattering; drive away: *Education alone can dispel this fear.*

dis•pen•sa•ble |dĭ spĕn′sə bəl| *adj.* **1.** Capable of being dispensed with; not necessary or important: *Truth is never dispensable; rumor always is.* **2.** Capable of being overlooked or pardoned, as a sin. —**dis•pen′sa•bil′i•ty** *n.*

dis•pen•sa•ry |dĭ spĕn′sə rē| *n., pl.* **dis•pen•sa•ries.** **1.** An office in a hospital, school, or other institution where medicines and medical supplies are given out. **2.** A public institution that provides medical treatment and medicines; a clinic.

dis•pen•sa•tion |dĭs′pən sā′shən| *or* |-pĕn-| *n.* **1.** The act of dispensing or giving out; distribution. **2.** Something given out or distributed. **3.** Freedom or release from an obligation or rule, granted in a particular case.

dis•pense |dĭ spĕns′| *v.* **dis•pensed, dis•pens•ing.** **1.** To deal out or distribute in parts or portions. **2.** To prepare and give out (medicines). **3.** To carry out; administer: *the way in*

dismal

The earliest use of **dismal** *in Modern English was in the phrase* in the dismal, *"at an unlucky time" or "in the evil days." The concept of evil days appears in many early literary works. Also called "Egyptian days," the phrase refers to the two days a month that were considered unlucky and were said to have been discovered by Egyptian astrologers. Some medieval writers felt that the phrase referred to the plagues of ancient Egypt.* **Dismal** *ultimately comes from Latin* dies mali, *"evil days."*

ă **pat**/ā **pay**/â **care**/ä **father**/ĕ **pet**/ē **be**/ĭ **pit**/ī **pie**/î **fierce**/ŏ **pot**/ō **go**/ô **paw**, **for**/oi **oil**/ŏŏ **book**/ōō **boot**/ou **out**/ŭ **cut**/û **fur**/*th* **the**/th **thin**/hw **which**/**zh** vision/ə **ago**, item, pencil, atom, circus *which the king dispensed justice.* —**phrasal verb. dispense with.** To manage without; forgo: *dispensed with formality and got down to business.*

dis•pens•er |dĭ **spĕn′**sər| *n.* Someone or something that dispenses, especially a container that gives out paper cups, razor blades, etc.

dis•per•sal |dĭ **spûr′**səl| *n.* An act of dispersing or the condition of being dispersed; distribution; scattering: *the dispersal of a crowd.*

dis•perse |dĭ **spûrs′**| *v.* **dis•persed, dis•pers•ing. 1.** To move or distribute in different directions; scatter: *disperse a crowd. The crowd dispersed at the command of the police officer.* **2.** To cause to vanish or disappear; dispel: *Windstorms disperse the scent, making pursuit difficult.* **3.** To cause (light or other radiation) to separate into component parts, as in forming a spectrum.

dis•per•sion |dĭ **spûr′**zhən| *or* |-shən| *n.* **1.** The breaking up of light or other radiation into components, usually according to wavelength. **2.** A material system, such as a smoke or fog, made up of tiny particles of one substance distributed throughout another substance. **3.** The act of dispersing; a driving away: *a bright sun that caused dispersion of the fog.*

dis•pir•it |dĭ **spĭr′**ĭt| *v.* To lower in spirit; dishearten: *failure that dispirits mankind.*

dis•pir•it•ed |dĭ **spĭr′**ĭ tĭd| *adj.* Depressed; disheartened: *feeling tired and dispirited.* —**dis•pir′it•ed•ly** *adv.*

dis•place |dĭs **plās′**| *v.* **dis•placed, dis•plac•ing. 1.** To change the place or position of; put out of place. **2.** To take the place of; supplant: *people displaced by machines that have eased them out of their jobs.* **3.** To fill the space of (a quantity of liquid, gas, etc.).

displaced person. A person who has been driven from his home country by war.

dis•place•ment |dĭs **plās′**mənt| *n.* **1. a.** The weight or volume of fluid displaced by a body floating in it, often used as a measure of the weight or bulk of ships. **b.** The measure of the distance that a body has been moved through space, usually expressed as a vector. **c.** The volume displaced by the pistons of an engine in moving back and forth: *a V-8 engine with a 300-cubic-inch displacement.* **2.** A chemical reaction in which an atom or radical replaces another in a compound. **3.** The act of displacing or the condition of being displaced.

dis•play |dĭ **splā′**| *v.* **1.** To hold up to view or put on view; exhibit: *models displaying the latest fashions; libraries that display rare books.* **2.** To make noticeable; show evidence of: *ashamed to display his fear.* **3.** To spread out; unfurl: *Our flag should be displayed on appropriate holidays.* —*n.* **1.** The act of displaying: **a.** A public showing or exhibition: *a display of American paintings; a military display of the colors.* **b.** A demonstration of the existence of something: *an ugly display of temper.* **2.** Anything that is exhibited: *The display of Indian pottery continues through Friday.* **3.** A show designed to impress or to attract attention: *making a big display of his wealth.* —**modifier:** *a display window.*

dis•please |dĭs **plēz′**| *v.* **dis•pleased, dis•pleas•ing.** To cause annoyance or dissatisfaction to; gain the disapproval or dislike of; offend.

dis•pleas•ure |dĭs **plĕzh′**ər| *n.* The condition of being displeased; annoyance or anger; dissatisfaction. [SEE NOTE]

dis•port |dĭ **spôrt′**| *or* |**-spōrt′**| *v.* To entertain (oneself) by sport or play.

dis•pos•a•ble |dĭ **spō′**zə bəl| *adj.* Designed to be thrown away after use.

dis•pos•al |dĭ **spō′**zəl| *n.* **1.** The act of throwing out or away: *the problem of waste disposal.* **2.** An apparatus or machine for getting rid of something: *proper disposal of sewage; a garbage disposal.* **3.** The act or method of attending to or settling a matter: *the principal's disposal of my application.* **4.** The act of transferring ownership by sale or gift: *the disposal of a bankrupt company's assets.* **5.** The liberty or power to use something: *limousines put at their disposal; knowledge at modern man's disposal.*

dis•pose |dĭ **spōz′**| *v.* **dis•posed, dis•pos•ing. 1.** To place or set in a particular order; arrange: *disposed his bomber squadron with great skill.* **2.** To settle or decide something: *Man proposes; God disposes.* **3.** To make willing or receptive for; incline: *feeling half disposed to object.* **4.** —**dispose of.** To get rid of, as by attending to or settling, giving or selling, destroying or throwing away, or eating or drinking: *old business disposed of. The boy greedily disposed of his food.*

dis•po•si•tion |dĭs′pə **zĭsh′**ən| *n.* **1.** One's usual mood or attitude; temperament: *an affectionate disposition; a warlike disposition.* **2.** A tendency or inclination to behave in a certain way: *He showed a disposition to rebel at any authority.* **3.** Arrangement or distribution: *the disposition of books on the library shelves.* **4.** An act of settling; settlement: *disposition of your legal problems.* **5.** An act of disposing of, as by transferring ownership or throwing away: *the disposition of his stocks and bonds.*

dis•pos•sess |dĭs′pə **zĕs′**| *v.* To deprive (someone) of the possession of something, such as land or buildings. —**dis′pos•ses′sion** *n.*

dis•proof |dĭs **pro͞of′**| *n.* **1.** An act of disproving. **2.** Evidence that disproves.

dis•pro•por•tion |dĭs′prə **pôr′**shən| *or* |**-pōr′-**| *n.* An absence of proper proportion; lack of balance or harmonious relationship.

dis•pro•por•tion•ate |dĭs′prə **pôr′**shə nĭt| *or* |**-pōr′-**| *adj.* Out of proportion to something else, as in size or shape; not proportionate. —**dis′pro•por′tion•ate•ly** *adv.*

dis•prove |dĭs **pro͞ov′**| *v.* **dis•proved, dis•prov•ing.** To prove (something) to be false, invalid, or in error; refute.

dis•put•a•ble |dĭ **spyo͞o′**tə bəl| *or* |**dĭs′**pyo͝o-| *adj.* Capable of being disputed or questioned; debatable. —**dis•put′a•bil′i•ty** *n.*

dis•pu•tant |dĭ **spyo͞ot′**nt| *or* |**dĭs′**pyo͝o tənt| *n.* A person taking part in an argument, debate, or quarrel.

dis•pu•ta•tion |dĭs′pyo͝o **tā′**shən| *n.* An act of disputing; an argument or debate.

dis•pute |dĭ **spyo͞ot′**| *v.* **dis•put•ed, dis•put•ing. 1.** To argue about; debate: *disputing the humanities' role in a scientific age; men forever disputing in their search for truth.* **2.** To question the truth or validity of; doubt: *Harvey disputed the ancient belief about the flow of blood in the human body.* **3.** To quarrel: *like children disputing over which should have a larger portion of food.* —*n.* **1.** A

displeasure

Following is a small selection of the expressions listed under "interjections of displeasure" in the American Thesaurus of Slang *(1962), by Lester V. Berrey and Melvin Van Den Bark:*
Ai, yai, yai!, ain't it the limit!, botheration!, fiddlesticks!, fooey!, (aw) fudge!, how do you like that!, it shouldn't happen to a dog!, the hell with it!, (oh) murder!, nuts!, of all the nutty snobblewozzles! . . . Aa, yer fadder's mustache!, don't be like that!, don't give me that!, drop dead!, (aw) get along with you!, of all the!, what's the big idea?

verbal controversy; debate; argument; disagreement: *a theory in dispute; a dispute as to how turkeys originated.* **2.** A quarrel: *family disputes.*

dis•qual•i•fi•ca•tion |dĭs kwŏl′ə fĭ **kā′**shən| *n.* **1.** The act of disqualifying or the condition of being disqualified. **2.** Something that disqualifies: *A prison record is not always a disqualification for employment.*

dis•qual•i•fy |dĭs **kwŏl′**ə fī′| *v.* **dis•qual•i•fied, dis•qual•i•fy•ing, dis•qual•i•fies. 1.** To make unfit; disable: *Lack of perfect eyesight disqualified him for training as a Marine pilot.* **2.** To declare to be ineligible, unsuitable, or unworthy, as to hold a position or win a contest: *rules that disqualify one for jury duty in certain cases.*

dis•qui•et |dĭs **kwī′**ĭt| *v.* To make uneasy; trouble; worry. **—dis•qui′et•ing** *adj.: disquieting news.* *—n.* The absence of peace of mind; uneasiness.

dis•qui•e•tude |dĭs **kwī′**ĭ to͞od′| *or* |-tyo͞od′| *n.* Worry; uneasiness; anxiety.

dis•qui•si•tion |dĭs′kwĭ **zĭsh′**ən| *n.* A formal discussion or account of a subject.

Dis•rae•li |dĭz **rā′**lē|, **Benjamin.** 1804–1881. British statesman; prime minister (1868 and 1874–80).

dis•re•gard |dĭs′rĭ **gärd′**| *v.* To pay little or no attention to; fail to consider or heed: *disregard danger; disregard stop signs; disregard property rights.* *—n.* Lack of attentiveness to or due respect for something: *a disregard for rules of safety; disregard of their own health.*

dis•re•pair |dĭs′rĭ **pâr′**| *n.* The condition of being neglected or in need of repair.

dis•rep•u•ta•ble |dĭs **rĕp′**yə tə bəl| *adj.* **1.** Lacking a good reputation: *a disreputable place of business.* **2.** Not respectable in appearance or character: *His manner of dress was casual to the point of being disreputable.* **—dis•rep′u•ta•ble•ness** *n.* **—dis•rep′u•ta•bly** *adv.*

dis•re•pute |dĭs′rĭ **pyo͞ot′**| *n.* The absence or loss of reputation; low regard; discredit.

dis•re•spect |dĭs′rĭ **spĕkt′**| *n.* Lack of respect or courtesy; rudeness.

dis•re•spect•ful |dĭs′rĭ **spĕkt′**fəl| *adj.* Having or showing a lack of respect; rude; discourteous. **—dis′re•spect′ful•ly** *adv.*

dis•robe |dĭs **rōb′**| *v.* **dis•robed, dis•rob•ing.** To undress: *She disrobed the doll. The doctor asked the patient to disrobe.*

dis•rupt |dĭs **rŭpt′**| *v.* **1.** To upset the order of; throw into confusion or disorder: *a storm that disrupted the lives of hundreds.* **2.** To interrupt or block the progress or functioning of: *Floods disrupted transportation and communication.* **—dis•rup′tion** *n.*

dis•rup•tive |dĭs **rŭp′**tĭv| *adj.* Causing or likely to cause disorder, interference, or discord.

dis•sat•is•fac•tion |dĭs săt′ĭs **făk′**shən| *n.* The feeling of being displeased or dissatisfied.

dis•sat•is•fied |dĭs **săt′**ĭs fīd′| *adj.* Feeling or showing a lack of contentment; displeased; discontented: *dissatisfied with his work.*

dis•sat•is•fy |dĭs **săt′**ĭs fī′| *v.* **dis•sat•is•fied, dis•sat•is•fy•ing, dis•sat•is•fies.** To fail to meet the expectation of or fulfill the desires of.

dis•sect |dĭ **sĕkt′**| *or* |dī-| *v.* **1.** To cut apart or separate (tissue), as in surgery or the study of anatomy. **2.** To examine, analyze, or criticize with great care.

dis•sec•tion |dĭ **sĕk′**shən| *or* |dī-| *n.* **1.** The act or process of dissecting. **2.** Something that has been dissected, as a tissue being studied.

dis•sem•ble |dĭ **sĕm′**bəl| *v.* **dis•sem•bled, dis•sem•bling. 1.** To conceal or hide behind a false appearance or manner: *dissembled his disappointment with a show of gaiety.* **2.** To make a false show of; pretend; feign: *dissembling sympathy.* **—dis•sem′bler** *n.* [SEE NOTE]

dis•sem•i•nate |dĭ **sĕm′**ə nāt′| *v.* **dis•sem•i•nat•ed, dis•sem•i•nat•ing.** To make known widely; spread abroad: *disseminating knowledge.* **—dis•sem′i•na′tion** *n.*

dis•sen•sion |dĭ **sĕn′**shən| *n.* A difference of opinion, especially one that causes a dispute or prevents harmony within a group.

dis•sent |dĭ **sĕnt′**| *v.* To think or feel differently; disagree; differ: *your right to dissent from the majority view.* **—dis•sent′ing** *adj.: a dissenting opinion.* *—n.* **1.** Difference of opinion or feeling; disagreement. **2.** The refusal to conform to the authority or rules of a government or church. ¶*These sound alike* **dissent, descent.**

dis•sent•er |dĭ **sĕn′**tər| *n.* **1.** A person who dissents. **2.** Often **Dissenter.** A person who refuses to accept the beliefs and practices of an established or national church, as an English Protestant who dissents from the Church of England.

dis•ser•ta•tion |dĭs′ər **tā′**shən| *n.* A lengthy and formal discussion or written treatment of a subject, as one prepared by a candidate for an advanced degree at a university.

dis•serv•ice |dĭs **sûr′**vĭs| *n.* A harmful action; an ill turn.

dis•sev•er |dĭ **sĕv′**ər| *v.* To separate or divide into parts.

dis•si•dent |**dĭs′**ĭ dənt| *adj.* Disagreeing, as in opinion or belief; dissenting. *—n.* A person who disagrees; a dissenter. **—dis′si•dence** *n.*

dis•sim•i•lar |dĭ **sĭm′**ə lər| *or* |dĭs **sĭm′**-| *adj.* Unlike; different; distinct. **—dis•sim′i•lar•ly** *adv.*

dis•sim•i•lar•i•ty |dĭ sĭm′ə **lăr′**ĭ tē| *n., pl.* **dis•sim•i•lar•i•ties. 1.** The condition or quality of being distinct or unlike; difference. **2.** A point of distinction or difference: *Even so-called identical twins have dissimilarities.*

dis•sim•u•late |dĭ **sĭm′**yə lāt′| *v.* **dis•sim•u•lat•ed, dis•sim•u•lat•ing.** To hide one's true feelings or intentions; dissemble. **—dis•sim′u•la′tion** *n.* [SEE NOTE]

dis•si•pate |**dĭs′**ə pāt′| *v.* **dis•si•pat•ed, dis•si•pat•ing. 1.** To drive away by or as if by dispersing; rout; scatter: *A strong wind dissipated the clouds.* **2.** To vanish by dispersion; disappear: *Upon escaping into the air, steam dissipates. His anger soon dissipated in her presence.* **3.** To use up unwisely; waste; squander: *He dissipated his money and strength on the project.* **4.** To indulge in pleasure harmfully or too freely; carouse.

dis•si•pat•ed |**dĭs′**ə pā′tĭd| *adj.* **1.** Indulging in pleasure to a degree harmful to health or morals; dissolute: *arrogant and dissipated young men.* **2.** Wasted; squandered: *a dissipated fortune.*

dis•si•pa•tion |dĭs′ə **pā′**shən| *n.* **1.** The act of scattering or the condition of being scattered; dispersion. **2.** Wasteful use or expenditure, as of money, energy, or time. **3.** Overindulgence in pleasure; intemperance.

dis•so•ci•ate |dĭ **sō′**shē āt′| *or* |-sē-| *v.* **dis•so•**

dissemble

"If you dissemble sometimes your knowledge of that [which] you are thought to know, you shall be thought, another time, to know that [which] you know not." — Francis Bacon (1561–1626).

dissimulate

Dissimulate *is from Latin* dissimulāre, *"to pretend that something is different from what it really is, disguise":* dis-, *"not, opposite,"* + simulāre, *"to pretend." Separately, Latin* dissimulāre *became* dessembler *in Old French, and this was borrowed into English as* **dissemble. Dissimulate** *and* **dissemble** *thus have not only the same basic meaning but also the same origin; they are homonymous doublets.*

ci•at•ed, dis•so•ci•at•ing. 1. To remove from association or cease associating; separate; part. **2.** To undergo or cause to undergo dissociation.

dis•so•ci•a•tion |dĭ sō'sē **ā'**shən| *or* |-shē-| *n.* **1.** A chemical process in which some physical influence, such as heat or the presence of a solvent, causes a molecule to split apart into simpler groups of atoms, single atoms, or ions. **2.** A disorder in which various parts of a person's mental activity become separated from each other. **3.** The act of breaking away or separating.

dis•sol•u•ble |dĭ **sŏl'**yə bəl| *adj.* Capable of being dissolved.

dis•so•lute |**dĭs'**ə lo͞ot'| *adj.* Lacking in moral restraint; immoral. **—dis'so•lute'ly** *adv.* **—dis'so•lute'ness** *n.*

dis•so•lu•tion |dĭs'ə **lo͞o'**shən| *n.* **1.** The act or process of breaking up into parts; disintegration. **2.** An act of ending a formal or legal bond or tie; annulment; termination: *dissolution of a contract; dissolution of a marriage.* **3.** The act or process of changing from a solid to a liquid.

dis•solve |dĭ **zŏlv'**| *v.* **dis•solved, dis•solv•ing. 1.** To be taken up or cause to be taken up into a solution: *Alcohol dissolves in water. Dissolve the powder in water.* **2.** To absorb into a solution: *Water dissolves sugar.* **3.** To change from a solid to a liquid; melt. **4.** To bring to an end, as a marriage, union, or partnership; terminate; annul. **5.** To dismiss (a meeting or lawmaking body). **6.** To fade away or cause to disappear; melt: *resentment that dissolves into a willingness to help; dissolving her anger with kind words.* **7.** To be overcome emotionally: *My reaction to a crisis was to dissolve into tears.* **—dis•solv'a•ble** *adj.*

dis•so•nance |**dĭs'**ə nəns| *n.* **1.** In music: **a.** A combination of tones that sounds harsh in comparison to the combinations before it and that is resolved when followed by an appropriate consonance. **b.** The condition or quality of being dissonant. **2.** Lack of agreement or consistency.

dis•so•nant |**dĭs'**ə nənt| *adj.* **1.** Of or having dissonance or dissonances. **2.** Having many dissonances: *dissonant music.* **—dis'so•nant•ly** *adv.*

dis•suade |dĭ **swād'**| *v.* **dis•suad•ed, dis•suad•ing.** To discourage or keep (someone) from a purpose or course of action: *His invitation dissuaded her from leaving early.* **—dis•sua'sion** |dĭ-**swā'**zhən| *n.*

dis•taff |**dĭs'**tăf'| *or* |-täf'| *n.* A stick holding flax or wool to be drawn off onto a spindle and spun into thread or yarn. [SEE PICTURE]

distaff side. The female side or branch of a family. [SEE NOTE]

dis•tance |**dĭs'**təns| *n.* **1. a.** The length of a path, especially a straight line segment, that joins two points. **b.** The length of the shortest line segment that can connect a given point and a given line, a given point and a given surface, a pair of given lines, or a pair of given surfaces. **2.** A stretch of space without definite limits: *a plane flying some distance off its course.* **3.** The condition of being apart in space or time: *"Distance only lends enchantment"* (Arthur Gillespie).

***Idioms.* in the distance.** In a space far removed: *Ocean Park seemed small in the distance.* **keep (one's) distance. 1.** To remain apart from; stay away from. **2.** To be aloof or unfriendly.

dis•tant |**dĭs'**tənt| *adj.* **1.** Far removed in space or time: *a distant peak; the distant past.* **2.** Far apart in relationship: *a distant cousin.* **3.** Unfriendly in manner; aloof: *appearing cold and distant.* *—adv.* At or to a distance; away: *a house only eight miles distant.* **—dis'tant•ly** *adv.*

dis•taste |dĭs **tāst'**| *n.* A dislike or aversion: *a distaste for music.*

dis•taste•ful |dĭs **tāst'**fəl| *adj.* Unpleasant; disagreeable: *distasteful remarks.* **—dis•taste'ful•ly** *adv.* **—dis•taste'ful•ness** *n.*

dis•tem•per |dĭs **tĕm'**pər| *n.* An infectious, often fatal disease of dogs, cats, and other animals.

dis•tend |dĭ **stĕnd'**| *v.* To swell or stretch by or as if by internal pressure: *They ate until their stomachs distended. Fluid distended the blister.*

dis•ten•tion, also **dis•ten•sion** |dĭ **stĕn'**shən| *n.* **1.** The act or process of distending. **2.** The condition of being distended.

dis•till |dĭ **stĭl'**| *v.* **dis•tilled, dis•till•ing. 1.** To treat (a substance) by the process of distillation. **2.** To separate (a substance) from a mixture by distillation. **3.** To undergo or be produced by distillation.

dis•til•late |**dĭs'**tə lĭt| *or* |-lāt'| *or* |dĭ **stĭl'**ĭt| *n.* The substance condensed from vapor in distillation.

dis•til•la•tion |dĭs'tə **lā'**shən| *n.* **1.** Any one of several processes in which a complex mixture or substance is broken up into relatively pure components by being heated until the components vaporize one by one and are made to condense individually. **2.** A distillate.

dis•till•er |dĭ **stĭl'**ər| *n.* Someone or something that distills, especially a producer of alcoholic liquors by distillation.

dis•till•er•y |dĭ **stĭl'**ə rē| *n., pl.* **dis•till•er•ies.** An establishment or plant for distilling, especially alcoholic liquors.

dis•tinct |dĭ **stĭngkt'**| *adj.* **1.** Having an identity of its own; not identical; individual: *each having its own distinct personality.* **2.** Not similar; different: *lines having distinct thicknesses.* **3.** Easily perceived by the senses or mind; unmistakable: *a distinct odor.* **4.** Clear; well-defined; definite: *distinct vision; a distinct outline; a distinct disadvantage.* **—dis•tinct'ly** *adv.* **—dis•tinct'ness** *n.*

dis•tinc•tion |dĭ **stĭngk'**shən| *n.* **1.** The act of distinguishing; discrimination: *Employers must make no distinction because of race in hiring.* **2.** The condition or fact of being distinct; a difference; unlikeness: *a distinction between capital letters and small ones.* **3.** Something that sets one apart; a distinguishing mark or experience: *Franklin had the distinction of serving as postmaster general under the British and the Continental Congress.* **4.** Excellence: *composers of distinction.* **5.** Recognition of achievement or superiority; honor: *won prizes and distinction.*

dis•tinc•tive |dĭ **stĭngk'**tĭv| *adj.* Serving to identify, characterize, or set apart from others: *Red berries are a distinctive feature of this plant.* **—dis•tinc'tive•ly** *adv.* **—dis•tinc'tive•ness** *n.*

dis•tin•guish |dĭ **stĭng'**gwĭsh| *v.* **1. a.** To recognize as being different or distinct: *a way to distinguish spiders from ants.* **b.** To recognize differences; make a clear distinction; discriminate: *distinguish between fact and opinion.* **2.** To perceive distinctly; make out; discern: *the ear's*

distaff
Spinning wheel, showing the distaff (circled) in position

Before the Industrial Revolution, spinning at home was a permanent daily occupation for many women. The machinery of spinning was a universally familiar piece of household furniture. The **distaff** *thus became a symbol of women's work and of women themselves. This is the explanation of* **distaff side,** *an old-fashioned phrase that probably now only occurs in literature.* **Distaff** *was* distæf *in Old English and means "flax-staff":* dis-, *"bundle of flax,"* + stæf, *"a staff."*

distributive property
Careful examination of the equation given will show that it is correct if we replace ♦ with × or ÷ but incorrect if we replace ♦ with + or − and ● with × or ÷. Therefore we can say that multiplication and division have the **distributive property** *with respect to addition and subtraction but not vice versa.*

ability to distinguish tones. **3.** To make noticeable or different; set apart: *simple, clean-cut forms that distinguish the work of this architect.* **4.** To cause (oneself) to gain fame, esteem, or honor: *He distinguished himself both as a composer and as a painter.* —**dis•tin'guish•a•ble** *adj.*

dis•tin•guished |dĭ **stĭng'**gwĭsht| *adj.* **1.** Recognized as excellent; eminent; famous; renowned: *a distinguished composer.* **2.** Dignified in conduct or appearance.

dis•tort |dĭ **stôrt'**| *v.* **1.** To twist (something) out of the usual shape; contort: *a grin that distorted his face.* **2.** To give a false account of; misrepresent: *The reporters distorted his statement.*

dis•tor•tion |dĭ **stôr'**shən| *n.* **1. a.** The act of distorting. **b.** The condition of being distorted. **2.** Something distorted: *His account of what happened was full of distortions.* **3.** Any unwanted change in the shape or color of an image produced by a lens or other optical system. **4.** Any unwanted change in an electrical or electromagnetic signal.

dis•tract |dĭ **străkt'**| *v.* To draw the attention of away from something; divert.

dis•tract•ed |dĭ **străk'**tĭd| *adj.* **1.** Very confused or bewildered: *distracted between joy and sorrow.* **2.** Violently upset in mind, especially by grief.

dis•trac•tion |dĭ **străk'**shən| *n.* **1.** Something that distracts: *too many distractions while studying.* **2.** Great mental agitation: *Worry drove me to distraction.*

dis•traught |dĭ **strôt'**| *adj.* **1.** Anxious or agitated; worried. **2.** Crazed; mad.

dis•tress |dĭ **strĕs'**| *n.* **1.** Pain or suffering of mind or body resulting from worry, anxiety, or sickness. **2.** The condition of being in need of immediate assistance: *swimmers in distress.* —***modifier:*** *a distress call; distress signals.* —*v.* To cause (someone) to suffer in mind or body.

dis•tress•ful |dĭ **strĕs'**fəl| *adj.* Causing, experiencing, or showing distress. —**dis•tress'ful•ly** *adv.*

dis•trib•ute |dĭ **strĭb'**yo͞ot| *v.* **dis•trib•ut•ed, dis•trib•ut•ing. 1.** To divide and give out in portions; parcel out: *distribute sheets of paper among the class.* **2.** To pass or send out; deliver: *companies that distribute oil to other parts of the country.* **3.** To spread or scatter over an area: *Cotton plantations were not distributed generally over the Union but located in the South.* **4.** To deal in, especially as a wholesaler. **5. a.** To apply (multiplication by a given factor) to each of the terms that make up a mathematical expression. For example, if $Q = t_1 + t_2 + \ldots t_n$, where each t is an individual term, then $MQ = M(t_1 + t_2 + \ldots t_n) = Mt_1 + Mt_2 + \ldots Mt_n$. **b.** To be capable of being distributed in this way: *Multiplication distributes over addition.* See **distributive property.**

dis•tri•bu•tion |dĭs'trə **byo͞o'**shən| *n.* **1.** The act of distributing. **2.** The way in which a thing is distributed: *a map showing the distribution of wildlife in America.* **3.** The process or system by which goods reach consumers; marketing; merchandising.

dis•trib•u•tive |dĭ **strĭb'**yə tĭv| *adj.* **1.** Of distribution: *the distributive function of the blood stream.* **2.** Of or having the distributive property. —**dis•trib'u•tive•ly** *adv.*

distributive property. The property of a mathematical operation, ♦, that with respect to another operation, ●, is stated as $(a ♦ b) ● (a ♦ c) = a ♦ (b ● c)$. [SEE NOTE]

dis•trib•u•tor |dĭ **strĭb'**yə tər| *n.* **1.** Someone or something that distributes. **2.** A person who or company that markets or sells merchandise, especially a wholesaler. **3.** In certain internal-combustion engines, a device that switches electricity to each spark plug at the correct time.

dis•trict |**dĭs'**trĭkt| *n.* **1.** A part of a geographical unit, such as a city or state, marked out by law for a particular purpose: *our school district; voters of the tenth electoral district.* **2.** An area, especially one having a particular characteristic or function: *the theater district; a shopping district.* —*v.* To mark off or divide into districts.

district attorney. The prosecuting attorney of a judicial district.

District of Columbia. The Federal District of the United States, wholly occupied by the capital city of Washington.

dis•trust |dĭs **trŭst'**| *n.* Lack of trust; suspicion. —*v.* To lack confidence in; doubt; suspect.

dis•trust•ful |dĭs **trŭst'**fəl| *adj.* Feeling doubt; suspicious. —**dis•trust'ful•ly** *adv.* —**dis•trust'ful•ness** *n.*

dis•turb |dĭ **stûrb'**| *v.* **1.** To break up or destroy the peace, order, or settled state of: *strong winds disturbing the surface of the lake.* **2.** To trouble emotionally or mentally; upset: *disturbed by lack of word from you.* **3.** To intrude upon; bother: *visitors constantly disturbing him; a radio that disturbed our sleep.*

dis•tur•bance |dĭ **stûr'**bəns| *n.* **1. a.** The act or process of disturbing: *the disturbance of a chemical reaction by light.* **b.** The condition of being disturbed: *a disturbance of radio communications.* **2.** A concentration of energy or mass in a small part of something that is otherwise fairly uniform: *A storm is an atmospheric disturbance.* **3.** Something that disturbs; an interruption or intrusion. **4. a.** A commotion or scuffle: *creating a disturbance on the bus.* **b.** An outbreak of disorder: *student disturbances on college campuses; a border disturbance.* **5.** Abnormal or improper function; malfunction; disorder: *emotional disturbances; a glandular disturbance.*

di•sul•fide |dī **sŭl'**fīd'| *n.* A chemical compound that contains two atoms of sulfur combined with a single other element or radical.

dis•un•ion |dĭs **yo͞on'**yən| *n.* **1.** The condition of being disunited; separation. **2.** Lack of unity or agreement; discord.

dis•u•nite |dĭs'yo͞o **nīt'**| *v.* **dis•u•nit•ed, dis•u•nit•ing.** To make or become separate or divided: *differences of opinion that disunited our club; when the party threatened to disunite over the question of new taxes.*

dis•u•ni•ty |dĭs **yo͞o'**nĭ tē| *n., pl.* **dis•u•ni•ties.** Lack of unity or agreement; discord; dissension.

dis•use |dĭs **yo͞os'**| *n.* The condition of not being used or of being no longer in use.

ditch |dĭch| *n.* A long, narrow trench dug in the ground. —*v.* **1.** To dig or make a ditch in or around. **2.** To drive (a vehicle) into a ditch. **3.** *Slang.* To throw aside; get rid of. **4.** *Slang.* To bring (a land-based airplane) to a forced landing on water.

dith•er |dĭth'ər| *n.* A condition of nervous excitement or indecision.

dit•to |dĭt'ō| *n., pl.* **dit•tos.** **1.** The same as stated above or before. Used to avoid repeating a word and indicated by a pair of small marks (″) placed under the word that would otherwise be repeated. **2.** A duplicate or copy.

dit•ty |dĭt'ē| *n., pl.* **dit•ties.** A simple song.

di•ur•nal |dī ûr'nəl| *adj.* **1.** Occurring in a day or each day; daily. **2.** Occurring or active during the daytime rather than at night: *diurnal birds of prey.* **—di•ur'nal•ly** *adv.*

di•van |dĭ văn'| *or* |dī'văn'| *n.* A long couch, usually without a back or arms.

dive |dīv| *v.* **dived** or **dove** |dōv|, **dived, div•ing.** **1.** To plunge headfirst into water. **2.** To go or cause to go underwater; submerge: *The submarine dived. He defied orders not to dive the submarine.* **3.** To plunge or fall headfirst through the air: *He dived from the tenth floor in a suicide attempt.* **4.** To plunge or cause to plunge rapidly and nose down: *watching the airplanes dive; dived his plane into the enemy formation.* **5.** To drop sharply and rapidly: *Stock prices dived after the President made his announcement.* **6.** To rush headlong or plunge into: *dived into the crowd of students; training that prepared him to dive into his new duties.* *—n.* **1.** A headlong plunge into water. **2.** A sharp downward movement through space or water, as of an airplane or submarine. **3.** A sudden drop or fall.

dive bomber. A bomber that releases its bombs at the end of a steep dive toward its target.

div•er |dī'vər| *n.* **1.** A person who dives into water: *a champion diver.* **2.** A person who works underwater, as in gathering pearl oysters or performing salvage operations.

di•verge |dĭ vûrj'| *or* |dī-| *v.* **di•verged, di•verg•ing.** **1.** To go or extend in different directions from a common point; branch out: *a road that suddenly diverged into paths like branches of the letter "Y."* **2.** To turn aside or depart from a set course, standard, or norm; deviate. **3.** To differ, as in opinion or manner. **4.** In mathematics, to fail to converge.

di•ver•gence |dĭ vûr'jəns| *or* |dī-| *n.* **1.** The act of diverging. **2.** Departure from an established course, pattern, or standard. **3.** Difference, as of opinion.

di•ver•gent |dĭ vûr'jənt| *or* |dī-| *adj.* **1.** Drawing apart from a common point; diverging. **2.** Differing: *widely divergent trends.* **3.** In mathematics, not convergent. **—di•ver'gent•ly** *adv.*

di•vers |dī'vərz| *adj.* Various; several. [SEE NOTE]

di•verse |dĭ vûrs'| *or* |dī-| *or* |dī'vûrs'| *adj.* **1.** Distinct in kind; different: *The personalities of Bob and Jim are diverse.* **2.** Of several or many kinds: *America is a land of diverse people.* **—di•verse'ly** *adv.* **—di•verse'ness** *n.* [SEE NOTE]

di•ver•si•fi•ca•tion |dĭ vûr'sə fĭ kā'shən| *n.* The act of diversifying or the condition of being diversified.

di•ver•si•fy |dĭ vûr'sə fī'| *or* |dī-| *v.* **di•ver•si•fied, di•ver•si•fy•ing, di•ver•si•fies.** **1.** To give diversity or variety to: *inventions that have diversified our lives.* **2.** To spread out over a wide range; make or become varied in form, character, or activity: *He diversified his investments to reduce the risk of heavy financial losses.*

di•ver•sion |dĭ vûr'zhən| *or* |-shən| *or* |dī-| *n.* **1.** The act of diverting: *the diversion of a river through the construction of dams.* **2.** Something that relaxes or entertains; recreation: *the diversion of a royal hunt.* **3.** The act or an example of drawing the attention to a different course, direction, etc.

di•ver•si•ty |dĭ vûr'sĭ tē| *or* |dī-| *n., pl.* **di•ver•si•ties.** **1.** Difference: *In a democracy, diversity in our ways of thinking is to be expected.* **2.** Variety: *Not even insects can match the fishes' diversity in size and shape.*

di•vert |dĭ vûrt'| *or* |dī-| *v.* **1.** To turn aside from a course or direction; deflect: *dams built to divert the river water into canals.* **2.** To draw (the mind or attention) to another direction: *amusements that divert their attention from study.* **3.** To amuse or entertain.

di•ver•ti•men•to |dĭ vûr'tə mĕn'tō| *n., pl.* **di•ver•ti•men•tos.** A chamber music form, usually in several movements, commonly written during the 18th century.

di•vert•ing |dĭ vûr'tĭng| *or* |dī-| *adj.* Amusing; entertaining: *a diverting short story.* **—di•vert'ing•ly** *adv.*

di•vest |dĭ vĕst'| *or* |dī-| *v.* **1.** To strip, as of clothes: *He divested himself of his boots before coming in.* **2.** To deprive, as of rights or property: *The noblemen divested the king of his power.*

di•vide |dĭ vīd'| *v.* **di•vid•ed, di•vid•ing.** **1.** To separate or become separated into parts, groups, or branches; split: *divide a cake. The river divides here.* **2.** To separate into opposing factions; disunite: *Bad feelings have divided the team.* **3.** To separate from; cut off; keep apart: *A mountain chain divides France and Spain.* **4.** To classify according to kind; group: *divide books into fiction and nonfiction.* **5.** To apportion or distribute among a number: *The workers divided the money among themselves.* **6. a.** To perform the operation of division on (a number): *divide 10 by 2. This machine multiplies and divides.* **b.** To be an exact factor of: *5 divides 15.* *—n.* A ridge separating two areas of land each drained by a different river system.

div•i•dend |dĭv'ĭ dĕnd'| *n.* **1.** A number that is to be divided. **2.** A share of profits paid to a stockholder. **3.** *Informal.* A share of a surplus; bonus: *Doing it that way will bring dividends.*

di•vid•er |dĭ vī'dər| *n.* **1.** Something that divides, especially a screen or other partition: *a room divider.* **2. dividers.** A device that is something like a compass, used for dividing lines and transferring measurements. [SEE PICTURE]

div•i•na•tion |dĭv'ə nā'shən| *n.* **1.** The art of foretelling the future or discovering concealed knowledge through supposedly supernatural means. **2.** A clever guess.

di•vine¹ |dĭ vīn'| *adj.* **1.** Of, from, or like God or a god: *divine love. "To err is human, to forgive divine."* **2.** Being or having the nature of a god: *a divine being.* **3.** In the service or worship of God or a god; sacred; holy: *divine rites.* **4.** *Informal.* Wonderful; excellent: *This cake is divine!* *—n.* **1.** A clergyman. **2.** A person learned in theology. **—di•vine'ly** *adv.*

di•vine² |dĭ vīn'| *v.* **di•vined, di•vin•ing.** **1.** To foretell or prophesy. **2.** To guess: *He shot out of*

divers/diverse

Latin dīvertere, *"to turn aside, to turn in different directions"* (dis-, *"apart,"* + vertere, *"to turn"*), *formed the adjective* dīversus, *"different, various." This passed into Old French as* divers, *which was borrowed into Middle English as* **divers** *or* **diverse**. *The two variant forms still exist, but* **divers** *is becoming obsolete.* **Diverse** *is a more normal spelling, since it is of the same origin as* **adverse, inverse, reverse,** *etc.*

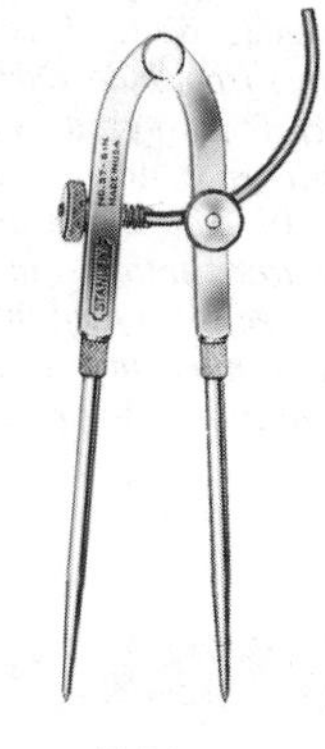

dividers

divining rod
Sixteenth-century woodcut

do¹⁻²
Do¹ *was* dō-n *in Old English, descending unchanged from prehistoric Germanic* dō-n. *This ultimately comes from Indo-European* dhō-, *which is an o-grade variant of the basic root* dhē-, *"to set, put, do." (An Indo-European* dh- *regularly turned into* d- *in Germanic; in Greek it turned into* th- *and in Latin into either* f- *or* d-.) **Do²** *is from Italian* do *or* du.

Doberman pinscher
The **Doberman pinscher** was bred by Ludwig *Doberman,* a nineteenth-century German dog-breeder; *pinscher* is the German word for "terrier."

ă pat/ā pay/â care/ä father/ĕ pet/ ē be/ĭ pit/ī pie/î fierce/ŏ pot/ ō go/ô paw, for/oi oil/ŏŏ book/ ōō boot/ou out/ŭ cut/û fur/ *th* the/th thin/hw which/zh vision/ ə ago, item, pencil, atom, circus

the stalled car and immediately divined the cause of the trouble. —**di•vin'er** *n.*

diving bell. A large vessel used to house persons working underwater. It is raised and lowered by means of a cable and is supplied with air under pressure.

diving suit. A heavy waterproof garment with a detachable air-fed helmet, used for underwater work.

divining rod. A forked stick believed to indicate the presence of underground water or minerals by bending downward when held over a source. [SEE PICTURE]

di•vin•i•ty |dĭ vĭn'ĭ tē| *n., pl.* **di•vin•i•ties. 1.** The condition or quality of being divine. **2. a. the Divinity.** God. **b.** A god or goddess. **3.** The study of God and religion; theology.

di•vis•i•ble |dĭ vĭz'ə bəl| *adj.* **1.** Capable of being divided. **2.** Containing a given integer as one of its factors: *16 is divisible by 4.* —**di•vis'i•bil'i•ty** *n.* —**di•vis'i•bly** *adv.*

di•vi•sion |dĭ vĭzh'ən| *n.* **1.** The mathematical process of determining the factor by which a given number must be multiplied in order to make a second given number. **2.** The act of dividing or the condition of being divided; separation into parts. **3.** One of the parts or groups into which something is divided: *Our team has been in the first division most of the season.* **4.** Something that divides or keeps separate; a partition. **5.** Disagreement; disunity: *The meeting was marked by division.* **6.** An army unit composed of a number of battalions.

division sign. The symbol (÷) placed between two numbers to indicate that the first is to be divided by the second.

di•vi•sive |dĭ vī'sĭv| *adj.* Creating or tending to create disagreement or disunity: *A divisive political issue.* —**di•vi'sive•ly** *adv.* —**di•vi'sive•ness** *n.*

di•vi•sor |dĭ vī'zər| *n.* The number by which another number is to be divided.

di•vorce |dĭ vôrs'| *or* |-vōrs'| *n.* **1.** The legal termination of a marriage. **2.** The complete separation of things: *the divorce of the courts and politics.* —*v.* **di•vorced, di•vor•cing. 1.** To end the marriage of (persons). **2.** To rid oneself of (a husband or wife) by legal divorce. **3.** To separate or remove (a thing or things).

div•ot |dĭv'ət| *n.* A piece of turf torn up by a golf club in hitting the ball.

di•vulge |dĭ vŭlj'| *v.* **di•vulged, di•vulg•ing.** To make known; reveal; tell: *divulge a secret.* —**di•vulg'er** *n.*

Dix•ie |dĭk'sē|. The Southern states of the United States, especially those that joined the Confederacy during the Civil War. Also called *Dixie Land.*

diz•zy |dĭz'ē| *adj.* **diz•zi•er, diz•zi•est. 1.** Having a sensation of whirling or feeling a tendency to fall; giddy. **2.** Producing or tending to produce giddiness: *a dizzy height.* **3.** *Informal.* Scatterbrained; silly; foolish. —*v.* **diz•zied, diz•zy•ing, diz•zies.** To make dizzy; confuse; bewilder. —**diz'zy•ing** *adj.: a dizzying pace.* —**diz'zi•ly** *adv.* —**diz'zi•ness** *n.*

Dja•kar•ta |jə kär'tə|. The capital of Indonesia. Population, 4,576,000.

Dji•bou•ti |jĭ bōō'tē|. A country on the coast of northeastern Africa. Population, 386,000. Capital, Djibouti (population, 96,000).

DMZ Demilitarized zone.

DNA A nucleic acid having a very complicated structure and forming the main constituent of the chromosomes of living cells; deoxyribonucleic acid.

do¹ |dōō| *v.* **did** |dĭd|, **done** |dŭn|, **do•ing, does** |dŭz|. **1.** To perform or accomplish: *do a good job.* **2.** To carry out the requirements of; fulfill or complete: *Do your duty. He is doing his military service.* **3.** To create, compose, or make: *He is doing a painting for me. Do five copies of this letter.* **4.** To bring about; effect: *Crying won't do any good.* **5.** To put into action; exert: *I'll do everything in my power to help you.* **6.** To deal with as is necessary: *I have a lot of work to do. "The barber will do you next, Mr. Smith."* **7.** To render or give: *I wish he would do me the courtesy of calling back.* **8.** To work at for a living: *What do you do?* **9.** To work out the details of; solve (a problem): *To do this equation takes a while.* **10.** To present or perform (a play, dramatic reading, etc.); stage. **11.** To have the role of; play. **12.** To cover (a specified distance) in traveling: *We can't do a mile in less than 10 minutes.* **13.** To tour: *do Europe on five dollars a day.* **14.** To be sufficient or convenient for; suffice: *This room will do us very nicely.* **15.** To set or style (the hair): *do one's hair.* **16.** *Informal.* To serve (a prison term): *He did time on Riker's Island.* **17.** *Slang.* To cheat: *do someone out of his inheritance.* **18.** To act or strive effectively or energetically: *Do or die.* **19.** —Used as an auxiliary: **a.** To indicate the tense in questions, negative statements, and inverted phrases: *Do you understand? I did not sleep well. Little did he suspect.* **b.** As a substitute for an antecedent verb: *She tries as hard as they do.* **c.** For emphasis: *I do want to be sure.* —***phrasal verbs.*** **do away with. 1.** To eliminate; dispose of. **2.** To kill or destroy. **do by.** To behave toward; deal with: *She hasn't done very well by me.* **do for.** To take care of. **do in.** *Slang.* **1.** To exhaust: *That run really did me in.* **2.** To kill: *Nobody really knows who did him in.* **do over.** *Informal.* To redecorate: *Professionals are doing over their house.* **do up. 1.** To dress lavishly. **2.** To wrap and tie (a package). **do without.** To manage without something. —*n., pl.* **do's** or **dos.** A statement of what should be done: *do's and dont's.* ¶*These sound alike* **do, dew, due.** [SEE NOTE]

Idioms. **do one's thing.** To do what one does best or finds most enjoyable. **have to do with. 1.** To have a relation or relationship with. **2.** To be concerned with; have as subject matter: *a book having to do with religion.* **make do.** To manage (with whatever one has or whatever is at hand).

do² |dō| *n., pl.* **dos.** A syllable used in music to represent the keynote of a major scale or sometimes the tone C. ¶*These sound alike* **do, doe, dough.** [SEE NOTE]

dob•bin |dŏb'ĭn| *n.* A horse, especially an old or plodding work horse.

Do•ber•man pin•scher |dō'bər mən pĭn'shər|. A fairly large dog of a breed originally developed in Germany, having a short, smooth, usually black coat. [SEE PICTURE]

doc•ile |dŏs'əl| *adj.* Easy to train or handle; tractable; submissive: *a docile horse; a docile child.* —**doc'ile•ly** *adv.* —**do•cil'i•ty** |dŏ sĭl'ĭ tē| *or* |dō-| *n.*

dock¹ |dŏk| *n.* **1. a.** A landing pier for ships or

boats. **b.** A loading platform for trucks or trains. **2.** Often **docks.** The landing area in a harbor. **3.** The waterway between or alongside piers that receives a ship for loading, unloading, etc. *—v.* **1.** To maneuver or come into a dock: *dock a big liner. The freighter docked at noon.* **2.** To join together (two or more spacecraft) while in space. [SEE NOTE]

dock[2] |dŏk| *v.* **1.** To clip or cut off, as an animal's tail. **2. a.** To withhold a part of (a salary). **b.** To penalize (a worker) by such deduction. [SEE NOTE]

dock[3] |dŏk| *n.* An enclosed place where the defendant stands or sits in a criminal court. [SEE NOTE]

dock[4] |dŏk| *n.* A weedy plant with clusters of small greenish or reddish flowers. [SEE NOTE]

dock•et |**dŏk**′ĭt| *n.* **1.** A calendar of cases awaiting court action. **2.** Any list of things to be done; an agenda. **3.** A label or ticket attached to a package and listing its contents. *—v.* **1.** To enter in a docket; schedule. **2.** To label or ticket (a parcel).

dock•yard |**dŏk**′yärd′| *n.* **1.** A shipyard. **2.** *British.* A **navy yard.**

doc•tor |**dŏk**′tər| *n.* **1.** A person who is trained and licensed to practice medicine, surgery, dentistry, etc. **2.** A person who holds the highest degree given by a university. *—v. Informal.* **1.** To give medical treatment to. **2.** To tamper with or falsify: *doctor the evidence.*

doc•tor•al |**dŏk**′tər əl| *adj.* Of a doctor or doctorate: *a doctoral dissertation.*

doc•tor•ate |**dŏk**′tər ĭt| *n.* The degree or status of a doctor as awarded by a university: *a doctorate in English literature.*

doc•tri•naire |dŏk′trə **nâr**′| *n.* A person who is rigidly attached to a practice or theory without considering whether it is practical, applicable, etc. *—adj.* Of or like a doctrinaire; dogmatic.

doc•trine |**dŏk**′trĭn| *n.* A principle or set of principles held and put forward by a religious, political, or other group; dogma: *the doctrine of Dutch Calvinism; the Monroe Doctrine; a constitutional doctrine.* **—doc′trin•al** *adj.*

doc•u•ment |**dŏk**′yə mənt| *n.* An official paper that can be used to furnish evidence or information. *—v.* |**dŏk**′yə mĕnt′|. To prove or support with evidence: *document a report.*

doc•u•men•ta•ry |dŏk′yə **mĕn**′tə rē| *adj.* Of or based on documents: *documentary evidence. —n., pl.* **doc•u•men•ta•ries.** A motion picture giving a factual account of some subject and often showing actual events.

doc•u•men•ta•tion |dŏk′yə mĕn **tā**′shən| *n.* **1.** The provision of documents or references. **2.** The documents or references provided.

dod•der[1] |**dŏd**′ər| *v.* To tremble or move shakily, as from old age; totter. [SEE NOTE]

dod•der[2] |**dŏd**′ər| *n.* A plant with tiny, inconspicuous leaves and flowers and slender, yellowish stems that twine around and absorb nourishment from other plants. [SEE NOTE]

do•dec•a•gon |dō **dĕk**′ə gŏn′| *n.* A plane geometric figure having 12 sides and 12 angles.

do•dec•a•he•dron |dō dĕk′ə **hē**′drən| *or* |dō′dĕk-| *n., pl.* **do•dec•a•he•drons** or **do•dec•a•he•dra** |dō dĕk′ə **hē**′drə| *or* |dō′dĕk-|. A solid geometric figure having 12 plane faces.

dodge |dŏj| *v.* **dodged, dodg•ing. 1.** To avoid by moving quickly aside or out of the way; shift suddenly: *She dodged the pillow that was thrown at her. He dodged when I tried to catch him.* **2.** To evade by cunning, trickery, etc.: *The candidate dodged the issue. —n.* **1.** A quick move or shift. **2.** A clever way or method of avoiding something; trick: *a tax dodge.* **—dodg′er** *n.*

do•do |**dō**′dō| *n., pl.* **do•does** or **do•dos.** A large, heavy-set bird that formerly lived on an island in the Indian Ocean but has been extinct for about 300 years. It had very short wings and was unable to fly. [SEE PICTURE]

doe |dō| *n.* **1.** A female deer. **2.** The female of certain other animals, such as the hare or kangaroo. ¶*These sound alike* **doe, do[2], dough.**

do•er |**dōō**′ər| *n.* **1.** A person who does something. **2.** An especially active person.

does |dŭz|. Third person singular present tense of **do.**

doe•skin |**dō**′skĭn′| *n.* **1.** The skin of a female deer or of a sheep or lamb. **2.** Soft leather made from such skin, used for gloves. **3.** A soft, smooth woolen fabric with a nap on it.

does•n't |**dŭz**′ənt|. Does not.

doff |dôf| *or* |dŏf| *v.* **1.** To take off (clothing): *She doffed her coat.* **2.** To lift (one's hat) in greeting: *He doffed his hat.*

dog |dôg| *or* |dŏg| *n.* **1.** An animal that is related to the wolves and foxes and that has from earliest times been kept as a pet or trained for hunting, guarding, etc. **2.** *Informal.* A fellow: *You lucky dog!* **3.** *Slang.* **a.** An uninteresting or unattractive person: *a date with a real dog.* **b.** A very inferior product, creation, etc.: *That show was a dog. —v.* **dogged, dog•ging.** To follow after like a dog; trail persistently: *My little brother has been dogging me all afternoon.*

dog•cart |**dôg**′kärt′| *or* |**dŏg**′-| *n.* **1.** A vehicle drawn by one horse and accommodating two persons seated back to back. **2.** A small cart pulled by dogs.

dog days. The hot, sultry period between mid-July and September.

doge |dōj| *n.* The elected chief magistrate of the former republics of Venice and Genoa.

dog-ear |**dôg**′îr′| *or* |**dŏg**′-| *n.* A turned-down corner of a page of a book. *—v.* To turn down the corner of (a book page).

dog•gie or **dog•gy** |**dô**′gē| *or* |**dŏg**′ē| *n., pl.* **dog•gies.** A dog, especially a small one.

doggie bag or **doggy bag.** A bag for leftover food taken home from a restaurant.

dog•fight |**dôg**′fīt′| *or* |**dŏg**′-| *n.* **1.** A violent fight between or as if between dogs; a brawl. **2.** A battle between fighter planes.

dog•fish |**dôg**′fĭsh′| *or* |**dŏg**′-| *n., pl.* **dog•fish** or **dog•fish•es.** Any of several small sharks.

dog•ged |**dô**′gĭd| *or* |**dŏg**′ĭd| *adj.* Not giving up easily; willful; stubborn: *dogged efforts.* **—dog′ged•ly** *adv.* **—dog′ged•ness** *n.*

dog•ger•el |**dô**′gər əl| *or* |**dŏg**′ər-| *n.* Verse of a loose, irregular rhythm or of a trivial nature.

dog•house |**dôg**′hous′| *or* |**dŏg**′-| *n., pl.* **-hous•es** |-hou′zĭz|. A small house or shelter for a dog.

do•gie |**dō**′gē| *n.* In the western United States, a motherless or stray calf.

dog•ma |**dôg**′mə| *or* |**dŏg**′-| *n.* **1.** A system of doctrines proclaimed true, as by a religious sect:

dock[1-2-3-4]

Dock[1] *originally meant "the trench or pool in which a boat lies at low tide," then "a man-made channel for a boat," then "a built-up ship basin with facilities for loading and repairing." It is from Dutch* docke, *which probably comes from Late Latin* ductia, *"channel," a variant of* ductus, *"duct."* **Dock[2]**, *"to cut an animal's tail," was originally a noun meaning "the fleshy stump of a horse's tail"; it probably comes from a Germanic word meaning "lump, bundle."* **Dock[3]**, *"enclosure for a defendant," was originally a thieves' slang word in the sixteenth century, coming from Flemish* docke, *"chicken pen."* **Dock[4]**, *the plant, is an Old English word, originally spelled* docce.

dodder[1-2]

Dodder[1] *is probably from some unknown Scandinavian word related to Norwegian* dudra, *"to quiver."* **Dodder[2]** *probably comes from a similar source, originally meaning "quivering plant."*

dodo

Roman Catholic dogma. **2.** A principle, belief, or idea, especially one considered to be absolute truth: *the dogma that all men are created equal.*

dog•mat•ic |dôg **măt′**ĭk| *or* |dŏg-| *adj.* **1.** Of or relating to dogma: *a dogmatic idea.* **2.** Asserting or expressing principles, beliefs, etc., in an authoritative, often arrogant way; overpositive: *a dogmatic person.* —**dog•mat′i•cal•ly** *adv.*

dog•ma•tism |**dôg′**mə tĭz′əm| *or* |**dŏg′**-| *n.* Dogmatic assertion of an opinion or belief.

do-good•er |**do͞o′**go͝od′ər| *n. Informal.* A person who is too eager to make reforms and help people.

Dog Star. Sirius.

dog•tooth violet |**dôg′**to͞oth′| *or* |**dŏg′**-|. A North American plant having leaves with reddish blotches and nodding, lilylike yellow flowers.

dog•trot |**dôg′**trŏt′| *or* |**dŏg′**-| *n.* A steady trot like that of a dog.

dog•watch |**dôg′**wŏch′| *or* |-wôch′| *or* |**dŏg′**-| *n.* Either of two periods of watch aboard a ship, from 4 to 6 p.m. or from 6 to 8 p.m.

dog•wood |**dôg′**wo͝od′| *or* |**dŏg′**-| *n.* A tree with small greenish flowers surrounded by showy white or pink petallike leaves.

Do•ha |**dō′**hə|. The capital of Qatar. Population, 150,000.

doi•ly |**doi′**lē| *n., pl.* **doi•lies.** A small, fancy mat, as of lace, linen, or paper, often put under a dish, vase, etc., to protect or decorate a table top.

do•ings |**do͞o′**ĭngz| *pl.n.* Activities, especially social activities: *doings at the church.*

do-it-your•self |**do͞o′**ĭt yər **sĕlf′**| *adj. Informal.* Of or designed to be done or assembled by an amateur without professional help.

dol•drums |**dōl′**drəmz| *or* |**dôl′**-| *or* |**dŏl′**-| *pl.n.* **1.** The ocean regions near the equator where there is little or no wind. **2.** A period or condition of depression or inactivity.

dole |dōl| *n.* **1.** The distribution of goods, especially of money, food, or clothing as charity. **2.** A gift or share of money, food, or clothing distributed as charity. —*v.* **doled, dol•ing.** To distribute in small portions; give out sparingly: *My mother doles out my allowance.*

dole•ful |**dōl′**fəl| *adj.* Very sad; mournful: *a doleful expression.* —**dole′ful•ly** *adv.*

doll |dŏl| *n.* **1.** A child's toy representing a baby or other human being. **2.** *Informal.* A pretty child or young woman. **3.** *Slang.* A person regarded with fond familiarity: *She is a living doll!* —**phrasal verb. doll up.** *Informal.* To dress up smartly, as for a special occasion.

dol•lar |**dŏl′**ər| *n.* The basic unit of money in the United States, Australia, Canada, Ethiopia, Guyana, Jamaica, Liberia, Malaysia, New Zealand, Trinidad and Tobago, Barbados, Zimbabwe, Hong Kong, and Singapore, equal to 100 cents.

dol•lop |**dŏl′**əp| *n.* A large lump, portion, or helping: *a dollop of ice cream.*

dol•ly |**dŏl′**ē| *n., pl.* **dol•lies. 1.** A child's term for a doll. **2.** A low platform that moves on small wheels or rollers, used for moving heavy loads.

dol•man |**dōl′**mən| *or* |**dōl′**-| *n.* A long, open Turkish robe with sleeves. ¶*These sound alike* **dolman, dolmen.**

dol•men |**dōl′**mən| *or* |**dŏl′**-| *n.* A prehistoric structure made up of two or more massive upright stones supporting a horizontal stone, often forming a chamber; a cromlech. ¶*These sound alike* **dolmen, dolman.**

do•lo•mite |**dō′**lə mīt′| *or* |**dŏl′**ə-| *n.* A gray, pink, or white mineral consisting mainly of a carbonate of calcium and magnesium.

do•lor•ous |**dō′**lər əs| *or* |**dŏl′**ər-| *adj.* Sorrowful; sad. —**do′lor•ous•ly** *adv.*

dol•phin |**dŏl′**fĭn| *or* |**dôl′**-| *n.* **1.** A sea animal related to the whales but smaller and with a beaklike snout. **2.** An ocean fish with rainbowlike coloring. [SEE PICTURES & NOTE]

dolman sleeve. A sleeve that is very wide at the armhole and narrow at the wrist.

dolt |dōlt| *n.* A dull or stupid person.

dolt•ish |**dōl′**tĭsh| *adj.* Dull; stupid. —**dolt′ish•ly** *adv.* —**dolt′ish•ness** *n.*

-dom. A suffix that forms nouns: **freedom; kingdom.**

do•main |dō **mān′**| *n.* **1.** A territory or range of rule or control; realm: *the duke's domains; the lion's domain.* **2.** A sphere of interest or activity; field: *That professor's domain is history.* **3.** The set of all the values that an independent variable of a mathematical function can have.

dome |dōm| *n.* **1.** A hemispheric roof or vault. **2.** Any object or structure that looks like this.

domed |dōmd| *adj.* **1.** Shaped like a dome: *his domed forehead.* **2.** Having a dome: *the domed Capitol building.*

do•mes•tic |də **mĕs′**tĭk| *adj.* **1.** Of a home, household, or family life: *domestic chores; domestic joys.* **2.** Enjoying or interested in home life and household affairs: *Because of Abby's musical talent, her parents did not expect her to be domestic.* **3.** Used to living with human beings; not wild; tame: *cats, dogs, and other domestic animals.* **4.** Of the policies, activities, or life within a country: *The President makes important decisions in both domestic and foreign affairs.* **5.** Of, within, or originating within a particular country; not foreign or imported: *domestic cars; a domestic airline route.* —*n.* A household servant, such as a maid or cook.

do•mes•ti•cate |də **mĕs′**tĭ kāt′| *v.* **do•mes•ti•cat•ed, do•mes•ti•cat•ing. 1.** To train to live with and be of use to human beings; tame: *Dogs had been domesticated in America before the arrival of explorers from Europe.* **2.** To make (someone) comfortable with or adjusted to home life. —**do•mes′ti•ca′tion** *n.*

do•mes•tic•i•ty |dō′mĕ **stĭs′**ĭ tē| *n.* **1.** The quality or condition of being domestic. **2.** Home life or devotion to it.

dom•i•cile |**dŏm′**ĭ sīl′| *or* |-səl| *or* |**dō′**mĭ-| *n.* **1.** A residence; home. **2.** One's legal residence. —*v.* **dom•i•ciled, dom•i•cil•ing.** To dwell: *For years he domiciled with his aunt.*

dom•i•nance |**dŏm′**ə nəns| *n.* The condition or fact of being dominant.

dom•i•nant |**dŏm′**ə nənt| *adj.* **1.** Having the most influence or control; governing: *the dominant person in a partnership.* **2.** Most prominent: *the dominant building in New York's skyline.* **3.** Producing a typical effect even when paired with an unlike gene for the same characteristic: *In fruit flies the gene for red eyes is dominant over the gene for white eyes.* **4.** Of or based on the fifth tone of a major or minor scale. —*n.* The fifth tone of a major or minor scale.

dolphin
Above: Sense 1
Below: Sense 2

There are two difficulties with the word **dolphin.** *(1) The animal is very similar to the porpoise, to which it is closely related (but the porpoise has a shorter snout). As a result,* **porpoise** *and* **dolphin** *are often loosely used interchangeably. (2) When European sailors in the sixteenth century encountered the colored fish of sense 2, they called it a dolphin, although it is in no way related to the animal, which is a mammal, not a fish.*

ă **pat**/ā **pay**/â **care**/ä **father**/ĕ **pet**/ ē **be**/ĭ **pit**/ī **pie**/î **fierce**/ŏ **pot**/ ō **go**/ô **paw, for**/oi **oil**/o͝o **book**/ o͞o **boot**/ou **out**/ŭ **cut**/û **fur**/ *th* **the**/th **thin**/hw **which**/**zh** vision/ ə **ago**, item, pencil, atom, circus

dom•i•nate |dŏm′ə nāt′| *v.* **dom•i•nat•ed, dom•i•nat•ing. 1.** To control, govern, or rule by superior power or strength; be dominant in position or authority: *No country can dominate the world. He had an uncontrollable desire to dominate.* **2.** To occupy the most prominent position in or over: *Wheat fields dominate the landscape of the region.* —**dom′i•na′tion** *n.*

dom•i•neer |dŏm′ə nîr′| *v.* To rule over arbitrarily or arrogantly; tyrannize.

Dom•i•ni•ca |dŏm′ĭ nē′kə| *or* |də mĭn′ĭ kə|. An island country in the eastern Caribbean Sea. Population, 74,000. Capital, Roseau.

Do•min•i•can Republic |də mĭn′ĭ kən|. A country in the West Indies, occupying the eastern two thirds of the island of Hispaniola. Population, 4,562,000. Capital, Santo Domingo. —**Do•min′i•can** *adj. & n.*

dom•i•nie |dŏm′ə nē| *or* |dō′mə-| *n. Scottish.* A schoolteacher.

do•min•ion |də mĭn′yən| *n.* **1.** Control or the exercise of control; rule; sovereignty. **2.** A territory or sphere of influence or control; domain: *the dominions of the king.* **3. Dominion.** One of certain self-governing nations within the Commonwealth of Nations.

Dominion Day. A national holiday in Canada, celebrated on July 1 in honor of the anniversary of the formation of the Dominion in 1867.

dom•i•no[1] |dŏm′ə nō′| *n., pl.* **dom•i•noes** or **dom•i•nos. 1.** A masquerade costume made up of a cloak with a hood and a mask worn over the top half of the face. **2.** The mask itself. **3.** A person wearing such a costume or mask. [SEE NOTE & PICTURE]

dom•i•no[2] |dŏm′ə nō′| *n., pl.* **dom•i•noes** or **dom•i•nos. 1.** A small, rectangular block, the face of which is divided into halves, each half blank or marked by one to six dots. **2. dominoes** *(used with a singular verb).* The game played with a set of these pieces. [SEE NOTE & PICTURE]

don[1] |dŏn| *n.* **1. Don.** A Spanish word similar to Sir, used before the first name of a man in speaking to or of him. **2.** A college or university teacher in England.

don[2] |dŏn| *v.* **donned, don•ning.** To put on; dress in: *don a coat.*

do•nate |dō′nāt′| *or* |dō nāt′| *v.* **do•nat•ed, do•nat•ing.** To present as a gift to a fund or cause; contribute: *donate a dollar to the Red Cross.*

do•na•tion |dō nā′shən| *n.* **1.** The act of donating. **2.** Something donated; a contribution.

done |dŭn|. Past participle of **do.** —*adj.* **1.** Completely accomplished or finished. **2.** Cooked adequately: *Is the fish done?* **3.** Socially acceptable: *That's not done in polite society.* ¶ *These sound alike* **done, dun.**

Idiom. **done for. 1.** Doomed; dying. **2.** Exhausted.

don•jon |dŭn′jən| *or* |dŏn′-| *n.* The main tower of a castle; a keep. ¶ *These sound alike* **donjon, dungeon.**

don•key |dŏng′kē| *or* |dŭng′-| *or* |dông′-| *n., pl.* **don•keys. 1.** An animal related to the horse but smaller and with longer ears. **2.** A stubborn or stupid person.

donkey engine. A small steam engine used for lifting or pumping, especially aboard ship.

Don•na |dŏn′ə| *n.* An Italian word similar to Lady or Madam, used before the first name of a woman in speaking to or of her.

don•nish |dŏn′ĭsh| *adj.* Like a university don; very learned; bookish.

don•ny•brook |dŏn′ē brook′| *n.* A brawl.

do•nor |dō′nər| *n.* **1.** A person who gives or contributes something, such as money to a cause or fund. **2.** A person or animal from whom blood, tissue, an organ, etc., is taken for use in a transfusion or a transplant.

do-noth•ing |do͞o′nŭth′ĭng| *adj.* Making no effort for change or improvement: *a do-nothing mayor.*

don't |dōnt|. Do not.

doo•dad |do͞o′dăd′| *n. Informal.* Any unnamed or nameless gadget or trinket.

doo•dle |do͞od′l| *v.* **doo•dled, doo•dling.** To scribble (a design or figure) while thinking about something else. —*n.* A design or figure drawn while thinking about something else.

doo•dle•bug |do͞od′l bŭg′| *n.* The larva of an insect, the **ant lion.**

doo•hick•ey |do͞o′hĭk′ē| *n., pl.* **doo•hick•eys.** *Informal.* Any gadget or mechanical part whose name one cannot recall.

doom |do͞om| *n.* A terrible fate, especially death or extinction: *send a person to his doom.* —*v.* To destine to an unhappy end, especially to death: *doomed to die soon.*

dooms•day |do͞omz′dā′| *n.* **1.** The day of the Last Judgment. **2.** Any dreaded day of judgment or reckoning.

door |dôr| *or* |dōr| *n.* **1.** A movable panel on hinges, used to open or close an entrance to a room, building, vehicle, etc. **2.** An entrance or passage. **3.** A means of access. **4.** The room or building to which a door belongs: *She lives three doors down the street from here.*

door•jamb |dôr′jăm′| *or* |dōr′-| *n.* Either of the two vertical pieces framing a doorway.

door•man |dôr′măn′| *or* |-mən| *or* |dōr′-| *n., pl.* **-men** |-mĕn′| *or* |-mən|. A man hired to attend the entrance of a hotel, apartment house, or office building.

door•mat |dôr′măt′| *or* |dōr′-| *n.* **1.** A mat outside a door, used to wipe wet or dirty shoes on. **2.** *Slang.* A person who lets himself be mistreated without fighting back.

door•nail |dôr′nāl′| *or* |dōr′-| *n.* A type of large-headed nail.

Idiom. **dead as a doornail.** Undoubtedly dead.

door•step |dôr′stĕp′| *or* |dōr′-| *n.* A step leading to a door.

door•stop |dôr′stŏp′| *or* |dōr′-| *n.* **1.** A wedge inserted beneath a door to hold it open. **2.** A weight or spring that prevents a door from slamming. **3.** A rubber-tipped projection attached to a wall to protect it from the impact of an opening door.

door•way |dôr′wā′| *or* |dōr′-| *n.* The entrance to a room or building.

door•yard |dôr′yärd′| *or* |dōr′-| *n.* A yard in front of the door of a house.

dope |dōp| *n.* **1.** Any one of many chiefly liquid preparations added or applied to things in order to produce desired properties; an additive or conditioner. **2.** *Informal.* Any of several narcotics, stimulants, and other drugs, especially those sold and used illegally, as by addicts. **3.** *Slang.*

domino[1·2]

Domino[1] *originally meant "a hooded cloak worn by priests." In Latin,* dominō *is an inflected form of* dominus, *"lord"; it occurs in various phrases in the Catholic liturgy, such as* Benedicāmus Dominō, *"Let us bless the Lord." It is assumed that both* **domino[1]** *and* **domino[2]** *somehow come from Latin* dominō, *but it is not known how.*

domino[1]

domino[2]

Doppler effect
This effect was discovered by Christian Johann Doppler *(1803–1853), Austrian physicist.*

dormer

dormouse

A very stupid person. **4.** *Slang.* Information. —*v.* **doped, dop•ing. 1.** To treat with an additive, conditioner, or similar preparation. **2.** *Informal.* To administer a narcotic or stimulant to, especially in secret; drug.

Dop•pler effect |dŏp′lər|. A change in the observed frequency of a wave, as of sound or light, that occurs when there is relative motion between the observer and the source of the wave. If the source and observer are approaching each other, the frequency is raised. If the source and observer are moving apart, the frequency is lowered. [SEE NOTE]

Dor•ic |dôr′ĭk| *or* |dŏr′-| *adj.* Of or belonging to an order of ancient Greek and Roman architecture characterized by a heavy column with a plain, saucer-shaped top, or capital: *a Doric column; a Doric capital.*

dorm |dôrm| *n. Informal.* A dormitory.

dor•mant |dôr′mənt| *adj.* **1.** In an inactive, often sleeplike condition during which life processes slow down or are suspended: *a dormant snake coiled up in its winter hideaway.* **2.** Not active but capable of renewed activity: *a dormant volcano.* —**dor′man•cy** *n.*

dor•mer |dôr′mər| *n.* **1.** A window set in a small gable projecting from a roof. **2.** The gable holding such a window. [SEE PICTURE]

dor•mi•to•ry |dôr′mĭ tôr′ē| *or* |-tōr′ē| *n., pl.* **dor•mi•to•ries. 1.** A large room providing sleeping quarters for a number of people. **2.** A building for housing a number of persons, as at a school.

dor•mouse |dôr′mous′| *n., pl.* **-mice** |-mīs′|. A small, squirrellike animal of Europe, Asia, and northern Africa. [SEE PICTURE]

dor•sal |dôr′səl| *adj.* Of, toward, on, in, or near the back of an animal. —**dor′sal•ly** *adv.*

do•ry |dôr′ē| *or* |dōr′ē| *n., pl.* **do•ries.** A flat-bottomed boat with high flaring sides, used in offshore fishing.

dos•age |dō′sĭj| *n.* **1.** The administration or application of medicine or something that acts on living organisms in regulated amounts. **2.** The amount administered or applied.

dose |dōs| *n.* **1.** An amount of something that acts on a living organism: *a dose of medicine; a dose of radiation.* **2.** *Informal.* An amount, especially of something unpleasant, to which one is subjected: *a dose of hard luck.* —*v.* **dosed, dos•ing.** To administer something to (a person or organism) in doses.

do•sim•e•ter |dō sĭm′ĭ tər| *n.* An instrument or device that measures and indicates the amount of radioactivity or x-rays to which an individual has been exposed.

dos•si•er |dŏs′ē ā| *or* |-ē ər| *or* |dô′sē ā| *or* |-sē ər| *n.* A collection of papers or documents pertaining to a particular person or subject.

dost |dŭst|. *Archaic.* A form of the present tense of **do**, used with *thou.* ¶*These sound alike* **dost, dust.**

Dos•to•yev•sky |dôs′tô yĕf′skē|, **Fyodor.** 1821–1881. Russian novelist.

dot |dŏt| *n.* **1.** A small, round mark; a spot; point. **2.** A short signal in Morse code, used in combination with a dash, as long signal, to represent letters and numbers. —*v.* **dot•ted, dot•ting.** To mark or cover with or as if with dots.

Idiom. **on the dot.** Exactly on time: *We arrived on the dot.*

do•tage |dō′tĭj| *n.* A condition marked by feeble-mindedness and foolish behavior, sometimes caused by old age.

do•tard |dō′tərd| *n.* A person in his dotage.

dote |dōt| *v.* **dot•ed, dot•ing. 1.** To lavish excessive fondness or affection: *His parents doted on him.* **2.** To be foolish or feeble-minded, especially in old age.

doth |dŭth|. *Archaic.* A form of the present tense of **do**, used with *he, she,* or *it.*

dotted swiss. A light, crisp cotton fabric with a design of raised, spaced dots, used for dresses, curtains, etc.

dot•ty |dŏt′ē| *adj.* **dot•ti•er, dot•ti•est.** Very eccentric or crazy: *a dotty old lady.* —**dot′ti•ness** *n.*

dou•ble |dŭb′əl| *adj.* **1.** Twice as much in size, strength, number, or amount: *a double dose.* **2.** Composed of two like parts; in a pair: *double doors.* **3.** Composed of two unlike parts; combining two; dual: *a double meaning.* **4.** Accommodating or designed for two: *a double bed.* **5.** Acting two parts: *a double agent.* **6.** Having many more than the usual number of petals, usually in a crowded or overlapping arrangement: *a double chrysanthemum.* —*adv.* **1.** Two together: *ride double on a horse.* **2.** In two: *bent double.* —*n.* **1.** Someone or something that resembles another; a duplicate. **2.** A hit in baseball that enables the batter to reach second base safely. **3. doubles.** A match between two pairs of players, as in tennis or handball. —*v.* **dou•bled, dou•bling. 1.** To make or become twice as great: *Double the amount if both of you go. The population doubled in that town.* **2.** To fold in two: *double the blanket.* **3.** To duplicate; repeat: *Double the "t" in "hit" when you spell the participle "hitting."* **4.** To serve an additional purpose: *My bed doubles as a couch.* **5.** To replace or be a substitute for: *That actor can double for the star if need be.* **6.** To hit a double; reverse: *double back on one's trail.* —***phrasal verb.*** **double up. 1.** To bend suddenly, as in pain or laughter. **2.** To share accommodations meant for one person.

Idiom. **on the double.** Immediately or quickly.

double bar. A pair of vertical lines drawn across one or more musical staves to indicate the end of a large section of a composition.

dou•ble-bar•reled |dŭb′əl băr′əld| *adj.* **1.** Having two barrels mounted side by side: *a double-barreled shotgun.* **2.** Serving two purposes; twofold: *a double-barreled question.*

double bass |bās|. The largest and lowest pitched of the stringed instruments that are normally played with a bow.

double bassoon. A contrabassoon.

double boiler. A cooking utensil consisting of two pots, one of which fits part way into the other. Water boiling in the lower pot cooks food in the upper.

dou•ble-breast•ed |dŭb′əl brĕs′tĭd| *adj.* Describing a coat or jacket, usually with two rows of buttons, that is fastened down the front by lapping one side over the other across the breast.

dou•ble-check |dŭb′əl chĕk′| *v.* To check (something) again to make sure it is right: *double-check one's addition.*

ă **pat**/ā **pay**/â **care**/ä **father**/ĕ **pet**/ē **be**/ĭ **pit**/ī **pie**/î **fierce**/ŏ **pot**/ō **go**/ô **paw**, **for**/oi **oil**/ŏŏ **book**/ōō **boot**/ou **out**/ŭ **cut**/û **fur**/*th* **the**/th **thin**/hw **which**/**zh** vision/ə **ago**, item, pencil, atom, circus

double chin. A fold of fatty flesh beneath the chin.

dou•ble-cross |dŭb′əl krôs′| *or* |-krŏs′|. *Slang. v.* To betray (someone) by doing the opposite of what was agreed on. —*n.* An act of double-crossing; betrayal. —**dou′ble-cross′er** *n.*

dou•ble-deal•ing |dŭb′əl dē′lĭng| *adj.* Deceitful; treacherous. —*n.* Deceitfulness; treachery. —**dou′ble-deal′er** *n.*

dou•ble-deck•er |dŭb′əl dĕk′ər| *n.* **1.** A vehicle, such as a bus or railway car, having two decks or tiers for passengers. **2.** Two beds, one built above the other. **3.** *Informal.* A sandwich having three slices of bread and two layers of filling. —***modifier:*** *a double-decker bus; a double-decker bed; a double-decker sandwich.*

dou•ble-dig•it |dŭb′əl dĭj′ĭt| *adj.* Of or relating to percentage rates between 10 and 99 percent: *double-digit inflation.*

dou•ble-edged |dŭb′əl ĕjd′| *adj.* **1.** Having two cutting edges, as some razor blades. **2.** Capable of being effective or interpreted in two ways: *double-edged praise.*

dou•ble-head•er |dŭb′əl hĕd′ər| *n.* Two games played one after the other on the same day, as in professional baseball.

dou•ble-joint•ed |dŭb′əl join′tĭd| *adj.* Having unusually flexible joints permitting connected parts, such as limbs or fingers, to be bent at unusual angles.

double knit. A jerseylike fabric knitted on a machine equipped with two sets of needles so that a double thickness of fabric is produced in which the two sides of the fabric are interlocked. —***modifier:*** **(double-knit):** *double-knit suit.*

double negative. A construction in which two negatives are used when only one should be; for example, the sentence *He didn't say nothing* contains a double negative.

dou•ble-park |dŭb′əl pärk′| *v.* To park (a car or vehicle) alongside another vehicle already parked parallel to the curb.

double pneumonia. Pneumonia in which both lungs are affected.

dou•ble-quick |dŭb′əl kwĭk′| *adj.* Very quick; rapid. —*n.* A marching pace, **double time.**

dou•ble-reed |dŭb′əl rēd′| *adj.* Of any of the wind instruments, such as the bassoon, whose mouthpieces are formed of two joined reeds that vibrate against each other.

double star. A **binary star.**

dou•blet |dŭb′lĭt| *n.* **1.** A close-fitting jacket, with or without sleeves, worn by men between the 15th and 17th centuries. **2.** One of two words derived ultimately from the same source but not through the same route, for example, *skirt* and *shirt.* [SEE NOTE & PICTURE]

double take. A delayed reaction to something unusual: *He did a double take when he saw her strange costume.*

double talk. Meaningless speech that consists of nonsense syllables mixed with real words.

double time. 1. A rapid marching pace of 180 three-foot steps per minute. **2.** A wage rate that is double the normal rate.

dou•bloon |dŭ blo͞on′| *n.* An obsolete Spanish gold coin.

dou•bly |dŭb′lē| *adv.* To a double degree; twice: *doubly sure.*

doubt |dout| *v.* **1.** To be uncertain or unsure about: *Many people doubt that he will make the trip.* **2.** To be suspicious of; distrust: *She does not doubt her son's word.* —*n.* **1.** Often **doubts.** A lack of conviction or certainty: *He had doubts about the kind of role he was intended to play.* **2.** An uncertain condition or state of affairs: *When in doubt, look up the word in the dictionary.* —**doubt′er** *n.*

Idioms. **beyond doubt.** Unquestionably; definitely. **no doubt.** Certainly: *No doubt you already know the answer.* **without doubt.** Certainly.

doubt•ful |dout′fəl| *adj.* **1.** Not sure; uncertain: *The outcome of the game looks very doubtful.* **2.** Having or showing doubt; questioning: *a doubtful expression.* **3.** Questionable; suspicious: *a man with a doubtful past.* —**doubt′ful•ly** *adv.*

doubt•less |dout′lĭs| *adv.* **1.** Certainly; assuredly: *The spine is doubtless a protective device.* **2.** Presumably; probably: *This will doubtless reach him in time.* —**doubt′less•ly** *adv.*

douche |do͞osh| *n.* **1.** A stream of liquid or air applied to a part or cavity of the body in order to cleanse or apply medication. **2.** A syringe or other instrument used for applying a douche. —*v.* **douched, douch•ing.** To cleanse or treat with a douche.

dough |dō| *n.* **1.** A soft, thick mixture, as of flour and liquids, that is baked as bread, pastry, etc. **2.** *Slang.* Money. ¶*These sound alike* **dough, do²,** **doe.**

dough•nut |dō′nŭt′| *or* |-nət| *n.* A small, ring-shaped cake made of sweetened dough that is fried in deep fat.

dough•ty |dou′tē| *adj.* **dough•ti•er, dough•ti•est.** Brave; courageous: *a doughty general.* —**dough′ti•ness** *n.*

dough•y |dō′ē| *adj.* **dough•i•er, dough•i•est.** Having the appearance or consistency of dough. —**dough′i•ness** *n.*

Doug•las fir |dŭg′ləs|. A tall evergreen tree of western North America, having strong, heavy wood valuable as lumber.

dour |do͝or| *or* |dour| *adj.* **1.** Stern and forbidding: *a dour and ascetic minister.* **2.** Gloomy; sullen: *a dour expression on his face.* —**dour′ly** *adv.* —**dour′ness** *n.*

douse |dous| *v.* **doused, dous•ing. 1.** To plunge into liquid; immerse: *douse the shirts in clean water.* **2.** To make thoroughly wet; drench: *They doused their friends with a garden hose.*

dove¹ |dŭv| *n.* **1.** A pigeon or related bird, especially one of a kind that lives in a naturally wild state. **2.** A person who advocates peace and a general reduction in military expenditures.

dove² |dōv|. A past tense of **dive.**

dove•cote |dŭv′kōt′| *n.* A roost for domesticated pigeons.

Do•ver |dō′vər|. The capital of Delaware. Population, 23,512.

dove•tail |dŭv′tāl′| *n.* **1.** A fan-shaped tenon that forms a tight joint when fitted into a corresponding mortise. **2.** A joint formed by interlocking one or more such tenons and mortises. —*v.* **1.** To join by means of dovetails. **2.** To connect or combine precisely and harmoniously. [SEE PICTURE]

dow•a•ger |dou′ə jər| *n.* **1.** A widow who holds a title or property from her dead husband: *a*

doublet

English borrows words so freely from other languages that it has often borrowed the same foreign word twice at different times, thus producing a pair of **doublets.** *Some examples:* **abbreviate/abridge, adamant/diamond, cattle/chattel, castle/chateau.** *A more remote kind of doublet occurs when English borrows a foreign word that turns out to have the same ancestral Indo-European origin as an already existing English word.*

doublet

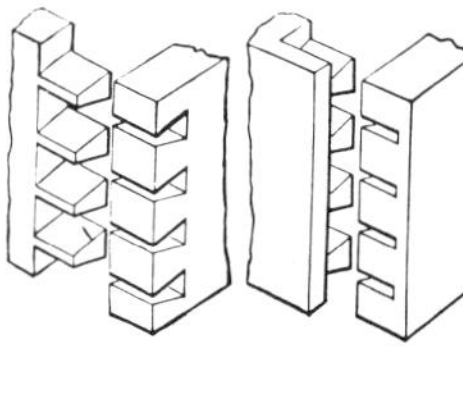

dovetail

down[1-2-3]

A **down**³ *is not* **down**¹ *but an* **up***land; and yet* **down**¹ *is derived from* **down**³. **Down**³ *was* dūn, *"hill," in Old English. (***Dune** *comes from the related Dutch word* dune, *"hill of sand.") Old English* dūn *was used in the expression* ofdūne, *"from the hill," that is, "downward."* Ofdūne *became* adūne *and then* dūne, *which became* **down**¹ *in Modern English.* **Down**² *is separate; it was borrowed from Old Norse* dūnn, *of the same meaning.*

dozen

To count in **dozens** *(as in inches to the foot) is to use a* **duodecimal** *system. The Latin word for "twelve" was* duodecim *(*duo, *"two," +* decem, *"ten").* **Duodecimal** *is borrowed straight from this. In Old French,* duodecim *became* doze; *from this was formed* dozeine, *"a group of twelve," which was borrowed into English as* **dozen**.

ă **pat**/ā **pay**/â **care**/ä **father**/ĕ **pet**/ ē **be**/ĭ **pit**/ī **pie**/î **fierce**/ŏ **pot**/ ō **go**/ô **paw**, **for**/oi **oil**/ŏŏ **book**/ ōō **boot**/ou **out**/ŭ **cut**/û **fur**/ *th* **the**/th **thin**/hw **which**/**zh** **vision**/ ə **ago**, **item**, **pencil**, **atom**, **circus**

dowager empress. **2.** An elderly woman of high social rank.

dow•dy |**dou'**dē| *adj.* **dow•di•er, dow•di•est.** Lacking in stylishness or neatness; shabby: *dowdy clothes; a dowdy girl.* —**dow'di•ly** *adv.* —**dow'di•ness** *n.*

dow•el |**dou'**əl| *n.* A round wooden pin that fits into a corresponding hole to fasten or align two adjacent pieces. —*v.* **dow•eled** or **dow•elled, dow•el•ing** or **dow•el•ling.** To fasten or align with dowels.

dow•er |**dou'**ər| *n.* The part of a deceased man's estate allotted by law to his widow for her lifetime.

down¹ |doun| *adv.* **1. a.** From a higher to a lower place: *pull down the shades; climb down.* **b.** From an upright position to a horizontal position: *The man was knocked down by a car.* **2.** In or to a lower position, point, condition, quantity, etc.: *getting ready to sit down; going down to Florida. Stock prices are coming down. Boil the syrup down.* **3.** From an earlier to a later time: *looking down through the ages.* **4.** In partial payment at the time of purchase: *five dollars down.* **5.** In writing: *taking a statement down.* **6.** To the source: *tracking a rumor down.* **7.** Seriously; intensely: *get down to work.* —*adj.* **1. a.** Moving or directed downward: *a down elevator.* **b.** In a low position; not up: *The blinds are down.* **2.** Sick; not feeling well: *She is down with a bad cold.* **3.** In certain games, trailing an opponent by a specified number of points, goals, or strokes: *down two.* **4.** Being the first installment in a series of payments: *a down payment.* —*prep.* In a descending direction upon, along, through, or into: *down the stairs; down the road; down the years.* —*n.* **1. a.** A downward movement; descent. **b.** A low or bad phase: *ups and downs.* **2.** Any of a series of four plays in football during which a team must advance at least ten yards to retain possession of the ball. —*v.* **1.** To bring, strike, or throw down: *He downed his opponent in the second round.* **2.** To swallow hastily; gulp: *down an extra cup of coffee.* [SEE NOTE]

Idioms. **down and out.** Lacking friends or resources; destitute. **down in the mouth.** Discouraged; sad. **down on.** *Informal.* Hostile toward; out of patience with. **down with. 1.** To a lower or inferior position. **2.** Away with; put down or overthrow: *Down with the monarchy!*

down² |doun| *n.* **1.** Fine, soft, fluffy feathers. **2.** A similar soft, fine covering or substance: *the down on a peach.* —***modifier:*** *a down pillow.* [SEE NOTE]

down³ |doun| *n.* Often **downs.** An expanse of grassy upland used for grazing, especially in southern England. [SEE NOTE]

down•beat |**doun'**bēt'| *n.* **1.** The downward hand movement made by a conductor to indicate the first beat of a musical measure. **2.** The first beat of a musical measure.

down•cast |**doun'**kăst'| *or* |-käst'| *adj.* **1.** Directed downward: *downcast eyes.* **2.** Depressed; sad: *feeling sullen and downcast.*

down•fall |**doun'**fôl'| *n.* **1.** A sudden loss, as of wealth, reputation, or status; ruin: *the downfall of Napoleon.* **2.** Something causing this: *Greed was her downfall.*

down•grade |**doun'**grād'| *n.* A descending slope in a road. —*v.* **down•grad•ed, down•grad•ing. 1.** To lower the status and salary of: *downgrade an employee.* **2.** To lower or minimize the importance or reputation of: *The press downgraded him as a player because of his injured knee.*

down•heart•ed |**doun'här'**tĭd| *adj.* Low in spirits; sad; depressed: *downhearted losers.* —**down'heart'ed•ly** *adv.* —**down'heart'ed•ness** *n.*

down•hill |**doun'hĭl'**| *adv.* Down the slope of a hill; in a downward direction: *We raced downhill. His health went downhill.* —*adj.* |**doun'**hĭl'|: *a downhill direction.*

Down•ing Street |**dou'**nĭng|. The British Prime Minister's residence and office.

down•pour |**doun'**pôr'| *or* |-pōr'| *n.* A heavy fall of rain.

down•right |**doun'**rīt'| *adj.* **1.** Thoroughgoing; out-and-out; complete: *a downright coward; a downright lie.* **2.** Straightforward; candid: *a downright answer.* —*adv.* Thoroughly; absolutely: *He was downright unpleasant.*

down•stairs |**doun'stârz'**| *adv.* **1.** Down the stairs. **2.** To or on a lower floor. —*adj.* |**doun'**stârz'|: *a downstairs bedroom.* —*n.* |**doun'stârz'**| *(used with a singular verb).* The lower or main floor of a building.

down•stream |**doun'strēm'**| *adv.* In the direction of a stream's current: *He swam downstream.* —*adj.* |**doun'**strēm'|: *a downstream boat race.*

down-to-earth |**doun'**tōō **ûrth'**| *or* |-tə-| *adj.* Realistic; sensible: *a down-to-earth person.*

down•town |**doun'toun'**| *adv.* Toward or in the lower part or business center of a town or city: *She went downtown.* —*adj.* |**doun'**toun'|: *the downtown area; downtown Tokyo.*

down•trod•den |**doun'**trŏd'n| *adj.* Oppressed; tyrannized: *a downtrodden person.*

down•turn |**doun'**tûrn'| *n.* A tendency downward, especially in business or economic activity.

down•ward |**doun'**wərd| *adv.* Also **down•wards** |**doun'**wərdz|. **1.** From a higher to a lower place, level, or condition: *Cool air moves downward.* **2.** From an earlier to a more recent time: *Man has studied nature downward through history.* —*adj.* Descending from a higher to a lower place, level, or condition: *a downward movement.*

down•y |**dou'**nē| *adj.* **down•i•er, down•i•est. 1.** Of or like down; soft and fluffy. **2.** Covered or filled with down.

dow•ry |**dou'**rē| *n., pl.* **dow•ries.** Money or property brought by a bride to her husband.

dowse |douz| *v.* **dowsed, dows•ing.** To use a divining rod to attempt to find underground water or minerals. —**dows'er** *n.*

dowsing rod. A **divining rod.**

dox•ol•o•gy |dŏk **sŏl'**ə jē| *n., pl.* **dox•ol•o•gies.** A hymn or verse in praise of God.

doz. dozen.

doze |dōz| *v.* **dozed, doz•ing. 1.** To sleep or appear to sleep lightly; nap: *He dozed away the afternoon hours. He dozed on the porch where the sun was hot.* **2.** To fall into a light sleep: *She dozed off during the play's first act.* —*n.* A short, light sleep; a nap.

doz•en |**dŭz'**ən| *n.* **1.** *pl.* **dozen.** A set of 12: *Twelve dozen equal one gross. How many eggs are there in four dozen?* **2.** *pl.* **dozens.** A large, undetermined amount: *Dozens of salmon churned* *the water.* —*adj.* Twelve: *a dozen eggs; two dozen eggs.* [SEE NOTE on p. 278]

doz•enth |**dŭz′**ənth| *adj.* Twelfth.

DP, D.P. displaced person.

Dr. **1.** doctor. **2.** drive (in street names).

drab |drăb| *adj.* **drab•ber, drab•best.** **1.** Dull; commonplace; dreary: *a drab house; a drab day.* **2. a.** Light dull brown or grayish brown: *drab shorts.* **b.** Light olive brown; khaki-colored: *a drab uniform.* —*n.* **1.** A light dull brown or grayish brown. **2.** A light olive brown; khaki color. —**drab′ly** *adv.* —**drab′ness** *n.*

drach•ma |**drăk′**mə| *n., pl.* **drach•mas** or **drach•mae** |**drăk′**mē|. **1.** The basic unit of money in modern Greece. **2.** An ancient Greek coin.

draft |drăft| *or* |dräft| *n.* **1.** A current of air, especially in an enclosed area. **2.** A device in a flue that controls the circulation of air. **3.** A pull or traction of a load, as by horses or oxen: *buy two horses for draft.* **4. a.** The act or an example of drawing in a fishnet. **b.** The amount of fish drawn in. **5.** A preliminary outline, plan, or picture; a version: *a rough draft of the paragraph; a draft of the architect's plans.* **6.** The selection of personnel for a specific duty: *They hoped for the draft of a fine quarterback.* **7. a.** Compulsory assignment to military service: *The draft may be replaced by an all-volunteer army.* **b.** The group of men so assigned. **8. a.** A gulp, swallow, or drink of something. **b.** The amount taken in in a single swallow. **9.** A document for the transfer of money: *a bank draft.* **10.** The depth of a vessel's keel below the water line. —***modifier:*** *a draft card; the army's draft quota; a team of draft horses.* —*v.* **1. a.** To select for a specific duty: *They drafted the new candidate.* **b.** To assign to military service: *Married men are generally drafted after single men.* **2.** To draw up a preliminary plan, sketch, or version of: *He drafted a new tax-law.*

draft•ee |drăf **tē′**| *or* |dräf-| *n.* A man who is drafted into the armed forces.

draft•ing |**drăf′**tĭng| *or* |**dräf′**-| *n.* Drawing that systematically represents mechanical and architectural structures, giving all important details and measurements. —***modifier:*** *a drafting board.*

drafts•man |**drăfts′**mən| *or* |**dräfts′**-| *n., pl.* **-men** |-mən|. **1.** A person who draws plans or designs, as of buildings or machinery, for a living. **2.** Someone who excels in drawing.

draft•y |**drăf′**tē| *or* |**dräf′**-| *adj.* **draft•i•er, draft•i•est.** Having or exposed to drafts of air: *a drafty house.* —**draft′i•ness** *n.*

drag |drăg| *v.* **dragged, drag•ging.** **1.** To draw along, pull, or haul by force: *It is easier to roll a log than to drag it.* **2.** To trail or cause to trail along the ground: *His coat drags behind him because it is too long. Don't drag the clothes in the mud.* **3.** To search the bottom of (a body of water), as with a hook or net: *They dragged the river looking for the body of the man thought to have drowned.* **4.** To move with reluctance or difficulty: *Don't drag around looking half dead.* **5.** To pass or proceed slowly: *Time dragged. The war dragged on and on.* **6.** To prolong unnecessarily or tediously: *They dragged out the discussion.* —***phrasal verb.*** **drag in.** To introduce into a discussion: *She dragged in things that had happened ten years before.* —*n.* **1.** Something pulled along the ground, especially something for carrying loads: *The horse was harnessed to the drag.* **2.** Something that slows or stops motion: *He had a drag on his fishing reel.* **3.** *Slang.* Something or someone especially bothersome. **4.** *Slang.* A puff on a cigarette. **5.** The force that tends to slow a body that is in motion through a fluid, as air or water.

Idiom. **drag (one's) feet.** To act, work, or move with intentional slowness.

drag•gle |**drăg′**əl| *v.* **drag•gled, drag•gling.** To make or become wet and muddy by or as if by dragging along the ground.

drag•net |**drăg′**nĕt′| *n.* **1.** A large net of conical shape towed along a river or sea bottom to catch fish or to search for something. **2.** A system of search, employed by the police, in which all available resources are used.

drag•on |**drăg′**ən| *n.* An imaginary giant reptile of stories, legends, etc., often represented as a winged, fire-breathing monster. [SEE PICTURE]

drag•on•fly |**drăg′**ən flī′| *n., pl.* **-flies.** A large insect with a long body and four narrow, clear wings with netlike veins. [SEE PICTURE]

dra•goon |drə **go͞on′**| *or* |dră-| *n.* A heavily armed soldier in some armies of the 17th and 18th centuries.

drag race. A race between cars to determine which can accelerate faster from a standstill.

drain |drān| *v.* **1.** To draw off (a liquid) gradually: *Dig ditches to drain the water away.* **2.** To make or become dry or less wet as the result of the flowing away of water or the drawing off of liquid: *Drain the sink. The bacon will drain well on paper towels.* **3.** To pour forth contents; discharge; flow off: *The river drains into the sea.* **4.** To remove water through natural channels from (a given region or tract of land): *The Amazon drains an area of more than two and a half million square miles.* **5.** To exhaust; consume totally: *The hectic life he pursued began to drain his resources.* **6.** To drink all the contents of: *Hank drained the coffee cup.* —*n.* **1.** A pipe or channel by which liquid is drained off: *Try not to clog up the drain.* **2.** Something that drains or exhausts: *The building of the new plant is a drain on the company's resources.*

drain•age |**drā′**nĭj| *n.* **1.** The action or a given method of draining, especially water or waste material. **2.** A natural or artificial system of drains. **3.** Material that is drained off. —***modifier:*** *a drainage ditch; a drainage system.*

drake |drāk| *n.* A male duck.

dram |drăm| *n.* **1. a.** A unit of avoirdupois weight equal to 0.0625 ounce. **b.** A unit of apothecary weight equal to 60 grains. **2.** A small drink, as of alcohol.

dra•ma |**drä′**mə| *or* |**drăm′**ə| *n.* **1.** A play in prose or verse, especially one telling a serious story. **2.** A play or plays of a given type or period: *poetic drama; Elizabethan drama.* **3.** The art and practice of writing and producing works for the stage. **4.** A situation in real life or a series of events that resemble a play, especially in building to a climax. **5.** The quality of being dramatic and therefore able to stir a person's feelings. —***modifier:*** *a drama critic.*

dra•mat•ic |drə **măt′**ĭk| *adj.* **1.** Of drama or the theater: *dramatic performances.* **2.** Resembling a

dragon

dragonfly

drama; building to a climax: *the dramatic events that led to his election.* **3.** Striking in appearance or effect; stirring: *The mountains, blue-green glaciers, and other dramatic sights are attracting more and more tourists each year.* —**dra•mat'i•cal•ly** *adv.*

dra•mat•ics |drə măt'ĭks| *n.* **1.** *(used with a singular or plural verb).* The art or practice of acting in or staging plays: *Dramatics is his main hobby.* **2.** *(used with a plural verb).* Exaggerated behavior appropriate to the stage: *His dramatics become less amusing every day.* —***modifier:*** *a dramatics teacher.*

dram•a•tis per•so•nae |drăm'ə tĭs pər sō'nē| *or* |drä'mə-|. The characters in a play or story.

dram•a•tist |drăm'ə tĭst| *or* |drä'mə-| *n.* A person who writes plays; a playwright.

dram•a•tize |drăm'ə tīz'| *or* |drä'mə-| *v.* **dram•a•tized, dram•a•tiz•ing. 1.** To make (something) into a play or screenplay. **2.** To present or view in a dramatic or highly emotional way: *She likes to dramatize her problems.* **3.** To make (something) seem striking or vivid; portray emphatically: *The report dramatizes the suffering of the flood victims.* —**dram'a•ti•za'tion** *n.*

drank |drăngk|. Past tense of **drink.**

drape |drāp| *v.* **draped, drap•ing. 1.** To cover or hang with cloth in loose folds: *He draped the unfinished painting.* **2.** To arrange or hang in loose, graceful folds: *She draped the veil over her head. Silk drapes easily.* **3.** To hang loosely: *He draped his legs over the chair.* —*n.* **1.** Often **drapes.** Long, heavy curtains that hang straight in loose folds. **2.** The way in which cloth falls or hangs: *the drape of a Roman toga.*

drap•er |drā'pər| *n. British.* A dealer in cloth or dry goods.

drap•er•y |drā'pə rē| *n., pl.* **drap•er•ies. 1.** Cloth arranged in loose folds, especially when represented in painting or sculpture. **2.** Often **draperies.** Long, heavy curtains that hang straight in loose folds; drapes.

dras•tic |drăs'tĭk| *adj.* Violently effective; extreme or severe: *drastic measures to curb inflation.* —**dras'ti•cal•ly** *adv.*

drat |drăt| *interj.* A word used to express annoyance.

draught |drăft| *or* |dräft| *n. & v.* Chiefly British form of the word **draft.**

draughts |drăfts| *or* |dräfts| *n. (used with a singular verb). Chiefly British.* The game of checkers.

draw |drô| *v.* **drew** |drōō|, **drawn** |drôn|, **draw•ing. 1. a.** To pull or move (something) in a given direction or to a given position: *The dog draws his tail in when frightened. Draw the belt through the loops.* **b.** To pull or move so as to cover or uncover: *draw the drapes; drew the blankets up to her neck.* **c.** To cause to move, as by pulling or hauling: *Will fireflies draw the tiny golden chariots of the fairies?* **2. a.** To pull out; extract; remove: *Try to draw two balls from the box at the same time.* **b.** To take out, as from a scabbard, sheath, or holster: *draw swords; draw a gun.* **c.** To earn; bring: *draw interest.* **d.** To withdraw (money): *He drew $20 from his account.* **3.** To cause to flow: *draw blood; draw water; drew a cup of coffee from the urn.* **4.** To suck or take in (air or water): *He drew a breath. Elephants draw up the cool water in their trunks and squirt it over their backs.* **5.** To move or cause to move in a given direction: *The boat drew near the shore. She drew them into the semidarkness of the room.* **6. a.** To produce by marking a surface with a pen, pencil, crayon, etc.: *Draw a line under the right answer.* **b.** To represent (figures or pictures) by marking in such a way; sketch: *Draw a landscape. She draws well.* **7.** To represent in words: *He drew an elaborate campaign plan for his audience.* **8. a.** To get as a response; elicit: *He drew laughter from the audience.* **b.** To get in return for (services, efforts, etc.): *draw a salary.* **9. a.** To get by chance or in a chance drawing: *We drew the lucky number.* **b.** To participate in a chance drawing: *We draw in order to decide who goes first.* **10.** To attract; entice: *The coolness and quiet drew summer visitors.* **11.** To deduce from evidence at hand; formulate: *Draw a conclusion from the facts you have already gathered.* **12.** To remove the intestines of (an animal); disembowel: *After drawing the venison, we prepared it for cooking.* —***phrasal verbs.*** **draw back.** To pull back; retreat: *The dog drew back in fear. He drew back his arm.* **draw on** (or **upon**). To use as a source; call upon: *They drew on these developments to examine the matter.* **draw out. 1.** To extend in length; stretch: *fibers drawn out into long strands.* **2.** To extend unnecessarily in time: *She drew out the discussion until we were bored stiff.* **draw up. 1.** To write up in a set form; compose: *draw up a list.* **2.** To make (oneself) stand erect: *He drew himself up to his fullest height.* —*n.* **1.** An act of drawing: *Wild Bill was quick on the draw.* **2.** A contest ending in a tie.

Idioms. **draw a blank. 1.** To be unsuccessful; lose. **2.** To fail to find something, especially to forget something completely. **draw and quarter.** To execute by tying each limb to a horse and driving the horses in different directions. **draw the line.** To set a limit, as on behavior.

draw•back |drô'băk'| *n.* A disadvantage or inconvenience.

draw•bridge |drô'brĭj'| *n.* A bridge that can be raised or turned aside, either to prevent its being crossed or to allow ships to pass beneath it.

draw•er. *n.* **1.** |drô'ər|. A person who draws. **2.** |drôr|. A boxlike compartment in a bureau or table that can be pulled in and out on slides. **3. drawers** |drôrz|. Underpants.

draw•ing |drô'ĭng| *n.* **1.** The act or an example of drawing. **2.** The art of representing forms and figures on a surface by means of lines. **3.** A portrayal of forms and figures by means of lines. **4.** A selection of tickets, slips, numbers, etc., at a raffle or lottery.

drawing room. A living room or parlor in a private house.

draw•knife |drô'nīf'| *n., pl.* **-knives** |-nīvz'|. A woodworking tool that has a blade and two handles, used for shaving wood surfaces. [SEE PICTURE]

drawl |drôl| *v.* To speak or utter with lengthened or drawn-out vowels. —*n.* The speech or manner of speaking of one who drawls: *a southern drawl.*

drawn |drôn|. Past participle of **draw.** —*adj.* Worn-looking; haggard: *He looked drawn after his illness.*

drawknife

ă **pat**/ā **pay**/â **care**/ä **father**/ĕ **pet**/ē **be**/ĭ **pit**/ī **pie**/î **fierce**/ŏ **pot**/ō **go**/ô **paw**, **for**/oi **oil**/ŏŏ **book**/ōō **boot**/ou **out**/ŭ **cut**/û **fur**/*th* **the**/th **thin**/hw **which**/zh **vision**/ə **ago**, **item**, **pencil**, **atom**, **circus**

drawn butter. The clear butter that separates from the heavier solids after melting.

draw•string |drô'strĭng'| *n.* A cord or ribbon run through a hem or casing and pulled to tighten or close an opening.

dray |drā| *n.* A low, heavy cart without sides, used for hauling.

dread |drĕd| *n.* A great fear, as of something about to happen: *They lived in dread of attack.* —*v.* To be in terror of; fear greatly: *After we moved away came her surprise visits that we used to dread. Cats dread water.* —**dread'ed** *adj.: a dreaded disease.* —*adj.* Inspiring great fear: *hearing the dread sound approaching; the most dangerous of all South American fishes, the dread piranha.*

dread•ful |drĕd'fəl| *adj.* **1.** Inspiring dread or great fear; terrible: *a dreadful disease. Dreadful things happened in the city during the siege.* **2.** Arousing pity, sympathy, etc.; tragic: *a dreadful disappointment. "It's so dreadful to be poor!" sighed Meg.* **3.** Of poor quality or in poor taste, etc.: *dreadful furniture; dreadful clothes.* **4.** Offensive to good manners, taste, etc.; distasteful; shocking: *dreadful behavior.* —**dread'ful•ly** *adv.* —**dread'ful•ness** *n.*

dread•nought |drĕd'nôt'| *n.* A heavily armed battleship.

dream |drēm| *n.* **1.** A series of mental images, ideas, and emotions occurring during sleep: *He escaped now and then into dreams in which he was a hero.* **2.** A daydream. **3.** A dreamlike condition; a trance: *She walked around in a dream.* **4.** A hope or aspiration: *dreams of peace, equality, and justice.* **5.** Something especially lovely or pleasant: *a dream of a dress. Our evening was a dream.* —**modifier:** *a dream world; a dream house.* —*v.* **dreamed** or **dreamt** |drĕmt|, **dream•ing. 1. a.** To have a dream or dreams while sleeping: *Lovers dream of love. Normally, a person dreams from one to two hours every night.* **b.** To imagine in a dream: *I dreamed that the law was after me.* **2.** To daydream. **3.** To hope for (something); have aspirations for: *The Quakers dreamed of building a colony where men would be free to worship as they pleased.* **4.** To give serious consideration to; consider possible: *I wouldn't dream of following such a suggestion. Anne never dreamed that her diary would be published.* —***phrasal verb.*** **dream up.** To invent; contrive; concoct: *Henry dreams up most of the schemes that we get involved in.* —**dream'er** *n.*

dream•boat |drēm'bōt'| *n. Slang.* Someone or something regarded as notable for its beauty, excellence, remarkable qualities, etc.: *That actor is a real dreamboat. It's a dreamboat of a car.*

dream•land |drēm'lănd'| *n.* An ideal or imaginary land.

dreamt |drĕmt|. A past tense and past participle of **dream**.

dream•y |drē'mē| *adj.* **dream•i•er, dream•i•est. 1.** Like a dream; vague; hazy: *a dreamy state; a dreamy look.* **2.** Given to daydreams: *The dreamy boy did not pay attention in class.* **3.** Soothing; quiet; pleasant: *dreamy music.* —**dream'i•ly** *adv.* —**dream'i•ness** *n.*

drear |drîr| *adj.* Dreary. Used chiefly in poetry.

drear•y |drîr'ē| *adj.* **drear•i•er, drear•i•est. 1.** Gloomy; dismal: *a dreary January rain.* **2.** Boring; dull: *The girls tried to do their dreary tasks cheerfully.* —**drear'i•ly** *adv.* —**drear'i•ness** *n.*

dredge[1] |drĕj| *n.* **1.** A machine that uses scooping or suction devices to remove mud, silt, etc., from the bottom of a body of water. **2.** A ship or barge equipped with such a machine. —*v.* **dredged, dredg•ing. 1.** To clean out or deepen the bed of (a harbor or channel). **2.** To fish up from or as if from the bottom of a river, lake, etc., with a dredge: *dredging up forgotten grievances. They dredged an old car out of the river.* **3.** To use a dredge: *dredging for oysters.* [SEE NOTE & PICTURE]

dredge[2] |drĕj| *v.* **dredged, dredg•ing.** To coat (food) by sprinkling with flour, sugar, etc. [SEE NOTE]

dregs |drĕgz| *pl.n.* **1.** The sediment of a liquid. **2.** The least desirable portion of something: *the dregs of society.*

drench |drĕnch| *v.* To wet through and through; saturate: *Occasionally a cloudburst will drench the desert.*

Dres•den |drĕz'dən|. A city in southeastern East Germany. Population, 500,000.

Dresden china. A kind of china, **Meissen ware.**

dress |drĕs| *n.* **1.** An outer garment worn by women and girls, consisting of a top and skirt, usually in one piece. **2.** Any clothing, apparel, or attire: *formal dress; fancy dress.* —**modifier:** *a dress designer.* —*v.* **1.** To put clothes on: *Dress the baby. She dressed hurriedly.* **2.** To choose clothes and wear them: *He dresses with elegance.* **3.** To decorate or arrange a display in: *dress a store window.* **4.** To arrange or style (the hair). **5.** To apply medicine, bandages, etc., to (a wound). **6.** To groom; curry: *Birds use their beaks to dress their feathers.* **7.** To make ready for use: *dress a hide; dress lumber.* **8.** To prepare (fish or poultry) for cooking or sale: *dress a turkey.* **9.** To arrange (troops). —***phrasal verb.*** **dress up. 1.** To put on formal or fancy clothes. **2.** To make more interesting; embellish: *Oil and vinegar dress up a salad.* —*adj.* **1.** Suitable for formal occasions or business wear: *a dress shirt, not a sport shirt.* **2.** Calling for formal clothes: *a dress reception.* [SEE NOTE]

dress circle. A section of seats in a theater or opera house, usually the first tier above the orchestra.

dress•er |drĕs'ər| *n.* **1.** A chest of drawers, usually with a mirror above it. **2.** A cupboard or set of shelves for dishes or kitchen utensils.

dress•ing |drĕs'ĭng| *n.* **1.** Medicine, bandages, etc., applied to a wound. **2.** A sauce for certain dishes, such as salads. **3.** A stuffing, as for poultry or fish.

dressing gown. A robe worn informally at home.

dressing room. A room in a theater or a home for changing costumes or clothes and making up.

dress•mak•er |drĕs'mā'kər| *n.* A person who makes dresses and other garments for women. —**dress'mak'ing** *n.*

dress rehearsal. A final rehearsal, as of a play, with costumes and stage properties.

dress•y |drĕs'ē| *adj.* **dress•i•er, dress•i•est. 1.** Formal or fancy, as clothing: *a dressy dress.* **2.** Wearing or calling for elegant, stylish clothes: *a dressy occasion.* —**dress'i•ly** *adv.*

dredge[1-2]
Dredge[1] *first appears in the sixteenth century. Its previous history is obscure, but it may be related to* **drag. Dredge[2]** *is from an obsolete noun meaning "a sweetmeat," which was borrowed from Old French* dragee.

dredge[1]

dress
"Take great care always to be dressed like the reasonable people of your own age, in the place where you are; whose dress is never spoken of one way or the other, as either too negligent or too much studied." —*Lord Chesterfield, letter to his son (1746).*

dribble

drill[1-2]
Drill[1] *is from Dutch* dril. **Drill**[2] *is a shortening of the earlier form* drilling, *which is from German* drillich, *"twilled cloth."*

drill press

drew |dro͞o|. Past tense of **draw.**

drib·ble |drĭb′əl| *v.* **drib·bled, drib·bling. 1.** To drip or cause to drip; trickle: *The water dribbled out of the faucet. He dribbled a little water into the pan.* **2.** To slobber; drool: *She dribbled orange juice all over her blouse. Most babies dribble when they eat.* **3.** To move (a ball) by bouncing or kicking repeatedly, as in basketball or soccer: *He dribbles the ball. He dribbles quickly.* —*n.* **1.** A small quantity; a drop: *a dribble of milk. Put just a dribble of paint on the paper.* **2.** The action of dribbling a ball. —**drib′bler** *n.* [SEE PICTURE]

drib·let |drĭb′lĭt| *n.* A small amount or portion.

dried-up |drīd′ŭp′| *adj.* Completely dry: *a dried-up flower.*

dri·er[1] |drī′ər| *n.* **1.** A substance added to a paint, varnish, ink, etc., to make it harden or dry more quickly. **2.** A form of the word **dryer** (an appliance).

dri·er[2] |drī′ər| *adj.* A comparative of **dry.**

dri·est |drī′ĭst| *adj.* A superlative of **dry.**

drift |drĭft| *v.* **1.** To be or cause to be carried along by or as if by a current of water or air: *The boat drifted toward shore. The fishermen drifted their nets. The smoke drifted out through the window.* **2. a.** To move unhurriedly with no apparent effort: *The bystanders gradually drifted away.* **b.** To live or move, as from place to place or job to job, without definite goals: *Many people just drift through life.* **c.** To roam about: *Bison drift before storms.* **3.** To move from a set course: *His mind drifted away from the subject.* **4.** To accumulate or cause to accumulate in piles: *The snow drifts deeply in the valley. The wind drifted the snow.* —*n.* **1.** The act or process of drifting. **2.** Something that drifts, as a current of water or air. **3.** The amount by which something drifts away from a set or proper course. **4.** A mass of material, such as sand or snow, deposited by a current of air or water. **5.** Fragments of rock that are carried and deposited by a glacier. **6.** A general meaning or direction: *the drift of her conversation.*

drift·er |drĭf′tər| *n.* A person who lives or moves, as from place to place or from job to job, without definite goals.

drift·wood |drĭft′wo͝od′| *n.* Wood floating in or washed ashore by the water.

drill[1] |drĭl| *n.* **1. a.** Any of several tools used to make holes in solid materials, usually by a rotating action or by repeated striking. **b.** The piece of machinery, often held or guided by hand, that provides the rotary or striking action. **2.** A means of teaching or training involving continuous repetition of a single physical or mental exercise. **3.** A specific exercise meant to develop a skill or make someone more familiar with a procedure: *a fire drill.* —*v.* **1.** To make (a hole) with a drill. **2.** To teach or train by continuous repetition. **3.** To engage in repetitious physical or mental exercises. [SEE NOTE]

drill[2] |drĭl| *n.* A strong cotton or linen twilled cloth, used for work clothes. [SEE NOTE]

drill press. A stationary, power-driven drilling machine, used mainly on metals, in which the drill is forced into the metal automatically or by a hand lever. [SEE PICTURE]

drink |drĭngk| *v.* **drank** |drăngk|, **drunk** |drŭngk|, **drink·ing. 1.** To take into the mouth and swallow (liquid): *He drinks a quart of milk a day. His guests drank from goblets.* **2.** To soak up (liquid or moisture); absorb: *The parched earth drank up the rain.* **3.** To swallow the liquid contents of (a glass, cup, etc.): *I drank a cup of coffee.* **4. a.** To propose (a toast): *We drank many toasts at the dinner.* **b.** To toast (something or someone): *I won't drink the health of such an odious man as Scrooge.* **c.** To salute with a toast: *We drank to him on his birthday.* **5.** To use alcoholic beverages, especially in excess: *He drank to bolster his courage.* **6.** To take in eagerly; receive with pleasure: *"Juliet, my ears have not yet drunk a hundred words of thy tongue's utterance, yet I know the sound"* (Shakespeare). —*n.* **1. a.** A liquid for drinking; a beverage: *a soft drink.* **b.** An alcoholic beverage: *I have a drink before dinner.* **2.** Beverages in general: *food and drink.* **3.** An amount of liquid swallowed, as a glassful: *a drink of water.* **4.** Excessive use of alcoholic beverages: *His depression drove him to drink.* —**drink′a·ble** *adj.* —**drink′er** *n.*

drink·ing |drĭng′kĭng| *n.* **1.** The act or process of taking liquids. **2.** The use of alcoholic beverages, especially to excess. —***modifier:*** *drinking water.*

drip |drĭp| *v.* **dripped, drip·ping.** To fall or let fall in drops: *Water dripped from the faucet. Drip some hot wax in a holder to secure the candle.* —*n.* **1.** Liquid or moisture that falls in drops. **2.** The sound made by dripping liquid. **3.** The process of falling in drops. **4.** *Slang.* An unpleasant or boring person.

drip-dry |drĭp′drī′| *adj.* Made of a fabric that will not wrinkle if hung up dripping wet to dry without being wrung out: *a drip-dry dress.* —*v.* |drĭp′drī′| *or* |drĭp′drī′| **-dried, -dry·ing, -dries.** To dry by hanging up wet, without wringing out: *drip-dry a dress; let a shirt drip-dry.*

drip·pings |drĭp′ĭngz| *pl.n.* The fat and juice from roasting meat, often used in making gravy.

drive |drīv| *v.* **drove** |drōv|, **driv·en** |drĭv′ən|, **driv·ing. 1. a.** To set and keep in motion; propel by force: *The wind drove the snow in our faces.* **b.** To move by or as if by prodding: *They drove the cattle down to the pasture.* **c.** To force to leave or retreat; expel; repulse: *Germanic tribes slowly drove out the Celts. They drove back the enemy.* **2. a.** To force into a particular state, usually of distress: *The gadfly supposedly drives cattle mad.* **b.** To be or supply the motivating force to; spur: *The desire for a new challenge drives some people to climb new peaks. He drove himself too hard at work.* **3.** To force to penetrate or penetrate: *drive a nail into wood. It drove right through the bottom.* **4. a.** To guide, control, and direct (a vehicle): *He drives a car to work every day.* **b.** To operate a vehicle: *She drives well. Drive safely.* **c.** To transport in a vehicle: *He drove me to work.* **5.** To supply the power to move: *The internal-combustion engine drives our cars.* **6.** To hit (a ball) hard in a game: *He drives the ball to center field. He drove in two runs.* —*n.* **1.** A ride, trip, or journey in a vehicle, such as an automobile: *a Sunday drive; a four-hundred-mile drive.* **2. a.** A road for automobiles. **b.** A driveway. **3. a.** The means for transmitting motion to a machine. **b.** The means by which automotive power is applied to a roadway: *four-wheel drive.*

4. a. An organized effort to accomplish something: *a charity drive; a drive to find a cancer cure.* b. A massive and sustained military offensive: *the British drive into Libya.* 5. a. Energy; push; initiative: *Her drive and ambition will help her get ahead.* b. A strong motivating instinct: *All basic human drives can be utilized to advantage.* 6. A ball hit hard in a game. 7. a. The act of rounding up and driving cattle, as to new pastures. b. The act of driving logs down a river.
Idioms. **drive at.** To mean to do or say. **drive home.** To cause to be evident or obvious through force, repetition, emphasis, etc.

drive-in |drīv′ĭn′| *n.* A restaurant, movie theater, or other business establishment designed so that customers can stay in their cars while eating, watching a picture, etc.

driv•el |drĭv′əl| *v.* **driv•eled** or **driv•elled, driv•el•ing** or **driv•el•ling.** 1. To slobber; drool. 2. To talk stupidly, childishly, or senselessly. —*n.* 1. Saliva flowing from the mouth. 2. Stupid or childish talk. —**driv′el•er, driv′el•ler** *n.*

driv•er |drī′vər| *n.* 1. A person who drives a car, truck, or other vehicle. 2. A wooden-headed golf club used for making long shots from the tee. 3. Any tool or machine part that transmits force, motion, or energy to something else.

drive shaft. A turning shaft that transmits mechanical power to the place where it is applied.

drive•way |drīv′wā′| *n.* A private road connecting a house, garage, or other building with the street.

driz•zle |drĭz′əl| *v.* **driz•zled, driz•zling.** 1. To rain gently in fine, mistlike drops. 2. To let fall in fine drops or particles: *Drizzle fat evenly over the chicken.* —*n.* A fine, gentle, misty rain.

drogue |drōg| *n.* 1. A sea anchor. 2. A **drogue parachute.**

drogue parachute. A parachute used to slow down a fast-moving object, especially a small parachute used to slow down a space vehicle during re-entry. [SEE PICTURE]

droll |drōl| *adj.* Amusingly odd; comical: *a droll old man.* —**droll′ness** *n.*

droll•er•y |drō′lə rē| *n., pl.* **droll•er•ies.** 1. A droll quality. 2. An odd or quaint way of acting, behaving, etc. 3. Something droll, as a tale.

drom•e•dar•y |drŏm′ĭ dĕr′ē| *or* |drŭm′-| *n., pl.* **drom•e•dar•ies.** The one-humped camel widely used for riding and carrying loads in northern Africa and southwestern Asia. [SEE PICTURE at **camel**]

drone[1] |drōn| *n.* 1. A male bee, especially a honeybee. Drones have no stings, do no work, and do not produce honey. 2. Someone who is lazy; a loafer. 3. An unmanned aircraft operated by remote control. [SEE NOTE]

drone[2] |drōn| *v.* **droned, dron•ing.** 1. To make a continuous low, dull humming sound: *An airplane droned far overhead.* 2. To speak in a monotonous tone. —*n.* 1. A continuous low humming or buzzing sound. 2. a. A single tone sustained throughout a musical composition or one of its sections, especially in the bass. b. Something, such as one of the pipes of a bagpipe, that produces such a tone. [SEE NOTE]

drool |dro͞ol| *v.* 1. To let saliva dribble or drop from the mouth, as a baby does. 2. To show great appreciation, as if watering at the mouth: *He drooled over the sports car in the showroom.* —*n.* Saliva flowing from the mouth; dribble: *She wiped the drool from the baby's chin.*

droop |dro͞op| *v.* 1. To bend or hang downward; sag: *The flowers are beginning to droop. The dog drooped his ears.* 2. To become weak or depressed; languish: *His spirits drooped.* —*n.* The act or condition of drooping: *the droop of his head.* ¶*These sound alike* **droop, drupe.**

droop•y |dro͞o′pē| *adj.* **droop•i•er, droop•i•est.** 1. Bending or hanging downward; sagging: *droopy eyelids.* 2. Sad; dejected: *a droopy look.* —**droop′i•ly** *adv.* —**droop′i•ness** *n.*

drop |drŏp| *v.* **dropped, drop•ping.** 1. To fall or let fall from a higher to a lower place or position: *A penny dropped from his pocket. She dropped a dish on the floor.* 2. To lower, as by a rope: *drop anchor; drop the blinds.* 3. a. To decrease; become less, as in amount, number, etc.: *The price of milk dropped.* b. To lower the level of: *drop one's voice.* 4. a. To descend; sink: *The sun dropped toward the western hills.* b. To form a steep decline: *The cliffs dropped to the ocean.* 5. To leave out; omit: *drop a letter from a word.* 6. To set down at a particular place; deliver: *drop a passenger at his destination. The postman dropped off a package at our house.* 7. To retreat a short distance: *The quarterback dropped back to pass.* 8. To fail to keep up, as in a race: *The runner dropped behind.* 9. To resign from; officially quit: *drop a course in school.* 10. To take away one's membership; remove: *The coach dropped him from the team.* 11. To fall or sink into a state of exhaustion: *drop from overexertion.* 12. To dissociate oneself from; reject: *drop one's friends.* 13. To cease consideration or treatment of; have done with: *Let's drop the matter.* 14. To say or offer casually: *drop a hint.* 15. To write and send off at leisure: *drop a postcard to a friend.* 16. To shoot down: *He dropped the outlaw with a single shot.* —***phrasal verbs.*** **drop in** (or **over** or **by**). To visit informally. **drop off.** 1. To fall asleep. 2. To decrease. **drop out.** To withdraw from participation in a school, club, game, or organized society. —*n.* 1. A tiny mass of liquid that is rounded or pear-shaped: *a drop of rain.* 2. Something resembling this in shape or size: *a lemon drop; a cough drop.* 3. A small amount of liquid: *drink a cup to the last drop.* 4. A sudden fall or decrease: *a drop in temperature; a drop in prices.* 5. a. A steep or sheer descent: *The hikers avoided the drop.* b. The distance of such a descent: *a drop of 200 feet.* 6. Something arranged to fall or be lowered, as a drop curtain. 7. A delivery by parachute.
Idioms. **a drop in the bucket.** A trifling portion of what is needed. **at the drop of a hat.** Immediately and willingly.

drop cloth. A large cloth that painters use to cover and protect furniture and floors while they are painting a room.

drop kick. A kick made by dropping a football and kicking it just as it starts to rebound.

drop leaf. A wing or extension on a table, hinged for folding down when not in use. —***modifier:*** **(drop-leaf):** *a drop-leaf table.*

drop•let |drŏp′lĭt| *n.* A tiny drop.

drop•out |drŏp′out′| *n.* 1. A person who quits school before completing a course of instruction.

drogue parachute
A drogue parachute used to slow a jet aircraft in landing

drone[1-2]
Drone[1] *was* drān *in Old English. It comes from a root meaning "to buzz."* **Drone**[2] *first appears in the sixteenth century. It seems to be an extension of* **drone**[1], *reverting to the original meaning of the root.*

Druid
Trees were important in Celtic religion. The Celts had no temples in their towns, but held their ceremonies in sacred woods. Their priests were called Druides, *which means "they who know trees":* dru-, *"tree,"* + wid-, *"know."*

2. A person who withdraws from organized society, usually in protest against its values.

drop•per |drŏp′ər| *n.* A small tube with a suction bulb at one end for drawing in a liquid and releasing it in drops.

drop•ping |drŏp′ĭng| *n.* **1.** Something dropped. **2. drop•pings.** The dung of animals.

drop•sy |drŏp′sē| *n.* A diseased condition in which abnormally large amounts of fluid collect in body tissues and cavities.

dro•soph•i•la |drō sŏf′ə lə| *or* |drə-| *n.* A small fruit fly of a kind much used by scientists in studies of inheritance.

dross |drôs| *or* |drŏs| *n.* **1.** The waste material that rises to the surface of a molten metal as it is being smelted or refined. **2.** Worthless material mixed with or contained in a substance; impurity: *the dross in a bushel of corn.*

drought |drout| *n.* A long period with little or no rain.

drouth |drouth| *n.* A form of the word **drought.**

drove[1] |drōv|. Past tense of **drive.**

drove[2] |drōv| *n.* **1.** A number of cattle, sheep, horses, etc., being driven in a group. **2.** A crowd; throng: *droves of visitors.*

dro•ver |drō′vər| *n.* A person who drives cattle, sheep, horses, etc., to market or to grazing lands.

drown |droun| *v.* **1.** To kill or die by submerging and suffocating in water or other liquid: *Flash floods drowned many large flocks of sheep.* **2.** To drench thoroughly or cover with a liquid: *She drowned him with a deluge of cold water. He drowned the peas in butter.* **3.** To erase the traces of, as by immersion; drive out; extinguish: *The rainstorm drowned the scent of the leopard.* **4.** To be strong enough to overpower or blur another sound: *The sound of their laughter drowned out his voice.*

drowse |drouz| *v.* **drowsed, drows•ing.** To be half asleep; doze: *A dog drowsed in the sun.* —*n.* The condition of being half asleep.

drows•y |drou′zē| *adj.* **drows•i•er, drows•i•est. 1.** Sleepy. **2.** Causing sleepiness: *a drowsy lullaby.* —**drows′i•ly** *adv.* —**drows′i•ness** *n.*

drub |drŭb| *v.* **drubbed, drub•bing. 1.** To beat with or as if with a stick; thrash. **2.** To defeat thoroughly: *drub an opposing team.*

drub•bing |drŭb′ĭng| *n.* **1.** A beating with or as if with a stick: *get a drubbing for stealing cookies.* **2.** A thorough defeat: *take a drubbing in a football game.*

drudge |drŭj| *n.* A person who does hard, tiresome, or menial work: *Cinderella was the drudge of the household.* —*v.* **drudged, drudg•ing.** To do hard, tiresome, or menial work.

drudg•er•y |drŭj′ə rē| *n., pl.* **drudg•er•ies.** Hard, tiresome, or menial work: *household drudgery.*

drug |drŭg| *n.* **1.** A substance that has some special effect on the life processes of an organism, especially a substance used in medicine, as for curing disease or relieving symptoms. **2.** A narcotic or other substance whose main effect is on the nervous system, especially one whose use tends to become habitual. —*v.* **drugged, drug•ging. 1.** To administer a drug to. **2.** To mix a drug into (food or drink). **3.** To make dull or sleepy as if with a drug.

drug addict. A person addicted to the use of a narcotic or similar drug.

drug•gist |drŭg′ĭst| *n.* **1.** A pharmacist. **2.** Someone who owns or operates a drugstore.

drug•store |drŭg′stôr′| *or* |-stōr′| *n.* Also **drug store.** A store where prescriptions are filled and drugs that are legally available are sold.

dru•id |drōō′ĭd| *n.* Often **Druid.** A member of the priesthood of the ancient Celtic religion of Britain and Gaul. [SEE NOTE]

drum |drŭm| *n.* **1.** A musical instrument consisting of a hollow container, such as a tube or bowl, with a membrane stretched across one or more of its openings. It is played by beating on the membrane, either with the hands or with sticks. **2.** Anything having a generally cylindrical shape, such as a large oil container, a large spool of wire, or a machine part. —*v.* **drummed, drum•ming. 1.** To play a drum. **2.** To perform (a musical part or piece) on a drum. **3.** To thump or tap rhythmically or continually: *His fingers drummed on the table.* **4.** To make known by constant repetition: *Facts and figures were drummed into their heads.* —***phrasal verb.*** **drum up.** To obtain, stimulate, or create (business, sales, etc.): *Young people drummed up support for the candidate.*

drum•lin |drŭm′lĭn| *n.* A long, low hill, rounded at one end and pointed at the other, formed from material left by a glacier.

drum major. A man in a costume and tall helmet who leads a marching band, often prancing before it and keeping time with a baton.

drum majorette. A girl in a costume who prances and twirls a baton at the head of a marching band.

drum•mer |drŭm′ər| *n.* **1.** A person who plays a drum. **2.** A traveling salesman.

drum•stick |drŭm′stĭk′| *n.* **1.** A stick for beating a drum. **2.** The lower part of the leg of a cooked chicken, turkey, etc.

drunk |drŭngk|. Past participle of **drink.** —*adj.* **1.** Overcome by alcohol; intoxicated. **2.** Overcome by emotion: *She was drunk with happiness.* —*n.* **1.** A drunken person, especially a drunkard. **2.** A drinking spree.

drunk•ard |drŭng′kərd| *n.* A person who is habitually drunk.

drunk•en |drŭng′kən| *adj.* **1.** Drunk; intoxicated: *a drunken driver.* **2.** Caused by intoxication: *a drunken rage.* **3.** Of or happening during intoxication: *a drunken party; drunken driving.* —**drunk′en•ly** *adv.* —**drunk′en•ness** *n.*

drunk•om•e•ter |drŭng **kŏm**′ĭ tər| *n.* An instrument that indicates the amount of alcohol in the blood of a person suspected of drunkenness by analyzing his breath.

drupe |drōōp| *n.* A fleshy fruit, such as a cherry, plum, or peach, with a single hard stone. ¶ *These sound alike* **drupe, droop.**

dry |drī| *adj.* **dri•er** or **dry•er, dri•est** or **dry•est. 1.** Free from liquid or moisture; not wet or damp: *change into dry clothes. The laundry should be dry by now.* **2.** Containing or bearing relatively little moisture: *dry air; a dry wind.* **3.** Not under water: *dry land.* **4.** Not liquid; solid: *dry foods.* **5.** Marked by little or no rainfall; arid: *the dry season.* **6.** Parched, so as to produce thirst: *My throat is dry.* **7.** Having all or almost all the water drained away, evaporated, etc.: *a dry riverbed.* **8.** Not shedding tears: *dry eyes.*

ă pat/ā pay/â care/ä father/ĕ pet/ ē be/ĭ pit/ī pie/î fierce/ŏ pot/ ō go/ô paw, for/oi oil/ŏŏ book/ ōō boot/ou out/ŭ cut/û fur/ *th* the/th thin/hw which/zh vision/ ə ago, item, pencil, atom, circus

9. Brittle from drying out: *Dry branches snapped under his feet.* **10.** Without butter, jelly, etc.: *dry toast.* **11.** Quietly ironic: *a dry wit.* **12.** Matter-of-fact; tedious: *a dry lecturer.* **13.** Plain; unadorned: *dry facts.* **14.** Not sweet: *a dry wine.* **15.** *Informal.* Prohibiting the sale of alcoholic beverages: *a dry county.* —*v.* **dried, dry•ing.** To make or become dry: *She dried the dishes after supper. His socks dried off.* —**dried'** *adj.: dried fruits; dried mud.* —***phrasal verb.*** **dry up. 1.** To become empty of water: *The river dried up.* **2.** *Slang.* To stop talking; shut up: *Why don't you just dry up?* —**dry'ly** *adv.* —**dry'ness** *n.*

dry•ad |**drī'**əd| *or* |-ăd'| *n.* Often **Dryad.** In Greek mythology, a wood nymph.

dry cell. An electric cell that has an electrolyte in the form of a moist paste and that is sealed to prevent spilling.

dry-clean |**drī'klēn'**| *v.* To clean (clothing or fabrics) by using chemicals that dissolve or absorb dirt and grease, as opposed to washing with water.

dry cleaner. A person or an establishment that dry-cleans clothes.

dry dock. A large floating or stationary basin into which a ship can be moved and the water pumped out.

dry-dock |**drī'**dŏk'| *v.* To place (a ship) in a dry dock, as for repairs.

dry•er |**drī'**ər| *n.* **1.** An appliance that removes moisture: *a hair dryer.* **2.** A form of the word **drier** (a drying substance).

dry goods. Cloth, clothing, linens, sewing articles, etc., as opposed to liquids, hardware, etc.

Dry Ice. A trademark for solid carbon dioxide used as a cooling agent.

dry measure. A system of units for measuring solids, such as grains, fruits, and vegetables, by volume.

dry rot. A condition in which fungi attack timbers, which actually must be damp, causing them to become soft and crumble.

dry run. A trial run or rehearsal, as a military exercise without the use of live ammunition.

DST, D.S.T. daylight-saving time.

du•al |**dōō'**əl| *or* |**dyōō'**-| *adj.* Composed of two parts; double; twofold: *a dual monarchy; a dual role.* ¶*These sound alike* **dual, duel.** —**du'al•ly** *adv.*

du•al•i•ty |dōō **ăl'**ĭ tē| *or* |dyōō-| *n.* The quality or condition of being twofold.

dub[1] |dŭb| *v.* **dubbed, dub•bing. 1.** To confer knighthood on (a person) by touching him on the shoulder with a sword. **2.** To give a nickname to: *The tiny one-man submarines were dubbed "Sea Fleas" by the sailors.* [SEE NOTE]

dub[2] |dŭb| *v.* **dubbed, dub•bing. 1.** To insert (new sounds) into an existing recording, as on magnetic tape or the sound track of a film. **2.** To provide (a film) with a new sound track, often with the dialogue in a different language. **3.** To copy (a recording) in order to make changes, cuts, or additions. [SEE NOTE]

du•bi•ous |**dōō'**bē əs| *or* |**dyōō'**-| *adj.* **1.** Doubtful; uncertain: *a dubious future. I am dubious of the outcome.* **2.** Questionable; shady; suspicious: *a dubious character.* —**du'bi•ous•ly** *adv.* —**du'bi•ous•ness** *n.*

Dub•lin |**dŭb'**lĭn|. The capital of Ireland. Population, 570,000.

du•cal |**dōō'**kəl| *or* |**dyōō'**-| *adj.* Of a duke or dukedom.

duc•at |**dŭk'**ət| *n.* Any of various gold coins formerly used in Europe.

duch•ess |**dŭch'**ĭs| *n.* **1.** The wife of a duke. **2.** A woman holding a rank equal to that of a duke in her own right.

duch•y |**dŭch'**ē| *n., pl.* **duch•ies.** The rank or domain of a duke or duchess.

duck[1] |dŭk| *n.* **1.** Any of several kinds of wild or domesticated water birds with a broad, flat bill, short legs, and webbed feet. **2.** The meat of such a bird, used as food. [SEE NOTE & PICTURES]

duck[2] |dŭk| *v.* **1.** To lower (the head and body) quickly, especially to avoid being hit or observed: *He ducked when the snowball was thrown at him. She ducked her head getting into the car.* **2.** To evade; dodge: *duck a responsibility. He ducked the snowball.* **3.** To push suddenly under water: *boys ducking each other in the pool.* **4.** *Informal.* To enter or leave quickly or temporarily: *duck out of a meeting.* —*n.* The act of ducking. [SEE NOTE]

duck[3] |dŭk| *n.* **1.** A strong cotton or linen cloth, lighter than canvas. **2. ducks.** Trousers, especially white ones, made of this fabric. —***modifier:*** *duck trousers.* [SEE NOTE]

duck•bill |**dŭk'**bĭl'| *n.* An animal, the platypus.

duck•billed |**dŭk'**bĭld'| *adj.* Having a bill or projecting part that resembles a duck's bill: *a duckbilled dinosaur.*

duck hawk. A bird, the **peregrine falcon.**

ducking stool. A device formerly used in Europe and New England for punishment, consisting of a chair in which an offender was tied and ducked into water.

duck•ling |**dŭk'**lĭng| *n.* A young duck.

duck•pins |**dŭk'**pĭnz'| *n. (used with a singular verb).* A game similar to bowling but played with smaller pins and balls.

duck•weed |**dŭk'**wēd'| *n.* A small, stemless water plant that forms floating masses on the surface of ponds and other quiet waters.

duct |dŭkt| *n.* **1.** Any tube through which something flows. **2.** A tube in the body through which a fluid passes. **3.** A tube or pipe that carries electric cables or wires.

duc•tile |**dŭk'**tĭl| *adj.* Capable of being drawn out into a fine strand or wire: *a ductile metal.*

duct•less gland |**dŭkt'**lĭs|. An **endocrine gland.**

dud |dŭd| *n. Informal.* **1.** A bomb or shell that fails to explode when it should. **2.** Someone or something that turns out to be a failure: *Our plan was a real dud.*

dude |dōōd| *or* |dyōōd| *n.* **1.** A visitor or newcomer to the American West, especially a guest at a dude ranch. **2.** *Informal.* An overdressed man; a dandy. **3.** *Slang.* A fellow; chap.

dude ranch. A resort patterned after a Western ranch, featuring horseback riding and other outdoor activities.

dudg•eon |**dŭj'**ən| *n.* Anger; resentment: *The old lady stalked off in high dudgeon.*

duds |dŭdz| *pl.n. Informal.* Clothes or belongings.

due |dōō| *or* |dyōō| *adj.* **1.** Payable immediately or on demand. **2.** Owed as a debt; owing: *the amount still due.* **3.** Fitting or appropriate:

dub[1-2]

Dub[1] *was* dubbian, *"to tap," in Old English.* **Dub[2]** *comes from the slang of recording technicians. It is a shortening of* **double,** *since "to make a copy of a recording" is "to make a duplicate or double."*

duck[1-2-3]

Duck[2] *was* douken *in Middle English. It must have existed in Old English, but it happens not to have been preserved in any documents. It has been possible to reconstruct it by comparing the Middle English form with several obviously related words in the other Germanic languages, words such as Old Frisian* dūka *and Old Low German* dūken, *both meaning "to dive or plunge." All the evidence thus points to a normal Old English verb* dūcan. *This is further supported by the fact that* **duck[1],** *which was* dūce *in Old English, obviously meant "diving bird" and is directly derived from the reconstructed verb* dūcan. **Duck[3]** *is not related; it comes from Dutch* doek, *"linen cloth."*

duck[1]
Above: Female mallard duck and ducklings
Below: Domesticated duck and ducklings

dugong

He was shown due esteem. **4.** Sufficient; adequate: *We have due cause to be upset about the new zoning law.* **5.** Expected or scheduled: *When is the train due to arrive?* —*n.* **1.** Something that is owed or deserved: *Give the Devil his due.* **2. dues.** A charge or fee for membership, as in a club. —*adv.* Straight; directly: *due west.* —*Note: Due* is often used followed by *to* to form the prepositional group **due to. 1.** Caused by: *His hesitation was due to fear.* **2.** Because of: *The game was called off due to rain.* ¶*These sound alike* **due, dew, do**[1].

du•el |dōō′əl| *or* |dyōō′-| *n.* **1.** A prearranged combat between two men, fought with deadly weapons to settle a point of honor. **2.** Any contest between two opponents: *a duel of wits in the courtroom.* —*v.* **du•eled** or **du•elled, du•el•ing** or **du•el•ling.** To fight in a duel. ¶*These sound alike* **duel, dual.** —**du′el•er, du′el•ist** *n.*

due process of law. A manner of proceeding in judicial or other governmental activity that does not violate the legal rights of the individual.

du•et |dōō ĕt′| *or* |dyōō-| *n.* **1.** A musical composition for two voices or two instruments. **2.** The two performers who present such a composition.

duff |dŭf| *n.* A stiff flour pudding boiled in a cloth bag or steamed.

duf•fel |dŭf′əl| *n.* **1.** A coarse woolen cloth with a nap on both sides. **2.** Clothing and equipment carried when camping.

duffel bag. A large, heavy cloth bag, often shaped like a cylinder, used to carry clothes and personal belongings.

duf•fer |dŭf′ər| *n.* **1.** *Informal.* A dull-witted or stupid person. **2.** A person who is inept, as at a certain sport or game.

dug[1] |dŭg|. Past tense and past participle of **dig.**

dug[2] |dŭg| *n.* An udder, breast, or teat of a female animal.

du•gong |dōō′gŏng′| *n.* A plant-eating tropical sea mammal with flipperlike front limbs and a flat, fanlike tail. [SEE PICTURE]

dug•out |dŭg′out′| *n.* **1.** A boat or canoe made by hollowing out a log. **2.** A rough shelter dug into the ground or on a hillside and used especially in battle for protection from artillery. **3.** A long, low shelter at the side of a baseball field for the players.

duke |dōōk| *or* |dyōōk| *n.* **1.** A member of the highest level of the British peerage, holding a title and rank above that of a marquis. **2.** A man who rules an independent duchy.

duke•dom |dōōk′dəm| *or* |dyōōk′-| *n.* The rank or domain of a duke.

dukes |dōōks| *or* |dyōōks| *pl.n. Slang.* The fists: *Put up your dukes!*

dul•cet |dŭl′sĭt| *adj.* Pleasing to the ear; gently melodious: *sweet dulcet tones.*

dul•ci•mer |dŭl′sə mər| *n.* A musical instrument consisting of a set of strings of different lengths stretched across a sound box or sounding board and played with two small hammers.

dull |dŭl| *adj.* **dull•er, dull•est. 1.** Not having a sharp edge or point; blunt: *a dull knife; a dull pencil.* **2.** Not keenly or intensely felt: *a dull ache.* **3.** Unexciting; boring: *a dull book; dull work.* **4.** Not brisk or active; sluggish: *Business is dull.* **5.** Slow to learn: *a dull student.* **6.** Not bright or vivid; dim: *a dull sky; a dull color.* **7.** Not loud or piercing; muffled: *a dull sound.* —*v.* To make or become dull: *dull a knife. His mind dulled as he grew more and more sleepy.* —**dull′ness** *n.* —**dull′y** *adv.*

dull•ard |dŭl′ərd| *n.* A dull or stupid person.

du•ly |dōō′lē| *or* |dyōō′-| *adv.* **1.** In a proper manner; rightfully: *a duly elected candidate.* **2.** At the expected time; punctually: *The loan was duly repaid.*

dumb |dŭm| *adj.* **dumb•er, dumb•est. 1.** Unable to speak; mute: *a deaf and dumb person.* **2.** Unwilling to speak; silent: *She remained dumb under questioning.* **3.** Temporarily speechless, as from shock: *He was dumb with surprise.* **4.** *Informal.* Stupid or silly: *You have some really dumb friends. That's a pretty dumb game you're playing.* —**dumb′ly** *adv.* —**dumb′ness** *n.*

dumb•bell |dŭm′bĕl′| *n.* **1.** A weight, lifted for exercise, consisting of a short bar with a metal ball at each end. **2.** *Slang.* A stupid or ignorant person.

dumb•wait•er |dŭm′wā′tər| *n.* A small elevator used to convey food, dishes, or other goods from one floor to another.

dum•dum bullet |dŭm′dŭm′|. A bullet with a soft tip that is designed to expand on contact and produce a large, gaping wound.

dum•found, also **dumb•found** |dŭm′found′| *v.* To make speechless with astonishment; stun: *His performance dumfounded the experts.*

dum•my |dŭm′ē| *n., pl.* **dum•mies. 1.** A model of the human figure, as one used to display clothes or to shoot at or tackle as a target: *a dressmaker's dummy.* **2.** A doll or puppet used by a ventriloquist. **3.** *Slang.* A stupid or foolish person. **4.** In printing: **a.** A model of a book to be printed. **b.** A model of a page with text and pictures pasted into place to direct the printer; a layout.

dump |dŭmp| *v.* **1.** To release, throw down, or discard in a mass: *The factory dumped waste into the river. The boy dumped his books on the table.* **2. a.** To empty (material) out of a container or vehicle: *dump garbage from a truck.* **b.** To empty out (a container or vehicle): *dump a wastebasket.* **3.** To place (goods) on the market, especially in a foreign country, in large quantities and at a low price. —*n.* **1.** A place where garbage or trash is permanently discarded. **2.** A military storage place: *an ammunition dump.* **3.** *Slang.* A poorly maintained place.

dump•ling |dŭmp′lĭng| *n.* **1.** A small ball of dough cooked in stew or soup. **2.** Sweetened dough wrapped around an apple or other fruit, baked and served as dessert.

dumps |dŭmps| *pl.n.* Low, gloomy spirits; depression: *down in the dumps.*

dump•y |dŭm′pē| *adj.* **dump•i•er, dump•i•est.** Short and plump; squat. —**dump′i•ly** *adv.* —**dump′i•ness** *n.*

dun[1] |dŭn| *v.* **dunned, dun•ning.** To ask (a debtor) persistently for payment. ¶*These sound alike* **dun, done.** [SEE NOTE]

dun[2] |dŭn| *n.* **1.** A dull grayish brown. **2.** A dun-colored horse. —*adj.* Dull grayish brown: *a dun pony; the yellow and dun hills at sunset.* ¶*These sound alike* **dun, done.** [SEE NOTE]

dunce |dŭns| *n.* A stupid person; a numskull.

dun[1-2]

Dun[1] *is of obscure origin.* **Dun**[2] *was* dunn *in Old English, meaning "dark brown." It was probably borrowed from Celtic; the Welsh equivalent is* dwn, *"dull brown." (Note that* w *represents a vowel, approximately* ü, *in Welsh.)*

ă **pat**/ā **pay**/â **care**/ä **father**/ĕ **pet**/ ē **be**/ĭ **pit**/ī **pie**/î **fierce**/ŏ **pot**/ ō **go**/ô **paw, for**/oi **oil**/ŏŏ **book**/ ōō **boot**/ou **out**/ŭ **cut**/û **fur**/ *th* **the**/th **thin**/hw **which**/zh **vision**/ ə **ago,** item, pencil, atom, circus

dune |do͞on| *or* |dyo͞on| *n.* A hill or ridge of wind-blown sand.

dune buggy. A small, light automobile, generally having a rear-engine chassis and a molded fiber-glass frame without doors and roof, and usually equipped with a souped-up engine and oversize tires for driving on sand dunes.

dung |dŭng| *n.* Solid waste material excreted by animals; manure.

dun•ga•ree |dŭng′gə **rē′**| *n.* **1.** A sturdy blue denim fabric. **2. dungarees.** Overalls or trousers made from this fabric; blue jeans.

dun•geon |**dŭn′**jən| *n.* A dark underground prison. ¶*These sound alike* **dungeon, donjon.**

dunk |dŭngk| *v.* **1.** To dip or briefly submerge (something) in a liquid: *dunk a doughnut; dunk the Easter eggs in the coloring.* **2.** To submerge (someone) playfully, as in a swimming pool.

du•o |**do͞o′**ō| *or* |**dyo͞o′**ō| *n., pl.* **du•os. 1.** A duet, as of musical performers. **2.** A couple; pair.

du•o•dec•i•mal |do͞o′ō **dĕs′**ə məl| *or* |dyo͞o′-| *adj.* **1.** Of or based on the number 12. **2.** Used in the duodecimal numeration system: *a duodecimal digit.*

duodecimal numeration system. A system of numeration in which 12 is the base. In this system the number represented as 144 in the decimal system would be represented as 100.

du•o•de•num |do͞o′ə **dē′**nəm| *or* |dyo͞o′-| *or* |do͞o **ŏd′**n əm| *or* |dyo͞o-| *n., pl.* **du•o•de•na** |do͞o′ə **dē′**nə| *or* |dyo͞o′-| *or* |do͞o **ŏd′**n ə| *or* |dyo͞o-|. The beginning portion of the small intestine.

dupe |do͞op| *or* |dyo͞op| *n.* A person who is used or taken advantage of through deception and trickery. *—v.* **duped, dup•ing.** To deceive; trick; fool.

du•ple |**do͞o′**pəl| *or* |**dyo͞o′**-| *adj.* Consisting of two parts or units; double.

du•plex |**do͞o′**plĕks′| *or* |**dyo͞o′**-| *adj.* **1.** Twofold. **2.** Consisting of two identical units that can operate either together or separately: *a duplex electrical outlet.* **3.** In electrical or electronic communications: **a.** Capable of transmitting and receiving at the same time. **b.** Capable of going from transmitting to receiving and vice versa without being switched by hand. *—n.* A duplex apartment or house.

duplex apartment. An apartment that has rooms on two floors connected by an inner staircase.

duplex house. A house divided into two separate units for two families.

du•pli•cate |**do͞o′**plĭ kĭt| *or* |**dyo͞o′**-| *n.* **1.** Either of two things that are exactly alike: *These reports are duplicates of each other.* **2.** An exact copy of an original: *The files contain a duplicate of his letter.* **—modifier:** *a duplicate key.* *—v.* |**do͞o′**plĭ kāt′| *or* |**dyo͞o′**-| **du•pli•cat•ed, du•pli•cat•ing. 1.** To make an exact copy of: *duplicate a key.* **2.** To do or perform again; repeat: *duplicate an experiment.* **—du′pli•ca′tion** *n.*

du•pli•ca•tor |**do͞o′**plĭ kā′tər| *or* |**dyo͞o′**-| *n.* A machine that makes copies of printed or written material.

du•plic•i•ty |do͞o **plĭs′**ĭ tē| *or* |dyo͞o-| *n., pl.* **du•plic•i•ties.** Deceit; double-dealing.

du•ra•ble |**do͝or′**ə bəl| *or* |**dyo͝or′**-| *adj.* Able to withstand wear and tear; sturdy; lasting: *a raincoat made of durable plastic.* **—du′ra•bil′i•ty** *n.* **—du′ra•bly** *adv.*

du•ra ma•ter |**do͝or′**ə **mā′**tər| *or* |**dyo͝or′**ə|. The tough, fibrous membrane that forms the outer covering of the brain and spinal cord.

du•ra•tion |do͞o **rā′**shən| *or* |dyo͞o-| *n.* **1.** The period of time during which something exists or persists: *the duration of a storm.* **2.** Continuance in time: *a life of long duration.*

du•ress |do͞o **rĕs′**| *or* |dyo͞o-| *or* |**do͝or′**ĭs| *or* |**dyo͝or′**-| *n.* Constraint by threat; coercion: *The prisoner confessed only under extreme duress.*

dur•ing |**do͝or′**ĭng| *or* |**dyo͝or′**-| *prep.* **1.** Throughout the course or duration of: *during the entire evening.* **2.** Within the time of; at some time in: *born sometime during the 19th century.*

durst |dûrst|. *Archaic.* A past tense of **dare.**

du•rum |**do͝or′**əm| *or* |**dyo͝or′**-| *n.* Also **durum wheat.** A kind of wheat with hard grains, used chiefly in making spaghetti, macaroni, etc.

dusk |dŭsk| *n.* **1.** The time of evening immediately before darkness; the darker stage of twilight. **2.** Partial darkness: *in the dusk of a forest.*

dusk•y |**dŭs′**kē| *adj.* **dusk•i•er, dusk•i•est. 1.** Rather dark in color: *a dusky brown.* **2. a.** Lacking adequate light; dim: *a dusky room.* **b.** Tending to darkness, as from the approach of night: *It's getting dusky outside.* **—dusk′i•ly** *adv.* **—dusk′i•ness** *n.*

dust |dŭst| *n.* **1.** Matter in the form of fine, dry particles: *gold dust; the dust on the furniture.* **2.** A cloud of such matter: *the reddish dust raised by the horses' hooves.* **—modifier:** *a dust storm.* *—v.* **1.** To remove dust from by wiping, brushing, or beating: *dust the furniture. She dusts every day.* **2.** To sprinkle with a powdery substance: *dust the cookies with sugar. Snow dusted the trees.* ¶*These sound alike* **dust, dost.**

dust bowl. A region in which dry weather and dust storms have produced conditions like those of a desert.

dust•er |**dŭs′**tər| *n.* **1.** Someone or something that dusts. **2.** A cloth, feather brush, etc., used to remove dust. **3.** A device for spreading powder, insecticide, etc. **4.** A loose, lightweight coat or smock, as one worn to keep dust off the clothes.

dust•pan |**dŭst′**păn′| *n.* A short-handled, shovellike pan into which dust is swept.

dust•y |**dŭs′**tē| *adj.* **dust•i•er, dust•i•est. 1.** Covered or filled with dust: *a dusty road; a dusty room.* **2.** Of the color of dust; grayish. **3.** Like dust; powdery: *dusty soil.* **—dust′i•ness** *n.*

Dutch |dŭch| *n.* **1. the Dutch** *(used with a plural verb).* The people of the Netherlands. **2.** The Germanic language of the Netherlands. *—adj.* Of the Netherlands, the Dutch, or their language. *—adv.* So that each person pays his own way: *go Dutch to the movies.* [SEE NOTE]

Dutch door. A door divided in half horizontally so that either part may be left open or closed.

Dutch Guiana. A former name for **Surinam.**

Dutch•man |**dŭch′**mən| *n., pl.* **-men** |-mən|. A man who is a native or inhabitant of the Netherlands.

Dutch•man's-breech•es |**dŭch′**mənz **brĭch′**ĭz| *n., pl.* **Dutch•man's-breech•es.** A woodland plant with feathery leaves and whitish flowers with two pointed projections. [SEE PICTURE]

Dutch

The name **Dutch** *comes from Dutch* dutsch, *but it did not originally mean "of the Netherlands." Its original meaning was "German" in the larger sense, including both the "High German" people of Germany and their relatives the "Low German" people of the Netherlands. In the seventeenth century the English began to call the High Germans* **German** *and to keep* **Dutch** *for the Low Germans, or Netherlanders. Note that the related German word* deutsch *still means "German," and that the German word for Germany is* Deutschland. *See also* **Pennsylvania Dutch.**

Dutchman's-breeches

Dutch oven. **1.** A large, heavy pot or kettle with a tight lid, used for slow cooking. **2.** A wall oven in which food is baked by means of preheated brick walls.

Dutch treat. *Informal.* An outing, as for dinner or a movie, for which each person pays his own share of the cost.

du•te•ous |**dōō'**tē əs| *or* |**dyōō'**-| *adj.* Obedient; dutiful: *a duteous servant.* —**du'te•ous•ly** *adv.*

du•ti•a•ble |**dōō'**tē ə bəl| *or* |**dyōō'**-| *adj.* Subject to import tax: *dutiable goods.*

du•ti•ful |**dōō'**tĭ fəl| *or* |**dyōō'**-| *adj.* **1.** Careful to perform one's duty: *a dutiful citizen.* **2.** Expressing a sense of duty: *dutiful words.* —**du'ti•ful•ly** *adv.* —**du'ti•ful•ness** *n.*

du•ty |**dōō'**tē| *or* |**dyōō'**-| *n., pl.* **du•ties.** **1.** Something that a person ought to or must do: *the duty of defending one's country.* **2. a.** Moral obligation: *a strong sense of duty.* **b.** The compulsion felt to meet such obligation: *the call of duty.* **3.** A task, assignment, or function: *household duties; the duties of a senator.* **4.** Military service: *on active duty.* **5.** A tax charged by a government, especially on imports.

Idioms. **off duty.** Not at one's work or assignment. **on duty.** At one's work or assignment.

Dvoř•ák |**dvôr'**zhăk|, **Anton.** 1841–1904. Czech composer.

dwarf |dwôrf| *n., pl.* **dwarfs** or **dwarves** |dwôrvz|. **1.** A person whose size is very much smaller than normal. **2.** In fairy tales and legends, a tiny, often ugly, person sometimes possessing magical powers. **3.** A **dwarf star.** —*v.* **1.** To check the natural growth of; stunt. **2.** To make seem small by comparison: *The liner dwarfed the tugboats.* —*adj.* Of an unusually small type or variety: *a dwarf tree.*

dwarf star. A star, such as the sun, whose mass is relatively small and whose output of light is average or below average.

dwarves |dwôrvz| *n.* A plural of **dwarf.**

dwell |dwĕl| *v.* **dwelt** |dwĕlt| or **dwelled, dwell•ing.** **1.** To live as a resident; reside: *dwell in a city.* **2.** To linger over or emphasize in thought, speech, or writing: *Don't dwell on past mistakes.* —**dwell'er** *n.*

dwell•ing |**dwĕl'**ĭng| *n.* A place to live in; a residence; abode.

dwelt |dwĕlt|. A past tense of **dwell.**

dwin•dle |**dwĭn'**dəl| *v.* **dwin•dled, dwin•dling.** To waste away; diminish: *Our savings dwindled away.*

Dy The symbol for the element dysprosium.

dye |dī| *n.* **1.** Any coloring matter used to change the color of hair, cloth, etc. **2.** A color imparted by dyeing. —*v.* **dyed, dye•ing.** To color with or become colored by a dye: *She dyed her hair red. This fabric dyes easily.* ¶*These sound alike* **dye, die.** —**dy'er** *n.*

dyed-in-the-wool |**dīd'**ĭn *th*ə **wŏŏl'**| *adj.* Thoroughgoing; outright: *a dyed-in-the-wool conservative politician.*

dye•stuff |**dī'**stŭf'| *n.* Any material used as or yielding a dye.

dy•ing |**dī'**ĭng| *adj.* **1.** About to die: *a dying man.* **2.** Drawing to an end: *a dying day.* **3.** Done or uttered just before death: *his dying words.*

dyke |dīk| *n.* A form of the word **dike.**

dy•nam•ic |dī **năm'**ĭk| or **dy•nam•i•cal** |dī **năm'**ĭ kəl| *adj.* **1.** Energetic; vigorous: *a dynamic President.* **2.** Marked by or tending to produce progress: *a dynamic social system.* **3.** Of energy, force, or motion in relation to force. **4.** Of or indicating musical dynamics: *dynamic markings.* —**dy•nam'i•cal•ly** *adv.*

dy•nam•ics |dī **năm'**ĭks| *n.* **1.** *(used with a singular verb).* The branch of physics that deals with forces, energy, and motion and the relationships between them: *A knowledge of dynamics is useful in designing machines.* **2.** *(used with a plural verb).* The relationships between causes and effects in any given system: *The dynamics of a society are often complex.* **3.** *(used with a singular verb).* Variation in force and intensity, especially in musical sound.

dy•na•mism |**dī'**nə mĭz'əm| *n.* The quality or condition of being dynamic; vigor: *the dynamism of the new Administration.*

dy•na•mite |**dī'**nə mīt'| *n.* A powerful explosive composed of nitroglycerin or ammonium nitrate combined with an absorbent material and usually packaged in sticks. —*v.* **dy•na•mit•ed, dy•na•mit•ing.** To blow up with or as if with dynamite. —**dy'na•mit'er** *n.* [SEE NOTE]

dynamite
Dynamite *was invented by Alfred Nobel. He patented it in 1867 and coined the Swedish name,* dynamit, *from Greek* dunamis, *"force, power."*

dy•na•mo |**dī'**nə mō'| *n., pl.* **dy•na•mos.** **1.** An electric generator, especially one that produces direct current. **2.** *Informal.* An extremely energetic and forceful person.

dy•na•mo•e•lec•tric |dī'nə mō'ĭ **lĕk'**trĭk| *adj.* Of or performing the conversion of mechanical energy into electrical energy or vice versa.

dy•na•mom•e•ter |dī'nə **mŏm'**ĭ tər| *n.* An instrument used to measure mechanical power or force.

dy•nast |**dī'**năst'| *or* |-nəst| *n.* A ruler, especially one belonging to a dynasty.

dy•nas•tic |dī **năs'**tĭk| *adj.* Of a dynasty: *rules for dynastic succession.*

dy•nas•ty |**dī'**nə stē| *n., pl.* **dy•nas•ties.** **1.** A succession of rulers from the same family or line: *the Hapsburg dynasty.* **2.** A family or group that maintains great power, wealth, or position for several generations.

dyne |dīn| *n.* A unit of force equal to one hundred-thousandth (10^{-5}) of a newton. ¶*These sound alike* **dyne, dine.**

dys•en•ter•y |**dĭs'**ən tĕr'ē| *n.* An infection of the lower intestines that produces pain, fever, and severe diarrhea.

dys•func•tion |dĭs **fŭngk'**shən| *n.* Any disorder in the functioning of a system or organ of the body.

dys•gen•ic |dĭs **jĕn'**ĭk| *adj.* Of or causing the deterioration of inherited characteristics: *a dysgenic mutation.*

dys•pep•sia |dĭs **pĕp'**shə| *or* |-sē ə| *n.* Digestion that is poor or disordered in some way; indigestion.

dys•pep•tic |dĭs **pĕp'**tĭk| *adj.* Of or suffering from dyspepsia. —*n.* A person who often suffers from dyspepsia. —**dys•pep'ti•cal•ly** *adv.*

dys•pro•si•um |dĭs **prō'**zē əm| *n.* Symbol **Dy** One of the elements, a soft, silvery rare-earth metal. Atomic number 66; atomic weight 162.50; valence +3; melting point 1,407°C; boiling point 2,600°C.

dz. dozen.

ă pat/ā pay/â care/ä father/ĕ pet/ ē be/ĭ pit/ī pie/î fierce/ŏ pot/ ō go/ô paw, for/oi oil/ŏŏ book/ ōō boot/ou out/ŭ cut/û fur/ *th* the/th thin/hw which/zh vision/ ə ago, item, pencil, atom, circus

Ee

e, E |ē| *n., pl.* **e's** or **E's** **1.** The fifth letter of the English alphabet. **2. E** In music, the third tone in the scale of C major. [SEE NOTE]

e, E, e., E. east; eastern.

ea. each

each |ēch| *adj.* One of two or more persons or things; every: *He talked to each one of us. He sat down and looked at the people on each side of him.* —*pron.* Every one of a group of persons, objects, or things: *Each presented his gift.* —*adv.* For or to each one; apiece: *pay ten cents each. He gave the boys a dollar each.*

each other. **1.** Each the other. Used as a compound reciprocal pronoun: *They met each other at the beach. We see each other every day.* **2.** *Informal.* One another.

ea•ger |ē′gər| *adj.* **eag•er•er, ea•ger•est.** **1.** Full of strong and impatient desire: *explorers burning with curiosity and eager for fame and fortune.* **2.** Enthusiastically expectant; keenly interested: *Thousands of eager sports fans cheered the players.* —**ea′ger•ly** *adv.* —**ea′ger•ness** *n.*

ea•gle |ē′gəl| *n.* Any of several large birds of prey with a hooked bill, broad, strong wings, and soaring flight.

eagle eye. **1.** A very sharp watch: *keeping an eagle eye on the captives.* **2.** A keen sense of sight or observation: *an eagle eye for details.*

ea•gle-eyed |ē′gəl īd′| *adj.* Having very keen eyesight.

ea•glet |ē′glĭt| *n.* A young eagle.

ear[1] |îr| *n.* **1. a.** In human beings and other animals, the organ of the body that is most sensitive to sounds; the organ of hearing. See **inner ear, middle ear, outer ear. b.** The part of this organ that shows on the outside of the body. **2.** The sense of hearing: *sounds pleasant to the ear.* **3.** The ability to distinguish tunes or sounds very accurately or acutely: *the precise ear of a musician.* **4.** Attention; heed: *Give me your ear a little longer.* **5.** A part that resembles an ear, as the handle of a cup or pitcher. [SEE NOTE & PICTURE]

Idiom. **all ears.** Listening eagerly; paying careful attention.

ear[2] |îr| *n.* The seed-bearing part of a grain plant such as corn or wheat. [SEE NOTE]

ear•ache |îr′āk′| *n.* A pain in the ear.

ear•drum |îr′drŭm′| *n.* **1.** The membrane that forms the outer boundary of the cavity of the middle ear; the tympanic membrane. **2.** The cavity of the middle ear; the tympanum.

eared |îrd| *adj.* **1.** Having an ear or ears: *an eared pitcher.* **2.** Having a certain kind or number of ears: *long-eared.*

ear•flap |îr′flăp′| *n.* A cloth or fur tab on a cap that can be turned down to cover the ear or ears.

ear•ful |îr′fo͝ol′| *n.* **1.** A flow of gossip or information. **2.** A scolding.

earl |ûrl| *n.* A member of the British peerage holding a title and rank below that of a marquis and above that of a viscount.

ear•lap |îr′lăp′| *n.* An earflap.

earl•dom |ûrl′dəm| *n.* The rank or domain of an earl.

ear•lobe |îr′lōb′| *n.* The soft, fleshy part at the bottom of the outer portion of the human ear.

ear•ly |ûr′lē| *adj.* **ear•li•er, ear•li•est.** **1.** Of, belonging to, or happening near the beginning of a time period, series, course of development, etc.: *the early morning; a man in his early twenties; the early stages of an animal's growth.* **2.** Of a long-ago or primitive time; ancient: *Early man learned to use boats thousands of years ago.* **3.** Arriving on or happening before the usual or expected time: *a few early robins hopping in the snow.* **4.** In the near future: *Union leaders predict an early settlement of the strike.* —*adv.* **ear•li•er, ear•li•est.** **1.** At or near the beginning of a time period, series of events, course of development, etc.: *The hikers set out early in the morning. He was wounded early in the battle.* **2.** Before the usual or expected time: *arrive early.* **3.** Far back in time; long ago: *The island of Delos was probably inhabited as early as the tenth century before the Christian era.* **4.** So as to allow enough time: *send your invitations early.*

early bird. *Informal.* A person who wakes up, arrives, or starts being active before most others.

ear•mark |îr′märk′| *n.* **1.** A notch or other mark made in the ear of an animal so that it can be recognized as belonging to a particular person: *At roundup time the rancher found his cattle by their earmarks.* **2.** Any sign, mark, or special quality by which something is known or recognized: *Careful observation of details is one of the earmarks of a good scientist.* —*v.* **1.** To mark the ear of (an animal) with an identifying notch, mark, etc. **2.** To set aside for some purpose: *Mrs. Espinosa earmarked part of her earnings for a summer vacation.*

ear•muff |îr′mŭf′| *n.* One of a pair of warm fur or cloth coverings for the ears, often on an adjustable headband.

earn |ûrn| *v.* **1.** To get or gain (money, wages, etc.) by working or by supplying a product or service: *Bob earns a living by catching and selling lobsters.* **2.** To deserve or win by one's efforts or behavior: *The chief earned his right to lead by his bravery and wisdom. The novelist's original ideas have*

The letter **E** *comes originally from the Phoenician* hē *(1), which stood for the consonant* h. *When the Greeks borrowed the sign, they reversed its direction (2) and used it to stand for the vowel* e, *calling it* e-psilon, *"short e." The Romans took it over from the Greeks and gave it the shape (3) that it still has.*

ear[1-2]

Ear[1] *and* **ear[2]** *are both native Old English words, but they were originally very dissimilar, and are not related.* **Ear[1]** *was* ēare *in Old English, and* **ear[2]** *was* æhher.

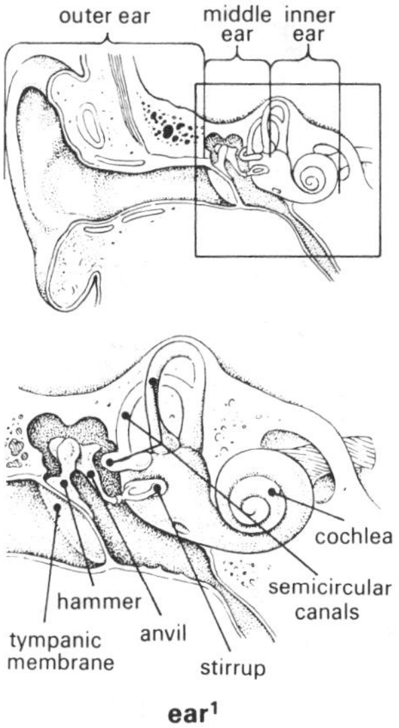

ear[1]
The human ear

earnest[1-2]

Earnest[1] *was originally a noun meaning "seriousness"; this now exists only in the phrase* in earnest. *In Old English the word was* eornost, *meaning "fighting spirit, fierceness in battle." (The masculine given name* Ernest *comes from German* Ernst, *which is closely related to* **earnest** *and had the same original meaning.)* **Earnest[2]** *originally meant "installment of money paid in advance, a down payment." It ultimately comes, through Old French, Latin, and Greek, from a Hebrew word meaning "security, pledge."*

earring

easel

ă pat/ā pay/â care/ä father/ĕ pet/ ē be/ĭ pit/ī pie/î fierce/ŏ pot/ ō go/ô paw, for/oi oil/ŏŏ book/ ōō boot/ou out/ŭ cut/û fur/ *th* the/th thin/hw which/zh vision/ ə ago, item, pencil, atom, circus

earned him the reputation of a fine writer. **3.** To produce (interest, profit, etc.): *additional income earned by money in a savings account.* ¶*These sound alike* **earn, urn.**

ear•nest[1] |ûr′nĭst| *adj.* **1.** Showing or expressing deep, sincere feeling: *The king knelt in earnest prayer.* **2.** Serious and determined in purpose: *groups of earnest students.* **—ear′nest•ly** *adv.* **—ear′nest•ness** *n.* [SEE NOTE]

***Idiom.* in earnest. 1.** With serious purpose or intent: *After a halfhearted start, we began working in earnest.* **2.** In fact or in truth; really: *The audience had at first clapped politely but were now laughing in earnest.*

ear•nest[2] |ûr′nĭst| *n.* Something, as a promise or assurance, given or offered as a sign or indication of one's intentions. [SEE NOTE]

earn•ings |ûr′nĭngz| *pl.n.* Money earned in payment for work or as profit.

ear•phone |îr′fōn′| *n.* A device that changes electrical signals into audible sound and that is made to be worn near or in contact with the ear.

ear•ring |îr′rĭng| *or* |-ĭng| *n.* A piece of jewelry worn clipped to or hanging from the lobe of the ear. [SEE PICTURE]

ear•shot |îr′shŏt′| *n.* The range or distance within which sound can be heard.

earth |ûrth| *n.* **1.** Often **Earth.** The planet on which human beings live, the third planet of the solar system in order of increasing distance from the sun. Its diameter is about 7,900 miles, its average distance from the sun is about 93 million miles, and it takes 365.26 days to complete an orbit of the sun. **2.** The world, especially the physical world regarded as the place where people live: *Magellan's crew were afraid they might sail off the edge of a flat earth.* **3. a.** The part of the planet Earth that has a solid surface, as distinguished from the oceans and the air; land. **b.** The surface of the land; ground: *snowflakes falling to the earth.* **c.** The soft, crumbly, or powdery substance forming much of this surface; soil: *seeds sprouting in the moist earth.* **—*modifier:*** *an earth satellite.*

***Idiom.* down to earth.** Sensible; realistic.

earth•bound |ûrth′bound′| *adj.* **1.** Unable to leave the surface of the earth: *Until recent times, people were earthbound, moving in horse-drawn vehicles, boats, and slow trains.* **2.** Heading toward the earth: *an earthbound spaceship.*

earth•en |ûr′thən| *adj.* **1.** Made of or consisting of earth or soil: *the earthen floor of the cabin.* **2.** Made of clay, usually hardened and fused by heat: *an earthen jar.*

earth•en•ware |ûr′thən wâr′| *n.* Dishes, containers, etc., made from coarse or heavy clay hardened and fused by heat and often left unglazed. **—*modifier:*** *an earthenware teapot.*

earth•light |ûrth′līt′| *n.* The light of the sun reflected from the earth, as seen from a place far from the earth: *The mountains of the moon make jagged shadows in the bright earthlight.*

earth•ling |ûrth′lĭng| *n.* A person who lives on the earth; a human being.

earth•ly |ûrth′lē| *adj.* **1.** Of the earth, especially of the material world, rather than heavenly or spiritual. **2.** Possible; imaginable: *nonsense with no earthly meaning.* **—earth′li•ness** *n.*

earth•quake |ûrth′kwāk′| *n.* A series of waves or vibrations that pass through the crust of the earth, causing movements, often of violent force, at the surface. Earthquakes are caused by volcanic action or by the sudden breaking loose of rock under great strain or pressure.

earth satellite. A satellite, especially an artificial satellite, in orbit around the earth.

earth science. Any of several sciences, such as geology and meteorology, that are concerned with the physical nature and origin of the earth.

earth•ward |ûrth′wərd| *adv.* Also **earth•wards** |ûrth′wərdz|. To or toward the earth: *Feathery snowflakes drifted earthward.* *—adj.: the earthward fall of a meteorite.*

earth•work |ûrth′wûrk′| *n.* Often **earthworks.** Earth piled up into a bank or wall, as for military defense or in building and construction.

earth•worm |ûrth′wûrm′| *n.* A common worm that has a body divided into many ringlike segments and that burrows in soil.

earth•y |ûr′thē| *adj.* **earth•i•er, earth•i•est. 1.** Of or like earth or soil: *the earthy smell of the woods after rain.* **2.** Hearty, uninhibited, and sometimes considered crude: *earthy humor.* **—earth′i•ness** *n.*

ear•wig |îr′wĭg′| *n.* An insect with a pair of pincerlike parts protruding from the rear of the body.

ear•worm |îr′wûrm′| *n.* A moth caterpillar that feeds on and damages ears of corn and other plant products: *a corn earworm.*

ease |ēz| *n.* **1.** Freedom from difficulty, strain, trouble, etc.; easiness: *Arrange your equipment for convenience and ease in working.* **2.** Relief, as from pain or worry: *give ease to his troubled heart.* **3.** Practiced or effortless skill or self-assurance: *She rode sidesaddle with grace and ease.* **4.** Comfort; luxury: *a life of ease and pleasure.* **5.** Fullness or extra material that permits freedom of movement: *Allow a few inches of ease across the shoulders of the dress.* **—*v.* eased, eas•ing. 1.** To make less troublesome or difficult; make easier: *Use short cuts to ease and speed your work.* **2.** To relieve; comfort: *The nurse gave the sick man medicine to ease his pain.* **3.** To move slowly and carefully: *The tug eased into the narrow docking space. Use a shoehorn to ease your foot into a new shoe.* **4.** To relax; let up: *The pull of the current eased as the tide turned. His foot eased up on the gas pedal.* **5.** To provide with enough fullness to allow freedom of movement: *Ease the sleeves at the armholes.*

***Idiom.* at ease. 1.** Free from strain or discomfort; relaxed; comfortable: *The guests were all at ease and enjoying themselves.* **2.** In a standing position with the legs apart, the hands clasped behind the back, and maintaining silence.

ea•sel |ē′zəl| *n.* An upright stand or rack used to support the canvas or other material painted on by an artist or to display a picture or sign. [SEE PICTURE]

eas•i•ly |ē′zə lē| *adv.* **1.** Without difficulty; with ease; readily: *Libraries are arranged so that you can find books easily.* **2.** Without doubt; surely: *That is easily the best meal I have ever eaten.* **3.** Possibly; very likely: *If he runs so fast, he might easily trip and fall.*

east |ēst| *n.* **1.** The direction toward which the earth rotates on its axis; the direction from which the sun is seen to rise: *a wind blowing from the east.* **2.** Often **East.** A region or part of the earth in this direction: *the Brazilian highlands of the east.* **3. the East. a.** Asia and the nearby islands of the Indian and Pacific oceans; the Orient. **b.** The part of the United States along or near the Atlantic coast. *—adj.* **1.** Of, in, or toward the east: *the east bank of the river.* **2.** Often **East.** Forming or belonging to a region, country, etc., toward the east: *East Germany.* **3.** From the east: *An east wind is blowing.* *—adv.* In a direction to, from, or toward the east: *a river flowing east.*

East Berlin. The capital of the German Democratic Republic. Population, 1,100,000.

East·er |ē′stər| *n.* A Christian festival celebrating the Resurrection of Christ. It is held on the first Sunday following the first full moon on or after March 21. *—**modifier:** Easter vacation.*

Easter egg. A dyed or painted egg traditionally given as a gift or hidden and hunted for by children at Easter time.

Easter Island. An island of Chile in the South Pacific Ocean, 2,200 miles west of South America, famous for its numerous ancient massive heads carved in stone.

east·er·ly |ē′stər lē| *adj.* **1.** In or toward the east: *the most easterly point of the continent; a plane flying in an easterly direction.* **2.** From the east: *easterly winds.* *—adv.: winds blowing easterly.* *—n., pl.* **east·er·lies.** A storm or wind from the east.

east·ern |ē′stərn| *adj.* **1.** Often **Eastern.** Of, in, or toward the east: *eastern Europe.* **2.** From the east: *an eastern wind.*

Eastern Daylight-Saving Time. Daylight-saving time as reckoned in the region between the meridians at 67.5° and 82.5° west of Greenwich, England. The eastern United States is in this region. See **time zone.**

east·ern·er |ē′stə nər| *n.* Often **Easterner.** A person who lives in or comes from the east, especially the eastern United States.

Eastern Hemisphere. The half of the earth that includes Europe, Africa, Asia, and Australia.

east·ern·most |ē′stərn mōst′| *adj.* Farthest east.

Eastern Orthodox Church. A group of present-day churches, including the Greek Orthodox and the Russian Orthodox, that trace their origin to the early Christian Church established during the Byzantine Empire.

Eastern Standard Time. Standard time as reckoned in the region between the meridians at 67.5° and 82.5° west of Greenwich, England. The eastern United States is in this region. See **time zone.**

East·er·tide |ē′stər tīd′| *n.* The Easter season.

East Germany. The unofficial name for the German Democratic Republic.

East In·dies |ĭn′dēz|. The islands southeast of Asia in what is now Indonesia. *—***East Indian.**

east·ward |ēst′wərd| *adv.* Also **east·wards** |ēst′wərdz|. To or toward the east: *a river flowing eastward.* *—adj.: the eastward flow of the current.* *—n.* A direction or region to the east: *the sun rising to the eastward.*

eas·y |ē′zē| *adj.* **eas·i·er, eas·i·est. 1.** Not difficult; requiring little or no effort, trouble, etc.: *an easy task; handwriting that is easy to read.* **2.** Free from worry, strain, or pain: *an easy mind and a happy disposition.* **3.** Not forced, hurried, or strenuous: *within easy walking distance.* **4.** Relaxed; comfortable: *a natural, easy manner.* **5.** Not strict or demanding; lenient: *A teacher who gives only A's is an easy marker.* *—adv. Informal.* Without strain or difficulty; in a relaxed, comfortable manner. *—***eas′i·ness** *n.*

Idioms. **go easy (on). 1.** To be moderate, restrained, or sparing: *go easy on the whipped cream.* **2.** To be lenient or sympathetic: *go easy on first offenders.* **take it** (or **things**) **easy.** To remain calm and unruffled; relax.

easy chair. A large, comfortable upholstered chair.

eas·y·go·ing |ē′zē gō′ĭng| *adj.* **1.** Relaxed; carefree: *an easygoing life; the easygoing sports editor of the school newspaper.* **2.** Going at an even, relaxed pace: *easygoing horses.*

eat |ēt| *v.* **ate** |āt|, **eat·en** |ēt′n|, **eat·ing. 1.** To take (solid food) into the body as nourishment by swallowing: *Owls eat mice. Eat slowly and chew well.* **2.** To have (a meal): *The Pilgrims and Indians ate together at long tables. We always eat dinner at six o'clock.* **3.** To wear, corrode, break, etc., by or as if by eating or gnawing: *The worm ate its way into the apple. Rust ate away the iron pipes. Unexpected expenses ate into his savings.* *—**phrasal verb.*** **eat up. 1.** To use up; consume: *Wage increases were eaten up by the rise in the cost of living.* **2.** *Informal.* To enjoy greatly; be greedy for: *She eats up compliments.* *—n.* **eats.** *Slang.* Food. *—***eat′er** *n.*

eat·a·ble |ē′tə bəl| *adj.* Fit for eating; edible. *—n.* Often **eatables.** Food.

eau de co·logne |ō′ də kə lōn′|. *pl.* **eaux de co·logne** |ō′ də kə lōn′| *or* |ōz′|. A lightly perfumed liquid; cologne.

eaves |ēvz| *n.* *(used with a plural verb).* The part of a roof that forms the lower edge and projects beyond the walls. [SEE PICTURE]

eaves

eaves·drop |ēvz′drŏp′| *v.* **eaves·dropped, eaves·drop·ping.** To listen secretly to the private conversation of others: *hidden behind the door to eavesdrop.* *—***eaves′drop′per** *n.*

ebb |ĕb| *v.* **1.** To flow or fall back, as the tide does after reaching its highest point; recede. **2.** To fade or fall away; weaken; fail: *The hooked fish struggled more and more weakly as its strength ebbed.* *—n.* **1.** A retreating or receding motion, as of the tide as it falls back from its highest point. **2.** A low point: *His fortunes were at their lowest ebb.*

ebb tide. 1. The tide when it is moving back after reaching its highest point. **2.** The period between high tide and low tide.

eb·on |ĕb′ən| *adj.* Black. Used chiefly in poetry.

eb·on·ite |ĕb′ən īt′| *n.* A type of **hard rubber,** especially one that is colored black.

eb·on·y |ĕb′ə nē| *n., pl.* **eb·on·ies.** The hard black or blackish wood of a tropical tree, used especially for piano keys. *—**modifier:** an ebony cabinet.* *—adj.* Black: *ebony hair.*

e·bul·lient |ĭ bŭl′yənt| *adj.* Full of bubbling excitement, enthusiasm, or high spirits. *—***e·bul′lience** *n.*

eb·ul·li·tion |ĕb′ə lĭsh′ən| *n.* The bubbling or boiling of a liquid.

echelon

eclipse
Total eclipse of the sun photographed in Peru, November 12, 1966.

ecology/economy

Economy *is from Greek* oikonomia, *"household management":* oikos, *"house, home,"* + -nomia, *"management."* **Ecology** *is from a nineteenth-century German word,* ökologie, *meaning "habitat study," or "environment science." It was made up from the same Greek word* oikos, *"house" (this time used to mean "the place and conditions in which animals and plants live"),* + *Greek* -logia, *"study, science."*

ă **pat**/ā **pay**/â **care**/ä **father**/ĕ **pet**/ ē **be**/ĭ **pit**/ī **pie**/î **fierce**/ŏ **pot**/ ō **go**/ô **paw**, **for**/oi **oil**/ŏŏ **book**/ ōō **boot**/ou **out**/ŭ **cut**/û **fur**/ *th* **the**/th **thin**/hw **which**/zh **vision**/ ə **ago**, **item**, **pencil**, **atom**, **circus**

ec•cen•tric |ĭk **sĕn**'trĭk| *adj.* **1.** Odd or unusual in appearance, behavior, etc.; strange; peculiar: *an eccentric hat; an eccentric person; an eccentric habit.* **2.** Deviating from the form of a circle in the way that an ellipse does: *a very eccentric orbit.* **3.** Not in or at the center: *an eccentric pivot.* **4.** Revolving on an eccentric pivot or shaft: *an eccentric wheel.* **5.** Having different centers, as a pair of geometric figures, especially circles. *—n.* **1.** A person who is odd in behavior. **2.** An eccentric machine part, especially a disk or wheel. **—ec•cen'tri•cal•ly** *adv.*

ec•cen•tric•i•ty |ĕk'sĕn **trĭs'**ĭ tē| *n., pl.* **ec•cen•tric•i•ties. 1.** The condition or quality of being eccentric. **2.** The degree by which something is eccentric.

ec•cle•si•as•tic |ĭ klē'zē **ăs'**tĭk| *adj.* Ecclesiastical. *—n.* A clergyman; priest.

ec•cle•si•as•ti•cal |ĭ klē'zē **ăs'**tĭ kəl| *adj.* Of a church, especially as an organized institution; clerical: *Ireland was a center of ecclesiastical learning during the Dark Ages.*

ech•e•lon |**ĕsh'**ə lŏn'| *n.* **1.** A steplike formation of military aircraft, naval vessels, etc. **2.** A section or part of a military or naval force. **3.** A level of command or authority: *He was a member of the lowest echelon in his firm.* [SEE PICTURE]

e•chi•no•derm |ĭ **kī'**nə dûrm'| *n.* Any of a large group of sea animals, such as a starfish or sea urchin, having a spiny or rough outer covering and parts that radiate from a center.

ech•o |**ĕk'**ō| *n., pl.* **ech•oes. 1. a.** A reflected sound wave or series of reflected sound waves that reaches an observer with a long enough delay to be heard as distinct from the original direct sound wave. **b.** A sound produced in this way. **2.** Any reflected wave, as in radio or, especially, in radar. **3.** Any repetition or imitation of something, as of the opinions, speech, or dress of another. *—v.* **1.** To repeat or be repeated by or as if by an echo; send back the sound of: *The canyon echoed her cry. His shouts echoed from one mountain to the next. The speech echoed in her ears.* **2.** To resound with or emit an echo; reverberate: *The long hallway echoed with his footsteps.* **3.** To repeat or imitate: *followers echoing the thoughts of a leader.*

ech•o•lo•ca•tion |ĕk'ō lō **kā'**shən| *n.* **1.** The ability of certain animals, such as bats and dolphins, to judge their positions in relation to their surroundings by emitting high-frequency sounds and listening to the echoes. **2.** The use of a similar method, in which electronic instruments are employed, by human beings.

é•clair |ā **klâr'**| *or* |**ā'**klâr'| *n.* A light, oblong pastry with a cream or custard filling, usually iced with chocolate.

é•clat |ā **klä'**| *n.* **1.** Great brilliance, as of performance or achievement: *She played the sonata with éclat.* **2.** Great success or acclaim: *He longed for glory and the éclat that came with it.*

ec•lec•tic |ĭ **klĕk'**tĭk| *adj.* Choosing or consisting of what appears to be the best from various sources, systems, or styles: *an eclectic musician; eclectic architecture.* *—n.* A person whose opinions and beliefs are drawn from several sources. **—ec•lec'ti•cal•ly** *adv.*

e•clipse |ĭ **klĭps'**| *n.* **1. a.** The blocking by another celestial body of part or all of the light that reaches an observer from a given celestial body. **b.** The time during which such a blocking occurs. **2.** A decline; downfall: *His fame has suffered an eclipse.* *—v.* **e•clipsed, e•clips•ing. 1.** To block the light of: *as one of a pair of binary stars eclipses the other.* **2.** To obscure or overshadow the importance, fame, or reputation of; reduce in importance by comparison: *This news eclipses everything. Columbus was destined to eclipse his fellow navigators completely.* [SEE PICTURE]

e•clip•tic |ĭ **klĭp'**tĭk| *n.* The circle formed by the intersection of the plane of the earth's orbit and the celestial sphere.

ec•o•log•i•cal |ĕk'ə **lŏj'**ĭ kəl| *or* |ē'kə-| or **ec•o•log•ic** |ĕk'ə **lŏj'**ĭk| *or* |ē'kə-| *adj.* Of ecology. **—ec'o•log'i•cal•ly** *adv.*

e•col•o•gist |ĭ **kŏl'**ə jĭst| *n.* A scientist who specializes in ecology.

e•col•o•gy |ĭ **kŏl'**ə jē| *n.* **1.** The science of the relationships between living things and their environment. **2.** The relationship between living things and their environment. [SEE NOTE]

e•co•nom•ic |ē'kə **nŏm'**ĭk| *or* |ĕk'ə-| *adj.* **1.** Of the production, development, and management of material wealth, as of a country, household, or business enterprise: *the government's economic policy.* **2.** Showing or related to the basic activities of a nation as expressed through its economy: *an economic map.* **3.** Of the science of economics: *economic doctrines.*

e•co•nom•i•cal |ē'kə **nŏm'**ĭ kəl| *or* |ĕk'ə-| *adj.* Not wasteful or extravagant; prudent; using only a necessary amount, as of money, fuel, etc.: *an economical person; an economical engine.*

e•co•nom•i•cal•ly |ē'kə **nŏm'**ĭ kə lē| *or* |ĕk'ə-| *adv.* **1.** In an economic way; financially: *Every country wants to be economically independent.* **2.** Sparingly: *Use things economically.*

e•co•nom•ics |ē'kə **nŏm'**ĭks| *or* |ĕk'ə-| *n.* **1.** *(used with a singular verb).* The science that deals with the production, distribution, development, and consumption of goods and services. **2.** *(used with a plural verb).* Economic condition or an aspect of it, as of a country, individual, etc.: *the economics of a large agricultural region. The economics of his investments are hard to understand.*

e•con•o•mist |ĭ **kŏn'**ə mĭst| *n.* A person who specializes in economics.

e•con•o•my |ĭ **kŏn'**ə mē| *n., pl.* **e•con•o•mies. 1.** The careful or thrifty use or management of resources, as of income, materials, or labor: *One must practice economy in buying new clothes.* **2.** An example of this; a saving: *the economies of mass production.* **3.** The management of the resources of a country, community, or business: *the American economy.* **4. a.** A system for the management and development of resources: *an agricultural economy.* **b.** The economic system of a country, region, state, etc.: *Tobacco is the center of their economy.* [SEE NOTE]

ec•o•sys•tem |**ĕk'**ō sĭs'təm| *n.* The plants and animals of an ecological community, together with their environment, forming an interacting system of activities and functions regarded as a unit: *Far from being a wholly dangerous and destructive influence in the natural world, the crocodile is a useful member of a complex ecosystem.*

ec•sta•sy |ĕk′stə sē| *n., pl.* **ec•sta•sies.** A state of intense emotion, especially of joy or delight.

ec•stat•ic |ĕk stăt′ĭk| *adj.* **1.** Of, producing, experiencing, or showing great joy or delight: *answering with an ecstatic voice. I was ecstatic over the good news.* **2.** In a state of ecstasy; enraptured: *He bounded about the room in ecstatic delight.* —**ec•stat′i•cal•ly** *adv.*

ec•to•derm |ĕk′tə dûrm′| *n.* The outermost of the three layers of cells found in an early embryo, developing in time into the outer skin and nervous system.

Ec•ua•dor |ĕk′wə dôr′|. A country on the western coast of South America between Colombia and Peru. Population, 6,951,000. Capital, Quito.

ec•u•men•i•cal |ĕk′yo͞o mĕn′ĭ kəl| *adj.* Of the worldwide Christian church, especially in regard to unity: *an ecumenical council; the ecumenical movement.* —**ec′u•men′i•cal•ly** *adv.*

ec•ze•ma |ĕk′sə mə| *or* |ĕg′-| *or* |ĭg zē′-| *n.* An inflammation of the skin, marked by redness, itching, and the formation of sores that discharge fluid and become crusted and scaly. It is not contagious.

-ed[1]. A suffix that forms the past tense and past participle of verbs: **cared; carried; carted.**

-ed[2]. A suffix that forms adjectives from nouns: *a footed vase.*

ed. **1.** edition; editor. **2.** education.

E•dam cheese |ē′dəm| *or* |ē′dăm′|. A mild, yellow Dutch cheese, pressed into balls and usually covered with red paraffin.

Ed•da |ĕd′ə| *n.* **1.** A collection of Old Norse poems called the Elder or Poetic Edda, assembled in the early 13th century. **2.** A manual of Icelandic poetry, called the Younger or Prose Edda, compiled a generation later.

ed•dy |ĕd′ē| *n., pl.* **ed•dies.** A current, as of a liquid or gas, that moves contrary to the direction of a main current, especially in a circular motion. —*v.* **ed•died, ed•dy•ing, ed•dies.** To move in or as if in an eddy.

Ed•dy |ĕd′ē|, **Mary Baker.** 1821–1910. American religious leader; founder of the Church of Christ, Scientist.

e•del•weiss |ād′l vīs′| *or* |-wīs′| *n.* A plant that grows high in the Alps. It is covered with whitish down, and has small flowers surrounded by petallike leaves. [SEE PICTURE]

e•de•ma |ĭ dē′mə| *n.* A diseased condition in which an excess of fluid collects in tissue and causes it to swell.

E•den |ēd′n| *n.* In the Bible, the first home of Adam and Eve; Paradise. Also called *Garden of Eden.*

edge |ĕj| *n.* **1.** The line or point where an object, area, etc., begins or ends: *a cottage on the edge of a forest; the edge of a lake; the edge of a sheet of paper.* **2.** A dividing line or point of transition; a border: *Science stood on the edge of another major discovery.* **3.** A rim, brink, or crest, as of a cliff or ridge. **4.** The usually thin, sharpened side of the blade of a knife, tool, etc. **5.** A margin of superiority; an advantage: *We had a slight edge over the other team.* **6.** A line or line segment formed by the intersection of two surfaces of a three-dimensional figure, as a polyhedron: *the edge of a brick.* **7.** A trace of hardness or harshness, often expressive of annoyance, displeasure, etc.: *His voice had a menacing edge when he addressed the class.* —*v.* **edged, edg•ing. 1.** To advance or move gradually: *He edged his way through the crowd. The tide edged slowly across the marsh.* **2.** To give an edge to; sharpen. **3.** To be on or near an edge of: *Trees edged the lawn.* **4.** To put a border or edge on: *She edged the sleeve with lace.*

Idioms. on edge. Tense or nervous; irritable. **set (someone's) teeth on edge.** To annoy or irritate strongly. **take the edge off.** To soften or dull, as the pleasure or force of: *Crackers will take the edge off your appetite.*

edg•ing |ĕj′ĭng| *n.* A border or trimming on or along an edge: *an edging of lace on a slip.*

edg•y |ĕj′ē| *adj.* **edg•i•er, edg•i•est.** On edge; tense; nervous. —**edg′i•ness** *n.*

ed•i•ble |ĕd′ə bəl| *adj.* Capable of being eaten; fit to eat: *edible roots; edible mushrooms.* —*n.* Often **edibles.** Something to be eaten; food.

e•dict |ē′dĭkt′| *n.* A decree or proclamation issued by an authority.

ed•i•fi•ca•tion |ĕd′ə fĭ kā′shən| *n.* Intellectual, moral, or spiritual improvement; enlightenment: *a book written for the edification of youth.*

ed•i•fice |ĕd′ə fĭs| *n.* A building, especially one that is very imposing in size or appearance.

ed•i•fy |ĕd′ə fī′| *v.* **ed•i•fied, ed•i•fy•ing, ed•i•fies.** To instruct or enlighten so as to encourage intellectual, moral, or spiritual improvement.

Ed•in•burgh |ĕd′n bûr′ō| *or* |-bûr′ə|. The capital of Scotland. Population, 475,000.

Ed•i•son |ĕd′ĭ sən|, **Thomas Alva.** 1847–1931. American inventor; obtained 1,100 patents in such fields as telegraphy, phonography, electric lighting, and photography.

ed•it |ĕd′ĭt| *v.* **1.** To make (written material) ready for publication by correcting, revising, or marking directions for a printer. **2.** To select or arrange for publication. **3.** To supervise the publication of (a newspaper or magazine). **4.** To eliminate; delete: *Someone edited out her remarks about religion.* **5.** To select and put together the parts of (a motion picture, electronic tape, or soundtrack).

edit. edition; editor.

e•di•tion |ĭ dĭsh′ən| *n.* **1. a.** The entire number of copies of a book or newspaper printed at one time and having the same content. **b.** A single copy of such a number. **2.** Any of the various forms in which something is issued or produced: *a paperback edition of her novel.*

ed•i•tor |ĕd′ĭ tər| *n.* **1.** A person who prepares written material for publication, often by revising or correcting it. **2.** A person who prepares a motion picture, electronic tape, or soundtrack for viewing or hearing by selecting its parts. **3.** A person who directs the writing and layout of a newspaper or magazine or supervises one of its departments. [SEE NOTE]

ed•i•to•ri•al |ĕd′ĭ tôr′ē əl| *or* |-tōr′-| *n.* An article in a newspaper or magazine expressing the opinions of its editors or publisher. —*adj.* **1.** Of an editor or editors. **2.** Expressing opinion rather than reporting news: *the editorial page of the newspaper.* —**ed′i•to′ri•al•ly** *adv.*

ed•i•to•ri•al•ize |ĕd′ĭ tôr′ē ə līz′| *or* |-tōr′-| *v.* **ed•i•to•ri•al•ized, ed•i•to•ri•al•iz•ing. 1.** To express an opinion in or as if in an editorial. **2.** To

edelweiss

editor

The word **editor** *originally meant "publisher" and comes from Latin* ēditor, *"he who brings out or publishes," which is from* ēdere, *"to bring out":* ē-, *"out,"* + -dere, *"to bring."* **Edit** *is a back-formation from* **editor**.

educate
It has often been said that **education** *literally means "a drawing out" of a person's talent as opposed to "a putting in" of knowledge or instruction. This is an interesting idea, but it is not quite true in terms of the etymology of the word.* **Educate** *comes from Latin* ēducāre, *"to lead or bring out":* ē-, *"out," +* dūcere, *"to lead or bring." This word originally referred to the midwife, who helps bring a baby out of the womb at birth. Later it began to mean "to bring a young person out into the world, to bring up, to educate."*

eel
Many eels spend their lives in oceans and seas, but the common eels of North America and Europe hatch in a part of the Atlantic Ocean called the Sargasso Sea and then migrate up rivers to fresh water, where they spend most of their lives. When they are ready to breed, they swim back to the Sargasso Sea.

ă pat/ā pay/â care/ä father/ĕ pet/ē be/ĭ pit/ī pie/î fierce/ŏ pot/ō go/ô paw, for/oi oil/ŏŏ book/ōō boot/ou out/ŭ cut/û fur/*th* the/th thin/hw which/zh vision/ə ago, item, pencil, atom, circus

express an opinion or opinions in what is supposed to be a report of facts.

ed•i•tor•ship |ĕd'ĭ tər shĭp'| *n.* **1.** The position or activity of an editor. **2.** The guidance or direction of an editor.

Ed•mon•ton |ĕd'mən tən|. The capital of Alberta, Canada. Population, 518,000.

EDST, E.D.S.T. Eastern Daylight-Saving Time.

ed•u•ca•ble |ĕj'ŏŏ kə bəl| *adj.* Capable of being educated.

ed•u•cate |ĕj'ŏŏ kāt'| *v.* **ed•u•cat•ed, ed•u•cat•ing.** To provide with knowledge or training, especially through formal schooling; teach: *It is the responsibility of a community to educate each child. Their purpose is to educate through the use of visual aids.* [SEE NOTE]

ed•u•cat•ed |ĕj'ŏŏ kā'tĭd| *adj.* **1.** Having an education, especially one above the average. **2.** Based on experience and some factual knowledge: *an educated guess.*

ed•u•ca•tion |ĕj'ŏŏ kā'shən| *n.* **1. a.** The process of imparting or obtaining knowledge or skill; systematic instruction: *A new method of printing books started one of the world's greatest advances in education. He wanted to continue his education after high school.* **b.** The knowledge or skill obtained by such a process; learning: *A boy in 18th-century England without parents, education, or money ended up in the grim and ugly mills.* **2.** A program of instruction of a specified kind or level: *driver education; a college education.* **3.** The field of study that is concerned with teaching and learning; the theory of teaching: *Many teachers are graduates of schools of education.*

ed•u•ca•tion•al |ĕj'ŏŏ kā'shə nəl| *adj.* **1.** Of education: *educational standards; an educational system.* **2.** Serving to give knowledge or skill; instructive: *an educational hobby.* —**ed'u•ca'tion•al•ly** *adv.*

ed•u•ca•tor |ĕj'ŏŏ kā'tər| *n.* **1.** A teacher. **2.** A specialist in the theory and practice of education.

e•duce |ĭ dōōs'| *or* |ĭ dyōōs'| *v.* **e•duced, e•duc•ing.** To draw or bring out; elicit: *A teacher should try to educe the best in each student.* —**e•duc'i•ble** *adj.*

-ee. A suffix that forms nouns from verbs: **draftee; trainee.**

eel |ēl| *n.* Any of several long, slippery, snakelike fishes. [SEE PICTURE]

e'en¹ |ēn| *n.* Evening. Used chiefly in poetry.

e'en² |ēn| *adv.* Even. Used chiefly in poetry.

e'er |âr| *adv.* Ever. Used chiefly in poetry. ¶*These sound alike* **e'er, air, are², ere, heir.**

-eer. A suffix meaning "someone who works, makes, is involved in, etc.": **auctioneer; racketeer.**

ee•rie, also **ee•ry** |îr'ē| *adj.* **ee•ri•er, ee•ri•est. 1.** Inspiring fear without being openly threatening; strangely unsettling; weird: *The entire countryside was bathed in an eerie, crimson light.* **2.** Supernatural in aspect or character; mysterious; uncanny: *Eerie noises in the ghostly chamber petrified the nervous visitors.* —**ee'ri•ly** *adv.* —**ee'ri•ness** *n.*

ef•face |ĭ fās'| *v.* **ef•faced, ef•fac•ing.** To remove by or as if by rubbing out; obliterate; erase: *a giant effort to efface the traces of the forest fire.* —**ef•face'ment** *n.*

ef•fect |ĭ fĕkt'| *n.* **1.** Something brought about by a cause or agent; a result: *The effect of advertising should be an increase in sales.* **2.** The power or capacity to bring about a desired result; influence: *Advice has no effect on him.* **3. a.** An artistic technique that produces a specific impression: *A great many special effects can be used in making a movie.* **b.** The impression produced by an artistic technique, a way of behaving, etc.: *He created an effect of sunlight in the painting. She cries just for effect.* **4. effects.** Physical belongings; goods; property. —*v.* To produce as a result; cause to occur: *Science and technology have effected many changes in society.*

Idioms. in effect. 1. In fact; actually: *What is he in effect saying?* **2.** In active force: *The new law is now in effect.* **take effect.** To become operative; gain active force: *The tranquilizer takes effect quickly.* **to the** (or **that**) **effect.** Having the (or that) meaning: *He said he approved, or something to that effect.*

ef•fec•tive |ĭ fĕk'tĭv| *adj.* **1.** Having or producing the intended or desired effect; serving the purpose: *There are two kinds of vaccine effective against polio. A writer must make effective use of adjectives.* **2.** Operative; in effect: *The law will be effective immediately.* —**ef•fec'tive•ly** *adv.* —**ef•fec'tive•ness** *n.*

ef•fec•tu•al |ĭ fĕk'chōō əl| *adj.* Producing or sufficient to produce a desired effect; fully adequate: *effectual methods.* —**ef•fec'tu•al•ly** *adv.* —**ef•fec'tu•al•ness** *n.*

ef•fem•i•nate |ĭ fĕm'ə nĭt| *adj.* Having qualities associated with women rather than men; unmanly: *an effeminate man.* —**ef•fem'i•na•cy** |ĭ fĕm'ə nə sē|, **ef•fem'i•nate•ness** *n.* —**ef•fem'i•nate•ly** *adv.*

ef•fer•vesce |ĕf'ər vĕs'| *v.* **ef•fer•vesced, ef•fer•vesc•ing. 1.** To give off gas in small bubbles, as a liquid that is fermenting or carbonated does. **2.** To come out of a liquid in small bubbles. **3.** To show high spirits; be lively.

ef•fer•ves•cence |ĕf'ər vĕs'əns| *n.* **1.** The process or capability of giving off gas in small bubbles. **2.** Sparkling high spirits; vivacity.

ef•fer•ves•cent |ĕf'ər vĕs'ənt| *adj.* **1.** Having effervescence or produced by effervescing. **2.** High-spirited; lively.

ef•fete |ĭ fēt'| *adj.* **1.** Having lost vitality, strength, character, vigor, etc.; spent; degenerate: *an effete civilization; an effete romantic style.* **2.** Decadent and soft as a result of self-indulgence and lack of discipline: *an effete man; an effete people.* —**ef•fete'ly** *adv.* —**ef•fete'ness** *n.*

ef•fi•ca•cious |ĕf'ĭ kā'shəs| *adj.* Capable of producing the desired effect. —**ef'fi•ca'cious•ly** *adv.* —**ef'fi•ca'cious•ness** *n.*

ef•fi•ca•cy |ĕf'ĭ kə sē| *n.* Power or capacity to produce the desired effect; effectiveness.

ef•fi•cien•cy |ĭ fĭsh'ən sē| *n., pl.* **ef•fi•cien•cies. 1.** The condition or quality of being efficient. **2.** The effectiveness of something; the measure of how well something operates. **3.** The fraction of the energy put into a machine that appears in the form of useful output. **4.** *Informal.* A furnished apartment with cooking facilities for short-term rental, especially one in a resort area.

efficiency expert. An expert in the analysis and improvement of industrial efficiency and productivity.

ef·fi·cient |ĭ fĭsh′ənt| *adj.* Acting or producing effectively with a minimum of waste, expense, or effort: *James Watt designed the first efficient steam engine. She is an efficient secretary.* —**ef·fi′cient·ly** *adv.*

ef·fi·gy |ĕf′ĭ jē| *n., pl.* **ef·fi·gies. 1.** A painted or sculptured likeness of a person, as on a stone wall or monument. **2.** A crude image or dummy fashioned in the likeness of a hated or despised person.

Idiom. **hang** (or **burn**) **in effigy.** To hang (or burn) publicly the image of a disliked person.

ef·flo·resce |ĕf′lə rĕs′| *v.* **ef·flo·resced, ef·flo·resc·ing.** In chemistry, to lose water of crystallization and become a powder: *Sodium carbonate effloresces in air.* —**ef′flo·res′cence** *n.*

ef·flu·ent |ĕf′lo͞o ənt| *adj.* Flowing out or forth. —*n.* **1.** Something that flows out or forth, as water that flows from a lake. **2.** The liquid matter that flows from a sewer or waste pipe: *The effluent from the mill polluted the stream.*

ef·flu·vi·um |ĭ flo͞o′vē əm| *n., pl.* **ef·flu·vi·a** |ĭ-flo͞o′vē ə|. An invisible or barely visible flow of gas or smoke, especially one that is foul or harmful.

ef·fort |ĕf′ərt| *n.* **1.** The use of physical or mental energy to do something; exertion: *Doing it this way will save time and effort.* **2. a.** A difficult or tiring exertion of strength or will: *It was an effort to get up.* **b.** An attempt, especially an earnest attempt: *Make an effort to arrive promptly!* **3.** Something done or produced through exertion; an achievement: *This painting is his latest effort.*

ef·fort·less |ĕf′ərt lĭs| *adj.* Requiring or showing little or no effort: *an effortless activity.* —**ef′fort·less·ly** *adv.* —**ef′fort·less·ness** *n.*

ef·fron·ter·y |ĭ frŭn′tə rē| *n., pl.* **ef·fron·ter·ies.** Shameless or insulting boldness; audacity.

ef·ful·gent |ĭ fo͝ol′jənt| *adj.* Shining brilliantly; radiant: *the effulgent sun.* —**ef·ful′gence** |ĭ fo͝ol′-jəns| *n.* —**ef·ful′gent·ly** *adv.*

ef·fu·sion |ĭ fyo͞o′zhən| *n.* **1.** The passage of a gas through tiny holes as a result of pressure applied to it. **2.** A seepage of fluid into a cavity of the body. **3.** An unrestrained outpouring of feeling, as in speech or writing.

ef·fu·sive |ĭ fyo͞o′sĭv| *adj.* Unrestrained or excessive in emotional expression; gushy: *an effusive display of gratitude.* —**ef·fu′sive·ly** *adv.* —**ef·fu′sive·ness** *n.*

eft |ĕft| *n.* A newt, especially one in an immature stage that lives on land rather than in water.

e.g. for example. *E.g.* stands for Latin *exempli gratia,* "for the sake of example, for example." [SEE NOTE]

egg¹ |ĕg| *n.* **1.** Also **egg cell.** One of the female sex cells of a plant or animal, uniting with a male sex cell in the process of sexual reproduction. **2.** A female sex cell of any of many kinds of animals, generally containing nutrient material and covered with a protective coating, and often deposited outside the mother's body to hatch. Insects, frogs, fish, turtles, and birds are among the animals that lay eggs. **3.** The hard-shelled egg of a bird, especially one produced by a chicken and used as food. **4.** *Informal.* A fellow: *He's a good egg.* —**modifier:** *a spider's egg case; egg yolks.* [SEE NOTE & PICTURE]

egg² |ĕg| *v.* —**egg on.** To encourage or incite with taunts, dares, etc.; urge: *Egged on by him and quite willing on my own, I played a shameful trick on the old man.* [SEE NOTE]

egg·beat·er |ĕg′bē′tər| *n.* A kitchen utensil with rotating blades for beating eggs, whipping cream, or mixing together cooking ingredients.

egg·head |ĕg′hĕd′| *n. Slang.* An intellectual.

egg·nog |ĕg′nŏg′| *n.* A drink of milk and beaten eggs, often mixed with rum, brandy, or other liquor.

egg·plant |ĕg′plănt′| *or* |-plänt′| *n.* **1.** A plant with large, egg-shaped, purple-skinned fruit. **2.** The fruit of this plant, eaten as a vegetable.

egg roll. A Chinese-American food consisting of an egg pastry rolled around minced vegetables, sometimes with seafood, and fried.

egg·shell |ĕg′shĕl′| *n.* **1.** The thin, breakable outer covering of a bird's egg. **2.** A light, yellowish tan. —*adj.* Light, yellowish tan.

egg white. The albumen of an egg.

eg·lan·tine |ĕg′lən tīn′| *or* |-tēn′| *n.* A rose, the sweetbrier.

e·go |ē′gō| *or* |ĕg′ō| *n., pl.* **e·gos. 1.** The part of a human mind or personality that is aware of itself as different from other things and calls itself "I." **2.** Egotism; conceit.

e·go·cen·tric |ē′gō sĕn′trĭk| *or* |ĕg′ō-| *adj.* Concerned too much with oneself; selfish; self-centered.

e·go·ism |ē′gō ĭz′əm| *or* |ĕg′ō-| *n.* **1.** The condition or quality of thinking or acting with only oneself and one's own interests in mind; preoccupation with one's own welfare and advancement. **2.** Conceit; egotism. —**e′go·ist** *n.*

e·go·tism |ē′gə tĭz′əm| *or* |ĕg′ə-| *n.* **1.** The tendency to talk about oneself excessively and boastfully. **2.** An inordinately large sense of self-importance; egoism. —**e′go·tist** *n.*

e·go·tis·ti·cal |ē′gə tĭs′tĭ kəl| *or* |ĕg′ə-| or **e·go·tis·tic** |ē′gə tĭs′tĭk| *or* |ĕg′ə-| *adj.* **1.** Thinking too highly of oneself; conceited. **2.** Selfish; self-centered. —**e′go·tis′ti·cal·ly** *adv.*

ego trip. *Slang.* **1.** An experience that boosts or gratifies the ego. **2.** An act of self-aggrandizement or self-indulgence.

e·go-trip |ē′gō trĭp′| *v.* **e·go-tripped, e·go-trip·ping.** *Slang.* To seek ego gratification, as by self-aggrandizement or self-indulgence.

e·gre·gious |ĭ grē′jəs| *or* |-jē əs| *adj.* Outstandingly bad; outrageous; flagrant: *an egregious error.* —**e·gre′gious·ly** *adv.* —**e·gre′gious·ness** *n.*

e·gress |ē′grĕs′| *n.* **1.** A path or means of going out; an exit. **2.** The right to go out: *He was denied egress.* **3.** The act of going out.

e·gret |ē′grĭt| *or* |ĕg′rĭt| *n.* **1.** A usually white wading bird with a long neck and a long, pointed bill. Many egrets have long, lacy, drooping plumes during the breeding season. **2.** A tuft of plumes from an egret's tail; an aigrette.

E·gypt |ē′jĭpt|. A country in northeastern Africa, bounded on the north by the Mediterranean Sea and on the east by the Red Sea. Population, 41,572,000. Capital, Cairo.

E·gyp·tian |ĭ jĭp′shən| *n.* **1.** A native or inhabitant of Egypt. **2.** The language of the ancient Egyptians. —*adj.* Of Egypt or the Egyptians.

eh |ā| *or* |ĕ| *interj.* **1.** A word used in asking for

e.g.

E.g. *is short for the Latin phrase* exemplī grātiā, *"for example" or "for the sake of an example":* exemplī, *possessive case of* exemplum, *"an example,"* + grātiā, *"for the sake," from* grātia, *"grace, sake."*

egg¹·²

Egg¹ *is from Old Norse* egg, *which is descended from prehistoric Germanic* ajja- *and ultimately from the Indo-European word for "bird." (In Indo-European terms, therefore, we have an answer to the old question "Which came first, the chicken or the egg?")* **Egg²** *also comes from an Old Norse word,* eggja, *"to goad."*

egg¹
Above: Eggs of a bird, the black skimmer
Below: Grasshopper eggs

eland
Although the **eland** *is an African animal, its name comes ultimately from Northern Europe. The Lithuanian word for "stag" was* elenis, *which was borrowed into German as* elen *and thence into Dutch and Afrikaans as* eland. *The South African Dutch (Afrikaners) applied the name to an African antelope, and it was borrowed into English as* **eland**.

ă pat/ā pay/â care/ä father/ĕ pet/ ē be/ĭ pit/ī pie/î fierce/ŏ pot/ ō go/ô paw, for/oi oil/ŏŏ book/ ōō boot/ou out/ŭ cut/û fur/ *th* the/th thin/hw which/zh vision/ ə ago, item, pencil, atom, circus

agreement, confirmation, etc.: *Didn't give you a chance, eh?* **2.** A word used as a question: *Eh? What was that?*

ei•der |ī′dər| *n.* A sea duck of northern regions, having very soft, downy feathers on its breast.

ei•der•down |ī′dər doun′| *n.* **1.** The soft, light down of the eider duck, used for stuffing quilts, pillows, and sleeping bags. **2.** A quilt stuffed with this down.

Eif•fel Tower |ī′fəl|. A tower, 984 feet high, in Paris, France, designed and originally erected for the Paris Exposition (1889).

eight |āt| *n.* A number, written 8 in Arabic numerals, that is equal to the sum of 7 + 1. It is the positive integer that immediately follows 7. ¶*These sound alike* **eight, ate.** —**eight** *adj. & pron.*

eight•een |ā′tēn′| *n.* A number, written 18 in Arabic numerals, equal to the sum of 17 + 1. It is the positive integer that immediately follows 17. —**eight′een′** *adj. & pron.*

eight•eenth |ā′tēnth′| *n.* **1.** In a set of items arranged to match the natural numbers in a one-to-one correspondence, the item that matches the number eighteen. **2.** One of eighteen equal parts of a unit, written $^1/_{18}$. —**eight′eenth′** *adj. & adv.*

eighth |ātth| *n.* **1.** In a set of items arranged to match the natural numbers in a one-to-one correspondence, the item that corresponds to the number eight. **2.** One of eight equal parts of a unit, written $^1/_8$. —**eighth** *adj. & adv.*

eighth note. A musical note that lasts half as long as a quarter note and twice as long as a sixteenth note.

eight•i•eth |ā′tē ĭth| *n.* **1.** In a set of items arranged to match the natural numbers in a one-to-one correspondence, the item that matches the number eighty. **2.** One of eighty equal parts of a unit, written $^1/_{80}$. —**eight′i•eth** *adj. & adv.*

eight•y |ā′tē| *n., pl.* **eight•ies.** A number, written 80 in Arabic numerals, that is equal to the product of 8 × 10. It is the tenth positive integer after 70. —**eight′y** *adj. & pron.*

Ein•stein |īn′stīn′|, **Albert.** 1879–1955. German-born American theoretical physicist; formulated the theory of relativity.

ein•stein•i•um |īn stī′nē əm| *n.* Symbol **Es** One of the elements, a metal first discovered in the debris of a hydrogen-bomb explosion and later produced by nuclear bombardment. It has 12 isotopes with half-lives ranging from 1.2 minutes to 270 days and mass numbers ranging from 245 to 256. Atomic number 99.

Ei•sen•how•er |ī′zən hou′ər|, **Dwight David.** 1890–1969. Thirty-fourth President of the United States (1953–61).

ei•ther |ē′*th*ər| *or* |ī′*th*ər| *pron.* One or the other of two: *Neither team had scored, and there seemed little likelihood that either would. They went a mile before either of them spoke.* —*adj.* **1.** One or the other; any one of two: *When two words are joined in a compound, the spelling of either word is seldom changed.* **2.** Each of the two: *Candles stood on either side of the centerpiece.* —*conj.* —Used correlatively with *or* to introduce alternatives: *A statement using an equals sign may be either true or false.* —*adv.* Likewise; also; any more than the other. Used as an intensive following negative statements: *He didn't want to be late for school, but he didn't want to meet those boys again either.*

e•jac•u•late |ĭ jăk′yə lāt′| *v.* **e•jac•u•lat•ed, e•jac•u•lat•ing. 1.** To produce a short, sudden spurt of (a fluid). **2.** To utter suddenly and passionately; exclaim: *"What on earth does this mean?" I ejaculated.*

e•jac•u•la•tion |ĭ jăk′yə lā′shən| *n.* **1.** The act or process of ejaculating. **2.** A sudden utterance; an exclamation.

e•ject |ĭ jĕkt′| *n.* **1.** To throw out forcefully; expel: *The rifle ejects empty shells after firing.* **2.** To compel to leave; evict: *The board of directors ejected Mr. Jones from the club.* **3.** To catapult oneself from a disabled aircraft: *The pilot ejected over water.* —**e•jec′tion** *n.*

ejection seat. A seat designed to eject clear of an aircraft and parachute to the ground in an emergency.

e•jec•tor |ĭ jĕk′tər| *n.* Something or someone that ejects, especially a part of a machine that ejects waste or spent material.

eke[1] |ēk| *v.* **eked, ek•ing. 1.** To make (money, a living, etc.) with great effort or strain: *eke out a livelihood.* **2.** To supplement with great effort; strain to fill out: *He eked out his income by working at night.*

eke[2] |ēk| *adv. Archaic.* Also.

EKG electrocardiogram; electrocardiograph.

el. elevation.

e•lab•o•rate |ĭ lăb′ər ĭt| *adj.* Planned or made with great attention to numerous parts or details; complicated but carefully wrought; intricate: *elaborate preparations for the festivities; a play with elaborate scenery and costumes.* —*v.* |ĭ lăb′ə rāt′| **e•lab•o•rat•ed, e•lab•o•rat•ing. 1.** To express oneself at greater length or in greater detail; provide further information: *After receiving only a brief answer to our question, we asked him to elaborate.* **2.** To work out with care and detail; develop thoroughly: *It may take a scientist years to elaborate a theory.* —**e•lab′o•rate•ly** *adv.* —**e•lab′o•rate•ness** *n.* —**e•lab′o•ra′tion** *n.*

é•lan |ā län′| *n.* **1.** Zest; dash. **2.** Style; flair: *She plays the piano with élan.*

e•land |ē′lənd| *n.* A large African antelope with twisted horns. [SEE PICTURE]

e•lapse |ĭ lăps′| *v.* **e•lapsed, e•laps•ing.** To pass; go by: *Months elapsed before I heard from my friend again.*

e•las•tic |ĭ lăs′tĭk| *adj.* **1. a.** Returning to a normal shape or arrangement after being stretched, compressed, or otherwise deformed. **b.** Occurring without loss of momentum: *an elastic collision.* **2.** Capable of adapting or being adapted to change or a variety of circumstances; flexible: *an elastic clause in the contract.* **3.** Quick to recover or revive: *an elastic spirit.* —*n.* **1.** A fabric or tape woven with strands of real or imitation rubber to make it stretch: *Garters and girdles are made of elastic. She ran a piece of elastic through the waistband.* **2.** A **rubber band.**

e•las•tic•i•ty |ĭ lă stĭs′ĭ tē| *or* |ē′lă-| *n.* **1.** The condition or property of being elastic. **2.** The degree to which something has this property.

e•late |ĭ lāt′| *v.* **e•lat•ed, e•lat•ing.** To raise the spirits of; make very happy or joyful: *The news of his victory elated his faithful supporters.* —**e•lat′ed**

adj.: an elated feeling.

e•la•tion |ĭ lā′shən| *n.* An intense feeling of happiness or joy: *the elation that a musician or an athlete feels after a good performance.*

E layer. A region of the ionosphere occurring between about 55 and 95 miles above the earth. It influences long-distance radio communications by reflecting certain radio waves strongly.

El•be |ĕl′bə| *or* |ĕlb|. A river rising in Czechoslovakia and flowing through Germany to the North Sea.

el•bow |ĕl′bō| *n.* **1. a.** The joint or bend between the forearm and the upper arm. **b.** The bone that projects at the outer part of this joint. **2.** Anything that bends sharply or has a sharp angle in it, especially a length of pipe. **3.** The part of a sleeve that covers the elbow: *a jacket with worn elbows.* —*v.* **1.** To push, jostle, or shove with or as if with the elbows. **2.** To make (one's way) by pushing, jostling, or shoving: *He elbowed his way through the crowd.*

Idiom. **rub elbows with. 1.** To mingle socially with (wealthy or prominent people). **2.** To come in contact with: *Peasants in native garb rub elbows in the streets of Cairo with office workers in business suits.*

elbow grease. *Informal.* Strenuous physical effort: *Polishing a car requires elbow grease.*

el•bow•room |ĕl′bō ro͞om′| *or* |-ro͝om′| *n.* Room to move around or function in; ample space: *Many people living in the city don't feel that they have enough elbowroom.*

eld•er¹ |ĕl′dər| *adj.* A comparative of **old,** used only of persons who are relatives: *her elder sister.* —*n.* **1.** An older person: *Relationships between boys and their well-meaning elders have changed very little with the passing of time.* **2.** An older, influential man of a tribe, community, etc.: *The administration of justice lay mostly in the hands of the local elders.* **3.** One of the governing officers of certain churches. [SEE NOTE]

el•der² |ĕl′dər| *n.* A shrub with clusters of small white flowers and blackish or red berries. [SEE NOTE]

el•der•ber•ry |ĕl′dər bĕr′ē| *n., pl.* **-ber•ries. 1.** The small, round fruit of an elder, sometimes used to make wine or preserves. **2.** The elder (shrub). [SEE PICTURE]

eld•er•ly |ĕl′dər lē| *adj.* Approaching old age: *an elderly gentleman.* —**eld′er•li•ness** *n.*

eld•est |ĕl′dĭst| *adj.* A superlative of **old,** used only of persons who are relatives: *the king's eldest son.*

El Do•ra•do |ĕl′ də rä′dō|. **1.** A legendary city of great wealth in South America, eagerly sought after by early explorers. **2.** Any place of fabulous wealth.

e•lect |ĭ lĕkt′| *v.* **1.** To choose by vote for an office: *elect a senator.* **2.** To choose or make a choice; decide: *elect an art course. I elected to go.* —*adj.* Elected but not yet installed in office: *the governor-elect.*

e•lec•tion |ĭ lĕk′shən| *n.* **1.** The act or process of choosing by vote among candidates to fill an office or position: *the election of representatives; the Presidential election of 1972.* **2.** The fact of being so chosen: *His election to Congress pleased all his supporters.*

e•lec•tion•eer |ĭ lĕk′shə nîr′| *v.* To work actively to gain votes for a particular candidate or party.

e•lec•tive |ĭ lĕk′tĭv| *adj.* **1.** Filled or obtained by election: *an elective office.* **2.** Chosen by election: *an elective official.* **3.** Capable of being chosen; optional: *Art is an elective course in my school.* —*n.* An optional course in school.

e•lec•tor |ĭ lĕk′tər| *n.* **1.** A qualified voter. **2.** A member of the electoral College of the United States. **3. Elector.** One of the German princes in the Holy Roman Empire with the right to elect the emperor.

e•lec•tor•al |ĭ lĕk′tər əl| *adj.* **1.** Of or composed of electors, especially the members of the Electoral College: *The President swept 41 states with an electoral vote of 457.* **2.** Of or pertaining to election: *electoral reforms.*

Electoral College. A group of persons, called electors, chosen by the states and the District of Columbia to elect the President and Vice President of the United States. The number of electors allotted to each state is based on population.

e•lec•tor•ate |ĭ lĕk′tər ĭt| *n.* All those persons qualified to vote in an election.

e•lec•tric |ĭ lĕk′trĭk| or **e•lec•tri•cal** |ĭ lĕk′trĭ kəl| *adj.* **1. a.** Of, derived from, producing, or produced by electricity. **b.** Powered or operated by electricity. **2.** Charged with emotion; exciting; thrilling: *the electric feeling of watching the clock tick off the last seconds of the game.* —*n.* Something that is powered by electricity, especially an automobile or locomotive. —**e•lec′tri•cal•ly** *adv.* [SEE NOTE]

electrical engineering. Engineering that deals with the practical use of electricity and its effects. —**electrical engineer.**

electric arc. An arc (bright streak or spark).

electric cell. A device in which chemical energy is changed into electrical energy, usually consisting of electrodes of dissimilar substances immersed in an electrolyte. A cell whose action cannot easily be reversed is called a **primary cell,** while one whose action can be reversed is called a **secondary cell.**

electric chair. 1. A chair used to restrain and electrocute a person sentenced to death. **2.** Execution by electrocution.

electric charge. 1. The basic property of matter from which electric phenomena result; charge. **2.** The measure of this property.

electric current. A flow of particles of matter most of which have an electric charge of the same kind; current.

electric eel. An eellike South American freshwater fish that can produce an electric discharge capable of giving a strong shock.

electric eye. A **photoelectric cell.**

electric field. A region of space, such as that around an object that has collected an electric charge, in which a unit of electric charge is acted on by a measurable force at any point.

electric guitar. A guitar whose notes are turned into electrical signals by pickups placed under the strings, the signals being amplified and sent to a loudspeaker.

e•lec•tri•cian |ĭ lĕk trĭsh′ən| *or* |ē′lĕk-| *n.* A person whose work is installing, maintaining, repairing, or operating electric equipment. [SEE PICTURE]

elder¹⁻²

Elder¹ *and* **eldest** *were* eldra *and* eldesta *in Old English. They are the original regular comparative and superlative of Old English* eald *or* ald, *"old." The forms* **older** *and* **oldest,** *which are regular in terms of modern English, are actually later.* **Elder²** *was* ellen *in Old English. The elder tree is not related to the alder tree, but the two names are probably related, both coming from a root* el-, *meaning "red-brown."*

elderberry

electric/electrical

Sometimes **electric** *is used to refer to physical effects of electricity* (electric discharge, electric power), *while* **electrical** *refers to someone or something having to do with electricity* (electrical engineer, electrical repairs). *But this is not a clear, positive rule.*

electrician

electro-
Since prehistoric times, it has been noticed that amber, when rubbed, attracts small bits of straw, wood, etc. This electromagnetic effect was one of the first to be scientifically studied, in the early seventeenth century. It is for this reason that the words **electric, electricity,** *etc., were coined from* ēlektron, *the Greek word for "amber."*

electromagnet
Electromagnet lifting scrap iron

ă pat/ā pay/â care/ä father/ĕ pet/ē be/ĭ pit/ī pie/î fierce/ŏ pot/ō go/ô paw, for/oi oil/ŏŏ book/ōō boot/ou out/ŭ cut/û fur/*th* the/th thin/hw which/zh vision/ə ago, item, pencil, atom, circus

e•lec•tric•i•ty |ĭ lĕk **trĭs′**ĭ tē| *or* |ē′lĕk-| *n.* **1.** The physical phenomena that arise from the existence of electric charges and interactions that involve them. **2.** The scientific study of these phenomena. **3.** Power that is transmitted by electrical means; electric power. **4.** Emotional excitement; thrill: *Many television viewers felt the electricity of the moment the astronaut set foot on the moon's surface.*

electric potential. The work needed per unit of charge to move an electrically charged body from one point in an electric field to another.

electric power. Power that is transmitted in the form of electrically charged particles, mainly electrons, flowing through wires or other conductors.

e•lec•tri•fy |ĭ **lĕk′**trə fī′| *v.* **e•lec•tri•fied, e•lec•tri•fy•ing, e•lec•tri•fies. 1.** To give an electric charge to. **2. a.** To wire or equip (a building, room, etc.) for the use of electric power. **b.** To supply with electric power. **3.** To thrill, startle, or shock: *The speaker electrified the audience by describing what he had seen in the jungles of South America.* —**e•lec′tri•fi•ca′tion** *n.*

electro–. A word element meaning "electric, electrically, or electricity": **electrocardiograph.** [SEE NOTE]

e•lec•tro•car•di•o•gram |ĭ lĕk′trō **kär′**dē ə-grăm′| *n.* The curve traced by an electrocardiograph, used in studying the heart and diagnosing its diseases.

e•lec•tro•car•di•o•graph |ĭ lĕk′trō **kär′**dē-ə grăf′| *or* |-grăf′| *n.* An instrument that records the electrical activity of the heart, usually in the form of a curve traced on a chart.

e•lec•tro•chem•i•cal |ĭ lĕk′trō **kĕm′**ĭ kəl| *adj.* **1.** Of or involved in electrochemistry: *electrochemical research.* **2.** Involving both electricity and chemistry: *an electrochemical effect.* —**e•lec′tro•chem′i•cal•ly** *adv.*

e•lec•tro•chem•is•try |ĭ lĕk′trō **kĕm′**ĭ strē| *n.* The scientific study of phenomena that involve electricity and chemistry.

e•lec•tro•cute |ĭ **lĕk′**trə kyōōt′| *v.* **e•lec•tro•cut•ed, e•lec•tro•cut•ing.** To kill with electricity, especially to execute by sending an electric current through the body of.

e•lec•tro•cu•tion |ĭ lĕk′trə **kyōō′**shən| *n.* Death caused by an electric current, especially execution by the electric chair.

e•lec•trode |ĭ **lĕk′**trōd′| *n.* A conductor that transfers electric charges into or out of another conducting medium or that influences the flow of current in another conducting medium.

e•lec•tro•dy•nam•ics |ĭ lĕk′trō dī **năm′**ĭks| *n.* *(used with a singular verb).* The scientific study of the relationships between electric, magnetic, and mechanical phenomena.

e•lec•tro•en•ceph•a•lo•gram |ĭ lĕk′trō ĕn-**sĕf′**ə lə grăm′| *n.* The curve traced by an electroencephalograph, used in studying the brain and diagnosing its diseases.

e•lec•tro•en•ceph•a•lo•graph |ĭ lĕk′trō ĕn-**sĕf′**ə lə grăf′| *or* |-grăf′| *n.* An instrument that records the electrical activity of the brain, usually in the form of a curve on a graph.

e•lec•trol•y•sis |ĭ lĕk **trŏl′**ĭ sĭs| *or* |ē′lĕk-| *n.* **1.** A chemical change, especially decomposition, produced in an electrolyte by an electric current. **2.** Destruction of living tissue, such as the roots of hairs, by an electric current.

e•lec•tro•lyte |ĭ **lĕk′**trə līt′| *n.* **1.** A substance that when dissolved or melted becomes electrically conductive by breaking apart into ions. **2.** A solution that conducts electricity, especially a solution used in an electric cell or battery.

e•lec•tro•lyt•ic |ĭ lĕk′trə **lĭt′**ĭk| *adj.* **1.** Of or caused by electrolysis. **2.** Of or using an electrolyte. —**e•lec′tro•lyt′i•cal•ly** *adv.*

e•lec•tro•lyze |ĭ **lĕk′**trə līz′| *v.* **e•lec•tro•lyzed, e•lec•tro•lyz•ing.** To decompose by electrolysis.

e•lec•tro•mag•net |ĭ lĕk′trō **măg′**nĭt| *n.* A device consisting essentially of a soft-iron core with a coil of insulated wire wound onto it. When an electric current passes through the coil, the core of the coil becomes a magnet. [SEE PICTURE]

e•lec•tro•mag•net•ic |ĭ lĕk′trō măg **nĕt′**ĭk| *adj.* Of or involving electromagnetism.

electromagnetic wave. A wave that travels through space as a system of electric and magnetic fields that vary periodically with position and time. Waves of this kind include radio waves, light waves, x-rays, and gamma rays.

e•lec•tro•mag•net•ism |ĭ lĕk′trō **măg′**nĭ tĭz′-əm| *n.* **1.** Magnetism that arises from the motion of an electric charge. **2.** The scientific study of electricity and magnetism and the relationships between them.

e•lec•trom•e•ter |ĭ lĕk **trŏm′**ĭ tər| *or* |ē′lĕk-| *n.* Any one of several instruments used to detect and measure electric charges and differences of electric potential.

e•lec•tro•mo•tive |ĭ lĕk′trō **mō′**tĭv| *adj.* Of or tending to produce an electric current.

electromotive force. 1. A force that tends to produce an electric current. **2.** The energy per unit of charge that is converted into electrical form by a battery, generator, or any other similar device. **3.** A difference of electric potential; voltage.

e•lec•tron |ĭ **lĕk′**trŏn′| *n.* A subatomic particle commonly found as one of a group surrounding the nucleus of an atom. It has a unit negative electric charge of about 1.602×10^{-19} coulomb and a mass, when at rest, of 9.1066×10^{-28} gram.

electron gun. A source of electrons and a series of electrodes that forms the electrons into a high-speed beam, as in a cathode-ray tube.

e•lec•tron•ic |ĭ lĕk **trŏn′**ĭk| *or* |ē′lĕk-| *adj.* **1.** Of or involving electrons. **2.** Of, based on, or operated by a controlled flow of electrons or other carriers of electric charge, as in an electron tube or semiconductor. **3.** Of or involved in electronics: *an electronic technician.* —**e•lec•tron′i•cal•ly** *adv.*

electronic music. Music produced entirely or in part by manipulating natural or artificial sounds with tape recorders or other electronic devices.

e•lec•tron•ics |ĭ lĕk **trŏn′**ĭks| *or* |ē′lĕk-| *n.* **1.** *(used with a singular verb).* **a.** The science and technology concerned with the development and practical application of electronic devices and systems: *Electronics has made space flight possible.* **b.** The commercial industry of electronic devices and systems. **2.** *(used with a plural verb).* The part of something that is composed mainly of electronic devices: *The electronics of the phonograph were faulty.* —**modifier:** *an electronics manufacturing plant; an electronics engineer.*

electron microscope. An instrument that is similar in principle to an ordinary microscope but in which a beam of electrons focused by magnetic fields is used instead of a beam of light focused by lenses. An electron microscope can make visible objects that are too small to be seen with an ordinary microscope.

electron tube. A sealed, enclosed space, containing either a vacuum or a small amount of gas, in which electrons act as the main carriers of current between at least two electrodes, often with one or more other electrodes controlling the electron flow.

electron volt. A unit of energy equal to the energy gained by an electron that is accelerated by a potential difference of one volt. An electron volt equals about 1.602×10^{-19} joule.

e•lec•tro•plate |ĭ **lĕk'**trə plāt'| *v.* **e•lec•tro•plat•ed, e•lec•tro•plat•ing.** To cover or coat with a thin layer of metal by means of an electrolytic process.

e•lec•tro•scope |ĭ **lĕk'**trə skōp'| *n.* An instrument used to detect the presence of electric charges and to determine whether they are positive or negative.

e•lec•tro•stat•ic |ĭ lĕk'trō **stăt'**ĭk| *adj.* **1.** Of, produced by, or caused by stationary electric charges. **2.** Of or involving electrostatics.

electrostatic generator. Any one of several machines that collect large amounts of static electric charge, creating large differences of electric potential.

e•lec•tro•stat•ics |ĭ lĕk'trō **stăt'**ĭks| *n.* *(used with a singular verb).* The scientific study of the phenomena associated with static electric charges.

e•lec•tro•ther•a•py |ĭ lĕk'trō **thĕr'**ə pē| *n.* Any form of medical treatment in which electric currents, radio waves, etc., are applied to body tissues.

e•lec•tro•type |ĭ **lĕk'**trə tīp'| *n.* **1.** A duplicate metal plate used in printing, made by electroplating a mold of the original plate. **2.** The process of making such a duplicate plate. —*v.* **e•lec•tro•typed, e•lec•tro•typ•ing.** To make an electrotype of.

el•e•gance |**ĕl'**ĭ gəns| *n.* **1.** Refinement and grace in appearance or manner: *He noticed her unaffected elegance the moment she entered the ballroom.* **2.** Tasteful richness in form, decoration, or presentation: *signs of past elegance in the doorways of the delapidated building.* **3.** Something that is a luxury: *At that time roast beef was an elegance we could not afford.*

el•e•gant |**ĕl'**ĭ gənt| *adj.* **1.** Marked by elegance; refined or tastefully lavish: *elegant society; an elegant restaurant.* **2.** Excellent; splendid: *an elegant idea; a hardy, elegant little tree.* —**el'e•gant•ly** *adv.*

el•e•gy |**ĕl'**ə jē| *n., pl.* **el•e•gies.** A poem or song that expresses sorrow, especially one to lament a death.

el•e•ment |**ĕl'**ə mənt| *n.* **1.** A fundamental or essential part of a whole; a necessary feature: *the elements of a sentence; the basic elements of music.* **2.** A trace or suggestion: *A distinct element of mystery pervades the whole story.* **3.** Any substance composed of atoms that all have the same number of protons in their nuclei. An element is a substance that cannot be broken down by chemical means. **4.** In mathematics, any one of the members of a set. **5. a.** Any line on the surface of a cone that passes through its vertex. **b.** Any of the straight lines contained in the curved surface of a cylinder. **6. elements.** The force or forces of weather, as cold, wind, rain, etc.: *He braved the elements to walk ten miles to the schoolhouse.* **7.** An environment to which someone or something is suited or adapted: *The sea was as much his element as the land.* **8. elements.** The bread and wine of the Eucharist. [SEE NOTE]

el•e•men•tal |ĕl'ə **mĕn'**tl| *adj.* **1.** Not complex or refined; basic; primitive; earthy: *The man felt as if he had become once more an elemental being, passionate and wild, defying the heavens.* **2.** Of or resembling a force of nature in power or effect: *the elemental fury of the hurricane.*

el•e•men•ta•ry |ĕl'ə **mĕn'**tə rē| *or* |-trē| *adj.* Of, involving, or introducing the fundamental or simplest aspects of a subject: *an elementary textbook; elementary education.*

elementary particle. A subatomic particle that is thought not to be divisible into smaller particles.

elementary school. A school attended for the first six to eight years of a child's formal classroom instruction.

el•e•phant |**ĕl'**ə fənt| *n.* A very large Asian or African animal with a long, flexible trunk and long tusks. [SEE PICTURE]

el•e•phan•ti•a•sis |ĕl'ə fən **tī'**ə sĭs| *or* |-făn-| *n.* A disease in which parts of the body, especially the lower parts, become enlarged, often to extreme proportions, as a result of the blockage of lymph ducts by parasitic worms.

el•e•vate |**ĕl'**ə vāt'| *v.* **el•e•vat•ed, el•e•vat•ing.** **1.** To raise to a higher place or position; lift up: *A nurse elevated the head of the bed so that the patient could sit up to read.* **2.** To promote to a higher rank: *The queen elevated him to the peerage.* **3.** To bring to a higher moral, cultural, or intellectual level: *He elevated the simple folk song to heights of great beauty.*

el•e•vat•ed |**ĕl'**ə vā'tĭd| *adj.* **1.** Raised or placed above a given level: *the elevated throne of the Pharaoh.* **2.** Exalted; lofty: *elevated praise; elevated thought.* —*n. Informal.* A train that operates on a track raised high enough above the ground so that vehicles and pedestrians can pass beneath.

el•e•va•tion |ĕl'ə **vā'**shən| *n.* **1.** An elevated place or position: *a slight elevation called the pitcher's mound.* **2.** The height to which something is elevated: *Vapors move rapidly from the earth's surface to a considerable elevation in the atmosphere.* **3.** A height, especially as measured from some special reference, such as sea level: *The elevation of that peak is 5,227 feet.* **4.** Loftiness, grandeur, or dignity, as of thought. **5.** A scale drawing of the side, front, or rear of a structure.

el•e•va•tor |**ĕl'**ə vā'tər| *n.* **1.** A platform or enclosure raised or lowered in a vertical shaft to transport freight or people. **2.** A granary

element

The idea that all things are made up of combinations of simple substances is very old. The ancient Greeks and Romans, and the Europeans of the Middle Ages, identified earth, air, fire, and water as these substances. Modern science has identified over one hundred substances, such as iron, carbon, oxygen, etc., from which the entire universe appears to be made. They do not appear, however, to be simple, nor is there reason to believe that all of them are known.

elephant

Elephants are the largest land animals now in existence. The African elephant *(above)* is somewhat larger than the Asian elephant and has large, fanlike ears.

elk
American elk, or wapiti

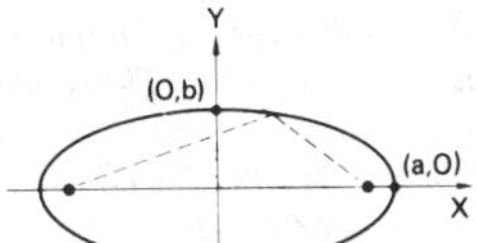

ellipse
The graph of the equation
$\frac{x^2}{a^2} + \frac{y^2}{b^2} = 1$ is an **ellipse,**
where *a* and *b* are constants that are not equal and neither of them is zero.

elm
American elm, with drawing of leaf (above)

ă pat/ā pay/â care/ä father/ĕ pet/ ē be/ĭ pit/ī pie/î fierce/ŏ pot/ ō go/ô paw, for/oi oil/ŏŏ book/ ōō boot/ou out/ŭ cut/û fur/ *th* the/th thin/hw which/zh vision/ ə ago, item, pencil, atom, circus

equipped for hoisting and discharging grain. **3.** A movable airfoil, usually attached to a horizontal part of the tail assembly of an aircraft, used to turn the nose of the craft upward or downward. **—modifier:** *an elevator operator; an elevator ride; an elevator door.*

e•lev•en |ĭ **lĕv'**ən| *n.* A number, written 11 in Arabic numerals, that is equal to the sum of 10 + 1. It is the positive integer that immediately follows 10. **—e•lev'en** *adj. & pron.*

e•lev•enth |ĭ **lĕv'**ənth| *n.* **1.** In a set of items arranged to match the natural numbers in a one-to-one correspondence, the item that matches the number eleven. **2.** One of eleven equal parts of a unit, written $^1/_{11}$. **—e•lev'enth** *adj. & adv.*

elf |ĕlf| *n., pl.* **elves** |ĕlvz|. In Germanic folklore, a tiny, magic-wielding creature, often mischievous but rarely evil.

elf•in |**ĕl'**fĭn| *adj.* **1.** Of an elf or elves: *the elfin king.* **2.** Suggestive of an elf or elves; sprightly, prankish, or mischievous: *an elfin smile.*

elf•ish |**ĕl'**fĭsh| *adj.* Of or resembling an elf or elves: *elfish tricks; an elfish dance.* **—elf'ish•ly** *adv.* **—elf'ish•ness** *n.*

e•lic•it |ĭ **lĭs'**ĭt| *v.* To bring out; evoke: *He elicited the truth from the witness.* ¶*These sound alike* **elicit, illicit.**

el•i•gi•ble |**ĕl'**ĭ jə bəl| *adj.* **1.** Qualified for a group, position, privilege, etc.: *eligible voters; an eligible player for a varsity sport.* **2.** Suited to and desirable, especially for marriage: *Their daughter was of marriageable age and ready to be introduced to eligible men.* **—el'i•gi•bil'i•ty** *n.*

E•li•jah |ĭ **lī'**jə|. In the Bible, a Hebrew prophet and hero who performed many miracles and denounced idol worshipers.

e•lim•i•nate |ĭ **lĭm'**ə nāt'| *v.* **e•lim•i•nat•ed, e•lim•i•nat•ing. 1.** To get rid of; remove: *efforts to eliminate poverty.* **2.** To leave out or omit from consideration; reject: *List the separate events in the story and eliminate those not closely related to the point of the story.* **3.** To remove or disqualify, as by defeat in a contest: *Her misspelling of that word eliminated her from the contest.* **4.** To rid the body of (waste products).

e•lim•i•na•tion |ĭ lĭm'ə **nā'**shən| *n.* **1.** The act or process of eliminating: *the elimination of waste bodily products. The elimination of language barriers presents a challenge.* **2.** An example of eliminating: *He was distressed by his elimination from the contest.*

E•li•sha |ĭ **lī'**shə|. In the Bible, a Hebrew prophet who was anointed by Elijah and succeeded him as prophet to Israel.

e•lite, also **é•lite** |ĭ **lēt'**| *or* |ā **lēt'**| *n.* **1.** *(used with a plural verb).* The best or superior members of a society or group: *an educational elite. They were the elite of the sports world.* **2.** A size of type on a typewriter equal to ten points. **—modifier:** *the emperor's elite personal troops; a line of elite type.*

e•lix•ir |ĭ **lĭk'**sər| *n.* **1.** A sweetened and flavored solution of alcohol and water containing one or more medicinal substances. **2.** In medieval alchemy, a much sought-after preparation that supposedly had the power to change base metals into gold, cure all human disorders, and maintain life indefinitely.

E•liz•a•beth I |ĭ **lĭz'**ə bəth|. 1533–1603. Queen of England and Ireland (1558–1603).

Elizabeth II. Born 1926. Queen of Great Britain and Northern Ireland (since 1952).

E•liz•a•be•than |ĭ lĭz'ə **bē'**thən| *or* |**-bĕth'**ən| *adj.* Of, characteristic, or representative of the reign of Elizabeth I: *Elizabethan styles; Elizabethan drama.* **—n.** An Englishman living during the reign of Elizabeth I.

elk |ĕlk| *n., pl.* **elks** or **elk. 1.** A large North American deer, the wapiti. **2.** The European moose. [SEE PICTURE]

ell¹ |ĕl| *n.* A wing of a building at right angles to the main structure.

ell² |ĕl| *n.* An old English measure of length, used mainly in measuring cloth.

el•lipse |ĭ **lĭps'**| *n.* A closed plane curve composed of all the points that have the sum of their distances from two fixed points equal to a constant. [SEE PICTURE]

el•lip•sis |ĭ **lĭp'**sĭs| *n., pl.* **el•lip•ses** |ĭ **lĭp'**sēz'|. **1.** In grammar, the omission of a word or phrase needed to make the sentence syntactically complete but not necessary for understanding it; for example, the sentence *Stop laughing,* meaning *You stop laughing,* shows ellipsis. **2.** A mark or series of marks (. . .) used in writing or printing to indicate an omission of a word or words.

el•lip•tic |ĭ **lĭp'**tĭk| or **el•lip•ti•cal** |ĭ **lĭp'**tĭ kəl| *adj.* **1.** Of, shaped like, or related to an ellipse. **2.** In grammar, containing an ellipsis; having a word or words omitted: *an elliptic clause.* **—el•lip'ti•cal•ly** *adv.*

elm |ĕlm| *n.* **1.** A tall shade tree with arching or curving branches. **2.** The hard, strong wood of such a tree. [SEE PICTURE]

el•o•cu•tion |ĕl'ə **kyōō'**shən| *n.* The art or style of public speaking that emphasizes gestures and vocal delivery. **—modifier:** *an elocution class.*

e•lon•gate |ĭ **lông'**gāt'| *or* |ĭ **lŏng'**-| *or* |ē'lông-gāt'| *or* |ē'lŏng-| *v.* **e•lon•gat•ed, e•lon•gat•ing.** To make or become longer; lengthen: *The artist elongated the face and figure in his paintings. The tip of the stem elongates slowly at first.* **—e•lon'gat'ed** *adj.*: *the elongated orbits of comets; elongated crystals.*

e•lon•ga•tion |ĭ lông **gā'**shən| *or* |ĭ lŏng-| *or* |ē'lông-| *or* |ē'lŏng-| *n.* **1.** The act of elongating or the condition of being elongated. **2.** Something that elongates or lengthens; an extension: *He often felt that his pen was an elongation of his hand.*

e•lope |ĭ **lōp'**| *v.* **e•loped, e•lop•ing.** To go or run away with a lover, especially with the intention of getting married without the consent of parents: *Robert and Elizabeth eloped and went to Italy.* **—e•lope'ment** *n.*

el•o•quence |**ĕl'**ə kwəns| *n.* **1.** Fluent, persuasive, and expressive discourse: *His masterly speech rolled on in mighty surges of eloquence.* **2.** The ability to express an intended meaning or to persuade: *He was carried away by the crowd's enthusiasm and his own eloquence.*

el•o•quent |**ĕl'**ə kwənt| *adj.* **1.** Fluent, persuasive, and expressive in discourse: *eloquent language; an eloquent appeal for human rights.* **2.** Clearly and movingly expressive of some emotion, condition, etc.: *an eloquent smile.* **—el'o•quent•ly** *adv.*

El Sal•va•dor |ĕl săl'və dôr'|. A country on the Pacific coast of Central America. Population, 3,980,000. Capital, San Salvador.

else |ĕls| *adj.* **1.** Other; different: *somebody else.* **2.** In addition; more: *Would you like anything else?* —*adv.* **1.** Differently: *How else could it have been done?* **2.** Otherwise: *Be careful, else you will make a mistake. Run, or else you will be caught in the rain.*

else•where |ĕls'hwâr'| *or* |-wâr'| *adv.* Somewhere or anywhere else: *He decided to go elsewhere.*

e•lu•ci•date |ĭ lo͞o'sĭ dāt'| *v.* **e•lu•ci•dat•ed, e•lu•ci•dat•ing.** To make clear or plain; clarify: *elucidate the meaning of the phrase. Study the text and elucidate.* —**e•lu'ci•da'tion** *n.*

e•lude |ĭ lo͞od'| *v.* **e•lud•ed, e•lud•ing. 1.** To avoid or escape, as by artfulness, cunning, or daring; evade: *He eluded the attacks of the beast. The fox eludes as the dogs pursue.* **2.** To escape understanding or detection by; baffle: *Minute things elude the naked eye.*

e•lu•sion |ĭ lo͞o'zhən| *n.* The act or an example of eluding; escape or evasion: *the fox's elusion of the hounds.* ¶*These sound alike* **elusion, illusion.**

e•lu•sive |ĭ lo͞o'sĭv| *adj.* Tending to elude: *elusive little butterflies.* ¶*These sound alike* **elusive, illusive.**

el•ver |ĕl'vər| *n.* A young eel.

elves |ĕlvz| *n.* Plural of **elf.**

em–. See **en–.**

e•ma•ci•ate |ĭ mā'shē āt'| *v.* **e•ma•ci•at•ed, e•ma•ci•at•ing.** To make (a person or animal) thin and wasted, as by starvation or illness. —**e•ma'ci•at'ed** *adj.: an emaciated child.* —**e•ma'ci•a'tion** *n.*

em•a•nate |ĕm'ə nāt'| *v.* **em•a•nat•ed, em•a•nat•ing.** To come or send forth, as from a source or origin; issue or emit: *Sweet sounds emanated from a hidden cove. Radioactive substances emanate gamma rays.*

em•a•na•tion |ĕm'ə nā'shən| *n.* **1.** An act or an example of emanating: *the emanation of heat from the fire.* **2.** Something that emanates from a source: *the heavy, sweet emanations of magnolias.*

e•man•ci•pate |ĭ măn'sə pāt'| *v.* **e•man•ci•pat•ed, e•man•ci•pat•ing.** To free from bondage, oppression, or restraint; liberate: *emancipate serfs.*

e•man•ci•pa•tion |ĭ măn'sə pā'shən| *n.* **1.** The act of emancipating or the condition of being emancipated: *the emancipation of slaves.* **2.** Often **Emancipation.** In the United States, the formal abolition of slavery.

Emancipation Proclamation. A proclamation issued during the Civil War by President Abraham Lincoln, effective January 1, 1863, freeing slaves in those areas still fighting against the Union.

e•man•ci•pa•tor |ĭ măn'sə pā'tər| *n.* Someone or something that emancipates.

e•mas•cu•late |ĭ măs'kyə lāt'| *v.* **e•mas•cu•lat•ed, e•mas•cu•lat•ing. 1.** To castrate (a male animal). **2.** To deprive of strength; make weak: *emasculate a language; emasculate a law.* —**e•mas'cu•la'tion** *n.*

em•balm |ĕm bäm'| *v.* To treat (a corpse) with substances that prevent or retard decay. —**em•balm'er** *n.*

em•bank•ment |ĕm băngk'mənt| *n.* A mound of earth or stone built up to hold back water or to support a roadway.

em•bar•go |ĕm bär'gō| *n., pl.* **em•bar•goes. 1.** An order by a government prohibiting merchant ships from entering or leaving its ports: *New England ports were especially hard hit by the embargo imposed by Congress.* **2.** A suspension by a government of foreign trade or of foreign trade in a particular commodity: *the U.S. embargo on Cuban exports; an embargo on sugar.* —*v.* **em•bar•goed, em•bar•go•ing, em•bar•goes.** To place an embargo upon.

em•bark |ĕm bärk'| *v.* **1.** To board or cause to board a vessel, especially at the start of a journey: *He embarked for the 10-mile trip by water. He embarked her from Southampton.* **2.** To set out on a venture; commence: *They embarked on a nationwide campaign to educate the people. He embarked upon the composition of a large musical work.* —**em'bar•ka'tion** |ĕm'bär kā'shən| *n.*

em•bar•rass |ĕm băr'əs| *v.* **1.** To feel or cause to feel self-conscious or ill at ease; disconcert: *She embarrasses easily. They embarrassed him by poking fun at his red, curly hair.* **2. a.** To hamper with financial difficulties: *The king's servants were much embarrassed for lack of the wages due them.* **b.** To beset with difficulties; impede: *Pride, envy, greed, and selfishness embarrass the human race.* —**em•bar'rassed** *adj.: low, embarrassed voices.* —**em•bar'rass•ing** *adj.: an embarrassing spelling mistake; an embarrassing situation.*

em•bar•rass•ment |ĕm băr'əs mənt| *n.* **1.** The condition of being embarrassed: *constant financial embarrassment. Her face turned red with embarrassment.* **2.** Something that embarrasses: *Coughing loudly at a concert can be a great embarrassment.*

em•bas•sy |ĕm'bə sē| *n., pl.* **em•bas•sies. 1.** The position, function, or assignment of an ambassador. **2.** A mission to a foreign government headed by an ambassador. **3.** An ambassador and his staff. **4.** The official headquarters of an ambassador and his staff.

em•bat•tled |ĕm băt'ld| *adj.* In readiness for battle or in a state of war: *They had to get supplies across the submarine-infested Atlantic to embattled Britain and Soviet Russia.*

em•bed |ĕm bĕd'| *v.* **em•bed•ded, em•bed•ding. 1.** To fix or become fixed firmly in a surrounding mass: *They embedded the pilings deep into the subsoil. The sea urchin spines broke off and embedded in the diver's skin.* **2.** To fix in the memory: *He has embedded his name in the minds of millions of people.* —**em•bed'ded** *adj.: an embedded splinter.*

em•bel•lish |ĕm bĕl'ĭsh| *v.* **1.** To ornament or adorn in order to make more beautiful: *She embellished the wall with pictures.* **2.** To add fanciful or fictitious details to: *embellish the truth.* —**em•bel'lish•ment** *n.* [SEE NOTE]

em•ber |ĕm'bər| *n.* **1.** A piece of live coal or wood, as in a dying fire. **2. embers.** The smoldering coal or ash of a dying fire: *Embers still glowed in the fireplace.*

em•bez•zle |ĕm bĕz'əl| *v.* **em•bez•zled, em•bez•zling.** To take (money or property) for one's own use in violation of a trust: *He embezzled the*

embellish

Embellish, *which comes from the French verb* embelliss-, embellir, *"to make (something) beautiful," breaks up neatly into three syllables that are, respectively, prefix, root, and ending. The prefix* em- *is a variant of the* en- *in* endanger, enslave, ensure; *it is used to form verbs meaning "to cause (something) to become (such)." The root* bel- *means "beautiful," as in* **belle.** *The ending* -ish, *which has no special meaning, occurs with a class of verbs borrowed from French; other examples are* **abolish, finish, vanish.**

embroidery

emcee

Emcee *is an unusual kind of word, formed from the* sounds *of the letters of an abbreviation (*m.c. *stands for* master of ceremonies*).*

emerge/emergency

Emerge *is from Latin* ēmergere, *"to un-sink, to rise to the surface, to come out":* ē-, *"out,"* + mergere, *"to sink." The word* **emergency** *first appeared in the seventeenth century; it originally meant "the rising of something out of water" but later came to mean "something that comes up unexpectedly, a sudden event, an urgent happening."*

ă pat/ā pay/â care/ä father/ĕ pet/ē be/ĭ pit/ī pie/î fierce/ŏ pot/ō go/ô paw, for/oi oil/o͝o book/o͞o boot/ou out/ŭ cut/û fur/*th* the/th thin/hw which/zh vision/ə ago, item, pencil, atom, circus

money from his firm. —**em•bez'zle•ment** *n.* —**em•bez'zler** *n.*

em•bit•ter |ĕm **bĭt'**ər| *v.* To cause bitter feelings, harsh resentments, and animosities in: *The Civil War embittered the American people.* —**em•bit'tered** *adj.: an embittered generation.*

em•bla•zon |ĕm **blā'**zən| *v.* **1.** To ornament richly, as with heraldic devices: *emblazon a tapestry with fleurs-de-lis.* **2.** To make brilliant with colors: *Fireworks emblazoned the night.*

em•blem |**ĕm'**bləm| *n.* An object or picture that comes to represent something else; a symbol: *The bald eagle is the national emblem of the United States.*

em•bod•i•ment |ĕm **bŏd'**ē mənt| *n.* Someone or something that embodies something else; a perfect example: *She was thought to be the embodiment of kindness.*

em•bod•y |ĕm **bŏd'**ē| *v.* **em•bod•ied, em•bod•y•ing, em•bod•ies. 1.** To represent in or as if in bodily form; personify: *The general embodied the spirit of revolution and freedom.* **2.** To make or include as part of a united whole: *Many modern western governments embody the ideas and teachings of ancient Greek philosophies.*

em•bo•li |**ĕm'**bə lī'| *n.* Plural of **embolus.**

em•bo•lism |**ĕm'**bə lĭz'əm| *n.* The obstruction of a blood vessel by an embolus.

em•bo•lus |**ĕm'**bə ləs| *n., pl.* **em•bo•li** |**ĕm'**bə-lī'|. An air bubble, blood clot, or other mass of material that blocks a blood vessel.

em•bon•point |äɴ bôɴ **pwăɴ'**| *n. French.* A well-fed appearance; plumpness.

em•bos•om |ĕm **bo͝oz'**əm| *or* |**-bo͞o'**zəm| *v.* **1.** To clasp to or hold as if in the bosom or close to the heart; cherish: *She embosomed the cause of freedom with great fervor.* **2.** To enclose protectively; surround or shelter: *A spacious valley was embosomed by lofty, snow-capped mountains.*

em•boss |ĕm **bôs'**| *or* |**-bŏs'**| *v.* **1.** To cause (a design) to stand out by raising it above the surrounding surface: *emboss a head on a coin.* **2.** To decorate with a raised design: *emboss leather.* —**em•bossed'** *adj.: an embossed design.*

em•bou•chure |äm'bo͞o **sho͝or'**| *n.* **1.** The mouthpiece of a musical wind instrument. **2.** The way in which the lips and tongue are applied to such a mouthpiece.

em•brace |ĕm **brās'**| *v.* **em•braced, em•brac•ing. 1.** To clasp or hold with the arms as a sign of affection: *embrace a child. They ran toward each other and embraced.* **2.** To encircle or surround: *Nerves embrace the body from head to toe. Shadows embraced the room.* **3.** To take up willingly; adopt wholeheartedly: *He left the farm and embraced the hectic life of the big city.* **4.** To include within its bounds; encompass: *a territory embracing the seacoast and several islands. His education embraced all the sciences.* —*n.* The act of embracing.

em•bra•sure |ĕm **brā'**zhər| *n.* **1.** An opening in a wall for a window or door. **2.** An opening for a gun in a wall or parapet.

em•broi•der |ĕm **broi'**dər| *v.* **1.** To work (a design) into cloth with a needle and thread: *embroider flowers on a handkerchief.* **2.** To decorate (cloth) by sewing on designs with thread: *embroider a sampler. She embroiders beautifully.* **3.** To add imaginary, made-up details to (a story) for added interest; exaggerate: *She embroidered her autobiography heavily.* —**em•broi'dered** *adj.: an embroidered handkerchief.*

em•broi•der•y |ĕm **broi'**də rē| *n., pl.* **em•broi•der•ies. 1.** The art or act of embroidering. **2.** An embroidered fabric or design. —***modifier:*** *an embroidery needle.* [SEE PICTURE]

em•broil |ĕm **broil'**| *v.* To involve or entangle in argument, contention, or conflict.

em•bry•o |**ĕm'**brē ō'| *n., pl.* **em•bry•os. 1.** An organism in its earliest stages of growth, just after its development from an egg cell. **2.** An early or beginning stage.

em•bry•ol•o•gist |ĕm'brē **ŏl'**ə jĭst| *n.* A scientist who specializes in embryology.

em•bry•ol•o•gy |ĕm'brē **ŏl'**ə jē| *n.* The scientific study of embryos and their development. —**em'bry•o•log'i•cal** |ĕm'brē ə **lŏj'**ĭ kəl|, **em'bry•o•log'ic** |ĕm'brē ə **lŏj'**ĭk| *adj.*

em•bry•on•ic |ĕm'brē **ŏn'**ĭk| *adj.* **1.** Of or in the condition of being an embryo. **2.** In an early, undeveloped state: *What can be said about the earth's first, embryonic days?*

em•cee |**ĕm'sē'**|. *Informal. n.* A **master of ceremonies.** —*v.* **em•ceed, em•cee•ing.** To serve as master of ceremonies of: *He emcees a quiz program. He emceed at a benefit performance.* [SEE NOTE]

em•er•ald |**ĕm'**ər əld| *or* |**ĕm'**rəld| *n.* **1.** A bright-green, transparent form of beryl that is used as a gem. **2.** A dark yellowish green. —***modifier:*** *an emerald necklace.* —*adj.* Dark yellowish green.

e•merge |ĭ **mûrj'**| *v.* **e•merged, e•merg•ing. 1.** To come into view; appear: *The butterfly emerged from the cocoon.* **2.** To come into existence; crop up: *A new spirit of freedom emerged.* **3.** To become known, revealed, or evident: *The young country has emerged as a world power.* [SEE NOTE]

e•mer•gence |ĭ **mûr'**jəns| *n.* The act or process of emerging: *the emergence of a butterfly from a cocoon. The 18th century marks the emergence of an influential middle class.*

e•mer•gen•cy |ĭ **mûr'**jən sē| *n., pl.* **e•mer•gen•cies.** A serious situation or occurrence that develops suddenly and calls for immediate action. —***modifier:*** *an emergency signal; an emergency aircraft landing.* [SEE NOTE]

e•mer•i•tus |ĭ **mĕr'**ĭ təs| *adj.* Retired but retaining an honorary title corresponding to that held before retirement: *president emeritus of the university.*

Em•er•son |**ĕm'**ər sən|, **Ralph Waldo.** 1803–1882. American essayist and poet.

em•er•y |**ĕm'**ə rē| *or* |**ĕm'**rē| *n.* An impure form of the mineral corundum used in grinding and polishing.

emery board. A flat cardboard or wooden strip coated with powdered emery and used to file the fingernails.

e•met•ic |ĭ **mĕt'**ĭk| *adj.* Causing vomiting. —*n.* An emetic drug or medicine.

emf, EMF electromotive force.

em•i•grant |**ĕm'**ĭ grənt| *n.* Someone who leaves a native country or region to settle in another: *wagon trains of emigrants from the East.* —***modifier:*** *an emigrant family.*

em•i•grate |**ĕm'**ĭ grāt'| *v.* **em•i•grat•ed, em•i•**

grat•ing. To leave a native country or region to settle in another: *In 1908 he emigrated from Italy.* —**em'i•gra'tion** *n.*

é•mi•gré |ĕm'ĭ grā'| *n.* An emigrant, especially a person who has fled his country because of political upheaval: *the Royalist émigrés during the French Revolution.*

em•i•nence |ĕm'ə nəns| *n.* **1.** A position of great distinction or superiority in achievement, rank, etc.: *a man of eminence in medicine. The city owes its eminence to education and industry.* **2.** A rise or elevation of ground; a hill: *The pioneers halted the wagons at an eminence called Coogan's Hill.* **3. Eminence.** A title of respect used when speaking to or of a cardinal in the Roman Catholic Church: *Your Eminence; His Eminence.*

em•i•nent |ĕm'ə nənt| *adj.* **1.** Outstanding in performance, character, or rank; distinguished: *an eminent scientist.* **2.** Remarkable; noteworthy: *the eminent history of his journeys.* —**em'i•nent•ly** *adv.*

e•mir |ĕ mîr'| *n.* **1.** An Arabian prince, chieftain, or governor. **2.** A title of honor given to the descendants of Mohammed.

e•mir•ate |ĕ mîr'ĭt| *or* |-āt'| *n.* The rank or domain of an emir.

em•is•sar•y |ĕm'ĭ sĕr'ē| *n., pl.* **em•is•sar•ies.** A person sent on a mission or errand as the representative of another.

e•mis•sion |ĭ mĭsh'ən| *n.* **1.** The act or process of emitting. **2.** Something that is emitted: *the harmful emissions of radium.*

emission spectrum. The spectrum, often a series of bright lines or bands of color, formed when a substance is excited, as by heating, to the point where it emits radiation. The characteristics of such a spectrum depend in general on the nature of the radiating body and the degree to which it is excited.

e•mis•sive |ĭ mĭs'ĭv| *adj.* Emitting or tending to emit; radiating: *a hot, highly emissive star.*

e•mit |ĭ mĭt'| *v.* **e•mit•ted, e•mit•ting.** **1.** To release, give off, or send out (light, heat, etc.). **2.** To utter; express: *The baby emitted a cry.*

e•mit•ter |ĭ mĭt'ər| *n.* **1.** Someone or something that emits. **2.** The terminal of a transistor that corresponds most closely to the cathode of an electron tube.

e•mol•lient |ĭ mŏl'yənt| *adj.* Acting to produce softness and smoothness, especially of the skin. —*n.* A substance applied to the skin to make it soft and smooth.

e•mo•tion |ĭ mō'shən| *n.* **1.** Any strong excitement or stimulation, such as fright, rage, joy, etc., often involving characteristic chemical and physical changes in the function of the body. **2.** A strong, complex feeling, such as love, sorrow, hate, etc.

e•mo•tion•al |ĭ mō'shə nəl| *adj.* **1.** Of emotion: *emotional conflict; emotional satisfaction.* **2.** Easily stirred by emotion: *a lively, emotional people.* **3.** Capable of affecting the emotions: *the emotional power of language.* **4.** Showing emotion: *an emotional response to music.* —**e•mo'tion•al•ly** *adv.*

e•mo•tion•al•ism |ĭ mō'shə nə lĭz'əm| *n.* **1.** A tendency to encourage or to yield to emotion: *the emotionalism of adolescent girls.* **2.** A tendency, especially as expressed in the arts, to make an undue display of emotion: *the emotionalism of the romantic composers.*

em•pa•thy |ĕm'pə thē| *n.* Identification with and involvement in another's situation, especially with sincere understanding and deep concern.

em•per•or |ĕm'pər ər| *n.* A male ruler of an empire. [SEE NOTE]

em•pha•sis |ĕm'fə sĭs| *n., pl.* **em•pha•ses** |ĕm'fə sēz'|. **1.** Special importance or significance placed upon or imparted to something: *a strong emphasis on foreign languages; increased emphasis on quality rather than quantity.* **2.** Stress given to a particular syllable, word, or phrase.

em•pha•size |ĕm'fə sīz'| *v.* **em•pha•sized, em•pha•siz•ing.** To give emphasis to; stress: *emphasize a word by repeating it. We emphasize freedom and independence at this school.*

em•phat•ic |ĕm făt'ĭk| *adj.* **1.** Expressed or performed with emphasis: *an emphatic shake of the head.* **2.** Bold and definite in expression or action: *an emphatic person.* —**em•phat'i•cal•ly** *adv.*

em•phy•se•ma |ĕm'fĭ sē'mə| *n.* A disease in which the alveoli of the lungs become stretched to an excessive degree and lose their elasticity, resulting in an often severe loss of breathing ability.

em•pire |ĕm'pīr'| *n.* **1.** A group of territories or nations headed by one single central government: *the empire of Alexander the Great.* **2.** Absolute imperial dominion and authority: *Much of the ancient world was under the empire of Rome.* **3.** An extensive enterprise or group of enterprises owned or controlled by a single person, family, or financial group: *a vast publishing empire; a billion-dollar automotive empire.*

em•pir•i•cal |ĕm pîr'ĭ kəl| *adj.* Relying upon or based on observation or experiment rather than theory: *empirical thought; empirical knowledge.* —**em•pir'i•cal•ly** *adv.*

em•place•ment |ĕm plās'mənt| *n.* A position for guns, as a mounting or platform, within a fortification.

em•ploy |ĕm ploi'| *v.* **1.** To engage the services of; provide with a job and livelihood: *He employs many workers.* **2.** To make use of; put to use: *They employed all their skills to build the bridge.* **3.** To devote or apply (one's time or energies) to some activity: *He employed all his leisure in fishing and golfing. The apprentices were busily employed hewing out the timbers.* —*n.* The condition of being employed: *He was in the employ of the government.*

em•ploy•ee |ĕm ploi'ē| *or* |ĕm'ploi ē'| *n.* A person who works for another person or a corporation in return for wages or a salary.

em•ploy•er |ĕm ploi'ər| *n.* A person or corporation that employs people for wages or a salary.

em•ploy•ment |ĕm ploi'mənt| *n.* **1.** A job or activity: *He got regular employment on a fishing vessel.* **2.** The act of employing or of putting to use or work: *the employment of ferries to cross rivers.* **3.** The condition of being employed: *a high level of employment in that country.* —**modifier:** *an employment agency.*

em•po•ri•um |ĕm pôr'ē əm| *or* |-pōr'-| *n., pl.* **em•po•ri•ums** or **em•po•ri•a** |ĕm pôr'ē ə| *or* |-pōr'-|. A large store carrying a wide variety of merchandise.

emperor

The Roman republic, like many a modern republic, was subverted and taken over by army commanders who became the sole rulers. We now call these rulers "emperors," but this was not their political title. The word comes from Old French empereor, *which is from Latin* imperātor, *"general, commander in chief." The Roman ruler always held the rank of general, but his civilian titles as head of state were* princeps, *"prince,"* Augustus *(see note at* **august**), *and* Caesar *(after Julius Caesar).*

emu

em•pow•er |ĕm pou′ər| *v.* To give legal power to; authorize: *The state legislature empowered the governor to levy new taxes.*

em•press |ĕm′prĭs| *n.* **1.** A female ruler of an empire. **2.** The wife or widow of an emperor.

emp•ty |ĕmp′tē| *adj.* **emp•ti•er, emp•ti•est. 1.** Containing nothing: *an empty box; an empty gas tank.* **2.** Having no occupants or inhabitants; vacant; unoccupied: *the empty continent of Antarctica; an empty house; an empty lot; an empty bus.* **3.** Lacking purpose or substance: *an empty life.* **4.** Not having something; devoid; lacking: *a life empty of adventure; streets empty of traffic.* **5.** Having no value or meaning; meaningless or vain: *empty promises; empty pleasures.* **6.** Needing food; hungry: *an empty stomach.* —*v.* **emp•tied, emp•ty•ing, emp•ties. 1.** To make or become empty: *empty an ashtray. At the shout of "fire" the theater emptied immediately.* **2.** To transfer or pour off: *Please empty the contents of the can into a cooking pot.* **3.** To discharge or flow: *The Ohio River empties into the Mississippi.* —**emp′ti•ly** *adv.* —**emp′ti•ness** *n.*

emp•ty-hand•ed |ĕmp′tē hăn′dĭd| *adj.* **1.** Bearing no gifts, possessions, etc.: *They arrived empty-handed at the birthday party.* **2.** Having accomplished nothing; with nothing to show for one's efforts: *They returned from the hunt empty-handed.*

empty set. The set that has no members; the null set.

em•py•re•an |ĕm′pī rē′ən| *or* |ĕm pîr′ē ən| *n.* The highest reaches of heaven. —*adj.* Heavenly; celestial.

e•mu |ē′myo͞o| *n., pl.* **e•mus.** A large Australian bird related to and resembling the ostrich. [SEE PICTURE]

em•u•late |ĕm′yə lāt′| *v.* **em•u•lat•ed, em•u•lat•ing.** To strive to equal or excel, especially through imitation: *He is trying to emulate the success of his famous father.* —**em′u•la′tion** *n.*

e•mul•si•fy |ĭ mŭl′sə fī′| *v.* **e•mul•si•fied, e•mul•si•fy•ing, e•mul•si•fies.** To make into an emulsion: *Soap emulsifies fats in water.* —**e•mul′si•fi•ca′tion** *n.*

e•mul•sion |ĭ mŭl′shən| *n.* **1.** A suspension of tiny droplets of one liquid in a second liquid with which the first does not mix, as the suspension of cream in homogenized milk. **2.** The light-sensitive coating of a photographic film or plate, usually made of fine grains of a silver salt suspended in a thin layer of gelatin.

en–. A prefix that forms verbs: **encompass; endanger.** When *en-* is followed by *b, m,* or *p,* it becomes *em-.*

–en[1]. A suffix that forms verbs from adjectives: **cheapen, lengthen.**

–en[2]. A suffix that forms adjectives from nouns: **earthen; wooden.**

en•a•ble |ĕn ā′bəl| *v.* **en•a•bled, en•a•bling.** To give the means, ability, or opportunity to do something: *Science has enabled man to probe the secrets of the universe.*

en•act |ĕn ăkt′| *v.* **1.** To establish by law; decree: *The Senate enacted legislation to curb the use of drugs.* **2.** To act out as on a stage; represent: *The children enacted the final scene of the play.* —**en•act′ment** *n.*

e•nam•el |ĭ năm′əl| *n.* **1.** A colorful substance baked onto the surface of metal, porcelain, pottery, etc., for decoration or protection. **2.** A paint that dries to a hard, glossy, surface. **3.** The hard substance that covers the exposed part of a tooth. —***modifier:*** *an enamel plate; enamel bracelets.* —*v.* **e•nam•eled** or **e•nam•elled, e•nam•el•ing** or **e•nam•el•ling.** To coat, inlay, or decorate with enamel.

e•nam•el•ware |ĭ năm′əl wâr′| *n.* Objects of metal, porcelain, etc., coated with enamel for protection.

en•am•ored |ĭ năm′ərd| *adj.* Very fond of or in love with.

en•camp |ĕn kămp′| *v.* To set up or live in a camp.

en•camp•ment |ĕn kămp′mənt| *n.* **1.** The act of setting up a camp. **2.** The condition of living in a camp. **3.** A camp or campsite.

en•cap•su•late |ĕn kăp′sə lāt′| *v.* **en•cap•su•lat•ed, en•cap•su•lat•ing.** To enclose or become enclosed in or as if in a capsule. —**en•cap′su•la′tion** *n.*

en•case |ĕn kās′| *v.* **en•cased, en•cas•ing.** To enclose in or as if in a case: *The bones of the skull encase the brain.*

–ence. A suffix that forms nouns from verbs: **emergence; reference.**

en•ceph•a•la |ĕn sĕf′ə lə| *n.* Plural of **encephalon.**

en•ceph•a•li•tis |ĕn sĕf′ə lī′tĭs| *n.* Inflammation of the brain.

en•ceph•a•lon |ĕn sĕf′ə lŏn′| *n., pl.* **en•ceph•a•la** |ĕn sĕf′ə lə|. The brain of a vertebrate animal.

en•chant |ĕn chănt′| *or* |-chänt′| *v.* **1.** To cast under a spell; bewitch. **2.** To delight utterly; charm: *Her green eyes enchanted him.* —**en•chant′ing** *adj.: an enchanting smile; an enchanting girl.* —**en•chant′er** *n.*

en•chant•ment |ĕn chănt′mənt| *or* |-chänt′-| *n.* **1.** An act of enchanting: *"This flower is the product of enchantment," said the witch.* **2.** The condition or quality of being enchanted; fascination: *Her dancing lent enchantment to a dull ballet.* **3.** Something that enchants; a magic spell: *The genie's enchantments kept the princess asleep for a hundred years.*

en•chant•ress |ĕn chăn′trĭs| *or* |-chän′-| *n.* **1.** A sorceress. **2.** A very appealing or charming woman.

en•chi•la•da |ĕn′chə lä′də| *n.* A rolled tortilla with a cheese or meat filling, served with a spicy sauce.

en•ci•pher |ĕn sī′fər| *v.* To put a message into cipher. —**en•ci′pher•ment** *n.*

en•cir•cle |ĕn sûr′kəl| *v.* **en•cir•cled, en•cir•cling. 1.** To form a circle around; surround: *The students encircled the basketball team after the game.* **2.** To move or go around; make a circuit of: *It takes the earth one year to encircle to the sun.* —**en•cir′cle•ment** *n.*

en•clave |ĕn′klāv′| *n.* **1.** A small territory lying entirely within the boundaries of another country. **2.** A small area within a city or country, inhabited by a minority group.

en•close |ĕn klōz′| *v.* **en•closed, en•clos•ing. 1.** To surround on all sides; close in: *A high fence encloses the field. You should always enclose the title of a poem in quotation marks.* **2.** To insert in the same envelope or package with the main letter: *I enclose a check for twenty-five dollars.*

en•clo•sure |ĕn **klō′**zhər| *n.* **1.** The act or process of enclosing. **2.** Something that encloses, as a wall or fence. **3.** An area surrounded by a fence, gate, etc. **4.** An additional item inserted in a letter or package.

en•code |ĕn **kōd′**| *v.* **en•cod•ed, en•cod•ing.** To put (information, a message, etc.) into code. —**en•cod′er** *n.*

en•co•mi•um |ĕn **kō′**mē əm| *n., pl.* **en•co•mi•ums** or **en•co•mi•a** |ĕn **kō′**mē ə|. A statement or formal expression of high praise; a tribute.

en•com•pass |ĕn **kŭm′**pəs| *v.* **1.** To take in; include; comprise: *The report encompassed a wide variety of subjects.* **2.** To form a circle or ring about; surround.

en•core |**äng′**kôr′| *or* |-kōr′| *or* |**än′**-| *n.* **1.** A request by an audience, expressed by prolonged applause, to a singer, orchestra, etc., for an additional performance. **2.** An additional performance in response to such a request. —*interj.* A word used to express a request for an additional performance.

en•coun•ter |ĕn **koun′**tər| *n.* **1.** A chance or unexpected meeting: *an encounter with a bear in the woods.* **2.** A clash, battle, or fight: *a brief encounter with the enemy.* —*v.* **1.** To meet or come upon, especially unexpectedly: *encounter many new words in a book.* **2.** To be faced with: *encounter difficulties; encounter many problems.* **3.** To meet in battle: *encounter enemy troops.*

en•cour•age |ĕn **kûr′**ĭj| *or* |**-kŭr′-**| *v.* **en•cour•aged, en•cour•ag•ing.** **1.** To give hope or confidence to; hearten: *The doctor's report encouraged me somewhat.* **2.** To urge or inspire; stimulate: *The teacher encouraged the students to make use of the library.* **3.** To help bring about; foster: *Some people feel that violence on television encourages real violence.* —**en•cour′ag•ing** *adj.:* *encouraging news; an encouraging sign.*

en•cour•age•ment |ĕn **kûr′**ĭj mənt| *or* |**-kŭr′-**| *n.* **1.** The act of encouraging: *cries of encouragement. In his profession they believe in the encouragement of individual initiative.* **2.** Something that encourages: *Kind words are an encouragement.*

en•croach |ĕn **krōch′**| *v.* To intrude or infringe upon the rights or property of another: *encroach on the fields of a neighboring farm.* —**en•croach′ment** *n.*

en•crust |ĕn **krŭst′**| *v.* **1.** To cover with a crust or hard layer: *Ice encrusted the windowsill.* **2.** To adorn with a solid covering of jewels or other ornaments: *encrust a crown with diamonds.* —**en′crus•ta′tion** *n.*

en•cum•ber |ĕn **kŭm′**bər| *v.* To burden or clutter so as to hinder or impede: *a knight encumbered with heavy armor.*

en•cum•brance |ĕn **kŭm′**brəns| *n.* Someone or something that encumbers or hinders; a burden or obstacle.

-ency. A suffix that forms nouns from verbs: **dependency; emergency.**

en•cyc•li•cal |ĕn **sĭk′**lĭ kəl| *n.* A letter from the pope on a specific subject, addressed to the bishops of the Roman Catholic Church.

en•cy•clo•pe•di•a, also **en•cy•clo•pae•di•a** |ĕn sī′klə **pē′**dē ə| *n.* A book or set of books containing articles arranged in alphabetical order and covering one particular field or a wide variety of subjects. [SEE NOTE]

encyclopedia
The word **encyclopedia** *is from Greek* enkuklios paideia, *"general education":* enkuklios, *"circular, all-round, general" (from* kuklos, *"circle"),* + paideia, *"education" (from* pais, paid-, *"young person").*

en•cy•clo•pe•dic, also **en•cy•clo•pae•dic** |ĕn sī′klə **pē′**dĭk| *adj.* **1.** Of or like an encyclopedia. **2.** Having or covering a wide range of information; comprehensive: *encyclopedic knowledge.*

en•cyst |ĕn **sĭst′**| *v.* To enclose or become enclosed in a cyst or sac.

end |ĕnd| *n.* **1. a.** Either extremity of something that has length: *They sat at opposite ends of the table.* **b.** The extreme edge or limit of a space, area, etc.: *Buffalo lies at the eastern end of Lake Erie.* **2.** The finish or conclusion of something: *Summer is coming to an end. I'll be able to pay you at the end of the month.* **3.** The point that marks the extent of something; a final limit: *He is at the end of his resources.* **4.** A purpose or goal: *The end justifies the means.* **5.** Death or ruin: *meet a violent end; the end of civilization.* **6.** In football, either of two players stationed at the ends of a team's line. —***modifier:*** *the end room of a corridor; the end result; the end product.* —*v.* To bring or come to an end: *a nice way to end a trip.* —***phrasal verb.*** **end up.** To finish or wind up in a certain situation or place: *end up a millionaire; end up in jail; end up looking foolish.*

Idioms. **hold** (or **keep**) **(one's) end up.** To do one's share. **make (both) ends meet.** To manage to live within one's means. **on end. 1.** In an upright position: *His hair stood on end.* **2.** Without interruption; continuously: *working for weeks on end.*

en•dan•ger |ĕn **dān′**jər| *v.* To put in danger; imperil; jeopardize: *The oil spill endangered thousands of birds.* —**en•dan′gered** *adj.:* *an endangered species.*

en•dear |ĕn **dîr′**| *v.* To make dear, admired, or well-liked: *The actor quickly endeared himself to the audience.* —**en•dear′ing** *adj.:* *endearing qualities.*

en•dear•ment |ĕn **dîr′**mənt| *n.* An expression of affection.

en•deav•or |ĕn **dĕv′**ər| *v.* To make an effort; attempt; strive: *The duke still endeavored to keep up some show of former wealth.* —*n.* **1.** A major effort or attempt. **2.** An undertaking: *a new business endeavor.*

en•deav•our |ĕn **dĕv′**ər| *v.* & *n.* British form of the word **endeavor.**

en•dem•ic |ĕn **dĕm′**ĭk| *adj.* Common in and restricted to a particular region, area, country, or group of people: *an endemic disease of Southeast Asia.*

end•ing |**ĕn′**dĭng| *n.* **1.** The concluding part, especially of a book, play, or film: *a happy ending.* **2.** A letter or letters added to the end of a word, especially to make an inflected form.

en•dive |**ĕn′**dīv′| *or* |**än′**dēv′| *n.* **1.** A plant with crisp, curly or wavy leaves used in salads. **2.** A related plant with a narrow, pointed cluster of whitish leaves. [SEE PICTURE]

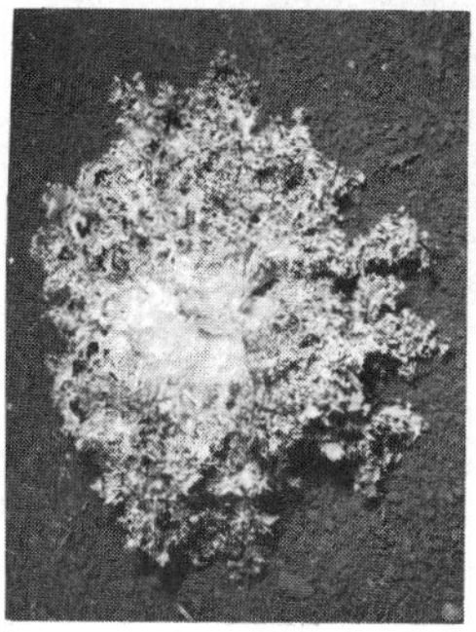

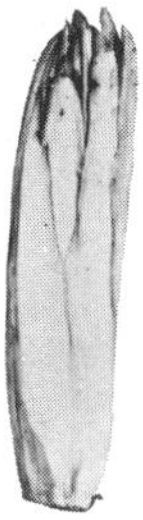

endive
Above: Sense 1
Below: Sense 2

end•less |**ĕnd′**lĭs| *adj.* **1.** Having or seeming to have no end; infinite: *endless stretches of sandy beaches.* **2.** Constant; incessant: *endless arguments.* —**end′less•ly** *adv.* —**end′less•ness** *n.*

en•do•crine |**ĕn′**də krĭn| *or* |-krēn′| *or* |-krīn′| *adj.* **1.** Secreting internally rather than through a duct. **2.** Of an endocrine gland or glands: *en-*

docrine secretions; an endocrine disease. —*n.* An **endocrine gland.**

endocrine gland. Any of the ductless glands, such as the thyroid gland and adrenal gland, whose secretions pass directly into the bloodstream. [SEE PICTURE]

en•do•cri•nol•o•gist |ĕn′də krə **nŏl′**ə jĭst| *n.* A physician or scientist who specializes in endocrinology.

en•do•cri•nol•o•gy |ĕn′də krə **nŏl′**ə jē| *n.* The scientific and medical study of the endocrine glands, their functions, and their diseases.

en•do•derm |**ĕn′**də dûrm′| *n.* The innermost of the three layers of cells found in an early embryo, developing in time into the digestive and breathing tubes and the glands.

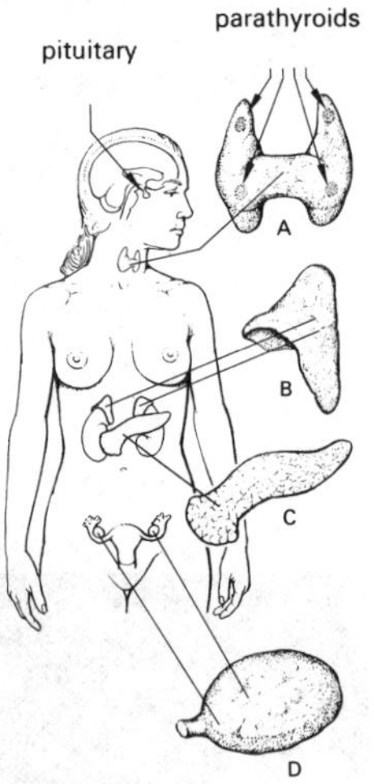

endocrine glands
Endocrine glands of human female
A. Thyroid
B. Adrenal gland
C. Islands of Langerhans
D. Ovary

en•dorse |ĕn **dôrs′**| *v.* **en•dorsed, en•dors•ing.** **1.** To write one's signature on the back of (a check) in order to receive or be credited with the money indicated on its front. **2.** To give approval of; support: *Many senators have already endorsed the new bill.*

en•dorse•ment |ĕn **dôrs′**mənt| *n.* **1.** A signature on the back of a check. **2.** Approval; support: *The plan has my endorsement.*

en•do•skel•e•ton |ĕn′dō **skĕl′**ĭ tn| *n.* A supporting structure or framework within the body, as the skeleton in man and other vertebrates.

en•do•sperm |**ĕn′**də spûrm′| *n.* A part of a plant seed that contains stored food and supplies nourishment for the developing embryo.

en•do•ther•mic |ĕn′dō **thûr′**mĭk| *adj.* Causing or characterized by absorption of heat: *an endothermic chemical reaction.*

en•dow |ĕn **dou′**| *v.* **1.** To provide with property, income, or a source of income: *endow a college.* **2.** To provide or invest with certain talents, qualities, rights, etc.: *Nature has endowed her with both beauty and charm.*

en•dow•ment |ĕn **dou′**mənt| *n.* **1.** Money or property donated to an institution or person as a source of income. **2.** A natural gift or quality, such as beauty or talent.

end point. **1.** The point at which a process reaches its end or completion; a final point. **2. a.** Either of the points that mark the ends of a line segment, arc, etc. **b.** The point from which a ray extends.

end table. A small table, usually placed at either end of a couch.

en•dur•ance |ĕn **dŏŏr′**əns| *or* |**-dyŏŏr′-**| *n.* The ability to withstand strain, stress, hardship, use, etc.: *Climbing that mountain is a real test of a person's endurance.* —**modifier:** *an endurance test; an endurance record.*

en•dure |ĕn **dŏŏr′**| *or* |**-dyŏŏr′**| *v.* **en•dured, en•dur•ing.** **1.** To undergo; bear up under: *The early settlers of America endured great hardships.* **2.** To continue to exist; last: *His name will endure forever.* **3.** To bear with tolerance; put up with: *He could no longer endure her rudeness.* —**en•dur′ing** *adj.: enduring fame; of enduring value.* —**en•dur′a•ble** *adj.*

end•ways |**ĕnd′**wāz′| *adv.* A form of the word **endwise.**

end•wise |**ĕnd′**wīz′| *adv.* **1.** On end; erect: *Stand the books endwise.* **2.** With the end foremost: *a bookcase standing endwise against a wall.* **3.** Lengthwise: *a sofa placed endwise along a wall.* **4.** End to end: *Lay the bricks endwise.*

end zone. In football, the area beyond the goal line at each end of the field.

en•e•ma |**ĕn′**ə mə| *n.* **1.** The injection of a liquid into the rectum through the anus for cleansing, as a laxative, or for other therapeutic purposes. **2.** The liquid used in this way.

en•e•my |**ĕn′**ə mē| *n., pl.* **en•e•mies.** **1.** A person, animal, group, etc., that shows hostility toward, or opposes the purposes or interests of, another; a foe: *Ecologists are enemies of air pollution. Cats, hawks, and owls are enemies of mice.* **2.** A hostile power or force or a member or a unit of such a force: *In World War II the enemy was Germany, with its friends in Europe, and Japan. It was difficult for an enemy to cross the waters and set foot on British soil.* **3.** Something harmful or injurious in its effects: *Weather is sometimes the farmer's worst enemy.* —**modifier:** *enemy soldiers; an enemy aircraft.*

en•er•get•ic |ĕn′ər **jĕt′**ĭk| *adj.* Full of energy; vigorous. —**en′er•get′i•cal•ly** *adv.*

en•er•gize |**ĕn′**ər jīz′| *v.* **en•er•gized, en•er•giz•ing.** To supply energy or power to; make active: *This switch energizes the electric circuit.* —**en′er•giz′er** *n.*

en•er•gy |**ĕn′**ər jē| *n., pl.* **en•er•gies.** **1.** The capability for doing work, especially the work that a material body or system can perform on another such body by undergoing a change in state. **2.** The ability to act or put forth effort either with the mind or body: *He lacked energy to finish the job.* **3.** Strength and vigor: *Good food helps give us energy.* **4. energies.** Powers available for working or efficiently put to work: *He devoted all his energies to a worthy cause.*

en•er•vate |**ĕn′**ər vāt′| *v.* **en•er•vat•ed, en•er•vat•ing.** To deprive of strength or vitality; weaken. —**en′er•vat′ing** *adj.: enervating weather.*

en•fee•ble |ĕn **fē′**bəl| *v.* **en•fee•bled, en•fee•bling.** To make feeble; weaken. —**en•fee′ble•ment** *n.*

en•fold |ĕn **fōld′**| *v.* **1.** To surround with a covering: *enfold a pillow in a pillowcase.* **2.** To embrace: *He enfolded her in his arms.*

en•force |ĕn **fôrs′**| *or* |**-fōrs′**| *v.* **en•forced, en•forc•ing.** **1.** To compel observance of or obedience to: *enforce the provisions of a law.* **2.** To give force to; reinforce: *enforce one's opinion with numerous arguments.* —**en•force′a•ble** *adj.*

en•force•ment |ĕn **fôrs′**mənt| *or* |**-fōrs′-**| *n.* The act or process of enforcing: *strict enforcement of the law.*

en•fran•chise |ĕn **frăn′**chīz′| *v.* **en•fran•chised, en•fran•chis•ing.** To give (someone) the rights of citizenship, especially the right to vote. —**en•fran′chise•ment** |ĕn **frăn′**chĭz mənt| *n.*

Eng. England; English.

en•gage |ĕn **gāj′**| *v.* **en•gaged, en•gag•ing.** **1.** To contract for the services of; hire; employ: *engage a lawyer; engage a servant.* **2.** To contract for the use of; reserve: *engage a hotel room.* **3.** To attract; hold: *Her attention was engaged by the fashion show on the main floor of the store.* **4. a.** To take part; involve oneself in: *A number of scientists engaged in atomic research in different countries.* **b.** To be busy with; work at: *She was engaged in knitting. The man was engaged in advertising Dr. Bradford's tonic.* **5.** To draw into;

ă **pat**/ā **pay**/â **care**/ä **father**/ĕ **pet**/ē **be**/ĭ **pit**/ī **pie**/î **fierce**/ŏ **pot**/ō **go**/ô **paw, for**/oi **oil**/ŏŏ **book**/ōō **boot**/ou **out**/ŭ **cut**/û **fur**/*th* **the**/th **thin**/hw **which**/zh **vision**/ə **ago,** item, pencil, atom, circus involve: *engage someone in conversation.* **6.** To begin fighting with: *The admiral with his six ships engaged the Spanish fleet, and by noon the battle was over.* **7.** To promise or agree to marry: *Anne is engaged to Harry.* **8.** To come or cause to come into an arrangement that allows power to be transmitted: *engage the gears. The clutch engages poorly.*

en•gaged |ĕn **gājd′**| *adj.* **1.** Pledged to marry; betrothed: *an engaged couple.* **2.** Employed; occupied; busy: *This taxicab is engaged.* **3.** In conflict or battle: *Our fleet was heavily engaged in the Pacific Ocean.* **4.** Arranged so as to transmit power, as gears or mechanical parts.

en•gage•ment |ĕn **gāj′**mənt| *n.* **1.** An act of engaging or the condition of being engaged. **2. a.** A pledge to marry; betrothal. **b.** The period during which one is so pledged. **3.** A promise to appear at a certain time, as for business or social activity; an appointment: *a dinner engagement.* **4.** Employment, especially for a set length of time: *an actors' two-week engagement.* **5.** A battle; military encounter.

en•gag•ing |ĕn **gā′**jĭng| *adj.* Winning; pleasing; charming: *an engaging smile.*

en•gen•der |ĕn **jĕn′**dər| *v.* To give rise to; cause; produce: *His manner is not the kind that engenders confidence or respect.*

en•gine |**ĕn′**jən| *n.* **1.** A machine that turns energy into mechanical motion, especially one that gets its energy from a source of heat, as the burning of a fuel. **2.** Any machine or mechanical device: *engines of destruction.* **3.** A locomotive.

en•gi•neer |ĕn′jə **nîr′**| *n.* **1.** A person who works in a branch of engineering, especially someone having a special training at the college level or beyond. **2.** A person who operates complicated equipment: *a recording engineer.* **3.** A person who runs a locomotive. —*v.* **1.** To plan and supervise the construction of (a project, device, etc.), especially by the use of scientific principles. **2.** To plan or accomplish by skill or trickery; maneuver. [SEE PICTURE]

en•gi•neer•ing |ĕn′jə **nîr′**ĭng| *n.* The use of scientific knowledge and principles for practical purposes, as in designing and building structures, machinery, and transportation systems and in making industrial products.

Eng•land |**ĭng′**glənd|. The largest division of the United Kingdom, occupying the southern part of the island of Great Britain. Population, 46,000,000. Capital, London. [SEE NOTE]

Eng•lish |**ĭng′**glĭsh| *n.* **1.** The Germanic language of Britain, the United States, and many other countries. English is divided historically into **Old English, Middle English,** and (modern) **English. 2. the English** *(used with a plural verb).* The people of England. —*adj.* Of England, the English, or their language.

English Channel. A channel between England and France, connecting the North Sea with the Atlantic Ocean.

English horn. A woodwind musical instrument similar to but larger than the oboe, pitched a fifth below it and having a more somber tone. [SEE PICTURE]

Eng•lish•man |**ĭng′**glĭsh mən| *n., pl.* **-men** |-mən|. A man who is a native or inhabitant of England.

English muffin. A griddle-baked muffin made of yeast dough, usually served toasted.

en•graft |ĕn **grăft′**| *or* |**-gräft′**| *v.* To graft (a shoot) onto a tree or plant.

en•grave |ĕn **grāv′**| *v.* **en•graved, en•grav•ing. 1.** To carve, cut, or etch (a design or letters) into a surface: *engrave a name on a plaque.* **2.** To carve, cut, or etch a design or letters into (a surface): *engrave a marble stone with a coat of arms; engrave a plate.* **3.** To impress deeply; fix permanently: *engrave rules of conduct on a child's mind.* —**en•grav′er** *n.*

en•grav•ing |ĕn **grā′**vĭng| *n.* **1.** The art or technique of cutting letters or designs into a surface. **2.** An engraved surface used for printing. **3.** A print made from an engraved plate.

en•gross |ĕn **grōs′**| *v.* To occupy the complete attention of; absorb wholly: *He is engrossed in a new book.* —**en•gross′ing** *adj.*: *an engrossing novel.*

en•gulf |ĕn **gŭlf′**| *v.* To cause to disappear by or as if by overflowing and enclosing; swallow up: *The flood waters engulfed the surrounding farmlands.*

en•hance |ĕn **hăns′**| *or* |**-häns′**| *v.* **en•hanced, en•hanc•ing.** To add to; make greater; increase, as in value, cost, beauty, etc.: *The success of the season enhanced his prestige as coach of the football team. The new garden has greatly enhanced his house.* —**en•hance′ment** *n.*

en•har•mon•ic |ĕn′här **mŏn′**ĭk| *adj.* Of or involving the use of two different names, such as F♯ and G♭ or C♯ and D♭, for the same musical tone.

e•nig•ma |ĭ **nĭg′**mə| *n.* Someone or something that is hard to figure out; a puzzle.

en•ig•mat•ic |ĕn′ĭg **măt′**ĭk| or **en•ig•mat•i•cal** |ĕn′ĭg **măt′**ĭ kəl| *adj.* Hard to figure out; puzzling; baffling; mysterious: *enigmatic behavior.* —**en′ig•mat′i•cal•ly** *adv.*

en•join |ĕn **join′**| *v.* **1.** To order (someone) to do something, especially formally or officially; command. **2.** To prohibit or forbid, especially by legal order: *The company was enjoined from merging with its competitor.*

en•joy |ĕn **joi′**| *v.* **1.** To receive pleasure from; relish: *enjoy life. Did you enjoy the movie? I enjoy living in the country.* **2.** To have the benefit of: *enjoy good health. Hawaii enjoys good weather the year round.* **3. —enjoy oneself.** To have a good time.

en•joy•a•ble |ĕn **joi′**ə bəl| *adj.* Giving enjoyment; pleasant; agreeable: *We had a very enjoyable time.* —**en•joy′a•ble•ness** *n.* —**en•joy′a•bly** *adv.*

en•joy•ment |ĕn **joi′**mənt| *n.* **1.** The act or condition of experiencing pleasure in something: *the enjoyment of good food.* **2.** Pleasure; joy: *He works in the garden for enjoyment.* **3.** The use or possession of something beneficial or pleasurable: *the enjoyment of good health.*

en•large |ĕn **lärj′**| *v.* **en•larged, en•larg•ing. 1.** To make or become larger: *enlarge a hole; enlarge a picture. The city has greatly enlarged in recent years.* **2.** To discuss or analyze in greater detail; expand: *I should like to enlarge a bit on this point.*

en•large•ment |ĕn **lärj′**mənt| *n.* **1.** The act of

engineer

England

The name **England** *does not apply to the island of Britain as a whole, but only to the largest part of it, in the south. The kingdom of England was not founded until the ninth century* A.D. *It was a separate nation until 1701, when it was united with Scotland to form* **Great Britain.** *England is still technically a kingdom. The name is also often used for the whole country of Great Britain; but this is not correct, and is likely to be resented by some of the Scots and the Welsh. See note at* **Great Britain.**

English horn

enlarging or the condition of being enlarged. **2.** Something that enlarges another thing. **3.** Something enlarged, especially a magnified print of a photographic negative.

en•larg•er |ĕn lär'jər| *n.* Someone or something that enlarges, especially an optical device used to make enlargements of photographic negatives.

en•light•en |ĕn līt'n| *v.* **1.** To give knowledge or insight to; instruct. **2.** To give information to; inform. **—en•light'ened** *adj.: enlightened leadership; an enlightened people.* **—en•light'en•ing** *adj.: an enlightening discussion.*

en•light•en•ment |ĕn līt'n mənt| *n.* **1.** The act of enlightening or the condition of being enlightened. **2. the Enlightenment.** A movement of the 18th century that called for critical examination of previously unchallenged doctrines and beliefs.

en•list |ĕn lĭst'| *v.* **1.** To take into or join the armed forces: *enlist men for the army. He enlisted in the army after high school.* **2.** To gain or secure (help or support): *enlist supporters for a cause.*

enlisted man. Any man in the armed forces who is not a warrant officer or a commissioned officer.

en•list•ment |ĕn lĭst'mənt| *n.* **1.** The act of enlisting in the armed forces. **2.** The period of time for which one enlists: *a two-year enlistment.*

en•li•ven |ĕn lī'vən| *v.* To make lively or spirited; animate: *enliven the party with music.*

en masse |än măs'| *or* |ĕn|. In a group or body; all together.

en•mesh |ĕn mĕsh'| *v.* To catch in or as if in a net or mesh; entangle: *He was enmeshed in a family quarrel.*

en•mi•ty |ĕn'mĭ tē| *n., pl.* **en•mi•ties.** Deep hatred or hostility, as between enemies or opponents; antagonism.

en•no•ble |ĕn nō'bəl| *v.* **en•no•bled, en•no•bling. 1.** To give a noble or lofty quality to. **2.** To raise to the rank of nobleman.

en•nui |än wē'| *or* |än'wē'| *n.* Dissatisfaction resulting from inactivity or lack of interest; boredom.

e•nor•mi•ty |ĭ nôr'mĭ tē| *n., pl.* **e•nor•mi•ties. 1.** Great wickedness; outrageousness: *the enormity of a crime.* **2.** A monstrous act or crime; an outrage.

e•nor•mous |ĭ nôr'məs| *adj.* Of very great size, extent, number, or degree; huge; immense: *an enormous dog; the enormous cost of the project.* **—e•nor'mous•ly** *adv.* **—e•nor'mous•ness** *n.*

e•nough |ĭ nŭf'| *adj.* Sufficient to meet a need or satisfy a desire: *There is enough food for everybody. Will $10 be enough to pay for the tickets?* *—n.* An adequate quantity: *He ate enough for two.* *—adv.* **1.** To a satisfactory amount or degree; sufficiently: *Are you warm enough?* **2.** Very; fully; quite: *We were glad enough to leave.* **3.** Tolerably; rather: *She sang well enough, but the show was a failure.*

en•quire |ĕn kwīr'| *v.* **en•quired, en•quir•ing.** A form of the word **inquire.** [SEE NOTE]

en•quir•y |ĕn kwīr'ē| *n., pl.* **en•quir•ies.** A form of the word **inquiry.**

en•rage |ĕn rāj'| *v.* **en•raged, en•rag•ing.** To send into a rage; make very angry; infuriate: *His statement enraged Republicans and Democrats alike.*

en•rap•ture |ĕn răp'chər| *v.* **en•rap•tured, en•rap•tur•ing.** To fill with delight; captivate; enchant.

en•rich |ĕn rĭch'| *v.* **1.** To make rich or richer: *enrich oneself at the expense of the poor.* **2.** To make fuller, more meaningful, or more rewarding: *Religion enriches many people's lives. Foreign words have enriched the English language.* **3.** To improve the quality of by adding certain elements or ingredients: *Fertilizer enriches the soil. Milk may be enriched by adding vitamin D.* **4.** To treat (a substance) so as to increase its concentration of a desired component: *enrich uranium.* **—en•rich'ing** *adj.: an enriching experience.* **—en•rich'ment** *n.*

en•roll |ĕn rōl'| *v.* To sign up; register; enter; enlist: *enroll men in the army. I have decided to enroll in an art course.*

en•roll•ment |ĕn rōl'mənt| *n.* **1.** The act of enrolling: *College enrollment begins tomorrow.* **2.** The number of people enrolled: *The school has an enrollment of six hundred.*

en route |än ro͞ot'| *or* |ĕn|. On or along the way: *We'll pick you up en route to the theater.*

en•sconce |ĕn skŏns'| *v.* **en•sconced, en•sconc•ing.** To settle comfortably or snugly: *She ensconced herself in the armchair.*

en•sem•ble |än säm'bəl| *n.* **1.** A complete outfit made up of parts that match or go together: *Her spring ensemble consisted of a suit, hat, shoes, gloves, and bag.* **2.** A group of musicians who perform together. [SEE PICTURE]

en•shrine |ĕn shrīn'| *v.* **en•shrined, en•shrin•ing. 1.** To place or preserve in a shrine. **2.** To preserve or cherish as sacred: *His name is enshrined in our hearts forever.*

en•shroud |ĕn shroud'| *v.* To cover; veil; obscure: *Fog enshrouded the city. His life is enshrouded in secrecy.*

en•sign |ĕn'sən| *n.* **1.** |*also* ĕn'sīn'|. A national flag or banner, often having a special insignia, displayed on ships. **2.** |*also* ĕn'sīn'|. Any badge, symbol, or token of office. **3.** An officer in the U.S. Navy ranking below a lieutenant.

en•si•lage |ĕn'sə lĭj| *n.* Fodder preserved in a silo; silage.

en•slave |ĕn slāv'| *v.* **en•slaved, en•slav•ing.** To make a slave of; force into slavery. **—en•slave'ment** *n.*

en•snare |ĕn snâr'| *v.* **en•snared, en•snar•ing.** To catch in or as if in a trap or snare.

en•sue |ĕn so͞o'| *v.* **en•sued, en•su•ing.** To follow as a consequence; result: *Angry words were exchanged, and a fight ensued.*

en•sure |ĕn sho͝or'| *v.* **en•sured, en•sur•ing.** To make sure or certain of; guarantee; insure: *Few people take measures to ensure good health and safety.* [SEE NOTE]

-ent. A suffix that forms adjectives and nouns: **effervescent; resident.**

en•tab•la•ture |ĕn tăb'lə chər| *n.* In Greek and Roman architecture, the upper section of a structure, resting on the capital and including the architrave, frieze, and cornice.

en•tail |ĕn tāl'| *v.* To have as a result; involve: *The new project will entail great expense.*

en•tan•gle |ĕn tăng'gəl| *v.* **en•tan•gled, en•tan•gling. 1.** To make tangled; snarl: *The fishing line has become entangled.* **2.** To involve, as in some-

enquire/inquire

In the materials on which this Dictionary was based, **enquire** *and* **enquiry** *occurred only 5 times in all, while* **inquire** *and* **inquiry** *occurred 75 times.* **Enquire** *is obviously a rather rare variant, but not so rare that it can be ignored.*

ensemble

ensure/insure

Ensure *and* **insure** *have the same origin (from* **sure***) and the same basic meaning, "to make safe or certain." In this sense, they are nearly equal variants, but* **insure** *seems to be slightly more popular. In addition,* **insure** *has a second meaning, "to protect by financial insurance";* **ensure** *is never used in this sense.*

ă pat/ā pay/â care/ä father/ĕ pet/ē be/ĭ pit/ī pie/î fierce/ŏ pot/ō go/ô paw, for/oi oil/o͝o book/o͞o boot/ou out/ŭ cut/û fur/*th* the/th thin/hw which/zh vision/ə ago, item, pencil, atom, circus

thing complicated or difficult: *He became entangled in a long legal dispute.*

en•tan•gle•ment |ĕn **tăng′**gəl mənt| *n.* **1.** An act or example of becoming entangled: *the entanglement of a fishing line.* **2.** Something that entangles, especially barbed wire. **3.** An involvement in a complicated situation or relationship: *a romantic entanglement. The country's policy was to avoid foreign entanglements.*

en•ter |**ĕn′**tər| *v.* **1.** To come or go in or into: *Knock and enter! The ship entered the harbor. The thought never entered my head.* **2.** To pierce; penetrate: *The bullet entered his lung.* **3.** To come onstage: *Anthony enters dressed as a beggar.* **4.** To begin; embark upon: *Our work is now entering a new phase.* **5.** To become a member of or participant in: *Colorado entered the Union in 1876.* **6.** To take up; make a beginning in: *enter the profession of one's choice.* **7.** To register or enroll: *We have decided to enter him in a private school.* **8.** To inscribe; record: *Enter the total amount in the box below.* **9.** To register in a contest: *enter a beauty contest; enter a horse in a race.* **10.** To submit formally for consideration: *We entered a protest against the other team's conduct.* —***phrasal verb.*** **enter into. 1.** To take part in: *enter into a conversation.* **2.** To be a factor: *Many considerations entered into the decision.*

en•ter•i•tis |ĕn′tə **rī′**tĭs| *n.* Inflammation of the intestinal tract.

en•ter•prise |**ĕn′**tər prīz′| *n.* **1.** An undertaking or venture: *a new business enterprise.* **2.** Economic activity: *free enterprise; private enterprise.* **3.** Initiative in undertaking new projects; adventurous spirit.

en•ter•pris•ing |**ĕn′**tər prī′zĭng| *adj.* Showing imagination, initiative, and willingness to undertake new and challenging projects. —**en′ter•pris′ing•ly** *adv.*

en•ter•tain |ĕn′tər **tān′**| *v.* **1.** To hold the attention of; amuse. **2.** To have (a person) as a guest: *entertained her at dinner. Our family entertains often.* **3.** To consider: *He will entertain no more offers.* **4.** To hold in mind: *I entertain few illusions.*

en•ter•tain•er |ĕn′tər **tā′**nər| *n.* A person, such as a singer, dancer, or comedian, who performs for an audience.

en•ter•tain•ing |ĕn′tər **tā′**nĭng| *adj.* Amusing; agreeably diverting. —**en′ter•tain′ing•ly** *adv.*

en•ter•tain•ment |ĕn′tər **tān′**mənt| *n.* **1.** The act of entertaining. **2.** Something intended to amuse or divert, as a show, nightclub act, etc. **3.** The pleasure that comes from being entertained; amusement.

en•thrall, also **en•thral** |ĕn **thrôl′**| *v.* **en•thralled, en•thrall•ing.** To hold spellbound; captivate: *The magic and power of his voice enthralled all who heard it.*

en•throne |ĕn **thrōn′**| *v.* **en•throned, en•thron•ing. 1.** To place on a throne; invest with sovereign power. **2.** To give a high place to, as in one's affection; revere. —**en•throne′ment** *n.*

en•thuse |ĕn **thōōz′**| *v.* **en•thused, en•thus•ing.** *Informal.* To make or become enthusiastic. [SEE NOTE]

en•thu•si•asm |ĕn **thōō′**zē ăz′əm| *n.* Great interest, excitement, or admiration: *The idea did not arouse much enthusiasm.*

en•thu•si•ast |ĕn **thōō′**zē ăst′| *n.* A person with a keen interest in a particular hobby or activity: *a tennis enthusiast.*

en•thu•si•as•tic |ĕn thōō′zē **ăs′**tĭk| *adj.* Showing or having enthusiasm; eager: *an enthusiastic welcome. He was not enthusiastic about his team's chances.* —**en•thu′si•as′ti•cal•ly** *adv.*

en•tice |ĕn **tīs′**| *v.* **en•ticed, en•tic•ing.** To attract by offering something tempting; lure: *They enticed him into investing money in stocks.* —**en•tic′ing** *adj.: an enticing offer.* —**en•tice′ment** *n.*

en•tire |ĕn **tīr′**| *adj.* **1.** Having no part missing or excepted; whole: *the entire country; his entire savings; the entire class.* **2.** Without reservation or limitation; total; complete: *my entire approval.* —**en•tire′ly** *adv.*

en•tire•ty |ĕn **tīr′**tē| *n., pl.* **en•tire•ties. 1.** The condition of being entire; completeness. **2.** Something that is entire; a whole.

Idiom. **in its entirety.** As a whole: *We must examine the problem in its entirety.*

en•ti•tle |ĕn **tīt′**l| *v.* **en•ti•tled, en•ti•tling. 1.** To give a name or title to; designate: *entitle a book.* **2.** To give a right or privilege: *This coupon entitles you to a 10 per cent discount. Everyone is entitled to his opinion.*

en•ti•ty |**ĕn′**tĭ tē| *n., pl.* **en•ti•ties.** Something that exists and may be distinguished from other things: *American English and British English are often considered separate entities.*

en•tomb |ĕn **tōōm′**| *v.* To place in or as if in a tomb or grave; bury: *The explosion entombed 28 coal miners.* —**en•tomb′ment** *n.*

en•to•mo•log•i•cal |ĕn′tə mə **lŏj′**ĭ kəl| *adj.* Of or relating to entomology.

en•to•mol•o•gist |ĕn′tə **mŏl′**ə jĭst| *n.* A scientist who specializes in entomology.

en•to•mol•o•gy |ĕn′tə **mŏl′**ə jē| *n.* The scientific study of insects. [SEE NOTE]

en•tou•rage |ăn′tōō **räzh′**| *n.* A group of people, such as associates or attendants, who accompany an important person.

en•trails |**ĕn′**trālz′| *or* |-trəlz| *pl.n.* The internal organs of the body, especially the intestines.

en•train |ĕn **trān′**| *v.* To board or put on board a train.

en•trance[1] |**ĕn′**trəns| *n.* **1.** The act or an example of entering: *an actor's entrance onstage; a candidate's entrance into politics.* **2.** A door or passageway through which one enters: *the back entrance of a building.* **3.** The permission, right, or ability to enter; admission: *He was denied entrance to the meeting.* —***modifier:*** *an entrance examination.* [SEE NOTE]

en•trance[2] |ĕn **trăns′**| *or* |**-träns′**| *v.* **en•tranced, en•tranc•ing. 1.** To put into a trance. **2.** To fill with great pleasure or wonder; fascinate. —**en•tranc′ing** *adj.: an entrancing sight; an entrancing young lady.* [SEE NOTE]

en•trant |**ĕn′**trənt| *n.* A person who enters a competition, such as a race or contest.

en•trap |ĕn **trăp′**| *v.* **en•trapped, en•trap•ping.** To catch in or as if in a trap. —**en•trap′ment** *n.*

en•treat |ĕn **trēt′**| *v.* To ask earnestly; beg; implore: *"Help me, I entreat you!"*

en•treat•y |ĕn **trē′**tē| *n., pl.* **en•treat•ies.** An earnest request; a plea.

en•trée, also **en•tree** |**ăn′**trā| *n.* **1.** The right, permission, or liberty to enter; entrance; admit-

enthuse

Enthuse, *a back-formation from* **enthusiasm,** *is not yet accepted as a serious word. The American Heritage Usage Panel disapproves of it by a vote of three to one (example:* The majority leader enthused over his party's gains*). In addition, the word did not appear at all in the five million words of school literature on which this Dictionary is based.*

entomology/etymology

Etymologists, *including the writer of this note, are distressed when they are mistaken for* **entomologists,** *and vice versa. The etymology of the word* **entomology** *is: from Greek* entomon, *"an insect," which is from* entomos, *"cut into pieces, divided up" (because insects are divided into three segments: head, thorax, and abdomen). The etymology of* **etymology** *is given in the note at* **etymology.**

entrance[1-2]

Entrance[1] *is from* **enter,** *and* **entrance**[2] *is from* **trance.** *Notice that in the pronunciation of each word the stress is on the root, which contains the main idea of the word. The unstressed* -ance *of* **entrance**[1] *is the common noun ending* -ance *as in* **appearance, tolerance.** *The unstressed* en- *of* **entrance**[2] *is the common prefix* en- *(a variant of* in-*) as in* **enable, encamp.**

tance: *gain entrée to a meeting.* **2.** The main course of a meal.

en•trench |ĕn **trĕnch′**| *v.* **1.** To place in a trench or strong defensive position: *The soldiers entrenched themselves in the bunker.* **2.** To implant or establish firmly: *ideas firmly entrenched in his mind.*

en•trench•ment |ĕn **trĕnch′**mənt| *n.* **1.** The act of entrenching or the condition of being entrenched. **2.** A system of trenches and mounds used for defense.

en•tre•pre•neur |ăn′trə prə **nûr′**| *or* |**-nŏŏr′**| *n.* A person who organizes and operates a business enterprise.

en•trust |ĕn **trŭst′**| *v.* **1.** To turn over (something) for safekeeping, care, or action: *entrust a sale to a broker.* **2.** To charge (someone) with a task or responsibility involving trust: *entrust someone with a difficult assignment.*

en•try |**ĕn′**trē| *n., pl.* **en•tries. 1. a.** The act or right of entering; entrance: *A visa is needed for entry into the country.* **b.** A passage or opening affording entrance. **2. a.** The inclusion of an item in a diary, register, list, or other record. **b.** An item thus entered. **3.** A word, phrase, or term entered and defined in a dictionary or encyclopedia. **4.** Someone or something entered in a race or contest.

en•try•way |**ĕn′**trē wā′| *n.* A passage or opening serving as an entrance.

en•twine |ĕn **twīn′**| *v.* **en•twined, en•twin•ing.** To wind or twine around or about: *Ivy entwined the front of the house.*

e•nu•mer•ate |ĭ **nōō′**mə rāt′| *or* |ĭ **nyōō′**-| *v.* **e•nu•mer•at•ed, e•nu•mer•at•ing. 1.** To count off or name one by one; list: *The details are too long to enumerate.* **2.** To match (the members of a set) one by one with the natural numbers; count.

e•nu•mer•a•tion |ĭ nōō′mə **rā′**shən| *or* |ĭ-nyōō′-| *n.* **1.** The act or process of enumerating. **2.** A detailed list of items.

e•nun•ci•ate |ĭ **nŭn′**sē āt′| *or* |-shē-| *v.* **e•nun•ci•at•ed, e•nun•ci•at•ing. 1.** To pronounce (words), especially in a clear and distinct manner: *You must try to enunciate more clearly.* **2.** To state or set forth thoroughly and systematically: *The President enunciated his program for tax reform.* **3.** To announce; proclaim.

e•nun•ci•a•tion |ĭ nŭn′sē **ā′**shən| *or* |-shē-| *n.* **1.** The way in which a person pronounces words or speech sounds. **2.** An announcement, declaration, or similar official statement.

en•vel•op |ĕn **vĕl′**əp| *v.* **1.** To enclose completely with or as if with a covering: *envelop a baby in a blanket. Legend and myth have long enveloped the origins of the city of Rome. The tornado funnel enveloped the barn.* **2.** To surround; encircle: *Union soldiers attempted to envelop Lee's troops.*

en•ve•lope |**ĕn′**və lōp′| *or* |**ăn′**-| *n.* **1.** A flat paper wrapper with a gummed flap, used chiefly for mailing letters. **2.** The section of a dirigible or balloon that is filled with gas.

en•vi•a•ble |**ĕn′**vē ə bəl| *adj.* Admirable or desirable enough to be envied: *an enviable reputation; an enviable achievement.* **—en′vi•a•ble•ness** *n.* **—en′vi•a•bly** *adv.*

en•vi•ous |**ĕn′**vē əs| *adj.* Feeling or expressing envy: *I am envious of your achievements. She had an envious look on her face.* **—en′vi•ous•ly** *adv.* **—en′vi•ous•ness** *n.*

en•vi•ron•ment |ĕn **vī′**rən mənt| *or* |**-vī′**ərn-| *n.* **1.** Surroundings and conditions that affect natural processes and the growth and development of living things: *Fish and birds, like all living things, are adapted to special habitats within their environment. The children grew up in a family with a warm and loving environment.* **2.** A special kind or combination of such surroundings or conditions: *The desert is not the right environment for a maple tree.*

en•vi•ron•men•tal |ĕn vī′rən **mĕn′**tl| *or* |-vī′-ərn-| *adj.* Of the environment: *Climate is an important environmental factor affecting plant and animal life. Our class often goes on field trips as part of our environmental study program.*

en•vi•rons |ĕn **vī′**rənz| *or* |**-vī′**ərnz| *or* |**ĕn′**vər-ənz| *pl.n.* The surrounding areas, especially of a city; suburbs.

en•vis•age |ĕn **vĭz′**ĭj| *v.* **en•vis•aged, en•vis•ag•ing. 1.** To picture in the mind; imagine: *It takes no great stretch of the imagination to envisage the feather as a modified reptile's scale.* **2.** To expect or contemplate, especially as a future possibility or goal: *It is difficult to envisage a change in foreign policy.*

en•vi•sion |ĕn **vĭzh′**ən| *v.* To picture in one's mind; imagine: *He envisioned himself as president of the club.*

en•voy |**ĕn′**voi′| *or* |**ăn′**-| *n.* **1.** A person sent on an errand or mission. **2.** A person sent to represent his government in a particular dealing with another government. **3.** A person ranking next below an ambassador who represents his government in a foreign country.

en•vy |**ĕn′**vē| *n., pl.* **en•vies. 1.** A feeling of discontent and resentment aroused by the abilities, qualities, or achievements of another, with a strong desire to have them for oneself. **2.** The object of such a feeling: *He is the envy of his classmates. His new car was the envy of all his friends.* —*v.* **en•vied, en•vy•ing, en•vies.** To feel envy toward: *I envy you your curly hair. She has a figure that any girl would envy.*

en•wrap |ĕn **răp′**| *v.* **en•wrapped, en•wrap•ping.** To wrap or enclose in something, such as a garment or other covering.

en•zyme |**ĕn′**zīm′| *n.* **1.** Any of a large number of proteins that act as catalysts in the chemical processes that go on in living organisms. **2.** A commercially produced protein of this type used in chemical processes and in many household detergents.

E•o•cene |**ē′**ə sēn′| *n.* Also **Eocene epoch.** The geologic epoch that began about 58 million years ago and ended about 36 million years ago, characterized by the rise of mammals. ***—modifier:*** *an Eocene fossil.*

e•o•hip•pus |ē′ō **hĭp′**əs| *n.* A small, extinct animal that lived millions of years ago and was an ancestor of the horses of today. [SEE PICTURE]

E•o•lith•ic |ē′ə **lĭth′**ĭk| *n.* The era considered to be the earliest period of human culture preceding the Paleolithic; the earliest part of the Stone Age. ***—modifier:*** *an Eolithic flint.*

e•on |**ē′**ŏn′| *or* |**ē′**ən| *n.* **1.** An extremely long period of time; an age; eternity. **2.** A division of geologic time that contains two or more eras.

eohippus

ă **pat**/ā **pay**/â **care**/ä **father**/ĕ **pet**/ ē **be**/ĭ **pit**/ī **pie**/î **fierce**/ŏ **pot**/ ō **go**/ô **paw**, **for**/oi **oil**/ŏŏ **book**/ ōō **boot**/ou **out**/ŭ **cut**/û **fur**/ *th* **the**/th **thin**/hw **which**/zh **vision**/ ə **ago**, item, pencil, atom, circus

ep•au•let or **ep•au•lette** |ĕp′ə lĕt′| *or* |ĕp′ə-lĕt′| *n.* An ornamental strap worn on the shoulder of an officer's uniform.

é•pée, also **e•pee** |ā pā′| *n.* A fencing sword with a bowl-shaped guard and a long, narrow blade that has no cutting edge and tapers to a blunt point.

e•phed•rine |ĭ fĕd′rĭn| *or* |ĕf′ĭ drēn′| *n.* A white, odorless alkaloid composed of carbon, hydrogen, nitrogen, and oxygen in the proportions $C_{10}H_{15}NO$. It is extracted from the leaves of a shrub and also made synthetically. When it is used as a drug, its actions and uses are similar to those of adrenalin.

e•phem•er•al |ĭ fĕm′ər əl| *adj.* Lasting only a brief time; short-lived: *Fame and glory are often ephemeral.* —**e•phem′er•al•ly** *adv.*

epi–. A prefix meaning "on, upon, near, toward, or over": **epicenter; epidermis.**

ep•ic |ĕp′ĭk| *n.* A long poem or literary work about heroic characters who perform outstanding deeds. —*adj.* **1.** Of or resembling an epic: *an epic poem.* **2.** Like something described in an epic; tremendous: *an epic achievement.*

ep•i•can•thic fold |ĕp′ĭ kăn′thĭk|. A fold of skin on the upper eyelid that tends to cover the inner corner of the eye, found in the Chinese and many other Mongolian peoples.

ep•i•cen•ter |ĕp′ĭ sĕn′tər| *n.* The part of the earth's surface that is directly above the point where an earthquake begins.

ep•i•cure |ĕp′ĭ kyo͝or′| *n.* **1.** A person with refined tastes in food, wine, etc. **2.** *Archaic.* A person devoted to sensuous pleasure and luxurious living.

ep•i•cu•re•an |ĕp′ĭ kyo͝o rē′ən| *adj.* **1.** Devoted to the pursuit of sensuous pleasure and luxury. **2.** Suited to the tastes of an epicure: *an epicurean meal.* —*n.* An epicure.

ep•i•dem•ic |ĕp′ĭ dĕm′ĭk| *adj.* Spreading rapidly and widely among the inhabitants of an area: *an epidemic disease.* —*n.* **1.** A contagious disease that spreads rapidly: *an influenza epidemic.* **2.** A rapid spread or development: *an epidemic of bank robberies.*

ep•i•der•mis |ĕp′ĭ dûr′mĭs| *n.* An outer protective layer of cells, as of the human skin or the leaves, stems, and roots of plants.

ep•i•glot•tis |ĕp′ĭ glŏt′ĭs| *n.* An elastic flap of cartilage found at the base of the tongue. It covers the glottis during swallowing to keep food from entering the windpipe.

ep•i•gram |ĕp′ĭ grăm′| *n.* A brief witty saying, often with an ironic twist.

ep•i•gram•mat•ic |ĕp′ĭ grə măt′ĭk| *adj.* Of or like an epigram; terse; witty. —**ep′i•gram•mat′i•cal•ly** *adv.*

ep•i•graph |ĕp′ĭ grăf′| *or* |-gräf′| *n.* **1.** An inscription, as on a building, monument, etc. **2.** A quotation at the beginning of a book or a chapter of a book.

ep•i•lep•sy |ĕp′ə lĕp′sē| *n.* A disorder of the nervous system in which there are recurring seizures marked by disturbances of consciousness or convulsions or both. In its milder form the attacks are very short.

ep•i•lep•tic |ĕp′ə lĕp′tĭk| *adj.* Of or suffering from epilepsy. —*n.* A person who has epilepsy.

ep•i•logue, also **ep•i•log** |ĕp′ə lôg′| *or* |-lŏg′| *n.* **1.** A short poem or speech spoken directly to the audience at the end of a play. **2.** A short section at the end of any literary work, often dealing with the future of its characters.

ep•i•neph•rin |ĕp′ə nĕf′rĭn| *n.* A form of the word **epinephrine.**

ep•i•neph•rine |ĕp′ə nĕf′rēn′| *or* |-rĭn| *n.* Adrenalin, a hormone.

E•piph•a•ny |ĭ pĭf′ə nē| *n.* A Christian festival occurring on January 6 and celebrating the visit of the Magi to the Christ child, the first revelation of Christ to the Gentiles.

ep•i•phyte |ĕp′ə fīt′| *n.* A plant that grows on another plant or object that provides support but not nourishment. Spanish moss and certain orchids are epiphytes.

ep•i•phyt•ic |ĕp′ə fĭt′ĭk| *adj.* Of or relating to an epiphyte.

e•pis•co•pal |ĭ pĭs′kə pəl| *adj.* **1.** Of or governed by bishops. **2. Episcopal.** Of, belonging to, or having to do with the Protestant Episcopal Church.

Episcopal Church. The **Protestant Episcopal Church.**

E•pis•co•pa•lian |ĭ pĭs′kə pāl′yən| *or* |-pā′lē-ən| *n.* A member of the Protestant Episcopal Church. —*adj.* Of, belonging to, or having to do with the Protestant Episcopal Church.

ep•i•sode |ĕp′ĭ sōd′| *n.* **1. a.** An event or series of related events in the course of a continuous experience: *an episode of her childhood.* **b.** An incident that forms a distinct part of a story. **2.** An installment in a serialized novel, play, or radio or television program.

ep•i•sod•ic |ĕp′ĭ sŏd′ĭk| *adj.* Presented in episodes; somewhat uneven or disjointed: *an episodic narrative.* —**ep′i•sod′i•cal•ly** *adv.*

e•pis•te•mol•o•gy |ĭ pĭs′tə mŏl′ə jē| *n.* The branch of philosophy that deals with the origin and nature of knowledge.

e•pis•tle |ĭ pĭs′əl| *n.* **1.** A letter, especially a formal one. **2.** Often **Epistle.** One of the letters written by the Apostles and forming part of the New Testament.

ep•i•taph |ĕp′ĭ tăf′| *or* |-täf′| *n.* An inscription on a tombstone or monument in memory of the person buried there. [SEE NOTE]

ep•i•the•li•um |ĕp′ə thē′lē əm| *n., pl.* **ep•i•the•li•ums** or **ep•i•the•li•a** |ĕp′ə thē′lē ə|. The thin, membranous tissue that covers most of the internal surfaces and organs of an animal body and the outer surface as well. —**ep′i•the′li•al** |ĕp′ə thē′lē əl| *adj.*

ep•i•thet |ĕp′ə thĕt′| *n.* **1.** A term used to describe the nature of someone or something; for example, *the Lion-Hearted* in *Richard the Lion-Hearted* is an epithet. **2.** An abusive or insulting word or phrase.

e•pit•o•me |ĭ pĭt′ə mē| *n.* **1.** Someone or something that is the perfect example of an entire group or class; embodiment: *His answer was the epitome of tactfulness and diplomacy.* **2.** A summary of a book, article, etc.

e•pit•o•mize |ĭ pĭt′ə mīz′| *v.* **e•pit•o•mized, e•pit•o•miz•ing.** **1.** To typify or represent perfectly an entire group or class. **2.** To make a summary of.

ep•och |ĕp′ək| *n.* **1.** A unit of geologic time that is a division of a period. **2.** A particular period

epitaph

Two inscriptions on English graves: "Here lie the remains of James Pady, brick-maker, in hope that his clay will be remoulded in a workmanlike manner, far superior to his former perishable materials."

"Here lie I, Martin Elginbrodde,
Have mercy on my soul, Lord God.
As I would do were I Lord God,
And you were Martin Elginbrodde."

equal
The mathematical relation ♦ is the relation of equality or equivalence if: (1) a ♦ a, *(2)* a ♦ b *means also that* b ♦ a, *and (3)* a ♦ b ♦ c *together mean that* a ♦ c. *In mathematical notation, "is equal to" is abbreviated* = a = b; *2 + 2 = 4.*

equestrian
Equestrian *comes from Latin* equus, *"horse," which is descended from* ekwos, *the prehistoric Indo-European word for "horse." This word was probably in use before the horse was tamed or trained by man. Indo-European peoples seem to have played a leading part in developing the arts of driving and riding, from about 2500* B.C. *onward. The Greeks, the Celts, the Scythians, the Persians, and the Aryans of India had very strong traditions of horsemanship and even horse-worship.*

equestrian statue

ă pat/ā pay/â care/ä father/ĕ pet/ ē be/ĭ pit/ī pie/î fierce/ŏ pot/ ō go/ô paw, for/oi oil/ŏŏ book/ ōō boot/ou out/ŭ cut/û fur/ *th* the/th thin/hw which/zh vision/ ə ago, item, pencil, atom, circus

in history marked by certain important events or developments; an era: *the feudal epoch; the epoch of space exploration.*

ep•och•al |ĕp′ə kəl| *adj.* **1.** Of or characteristic of a geologic epoch. **2.** Opening a new era; highly important or significant; momentous: *The mission of Apollo 11 ranks as one of the epochal voyages of all time.*

ep•och-mak•ing |ĕp′ək mā′kĭng| *adj.* Opening a new era; highly important or significant; momentous: *epoch-making events that changed the whole course of civilization.*

ep•ox•y |ĭ pŏk′sē| *n., pl.* **ep•ox•ies.** Any one of a number of synthetic resins that set to form tough, resistant, and strongly adhesive materials, used in making paints, varnishes, lacquers, and adhesives. ***—modifier:*** *an epoxy cement.*

ep•si•lon |ĕp′sə lŏn′| *n.* The fifth letter of the Greek alphabet, written Ε, ε. In English it is represented as *E, e.*

Ep•som salts |ĕp′səm|. Hydrated magnesium sulfate, used in medicine as a cathartic and for bathing inflamed or sore parts of the body and in the leather and textile industries.

eq. 1. equal. **2.** equation. **3.** equivalent.

eq•ua•ble |ĕk′wə bəl| *or* |ē′kwə-| *adj.* **1.** Unvarying; steady; even: *an equable climate.* **2.** Even-tempered; not readily upset; serene: *He has an equable disposition.* **—eq′ua•bil′i•ty** *n.* **—eq′ua•bly** *adv.*

e•qual |ē′kwəl| *adj.* **1.** Having the same capability, amount, extent, etc., as another: *equal strength; equal importance; equal damage.* **2.** In mathematics: **a.** Having the same meaning or value: *3 + 2 and 5 are equal.* **b.** Capable of being substituted one for the other. **3.** Having the same privileges, status, or rights: *All men are created equal.* **4.** Having the necessary strength, ability, or determination; qualified: *equal to the task.* *—n.* Someone or something that is equal to another: *treat him as an equal.* *—v.* **e•qualed** or **e•qualled, e•qual•ing** or **e•qual•ling. 1.** To be equal to, as in value: a *equals* b. *My ability equals his.* **2.** To do, make, or produce something equal to: *He equaled the world's record in the mile run.* ***—phrasal verb.*** **equal out.** To be of equal value; reach a balance: *The pros and cons equal out.* **—e′qual•ly** *adv.* [SEE NOTE]

e•qual•i•ty |ĭ kwŏl′ĭ tē| *n., pl.* **e•qual•i•ties. 1.** The condition of being equal, especially the condition of enjoying equal rights, as political, economic, and social rights. **2.** A mathematical statement that two things are equal.

e•qual•ize |ē′kwə līz′| *v.* **e•qual•ized, e•qual•iz•ing.** To make or become equal: *This equalizes the temperatures. Wait until the pressures equalize.* **—e′qual•i•za′tion** *n.* **—e′qual•iz′er** *n.*

equal sign. The symbol (=) used in mathematics to indicate that things are equal, as in $a = b$ and $2 + 2 = 4$.

equal temperament. The tuning of a musical instrument so that all semitones are equal in size.

e•qua•nim•i•ty |ē′kwə nĭm′ĭ tē| *or* |ĕk′wə-| *n.* The condition or quality of being calm and even-tempered; composure.

e•quate |ĭ kwāt′| *v.* **e•quat•ed, e•quat•ing.** To make equal or consider to be equal: *Many people equate wisdom with old age.*

e•qua•tion |ĭ kwā′zhən| *or* |-shən| *n.* A mathematical statement that two expressions are equal. For example, $3 + 2 = 5$, $3 \times 2 = 6$, $y = 2 + 8$, and $x + y = 18$ are all equations.

e•qua•tor |ĭ kwā′tər| *n.* **1.** The great circle whose plane is perpendicular to the earth's axis of rotation and whose circumference coincides with the earth's surface. It divides the earth into the Northern Hemisphere and the Southern Hemisphere. **2.** A similar circle on any celestial body: *the sun's equator.* **3.** The **celestial equator.**

e•qua•to•ri•al |ē′kwə tôr′ē əl| *or* |-tōr′-| *or* |ĕk′wə-| *adj.* **1.** Of or near the equator. **2.** Characteristic of the equator or the regions near it: *equatorial heat.*

Equatorial Guin•ea |gĭn′ē|. A small country in western Africa, consisting of Río Muni on the mainland and the island of Bioko and smaller islands in the Gulf of Guinea. Population, 244,000. Capital, Malabo (on the island of Bioko).

eq•uer•ry |ĕk′wə rē| *n., pl.* **eq•uer•ries. 1.** An officer in charge of the horses in a royal or noble household. **2.** In England, a personal attendant to a member of the royal family.

e•ques•tri•an |ĭ kwĕs′trē ən| *adj.* **1.** Of horseback riding: *equestrian ability.* **2.** Represented on horseback: *an equestrian statue of General Grant.* *—n.* A person who rides a horse or performs on horseback. [SEE NOTE & PICTURE]

e•ques•tri•enne |ĭ kwĕs′trē ĕn′| *n.* A female equestrian.

equi–. A word element meaning "equal or equally": **equidistant.**

e•qui•an•gu•lar |ē′kwē ăng′gyə lər| *adj.* Having all angles equal: *an equiangular triangle.*

e•qui•dis•tant |ē′kwĭ dĭs′tənt| *adj.* Equally distant. **—e′qui•dis′tant•ly** *adv.*

e•qui•lat•e•ral |ē′kwə lăt′ər əl| *adj.* Having all sides equal, as a geometric figure. **—e′qui•lat′er•al•ly** *adv.*

e•qui•lib•ri•um |ē′kwə lĭb′rē əm| *n.* **1.** A condition of balance between opposites: *The death rate and the birth rate were in equilibrium.* **2.** Mental or emotional stability. **3.** A condition in which all the forces and torques acting on a physical system cancel each other and the net result is the same as if there were no force or torque at all. **4.** A condition in which a chemical reaction and its corresponding reverse reaction go on at equal rates, leaving the concentrations of the reacting substances the same.

e•quine |ē′kwīn′| *adj.* Of, related to, or characteristic of a horse.

e•qui•noc•tial |ē′kwə nŏk′shəl| *or* |ĕk′wə-| *adj.* **1.** Of an equinox or the equinoxes. **2.** Occurring at or near the time of an equinox: *an equinoctial storm.*

e•qui•nox |ē′kwə nŏks′| *or* |ĕk′wə-| *n.* **1.** Either of the times of year at which the sun crosses the celestial equator and day and night are about equal in length; the autumnal equinox or the vernal equinox. **2.** The position of the sun at these times; the points where the ecliptic and the celestial equator intersect.

e•quip |ĭ kwĭp′| *v.* **e•quipped, e•quip•ping.** To supply with what is needed or wanted; provide: *We equipped ourselves with sleeping bags for the long hike.*

eq•ui•page |ĕk′wə pĭj| *n.* **1.** Equipment, as of

an army. **2.** An elegantly equipped horse-drawn carriage, usually attended by footmen.

e•quip•ment |ĭ **kwĭp′**mənt| *n.* **1.** The things needed or used for a particular purpose: *camping equipment.* **2.** The act of equipping.

e•qui•poise |**ē′**kwə poiz′| *or* |**ĕk′**wə-| *n.* **1.** Equality in distribution, as of weight, forces, etc.; balance; equilibrium. **2.** A weight or force that balances another; a counterbalance.

eq•ui•ta•ble |**ĕk′**wĭ tə bəl| *adj.* Just and fair; impartial: *an equitable decision.* **—eq′ui•ta•bly** *adv.*

eq•ui•ty |**ĕk′**wĭ tē| *n., pl.* **eq•ui•ties. 1.** Justice; fairness; impartiality. **2.** Legal justice applied in circumstances not covered by a law or laws: *a court of equity.* **3.** The value of a business or property after the debts, mortgages, etc., on it are deducted.

e•quiv•a•lence |ĭ **kwĭv′**ə ləns| *n.* The condition or property of being equivalent.

e•quiv•a•lent |ĭ **kwĭv′**ə lənt| *adj.* **1.** Equal in amount, value, meaning, force, etc. **2. a.** Capable of having elements matched in a one-to-one correspondence: *equivalent sets.* **b.** Equal in measure and matching part for part: *equivalent figures.* **c.** Equal in numerical value. *—n.* Something that is equivalent: *A dime is the equivalent of two nickels.*

e•quiv•o•cal |ĭ **kwĭv′**ə kəl| *adj.* **1.** Capable of being interpreted in two ways; ambiguous: *an equivocal answer.* **2.** Of uncertain outcome or worth; inconclusive: *an equivocal result.* **—e•quiv′o•cal•ly** *adv.* **—e•quiv′o•cal•ness** *n.*

e•quiv•o•cate |ĭ **kwĭv′**ə kāt′| *v.* **e•quiv•o•cat•ed, e•quiv•o•cat•ing.** To use equivocal language intentionally; speak ambiguously; hedge. **—e•quiv′o•ca′tion** *n.*

Er The symbol for the element erbium.

-er[1]. A suffix that forms the comparative of adjectives and adverbs: **neater; whiter; slower.**

-er[2]. A suffix that forms nouns: **blender; foreigner; helper; photographer.**

e•ra |**îr′**ə| *or* |**ĕr′**ə| *n.* **1.** A period of time that utilizes a specific point in history as its beginning: *the Christian era; the Colonial era in U.S. history; the era of the atom.* **2.** The longest division of geologic time, containing one or more periods.

e•rad•i•cate |ĭ **răd′**ĭ kāt′| *v.* **e•rad•i•cat•ed, e•rad•i•cat•ing.** To remove all traces of; destroy completely: *Can we eradicate poverty?* **—e•rad′i•ca′tion** *n.*

e•rase |ĭ **rās′**| *v.* **e•rased, e•ras•ing. 1.** To remove (something written or drawn) by rubbing or wiping: *erase a mistake.* **2.** To remove writing or a recording from: *erase a blackboard; erase a tape.* **3.** To remove all traces of; eradicate: *Time erases hurt feelings.* **4.** To be capable of being erased: *a paper that erases easily.*

e•ras•er |ĭ **rā′**sər| *n.* Something that erases, as a piece of rubber, cloth, or felt: *a blackboard eraser.* [SEE PICTURE]

E•ras•mus |ĭ **răz′**məs|, **Desiderius.** 1466?–1536. Dutch theologian and scholar.

e•ras•ure |ĭ **rā′**shər| *n.* **1.** The act of erasing. **2.** The trace or mark remaining on a surface from which something has been erased.

er•bi•um |**ûr′**bē əm| *n.* Symbol **Er** One of the elements, a soft, silvery rare-earth element. Atomic number 68; atomic weight 167.26; valence +3; melting point 1,497°C; boiling point 2,900°C.

ere |âr|. *Archaic. prep.* Previous to; before. *—conj.* **1.** Before. **2.** Sooner than; rather than. ¶*These sound alike* **ere, air, are[2], e'er, heir.**

e•rect |ĭ **rĕkt′**| *adj.* Directed or pointing upward; standing upright; vertical: *erect posture.* *—v.* **1.** To build; put up; construct: *erect a skyscraper; erect a monument.* **2.** To raise upright; set on end: *erect a Christmas tree for decorating.* **3.** To set up; establish: *Countries erected customs barriers to limit imports.* **—e•rect′ly** *adv.* **—e•rect′ness** *n.*

e•rec•tion |ĭ **rĕk′**shən| *n.* **1.** The act of erecting, building, or raising upright. **2.** Something erected, as a building.

e•rec•tor |ĭ **rĕk′**tər| *n.* Someone or something that erects.

erg |ûrg| *n.* A unit of energy or work equal to one ten-millionth (10^{-7}) of a joule.

er•go |**ûr′**gō| *or* |**âr′**-| *conj. & adv.* Consequently; therefore.

er•got |**ûr′**gət| *or* |-gŏt′| *n.* A fungus that infects rye, wheat, and other grain plants, forming black masses among the seeds. Grain infected with ergot is poisonous, and can cause serious illness.

er•got•ism |**ûr′**gə tĭz′əm| *n.* Poisoning that results from eating grain that is infected with ergot.

Er•ic•son |**ĕr′**ĭk sən|, **Leif.** Norwegian navigator, believed to have landed in North America in about the year A.D. 1000.

E•rie |**îr′**ē| *n., pl.* **E•rie** or **E•ries. 1.** A North American Indian tribe formerly living in the region around Lake Erie. **2.** A member of this tribe. **3.** The Iroquoian language of this tribe.

E•rie, Lake |**îr′**ē|. One of the Great Lakes, bounded by Michigan, Ohio, Pennsylvania, New York, and Ontario, Canada.

Er•in |**ĕr′**ĭn|. Ireland. Used chiefly in poetry.

erl•king |**ûrl′**kĭng′| *n.* An evil spirit of Germanic folklore who plays cruel tricks on children.

er•mine |**ûr′**mĭn| *n.* **1.** A weasel with brownish fur that in winter turns to white with a black tail tip. **2.** The white fur of this animal. [SEE PICTURES & NOTE]

e•rode |ĭ **rōd′**| *v.* **e•rod•ed, e•rod•ing. 1.** To wear away or become worn away by or as if by rubbing or bombardment with small particles: *Wind eroded the hillside. The slope erodes when it rains.* **2.** To form by wearing away earth or rock in this way: *The river eroded a deep gorge.*

Er•os |**îr′**ŏs′| *or* |**ĕr′**-|. The Greek god of love.

e•ro•sion |ĭ **rō′**zhən| *n.* The process of eroding or the condition of being eroded, especially by means of natural agents such as wind, water, and weather.

e•ro•sive |ĭ **rō′**sĭv| *adj.* Acting or tending to erode: *erosive winds.*

e•rot•ic |ĭ **rŏt′**ĭk| *adj.* Of or arousing sexual desire. **—e•rot′i•cal•ly** *adv.*

e•rot•i•cism |ĭ **rŏt′**ĭ sĭz′əm| *n.* Erotic quality or nature.

err |ûr| *or* |ĕr| *v.* To make a mistake or error; be incorrect: *He erred when he said that pollution wasn't a problem.*

er•rand |**ĕr′**ənd| *n.* **1.** A short trip taken to perform a specified task. **2.** The purpose or

eraser

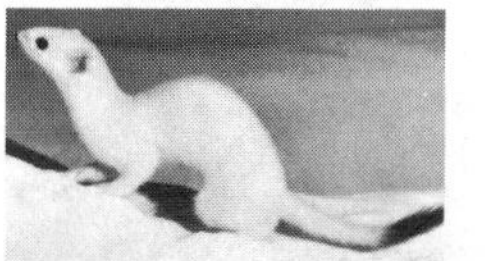

ermine
Above: Ermine in winter coat
Below: Ermine robes of King George III of England

ermine
In the Middle Ages, rich clothes were sometimes trimmed with the white furs of ermines, with the black tails showing as a pattern. Ermine is still worn in England on the state robes of royalty, and peers, and some judges and mayors.

object of such a trip: *His errand was to mail a letter.* —**modifier:** *an errand boy.*

er•ra•ta |ĭ rä'tə| *or* |ĭ rā'-| *pl.n.* The less frequently used singular is **er•ra•tum** |ĭ rä'təm| *or* |ĭ rā'-|. A list of corrections at the beginning or end of a book.

er•rat•ic |ĭ răt'ĭk| *adj.* **1.** Irregular or uneven in quality, progress, etc.: *His work has been erratic.* **2.** Odd; eccentric: *erratic behavior.* —**er•rat'i•cal•ly** *adv.*

er•ro•ne•ous |ĭ rō'nē əs| *adj.* Containing or derived from error; mistaken; false: *an erroneous conclusion.* —**er•ro'ne•ous•ly** *adv.*

er•ror |ĕr'ər| *n.* **1.** Something that is incorrect or wrong; a mistake: *an error in addition.* **2.** The condition of being incorrect or wrong: *His statement is in error.* **3. a.** The difference between a value that is measured or computed and the value that is correct or probably correct. **b.** The difference between what a machine or device is set to do by its controls and what it actually does: *an error in a thermostat.* **c.** Any mistake or inaccuracy, especially one that can be expressed as a number. **4.** The failure of a fielder in baseball to make a defensive play that could normally have been made and that would have resulted in an out or prevented a runner from advancing.

er•satz |ĕr'zäts'| *adj.* Substitute; artificial: *ersatz mink.*

erst•while |ûrst'hwīl'| *or* |-wīl'| *adj.* Former: *her erstwhile husband.* —*adv. Archaic.* In times past; formerly.

er•u•dite |ĕr'yo͝o dīt'| *or* |ĕr'o͝o-| *adj.* Having or marked by erudition; learned: *an erudite book.* —**er'u•dite'ly** *adv.*

er•u•di•tion |ĕr'yo͝o **dĭsh'**ən| *or* |ĕr'o͝o-| *n.* Great knowledge or learning: *a scholar's erudition.*

escape velocity
For a body located on the surface of the earth, **escape velocity** *is about 7 miles per second in a vertical direction.*

e•rupt |ĭ **rŭpt'**| *v.* **1.** To shoot forth (lava, steam, etc.), as a volcano or geyser does: *A volcano may continue to erupt lava for many years. The volcano was threatening to erupt.* **2.** To appear or develop suddenly and violently: *a regional conflict that in another decade would erupt into violent warfare.* **3.** To appear on the skin: *Boils erupted on his back.*

e•rup•tion |ĭ **rŭp'**shən| *n.* **1.** The fact or an example of erupting: *The frequency of eruption varies among different geysers. The eruption of the volcano went on for over nine years.* **2.** A sudden, often violent outburst: *the eruption of a disease.* **3.** A rash or blemish on the skin or on a mucous membrane.

e•rup•tive |ĭ **rŭp'**tĭv| *adj.* Characterized by an eruption or eruptions, as of the skin: *an eruptive disease.*

-ery. A suffix that forms nouns from verbs or other nouns: **bakery; greenery; savagery; snobbery.**

er•y•sip•e•las |ĕr'ĭ **sĭp'**ə ləs| *or* |îr'ĭ-| *n.* A spreading inflammation of the skin and the tissue just under it, caused by bacteria.

e•ryth•ro•blast |ĭ **rĭth'**rə blăst'| *n.* Any of the cells in the bone marrow that have nuclei and that develop into red blood cells.

e•ryth•ro•cyte |ĭ **rĭth'**rə sīt'| *n.* A red blood cell.

-es[1]. A suffix that forms the plural of nouns ending in *-s, -z, -sh, -ch,* and some ending in *-y* or *-f*: **twitches; ladies.**

-es[2]. A suffix that forms the third person singular form of the present tense of verbs ending in *-s, -z, -sh, -ch,* and some ending in *-y*: **amasses; fizzes; defies.**

Es The symbol for the element einsteinium.

es•ca•late |ĕs'kə lāt'| *v.* **es•ca•lat•ed, es•ca•lat•ing.** To increase or cause to increase in value, scope, intensity, etc.: *Both sides have escalated the war. Food prices and rents have escalated.* —**es'ca•la'tion** *n.*

es•ca•la•tor |ĕs'kə lā'tər| *n.* A moving stairway consisting of steps attached to a continuously circulating belt.

es•cal•lop |ĭ **skŏl'**əp| *or* |ĭ **skăl'**-| *v.* A form of the word **scallop.**

es•ca•pade |ĕs'kə pād'| *n.* A carefree or reckless adventure; a fling; caper.

es•cape |ĭ **skāp'**| *v.* **es•caped, es•cap•ing.** **1.** To break loose from confinement; get free: *escape from prison. The prisoners escaped by climbing the wall.* **2.** To succeed in avoiding (capture, danger, harm, etc.): *escape injury.* **3.** To leak or seep out: *All the air escaped from the balloon.* **4.** To elude the memory or mind of; be forgotten or unnoticed by: *His name escapes me.* **5.** To issue from involuntarily: *A sigh escaped her lips.* —*n.* **1.** The act or an example of escaping: *prisoners planning an escape.* **2.** A means of escaping: *a fire escape.* **3.** A means of obtaining temporary freedom from worry, care, etc.: *Television is his escape from business problems.* —**modifier:** *an escape hatch.*

es•cape•ment |ĭ **skāp'**mənt| *n.* **1.** A device somewhat similar to a ratchet, used in watches and clocks to control the speed at which the movement runs. **2.** Any similar device in which a movable catch engages a series of notches.

escape velocity. The smallest velocity with which a body can escape from the gravitational attraction of another body. [SEE NOTE]

es•cap•ism |ĭ **skā'**pĭz'əm| *n.* The habit or practice of avoiding reality by engaging in fantasy, daydreams, entertainment, or other forms of distraction. —**es•cap'ist** *n.*

es•car•got |ĕ skär **gō'**| *n., pl.* **es•car•gots** |ĕ-skär **gō'**|. An edible snail, especially when cooked.

es•ca•role |ĕs'kə rōl'| *n.* A plant with densely clustered, ruffled leaves used in salads.

es•carp•ment |ĭ **skärp'**mənt| *n.* **1.** A steep slope or long cliff formed by erosion or by vertical movement of the earth's crust along a fault. **2.** A steep slope or embankment in front of a fortification.

-escence. A suffix that forms nouns: **convalescence.**

-escent. A suffix that forms adjectives: **convalescent.**

es•chew |ĕs **cho͞o'**| *v.* To take care to avoid; shun: *eschew evil.*

es•cort |ĕs'kôrt'| *n.* **1.** One or more persons accompanying another to give protection or guidance or to pay honor. **2.** One or more planes, ships, etc., accompanying another or others to provide protection. **3.** A man who acts as the companion of a woman in public. —*v.* |ĭ **skôrt'**|. To accompany as an escort: *Police*

ă **pat**/ā **pay**/â **care**/ä **father**/ĕ **pet**/ē **be**/ĭ **pit**/ī **pie**/î **fierce**/ŏ **pot**/ō **go**/ô **paw**, **for**/oi **oil**/o͝o **book**/o͞o **boot**/ou **out**/ŭ **cut**/û **fur**/*th* **the**/th **thin**/hw **which**/**zh** vision/ə **ago**, item, pencil, atom, circus *escorted the President during the parade. I escorted her home.*

es•crow |ĕs′krō′| *or* |ĭ **skrō′**| *n.* The condition of a written agreement, such as a deed, bond, etc., put into the custody of a third party until certain conditions are fulfilled: *The bank is holding the deed in escrow until the heir reaches his twenty-first birthday.*

es•cu•do |ĕ **skōō′**dō| *n., pl.* **es•cu•dos.** The basic unit of money of Portugal and Chile.

es•cutch•eon |ĭ **skŭch′**ən| *n.* A shield or shield-shaped emblem bearing a coat of arms.

–ese. A suffix that forms nouns and adjectives: **Chinese.**

es•ker |ĕs′kər| *n.* A ridge of coarse gravel deposited by a stream flowing in a trough or tunnel in a melting sheet of glacial ice.

Es•ki•mo |ĕs′kə mō′| *n., pl.* **Es•ki•mos** or **Es•ki•mo. 1.** A member of a people native to the Arctic coastal regions of North America, parts of Greenland, and Siberia. **2.** The language of these people. *—adj.* Of the Eskimos or their language.

Eskimo dog. A large dog with a thick coat and a plumelike tail, used to pull sleds.

e•soph•a•gus |ĭ **sŏf′**ə gəs| *n., pl.* **e•soph•a•gi** |ĭ **sŏf′**ə jī′|. The tube of the alimentary canal that connects the throat and stomach; the gullet. [SEE PICTURE]

es•o•ter•ic |ĕs′ə **tĕr′**ĭk| *adj.* Intended for or understood by only a small group: *an esoteric book.* **—es′o•ter′i•cal•ly** *adv.*

ESP extrasensory perception.

esp. especially.

es•pa•drille |ĕs′pə drĭl′| *n.* A sandal having a rope sole and a canvas upper part.

es•pe•cial |ĭ **spĕsh′**əl| *adj.* Standing above others; particular; exceptional: *an especial friend.*

es•pe•cial•ly |ĭ **spĕsh′**ə lē| *adv.* To an extent or degree deserving of special emphasis; particularly: *In what way is the helicopter especially useful? His songs are especially well known.*

Es•pe•ran•to |ĕs′pə **rän′**tō| *or* |**-răn′**-| *n.* An artificial international language based on word roots common to many European languages.

es•pi•o•nage |ĕs′pē ə näzh′| *or* |-nĭj| *n.* **1.** The act or practice of spying. **2.** The use of spies by a government to gain secret information about another country.

es•pla•nade |ĕs′plə nād′| *or* |-näd′| *n.* A flat, open stretch of pavement or grass used as a promenade.

es•pou•sal |ĭ **spou′**zəl| *n.* **1.** Adoption of or support for an idea or cause: *espousal of women's rights.* **2.** Often **espousals. a.** An engagement; betrothal. **b.** A wedding ceremony.

es•pouse |ĭ **spouz′**| *v.* **es•poused, es•pous•ing. 1.** To give loyalty or support to (an idea or cause); adopt: *espouse free elections.* **2.** To marry. **3.** To give (a woman) in marriage.

es•pres•so |ĕ **sprĕs′**ō| *n., pl.* **es•pres•sos.** A strong coffee brewed by forcing steam through long-roasted, powdered beans.

es•prit |ĕ **sprē′**| *n.* Liveliness of mind and expression; wit.

es•prit de corps |ĕ **sprē′** də **kôr′**|. A spirit of devotion and enthusiasm among members of a group for one another, their group, and its purposes.

es•py |ĭ **spī′**| *v.* **es•pied, es•py•ing, es•pies.** To catch sight of; glimpse: *I espied the building in the distance.*

Esq. Esquire (title).

–esque. A suffix that forms adjectives: **statuesque.**

es•quire |ĕ **skwīr′**| *or* |ĕs′kwīr′| *n.* **1.** A member of the English gentry ranking just below a knight. **2. Esquire.** A title of courtesy used after a man's full name: *Martin Chuzzlewit, Esq.* [SEE NOTE]

–ess. A suffix meaning "a female": **heiress.**

es•say. *n.* **1.** |ĕs′ā′|. A short literary composition on a single subject, usually presenting the personal views of the author. **2.** |ĕs′ā′| *or* |ĕ **sā′**|. An attempt; try: *He made an essay at climbing the mountain.* *—v.* |ĕ **sā′**|. To make an attempt at; try: *Often his lips had essayed to speak, imploring for pardon.*

es•say•ist |ĕs′ā′ĭst| *n.* A writer of essays.

es•sence |ĕs′əns| *n.* **1.** The quality or qualities of a thing that give it its identity: *The essence of democracy is faith in the people.* **2. a.** An extract made from a substance and retaining its basic or most desirable properties in concentrated form. **b.** An alcohol solution of such an extract. **3.** A perfume or scent.

es•sen•tial |ĭ **sĕn′**shəl| *adj.* **1.** Of the greatest importance; indispensable; basic: *Each part is essential to the whole. The microscope is an essential tool of science.* **2.** Of, being, or containing an essence, as of a plant or spice. *—n.* A fundamental, necessary, or indispensable part, item, principle, etc.: *Take along only essentials when traveling.* **—es•sen′tial•ly** *adv.*

essential oil. An easily evaporated oil, usually having the odor or flavor of the plant from which it is taken, used in making perfumes and flavorings.

–est. A suffix that forms the superlative of adjectives and adverbs: **warmest; latest.**

EST, E.S.T. Eastern Standard Time.

es•tab•lish |ĭ **stăb′**lĭsh| *v.* **1.** To settle securely in a position, condition, etc.; install: *I've established myself in this town.* **2.** To begin or set up, as a business; found; create: *His grandfather established the company in 1889.* **3.** To show to be true; prove: *establish one's innocence.* **4.** To cause to be recognized and accepted without question: *His flight established Lindbergh as a national hero.*

es•tab•lish•ment |ĭ **stăb′**lĭsh mənt| *n.* **1.** The act of establishing or condition of being established. **2. a.** A business firm, club, or home, including its members or residents. **b.** A place of business, including the property and employees. **3. the Establishment.** An exclusive or powerful group in control of society or a field of activity.

es•tate |ĭ **stāt′**| *n.* **1.** A large piece of rural land, usually with a large house. **2.** Everything one owns, especially all of the property and debts left by a deceased person. **3.** A condition of life or wealth; status; rank: *one's estate in life.* **4.** Often **Estate.** A class of citizens within a nation with distinct political rights: *the three Estates of 18th-century France.*

es•teem |ĭ **stēm′**| *v.* **1.** To think highly of; respect; prize: *I esteem an honest man.* **2.** To judge

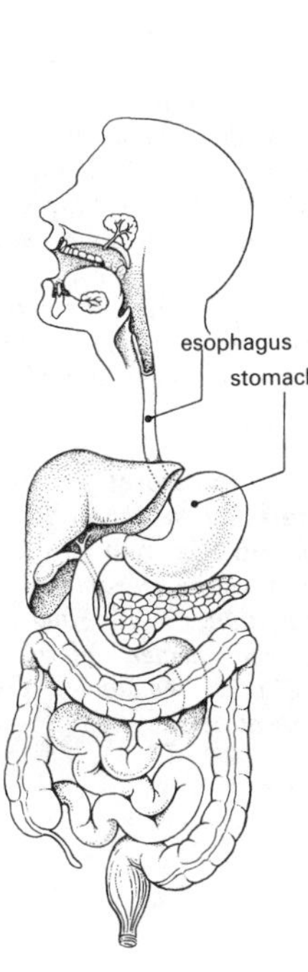

esophagus

esquire

The Late Latin word scūtārius, *"shield-bearer" (from* scūtum, *"shield"), became* escuier *in Old French, with meaning "the attendant and shield-bearer of a knight."* Escuier *was borrowed into English as* **esquire,** *and became the title for gentlemen who had coats of arms but were not knights. In modern British usage it survives as a formal title for any man. The British use* **Mr.** *in the same way that it is used in America, except that in the address of a letter (and in some legal documents)* Mr. David Frost *is referred to as* David Frost, Esq.

to be; regard as; consider: *That was esteemed the best.* —*n.* Favorable regard; respect: *He is held in high esteem.*

es•ter |ĕs'tər| *n.* Any one of the large group of chemical compounds formed when an acid and an alcohol interact so that the hydrogen characteristic of the acid and the hydroxyl group of the alcohol combine to form water, leaving the remaining radicals or groups bound together.

Es•ther |ĕs'tər|. In the Bible, the Jewish wife of a king of Persia who saved her people from massacre.

es•thete |ĕs'thēt'| *n.* **1.** A person who appreciates and admires what is beautiful, as in art. **2.** A person whose appreciation and admiration of beauty are thought to be affected or excessive.

es•thet•ic |ĕs thĕt'ĭk| *adj.* **1.** Of esthetics. **2.** Of or sensitive to what is beautiful; artistic. —**es•thet'i•cal•ly** *adv.*

es•thet•ics |ĕs thĕt'ĭks| *n.* *(used with a singular verb).* The branch of philosophy that provides a theory of the beautiful and of the fine arts.

es•ti•ma•ble |ĕs'tə mə bəl| *adj.* **1.** Capable of being calculated. **2.** Worthy; admirable: *an estimable person.* —**es'ti•ma•bly** *adv.*

es•ti•mate |ĕs'tə māt'| *v.* **es•ti•mat•ed, es•ti•mat•ing. 1.** To make a judgment as to the likely or approximate cost, quantity, or extent of; calculate roughly: *I estimate that 25 people will come to the party.* **2.** To form an opinion about; evaluate. —*n.* |ĕs'tə mĭt| *or* |-māt'|. **1.** A rough calculation. **2.** A preliminary calculation, especially one made by a repairman, businessman, etc., about the cost of work to be undertaken. **3.** An opinion; evaluation.

es•ti•ma•tion |ĕs'tə mā'shən| *n.* **1.** The act or an example of estimating. **2.** An opinion; judgment: *He is a fine person in my estimation.* **3.** High regard; esteem: *She is held in estimation by those who know her.*

Es•to•ni•a |ĕ stō'nē ə|. A former country on the Baltic Sea, now a part of the Soviet Union.

Es•to•ni•an |ĕ stō'nē ən| *n.* **1.** A native or inhabitant of Estonia. **2.** The language of Estonia, related to Finnish. —*adj.* Of Estonia, the Estonians, or their language.

es•trange |ĭ strānj'| *v.* **es•tranged, es•trang•ing.** To give rise to hostility or indifference in where there had originally been a friendly or affectionate relationship: *estrange a wife from her husband.* —**es•trange'ment** *n.*

es•tro•gen |ĕs'trə jən| *n.* Any of several hormones, produced mainly in the ovaries, that act to regulate certain female reproductive functions and maintain female secondary sex characteristics.

es•trous |ĕs'trəs| *adj.* **1.** Of or having to do with estrus. **2.** In heat: *an estrous bitch.*

es•trus |ĕs'trəs| *n.* Any of the regularly recurring periods during which a female mammal, other than a human being, produces one or more egg cells and is ready to mate; heat.

es•tu•ar•y |ĕs'chōō ĕr'ē| *n., pl.* **es•tu•ar•ies.** The wide lower part of a river where its current is met and influenced by the tides of the ocean.

-et. A suffix that forms nouns: **baronet; octet.**

e•ta |ā'tə| *or* |ē'tə| *n.* The seventh letter of the Greek alphabet, written Η, η. In English it is represented as long *e.*

et al. and others. An abbreviation for the Latin expression *et alii.* [SEE NOTE]

etc. and so forth. An abbreviation for the Latin phrase *et cetera.*

et cet•er•a |ĕt sĕt'ər ə| *or* |sĕt'rə|. And other things of the same type; and so forth. This was originally a Latin expression. [SEE NOTE]

etch |ĕch| *v.* **1.** To eat away (metal, glass, etc.) with or as if with acid. **2.** To make (a shape or pattern) on a metal plate by dissolving parts of it with acid. **3.** To practice the art of etching. **4.** To impress or imprint clearly.

etch•ing |ĕch'ĭng| *n.* **1.** The art or technique of making etched metal plates and using them to print pictures and designs. **2.** A design or picture etched on such a plate. **3.** A print made from such a plate.

e•ter•nal |ĭ tûr'nəl| *adj.* **1.** Without beginning or end; existing outside of time: *God, the eternal Father.* **2.** Unaffected by time; lasting; timeless: *Rome, the Eternal City.* **3.** Seemingly endless; incessant: *eternal complaining.* —*n.* **1.** Something that is eternal. **2. the Eternal.** God. —**e•ter'nal•ly** *adv.*

e•ter•ni•ty |ĭ tûr'nĭ tē| *n., pl.* **e•ter•ni•ties. 1.** All of time without beginning or end; infinite time. **2. a.** The endless period of time following death. **b.** The afterlife; immortality. **3.** A very long or seemingly very long time: *It was an eternity before he arrived!*

-eth[1]. A suffix that forms the archaic third person singular form of the present tense of verbs: *goeth.*

-eth[2]. A form of the number suffix **-th.**

eth•ane |ĕth'ān'| *n.* A colorless, odorless gas composed of carbon and hydrogen and having the formula C_2H_6. It occurs in natural gas, and is used as a fuel and in refrigeration.

eth•a•nol |ĕth'ə nôl'| *or* |-nōl'| *or* |-nŏl'| *n.* An alcohol composed of carbon, hydrogen, and oxygen in the proportions C_2H_6O. It is obtained from the fermentation of sugars and starches and is also made artificially. It is used in drugs, explosives, and drinks such as beer, wine, and whiskey; it is also widely used as a solvent.

e•ther |ē'thər| *n.* **1.** Any one of a class of organic chemical compounds composed of two hydrocarbon groups linked by an oxygen atom to form the general structure R-O-R, where R is any hydrocarbon group. Ethers are often formed by joining two molecules of an alcohol and extracting a water molecule. **2.** The ether formed from ethanol, containing carbon, hydrogen, and oxygen in the proportions $C_4H_{10}O$. It evaporates easily, is very flammable, and is used as a solvent and in medicine as an anesthetic. **3.** A massless material, now known to be nonexistent, once thought to fill space and act as a medium for electromagnetic waves. **4.** The clear sky; the heavens.

e•the•re•al |ĭ thîr'ē əl| *adj.* **1.** Delicate; exquisite: *ethereal music.* **2.** Of heaven; heavenly: *ethereal beings.* —**e•the're•al•ly** *adv.*

e•ther•ize |ē'thə rīz'| *v.* **e•ther•ized, e•ther•iz•ing.** To drug (a person or animal) with ether, especially as an anesthetic.

eth•ic |ĕth'ĭk| *n.* A principle of right or good conduct or a body of such principles.

eth•i•cal |ĕth'ĭ kəl| *adj.* **1.** Conforming to ac-

et al.

Et al. *is the equivalent of* **et cetera,** *but is only used to refer to people. It is short for the Latin phrases* et alii *or* et aliae, *meaning "and the other people":* et, *"and,"* + alii *or* aliae, *the masculine and feminine plural forms, respectively, of* alius, *"other."*

et cetera

Et cetera, *often abbreviated to* **etc.** *or* **&c.,** *is from the Latin phrase* et cētera, *meaning "and the other things":* et, *"and,"* + cētera, *the neuter plural of* cēterus, *"other, remaining." Compare note at* **et al.**

ă pat/ā pay/â care/ä father/ĕ pet/ ē be/ĭ pit/ī pie/î fierce/ŏ pot/ ō go/ô paw, for/oi oil/ŏŏ book/ ōō boot/ou out/ŭ cut/û fur/ *th* the/th thin/hw which/zh vision/ ə ago, item, pencil, atom, circus

cepted standards of right behavior or conduct. **2.** Of or dealing with ethics. —**eth'i•cal•ly** *adv.*

eth•ics |ĕth'ĭks| *n.* **1.** *(used with a singular verb).* The branch of philosophy that deals with the rules of right and wrong conduct. **2.** Standards of right behavior or conduct; moral principles: *a code of ethics; the ethics of the medical profession.* **3.** The moral quality of a course of action; fitness: *I question the ethics of his decision.*

E•thi•o•pi•a |ē'thē ō'pē ə|. A country in eastern Africa, on the Red Sea. Population, 27,239,000. Capital, Addis Ababa. —**E'thi•o'pi•an** *adj.* & *n.*

eth•nic |ĕth'nĭk| *adj.* Of or being a group of people that can be identified within a larger culture or society on the basis of such factors as religion, language, ancestry, and physical traits. —**eth'ni•cal•ly** *adv.*

eth•nol•o•gy |ĕth nŏl'ə jē| *n.* **1.** The branch of anthropology that studies and compares the characteristics, history, and development of human cultures. **2.** The branch of anthropology that studies the characteristics and origins of ethnic groups and the relations among them.

eth•yl |ĕth'əl| *n.* The organic radical that has the formula C_2H_5 and a valence of 1.

ethyl alcohol. Ethanol.

eth•yl•ene |ĕth'ə lēn'| *n.* A colorless, flammable gas composed of carbon and hydrogen and having the formula C_2H_4. It is obtained from petroleum and natural gas and is used as a fuel and in making other organic compounds.

ethylene gly•col |glī'kôl'| *or* |-kōl'| *or* |-kŏl'|. A poisonous, syrupy, colorless alcohol composed of carbon, hydrogen, and oxygen and having the formula $C_2H_6O_2$. It is often used as an antifreeze in heating and cooling systems that use water.

e•ti•ol•o•gy |ē'tē ŏl'ə jē| *n., pl.* **e•ti•ol•o•gies.** **1.** The scientific and medical study of the causes of diseases. **2.** The cause or origin of a disease.

et•i•quette |ĕt'ĭ kĭt| *or* |-kĕt'| *n.* Rules of correct behavior among people, in a profession, etc.: *court etiquette; military etiquette.*

E•ton collar |ēt'n|. A wide, stiff white collar originally worn overlapping the lapels of an Eton jacket. [SEE PICTURE]

Eton jacket. A waist-length jacket with wide lapels, open down the front.

E•trus•can |ĭ trŭs'kən| *n.* **1.** A member of an ancient people who lived in what is now west-central Italy. **2.** The language of this people. —**E•trus'can** *adj.*

-ette. A suffix meaning: **1.** Small: **kitchenette.** **2.** Imitation or substitute: *Leatherette.* **3.** Female: **usherette.**

é•tude, also **e•tude** |ā'to͞od'| *or* |ā'tyo͞od'| *n.* **1.** A piece of music meant to be used for practice in developing a given point of technique. **2.** A piece of music embodying some point of technique but meant to be played for an audience.

et•y•mol•o•gist |ĕt'ə mŏl'ə jĭst| *n.* A person who specializes in etymology.

et•y•mol•o•gy |ĕt'ə mŏl'ə jē| *n., pl.* **et•y•mol•o•gies.** **1.** The origin and development of a word as shown by its earliest use and changes in form and meaning. **2.** An account of the development of a specific word. **3.** The study of such developments. —**et'y•mo•log'i•cal** |ĕt'ə mə lŏj'ĭ kəl| *adj.* [SEE NOTE]

eu-. A prefix meaning "good, well": **euphonious.**

Eu The symbol for the element europium.

eu•ca•lyp•tus |yo͞o'kə lĭp'təs| *n., pl.* **eu•ca•lyp•tus•es.** Any of several tall Australian trees with leaves that yield a strong-smelling oil used in medicine, and wood used as timber.

Eu•cha•rist |yo͞o'kər ĭst| *n.* **1.** The Christian sacrament commemorating Christ's Last Supper; Communion. **2.** The consecrated bread and wine used in this sacrament.

Eu•clid |yo͞o'klĭd|. Greek mathematician of the third century B.C.

eu•gen•ics |yo͞o jĕn'ĭks| *n.* *(used with a singular verb).* The scientific study of and methods for improving a species, especially human beings, by applying genetic principles.

eu•gle•na |yo͞o glē'nə| *n.* A tiny one-celled water organism that moves by means of a long, whiplike part and has green coloring like that of a plant.

eu•lo•gize |yo͞o'lə jīz'| *v.* **eu•lo•gized, eu•lo•giz•ing.** To write or deliver a eulogy about; praise highly; extol.

eu•lo•gy |yo͞o'lə jē| *n., pl.* **eu•lo•gies.** A speech or written tribute praising a person or thing, especially a person who has just died.

eu•nuch |yo͞o'nək| *n.* A castrated man, especially one who was employed as a harem attendant in certain Oriental courts.

eu•phe•mism |yo͞o'fə mĭz'əm| *n.* An inoffensive term substituted for one considered offensive or too forthright; for example, *pass away* is a euphemism for *die.*

eu•phe•mis•tic |yo͞o'fə mĭs'tĭk| *adj.* Being a euphemism: *a euphemistic expression.*

eu•pho•ni•ous |yo͞o fō'nē əs| *adj.* Pleasing in sound; agreeable to the ear: *euphonious music.* —**eu•pho'ni•ous•ly** *adv.*

eu•pho•ni•um |yo͞o fō'nē əm| *n.* A brass wind instrument that is something like a tuba but higher in pitch.

eu•pho•ny |yo͞o'fə nē| *n., pl.* **eu•pho•nies.** Agreeable sound, especially in the use of words.

eu•pho•ri•a |yo͞o fôr'ē ə| *or* |-fōr'-| *n.* **1.** A feeling of happiness and well-being. **2.** An exaggerated feeling of this kind caused by a drug or found as a symptom of a disease.

Eu•phra•tes |yo͞o frā'tēz|. A river of southwestern Asia, flowing from central Turkey through Syria and Iraq to join the Tigris.

Eur•a•sia |yo͞o rā'zhə| *or* |-shə|. The large land mass comprising Europe and Asia.

Eur•a•sian |yo͞o rā'zhən| *or* |-shən| *n.* A person of mixed European and Asian ancestry. —*adj.* Of Eurasia or the Eurasians.

eu•re•ka |yo͞o rē'kə| *interj.* A word used to express triumph upon discovering something.

Eu•rope |yo͝or'əp|. A continent extending from the Atlantic Ocean to Asia.

Eu•ro•pe•an |yo͝or'ə pē'ən| *n.* **1.** A native or inhabitant of Europe. **2.** A person of European descent. —*adj.* Of Europe, the Europeans, or their languages and cultures.

European plan. A system of hotel management in which the amount charged a guest per day covers only the room and service and does not include meals. See **American plan.**

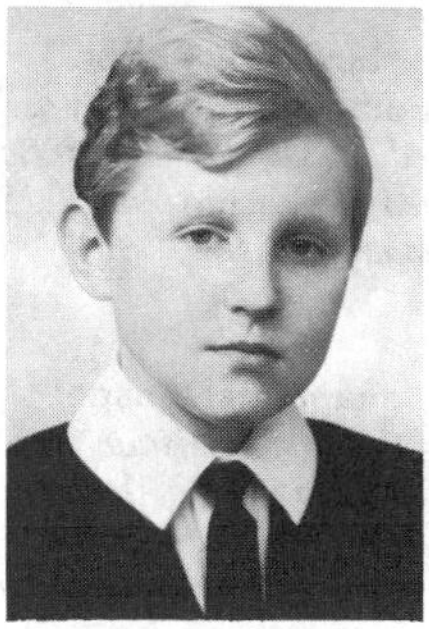

Eton collar

etymology

This is the etymology of the word **etymology**; *it comes from Greek* etumologia, *"explanation of true meaning"* (etumon, *"true meaning,"* + -logia, *"explanation or study"*). *But in fact the etymology of a word does not necessarily explain its "true" meaning at all, only its earlier meaning. For example, the word* **idiot** *originally meant "an ordinary person." The real value of etymology is that it is a kind of miniature history; like other kinds of history, it is not always useful, but it is nearly always interesting in one way or another.*

Eustachian tube
The **Eustachian tube** *was discovered by and named for Bartolommeo* Eustachio *(died 1574), Italian anatomist.*

evangelist/gospel
When the first Christian missionaries came to Britain, they brought (in Latin) the euangelium, *"the good news" of Christ (from Greek* eu-, *"good,"* + angellein, *"to announce news"). For the benefit of the natives of Britain,* euangelium *was translated into Old English as* gōdspel, *"good news":* gōd, *"good,"* + spel, *"news."* Gōdspel *became* **gospel** *in modern English. In the Middle English period,* euangelium *was borrowed directly to make the word* **evangelist,** *"one who tells the good news or gospel."*

even[1-2], etc.
Even[1] *was* efen, *"level," in Old English.* **Even**[2] *was* æfen *in Old English, and it originally meant "the after or later time (of day)"; it is related to* **after.** *The longer form* **evening** *began to displace* **even**[2] *in the Middle English period (at the same time that* **morning** *replaced* **morn**). *The poetic shorter form* **eve** *dates from the same time. The name* **Eve** *(in the Bible) is from Latin* Eva, *which is from Hebrew* Hawwah, *which meant "living."*

ă pat/ā pay/â care/ä father/ĕ pet/ ē be/ĭ pit/ī pie/î fierce/ŏ pot/ ō go/ô paw, for/oi oil/o͝o book/ o͞o boot/ou out/ŭ cut/û fur/ *th* the/th thin/hw which/zh vision/ ə ago, item, pencil, atom, circus

eu•ro•pi•um |yo͞o rō′pē əm| *n.* Symbol **Eu** One of the elements, a soft, silvery-white rare-earth metal. Atomic number 63; atomic weight 151.96; valences +2, +3; melting point 826°C; boiling point 1439°C.

Eu•sta•chian tube |yo͞o stā′shən| *or* |-stā′kē-ən|. The narrow tube that connects the middle ear and the pharynx and allows the pressures on both sides of the eardrum to equalize. [SEE NOTE]

eu•tha•na•sia |yo͞o′thə nā′zhə| *or* |-zhē ə| *n.* The act of killing a person thought to be incurably ill or injured in order to spare him suffering.

eu•then•ics |yo͞o thĕn′ĭks| *n. (used with a singular verb).* The scientific study of ways to help human beings to function better and live more happily by adjustment of environment.

e•vac•u•ate |ĭ văk′yo͞o āt′| *v.* **e•vac•u•at•ed, e•vac•u•at•ing. 1.** To send away or withdraw (inhabitants or troops) from an area: *evacuate a city threatened by a forest fire.* **2.** To withdraw or depart from; vacate: *The firemen quickly evacuated the burning building.* **3.** To create a vacuum in (a container). **4.** To expel or discharge (waste matter), especially from the bowels. **—e•vac′u•a′tion** *n.*

e•vade |ĭ vād′| *v.* **e•vad•ed, e•vad•ing. 1.** To escape or avoid, as by cleverness or deceit: *evade arrest; evade a blow.* **2.** To avoid fulfilling, answering, etc.: *evade responsibility; evade a question.*

e•val•u•ate |ĭ văl′yo͞o āt′| *v.* **e•val•u•at•ed, e•val•u•at•ing. 1.** To find out, judge, or estimate the value or worth of; examine and appraise: *evaluate a course; evaluate a book. Records make it possible to evaluate your expenditures.* **2.** To find the numerical value of (an algebraic expression).

e•val•u•a•tion |ĭ văl′yo͞o ā′shən| *n.* **1.** The act of evaluating or judging: *Evaluation requires you to use all of your thought processes.* **2.** The result of evaluating; a judgment or appraisal: *Biographers do not always agree in their evaluation of men and their actions.*

ev•a•nes•cent |ĕv′ə nĕs′ənt| *adj.* Tending to vanish or last only a short time; fleeting: *evanescent spring flowers.* **—ev′a•nes′cence** |ĕv′ə nĕs′əns| *n.* **—ev′a•nes′cent•ly** *adv.*

e•van•gel•i•cal |ē′văn jĕl′ĭ kəl| or **e•van•gel•ic** |ē′văn jĕl′ĭk| *adj.* **1.** Of or in accordance with the Christian gospel, especially the four Gospels of the New Testament. **2.** Of or being a Protestant group stressing the belief that salvation is achieved through faith in Christ. **—e′van•gel′i•cal•ly** *adv.*

e•van•gel•ism |ĭ văn′jə lĭz′əm| *n.* The practice of zealously preaching and spreading the gospel, as through missionary work.

e•van•gel•ist |ĭ văn′jə lĭst| *n.* **1.** Often **Evangelist.** Any of the authors of the New Testament Gospels; Matthew, Mark, Luke, or John. **2.** A zealous preacher. **3.** A Mormon patriarch. [SEE NOTE]

e•van•gel•ize |ĭ văn′jə līz′| *v.* **e•van•gel•ized, e•van•gel•iz•ing.** To preach and spread the gospel. **—e•van′gel•i•za′tion** *n.*

e•vap•o•rate |ĭ văp′ə rāt′| *v.* **e•vap•o•rat•ed, e•vap•o•rat•ing. 1.** To change into the form of a vapor or gas: *Alcohol evaporates quickly. The sun evaporates water from the ocean.* **2.** To dry or thicken (a substance) by extracting water vapor from it. **3.** To disappear; vanish; fade: *His confidence evaporated as the airplane was about to land.* **—e•vap′o•ra′tion** *n.*

evaporated milk. Unsweetened milk that has been slightly thickened by evaporation.

e•va•sion |ĭ vā′zhən| *n.* **1. a.** The act of avoiding, evading, or escaping; dodging. **b.** Illegal avoidance of a responsibility: *tax evasion.* **2.** A means of evading; an excuse.

e•va•sive |ĭ vā′sĭv| *adj.* Tending to evade; not straightforward; not direct or frank; vague: *He always gives evasive answers.* **—e•va′sive•ly** *adv.* **—e•va′sive•ness** *n.*

eve |ēv| *n.* **1.** Often **Eve.** The evening or day preceding a special day: *New Year's Eve.* **2.** The period immediately preceding a certain event: *the eve of the game.* **3.** Evening. Used chiefly in poetry.

Eve |ēv|. In the Bible, the first woman, wife of Adam.

e•ven[1] |ē′vən| *adj.* **1. a.** Having a horizontal surface; flat: *The floor is even.* **b.** Having no roughness, indentations, etc.; smooth: *an even board.* **c.** At the same height or depth; parallel; level: *The picture is even with the window.* **2.** Having no variations; uniform: *an even rate of speed.* **3.** Calm; peaceful: *an even temper.* **4. a.** Equally matched: *an even fight.* **b.** Equal in degree, extent, or amount: *even amounts of oil and vinegar.* **5.** Containing 2 as a factor; exactly divisible by 2: *even integers.* **6.** Having equal probability: *an even chance of winning the race.* **7. a.** Having an equal score: *The teams are even.* **b.** Being equal for each opponent: *an even score.* **8.** Having nothing due: *Give him one dollar, and you are even.* **9.** Having an exact amount, extent, or number: *an even pound.* —*adv.* **1.** To a higher or greater degree; yet; still: *an even worse condition.* **2.** At the same time as; just: *Even as we watched, the building collapsed.* **3.** In spite of; notwithstanding: *Even with his head start, I overtook him.* **4.** In fact; moreover: *unhappy, even weeping.* —*v.* To make or become even: *even a score; even out the ground with a grader. His apology will even things up. Odds have evened between the contestants for the championship.* **—e′ven•ly** *adv.* **—e′ven•ness** *n.* [SEE NOTE]

***Idioms.* break even.** *Informal.* To have neither losses nor gains. **get even.** To take revenge.

e•ven[2] |ē′vən| *n. Archaic.* Evening. [SEE NOTE]

eve•ning |ēv′nĭng| *n.* **1.** The period just after sunset; early night. **2.** This period spent in a specified way: *a musical evening.* **—modifier:** *an evening bath; an evening meal.*

evening clothes. Clothing designed for evening wear on formal or semiformal occasions, as a man's tuxedo or white tie and tails or a woman's evening gown.

evening dress. 1. Evening clothes. 2. An evening gown.

evening gown. A woman's formal dress, usually long, low-cut, and sleeveless.

evening star. A planet, especially Mercury or Venus, that shines brightly in the western sky shortly after sunset.

even number. Any whole number that is a multiple of 2.

e•vent |ĭ vĕnt′| *n.* **1.** An occurrence, incident, or experience, especially one of significance: *the course of human events.* **2.** An item in a program of sports: *the event for ten-year-old swimmers.*
Idioms. **at all events.** In any case; anyhow. **in any event.** In any case; anyhow. **in the event.** In case; if it should happen: *in the event of the President's death.*

e•vent•ful |ĭ vĕnt′fəl| *adj.* **1.** Full of events: *an eventful afternoon.* **2.** Important; momentous: *an eventful decision.* —**e•vent′ful•ly** *adv.* —**e•vent′ful•ness** *n.*

e•ven•tide |ē′vən tīd′| *n.* Evening. Used chiefly in poetry.

e•ven•tu•al |ĭ vĕn′cho͞o əl| *adj.* Occurring at an unspecified future time; ultimate: *He never lost hope of eventual victory.* —**e•ven′tu•al•ly** *adv.*

e•ven•tu•al•i•ty |ĭ vĕn′ cho͞o ăl′ĭ tē| *n., pl.* **e•ven•tu•al•i•ties.** Something that may occur; a possibility.

ev•er |ĕv′ər| *adv.* **1.** At all times; always: *He is ever courteous.* **2.** At any time: *Have you ever seen him?* **3.** By any chance; in any possible case or way: *I don't know how he ever thought he was going to get away with that.*
Idioms. **ever so.** *Informal.* Extremely; very: *I'm ever so glad to see you.* **ever so often.** Frequently.

Ev•er•est, Mount |ĕv′ər ĭst|. The highest peak (29,028 feet) in the world, in the Himalaya Mountains on the border of Nepal and Tibet.

ev•er•glade |ĕv′ər glād′| *n.* An area of low, marshy land; a swamp.

Ev•er•glades, The |ĕv′ər glādz′|. A swampy region in southern Florida, abundant in wildlife and tropical plants.

ev•er•green |ĕv′ər grēn′| *adj.* **1.** Having leaves or needles that remain green all year: *evergreen trees.* **2.** Remaining green all year: *evergreen leaves.* —*n.* An evergreen tree, shrub, or plant, such as a pine, holly, or rhododendron. —***modifier:*** *an evergreen forest.*

ev•er•last•ing |ĕv′ər lăs′tĭng| *or* |-lä′stĭng| *adj.* **1.** Lasting forever; eternal: *everlasting God.* **2.** Continuing indefinitely; seemingly unending: *everlasting bliss.* —*n.* Any of several plants with flowers that keep their color and fresh appearance when dried. —**ev′er•last′ing•ly** *adv.*

ev•er•more |ĕv′ər môr′| *or* |-mōr′| *adv.* —**for evermore.** Forever.

eve•ry |ĕv′rē| *adj.* **1.** Each without exception: *every student in the class.* **2.** Each in a specified series: *every third seat; every two hours.* **3.** The utmost: *She was given every care.* —*adv.* More or less; periodically: *every once in a while.*
Idioms. **every bit.** *Informal.* In all ways; quite; equally: *He is every bit as mean as she is.* **every other.** Each alternate; each second: *every other seat.* **every so often.** Occasionally. **every which way.** *Informal.* In complete disorder.

eve•ry•bod•y |ĕv′rē bŏd′ē| *pron.* Every person; everyone. [SEE NOTE]

eve•ry•day |ĕv′rē dā′| *adj.* Ordinary; usual: *everyday dress; everyday cares.*

eve•ry•one |ĕv′rē wŭn′| *pron.* Every person; everybody. [SEE NOTE]

eve•ry•place |ĕv′rē plās′| *adv. Informal.* Everywhere.

eve•ry•thing |ĕv′rē thĭng′| *pron.* **1.** The totality or entirety: *everything in this room.* **2.** All relevant items or factors: *Tell him everything.* **3.** The most important fact or consideration: *Her children are everything to her.* **4.** All aspects of something; things in general: *Everything went wrong.*

eve•ry•where |ĕv′rē hwâr′| *or* |-wâr′| *adv.* In any or every place; in all places.

eve•ry•wheres |ĕv′rē hwârz′| *or* |-wârz′| *adv.* A dialectal form of the word **everywhere.**

e•vict |ĭ vĭkt′| *v.* To put out (a tenant) by legal process: *They evicted the family for nonpayment of rent.* —**e•vic′tion** *n.*

ev•i•dence |ĕv′ĭ dəns| *n.* **1.** Something that furnishes proof; the data on which a conclusion is based: *What evidence do you have that he left yesterday?* **2.** The statements and objects examined for judgment in a court of law: *The evidence against him was only the old lady's hearsay and a blood-stained shirt.* —*v.* **ev•i•denced, ev•i•denc•ing.** To indicate clearly; prove: *The history of the region goes back more than 5,000 years, as evidenced by the archaeological finds of modern times.*

ev•i•dent |ĕv′ĭ dənt| *adj.* Obvious; clear; plain: *He has the evident intention of taking the shorter route.*

ev•i•dent•ly |ĕv′ĭ dənt lē| *or* |-dĕnt′-| *adv.* **1.** Obviously; clearly: *She is evidently a bad singer.* **2.** Apparently or seemingly; probably: *The train evidently is going to be late.*

e•vil |ē′vəl| *adj.* **e•vil•er, e•vil•est.** **1.** Morally bad or wrong; wicked; sinful: *an evil man; evil deeds.* **2.** Causing harm, disaster, misfortune, etc.; harmful: *evil spirits.* **3.** Indicating future misfortune: *evil omens.* **4.** Angry or spiteful; malicious: *an evil temper.* —*n.* **1.** Wickedness; sin: *Deliver us from evil.* **2.** Evil deeds, acts, etc.: *"The evil that men do lives after them"* (Shakespeare). **3.** Often **evils.** Anything undesirable because of its harmful nature or effect: *social evils; political evils.* —**e′vil•ly** *adv.* —**e′vil•ness** *n.*

e•vil•do•er |ē′vəl do͞o′ər| *n.* A person who does evil things.

evil eye. A gaze or stare believed to cause injury or misfortune.

e•vince |ĭ vĭns′| *v.* **e•vinced, e•vinc•ing.** To show or demonstrate clearly; manifest; exhibit: *She evinced surprise at his statement.*

e•vis•cer•ate |ĭ vĭs′ə rāt′| *v.* **e•vis•cer•at•ed, e•vis•cer•at•ing.** To take out the intestines or other internal organs of. —**e•vis′cer•a′tion** *n.*

ev•o•ca•tion |ĕv′ə kā′shən| *n.* The act of calling forth: *the evocation of pleasant childhood memories.*

e•voc•a•tive |ĭ vŏk′ə tĭv| *adj.* Tending to evoke: *The word "energy" is highly evocative of motion, vitality, and strength.*

e•voke |ĭ vōk′| *v.* **e•voked, e•vok•ing.** To summon or call forth; inspire: *Not so very long ago tropical Africa evoked thoughts only of the exotic and adventurous.*

ev•o•lu•tion |ĕv′ə lo͞o′shən| *n.* **1.** A gradual process by which something changes into a different form: *the evolution of modern science; the evolution of jazz.* **2.** The biological theory that groups of organisms, such as species, can change over a long period of time and through natural processes, so that descendants become less like their ancestors. **3.** The historical development of a related group of organisms: *plant evolution.*

everybody/everyone
Everybody *and* **everyone** *seem to have exactly the same meaning, but in the materials on which this Dictionary was based,* **everyone** *occurs about two and one-half times as often as* **everybody.**

evolve/evolution

Evolve *comes from Latin* ēvolvere, *"to roll out, to unfold":* ē-, *"out,"* + volvere, *"to roll." The past participle of* ēvolvere *was* ēvolūtus *(in Latin, the letter* v *was pronounced /w/, and this sound can change to /u/). From this was formed the noun* ēvolūtiō, *"an unrolling," from which we have* **evolution.** *Notice the similarity of* **revolve/revolution** *(which are from the same Latin verb) and* **solve/solution** *(which are from a different but similar verb).*

ewe

Ewe *was* ēowu *in Old English and* awiz *in prehistoric Germanic. It is descended from* owis, *the original Indo-European word for "sheep."*

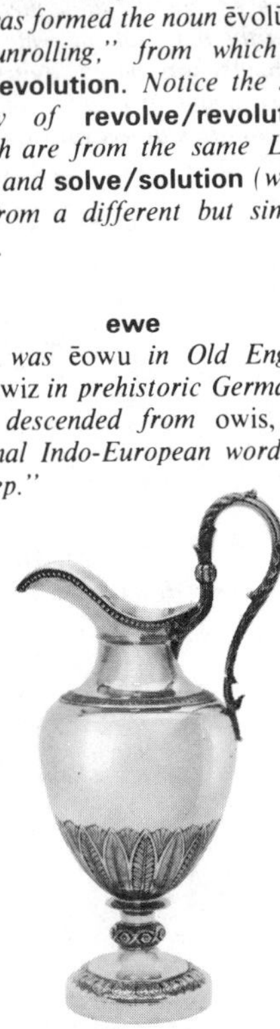

ewer

excavate

ă pat/ā pay/â care/ä father/ĕ pet/ ē be/ĭ pit/ī pie/î fierce/ŏ pot/ ō go/ô paw, for/oi oil/o͝o book/ o͞o boot/ou out/ŭ cut/û fur/ *th* the/th thin/hw which/zh vision/ ə ago, item, pencil, atom, circus

4. The mathematical operation of finding a square root, cube root, or other root of a number. [SEE NOTE]

ev•o•lu•tion•ar•y |ĕv'ə **lo͞o'**shə nĕr'ē| *adj.* **1.** Of or involving evolution. **2.** Of or in accord with the biological theory of evolution.

e•volve |ĭ **vŏlv'**| *v.* **e•volved, e•volv•ing. 1.** To develop or emerge; arrive at gradually: *Jackson evolved a plan. The method of coping with the disaster evolved gradually.* **2.** To develop by evolutionary processes, especially from a simple or primitive form to a complex or highly organized one. **3.** To yield or give off; set free: *a reaction that evolves heat.* [SEE NOTE]

ewe |yo͞o| *n.* A female sheep. ¶*These sound alike* **eye, yew, you.** [SEE NOTE]

ew•er |**yo͞o'**ər| *n.* A large, wide-mouthed pitcher or jug. [SEE PICTURE]

ex. example.

ex–. A prefix meaning: **1.** Out; out of: **excommunicate.** When *ex-* is followed by *f,* it becomes *ef-.* **2.** Former: *ex-congressman.*

ex•ac•er•bate |ĭg **zăs'**ər bāt'| *or* |ĭk **săs'**-| *v.* **ex•ac•er•bat•ed, ex•ac•er•bat•ing.** To increase the severity of; aggravate: *exacerbate tensions.* —**ex•ac'er•ba'tion** *n.*

ex•act |ĭg **zăkt'**| *adj.* **1.** Precise in all details; completely correct; accurate: *a person's exact words; an exact description.* **2.** Characterized by precision: *the exact sciences; an exact reading.* **3.** Leaving no remainder: *an exact divisor.* —*v.* To call for; require; demand: *exact payment; exact great effort.* —**ex•act'ness** *n.*

ex•act•ing |ĭg **zăk'**tĭng| *adj.* **1.** Making great demands: *an exacting teacher.* **2.** Requiring great effort or care: *an exacting task.* —**ex•act'ing•ly** *adv.*

ex•ac•tion |ĭg **zăk'**shən| *n.* **1.** The act of exacting or demanding. **2.** Something exacted or demanded, as a tax considered to be excessive.

ex•act•i•tude |ĭg **zăk'**tĭ to͞od'| *or* |-tyo͞od'| *n.* The condition or quality of being exact.

ex•act•ly |ĭg **zăkt'**lē| *adv.* **1.** In an exact manner; precisely: *Follow the recipe exactly.* **2.** In all respects; just: *Do exactly what you please.* **3.** Quite so; as you say: *"Exactly," he replied, "I feel the same way."* **4.** Without a remainder: *Even numbers are exactly divisible by 2.*

ex•ag•ger•ate |ĭg **zăj'**ə rāt'| *v.* **ex•ag•ger•at•ed, ex•ag•ger•at•ing. 1.** To enlarge beyond normal bounds: *A map using the Mercator projection exaggerates the size of areas of high latitude. Some glandular disorders exaggerate growth.* **2.** To enlarge or magnify beyond the truth; overstate: *Often people will exaggerate a real story until it becomes a "tall tale." Don't exaggerate your accomplishments just to get attention.*

ex•ag•ger•a•tion |ĭg zăj'ə **rā'**shən| *n.* **1.** The act of exaggerating. **2.** An example of exaggeration; an overstatement.

ex•alt |ĭg **zôlt'**| *v.* **1.** To raise in position, status, rank, etc.; elevate: *The emperor exalted his general to a place among the peers of the realm.* **2.** To praise; honor; glorify: *Exalt the word of God.* —**ex'al•ta'tion** |ĕg'zôl **tā'**shən| *n.*

ex•alt•ed |ĭg **zôl'**tĭd| *adj.* **1.** Having high rank; dignified: *an exalted personage.* **2.** Lofty; noble: *an exalted literary style.*

ex•am |ĭg **zăm'**| *n. Informal.* An examination.

ex•am•i•na•tion |ĭg zăm'ə **nā'**shən| *n.* **1.** The act of examining; investigation; analysis. **2.** A set of written or oral questions or exercises designed to test knowledge or skills; a test. **3.** An inspection of part or all of the body, as by a dentist or physician. **4.** A formal interrogation: *examination of the witness.*

ex•am•ine |ĭg **zăm'**ĭn| *v.* **ex•am•ined, ex•am•in•ing. 1.** To investigate (someone or something) in detail; observe carefully: *Examine the plant cells under a microscope. The inspector examined the accounts.* **2.** To inspect or observe for evidence of disease, abnormality, etc.: *The doctor examined the babies.* **3.** To interrogate or question formally to obtain information, facts, etc.: *The prosecutor examined the witness.* **4.** To present questions to in order to test knowledge. —**ex•am'in•er** *n.*

ex•am•ple |ĭg **zăm'**pəl| *or* |-**zäm'**-| *n.* **1.** One case, item, fact, incident, etc., that is typical of a whole class or group; a sample or specimen: *Water is one example of matter.* **2.** Someone or something worthy of imitation; a model: *His life is an example of dedication.* **3.** Someone or something that serves or is intended to serve as a warning: *Let his punishment be an example to you.* **4.** A problem or exercise shown with its solution to serve as a model or to illustrate a principle or method: *This example illustrates multiplication with fractions.*

Idioms. **for example.** Serving as an illustration, a model, etc. **set an example.** To be a model of behavior worthy of imitation.

ex•as•per•ate |ĭg **zăs'**pə rāt'| *v.* **ex•as•per•at•ed, ex•as•per•at•ing.** To irritate greatly; try the patience of; irk: *Her shrill voice always exasperated him.*

ex•as•per•a•tion |ĭg zăs'pə **rā'**shən| *n.* The condition of being exasperated; extreme irritation.

Ex•cal•i•bur |ĕk **skăl'**ə bər| *n.* In medieval legend, the sword of King Arthur.

ex•ca•vate |**ĕks'**kə vāt'| *v.* **ex•ca•vat•ed, ex•ca•vat•ing. 1.** To dig or dig out; hollow out: *The workmen excavated the swimming pool. Archaeologists excavate for many years trying to find ruins.* **2.** To uncover by digging; expose to view: *They excavated the ruins of Pompeii out of lava under which it had been buried.* [SEE PICTURE]

ex•ca•va•tion |ĕks'kə **vā'**shən| *n.* **1.** The act or process of excavating. **2.** A cavity formed by excavating. **3.** Something, such as ruins, uncovered by excavating.

ex•ceed |ĭk **sēd'**| *v.* **1.** To be greater than; surpass: *When supply exceeds demand, prices tend to go down.* **2.** To go beyond the limits of: *The command exceeded his authority.*

ex•ceed•ing |ĭk **sē'**dĭng| *adj.* Extreme: *handle with exceeding care.* —*adv. Archaic.* Exceedingly.

ex•ceed•ing•ly |ĭk **sē'**dĭng lē| *adv.* To an unusual degree; extremely: *exceedingly bright; exceedingly bad.*

ex•cel |ĭk **sĕl'**| *v.* **ex•celled, ex•cel•ling.** To be better than or superior to (others); surpass: *She excels in wit. Her beauty excels that of the other girls.*

ex•cel•lence |**ĕk'**sə ləns| *n.* The condition or quality of being excellent; superiority: *artistic excellence.*

Ex•cel•len•cy |ĕk′sə lən sē| *n., pl.* **Ex•cel•len•cies.** A title used in speaking of or to certain high officials, such as ambassadors, governors, or bishops: *His Excellency; Your Excellency.*

ex•cel•lent |ĕk′sə lənt| *adj.* Of the highest quality; very fine; superb: *an excellent reason; an excellent book.* —**ex′cel•lent•ly** *adv.*

ex•cept |ĭk sĕpt′| *prep.* Other than; but: *All the eggs except one are broken. Everybody went to the movies except for me.* —*conj.* **1.** If it were not for the fact that; only: *I could leave early except I don't want to.* **2.** Otherwise than: *He would not open his mouth except to yell.* —*v.* To leave out or exclude: *When I say that everybody was late, I except Dick and Jane.*

ex•cept•ing |ĭk sĕp′tĭng| *prep.* Except: *No one was permitted to enter that room, excepting the housekeeper.*

ex•cep•tion |ĭk sĕp′shən| *n.* **1.** An exclusion or omission: *Everyone is here without exception.* **2.** A case that does not conform to normal rules: *In 1968 shutouts by the pitcher were more the rule than the exception.*

Idiom. **take exception.** To object to; take issue with.

ex•cep•tion•al |ĭk sĕp′shə nəl| *adj.* Being an exception; unusual; extraordinary: *exceptional beauty.* —**ex•cep′tion•al•ly** *adv.*

ex•cerpt |ĕk′sûrpt′| *n.* A passage or scene selected from a book, film, musical work, speech, etc. —*v.* |ĭk **sûrpt′**|. To select, quote, or take out (a passage or scene) from a book, film, musical work, speech, etc.

ex•cess |ĭk sĕs′| *or* |ĕk′sĕs′| *n.* **1.** The condition of exceeding what is normal or sufficient: *overcome by an excess of grief.* **2.** Something that exceeds what is normal or sufficient: *She responded eagerly with an excess of superlatives.* **3.** An amount or quantity by which something exceeds another: *an excess of two gallons over what the container would hold; an excess of imports over exports.* —*adj.* Exceeding what is normal or required: *Shake off the excess water.*

Idioms. **in excess of.** More than; greater than. **to excess.** To an extreme degree; too much: *generous to excess.*

ex•ces•sive |ĭk sĕs′ĭv| *adj.* Exceeding what is normal, proper, reasonable, or necessary; immoderate; extreme: *Excessive intake of alcohol leads to drunkenness.* —**ex•ces′sive•ly** *adv.* —**ex•ces′sive•ness** *n.*

ex•change |ĭks **chānj′**| *v.* **ex•changed, ex•chang•ing. 1.** To give, provide, or transfer (one thing for another); trade: *They traded with the Indians, exchanging cheap trinkets for valuable furs.* **2.** To replace (something unsatisfactory) with something else: *The store exchanged the tie for a belt. I'm sure you can exchange the gift.* **3.** To give and receive reciprocally; interchange: *exchange glances; exchange words; exchange letters.* —*n.* **1. a.** An act or example of exchanging: *an exchange of gifts; an exchange of ideas; a cultural exchange.* **b.** A verbal interchange: *The heated exchange brought out their feelings.* **2.** A place where things, especially stocks or commodities, are exchanged or traded: *a stock exchange; a grain exchange; a commodities exchange.* **3. a.** A system of payments in which checks, drafts, or bills are used instead of money and in which a percentage is charged for the exchange into currency. **b.** The percentage charged. **4.** A **telephone exchange.** —***modifier:*** *the exchange rates of currency; exchange controls.* —**ex•change′a•ble** *adj.* —**ex•chang′er** *n.*

Idiom. **in exchange (for).** As a substitute.

Ex•cheq•uer |ĕks′chĕk′ər| *or* |ĭks **chĕk′**ər| *n.* The British governmental department in charge of the national revenue.

ex•cise¹ |ĕk′sīz′| *n.* An **excise tax.** [SEE NOTE]

ex•cise² |ĭk **sīz′**| *v.* **ex•cised, ex•cis•ing.** To remove by or as if by cutting, especially as a surgical procedure. —**ex•ci′sion** |ĕk **sĭzh′**ən| *or* |ĭk-| *n.* [SEE NOTE]

excise tax. A tax on the production, sale, or consumption of certain commodities within a country.

ex•cit•a•ble |ĭk **sī′**tə bəl| *adj.* **1.** Capable of being excited. **2.** Easily excited: *a nervous and excitable person.* —**ex•cit′a•bil′i•ty, ex•cit′a•ble•ness** *n.* —**ex•cit′a•bly** *adv.*

ex•ci•ta•tion |ĕk′sī **tā′**shən| *n.* **1. a.** A process in which an atom, molecule, or other physical system absorbs energy and changes its internal structure. **b.** The condition of an atom, molecule, etc., that has undergone this process. **2.** Stimulation, as of a nerve, muscle, etc.

ex•cite |ĭk **sīt′**| *v.* **ex•cit•ed, ex•cit•ing. 1.** To stir up; arouse; stimulate: *excite the imagination. Strange stories excite the children.* **2.** To call forth, draw out, or elicit as a reaction: *excite a response; excite pity.* **3.** To make (an organism or one of its parts) more active; stimulate. **4.** To increase the energy of (an atom, molecule, or other physical system).

ex•cit•ed |ĭk **sī′**tĭd| *adj.* **1.** In a condition of excitement: *They were very excited about their discoveries in the field of electronics.* **2.** In physics, having more than the minimum amount of energy possible: *an excited atom.* —**ex•cit′ed•ly** *adv.*

ex•cite•ment |ĭk **sīt′**mənt| *n.* **1.** The condition of being excited; agitation; confusion; commotion: *As the countdown continued, the excitement increased. In the excitement, many people were injured.* **2.** Something that excites: *the excitement of a first trip to Europe.*

ex•cit•ing |ĭk **sī′**tĭng| *adj.* Creating excitement; rousing: *an exciting adventure; an exciting trip.* —**ex•cit′ing•ly** *adv.*

ex•claim |ĭk **sklām′**| *v.* To cry out or speak suddenly, as from surprise: *"Tin soldiers," exclaimed the little boy happily. She couldn't help exclaiming at Grandma's appearance.*

ex•cla•ma•tion |ĕk′sklə **mā′**shən| *n.* **1.** An abrupt, sudden utterance; an outcry: *an exclamation of pain; exclamations of pleasure.* **2.** An interjection.

exclamation mark. An **exclamation point.**

exclamation point. A punctuation mark (!) used after an exclamation.

ex•clam•a•to•ry |ĭk **sklăm′**ə tôr′ē| *or* |-tōr′ē| *adj.* Of, containing, or being an exclamation.

ex•clude |ĭk **sklōōd′**| *v.* **ex•clud•ed, ex•clud•ing. 1.** To prevent or keep from entering a place, group, activity, club, etc.; bar: *exclude a person from a job.* **2.** To leave out; omit; disregard: *Let's not exclude the possibility of rain during the weekend.*

excise¹ ²

Excise¹ *is from Dutch* excijs, *"tax." This is probably from Old French* acceis, *which is from a Late Latin word,* accēnsum, *"tax" (related to* cēnsus, *"census").* **Excise²** *is from Latin* excīdere, *"to cut out":* ex-, *"out,"* + caedere, *"to cut."*

execute
Execute *is from Medieval Latin* execūtāre, *"to follow out"* (ex-, *"out,"* + secūt-, *"follow"*). *Its basic meaning was "to follow a thing through, to carry out a task or order." But it also meant "to go after someone, to pursue" and hence "to pursue someone with justice or punishment," which accounts for sense 4 of* **execute** *and sense 3 of* **execution**.

ex•clu•sion |ĭk sklo͞o′zhən| *n.* **1.** The act of excluding: *At its inception, the Republican Party stood for exclusion of slavery from all territories of the United States.* **2.** The condition of being excluded.

ex•clu•sive |ĭk sklo͞o′sĭv| *adv.* **1.** Not divided or shared with others: *exclusive publishing rights.* **2.** Undivided; concentrated: *giving the class his exclusive attention.* **3. a.** Admitting only certain people to membership, participation, etc.; socially restricted: *an exclusive country club; an exclusive school.* **b.** Catering to wealthy people; chic: *an exclusive antique shop; an exclusive dress designer.* **4.** Regarded as unrelated; separate: *These two ideas are mutually exclusive.* —*n.* A newspaper story granted to or obtained by only one person or source. —**ex•clu′sive•ly** *adv.* —**ex•clu′sive•ness** *n.*

Idiom. **exclusive of.** Not including; besides: *exclusive of these factors.*

ex•com•mu•ni•cate |ĕks′kə myo͞o′nĭ kāt′| *v.* **ex•com•mu•ni•cat•ed, ex•com•mu•ni•cat•ing.** To cut off from religious participation in a church. —**ex′com•mu′ni•ca′tion** *n.*

ex•cre•ment |ĕk′skrə mənt| *n.* Waste matter that passes from the body after digestion, especially from the intestinal tract.

ex•cres•cence |ĭk skrĕs′əns| *n.* **1.** An abnormal or disfiguring growth on the body. **2.** A normal outgrowth of the body, as hair or a toenail.

ex•cres•cent |ĭk skrĕs′ənt| *adj.* Of or forming an excrescence, especially one that is abnormal: *excrescent tissue.*

ex•crete |ĭk skrēt′| *v.* **ex•cret•ed, ex•cret•ing.** To eliminate (waste matter) from tissues or organs, as of the body.

ex•cre•tion |ĭk skrē′shən| *n.* **1.** The act or process of excreting. **2.** The waste matter that is excreted.

ex•cre•to•ry |ĕk′skrĭ tôr′ē| *or* |-tōr′ē| *adj.* Of, involving, or used in excretion.

ex•cru•ci•at•ing |ĭk skro͞o′shē ā′tĭng| *adj.* Intensely painful; agonizing: *excruciating pain in his left hand; an excruciating headache.* —**ex•cru′ci•at′ing•ly** *adv.*

ex•cur•sion |ĭk skûr′zhən| *n.* **1.** A short, brief journey, especially a tour made for pleasure with a group; an outing. **2.** A trip, as on a boat, bus, or train, at a special reduced fare. **3. a.** A movement or deviation from an average position or condition or from a state of rest. **b.** The measure or magnitude of such a deviation. —***modifier:*** *an excursion boat; excursion fares; round-trip excursion tickets.*

ex•cuse |ĭk skyo͞oz′| *v.* **ex•cused, ex•cus•ing. 1. a.** To pardon; forgive: *I beg you to excuse me for what I did yesterday.* **b.** To make allowance for; overlook: *Please excuse my late arrival.* **2.** To serve as an apology for; justify: *Nothing excuses such rudeness.* **3.** To free or release from a duty, activity, obligation, etc.: *All seniors will be excused from school at 1:00 today.* —*n.* |ĭk skyo͞os′|. **1.** Something offered as grounds for excusing; a reason or explanation: *You must bring a written excuse when you are absent from school.* **2.** Something that serves to excuse; a justification: *There is no excuse for such behavior.* **3.** *Informal.* Something falling short of expectations: *He is a poor excuse for a poet.* —**ex•cus′a•ble** *adj.* —**ex•cus′a•ble•ness** *n.* —**ex•cus′a•bly** *adv.* —**ex•cus′er** *n.*

exec. executive.

ex•e•crate |ĕk′sĭ krāt′| *v.* **ex•e•crat•ed, ex•e•crat•ing. 1.** To protest vehemently against; denounce. **2.** To loathe; hate; detest. —**ex′e•cra′tion** *n.*

ex•e•cute |ĕk′sĭ kyo͞ot′| *v.* **ex•e•cut•ed, ex•e•cut•ing. 1.** To perform; do: *execute a difficult dance step; execute an assault.* **2. a.** To put into effect: *execute a law.* **b.** To carry out what is required by: *execute a will.* **3.** To make or produce (a work of art), especially according to a design: *Michelangelo executed many pieces of sculpture.* **4.** To subject to capital punishment: *execute a criminal.* **5.** To make valid; legalize, as by signing: *execute a deed.* [SEE NOTE]

ex•e•cu•tion |ĕk′sĭ kyo͞o′shən| *n.* **1.** The act or process of executing or carrying out: *creating obstructions to the execution of the law; the flawless execution of a piece of pottery.* **2.** The manner, style, or result of carrying out: *cleverness of design and execution.* **3. a.** The infliction of capital punishment: *execution by hanging.* **b.** An example of this: *three executions in one day. People assembled to witness the execution.*

ex•e•cu•tion•er |ĕk′sĭ kyo͞o′shə nər| *n.* Someone who executes a condemned person.

ex•ec•u•tive |ĭg zĕk′yə tĭv| *n.* **1.** A person or group that has administrative or managerial authority in an organization, especially in a corporation. **2.** The chief officer of a government or political division. **3.** The branch of government concerned with putting the country's laws into effect. —*adj.* **1.** Of or capable of carrying out plans, duties, etc.: *an executive committee; an executive board.* **2.** Of the branch of government concerned with putting laws into effect: *executive powers; an executive order.* **3.** Of or working for an executive: *executive offices; an executive secretary.*

ex•ec•u•tor |ĭg zĕk′yə tər| *n.* A person designated to execute the terms of a will.

ex•em•pla•ry |ĭg zĕm′plə rē| *adj.* **1.** Worthy of imitation; commendable: *exemplary behavior.* **2.** Serving as a warning: *exemplary punishment.* —**ex•em′pla•ri•ly** *adv.*

ex•em•pli•fy |ĭg zĕm′plə fī′| *v.* **ex•em•pli•fied, ex•em•pli•fy•ing, ex•em•pli•fies.** To serve as an example of; illustrate; show: *The glitter of court life and the poverty of the lower classes exemplified the extreme contrasts of the period.* —**ex•em′pli•fi•ca′tion** *n.*

ex•empt |ĭg zĕmpt′| *v.* To free from a duty or obligation required of others; excuse: *Some laws exempt churches and charities from taxes.* —*adj.* Freed from a duty or obligation required of others; excused: *exempt from criticism.* —**ex•empt′i•ble** *adj.*

ex•emp•tion |ĭg zĕmp′shən| *n.* **1.** The act of exempting or the condition of being exempt. **2.** A fixed sum that a taxpayer is allowed to deduct from his annual taxable income for himself and for each of his dependents.

ex•er•cise |ĕk′sər sīz′| *n.* **1.** An act or example of using or putting into play or effect: *the exercise of restraint; the exercise of power.* **2.** The fulfillment or performance of (a duty, office, function, etc.): *the exercise of their official duties.* **3.**

exercise
"Not less than two hours a day should be devoted to exercise."—Thomas Jefferson (1786). "Reading is to the mind what exercise is to the body."—Sir Richard Steele (1672–1729).

ă **pat**/ā **pay**/â **care**/ä **father**/ĕ **pet**/ ē **be**/ĭ **pit**/ī **pie**/î **fierce**/ŏ **pot**/ ō **go**/ô **paw**, **for**/oi **oil**/o͝o **book**/ o͞o **boot**/ou **out**/ŭ **cut**/û **fur**/ *th* **the**/th **thin**/hw **which**/zh **vision**/ ə **ago**, **item**, **pencil**, **atom**, **circus**

An activity requiring physical exertion, usually done to maintain or develop physical fitness. **4.** A lesson, problem, task, etc., designed to develop or improve understanding or skill: *Do the vocabulary exercises at the end of this chapter.* **5. exercises.** A ceremony with speeches, awards, etc.: *commencement exercises.* —*v.* **ex•er•cised, ex•er•cis•ing. 1.** To put into play or operation; use: *exercised his rights as a citizen; exercise restraint.* **2. a.** To do exercise, especially that which involves physical exertion: *He exercises for an hour daily.* **b.** To subject to physical exercise: *exercise a horse; exercised his stiff muscles.* [SEE NOTE on p. 322]

ex•ert |ĭg zûrt′| *v.* **1.** To put into effect; bring to bear: *Air exerts pressure. Architects exert a great influence on our daily lives.* **2. —exert (oneself).** To make a strenuous effort: *She exerted herself trying to say the right thing to everybody.*

ex•er•tion |ĭg zûr′shən| *n.* The act or an example of exerting, especially a strenuous effort: *You can sometimes do a lot with little exertion.*

ex•e•unt |ĕk′sē ənt| *or* |-o͞ont′|. *Latin.* They go out. Used as a stage direction to indicate that two or more actors leave the stage.

ex•ha•la•tion |ĕks′hə lā′shən| *or* |ĕk′sə-| *n.* **1.** The act or process of exhaling. **2.** Something, such as air or vapor, that is exhaled.

ex•hale |ĕks hāl′| *or* |ĕk sāl′| *v.* **ex•haled, ex•hal•ing. 1.** To breathe out: *After a minute under water you must come up and exhale.* **2.** To give off (gas, a gaseous mixture, or vapor) by or as if by breathing out: *She exhaled air.*

ex•haust |ĭg zôst′| *v.* **1.** To draw off or release (a liquid or gas). **2.** To drain the contents of; empty: *exhaust the fuel tank.* **3.** To use up; consume: *The diver exhausted his air supply.* **4.** To wear out completely; tire: *She exhausts herself with work. Overwork exhausts even the most energetic people.* **5.** To study, discuss, investigate, or deal with completely and comprehensively: *exhaust a topic; exhaust all possibilities.* **—ex•haust′ed** *adj.: an exhausted swimmer; an exhausted sleep.* **—ex•haus′ting** *adj.: exhausting work.* —*n.* **1.** The escape or release of waste gases or vapors, as from an engine. **2.** The vapors or gases released. **3.** A device, system, or part that pumps such gases out or allows them to escape: *a faulty automobile exhaust.* ***—modifier:*** *an exhaust fan; an exhaust pipe.*

ex•haus•tion |ĭg zôs′chən| *n.* **1.** An act or example of exhausting, especially the complete using up of a supply. **2.** A condition in which an organism is drained of energy, strength, or vitality; extreme fatigue: *nervous exhaustion.*

ex•haus•tive |ĭg zôs′tĭv| *adj.* Comprehensive; thorough: *exhaustive tests.*

ex•hib•it |ĭg zĭb′ĭt| *v.* **1.** To give evidence of; show; demonstrate: *a great opportunity to exhibit their courage in battle.* **2.** To present for the public to view; display: *He exhibits his works at a gallery. She exhibits twice a year at a gallery.* —*n.* **1.** Something exhibited; a display: *a museum exhibit.* **2.** Something formally introduced as evidence in a court of law. [SEE NOTE]

***Idiom.* on exhibit.** Available for public viewing; on display.

ex•hi•bi•tion |ĕk′sə bĭsh′ən| *n.* **1.** An act or example of exhibiting; a display: *an exhibition of strength; the flying exhibition at the airfield.* **2.** A display for the public, as of art works, industrial products, etc.: *a museum exhibition.* ***—modifier:*** *exhibition buildings; an exhibition game.*

***Idiom.* on exhibition.** Available for public viewing or display.

ex•hi•bi•tion•ism |ĕk′sə bĭsh′ə nĭz′əm| *n.* The act or practice of behaving in a way that is meant to attract attention. **—ex′hi•bi′tion•ist** *n.*

ex•hil•a•rate |ĭg zĭl′ə rāt′| *v.* **ex•hil•a•rat•ed, ex•hil•a•rat•ing. 1.** To make very happy; elate: *Challenges can both exhilarate and frighten us.* **2.** To refresh; invigorate: *Cold northern air exhilarates us.* **—ex•hil′a•ra′tion** *n.*

ex•hort |ĭg zôrt′| *v.* To urge by strong argument, appeal, etc.; admonish: *The preacher exhorted the crowd to repent.*

ex•hor•ta•tion |ĕg′zôr tā′shən| *or* |ĕk′sôr-| *n.* **1.** An act or example of exhorting: *an exhortation of religious fervor to the congregation.* **2.** A speech intended to advise or encourage: *his final exhortation to his aides.*

ex•hume |ĭg zyo͞om′| *or* |ĕks hyo͞om′| *v.* **ex•humed, ex•hum•ing. 1.** To dig up or remove from a grave. **2.** To bring to light; uncover: *exhume old superstitions.*

ex•i•gen•cy |ĕk′sĭ jən sē| *n., pl.* **ex•i•gen•cies. 1.** A situation demanding swift attention. **2.** Often **exigencies.** Urgent demands or requirements; pressing needs.

ex•i•gent |ĕk′sĭ jənt| *adj.* Requiring immediate attention; urgent: *exigent demands.*

ex•ile |ĕg′zīl′| *or* |ĕk′sīl′| *n.* **1. a.** Enforced removal from one's native country; banishment: *Exile was the punishment for his political activities.* **b.** Voluntary separation from one's native country: *Many chose exile over Nazism.* **2.** Someone who is or has been banished from his country, either by force or voluntarily. **3.** A condition of being banished from one's country: *He was in exile for ten years.* **4.** Banishment from an organization, sphere of influence, activity, etc.: *The scandal was the cause of his exile from the National Basketball Association.* —*v.* **ex•iled, ex•il•ing.** To send (someone) into exile; banish: *Soon after the coronation the king proceeded to imprison, exile, or execute his enemies.*

ex•ist |ĭg zĭst′| *v.* **1.** To have material or spiritual being: *You cannot photograph something that does not exist.* **2. a.** To have life; live: *Dinosaurs existed millions of years ago.* **b.** To continue to live: *Man cannot exist without food and water.* **3.** To be present; occur: *Completely free trade has never existed.*

ex•is•tence |ĭg zĭs′təns| *n.* **1.** The fact or condition of existing; being: *The voice is the most efficient sound producer in existence.* **2.** The fact or condition of continued being; life: *Wheels have revolutionized man's existence.* **3.** A manner of existing: *an ordinary existence; a meager existence.* **4.** Occurrence; presence: *the existence of life on other planets.*

ex•is•tent |ĭg zĭs′tənt| *adj.* **1.** Having life or being; existing: *existent creatures.* **2.** Occurring at the present time; current: *existent rules and regulations.*

ex•is•ten•tial•ism |ĕg′zĭ stĕn′shə lĭz′əm| *or* |ĕk′sĭ-| *n.* A 20th-century philosophy that views the individual as being unique and alone in an

exhibit

Exhibit *is from Latin* exhibēre *(past participle* exhibitus*), "to hold (something) out, to offer, to display":* ex-, *"out,"* + habēre, *"to hold." This verb formed the noun* exhibitiō, *"a showing," from which we have* **exhibition.** *Notice that in compounds,* habēre *changes to* -hibēre. *We have two other verbs from exactly parallel compounds of* habēre, *each taking its ending from the past participle ending in* -hibitus *and its noun from the noun ending in* -hibitiō. **Inhibit** *is from Latin* inhibēre, *"to hold onto, to hold back, to keep in"* (in-, *"in or on"*). **Prohibit** *is from Latin* prohibēre, *"to hold (a person) from the front, to prevent, to forbid"* (pro-, *"in front"*).

indifferent and even hostile universe, regards human existence as unexplainable, and stresses man's freedom of choice. —**ex'is•ten'tial•ist** *n.*

ex•it[1] |ĕg'zĭt| *or* |ĕk'sĭt|. *Latin.* She (or he) goes out. Used as a stage direction. [SEE NOTE]

ex•it[2] |ĕg'zĭt| *or* |ĕk'sĭt| *n.* **1.** A passage or way out. **2.** The act of going away or out. **3.** A performer's departure from the stage. —*v.* **1.** To make one's exit; depart. **2.** To leave the stage. [SEE NOTE]

ex•o•bi•ol•o•gist |ĕk'sō bī ŏl'ə jĭst| *n.* A scientist who specializes in exobiology.

ex•o•bi•ol•o•gy |ĕk'sō bī ŏl'ə jē| *n.* **1.** The scientific search for and study of organisms that do not live on the earth or in its atmosphere. **2.** The scientific study of the effects that travel in space has on living organisms.

ex•o•dus |ĕk'sə dəs| *n.* **1.** Any mass departure or wave of emigration: *the Negro exodus from the South.* **2. a. the Exodus.** In the Bible, the flight from Egypt of the Israelites, led by Moses. **b. Exodus.** The second book of the Old Testament, which tells of this flight.

ex of•fi•ci•o |ĕks' ə fĭsh'ē ō'|. By virtue of one's office or position: *The mayor is ex officio a member of the city council.* This expression was originally a Latin phrase.

ex•on•er•ate |ĭg zŏn'ə rāt'| *v.* **ex•on•er•at•ed, ex•on•er•at•ing.** To free from a charge; declare blameless: *The court exonerated the defendant.* —**ex•on'er•a'tion** *n.*

ex•or•bi•tant |ĭg zôr'bĭ tənt| *adj.* Exceeding reasonable limits; excessive; extravagant: *Exorbitant prices discourage potential buyers.* —**ex•or'bi•tance** |ĭg zôr'bĭ təns| *n.* —**ex•or'bi•tant•ly** *adv.*

ex•or•cise |ĕk'sôr sīz'| *v.* **ex•or•cised, ex•or•cis•ing.** **1.** To expel (an evil spirit) by or as if by prayer or magic. **2.** To free from evil spirits: *The priests tried to exorcise the girl, whom they considered a witch.* —**ex'or•cis'er** *n.*

ex•or•cism |ĕk'sôr sĭz'əm| *n.* The act or practice of exorcising.

ex•o•skel•e•ton |ĕk'sō skĕl'ĭ tn| *n.* A tough, protective outer body covering, as of a crustacean; an external skeleton. [SEE NOTE]

ex•o•sphere |ĕk'sō sfîr'| *n.* The outermost layer of the atmosphere, considered to begin 300 to 600 miles above the earth.

ex•o•ther•mic |ĕk'sō thûr'mĭk| *adj.* Releasing or giving off heat: *an exothermic chemical reaction.*

ex•ot•ic |ĭg zŏt'ĭk| *adj.* **1.** From another part of the world; not native; foreign: *exotic birds; exotic customs.* **2.** Having the charm of the unfamiliar; strikingly or intriguingly unusual: *She is an exotic beauty.* [SEE NOTE]

ex•pand |ĭk spănd'| *v.* **1.** To increase in one or more physical dimensions, as length or volume: *Gases expand when heated.* **2.** To increase or undergo an increase in extent, size, number, volume, etc.; grow or develop: *He expanded his business into new areas. Try to expand your knowledge. His business expanded rapidly.* **3.** To speak or write fully and in detail; expatiate: *He will expand on the problem at the meeting.* **4.** To write (a number or mathematical expression) in an extended form: *We expand 452 by writing it as 400 + 50 + 2.* —**ex•pand'a•ble** *adj.*

expanded numeral. A numeral written in the form $a_m b^m + a_{m-1} b^{m-1} + \ldots + a_0 b^0$, where b is the base of the system of numeration and a_m through a_0 are whole numbers less than the base. For example, the expanded form of 973 (base ten) is $9 \times 10^2 + 7 \times 10^1 + 3 \times 10^0$, or $900 + 70 + 3$.

expanding universe theory. The theory that the entire material universe is expanding with all of its parts moving outward from a central point and that the parts most distant from this point have the greatest velocities. The theory is based on an interpretation of the properties of light from distant galaxies that suggests that they are rapidly moving away from the earth.

ex•panse |ĭk spăns'| *n.* A wide and open extent, as of land, air, or water: *a vast expanse of desert; a majestic expanse of ocean.*

ex•pan•sion |ĭk spăn'shən| *n.* **1.** The act or process of expanding; an increase in extent, size, number, volume, etc.: *an aggressive policy of territorial expansion; the growth and expansion of Italy's industry; a rapid expansion of the population; the expansion of a liquid as a gauge of temperature.* **2.** Something formed or produced by expansion: *The suburbs are now becoming thickly settled as expansions of the cities.* **3.** The extent or amount by which something has expanded: *a westward expansion of 400 miles.* **4. a.** A number or other mathematical expression written in an extended form; for example, $a^2 + 2ab + b^2$ is the expansion of $(a + b)^2$. **b.** The process of finding this extended form.

ex•pan•sion•ist |ĭk spăn'shə nĭst| *adj.* Of or in favor of territorial or economic expansion: *the expansionist spirit of the 1840's in America.*

ex•pan•sive |ĭk spăn'sĭv| *adj.* **1.** Having considerable sweep; broad; wide: *the calm, expansive lake.* **2. a.** Kind and generous; outgoing: *Father was in an expansive mood and gave us a raise in allowance.* **b.** Marked by euphoria and exaggerated self-importance: *His expansive behavior indicated his need for psychiatric care.* **3.** Capable of expanding or tending to expand. **4.** Grand in scale: *his expansive style of living.* —**ex•pan'sive•ly** *adv.* —**ex•pan'sive•ness** *n.*

ex•pa•ti•ate |ĭk spā'shē āt'| *v.* **ex•pa•ti•at•ed, ex•pa•ti•at•ing.** To speak or write at length; elaborate: *He expatiated freely on the subjects about which he was most knowledgeable.* —**ex•pa'ti•a'tion** *n.*

ex•pa•tri•ate |ĕks pā'trē āt'| *v.* **ex•pa•tri•at•ed, ex•pa•tri•at•ing.** **1.** To banish (a person) from his native land; exile: *The government expatriated the most active members of the opposition.* **2.** To banish (oneself) from one's native land to reside in another country: *Many American writers expatriated themselves to France in the 1920's. Some expatriated to England.* —*n.* |ĕks pā'trē ĭt| *or* |-āt'|. An expatriated person: *Many American expatriates live in France.* —**modifier:** *an expatriate poet.* —**ex•pa'tri•a'tion** *n.*

ex•pect |ĭk spĕkt'| *v.* **1.** To look forward to the occurrence of something; think or believe that something or someone will happen, come, appear, etc.: *The adventurer expects danger. The farmer expects to plant corn. We have been expecting you all morning.* **2. a.** To consider reasonable, proper, or just: *expect an apology.* **b.** To consider necessary; require: *The emperors ex-*

exit[1-2]

Exit[1] *is from Latin* exit, *"he or she goes out," the third person singular of the present tense of* exīre, *"to go out":* ex-, *"out,"* + īre, *"to go."* **Exeunt** *is from the third person plural of the same tense.* **Exit[2]** *is from Latin* exitus, *"a going out, a way out," which is a noun formed from the same verb* exīre.

exoskeleton, etc.

The exo- *of* **exoskeleton** *and other words is from Greek* exō, *"outside," which is an extension of* ex, *"out of." The Latin preposition meaning "out of" is also* ex. *Both the Latin* ex *and the Greek* ex *are obviously descended from the prehistoric Indo-European word for "out," which has been reconstructed as* eghs.

exotic

Exotic *comes from Greek* exōtikos, *"coming from outside, foreign," which is from* exō, *"outside" (see note at* **exoskeleton***). Most words for "foreign," including the word* **foreign** *itself and the word* **alien**, *tend to have an adverse flavor, expressing a general mistrust of unfamiliar things. Sense 2 of* **exotic** *is an interesting exception, stressing the romantic or even mysterious appeal of strangeness. Compare the notes at* **barbarous** *and* **strange**.

ă **pat**/ā **pay**/â **care**/ä **father**/ĕ **pet**/ ē **be**/ĭ **pit**/ī **pie**/î **fierce**/ŏ **pot**/ ō **go**/ô **paw**, **for**/oi **oil**/ŏŏ **book**/ ōō **boot**/ou **out**/ŭ **cut**/û **fur**/ *th* **the**/th **thin**/hw **which**/zh **vision**/ ə **ago**, item, pencil, atom, circus *pected absolute obedience.* **3.** *Informal.* To suppose or think: *I expect you're right.*

ex•pect•an•cy |ĭk **spĕk′**tən sē| *n., pl.* **ex•pect•an•cies. 1.** The act or condition of expecting; anticipation: *Tension and expectancy gripped the fans in the last moments of the game.* **2.** Something expected, especially as a result of calculation from known facts or statistics: *a life expectancy of 70 years.*

ex•pect•ant |ĭk **spĕk′**tnt| *adj.* **1.** Filled with or marked by expectation: *A hush fell over the expectant audience.* **2.** Awaiting the birth of a child: *an expectant mother.* —**ex•pect′ant•ly** *adv.*

ex•pec•ta•tion |ĕk′spĕk **tā′**shən| *n.* **1.** The act or condition of expecting; anticipation: *the expectation of success. Rufus waved his tail in expectation.* **2. expectations.** Prospects; hopes: *The trade agreement fell short of expectations.*

ex•pec•to•rant |ĭk **spĕk′**tər ənt| *adj.* Easing or increasing secretion or discharge from the mucous membranes of the throat and respiratory system. —*n.* An expectorant medicine or drug.

ex•pec•to•rate |ĭk **spĕk′**tə rāt′| *v.* **ex•pec•to•rat•ed, ex•pec•to•rat•ing. 1.** To force (something) from the mouth by action of the tongue and lips; spit. **2.** To cough up and discharge by spitting. **3.** To clear the chest or lungs by coughing and spitting. —**ex•pec′to•ra′tion** *n.*

ex•pe•di•ence |ĭk **spē′**dē əns| *n.* A form of the word **expediency.**

ex•pe•di•en•cy |ĭk **spē′**dē ən sē| *n., pl.* **ex•pe•di•en•cies. 1.** Appropriateness to the purpose at hand. **2.** Selfish practicality: *His plans were based on sheer expediency.*

ex•pe•di•ent |ĭk **spē′**dē ənt| *n.* Something that answers a particular purpose; a means to an end: *Flight is the most common expedient adopted by those mammals that are the hunted rather than the hunter.* —*adj.* **1.** Suited to a particular purpose; appropriate: *The generals decided it would not be expedient to attack yet.* **2.** Serving narrow or selfish interests; useful and practical though perhaps unprincipled: *As a politician, he always did what was expedient.* —**ex•pe′di•ent•ly** *adv.*

ex•pe•dite |**ĕk′**spĭ dīt′| *v.* **ex•pe•dit•ed, ex•pe•dit•ing. 1.** To speed or ease the progress of; facilitate: *He expedited my job application by a phone call to the manager.* **2.** To perform quickly and efficiently: *expedite an assignment.*

ex•pe•di•tion |ĕk′spĭ **dĭsh′**ən| *n.* **1.** A trip made by an organized group of people with a definite purpose: *a map-making expedition; an expedition to the South Pole.* **2.** A group making such a trip: *The expedition finally arrived.*

ex•pe•di•tion•ar•y |ĕk′spĭ **dĭsh′**ə nĕr′ē| *adj.* Of or being a military expedition: *an expeditionary force.*

ex•pe•di•tious |ĕk′spĭ **dĭsh′**əs| *adj.* Acting or done with speed and efficiency: *The most expeditious handling and transportation available will be used for fastest delivery of mail.* —**ex′pe•di′tious•ly** *adv.* —**ex′pe•di′tious•ness** *n.*

ex•pel |ĭk **spĕl′**| *v.* **ex•pelled, ex•pel•ling. 1.** To force or drive out; eject forcefully: *expel air from the lungs.* **2.** To dismiss by official decision: *The principal decided to expel Tom from school.*

ex•pend |ĭk **spĕnd′**| *v.* To use up; consume; spend: *expend one's time and money on a futile project.*

ex•pend•a•ble |ĭk **spĕn′**də bəl| *adj.* Subject to being sacrificed or used up to gain an objective: *Army headquarters decided that our regiment was expendable.*

ex•pen•di•ture |ĭk **spĕn′**dĭ chər| *n.* **1.** The act or process of expending. **2.** Something that is expended: *enormous expenditures of money for the new highway.*

ex•pense |ĭk **spĕns′**| *n.* **1.** The cost involved in some activity; a price: *the expense involved in landing a man on the moon.* **2.** Something requiring the expenditure of money: *Maintaining a car can be a heavy expense.* **3.** Loss; sacrifice: *He finished the project on time but at the expense of his health.* **4. expenses. a.** Charges incurred in carrying out an assignment: *a salesman's expenses.* **b.** Money set aside to pay such charges: *He received a salary plus expenses.*

ex•pen•sive |ĭk **spĕn′**sĭv| *adj.* **1.** High-priced; costly: *an expensive dress.* **2.** Achieved or gained at great loss or sacrifice: *Gettysburg was an expensive victory for the Union army.* —**ex•pen′sive•ly** *adv.* —**ex•pen′sive•ness** *n.*

ex•pe•ri•ence |ĭk **spîr′**ē əns| *n.* **1.** An event or series of events participated in or lived through: *the experience of being in an earthquake. He had an exciting experience at the fair.* **2.** Knowledge or skill gained through direct activity or practice: *He gained much experience on his previous job.* —*v.* **ex•pe•ri•enced, ex•pe•ri•enc•ing.** To participate in personally; live through: *experience a great personal loss.* [SEE NOTE]

ex•pe•ri•enced |ĭk **spîr′**ē ənst| *adj.* Skilled or knowledgeable through much experience: *an experienced teacher.*

ex•per•i•ment |ĭk **spĕr′**ə mənt| *or* |-mĕnt′| *n.* Something done to demonstrate a known fact, check the correctness of a theory, or see how well a new thing works; a test. —*v.* To conduct an experiment or experiments; make tests or trials. —**ex•per′i•ment′er** *n.* [SEE PICTURE & NOTE]

ex•per•i•men•tal |ĭk spĕr′ə **mĕn′**tl| *adj.* **1.** Of or based on experiments: *experimental evidence; experimental procedures; experimental science.* **2.** New and being tested: *an experimental drug.* —**ex•per′i•men′tal•ly** *adv.*

ex•per•i•men•ta•tion |ĭk spĕr′ə mĕn **tā′**shən| *n.* The act, process, or practice of experimenting.

ex•pert |**ĕk′**spûrt′| *n.* A person with great knowledge, skill, and experience in a particular field: *He is one of the nation's leading foreign-policy experts.* —*adj.* |ĭk **spûrt′**| *or* |**ĕk′**spûrt′|. **1.** Having great knowledge, skill, and experience in a particular field: *an expert photographer.* **2.** Given by an expert: *expert advice; an expert opinion.* —**ex•pert′ly** *adv.* —**ex•pert′ness** *n.* [SEE NOTE]

ex•per•tise |ĕk′spər **tēz′**| *n.* Expert skill or knowledge.

ex•pi•ate |**ĕk′**spē āt′| *v.* **ex•pi•at•ed, ex•pi•at•ing.** To atone or make amends for: *expiate a crime.* —**ex′pi•a′tion** *n.*

ex•pi•ra•tion |ĕk′spə **rā′**shən| *n.* **1.** The act or process of breathing out. **2.** The process of coming to a close; termination: *the expiration of a lease.* —***modifier:*** *an expiration date.*

ex•pire |ĭk **spīr′**| *v.* **ex•pired, ex•pir•ing. 1.** To breathe out; exhale. **2.** To stop breathing permanently; die. **3.** To come to an end; termi-

experience/experiment/expert
Experiment *is from Latin* experīmentum, *"a trying out, a test, an experiment." This is a noun formed from the verb* experīrī, *"to try out, to test, to learn by testing":* ex-, *"out,"* + perīrī, "to try." There was also another noun formed from this verb: experientia, *"knowledge gained by trying or testing," from which we have* **experience.** *And the verb's past participle was* expertus, *"proved by experience," from which we have* **expert.** *These are the etymological meanings and relationships of the three words, but notice that they have developed rather differently in English. Experience is gained in the general course of life, not especially by experiments; and expert is not exactly synonymous with experienced.*

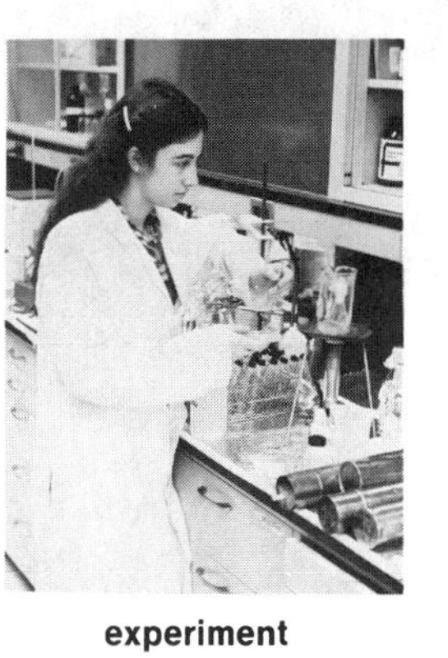

experiment

nate; cease to be effective: *His driver's license expired last month.*

ex•plain |ĭk **splān'**| *v.* **1.** To make plain or clear; clarify: *explain the rules of a game; explain the meaning of a poem.* **2.** To offer reasons for; account for: *He was asked to explain his erratic attendance.* **3.** To give an explanation: *Please give me a chance to explain.* —***phrasal verb.* explain away.** To give an excuse or contrived explanation for. —**ex•plain'a•ble** *adj.* —**ex•plain'er** *n.* [SEE NOTE]

ex•pla•na•tion |ĕk'splə **nā'**shən| *n.* **1.** The act or process of explaining; clarification: *the explanation of a theory.* **2.** A statement, fact, etc., that serves to explain: *Give your class an explanation of how to make a kite.* **3.** A meaning; reason; interpretation: *The police sought an explanation for the murder.*

ex•plan•a•to•ry |ĭk **splăn'**ə tôr'ē| *or* |-tōr'ē| *adj.* Serving or intended to explain: *This book includes explanatory notes.*

ex•ple•tive |**ĕk'**splĭ tĭv| *n.* An exclamation or oath, especially one that is profane or obscene; for example, *damn* is an expletive.

ex•pli•ca•ble |**ĕk'**splĭ kə bəl| *adj.* Capable of being explained; explainable: *Ghosts are simply not explicable in scientific terms.*

ex•pli•cate |**ĕk'**splĭ kāt'| *v.* **ex•pli•cat•ed, ex•pli•cat•ing.** To make clear the meaning of; explain: *explicate a scientific theory.* [SEE NOTE]

explain/explicate

The two words mean approximately the same thing, but with subtly different nuances. Their etymologies are helpful in understanding this. **Explain** *is from Latin* explānāre, *"to make (something) plain or clear": ex-, "out," +* plānus, *"plain, clear."* **Explicate** *is from Latin* explicāre, *"to unfold, untie, disentangle," hence "to describe (something difficult), to interpret": ex-, "out, un-," +* plicāre, *"to fold."*

ex•pli•ca•tion |ĕk'splĭ **kā'**shən| *n.* **1.** The act of explicating. **2.** A detailed analysis or interpretation: *an explication of a literary text.*

ex•plic•it |ĭk **splĭs'**ĭt| *adj.* Clearly defined; specific; precise: *The doctor asked her to be explicit in describing her symptoms.* —**ex•plic'it•ly** *adv.* —**ex•plic'it•ness** *n.*

ex•plode |ĭk **splōd'**| *v.* **ex•plod•ed, ex•plod•ing. 1.** To undergo or release energy in an explosion: *Bombs exploded all around.* **2.** To break apart and be destroyed by an explosion: *Suddenly the tank exploded.* **3.** To cause to undergo an explosion; detonate: *The heat exploded the ammunition.* **4.** To burst forth or break out suddenly: *Father exploded with anger when he saw my report card.* **5.** To increase sharply: *The population of Latin America is exploding.* **6.** To expose as false; refute: *Copernicus exploded the theory that the earth is the center of the universe.* —**ex•plod'er** *n.*

ex•ploit |**ĕk'**sploit'| *n.* An act or deed, especially a brilliant or heroic feat: *the exploits of Robin Hood.* —*v.* |ĭk **sploit'**|. **1.** To make the greatest possible use of; turn to advantage: *exploit the nation's timber resources; exploit an idea.* **2.** To make use of selfishly or unethically: *The plantation owners often exploited their slaves ruthlessly.* —**ex•ploit'a•ble** *adj.* —**ex•ploit'er** *n.*

ex•ploi•ta•tion |ĕk'sploi **tā'**shən| *n.* **1.** The act of exploiting: *the exploitation of our oil reserves.* **2.** The utilization of another person for selfish purposes: *the exploitation of free labor.*

ex•plo•ra•tion |ĕk'splə **rā'**shən| *n.* **1.** The act of exploring: *Spain began the exploration of the New World.* **2.** A medical examination of an organ or part of the body, especially one that cannot normally be seen.

ex•plor•a•to•ry |ĭk **splôr'**ə tôr'ē| *or* |-**splōr'**ə tōr'ē| *adj.* Of or for exploration: *an exploratory trip; exploratory surgery.*

ex•plore |ĭk **splôr'**| *or* |-**splōr'**| *v.* **ex•plored, ex•plor•ing. 1.** To travel into or wander through (an unknown or unfamiliar place, region, etc.) for the purpose of discovery: *DeSoto explored a vast region in North America. The children decided to explore the attic.* **2.** To conduct a systematic search: *The geologists explored for oil on our farm.* **3.** To look into; investigate: *explore the possibilities of a cease-fire.* **4.** To make a medical examination of (an organ or part of the body).

ex•plor•er |ĭk **splôr'**ər| *or* |-**splōr'**-| *n.* **1.** A person who explores unknown or little-known places. **2. Explorer.** An **Explorer Scout.**

Explorer Scout. A member of the Explorer Scouts, a division of the Boy Scouts for boys of 14 or over.

ex•plo•sion |ĭk **splō'**zhən| *n.* **1. a.** A sudden, violent release of energy from a confined space, especially with the production of a shock wave and a loud, sharp sound, as well as heat, light, flames, and flying debris. **b.** The loud, sharp sound made by such a release of energy. **2.** A sudden outbreak: *an explosion of laughter.* **3.** A sudden and sharp increase: *the population explosion.*

ex•plo•sive |ĭk **splō'**sĭv| *adj.* **1.** Of or like an explosion: *an explosive release of energy.* **2.** Capable of exploding or tending to explode: *an explosive substance.* —*n.* A substance, especially a prepared chemical, that tends to explode or is capable of exploding. —**ex•plo'sive•ly** *adv.* —**ex•plo'sive•ness** *n.*

ex•po•nent |ĭk **spō'**nənt| *n.* **1.** A person who explains or interprets something: *a leading exponent of new teaching methods.* **2.** A person who speaks for, represents, or advocates: *a consistent exponent of moderation in politics.* **3.** Any number or symbol, such as the *2* in $(x + y)^2$, that indicates the number of times a mathematical expression is used as a factor. The symbol is usually written above and to the right of the expression to which it applies.

ex•po•nen•tial |ĕk'spō **nĕn'**shəl| *adj.* **1.** Of, containing, or involving one or more exponents. **2.** Of or defined by a mathematical function that has an independent variable as an exponent: *an exponential increase.* —*n.* Also **exponential function.** A mathematical function, such as $f(x) = ab^x$, that contains an independent variable used as an exponent.

ex•port |ĭk **spôrt'**| *or* |-**spōrt'**| *or* |**ĕk'**spôrt'| *or* |-spōrt'| *v.* To send or carry (goods, products, etc.) to another country for trade or sale: *Argentina exports beef. America exports to many lands.* —*n.* |**ĕk'**spôrt'| *or* |-spōrt'|. **1.** The act or process of exporting: *the export of raw materials.* **2.** Something that is exported: *Oil is the major export of the Arab countries.* —***modifier:*** *an export tax; the export trade.* —**ex•port'a•ble** *adj.* —**ex•port'er** *n.*

ex•por•ta•tion |ĕk'spôr **tā'**shən| *or* |-spōr-| *n.* The act or process of exporting.

ex•pose |ĭk **spōz'**| *v.* **ex•posed, ex•pos•ing. 1.** To uncover; lay bare: *expose one's back to the sun.* **2.** To lay open or subject, as to a force, influence, etc.: *expose a child to books at the earliest possible age; expose an opponent to ridicule.* **3.** To make visible; reveal: *Cleaning has ex-*

posed the grain of the wood. **4. a.** To disclose; make known: *expose a plot.* **b.** To reveal the guilt or misdeeds of: *expose a thief; expose a dishonest employee.* **5.** To subject (a photographic film or plate) to the action of light.

ex•po•sé |ĕk'spō **zā'**| *n.* An exposure or revelation, as through a newspaper article, of a fraud, crime, etc.

ex•po•si•tion |ĕk'spə **zĭsh'**ən| *n.* **1.** A written or oral presentation of informative or explanatory material. **2.** Often **Exposition.** A large public exhibition or fair: *the Chicago Exposition.* **3.** The opening section of a musical composition, such as a sonata or fugue, in which the themes are first stated.

ex•pos•i•tor |ĭk **spŏz'**ĭ tər| *n.* A person who expounds or explains something.

ex•pos•i•to•ry |ĭk **spŏz'**ĭ tôr'ē| *or* |-tōr'ē| *adj.* Serving to inform or explain: *expository writing.*

ex post fac•to |**ĕks'** pōst' **făk'**tō|. Enacted after an event but applying to it nonetheless; retroactive: *an ex post facto law.* This expression was originally a Latin phrase.

ex•pos•tu•late |ĭk **spŏs'**chə lāt'| *v.* **ex•pos•tu•lat•ed, ex•pos•tu•lat•ing.** To reason earnestly with someone, especially in an effort to dissuade, correct, etc.; remonstrate. —**ex•pos'tu•la'tion** *n.*

ex•po•sure |ĭk **spō'**zhər| *n.* **1.** The act or an example of exposing: *a newspaper's exposure of a scandal.* **2.** The condition of being exposed: *a child's exposure to measles; India's exposure to Western ideas.* **3.** A location or position in relation to the sun, winds, points of the compass, etc.: *a house with a northern exposure.* **4. a.** The act or process of exposing a photographic film or plate. **b.** The length of time for which such a film or plate is exposed: *a long exposure.* **c.** The amount of light to which a film or plate is exposed. **d.** An exposed film or plate or an exposed section of a roll of film.

exposure meter. An instrument that indicates the intensity of light from a source, often equipped with scales for computing the correct adjustments for a camera and film to be used in photographing that source.

ex•pound |ĭk **spound'**| *v.* To set forth or explain in detail: *He always expounds his viewpoint in a vigorous manner.* —**ex•pound'er** *n.*

ex•press |ĭk **sprĕs'**| *v.* **1.** To make known; show; reveal: *His face expressed great joy. This painting expresses the artist's inner doubts and conflicts.* **2.** To put into words; state: *She certainly expresses her ideas clearly.* **3.** To be a sign of; signify: *In arithmetic, the minus sign expresses subtraction.* **4.** —**express (oneself). a.** To put one's thoughts into words. **b.** *Informal.* To give expression or vent to one's thoughts, feelings, dreams, etc. —*adj.* **1.** Clearly stated; explicit; definite: *an express reason; one's express wishes; an express command.* **2.** Of or sent out by rapid direct transportation: *an express highway; an express package.* **3.** Direct, rapid, and usually not making local stops: *an express train.* —*adv.* By express transportation: *send a package express.* —*n.* **1.** An express train, bus, etc. **2. a.** A rapid, efficient system for the delivery of goods and mail. **b.** A company that deals in such transport. [SEE NOTE]

ex•press•i•ble |ĭk **sprĕs'**ə bəl| *adj.* Capable of being expressed: *His thoughts were so confused as to be barely expressible.*

ex•pres•sion |ĭk **sprĕsh'**ən| *n.* **1.** The act or process of expressing: *the expression of one's opinion through the ballot box.* **2. a.** Anything that serves to express an idea, feeling, etc.: *sending flowers as an expression of thanks.* **b.** A facial aspect or look that indicates a certain mood or feeling: *an expression of anger in his eyes; a worried expression.* **3.** A particular word, phrase, or saying: *"Burnt to a crisp" is a familiar expression.* **4.** A vivid or emphatic manner of speaking: *He tried to put expression in his voice.* **5.** A mathematical symbol or an arrangement of mathematical symbols that has some meaning: *an algebraic expression.*

ex•pres•sion•ism |ĭk **sprĕsh'**ə nĭz'əm| *n.* A movement in the fine arts during the latter part of the 19th century and early part of the 20th century that used color, symbols, and other devices to portray emotion.

ex•pres•sion•less |ĭk **sprĕsh'**ən lĭs| *adj.* Not revealing feelings or emotion; impassive: *His face was completely expressionless.*

ex•pres•sive |ĭk **sprĕs'**ĭv| *adj.* **1.** Expressing or tending to express: *music expressive of one's mood.* **2.** Full of meaning; significant: *an expressive glance.* —**ex•pres'sive•ly** *adv.* —**ex•pres'sive•ness** *n.*

ex•press•ly |ĭk **sprĕs'**lē| *adv.* **1.** Especially; particularly: *a ship designed expressly for exploring the Arctic waters.* **2.** Without any doubt; definitely; plainly; explicitly: *The rules expressly forbid it.*

ex•press•man |ĭk **sprĕs'**mən| *n., pl.* **-men** |-mən|. A man, usually a truck driver who makes collections or deliveries, employed by an express company.

ex•press•way |ĭk **sprĕs'**wā'| *n.* A multilane highway designed for high-speed travel.

ex•pro•pri•ate |ĕks **prō'**prē āt'| *v.* **ex•pro•pri•at•ed, ex•pro•pri•at•ing.** **1.** To acquire (land or other property), especially for public use, by taking it away from the original owner: *The new government expropriated the copper mines.* **2.** To take away the property of; dispossess: *The discontented peasants expropriated the landlords.* —**ex•pro'pri•a'tion** *n.*

ex•pul•sion |ĭk **spŭl'**shən| *n.* **1.** The act of expelling: *the expulsion of waste from the body.* **2.** The condition of being expelled: *He was threatened with expulsion from school.*

ex•punge |ĭk **spŭnj'**| *v.* **ex•punged, ex•pung•ing.** To remove completely; delete; erase: *expunge a statement from the records.*

ex•pur•gate |**ĕk'**spər gāt'| *v.* **ex•pur•gat•ed, ex•pur•gat•ing.** To remove obscene or otherwise objectionable passages from (a published work): *expurgate a novel; expurgate a play.* —**ex'pur•ga'tion** *n.*

ex•qui•site |**ĕk'**skwĭz ĭt| *or* |ĭk **skwĭz'**ĭt| *adj.* **1.** Of special beauty, charm, elegance, etc.: *an exquisite vase.* **2.** Intense; keen: *He takes exquisite pleasure in his meals.* **3.** Keenly sensitive; discriminating: *She has exquisite taste in art.* —**ex'qui•site•ly** *adv.* [SEE NOTE]

ex•tant |**ĕk'**stənt| *or* |ĭk **stănt'**| *adj.* Still in existence; not destroyed, lost, or extinct: *the extant plays of Shakespeare.*

express
Senses 2 and 3 of the adjective **express** *arose from sense 1. An* express messenger *was one sent for a single* express, or *"specially stated," purpose. An* express train *was originally a train hired by a group of people to make one* express *journey.*

exquisite
Exquisite *is from Latin* exquisitus, *"carefully sought out, very choice, excellent"; this is from* exquirere, *"to seek out":* ex-, *"out,"* + quaerere, *"to seek."*

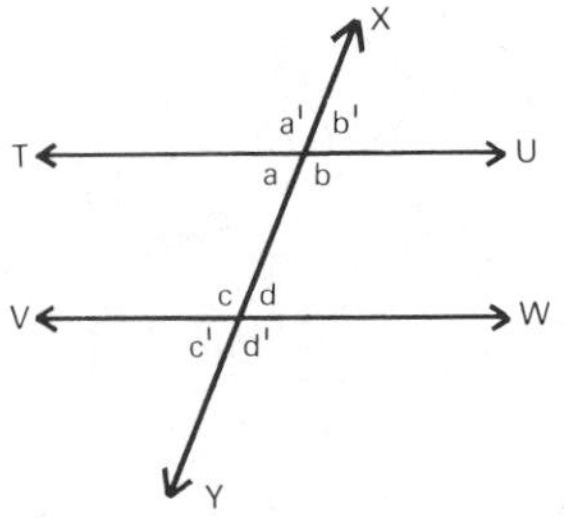

exterior angles
Angles a′, b′, c′, d′ are exterior angles of the parallel lines TU, VW cut by the transversal XY

extinguish/extinct
Extinguish *is from Latin* exstinguere, *"to put out (a fire)," also "to kill, to destroy": ex-, "out," +* stinguere, *"to quench." The past participle of this verb was* exstinctus, *"put out, destroyed," from which we have* **extinct**.

extort
Extort *is from Latin* extorquēre, *"to pull (something) out with a twist, to torture (a person), to get (something from a person) by force":* ex-, *"out,"* + torquēre, *"to twist."*

ă pat/ā pay/â care/ä father/ĕ pet/ ē be/ĭ pit/ī pie/î fierce/ŏ pot/ ō go/ô paw, for/oi oil/o͝o book/ o͞o boot/ou out/ŭ cut/û fur/ *th* the/th thin/hw which/zh vision/ ə ago, item, pencil, atom, circus

ex•tem•po•ra•ne•ous |ĭk stĕm′pə **rā′**nē əs| *adj.* Done or made with little or no advance preparation; impromptu: *an extemporaneous speech; extemporaneous remarks.* —**ex•tem′po•ra′ne•ous•ly** *adv.*

ex•tend |ĭk **stĕnd′**| *v.* **1.** To make longer; lengthen; prolong: *extend the sides of an angle; extend the average life span.* **2.** To reach or go: *The curve extends from point A to point B. The beach extends for miles.* **3.** To make greater; enlarge: *extend the boundaries of the empire; extended his personal influence.* **4.** To offer or grant: *extend congratulations to the newlyweds; extend aid to an underdeveloped country.* **5.** To straighten or reach out with (a body part): *Extend your left arm.* **6.** To grant additional time for payment or delivery of: *The bank extended his loan for a few more months. The editor extended the deadline on my article.*

***Idiom.* extend (oneself).** To exert oneself greatly; make a serious effort.

ex•tend•ed |ĭk **stĕn′**dĭd| *adj.* **1.** Stretched or spread out: *extended arms.* **2.** Continued for a long period of time; prolonged: *extended peace talks.* **3.** Extensive in scope, meaning, etc.; widespread: *extended television coverage.* —**ex•tend′ed•ly** *adv.*

ex•ten•sion |ĭk **stĕn′**shən| *n.* **1.** The act of extending or the condition of being extended: *the extension of the income tax surcharge until the end of the year. He advocated the extension of the powers of the Federal Government to curb unfair business practices.* **2. a.** A part that extends from a main part; a prolongation: *The Atlas Mountains are considered an extension of the European Alps.* **b.** A structure that is built onto a main structure; an addition: *start work on the new extension to our house.* **3.** Something that develops, grows, or follows from something else: *a logical extension of his ideas. Music began among primitive people as an extension of speech.* **4.** An additional period of time granted, as for meeting an obligation: *an extension on a loan.* **5.** The act of straightening or extending a part of the body. **6. a.** Any one of a set of telephones that can be reached by dialing the same telephone number. **b.** Any one of a network of telephones to which calls can be directed through a switchboard and that can call each other. —***modifier:*** *an extension cord.*

ex•ten•sive |ĭk **stĕn′**sĭv| *adj.* **1.** Large in area, amount, etc.; vast: *He owns extensive tracts of land near the ocean.* **2.** Broad in scope; far-reaching; comprehensive: *make extensive changes in the school curriculum.* —**ex•ten′sive•ly** *adv.* —**ex•ten′sive•ness** *n.*

ex•ten•sor |ĭk **stĕn′**sər| *n.* Any muscle that causes a joint to straighten and so extends a body part.

ex•tent |ĭk **stĕnt′**| *n.* **1. a.** The area or distance over which something extends; size: *a land of vast extent.* **b.** A particular area; expanse: *The farm included an extent of pine forest.* **2.** The scope or range of something: *The extent of scientific knowledge has increased vastly since Benjamin Franklin's time.* **3.** The point or degree to which something extends: *To a certain extent, he led a happy life.*

ex•ten•u•ate |ĭk **stĕn′**yo͞o āt′| *v.* **ex•ten•u•at•ed, ex•ten•u•at•ing.** To make (an offense, error, etc.) seem less serious by providing partial excuses or justifications. —**ex•ten′u•a′tion** *n.* —**ex•ten′u•a′tor** *n.* —**ex•ten′u•a•to′ry** |-ə tôr′ē| *or* |-tōr′ē| *adj.*

ex•ten•u•at•ing |ĭk **stĕn′**yo͞o ā′tĭng| *adj.* Serving as a partial excuse or justification for an offense, error, etc: *The judge took into consideration the extenuating circumstances.*

ex•te•ri•or |ĭk **stîr′**ē ər| *adj.* **1.** Outer; external: *an exterior wall.* **2.** Suitable for use outside: *an exterior paint.* —*n.* **1.** A part or surface that is outside: *the exterior of a house.* **2.** An outward appearance; aspect: *a friendly exterior.*

exterior angle. The angle formed between a side of a polygon and an extended adjacent side. [SEE PICTURE]

ex•ter•mi•nate |ĭk **stûr′**mə nāt′| *v.* **ex•ter•mi•nat•ed, ex•ter•mi•nat•ing.** To get rid of by destroying completely; wipe out: *exterminate a colony of termites.* —**ex•ter′mi•na′tion** *n.*

ex•ter•mi•na•tor |ĭk **stûr′**mə nā′tər| *n.* A person whose work or business is exterminating rats, cockroaches, etc.

ex•ter•nal |ĭk **stûr′**nəl| *adj.* **1.** Of, on, or for the outside or an outer part; exterior: *external repairs on a house.* **2.** Acting or coming from the outside: *A moving body will continue in its direction of motion unless subjected to an external force.* **3.** For outward show; superficial: *an external display of politeness.* **4.** Of, on, or for the outer surface of the body: *an external growth; a medicine for external use only.* —*n.* **externals.** Outward appearances: *the externals of religion. Don't judge people by mere externals.* —**ex•ter′nal•ly** *adv.*

external ear. The parts of the ear that are outside of the head; the outer ear.

ex•tinct |ĭk **stĭngkt′**| *adj.* **1.** No longer existing in living form: *extinct animals such as dinosaurs and mastodons.* **2.** Not likely to erupt; inactive: *an extinct volcano.* **3.** Not burning: *The flames were extinct at last.* [SEE NOTE]

ex•tinc•tion |ĭk **stĭngk′**shən| *n.* **1.** The act or process of extinguishing or making extinct: *the extinction of a fire; causing the extinction of all plant life in the area.* **2.** The condition of being extinguished or extinct: *Man hunted and pursued the buffalo to the brink of extinction.*

ex•tin•guish |ĭk **stĭng′**gwĭsh| *v.* **ex•tin•guished, ex•tin•guish•ing.** **1.** To put out (a fire or flame); quench: *extinguish a candle.* **2.** To put an end to; destroy: *extinguish a person's last hope.* —**ex•tin′guish•a•ble** *adj.* [SEE NOTE]

ex•tin•guish•er |ĭk **stĭng′**gwĭ shər| *n.* Any device used to put out or fight fires, especially a tube or canister from which chemicals are sprayed on the fire.

ex•tir•pate |**ĕk′**stər pāt′| *or* |ĭk **stûr′**-| *v.* **ex•tir•pat•ed, ex•tir•pat•ing.** **1.** To remove completely by rooting up or cutting out: *extirpate a tumor.* **2.** To destroy; exterminate: *extirpate an evil.* —**ex′tir•pa′tion** *n.*

ex•tol, also **ex•toll** |ĭk **stōl′**| *v.* **ex•tolled, ex•tol•ling.** To praise highly; laud: *extol someone's merits.* —**ex•tol′ler** *n.*

ex•tort |ĭk **stôrt′**| *v.* To obtain by threats or other coercive means; exact; wring: *extort a confession from a prisoner.* [SEE NOTE]

ex•tor•tion |ĭk **stôr′**shən| *n.* The act or crime of extorting money, information, etc., by threats or other coercive means. —**ex•tor′tion•ist** *n.*

ex•tor•tion•ate |ĭk stôr′shə nĭt| *adj.* **1.** Too high; exorbitant: *extortionate prices.* **2.** Of, marked by, or like extortion: *the extortionate demands of the student rebels.* —**ex•tor′tion•ate•ly** *adv.*

ex•tra |ĕk′strə| *adj.* More than what is usual, expected, etc.; additional: *earn extra money.* —*adv.* **1.** Especially; unusually: *The children were extra quiet today.* **2.** In addition: *pay extra.* —*n.* **1.** Often **extras.** Something additional, as an accessory for which an added charge is made: *Dad bought all the extras with his new car.* **2.** A special edition of a newspaper. **3.** A motion-picture actor hired to play a minor part, as in a crowd scene. [SEE NOTE]

extra–. A prefix meaning "outside or beyond a boundary": **extraordinary.** [SEE NOTE]

ex•tract |ĭk străkt′| *v.* **1.** To draw out or forth forcibly; pull out: *extract a tooth.* **2.** To obtain despite resistance, as by a threat: *extract a confession.* **3.** To obtain by a chemical or physical process: *extract a metal from an ore.* **4.** To find or calculate (a root of a number). —*n.* |ĕk′străkt′|. **1.** A concentrated substance prepared from a natural substance, such as a food or flavoring; essence: *vanilla extract.* **2.** A passage from a literary work; an excerpt.

ex•trac•tion |ĭk străk′shən| *n.* **1.** The act or process of extracting: *the extraction of square roots.* **2.** Something extracted; an extract. **3.** Descent; origin: *of Italian extraction.*

ex•trac•tive |ĭk străk′tĭv| *adj.* Of, involving, or resulting from extraction: *an extractive product. Mining is an extractive industry.*

ex•trac•tor |ĭk străk′tər| *n.* Someone or something that extracts, especially a tool or mechanical device.

ex•tra•cur•ric•u•lar |ĕk′strə kə rĭk′yə lər| *adj.* Not part of the regular course of study: *Debating is an extracurricular activity in our school.*

ex•tra•dite |ĕk′strə dīt′| *v.* **ex•tra•dit•ed, ex•tra•dit•ing.** To surrender or obtain the surrender of (an alleged criminal) for trial by another judicial authority. —**ex′tra•di′tion** |ĕk′strə dĭsh′ən| *n.*

ex•tra•ne•ous |ĭk strā′nē əs| *adj.* Irrelevant; not essential: *These facts are completely extraneous to the issue at hand.* —**ex•tra′ne•ous•ly** *adv.* —**ex•tra′ne•ous•ness** *n.*

ex•traor•di•nar•y |ĭk strôr′dn ĕr′ē| *or* |ĕk′strə-ôr′-| *adj.* Very unusual; exceptional; remarkable: *an extraordinary person; an extraordinary event.* —**ex•traor′di•nar′i•ly** *adv.*

ex•trap•o•late |ĭk străp′ə lāt′| *v.* **ex•trap•o•lat•ed, ex•trap•o•lat•ing. 1.** To estimate a value of (a function) that corresponds to a value of the independent variable that is either greater or smaller than any of the values for which the value of the function is known. **2.** To make an estimate or prediction of (unknown data) on the basis of available data. —**ex•trap′o•la′tion** *n.*

ex•tra•sen•so•ry |ĕk′strə sĕn′sə rē| *adj.* Outside the range of normal human senses.

extrasensory perception. Perception by means other than the normal human senses, especially by supernatural means.

ex•tra•ter•res•tri•al |ĕk′strə tə rĕs′trē əl| *adj.* From or located outside the earth or its atmosphere.

ex•trav•a•gance |ĭk străv′ə gəns| *n.* **1.** Lack of restraint, especially in the spending of money: *His extravagance led him into debt.* **2.** Something that is excessively costly: *waste money on extravagances.*

ex•trav•a•gant |ĭk străv′ə gənt| *adj.* **1.** Wasteful or lavish; unrestrained: *My sister goes on extravagant buying sprees.* **2.** Going beyond reasonable bounds; excessive: *He makes extravagant demands on his friends.* —**ex•trav′a•gant•ly** *adv.*

ex•trav•a•gan•za |ĭk străv′ə găn′zə| *n.* A lavish stage or screen production; a spectacular.

ex•treme |ĭk strēm′| *adj.* **1.** Very great or intense; utmost: *exercise extreme caution; suffer from the extreme cold.* **2.** Farthest; outermost: *the extreme end of the room; the extreme edge of a cliff.* **3.** Drastic; severe: *extreme measures.* **4.** Far from moderate; radical: *He holds extreme opinions in politics.* **5.** Out of the ordinary; unconventional: *She wears extreme dresses.* —*n.* **1.** Either of two ends of a scale, range, etc.: *swing from one extreme to another; the extremes of wealth and poverty.* **2. a.** The greatest or utmost degree: *eager to the extreme.* **b.** Often **extremes.** Great excess: *He, too, expressed himself on the extremes of fashion.* **3.** A drastic expedient: *resort to extremes in an emergency.* **4. extremes.** In mathematics, the first and last terms of a proportion. —**ex•treme′ly** *adv.* —**ex•treme′ness** *n.*

***Idiom.* in the extreme.** To the greatest or utmost degree.

extremely high frequency. A radio-wave frequency between 30,000 and 300,000 megahertz.

extreme unction. In the Roman Catholic Church, the sacrament administered to a seriously ill or dying person.

ex•trem•ism |ĭk strē′mĭz′əm| *n.* In politics, extreme or radical views.

ex•trem•ist |ĭk strē′mĭst| *n.* A person with extreme views, especially in politics; a radical. —*modifier:* *an extremist position on home rule.*

ex•trem•i•ty |ĭk strĕm′ĭ tē| *n., pl.* **ex•trem•i•ties. 1.** The farthest point; end: *Patagonia is at the southern extremity of South America.* **2.** Extreme danger, distress, or need: *The victims of the fire cried for help in their extremity.* **3.** A drastic measure: *resort to extremities in a crisis.* **4. extremities.** The hands or feet.

ex•tri•cate |ĕk′strĭ kāt′| *v.* **ex•tri•cat•ed, ex•tri•cat•ing.** To set free from (an entanglement, difficulty, etc.); disengage: *extricate oneself from an embarrassing situation.* —**ex′tri•ca′tion** *n.*

ex•trin•sic |ĭk strĭn′sĭk| *adj.* **1.** Not coming from within a thing; not essential or basic: *an extrinsic personality trait.* **2.** Originating from the outside; external: *study the extrinsic forces acting on a process.* —**ex•trin′si•cal•ly** *adv.*

ex•tro•vert |ĕk′strə vûrt′| *n.* A person whose interest tends to center on the people and things around him rather than on his own inner thoughts and feelings; an outgoing person.

ex•trude |ĭk strōōd′| *v.* **ex•trud•ed, ex•trud•ing. 1.** To push or thrust out: *Expansion extruded the lava. Molten metal extruded from the crack.* **2.** To shape (metal, plastic, etc.) by forcing through a die.

ex•tru•sion |ĭk strōō′zhən| *n.* **1.** The act or process of extruding. **2.** Something that has been extruded.

extra/extra-

The adjective and adverb **extra** *mean almost the opposite of the prefix* **extra-**. *The word* **extraterrestrial** *does not mean what the phrase* extra terrestrial *would mean;* **extraterrestrial** *means "outside the earth," or "not terrestrial," while* extra terrestrial *(if such a phrase could exist) would mean "especially terrestrial." the reason is this: The prefix* **extra-** *comes from Latin* extrā, *"outside or beyond." One of the words formed with this prefix is* **extraordinary,** *meaning "outside the ordinary, exceptional, additional." The adjective* **extra** *is not directly from the prefix, but is a shortened form of* **extraordinary** *and thus means "additional."*

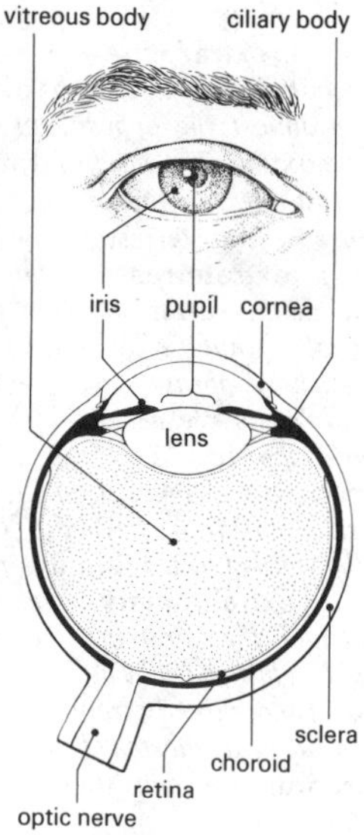

eye
The human eye seen from the front and in cross section

eyestalk
Eyestalks of a fiddler crab

ă pat/ā pay/â care/ä father/ĕ pet/ ē be/ĭ pit/ī pie/î fierce/ŏ pot/ ō go/ô paw, for/oi oil/ŏŏ book/ ōō boot/ou out/ŭ cut/û fur/ *th* the/th thin/hw which/zh vision/ ə ago, item, pencil, atom, circus

ex•u•ber•ance |ĭg zōō'bər əns| *n.* The condition or quality of being exuberant: *sing with wild exuberance.*

ex•u•ber•ant |ĭg zōō'bər ənt| *adj.* Lively and joyous; high-spirited: *The crowd was in an exuberant mood.* —**ex•u'ber•ant•ly** *adv.*

ex•ude |ĭg zōōd'| *or* |ĭk sōōd'| *v.* **ex•ud•ed, ex•ud•ing.** To give or come forth, by or as if by oozing: *exude sweat. Confidence exuded from his every pore.*

ex•ult |ĭg zŭlt'| *v.* To rejoice greatly, as in triumph; be jubilant: *The entire student body exulted over the team's victory.*

ex•ult•ant |ĭg zŭl'tnt| *adj.* Feeling great joy; jubilant: *an exultant victor.* —**ex•ult'ant•ly** *adv.*

ex•ul•ta•tion |ĕg'zŭl tā'shən| *or* |ĕk'sŭl-| *n.* Great joy; jubilation: *shout with sheer exultation.*

eye |ī| *n.* **1. a.** An organ by means of which an animal is able to see or sense light. **b.** Either of the pair of organs by which vertebrates see, consisting of a hollow structure that contains a photosensitive retina on which a lens focuses incoming light. **c.** The outer, visible part of this organ together with the structures around it, as the eyelids, eyelashes, and eyebrows. **2.** Sight; vision: *A marksman must have a sharp eye.* **3.** A look; gaze: *cast a disdainful eye at the inept fellow.* **4.** The ability to estimate, judge, etc.: *The coach had an eye for new talent.* **5.** A way of regarding something; point of view: *saw the world with a cynical eye.* **6.** A marking that resembles or seems like an eye, as a bud on a potato or a spot on a peacock's tail feather. **7.** The hole in a needle through which the thread goes. **8.** The loop to which a hook is linked for fastening. **9.** The relatively calm area at the center of a hurricane or similar storm. —*v.* **eyed, eye•ing.** To look at; regard: *eyed him suspiciously.* ¶*These sound alike* **eye, aye, I.** [SEE PICTURE]

Idioms. **catch (someone's) eye.** To attract someone's attention. **in the eyes of.** In the opinion or judgment of. **keep an eye on.** To watch carefully; look after. **make eyes at.** *Informal.* To gaze at flirtatiously. **see eye to eye.** To be in complete agreement. **set eyes on.** To see. **with an eye to.** With the aim or intent of.

eye•ball |ī'bôl'| *n.* **1.** The ball-shaped part of the eye, enclosed by the socket and eyelids and connected at the rear to the optic nerve. **2.** The eye itself.

eye•brow |ī'brou'| *n.* **1.** The bony ridge of the skull that extends over the eye. **2.** The arch of short hairs covering this ridge.

eyebrow pencil. A cosmetic in pencil form used for darkening the eyebrows.

eye•cup |ī'kŭp'| *n.* A small cup with a rim shaped to fit over the eye, used for washing the eye or applying liquid medicine to it.

eye•drop•per |ī'drŏp'ər| *n.* A dropper for applying liquid medicine to the eye.

eye•ful |ī'fŏŏl'| *n.* **1.** An amount of something that covers the eye: *an eyeful of sand.* **2.** A satisfying or revealing look; a good look: *He got a real eyeful during his tour of the school.* **3.** *Informal.* A pleasing sight: *What an eyeful that gal is!*

eye•glass |ī'glăs'| *or* |ī'gläs'| *n.* **1. a. eyeglasses.** A pair of lenses worn in front of the eyes to improve faulty vision; glasses; spectacles. **b.** A lens, such as a monocle, worn or held in front of an eye to improve vision. **2.** An eyepiece, as of a microscope or telescope.

eye•lash |ī'lăsh'| *n.* **1.** A row of hairs that forms a fringe on the edge of an eyelid. **2.** Any one of the hairs in this row.

eye•let |ī'lĭt| *n.* **1. a.** A small hole for a lace, cord, or hook to fit through: *Shoelaces are threaded through eyelets in a shoe.* **b.** A metal ring used as a rim to strengthen such a hole. **2.** A small hole in embroidery with fancy stitches around the edge. ¶*These sound alike* **eyelet, islet.**

eye•lid |ī'lĭd'| *n.* Either one of a pair of folds of skin and muscle that can be brought together to cover an eye.

eye liner. A cosmetic used to draw a line along the rim of the eyelid.

eye opener. Something that gives a person startling new insights; a revelation.

eye•piece |ī'pēs'| *n.* The lens or group of lenses closest to the eye in a telescope, microscope, or similar optical instrument.

eye shadow. A cosmetic used to color the eyelids.

eye•shot |ī'shŏt'| *n.* The distance that the eye can see; range of vision: *The mountains gradually came within eyeshot.*

eye•sight |ī'sīt'| *n.* **1.** The ability to see; vision. **2.** The range of vision; view: *a hill within eyesight of the road.*

eye•sore |ī'sôr'| *or* |ī'sōr'| *n.* An ugly or unpleasant sight: *That junkyard is the biggest eyesore in town.*

eye•spot |ī'spŏt'| *n.* **1.** In certain one-celled organisms, a colored area that is sensitive to light and functions somewhat like an eye. **2.** A rounded, eyelike marking, as on a butterfly's wing or a peacock's tail feather.

eye•stalk |ī'stôk'| *n.* A movable stalklike part having at its tip one of the eyes of a crab, lobster, etc. [SEE PICTURE]

eye•strain |ī'strān'| *n.* Fatigue of one or more of the muscles of the eye, resulting from weakness or errors of refraction.

eye•tooth |ī'tōōth'| *n., pl.* **-teeth** |-tēth'|. Either of the canine teeth of the upper jaw.

eye•wash |ī'wŏsh'| *or* |ī'wôsh'| *n.* A medicated solution used for washing the eyes.

eye•wit•ness |ī'wĭt'nĭs| *or* |ī'wĭt'-| *n.* A person who has personally seen someone or something, such as an accident or a crime, and can bear witness to the fact. —***modifier:*** *an eyewitness account of the crime.*

ey•rie or **ey•ry** |âr'ē| *or* |îr'ē| *n., pl.* **ey•ries. 1.** The nest of an eagle or other predatory bird, built on a crag or other high place. **2.** A house or stronghold built on a height. ¶*These sound alike* **eyrie, airy.**

E•ze•ki•el |ĭ zē'kē əl|. A Hebrew prophet of the sixth century B.C.

Ez•ra |ĕz'rə|. A Hebrew high priest of the fifth century B.C.

Ff

f, F |ĕf| *n., pl.* **f's** or **F's.** **1.** The sixth letter of the English alphabet. **2. F** In music, the fourth tone in the scale of C major. **3. F** A failing grade, as in school. [SEE NOTE]

F **1.** Fahrenheit. **2.** The symbol for the element fluorine.

fa |fä| *n.* A syllable used in music to represent the fourth tone of a major scale or sometimes the tone F.

fa•ble |fā'bəl| *n.* A brief tale or story, often with animal characters that speak and act like human beings, that teaches a useful lesson about human nature.

fa•bled |fā'bəld| *adj.* **1.** Described in stories but perhaps only legendary: *in search of the fabled city of El Dorado, which was supposed to be made of solid gold.* **2.** Famous in legend, history, etc.: *The most exciting place in Turkey is the fabled city of Istanbul.*

fab•ric |făb'rĭk| *n.* **1.** Cloth or other material produced by joining fibers together, often in a special way: *Lace, felt, and jersey are different types of fabric.* **2.** Material resembling cloth, as plastic in sheet form: *vinyl upholstery fabric.*

fab•ri•cate |făb'rĭ kāt'| *v.* **fab•ri•cat•ed, fab•ri•cat•ing.** **1. a.** To manufacture; fashion or make: *fabricate metal into pins.* **b.** To construct; build. **2.** To make up; invent: *fabricate a tale.* **—fab'ri•ca'tion** *n.*

fab•u•list |făb'yə lĭst| *n.* A composer of fables.

fab•u•lous |făb'yə ləs| *adj.* **1.** Belonging to legend; mythical: *the fabulous Phoenix.* **2.** Famous in old stories; fabled: *the fabulous lands of Asia.* **3.** *Informal.* Extremely exciting or excellent; of amazing quantity or quality; wonderful: *a fabulous harvest. Come to fabulous New York City.* **—fab'u•lous•ly** *adv.* [SEE NOTE]

fa•çade, also **fa•cade** |fə säd'| *n.* **1.** The main face or front of a building. **2.** The front part of anything, especially an artificial or false front.

face |fās| *n.* **1.** The surface of the front of the head from the top of the forehead to the bottom of the chin and from ear to ear. **2. a.** The expression of the features of this part of the head: *a sad face.* **b.** An exaggerated expression: *Don't make faces.* **3.** The surface presented to view; the front: *the face of a building; the sheer face of a mountain.* **4.** The upper or marked side of something, such as a clock or playing card. **5.** A plane surface that bounds a solid geometric figure. **6.** The outward appearance of something; aspect; look: *The face of the city has changed.* **7.** Value or standing in the eyes of others; dignity; prestige: *They hushed up the affair to save face.* **8.** In printing, typeface. *—modifier: face powder; a face towel; a face mask.* *—v.* **faced, fac•ing.** **1.** To have or turn the face to or in a certain direction: *Turn around and face the class. Turn and face left.* **2.** To have the front directly opposite to; look out on; front on: *The cathedral faces the square.* **3.** To confront or deal with boldly or bravely: *He has faced danger many times. We must face the situation calmly.* **4.** To meet in competition: *The White Sox face the Orioles today.* **5.** To be or have in store: *Many problems face space travelers. We are facing a serious food crisis.* **6.** To recognize; realize: *You've got to face the facts.* **7. a.** To furnish with a surface or cover of a different material: *face the walls of a building with white marble.* **b.** To provide the edge or edges of (a cloth garment) with finishing and trimming: *face a cloth collar with leather.* *—phrasal verb.* **face up to.** To confront bravely: *You must face up to the crisis.*

Idioms. **face to face.** **1.** In each other's presence. **2.** Directly confronting: *face to face with danger.* **on the face of it.** From all appearances; apparently. **to (one's) face.** In one's presence.

face•less |fās'lĭs| *adj.* **1.** Having no face. **2.** Unidentified or unidentifiable; anonymous: *faceless lawmakers of the country.*

face lifting. **1.** Plastic surgery to tighten sagging facial muscles and improve the appearance of facial skin. **2.** An extensive alteration or renovation of an outward appearance, especially of the exterior of a building.

fac•et |făs'ĭt| *n.* **1.** One of the flat, polished surfaces cut on a gem to catch the light. **2.** A separate side or aspect of anything: *the many facets of a problem.* **3.** A small, smooth, flat or rounded surface on a bone or tooth.

fa•ce•tious |fə sē'shəs| *adj.* Meant to be funny; humorous: *a facetious remark.* **—fa•ce'tious•ly** *adv.* **—fa•ce'tious•ness** *n.*

face value. The value printed or written on a bill, bond, coin, postage stamp, etc.

Idiom. **take** (or **accept**) **at face value.** To accept as genuine without checking further.

fa•cial |fā'shəl| *adj.* Of the face. *—n.* A treatment for the face, usually consisting of a massage and the application of cosmetic creams.

fac•ile |făs'əl| *adj.* **1.** Done with little effort or difficulty; easy: *a facile task.* **2.** Working, acting, or speaking effortlessly; fluent: *a facile speaker.* **3.** Arrived at without due care or effort; superficial: *a facile solution.*

fa•cil•i•tate |fə sĭl'ĭ tāt'| *v.* **fa•cil•i•tat•ed, fa•cil•i•tat•ing.** To make easier; aid; assist: *New equipment would greatly facilitate the task of the workers.* **—fa•cil'i•ta'tion** *n.*

(1) (2) (3)

The letter **F** *comes originally from the Phoenician letter* wāw *(1), which stood for a kind of /w/ sound. This was borrowed by the Greeks as* digamma *(2), a letter that later disappeared from Greek.* Digamma *was borrowed from the Greeks by the Romans (3), and was used to stand for /f/; its shape remains basically unchanged in our modern alphabet.*

fabulous

In informal or slang speech, sense 3 of **fabulous** *is often extended to apply to almost anything:* Have a fabulous time. It's fabulous of you. *It is often pointed out that this kind of loose exaggeration leads to the devaluation of words;* **fabulous** *may have lost some of its earlier exotic impact in this way. But rhetorical overstatement is an old and perhaps universal tendency.* **Fabulous** *itself comes from Latin* fābulōsus, *"fabled, mythical" (from* fābula, *"fable"); and already in Late Latin* fābulōsus *was being used to mean "incredible," as in "a fabulous number of people."*

facsimile/factotum
Both of these words are from Latin phrases beginning with the word fac, *which is the imperative of* facere, *"to make or do."* Fac simile *means "make it the same!";* fac tōtum *means "do everything!"*

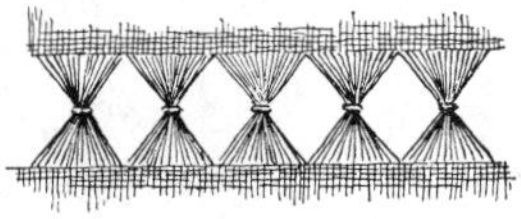

fagoting

Fahrenheit
The **Fahrenheit** *temperature scale was developed by Gabriel Daniel* Fahrenheit *(1686–1736), German physicist.*

ă pat/ā pay/â care/ä father/ĕ pet/ē be/ĭ pit/ī pie/î fierce/ŏ pot/ō go/ô paw, for/oi oil/ŏŏ book/ōō boot/ou out/ŭ cut/û fur/*th* the/th thin/hw which/zh vision/ə ago, item, pencil, atom, circus

fa•cil•i•ty |fə sĭl'ĭ tē| *n., pl.* **fa•cil•i•ties. 1.** Ease in moving, acting, or doing, resulting from skill or aptitude: *He reads music with great facility.* **2.** Often **facilities.** Something built to provide a service or convenience: *storage facilities.*

fac•ing |fā'sĭng| *n.* **1.** A lining or trimming that covers a cloth edge, especially an inner edge that shows because it is turned back: *suede facings on cuffs and lapels.* **2.** An outer layer of different material applied to a surface as a decoration or protection: *a stone wall with wood facing.*

fac•sim•i•le |făk sĭm'ə lē| *n.* An exact copy or reproduction, as of a document, book, painting, etc. [SEE NOTE]

fact |făkt| *n.* **1.** Something known with certainty: *stick to the facts.* **2.** Something asserted as certain: *Be sure to check the facts.* **3.** Something having real, demonstrable existence: *You must learn to distinguish between fact and fiction.*
Idiom. **as a matter of fact.** In truth; actually. **in fact.** In reality; in truth.

fac•tion |făk'shən| *n.* **1.** A group of persons forming a united, usually discontented and troublesome, minority within a larger group. **2.** Internal discord; conflict within an organization or nation. —**fac'tion•al** *adj.*

fac•tious |făk'shəs| *adj.* Tending to cause conflict or discord; divisive: *factious quarrels.* —**fac'tious•ly** *adv.* —**fac'tious•ness** *n.*

fac•tor |făk'tər| *n.* **1.** Something that helps bring about a certain result; ingredient: *Many factors contributed to his success.* **2.** One of two or more numbers or expressions that have a given product; for example, 2 and 3 are factors of 6, and $a + b$ and $a - b$ are factors of $a^2 - b^2$. —*v.* To find the factors of (a number or expression).

fac•tor•a•ble |făk'tər ə bəl| *adj.* In mathematics, capable of being written as a product of two or more prime factors.

fac•to•ri•al |făk tôr'ē əl| *or* |-tōr'-| *n.* The product of all of the positive integers from 1 to a given positive integer. For example, the factorial of 4, usually written 4!, is equal to $1 \times 2 \times 3 \times 4 = 24$. By a necessary and useful mathematical convention, $0! = 1$. —*adj.* Of a factorial.

fac•tor•i•za•tion |făk'tər ĭ zā'shən| *n.* **1.** The act or process of factoring. **2.** A mathematical expression written in the form of a product and equivalent to another mathematical expression. For example, $5 \times 3 \times 2$ is a factorization of 30, and $(a + b)(a - b)$ is a factorization of $a^2 - b^2$.

fac•to•ry |făk'tə rē| *n., pl.* **fac•to•ries.** A building or group of buildings in which goods are manufactured; a plant. —***modifier:*** *factory workers.*

fac•to•tum |făk tō'təm| *n.* An assistant with a wide range of duties. [SEE NOTE]

fac•tu•al |făk'chōō əl| *adj.* Based on or containing facts: *factual information; a factual account of what happened.* —**fac'tu•al•ly** *adv.*

fac•ul•ty |făk'əl tē| *n., pl.* **fac•ul•ties. 1.** One of the powers of the mind: *the faculty of speech. He is still in full possession of his faculties.* **2.** A special ability or aptitude; skill: *He has a faculty for languages.* **3. a.** The teaching staff of a school, college, or university. **b.** One of the divisions or departments of learning at a college or university: *the faculty of law.* —***modifier:*** *a faculty member; a faculty tea.*

fad |făd| *n.* A fashion, as in dress, behavior, or speech, that enjoys brief popularity.

fade |fād| *v.* **fad•ed, fad•ing. 1.** To cause to lose or to lose brightness; dim: *Sunlight faded the colors. The material faded in the wash.* **2.** To lose freshness; wither: *The flowers are beginning to fade.* **3.** To become faint or inaudible; die out: *The sound of his footsteps gradually faded away.* **4.** To disappear slowly; vanish: *The riders faded into the distance. Hope faded for the trapped coal miners.* —**fad'ed** *adj.: a faded shirt.* —***phrasal verbs.*** **fade in. 1.** To make (an image or sound) appear gradually, as in television, films, or radio broadcasting. **2.** To become visible or audible gradually. **fade out. 1.** To make (an image or sound) disappear gradually, as in television, films, or radio broadcasting. **2.** To become invisible or inaudible gradually. —*n.* A fade-in or fade-out, as in television, films, or radio broadcasting.

fade-in |fād'ĭn'| *n.* **1.** The act or process of fading in an image or sound. **2.** The result achieved by this.

fade-out |fād'out'| *n.* **1.** The act or process of fading out an image or sound. **2.** The result achieved by this.

fa•er•ie, also **fa•er•y** |fā'ə rē| *or* |fâr'ē| *n., pl.* **fa•er•ies.** *Archaic.* A fairy.

fag |făg| *v.* **fagged, fag•ging.** To exhaust from long work; fatigue: *Three hours on the tennis court fagged him out.*

fag end. 1. The frayed, worn, or untwisted end of a piece of cloth or rope. **2.** The last and least useful part of anything: *the fag end of an exhausting day.*

fag•ot, also **fag•got** |făg'ət| *n.* A bundle of twigs, sticks, or branches bound together, especially for firewood.

fag•ot•ing, also **fag•got•ing** |făg'ə tĭng| *n.* Fancy stitching in which threads are tied in hourglass-shaped bunches or crisscrossed between two edges, leaving open spaces in the fabric. [SEE PICTURE]

Fahr•en•heit |făr'ən hīt'| *adj.* Of or concerning a temperature scale that indicates the freezing point of water as 32° and the boiling point of water as 212° under normal atmospheric pressure. [SEE NOTE]

fail |fāl| *v.* **1.** To be unsuccessful in attempting to do something: *He succeeded where all others had failed. The League of Nations failed to establish world peace.* **2.** To neglect or not do (something): *The defendant failed to appear. I fail to see the difference.* **3.** To stop functioning correctly; break down: *The brakes on the car failed.* **4.** To disappoint or prove undependable to: *I won't fail you this time.* **5.** To abandon; forsake: *His courage failed him.* **6.** To decline in strength or effectiveness; wane; fade: *His health is failing. His strength began to fail.* **7. a.** To receive less than a passing academic grade in: *Many students failed the course. Under the new system, a student either passes or fails.* **b.** To give less than a passing academic grade to: *The teacher failed nearly half the class.* **8.** To become bankrupt: *A number of downtown stores have failed.* —**fail'ing** *adj.: a failing grade; an old lady in failing health.* —*n.* —**without fail.** Definitely; positively: *The job will be finished tomorrow without fail.*

fail•ing |fā′lĭng| *n.* A minor fault or weakness; shortcoming: *know one's own failings.* —*prep.* In the absence of; without: *Failing instructions, we shall proceed on our own.*

faille |fīl| *or* |fāl| *n.* A slightly ribbed, woven fabric of silk, cotton, or rayon, used for clothing. —***modifier:*** *a faille dress.* ¶*These sound alike* **faille, file.**

fail-safe |fāl′sāf′| *adj.* **1.** Capable of compensating automatically for a failure, as a mechanical device. **2.** Acting to stop a military attack on the occurrence of a variety of conditions established beforehand. [SEE NOTE]

fail•ure |fāl′yər| *n.* **1.** The condition or an example of failing; lack of success: *a crop failure. The experiment ended in failure.* **2.** An example of failing to do something, either through neglect or inability: *Failure to comply with the regulations may result in a penalty or fine.* **3.** An example of a suspension of proper functioning or performance: *heart failure; an electric power failure.* **4.** The act or an example of becoming bankrupt: *several bank failures.* **5.** A person who has failed: *I'm a failure as a writer.*

fain |fān|. *Archaic. adv.* Willingly; gladly: *I would fain risk my life for thee.* —*adj.* Willing; glad: *We are fain to leave.* ¶*These sound alike* **fain, feign.**

faint |fānt| *adj.* **faint•er, faint•est. 1.** Not clearly seen, sensed, or heard; indistinct: *a faint light; a faint odor; a faint sound.* **2.** Not great; slight: *a faint hope; a faint chance; a faint resemblance.* **3.** About to fall unconscious; dizzy and weak: *Hunger made him feel faint.* —*n.* A sudden, usually short loss of consciousness, often caused by a deficient flow of blood to the brain. —*v.* To lose consciousness for a short time; swoon. ¶*These sound alike* **faint, feint.** —**faint′ly** *adv.* —**faint′ness** *n.*

faint-heart•ed |fānt′här′tĭd| *adj.* Lacking courage; cowardly; timid. —**faint′-heart′ed•ly** *adv.* —**faint′-heart′ed•ness** *n.*

fair[1] |fâr| *adj.* **fair•er, fair•est. 1.** Pleasing to look at; beautiful; lovely: *a fair maiden.* **2.** Light in color: *fair hair; fair skin.* **3.** Clear and sunny; free of clouds or storms: *fair weather.* **4.** With consideration for everyone concerned; just: *fair play; a fair price; a fair trial.* **5.** Neither good nor bad; average: *a fair chance of winning. The movie was only fair.* **6.** In baseball, lying or falling within the foul lines: *fair territory; a fair ball.* —*adv.* In a fair manner; properly: *I believe in playing fair.* —*v.* To make (a curve or curved surface) smooth and continuous: *fair the lines of a boat.* ¶*These sound alike* **fair, fare.** —**fair′ness** *n.* [SEE NOTE]

Idioms. **bid fair.** To show promise. **fair and square.** Just and honest. **fair to middling.** Fairly good; so-so.

fair[2] |fâr| *n.* **1.** A gathering for the buying and selling of goods; a market. **2.** A display of farm and home products of a region: *a state fair.* **3.** A large exhibition or display of the products and culture of nations: *a world's fair.* ¶*These sound alike* **fair, fare.** [SEE NOTE]

fair•ground |fâr′ground′| *n.* Often **fair•grounds.** An open space of land where fairs, exhibitions, or other public events are held.

fair-haired |fâr′hârd′| *adj.* **1.** Having blond hair. **2.** Favorite: *the fair-haired boy of the neighborhood.*

fair•ly |fâr′lē| *adv.* **1.** In a fair or just manner: *treating everyone fairly.* **2.** Moderately; rather: *I am feeling fairly well today.* **3.** Actually: *The walls fairly shook with his screaming.*

fair-mind•ed |fâr′mīn′dĭd| *adj.* Just and impartial; unprejudiced. —**fair′-mind′ed•ness** *n.*

fair sex. Women in general.

fair•way |fâr′wā′| *n.* On a golf course, the mowed area of grass extending toward a putting green.

fair•y |fâr′ē| *n., pl.* **fair•ies.** A supernatural being in human form, who is supposed to have magical powers. —***modifier:*** *a fairy story.*

fair•y•land |fâr′ē lănd′| *n.* **1.** The place where fairies are supposed to live. **2.** An enchanting place; a wonderland.

fairy ring. A circle of mushrooms in a grassy area, superstitiously believed to be caused by dancing fairies. [SEE PICTURE]

fairy tale. A story about fairies, magical creatures, or unreal things.

fait ac•com•pli |fĕ tä kôN plē′| *pl.* **faits ac•com•plis** |fĕ tä kôN plē′|. *French.* An accomplished fact; something already done that cannot be undone.

faith |fāth| *n.* **1.** Confidence or trust in a person, idea, or thing: *You must have faith in yourself.* **2.** Belief in God: *a man of great faith.* **3.** A religion: *the Christian faith; people of every faith.* **4.** A promise or pledge of loyalty: *break faith with one's supporters.*

Idioms. **bad faith.** Deceit; insincerity. **good faith.** Sincerity; honesty: *a token of one's good faith.* **on faith.** With trust; confidently: *You'll have to accept my promise on faith.*

faith•ful |fāth′fəl| *adj.* **1.** Loyal and dutiful: *a faithful friend; faithful service.* **2.** Accurate; exact: *a faithful reproduction.* —*n.* —**the faithful. 1.** The practicing members of a religion. **2.** The loyal followers of a cause, group, etc. —**faith′ful•ly** *adv.* —**faith′ful•ness** *n.*

faith•less |fāth′lĭs| *adj.* **1.** Breaking faith; disloyal. **2.** Lacking religious faith. —**faith′less•ly** *adv.* —**faith′less•ness** *n.*

fake |fāk| *v.* **faked, fak•ing. 1.** To simulate or put on an act; pretend; feign: *fake illness. I'm not baking; you can guess in a minute I really am faking.* **2.** To make in order to deceive; counterfeit or forge: *fake a ten-dollar bill.* **3.** In sports, to make a deceptive maneuver: *The halfback faked to his left and ran to the right.* —*n.* **1.** A person who tries to deceive by pretending to be what he is not or by claiming falsely that he has something; a faker. **2.** Something, such as a story, work of art, etc., that looks authentic but is not; a forgery: *The experts discovered a great number of fakes in his art collection.* —*adj.* False; counterfeit: *a fake document; a fake piece of sculpture.* —**fak′er** *n.*

fak•er•y |fā′kə rē| *n., pl.* **fak•er•ies. 1.** The act or process of faking: *He was involved in the fakery of many paintings.* **2.** Something faked: *firmly convinced that the sculpture was fakery.*

fa•kir |fə kîr′| *or* |fā′kər| *n.* A Moslem or Hindu religious beggar, especially one who is regarded as a holy man or who performs feats of endurance or magic. [SEE NOTE]

fail-safe

It is often assumed that a **fail-safe** *system turns itself off if anything goes wrong with its controls. While this might be true of a furnace, for example, which is better turned off than running without thermostatic control, it is not true of all systems. An automatic lighting system might well be designed to turn itself on if anything went wrong with its controls.*

fair[1-2]

Fair[1] *was* fæger *in Old English; its basic meaning, then as now, was "beautiful, pleasing."* **Fair**[2] *is from Old French* feire, *which is from Latin* fēriae, *"holidays."*

fairy ring

fakir

The second pronunciation of **fakir** *seems to be widely used, but it is rather undesirable since it is homophonous with* **faker** *and thus tends to suggest that a fakir is necessarily a charlatan. The word* **fakir** *comes from Arabic* faqīr, *"poor man."*

falcon

ă pat/ā pay/â care/ä father/ĕ pet/ ē be/ĭ pit/ī pie/î fierce/ŏ pot/ ō go/ô paw, for/oi oil/ŏŏ book/ ōō boot/ou out/ŭ cut/û fur/ *th* the/th thin/hw which/zh vision/ ə ago, item, pencil, atom, circus

fal•con |făl′kən| *or* |fôl′-| *or* |fô′kən| *n.* Any of several long-winged, swift-flying hawks, especially one of a kind trained to hunt for and catch small animals and birds. [SEE PICTURE]

fal•con•er |făl′kə nər| *or* |fôl′-| *or* |fô′kə-| *n.* A person who raises, trains, or hunts with falcons.

fal•con•ry |făl′kən rē| *or* |fôl′-| *or* |fô′kən-| *n.* **1.** The sport of hunting with falcons. **2.** The art of training falcons for hunting.

fal•de•ral or **fal•de•rol** |făl′də răl′| *n.* Variants of **folderol.**

fall |fôl| *v.* **fell** |fĕl|, **fall•en** |fô′lən|, **fall•ing.** **1. a.** To descend or move toward the center of the earth or another body by gravitational attraction, especially with no restraining force present: *The bombs fell, and the flames sparkled. The snow fell silently to the ground.* **b.** To flow downward, usually rapidly and often with violent motion: *The streams fall down the sides of the mountains in the spring.* **2. a.** To come to the ground suddenly and involuntarily: *She slipped on the ice and fell.* **b.** To make a similar motion voluntarily: *She sighed and fell back against the pillow. He fell to his knees and begged for mercy.* **3.** To be wounded or killed: *Many soldiers fall in battle.* **4.** To come as if by descending suddenly: *Darkness fell upon the scene. A hush fell over the crowd.* **5.** To diminish, as in value, intensity, etc.: *Prices fell on the stock exchange. The temperature fell below freezing. Did your voice rise or fall at the end of the question? The tidewater in the river rises and falls periodically.* **6.** To decline, as in moral standing; err or sin: *Lucifer, son of the morning, how thou hast fallen!* **7.** To collapse, especially into fragments: *The shock of the earthquake caused many houses to fall to pieces. The toy fell apart after one week of use.* **8.** To suffer defeat, destruction, capture, etc.: *Paris fell in 1940. The Russian monarchy fell in 1917.* **9. a.** To become separated: *The first stage of the rocket falls off before the second boost.* **b.** To cease to be an integral part of: *Most mammals have two sets of teeth, the first of which falls out early in life.* **10.** To take or have a specified position; come to rest at a specified place: *His eyes fell on the tree. The major stress falls on the first vowel in the word "travel."* **11.** To come to pass; happen: *Disasters fell upon the tiny village.* **12.** To have as a date; occur: *Thanksgiving always falls on a Thursday.* **13.** To pass from one state or condition into another: *fall asleep. The deer fell victim to the wolves.* **14.** To come as a task, right, assignment, duty, etc.: *The testing of the new flying machine fell to Orville Wright. The estate fell to the eldest surviving son.* **15.** To come by chance: *fall into a trap. The papers fell into the enemy's hands. He fell into bad company.* **16.** To come under the influence or control of another: *The knight fell under the spell of the witch. The country fell under foreign domination.* **17. a.** To come within the limits, scope, or jurisdiction of another; be in a certain category or class: *The children fell under my own observation. Most languages fall into groups, or families.* **b.** To divide naturally: *Most cakes fall into two general categories: butter and sponge.* **18.** To be uttered, usually involuntarily: *A sigh fell from her lips.* **19.** To hang down freely: *The stallion's long mane fell smoothly on his neck.* **20.** To assume a look of disappointment, shame, hurt, etc.: *Thomas's face fell when he saw how sick the puppy looked.* —***phrasal verbs.*** **fall back.** To give ground; retreat. **fall back on.** To turn to for help; resort to. **fall behind.** To fail to keep up with: *He fell behind the group he was supposed to be marching with. He fell behind in his bills.* **fall for.** *Informal.* **1.** To become infatuated or fall in love with: *He falls for every girl he meets.* **2.** To be taken in by: *Some people fall for anything you say.* **fall in.** To take one's place in a military formation. **fall in with.** **1.** To meet by chance: *The boy fell in with another boy he liked very much.* **2.** To agree to: *He immediately fell in with my suggestions.* **fall off.** To become smaller or fewer; decline: *Class attendance fell off in the spring. Enthusiasm for the game is falling off.* **fall on** (or **upon**). To attack suddenly: *The troops fell upon the enemy at dusk.* **fall out.** **1.** To quarrel; become estranged: *She has fallen out with her next-door neighbors.* **2.** To leave one's place in a military formation. **fall through.** To fail; collapse: *Their plans for a vacation fell through.* **fall to.** To begin; start: *The villagers fell to work at daybreak.* —*n.* **1.** The motion of a body or the path that it takes under the influence of a gravitational attraction: *the fall of a spacecraft toward the moon.* **2.** A sudden drop from a relatively erect to a less erect position: *He took a bad fall.* **3.** The distance that something falls: *a fall of three stories.* **4.** Often **Fall.** Autumn. **5.** Often **falls.** A waterfall; cascade. **6.** A reduction in amount, value, etc.: *a fall in prices.* **7.** A capture, overthrow, or collapse: *the fall of the Alamo; the fall of the Roman Empire.* **8.** A woman's hair piece with long hair that hangs down loose. **9.** In wrestling, the act of pinning one's opponent to the ground. **10. the Fall.** In theology, Adam's sin of disobeying God by eating the forbidden fruit, having as a consequence the loss of grace of all his descendants. —***modifier:*** *fall fashions; a fall day.*

Idioms. **fall flat.** *Informal.* To produce no result; fail. **fall short.** To fail to reach or attain: *The campaign fell short of expectations.*

fal•la•cious |fə lā′shəs| *adj.* Containing fundamental errors in reasoning; illogical: *fallacious arguments.* —**fal•la′cious•ly** *adv.*

fal•la•cy |făl′ə sē| *n., pl.* **fal•la•cies. 1.** An idea or opinion based on mistaken assumptions or logic; a false notion. **2.** False reasoning, belief, argument, etc.

fall•en |fô′lən|. Past participle of **fall.**

fall guy. *Slang.* Someone left to take the blame or responsibility, as for a scheme that has miscarried; a scapegoat.

fal•li•ble |făl′ə bəl| *adj.* Capable of making mistakes: *Like all men, the President is a fallible human being.* —**fal′li•bil′i•ty** *n.* —**fal′li•bly** *adv.*

fall•ing-out |fô′lĭng out′| *n., pl.* **fall•ings-out** or **fall•ing-outs.** A quarrel that often leads to a broken or more distant relationship; an estrangement.

falling sickness. Epilepsy, especially in one of its severe forms.

falling star. A body, such as a meteoroid, that becomes visible as a bright streak in the sky by falling into the atmosphere and burning up from the resulting heat.

Fal•lo•pi•an tube |fə lō′pē ən|. Either of a pair of tubes found in the female reproductive system of human beings and some other vertebrates. They carry egg cells from the region near the ovaries to the uterus. [SEE NOTE]

fall•out |fôl′out′| *n.* **1.** The slow fall of tiny particles of radioactive material from the atmosphere after a nuclear explosion. **2.** The particles that fall in this way. [SEE NOTE]

fal•low |făl′ō| *adj.* Plowed and tilled but left unseeded during a growing season: *a fallow field.*

fallow deer. A European deer having broad, flattened antlers and a coat spotted with white in the summer. [SEE PICTURE]

false |fôls| *adj.* **fals•er, fals•est. 1.** Contrary to fact or truth; incorrect: *a false assumption. Is this statement true or false?* **2.** Untruthful: *a false accusation.* **3.** Insincere; deceitful: *false promises.* **4.** Unfaithful; disloyal: *a false friend.* **5.** Based on mistaken ideas or information: *The news bulletin raised false hopes for a time.* **6. a.** Not natural; artificial: *false teeth; false eyelashes.* **b.** Not real or genuine: *false tears; a false signature; live under a false name.* **7.** In music, of incorrect pitch. —**false′ly** *adv.* —**false′ness** *n.*

false-heart•ed |fôls′här′tĭd| *adj.* Disloyal; deceitful: *a false-hearted lover.*

false•hood |fôls′ho͝od′| *n.* An untrue statement; a lie.

false rib. Any of the five lower pairs of ribs that do not join directly with the breastbone.

fal•set•to |fôl sĕt′ō| *n., pl.* **fal•set•tos.** A way of singing, used especially by males to artificially produce tones in an upper register that are above the normal range and that are less strong and colorful than the full voice. —***modifier:*** *a falsetto tone.* —*adv.* In falsetto: *sing falsetto.*

fal•si•fy |fôl′sə fī′| *v.* **fal•si•fied, fal•si•fy•ing, fal•si•fies. 1.** To state or describe untruthfully; misrepresent: *falsify history; falsify the facts.* **2.** To alter (a document) in order to deceive: *falsify a passport.* —**fal′si•fi•ca′tion** *n.*

fal•si•ty |fôl′sĭ tē| *n., pl.* **fal•si•ties. 1.** The condition of being false; falseness. **2.** Something false; a lie or falsehood.

fal•ter |fôl′tər| *n.* **1.** To perform haltingly; lose strength or momentum: *The engine faltered. The economy is beginning to falter.* **2.** To speak hesitatingly; stammer. **3.** To waver in purpose or action; hesitate: *Her determination faltered.*

fame |fām| *n.* Great reputation and recognition; public esteem; renown.

famed |fāmd| *adj.* Having great fame; famous; renowned.

fa•mil•iar |fə mĭl′yər| *adj.* **1.** Known or reminding one of something: *The name is not familiar to me. His face looks familiar.* **2.** Well-known; often encountered; common: *a familiar sight; the familiar voice of the announcer.* **3.** Having a good knowledge of; well-acquainted: *I am not familiar with the details of the case.* **4.** Of established friendship; informal or intimate: *be on familiar terms with someone.* **5.** Unduly forward; bold: *He was criticized for being too familiar with his superiors.* —**fa•mil′iar•ly** *adv.*

fa•mil•i•ar•i•ty |fə mĭl′ē ăr′ĭ tē| *n., pl.* **fa•mil•i•ar•i•ties. 1.** Acquaintance with or knowledge of something: *His familiarity with the city's streets helped him get around.* **2.** Friendship or informality: *The army discourages familiarity between officers and enlisted men.* **3.** Undue liberty or forwardness.

fa•mil•iar•ize |fə mĭl′yə rīz′| *v.* **fa•mil•iar•ized, fa•mil•iar•iz•ing.** To make oneself or another familiar with something.

fam•i•ly |făm′ə lē| *or* |făm′lē| *n., pl.* **fam•i•lies. 1.** Parents and their children. **2.** A group of persons related by blood or marriage; relatives. **3.** The members of one household. **4.** Line of descent; ancestry. **5.** A group of things that are alike; class. **6.** A group of related plants or animals ranking between a genus and an order. Dogs, wolves, coyotes, and foxes belong to the same animal family. Daisies, sunflowers, and marigolds belong to the same plant family. **7.** A language group derived from the same parent language. —***modifier:*** *a family reunion.*

family name. A person's last name; surname.

family tree. A record of all the ancestors of a family and their descendants.

fam•ine |făm′ĭn| *n.* A serious shortage of food resulting in widespread hunger and starvation.

fam•ished |făm′ĭsht| *adj.* Extremely hungry; starving.

fa•mous |fā′məs| *adj.* Well-known; famed; renowned: *Many famous people were there. Switzerland is famous for its scenic beauty.*

fa•mous•ly |fā′məs lē| *adv. Informal.* Very well; excellently: *The two got along famously.*

fan¹ |făn| *n.* **1.** A light, flat implement, usually shaped like a wedge or circle and often folding up like an accordion, waved in the hand to create a cool breeze. **2.** An electrical device that stirs up air by means of rapidly rotating metal blades. —*v.* **fanned, fan•ning. 1.** To cause air to blow upon with or as if with a fan: *He sat fanning himself under a tree. The wind fanned the flames.* **2.** To activate; stir up: *fan resentment against oneself.* **3.** To spread like a fan: *The search parties fanned out in different directions.* **4.** In baseball, to strike out (a batter). [SEE NOTE]

fan² |făn| *n. Informal.* An enthusiastic devotee or admirer: *a baseball fan.* —***modifier:*** *fan mail; a fan club.* [SEE NOTE]

fa•nat•ic |fə năt′ĭk| *n.* A person whose views, as well as his attachment to them, are so extreme as to be beyond what is normal or reasonable. —*adj.* A form of the word **fanatical.**

fa•nat•i•cal |fə năt′ĭ kəl| *adj.* Extreme or unreasonable: *a fanatical religious sect; a fanatical belief in something.* —**fa•nat′i•cal•ly** *adv.*

fa•nat•i•cism |fə năt′ĭ sĭz′əm| *n.* Enthusiasm or devotion so strong as to be neither normal nor reasonable.

fan•ci•er |făn′sē ər| *n.* A person with a special interest in something: *a horse fancier.*

fan•ci•ful |făn′sĭ fəl| *adj.* **1.** Created in the mind; imaginary; unreal: *fanciful tales.* **2.** Tending to indulge in fancy: *a fanciful writer; a fanciful mind.* **3.** Quaint or original in design; imaginative: *fanciful ivory figures.* —**fan′ci•ful•ly** *adv.* —**fan′ci•ful•ness** *n.*

fan•cy |făn′sē| *n., pl.* **fan•cies. 1.** Imagination, especially of a playful or whimsical sort: *In the spring a young man's fancy turns to thoughts of love.* **2.** A capricious idea or thought; whim: *She has a sudden fancy to buy a new hat.* **3.** A liking, fondness, or inclination: *take a fancy to someone.*

Fallopian tube

The **Fallopian tubes** *were first described by Gabriello* Fallopio *(1523–1562), Italian anatomist.*

fallout

The word **fallout** *is sometimes used, especially in newspapers, in a new metaphorical sense, "incidental results," as in* the technological fallout of the space program. *It remains to be seen whether this sense will establish itself as a permanent part of the language.*

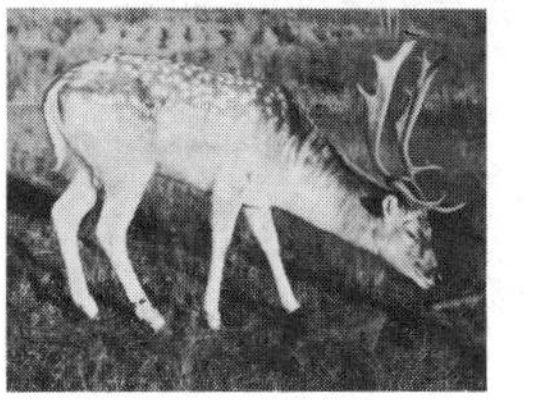

fallow deer

fan ¹·²

Fan¹ *was* fann *in Old English, and was borrowed from Latin* vannus. *It was originally the name of a device for separating chaff from grain; the device was a kind of basket in which the mixed grain and chaff were tossed in the air, while a draft was made by flaps so that the chaff was blown out and the grain stayed in. Later, the word* fann *was applied to any device for making an artificial draft.* **Fan²** *arose in the late nineteenth century in the United States; it is a shortening of* **fanatic,** *meaning "a fanatical supporter."*

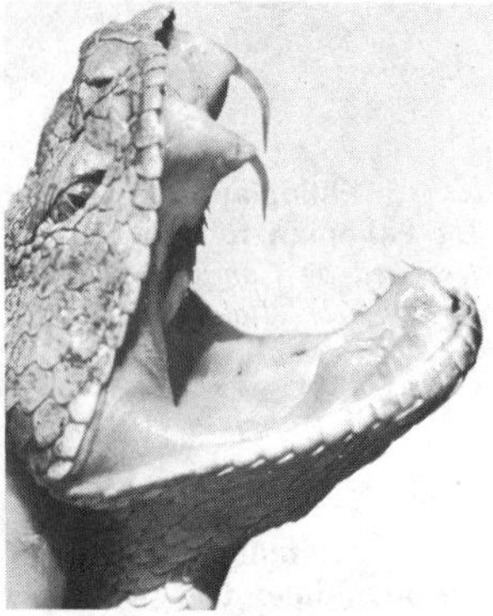

fang
Diamondback rattlesnake

fantail

far
The expression **as far as**, *meaning "to the extent that," introduces an adverbial clause:* As far as tennis is concerned, you can count me out. *In informal speech, the verb in this kind of clause is often left out:* As far as tennis, you can count me out. **As far as** *then becomes a prepositional phrase (directly governing a noun) meaning roughly "in the matter of." This is a quite logical development, but it has not yet been accepted as standard.*

ă pat/ā pay/â care/ä father/ĕ pet/ ē be/ĭ pit/ī pie/î fierce/ŏ pot/ ō go/ô paw, for/oi oil/o͝o book/ o͞o boot/ou out/ŭ cut/û fur/ *th* the/th thin/hw which/zh vision/ ə ago, item, pencil, atom, circus

He quickly caught the public's fancy. Do whatever strikes your fancy. —*adj.* **fan•ci•er, fan•ci•est. 1.** Not plain; elaborate in design: *fancy clothes; fancy woodwork.* **2.** Requiring or done with great skill; complex; intricate: *fancy diving; a boxer's fancy footwork.* **3.** Based on imagination, not fact; illusory: *fancy ideas.* **4.** Exorbitant; excessive: *That store charges very fancy prices.* —*v.* **fan•cied, fan•cy•ing, fan•cies. 1.** To picture in the mind; imagine: *Fancy that! He fancies himself as an actor.* **2.** To have a liking for; be fond of: *I don't fancy people who talk like that.* **3.** To feel like; feel inclined: *Do you fancy going to the movies?* **4.** To suppose; guess; surmise: *I fancy he'll be coming back soon.*

fan•fare |făn′fâr′| *n.* **1.** A short, rhythmic call played by one or more trumpets or similar brass instruments; a flourish. **2.** A spectacular public display, ceremony, or reaction; a stir.

fang |făng| *n.* A long, pointed tooth, such as one of the teeth with which a poisonous snake injects its venom or a meat-eating animal seizes and tears its prey. [SEE PICTURE]

fan•tail |făn′tāl′| *n.* **1.** A domesticated pigeon with a fan-shaped tail. **2.** A goldfish with a wide, fanlike double tail fin. [SEE PICTURE]

fan•tas•tic |făn tăs′tĭk| *adj.* **1.** Imagined or invented; unreal: *a fantastic story.* **2.** Weird; bizarre: *all sorts of fantastic figures and designs.* **3.** *Informal.* **a.** Remarkable; outstanding; superb: *He did a fantastic job.* **b.** Excessive or exorbitant: *fantastic prices.* —**fan•tas′ti•cal•ly** *adv.*

fan•ta•sy |făn′tə sē| *or* |-zē| *n., pl.* **fan•ta•sies. 1.** Mental invention and association; creative imagination; make-believe: *Modern technology has turned fantasy into fact.* **2.** Something that exists only in the mind or imagination; a daydream: *The idea was dismissed as sheer fantasy.* **3.** A story, play, etc., based on fantastic or unreal elements: *a romantic fantasy.*

far |făr| *adv.* **far•ther** |făr′*th*ər| or **fur•ther** |fûr′*th*ər|, **far•thest** |făr′*th*ĭst| or **fur•thest** |fûr′*th*ĭst|. **1.** To, from, or at a considerable distance: *How far did she go? She didn't go very far.* **2.** To or at a specific distance, degree, or position: *How far do you intend to take this argument?* **3.** To a considerable degree; much: *far better.* **4.** Not at all; anything but: *He's far from happy about the change.* —*adj.* **far•ther** or **fur•ther, far•thest** or **fur•thest. 1.** At considerable distance: *a far country.* **2.** More distant; opposite: *the far corner.* **3.** Extensive or long: *a far trek.* —*Note: Far* is often used with certain function words to form prepositional and adverbial groups. Some of the most frequent groups are: **as far as.** To the distance, extent, or degree that: *as far as I know.* **by far.** To a considerable degree: *His grades are better than hers by far.* **in so far** (or **insofar**) **as.** To the degree or extent that; as long as. **so far. 1.** Up to the present moment: *We haven't heard from him so far.* **2.** To a limited extent: *You can only go so far on 25 cents.* **so far as.** To the extent that: *so far as I can tell.* [SEE NOTE]

Idioms. **far and away.** Definitely; without a doubt: *He's far and away the best skier on the team.* **far and wide.** Everywhere. **far be it from me.** May I never: *Far be it from me to tell a lie.*

far•ad |făr′əd| *or* |-ăd′| *n.* A unit of capacitance equal to that of a capacitor that will accumulate a charge of 1 coulomb when a potential difference of 1 volt is applied to it.

far•a•day |făr′ə dā′| *n.* A unit of electric charge equal to the amount needed to dissolve or deposit an amount of a substance equal to its atomic or molecular weight multiplied by one gram, that is, say, 10 grams of a substance that has an atomic weight of 10. One faraday equals about 96,494 coulombs.

far•a•way |făr′ə wā′| *adj.* **1.** Very distant; remote: *faraway places.* **2.** Dreamy: *a faraway look in his eyes.*

farce |färs| *n.* **1.** A comic play with a story and characters greatly exaggerated to cause laughter. **2.** Something that is ridiculous or laughable, especially something supposed to be serious.

far•ci•cal |fär′sĭ kəl| *adj.* **1.** Of dramatic farce. **2.** Resembling farce; absurd; foolish.

fare |fâr| *n.* **1. a.** The cost of traveling by plane, train, bus, etc., from one place to another: *What is the fare to Chicago?* **b.** The money paid for such a trip or ride: *Pay your fare as you enter the bus.* **c.** A passenger who pays a fare: *The taxi stopped to pick up a fare.* **2.** Food and drink: *The fare at this lodge is very plain.* —*v.* **fared, far•ing.** To get along; progress; succeed: *How did he fare with his project?* ¶ *These sound alike* **fare, fair.**

Far East. 1. Eastern Asia, including China, Japan, and Korea. **2.** All Asian lands east of Afghanistan.

fare•well |fâr′wĕl′| *interj.* Good-by. —*n.* The act of saying good-by, usually with good wishes. —***modifier:*** *a farewell party.*

far-fetched |fär′fĕcht′| *adj.* Hard to believe; strained and improbable: *a far-fetched story; a far-fetched excuse.*

far-flung |fär′flŭng′| *adj.* Extending over a vast area: *a far-flung empire.*

fa•ri•na |fə rē′nə| *n.* A finely ground grain used as a cooked cereal or in puddings.

farm |färm| *n.* **1.** An area of land, including a house and barns, on which crops or animals are raised. **2.** Any land or water area used for raising a specified type of animal or vegetable life: *an oyster farm.* **3.** Also **farm club** or **farm team.** In baseball, a minor-league team affiliated with a major-league team for the purpose of training young or inexperienced players. —***modifier:*** *farm products.* —*v.* **1.** To engage in farming; grow crops or raise livestock. **2.** To cultivate or produce a crop on. —***phrasal verb.*** **farm out. 1.** To send (work) from a central point to be done elsewhere. **2.** In baseball, to assign (a player) to a farm team.

farm•er |fär′mər| *n.* A person who owns or operates a farm.

farm•house |färm′hous′| *n., pl.* **-hous•es** |-hou′zĭz|. The house on a farm in which the farmer lives.

farm•ing |fär′mĭng| *n.* The business of growing crops or raising livestock.

farm•stead |färm′stĕd′| *n.* A farm, including its land and buildings.

farm•yard |färm′yärd′| *n.* An area surrounded by or adjacent to farm buildings.

far-off |fär′ôf′| *or* |-ŏf′| *adj.* Faraway; distant.

far-out |fär′out′| *adj.* *Slang.* Exhibiting new and extremely unconventional ideas: *a far-out movie.*

far-reach•ing |fär′rē′chĭng| *adj.* Having a wide

influence or effect; extending far: *The decision had far-reaching consequences.*

far•row |făr′ō| *n.* A group of young pigs born at the same time of the same mother. —*v.* To give birth to young pigs.

far•see•ing |fär′sē′ĭng| *adj.* **1.** Able to see far; keen-sighted. **2.** Planning prudently for the future; foresighted.

far-sight•ed |fär′sī′tĭd| *adj.* **1.** Having a defect of vision in which parallel rays of light are brought to a focus behind the retina of the eye, making it easier to see distant objects than those that are nearby. **2.** Having or showing keen judgment of future events: *a far-sighted statesman; a far-sighted policy.* —**far′-sight′ed•ly** *adv.*

far•ther |fär′*th*ər| *adv.* **1.** To or at a greater distance: *He went farther than he had expected.* **2.** In addition. —*adj.* **1.** Remoter; more distant: *a house at the farther end of the street.* **2.** Longer or lengthier: *The trip there is farther than anyone expected.* [SEE NOTE on p. 377]

far•ther•most |fär′*th*ər mōst′| *adj.* Farthest; most remote: *the farthermost corners of the earth.*

far•thest |fär′*th*ĭst| *adj.* Most remote or distant: *the farthest regions of the Arctic.* —*adv.* To or at the greatest distance in space or time.

far•thing |fär′*th*ĭng| *n.* A former British coin worth one-fourth of a penny.

far•thin•gale |fär′*th*ĭng gāl′| *n.* **1.** A skirt with a hoop under it that makes it stand out around the waist, worn by women in the 16th and 17th centuries. **2.** A hoop worn under such a skirt.

fas•ci•nate |făs′ə nāt′| *v.* **fas•ci•nat•ed, fas•ci•nat•ing.** To capture and hold the interest and attention of; attract irresistibly. —**fas′ci•nat′ing** *adj.*: *a fascinating story.*

fas•ci•na•tion |făs′ə nā′shən| *n.* **1.** The condition of being fascinated: *Everyone watched in fascination.* **2.** The power of fascinating: *The sea has always held fascination for me.*

fas•cism |făsh′ĭz′əm| *n.* **1.** A dictatorship of the extreme right, marked by government control of the economy, strong appeals to nationalism, and suppression of all opposition. **2.** Any reactionary or totalitarian system of government.

fas•cist |făsh′ĭst| *n.* A person who advocates or practices fascism. —**modifier:** *a fascist regime.*

fash•ion |făsh′ən| *n.* **1.** A manner of performing; way: *Continue in this fashion until you have finished the job.* **2. a.** The style of dressing or way of behaving popular at a certain time: *the latest fashion; the fashions of the 1940's.* **b.** The current style: *out of fashion.* —**modifier:** *a fashion show.* —*v.* To make into a particular shape or form: *fashion figures from clay.*

Idiom. **after** (or **in**) **a fashion.** In some way or other; to some extent: *She sings after a fashion.*

fash•ion•a•ble |făsh′ə nə bəl| *adj.* **1.** Conforming to the current style; in fashion: *a fashionable society lady.* **2.** Frequented by or associated with persons who conform to the current fashion: *a fashionable hotel.* —**fash′ion•a•bly** *adv.*

fast[1] |făst| *or* |fäst| *adj.* **fast•er, fast•est.** **1.** Moving quickly; swift; rapid: *a fast runner; a fast train. Hockey is a fast game.* **2.** Done quickly: *a fast visit; a fast lunch.* **3.** Suitable for rapid movement: *the fast lane on a highway.* **4.** Ahead of time: *My watch is fast.* **5.** Firmly fixed or fastened: *Keep a fast grip on the rope.* **6.** Permanent; not liable to fade: *fast colors.* **7.** Loyal; firm: *fast friends.* **8.** Disregarding conventional or moral standards; dissipated: *a fast crowd; lead a fast life.* —*adv.* **1.** Quickly; rapidly: *You are driving too fast.* **2.** Firmly; securely: *Hold fast to the banister.* **3.** Deeply; soundly: *He is fast asleep.* [SEE NOTE]

fast[2] |făst| *or* |fäst| *v.* To go without all or certain foods, especially for religious reasons or as a form of protest. —*n.* The act or a period of fasting. —**modifier:** *a fast day.* [SEE NOTE]

fas•ten |făs′ən| *or* |fä′sən| *v.* **1. a.** To attach to something else; join; connect: *fasten a button to a skirt.* **b.** To take firm hold; cling fast: *The lid fastens onto the jar.* **2.** To make fast or secure: *Fasten your seat belts. The dress fastens in the back.* **3.** To fix or focus steadily: *His eyes fastened on the signature of the letter.*

fas•ten•er |făs′ə nər| *or* |fä′sə-| *n.* A device, such as a zipper, snap, etc., that holds separate things together. [SEE PICTURE]

fas•ten•ing |făs′ə nĭng| *or* |fä′sə-| *n.* Something, such as a lock, bolt, latch, catch, etc., used to fasten things together; a fastener.

fast-food |făst′fo͞od′| *or* |fäst′-| *adj.* Specializing in foods prepared and served quickly: *a fast-food restaurant.*

fas•tid•i•ous |fă stĭd′ē əs| *adj.* **1.** Careful in all details: *fastidious about one's appearance.* **2.** Overcritical: *a fastidious critic.* —**fas•tid′i•ous•ly** *adv.* —**fas•tid′i•ous•ness** *n.*

fast•ness |făst′nĭs| *or* |fäst′-| *n.* **1.** A remote or secure place, as a stronghold, fortress, etc.: *a mountain fastness.* **2.** The condition or quality of being fast and firm: *color fastness.*

fat |făt| *n.* **1.** Any one of a large number of oily compounds that are widely found in plant and animal tissues and that vary in form from soft solids to liquids. **2.** Tissue, especially of an animal, that contains a high proportion of such compounds. **3.** The best part of something: *live off the fat of the land.* —*adj.* **fat•ter, fat•test.** **1.** Having an excess of body fat; too plump; obese: *He decided to go on a diet because he was getting too fat.* **2.** Full of fat: *fat meat.* **3.** Big; ample; generous: *a fat paycheck.* **4.** *Slang.* Small; slight: *a fat chance.* —**fat′ness** *n.*

fa•tal |fāt′l| *adj.* **1.** Causing or capable of causing death; mortal: *a fatal illness; a fatal blow.* **2.** Causing ruin or destruction; disastrous: *a fatal blunder.* —**fa′tal•ly** *adv.*

fa•tal•ism |fāt′l ĭz′əm| *n.* **1.** The belief that all events are determined in advance by fate and cannot be altered by man. **2.** Acceptance of this belief; submission to fate. —**fa′tal•ist** *n.*

fa•tal•is•tic |fāt′l ĭs′tĭk| *adj.* Of, believing in, or given to fatalism: *a fatalistic attitude.* —**fa′tal•is′ti•cal•ly** *adv.*

fa•tal•i•ty |fā tăl′ĭ tē| *or* |fə-| *n., pl.* **fa•tal•i•ties.** **1.** A death caused by an accident or disaster. **2.** The ability to cause death: *diseases with a high degree of fatality.* —**modifier:** *fatality rate.*

fat•back |făt′băk′| *n.* Salt-cured fat from the upper part of a side of pork.

fate |fāt| *n.* **1.** The invisible force or power that is supposed to determine the course of events. **2.** Something that happens to or befalls a person or thing: *The fate of the plane's passengers is as yet unknown.* ¶*These sound alike* **fate, fete.**

fast[1-2]

Fast[1] *was* fæst *in Old English. Its original meaning was "firm, steady."* Fæst *as an adverb meant "firmly, tightly, closely, immediately"; with verbs of motion it came to mean "swiftly."* **Fast**[2] *is also a development of Old English* fæst; *the verb* fæstan *originally meant "to hold firm, to keep steady," and this came to mean specifically "to keep a vow of abstinence," whence, in Modern English,* **fast**[2].

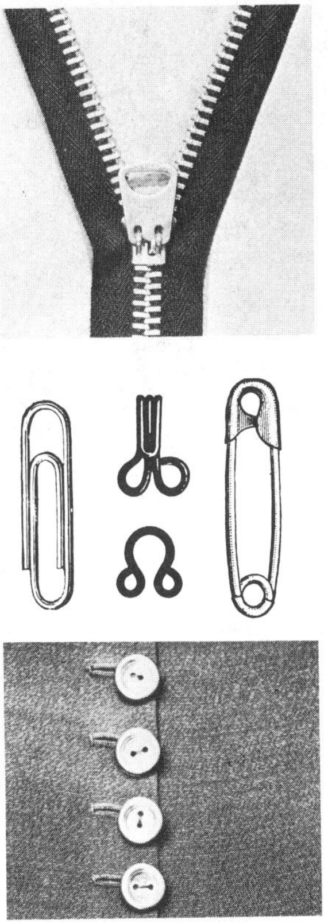

fasteners
Top: Zipper
Middle: Paper clip, hook and eye, safety pin
Bottom: Buttons

father

Father, *like most of the basic kinship terms, is descended directly from prehistoric Indo-European, and has easily recognizable cognates in other Indo-European languages.* **Father** *was* fæder *in Old English,* fadar *in prehistoric Germanic (whence also modern German* vater*), and* pəter *in Indo-European. Notice that an Indo-European* p- *regularly becomes* f- *in the Germanic languages.* Pəter *became* pater *in Latin (whence* **paternal,** *etc.), and* pater *in turn became* padre *in Spanish and Italian and* père *in French.*

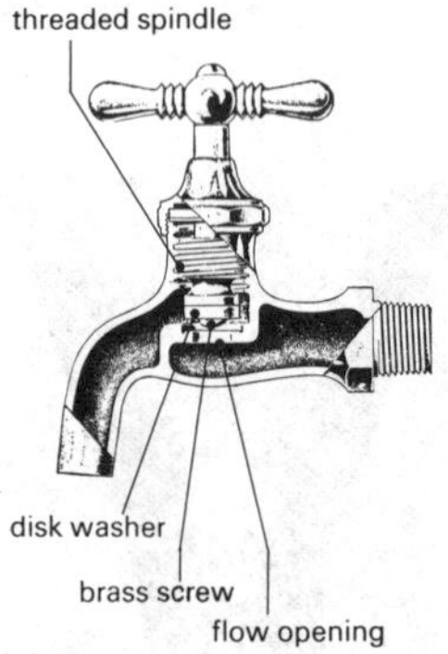

faucet

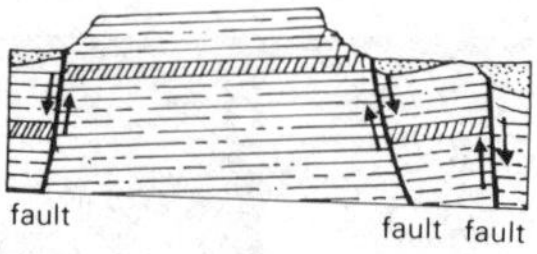

fault

ă pat/ā pay/â care/ä father/ĕ pet/ē be/ĭ pit/ī pie/î fierce/ŏ pot/ō go/ô paw, for/oi oil/ŏŏ book/ōō boot/ou out/ŭ cut/û fur/*th* the/th thin/hw which/zh vision/ə ago, item, pencil, atom, circus

fate•ful |**fāt**'fəl| *adj.* **1.** Decisively important; momentous: *the President's fateful decision to go to war.* **2.** Indicating approaching trouble or disaster; prophetic: *the first fateful signs that he was seriously ill.* —**fate'ful•ly** *adv.*

fa•ther |**fä'***th*ər| *n.* **1.** A male parent or guardian. **2.** Any male ancestor; forefather. **3.** A leader or official: *the city fathers.* **4.** A man who is a founder of or pioneer in something. **5. Father.** God. **6.** Often **Father.** A title of respect used when speaking to or of a priest or other clergyman. —*v.* **1.** To be the male parent of; beget. **2.** To create or found. [SEE NOTE]

fa•ther•hood |**fä'***th*ər ho͝od'| *n.* The condition of being a father; paternity.

fa•ther-in-law |**fä'***th*ər ĭn lô'| *n., pl.* **fa•thers-in-law.** The father of one's husband or wife.

fa•ther•land |**fä'***th*ər lănd'| *n.* A person's native land; the country of one's birth.

fa•ther•ly |**fä'***th*ər lē| *adj.* **1.** Of a father. **2.** Suited to a father: *a fatherly interest.* —**fa'ther•li•ness** *n.*

Father's Day. A holiday, celebrated on the third Sunday in June, in honor of fathers and fatherhood.

fath•om |**făth'**əm| *n., pl.* **fath•oms** or **fath•om.** A unit of length equal to six feet, used mainly in measuring and expressing depths in the ocean. —*v.* **1.** To measure the depth of; sound. **2.** To get to the bottom of; comprehend: *His motives are very difficult to fathom.* —**fath'om•a•ble** *adj.*

fath•om•less |**făth'**əm lĭs| *adj.* **1.** Too deep to be measured: *the fathomless oceans.* **2.** Too complicated to be understood: *the fathomless mysteries of the universe.*

fa•tigue |fə **tēg'**| *n.* **1.** Physical or mental weariness or exhaustion resulting from hard work or strain. **2.** Also **fatigue work.** Manual labor, such as barracks cleaning, assigned to soldiers. **3. fatigues.** Clothing worn by soldiers for heavy work or field duty. —*v.* **fa•tigued, fa•ti•guing.** To tire out; exhaust: *The march fatigued the man. He fatigues easily.* —**fa•ti'guing** *adj.*: *fatiguing work.*

fat•ten |**făt'**n| *v.* To make or become fat. —**fat'ten•ing** *adj.*: *fattening foods.*

fat•ty |**făt'**ē| *adj.* **fat•ti•er, fat•ti•est.** Of, like, or containing fat. —**fat'ti•ness** *n.*

fatty acid. Any one of a large group of organic acids that can be obtained by decomposing fats.

fat•u•ous |**făch'**ōō əs| *adj.* Foolish or silly; inane: *a fatuous remark; a fatuous smile.* —**fat'u•ous•ly** *adv.* —**fat'u•ous•ness** *n.*

fau•cet |**fô'**sĭt| *n.* A device with an adjustable valve for regulating the flow of liquid from a pipe; a tap. [SEE PICTURE]

fault |fôlt| *n.* **1.** Responsibility for a mistake, offense, etc.: *That is no fault of yours. The mix-up was all my fault.* **2.** A defect or shortcoming: *The book's one fault is that it is too long.* **3.** Something wrongly done; a mistake or error: *faults of grammar.* **4.** A break in a rock formation caused by a disturbance of the earth's crust that cracks the rock and shifts adjoining sections in a direction parallel to the crack. **5.** In tennis, a bad serve, two of which lose the point. —***modifier:*** *a fault line; a fault area.* —*v.* **1.** To find a fault in; criticize: *I cannot fault his performance.* **2.** To form a fault or faults: *rock that faulted in complex patterns.* [SEE PICTURE]

Idioms. **at fault.** Deserving of blame; guilty: *It is I who am at fault, not you.* **find fault with.** To seek and find faults in someone or something. **to a fault.** Excessively: *He is polite to a fault.*

fault•find•er |**fôlt'**fīn'dər| *n.* A person who continually seeks to find fault with others. —**fault'find'ing** *n.*

fault•less |**fôlt'**lĭs| *adj.* Without fault or flaw; perfect. —**fault'less•ly** *adv.* —**fault'less•ness** *n.*

fault•y |**fôl'**tē| *adj.* **fault•i•er, fault•i•est.** Having a fault or faults; imperfect or defective. —**fault'i•ly** *adv.* —**fault'i•ness** *n.*

faun |fôn| *n.* In Roman mythology, a woodland creature, half man and half goat. ¶*These sound alike* **faun, fawn.**

fau•na |**fô'**nə| *n.* The animals of a particular region or time period: *tropical fauna.*

Faust |foust|. A legendary German scholar and magician who sold his soul to the Devil in exchange for worldly power and knowledge.

fa•vor |**fā'**vər| *n.* **1.** A kind or helpful act: *He agreed to do it for me as a special favor.* **2.** Approval or support; sanction: *The idea of a national health plan is gaining favor with many congressmen.* **3.** A small gift given to each guest at a party or ball. **4.** Friendly regard shown by someone; partiality. **5.** Advantage; benefit: *a balance in our favor.* —*v.* **1.** To perform a kindness for; oblige: *Would you favor us with another song?* **2.** To be for; support; advocate: *I favor Harris for the job of director.* **3.** To show partiality toward; indulge: *He always seemed to favor his youngest daughter.* **4.** To be beneficial to; aid; promote: *The climate there favors the growing of fruit trees.* **5.** To resemble in appearance: *She seems to favor her father more than her mother.* **6.** To be gentle with; treat with care: *Johnny favored his sprained ankle as he walked.*

Idioms. **in favor of.** For; in support of: *All those in favor of the motion say "aye."* **in (someone's) favor.** To (someone's) advantage.

fa•vor•a•ble |**fā'**vər ə bəl| *adj.* **1.** Helpful; advantageous: *favorable winds; a favorable climate.* **2.** Encouraging; promising: *favorable signs of recovery.* **3.** Expressing approval or satisfaction: *The reviews of the movie were very favorable.* **4.** Pleasing; positive: *The new teacher has made a favorable impression so far.* **5.** Affirmative; as wished for: *hoping to receive a favorable reply.* —**fa'vor•a•bly** *adv.*

fa•vor•ite |**fā'**vər ĭt| *n.* **1.** Someone or something liked or preferred above all others: *That song is a favorite of mine.* **2.** A contestant considered most likely to win: *Notre Dame is the favorite in today's game.* —*adj.* Liked best; preferred above all others: *Green is my favorite color.*

fa•vor•it•ism |**fā'**vər ĭ tĭz'əm| *n.* Partiality, especially when unjust, shown toward one person or group over another.

fawn[1] |fôn| *n.* **1.** A young deer, especially one less than a year old. **2.** A light yellowish brown. —*adj.* Light yellowish brown. ¶*These sound alike* **fawn, faun.**

fawn[2] |fôn| *v.* **1.** To show friendliness or affection, as a dog does by coming close, licking, wagging its tail, etc.: *The friendly puppy fawned on its new owner.* **2.** To seek favor by flattery: *The ministers fawned on the young prince.* ¶*These sound alike* **fawn, faun.**

fay |fā| *n.* A fairy or elf. ¶*These sound alike* **fay, fey.**
faze |fāz| *v.* **fazed, faz•ing.** To upset; disconcert: *He never lets anything faze him.* ¶*These sound alike* **faze, phase.**
FBI, F.B.I. Federal Bureau of Investigation.
FCC Federal Communications Commission.
F clef. A musical clef, especially a bass clef, that shows the position of the F below middle C.
Fe The symbol for the element iron.
fe•al•ty |fē'əl tē| *n., pl.* **fe•al•ties. 1.** In feudal times, the loyalty owed by a vassal to his lord. **2.** Loyalty; fidelity; allegiance.
fear |fîr| *n.* **1.** A feeling of alarm or fright caused by the expectation of danger, pain, etc.; terror; dread: *fear of the unknown.* **2.** Reverence or awe: *fear of God.* **3.** A cause or ground for fear. *—v.* **1.** To be afraid; be frightened of: *You have nothing to fear. I feared you would never come. I fear for his life.* **2.** To be in awe; revere: *fear God.* **3.** To suspect or conclude regretfully: *I fear there is some mistake.*
fear•ful |fîr'fəl| *adj.* **1.** Feeling fear; afraid: *I was fearful of losing my way in the forest.* **2.** Causing fear; terrible: *the sound of a fearful explosion; a fearful noise.* **—fear'ful•ly** *adv.* **—fear'ful•ness** *n.*
fear•less |fîr'lĭs| *adj.* Having no fear; unafraid; brave: *a fearless warrior.* **—fear'less•ly** *adv.* **—fear'less•ness** *n.*
fear•some |fîr'səm| *adj.* Causing or capable of causing fear; frightening; awesome: *The rhinocerous is a fearsome sight.* **—fear'some•ly** *adv.* **—fear'some•ness** *n.*
fea•si•ble |fē'zə bəl| *adj.* **1.** Capable of being accomplished or carried out; possible: *a feasible project.* **2.** Likely; logical: *His answer seems feasible enough.* **—fea'si•bil'i•ty** *n.* **—fea'si•bly** *adv.*
feast |fēst| *n.* **1.** A large, elaborately prepared meal; a banquet: *a wedding feast.* **2.** A religious festival: *The holiday of Chanukah is sometimes called the Feast of Lights.* **—modifier:** *a feast day.* *—v.* **1.** To give a feast for: *feasting all their friends.* **2.** To eat heartily or with pleasure: *feast on a juicy roast beef.* **3.** To give pleasure to; delight: *feast one's eyes on the landscape.*
feat |fēt| *n.* An outstanding deed or accomplishment; an exploit: *The new bridge is a remarkable feat of engineering.* ¶*These sound alike* **feat, feet.**
feath•er |fĕth'ər| *n.* One of the light specialized structures growing from the skin of birds and forming their outer covering. A feather has a narrow, hollow central part with many fine strands arranged close together on each side. **—modifier:** *a feather pillow; a feather mattress.* *—v.* **1.** To cover or fit with a feather or feathers: *feather an arrow.* **2.** To turn (an oar) so that its blade is parallel to the surface of the water between strokes. **3.** To turn the blades of (an aircraft propeller) so that they are parallel to the direction of flight. **—feath'ered** *adj.: a feathered headdress.* [SEE PICTURE]
Idioms. **a feather in (one's) cap.** A distinctive achievement of which one can be proud. **feather (one's) nest.** To amass wealth by taking advantage of circumstances. **in fine feather.** In excellent form, health, or humor.
feather bed. A soft mattress or quilt stuffed with feathers or down.
feath•er•bed•ding |fĕth'ər bĕd'ĭng| *n.* The practice of requiring an employer to hire more workers than are actually needed or to refrain from laying off workers whose jobs have become obsolete.
feath•er•weight |fĕth'ər wāt'| *n.* **1.** A boxer weighing between 118 and 127 pounds. **2.** A very small or unimportant person or thing. **—modifier:** *a featherweight boxing match.*
feath•er•y |fĕth'ə rē| *adj.* **1.** Made of or covered with feathers. **2.** Like a feather or feathers; light, soft, or delicate: *the feathery touch of her fingertips.*
fea•ture |fē'chər| *n.* **1.** A prominent part, quality, or characteristic: *Jagged rocks were a feature of the landscape.* **2. a.** Any of the distinct parts of the face. **b. features.** The make-up or appearance of the face or its parts. **3.** The main film of a motion-picture program. **4.** A prominent article in a newspaper or magazine, usually one that explains something in the news or describes a person in the news. **—modifier:** *the feature film; a feature article.* *—v.* **fea•tured, fea•tur•ing.** To give special attention to; offer prominently: *The exhibit features paintings of colonial times.*
Feb. February.
Feb•ru•ar•y |fĕb'rōō ĕr'ē| *or* |fĕb'yōō-| *n.* The second month of the year, after January and before March. It has 28 days except in leap year, when it has 29 days. **—modifier:** *a February morning.*
fe•ces |fē'sēz| *pl.n.* Waste material excreted from the bowels.
feck•less |fĕk'lĭs| *adj.* Careless and irresponsible: *a feckless youth.* **—feck'less•ness** *n.*
fe•cund |fē'kənd| *or* |fĕk'ənd| *adj.* Productive; fertile; fruitful: *fecund land.* **—fe•cund'i•ty** |fĭ-kŭn'dĭ tē| *n.*
fed |fĕd|. Past tense and past participle of **feed.**
fed•er•al |fĕd'ər əl| *adj.* **1. a.** Of a form of government in which separate states, each retaining certain regulatory powers, are united under and recognize one central authority. **b.** Of or regulated by the central government of such a union rather than by a state government: *federal courts; federal laws.* **2. a.** Often **Federal.** Of or controlled by the central government of the United States: *a Federal Reserve Bank; Federal income tax.* **b. Federal.** Of or supporting the Union during the Civil War: *Federal troops.* *—n.* **Federal.** A supporter of the Union during the Civil War. **—fed'er•al•ly** *adv.* [SEE NOTE]
Federal Bureau of Investigation. An agency of the U.S. Department of Justice responsible for investigating violations of Federal law.
fed•er•al•ism |fĕd'ər ə lĭz'əm| *n.* **1.** A form of government in which power is divided between a central authority and a number of constituent units, especially the form of government of the United States of America. **2.** A doctrine advocating such a form of government.
fed•er•al•ist |fĕd'ər ə lĭst| *n.* **1.** A person who advocates federalism. **2. Federalist.** A supporter of the Federalist Party: *the Federalists of New England.* **—modifier:** *a Federalist Congress.*
Federalist Party. An American political party that flourished in the 1790's under the leadership of Alexander Hamilton. It advocated a strong centralized federal government.

feather
With enlarged portion showing details

federal, etc.
Federal *and its group of words were not actually coined in America, but they were first widely used by Americans, at the time of the Revolution. They come from Latin* foeder-, foedus, *"league, treaty, agreement, contract." This word is related to Latin* fidēs, *"trust, faith," and* fīdere, *"to trust," from which we have* **fidelity, confide,** *and other words.*

feedback
In general, when **feedback** *is used to control a system, a sample of the output is taken and subtracted from the input. Thus, for example, if the output increases, the input is decreased so that the output tends to return to its correct value; this is called* negative feedback. Positive feedback *is feedback that is added to the input.*

feelers
Above: Feelers of a moth
Below: Feelers of a cat

ă pat/ā pay/â care/ä father/ĕ pet/ ē be/ĭ pit/ī pie/î fierce/ŏ pot/ ō go/ô paw, for/oi oil/ŏŏ book/ ōō boot/ou out/ŭ cut/û fur/ *th* the/th thin/hw which/zh vision/ ə ago, item, pencil, atom, circus

Federal Reserve System. A centralized U.S. banking system consisting of 12 Federal Reserve Banks, each representing member banks in a given Federal Reserve District.

fed•er•ate |fĕd′ə rāt′| *v.* **fed•er•at•ed, fed•er•at•ing.** To bring or join together in a league, federal union, or other association.

fed•er•a•tion |fĕd′ə **rā′**shən| *n.* **1.** The act of joining together in a league, federal union, or other association: *The next step was federation on a national basis.* **2.** A league or association formed by federating: *a federation of dairymen.*

fee |fē| *n.* **1.** A fixed charge: *an admission fee; tuition fees.* **2.** A payment for professional or special service: *a lawyer's fee.* **3.** In feudal times, an estate of land; a fief.

fee•ble |fē′bəl| *adj.* **fee•bler, fee•blest. 1. a.** Lacking strength; weak or frail: *a feeble old woman.* **b.** Indicating weakness or frailty: *a feeble handshake; a feeble voice.* **2.** Without adequate force, power, or intensity; inadequate: *a feeble attempt; a feeble defense of the fort.* —**fee′ble•ness** *n.* —**fee′bly** *adv.*

fee•ble-mind•ed |fē′bəl **mīn′**dĭd| *adj.* Mentally deficient; subnormal in intelligence. —**fee′ble•mind′ed•ly** *adv.* —**fee′ble•mind′ed•ness** *n.*

feed |fēd| *v.* **fed** |fĕd|, **feed•ing. 1.** To give food to; supply with nourishment: *She feeds the birds. He fed the goldfish.* **2.** To provide as food or nourishment: *He fed peanuts to the elephant.* **3. a.** To serve as food for: *a turkey large enough to feed a dozen. Grass feeds great herds of cattle.* **b.** To produce food for: *The country can't feed its large population.* **4. a.** To eat: *The sheep fed as they moved along.* **b.** To use as food: *Young turtles feed on insects and small water animals.* **5.** To supply (fuel, materials, power, etc.) to: *He fed more wood to the fire.* **6.** In sports, to pass (the ball or puck) to a teammate, especially in order to score: *We fed the ball to our center.* —*n.* Food for animals or birds; fodder.
Idiom. **be fed up.** To be out of patience and disgusted: *He was fed up with the whole situation.*

feed•back |**fēd′**băk′| *n.* **1.** The return of a sample of the output of a system or process to the input, especially in such a way that the output is automatically kept within desired limits. **2.** The sample of the output used in this way. **3.** *Informal.* A response or reaction. [SEE NOTE]

feed•er |fē′dər| *n.* **1.** Someone who feeds animals, especially domestic animals or wild animals in captivity. **2.** Something that ingests food: *Some caterpillars are voracious feeders that can ravage a midsummer forest.* **3.** Any device for holding feed for animals so that they can obtain the food easily: *a bird feeder on a tall pole.* **4.** Anything that feeds materials into a machine to be processed. **5.** Any branch or tributary, as of a river, railroad, or corporation.

feel |fēl| *v.* **felt** |fĕlt|, **feel•ing. 1. a.** To be aware of or perceive through the sense of touch: *feel a piece of velvet. She felt leaves brush against her cheek.* **b.** To touch to or as if to examine: *She felt his forehead to discover if he had a fever.* **c.** To try to find something by the sense of touch: *He felt in another pocket for his pipe. He felt around for a match.* **d.** To be guided by or as if by the sense of touch: *In the dark he felt his way to the barn.* **2. a.** To be aware of by a physical sensation: *He felt a stomach pain. They felt the warmth of the campfire.* **b.** To be in a certain physical or emotional condition: *feel sleepy; feel hot; feel sad.* **c.** To give or produce a certain physical sensation: *The water feels cold.* **3. a.** To experience (an emotion, attitude, etc.); be affected or moved by: *He felt sympathy for the sick child.* **b.** To have sympathy or compassion: *She felt deeply for him in his sorrow.* **4.** To hold as an opinion; believe or consider: *She feels strongly about equal rights for women.* **5.** To have or receive a vague overall impression: *He could feel their disappointment.* **6.** To appear to be to the senses or the emotions; seem: *This cloth feels like satin.* —*n.* **1.** Perception or sensation caused by physical touch: *the feel of raindrops.* **2.** A quality that can be perceived by touching: *a closely woven cloth with a firm feel.*
Idioms. **feel like.** *Informal.* To be in the mood for: *She did not feel like writing in her diary.* **feel (like) (oneself).** To be aware of oneself as being in the usual state of health or spirits: *She doesn't feel quite herself this morning.* **feel (someone) out.** To try cautiously to learn the viewpoint or wish of (a person). **feel up to.** To feel capable or ready for: *She did not feel up to the task.*

feel•er |fē′lər| *n.* **1.** A slender part, such as a cat's whisker or an insect's antenna, used for touching or feeling. **2.** A remark, question, proposal, etc., designed to bring out the attitude or intention of others. [SEE PICTURE]

feel•ing |fē′lĭng| *n.* **1.** The sense that perceives physical sensation through the skin; the sense of touch. **2.** A physical sensation: *a fluttery feeling in her stomach.* **3.** Emotion, especially a tender emotion such as pity, sympathy, compassion, etc.: *a deep feeling for her friends.* **4. feelings.** The complex combination of one's emotions; sensibilities: *He tried to hide his feelings.* **5.** An awareness caused by emotion, attitudes, beliefs, etc.: *a feeling of contentment.* **6.** A distinct impression or mood: *a feeling of danger; the feeling of remoteness.* **7.** Opinion, attitude, belief, or point of view, often based on complex emotions or sensitivities: *his religious feelings; their feeling about nature.*

feel•ing•ly |fē′lĭng lē| *adv.* With much emotion or sensitivity: *He spoke feelingly about his homeland.*

feet |fēt| *n.* Plural of **foot.** ¶*These sound alike* **feet, feat.**

feign |fān| *v.* To give a false appearance of; pretend: *feign illness.* ¶*These sound alike* **feign, fain.**

feint |fānt| *n.* A movement, attack, etc., that is feigned in order to deceive an opponent or divert his attention away from the real target or objective. —*v.* To pretend (an attack) in order to deceive an opponent: *He feinted a pass but dribbled the ball instead. He feinted with the ball as if to take a shot.* ¶*These sound alike* **feint, faint.**

feist |fīst| *n.* *Informal.* A small dog of mixed ancestry; a mongrel.

feis•ty |fī′stē| *adj.* **feis•ti•er, feis•ti•est.** *Informal.* Scrappy or frisky.

feld•spar |**fĕld′**spär′| *or* |**fĕl′**spär′| *n.* Any one of a large group of minerals that occur widely in various rocks and that are composed largely of silicates.

fe•lic•i•ta•tion |fĭ lĭs'ĭ tā'shən| *n.* Often **felicitations.** Congratulation: *Your friends join with me in felicitations on your outstanding victory.*

fe•lic•i•tous |fĭ lĭs'ĭ təs| *adj.* **1.** Well-chosen; apt; appropriate: *a felicitous use of words.* **2.** Having an agreeable manner or style: *a felicitous writer.* —**fe•lic'i•tous•ly** *adv.*

fe•lic•i•ty |fĭ lĭs'ĭ tē| *n., pl.* **fe•lic•i•ties. 1.** Great happiness. **2.** An appropriate and pleasing manner or style: *the felicity of a phrase.*

fe•line |fē'līn'| *adj.* **1.** Of or typical of a cat or related animal. **2.** Like a cat: *walk with feline grace.* —*n.* A cat or related animal, such as a lion, tiger, or leopard. [SEE NOTE]

fell[1] |fĕl| *v.* To cause to fall; cut or knock down: *They felled trees to build a cabin. He wanted to fell the other boxer quickly.* [SEE NOTE]

fell[2] |fĕl| *adj.* **1.** Of a cruel nature; fierce and ruthless: *the fell bands of bandits.* **2.** Able to destroy; lethal: *a fell potion.* [SEE NOTE]

fell[3] |fĕl|. Past tense of **fall.**

fel•lah |fĕl'ə| *n.* A peasant or agricultural laborer in an Arab country.

fel•low |fĕl'ō| *n.* **1.** A man or boy. **2.** Any human being. **3.** A comrade; a companion; an associate: *Robin Hood and his fellows hid in the forest.* **4.** *Informal.* A boy friend. **5.** A member of a learned society. **6.** A graduate student who, because of merit, receives a grant of money for further study. **7.** One of a matched pair; a counterpart. —***modifier:*** *our fellow creatures; his fellow workers.*

fellow man. *pl.* **fellow men.** Any person regarded as related to another through human experience.

fel•low•ship |fĕl'ō shĭp'| *n.* **1.** Friendly association of people; companionship: *He enjoyed the fellowship of the other workers.* **2. a.** A union of friends or groups sharing a common interest: *The organization is a fellowship of many different churches from 90 countries.* **b.** Membership in such a group: *admitted to fellowship.* **3.** A grant of money awarded a graduate student in a college or university.

fel•on |fĕl'ən| *n.* Someone who has committed a felony. [SEE NOTE]

fe•lo•ni•ous |fə lō'nē əs| *adj.* Of or having the nature of a felony: *with felonious intent.*

fel•o•ny |fĕl'ə nē| *n., pl.* **fel•o•nies.** A serious crime, such as murder, rape, or burglary.

felt[1] |fĕlt| *n.* A smooth, firm cloth made by pressing and matting wool, fur, or other fibers together instead of weaving them. —***modifier:*** *a felt hat.* —*v.* **1.** To make into felt: *felting fibers to make cloth.* **2.** To cover with felt: *They felted the billiard table.* —**felt'ed** *adj.: a felted fabric.*

felt[2] |fĕlt|. Past tense and past participle of **feel.**

fem. female; feminine.

fe•male |fē'māl'| *adj.* **1.** Of or characteristic of animals or plants of the sex that produces egg cells and, in some animals, gives birth to offspring. **2.** Of or being a woman or girl: *a female voice; a female student.* **3.** Of or having a part, such as a slot or groove, into which a projecting part, such as a plug or prong, is meant to fit. —*n.* A female animal or plant.

fem•i•nine |fĕm'ə nĭn| *adj.* **1.** Of or belonging to the female sex. **2.** Marked by or possessing qualities generally associated with women; womanly: *a musical, feminine laugh.* **3.** In grammar, indicating or belonging to the gender of words or grammatical forms that are classified as female; for example, *lioness, hen, princess,* and *her* are feminine words. —**fem'i•nine•ly** *adv.*

fem•i•nin•i•ty |fĕm'ə nĭn'ĭ tē| *n.* **1.** The quality or condition of being feminine. **2.** Women as a group.

fem•i•nism |fĕm'ə nĭz'əm| *n.* **1.** A doctrine that advocates that women be given the same rights and status as men. **2.** The movement in support of this doctrine. —**fem'i•nist** *n.*

fe•mur |fē'mər| *n., pl.* **fe•murs** or **fem•o•ra** |fĕm'ər ə|. **1.** The long uppermost bone of the rear or lower limb in vertebrates, located between the knee and pelvis in human beings; the thighbone. **2.** The thigh.

fen |fĕn| *n.* Low, swampy land; a marsh; a bog.

fence |fĕns| *n.* **1. a.** A structure made of boards, posts, wire, rails, etc., that serves as an enclosure or barrier. **b.** Something resembling a fence: *The monster's mouth gaped, exposing a fence of teeth.* **2.** A person who receives and sells stolen goods. —*v.* **fenced, fenc•ing. 1.** To surround or separate with or as if with a fence: *fence a pasture.* **2.** To engage in fencing. —**fenc'er** *n.* [SEE NOTE]

Idiom. **on** (or **straddling**) **the fence.** *Informal.* Not taking either side of an issue, argument, etc.

fenc•ing |fĕn'sĭng| *n.* **1.** The art or sport of using certain kinds of swords, especially foils, in attacking and defending. **2.** Material, such as wire, boards, rails, etc., used in constructing fences. [SEE NOTE]

fend |fĕnd| *v.* To defend oneself from; repel; resist: *He used an oar to fend off the sharks.*

Idiom. **fend for (oneself).** To get along without aid; manage without help: *The boys had to fend for themselves at an early age.*

fen•der |fĕn'dər| *n.* **1.** A cover or guard mounted above and around a wheel of an automobile, truck or other motor vehicle. **2.** A device at the front end of a locomotive or streetcar, designed to push aside objects blocking the tracks. **3.** A low screen or frame placed in front of a fireplace.

fen•nel |fĕn'əl| *n.* **1.** A plant with stems, leaves, and seeds that have a sweet flavor like that of licorice. The stalks are sometimes eaten as salad, and the seeds are used as flavoring. **2.** The stalks or seeds of this plant.

fer-de-lance |fĕr'də lăns'| *or* |-läns'| *n.* A poisonous snake of tropical America and the West Indies.

Fer•di•nand V |fûr'dn ănd'|. 1452–1516. King of Spain who helped Columbus.

fer•ment |fûr'mĕnt'| *n.* **1.** Anything that causes fermentation, as a yeast, mold, or enzyme. **2.** Fermentation. **3.** A state of agitation; unrest: *the ferment caused by the Industrial Revolution.* —*v.* |fər mĕnt'|. To undergo or cause to undergo fermentation: *When fruit juice is left standing, it ferments. Yeast ferments carbohydrates.* —**fer•ment'ed** *adj.: fermented cider.*

fer•men•ta•tion |fûr'mĕn tā'shən| *n.* Any one of a group of chemical reactions, caused by various microorganisms or enzymes, in which relatively complex organic compounds are broken down into simpler compounds, especially the process by which yeasts convert sugar to alcohol

feline

Feline *is from Latin* fēlis *or* fēlēs, *"cat." The Romans did not originally have domestic cats;* fēlis *meant "small European wild cat." See note at* **cat.**

fell[1-2]**/felon**

Fell[1] *was* fellan *in Old English; it is closely related to* **fall.** *Both* **fell**[2] *and* **felon** *stem from the Late Latin word* fellō, *"evil person, criminal"; this word was inherited into Old French as* fel, *"evil, cruel," and was later additionally borrowed into Old French as* felon, *"a criminal"; these two words were then borrowed into English as* **fell**[2] *and* **felon.**

fence/fencing

The noun **fence** *is a shortening of* **defense.** *The verb* **fence** *originally meant "to make a defense or fence" (sense 1), and then "to practice the art of defense with a sword" (sense 2).*

Ferris wheel
Photograph of the original Ferris wheel at the 1893 Chicago World's Fair. It was designed and built by the American engineer George Washington *Ferris* (1859–1896).

ferryboat

ă pat/ā pay/â care/ä father/ĕ pet/ē be/ĭ pit/ī pie/î fierce/ŏ pot/ō go/ô paw, for/oi oil/o͝o book/o͞o boot/ou out/ŭ cut/û fur/*th* the/th thin/hw which/zh vision/ə ago, item, pencil, atom, circus

and carbon dioxide in the absence of oxygen from the air.

fer•mi•um |fûr′mē əm| *n.* Symbol **Fm** One of the elements, a metal first discovered in the debris of a hydrogen-bomb explosion and later produced by nuclear bombardment. It has ten isotopes with mass numbers ranging from 248 to 257 and half-lives from 0.6 minutes to 100 days. Atomic number 100.

fern |fûrn| *n.* Any of a group of plants that have fronds divided into many leaflets and that reproduce by means of spores rather than by producing flowers and seeds.

fe•ro•cious |fə rō′shəs| *adj.* **1.** Extremely cruel and fierce; savage: *a ferocious dog.* **2.** Extreme; intense: *a ferocious speed.* **—fe•ro′cious•ly** *adv.*

fe•roc•i•ty |fə rŏs′ĭ tē| *n., pl.* **fe•roc•i•ties. 1.** Extreme cruelty and fierceness; savageness: *the ferocity of the barbarians.* **2.** Great force; intensity: *the ferocity of her will to survive.*

fer•ret |fĕr′ĭt| *n.* **1.** A usually white form of the European polecat, an animal related to the weasels. It is often trained to hunt for rats and rabbits. **2.** A weasellike North American animal with yellowish fur and dark feet. *—v.* **1.** To drive out; expel. **2.** To uncover and bring to light by searching: *ferret out a secret.*

fer•ric |fĕr′ĭk| *adj.* Of or containing iron, especially with a valence of +3.

Ferris wheel |fĕr′ĭs|. A large upright, rotating wheel with suspended seats on which people ride for amusement. [SEE PICTURE]

ferro–. A word element meaning "iron": **ferromagnetic.**

fer•ro•mag•net•ic |fĕr′ō măg **nĕt′**ĭk| *adj.* Having magnetic properties similar to those of iron.

fer•rous |fĕr′əs| *adj.* Of or containing iron, especially with a valence of +2.

fer•ry |fĕr′ē| *n., pl.* **fer•ries. 1.** A boat used to transport people, vehicles, goods, etc.; a ferryboat. **2.** A commercial service using ferryboats for transporting: *He established the ferry to that island.* **3.** The place where a ferryboat embarks: *There was a fight down at the ferry.* ***—modifier:*** *a ferry trip; a ferry dock.* *—v.* **fer•ried, fer•ry•ing, fer•ries. 1.** To transport (people, vehicles, etc.) across a body of water: *They ferried their wagon across the river.* **2.** To cross a body of water on or as if on a ferry. **3.** To transport (people or things) from one place to another.

fer•ry•boat |fĕr′ē bōt′| *n.* A boat used to transport passengers, vehicles, goods, etc. [SEE PICTURE]

fer•tile |fûr′tl| *adj.* **1.** Rich in material needed to support plant life; favorable to the growth of crops and plants: *fertile soil; a fertile valley.* **2.** Capable of producing offspring; able to reproduce. **3.** Capable of developing into a complete organism; fertilized: *a fertile egg.* **4.** Highly productive or active; inventive: *a fertile imagination.* **—fer•til′i•ty** |fər **tĭl′**ĭ tē| *n.*

fer•til•ize |fûr′tl īz′| *v.* **fer•til•ized, fer•til•iz•ing. 1.** To cause (an egg cell, plant, etc.) to become fertile, especially by supplying it with sperm or pollen. **2.** To make fertile, especially by using fertilizer. **—fer′til•i•za′tion** *n.*

fer•til•iz•er |fûr′tl ī′zər| *n.* Any material, such as manure, compost, or a chemical compound, added to soil to increase its fertility.

fer•ule |fĕr′əl| *or* |-o͞ol′| *n.* A flat stick or ruler used in punishing children, especially by striking them on the hand.

fer•vent |fûr′vənt| *adj.* **1.** Showing deep feeling or great emotion; earnest: *a fervent entreaty from the king.* **2.** Zealous; ardent: *the fervent leader of the movement.* **3.** Intensely hot: *a fervent August when even thoughts seemed to melt.* **—fer′ven•cy** *n.* **—fer′vent•ly** *adv.*

fer•vid |fûr′vĭd| *adj.* **1.** Extremely fervent; impassioned: *a fervid reply to her mild question; a fervid desire to play baseball.* **2.** Extremely hot; burning; glowing: *the fervid reflection of the sun on the water.* **—fer′vid•ly** *adv.* **—fer′vid•ness** *n.*

fer•vor |fûr′vər| *n.* Intensity of emotion; fervency; ardor: *religious fervor.*

fes•tal |fĕs′təl| *adj.* Of or like a feast or festival; festive: *The village had a festal appearance.*

fes•ter |fĕs′tər| *v.* **1.** To generate or become filled with pus, as an infected wound does. **2.** To be or become a source of resentment, irritation, or corruption; rankle: *Envy festered for years in her mind.*

fes•ti•val |fĕs′tə vəl| *n.* **1.** An occasion of great significance, celebrated with special rituals or customs: *the harvest festival; a religious festival.* **2.** A series of cultural presentations: *an international film festival; a dance festival; a music festival.* ***—modifier:*** *a festival day; the festival site.*

fes•tive |fĕs′tĭv| *adj.* **1.** Of or suited to a feast or festival: *Food was heaped high on a festive table.* **2.** Merry; joyous: *a festive party; a festive season.* **—fes′tive•ly** *adv.* **—fes′tive•ness** *n.*

fes•tiv•i•ty |fĕ **stĭv′**ĭ tē| *n., pl.* **fes•tiv•i•ties. 1.** Often **festivities.** The activities during a festival or feast: *The festivities included parades, banquets, and balls.* **2.** The joy and gaiety of a celebration or festival: *a holiday with much festivity.*

fes•toon |fĕ **sto͞on′**| *n.* **1.** A length or chain of leaves, flowers, ribbon, paper, etc., hung in a curve between two points for decoration. **2.** A sculptured ornament in this shape, used in architecture. *—v.* To decorate with festoons: *a hall festooned with holly and ivy.*

fe•tal |fēt′l| *adj.* Of or having to do with a fetus.

fetch |fĕch| *v.* **1.** To go after and return with; get: *Shall I fetch your bags for you?* **2.** *Informal.* To bring (an amount of money): *The work fetched us a dollar a day.*

fetch•ing |fĕch′ĭng| *adj. Informal.* Very attractive; charming; captivating: *a fetching smile.*

fete, also **fête** |fāt| *n.* A festival or feast. *—v.* **fet•ed, fet•ing.** To honor with a fete: *They feted the hero with dinners and a parade.* ¶*These sound alike* **fete, fate.**

fet•id |fĕt′ĭd| *or* |fē′tĭd| *adj.* Having an offensive odor; foul-smelling.

fet•ish |fĕt′ĭsh| *n.* **1.** An object that is believed to have magical power. **2.** Something to which excessive attention or reverence is given: *an age in which hygiene has become a fetish.*

fet•ish•ism |fĕt′ĭ shĭz′əm| *or* |fē′tĭ-| *n.* **1.** The worship of or belief in the magical powers of fetishes. **2.** Excessive attention to or attachment for something. **—fet′ish•ist** *n.*

fet•lock |fĕt′lŏk′| *n.* **1.** A projection above and behind the hoof of a horse or related animal. **2.** A tuft of hair on this projection.

fet•ter |fĕt′ər| *n.* **1.** A chain or shackle attached to the ankles to restrain movement. **2.** Often **fetters.** Anything that restricts or restrains. *—v.* To restrict or restrain with or as if with fetters.

fet•tle |fĕt′l| *n.* Proper or sound condition; good spirits: *The horse is in fine fettle today.*

fe•tus |fē′təs| *n., pl.* **fe•tus•es.** The unborn young of a mammal from the time at which the major features of its body have appeared, especially an unborn human baby after the eighth week of its development.

feud |fyōōd| *n.* A bitter, prolonged quarrel between two people or groups, often involving much strife and conflict: *an ancient feud between two families.* *—v.* To carry on a feud; quarrel. [SEE NOTE]

feu•dal |fyōōd′l| *adj.* Of or involving feudalism: *a feudal estate.* [SEE NOTE]

feu•dal•ism |fyōōd′l ĭz′əm| *n.* A political and economic system in Europe during the Middle Ages, under which land was granted by a landowner to a person called a vassal in exchange for military service and various other duties. **—feu′dal•is′tic** *adj.*

fe•ver |fē′vər| *n.* **1.** An abnormally high body temperature. **2.** A disease in which an abnormally high body temperature is one of the main symptoms. **3.** A condition of great agitation or enthusiasm; intensity: *He caught the fever of excitement from John.*

fever blister. A **cold sore.**

fe•ver•ish |fē′vər ĭsh| *adj.* **1. a.** Having a fever, especially one that is not very high. **b.** Caused by a fever. **2.** In an agitated state; intensely emotional or active: *a feverish desire to win.* **—fe′ver•ish•ly** *adv.* **—fe′ver•ish•ness** *n.*

few |fyōō| *adj.* **few•er, few•est.** Amounting to or consisting of a small number. *—n. (used with a plural verb).* **1.** An indefinitely small number of persons or things: *Only a few were able to come to my party.* **2.** A limited, often select or elite group: *the happy few.* *—pron. (used with a plural verb).* A small number of persons or things: *Few were able to read.*

fey |fā| *adj.* **1.** Having visionary powers. **2.** Appearing as if under a spell; enchanted. ¶ *These sound alike* **fey, fay.**

fez |fĕz| *n., pl.* **fez•zes.** A high felt cap, usually red with a black tassel, worn chiefly in eastern Mediterranean countries. [SEE PICTURE]

ff fortissimo.

fi•an•cé |fē′än sā′| *or* |fē än′sā′| *n.* A man to whom a woman is engaged to be married.

fi•an•cée |fē′än sā′| *or* |fē än′sā′| *n.* A woman to whom a man is engaged to be married.

fi•as•co |fē ăs′kō| *n., pl.* **fi•as•coes** or **fi•as•cos.** A complete failure: *His new book was the worst fiasco of the writer's career.*

fi•at |fī′ăt′| *or* |-ət| *or* |fē′ät′| *n.* **1.** An order or decree. **2.** Authorization; sanction.

fib |fĭb| *n.* A small or trivial lie: *She told a fib about her age.* *—v.* **fibbed, fib•bing.** To tell a small or trivial lie. **—fib′ber** *n.*

fi•ber |fī′bər| *n.* **1.** A slender, threadlike strand, as of plant or animal tissue or of man-made material: *Cotton, wool, and nylon fibers may be spun into yarn.* **2.** A number of fibers forming a single substance: *muscle fiber; flax fiber.* **3.** Inner strength; character: *He was lacking in moral fiber.* ***—modifier:*** *a fiber rope.*

fi•ber•board |fī′bər bôrd′| *or* |-bōrd′| *n.* **1.** Any of a number of building materials composed of wood fibers or other plant fibers cemented together and compressed into sheets. **2.** A sheet of such a material.

Fi•ber•glas |fī′bər glăs′| *or* |-gläs′| *n.* A trademark for a type of fiber glass.

fiber glass. **1.** Any of several materials made from glass fibers, especially cloth, thread, etc., to be used as building insulation. **2.** Any of several stiff or rigid materials composed of glass fibers bonded together in a synthetic resin.

fi•bre |fī′bər| *n.* Chiefly British form of the word **fiber.**

fi•bril |fī′brəl| *or* |fĭb′rəl| *n.* A tiny, slender, often microscopic fiber.

fib•ril•la•tion |fĭb′rə lā′shən| *n.* An uncoordinated twitching of the individual fibers of a muscle, especially the muscles of the ventricles of the heart.

fi•brin |fī′brĭn| *n.* An elastic, insoluble protein that forms a fibrous network that is the main substance of a blood clot.

fi•brin•o•gen |fī brĭn′ə jən| *n.* A soluble protein that is normally present in the plasma of the blood.

fi•brous |fī′brəs| *adj.* Of, like, or having fibers.

fib•u•la |fĭb′yə lə| *n., pl.* **fib•u•lae** |fĭb′yə lē′| or **fib•u•las.** The smaller of the two bones that support the lower section of the hind or lower limb of vertebrates, located between the ankle and knee in human beings.

-fic. A suffix that forms adjectives: **terrific.**

fick•le |fĭk′əl| *adj.* Changeable, as in affections or loyalties; inconstant. **—fick′le•ness** *n.*

fic•tion |fĭk′shən| *n.* **1.** A product of the imagination: *Legends are often mixtures of fact and fiction.* **2. a.** The category of literature with imaginary characters and events, including novels, short stories, etc. **b.** A work of this category. ***—modifier:*** *a fiction writer.*

fic•tion•al |fĭk′shə nəl| *adj.* Of or associated with fiction: *a fictional account of boyhood.* **—fic′tion•al•ly** *adv.*

fic•ti•tious |fĭk tĭsh′əs| *adj.* Of fiction; imaginary; unreal: *a fictitious happening.* **2.** Intentionally deceptive; false: *invented a fictitious list of ancestors in order to claim royal descent.* **—fic•ti′tious•ly** *adv.* **—fic•ti′tious•ness** *n.*

fid•dle |fĭd′l| *n. Informal.* A violin. *—v.* **fid•dled, fid•dling.** **1.** *Informal.* To play the violin. **2.** To tinker or play idly with something, using the hands or fingers; fidget: *He fiddled with the rope while talking.*

fid•dler |fĭd′lər| *n. Informal.* A person who plays the violin. [SEE PICTURE]

fiddler crab. A crab of which the male has one front claw much larger than the other. [SEE PICTURE]

fid•dle•sticks |fĭd′l stĭks′| *interj.* A word used to express mild annoyance or impatience.

fi•del•i•ty |fĭ dĕl′ĭ tē| *or* |fī-| *n., pl.* **fi•del•i•ties.** **1.** Faithfulness to a person, cause, etc.; loyalty: *the fidelity of the crew to the captain.* **2.** Truthfulness; accuracy: *the fidelity with which he described his experience.* **3.** The degree to which an electronic system, such as a radio or phonograph, reproduces sound without distortion.

fidg•et |fĭj′ĭt| *v.* To move uneasily, nervously, or

feud/feudal

Feud *and* **feudal** *are both from interesting medieval words, but they are not related.* **Feud** *is from Old French* feide, *which is from Old High German* fēhida, *"hostility." In this word, the* fēhi- *means "enemy," and it is closely related to the Old English word* ge-fāh, *"enemy," which became* **foe** *in Modern English; the ending* -da *is the same as* -th *in English words like* growth *and* width; fēhi-da *is thus the equivalent of* foe-ness, *"the condition of being a foe."* **Feudal** *is from Medieval Latin* feudum, *"real estate," especially "land granted by a lord in exchange for military service by the tenant"; the word is Germanic and is related to* **fee** *and* **fief.**

fez

fiddler

fiddler crab

field
Field *was* **feld** *in Old English. It is closely related to the Dutch word* veld *or* velt, *"field," which the Afrikaners applied to the grasslands of southern Africa, and was borrowed into English as* **veldt**.

field glasses

fife

fife/pipe
Fife *is from German* pfeife, *which descends from Old High German* pfiffa *and before that from prehistoric Germanic* pīpa. Pīpa *separately passed into Old English as* pīpa *and became* **pipe** *in Modern English. The Germanic word itself is a borrowing from Latin* pīpāre, *"to chirp (as a bird)."*

ă pat/ā pay/â care/ä father/ĕ pet/ ē be/ĭ pit/ī pie/î fierce/ŏ pot/ ō go/ô paw, for/oi oil/ŏŏ book/ ōō boot/ou out/ŭ cut/û fur/ *th* the/th thin/hw which/zh vision/ ə ago, item, pencil, atom, circus

restlessly: *The audience fidgeted until curtain time.* —*n.* **the fidgets.** A condition of nervousness or restlessness. —**fidg'et·y** *adj.*

fie |fī| *interj.* A word used to express distaste or shock.

fief |fēf| *n.* In feudal times, an estate given by a landowner to a vassal in exchange for military service and other duties.

field |fēld| *n.* **1.** A broad area of land without forests, mountains, or towns: *small animals of field, forest, and stream.* **2.** A cultivated area of land, especially one devoted to a particular crop: *cotton fields; getting the field ready for spring planting.* **3.** A meadow: *a field of tall grass; a field of forget-me-nots.* **4.** A range or category of interest, particular activity, or specialization: *the field of medicine.* **5. a.** A physical property or influence, such as gravitational attraction or magnetic force, whose values vary with position throughout a region of space. **b.** A region of space in which such a physical property or influence has significant values. **6.** The area in which the eye or some optical instrument, such as a camera or telescope, produces an image: *the field of vision.* **7.** A place containing a specified natural resource: *oil fields; a gold field.* **8.** A large, flat surface where aircraft can take off or land; an airfield: *The plane had to land at another field.* **9.** A scene or place of battle; a battlefield: *The soldier was honored for bravery in the field.* **10.** In sports, the playing area marked out on the ground. **11.** The number of participants in a race: *a large field in the Kentucky Derby.* **12.** A great expanse of ice on the sea, as in a polar region: *From the plane he saw ice fields that stretched endlessly below.* **13.** A background area, as on a flag, painting, etc.: *a banner with fifty white stars on a field of blue.* **14.** A scene of practical work or observation away from the formal atmosphere of a laboratory, classroom, etc.: *The geologist enjoyed working in the field, collecting rocks and observing rock formations.* —***modifier:*** *field hands planting cotton; a field hospital.* —*v.* In baseball, to catch (a batted ball that hits the ground) and throw it to the proper player: *The shortstop fielded the ball and threw it to the first baseman.* [SEE NOTE]

field day. **1.** A day spent outdoors in a planned activity such as athletic competition, nature study, etc. **2.** *Informal.* An opportunity for expressing or asserting oneself with great pleasure or triumph: *He had a field day answering questions about cowboy heroes.*

field·er |fēl'dər| *n.* In baseball, a player stationed defensively in the field.

field glasses. Portable binoculars designed for outdoor use. [SEE PICTURE]

field goal. **1.** In football, a score of three points made by a place kick that propels the ball above the crossbar of the opposing team's goal posts. **2.** In basketball, a score of two points made during regular play by throwing the ball through the basket defended by the opposing team.

field magnet. A magnet used to provide a magnetic field needed for the operation of a machine such as a motor or generator.

field marshal. An officer in some European armies, usually ranking just below the commander in chief.

field trip. An organized trip made by a group to observe and learn, as by visiting a museum.

fiend |fēnd| *n.* **1.** An evil spirit; demon: *Captain Hook at first thought Peter was some fiend fighting him.* **2.** An evil or wicked person. **3.** *Informal.* A person absorbed in, addicted to, or obsessed with a certain job, pastime, etc.: *a baseball fiend; a fresh-air fiend.*

fiend·ish |fēn'dĭsh| *adj.* Of or like a fiend; evil, savage, or cruel: *a fiendish weapon.* —**fiend'ish·ly** *adv.* —**fiend'ish·ness** *n.*

fierce |fîrs| *adj.* **fierc·er, fierc·est.** **1.** Wild and savage; ferocious: *a fierce beast; the fierce roar of the lion; a wild stallion with fierce eyes.* **2.** Extreme in degree; intense: *fierce loyalty.* —**fierce'ly** *adv.* —**fierce'ness** *n.*

fier·y |fīr'ē| *or* |fī'ə rē| *adj.* **fier·i·er, fier·i·est.** **1.** Of, containing, consisting of, or like fire: *the fiery crater of the volcano; the fiery path of a comet across the sky; a fiery sunset.* **2.** Very hot: *the fiery pavements of the city.* **3. a.** Emitting or appearing to emit sparks; glowing; gleaming: *two fiery eyes in the darkness.* **b.** Reddish in color, like fire: *a youth with fiery hair; the pheasant's fiery tail feathers.* **4. a.** Charged with emotion, spirit, etc.; high-spirited: *a fiery speech; knights on fiery steeds.* **b.** Easily stirred up or provoked; tempestuous: *a fiery temper.* —**fier'i·ly** *adv.* —**fier'i·ness** *n.*

fi·es·ta |fē ĕs'tə| *n.* **1.** A religious festival, especially one celebrated in Spanish-speaking countries. **2.** Any celebration or festive occasion.

fife |fīf| *n.* A small high-pitched musical instrument similar to a flute, often used with drums to accompany military music. [SEE NOTE & PICTURE]

fif·teen |fĭf tēn'| *n.* A number, written 15 in Arabic numerals, that is equal to the sum of 14 + 1. It is the positive integer that immediately follows 14. —**fif·teen'** *adj. & pron.*

fif·teenth |fĭf tēnth'| *n.* **1.** In a set of items arranged to match the natural numbers in a one-to-one correspondence, the item that matches the number fifteen. **2.** One of fifteen equal parts, written 1/15. —**fif·teenth'** *adj. & adv.*

fifth |fĭfth| *n.* **1.** In a set of items arranged to match the natural numbers in a one-to-one correspondence, the item that matches five. **2.** One of five equal parts, written 1/5. **3.** A measure of liquid capacity equal to one fifth of a gallon, used mainly for alcoholic beverages. **4. a.** The interval between two musical tones that are seven semitones apart. **b.** The musical tone five steps above the tonic of a diatonic scale; the dominant. —**fifth** *adj. & adv.*

fif·ti·eth |fĭf'tē ĭth| *n.* **1.** In a set of items arranged to match the natural numbers in a one-to-one correspondence, the item that matches the number fifty. **2.** One of fifty equal parts, written 1/50. —**fif'ti·eth** *adj. & adv.*

fif·ty |fĭf'tē| *n., pl.* **fif·ties.** A number, written 50 in Arabic numerals, that is equal to the product of 5 × 10. It is the tenth positive integer after 40. —**fif'ty** *adj. & pron.*

fif·ty-fif·ty |fĭf'tē fĭf'tē| *Informal. adj.* **1.** Equally balanced between favorable and unfavorable: *a fifty-fifty chance to win the game.* **2.** Divided or shared equally: *They agreed on a fifty-fifty split of* *the money.* —*adv.* Equally: *The cookies were divided fifty-fifty by the two children.*

fig[1] |fĭg| *n.* **1. a.** A sweet, pear-shaped, many-seeded fruit that grows in warm regions. **b.** A tree that bears such fruit. **2.** The least bit or amount: *I don't care a fig about that.* —**modifier:** *a fig tree.* [SEE NOTE & PICTURE]

fig[2] |fĭg| *n. Informal.* **1.** Dress; array: *in full fig for the prom.* **2.** Physical condition: *He was in good fig for the tennis match.* [SEE NOTE]

fig. figure.

fight |fīt| *v.* **fought** |fôt|, **fight•ing. 1. a.** To struggle against (something or someone) with the hands or with weapons: *The gladiator fought the bear in the arena. They fought bravely against the invaders.* **b.** To take part in a struggle, battle, etc.: *The troops fought with Grant against the Confederates at Vicksburg.* **2.** To carry on or engage in: *fight a battle; fight a duel.* **3.** To struggle in any way, as by using arguments, skill, will power, etc.; put forth much effort to accomplish something: *He fought for freedom. He fought to get the plan adopted.* **4.** To quarrel; argue: *The two brothers fought bitterly.* **5.** To strive to overcome, suppress, defeat, or destroy: *fight down panic; fight disease; fight a forest fire.* **6.** To box or wrestle in the ring. **7.** To make (one's way) with great difficulty, as by combat: *He fought his way through the dense brush. The actress fought her way to the top.* —**phrasal verb. fight off.** To battle or act successfully against (an enemy or other hostile force): *They fought off the invaders. The medicine fights off disease germs.* —*n.* **1. a.** A physical conflict involving two or more people or animals: *a fist fight; a dog fight.* **b.** A quarrel. **2.** A battle waged between two opposing forces: *one of the fiercest fights of that campaign.* **3.** A boxing or wrestling match; a bout: *tickets for the fight.* **4.** Any vigorous or difficult struggle: *the fight for freedom.* **5.** A contest of wits, skill, or power: *a fight over the issue in the Senate.* **6.** The power or will to battle or struggle: *The hunted animal was exhausted and had little fight left.*

Idioms. **fight it out.** To battle or struggle until one side has won or otherwise been totally successful: *The men stayed in the Alamo to fight it out.* **fight shy of.** To keep away from; avoid.

fight•er |fī'tər| *n.* **1.** A person or animal who fights: *brave fighters in the battle; a fish that is quite a fighter.* **2.** A boxer or wrestler. **3.** Anyone who struggles or battles with determination or vigor for or against something: *a fighter in the courts; fire fighters.* **4.** Also **fighter plane.** A fast, maneuverable aircraft used in combat.

fig•ment |fĭg'mənt| *n.* Something produced by the imagination.

fig•ur•a•tive |fĭg'yər ə tĭv| *adj.* Based on, using, or containing figures of speech; not literal; metaphorical: *the figurative language of poetry; a figurative use of a word.* —**fig'ur•a•tive•ly** *adv.*

fig•ure |fĭg'yər| *n.* **1.** A written symbol, especially a numeral, that is not part of an alphabet. **2. figures.** Calculations that involve numbers; arithmetic: *a good head for figures.* **3.** In geometry, a subset of a plane or of space, for example, a union of lines or line segments or a union of planes or portions of planes. **4.** An amount represented in numbers: *a population figure.* **5. a.** A diagram, picture, or illustration: *On that page the figure on the right shows a bird in flight.* **b.** A design or pattern, as on cloth. **6.** The shape or form of a human body, especially as to weight and proportions: *Each girl buys clothes to suit her figure.* **7.** A body or form that is recognized as human or animal, though not necessarily seen in detail: *a tall figure standing in the doorway.* **8.** A representation of a person or animal, as in sculpture or painting: *stone figures in the garden; lifelike figures in wax.* **9.** An individual; especially a well-known person: *an important public figure.* **10.** The impression someone makes through his appearance or actions: *He cuts a fine figure in his new suit.* **11.** A short melodic, rhythmic, or harmonic unit, often expanded into a larger musical phrase or structure; a motif: *the opening figure of Beethoven's Fifth Symphony.* **12.** A group of movements in a dance: *the lovely figures of the minuet.* **13.** A **figure of speech.** —*v.* **fig•ured, fig•ur•ing. 1. a.** To work out by mathematics; calculate: *figured the cost of something; figure out his income tax.* **b.** To reach a conclusion about; decide on: *He figured some way to get across the mountain. She figured out the pronunciation of a new word.* **2. a.** *Informal.* To believe, imagine, or conclude: *I figured that you'd want to play baseball.* **b.** *Informal.* To interpret or understand: *I can't figure that fellow.* **3. figure on.** To depend on, plan on, or look forward to: *You can always figure on him to be on time. He figured on fishing from the river bank.* **4.** *Slang.* To seem logical, reasonable, or normal: *They decided to work as a team, and it really figured because they worked well together.* **5.** To be a part of; have importance: *The little sister just did not figure in her brothers' plans to build a hut.*

fig•ured |fĭg'yərd| *adj.* Decorated with designs or with a pattern: *figured wallpaper.*

fig•ure•head |fĭg'yər hĕd'| *n.* **1.** A person who heads a country or organization in name only, lacking actual power. **2.** A carved, decorative figure on the prow of a ship. [SEE PICTURE]

figure of speech. An expression in which words are used, not in their literal meanings, but to create vivid or dramatic effects. For example, metaphor, simile, hyperbole, and personification are common figures of speech.

fig•u•rine |fĭg'yə rēn'| *n.* A small ornamental figure made of wood, porcelain, glass, etc.; a statuette.

Fi•ji |fē'jē|. A group of islands in the southwestern Pacific Ocean, constituting an independent country. Population, 560,000. Capital, Suva.

fil•a•gree |fĭl'ə grē'| *n.* & *v.* A form of the word **filigree.**

fil•a•ment |fĭl'ə mənt| *n.* **1. a.** A fine wire that is enclosed in the bulb of an electric lamp and that is heated by the passage of current until it gives off light. **b.** An electrically heated wire that heats the cathode of some electron tubes. **2.** Any fine or slender thread, strand, fiber, etc.

fil•bert |fĭl'bərt| *n.* A hazelnut of a kind cultivated for eating.

filch |fĭlch| *v.* To steal (something) furtively; pilfer.

file[1] |fīl| *n.* **1. a.** A collection of papers, cards, etc., arranged in order: *a picture file.* **b.** The

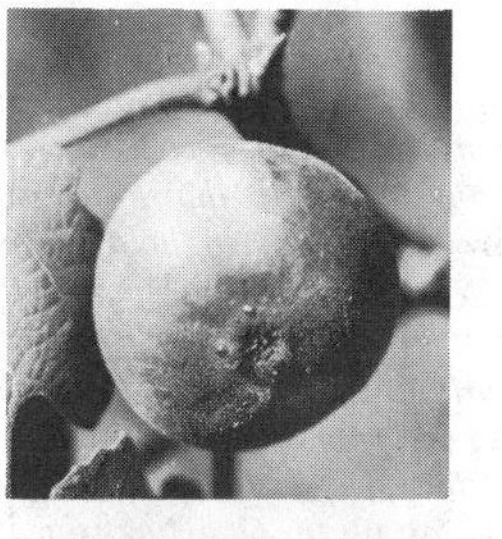

fig[1]
Above: Fruit
Below: Leaf

fig[1-2]
Fig[1] *is from Old French* figue, *which is ultimately from Latin* ficus, *"fig." The fig is native to the Mediterranean region, and it is probable that the word* ficus *was borrowed from the people who lived there before the ancestors of the Romans entered Italy.* **Fig[2]** *is of obscure origin; it first appeared in the nineteenth century.*

figurehead

file¹·²
The original office filing system (sense 1 of **file¹***) consisted of a string or wire that was stuck through papers to hold them in order. The word* **file¹** *comes from Old French* fil, *which is from Latin* filum, *"thread." (Sense 2 of* **file¹** *is from the Old French word, in the sense "line.")* **File²** *was* fēol *or* fīl *in Old English; it is descended from prehistoric Germanic* fīhala, *"cutting tool."*

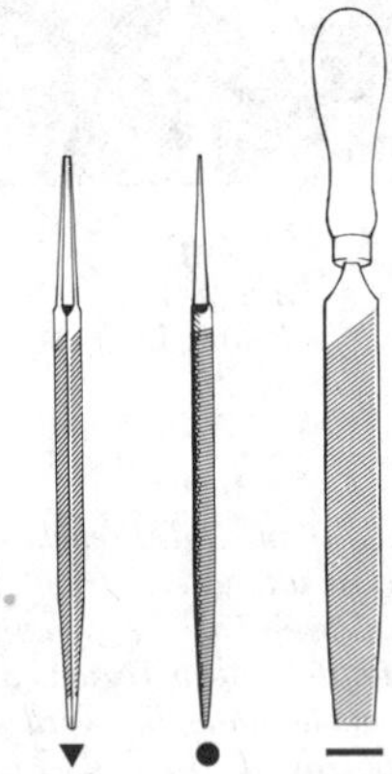

file²
Left to right: Taper file, round file, flat file (cross sections below)

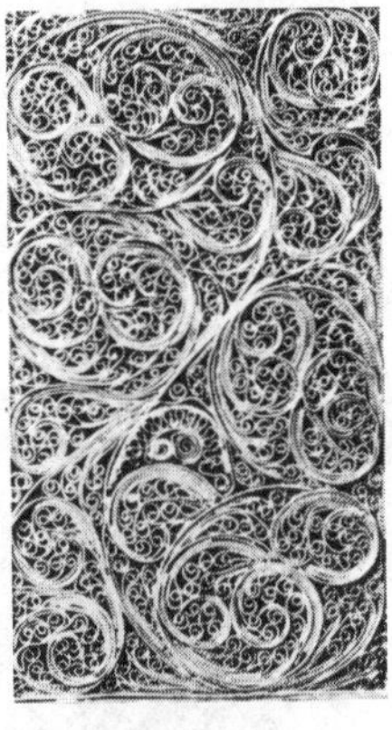

filigree

ă pat/ā pay/â care/ä father/ĕ pet/ ē be/ĭ pit/ī pie/î fierce/ŏ pot/ ō go/ô paw, for/oi oil/o͝o book/ o͞o boot/ou out/ŭ cut/û fur/ *th* the/th thin/hw which/zh vision/ ə ago, item, pencil, atom, circus

piece of furniture, drawer, box, or folder in which such a collection is kept: *The papers were stacked in huge files along the walls.* **2.** A collection of related data for a computer. **3.** A line of persons, animals, or things positioned one behind the other. *—modifier: a file card; a file clerk.* —*v.* **filed, fil•ing. 1.** To put or keep (papers, cards, etc.) in useful order; catalogue: *He filed reports, assignments, and library cards in a place where he could find them.* **2.** To submit (a story, report, etc.): *He rushed off to file his telegram to the newspapers.* **3.** To enter (a document) on public record or official record: *file a claim.* **4. a.** To present or hand in for consideration: *file an application for a job.* **b.** To apply: *file for a job.* **5.** To walk in a line or lines: *The nine justices, wearing black silk robes, filed in.* ¶*These sound alike* **file, faille.** [SEE NOTE]

file² |fīl| *n.* A steel tool having a series of sharp ridged edges, used in smoothing, shaping, or grinding down. —*v.* **filed, fil•ing.** To smooth, grind, or remove with a file. ¶*These sound alike* **file, faille.** [SEE NOTE & PICTURE]

fi•let¹ |fĭ lā′| *or* |fĭl′ā′| *n.* A net or lace with a background pattern of open squares over which designs may be darned.

fi•let² |fĭ lā′| *or* |fĭl′ā′| *n. & v.* A form of the word **fillet.**

fi•let mi•gnon |fĭ lā′ mĭn yŏn′|. A small, choice cut of beef from the loin.

fil•i•al |fĭl′ē əl| *adj.* Of or befitting a son or daughter in relation to a parent: *filial respect.* **—fil′i•al•ly** *adv.*

fil•i•bus•ter |fĭl′ə bŭs′tər| *n.* **1.** The tactic, used especially in the U.S. Senate, of delaying or trying to prevent the passage of legislation by making extremely prolonged speeches. **2.** An example of the use of this tactic: *The senator's filibuster against the bill failed in every respect.* —*v.* To use a filibuster in a legislative body.

fil•i•gree |fĭl′ĭ grē′| *n.* **1.** Lacelike ornamental work of twisted gold or silver wire. **2.** Any lacy, delicate design: *a filigree of light and shade. —modifier: filigree earrings; filigree frost.* —*v.* **fil•i•greed, fil•i•gree•ing.** To decorate with filigree: *Frost filigreed the glass.* [SEE PICTURE]

fil•ing |fī′lĭng| *n.* Often **filings.** Particles scraped off by a file.

Fil•i•pi•no |fĭl′ə pē′nō| *n., pl.* **Fil•i•pi•nos.** A native or inhabitant of the Philippines. —*adj.* Of the Philippines or the Filipinos.

fill |fĭl| *v.* **1.** To make or become full: *fill a glass; fill a theater. The boat sprang a leak and began to fill.* **2. a.** To occupy the whole of: *Smoke filled the room.* **b.** To be found throughout; pervade: *The valley was filled with the blue color of dusk.* **3.** To occupy or hold (a position, office, etc.): *He filled a new spot in the World Series.* **4.** To occupy the whole of (the mind, thoughts, etc.); consume: *The idea of the circus filled her with excitement.* **5.** To supply (a blank space) with writing, pictures, etc.: *Fill the blanks with the correct numerals.* **6.** To stop or plug up (an opening, hole, etc.): *fill a hole in the sidewalk with cement; fill teeth.* **7.** To satisfy or meet; fulfill: *fill the requirements for the job.* **8.** To supply or gather together the necessary materials for: *fill a prescription; fill an order for 20 books. —phrasal verbs.* **fill in. 1.** To make or become full or blocked, as with silt: *After many years, this soil filled in the sea.* **2.** To complete by writing in: *Take the form and fill in the blanks.* **3.** To substitute for: *The young Mantle filled in ably for DiMaggio.* **fill out.** To complete by writing in; fill in: *How did you know how to fill out the application?* **fill up.** To make or become full or overfull. —*n.* An amount that is needed to make full, complete, or satisfied: *I like baseball, but I've had my fill today. Eat your fill.*

Idioms. **fill (someone) in on.** *Informal.* To provide someone with new facts, details, etc. **fill (someone's) shoes.** To take someone's position and handle it properly.

fil•let. *n.* **1.** |fĭl′ĭt|. A narrow strip of material, especially a band or ribbon worn around the hair. **2.** |fĭ lā′| *or* |fĭl′ā′|. A boneless piece of meat or fish. —*v.* |fĭ lā′| *or* |fĭl′ā′| **fil•let•ed** |fĭ lād′| *or* |fĭl′ād′|, **fil•let•ing** |fĭ lā′ĭng| *or* |fĭl′ā′ĭng|. To remove the bones from (a piece of meat or fish).

fill-in |fĭl′ĭn′| *n.* Someone or something that fills in.

fill•ing |fĭl′ĭng| *n.* Something used to fill a space, cavity, or container: *a custard filling in a pie; a gold filling in a tooth.*

filling station. A **gas station.**

fil•lip |fĭl′əp| *n.* A mild incentive; stimulus: *Seven important summer festivals in the area provide an extra fillip for tourists.*

Fill•more |fĭl′môr′| *or* |-mōr′|, **Millard.** 1800–1874. Thirteenth President of the United States (1850–53).

fil•ly |fĭl′ē| *n., pl.* **fil•lies.** A young female horse; young mare.

film |fĭlm| *n.* **1.** A thin sheet or strip of flexible cellulose coated with materials that are sensitive to light, used in recording photographic images. **2. a.** A motion picture; movie. **b.** Motion pictures as an art; the cinema. **3.** A membranous covering: *The kittens' eyes were still covered with a bluish film.* **4.** A haze or mist: *Jellyfishes floated among the corals like a film of fog.* **5.** A thin coating, layer, or sheet: *a film of paint; a film of dust; a plastic film. —modifier: a film version of "Porgy and Bess."* —*v.* **1.** To make a movie of: *I filmed the porpoises in close-up while swimming alongside them.* **2.** To cover or become covered with or as if with a film.

film•strip |fĭlm′strĭp′| *n.* A strip of film for projection one picture or frame at a time.

film•y |fĭl′mē| *adj.* **film•i•er, film•i•est. 1.** Thin and transparent; gauzy: *filmy curtains.* **2.** Covered by or as if by a film; hazy or misty. **—film′i•ly** *adv.* **—film′i•ness** *n.*

fil•ter |fĭl′tər| *n.* **1. a.** A device containing a porous substance through which a liquid or gas is passed in order to remove unwanted components, especially suspended material. **b.** The porous material used in such a device. **2.** Any of a number of devices that operate on electric currents, electromagnetic waves, sound waves, etc., in a way that allows waves of certain frequencies to pass while those of other frequencies are blocked. —*v.* **1.** To pass or flow through or as if through a filter: *filter water; filter through enemy lines; light filtering through the shutters.* **2.** To remove or purify by means of a filter. ¶*These sound alike* **filter, philter.**

fil•ter•a•ble |fĭl′tər ə bəl| *adj.* **1.** Capable of being filtered. **2.** Small enough to pass through an exceedingly fine filter: *a filterable virus.*

filth |fĭlth| *n.* **1.** Foul or dirty matter: *Insects like flies carry filth that spreads disease germs.* **2.** A dirty, unhealthy, or corrupt condition; foulness: *diseases caused by filth, ignorance, and privation.* **3.** Anything that disgusts or offends, especially obscenity.

filth•y |**fĭl′**thē| *adj.* **filth•i•er, filth•i•est. 1.** Extremely dirty. **2. a.** Obscene: *a filthy picture.* **b.** Vile; nasty: *a filthy trick.* —**filth′i•ness** *n.*

fil•trate |**fĭl′**trāt′| *v.* **fil•trat•ed, fil•trat•ing.** To filter. —*n.* The part of the material that, when put into a filter, passes through it.

fil•tra•tion |fĭl **trā′**shən| *n.* The act or process of filtering.

fin[1] |fĭn| *n.* **1.** One of the thin, flat parts that extend from the body of a fish and are used for moving through and balancing in the water. Some whales and other water animals also have fins. **2.** A fixed or movable vane or airfoil used to stabilize an aircraft, missile, etc. **3.** A flexible piece of rubber attached to each foot to give added propulsion while swimming. [SEE NOTE & PICTURE]

fin[2] |fĭn| *n. Slang.* A five-dollar bill. [SEE NOTE]

fi•na•gle |fĭ **nā′**gəl| *v.* **fi•na•gled, fi•na•gling.** *Informal.* To get or achieve by tricky or crafty methods. —**fi•na′gler** *n.*

fi•nal |**fī′**nəl| *adj.* **1.** Coming at the end; last; concluding: *final preparations before leaving.* **2.** Ultimate and definitive; decisive: *the final struggle against Napoleon. The judge's decision is final.* **3.** *Informal.* Definite and absolute: *You're not going out tonight, and that's final.* —*n.* **1.** Often **finals.** The last game or games in a series of games or a tournament. **2.** The last examination of an academic course.

fi•na•le |fĭ **năl′**ē| *or* |-**nä′**lē| *n.* The final section of something that is performed, especially the ending of a musical composition.

fi•nal•ist |**fī′**nə lĭst| *n.* A contestant in the finals of a competition.

fi•nal•i•ty |fī **năl′**ĭ tē| *n., pl.* **fi•nal•i•ties.** The quality of being final; decisiveness: *The nurse spoke loudly and with finality.*

fi•nal•ize |**fī′**nə līz′| *v.* **fi•nal•ized, fi•nal•iz•ing.** To put into final form; complete. —**fi′nal•iz′er** *n.*

fi•nal•ly |**fī′**nə lē| *adv.* **1.** At last: *A taxi finally arrived to take us to the airport.* **2.** At the end; last.

fi•nance |fĭ **năns′**| *or* |**fī′**năns′| *n.* **1.** The management and use of funds, especially by government and big business. **2.** The science of the management of money and other assets: *the literature of finance.* **3. finances.** Money resources; funds: *His finances were getting low.* —*modifier: finance charges.* —*v.* **fi•nanced, fi•nanc•ing.** To provide funds or capital for.

fi•nan•cial |fĭ **năn′**shəl| *or* |fī-| *adj.* Of or having to do with finance or those who deal with finances: *a financial disaster; a financial backer.* —**fi•nan′cial•ly** *adv.*

fin•an•cier |fĭn′ən **sîr′**| *or* |fī′nən-| *n.* A person who is engaged in or expert in large-scale financial affairs.

finch |fĭnch| *n.* Any of several related birds with a short, thick bill used for cracking seeds. The cardinal, canary, and common house sparrow are finches.

find |fīnd| *v.* **found** |found|, **find•ing. 1.** To discover in a particular place; come upon by chance or accident: *I found this on the stairs.* **2.** To look for and discover: *Help Mary find her pen.* **3.** To learn: *Are you surprised to find that sound is a form of energy?* **4.** To get or come upon by investigating or calculating; determine: *Find the answers to these problems.* **5.** To meet with; encounter: *They found hot weather, fevers, and wild animals. Ants are found almost everywhere.* **6.** To recover (something lost): *Did you ever find your keys?* **7.** To reach; achieve: *It was through sports that his intense competitive spirit found an outlet.* **8.** To determine to be guilty or innocent: *The jury found him guilty.* —*phrasal verb.* **find out.** To get information about something; ascertain: *Scientists try to find out as much as they can about the world.* —*n.* Anything come upon or discovered: *news of rich gold and oil finds in the north.*

find•er |**fīn′**dər| *n.* **1.** Someone who finds something. **2.** A device, usually an auxiliary lens or telescope, used to see what a camera or large telescope is aimed at.

find•ing |**fīn′**dĭng| *n.* **1.** The act or an example of discovering. **2. findings. a.** The results or conclusions of an investigation. **b.** Discoveries; finds: *recent oil findings in the Sahara.* **3. findings.** Small articles used in a craft or trade.

fine[1] |fīn| *adj.* **fin•er, fin•est. 1.** Consisting of small particles; not coarse: *fine buckwheat flour; the fine spray of a garden hose.* **2.** Of very small thickness or weight: *fine silk; fine linen paper; fine hair.* **3.** Very thin or sharp; cut or honed to great sharpness: *a fine arrowpoint made by using small flaking tools; a blade with a fine edge.* **4.** Of delicate texture: *fine skin.* **5. a.** Delicately exacting and painstaking: *Cutting that stone was fine work, and he just had to sweat it out.* **b.** Marked by refinement and delicacy of workmanship: *She wanted to get him something really nice, something fine and rare.* **6.** Delicate and subtle in quality: *Irish hams are well known for their fine flavor.* **7.** Fashionably elegant: *all the branches of knowledge necessary to the education of a fine lady; fine new clothes.* **8.** Of superior quality, skill, or appearance; admirable; splendid: *a fine horse; a fine day; a fine performance.* **9.** In good health; quite well: *I'm fine, thank you.* **10.** —Used as an intensive: *This is a fine fix you have got us in!* —*interj.* A word used to indicate agreement or acquiescence: *How about taking in a movie? Fine!* —*adv.* Very well; splendidly: *The two of us are getting along just fine.* —**fine′ness** *n.* [SEE NOTE]

fine[2] |fīn| *n.* A sum of money imposed as a penalty for an offense. —*v.* **fined, fin•ing.** To impose a fine on. [SEE NOTE]

fine arts. The arts of painting, sculpture, and architecture, especially as presented in an academic curriculum.

fine-drawn |**fīn′drôn′**| *adj.* Drawn to the finest subtlety; extremely fine: *a fine-drawn analysis.*

fine•ly |**fīn′**lē| *adv.* **1.** In a fine manner; excellently; splendidly: *a finely dressed lady.* **2.** Delicately: *her finely chiseled features. The submerged leaves are finely lobed into threadlike segments.* **3.** In small pieces: *Sprinkle the soup with bits of crisp bacon and finely cut parsley.*

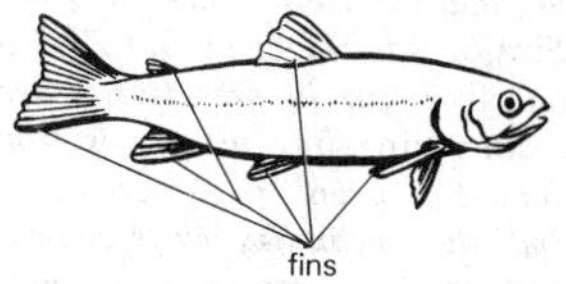

fin[1]
Fins of a fish

fin[1-2]
Fin[1] *was* finn *in Old English; its cognates in other West Germanic languages include German* finne *and Dutch* vin. **Fin[2]** *is an early twentieth-century slang borrowing from Yiddish* finf, *"five"; this is descended from Old High German* finf *or* funf *(modern German* fünf*) and is cognate with Old English* fīf, *"five." See note at* **five.**

fine[1-2]
These words are from Latin fīnis, *"end."* **Fine[2]** *is from Old French* fin, *meaning "end" and descended from* fīnis; *in medieval law,* fin *was used to mean "the end of a case" or "money paid to settle a case," hence the meaning of* **fine[2]**. **Fine[1]** *is from another Old French word* fin, *this one an adjective meaning "excellent"; this developed indirectly from Latin* fīnis, *which was sometimes used to mean "the summit, the ultimate."*

finger
The decimal system of counting derives from the fact that human beings have two hands with five digits each. The word **finger** *itself originally meant "one of five."* **Finger** *was* finger *in Old English and* fingwraz *in prehistoric Germanic.* Fingwraz *in turn is from Indo-European* penkweros *(an Indo-European* p- *always changes to* f- *in the Germanic languages).* Penkweros *meant "one of five," from* penkwe, *"five." See note at* **five**.

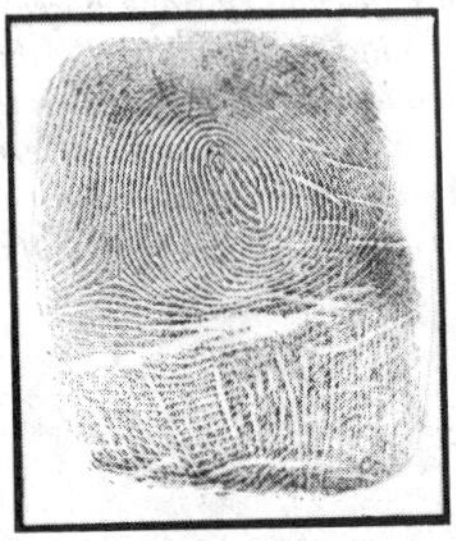

fingerprint
A right index finger

ă pat/ā pay/â care/ä father/ĕ pet/ ē be/ĭ pit/ī pie/î fierce/ŏ pot/ ō go/ô paw, for/oi oil/ŏŏ book/ ōō boot/ou out/ŭ cut/û fur/ *th* the/th thin/hw which/zh vision/ ə ago, item, pencil, atom, circus

fin•er•y |fī′nə rē| *n., pl.* **fin•er•ies.** Fine or fancy clothes and ornaments: *She came decked out in her spring finery.*

fi•nesse |fĭ nĕs′| *n.* **1.** Restraint and delicacy of performance or behavior: *His new sports car demands both finesse and strength to drive.* **2.** Subtlety; tact: *show finesse in handling a difficult situation.*

fin•ger |fĭng′gər| *n.* **1. a.** Any one of the five body parts that extend outward from the hand and that can be curled up, as in making a fist. **b.** One of these parts other than the thumb. **2.** The part of a glove that fits over a finger. **3.** Something resembling a finger. **4.** A controlling interest; concern. —*v.* **1.** To play (a musical instrument) by using the fingers in a particular way. **2.** To handle or feel with the fingers; touch: *The rancher stooped to finger the dry soil.* [SEE NOTE]
Idioms. **keep (one's) fingers crossed.** To hope for the best while watching out for the worst. **lay a finger on (someone).** To touch, especially with intent to harm. **put (one's) finger on.** To pin down or define.

finger bowl. A small bowl to hold water for rinsing the fingers at the table after a meal.

fin•ger•ing |fĭng′gər ĭng| *n.* **1.** The use of or technique of using the fingers in playing a musical instrument. **2.** Symbols in a musical score that indicate which fingers are to be used in playing.

fin•ger•ling |fĭng′gər lĭng| *n.* A young or small fish, such as a young salmon or trout.

fin•ger•nail |fĭng′gər nāl′| *n.* The thin sheet of horny, transparent material that covers and protects the back of the tip of each finger.

fin•ger•print |fĭng′gər prĭnt′| *n.* An impression formed by the curves in the ridges in the skin that covers the tip of the fingers, used as a way of identifying people. —*v.* To make a record of the fingerprints of. [SEE PICTURE]

finger tip. The extreme tip or end of a finger.

fin•ger•tip |fĭng′gər tĭp′| *n.* A form of the phrase **finger tip.**

fin•ick•y |fĭn′ĭ kē| *adj.* Very fussy; difficult to please.

fi•nis |fĭn′ĭs| *or* |fī′nĭs| *n.* The end.

fin•ish |fĭn′ĭsh| *v.* **1. a.** To cease or get done with doing (something): *All birds molt in late summer or early fall, after they finish nesting.* **b.** To reach the end of a task, course, etc.: *She started but never finished.* **2.** To complete: *Finish each of the following sentences.* **3.** To consume all of; use up: *finish a meal.* **4.** To kill, destroy, or wear out completely: *finish an enemy. That hike finished me.* **5.** To put the final touches on; perfect: *finish a painting.* **6.** To hem, trim, line, or decorate (a garment). **7.** To give (wood) a desired surface texture, as by treating with a finish: *Two cans of varnish are enough to finish that floor.* —*n.* **1.** The conclusion of something; the end: *His plan was crazy, but he was going to carry it off to the finish.* **2. a.** The last treatment or coating of a surface. **b.** The surface texture produced: *a smooth finish.* **3.** The material used in surfacing or finishing something.

fin•ished |fĭn′ĭsht| *adj.* **1.** Completed; ended. **2.** Skilled; accomplished. **3.** Perfected: *A final pressing should give your blouse a finished look.* **4.** Completely processed: *the finished product.*

finishing school. A private school where girls finish their education and are prepared for their entrance into society.

fi•nite |fī′nīt′| *adj.* **1.** Having bounds; not infinite; limited. **2. a.** Having a magnitude that is less than or equal to that of some number that can be reached by counting: *a finite sum.* **b.** Having a finite number as its measure: *a finite region.* **3.** In grammar, limited by person, number, and tense; for example, *am, is,* and *are* are finite verb forms as distinguished from *being* or *been.* —**fi′nite•ly** *adv.* —**fi′nite•ness** *n.*

Fin•land |fĭn′lənd|. A country of north-central Europe. Population, 4,692,000. Capital, Helsinki.

Finn |fĭn| *n.* A native or inhabitant of Finland.

finned |fĭnd| *adj.* **1.** Having a fin or fins: *a finned whale.* **2.** Having a certain kind or number of fins: *a spiny-finned fish.*

Fin•nish |fĭn′ĭsh| *n.* The language of Finland, related to Hungarian. —*adj.* Of Finland, the Finns, or their language.

fiord |fyôrd| *or* |fyōrd| *n.* A form of the word **fjord.**

fir |fûr| *n.* **1.** Any of several cone-bearing evergreen trees with rather flat needles. **2.** The wood of such a tree. —***modifier:*** *a fir forest.* ¶*These sound alike* **fir, fur.**

fire |fīr| *n.* **1.** A rapid, self-sustaining chemical reaction that releases light and heat, especially the burning of something in oxygen. **2.** A destructive burning: *a forest fire. He insured his house against fire.* **3.** Great enthusiasm; ardor. **4.** The discharge of a gun or guns: *artillery fire.* —*v.* **fired, fir•ing. 1.** To treat with or expose to heat, as by baking in a kiln or oven: *firing clay pottery.* **2.** To feed the fire of: *fire a furnace.* **3.** To detonate or shoot (a weapon): *fire a gun; fire at a target.* **4.** To launch (a rocket), usually by causing its fuel to start burning. **5.** To arouse; stimulate: *The lectures fired his enthusiasm.* **6.** *Informal.* To project or hurl suddenly and forcefully: *fire a ball at a batter; fire questions at a witness.* **7.** *Informal.* To discharge from a job; dismiss.
Idioms. **catch fire.** To become ignited. **hang fire. 1.** To fail to fire, as a gun. **2.** To be delayed, as an event or decision. **on fire.** Burning; ablaze; afire. **open fire.** To start shooting. **under fire.** Under attack: *The new law was under fire even before it was enforced.*

fire•arm |fīr′ärm′| *n.* Any weapon, especially a pistol or rifle, capable of firing a missile.

fire•ball |fīr′bôl′| *n.* **1.** The hot, brightly glowing, ball-shaped cloud of dust and gases formed by a nuclear explosion. **2.** A very bright meteor. **3.** Any bright, burning sphere, as a ball of fire or lightning. **4.** *Slang.* A very energetic person.

fire•brand |fīr′brănd′| *n.* **1.** A piece of burning wood. **2.** A person who stirs up trouble.

fire•bug |fīr′bŭg′| *n.* *Informal.* A person who deliberately sets fires; a pyromaniac.

fire•crack•er |fīr′krăk′ər| *n.* A small explosive charge in a cylinder of heavy paper, used to make noise, as at celebrations.

fire•damp |fīr′dămp′| *n.* A gas, chiefly methane, that occurs naturally in coal mines and forms an explosive mixture with air.

fire•dog |fīr′dôg′| *or* |-dŏg′| *n.* An andiron.

fire engine. A truck that carries firemen and equipment to fight a fire. [SEE PICTURE]
fire escape. A structure or device, such as an outside stairway attached to a building, used as an emergency exit in case of a fire. [SEE PICTURE]
fire extinguisher. A portable device containing chemicals that can be sprayed on a fire to put it out.
fire•fight•er |fīr′fī′tər| *n.* A person who fights fires, as a fireman. —**fire′fight′ing** *n.*
fire•fly |fīr′flī′| *n., pl.* **-flies.** A beetle that flies at night and gives off a flashing light from the rear part of its body.
fire•guard |fīr′gärd′| *n.* A **fire screen.**
fire•house |fīr′hous′| *n., pl.* **-hous•es** |-hou′zĭz|. A **fire station.**
fire irons. The equipment used to tend a fireplace, including a shovel, a poker, and tongs.
fire•less cooker |fīr′lĭs|. An insulated container that is preheated to permit the cooking of food.
fire•man |fīr′mən| *n., pl.* **-men** |-mən|. **1.** A man employed to fight fires. **2.** A man who feeds fuel to a fire in a furnace or locomotive engine; a stoker. **3.** An enlisted man in the U.S. Navy engaged in operating engineering machinery.
fire•place |fīr′plās′| *n.* An open recess for holding a fire at the base of a chimney.
fire•plug |fīr′plŭg′| *n.* A large upright pipe, usually on a curb, from which water can be drawn for fighting fires; a hydrant.
fire•proof |fīr′pro͞of′| *adj.* Made of material or materials that do not burn or that do not crack or break when exposed to heat or fire. —*v.* To make fireproof.
fire screen. A metal screen placed in front of an open fireplace to catch sparks.
fire•side |fīr′sīd′| *n.* **1.** The area surrounding a fireplace; hearth: *sitting about the fireside.* **2.** One's home: *A man has the right to the dignity of his own fireside after a day's work.*
fire station. A building for firefighting equipment and firemen.
fire•trap |fīr′trăp′| *n.* A building thought likely to catch fire easily or difficult to escape from in the event of fire.
fire truck. A **fire engine.**
fire•wa•ter |fīr′wô′tər| *or* |-wŏt′ər| *n. Slang.* Strong liquor, especially whiskey.
fire•weed |fīr′wēd′| *n.* A tall plant with reddish-purple flowers, often growing on ground that has recently been burned over.
fire•wood |fīr′wo͝od′| *n.* Wood used as fuel.
fire•works |fīr′wûrks′| *pl.n.* **1.** Explosives used to produce colored lights, smoke, and noise for entertainment at celebrations. **2.** A display of such devices.
firing line. **1.** The line of positions from which fire is directed against a target. **2.** The foremost position in an activity, controversy, etc.
firing pin. The part of the bolt of a firearm that strikes the primer and explodes the charge of the projectile.
fir•kin |fûr′kĭn| *n.* A small wooden barrel or keg, used especially for storing butter, cheese, or lard.
firm[1] |fûrm| *adj.* **firm•er, firm•est.** **1.** Unyielding to pressure; solid; hard: *firm ground.* **2.** Exhibiting the tone and resiliency characteristic of healthy tissue: *firm muscles. Plants need water to keep their leaves and stems firm.* **3.** Securely fixed in place: *In some parts of the skeleton two bones come together to form a firm, immovable structure.* **4.** Unwavering; steady: *a firm, brilliant tone.* **5.** Not changing; fixed: *a firm belief.* **6. a.** Constant and steady; not subject to dissolution: *a firm rapport with his employees; a firm partnership.* **b.** Strong and sure: *a firm grasp.* **7.** Steadfast: *a firm believer in athletics for everybody.* **8.** Showing or having resolution or determination: *a firm voice. I shall have to be firm about this subject.* —*adv.* Without wavering; resolutely: *The enemy stood firm and refused to surrender.* —*v.* To become firm: *Stock prices firmed up yesterday. The jelly firmed quickly.* —**firm′ly** *adv.* —**firm′ness** *n.* [SEE NOTE]
firm[2] |fûrm| *n.* A business establishment, especially one consisting of a partnership of two or more persons. [SEE NOTE]
fir•ma•ment |fûr′mə mənt| *n.* The heavens; sky.
first |fûrst| *adj.* **1.** Corresponding in order to the number one; coming before all others in time, order, rank, importance, etc.: *the first month of the year; the first chapter; the first in his class.* **2.** Highest in pitch or having the most important of a set of musical parts: *first soprano; first trumpet.* **3.** Of the transmission gear that produces the lowest speeds in an automobile. —*n.* **1.** In a set of items arranged to match the natural numbers in a one-to-one correspondence, the item that matches the number one. **2.** The beginning; outset: *At first I disliked spinach, but now I love it.* **3.** The first of a specified kind: *France boasts many aviation firsts.* **4.** The member of a set of similar voices or musical instruments that is highest in pitch or that has the principal part. **5.** The transmission gear in an automobile or truck that produces the lowest speeds. —*adv.* **1.** Before or above all others in time, rank, order, importance, etc.: *Who will speak first?* **2.** For the first time: *When did you first meet Mr. Jones?* **3.** Before some other specified or implied time: *First finish your work, then you may go.* **4.** In preference; rather: *He said he would quit first.*
first aid. Emergency care given to an injured or sick person before professional medical care is available.
first base. **1.** The first of the bases in the infield in baseball, counterclockwise from the home plate. **2.** The fielding position occupied by the first baseman. **3.** *Informal.* The first step in a project involving several steps: *The Senator's reform bill never got to first base.*
first-born |fûrst′bôrn′| *adj.* First in order of birth; born first. —*n.* The first-born child.
first class. **1.** The first, highest, or best group of some specified category. **2.** The most expensive class of accommodations on a train, ship, plane, etc. **3.** A class of mail including letters, post cards, and packages sealed against inspection.
first-class |fûrst′klăs′| *or* |-kläs′| *adj.* **1.** Of the first, highest, or best group of a certain category: *a first-class stateroom; first-class passengers.* **2.** Of the foremost excellence; fine: *a first-class mind.* —*adv.* **1.** In first-class accommodations:

fire engine

fire escape

firm[1·2]
Firm[1] *is from Latin* firmus, *"firm, steady, certain."* Firmus *produced the verb* firmāre, *"to make firm, to confirm, to promise." This remained in Italian as* firmare *and came to mean "to confirm something by signature, to sign with one's name." From* firmare *the noun* firma *was formed, meaning first "signature" and later "trademark, name of a business or partnership"; this was borrowed into English as* **firm**[2].

fisher

fishhook

fit[1-2]

Fit[1] *occurs first in the fourteenth century, as an adjective; its origin is obscure, but it seems to come from a verb* fitten, *meaning "to maneuver soldiers," hence perhaps "to arrange, to fit."* **Fit[2]** *originally meant "a painful or dangerous experience"; it was* fitt *in Old English, but it is unknown whether it is related to* **fit[1]**.

ă pat/ā pay/â care/ä father/ĕ pet/ ē be/ĭ pit/ī pie/î fierce/ŏ pot/ ō go/ô paw, for/oi oil/ŏŏ book/ ōō boot/ou out/ŭ cut/û fur/ *th* the/th thin/hw which/zh vision/ ə ago, item, pencil, atom, circus

They flew first-class. **2.** By first-class mail: *This box was mailed first-class.*

first•hand |**fûrst'hănd'**| *adj.* Received from the original source; direct: *firsthand observations; firsthand knowledge.* —*adv.* From the original source; by direct contact, observation, or experience: *learning firsthand about space.*

first•ly |**fûrst'**lē| *adv.* Before all others; in the first place; to begin with.

first person. **1. a.** A set of grammatical forms designating the speaker or writer of the sentence in which they appear. **b.** One of these forms; for example, *I* and *we* belong to this set. **2.** The style of storytelling in which such forms are used to tell the story: *a novel written in the first person.* —***modifier:*** **(first-person)***: a first-person account of the football game.*

first-rate |**fûrst'rāt'**| *adj.* **1.** Foremost in importance or rank: *a first-rate hotel.* **2.** Foremost in quality; excellent: *a first-rate mechanic.*

first-string |**fûrst'strĭng'**| *adj.* In sports, being the first choice to play a certain position on a team: *the first-string quarterback.*

first violin. A violin that plays the principal one of two or more violin parts.

firth |fûrth| *n.* A long, narrow inlet of the sea in Scotland.

fis•cal |**fĭs'**kəl| *adj.* **1.** Of the treasury or finances of a nation or branch of government: *an inflationary fiscal policy.* **2.** Of finances in general: *a fiscal agent.* —**fis'cal•ly** *adv.*

fiscal year. A 12-month period for which an organization plans the use of its funds.

fish |fĭsh| *n., pl.* **fish** or **fish•es.** **1.** Any of a large group of cold-blooded water animals having a backbone, fins, gills for breathing, and a streamlined body adapted for moving through water. **2.** The flesh of a fish, used as food. **3.** *Informal.* A person; fellow: *He's an odd fish.* —*v.* **1.** To catch or try to catch fish. **2.** To pull up or out in the manner of someone catching fish: *The children fished for coins in the fountain.* **3.** To seek by reaching into or groping in something: *She fished in her handbag for her keys.* **4.** To seek in a sly or indirect way: *He's always fishing for compliments.*

fish and chips. Fish fillets and sliced potatoes, both fried in deep fat.

fish•er |**fĭsh'**ər| *n.* **1.** Someone that fishes. **2.** A North American animal related to the mink and weasel and having thick, dark-brown fur. ¶*These sound alike* **fisher, fissure.** [SEE PICTURE]

fish•er•man |**fĭsh'**ər mən| *n., pl.* **-men** |-mən|. Someone who fishes as an occupation or for sport.

fish•er•y |**fĭsh'**ə rē| *n., pl.* **fish•er•ies.** **1.** The industry or occupation of fishing. **2.** A fishing ground: *the cod and haddock fisheries of the northwest Atlantic.*

fish•gig |**fĭsh'**gĭg'| *n.* A pronged fishing spear.

fish hawk. A bird, the osprey.

fish•hook |**fĭsh'**hŏŏk'| *n.* A barbed metal hook, attached to a line and baited, used for catching fish. [SEE PICTURE]

fish•ing |**fĭsh'**ĭng| *n.* The act or process of catching fish. —***modifier:*** *a fishing boat.*

fishing ground. A good place for fishing, especially for catching some particular kind of fish.

fishing rod. A long, slender rod with a hook, a line, and often a reel, used for catching fish.

fishing tackle. Equipment, such as hooks, lines, rods, reels, etc., used in catching fish.

fish•meal |**fĭsh'**mēl'| *n.* A mealy substance made from grinding up fish, especially menhaden. It is used as animal feed and fertilizer.

fish story. *Informal.* A boastful story that is probably not true.

fish•wife |**fĭsh'**wīf'| *n., pl.* **-wives** |-wīvz'|. **1.** *Archaic.* A woman who sells fish. **2.** A coarse, abusive woman; a shrew.

fish•y |**fĭsh'**ē| *adj.* **fish•i•er, fish•i•est.** **1.** Tasting or smelling of fish. **2.** Cold or expressionless: *fishy blue eyes.* **3.** *Informal.* Inspiring suspicion; unlikely; questionable: *something fishy about that excuse.*

fis•sion |**fĭsh'**ən| *n.* **1.** A reaction in which an atomic nucleus splits into fragments whose mass does not quite equal the mass of the original nucleus, the remaining mass being transformed into energy. **2.** A reproductive process in which a single cell splits to form two independent cells that later grow to full size.

fis•sion•a•ble |**fĭsh'**ə nə bəl| *adj.* Capable of undergoing nuclear fission.

fis•sure |**fĭsh'**ər| *n.* **1.** A long, narrow crack or opening, as in the face of a rock. **2.** A deep split, as in public opinion. ¶*These sound alike* **fissure, fisher.**

fist |fĭst| *n.* The hand closed tightly, with the fingers bent against the palm.

fist•ful |**fĭst'**fŏŏl'| *n., pl.* **fist•fuls.** A handful.

fist•i•cuffs |**fĭs'**tĭ kŭfs'| *pl.n.* **1.** Fighting with the fists. **2.** Boxing.

fis•tu•la |**fĭs'**chŏŏ lə| *n., pl.* **fis•tu•las** or **fis•tu•lae** |**fĭs'**chŏŏ lē'|. An abnormal passage from an abscess, cavity, or organ to the surface of the body or to another hollow organ.

fit[1] |fĭt| *v.* **fit•ted** or **fit, fit•ting.** **1.** To be the proper size and shape for (someone or something): *Does the shoe fit you? Yes, it fits.* **2.** To be appropriate or suitable to; be in keeping with: *His dignified appearance fitted his high office to perfection.* **3.** To adjust or alter to the size and shape desired: *The tailor fitted the suit on him.* **4.** To insert or adjust so as to be properly in place: *fit a handle on a door.* **5.** To equip or outfit: *fit out a ship for a long voyage; fit up a house with modern appliances.* **6. a.** To be in harmony with; agree: *His good mood fitted in with the joyousness of the occasion.* **b.** To be suited; belong: *She definitely does not fit in with those people.* —*n.* The way something fits: *a close fit; a perfect fit.* —*adj.* **fit•ter, fit•test.** **1.** Suited or adequate to a given circumstance or intention: *the fit time and place for the meeting. The dinner was not fit to eat.* **2.** Appropriate; proper: *Do it as you see fit. He did not think fit to follow my advice.* **3.** Physically sound; healthy: *keep fit.* [SEE NOTE]

fit[2] |fĭt| *n.* **1. a.** A sudden, violent appearance of a disease or a symptom of a disease: *a fit of malaria.* **b.** A convulsion. **2.** A sudden, violent spell of some emotion: *a fit of rage.* **3.** A sudden period of vigorous activity. [SEE NOTE]

Idiom. **by** (or **in**) **fits and starts.** With irregular intervals of action and inaction; intermittently.

fit•ful |**fĭt'**fəl| *adj.* **1.** Occurring in or as if in fits: *fitful coughing.* **2.** Interrupted by or as if by fits:

fitful sleep. —**fit'ful·ly** *adv.* —**fit'ful·ness** *n.*

fit·ter |fĭt'ər| *n.* **1.** A person who adjusts or alters clothes to make them fit. **2.** A person who installs or adjusts machinery.

fit·ting |fĭt'ĭng| *n.* **1.** A small, detachable part for a machine or mechanical device: *a pipe fitting.* **2.** A session of trying on clothes so that they can be made or adjusted to fit. —*adj.* Suitable; appropriate. —**fit'ting·ly** *adv.*

five |fīv| *n.* A number, written 5 in Arabic numerals, that is equal to the sum of 4 + 1. It is the positive integer that immediately follows 4. —**five** *adj. & pron.* [SEE NOTE]

five-and-dime |fīv'ən dīm'| *n.* A **five-and-ten-cent store.**

five-and-ten |fīv'ən tĕn'| *n.* A **five-and-ten-cent store.**

five-and-ten-cent store |fīv'ən tĕn'sĕnt'|. A variety store selling inexpensive commodities.

Five Nations. A confederation of five Iroquoian-speaking North American Indian tribes including the Mohawks, Oneidas, Onondagas, Cayugas, and Senecas.

fix |fĭks| *v.* **1.** To place or fasten securely: *fix a pole in the ground. "Fix bayonets" was the command.* **2.** To direct steadily: *She fixed her eyes on the screen.* **3.** To establish definitely; specify: *fix a time for the meeting.* **4.** To ascribe; place: *fix the blame.* **5.** To set right; repair: *fix a car; fix a drain.* **6.** To put together; make ready; prepare: *She is going to fix dinner for us.* **7.** To put in order; arrange: *She was tired of fixing her hair all the time.* **8.** To convert (nitrogen) into stable compounds that can be assimilated by living organisms. **9.** To mount (a specimen) for study under a microscope. **10.** To treat (a photographic image) with a chemical that prevents it from fading or changing color. **11.** To treat (a dyed material) with a substance that makes its color permanent. **12.** *Informal.* To get even with; take revenge upon: *"I'll fix him," she said in a rage.* **13.** *Informal.* To prearrange the outcome of by unlawful means: *fix a horse race; fix a fight.* —***phrasal verbs.*** **fix on** (or **upon**). To decide or agree on: *They fixed on Sunday the 15th as their wedding date.* **fix up.** *Informal.* **1.** To settle: *fix up an argument; fix up a contract.* **2.** To supply; provide: *We fixed him up with a new job.* **3.** To decorate or furnish: *She fixed up the room to serve as a guest bedroom.* —*n.* **1.** The position, as of a ship or aircraft, determined by observations or by radio. **2.** *Slang.* An injection of heroin or morphine.

fix·a·tion |fĭk sā'shən| *n.* **1.** The act or process of fixing: *fixation of nitrogen.* **2.** A strong attachment to a person or thing, usually formed in childhood or infancy and remaining as immature behavior in adulthood.

fix·a·tive |fĭk'sə tĭv| *n.* A substance used to treat something and make it permanent or resistant to change: *apply a fixative to the painting; add fixative to a perfume.*

fixed |fĭkst| *adj.* **1.** Firmly in position; immovable. **2.** Not subject to change or variation; constant. **3.** Firmly and often unreasonably held to: *a fixed idea.* **4.** *Informal.* Illegally prearranged as to outcome: *The game was fixed.* —**fix'ed·ly** |fĭk'sĭd lē| *adv.*

fixed star. A star so distant from the earth that its position with respect to other stars, unlike the positions of planets, always seems the same.

fix·ings |fĭk'sĭngz| *pl.n.* Accessories; trimmings: *"Ruffles! That's ladies' fixings," he snorted.*

fix·ture |fĭks'chər| *n.* **1.** An appliance or device, especially a part of a larger system, that is installed in a permanent location: *a plumbing fixture; an electrical fixture.* **2.** Someone or something likened to a fixture because permanently associated with a specified place, position, or function.

fizz |fĭz| *v.* To make a hissing or bubbling sound: *Limestone will fizz if you pour vinegar on it.* —*n.* **1.** A hissing or bubbling sound. **2.** A bubbly beverage: *a brandy fizz.*

fiz·zle |fĭz'əl| *v.* **fiz·zled, fiz·zling.** **1.** To make a hissing or sputtering sound, especially when going out: *The hot coals fizzled out in the water.* **2.** *Informal.* To fail or peter out, especially after a hopeful beginning: *The sales campaign fizzled almost before it began.* —*n. Informal.* A failure; fiasco.

fjord |fyôrd| *or* |fyōrd| *n.* A long, narrow inlet from the sea between steep cliffs or slopes.

fl, fl. fluid.

Fla. Florida.

flab·ber·gast |flăb'ər găst'| *v.* To confound or overwhelm with astonishment; astound.

flab·by |flăb'ē| *adj.* **flab·bi·er, flab·bi·est.** Lacking firmness; loose and soft: *flabby skin; flabby muscles.* —**flab'bi·ly** *adv.* —**flab'bi·ness** *n.*

flac·cid |flăk'sĭd| *or* |flăs'ĭd| *n.* Lacking firmness; soft and limp; flabby: *flaccid muscles.* —**flac·cid'i·ty, flac'cid·ness** *n.* —**flac'cid·ly** *adv.*

flac·on |flăk'ən| *n.* A small stoppered bottle, as for perfume.

flag¹ |flăg| *n.* A piece of cloth varying in size, color, and design, used as a symbol, signal, emblem, etc. —*v.* **flagged, flag·ging.** To signal with or as if with a flag. —***phrasal verb.*** **flag down.** To call and signal to stop; hail: *flag down a taxi.* [SEE NOTE]

flag² |flăg| *v.* **flagged, flag·ging.** To decline in vigor; slacken: *Our spirits flagged when we fell behind by two touchdowns.* [SEE NOTE]

flag³ |flăg| *n.* A wild iris or similar plant. [SEE NOTE]

flag⁴ |flăg| *n.* **1.** A slab of flagstone used for paving. **2.** Flagstone. [SEE NOTE]

fla·gel·la |flə jĕl'ə| *n.* Plural of **flagellum.**

flag·el·late |flăj'ə lāt'| *v.* **flag·el·lat·ed, flag·el·lat·ing.** To whip; flog. —*adj.* |flăj'ə lĭt| *or* |-lāt'|. **1.** Having a slender, whiplike projecting part, as certain one-celled organisms do. **2.** Slender and whiplike. —*n.* |flăj'ə lĭt| *or* |-lāt'|. A single-celled organism, such as a euglena, having one or more slender, whiplike projections used for moving through the water. —**flag'el·la'tion** *n.*

fla·gel·lum |flə jĕl'əm| *n., pl.* **fla·gel·la** |flə jĕl'ə|. A slender, whiplike strand extending from certain one-celled organisms and usually lashed back and forth as a means of moving through the water.

flag·eo·let |flăj'ə lĕt'| *or* |-lā'| *n.* A type of small flute having its mouthpiece at the extreme end rather than on the side.

flag·on |flăg'ən| *n.* A container for wine or other liquors, having a handle, a spout, and often a lid.

five

The prehistoric Indo-European word for "five" was penkwe, *with a variant form* pempe. *In Germanic,* pempe *changed to* fimfi, *and in Old English* fimfi *changed to* fīf, *which became* **five** *in Modern English. See also notes at* **fin²** *and* **finger.**

flag¹·²·³·⁴

Flag¹ *and* **flag²** *both first appear in the sixteenth century; they are both of unknown origin, but they may possibly be related to each other, since* **flag²** *originally meant "to hang down limply."* **Flag³** *first appears in the fourteenth century and is also of unknown origin. The earliest recorded meaning of* **flag⁴** *is "a cut piece of turf or sod," but the meaning "flat stone" may have existed earlier, and the word seems to have been borrowed from Old Norse* flaga, *"flat stone."*

flag•pole |flăg′pōl′| *n.* A pole on which a flag is hoisted and flown.

fla•grant |flā′grənt| *adj.* Extremely or deliberately noticeable; shocking: *a flagrant error.*

flag•ship |flăg′shĭp′| *n.* A ship carrying a fleet or squadron commander and flying his flag.

flag•staff |flăg′stăf′| *or* |-stäf′| *n., pl.* **-staffs** or **-staves** |-stāvz′|. A flagpole.

flag•stone |flăg′stōn′| *n.* A flat, fine-grained, evenly layered stone split into slabs for paving.

flail |flāl| *n.* A tool for threshing grain, consisting of a long wooden handle and a shorter, free-swinging stick attached to its end. —*v.* To thresh or beat with or as if with a flail.

flair |flâr| *n.* A natural talent or aptitude; knack: *a flair for writing.* ¶*These sound alike* **flair, flare.**

flak |flăk| *n.* **1. a.** Antiaircraft artillery. **b.** The bursting shells fired from such artillery. **2.** *Slang.* Excessive criticism; abuse: *My mother gives me a lot of flak about being messy.*

flake |flāk| *n.* **1.** A small, thin piece or particle of something: *a soap flake.* **2.** *Slang.* A person who is somewhat eccentric. —*v.* **flaked, flak•ing.** To come off in flakes; chip off: *The paint is flaking.*

flak•y |flā′kē| *adj.* **flak•i•er, flak•i•est. 1.** Made of or tending to form flakes or thin, crisp fragments: *a flaky pie crust.* **2.** *Slang.* Eccentric; odd. —**flak′i•ness** *n.*

flam•boy•ant |flăm boi′ənt| *adj.* **1.** Highly elaborate; ornate: *a flamboyant literary style.* **2.** Exaggerated or high-flown in style, manner, etc.; showy: *a flamboyant Shakespearean actor.* **3.** Brilliant; vivid: *flamboyant colors.* —**flam•boy′ance, flam•boy′an•cy** *n.* —**flam•boy′ant•ly** *adv.*

flamingo

flame |flām| *n.* **1.** The often bright zone of burning gases and fine suspended particles that forms as a result of a fire. **2.** Often **flames.** The condition of active, blazing combustion: *burst into flames.* **3.** *Informal.* A sweetheart. —*v.* **flamed, flam•ing. 1.** To burn brightly; blaze: *the logs flamed up.* **2.** To flash suddenly like a flame: *Hatred flamed in his eyes.*

fla•men•co |flə mĕng′kō| *n.* **1.** A dance style of the Spanish Gypsies that is characterized by forceful rhythms. **2.** The guitar music for this dance style. —***modifier:*** *a flamenco dancer.*

flam•ing |flā′mĭng| *adj.* **1.** On fire; in flames; blazing: *flaming logs.* **2.** Brilliantly colored, especially red or yellow: *the flaming colors of autumn leaves.* **3.** Burning as if with flame; flushed or passionate: *flaming cheeks; a flaming rage.*

fla•min•go |flə mĭng′gō| *n., pl.* **fla•min•gos** or **fla•min•goes.** A long-legged, long-necked tropical wading bird with reddish or pinkish feathers. [SEE PICTURE]

flam•ma•ble |flăm′ə bəl| *adj.* Easy to set fire to and capable of burning very rapidly: *Gasoline is very flammable.*

Flan•ders |flăn′dərz|. A region of Europe extending along the North Sea, located primarily in Belgium but including adjacent parts of France.

flange |flănj| *n.* A rim or edge that projects from something, such as a wheel or a pipe, used to strengthen it, hold it in place, or attach it to something. —*v.* **flanged, flang•ing.** To equip with a flange.

flank |flăngk| *n.* **1. a.** The fleshy part of the body between the ribs and the hip. **b.** A cut of meat from this part of an animal. **2.** A side or lateral part: *the flank of a mountain.* **3.** The right or left side of a military formation. —*v.* **1.** To attack or maneuver around the flank of: *flank an enemy army.* **2.** To be placed or situated at the side of: *Two chairs flanked the couch.*

flank•er |flăng′kər| *n.* **1.** A person or persons that protect a flank. **2.** In football, a halfback stationed just behind the line of scrimmage and to the right of his team's right end.

flan•nel |flăn′əl| *n.* **1.** A soft woven cloth with a nap, made of wool, cotton, or a blend of wool and other fibers. **2. flannels.** Trousers, underwear, or other garments made of flannel. —***modifier:*** *long red flannel underwear.*

flap |flăp| *v.* **flapped, flap•ping. 1.** To move or cause to move (the wings or arms) up and down; beat. **2.** To wave about while attached to something stationary; flutter: *a flag flapping in the wind.* —*n.* **1.** A flat piece attached along one side and hanging loose on the other, often over an opening: *the flap of a pocket.* **2.** A section of the rear edge of an aircraft wing that can be swung up and down in order to control the lift and drag of the wing. **3.** The sound or action of flapping: *the flap of wings.* **4.** *Slang.* A state of agitation, nervous excitement, etc.

flap•jack |flăp′jăk′| *n.* A pancake.

flap•per |flăp′ər| *n.* A young woman of the 1920's who was disdainful of conventional dress and behavior.

flare |flâr| *v.* **flared, flar•ing. 1.** To burn with a sudden or unsteady flame: *The candles flared briefly before going out.* **2.** To burst out like a flame: *Tempers flared during the discussion.* **3.** To spread outward in a shape like that of a cone. —***phrasal verb.*** **flare up. 1.** To break into flame suddenly. **2.** To become suddenly angry, excited, etc. —*n.* **1.** A sudden or unsteady blaze of light. **2.** Any one of several devices that produce a bright flame for signaling, illumination, etc. **3.** A **solar flare. 4.** A shape or form that spreads out something like a cone: *The flare of a trumpet.* ¶*These sound alike* **flare, flair.**

flare-up |flâr′ŭp′| *n.* **1.** A sudden outbreak of flame or light. **2.** An outburst or eruption: *a flare-up of anger.*

flash |flăsh| *v.* **1.** To send forth instantly or suddenly: *flash a light in her eyes; flash a signal. The mother flashed the child a disapproving look.* **2.** To appear, occur, or be perceived for an instant only: *A knife flashed in the sun. A thought flashed through his mind.* **3.** To be lighted on and off; sparkle: *The lighthouse flashed in the distance.* **4.** To give out a sudden, bright light: *The fireworks flashed across the sky.* **5.** To move rapidly: *A car flashed by.* **6.** To send (a message) at great speed, as by telegraph: *flashing a bulletin to catch the last edition of a newspaper.* —*n.* **1.** A short, sudden burst of light or other radiation: *a flash of lightning.* **2.** A sudden, brief burst: *a flash of insight; a flash of humor.* **3.** A split second; an instant: *in a flash.* **4.** A brief, important news item sent to a newspaper, radio station, etc.

Idiom. **flash in the pan.** Someone or something that promises great success but fails.

flash•back |flăsh′băk′| *n.* The interruption of a story, motion picture, etc., to show or tell about an incident or scene from the past.

ă pat/ā pay/â care/ä father/ĕ pet/ē be/ĭ pit/ī pie/î fierce/ŏ pot/ō go/ô paw, for/oi oil/o͝o book/o͞o boot/ou out/ŭ cut/û fur/*th* the/th thin/hw which/zh vision/ə ago, item, pencil, atom, circus

flash bulb. A glass bulb coated with plastic that is ignited by electricity and produces a bright flash of light for photography.

flash card. One of a set of cards marked with words, numbers, etc., displayed briefly by a teacher to a class in a drill.

flash•cube |**flăsh'**kyo͞ob'| *n.* A small cube that contains four flash bulbs and rotates automatically for taking four photographs in succession.

flash flood. A sudden, violent flood after a heavy rain.

flash gun. A portable device used in photography to hold a flash bulb and fire it electrically.

flash•light |**flăsh'**līt'| *n.* **1.** A small, portable electric lamp consisting of a bulb, a switch, and a power source of several small dry cells all enclosed in a metal or plastic case. **2.** A short, bright flash of light, as from a flash bulb.

flash•y |**flăsh'**ē| *adj.* **flash•i•er, flash•i•est. 1.** Giving a superficial impression of brilliance: *a flashy performance.* **2.** Cheap and showy; gaudy: *a flashy tie.* **—flash'i•ly** *adv.* **—flash'i•ness** *n.*

flask |flăsk| *or* |fläsk| *n.* A bottle or other container with a narrow neck, especially a round or cone-shaped container with a long, narrow neck, used in laboratories.

flat[1] |flăt| *adj.* **flat•ter, flat•test. 1.** Having a smooth, even surface; level: *flat land.* **2.** Not round: *The earth was once thought to be flat.* **3.** Extending or lying completely in a plane: *a flat geometric figure.* **4.** Horizontal or nearly horizontal: *flat on one's back.* **5.** Not deep or high; shallow: *a flat dish.* **6.** Having lost contained air; deflated: *a flat tire.* **7.** Without sparkle or liveliness: *a flat performance. The soda is flat.* **8.** Downright; absolute: *a flat refusal.* **9.** Unvarying; fixed: *a flat rate.* **10.** Not glossy: *a flat paint.* **11. a.** Lower in pitch than is correct: *a flat note; a flat musical instrument.* **b.** Being one half step lower than the corresponding natural tone or key: *D flat.* *—adv.* **1.** So as to be flat: *press dough flat.* **2.** Exactly: *He ran the race in 50 seconds flat.* **3.** Completely: *I'm flat broke.* **4.** Below the correct pitch: *Don't sing flat.* *—n.* **1.** A flat surface or part. **2.** Often **flats.** An area of level, low-lying ground. **3.** A deflated tire. **4. a.** A sign (♭) attached to a musical note to show that its pitch is one half step lower than usual. **b.** A note that is lowered in this way: *an E flat.* *—v.* **flat•ted, flat•ting.** To sing or play flat. **—flat'ly** *adv.* **—flat'ness** *n.* [SEE NOTE]

flat[2] |flăt| *n. British.* An apartment on one floor of a building. [SEE NOTE]

flat•boat |**flăt'**bōt'| *n.* A flat-bottomed barge for transporting freight in shallow inland waters. [SEE PICTURE]

flat•car |**flăt'**kär'| *n.* A railroad car without sides or a roof, used for carrying freight.

flat•fish |**flăt'**fĭsh'| *n., pl.* **-fish** or **-fish•es.** A fish, such as a flounder or sole, having a flattened body with the eyes on the upper side.

flat•foot |**flăt'**fo͝ot'| *n.* **1.** *pl.* **flat•feet** |**flăt'**fēt'|. A condition in which the arch of the foot is broken down and the entire sole touches the ground. **2.** *pl.* **flat•foots.** *Slang.* A policeman.

flat-foot•ed |**flăt'fo͝ot'**ĭd| *adj.* **1.** Of or suffering from flatfoot. **2.** Unprepared; unable to react quickly: *catch one flat-footed.* **—flat'-foot'ed•ly** *adv.* **—flat'-foot'ed•ness** *n.*

Flat•head |**flăt'**hĕd'| *n., pl.* **Flat•head** or **Flat•heads. 1. a.** Any of several North American Indian tribes who were said to have a custom of deforming their heads. **b.** A member of any of these tribes. **2. a.** A North American Indian tribe of Montana that did not practice the custom of deforming their heads. **b.** A member of this tribe. **c.** The Salish language of this tribe.

flat•i•ron |**flăt'**ī'ərn| *n.* An externally heated iron for pressing clothes.

flat•ten |**flăt'**n| *v.* **1.** To make or become flat or flatter. **2.** To knock down, as in a fight.

flat•ter |**flăt'**ər| *v.* **1.** To compliment (someone) excessively and often insincerely, especially in order to win favor. **2.** To please or gratify: *Receiving the award flattered me.* **3.** To make more attractive than is actually the case: *The photograph flatters her.* **—flat'ter•ing** *adj.: flattering remarks; a flattering hat.* **—flat'ter•er** *n.*

flat•ter•y |**flăt'**ə rē| *n., pl.* **flat•ter•ies.** Excessive and insincere praise.

flat•top |**flăt'**tŏp'| *n. Informal.* An aircraft carrier.

flat•u•lent |**flăch'**o͞o lənt| *adj.* **1.** Afflicted with excessive gas in the digestive tract. **2.** Pompous; pretentious. **—flat'u•lence** *n.*

flat•ware |**flăt'**wâr'| *n.* Tableware that is fairly flat, especially silver or steel utensils such as knives, forks, and spoons.

flat•worm |**flăt'**wûrm'| *n.* Any of a group of worms having a flattened body, as a tapeworm or planarian. Many flatworms are parasites that live within the bodies of other animals, including human beings.

flaunt |flônt| *v.* **1.** To show off: *flaunt one's knowledge.* **2.** To wave proudly: *a flag flaunting in the wind.* [SEE NOTE]

flau•tist |**flô'**tĭst| *or* |**flou'-**| *n.* A flutist.

fla•vor |**flā'**vər| *n.* **1.** Distinctive taste of something; savor: *a flavor of smoke in bacon.* **2.** A seasoning; flavoring: *natural and artificial flavors for candies and ice creams.* **3.** A quality felt to be characteristic of a thing: *the mysterious flavor of the Orient.* *—v.* To give flavor to. **—fla'vor•ful** *adj.* **—fla'vor•less** *adj.*

fla•vor•ing |**flā'**vər ĭng| *n.* A substance, such as an extract or a spice, used to flavor food.

flaw |flô| *n.* A blemish, crack, or other defect; an imperfection: *a flaw in a diamond; a flaw in an argument; a flaw in his character.* *—v.* To make or become defective.

flaw•less |**flô'**lĭs| *adj.* Without a flaw; perfect. **—flaw'less•ly** *adv.* **—flaw'less•ness** *n.*

flax |flăks| *n.* **1.** A plant with blue flowers, seeds that yield linseed oil, and stems that yield a light-colored fiber from which linen is made. **2.** The fiber obtained from this plant.

flax•en |**flăk'**sən| *adj.* **1.** Made of flax: *flaxen thread.* **2.** Having the pale-yellow color of flax fiber: *flaxen hair.*

flax•seed |**flăks'**sēd'| *n.* The seeds of flax, from which linseed oil is pressed.

flay |flā| *v.* **1.** To strip off the skin of: *flay a deer.* **2.** To criticize or scold harshly.

F layer. The highest zone of the ionosphere, extending variously from about 90 or 120 miles upward to about 250 miles above the earth.

flea |flē| *n.* Any of several small, wingless, jumping insects that live on and suck blood from

flat[1-2]

Flat[1] *is from Old Norse* flatr, *"level, flat."* **Flat**[2] *was originally a Scottish word, spelled* flet, *meaning "floor, a single floor of a house"; it comes from Old English* flett, *"floor, ground," which is related to Old Norse* flatr, **flat**[1]. *In addition, the modern use of the word has obviously been directly influenced by* **flat**[1], *since an apartment on one floor is "flat."*

flatboat

flaunt/flout

These two words are unrelated and have very different meanings. But because they are similar, and because they can be used of different aspects of the same context, **flaunt** *is sometimes unconsciously used for* **flout.** *If you* **flout** *public opinion, you can be said to* **flaunt** *your contempt for public opinion. This is not the same as saying that you* **flaunt** *public opinion, which 91 per cent of the American Heritage Usage Panel considers to be an outright mistake.*

fleet[1-2]/float
Old English flēotan, *"to float," became* fleten, *"to flow, go swiftly," in Middle English and* **fleet[2]** *in Modern English.* Flēotan *also formed the noun* flēot, *"a floating, a collection of ships," which became* **fleet[1]**. *Closely related to* flēotan *is Old English* flotian, *also meaning "to float"; this became* **float** *in Modern English.*

fleur-de-lis

flick[1-2]/flicker[1-2]
Flick[1] *first appears in the fifteenth century and is apparently an imitative word, formed to resemble the sound or "feel" of the thing it describes.* **Flicker[1]** *was* flicorian *in Old English, meaning "to flutter or hover"; this also seems somewhat imitative.* **Flick[2]** *is shortened from* **flicker[1]**, *which was an early slang word for a movie (because of the flickering light).* **Flicker[2]** *is probably "the bird that moves as fast as a flick," from* **flick[1]**

ă pat/ā pay/â care/ä father/ĕ pet/ē be/ĭ pit/ī pie/î fierce/ŏ pot/ō go/ô paw, for/oi oil/ŏŏ book/ōō boot/ou out/ŭ cut/û fur/*th* the/th thin/hw which/zh vision/ə ago, item, pencil, atom, circus

the bodies of animals, including human beings. ¶*These sound alike* **flea, flee.**

fleck |flĕk| *n.* **1.** A small, irregular mark, spot, flake, etc.: *a fleck of dirt.* **2.** A small patch of color or light: *a fleck of sunlight.* —*v.* To mark with flecks; spot: *a path flecked with light.*

fled |flĕd|. Past tense and past participle of **flee.**

fledge |flĕj| *v.* **fledged, fledg•ing. 1.** To become covered with adult feathers and be able to fly, as a young bird. **2.** To cover with or as if with feathers. —**fledged'** *adj.*: *a newly fledged bird.*

fledg•ling, also **fledge•ling** |**flĕj'**lĭng| *n.* **1.** A young bird that has just grown its flying feathers and is learning to fly. **2.** Someone or something that is just developing and has had little experience.

flee |flē| *v.* **fled** |flĕd|, **flee•ing. 1.** To run away, as from trouble or danger: *The burglar fled when the alarm went off.* **2.** To run away from: *The family fled the burning house.* **3.** To pass swiftly by or away; vanish: *His hopes fled when he learned what had happened.* ¶*These sound alike* **flee, flea.** [SEE NOTE on p. 358]

fleece |flēs| *n.* The wool forming the coat of a sheep or similar animal. —*v.* **fleeced, fleec•ing. 1.** To shear the fleece from. **2.** *Informal.* To defraud (a person) of money or property.

fleec•y |**flē'**sē| *adj.* **fleec•i•er, fleec•i•est. 1.** Of fleece or similar material; warm and soft: *fleecy blankets.* **2.** Resembling fleece: *fleecy clouds.* —**fleec'i•ness** *n.*

fleet[1] |flēt| *n.* **1. a.** A group of as many warships as are needed for a major operation, under the command of an admiral. **b.** The entire navy of a government. **2. a.** A large number of boats, ships, etc., operating as a more or less organized group: *a fishing fleet.* **b.** A large group of vehicles operating under one management: *a fleet of taxicabs.* [SEE NOTE]

fleet[2] |flēt| *adj.* **fleet•er, fleet•est.** Moving or able to move swiftly; nimble: *a fleet animal.* —*v.* To move or pass swiftly: *clouds fleeting across the sky.* —**fleet'ly** *adv.* —**fleet'ness** *n.* [SEE NOTE]

fleet•ing |**flē'**tĭng| *adj.* Passing quickly; very brief: *a fleeting glimpse.* —**fleet'ing•ly** *adv.*

Flem•ish |**flĕm'**ĭsh| *n.* **1. the Flemish** *(used with a plural verb).* The people of Flanders. **2.** The Germanic language of these people, related to Dutch. —*adj.* Of Flanders, the Flemish, or their language.

flense |flĕns| *v.* **flensed, flens•ing** To strip the blubber or skin from: *flense a whale.*

flesh |flĕsh| *n.* **1.** The soft tissue of the body, especially the skeletal muscles as distinguished from the bones and internal organs. **2.** The meat of animals, as distinguished from the edible parts of fish, used as food. **3.** The pulpy, usually edible part of a fruit or vegetable. **4.** Man's body as opposed to the mind or soul: *The spirit is willing, but the flesh is weak.*

Idioms. **flesh and blood.** A blood relative or relatives; kin. **in the flesh.** In person; actually present.

flesh•ly |**flĕsh'**lē| *adj.* **flesh•li•er, flesh•li•est. 1.** Of the body; physical. **2.** Not spiritual; worldly.

flesh•y |**flĕsh'**ē| *adj.* **flesh•i•er, flesh•i•est. 1.** Of or like flesh. **2.** Having much or too much flesh; plump: *fleshy jowls; a fleshy fruit.*

fleur-de-lis or **fleur-de-lys** |flûr'də **lē'**| *or* |flŏŏr'-| *n., pl.* **fleurs-de-lis** or **fleurs-de-lys** |flûr'də **lēz'**| *or* |flŏŏr'-|. A design that has three petallike parts and somewhat resembles an iris flower. [SEE PICTURE]

flew |flōō|. Past tense of **fly.** ¶*These sound alike* **flew, flu, flue.**

flex |flĕks| *v.* **1.** To bend or cause to bend: *His toes flexed repeatedly. Flex your elbow.* **2.** To cause (a muscle) to contract.

flex•i•ble |**flĕk'**sə bəl| *adj.* **1.** Capable of bending or being bent; supple; pliable. **2.** Capable of or responsive to change; adaptable: *flexible plans.* —**flex'i•bil'i•ty** *n.* —**flex'i•bly** *adv.*

flick[1] |flĭk| *n.* A light, quick blow or stroke: *a flick of a whip.* —*v.* **1.** To hit or remove with a light, quick blow, especially with the tips of the fingers: *He flicked the dust off his pants.* **2.** To strike with a light, quick blow: *flick a horse with a whip.* **3.** To move or cause to move with a flick: *The birds flicked off the branch and were out of sight in an instant. The snake flicked its tongue.* [SEE NOTE]

flick[2] |flĭk| *n. Slang.* A motion picture. [SEE NOTE]

flick•er[1] |**flĭk'**ər| *v.* **1.** To give off light that burns or shines unsteadily: *The candles flickered in the breeze.* **2.** To move waveringly; flutter: *Shadows flickered on the wall.* —*n.* **1.** An uneven or unsteady light. **2.** A brief or slight sensation or expression, as of an emotion: *I saw a flicker of disappointment on his face.* **3.** A tremor or flutter. [SEE NOTE]

flick•er[2] |**flĭk'**ər| *n.* A North American woodpecker with a brown back and a spotted breast. [SEE NOTE]

flied |flīd|. Past tense and past participle of **fly** (to hit a baseball).

fli•er |**flī'**ər| *n.* **1.** Anything that flies, especially a pilot or aviator. **2.** *Informal.* A daring or risky financial venture. **3.** *Informal.* A pamphlet or circular prepared for mass distribution.

flies |flīz|. **1.** Plural of the noun **fly. 2.** Third person singular present tense of the verb **fly.**

flight[1] |flīt| *n.* **1.** The act or process of flying: *a bird's flight.* **2.** A scheduled airline trip or the plane making it. **3.** A group, especially of birds or aircraft, flying together. **4.** An effort that surpasses the usual bounds; a soaring: *a flight of the imagination.* **5.** Any swift passage or movement: *the flight of time.* **6.** A series of stairs, as between floors. —***modifier:*** *flight instruction; a flight crew.* [SEE NOTE on p. 358]

flight[2] |flīt| *n.* An act of running away; escape. [SEE NOTE on p. 358]

Idioms. **put to flight.** To drive or frighten away. **take flight.** To run away.

flight•less |**flīt'**lĭs| *adj.* Unable to fly: *Ostriches and penguins are flightless birds.*

flight•y |**flī'**tē| *adj.* **flight•i•er, flight•i•est.** Going from one idea, interest, etc., to another, giving little thought to any of them; unsteady or fickle; giddy. —**flight'i•ness** *n.*

flim•sy |**flĭm'**zē| *adj.* **flim•si•er, flim•si•est. 1.** Lacking solidity or strength: *a flimsy house; flimsy cloth.* **2.** Implausible; unconvincing: *a flimsy excuse.* —**flim'si•ly** *adv.* —**flim'si•ness** *n.*

flinch |flĭnch| *v.* To shrink or wince, as from pain or fear.

fling |flĭng| *v.* **flung** |flŭng|, **fling•ing. 1.** To throw violently; toss or hurl: *He flung his coat on the chair.* **2.** To move quickly, violently, or impulsively: *She flung her head back in disdain.* **3.** To put or send suddenly or unexpectedly: *The dictator flung his enemies into prison.* **4.** To go angrily; rush: *She flung out of the room without saying good-by.* —*n.* **1.** An act of flinging or hurling; a throw; toss. **2.** A lively dance of the Scottish Highlands. **3.** A brief period of indulging one's impulses; a spree. **4.** *Informal.* A brief attempt or try: *a fling at skiing.*

flint |flĭnt| *n.* **1.** A very hard, fine-grained type of quartz that makes sparks when struck with steel. **2.** A small cylinder of an alloy that makes sparks when scratched or scraped, used in lighters to ignite fuel.

flint•lock |**flĭnt**′lŏk′| *n.* **1.** A gunlock in which a flint strikes a metal plate, thus producing sparks that ignite the gunpowder. **2.** An old type of gun having such a gunlock. [SEE PICTURE]

flint•y |**flĭn**′tē| *adj.* **flint•i•er, flint•i•est. 1.** Composed of or containing flint. **2.** Unyielding; stony: *a flinty look.* —**flint′i•ness** *n.*

flip |flĭp| *v.* **flipped, flip•ping. 1.** To toss (a coin) vertically in the air, giving it a spin: *Let's flip a coin to decide who goes first.* **2.** To strike with a light, quick blow; flick: *Don't flip the ashes of your cigar on the rug.* **3.** To reverse or overturn quickly by or as if by turning over or around: *flip a pancake.* **4.** *Slang.* To be overwhelmed: *They flipped when they saw the new car.* —*n.* **1.** An act of flipping, especially a quick, turning movement: *give the hamburger a flip.* **2.** A somersault. **3.** A mixed drink made with any of the various alcoholic beverages, often including beaten eggs. —*adj. Informal.* Flippant: *a flip attitude.*

flip•pant |**flĭp**′ənt| *adj.* Casually or humorously disrespectful; saucy: *flippant remarks.* —**flip′pan•cy** *n.* —**flip′pant•ly** *adv.*

flip•per |**flĭp**′ər| *n.* **1.** A wide, flat, finlike limb, as of a seal or walrus, adapted for swimming. **2.** A wide, flat, finlike rubber shoe worn for swimming and skin diving. [SEE PICTURE]

flirt |flûrt| *v.* **1.** To play lightheartedly at courtship: *Jack likes to flirt with pretty girls.* **2.** To deal triflingly; toy: *flirt with danger.* **3.** To toss or move abruptly or jerkily; flick: *The bird flirted its tail.* —*n.* **1.** A person given to romantic flirting. **2.** An abrupt, jerking movement.

flir•ta•tion |flûr **tā**′shən| *n.* **1.** The act or practice of flirting. **2.** A casual or brief romance.

flir•ta•tious |flûr **tā**′shəs| *adj.* Lightheartedly romantic: *a flirtatious look; a flirtatious girl.* —**flir•ta′tious•ly** *adv.* —**flir•ta′tious•ness** *n.*

flit |flĭt| *v.* **flit•ted, flit•ting. 1.** To move quickly and nimbly: *Birds flitted about.* **2.** To move or pass quickly: *A smile flitted across his face.*

float |flōt| *v.* **1.** To remain or cause to remain suspended in or at the top of a mass of liquid or gas without sinking: *Balloons filled with helium float in the air. Divers worked to float the sunken ship.* **2.** To move or cause to move lightly and easily, as on water or in the air: *Lumberjacks floated logs down the river.* **3.** To move or go from place to place with little purpose; drift: *That man floats from town to town.* **4. a.** To set up (a business, company, etc.) by selling stocks: *float an oil company.* **b.** To offer for sale: *float a bond issue.* —*n.* **1.** Any object designed to float: **a.** A cork or other floating object on a fishing line. **b.** An anchored raft used by swimmers. **2.** A large, flat vehicle bearing an exhibit in a parade. **3.** A soft drink with ice cream floating in it. [SEE NOTE on p. 354]

floating rib. One of the four lower ribs that, unlike the other ribs, are not connected at the front.

flock |flŏk| *n.* **1.** A group of animals, such as birds or sheep, that live, travel, or feed together. **2.** A group of people under the leadership of one person, especially the members of a church. —*v.* To gather or travel in a flock or crowd: *People flocked to the cities.* [SEE NOTE]

floe |flō| *n.* A large, flat mass of ice formed on the surface of a body of water. ¶*These sound alike* **floe, flow.**

flog |flŏg| *or* |flôg| *v.* **flogged, flog•ging.** To beat harshly with a whip or rod. —**flog′ger** *n.*

flood |flŭd| *n.* **1.** The covering or filling with water of a place that is normally dry; a great overflow of water. **2.** Any large flow or outpouring: *a flood of tears; the flood of settlers from Europe.* **3. the Flood.** The universal overflowing of the land by water recorded in the Bible as having occurred in the days of Noah. —*v.* **1.** To fill or cover with or as if with a flood: *The rains flooded the cellar. When it rains the yard always floods.* **2.** To fill or overwhelm with an abundance or excess: *Letters flooded the main office with complaints.* **3.** To overflow; pour forth: *The river floods in the spring.*

flood•gate |**flŭd**′gāt′| *n.* A gate used to control the flow from a large body of water, such as a reservoir or an artificial lake.

flood•light |**flŭd**′līt′| *n.* An electric lamp that produces a broad and very bright beam of light.

flood tide. The incoming or rising tide.

floor |flôr| *or* |flōr| *n.* **1.** The surface of a room on which one stands. **2.** The ground or lowermost surface, as of a forest or ocean. **3.** The lower part of a room, such as a legislative chamber, where business is conducted. **4.** The right to address an assembly: *Mr. Smith has the floor.* **5.** A story or level of a building: *living on the fifth floor.* —*v.* **1.** To provide with a floor. **2.** To knock down: *He floored his opponent.* **3.** To stun; overwhelm: *The news floored me.*

floor•ing |**flôr**′ĭng| *or* |**flōr**′-| *n.* **1.** Material, such as lumber, used in making floors. **2.** A floor or floors.

floor show. The entertainment presented in a night club.

floor•walk•er |**flôr**′wô′kər| *or* |**flōr**′-| *n.* An employee of a department store who supervises sales personnel and assists customers in a designated area of the store.

flop |flŏp| *v.* **flopped, flop•ping. 1.** To fall heavily and noisily; plop: *He flopped down on the bed.* **2.** To move about in a clumsy, noisy way; flap: *The dog's ears flopped as it jogged along.* **3.** *Informal.* To fail utterly. —*n.* **1.** The action or sound of flopping. **2.** *Informal.* A complete failure: *The play was a flop.*

flop•py |**flŏp**′ē| *adj.* **flop•pi•er, flop•pi•est.** Tending to flop: *The dog had floppy ears.*

floppy disk. A flexible plastic disk coated with magnetic material used to store computer data.

flo•ra |**flôr**′ə| *or* |**flōr**′ə| *n.* The plants of a

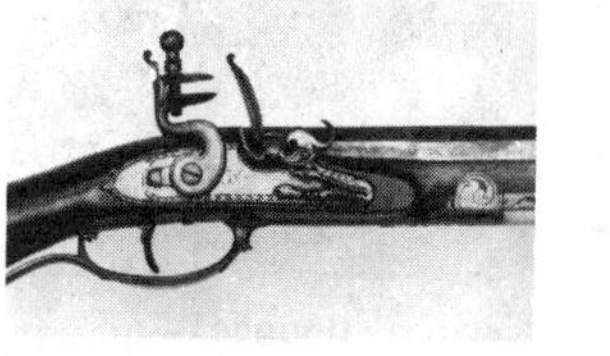

flintlock
Eighteenth-century American

flipper

flock

The English language has a great array of special terms for groups of animals. Below is a selection of the more important ones.

covey	*grouse, partridges*
drove	*cattle, sheep, geese, when being driven from place to place*
flock	*sheep, goats; birds, especially when on the ground*
gaggle	*geese*
gam[1]	*whales*
herd	*cattle; elephants, zebras; whales, seals*
pack	*wolves, hounds*
pride	*lions*
school *or* **shoal**	*fish; porpoises*
swarm	*insects, especially when migrating*

flounce[1]
Mid-nineteenth-century gown

flounce[1-2]
Flounce[1] *was originally* frounce *and comes from Old French* fronce, *"a wrinkle, a fold."* **Flounce**[2] *is of unknown origin.*

flounder[1-2]
Flounder[1] *is possibly a blend of* **blunder** *and* **founder**[2]. **Flounder**[2] *is from Norman French* floundre, *which is probably from an old Scandinavian word meaning "flat fish" (like modern Swedish* flundra, *"flounder").*

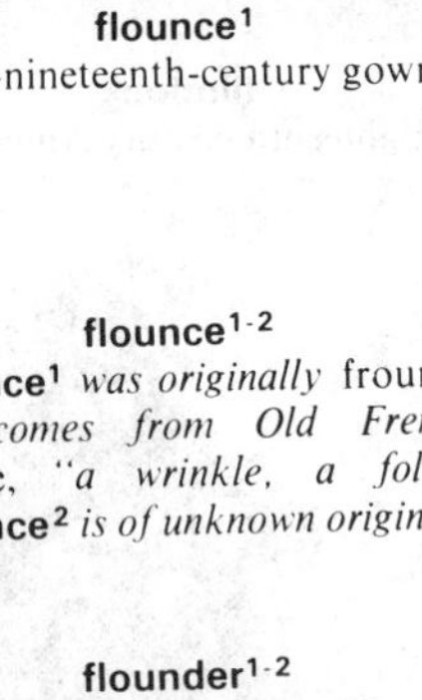

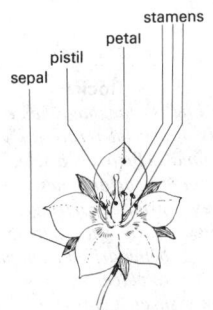

flower
Flower showing details

ă pat/ā pay/â care/ä father/ĕ pet/ ē be/ĭ pit/ī pie/î fierce/ŏ pot/ ō go/ô paw, for/oi oil/o͝o book/ o͞o boot/ou out/ŭ cut/û fur/ *th* the/th thin/hw which/zh vision/ ə ago, item, pencil, atom, circus

particular region or time period: *desert flora.*

flo•ral |**flôr′**əl| *or* |**flōr′**-| *adj.* Of or suggestive of flowers: *a floral arrangement; floral perfume.*

Flor•ence |**flôr′**əns| *or* |**flŏr′**-|. A city in north-central Italy. Population, 456,000. —**Flor′en•tine′** |**flôr′**ən tēn′| *or* |-tīn′| *or* |**flŏr′**-| *adj.* & *n.*

flo•ret |**flôr′**ĭt| *or* |**flōr′**-| *n.* A small flower that is usually part of a dense cluster, as that forming the central part of a daisy.

flor•id |**flôr′**ĭd| *or* |**flŏr′**-| *adj.* **1.** Flushed with rosy color; ruddy: *a florid complexion.* **2.** Heavily embellished; flowery: *a florid style of writing.*

Flor•i•da |**flôr′**ĭ də| *or* |**flŏr′**-|. The southeasternmost state of the United States. Population, 7,442,000. Capital, Tallahassee. —**Flo•rid′i•an** |flə **rĭd′**ē ən| *adj.* & *n.*

flo•rist |**flôr′**ĭst| *or* |**flōr′**-| *or* |**flŏr′**-| *n.* A person whose business is the raising or selling of flowers.

floss |flôs| *or* |flŏs| *n.* **1.** A soft, glossy, loosely twisted silk or cotton thread used in embroidery. **2.** Also **dental floss.** A strong waxed thread used to clean between the teeth. **3.** A mass or tuft of soft, silky fibers.

floss•y |**flô′**sē| *or* |**flŏs′**ē| *adj.* **floss•i•er, floss•i•est. 1.** Soft and silky or downy. **2.** *Slang.* Stylish and showy.

flo•til•la |flō **tĭl′**ə| *n.* **1.** A fleet of boats or other small vessels. **2.** A U.S. naval unit made up of two or more squadrons of submarines or light ships.

flot•sam |**flŏt′**səm| *n.* Floating wreckage or cargo from a shipwreck.
Idiom. **flotsam and jetsam. 1.** Anything washed ashore from ships. **2.** Odds and ends.

flounce[1] |flouns| *n.* A gathered or pleated strip of cloth, such as a ruffle, sewn along its upper edge to a skirt, curtain, etc. —*v.* **flounced, flounc•ing.** To trim with a flounce or flounces. [SEE NOTE & PICTURE]

flounce[2] |flouns| *v.* **flounced, flounc•ing.** To walk swiftly and angrily: *The woman flounced out of the room in a huff.* [SEE NOTE]

floun•der[1] |**floun′**dər| *v.* **1.** To move clumsily or with difficulty: *floundering through deep snow.* **2.** To proceed clumsily and in confusion: *flounder through a speech.* [SEE NOTE]

floun•der[2] |**floun′**dər| *n., pl.* **floun•der** or **floun•ders.** Any of several flatfishes often used as food. [SEE NOTE]

flour |flour| *n.* A fine, powdery substance made by grinding wheat or another grain. —*v.* To cover or coat with flour.

flour•ish |**flûr′**ĭsh| *or* |**flŭr′**-| *v.* **1.** To grow well or luxuriantly; thrive: *Most flowers flourish in full sunlight.* **2.** To fare well; succeed; prosper: *The lawyer's practice flourished.* **3.** To wave vigorously or dramatically: *He flourished his hat before the cheering crowd.* —*n.* **1.** An act or example of waving something vigorously or dramatically: *a flourish of a sword.* **2.** An added, decorative touch; embellishment: *His handwriting has many flourishes.* **3.** A fanfare.

flout |flout| *v.* To show contempt for: *flout convention.* —**flout′er** *n.* [SEE NOTE on p. 353]

flow |flō| *v.* **1.** To move or run freely, as does a liquid or gas: *Tears flowed from her eyes. Air flowed in through the window.* **2.** To move or proceed steadily and continuously: *Traffic flowed through the tunnel.* **3.** To appear smooth, harmonious, and graceful: *Write paragraphs that flow.* **4.** To hang loosely and gracefully: *The cape flowed from his shoulders.* **5.** To come from; derive: *Several conclusions flow from his statement.* **6.** To come in; rise: *The tide began to flow.* —*n.* **1.** The act or process of flowing: *A dam stops the flow of water.* **2.** A flowing mass; a stream: *a lava flow.* **3.** A continuous movement or circulation; a current: *a flow of traffic; the flow of a river.* **4.** A continuous output or outpouring; a flood: *a flow of ideas.* **5.** The rising of the tide. ¶*These sound alike* **flow, floe.**

flow•er |**flou′**ər| *n.* **1.** The part of a seed-bearing plant that contains the organs of reproduction and that produces seeds. Flowers often have colorful or showy petals, but many kinds are small and inconspicuous. **2.** A plant that is noticeable chiefly for its flowers: *We planted pansies, marigolds, and other flowers.* **3.** The best example or representative of something: *They were the flower of their generation.* **4.** Often **flowers.** A fine powder produced by condensation or sublimation: *flowers of sulfur.* —***modifier:*** *a flower arrangement; a flower garden.* —*v.* **1.** To produce flowers; bloom. **2.** To develop fully; reach a peak. [SEE PICTURE]

flow•ered |**flou′**ərd| *adj.* Having flowers or a design of flowers: *flowered wallpaper.*

flow•er•y |**flou′**ə rē| *adj.* **flow•er•i•er, flow•er•i•est. 1.** Full of or suggestive of flowers: *flowery meadows; a flowery fragrance.* **2.** Full of fancy, high-sounding words or expressions: *a flowery speech.* —**flow′er•i•ness** *n.*

flown |flōn|. Past participle of **fly.**

flu |flo͞o| *n. Informal.* Often **the flu.** Influenza. —***modifier:*** *a flu epidemic.* ¶*These sound alike* **flu, flew, flue.**

fluc•tu•ate |**flŭk′**cho͞o āt′| *v.* **fluc•tu•at•ed, fluc•tu•at•ing.** To change or vary, as by moving back and forth from one level, condition, or direction to another: *Prices fluctuate according to supply and demand.* —**fluc′tu•a′tion** *n.*

flue |flo͞o| *n.* A pipe, tube, etc., through which smoke, steam, etc., may pass, as in a chimney or boiler. ¶*These sound alike* **flue, flew, flu.**

flu•en•cy |**flo͞o′**ən sē| *n.* Smoothness and effortless ease, especially in speaking or writing.

flu•ent |**flo͞o′**ənt| *adj.* **1.** Capable of speaking or writing a language smoothly, with effortless ease: *He was fluent in German and French.* **2.** Smoothly and naturally flowing: *He speaks fluent French.* —**flu′ent•ly** *adv.*

fluff |flŭf| *n.* Light, soft, downy substance: *The eaglets were round balls of white fluff.* —*v.* To make light and puffy by patting, poking, or shaking into a soft, loose mass: *She fluffed up her hair. Fluff rice with a fork. Fluff the patient's pillow.*

fluff•y |**flŭf′**ē| *adj.* **fluff•i•er, fluff•i•est.** Having fur, feathers, fibers, etc., that stand out in a soft, full mass: *fluffy kittens; the fluffy boll of a cotton plant.* —**fluff′i•ness** *n.*

flu•id |**flo͞o′**ĭd| *n.* A substance, such as air or water, that flows relatively easily and tends to take on the shape of its container. All liquids and gases are fluids. —***modifier:*** *a unit of fluid measure.* —*adj.* **1.** Capable of flowing; liquid or gaseous: *The waters of the lake remained fluid* *throughout the winter.* **2.** Easily changed or readily changing; adaptable: *fluid living space.*

fluid dram. A unit equal to $^1/_8$ of a fluid ounce.

flu•id•i•ty |flo͞o **id**′ĭ tē| *n.* The condition or property of being fluid.

fluid ounce. A unit of fluid volume or capacity equal to $^1/_{16}$ of a pint or about 1.8 cubic inches.

fluke[1] |flo͝ok| *n.* **1.** *pl.* **fluke** or **flukes.** Any of several flounders or similar flatfish. **2.** Any of various flatworms that are often harmful parasites living within the body of human beings and other animals. [SEE NOTE]

fluke[2] |flo͝ok| *n.* **1.** The triangular blade at the end of either arm of an anchor, designed to dig into the ocean bottom. **2.** The barbed head of a harpoon, lance, or arrow. **3.** One of the two flattened, finlike divisions of a whale's tail. [SEE NOTE & PICTURES]

fluke[3] |flo͝ok| *n.* An accidental stroke of good luck. [SEE NOTE]

flume |flo͞om| *n.* **1.** A narrow gorge with a stream flowing or rushing through it. **2.** An artificial channel for flowing water, used to float logs, divert a stream, furnish waterpower, etc.

flung |flŭng|. Past tense and past participle of **fling.**

flunk |flŭngk| *v. Informal.* **1.** To fail (a test, subject, or grade in school). **2.** To give (someone) a failing grade. —***phrasal verb.* flunk out.** To expel or be expelled from a school or course because of failing grades.

flun•key |**flŭng**′kē| *n., pl.* **flun•keys.** A form of the word **flunky.**

flun•ky |**flŭng**′kē| *n., pl.* **flun•kies. 1. a.** A uniformed manservant, footman, or lackey. **b.** Anyone who does a servant's work. **2.** A person who slavishly flatters and fawns on another to win favor. The word "flunky" is often considered insulting.

flu•o•resce |flo͞o′ə **rĕs**′| *or* |flo͞o **rĕs**′| *v.* **flu•o•resced, flu•o•resc•ing.** To absorb electromagnetic radiation and emit other electromagnetic radiation, especially visible light, for as long as the incoming radiation continues.

flu•o•res•cence |flo͞o′ə **rĕs**′əns| *or* |flo͞o **rĕs**′-| *n.* **1.** The action, process, or property of fluorescing. **2.** Electromagnetic radiation, especially visible light, produced by fluorescing.

flu•o•res•cent |flo͞o′ə **rĕs**′ənt| *or* |flo͞o **rĕs**′-| *adj.* Exhibiting fluorescence. —*n.* A **fluorescent lamp.**

fluorescent lamp. An electric lamp that generates light by means of an electric discharge through a gas-filled tube in which the ultraviolet light emitted by the discharge is converted to visible light by fluorescent material that coats the inside.

fluor•i•date |**flo͝or**′ĭ dāt′| *or* |**flôr**′-| *or* |**flōr**′-| *v.* **fluor•i•dat•ed, fluor•i•dat•ing.** To add a compound of fluorine to (drinking water) in order to prevent tooth decay. —**fluor′i•dat′ed** *adj.: fluoridated water.* —**fluor′i•da′tion** *n.*

flu•o•ride |**flo͞o**′ə rīd′| *or* |**flo͝or**′īd′| *or* |**flôr**′-| *or* |**flōr**′-| *n.* A chemical compound of fluorine and another element.

flu•o•rine |**flo͞o**′ə rēn′| *or* |-rĭn| *or* |**flo͝or**′ēn′| *or* |-ĭn| *or* |**flôr**′-| *or* |**flōr**′-| *n.* Symbol **F** One of the elements, a pale-yellow, highly poisonous, highly corrosive gas. Atomic number 9; atomic weight 18.998; valence –1; melting point –219.62°C; boiling point –188.14°C.

flu•o•rite |**flo͞o**′ə rīt′| *or* |**flo͝or**′īt′| *or* |**flôr**′-| *or* |**flōr**′-| *n.* A mineral that occurs in a variety of colors, composed chiefly of calcium fluoride, CaF_2, and that often fluoresces under ultraviolet light.

fluor•o•scope |**flo͝or**′ə skōp′| *or* |**flôr**′-| *or* |**flōr**′-| *or* |**flo͞o**′ər ə-| *n.* A device that contains a fluorescent screen on which the internal structure of the human body can be continuously studied by means of x-rays.

flu•or•spar |**flo͞o**′ər spär′| *n.* Fluorite.

flur•ry |**flûr**′ē| *or* |**flŭr**′ē| *n., pl.* **flur•ries. 1. a.** A sudden gust of wind. **b.** A brief, light fall of snow. **2.** A sudden burst of bustling activity; a stir: *a flurry of preparations.* —*v.* **flur•ried, flur•ry•ing, flur•ries.** To confuse, excite, or agitate; fluster: *Unexpected company flurried the hostess.*

flush[1] |flŭsh| *v.* **1. a.** To turn red in the face; blush: *She flushed with annoyance.* **b.** To turn red; redden: *His cheeks flushed with shame.* **c.** To glow: *I felt my face flush red.* **2.** To wash out, empty, or discharge with a sudden, rapid flow of water: *Flush the toilet. The toilet is flushing. Sewage and wastes are flushed into drainpipes.* **3.** To flow suddenly; flood: *Blood flushed into his face.* **4.** To excite; elate; exhilarate: *They were flushed with victory.* —**flushed′** *adj.: a flushed face; a flushed and breathless runner.* —*n.* **1.** A blush or rosy glow. **2.** A sudden flow or gush of liquid. **3.** A rush of strong feeling or lively excitement: *the first fine flush of enthusiasm.* —*adj.* **flush•er, flush•est. 1.** In line or on a level; even: *The first column is flush with the margin.* **2.** Supplied with plenty of money; prosperous: *He bought us candy when he was flush.* [SEE NOTE]

flush[2] |flŭsh| *v.* **1.** To startle (a hidden bird or animal) into sudden motion. **2.** To dart out or fly from a hiding place: *The dog chased the two grouse when they flushed.* [SEE NOTE]

flush[3] |flŭsh| *n.* A hand of cards in poker in which all of the cards are of the same suit. [SEE NOTE]

flus•ter |**flŭs**′tər| *v.* To make nervous, excited, or confused: *The staring faces flustered her.* —*n.* A nervous, excited, or confused condition.

flute |flo͞ot| *n.* **1.** A high-pitched woodwind instrument having mellow, velvety low tones and clear, silvery high tones. It is played by blowing across or into a whistlelike mouthpiece near or at one end. **2.** An ornamental groove, as in a pillar or a pleated ruffle. —*v.* **flut•ed, flut•ing. 1. a.** To play on a flute. **b.** To make a flutelike tone. **2.** To make ornamental grooves, pleats, or ridges in: *flute a pie crust.* —**flut′ed** *adj.: a fluted column.*

flut•ing |**flo͞o**′tĭng| *n.* A series of rounded grooves, as in an ornamented column.

flut•ist |**flo͞o**′tĭst| *n.* A person who plays the flute. [SEE PICTURE]

flut•ter |**flŭt**′ər| *v.* **1.** To flap the wings rapidly in flying or trying to fly: *A butterfly fluttered by.* **2.** To wave, flap, or beat rapidly: *The bird fluttered its wings. We saw its wings flutter. The wounded bird's heart was fluttering.* **3.** To move quickly in a nervous, restless, or excited way: *Linda fluttered around the room.* —**flut′ter•ing** *adj.: fluttering leaves; fluttering wings.* —*n.* **1.** A quick flapping, flickering, or vibrating motion:

fluke[1-2-3]

Fluke[1] *was* flōc *in Old English and originally meant "flat fish." It has been suggested that* **fluke**[2] *is taken from* **fluke**[1]*, since anchor flukes are flat in shape; but this is only guesswork.* **Fluke**[3] *is of unknown origin.*

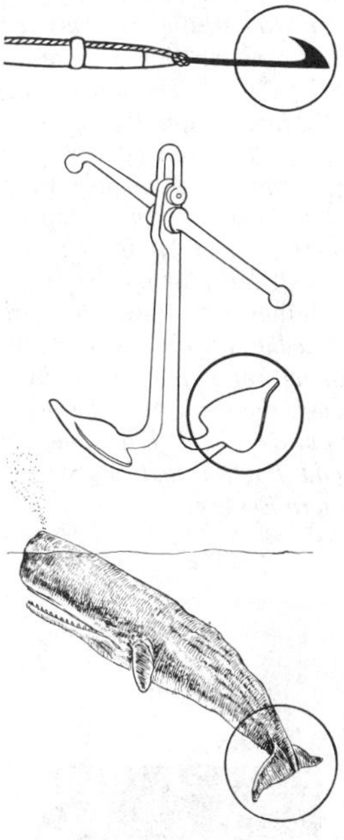

fluke[2]
From top: Flukes on a harpoon, of an anchor, and of a sperm whale

flush[1-2-3]

Flush[2] *was* flusshen *in Middle English; its original meaning was "to fly out suddenly" (sense 2); its origin is obscure.* **Flush**[1] *originally meant "to rush, as a liquid" (senses 2 and 3; sense 1 arose from sense 3); it probably comes from* **flush**[2]. **Flush**[3] *is from Old French* fluz, *"a flow."*

flutist

fly[1-2]/flee/flight[1-2]
All these words are native Old English words descended from one Germanic root, fliu- *or* flu-, *meaning "to go quickly, to fly." The basic Germanic verb was* fliugan, *"to fly through the air"; this became* flēogan *in Old English and* **fly[1]** *in Modern English. This verb formed a noun,* fliugjo, *"the one that flies, a fly," becoming* flēoge *in Old English and* **fly[2]** *in Modern English. A related verb,* fliuhan, *became Old English* flēon, *"to run away (from)," whence Modern English* **flee**. *The two Germanic verbs* fliugan, *"to* **fly[1]**,*" and* fliuhan, *"to* **flee,***" regularly formed the abstract noun* flugti-, *meaning both "the act of flying through the air" and "the act of running away"; both became* flyht *in Old English and* **flight[1-2]** *in Modern English.*

flying fish

fob[1-2]
Fob[1] *is probably from a dialectal German word,* fuppe, *"pocket."* **Fob[2]** *is of unknown origin.*

ă pat/ā pay/â care/ä father/ĕ pet/ ē be/ĭ pit/ī pie/î fierce/ŏ pot/ ō go/ô paw, for/oi oil/ŏŏ book/ ōō boot/ou out/ŭ cut/û fur/ *th* the/th thin/hw which/zh vision/ ə ago, item, pencil, atom, circus

the flutter of wings. **2.** A condition of nervous excitement.

flutter kick. A swimming kick in which the legs are held horizontally and alternately moved up and down in rapid strokes without bending the knees.

flu•vi•al |**flōō′**vē əl| *adj.* **1.** Of or living in a river or stream. **2.** Formed or produced by the action of flowing water: *fluvial erosion.*

flux |flŭks| *n.* **1.** Continual change or flow; shifting movement: *the flux and tempo of modern life.* **2.** A heavy discharge of a fluid from a body surface or cavity. **3. a.** A flow of matter or energy. **b.** The number of lines of force that pass through a given surface located in a magnetic field or electric field. **4. a.** A substance used in soldering and brazing to prevent oxide from forming on surfaces that are to be joined. **b.** A mineral used in a smelting furnace to make metals melt more easily or to prevent oxides from forming.

fly[1] |flī| *v.* **flew** |flōō|, **flown** |flōn|, **fly•ing, flies. 1.** To move through the air with the aid of wings or winglike parts: *Birds fly.* **2.** To travel through the air like a bird: *A plane flew over our house.* **3.** To travel through air or space in an aircraft or spacecraft: *Have you ever flown in a jet?* **4.** To operate or pilot (an aircraft or spacecraft): *fly a plane.* **5.** To pass over in flight: *The plane flew 500 miles in an hour.* **6.** To carry or transport by air: *Supplies were flown to the men.* **7.** To perform in an aircraft: *He flew 66 combat missions.* **8.** To display (a flag, pennant, etc.) by fastening one end to a staff and letting the other end hang or wave. **9.** To wave or flap in the air: *The flag flies from the flagpole.* **10.** To sail or float in the air: *Fly a kite. Will the kite fly?* **11.** *Past tense and past participle* **flied.** To hit a baseball high in the air so that it travels in an arc: *Davis flied out to the center fielder.* **12.** To be swept or blown away or off: *His hat flew off.* **13.** To move or go by swiftly; speed: *She flew to the door. Time flies.* **14.** To shoot or spray out: *Sparks flew in all directions.* **15.** To give sudden expression; burst: *fly into a rage.* —***phrasal verb.*** **fly at.** To rush at angrily. —*n., pl.* **flies. 1.** Also **fly ball.** A baseball hit high in the air. **2.** A cloth flap covering a zipper or set of buttons, especially one on the front of trousers. [SEE NOTE]

Idioms. **fly in the face** (or **teeth**) **of.** To defy openly or contradict completely: *He flew in the face of tradition.* **let fly.** To shoot, hurl, or propel (a missile, weapon, etc.). **on the fly. 1.** In flight; in the air. **2.** On the run; in a hurry.

fly[2] |flī| *n., pl.* **flies. 1.** Any of a large number of winged insects, especially one of a group that includes the common housefly and many others having a single pair of thin, clear wings. **2.** A fishhook made to look like such an insect, as by attaching bits of feathers. [SEE NOTE]

Idiom. **fly in the ointment.** A bad point or drawback that spoils something that would otherwise be pleasant.

fly•catch•er |**flī′**kăch′ər| *n.* Any of several birds that fly after and catch flying insects.

fly•er |**flī′**ər| *n.* A form of the word **flier.**

Fly•ers |**flī′**ərz|. The National Hockey League team from Philadelphia.

fly•ing |**flī′**ĭng| *adj.* **1.** Moving, traveling, or shooting through the air: *a flying insect; a flying carpet; flying glass.* **2.** Waving or fluttering in the air: *flying flags.* **3.** Swiftly moving: *flying fingers.* **4.** Brief; hurried: *a flying visit.* **5.** In or for flight or aviation: *flying time; flying lessons; a flying suit.* —*n.* **1.** Flight, as in an aircraft. **2.** The operation of an aircraft.

flying buttress. An arch extending from a separate supporting structure to brace part of the main structure of a building.

flying fish. An ocean fish with large side fins that are spread out like wings as it makes gliding leaps above the water. [SEE PICTURE]

flying saucer. Any of various unidentified flying objects, usually shaped like glowing disks, that certain persons have reported seeing.

flying squirrel. A squirrel that makes long, gliding leaps with the aid of broad, winglike folds of skin that stretch between the forelegs and the hind legs.

fly•leaf |**flī′**lēf′| *n., pl.* **-leaves** |-lēvz′|. A blank page at the beginning or end of a book.

fly•pa•per |**flī′**pā′pər| *n.* Paper coated with a sticky, sometimes poisonous substance, used to catch flies.

fly•speck |**flī′**spĕk′| *n.* **1.** A small stain or spot of dirt left by a fly. **2.** Any similar small spot.

fly•trap |**flī′**trăp′| *n.* See **Venus's-flytrap.**

fly•wheel |**flī′**hwēl′| *or* |-wēl′| *n.* A massive rotating wheel used to keep a shaft of a machine turning at a steady speed.

fm, FM frequency modulation. —***modifier:*** *an fm radio.*

Fm The symbol for the element fermium.

f-num•ber |**ĕf′**nŭm′bər| *n.* A number obtained as the quotient of the focal length of a lens divided by its diameter, used in photography as a measure of the effectiveness of the lens in collecting light.

foal |fōl| *n.* A young horse, zebra, or similar related animal, especially one less than a year old. —*v.* To give birth to (a foal): *foal a colt; a mare ready to foal.*

foam |fōm| *n.* A large collection of gas bubbles trapped in a film of liquid, as the light, frothy mass formed when a solution of a soap or detergent is shaken. —*v.* To form foam or come forth in foam; froth: *The mad dog foamed at the mouth. The water boiled and foamed.*

foam rubber. A light, spongy form of rubber made by forcing air bubbles into liquid rubber and letting it harden. —***modifier:*** **(foam-rubber):** *foam-rubber pillows.*

foam•y |**fō′**mē| *adj.* **foam•i•er, foam•i•est.** Of, like, full of, or covered with foam: *foamy suds; a foamy pool.* —**foam′i•ly** *adv.* —**foam′i•ness** *n.*

fob[1] |fŏb| *n.* **1.** A small front pocket in a man's trousers or vest, used to hold a watch. **2.** A short chain or ribbon attached to such a watch. **3.** An ornament dangling from such a chain or ribbon. [SEE NOTE]

fob[2] |fŏb| *v.* **fobbed, fob•bing.** —**fob off.** To put off or palm off by being tricky or dishonest: *fob off a reporter with a false lead; fob off a copy as an original.* [SEE NOTE]

f.o.b., F.O.B. free on board, a term meaning that something will be delivered onto a ship, train, etc., without charge, with the buyer paying all further shipping charges.

fo•cal |fō′kəl| *adj.* Of, at, or concerning a focus.

focal length. **1.** The distance from the surface of a lens to the focus located on that side of the lens. **2.** The distance from the surface of a reflector to its focus.

fo•ci |fō′sī′| *n.* A plural of **focus.**

fo'c's'le or **fo'c'sle,** also **fo'c's'tle** |fōk′səl| *n.* Forms of the word **forecastle.**

fo•cus |fō′kəs| *n., pl.* **fo•cus•es** or **fo•ci** |fō′sī′|. **1. a.** A point in a system of lenses or another optical system at which rays of light come together or from which they appear to spread. **b. Focal length. c.** The degree of clarity with which an eye or optical instrument produces an image: *a telescope with poor focus.* **d.** The condition or adjustment in which an eye or optical instrument gives its best image: *The camera is out of focus.* **2.** A center of interest, attention, or activity. **3.** Concentration or emphasis: *The narrator's focus shifts from mother to father to son.* **4.** Any central point or region, such as the point at which an earthquake starts or a region of the body in which an infection is largely confined. **5.** A fixed point or one of a pair of fixed points used in constructing a curve such as an ellipse, parabola, or hyperbola. —*v.* **fo•cused** or **fo•cussed, fo•cus•ing** or **fo•cus•sing. 1. a.** To produce a clear image of (an object, place, etc.) by adjusting the eyes or an optical instrument. **b.** To adjust (the eyes, a lens, instrument, etc.) in order to produce a clear image: *Focus the telescope on the moon.* **2.** To bring or come to a focus: *A camera lens focuses light on the film.* **3.** To concentrate or center; fix: *Focus your attention on the lesson. Public attention focused on the Olympics.*

fod•der |fŏd′ər| *n.* Food, such as chopped corn stalks or hay, for horses, cattle, etc. —***modifier:*** *fodder crops.*

foe |fō| *n.* An enemy, opponent, or adversary.

foe•tal |fēt′l| *adj.* A form of the word **fetal.**

foe•tus |fē′təs| *n., pl.* **foe•tus•es.** A form of the word **fetus.**

fog |fôg| *or* |fŏg| *n.* **1.** A cloudlike mass of condensed water vapor lying close to the surface of the ground or water. **2.** Any cloud of material, such as dust or smoke, that floats in the air: *a fog of insect spray.* **3.** A confused or unthinking condition: *All considerations vanished in the fog of his anger.* —*v.* **fogged, fog•ging. 1.** To cover or become covered with or as if with fog: *Steam fogged the bathroom mirror. The car windows fogged up.* **2.** To make uncertain or unclear; confuse: *Alcohol fogged his mind.*

fo•gey |fō′gē| *n., pl.* **fo•geys.** A form of the word **fogy.**

fog•gy |fô′gē| *or* |fŏg′ē| *adj.* **fog•gi•er, fog•gi•est. 1.** Full of or covered by fog: *foggy air; foggy islands.* **2.** Characterized by fog: *foggy weather.* **3.** Dim, blurred, or clouded: *a foggy image.* **4.** Confused or vague: *I don't have the foggiest notion.* —**fog′gi•ly** *adv.* —**fog′gi•ness** *n.*

fog•horn |fôg′hôrn′| *or* |fŏg′-| *n.* A horn, usually having a deep tone, blown to warn ships of danger in foggy weather.

fo•gy |fō′gē| *n., pl.* **fo•gies.** A person with old-fashioned or narrow-minded notions. —**fo′gy•ish** *adj.* —**fo′gy•ism** *n.*

foi•ble |foi′bəl| *n.* A minor personal fault, failing, or peculiarity that is easy to forgive.

foil^1 |foil| *v.* To prevent from being successful, as by outwitting; frustrate; thwart: *an alarm system to foil thieves.* [SEE NOTE]

foil^2 |foil| *n.* **1.** A thin, flexible sheet of metal: *aluminum foil.* **2.** Something that makes something else stand out by contrast: *He was a perfect foil for the comedian.* [SEE NOTE]

foil^3 |foil| *n.* A long, light, slender sword used in fencing, with a blunt point to prevent injury. [SEE PICTURE & NOTE]

foist |foist| *v.* To pass off (something inferior) as genuine, valuable, or worthy; palm off: *He tried to foist damaged merchandise on his customers.*

fold^1 |fōld| *v.* **1.** To bend together, double up, or crease so that one part lies over another: *Fold your paper in half. This stationery folds down the middle.* **2.** To close or flatten by bending, pressing, or doubling jointed or connected parts together: *The bird folded its wings. The fan folds up.* **3. a.** To bend (the arms) inward and hold or twine them together: *The Indians folded their arms over their chests.* **b.** To clasp (the hands) together, as when sitting still or praying: *Fold your hands in your lap.* **4.** To clasp or embrace: *She folded the infant in her arms.* **5.** To blend (an ingredient) into a mixture by gently spooning one part over another: *Fold the beaten egg whites into the batter.* **6.** To give way; collapse: *His wobbly legs folded under him.* **7.** *Informal.* To fail and close: *The show folded.* —**fold′ed** *adj.: a folded map; folded rocks.* —**fold′ing** *adj.: folding chairs; folding doors.* —***phrasal verb.* fold up.** *Informal.* To stop trying or become incapable of further action: *He hits a golf ball well until people start to watch him; then he folds up.* —*n.* **1.** A line or crease formed by folding: *Tear the paper along the fold.* **2.** A layer, hollow, or pleat formed by folding: *She hid in the folds of the curtain.* **3.** A folded edge or piece: *the fold of a hem.* [SEE NOTE]

fold^2 |fōld| *n.* **1.** A pen for sheep or other domestic animals. **2.** An established group, such as a church or political party, whose members share the same beliefs, aims, or interests. [SEE NOTE]

-fold. A suffix meaning: **1.** Multiplication by a specified number: *a tenfold increase; wealth that increases tenfold.* **2.** Having a specified number of parts: *a threefold problem.* [SEE NOTE]

fold•er |fōl′dər| *n.* **1. a.** A folded sheet of cardboard or heavy paper used as a holder for loose papers: *a file folder.* **b.** Any folded cover used as a container: *a folder of matches.* **2.** A booklet or pamphlet made of one or more folded sheets of paper: *travel folders.* **3.** A person or machine that folds things.

fol•de•rol |fŏl′də rŏl′| *n.* Foolish talk or behavior; nonsense.

fo•li•a |fō′lē ə| *n.* Plural of **folium.**

fo•li•age |fō′lē ĭj| *n.* The leaves of plants or trees; leaves in general.

fo•lic acid |fō′lĭk|. A member of the vitamin-B complex composed of carbon, hydrogen, nitrogen, and oxygen in the proportions $C_{19}H_{19}N_7O_6$. It occurs in green plants, fresh fruit, liver, and yeast, and is used to treat certain forms of anemia.

fo•li•o |fō′lē ō′| *n., pl.* **fo•li•os. 1. a.** A large sheet of paper folded once, making two leaves or four

foil^3

foil$^{1\text{-}2\text{-}3}$

Foil^1 *was* foilen *in Middle English and originally meant "to trample down, to tread on."* **Foil^2** *is from Old French* foile, *"leaf, thin sheet of metal," which is from Latin* folium, *"leaf." (Jewelers used to set a piece of bright metal foil behind a gemstone to make it more brilliant; hence sense 2 of* **foil^2**.*)* **Foil^3** *is of unknown origin.*

fold$^{1\text{-}2}$/-fold

Fold^1 *was* faldan *in Old English, and it is descended from prehistoric Germanic* falthan, *"to fold." The suffix* **-fold** *was Old English* -fald, *from Germanic* -falthaz, *"-times."* Falthan *and* -fald *are both from the Indo-European root* pelt-, *"fold."* **Fold^2** *was* fald *or* falod *in Old English and is not related.*

folk etymology

People have a tendency, often unconscious, to try to reshape an unfamiliar word to resemble something familiar. This sometimes results in a permanent change. See notes at **Betelgueuse, compound, coleslaw, crayfish.**

font[1]

font[1-2]

Font[1] *is related to* **fountain; font[2]** *is related to* **foundry. Font[1]** *was* font *in Old English and is an early Christian borrowing from Latin* fons, font-, *"a spring, a well." (In Late Latin,* fontāna, *an extended form of this word, was used;* fontāna *became* fontaine *in Old French, and was borrowed into English as* **fountain.**) **Font[2]** *is from Old French* font, *"a melting, a casting of metal, a single casting of metal type"; this is from* fondre, *"to melt, to cast metal," which is from Latin* fundere, *"to melt, to pour." See notes at* **found** *and* **fuse.**

ă pat/ā pay/â care/ä father/ĕ pet/ ē be/ĭ pit/ī pie/î fierce/ŏ pot/ ō go/ô paw, for/oi oil/ŏŏ book/ ōō boot/ou out/ŭ cut/û fur/ *th* the/th thin/hw which/zh vision/ ə ago, item, pencil, atom, circus

pages of a book. **b.** A book of the largest common size, consisting of such folded sheets. **2.** A page number in a book. *—modifier: folio pages; a folio edition.*

fo•li•um |fō′lē əm| *n., pl.* **fo•li•a** |fō′lē ə|. A thin layer or stratum of rock, especially metamorphic rock.

folk |fōk| *n., pl.* **folk** or *informal* **folks. 1.** A people or nation. **2. a.** People of a certain kind: *city folk; honest folk.* **b.** A group of creatures: *the forest folk.* **3. folks.** *Informal.* People in general: *The sign "Beware!" scared folks away.* **4. folks.** *Informal.* One's family or relatives: *her father's folks.* *—adj.* Of, belonging to, or coming from the common people, who preserve legends and traditions, develop arts and crafts, etc.: *a folk hero; a folk tune.*

-folk. A word element meaning "a specified group of people": **kinsfolk; womenfolk.**

folk dance. 1. A dance, often of unknown origin, that is traditional among the common people of a country or region. **2.** The music for such a dance. —**folk dancing.**

folk etymology. 1. Alteration of a word by influence of another word or words not related to the first. **2.** A word altered in this way. [SEE NOTE]

folk•lore |fōk′lôr′| *or* |-lōr′| *n.* The traditions, beliefs, legends, customs, etc., handed down by a people from generation to generation.

folk music. Music that is traditional among the common people of a country or region. It is usually passed from person to person without musical notation and is often of unknown origin.

folk rock. A variety of popular music that combines elements of rock 'n' roll and folk music.

folk singer. Someone who specializes in singing and, often, composing folk songs. —**folk singing.**

folk song. 1. A song that is part of the folk music of a people. **2.** A song composed in imitation of such a song.

folk•sy |fōk′sē| *adj.* **folk•si•er, folk•si•est.** *Informal.* **1.** Down to earth; free of pretense; simple and casual. **2.** Friendly; neighborly; sociable. —**folk′si•ness** *n.*

folk•tale |fōk′tāl′| *n.* Also **folk tale.** A traditional story or local legend handed down by the common people of a country or region from one generation to the next.

fol•li•cle |fŏl′ĭ kəl| *n.* **1.** A rounded clump of cells, sometimes containing a cavity. **2.** A tiny sac in the body, such as the depression in the skin from which a hair grows. **3.** One of the structures in an ovary in which the ova are contained.

fol•low |fŏl′ō| *v.* **1.** To go or come after: *Follow the usher. You lead; I'll follow.* **2.** To move behind, as when chasing or trailing: *Follow the suspect at a distance.* **3.** To move or go along: *follow a trail; a new path to follow.* **4.** To take the same course as: *They followed the river southward.* **5.** To come after in order, time, or position: *Night follows day. When the right foot precedes, the left foot follows.* **6. a.** To be the result of: *A fight followed the argument.* **b.** To come as a result: *If you break the rules, trouble will follow.* **7. a.** To act in agreement with; obey: *follow orders.* **b.** To keep to or stick to: *follow a recipe.* **c.** To use as a guide: *Follow the example. She had a map to follow.* **8.** To be a believer in or disciple of: *follow a religion.* **9.** To take as one's work or occupation: *follow a trade.* **10.** To listen to or watch closely: *Fans followed the ball game on radio and TV.* **11.** To keep up with; stay informed about: *follow new developments in a case.* **12.** To understand; grasp; comprehend: *Do you follow my logic? Your reasoning is hard to follow.* *—phrasal verbs.* **follow up. 1.** To make (a previous action) more effective by doing something else that adds to it: *He followed up a body blow with a knockout punch.* **2.** To act on or carry out: *follow up a suggestion.* **3.** To seek or give more information about: *follow up a news story.* **follow with. 1.** To put after: *Follow the sentence with a period.* **2.** To repeat the same basic action with: *He put three eggs on his plate and followed with three pieces of bacon.*

fol•low•er |fŏl′ō ər| *n.* Someone or something that follows another or a belief, theory, etc., as a supporter, disciple, or admirer.

fol•low•ing |fŏl′ō ĭng| *adj.* **1. a.** Next: *the following afternoon.* **b.** After: *on the day following.* **2.** Now to be mentioned or given: *Answer the following questions. Do the following exercise.* *—n.* **1.** A group of admirers, supporters, or disciples: *a politician with a large following.* **2. the following.** The items or ones to be mentioned next: *Please buy the following: milk, bread, and eggs.*

fol•low-the-lead•er |fŏl′ō *thə* lē′dər| *n.* A game in which players have to imitate each move the leader makes.

fol•low-up |fŏl′ō ŭp′| *n.* Something, such as a letter, procedure, or visit, that makes previous action more effective. *—modifier: a follow-up report.*

fol•ly |fŏl′ē| *n., pl.* **fol•lies. 1.** Lack of good sense or judgment; foolishness. **2.** A piece of foolishness, as a silly idea, plan, or action.

fo•ment |fō mĕnt′| *v.* To stir up; arouse; provoke: *foment a rebellion.*

fond |fŏnd| *adj.* **fond•er, fond•est. 1.** Loving or affectionate: *a fond heart; a fond good night.* **2.** Foolishly affectionate. **3.** Cherished; dear: *my fondest hopes.* —**fond′ly** *adv.*

Idiom. **fond of.** Having a liking for: *fond of pets; fond of fighting.*

fon•dle |fŏn′dl| *v.* **fon•dled, fon•dling.** To touch or stroke lovingly; caress: *fondle a puppy.*

fond•ness |fŏnd′nĭs| *n.* **1.** Liking or inclination: *a fondness for study.* **2.** Warm affection.

fon•due |fŏn dōō′| *n.* A hot dish made of melted cheese, eaten by dipping bits of bread into it.

font[1] |fŏnt| *n.* **1.** A basin that holds holy water or water used in baptizing. **2.** A source; a fountain: *The old man is a font of knowledge.* [SEE NOTE & PICTURE]

font[2] |fŏnt| *n.* A complete set of printing type of one size and style. [SEE NOTE]

food |fōōd| *n.* **1.** Any substance that a plant or animal can take in and use for energy and for material to maintain life and growth; nourishment. **2.** A supply of things to eat: *He brought them food and medicine.* **3.** A particular kind of nourishment: *plant food; dog food.* **4.** Nourishment in solid form: *food and drink.* **5.** Anything that stimulates or encourages some activity: *The sermon gave them food for thought.* *—modifier: a food fish; a food supply.*

food chain. A series of plants and animals within an environment, of which each kind serves as a source of nourishment for the next in the series.

food cycle. A group of food chains that constitutes all or most of the food relations in an ecological community.

food poisoning. Poisoning that results from eating food that has become contaminated with bacteria.

food processor. An appliance with interchangeable blades that processes food, as by slicing or shredding, at high speeds.

food stamp. A stamp issued by the government and sold or given to low-income persons to be redeemed for food.

food•stuff |fo͞od'stŭf'| *n.* Any substance that can be used or prepared for use as food.

food web. All the individual food chains that enable an ecological community to survive.

fool |fo͞ol| *n.* **1.** A stupid, silly, reckless, or thoughtless person. **2.** In olden days, a jester who entertained at the court of a king or nobleman by telling jokes, doing tricks, and clowning. *—adj. Informal.* Foolish; stupid: *some fool kid; a fool trick.* *—v.* **1.** To trick, deceive, or mislead: *You can't fool me. I'm not easy to fool.* **2.** To joke, pretend, or tease: *I'm not fooling; I'm serious.* ***—phrasal verbs.*** **fool around.** *Informal.* **1.** To waste time; idle. **2.** To mess around; play. **3.** To tease, joke, or kid. **fool with (or around with).** *Informal.* To play, tamper, or meddle with: *Don't fool with Dad's mower.*

fool•har•dy |fo͞ol'här'dē| *adj.* **fool•har•di•er, fool•har•di•est.** Foolishly bold; showing daring without foresight; rash and reckless: *a foolhardy beginner trying to ski down the highest slope.* **—fool'har'di•ness** *n.*

fool•ish |fo͞o'lĭsh| *adj.* **1. a.** Lacking in good sense or judgment: *foolish people.* **b.** Unwise: *a foolish choice.* **2.** Like a fool; silly; absurd: *He felt foolish.* **3.** Pointless; senseless: *"Fishing is foolish," said the disappointed child.* **—fool'ish•ly** *adv.* **—fool'ish•ness** *n.*

fool•proof |fo͞ol'pro͞of'| *adj.* So safe, effective, and reliable that even a fool could not keep it from working properly: *a foolproof burglar alarm; a foolproof plan.*

fools•cap |fo͞olz'kăp'| *n.* Writing paper in large sheets about 13 inches wide and 16 inches long.

fool's gold. Pyrite or any of several other minerals that are sometimes mistaken for gold.

foot |fo͝ot| *n., pl.* **feet** |fēt|. **1.** The part of the leg that rests on or touches the ground, floor, etc., in standing or walking. **2.** A similar part used for moving or attachment, as the muscular organ extending from the shell of a snail or clam. **3.** Any part or base resembling a foot, as the end of a table leg. **4.** The lowest part of something high or long; the bottom: *the foot of the stairs; the foot of the page.* **5.** The end opposite the head in position or rank: *the foot of the bed; the foot of the class.* **6.** The part of a boot or stocking that covers the foot. **7.** A unit of length equal to 1/3 of a yard or 12 inches. **8.** One of the parts into which a line of poetry is divided when counting off units of rhythm. "Mārў / hăd ă / lĭttle / lămb" is a line with four feet. **9.** The attachment on a sewing machine that clamps down and guides the cloth. **10.** Foot soldiers; infantry. ***—modifier:*** *a foot warmer.* *—v. Informal.* **1.** To pay: *I'll foot the bill.* **2.** To add; total: *You foot up the bill.* **—foot'less** *adj.* [SEE NOTES]

Idioms. **at the feet of** or **at (one's) feet.** Fascinated or enchanted by; under the spell of. **foot it.** To walk, dance, or run. **on foot. 1.** Walking or running rather than riding. **2.** Under way; in progress: *Plans were on foot for a party.* **on (or to) (one's) feet.** In (or to) a standing position: *He landed on his feet. We rose to our feet.* **put (one's) best foot forward.** *Informal.* To make a good first impression. **put (one's) foot down.** *Informal.* To take a firm stand; insist on being obeyed. **put (one's) foot in it.** To make an embarrassing blunder. **put (one's) foot in (one's) mouth** *Informal.* To say something by mistake that causes embarrassment or hurt feelings. **set foot. 1.** To take a single step into or onto: *Don't set foot in this room.* **2.** To arrive or land: *set foot on shore.* **under foot.** In danger of being stepped on.

foot•age |fo͝ot'ĭj| *n.* A length or amount of something as measured in feet: *film footage.*

foot-and-mouth disease |fo͝ot'n mouth'|. A highly contagious disease of cattle and other animals with cloven hoofs, marked by fever and the breaking out of blisters around the mouth and hoofs.

foot•ball |fo͝ot'bôl'| *n.* **1. a.** A game played by two teams of 11 players each on a long field with goals at either end, the object being to carry the ball across the opponent's goal line or to kick it between the opponent's goal posts. **b.** The inflated oval ball used in this game, made of a bladder covered with leather, often pigskin. **2.** *British.* **a.** Soccer or rugby. **b.** The ball used in soccer or rugby. ***—modifier:*** *a football team.*

foot-can•dle |fo͝ot'kăn'dl| *n.* A unit equal to the illumination of a surface that has each of its points one foot away from a source of light rated at one candela.

foot•ed |fo͝ot'ĭd| *adj.* **1.** Having a foot or feet: *a footed vase.* **2.** Having a certain kind or number of feet: *a four-footed animal.*

foot•fall |fo͝ot'fôl'| *n.* The sound made by a footstep.

foot•hill |fo͝ot'hĭl'| *n.* A low hill located near the base of a mountain or mountain range.

foot•hold |fo͝ot'hōld'| *n.* **1.** A place to put the foot so that it won't slip, especially when climbing. **2.** A small, secure position, often in alien surroundings, where it is safe to stay or from which it is possible to advance.

foot•ing |fo͝ot'ĭng| *n.* **1.** A firm placing of the feet allowing one to stand or move without falling: *lose one's footing.* **2.** A safe place on which to stand or step: *The icy walk offered us no footing.* **3.** The condition of a surface for walking or running: *The road was muddy and the footing treacherous.* **4.** A basis or standing: *You'll be on an equal footing with the others.*

foot•lights |fo͝ot'līts'| *pl.n.* Lights placed in a row along the front of a stage floor.

foot•man |fo͝ot'mən| *n., pl.* **-men** |-mən|. A male servant, usually in uniform, who opens doors, serves at the table, etc.

foot•note |fo͝ot'nōt'| *n.* A note at the bottom of a page explaining something or giving the source of a quotation, fact, or idea.

food chain

A food chain of ocean life begins with tiny plants and animals called plankton, which are eaten by small crustaceans, which in turn are eaten by small fish. These are fed on by larger fish, such as mackerel, which serve as food for still larger fish, such as tuna or swordfish. Another common food chain begins with grass, eaten by cattle, which supply food for human beings.

foot

Foot *was* fōt *in Old English,* fōt- *also in prehistoric Germanic, and* pōd- *in Indo-European. (Notice that Indo-European* p *always becomes* f *in the Germanic languages and that* d *always becomes* t.*)* Pōd- *itself in Indo-European is a variant of* ped-, *the basic word for "foot." It appears in Latin as* pēs, ped- *and in Greek as* pous, pod-

foot

The idiom **put one's foot in one's mouth** *probably results from an extension of the much older idiom* **put one's foot in it**. *A joke was devised consisting of an intentional mixture of two idioms, with ludicrous result (*to open one's mouth = *"to begin to speak"):* "He never opens his mouth but he puts his foot in it." *This joke has been so widely repeated that the resulting new idiom* **put one's foot in one's mouth** *seems to be actually replacing the earlier one.*

forasmuch as

The process of running phrases together to make compound prepositions, adverbs, and conjunctions is an archaic Germanic feature that English has inherited from its past. Probably the process is no longer actively operating, so that no new words will be formed in this way. Examples: **forasmuch as, inasmuch as, insofar as, therefore, notwithstanding, nonetheless.**

force

The idea of **force,** *while perhaps familiar in everyday experience, is difficult to express in a clear, scientific way. In physics, a force is defined more by what it does than by what it is. Thus, Sir Isaac Newton (1642–1727) defined force as* **F** = m**a**, *where* **F** *is force,* m *is mass, and* **a** *is acceleration.* **F** *and* **a** *are printed in boldface type to show that they are vectors, that is, that they have direction as well as magnitude.*

ă pat/ā pay/â care/ä father/ĕ pet/ ē be/ĭ pit/ī pie/î fierce/ŏ pot/ ō go/ô paw, for/oi oil/ŏŏ book/ ōō boot/ou out/ŭ cut/û fur/ *th* the/th thin/hw which/zh vision/ ə ago, item, pencil, atom, circus

foot•path |fo͝ot′păth′| *or* |-päth′| *n., pl.* **-paths** |-păthz′| *or* |-päthz′| *or* |-păths′| *or* |-päths′|. A narrow path for people to walk on.

foot-pound |fo͝ot′pound′| *n.* A unit equal to the work or energy needed to lift a one-pound weight a distance of 1 foot against the force of the earth's gravity.

foot•print |fo͝ot′prĭnt′| *n.* A mark or indented place left by a foot or shoe, as in sand, snow, etc.

foot•race |fo͝ot′rās′| *n.* A race run by people on foot.

foot•rest |fo͝ot′rĕst′| *n.* A low stool, metal bar, or other support on which to rest the feet.

foot soldier. An infantryman.

foot•sore |fo͝ot′sôr′| *or* |-sōr′| *adj.* Having sore, tired, or aching feet from much walking.

foot•step |fo͝ot′stĕp′| *n.* **1.** A step taken by a foot in walking or running. **2.** The sound of a step. **3.** A footprint.
Idiom. **follow in (someone's) footsteps.** To do the same thing or practice the same profession as someone who went before.

foot•stool |fo͝ot′sto͞ol′| *n.* A low stool on which to rest the feet while sitting.

foot•wear |fo͝ot′wâr′| *n.* Coverings for the feet, such as shoes, slippers, sandals, boots, etc.

foot•work |fo͝ot′wûrk′| *n.* Controlled movement of the feet, as in boxing or dancing: *fancy footwork.*

fop |fŏp| *n.* A man who is very vain about his fancy clothes and stylish appearance; a dandy.

for |fôr| *or* |fər *when unstressed*| *prep.* **1.** Directed or sent to: *a letter for you.* **2.** As a result of: *weep for joy.* **3.** To the extent or through the duration of: *sitting still for an hour.* **4.** In order to go to or reach: *starting for home.* **5. a.** With a view to: *swimming for fun.* **b.** So as to find, get, have, keep, or save: *looking for a bargain; fighting for one's life.* **6.** In order to serve in or as: *studying for the ministry.* **7.** In the amount or at the price of: *a bill for three dollars; buying a dog for ten dollars.* **8.** In response to: *I slapped him for saying that.* **9.** In view of the normal character of: *His book is pretty short for a novel.* **10.** At a stated time: *a date for one o'clock.* **11.** In the service or hire of: *working for a boss.* **12.** In spite of: *For all her experience, she does a poor job.* **13.** On behalf or in honor of: *a collection for the poor; a reception for the ambassador.* **14.** In place of: *using artificial flowers for real ones.* **15.** Together with: *one rotten apple for every good one.* **16.** As against: *pound for pound.* **17.** As being: *took him for a fool.* **18.** As the duty or task of; up to: *That's for you to decide.* —*conj.* Because; since. ¶*These sound alike* **for, fore, four.**

for•age |fôr′ĭj| *or* |fŏr′-| *n.* **1.** Food for horses, cattle, or other animals, as plants or grass eaten while grazing. **2.** A search to find available food or supplies. —*modifier: forage crops.* —*v.* **for•aged, for•ag•ing. 1.** To search for food: *Raccoons forage in garbage dumps.* **2.** To search or hunt about, as for anything needed or desired: *a boy foraging in a drawer for a sock.* **3.** To get, as food, by searching about: *The girls foraged cookies from the pantry.* —**for′ag•er** *n.*

for•as•much as |fôr′əz mŭch′|. Inasmuch as. [SEE NOTE]

for•ay |fôr′ā′| *or* |fŏr′ā′| *n.* **1.** A sudden raid, expedition, or invasion, as to fight someone. **2.** A first attempt or venture in some field: *her opening foray into politics.* —*v.* To make a raid, as for plunder: *foray into enemy territory.*

for•bad |fər băd′| *or* |fôr-|. A past tense of **forbid.**

for•bade |fər băd′| *or* |-bād′| *or* |fôr-|. A past tense of **forbid.**

for•bear[1] |fôr bâr′| *v.* **for•bore** |fôr bôr′| *or* |-bōr′|, **for•borne** |fôr bôrn′| *or* |-bōrn′|, **for•bear•ing. 1. a.** To keep from; refrain from; resist: *I could not forbear whispering.* **b.** To hold back; refrain: *forbear from replying.* **2.** To give up; stop; cease: *Forbear trading in the furs of endangered species.* **3.** To be patient or tolerant: *Forbear with my ignorance.* —**for•bear′ing** *adj.*: *forbearing parents.*

for•bear[2] |fôr′bâr′| *or* |fōr′-| *n.* A form of the word **forebear.**

for•bear•ance |fôr bâr′əns| *n.* Patience, tolerance, or restraint: *He appealed to his restless countrymen for more time and forbearance.*

for•bid |fər bĭd′| *or* |fôr-| *v.* **for•bade** |fər băd′| *or* |-bād′| *or* |fôr-| or **for•bad** |fər băd′| *or* |fôr-|, **for•bid•den** |fər bĭd′n| *or* |fôr-|, **for•bid•ding. 1.** To refuse to allow; prohibit or deny: *The law forbids robbery. The queen forbade them entry.* **2.** To order (someone) not to do something: *I forbid you to go.* **3.** To make (something) impossible; prevent: *Time forbids my continuing. Heaven forbid!*

for•bid•ding |fər bĭd′ĭng| *or* |fôr-| *adj.* Threatening, dangerous, or unfriendly in nature or appearance; frightening: *a forbidding desert; a fierce, forbidding scowl.*

for•bore |fôr bôr′| *or* |-bōr′|. Past tense of **forbear.**

for•borne |fôr bôrn′| *or* |-bōrn′|. Past participle of **forbear.**

force |fôrs| *or* |fōrs| *n.* **1.** Strength; power; energy: *the force of an explosion.* **2.** Power, pressure, or violence used on something or someone that resists: *use force in driving a nail; a confession obtained by force.* **3.** Something, such as a push or pull, that accelerates a given mass in the direction in which it is applied and has a measure equal to the product of the mass multiplied by the amount by which it is accelerated: *the force of the wind against a sail.* **4. a.** A group of people organized for a purpose, available for service, and considered a source of power: *a large labor force; a police force.* **b.** A military branch or unit: *the armed forces; a tank force.* **c. forces.** An army: *Napoleon's forces.* **5.** A strong influence acting as an urge or restraint: *forces affecting modern life.* **6.** Mental or moral strength: *sheer force of will.* **7.** The power to influence or persuade; effectiveness: *the force of an appeal.* **8.** Legal effectiveness; validity: *The contract was void and of no force.* —*v.* **forced, forc•ing. 1.** To make do something, as through pressure or necessity: *He forced the enemy to surrender.* **2.** To move, push, or drive by pressure: *The pump forces water up into the pipe.* **3.** To bring on or bring about through effort or pressure: *forcing a smile onto her face.* **4.** To make (one's way) by pushing, thrusting, breaking, etc.: *They forced their way through the thorn hedge.* **5.** To break or pry open by using violence: *force the door; force a lock.* **6.** To impose, inflict, or intrude: *He forced his ideas on them.* **7.** To cause to grow or bloom rapidly by artificial means: *force flowers in a greenhouse.* [SEE NOTE]

Idioms. **by** (or **from** or **through) force of.** As the result of: *ruined through force of circumstances.* **in force. 1.** In effect; in operation; valid: *a rule no longer in force.* **2.** In full strength: *The marching band turned out in force.*

forced |fôrst| *or* |fōrst| *adj.* **1.** Done under force, not by free choice; compulsory: *forced labor.* **2.** Not natural; strained: *forced laughter.* **3.** Required by an emergency: *a forced landing.*

force•ful |fôrs′fəl| *or* |fōrs′-| *adj.* Full of force; strong; powerful; effective: *a forceful speaker.* —**force′ful•ly** *adv.* —**force′ful•ness** *n.*

for•ceps |fôr′səps| *n. (used with a plural verb).* A pair of special pincers or tongs used by surgeons, dentists, jewelers, etc., for delicate grasping, holding, or pulling.

for•ci•ble |fôr′sə bəl| *or* |fōr′-| *adj.* Accomplished through the use of force: *a burglar's forcible entry.* —**for′ci•bly** *adv.*

ford |fôrd| *or* |fōrd| *n.* A shallow place in a stream or river where one can wade, ride, or drive across. —*v.* To cross (a stream or river) by wading, riding, or driving through a ford.

Ford |fôrd| *or* |fōrd|, **Gerald Rudolph.** Original name, Leslie Lynch King, Jr. Born 1913. Thirty-eighth President of the United States (1974–77).

Ford |fôrd| *or* |fōrd|, **Henry.** 1863–1947. American automobile manufacturer.

fore |fôr| *or* |fōr| *adj. & adv.* In, at, or toward the front. —*n.* The front part. —*interj.* A shout used by golfers to warn others on the course that the ball is about to be hit in their direction. ¶ *These sound alike* **fore, for, four.**

Idiom. **to the fore. 1.** In or to the front; forward: *In the seating plan used for concert bands, the woodwinds are to the fore.* **2.** In or into a prominent position: *New issues brought new leaders to the fore.*

fore–. A word element meaning: **1.** Earlier; before: **foresight; forefather. 2.** In front; front: **foreleg; forepaw. 3.** The front or first part of: **forehead; forearm. 4.** First in order or rank: **forefinger; foreman.** [SEE NOTE]

fore and aft. Lengthwise, in line with the center line of a ship: *sails rigged fore and aft.*

fore-and-aft |fôr′ən ăft′| *or* |-äft′| *or* |fōr′-| *adj.* Extending lengthwise along the center line of a ship, from bow to stern: *fore-and-aft sails.* [SEE PICTURE]

fore•arm¹ |fôr′ärm′| *or* |fōr′-| *n.* The part of the arm between the wrist and elbow.

fore•arm² |fôr **ärm′**| *or* |fōr-| *v.* To prepare in advance for coming danger or difficulty; arm beforehand: *Forewarned is forearmed.*

fore•bear |fôr′bâr′| *or* |fōr′-| *n.* An ancestor; forefather.

fore•bode |fôr **bōd**| *or* |fōr-| *v.* **fore•bod•ed, fore•bod•ing.** To give or have a hint or warning of (something bad to come): *The dark scowls on their faces foreboded a fight.*

fore•bod•ing |fôr **bō′**dĭng| *or* |fōr-| *n.* An uneasy feeling that something bad is going to happen.

fore•brain |fôr′brān′| *or* |fōr′-| *n.* **1.** The forward part of the brain of a vertebrate. **2.** The part of the brain of an embryo from which this develops.

fore•cast |fôr′kăst′| *or* |-käst′| *or* |fōr′-| *v.* **fore•cast** or **fore•cast•ed, fore•cast•ing. 1. a.** To tell in advance, especially after analyzing available data: *forecast an eclipse.* **b.** To tell (weather conditions) in advance. **2.** To serve as an advance indication of: *signs that forecast the end of winter.* —*n.* A prediction, as of coming events or conditions: *the weather forecast; population forecasts.* —**fore′cast′er** *n.*

fore•cas•tle |fōk′səl| *or* |fôr′kăs′əl| *or* |-kä′səl| *or* |fōr′-| *n.* **1.** The section of a ship's upper deck located at the bow, in front of the foremast. **2.** The crew's quarters in the front part of a merchant ship.

fore•close |fôr **klōz′**| *or* |fōr-| *v.* **fore•closed, fore•clos•ing.** To end (a mortgage), taking possession of the mortgaged property when regular payments on the mortgage loan are not met.

fore•clo•sure |fôr **klō′**zhər| *or* |fōr-| *n.* A legal proceeding by which a mortgage is foreclosed, enabling the holder of the mortgage to take or sell the mortgaged property to satisfy his claim for payment.

fore•fa•ther |fôr′fä′*th*ər| *or* |fōr′-| *n.* An ancestor.

fore•fin•ger |fôr′fĭng′gər| *or* |fōr′-| *n.* The finger next to the thumb; index finger.

fore•foot |fôr′fo͝ot′| *or* |fōr′-| *n., pl.* **-feet** |-fēt′|. **1.** One of the front feet of an animal. **2.** The part of a ship at which the prow joins the keel.

fore•front |fôr′frŭnt′| *or* |fōr′-| *n.* **1.** The part or area at the very front. **2.** The most important part or most advanced position: *He towered in the forefront of politics.*

fore•gath•er |fôr **găth′**ər| *or* |fōr-| *v.* A form of the word **forgather.**

fore•go |fôr **gō′**| *or* |fōr-| *v.* **fore•went** |fôr **wĕnt′**| *or* |fōr-|, **fore•gone** |fôr **gôn′**| *or* |**-gŏn′**| *or* |fōr-|, **fore•go•ing, fore•goes.** A form of the word **forgo.**

fore•go•ing |fôr **gō′**ĭng| *or* |fōr-| *or* |fôr′gō′-| *or* |fōr′-| *adj.* Said, written, or encountered just before; previous: *the foregoing statements.* —*n.* **the foregoing.** What has just been said, written, or discussed: *The foregoing represents a systematic approach to the problem.*

fore•gone |fôr **gôn′**| *or* |**-gŏn′**| *or* |fōr-|. Past participle of **forego.**

fore•gone conclusion |fôr′gôn′| *or* |-gŏn′| *or* |fōr′-|. A result, outcome, or decision seeming so certain that it can be known or agreed on in advance: *His nomination for the Presidency was a foregone conclusion.*

fore•ground |fôr′ground′| *or* |fōr′-| *n.* The part of a scene or picture that is or that seems to be closest to the person viewing it.

fore•hand |fôr′hănd′| *or* |fōr′-| *n.* In sports, a stroke, as of a racket, made with the palm of the hand turned forward. —***modifier:*** *a forehand stroke.* —*adv.* With a forehand stroke or motion: *hit the ball forehand.* [SEE PICTURE]

fore•head |fôr′ĭd| *or* |fŏr′-| *or* |fôr′hĕd′| *or* |fōr′-| *n.* The front part of the head above the eyes.

for•eign |fôr′ĭn| *or* |fŏr′-| *adj.* **1.** Being outside

for-/fore-

The prefix for-, *now surviving only in* **forbear¹, forbid, forget, forgive, forgo,** *and* **forswear,** *is common to the Germanic languages but is no longer active in English. Its meaning is hard to define precisely, but it contains the idea of excluding, rejecting, or doing without. Thus* **forbear¹** *is "to bear oneself without doing something that one could do";* **forbid** *is "to bid someone to keep away from something";* **forget** *is "not to get" or "to lose one's grasp on." Notice that some of the words with* for- *have variant spellings in* fore-. *But words containing the separate prefix* **fore-** *(meaning "before, in front") only have spellings in* fore-.

fore-and-aft

forehand

or different from one's own country: *a foreign country.* **2.** Of, from, by, with, or for another country or other countries: *a foreign language; a foreign government; foreign trade.* **3.** Dealing with other nations or governments: *foreign affairs.* **4.** Not naturally or normally belonging; alien: *Jealousy is foreign to her nature.*

for•eign•er |fôr′ə nər| *or* |fŏr′-| *n.* **1.** A person from a foreign country. **2.** Any outsider.

foreign exchange. The process of settling debts between people, businesses, or governments of different countries, involving the changing of money from one nation's currency for an equivalent value in another nation's currency.

fore•knowl•edge |fôr′nŏl′ĭj| *or* |fōr′-| *or* |fôr-nŏl′ĭj| *or* |fōr-| *n.* Knowledge of something before it happens or comes into existence.

fore•leg |fôr′lĕg′| *or* |fōr′-| *n.* One of the front legs of an animal.

fore•limb |fôr′lĭm′| *or* |fōr′-| *n.* A front part such as an arm, wing, foreleg, or flipper.

fore•lock |fôr′lŏk′| *or* |fōr′-| *n.* A lock of hair that grows or falls on the forehead.

fore•man |fôr′mən| *or* |fōr′-| *n., pl.* **-men** |-mən|. **1.** A person who has charge of a group of workers, as at a factory or ranch. **2.** The member of a jury who presides over the deliberations and announces the verdict to the court.

fore•mast |fôr′məst| *or* |-măst′| *or* |-mäst′| *or* |fōr′-| *n.* The mast closest to the bow of a sailing ship.

fore•most |fôr′mōst′| *or* |fōr′-| *adj.* First in rank or position; most important; leading; chief: *the world's foremost authority on the subject.*

fore•noon |fôr′no͞on′| *or* |fōr′-| *n.* The period of time between sunrise and noon; morning.

fore•or•dain |fôr′ôr **dān′**| *or* |fōr′-| *v.* To decide, determine, or decree beforehand; predestine: *They believed their fate was foreordained.*

fore•part |fôr′pärt′| *or* |fōr′-| *n.* The first or front part: *the forepart of a shell.*

fore•paw |fôr′pô′| *or* |fōr′-| *n.* A front paw.

fore•quar•ter |fôr′kwôr′tər| *or* |fōr′-| *n.* **1.** Often **forequarters.** The front legs, shoulders, etc., of a four-footed animal. **2.** The front leg and front part of a side of beef, lamb, etc.

fore•run•ner |fôr′rŭn′ər| *or* |fōr′-| *n.* Something that comes before another thing in time and that prepares the way for it or signals its approach: *The harpsichord was the forerunner of the piano.*

fore•sail |fôr′səl| *or* |-sāl′| *or* |fōr′-| *n.* **1.** The biggest and lowest sail on the foremast of a square-rigged ship. **2.** The principal fore-and-aft sail on the foremast of a schooner.

fore•saw |fôr **sô′**| *or* |fōr-|. Past tense of **foresee.**

fore•see |fôr **sē′**| *or* |fōr-| *v.* **fore•saw** |fôr **sô′**| *or* |fōr-|, **fore•seen** |fôr **sēn′**| *or* |fōr-|, **fore•see•ing.** To see, imagine, or realize in advance; anticipate: *a situation I had not foreseen.*

fore•see•a•ble |fôr **sē′**ə bəl| *or* |fōr-| *adj.* Capable of being anticipated or predicted: *within the foreseeable future.*

fore•seen |fôr **sēn′**| *or* |fōr-|. Past participle of **foresee.**

fore•shad•ow |fôr **shăd′**ō| *or* |fōr-| *v.* To give an advance warning, sign, or hint of (something to come).

fore•short•en |fôr **shôr′**tn| *or* |fōr-| *v.* To show the length of (a figure, design, etc.) by shortening certain lines so as to give the illusion of depth or distance. [SEE PICTURE]

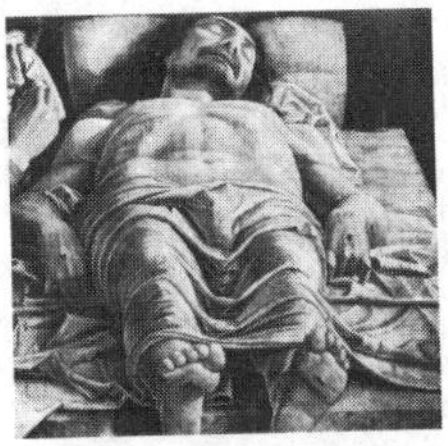

foreshorten

fore•sight |fôr′sīt′| *or* |fōr′-| *n.* The ability to look ahead, anticipate, and plan for the future before it comes. —**fore′sight′ed** *adj.*

fore•skin |fôr′skĭn′| *or* |fōr′-| *n.* The loose fold of skin that covers the end of the penis.

for•est |fôr′ĭst| *or* |fŏr′-| *n.* A dense growth of trees covering a large area. —***modifier:*** *a forest fire.*

fore•stall |fôr **stôl′**| *or* |fōr-| *v.* To prevent, put off, or cut off by taking effective action in advance: *He was curt with them to forestall any more questions.*

for•est•er |fôr′ĭ stər| *or* |fŏr′-| *n.* **1.** A person trained in forestry. **2.** An inhabitant of a forest.

for•est•ry |fôr′ĭ strē| *or* |fŏr′-| *n.* The science or work of developing and caring for forests.

fore•taste |fôr′tāst′| *or* |fōr′-| *n.* A first experience or sample of something to come in the future: *Her first published story gave her a foretaste of success.*

fore•tell |fôr **tĕl′**| *or* |fōr-| *v.* **fore•told** |fôr-**tōld′**| or |fōr-|, **fore•tell•ing.** To tell beforehand; predict: *Can a prophet foretell what will happen?*

fore•thought |fôr′thôt′| *or* |fōr′-| *n.* Thought, planning, or preparation for the future ahead of time.

fore•told |fôr **tōld′**| *or* |fōr-|. Past tense and past participle of **foretell.**

for•ev•er |fôr **ĕv′**ər| *or* |fər-| *adv.* **1.** For all time; eternally; always: *I'll love you forever.* **2.** At all times; constantly; incessantly: *Must you be forever complaining?*

for•ev•er•more |fôr ĕv′ər **môr′**| *or* |**-mōr′**| *or* |fər-| *adv.* Forever.

fore•warn |fôr **wôrn′**| *or* |fōr-| *v.* To warn in advance: *They were forewarned of their friend's arrival.*

fore•went |fôr **wĕnt′**| *or* |fōr-|. Past tense of **forego.**

fore•wing |fôr′wĭng′| *or* |fōr′-| *n.* A front wing, as of a moth, butterfly, or dragonfly.

fore•word |fôr′wûrd′| *or* |-wərd| *or* |fōr′-| *n.* An introduction at the beginning of a book or other piece of writing; a preface.

for•feit |fôr′fĭt| *v.* To lose or give up (something) as a penalty or fine for a failure, error, or offense: *By failing to appear and play, the opposing team forfeited the game.* —*n.* Something lost, given up, or paid as a penalty or fine: *pay a forfeit.*

for•fei•ture |fôr′fĭ chər| *n.* **1.** The loss or surrender of something as a penalty for a failure or offense. **2.** Something, such as property or money, lost or claimed as a forfeit.

for•gath•er |fôr **găth′**ər| *or* |fōr-| *v.* To gather together; assemble.

for•gave |fər **gāv′**| *or* |fôr-|. Past tense of **forgive.**

forge[1] |fôrj| *or* |fōrj| *n.* **1.** A furnace or hearth where metal is heated so that it can be worked more easily. **2.** The workshop of a blacksmith; a smithy. —*v.* **forged, forg•ing.** **1.** To work or shape (metal) by heating in a forge and hammering: *forge steel; forge a ring from gold.* **2.** To make, shape, or form as if by heating and ham-

forge[1]

forge[1-2]

Forge[1] *is from Old French* forge, *which is from Late Latin* faurga, *an altered form of* fabrica, *"blacksmith's workshop," from* faber, *"blacksmith, carpenter, craftsman." From* faber *also was formed the verb* fabricārī, *"to construct, to build," which was borrowed into English as* **fabricate.** *The origin of* **forge[2]** *is obscure; it has been suggested that it is a variant of the verb* **force,** *but there is no proof of this.*

ă pat/ā pay/â care/ä father/ĕ pet/ ē be/ĭ pit/ī pie/î fierce/ŏ pot/ ō go/ô paw, for/oi oil/o͝o book/ o͞o boot/ou out/ŭ cut/û fur/ *th* the/th thin/hw which/zh vision/ ə ago, item, pencil, atom, circus

mering metal: *The coach forged the team into a pennant winner.* **3.** To copy or imitate (a signature, piece of writing, etc.) with the intention of passing off the counterfeit as the real thing: *forge a check.* [SEE NOTE & PICTURE]

forge² |fôrj| *or* |fōrj| *v.* **forged, forg•ing.** To move forward gradually, by steady effort, or suddenly, with a burst of speed: *forge through a swamp; forge ahead in a race.* [SEE NOTE]

forg•er |fôr′jər| *or* |fōr′-| *n.* **1.** A person guilty of forging signatures, checks, documents, etc. **2.** A worker who forges metal; a smith.

for•ger•y |fôr′jə rē| *or* |fōr′-| *n., pl.* **for•ger•ies.** **1.** The act or crime of imitating a signature, document, painting, etc., with the intention of passing off the copy as the real thing. **2.** Something counterfeit, as a forged check.

for•get |fər gĕt′| *v.* **for•got** |fər gŏt′|, **for•got•ten** |fər gŏt′n| or **for•got, for•get•ting.** **1.** To be unable to remember or fail to remember: *He forgot her telephone number. Elephants never forget.* **2.** To stop remembering: *Uncle George forgot his troubles for a few happy hours.* **3.** To omit, disregard, or neglect: *I forgot to mention that detail.* —**for•get′ta•ble** *adj.* —**for•get′ter** *n.*

Idiom. **forget (oneself).** To lose one's inhibitions; act without restraint.

for•get•ful |fər gĕt′fəl| *adj.* **1.** Tending to forget or likely to forget: *a forgetful old man.* **2.** Neglectful; thoughtless: *The proud Indian was now dependent on a forgetful government.* —**for•get′ful•ly** *adv.* —**for•get′ful•ness** *n.*

for•get-me-not |fər gĕt′mē nŏt′| *n.* A low-growing plant with clusters of small blue flowers. [SEE PICTURE]

for•give |fər gĭv′| *v.* **for•gave** |fər gāv′|, **for•giv•en** |fər gĭv′ən|, **for•giv•ing.** **1.** To excuse for a fault, injury, or offense; pardon: *Forgive me for saying so, but you acted badly. They forgave his crime.* **2.** To grant forgiveness: *To err is human, to forgive divine.* —**for•giv′ing** *adj.*: *a forgiving nature.* —**for•giv′a•ble** *adj.*

for•give•ness |fər gĭv′nĭs| *n.* The act of forgiving; pardon.

for•go |fôr gō′| *v.* **for•went** |fôr wĕnt′|, **for•gone** |fôr gôn′| *or* |-gŏn′|, **for•go•ing.** To give up; relinquish; renounce: *Either you clean your room or you forgo your allowance.*

for•got |fər gŏt′|. Past tense and a past participle of **forget.**

for•got•ten |fər gŏt′n|. A past participle of **forget.**

for•int |fôr′ĭnt| *n.* The basic unit of money of Hungary.

fork |fôrk| *n.* **1.** A utensil with several sharp prongs or tines for use in eating food. **2.** A large farm tool of similar shape used in pitching hay or turning up ground; a pitchfork. **3. a.** A separation into two or more parts, as of the branches of a tree. **b.** One of these parts: *take the right fork of the road.* **4.** A **tuning fork.** —*v.* **1.** To raise, carry, pitch, or pierce with a fork. **2.** To divide into two or more branches.

Idiom. **fork over.** *Informal.* To hand over; pay: *Either fork over the money or we won't give you the car.*

forked |fôrkt| *adj.* **1.** Having or distinguished by a fork: *a forked stick; a forked road.* **2.** Shaped like a fork: *The snake flashed its forked tongue.* **3.** Ambiguous; deceitful: *He speaks with a forked tongue.*

fork lift. A small vehicle with wheels, equipped with a pair of prongs that can be slid under a load that is to be lifted and moved.

fork•lift |fôrk′lĭft′| *n.* A form of the phrase **fork lift.**

for•lorn |fôr lôrn′| *adj.* **1.** Deserted; forsaken; abandoned: *a forlorn house.* **2.** Wretched or pitiful in appearance or condition: *the forlorn little stray dog.* —**for•lorn′ly** *adv.* —**for•lorn′ness** *n.*

form |fôrm| *n.* **1.** The shape, structure, or contour of something; outward or visible appearance: *Geometry is concerned with the form of objects.* **2.** A person or animal as it can be seen, touched, etc.: *the human form. The place was alive with skulking furry forms.* **3. a.** The manner in which a thing exists; kind; variety; type: *Light is a form of energy.* **b.** The particular character or nature of something: *Diplomatic persuasion often takes the form of private talks.* **4.** A fixed or set procedure; a formula: *Some religions have substituted forms for meaningful content.* **5.** A document with blanks that are to be filled in: *an income-tax form.* **6. a.** Acceptable behavior: *It is not good form to whisper in the presence of others.* **b.** A usual manner of behaving: *True to form, they continued expanding their culture.* **7. a.** A meaningful linguistic element, as a prefix, suffix, etc. **b.** Any of the different shapes a word may take with regard to its inflection, pronunciation, etc.: *plural forms; inflected forms.* **8.** Fitness with regard to health or training: *She is in top form this season.* **9. a.** A model for making a mold: *Concrete is poured into forms.* **b.** A copy of the human figure used for fitting clothes. **10.** An artistic, musical, or literary style: *in sonata form.* **11.** A grade level in a British school or in some American private schools. —*v.* **1.** To give form to; make; produce: *When two or more atoms unite to form a substance, this substance is called a compound.* **2.** To come into or cause to come into being; appear; arise: *Buds form in the spring. Water forms rust on certain metals.* **3. a.** To make up; constitute: *Three rivers join to form the Missouri.* **b.** To organize: *form a students' committee.* **4. a.** To develop in the mind; conceive: *form an idea; form an impression.* **b.** To develop; acquire: *form a bad habit.* **c.** To develop by or as if by instructing: *form the minds of young children.* **5. a.** To produce (a tense, plural, etc.) by adding certain elements: *Most nouns form the plural by adding an -s to the singular.* **b.** To produce (a word) by derivation of the combination of elements: *form a new word by adding the suffix -tion to the root word.*

for•mal |fôr′məl| *adj.* **1. a.** Following accepted forms, conventions, or rules: *formal English.* **b.** Structured according to forms or conventions: *a formal meeting of the committee.* **c.** Officially made or stated: *a formal wedding announcement.* **2. a.** Calling for elegant clothes and fine manners: *a formal dance.* **b.** Suitable for occasions when elegant clothes and fine manners are called for: *formal dress.* **3.** Stiff; cold; ceremonious: *Her voice became stiff and formal.* —*n.* **1.** A dance at which women wear evening gowns and men wear tuxedos or white tie and tails. **2.** An **evening gown.** —**for′mal•ly** *adv.*

forget-me-not

fort

forte[1,2], etc.

Forte[1] *is from French* fort, *"strong," and* **forte**[2] *is from Italian* forte, *"strong." The French word and the Italian word are both descended from Latin* fortis, *"strong."* **Fort, fortify, fortitude,** *and* **fortress** *are all French derivatives of* fortis. **Fortissimo** *is from the Italian superlative of* forte.

ă pat/ā pay/â care/ä father/ĕ pet/ ē be/ĭ pit/ī pie/î fierce/ŏ pot/ ō go/ô paw, for/oi oil/ŏŏ book/ ōō boot/ou out/ŭ cut/û fur/ *th* the/th thin/hw which/zh vision/ ə ago, item, pencil, atom, circus

for•mal•de•hyde |fôr **măl'**də hīd'| *n.* A colorless, gaseous compound of carbon, hydrogen, and oxygen that has a sharp, suffocating odor and the formula CH_2O. It is used in making plastics, fertilizers, and dyes and as a preservative and disinfectant.

for•mal•ism |**fôr'**mə lĭz'əm| *n.* Strict observance of accepted or recognized forms.

for•mal•i•ty |fôr **măl'**ĭ tē| *n., pl.* **for•mal•i•ties. 1.** Rigorous observance of accepted rules or forms: *There was no formality at our dinner table.* **2.** An established rule, form, or custom: *the legal formalities of a trial.* **3.** Something done for the sake of form.

for•mal•ize |**fôr'**mə līz'| *v.* **for•mal•ized, for•mal•iz•ing. 1.** To give a definite structure or shape to: *formalize a style of writing.* **2.** To make formal or official: *They formalized the treaty.*

for•mat |**fôr'**măt'| *n.* **1.** A general plan for the organization or arrangement of a particular production: *the format of a new television series.* **2.** The form or layout of a publication.

for•ma•tion |fôr **mā'**shən| *n.* **1.** The act or process of forming; development: *the formation of labor unions.* **2. a.** Something formed: *a cloud formation.* **b.** Something formed geologically: *This formation is called a canyon.* **3.** A specific arrangement: *The team went into a T formation.*

form•a•tive |**fôr'**mə tĭv| *adj.* **1.** Of growth or development: *a formative period in China's history.* **2.** Forming or capable of forming: *a formative influence.*

for•mer |**fôr'**mər| *adj.* **1.** Occurring earlier in time or belonging to a period previous to the one specified: *former ages; our former President.* **2.** Coming before in place or order: *the former part of the book.* **3.** Being first or first mentioned of two: *Boston and Hartford are both big; the former city is the bigger of the two.* In this sense the word *former* is often used as a noun: *A garden plot was cleared by Jim and Fred on the former's land.*

for•mer•ly |**fôr'**mər lē| *adv.* At a former time; once: *Machines are used for work formerly done by men.*

For•mi•ca |fôr **mī'**kə| *n.* A trademark for several types of plastic sheets that are used especially for covering surfaces that must be resistant to chemicals and heat.

for•mic acid |**fôr'**mĭk|. A colorless corrosive fuming liquid compound of carbon, hydrogen, and oxygen having the formula CH_2O_2. It is used in dyeing and finishing textiles and paper and in making insect poisons and refrigerants.

for•mi•da•ble |**fôr'**mĭ də bəl| *adj.* **1.** Inspiring fear, dread, or alarm: *a formidable weapon; a formidable threat.* **2.** Able to impede progress or cause defeat; difficult to surmount; awesome: *a formidable task.* **3.** Admirable; awe-inspiring: *a formidable list of talents.* **—for'mi•da•bil'i•ty** *n.* **—for'mi•da•bly** *adv.*

form•less |**fôrm'**lĭs| *adj.* Having no specified form; shapeless: *formless mists and vapors.* **—form'less•ness** *n.*

For•mo•sa |fôr **mō'**sə|. The former name for Taiwan.

for•mu•la |**fôr'**myə lə| *n., pl.* **for•mu•las** or **for•mu•lae** |**fôr'**myə lē'|. **1.** An established set of words or rules for use in a ceremony, on a form, or in a procedure: *A formula for a business letter is often included in a secretary's manual.* **2.** A set of symbols that show the composition or the composition and structure of a chemical compound; for example, H_2O is the formula for water. **3.** A mathematical statement of a rule, principle, etc., especially in the form of an equation; for example, the formula for the area of a triangle is $a = {}^1/_2bh$, where *a* is the area, *b* the base, and *h* the altitude. **4.** A list of the ingredients and processes used in making something; a recipe: *the formula for a medicine.* **5.** A specially made liquid food for an infant.

for•mu•late |**fôr'**myə lāt'| *v.* **for•mu•lat•ed, for•mu•lat•ing.** To express in or as if in a formula; plan in an orderly way: *formulate an idea.* **—for'mu•la'tion** *n.*

for•ni•cate |**fôr'**nĭ kāt'| *v.* **for•ni•cat•ed, for•ni•cat•ing.** To have sexual intercourse with someone to whom one is not married. **—for'ni•ca'tion** *n.*

for•sake |fôr **sāk'**| *v.* **for•sook** |fôr **sŏŏk'**|, **for•sak•en** |fôr **sā'**kən|, **for•sak•ing. 1.** To give up; renounce: *They forsook their hunting skills for the life of settled farmers.* **2.** To leave; desert; abandon: *Do not forsake us in our time of need.* **—for•sak'en** *adj.: a lonely, forsaken place.*

for•sooth |fôr **sōōth'**| *adv. Archaic.* In truth; indeed.

for•swear |fôr **swâr'**| *v.* **for•swore** |fôr **swôr'**| *or* |**-swōr'**|, **for•sworn** |fôr **swôrn'**| *or* |**-swōrn'**|, **for•swear•ing.** To give up; renounce: *He forswore all evil.*

for•syth•i•a |fôr **sĭth'**ē ə| *or* |fər-| *n.* A garden shrub with yellow flowers that bloom early in spring.

fort |fôrt| *or* |fōrt| *n.* A fortified area or structure stationed with troops; a fortification. ¶*These sound alike* **fort, forte**[1]. [SEE PICTURE]

forte[1] |fôrt| *or* |fōrt| *n.* Something in which a person excels; a strong point. ¶*These sound alike* **forte**[1], **fort.** [SEE NOTE]

for•te[2] |**fôr'**tā'|. In music: *adj.* Loud. *—adv.* Loudly. *—n.* A musical passage that is or is to be performed loudly. [SEE NOTE]

forth |fôrth| *or* |fōrth| *adv.* **1. a.** Out into view, as from confinement or concealment: *At noon the young people poured forth from the schoolhouse.* **b.** Out: *Let the word go forth to friend and foe alike.* **2.** Forward or onward: *Putting forth all his strength, he bent the heavy bow.* ¶*These sound alike* **forth, fourth.**

Idioms. **and so forth.** And the like; et cetera: *We bought pencils, notebooks, and so forth.* **back and forth.** Backward and forward or to and fro: *The little bird darted back and forth.*

forth•com•ing |**fôrth'kŭm'**ĭng| *or* |**fōrth'-**| *adj.* **1.** About to appear; approaching: *his forthcoming book.* **2.** Available when required or as promised: *State aid was not forthcoming.*

forth•right |**fôrth'**rīt'| *or* |**fōrth'-**| *adj.* Straightforward; frank: *ask a forthright question.*

forth•with |fôrth'**wĭth'**| *or* |**-wĭth'**| *or* |fōrth'-| *adv.* At once; immediately: *You will report to headquarters forthwith.*

for•ti•eth |**fôr'**tē ĭth| *n.* **1.** In a set of items arranged to match the natural numbers in a one-to-one correspondence, the item that matches the number forty. **2.** One of forty equal parts of a unit, written ${}^1/_{40}$. **—for'ti•eth** *adj. & adv.*

for•ti•fi•ca•tion |fôr′tə fĭ kā′shən| *n.* **1.** The act or process of fortifying: *working on the fortification of the city against the invaders.* **2.** Something that fortifies or defends, as walls, moats, etc. **3.** Something fortified, especially a fort.

fortified wine. A wine to which a brandy or other spirit has been added.

for•ti•fy |fôr′tə fī′| *v.* **for•ti•fied, for•ti•fy•ing, for•ti•fies. 1.** To strengthen or secure (a position or structure) militarily: *They fortified the castle with deep moats.* **2.** To strengthen physically; invigorate: *The hikers fortified themselves with peanut-butter sandwiches.* **3.** To increase the amount of an important ingredient contained in (a food or other substance): *fortify bread with vitamins.* —**for′ti•fi′er** *n.*

for•tis•si•mo |fôr tĭs′ə mō′|. In music: *adj.* Very loud. —*adv.* Very loudly. —*n.* A musical passage, chord, etc., that is very loud or is to be performed very loudly.

for•ti•tude |fôr′tĭ to͞od′| *or* |-tyo͞od′| *n.* Strength to deal with pain or adversity.

fort•night |fôrt′nīt′| *or* |-nĭt| *n.* A period of two weeks.

fort•night•ly |fôrt′nīt′lē| *adj.* Happening once every two weeks. —*adv.* Once every two weeks.

for•tress |fôr′trĭs| *n.* A fort or other fortification.

for•tu•i•tous |fôr to͞o′ĭ təs| *or* |-tyo͞o′-| *adj.* **1.** Happening by accident or chance; unplanned. **2.** Lucky; fortunate: *a fortuitous happening.* —**for•tu′i•tous•ly** *adv.* —**for•tu′i•tous•ness** *n.* [SEE NOTE]

for•tu•nate |fôr′chə nĭt| *adj.* Having, bringing, or brought by good fortune; lucky: *a fortunate man; a fortunate choice.* —**for′tu•nate•ly** *adv.* [SEE NOTE]

for•tune |fôr′chən| *n.* **1.** The good or bad luck coming to a person or undertaking; chance: *I had the good fortune to meet nice people during my stay.* **2.** Destiny; fate: *Gypsy women tell fortunes for a few pennies.* **3.** An accumulation of material possessions or wealth; riches.

fortune cooky or **fortune cookie.** An Oriental cooky made of a thin layer of dough wrapped around a slip of paper on which a prediction of fortune or maxim is written.

fortune hunter. A person who seeks to become wealthy, especially through marriage.

for•tune•tell•er |fôr′chən tĕl′ər| *n.* A person who attempts to predict future events in the life of another. —**for′tune•tell′ing** *n.*

Fort Worth |wûrth|. A city of northeastern Texas. Population, 388,000.

for•ty |fôr′tē| *n., pl.* **for•ties.** A number, written 40 in Arabic numerals, that is equal to the product of 4 × 10. It is the tenth positive integer after 30. —**for′ty** *adj. & pron.*

for•ty-nin•er |fôr′tē nī′nər| *n.* A person who took part in the California gold rush of 1849.

fo•rum |fôr′əm| *or* |fōr′-| *n., pl.* **fo•rums. 1.** Often **Forum.** The public square of an ancient Roman city, especially the Forum of ancient Rome. **2.** Any public place or medium for open discussion. **3.** A court of law.

for•ward |fôr′wərd| *adj.* **1.** At, near, or belonging to the front of something: *the forward part of a train.* **2.** Going or moving toward a position in front: *He took a bad forward fall.* **3.** Presumptuous; bold: *I thought his manners were just a bit forward.* **4.** Progressive, especially in a political or economic way: *a forward young nation.* **5.** Mentally, physically, or socially advanced; precocious: *a forward child.* **6.** Prompt; eager: *forward with an offer to work late.* —*adv.* **1.** Also **for•wards** |fôr′wərdz|. Toward the front; frontward: *All volunteers please step forward.* **2.** In or toward the future: *I look forward to seeing you.* **3.** Into view; forth: *Come forward out of the shadows so that I can see you.* —*n.* **1.** A player in certain games, such as basketball or soccer, who is part of the front line of offense or defense. **2.** The position itself in one of these games. —*v.* **1.** To send on (something mailed) to a subsequent destination or address: *forward a letter. Please forward if not at the above address.* **2.** To send (something ordered) to a buyer: *We will forward the merchandise upon receipt of your check or money order.* **3.** To promote or advance: *always trying to forward their own interests.*

for•ward•ness |fôr′wərd nĭs| *n.* **1.** The condition or quality of being forward or well advanced. **2.** Insolence in behavior; boldness.

for•went |fôr wĕnt′|. Past tense of **forgo.**

fos•sil |fŏs′əl| *n.* **1.** The remains or traces of a plant or animal that lived long ago, embedded in the earth's crust. **2.** *Informal.* A person whose opinions are very old-fashioned or out-of-date. —***modifier:*** *fossil ferns.* [SEE PICTURES]

fos•sil•ize |fŏs′ə līz′| *v.* **fos•sil•ized, fos•sil•iz•ing.** To change into or become a fossil. —**fos′sil•i•za′tion** *n.*

fos•ter |fô′stər| *or* |fŏs′tər| *v.* **1.** To bring up; rear: *foster a child.* **2.** To promote the development or growth of; encourage; cultivate: *Good housing is important in fostering health in a community.* —*adj.* Receiving or giving parental care though not related by legal or blood ties: *a foster child; a foster parent.*

Fos•ter |fô′stər| *or* |fŏs′tər|, **Stephen Collins.** 1826–1864. American composer of songs.

fought |fôt|. Past tense and past participle of **fight.**

foul |foul| *adj.* **foul•er, foul•est. 1.** Offensive to the taste, smell, etc.; rotten; putrid: *a foul flavor; a foul smell.* **2.** Dirty; filthy: *foul hairs of the stray dog.* **3.** Morally offensive; wicked: *foul deeds; foul rumors.* **4.** Not according to accepted standards; dishonorable: *He used foul means to obtain his position of power.* **5.** Unpleasant; bad: *foul weather.* **6.** Vulgar; obscene: *foul language.* **7.** In sports, contrary to the rules of the game: *A foul blow in boxing is one below the waist.* **8.** In baseball, outside a foul line: *the foul zone.* —*adv.* In baseball, outside the base line: *The ball went foul.* —*n.* **1.** In sports, a violation of the rules of play: *a personal foul in a game of basketball.* **2.** In baseball, a **foul ball.** —*v.* **1.** To make or become foul: *Black factory smoke fouls the air. An unused room fouls with mustiness.* **2.** To commit a foul in a game. **3.** In baseball, to hit (a ball) beyond a foul line. —***phrasal verbs.*** **foul out.** To make an out in baseball by hitting a foul ball that is caught before it touches the ground. **foul up.** To ruin or spoil by making mistakes, using poor judgment, etc.; botch; bungle. ¶ *These sound alike* **foul, fowl.**

fou•lard |fo͞o lärd′| *n.* **1.** A lightweight silk or

fortunate/fortuitous

Fortune, *like luck, can be either good or bad, but* **fortunate,** *like lucky, means only "having good fortune."* **Fortune** *comes from Latin* fortūna, *which had precisely the same range of meanings as the English word, and* **fortunate** *is from Latin* fortunātus, *of which the same is true.* Fortūna *is based on the word* fors, fort-, *"chance, luck (good or bad)." This word had a separate adjective,* fortuitus, *meaning "happening by chance, accidental, unplanned," borrowed into English as* **fortuitous.** *The distinction between* **fortunate** *and* **fortuitous** *is both so clear and so useful that although* **fortuitous** *is sometimes used to mean "lucky" (sense 2), there are good grounds for avoiding this usage. Eighty-five per cent of the American Heritage Usage Panel regard it as unacceptable.*

fossil
Fossilized fern fronds *(above)* and trilobites *(below)*

found[2]/founder[1-2]/foundry
Found[2] *is from Old French* fonder, *which is from Latin* fundāre, *"to lay the foundation of," from* fundus, *"bottom, foundation."* Fundāre *also formed the noun* fundāmentum, *"foundation, groundwork, basis," from which we have* **fundamental**. **Founder[1]** *is, obviously, from* **found[2]**. **Founder[2]** *is from Old French* fondrer, *which is from Late Latin* fundorāre, *"to sink to the bottom, submerge," also from* fundus, *"bottom."* **Foundry** *is from French* fondrie, *"place for casting metal," from* fondre, *"to cast metal." See note at* **font**.

foundry

fox

satiny material, usually having a small printed pattern. **2.** A necktie, scarf, or handkerchief made of this material. *—modifier: a foulard tie.*

foul ball. In baseball, a batted ball landing or caught outside a foul line.

foul line. **1.** In basketball, a line, ten feet in front of the basket, at which a fouled player stands while shooting a free throw. **2.** In baseball, one of two lines extending from home plate to the outfield barriers to indicate the area in which a fair ball can be hit.

foul play. Unfair or treacherous action, especially when violent.

found[1] |found|. Past tense and past participle of **find**.

found[2] |found| *v.* To originate or establish (something); create; set up: *Booker T. Washington founded Tuskegee Institute.* [SEE NOTE]

foun•da•tion |foun dā′shən| *n.* **1.** The act of founding or establishing. **2. a.** The basis on which something stands or is developed; the underlying element or support: *the foundations of modern science.* **b.** The base on which a structure stands: *the foundation of a building.* **3. a.** Charitable funds used to endow schools, hospitals, etc. **b.** An institution that grants and is supported by such funds. **4.** A cosmetic used as a base for make-up.

foundation garment. A girdle or corset.

found•er[1] |foun′dər| *n.* A person who founds or helps to establish something: *the founders of the railroad company.* [SEE NOTE]

foun•der[2] |foun′dər| *v.* **1.** To fall or stumble: *The hunters foundered in the deep snow.* **2.** To fail utterly; collapse or break down. **3.** To sink: *The ships foundered in the gale.* [SEE NOTE]

found•ling |found′lĭng| *n.* A child found after being deserted by parents whose identity is not known. *—modifier: a foundling home.*

foun•dry |foun′drē| *n., pl.* **foun•dries.** A place in which metals are cast and molded. *—modifier: a foundry worker.* [SEE NOTE & PICTURE]

fount |fount| *n.* **1.** A source: *He was the fount of freedom to those helpless folk.* **2.** A fountain.

foun•tain |foun′tən| *n.* **1. a.** A spring of water from the earth. **b.** An upward jet of something: *A dozen brilliant fountains of lava shot forth from the volcano.* **2. a.** An artificially created stream of water. **b.** The structure or device in which such a stream rises and flows: *Rome has many elaborate fountains.* **c.** Such a device with a small jet of water suitable for drinking: *a drinking fountain.* **3.** A source; point of origin: *a fountain of knowledge.* **4.** A **soda fountain.**

foun•tain•head |foun′tən hĕd′| *n.* **1.** A spring that is the source of a stream. **2.** A primary source or origin.

fountain pen. A pen containing a reservoir of ink that automatically feeds the writing point.

four |fôr| *or* |fōr| *n.* A number, written 4 in Arabic numerals, that is equal to the sum of 3 + 1. It is the positive integer that immediately follows 3. ¶*These sound alike* **four, for, fore.** *—***four** *adj. & pron.*

Idiom. **on all fours.** On the hands and knees or on all four legs: *Babies crawl around on all fours.*

four bits. *Slang.* Fifty cents.

four-leaf clover |fôr′lēf′| *or* |fōr′-|. A clover leaf that has four leaflets instead of the usual three and is often considered a sign of good luck.

four-leaved clover |fôr′lēvd′| *or* |fōr′-|. A **four-leaf clover.**

four-o'clock |fôr′ə klŏk′| *or* |fōr′-| *n.* A garden plant with funnel-shaped, variously colored flowers that open in the late afternoon.

four-post•er |fôr′pō′stər| *or* |fōr′-| *n.* A bed with four tall corner posts originally intended to support curtains or a canopy.

four•score |fôr′skôr′| *or* |fōr′skōr′| *adj.* Four times twenty; eighty.

four•square |fôr′skwâr′| *or* |fōr′-| *adj.* **1.** Having four equal sides; square. **2.** Forthright.

four•teen |fôr′tēn′| *or* |fōr′-| *n.* A number, written 14 in Arabic numerals, that is equal to the sum of 13 + 1. It is the positive integer that immediately follows 13. *—***four′teen′** *adj. & pron.*

four•teenth |fôr′tēnth′| *or* |fōr′-| *n.* **1.** In a set of items arranged to match the natural numbers in a one-to-one correspondence, the item that matches the number fourteen. **2.** One of fourteen equal parts of a unit, written 1/14. *—***four′teenth′** *adj. & adv.*

fourth |fôrth| *or* |fōrth| *n.* **1.** In a set of items arranged to match the natural numbers in a one-to-one correspondence, the item that matches the number four. **2.** One of four equal parts of a unit, written 1/4; one-quarter. **3. a.** A musical interval of five half steps. **b.** The tone of a diatonic scale that is five half steps above the tonic; the subdominant. **4. the Fourth.** The **Fourth of July.** ¶*These sound alike* **fourth, forth.** *—***fourth** *adj. & adv.*

fourth dimension. A dimension other than the dimensions of length, width, and height, considered to be measured along an axis that meets at right angles all three axes of a three-dimensional coordinate system.

Fourth of July. **Independence Day.**

fo•ve•a |fō′vē ə| *n., pl.* **fo•ve•ae** |fō′vē ē′|. A shallow, cuplike depression in an organ of the body, especially a small depression in the retina of the eye where an image is received most clearly.

fowl |foul| *n., pl.* **fowl** or **fowls.** **1.** A bird, such as a chicken, duck, turkey, or pheasant, that is raised or hunted for food. **2.** A large full-grown chicken used for cooking. **3.** The meat of any of these birds. ¶*These sound alike* **fowl, foul.**

fox |fŏks| *n.* **1.** An animal related to the dogs and wolves, having a pointed snout, upright ears, and a long, bushy tail. **2.** The fur of a fox. **3.** A crafty or sly person. *—modifier: a fox hunt.* [SEE PICTURE]

fox•glove |fŏks′glŭv′| *n.* A plant with a long cluster of tube-shaped purplish, yellow, or white flowers.

fox•hole |fŏks′hōl′| *n.* A shallow pit dug by a soldier for protection in combat.

fox•hound |fŏks′hound′| *n.* A usually smooth-coated dog trained for fox hunting.

fox terrier. A small dog having a smooth or wiry white coat with dark markings.

fox trot. **1.** A ballroom dance composed of a mixture of fast and slow steps. **2.** Music for this dance, written in 2/4 or 4/4 time.

fox•y |fŏk′sē| *adj.* **fox•i•er, fox•i•est.** Sly or clever, as a fox is generally considered to be. *—***fox′i•ly** *adv.* *—***fox′i•ness** *n.*

ă pat/ā pay/â care/ä father/ĕ pet/ ē be/ĭ pit/ī pie/î fierce/ŏ pot/ ō go/ô paw, for/oi oil/ŏŏ book/ ōō boot/ou out/ŭ cut/û fur/ *th* the/th thin/hw which/zh vision/ ə ago, item, pencil, atom, circus

foy•er |foi'ər| *or* |foi'ā'| *n.* **1.** The lobby of a public building. **2.** The entrance hall of a private house or apartment.

Fr The symbol for the element francium.

Fr. France; French.

fra•cas |frā'kəs| *n.* A disorderly uproar.

frac•tion |frăk'shən| *n.* **1.** A number that is equal to a quotient of two other numbers, especially a quotient of two whole numbers, with the divisor not zero. **2.** A numeral written in the form $^a/_b$, where $b \neq 0$. **3. a.** Something that is less than a whole unit and that has a measure represented by a fraction: *a fraction of an inch.* **b.** Any subset of a set whose members can be counted: *A small fraction of the people voted.* **4.** In chemistry, one of the parts into which a mixture of substances can be separated. **5.** A piece of something; a part; a bit.

frac•tion•al |frăk'shə nəl| *adj.* **1.** Of or composed of a fraction or fractions. **2.** Very small; insignificant. **—frac'tion•al•ly** *adv.*

fractional distillation. A form of distillation in which the various components of a mixture are separated according to the temperatures at which they condense or vaporize.

frac•ture |frăk'chər| *n.* **1.** The act or process of breaking. **2.** A break or crack, as in bone. *—v.* **frac•tured, frac•tur•ing.** To break or cause to break. **—frac'tured** *adj.: fractured ribs.*

frag•ile |frăj'əl| *or* |-īl'| *adj.* **1.** Easily damaged or broken; brittle: *a fragile piece of crystal.* **2.** Lacking solidity; flimsy: *a fragile link between a nation and its history.* **3.** Physically weak; frail. **—frag'ile•ly** *adv.* **—fra•gil'i•ty** |frə jĭl'ĭ tē| *n.*

frag•ment |frăg'mənt| *n.* **1.** A piece or part broken off or detached from a whole: *a fragment of a china plate.* **2.** Something incomplete or unfinished: *a sentence fragment.* *—v.* To break into fragments.

frag•men•tar•y |frăg'mən tĕr'ē| *adj.* Consisting of fragments; broken; disconnected: *a fragmentary sentence.*

frag•men•ta•tion |frăg'mən **tā'**shən| *n.* The act or process of fragmenting or breaking into pieces: *the fragmentation of rocks.*

fra•grance |frā'grəns| *n.* A sweet or pleasant odor; scent: *the fragrance of pine.*

fra•grant |frā'grənt| *adj.* Having a pleasant odor; sweet-smelling: *a fragrant rose.*

frail |frāl| *adj.* **frail•er, frail•est.** **1.** Physically weak; not robust: *a frail old man.* **2.** Not strong; fragile: *a frail flower.*

frail•ty |frāl'tē| *n., pl.* **frail•ties.** **1.** The condition of being frail; weakness, especially of morality or character. **2.** Often **frailties.** A fault arising from human weakness; a failing: *human frailties.*

frame |frām| *n.* **1. a.** A basic or skeletal structure that shapes or supports: *a car frame.* **b.** An open structure or rim used to encase, hold, or border: *a door frame; a picture frame.* **c.** The human body: *He has a small frame.* **2.** The general structure of something; system: *the frame of government.* **3. a.** A round of play in some games, such as bowling. **b.** The box on a score sheet in which the score of such a round of play is entered. **c.** A similar box, as for entering answers: *Write the correct number in each frame.* **4.** An inning in baseball. **5.** A single exposure on a roll of movie film. *—v.* **framed, fram•ing.** **1.** To put together the various parts of; construct; build: *frame a treaty.* **2.** To put into words; phrase: *He framed his question in a funny way.* **3.** To provide with a frame; enclose or encircle: *frame a picture. Her fair hair framed her beautiful face.* **4.** *Slang.* To set up evidence so as to incriminate (someone) falsely: *He framed her by planting a gun in her bureau.* **—fram'er** *n.*

frame house. A house built with a wooden framework and usually covered with wood siding.

frame of mind. Mental state or attitude; mood.

frame of reference. **1.** A set or system of principles, rules, ideas, or values that serve as a basis for the formation of attitudes: *He has a very limited frame of reference due to his lack of education.* **2.** A system of coordinates used to describe position or motion, as in physics or mathematics.

frame-up |**frām'**ŭp'| *n. Slang.* A plot to make an innocent person appear guilty.

frame•work |**frām'**wûrk'| *n.* **1.** A skeletal structure that shapes or supports; a frame: *a framework of steel.* **2.** A basic arrangement, form system, or set of relationships.

franc |frăngk| *n.* The basic unit of money of France, Belgium, Burundi, Cameroon, Central African Republic, Chad, People's Republic of the Congo, Dahomey, Gabon, Ivory Coast, Luxembourg, Malagasy Republic, Mali, Niger, Rwanda, Senegal, Switzerland, Togo, Upper Volta, and of various overseas departments and territories of France. ¶*These sound alike* **franc, frank.** [SEE NOTE]

France |frăns| *or* |frāns|. A country in western Europe. Population, 52,507,000. Capital, Paris.

fran•chise |**frăn'**chīz'| *n.* **1.** The right to vote; suffrage. **2. a.** An authorization, right, or privilege granted to a person or group, as for selling a product within a district, governing a territory, etc. **b.** The limits or district within which such authorization is given.

fran•ci•um |**frăn'**sē əm| *n.* Symbol **Fr** One of the elements, an extremely unstable radioactive metal. It has several isotopes, the most stable of which is Fr 223 with a half-life of 21 minutes. Atomic number 87.

fran•gi•pan•i |frăn'jə **păn'**ē| *or* |-**pä'**nē| *n.* A tropical shrub with fragrant, variously colored flowers used in making perfume.

frank[1] |frăngk| *adj.* **frank•er, frank•est.** **1.** Open and sincere in expression; straightforward: *a frank discussion.* **2.** Undisguised; evident: *frank enjoyment.* *—v.* **1.** To put an official mark on (mail) so that it can be sent and delivered free of postage, through special official privilege. **2.** To send (mail) free of charge. *—n.* **1.** A mark placed on a piece of mail indicating that it is to be sent free of charge. **2.** The right to send mail free of charge. ¶*These sound alike* **frank, franc.** **—frank'ness** *n.* [SEE NOTE]

frank[2] |frăngk| *n. Informal.* A frankfurter. ¶*These sound alike* **frank, franc.** [SEE NOTE]

Frank |frăngk| *n.* A member of a Germanic tribe that conquered Gaul around A.D. 500 and established a large empire. [SEE NOTE]

Frank•fort |**frăngk'**fərt|. The capital of Kentucky. Population, 20,000.

frank•furt•er |**frăngk'**fər tər| *n.* A smoked sau-

franc/frank[1,2]

The gold coins of King John II of France (died 1364) bore the Latin inscription Rex Francorum, *"King of the Franks or French"; the coin came to be called a* **franc,** *and the name has stayed with later French coins. In the early period of Frankish rule in France, the national name* **Frank** *took on the meaning of "free man," since the ruling race was exempt from taxes. Thus the Old French adjective came to mean "free" and also "generous, open"; it was borrowed into English as* **frank**[1]. **Frank**[2] *is a shortening of* **frankfurter,** *a late nineteenth-century Americanism taken from* Frankfurt, *the German city on the river Main; and the name* Frankfurt *itself means "crossing or* **ford** *of the* **Franks.**"

Franks, etc.

In the time of the Roman Empire, a large group or confederacy of German tribes lived to the north of the river Main; they called themselves Frankon-, *the* **Franks,** *probably meaning "javelins." In the fifth century* A.D. *the Franks conquered the Roman province of Gaul and renamed it* Francia, *later* **France.** *During several centuries of ruling a Latin-speaking population, the conquerors lost their Germanic language* (**Frankish**) *and began to speak a kind of Latin. This Romance language, which borrowed many words from Frankish, was in Old English called* Frencisc, *later* **French.** *(We now call the early period* **Old French.**)

fraternal, etc.
This word and the next three entry words come from Latin frāter, *"brother."* Frāter *is descended from* bhrāter-, *the prehistoric Indo-European word for "brother." In Germanic,* bhrāter- *became* brōthar-, *which in Old English became* brōthor *and in Modern English* **brother**. *In Sanskrit,* bhrāter-.

fray¹⁻²
Fray¹ *is shortened from* affray, *an old word meaning "frighten," related to* **afraid**. **Fray**² *is from French* frayer, *which is from Latin* fricāre, *"to rub."*

freebooter
Freebooter *was originally a name for the pirates, of many nationalities, who plundered the colonies and shipping of the Caribbean in the sixteenth and seventeenth centuries. The word is from Dutch* vrijbuiter, *"a free plunderer, a roving robber":* vrij, *"free" (related to the word* **free**), + buiten, *"to plunder" (related to the word* **booty**).

ă pat/ā pay/â care/ä father/ĕ pet/ ē be/ĭ pit/ī pie/î fierce/ŏ pot/ ō go/ô paw, for/oi oil/ŏŏ book/ ōō boot/ou out/ŭ cut/û fur/ *th* the/th thin/hw which/zh vision/ ə ago, item, pencil, atom, circus

sage of beef or beef and pork. *—modifier: a frankfurter roll.*

frank•in•cense |frăngk'ĭn sĕns'| *n.* A gum with a pleasant, spicy odor, obtained from certain African and Asian trees and burned as incense.

Frank•ish |frăngk'ĭsh| *n.* The Germanic language of the Franks. *—adj.* Of the Franks or their language.

Frank•lin |frăngk'lĭn|, **Benjamin.** 1706–1790. American statesman, author, and scientist.

frank•ly |frăngk'lē| *adv.* **1.** In a frank manner; openly: *speaking frankly.* **2.** Honestly; in truth: *In your position, frankly, I would give up.*

fran•tic |frăn'tĭk| *adj.* Very excited with fear, anxiety, etc.; desperate; frenzied: *a frantic mob scene; a frantic scream.* **—fran'ti•cal•ly** *adv.*

fra•ter•nal |frə tûr'nəl| *adj.* **1. a.** Of brothers. **b.** Showing comradeship: *a fraternal greeting.* **2.** Consisting of persons linked by a common purpose or interest: *a fraternal society.* **3.** Of or concerning twins that develop from separately fertilized egg cells and that have distinct hereditary characteristics and often are of different sexes. **—fra•ter'nal•ly** *adv.* [SEE NOTE]

fra•ter•ni•ty |frə tûr'nĭ tē| *n., pl.* **fra•ter•ni•ties. 1.** A group of people associated or linked by similar interests, backgrounds, or occupations: *the drag-race fraternity; the medical fraternity.* **2.** A social organization of male college students. **3.** The relationship of a brother or brothers; brotherhood.

frat•er•nize |frăt'ər nīz'| *v.* **frat•er•nized, frat•er•niz•ing. 1.** To associate with (others) in a brotherly or friendly way. **2.** To mix intimately with the people of an enemy or conquered country. **—frat'er•ni•za'tion** *n.*

frat•ri•cide |frăt'rĭ sīd'| *n.* **1.** The act of killing one's own brother or sister. **2.** A person who kills his own brother or sister. **—frat'ri•ci'dal** *adj.*

fraud |frôd| *n.* **1.** A deliberate deception, often unlawful: *protecting the consumer against fraud.* **2.** A piece of trickery; a swindle. **3.** Someone who practices deception and trickery.

fraud•u•lent |frô'jə lənt| *adj.* Of, gained by, or using fraud: *a fraudulent scheme.* **—fraud'u•lence** *n.* **—fraud'u•lent•ly** *adv.*

fraught |frôt| *adj.* Filled; laden; loaded: *Every moment is fraught with significance.*

fray¹ |frā| *n.* A fight; brawl; battle. [SEE NOTE]

fray² |frā| *v.* To make or become ragged, worn, or raveled at the edge so that loose threads show. [SEE NOTE]

fraz•zle |frăz'əl| *v.* **fraz•zled, fraz•zling.** *Informal.* **1.** To fray, ravel, or tatter. **2.** To tire out completely. *—n.* **1.** A frayed or tattered condition. **2.** A ragged end or edge. **3.** A condition of total exhaustion: *He was worn to a frazzle.*

freak |frēk| *n.* **1.** A markedly abnormal organism, especially a person or animal that is considered a curiosity or monstrosity. **2.** A thing or an occurrence that is very unusual or irregular. *—modifier: a freak accident; a freak storm.*

freak•ish |frē'kĭsh| *adj.* Of or like a freak; markedly abnormal or unusual. **—freak'ish•ly** *adv.* **—freak'ish•ness** *n.*

freck•le |frĕk'əl| *n.* A small spot of dark pigment in the skin, often caused by exposure to the sun. *—v.* **freck•led, freck•ling.** To mark or become marked with freckles.

Fred•er•ic•ton |frĕd'rĭk tən|. The capital of New Brunswick, Canada. Population, 24,000.

free |frē| *adj.* **fre•er, fre•est. 1.** At liberty; not imprisoned or enslaved. **2.** Not controlled by obligation or the will of another: *felt free to go.* **3. a.** Having political independence: *a free country; a free people.* **b.** Having legal rights that a government may not violate: *a free press.* **4. a.** Not affected by a given condition: *free of germs; free from worry.* **b.** Not subject to a given condition; exempt: *tax-free income.* **5. a.** Not bound, confined, or fixed in position: *the free end of a chain.* **b.** Empty; not filled: *free space.* **6.** Not occupied or busy: *a free hour.* **7.** Costing nothing: *free meals.* **8.** Liberal or lavish: *very free with her money.* **9.** Not literal or exact: *a free translation.* *—adv.* **1.** In a free manner; freely: *The rope swung free.* **2.** Without charge: *We were admitted free.* *—v.* **freed, free•ing. 1.** To set at liberty. **2.** To rid or release: *freed from all suspicion of guilt.* **3.** To unfasten or untangle; detach. **—free'ly** *adv.* **—free'ness** *n.*

Idioms. **free and easy.** Informal; casual; easygoing. **make free with.** To take liberties with. **set free.** To liberate or release.

free association. 1. The associations that a person makes between ideas, memories, feelings, etc., when the normal rules of logic, meaningfulness, grammar, etc., are relaxed. **2.** A technique of psychoanalysis in which such associations are studied.

free•boot•er |frē'bōō'tər| *n.* A person who plunders, especially a pirate; a buccaneer. [SEE NOTE]

freed•man |frēd'mən| *n., pl.* **-men** |-mən|. A person who has been freed from slavery.

free•dom |frē'dəm| *n.* **1.** The condition of being free: *gave slaves their freedom; the Colonies' fight for freedom.* **2.** Ease of movement: *a skirt whose shortness gave freedom for long strides.* **3.** Frankness or boldness; lack of modesty or reserve: *the new freedom in movies.* **4.** The use of or access to something: *given the freedom of the city.*

free energy. The part of the energy of a physical system that can, in theory, be made available to do work.

free enterprise. The freedom of private businesses to operate in competition with one another with little government regulation.

free fall. The fall of a body toward the earth when the only retarding force acting on it is the drag produced by the atmosphere.

free-for-all |frē'fər ôl'| *n.* A noisy and disorganized quarrel, fight, or competition in which one and all take part.

free•hand |frē'hănd'| *adj.* Drawn by hand without the aid of tracing or drafting tools. *—adv.* By hand, without mechanical aids.

free lance. A person, especially a writer, editor, artist, or musician, who does not work for one employer only but sells his services to several employers as those services are needed. *—modifier:* **(free-lance):** *a free-lance job.*

free-lance |frē'lăns'| *or* |-läns'| *v.* **free-lanced, free-lanc•ing.** To work as a free lance. **—free'-lanc'er** *n.*

free•man |frē'mən| *n., pl.* **-men** |-mən|. **1.** A person not in slavery or serfdom. **2.** A person who possesses the rights and privileges of a citizen.

free•ma•son |frē′mā′sən| *n.* **1.** In the Middle Ages, a member of a guild of skilled traveling masons. **2. Freemason.** A member of the Free and Accepted Masons, an international secret fraternity.

free•ma•son•ry |frē′mā′sən rē| *n.* **1.** A sense of comradeship and sympathy among people; fellowship. **2. Freemasonry.** The Freemasons and their beliefs and practices.

fre•er |frē′ər| *adj.* Comparative of **free.**

free•si•a |frē′zhē ə| *or* |-zhə| *or* |-zē ə| *n.* A plant grown for its one-sided clusters of fragrant, variously colored flowers. [SEE PICTURE]

free-soil |frē′soil′| *adj.* **1.** Prohibiting slavery: *free-soil states.* **2. Free-Soil.** Of an American political party founded in 1848 to oppose the spread of slavery into United States Territories and the admission of slave states into the Union.

fre•est |frē′ĭst| *adj.* Superlative of **free.**

free•stone |frē′stōn′| *n.* **1.** A fruit, especially a peach, with pulp that separates easily from the stone. **2.** A stone, such as sandstone or limestone, soft enough to be cut easily without breaking. —***modifier:*** *a freestone peach.*

free•think•er |frē′thĭng′kər| *n.* A person who has rejected dogma and authority, especially in religious matters. —**free′think′ing** *adj. & n.*

free throw. In basketball, a throw from the foul line, awarded to a fouled player and scored as one point if successful.

Free•town |frē′toun′|. The capital of Sierra Leone. Population, 200,000.

free•way |frē′wā′| *n.* **1.** A highway having several lanes and no intersections or stoplights. **2.** A highway without tolls.

free wheel. A mechanical device, used in some bicycles and automobile transmissions, that allows a driven shaft to turn freely when its speed is greater than that of the shaft that drives it.

free•wheel•ing |frē′hwē′lĭng| *or* |frē′wē′-| *adj.* **1.** Of or equipped with free wheel. **2.** *Informal.* Free of restraints or formality and proceeding with unlimited energy: *a freewheeling real-estate promoter.*

free will. **1.** The power or opportunity to choose; free choice: *a decision made of his own free will.* **2.** The belief that man's choices are or can be determined by him and not by persons or things beyond his control.

free•will |frē′wĭl′| *adj.* Done of one's own will or choice; voluntary.

freeze |frēz| *v.* **froze** |frōz|, **froz•en** |frō′zən|, **freez•ing. 1.** To change from a liquid to a solid by loss or withdrawal of heat. **2.** To cause ice to form in or on. **3.** To stop work or be damaged as a result of the formation of ice: *The pipes froze.* **4.** To become covered or filled with ice: *The river froze.* **5.** To preserve (food) by cooling to a very low temperature. **6.** To make or become motionless or unable to move: *freeze with shock.* **7.** To be harmed or killed by cold, as persons or plants. **8.** To fix (prices or wages) at a certain level. —***phrasal verb.* freeze out.** To shut out or bar, as from a business or a social group: *chain stores freezing out small dealers.* —*n.* A period of very cold weather. ¶*These sound alike* **freeze, frieze.**

freez•er |frē′zər| *n.* Someone or something that freezes, especially a cold chamber in which perishable foods are frozen and stored.

freeze-dry |frēz′drī′| *v.* To preserve (foodstuffs) by freezing and then drying in a vacuum.

freezing point. The temperature at which a given liquid changes to a solid under a specified pressure, especially a pressure equal to that of the atmosphere.

freight |frāt| *n.* **1. a.** Goods carried by a vessel or vehicle, especially goods transported as cargo. **b.** The charge for transporting such goods. **2.** The commercial transportation of goods. **3.** A railway train carrying goods only. —***modifier:*** *a freight car; freight rates.* —*v.* **1.** To transport commercially as cargo. **2.** To load or fill: *ships waiting to be freighted.*

freight•er |frā′tər| *n.* **1.** A cargo ship. **2.** A shipper of cargo.

French |frĕnch| *n.* **1.** The Romance language of France and parts of Switzerland, Belgium, Canada, and other countries. **2. the French** *(used with a plural verb).* The people of France. —*adj.* Of France, the French, or their language. —*v.* **french.** To trim fat from (a chop).

French and Indian War. A war (1754–1763) fought in North America between England and France, the latter supported by its Indian allies.

French-Ca•na•di•an |frĕnch′kə nā′dē ən| *n.* A Canadian of French descent. —*adj.* Of or inhabited by Canadians of French ancestry.

French curve. A drawing or drafting instrument, flat with curved edges and scroll-shaped cutouts, used as a guide in connecting a set of points with a smooth curve. [SEE PICTURE]

French door. A door, usually one of a pair, with glass panes extending the full length.

French fries. Fried strips of potatoes.

French fry. To fry (potato strips, shrimp, etc.) in deep fat.

French Gui•an•a |gē ăn′ə| *or* |-ä′nə|. A French territory on the northern coast of South America. Population, 60,000. Capital, Cayenne.

French horn. A valved brass wind instrument with a long, coiled tube that flares from a narrow mouthpiece to a wide bell at the other end.

French•man |frĕnch′mən| *n., pl.* **-men** |-mən|. A man who is a native or inhabitant of France.

French Revolution. The revolution in France, lasting from 1789 to 1799, in which the monarchy and aristocracy were overthrown.

French toast. Sliced bread soaked in a milk-and-egg batter and fried.

fre•net•ic |frə nĕt′ĭk| *adj.* Full of violent excitement; frantic; frenzied. —**fre•net′i•cal•ly** *adv.*

fren•zied |frĕn′zēd| *adj.* Affected with or filled with frenzy; frantic. —**fren′zied•ly** *adv.*

fren•zy |frĕn′zē| *n., pl.* **fren•zies.** Wild excitement or a display of emotion suggesting madness, often accompanied by vigorous or violent activity: *sharks gone mad and dashing about in a blind frenzy.*

fre•quen•cy |frē′kwən sē| *n., pl.* **fre•quen•cies. 1.** The number of occurrences of a specified event within a given interval: **a.** The number of complete cycles of a wave that occur within a period of time. **b.** The number of complete oscillations or vibrations that a body undergoes in a given period of time. **2.** A fraction repre-

freesia

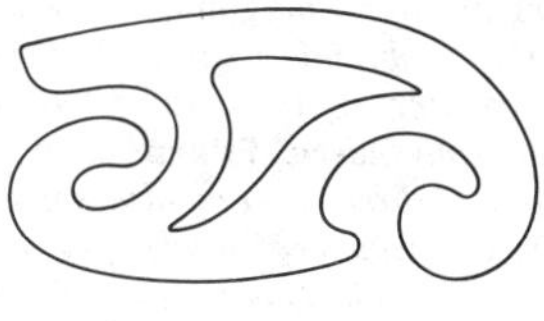

French curve

fret[1-2-3]
Fret[1] *was* fretan *in Old English; it originally meant "to eat up, devour," later "to irritate, to be irritated."* **Fret[2]** *is of obscure origin.* **Fret[3]** *is from Old French* frete, *"ornamental design, trellis-work."*

fret[3]

frieze[1-2]
Frieze[1] *and* **frieze[2]** *are not related, although their histories are rather similar.* **Frieze[1]** *is from French* frise, *which is from Medieval Latin* frisium *or* frigium, *"an embroidered edge or border on cloth"; this is a changed spelling of Latin* Phrygium, *"Phrygian cloth, embroidery," from* Phrygia, *a country in Asia Minor famous for embroidery.* **Frieze[2]** *is from an Old French word also spelled* frise, *meaning "woolen cloth," from Middle Dutch* vriese, *"Frisian cloth," from* Vriesland, *Friesland, a northern province of the Netherlands.*

frigate bird

ă pat/ā pay/â care/ä father/ĕ pet/ ē be/ĭ pit/ī pie/î fierce/ŏ pot/ ō go/ô paw, for/oi oil/ŏŏ book/ ōō boot/ou out/ŭ cut/û fur/ *th* the/th thin/hw which/zh vision/ ə ago, item, pencil, atom, circus

senting the number of times a particular event or value has occurred in a given number of opportunities for its occurrence. **3.** The condition of occurring repeatedly at short intervals: *The frequency of his calls is proof enough of his interest.*

frequency modulation. A method of modulation in which a carrier wave changes its frequency about a center value to an extent that corresponds to the strength of the modulating signal and at a rate that corresponds to the frequency of the modulating signal.

fre•quent |**frē′**kwənt| *adj.* Occurring or appearing quite often or at close intervals: *a frequent visitor in her home.* —*v.* |frĭ **kwĕnt′**| *or* |**frē′**kwənt|. To pay frequent visits to; be in or at often: *They frequented the museums.* —**fre′quent•ly** *adv.*

fres•co |**frĕs′**kō| *n., pl.* **fres•coes** or **fres•cos. 1.** The art of painting on wet plaster. **2.** A painting done in this manner.

fresh |frĕsh| *adj.* **fresh•er, fresh•est. 1.** Recently made, produced, or gathered; not stale, spoiled, or withered: *fresh bread; fresh wolf tracks.* **2.** Not preserved, as by canning, smoking, or freezing: *fresh fruit.* **3.** Containing only a small amount of dissolved salts, as compared with sea water: *fresh water.* **4.** New; additional: *fresh evidence; a fresh coat of whitewash.* **5.** New and unusual; different; original; novel: *a fresh approach to old problems.* **6.** Not yet used or soiled; free from impurity; clean: *fresh paper towels.* **7.** Bright and clear; not dull or faded: *a fresh memory.* **8.** Having just arrived; straight: *fresh from a visit to his boyhood home.* **9.** Refreshed; rested; revived: *fresh as a daisy after his afternoon nap.* **10.** Giving energy or strength; invigorating; bracing: *a fresh spring morning.* **11.** *Informal.* Bold; impudent. —*adv.* Recently; newly: *fresh-made rolls.* —**fresh′ly** *adv.* —**fresh′ness** *n.*
***Idiom.* fresh out.** *Informal.* Having just run out: *The storekeeper was fresh out of that item.*

fresh•en |**frĕsh′**ən| *v.* **1.** To make or become fresh. **2.** To make oneself clean: *freshening up after a long day at work.*

fresh•et |**frĕsh′**ĭt| *n.* **1.** A sudden overflow of a stream as a result of heavy rain or a thaw. **2.** A stream of fresh water that runs into a body of salt water.

fresh•man |**frĕsh′**mən| *n., pl.* **-men** |-mən|. A student in his first year at a high school or college. —***modifier:*** *the freshman class.*

fresh•wa•ter |**frĕsh′**wô′tər| *or* |-wŏt′ər| *adj.* Of, living in, or consisting of water that is not salty: *freshwater fish; a freshwater pond.*

fret[1] |frĕt| *v.* **fret•ted, fret•ting. 1.** To be or cause to be uneasy or troubled; worry: *One mother fretted about her son's clothes.* **2.** To gnaw or wear away; erode: *a river fretting a channel through the rock.* —*n.* A condition of being troubled; worry; irritation. [SEE NOTE]

fret[2] |frĕt| *n.* Any one of the ridges set across the fingerboard of a stringed instrument, such as a guitar, to help the player place his fingers correctly. —**fret′ted** *adj.* [SEE NOTE]

fret[3] |frĕt| *n.* An ornamental design within a band or border, consisting of repeated geometric designs. [SEE NOTE & PICTURE]

fret•ful |**frĕt′**fəl| *adj.* Feeling or showing irritation; peevish; discontented: *Small children are often fretful and whiny when they are hungry.* —**fret′ful•ly** *adv.* —**fret′ful•ness** *n.*

fret saw. A saw with a narrow, fine-toothed blade, used for cutting delicate ornamental patterns in thin wood or metal.

Freud |froid|, **Sigmund.** 1856–1939. Austrian physician, the founder of psychoanalysis.

Freud•i•an |**froi′**dē ən| *adj.* Of or in accord with the psychoanalytic theories and teachings of Sigmund Freud. —*n.* Someone who accepts and applies the psychoanalytic theories of Freud.

Fri. Friday.

fri•a•ble |**frī′**ə bəl| *adj.* Easily crumbled; brittle. —**fri′a•bil′i•ty, fri′a•ble•ness** *n.*

fri•ar |**frī′**ər| *n.* A man who is a member of certain Roman Catholic orders. ¶*These sound alike* **friar, fryer.**

fric•as•see |frĭk′ə **sē′**| *n.* Chicken cut into pieces, stewed, and served with a thick gravy. —*v.* To prepare as a fricassee.

fric•tion |**frĭk′**shən| *n.* **1.** The rubbing of one object or surface against another. **2.** A force that acts to resist or retard the relative motion of two objects that are in contact. **3.** A conflict or clash, as of persons having differing beliefs or personalities. —**fric′tion•less** *adj.*

fric•tion•al |**frĭk′**shə nəl| *adj.* Of or involving friction: *frictional heating.* —**fric′tion•al•ly** *adv.*

Fri•day |**frī′**dē| *or* |-dā′| *n.* The sixth day of the week, after Thursday and before Saturday. —***modifier:*** *a Friday ball game.*

friend |frĕnd| *n.* **1.** A person whom one knows and likes. **2.** Someone who supports a group, cause, or movement: *The congressman became known as a friend of conservationists.* **3. Friend.** A member of the Society of Friends; a Quaker.
***Idiom.* make friends with.** To enter into friendship with.

friend•less |**frĕnd′**lĭs| *adj.* Without friends. —**friend′less•ness** *n.*

friend•ly |**frĕnd′**lē| *adj.* **friend•li•er, friend•li•est. 1.** Of or suitable to a friend or friends: *friendly cooperation; a friendly letter.* **2.** Not feeling or showing enmity or hostility: *friendly as kittens.* **3.** Giving comfort or support; favorable: *friendly, warm sunlight.* —**friend′li•ness** *n.*

friend•ship |**frĕnd′**shĭp′| *n.* **1.** The condition of being friends. **2.** A feeling of warmth toward another; friendliness: *friendship between people who enjoy sharing many things.*

frieze[1] |frēz| *n.* **1.** In ancient Greek and Roman architecture, a plain or carved horizontal band of an entablature between the architrave and cornice. **2.** A decorative horizontal band along the upper part of a wall in a room. ¶*These sound alike* **frieze, freeze.** [SEE NOTE]

frieze[2] |frēz| *n.* A coarse, shaggy woolen cloth with an uncut nap, used for coats. ¶*These sound alike* **frieze, freeze.** [SEE NOTE]

frig•ate |**frĭg′**ĭt| *n.* **1.** Any of various fast-sailing square-rigged warships built between the 17th and the mid-19th centuries. **2.** An antisubmarine ship, used as an escort.

frigate bird. A tropical sea bird with long, powerful wings, dark feathers, and a forked tail. [SEE PICTURE]

Frig•ga |**frĭg′**ə|. In Norse mythology, the wife of Odin.

fright |frīt| *n.* **1.** Sudden, intense fear, as of

something immediately threatening; alarm. **2.** *Informal.* Something very ugly or alarming: *Her clothing is a fright.*

fright•en |frĭt'n| *v.* **1.** To make or become suddenly afraid; alarm or startle: *frighten a child. Her children frighten easily.* **2.** To drive or force by arousing fear: *His reputation as a bully frightened the younger boys away.*

fright•en•ing |frĭt'n ĭng| *adj.* Causing fright or sudden alarm. —**fright'en•ing•ly** *adv.*

fright•ful |frĭt'fəl| *adj.* **1.** Causing disgust or shock; horrifying: *a frightful slaughter of buffalo.* **2.** Causing fright; terrifying: *frightful masks.* **3.** *Informal.* Extreme; excessive: *a look of frightful contempt.* —**fright'ful•ly** *adv.*

frig•id |frĭj'ĭd| *adj.* **1.** Extremely cold: *a frigid room.* **2.** Stiff and formal in manner: *The faculty attended the commencement with a frigid dignity.* —**fri•gid'i•ty, frig'id•ness** *n.* —**frig'id•ly** *adv.*

Frigid Zone. Either of two zones on the earth's surface. The **North Frigid Zone** extends from the North Pole to the Arctic Circle. The **South Frigid Zone** extends from the South Pole to the Antarctic Circle.

fri•jol, also **fri•jole** |frē hōl'| *n., pl.* **fri•jo•les** |frē-hō'lēz|. A bean cultivated and used for food, especially in Mexico and the southwestern United States.

frill |frĭl| *n.* **1.** A gathered or pleated piece of fancy trimming, such as a lace ruffle: *frills on a doll's dress.* **2.** *Informal.* Something fancy but unnecessary, added on as an extra: *a basic course of study without any frills.* —*v.* To put a frill or frills on: *She frilled the skirt.*

frill•y |frĭl'ē| *adj.* **frill•i•er, frill•i•est.** Covered or decorated with frills: *a frilly party dress.*

fringe |frĭnj| *n.* **1.** A border or edging of hanging threads, cords, or strips, either loose, looped, or bunched, used for decoration. **2.** Something like fringe along an edge: *a fringe of eyelashes; a fringe of light.* **3.** An outer part; margin; edge: *on the fringe of the crowd.* **4.** Those members of a group or political party who hold extreme views: *"Every reform movement has a lunatic fringe."* (Theodore Roosevelt). —***modifier:*** *fringe groups.* —*v.* **fringed, fring•ing. 1.** To decorate with fringe. **2.** To form a fringe along the edge of: *Long lashes fringed her eyes.* —**fringed'** *adj.: a fringed curtain.* [SEE PICTURE]

fringe benefit. An employment benefit, such as medical care, given in addition to wages.

frip•per•y |frĭp'ə rē| *n., pl.* **frip•per•ies. 1.** Cheap, showy garments or ornaments. **2.** Any pretense or showing off, as in speech or behavior.

Fris•bee |frĭz'bē| *n.* A trademark for a saucer-shaped object that glides through the air when thrown and is tossed back and forth between players for recreation.

Fri•sian |frĭzh'ən| *or* |frē'zhən| *n.* **1.** A native or inhabitant of a northern province of the Netherlands. **2.** The Germanic language of these people. —**Fri'sian** *adj.*

frisk |frĭsk| *v.* **1.** To move about briskly and playfully; frolic: *Baby squirrels frisked in the trees.* **2.** To search (a person) for something concealed, especially weapons.

frisk•y |frĭs'kē| *adj.* **frisk•i•er, frisk•i•est.** Energetic, lively, and playful: *a frisky kitten.* —**frisk'i•ly** *adv.* —**frisk'i•ness** *n.*

frit•il•lar•y |frĭt'l ĕr'ē| *n., pl.* **frit•il•lar•ies. 1.** Any of several butterflies having brownish wings with black or silvery spots. **2.** A plant with nodding, bell-shaped, spotted or checkered flowers.

frit•ter¹ |frĭt'ər| *v.* —**fritter away.** To reduce or squander little by little; waste: *keep the boys from frittering away their time.* [SEE NOTE]

frit•ter² |frĭt'ər| *n.* A small fried cake of batter that often contains fruit, vegetables, or seafood. [SEE NOTE]

fri•vol•i•ty |frĭ vŏl'ĭ tē| *n., pl.* **fri•vol•i•ties. 1.** The condition or quality of being frivolous. **2.** A frivolous act or thing.

friv•o•lous |frĭv'ə ləs| *adj.* **1.** Not worthy of serious attention; insignificant; trivial: *wasting their time on frivolous ideas.* **2.** Not serious or sensible in manner or behavior; silly; flippant: *He seemed to be frivolous and unaware of the crisis.* —**friv'o•lous•ly** *adv.* —**friv'o•lous•ness** *n.*

frizz |frĭz| *v.* To curl (hair) in small, tight, crisp curls. —*n.* **1.** A tight, crisp curl. **2.** Kinky hair.

friz•zle¹ |frĭz'əl| *v.* **friz•zled, friz•zling.** To fry until crisp or curled. [SEE NOTE]

friz•zle² |frĭz'əl| *v.* **friz•zled, friz•zling.** To curl in small, tight, crisp ringlets. —*n.* A small, tight curl. [SEE NOTE]

friz•zly |frĭz'lē| *adj.* **friz•zli•er, friz•zli•est.** Frizzy; kinky.

friz•zy |frĭz'ē| *adj.* **friz•zi•er, friz•zi•est.** Full of tight, crisp little curls: *frizzy hair.*

fro |frō| *adv.* —**to and fro.** Back and forth: *watching the pendulum swing to and fro.*

frock |frŏk| *n.* **1.** A girl's or woman's dress. **2.** A long, loose outer garment, as a priest's, monk's, or friar's robe or a workman's smock.

frock coat. A man's double-breasted dress coat coming to the knees, worn in the 19th century.

frog |frôg| *or* |frŏg| *n.* **1.** An animal with smooth, moist skin, webbed feet, long hind legs used for leaping, and no tail when fully grown. Frogs are amphibians, and many kinds live chiefly in water. **2.** An ornamental fastener made of braid or cord with a looped piece that fits around a button. **3.** A device used where railroad tracks cross or join to allow wheels to roll smoothly. **4.** *Informal.* Hoarseness in one's throat. [SEE PICTURES]

frog kick. A swimming kick in which the legs are drawn up close beneath one, then thrust outward vigorously.

frog•man |frôg'măn'| *or* |-mən| *or* |frŏg'-| *n., pl.* **-men** |-mĕn'| *or* |-mən|. A swimmer provided with breathing apparatus and other equipment to execute underwater maneuvers, especially military maneuvers.

frol•ic |frŏl'ĭk| *n.* **1.** Gaiety; merriment: *"Frolic and an empty purse often go hand in hand," Benjamin Franklin wrote.* **2.** A gay, carefree time or entertainment: *an old-fashioned quilting frolic.* —*v.* **frol•icked, frol•ick•ing.** To behave playfully; romp.

frol•ic•some |frŏl'ĭk səm| *adj.* Full of fun; frisky; playful: *a frolicsome puppy.*

from |frŭm| *or* |frŏm| *or* |frəm *when unstressed*| *prep.* **1.** Beginning at a specified place or time: *walked home from the station; from midnight on.* **2.** With a specified time or point as the first of two limits: *from age four to age eight.* **3. a.** With

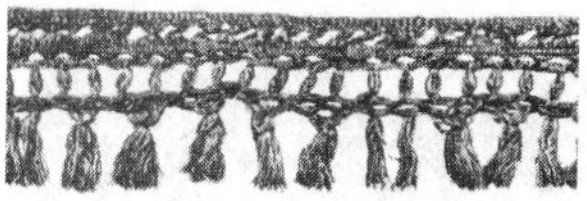

fringe

fritter¹·²

Fritter¹ *probably originally meant "to break in pieces or tear to rags," and may be related to a German word meaning "rags."* **Fritter²** *is from Old French* friture, *"something fried," and is related to* **fry¹**.

frizzle¹·²

Frizzle¹ *is probably a blend of* **fry¹** *and* **sizzle. Frizzle²** *is from* **frizz**, *which is from French* friser, *"to curl up, to shrivel."*

frog

Animal *(above)* and ornamental fastener *(below)*

frond

frontier
The second and third meanings of **frontier** *are special American developments. During most of American history, the edge of the settled country has been the place where unlimited cheap land was available to anyone willing to live the hard but independent life of the pioneer farmer. It has long been recognized that the experience of frontier life had a great part in shaping American society and character. Since the real frontier has disappeared, Americans have sometimes felt the need to find frontiers in other areas (sense 3) or even to invent new ones, such as "the New Frontier," which was the slogan of President Kennedy's administration.*

ă pat/ā pay/â care/ä father/ĕ pet/ē be/ĭ pit/ī pie/î fierce/ŏ pot/ō go/ô paw, for/oi oil/ŏŏ book/ōō boot/ou out/ŭ cut/û fur/*th* the/th thin/hw which/zh vision/ə ago, item, pencil, atom, circus

a person, place, or thing as the source, cause, or instrument: *a note from the teacher.* **b.** Because of: *faint from hunger.* **4.** Out of: *taking a book from the shelf.* **5.** Out of the jurisdiction, control, or possession of: *running away from home.* **6.** So as not to be engaged in: *kept from playing.* **7.** Measured by reference to: *away from home.* **8.** As opposed to: *knowing right from wrong.*

frond |frŏnd| *n.* The leaf of a fern, palm tree, etc., usually divided into smaller leaflets. [SEE PICTURE]

front |frŭnt| *n.* **1.** The forward part or surface of a thing or place: *a blouse with tucks down the front; a desk at the front of the room.* **2.** The area, location, or position directly before or ahead: *You are sure to find a crowd in front of the monkeys' cage.* **3.** A foremost position in rank, superiority, or leadership; forefront: *We are still in front scientifically.* **4.** The first part; beginning; opening: *the chart at the front of your book.* **5.** A person's manner or behavior when faced with a particular situation; demeanor or bearing: *trying to keep a brave front despite his misfortune.* **6.** A false appearance or manner; outward show: *He puts up a protective front among strangers.* **7.** Land bordering a lake, river, street, etc.: *a lake front.* **8.** In warfare, an area where major fighting is taking place. **9.** An area or scene of a particular activity: *laws showing greater concern for life on the home front.* **10.** The boundary between two masses of air that are at different temperatures: *a cold front.* **11.** A group or movement uniting persons or organizations that seek a common goal; a coalition. **12.** An outwardly respectable person or business that serves as a cover for secret or illegal activity. *—adj.* In or facing the front: *the front door; the front pages; the front view.* *—v.* To face or look out upon: *a building fronting on the street.*

front•age |**frŭn'**tĭj| *n.* **1. a.** The front part of a piece of property, as a lot or building. **b.** The dimensions of such a part. **2.** The land between a building and the street. **3.** The land next to a building, street, or body of water.

fron•tal |**frŭn'**tl| *adj.* **1.** Of, at, or concerning the front. **2.** Of the forehead. —**fron'tal•ly** *adv.*

frontal bone. A bone of the skull, consisting of a part that corresponds to the forehead and a part that forms the roof of the eye sockets and cavities of the nose.

fron•tier |frŭn **tîr'**| *n.* **1.** A boundary between countries or the land along such a boundary. **2.** A remote area within a country that marks the point of farthest settlement. **3.** Any undeveloped area or field of activity, interest, etc.: *exploring new frontiers in space.* —**modifier:** *frontier heroes; the frontier spirit.* [SEE NOTE]

fron•tiers•man |frŭn **tîrz'**mən| *n., pl.* **-men** |-mən|. A man who lives in an area just beyond which territory is not settled.

fron•tis•piece |**frŭn'**tĭs pēs'| *n.* An illustration that faces or comes just before the title page of a book.

frost |frôst| *or* |frŏst| *n.* **1.** A covering or deposit of small ice crystals formed from frozen water vapor. **2.** Weather conditions that favor or cause the formation of frost. *—v.* **1.** To cover with or as if with frost. **2.** To cover (a cake, cupcake, etc.) with icing.

frost•bite |**frôst'**bīt'| *or* |**frŏst'**-| *n.* Destruction of tissues in a part of the body as a result of freezing. *—v.* **-bit** |-bĭt'| or **-bit•ten** |-bĭt'n|, **-bit•ing.** To damage or destroy (tissues of the body) by freezing. —**frost'bit'ten** *adj.: frostbitten fingers.*

frost•ed |**frô'**stĭd| *or* |**frŏs'**tĭd| *adj.* **1.** Covered by frost or by a speckled surface resembling frost. **2.** Frostbitten. **3.** Covered with icing.

frost•ing |**frô'**stĭng| *or* |**frŏs'**tĭng| *n.* **1.** A sweet glaze of sugar and other ingredients, used to decorate cakes or cookies; icing. **2.** A roughened or speckled surface on glass or metal.

frost•y |**frô'**stē| *or* |**frŏs'**tē| *adj.* **frost•i•er, frost•i•est. 1.** Of or producing frost: *a frosty night.* **2.** Covered with or as if with frost: *the frosty bedroom window.* **3.** Cold in manner; unfriendly: *a frosty reply.* —**frost'i•ly** *adv.* —**frost'i•ness** *n.*

froth |frôth| *or* |frŏth| *n.* **1.** A mass of bubbles in or on a liquid; foam. **2.** Something lacking in substance or depth: *a play that is mere froth.* *—v.* To pour forth (a liquid) in the form of foam; foam: *They knew the dog was sick when it frothed at the mouth.*

froth•y |**frô'**thē| *or* |**frŏth'**ē| *adj.* **froth•i•er, froth•i•est. 1.** Of, like, or covered with froth: *a wave's frothy spray.* **2.** Light, frivolous, and playful: *a frothy comedy.* —**froth'i•ly** *adv.* —**froth'i•ness** *n.*

frown |froun| *v.* **1.** To wrinkle the brow, as in showing thought, puzzlement, or displeasure; scowl. **2.** To regard with disapproval or distaste. *—n.* The act of wrinkling the brow, as in showing thought, puzzlement, or displeasure; a scowl.

frow•zy |**frou'**zē| *adj.* **frow•zi•er, frow•zi•est. 1.** Untidy; slovenly; unkempt. **2.** Having an unpleasant smell; musty. —**frow'zi•ness** *n.*

froze |frōz|. Past tense of **freeze.**

fro•zen |**frō'**zən|. Past participle of **freeze.**

fruc•tose |**frŭk'**tōs'| *or* |**frŏŏk'**-| *n.* A very sweet sugar found in honey and in many fruits. It has the chemical formula $C_6H_{12}O_6$.

fru•gal |**frōō'**gəl| *adj.* **1.** Thrifty in managing money; not wasteful: *a frugal person.* **2.** Costing little or not very abundant: *the frugal fare on the farmers' tables.* **3.** Lacking richness, fertility, strength, or similar qualities; meager: *a frugal soil.* —**fru•gal'i•ty** |frōō **găl'**ĭ tē| *n.* —**fru'gal•ly** *adv.*

fruit |frōōt| *n., pl.* **fruit** or **fruits. 1. a.** The ripened, seed-bearing part of a flowering plant, as a pod, berry, or burr. **b.** A fleshy or juicy plant part of this kind, often sweet, as an apple, orange, or plum, eaten as food. **2.** A result or outcome; product: *enjoying at last the fruit of our years of labor.* —**modifier:** *fruit juice; fruit salad; fruit trees.* *—v.* To produce fruit.

fruit cake. A heavy, spiced cake containing various dried and preserved fruits and nuts.

fruit fly. A small fly whose larvae hatch in and feed on ripening or decaying fruit.

fruit•ful |**frōōt'**fəl| *adj.* **1.** Producing fruit. **2.** Productive or profitable: *General Eisenhower's long and fruitful life; that fruitful year of 1808.* —**fruit'ful•ly** *adv.* —**fruit'ful•ness** *n.*

fru•i•tion |frōō **ĭsh'**ən| *n.* **1.** The achievement of something desired or worked for; accomplishment: *Their plans never reached fruition.* **2.** The condition of bearing fruit.

fruit•less |**frōōt'**lĭs| *adj.* **1.** Having little or no result; unproductive: *dozens of fruitless experiments.* **2.** Producing no fruit. —**fruit'less•ly** *adv.* —**fruit'less•ness** *n.*

fruit sugar. Fructose.

fruit•y |frōō'tē| *adj.* **fruit•i•er, fruit•i•est.** Tasting or smelling of fruit. —**fruit'i•ness** *n.*

frus•trate |frŭs'trāt'| *v.* **frus•trat•ed, frus•trat•ing.** To prevent from accomplishing a purpose or goal; thwart or nullify. —**frus•tra'tion** *n.*

frus•tum |frŭs'təm| *n., pl.* **frus•tums** or **frus•ta** |frŭs'tə|. A part of a solid figure, such as a cone or pyramid, cut off by two parallel planes that cross all the lines contained in its surface, especially the section between the base and a plane parallel to it.

fry[1] |frī| *v.* **fried, fry•ing, fries.** To cook over direct heat in hot oil or fat: *He fried some chicken. The chicken is frying.* —*n., pl.* **fries.** A social meal of fried food: *a fish fry.* [SEE NOTE]

fry[2] |frī| *n., pl.* **fry.** A small fish, especially a recently hatched fish. [SEE NOTE]

fry•er |frī'ər| *n.* A small, young chicken suitable for frying. ¶*These sound alike* **fryer, friar.**

frying pan. A shallow pan with a long handle, used for frying food.

Idiom. **out of the frying pan into the fire.** Out of a difficult situation into an even worse one.

ft foot (unit of length).

fuch•sia |fyōō'shə| *n.* **1.** A plant grown for its drooping, often red and purple flowers. **2.** A bright purplish red. —*adj.* Bright purplish red. [SEE PICTURE]

fud•dle |fŭd'l| *v.* **fud•dled, fud•dling.** To muddle or confuse with or as if with liquor; intoxicate.

fudge |fŭj| *n.* A soft, rich candy, often flavored with chocolate.

fueh•rer |fyŏŏr'ər| *n.* A form of the word **führer.**

fu•el |fyōō'əl| *n.* **1.** Any substance, such as coal, wood, oil, or gas, that is burned or consumed in a chemical reaction in order to produce energy. **2.** A substance that can be made to undergo a nuclear reaction and produce energy. **3.** Anything that maintains, feeds, or increases an activity or strong feeling. —***modifier:*** *a fuel pump.* —*v.* **fu•eled** or **fu•elled, fu•el•ing** or **fu•el•ling.** To provide with fuel.

fuel cell. A device in which a fuel and an oxidizing agent react and release energy in the form of electricity.

fu•gi•tive |fyōō'jĭ tĭv| *adj.* **1.** Running or having run away, as from the law or justice: *a fugitive convict.* **2.** Passing quickly; fleeting or elusive: *trying to call back the fugitive hours.* —*n.* A person who flees; a runaway; refugee.

fugue |fyōōg| *n.* A musical composition in which one or more themes are stated and then developed by means of imitation and elaborate counterpoint.

füh•rer |fyŏŏr'ər| *n.* **1.** A leader, especially one who is a tyrant. **2. Führer.** The title of Adolf Hitler as leader of the German Nazis.

-ful. A suffix meaning: **1.** Full of: **eventful; playful. 2.** Characterized by: **boastful. 3.** Having a specified tendency or capability: **mournful; useful. 4.** An amount or quantity that will fill: **armful; cupful.**

ful•crum |fŏŏl'krəm| *or* |fŭl'-| *n., pl.* **ful•crums** or **ful•cra** |fŏŏl'krə| *or* |fŭl'-|. The point on which a lever turns.

ful•fill |fŏŏl fĭl'| *v.* **1.** To make come true: *determined to fulfill their ancient prophecies.* **2.** To carry out: *ordered to fulfill the terms of a contract.* **3.** To measure up to; satisfy: *fulfilling all requirements.* —**ful•fill'ment** *n.*

full |fŏŏl| *adj.* **full•er, full•est. 1.** Containing all that is normal or possible; filled: *a full bucket.* **2.** Not deficient or partial; complete: *your full attention; full employment.* **3.** Of highest degree or development: *at full speed; in full bloom.* **4.** Having a great many or a great deal of: *shelves full of books.* **5.** Charged or engrossed with: *a face full of helplessness and terror.* **6. a.** Totally qualified or accepted: *a full member of the club.* **b.** Required of an adult: *full fare.* **7.** Rounded in shape: *the fullest contours of the figure.* **8.** Not tight or narrow: *a full skirt.* **9.** Abundantly fed: *He was full to bursting.* **10.** Having depth and body; rich: *a full flavor.* **11.** Having its illuminated side completely facing the earth: *a full moon.* **12.** Having the same mother and father: *full brothers.* —*adv.* **1.** To a complete extent; entirely: *He knew full well that he was wrong.* **2.** Exactly; directly: *a blow that caught him full on the chin.* —**full'ness** *n.*

Idioms. **in full.** Completely: with nothing lacking: *paid in full; given in full.* **to the full** (or **fullest**). Completely: *enjoy to the full a new sensation.*

full•back |fŏŏl'băk'| *n.* **1.** In football, the player who, along with the halfbacks and quarterback, is in a team's offensive backfield. **2.** In soccer and field hockey, either of two players stationed near their team's goal.

full-blood•ed |fŏŏl'blŭd'ĭd| *adj.* **1.** Of unmixed ancestry; purebred; not hybrid. **2.** Full of vigor, drive, etc.; energetic.

full-blown |fŏŏl'blōn'| *adj.* **1.** In full bloom; fully open: *a full-blown tulip.* **2.** Fully matured or developed: *full-blown beauty.*

full dress. The kind of clothing required for very formal occasions or ceremonies, as a man's white tie and tails or a special uniform. —***modifier:*** **(full-dress):** *a full-dress uniform.*

fuller's earth. A very absorbent claylike substance used in talcum powder, in cleaning woolen cloth, and as a filtering material.

full-fledged |fŏŏl'flĕjd'| *adj.* **1.** Having the fully developed feathers of an adult bird. **2.** Having full standing or rank: *a full-fledged lawyer.*

full-grown |fŏŏl'grōn'| *adj.* Having reached full growth or development; fully mature: *a full-grown cat.*

full house. A hand of cards in poker consisting of three cards of one value and a pair.

full-length |fŏŏl'lĕngkth'| *or* |-lĕngth'| *adj.* **1.** Covering the entire length of someone or something: *a full-length mirror; a full-length wedding dress.* **2.** Of the normal or usual length: *a full-length motion picture; a full-length coat.*

full moon. 1. The phase of the moon when it is seen as a fully lighted disk. **2.** The time of the month when this occurs.

full nelson. A wrestling hold in which the hands are thrust under the opponent's arms from behind and pressed against the back of his neck.

full-scale |fŏŏl'skāl'| *adj.* Of the actual or full size; not reduced: *a full-scale model.*

full-size |fŏŏl'sīz'| *adj.* Of full or normal size: *a full-size pattern; a full-size man.*

fry[1·2]

Fry[1] *is from Old French* frire, *which is from Latin* frīgere, *"to roast or fry."* **Fry**[2] *is probably from Old French* frie, *"fish spawn," from* frier, *"to spawn."*

fuchsia

fulminate

Fulminate *is from Latin* fulmināre, *"to thunder, to throw lightning," from* fulmen, *"thunderbolt, lightning." The Latin verb was used of Jupiter throwing his thunderbolts at men and also of the Roman emperor, who was often compared to Jupiter. In the Middle Ages, the word was used of popes excommunicating people or otherwise blasting them. The English verb (in sense 2) remains a colorfully powerful word with a grandiose past.*

function

Strictly speaking, y = √x *is not a good definition of a* **function** *because for any value of* x *(take* x = 1, *for example) there are two values of* y *(in this case* y = 1 *and* y = −1*). This difficulty can be avoided by excluding negative values of* y*. Sometimes a function is not defined for all values of the independent variable. For example,* y = 1/x *is not defined for* x = 0.

funnel

ă pat/ā pay/â care/ä father/ĕ pet/ē be/ĭ pit/ī pie/î fierce/ŏ pot/ō go/ô paw, for/oi oil/o͝o book/o͞o boot/ou out/ŭ cut/û fur/*th* the/th thin/hw which/zh vision/ə ago, item, pencil, atom, circus

full-sized |**fo͝ol′sīzd′**| *adj.* A form of the word **full-size.**

full-time |**fo͝ol′tīm′**| *adj.* **1.** Occupying all of one's time: *full-time employment; a full-time course of instruction.* **2.** Devoting all of one's working time to a given job or duty: *a full-time nurse.* —**full′-time′** *adv.*

ful•ly |**fo͝ol′ē**| *adv.* **1.** Totally or completely: *fully aware that every place was occupied.* **2.** At least; no less than: *An even range of temperature is fully as important as a warm climate.*

ful•mi•nate |**fo͝ol′**mə nāt′| *v.* **ful•mi•nat•ed, ful•mi•nat•ing. 1.** To explode with sudden violence or force. **2.** To make a loud, strong verbal attack or denunciation. —*n.* Any of a number of salts that when dry explode violently at the slightest shock or friction. —**ful′mi•na′tion** *n.* [SEE NOTE]

ful•some |**fo͝ol′**səm| *adj.* Abundant to the point of being excessive or insincere: *fulsome praise.* —**ful′some•ly** *adv.* —**ful′some•ness** *n.*

fum•ble |**fŭm′**bəl| *v.* **fum•bled, fum•bling. 1.** To touch or handle unsteadily or idly: *He fumbled nervously with his keys.* **2.** To grope awkwardly to find or to accomplish: *fumbled for the lock.* **3.** To make a botch of; bungle: *He fumbled the job.* **4.** To handle clumsily or drop: *Our fullback fumbled the ball but managed to recover it.* —*n.* **1.** An act of fumbling. **2.** A football that has been dropped during play.

fume |fyo͞om| *n.* Any smoke, vapor, or gas, especially one that is irritating or has an unpleasant odor: *the fumes from a smokestack.* —*v.* **fumed, fum•ing. 1.** To produce or give off fumes. **2.** To treat or process (something) by exposure to fumes. **3.** To feel or show anger or agitation; seethe: *The big boy fretted and fumed.*

fu•mi•gate |**fyo͞o′**mĭ gāt′| *v.* **fu•mi•gat•ed, fu•mi•gat•ing.** To treat (a room or an object) with fumes in order to kill germs, insects, rats, or other pests. —**fu′mi•ga′tion** *n.*

fun |fŭn| *n.* Enjoyment, pleasure, or amusement. ***Idioms.* in fun.** As a joke; in jest. **make fun of.** To ridicule: *children making fun of the strange boy.* **poke fun at.** To ridicule.

func•tion |**fŭngk′**shən| *n.* **1.** The normal or proper activity of a person or thing: *the function of a teacher.* **2.** Something that is related to another thing and that depends on it for its existence, value, or meaning: *Growth is a function of nutrition.* **3. a.** A set of ordered pairs of numbers (*x*, *y*) having the property that for each value of *x* there is just one corresponding value of *y*. **b.** A set *D*, called the domain, and a second set *R*, called the range, together with a rule that associates exactly one element of *R* with each element of *D*. **4.** A very important or formal social gathering, official ceremony, etc. —*v.* To have or perform a function; serve: *This post functions as a support.* [SEE NOTE]

func•tion•al |**fŭngk′**shə nəl| *adj.* **1.** Of or concerning a function or functions. **2.** Designed for or adapted to a particular purpose, often avoiding unnecessary additions that are merely decorative; efficient and practical: *functional architecture.* **3.** Existing with no apparent change in the structure of an organism: *a functional disease.* —**func′tion•al•ly** *adv.*

func•tion•ar•y |**fŭngk′**shə nĕr′ē| *n., pl.* **func•tion•ar•ies.** A person who holds a position of authority or trust; an official.

function machine. An imaginary machine that gives the value of the function for which it is set when a member of the domain is fed in.

function rule. The rule by which the value of a function is determined from an element of the domain; for example, the rule $y = x + 5$ is a function rule.

function word. A word belonging to one of the following word classes: prepositions, auxiliary verbs, conjunctions, conjunctive adverbs, and relatives. Words belonging to these classes are called function words because they express grammatical function. They work as markers indicating relationships between words, clauses, and sentences, rather than as signs expressing content or meaning. In this Dictionary, determiners and all classes of pronouns are also treated as function words.

fund |fŭnd| *n.* **1.** A source of supply; a stock. **2.** A sum of money raised or set aside for a certain purpose: *an employee welfare fund.* **3. funds.** Available money; ready cash: *a club that often found itself out of funds.* —*v.* **1.** To furnish money for (a project, the operation of a program, etc.): *fund a housing project.* **2.** To make provision for paying off (a debt).

fun•da•men•tal |fŭn′də **mĕn′**tl| *adj.* **1.** Having to do with the foundation; elemental; basic; primary: *A fundamental knowledge of electricity should be part of everyone's education.* **2. a.** Of or concerning the component of a regularly recurring wave that is lowest in frequency. **b.** Of or concerning the frequency with which an object vibrates when it moves as a whole. —*n.* **1.** Something that is an elemental or basic part of a system, as a principle or law; an essential: *the fundamentals of mathematics.* **2.** A fundamental frequency, as of a wave or vibration. —**fun′da•men′tal•ly** *adv.*

fun•da•men•tal•ism |fŭn′də **mĕn′**tl ĭz′əm| *n.* **1.** Belief in the Bible as a historical record and statement of prophecy that is not to be questioned. **2.** Often **Fundamentalism.** A movement among Protestants based on this belief. —**fun′da•men′tal•ist** *n.* & *adj.*

fu•ner•al |**fyo͞o′**nər əl| *n.* The ceremonies held in connection with the burial or cremation of the dead. —***modifier:*** *a funeral director.*

fu•ne•re•al |fyo͞o **nîr′**ē əl| *adj.* **1.** Of or suitable for a funeral. **2.** Mournful; sorrowful. —**fu•ne′re•al•ly** *adv.*

fun•gi |**fŭn′**jī| *n.* A plural of **fungus.**

fun•gous |**fŭng′**gəs| *adj.* **1.** Of or typical of a fungus or fungi. **2.** Caused by a fungus: *a fungous plant disease.* ¶*These sound alike* **fungous, fungus.**

fun•gus |**fŭng′**gəs| *n., pl.* **fun•gi** |**fŭn′**jī′| or **fun•gus•es.** Any of a group of plants, such as a mushroom, mold, yeast, or mildew, that have no green coloring and that obtain their nourishment from living or dead plant or animal substances. ¶*These sound alike* **fungus, fungous.**

funk•y |**fŭng′**kē| *adj.* **funk•i•er, funk•i•est.** *Slang.* **1.** Having a lively, pulsating quality with a mixture of jazz, rock, and blues, often with soul-music overtones: *funky music.* **2.** Marked by self-expression and originality; modish and unconventional: *funky clothes.* **3.** Outlandishly vulgar or far-out in a humorous manner: *a funky movie.* —**funk'i•ness** *n.*

fun•nel |fŭn'əl| *n.* **1.** A utensil with a narrow open tube at one end, used in pouring liquids or other substances into a container with a small mouth. **2.** The smokestack of a ship or locomotive. **3.** Something shaped like a funnel, as a tornado, spider's web, etc. —*v.* **fun•neled** or **fun•nelled, fun•nel•ing** or **fun•nel•ling.** To move through or as if through a funnel. [SEE PICTURE]

fun•nies |fŭn'ēz| *pl.n. Informal.* Comic strips.

fun•ny |fŭn'ē| *adj.* **fun•ni•er, fun•ni•est. 1.** Causing laughter or amusement: *a funny clown; a funny show.* **2.** Strange; odd; curious: *"Pee Wee" seemed a funny name for a farmer.* —**fun'ni•ly** *adv.* —**fun'ni•ness** *n.*

funny bone. *Informal.* A point near the elbow where a nerve can be pressed against a bone, producing a numb or tingling feeling in the arm.

fur |fûr| *n.* **1.** The thick, soft hair covering the body of certain animals, such as a rabbit, cat, or fox. **2.** The hair-covered skin or skins of such animals, used for clothing, trimming, etc. **3.** A coat, cape, etc., made of fur. **4.** A fuzzy or fluffy covering that resembles fur. —***modifier:*** *a fur coat.* ¶*These sound alike* **fur, fir.**

fur•bish |fûr'bĭsh| *v.* To brighten by cleaning or rubbing; burnish.

Fu•ries |fyo͝or'ēz|. In Greek and Roman mythology, the three terrible winged goddesses who pursue and punish those who have committed crimes not already avenged.

fu•ri•ous |fyo͝or'ē əs| *adj.* **1.** Full of or marked by extreme anger; raging. **2.** Fierce; violent: *a furious speed; a furious battle.* —**fu'ri•ous•ly** *adv.* —**fu'ri•ous•ness** *n.*

furl |fûrl| *v.* To roll up and fasten (a flag or sail) to a pole, yard, or mast.

fur•long |fûr'lông'| *or* |-lŏng'| *n.* A unit of distance equal to 1/8 mile or 220 yards.

fur•lough |fûr'lō| *n.* A vacation or leave of absence from duty, especially one granted to enlisted personnel of the armed forces. —*v.* To grant a furlough to.

fur•nace |fûr'nĭs| *n.* **1.** An enclosed chamber in which a fuel is consumed, usually by burning, in order to produce heat. **2.** Any enclosed space that is extremely hot.

fur•nish |fûr'nĭsh| *v.* **1.** To equip with furniture: *furnishing a new home.* **2.** To supply; give: *furnish money.* —**fur'nished** *adj.: a furnished apartment.*

fur•nish•ings |fûr'nĭ shĭngz| *pl.n.* **1.** Furniture and other equipment for a home or office. **2.** Clothes and accessories: *men's furnishings.*

fur•ni•ture |fûr'nə chər| *n.* The movable articles, such as chairs, tables, etc., used to make a room or establishment fit for living or working.

fu•ror |fyo͝or'ôr'| *or* |-ōr'| *n.* A noisy outburst of anger, disapproval, enthusiasm, etc., as in a crowd; an uproar.

furred |fûrd| *adj.* **1.** Covered with, trimmed with, or dressed in fur: *a furred collar.* **2.** Having a certain kind of fur: *a long-furred animal.*

fur•ri•er |fûr'ē ər| *n.* A person who deals in fur or fur garments.

fur•row |fûr'ō| *or* |fŭr'ō| *n.* **1. a.** A long, narrow, shallow trench made in the ground by a plow or other tool. **b.** Any rut, groove, or depression similar to this: *furrows cut in the dirt road by water.* **2.** A deep wrinkle in the skin, as on the forehead. —*v.* To make furrows in: *Father furrowed the neat rows of the lettuce field. Anxiety furrowed his face.* [SEE PICTURE]

fur•ry |fûr'ē| *adj.* **fur•ri•er, fur•ri•est. 1.** Consisting of or covered with fur: *a furry coat; a furry animal.* **2.** Resembling fur; thick, soft, and fluffy: *cloth with a furry nap.* —**fur'ri•ness** *n.*

fur•ther |fûr'*th*ər| *adj.* **1.** More distant in time or degree: *You couldn't be further from the right idea.* **2.** Additional: *Keep tuned in for further bulletins.* —*adv.* **1.** To a greater extent; more: *He was going to explore the matter further.* **2.** In addition; furthermore; also: *We further see the importance of careful preparation.* **3.** At or to a more distant point in space or time: *Settlers who went to Colorado traveled further than those who stayed in Indiana.* —*v.* To help the progress of; forward; advance: *He furthered the careers of many composers.* [SEE NOTE]

fur•ther•ance |fûr'*th*ər əns|. The act of advancing or helping forward; advancement.

fur•ther•more |fûr'*th*ər môr'| *or* |-mōr'| *adv.* Moreover; in addition.

fur•ther•most |fûr'*th*ər mōst'| *adj.* Most distant or remote.

fur•thest |fûr'*th*ĭst| *adj.* Most distant in space, time, or degree: *the furthest corner of the earth.* —*adv.* **1.** To the greatest extent or degree: *went furthest toward finding an eventual solution.* **2.** At or to the most distant point in space or time: *traveled furthest but found true happiness back where he set out.*

fur•tive |fûr'tĭv| *adj.* Done or marked by stealth; shifty; sly: *a furtive glance.* —**fur'tive•ly** *adv.* —**fur'tive•ness** *n.*

fu•ry |fyo͝or'ē| *n., pl.* **fu•ries. 1.** Violent anger; rage. **2.** Violent and uncontrolled action; turbulence; agitation: *the blizzard's fury.* **3.** A person, especially a woman, who often has fits of violent anger.

furze |fûrz| *n.* A shrub, gorse.

fuse[1] |fyo͞oz| *n.* **1.** A length of easily burned material that is lighted at one end to carry a flame to and detonate an explosive charge at the other end. **2.** A form of the word **fuze.** —*v.* **fused, fus•ing.** To furnish (an explosive charge) with a fuse. [SEE NOTE]

fuse[2] |fyo͞oz| *v.* **fused, fus•ing. 1.** To make or become soft or liquid by heating or being heated; melt. **2.** To mix together or unite by or as if by melting; blend: *fuse separate images.* —*n.* A protective device for an electric circuit, consisting of an enclosed length of wire that heats up as the current through it increases, finally melting and opening the circuit when the current becomes too strong. [SEE NOTE]

fu•se•lage |fyo͞o'sə läzh'| *or* |-zə-| *n.* The main body of an airplane to which the wings and tail are attached.

fu•si•ble |fyo͞o'zə bəl| *adj.* Capable of being fused. —**fu'si•bil'i•ty** *n.*

fu•sil•lade |fyo͞o'sə lād'| *or* |-läd'| *or* |-zə-| *n.* **1.** The discharge of many guns at the same time or in rapid succession. **2.** Any rapid outburst: *a fusillade of insults.*

fu•sion |fyo͞o'zhən| *n.* **1.** The act or process of

furrow

further/farther

Farther *and* **further** *are historically variants; Old English* furthor, *"more far," split into* **farther** *and* **further** *in Middle English. They remain partly synonymous, but, as often happens with variants, each has tended to become specialized,* **farther** *for physical distance and* **further** *for figurative uses.* **Further** *thus has more different uses than* **farther,** *but* **farther** *still seems to be used more often; in the materials on which this Dictionary was based,* **farther** *occurs 443 times,* **further** *324 times.*

fuse1·2

Fuse[1] *is from Italian* fuso, *"spindle," later "fuse," which is from Latin* fūsus, *"spindle." (A spindle is a small wooden rod used in spinning; in the early days of gunpowder, bombs were ignited by small wooden tubes filled with steady-burning materials; these were similar to spindles, and were sometimes made of the same kind of wood; hence the transition of* fuso *in Italian.)* **Fuze** *is a variant of* **fuse**[1]. **Fuse**[2] *is from Latin* fūs-, *the past participial stem of* fundere, *"to pour, to melt metals."*

melting or mixing different things into one by heat. **2.** A mixture or blend formed by fusing two or more things: *An alloy is a fusion of several metals.* **3.** A reaction in which atomic nuclei combine to form more massive nuclei, generally leaving some excess mass that is converted into energy. **4.** A union formed by merging different things or groups.

fusion bomb. A bomb, especially a hydrogen bomb, that derives its energy mainly from the fusion of atomic nuclei.

fuss |fŭs| *n.* **1.** Needlessly nervous or useless activity; commotion; bustle: *leaving the building without noise or fuss.* **2.** A display of concern or worry over an unimportant matter: *Why make a fuss about a ridiculous dream?* **3.** A protest; complaint: *kick up a fuss over a meal.* —*v.* **1.** To get into or be in a state of nervous or useless activity: *She fussed over dinner.* **2.** To show excessive care or concern: *mothers fussing over children.* **3.** To protest; object; complain.

fuss•y |fŭs′ē| *adj.* **fuss•i•er, fuss•i•est.** **1.** Given to fussing; easily upset: *a fussy old lady.* **2.** Frequently complaining or making demands; discontented or dissatisfied: *a fussy eater.* **3.** Requiring or showing great attention to small details: *a fussy, time-consuming chore.* **4.** Having more small detail or fancy trimming than necessary: *a fussy dress.* —**fuss′i•ly** *adv.*

fus•ty |fŭs′tē| *adj.* **fus•ti•er, fus•ti•est.** **1.** Smelling of mildew or decay; musty; moldy. **2.** Old-fashioned; antique. —**fus′ti•ly** *adv.* —**fus′ti•ness** *n.*

fu•tile |**fyōōt′**l| *or* |**fyōō′**tĭl′| *adj.* Having no useful result; useless; vain: *futile efforts; engaging in futile conversation.* —**fu′tile•ly** *adv.*

fu•til•i•ty |fyōō **tĭl′**ĭ tē| *n., pl.* **fu•til•i•ties.** **1.** The condition or quality of being futile; uselessness; ineffectiveness: *Their protest was an exercise in futility.* **2.** Lack of importance or purpose: *laugh at the futility of life.*

fu•ture |**fyōō′**chər| *n.* **1.** The indefinite period of time yet to be; time that is to come: *plans for the future; doctors of the future.* **2.** That which will happen in time to come: *The state's future will depend on whether Alaskans can overcome the problems of their land.* **3.** The condition of a person or thing in time to come as predicted now: *a company whose future seemed shaky to its creditors.* **4.** Chance of success or advancement: *a land with a solid future.* **5.** Often **futures.** Commodities or stocks bought or sold upon agreement of delivery in time to come. **6.** The **future tense.** —*adj.* That will be or occur in time to come: *some future date; future generations.* [SEE NOTE]

future perfect tense. A verb tense expressing action completed by a stated time in the future. It is formed in English by combining *will have* or *shall have* with a past participle: *By noon tomorrow he will have arrived there.*

future tense. A verb tense used to express action in the future. It is formed in English with the help of the auxiliary verbs *shall* and *will: I shall be back tonight. They will leave in half an hour.*

fu•tur•is•tic |fyōō′chə **rĭs′**tĭk| *adj.* Suitable for a time far in the future: *such futuristic car components as fingernail-sized ignition systems.* —**fu′tur•is′ti•cal•ly** *adv.*

fu•tu•ri•ty |fyōō **tŏŏr′**ĭ tē| *or* |**-tyŏŏr′-**| *or* |**-chŏŏr′-**| *n., pl.* **fu•tu•ri•ties.** **1.** The future. **2.** The condition or quality of being in or of the future. **3.** A future event or possibility.

fuze |fyōōz| *n.* A mechanical or electrical device used to explode a bomb, grenade, or other explosive charge.

fuzz |fŭz| *n.* Soft, short fibers or hairs; fine down: *the fuzz on a peach.*

fuzz•y |fŭz′ē| *adj.* **fuzz•i•er, fuzz•i•est.** **1.** Covered with fuzz: *a fuzzy peach.* **2.** Of or like fuzz: *fuzzy hair.* **3.** Not clear; blurred: *a fuzzy snapshot.* —**fuzz′i•ly** *adv.* —**fuzz′i•ness** *n.*

-fy. A suffix that forms verbs: **simplify.**

future

"I like the dreams of the future better than the history of the past."—Thomas Jefferson (1816).

"I never think of the future. It comes soon enough." —Albert Einstein (1930).

"If we open a quarrel between the past and the present, we shall find we have lost the future." —Winston Churchill (1940).

ă pat/ā pay/â care/ä father/ĕ pet/
ē be/ĭ pit/ī pie/î fierce/ŏ pot/
ō go/ô paw, for/oi oil/ŏŏ book/
ōō boot/ou out/ŭ cut/û fur/
th the/th thin/hw which/zh vision/
ə ago, item, pencil, atom, circus

Gg

g, G |jē| *n., pl.* **g's** or **G's.** **1.** The seventh letter of the English alphabet. **2. G** In music, the fifth tone in the scale of C major. **3. G** A unit equal to the force exerted on a particular object by the earth's gravitational field. [SEE NOTE]
g **1.** acceleration of gravity. **2.** gram.
G |jē| *adj.* Indicating a rating given a motion picture deemed appropriate for all ages.
Ga The symbol for the element gallium.
Ga. Georgia.
gab |găb| *Informal. v.* **gabbed, gab•bing.** To talk idly and often at length; chatter. —*n.* Idle talk.
gab•ar•dine |găb′ər dēn′| *or* |găb′ər **dēn′**| *n.* **1.** A firm, woven cloth with a smooth surface and slanting ribs, used for coats, suits, etc. **2.** A cloak, the gaberdine. —***modifier:*** *a gabardine suit.*
gab•by |găb′ē| *adj.* **gab•bi•er, gab•bi•est.** *Informal.* Tending to talk too much. —**gab′bi•ness** *n.*
gab•er•dine |găb′ər dēn′| *or* |găb′ər **dēn′**| *n.* **1.** A long, loose cloak of coarse material, worn in the Middle Ages. **2.** The cloth gabardine.
ga•ble |gā′bəl| *n.* The triangular wall section between the two slopes of a roof. —**ga′bled** *adj.* [SEE PICTURE]
Ga•bon |gă **bôN′**|. A country on the west coast of central Africa. Population, 520,000. Capital, Libreville.
Gab•o•ro•ne |găb′ə **rō′**nə|. The capital of Botswana. Population, 18,000.
Ga•bri•el |gā′brē əl|. The Biblical archangel who acted as messenger of God.
gad |găd| *v.* **gad•ded, gad•ding.** To roam about seeking amusement or excitement; rove.
gad•a•bout |găd′ə bout′| *n.* A person who goes about seeking amusement or excitement.
gad•fly |găd′flī′| *n., pl.* **-flies.** **1.** A fly that bites or annoys cattle, horses, and other animals. **2.** A person who annoys or provokes others.
gadg•et |găj′ĭt| *n. Informal.* A small mechanical device; a contrivance. —***modifier:*** *a gadget store.*
gad•o•lin•i•um |găd′l **ĭn′**ē əm| *n.* Symbol **Gd** One of the elements, a silvery-white rare-earth metal. Atomic number 64; atomic weight 157.25; valence +3; melting point 1,312°C; boiling point approximately 3,000°C.
Gael |gāl| *n.* A Gaelic-speaking Celt of Scotland or Ireland.
Gael•ic |gā′lĭk| *n.* The Celtic languages of Ireland and Scotland. —*adj.* Of Gaelic or the Gaels.
gaff |găf| *n.* **1.** An iron hook set in a stick or handle, used for landing heavy fish. **2.** A spar used to support the top edge of a fore-and-aft sail. —*v.* To hook or land (a fish) with a gaff.
gaf•fer |găf′ər| *n. Informal.* An old man.
gag |găg| *n.* **1.** Something put into or over a person's mouth to prevent him from speaking or crying out. **2.** Something, such as a law or ruling, that limits or censors free speech, freedom of the press, etc. **3.** *Informal.* **a.** A humorous remark intended to make people laugh; a joke. **b.** A practical joke; a hoax. —*v.* **gagged, gag•ging.** **1.** To prevent from speaking or crying out by using a gag: *The soldiers bound and gagged their prisoners.* **2.** To prevent from speaking out or telling the truth; censor. **3.** To choke; retch: *I gagged on a piece of meat. The smell made me gag.*
gage¹ |gāj| *n.* Something deposited or given as security against an obligation; a pledge. ¶*These sound alike* **gage, gauge.** [SEE NOTE]
gage² |gāj| *n.* A form of the word **gauge.** [SEE NOTE]
gag•gle |găg′əl| *n.* A group or flock of geese.
gai•e•ty |gā′ĭ tē| *n.* **1.** The condition of being gay or merry; cheerfulness: *the gaiety of the cocktail party.* **2.** *pl.* **gai•e•ties.** Merrymaking; celebration: *Mardi gras is a season of gaiety.*
gai•ly |gā′lē| *adv.* **1.** In a joyful, cheerful, or happy manner; merrily. **2.** Brightly; colorfully; showily: *streets gaily decorated.*
gain |gān| *v.* **1.** To get possession, control, or ownership of, as by hard work, merit, imagination, struggle, etc.: *gain experience.* **2. a.** To develop or acquire gradually: *The movement gained strength.* **b.** To come to have: *Washington Irving was the first American writer to gain European acclaim.* **3. a.** To build up an increase of, as of weight, speed, time, etc.: *She gained 10 pounds just by eating chocolate.* **b.** To increase in weight: *She gained a lot.* **4. a.** To progress or advance: *The team gained 5 yards.* **b.** To arrive at; reach: *The troops gained the hill.* —*n.* **1.** Often **gains. a.** Something gained or acquired: *territorial gains.* **b.** Progress; advancement: *Economic gains were impressive last year.* **2.** Benefit; advantage: *using public funds for personal gain.*
Idioms. **gain ground.** To make progress; improve. **gain time.** To put off or delay in a roundabout way.
gain•er |gā′nər| *n.* **1.** Someone or something that gains. **2.** A dive in which the diver leaves the board facing forward, does a back somersault, and enters the water feet first.
gain•ful |gān′fəl| *adj.* Providing an income; profitable: *gainful employment.* —**gain′ful•ly** *adv.*
gain•say |gān′sā′| *v.* **gain•said** |gān′sĕd′|, **gain•say•ing.** To contradict; deny: *Do not gainsay him, even though you disagree.*
gait |gāt| *n.* **1.** A way of walking or running: *a slow gait; a clumsy gait.* **2.** One of the ways a

The letter **G** *comes originally from the Phoenician letter* gīmel *(1), which meant "camel." The Greeks borrowed it as* gamma, *turning it to face in the opposite direction (2); later its shape was altered (3). This shape was borrowed by the Romans (4), who used it both for the sound /g/ and for the sound /k/. Later they decided to distinguish between the two sounds, and so they added a small bar to the letter to stand for /g/ (5). This form is the source of our modern letter G. See also note at* **C.**

gable

gage¹·²/wage

Gage¹ *is from Old French* gage, *which is from Frankish* wadi, *"pledge." In the northern dialect of Old French,* wadi *became* wage, *"soldier's pay," and was borrowed into English as* **wage.** *(On the change of a Germanic* w *to an Old French* g, *see note at* **guard/ward.**) **Gage²**, *usually spelled* **gauge,** *is from northern Old French* gauge, *"measure, measuring instrument."*

galaxy

gall[1-2-3]

Gall[1] *was* gealla *in Old English; it is descended from a root meaning "yellow stuff."* **Gall**[2] *was also* gealla *in Old English, but this was a separate word from* **gall**[1] *and meant "sore on a horse"; it was probably borrowed from Latin* galla, *"swelling on a plant."* **Gall**[3] *is also borrowed from Latin* galla, *and it preserves the original meaning.*

gam[1-2]

Gam[1] *is a nineteenth-century Americanism; it was used to mean not only a school of whales but also a friendly meeting of whaling ships at sea. Its origin is obscure; it has been suggested that it may be related to* **game**[1]. **Gam**[2] *originally meant "leg of an animal" and is from northern Old French* gambe *(Modern French* jambe*).*

ă pat/ā pay/â care/ä father/ĕ pet/ ē be/ĭ pit/ī pie/î fierce/ŏ pot/ ō go/ô paw, for/oi oil/ŏŏ book/ ōō boot/ou out/ŭ cut/û fur/ *th* the/th thin/hw which/zh vision/ ə ago, item, pencil, atom, circus

horse moves by lifting the feet in a certain order or rhythm, as a walk, trot, or gallop. ¶ *These sound alike* **gait, gate.**

gai•ter |gā′tər| *n.* **1.** A leather or cloth covering for the lower leg or ankle, worn over part of the shoe; a spat. **2.** An ankle-high shoe with elastic sides. **3.** An overshoe with a cloth top.

gal |găl| *n. Informal.* A girl.

gal. gallon.

ga•la |gā′lə| *or* |găl′ə| *or* |gä′lə| *adj.* Festive: *There will be a gala dance on the last night of the voyage.* —*n.* A festive occasion or celebration.

ga•lac•tic |gə lăk′tĭk| *adj.* Of a galaxy or galaxies.

Gal•a•had |găl′ə hăd′|. In legends about King Arthur, the knight of pure heart who found the Grail.

gal•ax•y |găl′ək sē| *n., pl.* **gal•ax•ies. 1. a.** Any one of the many large collections of stars, gas, and dust that are found in the universe and that have one of a group of fairly definite forms. The average mass of a collection of this type is 100 billion times the mass of the sun. **b.** Often **the Galaxy.** The galaxy that contains the sun and solar system; the Milky Way. **2.** An assembly of brilliant, beautiful, or distinguished persons or things: *a galaxy of fireworks; a galaxy of television stars.* [SEE PICTURE]

gale |gāl| *n.* **1.** A very strong wind, especially one having a speed between 32 and 63 miles per hour. **2.** A noisy outburst: *gales of laughter.* —**modifier:** *gale winds.*

Ga•len |gā′lən|. 130?–201? Greek anatomist and physician.

ga•le•na |gə lē′nə| *n.* A gray mineral, essentially lead sulfide, that is the main ore of lead.

Gal•i•lee, Sea of |găl′ə lē′|. A freshwater lake bordered by Israel, Syria, and Jordan.

Gal•i•le•o |găl′ə lē′ō| *or* |-lā′ō|. 1564–1642. Italian physicist and astronomer.

gall[1] |gôl| *n.* **1.** Bile, a liquid produced by the liver. **2.** Bitterness of spirit; spite. **3.** Impudence; effrontery; nerve: *He had the gall to try to borrow money.* [SEE NOTE]

gall[2] |gôl| *n.* A sore caused by rubbing, as one under a horse's saddle. —*v.* **1.** To annoy. **2.** To make or become chafed. [SEE NOTE]

gall[3] |gôl| *n.* An abnormal swelling on a plant, caused by insects or disease organisms. [SEE NOTE]

gal•lant |găl′ənt| *adj.* **1.** Brave and noble; courageous; valorous: *a gallant knight; a gallant try.* **2.** |*also* gə **lănt′**| *or* |**-länt′**|. Polite and attentive to women; chivalrous: *his gallant manner.* —*n.* |gə**lănt′**| *or* |**-länt′**| *or* |**găl′**ənt|. **1.** A fashionable young man. **2.** A man who is polite and attentive to women. —**gal′lant•ly** *adv.*

gal•lant•ry |găl′ən trē| *n.* **1.** Heroic courage. **2.** Chivalrous attention to women; courtliness. **3.** *pl.* **gal•lant•ries.** A chivalrous act or action.

gall•blad•der |gôl′blăd′ər| *n.* Also **gall bladder.** A small, pear-shaped muscular sac that is located near the right lobe of the liver in which bile secreted by the liver is stored.

gal•le•on |găl′ē ən| *or* |găl′yən| *n.* A large three-masted sailing ship of the type much used by Spain during the 16th century.

gal•ler•y |găl′ə rē| *or* |găl′rē| *n., pl.* **gal•ler•ies. 1. a.** A long, narrow walk or passage, often with a roof and partly open at one side. **b.** Any enclosed passageway, especially one used for a specified purpose: *a shooting gallery.* **2. a.** The balcony in a theater or church. **b.** The seats in such a balcony. **c.** The people occupying these seats. **3.** Any large audience, as at a legislative assembly or sports event. **4.** A building or hall for displaying works of art. **5.** An underground tunnel or other passageway, as one dug for mining purposes.

gal•ley |găl′ē| *n.* **1.** A ship with a single deck, driven by sails and oars, much used in the Mediterranean until the 17th century. **2.** The kitchen on a ship or airliner. **3. a.** A long tray used by printers for holding metal type that has been set. **b.** A **galley proof.**

galley proof. A printer's proof taken from composed type before page composition to allow for the detection and correction of errors.

Gal•lic |găl′ĭk| *adj.* Of ancient Gaul or modern France.

gal•li•um |găl′ē əm| *n.* Symbol **Ga** One of the elements, a silvery metal. Atomic number 31; atomic weight 69.72; valences +2, +3; melting point 29.78°C; boiling point 2,403°C.

gal•li•vant |găl′ə vănt′| *v.* To travel or roam about in search of pleasure or amusement; gad.

gal•lon |găl′ən| *n.* A unit of liquid volume or capacity equal to 4 quarts or 231 cubic inches.

gal•lop |găl′əp| *n.* **1.** A fast gait of a horse, having a quick three-beat rhythm. **2.** A fast running pace. **3.** A ride on a horse going at a gallop. —*v.* **1.** To ride at a gallop. **2.** To run or dash.

gal•lows |găl′ōz| *n., pl.* **gal•lows•es** or **gal•lows. 1.** A framework with a suspended noose, used for execution by hanging. **2. the gallows.** Execution on a gallows or by hanging.

gall•stone |gôl′stōn′| *n.* A small, hard mass that forms in the gallbladder or in a bile duct.

ga•lore |gə **lôr′**| *or* |**-lōr′**| *adj. Informal.* In great numbers; in abundance: *bargains galore.*

ga•losh•es |gə **lŏsh′**ĭz| *n. (used with a plural verb).* Waterproof overshoes, often of rubber, worn in rainy or snowy weather.

gal•van•ic |găl **văn′**ĭk| *adj.* **1.** Of electricity that is produced by chemical means. **2.** Producing electricity by chemical means.

gal•va•nize |**găl′**və nīz′| *v.* **gal•va•nized, gal•va•niz•ing. 1.** To put a coating of zinc on (iron or steel) as protection against rust. **2.** To stir to action or awareness; spur: *galvanize the people into supporting the program.* —**gal′va•ni•za′tion** *n.*

gal•va•nom•e•ter |găl′və **nŏm′**ĭ tər| *n.* An instrument that detects and measures small electric currents.

gam[1] |găm| *n.* A school or herd of whales. [SEE NOTE]

gam[2] |găm| *n. Slang.* A person's leg, especially a shapely leg of a woman. [SEE NOTE]

Gam•bi•a |**găm′**bē ə|. A small country in western Africa on the Atlantic Ocean. Population, 601,000. Capital, Banjul.

gam•bit |**găm′**bĭt| *n.* **1.** A chess opening in which a pawn or piece is sacrificed in order to gain a favorable position. **2.** An opening action or remark: *a conversational gambit.*

gam•ble |**găm′**bəl| *v.* **gam•bled, gam•bling. 1.** To bet money on the outcome of a game, contest, or other event. **2.** To take a chance in the hope of gaining or achieving an advantage; speculate: *I'm* *gambling that stock prices will go up this year.* **3.** To lose by gambling: *He gambled away his entire inheritance.* —*n.* An act or undertaking of uncertain outcome; a risk. ¶*These sound alike* **gamble, gambol.** —**gam'bler** *n.*

gam•bling |**găm'**blĭng| *n.* **1.** The practice of betting money on the outcome of a game, contest, etc. **2.** The practice of taking risks for a possible advantage. —**modifier:** *a gambling debt.*

gam•bol |**găm'**bəl| *v.* **gam•boled** or **gam•bolled, gam•bol•ing** or **gam•bol•ling.** To skip about playfully; frolic. —*n.* The act or an example of skipping or frolicking about. ¶*These sound alike* **gambol, gamble.**

game¹ |găm| *n.* **1.** A sport or other form of play governed by specific rules: *Tennis is my favorite game.* **2.** A single contest between two opponents or teams: *a football game.* **3.** In tennis, bridge, etc., one of the brief contests that make up a set or match. **4.** The number of points needed to win a game. **5.** The equipment needed for playing certain games: *Pack the children's games in the suitcase.* **6.** A person's style or ability at a certain game: *He is off his game.* **7. a.** Animals, birds, or fish hunted for food or sport: *big game.* **b.** The flesh of such animals, used as food. **8.** A plan or scheme: *Do you think anyone will see through his game?* **9.** *Informal.* An occupation or profession: *the game of politics.* —**modifier:** *The pheasant is a game bird. We decided to build a game room in the basement.* —*adj.* **gam•er, gam•est. 1.** Courageous; plucky: *a game fighter.* **2.** *Informal.* Ready and willing: *I'm game for anything.* —**game'ly** *adv.* —**game'ness** *n.* [SEE NOTE]

game² |găm| *adj.* **gam•er, gam•est.** Lame: *landing with his game leg first.* [SEE NOTE]

game•cock |**găm'**kŏk'| *n.* A rooster trained for fighting.

game•keep•er |**găm'**kē'pər| *n.* A person employed to protect and maintain wildlife, especially on a country estate.

game•ster |**găm'**stər| *n.* A person who habitually gambles, as at cards.

gam•ete |**găm'**ēt'| *or* |gə **mēt'**| *n.* A germ cell that has half the normal number of chromosomes, especially a mature egg cell or sperm cell.

gam•ing |**gā'**mĭng| *n.* Gambling, as at cards.

gam•ma |**găm'**ə| *n.* **1.** The third letter of the Greek alphabet, written γ. In English it is represented as *n* before *g, k,* or *kh* or as *g.* **2.** A **gamma ray.**

gamma globulin. One of several globulins contained in human blood serum. It is known to contain antibodies against certain infectious diseases, such as measles and hepatitis, and it is sometimes used in their treatment.

gamma ray. Electromagnetic radiation that has, in general, wavelengths shorter than those of x-rays and correspondingly greater energy and penetrating power.

gam•ut |**găm'**ət| *n.* **1.** The entire range of musical tones. **2.** The complete range of anything.

gan•der |**găn'**dər| *n.* **1.** A male goose. **2.** *Slang.* A quick look.

Gan•dhi |**găn'**dē| *or* |**găn'**-|, **Mohandas K.** Called "Mahatma." 1869–1948. Hindu nationalist and spiritual leader.

gang |găng| *n.* **1.** A group of people, often young, who gather or associate together regularly. **2.** A group of young boys who band together to fight other such groups. **3.** An organized group of criminals. **4.** A group of laborers who work together under a single foreman: *a railroad gang; a chain gang.* —**modifier:** *a gang leader; gang warfare.* —*v.* To band together in a group or gang: *Everyone ganged around the mailman.* —**phrasal verb. gang up on.** *Informal.* To attack as a group. ¶*These sound alike* **gang, gangue.**

Gan•ges |**găn'**jēz|. A river in northern India and Bangladesh, sacred to Hindus, rising in the Himalaya Mountains and flowing generally southeast into the Indian Ocean.

gan•gli•a |**găng'**glē ə| *n.* A plural of **ganglion.**

gan•gling |**găng'**glĭng| *adj.* Tall, thin, and awkwardly built; lanky.

gan•gli•on |**găng'**glē ən| *n., pl.* **gan•gli•a** |**găng'**-glē ə| or **gan•gli•ons.** A compact group of nerve cells located outside the brain or spinal cord.

gang•plank |**găng'**plăngk'| *n.* A board or ramp used as a bridge between a ship and a pier.

gan•grene |**găng'**grēn'| *or* |găng **grēn'**| *n.* Death and decay of tissue in a living body, due to injury, disease, or failure of the blood supply. —**gan'gren•ous** |**găng'**grə nəs| *adj.*

gang•ster |**găng'**stər| *n.* A member of an organized group of criminals; a racketeer.

gangue |găng| *n.* The worthless rock or other material in which valuable minerals are found. ¶*These sound alike* **gangue, gang.**

gang•way |**găng'**wā'| *n.* **1. a.** A gangplank. **b.** An opening in a ship's bulwarks through which persons may board. **2.** A passage along either side of a ship's upper deck. **3.** *British.* An aisle.

gan•net |**găn'**ĭt| *n.* A large, mostly white sea bird that nests in large colonies on rocky coasts. [SEE PICTURE]

gant•let |**gănt'**lĭt| *or* |**gônt'**-| *n.* A form of the word **gauntlet.**

gan•try |**găn'**trē| *n., pl.* **gan•tries. 1. a.** A bridgelike framework on which a traveling crane moves. **b.** A similar structure that spans several railroad tracks and on which signals are mounted. **2.** A large vertical structure somewhat like a scaffold, used in assembling or servicing a rocket on its launching pad.

gaol |jāl| *n.* Chiefly British form of the word **jail.**

gap |găp| *n.* **1.** An opening or break, as in a wall, fence, etc.; a fissure: *a gap in the picket fence.* **2.** A break in the continuity of something; an interval: *There are obviously some gaps in your knowledge.* **3.** A break or pass through mountains. **4.** A difference; disparity: *the gap between spoken and written English.* **5.** A wide difference of ideas: *the generation gap; a credibility gap.* **6.** A separation between two conductors in an electric circuit across which a spark travels, as in an automobile spark plug.

gape |găp| *or* |găp| *v.* **gaped, gap•ing. 1.** To open the mouth wide, as if to bite or swallow. **2.** To stare in amazement, as with the mouth open. **3.** To open wide: *Cracks gaped on the levee after the flood.* —**gap'ing** *adj.: a gaping hole; a gaping wound.* —*n.* **1.** An act or example of gaping. **2.** A wide gap or opening.

gar |găr| *n.* A freshwater fish with a long, narrow body, sharp teeth, and long, narrow jaws.

game¹·²

Game¹ *was* gamen *in Old English; its original meaning was "fun, amusement, sport." In the medieval period and later, the favorite upper-class sport was hunting wild animals;* **game¹** *therefore came to mean "hunting" (a sense no longer in use) and also "wild animals or birds that are hunted" (sense 7).* **Gamble** *is a derivative of* **game¹**. **Game²** *probably comes from French* gambi, *"crooked."*

gannet

gargle/gargoyle/gurgle
A **gargoyle** *spouts out water from his mouth, and the resemblance to* **gargle** *and* **gurgle** *is no coincidence.* **Gargoyle** *is from Old French* gargouille, *"throat," hence also "gargoyle," which is from Latin* gurguliō, *"throat."* Gargouille *formed the verb* gargouiller, *"to make a gurgling noise in the throat"; this was borrowed into English as* **gargle**. **Gurgle** *seems to come more directly from Latin* gurguliō, *but the immediate source is unknown.*

gargoyle

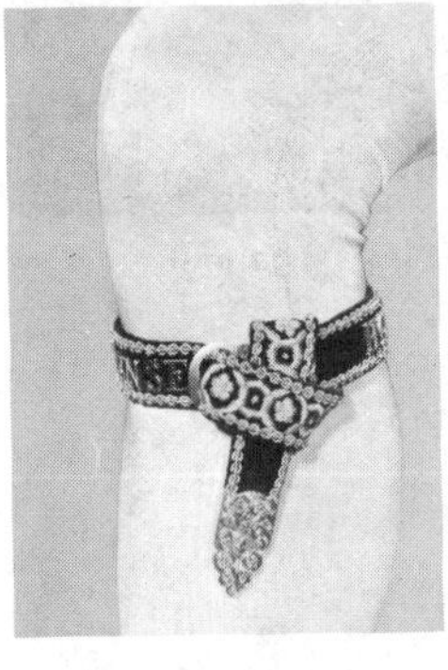

garter

ă pat/ā pay/â care/ä father/ĕ pet/ ē be/ĭ pit/ī pie/î fierce/ŏ pot/ ō go/ô paw, for/oi oil/ŏŏ book/ ōō boot/ou out/ŭ cut/û fur/ *th* the/th thin/hw which/zh vision/ ə ago, item, pencil, atom, circus

ga•rage |gə räzh′| *or* |-räj′| *n.* **1.** A shed or building in which to park a car or cars. **2.** A commercial establishment where cars are repaired and serviced. —**modifier:** *a garage door.* —*v.* **ga•raged, ga•rag•ing.** To put or keep in a garage.

garb |gärb| *n.* Clothing or way of dressing: *sailors' garb.* —*v.* To clothe or dress: *The judge was garbed in his robes.*

gar•bage |gär′bĭj| *n.* **1.** Food wastes, as from a kitchen. **2.** Anything that is worthless or inferior; trash. —**modifier:** *a garbage can.*

gar•ble |gär′bəl| *v.* **gar•bled, gar•bling. 1.** To distort or scramble (a message) in such a way that it cannot be understood. **2.** To pronounce indistinctly: *garble one's words.*

gar•den |gär′dn| *n.* **1.** A piece of land used for growing flowers, vegetables, or fruit. **2.** A park or similar place, often with animals or plants on public display: *a zoological garden.* —**modifier:** *a garden hose; a garden party.* —*v.* To care for plants or ground in a garden.

gar•den•er |gär′dn ər| *n.* A person who works in or takes care of a garden.

gar•de•nia |gär dē′nyə| *or* |-nē ə| *n.* **1.** A shrub with glossy evergreen leaves and large, fragrant white flowers. **2.** The flower of this shrub.

Garden of Eden. In the Bible, Eden.

Gar•field |gär′fēld′|, **James Abram.** 1831–1881. Twentieth President of the United States (1881); assassinated.

gar•fish |gär′fĭsh′| *n., pl.* **-fish** or **-fish•es.** A gar.

gar•gan•tu•an |gär găn′chōō ən| *adj.* Enormous; huge.

gar•gle |gär′gəl| *v.* **gar•gled, gar•gling. 1.** To tilt the head back and exhale air through a liquid held in the back of the mouth in order to wash the mouth or throat. **2.** To produce the sound of gargling. —*n.* **1.** A solution, often medicated, used for gargling. **2.** A sound made by gargling. [SEE NOTE]

gar•goyle |gär′goil′| *n.* A roof spout carved to represent a grotesque human or animal figure. [SEE NOTE & PICTURE]

gar•ish |gâr′ĭsh| *adj.* Too bright and flashy; loud and gaudy: *garish colors.* —**gar′ish•ly** *adv.*

gar•land |gär′lənd| *n.* A wreath or chain of flowers, leaves, etc., worn as a crown or used for ornament. —*v.* To decorate with a garland.

gar•lic |gär′lĭk| *n.* **1.** A plant related to the onion, having a bulb that is divided into sections and has a strong taste and odor. **2.** The bulb of this plant, used as seasoning. —**modifier:** *garlic dressing.*

gar•ment |gär′mənt| *n.* Any article of clothing. —**modifier:** *a garment bag.*

gar•ner |gär′nər| *v.* To gather and store: *garner grain; garner information.*

gar•net |gär′nĭt| *n.* Any of several common crystalline silicate minerals, usually red, that are used as gems and as abrasives. —**modifier:** *garnet earrings.*

gar•nish |gär′nĭsh| *v.* **1.** To adorn; embellish: *garnish a saddle with silver studs.* **2.** To add something to (a food or drink) for extra color or flavor: *garnish mashed potatoes with parsley.* —*n.* Something added to a food or drink to give it extra color or flavor.

gar•nish•ee |gär′nĭ shē′| *v.* **gar•nish•eed, gar•nish•ee•ing.** To attach (a debtor's pay, property, etc.) by garnishment.

gar•nish•ment |gär′nĭsh mənt| *n.* A legal proceeding in which money or property has been attached to satisfy a claim made against the holder of the money or property.

gar•ret |găr′ĭt| *n.* An attic.

gar•ri•son |găr′ĭ sən| *n.* **1.** A military post, especially a permanent one. **2.** The troops stationed at such a post. —*v.* To supply (a post) with troops.

gar•ru•lous |găr′ə ləs| *or* |găr′yə-| *adj.* Habitually talkative; chatty. —**gar′ru•lous•ness** *n.*

gar•ter |gär′tər| *n.* **1.** An elastic band or strap worn on the leg to hold up a stocking or sock. **2. Garter. a.** The badge of the Order of the Garter. **b.** The order itself. [SEE PICTURE]

garter snake. A nonpoisonous North American snake with lengthwise stripes.

gas |găs| *n., pl.* **gas•es** or **gas•ses. 1.** Any substance that is capable of expanding to fill any container completely and that takes on the shape of its container. **2.** Any substance that is a gas at normal temperatures under atmospheric pressure. **3.** Any of a number of gases that are burned as fuel. **4.** A poisonous, irritating, or choking gas used as a weapon: *tear gas.* **5.** Gasoline. —**modifier:** *a gas burner; a gas engine.* —*v.* **gassed, gas•sing, gas•es** or **gas•ses.** To injure or poison with gas.

gas chamber. A small, sealed room in which a condemned prisoner is executed by poison gas.

gas•e•ous |găs′ē əs| *or* |găs′yəs| *or* |găsh′əs| *adj.* Of, concerning, or existing as a gas: *The entire sun is in a gaseous state.*

gash |găsh| *v.* To make a long, deep cut or wound in: *gash a finger while sawing a piece of wood.* —*n.* A long, deep cut or wound.

gas•ket |găs′kĭt| *n.* A fitting or device, often of a soft or flexible material, placed between machine parts that fit together or in joints of pipes to form a seal.

gas•light |găs′līt′| *n.* Also **gas light. 1.** Light made by burning gas in a lamp. **2.** A lamp that uses gas as fuel.

gas mantle. A **Welsbach burner.**

gas mask. A mask that covers the face as protection against poisonous gases and that is equipped with an air filter.

gas•o•line |găs′ə lēn′| *or* |găs′ə lēn′| *n.* A highly flammable mixture of liquid hydrocarbons that evaporates very easily. It is used as a fuel for internal-combustion engines and as a solvent. —**modifier:** *a gasoline engine.*

gasp |găsp| *or* |gäsp| *v.* **1.** To inhale in a sudden, sharp way, as from shock or surprise: *The crowd gasped in amazement.* **2.** To make violent or fitful attempts at breathing: *He gasped for air.* **3.** To say in a breathless manner: *He gasped out a few words.* —*n.* A sudden, violent, or fitful intake of the breath.

gas station. An establishment at which vehicles are serviced, as with gasoline, water, etc.

gas•sy |găs′ē| *adj.* **gas•si•er, gas•si•est.** Of, like, containing, or filled with gas.

gas•tric |găs′trĭk| *adj.* Of or concerning the stomach.

gastric juice. The watery, acidic digestive fluid

secreted by the glands that line the inside of the stomach.

gas•tro•in•tes•ti•nal |găs′trō ĭn **tĕs′**tə nəl| *adj.* Of the stomach and intestines.

gas•tro•nom•ic |găs′trə **nŏm′**ĭk| *adj.* Of gastronomy.

gas•tron•o•my |gă **strŏn′**ə mē| *n.* The art or science of good eating. [SEE NOTE]

gas•tro•pod |**găs′**trə pŏd′| *n.* A snail or related mollusk having a single, usually coiled shell and a fleshy part with which it moves. [SEE NOTE]

gas•tru•la |**găs′**trōō lə| *n., pl.* **gas•tru•las** or **gas•tru•lae** |**găs′**trōō lē′|. The embryo at the stage following the blastula, when it forms a hollow structure open at one end with a layer of cells on both the inside and outside and with a third layer starting to form between these two.

gat[1] |găt| *n. Slang.* A pistol or revolver.

gat[2] |găt|. *Archaic.* A past tense of **get**.

gate |gāt| *n.* **1. a.** A hinged structure that serves as a door in a wall or fence. **b.** An opening in a wall or fence. **2.** A device for controlling the passage of water or gas through a dam or conduit. ¶*These sound alike* **gate, gait.**

gate•way |**gāt′**wā′| *n.* **1.** An opening, as in a wall or fence, that may be closed with a gate. **2.** Something that serves as a means of entrance or an access: *Denver is considered the gateway to the Rockies.*

gath•er |**găth′**ər| *v.* **1.** To bring or come together in a group; convene; assemble: *He gathered the students around him. The campers gathered around the fire.* **2. a.** To pick; collect: *Squirrels gather nuts.* **b.** To obtain from many places or sources; amass gradually: *gather information.* **3.** To summon up; muster (mental or physical powers): *It took him a few minutes to gather his wits.* **4.** To gain or increase by degrees: *gather speed.* **5.** To conclude; infer: *I gather you didn't care for the movie.* **6.** To run a thread through (cloth) so as to draw it up into small folds or pleats: *gather material at the waist of a full skirt.* —*n.* One of the soft, small folds or pleats made in cloth by gathering it. —**gath′er•er** *n.*

gath•er•ing |**găth′**ər ĭng| *n.* An assembly of persons; a meeting: *a family gathering.*

Gat•ling gun |**găt′**lĭng|. A machine gun having a cluster of barrels fired as the cluster is turned.

gauche |gōsh| *adj.* Lacking social grace; tactless; clumsy.

Gau•cho |**gou′**chō| *n., pl.* **Gau•chos.** A cowboy of the South American pampas.

gaud•y |**gô′**dē| *adj.* **gaud•i•er, gaud•i•est.** Too brightly colored and showy to be in good taste: *a gaudy red shirt.* —**gaud′i•ly** *adv.* —**gaud′i•ness** *n.*

gauge |gāj| *n.* **1.** A standard or scale of measurement. **2.** A standard dimension, size, etc.: **a.** The distance between two rails on a railroad. **b.** The size of the barrel of a shotgun. **c.** Thickness or diameter, as of sheet metal or wire. **3.** Any of a large number of devices or instruments used in making measurements or indicating measured values: *a pressure gauge.* —*v.* **gauged, gaug•ing. 1.** To measure precisely, especially by using a gauge: *gauge the depth of the ocean.* **2.** To evaluate or judge: *It is too early to gauge the damage caused by the hurricane.* ¶*These sound alike* **gauge, gage.**

Gaul[1] |gôl|. The name given in antiquity to the region corresponding approximately to present-day France and Belgium.

Gaul[2] |gôl| *n.* **1.** A Celt of ancient Gaul. **2.** A Frenchman.

Gaul•ish |**gô′**lĭsh| *n.* The Celtic language of ancient Gaul.

gaunt |gônt| *adj.* **gaunt•er, gaunt•est. 1.** Thin and bony; haggard; emaciated: *a gaunt face.* **2.** Bleak and desolate; stark: *the gaunt, forbidding mountains enclosing Death Valley.* —**gaunt′ly** *adv.* —**gaunt′ness** *n.*

gaunt•let[1] |**gônt′**lĭt| *or* |**gänt′**-| *n.* **1.** A glove, as of chain mail, worn with a suit of medieval armor to protect the hand. **2.** A heavy glove with a wide, flaring cuff that covers the wrist and part of the arm. **3.** A challenge, as to a fight: *He flung down the gauntlet.* [SEE NOTE]

gaunt•let[2] |**gônt′**lĭt| *or* |**gänt′**-| *n.* **1.** An old form of punishment in which a person was forced to run between two lines of men who struck him with clubs, sticks, or other weapons. **2.** A severe test, criticism, etc.; an ordeal: *The candidate had to run the gauntlet of questions from the press.* [SEE NOTE]

gauze |gôz| *n.* A loosely woven cloth that is thin enough to see through, used especially for bandages. —***modifier:*** *a gauze strip.*

gauz•y |**gô′**zē| *adj.* **gauz•i•er, gauz•i•est.** Of or like gauze; light, sheer, and thin enough to see through. —**gauz′i•ness** *n.*

gave |gāv|. Past tense of **give.**

gav•el |**găv′**əl| *n.* A small wooden mallet used by a presiding officer or auctioneer to signal for attention or order.

ga•vi•al |**gā′**vē əl| *n.* A reptile of southern Asia, related to the crocodiles and alligators but having a very long, slender snout. [SEE PICTURE]

ga•votte |gə **vŏt′**| *n.* **1.** A dance, originally a French peasant dance, somewhat resembling a minuet. **2.** Music written to accompany or as if to accompany this dance.

gawk |gôk| *v.* To stare stupidly; gape.

gawk•y |**gô′**kē| *adj.* **gawk•i•er, gawk•i•est.** Awkward; clumsy. —**gawk′i•ly** *adv.* —**gawk′i•ness** *n.*

gay |gā| *adj.* **gay•er, gay•est. 1.** Merry; lighthearted: *a gay mood; gay music.* **2.** Bright or lively, especially in color: *The package was tied with gay ribbons.*

gay•e•ty |**gā′**ĭ tē| *n., pl.* **gay•e•ties.** A form of the word **gaiety.**

gay•ly |**gā′**lē| *adv.* A form of the word **gaily.**

gaze |gāz| *v.* **gazed, gaz•ing.** To look intently, as with wonder or curiosity; stare: *The visitors gazed in awe at the wild beauty of the region.* —*n.* An intent, steady look.

ga•ze•bo |gə **zē′**bō| *or* |-**zā′**-| *n., pl.* **ga•ze•bos** or **ga•ze•boes.** An outdoor pavilion or small summerhouse.

ga•zelle |gə **zĕl′**| *n.* Any of several slender, swift-running horned animals of Africa and Asia.

ga•zette |gə **zĕt′**| *n.* **1.** A newspaper. **2.** An official journal or periodical.

gaz•et•teer |**găz′**ĭ **tîr′**| *n.* **1.** A book that lists alphabetically and describes briefly geographic terms, such as the names of countries, cities, mountains, and bodies of water. **2.** Such a list included in another book.

G clef. A **treble clef.**

gastronomy/gastropod

Some kinds of **gastropod** *are esteemed in* **gastronomy,** *especially in France, where they are called* **escargots**; *but this fact is irrelevant to the connection between the two words.* **Gastronomy** *is from French* gastronomie, *which is from Greek* gastronomia, *"the laws of the stomach, the science of good eating":* gastēr, *"stomach,"* + -nomia, *"laws, science."* **Gastropod** *is from Greek* gastēr + pous, pod-, *"foot"; the name means "stomach-foot," since snails use their stomach muscles for locomotion.*

gauntlet[1, 2]

Gauntlet[1] *is from Old French* gantelet, *"little glove, glovelet," diminutive of* gant, *"glove." Sense* **3** *arises from the medieval custom of throwing a glove down as a formal challenge to single combat.* **Gauntlet**[2] *was earlier* gantlope *(its present form results from the influence of* **gauntlet**[1]*); running* the gantlope, *or* gauntlet *was invented as a punishment for soldiers in the wars of the seventeenth century;* gantlope *comes from Swedish* gatlop, gatulop, *"passageway":* gata, *"road,"* + lop, *"course."*

gavial

Gd The symbol for the element gadolinium.
Ge The symbol for the element germanium.
gear |gîr| *n.* **1. a.** A toothed wheel or a similar mechanical device that interlocks with another toothed part in order to transmit motion. **b.** An arrangement of the gears of an automobile or other motor vehicle, used to match a range of road speeds to the possible speeds of the engine. **c.** An assembly of parts that does a particular job in a larger machine: *the landing gear of an aircraft.* **2.** Equipment, such as tools, clothing, etc., needed for a particular activity: *fishing gear.* —*v.* **1.** To provide with or connect by gears. **2.** To adjust or adapt: *The program must be geared to the audience.*
Idiom. **in** (or **out of**) **gear.** Having the gears that transmit power engaged (or not engaged).
gear•shift |gîr'shĭft'| *n.* A device for changing from one gear to another, as in an automobile.
gear•wheel |gîr'hwēl'| *or* |-wēl'| *n.* Also **gear wheel.** A wheel having teeth around its rim; a cogwheel.
geck•o |gĕk'ō| *n., pl.* **geck•os** or **geck•oes.** Any of several lizards having padded toe tips with which they can cling to and walk on walls, ceilings, etc. [SEE PICTURE]
gee[1] |jē| *interj.* A word used to express emphasis or as an exclamation of surprise.
gee[2] |jē| *interj.* A word used to command a horse or ox to turn to the right or to go forward.
geese |gēs| *n.* Plural of **goose.**
ge•fil•te fish |gə fĭl'tə|. Also **ge•füll•te fish.** Seasoned chopped fish mixed with crumbs and eggs, formed into balls, and cooked in a broth.
Gei•ger counter |gī'gər|. An instrument composed of a Geiger tube and an electronic device that counts the pulses of current it produces, used to detect and measure nuclear radiation, cosmic rays, etc.
Geiger tube. A gas-filled tube containing two electrodes across which there is almost enough voltage to make the gas conduct electricity. When a ray or particle enters the tube, it ionizes the gas and allows a short pulse of current to flow through the tube.
gei•sha |gā'shə| *or* |gē'-| *n., pl.* **gei•sha** or **gei•shas.** A Japanese girl trained to provide entertainment, such as singing, dancing, or amusing talk, especially for men.
gel |jĕl| *n.* A jellylike mixture, such as raw egg white, formed when the particles of a colloid become relatively large. ¶*These sound alike* **gel, jell.**
gel•a•tin, also **gel•a•tine** |jĕl'ə tən| *n.* **1.** A protein obtained by boiling the prepared skin, bones, and connective tissue of animals. It forms a gel when mixed with hot water and allowed to cool. It is used in foods, drugs, and photographic film. **2.** A jelly made with gelatin, popular as a dessert or salad base.
ge•lat•i•nous |jə lăt'n əs| *adj.* **1.** Similar in texture to a gel made from gelatin; thick and viscous. **2.** Of, like, or containing gelatin.
geld |gĕld| *v.* To remove the male sex glands of (a horse or other animal).
geld•ing |gĕl'dĭng| *n.* A castrated male animal, especially a horse.
gem |jĕm| *n.* **1.** A precious or semiprecious stone, especially one cut and polished as a jewel. **2.** Something or someone much admired or appreciated. —***modifier:*** *a gem dealer.*
Gem•i•ni |jĕm'ə nī'| *or* |-nē'|. The third sign of the zodiac.
gem•stone |jĕm'stōn'| *n.* A precious or semiprecious stone that may be used as a jewel when cut and polished.
Gen. **1.** general (military rank). **2.** Genesis.
gen•der |jĕn'dər| *n.* In grammar, one of a number of categories, such as masculine, feminine, and neuter, into which words are divided. In English, words denoting anything male are masculine, for example, *he, boy,* and *stallion;* those denoting anything female are feminine, for example, *she, girl,* and *mare;* and those denoting inanimate objects are neuter, for example, *it, book,* and *house.*
gene |jēn| *n.* A unit, located at a particular point on a chromosome, that controls or acts in the transmission of a hereditary characteristic, such as hair color or eye color in human beings, from parents to offspring.
ge•ne•a•log•i•cal |jē'nē ə lŏj'ĭ kəl| *or* |jĕn'ē-| *adj.* Of genealogy; showing lineage or family descent: *a genealogical tree.*
ge•ne•al•o•gy |jē'nē ăl'ə jē| *or* |-ŏl'-| *or* |jĕn'ē-| *n., pl.* **ge•ne•al•o•gies. 1.** A record or table of the descent of a family or person from an ancestor or ancestors. **2.** Direct descent from an ancestor or ancestors; lineage. **3.** The study of ancestry and family histories.
gen•e•ra |jĕn'ər ə| *n.* Plural of **genus.**
gen•er•al |jĕn'ər əl| *adj.* **1.** Applicable to or involving the whole or every member of a class or category: *a general meeting; a general strike.* **2.** Widespread; prevalent: *general discontent.* **3.** Not restricted or specialized: *a doctor with a general practice.* **4.** True or applicable in most, but not all, cases: *a general rule to follow.* **5.** Involving only the main or more obvious features of something; not precise or detailed: *discuss the matter in general terms.* **6.** Diversified: *a general store; a general education.* **7.** Highest or superior in rank: *the general manager.* —*n.* Any of several high-ranking officers in the Army, Air Force, or Marine Corps ranking above a colonel and including, in descending order of rank, **general, lieutenant general, major general,** and **brigadier general.** [SEE NOTE]
Idiom. **in general.** Generally; for the most part; on the whole.
General Assembly. The main body of the United Nations, in which each member nation is represented and has one vote.
general delivery. 1. A department of a post office that holds mail until it is called for. **2.** Mail sent to this department.
gen•er•al•is•si•mo |jĕn'ər ə lĭs'ə mō'| *n., pl.* **gen•er•al•is•si•mos.** The commander in chief of all the armed forces of certain countries.
gen•er•al•i•ty |jĕn'ə răl'ĭ tē| *n., pl.* **gen•er•al•i•ties.** A statement or idea that is general and imprecise rather than specific and to the point.
gen•er•al•i•za•tion |jĕn'ər ə lĭ zā'shən| *n.* **1.** The act of generalizing. **2.** A general statement; a generality.
gen•er•al•ize |jĕn'ər ə līz'| *v.* **gen•er•al•ized, gen•er•al•iz•ing. 1.** To make a general statement about a broad subject that is more or less appli-

gecko

general
General *is from Old French* general, *which is from Latin* generālis, *"belonging to a class or kind," from* genus, *"family, group, class, kind." The military noun meaning "officer of the highest rank" arose from the old title* captain general *or* general captain, *meaning "captain of the whole group, commander in chief."*

ă pat/ā pay/â care/ä father/ĕ pet/ ē be/ĭ pit/ī pie/î fierce/ŏ pot/ ō go/ô paw, for/oi oil/ŏŏ book/ ōō boot/ou out/ŭ cut/û fur/ *th* the/th thin/hw which/zh vision/ ə ago, item, pencil, atom, circus

cable to the whole. **2.** To bring into general use: *Dismantle originally meant "to remove a mantle or cloak from," but the word was generalized to include other senses.*

gen•er•al•ly |jĕn′ər ə lē| *adv.* **1.** Usually; as a rule: *I generally go for a walk before breakfast.* **2.** Widely; commonly: *The fact is not generally known.* **3.** In general terms: *Generally speaking, there are two ways to handle the problem.*

General of the Air Force. An officer having the highest rank in the U.S. Air Force.

General of the Army. An officer having the highest rank in the U.S. Army.

general relativity. The theory of gravitation developed by Albert Einstein, extending special relativity to frames of reference that are accelerated and introducing the principle that gravitational forces cannot be distinguished from those caused by inertia.

gen•er•al•ship |jĕn′ər əl shĭp′| *n.* **1.** The rank of general. **2.** Leadership or skill in the conduct of a war. **3.** Any skillful leadership or management.

gen•er•ate |jĕn′ə rāt′| *v.* **gen•er•at•ed, gen•er•at•ing. 1.** To produce by a physical or chemical process: *generate heat.* **2.** To cause; create: *generate worldwide interest.*

gen•e•ra•tion |jĕn′ə rā′shən| *n.* **1.** The act or process of generating: *the generation of electric power.* **2.** All of the offspring that are at the same stage of descent from a common ancestor. **3.** A group of people who grow up at about the same time, often thought to have similar ideas, customs, etc.: *the younger generation.* **4.** A class of things derived from an earlier class, usually by making improvements and refinements: *the new generation of computers.* **5.** The average length of time between the birth of parents and the birth of their children; a period of about thirty years.

gen•er•a•tive |jĕn′ə rā′tĭv| *or* |-ər ə tĭv| *adj.* Having the power to generate.

gen•er•a•tor |jĕn′ə rā′tər| *n.* **1.** Someone or something that generates. **2.** A machine or device that converts mechanical energy into electric energy, especially a rotary machine that works by electromagnetic induction. **3.** A chemical apparatus used to generate a gas or vapor.

ge•ner•ic |jə nĕr′ĭk| *adj.* **1.** Of, including, or indicating an entire group, class, or category; general rather than specific: *The generic word "sad" suggests specific words like "mournful," "grieving," and "downhearted."* **2.** Not protected by a trademark and therefore applicable to an entire class of products: *the generic name for a widely prescribed drug.* **—ge•ner′i•cal•ly** *adv.*

gen•er•os•i•ty |jĕn′ə rŏs′ĭ tē| *n.* The condition or quality of being generous; willingness in giving or sharing.

gen•er•ous |jĕn′ər əs| *adj.* **1. a.** Willing to give or share; unselfish: *a generous contributor to worthy causes.* **b.** Showing or reflecting generosity: *a generous gift.* **2.** Large; abundant; ample: *This restaurant serves very generous portions.* **3.** Lacking pettiness or meanness in thought or behavior; kind: *a generous judge; a generous critic.* **—gen′er•ous•ly** *adv.* [SEE NOTE]

gen•e•sis |jĕn′ĭ sĭs| *n., pl.* **gen•e•ses** |jĕn′ĭ sēz′|. **1.** The coming into being of anything; beginning; origin: *the genesis of a new nation.* **2. Genesis.** The first book of the Bible, describing God's creation of the world.

gen•et |jĕn′ĭt| *or* |jə nĕt′| *n.* A catlike Old World animal related to the mongoose, having spotted fur and a long tail. [SEE PICTURE]

ge•net•ic |jə nĕt′ĭk| or **ge•net•i•cal** |jə nĕt′ĭ kəl| *adj.* **1.** Of genetics. **2.** Of, affecting, or affected by a gene or genes: *genetic traits.* **—ge•net′i•cal•ly** *adv.*

ge•net•i•cist |jə nĕt′ĭ sĭst| *n.* A scientist who specializes in genetics.

ge•net•ics |jə nĕt′ĭks| *n.* **1.** *(used with a singular verb).* The scientific study of the biological processes involved in the transmission of characteristics from an organism to its offspring. **2.** *(used with a plural verb).* The genetic make-up of an individual or group.

Ge•ne•va |jə nē′və|. A city in Switzerland. Population, 170,000.

Gen•ghis Khan |jĕng′gĭs kän′| *or* |gĕng′gĭs|. 1162?–1227. Mongol conqueror of central Asia.

gen•ial |jēn′yəl| *or* |jē′nē əl| *adj.* **1.** Cheerful, friendly, and good-humored: *her genial personality.* **2.** Favorable to health or growth; warm and pleasant: *the genial sunshine.* **—ge′ni•al′i•ty** *n.* **—gen′ial•ly** *adv.*

ge•nie |jē′nē| *n., pl.* **ge•nies** or **ge•ni•i** |jē′nē ī′|. **1.** A supernatural spirit who appears in human form and magically grants the wishes of the one who summons him. **2.** A form of the word **jinni.**

ge•ni•i |jē′nē ī′| *n.* **1.** A plural of **genius. 2.** A plural of **genie.**

gen•i•tal |jĕn′ĭ təl| *adj.* **1.** Of, involving, or involved in biological reproduction: *the genital organs.* **2.** Of the genitals.

gen•i•ta•li•a |jĕn′ĭ tā′lē ə| *or* |-tāl′yə| *pl.n.* The genitals.

gen•i•tals |jĕn′ĭ təlz| *pl.n.* The organs that function in biological reproduction, especially the external parts of the sex organs.

gen•i•to•u•ri•nar•y |jĕn′ĭ tō yo͝or′ə nĕr′ē| *adj.* Of the genital or urinary organs.

gen•ius |jēn′yəs| *n., pl.* **gen•ius•es. 1.** Brilliant mental ability or outstanding creative power: *the genius of Leonardo da Vinci.* **2.** A person of the highest mental ability or the greatest creative power. **3.** A strong natural talent or ability: *a genius for leadership.* **4.** Skill at imagining and inventing new things; ingenuity: *the genius of American technology.* **5.** A person who is extremely talented or clever at something; a wizard: *a mechanical genius.* **6.** *pl.* **ge•ni•i** |jē′nē ī′|. The guardian spirit of a person or place.

Gen•o•a |jĕn′ō ə|. A city and port in northwestern Italy. Population, 850,000. **—Gen′o•ese′** |jĕn′ō ēz′| *or* |-ēs′| *adj.* & *n.*

gen•o•cide |jĕn′ə sīd′| *n.* The deliberate wiping out or killing off of a racial, religious, political, or cultural group.

gen•re |zhän′rə| *n.* **1.** A particular type or class of literary, musical, or artistic composition: *The novel and the drama are different literary genres.* **2.** A realistic style of painting featuring scenes and subjects of everyday life. **—*modifier:*** *a genre painter.*

gent |jĕnt| *n. Informal.* A man or gentleman.

gen•teel |jĕn tēl′| *adj.* **1.** Polite, courteous, and refined. **2.** Trying to seem refined, but in an artificial or prudish way.

generous, etc.

Almost all of the words from **gender** *to* **gentry** *(excluding only* **genet, gentian,** *and the proper nouns)—nearly 50 main entries in all—are borrowed from Greek, Latin, and French words containing the root* gen-. *The basic meaning of this root is "to give birth, to have children"; the main derivatives fall into groups related to: (1) "birth, reproduction, production":* **gene, genesis, genetic, genital, generate;** *(2a) "family or race":* **genealogy, generation, genocide;** *(2b) "group, class, type":* **gender, general, generic, genre;** *(3) "old family, upper-class background," hence "honorable, courteous, good-natured":* **gentle, gentleman, gentry.**

genet

gentle/Gentile
Latin gēns, gent- *basically meant "family or clan" and secondarily "race, people, nation." Its adjective* gentilis *thus has two distinct meanings: (a) "belonging to the same family" and (b) "belonging to a foreign nation." In sense (a),* gentīlis *passed into Old French as* gentil, *with the meaning "belonging to a noble family, highborn." The code of chivalry required knights and nobles to be kind to the poor and weak, and thus* gentil *also meant "generous, courteous, kind," and was borrowed into English as* **gentle**. *Latin* gentīlis *in sense (b), "foreign," was used by Jews to refer to non-Jews and by the early Christians to refer to non-Christians; it was borrowed directly into English as* **Gentile**.

geo-
The word element **geo-** *is from Greek* gē, *"earth, land."* **Geography** *is "description of the earth";* **geology** *is "earth science";* **geometry** *is "measurement of land, surveying," hence "science of measuring spatial relationships." Even the name* **George** *contains the same element; it is from Greek* geōrgos, *"land-worker, farmer":* gē, *"land," +* erg-, *"work."*

ă pat/ā pay/â care/ä father/ĕ pet/ ē be/ĭ pit/ī pie/î fierce/ŏ pot/ ō go/ô paw, for/oi oil/ŏŏ book/ ōō boot/ou out/ŭ cut/û fur/ *th* the/th thin/hw which/zh vision/ ə ago, item, pencil, atom, circus

gen•tian |jĕn′shən| *n.* Any of several plants usually having showy deep-blue flowers.

Gen•tile, also **gen•tile** |jĕn′tīl′| *n.* **1.** A person who is not a Jew, especially a Christian. **2.** Among Mormons, a person who is not a Mormon. **3.** A heathen. *—adj.* **1.** Of the Gentiles; not Jewish. **2.** Not Mormon. [SEE NOTE]

gen•til•i•ty |jĕn tĭl′ĭ tē| *n.* **1.** Good manners, good breeding, and refinement. **2.** The condition of coming from a family of distinction or high social standing. **3.** The gentry.

gen•tle |jĕn′tl| *adj.* **gen•tler, gen•tlest. 1.** Mild and soft: *gentle eyes; a gentle breeze.* **2.** Kindly, peaceful, and patient in disposition: *Gentle people can be brave.* **3.** Easily managed; docile; tame: *a gentle pony.* **4.** Soft and tender in touching or soothing: *gentle hands; gentle words.* **5.** Light and easy; not forceful: *a gentle nudge; gentle pressure.* **6.** Gradual; not steep or sudden: *gentle slopes.* **7.** Of or from a family of distinction or high social standing. **—gen′tle•ness** *n.* **—gen′tly** *adv.* [SEE NOTE]

gen•tle•folk |jĕn′tl fōk′| *pl.n.* Well-bred people of good family and high social standing.

gen•tle•man |jĕn′tl mən| *n., pl.* **-men** |-mən|. **1.** A man of high or noble birth or of superior social standing. **2.** A man whose fine clothes, manners, and speech mark him as a refined, well-bred person. **3.** Any man spoken of in a polite way: *a very nice old gentleman.* **4. gentlemen.** A word used in speaking of or to or in writing to men as members of a group: *Good evening, ladies and gentlemen.*

gen•tle•man•ly |jĕn′tl mən lē| *adj.* Of or like a gentleman; courteous, proper, or polite: *gentlemanly behavior.* **—gen′tle•man•li•ness** *n.*

gen•tle•wom•an |jĕn′tl wŏŏm′ən| *n., pl.* **-wom•en** |-wĭm′ĭn|. **1.** A woman of high or noble birth or of superior social standing. **2.** A polite, gracious, or considerate woman; a lady.

gen•try |jĕn′trē| *n.* **1.** Well-bred people of good family and high social standing. **2.** A social class ranking next below the nobility.

gen•u•flect |jĕn′yə flĕkt′| *v.* To bend one knee to or toward the ground, as to show respect. **—gen′u•flec′tion** *n.*

gen•u•ine |jĕn′yōō ĭn| *adj.* Not false; real; true: *genuine enthusiasm; a genuine antique; genuine leather.* **—gen′u•ine•ly** *adv.*

ge•nus |jē′nəs| *n., pl.* **gen•e•ra** |jĕn′ər ə|. **1.** A group of quite closely related plants or animals usually including several species. Dogs, wolves, and coyotes belong to the same genus. **2.** Any type, kind, or class with common characteristics.

geo–. A word element meaning "earth": **geology.** [SEE NOTE]

ge•o•cen•tric |jē′ō sĕn′trĭk| *adj.* **1.** Of or observed in relation to the center of the earth. **2.** Having or considering the earth as the center: *a geocentric model of the solar system.*

ge•ode |jē′ōd′| *n.* A small, hollow, usually rounded rock lined on the inside with mineral crystals, such as quartz.

ge•o•des•ic |jē′ə dĕs′ĭk| *n.* Any curve on a surface having the property that for any two points on it, the distance along it between the points is shorter than that along any other curve on the surface between those points. For example, on the surface of a sphere the geodesics are all great circles. *—adj.* Of geodesics or the geometry of geodesics.

geodesic dome. A structure having approximately the shape of a hemisphere, made up of straight structural elements that form polygons that fit rigidly together.

ge•od•e•sy |jē ŏd′ĭ sē| *n.* The scientific study of the size and shape of the earth.

ge•o•det•ic |jē′ə dĕt′ĭk| *adj.* Of geodesy.

ge•og•ra•pher |jē ŏg′rə fər| *n.* A person who specializes in geography.

ge•o•graph•ic |jē′ə grăf′ĭk| or **ge•o•graph•i•cal** |jē′ə grăf′ĭ kəl| *adj.* Of or in geography: *geographic boundaries; geographical names.* **—ge′o•graph′i•cal•ly** *adv.*

geographic mile. A **nautical mile.**

ge•og•ra•phy |jē ŏg′rə fē| *n., pl.* **ge•og•ra•phies. 1.** The study of the earth and its features and the distribution on the earth of life, including the position of continents, mountains, oceans, and rivers, the arrangement and boundaries of countries, states, and cities, and the effect of location on climate, resources, population, products, etc. **2.** The location, arrangement, or physical features of a region or place: *Study the geography of California.* **3.** A book on geography. **—*modifier:*** *a geography book.*

ge•o•log•ic |jē′ə lŏj′ĭk| or **ge•o•log•i•cal** |jē′ə lŏj′ĭ kəl| *adj.* Of geology. **—ge′o•log′i•cal•ly** *adv.*

ge•ol•o•gist |jē ŏl′ə jĭst| *n.* A scientist who specializes in geology.

ge•ol•o•gy |jē ŏl′ə jē| *n.* **1.** The scientific study of the origin, history, behavior, and structure of the earth. **2.** The geological study, analysis, properties, etc., of the earth or, especially, of one of its regions: *the geology of Antarctica.*

ge•om•e•ter |jē ŏm′ĭ tər| *n.* A mathematician who specializes in geometry.

ge•o•met•ric |jē′ə mĕt′rĭk| or **ge•o•met•ri•cal** |jē′ə mĕt′rĭ kəl| *adj.* **1.** Of geometry and its methods and principles: *a geometric axiom.* **2.** Consisting of or using simple shapes formed from straight lines or curves: *geometric figures; a geometric design.* **—ge′o•met′ri•cal•ly** *adv.*

ge•om•e•tri•cian |jē ŏm′ĭ trĭsh′ən| *or* |jē′ə-mĭ-| *n.* A geometer.

geometric mean. The positive, real n^{th} root of a product of n positive real numbers. For example, the geometric mean of 2, 4, and 8 is $\sqrt[3]{2\times4\times8} = \sqrt[3]{64} = 4$.

geometric progression. A sequence of numbers such as 5, 25, 125, 625 . . . , or, in general, a, $b \times a$, $b^2 \times a$, $b^3 \times a$, . . . , in which each term is the product of a constant factor and the preceding term.

ge•om•e•try |jē ŏm′ĭ trē| *n., pl.* **ge•om•e•tries. 1. a.** The mathematical study of the properties, measurement, and relationships of points, lines, planes, surfaces, and angles and of figures composed of combinations of them. **b.** A particular system of geometry. **c.** A geometry that deals only with a certain set of objects or problems: *solid geometry.* **2.** An overall shape or arrangement of parts, as in a design: *the geometry of an airplane.*

ge•o•mor•phol•o•gy |jē′ō môr fŏl′ə jē| *n.* The scientific study of the arrangement and evolution of the land masses of the earth.

ge•o•phys•i•cal |jē′ō fĭz′ĭ kəl| *adj.* Of or dealing with geophysics: *geophysical research.*

ge•o•phys•ics |jē′ō fĭz′ĭks| *n.* *(used with a singular verb).* The application of physics to the study of geology.

George III |jôrj|. 1738–1820. King of England during the American Revolution.

George, Saint Christian martyr of the early fourth century A.D.; patron saint of England.

George•town |jôrj′toun′|. The capital of Guyana. Population, 150,000.

Geor•gia |jôr′jə|. **1.** A Southern Atlantic state of the United States. Population, 5,464,265. Capital, Atlanta. **2.** A region on the southeastern shore of the Black Sea, now a republic of the Soviet Union.

Geor•gian |jôr′jən| *adj.* **1.** Of, during, or characteristic of the reigns of the four kings of England named George who ruled from 1714 to 1830: *Georgian architecture.* **2.** Of the U.S. state of Georgia or its inhabitants. **3.** Of the Soviet republic of Georgia, its people, or their language. *—n.* **1.** A native of the state of Georgia. **2.** A native of the republic of Georgia in the Soviet Union. **3.** The language spoken in the Soviet republic of Georgia.

ge•o•tro•pism |jē′ə trō′pĭz′əm| *or* |jē ŏt′rə pĭz′əm| *n.* The movement or growth of a living organism in response to the earth's gravity. An example is the downward growth of plant roots.

Ger. German; Germany.

ge•ra•ni•um |jĭ rā′nē əm| *n.* **1.** A plant with rounded leaves and showy clusters of red, pink, or white flowers, often grown as a potted plant. **2.** A related plant with pink or purplish flowers.

ger•bil |jûr′bĭl| *n.* A mouselike animal with long hind legs and a long tail. [SEE PICTURE]

ger•fal•con |jûr′făl′kən| *or* |-fôl′kən| *or* |-fô′kən| *n.* A form of the word **gyrfalcon.**

ger•i•at•rics |jĕr′ē ăt′rĭks| *n.* *(used with a singular verb).* The scientific and medical study of the biological processes and diseases of old age.

germ |jûrm| *n.* **1.** Any of various kinds of tiny organisms that cause disease. Certain bacteria, protozoans, and viruses are among the microorganisms considered to be germs. **2. a.** A tiny living cell or structure from which a new organism may develop. **b.** The part of a kernel of wheat or other cereal grain that can sprout to form a new plant. It is rich in vitamins and valued as a food supplement. **3.** The beginning or first form from which something larger or more complex develops: *the germ of a new theory.*

Ger•man |jûr′mən| *n.* **1.** A native or inhabitant of Germany. **2.** The Germanic language of Germany, Austria, and part of Switzerland. *—adj.* Of Germany, the Germans, or their language.

ger•mane |jər mān′| *adj.* Closely or naturally related to the thing in question; appropriate.

Ger•man•ic |jər măn′ĭk| *adj.* **1.** German. **2.** Of the branch of Indo-European from which English, German, the Scandinavian languages, and several other important languages are descended. **3.** Of any people who speak a Germanic language. **4.** Teutonic. *—n.* The branch of Indo-European including the Germanic languages.

ger•ma•ni•um |jər mā′nē əm| *n.* Symbol **Ge** One of the elements, a brittle, gray semiconducting metal. Atomic number 32; atomic weight 72.59; valences −4, +2, +4; melting point 937.4°C; boiling point 2,830°C.

German measles. A mild infectious disease whose symptoms include sore throat, fever, and skin rash.

German shepherd. A dog with a thick black or brownish coat, often trained to help police workers or blind people. [SEE PICTURE]

Ger•ma•ny |jûr′mə nē|. A former country in central Europe, since 1949 divided into two countries: **a.** The **German Federal Republic** (West Germany). Population, 62,048,000. Capital, Bonn. **b.** The **German Democratic Republic** (East Germany). Population, 17,170,000. Capital, East Berlin.

germ cell. A plant or animal cell, such as an egg or a sperm, that takes part in the process of reproduction.

ger•mi•cide |jûr′mĭ sīd′| *n.* A substance that is effective in killing germs.

ger•mi•nal |jûr′mə nəl| *adj.* **1.** Of or like a germ cell. **2.** Of or in an early stage of development.

ger•mi•nate |jûr′mə nāt′| *v.* **ger•mi•nat•ed, ger•mi•nat•ing.** To begin or cause to begin to grow; sprout: *Seeds need water and warmth to germinate. Try the experiment of germinating seeds at three different temperatures.* **—ger′mi•na′tion** *n.*

ger•ry•man•der |jĕr′ē măn′dər| *v.* To divide (a voting area) in such a way as to give unfair advantage to one political party. *—n.* An act or example of gerrymandering. [SEE NOTE]

ger•und |jĕr′ənd| *n.* The form of the verb ending in *ing* when it is used as a noun; a verbal noun. In the sentence *Hitting a ball hard requires strength,* the word *hitting* is a gerund. Like a noun, a gerund may be the subject of a sentence, but like a verb it may have a direct object *(ball)* and be modified by an adverb *(hard).*

Ge•sta•po |gə stä′pō| *n.* The secret police force of Nazi Germany, notorious for its ruthlessness.

ges•ta•tion |jĕ stā′shən| *n.* **1.** The development of a young animal in the uterus before birth. **2.** The development of a plan or idea in the mind. ***—modifier:*** *a gestation period.*

ges•tic•u•late |jĕ stĭk′yə lāt′| *v.* **ges•tic•u•lat•ed, ges•tic•u•lat•ing.** To make motions, as by waving the arms while speaking, in order to emphasize one's meaning or express one's feelings. **—ges•tic′u•la′tion** *n.*

ges•ture |jĕs′chər| *n.* **1.** A motion of the hands, arms, head, or body used while speaking or in place of speech to help express one's meaning: *The speaker used dramatic gestures.* **2.** An outward show of something, such as courtesy, respect, or friendship, whether sincere or done only for effect: *a thoughtful gesture.* *—v.* **ges•tured, ges•tur•ing.** To motion, signal, indicate, or point, using a gesture or gestures.

get |gĕt| *v.* **got** |gŏt|, **got** or **got•ten** |gŏt′n|, **get•ting.** **1.** To become or grow: *getting well after a long illness.* **2.** —Used in the same way as *be* in some passive constructions: *I got caught out in the rain.* **3.** To arrive: *When will we get to New York?* **4. a.** To betake oneself: *Get out!* **b.** *Informal.* To start: *Get going!* **c.** |gĭt|. To be off; depart: *Now get!* Used chiefly in regional speech. **5. a.** —Used in the perfect tense in the sense of *have: I've got all that I need.* **b.** —Used in the

gerbil

German shepherd

gerrymander

The word **gerrymander** *is one of the most famous of all Americanisms. In 1812, Elbridge Gerry (pronounced /***gĕr′ē***/) was governor of Massachusetts, and his party openly redrew election districts to keep themselves in power. The resulting shape on the map of one of the districts was so extremely irregular that an artist, Gilbert Stuart, was able to add wings, claws, and a head to it and turn it into a salamander or lizard. It is said to have been a newspaper editor who blended in the governor's name to coin the word* **gerrymander.**

get
The alternate past participle **gotten** *is old and regular; it is used, for example, in the* King James Bible *(1611). But while it has survived as an alternate in American English,* **gotten** *has completely disappeared in England. (Notice, however, that for the compound verb* **forget,** *the standard past participle, both in America and England, is* **forgotten.**)

geyser

ghost, etc.
Ghost *was* gāst *in Old English: its original meaning was "spirit or soul" in general; but later the meaning "visible spirit of a dead person" took over, and the original sense survives only in "the Holy Ghost." Different shades of meaning produced the adjectives* **ghastly** *and* **ghostly**. *The rather similar word* **ghoul** *is completely unrelated; its original meaning was sense 3, and it comes from Arabic* ghūl.

ă **pat**/ā **pay**/â **care**/ä **father**/ĕ **pet**/ē **be**/ĭ **pit**/ī **pie**/î **fierce**/ŏ **pot**/ō **go**/ô **paw**, **for**/oi **oil**/o͝o **book**/o͞o **boot**/ou **out**/ŭ **cut**/û **fur**/*th* **the**/th **thin**/hw **which**/**zh** vision/ə **ago**, item, pencil, atom, circus

perfect tense with an infinitive in the sense of *must: I've got to go now.* **6.** To obtain or acquire: *trying to get the money for a car.* **7.** To be able or allowed to (do something): *Do I get to practice later if I do this for you now?* **8.** To go after; fetch; retrieve: *Don't forget to get my books.* **9.** To reach or make contact with by or as if by radio or telephone: *Didn't you get that number?* **10.** To earn; gain: *He's getting a high salary for the job.* **11.** To receive: *get a telegram.* **12.** To buy: *I got this hat at a rummage sale.* **13.** To incur: *He got a tongue-lashing for that last trick.* **14.** To meet with; suffer: *If they don't behave themselves, they will get what is coming to them.* **15.** To come down with (a sickness); contract: *get the measles.* **16. a.** To capture or catch: *We chased him and finally got him.* **b.** *Informal.* To catch and cause harm to: *I'm going to get you sooner or later, just you wait and see!* **17.** To have or reach by calculation: *get a sum.* **18.** To understand; comprehend: *get the gist of what he said.* **19.** To prepare or make ready: *getting supper.* **20.** To cause to become or be in a specified condition: *getting the car started.* **21.** To cause to move, come, or go: *Get that cat out of here at once.* —***phrasal verbs.*** **get about** (or **around**). **1.** To move around, as in convalescence. **2.** *Informal.* To be socially active: *She really gets around.* **3.** To spread or travel, as gossip or news. **get across.** To be or make understood: *I'm just not getting across, I guess.* **get along. 1.** To be or remain on friendly terms with. **2.** To manage with reasonable success: *broke as usual, but getting along.* **3.** To advance; make progress: *How's your project getting along?* **4.** To move along; leave: *I think I'll be getting along now.* **get around. 1.** To evade; circumvent: *She is constantly trying to get around the rules.* **2.** *Informal.* To win (someone) over, as by cajolery or flattery: *She never fails to get around me.* **get at. 1.** To find a way to; reach: *The sponge fell behind the sink where I can't get at it.* **2.** To lead up to (a meaning): *Do you understand what I am getting at?* **get away.** To escape. **get away with.** To succeed in doing something disapproved without being punished or found out. **get back. 1.** To return to or take up again: *Let's get back to work.* **2.** To regain: *I lent it out and never got it back.* **get back at.** To have revenge against. **get by. 1.** To manage; survive: *They were poor but always got by somehow.* **2.** To pass within range of without drawing unfavorable attention. **get down to.** To turn the attention to; concentrate on: *Let's get down to business.* **get in. 1.** To enter or be allowed to enter: *Can we get in?* **2.** To arrive: *The plane gets in at midnight.* **3.** To manage to say, as in conversation: *get in a word.* **get in with.** *Informal.* To gain the favor of: *trying to get in with the new teacher.* **get off. 1.** To get down from or out of: *get off the train.* **2.** To escape, as punishment or labor: *getting off scot-free.* **3.** To remove; take away: *Get that cap off and stand up straight!* **get on. 1.** To climb up onto or into; enter: *Get on the train!* **2.** To be on friendly terms: *Bob and Dick got on for years and then suddenly had a fight.* **3.** To advance: *He's getting on in years.* **get out.** To leave. **get out of. 1.** To escape from or be released from: *The dog somehow got out of the kennel.* **2.** To move out of (sight, range, etc.): *Get out of my way.* **3.** To avoid or get around: *trying to get out of his homework.* **4.** To derive: *He's getting as much out of it as he can.* **get over. 1.** To get across; convey: *I wish I could get this over to you.* **2.** To recover from (a sickness, sorrow, etc.). **get through. 1.** To finish. **2.** To undergo and survive: *trying to get through a cold, hungry winter.* **get through to.** To make contact with: *The radio operator is trying to get through to the coast guard.* **get to. 1.** To reach: *We never quite got to that question.* **2.** To make contact with or communicate with: *Your message is getting to me at last.* **3.** *Slang.* To annoy: *Man, this kind of talk really gets to me.* **get together.** To meet; assemble: *getting together for supper tonight.* **get up.** To arise from bed. —**get'ter** *n.* [SEE NOTE]

Idioms. **get it. 1.** To understand; comprehend: *I just don't get it.* **2.** *Informal.* To be punished or scolded: *You're really going to get it when I catch you.* **get nowhere.** To make no progress or have no success: *She tried but got nowhere with Latin.* **get there.** *Informal.* To attain one's goal.

get•a•way |**gĕt'**ə wā'| *n.* **1.** The act or an example of escaping. **2.** The start, as of a race.

Geth•sem•a•ne |gĕth **sĕm'**ə nē|. In the New Testament, the garden where Christ suffered his agony and was betrayed and arrested.

get-to•geth•er |**gĕt'**tə gĕth'ər| *n. Informal.* A small party or gathering.

Get•tys•burg |**gĕt'**ĭz bûrg'|. A town in southern Pennsylvania, the site of a great battle in the Civil War.

get-up |**gĕt'**ŭp'| *n. Informal.* An outfit or costume, especially one that is odd or different.

get-up-and-go |**gĕt'**ŭp'ən **gō'**| *n. Informal.* Ambition and energy.

gew•gaw |**gyo͞o'**gô'| *n.* A showy trinket of little value; a bauble.

gey•ser |**gī'**zər| *n.* A natural hot spring that throws out a spray of steam and water from time to time. [SEE PICTURE]

Gha•na |**gä'**nə|. A country on the southern coast of West Africa. Population, 9,607,000. Capital, Accra. —**Gha'na•ian, Gha'ni•an** *adj.* & *n.*

ghast•ly |**găst'**lē| *or* |**gäst'**-| *adj.* **ghast•li•er, ghast•li•est. 1.** Terrifying; dreadful: *ghastly tales of starvation and disease.* **2.** Having a deathlike pallor or similar signs of being very sick: *The fever has gone down, but she looks ghastly.* **3.** Extremely unpleasant or bad: *a ghastly little person.* —**ghast'li•ness** *n.*

gher•kin |**gûr'**kĭn| *n.* A small cucumber used for pickling.

ghet•to |**gĕt'**ō| *n., pl.* **ghet•tos** or **ghet•toes. 1.** A slum section of an American city occupied predominantly by black or Spanish-speaking people. **2.** A section or quarter in a European city to which Jews are or were restricted. —***modifier:*** *ghetto dwellers; ghetto children.*

ghost |gōst| *n.* **1.** The spirit of a dead person, supposed to haunt or appear to living persons; a phantom; specter. **2.** A slight trace or hint; a vestige: *a ghost of a smile.* **3.** A false image, often faint, produced along with the correct image, as in television or photography. —*v.* To write (something) as a ghostwriter: *I want to introduce you to the man who ghosted the President's campaign speeches.* [SEE NOTE]

Idiom. **give up the ghost.** To die.

ghost•ly |gōst′lē| *adj.* **ghost•li•er, ghost•li•est.** Of or like a ghost: *a ghostly apparition.* —**ghost′li•ness** *n.*

ghost•write |gōst′rīt′| *v.* **ghost•wrote** |gōst′rōt′|, **ghost•writ•ten** |gōst′rĭt′n|, **ghost•writ•ing.** To write as a ghostwriter.

ghost•writ•er |gōst′rī′tər| *n.* A person who writes for and gives credit of authorship to another person who has hired him.

ghoul |go͞ol| *n.* **1.** A person who robs graves. **2.** A person who delights in loathsome things. **3.** In Islamic folklore, an evil spirit said to plunder graves and feast on corpses. —**ghoul′ish** *adj.*

GI |jē′ī′| *n., pl.* **GIs** or **GI's.** An enlisted man in any of the U.S. armed forces. —***modifier:*** *a GI uniform.*

GI or **G.I. 1.** Government Issue. **2.** gastrointestinal.

gi•ant |jī′ənt| *n.* **1.** Someone or something of great size. **2.** Someone of extraordinary importance: *a musical giant.* **3.** One of the manlike beings of extraordinary size and strength in myth or folklore. —*adj.* Gigantic; huge: *a giant department store; one giant leap for mankind.*

gib•ber |jĭb′ər| *v.* To speak rapidly and unintelligibly; chatter. —*n.* Gibberish.

gib•ber•ish |jĭb′ər ĭsh| *or* |gĭb′-| *n.* Unintelligible or nonsensical chatter; prattle.

gib•bet |jĭb′ĭt| *n.* A kind of gallows from which the bodies of executed criminals were hung for public viewing. —*v.* **gib•bet•ed** or **gib•bet•ted, gib•bet•ing** or **gib•bet•ting.** To hang or execute on a gibbet.

gib•bon |gĭb′ən| *n.* A tropical Asian ape with a slender body and long arms.

gib•bous |gĭb′əs| *adj.* Illuminated over more than half but less than all of its disk: *the gibbous moon.*

gibe |jīb| *n.* A derisive remark; a jeer: *The cruelest gibes came from his former friends.* —*v.* **gibed, gib•ing.** To make heckling or jeering remarks. ¶*These sound alike* **gibe, jibe.**

gib•let |jĭb′lĭt| *n.* Often **giblets.** The heart, liver, and gizzard of a fowl.

Gi•bral•tar |jĭ brôl′tər|. A British colony occupying about two square miles near the southern tip of Spain. Population, 25,000.

gid•dap |gĭ dăp′| *v.* To go ahead or go faster. Used as a command to a horse.

gid•dy |gĭd′ē| *adj.* **gid•di•er, gid•di•est. 1. a.** Having a lightheaded or whirling sensation; dizzy: *He was giddy with thirst.* **b.** Causing or capable of causing dizziness: *at a giddy speed.* **2.** Frivolous; lighthearted: *a giddy mood.* —**gid′di•ly** *adv.* —**gid′di•ness** *n.*

gid•dy•ap |gĭd′ē ăp′| *v.* A form of the word **giddap.**

gift |gĭft| *n.* **1.** Something given; a present: *a gift for our mother on Mother's Day.* **2.** A special talent, aptitude, faculty, or bent: *a gift for mathematics; the gift of sight; a girl with many gifts.*

gift•ed |gĭf′tĭd| *adj.* Endowed with natural ability; talented: *a gifted athlete.*

gift-wrap |gĭft′răp′| *v.* **-wrapped, -wrap•ping.** To cover or envelop (something intended as a gift) in a fancy wrapping.

gig[1] |gĭg| *n.* **1.** A light two-wheeled carriage drawn by one horse. **2.** A narrow ship's boat reserved for the captain's use. [SEE NOTE]

gig[2] |gĭg| *n.* A set of hooks that is dragged through a school of fish to hook them in the bodies. —*v.* **gigged, gig•ging.** To fish with a gig. [SEE NOTE]

gig[3] |gĭg| *n. Slang.* A job, especially an engagement for a musician.

gi•gan•tic |jī găn′tĭk| *adj.* **1.** Like or as big as a giant: *a gigantic sailor.* **2.** Of extraordinary strength, size, power, etc.; huge: *an outburst of gigantic rage; gigantic rocks.* —**gi•gan′ti•cal•ly** *adv.*

gig•gle |gĭg′əl| *v.* **gig•gled, gig•gling.** To laugh in a half-suppressed or nervous way; titter or chuckle. —*n.* A short, silly laugh.

gigue |zhēg| *n.* **1.** A dance, the jig. **2.** A lively musical composition, often the last movement of a suite, written to or as if to accompany a jig.

Gi•la monster |hē′lə|. A poisonous lizard of the southwestern United States, having a thick body with black and pinkish or yellowish markings. [SEE PICTURE]

gild |gĭld| *v.* **gild•ed** or **gilt** |gĭlt|, **gild•ing. 1.** To cover with a thin layer of gold: *gild the frame of a mirror.* **2.** To spread golden light across: *The lanterns gilded the green leaves.* ¶*These sound alike* **gild, guild.**

gill[1] |gĭl| *n.* **1.** The breathing organ by means of which fish and certain other water animals take oxygen from the water. **2.** One of the thin, closely crowded bladelike parts on the underside of a mushroom cap. [SEE NOTE]

gill[2] |jĭl| *n.* A unit of volume or capacity used mainly for liquids. It is equal to 4 ounces or 7.216 cubic inches. [SEE NOTE]

gil•ly•flow•er |jĭl′ē flou′ər| *n.* A carnation or other plant with fragrant flowers.

gilt |gĭlt| *n.* A thin layer of gold, such as gold leaf or gold-colored paint, applied to a surface. ¶*These sound alike* **gilt, guilt.**

gim•bals |jĭm′bəlz| *or* |gĭm′-| *pl.n.* A device consisting of a pair of rings mounted together so that each is free to turn about an axis at right angles to the motion of the other, used to keep something, such as a ship's compass, level in spite of rolling and pitching motion.

gim•crack |jĭm′krăk′| *n.* A cheap and showy object of little or no use.

gim•let |gĭm′lĭt| *n.* A small hand tool with a pointed spiral tip, used for boring holes.

gim•mick |gĭm′ĭk| *n. Slang.* **1.** A clever idea, catchword, scheme, innovation, etc., used to promote something: *an advertising gimmick.* **2.** A gadget.

gimp |gĭmp| *n.* A narrow braid or cord used to trim clothes, curtains, or furniture covers.

gin[1] |jĭn| *n.* A strong, clear alcoholic liquor distilled from grain and flavored with juniper berries. [SEE NOTE]

gin[2] |jĭn| *n.* A machine that separates the seeds from the fibers of cotton; a cotton gin. —*v.* **ginned, gin•ning.** To remove the seeds from (cotton) with a gin. —**gin′ner** *n.* [SEE NOTE]

gin•ger |jĭn′jər| *n.* **1. a.** A tropical plant having a root with a strong, sharp, spicy flavor. **b.** The root of this plant, often preserved with sugar or powdered and used for flavoring. **2.** *Informal.* Liveliness; pep. **3.** A reddish brown. —***modifier:*** *a ginger cooky.* —*adj.* Reddish brown: *a big ginger tomcat.*

gig[1-2]

Gig[1] *first occurs in the Middle English period, with the meaning "a spinning top" or "anything that spins around."* **Gig**[2] *is a shortening of* **fishgig**, *a barbed spear for catching fish; this word is borrowed from Spanish* fisga; *the alteration to* **fishgig** *is a piece of "folk etymology," suggested by the word* **fish.**

Gila monster

gill[1-2]

Gill[1] *is probably from Old Norse* gil, *which originally meant "jaw, cheek."* **Gill**[2] *is from Old French* gille, *which is from Late Latin* gillō, *"water pot."*

gin[1-2]

Gin[1] *was a Dutch invention; the word comes from Dutch* jenever, genever, *which is from Latin* jūniperus, *"juniper."* **Gin**[2] *is a shortening of* **engine.**

ginkgo

giraffe

ginger ale. A soft drink flavored with ginger.
ginger beer. A soft drink similar to ginger ale but flavored with fermented ginger.
gin•ger•bread |jĭn′jər brĕd′| *n.* A cake or cooky flavored with ginger and molasses.
gin•ger•ly |jĭn′jər lē| *adv.* Cautiously; carefully; warily: *He walked over to the brown horse and patted him gingerly.* —*adj.* Cautious; careful: *offering advice in a gingerly fashion.*
gin•ger•snap |jĭn′jər snăp′| *n.* A flat, brittle cooky made with molasses and ginger.
ging•ham |gĭng′əm| *n.* A light cotton cloth woven in checks, stripes, plaids, or solid colors. —**modifier:** *a gingham dress.*
gink•go |gĭng′kō| *n., pl.* **gink•goes.** A tree with straight branches and fan-shaped leaves, originally from China and often planted in city streets and parks. [SEE PICTURE]
gin rummy. A kind of rummy for two or more persons in which a person may win by matching all his cards or may end the game by melding when his unmatched cards add up to ten points or less.
gin•seng |jĭn′sĕng′| *n.* **1.** A plant with small greenish flowers and a forked root. **2.** The root of this plant, used especially by the Chinese as a medicine.
Gip•sy |jĭp′sē| *n. & adj.* A form of the word **Gypsy.**
gi•raffe |jĭ răf′| *or* |-räf′| *n.* A tall African animal with a very long neck and legs, a tan coat with brown blotches, and short horns. [SEE PICTURE]
gird |gûrd| *v.* **gird•ed** or **girt** |gûrt|, **gird•ing.** **1.** To encircle or attach with a belt, band, etc.: *gird on their trusty swords.* **2.** To prepare (oneself) for action: *I shall bring you arms to gird yourselves for battle.* **3.** To encircle or surround: *fields girded by railroad tracks.*
gird•er |gûr′dər| *n.* A horizontal beam, as of steel or wood, that acts as one of the main supports of a building or other structure.
gir•dle |gûr′dl| *n.* **1.** A belt, sash, or band worn around the waist. **2.** An elastic undergarment, lighter than a corset, worn by women to hold in the waist and hips. **3.** Anything that surrounds like a belt: *Just beyond the four inner planets is a girdle of small ones, the asteroids.* —*v.* **gir•dled, gir•dling.** **1.** To put a belt around: *He girdled his waist.* **2.** To encircle or surround: *A moat girdled the castle.* **3.** To remove a beltlike strip of bark from around the trunk of (a tree).
girl |gûrl| *n.* **1.** A female who has not yet reached womanhood. **2.** A young woman. **3.** A daughter: *the Jones girl. She's my sister's girl.* **4.** *Informal.* A female servant: *A new girl is reporting for work this morning.* **5.** *Informal.* A female friend or chum: *a bridge game with the girls.* **6.** *Informal.* A sweetheart or girlfriend: *She's my girl, and you can't dance with her.* [SEE NOTE]
girl•friend |gûrl′frĕnd′| *n.* Also **girl friend.** **1.** A female friend. **2.** *Informal.* A sweetheart or favored female companion of a man.
girl•hood |gûrl′ho͝od′| *n.* The time of being a girl.
girl•ish |gûr′lĭsh| *adj.* Of, like, or suitable for a girl. —**girl′ish•ly** *adv.* —**girl′ish•ness** *n.*
Girl Scout. A member of the Girl Scouts, an organization for girls between 7 and 17 that helps to develop physical fitness, good character, and homemaking ability.
girt |gûrt|. A past tense and past participle of **gird.**
girth |gûrth| *n.* **1.** The distance or measurement around something; circumference. **2.** A strap encircling the body of a horse or pack animal to secure a load or saddle on its back.
gist |jĭst| *n.* The central idea of something, such as a speech; essence: *the gist of a message.*
give |gĭv| *v.* **gave** |gāv|, **giv•en** |gĭv′ən|, **giv•ing.** **1.** To make a present of: *My sister gave me a new watch.* **2.** To make gifts or donations: *She gives generously to the town's charities.* **3.** To deliver in exchange or in payment; pay: *What will you give me for the car?* **4.** To place in the hands of; hand over; pass: *Please give me the salt.* **5.** To bestow; confer: *the freedom God gives to us.* **6.** To award as due: *They gave her a standing ovation.* **7.** To contribute; furnish; donate: *Give me a hand here.* **8.** To devote; apply: *giving it special attention.* **9. a.** To provide; furnish: *follow the directions given.* **b.** To provide (something required or expected): *With your tuning fork, give me "A."* **10.** To be a source of; supply: *Green vegetables give us vitamins and minerals.* **11.** To grant: *She gave her permission willingly.* **12.** To grant a share or degree of; impart; lend: *Blue lights gave the corridor a ghastly glow.* **13.** To permit; allow: *My tasks give me no rest.* **14.** To allot; assign: *a treaty that gave the Russians three Latvian ports to use.* **15.** To designate; name; specify: *Give a starting time for the race.* **16.** To offer or proffer: *She gave a prayer of thanks.* **17.** To emit or issue; give forth: *give an order.* **18.** To reveal; manifest: *His adolescence gave little indication of his future greatness.* **19.** To deliver; render: *She gave her recitation shyly.* **20. a.** To present; stage; put on: *The festival is giving all of Wagner's operas this year.* **b.** To cause to take place: *She gives very good parties.* **21.** To produce: *Their cows gave milk and cream.* **22. a.** To convey; deliver: *Give this envelope to your mother from me.* **b.** To transmit; communicate: *give her my regards. She kept the boys from giving German measles to their sisters.* **23.** To inflict on; mete; deal: *give him a nice, sharp blow on the head.* **24.** To administer: *She gave him his cough syrup.* **25.** To perform; execute: *The girl gave a little hop and kick.* **26.** To yield, as to pressure: *give ground to the enemy.* **27.** To permit a view of or access to; open: *a low door, which gave into another, rather small, room.* —***phrasal verbs.*** **give away.** **1.** To make a gift of. **2.** To present (a bride) to the bridegroom at a wedding ceremony. **3.** To reveal or make known, often by accident. **give back.** To return: *Give me back my book.* **give in.** To surrender; yield. **give off.** To send forth; emit; discharge: *Some chemical changes give off energy.* **give out.** **1.** To let (something) be known: *gave out the bad news.* **2.** To distribute: *give out surplus food to the needy.* **3.** To break down; fail: *My watch gave out.* **4.** To become used up; run out: *His supply of gloves gave out.* **give over.** **1.** To hand over. **2.** To devote; make available for a purpose: *The last part of the program is given over to questions from the audience.* **give up.** **1.** To surrender; admit defeat. **2.** To stop; leave off: *give*

girl

Girl *first appeared in the Middle English period, as* girle, gerle, *or* gurle. *It originally meant "young person of either sex," but by the sixteenth century it only meant "young female person." It is of entirely unknown origin.*

ă pat/ā pay/â care/ä father/ĕ pet/ē be/ĭ pit/ī pie/î fierce/ŏ pot/ō go/ô paw, for/oi oil/o͝o book/o͞o boot/ou out/ŭ cut/û fur/*th* the/th thin/hw which/zh vision/ə ago, item, pencil, atom, circus

up smoking. **3.** To part with; relinquish. **4.** To abandon hope for. **give way. 1.** To withdraw; retreat. **2.** To yield; make room for: *You must give way to the flow of cars coming in from the bridge.* **3.** To abandon oneself: *told himself he would not give way to his fears.* **4.** To collapse; break; fail: *The flooring threatened to give way.* —*n. Informal.* The quality or condition of being able to accommodate to pressure; elasticity; springiness: *the give in a metal antenna suspended from the building.* —**giv'er** *n.*

give-and-take |gĭv'ən tāk'| *n.* **1.** Willingness on both sides to make concessions; compromise. **2.** A lively exchange: *the give-and-take of our student debates.*

give•a•way |gĭv'ə wā'| *n. Informal.* **1.** Something given away at no charge. **2.** Something that betrays or exposes, often by accident.

giv•en |gĭv'ən|. Past participle of **give.** —*adj.* **1.** Specified; named; stated: *obtain all the facts on one given country.* **2.** Having a tendency; inclined: *given to sulking.* **3.** Presented; bestowed: *ideas freely given.*

given name. The name given to a person at birth or at baptism.

giz•zard |gĭz'ərd| *n.* **1.** An enlarged, muscular part in the digestive tract of a bird, in which bits of sand or gravel collect and in which food is ground and digested. **2.** A similar part in the digestive tract of an earthworm, insect, etc.

gla•cé |glă sā'| *adj.* Coated with a sugar glaze; candied.

gla•cial |glā'shəl| *adj.* **1.** Of, from, or having to do with a glacier. **2.** Often **Glacial.** Of or concerning the times in the Pleistocene epoch when glaciers covered much of the earth's surface.

gla•cier |glā'shər| *n.* A large mass of slowly moving ice, formed from snow packed together by the weight of snow above it.

glad |glăd| *adj.* **glad•der, glad•dest. 1.** Causing, bringing, or showing joy and pleasure: *glad news. He looked glad to see her.* **2.** Pleased; willing: *glad to give approval; glad to do the work.* **3.** Grateful: *glad for his help.* —**glad'ly** *adv.* —**glad'ness** *n.*

glad•den |glăd'n| *v.* To make glad.

glade |glād| *n.* An open space in a forest.

glad•i•a•tor |glăd'ē ā'tər| *n.* In ancient Rome, a man, especially a slave, captive, or criminal, who engaged in mortal combat in an arena to entertain the public. [SEE NOTE]

glad•i•o•la |glăd'ē ō'lə| *n.* A gladiolus.

glad•i•o•lus |glăd'ē ō'ləs| *n., pl.* **glad•i•o•li** |glăd'ē ō'lī'| *or* |-lē'| or **glad•i•o•lus•es.** A plant with sword-shaped leaves and a long cluster of showy, variously colored flowers. [SEE NOTE & PICTURE]

glam•or |glăm'ər| *n.* A form of the word **glamour.**

glam•or•ize |glăm'ə rīz'| *v.* **glam•or•ized, glam•or•iz•ing.** To make glamorous.

glam•or•ous |glăm'ər əs| *adj.* Having or showing glamour: *a glamorous actress.* —**glam'or•ous•ly** *adv.* —**glam'or•ous•ness** *n.*

glam•our |glăm'ər| *n.* An air of romantic charm or excitement surrounding a person or thing and capable of attracting the interest of a wide public; allure: *the glamour of the theater.*

glance |glăns| *or* |glāns| *v.* **glanced, glanc•ing. 1.** To look briefly or hastily: *She didn't even glance at his new outfit.* **2.** To strike a surface at such an angle as to fly off to one side: *The ax blade glanced and missed the log.* —*n.* A brief or hasty look: *a quick glance over his shoulder.*

gland |glănd| *n.* **1.** Any of a number of organs in the body whose main function is to produce some special substance, such as a hormone or enzyme, that the body uses in some way. **2.** An organ of the body, such as a lymph node, that resembles a gland in some way.

glan•ders |glăn'dərz| *n.* *(used with a singular verb).* A contagious disease of horses and other animals, caused by bacteria.

glan•du•lar |glăn'jə lər| *adj.* Of, like, or affecting a gland or its secretion.

glare |glâr| *v.* **glared, glar•ing. 1.** To stare fiercely or angrily: *glared at him with resentment.* **2.** To shine intensely; dazzle: *A searing sun glares down on the dunes.* —*n.* **1.** A fixed, angry stare. **2.** A very strong and blinding light: *the sun's glare.*

glar•ing |glâr'ĭng| *adj.* **1.** Staring fiercely or angrily: *a big setter with frightfully glaring eyes.* **2.** Shining intensely: *a glaring sun.* **3.** Too bright or intense; gaudy: *painted a glaring red.* **4.** Unmistakable; obvious; conspicuous: *a glaring error.* —**glar'ing•ly** *adv.*

Glas•gow |glăs'gō| *or* |-kō|. The largest city in Scotland. Population, 950,000.

glass |glăs| *or* |glās| *n.* **1.** Any of a large class of materials that harden from the molten state without crystallizing and becoming true solids. They are generally transparent or translucent and often break or shatter easily. **2. a.** Something made of glass, as a container for drinking or a mirror. **b.** A collection of such objects; glassware. **3. a.** A glass with something in it: *a glass of water.* **b.** The amount that a glass holds: *drink a glass of milk.* **4. glasses.** Any device containing a lens of glass and used to aid vision, especially eyeglasses. —***modifier:*** *a glass door.*

glass blowing. The art or process of shaping an object from a mass of molten glass by blowing air into it through a tube. —**glass blower.** [SEE PICTURE]

glass snake. A legless lizard that looks like a snake and has a tail that breaks off very easily.

glass•ware |glăs'wâr'| *or* |glās'-| *n.* Objects, especially containers, made of glass.

glass•y |glăs'ē| *or* |glā'sē| *adj.* **glass•i•er, glass•i•est. 1.** Like glass: *glassy rocks.* **2.** Without expression; lifeless; blank: *a glassy stare.* —**glass'i•ly** *adv.* —**glass'i•ness** *n.*

glau•co•ma |glô kō'mə| *or* |glou-| *n.* An eye disease in which the pressure of fluid inside the eyeball becomes abnormally high, creating damage that leads eventually to loss of sight.

glaze |glāz| *n.* **1.** A thin, smooth, shiny coating, as on paper or fabric. **2.** A thin, glassy coating of ice. **3.** A coating applied to ceramics before baking or firing in a kiln. **4.** A coating, as of syrup, applied to food. **5.** A glassy film, as over the eyes. —*v.* **glazed, glaz•ing. 1.** To fit or furnish with glass: *glaze a window.* **2.** To apply a glaze to: *glaze paper; glaze strawberries and top them with whipped cream.* **3.** To make or become coated with thin ice: *Sleet glazed the highway. The roads glazed, and all traffic was stopped.*

gladiator/gladiolus

Gladiator *is from Latin* gladiātor, *"swordsman," from* gladius, *"sword."* **Gladiolus** *is from Latin* gladiolus, *"little sword," diminutive of* gladius, *"sword"; the reference is to the shape of the plant's leaves.*

gladiolus

glass blower

glider

glockenspiel

ă pat/ā pay/â care/ä father/ĕ pet/ ē be/ĭ pit/ī pie/î fierce/ŏ pot/ ō go/ô paw, for/oi oil/ŏŏ book/ ōō boot/ou out/ŭ cut/û fur/ *th* the/th thin/hw which/zh vision/ ə ago, item, pencil, atom, circus

4. To become covered with a glassy film, as from injury or fatigue: *eyes glazing suddenly.*

gla•zier |glā'zhər| *n.* A person who cuts and fits glass for windows, doors, etc.

gleam |glēm| *n.* **1.** A beam or flash of light that soon disappears: *faint gleams of sunshine.* **2.** A steady glow; a glint: *the soft pale gleam of moonlight.* **3.** A brief or faint indication; a trace; token: *a gleam of hope.* —*v.* To give off a gleam; shine brightly: *frost and dew gleaming like diamonds.*

glean |glēn| *v.* **1.** To gather (grain) left behind by reapers. **2.** To gather (knowledge or information) bit by bit. —**glean'er** *n.*

glee |glē| *n.* **1.** Merriment; joy. **2.** An unaccompanied song for three or more male voices, popular in the 18th century.

glee club. A group of singers who perform usually short pieces of choral music.

glee•ful |glē'fəl| *adj.* Full of glee; merry. —**glee'ful•ly** *adv.* —**glee'ful•ness** *n.*

glen |glĕn| *n.* A valley.

Glen•gar•ry |glĕn găr'ē| *n., pl.* **Glen•gar•ries.** A Scottish cap creased lengthwise across the top, often with streamers in back.

glib |glĭb| *adj.* **glib•ber, glib•best. 1.** Speaking or writing readily but suggesting lack of thought or sincerity: *glib politicians accustomed to promising the moon in an election year.* **2.** Smooth and flowing but shallow or insincere in meaning: *a glib reply.* —**glib'ly** *adv.* —**glib'ness** *n.*

glide |glīd| *v.* **glid•ed, glid•ing. 1.** To move or cause to move smoothly and with little effort: *The sub glided through the Arctic waters. He glided his fingers along the strings of the instrument.* **2.** To pass or occur without notice: *Precious time had glided by.* **3.** To fly or soar without using propelling power, often taking advantage of favorable winds or air currents. **4.** To go or pass from one vowel or pitch to another without a break in the sound. —*n.* **1.** The act or process of gliding. **2.** A sound produced by gliding.

glid•er |glī'dər| *n.* **1.** An aircraft having wings and controls similar to those of an airplane but lacking an engine. It is designed to glide after being towed aloft by an airplane or launched from a catapult. **2.** A swinging couch that hangs in a vertical frame. [SEE PICTURE]

glim•mer |glĭm'ər| *n.* **1.** A dim or unsteady light; a flicker: *the glimmer of fireflies.* **2.** A faint trace or indication; a glimpse: *a glimmer of her old sense of humor.* —*v.* **1.** To give off a dim or flickering light: *a single lamp seen glimmering through the window.* **2.** To appear or be indicated faintly: *The Colorado River from the plane seemed a greenish snake glimmering far below.*

glimpse |glĭmps| *n.* A brief, incomplete view or look: *a glimpse of the town.* —*v.* **glimpsed, glimps•ing. 1.** To obtain a brief, incomplete view of: *glimpsed a passing car.* **2.** To look for a moment: *glimpse at the new furnishings.*

glint |glĭnt| *n.* **1.** A brief flash of light; a sparkle: *a cold glint in her eyes.* **2.** A faint or brief indication; a trace: *a glint of rising hate.* —*v.* To gleam or flash; sparkle: *Vermilion Creek, glinting like quicksilver in the moonlight.*

glis•san•do |glĭ sän'dō| *n., pl.* **glis•san•dos.** In music, a rapid glide from one tone to another.

glis•ten |glĭs'ən| *v.* To shine with reflected light: *Sunshine made the snow glisten on the mountains.* —*n.* A shine or sparkle.

glis•ter |glĭs'tər| *v.* To glisten: *"All that glisters is not gold."* Used chiefly in poetry.

glit•ter |glĭt'ər| *n.* **1.** A sparkling light or brightness that suggests a succession of brilliant flashes: *the winter world with its frosty glitter; a glitter in his eyes.* **2.** The condition or quality of being attractive in a brilliant or showy way; fascination: *the pomp and glitter of the queen's coronation.* —*v.* **1.** To sparkle brilliantly: *The stars glittered and winked.* **2.** To be brilliantly attractive: *a ballroom that glittered with chandeliers and tapestries.*

gloam•ing |glō'mĭng| *n.* Twilight. Used chiefly in poetry.

gloat |glōt| *v.* To look on or consider with great pleasure or with selfish or spiteful satisfaction.

glob |glŏb| *n.* A small drop or lump.

glob•al |glō'bəl| *adj.* **1.** Shaped like a globe; spherical. **2.** Of the entire earth; worldwide: *a low population figure by global standards.* —**glob'al•ly** *adv.*

globe |glōb| *n.* **1.** Any object having the general shape of a sphere, especially a representation of the earth or the celestial sphere. **2.** The earth. **3.** An object resembling a globe, as a glass sphere covering a light bulb.

glob•u•lar |glŏb'yə lər| *adj.* **1.** Like a globe or globule in shape. **2.** Made up of globules.

glob•ule |glŏb'yōōl| *n.* A tiny spherical mass, especially a small drop of liquid.

glob•u•lin |glŏb'yə lĭn| *n.* Any of a class of simple proteins that are widely found in blood, milk, muscle tissue, and plant seeds. They are soluble in dilute salt solutions and coagulate when heated.

glock•en•spiel |glŏk'ən spēl'| *or* |-shpēl'| *n.* A musical instrument consisting of a series of metal bars tuned to the tones of the chromatic scale. It is played by being struck with two light hammers. [SEE PICTURE]

gloom |glōōm| *n.* **1.** Partial or total darkness; dimness: *He peered into the gloom.* **2.** Lowness of spirit; sadness; depression: *the gloom that defeat always brings.*

gloom•y |glōō'mē| *adj.* **gloom•i•er, gloom•i•est. 1.** Dismal, dark, or dreary: *a gloomy, deserted castle.* **2.** Showing or filled with gloom; dejected: *sullen and gloomy in defeat.* **3.** Causing low spirits; depressing: *a gloomy tale.* **4.** Without hope; pessimistic: *gloomy about his future.* —**gloom'i•ly** *adv.* —**gloom'i•ness** *n.*

Glo•ri•a |glôr'ē ə| *or* |glōr'-| *n.* **1.** Any of the Christian hymns of praise to God that begin with the Latin word *"Glōria,"* meaning "glory." **2.** The music to which one of these hymns is set.

glo•ri•fi•ca•tion |glôr'ə fĭ kā'shən| *or* |glōr'-| *n.* An act of glorifying or the condition of being glorified; exaltation.

glo•ri•fy |glôr'ə fī'| *or* |glōr'-| *v.* **glo•ri•fied, glo•ri•fy•ing, glo•ri•fies. 1.** To give honor or high praise to; acclaim: *glorified their king by building a pyramid.* **2.** To give glory or honor to through worship: *glorify God.* **3.** To make seem more glorious or excellent than is actually the case: *Lumbering has been glorified in song and story.*

glo•ri•ous |glôr'ē əs| *or* |glōr'-| *adj.* **1.** Having or deserving glory; illustrious: *their glorious past.*

2. Giving or advancing glory: *a glorious victory.* 3. Having great beauty or splendor; magnificent: *a glorious sunset.* —**glo'ri•ous•ly** *adv.*

glo•ry |glôr'ē| *or* |glōr'ē| *n., pl.* **glo•ries. 1.** Great honor or praise granted by common consent; renown: *the days of Solomon's might and glory.* **2.** Something that brings honor, high regard, respect, or renown. **3.** Adoration or praise offered in worship: *"Glory to God in the highest."* **4.** Great beauty: *The sun was setting in a blaze of glory.* **5.** A condition of splendor, as a period of highest achievement or prosperity: *Paris in its greatest glory.* —*v.* **glo•ried, glo•ry•ing, glo•ries.** To rejoice: *Prussia had a number of strong kings who gloried in war.*

gloss¹ |glôs| *or* |glŏs| *n.* **1.** A bright, smooth shine on a surface; sheen: *the gloss of patent leather.* **2.** An attractive appearance intended to hide the real nature of something. —*v.* **1.** To give a bright shine or luster to. **2.** To make attractive or acceptable by concealing or misrepresenting: *gloss over problems.* [SEE NOTE]

gloss² |glôs| *or* |glŏs| *n.* **1.** A brief note that explains or translates a difficult word, phrase, or section of a text or manuscript. **2.** A collection of such notes; a glossary. —*v.* To provide (a text) with glosses. [SEE NOTE]

glos•sa•ry |glô'sə rē| *or* |glŏs'ə-| *n., pl.* **glos•sa•ries.** A collection of glosses, especially a list of specialized words with their definitions.

gloss•y |glô'sē| *or* |glŏs'ē| *adj.* **gloss•i•er, gloss•i•est.** Smooth and shiny: *Satin is a glossy fabric.* —**gloss'i•ly** *adv.* —**gloss'i•ness** *n.*

glot•tal |glŏt'l| *adj.* Of the glottis.

glot•tis |glŏt'ĭs| *n., pl.* **glot•tis•es** or **glot•ti•des** |glŏt'ĭ dēz'|. The space at the upper part of the larynx between the vocal cords.

glove |glŭv| *n.* **1.** A covering that fits the hand, with a separate section for each finger and the thumb. **2.** A padded leather covering worn over the hand to protect it, as when catching a baseball. **3.** A **boxing glove.** —*v.* **gloved, glov•ing.** To cover with a glove.

glov•er |glŭv'ər| *n.* A person who makes or sells gloves.

glow |glō| *v.* **1.** To shine brightly and steadily, especially with accompanying heat but without a flame: *The embers in the fireplace glowed.* **2.** To shine without giving off heat: *Some insects glow in the dark.* **3.** To have a bright, warm color: *The trees glowed in the bright sunlight.* **4.** To have a healthful, ruddy color: *His cheeks glowed.* **5.** To be bright or radiant; shine forth: *His face glowed with pride.* —*n.* **1.** A light produced by any physical source, such as fire, electricity, an organism, a heavenly body, etc. **2.** A shine of reflected light: *a glow in her dark eyes.* **3.** A brilliance or warmth of color: *metal with a radiant glow of gold.* **4.** Radiance or warmth caused by emotion: *the glow that's seen on happy faces.*

glow•er |glou'ər| *v.* To look or stare angrily. —*n.* An angry or threatening stare.

glow•ing |glō'ĭng| *adj.* **1.** Giving or reflecting brilliant light: *glowing coals; glowing green earrings.* **2.** Having a rich, warm color, as from health or strong emotion: *a glowing complexion.* **3.** Enthusiastic; highly favorable: *the glowing reports we've had about you.* —**glow'ing•ly** *adv.*

glow•worm |glō'wûrm'| *n.* The larva or grublike female of a firefly or similar insect, giving off a glowing light in the dark.

glu•cose |glo͞o'kōs'| *n.* Dextrose.

glue |glo͞o| *n.* **1.** Any of a large number of adhesive substances or solutions; a thick, sticky substance used to join things together. **2.** A glue obtained by boiling certain animal proteins. —*modifier: a glue pot; a glue factory.* —*v.* **glued, glu•ing. 1.** To stick or fasten together with glue. **2.** To fix or hold firmly as if with glue: *The hunters had their eyes glued to a far hilltop.*

glum |glŭm| *adj.* **glum•mer, glum•mest.** In low spirits; dejected; gloomy. —**glum'ly** *adv.* —**glum'ness** *n.*

glut |glŭt| *v.* **glut•ted, glut•ting. 1.** To fill, feed, or eat beyond capacity: *glutted himself with fine food.* **2.** To provide (a market) with goods so that the supply is much greater than the demand. —*n.* An oversupply.

glu•ten |glo͞ot'n| *n.* A mixture of plant proteins found in cereal grains such as corn and wheat, used as an adhesive and as a substitute for flour.

glu•ti•nous |glo͞ot'n əs| *adj.* Like or resembling glue; thick and sticky.

glut•ton |glŭt'n| *n.* **1.** A person who eats to excess. **2.** A person with an unusually great capacity to receive or withstand something: *a glutton for punishment.* —**glut'ton•ous** *adj.*

glut•ton•y |glŭt'n ē| *n., pl.* **glut•ton•ies.** Excess in eating or drinking.

glyc•er•in |glĭs'ər ĭn| *n.* Glycerol.

glyc•er•ine |glĭs'ər ĭn| *or* |-ə rēn'| *n.* A form of the word **glycerin.**

glyc•er•ol |glĭs'ə rôl'| *or* |-rōl'| *or* |-rŏl'| *n.* A sweet, syrupy alcohol having the formula $C_3H_8O_3$. It is obtained from fats and oils as a by-product of the manufacture of soaps and is used as a solvent, a sweetener, and an antifreeze and in the manufacture of explosives and other industrial products.

gly•co•gen |glī'kə jən| *n.* A sweet-tasting carbohydrate having the formula $(C_6H_{10}O_5)_n$. It is stored in the muscles, especially in the liver of animals, and is readily converted to dextrose.

gm, gm. gram.

G-man |jē'măn'| *n., pl.* **-men** |-mĕn'|. An agent of the Federal Bureau of Investigation.

gnarl |närl| *n.* A knot on a tree. —*v.* To make knotted or deformed; twist. [SEE NOTE]

gnarled |närld| *adj.* Having gnarls; knotty and misshapen.

gnash |năsh| *v.* To grind (the teeth) together. —*n.* An act of gnashing. [SEE NOTE]

gnat |năt| *n.* Any of several small, winged, biting insects.

gnaw |nô| *v.* **gnawed, gnawed** or **gnawn** |nôn|, **gnaw•ing. 1.** To bite, chew, or erode with the teeth: *animals gnawing the bark of trees.* **2.** To produce by gnawing: *Rats had gnawed a hole in the fence.* **3.** To wear away: *waves gnawing the rocky shore.* **4.** To trouble or cause distress: *Fear gnawed at the pit of his stomach.* —**gnaw'ing** *adj.: gnawing hunger.* ¶*These sound alike* **gnaw, naw.**

gneiss |nīs| *n.* A type of metamorphic rock having a composition about the same as that of granite but having the minerals that compose it arranged in layers. ¶*These sound alike* **gneiss, nice.**

gloss¹·²
Gloss¹ *is probably from a lost Scandinavian word related to Icelandic* glossi, *"spark," and more distantly to* **gleam** *and* **glow. Gloss²** *is from Greek* glōssa, *"tongue, language," also meaning "foreign or difficult word."*

gnarl, gnash, etc.
The combination gn- *at the beginning of a word, in which the /g/ is never pronounced, is rare in English.* **Gnarl** *was originally spelled with* kn-. **Gnash** *is borrowed from Old Norse* gnastan, *"gnashing."* **Gnat** *and* **gnaw** *are related Old English words, originally* gnæt *and* gnagan, *respectively; they are descended from a root,* ghen-, *"to bite."* **Gneiss** *is from German* gneiss. **Gnome** *was made up, from unknown sources, by the alchemist Paracelsus (1493-1541). And* **gnu** *is from Bantu* nqu.

gnu

go

Go *was* gān *or* gegān *in Old English; it is descended from prehistoric Germanic* gēn, *which in turn is from Indo-European* ghē-, *"to go." Apparently this verb did not originally have a past tense of its own and so "captured" one from another verb. The Middle English verb* wenden, *"to turn, to go," had the past tense* wente; *this past tense was increasingly used to mean "did go," and not "did turn," and eventually it was detached from* wenden *and attached to* **go**; *it became* **went** *in Modern English. Meanwhile,* wenden *became* **wend** *in Modern English, and having lost its old past tense was forced to form a new one,* **wended**.

ă pat/ā pay/â care/ä father/ĕ pet/ ē be/ĭ pit/ī pie/î fierce/ŏ pot/ ō go/ô paw, for/oi oil/ŏŏ book/ ōō boot/ou out/ŭ cut/û fur/ *th* the/th thin/hw which/zh vision/ ə ago, item, pencil, atom, circus

gnome |nōm| *n.* **1.** One of a fabled dwarflike race dwelling underground and possessing treasure hordes. **2.** A shriveled old man.

gnu |nōō| *or* |nyōō| *n., pl.* **gnus.** A large African antelope with a beard and mane, a long, tufted tail, and curved horns. ¶*These sound alike* **gnu, knew, new.** [SEE PICTURE]

go |gō| *v.* **went** |wĕnt|, **gone** |gôn| *or* |gŏn|, **go•ing. 1.** To move along; proceed: *We're going on a walk; do you want to go, too?* **2.** To move or proceed to a specified place: *The poor kid hasn't got any place he wants to go.* **3.** To move from a place; depart: *We must go at once.* **4.** To start to move away; begin to move: *He has been going for the past five minutes, but he hasn't got his coat.* **5. a.** To get out of sight; move out of someone's presence: *He'd better go before I really get mad.* **b.** To be free or move freely after being held: *She gradually let him go.* **6.** To start to function, operate, move, etc.: *The car wouldn't go.* **7.** —Used in the form *be going* in the sense of *will* to indicate an indefinite future: *I'm going to get us a house on the bay.* **8.** —Used with the present participle of the verb denoting the action to indicate the act of engaging in an activity: *Let's go swimming.* **9.** To make a specified sound: *The cannon went boom.* **10.** To belong in a definite place or position: *This book goes here.* **11.** To extend from one place or thing to another: *The drapes go from the ceiling to the floor.* **12.** To pass or be given to someone: *The bulk of the estate went to the nephew.* **13.** To be allotted: *This money goes for groceries.* **14.** To serve; help: *It all goes to show he was right in the first place.* **15.** To be compatible; harmonize: *Those colors go well with the shoes.* **16.** To proceed in a particular form or sequence: *How does the rest of the story go?* **17.** To be in a specified state of dress or undress: *They go barefoot the whole year through.* **18.** To die: *When did Grandpa go?* **19.** To come apart; cave in: *That wall looks just about ready to go.* **20.** To fail, as the eyes or ears: *My eyes are going.* **21.** To be consumed or used up: *The supplies went, and we were scared that we might starve.* **22.** To be sold or auctioned off: *Most of our stock went.* **23.** To enter into a specified condition; become: *The tire went flat.* **24.** To be or continue to be in a specified condition: *Outrages against our citizens abroad will not go unpunished.* **25.** To turn out; fare: *How did your day go?* **26.** To be thought of; be rated: *As dogs go, this one is very mean.* **27.** To pursue a course: *go to a lot of trouble; go too far.* **28.** To act, as under guidance or on advice: *Go on my word.* **29.** To hold out; endure: *Penguins can go for a month without food.* **—phrasal verbs. go about. 1.** To busy oneself with or manage: *How does one go about learning the piano?* **2.** To circulate; be current: *There's a rumor going about that she's leaving town.* **3.** To change direction in a sailing vessel; tack. **go ahead.** To start or proceed, especially without hesitation: *Go ahead, tell me about it.* **go along. 1.** To progress or proceed: *This job gets easier as you go along.* **2.** To depart; leave: *I think we ought to be going along.* **go along with.** To agree or act in agreement with. **go around.** To circulate; go about: *gossip that has been going around.* **go at.** To work at diligently or energetically: *When he does get down to work, he goes at it.* **go away. 1.** To depart from a place. **2.** To come to an end: *I wish this fever would go away.* **go back. 1.** To return. **2.** To extend back in space or time: *Her family goes back to the Mayflower.* **go back on. 1.** To withdraw from (a promise or obligation); abandon: *I could never go back on my word.* **2.** To betray: *go back on an old friend.* **go by. 1.** To pass or go past: *Don't let this chance go by.* **2.** To elapse, as time: *Years went by before we met again.* **go down. 1.** To descend. **2.** To be remembered: *She will go down as one of the great stars of our age.* **3.** To be defeated. **4.** To be believed or accepted: *His version of the incident doesn't go down with me.* **go for. 1.** To try to get or catch: *I went for the ball and missed it.* **2.** *Informal.* To appreciate or enjoy: *They both go for rock music.* **3.** To be sold for: *This shirt goes for $5.* **go in.** To enter. **go in for.** To indulge or participate in: *She never did go in for make-up.* **go into.** To take up or enter as an occupation, study, or pastime: *going into the ministry; go into the classics.* **go off. 1.** To leave, depart, or set out: *going off in search of firewood.* **2.** To fall into a specified state: *going off to sleep.* **3.** To be discharged, as firearms and explosives; explode: *The pistol went off by accident.* **4.** To start ringing, as a bell: *The alarm went off at 6 o'clock.* **5.** To happen: *Our party was a last-minute affair, but everything went off fine.* **6.** To err or deviate from the proper course: *I like most of the book, but in the final chapter the author really goes off.* **go on. 1. a.** To proceed, as in words or action: *Please go on with what you were saying.* **b.** To continue to exist: *Bee cities sometimes go on for hundreds of years.* **2.** To behave: *He ranted and raved and went on like a lunatic.* **3.** To happen: *He never really knows what's going on.* **4.** To begin to work, operate, etc.: *A light went on in the dark house.* **5.** To appear on the stage, as in a play: *Jim has got to learn to wait for his cue before going on.* **6.** To approach or almost be a specified age or length of time: *She's 10, going on 11.* **go out. 1.** To go outside, especially from one's home. **2.** To go to parties or public entertainments: *My parents no longer get a sitter for me when they go out.* **3.** To stop work, as in a strike: *The workers all went out on strike.* **4.** To be extinguished; end: *All the lights went out.* **5.** To become obsolete: *The Ivy League look went out years ago.* **6.** To be drawn or move to, as in affection or sympathy: *My heart goes out to you, and I understand.* **7.** To participate in (a sport): *going out for football.* **go over. 1.** To pass from one side to another: *Our best players went over to their team.* **2.** To study or examine in detail: *go over accounts.* **go through. 1.** To proceed through a place: *I opened the front door, and we went through to the back.* **2.** To be passed or approved: *Our proposal has gone through.* **3.** To search or examine in detail: *go through his belongings.* **4.** To undergo: *going through changes in color.* **go through with.** To complete or not leave undone: *They decided to go through with the original wedding plans.* **go together. 1.** To be suitable to each other; harmonize. **2.** To be sweethearts. **go under. 1.** To fail or be ruined: *My uncle's business almost went under.* **2.** To lose consciousness under an anesthetic: *I went under so fast I didn't know what had hit me.* **go up. 1.** To rise; ascend. **2.** To be uttered or emitted: *A* *shout went up when he appeared.* **3.** To be put up or built: *New homes are going up all over the place.* **4.** To be blown up, destroyed, etc.: *The woodshed went up in flames.* **go with.** To belong to or be a proper accompaniment of: *Potatoes go with steak.* —*n.* **1.** *Informal.* A try; venture: *Let's have a go at it.* **2.** *Informal.* A bargain; agreement; deal: *You bring the money and pay cash and it's a go.* **3.** *Informal.* Energy; vitality: *That kid has sure got a lot of go and will be successful.* —*adj. Informal.* Ready for action and in good shape: *Fuel is go.* [SEE NOTE on p. 394]

Idioms. **from the word go.** *Informal.* From the very beginning or from the bottom of the heart: *They're staunch Republicans from the word go.* **go far.** To succeed; prosper greatly: *Speak softly and carry a big stick; you will go far.* **go (someone) one better.** To surpass or outdo in some specified way. **no go.** *Informal.* Ineffective; useless. **on the go.** *Informal.* Perpetually busy. **to go.** To be taken out, as restaurant food and drink: *We want coffee and sandwiches to go.*

goad |gōd| *n.* **1.** A long stick with a pointed end used for prodding animals. **2.** Something that prods or urges; a stimulus or irritating incentive: *His rival's success was a goad to his imagination.* —*v.* To prod with or as if with a goad; give impetus to; incite.

go-a•head |gō'ə hĕd'| *n. Informal.* Permission to go ahead or proceed.

goal |gōl| *n.* **1.** A desired result or purpose toward which one is working; an objective. **2.** A place one is trying to reach: *His goal was California.* **3.** The finish line of a race. **4. a.** In certain sports, a structure or area into which players must propel the ball or puck in order to score. **b.** The score awarded for this. —***modifier:*** *a goal line; a goal post.*

goal•ie |gō'lē| *n. Informal.* A goalkeeper.

goal•keep•er |gōl'kē'pər| *n.* In soccer, hockey, etc., the player stationed at his team's goal to ward off shots made by the opposing team.

goat |gōt| *n.* A hoofed animal with horns and a beard, raised in many parts of the world for milk, meat, leather, and for the soft, warm hair of some kinds. [SEE PICTURE]

Idiom. **get (someone's) goat.** *Slang.* To make angry or annoyed.

goat•ee |gō tē'| *n.* A small beard ending in a point just below a man's chin. [SEE PICTURE]

goat•herd |gōt'hûrd'| *n.* A person who watches over or cares for a flock of goats.

goat•skin |gōt'skĭn'| *n.* **1.** The skin of a goat. **2.** Leather made from the skin. **3.** A container for wine or water made out of this leather. —***modifier:*** *a goatskin binding.*

gob¹ |gŏb| *n.* **1.** A small piece or lump: *a gob of wax; a gob of molten glass.* **2. gobs.** *Informal.* A large quantity, as of money.

gob² |gŏb| *n. Slang.* A sailor.

gob•ble¹ |gŏb'əl| *v.* **gob•bled, gob•bling.** To devour in big greedy gulps.

gob•ble² |gŏb'əl| *n.* The throaty, chuckling sound made by a male turkey. —*v.* **gob•bled, gob•bling.** To make this sound.

gob•bler |gŏb'lər| *n.* A male turkey.

go-be•tween |gō'bĭ twēn'| *n.* A person who helps to arrange an agreement between two sides by acting as the representative of each in its negotiations with the other.

Go•bi Desert |gō'bē|. A large desert in Asia, mostly in Mongolia.

gob•let |gŏb'lĭt| *n.* A drinking glass with a stem and base.

gob•lin |gŏb'lĭn| *n.* A grotesque, elfin creature of folklore, thought to work mischief or evil.

go-cart |gō'kärt'| *n.* **1.** A small wagon for children to ride in, drive, or pull. **2.** A small frame on casters designed to help support a child learning to walk. **3.** A handcart.

god |gŏd| *n.* **1. God.** A being regarded as the supreme creator and ruler of the universe, forming the object of worship in many religions. **2.** A male deity. **3.** An image or idol of a god. **4.** Something considered to be of great value, importance, etc.: *Absolute power was his god.* [SEE NOTE]

god•child |gŏd'chīld'| *n., pl.* **-chil•dren** |-chĭl'drən|. A child other than one's own for whom one serves as sponsor at baptism and whose religious training one promises to oversee.

god•daugh•ter |gŏd'dô'tər| *n.* A female godchild.

god•dess |gŏd'ĭs| *n.* **1.** A female deity: *Venus, goddess of love.* **2.** A woman of great beauty or grace.

god•fa•ther |gŏd'fä'*th*ər| *n.* A man who acts as sponsor of a child when the child is baptized and who promises to oversee the child's religious training.

God•head |gŏd'hĕd'| *n.* **the Godhead.** The essential and divine nature of God.

god•less |gŏd'lĭs| *adj.* **1.** Not believing in or worshiping God. **2.** Irreverent; wicked. —**god'less•ly** *adv.* —**god'less•ness** *n.*

god•like |gŏd'līk'| *adj.* Resembling or of the nature of god; divine.

god•ly |gŏd'lē| *adj.* **god•li•er, god•li•est.** Having great reverence for God; pious: *simple, godly people.* —**god'li•ness** *n.*

god•moth•er |gŏd'mŭ*th*'ər| *n.* A woman who acts as sponsor of a child when the child is baptized and who promises to oversee the child's religious training.

god•par•ent |gŏd'pâr'ənt| *or* |-păr'-| *n.* A godfather or godmother.

god•send |gŏd'sĕnd'| *n.* An unexpected piece of luck; a windfall.

God•speed |gŏd'spēd'| *n.* Success or good fortune: *He wished me Godspeed, and I left.*

Godt•håb |gôt'hôp'|. The capital of Greenland. Population, 9,000.

Goe•the |gœ'tə|, **Johann Wolfgang von.** 1749–1832. German poet and dramatist.

go-get•ter |gō'gĕt'ər| *n. Informal.* An enterprising, ambitious person.

gog•gle |gŏg'əl| *v.* **gog•gled, gog•gling.** To stare with wide and bulging eyes. —*n.* **1.** A stare or leer. **2. goggles.** A pair of large eyeglasses worn tight against the head as a protection against wind, glare, mud, etc.

go•ing |gō'ĭng| *n.* **1.** The act of leaving or moving away; departure: *comings and goings.* **2.** The condition underfoot as it affects one's headway in walking or riding: *It was rough going to get there, but we made it.* —*adj.* **1.** In full operation; flourishing: *Our business is at last a going concern.* **2.** Available or now in existence: *We make the best bikes going.*

goat

goatee

god/good

God *is* **good,** *and both words are native Old English; but they are not related, and their original meanings were quite different.* **Good** *was* gōd *in Old English; it is descended from prehistoric Germanic* gōdaz, *"fitting, suitable, good," which in turn is from Indo-European* ghedh-, *"to unite, join, fit."* **God** *was* god *in Old English,* gudam *in Germanic, and* ghuto- *in Indo-European; its original meaning was "he who is prayed to," from the root* gheu-, *"to call on, pray to."*

goldfish

gondola

goober
According to the Dictionary of Americanisms *(1951), the earliest known record of the word* **goober** *is in a Georgia newspaper of the year 1834; the word became widespread in the South and beyond. It is a vestige of the numerous Bantu languages once spoken in America by slaves brought from West Africa. In Angola to this day the word for "peanut" (also meaning "kidney") is* nguba.

ă pat/ā pay/â care/ä father/ĕ pet/ ē be/ĭ pit/ī pie/î fierce/ŏ pot/ ō go/ô paw, for/oi oil/ŏŏ book/ ōō boot/ou out/ŭ cut/û fur/ *th* the/th thin/hw which/zh vision/ ə ago, item, pencil, atom, circus

Idiom. **goings on.** Behavior or things happening, especially when regarded with disapproval.

goi•ter |goi′tər| *n.* A disease in which the thyroid gland becomes enlarged and is visible as a swelling at the front of the neck, often associated with a diet that contains too little iodine.

gold |gōld| *n.* **1.** Symbol **Au** One of the elements, a soft, yellow metal. Atomic number 79; atomic weight 196.97; valences +1, +3; melting point 1,063°C; boiling point 2,966°C. **2.** A deep, strong, or metallic yellow: *when leaves turn to red and gold.* **3.** Money, especially money in coins of gold. **4.** Something thought of as having great value or goodness: *a heart of gold.* —***modifier:*** *a gold ring; a gold coin.* —*adj.* Deep, strong, or metallic yellow.

gold•brick |gōld′brĭk′|. *Slang. n.* A person, especially a soldier, who avoids duties or work. —*v.* To shirk one's duties or work.

gold•en |gōl′dən| *adj.* **1.** Made of gold: *golden earrings.* **2.** Having the color of gold or a yellow color suggestive of gold: *a golden wheat field.* **3.** Of the greatest value or importance; precious: *golden memories of high school.* **4.** Marked by prosperity, expansion, and often creativeness: *the golden civilization of the Renaissance.* **5.** Very favorable; excellent: *a golden opportunity.*

golden age. **1.** In Greek and Roman mythology, a prehistoric age of peace and plenty. **2.** A period when a nation, art, science, etc., is at its height.

golden anniversary. A 50th anniversary.

golden calf. **1.** In the Bible, a golden image of a calf worshiped by the Israelites during one of Moses' absences on Sinai. **2.** Money as an idol.

Golden Fleece. In Greek mythology, the fleece of the golden ram, stolen by Jason and the Argonauts.

golden mean. A course between extremes; moderation.

gold•en•rod |gōl′dən rŏd′| *n.* A plant with plumelike clusters of small yellow flowers that bloom in late summer or fall.

golden rule. **1.** The teaching of Christ that one should behave toward others as one would have others behave toward oneself. **2.** Any basic rule or principle.

golden wedding. The 50th anniversary of a marriage.

gold-filled |gōld′fĭld′| *adj.* Made of a hard metal with an outer layer of gold: *a gold-filled watch.*

gold•finch |gōld′fĭnch′| *n.* **1.** A North American bird having yellow feathers with a black forehead, wings, and tail. **2.** A European bird with black, yellow, and red markings.

gold•fish |gōld′fĭsh′| *n., pl.* **-fish** or **-fish•es.** A small freshwater fish, usually golden-orange or reddish, often kept in home aquariums. [SEE PICTURE]

gold leaf. Gold beaten into extremely thin sheets, used for gilding.

gold•smith |gōld′smĭth′| *n.* A person who fashions or deals in objects of gold.

gold standard. A monetary standard under which the basic unit of money is equal in value to a specified amount of gold.

golf |gŏlf| *or* |gôlf| *n.* A game played over a large outdoor obstacle course having a series of 9 or 18 holes spaced far apart. A player, using various clubs, tries to take as few strokes as possible in hitting a ball into one hole after another. —***modifier:*** *a golf ball.* —*v.* To play golf. —**golf′er** *n.*

golf club. **1.** One of a set of clubs having a slender shaft and a head of wood or iron, used in golf. **2.** An association of golfers or the clubhouse and grounds belonging to it.

golf course. A large tract of land laid out for golf.

Gol•go•tha |gŏl′gə thə|. The place where Christ was crucified; Calvary.

Go•li•ath |gə lī′əth|. In the Bible, the giant Philistine slain by David with a slingshot.

Go•mor•rah |gə môr′ə| *or* |-mŏr′ə|. In the Bible, a city that God destroyed. See **Sodom.**

-gon. A word element meaning "a specified number of angles": **hexagon.**

go•nad |gō′năd′| *or* |gŏn′ăd′| *n.* An organ in which egg cells or sperm cells are produced; an ovary or testis.

gon•do•la |gŏn′dl ə| *n.* **1.** A long, narrow boat with a high pointed prow and stern and often a small cabin in the middle, used for public conveyance on the canals of Venice. **2.** An open, shallow freight car with low sides. **3. a.** The basket suspended from a balloon. **b.** The cabin of a dirigible. **4.** An enclosed car suspended from a cable used for transporting passengers, as up and down a ski slope. [SEE PICTURE]

gon•do•lier |gŏn′dl îr′| *n.* The boatman who stands at the stern of a gondola and propels it by sculling with a long oar.

gone |gôn| *or* |gŏn|. Past participle of **go.** —*adj.* **1.** Passed; bygone: *Winter was gone.* **2.** Away from a place; absent: *I'll be gone for a few days.* **3.** Dead: *When I am gone, you will wish I could be brought back to life.* **4.** Exhausted; used up: *Their strength was gone.*

gon•er |gô′nər| *or* |gŏn′ər| *n. Slang.* Someone or something that is ruined or doomed.

gong |gông| *or* |gŏng| *n.* A saucer-shaped metal disk that produces a loud, ringing tone when struck.

gon•o•coc•cus |gŏn′ə kŏk′əs| *n., pl.* **gon•o•coc•ci** |gŏn′ə kŏk′sī′|. A member of the species of bacteria that causes gonorrhea.

gon•or•rhe•a |gŏn′ə rē′ə| *n.* An infectious venereal disease of the genitourinary tract and, sometimes, the rectum.

goo |gōō| *n. Informal.* **1.** A sticky, wet substance. **2.** Sentimental drivel.

goo•ber |gōō′bər| *n.* A peanut. [SEE NOTE]

good |gŏŏd| *adj.* **bet•ter** |bĕt′ər|, **best** |bĕst|. **1.** Having positive or desirable qualities; not bad or poor: *a good book; good food.* **2. a.** Useful; suitable: *a good wood for shipbuilding.* **b.** Beneficial; helpful: *Earthworms are good for our soil.* **3.** Favorable: *good luck.* **4.** Enjoyable; pleasant: *a good time.* **5.** Superior to the average; competent; skilled: *a good painter.* **6. a.** Solid; sound: *a good reason; good mental health.* **b.** Not spoiled; usable: *Milk left in the refrigerator is usually good.* **7.** Selective; discriminating: *good taste.* **8. a.** Morally upright: *a good, honest person.* **b.** Honorable: *a good name.* **9. a.** Well-behaved; obedient: *good children.* **b.** Loyal; devoted: *a good friend.* **10.** Proper; correct: *good manners; good grammar.* **11.** Substantial; considerable: *a good income;*

a good profit. **12.** Not less than; full: *a good mile to the station.* **13.** Thorough; complete: *a good cry.* **14.** Fair; likely: *She has a good chance of becoming president.* **15.** Graded by U.S. Government standards as less than choice and prime: *good cuts of beef.* *—n.* **1.** Something good: *You must learn to accept the bad with the good.* **2.** Benefit; welfare: *for the good of the country.* **3.** Value; use: *What good is a birthday without a birthday cake?* [SEE NOTE on p. 395]
Idioms. a good deal. A lot; a considerable amount: *You learn a good deal when you collect stamps.* **as good as. 1.** Equal or equivalent to: *In some stores checks are as good as cash.* **2.** Nearly; almost: *This car is as good as new.* **for good.** Permanently; forever. **good and.** Very; entirely: *She is good and mad at him.* **good for. 1.** Able to serve or continue performing: *Our car is good for two more years.* **2.** Worth: *This ticket is good for two seats.* **make good.** To be successful: *He could never make good as an athlete.* **no good.** Useless: *It's no good arguing with him.* **to the good.** For the best.

good afternoon. A standard greeting used in the afternoon.

good-by or **good-bye** |go͝od'bī'| *interj.* A word used to express farewell. *—n.* An expression of farewell. *—modifier: a good-by kiss.*

good day. A standard greeting used during the day.

good evening. A standard greeting used in the evening.

good-for-noth•ing |go͝od'fər nŭth'ĭng| *or* |-nŭth'-| *n.* Someone considered worthless or useless. *—adj.* Having little worth; useless.

Good Friday. A church festival celebrated on the Friday before Easter in memory of the Crucifixion of Christ.

good•heart•ed |go͝od'här'tĭd| *adj.* Kind and generous: *a goodhearted person.* **—good'heart'ed•ly** *adv.* **—good'heart'ed•ness** *n.*

Good Hope, Cape of. A cape at the southern tip of Africa.

good-hu•mored |go͝od'hyo͞o'mərd| *adj.* Cheerful; amiable: *a good-humored disagreement.* **—good'-hu'mored•ly** *adv.*

good-look•ing |go͝od'lo͝ok'ĭng| *adj.* Having a pleasing appearance; attractive; handsome: *good-looking clothes; a good-looking girl.*

good•ly |go͝od'lē| *adj.* **good•li•er, good•li•est. 1.** Rather large; considerable: *a goodly number of people.* **2.** Pleasing in appearance, character, etc.: *a goodly house.*

good morning. A standard greeting used in the morning. *—modifier:* **(good-morning):** *a good-morning kiss.*

good-na•tured |go͝od'nā'chərd| *adj.* Having a pleasant disposition; cheerful: *a good-natured man; a good-natured face.* **—good'-na'tured•ly** *adv.*

good•ness |go͝od'nĭs| *n.* **1.** The quality or condition of being good; excellence: *the goodness of the fruit.* **2.** Kindness; benevolence: *Surely goodness and mercy shall follow me all the days of my life.* *—interj.* A word used in various phrases to express surprise: *For goodness sakes!*

good night. A standard greeting used at night. *—modifier:* **(good-night):** *a good-night kiss.*

goods |go͝odz| *pl.n.* **1.** Things that can be bought and sold; merchandise; wares: *manufactured goods.* **2.** Personal belongings. **3.** Cloth; fabric.

Good Sa•mar•i•tan |sə măr'ĭ tən|. **1.** In one of Christ's parables in the New Testament, the only passer-by who was willing to aid a man who had been beaten and robbed. **2.** A person who unselfishly helps others; a good neighbor.

good-sized |go͝od'sīzd'| *adj.* Of a fairly large size: *a good-sized rabbit.*

good•will |go͝od'wĭl'| *n.* Also **good will. 1.** An attitude of kindliness; friendliness. **2.** A good relationship of a nation with other nations or a business with its customers, considered as an asset that cannot be expressed in terms of money. *—modifier: a goodwill tour of Latin America.*

good•y¹ |go͝od'ē|. *Informal. n., pl.* **good•ies.** Something attractive or delectable, especially something good to eat. *—adj.* Goody-goody. *—interj.* A word used to express childish delight.

good•y² |go͝od'ē| *n. Archaic.* Often **Goody.** A polite title usually applied to a married woman of humble rank.

good•y-good•y |go͝od'ē go͝od'ē| *n., pl.* **good•y-good•ies.** A person who is affectedly good or sweet. *—adj.* Affectedly good or sweet.

goo•ey |go͞o'ē| *adj.* **goo•i•er, goo•i•est.** *Informal.* Sticky: *a cake with gooey chocolate icing.*

goof |go͞of|. *Slang. n.* **1.** A careless mistake; a slip. **2.** An incompetent or stupid person. *—v.* **1.** To make a careless mistake; blunder. **2.** To waste or kill time.

goof ball. *Slang.* Any barbiturate tablet or capsule, combined with a dose of amphetamine.

goof•y |go͞o'fē| *adj.* **goof•i•er, goof•i•est.** *Slang.* Silly; ridiculous. **—goof'i•ness** *n.*

goo•gol |go͞o'gŏl'| *n.* The number equal to 10 raised to the 100th power, written as 10^{100} or as 1 followed by 100 zeros.

gook |go͝ok| *n. Slang.* **1.** A dirty, slimy substance. **2.** An Oriental. The word "gook" is considered offensive.

goon |go͞on| *n. Slang.* **1.** A stupid or oafish person: *He thought of himself as an untalented goon.* **2.** A thug hired to intimidate or harm people, especially workers on strike.

goo•ney |go͞o'nē| *n., pl.* **goo•neys.** Also **gooney bird.** *Informal.* Any of several albatrosses common on islands of the Pacific.

goose |go͞os| *n., pl.* **geese** |gēs|. **1. a.** Any of several water birds related to the ducks but generally larger and with a longer neck and a shorter, more pointed bill. **b.** The female of such a bird. **c.** The meat of such a bird, used as food. **2.** *Informal.* A silly person. [SEE PICTURE]

goose•ber•ry |go͞os'bĕr'ē| *n., pl.* **-ber•ries. 1.** A juicy, greenish berry used chiefly for making jam or tarts. **2.** A spiny shrub that bears such berries. *—modifier: gooseberry jam.*

goose flesh. Also **goose bumps, goose pimples.** A roughness of the skin caused by tiny bumps that form in the areas surrounding the hairs on the skin as a reaction to cold, fear, etc.

G.O.P. Grand Old Party (the Republican Party).

go•pher |gō'fər| *n.* Any of several burrowing North American animals with pocketlike cheek pouches. [SEE PICTURE]

gore¹ |gôr| *or* |gōr| *v.* **gored, gor•ing.** To pierce or stab with a horn or tusk. [SEE NOTE]

gore² |gôr| *or* |gōr| *n.* A triangular piece of

goose

gopher

gore¹·²·³

Gore¹ *is from an old word for "spear," which was* gār *in Old English and is descended from prehistoric Germanic* gaiz-, *"spear, sharp point."* **Gore²** *originally meant "a triangular field, a wedge-shaped piece of land"; it was* gāra *in Old English, and is descended from the same Germanic word* gaiz-, *"sharp point," as above.* **Gore³** *was* gōr *in Old English, but it is not connected to* gār, *"spear"; its original meaning was "filth, slime," and it later came to mean "thick blood from a wound."*

gorilla

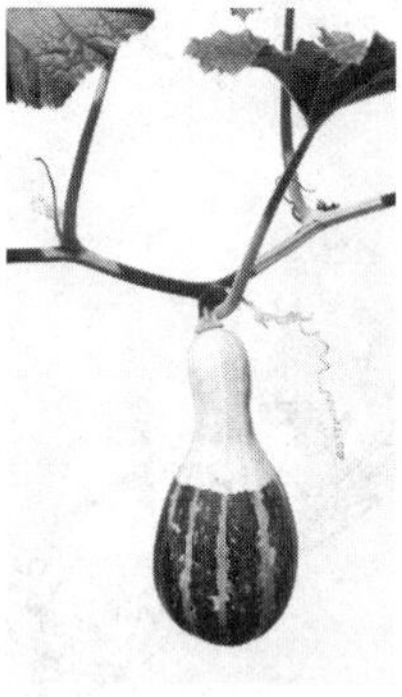

gourd

gourmand/gourmet
Gourmand *and* **gourmet** *are close in meaning (but not identical), and both come from French; it would be much neater if they were related to each other, but unfortunately they seem to be two independent words.* **Gourmand,** *first appearing in Old French in the fourteenth century, has always had its present meaning, "a hearty eater."* **Gourmet,** *occurring in Old French at the same period, originally meant "a wine merchant's servant"; by the influence of* gourmand *it later came to mean "a connoisseur of wine and food."*

ă pat/ā pay/â care/ä father/ĕ pet/ē be/ĭ pit/ī pie/î fierce/ŏ pot/ō go/ô paw, for/oi oil/o͝o book/o͞o boot/ou out/ŭ cut/û fur/*th* the/th thin/hw which/zh vision/ə ago, item, pencil, atom, circus

cloth, as one of those used in making umbrellas, sails, or certain skirts. —*v.* **gored, gor•ing.** To put a gore or gores in: *She gored the skirt.* [SEE NOTE on p. 397]

gore³ |gôr| *or* |gōr| *n.* Blood, especially dried blood from a wound. [SEE NOTE on p. 397]

gorge |gôrj| *n.* **1.** A deep, narrow passage with steep, rocky sides, as between mountains. **2.** The throat or gullet. —*v.* **gorged, gorg•ing. 1.** To stuff with food; satiate: *The woodchuck gorges himself in summer and sleeps in winter.* **2.** To eat gluttonously.

gor•geous |gôr'jəs| *adj.* **1.** Dazzlingly brilliant; magnificent: *gorgeous jewels.* **2.** Extremely beautiful: *a gorgeous girl.* —**gor'geous•ly** *adv.* —**gor'geous•ness** *n.*

go•ril•la |gə rĭl'ə| *n.* A large African ape with a heavy, stocky body and dark hair. ¶*These sound alike* **gorilla, guerrilla.** [SEE PICTURE]

gorse |gôrs| *n.* A spiny shrub with fragrant yellow flowers.

gor•y |gôr'ē| *or* |gōr'ē| *adj.* **gor•i•er, gor•i•est. 1.** Covered with or characterized by blood; bloody: *a gory battle.* **2.** Involving bloodshed and violence: *a gory movie.*

gosh |gŏsh| *interj.* A word used to express mild surprise, delight, disgust, etc.

gos•hawk |gŏs'hôk'| *n.* A large hawk with broad, rounded wings.

gos•ling |gŏz'lĭng| *n.* A young goose.

gos•pel |gŏs'pəl| *n.* **1.** The basic message of Christianity, that Christ came to the earth to save men. **2. Gospel.** Any of the four original accounts of the life of Christ in the New Testament, by Matthew, Mark, Luke, and John. **3.** *Informal.* Something unquestionably true: *He took their words as gospel.*

gos•sa•mer |gŏs'ə mər| *n.* **1.** Fine, silky strands spun by a spider. **2.** A soft, sheer, gauzy cloth. —*adj.* Light, thin, and delicate.

gos•sip |gŏs'əp| *n.* **1.** Trivial talk, often involving rumors of a personal or sensational nature. **2.** A person who habitually engages in such talk. —***modifier:*** *a gossip columnist.* —*v.* To engage in or spread gossip. —**gos'sip•y** *adj.*

got |gŏt|. Past tense and a past participle of **get.**

Goth |gŏth| *n.* A member of a Germanic people that invaded the Roman Empire in the third and fourth centuries A.D.

Goth•ic |gŏth'ĭk| *adj.* **1.** Of the Goths or their language or culture. **2.** Of a style of architecture prevalent in western Europe from the 12th through the 15th century, marked by pointed arches, flying buttresses, and much ornamental carving. **3.** Of a style of fiction of the 18th and 19th centuries that emphasized the grotesque and mysterious: *a Gothic novel.* —*n.* The Germanic language of the Goths.

got•ten |gŏt'n|. A past participle of **get.**

gouge |gouj| *n.* A chisel with a rounded blade in the shape of a long narrow scoop used for cutting grooves in wood. —*v.* **gouged, goug•ing. 1.** To cut, scoop out, or make grooves in with or as if with a gouge. **2.** To force out with one's thumb: *gouged out an eye.* **3.** To demand or extort extremely high prices from: *landlords gouging their tenants.* —**goug'er** *n.*

gou•lash |go͞o'läsh'| *or* |-lăsh'| *n.* A meat stew seasoned with paprika.

gou•ra•mi |go͝o rä'mē| *or* |go͝or'ə mē| *n., pl.* **gou•ra•mis.** Any of several freshwater fish of tropical Asia. Some kinds are brightly colored and are popular in home aquariums.

gourd |gôrd| *or* |gōrd| *or* |go͝ord| *n.* **1.** The fruit of a vine related to the pumpkin, squash, and cucumber, having a hard rind and often an irregular shape. **2.** The dried, hollowed-out shell of such a fruit, used as a ladle, bowl, etc. **3.** A vine that bears such fruit. [SEE PICTURE]

gour•mand |go͝or'mənd| *n.* A person who likes to eat well and heartily. [SEE NOTE]

gour•met |go͝or'mā'| *or* |go͝or mā'| *n.* A person who likes and knows fine food and drink. —***modifier:*** *gourmet foods.* [SEE NOTE]

gout |gout| *n.* A disease in which, as a result of faulty metabolism, hard deposits form in joints, especially of the big toe, causing arthritis.

gout•y |gou'tē| *adj.* **gout•i•er, gout•i•est. 1.** Of, like, or relating to gout. **2.** Suffering from or affected by gout. —**gout'i•ness** *n.*

Gov. governor.

gov•ern |gŭv'ərn| *v.* **1.** To direct or manage the public affairs of (a country, city, etc.); rule: *govern a country. The king governs well.* **2.** To control the actions, workings, or behavior of; direct: *The Torah contains the law that governs religious Jews.* **3.** To determine; guide: *The prices are governed by the demand for money and its supply.* **4.** In grammar, to require (a noun or verb) to be in a particular case or mood.

gov•ern•ess |gŭv'ər nĭs| *n.* A woman employed to teach and train the children of a private household.

gov•ern•ment |gŭv'ərn mənt| *n.* **1.** The act or process of governing, especially the political administration of an area: *the government of a state.* **2.** A system by which a political unit is governed: *democratic government.* **3.** A governing body or organization. —***modifier:*** *a government official.* —**gov'ern•ment'al** |gŭv'ərn mĕn'tl| *adj.*

gov•er•nor |gŭv'ər nər| *n.* **1.** The person elected chief executive of a state in the United States. **2.** An official appointed to govern a colony or territory. **3.** A person who directs the operation of a business or organization. **4.** A device that automatically regulates the operation of a machine.

gov•er•nor•ship |gŭv'ər nər shĭp'| *n.* The office of a governor or the period during which a governor is in office.

gown |goun| *n.* **1.** A long, loose, flowing garment, as a nightgown. **2.** A woman's dress, especially a formal or fancy one. **3.** A special robe for official ceremonies, worn by graduates, clergymen, judges, etc.

gr. gram.

grab |grăb| *v.* **grabbed, grab•bing. 1. a.** To take suddenly; snatch; seize: *The elephant grabbed the peanut out of her hand.* **b.** To make a snatch: *He grabbed at the chance of going to Europe.* **2.** To eat hurriedly: *He grabbed a sandwich.* —*n.* The act or an example of grabbing.

grab bag. A container filled with articles, such as party gifts, to be drawn sight unseen.

grace |grās| *n.* **1.** Effortless beauty of movement, form, etc.: *dance with grace.* **2.** A charming or pleasing quality or characteristic: *Courage is grace under pressure.* **3. a.** Favor; good will:

He hopes to stand high in his lady's grace. **b.** Divine favor; mercy: *God shed his grace on thee.* **4.** A short prayer of blessing or thanks before or after a meal. **5.** Extra time given to someone before requiring the fulfillment of an obligation, as the payment of a debt. **6. Grace.** A title used in speaking of or to a duke, duchess, or archbishop: *His Grace; Your Grace.* —*v.* **graced, grac•ing.** To honor; favor: *She graced the meeting with her regal presence.*

***Idioms.* by (the) grace of.** By reason or virtue of: *By grace of the jet, an executive can breakfast in New York and lunch in San Francisco.* **in the good** (or **bad**) **graces of.** In (or out) of favor with.

grace•ful |grās′fəl| *adj.* Showing grace of movement, form, or proportion: *a graceful dance.* —**grace′ful•ly** *adv.* —**grace′ful•ness** *n.*

grace note. A very short musical note added to a melody as an ornament, usually independent of the harmony.

gra•cious |grā′shəs| *adj.* **1.** Having or showing grace; kind; courteous: *a gracious host.* **2.** Graceful; delicate: *a gracious willow.* **3.** Elegant; leisurely: *a gracious dinner party.* —*interj.* A word used in various phrases to express surprise: *Goodness gracious! My gracious!* —**gra′cious•ly** *adv.* —**gra′cious•ness** *n.*

grack•le |grăk′əl| *n.* An American blackbird with iridescent, blackish feathers and a harsh, husky voice. [SEE PICTURE]

grad |grăd| *n. Informal.* A graduate of a school or college.

gra•da•tion |grā **dā′**shən| *n.* **1.** A series of gradual, successive stages or steps: *the gradations in shading from light to dark.* **2.** Any of the stages or steps in such a series.

grade |grād| *n.* **1.** One of a series of stages or degrees in quality, rank, value, etc.: *a poor grade of lumber; grade AA eggs. The rank of lieutenant is one grade lower than that of captain.* **2. a.** A slope or incline, as of a road. **b.** The degree to which something, such as a road or railroad track, slopes. **3.** A class or year in a school: *the fourth grade.* **4.** A mark showing the quality of a student's work: *He got a good grade in science.* —*v.* **grad•ed, grad•ing. 1.** To arrange or mark according to quality: *grade lumber.* **2.** To give a grade to: *grade term papers.* **3.** To arrange or adjust the slope of: *bulldozers grading a road.*

***Idiom.* make the grade.** *Informal.* To reach a goal; succeed.

grade crossing. An intersection at which two roads, two railroad tracks, or a road and a railroad track cross at the same level.

grad•er |grā′dər| *n.* **1.** A student in a specific grade at school: *a fifth grader; a seventh grader.* **2.** A person or machine that grades.

grade school. An **elementary school.**

gra•di•ent |grā′dē ənt| *n.* **1.** The degree to which something inclines; slope: *the steep gradient of the hillside.* **2.** A part that slopes upward or downward. **3.** The rate of change, often the maximum rate of change, of a variable such as temperature or pressure.

grad•u•al |grăj′o͞o əl| *adj.* Occurring in small stages or degrees or by even, continuous change: *the gradual slope of a road.* —**grad′u•al•ly** *adv.*

grad•u•ate |grăj′o͞o āt′| *v.* **grad•u•at•ed, grad•u•at•ing. 1.** To receive an academic degree or diploma: *He graduated from college.* **2.** To grant an academic degree or diploma: *The college graduated 100 students.* **3.** To go from one stage to another, usually to a higher or better one: *From his assignment in the branch office of the company he finally graduated to the main office.* **4.** To provide (a straightedge, container, etc.) with marks indicating measures, as of length or volume. —*n.* |**grăj′**o͞o ĭt| *or* |-āt′|. **1.** A person who has received an academic degree or diploma. **2.** A container marked with lines indicating how much it contains when filled to a certain level. —***modifier:*** *a graduate degree; graduate courses.* [SEE NOTE]

graduate school. A school of a university that offers studies beyond the bachelor's degree.

grad•u•a•tion |grăj′o͞o **ā′**shən| *n.* **1. a.** The act or process of completing a required phase of formal education and receiving an academic degree or a diploma. **b.** A ceremony for conferring academic degrees or diplomas. **2.** Any of the marks made on a container, instrument, etc., in order to graduate it: *marked with fine graduations that were hard to read.* —***modifier:*** *graduation day; graduation exercises.*

graf•fi•ti |grə **fē′**tē| *pl.n.* Anything drawn or written, as on a wall or door, so as to be seen by the public.

graft[1] |grăft| *or* |gräft| *v.* **1.** To join (a plant shoot or bud) to another living plant so that the two grow together as a single plant. **2.** To transplant or implant (tissue or an organ) into or onto a part of the body by surgery. —*n.* **1. a.** A shoot or bud that has been grafted onto another plant. **b.** The place or type of connection where such plant parts have been joined. **2.** An organ or a mass of tissue transplanted or implanted by surgery. [SEE NOTE]

graft[2] |grăft| *or* |gräft| *n.* **1.** The act of taking unscrupulous advantage of one's public position for private gain. **2.** The money, profit, or advantage gained by such an act. [SEE NOTE]

gra•ham |grā′əm| *adj.* Made from whole-wheat flour: *a graham cracker.*

Grail |grāl| *n.* In medieval legend, the cup or chalice used by Christ at the Last Supper.

grain |grān| *n.* **1. a.** A small, hard seed, especially of wheat, corn, rice, or other cereal plants. **b.** The seeds of such plants: *a harvest of grain.* **c.** Any small particle similar to a seed: *a grain of salt.* **2.** Cereal plants such as wheat or rye: *a field of grain.* **3.** A unit of weight equal to .0002285 ounce. **4. a.** The markings, pattern, or texture in wood, fabric, meat, etc. **b.** The direction of such markings. —***modifier:*** *grain storage.*

***Idioms.* go against (one's) grain.** To be contrary to one's natural disposition, inclination, etc. **with a grain of salt.** With reservations: *Take everything he says with a grain of salt.*

grain alcohol. Ethanol.

grain•y |grā′nē| *adj.* **grain•i•er, grain•i•est. 1.** Consisting of grains; granular: *grainy flour.* **2.** Having a surface pattern or grain: *grainy wood.*

gram |grăm| *n.* A unit of mass or weight in the metric system, equal to about $^{1}/_{28}$ ounce.

-gram[1]. A word element meaning "something written or drawn": **diagram; telegram.**

-gram[2]. A word element meaning "a gram": **kilogram.**

grackle

graduate

Sense 2 of this verb is older than sense 1. The original expression was He was graduated from college; *that is, the college did the graduating, and the student accepted graduation. But English verbs often switch from transitive to intransitive; the new construction* He graduated from college *is now accepted by 77 per cent of the American Heritage Usage Panel.*

graft[1-2]

Graft[1] *is from Old French* grafe, *which originally meant "pencil," then later "twig, shoot," and then especially "twig used for grafting."* **Graft[2]** *comes from nineteenth-century thieves' slang; it originally meant "work, piece of work," hence "a theft, a crime"; its further origin is unknown.*

gram-at•om |grăm′ăt′əm| *n.* The particular mass of an element whose measure in grams is numerically equal to the atomic weight.

gram•mar |grăm′ər| *n.* **1.** The system of rules used by the speakers of a language for making sentences in that language: *English grammar is quite different from Turkish grammar.* **2.** A description of the rules for making sentences in a given language: *I went out and bought a grammar of French.* **3.** Study of these rules or theory about them, especially as a school subject: *He can't spell but he's a whiz at math and grammar.* **4.** Usage judged with reference to an idea of standard usage: *If I write my paper the way I actually talk, the teacher will flunk me for bad grammar.* —**modifier:** *a grammar book.*

gram•mar•i•an |grə mâr′ē ən| *n.* A person who writes about or teaches grammar.

grammar school. **1.** An **elementary school.** **2.** *British.* A secondary or preparatory school.

gram•mat•i•cal |grə măt′ĭ kəl| *adj.* **1.** Of grammar: *grammatical principles.* **2.** Conforming to the rules of grammar: *a grammatical sentence.* —**gram•mat′i•cal•ly** *adv.*

gram molecule. A mole, an amount of a chemical compound.

grampus

gram•pus |grăm′pəs| *n., pl.* **gram•pus•es.** A sea animal related to the dolphins, porpoises, and whales. [SEE PICTURE]

gran•a•ry |grăn′ə rē| *or* |grā′nə-| *n., pl.* **gran•a•ries.** A building for storing grain.

grand |grănd| *adj.* **grand•er, grand•est.** **1.** Very pleasing; wonderful; fine: *a grand time.* **2. a.** Fine and impressive in appearance; stately; imposing: *The grand figure of the empress appeared at the royal box.* **b.** Magnificent; splendid: *a grand coronation ceremony.* **3.** Designating the highest in rank or most important of a category; main: *the grand prize; a grand ballroom.* **4.** Lofty; noble: *a grand purpose.* **5.** Including everything; comprehensive: *a grand total.* —*n.* **1.** A **grand piano.** **2.** *Slang.* A thousand dollars. —**grand′ly** *adv.* — **grand′ness** *n.*

grand•aunt |grănd′ănt′| *or* |-änt′| *n.* A sister of one's grandmother or grandfather; great-aunt.

Grand Canyon. A huge gorge, 4 to 18 miles wide and 1 mile deep, formed by the Colorado River in northern Arizona.

grand•child |grănd′chīld′| *or* |grăn′chīld′| *n., pl.* **-chil•dren** |-chĭl′drən|. A child of one's son or daughter.

grand•dad |grăn′dăd′| *n. Informal.* Grandfather.

grand•daugh•ter |grăn′dô′tər| *n.* The daughter of one's son or daughter.

grand duchess. **1.** The wife of a grand duke. **2.** A woman ruler of a grand duchy. **3.** A daughter of a czar or of one of his male descendants.

grand duchy. A territory ruled by a grand duke or a grand duchess.

grand duke. **1.** A nobleman ruling a grand duchy. **2.** A son of a czar or one of his male descendants.

gran•dee |grăn dē′| *n.* **1.** A nobleman of the highest rank in Spain or Portugal. **2.** Any person of high rank.

gran•deur |grăn′jər| *or* |-jŏŏr| *n.* Awe-inspiring greatness; splendor.

grand•fa•ther |grănd′fä′*th*ər| *or* |grăn′fä′-| *n.* The father of one's mother or father.

grand•fa•ther•ly |grănd′fä′*th*ər lē| *or* |grăn′-fä′-| *adj.* Typical of a grandfather; kindly; indulgent.

gran•di•ose |grăn′dē ōs′| *or* |grăn′dē ōs′| *adj.* **1.** Large or great in scope; grand: *a grandiose style.* **2.** Affectedly great; pompous. —**gran′di•ose′ly** *adv.* —**gran′di•os′i•ty** |grăn′dē ŏs′ĭ tē|, **gran′di•ose′ness** *n.*

grand jury. A jury of 12 to 23 persons that meets to examine evidence of a crime and determine whether an indictment should be made.

grand•ma |grănd′mä′| *or* |grăn′mä′| *or* |grăm′-mä′| *or* |grăm′ə| *n. Informal.* Grandmother.

grand•moth•er |grănd′mŭ*th*′ər| *or* |grăn′-mŭ*th*′-| *n.* The mother of one's father or mother.

grand•moth•er•ly |grănd′mŭ*th*′ər lē| *or* |grăn′-mŭ*th*′-| *adj.* Typical of a grandmother; affectionate; protective.

grand•neph•ew |grănd′nĕf′yōō| *or* |grăn′nĕf′-| *n.* A son of one's nephew or niece.

grand•niece |grănd′nēs′| *or* |grăn′nēs′| *n.* A daughter of one's nephew or niece.

grand opera. An opera, usually based on a serious subject, in which the entire text is set to music.

grand•pa |grănd′pä′| *or* |grăn′pä′| *or* |grăm′-pä′| *or* |grăm′pə| *n. Informal.* Grandfather.

grand•par•ent |grănd′pâr′ənt| *or* |-păr′-| *n.* A parent of one's mother or father.

grand piano. A piano built so that the strings are stretched out in a horizontal plane.

grand slam. **1.** In bridge, the taking of all the tricks. **2.** In baseball, a home run hit when three men are on base.

grand•son |grănd′sŭn′| *or* |grăn′sŭn′| *n.* The son of one's son or daughter.

grand•stand |grănd′stănd′| *or* |grăn′-| *n.* **1.** A roofed stand for spectators, as at a stadium. **2.** The spectators seated in such a stand.

grand•un•cle |grănd′ŭng′kəl| *n.* The uncle of one's father or mother; great-uncle.

Grange |grānj| *n.* **1.** The Patrons of Husbandry, a farmers' association founded in the United States in 1867. **2.** One of its branch lodges.

gran•ite |grăn′ĭt| *n.* A common, coarse-grained, hard rock composed mostly of quartz, feldspar, and mica. It is an igneous rock and is used in buildings and monuments. —**modifier:** *a granite monument.*

gran•ny or **gran•nie** |grăn′ē| *n., pl.* **gran•nies.** **1.** *Informal.* A grandmother. **2.** An old woman.

grant |grănt| *or* |gränt| *v.* **1.** To give or allow (something asked for): *grant a request.* **2.** To confer or bestow (a right, privilege, etc.) by a formal act: *The Constitution grants certain powers to the Supreme Court.* **3.** To admit as true; acknowledge: *I'll grant that he looks a lot better now.* —*n.* **1.** The act of or an example of granting. **2.** Something granted: *His grant covers five acres.*

Idiom. take for granted. **1.** To assume to be true, real, or accurate without question. **2.** To value too lightly: *We take for granted many of the wonders of electricity.*

Grant |grănt|, **Ulysses S(impson).** 1822–1885. Eighteenth President of the United States (1869–77).

ă pat/ā pay/â care/ä father/ĕ pet/ ē be/ĭ pit/ī pie/î fierce/ŏ pot/ ō go/ô paw, for/oi oil/ŏŏ book/ ōō boot/ou out/ŭ cut/û fur/ *th* the/th thin/hw which/zh vision/ ə ago, item, pencil, atom, circus

gran•u•lar |grăn'yə lər| *adj.* Of, like, or appearing to be made of grains or granules.

gran•u•late |grăn'yə lāt'| *v.* **gran•u•lat•ed, gran•u•lat•ing.** To make or become granular or grainy. —**gran'u•lat'ed** *adj.: granulated sugar.*

gran•u•la•tion |grăn'yə **lā**'shən| *n.* **1.** The act or process of granulating. **2.** The condition or appearance of being granulated. **3.** Something formed by the process of granulating: *a granulation on the skin.*

gran•ule |**grăn**'yōōl| *n.* A small grain or pellet.

grape |grāp| *n.* **1.** A juicy, smooth-skinned fruit that grows in clusters on a climbing vine. Grapes are eaten as fresh fruit and are used for making wine, raisins, and jelly or jam. **2.** A vine that bears such fruit. —***modifier:*** *grape jelly.* [SEE PICTURE]

grape•fruit |**grāp**'frōōt'| *n.* **1.** A large, round, yellow-skinned fruit related to the orange, having a somewhat sour taste. **2.** A tree that bears such fruit. —***modifier:*** *grapefruit juice.*

grape•shot |**grāp**'shŏt'| *n.* A cluster of small iron balls formerly used as a cannon charge. [SEE PICTURE]

grape•vine |**grāp**'vīn'| *n.* **1.** A vine on which grapes grow. **2.** An informal means of transmitting gossip, rumor, or information.

graph |grăf| *or* |grăf| *n.* **1.** A drawing of a set of points that represents a set of ordered pairs of numbers, made by using the first number of each pair as the *x* coordinate of each point and the second as the *y* coordinate. **2.** Any drawing or diagram used to present numerical data.

-graph. A word element meaning: **1.** Something that writes or records: **seismograph; telegraph. 2.** Something written or drawn: **lithograph.**

graph•eme |**grăf**'ēm'| *n.* A letter or combination of letters that represents a single phoneme.

-grapher. A word element meaning "someone who writes or records": **geographer; stenographer.**

graph•ic |**grăf**'ĭk| *adj.* **1. a.** Of written or drawn representations. **b.** Of graphics. **c.** Of the graphic arts. **2.** Of or represented by or as if by a graph: *the graphic scale of a map.* **3.** Described in vivid detail: *a graphic description of the incident.* —**graph'i•cal•ly** *adv.*

graphic arts. The arts that involve representing, writing, or printing on flat surfaces, as painting, drawing, engraving, lithography, etc.

graph•ics |**grăf**'ĭks| *n. (used with a singular or plural verb).* **1.** The art of making drawings in accordance with the rules of mathematics, as in architecture. **2.** The **graphic arts.**

graph•ite |**grăf**'īt'| *n.* A crystalline form of carbon that is steel-gray to black in color and rather soft. It is used in making lubricants, paints, and electrodes. It is most familiar as the material used in lead pencils.

-graphy. A word element meaning: **1.** The process or method of writing or representing in a certain way: **photography. 2.** Science of a specific subject: **oceanography.**

grap•nel |**grăp**'nəl| *n.* A small anchor with three or more claws.

grap•ple |**grăp**'əl| *v.* **grap•pled, grap•pling. 1.** To grasp with or as if with a grappling iron. **2.** To struggle or appear to struggle; wrestle: *grapple with an enemy.* **3.** To attempt to cope: *grapple with a difficult problem.* —*n.* A **grappling iron.**

grappling iron. Also **grappling hook.** An iron bar with several claws at one end for grasping or holding something.

grasp |grăsp| *or* |gräsp| *v.* **1.** To seize and hold firmly with or as if with the hands: *He grasped the sardine by the tail.* **2.** To take hold of in the mind; understand: *You fail to grasp the problem.* —*n.* **1.** A firm hold or grip: *The pirate wriggled out of his grasp.* **2.** The ability to attain; reach: *The victory seemed within the team's grasp.* **3.** Understanding; comprehension: *He has a thorough grasp of our problems.*

grasp•ing |**grăs**'pĭng| *or* |**gräs**'-| *adj.* Eager for gain; greedy: *a grasping moneylender.* —**grasp'ing•ly** *adv.*

grass |grăs| *or* |gräs| *n.* **1.** Any of a large group of plants with narrow leaves, jointed stems, and clusters of small, scalelike flowers. **2.** Such plants in general. **3.** Ground, such as a lawn or pasture, covered with such plants. **4.** *Slang.* Marijuana.

grass•hop•per |**grăs**'hŏp'ər| *or* |**gräs**'-| *n.* Any of several insects with two pairs of wings, of which the front pair is long and narrow, and long hind legs used for jumping. [SEE PICTURE]

grass•land |**grăs**'lănd'| *or* |**gräs**'-| *n.* An area, such as a prairie, covered with grass.

grass•y |**grăs**'ē| *or* |**grä**'sē| *adj.* **grass•i•er, grass•i•est. 1.** Covered with grass. **2.** Of, resembling, or suggestive of grass: *a grassy green.*

grate¹ |grāt| *v.* **grat•ed, grat•ing. 1.** To fragment, shred, or powder by rubbing against an abrasive surface: *Grate the nutmegs into a fine powder.* **2.** To make or cause to make a harsh grinding or rasping sound by rubbing: *You grate like a jay and squeak like a mouse. He grated the two rocks together.* **3.** To irritate; annoy: *That sound grates on my nerves.* —**grat'ed** *adj.: grated cheese.* ¶*These sound alike* **grate, great.** [SEE NOTE]

grate² |grāt| *n.* **1.** A framework or network of parallel or interwoven bars or wires, used to block an opening or to separate things by straining them. **2.** A similar framework used to hold the fuel in a stove, furnace, or fireplace. ¶*These sound alike* **grate, great.** [SEE NOTE]

grate•ful |**grāt**'fəl| *adj.* **1. a.** Appreciative; thankful: *Captain Lewis was grateful to Sacajawea for her bravery.* **b.** Expressive of gratitude: *a grateful look.* **2.** Affording pleasure; agreeable: *grateful relief from the rays of the sun.* —**grate'ful•ly** *adv.* —**grate'ful•ness** *n.*

grat•er |**grā**'tər| *n.* A kitchen utensil with rough or sharp-edged slits and perforations on which to shred or grate food.

grat•i•fi•ca•tion |grăt'ə fĭ **kā**'shən| *n.* **1.** The condition of being gratified; satisfaction: *He had the gratification of seeing his father publicly honored.* **2.** A source of pleasure or satisfaction: *His triumph was a great gratification to his old teacher.*

grat•i•fy |**grăt**'ə fī'| *v.* **grat•i•fied, grat•i•fy•ing, grat•i•fies. 1.** To give or be a source of pleasure to: *They were all gratified with the results of the sales campaign.* **2.** To give what is desired to; indulge: *Man has only begun to gratify his curiosity about other worlds.*

grat•ing¹ |**grā**'tĭng| *adj.* **1.** Harsh or rasping in

grape
Bunch of grapes

grapeshot

grasshopper

grate¹·²/grating¹·²
Grate¹ *is from Old French* grater, *"to scratch"; it is distantly related to the word* **scratch. Grate²** *is from Old French* grate, *"grille," ultimately from Latin* crātis, *"frame, basket." It is related to* **crate. Grating¹** *is from* **grate¹**, *and* **grating²** *is from* **grate²**.

sound: *a grating cry.* **2.** Nerve-racking; irritating: *a grating incident.* [SEE NOTE on p. 401]

grat•ing[2] |grā′tĭng| *n.* **1.** A set of parallel bars set across an opening, such as a window or doorway, in order to block it; a grate. **2.** A **diffraction grating.** [SEE NOTE on p. 401]

grat•is |grăt′ĭs| *or* |grā′tĭs| *adv.* Freely; without charge: *The tickets are given to you gratis.* —*adj.* Free: *The tickets are gratis.*

grat•i•tude |grăt′ĭ to͞od′| *or* |-tyo͞od′| *n.* Appreciation or thankfulness, as for something received or kindness shown.

gra•tu•i•tous |grə to͞o′ĭ təs| *or* |-tyo͞o′-| *adj.* **1.** Given without cost or obligation; free: *gratuitous help.* **2.** Unnecessary; unjustified: *a gratuitous remark.* —**gra•tu′i•tous•ly** *adv.* —**gra•tu′i•tous•ness** *n.*

gra•tu•i•ty |grə to͞o′ĭ tē| *or* |-tyo͞o′-| *n., pl.* **gra•tu•i•ties.** A favor or gift, usually of money, in return for service; a tip.

grave[1] |grāv| *n.* **1.** An excavation for the burial of a corpse; a burial place. **2.** Any place of burial. **3.** Death or extinction. [SEE NOTE]

grave[2] |grāv| *adj.* **grav•er, grav•est. 1.** Extremely serious; critical: *a grave illness; grave danger.* **2.** Serious in appearance; solemn: *a grave man.* **3.** Involving serious consequences; grievous; dire: *a grave error.* —**grave′ly** *adv.* —**grave′ness** *n.* [SEE NOTE]

grave[3] |grāv| *v.* **graved, grav•en** |grā′vən|, **grav•ing.** To sculpt or carve; engrave. [SEE NOTE]

grave•dig•ger |grāv′dĭg′ər| *n.* A person whose work is digging graves.

grav•el |grăv′əl| *n.* A loose mixture of pebbles or small pieces of rock. —***modifier:*** *a gravel driveway.* —*v.* **grav•eled** or **grav•elled, grav•el•ing** or **grav•el•ling.** To cover with a surface of gravel: *gravel a driveway.*

grav•el•ly |grăv′ə lē| *adj.* **1.** Of or containing gravel: *gravelly soil.* **2.** Harsh and irritating in sound: *a gravelly voice.*

grav•en |grā′vən|. Past participle of **grave.** —*adj.* —**graven image.** An idol carved of wood or stone: *"Thou shalt not make unto thee any graven image"* (The Bible, Exodus 20:4).

grave•stone |grāv′stōn′| *n.* A stone placed over a grave as a marker; a tombstone.

grave•yard |grāv′yärd′| *n.* A cemetery.

grav•i•tate |grăv′ĭ tāt′| *v.* **grav•i•tat•ed, grav•i•tat•ing.** To move under or as if under the influence of gravity.

grav•i•ta•tion |grăv′ĭ tā′shən| *n.* **1. a.** The attraction that tends to draw together any pair of material objects. **b.** The force involved in this attraction; gravity. **2.** The act or process of gravitating. —**grav′i•ta′tion•al** *adj.*

grav•i•ty |grăv′ĭ tē| *n.* **1. a.** The force of gravitation, having a magnitude (F) that is proportional to the product of the masses (m_1, m_2) divided by the square (s^2) of the distance between them. In mathematical notation $F = G (m_1 m_2/s^2)$, where G is a constant. **b.** The force that the earth or another celestial body exerts on any small mass close to its surface. **2.** Seriousness; importance: *It was then that the gravity of our deed fell upon us.*

gra•vy |grā′vē| *n., pl.* **gra•vies. 1. a.** The juices that drip from cooking meat. **b.** A sauce made from these juices. **2.** *Slang.* Easy money or profit: *Half is for expenses; the rest is gravy.* —***modifier:*** *a gravy bowl.*

gravy train. *Slang.* A job that requires little effort and pays well.

gray |grā| *n.* **1.** Any of the colors, all of which have brightness but lack hue, that can be made by mixing black and white in various proportions. **2.** Often **Gray. a.** A Confederate soldier in the U.S. Civil War. **b.** The Confederate Army. —*adj.* **1.** Of the color gray. **2.** Having gray hair: *an old gray head.* **3.** Lacking in cheer; gloomy: *a gray day.* —*v.* To make or become gray: *Suffering and anxiety grayed her hair. The driftwood grayed in the sand.* —**gray′ing** *adj.*: *graying hair.* —**gray′ness** *n.*

gray•beard |grā′bîrd′| *n.* An old man.

gray•ish |grā′ĭsh| *adj.* Somewhat gray.

gray•ling |grā′lĭng| *n., pl.* **gray•ling** or **gray•lings.** A freshwater fish related to the trout and salmon, having a large back fin.

gray matter. The brownish-gray tissue of the brain and spinal cord, made up of nerve cells and fibers and some supporting tissue.

graze[1] |grāz| *v.* **grazed, graz•ing. 1.** To feed on growing grasses and herbage: *Cattle graze on the grass.* **2.** To put (livestock) out to feed: *They graze cattle and sheep on the plains.*

graze[2] |grāz| *v.* **grazed, graz•ing.** To touch or scrape lightly in passing: *The suitcase grazed her leg and tore her stocking.* —*n.* A light touch or scrape in passing.

graz•ing |grā′zĭng| *n.* **1.** The act or process of raising livestock that feed on grasses and herbage. **2.** Land used for feeding; pasturage. —***modifier:*** *grazing lands; grazing animals.*

grease |grēs| *n.* **1.** Animal fat when melted or soft. **2.** Any thick, sticky oil or similar material, especially one used to lubricate moving parts. —***modifier:*** *a grease spot.* —*v.* **greased, greas•ing.** To apply grease to.

grease paint. Make-up worn by actors, clowns, and other performers in the theater. [SEE PICTURE]

grease•wood |grēs′wo͝od′| *n.* Any of several shrubs that grow in dry regions of western North America.

greas•y |grē′sē| *or* |-zē| *adj.* **greas•i•er, greas•i•est. 1.** Coated or soiled with grease: *greasy pots and pans.* **2.** Containing grease; oily: *greasy chicken soup.* —**greas′i•ly** *adv.* —**greas′i•ness** *n.* [SEE NOTE]

great |grāt| *adj.* **great•er, great•est. 1. a.** Large in size; notably big: *a great prairie.* **b.** Large in quantity or number: *great herds of animals.* **c.** Larger than others of the same or a similar kind: *a great horned owl.* **2.** Remarkable or outstanding in degree, extent, etc.: *a great crisis.* **3.** Important; significant: *a great work of art.* **4.** Prominent; famous; distinguished: *a great man.* **5.** Elaborate; intricate: *in great detail.* **6. a.** Doing something very skillfully: *a great tennis player.* **b.** Being something to a high degree: *a great eater.* **7.** *Informal.* Wonderful; very good: *a great party; a great time.* —*n.* Someone or something that is great: *one of the all-time greats of college football.* ¶*These sound alike* **great, grate.** —**great′ness** *n.*

great-aunt |grāt′ănt′| *or* |-änt′| *n.* A grandaunt.

Great Brit•ain |brĭt′n|. An island off the west-

grave[1-2-3]

Grave[1] *was* græf *in Old English; it is descended from prehistoric Germanic* graba, *"a digging, a dug-out hole, a burial."* **Grave[3]** *was* grafan *in Old English, from Germanic* graban, *"to dig or carve."* Graba *and* graban *are closely related.* **Grave[2]** *is from Latin* gravis, *"heavy," also "weighty, serious, solemn."*

grease paint

greasy

Two pronunciations are shown for this word: /grē′sē/ *and* /grē′zē/. *Specialists in American dialects showed long ago that in general the North prefers* /grē′sē/, *and the South prefers* /grē′zē/. *It has even been possible to draw on the map a continuous line, called an* **isogloss,** *stretching (so far) from New York State to Nebraska, north of which the pronunciation* /grē′sē/ *is most common and south of which you find* /grē′zē/.

ă pat/ā pay/â care/ä father/ĕ pet/ ē be/ĭ pit/ī pie/î fierce/ŏ pot/ ō go/ô paw, for/oi oil/o͝o book/ o͞o boot/ou out/ŭ cut/û fur/ *th* the/th thin/hw which/zh vision/ ə ago, item, pencil, atom, circus

ern coast of Europe, comprising England, Scotland, and Wales. [SEE NOTE]

great circle. A circle drawn on a sphere in such a way that one of its diameters passes through the center of the sphere.

great•coat |**grāt'**kōt'| *n.* A heavy overcoat.

Great Dane. A large, powerful dog with a smooth, short coat. [SEE PICTURE]

great-grand•child |grāt'**grănd'**chīld'| *or* |-**grăn'**-chīld'| *n., pl.* **-chil•dren** |-chĭl'drən|. Any of the children of a grandchild.

great-grand•daugh•ter |grāt'**grăn'**dô'tər| *n.* A daughter of a grandchild.

great-grand•fa•ther |grāt'**grănd'**fä'*th*ər| *or* |-**grăn'**fä'-| *n.* The father of any of one's grandparents.

great-grand•moth•er |grāt'**grănd'**mŭ*th'*ər| *or* |-**grăn'**mŭ*th'*-| *n.* The mother of any of one's grandparents.

great-grand•par•ent |grāt'**grănd'**pâr'ənt| *or* |-păr'-| *n.* The mother or father of any grandparent.

great-grand•son |grāt'**grănd'**sŭn'| *or* |-**grăn'**sŭn'| *n.* Any of the sons of a grandchild.

great-heart•ed |**grāt'hăr'**tĭd| *adj.* **1.** Courageous; brave. **2.** Generous; magnanimous: *a great-hearted person.* —**great'-heart'ed•ness** *n.*

Great Lakes. A group of five large lakes in the United States and Canada, comprising lakes Superior, Michigan, Huron, Erie, and Ontario.

great•ly |**grāt'**lē| *adv.* To a great degree; very much: *Families vary greatly in size.*

Great Salt Lake. A salt lake in northwestern Utah.

Great Spirit. A name used by white men for the principal god of any North American Indian tribe.

great-un•cle |**grāt'**ŭng'kəl| *n.* A granduncle.

grebe |grēb| *n.* A diving bird with a pointed bill and fleshy flaps along each toe. [SEE PICTURE]

Gre•cian |**grē'**shən| *adj.* Greek. —*n.* A native of Greece.

Greece |grēs|. A country in southeastern Europe, bounded by the Mediterranean, Ionian, and Aegean seas. Population, 9,000,000. Capital, Athens.

greed |grēd| *n.* A selfish desire for more than one needs or deserves, as of food, wealth, etc.

greed•y |**grē'**dē| *adj.* **greed•i•er, greed•i•est. 1.** Filled with greed; avaricious: *a man greedy for money and power.* **2.** Wanting to eat or drink more than is reasonable; gluttonous. —**greed'i•ly** *adv.* —**greed'i•ness** *n.*

Greek |grēk| *n.* **1.** A native or inhabitant of Greece. **2.** The ancient or modern language of the Greeks. —*adj.* Of Greece, the ancient or modern Greeks, or their language and culture.

Greek Orthodox Church. The **Eastern Orthodox Church.**

green |grēn| *n.* **1.** The color of most plant leaves and growing grass. **2. greens. a.** The branches and leaves of green plants used for decoration: *Christmas greens.* **b.** Leafy plants or plant parts eaten as vegetables: *salad greens; turnip greens.* **3.** A grassy lawn or park in the center of a village or town: *the village green.* **4.** On a golf course, the closely mowed area of grass surrounding a cup. —*adj.* **green•er, green•est. 1.** Of the color green. **2.** Covered with green growth or foliage: *green meadows.* **3.** Not ripe: *a green banana.* **4.** Lacking training or experience; unschooled: *green players.* **5.** Not aged or seasoned: *green wood.* **6.** Pale and sickly in appearance; wan: *He turned green at the thought.* —**green'ness** *n.*

green•back |**grēn'**băk'| *n.* A legal-tender note of U.S. currency.

green bean. The string bean.

green•er•y |**grē'**nə rē| *n.* Green plants or leaves.

green•gage |**grēn'**gāj'| *n.* A sweet plum with yellowish-green skin.

green•gro•cer |**grēn'**grō'sər| *n. Chiefly British.* A person who sells fresh fruit and vegetables.

green•horn |**grēn'**hôrn'| *n.* An inexperienced or immature person who is easily fooled.

green•house |**grēn'**hous'| *n., pl.* **-hous•es** |-hou'-zĭz|. A room or building with a glass roof and sides, used for growing plants that need an even, usually warm temperature.

greenhouse effect. The heating of the earth's atmosphere that occurs when infrared radiation from the sun passes through the atomosphere and strikes the earth's surface. This radiation loses some of its energy and rebounds with a longer wavelength that causes it to be absorbed in the atmosphere instead of passing out again.

green•ish |**grē'**nĭsh| *adj.* Somewhat green.

Green•land |**grēn'**lənd| *or* |-lănd'|. A large island in the North Atlantic Ocean, belonging to Denmark. Capital, Godthåb.

green•sward |**grēn'**swôrd'| *n.* Turf covered with green grass.

green thumb. A knack for making plants grow well.

Green•wich time |**grĭn'**ĭj| *or* |-ĭch| *or* |**grĕn'**-|. The time at the meridian at Greenwich, England (0° longitude), used as a basis for reckoning time throughout most of the world.

green•wood |**grēn'**wŏŏd'| *n.* A leafy wood or forest.

greet |grēt| *v.* **1.** To address in a friendly way; welcome; salute: *a hostess greeting her guests.* **2.** To receive or meet with a specified reaction: *Our parents greeted the news with great joy.* **3.** To present itself to; be perceived by: *A shocking scene greeted our eyes.*

greet•ing |**grē'**tĭng| *n.* A gesture, word, or message of welcome; a salutation.

gre•gar•i•ous |grĭ **gâr'**ē əs| *adj.* **1.** Living in flocks, herds, colonies, or similar groups with others of the same kind: *Zebras are gregarious.* **2.** Seeking out and enjoying the company of others; sociable: *a gregarious man.* —**gre•gar'i•ous•ly** *adv.* —**gre•gar'i•ous•ness** *n.*

Gre•go•ri•an calendar |grĭ **gôr'**ē ən| *or* |-**gōr'**-|. A calendar introduced by Pope Gregory XIII in 1582. It was adopted by England and the American colonies in 1752 and is the most widely used calendar today.

Gregorian chant. The type of plainsong used in the Roman Catholic Church.

grem•lin |**grĕm'**lĭn| *n.* **1.** One of an imaginary tribe of elves whose mischief is said to cause mechanical failures and malfunctions in aircraft. **2.** A mischief-maker.

Gre•na•da |grə **nā'**də|. An island country off the northern coast of South America. Population, 96,000. Capital, St. George's.

Great Britain

In 1707 the kingdoms of England and Scotland were united under the name **Great Britain** *("great" because for the first time the whole island of Britain was one country). In 1801, Ireland was united with Great Britain under the name* **the United Kingdom of Great Britain and Ireland.** *In 1922 the Irish republic became independent, and the full official name was adjusted to* **the United Kingdom of Great Britain and Northern Ireland.** *The following shorter names are also correct:* **the United Kingdom** *(informally* **the U.K.**), **Great Britain, Britain.** *See also note at* **England.**

Great Dane

grebe

greyhound

grinding
Mexican woman grinding cornmeal for tortillas

grip¹/gripe/grippe
These three words are related. **Grip¹** *was* gripa, *meaning "grasp," in Old English. The modern senses of* **gripe** *come from sense 2 of the noun (the* **gripes***); this originally meant "pinched feelings in the bowels" and comes from Old English* grīpan, *"to grasp at."* **Grippe** *is from French* grippe, *"a seizure," which is from Frankish* grīpan, *"to seize." All three words are ultimately from prehistoric Germanic* grip-, *"to grasp."*

ă pat/ā pay/â care/ä father/ĕ pet/ ē be/ĭ pit/ī pie/î fierce/ŏ pot/ ō go/ô paw, for/oi oil/ŏŏ book/ ōō boot/ou out/ŭ cut/û fur/ *th* the/th thin/hw which/zh vision/ ə ago, item, pencil, atom, circus

gre•nade |grə **nād′**| *n.* A small bomb detonated by a fuse and usually thrown by hand.

gren•a•dier |grĕn′ə **dîr′**| *n.* **1.** A soldier formerly bearing grenades. **2.** A member of the British Grenadier Guards, the first regiment of the royal household infantry.

grew |grōō|. Past tense of **grow.**

grey |grā| *n., adj., & v.* A form of the word **gray.**

grey•hound |**grā′**hound′| *n.* A slender, swift-running dog with long legs, a smooth coat, and a narrow head. [SEE PICTURE]

grid |grĭd| *n.* **1.** A framework of parallel or crisscrossed bars. **2.** Any pattern or network of crossing lines or elements, especially when they are arranged in parallel sets: *a grid on a map.* **3. a.** A fine wire screen or coil placed between the cathode and anode of an electron tube in a way that allows the voltage applied to it to control the passage of electrons through the tube. **b.** The terminal of an electron tube that connects to its grid.

grid•dle |**grĭd′**l| *n.* A flat pan or flat metal surface using for cooking pancakes, bacon, etc.

grid•dle•cake |**grĭd′**l kāk′| *n.* A pancake.

grid•i•ron |**grĭd′**ī′ərn| *n.* **1.** A framework of parallel metal bars on which meat or fish may be broiled. **2.** A football field.

grief |grēf| *n.* **1.** Intense sorrow; mental anguish. **2.** A cause of disappointment or sorrow.
***Idiom.* come to grief.** To meet with failure or defeat.

Grieg |grĕg|, **Edvard.** 1843–1907. Norwegian composer.

griev•ance |**grē′**vəns| *n.* **1.** A circumstance regarded as a cause for protest: *legislation aimed at the remedy of basic grievances.* **2.** A complaint based on such a circumstance.

grieve |grēv| *v.* **grieved, griev•ing. 1.** To feel grief; mourn: *She grieved for her dead child.* **2.** To cause to feel grief; distress: *The news grieved her deeply.*

griev•ous |**grē′**vəs| *adj.* **1.** Causing grief, pain, or anguish: *a grievous wound.* **2.** Extremely serious; grave; dire: *commit a grievous crime.* **—griev′ous•ly** *adv.* **—griev′ous•ness** *n.*

grif•fin |**grĭf′**ĭn| *n.* A fabled beast with the head and wings of an eagle and the body of a lion.

grill |grĭl| *n.* **1.** A cooking utensil with parallel thin metal bars on which meat or fish may be broiled. **2.** Food cooked by broiling or grilling. **3.** A form of the word **grille.** —*v.* **1.** To cook on a grill. **2.** *Informal.* To question closely and relentlessly; cross-examine.

grille |grĭl| *n.* A metal grating, often of decorative design, covering a door, window, or other opening.

grill•work |**grĭl′**wûrk′| *n.* Metalwork forming a grille.

grim |grĭm| *adj.* **grim•mer, grim•mest. 1.** Harsh; forbidding; stern: *a man with a grim countenance.* **2.** Uncompromising; relentless; fierce: *a grim determination to succeed.* **3.** Ghastly; grisly: *a grim reminder of the horrors of war.* **4.** Worried; gloomy: *He's in a grim mood today.* **—grim′ly** *adv.* **—grim′ness** *n.*

grim•ace |**grĭm′**əs| *or* |grĭ **mās′**| *n.* A facial contortion expressive of pain, disgust, etc. —*v.* **grim•aced, grim•ac•ing.** To make a grimace: *Father grimaced when he saw my report card.*

grime |grīm| *n.* Black dirt or soot, especially such dirt clinging to or ingrained in a surface.

Grimm |grĭm|, **Jakob.** 1785–1863. He and his brother **Wilhelm** (1786–1859) were German philologists and collectors of fairy tales.

grim•y |**grī′**mē| *adj.* **grim•i•er, grim•i•est.** Covered or ingrained with grime: *The window was so grimy she could barely peer through it.* **—grim′i•ly** *adv.* **—grim′i•ness** *n.*

grin |grĭn| *v.* **grinned, grin•ning. 1.** To smile broadly, showing the teeth: *grin with delight.* **2.** To say or express with a grin: *"Hello there," he grinned. The audience grinned its approval.* —*n.* The facial expression produced by grinning.

grind |grīnd| *v.* **ground** |ground|, **grind•ing. 1. a.** To crush into fine particles: *grind coffee beans.* **b.** To change into or produce by crushing: *grind wheat into flour; grind cornmeal.* **2.** To shape, sharpen, or refine by rubbing or wearing away a part of the material of: *grind a lens; grind a knife blade.* **3.** To rub together; gnash: *He ground his teeth in rage.* **4.** To operate by turning a crank: *grind a pepper mill.* **—*phrasal verb.* grind out. 1.** To produce by turning a crank: *grind out music on a hand organ.* **2.** To produce mechanically or without inspiration, as if by turning a crank: *grind out a book.* —*n.* **1.** A particular degree of pulverization, as of coffee beans: *a fine grind of coffee.* **2.** *Informal.* A laborious course or routine: *tired of the daily grind of classes.* **3.** *Informal.* A student who studies very hard to the exclusion of other activities: *His classmates think he's a grind.* [SEE PICTURE]

grind•er |**grīn′**dər| *n.* **1.** Someone who grinds, especially a person who sharpens scissors, knives, etc. **2.** Something that grinds, especially a power-operated grindstone.

grind•stone |**grīnd′**stōn′| *n.* A round, flat stone that spins on a shaft, used for grinding, polishing, or sharpening tools.
***Idiom.* keep (one's) nose to the grindstone.** To work hard and steadily.

grin•go |**grĭng′**gō| *n., pl.* **grin•gos.** *Slang.* In Latin America, a foreigner, especially an American or Englishman. The word "gringo" is often considered offensive.

grip¹ |grĭp| *n.* **1.** A tight hold; a firm grasp: *a good grip on the steering wheel.* **2.** A manner or power of grasping: *With age, his hands had lost their grip.* **3.** A part designed to be grasped and held; a handle. **4.** Control; power: *firm grip on one's emotions.* **5.** A prescribed method of clasping hands, used by members of a fraternal society. **6.** A suitcase or valise. **7.** Understanding; mastery: *a good grip on French grammar.* —*v.* **gripped, grip•ping. 1.** To grasp and maintain a hold on; seize firmly. **2.** To hold the attention of: *a scene that gripped the entire audience.* ¶*These sound alike* **grip, grippe.** [SEE NOTE]
***Idiom.* come to grips. 1.** To engage in combat; fight. **2.** To confront; try to deal with: *He finally came to grips with his problems.*

grip² |grĭp| *n.* A form of the word **grippe.**

gripe |grīp| *v.* **griped, grip•ing. 1.** *Informal.* To complain in a nagging manner; grumble. **2.** *Informal.* To irritate; annoy: *The new regulations griped the baseball players in all the leagues.* **3.** To have or cause to have sharp pains in the bowels. —*n.* **1.** *Informal.* A complaint; grievance. **2. gripes.** Sharp, repeated pains in the bowels. [SEE NOTE on p. 404]

grippe |grĭp| *n.* Influenza. ¶*These sound alike* **grippe, grip.** [SEE NOTE on p. 404]

gris•ly |grĭz′lē| *adj.* **gris•li•er, gris•li•est.** Horrifying; gruesome; grim: *a grisly murder.* ¶*These sound alike* **grisly, grizzly.**

grist |grĭst| *n.* **1.** Grain or a quantity of grain for grinding. **2.** Grain already ground.
Idiom. **grist for (one's) mill.** Anything that can be turned to one's advantage.

gris•tle |grĭs′əl| *n.* Cartilage, especially when found in meat.

gris•tly |grĭs′lē| *adj.* **gris•tli•er, gris•tli•est.** Of, like, or containing gristle.

grist•mill |grĭst′mĭl′| *n.* A mill for grinding grain.

grit |grĭt| *n.* **1.** Tiny rough particles, as of sand or stone. **2.** *Informal.* Perseverance; pluck: *A good quarterback needs plenty of courage and grit.* —*v.* **grit•ted, grit•ting.** To clamp or grind (the teeth) together, as in anger or determination.

grits |grĭts| *pl.n.* Coarsely ground grain, especially corn.

grit•ty |grĭt′ē| *adj.* **grit•ti•er, grit•ti•est.** Of, like, or containing grit.

griz•zled |grĭz′əld| *adj.* **1.** Streaked with gray; partly gray: *a grizzled beard.* **2.** Having gray hair or other marks of age: *a grizzled war veteran.*

griz•zly |grĭz′lē| *adj.* **griz•zli•er, griz•zli•est.** Grayish or flecked with gray. —*n., pl.* **griz•zlies.** A **grizzly bear.** ¶*These sound alike* **grizzly, grisly.**

grizzly bear. A large, grayish bear of western North America. [SEE PICTURE]

groan |grōn| *v.* **1.** To utter a deep, prolonged sound expressive of pain, grief, annoyance, etc.: *He groaned and groaned, but his toothache wouldn't disappear.* **2.** To make a low creaking sound resembling this: *The oaks groaned in the wind.* —*n.* **1.** The sound made in groaning; a moan: *the groans of wounded men.* **2.** A sound resembling this: *the creaks and groans of the deserted mill.* ¶*These sound alike* **groan, grown.**

groats |grōts| *pl.n.* Hulled, crushed grain, especially oats.

gro•cer |grō′sər| *n.* A storekeeper who sells foodstuffs and household supplies.

gro•cer•y |grō′sə rē| *n., pl.* **gro•cer•ies. 1.** A store selling foodstuffs and household supplies. **2. groceries.** The goods sold by a grocer. —***modifier:*** *a grocery list.*

gro•cer•y•man |grō′sə rē mən| *or* |-măn′| *n., pl.* **-men** |-mən| *or* |-mĕn′|. A grocer.

grog |grŏg| *n.* Rum or other alcoholic liquor diluted with water.

grog•gy |grŏg′ē| *adj.* **grog•gi•er, grog•gi•est.** Unsteady and dazed, as from an illness, a blow, lack of sleep, etc.: *groggy from the flu.* —**grog′gi•ly** *adv.* —**grog′gi•ness** *n.*

groin |groin| *n.* **1.** The fold or crease where the thigh joins the trunk, together with the area nearby. **2.** In architecture, the curved line of intersection of two ceiling vaults.

groom |grōōm| *or* |grŏŏm| *n.* **1.** A man or boy who takes care of horses. **2.** A bridegroom. —*v.* **1.** To make neat. **2.** To clean and brush (an animal). **3.** To train (a person), as for a certain job or position. [SEE NOTE]

grooms•man |grōōmz′mən| *or* |grŏŏmz′-| *n., pl.* **-men** |-mən|. A man who attends the bridegroom at his wedding.

groove |grōōv| *n.* **1.** A narrow furrow or channel: *a drawer that moves in and out on grooves. He has deep grooves of suffering in his face.* **2.** The track on a phonograph record that the needle follows. **3.** A settled, humdrum way of doing things; a routine or rut. —*v.* **grooved, groov•ing.** To cut a groove in. —**grooved′** *adj.: a grooved seam; the grooved surface of a record.*

groov•y |grōō′vē| *adj.* **groov•i•er, groov•i•est.** *Slang.* Delightful; exciting. —**groov′i•ly** *adv.* —**groov′i•ness** *n.*

grope |grōp| *v.* **groped, grop•ing. 1.** To reach about or search blindly or uncertainly: *grope for the light switch; grope for an answer.* **2.** To make (one's way) by groping.

gros•beak |grōs′bēk′| *n.* Any of several often colorful birds with a thick, rounded bill. [SEE PICTURE]

gros•grain |grō′grān′| *n.* **1.** A heavy silk or rayon fabric with narrow horizontal ribs. **2.** A ribbon made of this. —***modifier:*** *a grosgrain tie.*

gross |grōs| *adj.* **gross•er, gross•est. 1.** Exclusive of deductions; total: *gross income.* **2.** Flagrant; glaring: *a gross error.* **3.** Vulgar; coarse: *a gross remark.* —*n., pl.* **gross. 1.** Twelve dozen. **2.** A group of 12 dozen items: *buy a gross of oranges.* —*v.* To earn as a total income or profit before deducting expenses: *Our company grossed ten million dollars last year.*

gross national product. The total market value of all goods and services produced by a nation during a specified period.

gro•tesque |grō tĕsk′| *adj.* **1.** Ludicrously distorted and odd; horrible: *a grotesque monster.* **2.** Outlandish; bizarre: *a grotesque appearance.* —**gro•tesque′ly** *adv.* —**gro•tesque′ness** *n.*

grot•to |grŏt′ō| *n., pl.* **grot•toes** *or* **grot•tos.** A small cave or cavern or a structure built to resemble one.

grouch |grouch| *v.* To complain; grumble: *constantly grouching about the weather.* —*n.* **1.** A person who habitually complains or grumbles. **2.** A grumbling or sulky mood.

grouch•y |grou′chē| *adj.* **grouch•i•er, grouch•i•est.** Sulky; irritable; peevish: *a grouchy tone of voice; a grouchy old man.* —**grouch′i•ly** *adv.* —**grouch′i•ness** *n.*

ground¹ |ground| *n.* **1.** The solid surface of the earth; land; soil. **2.** Often **grounds.** An area or plot of land set aside or designated for a special purpose: *a burial ground.* **3.** Often **grounds.** The land surrounding or forming part of a house or other building: *the school grounds; the grounds of an estate.* **4. grounds.** The basis or reason for a belief, action, etc. **5. grounds.** The sediment at the bottom of a liquid, especially coffee. **6. a.** An electrical conductor that is at the same potential as the earth, especially one that makes contact with the earth. **b.** A large conductor used as a return path for several electric currents and considered to be at zero potential. —***modifier:*** *ground forces; ground transportation.* —*v.* **1.** To run or cause to run aground: *The schooner grounded in shallow water. We grounded our boat by accident.* **2.** To instruct in fundamentals; school: *ground a pupil in the rules of spelling.* **3.** To establish or base (a belief, claim, etc.): *He*

grizzly bear

groom/bridegroom

Groom *originally meant "boy or servant" and is of unknown origin.* **Bridegroom** *was* brȳd-guma, *"bride-man," in Old English; the word* guma, *"man," is not related to* **groom,** *but since* guma *died out as a separate word,* brȳd-guma *was mistakenly changed to* **bridegroom.** *Noah Webster, who knew that this was a mistake, wrote an angry note in his* American Dictionary *(1828): "Such a gross corruption or blunder ought not to remain a reproach to philology," and he tried to change the word back to* bridegoom. *This was one of his less successful reforms.*

grosbeak

ground-hog day
The old belief is that this is the day when the ground hog first comes out of hibernation. If the day is sunny, it will see its shadow and run back into its burrow; this is a sign of more cold weather to come.

ground squirrel

grouse¹

grouse¹·²
Both of these words are of unknown origin, and there seems to be no connection between them.

ă pat/ā pay/â care/ä father/ĕ pet/ ē be/ĭ pit/ī pie/î fierce/ŏ pot/ ō go/ô paw, for/oi oil/o͝o book/ o͞o boot/ou out/ŭ cut/û fur/ *th* the/th thin/hw which/zh vision/ ə ago, item, pencil, atom, circus

grounded his argument on hard, cold facts. **4.** To connect (an electric circuit or conductor) to a ground. **5.** To prevent (an aircraft or pilot) from flying. **6.** In baseball, to hit (a ball) along the ground.

Idioms. **break ground. 1.** To cut or dig into the soil, as in excavating. **2.** To start in on an undertaking. **cover ground. 1.** To move about or travel, especially over a considerable distance or area. **2.** To make headway in some work; accomplish a great deal. **cut the ground from under (someone's) feet.** To ruin someone's argument or defense. **from the ground up.** Leaving out nothing; completely; thoroughly: *learn a subject from the ground up.* **gain ground. 1.** To move forward; make progress. **2.** To gain favor or popularity. **hold** (or **stand) (one's) ground.** To hold one's position in the face of attack or opposition. **lose ground.** To be forced back; retreat. **run into the ground.** To overdo; overemphasize. **shift (one's) ground.** To change one's argument, tactics, etc.

ground² |ground|. Past tense and past participle of **grind.**

ground crew. The people responsible for maintaining and servicing aircraft on the ground.

ground floor. The floor of a building at ground level.

Idiom. **get in on the ground floor.** *Informal.* To work with a project or business from the very start.

ground hog. A burrowing animal, the woodchuck.

ground-hog day |**ground'**hôg'| *or* |-hŏg'|. A day, February 2, that traditionally indicates a late or early spring. [SEE NOTE]

ground•less |**ground'**lĭs| *adj.* Having no ground or foundation; unsupported by the facts: *a groundless accusation.* —**ground'less•ly** *adv.* —**ground'less•ness** *n.*

ground pine. A kind of club moss with stalks that resemble small pine trees and are often used for Christmas decorations.

ground squirrel. Any of several small, burrowing animals related to and resembling the chipmunks. [SEE PICTURE]

ground swell. A movement of the ocean in deep, rolling waves, often resulting from a distant storm or earthquake.

ground water. Water that collects beneath the surface of the earth, some of which feeds wells, springs, etc.

ground wave. A radio wave whose path follows the surface of the earth.

ground wire. A wire that is connected to the ground in an electric circuit.

ground•work |**ground'**wûrk'| *n.* Preliminary work that lays the basis for something; a foundation.

group |gro͞op| *n.* **1.** A number of persons or things gathered or located together: *a group of men on a street corner; a group of islands off the coast of Alaska.* **2.** A number of things classed together because of similar qualities: *a language group.* **3.** A structure formed of two or more atoms bound together in a particular way that acts as a unit and is found in a number of chemical compounds: *a hydroxyl group.* —***modifier:*** *a group discussion.* —*v.* **1.** To arrange or gather in a group or groups: *grouping blocks according to shape. They grouped on the steps of the library.* **2.** To divide, arrange, or classify: *group a class according to reading ability.*

group•er |**gro͞o'**pər| *n.* Any of several large, mostly tropical ocean fishes.

group•ing |**gro͞o'**pĭng| *n.* **1.** The act or process of arranging in groups: *Our system of numerals is based on grouping by tens.* **2.** A collection or assemblage of things, persons, etc.

grouse¹ |grous| *n., pl.* **grouse.** Any of several plump, chickenlike birds with mottled brown or grayish feathers. [SEE NOTE & PICTURE]

grouse² |grous| *v.* **groused, grous•ing.** *Informal.* To complain; grumble; grouch: *The guests groused about the hotel service.* —*n.* A cause for complaint; a grievance. [SEE NOTE]

grove |grōv| *n.* A group of trees with open ground between them.

grov•el |grŭv'əl| *or* |grŏv'-| *v.* **grov•eled** or **grov•elled, grov•el•ing** or **grov•el•ling. 1.** To lie flat or crawl on one's belly, as in abasement; humble oneself: *a slave forced to grovel at his master's feet.* **2.** To behave in a servile or abject manner; cringe: *Tommy groveled before the bully.* —**grov'el•er** *n.*

grow |grō| *v.* **grew** |gro͞o|, **grown** |grōn|, **grow•ing. 1.** To become larger in size as a result of some natural process: *a wart that grew on his finger. Our class studied how crystals grow.* **2.** To develop and reach maturity or adulthood: *The seeds won't grow unless you water them.* **3.** To be capable of growth; flourish: *Banana trees grow in humid, tropical countries.* **4.** To cause to grow; cultivate: *grow vegetables in a garden.* **5.** To produce as a crop: *Our farm grows tobacco.* **6.** To allow to grow on the body: *My big brother decided to grow a mustache.* **7.** To expand; increase: *The market for our company's products is growing.* **8.** To become: *It was growing dark outside.* —***phrasal verbs.*** **grow out of. 1.** To outgrow. **2.** To result or develop from. **grow up.** To develop and reach maturity or adulthood.

grow•er |**grō'**ər| *n.* A person who grows something, especially a farmer who grows a particular crop for sale: *a tobacco grower.*

growl |groul| *n.* A low, throaty sound such as that made by an angry dog. —*v.* **1.** To make such a sound. **2.** To speak in a gruff, angry manner.

grown |grōn|. Past participle of **grow.** —*adj.* Having reached adulthood; mature: *He's a grown man now.* ¶*These sound alike* **grown, groan.**

grown-up |**grōn'**ŭp'| *adj.* **1.** Adult; mature: *She's a grown-up lady now.* **2.** For or characteristic of adults: *behave in a grown-up manner.*

grown•up, also **grown-up** |**grōn'**ŭp'| *n.* An adult.

growth |grōth| *n.* **1.** The process of growing: *the growth of a child; the growth of India's population.* **2.** Complete development; maturity: *full growth.* **3.** Something that grows or has grown: *A thick growth of weeds covered the yard.* **4.** An abnormal mass of tissue growing in or on a living organism. —***modifier:*** *a growth rate.*

grub |grŭb| *v.* **grubbed, grub•bing. 1.** To dig in the ground: *grub for potatoes.* **2.** To work hard; drudge: *grub for a living.* **3.** *Slang.* To obtain by a plaintive request, as if begging: *grub a cigarette.* —*n.* **1.** The thick, wormlike larva of certain beetles and other insects. **2.** *Slang.* Food; victuals: *buy the grub for a camping trip.*

grub•by |grŭb′ē| *adj.* **grub•bi•er, grub•bi•est. 1.** Dirty; unkempt: *wearing grubby clothes.* **2.** *Slang.* Grimy; filthy. —**grub′bi•ly** *adv.* —**grub′bi•ness** *n.*

grub•stake |grŭb′stāk′| *n.* Supplies or funds advanced to a mining prospector or a person starting a business, in return for a promised share of the profits. —*v.* **grub•staked, grub•stak•ing.** To supply with a grubstake.

grudge |grŭj| *n.* A feeling of resentment or rancor: *nurse a grudge against a classmate.* —*v.* **grudged, grudg•ing.** To be reluctant to give or allow; begrudge: *Don't grudge her a few moments of happiness.*

grudg•ing•ly |grŭj′ĭng lē| *adv.* In a reluctant manner: *He grudgingly conceded defeat.*

gru•el |grōō′əl| *n.* A thin, watery porridge.

gru•el•ing |grōō′ə lĭng| *adj.* Exhausting; extremely tiring.

grue•some |grōō′səm| *adj.* Horrible; grisly; shocking: *a gruesome murder.* —**grue′some•ly** *adv.* —**grue′some•ness** *n.*

gruff |grŭf| *adj.* **gruff•er, gruff•est. 1.** Harsh-sounding; hoarse: *a gruff voice.* **2.** Stern; surly: *a gruff manner.* —**gruff′ly** *adv.* —**gruff′ness** *n.*

grum•ble |grŭm′bəl| *v.* **grum•bled, grum•bling.** To complain in a surly manner; mutter in discontent. —*n.* A muttered complaint. —**grum′bler** *n.*

grump•y |grŭm′pē| *adj.* **grump•i•er, grump•i•est.** Irritable; peevish: *Grandpa's in a grumpy mood today.* —**grump′i•ly** *adv.* —**grump′i•ness** *n.*

grunt |grŭnt| *n.* **1.** A short, low, throaty sound, such as that made by a pig. **2.** Any of several chiefly tropical ocean fishes that make such sounds. —*v.* **1.** To make a short, low, throaty sound. **2.** To speak or say with a sound similar to this. [SEE PICTURE]

gryph•on |grĭf′ən| *n.* A form of the word **griffin.**

Gua•da•la•ja•ra |gwäd′l ə hä′rə|. The second-largest city in Mexico. Population, 1,500,000.

Guam |gwäm|. An island in the western Pacific Ocean, a territory of the United States. Population, 105,821. Capital, Agana.

gua•na•co |gwə nä′kō| *n., pl.* **gua•na•cos.** A brownish South American animal related to and resembling the llama.

gua•no |gwä′nō| *n.* The dung of certain sea birds or bats, used to enrich the soil.

gua•ra•ni |gwä′rə nē′| *n., pl.* **gua•ra•ni** or **gua•ra•nis.** The basic unit of money of Paraguay.

Gua•ra•ni |gwä′rə nē′| *n., pl.* **Gua•ra•ni** or **Gua•ra•nis. 1.** One of various tribes of South American Indians of Paraguay, Bolivia, and southern Brazil. **2.** A member of any of these tribes. **3.** The language of this people, related to Tupi.

guar•an•tee |găr′ən tē′| *n.* **1.** Anything that makes certain a particular condition or outcome: *Money is not always a guarantee of happiness.* **2.** A personal promise or assurance: *You have my guarantee that I'll finish the job on time.* **3.** A promise or assurance, such as one given by a manufacturer as to the quality or durability of a product. **4.** A guaranty. —*v.* **guar•an•teed, guar•an•tee•ing. 1.** To render certain; make sure: *His family connections guaranteed his success in business.* **2.** To undertake to accomplish something; promise: *His uncle guaranteed to put him through college.* **3.** To give a guarantee for; assume responsibility for: *guarantee a loan.*

guar•an•tor |găr′ən tər| *or* |-tôr′| *n.* A person who promises to be liable for another's debts or obligations in the event of default.

guar•an•ty |găr′ən tē| *n., pl.* **guar•an•ties. 1.** An agreement by which a person assumes the responsibility of paying or fulfilling another person's debts or obligations. **2.** Anything held or given as security for the fulfillment of an obligation, the payment of a debt, etc. —*v.* **guar•an•tied, guar•an•ty•ing, guar•an•ties.** To assume responsibility for; guarantee.

guard |gärd| *v.* **1.** To protect from harm; watch over; defend: *guard a palace; guard the president.* **2.** To watch over or supervise, as to prevent escape: *guard a prisoner.* **3.** To take precautions: *guard against polio by taking a vaccine.* —*n.* **1.** Something that gives protection; a safeguard; defense: *a guard against tooth decay.* **2.** A person who keeps watch, protects, or controls, as in a prison. **3.** Protection; watch; control: *the prisoner is under close guard.* **4.** A special body of troops, as those connected with the household of a sovereign: *the palace guard.* **5.** Any device attached to a tool, especially a power tool, to protect the person who operates it. **6.** In football, either of the two players on a team's offensive line on each side of the center. **7.** In basketball, either of two players stationed farthest from the opponents' basket. —***modifier:*** *guard duty.* [SEE NOTE]

Idioms. **off (one's) guard.** Unprepared; not alert. **on (one's) guard.** Alert and watchful; cautious. **stand guard. 1.** To act as a sentry. **2.** To keep watch over.

guard cell. Either of a pair of crescent-shaped cells that control the opening and closing of one of the tiny pores on the outer surface of a leaf.

guard•ed |gär′dĭd| *adj.* **1.** Watched; protected: *a heavily guarded border.* **2.** Cautious; restrained; prudent: *guarded words.* —**guard′ed•ly** *adv.*

guard•house |gärd′hous′| *n., pl.* **-hous•es** |-hou′zĭz|. **1.** A military jail for soldiers guilty of minor offenses. **2.** A building that accommodates guards.

guard•i•an |gär′dē ən| *n.* **1.** Someone or something that guards, protects, or defends: *guardians of law and order.* **2.** A person who is legally responsible for the person or property of another person, such as a child, who cannot manage his affairs.

guard•room |gärd′rōōm′| *or* |-rŏŏm′| *n.* A room used by guards on duty.

Gua•te•ma•la |gwä′tə mä′lə|. **1.** A country in northwestern Central America. Population, 5,540,000. **2.** Also **Guatemala City.** The capital of this country. Population, 790,000. —**Gua′te•ma′lan** *adj. & n.*

gua•va |gwä′və| *n.* The sweet, yellow-skinned fruit of a tropical American tree, used to make jelly and preserves. —***modifier:*** *guava jelly.*

gu•ber•na•to•ri•al |gōō′bər nə tôr′ē əl| *or* |-tōr′-| *or* |gyōō′-| *adj.* Of a governor or the office of a governor: *a gubernatorial candidate.*

gudg•eon |gŭj′ən| *n.* A small freshwater fish of Europe and Asia.

grunt

guard/ward

The prehistoric Germanic word ward- *meant "a guard" or "to guard." It became* weard *in Old English and* **ward** *in Modern English. Separately,* ward- *was borrowed into Old French as* guarder, *"to guard";* guarder *was borrowed into English as* **guard.** *Notice that a Germanic* w- *when borrowed into Old French became a hard* g-. *This rule applied only to speech patterns south of a line that could be drawn across France. In the northern dialect of Old French, a Germanic* w- *remained a* w-. *For another example of this rule as shown in English words, see note at* **gage/wage.**

guillotine

guinea fowl

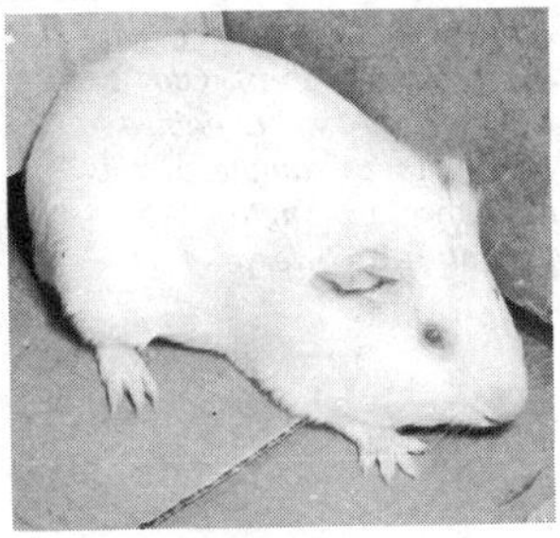

guinea pig

Guern•sey |gûrn'zē| *n., pl.* **Guern•seys.** One of a breed of brown and white cattle raised for milk.

guer•ril•la or **gue•ril•la** |gə rĭl'ə| *n.* A member of an irregular military force that uses harassing tactics against an enemy army, usually with the support of the local population. *—modifier: guerrilla warfare; guerrilla tactics.* ¶*These sound alike* **guerrilla, gorilla.**

guess |gĕs| *v.* **1.** To give an answer, make a statement or prediction, etc., without sufficient information: *He guessed that the Giants would win the series.* **2.** To estimate, judge, or surmise by intuition or hunch: *Guess what I'm thinking. We can only guess at his motives for the crime.* **3.** To suppose; think; believe: *I guess you're right.* **4.** To judge, choose, etc., correctly: *The detective finally guessed who the murderer was.* *—n.* A judgment or estimate arrived at by guessing; a conjecture: *If you're not sure of the answer, at least make a guess.* —**guess'er** *n.*

guess•work |gĕs'wûrk'| *n.* The process or result of making guesses; conjecture.

guest |gĕst| *n.* **1.** A visitor who receives hospitality at the home, table, etc., of another: *Mother invited guests for dinner.* **2.** A patron of a hotel, restaurant, etc. **3.** A visiting participant, as in a television program. *—modifier: a guest house; a guest speaker.*

guff |gŭf| *n. Slang.* Foolish talk; nonsense.

guf•faw |gə fô'| *n.* A hearty or coarse burst of laughter, often expressive of derision or disbelief. *—v.* To laugh heartily or coarsely.

guid•ance |gīd'ns| *n.* **1.** The act or an example of guiding: *The safari depended on the guidance of their African scouts.* **2.** Counseling, as on vocational, educational, or marital problems. **3.** Leadership, supervision: *a program under the direct guidance of the White House.* **4.** Advice or inspiration: *Pray for divine guidance.* **5.** Any of the various means by which the course of a missile in flight can be controlled or corrected.

guide |gīd| *n.* **1.** Something or someone that shows the way, directs, leads, controls, etc.: *a guide to spelling. Her mother was her guide in how to dress.* **2.** A person employed to guide a tour, expedition, etc. **3.** A guidebook or manual. **4. a.** A device, such as a ruler or compass, used to regulate the motion of the hand or to provide a reference, as in drawing. **b.** A device that keeps a cable or machine part from making any but the correct motions. *—modifier: a guide rope.* *—v.* **guid•ed, guid•ing. 1. a.** To direct; lead: *The scout guided them to the secret meeting place.* **b.** To serve as a guide for: *The ranger agreed to guide our expedition.* **2.** To direct the course of; steer: *guide a car down a narrow street.* **3.** To manage the affairs of; govern: *Lincoln guided our nation through a great crisis.* —**guid'ed** *adj.: a guided tour.* —**guid'ing** *adj.: a guiding principle of government; a guiding hand.*

guide•book |gīd'bo͝ok'| *n.* A handbook of information, especially for tourists.

guided missile. A missile whose course can be controlled while it is in flight.

guide•line |gīd'līn'| *n.* A policy or rule, or a statement of such a policy or rule, intended to give practical guidance: *The President presented his new guidelines for the economy.*

guide•post |gīd'pōst'| *n.* A post with a sign to give directions, placed at a fork in a road.

guild |gĭld| *n.* **1.** In medieval times, an association of merchants or artisans belonging to a particular trade or craft. **2.** An association of persons of the same trade, occupation, etc., formed for the mutual benefit of its members, as a trade union: *The American Newspaper Guild.* ¶*These sound alike* **guild, gild.**

guil•der |gĭl'dər| *n.* The basic unit of money of the Netherlands, Surinam, and the Netherlands Antilles.

guild•hall |gĭld'hôl'| *n.* **1.** The meeting hall of a guild. **2.** A town hall.

guile |gīl| *n.* Slyness; craftiness.

guile•ful |gīl'fəl| *adj.* Full of guile; crafty.

guile•less |gīl'lĭs| *adj.* Free of guile; simple; innocent; naive.

guil•lo•tine |gĭl'ə tēn'| *or* |gē'ə-| *n.* A machine for beheading a condemned prisoner, consisting of a heavy blade that falls freely between two upright posts. *—v.* |gĭl'ə **tēn'**| **guil•lo•tined, guil•lo•tin•ing.** To behead with a guillotine. [See Picture]

guilt |gĭlt| *n.* **1.** The fact of being responsible for a crime or wrongdoing. **2.** Sorrowful awareness of having done something wrong; remorse: *He could not bear the guilt of his sins.* ¶*These sound alike* **guilt, gilt.**

guilt•less |gĭlt'lĭs| *adj.* Free from guilt; innocent: *a guiltless person.*

guilt•y |gĭl'tē| *adj.* **guilt•i•er, guilt•i•est. 1.** Responsible for wrongdoing or a crime: *The jury found him not guilty.* **2.** Burdened with or showing a sense of guilt: *a guilty conscience.* —**guilt'i•ly** *adv.* —**guilt'i•ness** *n.*

guin•ea |gĭn'ē| *n.* **1.** A British unit of money equal to one pound and one shilling. **2.** A former gold coin worth this amount.

Guin•ea |gĭn'ē|. A country in western Africa, on the Atlantic Ocean. Population, 4,310,000. Capital, Conakry.

Guin•ea-Bis•sau |gĭn'ə bĭ **sou'**|. A country in western Africa, on the Atlantic Ocean. Population, 530,000. Capital, Bissau.

guinea fowl. Also **guinea hen.** A chickenlike bird that has blackish feathers with many small white spots and is raised for food. [See Picture]

guinea pig. An animal related to the woodchucks, mice, and squirrels, having short ears, short legs, and a tail so short as to be considered nonexistent. It is often kept as a pet or used in scientific experiments. [See Picture]

Guin•e•vere |gwĭn'ə vîr'|. In legends about King Arthur, King Arthur's wife.

gui•ro |gwîr'ō| *n., pl.* **gui•ros.** A percussion instrument that originated in Latin America, made of a gourd with a notched surface over which a stick is scraped to make a sound.

guise |gīz| *n.* **1.** Outward appearance; aspect: *entered the enemy castle in the guise of a beggar.* **2.** False appearance; pretense: *He tricked his partners under the guise of impeccable honesty.*

gui•tar |gĭ **tär'**| *n.* A musical instrument having a long fretted neck and a large, pear-shaped sound box with a flat back. It has six strings that are played by plucking or strumming. *—modifier: a guitar string.*

gui•tar•ist |gĭ **tär'**ĭst| *n.* A person who plays the guitar.

gulch |gŭlch| *n.* A small, shallow canyon or ravine.

gulf |gŭlf| *n.* **1.** A large area of a sea or ocean that is partly surrounded by land. **2.** A deep, wide chasm; an abyss: *the gulf that yawned beyond the cliff's edge.* **3.** A vast difference; a wide gap: *a gulf between generations.*

Gulf Stream. A warm ocean current flowing from the Gulf of Mexico along the eastern coast of the United States and then northeast toward Europe.

gull |gŭl| *n.* Any of several water birds found chiefly along coasts and having webbed feet, long wings, and usually gray and white feathers. [SEE PICTURE]

gul•let |**gŭl**′ĭt| *n.* **1.** The tube that connects the throat and stomach; the esophagus. **2.** The throat.

gul•li•ble |**gŭl**′ə bəl| *adj.* Easily fooled; credulous: *the sale of quack medicines to gullible people.* —**gul′li•bil′i•ty** *n.*

gul•ly |**gŭl**′ē| *n., pl.* **gul•lies.** A ditch or channel cut in the earth by running water, especially after a rain.

gulp |gŭlp| *v.* **1.** To swallow (food or drink) greedily or rapidly in large amounts: *He gulped down his lunch. Taste your food, don't gulp.* **2.** To breathe (air) in deep and hurried gasps. **3.** To utter with a gulp: *"Oh, no!" he gulped.* —*n.* **1.** The act of gulping: *Her ice-cream cone disappeared in one gulp.* **2.** An amount swallowed by gulping: *a large gulp of coffee.* **3.** A deep breath: *take a gulp of fresh air.*

gum[1] |gŭm| *n.* **1. a.** Any of a large number of thick, sticky substances that are produced by various plants and trees and that dry into brittle, noncrystalline solids that dissolve in water. **b.** Any similar substance, such as resin, produced by a plant. **c.** A product, such as rubber, made from such a plant substance. **d.** Also **gum tree.** Any of several trees that yield such a substance. **2. Chewing gum.** —*v.* **gummed, gum•ming. 1.** To cover, smear, seal, fill, or fasten in place with or as if with gum. **2.** To become sticky or clogged with or as if with gum. [SEE NOTE]

Idiom. **gum up the works.** *Slang.* To bungle.

gum[2] |gŭm| *n.* The firm connective tissue that surrounds and supports the bases of the teeth. [SEE NOTE]

gum arabic. A gum produced by certain African trees, used in making pills, emulsions, various foods, candies, etc., and in mucilage.

gum•bo |**gŭm**′bō| *n., pl.* **gum•bos.** A thick soup with okra and other vegetables and meat or seafood.

gum•boil |**gŭm**′boil′| *n.* A small boil or abscess on the gum.

gum•drop |**gŭm**′drŏp′| *n.* A small, sugar-coated candy made of sweetened gum arabic or gelatin.

gum•my |**gŭm**′ē| *adj.* **gum•mi•er, gum•mi•est. 1.** Of, like, filled with, or containing gum. **2.** Coated or covered with gum or a similar material. **3.** Thick and sticky. —**gum′mi•ness** *n.*

gump•tion |**gŭmp**′shən| *n. Informal.* Boldness; initiative; energy.

gum resin. A mixture of gum and resin produced by various plants or trees.

gum•wood |**gŭm**′wo͝od′| *n.* The wood of a gum tree.

gun |gŭn| *n.* **1.** A weapon that fires bullets or other projectiles, usually by the explosion of gunpowder. **2.** Any tool or device that shoots or forces something out: *a spray gun; an electron gun.* **3.** A discharge of a gun as a signal or salute. —*v.* **gunned, gun•ning. 1.** To shoot with a gun: *gun down an escaping prisoner.* **2.** To open the throttle of so as to accelerate: *gun the engine.* —***phrasal verb.*** **gun for. 1.** To seek to catch, overcome, or destroy: *Black Bart is gunning for the marshal.* **2.** To work or aim to gain: *The mayor is gunning for higher office.*

Idioms. **go great guns.** *Slang.* To do or proceed extremely well; be efficient: *His campaign is going great guns.* **jump the gun.** To begin a race before the starting signal. **stick to (one's) guns.** To hold firmly to an opinion or course of action.

gun•boat |**gŭn**′bōt′| *n.* A light vessel equipped with guns.

gun•cot•ton |**gŭn**′kŏt′n| *n.* Nitrocellulose.

gun•fight |**gŭn**′fīt′| *n.* A duel or battle with firearms. —*v.* **gun•fought** |**gŭn**′fôt′|, **gun•fight•ing.** To engage in a gunfight. —**gun′fight′er** *n.*

gun•fire |**gŭn**′fīr′| *n.* The firing of guns.

gung-ho |**gŭng′hō**′| *adj. Slang.* Extremely dedicated or enthusiastic: *a gung-ho worker.*

gun•lock |**gŭn**′lŏk′| *n.* The mechanism in some guns that ignites the gunpowder.

gun•man |**gŭn**′mən| *n., pl.* **-men** |-mən|. **1.** A gunfighter or professional killer. **2.** A criminal armed with a gun.

gun metal. 1. An alloy of copper with ten per cent tin, once widely used in making guns. **2.** Any metal used mainly in making guns.

gun•met•al |**gŭn**′mĕt′l| *n.* A dark gray. —*adj.* Dark gray.

gun•ner |**gŭn**′ər| *n.* **1.** A soldier, sailor, or airman who aims or fires a gun. **2.** In the U.S. Navy, a warrant officer in charge of a ship's guns.

gun•ner•y |**gŭn**′ə rē| *n.* **1.** The art and science of constructing and operating guns. **2.** The use of guns.

gun•ny |**gŭn**′ē| *n.* **1.** A strong, coarse cloth made of jute or hemp, used for sacks. **2.** Burlap.

gunny sack. A sack made of burlap or gunny.

gun•pow•der |**gŭn**′pou′dər| *n.* Any of several explosive powders used to propel projectiles from guns, especially a mixture of potassium nitrate, charcoal, and sulfur.

gun•shot |**gŭn**′shŏt′| *n.* **1.** Shot fired from a gun. **2.** The range of a firearm: *within gunshot.* —***modifier:*** *a gunshot wound.*

gun•sling•er |**gŭn**′slĭng′ər| *n.* A gunfighter, especially one of the old West; a gunman.

gun•smith |**gŭn**′smĭth′| *n.* A person who makes or repairs firearms.

gun•wale |**gŭn**′əl| *n.* The upper edge of the side of a ship or boat.

gup•py |**gŭp**′ē| *n., pl.* **gup•pies.** A small, brightly colored tropical freshwater fish that is often kept in home aquariums. [SEE PICTURE]

gur•gle |**gûr**′gəl| *v.* **gur•gled, gur•gling. 1.** To flow, making a low sound: *A stream gurgled through the woods.* **2.** To make such sounds: *The baby gurgled in its mother's arms.* —*n.* The act or sound of gurgling. [SEE NOTE on p. 382]

gu•ru |**go͞o**′ro͞o′| *or* |go͞o **ro͞o**′| *n.* **1.** Often **Guru.** A Hindu spiritual teacher. **2.** A person who is

gull

gum[1-2]

Gum[1] *is from Latin* gummi, *which is from Greek* kommi, *ultimately from Egyptian* kemai, *"gum."* **Gum**[2] *was* gōma *in Old English and originally meant "jaw" or "roof of the mouth."*

guppy

The **guppy** is named after R.J.L. *Guppy* of Trinidad, who took the first specimens to England.

guy[1-2]

Guy[1] *is probably from Dutch* gei, *"rope used in sail rigging."* **Guy[2]** *has a very odd history. On November 5, 1605, a group of English Catholics led by* Guy Fawkes *nearly succeeded in blowing up the Protestant King and Parliament with gunpowder. In most of England ever since, November 5 has been* Guy Fawkes Night, *celebrated rather like Halloween. Children make figures called* **guys** *out of rags and old clothes, collect money for fireworks, and burn the guys on bonfires. From this,* **guy** *also came to mean "a ragged, weird-looking person," and at the end of the nineteenth century it became an American slang word for "man."*

ă pat/ā pay/â care/ä father/ĕ pet/ ē be/ĭ pit/ī pie/î fierce/ŏ pot/ ō go/ô paw, for/oi oil/ŏŏ book/ ōō boot/ou out/ŭ cut/û fur/ *th* the/th thin/hw which/zh vision/ ə ago, item, pencil, atom, circus

followed as a teacher and regarded as having special knowledge or insight.

gush |gŭsh| *v.* **1.** To flow forth suddenly, violently, or abundantly: *Water gushed from the open fire hydrant.* **2.** To make an excessive display of enthusiasm, sentiment, etc.: *Be sincere when thanking someone, but don't gush.* —*n.* **1.** A sudden, violent, or abundant flow: *a gush of tears.* **2.** An excessive display of enthusiasm, sentiment, etc.

gush•er |**gŭsh'**ər| *n.* A well from which petroleum or natural gas pours forth abundantly without being pumped.

gush•y |**gŭsh'**ē| *adj.* **gush•i•er, gush•i•est.** Given to talking with excessive enthusiasm or sentiment. —**gush'i•ly** *adv.* —**gush'i•ness** *n.*

gust |gŭst| *n.* **1.** A sudden, strong rush of wind. **2.** An outburst of emotion: *a gust of rage.*

gus•to |**gŭs'**tō| *n.* Great enjoyment; zest: *He ate the hot dog with gusto.*

gust•y |**gŭs'**tē| *adj.* **gust•i•er, gust•i•est.** Marked by gusts of wind: *gusty weather.* —**gust'i•ly** *adv.* —**gust'i•ness** *n.*

gut |gŭt| *n.* **1.** The alimentary canal or any of its parts, especially the stomach or intestine. **2. guts.** The internal organs of the abdomen; bowels. **3.** The intestines of certain animals when processed for use as strings for musical instruments or as surgical sutures. **4. guts.** *Slang.* Courage; fortitude. —*v.* **gut•ted, gut•ting. 1.** To remove the intestines or entrails of; disembowel. **2.** To destroy the contents or interior of: *The fire gutted the house.*

gut•less |**gŭt'**lĭs| *adj. Slang.* Lacking courage or fortitude. —**gut'less•ness** *n.*

gut•ta-per•cha |gŭt'ə **pûr'**chə| *n.* A rubbery substance made from the sap of certain tropical trees, used in waterproofing and as electrical insulation.

gut•ter |**gŭt'**ər| *n.* **1. a.** A channel for draining off water at the edge of a street. **b.** A pipe or trough for draining off water under the border of a roof. **2.** A furrow or groove formed by running water. **3.** The trough on either side of a bowling alley. **4.** The lowest social class of a city: *language of the gutter.* —**modifier:** *gutter language.* —*v.* **1.** To form gutters or channels in: *Rain guttered the hillside.* **2.** To melt away rapidly, as a candle.

gut•ter•snipe |**gŭt'**ər snĭp'| *n.* A poor, homeless child forced to live in the streets.

gut•tur•al |**gŭt'**ər əl| *adj.* **1.** Of or concerning the throat. **2.** Produced in the throat. —*n.* A sound produced in or near the throat, as the *g* in *good.* —**gut'tur•al•ly** *adv.*

guy[1] |gī| *n.* A rope, cord, or cable used to steady, guide, or hold something. —*v.* To fasten, guide, or hold with a guy. [SEE NOTE]

guy[2] |gī| *n. Informal.* A man; fellow; chap. [SEE NOTE]

Guy•a•na |gī **ăn'**ə|. A country on the northern coast of South America. Population, 770,000. Capital, Georgetown.

guz•zle |**gŭz'**əl| *v.* **guz•zled, guz•zling.** To drink greedily or excessively. —**guz'zler** *n.*

gym |jĭm| *n. Informal.* **1.** A gymnasium. **2.** A class in physical education: *I have gym at 10:15.* —**modifier:** *gym shoes; a gym teacher.*

gym•na•si•um. *n., pl.* **gym•na•si•ums** or **gym•na•si•a** |jĭm **nā'**zē ə| *or* |gĭm **nä'**zē ə|. **1.** |jĭm**nā'**zē əm|. A room or building equipped for gymnastics and sports. **2.** |gĭm **nä'**zē ōōm'|. A high school in some European countries, especially Germany.

gym•nast |**jĭm'**năst'| *n.* A person skilled in gymnastics.

gym•nas•tic |jĭm **năs'**tĭk| *adj.* Of gymnastics.

gym•nas•tics |jĭm **năs'**tĭks| *n.* Body-building exercises requiring training and skill, especially those performed with special apparatus in a gymnasium.

gym•no•sperm |**jĭm'**nə spûrm'| *n.* Any of a group of plants, including the pines and other cone-bearing trees, that produce seeds that are not enclosed in a fruit.

gy•ne•col•o•gist |gī'nə **kŏl'**ə jĭst| *or* |jĭ'-| *or* |jĭn'ə-| *n.* A physician who specializes in gynecology.

gy•ne•col•o•gy |gī'nə **kŏl'**ə jē| *or* |jī'-| *or* |jĭn'ə-| *n.* The scientific and medical study of the functions and disorders of the female reproductive system and the parts of the endocrine system associated with it.

gyp |jĭp|. *Informal. v.* **gypped, gyp•ping.** To swindle, cheat, or defraud. —*n.* **1.** A person who gyps; a swindler. **2.** The act or an example of gypping; a swindle.

gyp•sum |**jĭp'**səm| *n.* A white mineral consisting mainly of a hydrated calcium compound that also contains sulfur and oxygen and has the formula $CaSO_4 \cdot 2H_2O$. It is used in manufacturing plaster of Paris, plasterboard, Portland cement, and fertilizers.

Gyp•sy, also **gyp•sy** |**jĭp'**sē| *n., pl.* **Gyp•sies. 1.** A member of a nomadic people that originally migrated to Europe from India in the 14th and 15th centuries. **2.** The language of this people, related to the Indo-European languages of India. —**Gyp'sy** *adj.*

gypsy moth. A small moth having hairy caterpillars that feed on leaves and do great damage to trees.

gy•rate |**jī'**rāt'| *v.* **gy•rat•ed, gy•rat•ing. 1.** To revolve or rotate on or around a center or axis. **2.** To move in a spiral or circular path. —**gy•ra'tion** *n.*

gyr•fal•con |**jûr'**făl'kən| *or* |-fôl'kən| *or* |-fô'kən| *n.* A large falcon of northern regions, with white or grayish feathers.

gy•ro |**jī'**rō| *n., pl.* **gy•ros.** A gyroscope.

gy•ro•com•pass |**jī'**rō kŭm'pəs| *n.* A device in which a gyroscope acts to keep a pointer aligned in the direction from south to north, giving a reference for use in navigation.

gy•ro•scope |**jī'**rə skōp'| *n.* A device consisting essentially of a disk or wheel that spins rapidly about an axis. Because the spinning motion tends to keep the line of the axis fixed, the device is often used to provide a directional reference, as in navigation instruments, missile guidance systems, etc.

gy•ro•scop•ic |jī'rə **skŏp'**ĭk| *adj.* **1.** Of a gyroscope or its physical action. **2.** Operating by means of a gyroscope: *a gyroscopic control system.* —**gy'ro•scop'i•cal•ly** *adv.*

gyve |jīv|. *Archaic. n.* Often **gyves.** A shackle or fetter, especially for the leg. —*v.* **gyved, gyv•ing.** To shackle. ¶*These sound alike* **gyve, jive.**

Hh

h, H |āch| *n., pl.* **h's** or **H's.** The eighth letter of the English alphabet. [SEE NOTE]
H The symbol for the element hydrogen.
ha |hä| *interj.* A word used to express laughter, surprise, triumph, etc.
ha•be•as cor•pus |hā′bē əs kôr′pəs|. One of various writs that may be issued to bring a person before a court or judge, especially to determine the right of the law to keep him in prison.
hab•er•dash•er |hăb′ər dăsh′ər| *n.* A dealer in men's furnishings, such as hats, shirts, socks, etc.
hab•er•dash•er•y |hăb′ər dăsh′ə rē| *n., pl.* **hab•er•dash•er•ies. 1.** The goods a haberdasher sells. **2.** A haberdasher's shop.
hab•it |hăb′ĭt| *n.* **1.** An activity so well established and repeated so frequently that it is done without thinking: *The teacher was pulling at his cheek, a habit that meant he was disturbed.* **2.** Customary practice or manner. **3.** An addiction: *a drug habit.* **4. a.** The clothing or costume worn by members of a religious order: *a nun's habit.* **b.** Also **riding habit.** A special outfit worn by a horseback rider. *—v.* To clothe; dress.
hab•it•a•ble |hăb′ĭ tə bəl| *adj.* Suitable to live in: *Is the old house habitable?* **—hab′it•a•bil′i•ty** *n.*
hab•i•tat |hăb′ĭ tăt′| *n.* The area or natural environment in which an animal or plant normally lives or grows.
hab•i•ta•tion |hăb′ĭ tā′shən| *n.* **1.** A place in which to live; a dwelling; house. **2.** The act of inhabiting or the condition of being inhabited: *Scientists expect that nuclear energy may open Antarctica to human habitation.*
hab•it-form•ing |hăb′ĭt fôr′mĭng| *adj.* Leading to or causing addiction: *a habit-forming drug.*
ha•bit•u•al |hə bĭch′o͞o əl| *adj.* **1. a.** Of the nature of a habit; done constantly or repeatedly: *habitual drunkenness.* **b.** By habit: *a habitual smoker; a habitual early riser.* **2.** Customary; usual: *He took his habitual place at the table.* **—ha•bit′u•al•ly** *adv.*
ha•bit•u•ate |hə bĭch′o͞o āt′| *v.* **ha•bit•u•at•ed, ha•bit•u•at•ing.** To familiarize with (something) by repetition or constant exposure; accustom: *We are habituated to the idea that our air and water are polluted.* **—ha•bit′u•a′tion** *n.*
ha•bit•u•é |hə bĭch′o͞o ā′| *or* |-bĭch′o͞o ā′| *n.* A person who visits a particular place of entertainment frequently: *a habitué of nightclubs.*
ha•ci•en•da |hä′sē ĕn′də| *n.* **1.** In Spanish-speaking countries, a large estate; a plantation or large ranch. **2.** The main house on such an estate, used as the owner's residence.
hack[1] |hăk| *v.* **1.** To cut with heavy and irregular blows; chop roughly with an ax, knife, etc.: *He hacked off a branch of the tree. They hacked their way through the jungle.* **2.** To cough roughly and harshly. **3.** To strike the arm of (an opponent), especially in basketball. *—n.* **1.** A rough, irregular cut or notch. **2.** A chopping blow. **3.** A rough cough. **—hack′er** *n.* [SEE NOTE]
hack[2] |hăk| *n.* **1.** A horse or a horse and carriage for hire. **2.** A worn-out, overworked horse. **3.** A person, especially a writer, who does routine work for hire. **4.** *Informal.* A taxicab. *—adj.* **1.** Done by or working as a hack: *hack work; a hack writer.* **2.** For a taxi or taxis: *a hack stand.* [SEE NOTE]
hack•le |hăk′əl| *n.* **1.** One of the long, slender, often glossy feathers on the neck of a rooster or other bird. **2. hackles.** Hairs on the back of the neck that can rise and bristle out with anger or fear: *The angry dog snarled, and its hackles rose.* [SEE PICTURE]
hack•ney |hăk′nē| *n., pl.* **hack•neys. 1.** A horse used for riding or driving. **2.** A coach or carriage for hire.
hack•neyed |hăk′nēd| *adj.* Overused and thus cheapened; trite; banal.
hack•saw |hăk′sô′| *n.* A saw with a tough, fine-toothed blade stretched taut in a frame, used for cutting metal. [SEE PICTURE]
had |hăd|. Past tense and past participle of **have.**
had•dock |hăd′ək| *n., pl.* **had•dock** or **had•docks.** A food fish of the northern Atlantic Ocean, related to and resembling the cod.
ha•des, also **Ha•des** |hā′dēz| *n.* Hell.
Ha•des |hā′dēz|. **1.** The Greek god of the underworld, identified with the Roman god Pluto. **2.** The underworld kingdom of this god.
had•n't |hăd′nt|. Had not.
hadst |hădst|. *Archaic.* A form of the past tense of **have,** used with *thou.*
haf•ni•um |hăf′nē əm| *n.* Symbol **Hf** One of the elements, a silvery metal. Atomic number 72; atomic weight 178.49; valence +4; melting point 2,150°C; boiling point 5,400°C.
haft |hăft| *or* |häft| *n.* The handle of a sword, knife, sickle, or other cutting instrument.
hag |hăg| *n.* **1.** An ugly, frightful old woman; a crone. **2.** A witch; sorceress.
hag•gard |hăg′ərd| *adj.* Appearing worn and exhausted because of suffering, worry, etc.; gaunt: *a haggard face.* **—hag′gard•ly** *adv.*
hag•gle |hăg′əl| *v.* **hag•gled, hag•gling. 1.** To bargain, as over the price of something. **2.** To argue in an attempt to come to terms: *The warring countries haggled over the site for peace talks.* **—hag′gler** *n.*

(1) (2) (3)

The letter **H** *comes originally from the Phoenician letter* hēth *(1). This was borrowed by the Greeks as* ēta *(2) and was used to stand for /h/ (and later for /ē/). The Romans borrowed it from the Greeks (3), and its shape has remained unchanged.*

hack[1·2]
Hack[1] *was* haccian *in Old English.* **Hack**[2] *is a shortening of* **hackney,** *which in turn is from* Hackney, *a place near London where horses were bred.*

hackle
Hackles of a rooster

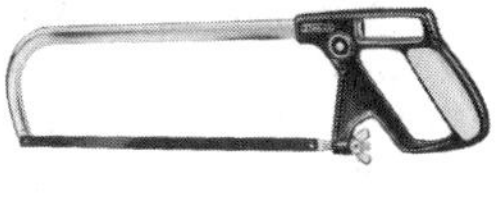

hacksaw

hail[1-2]

Hail[1] *was* hagol *in Old English. Like the modern good-by expressions "Keep well" and "Look after yourself,"* **hail[2]** *originally meant "Be healthy!" It comes from Old Norse* heil, *"healthy," which is closely related to* **hale** *and to* **health.**

Hague, The |hāg|. The seat of government of the Netherlands. Population, 570,000.

hah |hä| *interj.* A form of the word **ha.**

Hai•da |**hī′**də| *n., pl.* **Hai•da** or **Hai•das. 1.** Any of several tribes of North American Indians of several islands off the coasts of British Columbia and Alaska. **2.** A member of any of these tribes. **3.** The language of these tribes. —**Hai′dan** *adj.*

hail[1] |hāl| *n.* **1.** Water that falls to earth as pellets of ice or snow, usually during thunderstorms. **2.** Something that falls with the force and quantity of a shower of hail: *a hail of bullets; a hail of criticism.* —*v.* **1.** To fall as hail: *It hailed all afternoon.* **2.** To pour down or forth: *He hailed insults at his opponents.* ¶*These sound alike* **hail, hale.** [SEE NOTE]

hail[2] |hāl| *v.* **1.** To call to in greeting, welcome, etc.: *hail a friend.* **2.** To signal to in order to catch the attention of: *hail a cab.* **3.** To designate by tribute: *They hailed the old man their leader.* —***phrasal verb.*** **hail from.** To come or originate from: *He hails from Ohio.* —*n.* A shout made to greet or catch the attention of someone. —*interj.* A word used to express tribute or greeting. ¶*These sound alike* **hail, hale.** [SEE NOTE]

hail•stone |**hāl′**stōn′| *n.* Any of the pellets of snow or ice that form hail.

hail•storm |**hāl′**stôrm′| *n.* A storm in which hail falls.

hair |hâr| *n.* **1. a.** One of the fine, threadlike strands that grow from the skin of mammals, including human beings. **b.** A similar fine strand, as on a plant or insect. **2.** A covering of such strands, as on the human head. **3.** A tiny distance or narrow margin: *win by a hair.* ¶*These sound alike* **hair, hare.**

Idioms. **get in (someone's) hair.** To upset or annoy. **split hairs.** To make distinctions that are too small to be important.

hair•breadth |**hâr′**brĕdth′| *adj.* Extremely close: *a hairbreadth escape.* —*n.* A form of the word **hairsbreadth.**

hair•brush |**hâr′**brŭsh′| *n.* A brush for grooming the hair.

hair•cloth |**hâr′**klôth′| *or* |-klŏth′| *n.* A stiff, wiry, scratchy fabric with horsehair or camel's hair woven into it, used for upholstering furniture, stiffening garments, etc.

hair•cut |**hâr′**kŭt′| *n.* **1.** A shortening or shaping of the hair by cutting it: *You need a haircut.* **2.** The style in which the hair is cut: *a short haircut.*

hair•do |**hâr′**do͞o′| *n., pl.* **hair•dos.** A woman's hair style; coiffure.

hair•dress•er |**hâr′**drĕs′ər| *n.* A person who cuts or arranges women's hair.

hair•dress•ing |**hâr′**drĕs′ĭng| *n.* **1.** The occupation of a hairdresser. **2.** The act of dressing or arranging the hair. **3.** A preparation used in dressing or arranging the hair. —***modifier:*** *a hairdressing school.*

hair•less |**hâr′**lĭs| *adj.* Having little or no hair.

hair•line |**hâr′**līn′| *n.* **1.** The front edge of hair growing above the forehead or on the head. **2.** A very thin line.

hair piece. A small wig or thick bunch of real or artificial hair, as a toupee or fall, worn over a bald spot or as part of a hairdo.

hair•pin |**hâr′**pĭn′| *n.* A thin, U-shaped pin of metal, plastic, etc., with open ends, used to hold the hair in place. —*adj.* Doubled back in a deep U: *a hairpin curve.*

hair-rais•ing |**hâr′**rā′zĭng| *adj.* Horrifying; terrifying: *a hair-raising experience.*

hairs•breadth or **hair's-breadth** |**hârz′**-brĕdth′| *n.* A small space or distance; a narrow margin: *Their team won by a hairsbreadth.*

hair•split•ting |**hâr′**splĭt′ĭng| *n.* The act or process of making distinctions that are too small to be important. —**hair′split′ter** *n.*

hair spray. A preparation sprayed on the hair to keep the hair style neat.

hair•spring |**hâr′**sprĭng′| *n.* A fine spring that is alternately wound and unwound by the balance wheel of a watch or clock.

hair•y |**hâr′**ē| *adj.* **hair•i•er, hair•i•est. 1.** Covered with hair: *a hairy bear; hairy leaves.* **2.** Made of hair: *a hairy coat.* **3.** *Slang.* Difficult; dangerous: *a hairy escape.* —**hair′i•ness** *n.*

Hai•ti |**hā′**tē|. A country in the West Indies, occupying the western third of the island of Hispaniola. Population, 5,000,000. Capital, Port-au-Prince. —**Hai′tian** |**hā′**shən| *or* |-tē ən| *adj.* & *n.*

hake |hāk| *n., pl.* **hake** or **hakes.** An ocean fish related to the cod, used for food.

hal•berd |**hăl′**bərd| *or* |**hôl′**-| *or* |**hōl′**-| *n.* A weapon, used in the Middle Ages, consisting of a long pole with both a steel spike and an axlike blade mounted as a single piece at one end. [SEE PICTURE]

hal•cy•on |**hăl′**sē ən| *n.* A fabled bird, identified with the kingfisher, that was supposed to have the power to calm the wind and the waves while it nested on the sea. —*adj.* **1.** Calm and peaceful; tranquil. **2.** Prosperous: *halcyon years.*

hale |hāl| *adj.* **hal•er, hal•est.** Healthy; vigorous; robust. ¶*These sound alike* **hale, hail.**

Hale |hāl|, **Nathan.** 1755–1776. American army officer; hanged by the British for spying.

half |hăf| *or* |häf| *n., pl.* **halves** |hăvz| *or* |hävz|. **1. a.** Either of two equal parts into which a thing can be divided, especially either of a pair of subsets whose measure is equal and that form a unit set when taken together. **b.** A part of something approximately equal to the remainder: *the smaller half of a candy bar.* **2.** A half-hour. **3.** In football and other sports, either of the two time periods that make up a game. **4.** In football, a halfback. —*adj.* **1. a.** Being a half: *a half hour.* **b.** Being approximately a half. **2.** Partial; incomplete: *a half-truth.* **3.** Having only one parent in common with another person: *a half sister.* —*adv.* **1.** To the extent of exactly or nearly 50 per cent: *a half-empty tank.* **2.** Not completely; partly: *only half prepared; half asleep.*

Idioms. **better half.** *Informal.* One's spouse, especially one's wife. **by halves.** Partially; imperfectly: *Don't do things by halves.* **go halves.** To share equally. **in half.** Into halves.

half-and-half |**hăf′**ən **hăf′**| *or* |**häf′**ən **häf′**| *adj.* Being half one thing and half another. —*adv.* In equal portions. —*n.* A mixture of two things in equal portions.

half•back |**hăf′**băk′| *or* |**häf′**-| *n.* **1.** In football, either of the two players who, along with the fullback and quarterback, make up a team's offensive backfield. **2.** In soccer and field hock-

halberd

ă pat/ā pay/â care/ä father/ĕ pet/ ē be/ĭ pit/ī pie/î fierce/ŏ pot/ ō go/ô paw, for/oi oil/o͝o book/ o͞o boot/ou out/ŭ cut/û fur/ *th* the/th thin/hw which/zh vision/ ə ago, item, pencil, atom, circus

ey, any of the three players stationed at the beginning of play about halfway between the front line of players and the fullbacks.

half-baked |hăf′bākt′| *or* |häf′-| *adj.* **1.** Only partly baked; not cooked through. **2.** *Informal.* Not fully thought out; foolish: *a half-baked idea.*

half-breed |hăf′brēd′| *or* |häf′-| *n.* A person having parents of different ethnic types, especially one born of a Caucasian and an American Indian.

half brother. A brother related to one through only one parent.

half-caste |hăf′kăst′| *or* |häf′käst′| *n.* A person whose parents are of different racial groups, especially one born of a European and an Asian.

half dollar. A U.S. coin worth fifty cents.

half gainer. A dive in which the diver springs from the board facing forward, rotates backward in the air in a half backward somersault, and enters the water headfirst, facing the board.

half•heart•ed |hăf′här′tĭd| *or* |häf′-| *adj.* Done with or having little enthusiasm or interest; uninspired: *She made a halfhearted attempt at painting.* —**half′heart′ed•ly** *adv.*

half-hour |hăf′our′| *or* |häf′-| *n.* **1.** A period of time equal to 30 minutes. **2.** The point in time halfway between one hour and the next. —***modifier:*** *a half-hour broadcast.*

half-life |hăf′līf′| *or* |häf′-| *n.* The time required for half of the nuclei in a sample of radioactive material to undergo decay.

half-mast |hăf′măst′| *or* |häf′mäst′| *n.* The position about halfway up a mast or pole at which a flag is flown as a symbol of mourning for the dead or as a signal of distress.

half-moon |hăf′mo͞on′| *or* |häf′-| *n.* The moon when just half of its disk is visibly lighted.

half nelson. A wrestling hold in which one arm is passed under the opponent's arm from behind to the back of his neck.

half note. A musical note that lasts twice as long as a quarter note and half as long as a whole note.

half sister. A sister related to one through only one parent.

half-staff |hăf′stăf′| *or* |häf′stäf′| *n.* A half-mast.

half step. A unit of musical pitch equal to about the interval between a B and the neighboring C; a semitone.

half tone. A half step; semitone.

half•tone |hăf′tōn′| *or* |häf′-| *n.* **1.** A picture in which the various shades of light and dark used are produced by tiny dots that are dark and close together where a dark shade appears and lighter and more widely spaced to make lighter shades. **2.** The method or technique by which such a picture is prepared. **3.** The plate from which such a picture is printed.

half•way |hăf′wā′| *or* |häf′-| *adj.* **1.** Midway between two points or conditions; in the middle: *We were halfway between New York and Boston.* **2.** Reaching or including only half a portion; partial: *halfway measures.* —*adv.* |hăf′wā′| *or* |häf′-|. **1.** To or at half the distance: *I'll meet you halfway between your house and mine.* **2.** Very nearly; almost: *She halfway yielded to their requests.*

Idiom. **meet (someone) halfway.** To give up some of one's demands in order to reach agreement; compromise with.

half-wit |hăf′wĭt′| *or* |häf′-| *n.* **1.** A mentally retarded person. **2.** A stupid or foolish person; a simpleton. —**half′-wit′ted** *adj.*

hal•i•but |hăl′ə bət| *or* |hŏl′-| *n., pl.* **hal•i•but** or **hal•i•buts.** A large flatfish of northern ocean waters, used as a food. [SEE PICTURE]

Hal•i•fax |hăl′ə făks′|. The capital of Nova Scotia, Canada. Population, 117,882.

hal•ite |hăl′īt′| *or* |hā′līt′| *n.* **Rock salt.**

hal•i•to•sis |hăl′ĭ tō′sĭs| *n.* Breath that smells unpleasant.

hall |hôl| *n.* **1.** A corridor or passageway in a house, hotel, or other building. **2.** A large entrance room or vestibule in a building; a lobby. **3. a.** A large building for public gatherings or entertainments, as concerts, lectures, etc. **b.** The large room in which such events are held. **4.** A building used for the meetings of a social or religious organization. **5.** A large room for meetings, meals, etc. **6.** A college or university building. **7.** The main house on a landed estate. ¶*These sound alike* **hall, haul.**

hal•lah |KHä′lə| *n.* A form of the word **challah.**

hal•le•lu•jah |hăl′ə lo͞o′yə| *interj.* A word used to express praise or joy. —*n.* The exclamation of "hallelujah."

hall•mark |hôl′märk′| *n.* **1.** A mark used in England to stamp gold and silver articles that meet established standards of purity. **2.** Any mark indicating excellence or quality. **3.** Any distinguishing characteristic, feature, or trait.

hal•loo |hə lo͞o′| *interj.* A word used to get someone's attention: *"Halloo!" he shouted.* —*n.* A shout or call of "halloo": *He gave such a halloo that the men came running from the castle.* —*v.* **hal•looed, hal•loo•ing.** To shout "halloo": *hunters hallooing to their hounds in the woods.*

hal•low |hăl′ō| *v.* **1.** To make or set apart as holy; sanctify: *"We cannot dedicate—we cannot consecrate—we cannot hallow this ground. The brave men, living and dead, who struggled here have consecrated it"* (Abraham Lincoln). **2.** To honor as being holy; revere; adore: *"Our Father which art in heaven, Hallowed be thy name"* (The Bible, Matthew 6:9). —**hal′lowed** *adj: hallowed ground.*

Hal•low•een, also **Hal•low•e'en** |hăl′ō ēn| *or* |hŏl′-| *n.* A holiday occurring on October 31, the eve of All Saints' day. This holiday is often celebrated with pranks and merrymaking by children who wear masks and costumes. —***modifier:*** *Halloween masks.* [SEE NOTE]

hal•lu•ci•na•tion |hə lo͞o′sə nā′shən| *n.* **1.** An illusion of seeing, hearing, or otherwise sensing something that does not really exist; false perception. **2.** A vision, image, etc., that occurs as such an illusion.

hal•lu•ci•na•to•ry |hə lo͞o′sə nə tôr′ē| *or* |-tōr′ē| *adj.* **1.** Marked by hallucination: *a hallucinatory vision.* **2.** Hallucinogenic.

hal•lu•cin•o•gen |hə lo͞o′sə nə jən| *n.* A drug that induces hallucination.

hal•lu•ci•no•gen•ic |hə lo͞o′sə nə jĕn′ĭk| *adj.* Producing or tending to produce hallucinations: *a hallucinogenic drug.*

hall•way |hôl′wā′| *n.* **1.** A corridor, passageway, or hall in a building. **2.** An entrance hall; foyer.

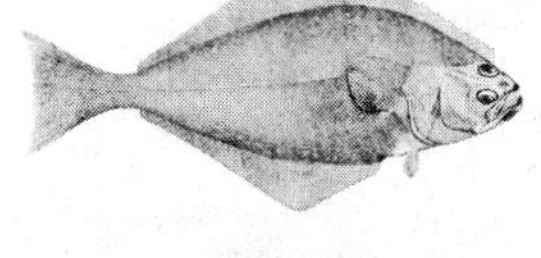

halibut

Halloween

In the old Celtic religion, the last day of the year was October 31, and that night was the feast of witches and spirits. The Church tried to suppress this ancient festival by making November 1 All Saints' Day, *or* All Hallows, *so that the night before became the* Eve of All Saints, *or* **Halloween.** *But the saints have not driven out the witches. The traditional customs of Halloween are a true survival of a religion older than Christianity. Children who dress up and demand "Trick or treat" are acting the roles of spirits in an ancient ritual.*

halo

halt[1-2]

Halt[1] *is from German* halt, *"Stop!"* **Halt[2]** *was* healtian *in Old English and originally meant "to walk as if with a broken leg."*

halter

hamper[1-2]

Hamper[1] *first appeared in the fourteenth century; its origin is unknown.* **Hamper[2]** *is from Norman French* hanaper, *"a kind of wicker basket."*

ă pat/ā pay/â care/ä father/ĕ pet/ ē be/ĭ pit/ī pie/î fierce/ŏ pot/ ō go/ô paw, for/oi oil/ŏŏ book/ ōō boot/ou out/ŭ cut/û fur/ *th* the/th thin/hw which/zh vision/ ə ago, item, pencil, atom, circus

ha•lo |hā'lō| *n., pl.* **ha•los** or **ha•loes. 1.** A circular band of light that surrounds the image of a light source, resulting from various effects such as reflection and refraction. **2.** A ring of light surrounding the heads or bodies of sacred figures, as in religious paintings. [SEE PICTURE]

hal•o•gen |hăl'ə jən| *n.* A group of elements composed of fluorine, chlorine, bromine, iodine, and astatine. These are considered a group because of similarities in their chemical and physical properties.

halt[1] |hôlt| *n.* A suspension of movement or progress; a temporary stop; a pause. —*v.* To come or bring to a stop: *The army halted for two days of rest. The government hopes to halt inflation this year.* [SEE NOTE]

halt[2] |hôlt| *v.* **1.** To proceed or act with uncertainty or indecision; waver. **2.** To limp or hobble, as a cripple. —**halt'ing** *adj.: a halting voice.* —*adj. Archaic.* Lame; crippled. [SEE NOTE]

hal•ter |hôl'tər| *n.* **1.** A device of rope or leather straps that fits around the head or neck of an animal, such as a horse, and can be used to lead or secure it. **2.** A rope with a noose used for execution by hanging. **3.** A blouse with a band that loops around the neck, leaving the back, arms, and shoulders bare. [SEE PICTURE]

halve |hăv| *or* |häv| *v.* **halved, halv•ing. 1. a.** To divide or separate into two equal portions or parts: *halve a cake.* **b.** To divide by two: *halve a number.* **2.** To reduce or lessen by half: *halve prices.* ¶ *These sound alike* **halve, have.**

halves |hăvz| *or* |hävz| *n.* Plural of **half.**

hal•yard |hăl'yərd| *n.* A rope used to raise or lower a sail or flag.

ham |hăm| *n.* **1.** The thigh of the hind leg of certain animals, especially of a hog. **2.** The meat from the thigh of a hog, often smoked or dried. **3.** The back of the knee or thigh. **4.** *Slang.* **a.** An actor who overacts or a performer who exaggerates. **b.** Any person who, liking attention, makes himself ridiculous or conspicuous. **5.** *Informal.* A person licensed to operate an amateur radio station. —***modifier:*** *a ham roast; a ham actor.* —*v.* **hammed, ham•ming.** *Slang.* To exaggerate or overdo (a role, line, etc.); overact.

Ham•burg |hăm'bûrg'|. A city of northern West Germany. Population, 1,850,000.

ham•burg•er |hăm'bûr'gər| *n.* **1.** Ground meat, usually beef. **2.** A cooked patty of such meat. **3.** A sandwich made with such a patty, usually in a roll or bun. —***modifier:*** *a hamburger bun.*

hame |hām| *n.* One of the two curved wooden or metal pieces of a harness that fit around the neck of a draft animal and to which the traces are attached.

Ham•il•ton |hăm'əl tən|. The capital of Bermuda. Population, 2,800.

Ham•il•ton |hăm'əl tən|, **Alexander.** 1755–1804. American Revolutionary statesman; first Secretary of the Treasury.

ham•let |hăm'lĭt| *n.* A small village.

Ham•let |hăm'lĭt|. The hero of Shakespeare's tragedy *Hamlet.*

ham•mer |hăm'ər| *n.* **1.** A hand tool consisting of an iron head attached to a wooden handle, used chiefly for driving in nails or for pounding and shaping metals. **2.** Any of a number of similar devices: **a.** The part of a gun that strikes the firing pin or percussion cap, causing it to go off. **b.** One of the padded wooden pieces that strike the strings of a piano. **c.** A device for striking a bell or gong. **3.** A metal ball weighing 16 pounds and having a long wire handle by which it is thrown for distance in an athletic contest. **4.** The largest of three small bones in the middle ear that transmit vibrations to the inner ear. —*v.* **1.** To pound or drive in with a hammer: *hammer a nail.* **2.** To beat into shape or flatten with a hammer: *hammer out a dent in a fender.* **3.** To deal repeated blows; pummel: *hammer on a door.* **4.** To impress by continual repetition. **5.** *Informal.* To work diligently and persistently: *He hammered away at his homework.* **6.** *Informal.* To fashion or devise after great effort: *The diplomats hammered out all the difficulties before the treaty was signed.*

ham•mer•head |hăm'ər hĕd'| *n.* Also **hammerhead shark.** A large shark having at each side of the head a long, sideways projection with an eye at the end.

hammer lock. A wrestling hold in which the opponent's arm is pulled behind his back and twisted upward.

ham•mock[1] |hăm'ək| *n.* A hanging bed or couch made of strong fabric suspended by cords between two supports.

ham•mock[2] |hăm'ək| *n.* A form of the word **hummock.**

ham•per[1] |hăm'pər| *v.* To prevent the progress, free movement, or action of; impede: *Complex economic problems hamper the nation's development.* [SEE NOTE]

ham•per[2] |hăm'pər| *n.* A large basket or similar container, usually with a cover, used for holding laundry or carrying food. [SEE NOTE]

ham•ster |hăm'stər| *n.* A small animal with soft fur, large cheek pouches and a short tail, often kept as a pet or used in scientific experiments.

ham•string |hăm'strĭng'| *n.* **1.** Either of two large tendons at the back of the human knee. **2.** A large tendon at the back of the hind leg of a horse or other four-footed animal. —*v.* **ham•strung** |hăm'strŭng'|, **ham•string•ing. 1.** To cripple (a person or animal) by cutting a hamstring. **2.** To destroy or hinder the efficiency of (someone or something); frustrate.

Han•cock |hăn'kŏk'|, **John.** 1737–1793. American revolutionary statesman; first signer of the Declaration of Independence.

hand |hănd| *n.* **1.** In human beings and similar animals, such as apes and monkeys, the part of the arm that is below the wrist. It consists of a palm to which four fingers and a thumb are attached, and is used for holding or grasping. **2.** A pointer that moves over a circular dial, as in a clock, meter, or gauge. **3.** A style of handwriting; penmanship: *The message was written in a good, clear hand.* **4. a.** Side or direction specified according to the way in which one is facing: *At my right hand you see a box.* **b.** One of the two sides of an argument, discussion, issue, etc.: *On the one hand I think you should go; on the other I think you should stay.* **5.** Physical assistance; help: *Give me a hand with this carton.* **6.** A person who does manual labor: *a hired hand.* **7.** A member of a ship's crew: *All hands on deck!* **8. a.** A person who is relatively skilled in a particular field: *He is quite a hand at plumbing.* **b.** Workmanship; skill; touch: *a master's hand.* **c.** A manner or way of doing or handling something: *She has a delicate hand with animals.* **9.** *Informal.* A round of applause: *The audience gave her a tremendous hand.* **10. a.** A pledge of marriage or permission to marry: *He asked for the hand of the viscount's daughter.* **b.** An agreement, especially a business agreement, in which something is pledged with a handshake: *You have my hand on that.* **11.** In card games: **a.** A player: *We need four hands for bridge.* **b.** The cards dealt to and held by a player: *Don't look at my hand.* **c.** One round of a game in which all the cards distributed are played out: *I'll sit out for this hand.* **12.** Often **hands. a.** Possession: *These books should be in her hands by noon.* **b.** Control; jurisdiction: *You are in good hands.* **13.** Participation; involvement: *One can see the hand of organized crime in the casino's operation.* **14.** A unit of length equal to four inches, used especially to indicate the height of horses. ***—modifier:*** *a hand mirror; hand signals; hand tools.* *—v.* To give or pass with or as if with the hands; transmit: *Hand me the flashlight. He handed the teacher a note.* ***—phrasal verbs.*** **hand down. 1.** To give or pass on, as from father to son: *The tribe handed down the legend from generation to generation.* **2.** To deliver or render (a verdict): *The court handed down a number of important decisions.* **hand in.** To turn in; submit: *Hand in your term papers by May 1.* **hand out.** To give out; distribute: *He stood on the corner, handing out leaflets to passers-by.* **hand over.** To yield control of; deliver up: *Hand over the money.*

Idioms. **at hand. 1.** Close by; near: *remain close at hand.* **2.** About to occur: *Spring is nearly at hand.* **3.** Presently being dealt with: *Let us return to the business at hand.* **at the hand** (or **hands**) **of.** By the action of: *He died at the hands of an assassin.* **by hand.** By using one's hands: *These dresses have been sewn by hand.* **force (someone's) hand.** To force someone to commit himself before he is ready to do so. **from hand to hand.** From one person to another in succession. **from hand to mouth.** With just enough for each day; with nothing set aside for the future: *live from hand to mouth.* **hand and foot. 1.** So as to prevent movement or escape: *They bound him hand and foot.* **2.** In every way; slavishly: *She waits on him hand and foot.* **hand in glove.** In close association: *They worked together hand in glove.* **hand in hand. 1.** Holding each other's hand. **2.** Closely linked or associated; jointly: *Proper diet and good health go hand in hand.* **hand it to.** *Informal.* To give credit to: *You've really got to hand it to him for his initiative.* **hand over fist.** *Informal.* At a tremendous rate: *He is making money hand over fist.* **hands down.** By a comfortable margin; easily: *She's sure to win the beauty contest hands down.* **have a hand in.** To have a share or part in: *I can see you had a hand in this. He wants to have a bigger hand in policy making.* **have (one's) hands full.** To be fully occupied; be unable to take on more duties or responsibilities. **in hand.** Under control: *He succeeded in keeping the situation in hand.* **lay hands** (or **a hand**) **on. 1.** To grasp or seize. **2.** To touch or handle, especially so as to harm. **off (one's) hands.** Out of one's care or responsibility: *At last we were able to get him off our hands.* **on hand.** Available for use: *We always keep a supply of food on hand.* **on (one's) hands.** In one's care or possession, usually as a responsibility or burden: *We've got my mother-in-law on our hands for the weekend.* **out of hand.** Out of control: *The situation is getting out of hand.* **out of (one's) hands.** Not under one's control or jurisdiction: *The matter is completely out of my hands.* **show** (or **tip**) **(one's) hand.** To reveal one's intentions in a given situation. **take in hand.** To take control of; handle; deal with: *We must try to take the boy in hand.* **throw up (one's) hands.** To give up in despair; concede.

hand•bag |hănd′băg′| *n.* **1.** A pocketbook carried in the hand or on the arm, used to hold money, papers, keys, etc. **2.** A small suitcase.

hand•ball |hănd′bôl′| *n.* **1.** A game in which the players hit a ball against a wall or walls with the hand. **2.** The small rubber ball used in this game. ***—modifier:*** *a handball court.*

hand•bill |hănd′bĭl′| *n.* A printed sheet or pamphlet distributed by hand; a leaflet.

hand•book |hănd′bo͝ok′| *n.* A small reference book or manual providing specific information on a certain subject.

hand•cart |hănd′kärt′| *n.* A small, usually two-wheeled cart pushed or pulled by hand.

hand•cuff |hănd′kŭf′| *n.* Often **handcuffs.** One of a pair of metal bracelets that are chained together and that can be locked around the wrists; manacle. *—v.* To put a handcuff or handcuffs on: *The sheriff handcuffed the prisoner.* [SEE PICTURE]

handcuff

hand•ed |hăn′dĭd| *adj.* **1.** Using or designed for use by one hand in preference to the other: *a left-handed pitcher; a left-handed golf club.* **2.** Having or requiring a particular number of hands: *a four-handed card game.*

Han•del |hăn′dl|, **George Frederick.** 1685–1759. German-born British composer.

hand•ful |hănd′fo͝ol′| *n.* **1.** The approximate amount or number of something that can be held in the hand: *a handful of coins.* **2.** A small but unspecified quantity or number: *a handful of people.* **3.** *Informal.* Someone or something that is too difficult to control or handle easily.

hand•i•cap |hăn′dē kăp′| *n.* **1.** In sports, an advantage in points, position, etc., given to a contestant who is considered to have less chance of winning than another: *His golf handicap is two strokes.* **2.** A horse race in which weights are assigned according to each horse's estimated chance of winning. The better his chance of winning, the more weight he must carry. **3.** Any defect in the structure or functioning of the body or mind that prevents someone from living normally; a disability. **4.** A disadvantage that makes progress or success more difficult; a hindrance: *We achieved our goal despite many handicaps.* *—v.* **hand•i•capped, hand•i•cap•ping.** To put at a disadvantage; hinder; impede.

hand•i•capped |hăn′dē kăpt′| *adj.* Suffering from or affected with a handicap; disabled or crippled. *—n.* Handicapped persons in general.

hand•i•craft |hăn′dē krăft′| *or* |-kräft′| *n.* **1.** A trade, craft, or occupation requiring skilled use of the hands, as weaving, basketry, etc. **2.** Often

handlebar mustache

handstand

handicrafts. The work produced by hand: *The shop sells handicrafts from many countries.*

hand•i•ly |hăn′dĭ lē| *or* |hăn′dl ē| *adv.* **1.** In a skillful manner: *He steered the sleigh handily.* **2.** Easily: *He won the race handily.*

hand•i•work |hăn′dē wûrk′| *n.* **1.** Work performed by hand or the objects produced by hand. **2. a.** Something accomplished by a single person's efforts: *The plot showed the handiwork of a great politician.* **b.** The result of such work: *This quilt was the handiwork of her grandmother.*

hand•ker•chief |hăng′kər chĭf| *or* |-chēf′| *n.* **1.** A small square of cloth used to wipe the nose, eyes, brow, etc., sometimes carried for decoration. **2.** A kerchief or scarf.

han•dle |hăn′dl| *n.* The part of a tool, door, container, etc., that is held, turned, or pulled with the hand. —*v.* **han•dled, han•dling. 1.** To touch, hold, or turn with the hands: *Please do not handle the merchandise.* **2.** To operate with the hands; manipulate: *If you eat in a Japanese restaurant, you must know how to handle chopsticks.* **3.** To be capable of being operated, manipulated, etc.: *The car handles easily.* **4.** To deal in; buy and sell: *Drugstores handle a wide variety of goods.* **5.** To deal with; cope with: *How do you handle a problem like this?*

***Idiom.* fly off the handle.** *Informal.* To fly into a rage; lose one's temper.

han•dle•bar |hăn′dl bär′| *n.* **1.** Often **handlebars.** A curved metal bar for steering a bicycle, motorcycle, etc. **2.** Also **handlebar mustache.** A long, curved mustache resembling a handlebar. [SEE PICTURE]

han•dler |hănd′lər| *n.* **1.** A person who handles someone or something. **2.** A person who trains a dog, horse, etc., and exhibits him in shows. **3.** A person who acts as the trainer or second of a boxer.

hand•made |hănd′mād′| *adj.* Made or prepared by hand rather than by machine.

hand•maid•en |hănd′mād′n| *n.* A female servant or attendant; a personal maid.

hand-me-down |hănd′mē doun′| *n. Informal.* Something, especially an article of clothing, passed on from one person to another.

hand•out |hănd′out′| *n.* **1.** Food, clothing, or money given to a beggar. **2.** A folder or leaflet circulated free of charge.

hand-pick |hănd′pĭk′| *v.* To select carefully for a special purpose. —**hand′-picked′** *adj.*: *a hand-picked committee.*

hand•rail |hănd′rāl′| *n.* A narrow rail to be grasped with the hand for support.

hand•saw |hănd′sô′| *n.* A saw used with one hand.

hand•shake |hănd′shāk′| *n.* The act or an example of grasping a person's right hand as a gesture of greeting, congratulation, etc.

hand•some |hăn′səm| *adj.* **hand•som•er, hand•som•est. 1.** Pleasing in appearance; good-looking: *a handsome lad; a handsome couple; a handsome new suit.* **2.** Generous; liberal: *a handsome reward.* ¶*These sound alike* **handsome, hansom.** —**hand′some•ly** *adv.* —**hand′some•ness** *n.*

hand•spring |hănd′sprĭng′| *n.* The act of flipping the body completely forward or backward from an upright position, landing first on the hands and then on the feet.

hand•stand |hănd′stănd′| *n.* The act of balancing on the hands with one's feet in the air. [SEE PICTURE]

hand-to-hand |hănd′tə hănd′| *adj.* At close quarters: *hand-to-hand combat.*

hand-to-mouth |hănd′tə mouth′| *adj.* Having barely enough; having nothing to spare: *a hand-to-mouth existence.*

hand•writ•ing |hănd′rī′tĭng| *n.* **1.** Writing done with the hand. **2.** The style of writing of a particular person.

hand•y |hăn′dē| *adj.* **hand•i•er, hand•i•est. 1.** Skillful in using one's hands, especially in a variety of ways: *He is very handy with a chisel. My father is very handy about the house.* **2.** Within easy reach; accessible: *a handy supply of medicine. Leave the dictionary on the table where it will be handy.* **3.** Useful; convenient: *An alarm clock is a handy thing to have when traveling.* **4.** Easy to use or handle: *a handy reference book.*

***Idiom.* come in handy.** To be useful, especially at some specified time: *The money is bound to come in handy someday.*

hand•y•man |hăn′dē măn′| *n., pl.* **-men** |-mĕn′|. A person hired to perform various odd jobs.

hang |hăng| *v.* **hung** |hŭng|, **hang•ing. 1.** To fasten or be attached from above with no support from below; suspend: *hang the clothes on the line. A sign hung over the door.* **2.** To fasten or become fastened so as to allow free movement at or about the point of suspension: *hang a door. The gate hangs on its hinges.* **3.** *Past tense & past participle* **hanged.** To execute or be executed by suspending or being suspended by the neck: *The British hanged Nathan Hale for spying. He will hang at dawn.* **4.** To hold or bend downward; let droop: *hang one's head in sorrow.* **5.** To incline downward; droop: *The spectators hung over the rail.* **6.** To remain suspended over a place or object; hover: *Smog hangs over many of our cities.* **7.** To attach to a wall: *hang wallpaper.* **8.** To furnish or decorate by suspending objects around or about: *We've decided to hang the walls with pictures.* **9.** To exhibit or be exhibited: *The museum hung the new paintings in the left wing. Several of his paintings hang in the National Gallery.* **10.** To depend; be dependent: *A great deal hangs on his decision.* **11.** To pay strict attention: *He hung on every word.* —***phrasal verbs.* hang around.** *Informal.* **1.** To spend time idly; loiter: *I think I'll hang around a while.* **2.** To keep company: *hang around with odd characters.* **hang back.** To show unwillingness to do something; hesitate; hold back. **hang on. 1.** To cling tightly to something: *"Hang on to the rope," the guide said.* **2.** To remain on the telephone; hold the line. **3.** To last; continue: *This fever keeps hanging on.* **hang onto.** To hold or cling tightly to something: *Hang onto the rope.* **hang out.** *Slang.* To spend one's free time in a certain place. **hang up.** To end a telephone conversation. —*n.* **1.** The way in which something hangs. **2.** *Informal.* The proper way of doing or using something; knack: *I can't get the hang of this new bicycle.*

***Idioms.* hang by a thread.** To be in an extremely precarious position. **hang fire.** To be slow in firing, as a gun. **hang over (one's) head.** To be or seem to be an imminent danger, threat, etc., to.

ă pat/ā pay/â care/ä father/ĕ pet/ē be/ĭ pit/ī pie/î fierce/ŏ pot/ō go/ô paw, for/oi oil/ŏŏ book/ōō boot/ou out/ŭ cut/û fur/*th* the/th thin/hw which/zh vision/ə ago, item, pencil, atom, circus

han•gar |hăng′ər| *n.* A building used for housing or repairing aircraft. ¶*These sound alike* **hangar, hanger.**

hang•dog |hăng′dôg′| *or* |-dŏg′| *adj.* **1.** Ashamed or guilty: *a hangdog look on his face.* **2.** Downcast; intimidated.

hang•er |hăng′ər| *n.* **1.** A frame, hook, or trap on which an article of clothing can be hung. **2.** A person who hangs something. ¶*These sound alike* **hanger, hangar.**

hang•er-on |hăng′ər ŏn′| *or* |-ôn′| *n., pl.* **hang•ers-on.** A person who cultivates the friendship of another, more influential person in the hope of achieving personal gain; a parasite.

hang•ing |hăng′ĭng| *n.* **1.** Execution on the gallows: *death by hanging; witness a hanging.* **2.** Often **hangings.** Something hung, as curtains, drapes, or tapestries: *wall hangings.* —*adj.* **1.** Suspended from above: *a hanging lamp; hanging moss.* **2.** Situated on a steep slope or on top of a building or some other high place: *the Hanging Gardens of Babylon.*

hang•man |hăng′mən| *n., pl.* **-men** |-mən|. A man who is employed to execute convicted criminals by hanging.

hang•nail |hăng′nāl′| *n.* A small flap of dead skin that hangs from the side or base of a fingernail.

hang•out |hăng′out′| *n. Informal.* A place often visited by a person or group: *The corner drugstore is a favorite hangout of teenagers.*

hang•o•ver |hăng′ō′vər| *n.* **1.** The unpleasant symptoms that sometimes remain after the effects produced by drinking large amounts of alcohol have worn off. **2.** Something left from an earlier time; a holdover.

hang-up |hăng′ŭp′| *n. Informal.* **1.** An inhibition. **2.** An abnormal preoccupation with something. **3.** An obstacle; inconvenience.

hank |hăngk| *n.* **1.** A coil or loop: *a hank of hair.* **2.** A looped bundle, as of yarn; a skein.

han•ker |hăng′kər| *v.* To have a longing or yearning; crave: *hanker to travel abroad.*

han•ky |hăng′kē| *n., pl.* **han•kies.** *Informal.* A handkerchief.

han•ky-pan•ky |hăng′kē păng′kē| *n. Informal.* Dishonest or mischievous activity.

Ha•noi |hä noi′| *or* |hă-|. The capital of Vietnam. Population, 2,571,000.

Han•sen's disease |hăn′sənz|. Leprosy.

han•som |hăn′səm| *n.* A two-wheeled horsedrawn carriage with the driver's seat high up at the rear. ¶*These sound alike* **hansom, handsome.** [SEE PICTURE]

Ha•nuk•kah or **Ha•nu•kah** |KHä′nŏŏ kä′| *or* |-nə kə| *or* |hä′-| *n.* A form of the word **Chanukah.**

hap•haz•ard |hăp hăz′ərd| *adj.* Lacking any definite plan or order; left to chance; random. —**hap•haz′ard•ly** *adv.*

hap•less |hăp′lĭs| *adj.* Unfortunate; unlucky. —**hap′less•ly** *adv.* [SEE NOTE]

hap•loid |hăp′loid′| *adj.* Having a number of chromosomes that is equal to half the number found in a normal body cell of a given species: *Germ cells are usually haploid.* —*n.* A haploid cell or individual.

hap•pen |hăp′ən| *v.* **1.** To come or pass, occur; take place: *Strange things happen in this world.* **2.** To have the luck; have the good or indifferent fortune: *Did you happen to see Steve anywhere?* **3.** To come upon by chance: *I happened upon an interesting article in the newspaper last week.* **4. a.** To be the fate of; become of: *What will happen to me?* **b.** To be the experience of; befall: *Nothing very exciting ever happens to me.* [SEE NOTE]

hap•pen•ing |hăp′ə nĭng| *n.* Something that happens; an event or occurrence.

hap•pen•stance |hăp′ən stăns′| *n.* A chance occurrence; accident: *by a curious happenstance.*

hap•py |hăp′ē| *adj.* **hap•pi•er, hap•pi•est. 1.** Having, showing, or marked by a feeling of joy or pleasure: *a happy child. This is the happiest day of my life.* **2.** Fortunate; favorable: *The story had a happy ending.* **3.** Apt; appropriate; suitable: *That was not a happy choice of words.* —**hap′pi•ly** *adv.* —**hap′pi•ess** *n.* [SEE NOTE]

hap•py-go-luck•y |hăp′ē gō lŭk′ē| *adj.* Easygoing; lighthearted; carefree.

ha•ra-ki•ri |hä′rə kîr′ē| *or* |hăr′ə-| *n.* Suicide by cutting open the abdomen with a dagger or knife, formerly practiced by the Japanese upper classes.

ha•rangue |hə răng′| *n.* A long, loud speech, often one in which the speaker denounces someone or something; a tirade. —*v.* **ha•rangued, ha•rangu•ing.** To address (a person, group of people, etc.) in a harangue.

har•ass |hăr′əs| *or* |hə răs′| *v.* **1.** To bother or torment with repeated interruptions, attacks, etc.: *harass a speaker with whistles and shouts.* **2.** To carry out repeated attacks or raids against: *Submarines continued to harass enemy shipping.* —**har′ass•ment** *n.*

har•bin•ger |här′bĭn jər| *n.* Something that indicates what is about to happen; a forerunner: *The robin is one of the harbingers of spring.*

har•bor |här′bər| *n.* **1.** A sheltered place serving as a port for ships. **2.** Any place of shelter or refuge: *home and harbor.* —*v.* **1.** To give shelter and lodging to; take in: *harbor an outlaw.* **2.** To have a specified thought or feeling: *harboring a grudge against one's neighbor.*

hard |härd| *adj.* **hard•er, hard•est. 1.** Resistant to pressure; firm; rigid: *a hard surface.* **2.** Difficult to understand, express, or convey: *a hard question.* **3.** Requiring great effort; arduous: *The book represents years of hard work by the author.* **4.** Energetic; industrious; diligent: *He's a very hard worker.* **5.** Intense; forceful: *a hard blow. Give the knob a hard twist.* **6.** Difficult to endure; trying: *a hard life.* **7.** Severe; harsh: *a hard winter.* **8.** Stern; strict; unrelenting: *a hard taskmaster.* **9.** Making few or no concessions: *a hard bargain; a hard line in foreign policy.* **10.** Sharp; probing; searching: *He promised to take a hard look at the entire situation.* **11.** Unchangeable; real: *hard facts; hard evidence.* **12.** Causing damage to; tending to wear down quickly: *Freezing weather is very hard on a car.* **13.** Bad: *a victim of very hard luck.* **14.** Bitter; rancorous; resentful: *No hard feelings, I hope!* **15. a.** Designating currency as against checks, notes, etc.: *hard cash.* **b.** Backed by and thus exchangeable for gold: *hard currency.* **16.** Designating the sound of the letters *c* and *g* as they are pronounced in *cat* and *go.* **17.** Having high alcoholic content; intoxicating: *no hard liquor.* **18.** Having or designating a cloth, card-

hansom

hapless, happy, happen
These are based on hap, *an old word meaning "luck, chance," which is from Old Norse* happ. **Hapless** *is "luckless, unlucky,"* **happy** *is "lucky, prosperous," and* **happen** *is "to occur by chance."*

hare

harlequin

harmonica

ă pat/ā pay/â care/ä father/ĕ pet/ ē be/ĭ pit/ī pie/î fierce/ŏ pot/ ō go/ô paw, for/oi oil/o͝o book/ o͞o boot/ou out/ŭ cut/û fur/ *th* the/th thin/hw which/zh vision/ ə ago, item, pencil, atom, circus

board, or leather binding: *a hard-bound book.* **19.** Containing dissolved salts that interfere with the action of soap: *hard water.* **20.** In physics, having high energy and great penetrating power: *hard x-rays.* —*adv.* **1.** Intently; earnestly: *work hard.* **2.** With great force, vigor, energy, etc.: *Press hard on the lever. She laughed hard at his jokes.* **3.** In such a way as to cause great damage: *A number of towns were hard hit by the storm.* **4.** With great distress, grief, etc.: *She took the news very hard.* **5.** With resistance; reluctantly: *Old superstitions die hard.* **6.** Toward or into a solid condition: *The cement will set hard within a day.*

Idioms. be hard put. To have great difficulty in doing something: *He was hard put to come up with an answer.* **hard and fast.** Fixed; rigid: *hard and fast rules.* **hard by.** Close to; near to: *The village lies hard by the river.* **hard of hearing.** Partially deaf. **hard up.** *Informal.* Short of or in need of money.

hard-boiled |**härd′boild′**| *adj.* **1.** Cooked by boiling to a solid consistency: *hard-boiled eggs.* **2.** *Informal.* Tough: *a hard-boiled policeman.*

hard coal. Anthracite.

hard-core |**härd′kôr′**| *adj.* **1.** Stubbornly resistant; inveterate: *the hard-core criminal element.* **2.** Deeply entrenched and difficult to remedy: *hard-core poverty cases.*

hard•en |**här′**dn| *v.* **1.** To make or become hard or harder: *harden steel. Allow the mixture to cool until it hardens.* **2.** To toughen; make rugged: *harden the troops by all-day marches.* **3.** To make or become unfeeling or cold in spirit: *War hardens the hearts of men. Difficult living conditions made their children harden early.* —**hard′ened** *adj.*: *hardened steel; a hardened criminal.*

hard-hat |**härd′**hăt| *n. Informal.* A construction worker.

hard•head•ed |**härd′hĕd′**ĭd| *adj.* **1.** Stubborn; willful. **2.** Coldly practical or realistic: *a hard-headed businessman.* —**hard′head′ed•ly** *adv.* —**hard′head′ed•ness** *n.*

hard•heart•ed |**härd′här′**tĭd| *adj.* Lacking feeling or sympathy; cold. —**hard′heart′ed•ly** *adv.* —**hard′heart′ed•ness** *n.*

har•di•hood |**här′**dē ho͝od′| *n.* Boldness and daring; audacity: *The lad wanted to prove his hardihood by attacking the Indians in their camp.*

Har•ding |**här′**dĭng|, **Warren Gamaliel.** 1865–1923. Twenty-ninth President of the United States (1921–23); died in office.

hard line. A firm, inflexible position or attitude regarding an issue, such as foreign policy, crime, etc. —***modifier:* (hard-line):** *a hard-line police commissioner.*

hard•ly |**härd′**lē| *adv.* **1.** Barely; only just: *He hardly noticed me.* **2.** Almost not at all: *She hardly spoke to him.* **3.** Probably not: *One would hardly expect a gift from them.*

hard•ness |**härd′**nĭs| *n.* **1.** The quality or condition of being hard. **2.** The degree to which a substance resists being scratched or being changed in shape by applied pressure.

hard palate. The rather hard, bony forward part of the palate.

hard rubber. A relatively inelastic rubber made with 30 to 50 per cent sulfur.

hard sell. *Informal.* Aggressive or high-pressure advertising or salesmanship.

hard•ship |**härd′**shĭp′| *n.* Something that causes suffering or difficulty: *The settlers at Jamestown suffered great hardships.*

hard•tack |**härd′**tăk′| *n.* A hard biscuit made only of flour and water; sea biscuit.

hard•top |**härd′**tŏp′| *n.* An automobile that looks like a convertible but has a fixed hard top.

hard•ware |**härd′**wâr′| *n.* **1.** Articles made of metal, as tools, nails, locks, cutlery, utensils, etc. **2.** The physical equipment used or needed to perform a particular task, especially such equipment as computers, instruments, electronic gear, etc. —***modifier:*** *a hardware store.*

hard•wood |**härd′**wo͝od′| *n.* **1.** A flowering tree with broad leaves as distinguished from a tree that has cones and needles. **2.** The wood of such a tree. —***modifier:*** *hardwood floors.*

har•dy |**här′**dē| *adj.* **har•di•er, har•di•est. 1.** Strong; robust: *a hardy mountain climber.* **2.** Bold; daring: *hardy travelers.* **3.** Able to withstand unfavorable conditions, such as cold weather: *a hardy rosebush.* —**har′di•ness** *n.*

hare |hâr| *n.* An animal related to and resembling the rabbits, but usually with longer ears and legs. ¶*These sound alike* **hare, hair.** [SEE PICTURE]

hare•bell |**hâr′**bĕl′| *n.* A plant with slender stems, narrow leaves, and blue, bell-shaped flowers.

hare•brained |**hâr′**brānd′| *adj.* Foolish; flighty: *harebrained schemes.*

hare•lip |**hâr′**lĭp′| *n.* A condition, existing from birth, in which the upper lip is divided into two or more parts.

har•em |**hâr′**əm| *or* |**hăr′**-| *n.* **1.** The part of a Moslem palace or house in which the women live. **2.** The women who live in a harem.

hark |härk| *v.* To listen carefully: *"Hark, the herald angels sing."* —***phrasal verb.* hark back. 1.** To return to a previous point, as in a narrative. **2.** To go back to an origin or source.

hark•en |**här′**kən| *v.* A form of the word **hearken.**

har•le•quin |**här′**lə kwən| *or* |-kən| *n.* **1.** Often **Harlequin.** A comic pantomime character, usually appearing in a mask and a costume of many colors. **2.** A clown; buffoon. [SEE PICTURE]

har•lot |**här′**lət| *n.* A prostitute.

harm |härm| *n.* Injury or damage: *Locusts often cause great harm to crops.* —*v.* To cause harm to; hurt: *The sun's light can harm your eyes.*

harm•ful |**härm′**fəl| *adj.* Causing or able to cause harm; injurious: *Birds devour harmful insects.* —**harm′ful•ly** *adv.* —**harm′ful•ness** *n.*

harm•less |**härm′**lĭs| *adj.* Causing little or no harm; inoffensive: *a harmless joke. Lambs are harmless.* —**harm′less•ly** *adv.* —**harm′less•ness** *n.*

har•mon•ic |här **mŏn′**ĭk| *n.* **1.** Any of the pure tones having frequencies that are whole-number multiples (twice, three times, four times, etc.) of a fundamental frequency and that sounding together with the fundamental make up a tone, as of a musical instrument. **2.** Any wave whose frequency is a whole-number multiple of that of another. —*adj.* **1.** Of harmonic motion. **2.** Of musical harmony. —**har•mon′i•cal•ly** *adv.*

har•mon•i•ca |här **mŏn′**ĭ kə| *n.* A small, rectangular musical instrument consisting of a series of tuned metal reeds that are made to vibrate by the player's breath.

harmonic motion. A type of vibrating motion, the simplest type possible, in which a body moves back and forth across a cental point under the influence of a force that tends to return it to that point. The motion of a pendulum is approximately of this type.

har•mo•ni•ous |här mō′nē əs| *adj.* **1.** Marked by agreement and good will; friendly: *a harmonious meeting.* **2.** Having elements pleasingly or appropriately combined: *harmonious colors.* **3.** Pleasing to the ear; melodious: *harmonious sounds.* —**har•mo′ni•ous•ly** *adv.*

har•mo•nize |här′mə nīz′| *v.* **har•mo•nized, har•mo•niz•ing. 1.** To provide harmony for (a melody). **2.** To sing or play in harmony. **3.** To be in or bring into agreement or harmony; be or make harmonious: *The tablecloth should harmonize with the dishes and centerpiece.* —**har′mo•ni•za′tion** *n.*

har•mo•ny |här′mə nē| *n., pl.* **har•mo•nies. 1. a.** A sequence of chords used to accompany a melody: *The piano fills in the harmony.* **b.** The study of the structure, succession, and relationships of combinations of tones that sound at the same time in music. **c.** The structure of music as seen in terms of this study. **d.** A particular chord or a passage based on it: *The tonic harmony persists for six measures.* **2.** A combination of musical sounds considered to be pleasing. **3.** A pleasing combination of the elements that form a whole: *color harmony; the order and harmony of the universe.* **4.** Agreement in feeling or opinion; good will; accord: *live in harmony.* —***modifier:*** *a harmony class; a harmony book.*

har•ness |här′nĭs| *n.* A set of leather straps and metal pieces by which an animal is attached to a vehicle or plow. —*v.* **1. a.** To put a harness on. **b.** To attach by means of a harness. **2.** To bring under control and direct the force of: *harness the energy of the sun.* [SEE PICTURE]

harp |härp| *n.* A musical instrument consisting of a triangular frame on which a series of strings varying in pitch are stretched. The player creates a sound by plucking the strings or brushing them with his fingers. —***modifier:*** *a harp concerto.* —*v.* —**harp on.** To write or talk about to an excessive or tedious degree. [SEE PICTURE]

harp•ist |här′pĭst| *n.* A person who plays the harp.

har•poon |här po͞on′| *n.* A spear with a rope attached and a barbed head with toggle action that is hurled by hand or shot from a gun, used in hunting whales and large fish. —*v.* To strike, kill, or take with a harpoon. —**har•poon′er** *n.*

harpoon gun. A gun that fires harpoons.

harp•si•chord |härp′sĭ kôrd′| *n.* A keyboard instrument that is somewhat similar to the piano except that its strings are plucked by small leather picks or quills rather than being struck by hammers. —***modifier:*** *a harpsichord suite.*

Har•py |här′pē| *n., pl.* **Har•pies. 1.** In Greek mythology, a hideous monster with a woman's head and trunk and a bird's tail, wings, and claws. **2. harpy.** A nasty or greedy person. **3. harpy.** A mean, scolding woman.

har•que•bus |här′kə bəs| *or* |-kwə-| *n.* A heavy, portable gun used in the Middle Ages.

har•ri•dan |hăr′ĭ dən| *n.* A mean, nasty old woman.

Har•ris•burg |hăr′ĭs bûrg′|. The capital of Pennsylvania. Population, 53,264.

Har•ri•son |hăr′ĭ sən|. **1. William Henry.** 1773–1841. Ninth President of the United States (1841); died in office. **2. Benjamin.** 1833–1901. Twenty-third President of the United States (1889–93); grandson of William Henry Harrison.

har•row |hăr′ō| *n.* A farm implement consisting of a heavy frame with sharp teeth or upright disks, used to break up and even off plowed ground. —*v.* To break up and level (soil or land) with a harrow.

har•row•ing |hăr′ō ĭng| *adj.* Distressing; agonizing: *a harrowing experience.*

har•ry |hăr′ē| *v.* **har•ried, har•ry•ing, har•ries. 1.** To raid, as in a war; pillage. **2.** To disturb by constant attacks; harass: *The readers harried the newspaper with constant phone calls.*

harsh |härsh| *adj.* **harsh•er, harsh•est. 1.** Unpleasant to the senses: *a harsh voice; a harsh odor; harsh colors.* **2.** Extremely severe or exacting; rigorous: *harsh treatment; a harsh climate.* —**harsh′ly** *adv.* —**harsh′ness** *n.*

hart |härt| *n.* A full-grown male deer, especially of the European red deer. ¶*These sound alike* **hart, heart.**

har•te•beest |här′tə bēst′| *or* |härt′bēst′| *n.* An African antelope with a brownish coat and outward-curving horns with ringlike ridges.

Hart•ford |härt′fərd|. The capital of Connecticut. Population, 136,392.

har•um-scar•um |hâr′əm skâr′əm| *or* |hăr′əm-skăr′əm| *adv.* In a wild or reckless way: *The children were running harum-scarum around the yard.* —*adj.* Irresponsible; reckless.

har•vest |här′vĭst| *n.* **1.** The act or process of gathering a crop: *The farmer hired extra hands for the harvest.* **2.** The crop thus gathered: *Everyone helped to bring in the harvest.* **3.** The amount or measure of the crop thus gathered: *a bumper harvest of wheat.* **4.** The result or consequence of any action: *The trip yielded a rich harvest of memories.* —***modifier:*** *harvest time.* —*v.* **1.** To gather (a crop). **2.** To receive (the benefits or consequences of an action).

har•vest•er |här′vĭ stər| *n.* **1.** A person who gathers a crop. **2.** A machine for harvesting crops; a reaper.

har•vest•man |här′vĭst mən| *n., pl.* **-men** |-mən|. A spiderlike animal, the **daddy longlegs.**

harvest moon. The full moon that occurs nearest the beginning of autumn.

has-been |hăz′bĭn′| *n. Informal.* A person once but no longer famous, popular, or successful.

hash |hăsh| *n.* **1.** Chopped meat and potatoes browned and cooked together. **2.** A jumble or hodgepodge. **3.** *Slang.* Hashish. —*v.* **1.** To chop into small pieces; mince. **2.** To discuss carefully; review: *hash over a problem.*

ha•sheesh |hä′shēsh′| *n.* A form of the word **hashish.**

hash•ish |hăsh′ēsh′| *or* |-ĭsh| *n.* A dry, resinous extract prepared from the hemp plant, smoked or chewed as an intoxicating drug.

Ha•si•dim |KHä sē′dĭm| *pl.n.* The less frequently used singular is **Ha•sid** |KHä′sĭd|. A form of the word **Chassidim.**

harness

harp

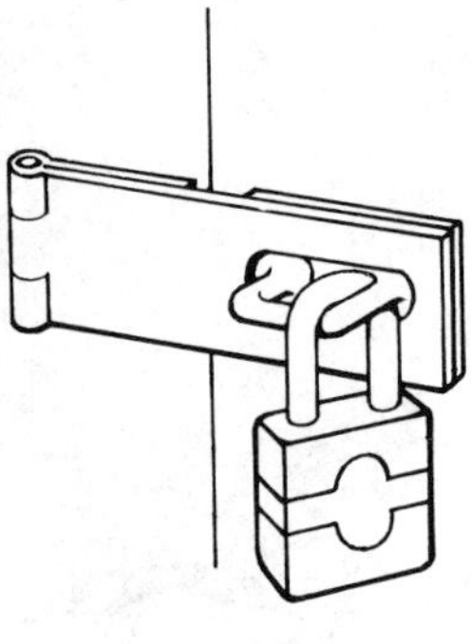

hasp

hatch[1-2]

***Hatch**[1] was* hæccan *in Old English, meaning "to produce chicks from eggs."* **Hatch**[2] *was Old English* hæc, *"small doorway." The two words are unrelated.*

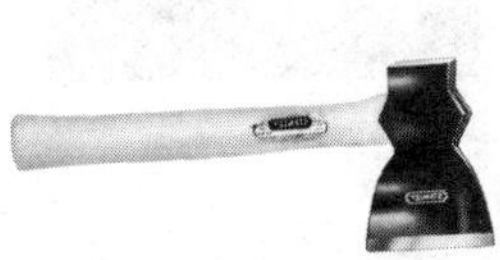

hatchet

ă pat/ā pay/â care/ä father/ĕ pet/ ē be/ĭ pit/ī pie/î fierce/ŏ pot/ ō go/ô paw, for/oi oil/ŏŏ book/ ōō boot/ou out/ŭ cut/û fur/ *th* the/th thin/hw which/zh vision/ ə ago, item, pencil, atom, circus

hasp |hăsp| *or* |häsp| *n.* A hinged fastener for a door that is passed over a staple and secured by a pin, bolt, or padlock. [SEE PICTURE]

Has•si•dim |KHä sē'dĭm| *pl.n.* The less frequently used singular is **Has•sid** |KHä'sĭd|. A form of the word **Chassidim.**

has•sle |hăs'əl|. *Informal. n.* **1.** An argument or squabble. **2.** Trouble; bother. *—v.* **has•sled, has•sling.** To argue or squabble.

has•sock |hăs'ək| *n.* A thick, firm cushion used as a footstool.

hast |hăst|. *Archaic.* A form of the present tense of **have,** used with *thou.*

haste |hāst| *n.* Swiftness of motion or action; rapidity; a hurry.

has•ten |hā'sən| *v.* **1.** To move or act swiftly; hurry: *He hastened home to tell the family the news.* **2.** To cause (something) to happen faster or sooner.

hast•y |hā'stē| *adj.* **hast•i•er, hast•i•est. 1.** Marked by speed; swift; rapid: *a hasty retreat.* **2.** Done or made too quickly to be accurate or wise; rash: *hasty judgments.* **—hast'i•ly** *adv.* **—hast'i•ness** *n.*

hasty pudding. 1. Cornmeal mush. **2.** *British.* A flour or oatmeal porridge.

hat |hăt| *n.* A covering for the head, especially one with a crown and brim. *—v.* **hat•ted, hat•ting.** To supply or cover with a hat.
Idioms. **at the drop of a hat.** At the slightest pretext or provocation. **pass the hat.** To take up a collection of money. **take (one's) hat off to.** To respect, admire, or congratulate. **talk through (one's) hat.** To talk nonsense. **under (one's) hat.** As a secret or in confidence.

hatch[1] |hăch| *v.* **1.** To come or cause to come out of an egg or eggs: *Ten chicks hatched today. The hen hatched a brood of ten chicks.* **2.** To break or open to produce young: *A robin's egg hatches in about 14 days.* **3.** To cause (an egg or eggs) to produce young: *The warmth of the sun hatches the eggs.* **4.** To devise or plot: *hatching an elaborate plan of escape.* [SEE NOTE]

hatch[2] |hăch| *n.* **1.** A small door: *an escape hatch.* **2. a.** A trap door, especially one covering a hatchway on a ship. **b.** Any door or doorway on shipboard. [SEE NOTE]

hatch•er•y |hăch'ə rē| *n., pl.* **hatch•er•ies.** A place where eggs, especially of fish or chickens, are hatched.

hatch•et |hăch'ĭt| *n.* A small ax with a short handle, used with one hand. [SEE PICTURE]
Idiom. **bury the hatchet.** To stop fighting; make peace.

hatch•way |hăch'wā'| *n.* **1.** An opening in a ship's deck giving access to a lower deck or to the hold. **2.** Any doorway on shipboard.

hate |hāt| *v.* **hat•ed, hat•ing. 1.** To feel aversion or enmity toward; regard with hostility: *"I hate you," he screamed at her.* **2. a.** To have a great dislike for; detest: *I hate spinach. He hates to lose.* **b.** To wish to avoid: *I'd hate to be in your shoes.* **3.** To regret: *I hate to interrupt, but we must go.* *—n.* Intense dislike; hatred.

hate•ful |hāt'fəl| *adj.* Arousing hatred; detestable. **—hate'ful•ly** *adv.* **—hate'ful•ness** *n.*

hath |hăth|. *Archaic.* A form of **has.**

ha•tred |hā'trĭd| *n.* Deep-seated antagonism or enmity; violent dislike or ill will; hate.

hat•ter |hăt'ər| *n.* A person who makes, sells, or repairs hats.

haugh•ty |hô'tē| *adj.* **haugh•ti•er, haugh•ti•est.** Proud and vain to the point of arrogance. **—haugh'ti•ly** *adv.* **—haugh'ti•ness** *n.*

haul |hôl| *v.* **1.** To pull, drag, or carry; tug: *We hauled the wood into the shed.* **2.** To transport, as with a truck or wagon; cart: *haul freight. Huge trucks were used to haul away the dirt and debris.* *—n.* **1.** The act of pulling, dragging, or carrying. **2.** A distance, especially the distance over which something is transported or someone travels: *a long haul across country.* **3.** Everything collected or acquired by a single effort; the take: *I hear you made quite a haul at the races today.* ¶*These sound alike* **haul, hall.**

haunch |hônch| *or* |hänch| *n.* **1.** The hip, buttock, and upper thigh of a person or animal: *The dog settled back on his haunches.* **2.** The loin and leg of an animal as used for food.

haunt |hônt| *or* |hänt| *v.* **1.** To visit or inhabit in the form of a ghost or other supernatural being. **2.** To linger in the mind; obsess: *The thought has haunted me ever since.* **3.** To visit often; frequent: *haunting the local bookstores.* **—haunt'ing** *adj.: a haunting melody.* *—n.* A place that is visited often: *a favorite haunt of artists.*

Hau•sa |hou'sə| *or* |-zə| *n., pl.* **Hau•sa. 1.** A member of a Negroid people of northern Nigeria and surrounding areas. **2.** Their language.

haut•boy |hō'boi'| *or* |ō'boi'| *n.* An oboe.

Ha•van•a |hə văn'ə|. The capital of Cuba. Population, 1,000,000.

have |hăv| *v.*

	1st person	2nd person	3rd person
Present Tense			
singular	**have**	**have**	**has** (hăz)
plural	**have**	**have**	**have**

Archaic 2nd person singular **hast** (hăst)
Archaic 3rd person singular **hath** (hăth)

Past Tense			
singular	**had** (hăd)	**had**	**had**
plural	**had**	**had**	**had**

Archaic 2nd person singular **hadst** (hădst)

Present Participle: **having** (hăv'ĭng)

Past Participle: **had** **1.**-Used as an auxiliary verb with a past participle to form the following tenses indicating completed action in the present, past, or future: **a.** Present perfect: *They have already had their supper.* **b.** Past perfect: *We had just finished supper when he arrived.* **c.** Future perfect: *I will have finished supper by the time they arrive.* **2.** —Used as an auxiliary verb to indicate necessity, obligation, or compulsion: **a.** With an infinitive: *I have to go.* **b.** With *got* followed by an infinitive: *I've got to go.* **3.** —Used as an auxiliary verb with *got* followed by an object in the present-tense sense of "have, possess, or own": *Burglars stay away because I have got nothing worth stealing.* **4.** To be in possession of; own: *She has two cars.* **5.** To be related or in a particular relationship to: *I have two brothers and one sister.* **6.** To be in a specified relationship to some action: *Do you have time to play?* **7.** To hold in one's mind; entertain: *I have my doubts about the wisdom of this plan.* **8.** To receive or get: *She had more than a dozen cards on her birthday.* **9.** To accept or take: *I'll have that gray jacket.* **10.** To suffer, experience, or undergo: *having a cold. I had a good summer.* **11.** To allow; permit: *I won't have any child of mine talk like that.* **12.** To cause (something) to be done: *He had a big cake made for the party.* **13.** To induce, order, or compel to: *have him go home before I throw him out.* **14.** *Informal.* To beat or cheat; get the better of: *I feel I've been had.* **15.** To infer or receive as a fact: *I have it on good authority that negotiations are already under way.* **16.** To imply: *Rumor had it that the ailing leader was actually dead.* **17. a.** To be a parent of: *have children.* **b.** To give birth to; bear: *She's having a baby next month.* —***phrasal verb.*** **have on. 1.** To be wearing: *She has on a red dress and black shoes.* **2.** *Informal.* To be scheduled for: *I have a dinner party on for tomorrow night.* ¶ *These sound alike* **have, halve.**

Idioms. **had just as well.** Might as well: *I'd just as well go now.* **have done with.** To be through with; finish: *Let's have done with this business once and for all.* **have had it.** To have endured all that one can. **have it in for.** To have a grudge against: *I've had it in for him ever since he told on me.* **have it out.** To settle a disagreement; fight it out to the end. **have to do with. 1.** To associate with. **2.** To deal or be concerned with: *The book has to do with the Civil War.*

ha•ven |hā′vən| *n.* **1.** A sheltered harbor. **2.** A place of refuge or rest; a safe shelter; sanctuary.

have-not |hăv′nŏt′| *n.* Often **have-nots.** A person or country having little or nothing in the way of material wealth.

hav•oc |hăv′ək| *n.* Devastation; destruction.

haw¹ |hô| *n.* **1.** The small red fruit of a hawthorn. **2.** A hawthorn or similar tree. [SEE NOTE]

haw² |hô| *interj.* A word used to command a horse or ox to turn to the left. [SEE NOTE]

Ha•wai•i |hə wä′ē| *or* |-wä′yə|. A state of the United States, consisting of a group of islands in the Pacific Ocean. Population, 965,000. Capital, Honolulu.

Ha•wai•ian |hə wä′yən| *n.* **1.** A native or inhabitant of Hawaii. **2.** The Polynesian language of the Hawaiians. —*adj.* Of Hawaii, the Hawaiians, or their language.

hawk¹ |hôk| *n.* **1.** Any of several birds with a short, hooked bill and strong claws with which they catch small birds and animals for food. **2.** *Informal.* A person who favors an aggressive, warlike version of his country's foreign policy. [SEE NOTE & PICTURE]

hawk² |hôk| *v.* To cry (goods) in the street; peddle. —**hawk′er** *n.* [SEE NOTE]

hawk³ |hôk| *v.* To clear or try to clear (the throat) by coughing up phlegm. [SEE NOTE]

hawk-eyed |hôk′īd′| *adj.* Having very strong eyesight.

hawks•bill |hôks′bĭl′| *n.* A tropical sea turtle valued as a source of tortoiseshell.

haw•ser |hô′zər| *n.* A heavy line or cable used in mooring or towing a ship.

haw•thorn |hô′thôrn′| *n.* A thorny shrub with white or pinkish flowers and red berries.

Haw•thorne |hô′thôrn′|, **Nathaniel.** 1804–1864. American writer.

hay |hā| *n.* Grass and other plants, such as clover, cut and dried and used chiefly as food for horses, cattle, etc. —*v.* To cut and dry grass or other plants so as to make them into hay. ¶ *These sound alike* **hay, hey.**

Idioms. **hit the hay.** *Slang.* To go to bed. **make hay.** To make the most of every opportunity.

hay•cock |hā′kŏk′| *n.* A cone-shaped mound of hay in a field.

Hay•dn |hīd′n|, **Franz Joseph.** 1732–1809. Austrian composer.

Hayes |hāz|, **Rutherford B(irchard).** 1822–1893. Nineteenth President of the United States (1877–81).

hay fever. A severe irritation of the eyes, nose, and breathing passages, caused by an intense allergy to various pollens that are blown about in the air.

hay•loft |hā′lôft′| *or* |-lŏft′| *n.* A loft in a barn or stable for storing hay.

hay•mow |hā′mou′| *n.* **1.** A hayloft. **2.** The hay stored in a hayloft.

hay•ride |hā′rīd′| *n.* A ride taken for pleasure in a wagon partly filled with hay.

hay•seed |hā′sēd′| *n.* **1.** Grass seed that is shaken out of hay. **2.** A country bumpkin.

hay•stack |hā′stăk′| *n.* A large stack of hay that stands out in the open in the winter.

hay•wire |hā′wīr′| *n.* Wire used for tying up bales of hay or straw. —*adj. Informal.* **1.** Not functioning properly; out of order or control: *The ship's compasses have gone haywire.* **2.** Emotionally upset; excited: *The players went haywire after losing the game.*

haz•ard |hăz′ərd| *n.* **1. a.** A chance of being injured, lost, etc.; danger; risk: *Space travel is full of hazards.* **b.** Something or someone that is likely to cause harm; a possible source of danger: *a fire hazard.* **2.** A sandtrap, pond, or other obstacle on a golf course. —*v.* **1.** To expose to danger; risk: *The sergeant hazarded his life for the safety of his men.* **2.** To take a chance and give; venture: *hazard a guess.*

haz•ard•ous |hăz′ər dəs| *adj.* Dangerous; perilous: *a hazardous voyage.*

haze¹ |hāz| *n.* **1.** A foglike mixture of dust, smoke, and vapor suspended in the air. **2.** A vague or confused state of mind. [SEE NOTE]

haze² |hāz| *v.* **hazed, haz•ing.** To harass with humiliating, silly, or unpleasant tasks: *haze freshmen in some colleges.* [SEE NOTE]

ha•zel |hā′zəl| *n.* **1.** A shrub or small tree that bears edible nuts enclosed in a leafy husk. **2.** A light, yellowish brown. —*adj.* Light, yellowish brown: *hazel eyes.*

ha•zel•nut |hā′zəl nŭt′| *n.* The nut of a hazel, having a smooth brown shell.

haz•y |hā′zē| *adj.* **haz•i•er, haz•i•est. 1.** Marked by the presence of haze; foggy: *a hazy sun.* **2.** Not clear; vague: *A hazy recollection of the incident.* —**haz′i•ly** *adv.* —**haz′i•ness** *n.*

H-bomb |āch′bŏm′| *n.* A **hydrogen bomb.**

he |hē| *pron.* **1.** The male person or animal last mentioned: *Tom worked here last summer, but now he is back in school. Though the mule often tried our patience, it was he who saved our lives.* **2.** Any person whose sex is not specified; that person; one: *He who looks for trouble usually hasn't far to search. Each of us is likely to feel that it is he alone who is right.* —*n.* A male animal or person: *If the puppy is a he, we'll call him Chief.* —*Note:* As a pronoun, *he* is in the nominative

haw¹·²
Haw¹ *was* haga *in Old English, meaning "hawthorn bush or hedge." It is related to the word* **hedge. Haw²,** *like* **gee** *(the traditional command to a horse to turn* right*), is old but of unknown origin.*

hawk¹·²·³
Hawk¹ *was* heafoc *in Old English.* **Hawk²** *is from* hawker, *an old word for "a street peddler," which is from Low German* höker. **Hawk³** *is imitative of the sound.*

hawk¹

haze¹·²
These two words are unrelated, but nothing very useful can be said about their origins. **Haze¹** *first appears in the eighteenth century; it is a back-formation from* **hazy,** *which appears a century earlier but is itself of unknown origin.* **Haze²** *is also of unknown origin.*

head

Head *was* heafod *in Old English. It is descended from prehistoric Germanic* haubud-, *which in turn is from Indo-European* kaput-, *"head." (An Indo-European* k- *always became* h- *in Germanic.) In Latin,* kaput- *became* caput, *still meaning "head"; from* caput, *other words, such as* **capital**, *have been borrowed into English.*

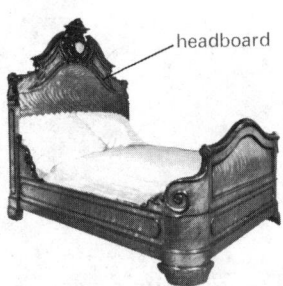

headboard

ă pat/ā pay/â care/ä father/ĕ pet/ ē be/ĭ pit/ī pie/î fierce/ŏ pot/ ō go/ô paw, for/oi oil/ŏŏ book/ ōō boot/ou out/ŭ cut/û fur/ *th* the/th thin/hw which/zh vision/ ə ago, item, pencil, atom, circus

case and serves either as the subject of a verb or as a predicate nominative following a form of the verb *be.* In each of the first examples given at 1 and 2, *he* is a subject; in each of the second examples, *he* is a predicate nominative.

He The symbol for the element helium.

head |hĕd| *n.* **1.** The uppermost or forwardmost part of the body of a vertebrate, containing the brain or principal nerve centers and the eyes, ears, nose, mouth, and jaws. **2.** The seat of the faculty of reason; intelligence, intellect, or mind: *I can do all the figuring in my head.* **3.** A mental ability or aptitude: *He has a good head for mathematics.* **4.** A projection, weight, or fixture at the end of an elongated object: *the head of a pin.* **5.** The working part of a tool: *the head of a hammer.* **6.** A rounded, tightly clustered mass of leaves, buds, or flowers: *a head of cabbage.* **7.** A person who leads, rules, or is in charge of something; a leader; director: *heads of state.* **8.** The foremost or leading position: *The bugler marched at the head of the column.* **9.** The uppermost part of something; the top: *Place the appropriate name at the head of each column.* **10.** The end considered the most important: *The host usually sits at the head of the table.* **11.** *pl.* **head.** A single animal or person: *seven head of cattle. The cost was ten dollars a head.* **12.** Often **heads** (*used with a singular verb*). The side of a coin having the principal design and the date. **13.** Any portrait or image of a person's head. **14.** The tip of a boil, pimple, or abscess, in which pus forms. **15.** The pressure exerted by a liquid or gas: *a head of steam.* **16.** The froth or foam on beer or ale that has just been poured. **17.** The membrane or skin stretched across a drum, tambourine, etc. **18.** An electromagnetic device used in recording or playing back a magnetic tape: *a tape recorder with three heads.* **19.** *Slang.* A habitual drug user: *an acid head.* —***modifier:*** *a head covering; a head injury.* —*adj.* Most important; ranking first: *the head librarian; the head coach.* —*v.* **1.** To proceed or set out in a certain direction: *head for home.* **2.** To aim, point, or turn in a certain direction: *He headed the team of horses up the hill.* **3.** To be in charge of; lead: *The minister headed the delegation.* **4.** To be in the first or foremost position of: *Collins heads the list of candidates for the job.* **5.** To place a heading on: *head each column with a number.* **6.** In soccer, to hit (a ball) into the air with one's head. —***phrasal verb.*** **head off.** To block the progress or completion of; intercept: *I'll try to head him off before he gets home.* [SEE NOTE]

Idioms. **come to a head. 1.** To fill with or give off pus, as a boil or abscess. **2.** To reach a critical point: *The crisis is coming to a head.* **go to (one's) head. 1.** To make one lightheaded or drunk: *Wine goes to my head.* **2.** To increase one's pride or conceit: *Success went to his head.* **head and shoulders above.** Far superior to: *He is head and shoulders above his classmates in reading ability.* **head over heels. 1.** Rolling, as in a somersault: *He tripped and fell head over heels.* **2.** Completely; hopelessly: *head over heels in love.* **keep (one's) head.** To remain calm; not lose control of oneself. **lose (one's) head.** To lose one's poise or self-control. **make head or tail of.** To make sense of: *I can't make head or tail of what he is saying.* **off** (or **out of**) **(one's) head.** Insane; crazy. **(one's) head off.** *Informal.* To an excessive or extreme degree: *She talked her head off.* **over (one's) head. 1.** Beyond one's ability to understand or deal with: *The conversation was completely over my head.* **2.** To a higher ranking person: *He went over his boss's head and spoke to the manager.* **put heads together.** To consult and plan together. **take it into (one's) head.** To decide suddenly. **turn (one's) head.** To make conceited.

head•ache |hĕd′āk′| *n.* **1.** A pain in the head. **2.** *Informal.* Something that causes trouble.

head•board |hĕd′bôrd′| *or* |-bōrd′| *n.* A board, frame, or panel that stands at the head of a bed. [SEE PICTURE]

head•dress |hĕd′drĕs′| *n.* **1.** A fancy covering or elaborate ornament worn on the head: *an Indian headdress of feathers.* **2.** A fancy way of arranging the hair, as with ribbons or combs.

head•ed |hĕd′ĭd| *adj.* **1.** Having a specified kind of head: *a flat-headed person.* **2.** Having hair of a certain color: *a red-headed boy.* **3.** Having a specified kind of disposition: *a hot-headed boy.* **4.** Having a specified number of heads: *a three-headed monster.*

head•first |hĕd′fûrst′| *adv.* **1.** With the head leading; headlong. **2.** Hastily; rashly: *He plunged headfirst into the new project.*

head•gear |hĕd′gîr′| *n.* **1.** A covering for the head, as a hat or helmet. **2.** The part of a harness that fits about a horse's head.

head-hunt•er |hĕd′hŭn′tər| *n.* A member of any primitive tribe having the custom of taking and preserving human heads as trophies or magical objects. —**head′-hunt′ing** *n.*

head•ing |hĕd′ĭng| *n.* **1.** The title, subtitle, or topic put at the head of a page, chapter, etc. **2.** The direction in which a ship or aircraft is moving; course.

head•land |hĕd′lănd′| *n.* A point of land, usually high and with a sheer drop, extending out into a body of water; a promontory.

head•light |hĕd′līt′| *n.* A lamp mounted on the front of an automobile, truck, train, etc.

head•line |hĕd′līn′| *n.* A group of words that is printed in large type over a newspaper article and tells what the article is about.

head•lock |hĕd′lŏk′| *n.* A wrestling hold in which the head of one wrestler is held tightly under the arm of the other.

head•long |hĕd′lông′| *or* |-lŏng′| *adv.* **1.** With the head leading; headfirst: *She slipped on a mossy stone and tumbled headlong into the water.* **2.** At reckless speed or with uncontrolled force: *He rode headlong in pursuit.* —*adj.* |hĕd′lông′| *or* |-lŏng′|. **1.** Done with the head leading: *a headlong fall.* **2.** Recklessly fast or uncontrollably forceful: *a headlong race; a headlong attack.*

head•man |hĕd′măn′| *n., pl.* **-men** |-mĕn′|. A man of highest rank or authority, as in a tribe.

head•mas•ter |hĕd′măs′tər| *or* |-mä′stər| *n.* A man who is a school principal, usually of a private school.

head•mis•tress |hĕd′mĭs′trĭs| *n.* A woman who is a school principal, usually of a private school.

head-on |hĕd′ŏn′| *or* |-ôn′| *adj.* **1.** Having the front end exposed and receiving the impact: *the head-on crash of the two trains.* **2.** Not deviating; direct: *the head-on fury of the storm.* —*adv.*

|hĕd′ŏn′| *or* |-ôn′|. **1.** With the front directed toward something: *The truck ran head-on into the building.* **2.** Without deviating; directly: *He attacked the idea head-on.*

head•piece |hĕd′pēs′| *n.* A helmet or cap worn to protect the head.

head•quar•ters |hĕd′kwôr′tərz| *pl.n.* **1.** The offices of a commander, as of a military unit, from which official orders are issued. **2.** Any center of operations: *the headquarters of the company.*

head•stand |hĕd′stănd′| *n.* An upside-down position in which a person balances himself with all his weight resting on his arms and on the top of his head. [SEE PICTURE]

head start. An early start giving an advantage, as a start before other competitors in a race.

head•stone |hĕd′stōn′| *n.* A memorial stone set at the head of a grave.

head•strong |hĕd′strông′| *or* |-strŏng′| *adj.* Inclined to insist on having one's own way; rashly willful; obstinate: *a proud and headstrong boy.*

head•wa•ters |hĕd′wô′tərz| *or* |-wŏt′ərz| *pl.n.* The bodies of water that form the source of a river.

head•way |hĕd′wā′| *n.* **1.** Movement forward; advance: *Against the current, he barely made headway in the light canoe.* **2.** Progress toward a goal: *They made little headway in the ticket sales.* **3.** The amount of time or distance that separates two vehicles traveling along the same route.

head wind. A wind blowing in the direction that directly opposes the course of a ship, aircraft, or other vehicle.

head•y |hĕd′ē| *adj.* **head•i•er, head•i•est. 1.** Tending to upset the balance of the senses or logic; intoxicating: *such heady success; the heady possibilities of the scheme.* **2.** Headstrong; willful: *her heady notions of what to do.* **—head′i•ly** *adv.* **—head′i•ness** *n.*

heal |hēl| *v.* **1.** To make or become healthy and sound: *heal the sick. His wound healed quickly.* **2.** To set right; amend: *healed the rift between the two friends.* ¶*These sound alike* **heal, heel, he'll. —heal′er** *n.*

health |hĕlth| *n.* **1.** The overall condition or functioning of the life processes of an organism at any particular time: *She is in poor health.* **2.** The normal functioning of an organism that is free of disease, injury, or defects: *a speedy return to health.* **3.** A wish for someone's well-being, often expressed as a toast. **—modifier:** *high health standards; a health hazard.*

health•ful |hĕlth′fəl| *adj.* Tending to promote good health; beneficial: *a healthful diet.* **—health′ful•ly** *adv.* **—health′ful•ness** *n.*

health•y |hĕl′thē| *adj.* **health•i•er, health•i•est. 1.** In a state of good health: *a healthy student.* **2.** Promoting good health; healthful: *a healthy climate.* **3.** Indicating or characteristic of good health in mind or body: *a healthy attitude.* **4.** Sizable: *a healthy portion.* **5.** Functioning or operating well; normal; stable: *a healthy economy.* **—health′i•ly** *adv.*

heap |hēp| *n.* **1.** A collection of things massed together; a pile: *a rubbish heap.* **2.** Often **heaps.** *Informal.* A great amount; a lot: *The game was heaps of fun.* **3.** *Slang.* An old or run-down car: *I can't race in this heap.* —*v.* **1.** To put, throw, or rise in a heap; pile up: *They heaped wood by the fireplace. Sand heaped up against the cabin wall.* **2.** To fill to overflowing; pile high: *They heaped the cart with old clothes.* **3.** To give or bestow in abundance: *They heaped insults upon him.*

hear |hîr| *v.* **heard** |hûrd|, **hear•ing. 1.** To detect, be aware of, or receive (sound) by the use of one's ears: *hear noises. He doesn't hear well.* **2.** To listen to attentively: *He loved to hear the tales told by the old sailor.* **3. a.** To get as information; learn: *He heard the news from a friend.* **b.** To receive communication, as by letter, telephone, etc.: *We have not heard from her lately.* **4.** To be familiar with; know of: *We've heard about that town.* **5.** To listen to in order to examine officially or formally: *The judge will hear the case in court.* **6.** *Informal.* To get a scolding: *If you don't sweep the floor, you'll hear from Mother.* ¶*These sound alike* **hear, here. —hear′er** *n.*

heard |hûrd|. Past tense and past participle of **hear.** ¶*These sound alike* **heard, herd.**

hear•ing |hîr′ĭng| *n.* **1.** The sense by which sound is detected; the capacity to hear. **2.** The region within which sounds from a particular location can be heard; earshot. **3.** An opportunity to be heard. **4.** A formal session for listening to testimony, arguments, etc.

hearing aid. A small electronic amplifying device used to aid the hearing of persons who are partially deaf.

heark•en |här′kən| *v.* To listen attentively; give heed: *They hearkened to the voice of the oracle.*

hear•say |hîr′sā′| *n.* Information or news heard from another person.

hearse |hûrs| *n.* A vehicle for carrying a dead person to a church or cemetery.

heart |härt| *n.* **1. a.** The hollow, muscular organ in vertebrates that receives blood from the veins and pumps it into the arteries by regular, rhythmic contraction. **b.** A similar organ in invertebrate animals. **2.** The approximate location of this organ in the chest; the bosom. **3.** The vital center of someone's being, emotions, sensitivity, and spirit: *With joy in his heart, he sailed up the river.* **4. a.** Emotional state, disposition, or mood: *having a change of heart.* **b.** Love; affection: *The children won his heart.* **c.** The capacity to feel sympathy, kindness, concern, etc.; compassion: *He has great heart.* **5.** Inner strength; courage: *The captain's talk gave him heart.* **6. a.** The central part; the center: *the heart of the city.* **b.** The essential part; the basis: *the heart of the matter.* **7.** Enthusiasm; energy: *His heart is not in his work.* **8.** Someone loved or respected: *a dear heart.* **9.** A two-lobed representation of the heart, usually colored red. **10. a.** A red figure, shaped like a heart, on a playing card. **b.** A card bearing this figure. **c. hearts.** The suit in a deck of cards having this figure as its symbol. **—modifier:** *a heart disease; a heart transplant.* ¶*These sound alike* **heart, hart.** [SEE PICTURES]

***Idioms.* after (one's) own heart.** Meeting one's preferences or desires; to one's liking: *He ran away to sea and found a life after his own heart.* **at heart.** Basically; fundamentally: *She is a good friend at heart.* **break (someone's) heart.** To cause someone much disappointment or grief. **by heart.** Entirely by memory: *He knew the poem by heart.* **have a heart.** Have sympathy; be considerate:

headstand

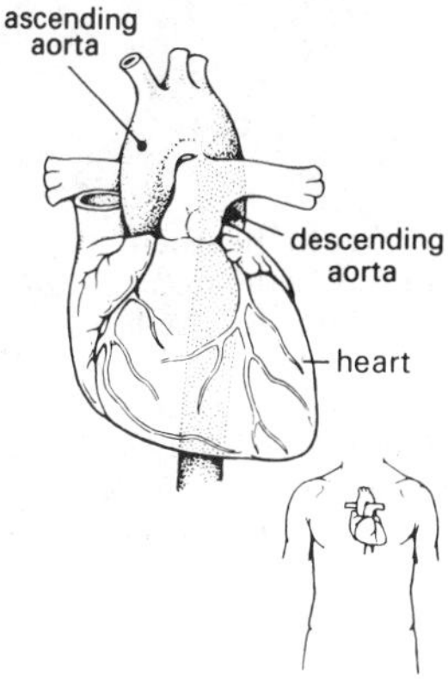

heart
Above: Human heart
Below: Playing card

Have a heart, John; we can't finish the job today. **have (one's) heart in the right place.** To be sincerely concerned or interested; have good intentions. **have the heart.** To have the will to do something unpleasant. **heart and soul.** All one's being: *She put heart and soul into the task.* **near (close, or dear) to (one's) heart.** Important to or cherished by a person: *That subject is near to her heart.* **set** (or **have**) **(one's) heart on.** To want more than anything else: *She set her heart on winning the prize.* **take to heart.** To be deeply affected or troubled by: *She took their mocking laughter to heart.* **to (one's) heart's content.** To one's entire satisfaction; as much as one wants: *There you may paint to your heart's content.* **wear (one's) heart on (one's) sleeve.** To show one's feelings easily.

heart•ache |**härt**'āk'| *n.* Emotional anguish; deep sorrow.

heart attack. A condition or seizure in which the functioning of the heart is impaired or interrupted, often because of an insufficient supply of blood to the tissues of the heart itself.

heart•beat |**härt**'bēt'| *n.* **1.** A single cycle of contraction and relaxation of the heart. **2.** The general nature of the heart's contractions or the rate at which they occur: *a weak, rapid heartbeat.*

heart•break |**härt**'brāk'| *n.* Great sorrow or grief; crushing disappointment: *The new nation was built on hardship and heartbreak.*

heart•break•ing |**härt**'brā'kĭng| *adj.* Causing great sorrow, grief, or disappointment: *heartbreaking news.* —**heart'break'ing•ly** *adv.*

heart•bro•ken |**härt**'brō'kən| *adj.* **1.** Suffering from great sorrow, grief, or disappointment; overcome by grief or despair: *a heartbroken widow.* **2.** Showing great sorrow, grief, or disappointment: *heartbroken cries; a heartbroken sob.* —**heart'bro'ken•ly** *adv.*

heart•burn |**härt**'bûrn'| *n.* A feeling of burning in the stomach and esophagus, usually caused by an excess of acid secreted in the stomach.

heart•ed |**här**'tĭd| *adj.* Having a specified kind of heart: *lighthearted; faint-hearted.*

heart•en |**här**'tn| *v.* To give strength or courage to; encourage; cheer: *She heartened the wounded and the weary.*

heart failure. A condition in which the heart loses some of its ability to pump blood to body tissues.

heart•felt |**härt**'fĕlt'| *adj.* Deeply felt; sincere; earnest: *heartfelt thanks; my heartfelt wishes.*

hearth |**härth**| *n.* **1.** The floor of a fireplace, usually extending into a room. **2.** The fireside as a symbol of family life or the home. **3.** The lower part of a refinery furnace, in which a metal or ore is treated by exposure to heat.

hearth•stone |**härth**'stōn'| *n.* **1.** Stone used in the construction of a hearth. **2.** The fireside; home.

heart•i•ly |**här**'tl ē| *adv.* **1.** In a warm and friendly manner; sincerely: *They welcomed him heartily.* **2.** With vigor or enthusiasm: *They plunged heartily into the game.* **3.** Thoroughly; completely: *She disapproved heartily of the plan. They heartily agreed.* **4.** With much appetite or enjoyment: *He had eaten heartily.*

heart•land |**härt**'lănd'| *n.* An important central region, especially a region considered vital economically or strategically to a nation.

heart•less |**härt**'lĭs| *adj.* Without sympathy or compassion; pitiless; cruel: *a heartless man beating a starving animal.* —**heart'less•ly** *adv.* —**heart'less•ness** *n.*

heart-rend•ing |**härt**'rĕn'dĭng| *adj.* Causing grief, anguish, or suffering: *a heart-rending conflict.* —**heart'-rend'ing•ly** *adv.*

hearts•ease |**härts**'ēz'| *n.* An old-fashioned name for several flowers, especially the Johnny-jump-up or the pansy.

heart•sick |**härt**'sĭk'| *adj.* Profoundly disappointed; very despondent: *a heartsick prisoner.*

heart•strings |**härt**'strĭngz'| *pl.n.* The deepest feelings of pity, sympathy, affection, etc.: *The story touched her heartstrings.*

heart-to-heart |**härt**'tə **härt**'| *adj.* Personal and sincere; frank: *a heart-to-heart talk.*

heart•wood |**härt**'wŏŏd'| *n.* The inner, older, usually darker wood of a tree, no longer active in conducting sap.

heart•y |**här**'tē| *adj.* **heart•i•er, heart•i•est.** **1.** Showing warmth of feeling; cheerful and friendly: *a hearty laugh.* **2. a.** Having vigor and strength; healthy; robust: *hearty settlers.* **b.** Vigorous; forceful: *a hearty thump on the back.* **3. a.** Giving much nourishment; substantial: *a hearty soup.* **b.** Enjoying or requiring much food: *a hearty appetite.* **4.** Openly and thoroughly sincere or enthusiastic: *our hearty congratulations.* —*n., pl.* **heart•ies.** A good fellow; a comrade, especially a sailor: *Bear a hand with the rowing, my hearties.* —**heart'i•ness** *n.*

heat |**hēt**| *n.* **1.** The energy associated with the rapid, unorganized motion of the atoms or molecules that make up a body. It can be transmitted through a solid or fluid medium by conduction, through a fluid medium by convection, or through space as infrared radiation. **2.** The sensations or effects that this energy produces in an organism, especially a feeling of being warm. **3.** Intense or excessive warmth: *escaping the summer heat.* **4.** The warmth provided for a building or room, as from a furnace, fireplace, etc.: *tenement buildings with no heat and no hot water.* **5.** An intense, exciting moment or period, as caused by emotion, stress, etc.; a height of feeling or energy: *in the heat of their discussion.* **6.** A time in which a female mammal, other than a woman, is ready to mate. **7.** A single course in a race or competition: *restless horses waiting for the first heat.* —**modifier:** *heat energy.* —*v.* **1.** To make or become warm or hot: *The sun heats the earth. The soup heated slowly.* **2.** To make emotionally or intellectually excited: *His arguments heated the crowd more than ever.* —**heat'ed** *adj.*: *a heated room; a heated debate.*

heat•er |**hē**'tər| *n.* A device that supplies heat for some purpose, such as keeping the inside of a house comfortable in cold weather.

heat exchanger. A device in which two fluids are brought close enough together so that heat can pass from one to the other, but without any mixing of the fluids.

heath |**hēth**| *n.* **1.** An open, uncultivated stretch of land covered with low-growing shrubs or plants, such as heather. **2.** A plant that grows on such land. [SEE NOTE]

hea•then |**hē**'*th*ən| *n., pl.* **hea•thens** or **hea•then.**

heath/heathen

Heath *was* hǣth *in Old English, and* **heathen** *was* hǣthen. *The two words are closely related;* hǣthen *originally meant "person who lives on the heaths or in the wilderness, savage, barbarian"; later it came to mean "non-Christian."*

ă pat/ā pay/â care/ä father/ĕ pet/ ē be/ĭ pit/ī pie/î fierce/ŏ pot/ ō go/ô paw, for/oi oil/ŏŏ book/ ōō boot/ou out/ŭ cut/û fur/ *th* the/th thin/hw which/zh vision/ ə ago, item, pencil, atom, circus

1. a. A person who is a member of a people, nation, etc., that does not acknowledge the God of Judaism, Christianity, or Islam. **b.** Such persons regarded as a group: *He wanted to help the heathen.* **2.** Anyone regarded as uncivilized or undisciplined. *—modifier: old heathen beliefs; a heathen land.* [SEE NOTE on p. 424]

heath•er |hĕth′ər| *n.* A low-growing shrub that has tiny evergreen leaves and small, bell-shaped purplish flowers and often grows in dense masses. [SEE PICTURE]

heat of fusion. The amount of heat needed to change a unit mass of a substance from solid to liquid form without changing its temperature. [SEE NOTE]

heat of vaporization. The amount of heat needed to change a unit mass of a substance from liquid to gaseous form without changing its temperature. [SEE NOTE]

heat shield. A device that protects something, such as a spacecraft, from heat.

heat stroke. A severe illness caused by exposure to too much heat. Its symptoms include headache, fever, hot and dry skin, and sometimes complete collapse.

heave |hēv| *v.* **heaved** or *chiefly nautical* **hove** |hōv|, **heav•ing. 1.** To raise or lift, especially with great effort or force; hoist: *heaved the pack onto his back.* **2.** To throw with or as if with great effort; hurl: *They heaved the sacks of cement onto the truck.* **3.** To utter painfully, unhappily, or with effort: *heave a sigh.* **4.** *Informal.* To vomit. **5.** To push or pull on a capstan bar or line: *heave around on the anchor.* **6.** To pull into a specified position: *A tugboat hove alongside.* **7.** To rise and fall, often with a kind of rhythm: *Seaweed heaved and swung on the gentle waves.* **8.** To rise up, bulge, or be forced upward, as through some outside force or medium: *Through the years the old town's sidewalks had heaved in many places.* **—phrasal verb. heave to.** To bring a ship at sea to a standstill. *—n.* **1.** An act or effort of heaving: *Each heave on the line loosened the anchor.* **2.** A throw: *give it a heave.* **3. heaves** (*used with a singular or plural verb*). A disease of horses affecting the lungs and characterized by coughing and difficulty in breathing.

***Idiom.* heave into sight** (or **view**). To rise or seemingly rise into view, as land or a ship does; become visible.

heav•en |hĕv′ən| *n.* **1.** Often **heavens.** The sky or universe as seen from the earth. **2.** In many religions, the abode of God, holy celestial beings, and the blessed dead. **3. Heaven.** The divine Providence; God: *Thank Heaven for your safety.* **4.** Often **heavens.** Used in exclamations: *Good heavens! Look at that crowd!* **5. a.** Great happiness; bliss: *It'll be heaven to visit that park.* **b.** A wonderful thing or place; a delight: *Her kitchen, fragrant from baking, was heaven.*

***Idioms.* in seventh heaven.** Supremely happy: *She is in seventh heaven now that she has a piano.* **move heaven and earth.** To do everything possible: *He'll move heaven and earth in order to find the lost letter.*

heav•en•ly |hĕv′ən lē| *adj.* **1.** Of or in the heavens; celestial: *the planets and other heavenly bodies.* **2. a.** Of the abode of God: *the heavenly hosts; the heavenly assembly.* **b.** Of or suitable for beings in heaven; divine; blessed: *in heavenly peace.* **3.** Very pleasing; delightful; lovely: *a heavenly day.*

heav•en•ward |hĕv′ən wərd| *adv.* Also **heav•en•wards** |hĕv′ən wərdz|. Toward heaven: *The prophet directed his plea heavenward. —adj.: the heavenward flight of the eagle.*

Heav•i•side layer |hĕv′ē sīd′|. The **E layer.** [SEE NOTE]

heav•y |hĕv′ē| *adj.* **heav•i•er, heav•i•est. 1.** Having relatively great weight: *a heavy skillet; a heavy rock.* **2. a.** Having a relatively large atomic mass: *lead and other heavy metals.* **b.** Having a larger atomic mass than other atoms of the same element: *heavy hydrogen.* **3.** Large in amount, yield, output, etc.; substantial: *a heavy rain; heavy traffic.* **4.** Having considerable thickness, body, or strength: *heavy winter clothing; some heavy thread.* **5.** Very dense or thick: *a heavy mist; a heavy growth of algae.* **6.** Written, drawn, or printed noticeably darkly or thickly: *a heavy accent mark; the heavy lines on a drawing.* **7.** Requiring much effort to accomplish; arduous: *heavy work.* **8.** In turmoil; rough; violent: *heavy seas.* **9.** Intense or sustained: *heavy fighting; a heavy attack.* **10.** Causing pain, suffering, or hardship; severe or burdensome: *heavy losses; a heavy penalty; heavy taxes.* **11.** Deeply concerned or sad: *a heavy heart.* **12.** Profound; deep: *a heavy sleep.* **13.** Weighed down, as from weariness or weight: *heavy eyelids from lack of sleep; branches heavy with apples.* **14.** Strong and pervasive; pungent: *a heavy scent.* **15. a.** Substantial; hearty: *a heavy lunch.* **b.** Not easily or quickly digested: *a heavy dessert.* **16.** Marked by strength, power, or force: *a heavy blow.* **17.** Involving large-scale manufacturing, as of machinery: *heavy industry.* **18.** Relatively loud; distinctly audible: *heavy breathing; a heavy sigh.* **19.** Indulging in to a great degree; chronic: *a heavy eater; a heavy reader. —n., pl.* **heav•ies. 1.** A villain in a story or play. **2. a.** A serious or tragic role in a dramatic presentation. **b.** An actor playing such a role. *—adv.* In a heavy manner; with great weight, amount, intensity, etc.: *Night lay heavy on the countryside.* **—heav′i•ly** *adv.* **—heav′i•ness** *n.*

***Idiom.* hang heavy.** To pass slowly or tediously: *Time hung heavy on his hands.*

heav•y-du•ty |hĕv′ē do͞o′tē| *or* |-dyo͞o′-| *adj.* Made to withstand hard use or wear.

heav•y-hand•ed |hĕv′ē hăn′dĭd| *adj.* **1.** Not skillful or graceful; awkward or clumsy in manner or style: *a heavy-handed painter.* **2.** Very strict in correcting or punishing: *a heavy-handed teacher.* **—heav′y-hand′ed•ness** *n.*

heav•y-heart•ed |hĕv′ē här′tĭd| *adj.* Melancholy; sad; depressed: *a heavy-hearted wanderer, far from home.* **—heav′y-heart′ed•ness** *n.*

heavy hydrogen. An isotope of hydrogen having a mass number greater than 1; deuterium or tritium.

heav•y•set |hĕv′ē sĕt′| *adj.* Having a heavy, compact build: *a heavyset, muscular fellow.*

heavy water. Water in which the isotope of hydrogen present is deuterium or, sometimes, tritium.

hea•vy•weight |hĕv′ē wāt′| *n.* **1.** Something or someone of more than average weight. **2.** A

heather

heat of fusion

One gram of ice at 0° C absorbs 80 calories in changing into one gram of liquid water at the same temperature under normal atmospheric pressure. Thus the **heat of fusion** *of water is 80 calories per gram.*

heat of vaporization

One gram of water at 100° C absorbs 539 calories in changing into one gram of steam at the same temperature under normal atmospheric pressure. Thus the **heat of vaporization** *of water is 539 calories per gram.*

Heaviside layer

The **Heaviside layer** *was named after Oliver* Heaviside *(died 1925), British physicist.*

hedgehog

heebie-jeebies
The expression **heebie-jeebies** *was coined by Billy De Beck (1890–1942), American cartoonist, in his comic strip* Barney Google.

heel[1-2]
Heel[1] *and* **heel[2]** *are both Old English words, but they are not related.* **Heel[1]** *was* hēla, *and* **heel[2]** *was* hieldan.

boxer weighing more than 175 pounds. —**modifier:** *a heavyweight fabric; a heavyweight champion.*

He•bra•ic |hĭ brā′ĭk| *adj.* Hebrew.

He•brew |hē′bro͞o| *n.* **1.** A member of the Semitic people claiming descent from Abraham, Isaac, and Jacob; an Israelite. **2. a.** The Semitic language of the ancient Hebrews, in which most of the Old Testament is written. **b.** The modern form of this language, which is the language of Israel. —*adj.* Of the Hebrews or their language.

Hebrew Scriptures. The older part of the Bible, containing the covenant between God and the Jewish people that is the foundation and Bible of Judaism, while constituting for Christians the Old Testament.

heck•le |hĕk′əl| *v.* **heck•led, heck•ling.** To harass or bother, as with questions, annoying interruptions, or mocking yells: *The crowd heckled the speaker at the rally.* —**heck′ler** *n.*

hec•tare |hĕk′târ′| *n.* A unit of area in the metric system, equal to 100 ares or 2.471 acres.

hec•tic |hĕk′tĭk| *adj.* **1.** Marked by intense activity, confusion, or turmoil: *a hectic day.* **2.** Feverish and flushed. —**hec′tic•al•ly** *adv.*

hecto–. A word element meaning "hundred": **hectometer.**

hec•to•me•ter |hĕk′tə mē′tər| *n.* A unit of length in the metric system, equal to 100 meters.

Hec•tor |hĕk′tər|. In Homer's *Iliad,* a Trojan prince killed by Achilles.

he'd |hēd|. **1.** He had. **2.** He would. ¶*These sound alike* **he'd, heed.**

hedge |hĕj| *n.* **1.** A row of closely planted shrubs or small trees forming a fence or boundary. **2.** Anything that serves as a means of protection or defense: *measures that are a direct hedge against pollution.* —*v.* **hedged, hedg•ing. 1.** To enclose or bound with or as if with a hedge or hedges. **2.** To restrict or confine; hem in: *The flooded river hedged us in on one side.* **3.** To avoid making a clear, direct answer or comment: *He also hedges on that issue.*

hedge•hog |hĕj′hôg′| *or* |-hŏg′| *n.* A small animal of Europe, Asia, and Africa, having the back covered with short, stiff spines. It rolls itself into a ball to protect itself. [SEE PICTURE]

hedge•row |hĕj′rō′| *n.* A row of bushes or trees forming a hedge.

he•don•ism |hēd′n ĭz′əm| *n.* **1.** Pursuit of pleasure. **2.** The belief that only that which gives or brings pleasure is good. —**he′don•ist** *n.*

hee•bie-jee•bies |hē′bē jē′bēz| *pl.n. Slang.* A feeling of uneasiness. [SEE NOTE]

heed |hēd| *v.* To pay attention to (a warning, advice, etc.); listen to and consider. —*n.* **1.** Close attention or consideration: *He gave no heed to her greeting.* **2.** Caution; care: *Take heed while crossing the narrow bridge.* ¶*These sound alike* **heed, he'd.**

heed•ful |hēd′fəl| *adj.* Paying close attention; mindful: *He was heedful of their advice.*

heed•less |hēd′lĭs| *adj.* Paying little or no attention; not taking heed; unmindful: *She was heedless of their scornful remarks.* —**heed′less•ly** *adv.* —**heed′less•ness** *n.*

hee•haw |hē′hô′| *n.* The loud, harsh sound made by a braying donkey. —*v.* To make such a sound.

heel[1] |hēl| *n.* **1. a.** The rounded rear portion of the human foot, under and behind the ankle. **b.** A similar part of the hind foot of some other vertebrates. **c.** A similar body part, such as the rounded, fleshy base of the human palm. **2.** The part of a sock, shoe, or stocking that covers the heel. **3. a.** The built-up part of a shoe or boot under the heel of the foot: *shoes with low heels.* **b. heels.** Shoes having heels of a certain height: *buy a pair of high heels.* **4.** The rear part of the working surface of a tool, such as a file or plane. **5.** One of the crusty ends of a loaf of bread. **6.** *Slang.* An insensitive or dishonorable man; a cad. —*v.* **1.** To put a heel or heels on. **2.** To follow closely behind: *told his dog to heel.* ¶*These sound alike* **heel, heal, he'll.** [SEE NOTE]

Idioms. **at (one's) heels.** Following closely behind: *He came into the kitchen with the child at his heels.* **down at the heels. 1.** Having one's shoe heels worn down. **2.** Not neat, tidy, or new in appearance; shabby. **on** (or **upon**) **the heels of. 1.** Directly behind. **2.** Immediately following: *the first spring birds on the heels of winter.* **take to (one's) heels.** To run away; flee: *When the children saw the bull, they took to their heels.*

heel[2] |hēl| *v.* To tilt or become tilted to one side: *heel a ship. The schooner's cargo shifted, and she heeled over dangerously.* ¶*These sound alike* **heel, heal, he'll.** [SEE NOTE]

heft |hĕft| *v.* **1.** To lift; hoist up: *He hefted the pick and went to work.* **2.** To estimate or test the weight of by lifting: *He hefted a parcel.* —*n. Informal.* Weight; heaviness; bulk.

heft•y |hĕf′tē| *adj.* **heft•i•er, heft•i•est. 1.** Having relatively great weight; heavy: *a hefty calf.* **2.** Big and strong: *a hefty sailor.* **3.** Great in force; powerful: *a hefty jolt.* **4.** Large or abundant; ample: *a hefty meal.*

he•gem•o•ny |hĭ jĕm′ə nē| *or* |hĕj′ə mō′nē| *n., pl.* **he•gem•o•nies.** Dominance, especially great influence of one state over another.

He•gi•ra |hĭ jī′rə| *or* |hĕj′ər ə| *n.* **1. a.** The flight of Mohammed from Mecca to Medina in A.D. 622. **b.** The Moslem era, which is reckoned from this date. **2. hegira.** Any flight, as from danger or hardship.

heif•er |hĕf′ər| *n.* A young cow, especially one that has not given birth to a calf.

height |hīt| *n.* **1. a.** The elevation of something above a given level, as above sea level or the ground; altitude: *What is the height of that mountain?* **b.** The distance from the base to the top or apex of something: *the height of a triangle.* **2.** A place, spot, or area a certain distance above or below a given level: *He aimed the rock at a height just above her window.* **3. a.** The extent of elevation above a certain level: *the height of the water in a canal.* **b.** Measurement from head to foot of the body in a normal stance; stature: *The boys compared their heights. The penguin was over three feet in height.* **4.** Often **heights.** A high place or an area of relatively great altitude: *not afraid of heights.* **5.** The highest or uppermost point; summit: *He looked down from the height of the bell tower.* **6. a.** The highest or most advanced degree; zenith: *the height of the power of ancient Egypt.* **b.** The point of greatest activity or intensity; climax: *the height of the tourist season.*

height•en |hīt′n| *v.* **1.** To increase or rise in

ă pat/ā pay/â care/ä father/ĕ pet/ ē be/ĭ pit/ī pie/î fierce/ŏ pot/ ō go/ô paw, for/oi oil/o͝o book/ o͞o boot/ou out/ŭ cut/û fur/ *th* the/th thin/hw which/zh vision/ ə ago, item, pencil, atom, circus

degree or quantity; intensify: *Figures of speech are used to heighten description. Their alarm heightened as the hours passed.* **2.** To make or become high or higher; raise or be raised: *He heightened the chair for the little girl. The cloud from the powerful bomb heightened and expanded.*

hei•nous |hā′nəs| *adj.* Very wicked or evil; abominable; odious: *a heinous crime.* —**hei′nous•ly** *adv.* —**hei′nous•ness** *n.*

heir |âr| *n.* A person who inherits or is legally entitled to inherit the property, rank, title, or office of another. ¶*These sound alike* **heir, air, are[2], e'er, ere.**

heir apparent. *pl.* **heirs apparent.** An heir whose right to inherit is certain provided he survives his ancestor.

heir•ess |âr′ĭs| *n.* A female heir.

heir•loom |âr′lo͞om′| *n.* A possession valued by members of a family and passed down through succeeding generations.

heir pre•sump•tive |prĭ zŭmp′tĭv|. *pl.* **heirs presumptive.** An heir whose right to inherit may be cancelled by the birth of a relative with stronger legal claim to the inheritance.

He•ji•ra |hĭ jī′rə| *or* |hĕj′ər ə| *n.* A form of the word **Hegira.**

held |hĕld|. Past tense and past participle of **hold.**

Hel•e•na |hĕl′ə nə|. The capital of Montana. Population, 22,500.

Hel•en of Troy |hĕl′ən|. In Greek mythology, the wife of Menelaus. Her abduction by Paris caused the Trojan War.

hel•i•cal |hĕl′ĭ kəl| *adj.* Shaped like or nearly like a helix. —**hel′i•cal•ly** *adv.*

hel•i•ces |hĕl′ĭ sēz′| *or* |hē′lĭ-|. A plural of **helix.**

hel•i•con |hĕl′ĭ kŏn′| *or* |-kən| *n.* A large circular tuba that fits around the player's shoulder. [SEE PICTURE]

hel•i•cop•ter |hĕl′ĭ kŏp′tər| *or* |hē′lĭ-| *n.* An aircraft whose lift is provided by one or more sets of vanes, mounted on its top side, that rotate about a roughly vertical axis.

he•li•o•cen•tric |hē′lē ō sĕn′trĭk| *adj.* **1.** Relative to the sun: *the heliocentric position of a planet.* **2.** Having the sun as center: *a heliocentric model of the solar system.*

he•li•o•graph |hē′lē ə grăf′| *or* |-gräf′| *n.* **1.** An instrument once used in photographing the sun. **2.** A signaling device consisting essentially of a movable mirror, used to flash messages by reflected sunlight.

he•li•o•trope |hē′lē ə trōp′| *or* |hēl′yə-| *n.* **1.** A garden plant with small, fragrant, purplish flowers. **2.** A light, reddish purple. —*adj.* Light, reddish purple.

hel•i•port |hĕl′ə pôrt′| *or* |-pōrt′| *n.* An airport for helicopters.

he•li•um |hē′lē əm| *n.* Symbol **He** One of the elements, a colorless, odorless inert gas. Atomic number 2; atomic weight 4.00; melting point −272.2°C; boiling point −268.6°C.

he•lix |hē′lĭks| *n., pl.* **he•lix•es** or **hel•i•ces** |hĕl′ĭ-sēz′| *or* |hē′lĭ-|. **1.** A curve drawn on the surface of a cone or cylinder so that it cuts each element of the figure at the same angle. **2.** Any spiral form or structure. [SEE PICTURES]

hell |hĕl| *n.* **1.** In ancient traditions, the abode of the dead; the underworld. **2.** Often **Hell.** In many religions, the abode of condemned souls and devils; the place of punishment of the wicked after death. **3.** Any place or situation of evil, misery, discord, or destruction: *into the hell of battle.* **4. a.** Torment; anguish: *She went through hell in that job.* **b.** Someone or something that causes trouble, agony, etc.: *He's hell when a job is not properly done.* **5.** Used as an oath: *How the hell can I do that? To hell with it!* —*interj.* A word used to express anger, impatience, dismay, etc.

he'll |hēl|. **1.** He will. **2.** He shall. ¶*These sound alike* **he'll, heal, heel.**

hell•bend•er |hĕl′bĕn′dər| *n.* A large salamander of rivers and streams of the eastern and central United States.

hell-bent |hĕl′bĕnt′| *adj.* Impetuously or recklessly determined to do or achieve something: *He was hell-bent on winning the prize.* —*adv.* Recklessly and determinedly: *He jumped hell-bent across the creek.*

hell•cat |hĕl′kăt′| *n.* **1.** A shrewish or quarrelsome woman; a vixen. **2.** A fiendish person.

hel•le•bore |hĕl′ə bôr′| *or* |-bōr′| *n.* Any of several poisonous plants with white or greenish flowers.

Hel•lene |hĕl′ēn′| *n.* A Greek.

Hel•len•ic |hĕ lĕn′ĭk| *adj.* Of the Greeks or their language and culture.

Hel•le•nis•tic |hĕl′ə nĭs′tĭk| *adj.* Of the Greeks or their language and culture from the time of Alexander the Great into the first century B.C.

hell•gram•mite |hĕl′grə mīt′| *n.* A large, brownish insect larva that lives in water and is often used as fishing bait.

hel•lion |hĕl′yən| *n. Informal.* A mischievous person, especially a young person or child.

hell•ish |hĕl′ĭsh| *adj.* **1.** Of hell. **2.** Like or worthy of hell; devilish; terrible: *a hellish racket; a hellish laugh.* —**hell′ish•ly** *adv.*

hel•lo |hĕ lō′| *or* |hə-| *or* |hĕl′ō| *interj.* A word used to greet someone, answer the telephone, or attract attention. —*n., pl.* **hel•los.** A call or greeting of "hello."

helm[1] |hĕlm| *n.* **1.** The steering gear of a ship, especially the tiller or wheel. **2.** A position of leadership or control. [SEE NOTE]

helm[2] |hĕlm| *n. Archaic.* A helmet. [SEE NOTE]

hel•met |hĕl′mĭt| *n.* A head covering of metal, plastic, or other hard material worn to protect the head, as in battle, work, or sports. —*v.* To provide with a helmet.

helms•man |hĕlmz′mən| *n., pl.* **-men** |-mən|. A person who steers a ship.

help |hĕlp| *v.* **1. a.** To give assistance or support to; aid: *She helped him with the farming.* **b.** To be of service; give assistance: *Do what you can to help.* **c.** To lend a hand to; assist: *She helped him into his coat.* **2.** To contribute to; further the progress or advancement of: *His attitude did not help heal the rift between them.* **3. a.** To give relief to: *help the poor.* **b.** To relieve; ease: *This medicine will help your cold.* **4.** To be able to prevent or change: *I cannot help what happened.* **5.** To refrain from; avoid: *He couldn't help laughing.* **6.** To wait on, as in a store or restaurant: *A very pleasant young man helped me in the sports department.* —***phrasal verb.*** **help out.** To aid with a

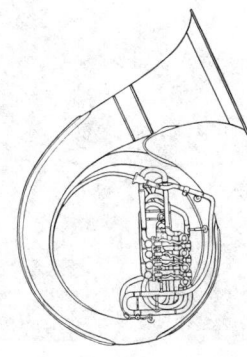

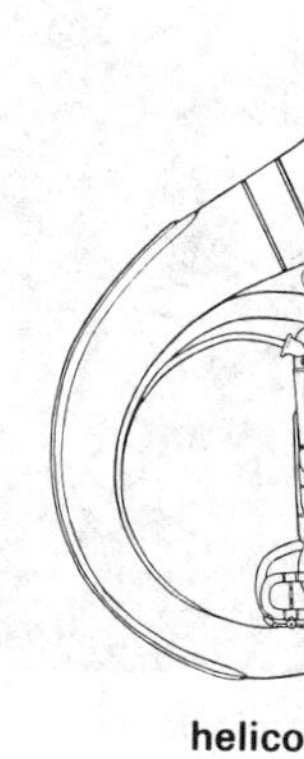

helicon

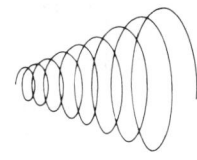

helix
Above: Conical helix
Below: Cylindrical helix

helm[1-2]
Helm[1] *was* helma, *"rudder or tiller," in Old English.* **Helm[2]** *is unchanged from its Old English form. It is now only a poetic and archaic word; for most purposes it has been replaced by its derivative* **helmet.**

hemlock
Needles and cones

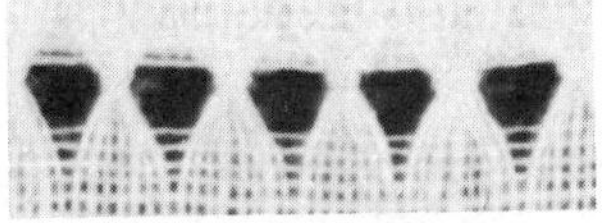

hemstitch

problem or difficulty. —*n.* **1. a.** The act or an example of helping: *We appreciate your help.* **b.** Assistance; aid: *With the help of a dictionary, you can understand words better.* **2.** Someone or something that helps: *She was always a great help to him.* **3. a.** Someone employed to serve in assisting, as a farm hand or servant. **b.** Such people in general: *Help is hard to find these days.* **4.** Relief; remedy: *There is no help for certain diseases.* —**help'er** *n.*

Idioms. **cannot help but.** To be compelled to; be unable to avoid or resist: *He cannot help but do what they ask.* **help (oneself) to. 1.** To serve oneself: *Help yourself to the food.* **2.** To take without asking permission: *Guests at motels frequently help themselves to the towels.*

help•ful |**hĕlp'**fəl| *adj.* Providing help; useful: *a helpful person; helpful methods.* —**help'ful•ly** *adv.* —**help'ful•ness** *n.*

help•ing |**hĕl'**pĭng| *n.* A portion of food for one person.

help•less |**hĕlp'**lĭs| *adj.* **1.** Unable to manage by oneself; dependent upon others: *a helpless old man; as helpless as a baby.* **2.** Indicating such a condition: *a helpless glance; a helpless gesture.* **3.** In a powerless or bewildered condition; incapable of action: *The councilors looked helpless when the king asked them how to weigh the elephant.* **4.** Unable to be remedied: *in a helpless situation.* —**help'less•ly** *adv.* —**help'less•ness** *n.*

help•mate |**hĕlp'**māt'| *n.* A helper or helpful companion, especially a spouse.

help•meet |**hĕlp'**mēt'| *n.* A form of the word **helpmate.**

Hel•sin•ki |**hĕl'**sĭng'kē|. The capital of Finland. Population, 550,000.

hel•ter-skel•ter |**hĕl'**tər **skĕl'**tər| *adv.* **1.** In disorderly haste: *They ran helter-skelter out of school.* **2.** Haphazardly: *Everything had been left helter-skelter on the sand.* —*adj.* Carelessly hurried and confused: *a helter-skelter retreat.*

helve |hĕlv| *n.* A handle of a wagon or tool, such as an ax, chisel, or hammer.

hem[1] |hĕm| *n.* A smooth, even edge of a garment or piece of cloth, made by folding the raw edge under and sewing it down. —*v.* **hemmed, hem•ming.** To fold back and sew down the edge of: *She hemmed her skirt.* —*phrasal verb.* **hem in.** To surround and shut in; enclose: *a valley hemmed in by mountains.*

hem[2] |hĕm| *n.* A short cough or clearing of the throat made to gain attention, hide embarrassment, etc. —*v.* **hemmed, hem•ming. 1.** To make this sound. **2.** To hesitate in speech.

Idiom. **hem and haw.** To be hesitant and indecisive.

he-man |**hē'**măn'| *n., pl.* **-men** |-mĕn'|. *Informal.* A muscular, rugged-looking man.

hem•a•tite |**hĕm'**ə tīt'| *or* |**hē'**mə-| *n.* A reddish mineral that consists mainly of a compound of iron and oxygen. It is the chief ore of iron.

hemi–. A prefix meaning "half": **hemisphere.**

Hem•ing•way |**hĕm'**ĭng wā'|, **Ernest.** 1899–1961. American novelist.

hem•i•sphere |**hĕm'**ĭ sfîr'| *n.* **1. a.** Either of the two halves into which a sphere is divided by a plane that passes through its center. **b.** Either half of a symmetrical object whose shape is roughly that of a sphere: *a hemisphere of the brain.* **2.** Either of the halves into which the earth is divided by the equator or by a great circle that passes through the poles.

hem•i•spher•ic |hĕm'ĭ **sfîr'**ĭk| *or* |**-sfĕr'**-| or **hem•i•spher•i•cal** |hĕm'ĭ **sfîr'**ĭ kəl| *or* |-**sfĕr'**-| *adj.* Of or shaped like a hemisphere.

hem•lock |**hĕm'**lŏk'| *n.* **1. a.** An evergreen tree with short, flat needles and small cones. **b.** The wood of such a tree. **2. a.** A poisonous plant with featherlike leaves and flat clusters of small, whitish flowers. **b.** A poison extracted from this plant. [SEE PICTURE]

hemo–. A word element meaning "blood": **hemoglobin.**

he•mo•glo•bin |**hē'**mə glō'bĭn| *or* |**hĕm'**ə-| *n.* The protein that gives the red blood cells of vertebrates their characteristic color. It has a very complex structure and contains iron. It acts in carrying oxygen from the lungs to other body tissues.

he•mo•phil•i•a |hē'mə **fĭl'**ē ə| *or* |-**fĭl'**yə| *or* |hĕm'ə-| *n.* An inherited blood disease, affecting principally males, in which some of the factors needed for proper clotting are absent. It causes heavy bleeding from even tiny wounds and sometimes bleeding when there is no wound at all.

he•mo•phil•i•ac |hē'mə **fĭl'**ē ăk'| *or* |hĕm'ə-| *n.* A person who suffers from hemophilia.

hem•or•rhage |**hĕm'**ər ĭj| *n.* Bleeding, especially heavy bleeding. —*v.* **hem•or•rhaged, hem•or•rhag•ing.** To have a hemorrhage; bleed heavily.

hem•or•rhoid |**hĕm'**ə roid'| *n.* **1.** A painful or itching mass of swollen, inflamed tissue and dilated veins in the region of the anus. **2. hemorrhoids.** The diseased condition in which such masses of tissue occur; piles.

hemp |hĕmp| *n.* **1. a.** A tall plant with stems that yield a tough fiber used for making rope, cord, etc. **b.** The fiber of this plant. **2.** Any drug, such as hashish, extracted from this plant.

hemp•en |**hĕm'**pən| *adj.* Made of or resembling hemp.

hem•stitch |**hĕm'**stĭch'| *n.* A fancy stitch that leaves an open design in cloth, made by pulling out several parallel threads and drawing the remaining threads together in even bunches. —*v.* To decorate with this stitch. [SEE PICTURE]

hen |hĕn| *n.* **1.** A full-grown female chicken. **2.** The female of various other birds. **3.** *Slang.* A woman, especially a fussy old woman.

hence |hĕns| *adv.* **1.** For this reason; therefore: *before the invention of writing when there were no records and hence no history.* **2.** From now: *30 years hence.* **3.** *Archaic.* Out of here; away from here: *Get thee hence!* —*interj.* *Archaic.* Go; get out: *Hence, away!*

hence•forth |**hĕns'**fôrth'| *adv.* From this or that time on: *Henceforth they would serve as slaves in the countries to which they were taken.*

hence•for•ward |hĕns **fôr'**wərd| *adv.* Henceforth.

hench•man |**hĕnch'**mən| *n., pl.* **-men** |-mən|. **1.** A loyal and trusted political follower who obeys unquestioningly the orders of his leader. **2.** A member of a criminal gang.

hen•na |**hĕn'**ə| *n.* **1. a.** A brownish-red dye obtained from the leaves of an Asian or African shrub. **b.** The shrub that yields this dye. **2.** A brownish red. —*adj.* Brownish red. —*v.* To dye or color with henna.

hen-pecked, also **hen•pecked** |hĕn′pĕkt′| *adj.* Dominated or constantly harassed by a wife: *a hen-pecked husband.*

hen•ry |hĕn′rē| *n., pl.* **hen•ries** or **hen•rys.** The measure of inductance, a unit equal to the inductance of an electric-circuit element across which an electromotive force of one volt is induced when the current through it changes at a rate of one ampere per second. [SEE NOTE]

Hen•ry VIII |hĕn′rē|. 1491–1547. King of England (1509–47).

Hen•ry |hĕn′rē|, **Patrick.** 1736–1799. American Revolutionary statesman and orator.

hep |hĕp| *adj.* A form of the word **hip** (aware).

he•pat•i•ca |hĭ păt′ĭ kə| *n.* A woodland plant with three-lobed leaves and lavender, white, or pink flowers. [SEE PICTURE]

hep•a•ti•tis |hĕp′ə tī′tĭs| *n.* Inflammation of the liver, caused by infection or poisoning.

hep•ta•gon |hĕp′tə gŏn′| *n.* A geometric figure that lies in a plane and is bounded by seven line segments.

hep•tag•o•nal |hĕp tăg′ə nəl| *adj.* Having the general shape of a heptagon; seven-sided.

her |hûr| *or* |hər *when unstressed*| *or* |ər *when unstressed*| *pron.* **1.** The objective case of **she.** —*Note*: *Her* has three main uses. It can be the direct object of a verb: *He touched her on the arm.* It can be the indirect object of a verb: *They gave her sound advice.* It can also be the object of a preposition: *The doorman left the keys with her.* **2.** A possessive form of **she.** —*Note: Her* is also used before nouns that it modifies to show possession or agency. *Her* means *of or belonging to her* (possession) in these examples: *her hat. The schooner had her decks washed by huge waves. Her* means *done or performed by her* (agency) in these examples: *her first job. The "Queen Elizabeth" was on her regular run between New York and Southampton. Her* also means the feminine person, animal, or thing that is the recipient of an action, as in this example: *She suffered her final disappointment and left.*

He•ra |hîr′ə|. In Greek mythology, the sister and wife of Zeus.

her•ald |hĕr′əld| *n.* **1.** A person in past times whose duty it was to convey messages or make announcements, as for a king. **2.** A person or thing that announces or gives indication of something to come; a harbinger: *"the lark, the herald of the morn"* (Shakespeare). —*v.* To indicate the coming of; foretell; announce: *Dark clouds heralded a thunderstorm.*

he•ral•dic |hĕ răl′dĭk| *adj.* Of heralds or heraldry.

her•ald•ry |hĕr′əl drē| *n.* The profession of studying, granting, and designing coats of arms and tracing and studying the descent and history of old families.

herb |ûrb| *or* |hûrb| *n.* **1.** A plant with leaves, roots, or other parts used to flavor food or as medicine. **2.** A plant with fleshy or comparatively soft stems as distinguished from one with woody stems and bark.

her•ba•ceous |hûr bā′shəs| *adj.* Of, like, or consisting of herbs: *a herbaceous plant; a herbaceous border around a flower bed.*

herb•age |ûr′bĭj| *or* |hûr′-| *n.* Growing grass or other soft-stemmed leafy plants, especially when eaten by grazing animals.

herb•al |hûr′bəl| *or* |ûr′-| *adj.* Of or relating to herbs used in cooking or medicine. —*n.* A book about such herbs.

herb•al•ist |hûr′bə lĭst| *or* |ûr′-| *n.* A person who grows, collects, or specializes in the use of herbs, especially medicinal herbs.

her•bar•i•um |hûr bâr′ē əm| *n., pl.* **her•bar•i•ums** or **her•bar•i•a** |hûr bâr′ē ə|. **1.** A collection of dried plants mounted and labeled for use in scientific study. **2.** A place or institution where such a collection is kept.

her•bi•vore |hûr′bə vôr′| *or* |-vōr′| *n.* An animal that feeds entirely on plants or plant parts.

her•biv•o•rous |hər bĭv′ər əs| *adj.* Feeding entirely on plants or plant parts: *Cattle, deer, and rabbits are herbivorous animals.*

her•cu•le•an |hûr′kyə lē′ən| *or* |hûr kyoo͞′lē-ən| *adj.* **1.** Tremendously difficult or demanding: *a herculean task.* **2.** Often **Herculean.** Of or resembling Hercules: *Herculean strength.*

Her•cu•les |hûr′kyə lēz′|. In Greek mythology, a mortal son of Zeus known for his great strength and courage.

herd |hûrd| *n.* **1.** A group of animals, such as cattle or elephants, that stay or are kept together. **2.** A number of people grouped together by some common factor: *A herd of shoppers waited to enter the store.* —*v.* **1.** To gather, keep, or drive together: *Men herded the cattle into railroad cars. Buffalo herded together on the plains.* **2.** To tend or watch over (a group of sheep, goats, etc.). ¶*These sound alike* **herd, heard.**

herd•er |hûr′dər| *n.* **1.** A person who tends or drives a herd, as of sheep or cattle. **2.** A person who owns or breeds livestock.

herds•man |hûrdz′mən| *n., pl.* **-men** |-mən|. A herder.

here |hîr| *adv.* **1.** At or in this place: *put it here.* **2.** At this time; now: *I think I'll call for a vote here.* **3.** At or on this point, detail, or item: *There is great disagreement here.* **4.** To this place; hither: *Come here.* **5.** —Used for emphasis: **a.** After a demonstrative pronoun: *Which word? This here.* **b.** After a noun or pronoun modified by a demonstrative pronoun: *this word here; this one here.* —*interj.* A word used as a response to a roll call, as a command to an animal, etc. ¶*These sound alike* **here, hear.**

here•a•bouts |hîr′ə bouts′| *adv.* In this area; around here.

here•af•ter |hîr ăf′tər| *or* |-äf′-| *adv.* From now on; after this: *I see that I hurt your feelings, so I will be kind to you hereafter.* —*n.* The world to come; life after death.

here•by |hîr bī′| *or* |hîr′bī′| *adv.* By virtue of this act, decree, document, etc.; by this means: *All persons are hereby commanded to comply with the requirements of this proclamation.*

he•red•i•tar•y |hə rĕd′ĭ tĕr′ē| *adj.* **1.** Passed or capable of being passed from parent to offspring by biological inheritance. **2.** Passing from an ancestor to a legal heir; inherited by law: *a hereditary estate.*

he•red•i•ty |hə rĕd′ĭ tē| *n., pl.* **he•red•i•ties. 1.** The passage of physical traits from parents to offspring by biological inheritance; genetic

henry
This unit is named for Joseph Henry *(1797–1878), American physicist.*

hepatica

hermit crab

heron

herringbone

ă pat/ā pay/â care/ä father/ĕ pet/ ē be/ĭ pit/ī pie/î fierce/ŏ pot/ ō go/ô paw, for/oi oil/o͝o book/ o͞o boot/ou out/ŭ cut/û fur/ *th* the/th thin/hw which/zh vision/ ə ago, item, pencil, atom, circus

transmission. **2.** The complete set of traits passed to an organism in this way.

Here•ford |**hûr′**fərd| *or* |**hĕr′**ə-| *n.* One of a breed of reddish-brown and white cattle originally developed in England.

here•in |hîr **ĭn′**| *adv.* In this thing, fact, or place: *After his wife died, he took to reading; herein he found his only consolation.*

here•of |hîr **ŭv′**| *or* |**-ŏv′**| *adv.* Of or concerning this.

here•on |hîr **ŏn′**| *or* |**-ôn′**| *adv.* On this basis or matter: *This is the Constitution; all of our laws are founded hereon.*

here's |hîrz|. Here is.

her•e•sy |**hĕr′**ĭ sē| *n., pl.* **her•e•sies. 1.** An opinion or doctrine in disagreement with established beliefs, especially religious beliefs. **2.** Adherence to such an opinion or doctrine.

her•e•tic |**hĕr′**ĭ tĭk| *n.* A person who holds opinions that differ from established beliefs, especially religious beliefs.

he•ret•i•cal |hə **rĕt′**ĭ kəl| *adj.* Of heresy or heretics: *a heretical movement; a heretical belief.*

here•to |hîr **to͞o′**| *adv.* To this document, place, etc.; to this: *Attached hereto is my voucher.*

here•to•fore |**hîr′**tə fôr′| *or* |-fōr′| *adv.* Before this; previously: *No vessel of such a size had heretofore been seen in the world.*

here•un•to |hîr **ŭn′**to͞o| *or* |hîr′ŭn **to͞o′**| *adv.* Hereto.

here•up•on |**hîr′**ə pŏn′| *or* |-pôn′| *adv.* Immediately after this; at this: *The troops opened fire; hereupon there was a bloody uprising.*

here•with |hîr **wĭth′**| *or* |**-wĭth′**| *adv.* **1.** Together with this: *I am sending herewith a snapshot of the baby.* **2.** By means of this; hereby: *I herewith renounce all claim to the estate.*

her•i•tage |**hĕr′**ĭ tĭj| *n.* **1.** Property that is or can be inherited. **2.** Something other than property passed down from preceding generations; legacy; tradition: *Every country has its heritage of folk music.*

her•maph•ro•dite |hər **măf′**rə dīt′| *n.* **1.** Someone who has the sex organs and secondary sex characteristics of both male and female. **2.** An organism, such as an earthworm or many plants, having both male and female sex organs in a single individual.

Her•mes |**hûr′**mēz′|. In Greek mythology, the messenger of the gods and patron of travelers, thieves, and commerce.

her•met•ic |hər **mĕt′**ĭk| or **her•met•i•cal** |hər **mĕt′**ĭ kəl| *adj.* Sealed so that air cannot enter or escape; airtight. —**her•met′i•cal•ly** *adv.*

her•mit |**hûr′**mĭt| *n.* A person who has withdrawn from society and lives a solitary existence.

her•mit•age |**hûr′**mĭ tĭj| *n.* **1.** The home of a hermit. **2.** A monastery.

hermit crab. A crab that uses an empty snail shell or similar shell to protect its own soft, unarmored body. [See Picture]

hermit thrush. A North American bird having a brownish back, a spotted breast, and a melodious song.

her•ni•a |**hûr′**nē ə| *n., pl.* **her•ni•as** or **her•ni•ae** |**hûr′**nē ē′|. A condition in which an organ or other structure of the body protrudes through an abnormal opening in the wall that normally contains it; a rupture.

he•ro |**hîr′**ō| *n., pl.* **he•roes. 1.** A man noted for his courage, special achievements, etc.: *a war hero; a sports hero.* **2.** The main male character in a novel, poem, movie, etc. **3.** A large sandwich made with a long, crusty roll or a loaf of bread split lengthwise.

Her•od An•ti•pas |**hĕr′**əd **ăn′**tĭ păs′|. Tetrarch of Galilee (4 B.C.–A.D. 40); examined Christ at the request of Pilate.

he•ro•ic |hĭ **rō′**ĭk| or **he•ro•i•cal** |hĭ **rō′**ĭ kəl| *adj.* **1.** Having or showing the qualities of a hero; courageous; noble: *heroic deeds; the heroic voyage of Magellan's men.* **2.** Having to do with or dealing with persons of great courage and deeds: *a heroic age in history.* —**he•ro′i•cal•ly** *adv.*

he•ro•ics |hĭ **rō′**ĭks| *n.* (*used with a plural verb*). Melodramatic behavior or language.

her•o•in |**hĕr′**ō ĭn| *n.* A bitter, white crystalline chemical compound derived from morphine. It is a powerful, very poisonous narcotic drug that is also very addictive. ¶*These sound alike* **heroin, heroine.**

her•o•ine |**hĕr′**ō ĭn| *n.* **1.** The female counterpart of a hero. **2.** The main female character in a novel, poem, movie, etc. ¶*These sound alike* **heroine, heroin.**

her•o•ism |**hĕr′**ō ĭz′əm| *n.* Heroic conduct or action; courage; bravery: *a great display of heroism on the battlefield.*

her•on |**hĕr′**ən| *n.* Any of several wading birds with a long neck, long legs, and a long, pointed bill. [See Picture]

her•pes |**hûr′**pēz′| *n.* Any of several diseases, caused by viruses, in which there is an eruption of the skin or mucous membrane.

her•pe•tol•o•gy |hûr′pĭ **tŏl′**ə jē| *n.* The scientific study of reptiles and amphibians.

her•ring |**hĕr′**ĭng| *n., pl.* **her•ring** or **her•rings. 1.** A fish of northern Atlantic waters, caught in large numbers for canning, pickling, or smoking. **2.** Any of several related fish.

her•ring•bone |**hĕr′**ĭng bōn′| *n.* **1.** A zigzag pattern made up of short parallel lines arranged in rows that slant first one way, then another. **2.** Cloth woven in this pattern. ***—modifier:*** *a herringbone tweed.* [See Picture]

hers |hûrz| *pron.* A possessive form of **she. 1.** —Used to indicate that something or someone belongs or pertains to her: *The large package is hers. He is no friend of hers.* **2.** —Used to indicate the one or ones belonging to her: *If his desk is occupied, use hers.*

her•self |hər **sĕlf′**| *pron.* A special form of **her.** It is used: **1.** In place of *her,* serving as a direct object, indirect object, or object of a preposition, to show that the action of a reflexive verb refers back to the subject: *She blamed herself* (direct object). *Jean always gives herself* (indirect object) *too much credit. She has saved it all for herself* (object of a preposition). **2.** Following or referring to a noun or the pronoun *she,* to give emphasis: *Mother herself is going. She herself saw it.* **3.** Referring to the subject, to mean *her real, normal, or healthy self: She has not been herself since the accident.*

Idiom. **by herself. 1.** Alone: *went to the party by herself.* **2.** Without help: *did all the work by herself.*

hertz |hûrtz| *n., pl.* **hertz** or **hertz•es.** A unit of frequency equal to one cycle per second.

he's |hēz|. **1.** He is. **2.** He has.

hes•i•tan•cy |hĕz′ĭ tən sē| *n., pl.* **hes•i•tan•cies. 1.** The condition or quality of being hesitant; indecision. **2.** An example of hesitating.

hes•i•tant |hĕz′ĭ tənt| *adj.* Inclined or tending to hesitate: *Stephen didn't know what to do and stood, hesitant, beside the sink.* —**hes′i•tant•ly** *adv.*

hes•i•tate |hĕz′ĭ tāt′| *v.* **hes•i•tat•ed, hes•i•tat•ing. 1.** To be slow to act, speak, or decide; pause in doubt or uncertainty; waver. **2.** To speak haltingly; falter.

hes•i•ta•tion |hĕz′ĭ tā′shən| *n.* **1.** The act or an example of hesitating. **2.** The condition of being hesitant: *Trying to conceal his hesitation, Buffalo Bill entered.* **3.** A pause in speech.

Hes•sian |hĕsh′ən| *n.* **1.**An inhabitant of **Hesse** |hĕs|, a state in Germany. **2.** A Hessian soldier who was hired to fight in the British army in America during the Revolutionary War. —*adj.* Of Hesse or its people.

hetero–. A word element meaning "other, different": **heterogeneous.**

het•er•o•dox |hĕt′ər ə dŏks′| *adj.* Not in agreement with accepted beliefs, especially in religion.

het•er•o•dox•y |hĕt′ər ə dŏk′sē| *n., pl.* **het•er•o•dox•ies. 1.** The condition of being heterodox. **2.** A heterodox belief.

het•er•o•ge•ne•ous |hĕt′ər ə jē′nē əs| *or* |-jēn′yəs| *adj.* Consisting of parts that are not alike; having dissimilar elements; not homogeneous: *a heterogeneous collection.* —**het′er•o•ge′ne•ous•ly** *adv.* —**het′er•o•ge′ne•ous•ness** *n.*

het•er•o•sex•u•al |hĕt′ər ə sĕk′sho͞o əl| *adj.* **1.** Marked by attraction to the opposite sex. **2.** Of different sexes. —*n.* A heterosexual person. —**het′er•o•sex′u•al′i•ty** *n.*

hew |hyo͞o| *v.* **hewed, hewn** |hyo͞on| or **hewed, hew•ing. 1.** To make or shape with an ax, knife, etc.: *hunters hewing their way through dense jungle.* **2.** To cut down with an ax; fell: *hew down an oak.* **3.** To strike or cut; chop: *hewed in pieces.* **4.** To adhere; keep; hold: *The new chairman will probably hew closely to the policies of his predecessor.* ¶*These sound alike* **hew, hue.**

hex |hĕks| *n.* **1.** An evil spell; a curse. **2.** Someone or something that brings bad luck. —*v.* **1.** To work evil on; bewitch. **2.** To wish or bring bad luck to.

hex•a•gon |hĕk′sə gŏn′| *n.* A geometric figure that lies in a plane and is bounded by six line segments. [SEE PICTURE]

hex•ag•o•nal |hĕk săg′ə nəl| *adj.* Having the general form of a hexagon; six-sided.

hey |hā| *interj.* **1.** A word used to express surprise, appreciation, wonder, etc.: *Hey, that's nice!* **2.** A word used to attract attention: *Hey, you!* ¶*These sound alike* **hey, hay.**

hey•day |hā′dā′| *n.* The period of greatest popularity, success, fashion, power, etc.; prime: *Piano ragtime reached its heyday toward the end of World War I.*

Hf The symbol for the element hafnium.

Hg The symbol for the element mercury.

hi |hī| *interj. Informal.* A word used as a greeting. ¶*These sound alike* **hi, hie, high.**

H.I. Hawaiian Islands.

hi•a•tus |hī ā′təs| *n., pl.* **hi•a•tus•es. 1.** A gap; missing section: *a hiatus in a manuscript.* **2.** Any loss or interruption in time or continuity.

Hi•a•wath•a |hī′ə wŏth′ə| *or* |-wô′thə|. The North American Indian hero of Longfellow's narrative poem *The Song of Hiawatha* (1855).

hi•ba•chi |hĭ bä′chē| *n.* A small charcoal-burning stove of Japanese origin. [SEE PICTURE]

hi•ber•nate |hī′bər nāt′| *v.* **hi•ber•nat•ed, hi•ber•nat•ing.** To spend the winter in an inactive state resembling deep sleep, during which the body temperature is lower than normal and breathing and other body processes slow down. —**hi′ber•na′tion** *n.* [SEE NOTE on p. 433]

Hi•ber•ni•a |hī bûr′nē ə|. *Latin.* Ireland.

hi•bis•cus |hī bĭs′kəs| *or* |hĭ-| *n., pl.* **hi•bis•cus•es.** Any of several tropical plants with large, showy, variously colored flowers.

hic•cup, also **hic•cough** |hĭk′ŭp| *n.* **1.** A spasm of the diaphragm that causes a sudden inhalation that is quickly cut off by another spasm in the glottis. **2. the hiccups.** An attack in which spasms of this kind occur repeatedly. —*v.* **hic•cupped, hic•cup•ping. 1.** To make the sound of a hiccup. **2.** To have the hiccups.

hick |hĭk|. *Informal. n.* A gullible, provincial person; a yokel. —*adj.* Rural: *a hick town.* The word "hick" is often considered contemptuous.

hick•o•ry |hĭk′ə rē| *n., pl.* **hick•o•ries. 1.** Any of several North American trees that have hard wood and that bear edible nuts with a smooth, hard shell. **2.** The wood of such a tree.

hid |hĭd|. Past tense and a past participle of **hide** (put out of sight).

hid•den |hĭd′n|. A past participle of **hide.** —*adj.* Out of sight, view, etc.; concealed: *a hidden driveway; a hidden meaning.*

hide¹ |hīd| *v.* **hid** |hĭd|, **hid•den** |hĭd′n| or **hid, hid•ing. 1.** To put or keep out of sight; secrete: *hide the Christmas gifts in the closet.* **2.** To prevent from being known; conceal: *She could barely hide her horror.* **3.** To cut off from sight; cover up: *Clouds hid the stars.* [SEE NOTE]

hide² |hīd| *n.* The skin of an animal, especially the thick, tough skin of a large animal. [SEE NOTE]

hide-and-seek |hīd′n sēk′| *n.* A children's game in which one player tries to find and catch others who are hiding.

hide•a•way |hīd′ə wā′| *n.* **1.** A hide-out. **2.** A secluded or isolated place.

hide•bound |hīd′bound′| *adj.* Adhering too much to one's own opinions or prejudices; narrow-minded.

hid•e•ous |hĭd′ē əs| *adj.* **1.** Horribly ugly; revolting: *a hideous mask.* **2.** Repugnant to the moral sense; despicable; odious: *a hideous murder.* —**hid′e•ous•ly** *adv.*

hide-out |hīd′out′| *n.* A place of shelter or concealment.

hid•ing¹ |hī′dĭng| *n.* The condition of being hidden: *go into hiding.* [SEE NOTE]

hid•ing² |hī′dĭng| *n. Informal.* A beating or thrashing. [SEE NOTE]

hie |hī| *v.* **hied, hie•ing** or **hy•ing.** *Archaic.* To hasten; hurry. ¶*These sound alike* **hie, hi, high.**

hi•er•ar•chi•cal |hī′ə rär′kĭ kəl| *or* |hī rär′-| or **hi•er•ar•chic** |hī′ə rär′kĭk| *or* |hī rär′-| *adj.* Of a hierarchy. —**hi′er•ar′chi•cal•ly** *adv.*

hi•er•ar•chy |hī′ə rär′kē| *or* |hī′rär′-| *n., pl.* **hi•er•ar•chies.** A body of persons, especially clergy,

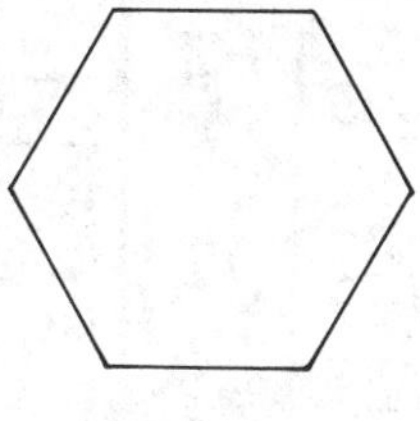

hexagon

hibachi

hide¹·²/hiding¹·²

Hide¹ *and* **hide²** *are both Old English words, and they are fairly closely related.* **Hide¹** *was Old English* hȳdan, *and is descended from a prehistoric Germanic root meaning "to cover over, to conceal."* **Hide²** *was Old English* hȳd *and is from the same root in the sense "a covering, a skin or pelt."* **Hiding¹** *and* **hiding²** *are thus also related;* **hiding¹** *needs no explanation, and* **hiding²** *means "a beating of the hide or skin."*

hieroglyphic

hi-fi

Hi-fi *is a rare example of a radical spelling simplification tha has been fully accepted. Usually such simplifications are considered informal, like* el-hi *for "elementary and high school."*

high jump

ă pat/ā pay/â care/ä father/ĕ pet/ ē be/ĭ pit/ī pie/î fierce/ŏ pot/ ō go/ô paw, for/oi oil/ŏŏ book/ ōō boot/ou out/ŭ cut/û fur/ *th* the/th thin/hw which/zh vision/ ə ago, item, pencil, atom, circus

organized or classified according to rank, capacity, or authority.

hi•er•o•glyph |hī'ər ə glĭf'| *or* |hī'rə glĭf'| *n.* A form of the word **hieroglyphic.**

hi•er•o•glyph•ic |hī'ər ə glĭf'ĭk| *or* |hī'rə-| or **hi•er•o•glyph•i•cal** |hī'ər ə glĭf'ĭ kəl| *or* |hī'rə-| *adj.* Of or written in a system of writing, used in ancient Egypt, in which pictures or symbols are used to represent words or sounds. *—n.* **1.** A picture or symbol used in hieroglyphic writing. **2. hieroglyphics.** Hieroglyphic writing. [SEE PICTURE]

hi•fa•lu•tin |hī'fə lōōt'n| *adj. Informal.* A form of the word **highfalutin.**

hi-fi |hī'fī'| *n.* **1. High fidelity. 2.** A system that produces realistic reproduction of sound from a radio, record, or magnetic tape. ***—modifier:*** *a hi-fi system.* [SEE NOTE]

hig•gle•dy-pig•gle•dy |hĭg'əl dē pĭg'əl dē| *adv.* In utter disorder or confusion. *—adj.* Disordered; jumbled.

high |hī| *adj.* **high•er, high•est. 1. a.** Having a relatively great elevation; extending far upward: *a high mountain; a high stool.* **b.** Extending a specified distance upward: *a cabinet 4 feet high and 2 feet wide.* **2.** Far above the horizon: *The sun is high in the sky.* **3.** Far from the equator: *the high latitudes.* **4.** Above average, as in degree, amount, quality, or intensity: *high temperature; higher wages; a high standard of living.* **5. a.** Having a musical pitch that corresponds to a relatively great number of cycles per second: *the high tones of a flute.* **b.** Not soft or hushed; piercing: *a high voice.* **6.** Being at or near its peak: *high noon.* **7.** Eminent in rank or status: *a high official.* **8.** Of great importance: *a high priority.* **9.** Excited; elated: *high spirits.* **10.** *Slang.* Intoxicated by alcohol or a narcotic. **11.** Relatively well-developed; complex: *the world of high finance.* **12.** At an advanced stage of development or complexity: *higher forms of animal life.* **13.** Favorable: *a high opinion of himself.* **14.** Allowing the greatest output speed: *high gear.* **15.** Luxurious; extravagant: *high living.* *—adv.* At, in, or to a high position, price, or level: *fly high in the sky.* *—n.* **1.** A high degree, level, point, etc.: *Prices reached a new high.* **2.** A mass of atmospheric air that exerts greater pressure than the air in the regions surrounding it; anticyclone. **3.** The transmission gear, as of an automobile, truck, etc., that gives the greatest output speed for a given engine speed. **4.** *Informal.* Intoxication or euphoria induced by a stimulant, narcotic, or other drug. ¶*These sound alike* **high, hi, hie.**

Idioms. **high and dry. 1.** Helpless; alone: *He left me high and dry.* **2.** Out of water, as a ship. **high and low.** Here and there; everywhere. **high and mighty.** Arrogant; domineering.

high•ball |hī'bôl'| *n.* An alcoholic beverage mixed with water or soda and served in a tall glass. ***—modifier:*** *a highball glass.*

high•boy |hī'boi'| *n.* A tall chest of drawers divided into two sections and supported on four legs.

High-Church |hī'chûrch'| *adj.* Of a faction of a Protestant Church that favors the orthodox ceremony and tradition of the Roman Catholic Church.

high explosive. An explosive that detonates rapidly and with great force.

high•fa•lu•tin |hī'fə lōōt'n| *adj. Informal.* Pompous or pretentious: *highfalutin notions.*

high fidelity. The reproduction and processing of electrical signals, especially those that represent sounds, as on records or magnetic tape, with little or no undesired change. ***—modifier:*** **(high-fidelity):** *high-fidelity equipment.*

high-flown |hī'flōn'| *adj.* **1.** Lofty; exalted: *high-flown ideals.* **2.** Pretentious; inflated.

high frequency. Any radio-wave frequency in the range between 3 megahertz (millions of cycles per second) and 30 megahertz. ***—modifier:*** **(high-frequency):** *high-frequency radio waves.*

high•hand•ed |hī'hăn'dĭd| *adj.* In an arrogant or arbitrary manner: *a highhanded reply.* **—high'hand'ed•ly** *adv.*

high jump. 1. A jump for height made over an adjustable horizontal bar in a field contest. **2.** Such a contest. [SEE PICTURE]

high•land |hī'lənd| *n.* **1.** Elevated land. **2. highlands.** A mountainous region or part of a country. **3. the Highlands.** A mountainous region of northern and western Scotland. ***—modifier:*** *a highland area; Highland traditions.*

High•land•er |hī'lən dər| *n.* A native of the Scottish Highlands.

Highland fling. A folk dance of the Highlands.

high•light |hī'līt'| *n.* **1.** A light or brilliantly lighted area, as in a painting or photograph. **2.** An outstanding event or part: *the highlight of one's career; the highlights of a story.* *—v.* **high•light•ed, high•light•ing.** To give prominence to, as by light; emphasize.

high•ly |hī'lē| *adv.* **1.** To a great degree; extremely; very: *highly developed; highly valued; highly amusing.* **2.** In a good or favorable way: *I think highly of him.* **3.** In a high position or rank: *a highly placed official.* **4.** At a high salary, cost, etc.: *a highly paid executive.*

high-mind•ed |hī'mīn'dĭd| *adj.* Noble; idealistic. **—high'-mind'ed•ness** *n.*

high•ness |hī'nĭs| *n.* **1.** Tallness; height. **2. Highness.** A title used in speaking of or to a member of a royal family: *Your Highness; His Royal Highness the Duke of Kent.*

high-pitched |hī'pĭcht'| *adj.* **1.** High in pitch, as a voice or musical tone. **2.** Steeply sloped, as a roof.

high-rise |hī'rīz'| *adj.* Designating a tall building with many stories reached by elevators. *—n.* A high-rise building.

high•road |hī'rōd'| *n. British.* A main road; highway.

high school. A secondary school including grades 9 or 10 through 12 or 7 through 12. ***—modifier:*** **(high-school):** *a high-school teacher.*

high seas. The open waters of an ocean or sea beyond the limits of a nation's jurisdiction.

high-spir•it•ed |hī'spĭr'ĭ tĭd| *adj.* **1.** Having a proud or unbroken spirit; brave. **2.** Lively; vivacious.

high-strung |hī'strŭng'| *adj.* Tending to be very nervous and sensitive.

high tide. 1. The tide when the water reaches its highest level. **2.** The time at which this occurs.

high time. 1. A time almost too late; fully time: *It's high time we went.* **2.** *Informal.* A good time.

high treason. Treason against one's country or sovereign.

high-wa•ter mark |hī'wô'tər| *or* |-wŏt'ər|. **1.** A mark showing the highest level reached by a body of water. **2.** The highest point, as of achievement; apex.

high•way |hī'wā'| *n.* **1.** A main public road, especially one connecting towns or cities. **2.** Any main route on land, over water, or in the air. *—modifier: a highway patrol.*

high•way•man |hī'wā'mən| *n., pl.* **-men** |-mən|. A robber who holds up travelers on a highway, especially one of former times in England.

high wire. A rope, usually of wire, tightly stretched high above the ground, upon which acrobats perform; a tightrope.

hi•jack |hī'jăk'| *v.* **1.** To rob (a truck, train, etc.) by stopping it in transit. **2.** To steal (goods) from a vehicle by stopping it in transit. **3.** To seize or take control of (a moving vehicle, such as a truck, aircraft, etc.). **—hi'jack'er** *n.*

hike |hīk| *v.* **hiked, hik•ing. 1.** To go on an extended walk, especially for pleasure; tramp. **2.** To pull or raise, especially with a sudden motion; hitch: *He hiked up his pants.* **3.** To rise or raise in amount: *hike up prices.* **—hik'ing** *adj.: a hiking trail.* *—n.* **1.** A long walk or trip on foot, as over countryside. **2.** A rise, as in prices. **—hik'er** *n.*

hi•lar•i•ous |hĭ lâr'ē əs| *or* |-lăr'-| *or* |hī-| *adj.* Boisterously funny; provoking much laughter: *a hilarious story.* **—hi•lar'i•ous•ly** *adv.*

hi•lar•i•ty |hĭ lăr'ĭ tē| *or* |-lâr'-| *or* |hī-| *n.* Boisterous merriment, fun, etc.

hill |hĭl| *n.* **1. a.** A feature of the earth's surface consisting of an elevated point, not as high as the top of a mountain, from which the land slopes away in all directions. **b. hills.** A range or group of features of this kind. **2.** An incline, especially in a road; a slope. **3.** A mound of earth.

hill•bil•ly |hĭl'bĭl'ē| *n., pl.* **hill•bil•lies.** *Informal.* A person who lives in or comes from a mountain area far from cities, especially in the southeastern United States. The word "hillbilly" is often considered offensive. *—modifier: hillbilly music.*

hill•ock |hĭl'ək| *n.* A small hill.

hill•side |hĭl'sīd'| *n.* The side of a hill.

hill•top |hĭl'tŏp'| *n.* The top of a hill.

hill•y |hĭl'ē| *adj.* **hill•i•er, hill•i•est.** Having many hills: *Puerto Rico is a hilly island.*

hilt |hĭlt| *n.* The handle of a sword or dagger.
Idiom. **to the hilt.** To the limit; completely: *He was in debt to the hilt.*

him |hĭm| *pron.* The objective case of **he.** *—Note:* *Him* has three main uses. It can be the direct object of a verb: *Everyone liked him.* It can be the indirect object of a verb: *Mary gave him the wallet.* It can also be the object of a preposition: *The garage attendant left your car keys with him.* ¶*These sound alike* **him, hymn.**

Him•a•la•yas |hĭm'ə lā'əz| *or* |hĭ măl'yəz|. Also **Himalaya Mountains.** A chain of mountains along the border between India and Tibet, having the highest peaks in the world. **—Him'a•la'yan** *adj.* [SEE NOTE]

him•self |hĭm sĕlf'| *pron.* A special form of **him.** It is used: **1.** In place of *him,* serving as a direct object, indirect object, or object of a preposition, to show that the action of a reflexive verb refers back to the subject: *He hit himself* (direct object) *with the hammer. John gave himself* (indirect object) *the benefit of the doubt. He put the blame on himself* (object of a preposition). **2.** Following or referring to a noun or the pronoun *he,* to give emphasis: *The boy himself admitted it. He himself did it.* **3.** Referring to the subject, to mean *his real, normal, or healthy self: Bill was not himself when he spoke so rudely. He looks more like himself after the vacation.*
Idiom. **by himself. 1.** Alone: *seated in a corner by himself.* **2.** Without help: *He wrote the speech by himself.*

hind¹ |hīnd| *adj.* At the rear or back part, especially of an animal: *hind legs.* [SEE NOTE]

hind² |hīnd| *n.* The female of the European red deer. [SEE NOTE]

hin•der¹ |hĭn'dər| *v.* To interfere with or prevent the action or progress of; get in the way of: *Rain hindered highway construction.* [SEE NOTE]

hind•er² |hīn'dər| *adj.* Toward the rear: *one of the hinder legs of a caterpillar.* [SEE NOTE]

Hin•di |hĭn'dē| *n.* An Indo-European language widely spoken in northern India. **—Hin'di** *adj.*

hind•most |hīnd'mōst'| *adj.* Farthest to the rear.

hind•quar•ter |hīnd'kwôr'tər| *n.* **1.** Often **hindquarters.** The rump or haunches of a four-footed animal. **2.** The hind leg and rear part of the body of an animal prepared for use as meat.

hin•drance |hĭn'drəns| *n.* **1.** Something or someone that hinders; an obstacle: *Strong winds are a hindrance to mountain climbers.* **2.** An act of hindering or a condition of being hindered: *unable to proceed without hindrance.*

hind•sight |hīnd'sīt'| *n.* A looking back to past events with full understanding or knowledge that was lacking when they occurred.

Hin•du |hĭn'dōō| *n.* A native or inhabitant of India, especially a believer in Hinduism. *—adj.* Of the Hindus or Hinduism.

Hin•du-Ar•a•bic numerals |hĭn'dōō ăr'ə bĭk|. **Arabic numerals.**

Hin•du•ism |hĭn'dōō ĭz'əm| *n.* The major religion of India, based on belief in a supreme being of many forms and natures. This religion has a complex system of philosophical and social doctrines.

hinge |hĭnj| *n.* **1.** A jointed device on which a door, gate, lid, etc., turns or swings. **2.** A similar structure joining two movable parts, such as the elbow or knee joint or the connecting joint on each of the two halves of a clam shell, oyster shell, etc. *—v.* **hinged, hing•ing. 1.** To attach by means of a hinge or hinges. **2. —hinge on** or **upon.** To depend: *A great deal hinges on this decision.* **—hinged'** *adj.: a box with a hinged lid.*

hin•ny |hĭn'ē| *n., pl.* **hin•nies.** A hybrid animal that is the offspring of a female donkey and a male horse. See **mule.**

hint |hĭnt| *n.* **1.** A slight indication or indirect suggestion: *Her smile gave no hint of how angry she felt.* **2.** A piece of useful information; a clue: *Listed below are some hints to help you solve the math problems.* **3.** A small amount; trace: *an almost white horse with just a hint of color.* *—v.* To make known or suggest by a hint or hints: *Our hostess hinted that it was time to leave.*

hin•ter•land |hĭn'tər lănd'| *n.* **1.** Land not bordering on a seacoast; an inland area. **2.** An

Himalayas/hibernate
The name **Himalaya** *means "the place of snow" in Sanskrit:* himā-, *"snow,"* + ālaya, *"place, abode." The Sanskrit word* himā-, *"snow, winter," is descended from the prehistoric Indo-European word* ghiem-, *also meaning "snow, winter." This word separately survived in Latin as* hībernus, *an adjective meaning "of the winter."* Hībernus *formed a verb* hībernāre, *"to pass the winter," which was borrowed into English as* **hibernate.**

hind¹⁻²/hinder¹⁻²
Hind¹ *and* **hinder²** *are shortenings of Old English* hindeweard *and* hinderweard, *"backward, toward the back," from a root* hind- *meaning "back."* **Behind** *is also from this root.* **Hinder¹** *was* hindrian *in Old English; it originally meant "to keep someone back" and is from the same root.* **Hind²** *is not related; it was* hind *in Old English, and it is descended from a root meaning "hornless animal" (the stag has antlers but the hind does not).*

hip$^{1\text{-}2\text{-}3\text{-}4}$

Hip^1 *and* **hip^2** *are unrelated Old English words; they were originally* hype *and* hēope, *respectively.* **Hip^3**, *according to the* Dictionary of American Slang *(1967), by Harold Wentworth and Stuart Berg Flexner, is a variant of* **hep**. **Hep**, *or* **hip^3**, *emerged around 1915; in the thirties it became especially associated with jazz and swing music; in the forties* **hip** *displaced* **hep**, *then* **hep cat** *gave way to* **hipster**, *and in the sixties the* **hippie** *was born. But the ultimate origin of* **hip^3**, *or* **hep**, *is unknown. The origin of* **hip^4** *is unknown.*

hippopotamus

Hippopotamus *comes from Greek* hippopotamos, *"river-horse":* hippos, *"horse,"* + potamos, *"river."* Hippos *is descended from* ekwos, *the prehistoric Indo-European word for "horse" (an Indo-European* kw *regularly became a* p *in Greek). See also note at* **equestrian**.

ă pat/ā pay/â care/ä father/ĕ pet/ ē be/ĭ pit/ī pie/î fierce/ŏ pot/ ō go/ô paw, for/oi oil/ŏŏ book/ ōō boot/ou out/ŭ cut/û fur/ *th* the/th thin/hw which/zh vision/ ə ago, item, pencil, atom, circus

area far from cities or towns; back country.

hip^1 |hĭp| *n.* **1.** The part of the body that projects outward over the hipbone between the waist and thigh. **2.** The hipbone or the hip joint. —***modifier:*** *a hip pocket.* [SEE NOTE]

hip^2 |hĭp| *n.* The berrylike, often bright-red seed case of a rose. [SEE NOTE]

hip^3 |hĭp| *adj.* **hip•per, hip•pest.** *Slang.* Well acquainted with new, often unconventional ideas or ways of behaving. [SEE NOTE]

hip^4 |hĭp| *interj.* Used in giving a cheer: *Hip, hip, hurrah!* [SEE NOTE]

hip•bone |**hĭp'**bōn'| *n.* Either of the large, flat, irregularly shaped bones that form the two halves of the pelvis.

hip joint. The joint between the hipbone and the femur, or thighbone.

hip•pie |**hĭp'**ē| *n. Informal.* A usually young person who joins with others in ideas, behavior, and a style of dress that express opposition to and rejection of conventional standards.

hip•po |**hĭp'**ō| *n., pl.* **hip•pos.** *Informal.* A hippopotamus.

Hip•poc•ra•tes |hĭ **pŏk'**rə tēz'|. 460?–377? B.C. Greek physician.

Hip•po•crat•ic oath |hĭp'ə **krăt'**ĭk|. A statement, dating from ancient times, in which newly qualified physicians swear to abide by the ethical principles of the medical profession.

hip•po•drome |**hĭp'**ə drōm'| *n.* **1.** A stadium with an oval racetrack, used for chariot races in ancient Greece and Rome. **2.** An arena used for horse shows and similar spectacles.

hip•po•pot•a•mus |hĭp'ə **pŏt'**ə məs| *n., pl.* **hip•po•pot•a•mus•es** or **hip•po•pot•a•mi** |hĭp'ə **pŏt'**ə mī'|. A large African river animal with dark, almost hairless skin, short legs, a broad snout, and a wide mouth. [SEE NOTE & PICTURE]

hire |hīr| *v.* **hired, hir•ing. 1.** To pay (a person or persons) for working or performing a service; employ: *hire workers.* **2.** To pay for the use of (something) for a limited time; rent: *hire a car.* —**hired'** *adj.: hired help; a hired car.* —***phrasal verb.*** **hire out.** To work or allow to be used for pay: *Phil hired out as a farm worker. Pablo hired out his donkey cart to the tourists.* —*n.* **1.** Money given as payment for doing work or for the use of something: *The day's hire for the car is ten dollars.* **2.** The act or fact of hiring; employment: *With the hire of the two assistants, the work became easier.*

Idiom. **for hire.** Available for use in exchange for payment.

hire•ling |**hīr'**lĭng| *n.* A person who works for pay, especially one willing to do any kind of work, however hateful or unpleasant, for money.

Hi•ro•shi•ma |hîr'ō **shē'**mə| *or* |hĭ **rō'**shĭ mə|. A port city in southwestern Japan, devastated by the first atomic bomb used in warfare (1945). Population, 550,000.

hir•sute |**hûr'**sōōt'| *adj.* Hairy.

his |hĭz| *pron.* The possessive form of **he**. **1.** —Used to indicate that someone or something belongs or pertains to him: *The book is his. I am a friend of his.* **2.** —Used to indicate the one or ones belonging to him: *If you can't find your hat, take his.* —*Note: His* is also used before nouns that it modifies to show possession or agency. *His* means *of or belonging to him* (possession) in this example: *His house was not far from ours. His* means *done or performed by him* (agency) in this example: *The boy was careful to see that his studies came first. His* also means the masculine person, animal, or thing that is the recipient of an action, as in this example: *The general suffered his final defeat and was sent into exile.*

His•pan•ic |hĭ **spăn'**ĭk| *adj.* Of or relating to the language, people, or culture of Spain, Portugal, or Latin America. —*n.* A person of Spanish or Latin-American origin or descent.

His•pan•io•la |hĭs'pən **yō'**lə|. An island in the West Indies, between Cuba and Puerto Rico. It is divided into Haiti, in the western part, and the Dominican Republic, in the eastern part.

hiss |hĭs| *n.* A drawn-out sound like that made by pronouncing the letter *s* or by gas escaping through a narrow opening: *the hiss of air escaping from a tire.* —*v.* **1.** To make such a sound. **2.** To say with such a sound: *"Shh," she hissed, "the mystery deepens."* **3.** To show dislike or scorn for (someone or something) by making such a sound: *The audience hissed the villain when he came on the stage.*

his•ta•mine |**hĭs'**tə mēn'| *or* |-mĭn| *n.* A chemical compound, $C_5H_9N_3$, found in plant and animal tissue. It stimulates gastric secretion, is thought to cause allergic reactions, and is used as a drug to cause dilation of blood vessels.

his•tol•o•gy |hĭ **stŏl'**ə jē| *n.* The scientific study of the detailed structure of plant and animal tissues as seen through a microscope.

his•to•ri•an |hĭ **stôr'**ē ən| *or* |-**stŏr'**-| *n.* A person who writes or specializes in the study of history.

his•tor•ic |hĭ **stôr'**ĭk| *or* |-**stŏr'**-| *adj.* **1.** Having importance in or influence on history; momentous: *a historic battle; a historic decision by the Supreme Court.* **2.** Famous or interesting because of past events, traditions, etc.: *The historic city of Williamsburg has been restored to its former condition.* **3.** Of or relating to history; historical.

his•tor•i•cal |hĭ **stôr'**ĭ kəl| *or* |-**stŏr'**-| *adj.* **1.** Of or taking place in history: *historical events; a historical period of great change.* **2.** Relating to or concerned with past events or the study of history: *a historical expedition to discover remains of an ancient civilization; a historical fiction; a painter of historical subjects.* **4.** Important in history; historic. —**his•tor'i•cal•ly** *adv.*

his•to•ry |**hĭs'**tə rē| *n., pl.* **his•to•ries. 1. a.** The continuing events of the past leading up to the present: *The invention of printing was one of the most important in history.* **b.** Such a series of events in the development of a country, time period, special subject, people, etc.: *United States history; the history of aviation.* **2.** An account or record of past events or information about the past, often in written form: *Governor William Bradford wrote a history of Plymouth Colony.* **3.** The study of past events as a special field of knowledge: *classes in arithmetic, history and science.* **4.** Something interesting or important that has happened and is likely to be remembered: *Joe Louis's powerful punches made boxing history.* —***modifier:*** *a history book; a history class.*

his•tri•on•ic |hĭs'trē **ŏn'**ĭk| *adj.* **1.** Dramatic in a showy or affected manner; excessively emotional. **2.** Of or typical of actors or acting. *—n.* **histrionics** *(used with a plural verb).* Showy, exaggerated emotional behavior.

hit |hĭt| *v.* **hit, hit•ting. 1.** To give a blow to; strike with a punch, slap, etc.: *hit someone; hit back in self-defense.* **2.** To strike or strike against with force; crash or crash into: *He fell and hit his head against the steps. The two boats hit in midstream.* **3.** To get to; reach: *hit a high note; going smoothly until we hit a bumpy road.* **4.** To strike with a bullet, arrow, or other missile: *hit the center of the target.* **5. a.** To drive (a ball or similar object) by striking with a bat, racket, etc.: *He hit the ball to center field. He hits, throws, and runs equally well.* **b.** In baseball, to get or achieve by doing this; bat: *He hit a home run. He hit .312 for the season.* **6.** To affect as if by a blow: *The bad news hit her hard.* **7.** To make an attack: *The enemy hit at midnight.* **8.** *Informal.* To set out on: *hit the trail.* **—phrasal verbs. hit on** (or **upon**). To reach or discover successfully; find: *hit on the right way to solve the problem.* **hit it off.** To get along well together. *—n.* **1.** A blow, shot, etc., that hits something: *a direct hit on the target.* **2.** A great or popular success: *the hit of the season.* **3.** In baseball, a ball so struck that the batter can reach at least first base safely. **—hit'ter** *n.*

hit-and-run |hĭt'n rŭn'| *adj.* **1.** Of, describing, or causing an automobile accident, attack, etc., in which someone causes harm or damage and leaves the scene immediately: *a hit-and-run driver.* **2.** Of a baseball play in which a player on base starts to run as the pitcher throws the ball and the batter tries to hit the ball.

hitch |hĭch| *v.* **1.** To tie or fasten to something with a rope, strap, loop, etc.: *The Eskimo trapper hitched his dog team to the sled. Get out the wagon and hitch up the old gray mare.* **2.** To raise or pull with a tug or jerk: *Lulu bent down to hitch up her socks. The hiker hitched the knapsack higher on his shoulders.* **3.** To move slowly and with difficulty: *hitched along the narrow, rocky ledge.* **4.** To get (a ride) by hitchhiking. *—n.* **1.** A short pull or jerk; a tug. **2.** A delay or difficulty; a snag: *a hitch in our plans.* **3.** Any of several kinds of knots used especially to fasten a rope to another object. **4.** A period of military service.

hitch•hike |hĭch'hīk'| *v.* **hitch•hiked, hitch•hik•ing.** To travel by getting a free ride from drivers of passing cars, trucks, etc. **—hitch'hik'er** *n.*

hith•er |hĭth'ər| *adv.* Here: *Little friends, how came ye hither?*

hith•er•to |hĭth'ər too'| *adv.* Until this time; up to now: *hitherto unobserved stars.*

Hit•ler |hĭt'lər|, **Adolf.** 1889–1945. Austrian-born Nazi leader; dictator of Germany (1933–45).

Hit•tite |hĭt'īt'| *n.* **1.** A member of a people who lived in Asia Minor and northern Syria from 2000 B.C. to 1200 B.C. **2.** The Indo-European language of this people. *—adj.* Of the Hittites or their language.

hive |hīv| *n.* **1. a.** A natural sheltering place or man-made container in which bees, especially honeybees, live. **b.** A colony of bees living in such a place. **2.** A crowded place full of busy activity. *—v.* **hived, hiv•ing.** To gather or live together in a hive. [SEE PICTURE]

hives |hīvz| *n. (used with a singular or plural verb).* Welts that itch severely, appearing on the skin as a result of an allergic reaction, a local infection, or some psychological cause.

hi•ya |hī'yə| *interj. Informal.* A word used as a friendly greeting.

h'm or **hm** |hmm| *interj.* Often **hmm, hmmm,** etc. Used to express a question, thoughtful concentration, hesitation prompted by doubt, etc.

H.M.S. His (or Her) Majesty's Ship.

ho |hō| *interj.* A word used to express surprise, triumph, discovery, laughter, etc. ¶*These sound alike* **ho, hoe.**

Ho The symbol for the element holmium.

hoa•gie or **hoa•gy** |hō'gē| *n., pl.* **hoa•gies.** *Slang.* A large sandwich made with a long roll or loaf of bread; a hero sandwich.

hoar |hôr| *or* |hōr| *adj.* White or gray; hoary. ¶*These sound alike* **hoar, whore.**

hoard |hôrd| *or* |hōrd| *n.* A hidden or saved-up supply that is kept in secret or guarded carefully: *the miser's hoard of gold.* *—v.* To save, keep, or store away, often secretly or greedily. ¶*These sound alike* **hoard, horde. —hoard'er** *n.*

hoar•frost |hôr'frôst'| *or* |-frŏst'| *or* |hōr'-| *n.* A deposit of ice crystals that forms on an object exposed to moist air, much as dew forms, except that the exposed object must be at a temperature below freezing.

hoar•hound |hôr'hound'| *or* |hōr'-| *n.* A form of the word **horehound.**

hoarse |hôrs| *or* |hōrs| *adj.* **hoars•er, hoars•est. 1.** Low and gruff in sound; husky: *a hoarse whisper; a hoarse voice.* **2.** Producing such a sound: *They shouted until they were hoarse.* ¶*These sound alike* **hoarse, horse. —hoarse'ly** *adv.* **—hoarse'ness** *n.*

hoar•y |hôr'ē| *or* |hōr'ē| *adj.* **hoar•i•er, hoar•i•est. 1.** White or grayish: *old men with hoary hair; a plant with hoary leaves.* **2.** Very old; aged: *hoary grandsires.*

hoax |hōks| *n.* A trick or action intended to deceive others, often in the form of a practical joke, false report, etc., that fools the public. *—v.* To deceive or cheat by a hoax.

hob¹ |hŏb| *n.* A shelf at the back or side of the inside of a fireplace, for keeping things warm. [SEE NOTE]

hob² |hŏb| *n.* **—play hob (with).** To cause trouble or mischief: *Closing Main Street for road repairs played hob with the traffic.* [SEE NOTE]

hob•ble |hŏb'əl| *v.* **hob•bled, hob•bling. 1.** To walk with a limp or with a slow, awkward motion, as an injured person does. **2.** To put a rope, strap, etc., around the legs of (an animal) to hamper but not completely prevent movement. **3.** To interfere with the action or progress of: *Injuries hobbled our star outfielder.* *—n.* **1.** A limp or slow, awkward motion in walking. **2.** A rope, strap, etc., used to hobble an animal.

hob•ble•de•hoy |hŏb'əl dē hoi'| *n.* A gawky, awkward boy or young man.

hob•by |hŏb'ē| *n., pl.* **hob•bies.** An interesting or enjoyable activity, such as collecting stamps or gardening, engaged in for one's own pleasure or satisfaction. **—modifier:** *a hobby show; a hobby shop.*

hob•by•horse |hŏb'ē hôrs'| *n.* **1.** A toy, plaything, etc., made to look like and be ridden like a

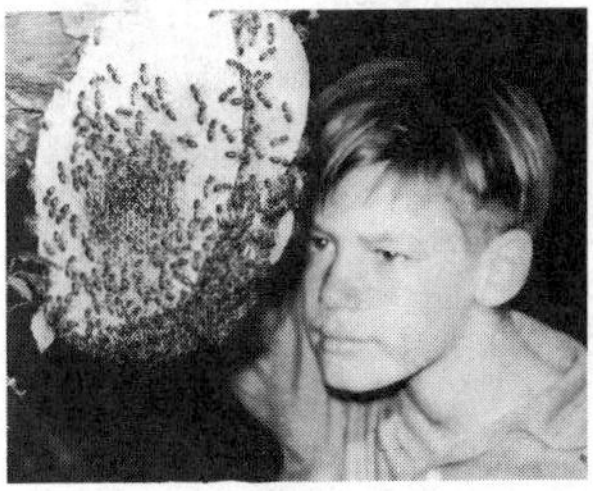

hive

hob¹⁻²/hobgoblin

Hob¹ *is of unknown origin.* **Hob²** *was originally a pet name for the name* Rob *or* Robin. *In medieval England, country people believed in an evil demon or spirit called* Puck; *by Shakespeare's time,* Puck *had become* Robin Goodfellow, *a mischievous but basically friendly spirit who played tricks like skimming the cream off milk and leading travelers astray at night. He was often known as* Hob *or* Hob-goblin, *hence the word* **hobgoblin,** *and the expression* **play hob with** *thus meant "to play the devil with" or "to play tricks with."*

hock[1-2]

Hock[1] *was* hōh, *"heel," in Old English.* ***Hock[2]*** *is an Americanism that is first recorded from the middle of the nineteenth century in the slang phrase* in hock, *which originally meant "in trouble" or "in prison." It is a borrowing from Dutch* hok, *"trouble, prison, doghouse." Later,* in hock *came to mean only "in pawn," and from this the verb* ***hock[2]*** *was formed.*

hockey

hold[1-2]

Hold[1] *was* healden *in Old English.* ***Hold[2]****, the lowest part of the inside of a ship, was originally the* ***hole****, but in the sixteenth century the word changed to* ***hold[2]****, doubtless by influence of* ***hold[1]****, since the space is used to* hold *cargo.*

ă pat/ā pay/â care/ä father/ĕ pet/ ē be/ĭ pit/ī pie/î fierce/ŏ pot/ ō go/ô paw, for/oi oil/ŏŏ book/ ōō boot/ou out/ŭ cut/û fur/ *th* the/th thin/hw which/zh vision/ ə ago, item, pencil, atom, circus

horse. **2.** A favorite subject of interest.

hob•gob•lin |hŏb'gŏb'lĭn| *n.* **1.** A mischievous or troublesome elf; goblin. **2.** An imaginary source of fear or horror. [SEE NOTE on p. 435]

hob•nail |hŏb'nāl'| *n.* One of the short nails with thick heads that are put on the soles of heavy shoes or boots to make them grip better or last longer.

hob•nob |hŏb'nŏb'| *v.* **hob•nobbed, hob•nob•bing.** To meet, talk, or spend time together in a friendly, familiar manner: *hobnobbing with the boys down at the clubhouse.*

ho•bo |hō'bō| *n., pl.* **ho•boes** or **ho•bos.** A person who wanders about from place to place, doing odd jobs and begging for a living; a tramp.

Ho Chi Minh City |hō' chē' mĭn'|. A city in southern Vietnam. Population, 3,420,000.

hock[1] |hŏk| *n.* **1.** The joint of the hind leg of a horse or other four-footed animal that corresponds to the ankle. **2.** A cut of meat from this apart, especially of a hog. [SEE NOTE]

hock[2] |hŏk|. *Informal. v.* To pawn. *—n.* The condition of being held by a pawnbroker: *Her diamonds are in hock.* [SEE NOTE]

hock•ey |hŏk'ē| *n.* **1.** Also **ice hockey.** A game played on ice, in which two opposing teams of skaters, using curved sticks, try to drive a flat disk, or puck, into the goal of the opponents' team. **2.** Also **field hockey.** A similar game played on a field with a ball instead of a puck. ***—modifier:*** *a hockey stick; hockey players.* [SEE PICTURE]

ho•cus-po•cus |hō'kəs pō'kəs| *n.* **1.** Nonsense syllables or words used in performing tricks of magic. **2.** A trick by a magician or juggler. **3.** Any deception or trickery.

hod |hŏd| *n.* **1.** A V-shaped trough on a long handle, held over the shoulder for carrying bricks, cement, etc. **2.** A pail for carrying coal; a coal scuttle.

hodge•podge |hŏj'pŏj'| *n.* A confused or haphazard mixture; a jumble.

hoe |hō| *n.* A tool with a flat blade on a long handle, used for breaking up soil, weeding, cultivating plants, etc. *—v.* **hoed, hoe•ing.** To dig, weed, etc., with a hoe. ¶ *These sound alike* **hoe, ho.**

hoe•down |hō'doun'| *n.* **1.** A square dance. **2.** A party at which such dancing is done. **3.** The music for such a dance.

hog |hôg| *or* |hŏg| *n.* **1.** A pig, especially a full-grown pig raised for meat. **2.** See **ground hog. 3.** *Informal.* A greedy or selfish person. ***—modifier:*** *hog meat; a hog farm. —v.* **hogged, hog•ging.** *Informal.* To take or use more than one's fair share of; monopolize greedily or selfishly: *hogging the middle of the road.*

hog•back |hôg'băk'| *or* |hŏg'-| *n.* A sharp ridge with steeply sloping sides, formed by the erosion of rock strata that are sharply tilted.

hogs•head |hôgz'hĕd'| *or* |hŏgz'-| *n.* **1.** A large barrel or cask, especially one that holds from 62 to 140 gallons. **2.** Any one of several measures of liquid volume or capacity ranging from 62.5 gallons to 140 gallons, especially one equal to 63 gallons.

hog•wash |hôg'wŏsh'| *or* |-wôsh'| *or* |hŏg'-| *n.* **1.** Garbage or slop fed to hogs. **2.** *Informal.* False or ridiculous talk, statements, etc.

ho-hum |hō'hŭm'| *interj.* Also **ho hum.** Used to imitate a yawn, express boredom, etc.

hoi pol•loi |hoi'pə loi'|. The common people, especially when regarded as of low social standing or lacking education or refinement.

hoist |hoist| *v.* To raise or haul up, often with the help of some mechanical apparatus: *Hoist the sails! —n.* **1.** A device, such as a crane, winch, or tackle, for hoisting. **2.** A pull or lift: *give the log a hoist onto the wagon.*

hoi•ty-toi•ty |hoi'tē toi'tē| *adj. Informal.* Pretentiously self-important; haughty; proud; stuck-up.

Hok•kai•do |hŏ kī'dō|. The second largest and northernmost of the main islands of Japan.

ho•kum |hō'kəm| *n. Informal.* Silly, insincere, or deceptive talk, actions, etc.; nonsense; humbug.

hold[1] |hōld| *v.* **held** |hĕld|, **hold•ing. 1. a.** To take and keep in one's hand, arms, or some other part or device that grips or clasps; grasp: *She held three pennies in her hand.* **b.** To cling: *The vines held to the wall.* **c.** To keep a grasp on: *holding tightly to a rope.* **2. a.** To take or have in control; restrain; check: *hold the horses.* **b.** To keep confined; detain: *They held the captured king in prison.* **3.** To keep or put in a certain way, place, position, etc.: *She walked into the room with her head held high.* **4.** To have or take as contents; contain: *This box holds a dozen cookes.* **5.** To bear; support: *Will that rope hold such a heavy load?* **6. a.** To remain firm or secure: *This knot will not hold.* **b.** To remain; stay: *Hold still while I comb your hair.* **7.** To keep; maintain: *holding a course to the north.* **8.** To have, be in, or occupy (a job, position, political office, etc.): *Thomas Jefferson held the office of President for two terms.* **9.** To cause to take place; conduct: *hold elections.* **10.** To have or keep in one's possession: *He holds many acres of land.* **11.** To defend against attack or capture: *Our soldiers held the fort.* **12.** To retain the interest or attention of; capture: *The magician held his audience with his amazing tricks.* **13. a.** To believe; consider: *"We hold these truths to be self-evident, that all men are created equal . . ."* (The Declaration of Independence). **b.** To claim; assert: *The police hold that the victim was murdered in cold blood.* **14.** To be loyal or faithful; stick: *hold firmly to one's beliefs.* **15.** To be true, correct, or usable: *This basic theory holds in all cases.* **16.** To stop or delay: *Hold dinner until I get home.* ***—phrasal verbs.*** **hold forth.** To talk at great length; make a long speech. **hold off.** To delay or wait: *I hope the rain holds off until after the picnic.* **hold on. 1.** To keep a grip; cling. **2.** To stop or wait for someone or something: *Hold on a minute.* **3.** To continue what one is doing; persevere: *The men in the fort held on in spite of enemy fire.* **hold (one's) own.** To stand one's ground; not yield or falter. **hold out.** To last: *How long will our water supply hold out?* **hold over. 1.** To keep longer than planned or expected: *The show has been held over for an extra week.* **2.** To put off; postpone. **hold up. 1.** To stop or interfere with; delay. **2.** To last; remain in good condition: *This car should hold up for many years.* **3.** To rob by threatening with harm or force. *—n.* **1.** An act or means of holding something; grasp; grip: *keep a firm hold; a wrestling hold.* **2.** Something held or used for support, as in climbing or clinging. **3.** A very strong influence or power: *Eng-*

land's hold over the American colonies. **4.** In music, a symbol placed near a note or, often, near a rest to indicate that the performer is to hold it beyond its given time value. [SEE NOTE on p. 436]

***Idioms.* get hold of.** To detain or reach (someone). **take (get, catch,** etc.) **hold of. 1.** To get a firm grasp or grip on. **2.** To have a powerful effect on; overcome: *A strange fear took hold of us.*

hold[2] |hōld| *n.* The lower inside of a ship or airplane, where cargo is stored. [SEE NOTE on p. 436]

hold•er |hōl'dər| *n.* **1.** A person who holds, owns, or possesses something: *a ticket holder; a job holder.* **2.** A thing or device for holding something: *a pot holder; a cigarette holder.*

hold•ing |hōl'dĭng| *n.* **1. holdings. a.** Property, such as land, money, or stocks, owned by a person, company, nation, etc.: *fair-sized holdings in Mexico.* **b.** Land rented or leased from another: *U.S. oil holdings in Arab countries.* **2.** In football and some other sports, an illegal hampering of an opponent's movements with the hands or arms.

holding company. A business organization that controls partial or complete interest in other companies.

hold•o•ver |hōld'ō'vər| *n.* Something or someone kept or remaining from an earlier time.

hold•up |hōld'ŭp'| *n.* **1.** A robbery committed by someone who is armed. **2.** A stopping of progress or activity; a delay.

hole |hōl| *n.* **1.** An opening or hollow made by or as if by digging, boring, cutting, poking, etc., into or through something: *tore a hole in her stocking.* **2.** A gap or space, especially one through which something or someone can pass: *The batter hit the ball through the hole between second and third base.* **3.** An animal's burrow or similar snug shelter: *a mouse's hole in the wall.* **4.** A fault, error, or omitted part: *the holes in his argument.* **5.** A bad or troublesome situation; a difficulty: *help a friend out of a hole.* **6.** An ugly, cramped, depressing place, such as a dungeon or hovel. **7. a.** On a golf course, one of the small hollows lined with a cup into which the ball must be hit. **b.** One of the 9 or 18 divisions of a golf course, from tee to cup. *—v.* **holed, hol•ing.** To propel (a golf ball) into the hole. ***—phrasal verbs.* hole out.** To finish play on a golf hole by sending the ball into the cup. **hole up** (or **in**). To sleep, hide, or take shelter in or as if in a burrow or similar hiding place. ¶*These sound alike* **hole, whole.**

***Idiom.* hole in one.** The driving of a golf ball from the tee to the hole in only one stroke.

hol•i•day |hŏl'ĭ dā'| *n.* **1.** A day or period set aside by law, religious custom, or tradition to celebrate a special event, honor someone, etc. **2.** A day or period of time for relaxing away from work; a vacation. ***—modifier:*** *a holiday dinner; holiday traffic.*

ho•li•ness |hō'lē nĭs| *n.* **1.** The condition or quality of being holy. **2. Holiness.** A title used in speaking of or to the pope.

Hol•land |hŏl'ənd|. A country, the Netherlands.

hol•lan•daise sauce |hŏl'ən dāz'| *or* |hŏl'ən-dāz'|. A rich, creamy sauce made with butter, egg yolks, and lemon juice or vinegar.

Hol•land•er |hŏl'ən dər| *n.* A native or inhabitant of the Netherlands.

hol•ler |hŏl'ər|. *Informal. v.* To shout; yell. *—n.* A shout or yell.

hol•low |hŏl'ō| *adj.* **hol•low•er, hol•low•est. 1.** Having or consisting of a space or opening inside: *a hollow log; a hollow rubber ball.* **2.** Shaped by or as if by scooping out; bowl-shaped or cup-shaped; concave: *a hollow basin under the waterfall.* **3.** Caved or dented in; sunken: *hollow cheeks.* **4.** Deep, low, and booming; echoing: *the hollow rumble of drums.* **5.** Without meaning or purpose; empty; useless: *a hollow life.* *—n.* **1.** An opening, space, or indentation in or within something. **2.** A small valley. *—v.* To make or become hollow, especially by or as if by scooping: *hollow out a log.* **—hol'low•ly** *adv.*

hol•ly |hŏl'ē| *n., pl.* **hol•lies. 1.** Any of several shrubs or trees having evergreen leaves with prickly edges and bright-red berries. **2.** Sprigs or branches of such a shrub or tree. ***—modifier:*** *a holly wreath.* [SEE PICTURE]

holly

hol•ly•hock |hŏl'ē hŏk'| *n.* A tall garden plant with a long cluster of showy, variously colored flowers. [SEE PICTURE]

hollyhock

Hol•ly•wood |hŏl'ē wo͝od'|. A district of Los Angeles, California, the center of the U.S. motion-picture industry.

hol•mi•um |hōl'mē əm| *n.* Symbol **Ho** One of the elements, a rare-earth metal. Atomic number 67; atomic weight 164.93; valence +3; melting point 1,461°C; boiling point 2,600°C.

hol•o•caust |hŏl'ə kôst'| *or* |hō'lə-| *n.* Great or total destruction, especially by fire.

Hol•o•cene |hŏl'ə sēn'| *or* |hō'lə-| *n.* Also **Hol•o•cene epoch.** The geologic epoch of the Cenozoic era that began about 11,000 years ago, extending from the end of the Pleistocene epoch to the present. ***—modifier:*** *a Holocene deposit; Holocene mammals.*

hol•o•graph |hŏl'ə grăf'| *or* |-gräf'| *n.* A document, such as a letter, will, etc., written entirely in the handwriting of the person who signs it.

Hol•stein |hōl'stīn'| *or* |-stēn'| *n.* One of a breed of black and white cattle raised for milk and milk products. [SEE PICTURE]

Holstein

hol•ster |hōl'stər| *n.* A leather case shaped to hold a pistol, usually worn on a belt.

ho•ly |hō'lē| *adj.* **ho•li•er, ho•li•est. 1.** Of or associated with God, a divine power, or religious beliefs and traditions, and therefore regarded with special reverence; sacred: *The Bible and the Koran are holy books.* **2.** Given a special influence or quality by or as if by God or a divine power; blessed: *a pure and holy feeling; freedom's holy light.* **3.** Living according to a strict or highly moral religious or spiritual system; saintly. **4.** Regarded with special respect or awe: *peace, education and other holy subjects of American politics.* ¶*These sound alike* **holy, wholly.**

Holy Father. One of the titles of the pope.

Holy Ghost. The third person of the Christian Trinity; the Holy Spirit.

Holy Land. Palestine.

Holy Roman Empire. A mostly Germanic empire of central Europe that lasted from the 10th through the 18th century.

Holy See. The official position, authority, or court of the pope.

hombre
Hombre *comes into American speech from the Southwest, where many people speak Spanish;* hombre *is the Spanish word for "man," and is directly descended from Latin* homo, *"man."*

homestead
In pioneering days, when the United States had enormous areas of unsettled land, many people believed that "the public lands of the United States belong to the people, and should not be sold to individuals nor granted to corporations, but should . . . be granted in limited quantities, free of cost, to landless settlers" (Free Soil Party, 1848). After much political argument, the Homestead Law of 1862 was passed by Congress, giving 160 acres of unsettled land to "any person who is the head of a family, or who has arrived at the age of twenty-one years, and is a citizen of the United States . . ."

ă pat/ā pay/â care/ä father/ĕ pet/ē be/ĭ pit/ī pie/î fierce/ŏ pot/ō go/ô paw, for/oi oil/o͝o book/o͞o boot/ou out/ŭ cut/û fur/*th* the/th thin/hw which/zh vision/ə ago, item, pencil, atom, circus

Holy Spirit. The third person of the Christian Trinity; the Holy Ghost.

ho•ly•stone |hō'lē stōn'| *n.* A piece of soft sandstone used for scouring the wooden decks of a ship. *—v.* **ho•ly•stoned, ho•ly•ston•ing.** To scrub or scour with a holystone.

Holy Thursday. **Maundy Thursday.**

Holy Week. The week before Easter.

hom•age |hŏm'ĭj| *or* |ŏm'-| *n.* **1.** Special honor or respect shown or expressed publicly: *The crowd cheered in homage to the great singer.* **2.** An action or ceremony, originating in feudal times, in which a person shows allegiance or loyalty to a ruler.

hom•bre |ŏm'brā'| *or* |-brē| *n. Slang.* A man; fellow. [SEE NOTE]

home |hōm| *n.* **1.** A house, apartment, or other building or shelter in which a person, animal, family, etc., lives. **2.** Such a dwelling place together with the family that lives there; a household. **3.** A place in which one was born or has lived a long time; one's true, permanent, or lovingly remembered dwelling place: *I'll wander no more, for Montana's my home.* **4.** The region or typical place in which an animal, plant, or thing is found: *The forest is the home of many birds and animals.* **5.** A place or institution for the care and shelter of those that need help: *a home for orphans; a home for stray animals.* **6.** In certain games, such as baseball or hide-and-seek, a goal or place of safety that the players try to reach. *—modifier: home life; home cooking.* *—adv.* **1.** To or at one's home: *The children raced home from school.* **2.** To the point or mark at which something is directed: *The arrow struck home.* *—v.* **homed, hom•ing. 1.** To return home: *crowds of tourists homing from abroad.* **2.** To be guided to a target or destination automatically or by some internal sense: *a missile that homes on a target.* **—home'less** *adj.*
***Idiom.* at home. 1.** Comfortable and relaxed; at ease: *at home with strangers.* **2.** Ready and expecting to have visitors: *We are at home every Thursday.*

home•com•ing |hōm'kŭm'ĭng| *n.* **1.** A return to one's home. **2.** In some high schools and colleges, a yearly celebration held for visiting alumni. *—modifier: the homecoming game.*

home economics. The art, skill, or science of managing a household, including cooking, sewing, child care, buying food and clothing, etc. **—home economist.**

home•land |hōm'lănd'| *n.* The country in which one was born or that one regards as one's true home.

home•like |hōm'līk'| *adj.* Typical of a home; comfortable and pleasant; cozy.

home•ly |hōm'lē| *adj.* **home•li•er, home•li•est. 1.** Typical of everyday life; familiar: *homely chores.* **2.** Not pretty; plain: *a homely child.*

home•made |hōm'mād'| *adj.* **1.** Made at home: *a delicious homemade pie.* **2.** Crudely or simply made, as if made at home: *homemade furniture.*

home•mak•er |hōm'mā'kər| *n.* A person who manages a household, as by planning and preparing meals, caring for children, and taking charge of the family budget. **—home'mak'ing** *n.*

home plate. In baseball, the base at which the batter stands and which must be touched by a runner after touching the other three bases to score a run.

hom•er |hō'mər| *n.* A **home run.** *—v.* To hit a home run: *Wilson homered over the left field wall.*

Ho•mer |hō'mər|. Greek epic poet who lived in about the eighth century B.C. He is generally believed to have been the author of the *Iliad* and the *Odyssey.* **—Ho•mer'ic** |hō mĕr'ĭk| *adj.*

home•room |hōm'ro͞om'| *or* |-ro͝om'| *n.* A classroom in which a group of pupils of the same grade gather each day, as in the morning before the start of classes, after lunch, or before dismissal.

home run. In baseball, a hit that travels a long distance, usually over the outfield barrier, and that allows the batter to touch all the bases and score a run. *—modifier:* **(home-run):** *one of the greatest home-run hitters of all time.*

home•sick |hōm'sĭk'| *adj.* Unhappy because one is away from one's home and family; longing for home. **—home'sick'ness** *n.*

home•spun |hōm'spŭn'| *n.* **1.** A plain, coarse, loosely woven cloth made of yarn that is spun at home. **2.** Any similar strong, coarse cloth. *—modifier: a homespun skirt.* *—adj.* **1.** Spun or woven at home: *homespun cloth.* **2.** Plain and simple in a folksy way: *homespun humor.*

home•stead |hōm'stĕd'| *n.* **1.** A house, especially a farmhouse or similar dwelling, together with the land and buildings belonging to it. **2.** A piece of land given by the government to a settler who claimed it and built a home on it. *—v.* To settle on land claimed as a homestead. **—home'stead'er** *n.* [SEE NOTE]

home•stretch |hōm'strĕch'| *n.* **1.** The part of a racetrack from the last turn to the finish line. **2.** The last stage of a journey or of an activity requiring time and effort.

home•ward |hōm'wərd| *adv.* Also **home•wards** |hōm'wərdz|. Toward home: *They turned their canoe and paddled homeward.* *—adj.: the homeward journey.*

home•work |hōm'wûrk'| *n.* Work, especially school assignments, to be done at home.

home•y |hō'mē| *adj.* **hom•i•er, hom•i•est.** Suggestive of home; pleasant, cheerful, and informal: *a restaurant with a homey atmosphere.*

hom•i•cide |hŏm'ĭ sīd'| *or* |hō'mĭ-| *n.* **1.** The killing of a person by another person. **2.** A person who kills another person. **—hom'i•ci'dal** *adj.*

hom•i•ly |hŏm'ə lē| *n., pl.* **hom•i•lies. 1.** A speech on a religious subject, delivered to a congregation; a sermon. **2.** A moralizing lecture.

homing pigeon. A pigeon trained to fly back to its home roost from great distances.

hom•i•ny |hŏm'ə nē| *n.* Hulled and dried kernels of corn, often ground into a coarse white meal called **hominy grits,** and cooked by boiling.

homo–. A word element meaning "same or similar": **homogeneous.**

ho•mo•ge•ne•ous |hō'mə jē'nē əs| *or* |-jēn'-yəs| *or* |hŏm'ə-| *adj.* Having or consisting of similar or related parts or elements forming a unified whole: *The performance combined music, poetry, acting, and dance into a homogeneous theatrical spectacle.* **—ho'mo•ge'ne•ous•ly** *adv.*

ho•mog•e•nize |hə mŏj'ə nīz'| *v.* **ho•mog•e•**

nized, ho•mog•e•niz•ing. To spread evenly through a fluid, especially to make (milk) uniform by breaking the fat it contains into tiny particles. **—ho•mog'e•nized'** *adj.: homogenized milk.* **—ho•mog'e•ni•za'tion** *n.*

hom•o•graph |hŏm'ə grăf'| *or* |-grăf'| *or* |hō'mə-| *n.* A word that has the same spelling as one or more other words but differs in meaning, origin, and sometimes in pronunciation; for example, *ring* (circle) and *ring* (sound); *bass* (fish) and *bass* (deep tone or voice) are homographs. [SEE NOTE]

ho•mol•o•gous |hə mŏl'ə gəs| *or* |hō-| *adj.* **1.** Similar and related in structure, evolutionary origin, etc., as the arm of a human being and the flipper of a seal. **2.** Of or indicating either of a pair of chromosomes whose genes are arranged in the same way.

hom•o•nym |hŏm'ə nĭm| *or* |hō'mə-| *n.* One of two or more words that have the same sound and often the same spelling but differ in meaning and origin; for example, *die* (to stop living), *die* (stamping or shaping device), and *dye* (color) are homonyms. **—ho•mon'y•mous** |hə mŏn'ə məs| *or* |hō-| *adj.* [SEE NOTE]

hom•o•phone |hŏm'ə fōn'| *or* |hō'mə-| *n.* A word that has the same sound as one or more other words but differs in spelling, meaning, and origin; for example, *for, fore,* and *four* are homophones. **—ho•moph'o•nous** |hə mŏf'ə nəs| *or* |hō-| *adj.* [SEE NOTE]

Ho•mo sa•pi•ens |hō'mō sā'pē ĕnz'| *or* |-ənz|. The scientific name for modern man, the only species of man still in existence.

ho•mo•sex•u•al |hō'mə sĕk'shōō əl| *or* |-mō-| *adj.* Of or having sexual relations with a member of the same sex. *—n.* Someone who has sexual relations with a member of the same sex. **—ho'mo•sex'u•al'i•ty** *n.*

hon |hŭn| *n. Informal.* Honey; sweetheart; dear. Often used as a term of address: *Hi, hon.*

Hon. Honorable (used in titles).

Hon•du•ras |hŏn dŏŏr'əs| *or* |-dyŏŏr'-|. A country in northern Central America. Population, 2,930,000. Capital, Tegucigalpa. **—Hon•du'ran** *adj.* & *n.*

hone |hōn| *v.* **honed, hon•ing.** To sharpen (a knife, razor, etc.) on or as if on a fine-grained stone. *—n.* A fine-grained stone used to sharpen knives, razors, tools, etc.

hon•est |ŏn'ĭst| *adj.* **1.** Truthful and trustworthy; not lying, stealing, cheating, etc. **2.** Not false; true: *Her answer sounded almost too simple, but it was honest.* **3.** Based on or using facts, truth, or reality; not deceptive: *a butcher who gives honest weight.* **4.** Not hiding anything; frank; sincere: *an honest opinion; an honest face.*

hon•est•ly |ŏn'ĭst lē| *adv.* **1.** In an honest manner: *products honestly labeled. Answer as honestly as you can.* **2.** Really; truly: *Do I honestly look like a magician who can pull rabbits out of a hat?*

hon•es•ty |ŏn'ĭ stē| *n.* The quality of being honest; truthfulness, sincerity, etc.

hon•ey |hŭn'ē| *n., pl.* **hon•eys. 1.** A sweet, thick, syrupy substance made by bees from the nectar of flowers and used as food. **2.** Sweetness; pleasantness. **3.** *Informal.* Darling. Often used as a term of address: *Hello, honey.*

hon•ey•bee |hŭn'ē bē'| *n.* A bee of a kind that lives in highly organized colonies and that produces honey.

hon•ey•comb |hŭn'ē kōm'| *n.* **1.** A wax structure with many small, six-sided compartments, made by honeybees to hold honey. **2.** Something full of openings or spaces like those in a honeycomb: *a great honeycomb of a building, full of storerooms, tunnels, and passages.* *—v.* To fill with openings or spaces like those in a honeycomb: *Tiny shops and stalls honeycombed the business district of the village.*

hon•ey•dew |hŭn'ē dōō'| *or* |-dyōō'| *n.* **1.** A sweet, sticky substance given off by aphids and certain other insects. **2.** A sweet, sticky substance sometimes found on plant leaves.

honeydew melon. A melon with a smooth, whitish rind and green flesh.

hon•eyed |hŭn'ēd| *adj.* Very sweet and intended to coax or please: *She was flattered by the rascal's honeyed words.*

hon•ey•moon |hŭn'ē mōōn'| *n.* A trip or vacation taken by a newly married couple. **—modifier:** *the honeymoon suite in a hotel.* *—v.* To spend a honeymoon. **—hon'ey•moon'er** *n.*

hon•ey•suck•le |hŭn'ē sŭk'əl| *n.* A vine or shrub with tube-shaped, often fragrant yellowish, white, or pink flowers. [SEE PICTURE]

Hong Kong |hŏng' kŏng'| *or* |hông' kông'|. A British colony on the coast of southeastern China. Population, 4,249,000.

honk |hôngk| *or* |hŏngk| *n.* A loud, harsh, resonant sound such as that made by a wild goose or an automobile horn. *—v.* To make or cause to make a honk: *A flock of geese honked overhead. The impatient driver honked his horn.* **—honk'er** *n.*

hon•ky or **hon•kie** |hông'kē| *or* |hŏng'-| *n., pl.* **hon•kies.** *Slang.* A white person. The word "honky" is considered offensive.

hon•ky-tonk |hông'kē tôngk'| *or* |hŏng'kē-tŏngk'| *n. Slang.* A cheap, noisy bar or dance hall.

Hon•o•lu•lu |hŏn'ə lōō'lōō|. The capital of Hawaii. Population, 320,000.

hon•or |ŏn'ər| *n.* **1.** Special respect or high regard: *displaying the flag to show honor to the United States.* **2. a.** A special privilege or mark of distinction: *Election to baseball's Hall of Fame is an honor that comes to few players.* **b.** A special way of showing respect or distinction: *the guest of honor at the banquet.* **3.** Someone or something that brings or shows high regard or special distinction: *Dr. Douglas is an honor to his profession.* **4.** Glory; credit; distinction: *The contests gave each brave a chance to win honor for himself and his tribe.* **5.** An inner sense of what is right; high principles; integrity: *bound by his honor and his conscience.* **6.** High standing among others; reputation; good name: *He fought to defend his honor.* **7.** Often **Honor.** A title of respect used when speaking to or of a judge, mayor, or other person of importance: *Your Honor; His Honor.* **8. honors.** Special recognition for unusual achievement in one's studies: *graduated from college with honors.* **—modifier:** *an honor student.* *—v.* **1.** To show special respect or recognition to: *The ancient Egyptians honored their rulers as gods.* **2.** To think highly of; esteem: *honored all over the world as a great phy-*

(1) **light[1]/light[2]** *(2)* **air/heir**
(3) **bass[1]**(băs)**/bass[2]**(bās)

homograph/ homonym/homophone

These words are made up of word elements based on Greek. Homo- *means "same," and* -graph, -onym, *and* -phone *mean, respectively, "spelling," "name," and "sound." In the diagram above, (1) and (3) are pairs of* **homographs,** *(1) and (2) are pairs of* **homonyms,** *and (2) is a pair of* **homophones.** *Put another way, set (1) is a pair of* **homonyms** *that are also* **homographs,** *set (2) is a pair of* **homonyms** *that are not also* **homographs,** *and are therefore called* **homophones,** *and set (3) is a pair of* **homographs** *that are not* **homonyms.**

honeysuckle

hood[1-2]

Hood[1] *was* hōd *in Old English; it is related to Old English* hætt, *which in Modern English became* **hat. Hood**[2] *is shortened from* **hoodlum,** *a word that first appeared in the late nineteenth century in American cities; its origin is obscure. The suffix* -hood, *as in* **manhood, childhood, falsehood,** *was* -hād *in Old English; it is descended from a separate Germanic noun,* haid-, *meaning "appearance, quality, condition."*

hoop

hoop skirt

ă pat/ā pay/â care/ä father/ĕ pet/ ē be/ĭ pit/ī pie/î fierce/ŏ pot/ ō go/ô paw, for/oi oil/ŏŏ book/ ōō boot/ou out/ŭ cut/û fur/ *th* the/th thin/hw which/zh vision/ ə ago, item, pencil, atom, circus

sician and scholar. **3.** To give honor or distinction to: *You honor us by your presence.* **4.** To accept as payment: *honor a check.* **—hon'ored** *adj.: an honored guest.*

Idioms. **do the honors.** To act as a host or hostess. **on (one's) honor.** As a solemn pledge.

hon•or•a•ble |ŏn'ər ə bəl| *adj.* **1.** Deserving honor or respect: *an honorable occupation.* **2.** Having or showing a strong sense of what is right or just: *an honorable man.* **3.** Showing or done with due honor or recognition of worth: *an honorable discharge from the army.* **4.** Often **Honorable.** A title of respect for certain high officials or people of importance: *the Honorable Justices of the Supreme Court.* **—hon'or•a•bly** *adv.*

hon•o•rar•i•um |ŏn'ə râr'ē əm| *n., pl.* **hon•o•rar•i•ums** or **hon•o•rar•i•a** |ŏn'ə râr'ē ə|. A payment made to a professional person for services for which fees are not legally or traditionally required.

hon•or•ar•y |ŏn'ə rĕr'ē| *adj.* Given or holding as an honor, without the fulfillment of the usual requirements: *an honorary college degree.* *—n., pl.* **hon•or•ar•ies.** An honorary degree.

honor system. A way of operating a school or other institution so that students or members are not kept under close supervision and are trusted to obey rules, take tests, do assignments, etc., without cheating.

hon•our |ŏn'ər| *n.* & *v.* Chiefly British form of the word **honor.**

hon•our•a•ble |ŏn'ər ə bəl| *adj.* Chiefly British form of the word **honorable.**

Hon•shu |hŏn'shōō|. The largest island of Japan.

hood[1] |hŏŏd| *n.* **1.** A soft, loose or fitted covering for the head and neck, often attached to a coat, cape, or robe. **2.** Something resembling this, such as a flower part or the skin around a cobra's neck. **3.** A hoodlike protective covering, such as the hinged metal lid over an automobile engine or the collapsible part of the head end of a baby carriage. *—v.* To cover or supply with or as if with a hood: *She hooded her head. Clouds hooded the mountain tops.* **—hood'ed** *adj.: a hooded cape; a hooded cobra.* [SEE NOTE]

hood[2] |hŏŏd| *n. Slang.* A thug or tough fellow; a hoodlum. [SEE NOTE]

hood•lum |hŏŏd'ləm| *or* |hōōd'-| *n.* **1.** A gangster or thug. **2.** A tough, wild, or destructive young fellow.

hood•wink |hŏŏd'wĭngk'| *v.* To deceive or mislead by trickery.

hoof |hŏŏf| *or* |hōōf| *n., pl.* **hoofs** or **hooves** |hŏŏvz| *or* |hōōvz|. The tough, horny case covering the toes or lower part of the foot of certain animals, such as horses, cattle, deer, and pigs. *—v.* **—hoof it.** *Slang.* **1.** To go on foot; walk. **2.** To dance.

Idiom. **on the hoof.** Alive; not yet butchered for meat: *cattle taken to market on the hoof.*

hoofed |hŏŏft| *or* |hōōft| *adj.* Having hoofs.

hook |hŏŏk| *n.* **1. a.** A curved or bent object or part, often of metal, used to catch, hold, fasten, or pull something: *catching fish with a rod and hook baited with worms; pots hung on hooks over the stove.* **b.** Something resembling such an object: *a narrow hook of land extending into the sea.* **2. a.** In baseball, basketball, golf, etc., a thrown or struck ball that moves in a curve. **b.** In boxing, a short, swinging blow delivered with a bent arm. *—v.* **1.** To fasten, link, etc., with or as if with a hook: *Make sure the passengers hook their safety belts. This dress hooks in back.* **2.** To catch, snare, or grab with a hook: *He hooked a 10-pound trout.* **3.** To move, throw, or extend in a curve or bend: *The golfer's drive hooked to the left. He hooked the ball into the basket.* **4.** To make (a rug) by looping yarn through canvas with a hook. **—hooked'** *adj.: the owl's hooked beak; a hooked spear; a hooked rug.* **—phrasal verb. hook up.** To assemble and connect (a device, especially an electric or electronic device) to a system or a source of power: *hook up a telephone.*

Idioms. **by hook or (by) crook.** By whatever means possible, fair or unfair. **hook, line, and sinker.** Without reservation; entirely; completely. **off the hook.** *Informal.* Free from a difficult situation or unpleasant obligation. **on (one's) own hook.** *Informal.* By one's own efforts.

hook•ah |hŏŏk'ə| *n.* A smoking pipe with a long tube passing through a container of water that cools the smoke as it is drawn through.

hook and eye. A fastener for clothes consisting of a small hook and loop which can be linked together.

hook•up |hŏŏk'ŭp'| *n.* An arrangement or connection of parts or devices acting as a unit, especially in an electric or electronic system.

hook•worm |hŏŏk'wûrm'| *n.* A parasitic worm having hooked mouth parts with which it fastens itself to the inside wall of the intestines of various animals, including human beings, causing serious disease.

hook•y |hŏŏk'ē| *n.* **—play hooky.** *Informal.* To be absent from school without permission or an acceptable excuse.

hoo•li•gan |hōō'lĭ gən| *n.* A hoodlum.

hoop |hōōp| *or* |hŏŏp| *n.* **1.** A circular band of wood, metal, etc., as one used as a plaything, in various sports, to spread out a full, circular skirt, or to hold together the staves forming the sides of a barrel. **2.** Something resembling such a band. ¶*These sound alike* **hoop, whoop.** [SEE PICTURE]

hoop•la |hōōp'lä'| *or* |hŏŏp'-| *n. Slang.* Noisy or confusing commotion or publicity.

hoo•poe |hōō'pōō| *n.* A bird of Europe, Asia, and Africa, having a fanlike crest and a long, slender bill.

hoop skirt. A long, full, bell-shaped skirt worn over a framework of connected hoops that spread it out. [SEE PICTURE]

hoo•ray |hōō rā'| *interj., n.,* & *v.* A form of the word **hurrah.**

hoot |hōōt| *n.* **1.** The deep, hollow cry of an owl or a similar sound. **2.** A shout of scorn or disapproval. *—v.* **1.** To make a deep, hollow cry or sound: *An owl hooted in the treetop. Foghorns hooted all night.* **2.** To shout, shout at, or drive away with scornful cries or jeers.

hoot•en•an•ny |hōōt'n ăn'ē| *n., pl.* **hoot•en•an•nies.** An informal performance by folk singers, usually with the audience joining in.

hooved |hŏŏvd| *or* |hōōvd| *adj.* A form of the word **hoofed.**

Hoo•ver |hōō'vər|, **Herbert Clark.** 1874–1964.

Thirty-first President of the United States (1929–33).

hooves |hŏŏvz| *or* |hōōvz| *n.* A plural of **hoof.**

hop¹ |hŏp| *v.* **hopped, hop•ping. 1.** To move with light, bounding leaps or skips or with a springing motion: *The frightened rabbit hopped away.* **2.** To jump on one foot. **3.** To move on, over, or onto by or as if by hopping: *hopped the fence in a single bound.* **4.** To make a quick trip, especially by air. *—n.* **1.** A motion made by or as if by hopping; a light, springy leap or bound: *She crossed the room in short hops.* **2.** A trip, especially by air: *a short hop between Boston and Cape Cod.* **3.** *Informal.* A dance.

hop² |hŏp| *n.* **1.** A twining vine with green flowers that resemble small pine cones. **2. hops.** The dried flowers of this plant, used as flavoring in making beer.

hope |hōp| *v.* **hoped, hop•ing. 1.** To look forward to something with a feeling of expectation or confidence; to want and expect: *He hopes his son will also become a farmer.* **2.** To wish earnestly: *Cyrus hoped he had not misspelled any of the words on the test.* **3.** To trust in or wish for a favorable outcome: *He wanted desperately to hope, but the chances of rescue seemed very slim.* *—n.* **1.** A feeling of confident expectation: *a young people full of pride, hope, and energy.* **2.** A reason for or cause of such a feeling: *You are the team's only hope for success.* **3.** What one wishes or hopes for; aspiration: *Have your aims and hopes changed often in the last few years?*

***Idiom.* hope against hope.** To hope that something will happen in spite of chances against it.

hope chest. A chest or large box in which a young woman collects household linens, silverware, etc., to use when she is married.

hope•ful |**hōp'**fəl| *adj.* **1.** Feeling, showing, or expressing hope; confidently expectant: *The immigrants arrived hopeful of a new and better life.* **2.** Inspiring hope; encouraging: *hopeful signs of peace.* *—n.* A person who wishes to succeed in something or who shows promise of succeeding: *Hundreds of hopefuls tried out for the role.* **—hope'ful•ly** *adv.* **—hope'ful•ness** *n.*

hope•less |**hōp'**lĭs| *adj.* **1.** Without hope; despairing: *The lost hikers felt hopeless.* **2.** Offering no hope; having or giving no chance of a successful or favorable outcome: *a hopeless search.* **3.** Beyond hope or expectation of improvement: *My room is a hopeless mess. He is a hopeless case.* **—hope'less•ly** *adv.* **—hope'less•ness** *n.*

Ho•pi |**hō'**pē| *n., pl.* **Ho•pi** or **Ho•pis. 1.** A North American Indian tribe now of northeastern Arizona. **2.** A member of this tribe. **3.** The Uto-Aztecan language of this tribe.

hop•per |**hŏp'**ər| *n.* **1.** Something or someone that hops, especially a hopping insect. **2.** A container for holding something such as coal, grain, or ashes, often having a wide, open top and a narrow bottom opening through which the contents can be removed.

hop•scotch |**hŏp'**skŏch'| *n.* A children's game in which players toss a small object into the numbered spaces of a pattern of rectangles marked on the ground, pavement, etc., and then hop or jump through the spaces to pick up the object and return.

horde |hôrd| *or* |hōrd| *n.* **1.** A large group, crowd, or swarm moving or doing something together: *hordes of people at the fair; an immense horde of winged insects.* **2.** A tribe or group of nomadic people: *In 1264 the Mongol hordes invaded China.* ¶*These sound alike* **horde, hoard.**

hore•hound |**hôr'**hound'| *or* |**hōr'**-| *n.* **1.** A strong-smelling plant that yields a bitter substance used in cough medicine and to flavor candy. **2.** An extract, medicine, or candy prepared from this plant.

ho•ri•zon |hə **rī'**zən| *n.* **1.** The line along which the earth and sky appear to meet. **2.** The range of one's experience, knowledge, interests, etc.: *people with narrow horizons.*

hor•i•zon•tal |hôr'ĭ **zŏn'**tl| *or* |hōr'-| *adj.* Parallel to or in the plane of the horizon; intersecting a vertical line or plane at right angles. *—n.* A horizontal line, plane, object, etc. **—hor'i•zon'tal•ly** *adv.*

hor•mone |**hôr'**mōn'| *n.* A substance that is produced by an organ of the body and carried, as by the blood, to another organ that it stimulates by chemical action.

horn |hôrn| *n.* **1.** One of a pair of hard, usually curved and pointed growths on the heads of cattle, sheep, goats, and related animals. **2.** A similar growth or projection, as on the head of a rhinoceros, giraffe, or snail. **3.** The hard, smooth substance forming the outer covering of the horns of cattle or related animals. **4. a.** A container made from an animal's horn: *a powder horn.* **b.** The amount held by such a container: *a horn of powder.* **5. a.** A **French horn. b.** *Informal.* Any wind instrument, especially a trumpet or other brass instrument. **c.** A wind instrument made of an animal horn. **6.** A flaring device used to project sound, as from a loudspeaker. **7.** A signaling device that produces a loud tone: *an automobile horn.* **—*modifier:*** *a horn knife handle; a horn player.* *—v.* **—horn in.** *Slang.* To join in without being invited. [SEE PICTURES]

Horn, Cape. The southernmost point of South America, on an island of Tierra del Fuego, Chile.

horn•bill |**hôrn'**bĭl'| *n.* Any of several birds of Africa and tropical Asia, having a large, curved bill, often with a bony projection on top.

horn•blende |**hôrn'**blĕnd'| *n.* A common, green to black mineral formed in the late stages of the cooling of igneous rock. It is a complex silicate of iron, calcium, magnesium, and other metals.

horned |hôrnd| *adj.* Having a horn, horns, or hornlike projections.

horned toad. Also **horned lizard.** A lizard of southwestern North America, having hornlike projections on the head, a broad, spiny body, and a short tail.

hor•net |**hôr'**nĭt| *n.* Any of several large stinging wasps that often build large, papery nests.

horn of plenty. A cornucopia.

horn•pipe |**hôrn'**pīp'| *n.* **1.** A lively, spirited dance, usually performed by one person. **2.** A musical composition written to accompany or as if to accompany this dance.

horn•y |**hôr'**nē| *adj.* **horn•i•er, horn•i•est. 1.** Made of horn or a similar substance. **2.** Having horns or hornlike projections. **3.** Tough and calloused: *horny hands; horny skin.*

hor•o•scope |**hôr'**ə skōp'| *or* |**hŏr'**-| *n.* **1.** The position of the planets and stars at a given

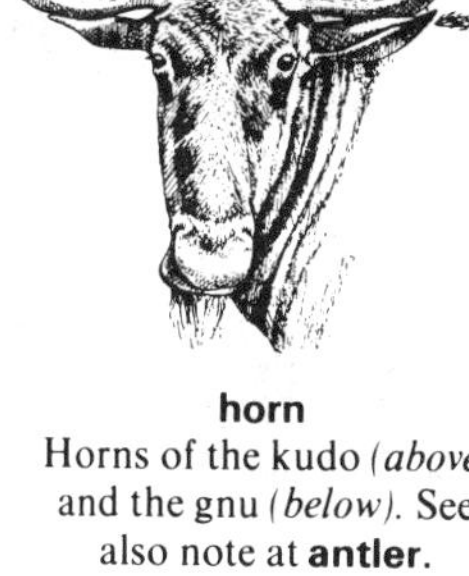

horn
Horns of the kudo *(above)* and the gnu *(below)*. See also note at **antler.**

horse chestnut
Above: Flower cluster
Below: Open bur

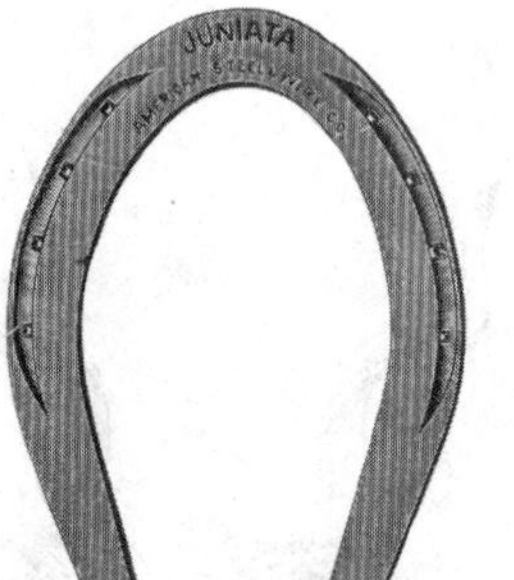

horseshoe

horseshoe crab

ă pat/ā pay/â care/ä father/ĕ pet/ ē be/ĭ pit/ī pie/î fierce/ŏ pot/ ō go/ô paw, for/oi oil/o͝o book/ o͞o boot/ou out/ŭ cut/û fur/ *th* the/th thin/hw which/zh vision/ ə ago, item, pencil, atom, circus

moment, such as the moment of a person's birth. **2.** A forecast, as of a person's future, based on the position of the planets and stars.

hor•ren•dous |hô **rĕn**′dəs| *or* |hŏ-| *adj.* Hideous; dreadful: *a horrendous story.* —**hor•ren′dous•ly** *adv.*

hor•ri•ble |**hôr**′ə bəl| *or* |**hŏr**′-| *adj.* **1.** Causing horror; dreadful: *a horrible crime.* **2.** Very unpleasant: *a horrible noise.* —**hor′ri•bly** *adv.*

hor•rid |**hôr**′ĭd| *or* |**hŏr**′-| *adj.* **1.** Causing horror: *The Chinese do not think of the dragon as a horrid monster.* **2.** Very unpleasant, disagreeable, bad, nasty, etc.: *horrid weather. He is a horrid person.* —**hor′rid•ly** *adv.* —**hor′rid•ness** *n.*

hor•ri•fy |**hôr**′ə fī′| *or* |**hŏr**′-| *v.* **hor•ri•fied, hor•ri•fy•ing, hor•ri•fies. 1.** To cause to feel horror: *The news horrified the people.* **2.** To shock: *The suggestion horrified him.* —**hor′ri•fy′ing** *adj.*: *a horrifying story.*

hor•ror |**hôr**′ər| *or* |**hŏr**′-| *n.* **1.** A feeling of repugnance and fear; terror: *Imagine his horror at the sight of the accident.* **2.** Something that causes such a feeling: *the horrors of slavery.* **3.** Intense dislike; loathing: *He had a horror of bees.* **4.** *Informal.* Something thought to be unpleasant, ugly, in bad taste, etc.: *Her dress is a horror.* —***modifier:*** *a horror story.*

hors d'oeuvre |ôr **dûrv**′|. *pl.* **hors d'oeuvres** |ôr **dûrvz**′| or **hors d'oeuvre.** Any of various appetizers served with cocktails or before a meal.

horse |hôrs| *n.* **1.** A large hoofed animal with a long mane and tail, used for riding and to pull vehicles or carry loads. **2.** A supportive frame or device consisting of a crossbar and four legs. **3.** A gymnastic device, used for vaulting and other exercises, consisting of an upholstered body supported by two legs. **4.** Soldiers on horseback; cavalry: *an army unit consisting of 100 horse.* —***modifier:*** *a horse show; a horse trainer.* —*v.* **horsed, hors•ing.** —**horse around.** *Informal.* To indulge in horseplay. ¶*These sound alike* **horse, hoarse.**

Idioms. **a horse of another** (or **a different**) **color.** *Informal.* Another matter entirely; something else. **be** (or **get**) **on (one's) high horse.** To be or become disdainful, conceited, etc. **from the horse's mouth.** From a reliable source of information. **hold (one's) horses.** To remain calm or patient; restrain oneself.

horse•back |**hôrs**′băk′| *n.* The back of a horse: *soldiers on horseback.* —***modifier:*** *horseback riding.* —*adv.* On the back of a horse: *ride horseback.*

horse chestnut. 1. A tree with upright clusters of white flowers and brown, shiny, inedible nuts enclosed in a spiny bur. **2.** The nut of such a tree. [SEE PICTURES]

horse•fly |**hôrs**′flī′| *n., pl.* **-flies.** Also **horse fly.** A large fly that bites and sucks blood from horses, cattle, and other animals.

horse•hair |**hôrs**′hâr′| *n.* **1.** The hair from a horse's mane or tail. **2.** Stiff cloth made of horsehair, used chiefly in upholstery.

horse latitudes. Either of two regions located over the oceans between about 30 and 35 degrees north and south latitudes. These regions are notable for high barometric pressure, calms, and light, changeable winds.

horse•man |**hôrs**′mən| *n., pl.* **-men** |-mən|. **1.** A man who rides a horse. **2.** A man skilled at horsemanship.

horse•man•ship |**hôrs**′mən shĭp′| *n.* The art of horseback riding.

horse opera. A movie, play, etc., about the U.S. West.

horse•play |**hôrs**′plā′| *n.* Rough, prankish play.

horse•pow•er |**hôrs**′pou′ər| *n., pl.* **horse•pow•er.** A unit of power equal to 745.7 watts or 33,000 foot-pounds per minute.

horse•rad•ish |**hôrs**′răd′ĭsh| *n.* **1.** A tall, coarse plant with a large, whitish, sharp-tasting root. **2.** The grated root of this plant, often mixed with vinegar and used as a relish.

horse•shoe |**hôrs**′sho͞o′| *or* |**hôrsh**′-| *n.* **1.** A U-shaped iron plate fitted and nailed to a horse's hoof. **2. horseshoes** *(used with a singular verb).* A game in which players try to toss horseshoes around a stake. **3.** Something shaped like a horseshoe. [SEE PICTURE]

horseshoe crab. A sea animal with a large, oval shell and a stiff, pointed tail. [SEE PICTURE]

horse•whip |**hôrs**′hwĭp′| *or* |-wĭp′| *n.* A whip used to control a horse. —*v.* **horse•whipped, horse•whip•ping.** To flog with a horsewhip.

horse•wom•an |**hôrs**′wo͝om′ən| *n., pl.* **-wom•en** |-wĭm′ĭn|. A woman skilled at horsemanship.

hors•y, also **hors•ey** |**hôr**′sē| *adj.* **hors•i•er, hors•i•est. 1.** Of or resembling a horse or horses. **2.** Fond of or interested in horses and horsemanship: *the horsy set at the racetrack.*

hor•ti•cul•ture |**hôr**′tĭ kŭl′chər| *n.* The science or art of raising and caring for plants, especially garden plants. —**hor′ti•cul′tur•al** *adj.*

hor•ti•cul•tur•ist |hôr′tĭ **kŭl**′chər ĭst| *n.* A person who specializes in horticulture.

ho•san•na |hō **zăn**′ə| *interj.* A word used to express praise to God or the Messiah. —*n.* A cry of "hosanna."

hose |hōz| *n.* **1.** *pl.* **hose.** Stockings or socks. **2.** *pl.* **hose.** Tights once worn by men as trousers. **3.** *pl.* **hos•es.** A long tube, usually of rubber, used for squirting or spraying water, conducting air, etc. —*v.* **hosed, hos•ing.** To wash or spray with water from a hose: *hose a lawn.*

Ho•se•a |hō **zē**′ə| *or* |-**zā**′ə|. A Hebrew prophet of the eighth century B.C.

ho•sier•y |**hō**′zhə rē| *n.* Stockings and socks; hose.

hos•pice |**hŏs**′pĭs| *n.* A shelter or lodging for travelers or very poor people, often maintained by a religious order.

hos•pi•ta•ble |**hŏs**′pĭ tə bəl| *or* |hŏ **spĭt**′ə bəl| *adj.* **1.** Cordial and generous to guests: *hospitable farmers.* **2.** Having an open mind; receptive: *hospitable to new ways of doing things.* —**hos′pi•ta•bly** *adv.*

hos•pi•tal |**hŏs**′pĭ təl| *or* |-pĭt′l| *n.* An institution providing medical or surgical care and treatment for the sick and injured. —***modifier:*** *hospital care.*

hos•pi•tal•i•ty |hŏs′pĭ **tăl**′ĭ tē| *n., pl.* **hos•pi•tal•i•ties. 1.** Cordial and generous reception of guests. **2.** An example of being hospitable.

hos•pi•tal•i•za•tion |hŏs′pĭ tə lĭ **zā**′shən| *n.* **1.** The fact or condition of being hospitalized: *Unnecessary hospitalization is a tremendous waste.* **2.** The length of time spent by a patient in a hospital. **3.** A form of insurance that completely or partially covers a patient's hospital expenses.

hos·pi·tal·ize |hŏs′pĭ tə līz′| *v.* **hos·pi·tal·ized, hos·pi·tal·iz·ing.** To put (a patient) into a hospital.

host¹ |hōst| *n.* **1.** A person, group, or institution that entertains guests: *He is our host for the weekend.* **2.** A living plant or animal on or in which a parasite or other organism lives and from which it usually gets its nourishment. —*v. Informal.* To serve as host for: *Chicago hosts many trade shows.* [SEE NOTE]

host² |hōst| *n.* **1.** An army. **2.** A great number: *a host of golden daffodils.* [SEE NOTE]

host³, also **Host** |hōst| *n.* The consecrated bread or wafer of the Eucharist. [SEE NOTE]

hos·tage |hŏs′tĭj| *n.* **1.** A person held as security for the fulfillment of certain terms. **2.** The condition of being so held.

hos·tel |hŏs′təl| *n.* An inexpensive lodging house for travelers and tourists of high-school or college age. ¶*These sound alike* **hostel, hostile.**

hos·tel·ry |hŏs′təl rē| *n., pl.* **hos·tel·ries.** An inn.

host·ess |hō′stĭs| *n.* **1.** A woman who acts as a host. **2.** A woman who greets and serves patrons, as at a restaurant, on an airplane, etc.

hos·tile |hŏs′təl| *or* |-tīl′| *adj.* **1.** Of an enemy: *hostile troops.* **2.** Feeling or showing opposition: *hostile to the suggestion.* **3.** Not hospitable: *a hostile environment.* ¶*These sound alike* **hostile, hostel.** —**hos′tile·ly** *adv.*

hos·til·i·ty |hŏ stĭl′ĭ tē| *n., pl.* **hos·til·i·ties.** **1.** The condition of being hostile; antagonism; enmity. **2. hostilities.** Open warfare.

hot |hŏt| *adj.* **hot·ter, hot·test.** **1. a.** Having or giving off great heat. **b.** Being at a high temperature. **2.** Being at a higher temperature than is normal or desirable: *a hot forehead.* **3.** Having a tropical or almost tropical climate: *a hot country.* **4.** Charged or energized with electricity: *the hot conductor of a circuit.* **5.** Radioactive, often dangerously so. **6.** Highly spiced: *hot mustard.* **7.** Explosive; fiery: *a hot contest.* **8.** *Informal.* Close to or having success: *He got hot in the second half of the game.* **9.** *Informal.* New; fresh: *hot off the press.* **10.** *Informal.* Currently popular: *a hot topic of conversation.* **11.** *Slang.* Recently stolen: *a hot television set.* —*adv.* At a higher temperature than normal or desirable: *an engine that runs hot.*

Idioms. **hot under the collar.** *Informal.* Angry. **in hot water.** *Informal.* In trouble.

hot·bed |hŏt′bĕd′| *n.* An environment lending itself to rapid and excessive growth, especially of something bad: *a hotbed of intrigue.*

hot cake. A pancake.

Idiom. **sell** (or **go**) **like hot cakes.** To be in great demand.

hot cross bun. A sweet bun made with raisins and topped with icing in the shape of a cross, traditionally eaten during Lent.

hot dog. A frankfurter, usually served in a long roll. —***modifier:*** **(hot-dog):** *a hot-dog stand.*

hot-dog |hŏt′dôg′| *or* |-dŏg′| *v.* **hot-dogged, hot-dog·ging.** *Slang.* To do stunts or acrobatic feats while skiing or surfing. —**hot′dog′ger** *n.*

ho·tel |hō tĕl′| *n.* A public house that provides lodging and often board and other services. —***modifier:*** *a hotel room.*

hot·foot |hŏt′fo͝ot′| *v.* To go in great haste; run: *hot foot it to the market and buy more milk.* —*adv.* In great haste.

hot·head·ed |hŏt′hĕd′ĭd| *adj.* **1.** Easily excited or angered; fiery: *Ethan Allen was a hotheaded Vermont farmer.* **2.** Impetuous; rash: *a hotheaded young fool.* —**hot′head′ed·ness** *n.*

hot·house |hŏt′hous′| *n., pl.* **-hous·es** |hou′zĭz|. A heated building or enclosure with a glass roof and sides, used for growing plants. —***modifier:*** *hothouse tomatoes.*

hot line. A direct communications link, as a telephone line between heads of government, for use in time of crisis.

hot·ly |hŏt′lē| *adv.* In a fiery manner; violently: *a hotly debated subject.*

hot plate. **1.** A table-top stove with one or two burners. **2.** An electrically heated plate or tray for cooking or keeping food warm.

hot rod. *Slang.* An automobile, usually old, that has been rebuilt or modified for greater power and speed. —***modifier:*** **(hot-rod):** *a hot-rod driver.*

hot·rod or **hot-rod** |hŏt′rŏd′| *n. Slang.* Forms of the phrase **hot rod.**

Hot·ten·tot |hŏt′n tŏt′| *n., pl.* **Hot·ten·tot** or **Hot·ten·tots.** **1.** A member of a people of southern Africa. **2.** The language of this people. —*adj.* Of the Hottentot or their language.

hound |hound| *n.* **1.** Any of several kinds of dogs originally bred and used for hunting. **2.** An enthusiast or addict: *a history hound.* —*v.* **1.** To pursue relentlessly. **2.** To urge insistently; nag: *His wife hounded him to get a new suit.*

hour |our| *n.* **1.** A unit of time equal to $^1/_{24}$ of the average interval between two successive points in time at which the sun is directly overhead; 60 minutes. **2. a.** One of the points on a clock or watch marking off successive periods of 60 minutes, either 12 periods from noon to midnight or 24 periods from noon to noon. **b.** The time of day as shown on a clock or watch marked with 12 hours: *The hour is 3 p.m.* **3. hours. a.** The time of day as shown on a clock or watch marked with 24 hours: *departing at 1700 hours.* **b.** The distance that can be traveled in an hour: *two hours from our destination.* **c.** A specified time: *office hours.* **4.** A customary time: *the dinner hour.* ¶*These sound alike* **hour, our.**

hour·glass |our′glăs′| *or* |-gläs′| *n.* An instrument for measuring time, consisting of two glass chambers with a narrow connecting channel and containing an amount of sand or mercury that passes from one chamber to the other in exactly one hour. [SEE PICTURE]

hour·ly |our′lē| *adj.* **1.** Occurring, done, taken, etc., every hour: *hourly temperature readings.* **2.** By the hour as a unit: *an hourly wage.* —*adv.* At or during every hour.

house |hous| *n., pl.* **hous·es** |hou′zĭz|. **1. a.** A building used by one or several families as a dwelling. **b.** A place of abode; a residence. **c.** A household. **2.** A building or other structure used for storage, shelter, etc.: *a birdhouse; a warehouse.* **3.** A building used for a specified purpose: *an opera house.* **4.** The number of people in an audience: *a full house.* **5.** Often **House.** A noble family: *House of Orange.* **6.** A commercial firm: *a banking house; a publishing house.* **7.** A legislative assembly. —***modifier:*** *house guests.* —*v.* |houz| **housed, hous·ing.** **1.** To pro-

host¹·²·³

Host¹ *is from Old French* hoste, *which is from Latin* hospes; *this word meant simultaneously "host" and "guest."* **Host²** *and* **hostile** *come from Latin* hostis, *"stranger."* **Host³** *is from Latin* hostia, *"something offered as a sacrifice."*

hourglass

houseboat

housing[1-2]
Housing[1] *is, obviously, from* **house. Housing**[2] *is from an Old French word,* houce, *meaning "covering."*

howdah

ă pat/ā pay/â care/ä father/ĕ pet/ ē be/ĭ pit/ī pie/î fierce/ŏ pot/ ō go/ô paw, for/oi oil/ŏŏ book/ ōō boot/ou out/ŭ cut/û fur/ *th* the/th thin/hw which/zh vision/ ə ago, item, pencil, atom, circus

vide living quarters for: *The cottage houses ten people.* **2.** To contain: *harbor.*

***Idioms.* bring down the house.** *Informal.* To receive enthusiastic applause from an audience: *His new act brought down the house.* **clean house. 1.** To take care of and clean a house. **2.** To get rid of undesirable or corrupt people, habits, etc. **keep house.** To clean and manage a house. **on the house.** As a gift from the management; free: *This soda is on the house.*

house•boat |**hous**'bōt'| *n.* A barge equipped for use as a home or cruiser. [SEE PICTURE]

house•break•er |**hous**'brā'kər| *n.* Someone who unlawfully breaks into another's house in order to commit a felony. —**house'break'ing** *n.*

house•bro•ken |**hous**'brō'kən| *adj.* Trained to live indoors: *a housebroken dog.*

house•fly |**hous**'flī'| *n., pl.* **-flies.** A common fly that is found in or around homes and that is a carrier of many diseases.

house•hold |**hous**'hōld'| *n.* The members of a family and others living together in a house or other place of residence. —***modifier:*** *household appliances.*

house•hold•er |**hous**'hōl'dər| *n.* **1.** Someone, especially the owner, who occupies a house. **2.** The head of a household.

house•keep•er |**hous**'kē'pər| *n.* A woman hired to take care of a home and perform such duties as cleaning, buying food, etc. —**house'keep'ing** *n.*

house•maid |**hous**'mād'| *n.* A woman employed to do housework.

House of Commons. 1. The lower house of Parliament in the United Kingdom. Its members are elected by the people and have the power to make laws. **2.** The lower house of the Canadian parliament.

house of correction. An institution housing persons convicted of minor criminal offenses.

House of Lords. The upper house of Parliament in the United Kingdom, made up of members of the nobility and high-ranking clergy.

House of Representatives. 1. The lower branch of the United States Congress, whose members are elected every two years. **2.** The lower branch of the legislature in most states of the United States.

house•top |**hous**'tŏp'| *n.* The roof of a house.

house•warm•ing |**hous**'wôr'mĭng| *n.* A party to celebrate the occupancy of a new house.

house•wife |**hous**'wīf'| *n., pl.* **-wives** |-wīvz'|. A married woman who manages her family's household.

house•work |**hous**'wûrk'| *n.* The tasks of housekeeping, as cleaning and cooking.

hous•ing[1] |**hou**'zĭng| *n.* **1.** Buildings or other shelters in which people live. **2.** Something that covers, contains, or protects a machine or any of its parts. —***modifier:*** *a housing development; a housing shortage.* [SEE NOTE]

hous•ing[2] |**hou**'zĭng| *n.* **1.** An ornamental or protective covering for a saddle. **2. housings.** Trappings, as for a horse. [SEE NOTE]

Hous•ton |**hyōō**'stən|. The largest city in Texas. Population, 1,594,086.

Hous•ton |**hyōō**'stən|, **Sam(uel).** 1793–1863. American political leader; first president of the Republic of Texas (1836–38 and 1841–44).

hove |hōv|. *Chiefly Nautical.* A past tense and past participle of **heave.**

hov•el |**hŭv**'əl| *or* |**hŏv**'-| *n.* A small, miserable dwelling.

hov•er |**hŭv**'ər| *or* |**hŏv**'-| *v.* **1.** To fly, soar, or float as if suspended: *Hummingbirds hover over the flowers they feed on.* **2.** To remain or linger close by: *Ann hovered around the baby's crib.* **3.** To be in a condition of uncertainty; waver: *They hovered between sadness and happiness.*

Hov•er•craft |**hŭv**'ər krăft'| *or* |-kräft'| *n.* A trademark for a vehicle designed to skim over land or water at a height of a few inches. This vehicle is held aloft by air forced downward by an engine-driven fan and propelled and steered by another such fan.

how |hou| *adv.* **1.** In what manner or way; by what means: *showing how it's done.* **2.** In what state or condition: *How does she look now that she's better?* **3.** To what extent, amount, or degree: *How do you like your new bike?* **4.** At what cost; for what price: *How do these things sell at wholesale as against retail?* **5.** What: *How is that again?* **6.** With what meaning: *How should I interpret this?* —*n.* The way something is done: *I am more interested in the how than the why of a thing.*

***Idioms.* how about? 1.** Would you like to have: *How about some ice cream?* **2.** What is your feeling or thought regarding: *How about her new dress?* **how come?** *Informal.* How is it that; why: *How come you got back so soon?*

how•dah |**hou**'də| *n.* A seat, usually fitted with a canopy and railing, placed on the back of an elephant or camel. [SEE PICTURE]

how do you do. A phrase used in greeting a person as an equivalent of the word "hello."

how•dy |**hou**'dē| *interj. Informal.* A word used to express greeting.

how•ev•er |hou **ĕv**'ər| *adv.* To whatever extent; no matter how: *However boring it may sound, it's actually an extremely interesting book.* —*conj.* Nevertheless; yet: *It was a difficult time; however, there were amusing moments.*

how•it•zer |**hou**'ĭt sər| *n.* A short cannon that fires shells in a high trajectory.

howl |houl| *n.* **1.** The long, wailing cry of a dog or wolf. **2.** An outcry, as of protest, pain, rage, etc. —*v.* **1.** to make a long, wailing cry or a similar sound: *The dogs howled at the moon.* **2.** To cry or wail loudly, especially in pain: *The old witch howled when Gretel pushed her into the oven.* **3.** *Slang.* To laugh heartily. —**howl'ing** *adj.: howling dogs.* —**howl'er** *n.*

how•so•ev•er |hou'sō **ĕv**'ər| *adv.* To whatever extent or degree; however.

hoy•den |**hoid**'n| *n.* A high-spirited, often boisterous girl or woman.

Hoyle |hoil| *n.* A standard reference book giving rules for card games and other indoor games.

***Idiom.* according to Hoyle.** According to accepted rules and without cheating.

hp horsepower.

HQ, h.q., H.Q. headquarters.

hr hour.

H.R.H. His (or Her) Royal Highness.

ht height.

hub |hŭb| *n.* **1.** The center part of a wheel, from which the spokes radiate. **2.** A center of activity; focal point: *the hub of a great empire.*

hub•bub |**hŭb**′ŭb′| *n.* Noisy confusion; uproar: *the hubbub of traffic.*

hub•cap |**hŭb**′kăp′| *n.* A round metal covering clamped over the hub of an automobile wheel.

huck•le•ber•ry |**hŭk**′əl bĕr′ē| *n., pl.* **-ber•ries.** **1.** A glossy, blackish, edible berry related to the blueberry. **2.** A shrub that bears such berries. —***modifier:*** *huckleberry pie.*

hud•dle |**hŭd**′l| *n.* **1.** A densely packed group or crowd: *a huddle of tiny tents.* **2.** In football, a brief gathering of a team's players behind the line of scrimmage to prepare for the next play. **3.** A small private conference. —*v.* **hud•dled, hud•dling. 1.** To crowd together, as from cold or fear; nestle: *The sheep huddled up against the fire. The adults huddled the children around the stove.* **2.** To draw oneself together; curl up: *The little brown rabbit huddled in a ball, afraid for its life.* **3. a.** In football, to gather in a huddle. **b.** To gather for a conference; meet.

Hud•son |**hŭd**′sən|. A river of New York State, flowing generally south to its mouth at New York City.

Hud•son |**hŭd**′sən|, **Henry.** Died 1611. English navigator; discovered the Hudson river and Hudson Bay.

Hud•son Bay |**hŭd**′sən|. An inland sea in north-central Canada.

hue[1] |hyo͞o| *n.* **1. a.** Color: *all the hues of the rainbow.* **b.** A particular color seen as distinct from other colors; a shade; tint. **2.** The property of color that is perceived and measured on a scale running from red through yellow, green, and blue to violet. ¶*These sound alike* **hue, hew.** [SEE NOTE]

hue[2] |hyo͞o| *n.* —**hue and cry.** A public clamor, as of protest or demand. ¶*These sound alike* **hue, hew.** [SEE NOTE]

huff |hŭf| *n.* A fit of anger or annoyance: *She left the room in a huff.* —*v.* To puff; blow, as from exhaustion: *They huffed and puffed all the way up the hill.*

huff•y |**hŭf**′ē| *adj.* **huff•i•er, huff•i•est. 1.** Easily offended; touchy: *He's very huffy today.* **2.** Arrogant; haughty: *It's not his place to get huffy with the customers.* —**huff′i•ly** *adv.* —**huff′i•ness** *n.*

hug |hŭg| *v.* **hugged, hug•ging. 1.** To clasp or hold closely; embrace: *hug a child.* **2.** To keep, remain, or be situated close to: *The plastic contact lens hugs the cornea.* **3.** To ascribe to (a belief, idea, principle, etc.); cherish. —*n.* An affectionate or tight embrace.

huge |hyo͞oj| *adj.* **hug•er, hug•est.** Of great size, extent, or quantity; tremendous: *a huge iceberg.* —**huge′ly** *adv.* —**huge′ness** *n.*

Hu•gue•not |**hyo͞o**′gə nŏt′| *n.* A French Protestant of the 16th and 17th centuries.

huh |hŭ| *interj.* Used in asking a question or to express surprise, scorn, etc.

hu•la |**ho͞o**′lə| *n.* A Hawaiian dance in which the wavy movements of the hips, arms, and hands tell a story.

hu•la-hu•la |**ho͞o**′lə **ho͞o**′lə| *n.* A form of the word **hula.**

hulk |hŭlk| *n.* **1.** A worn-out ship that is no longer able to move under its own power. **2.** A heavy, unwieldy ship. **3.** A clumsy and overweight person.

hulk•ing |**hŭl**′kĭng| *adj.* Unwieldy; clumsy; bulky: *a great, hulking mongrel.*

hull |hŭl| *n.* **1.** The framework of a ship or plane. **2.** The cluster of leaflets at the stem end of certain fruits, such as the strawberry. **3.** The outer covering of certain seeds, fruits, or nuts; a husk or pod. —*v.* To remove the hulls from: *hull strawberries.* [SEE PICTURES]

hul•la•ba•loo |**hŭl**′ə bə lo͞o′| *n.* Great noise or excitement; an uproar.

hul•lo |hə **lō**′| *interj.* & *n.* A form of the word **hello.**

hum |hŭm| *v.* **hummed, hum•ming. 1. a.** To produce (musical tones or a tune) as in singing but with the lips kept closed: *hum a song. She hummed softly to herself.* **b.** To put (someone) into a specified condition by so doing: *hum a child to sleep.* **2. a.** To emit the droning sound of an insect on the wing. **b.** To move about making such a sound: *The bees hummed around the flower.* **3.** To make a continuous low-pitched droning sound: *The television set hums when we turn it on.* **4.** To be full of or alive with activity: *The factories hum daily.* —*n.* **1.** The act or sound of humming: *the hum of bees. His hum grew to full song.* **2.** The confused noise of activity: *the hum of a sawmill.* —*interj.* A word used as a pause in speech or to indicate thought or express surprise, displeasure, etc.

hu•man |**hyo͞o**′mən| *adj.* **1.** Of or characteristic of the species to which man belongs or of man as a living thing: *the human body; a human voice.* **2.** Of or having the qualities of man or mankind: *human nature.* **3.** Made up of people: *a human bridge across the river.* —*n.* A person; a human being. —**hu′man•ness** *n.*

human being. A member of the species to which man belongs; a person.

hu•mane |hyo͞o **mān**′| *adj.* Kind; compassionate; merciful: *a doctor's humane concern.* —**hu•mane′ly** *adv.* —**hu•mane′ness** *n.*

hu•man•ism |**hyo͞o**′mə nĭz′əm| *n.* **1.** A philosophy, system of thought, or state of mind that is concerned with human beings, their achievements, interests, happiness, and improvement rather than with problems of theology, with abstract beings, concepts, etc. **2.** Often **Humanism.** A cultural and intellectual movement of the Renaissance that focused on the study of the ancient Greek and Roman arts.

hu•man•ist |**hyo͞o**′mə nĭst| *n.* **1.** Someone who studies the humanities. **2.** Someone who is concerned with the study and welfare of human beings. —*adj.* **1.** Of humanism or the humanities. **2.** Devoted to the study or welfare of man.

hu•man•i•tar•i•an |hyo͞o măn′ĭ **târ**′ē ən| *adj.* Concerned with human welfare and with the alleviation of human suffering: *humanitarian work in hospitals.* —*n.* Someone concerned with the promotion of human welfare and the advancement of social reforms; a philanthropist.

hu•man•i•tar•i•an•ism |hyo͞o măn′ĭ **târ**′ē ə-nĭz′əm| *n.* The belief that man has an obligation to work for the improvement of human welfare and for the alleviation of human suffering.

hu•man•i•ty |hyo͞o **măn**′ĭ tē| *n., pl.* **hu•man•i•ties. 1. a.** Human beings in general; mankind: *Some scientists serve humanity self-effacingly.* **b.** People; men: *On the street was a moving tide of*

hue[1·2]

Hue[1] *was Old English* hīw, *"appearance, beauty, color."* **Hue**[2] *is from Old French* hu, *"a shouting," from* huer, *"to shout."*

hull
Above: Hull of a boat
Below: Strawberry hull

hummingbird

hundred

Hundred *was* hund *or* hundred *in Old English; it is descended from prehistoric Germanic* hundan, *which in turn is from Indo-European* kəmtom. *An Indo-European* k- *always became a Germanic* h-, *but in Latin* k- *remained a hard* k- *sound. In Latin,* kəmtom *became* centum. *See note at* **century**.

ă pat/ā pay/â care/ä father/ĕ pet/ ē be/ĭ pit/ī pie/î fierce/ŏ pot/ ō go/ô paw, for/oi oil/ŏŏ book/ ōō boot/ou out/ŭ cut/û fur/ *th* the/th thin/hw which/zh vision/ ə ago, item, pencil, atom, circus

humanity. **2.** The quality or fact of being human: *Some denied the humanity of the slave because of his color.* **3.** The quality of being humane; kindness: *If man has a heart, he has some humanity in him.* **4. the humanities.** Those subjects, such as philosophy, literature, etc., concerned with man and his culture as opposed to the sciences.

hu•man•ize |hyōō′mə nīz′| *v.* **hu•man•ized, hu•man•iz•ing.** To make human or humane. —**hu′man•i•za′tion** *n.*

hu•man•ly |hyōō′mən lē| *adv.* **1.** In a human way: *She responded humanly to the cries for help.* **2.** By human means or capabilities: *as foolproof as is humanly possible.*

hu•man•oid |hyōō′mə noid′| *adj.* Resembling a human being in appearance. —*n.* A science-fiction character that resembles human beings.

hum•ble |hŭm′bəl| *adj.* **hum•bler, hum•blest. 1. a.** Having or showing feelings of humility rather than of pride; modest; meek. **b.** Expressed in a modest spirit: *humble thanks.* **2.** Of low social or political rank: *a humble clerk of the court.* —*v.* **hum•bled, hum•bling.** To make humble: *He humbled himself before the powerful and rich.* —**hum′ble•ness** *n.* —**hum′bly** *adv.*

hum•bug |hŭm′bŭg′| *n.* **1.** Something intended to deceive; a hoax. **2.** Someone who tries to trick or deceive; a charlatan. —*v.* **hum•bugged, hum•bug•ging.** To deceive or trick: *Grandfather was not easily humbugged by slick salesmen.*

hum•ding•er |hŭm′dĭng′ər| *n. Slang.* Someone or something excellent, remarkable, etc.

hum•drum |hŭm′drŭm′| *adj.* Without variety or change; monotonous; boring: *a humdrum existence.*

hu•mer•us |hyōō′mər əs| *n., pl.* **hu•mer•i** |hyōō′mə rī′|. **1.** The bone of the upper arm in human beings, extending from the shoulder to the elbow. **2.** A similar bone in other vertebrates. ¶*These sound alike* **humerus, humorous.**

hu•mid |hyōō′mĭd| *adj.* Having a large amount of water or water vapor; damp; moist: *humid air.*

hu•mid•i•fy |hyōō mĭd′ə fī′| *v.* **hu•mid•i•fied, hu•mid•i•fy•ing, hu•mid•i•fies.** To increase the amount of water vapor in (the air in an enclosed space). —**hu•mid′i•fi′er** *n.*

hu•mid•i•ty |hyōō mĭd′ĭ tē| *n.* Dampness, especially of the air. See **absolute humidity** and **relative humidity.**

hu•mi•dor |hyōō′mĭ dôr′| *n.* A container for cigars that has a device for maintaining the humidity at a constant level.

hu•mil•i•ate |hyōō mĭl′ē āt′| *v.* **hu•mil•i•at•ed, hu•mil•i•at•ing.** To lower the pride or status of; humble or disgrace.

hu•mil•i•a•tion |hyōō mĭl′ē ā′shən| *n.* **1.** The act of humiliating; degradation: *masters that delighted in the humiliation of their servants.* **2.** The condition of being humiliated; disgrace.

hu•mil•i•ty |hyōō mĭl′ĭ tē| *n.* The quality or condition of being humble; lack of pride; modesty: *handled it with tact and humility.*

hum•ming•bird |hŭm′ĭng bûrd′| *n.* Any of several very small, long-billed, often brightly colored birds. [See Picture]

hum•mock |hŭm′ək| *n.* A low mound or ridge, as of earth or snow.

hu•mor |hyōō′mər| *n.* **1.** The quality of being comical or funny: *adding to the humor of the story.* **2.** The ability to perceive, enjoy, or express what is comical or funny: *a sense of humor.* **3.** State of mind; mood; temper: *in a good humor.* **4. a.** Any clear or transparent body fluid, such as blood, lymph, or bile. **b.** The **aqueous humor. c.** The **vitreous humor.** —*v.* To comply with the wishes of (others); indulge: *The cowboys humored the cook good-naturedly.*

hu•mor•ist |hyōō′mər ĭst| *n.* Someone with a sharp sense of humor, especially a writer of comedy.

hu•mor•ous |hyōō′mər əs| *adj.* Having, marked by, or employing humor; funny: *a humorous writer; a humorous tale.* ¶*These sound alike* **humorous, humerus.** —**hu′mor•ous•ly** *adv.*

hu•mour |hyōō′mər| *n.* & *v.* British form of the word **humor.**

hump |hŭmp| *n.* **1.** A rounded lump or projecting part, as on the back of a camel or some cattle. **2.** A deformity of the back in which the spine curves in an abnormal way. —*v.* To rise in or form a hump; arch.

hump•back |hŭmp′băk′| *n.* **1.** A condition in which the back has a hump or an abnormal curvature. **2.** A person affected with such a condition; a hunchback. —**modifier:** *a humpback clown.* —**hump′backed′** *adj.*

humph |hŭmf| *interj.* Used to express contempt or displeasure.

hu•mus |hyōō′məs| *n.* A dark-colored substance that consists of decayed plant and animal material and forms a part of the soil necessary for plant nourishment.

Hun |hŭn| *n.* A member of a nomadic Asiatic people who invaded Europe in the fourth and fifth centuries A.D.

hunch |hŭnch| *n.* **1.** A strong feeling or guess, especially as to how something will turn out; a premonition: *I had a hunch this morning that today would be a great day.* **2.** A hump. —*v.* To draw up, arch, or bend into a hump: *He hunched his shoulders stubbornly. The horse hunched, reared, and threw the saddle off.*

hunch•back |hŭnch′băk′| *n.* **1.** An abnormally curved back. **2.** A person having such a back; a humpback. —**hunch′backed′** *adj.*

hun•dred |hŭn′drĭd| *n.* A number, written 100 in Arabic numerals, that is equal to the product of 10 × 10. It is the tenth positive integer after 90. —**hun′dred** *adj.* & *pron.* [See Note]

hun•dredth |hŭn′drĭdth| *n.* **1.** In a set of items arranged to match the natural numbers in a one-to-one correspondence, the item that matches the number one hundred. **2.** One of one hundred equal parts of a unit, written $^1/_{100}$, .01, or 10^{-2}. —**hun′dredth** *adj.* & *adv.*

hun•dred•weight |hŭn′drĭd wāt′| *n.* A unit of weight equal to 100 pounds.

hung |hŭng|. A past tense and past participle of **hang.**

Hun•gar•i•an |hŭng gâr′ē ən| *n.* **1.** A native or inhabitant of Hungary. **2.** The language of Hungary, related to Finnish. —*adj.* Of Hungary, the Hungarians, or their language.

Hun•ga•ry |hŭng′gə rē|. A country in central Europe. Population, 10,510,000. Capital, Budapest.

hun•ger |hŭng′gər| *n.* **1.** A strong desire for

food. **2.** A strong desire or craving for anything: *a hunger for learning.* —***modifier:*** *hunger pangs.* —*v.* **1.** To have a need or desire for food: *They hungered for something hot and delicious.* **2.** To have a strong desire or craving for anything: *The team hungered for victory.*

hun•gry |hŭng′grē| *adj.* **hun•gri•er, hun•gri•est. 1.** Desiring or craving food: *a hungry dog.* **2.** Desiring or craving anything: *hungry for affection.* **3.** Showing or feeling hunger, craving, need, etc.: *hungry eyes.* —**hun′gri•ly** *adv.*

hunk |hŭngk| *n. Informal.* A large piece; a chunk: *a hunk of freshly baked bread.*

Hun•nish |hŭn′ĭsh| *adj.* Of the Huns or their language. —*n.* The language of the Huns.

hunt |hŭnt| *v.* **1.** To pursue or seek to capture and kill (game or prey) for food or sport: *He hunts rabbits. The Indians hunt and fish.* **2. a.** To search for; seek out: *animals hunting food.* **b.** To conduct a thorough search; seek: *The posse hunted for the criminals.* **3.** To find, uncover, or get by searching thoroughly: *He hunted down the criminal and trapped him.* —*n.* **1.** The act or sport of hunting game. **2.** A hunting expedition, usually with horses and hounds: *a fox hunt.* **3.** A thorough search: *the hunt for the criminal.*

hunt•er |hŭn′tər| *n.* Someone or something that hunts game or prey for food or sport.

hunt•ing |hŭn′tĭng| *n.* The activity or sport of pursuing game or prey. —***modifier:*** *the hunting season.*

hunts•man |hŭnts′mən| *n., pl.* **-men** |-mən|. **1.** A hunter. **2.** Someone who has charge of the dogs for a hunt.

hur•dle |hûr′dl| *n.* **1. a.** A barrier used in obstacle races, usually consisting of a horizontal bar supported by two uprights. **b. hurdles** *(used with a singular verb).* A race in which such barriers must be jumped. **2.** An obstacle or problem that must be overcome. —***modifier:*** *a hurdle race.* —*v.* **hur•dled, hur•dling. 1.** To jump over something while running in or as if in a race. **2.** To surmount an obstacle, difficulty, etc. —**hur′dler** *n.* [SEE PICTURE]

hur•dy-gur•dy |hûr′dē gûr′dē| *or* |-gûr′-| *n., pl.* **hur•dy-gur•dies.** A musical instrument played by turning a crank, used most commonly by street musicians.

hurl |hûrl| *v.* **1.** To throw with great force; fling: *The water hurled the ice into the brook below.* **2.** To say or utter vehemently: *The witch doctor hurled angry words at the boy.* **3.** To move very fast; hurtle: *The train hurled past.* —*n.* The act of hurling; a forceful throw. —**hurl′er** *n.*

Hu•ron |hyo͝or′ən| *or* |-ŏn′| *n., pl.* **Hu•ron** or **Hu•rons. 1.** A confederation of four Iroquoian-speaking North American Indian tribes formerly living in the region east of Lake Huron and the St. Lawrence valley. **2.** A member of any of these tribes.

Hu•ron, Lake |hyo͝or′ən| *or* |-ŏn′|. One of the Great Lakes, lying between Michigan and Ontario, Canada.

hur•rah |ho͞o rä′| *or* |-rô′| *interj.* A word used to express approval, pleasure, or victory. —*n.* A shout of "hurrah." —*v.* To shout or cheer with "hurrah."

hur•ray |ho͞o rā′| *interj., n., & v.* A form of the word **hurrah.**

hur•ri•cane |hûr′ĭ kān′| *or* |hŭr′-| *n.* A severe, swirling tropical storm with heavy rains and winds exceeding 75 miles per hour, originating in the tropical parts of the Atlantic Ocean or the Caribbean Sea and moving generally northward. —***modifier:*** *the hurricane season.*

hur•ried |hûr′ēd| *or* |hŭr′-| *adj.* Done in great haste; rushed: *a hurried tour.* —**hur′ried•ly** *adv.*

hur•ry |hûr′ē| *or* |hŭr′ē| *v.* **hur•ried, hur•ry•ing, hur•ries.** To move or cause to move with great haste; rush: *People hurried to the grandstand. She hurried the smugglers out of the room. Hurry up or we will be late!* —*n.* The need or wish to hurry; a condition of urgency; a rush: *leave in a hurry. There's no need for hurry.*

hurt |hûrt| *v.* **hurt, hurt•ing. 1.** To cause physical damage or pain to; injure; wound: *Andy fell and hurt his ankle.* **2.** To have a feeling of pain or discomfort: *The doctor asked the player if his knees hurt.* **3.** To suffer or cause to suffer mental or emotional anguish; distress or offend: *I'm hurt that he didn't call. He hurt his mother's feelings.* **4.** To damage; harm: *This resistance began to hurt England's business.* —*n.* Something that hurts; a pain, injury, or wound.

hurt•ful |hûrt′fəl| *adj.* Causing hurt or injury; painful: *The truth is often hurtful.* —**hurt′ful•ly** *adv.* —**hurt′ful•ness** *n.*

hur•tle |hûr′tl| *v.* **hur•tled, hur•tling.** To move or cause to move with or as if with great speed: *He hurtled through the dust toward the highway. The weather hurtled leaves into the air.*

hus•band |hŭz′bənd| *n.* A man to whom a woman is married. —*v.* To spend or use economically and with care: *husband one's strength.* [SEE NOTE]

hus•band•ry |hŭz′bən drē| *n.* **1.** The work of raising crops and caring for farm animals; farming. **2.** Good or careful management.

hush |hŭsh| *v.* To make or become quiet: *hush a baby. The crowd hushed at the approach of the funeral train.* —**hushed′** *adj.: hushed voices.* —*n.* A silence or stillness; quiet.

hush•pup•py |hŭsh′pŭp′ē| *n., pl.* **hush•pup•pies.** A fried cornmeal fritter.

husk |hŭsk| *n.* The dry or leaflike outer covering of certain seeds or fruits, as of an ear of corn or a nut. —*v.* To remove the husk or husks from: *husk ears of corn.*

husk•y[1] |hŭs′kē| *adj.* **husk•i•er, husk•i•est.** Hoarse or deep: *a husky voice.* —**husk′i•ly** *adv.* —**husk′i•ness** *n.* [SEE NOTE]

husk•y[2] |hŭs′kē| *adj.* **husk•i•er, husk•i•est.** Rugged and strong; burly: *a husky, pigeon-toed football player.* —*n., pl.* **husk•ies.** A husky person. —**husk′i•ness** *n.* [SEE NOTE]

husk•y[3] |hŭs′kē| *n., pl.* **husk•ies.** Often **Husky.** A dog with a thick, furry coat, used in Arctic regions for pulling sleds. [SEE NOTE]

hus•sar |ho͞o zär′| *n.* A horseman of the light cavalry in some European armies.

hus•sy |hŭz′ē| *or* |hŭs′ē| *n., pl.* **hus•sies. 1.** A mischievous, impertinent girl. **2.** An immoral woman.

hus•tle |hŭs′əl| *v.* **hus•tled, hus•tling. 1.** To push or shove roughly: *The guards hustled me into a little office.* **2.** *Informal.* To hurry along; speed up: *He hustled the discussion to a conclusion and left.* **3.** *Informal.* To obtain business, money,

hurdle

husband

Husband *was* hūsbonda *in Old English and originally meant "master of the household":* hūs, *"house,"* + bonda, *"free farmer." In the materials on which this Dictionary was based,* **husband** *occurred 234 times, but* **wife** *occurred 636 times.*

husky[1-2-3]

Husky[1] *originally meant "dry as a husk" and comes from* **husk. Husky**[2] *apparently is a separate formation, also from* **husk,** *originally meaning "tough like a husk" (used of people like Indians and pioneers).* **Husky**[3] *was first used to mean "an Eskimo" and later "an Eskimo dog." The word is said to be an alteration of* **Eskimo.**

hyacinth

hydrofoil
Hydrofoil gunboat propelled by water jets

hyena

ă pat/ā pay/â care/ä father/ĕ pet/ ē be/ĭ pit/ī pie/î fierce/ŏ pot/ ō go/ô paw, for/oi oil/o͝o book/ o͞o boot/ou out/ŭ cut/û fur/ *th* the/th thin/hw which/zh vision/ ə ago, item, pencil, atom, circus

etc., by energetic activity; work busily and quickly: *A good waiter hustles and makes sure his customers are satisfied.* —*n.* **1.** The act of hustling; rough shoving: *the hustle and bustle of the crowds.* **2.** Energetic activity: *What he lacks in scoring ability, he makes up in hustle.* —**hust'ler** *n.*

hut |hŭt| *n.* A makeshift or crude dwelling or shelter; a shed; shack.

hutch |hŭch| *n.* **1.** A pen or coop for small animals, especially rabbits. **2.** A cupboard having open shelves above it.

hy•a•cinth |**hī'**ə sĭnth| *n.* A plant that grows from a bulb and has a cluster of fragrant, variously colored flowers. [SEE PICTURE]

hy•brid |**hī'**brĭd| *n.* **1.** A plant or animal that is the offspring of parents of different varieties or strains within a species or of different species. **2.** A plant or animal having an unlike pair of genes for the same inherited characteristic. **3.** Anything made by or resulting from combining things that are of different kinds. —*adj.* Made by or resulting from a combination of different types: *hybrid corn; a hybrid investment project.*

hy•brid•ize |**hī'**brĭ dīz'| *v.* **hy•brid•ized, hy•brid•iz•ing.** To produce or cause to produce a hybrid or hybrids; crossbreed. —**hy'brid•i•za'tion** *n.*

hy•dra |**hī'**drə| *n., pl.* **hy•dras.** A small freshwater animal with a tubelike body and a mouth opening surrounded by tentacles.

hy•dran•gea |hī **drān'**jə| *or* |-jē ə| *or* |-**drăn'**-| *n.* A shrub with large, rounded clusters of white, pink, or blue flowers.

hy•drant |**hī'**drənt| *n.* A large upright pipe, usually on a curb, from which water can be drawn for fighting fires; a fireplug.

hy•drate |**hī'**drāt'| *n.* A form of a chemical compound that contains water combined with it in definite proportions, the water forming a part of the crystalline or molecular structure. —*v.* **hy•drat•ed, hy•drat•ing.** To form a hydrate. —**hy•dra'tion** *n.*

hy•drau•lic |hī **drô'**lĭk| *adj.* **1.** Of, moved by, or operated by a liquid, especially water or oil under pressure: *a hydraulic jack.* **2.** Of hydraulics. **3.** Capable of hardening under water, as Portland cement. —**hy•drau'li•cal•ly** *adv.*

hy•drau•lics |hī **drô'**lĭks| *n.* *(used with a singular verb).* The scientific study and technological use of the behavior of fluids.

hydro–. A word element meaning: **1.** Water: **hydroelectric. 2.** Hydrogen: **hydrocarbon.**

hy•dro•car•bon |hī'drə **kär'**bən| *n.* Any member of the very large class of chemical compounds that contain only carbon and hydrogen. Benzene and butane are examples of hydrocarbons.

hy•dro•chlo•ric acid |hī'drə **klôr'**ĭk| *or* |-**klōr**-|. A colorless, fuming, corrosive solution of hydrogen chloride in water.

hy•dro•dy•nam•ic |hī'drō dī **năm'**ĭk| *adj.* **1.** Of or operated by a moving liquid. **2.** Of hydrodynamics. —**hy'dro•dy•nam'i•cal•ly** *adv.*

hy•dro•dy•nam•ics |hī'drō dī **năm'**ĭks| *n. (used with a singular verb).* The part of physics that deals with the behavior of fluids, especially fluids that cannot be compressed, in motion.

hy•dro•e•lec•tric |hī'drō ĭ **lĕk'**trĭk| *adj.* **1.** Generating electricity from the energy of running or falling water: *a hydroelectric power station.* **2.** Of or using the electricity generated in this way: *a hydroelectric power system.*

hy•dro•foil |**hī'**drə foil'| *n.* **1.** A structure shaped like a wing of an aircraft and attached to the hull of a boat below the water line so that at a certain speed the hull of the boat is lifted clear of the water, allowing the boat to travel faster and use less fuel. **2.** A boat equipped with such a device. [SEE PICTURE]

hy•dro•gen |**hī'**drə jən| *n.* Symbol **H** One of the elements, a colorless, highly flammable gas. Atomic number 1; atomic weight 1.008; valences –1, +1; melting point –259.14°C; boiling point –252.5°C.

hy•dro•gen•ate |**hī'**drə jə nāt'| *or* |hī **drŏj'**ə-| *v.* **hy•dro•gen•at•ed, hy•dro•gen•at•ing. 1.** To treat or combine chemically with hydrogen. **2.** To treat (a liquid vegetable oil) with hydrogen and convert it to a solid fat.

hydrogen bomb. An extremely destructive explosive weapon releasing energy derived from the fusion of nuclei of certain isotopes of hydrogen and nuclei of lithium.

hydrogen peroxide. A colorless, liquid chemical compound containing hydrogen and oxygen and having the formula H_2O_2. It is an unstable oxidizing agent, and is often used in a dilute water solution as an antiseptic.

hydrogen sulfide. A poisonous chemical compound containing hydrogen and sulfur and having the formula H_2S. It is a flammable gas having the characteristic odor of rotten eggs.

hy•drol•y•sis |hī **drŏl'**ĭ sĭs| *n.* A reaction in which the parts of a chemical compound are split apart by the action of water, as ions or as separate compounds.

hy•dro•lyze |**hī'**drə līz'| *v.* **hy•dro•lyzed, hy•dro•lyz•ing.** To subject to or undergo hydrolysis.

hy•drom•e•ter |hī **drŏm'**ĭ tər| *n.* An instrument used for measuring specific gravity, especially a sealed, graduated tube, weighted at one end, that sinks in a liquid to a depth used as a measure of the liquid's specific gravity.

hy•dro•pho•bi•a |hī'drə **fō'**bē ə| *n.* **1.** Rabies. **2.** Fear of water.

hy•dro•plane |**hī'**drə plān'| *n.* **1.** A motorboat designed so that only a small part of its hull touches the water at high speeds. **2.** A seaplane.

hy•dro•sphere |**hī'**drə sfîr'| *n.* The waters of the earth as distinguished from the atmosphere and the solid matter.

hy•dro•ther•a•py |hī'drə **thĕr'**ə pē| *n.* The medical use of water in the treatment of diseases.

hy•drox•ide |hī **drŏk'**sīd'| *n.* A chemical compound consisting of an element or radical joined to a hydroxyl group.

hydroxide ion. The negatively charged ion OH^-, characteristic of basic hydroxides.

hy•drox•yl |hī **drŏk'**sĭl| *n.* The radical or group OH, composed of hydrogen and oxygen and having a valence of 1. It is characteristic of bases, certain acids, and alcohols.

hy•e•na |hī **ē'**nə| *n.* A flesh-eating Asian or African animal with coarse, sometimes spotted or striped hair. [SEE PICTURE]

hy•giene |**hī'**jēn'| *n.* Scientific methods for the promotion of good health and the prevention of disease.

hy•gi•en•ic |hī'jē **ĕn'**ĭk| *adj.* **1.** Of hygiene. **2.**

Tending to promote good health: *hygienic practices.* **3.** Clean and free of germs; sanitary: *a hygienic kitchen.* —**hy′gi•en′i•cal•ly** *adv.*

hy•grom•e•ter |hī **grŏm′**ĭ tər| *n.* An instrument that measures atmospheric humidity.

hy•gro•scop•ic |hī′grə **skŏp′**ĭk| *adj.* Tending to absorb moisture readily, as from the atmosphere: *a hygroscopic salt.*

hy•ing |**hī′**ĭng|. A present participle of **hie.**

hy•men |**hī′**mən| *n.* A fold of membranous tissue that partially closes the external opening of the vagina.

hymn |hĭm| *n.* A song of joy, praise, or thanksgiving, especially one addressed to God. ¶*These sound alike* **hymn, him.**

hym•nal |**hĭm′**nəl| *n.* A book or collection of hymns.

hyper–. A prefix meaning: **1.** Over or in great amount: **hypercritical. 2.** Excessively: **hyperactive.**

hy•per•bo•la |hī **pûr′**bə lə| *n.* A plane curve, having two branches, composed of the set of all points such that the difference of their distances from the two fixed points is a constant.

hy•per•bo•le |hī **pûr′**bə lē| *n.* An exaggerated statement used as a figure of speech to make a strong effect; for example, *His recitation lasted a year* and *It rained last night; today our yard is a lake* make use of this figure of speech.

hy•per•bol•ic |hī′pər **bŏl′**ĭk| *adj.* **1.** Of or marked by hyperbole. **2.** Of or shaped like a hyperbola.

hy•per•crit•i•cal |hī′pər **krĭt′**ĭ kəl| *adj.* Given to finding fault too readily; overcritical; captious. —**hy′per•crit′i•cal•ly** *adv.*

hy•per•ten•sion |hī′pər **tĕn′**shən| *n.* A condition in which the pressure of the blood in the arteries is abnormally high.

hy•phen |**hī′**fən| *n.* A punctuation mark (-) used to connect the parts of a compound word or between syllables, especially of a word divided at the end of a line.

hy•phen•ate |**hī′**fə nāt′| *v.* **hy•phen•at•ed, hy•phen•at•ing.** To divide or connect with a hyphen. —**hy′phen•a′tion** *n.*

hyp•no•sis |hĭp **nō′**sĭs| *n., pl.* **hyp•no•ses** |hĭp**nō′**sēz′|. **1.** A sleeplike condition into which a person passes as a result of suggestions given by another person, becoming, once in that state, very responsive to further suggestions. **2.** Hypnotism.

hyp•not•ic |hĭp **nŏt′**ĭk| *adj.* **1.** Of, like, involving, or producing hypnosis. **2.** Of hypnotism. **3.** Causing or producing sleep. —*n.* A drug or other agent that produces sleep or a sleeplike state. —**hyp•not′i•cal•ly** *adv.*

hyp•no•tism |**hĭp′**nə tĭz′əm| *n.* The theory, method, or process of putting a person into a state of hypnosis.

hyp•no•tist |**hĭp′**nə tĭst| *n.* Someone who practices hypnotism.

hyp•no•tize |**hĭp′**nə tīz′| *v.* **hyp•no•tized, hyp•no•tiz•ing. 1.** To put (a person) into a state of hypnosis. **2.** To fascinate; captivate.

hy•po |**hī′**pō| *n. Informal.* A hypodermic needle, syringe, or injection.

hypo–. A prefix meaning "beneath, below": **hypodermic.**

hy•po•chon•dri•a |hī′pə **kŏn′**drē ə| *n.* A condition in which a person is convinced that he is ill or about to become ill and often feels real pain when there is, in fact, no illness present or likely.

hy•po•chon•dri•ac |hī′pə **kŏn′**drē ăk′| *n.* A person who is afflicted with hypochondria. —*adj.* Of or afflicted with hypochondria.

hy•poc•ri•sy |hĭ **pŏk′**rĭ sē| *n., pl.* **hy•poc•ri•sies.** A show or expression of feelings, beliefs, or qualities by a person who actually does not hold or possess them; insincerity.

hyp•o•crite |**hĭp′**ə krĭt′| *n.* A person who practices hypocrisy.

hyp•o•crit•i•cal |hĭp′ə **krĭt′**ĭ kəl| *adj.* Having the nature of a hypocrite or hypocrisy; insincere; false: *a hypocritical scoundrel; hypocritical speeches.* —**hyp′o•crit′i•cal•ly** *adv.*

hy•po•der•mic |hī′pə **dûr′**mĭk| *adj.* Injected beneath the skin, as a dose of medicine. —*n.* **1.** A hypodermic injection. **2. a.** A **hypodermic needle. b.** A **hypodermic syringe.**

hypodermic needle. A hollow, sharp-pointed needle that pierces the skin and through which a dose of medicine is injected from a hypodermic syringe.

hypodermic syringe. A syringe that is fitted with a hypodermic needle and holds a dose of medicine for a hypodermic injection.

hy•pot•e•nuse |hī **pŏt′**n o͞os′| *or* |-yo͞os′| *n.* The longest side of a triangle that contains an angle of 90 degrees. [SEE PICTURE]

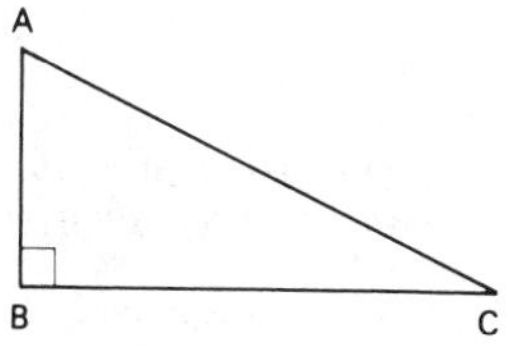

hypotenuse

hy•poth•e•sis |hī **pŏth′**ĭ sĭs| *n., pl.* **hy•poth•e•ses** |hī **pŏth′**ĭ sēz′|. **1.** An explanation or statement that accounts for all of a set of known facts but for which there is no direct supporting evidence: *the hypothesis that the solar system was formed from a cloud of dust.* **2.** Something that is assumed as a basis for action, discussion, etc.

hy•poth•e•size |hī **pŏth′**ĭ sīz′| *v.* **hy•poth•e•sized, hy•poth•e•siz•ing.** To put forth (a hypothesis).

hy•po•thet•i•cal |hī′pə **thĕt′**ĭ kəl| or **hy•po•thet•ic** |hī′pə **thĕt′**ĭk| *adj.* **1.** Of or based on a hypothesis. **2.** Of or depending on supposition; presumed: *Who was this hypothetical intruder?* —**hy′po•thet′i•cal•ly** *adv.*

hy•rax |**hī′**răks′| *n.* An animal of Africa and western Asia that resembles a woodchuck or rabbit but is more closely related to the hoofed animals. [SEE PICTURE]

hyrax

hys•sop |**hĭs′**əp| *n.* A pleasant-smelling plant with clusters of small blue flowers.

hys•te•ri•a |hĭ **stĕr′**ē ə| *or* |**-stîr′-**| *n.* **1.** A mental disorder in which physical symptoms as extreme as blindness or partial paralysis occur and in which the patient, although generally calm, may be subject to hallucinations, sleepwalking, or loss of memory. **2.** An extreme, uncontrollable fear or other strong emotion.

hys•ter•ic |hĭ **stĕr′**ĭk| *n.* Someone who suffers from hysteria. —*adj.* Hysterical.

hys•ter•i•cal |hĭ **stĕr′**ĭ kəl| *adj.* **1.** Of, resulting from, or characterized by hysteria. **2.** Having or subject to hysterics. **3.** Marked by uncontrolled emotion; violent or unrestrained: *laughing in hysterical relief.* —**hys•ter′i•cal•ly** *adv.*

hys•ter•ics |hĭ **stĕr′**ĭks| *n.* *(used with a singular verb).* **1.** A fit of uncontrolled laughing or crying or both. **2.** An attack of hysteria.

Hz hertz.

Ii

(1) (2) (3) (4)

The letter **I** *comes originally from the Phoenician letter* yōdh *(1), which meant "hand" and stood for the sound* y *as in* boy. *This was borrowed by the Greeks as* iota *(2, 3), which was used for the vowel* i. *The Romans borrowed it from the Greeks (4), and its shape has remained unchanged.*

ibis

ă **pat**/ā **pay**/â **care**/ä **father**/ĕ **pet**/ ē **be**/ĭ **pit**/ī **pie**/î **fierce**/ŏ **pot**/ ō **go**/ô **paw**, **for**/oi **oil**/o͝o **book**/ o͞o **boot**/ou **out**/ŭ **cut**/û **fur**/ *th* **the**/th **thin**/hw **which**/**zh** vision/ ə **ago**, item, pencil, atom, circus

i,I |ī| *n., pl.* **i's** or **I's. 1.** The ninth letter of the English alphabet. **2.** The Roman numeral for the number one. [SEE NOTE]

I |ī| *pron.* The person who is speaking or writing and who is referring to himself. *—Note: I,* which is in the nominative case, is used most often as the subject of a verb: *I expect to leave soon.* It can also be used as a predicate nominative following a form of the verb *be: It was I he had in mind when he made the complaint.* ¶ *These sound alike* **I, aye, eye.**

I The symbol for the element iodine.

i•amb |ī′ămb′| *n.* A unit of verse in which a stressed syllable follows an unstressed syllable. The following line from Shakespeare's *Julius Caesar* has five iambs: *O, párdon mé, thou bléeding piéce of eárth.* —**i•am′bic** *adj.*

-ian. A suffix that form nouns or adjectives: **Bostonian; pediatrician.**

I•be•ri•an Peninsula |ī bîr′ē ən|. A peninsula in southwestern Europe, comprising Spain and Portugal.

i•bex |ī′bĕks′| *n.* A wild goat of mountainous regions of Europe, Asia, and Africa, having long, curving horns.

ibid. In the same place. An abbreviation for the Latin word *ibidem.*

i•bis |ī′bĭs| *n.* A large wading bird with a long, downward-curving bill. [SEE PICTURE]

-ible. A form of the suffix **-able.**

-ic. A suffix that forms adjectives meaning "of or characteristic of": **allergic; atomic.**

ice |īs| *n.* **1.** Water frozen solid. **2.** A surface or mass of frozen water: *skated to the edge of the ice.* **3.** A dessert of sweetened and flavored crushed ice. —***modifier:*** *ice cubes.* —*v.* **iced, ic•ing. 1.** To chill with ice. **2.** To decorate (a cake, cookies, etc.) with icing. **3.** To freeze.

***Idiom.* break the ice.** To relax a tense or excessively formal atmosphere.

ice age. 1. Any of a series of cold periods, during which glaciers covered much of the earth. **2. Ice Age.** The Pleistocene or glacial epoch.

ice bag. A rubber bag filled with crushed ice and applied to sore or swollen parts of the body.

ice•berg |īs′bûrg′| *n.* **1.** A large, massive body of floating ice that has broken away from a glacier. **2.** *Informal.* A person whose manner is chilly, unfriendly, or aloof.

ice•bound |īs′bound′| *adj.* **1.** Locked in by ice: *an icebound ship.* **2.** Jammed or covered over by ice: *a harbor icebound during the winter.*

ice•box |īs′bŏks′| *n.* **1.** An insulated box into which ice is put to cool and preserve food. **2.** A refrigerator.

ice•break•er |īs′brā′kər| *n.* A sturdy ship built for breaking a passage through icebound waters.

ice cap. A mass of ice and snow that covers an area throughout the year.

ice cream. A smooth, sweet frozen food made of milk products, sugar, eggs, and flavoring. —***modifier:*** **(ice-cream):** *an ice-cream cone.*

Ice•land |īs′lənd|. An island nation in the North Atlantic Ocean east of Greenland. Population, 215,000. Capital, Reykjavik.

Ice•land•ic |īs lăn′dĭk| *n.* The Germanic language of Iceland. *—adj.* Of Iceland, its inhabitants, or their language.

ice pack. 1. A large mass of floating ice formed from small fragments that have pressed together and frozen solid. **2.** An **ice bag.**

ice pick. A hand tool with a sharply pointed spike, used for chipping or breaking ice.

ice skate. 1. A boot or shoe with a metal blade or runner mounted under it, worn for gliding over the ice. **2.** A metal blade or runner that is so used.

ice-skate |īs′skāt′| *v.* **ice-skat•ed, ice-skat•ing.** To skate on ice with ice skates.

ice skater. Someone who ice-skates.

ich•neu•mon |ĭk no͞o′mən| *or* |-nyo͞o′-| *n.* A mongoose of a kind common in Africa.

ichneumon fly. Also **ichneumon wasp.** A wasplike insect whose larvae feed on and destroy the larvae of other, often harmful insects.

ich•thy•ol•o•gist |ĭk′thē ŏl′ə jĭst| *n.* A scientist who specializes in ichthyology.

ich•thy•ol•o•gy |ĭk′thē ŏl′ə jē| *n.* The scientific study of fishes.

ich•thy•o•saur |ĭk′thē ə sôr′| *n.* An extinct fishlike sea reptile with long, narrow jaws and sharp teeth.

i•ci•cle |ī′sĭ kəl| *n.* A spike of ice hanging from a surface and formed by the freezing of dripping or falling water.

ic•ing |ī′sĭng| *n.* A sweet glaze of sugar, butter, and egg whites or milk, often flavored and cooked, used to decorate cakes or cookies.

i•con |ī′kŏn| *n.* A religious image painted on a panel.

i•con•o•clast |ī kŏn′ə klăst′| *n.* A person who attacks and seeks to overthrow popular or traditional ideas, beliefs, or practices. —**i•con′o•clas′tic** *adj.*

-ics. A suffix that forms nouns and means: **1.** The art or science of: **graphics. 2.** The activity or practice of: **hysterics.**

ic•y |ī′sē| *adj.* **ic•i•er, ic•i•est. 1.** Covered with ice; frozen: *an icy sidewalk.* **2.** Looking or feeling like ice; very cold: *icy feet.* **3.** Bitterly cold;

freezing: *the icy waters of the sea.* **4.** Very cold in manner; unfriendly: *an icy stare.* —**i'ci•ly** *adv.* —**i'ci•ness** *n.*

I'd |īd|. **1.** I had. **2.** I would. **3.** I should.

I•da•ho |ī'də hō'|. A Northwestern state of the United States. Population, 799,000. Capital, Boise.

i•de•a |ī dē'ə| *n.* **1. a.** Something formed carefully or fully; a thought; comprehension; understanding: *Do you have an idea of what is meant by a magnetic field?* **b.** Something formed sketchily; a notion; fancy: *He hadn't the vaguest idea of where to begin his search.* **2.** An opinion or belief; a view: *the idea that machinery alone can produce fine work.* **3.** A plan; a design: *a great idea for catching fish.*

i•de•al |ī dē'əl| *or* |ī dēl'| *n.* **1.** The condition of being perfect or an image of perfection in the mind. **2.** Someone or something regarded as a standard or model of perfection. —*adj.* **1.** Perfect or the best possible: *an ideal day for swimming.* **2.** Existing only as an idea that conforms perfectly to certain standards or laws: *under ideal conditions.* —**i•de'al•ly** *adv.*

i•de•al•ism |ī dē'ə lĭz'əm| *n.* **1.** The practice of seeing or representing things in ideal form rather than as they usually exist in real life. **2.** The practice of following or pursuing one's ideals. **3.** Any of several philosophical beliefs and systems that hold that reality consists of ideas or perceptions and that the material world we see around us is an illusion. —**i•de'al•ist** *n.*

i•de•al•is•tic |ī dē'ə lĭs'tĭk| *or* |ī'dē ə-| *adj.* Of or like idealism or an idealist: *an idealistic creed.* —**i•de'al•is'ti•cal•ly** *adv.*

i•de•al•ize |ī dē'ə līz'| *v.* **i•de•al•ized, i•de•al•iz•ing.** To regard as a model or standard of excellence: *an age that idealizes wealth as a mark of success.* —**i•de'al•i•za'tion** *n.*

i•den•ti•cal |ī dĕn'tĭ kəl| *adj.* **1.** Exactly equal and alike: *identical machine parts.* **2.** Being the very same: *the identical words the President used.* —**i•den'ti•cal•ly** *adv.*

identical twins. Human twins that develop from the same fertilized egg. They are always of the same sex and resemble each other very closely, having identical genetic traits.

i•den•ti•fi•ca•tion |ī dĕn'tə fĭ kā'shən| *n.* **1.** The act of identifying or the condition of being identified. **2.** Proof of someone's identity, as a card or letter bearing his name or position. —***modifier:*** *an identification tag.*

i•den•ti•fy |ī dĕn'tə fī'| *v.* **i•den•ti•fied, i•den•ti•fy•ing, i•den•ti•fies.** **1.** To establish the identity of: *Fingerprints are used to identify persons.* **2.** To consider as identical; equate: *identifying peace with the mere absence of war.* **3.** To associate or connect: *Grant was identified with Andrew Johnson's administration.* **4.** To feel closely associated or connected with a person, group, or place: *A Swiss always identifies with the canton where he was born.* —**i•den'ti•fi'a•ble** *adj.*

i•den•ti•ty |ī dĕn'tĭ tē| *n., pl.* **i•den•ti•ties.** **1.** The condition of being a certain person or thing and definitely recognizable as such. **2.** The condition of being exactly the same as something else: *The identity of the signatures was never in doubt.* **3. a.** A mathematical equation that remains true for all values of the variables that it contains. For example, $(x + y)^2 = x^2 + 2xy + y^2$ is true regardless of the values of x and y. **b.** An **identity element.**

identity element. The element of a set of numbers that when combined with another number in an operation leaves that number unchanged. For example, 0 is the identity element under addition for the real numbers, since, if a is any real number, $a + 0 = 0 + a = a$. Similarly, 1 is the identity element under multiplication for the real numbers, since $a \times 1 = 1 \times a = a$.

id•e•o•gram |ĭd'ē ə grăm'| *or* |ī'dē-| *n.* A character or symbol that represents an idea or thing but not a particular word or phrase for it. [SEE PICTURE]

id•e•o•graph |ĭd'ē ə grăf'| *or* |-gräf'| *or* |ī'dē-| *n.* An ideogram.

i•de•o•log•i•cal |ī'dē ə lŏj'ĭ kəl| *or* |ĭd'ē-| *adj.* Of or based on ideology: *ideological conflicts.* —**i'de•o•log'i•cal•ly** *adv.*

i•de•ol•o•gy |ī'dē ŏl'ə jē| *or* |ĭd'ē-| *n., pl.* **i•de•ol•o•gies.** A group of political and social ideas that help to determine the thinking and behavior of a class, party, nation, etc.

ides |īdz| *n.* *(used with a singular verb).* In the ancient Roman calendar, the 15th day of March, May, July, or October or the 13th day of the other months.

id•i•o•cy |ĭd'ē ə sē| *n., pl.* **id•i•o•cies.** **1.** A condition of extreme mental retardation. **2.** Foolish behavior.

id•i•om |ĭd'ē əm| *n.* **1.** An expression having a special meaning not obtainable or not clear from the usual meaning of the words in the expression; for example, *fly off the handle* (lose one's temper) and *on pins and needles* (in a condition of anxiety) are idioms. **2.** The accepted pattern of word usage within a language. For example, we say *acquiesce in a plan* rather than *acquiesce to a plan.* **3.** The language or other means of expression of a particular region, profession, etc.: *the colorful idiom of the Ozark Mountains.*

id•i•o•mat•ic |ĭd'ē ə măt'ĭk| *adj.* **1.** Being an idiom. **2.** In agreement with an accepted pattern of word usage. **3.** Using many idioms. —**id'i•o•mat'i•cal•ly** *adv.*

id•i•o•syn•cra•sy |ĭd'ē ō sĭng'krə sē| *or* |-sĭn'-| *n., pl.* **id•i•o•syn•cra•sies.** A peculiar trait or form of behavior.

id•i•o•syn•crat•ic |ĭd'ē ō sĭn krăt'ĭk| *adj.* Peculiar; eccentric: *idiosyncratic tastes in books.* —**id'i•o•syn•crat'i•cal•ly** *adv.*

id•i•ot |ĭd'ē ət| *n.* **1.** A mentally deficient person whose intelligence lies in the lowest range that can be measured. **2.** A very foolish or stupid person. [SEE NOTE]

id•i•ot•ic |ĭd'ē ŏt'ĭk| *adj.* **1.** Showing or suffering from idiocy. **2.** Of or like an idiot. —**id'i•ot'i•cal•ly** *adv.*

i•dle |īd'l| *adj.* **i•dler, i•dlest.** **1.** Not working or devoted to working or producing: *idle employees.* **2.** Avoiding work; lazy; shiftless: *idle boys who would do nothing but play.* **3.** Having no foundation in fact; worthless: *idle talk; no idle threat.* —*v.* **i•dled, i•dling.** **1.** To run at a low speed or out of gear: *The engine idled smoothly.* **2.** To cause to be unemployed or inactive: *a strike that idled the merchant fleet.* **3.** To pass (time) without working or in avoiding work. ¶*These sovnd*

ideogram

The first sign (1) below is the ancient ideogram for "tree," and next to it is its modern form. The character above (2) means "forest." The first sign above (3) is the ancient ideogram for "sun," with its modern form next to it. The character above (4) means "the sun seen in the trees," hence "the east."

(1)

(2)

(3)

(4)

idiot

Greek idiōtēs *(from* idios, *"private") meant "a private person, an ordinary person, someone with no special skill." This word was borrowed into Latin as* idiōta *and came to mean "an ignorant person." When the word was borrowed into English as* **idiot,** *the meaning degenerated even further.*

i.e.

I.e. *is short for the Latin phrase* id est, *"that is."*

igloo

Above: Sod igloo (summer)
Below: Snow igloo

iguana

ă pat/ā pay/â care/ä father/ĕ pet/ ē be/ĭ pit/ī pie/î fierce/ŏ pot/ ō go/ô paw, for/oi oil/o͝o book/ o͞o boot/ou out/ŭ cut/û fur/ *th* the/th thin/hw which/zh vision/ ə ago, item, pencil, atom, circus

alike **idle, idol, idyll.** —**i'dle•ness** *n.* —**i'dly** *adv.*

i•dler |īd'lər| *n.* A person who idles; a loafer.

i•dol |īd'l| *n.* **1.** An image that is worshiped as a god. **2.** A person or thing adored or greatly admired. ¶*These sound alike* **idol, idle, idyll.**

i•dol•a•ter |ī dŏl'ə tər| *n.* **1.** A person who worships an idol or idols. **2.** A person who admires or adores another beyond the limits of reason.

i•dol•a•try |ī dŏl'ə trē| *n., pl.* **i•dol•a•tries. 1.** The worship of idols. **2.** Blind admiration of or devotion to someone or something.

i•dol•ize |īd'l īz'| *v.* **i•dol•ized, i•dol•iz•ing. 1.** To regard with blind admiration or devotion: *idolized her son.* **2.** To worship or treat as an idol.

i•dyll, also **i•dyl** |īd'l| *n.* **1.** A short poem or prose piece about a pleasant scene of country life. **2.** A scene, experience, or relationship marked by supreme peacefulness and contentment. ¶*These sound alike* **idyll, idle, idol.**

i•dyl•lic |ī dĭl'ĭk| *adj.* Of or like an idyll; full of quiet beauty and peacefulness: *idyllic surroundings.* —**i•dyl'li•cal•ly** *adv.*

i.e. that is. An abbreviation for the Latin phrase *id est.* [SEE NOTE]

–ie. A suffix that forms nouns and means: **1.** Small; diminutive: **dearie. 2.** A person belonging to: **townie.**

if |ĭf| *conj.* **1.** In the event that: *If I were to go, I would be late.* **2.** Granting that; supposing: *Even if his story is true, what can we do about it?* **3.** On condition that: *I'll come only if you do.* **4.** Even though; although possibly: *a useless if handsome trinket.* **5.** Whether: *I asked if he was coming.* **6.** —Used to introduce an exclamatory clause indicating: **a.** Sharp regret or a strong wish: *If she had only come sooner!* **b.** Surprise, anger, or a similar feeling: *If you ever do that again!* —*n.* A possibility, condition, or stipulation: *I'm not listening to any ifs, ands, or buts.*

ig•loo |ĭg'lo͞o| *n.* An Eskimo house, sometimes built of blocks of ice. [SEE PICTURE]

ig•ne•ous |ĭg'nē əs| *adj.* **1.** Of or relating to fire. **2.** Formed, as certain rocks, by solidifying from a molten or partially molten state.

ig•nite |ĭg nīt'| *v.* **ig•nit•ed, ig•nit•ing.** To set fire to or catch fire.

ig•ni•tion |ĭg nĭsh'ən| *n.* **1.** The act or process of igniting. **2. a.** An electrical system that provides the spark that ignites the fuel mixture of an internal-combustion engine. **b.** A switch that activates this system.

ig•no•ble |ĭg nō'bəl| *adj.* **1.** Not having a noble character or purpose; dishonorable. **2.** Not of the nobility; common. —**ig•no'bly** *adv.*

ig•no•min•i•ous |ĭg'nə mĭn'ē əs| *adj.* **1.** Marked by shame or disgrace: *an ignominious failure.* **2.** Injuring dignity or pride; humiliating: *a slip, a fall, and an ignominious drenching in the pool.* —**ig'no•min'i•ous•ly** *adv.*

ig•no•min•y |ĭg'nə mĭn'ē| *n., pl.* **ig•no•min•ies. 1.** Disgrace; dishonor. **2.** Behavior or an act that brings dishonor.

ig•no•ra•mus |ĭg'nə rā'məs| *or* |-răm'əs| *n., pl.* **ig•no•ra•mus•es.** An ignorant person.

ig•no•rance |ĭg'nər əns| *n.* The condition of being ignorant; lack of knowledge.

ig•no•rant |ĭg'nər ənt| *adj.* **1.** Without education or knowledge. **2.** Showing lack of education or knowledge: *a note written in an ignorant hand.* **3.** Unaware or uninformed: *She was ignorant of what the postman had delivered that morning.* —**ig'no•rant•ly** *adv.*

ig•nore |ĭg nôr'| *or* |-nōr'| *v.* **ig•nored, ig•nor•ing.** To pay no attention to; disregard.

i•gua•na |ĭ gwä'nə| *n.* An often large tropical American lizard with a ridge of spines along the back. [SEE PICTURE]

il•e•um |ĭl'ē əm| *n., pl.* **il•e•a** |ĭl'ē ə|. The lowest section of the small intestine, extending from the jejunum to the beginning of the large intestine. ¶*These sound alike* **ileum, ilium.**

il•i•a |ĭl'ē ə| *n.* Plural of **ilium.**

Il•i•ad |ĭl'ē əd| *n.* An ancient Greek epic poem attributed to Homer, recounting the siege of Troy.

il•i•um |ĭl'ē əm| *n., pl.* **il•i•a** |ĭl'ē ə|. The uppermost of the three bones that make up each of the hipbones. ¶*These sound alike* **ilium, ileum.**

ilk |ĭlk| *n.* Type or kind: *He wanted no dealings with men of that ilk.*

ill |ĭl| *adj.* **worse** |wûrs|, **worst** |wûrst|. **1.** Not healthy; sick: *grew ill as the ship tossed.* **2.** Not normal; unsound: *ill health.* **3.** Not favorable or promising: *caused by ill luck.* **4.** Showing enmity, hostility, or bad feeling: *ill will.* **5.** Bringing harm or suffering: *escaped without ill effects.* —*adv.* **worse, worst. 1.** Not well; badly, wrongly, or cruelly: *ill repaid for your work.* **2.** Not favorably; unkindly: *took his words so ill.* **3.** Scarcely or with difficulty: *can ill afford the delay.* —*n.* **1.** Evil; wrongdoing; sin: *whether men do good or ill in this world.* **2.** Harm; disaster: *never suspecting the ill that lay in store for them.* **3.** Often **ills.** Something that causes suffering; an affliction; ailment: *seeking a cure for urban ills.*
Idiom. **ill at ease.** Nervous and uncomfortable.

I'll |īl|. **1.** I will. **2.** I shall. ¶*These sound alike* **I'll, aisle, isle.**

Ill. Illinois.

ill-bred |ĭl'brĕd'| *adj.* Badly brought up; bad-mannered; impolite.

il•le•gal |ĭ lē'gəl| *adj.* Prohibited by law or by official rules, as of a game. —**il'le•gal'i•ty** |ĭl'ē găl'ĭ tē| *n.* —**il•le'gal•ly** *adv.*

il•leg•i•ble |ĭ lĕj'ə bəl| *adj.* Not capable of being deciphered; not readable: *an illegible scrawl.* —**il•leg'i•bil'i•ty** *n.* —**il•leg'i•bly** *adv.*

il•le•git•i•mate |ĭl'ə jĭt'ə mĭt| *adj.* **1.** Against or not supported by the law; illegal: *an illegitimate deed; an illegitimate claim to property.* **2.** Born of parents not married to each other. —**il'le•git'i•ma•cy** *n.* —**il'le•git'i•mate•ly** *adv.*

ill-fat•ed |ĭl'fā'tĭd| *adj.* **1.** Destined for misfortune; doomed: *The ill-fated ship never reached her destination.* **2.** Marked by or causing misfortune; unlucky: *an ill-fated decision.*

ill-fa•vored |ĭl'fā'vərd| *adj.* Having an ugly or unattractive appearance.

ill-got•ten |ĭl'gŏt'n| *adj.* Obtained in an evil manner or by dishonest means: *ill-gotten wealth.*

ill-hu•mored |ĭl'hyo͞o'mərd| *adj.* Irritable; disagreeable; surly. —**ill'-hu'mored•ly** *adv.*

il•lib•er•al |ĭ lĭb'ər əl| *adj.* **1.** Narrow-minded; bigoted. **2.** *Archaic.* Ungenerous; stingy. —**il•lib'er•al•ly** *adv.*

il•lic•it |ĭ lĭs'ĭt| *adj.* Not permitted by law or custom; illegal; unlawful. ¶*These sound alike* **illicit, elicit.** —**il•lic'it•ly** *adv.* —**il•lic'it•ness** *n.*

il•lim•it•a•ble |ĭ lĭm′ĭ tə bəl| *adj.* Not capable of being limited; having no limit or boundaries: *the illimitable void of heaven.* —**il•lim′it•a•bly** *adv.*

Il•li•nois[1] |ĭl′ə **noi′**| *or* |**-noiz′**|. A Midwestern state of the United States. Population, 11,114,-000. Capital, Springfield.

Il•li•nois[2] |ĭl′ə **noi′**| *or* |**-noiz′**| *n., pl.* **Il•li•nois. 1.** A confederation of Algonquian-speaking North American Indian tribes of Illinois, Iowa, Wisconsin, and Missouri. **2.** A member of any of these tribes.

il•lit•er•a•cy |ĭ lĭt′ər ə sē| *n., pl.* **il•lit•er•a•cies.** The quality or condition of being unable to read and write.

il•lit•er•ate |ĭ lĭt′ər ĭt| *adj.* **1.** Unable to read and write. **2.** Showing a lack of education. —*n.* A person who is unable to read and write. —**il•lit′er•ate•ly** *adv.*

ill-man•nered |**ĭl′măn′**ərd| *adj.* Showing a lack of good manners; impolite; rude. —**ill′-man′nered•ly** *adv.*

ill-na•tured |**ĭl′nā′**chərd| *adj.* Disagreeable; surly. —**ill′-na′tured•ly** *adv.*

ill•ness |**ĭl′**nĭs| *n.* **1.** Sickness of body or mind. **2.** A particular sickness or disease; an ailment.

il•log•i•cal |ĭ **lŏj′**ĭ kəl| *adj.* Having or showing a lack of logic. —**il•log′i•cal•ly** *adv.*

ill-starred |**ĭl′stärd′**| *adj.* Unlucky; ill-fated.

ill-tem•pered |**ĭl′tĕm′**pərd| *adj.* Having or showing a bad temper. —**ill′-tem′pered•ly** *adv.*

ill-treat |**ĭl′trēt′**| *v.* To treat harmfully or cruelly.

il•lu•mi•nate |ĭ **lo͞o′**mə nāt′| *v.* **il•lu•mi•nat•ed, il•lu•mi•nat•ing. 1.** To provide with light; turn or focus light on: *a landscape illuminated by a full moon.* **2.** To make understandable; clarify; explain: *clues that illuminate the snarled story.* **3.** To decorate (a manuscript) with ornamental designs. —**il•lu′mi•na′tion** *n.* [SEE PICTURE]

il•lu•mine |ĭ **lo͞o′**mĭn| *v.* **il•lu•mined, il•lu•min•ing.** To give light to; light up; illuminate.

ill-us•age |**ĭl′**yo͞o′sĭj| *n.* Bad or unjust treatment.

ill-use |**ĭl′**yo͞oz′| *v.* **ill-used, ill-us•ing.** To treat badly; abuse.

il•lu•sion |ĭ **lo͞o′**zhən| *n.* **1.** An appearance or impression that has no real basis; false perception: *creating the illusion of depth in a painting.* **2.** A mistaken notion or belief. ¶*These sound alike* **illusion, elusion.**

il•lu•sive |ĭ **lo͞o′**sĭv| *adj.* Of or like an illusion; lacking reality. ¶*These sound alike* **illusive, elusive.** —**il•lu′sive•ly** *adv.* —**il•lu′sive•ness** *n.*

il•lu•so•ry |ĭ **lo͞o′**sə rē| *or* |-zə-| *adj.* Deceptive; not real; illusive.

il•lus•trate |**ĭl′**ə strāt′| *or* |ĭ **lŭs′**trāt′| *v.* **il•lus•trat•ed, il•lus•trat•ing. 1.** To clarify or explain by using examples, pictures, comparisons, etc.: *He illustrated his lecture by drawing charts on the blackboard.* **2.** To serve as an example, picture, or comparison of: *The diagram illustrates the arrangement of the solar system.* **3.** To provide (a book, magazine, etc.) with pictures, diagrams, examples, etc.

il•lus•tra•tion |ĭl′ə **strā′**shən| *n.* **1.** Something, such as a picture, diagram, chart, etc., serving to clarify, explain, or decorate. **2.** Something serving as an example, comparison, or proof: *A rock falling to the ground is an illustration of gravity.* **3.** The act of illustrating: *his step-by-step illustration of how to pitch a tent.*

il•lus•tra•tive |ĭ **lŭs′**trə tĭv| *or* |**ĭl′**ə strā′tĭv| *adj.* Serving as an illustration.

il•lus•tra•tor |**ĭl′**ə strā′tər| *n.* Someone who illustrates books, magazines, pamphlets, etc.

il•lus•tri•ous |ĭ **lŭs′**trē əs| *adj.* Famous; celebrated: *the illustrious commander.*

ill will. Unfriendly feeling; hostility; enmity.

I'm |īm|. I am.

im•age |**ĭm′**ĭj| *n.* **1.** A pattern of light and dark areas, often produced with color as well, that duplicates the appearance of some real object or objects, especially such a pattern formed by one or more lenses, mirrors, or other optical devices. **2.** A mental picture of something not present or real: *Images of snakes, lizards, and frogs came to his mind.* **3.** A reproduction of a person or thing, as a statue or a figure in a painting. **4. a.** A form distinctly like another; a close likeness: *"And God said, 'Let us make man in our image'"* (The Bible, Genesis 1:26). **b.** A person who resembles another: *the very image of his grandfather.* **5.** A general impression of a person or thing, as a concept that is held by the general public.

im•age•ry |**ĭm′**ĭj rē| *n.* The use of figures of speech or vivid descriptions in writing or speaking to produce mental images.

i•mag•i•na•ble |ĭ **măj′**ə nə bəl| *adj.* Capable of being imagined: *information on every imaginable topic.* —**i•mag′i•na•bly** *adv.*

i•mag•i•nar•y |ĭ **măj′**ə nĕr′ē| *adj.* Having existence only in the imagination; unreal; fictitious: *an imaginary illness.*

imaginary number. A number whose square is negative. The number whose square is -1 is usually written *i.* [SEE NOTE]

i•mag•i•na•tion |ĭ măj′ə **nā′**shən| *n.* **1. a.** The ability of the mind to conceive ideas or to form images of something not present; the power of mental conception. **b.** Such ability used creatively; inventiveness; creativity: *the lively imagination of the writer.* **2.** The ability to act effectively by using the creative power of the mind; resourcefulness: *The imagination of the men kept them alive in the Arctic wastes.*

i•mag•i•na•tive |ĭ **măj′**ə nə tĭv| *or* |-nā′-| *adj.* **1.** Having a strong imagination, especially creative imagination: *an imaginative person.* **2.** Created by or marked by originality and creativity: *imaginative writing.* —**i•mag′i•na•tive•ly** *adv.*

i•mag•ine |ĭ **măj′**ĭn| *v.* **i•mag•ined, i•mag•in•ing. 1.** To form a mental picture, idea, or impression of: *Can you imagine a blue horse with a yellow mane?* **2.** To make a guess; think; conjecture.

i•ma•go |ĭ **mā′**gō| *n., pl.* **i•ma•goes** or **i•ma•gi•nes** |ĭ **măj′**ə nēz′|. An insect in its fully developed adult stage.

i•mam |ĭ **mäm′**| *n.* **1.** A Moslem prayer leader. **2. Imam.** A religious or temporal leader claiming descent from Mohammed.

im•bal•ance |ĭm **băl′**əns| *n.* A lack of balance.

im•be•cile |**ĭm′**bĭ sĭl| *or* |-səl| *n.* **1.** A feeble-minded person, especially one less retarded than an idiot but more retarded than a moron. **2.** A stupid person. —*adj.* **1.** Lacking in mental ability. **2.** Stupid or foolish. —**im′be•cil′i•ty** *n.*

im•be•cil•ic |ĭm′bĭ **sĭl′**ĭk| *adj.* A form of the word **imbecile.**

im•bed |ĭm **bĕd′**| *v.* **im•bed•ded, im•bed•ding.** A form of the word **embed.**

illumination

imaginary number

The symbol i *and the fact that* $(a \times b)^2 = a^2 \times b^2$ *allows us to write the square root of any negative number. For instance,* $\sqrt{-4} = \sqrt{4 \times -1} = \sqrt{4} \times \sqrt{-1} = 2 \times i$.

imitative
All languages have **imitative** *words, words formed to imitate the sounds of the things that they represent. (Another term for* **imitative** *is* **onomatopoeic.**) *Examples: English* **bobwhite, Ping-Pong, whiz**; *French* ronron, *"purr of a cat,"* cricri, *"chirp of a cricket"; Latin* stloppus, *"slap on the cheek,"* susurrus, *"whisper"; Spanish* susurro, *"whisper"; Portuguese* piupiu, *"peep or cheep of a chick"; Japanese* gorogoro, *"purr of a cat."*

immanent/imminent
These two words, differing by only one letter, are both from Latin present participles. **Immanent** *is from Latin* immanēns, *"being or residing within (something)," from* immanēre, *"to be within":* in-, *"in,"* + manēre, *"to stay, reside."* **Imminent** *is from Latin* imminēns, *"impending, threatening to happen," from* imminēre, *"to impend, to threaten, to be near, to project toward":* in-, *"into, toward,"* + minēre, *"to stick out, project, overhang, threaten."*

immigrant
"All of our people all over the country—except the pure-blooded Indians—are immigrants or descendants of immigrants, including even those who came over here on the Mayflower." —Franklin Delano Roosevelt (1944).

ă pat/ā pay/â care/ä father/ĕ pet/ ē be/ĭ pit/ī pie/î fierce/ŏ pot/ ō go/ô paw, for/oi oil/o͝o book/ o͞o boot/ou out/ŭ cut/û fur/ *th* the/th thin/hw which/zh vision/ ə ago, item, pencil, atom, circus

im•bibe |ĭm **bīb'**| *v.* **im•bibed, im•bib•ing. 1.** To drink. **2.** To receive or absorb into the mind: *imbibe new ideas.* **—im•bib'er** *n.*

im•bro•glio |ĭm **brōl'**yō| *n., pl.* **im•bro•glios.** A confused or difficult situation; a predicament.

im•bue |ĭm **byo͞o'**| *v.* **im•bued, im•bu•ing. 1.** To inspire, permeate, or fill: *They were imbued with an interest in language.* **2.** To wet or soak thoroughly, as with a stain or dye.

im•i•ta•ble |**ĭm'**ĭ tə bəl| *adj.* Capable or worthy of being imitated.

im•i•tate |**ĭm'**ĭ tāt'| *v.* **im•i•tat•ed, im•i•tat•ing. 1.** To copy the actions, appearance, function, or sounds of: *Little children imitate their parents. He imitated bird calls.* **2.** To mimic playfully or mockingly: *She imitated the old woman's high-pitched laugh.* **3.** To look like; resemble: *Nylon can imitate many other materials.*

im•i•ta•tion |ĭm'ĭ **tā'**shən| *n.* **1.** The act or process of imitating or copying: *learning a song through imitation.* **2.** Something copied from or patterned after another: *The vase is an imitation of one in the museum.* **3.** An act of mimicking: *The comedian does imitations of television personalities.* **—modifier:** *imitation leather.*

im•i•ta•tive |**ĭm'**ĭ tā'tĭv| *adj.* **1.** Marked by imitation: *an imitative style.* **2.** Tending to imitate. **—im'i•ta'tive•ly** *adv.* [SEE NOTE]

im•i•ta•tor |**ĭm'**ĭ tā'tər| *n.* Someone or something that imitates.

im•mac•u•late |ĭ **măk'**yə lĭt| *adj.* **1.** Perfectly clean: *an immaculate coat.* **2.** Free from fault or error. **—im•mac'u•late•ly** *adv.*

Immaculate Conception. The Roman Catholic doctrine that the Virgin Mary was conceived in her mother's womb free from sin.

im•ma•nent |**ĭm'**ə nənt| *adj.* Existing within; inherent: *believed in a God immanent in human beings.* ¶*These sound alike* **immanent, imminent.** [SEE NOTE]

im•ma•te•ri•al |ĭm'ə **tîr'**ē əl| *adj.* **1.** Having no material body or form: *an immaterial phantom.* **2.** Of no importance or relevance; unimportant: *Now it is immaterial what she decides to do.* **—im'ma•te'ri•al•ly** *adv.*

im•ma•ture |ĭm'ə **to͝or'**| *or* |**-tyo͝or'**| *or* |**-cho͝or'**| *adj.* **1.** Not fully grown or developed; in an early or unripe stage: *immature corn.* **2.** Not behaving with normal maturity: *an immature girl.* **—im'ma•ture'ly** *adv.* **—im'ma•tur'i•ty** *n.*

im•meas•ur•a•ble |ĭ **mĕzh'**ər ə bəl| *adj.* Not capable of being measured: *his immeasurable surprise.* **—im•meas'ur•a•bly** *adv.*

im•me•di•ate |ĭ **mē'**dē ĭt| *adj.* **1.** Taking place at once or very soon; occurring without delay: *needing immediate medical care.* **2.** Close at hand; nearby: *our immediate surroundings.* **3.** Coming next or very soon: *the immediate future; an immediate danger.* **4.** Next in line or relation: *an immediate successor.* **—im•me'di•ate•ly** *adv.* **—im•me'di•ate•ness** *n.*

im•me•mo•ri•al |ĭm'ə **môr'**ē əl| *or* |**-mōr'-**| *adj.* Reaching beyond the limits of memory, tradition, or recorded history: *since time immemorial.* **—im'me•mo'ri•al•ly** *adv.*

im•mense |ĭ **mĕns'**| *adj.* Of great, often immeasurable, size, extent, degree, etc.: *immense rocks; an immense span of time.* **—im•mense'ly** *adv.* **—im•men'si•ty** *n.*

im•merse |ĭ **mûrs'**| *v.* **im•mersed, im•mers•ing. 1.** To cover completely in a liquid; submerge: *He immersed the pan in the stream.* **2.** To baptize by totally submerging in water. **3.** To involve deeply; absorb.

im•mer•sion |ĭ **mûr'**zhən| *or* |-shən| *n.* **1.** An act of immersing or the condition of being immersed. **2.** Baptism performed by immersing.

im•mi•grant |**ĭm'**ĭ grənt| *n.* A person who leaves his native country or region to settle in another. **—modifier:** *immigrant settlements; an immigrant family.* [SEE NOTE]

im•mi•grate |**ĭm'**ĭ grāt'| *v.* **im•mi•grat•ed, im•mi•grat•ing.** To move to and settle in a country or region to which one is not native. **—im'mi•gra'tion** *n.*

im•mi•nent |**ĭm'**ə nənt| *adj.* About to occur; impending: *an imminent crisis.* ¶*These sound alike* **imminent, immanent. —im'mi•nence** *n.* **—im'mi•nent•ly** *adv.* [SEE NOTE]

im•mo•bile |ĭ **mō'**bəl| *or* |-bēl'| *adj.* **1.** Not movable; fixed. **2.** Not moving; motionless. **—im'mo•bil'i•ty** *n.*

im•mo•bi•lize |ĭ **mō'**bə līz'| *v.* **im•mo•bi•lized, im•mo•bi•liz•ing.** To make immobile; render incapable of moving. **—im•mo'bi•li•za'tion** *n.*

im•mod•er•ate |ĭ **mŏd'**ər ĭt| *adj.* Not moderate: *an immoderate price.* **—im•mod'er•ate•ly** *adv.*

im•mod•est |ĭ **mŏd'**ĭst| *adj.* **1.** Conceited or arrogant: *his immodest description of his talents.* **2.** Not considered proper; indecent or offensive. **—im•mod'est•ly** *adv.* **—im•mod'es•ty** *n.*

im•mor•al |ĭ **môr'**əl| *or* |ĭ **mŏr'-**| *adj.* **1.** Not moral; contrary to what is considered just, right, or good: *the immoral system of slavery.* **2.** Not following accepted rules of conduct, especially sexual conduct. **—im•mor'al•ly** *adv.*

im•mo•ral•i•ty |ĭm'ə **răl'**ĭ tē| *or* |ĭm'ô-| *n., pl.* **im•mo•ral•i•ties. 1.** The quality or condition of being immoral. **2.** Behavior that is immoral: *guilty of immorality.*

im•mor•tal |ĭ **môr'**tl| *adj.* **1.** Not subject to death; living forever: *the immortal soul.* **2.** Having eternal fame: *an immortal poet.* **—n. 1.** Someone or something not subject to death. **2.** Someone with enduring fame: *an immortal in the field of baseball.* **—im•mor'tal•ly** *adv.*

im•mor•tal•i•ty |ĭm'ôr **tăl'**ĭ tē| *n.* **1.** The condition of being immortal. **2.** Enduring fame.

im•mor•tal•ize |ĭ **môr'**tl īz'| *v.* **im•mor•tal•ized, im•mor•tal•iz•ing.** To make immortal: *The poem immortalized the hero.*

im•mov•a•ble |ĭ **mo͞o'**və bəl| *adj.* **1.** Not capable of moving or of being moved. **2.** Unyielding; steadfast: *an immovable purpose.* **—n. immovables.** Property, such as real estate, that cannot be moved. **—im•mov'a•bly** *adv.*

im•mune |ĭ **myo͞on'**| *adj.* **1.** Not susceptible; resistant: *immune to a disease; immune to change.* **2.** Protected; guarded; safe: *immune from attack.*

im•mu•ni•ty |ĭ **myo͞o'**nĭ tē| *n., pl.* **im•mu•ni•ties. 1.** The ability of an animal or plant to resist a disease wholly or in part, especially a disease that is caused by microbes. **2.** Freedom from certain duties, penalties, etc.: *the rights and immunities enjoyed by citizens.*

im•mu•nize |**ĭm'**yə nīz'| *v.* **im•mu•nized, im•mu•niz•ing.** To produce immunity in, as by vaccination or inoculation. **—im'mu•ni•za'tion** *n.*

im•mu•nol•o•gist |ĭm'yə nŏl'ə jĭst| *n.* A physician who specializes in immunology.
im•mu•nol•o•gy |ĭm'yə nŏl'ə jē| *n.* The scientific and medical study and use of immunity.
im•mure |ĭ myo͝or'| *v.* **im•mured, im•mur•ing.** To confine within walls; imprison.
im•mu•ta•ble |ĭ myo͞o'tə bəl| *adj.* Not subject to change; unchangeable. **—im•mu'ta•bil'i•ty, im•mu'ta•ble•ness** *n.* **—im•mu'ta•bly** *adv.*
imp |ĭmp| *n.* **1.** A mischievous child. **2.** A small demon.
imp. **1.** imperative. **2.** imperfect. **3.** imperial. **4.** imported; importer.
im•pact |ĭm'păkt'| *n.* **1.** The action of one body striking against another; collision: *Neither car had been traveling fast at the time of impact.* **2.** The effect of something on the feelings or mind of the reader, spectator, etc.: *the emotional impact of a poem.*
im•pact•ed |ĭm păk'tĭd| *adj.* Located inside the gum in such a way that it will not come through the gum in a normal position: *an impacted tooth.*
im•pair |ĭm pâr'| *v.* To diminish in strength, quantity, or quality; weaken: *Fatigue had impaired his judgment.* **—im•pair'ment** *n.*
im•pa•la |ĭm pä'lə| *or* |-păl'ə| *n.* An African antelope that has curved, spreading horns and is able to make long, high leaps. [SEE PICTURE]
im•pale |ĭm pāl'| *v.* **im•paled, im•pal•ing.** **1.** To pierce with a sharp stake or point: *someone falling and impaling his hand on a nail.* **2.** To torture or kill by impaling. **—im•pale'ment** *n.*
im•pal•pa•ble |ĭm păl'pə bəl| *adj.* **1.** Not perceptible to the touch: *impalpable shadows.* **2.** Not easily grasped by the mind: *the impalpable complexity of relationships.* **—im•pal'pa•bil'i•ty** *n.* **—im•pal'pa•bly** *adv.*
im•pan•el |ĭm păn'əl| *v.* **im•pan•eled** or **im•pan•elled, im•pan•el•ing** or **im•pan•el•ling.** To enroll (a jury) upon a panel or list. **—im•pan'el•ment** *n.*
im•part |ĭm pärt'| *v.* **1.** To transmit; bestow: *imparted a backspin to the ball.* **2.** To make known; disclose; reveal: *She imparted her true feelings only to close friends.*
im•par•tial |ĭm pär'shəl| *adj.* Not favoring either side; unprejudiced: *an impartial witness.* **—im'par•ti•al'i•ty** |ĭm'pär shē ăl'ĭ tē| *n.* **—im•par'tial•ly** *adv.*
im•pass•a•ble |ĭm păs'ə bəl| *adj.* Impossible to travel across or over: *a deep, impassable gorge.* **—im•pass'a•bil'i•ty** *n.* **—im•pass'a•bly** *adv.*
im•passe |ĭm'păs'| *n.* A difficult situation from which there is no workable escape.
im•pas•sioned |ĭm păsh'ənd| *adj.* Filled with or expressive of intense feeling; ardent.
im•pas•sive |ĭm păs'ĭv| *adj.* Feeling or showing no emotion; calm: *an impassive face.* **—im•pas'sive•ly** *adv.* **—im•pas'sive•ness** *n.*
im•pa•tience |ĭm pā'shəns| *n.* **1.** The inability to wait patiently, endure irritation calmly, or show tolerant understanding: *his impatience with the whining puppy.* **2.** Restless eagerness: *their impatience to get to the river.*
im•pa•tient |ĭm pā'shənt| *adj.* **1.** Not patient. **2.** Suggesting impatience: *an impatient gesture.* **3.** Restlessly eager. **—im•pa'tient•ly** *adv.*
im•peach |ĭm pēch'| *v.* **1.** To charge (a public official) with misconduct in office before a proper court of justice. **2.** To challenge or discredit; attack: *impeach the truth of a report.* **—im•peach'ment** *n.*
im•pec•ca•ble |ĭm pĕk'ə bəl| *adj.* Without flaw; faultless: *impeccable table manners.* **—im•pec'ca•bly** *adv.* [SEE NOTE]
im•pe•cu•ni•ous |ĭm'pĭ kyo͞o'nē əs| *adj.* Without money; penniless. **—im'pe•cu'ni•ous•ly** *adv.*
im•ped•ance |ĭm pēd'ns| *n.* A measure of the total opposition to the flow of an electric current, especially in an alternating current.
im•pede |ĭm pēd'| *v.* **im•ped•ed, im•ped•ing.** To obstruct or slow down; block.
im•ped•i•ment |ĭm pĕd'ə mənt| *n.* **1.** A defect or malfunction: *a speech impediment.* **2.** A hindrance; obstruction: *His youth was no impediment to his success.*
im•pel |ĭm pĕl'| *v.* **im•pelled, im•pel•ling.** **1.** To urge to action; spur: *the curiosity that impels rock collectors to learn more about minerals.* **2.** To drive forward; propel.
im•pend |ĭm pĕnd'| *v.* To be about to take place; loom: *when the Civil War was impending.* **—im•pend'ing** *adj.*: *impending peril.*
im•pen•e•tra•ble |ĭm pĕn'ĭ trə bəl| *adj.* **1.** Not capable of being entered or penetrated: *an impenetrable swamp; an impenetrable thicket.* **2.** Not capable of being understood or discerned; incomprehensible; unfathomable: *her impenetrable secret.* **—im•pen'e•tra•bil'i•ty** *n.*
im•per•a•tive |ĭm pĕr'ə tĭv| *adj.* **1.** In grammar, of or being the mood of a verb that expresses a command, order, or request: *an imperative sentence; an imperative verb.* **2.** Expressive of a command or order; imperious: *an imperative manner.* **3.** Urgently essential; obligatory; mandatory: *For him, exercise was imperative.* *—n.* **1.** In grammar: **a.** The mood that expresses command, order, or request. **b.** A verb form of that mood. **2.** A command or order. **—im•per'a•tive•ly** *adv.* [SEE NOTE]
im•per•cep•ti•ble |ĭm'pər sĕp'tə bəl| *adj.* Not perceptible; not capable of being perceived by the senses or the mind: *an imperceptible movement.* **—im'per•cep'ti•bly** *adv.*
imperf. imperfect.
im•per•fect |ĭm pûr'fĭkt| *adj.* **1.** Not perfect; having faults, errors, gaps, etc.: *imperfect speech; an imperfect memory.* **2.** Of a set of verb forms used in certain languages to express incomplete or continuous action. *—n.* **1.** A set of verb forms used in certain languages to express incomplete or continuous action. **2.** A verb in one of these forms. **—im•per'fect•ly** *adv.*
im•per•fec•tion |ĭm'pər fĕk'shən| *n.* **1.** The condition or quality of being imperfect: *human imperfection.* **2.** A defect; a fault.
im•pe•ri•al |ĭm pîr'ē əl| *adj.* Of an empire, emperor, or empress: *the days of imperial Rome; the imperial court.* **—im•pe'ri•al•ly** *adv.*
im•pe•ri•al•ism |ĭm pîr'ē ə lĭz'əm| *n.* **1.** The policy of extending and increasing a nation's authority and power by acquiring territories or by establishing economic and political dominance over other nations. **2.** The system, policies, or practices of an imperial government. **—im•pe'ri•al•ist** *n.* & *adj.*
im•pe•ri•al•is•tic |ĭm pîr'ē ə lĭs'tĭk| *adj.* Of imperialism or imperialists. **—im•pe'ri•al•is'ti•cal•ly** *adv.*

impala

impeccable
Impeccable *was originally a religious word meaning "incapable of sinning." It comes from Latin* impeccābilis: in-, *"not,"* + peccāre, *"to sin." It is now chiefly applied to people who do something (choosing clothes, riding, writing letters, etc.) so perfectly that they cannot be criticized.*

imperative
The **imperative** *in English chiefly occurs in the second person, as in* You come here! Don't stop. Please go away. *First-person imperatives are usually formed with the auxiliary verb* **let,** *as in* Let us pray. Let's go. And let me say this . . . *Third-person imperatives exist in a number of special phrases, such as* So help me God. Long live the king. His blood be upon thy head. Serve him right. Far be it from me to say that . . . Suffice it to say that . . .

impetuous

Impetuous *is from Latin* impetuōsus, *"rushing onward violently," from* impetus, *"onrush, violent motion, attack."* Impetus, *from which we also have the English word* **impetus,** *is formed from* in-, *"into, onto, forward,"* + pet-, "go fast."

implore/deplore/explore

These come from two Latin compound verbs formed from plōrāre, *"to weep, to shout."* **Implore** *is from* implōrāre, *"to weep at (someone), to beg (someone for something) with tears"* (in-, *"toward, at"*). **Deplore** *is from* dēplōrāre, *"to lament bitterly"* (de-, *"very much"*). (**Explore** *is from Latin* explōrāre, *"to search out," which is probably not related to* plōrāre.)

ă pat/ā pay/â care/ä father/ĕ pet/ ē be/ĭ pit/ī pie/î fierce/ŏ pot/ ō go/ô paw, for/oi oil/o͝o book/ o͞o boot/ou out/ŭ cut/û fur/ *th* the/th thin/hw which/zh vision/ ə ago, item, pencil, atom, circus

im•per•il |ĭm pĕr′əl| *v.* **im•per•iled** or **im•per•illed, im•per•il•ing** or **im•per•il•ling.** To put in peril or danger; endanger: *Severe pollution imperils life on Earth.*

im•pe•ri•ous |ĭm pîr′ē əs| *adj.* **1.** Arrogant; overbearing; domineering. **2.** Compelling; urgent: *imperious demands of instinct.* —**im•pe′ri•ous•ly** *adv.* —**im•pe′ri•ous•ness** *n.*

im•per•ish•a•ble |ĭm pĕr′ĭ shə bəl| *adj.* Not likely to decay, become destroyed, or disappear.

im•per•me•a•ble |ĭm pûr′mē ə bəl| *adj.* Not permeable; not capable of being permeated, as by a liquid: *an impermeable raincoat.*

im•per•son•al |ĭm pûr′sə nəl| *adj.* **1.** Not referring to or intended for any particular person: *an impersonal remark.* **2.** Showing no emotion or personality: *an aloof, impersonal manner.* **3.** Not responsive to or expressive of human personalities; heartless: *a large, impersonal corporation.* —**im•per′son•al′i•ty** *n.* —**im•per′son•al•ly** *adv.*

im•per•son•ate |ĭm pûr′sə nāt′| *v.* **im•per•son•at•ed, im•per•son•at•ing.** To act the character or part of; pretend to be: *impersonated a British soldier in wartime.* —**im•per′son•a′tion** *n.* —**im•per′son•a′tor** *n.*

im•per•ti•nence |ĭm pûr′tn əns| *n.* **1.** Discourteousness; insolence. **2.** An impertinent act, statement, etc. **3.** Irrelevance.

im•per•ti•nent |ĭm pûr′tn ənt| *adj.* **1.** Impudent; rude: *an impertinent manner.* **2.** Irrelevant; not pertinent: *a question impertinent to the discussion.* —**im•per′ti•nent•ly** *adv.*

im•per•turb•a•ble |ĭm′pər tûr′bə bəl| *adj.* Not easily perturbed; unshakably calm and collected. —**im′per•turb′a•bil′i•ty** *n.* —**im′per•turb′a•bly** *adv.*

im•per•vi•ous |ĭm pûr′vē əs| *adj.* **1.** Not capable of being penetrated: *a material impervious to water.* **2.** Not capable of being affected; immune: *He seemed impervious to fear.* —**im•per′vi•ous•ly** *adv.* —**im•per′vi•ous•ness** *n.*

im•pet•u•os•i•ty |ĭm pĕch′o͞o ŏs′ĭ tē| *n., pl.* **im•pet•u•os•i•ties. 1.** The quality or condition of being impetuous: *the impetuosity of his rush into battle.* **2.** An impetuous act.

im•pet•u•ous |ĭm pĕch′o͞o əs| *adj.* **1.** Tending toward suddenness and boldness of action; impulsive: *an impetuous man.* **2.** Marked by violent movement: *the impetuous, storm-tossed seas.* —**im•pet′u•ous•ly** *adv.* [SEE NOTE]

im•pe•tus |ĭm′pĭ təs| *n., pl.* **im•pe•tus•es.** A driving force: *Blood circulates under the impetus of the heart's pumping action.*

im•pi•e•ty |ĭm pī′ĭ tē| *n., pl.* **im•pi•e•ties. 1.** The quality or condition of being impious; lack of due reverence: *impiety toward the religions of others.* **2.** An impious act.

im•pinge |ĭm pĭnj′| *v.* **im•pinged, im•ping•ing. 1.** To collide; strike: *Sound waves impinge on the insect's antennae.* **2.** To encroach; infringe; trespass: *impinged upon the rights of someone else.* —**im•pinge′ment** *n.* —**im•ping′er** *n.*

im•pi•ous |ĭm′pē əs| or |ĭm pī′-| *adj.* Not pious; lacking due reverence: *impious behavior in church.* —**im′pi•ous•ly** *adv.* —**im′pi•ous•ness** *n.*

imp•ish |ĭm′pĭsh| *adj.* Of or like an imp; playful; mischievous: *her impish humor; an impish grin.* —**imp′ish•ly** *adv.* —**imp′ish•ness** *n.*

im•pla•ca•ble |ĭm plā′kə bəl| or |-plăk′ə-| *adj.* Not easily calmed, pacified, or appeased: *an implacable fury; their implacable enemy.* —**im•pla′ca•bil′i•ty** *n.* —**im•pla′ca•bly** *adv.*

im•plant |ĭm plănt′| or |-plänt′| *v.* To establish firmly; instill; ingrain: *They tried to implant the old traditions among the people of the young nation.*

im•plau•si•ble |ĭm plô′zə bəl| *adj.* Not plausible; not believable or acceptable: *an implausible excuse.* —**im•plau′si•bly** *adv.*

im•ple•ment |ĭm′plə mənt| *n.* A tool, utensil, or instrument used in doing a task: *farm implements.* —*v.* |ĭm′plə mĕnt′|. To put into effect; carry out: *techniques and material for implementing an idea.* —**im′ple•men•ta′tion** *n.*

im•pli•cate |ĭm′plĭ kāt′| *v.* **im•pli•cat•ed, im•pli•cat•ing.** To involve or connect with a crime or other disapproved activity: *His testimony implicated several people in the scandal.*

im•pli•ca•tion |ĭm′plĭ kā′shən| *n.* **1.** Something implied: *the peaceful as well as military implications of artificial satellites.* **2.** The act of implying without direct explanation: *The writer conveyed his idea by implication.* **3.** The act of implicating or condition of being implicated: *denying his implication in the affair.*

im•plic•it |ĭm plĭs′ĭt| *adj.* **1.** Contained in the nature of something but not clearly apparent; inherent: *The butterfly is implicit in the caterpillar.* **2.** Implied or understood without being directly expressed: *Her opposition to war is implicit throughout her book.* **3.** So certain that it need not be affirmed; unquestioning; absolute: *implicit obedience.* —**im•plic′it•ly** *adv.*

im•plore |ĭm plôr′| or |-plōr′| *v.* **im•plored, im•plor•ing. 1.** To appeal to (someone) earnestly, anxiously, and humbly; entreat; beseech: *We implore you to help us.* **2.** To plead or beg for (something) earnestly and humbly: *He implored their pardon.* [SEE NOTE]

im•ply |ĭm plī′| *v.* **im•plied, im•ply•ing, im•plies. 1.** To say or convey indirectly; suggest without stating: *He turned down our request but implied that he might change his mind later.* **2.** To involve or suggest by logical necessity: *Life implies growth and death.*

im•po•lite |ĭm′pə līt′| *adj.* Not polite; discourteous; unmannerly: *an impolite remark; impolite behavior.* —**im′po•lite′ly** *adv.* —**im′po•lite′ness** *n.*

im•port |ĭm pôrt′| or |-pōrt′| or |ĭm′pôrt′| or |-pōrt′| *v.* **1.** To bring or carry in from an outside source, especially to bring in (goods) from another country for trade, sale, or use. **2.** To convey or indicate (something meaningful or significant); mean; signify: *They thought that comets imported great change for their country.* —**im•port′ed** *adj.: imported goods; an imported perfume.* —*n.* |ĭm′pôrt′| or |-pōrt′|. **1.** Something imported, as from another country. **2.** Importance; consequence: *an illness of serious import.* **3.** Meaning; signification: *the emotional import of music.* —***modifier:*** *the import trade; an import tax.*

im•por•tance |ĭm pôr′tns| *n.* The condition or quality of being important; significance.

im•por•tant |ĭm pôr′tnt| *adj.* **1.** Able to determine or change the course of events or the nature of things; significant: *an important seaport; an important crop; an important message.* **2.** Having rank, fame, or authority; prominent: *celebrities and other important people.* —**im•por′tant•ly** *adv.*

im•por•ta•tion |ĭm′pôr tā′shən| *or* |-pōr-| *n.* **1.** The act or practice of importing. **2.** Something imported; an import.

im•port•er |ĭm′pôr′tər| *or* |-pōr′-| *n.* A person, company, or country that imports goods from other countries.

im•por•tu•nate |ĭm pôr′chə nĭt| *adj.* Persistent in pressing a request or demand: *an importunate bill-collector.* —**im•por′tu•nate•ly** *adv.*

im•por•tune |ĭm′pôr to͞on′| *or* |-tyo͞on′| *or* |ĭm pôr′chən| *v.* **im•por•tuned, im•por•tun•ing.** To press with frequent requests; ask insistently. —**im′por•tu′ni•ty** *n.*

im•pose |ĭm pōz′| *v.* **im•posed, im•pos•ing. 1.** To place (something burdensome) on someone; inflict: *long hours of work that imposed a great strain on us.* **2.** To bring about by exercising authority; force to prevail: *impose a settlement.* **3.** To apply or enact (something to be paid, observed, or followed): *impose a tax.* —***phrasal verb.*** **impose on** (or **upon**). To take advantage of: *They did not wish to impose on us by staying too long.*

im•pos•ing |ĭm pō′zĭng| *adj.* Tending to excite awe, admiration, etc.; impressive. —**im•pos′ing•ly** *adv.*

im•po•si•tion |ĭm′pə zĭsh′ən| *n.* **1.** The act of imposing: *the imposition of fishing limits in offshore waters.* **2.** Something imposed, as a tax, burden, etc.: *The colonists resented such impositions as the tax on imported tea.* **3.** An unfair demand upon someone's time, friendship, hospitality, etc.

im•pos•si•bil•i•ty |ĭm pŏs′ə bĭl′ĭ tē| *n., pl.* **im•pos•si•bil•i•ties. 1.** The condition or quality of being impossible: *the impossibility of escape.* **2.** Something that is impossible.

im•pos•si•ble |ĭm pŏs′ə bəl| *adj.* **1.** Not capable of happening or existing: *It is impossible to be in two places at the same time.* **2.** Not likely to happen or be done: *It will be impossible to get there without taking the train.* **3.** Difficult to deal with or tolerate: *an impossible person.* —**im•pos′si•bly** *adv.*

im•post |ĭm′pōst′| *n.* Something imposed or levied, as a tax or duty.

im•pos•tor |ĭm pŏs′tər| *n.* A person who deceives by pretending to be someone else.

im•pos•ture |ĭm pŏs′chər| *n.* Deception or fraud, especially assumption of a false identity.

im•po•tent |ĭm′pə tənt| *adj.* Lacking strength, power, or force; unable to act. —**im′po•tence** *n.* —**im•po′tent•ly** *adv.*

im•pound |ĭm pound′| *v.* **1.** To seize and retain in legal custody. **2.** To confine in or as if in a pound: *The city impounds stray dogs.* **3.** To collect (water) in a natural or artificial lake.

im•pov•er•ish |ĭm pŏv′ər ĭsh| *or* |-pŏv′rĭsh| *v.* **1.** To reduce to poverty. **2.** To deplete of natural richness, strength, force, etc.: *Improper farming had impoverished the soil.* —**im•pov′er•ish•ment** *n.*

im•prac•ti•ca•ble |ĭm prăk′tĭ kə bəl| *adj.* Not capable of being done or carried out: *impracticable ideas for rural development.* —**im•prac′ti•ca•ble•ness** *n.* —**im•prac′ti•ca•bly** *adv.*

im•prac•ti•cal |ĭm prăk′tĭ kəl| *adj.* Not practical; unwise; foolish: *an impractical plan; a dreamy, impractical girl.* —**im•prac′ti•cal′i•ty** *n.*

im•pre•ca•tion |ĭm′prĭ kā′shən| *n.* A curse: *He yelled imprecations at the mob.*

im•pre•cise |ĭm′prĭ sīs′| *adj.* Not precise; not exact, definite, or clear: *speaking in imprecise terms.* —**im′pre•cise′ly** *adv.*

im•preg•na•ble |ĭm prĕg′nə bəl| *adj.* Safe against attack: *an impregnable fort.* —**im•preg′na•bly** *adv.*

im•preg•nate |ĭm prĕg′nāt′| *v.* **im•preg•nat•ed, im•preg•nat•ing. 1.** To make pregnant; fertilize. **2.** To fill completely; saturate: *The smell of liquor impregnated the room.* —**im′preg•na′tion** *n.*

im•pre•sa•ri•o |ĭm′prĭ sär′ē ō′| *or* |-sâr′-| *n., pl.* **im•pre•sa•ri•os.** A person who sponsors or produces entertainment, as operas, ballets, etc.

im•press¹ |ĭm prĕs′| *v.* **1.** To produce a vivid, often favorable effect on the mind or emotions of; seem remarkable to: *His performance impressed me.* **2.** To establish firmly in the mind, as by force or influence: *impressed upon the boys the spirit of good sportsmanship.* **3.** To mark or stamp with or as if with pressure: *impress a design upon a surface.* —*n.* |ĭm′prĕs′|. A mark or imprint made by pressure. [SEE NOTE]

im•press² |ĭm prĕs′| *v.* To force (a person) to serve in a military force. [SEE NOTE]

im•pres•sion |ĭm prĕsh′ən| *n.* **1.** A marked effect, image, or feeling retained in the mind: *early childhood impressions.* **2.** A vague notion, remembrance, belief, idea, etc.: *I had the impression that I had seen him before.* **3.** A mark or imprint made on a surface by pressure: *fossilized impressions of leaves.* **4.** A humorous imitation of someone's speech and manner: *He gave impressions of movie stars.* [SEE PICTURE]

im•pres•sion•a•ble |ĭm prĕsh′ə nə bəl| *adj.* Readily influenced or affected; suggestible. —**im•pres′sion•a•bil′i•ty** *n.*

im•pres•sion•ism, also **Im•pres•sion•ism** |ĭm prĕsh′ə nĭz′əm| *n.* **1.** A style of painting of the late 19th century, marked by concentration on the impression produced by a scene or object and the use of many small strokes to simulate reflected light. **2.** A musical style of the late 19th century, using rather vague but colorful harmonies and rhythms to suggest moods, places, and happenings. —**im•pres′sion•ist, Im•pres′sion•ist** *n.* & *adj.*

im•pres•sion•ist•ic, also **Im•pres•sion•ist•ic** |ĭm prĕsh′ə nĭs′tĭk| *adj.* Of impressionism or the impressionists.

im•pres•sive |ĭm prĕs′ĭv| *adj.* Making a strong or vivid impression; commanding attention: *an impressive monument; an impressive ceremony.* —**im•pres′sive•ly** *adv.* —**im•pres′sive•ness** *n.*

im•print |ĭm′prĭnt′| *n.* **1.** A mark or pattern made by something pressed on a surface: *an imprint of a foot in the sand.* **2.** A marked influence or effect: *South American countries show the imprint of Portuguese and Spanish colonization.* **3.** The publisher's name, often with date, address, and edition of a publication, printed on the title page. —*v.* |ĭm prĭnt′|. **1.** To produce (a mark, pattern, etc.) on a surface: *He imprinted his name on the card.* **2.** To establish firmly, as on the mind or memory.

im•pris•on |ĭm prĭz′ən| *v.* **1.** To put in prison. **2.** To enclose or confine: *Steep walls imprison the river in the narrow gorge.* —**im•pris′on•ment** *n.*

impress¹·²

Impress¹ *is from Latin* impremere, *"to press upon": in-, "into, onto," +* premere, *"to press." (The past participle of* premere *was* pressus, *and all the English derivatives, such as* **express,** *and* **press¹** *itself, have taken their forms from this.)* **Impress²** *was separately formed in English from the separate word* **press².**

impression
Impressions of fossilized fern fronds

improbable
"How often have I said to you that when you have eliminated the impossible, whatever remains, however improbable, *must be the truth?" (Sherlock Holmes to Dr. Watson). —Sir Arthur Conan Doyle (1859–1930).*

im•prob•a•ble |ĭm prŏb'ə bəl| *adj.* Not probable; unlikely: *an improbable tale.* —**im•prob'a•bil'i•ty** *n.* —**im•prob'a•bly** *adv.* [SEE NOTE]
im•promp•tu |ĭm prŏmp'to͞o| *or* |-tyo͞o| *adj.* Not prepared beforehand; not rehearsed: *an impromptu lecture.* —*adv.* Without rehearsal or preparation: *He sang impromptu for the children.* —*n.* Something made or done without rehearsal, as a musical composition or speech.
im•prop•er |ĭm prŏp'ər| *adj.* **1.** Not proper; incorrect: *the improper functioning of the machine; an improper diet.* **2.** Not conforming to social conventions: *improper behavior in church.* —**im•prop'er•ly** *adv.* —**im•prop'er•ness** *n.*
improper fraction. A fraction in which the numerator is greater than or equal to the denominator.
im•pro•pri•e•ty |ĭm'prə prī'ĭ tē| *n., pl.* **im•pro•pri•e•ties. 1.** The condition of being improper: *the impropriety of his behavior at the banquet.* **2.** An improper act, expression, etc.
im•prove |ĭm pro͞ov'| *v.* **im•proved, im•prov•ing.** To make or become better: *She improved her tennis serve by practicing. Living conditions improved.* —***phrasal verb.*** **improve on.** To change for the better or add to: *They improved on his method.*
im•prove•ment |ĭm pro͞ov'mənt| *n.* **1.** A change or addition that improves: *improvements in the wireless telegraph.* **2.** The act or process of improving: *There is always room for improvement.*
im•prov•i•dent |ĭm prŏv'ĭ dənt| *adj.* **1.** Not planning or providing for the future; careless of one's resources. **2.** Rash; heedless: *an improvident decision.* —**im•prov'i•dence** *n.* —**im•prov'i•dent•ly** *adv.*
im•prov•i•sa•tion |ĭm prŏv'ĭ zā'shən| *or* |ĭm'prə vĭ-| *n.* **1.** The act or process of improvising. **2.** Something improvised.
im•pro•vise |ĭm'prə vīz'| *v.* **im•pro•vised, im•pro•vis•ing. 1.** To invent or compose without preparation: *improvise a melody.* **2.** To make, build, or provide on the spur of the moment or from materials found nearby: *improvise a meal.* —**im'pro•vis'er** *n.*
im•pru•dent |ĭm pro͞od'nt| *adj.* Not prudent; unwise; rash. —**im•pru'dence** *n.* —**im•pru'dent•ly** *adv.*
im•pu•dent |ĭm'pyə dənt| *adj.* Bold and disrespectful; impertinent; rude: *the children's impudent remarks to the old man.* —**im'pu•dence** *n.* —**im'pu•dent•ly** *adv.*
im•pugn |ĭm pyo͞on'| *v.* To attack as false; cast doubt on: *impugned his right to the throne.*
im•pulse |ĭm'pŭls'| *n.* **1.** A short, sudden burst or flow, as of energy: *an electrical impulse.* **2.** A sudden inclination or urge; a whim: *acting on impulse.* **3.** A strong motivation; a drive or instinct: *A child has the impulse to utter audible sounds.* **4.** A driving force; a thrust; push; impetus: *a new impulse to the economy.*
im•pul•sive |ĭm pŭl'sĭv| *adj.* **1.** Tending to act on impulse rather than careful thought: *an impulsive shopper.* **2.** Caused by impulse; uncalculated: *an impulsive action.* **3.** Having the power to urge to action or drive forward. —**im•pul'sive•ly** *adv.* —**im•pul'sive•ness** *n.*
im•pu•ni•ty |ĭm pyo͞o'nĭ tē| *n., pl.* **im•pu•ni•ties.** Freedom from punishment, harm, or injury: *You cannot always play hooky with impunity.*
im•pure |ĭm pyo͝or'| *adj.* **1.** Not pure or clean; contaminated: *impure water.* **2.** Mixed with other substances: *Coal is impure carbon.* **3.** Morally imperfect; bad: *a belief that all human beings were impure by nature.* —**im•pure'ly** *adv.*
im•pu•ri•ty |ĭm pyo͝or'ĭ tē| *n., pl.* **im•pu•ri•ties. 1.** The condition or quality of being impure. **2.** A substance whose presence makes another substance impure: *water that contains impurities.*
im•pute |ĭm pyo͞ot'| *v.* **im•put•ed, im•put•ing.** To attribute to: *I impute my mistakes to my own carelessness.* —**im'pu•ta'tion** *n.*
in |ĭn| *prep.* **1. a.** Within the confines of; inside: *He's in his room.* Also used adverbially: *an old cigar box to keep pencils and crayons in.* **b.** Into a certain space: *couldn't get in the house.* Also used adverbially: *He couldn't get in.* **2.** Into the midst of or on the area of: *falling in the mud; playing in the street.* Also used adverbially: *went fishing on the river and fell in.* **3.** On or so as to affect: *punched him in the nose.* **4.** By the end of: *ready in a few minutes.* **5.** At the position of: *in command.* **6.** To or at the condition or situation of: *in trouble.* **7.** Following the pattern or form of: *going around in circles.* **8.** As part of the act or process of: *measures taken in defense.* **9.** As an expression of; out of: *said in anger.* **10.** By means of: *paid in cash.* **11.** With the use of: *drawings done in chalk.* **12.** Within the category or class of: *the latest thing in fashion.* **13.** According to: *in my opinion.* **14.** With reference to; as to: *different in color.* —*adv.* **1. a.** Indoors: *coming in out of the rain.* **b.** At home: *I don't expect to stay in after six o'clock.* **c.** To or into a certain place, especially in town: *When are you coming in?* **2.** Within some specified or understood situation: *He enlisted a couple of years ago, so he won't be in much longer.* **3.** Into a given activity together: *Count me in when you decide to start.* **4.** Inward: *caved in.* —*adj. Informal.* **1.** Fashionable; popular; prestigious: *Short haircuts are again the in look.* **2.** Having power; incumbent: *The in government was made up of a coalition.* **3.** Participating in or aware of: *She always wants to be in on everything that's happening.* —*n.* **1.** *Informal.* A means of access or favor: *He's got an in with the casting director.* **2.** Often **ins.** Those having power or inside influence: *The ins are always at an advantage over the outs.* —*Note: In* is often used followed by *that* to form the conjunctional phrase **in that.** Because; inasmuch as; since: *His arguments are unconvincing in that they are so obviously one-sided.* ¶*These sound alike* **in, inn.** [SEE NOTE]
Idioms. **all in.** *Informal.* Completely exhausted. **have it in for (someone).** *Informal.* To have a grudge against. **in for.** About to get or have: *He's in for a big surprise.* **ins and outs.** The details of an activity, process, etc.: *the ins and outs of local politics.*
in–¹. A prefix meaning "without, not": **inaccurate.** When *in-* is followed by *l* or *r*, it becomes *il-* or *ir-*, respectively. Before *b, m,* or *p*, it becomes *im-*. [SEE NOTE]
in–². A prefix meaning "in, within, or into": **inbound.** When *in-* is followed by *l* or *r*, it becomes *il-* or *ir-*, respectively. Before *b, m,* or *p*, it becomes *im-*. [SEE NOTE]

in
The Latin for "in" or "into" is in, *and this is not a coincidence. Both Latin* in *and the English word* **in** *are descended from the Indo-European word* en, *"in."*

in–¹·²
Both of these prefixes are from Latin, but they are not related. **In-¹** *is related to the English prefix* **un-**. **In-²** *is related to the English preposition* **in**. *See note at* **in**.

ă pat/ā pay/â care/ä father/ĕ pet/ē be/ĭ pit/ī pie/î fierce/ŏ pot/ō go/ô paw, for/oi oil/o͝o book/o͞o boot/ou out/ŭ cut/û fur/*th* the/th thin/hw which/zh vision/ə ago, item, pencil, atom, circus

in, in. inch.
In The symbol for the element indium.
in•a•bil•i•ty |ĭn′ə **bĭl′**ĭ tē| *n., pl.* **in•a•bil•i•ties.** Lack of ability or means: *inability to sleep.*
in•ac•ces•si•ble |ĭn′ăk **sĕs′**ə bəl| *adj.* Not accessible; unapproachable: *a nearly inaccessible place.* —**in′ac•ces′si•bly** *adv.*
in•ac•cu•ra•cy |ĭn **ăk′**yər ə sē| *n., pl.* **in•ac•cu•ra•cies. 1.** The quality or condition of being inaccurate: *the inaccuracy of his judgment.* **2.** An error; a mistake: *many inaccuracies in his report.*
in•ac•cu•rate |ĭn **ăk′**yər ĭt| *adj.* Not accurate; containing or making errors: *an inaccurate description.* —**in•ac′cu•rate•ly** *adv.*
in•ac•tion |ĭn **ăk′**shən| *n.* Lack or absence of action.
in•ac•tive |ĭn **ăk′**tĭv| *adj.* **1.** Not active or not tending to be active: *an inactive volcano; an inactive life.* **2.** Not available for full duties or service: *inactive players on a team.*
in•ad•e•qua•cy |ĭn **ăd′**ĭ kwə sē| *n., pl.* **in•ad•e•qua•cies. 1.** The quality or condition of being inadequate. **2.** A failing or lack; a defect.
in•ad•e•quate |ĭn **ăd′**ĭ kwĭt| *adj.* **1.** Not adequate; insufficient: *an inadequate diet; inadequate lubrication in a car.* **2.** Not able; incapable: *felt inadequate to the task.* —**in•ad′e•quate•ly** *adv.*
in•ad•mis•si•ble |ĭn′əd **mĭs′**ə bəl| *adj.* Not admissible or allowable: *inadmissible evidence in a court of law.* —**in′ad•mis′si•bil′i•ty** *n.*
in•ad•ver•tent |ĭn′əd **vûr′**tnt| *adj.* Accidental; unintentional. —**in′ad•ver′tence** *n.*
in•ad•vis•a•ble |ĭn′əd **vī′**zə bəl| *adj.* Unwise; not recommended. —**in′ad•vis′a•bil′i•ty** *n.*
in•al•ien•a•ble |ĭn **āl′**yə nə bəl| *adj.* Not capable of being given up or taken away: *an inalienable human right.* —**in•al′ien•a•bly** *adv.*
in•ane |ĭ **nān′**| *adj.* Lacking sense or meaning; empty; silly: *an inane comment.* —**in•ane′ly** *adv.*
in•an•i•mate |ĭn **ăn′**ə mĭt| *adj.* **1.** Not living: *an inanimate object.* **2.** Showing no sign of life; lifeless: *an inanimate body.* **3.** Not lively; listless. —**in•an′i•mate•ness** *n.*
in•an•i•ty |ĭ **năn′**ĭ tē| *n., pl.* **in•an•i•ties. 1.** The condition or quality of being inane. **2.** An inane statement, remark, etc.
in•ap•pli•ca•ble |ĭn **ăp′**lĭ kə bəl| *adj.* Not applicable: *That law is inapplicable in this case.* —**in•ap′pli•ca•bil′i•ty** *n.*
in•ap•pro•pri•ate |ĭn′ə **prō′**prē ĭt| *adj.* Not appropriate; unsuitable. —**in′ap•pro′pri•ate•ly** *adv.* —**in′ap•pro′pri•ate•ness** *n.*
in•ar•tic•u•late |ĭn′är **tĭk′**yə lĭt| *adj.* **1.** Uttered without the use of normal words or syllables: *an inarticulate cry.* **2.** Unable to speak; speechless: *inarticulate with astonishment.* **3.** Unable to speak with clarity or eloquence. —**in′ar•tic′u•late•ly** *adv.* —**in′ar•tic′u•late•ness** *n.*
in•as•much as |ĭn′əz **mŭch′**|. Because of the fact that; since.
in•at•ten•tion |ĭn′ə **tĕn′**shən| *n.* Lack of attention, notice, or regard; heedlessness.
in•at•ten•tive |ĭn′ə **tĕn′**tĭv| *adj.* Showing a lack of attention; negligent. —**in′at•ten′tive•ly** *n.* —**in′at•ten′tive•ness** *n.*
in•au•di•ble |ĭn **ô′**də bəl| *adj.* Incapable of being heard; not audible: *a nearly inaudible sound.* —**in•au′di•bly** *adv.*
in•au•gu•ral |ĭ **nô′**gyər əl| *adj.* **1.** Of an inauguration, especially a Presidential inauguration: *an inaugural address.* **2.** First; initial: *an inaugural flight.* —*n.* **1.** A speech made by a President of the United States at his inauguration. **2.** An inaugural ceremony or activity.
in•au•gu•rate |ĭ **nô′**gyə rāt′| *v.* **in•au•gu•rat•ed, in•au•gu•rat•ing. 1.** To install in office by a formal ceremony: *inaugurate a President.* **2.** To open or begin use of with a ceremony; dedicate: *inaugurate a highway.* —**in•au′gu•ra′tion** *n.*
in•aus•pi•cious |ĭn′ô **spĭsh′**əs| *adj.* Not auspicious; boding ill; unfavorable: *inauspicious circumstances.* —**in′aus•pi′cious•ly** *adv.* —**in′aus•pi′cious•ness** *n.*
in-be•tween |ĭn′bĭ **twēn′**| *adj.* Being in between; intermediate: *The color was an in-between shade, neither light nor dark.*
in•born |**ĭn′bôrn′**| *adj.* Present in a person or animal from birth: *an inborn trait.*
in•bound |**ĭn′bound′**| *adj.* Incoming; arriving: *an inbound ship.*
in•bred |**ĭn′brĕd′**| *adj.* **1.** Produced by or resulting from inbreeding. **2.** Existing from birth; inborn.
in•breed |**ĭn′**brēd′| *or* |ĭn **brēd′**| *v.* **in•bred** |**ĭn′**-brĕd′| or |ĭn **brĕd′**|, **in•breed•ing.** To breed by continued mating of closely related individuals so as to produce offspring with similar traits.
in•breed•ing |**ĭn′**brē′dĭng| *n.* **1.** The breeding or mating of closely related individuals. **2.** Intermarriage among people who are closely related or from the same social groups.
Inc. incorporated.
In•ca |**ĭng′**kə| *n., pl.* **In•ca** or **In•cas.** A member of the Quechua-speaking peoples who ruled Peru before the Spanish conquest in the 16th century.
in•cal•cu•la•ble |ĭn **kăl′**kyə lə bəl| *adj.* **1.** Too great to be calculated or described; enormous: *an incalculable number of ants.* **2.** Incapable of being foreseen: *an incalculable outcome.* —**in•cal′cu•la•bil′i•ty** *n.* —**in•cal′cu•la•bly** *adv.*
in•can•des•cent |ĭn′kən **dĕs′**ənt| *adj.* **1.** Giving off visible light as a result of being raised to a high temperature. **2.** Shining brilliantly; very bright. —**in′can•des′cence** *n.* —**in′can•des′cent•ly** *adv.*
incandescent lamp. An electric lamp in which a filament is heated to incandescence by a current that passes through it. [SEE PICTURE]
in•can•ta•tion |ĭn′kăn **tā′**shən| *n.* **1.** A formula of words or sounds recited or chanted to produce a magical effect. **2.** The act of reciting or chanting such a formula. [SEE NOTE]
in•ca•pa•ble |ĭn **kā′**pə bəl| *adj.* Not capable; lacking the necessary power or ability: *incapable of working by himself.* —**in•ca′pa•bil′i•ty** *n.*
in•ca•pac•i•tate |ĭn′kə **păs′**ĭ tāt′| *v.* **in•ca•pac•i•tat•ed, in•ca•pac•i•tat•ing.** To deprive of power or ability; disable: *An injury incapacitated our best player.*
in•ca•pac•i•ty |ĭn′kə **păs′**ĭ tē| *n., pl.* **in•ca•pac•i•ties. 1.** Lack of capacity; inadequate strength or ability: *incapacity for work.* **2.** A disability; a defect or handicap.
in•car•cer•ate |ĭn **kär′**sə rāt′| *v.* **in•car•cer•at•ed, in•car•cer•at•ing.** To put in jail; imprison. —**in•car′cer•a′tion** *n.*
in•car•nate |ĭn **kär′**nĭt| *or* |-nāt′| *adj.* **1.** In a bodily, especially human, form: *an incarnate*

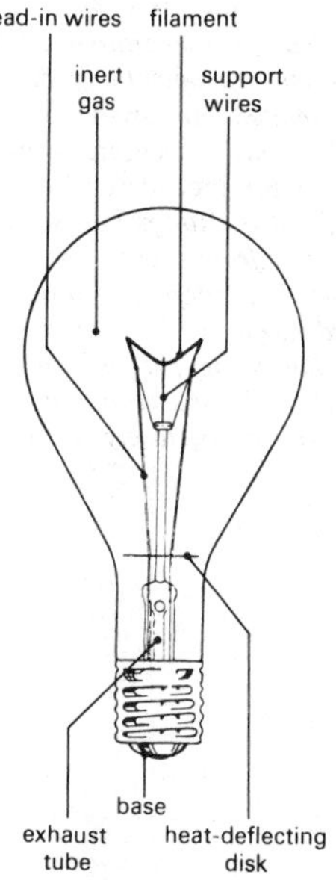

incandescent lamp

incantation/enchant
Incantation *is borrowed from Latin* incantāre, *"to sing at (someone), to put a magic spell on"; in-, "toward, at," +* cantāre, *"to sing." Separately,* incantāre *passed into Old French as* enchanter, *which was borrowed into English as* **enchant.** *Notice that* **incantation** *retains the sense of "singing, chanting," while* **enchant** *has lost this sense and refers only to magical effects.*

incense[1-2]
These are two separate words with different pronunciations, but they are related. **Incense[1]** *is from Old French* incenser, *which is from Latin* incendere, *"to set on fire," also "to make (someone) angry," from* cend- *or* cand-, *"hot."* Incendere *also formed the word* incensum, *"burnt material, substance for burning, incense," which is the source of* **incense[2]**. **Incendiary** *is closely related.*

inclined plane

inclose/enclose
In the five million words on which this Dictionary was based, there were only 3 occurrences of **inclose**, *as against 80 of* **enclose**.

ă pat/ā pay/â care/ä father/ĕ pet/ ē be/ĭ pit/ī pie/î fierce/ŏ pot/ ō go/ô paw, for/oi oil/ŏŏ book/ ōō boot/ou out/ŭ cut/û fur/ *th* the/th thin/hw which/zh vision/ ə ago, item, pencil, atom, circus

spirit. **2.** Personified: *He is wisdom incarnate.* —*v.* |ĭn **kär′**nāt′| **in•car•nat•ed, in•car•nat•ing.** To be a perfect embodiment of; personify: *a man who incarnated the ideals of his time.*

in•car•na•tion |ĭn′kär **nā′**shən| *n.* **1.** The act of incarnating or the condition of having taken on bodily form: *the incarnation of the devil in the form of a serpent.* **2. the Incarnation.** The embodiment of God in the human form of Christ. **3.** A person or thing thought to personify a quality or idea: *The wolverine has been considered the incarnation of everything evil.*

in•cau•tious |ĭn **kô′**shəs| *adj.* Not cautious; rash. —**in•cau′tious•ly** *adv.*

in•cen•di•ar•y |ĭn **sĕn′**dē ĕr′ē| *adj.* **1.** Starting or designed to start fires: *an incendiary bomb.* **2.** Of or involving arson: *an incendiary fire.* **3.** Tending to arouse passions or incite violent action; inflammatory: *incendiary pamphlets.* —*n., pl.* **in•cen•di•ar•ies. 1.** An arsonist. **2.** An incendiary bomb or other explosive.

in•cense[1] |ĭn **sĕns′**| *v.* **in•censed, in•cens•ing.** To make very angry; enrage. [SEE NOTE]

in•cense[2] |**ĭn′**sĕns′| *n.* **1.** A substance, as gum or wood, that burns with a pleasant odor. **2.** The smoke or odor produced by the burning of such a substance. [SEE NOTE]

in•cen•tive |ĭn **sĕn′**tĭv| *n.* Something inciting to action or effort; a stimulus.

in•cep•tion |ĭn **sĕp′**shən| *n.* The beginning of something; start.

in•ces•sant |ĭn **sĕs′**ənt| *adj.* Continuing without interruption; constant: *her incessant talk.* —**in•ces′sant•ly** *adv.*

in•cest |**ĭn′**sĕst′| *n.* Sexual union between persons who are so closely related that they cannot be legally married.

in•ces•tu•ous |ĭn **sĕs′**chōō əs| *adj.* **1.** Of incest. **2.** Having committed incest.

inch |ĭnch| *n.* A unit of length equal to 1/12 of a foot. —*v.* To move or proceed very slowly or by small degrees.

Idioms. **every inch.** In every detail; entirely: *He is every inch a hero.* **inch by inch.** Very gradually or slowly. **within an inch of.** Almost to the point of; very near.

in•cho•ate |ĭn **kō′**ĭt| *adj.* Not yet fully formed; just beginning to take shape: *A solution to the problem was inchoate in his mind.*

inch•worm |**ĭnch′**wûrm′| *n.* A caterpillar that moves by looping up its body and then stretching it out.

in•ci•dence |**ĭn′**sĭ dəns| *n.* The rate or frequency with which something occurs: *a high incidence of disease.*

in•ci•dent |**ĭn′**sĭ dənt| *n.* **1.** A definite, distinct occurrence; an event, especially a minor one. **2.** A disturbance or mishap that causes trouble or interrupts normal procedure: *The plane took off without incident.* —*adj.* Tending to happen or occur at the same time; accompanying: *the confusion incident to a quick change.*

in•ci•den•tal |ĭn sĭ **dĕn′**tl| *adj.* **1.** Likely to occur at the same time or as a minor consequence; attendant: *fleabites and other annoyances incidental to an African safari.* **2.** Of a minor, casual, or subordinate nature: *incidental expenses.* —*n.* Often **incidentals.** A minor item or expense.

in•ci•den•tal•ly |ĭn′sĭ **dĕn′**tl ē| *adv.* **1.** Apart from the main subject; by the way: *Incidentally, what time is it?* **2.** Casually or by chance.

in•cin•er•ate |ĭn **sĭn′**ə rāt′| *v.* **in•cin•er•at•ed, in•cin•er•at•ing.** To destroy by burning; burn up. —**in•cin′er•a′tion** *n.*

in•cin•er•a•tor |ĭn **sĭn′**ə rā′tər| *n.* A furnace or other device for burning waste.

in•cip•i•ent |ĭn **sĭp′**ē ənt| *adj.* In an initial or early stage; just beginning to exist or appear: *an incipient smile.* —**in•cip′i•en•cy, in•cip′i•ence** *n.*

in•cise |ĭn **sīz′**| *v.* **in•cised, in•cis•ing. 1.** To cut into (a surface) with or as if with a sharp tool: *incised the wood with the point of his chisel.* **2.** To cut (a design, writing, etc.) into a surface; carve.

in•ci•sion |ĭn **sĭzh′**ən| *n.* **1.** The act or an example of incising: *the incision of a design.* **2.** A thin, clean cut, especially in surgery.

in•ci•sive |ĭn **sī′**sĭv| *adj.* Sharp and clear; penetrating: *incisive comments; an incisive mind.* —**in•ci′sive•ly** *adv.* —**in•ci′sive•ness** *n.*

in•ci•sor |ĭn **sī′**zər| *n.* A tooth adapted for cutting, as one of the wedge-shaped teeth found in the front of the jaws of mammals.

in•cite |ĭn **sīt′**| *v.* **in•cit•ed, in•cit•ing.** To provoke to action; stir up; urge on: *He incited the people to violence.* —**in•cite′ment** *n.*

incl. including; inclusive.

in•clem•ent |ĭn **klĕm′**ənt| *adj.* **1.** Stormy; rough; severe: *inclement weather.* **2.** Unmerciful. —**in•clem′en•cy** *n.*

in•cli•na•tion |ĭn′klə **nā′**shən| *n.* **1. a.** A deviation from a particular direction, especially horizontal or vertical; a slant or slope. **b.** The amount or measure of such a deviation: *an inclination of 20 degrees.* **2.** A tendency to act in a certain way: *She has an inclination to observe and criticize the faults of others.* **3.** A natural or usual preference: *an inclination to skate.*

in•cline |ĭn **klīn′**| *v.* **in•clined, in•clin•ing. 1.** To depart or cause to depart from a true horizontal or vertical direction; to lean, slant, or slope: *a road that inclines steeply; incline the basement floor for better drainage.* **2.** To have a tendency or preference; tend: *She inclines to work hard.* **3.** To influence (someone) to have a certain preference, leaning, etc.; dispose: *This book might incline you to be more understanding.* **4.** To lower or bend (the head or body), as in a nod or bow. —*n.* |**ĭn′**klīn′|. A surface that inclines; a slope.

in•clined |ĭn **klīnd′**| *adj.* **1.** Deviating from horizontal or vertical; slanting. **2.** Having a preference or tendency; disposed: *He is inclined to make rather hasty judgments.*

inclined plane. A plane that meets the horizontal plane at an acute angle, especially a simple machine that has this form that allows a body to be raised by a force that is smaller than its weight. [SEE PICTURE]

in•cli•nom•e•ter |ĭn′klə **nŏm′**ĭ tər| *n.* **1.** An instrument used to determine the amount by which the direction of the earth's magnetic field deviates from horizontal at any point. **2.** An instrument that indicates the amount by which an aircraft or ship is tilted away from the true horizontal plane. **3.** An instrument used to measure the angle of an incline.

in•close |ĭn **klōz′**| *v.* **in•closed, in•clos•ing.** A form of the word **enclose.** [SEE NOTE]

in•clo•sure |ĭn klō′zhər| *n.* A form of the word **enclosure.**

in•clude |ĭn klōōd′| *v.* **in•clud•ed, in•clud•ing. 1.** To be made up of, at least in part; contain: *The collection includes some of her paintings.* **2.** To put into a group, class, or total: *Include in the basic statement all the necessary information.*

in•clud•ed |ĭn klōō′dĭd| *adj.* Formed and bounded by two intersecting straight lines, line segments, or rays: *an included angle.*

in•clu•sion |ĭn klōō′zhən| *n.* **1.** The act of including or the condition of being included. **2.** Something that is included.

in•clu•sive |ĭn klōō′sĭv| *adj.* **1.** Taking everything into account; including everything; comprehensive: *an inclusive fee.* **2.** Including the specified extremes or limits as well as the area between them: *numbers 1 to 50, inclusive.* —**in•clu′sive•ly** *adv.* —**in•clu′sive•ness** *n.*

in•cog•ni•to |ĭn kŏg′nĭ tō′| *or* |ĭn′kŏg nē′tō| *adv.* With one's identity hidden or disguised: *The movie star stayed at the hotel incognito.* [SEE NOTE]

in•co•her•ent |ĭn′kō hîr′ənt| *adj.* **1.** Not coherent; lacking orderly arrangement: *an incoherent explanation.* **2.** Unable to think or express one's thoughts in a clear or orderly manner: *She was incoherent with grief.* —**in′co•her′ence** *n.* —**in′co•her′ent•ly** *adv.*

in•com•bus•ti•ble |ĭn′kəm bŭs′tə bəl| *adj.* Not capable of being set afire or burned.

in•come |ĭn′kŭm′| *n.* The amount of money received during a period of time for labor or services, from the sale of property, etc.

income tax. A tax on a person's annual income, based on the amount of his income.

in•com•ing |ĭn′kŭm′ĭng| *adj.* **1.** Coming in; entering: *incoming mail.* **2.** About to come in; next in succession: *the incoming president.*

in•com•men•su•rate |ĭn′kə mĕn′shər ĭt| *or* |-sər ĭt| *adj.* Not commensurate; unequal; inadequate: *Her salary was incommensurate with her efforts.* —**in′com•men′su•rate•ly** *adv.*

in•com•mu•ni•ca•ble |ĭn′kə myōō′nĭ kə bəl| *adj.* Not capable of being communicated: *incommunicable wisdom.*

in•com•mu•ni•ca•do |ĭn′kə myōō′nĭ kä′dō| *adv.* Without the means or right of communicating with others: *a prisoner held incommunicado.* [SEE NOTE]

in•com•pa•ra•ble |ĭn kŏm′pər ə bəl| *adj.* **1.** Not capable of being compared: *incomparable amounts.* **2.** Above all comparison; unsurpassed. —**in•com′pa•ra•bly** *adv.*

in•com•pat•i•ble |ĭn′kəm păt′ə bəl| *adj.* **1.** Not compatible; not in harmony or agreement: *incompatible colors.* **2.** Not capable of living or working together happily or smoothly: *incompatible roommates.* —**in′com•pat′i•bil′i•ty** *n.* —**in′com•pat′i•bly** *adv.*

in•com•pe•tent |ĭn kŏm′pĭ tənt| *adj.* Not competent; not capable, as of doing a job: *an incompetent worker.* —**in•com′pe•tence** *n.* —**in•com′pe•tent•ly** *adv.*

in•com•plete |ĭn′kəm plēt′| *adj.* Not complete: *an incomplete set.* —**in′com•plete′ly** *adv.*

in•com•pre•hen•si•ble |ĭn′kŏm prĭ hĕn′sə bəl| *or* |ĭn kŏm′-| *adj.* Incapable of being understood or comprehended: *an incomprehensible sentence.* —**in′com•pre•hen′si•bil′i•ty** *n.* —**in′com•pre•hen′si•bly** *adv.*

in•com•press•i•ble |ĭn′kəm prĕs′ə bəl| *adj.* Not capable of being compressed. —**in′com•press′i•bil′i•ty** *n.*

in•con•ceiv•a•ble |ĭn′kən sē′və bəl| *adj.* Incapable of being thought of or imagined: *inconceivable difficulties.* —**in′con•ceiv′a•bly** *adv.*

in•con•clu•sive |ĭn′kən klōō′sĭv| *adj.* Not conclusive. —**in′con•clu′sive•ly** *adv.* —**in′con•clu′sive•ness** *n.*

in•con•gru•i•ty |ĭn′kŏng grōō′ĭ tē| *or* |ĭn′kən-| *n., pl.* **in•con•gru•i•ties. 1.** The condition or quality of being incongruous. **2.** Something that is incongruous.

in•con•gru•ous |ĭn kŏng′grōō əs| *adj.* **1.** Not consistent with what is logical, customary, or expected; inappropriate: *the incongruous cheerfulness of the executioner.* **2.** Made up of sharply different members, qualities, or parts: *an incongruous group of people.* —**in•con′gru•ous•ly** *adv.* —**in•con′gru•ous•ness** *n.*

in•con•se•quen•tial |ĭn kŏn′sĭ kwĕn′shəl| *adj.* Without consequence; lacking importance; petty: *an inconsequential and boring debate.* —**in•con′se•quen′tial•ly** *adv.*

in•con•sid•er•ate |ĭn′kən sĭd′ər ĭt| *adj.* Not considerate; thoughtless. —**in′con•sid′er•ate•ly** *adv.* —**in′con•sid′er•ate•ness** *n.*

in•con•sis•ten•cy |ĭn′kən sĭs′tən sē| *n., pl.* **in•con•sis•ten•cies. 1.** The condition or quality of being inconsistent. **2.** Something that is inconsistent: *inconsistencies in spelling.*

in•con•sis•tent |ĭn′kən sĭs′tənt| *adj.* Not consistent, especially: **1.** Not in agreement or harmony; incompatible: *an intersection inconsistent with the road map.* **2.** Lacking in correct logical relation; contradictory: *inconsistent statements.* —**in′con•sis′tent•ly** *adv.*

in•con•sol•a•ble |ĭn′kən sō′lə bəl| *adj.* Not capable of being consoled; despondent. —**in′con•sol′a•bly** *adv.*

in•con•spic•u•ous |ĭn′kən spĭk′yōō əs| *adj.* Not readily noticeable; not obvious: *The flowers of the oak and maple are inconspicuous.* —**in′con•spic′u•ous•ly** *adv.* —**in′con•spic′u•ous•ness** *n.*

in•con•stant |ĭn kŏn′stənt| *adj.* Not constant or steady; changeable or fickle. —**in•con′stan•cy** *n.* —**in•con′stant•ly** *adv.*

in•con•tro•vert•i•ble |ĭn′kŏn trə vûr′tə bəl| *adj.* Not capable of being disputed or denied; indisputable: *incontrovertible evidence.* —**in′con•tro•vert′i•bly** *adv.*

in•con•ven•ience |ĭn′kən vēn′yəns| *n.* **1.** Lack of ease or comfort; trouble; difficulty. **2.** Something that causes difficulty, trouble, or discomfort. —*v.* **in•con•ven•ienced, in•con•ven•ienc•ing.** To cause inconvenience for; trouble; bother.

in•con•ven•ient |ĭn′kən vēn′yənt| *adj.* Not convenient; causing difficulty. —**in′con•ven′ient•ly** *adv.*

in•cor•po•rate |ĭn kôr′pə rāt′| *v.* **in•cor•po•rat•ed, in•cor•po•rat•ing. 1.** To form into a legal corporation: *incorporate a business; decided to pool our capital and incorporate.* **2.** To combine or blend into a unified whole; unite: *a new car that incorporates the best features of past models.* **3.** To give a material form to; embody: *a bust that incorporates the sculptor's view of the subject.*

incognito/incommunicado
These two rather similar words are from quite different sources. **Incognito** *was borrowed from Italian in the early seventeenth century.* **Incommunicado** *is an Americanism, borrowed from Mexican Spanish in the early nineteenth century.*

incredible

Incredible *is from Latin* incrēdibilis, *"unbelievable": in-, "not,"* + crēd-, *"believe." Even in Latin it was often used exaggeratedly, to mean "extraordinary" or "amazing." It is now quite difficult to use the word in its literal sense.* He tells incredible stories *might be taken to mean that the stories are remarkable rather than impossible to believe. Much the same thing has happened with the word* **unbelievable.** *In the materials on which this Dictionary was based, the following statement turned up, from a magazine: "There are several unbelievable things about Elvis, but the most incredible is his staying power."*

incubator

indeed

Indeed *is a compound adverb, formed from the phrase* in deed, *"in fact, in reality." It became a single word in the seventeenth century.*

ă pat/ā pay/â care/ä father/ĕ pet/ ē be/ĭ pit/ī pie/î fierce/ŏ pot/ ō go/ô paw, for/oi oil/o͝o book/ o͞o boot/ou out/ŭ cut/û fur/ *th* the/th thin/hw which/zh vision/ ə ago, item, pencil, atom, circus

in•cor•po•rat•ed |ĭn **kôr**′pə rā′tĭd| *adj.* Organized and maintained as a legal business corporation: *an incorporated village.*

in•cor•rect |ĭn′kə **rĕkt′**| *adj.* Not correct; wrong or improper. **—in′cor•rect′ly** *adv.* **—in′cor•rect′ness** *n.*

in•cor•ri•gi•ble |ĭn **kôr**′ĭ jə bəl| *or* |**-kŏr′-**| *adj.* Not capable of being corrected or reformed. *—n.* A person who cannot be reformed. **—in•cor′ri•gi•bil′i•ty** *n.* **—in•cor′ri•gi•bly** *adv.*

in•cor•rupt•i•ble |ĭn′kə **rŭp′**tə bəl| *adj.* Not capable of being corrupted morally; not subject to corruption. **—in′cor•rupt′i•bil′i•ty** *n.* **—in′cor•rupt′i•bly** *adv.*

in•crease |ĭn **krēs′**| *v.* **in•creased, in•creas•ing.** To make or become greater or larger: *Machines increase production. The population increased rapidly.* *—n.* |**ĭn′**krēs′|. **1.** The act of increasing; growth: *the increase of leisure time.* **2.** The amount or rate by which something is increased: *a tax increase of 10 per cent.*

in•creas•ing•ly |ĭn **krē′**sĭng lē| *adv.* More and more: *increasingly difficult.*

in•cred•i•ble |ĭn **krĕd′**ə bəl| *adj.* **1.** Unbelievable: *an incredible excuse.* **2.** Astonishing; amazing: *Her pompadour rose to an incredible height.* [SEE NOTE]

in•cred•u•lous |ĭn **krĕj′**ə ləs| *adj.* **1.** Disbelieving; skeptical: *incredulous of flying-saucer stories.* **2.** Expressive of disbelief or astonishment: *He had an incredulous look on his face.* **—in′cre•du′li•ty** |ĭn′krĭ **do͞o′**lĭ tē| *or* |**-dyo͞o′-**| *n.* **—in•cred′u•lous•ly** *adv.*

in•cre•ment |**ĭn′**krə mənt| *n.* **1.** An increase in number, size, or amount; enlargement. **2.** An added amount, especially one of a series of regular, usually small, additions or stages. **3.** A change, especially a small change, in the value of a mathematical variable.

in•crim•i•nate |ĭn **krĭm′**ə nāt′| *v.* **in•crim•i•nat•ed, in•crim•i•nat•ing.** To charge with or involve in a crime or other wrongful act. **—in•crim′i•na′tion** *n.*

in•crust |ĭn **krŭst′**| *v.* A form of the word **encrust.**

in•cu•bate |**ĭn′**kyə bāt′| *or* |**ĭng′-**| *v.* **in•cu•bat•ed, in•cu•bat•ing.** **1.** To warm and hatch (eggs), as by the heat of a mother bird's body or an artificial source of heat. **2.** To develop; grow. **—in′cu•ba′tion** *n.*

in•cu•ba•tor |**ĭn′**kyə bā′tər| *or* |**ĭng′-**| *n.* **1.** An enclosed space in which a desired temperature can be maintained, used for incubating eggs, cultures of microorganisms, etc. **2.** A device used to supply a prematurely born infant with controlled conditions of temperature, humidity, and oxygen concentration. [SEE PICTURE]

in•cu•bus |**ĭn′**kyə bəs| *or* |**ĭng′-**| *n., pl.* **in•cu•bus•es.** **1.** An evil spirit believed to descend upon and have sexual intercourse with sleeping women. **2.** Anything burdensome.

in•cu•des |ĭn **kyo͞o′**dēz| *n.* Plural of **incus.**

in•cul•cate |ĭn **kŭl′**kāt′| *v.* **in•cul•cat•ed, in•cul•cat•ing.** To teach or impress by forceful urging or frequent repetition; instill: *inculcate a code of ethics.* **—in′cul•ca′tion** *n.*

in•cum•bent |ĭn **kŭm′**bənt| *adj.* **1.** Currently holding a specified office: *the incumbent mayor.* **2.** Imposed as an obligation or duty; required: *an incumbent duty.* *—n.* A person currently holding an office. **—in•cum′ben•cy** *n.*

in•cur |ĭn **kûr′**| *v.* **in•curred, in•cur•ring.** To become liable or subject to as a result of one's actions; bring upon oneself: *I incurred his dislike by telling him the truth.*

in•cur•a•ble |ĭn **kyo͝or′**ə bəl| *adj.* **1.** Not capable of being cured: *an incurable disease.* **2.** Not to be reformed or dissuaded; stubborn: *an incurable optimist.* **—in•cur′a•bly** *adv.*

in•cur•sion |ĭn **kûr′**zhən| *or* |-shən| *n.* A sudden attack on enemy territory; a raid.

in•cus |**ĭng′**kəs| *n., pl.* **in•cu•des** |ĭn **kyo͞o′**dēz|. One of the three small bones in the middle ear; the anvil.

Ind. Indiana.

in•debt•ed |ĭn **dĕt′**ĭd| *adj.* Obligated to another for a loan, gift, or useful service; beholden. **—in•debt′ed•ness** *n.*

in•de•cen•cy |ĭn **dē′**sən sē| *n., pl.* **in•de•cen•cies.** **1.** The condition or quality of being indecent. **2.** Something that is indecent.

in•de•cent |ĭn **dē′**sənt| *adj.* **1.** Offensive to good taste; unseemly. **2.** Offensive to public moral values; immodest. **—in•de′cent•ly** *adv.*

in•de•ci•sion |ĭn′dĭ **sĭzh′**ən| *n.* The condition of being unable to make up one's mind.

in•de•ci•sive |ĭn′dĭ **sī′**sĭv| *adj.* **1.** Not decisive; inconclusive: *an indecisive battle.* **2.** Tending to or marked by indecision; vacillating. **—in′de•ci′sive•ly** *adv.* **—in′de•ci′sive•ness** *n.*

in•dec•o•rous |ĭn **dĕk′**ər əs| *adj.* Lacking propriety; unseemly. **—in•dec′o•rous•ly** *adv.*

in•deed |ĭn **dēd′**| *adv.* **1.** In fact; in reality: *Her parents were indeed pleased with her marks.* **2.** —Used as an intensive: *Yes indeed, I do intend to go out tonight.* *—interj.* A word used to express surprise, irony, or angry or sarcastic disbelief: *We cannot take this money. Why not indeed?* [SEE NOTE]

indef. indefinite.

in•de•fat•i•ga•ble |ĭn′dĭ **făt′**ĭ gə bəl| *adj.* Untiring; tireless. **—in′de•fat′i•ga•bly** *adv.*

in•de•fen•si•ble |ĭn′dĭ **fĕn′**sə bəl| *adj.* Not capable of being defended: *an indefensible town; indefensible behavior.* **—in′de•fen′si•bly** *adv.*

in•de•fin•a•ble |ĭn′dĭ **fī′**nə bəl| *adj.* Not capable of being defined, described, or analyzed: *an indefinable feeling.* **—in′de•fin′a•bly** *adv.*

in•def•i•nite |ĭn **dĕf′**ə nĭt| *adj.* Not definite, especially: **1.** Not fixed: *an indefinite period of time.* **2.** Unclear; vague: *indefinite outlines.* **3.** Not decided; uncertain: *indefinite plans.* **—in•def′i•nite•ly** *adv.* **—in•def′i•nite•ness** *n.*

indefinite article. An article, in English either *a* or *an*, that does not fix the identity of the noun modified.

indefinite pronoun. A pronoun, as English *any* or *some*, that does not specify the identity of its object.

in•del•i•ble |ĭn **dĕl′**ə bəl| *adj.* **1.** Incapable of being removed, erased, or washed away; permanent. **2.** Making an indelible mark: *an indelible pen.* **—in•del′i•bil′i•ty, in•del′i•ble•ness** *n.* **—in•del′i•bly** *adv.*

in•del•i•cate |ĭn **dĕl′**ĭ kĭt| *adj.* **1.** Offensive to propriety; coarse: *an indelicate remark.* **2.** Tactless. **—in•del′i•ca•cy** *n.* **—in•del′i•cate•ly** *adv.*

in•dem•ni•fy |ĭn **dĕm′**nə fī′| *v.* **in•dem•ni•fied,**

in•dem•ni•fy•ing, in•dem•ni•fies. 1. To protect against possible damage, injury, etc.; insure. **2.** To make compensation to for damage or injury suffered. —**in•dem'ni•fi•ca'tion** *n.*

in•dem•ni•ty |ĭn dĕm'nĭ tē| *n., pl.* **in•dem•ni•ties. 1.** Insurance or other security against possible damage, loss, or injury. **2.** Compensation for damage, loss, or injury.

in•dent |ĭn dĕnt'| *v.* **1.** To set in (the first line of a paragraph) from the margin. **2.** To edge with notches or toothlike projections; make jagged: *Coves and capes indent the shoreline.* **3.** To make a dent, recess, or other impression in: *a potter's tool for indenting clay.* —**in•dent'ed** *adj.: an indented leaf.* —*n.* |ĭn'dĕnt'| *or* |ĭn dĕnt'|. An indentation. [SEE NOTE]

in•den•ta•tion |ĭn'dĕn tā'shən| *n.* **1.** The act of indenting or condition of being indented. **2.** The blank space between a margin and the beginning of an indented line. **3.** A deep recess along an edge or boundary. **4.** A notch or jagged cut in an edge, often one of a row forming toothlike projections.

in•den•ture |ĭn dĕn'chər| *n.* A deed or contract between two or more parties, especially one binding one party as a servant to another for a specified period of time. —*v.* **in•den•tured, in•den•tur•ing.** To bind by an indenture. —**in•den'tured** *adj.: indentured servants.*

in•de•pend•ence |ĭn'dĭ pĕn'dəns| *n.* The condition or quality of being independent.

Independence Day. A national holiday celebrated on July 4 in honor of the adoption of the Declaration of Independence in 1776.

in•de•pend•ent |ĭn'dĭ pĕn'dənt| *adj.* **1.** Politically autonomous; self-governing: *an independent country.* **2.** Free from the influence, control, or guidance of others; self-reliant: *an independent mind.* **3.** Not dependent on or connected with a larger or controlling group, system, etc.: *an independent food store.* **4.** Not committed to any one political party: *an independent voter.* **5.** Earning one's own living; self-supporting. **6.** Providing or being sufficient income to enable one to live without working: *a man of independent means.* —**in'de•pend'ent•ly** *adv.*

independent clause. A clause containing a subject, a verb, and sometimes an object and modifiers, capable of standing alone as a complete sentence.

independent variable. In a mathematical function, any of the set of variables, often containing but a single member, whose values, once fixed, determine a unique value of the dependent variable.

in-depth |ĭn'dĕpth'| *adj.* In greater detail than usual: *an in-depth television report.*

in•de•scrib•a•ble |ĭn'dĭ skrī'bə bəl| *adj.* **1.** Not capable of being described. **2.** Beyond description: *indescribable delight.* —**in'de•scrib'a•bly** *adv.*

in•de•struc•ti•ble |ĭn'dĭ strŭk'tə bəl| *adj.* Not capable of being destroyed. —**in'de•struc'ti•bly** *adv.*

in•de•ter•mi•nate |ĭn'dĭ tûr'mə nĭt| *adj.* Not capable of being determined; not precisely defined; vague: *a person of indeterminate age.*

in•dex |ĭn'dĕks'| *n., pl.* **in•dex•es** or **in•di•ces** |ĭn'dĭ-sēz'|. **1.** Anything that serves to guide, point out, or aid reference: **a.** An alphabetized listing of the names, places, and subjects in a printed work, giving the page on which each can be found. **b.** A series of notches cut into the edge of a book for easy access to chapters or other divisions. **c.** Any table, file, or catalogue. **2.** Anything that reveals or indicates; a sign: *A person's face is an index to his mood.* **3.** A small number that is positioned just above and to the left of a radical sign to show what root is to be extracted; for example, $\sqrt[4]{x}$ is read "the fourth root of *x*," the 4 being the index. If no index is written, then a 2 is understood. **4.** Something that serves as a reference or pointer, as in a scientific instrument. **5.** A ratio or coefficient used as a measure of some property or action, as in science. —*v.* **1.** To furnish with an index: *index a reference book.* **2.** To enter (an item) in an index.

in•dex•a•tion |ĭn'dĕk sā'shən| *n.* The linking of economic factors, as wages or prices, to a cost-of-living index so that they rise and fall within the rate of inflation.

index finger. The finger next to the thumb.

index of refraction. The quotient of the speed of light in a vacuum divided by the speed of light in a medium under consideration.

In•di•a |ĭn'dē ə|. The second most populous country in the world, located in southern Asia. Population, 550,000,000. Capital, New Delhi. [SEE NOTE]

India ink. A black liquid ink made from lampblack.

In•di•an |ĭn'dē ən| *n.* **1.** A native or inhabitant of India. **2.** An **American Indian.** —*adj.* **1.** Of India or its inhabitants. **2.** Of the American Indians or their languages and culture.

In•di•an•a |ĭn'dē ăn'ə|. A Midwestern state of the United States. Population, 5,490,179. Capital, Indianapolis.

In•di•an•ap•o•lis |ĭn'dē ə năp'ə lĭs|. The capital of Indiana. Population, 700,807.

Indian club. A bottle-shaped wooden club swung in the hand for gymnastic exercise.

Indian corn. *Chiefly British.* The kind of corn generally grown in North America; maize.

Indian meal. Cornmeal.

Indian Ocean. An ocean lying between Africa, Asia, Australia, and Antarctica.

Indian paintbrush. A plant with clusters of bright-red, petallike leaves surrounding the small, greenish flowers. [SEE PICTURE]

Indian summer. A period of mild weather occurring in late autumn or early winter.

Indian Territory. A former territory in the south-central United States administered by Indian tribes until its inclusion in the new state of Oklahoma in 1907.

in•di•cate |ĭn'dĭ kāt'| *v.* **in•di•cat•ed, in•di•cat•ing. 1.** To show or point out precisely: *indicate a route.* **2.** To serve as a sign or symptom of; signify: *dark clouds indicating rain.* **3.** To state or express briefly: *He indicated his wishes.*

in•di•ca•tion |ĭn'dĭ kā'shən| *n.* **1.** The act of indicating. **2.** Something that indicates; a sign, token, or symptom.

in•dic•a•tive |ĭn dĭk'ə tĭv| *adj.* **1.** Serving to point out or indicate: *an action indicative of his attitude.* **2.** Designating a verb mood that is used in a statement or question of fact; for example, *He*

indent

Indent *is from Old French* endenter, *"to make notches in":* en, *"in,"* + dent, *"tooth, tooth mark."* (Dent *is from Latin* dens, dent-, *"tooth," from which we have also* **dentist, trident,** *etc.*)

India, etc.

India *is named after the river Indus. In the Middle Ages, Europeans called the islands of Southeast Asia* the Indies. *When Columbus discovered the islands of Central America, it was believed that they were a part of the Indies. Later, when it was seen that this was a huge mistake, the old Indies were called the* **East Indies** *and the new ones the* **West Indies.** *Ever since Columbus's mistake, the native peoples of North and South America have been called* **Indians** *(*Indios *in Spanish).*

Indian paintbrush

went and *Did he go?* are in the indicative mood. —*n.* **1.** The indicative mood. **2.** A verb in this mood.

in•di•ca•tor |ĭn′dĭ kā′tər| *n.* **1.** Something that indicates, as a pointer or index. **2.** Any meter, gauge, warning light, etc., that tells something about the operation of a furnace, engine, or other machine or system. **3.** A chemical compound, such as litmus, that shows a characteristic change in color under certain known conditions, used in making chemical tests.

in•di•ces |ĭn′dĭ sēz′| *n.* A plural of **index.**

in•dict |ĭn dīt′| *v.* **1.** To accuse of a crime; charge. **2.** To make a formal accusation against by the findings of a grand jury.

in•dict•ment |ĭn dīt′mənt| *n.* **1. a.** The act of indicting: *the indictment of a suspect by a grand jury.* **b.** The condition of being indicted: *under indictment for murder.* **2.** A written statement, drawn up by the prosecuting attorney, listing the charges against an accused person.

in•dif•fer•ence |ĭn dĭf′ər əns| *or* |-dĭf′rəns| *n.* **1.** Lack of concern or interest. **2.** Lack of importance; insignificance: *a matter of indifference.*

in•dif•fer•ent |ĭn dĭf′ər ənt| *or* |-dĭf′rənt| *adj.* **1.** Having or showing no interest; not caring one way or the other. **2.** Showing no preference; impartial. **3.** Neither good nor bad; mediocre: *The musician gave an indifferent performance.* —**in•dif′fer•ent•ly** *adv.*

in•dig•e•nous |ĭn dĭj′ə nəs| *adj.* Of a kind or species originally living or growing in a region rather than coming or being brought from another part of the world: *The bison and the jack-in-the-pulpit are indigenous to North America.*

in•di•gent |ĭn′dĭ jənt| *adj.* Lacking the means to live; very poor; needy. —*n.* A very poor or needy person. —**in′di•gence** *n.*

in•di•gest•i•ble |ĭn′dĭ jĕs′tə bəl| *or* |-dī-| *adj.* Difficult or impossible to digest.

in•di•ges•tion |ĭn′dĭ jĕs′chən| *or* |-dī-| *n.* **1.** The inability to digest food. **2.** Discomfort or illness that accompanies this.

in•dig•nant |ĭn dĭg′nənt| *adj.* Feeling or expressing indignation: *indignant over her remarks.* —**in•dig′nant•ly** *adv.*

in•dig•na•tion |ĭn′dĭg nā′shən| *n.* Anger aroused by something unjust, mean, etc.

in•dig•ni•ty |ĭn dĭg′nĭ tē| *n., pl.* **in•dig•ni•ties.** Something that offends a person's pride and sense of dignity; an affront.

in•di•go |ĭn′dĭ gō′| *n., pl.* **in•di•gos** or **in•di•goes. 1. a.** A plant that yields a blue dye. **b.** A dark-blue dye obtained from this plant or an artificially made dye of the same color. **2.** A dark blue. —*adj.* Dark blue. [SEE NOTE]

indigo/indium

Indigo *comes from an earlier form,* indico, *and ultimately from Greek* indikon (pharmakon), *"the plant indigo" or "the blue dye indigo." The origin of the Greek word is Greek* Indikos, *"of India."* **Indium** *is from Latin* indicum, *"indigo" and is so called because of the indigo-blue color of its spectrum.*

in•di•rect |ĭn′də rĕkt′| *or* |-dī-| *adj.* **1.** Not taking a direct course; roundabout: *an indirect route.* **2.** Not straight to the point, as in talking. **3.** Not directly planned for; secondary: *indirect benefits.* —**in•di•rect′ly** *adv.* —**in•di•rect′ness** *n.*

indirect object. A grammatical object indirectly affected by the action of a verb; for example, *me* in *Sing me a song* and *turtle* in *He feeds the turtle lettuce* are indirect objects.

in•dis•creet |ĭn′dĭ skrēt′| *adj.* Lacking discretion; unwise or tactless. —**in′dis•creet′ly** *adv.*

in•dis•cre•tion |ĭn′dĭ skrĕsh′ən| *n.* **1.** Lack of discretion. **2.** An indiscreet act or remark.

in•dis•crim•i•nate |ĭn′dĭ skrĭm′ə nĭt| *adj.* **1.** Lacking in discrimination; exercising or showing no care in choosing: *an indiscriminate shopper.* **2.** Not sorted out or put in order; confused: *an indiscriminate pile of letters.* —**in′dis•crim′i•nate•ly** *adv.*

in•dis•pen•sa•ble |ĭn′dĭ spĕn′sə bəl| *adj.* Not capable of being dispensed with; essential; required: *Some bacteria are indispensable to man.* —**in′dis•pen′sa•bly** *adv.*

in•dis•posed |ĭn′dĭ spōzd′| *adj.* **1.** Mildly ill. **2.** Unwilling; averse: *indisposed to help.*

in•dis•po•si•tion |ĭn′dĭs pə zĭsh′ən| *n.* **1.** A minor ailment. **2.** Unwillingness.

in•dis•put•a•ble |ĭn′dĭ spyōō′tə bəl| *adj.* Not capable of being disputed; beyond doubt; undeniable. —**in′dis•put′a•bly** *adv.*

in•dis•sol•u•ble |ĭn′dĭ sŏl′yə bəl| *adj.* **1.** Not capable of being dissolved. **2.** Not capable of being broken or undone; permanent: *an indissoluble bond.* —**in′dis•sol′u•bly** *adv.*

in•dis•tinct |ĭn′dĭ stĭngkt′| *adj.* Not clearly heard, seen, or understood: *an indistinct sound.* —**in′dis•tinct′ly** *adv.* —**in′dis•tinct′ness** *n.*

in•dis•tin•guish•a•ble |ĭn′dĭ stĭng′gwĭ shə bəl| *adj.* **1.** Not capable of being perceived: *an indistinguishable difference.* **2.** Without distinctive qualities; hard to tell apart from others: *a small town indistinguishable from a thousand others.*

in•di•um |ĭn′dē əm| *n.* Symbol **In** One of the elements, a soft, silvery metal. Atomic number 49; atomic weight 114.82; valences +1, +2, +3; melting point 156.61°C; boiling point 2,000°C. [SEE NOTE]

in•di•vid•u•al |ĭn′də vĭj′ōō əl| *adj.* **1.** Existing as a distinct human being or thing; single; separate: *for each individual child; individual words.* **2.** Of, by, or for one person: *an individual portion.* **3.** Having a special quality; unique; distinct: *the individual aroma of cloves.* —*n.* **1.** A single person, plant, or animal considered separately from a group or from society. **2.** A particular person: *a disagreeable individual.*

in•di•vid•u•al•ism |ĭn′də vĭj′ōō ə lĭz′əm| *n.* **1.** The assertion of one's own will and personality; personal independence. **2.** Self-reliance. **3. a.** The theory that the individual is more important than the state or social group. **b.** The theory that the individual should be free to advance himself economically and should succeed by his own initiative.

in•di•vid•u•al•ist |ĭn′də vĭj′ōō ə lĭst| *n.* A person who is independent in thought and action.

in•di•vid•u•al•is•tic |ĭn′də vĭj′ōō ə lĭs′tĭk| *adj.* **1.** Different from others; distinctive: *an individualistic style.* **2.** Proudly independent in thought and action: *individualistic pioneers.* —**in′di•vid′u•al•is′ti•cal•ly** *adv.*

in•di•vid•u•al•i•ty |ĭn′də vĭj′ōō ăl′ĭ tē| *n., pl.* **in•di•vid•u•al•i•ties. 1.** The quality of being individual; distinctness: *music for two voices, each having individuality.* **2.** The qualities that make a person or thing different from others; distinctive identity: *expressing one's individuality.*

in•di•vid•u•al•ly |ĭn′də vĭj′ōō ə lē| *adv.* As individuals; singly; separately: *The principal knew all the students individually.*

in•di•vis•i•ble |ĭn′də vĭz′ə bəl| *adj.* **1.** Not capable of being divided. **2.** Not capable of being divided so as to give a quotient that is an integer and leave no remainder; for example, 7 is indivisible by 3. —**in'di·vis'i·bly** *adv.*

In·do·chi·na |ĭn'dō chē'nə|. The peninsula of southeastern Asia including Burma, Thailand, Laos, Cambodia, Vietnam, and the Malay Peninsula. —**In'do·chi·nese'** *adj. & n.*

in·doc·tri·nate |ĭn dŏk'trə nāt'| *v.* **in·doc·tri·nat·ed, in·doc·tri·nat·ing. 1.** To instruct in a body of doctrine. **2.** To teach to accept a system of thought uncritically. —**in·doc'tri·na'tion** *n.*

In·do-Eu·ro·pe·an |ĭn'dō yo͝or'ə pē'ən| *n.* **1.** A prehistoric language that is the ancestor of English, German, Russian, Gaelic, Latin, Greek, Persian, Sanskrit, and many other languages. **2.** One of the people who spoke this language. —*adj.* Of this ancestral language or the languages descended from it. [SEE NOTE]

in·do·lent |ĭn'də lənt| *adj.* **1.** Disinclined to work; habitually lazy. **2.** Suggesting a calm idleness and ease: *an indolent sigh.* —**in'do·lence** *n.*

in·dom·i·ta·ble |ĭn dŏm'ĭ tə bəl| *adj.* Not capable of being overcome or subdued; unconquerable. —**in·dom'i·ta·bly** *adv.*

In·do·ne·sia |ĭn'də nē'zhə| *or* |-shə|. A country in Southeast Asia, consisting of the islands of Sumatra, Java, Sulawesi, and many others, as well as parts of the islands of Borneo, Timor, and New Guinea. Population, 147,383,000. Capital, Djakarta. —**In'do·ne'sian** *adj. & n.*

in·door |ĭn'dôr'| *or* |-dōr'| *adj.* Of, situated in, or carried on within a house or other building: *an indoor pool; an indoor party.*

in·doors |ĭn dôrz'| *or* |-dōrz'| *adv.* In or into a house or other building: *staying indoors.*

in·dorse |ĭn dôrs'| *v.* **in·dorsed, in·dors·ing.** A form of the word **endorse.**

in·dorse·ment |ĭn dôrs'mənt| *n.* A form of the word **endorsement.**

in·du·bi·ta·ble |ĭn do͞o'bĭ tə bəl| *or* |-dyo͞o'-| *adj.* Too apparent to be doubted; unquestionable: *indubitable evidence.* —**in·du'bi·ta·bly** *adv.*

in·duce |ĭn do͞os'| *or* |-dyo͞os'| *v.* **in·duced, in·duc·ing. 1.** To persuade; influence; prevail upon: *Nothing could induce him to stay, and so he said good-by.* **2.** To cause or stimulate the occurrence of: *induce vomiting in a patient.* **3.** To reach (a conclusion or general law) by logical induction. **4.** To produce (electricity or magnetism) by induction.

in·duce·ment |ĭn do͞os'mənt| *or* |-dyo͞os'-| *n.* **1.** The act or process of inducing. **2.** Something that induces; an incentive; motive.

in·duct |ĭn dŭkt'| *v.* **1.** To place formally in office. **2.** To call into military service; draft.

in·duc·tance |ĭn dŭk'təns| *n.* **1.** An electric circuit element, typically a coil of wire, in which an electromotive force is produced by a magnetic field that varies with time. **2.** The measure of the characteristic electrical property of such a circuit element, expressed as the voltage induced per unit change in the magnetic field or as the voltage induced per unit change in the current.

in·duc·tee |ĭn'dŭk tē'| *n.* A person inducted or about to be inducted into the armed forces.

in·duc·tion |ĭn dŭk'shən| *n.* **1.** The act of inducting into office. **2.** The process of being enrolled in the armed forces. **3.** A method of reasoning or mathematical proof in which a conclusion is reached about all the members of a given set by examining just a few members of the set. **4. a.** The generation of an electromotive force across a circuit element by a magnetic field that changes with time. **b.** The generation of an electromotive force across a circuit element as a current that changes with time passes through it. **c.** The production of an electric charge in an uncharged body by bringing a charged body close to it. [SEE NOTE]

induction coil. A type of transformer, often used in automobile ignition systems, in which an interrupted direct current is changed into an interrupted high-voltage alternating current.

in·duc·tive |ĭn dŭk'tĭv| *adj.* **1.** Of or using induction: *inductive reasoning; an inductive proof.* **2.** Of, resulting from, or marked by electrical or electromagnetic inductance. —**in·duc'tive·ly** *adv.*

inductive reactance. The opposition to an electric current, especially a changing or alternating current, that is caused by an inductance in a circuit.

in·duc·tor |ĭn dŭk'tər| *n.* An electric circuit element, typically a coil of wire, having inductance as its principal property; an inductance.

in·dulge |ĭn dŭlj'| *v.* **in·dulged, in·dulg·ing. 1.** To yield to the desires of; pamper: *indulge a child.* **2.** To gratify or satisfy (a desire): *indulge a craving for chocolate.* **3.** To allow oneself some special pleasure: *indulge in an afternoon nap.* **4.** To engage; take part: *indulge in sports.*

in·dul·gence |ĭn dŭl'jəns| *n.* **1.** The act of indulging: *an occasional indulgence in rich food.* **2.** Something indulged in: *Sports cars are an expensive indulgence.* **3.** Liberal or lenient treatment: *parental indulgence.* **4.** In the Roman Catholic Church, the remission of punishment due for a sin after the guilt has been forgiven.

in·dul·gent |ĭn dŭl'jənt| *adj.* Showing, marked by, or given to indulgence; lenient: *an indulgent guardian.* —**in·dul'gent·ly** *adv.*

In·dus |ĭn'dəs|. A river rising in southwestern Tibet and flowing through Pakistan into the Indian Ocean.

in·dus·tri·al |ĭn dŭs'trē əl| *adj.* **1.** Of or having to do with industry: *industrial products.* **2.** Having highly developed industries: *an industrial nation.* **3.** Used in industry: *industrial diamonds.* —**in·dus'tri·al·ly** *adv.*

in·dus·tri·al·ist |ĭn dŭs'trē ə lĭst| *n.* A person who owns or runs a large industrial enterprise.

in·dus·tri·al·ize |ĭn dŭs'trē ə līz'| *v.* **in·dus·tri·al·ized, in·dus·tri·al·iz·ing.** To make industrial rather than agricultural; develop industries in. —**in·dus'tri·al·i·za'tion** *n.*

Industrial Revolution. A gradual shift from hand tools and home manufacturing to power-driven tools and large-scale factory production that began in England in about 1760 and continued into the 20th century.

in·dus·tri·ous |ĭn dŭs'trē əs| *adj.* Hard-working; diligent: *an industrious student.* —**in·dus'tri·ous·ly** *adv.* —**in·dus'tri·ous·ness** *n.*

in·dus·try |ĭn'də strē| *n., pl.* **in·dus·tries. 1. a.** The manufacture or production of goods on a large scale. **b.** A specific branch of such activity: *the motion-picture industry.* **2.** Hard work; steady effort: *I admire your industry.*

in·e·bri·ate |ĭ nē'brē āt'| *v.* **in·e·bri·at·ed, in·**

Indo-European

The original **Indo-European** *language was spoken in its original form as early as 4000* B.C.*—long before writing was invented. This language survived in many altered forms (Greek, Latin, Old English, etc.), which were written down in ancient times; thus many of the original words can be reconstructed by comparing the later forms. English, as one of the modern descendants of this prehistoric language, inherits numerous Indo-European words whose changing histories can be traced through six thousand years. English has also borrowed many other words from neighboring Indo-European languages such as French and German, so that often one ancestral word has been both* inherited *into English and later separately* borrowed *in another form. For examples, see the notes at* **acre, father, nose.**

induction

Mathematical **induction** *as a method of proof is applicable to a theorem that divides into a number of cases, each case corresponding to one of the natural numbers. If it can be shown that the theorem is true in the first case, and that if it is true for the* n*th case it must be true for the* n + *1st case, then it must be true for all cases. For example, if we observe that the sun rose today, and if we can prove that if the sun rises on any particular day, it must also rise the next day, it follows by mathematical induction that the sun must rise every day.*

infamy
On the day after Pearl Harbor Day, President Roosevelt broadcast to the nation: "Yesterday, December 7, 1941—a date that will live in infamy—the United States of America was suddenly and deliberately attacked by naval and air forces of the Empire of Japan." The original draft of the speech had read ". . . a day which will live in history . . ."; at the last moment, Roosevelt changed "history" to "infamy," which gives the whole passage a much stronger bite.

infant/infantry
Infant *is from Latin* infāns, infant-, *"baby, person who has not learned to speak":* in-, *"not, un-,"* + fā-, *"speak." In medieval Italian, Latin* infant- *became* infante *and took on the meaning "boy, young man," and then "young soldier, foot soldier." From* infante *in this sense was formed* infanteria, *"the foot soldiers collectively"; this was borrowed into English as* **infantry**.

ă pat/ā pay/â care/ä father/ĕ pet/ ē be/ĭ pit/ī pie/î fierce/ŏ pot/ ō go/ô paw, for/oi oil/ŏŏ book/ ōō boot/ou out/ŭ cut/û fur/ *th* the/th thin/hw which/zh vision/ ə ago, item, pencil, atom, circus

e•bri•at•ing. To intoxicate, as with alcohol; make drunk. —**in•e'bri•at'ed** *adj.: in an inebriated condition.* —*adj.* |ĭ **nē'**brē ĭt|. Intoxicated; drunken. —*n.* |ĭ **nē'**brē ĭt|. An intoxicated person, especially a drunkard.

in•ed•i•ble |ĭn **ĕd'**ə bəl| *adj.* Not edible; not suitable for food.

in•ef•fa•ble |ĭn **ĕf'**ə bəl| *adj.* **1.** Too great to express; beyond description: *ineffable joy.* **2.** Too sacred to be uttered: *the ineffable name of God.* —**in•ef'fa•bly** *adv.*

in•ef•fec•tive |ĭn'ĭ **fĕk'**tĭv| *adj.* **1.** Not effective; not producing results: *His attempt proved ineffective.* **2.** Not performing satisfactorily; incompetent: *an ineffective governor.* —**in'ef•fec'tive•ly** *adv.* —**in'ef•fec'tive•ness** *n.*

in•ef•fec•tu•al |ĭn'ĭ **fĕk'**chōō əl| *adj.* Not having the desired effect; vain: *Our protests proved ineffectual.* —**in'ef•fec'tu•al•ly** *adv.*

in•ef•fi•cien•cy |ĭn'ĭ **fĭsh'**ən sē| *n.* The condition, quality, or property of being inefficient.

in•ef•fi•cient |ĭn'ĭ **fĭsh'**ənt| *adj.* Wasteful of time, effort, materials, fuel, or energy: *an inefficient clerk; an inefficient machine.* —**in'ef•fi'cient•ly** *adv.*

in•e•las•tic |ĭn'ĭ **lăs'**tĭk| *adj.* Not capable of returning to its original shape or dimensions after being deformed; not elastic. —**in'e•las•tic'i•ty** *n.*

in•el•e•gant |ĭn **ĕl'**ĭ gənt| *adj.* Not elegant; lacking grace or good taste. —**in•el'e•gance** *n.* —**in•el'e•gant•ly** *adv.*

in•el•i•gi•ble |ĭn **ĕl'**ĭ jə bəl| *adj.* Not eligible; not qualified: *ineligible to vote; ineligible for citizenship.* —**in•el'i•gi•bil'i•ty** *n.*

in•ept |ĭn **ĕpt'**| *adj.* **1.** Lacking skill or competence: *an inept actor; an inept performance.* **2.** Inappropriate: *an inept suggestion.* —**in•ept'ly** *adv.*

in•ept•i•tude |ĭn **ĕp'**tĭ tōōd'| *or* |-tyōōd'| *n.* **1.** Lack of skill or competence. **2.** An inept act or remark.

in•e•qual•i•ty |ĭn'ĭ **kwŏl'**ĭ tē| *n., pl.* **in•e•qual•i•ties. 1.** The condition of being unequal: *the inequality of two line segments.* **2.** Lack of regularity; unevenness. **3. a.** A condition, as of society, in which some people or classes are favored over others. **b.** An example of this condition: *the inequalities that exist in housing, job opportunities, and education.* **4.** A mathematical statement that two numbers are not equal or that one is greater than or less than the other.

inequality sign. In mathematics, any of the signs $\neq$ (not equal), $>$ (greater than), or $<$ (less than), used in writing inequalities.

in•eq•ui•ta•ble |ĭn **ĕk'**wĭ tə bəl| *adj.* Not equitable; unfair; unjust: *an inequitable division of work.* —**in•eq'ui•ta•bly** *adv.*

in•ert |ĭ **nûrt'**| *adj.* **1.** Resisting change or motion; having inertia. **2.** Slow to move, act, or respond; sluggish. **3.** Incapable of reacting with other elements to form chemical compounds: *Helium is an inert gas.* —**in•ert'ly** *adv.*

in•er•tia |ĭ **nûr'**shə| *n.* **1.** The tendency of a physical body to remain at rest if at rest or, if moving, to continue moving in a straight line unless a force is applied to it. **2.** Resistance to move, act, or change.

in•er•tial guidance. |ĭ **nûr'**shəl|. Guidance, as for missiles, in which devices such as gyroscopes and pendulums are used to provide data or references for determining a course.

in•es•cap•a•ble |ĭn'ĭ **skā'**pə bəl| *adj.* Not capable of being avoided, denied, or overlooked: *inescapable duties.* —**in'es•cap'a•bly** *adv.*

in•es•ti•ma•ble |ĭn **ĕs'**tə mə bəl| *adj.* Too great or valuable to be estimated: *an inestimable service to all.* —**in•es'ti•ma•bly** *adv.*

in•ev•i•ta•ble |ĭn **ĕv'**ĭ tə bəl| *adj.* Not capable of being avoided or prevented: *an inevitable outcome.* —**in•ev'i•ta•bly** *adv.*

in•ex•act |ĭn'ĭg **zăkt'**| *adj.* Not exact; not quite accurate or precise. —**in'ex•act'ly** *adv.*

in•ex•cus•a•ble |ĭn'ĭk **skyōō'**zə bəl| *adj.* Impossible to excuse, pardon, or justify: *inexcusable behavior.* —**in'ex•cus'a•bly** *adv.*

in•ex•haust•i•ble |ĭn'ĭg **zô'**stə bəl| *adj.* Not capable of being used up; unlimited: *an inexhaustible supply of food.* —**in'ex•haust'i•bly** *adv.*

in•ex•o•ra•ble |ĭn **ĕk'**sər ə bəl| *adj.* **1.** Not capable of being persuaded or moderated by pleas: *The inexorable will of a dictator.* **2.** Not to be altered, avoided, or diverted; relentless: *inexorable doom.* —**in•ex'o•ra•bly** *adv.*

in•ex•pen•sive |ĭn'ĭk **spĕn'**sĭv| *adj.* Not expensive; low-priced; cheap. —**in'ex•pen'sive•ly** *adv.*

in•ex•pe•ri•ence |ĭn'ĭk **spîr'**ē əns| *n.* Lack of experience.

in•ex•pe•ri•enced |ĭn'ĭk **spîr'**ē ənst| *adj.* Lacking experience and the knowledge gained from experience.

in•ex•pert |ĭn **ĕk'**spûrt'| *adj.* Not expert; unskilled. —**in•ex'pert'ly** *adv.*

in•ex•pli•ca•ble |ĭn **ĕk'**splĭ kə bəl| *or* |ĭn'ĭk**splĭk'**ə bəl| *adj.* Not capable of being explained: *An inexplicable fear came over me.* —**in•ex'pli•ca•bly** *adv.*

in•ex•press•i•ble |ĭn'ĭk **sprĕs'**ə bəl| *adj.* Not capable of being expressed; indescribable: *inexpressible joy.* —**in'ex•press'i•bly** *adv.*

in•ex•tri•ca•ble |ĭn **ĕk'**strĭ kə bəl| *adj.* **1.** Not capable of being escaped from: *an inextricable trap.* **2.** Not capable of being untied or loosened: *an inextricable knot.* **3.** Not capable of being solved or set in order: *inextricable difficulties.* —**in•ex'tri•ca•bly** *adv.*

in•fal•li•ble |ĭn **făl'**ə bəl| *adj.* **1.** Not capable of making a mistake: *No man is infallible.* **2.** Not capable of failing: *an infallible cure for stage fright.* —**in•fal'li•bil'i•ty** *n.* —**in•fal'li•bly** *adv.*

in•fa•mous |**ĭn'**fə məs| *adj.* **1.** Having an exceedingly bad reputation; notorious: *an infamous racketeer.* **2.** Deserving universal condemnation; shocking; outrageous: *infamous deeds.* —**in'fa•mous•ly** *adv.*

in•fa•my |**ĭn'**fə mē| *n., pl.* **in•fa•mies. 1.** The condition of being infamous: *Franklin D. Roosevelt called December 7, 1941, "a day that will live in infamy."* **2.** Evil reputation. **3.** An infamous act; an outrage. [SEE NOTE]

in•fan•cy |**ĭn'**fən sē| *n., pl.* **in•fan•cies. 1.** The condition or time of being an infant. **2.** The earliest years or stage of something.

in•fant |**ĭn'**fənt| *n.* **1.** A child from the earliest period of its life up to about two years of age; a baby. **2.** In law, one who has not yet reached the age of majority; a minor. —***modifier:*** *an infant son; infant mortality.* [SEE NOTE]

in•fan•tile |ĭn′fən tīl′| *or* |-tĭl| *adj.* **1.** Of or having to do with infants or infancy: *infantile diseases.* **2.** Typical of what one would expect from an infant; childish: *infantile behavior.*

infantile paralysis. Poliomyelitis.

in•fan•til•ism |ĭn′fən tə lĭz′əm| *n.* A disorder in which a person reaches the age of adulthood but retains an infantile mentality, is stunted in growth, and is physically not mature.

in•fan•try |ĭn′fən trē| *n., pl.* **in•fan•tries.** The branch of an army made up of units trained to fight on foot. **—modifier:** *an infantry officer.* [SEE NOTE on p. 466]

in•fan•try•man |ĭn′fən trē mən| *n., pl.* **-men** |-mən|. A soldier in the infantry.

in•fat•u•ate |ĭn făch′o͞o āt′| *v.* **in•fat•u•at•ed, in•fat•u•at•ing.** To fill with a strong and foolish passion or attraction. **—in•fat′u•a′tion** *n.*

in•fect |ĭn fĕkt′| *v.* **1.** To contaminate or become contaminated with microorganisms that cause disease. **2.** To transmit a disease to.

in•fec•tion |ĭn fĕk′shən| *n.* **1. a.** The entry of microorganisms into the body or a part of the body, where they multiply and damage tissue or cause disease. **b.** The diseased condition resulting from this. **2.** An infectious disease.

in•fec•tious |ĭn fĕk′shəs| *adj.* **1.** Caused or spread by infection: *an infectious disease.* **2.** Tending to spread easily or catch on: *infectious laughter.* **—in•fec′tious•ly** *adv.*

in•fer |ĭn fûr′| *v.* **in•ferred, in•fer•ring.** To conclude from evidence; deduce. [SEE NOTE]

in•fer•ence |ĭn′fər əns| *or* |-frəns| *n.* **1.** The act or process of inferring: *arrive at a conclusion by inference.* **2.** Something inferred.

in•fe•ri•or |ĭn fîr′ē ər| *adj.* **1.** Low or lower in order, degree, or rank: *a person of inferior station; an inferior post in the company.* **2.** Low or lower in quality: *inferior merchandise.* **3.** Low or lower in ability, intelligence, etc.: *His brilliance makes me feel inferior.* **4.** Situated beneath or below; lower: *the inferior section of the spine.* **—n.** A person of lesser rank or status than others. [SEE NOTE]

in•fe•ri•or•i•ty |ĭn fîr′ē ôr′ĭ tē| *or* |-ŏr′-| *n.* The fact or quality of being inferior.

inferiority complex. A persistent feeling, and often the behavior arising from this feeling, of being an inadequate or worthless person.

in•fer•nal |ĭn fûr′nəl| *adj.* **1.** Of or resembling hell. **2.** Abominable; damnable: *an infernal nuisance.* **—in•fer′nal•ly** *adv.*

in•fer•no |ĭn fûr′nō| *n., pl.* **in•fer•nos.** A place resembling or suggesting hell, as in being chaotic, noisy, or intensely hot.

in•fest |ĭn fĕst′| *v.* To live in or overrun in large numbers so as to be harmful or unpleasant: *Rats infested the building.* **—in′fes•ta′tion** *n.*

in•fi•del |ĭn′fĭ dəl| *or* |-dĕl′| *n.* **1.** A person who is not a Christian. **2.** A person who is not a Moslem. **3.** A person who believes in no religion.

in•fi•del•i•ty |ĭn′fĭ dĕl′ĭ tē| *n., pl.* **in•fi•del•i•ties.** **1.** Unfaithfulness; disloyalty: *guilty of infidelity to his country.* **2.** Adultery. **3.** An unfaithful or adulterous act.

in•field |ĭn′fēld′| *n.* **1. a.** The area of a baseball field enclosed by the foul lines and the arc of the outfield grass just beyond the bases. **b.** The four infielders of a baseball team. **2.** The area inside a racetrack or running track.

in•field•er |ĭn′fēl′dər| *n.* A baseball player whose defensive position is in the infield; a first baseman, second baseman, shortstop, or third baseman.

in•fil•trate |ĭn fĭl′trāt′| *or* |ĭn′fĭl-| *v.* **in•fil•trat•ed, in•fil•trat•ing.** **1.** To pass (a liquid or gas) into something through tiny openings. **2.** To fill or saturate (something) by infiltrating a liquid or gas into it. **3.** To enter gradually or secretly: *Government agents infiltrated the organization.* **—in′fil•tra′tion** *n.*

in•fi•nite |ĭn′fə nĭt| *adj.* **1.** Having no limit in space, extent, number, or time; endless: *The universe is usually assumed to be infinite.* **2. a.** Greater in value than any specified number, however large: *an infinite number.* **b.** Having a measure that is infinite: *an infinite plane.* **3.** Seemingly without limit: *an infinite variety of colors.* **—n.** **1.** An infinite thing or quantity. **2. the infinite.** God. **—in′fi•nite•ly** *adv.*

in•fin•i•tes•i•mal |ĭn′fĭn ĭ tĕs′ə məl| *adj.* **1.** Extremely small; minute: *Matter is made up of infinitesimal units called atoms.* **2. a.** Exceeding zero by less than any specified number; as close to zero as one pleases. **b.** Having an infinitesimal measure: *an infinitesimal line segment.* **—n.** In mathematics, a function whose value becomes infinitesimal. **—in′fin•i•tes′i•mal•ly** *adv.*

in•fin•i•tive |ĭn fĭn′ĭ tĭv| *n.* A verb form that is not inflected to indicate person, number, or tense. In English, it is usually preceded by *to* or by an auxiliary verb. For example, in the phrases *wanted to leave* and *will play tomorrow, leave* and *play* are infinitives. **—adj.** Of or using the infinitive.

in•fin•i•ty |ĭn fĭn′ĭ tē| *n., pl.* **in•fin•i•ties.** **1.** A space, distance, period of time, or quantity that is or appears to be without limit or end. **2.** The quality or condition of being infinite. **3. a.** A quantity, not a number in the usual sense, whose value exceeds that of any chosen number, however large. **b.** A coordinate of a point that is considered to be an infinite distance away from a reference point. [SEE NOTE]

in•firm |ĭn fûrm′| *adj.* Weak in body, as from old age or sickness; feeble. **—in•firm′ly** *adv.*

in•fir•ma•ry |ĭn fûr′mə rē| *n., pl.* **in•fir•ma•ries.** A place for the care of sick or injured persons; a small hospital or dispensary.

in•fir•mi•ty |ĭn fûr′mĭ tē| *n., pl.* **in•fir•mi•ties.** **1.** The condition of being infirm; bodily weakness; frailty. **2.** A disease or disorder that causes this.

in•flame |ĭn flām′| *v.* **in•flamed, in•flam•ing.** **1. a.** To cause inflammation of (body tissues). **b.** To be affected by inflammation. **2.** To arouse to anger or other strong emotion: *His speech inflamed the crowd.* **—in•flamed′** *adj.: an inflamed membrane.*

in•flam•ma•ble |ĭn flăm′ə bəl| *adj.* **1.** Tending to catch fire easily and burn rapidly; flammable. **2.** Quickly or easily aroused to strong emotion.

in•flam•ma•tion |ĭn′flə mā′shən| *n.* Redness, swelling, heat, and pain in a part of the body, resulting from injury, infection, or irritation.

in•flam•ma•to•ry |ĭn flăm′ə tôr′ē| *or* |-tōr′ē| *adj.* **1.** Of or causing inflammation: *an inflammatory disease.* **2.** Tending to arouse strong

infer

Infer *has sometimes been used to mean "to hint indirectly." Over 90 per cent of the American Heritage Usage Panel considers that this usage is a mistake for* **imply.**

inferior, etc.

Inferior *is from Latin* īnferior, *"lower," from* īnferus, *"below." Closely related to this is Latin* īnfernus, *"the place below the earth, the lower world, hell," from which we have* **infernal.** *In Italian,* īnfernus *became* inferno, *"hell," borrowed into English as* **inferno.** *Also related to* īnferus *is Latin* īnfrā, *"below," from which we have* **infrared** *and* **infrasonic.**

infinity

It can be shown that there is more than one **infinity** *and that not all infinities are equal. They have special properties and require special care in treatment. Consider the infinity, which we shall here call* I, *that represents the measure of the set of natural numbers. It can be shown that a set of measure* I *can be put into a one-to-one correspondence with a proper subset of itself. For example, the even numbers are a subset of the natural numbers; yet by dividing each even number by 2 we generate a natural number, so there are twice as many even numbers as natural numbers.* I *also has the property of being neither even nor odd.*

emotion: *a speaker's inflammatory language.*

in•flat•a•ble |ĭn flā'tə bəl| *adj.* Made ready for use by inflating: *an inflatable rubber boat.*

in•flate |ĭn flāt'| *v.* **in•flat•ed, in•flat•ing. 1.** To fill with gas and expand: *Did he inflate the tires? The balloon inflated quickly.* **2.** To increase unduly; puff up: *The initial success inflated his hopes.* **3.** To raise (prices, wages, or currency) to an abnormally high degree. **—in•flat'ed** *adj.: inflated pillows; an inflated ego.*

in•fla•tion |ĭn flā'shən| *n.* **1. a.** The act or process of inflating. **b.** The condition or degree of being inflated. **2.** A sharp, continuing rise in the prices of goods and services, usually attributed to an abnormal increase in available currency and credit.

in•fla•tion•ar•y |ĭn flā'shə nĕr'ē| *adj.* Of or contributing to inflation: *inflationary prices.*

in•flect |ĭn flĕkt'| *v.* **in•flect•ed, in•flect•ing. 1.** To vary the pitch of (the voice), especially in speaking. **2.** To change the form of (a word) to indicate number, tense, person, degree, etc.; for example, *book* is inflected to *books* in the plural. **—in•flect'ed** *adj.: an inflected form.*

in•flec•tion |ĭn flĕk'shən| *n.* **1.** A change in the pitch of the voice, especially in speech: *Questions usually end with a rising inflection.* **2. a.** The process that changes a form of a word to indicate number, tense, person, degree, etc.; for example, the comparative *quicker* is formed from *quick* by inflection. **b.** A word derived by this process; an inflected form; for example, *drives, drove,* and *driven* are all inflections of the word *drive.* **c.** An affix involved in this process.

in•flex•i•ble |ĭn flĕk'sə bəl| *adj.* **1.** Not flexible; rigid. **2.** Not subject to change or modification: *an inflexible rule.* **3.** Refusing to change or modify one's views, attitude, or position: *inflexible in his demands.* **—in•flex'i•bil'i•ty** *n.*

in•flict |ĭn flĭkt'| *v.* **1.** To cause to be suffered or endured, as in an attack: *a kind of wasp that inflicts a severe bite.* **2.** To impose (something unwelcome): *inflict punishment.*

in•flu•ence |ĭn'flo͞o əns| *n.* **1.** The power to produce effects or changes: *a man with great influence in the government.* **2.** An effect or change produced by such power: *The book had a great influence on me.* **3.** Someone or something that brings about such an effect or change: *Travel has been a good influence on you.* —*v.* **in•flu•enced, in•flu•enc•ing.** To have an effect or impact upon: *The moon influences the tides. He tried to influence the jury with sensational disclosures.*

in•flu•en•tial |ĭn'flo͞o ĕn'shəl| *adj.* Having or exercising considerable influence: *an influential newspaper.* **—in'flu•en'tial•ly** *adv.*

in•flu•en•za |ĭn'flo͞o ĕn'zə| *n.* A disease caused by viruses. Its symptoms include fever, inflammation of the respiratory system, irritation of the intestines, and muscular pain. [SEE NOTE]

influenza
The first large epidemic of **influenza** *recorded in Europe was in 1743, when the* London Magazine *reported "News from Rome of a contagious distemper raging there called the Influenza."* **Influenza** *is the Italian word for "a pouring in, a mysterious influence, an epidemic disease." The worst outbreak of all was the worldwide epidemic of 1918 and 1919, in which 20 million people died.*

in•flux |ĭn'flŭks'| *n.* **1.** An inflow. **2.** A steady stream of people or things coming in.

in•form |ĭn fôrm'| *v.* **1.** To give information to; advise; notify. **2.** To give often incriminating information: *He informed on the other members of the gang.*

in•for•mal |ĭn fôr'məl| *adj.* **1.** Performed or made without set ceremonies, rules, etc.; unofficial: *an informal agreement.* **2.** Casual; relaxed: *an informal atmosphere.* **3.** Suitable for everyday use or for casual occasions: *informal dress.* **4.** Not suitable for formal writing but frequently used in conversation and ordinary writing; for example, *kid,* used to mean a child, and *mad,* as in *mad about rock music,* are informal. **—in•for'mal•ly** *adv.*

in•for•mal•i•ty |ĭn'fôr măl'ĭ tē| *n.* Lack of formality: *the informality of California social life.*

in•form•ant |ĭn fôr'mənt| *n.* A person who is a source of information.

in•for•ma•tion |ĭn'fər mā'shən| *n.* **1.** Facts or data about a certain event or subject: *a good source of general information.* **2.** The act or process of informing or the condition of being informed: *sent you a brochure for your information.* **—*modifier:*** *an information bureau.*

in•form•a•tive |ĭn fôr'mə tĭv| *adj.* Providing information; instructive: *an informative program.*

in•formed |ĭn fôrmd'| *adj.* Provided with information; knowledgeable: *He is very well informed.*

in•form•er |ĭn fôr'mər| *n.* A person who informs against others, especially to authorities.

in•frac•tion |ĭn frăk'shən| *n.* A breach or violation of a law, rule, or regulation.

in•fra•red |ĭn'frə rĕd'| *adj.* **1.** Having a wavelength longer than that of visible red light but shorter than those of microwaves: *infrared light.* **2.** Producing, using, or sensitive to infrared radiation: *an infrared camera.*

in•fra•son•ic |ĭn'frə sŏn'ĭk| *adj.* **1.** Of or using sound waves that are too low in frequency to be heard by human ears. **2.** Subsonic.

in•fre•quent |ĭn frē'kwənt| *adj.* Not frequent: *an infrequent visitor.* **—in•fre'quent•ly** *adv.*

in•fringe |ĭn frĭnj'| *v.* **in•fringed, in•fring•ing.** To break or ignore the terms of; violate: *infringe a law.* **—*phrasal verb.*** **infringe on** (or **upon**). To intrude or encroach upon: *infringing on other people's rights.* **—in•fringe'ment** *n.*

in•fu•ri•ate |ĭn fyo͝or'ē āt'| *v.* **in•fu•ri•at•ed, in•fu•ri•at•ing.** To make furious; enrage. **—in•fu'ri•at'ed** *adj.: an infuriated look.* **—in•fu'ri•at'ing** *adj.: an infuriating situation.*

in•fuse |ĭn fyo͞oz'| *v.* **in•fused, in•fus•ing. 1.** To fill; imbue; inspire: *The teacher infused the children with a great love of learning.* **2.** To impart or instill: *The coach infused a feeling of pride in his men.* **3.** To make an extract of by soaking or steeping without boiling: *infuse tea leaves.* **—in•fu'sion** *n.*

-ing¹. A suffix that forms the present participle of verbs: **being; happening; living.** [SEE NOTE]

-ing². A suffix that forms nouns and means: **1.** An action or process: **dancing; thinking. 2.** An example of an action or process: a **meeting. 3.** The result of an action or process: a **painting. 4.** Something used in an action or process: a **coating;** a **lining.** [SEE NOTE]

-ing¹·²
The suffix **-ing¹** *was originally* -ende *or* -inde *in Old English; it is related to the Latin suffix* -ant- *or* -ent-, *as in* **rampant, effluent.** *The suffix* **-ing²** *was* -ing *or* -ung *in Old English, and it is related to the modern German suffix* -ung, *as in* bildung, *"education."*

in•gen•ious |ĭn jēn'yəs| *adj.* **1.** Clever at devising things; creative: *an ingenious inventor.* **2.** Showing originality and resourcefulness: *an ingenious idea.* **—in•gen'ious•ly** *adv.*

in•ge•nu•i•ty |ĭn'jə no͞o'ĭ tē| *or* |-nyo͞o'-| *n.* Inventive skill or imagination; cleverness.

in•gen•u•ous |ĭn jĕn'yo͞o əs| *adj.* Frank and open; candid. artless: *an ingenuous answer.* **—in•**

ă pat/ā pay/â care/ä father/ĕ pet/ ē be/ĭ pit/ī pie/î fierce/ŏ pot/ ō go/ô paw, for/oi oil/o͝o book/ o͞o boot/ou out/ŭ cut/û fur/ *th* the/th thin/hw which/zh vision/ ə ago, item, pencil, atom, circus

gen'u•ous•ly *adv.* —**in•gen'u•ous•ness'** *n.*

in•gest |ĭn **jĕst'**| *v.* To take in (food) by or as if by swallowing. [SEE PICTURE]

in•got |**ĭng'**gət| *n.* A mass of metal shaped in the form of a bar or block.

in•grain |ĭn **grān'**| *v.* To impress deeply in the mind or nature; fix. —**in•grained'** *adj.*: *an ingrained habit.*

in•grate |**ĭn'**grāt'| *n.* An ungrateful person.

in•gra•ti•ate |ĭn **grā'**shē āt'| *v.* **in•gra•ti•at•ed, in•gra•ti•at•ing.** To work (oneself) into another's good graces; make (oneself) agreeable to another: *He tried to ingratiate himself with his teacher.* —**in•gra'ti•at'ing** *adj.*: *an ingratiating smile.*

in•grat•i•tude |ĭn **grăt'**ĭ to͞od'| *or* |-tyo͞od'| *n.* Lack of gratitude; ungratefulness.

in•gre•di•ent |ĭn **grē'**dē ənt| *n.* **1.** Something added or required to form a mixture or compound: *Lime is an ingredient of cement.* **2.** A basic factor or element; component: *Ambition and energy are important ingredients of success.*

in•gress |**ĭn'**grĕs'| *n.* **1.** A means or place of going in; an entrance. **2.** The right or permission to enter: *He was denied ingress to the building.* **3.** The act of going in or entering.

in•grown |**ĭn'**grōn'| *adj.* Grown abnormally into the skin or flesh: *an ingrown toenail.*

in•hab•it |ĭn **hăb'**ĭt| *v.* To live in; have as a dwelling place: *Dinosaurs inhabited the earth millions of years ago.*

in•hab•i•tant |ĭn **hăb'**ĭ tənt| *n.* A permanent resident of a particular place.

in•ha•la•tor |**ĭn'**hə lā'tər| *n.* A device that produces a vapor to be inhaled, either to ease breathing or to introduce medication.

in•hale |ĭn **hāl'**| *v.* **in•haled, in•hal•ing.** To draw in (air, smoke, etc.) by breathing; breathe in: *inhaling fresh air; inhale deeply.* —**in'ha•la'tion** |ĭn'hə **lā'**shən| *n.*

in•hal•er |ĭn **hā'**lər| *n.* **1.** Someone or something that inhales. **2.** An inhalator. **3.** A respirator.

in•har•mo•ni•ous |ĭn'här **mō'**nē əs| *adj.* **1.** Harsh or unpleasant in sound. **2.** Not in agreement; conflicting. —**in'har•mo'ni•ous•ly** *adv.*

in•her•ent |ĭn **hîr'**ənt| *or* |-**hĕr'**-| *adj.* Existing as a basic quality or characteristic; intrinsic: *inherent laziness.* —**in•her'ent•ly** *adv.*

in•her•it |ĭn **hĕr'**ĭt| *v.* **1.** To receive (property) from someone after he dies, usually as provided for in a will. **2.** To receive from a predecessor or former time: *As he took office the mayor inherited many serious problems.* **3.** To receive (a characteristic or trait) by or as if by genetic transmission from a parent or ancestor: *She inherited her father's dark eyes.* [SEE NOTE]

in•her•i•tance |ĭn **hĕr'**ĭ təns| *n.* **1.** The act or process of inheriting: *Noble titles are usually gained by inheritance.* **2.** Property, money, etc., that is received by an heir at a person's death. **3.** Something inherited; heritage: *Many American place names, foods, and legends are part of our inheritance from the Indians.*

in•hib•it |ĭn **hĭb'**ĭt| *v.* To restrain or hold back; prevent: *Shyness inhibited him from talking more freely.*

in•hi•bi•tion |ĭn'hĭ **bĭsh'**ən| *or* |ĭn'ĭ-| *n.* **1.** The act or process of inhibiting or the condition of being inhibited. **2.** The frequent or habitual suppression of a feeling, urge, biological drive, etc.: *His inhibitions made his life joyless and dull.*

in•hos•pi•ta•ble |ĭn **hŏs'**pĭ tə bəl| *or* |ĭn'hŏ**spĭt'**ə bəl| *adj.* **1.** Unfriendly: *an inhospitable neighbor.* **2.** Harsh; forbidding: *an inhospitable climate.* —**in•hos'pi•ta•bly** *adv.*

in•hu•man |ĭn **hyo͞o'**mən| *adj.* **1.** Not human; lacking or seeming to lack human qualities: *An inhuman figure lurked in the darkness.* **2.** Cruel; barbarous; brutal: *inhuman treatment.* —**in•hu'man•ly** *adv.*

in•hu•mane |ĭn'hyo͞o **mān'**| *adj.* Not humane; lacking mercy or kindness. —**in'hu•mane'ly** *adv.*

in•hu•man•i•ty |ĭn'hyo͞o **măn'**ĭ tē| *n.* The condition of being inhuman or inhumane: *man's inhumanity to his fellow man.*

in•im•i•cal |ĭ **nĭm'**ĭ kəl| *adj.* **1.** In opposition; adverse; detrimental: *actions inimical to the organization.* **2.** Unfriendly; hostile; antagonistic: *an inimical voice.* [SEE NOTE]

in•im•i•ta•ble |ĭ **nĭm'**ĭ tə bəl| *adj.* Impossible to imitate; unique: *a singer's inimitable style.* —**in•im'i•ta•bil'i•ty** *n.* —**in•im'i•ta•bly** *adv.*

in•iq•ui•tous |ĭ **nĭk'**wĭ təs| *adj.* Wicked; sinful: *an iniquitous act.*

in•iq•ui•ty |ĭ **nĭk'**wĭ tē| *n., pl.* **in•iq•ui•ties. 1.** Wickedness; evil. **2.** An immoral act; a sin.

in•i•tial |ĭ **nĭsh'**əl| *adj.* Of or occurring at the beginning; first: *The initial reaction was unenthusiastic.* —*n.* Often **initials.** The first letter or letters of a person's name or names, used as a shortened signature or for identification. —*v.* **in•i•tialed** or **in•i•tialled, in•i•tial•ing** or **in•i•tial•ling.** To mark or sign with one's initials. —**in•i'tial•ly** *adv.*

in•i•ti•ate |ĭ **nĭsh'**ē āt'| *v.* **in•i•ti•at•ed, in•i•ti•at•ing. 1.** To begin; originate: *initiate a campaign.* **2.** To introduce to a new subject, field, interest, etc.; guide: *A friend initiated me into the world of rock music.* **3.** To admit into membership, often with a special ceremony: *Ten new members were initiated into the fraternity.* —*n.* |ĭ **nĭsh'**ē ĭt|. A person who has been initiated.

in•i•ti•a•tion |ĭ nĭsh'ē **ā'**shən| *n.* **1.** The act or process of initiating. **2.** Admission into a club, society, or organization. **3.** A ceremony, ritual, etc., with which a new member is initiated. —***modifier:*** *an initiation fee.*

in•i•ti•a•tive |ĭ **nĭsh'**ē ə tĭv| *or* |ĭ **nĭsh'**ə-| *n.* **1.** The ability to begin or follow through with a plan of action or a task; enterprise and determination: *He acted on his own initiative.* **2.** The first step or action; opening move: *He took the initiative and wrote a letter to the city council.* **3.** The right or procedure by which citizens can propose a new law by petition and have it voted on by the electorate.

in•ject |ĭn **jĕkt'**| *v.* **1. a.** To force or drive (a liquid or gas) into something: *a mechanism that injects fuel into a cylinder of an engine.* **b.** To introduce (liquid medicine, serum, etc.) into the body, as by using a hypodermic syringe. **2.** To introduce into conversation or consideration: *I tried to inject a note of humor.*

in•jec•tion |ĭn **jĕk'**shən| *n.* **1.** The act or process of injecting. **2.** Something that is injected, especially a dose of a liquid medicine.

in•ju•di•cious |ĭn'jo͞o **dĭsh'**əs| *adj.* Showing a lack of judgment; imprudent: *an injudicious re-*

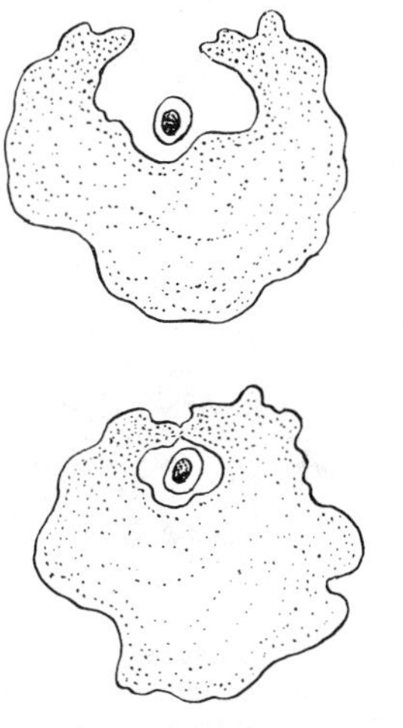

ingest
Ameba ingesting a food particle

inherit, etc.
Inherit *is from Latin* inhērēditāre, *or* hērēditāre, *"to receive as an heir," from* hērēs, hērēd-, *"an heir." In Old French,* hērēs *became* heir, *which was borrowed into English as* **heir.** Hērēs *is also the source of* **heritage, hereditary,** *and* **heredity.**

inimical/enemy
Inimical *is from Latin* inimīcus, *"unfriendly, hostile":* in-, *"not, un-,"* + amīcus, *"friend" (as in* **amicable***). Separately,* inimīcus *passed into Old French as* enemi, *which was borrowed into English as* **enemy.**

inkstand
Silver inkstand used by the signers of the Declaration of Independence

inlay

mark about them. —**in′ju·di′cious·ly** *adv.*

In·jun |ĭn′jən| *n.* An American Indian. The word "Injun" is considered offensive.

in·junc·tion |ĭn jŭngk′shən| *n.* **1.** An order or command. **2.** A court order prohibiting or requiring a specific course of action: *an injunction to delay a strike.*

in·jure |ĭn′jər| *v.* **in·jured, in·jur·ing.** To harm or damage; hurt: *He fell and injured his foot.*

in·ju·ri·ous |ĭn jo͝or′ē əs| *adj.* Causing injury or damage; harmful: *injurious chemicals.*

in·ju·ry |ĭn′jə rē| *n., pl.* **in·ju·ries. 1.** Damage to a person or thing; harm: *His reputation escaped injury.* **2.** A wound or other specific damage to the body: *a leg injury.*

in·jus·tice |ĭn jŭs′tĭs| *n.* **1.** Lack of justice; unfairness. **2.** A specific unjust act; a wrong.

ink |ĭngk| *n.* A colored liquid used especially for writing or printing. —***modifier:*** *an ink mark.* —*v.* To cover with ink; spread ink on: *The rubber stamp must be inked periodically.*

ink·blot |ĭngk′blŏt′| *n.* A blotted pattern of spilled ink.

ink·ling |ĭngk′lĭng| *n.* A slight indication; a hint; a vague idea: *This was the first inkling we had that something was wrong.*

ink·stand |ĭngk′stănd′| *n.* A tray or rack for bottles of ink, pens, and other writing implements. [SEE PICTURE]

ink·well |ĭngk′wĕl′| *n.* A small container for ink, usually on the top of a desk.

ink·y |ĭng′kē| *adj.* **ink·i·er, ink·i·est. 1.** Stained or smeared with ink: *inky fingers.* **2.** Dark; murky: *inky shadows.* —**ink′i·ness** *n.*

in·laid |ĭn′lād′| *or* |ĭn **lād′**| *adj.* **1.** Set smoothly into a surface to form a pattern or decoration: *a wall with inlaid mosaic tile.* **2.** Decorated with a pattern set into the surface: *an inlaid cabinet.*

in·land |ĭn′lənd| *adj.* Of or located in the interior of a country or region: *an inland waterway.* —*adv.* |ĭn′lənd| *or* |-lənd|. In, toward, or into the interior of a country or region.

in-law |ĭn′lô′| *n.* Any relative by marriage.

in·lay |ĭn′lā′| *or* |ĭn **lā′**| *v.* **in·laid** |ĭn′lād′| *or* |ĭn-**lād′**|, **in·lay·ing. 1.** To set (pieces of wood, ivory, metal, etc.) into a surface to form a design. **2.** To decorate by setting in such designs. —*n.* |ĭn′lā′|. **1.** Contrasting material set into a surface in pieces to form a design. **2.** An inlaid decoration or design. **3.** A filling, as of gold, molded to fit a cavity in a tooth and cemented into place. [SEE PICTURE]

in·let |ĭn′lĕt′| *or* |-lĭt| *n.* **1.** A bay, cove, estuary, or other recess along a coast. **2.** An opening providing a means of entrance.

in·mate |ĭn′māt′| *n.* A person confined to an institution such as a prison or asylum.

in·most |ĭn′mōst′| *adj.* Innermost.

inn |ĭn| *n.* **1.** A hotel or hostel. **2.** A tavern or restaurant. ¶ *These sound alike* **inn, in.**

in·nards |ĭn′ərdz| *pl.n. Informal.* **1.** The internal organs of the body, especially of the abdomen. **2.** The inner parts of a machine, structure, etc.

in·nate |ĭ **nāt′**| *or* |ĭn′āt′| *adj.* **1.** Possessed from birth: *an innate instinct.* **2.** Existing as a basic, seemingly inborn, characteristic: *an innate love of learning.* —**in·nate′ly** *adv.*

in·ner |ĭn′ər| *adj.* **1.** Located farther inside: *the inner core of the earth.* **2.** Of the spirit or mind: *inner peace.* **3.** More exclusive, private, or important: *the inner circles of government.*

inner city. The older central part of a city, especially when marked by crowded, run-down, low-income neighborhoods. —***modifier:*** **(inner-city):** *inner-city schools.*

inner ear. The innermost part of the ear of a vertebrate, consisting of the cochlea, vestibule, and semicircular canals.

in·ner·most |ĭn′ər mōst′| *adj.* Located farthest within: *the innermost ring of walls in a fortress.*

inner tube. A rubber tube placed inside certain kinds of tires to hold the air.

in·ning |ĭn′ĭng| *n.* One of the nine divisions of a baseball game during which each team comes to bat.

inn·keep·er |ĭn′kē′pər| *n.* A person who owns or manages an inn.

in·no·cence |ĭn′ə səns| *n.* The condition, quality, or fact of being innocent, especially freedom from guilt.

in·no·cent |ĭn′ə sənt| *adj.* **1.** Not guilty of a specific crime or fault: *The jury found him innocent.* **2.** Not experienced or worldly; naive: *an innocent child.* **3.** Not intended or intending to cause harm: *an innocent remark.* —*n.* A person, especially a child, who is free of evil or worldly knowledge. —**in′no·cent·ly** *adv.*

in·noc·u·ous |ĭ **nŏk′**yo͞o əs| *adj.* Harmless; innocent: *an innocuous remark.* —**in·noc′u·ous·ly** *adv.* —**in·noc′u·ous·ness** *n.*

in·no·vate |ĭn′ə vāt′| *v.* **in·no·vat·ed, in·no·vat·ing.** To be creative; begin or introduce (something new): *A good artist is always seeking to innovate.* —**in′no·va′tor** *n.*

in·no·va·tion |ĭn′ə **vā′**shən| *n.* **1.** The act or process of innovating: *an age of innovation.* **2.** Something newly introduced; a change: *challenging innovations in methods of teaching.*

in·nu·en·do |ĭn′yo͞o **ĕn′**dō| *n., pl.* **in·nu·en·does.** A subtle, veiled, often spiteful reference to someone or something not named; an insinuation.

in·nu·mer·a·ble |ĭ **no͞o′**mər ə bəl| *or* |ĭ **nyo͞o′**-| *adj.* Too numerous to be counted: *innumerable difficulties.* —**in·nu′mer·a·bly** *adv.*

in·oc·u·late |ĭ **nŏk′**yə lāt′| *v.* **in·oc·u·lat·ed, in·oc·u·lat·ing. 1.** To transmit a disease to by introducing bacteria or viruses into the body: *inoculate guinea pigs with viruses.* **2.** To introduce the microorganisms of a disease, antigens, vaccines, etc., into in order to immunize, cure, or experiment. —**in·oc′u·la′tion** *n.*

in·of·fen·sive |ĭn′ə **fĕn′**sĭv| *adj.* Giving no offense; harmless. —**in′of·fen′sive·ly** *adv.* —**in′of·fen′sive·ness** *n.*

in·op·er·a·ble |ĭn **ŏp′**ər ə bəl| *adj.* Not capable of being cured or corrected by surgery.

in·op·er·a·tive |ĭn **ŏp′**ər ə tĭv| *adj.* Not in working order: *an inoperative heater.*

in·op·por·tune |ĭn ŏp′ər **to͞on′**| *or* |**-tyo͞on′**| *adj.* Coming at the wrong time; inappropriate: *You called at a most inopportune moment.*

in·or·di·nate |ĭn **ôr′**dn ĭt| *adj.* Exceeding reasonable limits; immoderate; excessive: *a book of inordinate length.* —**in·or′di·nate·ly** *adv.*

in·or·gan·ic |ĭn′ôr **găn′**ĭk| *adj.* **1.** Not involving living organisms or the products of their life processes. **2.** Of mineral matter as opposed to the substance of things that are or were alive.

ă pat/ā pay/â care/ä father/ĕ pet/ ē be/ĭ pit/ī pie/î fierce/ŏ pot/ ō go/ô paw, for/oi oil/o͝o book/ o͞o boot/ou out/ŭ cut/û fur/ *th* the/th thin/hw which/zh vision/ ə ago, item, pencil, atom, circus

3. Of or involving chemical compounds that are not classified as organic: *inorganic chemistry.* —**in'or·gan'i·cal·ly** *adv.*

in·put |**ĭn'**pŏŏt'| *n.* **1.** Anything put into a device or system in order to produce a result or output: **a.** The power or energy used by the device or system in its operation. **b.** The data fed into a computer for processing. **2.** The part of a system or device at which power or data are received.

in·quest |**ĭn'**kwĕst'| *n.* **1.** A judicial inquiry, especially one made into the cause of a death. **2.** Any investigation.

in·quire |ĭn **kwīr'**| *v.* **in·quired, in·quir·ing. 1.** To ask in order to find out: *inquire the way to the station; inquire about the date of the sale.* **2.** To make a search or study; investigate: *inquire into a case.* —**in·quir'er** *n.* [SEE NOTE on p. 308]

in·quir·y |ĭn **kwīr'**ē| *or* |**ĭn'**kwə rē| *n., pl.* **in·quir·ies. 1.** The process of inquiring: *engaged in scientific inquiry.* **2.** A request for information: *many inquiries about the new mail rates.* **3.** A detailed examination of some matter; an investigation.

in·qui·si·tion |ĭn'kwĭ **zĭsh'**ən| *n.* **1. Inquisition.** In the Middle Ages, a tribunal of the Roman Catholic Church established to seek out and punish those people considered guilty of heresy. **2.** Any investigation that violates the privacy or rights of individuals.

in·quis·i·tive |ĭn **kwĭz'**ĭ tĭv| *adj.* **1.** Eager to learn: *an inquisitive child; an inquisitive mind.* **2.** Unduly curious; prying. —**in·quis'i·tive·ly** *adv.* —**in·quis'i·tive·ness** *n.*

in·quis·i·tor |ĭn **kwĭz'**ĭ tər| *n.* **1.** A person who conducts an official inquiry. **2. Inquisitor.** A member of the Inquisition. —**in·quis'i·to'ri·al** |ĭn kwĭz'ĭ **tôr'**ē əl| *or* |**-tōr'-**| *adj.*

in·road |**ĭn'**rōd'| *n.* **1.** A hostile invasion; a raid. **2.** An advance at the expense of something or someone else; an encroachment: *Japanese products have made huge inroads into the American economy.*

in·rush |**ĭn'**rŭsh'| *n.* A sudden rush in; an influx.

in·sane |ĭn **sān'**| *adj.* **1.** Of, showing, typical of, or affected by insanity: *an insane person.* **2.** Very foolish or irrational; wild. —**in·sane'ly** *adv.*

in·san·i·ty |ĭn **săn'**ĭ tē| *n., pl.* **in·san·i·ties. 1.** A serious mental illness or disorder. **2.** Extreme foolishness; utter folly: *Taking a chance like that would be sheer insanity.*

in·sa·tia·ble |ĭn **sā'**shə bəl| *or* |-shē ə-| *adj.* Not capable of being satiated; never satisfied: *an insatiable appetite.* —**in·sa'tia·bly** *adv.*

in·scribe |ĭn **skrīb'**| *v.* **in·scribed, in·scrib·ing. 1. a.** To write, print, carve, or engrave (words or letters) on or in a surface: *inscribe the winners' names on a plaque.* **b.** To mark or engrave (a surface) with words or letters: *inscribe a plaque with the names of the winners.* **2.** To sign or write a brief message in or on (a book or picture) when giving it as a gift. **3. a.** To enclose (a polygon, polyhedron, etc.) in another geometric figure so that every vertex of the enclosed figure touches the enclosing figure. **b.** To enclose (a circle, sphere, etc.) in another geometric figure so that every line or surface of the enclosing figure is tangent to the enclosed figure.

in·scrip·tion |ĭn **skrĭp'**shən| *n.* **1.** The act or an example of inscribing: *the inscription of the names of the war dead on a monument.* **2.** Something inscribed: *a wall covered with inscriptions.* **3.** A short, signed message in a book given as a gift.

in·scru·ta·ble |ĭn **skrōō'**tə bəl| *adj.* Difficult or impossible to understand or fathom; mysterious; enigmatic: *an inscrutable face.* —**in·scru'ta·bil'i·ty, in·scru'ta·ble·ness** *n.* —**in·scru'ta·bly** *adv.*

in·sect |**ĭn'**sĕkt'| *n.* Any of a large group of animals that have six legs, a body with three main divisions, and usually wings. Flies, bees, grasshoppers, butterflies, and moths are insects. [SEE PICTURES]

in·sec·ti·cide |ĭn **sĕk'**tĭ sīd'| *n.* Something, especially a poison, used to kill insects.

in·sec·tiv·o·rous |ĭn'sĕk **tĭv'**ər əs| *adj.* Feeding on insects: *insectivorous animals.*

in·se·cure |ĭn'sĭ **kyŏŏr'**| *adj.* **1.** Not secure or safe: *an insecure fortress.* **2.** Not firm or steady; shaky: *an insecure hold on the rock edge.* **3.** Apprehensive or lacking self-confidence: *feel very insecure.* —**in'se·cure'ly** *adv.*

in·se·cu·ri·ty |ĭn'sĭ **kyŏŏr'**ĭ tē| *n., pl.* **in·se·cu·ri·ties. 1.** Lack of security; the condition of being unsafe or unstable. **2.** Lack of assurance or self-confidence: *a feeling of insecurity.*

in·sem·i·nate |ĭn **sĕm'**ə nāt'| *v.* **in·sem·i·nat·ed, in·sem·i·nat·ing.** To introduce semen into the uterus of. —**in·sem'i·na'tion** *n.*

in·sen·sate |ĭn **sĕn'**sāt'| *or* |-sĭt| *adj.* **1.** Lifeless; inanimate. **2.** Cruel; savage; inhuman: *insensate slaughter.*

in·sen·si·ble |ĭn **sĕn'**sə bəl| *adj.* **1.** Deprived of sensation; unconscious or numb: *He lay insensible where he had fallen.* **2.** Unsusceptible; unaffected: *insensible to pain.* **3.** Not mindful; unheeding: *insensible to advice.* —**in·sen'si·bly** *adv.* —**in·sen'si·bil'i·ty** *n.*

in·sen·si·tive |ĭn **sĕn'**sĭ tĭv| *adj.* **1.** Not sensitive; numb: *render a tooth insensitive.* **2.** Not able to understand; unresponsive: *insensitive to the sufferings of others.* —**in·sen'si·tiv'i·ty** *n.*

in·sep·a·ra·ble |ĭn **sĕp'**ər ə bəl| *adj.* Not capable of being separated; always together: *inseparable friends.* —**in·sep'a·ra·bil'i·ty, in·sep'a·ra·ble·ness** *n.* —**in·sep'a·ra·bly** *adv.*

in·sert |ĭn **sûrt'**| *v.* To put or set in; introduce: *insert a key in a lock.* —*n.* |**ĭn'**sûrt'|. Something inserted or meant to be inserted, as into written material.

in·ser·tion |ĭn **sûr'**shən| *n.* **1.** The act of inserting: *the insertion of commas into the sentence.* **2.** Something inserted; an insert.

in·set |ĭn **sĕt'**| *v.* **in·set, in·set·ting.** To set in; insert. —*n.* |**ĭn'**sĕt'|. **1.** Something set in, as a small map or illustration set within the boundaries of a larger one. **2.** A piece of material, such as lace, set into a dress.

in·shore |**ĭn'**shôr'| *or* |-shōr'| *adv.* Toward the shore: *It was calm inshore.* —*adj.* Close to or coming toward the shore: *an inshore wind.*

in·side |**ĭn'**sīd'| *or* |ĭn **sīd'**| *n.* **1.** The inner part, side, surface, etc.: *the inside of a house.* **2. insides.** *Informal.* The inner organs, especially those of the abdomen; entrails. —*adj.* **1.** Inner; interior: *the inside pocket.* **2.** Of or coming from an authoritative source: *inside information.* **3.** Coming from a known group of employees or members: *The theft was definitely an inside job.*

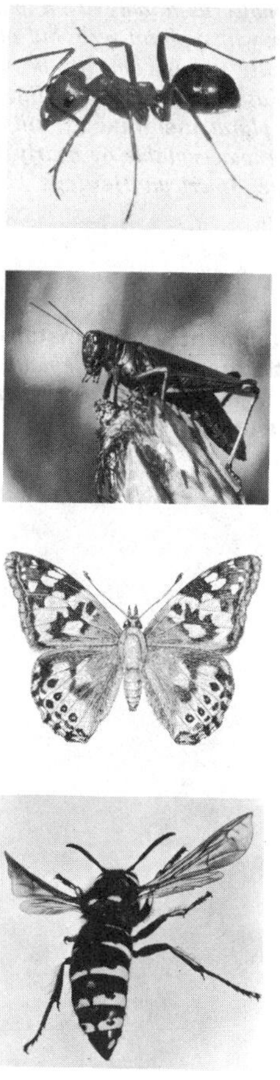

insects
Ant
Grasshopper
Butterfly
Hornet

insignia

Insignia *is from Latin* insignia, *a plural noun meaning "marks or badges of office, official decorations." In English,* **insignia** *was originally used only as a plural noun, with a plural verb, but more recently it has come to be used also as a singular noun. But the new plural* **insignias** *is still felt to be unacceptable by nearly half of the American Heritage Usage Panel.*

installment[1-2]

Installment[2] *is from* **install**, *but* **installment**[1] *was originally* es-tallment, *meaning "an agreed payment."*

ă pat/ā pay/â care/ä father/ĕ pet/ ē be/ĭ pit/ī pie/î fierce/ŏ pot/ ō go/ô paw, for/oi oil/o͝o book/ o͞o boot/ou out/ŭ cut/û fur/ *th* the/th thin/hw which/zh vision/ ə ago, item, pencil, atom, circus

4. In baseball, passing too near the body of the batter: *The first pitch was a fast ball, high and inside.* —*adv.* |ĭn **sīd'**|. Into or in the interior; within: *going inside; staying inside.* —*prep.* |ĭn **sīd'**|. **1.** On the inner side or part of: *inside the cave.* **2.** Into: *go inside the house.*

Idioms. **inside of.** Inside: *inside of the cave; inside of the door; inside of an hour; go inside of the house.* **inside out.** With the inner surface turned out; reversed: *wearing his socks inside out.*

in•sid•er |ĭn **sī'**dər| *n.* Someone who has special knowledge or access to private information.

in•sid•i•ous |ĭn **sĭd'**ē əs| *adj.* **1.** Intended to entrap; treacherous: *an insidious plot.* **2.** Working or spreading harmfully in a subtle or hidden manner: *insidious rumors; an insidious disease.* —**in•sid'i•ous•ly** *adv.* —**in•sid'i•ous•ness** *n.*

in•sight |**ĭn'**sīt'| *n.* **1.** The capacity to perceive the true nature of something: *insight into the workings of the system.* **2.** A perception of the true nature of something: *He had a brilliant insight about the meaning of the movie.*

in•sig•ni•a |ĭn **sĭg'**nē ə| *n., pl.* **in•sig•ni•a** or **in•sig•ni•as.** A badge of office, rank, nationality, membership, etc.; an emblem. [SEE NOTE]

in•sig•nif•i•cant |ĭn'sĭg **nĭf'**ĭ kənt| *adj.* Not significant, especially: **1.** Meaningless: *gestures insignificant to a foreigner.* **2.** Of no importance; trivial: *an insignificant detail.* **3.** Small in size, power, or value: *an insignificant country priest.* —**in'sig•nif'i•cance** *n.* —**in'sig•nif'i•cant•ly** *adv.*

in•sin•cere |ĭn'sĭn **sîr'**| *adj.* Not sincere; hypocritical: *an insincere apology.* —**in'sin•cere'ly** *adv.* —**in'sin•cer'i•ty** |ĭn'sĭn **sĕr'**ĭ tē| *n.*

in•sin•u•ate |ĭn **sĭn'**yo͞o āt'| *v.* **in•sin•u•at•ed, in•sin•u•at•ing. 1.** To introduce (ideas, thoughts, points of view, etc.) gradually and slyly: *She insinuated her political beliefs into the conversation.* **2.** To convey indirectly; hint covertly: *What are you insinuating?*

in•sin•u•a•tion |ĭn sĭn'yo͞o **ā'**shən| *n.* An indirect hint or suggestion.

in•sip•id |ĭn **sĭp'**ĭd| *adj.* **1.** Lacking flavor; bland: *an insipid meal.* **2.** Lacking excitement or interest; dull: *an insipid person; insipid remarks of a tour guide.* —**in•sip'id•ly** *adv.* —**in•sip'id•ness** *n.*

in•sist |ĭn **sĭst'**| *v.* **1.** To be firm in one's demand; take a strong stand: *I insist on watching the ball game.* **2.** To state or assert vehemently and persistently: *She insisted that he was wrong.*

in•sist•ent |ĭn **sĭs'**tənt| *adj.* **1.** Firm in asserting a demand or opinion: *He was very insistent that the water be boiled before use.* **2.** Repetitive or continual; persistent: *the wren's insistent melody.* —**in•sist'ence** *n.* —**in•sist'ent•ly** *adv.*

in•so•far as |ĭn'sō **fär'**|. To such an extent as: *Insofar as he can, the scientist excludes bias from his thinking.*

in•sole |**ĭn'**sōl'| *n.* **1.** The inner sole of a shoe or boot. **2.** An extra strip of material put inside a shoe for comfort or protection.

in•so•lent |**ĭn'**sə lənt| *adj.* Disrespectfully arrogant; impudent; rude: *an insolent reply.* —**in'so•lence** *n.* —**in'so•lent•ly** *adv.*

in•sol•u•ble |ĭn **sŏl'**yə bəl| *adj.* **1.** Not capable of being dissolved, especially in water: *an insoluble salt.* **2.** Not capable of being solved: *an insoluble puzzle.* —**in•sol'u•bil'i•ty** *n.*

in•sol•vent |ĭn **sŏl'**vənt| *adj.* Unable to meet one's debts; bankrupt. —**in•sol'ven•cy** *n.*

in•som•ni•a |ĭn **sŏm'**nē ə| *n.* Inability to sleep, especially when persistent.

in•so•much as |ĭn'sō **mŭch'**|. Inasmuch as; because; since.

in•spect |ĭn **spĕkt'**| *v.* **1.** To examine carefully and critically, especially for flaws: *The beavers swam back and forth, inspecting their dam.* **2.** To examine, review, or evaluate officially: *inspected the troops in his command every Saturday.*

in•spec•tion |ĭn **spĕk'**shən| *n.* **1.** The act or an example of inspecting: *An inspection of the wiring uncovered the source of the power failure.* **2.** An official examination or review: *Elevators must undergo an annual inspection.*

in•spec•tor |ĭn **spĕk'**tər| *n.* **1.** A person who inspects: *a customs inspector.* **2.** A police officer of high rank, usually in charge of several precincts.

in•spi•ra•tion |ĭn'spə **rā'**shən| *n.* **1.** A feeling of being inspired; stimulation of the mind, emotions, etc. **2.** Someone or something that inspires: *Bach was an inspiration to many other composers.* **3.** Something that is inspired; a sudden, original idea. **4.** The act or process of breathing in; inhalation. —**in'spi•ra'tion•al** *adj.*

in•spire |ĭn **spīr'**| *v.* **in•spired, in•spir•ing. 1.** To fill with noble or reverent emotion; exalt: *hymns that inspire the congregation.* **2.** To stimulate to creativity or action: *a worker inspired by fear of poverty.* **3.** To elicit or create (an emotion, attitude, etc.) in another or others: *tried to inspire confidence in the voters.* **4.** To be the cause or source of: *an invention that inspired many imitations.* **5.** To inhale (air): *inspiring the fresh country air.* —**in•spired'** *adj.*: *an inspired epic.* —**in•spir'ing** *adj.*: *an inspiring hymn.*

in•sta•bil•i•ty |ĭn'stə **bĭl'**ĭ tē| *n., pl.* **in•sta•bil•i•ties.** Lack of stability: *mental instability.*

in•stall |ĭn **stôl'**| *v.* **1.** To set in position and connect or adjust for use or service: *They installed the new phones yesterday.* **2.** To place in an office, rank, or position, usually with ceremony: *installed a new chairman.* **3.** To settle; place: *She installed herself in her favorite chair.*

in•stal•la•tion |ĭn'stə **lā'**shən| *n.* **1.** The act or process of installing: *the installation of telephones.* **2.** A system of machinery or other apparatus set up for use. **3.** A military base or camp.

in•stall•ment[1] |ĭn **stôl'**mənt| *n.* **1.** One of a series of payments in settlement of a debt. **2.** A portion or part of anything issued at intervals, especially a story in a magazine. —***modifier:*** *buying on the installment plan.* [SEE NOTE]

in•stall•ment[2] |ĭn **stôl'**mənt| *n.* The act or process of installing; installation. [SEE NOTE]

in•stance |**ĭn'**stəns| *n.* A case or example: *many instances of success.*

in•stant |**ĭn'**stənt| *n.* A period of time almost too brief to detect; a moment. —*adj.* **1.** Immediate: *an instant success.* **2.** Designed for quick preparation: *instant coffee.*

in•stan•ta•ne•ous |ĭn'stən **tā'**nē əs| *adj.* Happening without noticeable delay; immediate: *an instantaneous reaction.* —**in'stan•ta'ne•ous•ly** *adv.*

in•stant•ly |**ĭn'**stənt lē| *adv.* At once: *She recognized him instantly.*

in•stead |ĭn **stĕd'**| *adv.* In place of that previously mentioned; as an alternative: *They didn't have cider, so I got apple juice instead.*

***Idiom.* instead of.** In place of; rather than: *I'll go to the movies instead of you.*

in•step |**ĭn'**stĕp'| *n.* **1.** The arched middle part of the human foot. **2.** The part of a shoe or stocking covering this part of the foot.

in•sti•gate |**ĭn'**stĭ gāt'| *v.* **in•sti•gat•ed, in•sti•gat•ing. 1.** To stir up; foment: *instigate a rebellion.* **2.** To urge on; provoke: *taxes that instigated the colonies to revolt.* **—in'sti•ga'tion** *n.* **—in'sti•ga'tor** *n.*

in•still |ĭn **stĭl'**| *v.* To introduce by gradual, persistent efforts; implant: *Bobby Hull instills pure terror in the goalies by his great shooting.*

in•stinct |**ĭn'**stĭngkt'| *n.* **1.** An inner influence, feeling, or drive that is not learned and that results in complex animal behavior such as building of nests, incubation of eggs, nursing of young, etc. **2.** A natural talent or ability.

in•stinc•tive |ĭn **stĭngk'**tĭv| *adj.* Of or arising from instinct: *instinctive behavior.* **—in•stinc'tive•ly** *adv.*

in•sti•tute |**ĭn'**stĭ to͞ot'| *or* |-tyo͞ot'| *v.* **in•sti•tut•ed, in•sti•tut•ing. 1.** To establish, organize, and set in operation: *institute a parliamentary government.* **2.** To begin; initiate: *instituted a new policy on relations with China.* **—***n.* **1.** An educational institution: *a research institute.* **2.** The building or buildings of such an institution.

in•sti•tu•tion |ĭn'stĭ **to͞o'**shən| *or* |**-tyo͞o'**-| *n.* **1.** The act or process of instituting: *the institution of a new immigration quota.* **2.** An established custom, practice, or pattern of behavior that is important in the cultural life of a society: *the institution of marriage.* **3. a.** An organization or foundation, especially one dedicated to public service. **b.** The building or buildings housing such an organization. **—in'sti•tu'tion•al** *adj.*

in•struct |ĭn **strŭkt'**| *v.* **1.** To convey knowledge or skill to; teach: *The Indians instructed the white men in the growing and use of certain foods.* **2.** To give orders to; direct: *The sergeant instructed us to remain at attention.* [SEE NOTE]

in•struc•tion |ĭn **strŭk'**shən| *n.* **1.** Something that is taught; a lesson or series of lessons: *received instruction in classical music.* **2.** The act or profession of instructing; education: *a teacher's instruction of his pupils.* **3. instructions.** Directions; orders. **—in•struc'tion•al** *adj.*

in•struc•tive |ĭn **strŭk'**tĭv| *adj.* Used to instruct: *an instructive example.*

in•struc•tor |ĭn **strŭk'**tər| *n.* **1.** Someone who instructs; a teacher. **2.** A college or university teacher ranking below an assistant professor.

in•stru•ment |**ĭn'**strə mənt| *n.* **1.** A device designed to record, measure, indicate, etc. **2.** A mechanical tool or implement, especially one used by a physician, dentist, or scientist. **3.** A device used by a musician in making music. **4.** A means by which something is done: *Education can be used as an instrument for social change.* **5.** A person used and controlled by another: *The treasurer is a mere instrument of the president.*[SEE NOTE & PICTURES]

in•stru•men•tal |ĭn'strə **mĕn'**tl| *adj.* **1.** Serving as the means to bring something about; useful: *He was instrumental in acquiring the territory for his nation.* **2.** Performed on or written for musical instruments. **—in'stru•men'tal•ly** *adv.*

in•stru•men•tal•ist |ĭn'strə **mĕn'**tl ĭst| *n.* Someone who plays a musical instrument.

in•sub•or•di•nate |ĭn'sə **bôr'**dn ĭt| *adj.* Not submissive to authority; disobedient: *charged with being insubordinate to an officer.* **—in'sub•or'di•na'tion** |ĭn'sə bôr'dn **ā'**shən| *n.*

in•sub•stan•tial |ĭn'səb **stăn'**shəl| *adj.* **1.** Lacking substance or reality; imaginary: *an insubstantial vision of the future.* **2.** Lacking firmness or bulk; flimsy: *an insubstantial cardboard wall.* **—in'sub•stan'ti•al'i•ty** *n.*

in•suf•fer•a•ble |ĭn **sŭf'**ər ə bəl| *adj.* Not capable of being endured; intolerable: *insufferable manners.* **—in•suf'fer•a•bly** *adv.*

in•suf•fi•cien•cy |ĭn'sə **fĭsh'**ən sē| *n., pl.* **in•suf•fi•cien•cies. 1.** The quality or condition of being insufficient: *insufficiency of water.* **2.** Something insufficient: *This program has many insufficiencies.*

in•suf•fi•cient |ĭn'sə **fĭsh'**ənt| *adj.* Not sufficient; inadequate: *insufficient rainfall for the cultivation of fruit.* **—in'suf•fi'cient•ly** *adv.*

in•su•lar |**ĭn'**sə lər| *or* |**ĭns'**yə-| *adj.* **1.** Of, on, or forming an island or islands: *an insular nation.* **2. a.** Characteristic of the isolated life of an island people: *maintaining their insular customs.* **b.** Narrow; prejudiced: *insular opinions.* **—in'su•lar'i•ty** |ĭn'sə **lăr'**ĭ tē| *or* |ĭns'yə-| *n.*

in•su•late |**ĭn'**sə lāt'| *or* |**ĭns'**yə-| *v.* **in•su•lat•ed, in•su•lat•ing. 1.** To prevent the passage of heat, electricity, or sound into or out of, especially by surrounding or lining with something that blocks such a flow. **2.** To detach; isolate: *insulate a country from foreign influences.* **—in'su•lat'ing** *adj.: insulating material.*

in•su•la•tion |ĭn'sə **lā'**shən| *or* |ĭns'yə-| *n.* **1. a.** The act or process of insulating. **b.** The condition of being insulated: *kept warm by insulation.* **2.** Material that is used for insulating.

in•su•la•tor |**ĭn'**sə lā'tər| *or* |**ĭns'**yə-| *n.* A substance or device that insulates.

in•su•lin |**ĭn'**sə lĭn| *or* |**ĭns'**yə-| *n.* A hormone that is produced in the pancreas and acts to regulate the amount of sugar in the blood. Insulin is sometimes administered in the treatment of diabetes.

in•sult |ĭn **sŭlt'**| *v.* To speak to or treat with contempt; offend. **—in•sult'ing** *adj.: an insulting gesture.* **—***n.* |**ĭn'**sŭlt'|. An action or remark meant to insult.

in•su•per•a•ble |ĭn **so͞o'**pər ə bəl| *adj.* Not capable of being overcome; insurmountable: *an insuperable barrier.*

in•sup•port•a•ble |ĭn'sə **pôr'**tə bəl| *or* |**-pōr'**-| *adj.* Unbearable; intolerable: *insupportable pain.*

in•sur•ance |ĭn **sho͝or'**əns| *n.* **1.** The business of guaranteeing to cover specified losses in the future, as in case of accident, illness, theft, or death, in return for the continuing payment of regular sums of money. **2. a.** A contract making such guarantees to the party insured. **b.** The total amount to be paid to the party insured: *bought $10,000 of life insurance.* **c.** A periodic amount paid for such coverage; a premium: *We pay insurance on the first of the month.* **—*modifier:*** *an insurance company; insurance premiums.*

in•sure |ĭn **sho͝or'**| *v.* **in•sured, in•sur•ing. 1.** To cover with insurance: *insure a car.* **2.** To make

instruct/instrument

Instruct *is from Latin* instruct-, *a form of* instruere, *"to build up, to equip, to inform or teach (someone)":* in-, *"into, toward,* + struere, *"to build."* **Instrument** *is from Latin* instrūmentum, *"something used for building, equipping, or teaching, a tool,"* *which is also from* instruere.

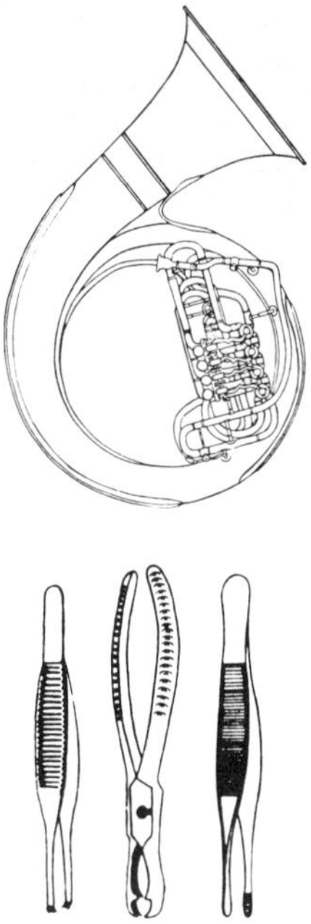

instruments
Above: Helicon
Below: Forceps

sure or certain of; guarantee: *insure the safety of the people.* —**in·sur'er** *n.* [SEE NOTE on p. 308]

in·sur·gent |ĭn sûr'jənt| *adj.* Rising in revolt: *The insurgent forces overthrew the government.* —*n.* Someone who revolts against authority.

in·sur·mount·a·ble |ĭn'sər **moun'**tə bəl| *adj.* Not capable of being surmounted; insuperable: *an insurmountable obstacle.*

in·sur·rec·tion |ĭn'sə **rĕk'**shən| *n.* The act or an example of open revolt against a civil authority or government; a rebellion.

in·tact |ĭn **tăkt'**| *adj.* Not impaired, injured, or damaged.

in·take |**ĭn'**tāk'| *n.* **1.** An opening by which a liquid or gas enters a container or pipe. **2. a.** The act or process of taking in: *an efficient air intake.* **b.** Something or the amount of something taken in: *an adequate intake of food.* —***modifier:*** *an intake valve.*

in·tan·gi·ble |ĭn **tăn'**jə bəl| *adj.* **1.** Not capable of being touched; lacking physical substance. **2.** Not capable of being perceived; vague; elusive: *an intangible change.* —*n.* Something intangible: *Beauty is an intangible in the art of design.* —**in·tan'gi·bly** *adv.*

in·te·ger |**ĭn'**tĭ jər| *n.* Any member of the set (. . . –2, –1, 0, +1, +2, . . .), including all of the positive whole numbers, all of the negative whole numbers, and zero. [SEE NOTE]

integer, etc.

Integer *was originally short for* integer number, *"a whole number"; this is from Latin* integer, *"untouched":* in-, *"not, un-,"* + teg-, *"touch."* Integer *also meant "unspoiled, complete, perfect, honest";* **integral, integrate,** *and* **integrity** *come from it in various of its senses. In Old French,* integer *became* entier, *which was borrowed into English as* **entire**.

in·te·gral |**ĭn'**tĭ grəl| *adj.* **1.** Necessary to form a whole: *Finland was once an integral part of Sweden.* **2.** Of, involving, or expressed as an integer or integers. —**in'te·gral·ly** *adv.*

in·te·grate |**ĭn'**tĭ grāt'| *v.* **in·te·grat·ed, in·te·grat·ing. 1.** To combine into a whole; unite: *All subjects were integrated into one course.* **2.** To eliminate racial or ethnic divisions in (a school system, neighborhood, etc.); desegregate. —**in'te·grat'ed** *adj.: an integrated neighborhood.* —**in'te·gra'tion** *n.*

in·teg·ri·ty |ĭn **tĕg'**rĭ tē| *n.* **1.** Strict personal honesty and independence: *a man of integrity.* **2.** Completeness; unity: *a movie shown without interruptions to maintain its integrity.*

in·teg·u·ment |ĭn **tĕg'**yə mənt| *n.* An outer covering, such as an animal's skin or a seed coat.

in·tel·lect |**ĭn'**tl ĕkt'| *n.* **1.** The capacity of the mind to think, reason, and learn. **2.** Someone of great intellectual ability.

in·tel·lec·tu·al |ĭn'tl **ĕk'**cho͞o əl| *adj.* **1.** Of or requiring use of the intellect: *intellectual activities; an intellectual discussion.* **2.** Having or seeming to have superior intelligence: *an intellectual person.* —*n.* A person of trained intelligence, especially a person devoted to the arts, letters, etc. —**in'tel·lec'tu·al·ly** *adv.*

in·tel·li·gence |ĭn **tĕl'**ə jəns| *n.* **1.** The capacity to learn, think, understand, and know; mental ability. **2.** Information; news, especially secret information about an enemy. —***modifier:*** *army intelligence reports.*

intelligence quotient. A number that relates actual age in years and mental age as measured by a test, derived by dividing the measured mental age by the age in years and multiplying the quotient by 100.

intelligence test. Any one of a number of standard tests used in measuring a person's intelligence or mental age.

in·tel·li·gent |ĭn **tĕl'**ə jənt| *adj.* **1.** Having intelligence: *an intelligent boy.* **2.** Showing intelligence; wise or thoughtful: *an intelligent decision.* —**in·tel'li·gent·ly** *adv.*

in·tel·li·gi·ble |ĭn **tĕl'**ə jə bəl| *adj.* Capable of being understood; comprehensible: *intelligible speech.* —**in·tel'li·gi·bly** *adv.*

in·tem·per·ance |ĭn **tĕm'**pər əns| *n.* Lack of temperance, as in the indulgence of an appetite or passion.

in·tem·per·ate |ĭn **tĕm'**pər ĭt| *adj.* Not temperate or moderate: *an intemperate drinker; intemperate language.* —**in·tem'per·ate·ly** *adv.*

in·tend |ĭn **tĕnd'**| *v.* **1.** To have as a design or purpose; have in mind; plan: *We intended to get an early start but were delayed.* **2.** To design for a specific purpose, function, or recipient: *For whom is this package intended?*

in·tend·ed |ĭn **tĕn'**dĭd| *adj.* **1.** Planned; intentional: *an intended insult.* **2.** Future; prospective: *his intended bride.* —*n. Informal.* Someone's prospective spouse: *her intended.*

in·tense |ĭn **tĕns'**| *adj.* **1.** Extremely deep, strong, forceful, or concentrated: *an intense blue; an intense odor; intense light.* **2.** Deeply felt; profound: *intense affection.* —**in·tense'ly** *adv.*

in·ten·si·fi·er |ĭn **tĕn'**sə fī'ər| *n.* **1.** Someone or something that intensifies. **2.** A word or word element that is used to add force or emphasis but contributes little or no new meaning; for example, the words *very* and *terribly* in *very pleased* and *terribly dark* are intensifiers.

in·ten·si·fy |ĭn **tĕn'**sə fī'| *v.* **in·ten·si·fied, in·ten·si·fy·ing, in·ten·si·fies.** To make or become intense or more intense: *The eerie music intensified the mystery of the movie. The battles intensified as the month wore on.*

in·ten·si·ty |ĭn **tĕn'**sĭ tē| *n., pl.* **in·ten·si·ties. 1.** The quality or condition of being intense; extreme depth, force, strength, or concentration: *emotional intensity; intensity of color.* **2.** Degree or amount of depth, force, strength, etc.: *The two colors vary in intensity.*

in·ten·sive |ĭn **tĕn'**sĭv| *adj.* Of or marked by intensity; concentrated: *intensive study; intensive thought.* —*n.* A word or word element used as an intensifier. —**in·ten'sive·ly** *adv.*

in·tent |ĭn **tĕnt'**| *adj.* **1.** Concentrated; intense: *an intent expression.* **2.** Having the mind fixed on some purpose; determined: *intent on securing their freedom.* —*n.* Aim; intention: *a hostile intent.* —**in·tent'ly** *adv.* —**in·tent'ness** *n.*

in·ten·tion |ĭn **tĕn'**shən| *n.* **1.** Something intended; a plan, purpose, etc. **2. intentions.** Purposes or motives in mind: *friendly intentions.*

in·ten·tion·al |ĭn **tĕn'**shə nəl| *adj.* Done deliberately; intended: *an intentional error.* —**in·ten'tion·al·ly** *adv.*

in·ter |ĭn **tûr'**| *v.* **in·terred, in·ter·ring.** To place in a grave; bury.

inter–. A prefix meaning: **1.** Between; among: **international. 2.** Mutually; together: **interact.** [SEE NOTE]

inter–/intra–

These are both Latin prefixes; inter *means "between (two or more things or people)," and* intrā *means "inside (one thing)." Thus in English* **interstate** *means "between two or more states," and* **intrastate** *means "inside one state."*

in·ter·act |ĭn'tər **ăkt'**| *v.* To act on or affect each other: *a pair of adjustments that interact; people who interact peacefully.* —**in'ter·ac'tion** *n.*

in·ter·cede |ĭn'tər **sēd'**| *v.* **in·ter·ced·ed, in·ter·ced·ing. 1.** To plead on another's behalf: *Mother interceded for her sister when grandfather was* *angry.* **2.** To mediate in a dispute: *Congress can intercede in certain labor disputes.*

in•ter•cept |ĭn′tər **sĕpt′**| *v.* **1.** To stop or interrupt the course or progress of: *intercept a messenger; intercept a quarterback's pass.* **2.** To cut off or bound part of (a line, plane, surface, or solid). —**in′ter•cep′tion** *n.*

in•ter•ces•sion |ĭn′tər **sĕsh′**ən| *n.* The act or an example of interceding.

in•ter•change |ĭn′tĕr **chānj′**| *v.* **-changed, -chang•ing. 1.** To switch each of (two things) into the place of the other. **2.** To give and receive mutually; exchange: *interchange ideas.* —*n.* |**ĭn′**tər chānj′|. **1.** The act or an example of interchanging: *the interchange of commodities.* **2.** A highway intersection that allows traffic to flow freely by means of separate levels from one road to another.

in•ter•change•a•ble |ĭn′tər **chān′**jə bəl| *adj.* Capable of being switched or interchanged: *Synonyms are interchangeable only in certain cases.* —**in′ter•change′a•bly** *adv.*

in•ter•col•le•giate |ĭn′tər kə **lē′**jĭt| *or* |-jē ĭt| *adj.* Involving two or more colleges: *an intercollegiate tournament.*

in•ter•con•ti•nen•tal |ĭn′tər kŏn′tə **nĕn′**tl| *adj.* **1.** Involving or extending between two continents: *intercontinental warfare.* **2.** Capable of flight from one continent to another: *an intercontinental ballistic missile.*

in•ter•course |**ĭn′**tər kôrs′| *or* |-kōrs′| *n.* **1.** Interchange between persons or groups; communication: *commercial intercourse between nations.* **2.** The act or process of mating, as between male and female mammals.

in•ter•de•nom•i•na•tion•al |ĭn′tər dĭ nŏm′ə **nā′**shə nəl| *adj.* Involving two or more denominations: *an interdenominational church.*

in•ter•de•pend•ent |ĭn′tər dĭ **pĕn′**dənt| *n.* Mutually dependent. —**in′ter•de•pend′ence** *n.*

in•ter•dict |ĭn′tər **dĭkt′**| *v.* **1.** To prohibit; forbid: *The Church interdicted use of certain words in prayer.* **2.** To impede; block: *bombed the trail to interdict enemy supply lines.* —*n.* |**ĭn′**tər dĭkt′|. An act of interdicting.

in•ter•est |**ĭn′**trĭst| *or* |-tər ĭst| *n.* **1. a.** Willingness to give special attention to something; active concern; curiosity: *arousing the reader's interest.* **b.** The quality of arousing such willingness: *a speech that lacked interest for me.* **c.** A subject that arouses such willingness: *Music, science fiction, and girls were among his interests.* **2.** Often **interests.** Advantage; benefit: *a government decision that is not in the public interest.* **3.** A right, claim, or legal share in something: *an interest in a business.* **4.** A charge paid for borrowing money, usually a percentage of the amount borrowed: *Bank interest is usually 5 per cent.* **5.** An excess or bonus beyond what is expected or due: *She paid back the insult with interest.* —**modifier:** *an interest rate of 7 per cent.* —*v.* **1.** To arouse interest in: *The teacher tries to interest her students in the subject.* **2.** To cause to become involved or concerned: *Can I interest you in buying a used car?*

in•ter•est•ed |**ĭn′**trĭ stĭd| *or* |-tər ĭ stĭd| *or* |-tə rĕs′tĭd| *adj.* **1.** Having or showing interest; disposed to participate, learn, or work: *She is interested in language study.* **2.** Having a right, claim, or share: *The interested parties met to settle the dispute.* —**in′ter•est•ed•ly** *adv.*

in•ter•est•ing |**ĭn′**trĭ stĭng| *or* |-tər ĭ stĭng| *or* |-tə rĕs′tĭng| *adj.* Arousing or holding interest or attention; absorbing: *an interesting legend.* —**in′ter•est•ing•ly** *adv.*

in•ter•fere |ĭn′tər **fîr′**| *v.* **in•ter•fered, in•ter•fer•ing. 1.** To act as an obstacle or hindrance; conflict: *Noises interfered with his concentration.* **2.** To intrude in the affairs of others; meddle.

in•ter•fer•ence |ĭn′tər **fîr′**əns| *n.* **1.** The act or an example of interfering: *our mindless interference with the vital life cycles of plants and animals.* **2.** In football: **a.** Illegal action against a player trying to catch a pass. **b.** The action of blocking for a ball carrier or the players providing such blocking. **3.** In various other sports, an illegal obstruction of a play or player. **4.** A physical effect in which two or more waves alternately reinforce and cancel each other at different points in space or time.

in•ter•im |**ĭn′**tər ĭm| *n.* An interval of time between two events, periods, or processes: *In the interim, he made do with odd jobs.* —*adj.* Of or during an interim; temporary: *an interim head of state.*

in•te•ri•or |ĭn **tîr′**ē ər| *n.* **1.** The inner part of something; the inside: *the interior of a house; the earth's interior.* **2.** The inland part of (a country, state, forest, etc.): *Eskimos in Alaska's interior get around on dog sleds.* —*adj.* **1.** Of or located in the inside; inner: *the interior surfaces of the heart.* **2.** Located away from a coast or border; inland: *Interior Canada is sparsely populated.* **3.** Of the interiors of houses and other structures: *an interior designer.*

interior angle. 1. Any of the innermost four of the eight angles formed when two straight lines are cut by a third straight line. **2.** An angle formed by two adjacent sides of a polygon and included within the polygon. [SEE PICTURE]

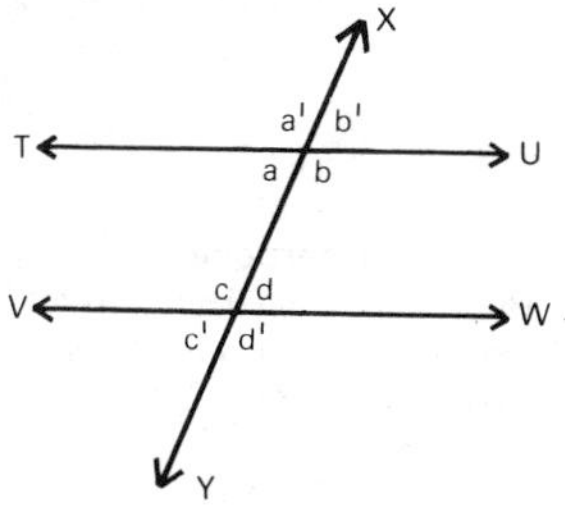

interior angle
The angles a, b, c, and d are the interior angles formed when the lines TU, VW are cut by the transversal XY

interj. interjection.

in•ter•ject |ĭn′tər **jĕkt′**| *v.* **1.** To put in between or among other things; insert briefly: *paused in his speech to interject a joke.* **2.** To exclaim: *"Hurry!" he interjected.*

in•ter•jec•tion |ĭn′tər **jĕk′**shən| *n.* **1.** The act of interjecting. **2.** A phrase or remark that is interjected. **3.** In grammar, a word that expresses some abrupt or momentary emotion and that stands alone grammatically; for example, the word *Ouch!* and the word *oh,* as in *Oh, what a feast,* are interjections. **4.** Any exclamation. —**in′ter•jec′tion•al** *adj.*

in•ter•lace |ĭn′tər **lās′**| *v.* **-laced, -lac•ing.** To weave, lace, or twine together: *She interlaced the ribbons. The leafy branches interlaced.*

in•ter•lard |ĭn′tər **lärd′**| *v.* To insert at intervals; intersperse: *He interlarded his opinions throughout the report.*

in•ter•lock |ĭn′tər **lŏk′**| *v.* To unite firmly or join closely: *The dancers form a circle and interlock hands. Our eyes interlocked.*

in•ter•lop•er |**ĭn′**tər lō′pər| *n.* Someone who intrudes or interferes wrongfully; a meddler: *No others may interfere, no interlopers from outside.*

in•ter•lude |**ĭn′**tər lo͞od′| *n.* **1.** Something, such as an event, episode, or period of time, that intervenes or interrupts the course of events.

2. A short piece of music that occurs between large sections of a long composition, acts of a play, parts of a religious service, etc.

in•ter•mar•ry |ĭn′tər măr′ē| *v.* **-mar•ried, -mar•ry•ing, -mar•ries. 1.** To marry someone of another religion, nationality, race, etc. **2.** To marry someone who is a member of one's own family, clan, tribe, etc. —**in′ter•mar′riage** *n.*

in•ter•me•di•ar•y |ĭn′tər mē′dē ĕr′ē| *n., pl.* **in•ter•me•di•ar•ies.** A person who acts as a mediator or go-between. —*adj.* In between; intermediate.

in•ter•me•di•ate |ĭn′tər mē′dē ĭt| *adj.* **1.** Lying or occurring between two extremes; in between; in the middle: *of intermediate size; an intermediate skier.* **2.** Of the grades between primary and secondary levels: *intermediate schools.* —*n.* Something intermediate.

in•ter•ment |ĭn tûr′mənt| *n.* The act or process of interring; burial.

in•ter•mez•zo |ĭn′tər mĕt′sō| *or* |-mĕd′zō| *n., pl.* **in•ter•mez•zos.** A piece of music heard between sections of a larger work, acts of a play or opera, etc.; an interlude.

in•ter•mi•na•ble |ĭn tûr′mə nə bəl| *adj.* Having or seeming to have no end; endless: *an interminable play.* —**in•ter′mi•na•bly** *adv.*

in•ter•min•gle |ĭn′tər mĭng′gəl| *v.* **-min•gled, -min•gling.** To mix or mingle.

in•ter•mis•sion |ĭn′tər mĭsh′ən| *n.* An interruption or recess, as between the acts of a play.

in•ter•mit•tent |ĭn′tər mĭt′nt| *adj.* Stopping and starting at intervals; not continuous: *intermittent noises.* —**in′ter•mit′tent•ly** *adv.*

in•tern |ĭn′tûrn′| *n.* A recent graduate of a medical school who is undergoing supervised practical training. —*v.* **1.** |ĭn′tûrn′|. To train or serve as an intern. **2.** |ĭn tûrn′|. To detain or confine, especially in wartime: *intern a ship.* —**in•tern′ment** *n.*

in•ter•nal |ĭn tûr′nəl| *adj.* **1.** Of or located within the limits or surface of something; inner; interior: *internal organs.* **2.** Of the domestic affairs of a country: *internal political divisions.* —**in•ter′nal•ly** *adv.*

in•ter•nal-com•bus•tion engine |ĭn tûr′nəl-kəm bŭs′chən|. An engine whose fuel is burned inside the engine itself rather than in an outside furnace or burner.

in•ter•na•tion•al |ĭn′tər năsh′ə nəl| *adj.* Of or between two or more nations or nationalities: *international trade.* —**in′ter•na′tion•al•ly** *adv.*

international candle. A candle, a unit of illumination.

International Date Line. An imaginary line through the Pacific Ocean roughly along the 180th meridian, to the east of which, by international agreement, the calendar date is one day earlier than to the west.

in•ter•na•tion•al•ize |ĭn′tər năsh′ə nə līz′| *v.* **in•ter•na•tion•al•ized, in•ter•na•tion•al•iz•ing.** To put under international control: *They internationalized the canal.*

in•terne |ĭn′tûrn′| *or* |ĭn tûrn′| *n. & v.* **in•terned, in•tern•ing.** A form of the word **intern.**

in•ter•nec•ine |ĭn′tər nĕs′ēn′| *or* |-ĭn′| *or* |-nē′sĭn′| *adj.* **1.** Destructive or fatal to both sides: *internecine warfare between rival clans.* **2.** Involving conflict within a group or nation; internally destructive: *an internecine struggle for leadership of the party.*

in•tern•ist |ĭn′tûr′nĭst| *or* |ĭn tûr′nĭst| *n.* A physician who specializes in internal medicine.

in•tern•ship |ĭn′tûrn shĭp′| *n.* A period of service as an intern.

in•ter•plan•e•tar•y |ĭn′tər plăn′ĭ tĕr′ē| *adj.* Between planets, especially of the solar system.

in•ter•play |ĭn′tər plā′| *n.* Mutual action, reaction, or influence; interaction: *There is constant interplay between soils and plants.*

in•ter•po•late |ĭn tûr′pə lāt′| *v.* **in•ter•po•lat•ed, in•ter•po•lat•ing. 1.** To determine an approximate value of (a mathematical function) between two known values, using some rule or procedure other than the function itself. **2.** To insert or add, as to a text. —**in•ter′po•la′tion** *n.*

in•ter•pose |ĭn′tər pōz′| *v.* **in•ter•posed, in•ter•pos•ing. 1.** To put or come between two parts, things, places, etc. **2.** To introduce (a remark, question, etc.) into a conversation; interject. **3.** To intervene, especially for the purpose of mediating. —**in′ter•po•si′tion** *n.* [SEE NOTE]

interpose
"Those who in quarrels interpose
Must often wipe a bloody nose."
—John Gay (1688–1732).

in•ter•pret |ĭn tûr′prĭt| *v.* **1.** To explain or clarify the meaning or significance of: *Scientists interpret data.* **2.** To see or understand in a certain way: *He interpreted the letter to mean that the deal was off.* **3.** To perform or present according to one's artistic understanding: *an actor interpreting a role.* **4.** To translate from one language to another.

in•ter•pre•ta•tion |ĭn tûr′prĭ tā′shən| *n.* **1. a.** The act or process of interpreting: *the interpretation of the law.* **b.** An example of interpreting; an explanation of the meaning of something unclear: *two different interpretations of a dream.* **2.** An artistic performance or presentation that expresses someone's understanding of the work. **3.** Translation, especially oral translation.

in•ter•pre•ta•tive |ĭn tûr′prĭ tā′tĭv| *adj.* Meant to explain: *an interpretative commentary.*

in•ter•pret•er |ĭn tûr′prĭ tər| *n.* **1.** A person who orally translates a conversation or speech from one language to another. **2.** A person who explains or expounds on a certain subject.

in•ter•pre•tive |ĭn tûr′prĭ tĭv| *adj.* A form of the word **interpretative.**

in•ter•ra•cial |ĭn′tər rā′shəl| *adj.* Of or between different races: *interracial cooperation.*

in•ter•re•lat•ed |ĭn′tər rĭ lā′tĭd| *adj.* Related to each other; affecting one another reciprocally.

in•ter•re•la•tion•ship |ĭn′tər rĭ lā′shən shĭp′| *n.* Mutual relationship: *the interrelationships among living things.*

in•ter•ro•gate |ĭn tĕr′ə gāt′| *v.* **in•ter•ro•gat•ed, in•ter•ro•gat•ing.** To question closely, as under formal conditions. —**in•ter′ro•ga′tor** *n.*

in•ter•ro•ga•tion |ĭn tĕr′ə gā′shən| *n.* **1.** The act of interrogating or the condition of being interrogated: *the interrogation of prisoners; confessed under interrogation.* **2.** An example of interrogating: *daily interrogations.*

in•ter•rog•a•tive |ĭn′tə rŏg′ə tĭv| *adj.* **1.** Of the nature of a question; asking a question: *an interrogative sentence.* **2.** Used in asking a question: *an interrogative pronoun.* —*n.* **1.** A word or form used in asking a question. **2.** A question.

in•ter•rog•a•to•ry |ĭn′tə rŏg′ə tôr′ē| *or* |-tōr′ē| *adj.* Interrogative.

ă pat/ā pay/â care/ä father/ĕ pet/ē be/ĭ pit/ī pie/î fierce/ŏ pot/ō go/ô paw, for/oi oil/ŏŏ book/ōō boot/ou out/ŭ cut/û fur/*th* the/th thin/hw which/zh vision/ə ago, item, pencil, atom, circus

in•ter•rupt |ĭn′tə **rŭpt′**| *v.* **1. a.** To break in upon: *interrupt a speech.* **b.** To stop the conversation, speech, or action of (someone) by breaking in: *Don't interrupt your betters.* **2.** To break the continuity of: *His father's illness interrupted his schooling.* —**in′ter•rup′tion** *n.* [SEE NOTE]

in•ter•sect |ĭn′tər **sĕkt′**| *v.* **1.** To be distinct from and have at least one point in common with (a line, curve, or geometric figure). **2.** To share elements in common with (another set). **3.** To cross: *roads that intersect north of town.*

in•ter•sec•tion |ĭn′tər **sĕk′**shən| *n.* **1.** The set of all points that are common to two or more geometric elements or figures: *the intersection of two straight lines.* **2. a.** The set of all the elements that are common to two other sets. **b.** The mathematical operation of forming or determining such a set: *The intersection of distinct sets forms the empty set.* **3. a.** The point where two or more things intersect. **b.** A corner where two or more roads intersect.

in•ter•sperse |ĭn′tər **spûrs′**| *v.* **in•ter•spersed, in•ter•spers•ing. 1.** To scatter here and there among other things: *We interspersed fern fronds among the flowers.* **2.** To give variety to by distributing things here and there: *interspersed the serious story with comic moments.*

in•ter•state |**ĭn′**tər stāt′| *adj.* Of, between, or connecting two or more states: *interstate commerce; an interstate highway.*

in•ter•stel•lar |ĭn′tər **stĕl′**ər| *adj.* Between the stars: *interstellar space.*

in•ter•twine |ĭn′tər **twīn′**| *v.* **-twined, -twin•ing.** To twist, twine, or link together: *intertwined the strands into a braid. Their arms intertwined.*

in•ter•val |**ĭn′**tər vəl| *n.* **1.** A period of time between two events or recurrences: *an interval of rest before resuming work.* **2.** A space between two points or objects: *Pierce the meat deeply at one-inch intervals.* **3. a.** The set of all numbers that lie between two given numbers, sometimes including either or both of the given numbers. **b.** A line segment that represents the numbers in this set. **4.** The difference in pitch between two musical tones.

in•ter•vene |ĭn′tər **vēn′**| *v.* **in•ter•vened, in•ter•ven•ing. 1.** To occur or come between two things, points, or events: *A day of calm intervened between the hectic weeks.* **2. a.** To enter a course of events so as to hinder or change it: *The governor intervened to delay the execution.* **b.** To interfere, usually with force, in the affairs of another nation.

in•ter•ven•tion |ĭn′tər **vĕn′**shən| *n.* **1.** The act or an example of intervening: *an intervention to settle an argument.* **2.** Interference in the affairs of another nation, usually with force.

in•ter•view |**ĭn′**tər vyōō′| *n.* **1.** A face-to-face meeting: *an interview for a job.* **2. a.** A conversation between a reporter and another person for the purpose of obtaining facts and statements. **b.** An account of such a conversation. —*v.* To have an interview with: *interview an actress.* —**in′ter•view′er** *n.*

in•ter•weave |ĭn′tər **wēv′**| *v.* **-wove** |-**wōv′**|, **-wo•ven** |-**wō′**vən|, **-weav•ing. 1.** To weave or twine together: *Cloth is made by interweaving threads. See how the vines interweave.* **2.** To connect or combine: *The author skillfully interweaves two plots in a single story.*

in•tes•tate |ĭn **tĕs′**tāt′| *or* |-tĭt| *adj.* **1.** Having made no legal will. **2.** Not disposed of by a legal will.

in•tes•ti•nal |ĭn **tĕs′**tə nəl| *adj.* Of, in, or involving the intestine: *an intestinal parasite.* —**in•tes′ti•nal•ly** *adv.*

in•tes•tine |ĭn **tĕs′**tĭn| *n.* The part of the alimentary canal that extends from the outlet of the stomach to the anus; the large intestine and small intestine. [SEE PICTURE]

in•ti•ma•cy |**ĭn′**tə mə sē| *n.* The condition of being intimate, especially close personal relationship.

in•ti•mate[1] |**ĭn′**tə mĭt| *adj.* **1.** Marked by a close and thorough acquaintance: *an intimate understanding of children.* **2.** Essential; innermost: *one's intimate thoughts.* **3.** Very personal; close: *an intimate friend.* —*n.* A close friend or confidant. —**in′ti•mate•ly** *adv.* [SEE NOTE]

in•ti•mate[2] |**ĭn′**tə māt′| *v.* **in•ti•mat•ed, in•ti•mat•ing.** To hint; imply: *He intimated that there was trouble ahead.* —**in′ti•ma′tion** *n.* [SEE NOTE]

in•tim•i•date |ĭn **tĭm′**ĭ dāt′| *v.* **in•tim•i•dat•ed, in•tim•i•dat•ing.** To frighten or inhibit by or as if by threats: *The advancing forces did not intimidate the Romans.* —**in•tim′i•da′tion** *n.*

in•to |**ĭn′**tōō| *prep.* **1.** To the inside of: *going into the house.* **2.** So as to be in or within: *enter into an agreement.* **3.** To the action or occupation of: *go into banking.* **4.** To the condition or form of: *break into pieces.* **5.** To a time or place in the course of: *It's getting well into the week.* **6.** Toward; in the direction of: *looking into the distance.* **7.** Against: *run into a tree.* **8.** *Informal.* Interested in or involved with: *They are into health foods.*

in•tol•er•a•ble |ĭn **tŏl′**ər ə bəl| *adj.* Not capable of being tolerated; unbearable: *an intolerable life of poverty.* —**in•tol′er•a•bly** *adv.*

in•tol•er•ance |ĭn **tŏl′**ər əns| *n.* The quality or condition of being intolerant.

in•tol•er•ant |ĭn **tŏl′**ər ənt| *adj.* **1.** Not tolerant, as of others; prejudiced: *an intolerant man.* **2.** Unable to endure: *intolerant of certain drugs.*

in•to•na•tion |ĭn′tō **nā′**shən| *n.* **1.** The way in which the speaking voice emphasizes words, makes pauses, or rises and falls in pitch in order to convey meaning. **2. a.** A particular quality or tone of voice: *an angry intonation.* **b.** Expression or expressiveness: *She spoke without intonation.* **3.** The manner in which musical tones are produced, sung, chanted, etc., especially with respect to accuracy of pitch.

in•tone |ĭn **tōn′**| *v.* **in•toned, in•ton•ing.** To recite in a singing or chanting voice, often on a single tone: *intoned prayers in church.*

in•tox•i•cant |ĭn **tŏk′**sĭ kənt| *n.* Something that intoxicates, especially an alcoholic drink.

in•tox•i•cate |ĭn **tŏk′**sĭ kāt′| *v.* **in•tox•i•cat•ed, in•tox•i•cat•ing. 1.** To make drunk. **2.** To fill with great excitement, enthusiasm, or delight; stimulate: *The idea intoxicated her.*

in•tox•i•cat•ed |ĭn **tŏk′**sĭ kā′tĭd| *adj.* **1.** Drunk or in a condition resembling drunkenness. **2.** Highly stimulated; elated; overjoyed.

in•tox•i•ca•tion |ĭn tŏk′sĭ **kā′**shən| *n.* **1.** The condition of being intoxicated; drunkenness. **2.** Great excitement, elation, or delight.

interrupt, etc.
Interrupt *is from Latin* interruptus, *the past participle of* interrumpere, *"to break apart, to break into the middle of":* inter-, *"between, in among,"* + rumpere, *"to break." Other English words derived from* rumpere *include* **abrupt** *("broken off short"),* **corrupt** *("ruined, morally destroyed"),* **disrupt** *("to break into pieces").*

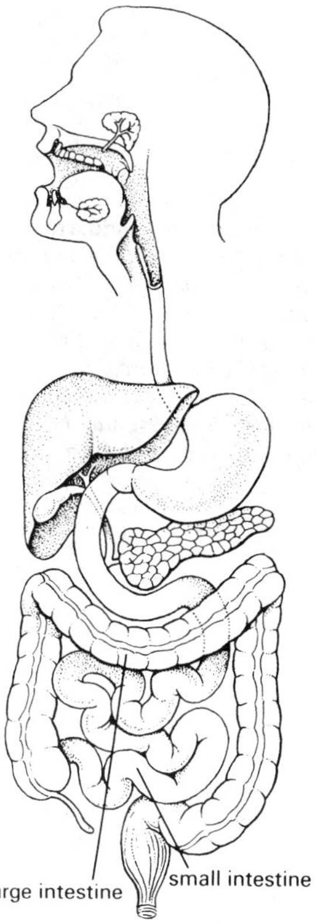

intestine

intimate[1-2]
Intimate[1] *is from Latin* intimātus, *"closely associated," from* intimus, *"inmost, deep, a close friend."* **Intimate**[2] *is from Latin* intimāre, *"to bring into someone's confidence, to announce," which is also from* intimus, *"inmost."*

intricate/intrigue
Intricate *is from Latin* intricātus, *"entangled," from* intricāre, *"to entangle, to perplex":* in-, *"into,"* + tricae, *"troubles."* Intricāre *separately passed into Italian as* intrigare, *which formed the noun* intrigo, *"a complication, a scheme"; this was borrowed into French as* intrigue *and thence into English as* **intrigue**.

inundate/undulate
Inundate *is from Latin* inundāre, *"to flow into, to overflow":* in-, *"into,"* + unda, *"wave."* Unda *also formed a diminutive noun,* undula, *"little wave," and a verb,* undulāre, *"to make a gentle wavy motion";* undulāre *was borrowed into English as* **undulate**.

invalid[1-2]
Invalid[2] *is from Latin* invalidus, *"not valid, weak":* in-, *"not, un-,"* + validus, *"valid, strong." In French* invalidus *became* invalide *and took on the special meaning "disabled or sick person"; this was borrowed into English as* **invalid[1]**.

ă pat/ā pay/â care/ä father/ĕ pet/ ē be/ĭ pit/ī pie/î fierce/ŏ pot/ ō go/ô paw, for/oi oil/ŏŏ book/ ōō boot/ou out/ŭ cut/û fur/ *th* the/th thin/hw which/zh vision/ ə ago, item, pencil, atom, circus

intra-. A prefix meaning "inside of, within": **intramural.** [SEE NOTE on p. 474]

in•trac•ta•ble |ĭn trăk'tə bəl| *adj.* Hard to manage or control; unmanageable; stubborn: *an intractable child.* —**in•trac'ta•bly** *adv.*

in•tra•mu•ral |ĭn'trə myŏŏr'əl| *adj.* Carried on within a school or other institution and involving no outsiders: *an intramural athletic program.*

in•tran•si•gent |ĭn trăn'sə jənt| *adj.* Refusing to compromise; stubborn. —**in•tran'si•gence** *n.* —**in•tran'si•gent•ly** *adv.*

in•tran•si•tive |ĭn trăn'sĭ tĭv| *adj.* Being or using a verb that does not require a direct object to complete its meaning; for example, in the sentence *The bell rang,* the verb *rang* is intransitive. —**in•tran'si•tive•ly** *adv.*

in•tra•u•ter•ine |ĭn'trə yōō'tər ĭn| *or* |-tə rīn'| *adj.* Within or for use within the uterus.

in•tra•ve•nous |ĭn'trə vē'nəs| *adj.* Within or into a vein: *an intravenous injection.* —**in'tra•ve'nous•ly** *adv.*

in•treat |ĭn trēt'| *v.* A form of the word **entreat.**

in•trench |ĭn trĕnch'| *v.* A form of the word **entrench.**

in•trench•ment |ĭn trĕnch'mənt| *n.* A form of the word **entrenchment.**

in•trep•id |ĭn trĕp'ĭd| *adj.* Brave, bold, and fearless; showing courage: *the intrepid pioneers.* —**in'tre•pid'i•ty** *n.* —**in•trep'id•ly** *adv.*

in•tri•ca•cy |ĭn'trĭ kə sē| *n., pl.* **in•tri•ca•cies. 1.** Complexity, as of design or structure: *the intricacy of a maze.* **2.** A complex part or arrangement of parts that helps to complicate the whole: *the intricacies of medicine.*

in•tri•cate |ĭn'trĭ kĭt| *adj.* **1.** Having a complicated structure, pattern, etc.; complex: *an intricate design.* **2.** Hard to understand: *intricate instructions.* —**in'tri•cate•ly** *adv.* [SEE NOTE]

in•trigue |ĭn trēg'| *v.* **in•trigued, in•tri•guing. 1.** To catch the interest or arouse the curiosity of; fascinate: *The mystery of hibernation has long intrigued biologists.* **2.** To plot or scheme secretly: *rivals intriguing against one another.* —**in•tri'guing** *adj.: an intriguing puzzle.* —*n.* |ĭn'trēg'| *or* |ĭn trēg'|. **1. a.** Plotting or scheming carried on in secret. **b.** A secret plot or scheme. **2.** A secret love affair. [SEE NOTE]

in•trin•sic |ĭn trĭn'sĭk| *adj.* Being part of the basic nature of a thing; fundamental; essential: *the intrinsic difficulty of mathematics.* —**in•trin'si•cal•ly** *adv.*

in•tro•duce |ĭn'trə dōōs'| *or* |-dyōōs'| *v.* **in•tro•duced, in•tro•duc•ing. 1.** To present (a person) by name to another or others in order to establish an acquaintance: *introduce a young person to a grownup.* **2.** To provide with a beginning knowledge or first experience of something: *This class will introduce you to tennis.* **3.** To open or begin: *She wrote a preface to introduce her book.* **4. a.** To bring or put in (something new or different); add: *introduce suspense into a story.* **b.** To bring in and establish in a new place or surroundings: *Dandelions were introduced from Europe.* **5.** To propose, create, or bring into use or acceptance for the first time: *introduce faster, safer methods; introduce legislation in Congress.* **6.** To put inside or into something; insert or inject: *introduce a vaccine into the body.*

in•tro•duc•tion |ĭn'trə dŭk'shən| *n.* **1.** A short section at the beginning of a book, speech, musical composition, play, etc., that leads into or prepares the way for what will follow. **2. a.** The act or process of introducing: *the introduction of the art of printing in the 15th century.* **b.** A particular act of introducing: *Alice made the introductions at the party.* **3.** Anything that introduces: *Rocks and minerals are fine introductions to the study of natural history.* **4.** A book or course of study that introduces students to a subject.

in•tro•duc•to•ry |ĭn'trə dŭk'tə rē| *adj.* Serving to introduce a subject, person, etc.: *an introductory paragraph; a few introductory remarks.*

in•tro•spec•tion |ĭn'trə spĕk'shən| *n.* The act or practice of looking inward to examine one's own thoughts and feelings.

in•tro•spec•tive |ĭn'trə spĕk'tĭv| *adj.* Having the habit or involving the practice of looking inward to examine one's own thoughts and feelings: *an introspective man; an introspective philosophy.* —**in'tro•spec'tive•ly** *adv.*

in•tro•vert |ĭn'trə vûrt'| *n.* A person whose interest tends to center on his own inner thoughts and feelings rather than on the people and things around him. —**in'tro•vert'ed** *adj.*

in•trude |ĭn trōōd'| *v.* **in•trud•ed, in•trud•ing.** To break, come, or force in without being wanted or asked: *Don't intrude on my privacy. Don't intrude your opinions into their argument.* —**in•trud'er** *n.*

in•tru•sion |ĭn trōō'zhən| *n.* **1.** The act of intruding: *Do you dare risk intrusion upon my privacy?* **2.** A particular act of intruding: *an annoying intrusion.*

in•tru•sive |ĭn trōō'sĭv| *adj.* Intruding or tending to intrude: *a rude, intrusive reporter.* —**in•tru'sive•ly** *adv.*

in•trust |ĭn trŭst'| *v.* A form of the word **entrust.**

in•tu•i•tion |ĭn'tōō ĭsh'ən| *or* |-tyōō-| *n.* **1.** The power of knowing or understanding something instantly, by instinct, without having to reason it out or to get proof. **2.** A perception based on insight or instinct.

in•tu•i•tive |ĭn tōō'ĭ tĭv| *or* |-tyōō'-| *adj.* **1.** Of or based on intuition: *intuitive powers; an intuitive understanding.* **2.** Having or using intuition: *an intuitive mind.* —**in•tu'i•tive•ly** *adv.*

in•un•date |ĭn'ŭn dāt'| *v.* **in•un•dat•ed, in•un•dat•ing. 1.** To cover with water; flood: *A tidal wave inundated the beach.* **2.** To overwhelm, as with a flood: *The courts are inundated with cases.* —**in'un•da'tion** *n.* [SEE NOTE]

in•ure |ĭn yŏŏr'| *v.* **in•ured, in•ur•ing.** To make used to something undesirable; accustom; harden: *Hard winters inured the pioneers to cold.*

in•vade |ĭn vād'| *v.* **in•vad•ed, in•vad•ing. 1.** To enter in order to attack, plunder, conquer, or take over: *The Romans invaded Britain.* **2.** To get into and spread harm through: *Viruses invade cells of the body. Locusts may invade our fields.* **3.** To enter in great numbers; overrun: *On winter weekends, skiers invade the mountain town.* **4.** To trespass or intrude upon; interfere with; violate: *invade someone's privacy.* —**in•vad'ing** *adj.: an invading army.* —**in•vad'er** *n.*

in•va•lid[1] |ĭn'və lĭd| *n.* A sick, weak, injured, or disabled person, especially someone in poor health for a long time. [SEE NOTE]

in•val•id[2] |ĭn văl'ĭd| *adj.* Not valid or proper;

without force, foundation, etc.: *an invalid will.* —**in•val'id•ly** *adv.* [SEE NOTE on p. 478]

in•val•i•date |ĭn văl'ĭ dāt'| *v.* **in•val•i•dat•ed, in•val•i•dat•ing.** To make void; nullify: *invalidated a will.*

in•val•u•a•ble |ĭn văl'yōō ə bəl| *adj.* Of a value greater than can be measured; very valuable: *invaluable art treasures; his invaluable help.* —**in•val'u•a•bly** *adv.*

in•var•i•a•ble |ĭn vâr'ē ə bəl| *adj.* Not changing or varying; constant; unchanging: *an invariable response.* —**in•var'i•a•bly** *adv.*

in•va•sion |ĭn vā'zhən| *n.* **1. a.** The act of invading: *the invasion of Italy by the Allies.* **b.** A particular act of invading, as a forceful entry or an attack, intrusion, onslaught, etc. **2.** The condition of being invaded: *a country in danger of invasion.* —**modifier:** *an invasion alert.*

in•vec•tive |ĭn vĕk'tĭv| *n.* Sharp, harsh, insulting words used to attack; violent denunciation or abuse.

in•veigh |ĭn vā'| *v.* To protest by speaking out violently and bitterly: *The tenants inveighed against higher rents.*

in•vei•gle |ĭn vē'gəl| *or* |-vā'-| *v.* **in•vei•gled, in•vei•gling.** To persuade, coax, or lure by flattering or deceiving: *They inveigled her into doing all the work.*

in•vent |ĭn vĕnt'| *v.* **1.** To think up and make, create, or devise (something that did not exist before): *invent new products; invent new words.* **2.** To make up: *invent an excuse.*

in•ven•tion |ĭn vĕn'shən| *n.* **1.** Something invented, as a device, system, or process that did not exist before: *Eli Whitney's cotton gin was an important invention.* **2.** The act of inventing: *the invention of the printing press.* **3.** The power or ability to invent: *a mystery writer of great invention.* **4.** Something that is made up or untrue: *His excuse was obviously an invention.*

in•ven•tive |ĭn vĕn'tĭv| *adj.* Having or showing the ability to think up new ideas, methods, etc.; creative; original: *a highly inventive mind.* —**in•ven'tive•ness** *n.*

in•ven•tor |ĭn vĕn'tər| *n.* An inventive person who thinks up new ideas and creates new things or methods.

in•ven•to•ry |ĭn'vən tôr'ē| *or* |-tōr'ē| *n., pl.* **in•ven•to•ries. 1.** A detailed list, as of goods or possessions. **2.** The process of making such a survey or list. **3.** The supply of goods on hand; stock: *The store's inventory is getting low.* —*v.* **in•ven•to•ried, in•ven•to•ry•ing, in•ven•to•ries.** To make an inventory of.

in•verse |ĭn vûrs'| *or* |ĭn'vûrs'| *adj.* **1.** Opposite, as in effect or character: *Addition and subtraction are inverse operations.* **2.** Reversed, as in order or sequence: *CBA is ABC in inverse order.* —*n.* **1.** Something opposite in effect or character: *Division is the inverse of multiplication.* **2.** An element x^* contained in a set S and related to another element x so that $x \blacklozenge x^* = I$, where $\blacklozenge$ is an operation defined for all pairs of elements in S and I is the identity element for that operation; an additive inverse or multiplicative inverse. —**in•verse'ly** *adv.*

inverse variation. A relationship between a pair of numbers x, y in which one decreases as the other increases, specifically the relationship expressed by $y = k/x$, where k is a constant.

in•ver•sion |ĭn vûr'zhən| *or* |-shən| *n.* **1.** The act of inverting or the condition of being inverted: *the inversion of "he was" in "a merry old soul was he."* **2.** Something inverted.

in•vert |ĭn vûrt'| *v.* **1.** To turn upside down: *Invert the jar and let it stand in a pan of water.* **2.** To reverse the order, position, or arrangement of: *invert a sentence by placing the predicate first.*

in•ver•te•brate |ĭn vûr'tə brĭt| *or* |-brāt'| *n.* An animal having no backbone, as a worm, clam, jellyfish, starfish, insect, or lobster. —*adj.* Having no backbone: *invertebrate animals.*

in•vest |ĭn vĕst'| *v.* **1.** To put (money) into something, such as property, stocks, or a business, in order to earn interest or make a profit: *She invested $18,000 in bonds.* **2.** To devote, spend, or use for future advantage or benefit: *They invested time and energy in the election campaign.* **3.** To entrust with a right or power: *invested with the authority to perform marriages.* **4.** To install in office with a formal ceremony: *invest a new bishop.* **5.** To provide, fill, or endow with a certain quality.

in•ves•ti•gate |ĭn vĕs'tĭ gāt'| *v.* **in•ves•ti•gat•ed, in•ves•ti•gat•ing. 1.** To look into or examine carefully in a search for facts, knowledge, or information: *investigate a burglary.* **2.** To make an investigation. [SEE NOTE]

in•ves•ti•ga•tion |ĭn vĕs'tĭ gā'shən| *n.* An examination, study, search, or inquiry conducted for the purpose of discovering facts or getting information.

in•ves•ti•ga•tor |ĭn vĕs'tĭ gā'tər| *n.* **1.** Someone who investigates. **2.** A detective.

in•vest•ment |ĭn vĕst'mənt| *n.* **1. a.** The act of investing: *the investment of money in new inventions.* **b.** A particular act of investing: *She made wise investments.* **2.** A sum of money invested: *interest earned on an investment.* **3.** Something in which money, time, or effort is invested: *Land is a good investment.*

in•ves•tor |ĭn vĕs'tər| *n.* A person, corporation, nation, etc., that invests money in the hope of making a profit.

in•vet•er•ate |ĭn vĕt'ər ĭt| *adj.* **1.** Fixed in a habit, custom, or practice; habitual; confirmed: *an inveterate reader.* **2.** Firmly established by having existed for a long time; long-standing; deep-rooted: *inveterate prejudice.*

in•vid•i•ous |ĭn vĭd'ē əs| *adj.* Likely to stir up bad feeling, envy, or resentment: *invidious comparisons between two children.* [SEE NOTE]

in•vig•or•ate |ĭn vĭg'ə rāt'| *v.* **in•vig•or•at•ed, in•vig•or•at•ing.** To fill with energy, strength, or vigor: *The crisp, cool autumn air invigorated her.* —**in•vig'or•at'ing** *adj.: an invigorating climate.*

in•vin•ci•ble |ĭn vĭn'sə bəl| *adj.* Too strong, powerful, or great to be defeated or overcome: *an invincible army; invincible courage.* —**in•vin'ci•bil'i•ty** *n.* —**in•vin'ci•bly** *adv.*

in•vi•o•la•ble |ĭn vī'ə lə bəl| *adj.* Regarded as sacred and not to be violated: *an inviolable sanctuary.*

in•vi•o•late |ĭn vī'ə lĭt| *adj.* Not violated, broken, invaded, or profaned; intact: *She kept her honor inviolate.*

in•vis•i•ble |ĭn vĭz'ə bəl| *adj.* Not capable of being seen; not visible: *Air is colorless and invis-*

investigate/vestige

Investigate *is from Latin* investīgāre, *"to trace out, to follow the tracks of (as a dog does)"*; in-, *"into,"* + vestīgium, *"tracks, footprints."* Vestīgium *was separately borrowed into English as* **vestige**.

invidious/envy

Invidious *is from Latin* invidiōsus, *"full of envy," from* invidia, *"envy," from* invidēre, *"to look at, to look at resentfully, to envy"*: in-, *"into, at,"* + vidēre, *"to look." Separately,* invidia *passed into Old French as* envie *and was borrowed into English as* **envy**.

ible. —**in•vis'i•bil'i•ty** *n.* —**in•vis'i•bly** *adv.*

in•vi•ta•tion |ĭn'vĭ **tā'**shən| *n.* **1.** A spoken or written request for someone to come somewhere or do something. **2.** The act of inviting.

in•vite |ĭn **vīt'**| *v.* **in•vit•ed, in•vit•ing. 1.** To ask (a person or persons) to come somewhere or do something: *invite guests to a wedding.* **2.** To ask formally: *The children invited the mayor to talk to their class.* **3.** To tend to bring on; provoke: *To drive recklessly is to invite disaster.* **4.** To tempt, lure, or entice: *The sun invites one to be out in the open air.*

in•vit•ing |ĭn **vī'**tĭng| *adj.* Attractive; tempting: *A swimming pool looks inviting on a hot day.*

in•vo•ca•tion |ĭn'və **kā'**shən| *n.* **1.** The act of invoking: *the people's prayerful invocation of their emperor.* **2.** An appeal for the presence or help of a higher power, as a prayer said at the opening of a religious service.

in•voice |**ĭn'**vois'| *n.* A detailed list of goods shipped to a buyer, with an account of all costs and charges. —*v.* **in•voiced, in•voic•ing.** To list or bill on an invoice: *invoice a shipment of books.* [SEE NOTE]

in•voke |ĭn **vōk'**| *v.* **in•voked, in•vok•ing. 1.** To call on (a higher power) for help, support, or inspiration: *The poet invoked the muse.* **2.** To ask or call for earnestly: *invoke divine blessing.* **3.** To use, apply, or put into effect: *The President invoked his power of veto.* **4.** To call up (a spirit) with magic words or spells.

in•vol•un•tar•y |ĭn **vŏl'**ən tĕr'ē| *adj.* **1.** Not subject to the control of the will: *an involuntary spasm.* **2.** Unintentional or accidental: *involuntary manslaughter.* —**in•vol'un•tar'i•ly** *adv.*

in•vo•lu•tion |ĭn'və **lōō'**shən| *n.* The operation of raising a number or mathematical expression to a power.

in•volve |ĭn **vŏlv'**| *v.* **in•volved, in•volv•ing. 1.** To call for; require: *Camping trips involve hard work.* **2.** To take in; include: *The plot of the play involves fairies, elves, and magic spells.* **3.** To have to do with; deal with: *Condensation involves the changing of a gas into a liquid.* **4.** To draw in; mix up; implicate: *He became involved in a smuggling ring.* **5.** To absorb completely; engross: *involved in her work.* —**in•volve'ment** *n.*

in•volved |ĭn **vŏlvd'**| *adj.* Complicated; complex; intricate: *a long, involved sentence.*

in•vul•ner•a•ble |ĭn **vŭl'**nər ə bəl| *adj.* Not capable of being hurt, wounded, attacked, etc.: *an invulnerable warrior; an invulnerable fort.* —**in•vul'ner•a•bil'i•ty** *n.* —**in•vul'ner•a•bly** *adv.*

in•ward |**ĭn'**wərd| *adv.* Also **in•wards** |**ĭn'**wərdz|. **1.** Toward the inside or center: *He swung the door inward. The spokes of the wheel run inward from the rim.* **2.** Toward one's own inner being: *She turned her thoughts inward.* —*adj.* Directed toward or located on the inside, center, or interior: *inward bleeding. With an inward pull she opened the door from within.*

in•ward•ly |**ĭn'**wərd lē| *adv.* **1.** On the inside; internally: *bleeding inwardly.* **2.** In the mind, heart, or spirit; within: *Inwardly, the boy was afraid.* **3.** To oneself; privately: *chuckling inwardly.*

i•o•dide |**ī'**ə dīd'| *n.* A chemical compound composed of iodine and another element or radical.

i•o•dine *n.* **1.** |**ī'**ə dēn'| *or* |**ī'**ə dīn'|. Symbol **I** One of the elements, a lustrous, gray, corrosive, poisonous solid. Atomic number 53; atomic weight 126.90; valences -1, +1, +3, +5, +7; melting point 113.5°C; boiling point 184.35°C. **2.** |**ī'**ə-dīn'|. An antiseptic solution of iodine and either sodium iodide (NaI) or potassium iodide (KI) dissolved in alcohol.

i•o•dize |**ī'**ə dīz'| *v.* **i•o•dized, i•o•diz•ing.** To treat or combine with iodine or an iodide. —**i'o•dized'** *adj.: iodized table salt.*

i•on |**ī'**ən| *or* |**ī'**ŏn'| *n.* An atom or group of atoms that, because it contains more or fewer electrons than protons, has an electric charge.

i•on•ic |ī **ŏn'**ĭk| *adj.* Of or containing ions.

I•on•ic |ī **ŏn'**ĭk| *adj.* Of or belonging to an order of ancient Greek and Roman architecture characterized by a column with spiral, scroll-like decorations at the top, or capital: *an Ionic column; an Ionic capital.*

i•on•i•za•tion |ī'ə nĭ **zā'**shən| *n.* **1.** The formation of ions; the gain or loss of electrons from atoms or groups of atoms that are electrically neutral. **2.** The separation of certain compounds into free ions, as when in solution or in liquid or gaseous form.

i•on•ize |**ī'**ə nīz'| *v.* **i•on•ized, i•on•iz•ing. 1.** To change into ions, wholly or in part. **2.** To break apart into ions: *A salt ionizes in solution.*

i•on•o•sphere |ī **ŏn'**ə sfîr'| *n.* A group of layers of the earth's atmosphere that are ionized by radiation from the sun and, therefore, are electrically conductive and capable of affecting certain radio waves. The ionosphere extends from about 30 miles to more than 250 miles above the earth, varying with the season and time of day.

i•o•ta |ī **ō'**tə| *n.* **1.** The ninth letter of the Greek alphabet, written *I, i.* In English it is represented as *I, i.* **2.** The least bit or smallest amount; a jot; particle: *There is not an iota of truth in that gossip.*

IOU |ī'ō **yōō'**| *n., pl.* **IOU's** or **IOUs.** A written promise to pay a debt, bearing the letters IOU, which stand for "I owe you," followed by the amount owed.

I•o•wa[1] |**ī'**ə wə|. A Midwestern state of the United States. Population, 2,852,000. Capital, Des Moines.

I•o•wa[2] |**ī'**ə wə| *n., pl.* **I•o•wa** or **I•o•was. 1.** A North American Indian tribe formerly living in Minnesota, Iowa, and Missouri. **2.** A member of this tribe. **3.** Their Siouan language.

ip•e•cac |**ĭp'**ĭ kăk'| *n.* **1.** A South American plant with roots used as medicine. **2.** The root of this plant or a medicine prepared from it.

IQ, I.Q. intelligence quotient.

Ir The symbol for the element iridium.

I•ran |ĭ **răn'**| *or* |ē **rän'**|. A country in southwestern Asia, south of the Caspian Sea. Population, 31,960,000. Capital Teheran. —**I•ra'ni•an** |ĭ **rā'**nē-ən| *adj. & n.*

I•raq |ĭ **răk'**| *or* |ē **räk'**|. A country in the Middle East. Population, 10,765,000. Capital, Baghdad. —**I•ra'qi** |ē **rä'**kē| *adj. & n.*

i•ras•ci•ble |ĭ **răs'**ə bəl| *or* |ī **răs'**-| *adj.* Having a hot temper; highly irritable: *an irascible man.*

i•rate |ī **rāt'**| *or* |**ī'**rāt'| *adj.* Angry; enraged: *"Get away from here!" shouted the irate farmer.* —**i•rate'ly** *adv.*

ire |īr| *n.* Anger; wrath.

invoice

Invoice *has nothing to do with the word* **voice**. *It was originally* invoys, *"lists of things sent," plural of* invoy, *"a list, something sent";* invoy *is from French* envoi, *"a sending, something sent," from* envoyer, *"to send."* Envoyer *also formed* envoyé, *"a person sent, a diplomatic officer," which was borrowed into English as* **envoy**.

ă pat/ā pay/â care/ä father/ĕ pet/ ē be/ĭ pit/ī pie/î fierce/ŏ pot/ ō go/ô paw, for/oi oil/ŏŏ book/ ōō boot/ou out/ŭ cut/û fur/ *th* the/th thin/hw which/zh vision/ ə ago, item, pencil, atom, circus

Ire•land |ĭr′lənd|. **1.** One of the British Isles, in the Atlantic Ocean west of Great Britain, divided into the Republic of Ireland, an independent country, and Northern Ireland, a part of the United Kingdom. **2.** The Republic of Ireland, which occupies most of the island of Ireland. Population, 3,086,000. Capital, Dublin.

ir•i•des•cence |ĭr′ĭ **dĕs′**əns| *n.* A display of rainbowlike colors, as in mother-of-pearl.

ir•i•des•cent |ĭr′ĭ **dĕs′**ənt| *adj.* Showing iridescence: *butterflies with iridescent wings.* —**ir′i•des′cent•ly** *adv.*

i•rid•i•um |ĭ **rĭd′**ē əm| *or* |ī **rĭd′**-| *n.* Symbol **Ir** One of the elements, a very hard and brittle, highly corrosion-resistant, yellowish metal. Atomic number 77; atomic weight 192.2; valences +3, +4; melting point 2,410°C; boiling point 4,527°C.

i•ris |**ī′**rĭs| *n.* **1.** The color membrane of the eye, located between the cornea and lens, that regulates the size of the pupil by expanding and contracting. **2.** Any of several plants with long, sword-shaped leaves and showy, often purplish-blue flowers. [SEE PICTURES]

I•rish |**ī′**rĭsh| *n.* **1. the Irish** *(used with a plural verb).* The people of Ireland or their descendants. **2.** The Celtic language of Ireland. —*adj.* Of Ireland, the Irish, or their language and culture.

I•rish•man |**ī′**rĭsh mən| *n., pl.* **-men** |-mən|. A man who is a native or inhabitant of Ireland.

Irish potato. The common white potato.

Irish Sea. The sea between Great Britain and Ireland.

irk |ûrk| *v.* To annoy, bother, or irritate: *Nothing irks him so much as to be kept waiting.*

irk•some |**ûrk′**səm| *adj.* Tiresome; tedious; annoying: *irksome homework.*

i•ron |**ī′**ərn| *n.* **1.** Symbol **Fe** One of the elements, a hard, gray, brittle metal, capable of being magnetized. Atomic number 26; atomic weight 55.85; valences +2, +3, +4, +6; melting point 1,535°C; boiling point 3,000°C. **2. a.** A metal appliance with a handle and flat bottom, used when heated to press cloth and clothing. **b.** Any of various other metal implements, especially those that are heated for use, as in branding cattle. **3. irons.** Shackles; fetters: *handcuffs and leg irons; put a prisoner in irons.* **4.** A golf club with a metal head. **5.** Great strength, firmness, or hardness: *clutching with a grip of iron.* **6.** Any hard, unyielding substance: *The heart in my breast is not of iron.* —***modifier:*** *an iron horseshoe.* —*adj.* **1.** Extremely hard, strong, or hardy: *a fighter's iron fist.* **2.** So strong and firm as to be unyielding: *an iron will.* —*v.* **1.** To press (clothing, linens, fabrics, etc.) with a heated iron or between heated rollers. **2.** To remove (creases) by pressing. —***phrasal verb.*** **iron out.** To work out; discuss and settle: *We must iron out our problems.*

Idiom. **strike while the iron is hot.** To seize a favorable opportunity for action.

Iron Age. The period in human history following the Stone Age and the Bronze Age, marked by the introduction of iron implements and weapons. In Europe it began around 1000 B.C.

i•ron•clad |**ī′**ərn klăd′| *adj.* **1.** Covered with iron plates for protection: *an ironclad ship.* **2.** Not to be broken or violated: *an ironclad rule.* —*n.* A 19th-century warship having sides armored with metal plates.

Iron Curtain. The invisible barrier of hostility, secrecy, censorship, etc., isolating the Soviet Union and the countries under its influence from the western European nations and the United States after World War II.

i•ron•ic |ī **rŏn′**ĭk| or **i•ron•i•cal** |ī **rŏn′**ĭ kəl| *adj.* Full of or showing irony; suggesting something different from what is expressed: *an ironic smile.* —**i•ron′i•cal•ly** *adv.*

iron lung. A metal tank in which the entire body except the head is enclosed and that, by means of regular changes in the pressure inside, provides artificial respiration for patients, such as polio victims, who need help in breathing.

i•ron•mon•ger |**ī′**ərn mŭng′gər| *or* |-mŏng′gər| *n. British.* A hardware merchant.

iron ore. Any of various minerals, such as hematite or magnetite, from which iron can be commercially extracted.

iron pyrites. Pyrite.

i•ron•stone |**ī′**ərn stōn′| *n.* **1.** Also **ironstone china.** A hard, usually plain white pottery used for dishes. **2.** Any of various types of iron ore.

i•ron•wood |**ī′**ərn wo͝od′| *n.* **1.** Any of several trees having very hard wood. **2.** The wood of such a tree.

i•ron•work |**ī′**ərn wûrk′| *n.* **1.** Work in iron, as gratings and rails. **2.** Articles made of iron. [SEE PICTURE]

i•ron•works |**ī′**ərn wûrks′| *n. (used with a singular verb).* A place where iron is smelted or heavy iron products are made.

i•ro•ny |**ī′**rə nē| *n., pl.* **i•ro•nies.** **1.** A wry, mocking way of using words or expressions so that they suggest the opposite of what they literally mean: *Using irony, Marc Antony called Caesar's assassins "honorable men."* **2.** A situation, outcome, or event that is opposite from or contrary to what might have been expected.

Ir•o•quoi•an |ĭr′ə **kwoi′**ən| *n.* **1.** A family of North American Indian languages spoken in Canada and the eastern United States. **2.** A member of a tribe speaking a language of this family. —**Ir′o•quoi′an** *adj.*

Ir•o•quois |**ĭr′**ə kwoi′| *or* |-kwoiz′| *n., pl.* **Ir•o•quois.** **1.** Any of the Iroquoian-speaking North American Indian tribes that formed the confederation known as the Five Nations. **2.** A member of any of these tribes.

ir•ra•di•ate |ĭ **rā′**dē āt′| *v.* **ir•ra•di•at•ed, ir•ra•di•at•ing.** **1.** To expose to or treat with light or other radiation. **2.** To fill with or as if with light; brighten; illuminate: *A smile irradiated her face.* —**ir•ra′di•a′tion** *n.*

ir•ra•tion•al |ĭ **răsh′**ə nəl| *adj.* **1.** Not capable of reasoning or thinking clearly. **2.** Not based on or guided by reason; unreasonable; illogical: *an irrational fear.* —**ir•ra′tion•al•ly** *adv.*

ir•ra•tion•al•i•ty |ĭ răsh′ə **năl′**ĭ tē| *n., pl.* **ir•ra•tion•al•i•ties.** **1.** The condition or quality of being irrational. **2.** An irrational action or idea.

irrational number. A number that cannot be written as a fraction whose numerator and denominator are both integers (whole numbers); for example, supposing that $q^2 = 2$, it can be shown that q cannot be written as a fraction using two integers.

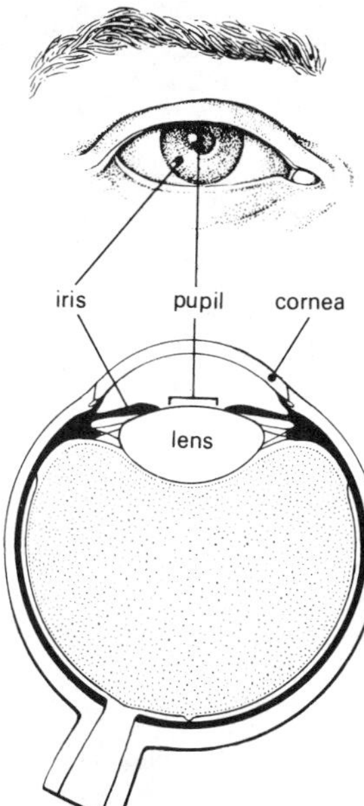

iris
Above: Sense 1
Below: Sense 2

ironwork
Railing and gate

ir•rec•on•cil•a•ble |ĭ rĕk′ən **sī′**lə bəl| *or* |ĭ **rĕk′**ən sī′-| *adj.* Not capable of being reconciled or brought into agreement: *irreconcilable enemies.*

ir•re•cov•er•a•ble |ĭr′ĭ **kŭv′**ər ə bəl| *adj.* Not capable of being recovered or redeemed: *irrecoverable losses.* **—ir′re•cov′er•a•bly** *adv.*

ir•re•deem•a•ble |ĭr′ĭ **dē′**mə bəl| *adj.* **1.** Not capable of being turned in for exchange: *an irredeemable coupon.* **2.** Not capable of being saved or reformed: *an irredeemable sinner.* **—ir′re•deem′a•bly** *adv.*

ir•re•duc•i•ble |ĭr′ĭ **dōō′**sə bəl| *or* |**-dyōō′**-| *adj.* Not capable of being reduced to a smaller or simpler amount or form: *an irreducible fraction.* **—ir′re•duc′i•bly** *adv.*

ir•ref•u•ta•ble |ĭ **rĕf′**yə tə bəl| *or* |ĭr′ĭ **fyōō′**tə bəl| *adj.* Not capable of being refuted: *irrefutable arguments.* **—ir•ref′u•ta•bly** *adv.*

ir•reg•u•lar |ĭ **rĕg′**yə lər| *adj.* **1.** Not standard or uniform, as in shape, size, length, or arrangement: *an irregular coastline; irregular splotches of color.* **2.** Not following a set pattern or regular schedule: *irregular rhythm.* **3.** Unusual or improper: *a highly irregular procedure.* **4.** In grammar, not following the standard pattern of inflected forms; for example, *do* is an irregular verb, with irregular principal parts. **5.** Not up to standard because of flaws or imperfections: *irregular merchandise.* **—ir•reg′u•lar•ly** *adv.*

ir•reg•u•lar•i•ty |ĭ rĕg′yə **lăr′**ĭ tē| *n., pl.* **ir•reg•u•lar•i•ties. 1.** The condition or quality of being irregular. **2.** An irregular feature, place, practice, etc.: *irregularities in the earth's surface; the irregularities of English spelling.*

ir•rel•e•vant |ĭ **rĕl′**ə vənt| *adj.* Having no relation to the subject or situation; not relevant or applicable: *an irrelevant question.* **—ir•rel′e•vance** *n.* **—ir•rel′e•vant•ly** *adv.*

ir•re•lig•ious |ĭr′ĭ **lĭj′**əs| *adj.* Indifferent or hostile to religion.

ir•re•me•di•a•ble |ĭr′ĭ **mē′**dē ə bəl| *adj.* Impossible to remedy, correct, cure, or repair: *irremediable harm.* **—ir′re•me′di•a•bly** *adv.*

ir•rep•a•ra•ble |ĭ **rĕp′**ər ə bəl| *adj.* Not capable of being repaired, remedied, undone, or set right: *irreparable damage.* **—ir•rep′a•ra•bly** *adv.*

ir•re•place•a•ble |ĭr′ĭ **plā′**sə bəl| *adj.* Not capable of being replaced: *irreplaceable supplies of coal and oil.*

ir•re•press•i•ble |ĭr′ĭ **prĕs′**ə bəl| *adj.* Impossible to hold back, control, or restrain: *irrepressible laughter.* **—ir′re•press′i•bly** *adv.*

ir•re•proach•a•ble |ĭr′ĭ **prō′**chə bəl| *adj.* Beyond reproach; blameless: *irreproachable manners.* **—ir′re•proach′a•bly** *adv.*

ir•re•sist•i•ble |ĭr′ĭ **zĭs′**tə bəl| *adj.* **1.** Too strong, powerful, or compelling to be resisted: *irresistible forces; an irresistible impulse.* **2.** Having an overpowering appeal: *irresistible beauty.* **—ir′re•sist′i•bil′i•ty** *n.* **—ir′re•sist′i•bly** *adv.*

ir•res•o•lute |ĭ **rĕz′**ə lōōt′| *adj.* Undecided or showing uncertainty about what to do; indecisive: *standing irresolute on the road; a good deal of irresolute discussion.* **—ir•res′o•lute′ly** *adv.*

ir•re•spec•tive |ĭr′ĭ **spĕk′**tĭv| *adj.* **—irrespective of.** Regardless of: *equal rights for all, irrespective of class or condition.*

ir•re•spon•si•bil•i•ty |ĭr′ĭ spŏn′sə **bĭl′**ĭ tē| *n.* Lack of responsibility or concern for consequences.

ir•re•spon•si•ble |ĭr′ĭ **spŏn′**sə bəl| *adj.* **1.** Showing no sense of responsibility or concern for consequences; not dependable, reliable, or trustworthy: *irresponsible liars.* **2.** Not capable of being called to account for one's actions: *A king with absolute power is irresponsible.* **—ir′re•spon′si•bly** *adv.*

ir•re•triev•a•ble |ĭr′ĭ **trē′**və bəl| *adj.* Not capable of being retrieved, recovered, or set right: *an irretrievable loss.* **—ir′re•triev′a•bly** *adv.*

ir•rev•er•ent |ĭ **rĕv′**ər ənt| *adj.* Showing a lack of reverence, as for someone or something held sacred or worthy of respect: *irreverent humor.* **—ir•rev′er•ence** *n.* **—ir•rev′er•ent•ly** *adv.*

ir•re•vers•i•ble |ĭr′ĭ **vûr′**sə bəl| *adj.* Not capable of being reversed: *an irreversible decision.* **—ir′re•vers′i•bly** *adv.*

ir•rev•o•ca•ble |ĭ **rĕv′**ə kə bəl| *adj.* Not capable of being changed or undone: *an irrevocable decision.* **—ir•rev′o•ca•bly** *adv.*

ir•ri•gate |**ĭr′**ĭ gāt′| *v.* **ir•ri•gat•ed, ir•ri•gat•ing. 1.** To supply (farmland, crops, etc.) with water by means of streams, ditches, pipes, canals, etc. **2.** To wash out (a wound or an opening of the body) with water, a medicated solution, etc. **—ir′ri•ga′tion** *n.* [SEE PICTURE]

irrigation

ir•ri•ta•ble |**ĭr′**ĭ tə bəl| *adj.* **1.** Easily annoyed, angered, or exasperated; cross; ill-tempered: *Lack of sleep made him nervous and irritable.* **2.** Abnormally sensitive: *raw, irritable skin.* **3.** Capable of responding to stimuli. **—ir′ri•ta•bil′i•ty** *n.* **—ir′ri•ta•bly** *adv.*

ir•ri•tant |**ĭr′**ĭ tənt| *adj.* Causing irritation; tending to irritate. *—n.* Something that irritates.

ir•ri•tate |**ĭr′**ĭ tāt′| *v.* **ir•ri•tat•ed, ir•ri•tat•ing. 1.** To make angry or impatient; annoy, bother, or exasperate: *His endless questions irritated me.* **2.** To cause to become sore or inflamed: *The heavy smoke irritated her eyes.* **—ir′ri•tat′ed** *adj.: an irritated customer; an irritated throat.* **—ir′ri•tat′ing** *adj.: an irritating habit; an irritating chemical.*

ir•ri•ta•tion |ĭr′ĭ **tā′**shən| *n.* **1.** The act or process of irritating. **2.** The condition of being irritated: *"Of course it's true!" he answered, with a show of irritation.* **3.** An annoyance or source of annoyance. **4.** Soreness, roughness, or tenderness of a bodily part.

Ir•ving |**ûr′**vĭng|, **Washington.** 1783–1859. American writer, historian, and humorist.

is |ĭz|. Third person singular present tense of **be.** ***Idiom.* as is.** In its present condition; without change, repair, etc.: *The shopworn merchandise will be sold as is.*

I•saac |**ī′**zək|. In the Bible, a Hebrew patriarch, son of Abraham and Sarah.

Is•a•bel•la I |ĭz′ə **bĕl′**ə|. 1451–1501. Queen of Castile and wife of Ferdinand V.

I•sa•iah |ī **zā′**ə|. A Hebrew prophet of the eighth century B.C.

is•chi•um |**ĭs′**kē əm| *n., pl.* **is•chi•a** |**ĭs′**kē ə|. The lowest of the three large bones that make up each of the hipbones.

-ise. Chiefly British form of the suffix **-ize.**

-ish. A suffix that forms adjectives and means: **1.** Of the nationality of: **Finnish. 2.** Having the characteristics or qualities of: **sheepish; woman-**

ă pat/ā pay/â care/ä father/ĕ pet/ē be/ĭ pit/ī pie/î fierce/ŏ pot/ō go/ô paw, for/oi oil/ŏŏ book/ōō boot/ou out/ŭ cut/û fur/*th* the/th thin/hw which/zh vision/ə ago, item, pencil, atom, circus

ish. 3. Preoccupied with: **selfish.** 4. *Informal.* Somewhere near; approximately: *He is fortyish.*

Ish•tar |ĭsh′tär′| *n.* In Assyrian and Babylonian mythology, the goddess of fertility and also of war.

i•sin•glass |ī′zĭng glăs′| *or* |-gläs′| *or* |ī′zən-| *n.* 1. A transparent, almost pure gelatin made from the air bladders of certain fishes, such as sturgeons. 2. The most common form of the mineral mica; muscovite.

I•sis |ī′sĭs|. In Egyptian mythology, a goddess of fertility.

Is•lam |ĭs′ləm| *or* |ĭz′-| *or* |ĭs läm′| *n.* 1. A religion based on the teachings of the prophet Mohammed, believing in one god, called Allah, and having a body of sacred laws revealed in the Koran; the Moslem religion. 2. a. The Moslem nations of the world. b. Moslems as a group or their civilization. —**Is•lam′ic** |ĭs lăm′ĭk| *or* |-lä′-mĭk| *or* |ĭz-| *adj.*

Is•lam•a•bad |ĭs lä′mə bäd′| *or* |ĭz-|. The capital of Pakistan. Population, 70,000.

is•land |ī′lənd| *n.* 1. A piece of land, especially one smaller than a continent, that is surrounded by water. 2. Anything like an island in being completely separated or different in character from what surrounds it. [SEE NOTE]

is•land•er |ī′lən dər| *n.* A person who lives on or was born on an island.

islands of Lang•er•hans |läng′ər häns′|. Any of the tiny masses of endocrine gland tissue that are spread through the pancreas and secrete the hormone insulin.

isle |īl| *n.* An island, especially a small one. ¶*These sound alike* **isle, aisle, I'll.** [SEE NOTE]

is•let |ī′lĭt| *n.* A very small island. ¶*These sound alike* **islet, eyelet.**

-ism. A suffix that forms nouns and means: 1. An act, practice, or process: **terrorism.** 2. A relationship or condition: **parallelism.** 3. Characteristic behavior or quality: **individualism.** 4. A word, phrase, idiom, or usage peculiar to a language, people, etc.: **Briticism.** 5. A doctrine, theory, system, or principle: **socialism.**

is•n't |ĭz′ənt|. Is not.

i•so•bar |ī′sə bär′| *n.* A line drawn on a weather map so that every point on the line has the same barometric pressure.

i•so•gloss |ī′sə glôs′| *or* |-glŏs′| *n.* A line on a map that separates areas in which linguistic features, such as a pronunciation or a form of word, differ.

i•so•late |ī′sə lāt′| *v.* **i•so•lat•ed, i•so•lat•ing.** 1. To separate from a group or whole and set apart. 2. To keep (someone with a contagious disease) from coming into contact with others who are not infected; quarantine.

i•so•la•tion |ī′sə lā′shən| *n.* 1. The condition of being isolated: *living in isolation from the world.* 2. The act or process of isolating: *the isolation of polio patients.*

i•so•la•tion•ism |ī′sə lā′shə nĭz′əm| *n.* A belief, or a policy based on the belief, that a nation should not take part in international affairs and alliances but should avoid entanglements with other countries. —**i′so•la′tion•ist** *n.*

i•so•mer |ī′sə mər| *n.* Any member of a set of chemical compounds that are identical in composition but, because their atoms are arranged in different ways, have different chemical and physical properties.

i•so•met•ric |ī′sə mĕt′rĭk| *adj.* Of or involving muscle contractions in which the ends of the muscle are held in place so that there is an increase in tension rather than a shortening of the muscle: *isometric exercises.*

i•sos•ce•les triangle |ī sŏs′ə lēz′|. A triangle in which two of the line segments bounding it are of equal length. [SEE PICTURE]

i•so•therm |ī′sə thûrm′| *n.* A line drawn on a weather map so that every point on the line has the same temperature at a given time or the same average temperature for a given period of time.

i•so•tope |ī′sə tōp′| *n.* Any of a set of atoms, or of a set of types of atoms, that contain in their nuclei the same number of protons but different numbers of neutrons. All isotopes of a given element have the same atomic number, but their atomic weights vary with the number of neutrons they contain. —**i′so•top′ic** |ī′sə tŏp′ĭk| *adj.*

Is•ra•el[1] |ĭz′rē əl|. 1. A country in the Middle East, established in 1948 in what was formerly Palestine. Population 3,318,000. Capital, Jerusalem. 2. An ancient Hebrew kingdom in northern Palestine.

Is•ra•el[2] |ĭz′rē əl| *n.* 1. In the Bible, the name given to Jacob by the angel with whom he wrestled. 2. The Jewish people as a whole, regarded as the descendants of Jacob.

Is•rae•li |ĭz rā′lē| *adj.* Of modern Israel or its people. —*n., pl.* **Is•rae•lis** or **Is•rae•li.** A native or inhabitant of modern Israel.

Is•ra•el•ite |ĭz′rē ə līt′| *n.* A Hebrew, regarded as a descendant of Jacob.

is•su•ance |ĭsh′o͞o əns| *n.* The act of issuing: *the issuance of hunting permits.*

is•sue |ĭsh′o͞o| *n.* 1. The act of putting out; release: *The date of issue is indicated on the first page.* 2. Something that is put into circulation: *a new issue of postage stamps.* 3. A single number of a newspaper or magazine: *the June issue.* 4. A subject being discussed or disputed; a question under debate: *the issue of school integration.* 5. An outflow or outpouring of water, air, smoke, etc.: *The lake has no issue to the sea.* 6. Offspring; children: *He died without issue.* —*v.* **is•sued, is•su•ing.** 1. To put out; announce: *issue orders.* 2. To put in circulation: *issue stamps.* 3. To give; extend; grant: *The government refused to issue him a patent.* 4. To give out; distribute: *Each soldier was issued a rifle and 100 rounds of ammunition.* 5. To come out; flow out: *Water issued from the broken pipe.*

Idioms. **at issue.** In question; in dispute: *Your past record is not at issue here.* **take issue with.** To disagree with; dispute: *Allow me to take issue with your last remark.*

-ist. A suffix that forms nouns and means: 1. Someone involved with a specified profession or thing: **dramatist; motorist.** 2. Someone who believes in a certain doctrine, system, etc.: **socialist.** 3. Someone characterized as having a particular trait: **romanticist.**

Is•tan•bul |ĭs′tăn bo͞ol′| *or* |-tän-|. The largest city in Turkey, a seaport in the European part of the country. Population, 2,248,000.

isth•mus |ĭs′məs| *n.* A narrow strip of land connecting two larger masses of land.

island/isle

These are basically unrelated words. **Island** *was* īland *or* īgland *in Old English; the* īg- *is from a Germanic word meaning "thing in the water."* **Isle** *is from Old French* isle, *which is from Latin* īnsula, *"island." The* -s- *in* **island** *was not originally there; it was added by the influence of* **isle** *(since people wrongly thought that the two words were related). Latin* īnsula *separately produced Italian* isolato, *"made into an island," from which we have* **isolate.**

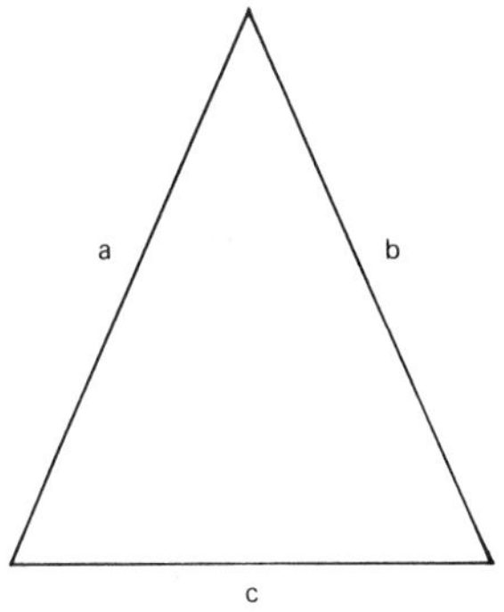

isosceles triangle
The sides a and b are equal

its

The possessive pronoun **its** *was formed from* **it** + *the possessive suffix* **'s**. *Although this pronoun was originally spelled* it's, *it is now only spelled* **its**, *since the spelling* **it's** *has been taken over by the contracted forms of* it is, it has.

ivy

it |ĭt| *pron.* The thing or nonhuman being last mentioned or thought to be understood: *He grabbed the snake and flung it into the brush. Whatever you choose, give it your best.* —*n.* In some children's games, the player who must perform a certain act, such as chasing the other players. —*Note:* As a pronoun, *it* often stands before a verb in the position normally occupied by the subject, but is not the subject. In the two following examples, no subject is expressed, and *it* represents a condition or fact: *It was very dark outside. It is nearly noon.* In the following examples, the subjects follow the verb: *It was my father on the phone* (the subject is a noun phrase, *my father*). *It was not true that he refused* (the subject is a clause, *that he refused*). *It is always easy to find fault* (the subject is an infinitive construction, *to find fault*). In such examples, *it* is an introductory word, or expletive.

It. Italian; Italy.

ital. italic.

I•tal•ian |ĭ **tăl'**yən| *n.* **1.** A native or inhabitant of Italy. **2.** The Romance language of Italy and a part of Switzerland. —*adj.* Of Italy, the Italians, or their language.

i•tal•ic |ĭ **tăl'**ĭk| *or* |ī **tăl'**-| *adj.* Being a style of printing type with the letters slanting to the right, used chiefly to set off a word or passage within a text of roman print: *This is italic print.* —*n.* Often **italics.** Italic print or typeface.

i•tal•i•cize |ĭ **tăl'**ĭ sīz'| *or* |ī **tăl'**-| *v.* **i•tal•i•cized, i•tal•i•ciz•ing.** To print in italic type; use italics: *italicize a word.*

It•a•ly |**ĭt'**l ē|. A country in southern Europe, projecting into the Mediterranean Sea. Population, 55,586,000. Capital, Rome.

itch |ĭch| *n.* **1.** A tickling or irritated feeling in the skin or a mucous membrane, especially a feeling that causes a desire to scratch. **2.** Any of a number of contagious skin diseases of which an intense itch is a characteristic symptom. **3.** A restless craving or desire: *Every spring I get an itch to go sailing.* —*v.* **1.** To feel, have, or cause to have an itch: *I itch all over.* **2.** To have a restless craving or desire: *She was just itching to show him what she had done.*

itch•y |**ĭch'**ē| *adj.* **itch•i•er, itch•i•est.** **1.** Of, having, or causing an itch: *an itchy palm; an itchy sweater.* **2.** Restless; jumpy: *a gunman with an itchy finger.* —**itch'i•ness** *n.*

-ite. A suffix that forms nouns and means: **1.** A native or resident of: *Brooklynite.* **2.** Someone involved with a specified movement, group, cause, etc.: **socialite.**

i•tem |**ī'**təm| *n.* **1.** A single article or unit: *an item of clothing. You must show a receipt for each item purchased.* **2.** A piece of news or information: *an interesting item in the newspaper.*

i•tem•ize |**ī'**tə mīz'| *v.* **i•tem•ized, i•tem•iz•ing.** To set down item by item; list: *itemizing all charges on the bill.*

i•tin•er•ant |ī **tĭn'**ər ənt| *or* |ĭ **tĭn'**-| *adj.* Traveling from place to place: *itinerant workers.* —*n.* A person who so travels.

i•tin•er•ar•y |ī **tĭn'**ə rĕr'ē| *or* |ĭ **tĭn'**-| *n., pl.* **i•tin•er•ar•ies.** **1.** A schedule of places to be visited in the course of a journey: *Their itinerary includes stops in Denver and Salt Lake City.* **2.** An account or record of a journey.

-itis. A suffix that forms nouns meaning "an inflammation of or an inflammatory disease": **bronchitis.**

it'll |**ĭt'**l|. **1.** It will. **2.** It shall.

its |ĭts| *pron.* The possessive case of **it.** —Used to indicate that someone or something belongs or pertains to it (the thing or animal mentioned). —*Note: Its* is usually used just before nouns that it modifies to show possession or agency. *Its* means *of or belonging to it* (possession) in this example: *Everything was in its place. Its* means *done or performed by it* (agency) in this example: *The spring is just below; its function is to exert pressure on the bolt. Its* also means the thing or animal that is the recipient of an action, as in this example: *At last the bull received its mortal wound.* Less often, possession or agency is indicated by *its* used absolutely, in place of the thing mentioned earlier: *They blamed the city planning commission, but many felt the fault was less its than the mayor's.* In every use, *its* is spelled without an apostrophe to distinguish the pronoun from the contraction *it's.* ¶*These sound alike* **its, it's.** [SEE NOTE]

it's |ĭts|. **1.** It is. **2.** It has. ¶*These sound alike* **it's, its.**

it•self |ĭt **sĕlf'**| *pron.* A special form of **it.** It is used: **1.** In place of *it*, serving as a direct object, indirect object, or object of a preposition, to show that the action of a reflexive verb refers back to the subject: *The team surprised itself* (direct object). *The commission voted itself* (indirect object) *a salary increase. In itself* (object of a preposition), *the ruling seems unimportant.* **2.** Following or referring to a noun or the pronoun *it*, to give emphasis: *The Constitution itself defines treason quite clearly.* **3.** Referring to the subject, to mean *its real or normal self: Old-time politics would not have been itself without rallies and parades.*

***Idiom.* by itself.** **1.** Alone: *A band of immigrants huddled by itself outside the customhouse.* **2.** Without help: *a refrigerator that defrosts by itself.*

-ity. A suffix that forms nouns meaning "a quality or condition": **authenticity.**

-ive¹. A suffix that forms adjectives meaning "tending toward, performing, or accomplishing something": **disruptive.**

-ive². A suffix that forms nouns meaning "something that performs or accomplishes something": **sedative.**

i•vo•ry |**ī'**və rē| *or* |**īv'**rē| *n., pl.* **i•vo•ries.** **1.** The hard, smooth, yellowish-white substance forming the tusks of elephants and certain other animals. It is used for making piano keys, decorative objects, etc. **2.** Something made or carved from this substance. **3.** A yellowish white. **4. ivories.** *Slang.* The keys of a piano. —***modifier:*** *ivory chess pieces.* —*adj.* Yellowish white.

Ivory Coast. A country on the southern coast of western Africa. Population, 4,770,000. Capital, Abidjan.

i•vy |**ī'**vē| *n., pl.* **i•vies.** **1.** A climbing or trailing plant with evergreen leaves. **2.** Any of several similar plants. See **poison ivy.** [SEE PICTURE]

-ize. A suffix that forms verbs and means: **1.** To become, cause to become, or form into: **Americanize; materialize.** **2.** To treat or affect with: **pasteurize; magnetize.**

ă **pat**/ā **pay**/â **care**/ä **father**/ĕ **pet**/ ē **be**/ĭ **pit**/ī **pie**/î **fierce**/ŏ **pot**/ ō **go**/ô **paw**, **for**/oi **oil**/ŏŏ **book**/ ōō **boot**/ou **out**/ŭ **cut**/û **fur**/ *th* **the**/th **thin**/hw **which**/zh **vision**/ ə **ago**, **item**, **pencil**, **atom**, **circus**

Jj

j, J |jā| *n., pl.* **j's** or **J's.** The tenth letter of the English alphabet. [SEE NOTE]

jab |jăb| *v.* **jabbed, jab•bing.** To poke or thrust, especially with something sharp: *He jabbed the needle into my arm. You accidentally jabbed me with your penknife.* —*n.* A poke or thrust.

jab•ber |**jăb′**ər| *v.* To talk rapidly and unintelligibly; chatter. —*n.* Rapid chatter.

ja•bot |zhă **bō′**| *or* |jă-| *n.* A series of frills or ruffles down the front of a shirt, blouse, or bodice.

jac•a•ran•da |jăk′ə **răn′**də| *n.* A tropical tree with feathery leaves and clusters of pale-purple flowers.

jack |jăk| *n.* **1.** A portable device used to raise slightly a heavy object, especially an automobile in order to change a tire. **2.** A socket into which a long, slender plug having a wire attached is inserted in order to make an electrical connection: *a telephone jack.* **3.** A playing card bearing the figure of a young man. It ranks above a ten and below a queen. **4. a. jacks** *(used with a singular verb).* A children's game played with a set of small six-pointed metal pieces and a small ball, the object being to pick up the pieces as the ball bounces. **b.** One of the pieces used in this game. **5.** A male donkey. **6.** A small flag flown at the bow of a ship to show nationality. **7.** *Slang.* Money: *Ten dollars is a lot of jack.* —*v.* —**jack up. 1.** To hoist by means of a jack. **2.** To raise: *jacked up rents.*

jack•al |**jăk′**əl| *or* |-ôl′| *n.* A doglike African or Asian animal that often feeds on the remains of animals killed by lions, leopards, etc.

jack•ass |**jăk′**ăs′| *n.* **1.** A male donkey. **2.** A foolish or stupid person.

jack•daw |**jăk′**dô′| *n.* A black crowlike bird of Europe and Asia.

jack•et |**jăk′**ĭt| *n.* **1.** A short coat, usually extending from the shoulders to the hips: *a sport jacket.* **2.** A protective cover for a book, phonograph record, etc. **3.** An outer covering or casing, as of an electric wire, a machine or machine part, or a bullet.

Jack Frost. Frost or cold weather personified.

jack•ham•mer |**jăk′**hăm′ər| *n.* A device for drilling through rock, held in the hands and operated by compressed air.

jack-in-the-box |**jăk′**ĭn *th*ə bŏks′| *n.* A toy consisting of a box from which a puppet springs when the lid is opened.

jack-in-the-pul•pit |**jăk′**ĭn *th*ə **pōōl′**pĭt| *or* |-**pŭl′**-| *n.* A North American plant with a leaflike, hood-shaped part enclosing a clublike flower stalk.

jack•knife |**jăk′**nīf′| *n., pl.* **-knives** |-nīvz′|. **1.** A large pocketknife with blades that can be folded back into the handle. **2.** A dive in which one bends over, touches the toes, and then straightens out before entering the water hands first.

jack-of-all-trades |jăk′əv **ôl′trādz′**| *n., pl.* **jacks-of-all-trades.** A person who can do many different kinds of work.

jack-o'-lan•tern |**jăk′**ə lăn′tərn| *n.* A lantern consisting of a hollowed-out pumpkin with a carved face and a light inside.

jack•pot |**jăk′**pŏt′| *n.* The largest possible award in various games or contests.
***Idiom.* hit the jackpot. 1.** To win a jackpot. **2.** To achieve sensational success.

jack rabbit. A long-eared, long-legged hare of western North America. [SEE PICTURE]

Jack•son[1] |**jăk′**sən|. The capital of Mississippi. Population, 150,000.

Jack•son[2] |**jăk′**sən|. **1. Andrew.** 1767–1845. Seventh President of the United States (1829–37). **2. Thomas Jonathan ("Stonewall").** 1824–1863. Confederate general in the Civil War.

jack•straw |**jăk′**strô′| *n.* **1. jackstraws** *(used with a singular verb).* A children's game played with a pile of straws or thin sticks in which the players try in turn to remove single sticks without disturbing the others. **2.** One of the straws or sticks used in this game.

Ja•cob |**jā′**kəb|. In the Bible, a Hebrew patriarch and father of the 12 sons who were the founders of the 12 tribes of Israel.

jac•quard, also **Jac•quard** |**jăk′**ärd′| *or* |jə-**kärd′**| *n.* **1.** A fabric with an intricate pattern woven into it on a special kind of loom called a **jacquard loom. 2.** Also **jacquard weave.** The kind of figured weave done on such a loom, used for brocade, damask, and tapestry.

jade[1] |jād| *n.* Either of two minerals that are usually white or pale green and are used as gemstones and as materials from which art objects are carved. —***modifier:*** *a jade bracelet.* [SEE NOTE]

jade[2] |jād| *n.* A broken-down or useless horse. [SEE NOTE]

jad•ed |**jā′**dĭd| *adj.* **1.** Tired or worn out: *a jaded face.* **2.** Dulled by having had too much of something: *jaded appetites.*

jag[1] |jăg| *n.* A sharp projecting point on an edge or surface. —*v.* **jag•ged, jag•ging.** To give an edge like that of a saw to; cut unevenly; notch.

jag[2] |jăg| *n. Slang.* A spree or binge: *a crying jag.*

jag•ged |**jăg′**ĭd| *adj.* **1.** Having notches; sharp, rough, and uneven: *jagged edges.* **2.** Having many indentations; irregular: *a jagged coastline.*

I J
(1) (2)

The letter **J** *is a medieval offshoot of the letter I. The Romans used I (1) both for the sound /i/ as in* bit *and for the sound /y/ as in* yet. *An example is the name IUPITER, pronounced /***yōō′***pĭtər/. In the Middle Ages, the original letter I was kept for the vowel, and for the y sound a new letter was made by adding a tail (2). In English, the j now stands for a different sound again, as in* judge /jŭj/; *but note that in German and some other languages, and in the International Phonetic Alphabet, j still stands for /y/.*

jack rabbit

jade[1-2]
Jade[1] *was once believed to cure kidney disease; the word is from French* jade, *shortened from Spanish* piedra de ijada, *"stone of the side" (*ijada, *"side of the body, flank"). The ultimate origin of* **jade[2]** *is unknown.*

jaguar

jam[1-2]

Jam[1] *and* ***jam[2]*** *both first appeared in the eighteenth century.* ***Jam[1]*** *is said to be an onomatopoeic word, formed to sound like what it means.* ***Jam[2]*** *is probably from* ***jam[1]****, since fruit is pounded or "jammed together" to make some kinds of preserves.*

jar[1-2]

Jar[1] *is ultimately from Arabic* jarrah, *"large pot."* ***Jar[2]*** *is probably an onomatopoeic word, formed to represent the sound of "jarring."*

ă pat/ā pay/â care/ä father/ĕ pet/ ē be/ĭ pit/ī pie/î fierce/ŏ pot/ ō go/ô paw, for/oi oil/ŏŏ book/ ōō boot/ou out/ŭ cut/û fur/ *th* the/th thin/hw which/zh vision/ ə ago, item, pencil, atom, circus

jag•uar |jăg′wär′| *n.* A large, leopardlike wild cat of tropical America. [SEE PICTURE]

jai a•lai |hī′ lī′| *or* |hī′ ə lī′| *or* |hī′ ə lī′|. A game, played on a court, in which the participants use a long hand-shaped basket strapped to the wrist to propel a ball against a wall.

jail |jāl| *n.* A place in which persons awaiting trial or serving a prison sentence are confined. —***modifier:*** *a jail term; a jail sentence.* —*v.* To put into jail; imprison.

jail•er |jā′lər| *n.* A person in charge of a jail.

jail•or |jā′lər| *n.* A form of the word **jailer**.

Ja•kar•ta |jə kär′tə|. See **Djakarta**.

ja•lop•y |jə lŏp′ē| *n., pl.* **ja•lop•ies.** *Informal.* An old automobile that barely runs.

jal•ou•sie |jăl′ə sē| *n.* A blind, shutter, window, or door with horizontal slats that can be tilted to admit or keep out light.

jam[1] |jăm| *v.* **jammed, jam•ming. 1. a.** To squeeze or wedge into a tight space: *jam a cork into a bottle.* **b.** To become wedged in a tight space; stick: *a rug that jams in a door.* **2.** To crowd or pack tightly: *Fifty thousand people jammed the stadium.* **3.** To force one's way into a crowded place: *Everyone jammed into the elevator.* **4.** To lock or cause to lock in an unworkable position: *The film jammed in the camera. Be careful not to jam the machine.* **5.** To catch accidentally between a moving object and a stationary one: *jam one's finger in the door.* **6.** To apply or thrust with great force: *jam on the brakes.* **7.** To make (radio signals) difficult or impossible to receive or demodulate, as by broadcasting an interfering signal. —*n.* **1.** A crush or congestion of people or things in a limited space so that movement becomes difficult or impossible: *a traffic jam; a log jam.* **2.** *Informal.* A difficult situation. ¶ *These sound alike* **jam, jamb.** [SEE NOTE]

jam[2] |jăm| *n.* A preserve made from whole fruit boiled to a pulp with sugar. ¶ *These sound alike* **jam, jamb.** [SEE NOTE]

Ja•mai•ca |jə mā′kə|. An island nation in the Caribbean Sea. Population, 2,000,000. Capital, Kingston. —**Ja•mai′can** *adj. & n.*

jamb |jăm| *n.* One of the vertical posts framing a door or window. ¶ *These sound alike* **jamb, jam.**

jam•ba•lay•a |jŭm′bə lī′ə| *n.* A Creole dish of oysters, shrimp, and chicken or ham, cooked with rice.

jam•bo•ree |jăm′bə rē′| *n.* **1.** A noisy party or celebration. **2.** A large assembly, often international, of Boy Scouts.

James |jāmz|, **Saint. 1.** Called "the Greater." One of the Twelve Apostles. **2.** Called "the Less." One of the Twelve Apostles; traditionally regarded as the half-brother of Jesus.

James•town |jāmz′toun′|. The first permanent English settlement in the United States, founded in 1607 in Virginia.

Jam•mu and Kash•mir |jŭm′ōō; kăsh mîr′| *or* |kăsh′mîr′|. The official name of Kashmir.

jam session. A gathering at which a group of jazz musicians improvise together.

Jan. January.

jan•gle |jăng′gəl| *v.* **jan•gled, jan•gling. 1.** To make or cause to make a harsh, metallic sound. **2.** To grate on or jar: *jangle one's nerves.* —*n.* A harsh, metallic sound.

jan•i•tor |jăn′ĭ tər| *n.* A person whose job it is to clean and take care of a building.

Jan•u•ar•y |jăn′yōō ĕr′ē| *n.* The first month of the year, after December and before February. It has 31 days. —***modifier:*** *a January day.*

Ja•nus |jā′nəs|. In Roman mythology, the god that protected doorways and city gates, depicted with two faces looking in opposite directions.

ja•pan |jə păn′| *n.* A black varnish, originally from the Orient, yielding a hard, brilliant finish on wood or metal. —*v.* **ja•panned, ja•pan•ning.** To varnish with japan.

Ja•pan |jə păn′|. A country consisting of four main islands and a number of lesser islands, off the eastern coast of Asia. Population, 110,000,000. Capital, Tokyo.

Jap•a•nese |jăp′ə nēz′| *or* |-nēs′| *n., pl.* **Jap•a•nese. 1.** A native or inhabitant of Japan. **2.** The language of Japan, unrelated to any other language so far as is known. —*adj.* Of Japan, the Japanese, or their language.

Japanese beetle. A green-and-brown beetle originally from eastern Asia but now common in North America.

jar[1] |jär| *n.* **1.** A cylindrical container of glass or earthenware, having a wide mouth and usually no handles. **2. a.** A jar with something in it: *buy a jar of jam.* **b.** The amount that a jar holds: *eat a jar of pickles.* [SEE NOTE]

jar[2] |jär| *v.* **jarred, jar•ring. 1.** To cause to shake violently; rock. **2.** To shock: *The news visibly jarred him.* **3.** To have an irritating effect: *The music jars on my nerves.* **4.** To come into conflict. —*n.* A jolt or shock. [SEE NOTE]

jar•gon |jär′gən| *n.* **1.** Nonsensical or meaningless talk; gibberish. **2.** A simplified or mixed language used by people who normally speak different languages. **3.** The specialized language of a trade, profession, or class.

jas•mine |jăz′mĭn| *n.* Any of several vines or shrubs with fragrant, usually yellow or white flowers.

Ja•son |jā′sən|. In Greek mythology, the leader of the Argonauts in quest of the Golden Fleece.

jas•per |jăs′pər| *n.* **1.** A reddish, brown, or yellow type of opaque quartz. **2.** Chalcedony, especially green chalcedony.

jaun•dice |jôn′dĭs| *or* |jän′-| *n.* An abnormal yellow coloration of the tissues and fluids of the body, resulting from bile pigments that accumulate when the liver does not function properly or when there are certain blood disorders.

jaun•diced |jôn′dĭst| *or* |jän′-| *adj.* **1.** Affected with jaundice. **2.** Showing or feeling jealousy, envy, etc.; prejudiced: *a jaundiced viewpoint.*

jaunt |jônt| *or* |jänt| *n.* A short trip or excursion; an outing.

jaun•ty |jôn′tē| *or* |jän′-| *adj.* **jaun•ti•er, jaun•ti•est. 1.** Having a carefree, self-confident air: *a jaunty gait.* **2.** Stylish or smart in appearance: *a jaunty hat.* —**jaun′ti•ly** *adv.*

ja•va |jä′və| *or* |jăv′ə| *n.* *Informal.* Brewed coffee.

Ja•va |jä′və| *or* |jăv′ə|. An island of Indonesia, southeast of Sumatra. It is the site of Djakarta, the country's capital. —**Ja′va•nese′** |jä′və nēz′| *or* |-nēs′| *adj. & n.*

jave•lin |jăv′lĭn| *or* |jăv′ə lĭn| *n.* A light spear that is thrown for distance in an athletic contest.

jaw |jô| *n.* **1.** Either of a pair of structures of

bone or cartilage that in most vertebrates form the framework of the mouth and hold the teeth. **2.** The parts of the body that form the walls of the mouth and serve to open and close it. **3. jaws.** Anything resembling a pair of jaws: *the jaws of a very large wrench.* —*v. Slang.* To talk in a gossipy manner.

jaw•bone |jô′bōn′| *n.* Any of the bones in the jaw, especially the bone of the lower jaw.

Jaws of Life. A trademark for a device used to provide access to persons trapped inside a crushed vehicle.

jay |jā| *n.* Any of several birds related to the crow, often having a crest, brightly colored feathers, and a loud, harsh call.

jay•walk |jā′wôk′| *v.* To cross a street in violation of the traffic rules, as in the middle of the block or when the light is red. —**jay′walk′er** *n.*

jazz |jăz| *n.* **1.** A type of music that was first played by Negro musicians in the southern United States. It has a strong rhythmic structure, makes frequent use of syncopation, and although it has evolved a great deal with passing time, retains a characteristic style of melody and harmony: *The musicians played jazz to a delighted audience.* **2.** *Slang.* Stuff; talk; nonsense: *clean living and all that jazz.* —**modifier:** *a jazz band; a jazz festival.*

jazz•y |jăz′ē| *adj.* **jazz•i•er, jazz•i•est. 1.** Resembling jazz. **2.** *Slang.* Showy; flashy: *a jazzy car.*

jeal•ous |jĕl′əs| *adj.* **1. a.** Fearful of losing someone's affection to another person: *a jealous husband.* **b.** Caused by such a fear: *jealous thoughts; a jealous rage.* **2.** Resenting another's success, advantages, etc.; envious: *She was always jealous of her older sister.* **3.** Careful or watchful in guarding something: *jealous of his good name.* —**jeal′ous•ly** *adv.* —**jeal′ous•ness** *n.*

jeal•ous•y |jĕl′ə sē| *n., pl.* **jeal•ous•ies. 1.** A jealous attitude or feeling. **2.** An act, statement, etc., that shows jealousy.

jeans |jēnz| *pl.n.* Boys' or girls' trousers of coarse, heavy, usually blue cotton cloth.

jeep |jēp| *n.* **1.** A small, rugged motor vehicle designed for military use. **2. Jeep.** A trademark for a line of automobiles and trucks designed for heavy-duty civilian use. [SEE PICTURE]

jeer |jîr| *v.* To shout at in a mocking way. —*n.* A loud mocking shout of disapproval: *The sound of jeers rocked the auditorium.*

Jef•fer•son |jĕf′ər sən|, **Thomas.** 1743–1826. Third President of the United States (1801–09).

Jefferson City. The capital of Missouri. Population, 33,619.

Je•ho•vah |jĭ hō′və|. In the Old Testament, God.

Jehovah's Witnesses. A religious sect predicting the imminent end of the world and opposed to war and to the authority of the government in matters of conscience.

je•june |jĭ jo͞on′| *adj.* Not interesting; dull: *a jejune story.*

je•ju•num |jĭ jo͞o′nəm| *n.* The part of the small intestine between the duodenum and the ileum.

jell |jĕl| *v.* **1.** To pass from a liquid to a semisolid state; congeal: *The custard has already jelled.* **2.** *Informal.* To take shape; crystallize: *Plans for the weekend haven't jelled yet.* ¶ *These sound alike* **jell, gel.**

Jell-O |jĕl′ō| *n.* A trademark for a gelatin dessert.

jel•ly |jĕl′ē| *n., pl.* **jel•lies. 1.** Soft, clear food that has a springy consistency, as one that is made by causing a liquid, such as fruit juice, to set by preparing it with pectin or gelatin. **2.** Any substance resembling this: *petroleum jelly.* —**modifier:** *jelly sandwiches; jelly jars.* —*v.* **jel•lied, jel•ly•ing, jel•lies.** To turn into jelly. —**jel′lied** *adj.*: *a jellied sauce.*

jel•ly•bean |jĕl′ē bēn′| *n.* A small, chewy, bean-shaped candy with a hard sugar coating.

jel•ly•fish |jĕl′ē fĭsh′| *n., pl.* **-fish** or **fish•es.** A sea animal with a jellylike, often umbrella-shaped body and tentacles that can cause an uncomfortable sting. [SEE PICTURE]

jen•net |jĕn′ĭt| *n.* **1.** A small Spanish horse used for riding. **2.** A female donkey.

jen•ny |jĕn′ē| *n., pl.* **jen•nies. 1.** A **spinning jenny. 2.** The female of certain animals, especially the donkey.

jeop•ard•ize |jĕp′ər dīz′| *v.* **jeop•ard•ized, jeop•ard•iz•ing.** To expose to loss or injury; endanger: *jeopardize one's health.*

jeop•ard•y |jĕp′ər dē| *n.* Danger of death, injury, or loss; peril: *The villagers' lives were constantly in jeopardy.*

jer•bo•a |jər bō′ə| *n.* A small, mouselike animal of Asia and northern Africa, having a long tail and long hind legs used for leaping.

Jer•e•mi•ah |jĕr′ə mī′ə|. A Hebrew prophet of the seventh and sixth centuries B.C.

jerk[1] |jûrk| *v.* **1.** To give (something) a quick pull, push, or twist. **2.** To make a sudden abrupt movement: *The fisherman felt his line suddenly jerk.* **3.** To move in sudden uneven motions: *The old streetcar jerked down the hill.* —*n.* **1.** A sudden, abrupt motion, such as a yank. **2.** *Slang.* A stupid person; a fool. [SEE NOTE]

jerk[2] |jûrk| *v.* To cut (meat) into strips and dry in the sun or cure with smoke. [SEE NOTE]

jer•kin |jûr′kĭn| *n.* A short, close-fitting jacket, usually sleeveless and often of leather, worn by men during the 16th and 17th centuries.

jerk•y[1] |jûr′kē| *adj.* **jerk•i•er, jerk•i•est. 1.** Making sudden starts and stops: *jerky movements.* **2.** *Slang.* Silly. —**jerk′i•ly** *adv.* —**jerk′i•ness** *n.* [SEE NOTE]

jerk•y[2] |jûr′kē| *n.* Meat, such as beef, that has been cut into strips and dried in the sun or cured with smoke. [SEE NOTE]

jer•ry-built |jĕr′ē bĭlt′| *adj.* Built hastily, cheaply, and poorly.

jer•sey |jûr′zē| *n., pl.* **jer•seys. 1.** A soft, elastic, knitted fabric of wool, cotton, rayon, etc., used for clothing. **2.** A garment, such as a pullover sweater or sport shirt, made of this fabric. **3. Jersey.** One of a breed of light-brown cattle raised for milk and milk products.

Je•ru•sa•lem |jə ro͞o′sə ləm|. The capital of ancient and modern Israel. Population, 301,000.

jes•sa•mine |jĕs′ə mĭn| *n.* A form of the word **jasmine**, used especially for the yellow-flowered climbing jasmine of the southeastern United States.

jest |jĕst| *n.* **1.** Something said or done for fun or amusement. **2.** A playful mood or manner: *He only said it in jest.* —*v.* To joke.

jest•er |jĕs′tər| *n.* **1.** A person who makes jokes.

jeep

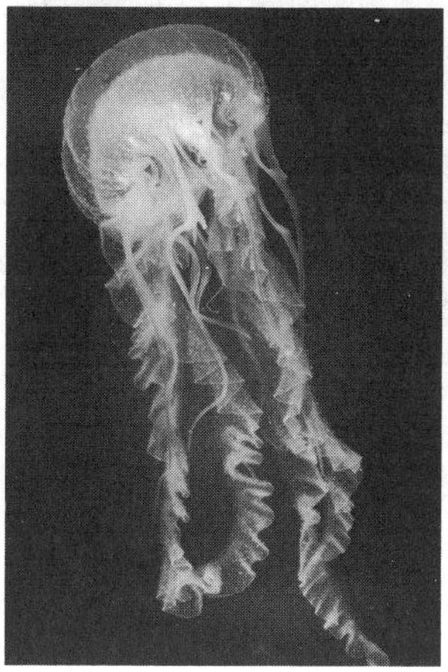

jellyfish

jerk[1-2]/jerky[1-2]

***Jerk*[1] *and* jerky[1] *are of unknown origin.* Jerk[2] *and* jerky[2] *are a completely separate group; this method of curing meat was invented by the Quechua, the people who ruled much of South America under the Inca Empire before the coming of the Spanish. The Quechua word for meat cured by this process was* ch'arki; *the Spanish borrowed this as* charqui, *and the English took it from the Spanish as* jerky[2]; jerk[2] *is a back-formation from* jerky[2].

2. In the Middle Ages, a person employed to entertain a king and his court.

Jes•u•it |jĕzh′o͝o ĭt| *or* |jĕz′yo͞o-| *n.* A member of the Society of Jesus, a Roman Catholic religious order. —*modifier: a Jesuit priest.*

Je•sus |jē′zəs|. Jesus of Nazareth, the founder of Christianity, considered by Christians as the Son of God and the Messiah; Christ.

jet[1] |jĕt| *n.* **1.** A dense black form of coal that can be polished to a bright shine and is used as a gem. **2.** A deep black. —*modifier: a jet necklace.* —*adj.* Deep black: *jet eyebrows.*

jet[2] |jĕt| *n.* **1.** A high-velocity stream of liquid or gas forced through a small opening or nozzle under pressure. **2.** An outlet or nozzle through which a stream is forced: *a gas jet.* **3. a.** A jet-propelled aircraft or other vehicle. **b.** A **jet engine.** —*modifier: a jet plane.* —*v.* **jet•ted, jet•ting.** To gush out; squirt: *Smoke jetted from the chimney.*

jet engine. Any engine that develops thrust by forcing out a jet, especially a jet composed of exhaust gases from material burned in the engine.

jet lag. The disruption of body rhythms resulting from high-speed air travel through several time zones.

jet-pro•pelled |jĕt′prə pĕld′| *adj.* Propelled by one or more jet engines: *a jet-propelled airplane.*

jet propulsion. The driving of a vehicle or other body by the thrust developed when a jet of gas or liquid is forced out, especially using a jet engine.

jet•sam |jĕt′səm| *n.* Things thrown overboard from a ship in distress. See **flotsam.**

jet stream. **1.** A strong wind, often reaching speeds of 175 miles an hour, that blows from a westerly direction at the base of the stratosphere. **2.** A rapidly moving stream of liquid or gas.

jet•ti•son |jĕt′ĭ sən| *or* |-zən| *v.* **1.** To cast (heavy objects) overboard, especially to lighten a ship in an emergency at sea. **2.** To discard (unwanted things).

jet•ty |jĕt′ē| *n., pl.* **jet•ties. 1.** A wharf or landing pier. **2.** A breakwater.

Jew |jo͞o| *n.* **1.** A person whose religion is Judaism. **2.** A descendant of the Hebrew people mentioned in the Bible.

jew•el |jo͞o′əl| *n.* **1.** A precious stone; a gem. **2.** A costly ornament, such as a ring or necklace, especially one of precious metal set with gems. **3.** A small gem used as a bearing in a watch. **4.** Something or someone that is greatly admired or valued: *The island is considered the jewel of the Caribbean. His wife is a jewel.* —*modifier: a jewel box.* —*v.* **jew•eled** or **jew•elled, jew•el•ing** or **jew•el•ling.** To decorate, adorn, or set with jewels. —**jew′eled** *adj.: a jeweled crown.*

jew•el•er, also **jew•el•ler** |jo͞o′ə lər| *n.* A person who makes, repairs, or sells jewelry.

jew•el•ry |jo͞o′əl rē| *n.* Ornaments to be worn, made of precious metals set with gems or from inexpensive or imitation materials.

jew•el•weed |jo͞o′əl wēd′| *n.* A plant having yellowish flowers with a narrow projection and seed pods that burst open at a touch when they are ripe.

Jew•ess |jo͞o′ĭs| *n.* A Jewish girl or woman. The word "Jewess" is often considered offensive.

Jew•ish |jo͞o′ĭsh| *adj.* Of the Jews, their religion, or their customs. —**Jew′ish•ness** *n.*

Jew•ry |jo͞o′rē| *n.* The Jewish people.

jew's-harp, also **jews'-harp** |jo͞oz′härp′| *n.* A small musical instrument consisting of a U-shaped frame to which a blade of springy metal is attached. The frame is held in the mouth, and the blade is plucked to produce twanging tones.

Jez•e•bel |jĕz′ə bĕl′| *or* |-bəl|. In the Bible, a queen of Israel who worshiped false idols.

jib |jĭb| *n.* **1.** A triangular sail set forward of the mast and stretching to the bow or bowsprit. **2. a.** The arm of a mechanical crane. **b.** The boom of a derrick.

jib boom. A spar that lengthens the bowsprit on some craft.

jibe[1] |jīb| *v.* **jibed, jib•ing. 1.** To swing or cause to swing (a fore-and-aft sail and its boom) hard from one side of the boat to the other when sailing before the wind. **2.** To change course so that the sail jibes. —*n.* The act of jibing. ¶ *These sound alike* **jibe, gibe.** [SEE NOTE]

jibe[2] |jīb| *v.* **jibed, jib•ing.** *Informal.* To be in accord; agree: *His story doesn't jibe with yours.* ¶ *These sound alike* **jibe, gibe.** [SEE NOTE]

jibe[3] |jīb| *n. & v.* A form of the word **gibe.**

jif•fy |jĭf′ē| *n., pl.* **jif•fies.** *Informal.* A moment; no time at all: *I'll have this fixed in a jiffy.*

jig |jĭg| *n.* **1. a.** Any of a number of fast, lively dances. **b.** A musical composition written to accompany or as if to accompany such a dance. **2.** Any of various devices used to guide a tool or hold work as it is fed to a tool. —*v.* **jigged, jig•ging. 1.** To dance a jig. **2.** To move up and down or to and fro in a quick, jerky way.

jig•ger |jĭg′ər| *n.* A small cup holding 1½ ounces of liquor.

jig•gle |jĭg′əl| *v.* **jig•gled, jig•gling.** To shake up and down or back and forth with short, quick jerks: *He was able to get the car started by jiggling the wires.* —*n.* A jiggling motion.

jig•saw |jĭg′sô′| *n.* A saw with a narrow blade fixed vertically in a frame, used for cutting along curved or wavy lines.

jigsaw puzzle. A mass of irregularly shaped pieces of wood or cardboard that are fitted together to form a picture.

jilt |jĭlt| *v.* To drop or cast aside (a boy friend or girl friend): *He jilted her in favor of Mary.*

Jim Crow |jĭm′krō′|. The practice of discriminating against and segregating black people.

jim•my |jĭm′ē| *n., pl.* **jim•mies.** A short crowbar with curved ends, often used by burglars to force open windows and doors. —*v.* **jim•mied, jim•my•ing, jim•mies.** To force open with a jimmy: *jimmy a door.*

jim•son•weed |jĭm′sən wēd′| *n.* A tall, coarse, poisonous plant with large, trumpet-shaped white or purplish flowers and prickly seed pods.

jin•gle |jĭng′gəl| *v.* **jin•gled, jin•gling.** To make or cause to make a tinkling or ringing metallic sound. —*n.* **1.** A tinkling or ringing sound made by small metal objects striking together. **2.** A simple, catchy rhyme or verse.

jin•ni |jĭn′ē| *or* |jĭ nē′| *n., pl.* **jinn** |jĭn|. In Moslem legend, a spirit able to appear in either human or animal form and to influence mankind for good or evil.

jin•rik•sha or **jin•rick•sha** |jĭn rĭk′shô′| *n.* A small two-wheeled carriage of the Orient, drawn by one or two men.

jibe[1,2]

The English and the Dutch have met each other on the sea for many centuries and have traded many technical nautical words to and fro. **Jibe**[1] *is one of these; it comes from the (now obsolete) Dutch word* giyben. *Other similarly related examples are* **freebooter, keelhaul, skipper, yacht. Jibe**[2] *is of unknown origin.*

ă pat/ā pay/â care/ä father/ĕ pet/ ē be/ĭ pit/ī pie/î fierce/ŏ pot/ ō go/ô paw, for/oi oil/o͝o book/ o͞o boot/ou out/ŭ cut/û fur/ *th* the/th thin/hw which/zh vision/ ə ago, item, pencil, atom, circus

jinx |jĭngks| *n. Informal.* **1.** An evil spell or any force or influence that is felt to bring bad luck. **2.** Someone or something supposed to bring bad luck. —*v. Informal.* To place a jinx on; bring bad luck to.

jit•ney |jĭt′nē| *n., pl.* **jit•neys.** A small bus that carries passengers for a low fare.

jit•ter•bug |jĭt′ər bŭg′| *n.* **1.** A vigorous, energetic dance perfomed to fast jazz or swing music, popular in the 1940's. **2.** *Informal.* A person who does such a dance. —*v.* **jit•ter•bugged, jit•ter•bug•ging.** To dance a jitterbug.

jit•ters |jĭt′ərz| *pl.n. Informal.* A fit of nervousness: *a case of the jitters.*

jit•ter•y |jĭt′ə rē| *adj. Informal.* Having the jitters; nervous.

jiu•jit•su |jo͞o jĭt′so͞o| *n.* A form of the word **jujitsu.**

jive |jīv| *n. Slang.* **1.** Jazz or swing music. **2.** The special words and speech used by jazz musicians and fans. ¶ *These sound alike* **jive, gyve.**

Joan of Arc |jōn′; ärk′|, **Saint.** 1412–1431. French heroine; condemned for witchcraft and heresy and burned at the stake; canonized 1920.

job |jŏb| *n.* **1. a.** A piece of work that needs to be done; a task. **b.** A completed task or assignment: *a job well done.* **2.** A position of employment: *a job in the bookstore.* **3.** A duty or responsibility: *Your job is to keep attendance.*

Job |jōb|. In the Bible, a man whose faith in God survived the test of great personal calamities.

job•ber |jŏb′ər| *n.* A person who buys merchandise from manufacturers and sells it to retailers at a profit.

jock |jŏk| *n. Slang.* **1.** A jockstrap. **2.** A male athlete, especially in college.

jock•ey |jŏk′ē| *n., pl.* **jock•eys.** A person who rides horses in races. —*v.* To maneuver in order to gain an advantage.

jock•strap |jŏk′străp′| *n.* Also **jock strap.** An **athletic supporter.**

jo•cose |jō kōs′| *adj.* Given to joking; merry; playful. —**jo•cose′ly** *adv.* —**jo•cose′ness, jo•cos′i•ty** |jō kŏs′ĭ tē| *n.*

joc•u•lar |jŏk′yə lər| *adj.* **1.** Given to joking: *a jocular fellow always ready to tease his friends.* **2.** Meant in jest: *a jocular remark.* —**joc′u•lar′i•ty** *n.* —**joc′u•lar•ly** *adv.*

joc•und |jŏk′ənd| *or* |jō′kənd| *adj.* Cheerful; pleasant; gay. —**jo•cun′di•ty** |jō kŭn′dĭ tē| *n.* —**joc′und•ly** *adv.*

jodh•purs |jŏd′pərz| *pl.n.* Breeches worn for horseback riding that fit loosely above the knees and tightly from the knees to the ankles.

Jo•el |jō′əl|. A Hebrew prophet of the fifth century B.C.

jog |jŏg| *v.* **jogged, jog•ging. 1.** To give a slight push to; nudge: *I felt someone jogging my elbow.* **2.** To stir or shake up: *Let's see if I can jog your memory.* **3.** To run or ride at a slow, steady trot: *He jogs every morning before breakfast.* —*n.* **1.** A slight push; a nudge. **2.** A slow, steady trot. [SEE PICTURE]

jog•gle |jŏg′əl| *v.* **jog•gled, jog•gling.** To shake slightly; nudge. —*n.* A shake or nudge.

Jo•han•nes•burg |jō hăn′ĭs bûrg′|. The largest city in South Africa. Population, 1,300,000.

John |jŏn| *n.* The fourth Gospel of the New Testament.

John, Saint. One of the Twelve Apostles; traditionally regarded as the author of the fourth Gospel.

John Bull. A personification of England or the English people. [SEE PICTURE]

John Doe. A made-up name used to refer to an unknown or unidentified person.

John Hancock. *Informal.* A person's signature, a term derived from the name of the first signer of the Declaration of Independence.

John Henry. 1. In U.S. folklore, a Negro laborer of great strength. **2.** A person's signature.

john•ny•cake |jŏn′ē kāk′| *n.* A thin, flat cornmeal bread, often baked on a griddle.

John•ny-jump-up |jŏn′ē jŭmp′ŭp′| *n.* A plant with small flowers that are shaped like violets and have the usually purple and yellow coloring of pansies.

John•ny Reb |jŏn′ē rĕb′|. A Confederate soldier.

John•son |jŏn′sən|. **1. Samuel.** 1709–1784. English critic and author; compiler of the first major dictionary of the English language. **2. Andrew.** 1808–1875. Seventeenth President of the United States (1865–69). **3. Lyndon Baines.** 1908–1972. Thirty-sixth President of the United States (1963–69).

John the Baptist. In the New Testament, the cousin of Jesus, whom he baptized.

join |join| *v.* **1.** To link or connect: *The Isthmus of Panama joins North and South America.* **2.** To put together in a continuous series: *The children joined hands in a circle.* **3.** To fasten or attach: *Solder is used to join metal parts together.* **4.** To unite: *Eleven states joined together to form the Confederacy.* **5.** To meet and unite with: *The Missouri River joins the Mississippi near St. Louis.* **6.** To become a member of: *join the Boy Scouts.* **7.** To enter into the company of: *Would you care to join us for lunch?* **8.** To become associated with: *If you can't lick 'em, join 'em.* **9.** To take part; participate: *join in the singing. Many nations have pledged to join the battle against hunger.* —***phrasal verb.*** **join up.** To enlist, especially in the armed forces.

join•er |joi′nər| *n.* **1.** A skilled workman who makes the inside woodwork, such as doors and stairs, for houses and other buildings **2.** *Informal.* A person inclined to join many groups or organizations.

joint |joint| *n.* **1.** A point at which movable body parts are connected or come together; for example, a connection between bones or a point at which parts of an insect's leg meet: *a knee joint.* **2.** Any place where two or more things come together: *a joint in a pipe.* **3.** Something used to join two parts or hold them together: *a ball-and-socket joint.* **4.** A part on a plant stem, often marked by a ridge or swelling, from which a leaf or stem may grow. **5.** A large cut of meat, as from the shoulder or leg. **6.** *Slang.* A cheap or shabby restaurant, bar, or public place. **7.** *Slang.* A marijuana cigarette. —*adj.* **1.** Undertaken or shared by two or more people or parties: *a joint effort; a joint bank account.* **2.** Sharing with someone else: *joint owners.* **3.** Involving both houses of a legislature: *a joint session of Congress.* —*v.* To provide with a joint.

Idiom. **out of joint. 1.** Not in place at the joint;

jog

John Bull

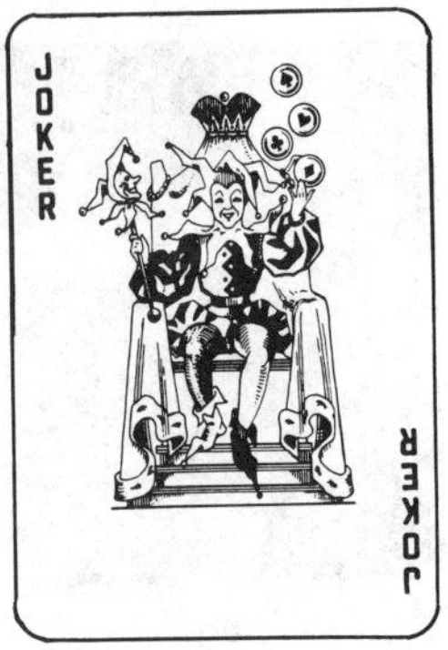

joker

joust

jowl[1-2]
Jowl[1] *and* **jowl[2]** *are unrelated Old English words, originally* ceafl, *"jaw," and* ceolu, *"throat," respectively.*

dislocated. **2.** In bad spirits; out of sorts. **3.** Out of order; in a state of disorder.

Joint Chiefs of Staff. The principal military advisory group to the President of the United States, composed of the chiefs of the Army, Navy, and Air Force.

joint•ed |**join′**tĭd| *adj.* **1.** Having a joint or joints: *the jointed legs of an insect.* **2.** Having a certain kind of joint: *double-jointed.*

joint•er |**join′**tər| *n.* A hand or power tool used to smooth sawed parts of wood before making joints.

joint•ly |**joint′**lē| *adv.* Together; in common.

joist |joist| *n.* A horizontal beam that supports the boards of a floor or ceiling.

joke |jōk| *n.* **1.** A short story designed to cause laughter. **2.** A mischievous trick; a prank: *a practical joke.* **3.** Something not to be taken seriously: *Can't you take a joke?* —*v.* **joked, jok•ing.** To say something as a joke; speak in fun.

jok•er |**jō′**kər| *n.* **1.** A person who tells or plays jokes. **2.** An extra playing card bearing the figure of a jester. If used in a game, it counts either as the highest card or as any card the holder desires. [SEE PICTURE]

joke•ster |**jōk′**stər| *n.* A joker.

jok•ing•ly |**jō′**kĭng lē| *adv.* As a joke; in jest.

jol•li•ty |**jŏl′**ĭ tē| *n.* Gaiety; merriment.

jol•ly |**jŏl′**ē| *adj.* **jol•li•er, jol•li•est.** Full of merriment and good spirits. —*adv. British Informal.* Very: *That's a jolly good idea!*

Jolly Rog•er |**rŏj′**ər|. A black flag on a pirate ship bearing a white skull and crossbones.

jolt |jōlt| *v.* **1.** To shake violently with a sudden sharp blow or movement. **2.** To move in a bumpy or jerky fashion: *The bus jolted to a stop.* —*n.* **1.** A sudden jerk or bump. **2.** Something that causes a sudden shock or surprise: *The news came as quite a jolt.*

Jo•nah |**jō′**nə|. In the Bible, a Hebrew prophet who was swallowed by a whale but disgorged unharmed later.

Jones |jōnz|, **John Paul.** 1747–1792. Scottish-born American naval commander in the Revolutionary War.

jon•quil |**jŏng′**kwĭl| *or* |**jŏn′**-| *n.* A garden plant having fragrant yellow flowers resembling those of the daffodil but with a shorter central part.

Jor•dan[1] |**jôr′**dn|. A country in the Middle East. Population, 2,646,000. Capital, Amman. —**Jor•da′ni•an** |jôr **dā′**nē ən| *adj.* & *n.*

Jor•dan[2] |**jôr′**dn|. The principal river of Israel and Jordan, flowing south from northern Israel to the Dead Sea.

Jo•seph |**jō′**zəf| *or* |-səf|. **1.** In the Old Testament, a son of Jacob who was sold into slavery in Egypt. **2.** In the New Testament, the husband of Mary and stepfather of Jesus.

josh |jŏsh| *v. Informal.* **1.** To tease in a light-hearted, playful way. **2.** To speak in jest; joke.

Josh•u•a |**jŏsh′**o͞o ə|. In the Bible, the leader of the Hebrews after Moses.

Joshua tree. A large treelike plant of desert regions of the southwestern United States, having clusters of stiff, pointed leaves at the ends of its branches.

jos•tle |**jŏs′**əl| *v.* **jos•tled, jos•tling.** **1.** To push or bump by running into suddenly: *The couples jostled each other on the dance floor.* **2.** To come into contact; crowd or brush against: *Thousands of people were jostling in the square.*

jot |jŏt| *v.* **jot•ted, jot•ting.** To write down briefly and hastily: *I jotted down a few notes on a pad.* —*n.* A tiny bit; iota: *They didn't care one jot.*

joule |jo͞ol| *or* |joul| *n.* A unit of energy or work equal to the work done by a force of one newton acting through a distance of one meter, or by one watt of power applied for a period of one second.

jounce |jouns| *v.* **jounced, jounc•ing.** To bounce up and down: *The bus jounced along the road.*

jour•nal |**jûr′**nəl| *n.* **1.** A daily record of events, business transactions, etc. **2.** A periodical containing news and articles in a particular field: *a medical journal.* **3.** A newspaper: *The Wall Street Journal.* **4.** The part of an axle or shaft that is supported by a bearing, as in a machine.

jour•nal•ism |**jûr′**nə lĭz′əm| *n.* The gathering and presentation of news, especially by newspapers and magazines.

jour•nal•ist |**jûr′**nə lĭst| *n.* A person employed in journalism, especially a reporter or editor.

jour•nal•is•tic |jûr′nə **lĭs′**tĭk| *adj.* Of or typical of journalism or journalists.

jour•ney |**jûr′**nē| *n., pl.* **jour•neys.** **1.** A trip, especially one over a great distance: *the long journey home.* **2.** The distance traveled on a journey or the time required for such a trip: *a thousand-mile journey; a three-day journey.* —*v.* To travel a great distance; make a long trip.

jour•ney•man |**jûr′**nē mən| *n., pl.* **-men** |-mən|. **1.** A person who has completed his apprenticeship in a trade or craft. **2.** A competent but undistinguished worker or performer.

joust |joust| *or* |jŭst| *or* |jo͞ost| *n.* A combat between two knights on horseback armed with lances and wearing armor. —*v.* To take part in a joust. [SEE PICTURE]

Jove |jōv|. Jupiter, the chief god of the Romans.

jo•vi•al |**jō′**vē əl| *adj.* Full of fun and good cheer; jolly: *a jovial old man.* —**jo′vi•al′i•ty** *n.* —**jo′vi•al•ly** *adv.*

jowl[1] |joul| *n.* **1.** The jaw, especially the lower jaw. **2.** The cheek. [SEE NOTE]

jowl[2] |joul| *n.* **1.** The flesh under the lower jaw, especially when plump or hanging loosely. **2.** Any loosely hanging flesh on or near the jaw of an animal: *the jowls of a bulldog.* [SEE NOTE]

joy |joi| *n.* **1.** A feeling of great happiness or delight: *shouts of joy.* **2.** A source or cause of joy: *the joys of motherhood.*

joy•ful |**joi′**fəl| *adj.* **1.** Full of joy: *a joyful occasion.* **2.** Showing or expressing joy: *a joyful song.* —**joy′ful•ly** *adv.* —**joy′ful•ness** *n.*

joy•ous |**joi′**əs| *adj.* Full of joy; joyful: *a joyous occasion.* —**joy′ous•ly** *adv.* —**joy′ous•ness** *n.*

jr., Jr. junior.

ju•bi•lant |**jo͞o′**bə lənt| *adj.* Full of joy; rejoicing: *a jubilant crowd.* —**ju′bi•lant•ly** *adv.*

ju•bi•la•tion |jo͞o′bə **lā′**shən| *n.* Great rejoicing: *The news was greeted with wild jubilation.*

ju•bi•lee |**jo͞o′**bə lē′| *n.* A special anniversary, such as the 25th or 50th, or the celebration of it.

Ju•dah |**jo͞o′**də|. An ancient Hebrew kingdom in southern Palestine.

Ju•da•ic |jo͞o **dā′**ĭk| *adj.* Of or relating to the Jews or Judaism.

Ju•da•ism |**jo͞o′**dē ĭz′əm| *n.* The religion of the

ă pat/ā pay/â care/ä father/ĕ pet/ ē be/ĭ pit/ī pie/î fierce/ŏ pot/ ō go/ô paw, for/oi oil/o͝o book/ o͞o boot/ou out/ŭ cut/û fur/ *th* the/th thin/hw which/zh vision/ ə ago, item, pencil, atom, circus

Jewish people, as set forth in the Old Testament and the Talmud, based on the belief in a single God.

Ju•das |**jo͞o**′dəs|. Called "Judas Iscariot." In the New Testament, the disciple who betrayed Jesus.

Ju•de•a |jo͞o **dē**′ə|. In Biblical times, southern Palestine.

judge |jŭj| *n.* **1.** A public official who hears and decides cases in a court of law. **2.** A person who watches over the proceedings during a contest and decides the winner. **3.** A person who gives an opinion about the value, quality, or outcome of something: *a good judge of character.* **4.** A leader of the Hebrews in the period of about 400 years between the death of Joshua and the crowning of King Saul. *—v.* **judged, judg•ing. 1.** To hear and pass judgment on in a court of law. **2.** To decide; settle (a contest or issue). **3.** To assign a value to; assess or appraise: *Let me smell one—that's the way to judge fruit. Until you speak, you are judged solely on your appearance.* **4.** To pass sentence upon; appraise harshly. **5.** To form an opinion about: *judge a person unfairly.*

judge•ship |**jŭj**′shĭp′| *n.* The office or jurisdiction of a judge or the period during which a judge is in office.

judg•ment, also **judge•ment** |**jŭj**′mənt| *n.* **1.** A decision reached after a careful weighing of evidence or choices, as in a court of law: *a judgment holding an act of Congress unconstitutional.* **2.** The ability to choose wisely; good sense: *trust his judgment.* **3.** The act or an instance of judging; the forming of a decision or opinion after due consideration: *The judgment of a legal case may require hours of research.*

Judgment Day. In religious tradition, the last day of the world, when God will pass final judgment on all souls. Also called *Day of Judgment.*

ju•di•cial |jo͞o **dĭsh**′əl| *adj.* **1.** Of courts of law or the administration of justice: *the judicial branch of government.* **2.** Decreed by a court: *a judicial decision.* *—***ju•di′cial•ly** *adv.*

ju•di•ci•ar•y |jo͞o **dĭsh**′ē ĕr′ē| *adj.* Of courts, judges, or the administration of justice. *—n., pl.* **ju•di•ci•ar•ies. 1.** The judicial branch of government. **2.** A system of courts of law and judges.

ju•di•cious |jo͞o **dĭsh**′əs| *adj.* Showing forethought and caution; prudent; sensible: *a more judicious use of resources.* *—***ju•di′cious•ly** *adv.*

ju•do |**jo͞o**′dō| *n.* A modern form of jujitsu using principles of balance, leverage, and movement in throwing an opponent from a standing position and in wrestling on the mat. It is studied as a method of physical and mental development and is also played as a sport.

jug |jŭg| *n.* **1.** A large container for storing and carrying liquids, having a narrow mouth and a small handle. **2.** *British.* A pitcher. **3. a.** A jug with something in it: *buy a jug of cider.* **b.** The amount that a jug holds: *drink a jug of water.*

jug•ger•naut |**jŭg**′ər nôt′| *n.* **1.** A belief or institution to which people sacrifice themselves in blind devotion. **2.** An advancing force or object that crushes anything in its path. [SEE NOTE]

jug•gle |**jŭg**′əl| *v.* **jug•gled, jug•gling. 1.** To keep (two or more objects) in the air at one time by alternately tossing and catching them. **2.** To handle with skill so as to balance or manage: *juggling his hat and camera.* **3.** To change or rearrange so as to mislead or cheat: *juggle figures on a report.*

jug•gler |**jŭg**′lər| *n.* **1.** An entertainer who juggles balls or other objects. **2.** One who uses tricks to mislead or cheat: *a juggler of figures.* [SEE PICTURE]

jug•u•lar |**jŭg**′yə lər| *adj.* Of, in, or involving the neck or throat. *—n.* A **jugular vein.**

jugular vein. Any of several large veins of the neck.

juice |jo͞os| *n.* **1.** The liquid contained in plant or animal tissue, especially in plant parts such as fruit, stems, or roots. **2.** A fluid secreted within an organ of the body: *digestive juices.* **3.** *Slang.* Electric current.

juic•er |**jo͞o**′sər| *n.* A kitchen appliance for extracting juice from fruits and vegetables.

juic•y |**jo͞o**′sē| *adj.* **juic•i•er, juic•i•est.** Full of juice: *juicy berries.*

ju•jit•su |jo͞o **jĭt**′so͞o| *n.* A Japanese art of unarmed self-defense in which an opponent is disabled or injured by means of techniques that force him to use his weight and strength against himself.

ju•jube |**jo͞o**′jo͞ob′| *n.* A chewy fruit-flavored candy.

juke box |jo͞ok|. A phonograph encased in a large cabinet, operated by inserting a coin and pressing a button for the desired record.

ju•lep |**jo͞o**′lĭp| *n.* A kind of mixed alcoholic drink, especially a mint julep.

Jul•ian calendar |**jo͞ol**′yən|. The calendar introduced in Rome by Julius Caesar in 46 B.C. It has been replaced by the Gregorian calendar.

ju•li•enne |jo͞o′lē **ĕn**′| *adj.* Cut into long thin strips: *julienne potatoes.*

Ju•li•et |**jo͞o**′lē ət| *or* |jo͞o′lē **ĕt**′|. The heroine and beloved of Romeo in Shakespeare's *Romeo and Juliet.*

Ju•ly |jo͞o **lī**′| *n.* The seventh month of the year, after June and before August. It has 31 days. *—**modifier:** a July holiday.*

jum•ble |**jŭm**′bəl| *v.* **jum•bled, jum•bling.** To mix without order or regularity; throw together: *big, little, and middle-sized girls all jumbled together.* *—n.* **1.** A confused, crowded grouping: *a jumble of modern automobiles and ancient ox carts.* **2.** A disordered state; a muddle: *a confused jumble in my mind.*

jum•bo |**jŭm**′bō| *n., pl.* **jum•bos.** Something very large of its kind. *—**modifier:** a jumbo frog.*

jump |jŭmp| *v.* **1.** To rise up off the ground by exerting the legs; spring; leap: *Grasshoppers have well-developed hind legs that allow them to jump.* **2. a.** To leap over: *A police dog can jump a wall more than nine feet tall.* **b.** *Informal.* To leap upon: *jumped a bus.* **3.** To cause to leap: *These magic shoes can jump you over rivers and houses.* **4.** To throw oneself off or from a place: *He jumped nimbly from the shore into a rowboat.* **5.** To move suddenly and in one motion: *The sailors jumped out of their bunks at the call of "Up all hands."* **6.** To pass quickly from one thing to another further on; skip: *Start counting, and jump by 5's to 50.* **7.** To start, as in fear or surprise: *colors so intense that they make your eyes jump.* **8.** To arrive at hastily: *jump to conclusions.* **9.**

juggernaut

Early accounts of India brought back by western travelers often included dramatic descriptions of an annual ceremony in which a large image of the god Krishna was pulled out on a huge wheeled platform, and it is said that worshipers would throw themselves in front of it to be crushed by the wheels. This scene, which seems to be exaggerated, impressed the European imagination so deeply that the word **juggernaut,** *which was one of Krishna's titles, has ever since been a powerful expression for a blind, crushing force.*

juggler

jumper[1-2]
Jumper[1] *is, obviously, from* **jump. Jumper[2]** *is probably from* jump *or* jup, *a British dialectal word for a short coat or top, which is from French* juppe.

jumping jack

junk[1-2]
Junk[1] *was originally a sailors' expression meaning "old worn-out bits of rope"; it goes back to the fifteenth century, but its origin is unknown.* **Junk[2]** *is from Dutch* jonk *and Portuguese* junco, *which are both borrowed from Malay* jong, *"seagoing ship."*

junk[2]
Model of a South China trading junk

ă pat/ā pay/â care/ä father/ĕ pet/ ē be/ĭ pit/ī pie/î fierce/ŏ pot/ ō go/ô paw, for/oi oil/o͝o book/ o͞o boot/ou out/ŭ cut/û fur/ *th* the/th thin/hw which/zh vision/ ə ago, item, pencil, atom, circus

To go up suddenly: *Prices jumped.* **10.** To respond eagerly: *We jumped at the chance.* **11.** To be dislodged from (a course or track): *Your needle may jump a groove when the sound is at low frequency.* —*n.* **1.** A leap off the ground. **2.** The distance or height achieved in a leap: *a jump of 16 feet.* **3.** An abrupt rise: *a jump in temperature.* **4.** An abrupt move to a different place or level: *Moving into a new block is a big jump for a Harlem kid.* **5.** A step: *He kept one jump ahead of the advancing frontier.* **6.** A sudden, involuntary movement; a jerk or start.

Idioms. **get** or **(have) the jump on.** *Slang.* To have an advantage over. **jump a claim.** To seize or use the rightful property of another. **jump bail.** To forfeit one's bail by not appearing in court when summoned. **jump the gun.** *Slang.* To start before the signal is given.

jump•er[1] |jŭm′pər| *n.* **1.** Someone or something that jumps: *a high jumper; a good jumper like a goat.* **2.** A short length of wire or other electrical conductor used to make a temporary connection. **3.** A long, heavy bar used to bore holes in rock or cement. [SEE NOTE]

jum•per[2] |jŭm′pər| *n.* **1.** A sleeveless dress worn over a blouse or sweater. **2.** A loose smock, blouse, or jacket worn over other clothes to protect them. [SEE NOTE]

jumping bean. A seed of any of certain Mexican plants, containing a moth larva whose movements cause the seed to twist and roll.

jumping jack. A toy figure with jointed limbs that can be made to dance by pulling an attached string. [SEE PICTURE]

jump rope. A rope held at both ends and turned so that one can jump over it as it touches the ground.

jump•y |jŭm′pē| *adj.* **jump•i•er, jump•i•est. 1.** Moving in jumps; jerky: *the jumpy movements of a flea.* **2.** Nervous; on edge.

jun•co |jŭng′kō| *n., pl.* **jun•cos.** A North American bird with mostly gray feathers.

junc•tion |jŭngk′shən| *n.* **1.** The act of joining or the condition of being joined: *the precise junction of two faces on a crystal.* **2.** The place at which two things join or meet: *The junction of the Mississippi and Illinois rivers.* **3.** The place at which railway tracks or roads cross and the settlement built there: *We pulled into the junction and headed straight for the station.*

junc•ture |jŭngk′chər| *n.* **1.** A joining; connection. **2.** The point, line, or seam at which two things join: *the junctures of different patterns in a quilt.* **3.** A point in time at which circumstances change: *At this juncture, a new government was formed.* **4.** A pause or break, as in speech: *Voice signals of pitch and juncture help give meaning to a sentence.*

June |jo͞on| *n.* The sixth month of the year, after May and before July. It has 30 days. —***modifier:*** *a June vacation.*

Ju•neau |jo͞o′nō|. The capital of Alaska. Population, 19,528.

jun•gle |jŭng′gəl| *n.* **1.** A dense growth of tropical trees and plants covering a large area. **2.** Any crowded space of uncontrolled growth; a profusion: *Certain mushrooms grow in a jungle among the ferns and palms.* **3.** A confusion; a tangle; maze: *the jungle of the marketplace.* —***modifier:*** *jungle sounds; a jungle doctor.*

Jungle gym. A trademark for a structure of poles and bars on which children can play.

jun•gly |jŭng′glē| *adj.* **jun•gli•er, jun•gli•est.** Characteristic of a jungle: *lush, jungly leaves.*

jun•ior |jo͞on′yər| *adj.* **1.** Of or for younger or smaller persons: *the junior skating championship; junior dress sizes.* **2. Junior.** A term used with the name of a son named after his father: *William, Junior, was the eldest son of the family.* **3.** Of lower rank or shorter length of service: *a junior partner.* **4.** Of the third year of a four-year high school or college: *the junior class.* —*n.* **1.** A person who is younger or of lesser rank than another: *She was sixteen years his junior.* **2.** A person of a younger age group. **3.** A student in his or her third year at a four-year high school or college: *The juniors gave the prom.* **4.** A range of sizes for girls' and women's clothes.

junior college. A school entered after high school that offers a two-year course of undergraduate training.

junior high school. A secondary school including the seventh, eighth, and sometimes ninth grades.

junior varsity. A high-school or college team that competes in sports with other schools on a level below that of a varsity team.

ju•ni•per |jo͞o′nə pər| *n.* An evergreen tree or shrub related to the pines, having small scalelike or prickly leaves and bluish, aromatic berries.

junk[1] |jŭngk| *n.* **1.** Bulky discarded materials, such as machine parts, rags, or paper. **2. a.** Something worn-out and discarded. **b.** *Informal.* Anything useless, cumbersome, or shoddy: *all that heavy chrome and junk on the new cars.* **3.** *Slang.* Heroin. —***modifier:*** *a junk shop; a junk dealer.* —*v.* To discard as worn-out or useless. [SEE NOTE]

junk[2] |jŭngk| *n.* A Chinese flat-bottomed ship with a high stern and battened sails. [SEE NOTE & PICTURE]

jun•ket |jŭng′kĭt| *n.* **1.** A sweet custardlike food made from flavored milk and rennet. **2.** A pleasure trip, especially one made by a government official at public expense.

junk•ie |jŭng′kē| *n. Slang.* A narcotics addict, especially one using heroin.

junk mail. Commercial advertisements sent to large numbers of people without their having requested them.

junk•yard |jŭngk′yärd′| *n.* A yard or other open area for the dumping of junk.

Ju•no |jo͞o′nō|. In Roman mythology, the wife of Jupiter.

jun•ta |ho͝on′tə| *or* |ho͞on′-| *or* |jŭn′-| *n.* A group of leaders who jointly govern a nation, especially such a group that is temporarily in power after a revolution.

Ju•pi•ter[1] |jo͞o′pĭ tər|. In Roman mythology, the ruler of the gods.

Ju•pi•ter[2] |jo͞o′pĭ tər| *n.* The fifth planet of the solar system in order of increasing distance from the sun. Its diameter is about 86,000 miles, its average distance from the sun is about 483 million miles, and it takes about 11 years and 315 days to make an orbit of the sun.

Ju•ras•sic |jo͞o răs′ĭk| *n.* Also **Jurassic period.** A geologic period that began 180 million years ago and ended 135 million years ago, characterized by the existence of dinosaurs and the appearance of primitive birds and mammals. *—modifier:* *a Jurassic fossil.*

ju•rid•i•cal |jo͞o rĭd′ĭ kəl| *adj.* Of the law or its administration; legal: *juridical authorities.* **—ju•rid′i•cal•ly** *adv.*

ju•ris•dic•tion |jo͝or′ĭs dĭk′shən| *n.* **1.** The authority to interpret and apply the law: *Federal courts have jurisdiction when a foreigner sues an American.* **2.** The range of such authority: *cases beyond the jurisdiction of state courts.* **3.** A geographic area under one legal or political authority.

ju•ris•pru•dence |jo͝or′ĭs pro͞od′ns| *n.* **1.** The science or philosophy of law. **2.** A system of laws: *17th-century jurisprudence.*

ju•rist |jo͝or′ĭst| *n.* A person, especially an eminent judge or lawyer, who is skilled in the law.

ju•ror |jo͝or′ər| *n.* A member of a jury.

ju•ry |jo͝or′ē| *n., pl.* **ju•ries. 1.** A panel of citizens sworn to hear and hand down verdicts on cases presented in a court of law: *the right to trial by jury.* **2.** A group of judges empowered to pick a winner or to award prizes. *—modifier:* *a jury trial; jury duty.*

ju•ry•man |jo͝or′ē mən| *n., pl.* **-men** |-mən|. A juror.

just |jŭst| *adj.* **1.** Showing honesty and impartiality; fair: *a just decision.* **2.** Consistent with what is right; proper; due: *a just resentment of her tormentors.* *—adv.* **1.** Exactly: *Everything went just as the old man said.* **2.** At that instant: *Just then a flash of lightning turned the whole room sharply white.* **3.** Quite recently: *We've just run out of it.* **4.** Barely; shortly: *Carl set out just after midnight.* **5.** Only a short distance; immediately: *The braids formed a loop just below her shoulders.* **6.** Simply; merely: *No boxer ever got to the top just by punching.* **7.** Really; certainly: *My brother makes me so mad I just boil inside.* **—just′ly** *adv.* **—just′ness** *n.*

Idioms. **just about.** Almost; very nearly. **just now. 1.** At this instant: *He's on the phone just now.* **2.** A moment ago: *They arrived just now.* **just the same.** Nevertheless: *The fence was not high, but just the same Willy gave him a push.*

jus•tice |jŭs′tĭs| *n.* **1.** The administration and procedure of law: *the Department of Justice.* **2.** A judge or justice of the peace: *The Supreme Court is made up of a Chief Justice and as many associate justices as Congress determines.* **3.** Fair treatment, in accordance with law or honor: *The civil judge must secure justice for the wronged person.* **4.** Rightness; morality: *a king who ruled with justice, love, and wisdom. Adams had a fiery temper and an ardent sense of justice.* **5.** Good reason; sound basis: *angry, and with justice.*

Idiom. **do justice. 1.** To apply the laws or standards of judgment fairly: *I hope to see justice done and credit given where credit is due.* **2.** To show to best advantage: *The photo doesn't do her justice.*

justice of the peace. A local magistrate having authority to act on minor offenses, perform marriages, and administer oaths.

jus•ti•fi•a•ble |jŭs′tə fī′ə bəl| *or* |jŭs′tə fī′-| *adj.* Capable of being justified; defensible: *It's a lot to pay for a car of this size, but justifiable when one considers the fine workmanship.* **—jus′ti•fi′a•bil′i•ty** *n.* **—jus′ti•fi′a•bly** *adv.*

jus•ti•fi•ca•tion |jŭs′tə fĭ kā′shən| *n.* **1.** The act of justifying or the condition of being justified. **2.** Something that justifies; a good reason.

jus•ti•fy |jŭs′tə fī′| *v.* **jus•ti•fied, jus•ti•fying, jus•ti•fies. 1.** To show or prove to be right or just: *making excuses to justify his actions in his own mind.* **2.** To show to be sound or sensible: *Do you believe a fear of snakes is justified?* **3.** To declare innocent; clear of blame: *confident that the court would justify him.*

jut |jŭt| *v.* **jut•ted, jut•ting.** To project sharply upward or outward; stick out: *buildings seemed to jut up as high as the heavens.* **—jut′ting** *adj.:* *jutting brows; a jutting rock.*

jute |jo͞ot| *n.* **1.** A tropical Asian plant that yields a fiber used to make rope, twine, and coarse cloth such as burlap. **2.** The fiber of this plant. [SEE PICTURE]

jute

Jute |jo͞ot| *n.* A member of a Germanic people who invaded Britain in the 5th century A.D. and became part of the Anglo-Saxon people.

ju•ve•nile |jo͞o′və nəl| *or* |-nīl′| *adj.* **1.** Young; immature; childish: *juvenile behavior. After a year the juvenile baboon is more independent of its mother.* **2.** Of or for young people: *Juvenile law courts hear cases involving young persons under 18 years of age.* *—n.* **1.** A young person or animal. **2.** An actor who plays the roles of children. **3.** A book for children.

juvenile delinquency. Antisocial or criminal behavior by children or adolescents.

juvenile delinquent. A child or adolescent guilty of juvenile delinquency.

jux•ta•pose |jŭk′stə pōz′| *v.* **jux•ta•posed, jux•ta•pos•ing.** To place side by side: *The artist juxtaposed the striped pattern of the zebra and the spotted pattern of the giraffe.* **—jux′ta•po•si′tion** *n.*

Kk

(1) (2) (3)

The letter **K** *comes originally from the Phoenician letter* kaph *(1), which meant "hollow of the hand" and stood for /k/. The Greeks borrowed it as* kappa *(2), with reversed orientation; from the Greeks it was borrowed by the Romans (3), although the Romans used it very little (they preferred C for a k sound). Our modern* **K** *is modeled on theirs.*

kangaroo

ă pat/ā pay/â care/ä father/ĕ pet/
ē be/ĭ pit/ī pie/î fierce/ŏ pot/
ō go/ô paw, for/oi oil/o͝o book/
o͞o boot/ou out/ŭ cut/û fur/
th the/th thin/hw which/zh vision/
ə ago, item, pencil, atom, circus

k, K |kā| *n., pl.* **k's** or **K's.** The 11th letter of the English alphabet. [SEE NOTE]

K 1. Kelvin. **2.** The symbol for the element potassium.

Kaa•ba |kä'bə| *or* |kä'ə bə| *n.* A shrine at Mecca, the goal of pilgrims and the focal point toward which Moslems throughout the world face when praying.

ka•bob |kə bŏb'| *n.* **Shish kebab.**

ka•bu•ki |kä bo͞o'kē| *or* |kə-| *n.* A kind of traditional Japanese drama with rich costumes and conventional gestures, dances, and songs. —***modifier:*** *kabuki plays; kabuki theaters.*

Ka•bul |kä'bo͝ol|. The capital of Afghanistan. Population, 534,000.

Kad•dish |kä'dĭsh| *n.* In Judaism, a prayer recited daily in the synagogue and by mourners after the death of a relative.

Kai•ser |kī'zər| *n.* The title of the emperors of Germany and Austria before 1918.

kale |kāl| *n.* A type of cabbage with crinkled leaves that do not form a tight head.

ka•lei•do•scope |kə lī'də skōp'| *n.* **1.** A tube-shaped toy in which bits of loose, colored glass contained at one end reflect light into changing patterns visible from a hole at the other end. **2.** A constantly changing variety: *This kaleidoscope of styles is a sign of health in the visual arts.*

ka•lei•do•scop•ic |kə lī'də skŏp'ĭk| *adj.* Vivid and rapidly changing: *Fantastic images and kaleidoscopic colors surged in upon me.* —**ka•lei'do•scop'i•cal•ly** *adv.*

Kam•pa•la |käm pä'lə|. The capital of Uganda. Population, 333,000.

kan•ga•roo |kăng'gə ro͞o'| *n.* An Australian animal with short forelegs, long hind legs used for leaping, and a long, tapering tail. The female kangaroo carries the newborn young in a pouch on the outside of her body. [SEE PICTURE]

kangaroo rat. A small, long-tailed animal of desert regions of southwestern North America, having long hind legs used for leaping.

Kan•sas |kăn'zəs|. A Midwestern state of the United States. Population, 2,363,208. Capital, Topeka. —**Kan'san** *adj. & n.*

Kansas City. 1. A city in western Missouri, on the Missouri River opposite Kansas City, Kansas. Population, 448,159. **2.** A city in northeastern Kansas, on the Missouri River opposite Kansas City, Missouri. Population, 161,087.

ka•o•lin |kā'ə lĭn| *n.* A fine white to yellowish or grayish clay used in making ceramics and as a filler and coating for paper and textiles.

ka•pok |kā'pŏk'| *n.* A silky fiber from the seed pods of a tropical tree, used for stuffing pillows, life preservers, etc. —***modifier:*** *a kapok pillow.*

kap•pa |kăp'ə| *n.* The tenth letter of the Greek alphabet, written Κ, κ. In English it is represented as *K, k.*

ka•put |kä po͞ot'| *or* |-po͞ot'| *or* |kə-| *adj. Informal.* **1.** In a hopeless position; defeated; lost. **2.** Not working; destroyed: *Our engine, lights, and radio were kaput.*

Ka•ra•chi |kə rä'chē|. Largest city in and former capital of Pakistan. Population, 3,499,000.

kar•a•kul |kăr'ə kəl| *n.* **1.** An Asian sheep bred for the curled, glossy fur of the young lambs. **2.** The fur itself. —***modifier:*** *a karakul hat.*

kar•at |kăr'ət| *n.* A measure of 24 parts used to indicate the proportion of pure gold contained in an alloy. For example, 12 karat gold is 50 per cent pure, and 18 karat gold is 75 per cent pure. ¶ *These sound alike* **karat, carrot.**

ka•ra•te |kə rä'tē| *n.* A form of unarmed fighting, developed in Japan, that stresses efficiently struck blows with the hands and feet. —***modifier:*** *a karate chop.*

kar•ma |kär'mə| *n.* **1.** In Hinduism and Buddhism, the belief that the fate of a soul in its current life is determined by its conduct in former lives. **2.** Fate; destiny.

ka•sha |kä'shə| *n.* Crushed buckwheat grain.

Kash•mir |kăsh mîr'| *or* |kăsh'mîr'|. A region between Pakistan, India, and China, disputed between India and Pakistan.

Kat•man•du |kät'män do͞o'|. The capital of Nepal. Population, 150,000.

ka•ty•did |kā'tē dĭd'| *n.* A green insect with long antennae, related to the grasshoppers. The males make vibrating sounds by rubbing together scrapers on the front wings.

kay•ak |kī'ăk'| *n.* **1.** A watertight Eskimo canoe made of skins stretched over a light wooden frame and having a deck covering that closes around the waist of the paddler. **2.** A lightweight canvas-covered canoe of the same design.

kay•o |kā'ō'| *v. & n.* A form of the word **KO.**

kc kilocycle.

Keats |kēts|, **John.** 1795–1821. English poet.

ke•bab, also **ke•bob** |kə bŏb'| *n.* **Shish kebab.**

kedge |kĕj| *n.* A small anchor.

keel |kēl| *n.* **1.** A strong timber, plate, or beam of metal running from stem to stern along the center line of a vessel and serving as the backbone to which the frames are attached. **2.** A fin extending lengthwise along the bottom of a sailboat or an airship to give the craft stability. **3.** A narrow, ridgelike part resembling a ship's keel. —*v.* **1.** To capsize: *A strong gale keeled the boat over. The sailboat pitched suddenly and then keeled over.*

2. *Informal.* To fall down; collapse: *She keeled over from sunstroke.*

***Idiom.* on an even keel.** Balanced; steady.

keel•haul |kēl′hôl′| *v.* **1.** To punish (a man) by hauling him under the keel of a ship from one side to the other or from stem to stern. **2.** To scold harshly.

keen[1] |kēn| *adj.* **keen•er, keen•est. 1.** Sharp at the edge or point: *a keen knife ripping through cloth.* **2.** Piercing; brisk: *The spring air was still a little keen for sitting long in comfort.* **3.** Intense; pointed; concentrated: *a keen glance; keen delight.* **4.** Acute; sensitive: *the keen eyes of the jackals.* **5.** Intellectually penetrating; astute; bright: *a keen observer of men.* **6.** Eager; avid: *a keen sports enthusiast.* **7.** *Slang.* Delightful; excellent: *My grandmother sends me keen presents.* —**keen′ly** *adv.* —**keen′ness** *n.* [SEE NOTE]

keen[2] |kēn| *n.* A crying or wailing in sorrow for the dead. —*v.* To cry in sorrow for the dead: *She's thinking of her lost baby and keening to herself.* [SEE NOTE]

keep |kēp| *v.* **kept** |kĕpt|, **keep•ing. 1.** To hold in one's possession; have and not give up; retain: *She kept locks of her friends' hair.* **2.** To cause to continue in a certain position or condition: *keeping her afloat despite the waves; keeping your eyes open.* **3. a.** To continue; stay: *keeping warm; keep busy; keeping touch.* **b.** To stay fresh or unspoiled: *Vegetables won't keep long.* **4.** To proceed in the same way or on the same course; adhere: *Traffic keeps to the left in Japan.* **5.** To maintain: *keeping a safe distance; keeping late hours.* **6. a.** To put for safety or convenience; store: *a camera that you can keep in your pocket.* **b.** To confine: *a fence to keep in the sheep.* **7.** To tend; manage: *She helps her mother keep house.* **8. a.** To raise and feed: *Most villagers keep ducks, geese, and pigs.* **b.** To provide for the needs of; support: *keeping a large family on a small income.* **9.** To make current entries in: *keep a record; keep a diary.* **10.** To perform attentively: *keeping watch; keeping count.* **11.** To observe faithfully: *keeping the Sabbath.* **12.** To carry out; fulfill (a promise or one's word). **13.** To prevent; stop: *kept the boat from overturning; keeping the soil around plants from drying out.* **14.** To detain or delay: *The teacher will keep him after school. I wonder what is keeping her.* —***phrasal verbs.* keep after.** To be persistent with: *You must keep after her or she will forget to clean her room.* **keep back. 1.** To refuse to give or tell; withhold. **2.** To prevent from getting in; hold back: *shutters to keep back the winter winds.* **keep from.** To avoid; prevent: *couldn't keep from grinning.* **keep on.** To continue without a pause; persist in: *He kept on trying until he passed his swimming test.* **keep up. 1.** To maintain the pace set by others: *keeping up with the rest of the class.* **2.** To keep in good condition; maintain: *keep up the property.* **3.** To continue: *The wind kept up.* —*n.* **1.** Care; custody: *in the keep of a foster parent.* **2.** One's living; means of support: *earning his keep by doing chores.* **3.** The stronghold of a castle.

***Idioms.* for keeps.** *Informal.* Permanently. **keep to (oneself). 1.** To avoid other people; remain alone. **2.** To tell no one about: *If he knows the answer, he's keeping it to himself.*

keep•er |kē′pər| *n.* **1.** A person who watches over or guards something; an attendant: *a zoo keeper; a lighthouse keeper.* **2.** A person who manages a certain kind of shop or business: *a tavern keeper.* **3.** A person who raises or cultivates something: *a keeper of bees.* **4.** A piece of iron that helps to preserve the magnetic power of magnets.

keep•ing |kē′pĭng| *n.* **1.** Care; custody: *documents in the keeping of his lawyer.* **2.** Agreement; conformity: *wearing a dress in keeping with the great occasion.*

keep•sake |kēp′sāk′| *n.* Something kept in memory of the person who gave it or the place from which it came; a memento.

keg |kĕg| *n.* **1.** A small barrel, usually one with a capacity of less than ten gallons. **2. a.** A keg with something in it: *a keg of mackerel in brine.* **b.** The amount that a keg holds: *drank two kegs of beer.*

Kel•ler |kĕl′ər|, **Helen Adams.** 1880–1968. American author and lecturer, blind and deaf from infancy.

kelp |kĕlp| *n.* Any of several brown, often very large seaweeds. [SEE PICTURE]

Kelt |kĕlt| *n.* A form of the word **Celt.**

Kelt•ic |kĕl′tĭk| *adj.* & *n.* A form of the word **Celtic.**

Kel•vin |kĕl′vĭn| *adj.* Of or involving the temperature scale that has its zero at absolute zero and uses degrees that are the same as those of the Celsius scale. [SEE NOTE]

ken |kĕn| *n.* **1.** Range of vision: *The 200-inch telescope brought billions of hitherto unobserved stars within man's ken.* **2.** Range of understanding; comprehension: *Some men of the late Renaissance were the last who could claim that they had all science within their ken.* [SEE NOTE]

Ken•ne•dy |kĕn′ĭ dē|, **John Fitzgerald.** 1917–1963. Thirty-fifth President of the United States (1961–63); assassinated.

ken•nel |kĕn′əl| *n.* **1.** A small shelter for a dog or dogs. **2.** Often **kennels.** An establishment for the breeding, training, or boarding of dogs.

Ken•tuck•y |kən tŭk′ē|. An east-central state of the United States. Population, 3,661,433. Capital, Frankfort. —**Ken•tuck′i•an** *adj.* & *n.*

Ken•ya |kĕn′yə| *or* |kēn′-|. A country in eastern Africa, on the Indian Ocean. Population, 12,912,000. Capital, Nairobi. —**Ken′yan** *adj.* & *n.*

ke•pi |kā′pē| *or* |kĕp′ē| *n.* A French military cap with a flat, round top and a visor.

Kep•ler |kĕp′lər|, **Johannes.** 1571–1630. German astronomer; developed the fundamental laws of planetary motion.

kept |kĕpt|. Past tense and past participle of **keep.**

ker•a•tin |kĕr′ə tĭn| *n.* A tough, fibrous protein that forms the outer layers of structures such as hair, nails, horns, and hoofs.

ker•chief |kûr′chĭf| *n.* **1.** A square scarf worn over the head or around the neck. **2.** A handkerchief.

ker•nel |kûr′nəl| *n.* **1.** A grain or seed, especially of corn, wheat, or a similar cereal plant. **2.** The often edible part inside the shell of a nut or the pit of a peach, plum, etc. **3.** The most important or essential part; core; heart: *the kernel of truth in a long-winded speech.* ¶*These sound alike* **kernel, colonel.**

keen[1-2]

Keen[1] *was* cēne *in Old English; it originally meant "wise, bold, powerful."* **Keen[2]** *is from Irish* caoninim, *"I weep and wail," which goes back to prehistoric Celtic* koinyo-.

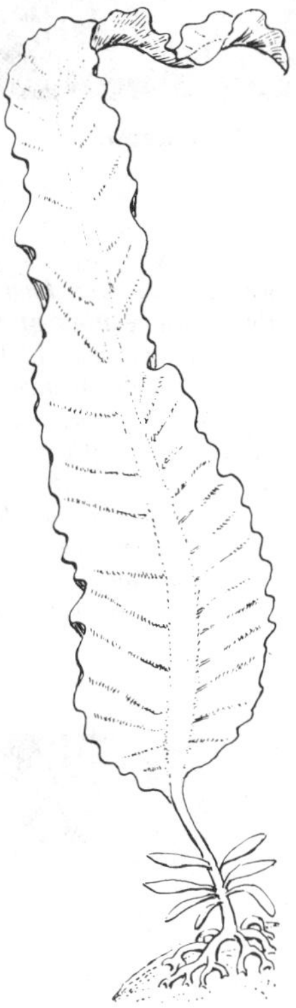

kelp

Kelvin

The **Kelvin** *scale is named for Lord* Kelvin *(1824–1907), British physicist and mathematician.*

ken

Ken *originally meant "knowledge" and is from the Scottish verb* ken, *"to know." This is descended from Old English* cennan, *"to make known," and is related to the word* **know.**

kettledrum

key[1-2]

Key[1] *was* cæg *in Old English. The only known relation of this word is in Frisian, the old language, very closely related to English, spoken in the islands on the North Sea coast of Germany. The Old Frisian for "key" was* kei. *But it is not known where the Frisians or the English got the word from.* **Key[2]** *is from Spanish* cayo, *"sandbar, small island."*

key[1]
Eighteenth-century key and keyhole

ă pat/ā pay/â care/ä father/ĕ pet/ ē be/ĭ pit/ī pie/î fierce/ŏ pot/ ō go/ô paw, for/oi oil/ŏŏ book/ ōō boot/ou out/ŭ cut/û fur/ *th* the/th thin/hw which/zh vision/ ə ago, item, pencil, atom, circus

ker•o•sene |kĕr′ə sēn′| *or* |kăr′-| *or* |kĕr′ ə **sēn′**| *or* |kăr′-| *n.* A thin, light-colored oil that is obtained mainly from petroleum and used chiefly as a fuel. —***modifier:*** *a kerosene lamp.*

kes•trel |kĕs′trəl| *n.* A small falcon with reddish-brown and gray feathers.

ketch |kĕch| *n.* A two-masted, fore-and-aft-rigged sailing vessel with the shorter mast placed aft.

ketch•up |kĕch′əp| *or* |kăch′-| *n.* A thick spicy sauce, usually made with tomatoes, used as a seasoning.

ket•tle |kĕt′l| *n.* **1.** A metal pot, usually with a lid, for boiling liquids or cooking. **2. a.** A kettle with something in it: *boiling a kettle of water for tea.* **b.** The amount that a kettle will hold: *The guests ate a whole kettle of chowder.*
***Idiom.* a fine kettle of fish.** A difficult situation; a predicament.

ket•tle•drum |kĕt′l drŭm′| *n.* A large drum having a bowl-shaped body of brass or copper and a parchment head that can be tuned by adjusting its tension. [SEE PICTURE]

key[1] |kē| *n.* **1.** A small piece of notched metal that is inserted into a lock to open or close it. **2. a.** A similar device for winding springs, as in toys and clocks. **b.** A small, slotted metal rod used to open cans. **3.** A means of gaining access, possession, or further understanding: *a key to the mystery.* **4.** A vital or crucial element: *The key to his success was his resistance to old-fashioned ideas.* **5.** Any explanatory table: **a.** One that explains the symbols and colors used on a map or chart. **b.** One that explains the meaning of various symbols or signs that appear in the text of a book: *a pronunciation key.* **c.** A set of answers to a test or to questions that are asked in a book. **6.** Any one of a set of buttons or levers moved by the fingers in operating a machine, playing a musical instrument, etc.: *a typewriter key; a piano key.* **7.** A group of musical tones related so that one of them is felt to be the primary tone to which the others gravitate, especially a tone and the major scale or minor scale based on it: *the key of D.* **8.** Correct musical pitch: *Tom often sings off key.* **9.** A general level of intensity or urgency: *After the formal interview the candidate spoke in a lower key to friends and newsmen.* **10.** A piece of wood inserted into a joint or corner to hold it firmly together. **11.** Also **key fruit.** A fruit, as of the maple, having a long, narrow, winglike part. —***modifier:*** *musical key changes; a key chain; the key word of a sentence; key states in an election campaign.* —*v.* **1.** To provide with an explanatory table: *an inset map that has been keyed separately.* **2.** To set (a piece of music) in a certain key. **3.** To adapt to special conditions; adjust: *Southeast Asian farming methods are keyed to the great variations in rainfall.* —***phrasal verb.* key up.** To make intense or nervous; excite: *too keyed up to think clearly.* ¶*These sound alike* **key, quay.** [SEE NOTE & PICTURE]

key[2] |kē| *n.* A low-lying island or reef along a coast, especially in the Gulf of Mexico. ¶*These sound alike* **key, quay.** [SEE NOTE]

Key |kē|, **Francis Scott.** 1779–1843. American lawyer; author of "The Star-Spangled Banner."

key•board |kē′bôrd′| *or* |-bōrd′| *n.* A set of keys, as on a piano, organ, or typewriter.

keyboard instrument. A musical instrument, such as a piano or harpsicord, in which keys struck by the fingers activate various mechanisms that produce sound.

keyed |kēd| *adj.* **1.** Equipped with keys: *a keyed flute.* **2.** Built with a keystone: *a keyed arch.*

key•hole |kē′hōl′| *n.* The hole in a lock into which a key fits.

key•note |kē′nōt′| *n.* **1.** The principal tone of a musical key; the tonic. **2.** The basic idea or theme, as of a speech, book, or political campaign.

key signature. The group of sharps or flats placed at the beginning of a musical staff to identify the key.

key•stone |kē′stōn′| *n.* **1.** The central wedge-shaped stone of an arch that locks the others together. **2.** The essential element that supports a whole: *The keystone of the early American spirit was freedom.* **3.** *Slang.* Second base on a baseball diamond.

Key West. City of extreme southern Florida, on **Key West Island,** westernmost of the Florida Keys in the Gulf of Mexico. Population, 24,292.

kg kilogram.

khak•i |kăk′ē| *or* |kä′kē| *n.* **1.** A yellowish brown. **2. a.** A strong, heavy, khaki-colored cloth, used for army uniforms. **b. khakis.** A uniform made of this cloth. —***modifier:*** *khaki trousers.* —*adj.* Yellowish-brown.

khan |kän| *or* |kăn| *n.* **1.** A title of courtesy in India and some countries of central Asia. **2. Khan.** The title of rulers of Mongol, Tatar, or Turkish tribes after the time of Genghis Khan.

Khar•toum |kär **tōōm′**|. The capital of Sudan. Population, 261,000.

kick |kĭk| *v.* **1.** To strike with the foot: *He kicked the table leg so hard he hurt his toe.* **2.** To lash out with the feet or hoofs: *Zebras kick as hard as mules, or harder.* **3.** To make repeated motions with the feet or legs, as in swimming: *Water birds have to paddle and kick for quite a while before they can take off.* **4.** To drive, thrust, or produce by vigorous motions of the legs: *kicked off their shoes to dance; a herd of cattle that kicked up swirls of dust.* **5.** In football: **a.** To punt. **b.** To score or achieve by punting or by means of a place kick: *kicked a 37-yard field goal.* **6.** To spring back suddenly; recoil: *He staggered when the musket kicked.* **7.** *Slang.* To defeat; overcome: *kicking a bad habit.* **8.** *Slang.* To complain; protest: *I didn't even kick when you borrowed my bicycle.* **9.** *Slang.* To thrive; prosper: *not only alive, but kicking.* —***phrasal verbs.* kick around.** *Slang.* **1.** To treat roughly; abuse. **2.** To discuss at leisure: *A few of the problems were kicked around some more after the conference.* **kick back.** *Informal.* To return (part of a payment) by agreement with the payer. **kick in.** *Informal.* To contribute (a share of money) to a common fund. **kick off.** In football, to put the ball in play by means of a place kick in the direction of the opposing team. **kick out.** *Slang.* To dismiss or eject: *He got kicked out of school for misbehavior.* **kick up.** *Informal.* To raise (trouble): *He kicked up a great fuss.* —*n.* **1.** A blow with the foot. **2.** Any one of several motions of the legs used in swimming: *a flutter kick.* **3. a.** The action of kicking a ball, as in a football kickoff or punt. **b.** The kicked ball: *Block that kick!* **c.** The distance covered by a kicked ball. **4.** The recoil of a cannon or firearm. **5.** *Slang.* Strength, force, or impact: *still some kick in the engine; a refreshing drink with a lot of kick in it.* **6.** *Slang.* A swift feeling of pleasure; a thrill: *She'll get a kick out of this greeting card.* **7.** *Slang.* A temporary enthusiasm for something: *on a Frisbee kick.*

kick•back |kĭk′băk′| *n.* **1.** A sharp reaction or recoil. **2.** *Informal.* A payment made to a person who controls or influences a source of income.

kick•ball |kĭk′bôl′| *n.* A children's game like baseball but played on a small diamond with an inflated ball that is kicked instead of batted.

kick•er |kĭk′ər| *n.* A person or animal that kicks, especially a football player who is called into the game to make kicks.

kick•off |kĭk′ôf′| *or* |-ŏf′| *n.* A kick in football or soccer with which play is begun.

kid |kĭd| *n.* **1. a.** A young goat. **b.** Leather made from the skin of a young goat; kidskin. **2.** *Informal.* A child or young person. **—*modifier:*** *kid gloves.* —*adj.* Younger: *my kid brother.* —*v.* **kid•ded, kid•ding.** *Informal.* **1.** To make fun of; tease: *The boys were kidding him enough about just being in the play.* **2.** To deceive for fun; fool: *Five hundred dollars? You must be kidding.* **3.** To be playful, amusing, or silly: *Stop kidding around.*

Kid•dush |kĭd′əsh| *or* |kĭ do͞osh′| *n.* A traditional Jewish ceremony performed on the eve of the Sabbath or a festival, consisting of the reciting of a prayer over a cup of wine or bread.

kid•nap |kĭd′năp′| *v.* **kid•naped** or **kid•napped, kid•nap•ing** or **kid•nap•ping.** To carry off and detain (a person or animal) by force, usually for ransom. **—kid′nap′er, kid′nap′per** *n.*

kid•ney |kĭd′nē| *n., pl.* **kid•neys. 1.** Either of a pair of organs that are located in the abdominal cavity of vertebrates close to the back. They act to keep the proper amount of water in the body and excrete wastes from the body in the form of urine. **2.** A similar excretory organ found in some invertebrates. **3.** The kidney of certain animals, eaten as food. **—*modifier:*** *kidney disorders.*

kidney bean. The reddish seed from the fully ripened pod of the common bean plant whose young, green pods are eaten as string beans.

kidney stone. A small, hard mass, usually of mineral salts from the urine, that forms in a kidney; a calculus.

kid•skin |kĭd′skĭn′| *n.* Soft leather made from the skin of a young goat. **—*modifier:*** *kidskin gloves.*

Ki•ev |kē′ĕf′| *or* |kē ĕv′|. A city of the Soviet Union, the capital of the Ukrainian S.S.R. Population, 1,827,000.

Ki•ga•li |kē gä′lē|. The capital of Rwanda. Population, 30,000.

Kil•i•man•ja•ro |kĭl′ə mən jä′rō|. The highest mountain (19,565 feet) in Africa, in northeastern Tanzania near the border with Kenya.

kill |kĭl| *v.* **1.** To cause the death of; deprive of life: *In eighteen months Buffalo Bill killed 4,280 buffaloes. Few animals kill for the sake of killing.* **2.** To put an end to: *His refusal to negotiate killed our hopes for peace.* **3.** To cause severe pain to; hurt intensely: *The narrow, stiff boots were killing his feet.* **4.** To make (time) pass in idle activity. **—*phrasal verb.* kill off.** To destroy totally or on a large scale: *Killing off one kind of animal or plant may upset the balance in nature.* —*n.* **1.** An act of killing: *The falcon made six kills on its first day of hunting.* **2.** Something that has just been killed: *Lions often dine on the kills of other predators.* ¶*These sound alike* **kill, kiln.**

kill•deer |kĭl′dîr′| *n., pl.* **kill•deers** or **kill•deer.** A North American bird with a banded breast and a call that sounds like its name. [SEE PICTURE]

kill•er |kĭl′ər| *n.* Someone or something that kills, especially: **1.** A murderer. **2.** A predator. **3.** A crazed or wounded animal that becomes dangerous or destructive: *Pain turns the best of tamed lions into killers.*

killer whale. A black and white whale that feeds on fish, seals, porpoises, etc.

kil•lie |kĭl′ē| *n.* A killifish.

kil•li•fish |kĭl′ē fĭsh′| *n., pl.* **-fish** or **-fish•es.** Any of several small freshwater or saltwater fishes often used as bait.

kill•ing |kĭl′ĭng| *n.* **1.** A murder. **2.** Something that has been hunted and killed; quarry: *a doe, a recent killing.* **3.** A sudden large profit: *A lottery, which he manipulated to his advantage, produced his first financial killing.* —*adj.* **1.** Apt to kill; fatal. **2.** Highly destructive: *a killing frost.*

kill•joy |kĭl′joi′| *n.* A person who spoils the fun of others.

kiln |kĭl| *or* |kĭln| *n.* Any of a variety of ovens used for hardening, burning, or drying things such as grain or lumber, especially a high-temperature oven used for firing pottery, porcelain, brick, etc. ¶*These sound alike* **kiln, kill.**

ki•lo |kē′lō| *or* |kĭl′ō| *n., pl.* **ki•los. 1.** A kilogram. **2.** A kilometer.

kilo–. A word element meaning "a thousand": **kilowatt.**

kil•o•cy•cle |kĭl′ə sī′kəl| *n.* **1.** A unit equal to 1,000 cycles. **2.** A kilohertz.

kil•o•gram |kĭl′ə grăm′| *n.* **1.** The basic unit of mass in the metric system. **2.** A force equal to the weight of one kilogram mass, equal to 2.2046 pounds.

kil•o•hertz |kĭl′ə hûrts′| *n.* A unit of frequency equal to 1,000 cycles per second.

kil•o•me•ter |kĭl′ə mē′tər| *or* |kĭ lŏm′ĭ tər| *n.* A unit of length equal to 1,000 meters or about 0.6214 mile.

kil•o•ton |kĭl′ə tŭn′| *n.* **1.** A unit of explosive force equal to the force with which 1,000 tons of TNT explode. This unit is used mainly in expressing the force of nuclear explosions. **2.** A thousand tons.

kil•o•watt |kĭl′ə wŏt′| *n.* A unit of power, especially electric power, equal to 1,000 watts.

kil•o•watt-hour |kĭl′ə wŏt′our′| *n.* A unit of energy, especially electrical energy, equivalent to one kilowatt acting for a period of one hour.

kilt |kĭlt| *n.* A knee-length pleated skirt, usually of a tartan wool, worn by men in the Scottish Highlands. [SEE PICTURE]

ki•mo•no |kĭ mō′nə| *or* |-nō| *n., pl.* **ki•mo•nos. 1.** A long, loose Japanese robe with wide sleeves and a broad sash, worn by men and women as an outer garment. **2.** A woman's dressing gown resembling such a robe. [SEE PICTURE]

kin |kĭn| *n.* **1.** A person's relatives; family. **2.**

killdeer

kilt

kimono

kind[1-2]

Kind[1] and kind[2] are related Old English words. **Kind[1]** *was* cynde, *"natural," also "of good family, well brought up, polite, generous."* **Kind[2]** *was* cynd, *"birth, nature," also "family, race" and hence "group, type." The connection is shown by the following statements: "She is a* **kind[1]** *person. She is one of our own* **kind[2]**.*" The words are closely related to Old English* cyn, *"family," which became* **kin** *in Modern English. They are all descended from prehistoric Germanic* kun-, *which is from Indo-European* gen-, *"to be born" (see note at* **gentle**).

kingfisher

kinkajou

ă pat/ā pay/â care/ä father/ĕ pet/ ē be/ĭ pit/ī pie/î fierce/ŏ pot/ ō go/ô paw, for/oi oil/ŏŏ book/ ōō boot/ou out/ŭ cut/û fur/ *th* the/th thin/hw which/zh vision/ ə ago, item, pencil, atom, circus

Fellow members of a group or kind: *Triceratops and their kin were fierce, horned dinosaurs.* —*adj.* Related; kindred: *fish that are not kin to any other known species.*

Idiom. **next of kin.** The person or persons most closely related.

kind[1] |kīnd| *adj.* **kind•er, kind•est. 1. a.** Inclined to help others and think of their welfare; generous in nature. **b.** Showing this inclination; helpful and considerate: *the kindest thing to do; kind words.* **2.** Courteous; thoughtful: *kind of you to write us.* [SEE NOTE]

kind[2] |kīnd| *n.* **1.** A group of similar things; a category: *Violins compose the largest single kind of instrument in the orchestra.* **2.** Sort; type: *looking for the kind of life that would make him happy.* **3.** A species: *Living things reproduce their own kind.* [SEE NOTE]

Idioms. **in kind. 1.** With goods rather than money: *paying in kind.* **2.** In nature or essence: *crimes that differ in degree but not in kind.* **kind of.** *Informal.* Rather: *It's getting kind of late.*

kin•der•gar•ten |kĭn'dər gär'tn| *n.* A class for children from four to six years of age, to prepare them for elementary school.

kind•heart•ed |kīnd'här'tĭd| *adj.* Unwilling to hurt others; gentle and generous by nature: *too kindhearted to scold his children.* —**kind'heart'ed•ly** *adv.* —**kind'heart'ed•ness** *n.*

kin•dle |kĭn'dl| *v.* **kin•dled, kin•dling. 1. a.** To build and start (a fire): *kindle a fire with matches.* **b.** To catch fire: *The paper kindled on the third match.* **2.** To glow; shine: *Her eyes kindled at the thought of home.* **3.** To arouse; excite: *The lecturer used a variety of appeals to kindle our interest in the subject.* —**kin'dler** *n.*

kin•dling |kĭnd'lĭng| *n.* Material, such as dry sticks of wood, for building a fire. —***modifier:*** *kindling wood.*

kind•ly |kīnd'lē| *adj.* **kind•li•er, kind•li•est. 1.** Considerate and gentle in nature; kind: *a kindly, warm-hearted woman.* **2.** Suggesting kindness; tender: *Kindly eyes smiled down into his.* **3.** Helpful; benevolent: *Not one kindly light shone from the shore to guide us.* —*adv.* **1.** Out of kindness: *He kindly offered to give us a lift.* **2.** In a kind way; cordially; warmly: *greeting them kindly.* **3.** Please: *Kindly read the message aloud.* —**kind'li•ness** *n.*

Idiom. **take kindly to.** To be receptive to; appreciate.

kind•ness |kīnd'nĭs| *n.* **1.** The quality of being kind; generosity. **2.** A kind act; a favor: *Johnny Appleseed did many kindnesses for the pioneers in addition to planting trees.*

kin•dred |kĭn'drĭd| *adj.* Having a similar origin or nature; related. —*n.* A group of related persons; a family, tribe, or clan.

kin•e•scope |kĭn'ĭ skōp'| *n.* **1.** The picture tube of a television receiver. **2.** A film of a television broadcast.

ki•net•ic |kĭ nĕt'ĭk| *adj.* Of, involving, or produced by motion.

kinetic energy. The energy that is associated with a body because of its motion. See **potential energy.**

kin•folk |kĭn'fōk'| *n.* A form of the word **kinsfolk.**

kin•folks |kĭn'fōks'| *n.* A form of the word **kinsfolk.**

king |kĭng| *n.* **1.** A man who alone rules a nation usually by inheritance of the office, and who leads his people either in fact or as a symbol of political authority; a male monarch. **2.** Someone who is treated with the greatest respect and honor: *The customer is king.* **3.** Someone or something that is regarded as the most powerful or outstanding: *The cowboy was the king of the range. Mont Blanc is king of the Alps.* **4.** The vital piece in the game of chess, able to move one square in any direction. **5.** In the game of checkers, a checker topped with another checker after reaching the opponent's side of the board and able to move both backward and forward. **6.** A playing card bearing the figure of a king. It ranks above a queen and below an ace.

King |kĭng|, **Martin Luther, Jr.** 1929–1968. American civil rights leader; assassinated.

king•bird |kĭng'bûrd'| *n.* Any of several grayish birds that often attack other birds.

king•bolt |kĭng'bōlt'| *n.* A vertical bolt connecting the front axle of a vehicle to the body and serving as a pivot when the vehicle turns; a kingpin.

king•dom |kĭng'dəm| *n.* **1.** A country that is ruled or headed by a king or queen. **2.** An area, province, or realm in which one thing is dominant: *in the kingdom of the imagination.* **3.** One of the large groups into which all living things and natural substances are divided: *the animal kingdom; the plant kingdom; the mineral kingdom.* **4.** In Christianity: **a.** Heaven. **b.** The world as it will be in the future when God's will is perfectly fulfilled: *"Thy kingdom come. Thy will be done on earth as it is in heaven"* (The Bible, Matthew 6:9–13).

king•fish•er |kĭng'fĭsh'ər| *n.* A large-billed bird that feeds on fish. [SEE PICTURE]

King James Bible. An Anglican translation of the Bible from Hebrew and Greek published in 1611 under the auspices of James I.

king•ly |kĭng'lē| *adj.* **king•li•er, king•li•est.** Of or befitting a king; regal —***modifier:*** *kingly throne; eating with kingly zest.* —**king'li•ness** *n.*

king•pin |kĭng'pĭn'| *n.* **1.** The foremost or central pin in the group of bowling pins to be knocked down. **2.** *Informal.* The most important or central person in an organization or operation. **3.** A kingbolt.

king•ship |kĭng'shĭp'| *n.* The office or length of rule of a king.

king-size |kĭng'sīz'|, also **king-sized** |kĭng'sīzd'| *adj.* Extra large: *a king-size container.*

King•ston |kĭng'stən|. The capital of Jamaica. Population, 123,000.

Kings•town |kĭngs'toun'|. The capital of St. Vincent and the Grenadines. Population, 17,000.

kink |kĭngk| *n.* **1.** A tight curl or sharp twist, as in a hair, wire, rope, etc. **2.** A painful stiffness or spasm of a muscle, as in the neck or back; a crick. **3.** A slight flaw, as in a plan. **4.** A curious, unpredictable act or turn of mind; a peculiarity. —*v.* To form or cause to form a kink; curl or twist sharply: *a tail that kinked at the end; kink yarn around knitting needles.*

kin•ka•jou |kĭng'kə jōō'| *n.* A furry, long-tailed tropical American animal that lives in trees. [SEE PICTURE]

kink•y |kĭng'kē| *adj.* **kink•i•er, kink•i•est. 1.** Full of tight, crisp little curls; frizzy: *kinky hair.* **2.** Peculiar; odd. **—kink'i•ness** *n.*

kin•ni•kin•nick |kĭn'ĭ kə **nĭk'**| *n.* **1.** A tobacco-like mixture of the dried leaves or bark of various plants, used by American Indians for smoking. **2.** A plant with leaves or bark used for such a preparation.

kins•folk |**kĭnz'**fōk'| *n.* Members of a family; relatives.

Kin•sha•sa |kĭn **shä'**sə|. The capital of Zaire. Population, 1,200,000.

kin•ship |**kĭn'**shĭp'| *n.* **1.** The condition of being related by blood or common origin: *the kinship of man with all other vertebrates.* **2.** A deep connection or similarity between persons or things: *As a composer he felt a special sense of kinship with Mozart.*

kins•man |**kĭnz'**mən| *n., pl.* **-men** |-mən|. A male relative.

kins•wom•an |**kĭnz'**wo͝om'ən| *n., pl.* **-wom•en** |-wĭm'ĭn|. A female relative.

ki•osk |**kē'**ŏsk'| *or* |kē **ŏsk'**| *n.* **1.** A small, sometimes ornamental structure used as a newsstand, refreshment booth, etc. **2.** A cylindrical structure, common on European sidewalks, on which advertisements are posted.

Ki•o•wa |**kī'**ō wä'| *or* |-ə wə| *n., pl.* **Ki•o•wa** or **Ki•o•was.** **1.** A tribe of Plains Indians of the south-central United States. **2.** A member of this tribe. **3.** The Uto-Aztecan language of this tribe.

kip |kĭp| *n., pl.* **kip.** The basic unit of money of Laos.

Kip•ling |**kĭp'**lĭng|, **Rudyard.** 1865–1936. English novelist and poet.

kip•per |**kĭp'**ər| *v.* To cure (fish) by splitting, salting, and drying. *—n.* A herring or salmon that has been cured by kippering.

kirk |kûrk| *n. Scottish.* A church.

kish•ke |**kĭsh'**kə| *n.* Beef casing stuffed with a seasoned mixture of matzo meal, onion, and suet; derma.

kis•met |**kĭz'**mĭt| *or* |**kĭs'**-| *n.* The fulfillment of destiny; fate.

kiss |kĭs| *v.* **1.** To touch and press with the lips as a sign of passion, affection, greeting, or reverence. **2.** To brush against; touch gently: *The tallest spires seemed to kiss heaven.* *—n.* **1. a.** An act of kissing; a caress with the lips. **b.** Such a caress regarded as a token of love, to be given, taken, kept, stolen, and sometimes blown across a distance. **2.** A small piece of candy.

kiss•er |**kĭs'**ər| *n.* **1.** A person who kisses. **2.** *Slang.* The mouth or face.

kit[1] |kĭt| *n.* **1.** A set of parts or materials to be assembled: *A radio receiver can be bought in a kit.* **2. a.** A compact set of tools and materials for a certain purpose: *a first-aid kit; a sewing kit.* **b.** A bag or other container for carrying such a set. [SEE NOTE]

kit[2] |kĭt| *n.* A young fur-bearing animal; a kitten or cub: *a panther kit; muskrat kits.* [SEE NOTE]

kitch•en |**kĭch'**ən| *n.* **1.** A room where food is cooked or prepared. **2.** The facilities and equipment used for preparing food: *setting up a camp kitchen.* ***—modifier:*** *a kitchen table.*

kitch•en•ette |kĭch'ə **nĕt'**| *n.* A small kitchen.

kitch•en•ware |**kĭch'**ən wâr'| *n.* Utensils, such as pots and pans, for use in the kitchen.

kite |kīt| *n.* **1.** A bird of prey with a long, often forked tail. **2.** A light frame, as of wood, covered with paper or similar material and flown in the wind at the end of a long string. *—v.* **kit•ed, kit•ing.** To fly swiftly like a kite: *The ducks kited back for the woods.* [SEE PICTURE]

kit•ten |**kĭt'**n| *n.* A young cat. [SEE NOTE]

kit•ty[1] |**kĭt'**ē| *n., pl.* **kit•ties.** *Informal.* A kitten or cat. [SEE NOTE]

kit•ty[2] |**kĭt'**ē| *n., pl.* **kit•ties.** A fund of money raised by the contributors to meet some group expense: *Everyone in the family put a part of his earnings into the vacation kitty.* [SEE NOTE]

ki•wi |**kē'**wē| *n.* A bird of New Zealand with a long, slender bill and brownish feathers. Its hidden wings are so small and undeveloped that it is unable to fly. [SEE PICTURE]

K.K.K. Ku Klux Klan.

Klan |klăn| *n.* The **Ku Klux Klan.**

Klans•man |**klănz'**mən| *n., pl.* **-men** |-mən|. A member of the Ku Klux Klan.

Kleen•ex |**klē'**nĕks'| *n.* A trademark for a soft paper cleansing tissue.

klep•to•ma•ni•a |klĕp'tə **mā'**nē ə| *or* |**-mān'**yə| *n.* An uncontrollable urge to steal, especially when there is no personal need or desire for the things stolen.

klep•to•ma•ni•ac |klĕp'tə **mā'**nē ăk'| *n.* A person who has kleptomania.

klieg light |klēg|. A powerful carbon-arc lamp used chiefly in making motion pictures.

Klon•dike |**klŏn'**dīk'|. A region in the Yukon Territory of Canada; the site of abundant gold deposits.

klutz |klŭts| *n. Slang.* A clumsy person.

km kilometer.

knack |năk| *n.* A special talent or skill: *He has the knack of getting along with people.*

knack•wurst |**nŏk'**wûrst'| *or* |-wo͝orst'| *n.* A short, thick sausage.

knap•sack |**năp'**săk'| *n.* A canvas or leather bag worn on the back to carry supplies on a hike or march.

knave |nāv| *n.* **1.** A dishonest, crafty man: *He played the knave in our business dealings.* **2.** *Archaic.* A male servant: *a lowly kitchen knave.* **3.** A playing card, the jack. ¶*These sound alike* **knave, nave.**

knav•er•y |**nā'**və rē| *n., pl.* **knav•er•ies.** Dishonesty; petty villainy.

knav•ish |**nā'**vĭsh| *adj.* Dishonest; unprincipled: *an evil-minded, knavish sort of fellow.* **—knav'ish•ly** *adv.* **—knav'ish•ness** *n.*

knead |nēd| *v.* **1.** To mix and work (a substance) into a plastic mass, as by folding, stretching, pressing, etc.: *The children watched the pizza man knead the dough.* **2.** To squeeze, press, or roll with the hands, as in massaging: *knead one's leg muscles to get the soreness out of them.* ¶*These sound alike* **knead, need.**

knee |nē| *n.* **1. a.** The joint at which the human thigh and lower leg come together. **b.** The region of the leg near and around this joint. **2.** A corresponding joint in the leg of another animal. **3.** Something that resembles a knee, as a point where something bends sharply. **4.** The part of a pair of trousers that covers the knee: *The knees of his overalls were patched.* *—v.* **kneed, knee•ing.** **1.** To push or strike with the knee: *He kneed the*

kit[1-2]/kitty[1-2]/kitten

Kit[1] *originally meant "soldier's equipment carried in a knapsack"; the word comes from Middle Dutch* kitte, *"tankard, wooden container."* **Kitty[2]** *originally meant "small bowl" and is from* **kit[1]**. **Kit[2]** *and* **kitty[1]** *are from* **kitten,** *which is related to the word* **cat.**

kite

kiwi

Knickerbocker, etc.
Washington Irving had a friend called Herman Knickerbocker, *who was descended from colonial Dutch settlers. When Irving wrote his humorous* History of New York *(1809), describing life in New Amsterdam, he used his friend Herman's family name and pretended that the book had been written by* Diedrich Knickerbocker. *The book was so popular that the name came first to be used for a Dutch New Yorker and then for baggy pants of the Dutch kind.*

knight

knitting

ă pat/ā pay/â care/ä father/ĕ pet/ē be/ĭ pit/ī pie/î fierce/ŏ pot/ō go/ô paw, for/oi oil/o͝o book/o͞o boot/ou out/ŭ cut/û fur/*th* the/th thin/hw which/zh vision/ə ago, item, pencil, atom, circus

door open. **2.** To press the flanks of (a riding horse) with the knees: *He kneed his pony to go faster.*
***Idiom.* force** (or **bring) (someone) to his knees.** To force to surrender; defeat: *American air power helped bring Germany to its knees.*

knee breeches. Short, fitted trousers ending at or just below the knee.

knee•cap |nē'kăp'| *n.* A small bone found at the front of the knee; the patella.

knee-deep |nē'dēp'| *adj.* **1.** As high as the knees: *The prairie grass was knee-deep.* **2.** Submerged to the knees: *The hikers were knee-deep in quicksand.* **3.** Deeply occupied: *I'm knee-deep in my studies this week.*

knee-high |nē'hī'| *adj.* As tall or high as the knee: *knee-high boots.*

kneel |nēl| *v.* **knelt** |nĕlt| or **kneeled, kneel•ing.** To rest or fall on one or both knees: *The doctor kneeled beside the patient's bed. The monks knelt in prayer.*

knee-length |nē'lĕngkth'| *or* |-lĕngth'| *adj.* As long or low as the knee: *knee-length pants.*

knee•pad |nē'păd'| *n.* A protective covering for the knee, as one used by a catcher in baseball.

knell |nĕl| *n.* The sound of a bell rung slowly and solemnly, as for a funeral. *—v.* **1.** To ring slowly and solemnly: *The church bells knelled all day.* **2.** To announce or summon by or as if by a knell: *The church bells were knelling the death of the young President.*

knelt |nĕlt|. A past tense and past participle of **kneel.**

Knes•set |knĕs'ĕt'| *n.* The Israeli Parliament.

knew |no͞o| *or* |nyo͞o|. Past tense of **know.** ¶ *These sound alike* **knew, gnu, new.**

Knick•er•bock•er |nĭk'ər bŏk'ər| *n.* **1.** A descendant of the Dutch settlers of New York. **2.** A New Yorker. [SEE NOTE]

knick•er•bock•ers |nĭk'ər bŏk'ərz| *pl.n.* Loose trousers with short legs that are gathered in a band just below the knee, such as those worn by the early Dutch settlers of New York.

knick•ers |nĭk'ərz| *pl.n.* Loose trousers with short legs that are gathered in with a band just below the knee.

knick•knack |nĭk'năk'| *n.* A small ornamental article; a trinket.

knife |nīf| *n., pl.* **knives** |nīvz|. **1.** A cutting instrument consisting of a sharp blade with a handle. **2.** A similar implement used as a weapon. *—v.* **knifed, knif•ing. 1.** To stab with a knife. **2.** *Informal.* To betray by underhand means. **3.** To cut or slash a way through: *the dorsal fin of a shark knifing through the water.*

knife-edge |nīf'ĕj'| *n.* **1.** The cutting edge of a blade. **2.** A sharp, knifelike edge.

knight |nīt| *n.* **1.** In feudal times, a mounted man-at-arms giving service to a king or other superior, especially such a man raised to an order of chivalry after training as a page and squire. **2.** In Great Britain, a man honored with a dignity by a sovereign for personal merit or service to the country. **3.** Either of two chess pieces that can be moved two squares horizontally and one vertically or two squares vertically and one horizontally. *—v.* To make (a person) a knight. ¶ *These sound alike* **knight, night.** [SEE PICTURE]

knight er•rant |ĕr'ənt|. *pl.* **knights errant.** In medieval times, a knight who wandered in search of adventure.

knight•hood |nīt'ho͝od'| *n.* **1.** The rank or dignity of a knight. **2.** The behavior or qualities suitable for a knight. **3.** Knights as a group.

knight•ly |nīt'lē| *adj.* Of or suitable for a knight. ¶ *These sound alike* **knightly, nightly.**

knish |knĭsh| *n.* A small piece of dough with a potato, cheese, kasha, or other filling, baked or fried.

knit |nĭt| *v.* **knit** or **knit•ted, knit•ting. 1.** To make (a fabric or garment) by interlocking yarn or thread in connected loops with special needles, either by hand or by machine: *She knit a sweater. Can you knit?* **2.** To knit with a plain, forward stitch: *Knit and purl. Knit one, purl two.* **3.** To draw together in wrinkles; furrow: *knit one's brows.* **4.** To grow or bind together: *a broken leg that fails to knit properly. A common heritage helped to knit the 13 colonies into a nation.* **—knit'ted** *adj.: a knitted fabric.* *—n.* A fabric or garment made by knitting: *a jersey knit.* ***—modifier:*** *a knit fabric; knit brows; a closely knit friendship.* ¶ *These sound alike* **knit, nit.**

knit•ting |nĭt'ĭng| *n.* **1.** The art or process of making knitted fabric: *She is good at knitting.* **2.** Fabric in the process of being knitted: *She brought along her knitting.* [SEE PICTURE]

knitting needle. One of two long, thin, pointed rods used in knitting by hand.

knit•wear |nĭt'wâr'| *n.* Articles of clothing knitted by hand or by machine.

knives |nīvz| *n.* Plural of **knife.**

knob |nŏb| *n.* **1.** A rounded mass at the end of a stick, post, etc.: *a brass knob on top of a bedpost; the knob of a walking stick.* **2.** A rounded mass extending from a surface, especially a rounded dial or handle: *a control knob on a television set; a knob for pulling open a drawer.* **3.** A doorknob: *Turn the knob and enter.*

knob•by |nŏb'ē| *adj.* **knob•bi•er, knob•bi•est.** Resembling a knob or knobs: *a skinny child with knobby knees; a few old, knobby hills.*

knock |nŏk| *v.* **1.** To hit; strike: *knock someone on the head; knock the ball clean out of the park.* **2.** To make a loud noise by hitting a hard surface; rap; bang: *knock on wood for luck. He knocked and knocked, but nobody came to the door.* **3.** To produce by a blow or blows: *knock a hole in the wall.* **4.** To collide or cause to collide; bump: *branches knocking together in the wind. He grabbed the two thugs by the collar and knocked their heads together.* **5.** To make a pounding or clanking noise: *Dad took the car to the garage when the engine started to knock.* **6.** To hit and cause to fall: *knock someone down in a fist fight. One of the guests accidentally knocked over a vase.* **7.** To remove, as by hitting, kicking, etc.: *knock the snow from one's shoes.* **8.** *Informal.* To criticize: *Her parents couldn't understand why she was always knocking her teachers.* **9.** To instill or render with or as if with a blow: *knock some sense into that boy's head. A gigantic wave almost knocked him senseless.* **10.** In baseball, to gain by a solid hit: *knock a home run.* ***—phrasal verbs.*** **knock about** (or **around).** *Informal.* **1.** To be rough or brutal with by or as if by beating with the fists. **2.** To wander from place to place. **knock off.** *Informal.* **1.** To cease; stop: *knock off work;*

knock off football practice. **2.** To accomplish; finish: *He knocked off his homework in no time flat.* **knock out. 1.** To render unconscious, as by a blow with the fist: *The champ knocked him out in the fourth round.* **2.** To drive out by a sharp blow: *knock someone's teeth out. He knocked the wind out of me.* **3.** To destroy or ruin: *knock out an enemy pillbox; knock out one's business competitors.* **4.** *Informal.* To exhaust completely: *That four-hour math exam really knocked me out.* **5.** *Informal.* To make or produce quickly or carelessly: *knock out a term paper in one evening.* **knock together.** *Informal.* To make or assemble, especially in a careless or crude fashion. *—n.* **1.** A sharp blow: *What he needs is a good knock on the head.* **2.** A rap, as on a door: *waited in terror for the Gestapo's knock.* **3.** A pounding or clanking noise, as of an engine in need of repairs.

***Idiom.* knock (someone) for a loop.** *Slang.* To shock or confuse greatly; astonish.

knock•a•bout |**nŏk'**ə bout'| *n.* A small sloop with a mainsail, a jib, and a keel, but no bowsprit. *—adj.* **1.** Rough and boisterous. **2.** Suitable for rough use.

knock•down |**nŏk'**doun'| *adj.* **1.** Strong enough to knock a person down: *a knockdown punch.* **2.** Violent; unrestrained: *a knockdown fight.*

knock•er |**nŏk'**ər| *n.* **1.** A person who knocks. **2.** A metal ring, knob, or hammer hinged to a door for use in knocking.

knock-knee |**nŏk'**nē'| *n.* An abnormal condition in which one or both legs are bent or twisted so that the knees are turned toward each other or touch each other. —**knock'-kneed'** *adj.*

knock•out |**nŏk'**out'| *n.* A blow that knocks a boxer to the canvas so that he cannot get up before the referee counts to ten.

knock•wurst |**nŏk'**wûrst'| *or* |-wŏŏrst'| *n.* A form of the word **knackwurst.**

knoll |nōl| *n.* A small, rounded hill; a hillock.

knot |nŏt| *n.* **1.** A compact interlacing of cord, rope, etc. **2.** A fastening made by tying string, rope, etc. **3.** A bow of ribbon, fabric, cord, or braid: *a lovers' knot.* **4.** A tightly twisted roll or coil of hair on a woman's head. **5.** A tight cluster of persons or things: *a knot of spectators.* **6.** A difficulty or complication: *The situation was full of knots.* **7.** A hard lump or bump on a part of the body, as resulting from a swelling, an enlarged gland, or an abnormal growth. **8.** A hard spot in wood, darker in color than the surrounding wood. **9.** A unit of speed equal to one nautical mile per hour, used especially by ships and aircraft. *—v.* **knot•ted, knot•ting. 1.** To tie or fasten in or with a knot: *She twisted the scarf smoothly over her forehead and knotted it in back. He knotted his sandal cords tighter.* **2.** To tense, as if into knots: *His stomach suddenly knotted with fear.* ¶*These sound alike* **knot, not.** [SEE PICTURES]

knot•hole |**nŏt'**hōl'| *n.* A hole in a piece of lumber where a knot has dropped out or been removed.

knot•ty |**nŏt'**ē| *adj.* **knot•ti•er, knot•ti•est. 1.** Tied or snarled in knots: *knotty cord.* **2.** Having many knots or knobs: *knotty lumber.* **3.** Difficult to solve: *a knotty problem in algebra.*

know |nō| *v.* **knew** |nōō| *or* |nyōō|, **known** |nōn|, **know•ing. 1.** To understand or have the facts about: *know the basic laws of physics. Do you know what causes thunder?* **2.** To be aware; realize; sense: *She somehow knows that we don't like her.* **3.** To be sure: *I know that I'm right.* **4.** To be acquainted or familiar with: *I know him very well; in fact, he's one of my closest friends. He knows the Rockies, having spent several summers there.* **5.** To recognize: *I know the tune, but I can't remember the words.* **6.** To have skill in or a practical grasp of: *She wished she knew how to make friends. Many people in France know two or more languages.* **7.** To have in the memory: *Jane knows the poem by heart.* **8.** To be able to distinguish: *Before they ate the apple, Adam and Eve didn't know good from evil.* **9.** To be subjected to: *He has known bitter hardship in his time. A virgin forest has never known the blade of an ax.* **10.** To find out; learn: *glad to know that the telegram had been a practical joke.* ¶*These sound alike* **know, no.** —**know'a•ble** *adj.* [SEE NOTE]

***Idiom.* in the know.** In possession of inside information.

know-how |**nō'**hou'| *n. Informal.* Practical knowledge; skill: *It took plenty of brains and know-how to build the pyramids of Egypt.*

know•ing |**nō'**ĭng| *adj.* **1.** Having knowledge or awareness. **2.** Having or reflecting shrewdness or discernment: *a knowing business investor.* **3.** Worldly-wise: *a knowing grin.* **4.** Suggestive of inside or secret information: *a knowing glance between mother and son.*

know•ing•ly |**nō'**ĭng lē| *adv.* **1.** In a manner suggestive of worldly or secret knowledge: *Sammy knowingly assured the other children that it would be easy to trick the teacher.* **2.** Deliberately: *A Hindu holy man will not knowingly harm any living creature.*

know-it-all |**nō'**ĭt ôl'| *n. Informal.* A person who acts as if he knew everything.

knowl•edge |**nŏl'**ĭj| *n.* **1.** Facts and ideas; information: *We must not despise new knowledge. Much of the world's technical knowledge is available only in English.* **2.** Awareness; understanding: *He gained a greater knowledge of the problems involved. Scientists add to our knowledge of the universe.* **3.** Learning; erudition: *The ancient Greeks valued knowledge for its own sake and were not interested in inventions.*

***Idiom.* to the best of (one's) knowledge.** As far as one knows.

knowl•edge•a•ble |**nŏl'**ĭ jə bəl| *adj.* Well-informed: *He is knowledgeable about foreign policy.*

known |nōn|. Past participle of **know.** *—adj.* **1.** Generally accepted: *It's a known fact that he's lazy.* **2.** Proven: *It's a known fact that light travels at 186,000 miles per second.* **3.** Explored: *Columbus sailed beyond the limits of the known world.*

know-noth•ing |**nō'**nŭth'ĭng| *n.* An ignorant person; ignoramus.

knuck•le |**nŭk'**əl| *n.* **1.** A joint of a finger, especially one of the joints connecting a finger to the hand. **2.** A cut of meat from a leg joint: *pig's knuckles.* *—v.* **knuck•led, knuck•ling.** To rub or press with the knuckles. *—**phrasal verbs.*** **knuckle down.** To set earnestly to work at a task. **knuckle under.** To give in; yield; submit.

knuckle ball. In baseball, a slow, fluttering pitch resulting from a special grip in which the knuck-

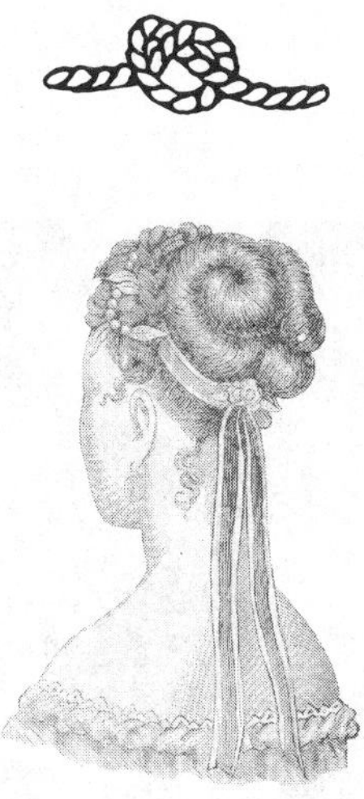

knots
Above: Overhand
Below: Chignon

know

The k- *in* **know,** *as in most other English words beginning with* kn-, *was originally fully pronounced.* **Know** *was* cnāwan *in Old English, descending from prehistoric Germanic* knōw- *and ultimately from Indo-European* gnōw-. *It is related to Latin* gnōscere, *"to get to know," appearing in* **notice** *and* **recognize,** *and to Greek* gnōnai, *"to know," appearing in* **diagnosis.**

koala

kosher

The Jewish dietary laws stem from ancient Biblical and rabbinic laws. For example, meat considered **kosher,** *or "proper," includes those animals, such as cattle, sheep, and goats, that have cloven hoofs and chew their cud. The animal must be killed in a certain way, and the meat must be drained of blood and salted before cooking. Meat is not eaten with milk or milk products. Of the animals that live in the water, only those with fins and scales are permitted.*

kudu

ă pat/ā pay/â care/ä father/ĕ pet/ ē be/ĭ pit/ī pie/î fierce/ŏ pot/ ō go/ô paw, for/oi oil/o͝o book/ o͞o boot/ou out/ŭ cut/û fur/ *th* the/th thin/hw which/zh vision/ ə ago, item, pencil, atom, circus

les of two or three fingers are bent in such a way that the ball is gripped by the nails rather than the fleshy tips of these fingers.

KO, also **K.O., k.o.** |kā′ō′| *v.* **KO'd, KO'ing, KO's.** *Slang.* To knock out. *—n., pl.* **KO's.** In boxing, a knockout.

ko•a•la |kō ä′lə| *n.* Also **koala bear.** A furry Australian animal that lives in eucalyptus trees and feeds almost entirely on their leaves and bark. [SEE PICTURE]

kohl |kōl| *n.* A cosmetic used in Moslem and Asian countries to darken the eyelids. ¶ *These sound alike* **kohl, coal.**

kohl•ra•bi |kōl rä′bē| *or* |kōl′rä′-| *n.* A plant with a thick, rounded, turniplike stem that is eaten as a vegetable.

ko•la |kō′lə| *n.* Either of two African trees bearing nuts containing caffeine that yield an extract used in beverages and medicines.

koo•doo |ko͞o′do͞o| *n.* A form of the word **kudu.**

kook |ko͞ok| *n. Slang.* An eccentric or zany person: *They labeled everyone who objected to the plan as radicals and kooks.*

kook•a•bur•ra |ko͝ok′ə bûr′ə| *n.* An Australian bird with a call that sounds like loud, harsh laughter.

kook•y |ko͞o′kē|. *Slang. adj.* **kook•i•er, kook•i•est.** Strange; zany: *When children watch violence on television, they can get kooky ideas. —adv.* In a zany or strange manner: *Why does she act kooky all the time?* **—kook′i•ness** *n.*

ko•peck |kō′pĕk′| *n.* A coin worth 1/100 of a rouble.

Ko•ran |kô răn′| *or* |-rän′| *or* |kō-| *or* |kôr′ăn′| *n.* The sacred book of Islam, believed to contain the words of Allah as revealed to the prophet Mohammed.

Ko•re•a |kô rē′ə| *or* |kō-|. A former country on a peninsula in eastern Asia, divided since 1948 into North Korea and South Korea.

Ko•re•an |kô rē′ən| *or* |kō-| *n.* **1.** A native or inhabitant of Korea. **2.** The language of Korea, which has many words of Chinese origin. *—adj.* Of Korea, the Koreans, or their language.

Korean War. A war fought between North Korea, aided by Communist China, and South Korea, aided by the United Nations, between 1950 and 1953.

ko•ru•na |kôr′ə nä′| *n. pl.* **ko•ru•ny** |kôr′ə nē| or **ko•ru•nas.** The basic unit of money of Czechoslovakia.

ko•sher |kō′shər| *adj.* **1.** Conforming to or prepared in accordance with Jewish dietary laws. **2.** Preparing or selling kosher food: *a kosher delicatessen.* [SEE NOTE]

ko•to |kō′tō| *n.* A traditional Japanese musical instrument having 13 strings stretched across an oblong sound box.

kow•tow |kow′tou′| *or* |-tou′| *v.* To show exaggerated respect or obedience; fawn: *a clerk who was always kowtowing to the office manager.*

Kr The symbol for the element krypton.

kraal |kräl| *n.* **1.** A village of southern Africa, usually consisting of huts surrounded by a stockade. **2.** An enclosure for livestock in southern Africa.

K ration. An emergency field ration, consisting of a single tightly packaged meal, developed for the use of American soldiers during World War II.

Krem•lin |krĕm′lĭn| *n.* **1.** The citadel of Moscow, housing major offices of the Soviet government. **2.** The Soviet government.

krill |krĭl| *n. (used with a singular or plural verb).* Very small, shrimplike sea animals that are the chief food of certain whales.

kris |krēs| *n.* A sword of East Indian origin having a wavy, double-edged blade.

Krish•na |krĭsh′nə|. The chief hero of Hindu mythology, worshiped as an incarnation of the god Vishnu.

Kriss Krin•gle |krĭs′ krĭng′gəl|. **Santa Claus.**

kro•na |krō′nə| *n.* **1.** *pl.* **kro•nor** |krō′nôr′|. The basic unit of money of Sweden. **2.** *pl.* **kro•nur** |krō′nər|. The basic unit of money of Iceland.

kro•ne |krō′nə| *n., pl.* **kro•ner** |krō′nər|. The basic unit of money of Denmark and Norway.

kro•nor |krō′nôr′| *n.* Plural of **krona** (Sweden).

kro•nur |krō′nər| *n.* Plural of **krona** (Iceland).

kryp•ton |krĭp′tŏn′| *n.* Symbol **Kr** One of the elements, an inert gas. Atomic number 36; atomic weight 83.80; melting point -156.6°C; boiling point -152.30°C.

Kua•la Lum•pur |kwä′lə lo͝om po͝or′|. The capital of Malaysia. Population, 452,000.

Ku•blai Khan |ko͞o′blī kän′|. 1216–1294. Mongol emperor of China.

ku•dos |ko͞o′dōz′| *or* |-dōs′| *or* |-dŏs′| *or* |kyo͞o′-| *n. (used with a singular verb).* Praise or acclaim as a result of exceptional achievement, performance, etc.: *a writer who has won many kudos for his recent work.*

ku•du |ko͞o′do͞o| *n.* An African antelope with long, spirally twisted horns. [SEE PICTURE]

Ku Klux Klan |ko͞o′ klŭks′ klăn′| *or* |kyo͞o′|. A secret society founded in the southern United States after the Civil War to enforce white supremacy, often with terroristic methods.

kum•quat |kŭm′kwŏt′| *n.* **1.** A small, thin-skinned, edible orangelike fruit. **2.** A tree that bears such fruit.

kung fu |ko͝ong′ fo͞o′| *or* |go͝ong′|. A Chinese system of self-defense resembling the Japanese system karate.

Ku•wait |ko͞o wāt′| *or* |-wīt′|. A country on the Arabian Peninsula, at the head of the Persian Gulf. Population, 929,000. Capital, Kuwait.

kw, kW, k.w. kilowatt.

kwa•cha |kwä′chä′| *n.* The basic unit of money of Zambia and Malawi.

kwh, kWh, k.w.h., K.W.H. kilowatt-hour.

Ky. Kentucky.

kyat |kyät| *or* |kē ät′| *n.* The basic unit of money of Burma.

Kyo•to |kē ō′tō|. A city in Japan; the capital of Japan until 1868. Population, 1,440,000.

Ll

l, L |ĕl| *n., pl.* **l's** or **L's.** **1.** The 12th letter of the English alphabet. **2.** The Roman numeral for the number 50. [SEE NOTE]

l., L. left.

l liter.

la |lä| *n.* A syllable used in music to represent the sixth tone of a major scale or sometimes the tone A.

La The symbol for the element lanthanum.

La. Louisiana.

lab |lăb| *n. Informal.* A laboratory.

la•bel |lā'bəl| *n.* **1.** A tag, sticker, etc., attached to an article or to a container or package to identify or give appropriate information about the article: *the label on a can of peaches.* **2.** A descriptive word, phrase, abbreviation, etc., used to classify or identify: *a part-of-speech label. He rapidly acquired the label "subversive."* —*v.* **la•beled** or **la•belled, la•bel•ing** or **la•bel•ling. 1.** To attach a label to: *label a package for mailing.* **2.** To identify or designate with a number, letter, word, etc.: *Draw a triangle and label the sides A, B, and C.* **3.** To describe or classify as: *Explorers labeled Africa the "Dark Continent."*

la•bi•al |lā'bē əl| *adj.* Of or involving the lips. [SEE NOTE]

la•bor |lā'bər| *n.* **1.** An exertion of physical or mental effort; work; toil: *the labor involved in climbing a hill.* **2.** A specific task: *the twelve labors of Hercules.* **3.** A particular form of work or method of working: *manual labor.* **4. a.** The working class: *the war between labor and capital.* **b.** The trade union movement, especially its officials: *Labor faithfully supports the White House on foreign policy.* **5.** The process by which a baby is pushed out of the uterus at birth. —***modifier:*** *a labor leader.* —*v.* **1.** To work; toil: *He labored for years on an auto assembly line.* **2.** To make a great effort: *laboring to make the meaning of every phrase clear.* **3.** To move slowly and with difficulty: *Our old jalopy labored over the mountain pass.*

lab•o•ra•to•ry |lăb'rə tôr'ē| *or* |-tōr'ē| *n., pl.* **lab•o•ra•to•ries. 1.** A room or building equipped for scientific research, experiments, or testing. **2.** A place where drugs or chemicals are manufactured. —***modifier:*** *laboratory tests.*

Labor Day. A holiday celebrated on the first Monday of September in honor of the working class.

la•bored |lā'bərd| *adj.* Showing obvious effort; strained: *a labored reply to a question.*

la•bor•er |lā'bər ər| *n.* A worker, especially one who does unskilled manual labor.

la•bo•ri•ous |lə bôr'ē əs| *or* |-bōr'-| *adj.* Demanding great effort; difficult: *a laborious task.* —**la•bo'ri•ous•ly** *adv.*

la•bor-sav•ing |lā'bər sā'vĭng| *adj.* Designed to conserve or diminish the amount of human labor needed: *labor-saving devices.*

labor union. An organization of people who work for wages, formed to protect and further their mutual interests, as better wages, working conditions, etc.; a trade union.

la•bour |lā'bər| *n.* & *v.* Chiefly British form of the word **labor.**

Lab•ra•dor |lăb'rə dôr'|. **1.** A peninsula of northeastern Canada, between Hudson Bay and the Atlantic Ocean. **2.** The northeastern part of this peninsula, part of Newfoundland.

la•bur•num |lə bûr'nəm| *n.* A tree or shrub planted for its drooping clusters of yellow flowers.

lab•y•rinth |lăb'ə rĭnth'| *n.* **1.** A network of winding, connected passages through which it is difficult to find one's way without help; a maze. **2. Labyrinth.** In Greek mythology, the maze in which the Minotaur was confined. **3.** The semicircular canals, cochlea, and vestibule of the inner ear. [SEE PICTURE]

lac |lăk| *n.* A resinous substance secreted by a tropical Asian insect and used in making shellac. ¶*These sound alike* **lac, lack.**

lace |lās| *n.* **1.** A delicate fabric of fine threads woven in an open, weblike pattern with fancy designs. **2.** A cord or string drawn through eyelets or around hooks to pull and tie opposite edges together. **3.** Gold or silver braid used as a trimming, as on uniforms. —***modifier:*** *a lace tablecloth.* —*v.* **laced, lac•ing. 1.** To fasten or tie with a lace or laces: *Lace up your shoes. Do your boots lace or zip?* **2.** To weave, twist, or twine together: *laced strands into a braid.*

lac•er•ate |lăs'ə rāt'| *v.* **lac•er•at•ed, lac•er•at•ing.** To rip or tear, especially in an injury. —**lac'er•a'tion** *n.*

lace•wing |lās'wĭng'| *n.* An insect that has four gauzy wings and feeds on and destroys aphids and other insect pests.

lach•ry•mal |lăk'rə məl| *adj.* Of tears or the glands that secrete tears. —*n.* **lachrymals.** The glands that secrete tears; the lachrymal glands.

lack |lăk| *n.* **1.** A deficiency; shortage: *a lack of communication between the brothers.* **2.** A complete absence: *The lack of electricity made life very hard.* **3.** Something that is needed: *Water is a lack of desert areas.* —*v.* **1.** To have very little of: *She lacks the will power to stay on her diet very long.* **2.** To be entirely without: *streets that often lacked trees.* **3.** To be wanting or deficient: *His*

(1) (2) (3) (4) (5)

The letter **L** *comes originally from the Phoenician letter* lāmedh *(1). The Greeks borrowed it as* lambda *(2, 3). In turn the Romans borrowed it from the Greeks (4) and later gave it the shape (5) that it still has.*

labial/lip

The resemblance between **lip** *and* **labial** *is not accidental.* **Labial** *is from Latin* labium, *which is descended from* leb-, *the prehistoric Indo-European word for "lip." In Germanic,* leb- *became* lep-, *appearing in Old English as* lippa; *this became* **lip** *in Modern English.*

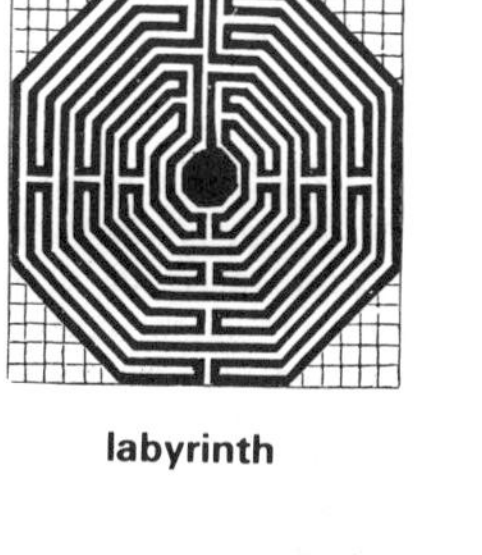

labyrinth

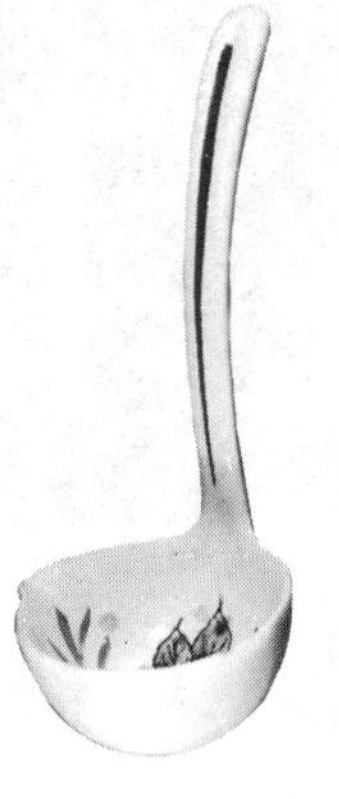

ladle

lady/lord

In Old English, the mistress of a great household was called lāf-dige, *"she who makes the bread," and the master was called* lāf-weard, *"he who keeps the bread." The first element in both titles is* lāf *or* hlāf, *"bread, loaf"; the second elements are* -dig-, *"to knead," and* weard, *"keeper, guard," respectively. In the feudal society of the Anglo-Saxons, the mistress and master "gave bread" (i.e., supplied food and livelihood in general) to their family, their vassals, and their slaves. In Middle English,* lāfdige *became* lafdi, *and* lāfweard *became* loverd; *in Modern English they became* **lady** *and* **lord**.

ladybug

ă pat/ā pay/â care/ä father/ĕ pet/ ē be/ĭ pit/ī pie/î fierce/ŏ pot/ ō go/ô paw, for/oi oil/ŏŏ book/ ōō boot/ou out/ŭ cut/û fur/ *th* the/th thin/hw which/zh vision/ ə ago, item, pencil, atom, circus

diet is lacking in protein. ¶ *These sound alike* **lack, lac.**

lack•a•dai•si•cal |lăk′ə **dā**′zĭ kəl| *adj.* Lacking spirit or interest: *a lackadaisical attitude toward one's schoolwork.* —**lack′a•dai′si•cal•ly** *adv.*

lack•ey |lăk′ē| *n., pl.* **lack•eys. 1.** A male servant in uniform; a footman. **2.** A servile follower who does whatever he is told to do.

lack•lus•ter |lăk′lŭs′tər| *adj.* Lacking luster, brightness, etc.; dull: *lackluster conversation.*

la•con•ic |lə kŏn′ĭk| *adj.* Terse; concise: *a laconic reply.* —**la•con′i•cal•ly** *adv.*

lac•quer |lăk′ər| *n.* Any material that is dissolved in a solvent and can be applied to a surface, drying to leave a glossy finish. —*v.* To coat with lacquer. —**lac′quered** *adj.: a lacquered tray.*

la•crosse |lə krôs′| *or* |-krŏs′| *n.* A game, played on a field, in which participants use a stick with a webbed pouch to maneuver a ball, the object being to propel the ball into the opposing team's goal.

lac•tase |lăk′tās′| *n.* An enzyme, found in some yeasts and in the digestive juices of mammals, that acts in the conversion of lactose into simpler sugars.

lac•tic |lăk′tĭk| *adj.* Of or derived from milk.

lactic acid. An organic acid, having the formula $C_3H_6O_3$, found in sour milk, molasses, wines, and various fruits, and used as a flavoring and preservative for foods.

lac•tose |lăk′tōs′| *n.* A white, crystalline sugar that is found in milk and has the formula $C_{12}H_{22}O_{11}$. It is used in infant foods, bakery products, and various sweets.

lac•y |lā′sē| *adj.* **lac•i•er, lac•i•est.** Of or like lace: *a table covered with a lacy white cloth.*

lad |lăd| *n.* A boy or young man.

lad•der |lăd′ər| *n.* **1.** A portable device for climbing up or down, consisting usually of two long, parallel side pieces or ropes crossed by equally spaced rungs. **2.** Anything likened to a ladder: *climbing the social ladder.*

lad•en |lăd′n| *adj.* **1.** Carrying a burden or cargo: *a heavily laden mule.* **2.** Loaded or filled with something: *a ship laden with silks and teas from China.* **3.** Oppressed; burdened: *a mother laden with grief.*

lad•ing |lā′dĭng| *n.* Cargo; freight: *a bill of lading.*

la•dle |lād′l| *n.* A long-handled utensil with a cup-shaped receptacle at one end, used for dipping out liquids. —*v.* **la•dled, la•dling.** To lift out and pour with a ladle. [SEE PICTURE]

la•dy |lā′dē| *n., pl.* **la•dies. 1.** A woman of breeding, culture, or high station. **2.** The wife of a man of high rank: *the colonel's lady.* **3. a.** A woman regarded as proper and virtuous. **b.** A well-behaved young girl: *She's a perfect little lady.* **4.** Any woman spoken of in a polite way: *the lady who lives next door.* **5. ladies.** A word used in speaking of or to or in writing to women as members of a group: *Ladies and gentlemen, I bid you welcome.* **6.** The female head of a household. **7. Lady.** *British.* The general female title of nobility or other rank. **8. my lady.** Used as a title of address for a lady. [SEE NOTE]

la•dy•bird |lā′dē bûrd′| *n.* An insect, the ladybug.

la•dy•bug |lā′dē bŭg′| *n.* A small beetle, often reddish with black spots, that feeds on and destroys aphids and other insect pests. [SEE PICTURE]

lady in waiting. *pl.* **ladies in waiting.** A lady of a court appointed to attend a queen or princess.

la•dy•like |lā′dē līk′| *adj.* Refined; well-bred; delicate: *Sally gave a short, ladylike sniffle.*

La•dy•ship |lā′dē shĭp′| *n.* A word used in speaking of or to a woman holding the rank of lady.

la•dy's-slip•per |lā′dēz slĭp′ər| *n.* Any of several orchids having flowers with a protruding, pouch-like part.

La•fay•ette |lä′fē **ĕt**′| *or* |lăf′ē-|, **Marquis de.** 1757–1834. French political leader; commanded American troops in the Revolutionary War.

lag |lăg| *v.* **lagged, lag•ging. 1.** To fall behind: *a soldier who lagged behind the rest of the column.* **2.** To weaken or diminish; slacken: *Our spirits began to lag.* —*n.* **1.** The act or condition of lagging: *the lag of one nation behind another.* **2.** The extent or degree of lagging; a gap: *a huge lag between one's beliefs and one's actions.*

la•ger |lä′gər| *n.* A type of beer that is stored to allow sedimentation.

lag•gard |lăg′ərd| *n.* A person who lags behind; a straggler. —*adj.* Lagging behind; slow: *a laggard runner.*

la•goon |lə **gōōn**′| *n.* A body of water, usually connecting with the ocean, especially one bounded by sandbars or coral reefs.

La•gos |lā′gŏs′| *or* |-gəs|. The capital of Nigeria. Population, 665,000.

laid |lād|. Past tense and past participle of **lay.**

laid-back |lād′băk′| *adj.* *Informal.* Casual or relaxed in atmosphere or character.

lain |lān|. Past participle of **lie.** ¶ *These sound alike* **lain, lane.**

lair |lâr| *n.* The den or dwelling place of a wild animal.

laird |lârd| *n.* *Scottish.* The owner of a landed estate.

la•i•ty |lā′ĭ tē| *n.* The laymen of a religious group as distinguished from the clergy.

lake |lāk| *n.* A large inland body of fresh or salt water.

lam |lăm| *n.* —**on the lam.** *Slang.* In flight from the law.

la•ma |lä′mə| *n.* A Buddhist monk of Tibet or Mongolia.

lamb |lăm| *n.* **1.** A young sheep. **2.** The flesh of a young sheep used as meat.

lam•baste |lăm **bāst**′| *v.* **lam•bast•ed, lam•bast•ing.** *Slang.* **1.** To thrash; beat. **2.** To scold; berate: *lambasted for his tardiness.*

lamb•da |lăm′də| *n.* The eleventh letter of the Greek alphabet, written Λ, λ. In English it is represented as *L, l.*

lam•bent |lăm′bənt| *adj.* Flickering or glowing gently: *a lambent flame; her lambent eyes.*

lamb•kin |lăm′kĭn| *n.* A little lamb.

lame |lām| *adj.* **lam•er, lam•est. 1.** Limping, as from exhaustion. **2.** Crippled in a leg or foot. **3.** Weak; unsatisfactory: *a lame excuse.* —*v.* **lamed, lam•ing.** To make lame; cripple. —**lame′ly** *adv.* —**lame′ness** *n.*

la•mé |lă **mā**′| *n.* A fabric in which flat metal threads of gold or silver are woven with threads of fiber such as silk. —**modifier:** *a lamé dress.*

la•ment |lə mĕnt′| *v.* To mourn over; grieve: *lament the death of a loved one; lament with a broken heart.* —*n.* **1.** An expression of grief: *shattering his heart with tears and laments.* **2.** A sorrowful song or poem.

lam•en•ta•ble |lăm′ən tə bəl| *or* |lə mĕn′-| *adj.* To be lamented; regrettable: *a lamentable mistake.* —**lam′en•ta•bly** *adv.*

lam•en•ta•tion |lăm′ən tā′shən| *n.* The act of lamenting; an expression of sorrow, grief, etc.

lam•i•nate |lăm′ə nāt′| *v.* **lam•i•nat•ed, lam•i•nat•ing. 1.** To beat or press into a thin plate or sheet. **2.** To split into thin layers. **3.** To make by joining several layers: *laminate plywood.* —*n.* Something made by joining layers together: *a plastic laminate.* —**lam′i•na′tion** *n.*

lamp |lămp| *n.* **1.** Any device using oil, gas, electricity, etc., to give light. **2.** A device generating and using light for purposes other than illumination: *a sun lamp.* —**modifier:** *a lamp shade.* [SEE NOTE]

lamp•black |lămp′blăk′| *n.* A gray or black pigment composed of finely divided carbon collected in the form of soot by letting a smoky flame contact a cold surface.

lam•poon |lăm po͞on′| *n.* **1.** A piece of writing or acting that uses ridicule to attack a person, institution, etc. **2.** A light, good-humored satire. —*v.* To ridicule or satirize with a lampoon: *a skit that lampoons the Pentagon.*

lam•prey |lăm′prē| *n., pl.* **lam•preys.** A fish with a long, eellike body and a round, jawless mouth used for sucking and clinging.

lance |lăns| *or* |läns| *n.* **1.** A weapon, such as one used by knights or warriors on horseback, consisting of a long shaft and a sharp metal head. **2.** An implement resembling such a weapon, as a surgeon's lancet or a spear used by whalers. —*v.* **lanced, lanc•ing.** To pierce or cut into with a lancet: *lance a boil.*

lance corporal. See **corporal** (military rank).

lance•let |lăns′lĭt| *or* |läns′-| *n.* A small, flat-bodied sea animal that has a strip of cartilage called a notochord along its back and that belongs to the same main group of animals as those having true backbones.

Lan•ce•lot |lăn′sə lət| *or* |-lŏt′| *or* |län′-|. In legends about King Arthur, the bravest knight of the Round Table.

lanc•er |lăn′sər| *or* |län′-| *n.* A cavalry soldier equipped with a lance.

lan•cet |lăn′sĭt| *or* |län′-| *n.* A surgical knife with a short, broad, double-edged blade that tapers to a point.

land |lănd| *n.* **1.** A part of the earth's surface not covered by water. **2.** A particular part of the earth; a region or country: *We paddled up the river to the land of the bison and beaver.* **3.** A country; a nation: *the highest elective office in the land.* **4.** Earth; ground: *plowing the land.* **5.** Property: *buy land in Hawaii.* —**modifier:** *land animals.* —*v.* **1. a.** To arrive after traveling, especially over water: *landed on a small island.* **b.** To bring or put down after traveling in such a manner: *landed the cargo on the dock.* **2.** To come down and come to rest: *He tripped and landed in an undignified heap.* **3.** To cause (an aircraft or similar vehicle) to descend and settle on a surface. **4.** To bring in, knock down, get, etc., by or as if by catching: *fished all morning and landed three sunfish.* **5.** To arrive or cause to arrive in a place or condition: *He landed in jail after a career of crime.* [SEE NOTE]

land•ed |lăn′dĭd| *adj.* **1.** Owning land: *the landed gentry.* **2.** Consisting of land in the form of property: *a landed estate.*

land grant. Public land given by a government for a railroad, state college, etc. —**modifier: (land-grant):** *land-grant colleges.*

land•hold•er |lănd′hōl′dər| *n.* Someone who owns or has possession of land.

land•hold•ing |lănd′hōl′dĭng| *n.* **1.** Often **landholdings.** Land owned or occupied by a landholder. **2.** The ownership or possession of land.

land•ing |lăn′dĭng| *n.* **1.** The act or process of coming to land or of coming to rest, as after a voyage or flight: *a landing on the moon.* **2.** A wharf or pier. **3.** A level area at the top or bottom of a set of stairs. —**modifier:** *landing instructions.*

landing field. An area of level land used by aircraft for landing and taking off.

landing gear. The structure attached to the underside of an airplane to support it when it is on land or, in the case of a seaplane, in water.

land•la•dy |lănd′lā′dē| *n., pl.* **-la•dies.** A woman who owns or is in charge of a house, apartment building, inn, boarding house, etc., with rooms or living space rented out to others.

land•locked |lănd′lŏkt′| *adj.* **1.** Entirely or almost entirely surrounded by land: *Switzerland is a landlocked country.* **2.** Living only in inland waters: *landlocked salmon.*

land•lord |lănd′lôrd′| *n.* **1.** A man who owns or is in charge of a house, apartment building, inn, boarding house, etc., with rooms or living space rented out to others. **2.** A landowner who rents land and homes to tenants.

land•lub•ber |lănd′lŭb′ər| *n.* A person unfamiliar with sailing or with life aboard a ship or boat.

land•mark |lănd′märk′| *n.* **1.** A fixed object, often an engraved concrete block, used to mark a boundary or indicate a position for travelers or surveyors. **2.** A familiar or easily recognized object, feature of the landscape, etc. **3.** A building or place preserved for its special historical importance or interest. **4.** An event, discovery, work, etc., that is important in the history or development of something.

land mine. A small bomb or similar device buried in the ground and set to explode when stepped on or run over by a vehicle.

land•own•er |lănd′ō′nər| *n.* A person who owns land.

land•scape |lănd′skāp′| *n.* **1.** A stretch of land or countryside forming a single scene or having its own special appearance or characteristics. **2.** A painting, photograph, etc., showing such a scene. —**modifier:** *landscape painting.* —*v.* **land•scaped, land•scap•ing.** To change or improve the appearance of (a piece of ground), as by forming slopes, planting trees, etc.

land•slide |lănd′slīd′| *n.* **1. a.** An occurrence in which a large mass of earth and rock breaks loose and falls or slides, as down a slope. **b.** The mass of earth and rock that moves in this way. **2.** A very large majority of votes resulting in

lamp/lantern

The Greek verb lampein, *"to shine or burn," formed two nouns meaning "a burning torch or lamp": (1)* lampas *and (2)* lamptēr. *These were borrowed into Latin as* lampas *and* lanterna, *respectively, thence into Old French as* lampe *and* lanterne, *and thence into English as* **lamp** *and* **lantern**.

land

The word **land** *has hardly changed for over two thousand years. It was* land *in Old English, and is descended from* landam *in prehistoric Germanic. It also appears as* land *in modern Dutch and German and in numerous Germanic place names, such as* **England,** *the* **Netherlands,** Deutschland *(Germany), etc.*

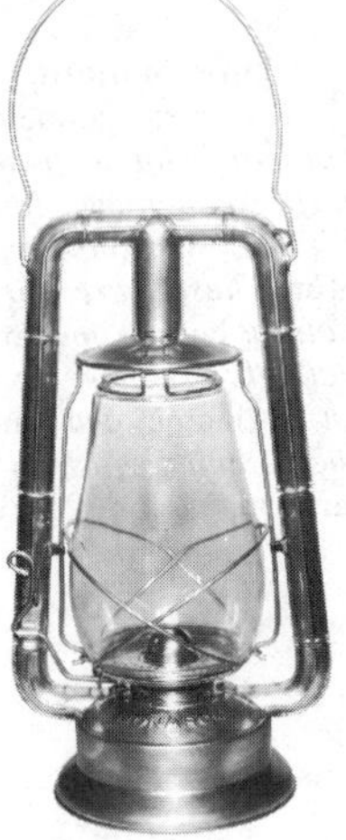

lantern

lap[1-2-3]

Lap[1] *was* læppa *in Old English; it originally meant "a fold or flap in clothes."* **Lap**[2] *("to fold or wrap") probably comes from* **lap**[1]. **Lap**[3] *is unrelated; it was* lapian *in Old English, and it originally meant "to smack one's lips."*

lapwing

ă pat/ā pay/â care/ä father/ĕ pet/ ē be/ĭ pit/ī pie/î fierce/ŏ pot/ ō go/ô paw, for/oi oil/ŏŏ book/ ōō boot/ou out/ŭ cut/û fur/ *th* the/th thin/hw which/zh vision/ ə ago, item, pencil, atom, circus

victory for a candidate or political party.

land•ward |lănd′wərd| *adv.* Also **land•wards** |lănd′wərdz|. To or toward land: *The boat drifted landward.* —*adj.: a landward course.*

lane |lān| *n.* **1.** A narrow path or road, often bordered by grass, hedges, trees, fences, or walls. **2.** A set course or way over water or through the air, used by ships or aircraft: *sky lanes for airplanes; the shipping lanes of the Atlantic.* **3.** A lengthwise division of a roadway, racecourse, etc.: *six lanes in a highway; the inside lane of the track.* **4.** A wood-surfaced passageway along which a bowling ball is rolled. ¶ *These sound alike* **lane, lain.**

lang |lăng| *adj. & adv. Scottish.* Long.

lan•guage |lăng′gwĭj| *n.* **1. a.** The use by human beings of voice sounds, and often of written symbols that represent these sounds, in organized combinations and patterns to express and communicate thoughts and feelings. **b.** A system of words formed from such combinations and patterns, used by the people of a particular country or by a group of people having a shared history or set of tradiitons: *Many languages are spoken in Africa.* **2.** Any system of signs, symbols, gestures, etc., for conveying information: *sign language; a computer language.* **3.** The special words, expression, or style used by members of a group, profession, etc.: *medical language.* **4.** A particular way or style of speaking or writing: *formal language.* —**modifier:** *a language problem; language studies.*

lan•guid |lăng′gwĭd| *adj.* **1.** Lazily slow or relaxed: *a languid wave of the hand.* **2.** Lacking spirit or energy: *She was languid after her long illness.* **3.** Causing a feeling of laziness or listlessness: *languid weather.* —**lan′guid•ly** *adv.*

lan•guish |lăng′gwĭsh| *v.* **1.** To lose strength or vigor; droop; flag: *languish from hunger.* **2.** To become listless and depressed; pine: *alone and languishing in his fine new home.* **3.** To remain under miserable or depressing conditions: *languished for years in a dungeon.*

lan•guor |lăng′gər| *n.* **1.** Lack of energy; fatigue; listlessness. **2.** A dreamy, lazy mood or quality: *the languor of a warm summer afternoon.* —**lan′guor•ous** *adj.*

lank |lăngk| *adj.* **lank•er, lank•est. 1.** Long and lean; gaunt: *his lank body.* **2.** Long, straight, and limp; stringy: *lank, fair hair.* —**lank′ly** *adv.*

lank•y |lăng′kē| *adj.* **lank•i•er, lank•i•est.** Tall, thin, and gawky: *a long, lanky fellow.* —**lank′i•ness** *n.*

lan•o•lin |lăn′ə lĭn| *n.* A yellowish-white fatty substance obtained from wool and used in soaps, cosmetics, and ointments.

Lan•sing |lăn′sĭng|. The capital of Michigan. Population, 129,000.

lan•tern |lăn′tərn| *n.* A case or container for holding and shielding a light, having sides or an opening through which the light can shine. [SEE NOTE on p. 505 & PICTURE]

lan•tha•nide |lăn′thə nīd′| *or* |-nĭd| *n.* Any **rare-earth element.**

lan•tha•num |lăn′thə nəm| *n.* Symbol **La** One of the elements, a soft, silvery rare-earth metal. Atomic number 57; atomic weight 138.91; valence +3; melting point 920°C; boiling point 3,469°C.

lan•yard |lăn′yərd| *n.* **1.** A short rope used on shipboard to secure the rigging. **2.** A cord worn around the neck for holding a knife, keys, etc.

La•os |lä′ōs′| *or* |lā′ŏs′|. A country in Southeast Asia, between Thailand and Vietnam. Population, 3,257,000. Capital, Vientiane. —**La•o′tian** |lā ō′shən| *adj. & n.*

lap[1] |lăp| *n.* **1.** The level place formed by the front part of the legs above the knees of a person who is sitting: *holding a puppy in his lap.* **2.** The part of a person's clothing that covers the lap: *the lap of a skirt.* **3.** Someone's care or responsibility: *He always dumps all his troubles in my lap.* [SEE NOTE]

lap[2] |lăp| *v.* **lapped, lap•ping. 1.** To fold or wrap over or around something: *Lap the pie dough over the filling.* **2.** To lie, place, or extend partly over something else; overlap: *Lap the shingles over one another.* —*n.* **1.** A part folded or extending over something else; an overlapping part. **2. a.** A single length or turn over or around something, as a racecourse: *dived into the pool and swam three laps.* **b.** A single part or stage, as of a journey. [SEE NOTE]

lap[3] |lăp| *v.* **lapped, lap•ping. 1.** To take up and swallow (a liquid) by using the tongue: *The kitten lapped up the milk.* **2.** To wash or splash with a light, slapping sound: *The sea lapped the shore gently. Ripples lapped against the dock.* —*n.* The sound or action of lapping: *the lap of the waves; each lap of the kitten's tongue.* [SEE NOTE]

La Paz |lə päz′| *or* |päz′|. The administrative capital of Bolivia. Population, 600,000.

lap dog. A small, easily held dog kept as a pet.

la•pel |lə pĕl′| *n.* One of the two flaps that extend down from the collar of a coat, jacket, etc., and fold back against the chest.

lap•i•dar•y |lăp′ĭ dĕr′ē| *n., pl.* **lap•i•dar•ies.** A person who works at cutting, engraving, or polishing gemstones. —*adj.* Of or relating to the work or art of a lapidary.

lap•is laz•u•li |lăp′ĭs lăz′yŏŏ lē| *or* |lăzh′ōō-|. An opaque, deep-blue mineral that is used as a gemstone.

Lap•land |lăp′lănd′|. A large area of northern Norway, Sweden, Finland, and the northwestern Soviet Union. —**Lap′land′er** *n.*

Lapp |lăp| *n.* **1.** One of the nomadic people who live in Lapland; a Laplander. **2.** The language of the Lapps.

lapse |lăps| *n.* **1.** A slip, error, or failure, especially a slight or unimportant one: *a lapse of memory.* **2.** A return or change to an earlier or different, often less desirable, condition: *a lapse into barbarism.* **3.** An interval or period of passing time: *a lapse of three months.* **4.** The termination of an agreement, right, privilege, custom, etc., through neglect, disuse, or the passage of time: *the lapse of a lease.* —*v.* **lapsed, lap•sing. 1.** To fall back or away into an earlier or different, often less desirable, condition: *lapsed into silence.* **2.** To be no longer in force because of neglect, disuse, the passage of time, etc.: *He allowed his insurance policy to lapse.*

lap•wing |lăp′wĭng′| *n.* A European bird with a narrow, wispy crest and a loud, piercing call. [SEE PICTURE]

lar•board |lär′bərd| *n.* The port side of a ship or boat. —*adj.* On the port side.

lar•ce•nous |lär′sə nəs| *adj.* **1.** Guilty of larceny; thieving. **2.** Of larceny.
lar•ce•ny |lär′sə nē| *n., pl.* **lar•ce•nies.** The crime of stealing; theft.
larch |lärch| *n.* **1.** A tall, cone-bearing tree that sheds its needles every year. **2.** The hard, strong wood of such a tree.
lard |lärd| *n.* The white waxy or greasy substance prepared from the melted-down fat of a pig. —*v.* **1.** To cover or coat with lard or a similar fat. **2.** To make or try to make (speech, writing, etc.) richer, more effective, or longer by adding something: *He larded his report with French quotations.*
lar•der |lär′dər| *n.* **1.** A room cupboard, etc., where food is stored. **2.** A supply of food.
large |lärj| *adj.* **larg•er, larg•est. 1.** Bigger than average in size, amount, number, etc.; not small: *large animals such as whales and elephants; a large sum of money.* **2.** Great; considerable: *Scientific discoveries have increased our knowledge to a large extent.* **3.** Understanding; tolerant; liberal: *a large and generous spirit.* —**large′ness** *n.*
Idioms. **at large. 1.** Not in confinement or captivity; at liberty; free: *a convict still at large.* **2.** As a whole; in general: *the country at large.* **3.** Not representing or assigned to a single country, district, etc.: *an ambassador at large.* **by and large.** For the most part; on the whole.
large intestine. The section of the intestine that extends from the end of the small intestine to the anus. It serves to absorb water from the waste matter left after food is digested.
large•ly |lärj′lē| *adv.* **1.** For the most part; mainly: *He is largely responsible for the accident.* **2.** On a large scale; amply: *They contributed largely to the pension fund.*
large-scale |lärj′skāl′| *adj.* **1.** Large or wide in scope, range, effect, etc.: *large-scale farming.* **2.** Drawn or made comparatively large, especially so as to show detail: *a large-scale map.*
lar•ghet•to |lär gĕt′ō|. In music: *adj.* Moderately slow; somewhat faster than largo. —*adv.* Moderately slowly; somewhat more quickly than largo. —*n., pl.* **lar•ghet•tos.** A moderately slow section of a composition.
lar•go |lär′gō|. In music: *adj.* Very slow. —*adv.* Very slowly. —*n., pl.* **lar•gos.** A very slow section of a composition.
lar•i•at |lăr′ē ət| *n.* A long rope with an adjustable noose at one end, used especially to catch horses and cattle; a lasso.
lark¹ |lärk| *n.* Any of several mostly European songbirds that often sing as they fly high in the air. [SEE NOTE]
lark² |lärk| *n.* A merry adventure, prank, or romp. —*v.* To engage in fun or merry pranks; frolic; romp. [SEE NOTE]
lark•spur |lärk′spûr′| *n.* A plant with a cluster of showy, usually blue flowers having a narrow, tubelike projecting part.
lar•va |lär′və| *n., pl.* **lar•vae** |lär′vē| or **lar•vas. 1.** The wingless, often wormlike immature form of a newly hatched insect. Caterpillars and grubs are insect larvae. **2.** The newly hatched earliest stage of certain other animals, having a form and appearance very different from that of the adult. —**lar′val** *adj.* [SEE PICTURE]
la•ryn•ges |lə rĭn′jēz| *n.* A plural of **larynx.**
lar•yn•gi•tis |lăr′ən jī′tĭs| *n.* Inflammation of the larynx, causing hoarseness and sometimes temporary loss of the voice.
lar•ynx |lăr′ĭngks| *n., pl.* **la•ryn•ges** |lə rĭn′jēz| or **lar•ynx•es.** The upper part of the respiratory tract between the pharynx and trachea, having walls of cartilage and containing the vocal cords.
las•civ•i•ous |lə sĭv′ē əs| *adj.* Sensual; lewd. —**las•civ′i•ous•ly** *adv.* —**las•civ′i•ous•ness** *n.*
la•ser |lā′zər| *n.* Any of a number of devices that use the radiating properties of systems of atoms or molecules to generate light that is of a single, precise wavelength, with all of the waves polarized, exactly aligned, and matching each other in their phases. —*modifier: a laser beam.*
lash¹ |lăsh| *n.* **1. a.** A whip. **b.** A narrow cord or strip of leather forming the striking end of a whip. **2.** A stroke or blow given with a whip. **3.** A whiplike motion or effect. **4.** An eyelash. —*v.* **1.** To strike with or as if with a whip: *I lashed my horse's flank with all the strength of my arm. The thorny brambles lashed across his body.* **2.** To wave, move, or strike with a thrashing, whiplike motion: *The cat crouched low and lashed his tail from side to side.* **3.** To use angry words to attack or criticize: *The senator lashed back at the reporters.* [SEE NOTE]
lash² |lăsh| *v.* To hold securely in place with rope, cord, straps, etc.: *Her captors lashed her to a tree so that she could not escape.* [SEE NOTE]
lass |lăs| *n.* A girl or young woman.
las•sie |lăs′ē| *n.* A girl; lass.
las•si•tude |lăs′ĭ to͞od′| *or* |-tyo͞od′| *n.* A condition or feeling of listless weakness or exhaustion.
las•so |lăs′ō| *or* |lă so͞o′| *n., pl.* **las•sos** or **las•soes.** A long rope with an adjustable noose at one end, used especially to catch horses and cattle; a lariat. —*v.* **las•soed, las•so•ing, las•soes.** To catch with a lasso: *lasso a runaway calf.*
last¹ |lăst| *or* |läst| *adj.* **1.** Coming, being, or placed after all others; final: *the last game of the season.* **2.** Being the only one or ones left; remaining: *We shot off the last Roman candle.* **3. a.** Just past: *last night.* **b.** Being the one just before: *The pictures on the last page are in color.* **4.** The latest possible: *waited until the last minute.* **5.** Least likely or expected: *the last person we would have suspected.* —*adv.* **1.** After all others: *Grandpa arrived last.* **2.** At the end; finally: *Beat the eggs, stir in the sugar, and last add the flour.* **3.** Most recently: *when I last saw her.* —*n.* **1.** Someone or something that is last: *ate all the chocolates but the last.* **2.** The end: *He held out to the last.* [SEE NOTE]
Idioms. **at last.** Finally. **at long last.** After a long time or wait.
last² |lăst| *or* |läst| *v.* **1.** To continue for a period of time: *The Wright brothers' first flight lasted twelve seconds.* **2.** To continue to be in existence; endure: *A few of the ancient Roman roads have lasted until today.* **3.** To be usable or enough for one's needs: *A battery like this lasts only a few weeks.* [SEE NOTE]
last³ |lăst| *or* |läst| *n.* A foot-shaped block used in making or repairing shoes. [SEE NOTE]
last•ing |lăs′tĭng| *or* |lä′stĭng| *adj.* Continuing or remaining for a long time; enduring: *a lasting peace between nations.*

lark¹⁻²
Lark¹ *was* lāwerce *in Old English.* **Lark²** *is probably a variant of an old dialectal word,* lake, *"to play."*

larva
Insect larvae

lash¹⁻²
Lash¹ *is of unknown origin, first appearing in the fourteenth century.* **Lash²** *is probably from Old French* lachier, *"to tie, entangle, ensnare"; it is related to* **lace.**

last¹⁻²⁻³
Last¹ *was* latost *in Old English;* latost *is the superlative of* læt, *"late," and* **last¹** *is therefore a doublet of* **latest** *(as* **latter** *is a doublet of* **later**). **Last²** *was* læstan *in Old English and meant "to go on, to continue"; it is descended from prehistoric Germanic* laistjan, *meaning "to follow a track or trail," from* laist-, *"track, trail, footprint."* **Last³** *was* läst *in Old English and meant "sole of the foot"; it is descended directly from Germanic* laist-, *"footprint," and is therefore a close relative of* **last².**

latch

latter

Many authorities, including most of the American Heritage Usage Panel, do not accept the use of **latter** *to refer to the* last-named *of three or more people or things. A rule of this kind, however, is more a matter of style than of grammatical correctness, and is often broken. The following sentence is from* A Christmas Carol, *by Charles Dickens: "Marley in his pigtail, usual waistcoat, tights, and boots; the tassels on the latter bristling, like his pigtail . . ."*

ă pat/ā pay/â care/ä father/ĕ pet/ ē be/ĭ pit/ī pie/î fierce/ŏ pot/ ō go/ô paw, for/oi oil/ŏŏ book/ ōō boot/ou out/ŭ cut/û fur/ *th* the/th thin/hw which/zh vision/ ə ago, item, pencil, atom, circus

last•ly |lăst′lē| *or* |läst′-| *adv.* At the end.

Last Supper. The last meal of Christ with his disciples before his arrest and crucifixion.

Las Ve•gas |läs vā′gəs|. A resort city in southern Nevada. Population, 125,000.

lat. latitude.

latch |lăch| *n.* A lock or catch consisting of a movable bar that fits into a notch or slot to fasten a door, gate, window, etc. —*v.* To close or lock with a latch: *Latch the door. Does the door latch securely?* [SEE PICTURE]

***Idiom.* latch on to** (or **onto**). To get hold of: *latch on to a new and popular political issue.*

latch•key |lăch′kē′| *n.* A key for opening a latch, especially one on a main or front door.

late |lāt| *adj.* **lat•er, lat•est. 1.** Coming, happening, or doing something after the expected, usual, or proper time; not on time or early; tardy: *late for his appointment.* **2.** Past or beyond the usual or accustomed time: *The road was dark and lonely, and it was very late.* **3.** Near or toward the end or more advanced part of a time period, series, etc.: *the late afternoon.* **4.** Of a time just past; recent: *This tractor is a late model.* **5.** Dead for a comparatively short time; recently deceased: *the late President Kennedy.* —*adv.* **lat•er, lat•est. 1.** After or beyond the usual, expected, or proper time: *The train arrived late.* **2.** At an advanced stage, place, etc.: *Our team scored the winning run late in the game.* **3.** Recently: *as late as last week.* —**late′ness** *n.*

***Idiom.* of late.** In the near past; recently.

late•com•er |lāt′kŭm′ər| *n.* Someone or something that arrives after the expected time or later than most or all others.

la•teen sail |lă tēn′|. A triangular sail hung on a long pole attached at an angle to a short mast.

Late Latin. Latin from the third to the seventh century A.D.

late•ly |lāt′lē| *adv.* Not long ago; recently.

la•tent |lāt′nt| *adj.* Present or capable of coming into existence but not evident or active: *latent talent; latent energy.* —**la′ten•cy** *n.*

latent heat. The heat gained or lost by a substance in changing between its solid and liquid states or liquid and gaseous states.

lat•er•al |lăt′ər əl| *adj.* On, of, toward, or from the side or sides: *a lateral motion of a machine part; a lateral pass in football.* —**lat′er•al•ly** *adv.*

la•tex |lā′tĕks′| *n.* **1.** The milky, sticky sap of certain trees and plants, such as the rubber tree. **2.** A synthetic preparation resembling this, used in paints, adhesives, and other products.

lath |lăth| *or* |läth| *n., pl.* **laths** |lă*th*z| *or* |lăths| *or* |lä*th*z| *or* |läths|. Any of a series of thin, narrow strips of wood or metal arranged to run parallel, usually as a supporting structure for plaster, shingles, tiles, etc.

lathe |lā*th*| *n.* A machine on which a piece of wood, metal, etc., is spun and shaped by a tool that cuts or wears it away. —*v.* **lathed, lath•ing.** To cut or shape on a lathe.

lath•er |lă*th*′ər| *n.* **1.** A thick, creamy foam formed by soap or detergent thoroughly mixed with water. **2.** Froth formed by heavy sweating, especially on a horse. **3.** *Informal.* A condition of impatient or troubled excitement. —*v.* **1.** To cover with lather: *lathered his chin and began shaving.* **2.** To produce or form lather.

Lat•in |lăt′n| *or* |-ĭn| *adj.* **1.** Of an ancient people of Italy who were among the original settlers of ancient Rome. **2.** Of or in the language of ancient Rome. **3.** Of those countries or peoples using the Romance languages that developed from the language of ancient Rome. —*n.* **1.** The Indo-European language of the ancient Romans. **2.** One of the people of southern Italy who were among the original settlers of ancient Rome. **3.** A member of a people who speak a Romance language.

Latin America. The countries of the Western Hemisphere south of the United States, having either Spanish or Portuguese as their official language. —**Latin American.**

Lat•in-A•mer•i•can |lăt′n ə mĕr′ĭ kən| *or* |lăt′-ĭn-| *adj.* Of Latin America.

lat•i•tude |lăt′ĭ to͞od′| *or* |-tyo͞od′| *n.* **1. a.** Distance north or south of the equator measured as the angle between the radius from the center of the earth to a point on its surface and the radius that intersects the equator and the meridian on which the point lies, usually expressed in degrees. **b.** A similar measure of angular distance applied to any more or less spherical celestial body, such as the moon or a planet. **2. latitudes.** A region of the earth indicated by its approximate latitude: *the polar latitudes; the middle latitudes.* **3.** Freedom from limitations, regulations, or restrictions; scope for action, making decisions, etc. —**lat′i•tu′di•nal** *adj.*

la•trine |lə trēn′| *n.* A communal toilet of the type often used in camps, military barracks, etc.

lat•ter |lăt′ər| *adj.* **1.** Being the second or second mentioned of two: *The latter place was easier to reach than the former.* In this sense the word *latter* is often used as a noun: *He worked closely with Theodore Roosevelt during the first years of the latter's Presidency.* **2.** Closer to the end: *the latter part of the book.* [SEE NOTE]

lat•ter-day |lăt′ər dā′| *adj.* Of the present or a time not long past; recent; modern: *television, computers, and other latter-day marvels.*

Latter-Day Saint. A Mormon.

lat•tice |lăt′ĭs| *n.* **1.** An open framework made of interwoven strips of wood, metal, etc., crossing at regular intervals. **2.** Something resembling this, as a window. —**lat′ticed** *adj.*

Lat•vi•a |lăt′vē ə|. A former country on the Baltic Sea, now a part of the Soviet Union.

Lat•vi•an |lăt′vē ən| *n.* **1.** A native or inhabitant of Latvia. **2.** The Baltic language of Latvia. —*adj.* Of Latvia, the Latvians, or their language.

laud |lôd| *v.* To praise highly.

laud•a•ble |lô′də bəl| *adj.* Deserving praise; praiseworthy; commendable: *Frankness is a laudable quality in a President.* —**laud′a•bly** *adv.*

lau•da•num |lôd′n əm| *n.* An alcohol solution of opium.

laud•a•to•ry |lô′də tôr′ē| *or* |-tōr′ē| *adj.* Expressing or giving praise: *laudatory remarks.*

laugh |lăf| *or* |läf| *v.* **1. a.** To make sounds and often face and body movements to express happiness, amusement, scorn, nervousness, etc. **b.** To say while making such sounds: *"You're so funny!" laughed Joel.* **2.** To make a sound resembling laughter: *Hyenas laughed in the distance.* **3.** To express or feel amusement, ridicule, or scorn: *Her eyes were laughing.* **4.** To drive by or as if by the force of laughter: *laugh your worries away.* —*n.* **1.** The act of laughing or a sound made in laughing. **2.** A cause or reason for laughing; a joke: *I just did it for a laugh.*

Idiom. **laugh up** (or **in**) **one's sleeve.** To be secretly amused, especially over the difficulties of another.

laugh•a•ble |lăf′ə bəl| *or* |lä′fə-| *adj.* Causing or likely to cause laughter, especially scornful laughter; ridiculous. —**laugh′a•bly** *adv.*

laughing gas. **Nitrous oxide.**

laughing jackass. A bird, the kookaburra.

laugh•ing•stock |lăf′ĭng stŏk′| *or* |lä′fĭng-| *n.* An object of mocking laughter, jokes, or ridicule.

laugh•ter |lăf′tər| *or* |läf′-| *n.* **1.** The act or sound of laughing. **2.** Happiness, amusement, etc., expressed by or as if by laughing: *The laughter in her eyes died when she saw him.*

launch[1] |lônch| *or* |länch| *v.* **1.** To move or set in motion with force: *launch a rocket into space.* **2.** To move (a boat or ship) into the water, either for the first time or after it has been out of water for a long period. **3. a.** To set or start into action: *launch a new research program.* **b.** To set out; make a start: *launched forth on a new career.* —*n.* The action or process of launching something, especially a rocket, spacecraft, etc. —***modifier:*** *launch operations.* [SEE NOTE]

launch[2] |lônch| *or* |länch| *n.* **1.** A relatively large open or partly covered motorboat. **2.** A large boat carried by ships of former times. [SEE NOTE]

launch pad. Also **launching pad.** The platform or base from which a rocket or space vehicle is launched.

launch vehicle. A booster for launching a spacecraft.

laun•der |lôn′dər| *or* |län′-| *v.* **1.** To wash or wash and iron (clothes, linens, etc.). **2.** To be capable of being washed: *This fabric launders easily and will not shrink.*

laun•dress |lôn′drĭs| *or* |län′-| *n.* A woman employed to wash and iron clothes, linens, etc.

Laun•dro•mat |lôn′drə măt′| *or* |län′-| *n.* A trademark for a commercial establishment to which people take their laundry to be washed and dried in coin-operated machines.

laun•dry |lôn′drē| *or* |län′-| *n., pl.* **laun•dries.** **1.** A place or business establishment where clothes, linens, etc., are washed. **2.** Clothes, linens, etc., that are to be washed or that have just been washed: *Sort the laundry by color.* —***modifier:*** *a laundry bag; the laundry room.*

lau•re•ate |lôr′ē ĭt| *n.* A person who has been awarded the highest honors for accomplishments in a field of endeavor, as in science or literature.

lau•rel |lôr′əl| *or* |lŏr′-| *n.* **1. a.** A shrub or tree with glossy, spicy-smelling evergreen leaves. **b.** Any of several similar shrubs or trees. See **mountain laurel.** **2. laurels.** Honors; glory; fame: *He won his laurels as a pioneer in space travel.* —***modifier:*** *a laurel wreath.* [SEE PICTURE]

Idioms. **look to (one's) laurels.** To guard against losing one's glory or high standing to another. **rest on (one's) laurels.** To remain satisfied with what one has already accomplished.

la•va |lä′və| *or* |lăv′ə| *n.* **1.** Molten rock that flows from a volcano or from a crack in the earth. **2.** The rock formed when this substance cools and hardens.

lav•a•to•ry |lăv′ə tôr′ē| *or* |-tōr′ē| *n., pl.* **lav•a•to•ries.** **1.** A room equipped with washing and toilet facilities, especially in a public building, institution, etc. **2.** A sink or washbowl used for washing the hands and face.

lave |lāv| *v.* **laved, lav•ing.** To wash or bathe.

lav•en•der |lăv′ən dər| *n.* **1. a.** A plant with small, fragrant purplish flowers that yield an oil used in making perfume. **b.** The fragrant dried flowers or leaves of this plant. **2.** A pale or light purple. —*adj.* Pale or light purple.

lav•ish |lăv′ĭsh| *adj.* **1.** Given or provided very plentifully: *a party with lavish refreshments.* **2.** Very generous or free in giving or using something: *Be lavish with praise.* **3.** Extravagantly luxurious, showy, etc.: *a lavish hotel.* —*v.* To give, bestow, spend, etc., freely, plentifully, or to excess: *She lavished praise and affection on her grandchildren.* —**lav′ish•ly** *adv.* —**lav′ish•ness** *n.*

law |lô| *n.* **1.** A rule established by a government, organized society, or another source of authority to regulate people's conduct or activities. **2.** A set or system of such rules. **3.** The force or authority of such a system of rules: *respect for law and order.* **4.** The study, body of knowledge, or profession relating to such rules and regulations: *a professor of law; the practice of law.* **5.** Someone or something representing the force or authority of the law: *a fugitive pursued by the law.* **6.** A statement or ruling that must be obeyed: *The king's word was law.* **7.** A generally accepted rule, principle, or practice: *the laws of grammar.* **8.** A scientific or mathematical statement or set of statements that is true under particular circumstances: *the law of gravity; the law of signs.* —***modifier:*** *law enforcement; a law student.*

Idiom. **lay down the law.** To make firm and authoritative statements that demand obedience or compliance.

law-a•bid•ing |lô′ə bī′dĭng| *adj.* Obeying or acting in accordance with the law: *law-abiding citizens.*

law•break•er |lô′brā′kər| *n.* A person who breaks the law.

law•ful |lô′fəl| *adj.* **1.** Allowed or established by law: *lawful acts.* **2.** Recognized by the law: *his lawful wife; a lawful marriage.* —**law′ful•ly** *adv.* —**law′ful•ness** *n.*

law•giv•er |lô′gĭv′ər| *n.* A person who establishes a set or system of laws for a people.

law•less |lô′lĭs| *adj.* **1.** Not governed or controlled by law: *There was a time when the West was wild and lawless.* **2.** Disregarding, disobeying, or violating the law: *a lawless mob; lawless acts.* —**law′less•ly** *adv.* —**law′less•ness** *n.*

law•mak•er |lô′mā′kər| *n.* A person who takes part in writing or passing laws; a legislator. —**law′mak′ing** *n.* & *adj.*

lawn[1] |lôn| *n.* A piece of ground, as near a house or in a park, planted with grass that is usually mowed regularly. [SEE NOTE]

lawn[2] |lôn| *n.* A very fine, thin fabric of cotton or linen. [SEE NOTE]

lawn•mow•er |lôn′mō′ər| *n.* Also **lawn mower.** A machine, either hand-operated or power-operated, for cutting grass.

launch[1-2]

Although one can **launch**[1] *a* **launch**[2], *the two words are completely unrelated.* **Launch**[1] *is from Old French* lancher *or* lancier, *"to throw"; it is related to* **lance. Launch**[2] *is from Portuguese* lancha, *"small, fast boat," which is from Malay* lancharan, *a kind of boat.*

laurels

lawn[1-2]

Lawn[1] *was earlier* laund, *and is borrowed from Old French* launde, *"rough grassy land, heath"; it is ultimately related to* **land. Lawn**[2] *is probably from* Laon, *the name of a linen-manufacturing town in France.*

law•ren•ci•um |lô rĕn′sē əm| *or* |lō-| *n.* Symbol **Lw** One of the elements, a metal first produced by bombarding californium isotopes with boron isotopes. It has a single isotope with mass number 257 and a half-life of 8 seconds. Atomic number 103.

law•suit |lô′so͞ot′| *n.* A question, claim, etc., brought before a court of law for settlement.

law•yer |lô′yər| *or* |loi′ər| *n.* A person who is trained and qualified to give legal advice to clients and represent them in court.

lax |lăks| *adj.* **lax•er, lax•est. 1.** Not strict; too lenient: *lax rules.* **2.** Careless; negligent: *lax about paying bills.* **3.** Loose; slack. **—lax′ly** *adv.* **—lax′ness** *n.*

lax•a•tive |lăk′sə tĭv| *n.* A medicine or a food that stimulates bowel movements. *—adj.* Having the effect of a laxative.

lax•i•ty |lăk′sĭ tē| *n.* The condition or quality of being lax; lack of strictness, careful concern, etc.

lay[1] |lā| *v.* **laid** |lād|, **lay•ing. 1. a.** To place or put, especially on a flat surface or in a horizontal position: *Ma laid the baby in the cradle.* **b.** To put or place in a certain position, condition, etc.: *Lay aside your hammer and rest awhile.* **2.** To place (oneself) in a lying or resting position: *Now I lay me down to sleep.* **3.** To put in place; install by putting down: *lay tiles for flooring.* **4.** To produce inside the body and bring forth (an egg or eggs): *lay eggs. Our hens stopped laying.* **5.** To cause to settle, subside, or stop being troublesome: *lay a ghost; lay the dust by hosing the driveway.* **6.** To arrange things on or for: *lay the table for dinner.* **7.** To form; prepare; establish: *We must lay our plans for tomorrow.* **8.** To set, as the action of a play or story. **9.** To impose: *lay a fine.* **10.** To put forth; present: *He laid his report before the Senate.* **11.** To place as important or significant: *lay emphasis on the differences between the words.* **12.** To assign; charge: *I lay the blame for the rumor on her gossiping.* **13.** To cause to be in a certain condition, relationship, etc.: *He laid himself open to trouble.* **14.** To knock down: *laid him on the ground with a single blow.* **15. a.** To place (a bet or wager): *laying bets on the outcome of the fight.* **b.** To bet; wager: *I'll lay $5 that his horse will win.* ***—phrasal verbs.*** **lay about** or **lay about (oneself).** To hit out in all directions. **lay aside.** To put away; abandon: *lay aside old prejudices.* **lay away. 1.** To save for future use. **2.** To reserve (merchandise) until wanted or paid for. **lay by.** To save for future needs. **lay down.** To set forth; establish: *lay down rules by which to live.* **lay in.** To get and store up (food, provisions, etc.): *laying in supplies for the winter.* **lay into.** *Informal.* To thrash or scold sharply. **lay low.** To bring to a condition of weakness, helplessness, or destruction. **lay off. 1.** To dismiss or suspend from a job. **2.** *Slang.* **a.** To stop teasing, criticizing, or picking on (someone). **b.** To stop using or doing something. **lay on.** To strike or attack with forceful blows. **lay open.** To slash or break open. **lay out. 1.** To arrange according to a plan: *laying out the streets and avenues of the nation's new capital.* **2.** To spend (money). **lay up. 1.** To store (supplies) for future needs. **2.** To keep in bed or out of action as a result of illness or injury. *—n.* **—lay of the land. 1.** The form or nature of an area of land. **2.** *Informal.* The general situation or outlook. ¶*These sound alike* **lay, lei[1]**. [SEE NOTE]

lay[1]/lie[1]
These two verbs, which in some contexts are easy to confuse, are closely related. The prehistoric Indo-European root leg- *had two meanings: (1) "to stretch oneself out on the ground, to recline" (intransitive); and (2) "to place (something) down on the ground, to put" (transitive). In Germanic, these two meanings were expressed by two separate verbs derived from the root* leg-*: (1)* ligjan *and (2)* lagjan; *they have remained separate but closely associated ever since. (1)* Ligjan *became Old English* licgan, *Middle English* ligen *or* lien, *Modern English* **lie[1]**. *(2)* Lagjan *became Old English* lecgan, *Middle English* leggen, *Modern English* **lay[1]**. **Lie[1]** *is still only* intransitive, **lay[1]** *is still only* transitive. *(***Lay[2]*** is the past tense of* **lie[1]**.*)*

lay[2] |lā|. Past tense of **lie** (recline or rest). ¶*These sound alike* **lay, lei[1]**.

lay[3] |lā| *adj.* **1.** Not of or belonging to the ordained religious clergy: *a lay missionary.* **2.** Not of or belonging to a particular profession requiring specialized knowledge or training: *a lay observer on the scientific expedition.* ¶*These sound alike* **lay, lei[1]**. [SEE NOTE]

lay[4] |lā| *n.* A poem or song that is simple in style and tells a story; a ballad. ¶*These sound alike* **lay, lei[1]**. [SEE NOTE]

lay[3-4]
Lay[3] *is from Old French* lai, *which is from Latin* lāicus, *from Greek* lāikos, *"of the people as opposed to priests," from* lāos, *"the people."* **Lay[4]** *is from Provençal* lais, *"ballad."*

lay•er |lā′ər| *n.* **1.** A single thickness, coating, or sheet of material spread out or covering a surface: *a layer of clouds; a cake with three layers.* **2.** Someone or something that lays something: *a carpet layer. That hen is a good layer.* *—v.* To form, arrange, or split into layers.

lay•ette |lā ĕt′| *n.* A complete set of clothing, bedding, and other supplies for a newborn child.

lay•man |lā′mən| *n., pl.* **-men** |-mən|. **1.** A person who does not have the specialized knowledge or training of a member of a profession or highly skilled occupation. **2.** A person who is not a member of the religious clergy.

lay•off |lā′ôf′| *or* |-ŏf′| *n.* **1. a.** A temporary dismissal of employees. **b.** The period of such unemployment. **2.** Any period of temporary inactivity: *His pitching was rusty because of the long layoff since last season.*

lay•out |lā′out′| *n.* A planned arrangement of parts or items, especially on a flat surface or single level: *the layout of an apartment; a page layout of printing and illustrations.*

laze |lāz| *v.* **lazed, laz•ing.** To lounge or relax lazily; loaf.

la•zy |lā′zē| *adj.* **la•zi•er, la•zi•est. 1.** Not willing to work or be energetic: *a lazy person.* **2.** Causing, expressing, or suggesting idleness or lack of energy: *lazy summer afternoons; a lazy yawn.* **3.** Slow-moving: *lazy clouds floating overhead.* **—la′zi•ly** *adv.* **—la′zi•ness** *n.*

lb, lb. pound (unit of weight).

l.c.d., L.C.D. lowest common denominator.

l.c.m., L.C.M. least common multiple.

lea |lē| *or* |lā| *n.* A meadow. ¶*These sound alike* **lea, lee.**

leach |lēch| *v.* **1.** To remove (soluble materials) from a substance by causing or allowing a liquid to wash through or over it: *Heavy rains leached minerals from the soil.* **2.** To cause or allow a liquid to wash through (a substance) and remove the soluble materials in it: *Heavy rains have leached the soil of minerals.* **3.** To pass (a liquid) through a substance so as to remove soluble materials. **4.** To be washed or washed out in this way. ¶*These sound alike* **leach, leech.**

lead[1] |lēd| *v.* **led** |lĕd|, **lead•ing. 1. a.** To show or guide along the way, as by going ahead or accompanying and giving directions: *The guide will lead us to the top of the mountain.* **b.** To show (the way) in this manner: *Betsy led the way. The scouts led, and we followed.* **2. a.** To guide or cause to move forward by taking by the hand, an attached rope or rein, etc. **b.** To be guided in this manner: *This pony is gentle and leads easily.* **3.** To be or form a way, route, or passage: *The trail leads to a little stream.* **4.** To guide as if by

ă pat/ā pay/â care/ä father/ĕ pet/ē be/ĭ pit/ī pie/î fierce/ŏ pot/ō go/ô paw, for/oi oil/o͝o book/o͞o boot/ou out/ŭ cut/û fur/*th* the/th thin/hw which/zh vision/ə ago, item, pencil, atom, circus

showing or taking along a way or route: *This path will lead us home.* **5.** To go at the head of a group: *lead a procession.* **6.** To be at the head of an undertaking or a group engaged in an undertaking, activity, etc.; act as leader of: *lead an expedition.* **7.** To be ahead of or ahead: *leading all the other runners; leading by a score of 10 to 4.* **8.** To cause to follow a line of thought, action, etc.; influence or direct: *His sincerity leads me to believe he is telling the truth.* **9. lead to.** To tend toward or result in: *Commerce led to the development of cities.* **10.** To live; experience: *He leads a rough and vigorous life.* **11.** To direct the performance of (a group of musicians); conduct: *lead an orchestra.* **12.** To make the first or beginning motion: *Gallop to the music, leading with your right foot.* —**phrasal verbs. lead off.** To begin; start; open. **lead (someone) on.** To tempt or lure (someone) into doing something unwise or believing something untrue. **lead up to.** To introduce or prepare the way for (something), as by a long series of hints or remarks. —*n.* **1.** The front, foremost, or winning position: *Our team took the lead in the game.* **2.** The amount by which one is ahead: *a five-point lead.* **3.** Action or a way of thinking that influences others to follow; leadership: *They followed his lead and voted against the amendment.* **4.** Something that serves as useful information; a clue or hint: *leads that helped solve the problem.* **5.** The main part in a play, moving picture, musical performance, etc. **6.** The opening sentence, lines, or paragraph of a news story. **7.** A rope, leash, etc., for leading an animal. **8.** An electrical conductor, usually a wire, by which a device or circuit element can be connected to other components of a circuit. —**modifier:** *the lead dog of a team; a lead rope.* ¶*These sound alike* **lead[1], lied.** [SEE NOTE]

lead[2] |lĕd| *n.* **1.** Symbol **Pb** One of the elements, a soft, heavy, dull-gray metal. Atomic number 82; atomic weight 207.19; valences +2, +4; melting point 327.5°C; boiling point 1,744°C. **2.** A material, often basically graphite, used as the writing substance in pencils. **3.** A piece of lead or other metal attached to a length of line, used in measuring depths. **4.** A strip of metal used in printing to separate lines of type or keep them in place. —**modifier:** *a lead tube; a lead mine; a lead pencil.* —*v.* To cover, join, weight, etc., with lead. —**lead'ed** *adj.*: *leaded window panes.* ¶*These sound alike* **lead[2], led.** [SEE NOTE]

lead arsenate. A poisonous white crystalline compound, $Pb_3(AsO_4)_2$, used in insecticides.

lead•en |lĕd'n| *adj.* **1.** Made of lead. **2.** Dull, dark gray: *leaden skies.* **3.** Feeling as if weighted, burdened, or heavy: *leaden feet.* **4.** Gloomy; depressing: *a leaden future.*

lead•er |lē'dər| *n.* Someone or something that leads: *the party's leader; a born leader.*

lead•er•ship |lē'dər shĭp'| *n.* **1.** The position of a leader. **2.** The guidance or command of a leader or leaders: *under the leadership of skillful engineers.* **3.** Ability to act as a leader: *He has shown strong leadership.*

lead•ing[1] |lē'dĭng| *adj.* **1.** In the first or front position: *the leading horse in a race.* **2.** Most important; main; foremost: *the leading countries in making cars.* **3.** Designed to encourage a desired response: *a leading question.* [SEE NOTE]

lead•ing[2] |lĕd'ĭng| *n.* Strips of lead used to join windowpanes or to separate lines of type or keep them in place. [SEE NOTE]

leaf |lēf| *n., pl.* **leaves** |lēvz|. **1.** A usually thin, flat, green plant part attached to a stem or stalk. The vital process of photosynthesis takes place mainly in the leaves of green plants. **2.** A leaflike part, such as a petal. **3.** The condition of having leaves: *trees bursting into leaf.* **4.** One of the sheets of paper forming the pages of a book, magazine, notebook, etc. **5.** A very thin sheet of metal: *gold leaf.* **6.** A flat, movable part, as one opened out from or put into a table to make it larger. —**modifier:** *leaf clusters; leaf tissue.* —*v.* **1.** To produce or put forth leaves. **2.** To turn or glance at pages, sheets of paper, etc.: *leaf through a book.* ¶*These sound alike* **leaf, lief.** —**leaf'less** *adj.* [SEE PICTURE]

***Idioms.* take a leaf from (someone's) book.** To follow someone's example. **turn over a new leaf.** To make a fresh start by deciding to improve one's ways.

leaf•let |lēf'lĭt| *n.* **1.** A small leaf or leaflike part, especially one of the divisions of a compound leaf, as of a clover. **2.** A booklet, small pamphlet, etc.

leaf•stalk |lēf'stôk'| *n.* The stalk by which a leaf is attached to a stem.

leaf•y |lē'fē| *adj.* **leaf•i•er, leaf•i•est. 1.** Having many leaves; covered with leaves: *leafy branches.* **2.** Consisting of leaves: *leafy vegetables.* **3.** Of or like leaves: *a leafy green.*

league[1] |lēg| *n.* **1.** A group of nations, people, organizations, etc., acting or working together in an alliance or association. **2.** An association of sports teams or clubs that compete chiefly among themselves: *the major baseball leagues.* —**modifier:** *the league champions.* —*v.* **leagued, lea•guing.** To form an association or alliance: *The tribes leagued together to assist one another.* [SEE NOTE]

***Idiom.* in league.** Joined or working together.

league[2] |lēg| *n.* Any of several approximately equal units of distance, especially one equal to three miles. [SEE NOTE]

League of Nations. An organization of nations established after World War I to preserve peace.

lea•guer |lē'gər| *n. Informal.* Someone who belongs to a sports league: *the Little Leaguers.*

leak |lēk| *n.* **1.** A hole, crack, or similar break or opening through which something meant to be kept in or out can escape or pass: *plug up the leak in the gas pipe.* **2.** An escape or passage of something through or as if through such an opening or break: *We can't stop the leak in the gas pipes. There was a leak in the security system.* —*v.* **1.** To escape or pass accidentally or unexpectedly through or as if through an opening or break: *Water leaked from the rusty pail.* **2.** To allow (something) to escape or pass through an opening or openings: *a pipe that leaks water. The boat struck a rock and began to leak.* **3.** To become or allow to be known through accident or a deliberate break in secrecy: *The news leaked out. He leaked the information to the newspapers.* ¶*These sound alike* **leak, leek.**

leak•age |lē'kĭj| *n.* **1.** The process of leaking.

lead[1-2]/leading[1-2]

Lead[1] *was* lǣdan *in Old English.* **Lead[2]** *was Old English* lēad, *and is probably borrowed from Celtic.* **Leading[1]** *and* **leading[2]** *are from* **lead[1]** *and* **lead[2]**, *respectively.*

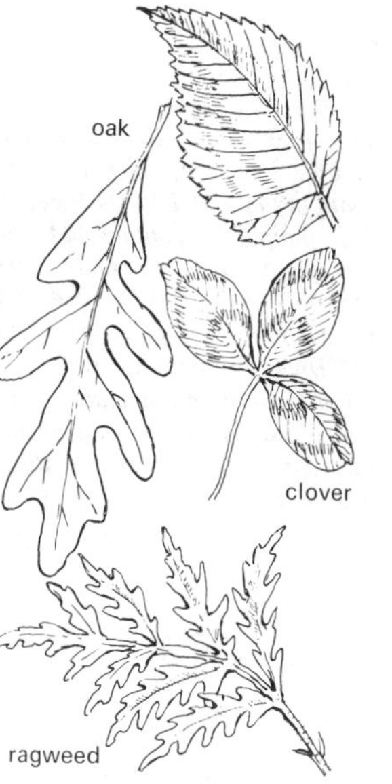

leaf

league[1-2]

League[1] *is from Old French* ligue, *which is from Italian* liga, *"a group that is tied together by promises"; it is related to* **ligature** *and* **oblige. League[2]** *is from Late Latin* leuga, *a Celtic measure of distance.*

lean[1-2]

Lean[1] *was* hlinian *in Old English; it is descended from prehistoric Germanic* hlin-, *which in turn is from the Indo-European root* klin-, *still meaning "to lean." Notice that an Indo-European* k- *always became a Germanic* h-. *Separately, the root* klin- *appears in Latin as* -clīnāre, *"to lean," from which we have* **decline, incline, recline**; *all these are thus cognates of* **lean[1]**. **Lean[2]** *was* hlæne *in Old English; it is not related to* **lean[1]**.

leap

The prehistoric Germanic verb hlaupa, *"to run, to jump," appears in (1) Old English* hlēapan, *"to jump," becoming Modern English* **leap**; *(2) Old Norse* hlaupa, *"to run," which was borrowed into English as* **lope**; *and (3) Dutch* lopen, *"to run." The original Germanic language often had a full* h *before consonants; this aspirate has entirely disappeared in Modern English and in most of the other modern Germanic languages.*

leapfrog

ă pat/ā pay/â care/ä father/ĕ pet/ē be/ĭ pit/ī pie/î fierce/ŏ pot/ō go/ô paw, for/oi **oil**/o͝o book/o͞o boot/ou **out**/ŭ cut/û **fur**/*th* **the**/th **thin**/hw **which**/**zh** vision/ə ago, item, pencil, atom, circus

2. a. Something that escapes or enters by leaking. **b.** The amount that leaks in or out.

leak•y |lē′kē| *adj.* **leak•i•er, leak•i•est.** Having, allowing, or tending to allow a leak or leaks: *a leaky container; a leaky valve.*

lean[1] |lēn| *v.* **leaned** or **leant** |lĕnt|, **lean•ing.** **1.** To bend or incline (the body or a part of the body): *leaned her head forward to hear better.* **2.** To slant from an upright or perpendicular position: *His handwriting leans to the right.* **3.** To rest one's weight or to place so as to be supported: *leaned heavily on his cane as he limped along.* **4.** To rely, as for assistance or support; depend: *He leans on his friends when he is in trouble.* **5.** To have a tendency or preference: *He leans toward socialism.* —*n.* A slant or inclination: *the lean of that high cliff.* ¶*These sound alike* **lean, lien.** [SEE NOTE]

lean[2] |lēn| *adj.* **lean•er, lean•est.** **1.** Not fat or fleshy; thin: *a lean cat.* **2.** Containing little or no fat: *lean meat.* **3.** Not productive, plentiful, or satisfying: *the lean years of the depression.* —*n.* Meat with little or no fat. ¶*These sound alike* **lean, lien.** —**lean′ness** *n.* [SEE NOTE]

lean•ing |lē′nĭng| *n.* A tendency; preference.

leant |lĕnt|. A past tense and past participle of **lean** (to bend or incline).

lean-to |lēn′to͞o′| *n., pl.* **lean-tos.** **1.** A shed with a sloping roof, built against a wall or the side of a building. **2.** A simple shelter, often having a sloping roof resting on the ground at one side and raised on poles at the other.

leap |lēp| *v.* **leaped** or **leapt** |lĕpt| *or* |lēpt|, **leap•ing.** **1.** To move with a sudden, springing motion; jump or bound. **2.** To move or seem to move with a similar sudden or rapid motion: *The fire leaped into flame. My heart leaps with joy.* **3. a.** To jump or spring over: *Salmon often leap waterfalls.* **b.** To cause to jump: *leap a horse over a fence.* —*n.* **1.** The act of leaping; a spring, jump, or bound. **2.** The distance covered or progress made by or as if by such a movement: *a leap of ten feet.* [SEE NOTE]

Idiom. **by leaps and bounds.** By increasing or advancing very rapidly: *The little orchestra grew by leaps and bounds.*

leap•frog |lēp′frŏg′| *or* |-frōg′| *n.* A game in which players take turns bending over and then leaping with the legs astraddle the next player. [SEE PICTURE]

leapt |lĕpt| *or* |lēpt|. A past tense and past participle of **leap.**

leap year. A year in which there are 366 days, the extra day, February 29, being added to make up for the fact that the astronomical year is about one quarter of a day longer than the usual calendar year.

learn |lûrn| *v.* **learned** or **learnt** |lûrnt|, **learn•ing.** **1. a.** To gain knowledge or skill through study or experience: *learning French; learning to swim.* **b.** To gain knowledge of or skill in: *Spoken English is the form of the language we learn first.* **2.** To become informed; find out: *learned from the newspaper that Sunday's game was a doubleheader.* **3.** To acquire through experience: *learning bad habits.* **4.** To fix in the mind; memorize: *After you have learned the tune, add the words.* —**learn′er** *n.*

learn•ed |lûr′nĭd| *adj.* Having or showing deep knowledge; scholarly. —**learn′ed•ly** *adv.*

learn•ing |lûr′nĭng| *n.* **1.** Instruction; education: *a real hunger for learning.* **2.** Thorough knowledge gained by study: *men of learning.*

learnt |lûrnt|. A past tense and past participle of **learn.**

lease |lēs| *n.* **1. a.** A written agreement by which an owner of property grants the use of it to someone else for a certain time in exchange for rent. **b.** The period of time specified in such an agreement. **2.** An extension with better prospects: *a new lease on life.* —*v.* **leased, leas•ing.** **1.** To grant the use of (property) by lease: *lease tractors.* **2.** To acquire or hold (property) by lease: *lease a house.*

leash |lēsh| *n.* A cord, chain, or strap attached to a collar or harness and used to hold or lead a dog or other animal. —*v.* **1.** To hold, lead, or restrain with a leash: *Leash your dog.* **2.** To limit the freedom of; control: *leashed his feelings.*

least |lēst|. A superlative of **little.** —*adj.* **1.** Smallest in degree or size: *I haven't got the least intention of doing that.* **2.** Lowest in importance or rank: *The prize money was scrupulously distributed to all according to rank down to the least cabin boy.* —*adv.* Superlative of **little.** To the smallest degree: *the least skillful carpenter around; liked vanilla ice cream best and strawberry least.* —*n.* **1.** The smallest in size or importance: *The least of them spoke up boldly when encouraged.* **2.** The smallest appropriate thing: *The least you could do would be to apologize.*

Idioms. **at least.** **1.** No less than: *I go to the post office at least once a day.* **2.** In any event; anyway: *At least he got home safe.* **in the least.** At all: *I don't mind in the least.*

least common denominator. A **lowest common denominator.**

least common multiple. The smallest number that is a common multiple of two other numbers; for example, 12 is the least common multiple of 3 and 4.

leath•er |lĕth′ər| *n.* A material made by cleaning and tanning the skin or hide of an animal and preparing it for use. —*modifier: a leather jacket.*

leath•ern |lĕth′ərn| *adj. Archaic.* Made of or resembling leather.

leath•er•y |lĕth′ə rē| *adj.* Like leather; tough and hardened: *leathery hands.*

leave[1] |lēv| *v.* **left** |lĕft|, **leav•ing.** **1.** To depart; go away from (a place): *leaving before the sun is up; left town on Thursday.* **2.** To go without taking; forget: *She left her umbrella on the train.* **3.** To allow to remain unchanged or unused: *Leave an opening in the front for the garment's neck.* **4.** To allow to remain in a certain condition or place: *left her bed unmade again.* **5.** To cause to remain after a loss or reduction: *all the strength left in him; no teeth left.* **6.** To affect in a specified way: *a fall that shook him up but left him unhurt.* **7.** To place, give, or deliver before going: *leave a pan of water in the yard for the birds.* **8.** To give to another to do or use; entrust: *leaving the mission in the hands of an assistant.* **9.** To give for the benefit of survivors or followers; bequeath: *left 400 paintings to the museum.* **10.** To deposit before going: *a fine, almost invisible thread left by a spider.* **11.** To have as a result or aftermath: *The hurricane left incalculable destruction in its wake.* —***phrasal verbs.*** **leave alone.** To stop annoying or troubling. **leave behind.** To go or advance well ahead of or beyond: *left behind the other runners; looked back as we were leaving the town behind.* **leave off.** To cease: *hard to know where one leaves off and another begins.* **leave out.** To fail to include; omit: *leaving out unimportant details.* [SEE NOTE]

leave[2] |lēv| *n.* **1.** Permission: *leave to stay out until midnight.* **2. a.** Official permission to be absent from duty for a fairly long time. **b.** An absence of this kind: *on leave.* **c.** The length of such an absence. **3.** A formal farewell: *took leave of his friends and departed.* [SEE NOTE]

leaved |lēvd| *adj.* Having a certain number or kind of leaves: *a four-leaved clover.*

leav•en |lĕv′ən| *n.* **1.** A fermenting substance, such as yeast, used to cause dough or batter to rise. **2.** Something added to lighten or enliven the whole: *the leaven of wit.* —*v.* **1.** To add yeast or another fermenting agent to (dough or batter). **2.** To enliven. —**leav′ened** *adj.: leavened bread.*

leav•en•ing |lĕv′ə nĭng| *n.* Leaven.

leaves |lēvz| *n.* Plural of **leaf.**

leave-tak•ing |lēv′tā′kĭng| *n.* An exchange of good-bys; a farewell.

leav•ings |lē′vĭngz| *pl.n.* Bits left over; remains: *the turkey leavings.*

Leb•a•non |lĕb′ə nən|. A country in the Middle East, at the eastern end of the Mediterranean Sea. Population, 3,000,000. Capital, Beirut. —**Leb′a•nese′** |lĕb′ə **nēz′**| *or* |**-nēs′**| *adj. & n.*

lech•er |lĕch′ər| *n.* A man given to excessive sexual activity.

lech•er•ous |lĕch′ər əs| *adj.* Preoccupied with thoughts of sexual activity. —**lech′er•ous•ly** *adv.* —**lech′er•ous•ness** *n.*

lech•er•y |lĕch′ə rē| *n.* Excessive sexual activity.

lec•tern |lĕk′tərn| *n.* A tall desk, often with a slanted top, that serves as a support for the notes or books of a speaker. [SEE PICTURE]

lec•ture |lĕk′chər| *n.* **1.** A speech providing information about a given subject, delivered before an audience or class. **2.** A serious, lengthy warning or reproof. —***modifier:*** *a lecture tour; a lecture hall.* —*v.* **lec•tured, lec•tur•ing. 1.** To deliver a lecture or lectures: *lecturing on electricity at the university.* **2.** To give a lecture to (a class or audience). **3.** To scold or warn at length. —**lec′tur•er** *n.*

led |lĕd|. Past tense and past participle of **lead** (show or guide). ¶*These sound alike* **led, lead[2].**

ledge |lĕj| *n.* **1.** A cut or projection forming a flat space on the side of a cliff or rock wall. **2.** The rim or edge of a cliff. **3.** A narrow shelf projecting from a wall: *a window ledge.* **4.** A raised edge serving to enclose or protect.

ledg•er |lĕj′ər| *n.* An account book in which sums of money received and paid out by a business are recorded.

lee |lē| *n.* The side that is turned away from the wind; the sheltered side: *a ship's lee; in the lee of the island.* —*adj.* **1.** Away from the wind: *Fires should be built on the lee side.* **2.** Lying on the side of a ship toward which the ship is being driven by the wind: *a dangerous lee shore.* ¶*These sound alike* **lee, lea.**

Lee |lē|, **Robert E(dward).** 1807–1870. Commander in chief of Confederate armies in the Civil War.

leech |lēch| *n.* **1.** A worm that lives in water and sucks blood from other animals, including human beings. **2.** A person who constantly clings to or gains profit from someone else; a parasite. ¶*These sound alike* **leech, leach.**

leek |lēk| *n.* A vegetable related to the onion, having a narrow white bulb and long, dark-green leaves. ¶*These sound alike* **leek, leak.**

leer |lîr| *n.* An insulting, lustful, or nasty look; an arrogant or contemptuous glance. —*v.* To look with a leer: *The torturer leered at his victim.*

leer•y |lîr′ē| *adj.* **leer•i•er, leer•i•est.** *Informal.* Suspicious; wary. —**leer′i•ly** *adv.*

lees |lēz| *pl.n.* Dregs that settle during fermentation, especially in wine.

lee•ward |lē′wərd| *or* |lo͞o′ərd| *adj.* Facing away from the wind; downwind: *the leeward quarter.* —*adv.: passing leeward of the reef.* —*n.* The lee side: *a whale to leeward of us.*

Lee•ward Islands |lē′wərd|. A group of islands in the West Indies, forming the northern half of the Lesser Antilles and including the Virgin Islands and other small islands.

lee•way |lē′wā′| *n.* **1.** The drift of a ship or plane to leeward of its course. **2.** Space or time free for maneuvering, changing plans, etc.

left[1] |lĕft| *n.* **1. a.** The side from which one begins to read a line of English. **b.** The corresponding side of anything: *The number 9 is on the left of a clock face.* **c.** The direction of this side: *The heart lies just behind and to the left of the breastbone.* **2.** Often **the Left.** The political parties and spokesmen that seek changes toward more social equality, greater power for citizens in government, or socialism, either by reform or by revolution. —*adj.* **1.** Located on the left: *the left hand.* **2.** Done to the left: *a left turn.* —*adv.* On or to the left. [SEE PICTURE]

left[2] |lĕft|. Past tense and past participle of **leave** (go away).

left field. 1. The third of the outfield in baseball that is to the left, looking from home plate. **2.** The position played by the left fielder.

left fielder. The baseball player who defends left field.

left-hand |lĕft′hănd′| *adj.* **1.** Located on the left: *the upper left-hand corner.* **2.** Turning from right to left: *a screw with left-hand threads.*

left-hand•ed |lĕft′hăn′dĭd| *adj.* **1.** Using the left hand, as for writing, working, or throwing, more easily and naturally than the right hand. **2.** Designed for use by the left hand: *a left-handed monkey wrench.* **3.** Turning or spiraling from right to left: *a left-handed conch.* **4.** Awkward; clumsy: *a left-handed apology.* **5.** Doubtful in meaning or sincerity; ambiguous: *a left-handed compliment.* —*adv.* With the left hand.

left-hand•er |lĕft′hăn′dər| *n.* A person who is left-handed.

left•ist |lĕf′tĭst| *n.* A person with political views associated with the left; a liberal or radical. —*adj.* Of the political left: *leftist publications.*

left•o•ver or **left-o•ver** |lĕft′ō′vər| *n.* Often **leftovers.** Something remaining unused or uneaten: *had leftovers for dinner.* —*adj.* Remaining unused or uneaten: *leftover fabric; leftover rice.*

leave[1-2]
Leave[1] *was* lǣfan *in Old English, and* **leave[2]** *was* lēaf; *they are not related.*

lectern
Eighteenth-century American

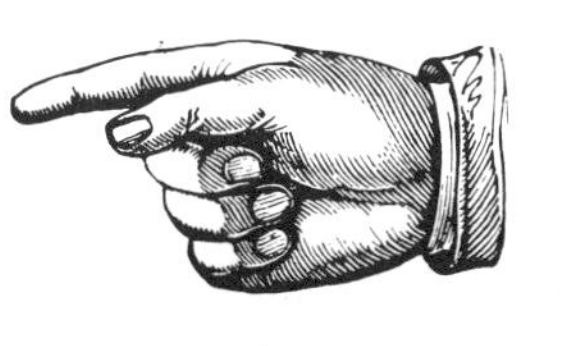

left[1]

left wing. **1.** The political left. **2.** Those people within any group who are relatively more active in seeking progressive change: *the Republican left wing.*

left-wing |lĕft′wĭng′| *adj.* Of the left wing: *a left-wing newspaper.*

left-wing•er |lĕft′wĭng′ər| *n.* A member of the left wing.

left•y |lĕf′tē| *n., pl.* **left•ies.** *Slang.* A person who is left-handed.

leg |lĕg| *n.* **1.** A limb or other projection of the body of an animal that the animal uses in supporting itself or in moving about. **2.** Either of the lower or hind limbs of a human being, ape, monkey, etc. **3.** One of the parts of a pair of trousers or stockings that fits around the leg. **4.** A projecting part of something on which it stands: *a table leg.* **5.** One of the extended parts of a forked or jointed object: *One leg of the compass holds a pencil.* **6.** Either of the sides of a right triangle that meet to form the right angle. **7.** A stage of a journey or course: *the first leg of a relay race.* —***modifier:*** *leg muscles.* —*v.* **legged, leg•ging.** To go on foot; walk or run: *I legged it over to the gymnasium.*

Idioms. **on (one's) last legs.** At the end of one's strength; ready to collapse. **pull (someone's) leg.** *Informal.* To deceive in fun; tease; kid.

leg•a•cy |lĕg′ə sē| *n., pl.* **leg•a•cies.** **1.** Money or property left to someone in a will. **2.** Something passed on to those who come later in time; heritage: *a legacy of military strength.*

le•gal |lē′gəl| *adj.* **1.** Of or for the administration, procedures, or profession of the law: *legal training.* **2.** Authorized or set down by law: *the legal heir.* **3.** Permitted by law: *legal activities.* —**le′gal•ly** *adv.*

le•gal•i•ty |lĭ găl′ĭ tē| *n., pl.* **le•gal•i•ties.** **1.** The fact of being legal; lawfulness. **2.** A requirement of the law.

le•gal•ize |lē′gə līz′| *v.* **le•gal•ized, le•gal•iz•ing.** To make legal. —**le′gal•i•za′tion** *n.*

legal tender. Currency that must legally be accepted in payment of a debt.

leg•ate |lĕg′ĭt| *n.* An official envoy or ambassador, especially one representing the pope.

le•ga•tion |lĭ gā′shən| *n.* **1.** A diplomatic mission in a foreign country, ranking below an embassy. **2.** The building occupied by such a mission.

le•ga•to |lə gä′tō|. In music: *adj.* In a smooth, even style of playing or singing. —*adv.* In a smooth, even manner. —*n., pl.* **le•ga•tos.** A style of performance in which the tones are joined smoothly.

leg•end |lĕj′ənd| *n.* **1. a.** A story of uncertain truthfulness handed down from earlier times. **b.** A group of such stories or all such stories of the remote past: *a giant in Norse legend.* **2.** An inscription on a coin, banner, or other object. **3.** An explanatory caption or note under a map, chart, etc.

leg•en•dar•y |lĕj′ən dĕr′ē| *adj.* **1.** Based on or told of in legends: *legendary history; legendary heroes.* **2.** Talked about frequently; famous: *His rages were legendary.*

leg•er•de•main |lĕj′ər də mān′| *n.* **1.** Tricks performed with the hands, as by a juggler or magician. **2.** Any deception or trickery.

leg•ged |lĕg′ĭd| *or* |lĕgd| *adj.* Having a certain kind or number of legs: *a bony-legged boy; four-legged animals.*

leg•gings |lĕg′ĭngz| *n.* A leg covering of cloth or leather, usually extending from the waist or knee to the ankle.

leg•gy |lĕg′ē| *adj.* **leg•gi•er, leg•gi•est.** **1.** Having long, awkward legs: *a gangling, leggy boy.* **2.** Having attractively long and slender legs.

leg•horn |lĕg′hôrn′| *or* |-ərn| *n.* Often **Leghorn.** One of a breed of white chickens raised especially for eggs.

leg•i•ble |lĕj′ə bəl| *adj.* Capable of being read: *legible handwriting.* —**leg′i•bil′i•ty, leg′i•ble•ness** *n.* —**leg′i•bly** *adv.*

le•gion |lē′jən| *n.* **1.** The major unit of the ancient Roman army, consisting of at least 3,000 foot soldiers and 100 calvalrymen. **2.** Any of several large military divisions of modern times. **3.** A large group or number of persons, things, etc.: *legions of insects.* **4.** Often **Legion.** Any of various military or citizens' organizations: *the American Legion; the Foreign Legion.*

leg•is•late |lĕj′ĭs lāt′| *v.* **leg•is•lat•ed, leg•is•lat•ing.** **1.** To pass laws. **2. a.** To enact into law: *legislate reforms in the housing code.* **b.** To bring about by enacting laws: *legislated a commission to investigate urban problems.*

leg•is•la•tion |lĕj′ĭs lā′shən| *n.* **1.** The act or process of making laws. **2.** A proposed or enacted law or group of laws: *legislation pending before Congress.*

leg•is•la•tive |lĕj′ĭs lā′tĭv| *adj.* **1.** Of making laws: *legislative powers.* **2.** Of or relating to a body of people who make laws: *legislative goals.* **3.** Having power to make laws: *the legislative branch of government.*

leg•is•la•tor |lĕj′ĭs lā′tər| *n.* A member of a body that makes laws: *our legislators in Congress.*

leg•is•la•ture |lĕj′ĭs lā′chər| *n.* A body of persons empowered to make and change the laws of a nation or state.

le•git•i•mate |lə jĭt′ə mĭt| *adj.* **1.** Being or acting in accordance with the law; lawful: *the legitimate monarch.* **2.** Supported by logic or common sense; reasonable: *legitimate reason for his absence.* **3.** Authentic; genuine; real: *voicing many legitimate complaints.* **4.** Born of legally married parents: *a legitimate child.* —**le•git′i•mate•ly** *adv.* —**le•git′i•ma•cy** |-mə sē| *n.*

leg•ume |lĕg′yo͞om′| *or* |lə gyo͞om′| *n.* **1.** Any of a group of related pod-bearing plants that includes the beans, peas, clover, and alfalfa. **2.** Often **legumes.** The pod or seeds of such a plant, especially when used as food. —**le•gu′mi•nous** *adj.*

leg warmers. Knitted leggings that extend from the ankles to the upper thighs.

lei[1] |lā| *or* |lā′ē| *n.* A garland of flowers such as is worn around the neck in Hawaii. ¶*These sound alike* **lei**[1], **lay.** [SEE PICTURE]

lei[1]

le•i[2] |lĕ′ĭ| *n.* Plural of **leu.**

lei•sure |lē′zhər| *or* |lĕzh′ər| *n.* Freedom from work or time-consuming tasks; time in which to do as one pleases: *devoting his leisure to stamp collecting.* —***modifier:*** *leisure time.*

Idioms. **at leisure.** **1.** Not occupied; free. **2.** In one's spare time. **at (one's) leisure.** At one's convenience; when one has free time.

ă pat/ā pay/â care/ä father/ĕ pet/ ē be/ĭ pit/ī pie/î fierce/ŏ pot/ ō go/ô paw, for/oi oil/o͝o book/ o͞o boot/ou out/ŭ cut/û fur/ *th* the/th thin/hw which/zh vision/ ə ago, item, pencil, atom, circus

lei•sure•ly |lē′zhər lē| *or* |**lĕzh′**ər-| *adj.* Without haste or exertion; unhurried: *a leisurely lunch.* —*adv.* At an unhurried pace; slowly: *cruised leisurely toward town.* —**lei′sure•li•ness** *n.*

lek |lĕk| *n.* The basic unit of money of Albania.

lem•ming |**lĕm′**ĭng| *n.* A short-tailed animal of northern regions, related to the rats and mice. [SEE PICTURE]

lem•on |**lĕm′**ən| *n.* **1. a.** An egg-shaped yellow fruit related to the orange, lime, and grapefruit, having sour, juicy pulp. **b.** A tree that bears such fruit. **2.** Also **lemon yellow.** A bright, clear yellow. **3.** *Informal.* Something or someone that turns out to be disappointing. —***modifier:*** *lemon juice; a lemon pie.* —*adj.* Bright, clear yellow.

lem•on•ade |lĕm′ə **nād′**| *n.* A drink made of lemon juice, water, and sugar.

lem•pi•ra |lĕm **pîr′**ə| *n.* The basic unit of money of Honduras.

le•mur |**lē′**mər| *n.* A small, monkeylike animal of the island of Madagascar, having large eyes, soft fur, and a long tail. [SEE PICTURE]

Len•a•pe |**lĕn′**ə pē| *n.* An Indian tribe, the Delaware.

lend |lĕnd| *v.* **lent** |lĕnt|, **lend•ing. 1.** To give or allow the use of (something) with the understanding that it is to be returned: *Mother lent me her pink shawl for the party.* **2.** To provide (money) temporarily, usually at a certain rate of interest. **3.** To contribute; impart: *Chlorophyll lends its green color to most plants.* **4.** To put to another's service or use: *The neighbors lent a helping hand.* —**lend′er** *n.*

Idiom. **lend (oneself) to.** To be suitable for: *laws that lend themselves to various interpretations.*

length |lĕngkth| *or* |lĕngth| *n.* **1.** The measured distance from one end of a thing to the other along its greatest dimension: *the length of a boat.* **2.** The full extent of something long or stretched out: *traveled the length of the Nile River.* **3.** An extent to which an action or policy is carried; an extreme: *The planners went to great lengths to restore Williamsburg in every important detail.* **4.** The measure of something used as a unit to estimate distances: *two arm's lengths.* **5.** A piece, usually measured to a certain size, cut from a larger piece: *a length of wire; a length of silk.* **6.** The extent or duration of something: *the length of a club meeting.*

Idioms. **at length. 1.** After some time; eventually. **2.** Without being restricted in time or space; fully: *spoke at length.* **keep at arm's length.** To treat with reserve or suspicion.

length•en |**lĕngk′**thən| *or* |**lĕng′**-| *v.* To make or become longer: *lengthen a dress; shadows that lengthen as sunset approaches.*

length•wise |**lĕngkth′**wīz′| *or* |**lĕngth′**-| *adv.* Along the direction of the length: *Fold a sheet of paper lengthwise.* —*adj.: lengthwise pleats.*

length•y |**lĕngk′**thē| *or* |**lĕng′**-| *adj.* **length•i•er, length•i•est. 1.** Lasting a long time: *a lengthy explanation.* **2.** Extending for a long distance or a great space: *a lengthy route.* —**length′i•ly** *adv.*

le•ni•ent |**lē′**nē ənt| *or* |**lēn′**yənt| *adj.* **1.** Inclined to forgive; merciful: *a lenient judge.* **2.** Not strict or demanding; generous: *lenient rules.* —**le′ni•en•cy, le′ni•ence** *n.* —**le′ni•ent•ly** *adv.*

Len•i-Len•a•pe |lĕn′ē **lĕn′**ə pē| *n.* A form of the word **Lenape.**

Len•in |**lĕn′**ĭn| *or* |-ēn′|, **Vladimir Ilyich.** 1870–1924. Russian revolutionary leader and founder of the modern Soviet state.

Len•in•grad |**lĕn′**ĭn grăd′|. The second-largest city in the Soviet Union. Population, 4,313,000.

lens |lĕnz| *n., pl.* **lens•es. 1. a.** A piece of glass or other transparent material that has been precisely shaped so as to cause parallel light rays that pass through it to concentrate to a focus or to spread out as if coming from a focus. **b.** A combination of two or more such lenses used to form or magnify an image, as in a camera or telescope. **2.** A transparent structure, found just behind the iris of the eye, that acts to focus light entering the eye on the retina. **3.** Any device that causes radiation other than light to concentrate or spread out in a manner like that of a lens: *an electron lens.*

lent |lĕnt|. Past tense and past participle of **lend.**

Lent |lĕnt| *n.* A time of fasting and penitence observed by Christians from Ash Wednesday until Easter. —**Lent′en** *adj.*

len•til |**lĕn′**təl| *or* |**lĕn′**tl| *n.* **1.** The round, flat, edible seed of a pod-bearing plant related to the beans and peas. **2.** A plant that bears such seeds.

Le•o |**lē′**ō| *n.* The fifth sign of the zodiac

Le•o•nar•do da Vin•ci |lē′ə **när′**dō də **vĭn′**chē|. See **da Vinci, Leonardo.**

le•one |lē **ōn′**| *n.* The basic unit of money of Sierra Leone.

le•o•nine |**lē′**ə nīn′| *adj.* Of or typical of a lion: *a leonine mane.*

leop•ard |**lĕp′**ərd| *n.* **1.** A large wild cat of Africa and Asia, usually having a tawny coat with black spots but sometimes all black. **2.** The fur of this animal. [SEE PICTURE]

le•o•tard |**lē′**ə tärd′| *n.* Often **leotards.** A tight-fitting garment, originally worn by dancers and acrobats. [SEE PICTURE]

lep•er |**lĕp′**ər| *n.* A person afflicted with leprosy. —***modifier:*** *a leper colony.*

lep•re•chaun |**lĕp′**rə kôn′| *or* |-kŏn′| *n.* In Irish folklore, one of a race of elves resembling tiny, wrinkle-faced old men.

lep•ro•sy |**lĕp′**rə sē| *n.* An infectious bacterial disease that causes ulcers and sores on the body and in its severe forms causes progressive destruction of tissue, with paralysis and loss of sensation.

lep•rous |**lĕp′**rəs| *adj.* **1.** Of or suggesting leprosy. **2.** Having leprosy.

le•sion |**lē′**zhən| *n.* **1.** A wound or injury. **2.** A small, well-defined area of the body in which tissue has changed in a way that is characteristic of some disease.

Le•so•tho |lə **sō′**tō|. A small country entirely surrounded by the Republic of South Africa. Population, 1,016,000. Capital, Maseru.

less |lĕs| *adj.* **1.** A comparative of **little.** Not as great in amount or quantity: *less time to spare.* **2.** Fewer: *The more law enforcement on the highway, the less accidents.* **3.** Lower in rank or importance: *The guest of honor at school today was no less a person than the First Lady.* —*adv.* Comparative of **little.** To a smaller extent, degree, or frequency: *He was less scared than his friend.* —*prep.* **1.** Minus; subtracting: *Six less 1 is 5.* **2.** Except for; excluding: *The shipment arrived*

lemming

lemur

leopard

Leopard is from Greek *leopardos,* "lion-panther": *leōn,* "lion," + *pardos,* "panther, pard" (see **pard**[1]). The Greeks thought that the leopard was a cross between the lion and the panther.

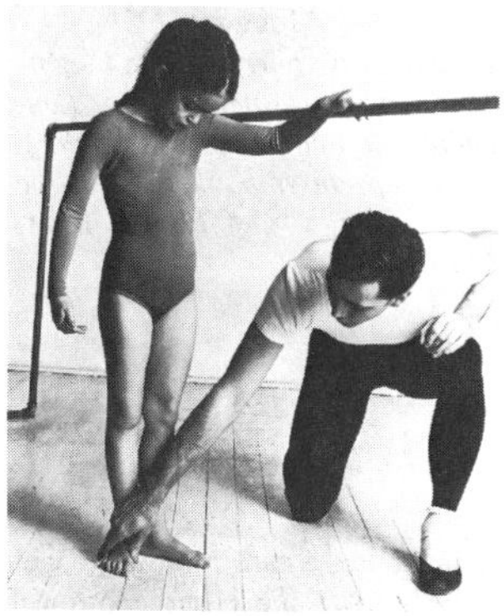

leotard

Leotard comes from the name of Jules *Léotard,* a French acrobat of the nineteenth century.

let[1·2]
Let[1] *was* lǣtan *in Old English and meant "to leave behind, to leave undone," hence "to allow."* **Let**[2] *is from Old English* lettan, *"to hinder, prevent," originally "to make late." It is ultimately related to* **let**[1].

levee
Levee *was borrowed in eighteenth-century America from Louisiana French* levée, *"something raised up, an embankment on the Mississippi," from French* lever, *"to raise."*

ă pat/ā pay/â care/ä father/ĕ pet/ ē be/ĭ pit/ī pie/î fierce/ŏ pot/ ō go/ô paw, **for**/oi **oil**/o͝o book/ o͞o boot/ou **out**/ŭ cut/û fur/ *th* **the**/th **thin**/hw **which**/**zh** vision/ ə ago, item, pencil, atom, circus

intact, less a couple of broken pots. —*n.* A smaller amount or share: *He got less than he asked for.* —*pron.* Fewer things or persons: *Many things begin badly; less end well.*

Idioms. **less than.** Not at all: *a less than satisfactory reply.* **much** (or **still**) **less.** Especially not: *I'm not accusing anybody in your family, much less your sister.*

–less. A suffix that forms adjectives meaning "without, free of": **motherless; nameless.**

les•see |lĕ sē′| *n.* A tenant holding a lease.

less•en |lĕs′ən| *v.* To make or become less: *a drug to lessen the pain. The pain lessened immediately.* ¶*These sound alike* **lessen, lesson.**

less•er |lĕs′ər| *adj.* **1.** Smaller in size, importance, etc.: *a lesser evil; lesser gods.* **2.** Of inferior quality: *I can take a lesser athlete and beat a better athlete with my program.* **3.** Of a smaller size than other similar forms: *The lesser anteater can hang in the trees by its long tail.*

les•son |lĕs′ən| *n.* **1.** Something to be learned: *The first lesson for your dog is to learn the meaning of the word "come."* **2.** An assignment or exercise in which something is to be learned: *an algebra textbook divided into 40 lessons.* **3.** A period of time devoted to teaching or learning a certain subject: *three piano lessons a week.* **4.** An example from which one can learn. **5.** A reading from the Bible given as part of a religious service. ¶*These sound alike* **lesson, lessen.**

les•sor |lĕs′ôr′| *or* |lĕ sôr′| *n.* A person who rents property to another by lease.

lest |lĕst| *conj.* **1.** For fear that; so as to prevent the possibility that: *Care should be taken lest the nails not be hammered in far enough to hold.* **2.** That: *Friends tried to discourage her in this ambition, fearing lest she be hurt.*

let[1] |lĕt| *v.* **let, let•ting. 1.** To grant permission to; allow: *She let him continue.* **2.** To cause; make: *Let me know what happened.* **3.** To allow as an assumption; suppose: *Let x equal 4.* **4.** To provide with an opportunity or means: *She let the pudding jell in the refrigerator.* **5.** To permit to move in a specified way: *Let me in. Let the cat out.* **6.** To permit to escape; release: *let the air out of the balloon.* **7.** To rent or lease: *He lets his extra rooms to students.* **8.** To assign or grant (work) to another: *letting a construction job to the lowest bidder.* **9.** —Used as an auxiliary verb in the imperative to indicate: **a.** Request, proposal, or command: *Let's get going!* **b.** Warning or threat: *Just let him try to lay his hands on me!* **c.** Acceptance of or resignation to the inevitable: *Let things fall as they may.* —***phrasal verbs.*** **let down. 1.** To slow down; ease up: *We've nearly finished, so don't let down now.* **2.** To fail to support or satisfy; disappoint: *They let me down.* **let off. 1.** To excuse from work or duty: *let the students off early.* **2.** To release with little or no punishment: *The principal let us off with a warning.* **let on.** To allow it to be known; reveal: *Don't let on that I talked to you about it.* **let out.** To loosen or widen by releasing material from a seam: *let out a tight dress.* **let up.** To become slower or less intense; diminish: *By evening the rain had let up a little.* [SEE NOTE]

let[2] |lĕt| *n.* **1.** Obstacle; obstruction: *free to investigate without let or hindrance.* **2.** A served ball in tennis and other net games that must be replayed because it has touched the net before falling into the proper court. [SEE NOTE]

–let. A suffix that forms nouns and means "small, diminutive": **booklet.**

let•down |lĕt′doun′| *n.* **1.** A decrease or decline, as in energy or effort. **2.** A disappointment.

le•thal |lē′thəl| *adj.* Causing or capable of causing death: *a lethal dose of a drug; a lethal weapon.* —**le′thal•ly** *adv.*

le•thar•gic |lə thär′jĭk| *adj.* Of, causing, or in a state of lethargy. —**le•thar′gi•cal•ly** *adv.*

leth•ar•gy |lĕth′ər jē| *n., pl.* **leth•ar•gies. 1.** Drowsy or sluggish indifference; apathy. **2.** An unconscious state resembling deep sleep.

let's |lĕts|. Let us.

let•ter |lĕt′ər| *n.* **1.** A written or printed mark that represents a speech sound and is used to spell words; one of the characters of an alphabet. **2.** An emblem bearing the initials of a school, awarded to athletes. **3.** A written message addressed to someone and usually sent by mail in an envelope. **4.** A document carried by a person and used for identification or to obtain privileges: *a safe-conduct letter.* **5. letters.** Literature: *a man of letters; English letters.* **6.** The strict, literal meaning: *following the letter of the law.* —***modifier:*** *a letter opener.* —*v.* To mark or write with letters: *letter a title.* —**let′ter•er** *n.*

let•ter•head |lĕt′ər hĕd′| *n.* **1.** A printed heading at the top of a sheet of letter paper, usually indicating the name and address of the sender. **2.** Letter paper with such headings.

let•ter•ing |lĕt′ər ĭng| *n.* **1.** The action or art of forming letters, as in the making of signs and posters. **2.** The letters inscribed on a sign, poster, greeting card, etc. —***modifier:*** *a lettering pen.*

let•ter-per•fect |lĕt′ər pûr′fĭkt| *adj.* Perfect in every detail.

let•ter•press |lĕt′ər prĕs′| *n.* **1.** The process of printing from type or some other raised, inked surface. **2.** Matter printed by this process. —***modifier:*** *letterpress printing.*

Let•tish |lĕt′ĭsh| *n.* **1.** Latvian. **2.** A Latvian. —*adj.* Latvian.

let•tuce |lĕt′ĭs| *n.* A plant cultivated for its edible light-green leaves, eaten as salad.

let•up |lĕt′ŭp′| *n.* **1.** A reduction in pace, force, or intensity: *no letup in the buffalo's pounding charge.* **2.** A pause or stop, as in work.

le•u |lĕ′o͞o| *n., pl.* **le•i** |lĕ′ĭ|. The basic unit of money of Rumania.

leu•co•cyte |lo͞o′kə sīt′| *n.* A form of the word **leukocyte.**

leu•ke•mi•a |lo͞o kē′mē ə| *n.* Any of a group of usually fatal diseases in which the white blood cells increase in uncontrolled numbers; cancer of the blood.

leu•ko•cyte |lo͞o′kə sīt′| *n.* A **white blood cell.**

lev |lĕf| *n., pl.* **lev•a** |lĕv′ə|. The basic unit of money of Bulgaria.

Le•vant |lə vănt′|. The countries bordering on the eastern Mediterranean Sea. —**Le′van•tine′** |lĕv′ən tēn′| *or* |-tīn′| *or* |lə văn′tĭn| *adj.* & *n.*

lev•ee |lĕv′ē| *n.* **1.** A bank of earth, concrete, or other material raised along a river to keep it from flooding. **2.** A landing place on a river. ¶*These sound alike* **levee, levy.** [SEE PICTURE]

lev•el |lĕv′əl| *n.* **1.** A height or depth: *A platform* *was erected at the level of Miss Liberty's knee for the statue dedication ceremony.* **2.** A standard elevation from which other heights and depths are measured: *Death Valley is 282 feet below sea level.* **3.** A grade or degree of anything that can be thought of as high or low: *a high level of education.* **4.** A relative position, rank, or class: *people of all levels of society.* **5.** A story or stage of a building or other structure. **6.** A stage in a series progressing toward greater difficulty, complexity, or development: *a deeper level of understanding.* **7.** Also **spirit level.** A liquid-filled tube containing an air bubble that moves to a center window when the tube is set on a perfectly horizontal surface. **8.** A line or plane joining points of equal height: *His head is on a level with my chin.* **9.** A flat, smooth stretch of land. *—adj.* **1.** Having a flat, smooth surface: *level farmland.* **2.** Horizontal: *The bill of my cap was on an angle rather than level.* **3.** Steady; uniform; unwavering: *a level tone.* **4.** Being at the same height, rank, or position; even: *a night table level with the bed.* *—v.* **lev•eled** or **lev•elled, lev•el•ing** or **lev•el•ling. 1.** To make or become smooth, flat, or horizontal: *leveling the ground for a new factory; land leveling out into broad plains.* **2.** To cut, tear, or knock down to the ground: *a tornado that leveled buildings.* **3.** To place on the same level; equalize. **4.** To aim carefully: *leveled his rifle for a third shot.* **5.** To direct forcefully toward someone: *leveled charges of dishonesty at the mayor.* **6.** *Informal.* To be frank and open: *The negotiators began by leveling with each other.* **—lev'el•er, lev'el•ler** *n.* **—lev'el•ly** *adv.* **—lev'el•ness** *n.*

Idioms. **(one's) level best.** The best one can do in an earnest attempt. **on the level.** *Informal.* Without deception or dishonesty.

lev•el•head•ed |lĕv′əl **hĕd′**ĭd| *adj.* Self-composed and sensible. **—lev'el•head'ed•ness** *n.*

lev•er |**lĕv′**ər| *or* |**lē′**vər| *n.* **1.** A simple machine consisting of a rigid bar or rod that turns on a fixed pivot or fulcrum. **2.** A projecting handle used to control, adjust, or operate a device or machine. [SEE PICTURE]

lev•er•age |**lĕv′**ər ĭj| *or* |**lē′**vər-| *n.* **1.** The action or mechanical advantage of a lever. **2.** An advantage in position or in means at one's disposal: *His private fortune gave him great political leverage in the campaign.*

le•vi•a•than |lə **vī′**ə thən| *n.* **1.** A huge sea creature mentioned in the Old Testament. **2.** Anything of enormous size or bulk.

Le•vis |**lē′**vīz′| *pl.n.* A trademark for close-fitting trousers of heavy denim.

lev•i•ty |**lĕv′**ĭ tē| *n., pl.* **lev•i•ties. 1.** A light, humorous manner or attitude, especially when inappropriate; frivolity. **2.** A humorous or careless remark made at the wrong time.

lev•y |**lĕv′**ē| *v.* **lev•ied, lev•y•ing, lev•ies. 1.** To impose or collect (a tax, tariff, or other fee). **2.** To draft into military service. **3.** To declare and wage: *"as free and independent states, they have full power to levy war"* (Declaration of Independence). *—n., pl.* **lev•ies. 1.** The act of levying. **2.** An imposed tax, tariff, or other fee. **3.** A body of troops drafted into military service. ¶*These sound alike* **levy, levee.**

lewd |lo͞od| *adj.* **lewd•er, lewd•est. 1.** Depicting or referring to sex in a coarse or insulting way; obscene; indecent. **2.** Preoccupied with sexual desire; lustful. **—lewd'ly** *adv.* **—lewd'ness** *n.*

lex•i•cal |**lĕk′**sĭ kəl| *adj.* **1.** Of or relating to the words or vocabulary of a language. **2.** Of a lexicon or lexicography. **—lex'i•cal•ly** *adv.*

lex•i•cog•ra•pher |lĕk′sĭ **kŏg′**rə fər| *n.* A person who writes or compiles a dictionary.

lex•i•co•graph•ic |lĕk′sĭ kō **grăf′**ĭk| or **lex•i•co•graph•i•cal** |lĕk′sĭ kō **grăf′**ĭ kəl| *adj.* Of lexicography. **—lex'i•co•graph'i•cal•ly** *adv.*

lex•i•cog•ra•phy |lĕk′sĭ **kŏg′**rə fē| *n.* The process or work of writing dictionaries.

lex•i•con |**lĕk′**sĭ kŏn′| *n.* **1.** A dictionary, especially one giving translations of words from an ancient language. **2.** A stock of terms used in a particular subject or profession.

Lex•ing•ton |**lĕk′**sĭng tən|. A town near Boston, Massachusetts, site of the first battle of the American Revolution.

Ley•den jar |**līd′**n|. An early form of capacitor consisting of a jar covered inside and out with metal foil, having a conductor that contacts the inner foil and passes out of the jar through an insulated stopper.

Li The symbol for the element lithium.

li•a•bil•i•ty |lī′ə **bĭl′**ĭ tē| *n., pl.* **li•a•bil•i•ties. 1.** Something that one owes; an obligation; debt. **2.** Legal responsibility to fulfill some contract or obligation. **3.** Something that holds one back; a handicap; disadvantage. **4.** A tendency; susceptibility.

li•a•ble |**lī′**ə bəl| *adj.* **1.** Legally obligated or responsible: *liable for the damages.* **2.** Able to incur or receive; subject: *We are liable to trial only by juries of our fellow citizens.* **3.** Susceptible; prone: *delicate eyes, especially liable to injury.* **4.** Likely: *liable to make mistakes.*

li•ai•son |lē′ā **zŏn′**| *or* |lē **ā′**zŏn′| *n.* **1.** Communication between different offices or units of an organization. **2.** A channel or means of communication: *He served as the President's liaison with Congress.*

li•an•a |lē **ăn′**ə| *or* |**-ä′**nə| *n.* A high-climbing tropical vine with woody stems.

li•ar |**lī′**ər| *n.* A person who tells lies.

li•bel |**lī′**bəl| *n.* **1.** A written or printed statement that unjustly damages a person's reputation or exposes him to ridicule. **2.** The act or crime of making such a statement. *—v.* **li•beled** or **li•belled, li•bel•ing** or **li•bel•ling.** To commit libel against. **—li'bel•er** *n.* **—li'bel•ous** *adj.*

lib•er•al |**lĭb′**ər əl| *or* |**lĭb′**rəl| *adj.* **1.** Tending to give generously: *a liberal benefactor.* **2.** Generous in amount; ample: *a liberal tip.* **3.** Loose; approximate: *a liberal adaptation of the novel for the screen.* **4.** Of or relating to the liberal arts. **5.** Respectful of different people and ideas; tolerant. **6.** Having or expressing political views that favor civil liberties, democratic reforms, and the use of governmental power to promote social progress. *—n.* A person with liberal political opinions. **—lib'er•al•ness** *n.*

liberal arts. College studies such as languages, history, and philosophy, rather than the sciences or technical studies.

lib•er•al•ism |**lĭb′**ər ə lĭz′əm| *or* |**lĭb′**rə-| *n.* Liberal political views and policies.

lib•er•al•i•ty |lĭb′ə **răl′**ĭ tē| *n., pl.* **lib•er•al•i•ties. 1.** Generosity. **2.** A generous gift or expense: *a*

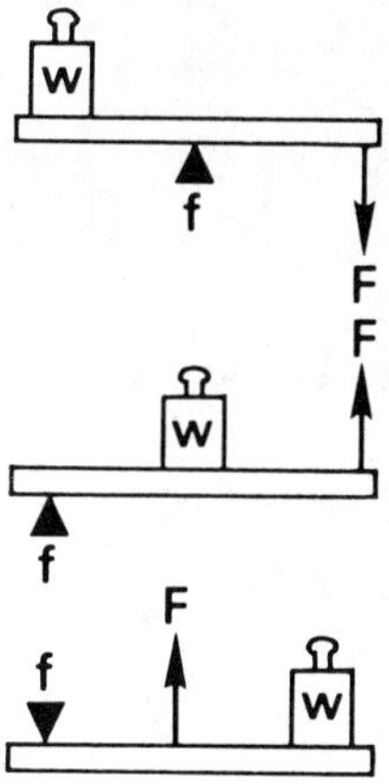

lever
Three basic types of lever; **f** is the fulcrum, and **F** is the force needed to raise a weight **W**

millionaire known for his liberalities. **3.** Openness of mind or attitude; tolerance.

lib•er•al•ize |lĭb′ər ə līz′| *or* |lĭb′rə-| *v.* **lib•er•al•ized, lib•er•al•i•zing. 1.** To make less restrictive: *liberalize the immigration policy.* **2.** To reform in accordance with liberal political principles. —**lib′er•al•i•za′tion** *n.*

lib•er•al•ly |lĭb′ər ə lē| *or* |lĭb′rə-| *adv.* **1.** Generously; amply: *liberally sprinkled with salt.* **2.** Loosely; approximately.

lib•er•ate |lĭb′ə rāt′| *v.* **lib•er•at•ed, lib•er•at•ing. 1.** To set free, as from confinement, foreign control, etc. **2.** *Slang.* To obtain by looting: *some fine French cognac we had liberated from the Germans.* —**lib′er•at′ed** *adj.: liberated women.* —**lib′er•a′tion** *n.* —**lib′er•a′tion•ist** *n.*

lib•er•a•tor |lĭb′ə rā′tər| *n.* A person who liberates, especially a person who wins freedom for a people.

Li•be•ri•a |lī bîr′ē ə|. A country in western Africa, on the Atlantic. Population, 1,670,000. Capital, Monrovia. —**Li•be′ri•an** *adj. & n.*

lib•er•tine |lĭb′ər tēn′| *n.* A person who lives an irresponsible, immoral life; a rake.

lib•er•ty |lĭb′ər tē| *n., pl.* **lib•er•ties. 1.** Freedom from confinement or forced labor. **2.** Freedom of action, belief, or expression. **3.** Political freedom from unjust or unrepresentative government: *The Magna Charta is known as the cornerstone of English liberty.* **4.** A legal right to engage in a certain kind of action without control or interference: *the civil liberties protected by the Bill of Rights.* **5.** Freedom to choose or to do as one pleases. **6.** Often **liberties.** A bold or disrespectful course of action: *take liberties.* **7.** A period during which a sailor is authorized to go ashore. [SEE NOTE]

***Idiom.* at liberty. 1.** Out of confinement; free. **2.** Allowed: *at liberty to leave.*

library/liberty, etc. **Library** *is from Latin* liber, *"a book."* **Liberty** *and its group, including* **liberal** *and* **liberate,** *are from Latin* līber, *"free."*

li•bi•do |lĭ bē′dō| *or* |-bī′-| *n., pl.* **li•bi•dos. 1.** The emotional and mental energy associated with basic biological urges or drives. **2. a.** Action or behavior that is derived from the sex drive. **b.** Sexual desire.

Li•bra |lī′brə| *or* |lē′-| *n.* The seventh sign of the zodiac.

li•brar•i•an |lī brâr′ē ən| *n.* A person who works in or is in charge of a library.

li•brar•y |lī′brĕr′ē| *n., pl.* **li•brar•ies. 1.** A place where books, magazines, records, and other reference materials are kept for reading or borrowing. **2.** Any large, permanent collection of reading matter. —***modifier:*** *library books; a library card.* [SEE NOTE]

li•bret•to |lĭ brĕt′ō| *n., pl.* **li•bret•tos** or **li•bret•ti** |lĭ brĕt′ē|. The text of an opera or other dramatic musical work.

Li•bre•ville |lē′brə vēl′|. The capital of Gabon. Population, 57,000.

Lib•y•a |lĭb′ē ə|. A country in northern Africa, on the Mediterranean Sea. Population, 2,240,000. Capital, Tripoli. —**Lib′y•an** *adj. & n.*

lice |līs| *n.* Plural of **louse.**

li•cense |lī′səns| *n.* **1. a.** Legal permission to do or own a specified thing. **b.** A document, card, plate, or other proof that such permission has been granted. **2.** Lack of due restraint; excessive freedom. **3.** Deviation from normal rules or procedures for a special purpose: *poetic license.* —***modifier:*** *license plates; a license number.* —*v.* **li•censed, li•cens•ing.** To grant a license to or for.

li•cen•tious |lī sĕn′shəs| *adj.* Defying all rules of conduct; unrestrained; immoral. —**li•cen′tious•ly** *adv.* —**li•cen′tious•ness** *n.*

li•chee |lē′chē| *n.* A form of the word **litchi.**

li•chen |lī′kən| *n.* A plant consisting of a fungus and an alga growing in close combination and forming a crustlike, scaly, or branching growth on rocks and tree trunks. ¶*These sound alike* **lichen, liken.**

lick |lĭk| *v.* **1.** To pass the tongue over. **2.** To move or flicker like a tongue: *watched the flames lick around the oak logs in the fireplace.* **3.** To defeat, as in a fight or competition: *Weight was not the only problem she licked that summer.* **4.** To punish with a beating; thrash. —*n.* **1.** A movement of the tongue over something. **2.** A deposit of exposed natural salt that is licked by passing animals. **3.** A blow.

lick•e•ty-split |lĭk′ĭ tē splĭt′| *adv. Informal.* Very quickly.

lic•o•rice |lĭk′ə rĭs| *or* |-ər ĭsh| *n.* **1.** A plant with a sweet, strong-tasting root used to flavor candy, medicine, etc. **2.** The root of this plant. **3.** A chewy, often black candy flavored with an extract from this root.

lid |lĭd| *n.* **1.** A removable cover for a hollow container: *the lid of a jar; the lid of a box.* **2.** An eyelid. —*v.* **lid•ded, lid•ding.** To cover with or as if with a lid: *crates tightly lidded for storage.*

lie¹ |lī| *v.* **lay** |lā|, **lain** |lān|, **ly•ing. 1.** To take a flat or resting position: *He lay down under an elm tree to sleep.* **2.** To be in a flat or resting position: *She was lying on the floor.* **3.** To be or rest on a horizontal surface: *Rocks have lain undisturbed on the lunar surface for many centuries.* **4.** To be located: *East of the Philippines lie many tiny islands.* **5.** To remain in a certain condition or position: *We let the land lie fallow.* **6.** To be inherent; exist: *The answer lay in further research.* **7.** To be buried: *a butterfly, bursting on brilliant wings from the tomb in which it has lain.* —***phrasal verb.* lie in.** To be in confinement for childbirth. —*n.* **1.** The surface or slope of a piece of land: *the irregular lie of a mountain pasture.* **2.** The position of something, such as a golf ball, that has come to a stop: *a difficult lie.* **3.** An animal's hiding place: *He fished carefully, making short casts to the likely lies.* ¶*These sound alike* **lie, lye.** [SEE NOTE; also SEE NOTE on p. 510]

***Idioms.* lie down on the job.** To do less than one can or should. **lie in wait. 1.** To remain alert or in readiness. **2.** To prepare an ambush. **lie low.** To keep oneself or one's plans hidden.

lie¹⁻² *For* **lie¹**, *see note at* **lay¹**. **Lie²** *was originally a verb; it was* lēogan *in Old English.*

lie² |lī| *n.* An untrue statement made by one who knows it to be untrue; a falsehood. —*v.* **lied, ly•ing. 1.** To tell a lie or lies. **2.** To create an illusion or false impression: *Even photographs can lie.* ¶*These sound alike* **lie, lye.** [SEE NOTE]

***Idiom.* give the lie to. 1.** To accuse of being untruthful. **2.** To show or prove to be untrue.

Liech•ten•stein |lĭk′tən stīn′|. A principality in central Europe between Austria and Switzerland. Population, 20,000. Capital, Vaduz.

lied |lēd| *n., pl.* **lie•der** |lē′dər|. A German lyric song. ¶*These sound alike* **lied, lead¹.**

lie detector. A polygraph.

ă pat/ā pay/â care/ä father/ĕ pet/ ē be/ĭ pit/ī pie/î fierce/ŏ pot/ ō go/ô paw, for/oi oil/ŏŏ book/ ōō boot/ou out/ŭ cut/û fur/ *th* the/th thin/hw which/zh vision/ ə ago, item, pencil, atom, circus

lief |lēf| *adv.* Readily; willingly: *I would as lief go now as later.* ¶*These sound alike* **lief, leaf.**

liege |lēj| *n.* **1.** A lord or sovereign in feudal times. **2.** A person owing allegiance and services to such a lord or sovereign; a vassal. —*adj.* Participating in the feudal relationship between a lord and his vassals: *a liege lord; a liege man.*

lien |lēn| *or* |lē′ən| *n.* The legal right to take or hold the property of someone who owes one money, either as payment or as security for the debt. ¶*These sound alike* **lien, lean.**

lieu |lo͞o| *n.* —**in lieu of.** In place of: *cash in lieu of a check.*

lieu•ten•ant |lo͞o tĕn′ənt| *n.* **1.** An officer in the Army, Air Force, or Marine Corps ranking below a captain. A **first lieutenant** ranks above a **second lieutenant.** **2.** An officer in the Navy ranking above an ensign and below a lieutenant commander. **3.** An officer in a police or fire department ranking below a captain. **4.** A chief assistant; deputy.

life |līf| *n., pl.* **lives** |līvz|. **1.** The property or quality that distinguishes living organisms from dead organisms and nonliving matter, shown in the ability to grow, carry on metabolism, respond to stimuli, and reproduce. **2.** The fact of being alive or remaining alive: *risk one's life.* **3.** The period of time between birth and death; lifetime: *He lived there for the rest of his life.* **4.** The time for which something exists or works: *the useful life of a car.* **5.** Living organisms in general: *plant life; marine life.* **6.** A living being: *The earthquake claimed hundreds of lives.* **7.** Human existence or activity in general: *city life; the problems we face in real life.* **8.** A way of living: *I prefer the outdoor life.* **9.** Liveliness or vitality: *His face was eager, bright, and full of life.* **10.** An account of a person's life; a biography. —***modifier:*** *life imprisonment; a person's life history.*

Idioms. **for dear life.** With desperate effort or speed: *hold on for dear life.* **not on your life.** *Informal.* Definitely not.

life belt. A life preserver worn like a belt.

life•boat |līf′bōt′| *n.* **1.** A boat carried on a ship for use if the ship has to be abandoned. **2.** A boat used for rescue service.

life buoy. A ring made of cork or other buoyant material for keeping a person afloat.

life cycle. The series of changes through which a living thing passes, from the time it begins to exist to the mature stage in which it can take part in the process of reproduction that will again start the series for a new organism or organisms.

life•guard |līf′gärd′| *n.* A person hired to look out for the safety of bathers at a beach or pool.

life insurance. Insurance on a person's life, paid for by regular premiums and guaranteeing a certain sum of money to a wife, child, etc., on the death of the holder.

life•less |līf′lĭs| *adj.* **1.** Without life; dead or inanimate. **2.** Not supporting life; without living organisms: *a lifeless planet.* **3.** Lacking spirit or brightness: *lifeless colors.*

life•like |līf′līk′| *adj.* **1.** Resembling a living thing: *a lifelike statue.* **2.** Accurately representing real life: *a lifelike description.*

life•line |līf′līn′| *n.* **1.** An anchored line thrown as a support to someone falling or drowning. **2.** A line shot to a ship in distress to allow it to haul aboard lifesaving equipment. **3.** A line used to raise and lower deep-sea divers. **4.** A means or route for transporting supplies.

life•long |līf′lông′| *or* |-lŏng′| *adj.* Lasting over a lifetime: *a lifelong friend; a lifelong ambition.*

life preserver. A buoyant device, usually a belt, jacket, etc., designed to keep a person afloat.

life-size |līf′sīz′| *adj.* Being of the same size as the person or object represented.

life-sized |līf′sīzd′| *adj.* A form of the word **life-size.**

life•style, also **life-style** |līf′stīl′| *n.* Also **life style.** A way of life or style of living: *the lifestyle of young people.*

life-sup•port system |līf′sə pôrt′| *or* |-pōrt′|. The equipment that supplies oxygen, regulates temperature, and generally keeps conditions in a spacecraft such that the crew can live.

life•time |līf′tīm′| *n.* The period of time during which someone or something remains alive, exists, etc.: *in our lifetime; the lifetime of a car.*

lift |lĭft| *v.* **1.** To raise into the air from a resting position; pick up: *lift the receiver of a telephone. The suitcase is too heavy to lift.* **2.** To move or direct upward; raise: *lift one's eyes.* **3.** To raise or improve in condition, status, etc.: *lift oneself out of the ghetto. The news lifted everybody's spirits.* **4.** To end; stop; suspend: *lift a siege.* **5.** To rise and disappear: *Waiting for the fog to lift.* **6.** *Informal.* To copy from something already published: *He lifted his term paper from a magazine article.* —***phrasal verb.*** **lift off.** To begin flight, as a rocket or spacecraft. —*n.* **1.** An example of lifting or being lifted: *Give me a lift into the saddle.* **2.** A short ride in a vehicle. **3.** The extent or height something is raised. **4.** An elevation of the spirit: *The news from home gave us all a big lift.* **5.** A cable with seats attached, used for carrying people up a slope: *a ski lift; a chair lift.* **6.** *British.* An elevator.

lift•off |lĭft′ôf′| *or* |-ŏf′| *n.* **1.** The first movement of a rocket or spacecraft in beginning its flight. **2.** The point in time at which this occurs.

lig•a•ment |lĭg′ə mənt| *n.* A sheet or band of tough, fibrous tissue that connects bones or cartilage or holds a muscle or body organ in place.

lig•a•ture |lĭg′ə chər| *n.* **1. a.** A slur used to join a group of musical notes. **b.** The notes joined in this way. **2.** In printing, a character of type combining two or more letters, as *æ.*

light[1] |līt| *n.* **1. a.** Any electromagnetic radiation that can be perceived by the normal, unaided human eye, having wavelengths between 3,900 angstroms and 7,700 angstroms. **b.** Electromagnetic radiation with wavelengths just beyond those of visible light: *infrared light; ultraviolet light.* **2.** A source of either of these types of radiation, especially an electric lamp: *Leave a light burning in the hallway.* **3.** Visible light considered necessary for seeing: *enough light to read by.* **4.** A source of fire, as a match: *Mister, have you got a light?* **5.** A famous or outstanding person: *one of the leading lights of the Broadway stage.* **6.** A way of looking at or considering a certain matter: *This puts the whole thing in a different light.* **7.** A light shade or color: *the lights and darks in an oil painting.* —***modifier:*** *a light bulb; light rays.* —*adj.* **light•er, light•est. 1.**

light[1·2]

These two words have always had their present basic meanings. **Light**[1] *was* līht *in Old English; it is descended from prehistoric Germanic* liuht-, *which in turn is from Indo-European* leukt-. *It is related to* **luminous, lustrous,** *and* **lucid. Light**[2] *was Old English* lēoht, *from Germanic* līht-, *from Indo-European* legwht-; *it is related to Latin* levis, *"light," from which we have* **levity. Lighten**[1] *and* **lightness**[1] *are from* **light**[1], *and* **lighten**[2] *and* **lightness**[2] *are from* **light**[2].

lighter¹⁻²
Lighter¹ *is from* **light¹**. **Lighter²** *is probably from Dutch; Dutch* lichten *(related to* **light²**) *means "to lighten, to unload," and could have formed a noun* lichter *meaning "unloader, barge used for unloading"; this word is not recorded, but it is a reasonable guess that it did exist and that it was the source of* **lighter²**.

like¹⁻²
Like¹ *was* līcian *in Old English, and it originally meant "to please, to have a pleasing appearance."* **Like²** *is from Old English* gelīc, *meaning "having the same form or appearance, similar." The two words are descended from prehistoric Germanic* līk-, *"form, appearance."*

ă pat/ā pay/â care/ä father/ĕ pet/ ē be/ĭ pit/ī pie/î fierce/ŏ pot/ ō go/ô paw, for/oi oil/ŏŏ book/ ōō boot/ou out/ŭ cut/û fur/ *th* the/th thin/hw which/zh vision/ ə ago, item, pencil, atom, circus

Bright; not dark: *It gets light here about 6 in the morning.* **2.** Pale in color: *light gray; light hair; a light complexion.* —*v.* **light•ed** or **lit** |lĭt|, **light•ing. 1. a.** To set burning; ignite: *light a fire.* **b.** To start to burn; be ignited: *The oven won't light.* **2.** To cause to give out light; turn on: *light a lamp.* **3.** To provide with light: *lit the room with candles.* **4.** To make lively or animated: *A smile lighted her face.* [SEE NOTE on p. 519]

Idioms. **come to light.** To be revealed; come to public attention: *New information has recently come to light.* **in (the) light of.** Considering; in view of: *re-examine a matter in the light of new information.* **see the light.** To understand or appreciate something for the first time.

light² |līt| *adj.* **light•er, light•est. 1.** Having little weight; not heavy: *a light suitcase; a light jacket.* **2.** Having little force or impact: *a light blow.* **3.** Small in intensity or amount: *a light breeze; a light lunch.* **4.** Intended as entertainment; not serious or profound: *light comedy.* **5.** Free from care or worry: *a light heart.* **6.** Moving easily and quickly; nimble: *light on one's feet.* **7.** Requiring little effort or exertion: *light household chores.* **8.** Somewhat unsteady or faint; dizzy: *feel light in the head.* **9.** Consuming relatively moderate amounts of something: *a light eater.* **10.** Containing relatively little alcohol: *a light wine.* **11.** Easily awakened or disturbed: *a light sleeper.* —*adv.* Lightly; with little baggage: *We always travel light.* —*v.* **light•ed** or **lit** |lĭt|, **light•ing. 1.** To come to rest; land; perch: *The bird lit on my shoulder.* **2.** To get down, as from a mount or vehicle; alight: *The truck stopped and six soldiers lighted from the rear compartment.* —***phrasal verbs.*** **light into.** *Informal.* To attack violently: *He lit into his opponent at the opening bell.* **light out.** *Informal.* To depart suddenly; take off: *The runner on third base lit out for home.* [SEE NOTE on p. 519]

Idiom. **make light of.** To treat as unimportant; minimize; play down: *make light of a danger.*

light•en¹ |līt'n| *v.* To make or become lighter or brighter: *Adding white will lighten any color. The sky is beginning to lighten.*

light•en² |līt'n| *v.* **1.** To make less heavy; reduce the weight of: *Leaving out those books will lighten your suitcase considerably.* **2.** To make less burdensome or oppressive: *new appliances that lighten household work.* **3.** To gladden or cheer: *a song to lighten everyone's heart.*

light•er¹ |lī'tər| *n.* **1.** A person who lights something: *a lighter of fires.* **2.** A device for lighting a cigarette, cigar, pipe, etc. [SEE NOTE]

light•er² |lī'tər| *n.* A big barge used for loading and unloading ships moored outside a harbor that is too shallow for them to enter. —*v.* To carry (cargo) in a lighter. [SEE NOTE]

light•face |līt'fās'| *n.* Type that has relatively thin, light lines. This definition is in lightface.

light-foot•ed |līt'fŏŏt'ĭd| *adj.* Moving with light and graceful steps; nimble.

light•head•ed |līt'hĕd'ĭd| *adj.* **1.** Giddy, dizzy, or faint, as because of drunkenness or illness. **2.** Silly or foolish in one's manner or behavior.

light•heart•ed |līt'här'tĭd| *adj.* Carefree and gay: *a lighthearted attitude; a lighthearted song.* —**light'heart'ed•ly** *adv.* —**light'heart'ed•ness** *n.*

light•house |līt'hous'| *n., pl.* **-hous•es** |-hou'zĭz|. A tower with a powerful light at the top, used to guide ships.

light•ing |lī'tĭng| *n.* **1.** Light supplied, as for a room or area; illumination: *the proper amount of lighting.* **2.** The means or equipment by which such light is provided: *electric lighting.*

light•ly |līt'lē| *adv.* **1.** With little pressure or force: *Tread lightly on the new carpet.* **2.** With a small, thin, or light amount of something: *dress lightly in summer.* **3.** To a small amount or degree: *lightly tarnished metal.* **4.** Not seriously; with little concern: *a matter not to be taken lightly.* **5.** With little or no penalty: *I think he got off too lightly.*

light meter. An **exposure meter.**

light•ness¹ |līt'nĭs| *n.* A property or quality of a color measured as the degree to which an object of that color reflects light or allows light to pass through; brightness or paleness.

light•ness² |līt'nĭs| *n.* **1.** The property or quality of having little weight or force. **2.** The quality of being light or nimble on one's feet. **3.** Lack of seriousness; levity.

light•ning |līt'nĭng| *n.* **1.** A large, high-voltage electrical discharge that occurs in the atmosphere from natural causes. **2.** The flash of light that accompanies such a discharge.

lightning bug. A firefly.

lightning rod. A pointed metal rod placed high on a building or structure and connected to the ground by a heavy wire or cable to give protection from lightning.

light•ship |līt'shĭp'| *n.* A ship with a powerful light or other warning signals, anchored in dangerous waters to alert and guide other vessels.

light•weight |līt'wāt'| *n.* A boxer weighing between 127 and 135 pounds. —*adj.* Not heavy; weighing relatively little: *a lightweight jacket.*

light-year |līt'yîr'| *n.* Also **light year.** A measure of distance equal to the distance light travels through empty space in a year; about 5.878 trillion (5.878×10^{12}) miles.

lig•nite |lĭg'nīt'| *n.* A soft, brownish-black form of coal that has relatively little fuel value.

lig•num vi•tae |lĭg'nəm vī'tē|. **1.** A tropical American tree with very hard, heavy wood. **2.** The wood of such a tree.

lik•a•ble |lī'kə bəl| *adj.* Easy to like; having a pleasing personality: *a likable fellow.*

like¹ |līk| *v.* **liked, lik•ing. 1.** To be fond of: *She likes Jim a lot but not enough to go steady.* **2.** To find pleasant; enjoy: *He liked the place so much he decided to stay.* **3.** To regard favorably: *Which dress do you like best?* **4.** To regard; feel about: *How do you like your new teacher?* **5.** To wish or want: *Take as much as you like.* —*n.* **likes.** The things one enjoys or prefers: *likes and dislikes.* [SEE NOTE]

like² |līk| *prep.* **1. a.** The same as or similar to, as in nature: *Habits are like measles in that they can be catching.* **b.** Similar to, as in appearance or sound: *There was a crash like thunder.* **2.** In the same or a similar manner as: *act like a man.* **3.** In character with: *It's not like him to fall down on the job.* **4.** Such as: *great peaks like Mt. Shasta or Mt. Rainier.* —*adj.* The same or nearly the same: *My uncle left $100 to me and my sister and a like sum to each of our cousins.* —*n.* Persons or things similar to the one or ones named: *denim, gabardine, and the like.* [SEE NOTE on p. 520]

-like. A suffix that forms adjectives and means: **1.** Similar to: **lifelike. 2.** Characteristic of: **ladylike.**

like•a•ble |lī'kə bəl| *adj.* A form of the word **likable.**

like•li•hood |līk'lē ho͝od'| *n.* The chance of a certain thing happening; probability: *The likelihood of his being there is very remote.*

like•ly |līk'lē| *adj.* **like•li•er, like•li•est. 1.** Having or showing a strong probability; apt: *It is likely to rain at any moment.* **2.** Probable: *Mr. Cummings seems the likely choice for the job.* **3.** Seeming to be true; credible: *a likely excuse.* **4.** Appropriate or suitable: *June 25 seems a likely date for the party.* **5.** Showing promise of success in future life: *a likely lad.* —*adv.* Probably: *Most likely it's just a passing fad.*

lik•en |lī'kən| *v.* To describe as resembling something else: *Politics has been likened to a game of chess.* ¶ *These sound alike* **liken, lichen.**

like•ness |līk'nĭs| *n.* **1.** Similarity or resemblance: *There is an amazing likeness between Edward and his father.* **2.** A copy or picture of someone or something: *The portrait is a perfect likeness of you.*

like•wise |līk'wīz'| *adj.* **1.** Similarly; in like manner: *The students watched him swim and did likewise.* **2.** Moreover; besides: *Likewise, the child knew many new words.*

lik•ing |lī'kĭng| *n.* **1.** A feeling of fondness or affection: *a special liking for ice cream.* **2.** Preference or taste: *I'll try to choose a name more to your liking.*

li•lac |lī'lək| *or* |-lŏk'| *or* |-lăk'| *n.* **1.** A shrub planted for its clusters of fragrant purplish or white flowers. **2.** A pale purple. —*adj.* Pale purple.

Lil•li•pu•tian |lĭl'ə pyo͞o'shən| *n.* **1.** One of the six-inch-high inhabitants of the imaginary country of Lilliput in Jonathan Swift's *Gulliver's Travels* (1726). **2.** Often **lilliputian.** A tiny person. —*adj.* Often **lilliputian.** Very small; tiny.

Li•long•we |lĭ **lông**'wā|. The capital of Malawi. Population, 103,000.

lilt |lĭlt| *n.* A pleasant, cheerful, rhythmic motion, of, suggested by, or suggesting music.

lilt•ing |lĭl'tĭng| *adj.* Characterized by a pleasant, lively rhythm; having a lilt: *a happy, lilting tune.*

lil•y |lĭl'ē| *n., pl.* **lil•ies. 1.** Any of several related plants with showy, trumpet-shaped flowers. **2.** The flower of such a plant. [SEE PICTURE]

lily of the valley. *pl.* **lilies of the valley.** A plant with a slender cluster of fragrant, bell-shaped white flowers. [SEE PICTURE]

lily pad. One of the broad, floating leaves of a water lily.

lil•y-white |lĭl'ē **hwīt'**| *or* |**-wīt'**| *adj.* **1.** White as a lily. **2.** Beyond reproach; innocent; pure.

Li•ma |lē'mə|. The capital of Peru. Population, 2,862,000.

li•ma bean |lī'mə|. **1.** A plant having flat pods containing large, light-green edible seeds. **2.** The seed of such a plant.

limb[1] |lĭm| *n.* **1.** A jointed animal part, such as a leg, arm, wing, or flipper. **2.** One of the larger branches of a tree. ¶ *These sound alike* **limb, limn.**

Idiom. **out on a limb.** In a dangerous or vulnerable position.

limb[2] |lĭm| *n.* The outer edge of the apparent disk of a celestial object. ¶ *These sound alike* **limb, limn.**

lim•ber |lĭm'bər| *adj.* **1.** Bending easily; pliable: *limber muscles.* **2.** Moving easily and nimbly; agile: *a limber athlete.* —*v.* To engage in light exercise so as to make the body more limber.

lim•bo |lĭm'bō| *n.* **1.** Often **Limbo.** In some Christian theologies, the abode of souls kept from heaven by circumstance, such as lack of baptism. **2.** A place or condition of neglect or stagnation.

Lim•burg•er cheese |lĭm'bûr'gər|. A soft or white cheese with a strong odor and flavor.

lime[1] |līm| *n.* **1.** A green-skinned fruit related to the lemon and orange, having sour juice used as flavoring. **2.** A tree that bears such fruit. —***modifier:*** *a lime pit.* [SEE NOTE]

lime[2] |līm| *n.* A European linden tree. [SEE NOTE]

lime[3] |līm| *n.* **Calcium oxide.** [SEE NOTE]

lime•light |līm'līt'| *n.* **1.** A brilliant light produced by heating lime. In earlier times it was used to illuminate stages of theaters. **2. the limelight.** The center of public attention: *The President is always in the limelight.*

lim•er•ick |lĭm'ər ĭk| *n.* A humorous five-line poem in which the first, second, and last lines rhyme with each other and the third line rhymes with the fourth.

lime•stone |līm'stōn'| *n.* A form of sedimentary rock that consists mainly of calcium carbonate with varying amounts of magnesium carbonate and quartz, used as a building material and in making lime and cement.

lim•it |lĭm'ĭt| *n.* **1.** A point or line beyond which one cannot go: *Fishing is not allowed within the 12-mile limit.* **2.** Often **limits.** The boundary surrounding a certain area: *within the city limits.* **3.** The greatest amount or number of something allowed: *a speed limit.* **4.** Something that restricts or keeps within bounds: *There are limits as to how much we can do.* **5.** The utmost extent; the breaking point: *press one's luck to the limit.* **6. the limit.** *Informal.* Something that exhausts one's patience; the last straw: *Their latest demands are simply the limit.* —*v.* To place a limit on; confine: *Try to limit your talk to ten minutes. Scientific research is not limited to the laboratory.*

lim•i•ta•tion |lĭm'ĭ **tā'**shən| *n.* **1.** Something that limits; a restriction: *The new constitution places severe limitations on the king's powers.* **2.** A shortcoming: *learn to accept one's limitations.*

lim•it•ed |lĭm'ĭ tĭd| *adj.* **1.** Confined within certain limits; not great in size or amount: *a person of limited experience.* **2.** Making few stops and carrying fewer passengers: *a limited train.* —*n.* A limited train: *the Twentieth Century Limited.*

limn |lĭm| *v. Archaic.* **1.** To draw or paint. **2.** To describe. ¶ *These sound alike* **limn, limb.**

lim•ou•sine |lĭm'ə zēn'| *or* |lĭm'ə **zēn'**| *n.* A large, luxurious automobile, often with a glass partition between the driver and the passengers.

limp |lĭmp| *v.* **1.** To walk in a lame or irregular way, as if unable to fully use one leg. **2.** To travel or proceed in a shaky or unpredictable way: *The damaged ship limped back to port.* —*n.*

lily

lily of the valley

lime[1-2-3]

Lime[1] *is from Arabic* līmah. **Lime[2]** *is a variant of* **linden. Lime[3]** *was* līm *in Old English; it originally meant "birdlime, slimy substance."*

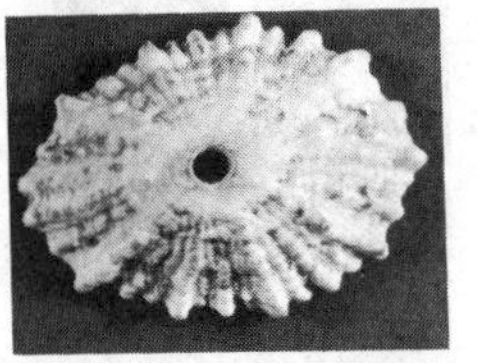

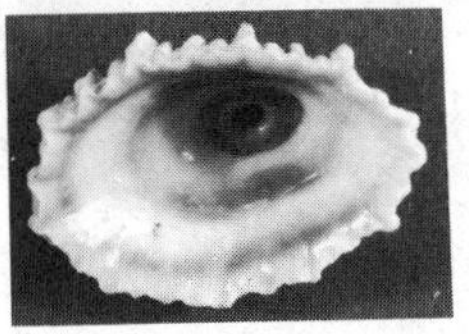

limpet

line[1-2], etc.

The flax plant has been cultivated since ancient times; it produces a fine fiber used to make cloth, and its seeds, called linseeds, are pressed to yield an oil. The Latin word for this plant was līnum. *(1)* Līnum *was borrowed into Old English as* līn, *from which we have* **linseed**. *From* līn *was formed the Middle English verb* linen, *meaning "to sew flax cloth onto, to reinforce a garment with flax cloth"; this became* **line**[2] *(hence* **lining***) in Modern English. Also from* līn *was formed the Old English adjective* līnen, *meaning "made of flax"; this became Modern English* **linen**. *(2) From Latin* līnum *was formed* līnea, *"a thread of flax"; this was borrowed into Old English as* līne, *which came to mean "cord, rope, long thin mark, long row of objects," etc., and in Modern English it became* **line**[1].

ă pat/ā pay/â care/ä father/ĕ pet/ ē be/ĭ pit/ī pie/î fierce/ŏ pot/ ō go/ô paw, for/oi oil/ŏŏ book/ ōō boot/ou out/ŭ cut/û fur/ *th* the/th thin/hw which/zh vision/ ə ago, item, pencil, atom, circus

An irregular, jerky, or awkward way of walking. *—adj.* Lacking or having lost stiffness or the ability to support itself: *a limp arm; a limp leaf.* **—limp'ly** *adv.* **—limp'ness** *n.*

lim•pet |lĭm'pĭt| *n.* A soft-bodied sea animal that has a tent-shaped shell and clings to rocks. [SEE PICTURES]

lim•pid |lĭm'pĭd| *adj.* Perfectly clear; transparent: *Her eyes were like limpid pools of water.*

lim•y |lī'mē| *adj.* **lim•i•er, lim•i•est.** Of lime.

linch•pin |lĭnch'pĭn'| *n.* An iron pin inserted in the end of an axle to prevent a wheel from slipping off.

Lin•coln |lĭng'kən|. The capital of Nebraska. Population, 148,000.

Lin•coln |lĭng'kən|, **Abraham.** 1809–1865. Sixteenth President of the United States (1861–65); assassinated.

Lincoln's Birthday. A holiday celebrated on February 12 in honor of the birthday of Abraham Lincoln.

Lind•bergh |lĭnd'bûrg'| *or* |lĭn'-|, **Charles Augustus.** 1902–1974. American aviator; the first to make a solo flight across the Atlantic Ocean (1927).

lin•den |lĭn'dən| *n.* Any of several trees with heart-shaped leaves and fragrant yellowish flowers, often planted for shade.

line[1] |līn| *n.* **1. a.** Any path taken by a point that is free to move: *a straight line; a curved line.* **b.** A path of this kind in which there is no change of direction. **2.** A long, thin, continuous mark, as one made on paper by a pen or pencil. **3. a.** A border or boundary: *the county line.* **b.** A movable or imaginary boundary: *The river is our first line of defense.* **c.** The starting or finishing point of a race. **d.** Any of the marks on a playing field or court indicating boundaries of play: *the foul lines.* **4.** Anything that serves to distinguish between two things: *We must draw the line between dissent and disruption.* **5.** A group of people or things arranged in a row: *He ordered his men to march in a line behind him.* **6.** Alignment: *Your rear wheels are out of line.* **7.** Often **lines.** Outline, contour, or styling: *the sleek lines of the new car.* **8.** A row of words printed or written across a page or column. **9. lines.** The words recited by an actor in a play: *He is busy memorizing his lines.* **10.** A wrinkle or crease on the skin, especially of the face or palm. **11.** A cable, rope, string, cord, wire, etc.: *a fishing line.* **12.** A course of progress or movement: *the line of flight.* **13.** An attitude or policy: *His party supported the compromise, but he took a different line.* **14.** A sequence of related ideas leading to a certain ending or conclusion: *a story line; a line of reasoning.* **15.** A system of transportation or a company owning such a system: *a bus line; a steamship line.* **16.** A system of wires or other conductors used to connect electricity, usually over long distances: *a power line; a telegraph line.* **17.** A telephone connection: *a party line.* **18.** A pipe or system of pipes used to carry water or other liquid: *a sewer line.* **19.** A brief letter; a note: *Drop me a line.* **20.** A succession of persons or animals descended from a common ancestor: *a long line of emperors.* **21.** In football, the seven players stationed at the line of scrimmage as a play begins. **22.** A range of merchandise having several styles and sizes: *a line of cars.* **23.** A person's trade or occupation: *What is your line of work?* **24.** The range of a person's ability or knowledge: *That sort of work is out of my line.* **25.** *Informal.* A false or exaggerated story intended to impress or deceive a listener. **26.** *Informal.* A piece of useful information: *See if you can get a line on what he's doing.* *—v.* **lined, lin•ing. 1.** To mark with lines: *line paper.* **2.** To form a line along: *Thousands of people lined the sidewalks.* **3.** To fill or cover: *The walls are lined with paintings.* **—lined'** *adj.: lined paper; her deeply lined face.* ***—phrasal verb.*** **line up. 1.** To arrange in a line; align. **2.** To form a line: *Planes must line up and wait their turn to take off.* **3.** To win over to a cause; secure; gain: *He has already lined up considerable support for the bill.* [SEE NOTE]

Idioms. **all along the line.** Throughout: *inefficiency all along the line.* **bring into line.** To persuade to agree or conform. **hold the line.** To maintain a firm position; not yield: *holding the line on new expenditures.* **in line.** Behaving properly: *keeping the children in line.* **in line for.** Due for: *in line for a promotion.* **in line with.** Conforming to; in accordance with: *The new proposal is in line with our general policy.* **lay it on the line.** *Informal.* To speak openly, concealing nothing. **on the line.** *Informal.* **1.** Immediately available; ready: *cash on the line.* **2.** At stake: *Your reputation is squarely on the line.* **out of line.** Improper; uncalled-for: *a remark somewhat out of line.* **read between the lines.** To seek a hidden meaning.

line[2] |līn| *v.* **lined, lin•ing. 1.** To cover the inside surface of with a layer of material: *The seamstress lined the dress with rayon.* **2.** To serve as a lining for or in: *Tissue paper lined the box.* [SEE NOTE]

lin•e•age |lĭn'ē ĭj| *n.* **1.** Direct descent from a particular ancestor; ancestry. **2.** All of the descendants of a particular ancestor.

lin•e•al |lĭn'ē əl| *adj.* **1.** In the direct line of descent. **2.** Linear. **—lin'e•al•ly** *adv.*

lin•e•a•ment |lĭn'ē ə mənt| *n.* A facial feature.

lin•e•ar |lĭn'ē ər| *adj.* **1. a.** Of, like, or involving a line, especially a straight line. **b.** Of or involving a linear equation. **2.** Consisting of or using lines: *a linear design.*

linear accelerator. An accelerator for particles, such as electrons, protons, or ions, in which the particles are accelerated in a straight line.

linear equation. An algebraic equation of the form $ax + by + c = 0$, where a, b, and c are constants and a and b are not both zero.

linear measure. 1. Measurement of length or distance. **2.** A unit or system of units for measuring length or distance.

line•back•er |līn'băk'ər| *n.* In football, a player stationed just behind a team's defensive line.

line•man |līn'mən| *n., pl.* **-men** |-mən|. **1.** A person whose job is to put up or repair telephone, telegraph, or other power lines. **2.** A person whose job is to inspect and repair railroad tracks. **3.** In football, a player stationed within one yard of a team's line of scrimmage.

lin•en |lĭn'ən| *n.* **1. a.** Strong, lustrous cloth made of flax fibers. **b.** Thread spun from flax. **2.** Often **linens.** Cloth articles or garments, such as sheets, tablecloths, shirts, etc., made of or once made of linen: *household linens.* —**modifier:** *a linen tablecloth; a linen closet.*

line of force. Any of a set of lines imagined to exist in a field of force so that a tangent to a line at any point gives the direction of the field at that point and the number of lines passing through a region represents the strength of the field in that region.

line of scrimmage. An imaginary line across a football field on which the ball rests and at which the teams line up for a new play.

lin•er[1] |lī′nər| *n.* A commercial ship or airplane carrying passengers on a regular route.

lin•er[2] |lī′nər| *n.* **1.** A person who makes or puts in linings. **2.** Something used as a lining.

line segment. The part of a line lying between two points that are chosen to be its ends. [SEE PICTURE]

lines•man |līnz′mən| *n., pl.* **-men** |-mən|. **1.** An official who assists a referee in football, ice hockey, tennis, and other sports. **2.** A telephone or telegraph lineman.

line spectrum. A spectrum consisting of a series of distinct, fairly narrow lines.

line-up, also **line•up** |līn′ŭp′| *n.* **1.** The members of a team actually playing in a game: *the starting line-up.* **2.** A group of persons lined up for purposes of identification: *a police line-up.*

-ling. A suffix that forms nouns and means: **1.** Someone in a specific condition: **hireling. 2.** Small, young, or inferior: **duckling;** *princeling.*

lin•ger |lĭng′gər| *v.* **1.** To remain in a place longer than usual, as if reluctant to leave: *linger over a cup of coffee.* **2.** To remain alive or in existence, even though close to death or extinction: *The patient continues to linger.* **3.** To be slow in acting: *linger over a decision.*

lin•ge•rie |län′zhə rē′| *or* |län′zhə rā′| *n.* Women's underwear and sleeping garments.

lin•go |lĭng′gō| *n., pl.* **lin•goes.** Language that is often difficult to understand, usually because it contains many specialized or unusual words: *Waiters and cooks have a lingo all their own.*

lin•gua |lĭng′gwə| *n., pl.* **lin•guae** |lĭng′gwē′|. The tongue or a similar organ.

lingua fran•ca |frăng′kə|. A language used between people who normally speak different languages: *English serves as the lingua franca of many African countries.*

lin•guist |lĭng′gwĭst| *n.* **1.** A person who speaks several languages fluently. **2.** A specialist in linguistics.

lin•guis•tic |lĭng gwĭs′tĭk| *adj.* Of language or lingusitics. —**lin•guis′ti•cal•ly** *adv.*

lin•guis•tics |lĭng gwĭs′tĭks| *n. (used with a singular verb).* The science of language; the study of the nature and structure of human speech.

lin•i•ment |lĭn′ə mənt| *n.* A liquid medicine rubbed on the skin to soothe or relieve pain.

lin•ing |lī′nĭng| *n.* **1.** An inner covering or coating: *the stomach lining.* **2.** A layer of material used on an inside surface: *a raincoat with a removable lining.* —**modifier:** *lining material.*

link |lĭngk| *n.* **1.** One of the rings or loops forming a chain: *A chain is only as strong as its weakest link.* **2.** Anything that joins or connects: *links with the past; a new rail link.* **3.** A unit of distance used in surveying land, equal to one hundredth of a chain, or 7.92 inches. —*v.* To connect: *The Suez Canal links the Mediterranean with the Indian Ocean.* [SEE PICTURE]

linking verb. A verb that, instead of expressing an action, simply connects the subject of a sentence with a word or phrase that tells something about the subject; for example, the verbs in the following sentences are linking verbs: *She was very happy. Arthur seemed uncertain about grammar. Then he became a truck driver. I got sleepy.*

links |lĭngks| *pl.n.* A **golf course.** ¶*These sound alike* **links, lynx.**

lin•net |lĭn′ĭt| *n.* A small, brownish European songbird.

li•no•le•um |lĭ nō′lē əm| *n.* A sturdy, washable material made in sheets by pressing a mixture of hot linseed oil, rosin, powdered cork, and coloring onto a cloth backing, used for covering floors and counters.

Lin•o•type |lī′nə tīp′| *n.* A trademark for a keyboard-operated machine that can set an entire line of type on a single metal slug.

lin•seed |lĭn′sēd′| *n.* The seed or seeds of the flax plant, pressed to obtain linseed oil.

linseed oil. A yellow-to-brown oil that thickens and hardens when exposed to air, extracted from flax seeds and used in paints and varnishes.

lint |lĭnt| *n.* **1.** Clinging bits of fiber and fluff from yarn or cloth. **2.** Downy material scraped from linen cloth and used to dress wounds.

lin•tel |lĭn′tl| *n.* The horizontal beam over the top of a door or window, supporting the weight of the structure above it.

lint•er |lĭn′tər| *n.* **1. linters.** The short fibers that cling to cotton seeds after the first ginning. **2.** A machine that removes linters from cotton seeds.

li•on |lī′ən| *n.* **1.** A very large wild cat of Africa and India, having a tawny coat and a heavy mane around the neck and shoulders in the male. **2.** See **mountain lion. 3.** A person of great strength or courage. **4.** A person who is a center of attention; a celebrity. [SEE PICTURE]

li•on•ess |lī′ə nĭs| *n.* A female lion.

li•on-heart•ed |lī′ən här′tĭd| *adj.* Extraordinarily courageous.

li•on•ize |lī′ə nīz′| *v.* **li•on•ized, li•on•iz•ing.** To look upon or treat as a celebrity.

lip |lĭp| *n.* **1.** Either of the fleshy, muscular folds of tissue that together surround the mouth. **2.** The rim of a container, wound, etc. **3.** A protruding part of certain flowers, such as an orchid or a snapdragon. [SEE NOTE on p. 503]

li•pase |lī′pās′| *or* |lĭp′ās′| *n.* Any one of several enzymes that decompose fats with water to form glycerol and fatty acids.

lip•id |lĭp′ĭd| *or* |lī′pĭd| *n.* Any of a large number of fats or fatty substances that are insoluble in water and soluble in organic solvents, and that are important structural materials of living cells.

lip•ide |lĭp′īd′| *or* |lī′pīd′| *n.* A form of the word **lipid.**

lip•stick |lĭp′stĭk′| *n.* A stick of waxy lip coloring enclosed in a small case.

liq•ue•fac•tion |lĭk′wə făk′shən| *n.* **1.** The act or process of liquefying. **2.** The condition of being liquefied.

liq•ue•fy |lĭk′wə fī′| *v.* **liq•ue•fied, liq•ue•fy•ing.** To make or become liquid. —**liq′ue•fi′er** *n.*

li•queur |lĭ kûr′| *n.* A sweet, syrupy alcoholic

line segment
The distance between points A and B is a line segment of the line between the two arrowheads

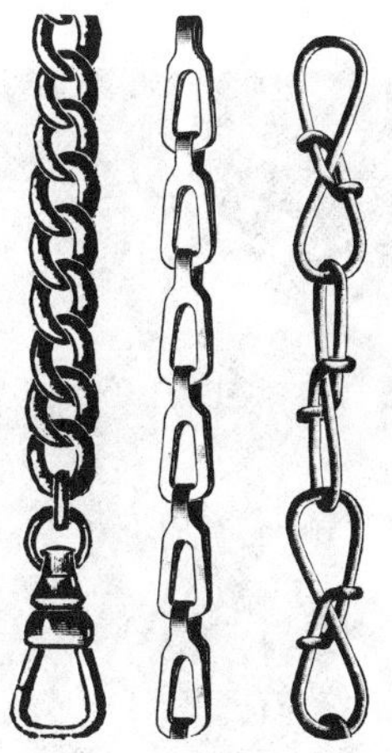

link

lion

list[1-2]
List[1] *is from Old French* liste, *"edge, strip of paper."* **List[2]** *is of unknown origin.*

litchi

beverage made with various aromatic ingredients, often with a brandy base; a cordial.

liq•uid |lĭk'wĭd| *n.* **1.** The state of matter in which a substance characteristically flows readily, has little tendency to break apart, and is difficult to compress. **2.** Matter or a particular body of matter in this state. *—adj.* **1.** In the state of a liquid: *a liquid rocket fuel.* **2.** Readily converted into cash: *liquid assets.*

liq•ui•date |lĭk'wĭ dāt'| *v.* **liq•ui•dat•ed, liq•ui•dat•ing. 1.** To pay off or settle: *liquidate one's debts.* **2.** To close down (a business firm) by settling its accounts and dividing up any remaining assets. **3.** To put to death; do away with; kill. —**liq'ui•da'tion** *n.*

liquid measure. 1. A unit or system of units for measuring liquid volume or capacity. **2.** A measure for liquids.

liq•uor |lĭk'ər| *n.* **1.** An alcoholic beverage made by distillation rather than by fermentation. **2.** Any juice or broth produced in cooking. **3.** A solution or liquid mixture used in chemistry.

lira |lîr'ə| *n., pl.* **li•re** |lîr'ā| *or* **li•ras.** The basic unit of money of Italy and Turkey.

Lis•bon |lĭz'bən|. The capital of Portugal. Population, 761,000.

lisle |līl| *n.* A fine, smooth, tightly twisted cotton thread or a fabric knitted from it. *—modifier: lisle socks.*

lisp |lĭsp| *n.* A speech defect in which *s* and *z* are pronounced *th.* *—v.* To speak with a lisp.

lis•some |lĭs'əm| *adj.* Moving or bending easily; lithe. —**lis'some•ly** *adv.*

list[1] |lĭst| *n.* A series of names of people or things, written or printed one after the other: *a guest list; a shopping list.* *—v.* **1.** To make a list of: *List your reasons. Listed below are the names of the candidates.* **2.** To include in a list: *He is not listed in the phone book.* [SEE NOTE]

list[2] |lĭst| *n.* A tilt to one side, as of a ship: *a sudden list to starboard.* *—v.* To tilt to one side, as a ship; heel. [SEE NOTE]

lis•ten |lĭs'ən| *v.* **1.** To make an effort to hear something: *If you listen carefully, you can just hear the ocean. I never listen to the radio.* **2.** To pay attention; heed: *Now listen to me!* *—phrasal verb.* **listen in. 1.** To tune in and listen to a broadcast. **2.** To listen to a conversation between other people; eavesdrop. —**lis'ten•er** *n.*

list•ing |lĭs'tĭng| *n.* **1.** A list. **2.** Something entered on a list or in a directory: *a telephone listing.*

list•less |lĭst'lĭs| *adj.* Lacking energy or enthusiasm; lethargic: *You will feel listless until the fever passes.* —**list'less•ly** *adv.* —**list'less•ness** *n.*

list price. A basic price published in a price list, often reduced by a dealer.

Liszt |lĭst|, **Franz.** 1811–1886. Hungarian composer and pianist.

lit |lĭt|. A past tense and past participle of **light.**

li•tchi |lē'chē| *n., pl.* **li•tchis. 1.** Also **litchi nut.** The sweet, thin-shelled fruit of a Chinese tree. **2.** The tree itself. [SEE PICTURE]

li•ter |lē'tər| *n.* A unit of volume that is equal to the volume of a cube that is one-tenth of a meter on each edge. A liter is equal to about 1.056 liquid quarts or 0.908 dry quart.

lit•er•a•cy |lĭt'ər ə sē| *n.* The ability to read or write, especially as it exists in a group, community, or country. *—modifier: a literacy test.*

lit•er•al |lĭt'ər əl| *adj.* **1.** Reflecting exactly what is meant by a word or group of words: *the literal meaning of a word.* **2.** Corresponding word for word: *a literal translation.*

lit•er•al•ly |lĭt'ər ə lē| *adv.* **1.** In the literal sense; in a literal manner: *Translated literally "carte blanche" means "blank card."* **2.** In the literal rather than the figurative sense of the word or words used: *Literally millions of lives were saved by the vaccine.*

lit•er•ar•y |lĭt'ə rĕr'ē| *adj.* **1.** Of literature or authors: *a literary critic; a literary agent.* **2.** Suited to literature rather than to everyday speech or writing: *a literary style.* **3.** Having knowledge of or attachment to literature.

lit•er•ate |lĭt'ər ĭt| *adj.* **1.** Able to read and write. **2.** Skillful in the use of words: *a literate style.* **3.** Educated in or familiar with literature. *—n.* A person who can read and write.

lit•er•a•ture |lĭt'ər ə chər| *n.* **1.** A body of writing in prose or verse. **2.** Imaginative or creative writing, especially writing having recognized artistic value. **3.** A body of writing on a given subject. **4.** Printed material of any kind, as for a political campaign.

lithe |līth| *adj.* **lith•er, lith•est.** Smooth and graceful in motion. —**lithe'ly** *adv.* —**lithe'ness** *n.*

lith•i•um |lĭth'ē əm| *n.* Symbol **Li** One of the elements, a soft, silvery, highly reactive metal. Atomic number 3; atomic weight 6.94; valence +1; melting point 179°C; boiling point 1,317°C.

lith•o•graph |lĭth'ə grăf'| *or* |-grăf'| *n.* A print produced by lithography. *—v.* To produce by lithography. —**li•thog'ra•pher** |lĭ thŏg'rə fər| *n.*

lith•o•graph•ic |lĭth'ə grăf'ĭk| *adj.* Of lithography. —**lith'o•graph'i•cal•ly** *adv.*

li•thog•ra•phy |lĭ thŏg'rə fē| *n.* A printing process in which the printing surface, often a metal plate, is treated so that ink will stick only to those parts that are to be printed.

lith•o•sphere |lĭth'ō sfîr'| *n.* **1.** The solid part of the earth, as distinguished from the hydrosphere and atmosphere. **2.** The rocky crust of the earth.

Lith•u•a•ni•a |lĭth'o͞o ā'nē ə|. A former country on the Baltic Sea, now a part of the Soviet Union.

Lith•u•a•ni•an |lĭth'o͞o ā'nē ən| *n.* **1.** A native or inhabitant of Lithuania. **2.** The Baltic language of Lithuania. *—adj.* Of Lithuania, the Lithuanians, or their language.

lit•i•ga•tion |lĭt'ĭ gā'shən| *n.* **1.** The process of carrying on a lawsuit: *prolonged litigation over a contested estate.* **2.** A legal case; lawsuit.

lit•mus |lĭt'məs| *n.* A blue powder, derived from certain lichens, that changes from blue to red in an acid solution and from red to blue in an alkaline solution.

litmus paper. Unsized white paper that has been treated with litmus, used to distinguish acid and alkaline solutions.

li•tre |lē'tər| *n.* British form of the word **liter.**

lit•ter |lĭt'ər| *n.* **1.** A couch mounted on poles and often covered by a canopy, used to carry a person from place to place. **2.** A stretcher used to carry a sick or wounded person. **3.** Straw, hay, etc., used as bedding for animals to sleep on. **4.** Young animals borne at one time by a single mother: *a litter of puppies.* **5.** Carelessly scattered scraps of paper or other waste material. —*v.* To make (a place) untidy by scattering things about: *No littering! Please don't litter the streets.*

lit•ter•bug |lĭt′ər bŭg′| *n. Informal.* A person who carelessly scatters waste material.

lit•tle |lĭt′l| *adj.* **lit•tler, lit•tlest** or **least** |lēst|. **1.** Small in size, quantity, or degree: *a stout little man.* **2. a.** Young: *All but the littlest of the children had to work hard.* **b.** Younger: *Archie was close to his little brother all their lives.* **3.** Also comparative **less** |lĕs|, superlative **least. a.** Short in extent or duration; brief: *little time.* **b.** Unimportant; trivial: *It makes little difference.* **4.** Without much force; weak: *The little cry came again and the searchers looked toward the cave.* —*adv.* **less, least.** Not much: *He sleeps very little.* —*n.* **1.** A small amount: *I asked him for some cake, and he gave me a little.* **2.** Something much less than all: *You know much; I know little.*

Idioms. **a little. 1.** Slightly: *I have to be a little careful of my diet.* **2.** A small amount of: *I wish I had a little flour to put in the pot.* **little by little.** Gradually: *He's getting better little by little.*

Little Dipper. A group of seven stars in the northern sky that form the outline of a dipper; the constellation Ursa Minor.

Little League. An organization of baseball teams for boys nine to twelve years old.

Little Rock. The capital of Arkansas. Population, 130,000.

li•tur•gi•cal |lĭ tûr′jĭ kəl| *adj.* Of or used in liturgy.

lit•ur•gy |lĭt′ər jē| *n., pl.* **lit•ur•gies.** The prescribed form for a religious service; ritual.

liv•a•ble |lĭv′ə bəl| *adj.* **1.** Suitable for living in: *a very livable house.* **2.** Bearable; endurable: *a life of hardship that was barely livable.*

live[1] |lĭv| *v.* **lived, liv•ing. 1.** To be alive; exist: *Fish cannot live long out of water.* **2.** To continue to remain alive: *Long live the king!* **3.** To support oneself; subsist: *Two can live as cheaply as one.* **4.** To reside or dwell: *Eskimos live in igloos.* **5.** To spend or pass (one's life): *He has lived his whole life here in Willow Falls.* **6.** To conduct one's life in a certain manner: *live happily.* **7.** To enjoy life to the utmost: *He really knows how to live!* —*phrasal verbs.* **live down.** To reduce or eliminate the shame of (a misdeed, scandal, etc.) over a period of time. **live up to. 1.** To live in accordance with: *live up to one's ideals.* **2.** To come up to; not disappoint: *live up to expectations.* **3.** To fulfill; carry out: *live up to one's end of a bargain.* **live with.** To put up with; resign oneself to; accept: *It's something you're going to have to learn to live with.* [SEE NOTE]

Idiom. **live it up.** *Informal.* To engage in pleasures one usually denies oneself.

live[2] |līv| *adj.* **1.** Alive; living: *live fishing bait; a real live monkey.* **2.** Glowing; burning: *a live coal.* **3.** Energized with electricity or carrying electric current: *a live circuit.* **4.** Not exploded; able to be fired: *live ammunition.* **5.** Of current interest or importance: *a live issue.* **6.** Broadcast while actually being performed: *a program coming live from New York.* [SEE NOTE]

live•li•hood |līv′lē ho͝od′| *n.* The way in which a person earns his living.

live•long |lĭv′lông′| *or* |-lŏng| *adj.* Whole; entire: *all the livelong day.*

live•ly |līv′lē| *adj.* **live•li•er, live•li•est. 1.** Full of life, energy, or activity: *a lively baby; a lively town.* **2.** Animated; spirited; stimulating: *a lively style of writing; a lively tune.* **3.** Keen; brisk: *lively trade between the two countries.* **4.** Rich; inventive: *a lively imagination.* **5.** Bright; vivid: *lively colors.* **6.** Tending to bounce or rebound stongly: *a lively baseball.* —*adv.* In a lively manner: *Step lively!* —**live′li•ness** *n.*

liv•en |lī′vən| *v.* To make or become lively.

live oak |līv|. An evergreen oak tree of the southern United States.

liv•er |lĭv′ər| *n.* **1.** A large glandular organ found in the abdomen of vertebrates. It secretes bile and acts in the formation of blood and in the metabolism of nutrients. **2.** A similar organ of invertebrate animals. **3.** The liver of an animal, used as food. —*modifier: liver pâté.*

liv•er•ied |lĭv′ə rēd| *or* |lĭv′rēd| *adj.* Wearing livery: *a liveried footman.*

Liv•er•pool |lĭv′ər po͞ol′|. A city and port in western England. Population, 700,000.

liv•er•wort |lĭv′ər wûrt′| *n.* **1.** Any of a group of green plants that are related to the mosses and that do not bear flowers. **2.** A flowering plant, the hepatica.

liv•er•y |lĭv′ə rē| *or* |lĭv′rē| *n., pl.* **liv•er•ies. 1.** A distinctive uniform worn by the male servants of a household, such as footmen or chauffeurs. **2.** The stabling and care of horses for a fee. —*modifier: a livery stable.*

live•stock |līv′stŏk′| *n.* Animals, such as cattle, horses, sheep, or pigs, raised and kept for human use, as on a farm.

live wire |līv|. **1.** A wire that is charged with electricity, usually dangerous to touch. **2.** *Slang.* An alert, energetic, or imaginative person.

liv•id |lĭv′ĭd| *adj.* **1.** Discolored, as from a bruise. **2.** Deathly pale or white, as from anger, fear, etc. **3.** Extremely angry; enraged.

liv•ing |lĭv′ĭng| *adj.* **1.** Alive: *famous living persons.* **2.** Currently existing or in use: *a living language.* **3.** True to life: *the living image of her mother.* **4.** *Informal.* Absolute: *You're just a living doll!* —*n.* **1.** The condition or action of maintaining life: *the high cost of living.* **2.** A manner or style of life: *plain living.* **3.** A means of maintaining life: *Eskimos make their living by hunting and trapping.* —*modifier: living conditions; living quarters.*

living room. A room for general use and the entertainment of guests in a household.

liz•ard |lĭz′ərd| *n.* **1.** Any of a group of reptiles having a scaly, often slender body, four legs, and a tapering tail. **2.** Leather made from lizard skin. —*modifier: a lizard belt.*

ll. lines.

lla•ma |lä′mə| *n.* A South American animal related to the camel, raised for its soft, fleecy wool and for carrying loads. [SEE PICTURE]

LM **lunar module.**

lo |lō| *interj.* A word used to call attention to something remarkable or important. ¶*These sound alike* **lo, low.**

load |lōd| *n.* **1.** A weight or mass that is carried, lifted, or supported. **2. a.** Anything that is carried, as by a vehicle, person, or animal: *a load of*

live[1-2]

Live[1] *was* lifian *in Old English; its original meaning was "to continue."* **Life** *was Old English* līf *and is closely related to* **live**[1]. **Alive** *comes from Old English* on līf, *"in life";* **live**[2] *is shortened from* **alive**.

llama

loaf[1-2]

Loaf[1] *was* hlāf *in Old English; it is descended from prehistoric Germanic* hlaibaz. **Loaf**[2] *is probably a back-formation from* **loafer**, *which is of obscure origin.*

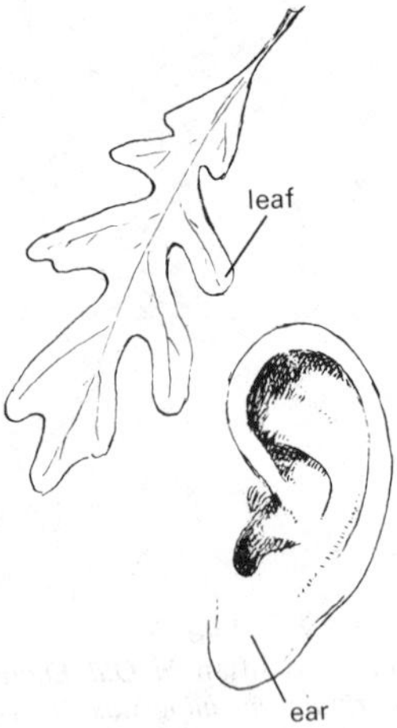

lobe
Above: Leaf lobe
Below: Ear lobe

lock[1-2]

Lock[1] *was Old English* loc, *and* **lock**[2] *was Old English* locc. *Probably the two words are ultimately the same; the original meanings may have been "turning, twisting device"* (**lock**[1]) *and "twist of hair"* (**lock**[2]).

ă pat/ā pay/â care/ä father/ĕ pet/ ē be/ĭ pit/ī pie/î fierce/ŏ pot/ ō go/ô paw, for/oi oil/ŏŏ book/ ōō boot/ou out/ŭ cut/û fur/ *th* the/th thin/hw which/zh vision/ ə ago, item, pencil, atom, circus

firewood. **b.** The quantity or amount carried: *a wagon with a full load of hay.* **3.** An object or device to which power is delivered, as by an electric circuit or mechanical system. **4.** The amount of work, duties, etc., done, performed, or produced by a person, machine, etc. **5.** A single charge of ammunition for a gun. **6.** Mental stress regarded as a depressing weight or burden: *That's a load off my mind.* **7.** Often **loads.** *Informal.* A great number or amount: *invited to loads of parties.* —*v.* **1. a.** To place (material to be carried) in or on a structure, machine, conveyance, etc.: *load grain onto a train.* **b.** To place material to be carried in or on: *load a ship.* **c.** To receive a load; take on cargo: *While in port, the ship loaded.* **2.** To provide or fill nearly to overflowing: *Grandmother loaded the table with food.* **3.** To weigh down; burden: *The wars loaded the people with cares.* **4.** To charge with ammunition: *load a gun.* **5. a.** To insert (film, tape, etc.) into a holder or magazine: *load film into a camera.* **b.** To insert film, tape, etc., into: *load a camera.* **6.** To subject (an engine, structure, electric power system, etc.) to a load. **7.** In baseball, to fill (the three bases) with base runners. **8.** To make (dice) heavier on one side. —**load'ing** *adj.: the loading platform.* ¶*These sound alike* **load, lode.** —**load'er** *n.*

Idiom. get a load of. *Slang.* To take notice of: *Get a load of that new car.*

loaf[1] |lōf| *n., pl.* **loaves** |lōvz|. **1.** A shaped mass of bread baked in one piece. **2.** Any shaped mass of food: *a meat loaf.* —**modifier:** *a loaf pan.* [SEE NOTE]

loaf[2] |lōf| *v.* To spend time lazily or aimlessly; idle: *We loafed all morning.* [SEE NOTE]

loaf•er |lō'fər| *n.* **1.** A person who spends time lazily or idly; an idler. **2.** A shoe for informal wear, shaped like a moccasin.

loam |lōm| *n.* A soil that contains mainly sand, clay, silt, and decayed plant matter.

loam•y |lō'mē| *adj.* **loam•i•er, loam•i•est.** Consisting of or containing loam: *loamy soil.*

loan |lōn| *n.* **1.** The act of lending: *the loan of a raincoat to a friend.* **2.** The condition or arrangement of being lent: *Some paintings are on loan from other museums.* **3. a.** Something borrowed: *That lamp is a loan from my neighbor.* **b.** A sum of money lent at interest: *a loan at the bank.* —**modifier:** *a loan company.* —*v.* To lend. ¶*These sound alike* **loan, lone.**

loan-word, also **loan•word** |lōn'wûrd'| *n.* Also **loan word.** A word that has been borrowed from one language for use in another; for example, *encore, spaghetti,* and *sombrero* are loan-words.

loath |lōth| *or* |lō*th*| *adj.* Not willing; reluctant; averse: *He was loath to accept the offer.*

loathe |lō*th*| *v.* **loathed, loath•ing.** To regard with intense dislike; detest: *loathe spinach.*

loath•ing |lō'*th*ĭng| *n.* Extreme dislike; aversion; abhorrence.

loath•some |lō*th*'səm| *or* |lōth'-| *adj.* Detestable; repulsive; disgusting.

loaves |lōvz| *n.* Plural of **loaf.**

lob |lŏb| *v.* **lobbed, lob•bing.** To hit, throw, or propel (a ball) in a high arc. —*n.* **1.** A ball hit or thrown in a high arc. **2.** A cricket ball thrown underhand in a slow arc.

lob•by |lŏb'ē| *n., pl.* **lob•bies. 1.** A hall or waiting room in a hotel, apartment house, or theater. **2.** A group of private persons engaged in trying to influence lawmakers in favor of some special interest. —*v.* **lob•bied, lob•by•ing, lob•bies.** To seek to influence lawmakers in favor of some special interest.

lob•by•ist |lŏb'ē ĭst| *n.* A person who lobbies.

lobe |lōb| *n.* A rounded, projecting part, as of a leaf or an organ of the body. —**lobed** *adj.* [SEE PICTURES]

lo•be•li•a |lō bē'lē ə| *or* |-bēl'yə| *n.* Any of several plants with clusters of blue, red, or purplish flowers.

lob•lol•ly pine |lŏb'lŏl'ē|. A pine tree of the southeastern United States, having strong wood used as lumber and for making paper pulp.

lob•ster |lŏb'stər| *n.* **1.** A sea animal related to the crabs and shrimps, having a long, hard-shelled body and five pairs of legs, of which the front pair are large and pincerlike. **2.** The meat of a lobster, used as food. —**modifier:** *lobster traps; a lobster boat.*

lo•cal |lō'kəl| *adj.* **1.** Of a limited area or place: *local governments; a local storm.* **2.** Making many stops; not express: *a local train.* **3.** Limited to part of the body rather than the entire system: *a local infection.* —*n.* **1.** A person who lives in a certain region or neighborhood: *The locals thought the new family was odd.* **2.** A local branch of an organization, especially of a labor union. **3.** A local train, bus, etc. —**lo'cal•ly** *adv.*

local anesthetic. An anesthetic that acts only on and around the point on the body where it is applied or injected.

lo•cale |lō kăl'| *or* |-käl'| *n.* The scene or setting, as of an event or a written work.

lo•cal•i•ty |lō kăl'ĭ tē| *n., pl.* **lo•cal•i•ties.** A certain neighborhood, place, or region.

lo•cal•ize |lō'kə līz'| *v.* **lo•cal•ized, lo•cal•iz•ing.** To make or become local: *localized the infection; panic that localized near the city hall.*

lo•cate |lō'kāt'| *or* |lō kāt'| *v.* **lo•cat•ed, lo•cat•ing. 1.** To determine and show the position or boundaries of: *locate Austria on a map.* **2.** To find by searching, inquiring, or examining: *locate food; locate information.* **3.** To place or situate: *Try to locate your vegetable plot in a sunny, fertile area.* **4.** To go and live somewhere: *The family has located in Iowa.*

lo•ca•tion |lō kā'shən| *n.* **1.** A place where something is located; a site or position: *the location of the hospital.* **2.** The act or process of locating: *the location of water by probing the earth.* **3.** The fact of being located or settled: *their sudden location in another state.* **4.** A site away from a motion-picture studio at which a scene is filmed: *shot on location in Spain.*

loch |lŏk| *or* |lŏKH| *n. Scottish.* A lake. ¶*These sound alike* **loch, lock.**

lo•ci |lō'sī'| *n.* Plural of **locus.**

lock[1] |lŏk| *n.* **1.** A device used to hold, close, or secure, especially a device operated by a key or combination that holds a door, lid, etc., shut. **2.** A section of a canal, closed off with gates, in which a ship can be raised or lowered by pumping water in or out. **3.** A mechanism in a firearm for exploding the charge. **4.** Any of several wrestling holds. **5.** An **air lock.** —*v.* **1.** To fasten shut or secure with a lock or locks:

lock the door. **2.** To hold, fasten, or bind securely in position: *The brakes locked the wheels. Energy is locked up in the atom.* **3.** To become tightly held, fastened, or secured: *This valve locks automatically under pressure.* **4.** To intertwine: *They locked arms and walked off.* **5.** To make and hold (eye contact): *He locked eyes with her. Their eyes locked in a cold, bold stare.* —**locked'** *adj.: a locked door.* —***phrasal verb.*** **lock out. 1.** To shut out, as by locking a door: *locked him out of their games.* **2.** To prevent (employees) from entering their place of work during a labor dispute. ¶*These sound alike* **lock, loch.** [SEE NOTE & PICTURES]

Idiom. **lock, stock, and barrel.** Together with everything; completely: *She left town with her possessions, lock, stock, and barrel.*

lock² |lŏk| *n.* **1.** A strand or curl of hair; a tress; ringlet. **2. locks.** The hair of the head: *She combed her long golden locks.* **3.** A small wisp or tuft of wool, cotton, etc. ¶*These sound alike* **lock, loch.** [SEE NOTE]

lock•er |**lŏk'**ər| *n.* **1.** A compartment in a gymnasium or public place for the safekeeping of clothes and valuables. **2.** A refrigerated cabinet or room for storing frozen foods for long periods of time. —***modifier:*** *a locker key.*

lock•et |**lŏk'**ĭt| *n.* A small, ornamental metal case for a picture, lock of hair, or other keepsake, usually worn on a chain around the neck.

lock•jaw |**lŏk'**jô'| *n.* **1.** Tetanus, a disease. **2.** A symptom of tetanus in which the jaw is held tightly closed by a spasm of muscles.

lock•out |**lŏk'**out'| *n.* The act of closing down a plant during a labor dispute in order to force employees to meet the employer's terms or modify their own terms.

lock•smith |**lŏk'**smĭth'| *n.* A person who makes or repairs locks.

lo•co•mo•tion |lō'kə **mō'**shən| *n.* **1.** The act or capability of moving from place to place. **2.** Locomotive power.

lo•co•mo•tive |lō'kə **mō'**tĭv| *n.* An engine, usually electric or diesel-powered, used to pull or push railroad cars along a track. —***modifier:*** *the locomotive whistle.* [SEE PICTURE]

lo•co•weed |**lō'**kō wēd'| *n.* Any of several western American plants that cause severe illness when eaten by cattle, sheep, etc.

lo•cus |**lō'**kəs| *n., pl.* **lo•ci** |**lō'**sī'|. The set or arrangement of all points that satisfy specified mathematical conditions.

lo•cust |**lō'**kəst| *n.* **1.** A grasshopper of a kind that travels in large swarms, often doing great damage to crops. **2.** Often **seventeen-year locust.** A cicada of a kind that remains underground in an immature stage for seventeen years. **3.** Any of several trees with featherlike leaves, drooping clusters of fragrant white flowers, and beanlike pods. [SEE PICTURE]

lode |lōd| *n.* A deposit of a metal-bearing ore, such as a vein clearly bounded by rock that is not ore. ¶*These sound alike* **lode, load.**

lode•star |**lōd'**stär'| *n.* A star used as a point of reference, especially Polaris, the North Star.

lode•stone |**lōd'**stōn'| *n.* A magnetized piece of magnetite.

lodge |lŏj| *n.* **1.** A cottage or cabin, especially one in a secluded place used as a temporary abode or shelter: *a ski lodge; a fishing lodge.* **2.** An inn. **3.** A local chapter or meeting place of a fraternal organization: *a Masonic lodge.* —***modifier:*** *the lodge gate.* —*v.* **lodged, lodg•ing. 1.** To provide with sleeping quarters. **2.** To establish or become established in a place. **3.** To live in a rented room or rooms. **4.** To be or become embedded: *A splinter lodged in his heel.* **5.** To present (a charge, complaint, etc.) to an appropriate official or office; register.

lodg•er |**lŏj'**ər| *n.* A person who rents a room or rooms in another person's house.

lodg•ing |**lŏj'**ĭng| *n.* **1.** A temporary place to sleep. **2. lodgings.** Rented living quarters.

lo•ess |**lō'**ĕs| *or* |lĕs| *or* |lŭs| *n.* A yellow to gray fine-grained silt or clay, thought to be deposited as dust blown by the wind.

loft |lôft| *or* |lŏft| *n.* **1.** A large, often unpartitioned floor in a commercial building. **2.** An open space under a roof; an attic or garret. **3.** A gallery or balcony, as in a church: *a choir loft.* **4.** A hayloft. —*v.* To send (a ball) in a high arc.

loft•y |**lôf'**tē| *or* |**lŏf'**-| *adj.* **loft•i•er, loft•i•est. 1.** Of great height; towering: *lofty mountains.* **2.** Elevated in character or spirit; exalted; noble: *lofty thoughts; lofty principles.* **3.** Arrogant; overbearing; haughty: *a lofty treatment of others.* —**loft'i•ly** *adv.* —**loft'i•ness** *n.*

log |lôg| *or* |lŏg| *n.* **1. a.** A large trunk of a tree that has fallen or been cut down. **b.** A cut length of such wood, used for building, firewood, or lumber. **2.** A device trailed from a ship to determine its speed through the water. **3. a.** An official record of speed, progress, and important events, kept on a ship or aircraft. **b.** Any journal or record. —***modifier:*** *a log fire; a log cabin.* —*v.* **logged, log•ging. 1.** To cut down the timber of (a section of land). **2.** To cut down, trim, and haul timber. **3.** To enter (something) in a logbook or other record. **4.** To travel (a certain distance or at a certain speed). —**log'ger** *n.*

Idiom. **sleep like a log.** To sleep soundly.

log logarithm.

lo•gan•ber•ry |**lō'**gən bĕr'ē| *n., pl.* **-ber•ries.** The edible dark-red fruit of a prickly plant related to the blackberry and the raspberry.

log•a•rithm |**lô'**gə rĭth'əm| *or* |**lŏg'**ə-| *n.* The exponent that indicates the power to which a fixed, positive number, called the base, must be raised to produce a given number; for example, if n is the base and $x = n^a$, then a is said to be the logarithm of x to the base n. See **common logarithm.** —**log'a•rith'mic** *adj.*

log•ger•head |**lô'**gər hĕd'| *or* |**lŏg'**ər-| *n.* **1.** A large sea turtle of warm waters. **2.** *Informal.* A person who acts in a stupid way; a blockhead.

Idiom. **at loggerheads.** In disagreement or in a dispute with; at odds.

log•ging |**lô'**gĭng| *or* |**lŏg'**ĭng| *n.* The work of cutting down trees and moving logs to a mill.

log•ic |**lŏj'**ĭk| *n.* **1.** The study of the principles of reasoning, especially of the forms and relationships between statements as distinguished from the content of statements. **2.** Rational thought; clear reasoning. **3.** A particular system or method of reasoning. **4.** A way of thinking or reasoning: *the political logic of frontier people.*

log•i•cal |**lŏj'**ĭ kəl| *adj.* **1.** Of, using, or agreeing

lock¹
Above: Padlock
Below: Locks on the Panama Canal

locomotive
Diesel locomotive

locust

long[1-2]

Long[1] *was* long *or* lang *in Old English.* **Long[2]** *was Old English* langian, *which originally meant "to grow longer"; it was used in phrases like* "it longs me for (something)," *meaning "it makes me wish for, I yearn for," and later* "to long for" *came to mean "to yearn for." The details are rather difficult to understand, but apparently the key idea is that when you deeply yearn for something, it makes the time seem to pass slowly.*

longhorn

with the principles of logic. **2.** Reasonable: *a logical choice.* **3.** Able to reason clearly and rationally: *a logical mind.* —**log'i•cal•ly** *adv.*

lo•gi•cian |lō **jĭsh'**ən| *n.* A person who practices or is skilled in logic.

lo•gis•tics |lō **jĭs'**tĭks| *n. (used with a singular verb).* The problems and methods of obtaining, distributing, maintaining, and replacing materiel and personnel, as in a military operation.

lo•gy |**lō'**gē| *adj.* **lo•gi•er, lo•gi•est.** Sluggish; lethargic.

-logy. A word element meaning: **1.** An oral or written expression: **phraseology. 2.** The science, theory, or study of: **sociology.**

loin |loin| *n.* **1. a.** Often **loins.** The part of the sides and back of the body between the ribs and hipbones. **b.** A cut of meat taken from this part of an animal. **2. loins. a.** The region of the thighs and groin. **b.** The reproductive organs.

loin•cloth |**loin'**klôth'| *or* |-klŏth'| *n., pl.* **-cloths** |-klôthz'| *or* |-klŏthz'| *or* |-klôths'| *or* |-klŏths'|. A strip of cloth worn around the loins as a garment.

loi•ter |**loi'**tər| *v.* **1.** To stand about idly; linger. **2.** To go slowly, stopping often: *She loitered on the way to the dentist.* —**loi'ter•er** *n.*

loll |lŏl| *v.* **1.** To move, stand, sit, or rest in a lazy way: *lolling about in dungarees at home.* **2.** To hang or let hang loosely or laxly: *The hunted wolf's quivering tongue lolled.*

lol•la•pa•loo•za |lŏl'ə pə **lōō'**zə| *n. Slang.* Something outstanding.

lol•li•pop, also **lol•ly•pop** |**lŏl'**ē pŏp'| *n.* A piece of hard candy on the end of a stick.

Lo•mé |lō **mā'**|. The capital of Togo. Population, 130,000.

Lon•don |**lŭn'**dən|. The capital of England and of the United Kingdom on the Thames River in southeastern England. Population, 8,000,000.

lone |lōn| *adj.* **1.** Single, solitary: *a lone horseman.* **2.** Remote; unfrequented: *the lone prairie.* ¶*These sound alike* **lone, loan.**

lone•ly |**lōn'**lē| *adj.* **lone•li•er, lone•li•est. 1.** Sad at being alone: *a lonely little boy with no friends.* **2.** Alone: *a lonely traveler.* **3.** Unfrequented; remote: *a lonely road.* —**lone'li•ness** *n.*

lone•some |**lōn'**səm| *adj.* **1.** Sad and depressed at feeling alone. **2.** Producing a feeling of loneliness: *a lonesome voyage.* **3.** Unfrequented; remote: *a lonesome mountain trail.*

long[1] |lông| *or* |lŏng| *adj.* **long•er, long•est. 1.** Having great length: *a long river; a long novel.* **2.** Of relatively great duration or extent: *a long time; a long journey.* **3.** Of a certain extent or duration: *The reptile was 30 feet long. His speech was an hour long.* **4.** Extending far into the future; far-reaching: *a long view of the situation.* **5.** Having an abundance of: *She is long on kindness.* **6.** Having a sound that is comparatively drawn out or prolonged; for example, the *a* in *pane* is a long vowel in contrast with the short *a* in *pan.* —*adv.* **1.** During or for an extended period of time: *Stay as long as you like.* **2.** For or throughout a specific period: *all night long.* **3.** At a very distant time: *long after Christmas; long ago.* [SEE NOTE]

long[2] |lông| *or* |lŏng| *v.* To have a strong desire; wish for very much; yearn: *She longed to go back home.* [SEE NOTE]

long. longitude.

long distance. An operator or system that places long-distance telephone calls.

long-dis•tance |**lông'**dĭs'təns| *or* |**lŏng'**-| *adj.* **1.** Covering or carried over a great distance: *a long-distance race.* **2.** Of communications by telephone to a distant station. —*adv.* By telephone to a distant station: *He talked long-distance.*

lon•gev•i•ty |lŏn **jĕv'**ĭ tē| *n.* Long life.

Long•fel•low |**lông'**fĕl'ō| *or* |**lŏng'**-|, **Henry Wadsworth.** 1807-1882. American poet.

long•hand |**lông'**hănd'| *or* |**lŏng'**-| *n.* Writing in which the letters of each word are joined together; ordinary handwriting.

long•horn |**lông'**hôrn'| *or* |**lŏng'**-| *n.* One of a breed of cattle with long, spreading horns, formerly raised in the southwestern United States. [SEE PICTURE]

long•ing |**lông'**ĭng| *or* |**lŏng'**-| *n.* A deep yearning; a strong desire. —*adj.* Showing a deep yearning: *a longing look.* —**long'ing•ly** *adv.*

Long Island. An island in New York State, projecting into the Atlantic Ocean.

lon•gi•tude |**lŏn'**jĭ tōōd'| *or* |-tyōōd'| *n.* Distance east and west of the meridian at Greenwich, England, measured as the angle between the plane that contains that meridian and the plane that contains the meridian through the point to which the distance is measured.

lon•gi•tu•di•nal |lŏn'jĭ **tōōd'**n əl| *or* |**-tyōōd'**-| *adj.* **1.** Of or involving length or longitude. **2.** Placed or running lengthwise: *longitudinal stripes.* —**lon'gi•tu'di•nal•ly** *adv.*

long-lived |**lông'**līvd'| *or* |-lĭvd'| *or* |**lŏng'**-| *adj.* Having a long life; existing for a long time.

long-play•ing |**lông'**plā'ĭng| *or* |**lŏng'**-| *adj.* Of a phonograph record with very fine grooves that plays for a long time, especially a record that turns at $33\frac{1}{3}$ revolutions per minute.

long-range |**lông'**rānj'| *or* |**lŏng'**-| *adj.* **1.** Involving a span of years; not immediate: *long-range plans.* **2.** Of or designed for great distances: *long-range bombers.*

long•shore•man |**lông'**shôr'mən| *or* |-shōr'-| *or* |**lŏng'**-| *n., pl.* **-men** |-mən|. A dock worker who loads and unloads ships.

long-suf•fer•ing |**lông'**sŭf'ər ĭng| *or* |**lŏng'**-| *adj.* Patiently enduring pain or difficulty.

long-term |**lông'**tûrm'| *or* |**lŏng'**-| *adj.* Involving a number of years: *a long-term investment.*

long-time |**lông'**tīm'| *or* |**lŏng'**-| *adj.* Having existed for a long time: *a long-time friend.*

long ton. A ton weighing 2,240 pounds.

long-wave |**lông'**wāv'| *or* |**lŏng'**-| *adj.* Of or having a relatively long wavelength.

long-wind•ed |**lông'**wĭn'dĭd| *or* |**lŏng'**-| *adj.* **1.** Writing or talking at great length. **2.** Not easily subject to loss of breath. —**long'-wind'ed•ly** *adv.* —**long'-wind'ed•ness** *n.*

look |lŏŏk| *v.* **1.** To use the eyes to see; perceive by sight. **2.** To focus one's gaze or attention: *She looked toward the river.* **3. a.** To appear; seem: *These bananas look ripe.* **b.** To appear to be: *She does not look her age.* **4.** To face in a certain direction: *The house looks on the sea.* **5.** —Used in the imperative as an intensive, to call attention, protest, etc.: *Look, I cannot be there tomorrow.* —**phrasal verbs. look after.** To take care of: *look after the baby.* **look at (on,** or

ă **pat**/ā **pay**/â **care**/ä **father**/ĕ **pet**/ ē **be**/ĭ **pit**/ī **pie**/î **fierce**/ŏ **pot**/ ō **go**/ô **paw, for**/oi **oil**/ŏŏ **book**/ ōō **boot**/ou **out**/ŭ **cut**/û **fur**/ *th* **the**/th **thin**/hw **which**/zh **vision**/ ə **ago, item, pencil, atom, circus** upon). **1.** To regard; consider: *a good way to look at the problem.* **2.** To examine: *look at the tires of my car.* **look down on** (or **upon**). To regard with contempt: *He looks down on women.* **look for.** **1.** To search for: *animals looking for food.* **2.** To expect: *look for profits.* **look forward to.** To anticipate, usually with pleasure: *I'm looking forward to my trip to Bermuda.* **look in on.** To make a brief visit with: *I'll look in on your grandmother tomorrow.* **look into.** To inquire into; investigate: *I'll look into it for you.* **look out (for).** To be on guard: *look out for snakes on the beach.* **look over.** To examine, often casually: *He looked over the report.* **look to.** **1.** To rely on: *We look to the farmers for food.* **2.** To attend to: *Please look to the chickens while I'm away.* **look up.** **1.** To search for: *look up a word in the dictionary.* **2.** To locate and call upon; visit: *Look us up when you are in town.* **3.** *Informal.* To improve: *Things are beginning to look up around here.* **look up to.** To admire and respect: *He looks up to the coach.* —*n.* **1.** The action of looking; a gaze or glance: *a quick look at the map.* **2.** An inspection or examination: *Take a look at the car to see what's wrong.* **3.** An expression or appearance: *a look of pain in her eyes.* **4. looks.** Personal appearance: *His good looks are legendary.*

looking glass. A mirror.

look•out |**lo͝ok**'out'| *n.* **1.** Someone assigned to watch for something. **2.** The fact of waiting and watching: *keeping a sharp lookout for the enemy.* **3.** A high place that commands a wide view for keeping watch. **4.** A particular problem or concern: *His plans are his own lookout.* —***modifier:*** *a lookout tower.*

loom[1] |lo͞om| *v.* **1.** To come into view or appear as a massive or indistinct image: *Clouds loomed behind the mountains.* **2.** To seem close at hand; be about to happen: *The day of battle loomed before us.* [SEE NOTE]

loom[2] |lo͞om| *n.* A machine or frame on which threads or yarns are woven to make cloth. [SEE NOTE & PICTURE]

loon[1] |lo͞on| *n.* A diving bird with a dark, speckled back, a pointed bill, and an eerie, laughlike cry. [SEE NOTE & PICTURE]

loon[2] |lo͞on| *n.* **1.** A simple-minded or mad person. **2.** An idler. [SEE NOTE]

loon•y |**lo͞o**'nē| *Informal. adj.* **loon•i•er, loon•i•est.** So odd as to appear insane or stupid. —*n., pl.* **loon•ies.** A simple-minded or mad person.

loop |lo͞op| *n.* **1.** A roughly circular or oval length of rope, thread, or wire joined at the ends. **2.** Any roughly circular or oval pattern or path that closes or nearly closes on itself: *The car made a loop around the town.* **3.** A closed path in an electric circuit. **4.** A maneuver in which an aircraft flies in a circle that lies in a vertical plane without changing the direction in which its wings point. —*v.* **1.** To make or form into a loop or loops. **2.** To fasten or join with a loop or loops: *looped the thread around the bobbin.* **3.** To fly (an aircraft) in a loop or loops.

loop•hole |**lo͞op**'hōl'| *n.* **1.** A small hole or slit in a wall for looking or shooting through. **2.** A means of escape, especially an omission or an unclear provision in a law or contract that provides a means of evasion.

loose |lo͞os| *adj.* **loos•er, loos•est.** **1.** Not tightly fastened or secured: *a loose shoelace; loose boards.* **2.** Free from confinement, bonds, fetters, etc.: *The stallion was loose.* **3.** Not tight-fitting or tightly fitted: *a loose robe; loose sleeves.* **4.** Not tightly stretched; flexible: *the loose skin of a turtle's neck.* **5.** Not tightly packed; not compact: *cloth with a loose weave.* **6.** Not bound, bundled, or joined together: *loose book pages.* **7.** Allied but not joined in a formal, rigid union: *a loose confederation.* **8.** Not strict or exact: *a loose style of writing; a loose count.* —*adv.* In a loose manner or condition: *The cows ran loose. Her hair hung loose.* —*v.* **loosed, loos•ing.** **1.** To set free; release. **2.** To make less tight, firm, or compact. **3.** To untie, undo, or unwrap. **4.** To discharge (a missile): *loose an arrow.* —**loose'ly** *adv.* —**loose'ness** *n.*

Idiom. **at loose ends.** Having no plans or direction: *After college, he was at loose ends.*

loose-leaf |**lo͞os**'lēf'| *adj.* Designed to hold easily removed pages: *a loose-leaf notebook.*

loos•en |**lo͞o**'sən| *v.* **1.** To make or become loose or looser: *loosen the guitar strings. When the rope loosens, the cowboy tightens it.* **2.** To free, untie, or release: *He loosened the calf from the bush.* **3.** To break into smaller pieces; make less compact: *loosen the soil with hoes.* **4.** To free or become free of restraint or strictness; relax: *Wine loosened her tongue.*

loot |lo͞ot| *n.* **1.** Valuable things pillaged in time of war; spoils. **2.** Stolen goods. **3.** *Slang.* Money. —*v.* To rob of valuable things by violent means; plunder; pillage. ¶*These sound alike* **loot, lute.** —**loot'er** *n.*

lop[1] |lŏp| *v.* **lopped, lop•ping.** To cut off a part from; trim: *lopped the shrub.*

lop[2] |lŏp| *v.* **lopped, lop•ping.** To hang loosely; droop: *The puppy's ears lopped.*

lope |lōp| *v.* **loped, lop•ing.** To run or ride with a steady, easy gait: *The horse loped along the trail.* —*n.* A steady, easy gait.

lop•sid•ed |**lŏp'sī'**dĭd| *adj.* Heavier, larger, or higher on one side than on the other: *a lopsided pumpkin.* —**lop'sid'ed•ly** *adv.* —**lop'sid'ed•ness** *n.*

lo•qua•cious |lō **kwā'**shəs| *adj.* Very talkative. —**lo•qua'cious•ly** *adv.* —**lo•qua'cious•ness** *n.*

lo•quac•i•ty |lō **kwăs'**ĭ tē| *n.* The condition of being loquacious.

lord |lôrd| *n.* **1.** In feudal times, a man of high rank, as a king or the owner of a manor. **2. Lord.** *British.* The general male title of nobility. **3.** Anyone with great authority or power. **4. my lord.** Used as a title of address for a lord. **5. Lord. a.** God. **b.** Christ. —*v.* To behave in a domineering, haughty, or patronizing manner: *a family lording it over the countryside; a matron who lorded over the club.* [SEE NOTE on p. 504]

lord•ly |**lôrd**'lē| *adj.* **lord•li•er, lord•li•est.** **1.** Of or suitable for a lord: *a lordly estate; a lordly deed.* **2.** Arrogant; haughty. —**lord'li•ness** *n.*

lord•ship |**lôrd**'shĭp'| *n.* **1. Lordship.** A form of address for a British nobleman, judge, or bishop: *your Lordship; his Lordship.* **2.** The rank or domain of a lord.

Lord's Prayer. The prayer taught by Christ to his disciples; the paternoster.

Lord's Supper. **1.** The **Last Supper.** **2.** The Eucharist.

lore |lôr| *or* |lōr| *n.* **1.** Accumulated fact, tra-

loom[1-2]

Loom[1] *is probably borrowed from some Low German word similar to Frisian* lōmen, *"to move slowly"; this is related to* **lame.** **Loom[2]** *is from Old English* geloma, *"a tool, a device."*

loom[2]

loon[1-2]

Loon[1] *is borrowed from Old Norse* lōmr, *"diving bird."* **Loon[2]** *is of unknown origin. It is recorded as early as the fifteenth century, and is not related to* **loony,** *which is a nineteenth-century slang word from* **lunatic.**

loon[1]

lotus

louse/mouse

These two words have hardly changed in the last six thousand years, and they have always rhymed with each other. They were lūs *and* mūs *in Old English, descending from* lūs *and* mūs *in prehistoric Germanic and, in turn, from* lūs *and* mūs *in Indo-European.*

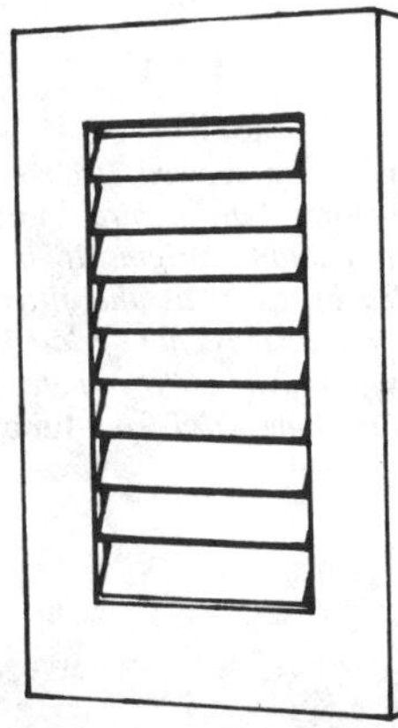

louver

ă pat/ā pay/â care/ä father/ĕ pet/ ē be/ĭ pit/ī pie/î fierce/ŏ pot/ ō go/ô paw, for/oi oil/ŏŏ book/ ōō boot/ou out/ŭ cut/û fur/ *th* the/th thin/hw which/zh vision/ ə ago, item, pencil, atom, circus

dition, or belief: *sea lore.* **2.** Knowledge gained by experience, tradition, or study.

lor•ry |lôr′ē| *or* |lŏr′ē| *n., pl.* **lor•ries.** *British.* A motor truck.

Los An•ge•les |lôs ăn′jə ləs| *or* |-lēz′| *or* |lŏs|. The largest city in California. Population, 2,966,763.

lose |lōōz| *v.* **lost** |lôst| *or* |lŏst|, **los•ing. 1.** To fail to find in the usual place; miss from one's possession: *I lost my geometry book.* **2.** To be unable to maintain, sustain, or keep: *lose one's balance.* **3. a.** To be deprived of by accident, death, etc.: *lose an arm in a car crash; lose a job.* **b.** To part with, give up, or shed through natural change, growth, or alteration: *Many trees lose their leaves in the autumn.* **4.** To fail to win or succeed: *lose a game.* **5.** To fail to take advantage of; waste: *lose precious minutes; lose a chance.* **6.** To rid oneself of: *lose weight.* **7.** To stray from and be unable to find again: *lose one's way.* **8.** To avoid and escape from; elude; evade: *The fox lost the hounds in the bush.* **9.** To fail to see, understand, keep track of, hear, etc.; miss: *lose the balloon in the clouds; lose track of time.* **10.** To cause the loss of: *His behavior lost him some friends.* —**los′ing** *adj.: a losing battle; the losing team.* —***phrasal verbs.*** **lose out.** To be defeated. **lose out on.** To miss: *lose out on an opportunity.* —**los′er** *n.*

loss |lôs| *or* |lŏs| *n., pl.* **loss•es. 1.** The act or fact of losing or having lost something: *a loss of memory; the loss of many ships; the loss of a game.* **2.** Someone or something that is lost. **3.** The suffering or hardship caused by losing or having lost something or someone. **4. losses.** Casualties or fatalities: *military losses.*

Idioms. **at a loss.** Perplexed; puzzled; bewildered: *She felt totally at a loss and did not know what to do.* **at (a) loss for.** Unable to bring forth or come up with: *never at loss for words.*

lost |lôst| *or* |lŏst| *adj.* **1.** Misplaced or strayed; missing: *a lost ring.* **2.** Not won or likely to be won: *a lost battle; a lost cause.* **3.** Ruined; destroyed: *All seemed lost.* **4.** No longer possessed; gone or passed away: *lost youth.* **5.** Occupied with; involved in: *lost in daydreams.* **6.** Uncertain; bewildered: *She felt lost in the new school.* **7.** Not used; wasted: *a lost opportunity.*

lot |lŏt| *n.* **1.** A large amount or number: *I have a lot of work to do.* **2.** A number of people or things of a kind: *He is the runt of the lot.* **3.** A kind, type, or sort: *The pirates are a bad lot of men.* **4. a.** A piece of land: *a lot behind the house.* **b.** A piece of land having a specific designation or size: *a parking lot.* **c.** A movie studio. **5.** An object used to determine or choose something by chance: *They drew lots to see who would go first.* **6.** Fortune in life; fate; luck: *the lot of the common people.*

lo•tion |lō′shən| *n.* **1.** A liquid medicine made to be applied to the skin, especially one that contains a substance in suspension. **2.** Any cosmetic liquid applied to the body: *hand lotion.*

lot•ter•y |lŏt′ə rē| *n., pl.* **lot•ter•ies.** A contest in which the winner is chosen in a drawing of lots. —***modifier:*** *a lottery ticket.*

lo•tus |lō′təs| *n., pl.* **lo•tus•es. 1.** Any of several plants related to the water lily, having large white, pink, or yellow flowers. **2.** In Greek mythology, a fruit that caused a state of dreamy idleness in those who ate it. [SEE PICTURE]

loud |loud| *adj.* **loud•er, loud•est. 1.** Of or having a very strong sound; having high volume and intensity: *loud music; a loud crash.* **2.** Producing or capable of producing loud sounds: *a loud instrument.* **3.** Gaudy; flashy: *a loud shirt.* —*adv.* **loud•er, loud•est.** In a loud manner. —**loud′ly** *adv.* —**loud′ness** *n.*

loud•speak•er, also **loud-speak•er** |loud′spē′kər| *n.* A device that converts an electrical signal into sound and projects the sound into the surrounding space.

Lou•is XIV |lōō′ē|. 1638–1715. King of France (1643–1715).

Louis XVI. 1754–1793. King of France (1774–92); guillotined during the French Revolution.

Lou•i•si•an•a |lōō ē′zē ăn′ə|. A Southern state of the United States. Population, 4,203,972. Capital, Baton Rouge.

Louisiana Purchase. The territory between the Mississippi River and the Rocky Mountains, purchased by the United States from France in 1803 for $15,000,000.

Lou•is•ville |lōō′ē vĭl′|. The largest city in Kentucky. Population, 298,451.

lounge |lounj| *v.* **lounged, loung•ing. 1.** To stand, sit, or lie in a lazy or relaxed way. **2.** To pass time idly: *She lounged around the house.* —*n.* **1. a.** A waiting room or bar in a hotel or theater. **b.** Any room for informal gathering: *the new student lounge.* **2.** A long couch.

lour |lou′ər| *n. & v.* A form of the word **lower** (scowl).

louse |lous| *n., pl.* **lice** |līs|. **1.** Any of a large number of small, wingless insects that often live as parasites on the bodies of various animals, including human beings. **2.** *pl.* **lous•es.** *Slang.* A mean or contemptible person. [SEE NOTE]

lous•y |lou′zē| *adj.* **lous•i•er, lous•i•est. 1.** Covered or overrun with lice. **2.** *Slang.* **a.** Mean; nasty. **b.** Inferior; worthless.

lout |lout| *n.* A foolish and stupid person.

lou•ver |lōō′vər| *n.* **1.** An opening, as in a wall, fitted with slats across it. **2.** Any of the slats used in such an opening. —***modifier:*** *a louver door.* —**lou′vered** *adj.* [SEE PICTURE]

lov•a•ble |lŭv′ə bəl| *adj.* Having qualities that attract affection; adorable: *Otters are smart, lovable animals.* —**lov′a•ble•ness** *n.* —**lov′a•bly** *adv.*

love |lŭv| *n.* **1.** Intense affection and warm feeling for another. **2.** Affectionate regards: *Give her my love.* **3.** Strong sexual desire for another person. **4.** Strong fondness for or devotion to something: *a love of money.* **5.** A beloved person. Often used as a term of address: *Come here, my love.* —***modifier:*** *a love song.* —*v.* **loved, lov•ing. 1.** To feel love or strong affection for. **2.** To desire (someone) sexually; feel deep passion for. **3.** To like enthusiastically; delight in: *Johnny loves to play hockey.*

love•bird |lŭv′bûrd′| *n.* A small parrot that is often kept as a cage bird and that seems to show great fondness for its mate.

love•lorn |lŭv′lôrn′| *adj.* Deprived of love or one's lover.

love•ly |lŭv′lē| *adj.* **love•li•er, love•li•est. 1.** Inspiring love and affection: *a lovely, sweet-natured person.* **2.** Having pleasing or attractive qualities; beautiful: *a lovely girl; a lovely house.* **3.** Enjoyable; delightful: *We spent a lovely evening at our friend's house.* —**love'li•ness** *n.*

lov•er |lŭv'ər| *n.* **1.** Someone who loves another person: *A false-hearted lover is worse than a thief.* **2.** Someone who is fond of or devoted to something: *a nature lover.*

lov•ing |lŭv'ĭng| *adj.* Feeling or showing love; devoted: *tender loving care.* —**lov'ing•ly** *adv.*

low[1] |lō| *adj.* **low•er, low•est. 1.** Having little relative height: *a low stool; a low sea cliff.* **2.** Of less than usual depth; shallow: *The river is low.* **3.** Near or at the horizon: *The moon is low in the sky.* **4.** Nearest to the equator: *the low latitudes.* **5.** Of the lowlands: *the Low Countries.* **6.** Below average, as in amount, degree, or intensity: *low wages; low cost; low temperature.* **7. a.** Having a musical pitch that corresponds to a relatively small number of cycles per second: *the low tones of a tuba.* **b.** Not loud; hushed: *a low voice.* **8.** Inadequate in amount: *Our supplies are low.* **9.** Having or denoting inferior social or cultural status: *a man of low birth. English was once considered a low language.* **10.** Of relatively simple structure in the scale of living things: *lower forms of animal life.* **11.** Dejected or depressed: *in low spirits.* **12.** Of small value or quality; disparaging: *a low opinion of her cousin's friends.* —*adv.* **1.** At, in, or to a low position, level, etc: *fly low.* **2.** With or at a low pitch: *an instrument that plays low.* **3.** Not loudly; softly: *speaking low.* —*n.* **1.** A low level, position, or degree: *The market hit a new low today.* **2.** The transmission gear, as of an automobile, truck, etc., that gives the smallest output speed for a given engine speed. **3.** A mass of atmospheric air that exerts less pressure than the air around it. ¶*These sound alike* **low, lo.** —**low'ness** *n.* [SEE NOTE]

low[2] |lō| *n.* The deep, long, throaty sound made by cattle; a moo. —*v.* To make such a sound; moo. ¶*These sound alike* **low, lo.** [SEE NOTE]

low•boy |lō'boi'| *n.* A low chest of drawers with a top that can be used as a table.

Low-Church |lō'chûrch'| *adj.* Of a faction in a Protestant Church that favors widespread preaching of the Gospel and simple ceremony.

Low Countries. The Netherlands, Belgium, and Luxembourg.

low•er[1] |lō'ər|. Comparative of **low.** —*adj.* Designating the larger and usually more representative house of a legislature with two houses: *the lower house.* —*v.* **1.** To let, bring, or move something down to a lower level: *lower the flag; lower one's head.* **2.** To make or become less in value, degree, or quality: *lower prices. Prices gradually lowered in the summer.* **3.** To reduce the volume of: *lower one's voice.*

low•er[2] |lou'ər| *v.* **1.** To look angry or sullen; scowl. **2.** To appear dark or threatening, as the sky or weather. —*n.* A sullen or angry look.

Lower California. A peninsula of northwestern Mexico, extending south from the U.S. border.

lower case. Small letters as distinguished from capital letters. —***modifier:*** **(lower-case):** *lower-case letters.*

low•er•most |lō'ər mōst'| *adj.* Lowest.

lowest common denominator. The least common multiple of the denominators of a set of fractions.

low frequency. Any radio-wave frequency in the range between 30 kilohertz and 300 kilohertz. —***modifier:*** **(low-frequency):** *low-frequency waves.*

Low German. Any of several dialects of German spoken in northern Germany.

low•land |lō'lənd| *n.* An area of land that is low in relation to the surrounding country.

low•ly |lō'lē| *adj.* **low•li•er, low•li•est.** Low in rank, position, etc.: *a person of lowly birth.* —**low'li•ness** *n.*

low tide. 1. The tide as it reaches its lowest point. **2.** The time at which this occurs.

lox[1] |lŏks| *n.* Smoked salmon. [SEE NOTE]

lox[2] |lŏks| *n.* Liquid oxygen, as when used as an oxidizer for rocket fuel. [SEE NOTE]

loy•al |loi'əl| *adj.* Faithful to a person, country, idea, custom, etc.: *Robin Hood's band of loyal men.* —**loy'al•ly** *adv.*

loy•al•ist |loi'ə lĭst| *n.* Often **Loyalist.** Someone who remains loyal to the established power, especially during a civil war or revolution.

loy•al•ty |loi'əl tē| *n.* The condition of being loyal; faithful and loyal conduct.

loz•enge |lŏz'ĭnj| *n.* **1.** A flat, diamond-shaped figure. **2.** A small piece of medicated candy often having this shape. [SEE PICTURE]

LP |ĕl'pē'| *adj.* Long-playing. —*n., pl.* **LP's** or **LPs.** A trademark for a long-playing phonograph record.

LSD |ĕl'ĕs'dē'| *n.* Also **LSD-25.** A powerful drug that induces hallucinations and other usually temporary mental abnormalities, such as illusions of hearing sounds or feeling colors.

Lt. lieutenant.

ltd., Ltd. limited.

Lu The symbol for the element lutetium.

Lu•an•da |lo͞o ăn'də|. The capital of Angola. Population, 245,000.

Luang Pra•bang |lwäng' prə bäng'|. A former capital of Laos. Population, 8,000.

lu•au |lo͞o ou'| *n.* A Hawaiian feast.

lub•ber |lŭb'ər| *n.* **1.** A clumsy fellow. **2.** An inexperienced sailor; a landlubber.

lu•bri•cant |lo͞o'brĭ kənt| *n.* Any of a number of slippery substances, such as oil, grease, or graphite, used as a coating for the surfaces of moving parts to reduce friction, wear, etc.

lu•bri•cate |lo͞o'brĭ kāt'| *v.* **lu•bri•cat•ed, lu•bri•cat•ing.** To apply or use a lubricant: *lubricate a car.* —**lu'bri•ca'tion** *n.* —**lu'bri•ca'tor** *n.*

lu•cid |lo͞o'sĭd| *adj.* **1.** Easily understood, clear: *a lucid explanation.* **2.** Mentally sound; sane; rational: *The senile man has his lucid hours.* —**lu•cid'i•ty, lu'cid•ness** *n.* —**lu'cid•ly** *adv.*

Lu•ci•fer |lo͞o'sə fər|. In Christian tradition, the archangel cast from Heaven for leading a revolt of angels; Satan.

Lu•cite |lo͞o'sīt'| *n.* A trademark for a transparent plastic resin sometimes used as a substitute for glass where breakage is a problem.

luck |lŭk| *n.* **1.** The chance happening of good or bad events; fate; fortune. **2.** Good fortune; success: *beginner's luck.*

Idioms. **down on (one's) luck.** Undergoing misfortune. **in luck.** Lucky. **out of luck.** Unlucky.

luck•i•ly |lŭk'ə lē| *adv.* With or by favorable chance; fortunately.

luck•less |lŭk'lĭs| *adj.* Having no luck.

luck•y |lŭk'ē| *adj.* **luck•i•er, luck•i•est. 1.** Hav-

low[1-2]

Low[1] *was* lowe *or* lah *in Middle English, and is borrowed from Old Norse* lāgr; *its original meaning was "lying flat," and it is related to* **lie**[1]. **Low**[2] *was* hlōwan *in Old English; it is descended from prehistoric Germanic* hlō-, *which is from Indo-European* klā-. *(For the change of* kl- *to* hl- *and then to* l-, *compare note at* **lean**[1].*) So, while the sound a cow makes may sound like* low *to us, to the Indo-Europeans it sounded like* klā.

lox[1-2]

Lox[1] *is from Yiddish* laks, *which is descended from Old High German* lahs, *"salmon."* **Lox**[2] *is an acronym from* liquid oxygen.

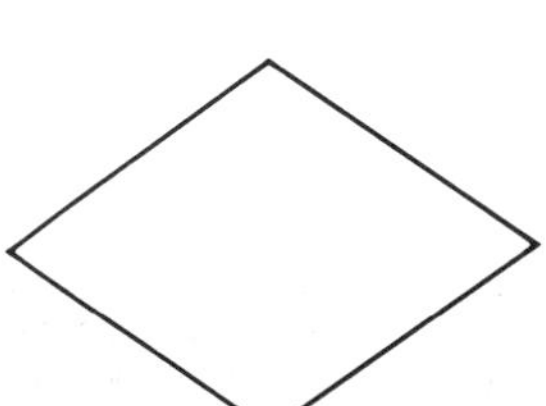

lozenge

ing good luck: *a lucky girl.* **2.** Bringing good luck: *a lucky penny; a lucky day.*

lu•cra•tive |lo͞o'krə tĭv| *adj.* Producing wealth; profitable: *a lucrative importing business.*

lu•cre |lo͞o'kər| *n.* Money; gain; profits.

lu•di•crous |lo͞o'dĭ krəs| *adj.* Obviously absurd; laughable: *the ludicrous costume of the clown.* —**lu'di•crous•ly** *adv.* —**lu'di•crous•ness** *n.*

lug¹ |lŭg| *v.* **lugged, lug•ging.** To drag or haul with great difficulty: *lug supplies.*

lug² |lŭg| *n.* An earlike part or projection, as on a machine, used to hold or support.

lug•gage |lŭg'ĭj| *n.* The bags, suitcases, boxes, etc., taken on a trip; baggage.

lu•gu•bri•ous |lo͝o go͞o'brē əs| *or* |-gyo͞o'-| *adj.* Sad or mournful, especially to a ridiculous degree: *the lugubrious face of a basset hound.* —**lu•gu'bri•ous•ly** *adv.*

Luke |lo͝ok|. The third Gospel of the New Testament.

Luke |lo͝ok|, **Saint.** A companion of the Apostle Paul, traditionally regarded as the author of the third Gospel.

luke•warm |lo͞ok'wôrm'| *adj.* **1.** Neither hot nor cold; mildly warm: *lukewarm water.* **2.** Lacking in enthusiasm; indifferent: *a lukewarm greeting.*

lull |lŭl| *v.* To cause to sleep or rest; calm; soothe: *a song to lull a child to sleep.* —*n.* A temporary lessening of activity, noise, etc.: *a lull in the storm; a lull in sales.*

lull•a•by |lŭl'ə bī'| *n., pl.* **lull•a•bies.** A soothing song meant to lull a child to sleep.

lum•ba•go |lŭm bā'gō| *n.* A painful form of rheumatism that affects the muscles and tendons of the lower back.

lum•bar |lŭm'bər| *or* |-bär'| *adj.* Of or located in the part of the back between the lowest ribs and the hips. ¶*These sound alike* **lumbar, lumber.**

lum•ber¹ |lŭm'bər| *n.* Timber sawed into boards and planks. —***modifier:*** *a lumber mill.* —*v.* To cut down and prepare timber for market. ¶*These sound alike* **lumber, lumbar.** [SEE NOTE]

lum•ber² |lŭm'bər| *v.* To walk or move with clumsiness and often great noise: *Twenty elephants lumbered slowly into the arena.* ¶*These sound alike* **lumber, lumbar.** [SEE NOTE]

lum•ber•jack |lŭm'bər jăk'| *n.* A man whose work is to chop down trees and transport the timber to a sawmill.

lu•men |lo͞o'mən| *n., pl.* **lu•mens** or **lu•mi•na** |lo͞o'mə nə|. **1.** The inner open space of a tubular organ, such as a blood vessel or intestine. **2.** A measure of the energy radiated by a source as light, equal to the light energy radiated by a source of one candela through a region of space that cuts off on the surface of a sphere an area equal to the square of the radius when the source is at the center of the sphere.

lu•mi•nar•y |lo͞o'mə nĕr'ē| *n., pl.* **lu•mi•nar•ies.** **1.** An object, especially a celestial body, that gives off light. **2.** A notable person in a specific field: *German medical luminaries.*

lu•mi•nes•cence |lo͞o'mə nĕs'əns| *n.* **1.** The production of light by a process that does not use heat or produce any significant amount of heat, as in fluorescence, phosphorescence, or bioluminescence. **2.** Light that is produced in this way. —**lu'mi•nes'cent** *adj.*

lu•mi•nos•i•ty |lo͞o'mə nŏs'ĭ tē| *n., pl.* **lu•mi•nos•i•ties.** **1.** The condition or property of being luminous. **2.** The fraction of the total energy radiated by a source that takes the form of visible light.

lu•mi•nous |lo͞o'mə nəs| *adj.* **1.** Giving off light, especially light that is self-generated rather than reflected; shining: *a luminous sign.* **2.** Easily understood; clear: *simple, luminous prose.*

lump¹ |lŭmp| *n.* **1.** An irregularly shaped mass or piece of compact material: *a lump of rock.* **2.** A small cube of sugar: *She takes two lumps in her coffee.* **3.** Any abnormal swelling or bump in a part of the body. —*adj.* **1.** Formed into lumps: *lump sugar.* **2.** Not divided into parts; whole: *a lump sum.* —*v.* **1.** To form or cause to form lumps: *The chocolate lumps when a cold liquid is added. Don't lump the flour with hot fat.* **2.** To put or consider together in a single group or pile: *Lump all these expenses under the heading of entertainment.* [SEE NOTE]

lump² |lŭmp| *v.* —**like it or lump it.** *Informal.* To endure or put up with something, whether one likes it or not. [SEE NOTE]

lump•y |lŭm'pē| *adj.* **lump•i•er, lump•i•est.** Full of lumps: *lumpy gravy.*

lu•na•cy |lo͞o'nə sē| *n., pl.* **lu•na•cies.** **1.** Mental derangement; insanity. **2.** Foolish and irresponsible conduct.

lu•nar |lo͞o'nər| *adj.* **1.** Of, caused by, or affecting the moon: *a lunar orbit.* **2.** Measured or determined by motions of the moon: *a lunar year.* **3.** On the moon: *a lunar landing.*

lunar module. A section of a spacecraft, designed for a moon mission, that can be detached from the main craft, landed on the moon, and finally rejoined with the main craft.

lu•na•tic |lo͞o'nə tĭk| *n.* An insane person; a madman. —*adj.* **1.** Suffering from madness; insane. **2.** Of or for the insane: *a lunatic asylum.* **3.** Wildly or recklessly foolish: *a lunatic idea.*

lunch |lŭnch| *n.* **1.** A meal eaten at midday. **2.** The food for this meal. —*v.* To eat lunch. —***modifier:*** *a lunch box; the lunch hour.*

lunch•eon |lŭn'chən| *n.* A midday meal; lunch.

lunch•room, also **lunch-room** |lŭnch'ro͞om'| *or* |-ro͝om'| *n.* The cafeteria or room in a building, such as a school, where lunch is eaten.

lung |lŭng| *n.* **1.** Either of two spongy, saclike organs that, along with the heart, occupy the chest cavity of most vertebrates. They draw air from the atmosphere, absorbing oxygen from it and discharging carbon dioxide into it. **2.** A similar organ found in some invertebrates, such as land snails. —***modifier:*** *lung diseases.*

lunge |lŭnj| *n.* A sudden, forceful movement forward; a plunge: *The fielder made a lunge for the ball.* —*v.* **lunged, lung•ing.** To make a sudden, forceful movement forward.

lung•fish |lŭng'fĭsh'| *n., pl.* **-fish** or **fish•es.** Any of several tropical freshwater fishes having a long narrow body and gills as well as lunglike organs that enable them to breathe out of water.

lu•pine, also **lu•pin** |lo͞o'pĭn| *n.* A plant having leaves with many leaflets and long clusters of variously colored flowers.

lurch¹ |lûrch| *n.* An unsteady or abrupt swaying movement. —*v.* To move unsteadily; stagger: *The big, bullying fellow lurched toward Jed.* [SEE NOTE on p. 533]

lumber¹⁻²

Lumber¹ *earlier meant "rough bits of wood" and originally "bits and pieces, odds and ends." It is said to come from* lumber house, *an old term for a pawnshop, where many small objects or "odds and ends" are kept in pawn. (*Lumber house *comes from a variant of* Lombard, *a person from* Lombardy *in northern Italy;* Lombards *were famous as bankers and moneylenders.)* **Lumber²** *is of obscure origin.*

lump¹⁻²

Lump¹ *is probably related to Dutch* lomp, *"a rag," and Low German* lump, *"coarse."* **Lump²** *is of unknown origin.*

ă pat/ā pay/â care/ä father/ĕ pet/ ē be/ĭ pit/ī pie/î fierce/ŏ pot/ ō go/ô paw, for/oi oil/o͝o book/ o͞o boot/ou out/ŭ cut/û fur/ *th* the/th thin/hw which/zh vision/ ə ago, item, pencil, atom, circus

lurch² |lûrch| *n.* —**in the lurch.** In a difficult or embarrassing position. [SEE NOTE]

lure |lo͝or| *n.* **1.** Something that attracts, appeals, or entices, especially with the promise of pleasure or a reward: *the lure of the sea.* **2.** Any of various small devices used by a fisherman to attract and catch fish. —*v.* **lured, lur•ing.** To attract, appeal to, or entice.

lu•rid |lo͝or'ĭd| *adj.* **1.** Causing shock or horror: *a lurid description of a train crash.* **2.** Glowing or glaring through a haze: *the lurid flames of a distant fire.* —**lu'rid•ly** *adv.*

lurk |lûrk| *v.* **1.** To be or keep out of view, lying in wait or ready to attack: *The river pirates lurked in caves along the banks.* **2.** To move about furtively; sneak: *A burglar lurked around the house.* —**lurk'er** *n.*

Lu•sa•ka |lo͞o sä'kə|. The capital of Zambia. Population, 374,000.

lus•cious |lŭsh'əs| *adj.* **1.** Having a delicious taste or smell: *a luscious peach.* **2.** Appealing to the senses: *singing with luscious beauty of tone.* —**lus'cious•ly** *adv.* —**lus'cious•ness** *n.*

lush¹ |lŭsh| *adj.* **lush•er, lush•est.** **1.** Having or forming a thick, plentiful plant growth: *lush green lawns; lush grass.* **2.** Luxurious; sumptuous: *a lush carpet.* [SEE NOTE]

lush² |lŭsh| *n. Slang.* An alcoholic. [SEE NOTE]

lust |lŭst| *n.* **1.** An intense sexual desire. **2.** Any overwhelming desire or craving: *a lust for power.* —*v.* **1.** To have an intense sexual desire. **2.** To have an overwhelming desire or craving.

lus•ter |lŭs'tər| *n.* **1.** Soft reflected light; sheen; gloss: *the luster of pearls.* **2.** The appearance of the surface of a mineral judged by its sheen or ability to reflect light. **3.** Glory; splendor: *His heroic deeds added luster to his name.* **4.** Any of various substances, such as wax, used to give an object gloss or polish.

lus•tre |lŭs'tər| *n.* British form of the word **luster.**

lus•trous |lŭs'trəs| *adj.* Having a gloss or sheen; gleaming: *lustrous Oriental silks; deep-set, lustrous eyes.* —**lus'trous•ly** *adv.* —**lus'trous•ness** *n.*

lust•y |lŭs'tē| *adj.* **lust•i•er, lust•i•est.** **1.** Full of vitality; robust: *a tall, lusty young man.* **2.** Strong; powerful: *Babe Ruth's lusty swing; a lusty country wine.* —**lust'i•ly** *adv.* —**lust'i•ness** *n.*

lute |lo͞ot| *n.* A stringed musical instrument with a body shaped like half a pear and usually a bent neck with a fingerboard that has frets. ¶*These sound alike* **lute, loot.**

lu•te•ti•um |lo͞o tē'shē əm| *n.* Symbol **Lu** One of the elements, a silvery rare-earth metal. Atomic number 71; atomic weight 174.97; valence +3; melting point 1,652°C; boiling point 3,327°C.

Lu•ther |lo͞o'thər|, **Martin.** 1483-1546. German theologian and religious reformer.

Lu•ther•an |lo͞o'thər ən| *adj.* Of Martin Luther or the branch of the Protestant Church founded on his belief that Christ is all-forgiving and that salvation can be attained through faith in the power of God.

Lu•ther•an•ism |lo͞o'thər ə nĭz'əm| *n.* The doctrines and forms of worship of Lutherans.

Lux•em•bourg |lŭk'səm bûrg'|. **1.** A small country in western Europe between France, Belgium, and West Germany. Population, 339,000. **2.** Also **Luxembourg City.** The capital of this country. Population, 77,000.

lux•u•ri•ant |lŭg zho͝or'ē ənt| *or* |lŭk sho͝or'-| *adj.* Growing abundantly; lush: *luxuriant vegetation.* —**lux•u'ri•ance** *n.* —**lux•u'ri•ant•ly** *adv.*

lux•u•ri•ate |lŭg zho͝or'ē āt'| *or* |lŭk sho͝or'-| *v.* **lux•u•ri•at•ed, lux•u•ri•at•ing.** To take great pleasure; indulge oneself: *luxuriate in the warm sunshine; luxuriate in one's own despair.*

lux•u•ri•ous |lŭg zho͝or'ē əs| *or* |lŭk sho͝or'-| *adj.* Marked by luxury; sumptuous: *a luxurious apartment.* —**lux•u'ri•ous•ly** *adv.*

lux•u•ry |lŭg'zhə rē| *or* |lŭk'shə-| *n., pl.* **lux•u•ries.** **1.** Something not considered essential but that gives great pleasure or enjoyment, especially something expensive, hard to get, etc.; an extravagance. **2.** A sumptuous environment or way of living: *live in luxury.* —*modifier: a luxury hotel.*

Lw The symbol for the element lawrencium.

-ly¹. A suffix that forms adjectives and means: **1.** Characteristic of: **sisterly.** **2.** Appearing or occurring at specified intervals: **weekly.**

-ly². A suffix that forms adverbs and means: **1.** In a specified manner: **gradually.** **2.** At a specified interval: **hourly.**

ly•ce•um |lī sē'əm| *n.* A hall in which lectures, concerts, etc., are presented.

lye |lī| *n.* **1.** The powerfully alkaline solution made by allowing water to wash through wood ashes. **2. Sodium hydroxide.** ¶*These sound alike* **lye, lie.**

ly•ing |lī'ĭng|. Present participle of **lie.**

lymph |lĭmf| *n.* The clear, watery, often slightly yellow liquid that is collected from the body tissues, flows through the lymphatic system and thoracic duct, and finally returns to the blood circulation. It contains white blood cells, a few red blood cells, droplets of fat, and some dissolved proteins.

lym•phat•ic |lĭm făt'ĭk| *adj.* Of or involving lymph, the vessels through which it flows, or lymph nodes.

lymphatic system. The connected system of spaces and vessels between tissues and organs of the body through which lymph circulates.

lymph node. Any of the numerous round or oval structures, located along the lymphatic vessels, that supply certain white blood cells to the body and remove bacteria and foreign particles from the lymph.

lym•pho•cyte |lĭm'fə sīt'| *n.* A white blood cell of the type that is formed in the lymph nodes.

lynch |lĭnch| *v.* To execute, especially by hanging, without due process of law. —**lynch'er** *n.*

lynx |lĭngks| *n.* A wild cat with thick, soft fur, tufted ears, and a short tail. ¶*These sound alike* **lynx, links.** [SEE PICTURE]

lyre |līr| *n.* An ancient stringed instrument, related to the harp.

lyre•bird |līr'bûrd'| *n.* An Australian bird of which the male has a long tail that is spread into the shape of a lyre when he courts the female. [SEE PICTURE]

lyr•ic |lĭr'ĭk| or **lyr•i•cal** |lĭr'ĭ kəl| *adj.* Of poetry that is a direct, often songlike expression of the poet's thoughts and feelings: *a lyric poem.* —*n.* **1.** A lyric poem or poet. **2. lyrics.** The words of a song. —**lyr'i•cal•ly** *adv.*

lurch¹·²

Lurch¹ *is of unknown origin.* **Lurch²** *was originally a special term used in an old board game something like checkers; the* lurch *was a losing position, so that "to leave someone in the lurch" was to defeat him. The game itself was also called* lurch, *and the name comes from French* lourche.

lush¹·²

Lush¹ *is probably a variant of* lasche, *an old word meaning "soft, watery," possibly related to* **lax,** *"loose."* **Lush²** *is of unknown origin.*

lynx

lyrebird

Mm

(1) (2) (3)

The letter **M** *comes originally from the Phoenician letter* mēm *(1), which meant "water" and stood for the consonant /m/. The Greeks borrowed it, turning it around (2) and renaming it* mu. *The Romans borrowed it from the Greeks, giving it a symmetrical shape (3) that is the basis of the modern letter* **M**.

macaw

mace1-2

Mace1 *is from Old French* masse, *"club"; it is related to* **mattock**. **Mace**2 *is from Greek* makir, *the name of a spice imported from the east.*

ă pat/ā pay/â care/ä father/ĕ pet/ ē be/ĭ pit/ī pie/î fierce/ŏ pot/ ō go/ô paw, for/oi oil/ŏŏ book/ ōō boot/ou out/ŭ cut/û fur/ *th* the/th thin/hw which/zh vision/ ə ago, item, pencil, atom, circus

m, M |ĕm| *n., pl.* **m's** or **M's. 1.** The 13th letter of the English alphabet. **2.** The Roman numeral for the number 1,000. [SEE NOTE]

m. 1. meter (measure). **2.** mile.

ma |mä| *n. Informal.* Mother.

M.A. Master of Arts.

Ma'am |măm| *n.* Madam.

ma•ca•bre |mə **kä'**brə| *or* |-bər| *adj.* Suggesting the horror of death and decay; gruesome; ghastly: *the macabre details of the murder.*

mac•ad•am |mə **kăd'**əm| *n.* A paving material made of layers of small stones packed together, now usually bound with asphalt or tar. *—modifier: a macadam road.*

mac•ad•am•ize |mə **kăd'**ə mīz'| *v.* **mac•ad•am•ized, mac•ad•am•iz•ing.** To build or pave (a road) with macadam.

ma•caque |mə **kăk'**| *or* |**-käk'**| *n.* Any of several short-tailed monkeys of Asia and northern Africa.

mac•a•ro•ni |măk'ə **rō'**nē| *n.* Dried pasta, usually in the shape of hollow tubes. *—modifier: a macaroni salad.*

mac•a•roon |măk'ə **rōōn'**| *n.* A chewy cooky made with sugar and egg whites and flavored with ground almonds or coconut.

Mac•Ar•thur |mək **är'**thər|, **Douglas.** 1880–1964. American General of the Army; supreme commander of Allied Forces in the Southwest Pacific during World War II.

ma•caw |mə **kô'**| *n.* A large, often brightly colored tropical American parrot with a long tail. [SEE PICTURE]

mace1 |mās| *n.* **1.** A heavy club with a spiked metal head, used in medieval times. **2.** A ceremonial staff carried or displayed as a symbol of authority. [SEE NOTE]

mace2 |mās| *n.* A spice made from the bright-red covering that partly encloses the seed of the nutmeg. [SEE NOTE]

Mace |mās| *n.* **Chemical Mace.**

Mac•e•do•ni•a |măs'ĭ **dō'**nē ə|. **1.** An ancient kingdom, north of Greece, that reached the height of its power under Alexander the Great. **2.** A region comprising parts of Greece, Bulgaria, and Yugoslavia. —**Mac'e•do'ni•an** *adj.* & *n.*

Mach, also **mach** |mäk| *n.* **Mach number.**

ma•chet•e |mə **shĕt'**ē| *or* |**-chĕt'**ē| *n.* A large, heavy knife with a broad blade, used especially in Latin America as a weapon and for clearing paths and cutting sugar cane.

Mach•i•a•vel•li |măk'ē ə **vĕl'**ē|, **Niccolò.** 1469–1527. Italian statesman and political theorist.

Mach•i•a•vel•li•an |măk'ē ə **vĕl'**ē ən| *adj.* Of or resembling the crafty practices of Niccolò Machiavelli, who believed that any means are justifiable for maintaining political power. *—n.* Someone who believes in Machiavellian principles.

mach•i•na•tion |măk'ə **nā'**shən| *or* |măsh'-| *n.* A hostile or evil scheme or plot.

ma•chine |mə **shēn'**| *n.* **1.** A system or device built to use energy in performing tasks: *a washing machine.* **2.** Any of several simple devices such as an inclined plane, lever, or screw that acts on an applied force so as to change its magnitude or direction or both. **3.** A person who acts or performs a task mechanically, without intelligence, etc. **4.** An organized group of people, usually run by one or more leaders, that controls the policies and activities of a political party in an area. *—modifier: machine parts.* *—v.* **ma•chined, ma•chin•ing.** To cut, shape, or finish by machine: *machine metal; a metal that machines easily.*

machine gun. A gun that fires rapidly and repeatedly when the trigger is pressed. *—modifier:* **(machine-gun):** *machine-gun fire.*

ma•chine-gun |mə **shēn'**gŭn'| *v.* **ma•chine-gunned, ma•chine-gun•ning.** To fire at or kill with a machine gun.

ma•chin•er•y |mə **shē'**nə rē| *n., pl.* **ma•chin•er•ies. 1.** Machines or machine parts as a group. **2.** The working parts of a particular machine: *the machinery of a clock.* **3.** Any system with related elements that operate together: *the complex machinery of modern society.*

ma•chin•ist |mə **shē'**nĭst| *n.* Someone skilled in the use of machine tools to work metal.

Mach number. The quotient of the speed of a body divided by the speed of sound in the surrounding medium; for example, an aircraft flying in air at twice the speed of sound has a Mach number of 2.

mac•in•tosh |**măk'**ĭn tŏsh'| *n.* A form of the word **mackintosh.**

mack•er•el |**măk'**ər əl| *or* |**măk'**rəl| *n., pl.* **mack•er•el** or **mack•er•els.** Any of several ocean fishes much used as food.

mackerel sky. A cloud formation that appears as a series of light and dark irregular bands resembling the markings of a mackerel.

mack•i•naw |**măk'**ə nô'| *n.* A short coat of heavy woolen material, usually plaid.

mack•in•tosh |**măk'**ĭn tŏsh'| *n. British.* A raincoat.

ma•cron |**mā'**krŏn'| *or* |-krən| *n.* A mark placed over a vowel to show that it has a long sound, as the (ā) in *make.*

mad |măd| *adj.* **mad·der, mad·dest. 1.** Having a diseased mind; insane. **2.** *Informal.* Very irritated; angry. **3.** Very foolish; rash: *a mad idea.* **4.** *Informal.* Very enthusiastic: *mad about basketball.* **5.** Marked by excitement or confusion; frantic: *a mad scramble for the bus.* **6.** Affected by rabies; rabid: *a mad dog.* —**mad'ly** *adj.* —**mad'ness** *n.* [SEE NOTE]

Mad·a·gas·car |măd'ə găs'kər|. An island off the southeastern coast of Africa, constituting an independent country. Population, 8,742,000. Capital, Antananarivo.

Mad·am |măd'əm| *n., pl.* **Mes·dames** |mā dăm'| *or* |-dăm'|. **1.** A word used alone as a title of courtesy in speaking to a woman. **2.** A word used as a title of courtesy before a woman's surname or before a title: *Madam Chairman.*

Mad·ame |măd'əm| *or* |mə dăm'| *n., pl.* **Mes·dames** |mā dăm'| *or* |-dăm'|. A French word similar to Mrs., used before a woman's name in speaking to or of her.

mad·cap |măd'kăp'| *n.* A rash or impulsive person, especially a girl. —*adj.* Not sensible; rash; impulsive: *a madcap idea.*

mad·den |măd'n| *v.* **1.** To make mad; drive insane. **2.** To make angry; infuriate.

mad·den·ing |măd'n ĭng| *adj.* Causing great anger; infuriating: *a maddening noise.* —**mad'den·ing·ly** *adv.*

mad·der |măd'ər| *n.* **1. a.** A plant with small yellow flowers and a fleshy red root that is the source of a dye. **b.** Any of several related plants. **2.** A red dye made from the root of the madder plant.

made |mād|. Past tense and past participle of **make.** ¶*These sound alike* **made, maid.**
 Idiom. **made for.** Perfectly suited for: *made for each other.*

Ma·dei·ra[1] |mə dîr'ə|. **1.** A group of Portuguese islands in the Atlantic Ocean off the northwest coast of Africa. **2.** The largest of these islands.

Ma·dei·ra[2] |mə dîr'ə| *n.* Any of several white fortified dessert wines.

Mad·e·moi·selle |măd'ə mə zĕl'| *or* |măd'mwə-| *n., pl.* **Mes·de·moi·selles** |mā'də mə zĕl'| *or* |mād'mwə-|. A French word similar to Miss, used before a woman's name in speaking to or of her.

made-up |măd'up'| *adj.* **1.** Not real; imaginary; invented: *made-up stories.* **2.** Adorned with cosmetics or make-up: *a made-up face.*

mad·house |măd'hous'| *n., pl.* **-hous·es** |-hou'zĭz|. **1.** An insane asylum. **2.** *Informal.* Any place of confusion or disorder.

Mad·i·son |măd'ĭ sən|. The capital of Wisconsin. Population, 170,000.

Mad·i·son |măd'ĭ sən|, **James.** 1751–1836. Fourth President of the United States (1809–17).

mad·man |măd'măn'| *or* |-mən| *n., pl.* **-men** |-mĕn'| *or* |-mən|. A man who is mad; a maniac.

Ma·don·na |mə dŏn'ə| *n.* An artistic representation, such as a statue or painting, of the Virgin Mary.

mad·ras |măd'rəs| *or* |mə drăs'| *or* |-dräs'| *n.* A fine cotton cloth, usually having a plaid, striped, or checked pattern. —*modifier:* *a madras shirt.*

Ma·drid |mə drĭd'|. The capital of Spain. Population, 3,146,000.

mad·ri·gal |măd'rĭ gəl| *n.* Any of various musical compositions written for two or more unaccompanied voices and popular in the early Renaissance in Italy and in Elizabethan England.

mael·strom |māl'strəm| *n.* **1.** A large and violent whirlpool. **2.** A situation that resembles such a whirlpool in violence, turbulence, etc.: *caught in the maelstrom of war.* [SEE NOTE]

maes·tro |mī'strō| *n., pl.* **maes·tros.** A master in an art, especially a famous conductor, composer, or music teacher.

Ma·fi·a |mä'fē ə| *n.* An alleged secret organization believed to be involved in criminal activities, especially in Italy and the United States, since the late 19th century.

mag. magazine.

mag·a·zine |măg'ə zēn'| *or* |măg'ə zēn'| *n.* **1.** A periodical containing written matter, such as articles or stories, and usually also illustrations and advertising. **2.** A building or room where ammunition is stored. **3.** In some firearms, a container in which cartridges are held until they pass into the chamber for firing. —*modifier:* *a magazine article.* [SEE NOTE]

Ma·gel·lan |mə jĕl'ən|, **Ferdinand.** 1480?–1521. Portuguese navigator in the service of Spain; he commanded the first expedition that sailed around the world.

ma·gen·ta |mə jĕn'tə| *n.* A bright purplish red. —*adj.* Bright purplish red.

mag·got | |măg'ət| *n.* The soft-bodied, wormlike larva of a fly, such as the housefly, usually found in decaying matter or as a parasite.

Ma·gi |mā'jī'| *pl.n.* In the Bible, the three wise men of the East who traveled to Bethlehem to worship the infant Jesus.

mag·ic |măj'ĭk| *n.* **1. a.** The art or alleged art of controlling natural events, effects, or forces by invoking supernatural powers through charms, spells, etc.; witchcraft. **b.** The charms, spells, etc., used to invoke such aid. **2.** The use of sleight of hand and other tricks to produce entertaining and baffling effects. **3.** Any mysterious quality that seems to enchant; a special charm: *the magic of the woods in the fall.* —*adj.* **1.** Of or having to do with magic and its practice: *magic words; a magic trick.* **2.** Possessing supernatural powers: *a magic wand.*

mag·i·cal |măj'ĭ kəl| *adj.* **1.** Of or produced by magic: *a magical spell; the magical transformation of mice into horses.* **2.** Resembling magic in qualities of enchantment, mystery, etc.: *the magical moments of a spring day.* —**mag'i·cal·ly** *adv.*

ma·gi·cian |mə jĭsh'ən| *n.* **1.** A person who uses magic; a sorcerer; wizard. **2.** An entertainer who performs tricks of magic.

magic lantern. An early kind of slide projector.

mag·is·te·ri·al |măj'ĭ stîr'ē əl| *adj.* **1.** Of a magistrate or his official functions: *magisterial duties.* **2.** Having or showing authority; commanding: *His finger sliced the air with a magisterial gesture.* —**mag'is·te'ri·al·ly** *adv.*

mag·is·tra·cy |măj'ĭ strə sē| *n., pl.* **mag·is·tra·cies. 1.** The position, duties, or term of office of a magistrate. **2.** A body of magistrates.

mag·is·trate |măj'ĭ strāt'| *or* |-strĭt| *n.* **1.** A civil official with the authority to administer the

mad

The obsolete verb mad, *meaning "to act like a madman, to rush around crazily," happens to have been preserved in one very famous quotation: "Far from the madding crowd's ignoble strife" (Thomas Gray, 1716–1771). The quotation refers to the peaceful life of the country, far from the insane competition of the city.* Far From the Madding Crowd *was also used by Thomas Hardy (1840–1928) as the title of a novel set in the remote countryside of the west of England. The word* madding *is often misquoted as* maddening.

maelstrom

The original **maelstrom** *is a whirlpool caused by tides off the coast of Norway. The word comes from Dutch* maelstrom, *"whirlstream":* malen, *"to whirl,"* + stroom, *"a current, stream."*

magazine

It would be hard to guess the connection between the different meanings of **magazine,** *because the original meaning has disappeared. The word originally meant "a storehouse, a warehouse"; sense* **2** *is a simple specialized use of this, and sense* **3** *is a technical extension. Sense* **1,** *which is now by far the commonest, comes from papers like* The Gentleman's Magazine, *first published in 1731; this title meant that the paper was a "storehouse" of different kinds of writing; later the word came to mean "any periodical paper."*

magnesium/magnet
The word **magnesium** *comes from Greek* magnēsia, *which meant "metal from Magnesia";* Magnesia *was the name of a mining region north of Greece.* **Magnesium** *is used in various alloys, in flash photography, and in incendiary bombs. Magnesium has nothing to do with magnets, but the word* **magnesium** *is related to the word* **magnet. Magnet** *comes from Greek* Magnēs, *which meant "stone from Magnesia"; the Greeks regarded magnetic iron as a special kind of stone, and they apparently also associated it with the same mining region,* Magnesia.

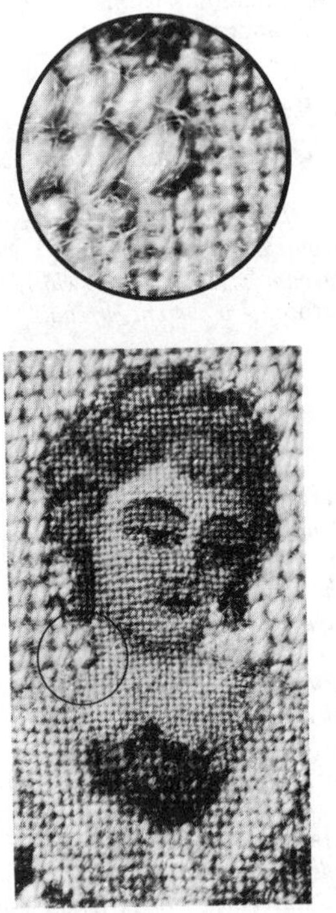

magnification

ă pat/ā pay/â care/ä father/ĕ pet/ ē be/ĭ pit/ī pie/î fierce/ŏ pot/ ō go/ô paw, for/oi oil/ŏŏ book/ ōō boot/ou out/ŭ cut/û fur/ *th* the/th thin/hw which/zh vision/ ə ago, item, pencil, atom, circus

law. **2.** A minor law official, such as a justice of the peace or the judge of a police court.

mag•ma |**măg′**mə| *n.* The hot molten material under the earth's crust that often cools and hardens to form igneous rock.

Mag•na Char•ta or **Mag•na Car•ta** |**măg′**-nə **kär′**tə|. A document of English political and civil liberties granted by King John in 1215.

mag•na cum lau•de |**mäg′**nä kōōm **lou′**dā| *or* |**măg′**nə kōōm **lô′**də|. With great praise. This was originally a Latin expression.

mag•na•nim•i•ty |măg′nə **nĭm′**ĭ tē| *n.* The quality of being magnanimous.

mag•nan•i•mous |măg **năn′**ə məs| *adj.* Noble in heart and mind; generous; unselfish and gracious: *a magnanimous gesture; a magnanimous person.* **—mag•nan′i•mous•ly** *adv.*

mag•nate |**măg′**nāt′| *or* |-nĭt| *n.* A powerful and influential person, especially in business.

mag•ne•sia |măg **nē′**zhə| *or* |-shə| *n.* Magnesium oxide, especially when processed for purity.

mag•ne•si•um |măg **nē′**zē əm| *or* |-zhəm| *n.* Symbol **Mg** One of the elements, a lightweight, moderately hard, silvery metal that burns with an intense flame. Atomic number 12; atomic weight 24.31; valence +2; melting point 651°C; boiling point 1,107°C. [SEE NOTE]

mag•net |**măg′**nĭt| *n.* **1.** Something, such as a piece of metal, an ore, etc., that attracts iron and other substances. **2.** An electromagnet. **3.** A person, place, etc., that exerts a powerful attraction. [SEE NOTE]

mag•net•ic |măg **nĕt′**ĭk| *adj.* **1.** Of magnetism or magnets. **2.** Having the properties of a magnet; showing magnetism. **3.** Of or relative to the magnetic poles of the earth: *magnetic north.* **4.** Operating by magnetism: *magnetic recording.* **5.** Having the power to attract or charm: *a motion-picture star with a magnetic personality.* **—mag•net′i•cal•ly** *adv.*

magnetic compass. An instrument in which a magnetic needle is used to determine directions in relation to the earth's magnetic field.

magnetic declination. The angle that a meridian passing through the geographic poles makes with a meridian passing through the magnetic poles at any point on the earth.

magnetic field. A region of space, as that around a magnet or an electric current, in which a detectable force is exerted on a magnetic body at any point.

magnetic flux. The total number of magnetic lines of force that pass through a bounded area that is cut by a magnetic field.

magnetic mine. An explosive underwater mine that is detonated when a large magnetic mass, such as the steel hull of a ship, comes near it.

magnetic needle. A light, needle-shaped magnet, usually suspended from a pivot, that aligns itself with any magnetic field around it, used in magnetic compasses.

magnetic north. The direction in which the north-seeking pole of a magnetic needle points.

magnetic pole. **1.** Either of two points or regions at or near the ends of a magnet where the magnetic field is strongest. **2.** Either of two variable points on the earth's surface, close to but not the same as the geographic poles, at which the earth's magnetic field is strongest. See **north pole, north-seeking pole, south pole, south-seeking pole.**

magnetic tape. A plastic or paper tape coated with tiny magnetic particles for use in recording.

mag•net•ism |**măg′**nĭ tĭz′əm| *n.* **1.** The properties, effects, etc., associated with the presence of magnetic fields. **2.** The study of magnets and their effects. **3.** The force produced by a magnetic field. **4.** An unusual power to attract, influence, etc.: *the magnetism of the actor's personality.*

mag•net•ite |**măg′**nĭ tīt′| *n.* The mineral form of black iron oxide, Fe_3O_4, that is an important iron ore.

mag•net•ize |**măg′**nĭ tīz′| *v.* **mag•net•ized, mag•net•iz•ing. 1.** To make (an object) into a magnet, temporarily or permanently. **2.** To exert a strong attraction or influence upon (someone): *Her performance magnetized the audience.* **—mag′net•i•za′tion** *n.*

mag•ne•to |măg **nē′**tō| *n., pl.* **mag•ne•tos.** A small alternator that works by means of permanent magnets, used to generate the electricity for the spark in some engines.

mag•ne•to•sphere |măg **nē′**tō sfîr′| *n.* A region of space surrounding the earth in which charged atomic particles are trapped by the earth's magnetic field. See **Van Allen belt.**

magnet school. A school that draws students from a wide geographic area that crosses district boundaries and offers an educational program with a major theme or focus, as science, the humanities, creative writing, etc.

mag•ni•fi•ca•tion |măg′nə fĭ **kā′**shən| *n.* **1.** The act or process of magnifying. **2.** The degree to which something is magnified, especially the quotient of the size of an image divided by the size of the object. [SEE PICTURES]

mag•nif•i•cent |măg **nĭf′**ĭ sənt| *adj.* **1.** Splendid in appearance; grand; remarkable: *a magnificent cathedral.* **2.** Outstanding of its kind; excellent: *a magnificent hunting dog.* **—mag•nif′i•cence** *n.* **—mag•nif′i•cent•ly** *adv.*

mag•ni•fy |**măg′**nə fī′| *v.* **mag•ni•fied, mag•ni•fy•ing, mag•ni•fies. 1.** To cause to appear greater or seem more important; exaggerate: *Don't magnify small problems into large ones.* **2. a.** To make (an object) appear larger than it really is, especially by the use of one or more lenses. **b.** To be capable of doing this: *a lens that magnifies.* **—mag′ni•fi′er** *n.*

magnifying glass. A lens, usually equipped with a frame and handle, that makes objects seen through it appear larger.

mag•ni•tude |**măg′**nĭ tōōd′| *or* |-tyōōd′| *n.* **1.** Greatness, as of position, size, influence, etc.: *the magnitude of his achievements; failing to realize the magnitude of the problem.* **2. a.** A property, such as the volume of a solid, the length of a line segment, or the strength of a force, that can be measured and expressed as a number. **b.** The numerical measure of such a property, especially when its sign, positive or negative, is ignored: *the magnitude of an electric charge.* **3.** The relative brightness of a celestial body measured on a numerical scale.

mag•no•lia |măg **nōl′**yə| *or* |**-nō′**lē ə| *n.* **1.** A tree or shrub with large, showy, usually white or pink flowers. **2.** The flower of such a tree or shrub. [SEE PICTURE]

mag•pie |**măg′**pī′| *n.* **1.** A long-tailed, noisy, black and white bird related to the crows and jays. **2.** A person who chatters. [SEE PICTURE]

ma•guey |mə **gā′**| *or* |**măg′**wā′| *n., pl.* **ma•gueys.** **1.** A tropical American plant with large, stiff leaves that yield a fiber used for making rope, twine, etc. **2.** The fiber of this plant.

Mag•yar |**măg′**yär′| *or* |**mäg′**-| *n.* **1.** A Hungarian. **2.** A language, Hungarian. —**Mag′yar** *adj.*

ma•ha•ra•jah or **ma•ha•ra•ja** |mä′hə **rä′**jə| *or* |-zhə| *n.* A former king or prince in India.

ma•ha•ra•ni or **ma•ha•ra•nee** |mä′hə **rä′**nē| *n.* **1.** The wife of a maharajah. **2.** A former queen or princess in India.

Ma•hat•ma |mə **hät′**mə| *or* |-**hăt′**-| *n.* A Hindu title of respect for a holy man.

Ma•hi•can |mə **hē′**kən| *n., pl.* **Ma•hi•can** or **Ma•hi•cans.** **1.** A North American Indian tribe formerly living in the area of the upper Hudson River valley and Lake Champlain. **2.** A member of this tribe. **3.** Their Algonquian language.

mah•jong, also **mah•jongg** |**mä′jông′**| *or* |-**jŏng′**| *or* |-**zhông′**| *or* |-**zhŏng′**| *n.* A game usually played by four persons using tiles bearing various designs.

ma•hog•a•ny |mə **hŏg′**ə nē| *n., pl.* **ma•hog•a•nies.** **1. a.** A tropical American tree with hard, reddish-brown wood. **b.** The wood of such a tree, much used for making furniture. **2.** Any of several similar trees or their wood. **3.** A reddish brown. —***modifier:*** *a mahogany table.* —*adj.* Reddish brown.

Ma•hom•et |mə **hŏm′**ĭt|. A form of the name **Mohammed.**

ma•hout |mə **hout′**| *n.* The keeper and driver of an elephant.

maid |mād| *n.* **1.** A girl or an unmarried woman. **2.** A female servant. ¶*These sound alike* **maid, made.**

maid•en |**mād′**n| *n.* An unmarried girl or woman. —*adj.* **1. a.** Of a maiden. **b.** Suited to a maiden: *maiden innocence.* **2.** Unmarried: *a maiden aunt.* **3.** First or earliest: *a ship's maiden voyage.*

maid•en•hair |**măd′**n hâr′| *n.* Also **maidenhair fern.** A fern having thin, dark stems and feathery fronds with fan-shaped leaflets.

maid•en•hood |**măd′**n ho͝od′| *n.* The condition or time of being a maiden.

maiden name. A woman's family name before marriage.

maid in waiting. *pl.* **maids in waiting.** An unmarried girl or woman who attends a queen or princess.

maid of honor. *pl.* **maids of honor.** **1.** The chief unmarried female attendant of the bride at a wedding. **2.** An unmarried noblewoman who attends a queen or princess.

maid•ser•vant |**mād′**sûr′vənt| *n.* A female servant.

Mai•du |**mī′**do͞o| *n., pl.* **Mai•du** or **Mai•dus.** **1.** A North American Indian tribe of the Sacramento Valley area of California. **2.** A member of this tribe. **3.** The Penutian language of this tribe.

mail¹ |māl| *n.* **1. a.** Materials, such as letters and packages, handled in the postal system of a country. **b.** Materials processed for distribution from a post office at a specified time: *the morning mail.* **c.** Postal material for a specified person or organization: *What did we get in the mail today?* **2.** A governmental system that handles the postal materials of a country. —***modifier:*** *a mail plane; a mail truck.* —*v.* To send by mail. ¶*These sound alike* **mail, male.** [SEE NOTE]

mail² |māl| *n.* Armor that will bend, made of connected metal rings, loops of chain, or overlapping scales, worn to protect the body in battle. —*v.* To cover with such armor. ¶*These sound alike* **mail, male.** [SEE NOTE]

mail•box |**māl′**bŏks′| *n.* **1.** A public box in which outgoing mail is deposited. **2.** A private box for incoming mail.

mail•man |**māl′**măn′| *n., pl.* **-men** |-mĕn′|. A person who carries and delivers mail; a postman.

mail order. A request for goods or services that is received and usually filled through the mail. —***modifier:*** **(mail-order):** *a mail-order catalogue.*

maim |mām| *v.* To disable, usually by depriving of the use of a limb; cripple: *Car accidents kill or maim many people every year.*

main |mān| *adj.* Most important; principal; major: *Look for the main idea in each paragraph.* —*n.* **1.** A large pipe, duct, conduit, or conductor used to carry water, oil, gas, or electricity. **2.** Also **Spanish Main.** The mainland as opposed to islands. Used chiefly in historical texts. **3.** The open sea. Used chiefly in poetry. ¶*These sound alike* **main, mane.**

Idiom. **in the main.** For the most part; on the whole.

Maine |mān|. A state of the United States, in the extreme northeast of the country. Population, 1,000,000. Capital, Augusta.

main•land |**mān′**lănd′| *or* |-lənd| *n.* The principal land mass of a country, territory, or continent as opposed to its islands or peninsulas.

main•ly |**mān′**lē| *adv.* Most importantly; for the most part.

main•mast |**mān′**məst| *n.* The principal mast of a sailing ship.

main•sail |**mān′**səl| *n.* The largest sail set on the mainmast of a sailing ship.

main•spring |**mān′**sprĭng′| *n.* **1.** The spring that stores the power that drives a mechanism, especially a clock or watch. **2.** An impelling cause; motivating force: *A desire for revenge was the mainspring of his plan.*

main•stay |**mān′**stā′| *n.* **1.** A strong rope or cable that holds in place the mainmast of a sailing vessel. **2.** A main support: *He is the mainstay of the team.*

main•stream |**mān′**strēm′| *n.* The prevailing current or direction of a movement or influence: *writers in the mainstream of 19th-century thought.*

main•tain |mān **tān′**| *v.* **1.** To keep up; carry on; continue: *The train maintains a moderate speed on upgrades. The troops maintained order.* **2.** To keep in a desirable condition; keep from changing, declining, etc.: *maintain public roads; maintain order.* **3.** To provide for the upkeep of; bear the expenses of: *maintain a large family.* **4.** To uphold against attack or danger; defend: *maintain one's rights.* **5.** To assert as true; declare: *maintain one's innocence.*

main•te•nance |**mān′**tə nəns| *n.* **1.** The act of

magnolia

magpie

mail¹·²

Mail¹ *originally meant "a bag for carrying letters, a mailbag"; it comes from Old French* maile, *"pouch, bag."* **Mail²** *is from Old French* maille, *"mesh, network."*

maintaining, as by supporting, upholding, preserving, etc. **2.** The work involved in maintaining; care; upkeep. **3.** Means of support or livelihood.

main•top |mān'tŏp'| *n.* A platform at the head of the mainmast on a square-rigged ship.

main yard. The yard on which the mainsail of a sailing ship is extended.

maî•tre d' |mā'trə dē'|. *Informal.* A headwaiter. [SEE NOTE]

maize |māz| *n.* **1.** The corn plant or its edible kernels. **2.** A light to strong yellow. *—adj.* Light to strong yellow. ¶*These sound alike* **maize, maze.**

maître d'

Maitre d' *is a shortening of French* maître d'hôtel; *this phrase, literally meaning "master of the inn," is the French term for "headwaiter" or "manager of a restaurant."*

Maj. major (military rank).

ma•jes•tic |mə jĕs'tĭk| *adj.* **1.** Full of majesty; stately; dignified: *The queen gave a majestic wave of the hand.* **2.** Imposing; splendid: *a majestic oak.* **—ma•jes'tic•al•ly** *adv.*

maj•es•ty |măj'ĭ stē| *n., pl.* **maj•es•ties. 1.** The greatness, power, and dignity of a sovereign. **2.** A quality of stateliness, splendor, or grandeur: *the majesty of the Rocky Mountains.* **3. Majesty.** A title used in speaking of or to a sovereign, such as a king or queen: *Her Majesty.*

Maj. Gen. major general.

ma•jor |mā'jər| *adj.* **1. a.** Large and important: *the Colorado, a major American river.* **b.** Important or considerable; leading: *a major symphony orchestra. The hand crossbow played a major role in the campaigns of the Middle Ages.* **2. a.** Larger or largest: *the major portion of the liquid. The major divisions of the ruler are inches.* **b.** Most important; chief; main: *The major export of Ethiopia is coffee. An ordinary television set has five major control knobs.* **3. a.** Of a major scale or the pattern of intervals in it. **b.** Containing as many semitones as the interval of that type formed by the tonic of a major scale and one of the tones above it: *a major third; a major sixth; a major seventh.* **c.** Containing a major third: *a major triad.* **d.** Based on a major scale: *a major key.* *—n.* **1.** An officer in the Army, Air Force, or Marine Corps ranking above a captain and below a lieutenant colonel. **2. a.** In schools and colleges, a field of study chosen. **b.** A student studying a particular subject: *an English major.* **3.** *Informal.* **the majors.** The major leagues of a sport in general. **4.** A major scale, key, interval, etc. *—v.* To be a student in a particular subject: *She is majoring in Spanish.*

majorette

Ma•jor•ca |mə jôr'kə| *or* |-yôr'-|. The largest of the Balearic Islands. Population, 375,000.

ma•jor-do•mo |mā'jər dō'mō| *n., pl.* **ma•jor-do•mos.** A head steward or butler, as one in the household of a great nobleman.

ma•jor•ette |mā'jə rĕt'| *n.* A **drum majorette.** [SEE PICTURE]

major general. An officer in the Army, Air Force, or Marine Corps ranking above a brigadier general and below a lieutenant general.

ma•jor•i•ty |mə jôr'ĭ tē| *or* |-jŏr'-| *n., pl.* **ma•jor•i•ties. 1.** The greater number or part of something; a number more than half of a total: *the majority of the class.* **2.** The excess of a greater number over a smaller number; margin: *won by a majority of 5,000 votes.* **3.** The status of having reached the age of legal responsibility.

major league. 1. Either of the two principal groups of baseball teams in the United States; the American League or the National League. **2.** Any league of principal importance in professional sports.

ma•jor-league |mā'jər lēg'| *adj.* **1.** Of a major league: *a major-league player.* **2.** Outstanding of its kind: *a major-league performance.*

ma•jor-lea•guer |mā'jər lē'gər| *n.* A major-league player.

major scale. A musical scale in which the third and fourth tones and seventh and eighth tones are separated by half steps and all others are separated by whole steps.

make |māk| *v.* **made** |mād|, **mak•ing. 1.** To bring into being or construct by or as if by forming, shaping, combining materials, etc.: *make a dress.* **2.** To bring about or cause to exist or appear: *Don't make such a fuss. Bees make honey.* **3. a.** To cause to be in a certain state or condition; cause to become: *make the puppy unhappy.* **b.** To cause to behave in a particular manner: *Slamming the oven door makes the cake fall.* **c.** To compel: *make him go with you.* **4.** To carry out, engage in, or perform (an action): *make an attempt; make war.* **5. a.** To be capable of being used for or transformed into: *The point where a river meets the ocean often makes a good harbor.* **b.** To develop into: *He will make a fine executive.* **6. a.** To formulate in one's mind: *make plans.* **b.** To arrive at: *make decisions.* **7.** To form as one's own; acquire: *make friends.* **8.** To form or amount to; constitute: *Two halves make a whole.* **9.** To set up or in order; prepare: *make a bed; make coffee.* **10.** To gain or earn: *make money.* **11.** To score; achieve: *make a home run.* **12.** To manage to reach: *make a train.* **13. a.** *Informal.* To achieve the rank of: *make lieutenant.* **b.** To succeed in becoming a member of: *make the team.* **14.** To provide: *make room.* **15. a.** To calculate as being; estimate: *We make the house to be about 100 years old.* **b.** To regard as the meaning or nature: *What do you make of her letter?* **16.** To be the thing that completes or satisfies: *The scenery makes the movie.* **—phrasal verbs. make for.** To set out in the direction of; head for: *The bandits made for the hills.* **make out. 1.** To see and identify, especially with difficulty: *I can make out a sign ahead.* **2.** To understand: *I can't make out the words of the song.* **3. a.** To write out: *make out a list.* **b.** To fill in by writing: *make out an application.* **4.** *Slang.* To get along well; succeed: *make out in school.* **make over. 1.** To change or redo; renovate. **2.** To change or transfer the ownership of: *make over the property to his son.* **make up. 1.** To construct fictionally or falsely: *make up a story.* **2.** To constitute: *This city is made up of many different kinds of people.* **3. a.** To compensate, as for a mistake or omission: *make up for my lapse of memory.* **b.** To satisfy a grievance or debt: *I promise I'll make it up to you.* **c.** To make good (a lack): *make up the difference.* **4.** To resolve a personal quarrel: *Let's kiss and make up.* **5.** To repeat (an examination missed or failed). **6.** To apply cosmetics to. **7.** To settle; decide: *make up one's mind.* *—n.* **1.** A style or manner in which something is made: *a machine of intricate make.* **2.** A specific line of manufactured goods; a brand: *a make of stereo records.*

ă pat/ā pay/â care/ä father/ĕ pet/ ē be/ĭ pit/ī pie/î fierce/ŏ pot/ ō go/ô paw, for/oi oil/ŏŏ book/ ōō boot/ou out/ŭ cut/û fur/ *th* the/th thin/hw which/zh vision/ ə ago, item, pencil, atom, circus

Idioms. **make away** (or **off**) **with.** To carry off, especially by stealing. **make it.** To succeed, as in reaching: *I don't think I can make it back to the house.*

make-be•lieve |māk′bĭ lēv′| *n.* Playful pretense; fiction. —*adj.* Pretended; fictional: *a make-believe land.*

mak•er |mā′kər| *n.* **1.** Someone or something that makes. **2. Maker.** God: *our Maker.*

make•shift |māk′shĭft′| *n.* Something used or assembled as a temporary substitute. —*adj.* Serving as a temporary substitute: *a makeshift shelter.*

make-up, also **make•up** |māk′ŭp′| *n.* **1.** The way in which something is composed or arranged; construction: *its biological make-up.* **2.** The qualities or temperament that make up a personality; disposition: *His troubles are in his make-up.* **3.** Cosmetics applied especially to the face. **4.** A special examination given to a student who has missed or failed a previous one. —*modifier:* *a make-up kit; make-up remover.*

mal–. A prefix meaning "bad, wrongly": **malpractice; malformed.**

Ma•la•bo |mä lä′bō| *or* |măl′ə bō′|. The capital of Equatorial Guinea. Population, 37,000.

mal•a•chite |măl′ə kīt′| *n.* A green to nearly black mineral consisting mainly of a carbonate of copper, used as an ore of copper and for ornamental stoneware.

mal•ad•just•ed |măl′ə jŭs′tĭd| *adj.* Poorly adjusted to one's environment or to one's circumstances.

mal•a•droit |măl′ə **droit′**| *adj.* Lacking dexterity or skill; clumsy: *a maladroit movement of the hand.* —**mal′a•droit′ly** *adv.* —**mal′a•droit′ness** *n.*

mal•a•dy |măl′ə dē| *n., pl.* **mal•a•dies.** A disease, disorder, or ailment; a sickness.

Mal•a•gas•y Republic |măl′ə găs′ē|. The former name for **Madagascar.**

ma•la•mute |măl′ə myōōt′| *n.* A dog developed in Alaska as a sled dog, with a thick coat and a bushy tail.

ma•lar•i•a |mə lâr′ē ə| *n.* A severe infectious disease whose symptoms are typically cycles of chills, fever, and sweating. It is caused by protozoan parasites that attack red blood cells and that are transmitted by the bite of the female anopheles mosquito. —**ma•lar′i•al** *adj.*

Ma•la•wi |mä lä′wē|. A country in southeastern Africa. Population, 4,900,000. Capital, Lilongwe.

Ma•lay |mā′lā′| *or* |mə lā′| *n.* **1.** A member of a people of the Malay Peninsula and some adjacent areas. **2.** The language of this people. —*adj.* Of the Malays or their language. —**Ma•lay′an** |mə-lā′ən| *adj. & n.*

Ma•lay•a |mə lā′ə|. The Malay Peninsula.

Malay Peninsula. A long, narrow peninsula in Southeast Asia, composed of parts of Malaysia, Thailand, and Burma.

Ma•lay•sia |mə lā′zhə| *or* |-shə|. A country in Southeast Asia consisting of the southern part of the Malay Peninsula and the northern part of the island of Borneo. Population, 13,436,000. Capital, Kuala Lumpur. —**Ma•lay′sian** *adj. & n.*

mal•con•tent |măl′kən tĕnt′| *adj.* Dissatisfied, especially with established authority. —*n.* A malcontent person.

Mal•dives |măl′dīvz′|. A group of islands in the Indian Ocean, southwest of India, constituting an independent country. Population, 143,000. Capital, Male.

male |māl| *adj.* **1.** Of or characteristic of animals or plants of the sex that is equipped with organs that produce sperm cells for fertilizing egg cells. **2.** Of or being a man or boy: *a male voice; a male student.* **3.** Designed to make a connection by fitting into a matching socket or opening: *a male plug; a male thread on a bolt.* —*n.* **1.** A male animal or plant. **2.** A man or boy. ¶ *These sound alike* **male, mail.**

Ma•le |mä′lē|. The capital of the Maldive Islands. Population, 12,000.

mal•e•dic•tion |măl′ĭ **dĭk′**shən| *n.* An appeal, as to a supernatural power, for evil to fall on someone; a curse.

mal•e•fac•tor |măl′ə făk′tər| *n.* **1.** A person who has committed a crime; a criminal. **2.** An evildoer.

ma•lev•o•lent |mə lĕv′ə lənt| *adj.* Wishing harm to others; malicious: *a malevolent old man.* —**ma•lev′o•lence** *n.* —**ma•lev′o•lent•ly** *adv.*

mal•fea•sance |măl fē′zəns| *n.* Wrongdoing or misconduct, especially by a public official.

mal•for•ma•tion |măl′fôr **mā′**shən| *n.* **1.** The condition of being malformed. **2.** An abnormal structure or form, as of a part of the body.

mal•formed |măl **fôrmd′**| *adj.* Having a faulty or abnormal form: *a malformed leg.*

mal•func•tion |măl **fŭngk′**shən| *v.* **1.** To fail to function. **2.** To function in an abnormal or improper way. —*n.* The process of malfunctioning or an example of malfunctioning.

Ma•li |mä′lē|. A country in western Africa. Population, 5,560,000. Capital, Bamako.

mal•ice |măl′ĭs| *n.* The desire to harm others or to see others suffer; ill will; spite.

ma•li•cious |mə **lĭsh′**əs| *adj.* Having, showing, or motivated by malice; spiteful: *a malicious woman; a malicious lie.* —**ma•li′cious•ly** *adv.* —**ma•li′cious•ness** *n.*

ma•lign |mə **līn′**| *v.* To speak evil of; slander: *malign a person with vicious gossip.* —*adj.* **1.** Showing or having malice: *a malign look.* **2.** Evil in nature; injurious: *a malign influence.*

ma•lig•nan•cy |mə **lĭg′**nən sē| *n., pl.* **ma•lig•nan•cies. 1.** The condition or quality of being malignant. **2.** A malignant tumor.

ma•lig•nant |mə **lĭg′**nənt| *adj.* **1.** Having or showing ill will; malicious. **2. a.** Threatening to life or health: *a malignant disease.* **b.** Tending to grow and spread throughout the body, eventually causing death: *a malignant growth.* —**ma•lig′nant•ly** *adv.*

ma•lig•ni•ty |mə **lĭg′**nĭ tē| *n., pl.* **ma•lig•ni•ties. 1.** Deep-rooted ill will; malice. **2.** An act of great malice.

ma•lin•ger |mə **lĭng′**gər| *v.* To pretend to be ill or injured in order to avoid work or duty. —**ma•lin′ger•er** *n.*

mall |môl| *or* |măl| *n.* **1.** A shady public walk or promenade. **2. a.** A street lined with shops and closed to vehicles. **b.** A **shopping center. 3.** A center strip dividing a road or highway. ¶ *These sound alike* **mall, maul.**

mal•lard |măl′ərd| *n.* A wild duck of which the male has a glossy green head and neck. [SEE PICTURE]

mallard

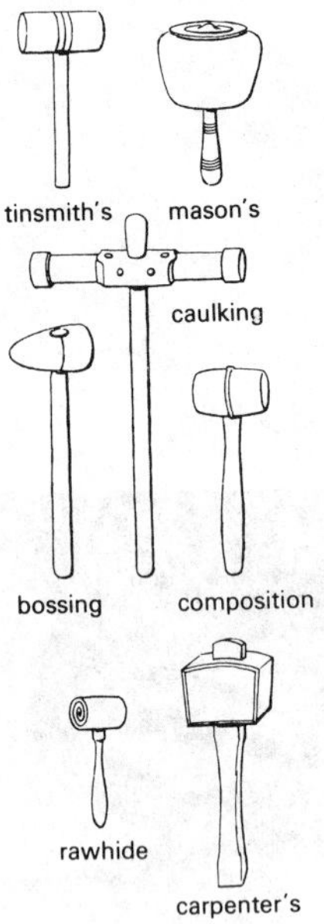

mallet

mammoth

ă pat/ā pay/â care/ä father/ĕ pet/ ē be/ĭ pit/ī pie/î fierce/ŏ pot/ ō go/ô paw, for/oi oil/o͝o book/ o͞o boot/ou out/ŭ cut/û fur/ *th* the/th thin/hw which/zh vision/ ə ago, item, pencil, atom, circus

mal•le•a•ble |măl′ē ə bəl| *adj.* **1.** Capable of being shaped or formed, as by pressure or hammering: *a malleable metal.* **2.** Capable of being changed or influenced; pliable: *the malleable mind and personality of a young child.* —**mal′le•a•bil′i•ty** *n.*

mal•le•i |măl′ē ī′| *or* |-ē ē′| *n.* Plural of **malleus.**

mal•let |măl′ĭt| *n.* **1.** A hammer with a cylindrical wooden head and a short handle. **2.** A similar, longer-handled implement used to strike the ball in croquet and polo. [SEE PICTURE]

mal•le•us |măl′ē əs| *n., pl.* **mal•le•i** |măl′ē ī′| *or* |-ē ē′|. The largest of three small bones in the middle ear; the hammer.

mal•low |măl′ō| *n.* Any of several related plants with flowers that are usually pink or white and often large and showy.

malm•sey |mäm′zē| *n., pl.* **malm•seys.** A fortified sweet white wine.

mal•nu•tri•tion |măl′no͞o **trĭsh′**ən| *or* |-nyo͞o-| *n.* A condition in which, as a result of a poor diet, too little food, or faulty digestion or assimilation, the body is not supplied with essential nutrients.

mal•oc•clu•sion |măl′ə **klo͞o′**zhən| *n.* A condition in which the upper and lower teeth fail to meet properly; a faulty bite.

mal•prac•tice |măl **prăk′**tĭs| *n.* **1.** Improper or careless treatment of a patient by a physician. **2.** Any improper conduct by someone holding a professional position.

malt |môlt| *n.* Barley or other grain that has been allowed to sprout and then dried. It is used chiefly in making beer, whiskey, etc. —*v.* **1.** To make (grain) into malt. **2.** To mix or prepare with malt.

Mal•ta |môl′tə|. An island nation in the Mediterranean Sea, south of Sicily. Population, 321,000. Capital, Valletta. —**Mal•tese′** |môl **tēz′**| *or* |-**tēs′**| *adj.* & *n.*

mal•tase |môl′tās′| *n.* An enzyme that converts maltose to glucose.

malt•ed |môl′tĭd| *n.* A drink, **malted milk.**

malted milk. **1.** A soluble powder made of dried milk, malted barley, and wheat flour. **2.** A drink made of this powder mixed with milk, ice cream, and flavoring.

Maltese cat. A cat with short, bluish-gray fur, often kept as a pet.

Maltese cross. A cross having the form of four arrowheads placed with their points toward the center of a circle.

mal•tose |môl′tōs′| *n.* A sugar that has the formula $C_{12}H_{22}O_{11}$, found in malt.

mal•treat |măl **trēt′**| *v.* To treat cruelly; handle roughly: *Do not maltreat animals.* —**mal•treat′ment** *n.*

ma•ma |mä′mə| *or* |mə **mä′**| *n.* Mother. Used chiefly by children.

mam•bo |mäm′bō| *n., pl.* **mam•bos.** **1.** A Latin-American dance resembling the rumba. **2.** The music for this dance. —*v.* To dance the mambo.

mam•ma |mä′mə| *or* |mə **mä′**| *n.* A form of the word **mama.**

mam•mal |măm′əl| *n.* Any of a group of animals that have hair or fur on their bodies and, in the females, special glands that produce milk for feeding their young. Cats, dogs, cows, elephants, mice, bats, whales, and human beings are all mammals. —**mam•ma′li•an** |mə **mā′**lē ən| *or* |-**māl′**yən| *adj.*

mam•ma•ry |măm′ə rē| *adj.* Of a breast or milk-producing gland.

mammary gland. One of the special milk-producing glands, such as a breast or udder, in female mammals.

Mam•mon |măm′ən| *n.* **1.** In the New Testament, riches and avarice personified as a false god. **2.** Often **mammon.** Riches regarded as an object of worship or an evil influence.

mam•moth |măm′əth| *n.* An extinct elephant that had long tusks and thick hair and that lived throughout the Northern Hemisphere during the Ice Age. —*adj.* Huge; gigantic: *a feeble fire in a mammoth fireplace.* [SEE PICTURE]

mam•my |măm′ē| *n., pl.* **mam•mies.** **1.** Mother. **2.** A black woman in the southern United States hired as a nurse for white children. The word "mammy" is often considered offensive.

man |măn| *n., pl.* **men** |mĕn|. **1.** A full-grown male human being. **2.** Human beings in general; humanity; mankind: *the history of man.* **3.** Human beings considered as a kind of organism; the human species: *Man is a mammal.* **4. a.** A male person regarded as physically strong, brave, potent, etc.: *He enlisted in the Marine Corps, hoping it would make a man out of him.* **b.** A male person regarded as having strong moral qualities: *Are you enough of a man to accept the responsibility of leadership?* **5.** The male head of a household: *When his father died, Tom became the man of the family.* **6.** A husband, lover, or sweetheart. **7.** A male servant, employee, worker, etc.: *Robinson Crusoe and his man Friday; ten men on the job.* **8.** *Informal.* Fellow. **9.** Any of the pieces used in chess, checkers, and similar board games. —*v.* **manned, man•ning. 1.** To take one's place for work at or take one's post at: *man the oars. The first mate manned the bridge.* **2.** To supply with men: *The captain manned his ship with a crew of Greek sailors.* —*interj.* A word used to express excitement or to draw attention: *Man! It's a hot day.*

Idioms. **as one man.** In unison; unanimously. **be (one's) own man.** To have control over one's own life; be independent. **to a man.** Including everyone; without exceptions.

Man, Isle of |măn|. A British island in the Irish Sea.

man•a•cle |măn′ə kəl| *n.* One of a pair of strong, connected rings that can be locked around the wrists of a prisoner; a handcuff. —*v.* **man•a•cled, man•a•cling.** To restrain with manacles.

man•age |măn′ĭj| *v.* **man•aged, man•ag•ing. 1.** To exert control over: *a horse that is hard to manage. It is never easy to manage one's fears.* **2.** To operate, drive, etc.: *manage a bulldozer.* **3.** To succeed in doing or accomplishing; contrive or arrange: *Cuckoos manage to get along without having to build nests.* **4.** To be in charge of; direct: *manage a household.*

man•age•a•ble |măn′ĭ jə bəl| *adj.* Capable of being managed or controlled: *For once, I was baby-sitting for a manageable child.* —**man′age•a•bil′i•ty** *n.*

man•age•ment |măn′ĭj mənt| *n.* **1.** The act or process of managing: *careful management of the* *family budget.* **2.** The practice of managing: *He studied hotel management.* **3.** The managers, supervisors, etc., of a business, organization, etc.: *At the factory where Dad works, the management has been laying people off.*

man•ag•er |**măn'**ĭ jər| *n.* **1.** A person who manages a business or other enterprise. **2. a.** A person in charge of the training and performance of an athlete or athletic team. **b.** A student in charge of the equipment, uniforms, etc., of a school or college team.

man•a•ge•ri•al |măn'ĭ **jîr'**ē əl| *adj.* Of a manager or management: *learn managerial skills.*

managing editor. A person who supervises and coordinates all phases of work on a newspaper, magazine, book, etc.

Ma•na•gua |mä **nä'**gwä|. The capital of Nicaragua. Population, 275,000.

ma•ña•na |mä **nyä'**nä|. *Spanish. adv.* **1.** Tomorrow. **2.** In the future. —*n.* The next day or some indefinite time in the future.

man-at-arms |**măn'**ət **ärmz'**| *n., pl.* **men-at-arms** |**mĕn'**ət **ärmz'**|. A soldier, especially a heavily armed mounted soldier in the Middle Ages.

man•a•tee |**măn'**ə tē'| *n.* A plant-eating water mammal of rivers and bays along the tropical Atlantic coast, having flippers near the head and a paddlelike tail. [SEE PICTURE]

Man•ches•ter |**măn'**chĕs'tər| *or* |-chĭ stər|. **1.** A city in central England. Population, 600,000. **2.** The largest city in New Hampshire. Population, 90,936.

Man•chu |**măn'**chōō| *or* |măn **chōō'**| *n., pl.* **Man•chu** or **Man•chus. 1.** A member of a nomadic people, native to Manchuria, who ruled China from 1644 to 1911. **2.** The language of the Manchu. —*adj.* **1.** Of the Manchu or their language. **2.** Of Manchuria.

Man•chu•ri•a |măn **chŏŏr'**ē ə|. A region in northeastern China. —**Man•chu'ri•an** *adj. & n.*

Man•dan |**măn'**dăn'| *n., pl.* **Man•dan** or **Man•dans. 1.** A North American Indian tribe formerly living in North Dakata. **2.** A member of this tribe. **3.** The Siouan language of this tribe.

man•da•rin |**măn'**də rĭn| *n.* **1.** In imperial China, a high public official. **2. Mandarin.** The national language of China, based on the principal dialect spoken in and around Peking. In imperial China, Mandarin was the court language.

man•date |**măn'**dāt'| *n.* **1.** The results of a political election, regarded as expressing the true wishes of the voting public and thus used to justify the policies of the elected officials: *President Kennedy felt the American people had given him a mandate for vigorous action.* **2. a.** Control over a territory, as granted by the League of Nations (1920–46) to one of its member nations. **b.** A territory under such control.

man•da•to•ry |**măn'**də tôr'ē| *or* |-tōr'ē| *adj.* Required; obligatory: *A college degree is mandatory for most teaching jobs.*

man•di•ble |**măn'**də bəl| *n.* **1.** A jaw of a vertebrate, especially the lower jaw. **2.** Any of the parts that form the mouth opening of an animal.

man•do•lin |**măn'**dl ĭn'| *or* |măn'dl **ĭn'**| *n.* A musical instrument having a pear-shaped body and a neck that has frets over which four pairs of strings are stretched.

man•drake |**măn'**drāk'| *n.* **1.** A plant with a forked root that resembles the human body and was formerly believed to have magical powers. **2.** A North American plant, the **May apple.**

man•drel or **man•dril** |**măn'**drəl| *n.* **1.** A spindle or shaft used to hold material that is being shaped on a lathe. **2.** A rotary shaft on which a working tool is mounted.

man•drill |**măn'**drĭl| *n.* A large African monkey with brightly colored patches of skin on the face and buttocks. [SEE PICTURE]

mane |mān| *n.* The long hair growing from the neck and head of certain animals, such as a horse or a male lion. ¶*These sound alike* **mane, main.** —**maned** *adj.*

ma•neu•ver |mə **nōō'**vər| *or* |-**nyōō'**-| *n.* **1.** A change in the course or position of a vehicle, as an aircraft, automobile, etc. **2.** A calculated act; trick; stratagem: *The lawyer used various legal maneuvers to outwit the prosecutor.* **3. a.** A tactical or strategic movement, as of troops, warships, etc.: *By a series of brilliant maneuvers, the general outwitted the enemy.* **b. maneuvers.** A large-scale military exercise in which such movements are practiced: *The regiment is on maneuvers.* —*v.* **1.** To make or cause to make one or more changes in course or position: *The "Nautilus" had to maneuver very carefully to avoid the icebergs. The Ski Patrolmen showed the boys how to maneuver a stretcher case down a cliff.* **2.** To make one or more changes in tactics or approach: *Our lawyer maneuvered to get the trial postponed.* **3.** To manipulate, as by trickery: *She finally maneuvered him into proposing marriage.* **4.** To carry out a military maneuver: *an army bottled up and unable to maneuver.* —**ma•neu'ver•a•bil'i•ty** *n.* —**ma•neu'ver•a•ble** *adj.*

man•ful |**măn'**fəl| *adj.* Brave; resolute; manly. —**man'ful•ly** *adv.* —**man'ful•ness** *n.*

man•ga•nese |**măng'**gə nēz'| *or* |-nēs'| *n.* Symbol **Mn** One of the elements, a gray, brittle metal. It is found in minerals and is used in steel alloys to improve their strength, hardness, and resistance to wear. Atomic number 25; atomic weight 54.94; valences +1, +2, +3, +4, +6, +7; melting point 1,244°C; boiling point 2,097°C.

mange |mānj| *n.* A skin disease of dogs and other mammals, characterized by itching and loss of hair.

man•ger |**mān'**jər| *n.* A trough or open box in which feed for horses or cattle is placed.

man•gle¹ |**măng'**gəl| *v.* **man•gled, man•gling. 1.** To disfigure by crushing, hacking, etc.: *The worker mangled his arm in an accident.* **2.** To ruin, spoil: *The musicians completely mangled the symphony for lack of rehearsal.* [SEE NOTE]

man•gle² |**măng'**gəl| *n.* A laundry machine that presses fabrics, clothes, and household linens by running them between heated rollers. —*v.* **man•gled, man•gling.** To smooth or press with a mangle: *mangle the sheets.* [SEE NOTE]

man•go |**măng'**gō| *n., pl.* **man•goes** or **man•gos. 1.** A tropical fruit with a smooth rind and sweet, juicy, yellow-orange flesh. **2.** A tree that bears such fruit.

man•grove |**măn'**grōv'| *or* |**măng'**grōv'| *n.* A tropical tree or shrub that has many stiltlike roots growing above the ground and forms dense

manatee

mandrill

mangle¹⁻²
Mangle¹ *is from Norman French* mahangler, *"to wound."* **Mangle²** *is from Dutch* mangel, *"machine for wringing out clothes."*

thickets in marshes and along shores.

man•gy |măn′jē| *adj.* **man•gi•er, man•gi•est.** **1.** Having or appearing to have mange: *a pack of barking, mangy dogs.* **2.** Having many bare spots; shabby: *a mangy old fur coat.*

man•han•dle |măn′hăn′dl| *v.* **man•han•dled, man•han•dling.** To handle in a rough manner; treat with brutality.

Man•hat•tan |măn **hăt′**n| *or* |mən-|. An island in the Hudson River, forming a borough of New York City.

man•hole |**măn′**hōl′| *n.* A hole in a street, with a removable cover, through which an underground sewer, pipe, conduit, etc., can be entered for repair work or inspection.

man•hood |**măn′**ho͝od′| *n.* **1.** The condition of being an adult male person: *watched her son grow to manhood.* **2.** Possession of the qualities expected of an adult man, as courage and vigor: *Sammy enlisted in the Marines to prove his manhood.* **3.** Men in general: *the manhood of the country.*

man-hour |**măn′**our′| *n.* A unit of labor equal to one person working for one hour, used in expressing and estimating industrial production and costs.

ma•ni•a |**mā′**nē ə| *or* |**mān′**yə| *n.* **1.** A form of mental disturbance associated with psychosis, in which a patient becomes excessively active and gay and experiences a rapid stream of changing ideas. **2.** An intense enthusiasm; craze: *He has a mania for stamp and coin collecting.* —**man′ic** |**măn′**ĭk| *adj.*

ma•ni•ac |**mā′**nē ăk′| *n.* A mentally ill person, especially one who acts violent.

ma•ni•a•cal |mə **nī′**ə kəl| *adj.* Mentally ill and extremely violent; mad; crazy: *a maniacal killer held by the guards.*

man•i•cure |**măn′**ĭ kyo͝or′| *n.* A cosmetic treatment for the hands and fingernails. —*v.* **man•i•cured, man•i•cur•ing.** To care for (the fingernails) by shaping, cleaning, and polishing. —**man′i•cur′•ist** *n.* [SEE NOTE]

manicure
Manicure *is from French* manicure, *which was formed from Latin* manus, *"hand,"* + cūra, *care."*

man•i•fest |**măn′**ə fĕst′| *adj.* Obvious; clear; apparent: *It is strange that so manifest a hoax has been able to fool so many people.* —*v.* To reveal; show; display: *manifest a desire to leave.* —*n.* A list of cargo or passengers: *a ship's manifest.* —**man′i•fest•ly** *adv.*

man•i•fes•ta•tion |măn′ə fē **stā′**shən| *n.* **1.** The act of showing, demonstrating, or proving: *his excessive manifestations of affection.* **2.** Something that reveals something else: *Heat was recognized as a manifestation of motion among tiny molecules.*

man•i•fes•to |măn′ə **fĕs′**tō| *n., pl.* **man•i•fes•toes** or **man•i•fes•tos.** A public declaration of principles and aims, especially those of a political nature.

man•i•fold |**măn′**ə fōld′| *adj.* **1.** Of many kinds; varied: *The village woke from its sleep and arose to begin its manifold labors.* **2.** Having many parts, forms, or aspects: *God's manifold creation.* —*n.* A pipe or tube that has several openings for making multiple connections: *the exhaust manifold of an automobile.*

man•i•kin |**măn′**ĭ kĭn| *n.* A form of the word **mannequin.**

Ma•nil•a |mə **nĭl′**ə|. The largest city and de facto capital of the Philippines. Population, 1,626,000.

man•i•oc |**măn′**ē ŏk′| *n.* A tropical plant, the cassava.

ma•nip•u•late |mə **nĭp′**yə lāt′| *v.* **ma•nip•u•lat•ed, ma•nip•u•lat•ing.** **1.** To operate or arrange with the hands: *manipulate the controls on an airplane.* **2.** To influence or manage in a clever or devious way: *He was clever enough to manipulate his partners.* **3.** To control (an intricate process), as if by the dexterity of human hands: *Electronic music consists of sounds manipulated by electronic equipment.* —**ma•nip′u•lat′ive** *adj.*

ma•nip•u•la•tion |mə nĭp′yə **lā′**shən| *n.* **1.** The act of manipulating: *You'll find it sheer fascination to watch a block of wood take shape under the deft manipulation of a lathe chisel.* **2.** Clever or devious management: *manipulation of public opinion.*

ma•nip•u•la•tor |mə **nĭp′**yə lā′tər| *n.* **1.** Someone or something that manipulates. **2.** A person who is clever or devious at influencing or controlling others: *He's a born manipulator.*

Man•i•to•ba |măn′ĭ **tō′**bə|. A province of south-central Canada. Population, 1,000,000. Capital, Winnipeg.

man•kind |**măn′kīnd′**| *or* |-kīnd′| *n.* Human beings in general; the human species.

man•ly |**măn′**lē| *adj.* **man•li•er, man•li•est.** **1.** Having qualities, such as courage and vigor, expected of a man: *teach young boys how to be manly.* **2.** Of or befitting a man: *He spoke up in a firm and manly voice.* —**man′li•ness** *n.*

man-made |**măn′mād′**| *adj.* Made by man rather than by nature; synthetic: *a man-made satellite in the sky.*

man•na |**măn′**ə| *n.* In the Bible, the food miraculously provided for the Israelites during their flight from Egypt.

man•ne•quin |**măn′**ĭ kĭn| *n.* **1.** A life-size model of the human body, used mainly for displaying clothes. **2.** A woman who models clothes; a model.

man•ner |**măn′**ər| *n.* **1. a.** A way or style of doing things: *proceed in the usual manner.* **b.** The way in which something is done or happens: *shook his head in a mournful manner. There was something suspicious about the manner of his death.* **2.** A style of personal behavior: *Casual in manner, Miss Brooks prefers plain, direct talk.* **3. manners. a.** Socially proper behavior; etiquette: *Mind your manners, child!* **b.** The customs of a society or period: *a novel of Victorian manners and morals.* **4.** Kind; sort: *What strange manner of beast is this?* ¶ *These sound alike* **manner, manor.**

Idioms. **all manner of.** All kinds of. **in a manner of speaking.** In a way; so to speak.

man•ner•ism |**măn′**ə rĭz′əm| *n.* **1.** A distinctive personal trait; quirk: *He has a mannerism of scratching his chin.* **2.** A habit or stylistic flourish that is regarded as exaggerated or affected: *He gradually rid his speech of mannerisms.*

man•ner•ly |**măn′**ər lē| *adj.* Having good manners; polite: *a mannerly old gentleman.* —*adv.* With good manners; politely: *He greeted us mannerly.*

man•nish |**măn′**ĭsh| *adj.* **1.** Characteristic of a man: *her low, mannish voice.* **2.** More suitable for a man than for a woman; masculine: *She prefers a mannish style of dress.* —**man′nish•ly** *adv.*

ma•noeu•vre |mə no͞o′vər| *or* |-nyo͞o′-| *n.* & *v.* **ma•noeu•vred, ma•noeu•vring.** British form of the word **maneuver.**

man-of-war |măn′ə wôr′| *or* |măn′əv-| *n., pl.* **men-of-war** |mĕn′-|. **1.** A warship. **2.** See **Portuguese man-of-war.**

ma•nom•e•ter |mə nŏm′ĭ tər| *n.* An instrument that measures and indicates the pressure of a liquid or gas.

man•or |măn′ər| *n.* **1.** The estate of a feudal lord. **2.** Any landed estate. **3.** The main house on an estate. ¶ *These sound alike* **manor, manner.**

ma•no•ri•al |mə nôr′ē əl| *or* |-nōr′-| *adj.* Of or being a manor: *a manorial estate.*

man-o'-war bird |măn′ə wôr′|. The **frigate bird.**

man•pow•er |măn′pou′ər| *n.* **1.** The power supplied by human physical effort: *The men of bygone days had only the simplest tools and devices, and they relied largely on manpower.* **2.** The number of people working or available for work, especially on a particular task.

man•sard |măn′särd′| *n.* A roof having two slopes on all four sides, with the lower slope steeper than the upper.

man•serv•ant |măn′sûr′vənt| *n., pl.* **men•serv•ants** |mĕn′sûr′vənts|. A male servant.

man•sion |măn′shən| *n.* A large, stately house.

man•slaugh•ter |măn′slô′tər| *n.* **1.** The act of killing a fellow human being without intending to do so. **2.** This act regarded as a crime, as, for example, when a motorist kills a pedestrian through negligence.

man•ta |măn′tə| *n.* Often **manta ray.** A large ocean fish having a flattened body with winglike extensions at the sides.

man•tel |măn′tl| *n.* **1.** An ornamental facing around a fireplace. **2.** A mantlepiece.

man•tel•piece |măn′tl pēs′| *n.* The shelf over a fireplace.

man•tid |măn′tĭd| *n.* An insect, the mantis.

man•til•la |măn tē′yə| *or* |-tĭl′ə| *n.* A scarf, usually of lace, worn over the head and shoulders by women in Spain and Latin America.

man•tis |măn′tĭs| *n.* Often **praying mantis.** A large, grasshopperlike insect that preys on other insects and that holds its front legs folded up as if praying. [SEE PICTURE]

man•tis•sa |măn tĭs′ə| *n.* The fractional part of a logarithm to the base ten. For example, if 2.749 is a logarithm, .749 is the mantissa.

man•tle |măn′tl| *n.* **1.** A loose, sleeveless cloak worn over outer garments. **2.** Anything that covers or conceals, likened to a cloak: *a soft mantle of snow; a mantle of official secrecy.* **3.** The layer of the earth between the crust and the core. **4.** A **Welsbach burner. 5.** The layer of soft tissue that covers the body of a clam, oyster, or other mollusk and secretes the material that forms the shell. **6.** A form of the word **mantel.** —*v.* **man•tled, man•tling.** To cover with or as if with a cloak: *Night mantled the earth.*

man•tle•piece |măn′tl pēs′| *n.* A form of the word **mantelpiece.**

man•u•al |măn′yo͞o əl| *adj.* **1.** Of the hands: *manual dexterity.* **2.** Used by or operated with the hands: *a manual keyboard; manual controls.* **3.** Requiring physical rather than mental effort: *manual labor.* —*n.* A small book of instructions; a guidebook; handbook: *a carpentry manual.* —**man′u•al•ly** *adv.*

manual alphabet. An alphabet of hand signs used by deaf-mutes. [SEE PICTURE]

man•u•fac•ture |măn′yə făk′chər| *v.* **man•u•fac•tured, man•u•fac•tur•ing. 1.** To make or process (a product), especially with the use of industrial machines: *a company that manufactures cars.* **2.** To make up; concoct; fabricate: *Your Honor, the prosecution has manufactured this evidence against my client.* —*n.* The act or process of manufacturing. —**man′u•fac′tur•er** *n.*

ma•nure |mə no͝or′| *or* |-nyo͝or′| *n.* Animal dung, especially the dung of cattle, collected for use as fertilizer. —*v.* **ma•nured, ma•nur•ing.** To apply manure to: *In the springtime the farmer manures and plows his fields and sows seeds.*

man•u•script |măn′yə skrĭpt′| *n.* **1.** A handwritten or typewritten book, paper, article, etc., as distinguished from a printed copy: *submit a manuscript to a publisher.* **2.** Handwriting as opposed to printing.

Manx |măngks| *n.* **1.** A native or inhabitant of the Isle of Man. **2.** The extinct Celtic language of the Isle of Man. —*adj.* Of the Isle of Man, its inhabitants, or their language.

Manx cat. A cat of a domestic breed having short hair and a tail so short as to be invisible. [SEE PICTURE]

man•y |mĕn′ē| *adj.* **more** |môr| *or* |mōr|, **most** |mōst|. **1.** Numerous; a large number of: *many rules.* **2.** Being one of a large number. Used especially before *a* or *an: many a man.* —*n. (used with a plural verb).* **1.** A large number of persons or things: *Many of us were at the party.* Also used as a pronoun: *Many were invited, but only a few came.* **2. the many.** The majority of the people: *Democracy is the rule of the many.*

Mao•ism |mou′ĭz′əm| *n.* The interpretation of Marxism-Leninism adhered to by Chinese Communists and their international followers.

Mao•ri |mou′rē| *n., pl.* **Mao•ri** or **Mao•ris. 1.** A member of the native population of New Zealand. **2.** The language of this people. —**Mao′ri** *adj.*

Mao Ze•dong |mou′ dzŭ′do͝ong′|. also **Mao Tse-tung** |tsĭ to͝ong′|. 1893–1976. Chinese Communist leader.

map |măp| *n.* **1. a.** A drawing or chart of all or part of the earth's surface, showing countries, cities, oceans, rivers, mountains, etc. **b.** Such a drawing giving highly specialized information: *a weather map.* **2.** A drawing or chart of the moon, a planet, etc. **3.** A chart of space, showing the relative position of stars, planets, etc. **4.** Any maplike representation: *The burglars had a detailed map of the building and its alarm system.* —*v.* **mapped, map•ping. 1.** To survey in detail for the purpose of making a map: *Scientists are using sonar to map the ocean floor.* **2.** To represent on a map: *a method of projection to map large areas.* **3.** To plan in detail: *a full day's program mapped out in advance; map the strategy for a military campaign.* **4.** To establish a mapping between a set and another set: *map the real numbers onto the points of a line.*

ma•ple |mā′pəl| *n.* **1.** Any of several trees having broad leaves with pointed lobes and paired seeds with narrow, winglike extensions. One North American kind, the **sugar maple,** has sap

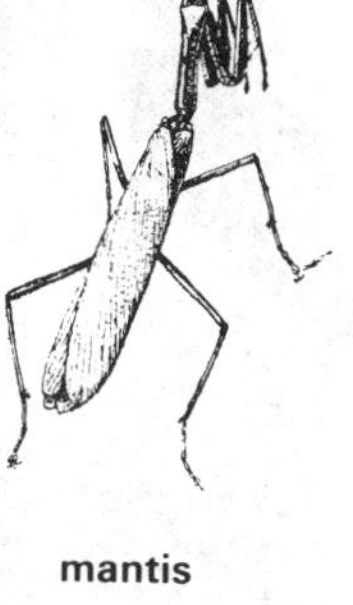

mantis

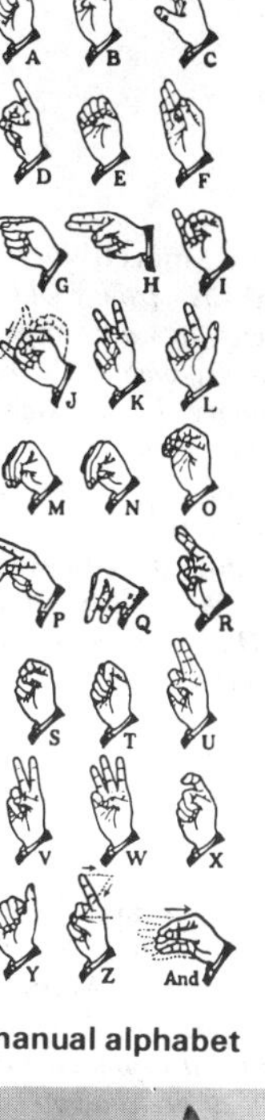

manual alphabet

Manx cat

marabou

march[1-2]

March[1] *is from Old French* marcher, *"to walk, to pace out"; it originally meant "to mark out a boundary by walking around it." Before maps were common, a traditional way of making sure that property lines were known was to have witnesses walk around them once a year.* **March[2]** *is from Old French* marche, *"a boundary, a frontier." See note at* **mark**.

mare[1-2]

Mare[1] *was* mēre, *"female horse," in Old English.* **Mare[2]** *is from Latin* mare, *"sea"; early astronomers liked to imagine that these dark lunar areas might be water.*

ă pat/ā pay/â care/ä father/ĕ pet/ ē be/ĭ pit/ī pie/î fierce/ŏ pot/ ō go/ô paw, for/oi oil/ŏŏ book/ ōō boot/ou out/ŭ cut/û fur/ *th* the/th thin/hw which/zh vision/ ə ago, item, pencil, atom, circus

that is boiled to produce **maple syrup** and **maple sugar**, both of which are used for sweetening and flavoring. **2.** The wood of a maple, often used for furniture. —***modifier:*** *a maple chair.*

map•ping |**măp′**ĭng| *n.* A mathematical rule that establishes a correspondence between each member of a set and a single member of a second set.

Ma•pu•to |mə **pōō′**tō|. The capital of Mozambique. Population, 755,000.

Mar. March.

mar |măr| *v.* **marred, mar•ring. 1.** To deface or make a dent in; damage: *mar the surface of a lacquered table.* **2.** To spoil; ruin: *Rain marred their visit to the beach.*

mar•a•bou |**măr′**ə bōō′| *n.* **1.** A large African stork having fluffy down used to trim clothing. **2.** The down of this bird. [SEE PICTURE]

ma•ra•ca |mə rä′kə| *or* |**-răk′**ə| *n.* A musical percussion instrument consisting of a hollow, gourdlike rattle containing pebbles or dried beans. Maracas are often played in pairs.

mar•a•schi•no |**măr′**ə **skē′**nō| *or* |**-shē′**-| *n.* A liqueur made from the fermented juice and crushed pits of a European cherry.

maraschino cherry. A preserved cherry flavored with maraschino.

mar•a•thon |**măr′**ə thŏn′| *n.* **1.** A cross-country foot race of 26 miles, 385 yards. It is an event in the Olympic games. **2.** Any long-distance race: *a swimming marathon.* **3.** A contest of endurance: *a dance marathon.*

ma•raud•ing |mə **rô′**dĭng| *adj.* Roving in search of or raiding to seize booty: *marauding grizzlies in Yellowstone Park.*

mar•ble |**mär′**bəl| *n.* **1.** Any of several crystalline rocks composed mainly of calcium carbonate, often having irregularly colored marks due to impurities. It is of metamorphic origin and is used in buildings and in making ornaments. **2. a.** A little ball made of a hard substance such as glass. **b. marbles** *(used with a singular verb).* A children's game played with such balls. Usually the object of the game is to knock marbles out of a circle marked on the ground with a marble shot by a flick of the thumb. —***modifier:*** *a marble statue; a marble floor; a marbles tournament.* —*adj.* **1.** Having irregularly colored markings like marble: *marble ice cream.* **2.** White and smooth: *her marble brow.*

march[1] |märch| *v.* **1.** To walk with measured steps at a steady rate, as in a parade: *And then with music and with song/How cheerfully we'll march along.* **2.** To cause to move or move in or as if in a military formation: *march the students into chapel. Napoleon's armies marched east.* **3.** To walk in a purposeful or determined manner; stride: *He marched right up to the police officer and asked the name of the street.* **4.** To advance with a steady movement: *Time marches on.* —*n.* **1.** The steady forward movement of a body of troops: *Sherman's march through Georgia to the sea.* **2.** A journey by foot: *a march of ten miles.* **3.** The distance covered by marching: *Their objective was only two days' march away.* **4.** Forward movement; progression: *the dramatic march of modern science.* **5.** A protest demonstration in the form of a parade: *a peace march.* **6.** Music written to accompany or as if to accompany marching. [SEE NOTE]

Idioms. **on the march.** Moving ahead; advancing. **steal a march on.** To get ahead of, especially by quiet efforts or a discreet move.

march[2] |märch| *n.* A border region: *guarded the marches of the Empire from barbarian tribes.* [SEE NOTE]

March |märch| *n.* The third month of the year, after February and before April. It has 31 days. —***modifier:*** *March winds.*

mar•chion•ess |**mär′**shə nĭs| *or* |**mär′**shə **nĕs′**| *n.* **1.** The wife of a marquis. **2.** A woman holding a rank equal to that of a marquis in her own right.

Mar•co•ni |mär **kō′**nē|, **Guglielmo.** 1874–1937. Italian inventor; developed the wireless telegraph.

Mar•di gras |**mär′**dē grä′| *or* |**grä′**|. A day of merrymaking celebrated on the last day before Lent, the Tuesday before Ash Wednesday.

mare[1] |mâr| *n.* A female horse, zebra, or other related animal. [SEE NOTE]

ma•re[2] |**mä′**rā| *n., pl.* **ma•ri•a** |**mä′**rē ə|. Any of the large regions of the moon's surface that appear darker than the surrounding regions. [SEE NOTE]

mar•ga•rine |**mär′**jər ĭn| *or* |-jə **rēn′**| *n.* A fatty mixture composed of vegetable oils that have been treated with hydrogen to make them solid, vitamins, coloring, flavoring, and other ingredients, used as a substitute for butter.

mar•gin |**mär′**jĭn| *n.* **1.** An edge; border; verge: *the margin of a pond.* **2.** The blank space bordering the written or printed area on a page. **3.** An extra amount, as of time, money, etc., allowed beyond what is needed. **4.** A quantity or degree of advantage: *a 500-vote margin.*

mar•gin•al |**mär′**jə nəl| *adj.* **1.** Written or printed in the margin of a book: *a marginal note.* **2.** Situated on the border or edge: *states marginal to Canada.* **3.** Producing goods at a rate that barely covers production costs; making a very small profit: *All the firms in the area became marginal operations.* —**mar′gin•al•ly** *adv.*

mar•gi•na•li•a |mär′jə **nā′**lē ə| *or* |**-nāl′**yə| *pl.n.* Notes in a book margin.

mar•gue•rite |mär′gə **rēt′**| *or* |-gyə-| *n.* A daisy or a similar plant with yellow and white flowers.

ma•ri•a |**mä′**rē ə| *n.* Plural of **mare** (region of the moon).

Ma•rie An•toi•nette |mə **rē′** ăn′twə **nĕt′**|. 1755–1793. Queen of France; wife (1770) of Louis XVI; guillotined.

mar•i•gold |**măr′**ĭ gōld′| *or* |**mâr′**-| *n.* **1.** A garden plant with showy orange, yellow, or reddish flowers. **2.** See **marsh marigold.**

mar•i•jua•na, also **mar•i•hua•na** |măr′ə **wä′** nə| *or* |**-hwä′**-| *n.* **1.** The hemp plant. **2.** The dried leaves or flowers of the hemp plant, which contain an intoxicating drug.

ma•rim•ba |mə **rĭm′**bə| *n.* A large xylophone having a resonant tube beneath each of the tuned wooden bars.

ma•ri•na |mə **rē′**nə| *n.* A boat basin that has docks, moorings, supplies, and repair facilities for sailboats and motorboats.

mar•i•nade |**măr′**ə **nād′**| *n.* A liquid, such as vinegar or wine, with various spices, used for soaking meat or fish before cooking.

mar•i•nate |măr′ə nāt′| *v.* **mar•i•nat•ed, mar•i•nat•ing.** To soak (meat or fish) in a marinade.

ma•rine |mə rēn′| *adj.* **1.** Of the sea: *marine biology.* **2.** Native to the sea: *marine life.* **3.** Of shipping or navigation; maritime: *marine engineering; marine insurance.* —*n.* **1.** A soldier serving on a ship or at a naval base. **2. Marine.** A member of the U.S. Marine Corps.

Marine Corps. A branch of the U.S. armed forces whose troops are specially trained for amphibious landings and for combat on both land and water.

mar•i•ner |măr′ə nər| *n.* A sailor.

mar•i•o•nette |măr′ē ə nět′| *n.* A small wooden figure resembling a person and fitted with strings that are moved from above. Marionettes are used to perform shows on a small stage. [SEE PICTURE]

mar•i•tal |măr′ĭ təl| *adj.* Of or relating to marriage: *marital vows; marital problems.*

mar•i•time |măr′ĭ tīm′| *adj.* **1.** Located on or near the sea: *a maritime province.* **2.** Of shipping or navigation: *maritime law.*

Maritime Provinces. Three provinces on the Atlantic coast of Canada, Nova Scotia, New Brunswick, and Prince Edward Island.

mar•jo•ram |mär′jər əm| *n.* A plant with spicy, pleasant-smelling leaves used as flavoring.

mark[1] |märk| *n.* **1.** A scratch, dent, stain, etc., on a surface: *The cat left claw marks on my arm.* **2. a.** A line, dot, or other simple marking made by hand: *made a mark beside the name of each player to be fined.* **b.** A standard written or printed symbol: *a punctuation mark; an accent mark.* **c.** A cross or other sign made in place of a signature by someone who is unable to write. **3.** An object used to indicate position; a marker: *a bookmark.* **4.** An indication of some quality or condition: *Taking responsibility for your own personal finances is a mark of maturity.* **5.** A lasting impression: *The Crusades left their mark on Western civilization.* **6.** Something that is aimed at; a target: *The arrow found its mark.* **7.** A label, seal, etc., placed on an article: *our company's mark of quality.* **8.** A recognized standard of quality: *His work is not up to the mark.* **9.** A grade; rating: *poor marks in arithmetic.* **10.** A figure registering a point or level that has been or will be reached: *He had passed the 200-pound mark during his early thirties.* **11.** A starting line or position, as in a track event: *"On your mark! Get set! Go!"* —*v.* **1.** To make a mark on: *His greasy fingers marked the cover of the book.* **2.** To show by a mark: *Mark your answer in either the true or false box.* **3.** To give evidence of; reveal: *signs in nature that sadly mark the end of summer.* **4.** To be a feature of; distinguish; characterize: *the palm trees that mark the hotel.* **5.** To single out: *The company marked her for promotion.* **6.** To heed; note: *Mark my words, you're in for trouble.* **7.** To grade: *The teacher sat up all night marking papers. Miss Brooks marks strictly.* —***phrasal verbs.* mark down.** **1.** To make a note of. **2.** To mark with a lower sales price. **mark off.** To mark the dimensions or limits of. **mark up.** **1.** To cover with markings. **2.** To mark with a higher sales price. [SEE NOTE]

***Idioms.* beside** (or **wide of**) **the mark.** Not to the point; irrelevant. **make (one's) mark.** To achieve success; become famous. **mark time.** To make no progress for a period of time. **of mark.** Of importance: *a man of mark.*

mark[2] |märk| *n.* The basic unit of money of Germany. See **Deutsche mark** and **ostmark.** [SEE NOTE]

Mark |märk| *n.* The second Gospel of the New Testament.

Mark, Saint. A companion of the Apostle Peter, traditionally regarded as the author of the second Gospel.

marked |märkt| *adj.* **1.** Having a mark or marks: *Pedestrians should use the marked crosswalk.* **2.** Noticeable; distinct; clear: *a marked difference in price.* **3.** Singled out, as for a dire fate: *He's a marked man.* —**mark′ed•ly** |mär′kĭd lē| *adv.*

mark•er |mär′kər| *n.* **1.** Something used to draw marks on a surface: *The children bought poster paper and markers to make signs for their bazaar.* **2.** Something that distinguishes or reveals something else, as a bookmark, milestone, etc.

mar•ket |mär′kĭt| *n.* **1. a.** A public gathering for buying and selling goods: *The farmer took his cheese to market.* **b.** The place for such a gathering: *He set up a stall in the market.* **2.** A store that sells a particular type of merchandise: *a fish market.* **3.** A **stock market.** **4.** The process of buying and selling a particular product: *the international coffee market.* **5. a.** A region or country where goods may be sold: *a foreign market for American consumer goods.* **b.** A particular type or group of buyers: *advertising aimed at the college market.* **6.** A desire to buy; demand: *Is there a market for our product?* —**modifier:** *a market town; the market price.* —*v.* **1.** To sell or offer for sale: *The co-op marketed its grain through a central sales agency.* **2.** To buy food and household supplies: *Mother markets on Friday.* —**mar′ket•er** *n.*

***Idioms.* be in the market for.** To desire to buy. **play the market.** To speculate on the stock market. **put on the market.** To offer for sale.

mar•ket•ing |mär′kĭ tĭng| *n.* The branch of the science of business administration dealing with advertising, sales techniques, etc.

mar•ket•place |mär′kĭt plās′| *n.* Also **market place.** **1.** A public square or other place in which a market is set up. **2. a.** The general process of buying and selling, regarded as taking place in a market. **b.** Any general process of exchange: *the marketplace of ideas.*

mark•ing |mär′kĭng| *n.* **1.** A mark or marks: *The Indians had left tree markings along the trail. The planet Mars has craters, polar caps, and strange markings.* **2.** The special way in which the fur, plumage, etc., of an animal is colored: *a bird with beautiful markings.*

mark•ka |mär′kä′| *n., pl.* **mark•kaa** |mär′kä′|. The basic unit of money of Finland.

marks•man |märks′mən| *n., pl.* **-men** |-mən|. A person skilled at shooting a gun or other weapon. —**marks′man•ship′** *n.*

mark•up |märk′ŭp′| *n.* **1.** A raise in the price of an article. **2.** The amount added to the cost of an item to figure its selling price.

marl |märl| *n.* A loose soil mixture containing clay, sand, shells, etc., sometimes used as fertilizer.

marionette
Jackson, the famous
Bil Baird marionette

mark[1-2]

The prehistoric Germanic word mark- *basically meant "boundary, property line, border"; it came also to mean "something that identifies a boundary, a landmark"; later it also meant "a mark or sign in general, especially an official mark on a bar of metal," and hence finally "a unit of weight or currency."* Mark- *appears in the following words: (1) Old English* mearc, *which had all of the meanings listed above, becoming Modern English* **mark**[1]; *(2) German* mark, *"unit of currency," borrowed into English as* **mark**[2]; *(3) Old French* marche, *"boundary, frontier," and* marcher, *"to pace out a boundary"; see note at* **march.**

marmoset

mar·lin |mär′lĭn| *n.* A large ocean fish resembling the swordfish, often caught for sport. ¶*These sound alike* **marlin, marline.**

mar·line |mär′lĭn| *n.* A light rope made of two loosely twisted strands, used on ships. ¶*These sound alike* **marline, marlin.**

mar·ma·lade |mär′mə lād′| *n.* A preserve made from the pulp and rind of fruits.

Mar·ma·ra, Sea of |mär′mər ə|. A sea between European and Asiatic Turkey.

mar·mo·set |mär′mə sĕt′| *or* |-zĕt′| *n.* A small tropical American monkey with thick, soft fur and a long tail. [SEE PICTURE]

mar·mot |mär′mət| *n.* A short-legged burrowing animal, such as the woodchuck or any of several related animals of western North America.

ma·roon¹ |mə ro͞on′| *v.* To abandon or isolate (someone), as on a deserted island, with little hope of rescue or escape. [SEE NOTE]

ma·roon² |mə ro͞on′| *n.* A dark purplish red. —*adj.* Dark purplish red. [SEE NOTE]

mar·quee |mär kē′| *n.* A structure that projects over the entrance to a building, such as a theater, and is usually equipped with a signboard.

mar·quess |mär′kwĭs| *n.* Chiefly British form of the word **marquis.**

mar·quis. *n., pl.* **mar·quis** or **mar·quis·es. 1.** |mär′kwĭs|. A member of the British peerage holding a title and rank below that of a duke and above that of an earl. **2.** |mär kē′|. A nobleman of similar rank in certain other countries.

mar·quise |mär kēz′| *n.* A marchioness.

mar·riage |măr′ĭj| *n.* **1.** The state of being husband and wife. **2. a.** The act of marrying. **b.** The ceremony involved; a wedding. **3.** Any close union: *a marriage of minds.* —**modifier:** *marriage vows.*

mar·riage·a·ble |măr′ĭ jə bəl| *adj.* Suitable for marriage.

mar·ried |măr′ēd| *adj.* **1.** Having a husband or wife. **2.** Joined by marriage: *a married couple.* **3.** Resulting from marriage: *married life; her married name.* —*n.* Often **marrieds.** A married person: *young marrieds.*

mar·row |măr′ō| *n.* **1.** The soft material that fills the cavities inside bones, consisting of fat cells and maturing blood cells together with connective tissue and blood vessels. **2.** The nerve tissue that fills the interior of the bones of the spine; the spinal cord. **3.** The essential part; pith: *She was a country girl to the very marrow.*

mar·ry¹ |măr′ē| *v.* **mar·ried, mar·ry·ing, mar·ries. 1.** To take (someone) as a husband or wife; enter into marriage: *He married my sister. She has no plans to marry.* **2.** To unite (a couple) as husband and wife: *The rabbi married them.* **3.** To give in marriage: *married off his daughters.* [SEE NOTE]

mar·ry² |măr′ē| *interj. Archaic.* A word used to express surprise or emphasis. [SEE NOTE]

Mars¹ |märz|. The Roman god of war.

Mars² |märz| *n.* The fourth planet of the solar system in order of increasing distance from the sun. Its diameter is about 4,200 miles, its average distance from the sun is about 142 million miles, and it takes about 687 days to complete an orbit of the sun.

Mar·seille |mär sā′|. Also **Mar·seilles** |mär sā′| *or* |-sālz′|. The oldest city in France and its principal seaport, located on the Mediterranean coast. Population, 900,000.

marsh |märsh| *n.* An area of low-lying, wet land; a swamp or bog.

mar·shal |mär′shəl| *n.* **1.** In some countries, a military officer of the highest rank. **2.** In the United States: **a.** A Federal or city officer who carries out court orders. **b.** The head of a police or fire department. **3.** A person in charge of a ceremony or parade. —*v.* **mar·shaled** or **mar·shalled, mar·shal·ing** or **mar·shal·ling. 1.** To place in methodical order; organize: *The research team marshaled facts for the great debate.* **2.** To enlist and organize for a specified purpose: *We marshaled our best brains to put a man on the moon.* ¶*These sound alike* **marshal, martial.**

Mar·shall |mär′shəl|, **John.** 1755–1835. American jurist; Chief Justice of the United States (1801–35).

marsh gas. Impure methane that occurs naturally in swamps.

marsh·land |märsh′lănd′| *n.* A marshy area.

marsh·mal·low |märsh′mĕl′ō| *or* |-măl′ō| *n.* A soft white candy with a spongy texture.

marsh marigold. A North American plant that grows in wet places and has bright-yellow flowers resembling those of the buttercup.

marsh·y |mär′shē| *adj.* **marsh·i·er, marsh·i·est.** Wet and swampy like a marsh.

mar·su·pi·al |mär so͞o′pē əl| *n.* Any of a group of animals, such as a kangaroo, of which the females have a pocketlike pouch in which the newborn young are nursed and carried.

mart |märt| *n.* A market or trading center.

mar·ten |mär′tn| *n.* **1.** An animal related to the weasel and the mink, having thick, soft brown fur. **2.** The fur of such an animal. ¶*These sound alike* **marten, martin.**

mar·tial |mär′shəl| *adj.* Of war; warlike: *the martial character of his ancestors; martial music.* ¶*These sound alike* **martial, marshal.**

martial law. Temporary military rule of a civilian population imposed in an emergency, as in time of war.

Mar·tian |mär′shən| *adj.* Of the planet Mars. —*n.* A being that supposedly lives on the planet Mars.

mar·tin |mär′tn| *n.* A bird related to the swallows, as the **purple martin** of North America, which has glossy blue-black feathers and a forked tail. ¶*These sound alike* **martin, marten.**

mar·ti·net |mär′tn ĕt′| *n.* A person who demands strict obedience to rules, especially in the military.

mar·ti·ni |mär tē′nē| *n.* A cocktail of gin and dry vermouth.

mar·tyr |mär′tər| *n.* **1.** A person who chooses to suffer death or torture rather than give up religious principles. **2.** A person who sacrifices something important to him to further a belief, cause, or principle. **3.** A person who endures great suffering. —*v.* To make a martyr of.

mar·tyr·dom |mär′tər dəm| *n.* The condition of being a martyr.

mar·vel |mär′vəl| *n.* Someone or something that causes surprise, astonishment, or wonder: *The space capsules are a marvel of technology.* —*v.* **mar·veled** or **mar·velled, mar·vel·ing** or **mar·vel·ling.** To be filled with surprise, astonishment, or

maroon¹⁻²

In the Caribbean islands in the seventeenth century, many slaves escaped and formed free communities living in the forests and hills; ex-slaves were called maroons *(from Spanish* cimarron, *"wild"). From this came the verb* **maroon¹**, *at first meaning "to escape into the wilds" and later used by the buccaneers to mean "to put someone into the wilds (as a punishment)." (To this day in Jamaica the descendants of those escaped slaves are called the* Maroons.*)* **Maroon²** *is from French* marron, *"chestnut," hence the color of chestnut blossom.*

marry¹⁻²

Marry¹ *is from Old French* marier, *from Latin* maritus, *"husband."* **Marry²** *is a variant of* Mary! *(an oath in the name of the Virgin Mary).*

ă pat/ā pay/â care/ä father/ĕ pet/ ē be/ĭ pit/ī pie/î fierce/ŏ pot/ ō go/ô paw, for/oi oil/o͝o book/ o͞o boot/ou out/ŭ cut/û fur/ *th* the/th thin/hw which/zh vision/ ə ago, item, pencil, atom, circus

wonder: *The space capsules are a marvel of technology.* —*v.* **mar•veled** or **mar•velled, mar•vel•ing** or **mar•vel•ling.** To be filled with surprise, astonishment, or wonder: *marvel at seeing the snowy peaks of the Rocky Mountains.*

mar•vel•ous, also **mar•vel•lous** |mär'və ləs| *adj.* Causing wonder; notably superior: *the marvelous gorge cut out by the Colorado River.* —**mar'vel•ous•ly** *adv.* —**mar'vel•ous•ness** *n.*

Marx |märks|, **Karl.** 1818–1883. German philosopher and political economist; the founder of Communism.

Marx•ism |märk'sĭz'əm| *n.* The system of thought developed by Karl Marx and others that gives class struggle the primary role in leading society from capitalism to communism. —**Marx'ist** *n.*

Marx•ism-Len•in•ism |märk'sĭz'əm lĕn'ə nĭz'əm| *n.* The official doctrine of the world Communist movement, developed as an expansion of Marxism to include Lenin's concept of imperialism as the final form of capitalism.

Mar•y |mâr'ē|. The mother of Christ.

Mar•y•land |mâr'ə lənd| *or* |mĕr'-|. A Middle Atlantic state of the United States. Population, 4,216,446. Capital, Annapolis.

Mary Mag•da•lene |măg'də lēn'| *or* |-lən| *or* |măg'də lē'nē|. In the New Testament, a woman who became a disciple of Christ after he cured her of evil spirits. She is traditionally identified with the repentant sinful woman whom Christ forgave.

mar•zi•pan |mär'zə păn'| *or* |märt'sə-| *n.* A confection flavored with ground almonds and often molded into decorative shapes.

masc. masculine.

mas•car•a |mă skăr'ə| *n.* A cosmetic used to darken the eyelashes or eyebrows.

mas•cot |măs'kŏt'| *or* |-kət| *n.* Someone or something believed to bring good luck: *The team mascot is a donkey.*

mas•cu•line |măs'kyə lĭn| *adj.* **1.** Of boys or men: *masculine qualities.* **2.** Considered mannish: *a masculine hairdo.* **3.** In grammar, belonging to or indicating the gender of nouns classified as male; for example, the word *actor* is a masculine noun.

mas•cu•lin•i•ty |măs'kyə lĭn'ĭ tē| *n.* The quality or condition of being masculine.

ma•ser |mā'zər| *n.* Any of several devices that are similar in principle to the laser but operate with microwaves rather than with light.

Mas•e•ru |măz'ə ro͞o'|. The capital of Lesotho. Population, 20,000.

mash |măsh| *n.* **1.** A mixture of crushed grain that ferments and is used to distill alcohol or spirits. **2.** Any soft, pulpy mixture, especially one meant to be fed to livestock. —*v.* **1.** To convert (grain) into mash. **2.** To convert into a soft, pulpy mixture: *mash potatoes.* **3.** To crush; smash. —**mashed'** *adj.*: *mashed potatoes.*

mask |măsk| *or* |mäsk| *n.* **1. a.** A covering, often having openings for the eyes, worn over part or all of the face as a disguise: *a Halloween mask.* **b.** A facial covering worn for ritual. **c.** A representation of a face, especially in a particular pose: *a tragic mask.* **2.** A protective covering for the face: *gas mask; oxygen mask.* **3.** A face that resembles a mask in certain characteristics as immobility, lack of expression, etc.: *Hopalong's face was a gray mask in the moonlight.* **4.** Anything that disguises or conceals. —*v.* **1.** To cover with or as if with a mask: *He masked his face. The grating masks the large opening to the tunnel.* **2.** To put a mask on for disguise: *He masked himself at midnight.* —**masked'** *adj.*: *a masked bandit.* ¶*These sound alike* **mask, masque.** [SEE PICTURES]

masking tape. A tape with adhesive on one side used for securing objects, covering areas not to be painted, decorating, etc.

mas•o•chism |măs'ə kĭz'əm| *or* |măz'-| *n.* An emotional disorder in which a person gets excitement and satisfaction by being abused, mistreated, or subjected to pain. —**mas'o•chist** *n.*

ma•son |mā'sən| *n.* **1.** A person who builds or works with stone or brick. **2. Mason.** A Freemason.

Ma•son-Dix•on line |mā'sən dĭk'sən|. The boundary between Pennsylvania and Maryland, generally thought of as dividing the North from the South.

Ma•son•ic |mə sŏn'ĭk| *adj.* Of Freemasons or Freemasonry.

Ma•son jar |mā'sən|. A wide-mouthed glass jar used especially for home canning and preserving.

ma•son•ry |mā'sən rē| *n.* **1.** The trade or work of a mason. **2.** Stonework or brickwork. **3. Masonry.** Freemasonry. —***modifier:*** *a masonry wall.*

masque |măsk| *or* |mäsk| *n.* **1.** A dramatic presentation popular in Europe in the 16th and 17th centuries as a court entertainment. **2.** A masquerade party; a masked ball. ¶*These sound alike* **masque, mask.**

mas•quer•ade |măs'kə rād'| *n.* **1. a.** A dance or party at which masks and fancy costumes are worn. **b.** The costume worn. **2.** Any disguise or false pretense. —***modifier:*** *a masquerade costume.* —*v.* **mas•quer•ad•ed, mas•quer•ad•ing. 1.** To dress up in a special costume or disguise: *The queen masqueraded as a shepherdess.* **2.** To have a deceptive appearance: *It is a sermon masquerading as a novel.*

mass |măs| *n.* **1.** A unified body of matter with no specific shape: *a mass of clay.* **2.** Any large amount or number that is not specified: *I got masses of presents for my birthday.* **3.** The major part of something: *the great mass of our national wealth.* **4.** The physical bulk of a solid body: *The huge mass of the central towers slowly appeared on the horizon.* **5.** A measure of the amount of matter contained in a physical body, equivalent to the quotient of a force acting on the body divided by the acceleration that the body undergoes as a result of that force. **6. the masses.** The body of common people. —*v.* To gather into or assemble in a mass: *The army massed its troops at the frontier. The people massed downtown to watch the parade.* —*adj.* **1.** Of, involving, or attended by large numbers of people: *a mass meeting.* **2.** Done on a large scale: *mass production.*

Mass, also **mass** |măs| *n.* **1. a.** In Roman Catholic and certain Protestant churches, the celebration of the Eucharist. **b.** The service including this celebration. **2.** A musical setting for the words of certain parts of the Mass.

Mass. Massachusetts.

Mas•sa•chu•set |măs'ə cho͞o'sĭt| *or* |-zĭt| *n., pl.* **Mas•sa•chu•set** or **Mas•sa•chu•sets. 1.** A North American Indian tribe of the Massachusetts

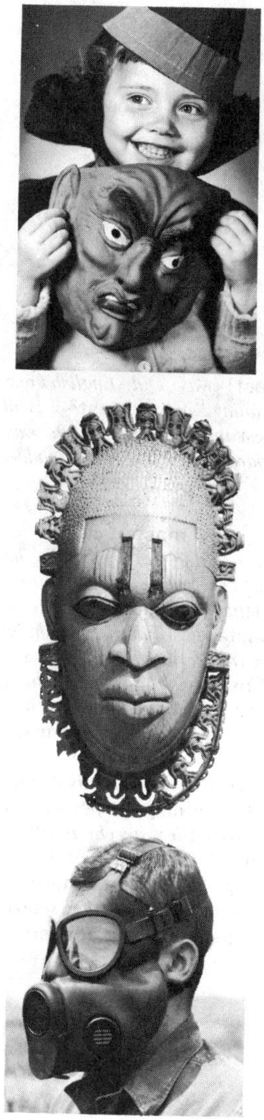

mask
Halloween mask
Nigerian ivory mask
Gas mask

coastal area. **2.** A member of this tribe. **3.** The Algonquian language of this tribe.

Mas•sa•chu•sett |măs'ə **cho͞o**'sĭt| *or* |-zĭt| *n., pl.* **Mas•sa•chu•sett** or **Mas•sa•chu•setts.** A form of the word **Massachuset.**

Mas•sa•chu•setts |măs'ə **cho͞o**'sĭts| *or* |-zĭts|. A New England state of the United States. Population, 5,725,000. Capital, Boston.

mas•sa•cre |**măs**'ə kər| *n.* **1.** A savage slaughter of a considerable number of people or animals. **2.** *Informal.* A severe defeat, as in sports. —*v.* **mas•sa•cred, mas•sa•cring. 1.** To slaughter a number of people or animals savagely. **2.** *Informal.* To defeat severely in a sport: *The Mets massacred their opponents.*

mas•sage |mə **säzh**'| *or* |-**säj**'| *n.* A body rub given to improve circulation and relax muscles. —*v.* **mas•saged, mas•sag•ing.** To give a massage to.

mass-en•er•gy |**măs'ĕn**'ər jē| *n.* Mass and energy considered as equivalent and interchangeable, as shown in the equation $E = mc^2$, where E is energy, m mass, and c the speed of light.

mas•seur |mă **sûr**'| *or* |mə-| *n.* A man who gives massages professionally.

mas•seuse |mă **so͞os**'| *or* |-**so͞oz**'| *or* |mə-| *n.* A woman who gives massages professionally.

mas•sive |**măs**'ĭv| *adj.* **1.** Large; heavy and solid; bulky: *a massive elephant.* **2. a.** Unusually large or impressive: *a massive head.* **b.** Larger than normal in amount: *a massive dose of medicine.* **3.** Large in scope, intensity, degree, scale, etc.: *a massive movement toward the West.* —**mas'sive•ly** *adv.* —**mas'sive•ness** *n.*

mass media. The various media of public communication, such as television, radio, films, newspapers, etc.

mass number. The total of the neutrons and protons present in an atomic nucleus.

mass-pro•duce |**măs**'prə **do͞os**'| *or* |-**dyo͞os**'| *v.* **-pro•duced, -pro•duc•ing.** To produce in large quantities: *mass-produce high-quality products.* —**mass'-pro•duced'** *adj.*: *mass-produced cars.*

mast[1] |măst| *or* |mäst| *n.* **1.** An upright pole that supports the sails, rigging, etc., of a ship or boat. **2.** Any upright pole. [SEE NOTE]

***Idiom.* before the mast.** Serving as a common sailor.

mast[2] |măst| *or* |mäst| *n.* The fallen nuts of forest trees, such as oaks or beeches, used especially to feed pigs. [SEE NOTE]

mas•ter |**măs**'tər| *or* |**mä**'stər| *n.* **1. a.** Someone who directs, rules, or controls others; a ruler: *Philip of Macedon became master of Greece.* **b.** Someone in control of something: *the master of the house. He thought of himself as master of the plantation.* **2.** The captain of a ship. **3.** The owner of a slave or animal. **4.** Someone who employs others, especially someone who takes on apprentices. **5.** A teacher; schoolmaster or tutor. **6.** Someone of great learning, skill, ability, etc.; an expert: *a master in design.* **7. a.** A person who has received a college or university degree after completing at least one year of graduate study. **b. Master.** The title of a person with this degree: *Master of Arts; Master of Science.* **8. Master.** A word used in speaking of or to a boy or youth not considered old enough to be addressed as Mister. **9.** An original, as of a record or document, from which copies are made. —*adj.* **1.** Ruling over others; dominant: *a master race.* **2.** Being the principal or chief one: *a master bedroom.* **3.** Being a master at something; fully skilled; expert: *a master composer; a master plumber.* **4.** Being the original from which copies are made: *a master recording.* —*v.* **1.** To become the master of; bring under control: *master one's emotions.* **2.** To become skilled in the use of: *Helen Keller mastered sign language and later learned to speak.* [SEE NOTE]

mas•ter-at-arms |**măs**'tər ət **ärmz**'| *or* |**mä**'stər-| *n., pl.* **mas•ters-at-arms.** A naval petty officer assigned to maintain law and order.

mas•ter•ful |**măs**'tər fəl| *or* |**mä**'stər-| *adj.* **1.** Like a master; domineering: *a masterful woman.* **2.** Expert; skillful: *a masterful rendition of the piano concerto.* —**mas'ter•ful•ly** *adv.* —**mas'ter•ful•ness** *n.*

mas•ter•ly |**măs**'tər lē| *or* |**mä**'stər-| *adj.* Knowledgeable and skillful like a master: *a masterly diplomatic stroke.*

mas•ter•mind |**măs**'tər mīnd'| *or* |**mä**'stər-| *n.* Someone who plans or directs something. —*v.* To plan or direct (something): *mastermind the team's defense.*

master of ceremonies. A person who introduces the various events and people on the program at a banquet dinner, an entertainment show, etc.

mas•ter•piece |**măs**'tər pēs'| *or* |**mä**'stər-| *n.* **1.** An outstanding work of art or craft. **2.** Something done with skill or brilliance: *His plan was a masterpiece of ingenuity.*

master sergeant. A noncommissioned officer of the next to the highest rating in the U.S. Army, Air Force, and Marine Corps.

mas•ter•y |**măs**'tə rē| *or* |**mä**'stə-| *n.* **1.** Complete control or domination: *striving to attain mastery over his emotions.* **2.** Possession of great skill, knowledge, or technique: *his great mastery of the mechanics of writing.*

mast•head |**măst**'hĕd'| *or* |**mäst**'-| *n.* **1.** The top of a ship's mast. **2.** The listing in a newspaper, magazine, or other publication of its owners and chief editors and information about its operation.

mas•ti•cate |**măs**'tĭ kāt'| *v.* **mas•ti•cat•ed, mas•ti•cat•ing.** To chew (food). —**mas'ti•ca'tion** *n.*

mas•tiff |**măs**'tĭf| *n.* A large dog with a short brownish coat and short, square jaws.

mas•to•don |**măs**'tə dŏn'| *n.* An extinct animal related to and resembling the elephant. Mastodons lived in North America until the end of the Ice Age.

mas•tur•bate |**măs**'tər bāt'| *v.* **mas•tur•bat•ed, mas•tur•bat•ing.** To perform an act of masturbation.

mas•tur•ba•tion |măs'tər **bā**'shən| *n.* The act of exciting the genitals, usually to orgasm, by means other than sexual intercourse.

mat[1] |măt| *n.* **1.** A flat piece of coarse material, often woven of straw, hemp, rushes, etc., used as a floor covering or as a pad or cushion. **2.** A kind of small rug, as one used to wipe the shoes on or to keep the bathroom floor from getting wet. **3.** A small piece of material put under a dish, vase, etc., to protect or decorate the surface of a table. **4.** A thick pad or firm mattress used

mast[1-2]

Mast[1] *was Old English* mæst, *meaning "pole."* **Mast[2]** *was also* mæst *in Old English but was a separate word, meaning "fodder."*

master, etc.

Latin magister, *"chief, head, master," was borrowed into Old English as* magister, *becoming* **master** *in Modern English.* **Mister** *(abbreviated* **Mr.***) is a variant of* **master. Mistress** *is the feminine form of* **mister.** *In Italian, Latin* magister *became* maestro, *which was borrowed into English (in artistic contexts) as* **maestro.** *In French,* magister *became* maître *(a circumflex accent is often the sign of an old* s *that has been dropped), whence* **maitre d'.** Magister *is also the source of* **magistrate** *and* **magisterial.**

ă pat/ā pay/â care/ä father/ĕ pet/ ē be/ĭ pit/ī pie/î fierce/ŏ pot/ ō go/ô paw, for/oi oil/o͝o book/ o͞o boot/ou out/ŭ cut/û fur/ *th* the/th thin/hw which/zh vision/ ə ago, item, pencil, atom, circus

on the floor for tumbling, wrestling, or acrobatics. **5.** A dense or tangled mass: *a mat of hair.* —*v.* **mat•ted, mat•ting. 1.** To tangle into a thick, compact mass: *Felt is made by matting fibers together. The cat's fur got wet and matted.* **2.** To cover with a mat or with matting: *They matted the floor of the hut.* —**mat'ted** *adj.: matted underbrush; a matted floor.* ¶*These sound alike* **mat, matte.** [SEE NOTE]

mat[2] |măt| *n.* **1.** A decorative border, as of cardboard, placed around a picture to serve as a frame or contrast between the picture and a frame. **2.** A dull finish; matte. —*v.* **mat•ted, mat•ting.** To put a mat around (a picture). ¶*These sound alike* **mat, matte.** [SEE NOTE]

mat•a•dor |măt'ə dôr'| *n.* A person who fights and kills the bull in a bullfight.

match[1] |măch| *n.* **1. a.** Someone or something exactly like another: *Find the match for this color.* **b.** Someone or something that is similar to or harmonizes well with another: *This tie is a good match for your striped shirt.* **2.** Something or someone with equal or near equal capabilities: *The mink was no match for the otter.* **3.** A sports contest: *a shooting match; a wrestling match.* **4. a.** A marriage. **b.** Someone viewed as a marriage prospect: *All girls consider him a good match.* —*v.* **1. a.** To be alike: *The two colors match exactly.* **b.** To be similar to in certain ways: *No one can match his hunting skill.* **2. a.** To go well or harmonize with; be suitable for: *His shirt matches his slacks.* **b.** To fit together: *Match the edges of the seam and baste.* **3. a.** To correspond to: *The words below match the items in the picture.* **b.** To put two like or similar things together; pair: *Match up your socks.* **4. a.** To provide with an opponent or competitor: *He matched one group against the other in a spelling bee.* **b.** To place in competition; pit: *They matched wits.* [SEE NOTE]

match[2] |măch| *n.* A strip of wood, cardboard, or wax coated at one end with a substance that catches fire when rubbed on a rough surface or on a specially treated surface. [SEE NOTE]

match•book |**măch'**bo͝ok'| *n.* A small cardboard folder containing safety matches.

match•box |**măch'**bŏks'| *n.* A box for matches.

match•less |**măch'**lĭs| *adj.* Having no match or equal: *her matchless intelligence.*

match•lock |**măch'**lŏk'| *n.* A kind of musket in which the powder charge was ignited by a cord or wick.

match•mak•er |**măch'**mā'kər| *n.* **1.** Someone who arranges or habitually tries to arrange marriages. **2.** Someone who arranges athletic competitions. —**match'mak'ing** *adj.* & *n.*

mate[1] |māt| *n.* **1.** One of a matched pair: *Find the mate to this sock.* **2.** A spouse; a husband or wife. **3.** The male or female of a pair of animals or birds. **4.** A close associate; partner: *He needs more help from his mates to finish the job.* **5. a.** An officer on a merchant ship ranking below the captain. **b.** A naval officer ranking below and assisting a warrant officer. —*v.* **mat•ed, mat•ing. 1.** To join closely; pair. **2.** To pair or cause to pair (a male and a female animal) and allow them to breed: *mate cats. Many animals mate in the spring.* —**mat'ing** *adj.: a mating call; mating season.* [SEE NOTE]

mate[2] |māt| *n.* In chess, a checkmate. —*v.* **mat•ed, mat•ing.** To checkmate. [SEE NOTE]

ma•té |**mä'**tā'| *n.* **1.** A South American shrub with evergreen leaves used to make a drink that resembles tea. **2.** The drink made from these leaves.

ma•te•ri•al |mə **tîr'**ē əl| *n.* **1.** The substance or thing from which something is or can be made: *Hemp is often used as material for ropes.* **2.** Cloth or fabric. **3.** Something, as facts, information, observations, etc., that may be refined, analyzed, or otherwise reworked and made or incorporated into a finished product: *gathering material for a book on sheep dogs; material for a comedy.* **4. materials.** Tools or apparatus for the performance of a certain task: *writing materials; building materials.* —*adj.* **1.** Of or existing in the form of matter. **2.** Of or affecting physical well-being: *material comforts.* **3.** Of the physical as opposed to the spiritual or intellectual: *She did it not for material gain but for spiritual satisfaction.*

ma•te•ri•al•ism |mə **tîr'**ē ə lĭz'əm| *n.* **1.** The philosophical doctrine that physical matter is the only reality in the universe and that everything else, including man, his thoughts, feelings, mind, and will can be explained in terms of physical laws. **2.** The doctrine that physical well-being and worldly possessions make up the greatest good and highest value in life. **3.** Excessive concern with money and possessions to the exclusion of spiritual or intellectual things. —**ma•te'ri•al•ist** *n.*

ma•te•ri•al•is•tic |mə tîr'ē ə **lĭs'**tĭk| *adj.* **1.** Of the doctrines of materialism. **2.** Excessively concerned with money and possessions to the exclusion of spiritual or intelleotual things. —**ma•te'ri•al•is'tic•al•ly** *adv.*

ma•te•ri•al•ize |mə **tîr'**ē ə līz'| *v.* **ma•te•ri•al•ized, ma•te•ri•al•iz•ing. 1.** To become real or actual; take material form; become a fact: *If her dreams materialize, life will be much more peaceful. The support for the project never materialized.* **2.** To appear as if from nowhere: *A red fish materialized alongside the canoe.*

ma•te•ri•al•ly |mə **tîr'**ē ə lē| *adv.* **1.** To a significant extent or degree; considerably: *His cooperation aided materially in the successful completion of the experiment.* **2. a.** So far as what promotes physical well-being is concerned: *a couple that lives materially well.* **b.** In a material way: *strong materially but weak in determination.*

ma•te•ri•el or **ma•té•ri•el** |mə tîr'ē **ĕl'**| *n.* Equipment, apparatus, and supplies, especially the guns and ammunition of a military force.

ma•ter•nal |mə **tûr'** nəl| *adj.* **1.** Of a mother or motherhood: *a maternal instinct.* **2.** Inherited from one's mother: *a maternal trait.* **3.** Related to through one's mother. —**ma•ter'nal•ly** *adv.*

ma•ter•ni•ty |mə **tûr'**nĭ tē| *n.* The state of being a mother. —*adj.* Connected with pregnancy and childbirth: *a maternity dress; maternity care.*

math |măth| *n.* Mathematics. —**modifier:** *a math quiz.*

math•e•mat•i•cal |măth'ə **măt'**ĭ kəl| *adj.* Of, involved in, or characteristic of mathematics. —**math'e•mat'i•cal•ly** *adv.*

math•e•ma•ti•cian |măth'ə mə **tĭsh'**ən| *n.* A person who is skilled in or who specializes in mathematics.

mat[1-2]

Mat[1] *was* matt- *in Old English; it was borrowed from Latin* matta, *which is probably borrowed from Carthaginian* maṭṭa, *"a mat."* **Mat[2]** *is a variant of* **matte**; *it originally meant "a dull surface (as opposed to a shiny finish) on materials such as paper," and it later came to mean "a paper or cardboard border" (see sense 1); it is borrowed from French* mat, *"dull, not shiny."*

match[1-2]

Match[1] *was* gemæcca, *"companion, one of a pair," in Old English.* **Match[2]** *originally meant "lamp wick," and is borrowed from Old French* meiche.

mate[1-2]

Mate[1] *is from Low German* mate, *earlier* gemate; *its original meaning was "messmate, person with whom one shares one's meat or food" (ge- in the Germanic languages often means "together," and* mat- *is related to* **meat**). **Mate[2]** *is shortened from* **checkmate,** *which ultimately comes from Arabic* shāh māt, *"the king is dead."*

math•e•mat•ics |măth′ə măt′ĭks| *n. (used with a singular verb).* The study of numbers, forms, arrangements, and sets, and of their relationships and properties. Arithmetic, algebra, and geometry are three branches of mathematics.

mat•i•nee or **mat•i•née** |măt′n ā′| *n.* A theatrical performance given in the afternoon.

ma•tri•arch |mā′trē ärk′| *n.* A woman who rules a family, clan, or tribe. —**ma′tri•ar′chal** *adj.*

ma•tri•ar•chy |mā′trē är′kē| *n., pl.* **ma•tri•ar•chies. 1.** A social system in which descent is traced through the mother's side of the family. **2.** A society in which women have most of the authority.

ma•tri•ces |mā′trĭ sēz′| *or* |măt′rĭ-| *n.* Plural of **matrix.**

mat•ri•cide |măt′rĭ sīd′| *or* |mā′trĭ-| *n.* **1.** The act of killing one's mother. **2.** A person who kills his mother. —**mat′ri•ci′dal** *adj.*

ma•tric•u•late |mə trĭk′yə lāt′| *v.* **ma•tric•u•lat•ed, ma•tric•u•lat•ing.** To register or allow to register in a college or university. —**ma•tric′u•la′tion** *n.*

mat•ri•mo•ny |măt′rə mō′nē| *n., pl.* **mat•ri•mo•nies.** The condition of being married; marriage. —**mat′ri•mo′ni•al** *adj.*

ma•trix |mā′trĭks| *n., pl.* **ma•tri•ces** |mā′trĭ sēz′| *or* |măt′rĭ-|. **1.** A situation, substance, object, etc., within which something is contained, originates, or develops: *an understanding atmosphere that is the matrix of peace.* **2.** The uterus; womb. **3.** The group of cells from which a fingernail, toenail, or tooth grows. **4.** The solid matter in which a fossil or crystal is embedded. **5.** A mold or die, as for casting or shaping metal.

ma•tron |mā′trən| *n.* **1.** A married woman, especially one in middle age or older. **2.** A woman official of a public institution, such as a school or prison. [SEE NOTE]

matron, etc.
The Indo-European word for "mother" was māter-. *It became: (1) Old English* mōdor, *becoming Modern English* **mother**; *(2) Latin* māter, *"mother," with its derivatives* māternus, *"motherly," and* mātrōna, *"married woman," from which we have* **matriarch, matricide, maternal, maternity,** *and* **matron**; *and (3) Greek* mētēr, *"mother"; see note at* **metropolis.**

ma•tron•ly |mā′trən lē| *adj.* **1.** Of a matron. **2.** Suitable for a matron.

matron of honor. *pl.* **matrons of honor.** A married woman serving as chief attendant of the bride at a wedding.

matte |măt| *n.* A dull finish, as on glass, paper, or metal. ¶*These sound alike* **matte, mat.**

mat•ter |măt′ər| *n.* **1. a.** Anything that occupies space and displays the properties of inertia and gravitation when at rest as well as when in motion; the stuff of which the physical bodies of the universe are made. **b.** A specific type of substance: *organic matter.* **2.** The substance or content of something: *the subject matter for a news report.* **3. a.** Something that is a subject of concern, feeling, action, etc.: *A fire is a serious matter.* **b.** Business, affair, or thing: *I took the matter up with my superiors.* **4. the matter.** An unpleasant or disagreeable circumstance or thing; a problem; trouble; difficulty: *What's the matter with him?* **5.** A certain quantity, amount, or extent: *It was only a matter of minutes before the lights went out.* **6.** Something written or printed or to be written or printed: *reading matter.* —*v.* To be of importance: *We tried to pretend that it didn't matter at all.*

***Idioms.* as a matter of course.** Naturally; logically: *You accept good health as a matter of course throughout your life.* **as a matter of fact.** In fact; actually. **for that matter.** So far as that is concerned; as for that. **no matter.** Of no importance or consequence; regardless of: *No matter how hard we try, we cannot achieve our goals.* **the fact of the matter is.** Actually.

Mat•ter•horn |măt′ər hôrn′|. A mountain peak in the Alps, on the Italian-Swiss frontier.

mat•ter-of-fact |măt′ər əv făkt′| *adj.* **1.** Adhering strictly to the facts; not imaginative; literal: *a matter-of-fact description of the party.* **2.** Free from emotion, affection, etc.: *a matter-of-fact tone of voice.* —**mat′ter-of-fact′ly** *adv.*

Mat•thew |măth′yo͞o| *n.* The first Gospel of the New Testament.

Mat•thew, Saint. One of the twelve Apostles, traditionally regarded as the author of the first Gospel.

mat•ting |măt′ĭng| *n.* **1.** A coarse fabric of woven straw, hemp, rushes, etc., used especially for making mats or covering floors. **2.** Mats in general.

mat•tock |măt′ək| *n.* A gardening tool with the blade set at right angles to the handle, used for cutting roots or breaking up soil.

mat•tress |măt′rĭs| *n.* A pad of heavy cloth filled with soft material and sometimes containing springs, used on or as a bed. —***modifier:*** *a mattress pad.*

mat•u•ra•tion |măch′o͝o rā′shən| *n.* **1.** The process of becoming mature. **2.** Discharge of pus, as from a boil.

ma•ture |mə to͝or′| *or* |-tyo͝or′| *or* |-cho͝or′| *adj.* **1.** Having reached full growth or development: *a mature plant.* **2.** Having reached a certain stage of development after a process: *a mature wine.* **3.** Having the mental and emotional qualities associated with an adult: *a mature woman; a mature youngster.* **4.** Having characteristics associated with full development: *mature hands; mature art.* —*v.* **ma•tured, ma•tur•ing. 1.** To reach full growth or development. **2.** To become ripe. **3.** To advance mentally and emotionally: *As the composer matured, he developed his own style.* **4.** To become due, as a bond or note: *This bond matures in ten years.*

ma•tur•i•ty |mə to͝or′ĭ tē| *or* |-tyo͝or′-| *or* |-cho͝or′-| *n.* **1.** The condition of being mature; full growth or development. **2.** The time at which a note or bond becomes due.

mat•zo |mät′sə| *n., pl.* **mat•zoth** |mät′sōt′| *or* |-sōs′| or **mat•zos** |mät′səz| *or* |-səs|. A brittle, flat piece of unleavened bread, eaten especially during Passover.

maud•lin |môd′lĭn| *adj.* Excessively sentimental.

maul |môl| *n.* A heavy hammer with a long handle, used to drive stakes, piles, or wedges. —*v.* To injure or damage by or as if by beating, tearing, or handling roughly: *The tiger mauled the boy. The Giants mauled the opposing team.* ¶*These sound alike* **maul, mall.**

maun•der |môn′dər| *v.* **1.** To talk incoherently or aimlessly. **2.** To wander about aimlessly or vaguely.

Maun•dy Thursday |môn′dē|. A church festival celebrated on the Thursday before Easter in memory of Christ's Last Supper and betrayal.

Mau•ri•ta•ni•a |môr′ĭ tā′nē ə|. A country in northwestern Africa, on the Atlantic Ocean. Population, 1,290,000. Capital, Nouakchott.

Mau•ri•ti•us |mô rĭsh′ē əs| *or* |-rĭsh′əs|. An

ă pat/ā pay/â care/ä father/ĕ pet/ ē be/ĭ pit/ī pie/î fierce/ŏ pot/ ō go/ô paw, for/oi oil/o͝o book/ o͞o boot/ou out/ŭ cut/û fur/ *th* the/th thin/hw which/zh vision/ ə ago, item, pencil, atom, circus

island country in the Indian Ocean, about 500 miles east of Madagascar. Population, 959,000. Capital, Port Louis.

mau•so•le•um |mô′sə lē′əm| *or* |-zə-| *n., pl.* **mau•so•le•ums** or **mau•so•le•a** |mô′sə lē′ə| *or* |-zə-|. A large and stately tomb.

mauve |mōv| *n.* A light reddish or grayish purple. *—adj.* Light reddish or grayish purple.

mav•er•ick |măv′ər ĭk| *or* |măv′rĭk| *n.* **1.** An unbranded calf or colt, traditionally belonging to the first person to brand it. **2.** A person who refuses to go along with the policies, views, etc., of his group. *—**modifier:** a maverick politician.*

ma•vis |mā′vĭs| *n.* A European thrush with a clear, musical song.

maw |mô| *n.* The mouth, gullet, or stomach of a hungry or ferocious animal.

mawk•ish |mô′kĭsh| *adj.* Excessively and obnoxiously sentimental: *a mawkish person.* —**mawk′ish•ly** *adv.* —**mawk′ish•ness** *n.*

max. maximum.

max•im |măk′sĭm| *n.* A brief formulation of a basic principle or rule of conduct; for example, *Early to bed, early to rise, makes a man healthy, wealthy, and wise* is a maxim.

max•i•ma |măk′sə mə| *n.* A plural of **maximum.**

max•i•mize |măk′sə mīz′| *v.* **max•i•mized, max•i•miz•ing.** To make as great or large as possible; increase to a maximum.

max•i•mum |măk′sə məm| *n., pl.* **max•i•mums** or **max•i•ma** |măk′sə mə|. The greatest or greatest possible number, measure, quantity, or degree: *The temperature reached a maximum at noon.* *—adj.* Of or having the greatest number, measure, quantity, or degree that has been reached or can be reached: *The train has a maximum speed of 80 miles per hour.*

may¹ |mā| *v.* Past **might** |mīt|. —Used as an auxiliary to indicate: **1.** Possibility: *It may rain. It looked as if it might rain.* **2.** An asking or giving of permission: *May I take a swim? You may.* **3.** Ability or capacity, with the force of can: *I wonder if I may be of some use around here. I came here thinking I might be of service to you.* **4.** Purpose or result. Used in clauses introduced by *so that: I make my stories lively and simple so that the smallest child may enjoy them. He drew a diagram so that I might understand what he was talking about.* **5.** Desire or fervent wish. Used in exclamations: *Long may he live! May he live to regret this day!* [SEE NOTE]

may² |mā| *n. British.* The blossoms of the hawthorn: *Here we go gathering nuts and may.* [SEE NOTE]

May |mā| *n.* The fifth month of the year, after April and before June. It has 31 days. *—**modifier:** May flowers.* [SEE NOTE]

Ma•ya |mä′yə| *or* |mī′ə| *n., pl.* **Ma•yas** or **Ma•ya.** A member of a Mayan-speaking people of Central America and southern Mexico whose civilization reached its height around A.D. 1000.

Ma•yan |mä′yən| *or* |mī′ən| *n.* **1.** A Maya. **2.** A family of Indian languages spoken in Central America. *—adj.* **1.** Of Mayan. **2.** Of the Mayas or their language and culture.

May apple. A North American plant with a single, nodding white flower and an oval yellow fruit. The roots, leaves, and seeds of the May apple are poisonous.

may•be |mā′bē| *adv.* Possibly; perhaps: *Maybe we can go sailing tomorrow.*

May Day. 1. A traditional holiday occurring on May 1, in celebration of spring. **2.** A day regarded in many places as an international holiday celebrated on May 1 to honor workers.

may•day |mā′dā′| *n.* An international radiotelephone signal word used by airplanes and ships in trouble. [SEE NOTE]

may•flow•er |mā′flou′ər| *n.* Any of several plants that bloom in spring, especially the arbutus.

May•flow•er |mā′flou′ər|. The ship on which the Pilgrims sailed to America from England in 1620.

may•fly |mā′flī′| *n., pl.* **-flies.** An insect with transparent wings and long, hairlike parts extending from the end of the body. Fully developed mayflies live for only a day or two.

may•hem |mā′hĕm′| *or* |mā′əm| *n.* **1.** In law, the willful maiming or crippling of a person. **2.** A state of violent confusion.

may•n't |mā′ənt| *or* |mānt|. May not.

may•on•naise |mā′ə nāz′| *or* |mā′ə nāz′| *n.* A dressing made of beaten raw egg yolk, oil, lemon juice or vinegar, and seasonings.

may•or |mā′ər| *or* |mâr| *n.* The chief government official of a city or town. —**may′or•al** *adj.*

may•or•al•ty |mā′ər əl tē| *or* |mâr′əl-| *n., pl.* **may•or•al•ties. 1.** The position of a mayor. **2.** The term of office of a mayor or the period during which he serves.

May•pole, also **may•pole** |mā′pōl′| *n.* A pole decorated with streamers, ribbons, garlands, flowers, etc., around which people dance on May Day. [SEE PICTURE]

maze |māz| *n.* **1.** A complicated, usually confusing network of passageways or pathways. **2.** Any state of confusion or bewilderment. ¶*These sound alike* **maze, maize.** [SEE PICTURE]

ma•zur•ka |mə zûr′kə| *or* |-zo͝or′-| *n.* **1.** A lively Polish dance that resembles a polka. **2.** Music written to accompany or as if to accompany this dance.

Mba•bane |əm bə bän′|. The capital of Swaziland. Population, 23,000.

M.C. 1. Master of Ceremonies. **2.** Member of Congress.

Mc•Kin•ley, Mount |mə kĭn′lē|. The highest mountain (20,320 feet) in North America, in Alaska.

Mc•Kin•ley |mə kĭn′lē|, **William.** 1843–1901. Twenty-fifth President of the United States (1897–1901); assassinated.

Md The symbol for the element mendelevium.

Md. Maryland.

M.D. Doctor of Medicine.

me |mē| *pron.* The objective case of **I.**—*Note: Me* has three main uses. It can be the direct object of a verb: *They blamed me.* It can be the indirect object of a verb: *Give me the letter.* It can also be the object of a preposition: *She addressed it to me.* As an objective pronoun, *me* would not normally follow a form of the verb *be,* according to the rules of grammar. But in the expression *It's me* or examples patterned on it *(The one you forgot to mention was me),* most persons would find I much less natural than *me.* In such examples, *me* is an acceptable substitute for *I,*

may¹·²/May

The Old English verb magan *meant "to be strong, to be able (to do something)"; "I am able" and "he is able" were* mæg, *and the past tense, "was able," was* mighte; mæg *and* mighte *became* **may¹** *and* **might²**, *respectively, in Modern English.* **May²** *is from the month of* **May** *(which is when the hawthorn blooms in England).* **May** *is from Latin* Maius mensis, *"Maia's month";* Maia *was an ancient Italian goddess.*

mayday

The signal word **mayday** *is an English spelling of the French phrase* m'aider, *"help me."*

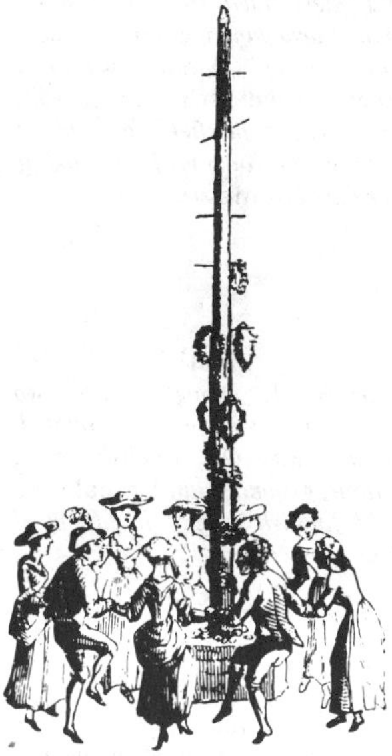

Maypole

maze

especially in speech and informal writing. ¶*These sound alike* **me, mi.**

Me. Maine (unofficial).

mead¹ |mēd| *n.* An alcoholic beverage made of fermented honey and water. ¶*These sound alike* **mead, meed.** [SEE NOTE]

mead² |mēd| *n. Archaic.* A meadow. ¶*These sound alike* **mead, meed.** [SEE NOTE]

mead•ow |mĕd'ō| *n.* A stretch of grassy ground, such as one used as a pasture or for growing hay.

mead•ow•lark |mĕd'ō lärk'| *n.* A North American songbird having a brownish back and a yellow breast with a V-shaped black marking.

mea•ger |mē'gər| *adj.* **1.** Having little flesh; thin: *a meager face.* **2.** Lacking in quantity or richness; scanty: *a meager living scraped from the soil.* **3.** Lacking in fertility; barren: *pastures too meager to be farmed.* —**mea'ger•ly** *adv.* —**mea'ger•ness** *n.*

meal¹ |mēl| *n.* Grain that has been coarsely ground. [SEE NOTE]

meal² |mēl| *n.* **1.** The food served and eaten in one sitting. **2.** The customary time for eating: *Don't eat between meals.* [SEE NOTE]

meal•y |mē'lē| *adj.* **meal•i•er, meal•i•est. 1.** Like meal in consistency; granular: *mealy flecks of potato.* **2.** Containing or covered with meal. **3.** Lacking color; pale: *a mealy complexion.* **4.** Mealy-mouthed.

meal•y-mouthed |mē'lē mouthd'| *or* |-moutht'| *adj.* Unwilling to speak directly or simply; deviously indirect.

mean¹ |mēn| *v.* **meant** |mĕnt|, **mean•ing. 1.** To have the sense of; signify: *Do you know what the word "beauty" means? Your dictionary tells you what words mean.* **2.** To act as a symbol of; represent: *In his poems the budding flower means youth.* **3.** To be likely to result in; be attended by: *Dark clouds often mean a storm.* **4.** To bring about or have as a consequence: *Friction means heat.* **5.** To intend to convey or indicate: *What do you mean by that look?* **6.** To have as a purpose or intention: *He means no harm.* **7.** To design or intend for a certain purpose or end: *a tall building meant for grain storage.* **8.** To be of a specified importance; matter: *His friendship meant a great deal to her.* ¶*These sound alike* **mean, mien.** [SEE NOTE]

Idioms. **mean well.** To have good intentions. **mean well by.** To have good intentions toward.

mean² |mēn| *adj.* **mean•er, mean•est. 1.** Common, ordinary, or low, as in rank, quality, value, appearance, etc.: *of mean intelligence; living in a mean cottage.* **2.** Lacking kindness and good will; cruel; spiteful: *a mean remark. The three women were as mean as they could be to Cinderella.* **3.** Miserly; stingy: *He was too mean to have electricity installed on the farm.* **4.** *Informal.* Ill-tempered: *He was a mean old bull.* **5.** *Slang.* Impressive; excellent: *She plays a mean game of baseball.* ¶*These sound alike* **mean, mien.** —**mean'ness** *n.* [SEE NOTE]

mean³ |mēn| *n.* **1.** A middle point, state, person, thing, etc., between two extremes. **2. a.** A number that is considered to represent an entire set of numbers, determined from the set in any of several ways; average. **b.** An **arithmetic mean. 3. means. a.** Something, such as a method or course of action, by which an act or end is achieved: *searching for a practical means of capturing the sun's energy.* **b.** Money, property, or other wealth: *a woman of means.* —*adj.* **1.** Occupying a middle or intermediate position between two extremes. **2.** Intermediate in size, extent, degree, etc.; medium: *a mean temperature; the mean height of the children in the class.* ¶*These sound alike* **mean, mien.** [SEE NOTE]

Idioms. **by all means.** Without fail; certainly. **by any means.** In any case: *She is not by any means unqualified.* **by means of.** With the use of; through. **by no means.** Certainly not.

me•an•der |mē ăn'dər| *v.* **1.** To follow a winding and turning course: *The river meanders through the town.* **2.** To wander aimlessly and idly. —**me•an'der•ing** *adj.: a meandering stream.* —*n.* Often **meanders.** A winding and turning course, as of a stream or path.

mean•ing |mē'nĭng| *n.* **1.** That which something, as a word or sentence, means or signifies: *Look up the meaning of the word "beauty" in your dictionary.* **2.** That which something intends to show, convey, or indicate: *What was the meaning of that remark?* —*adj.* **1.** Full of meaning; expressive: *a meaning smile.* **2.** Having a specified purpose or intent: *a well-meaning woman.*

mean•ing•ful |mē'nĭng fəl| *adj.* **1.** Having a meaning or function; capable of being interpreted, understood, etc.: *meaningful sounds.* **2.** Full of meaning; significant: *a meaningful discussion.* —**mean'ing•ful•ly** *adv.*

mean•ing•less |mē'nĭng lĭs| *adj.* Having no meaning or significance: *a meaningless phrase; a meaningless expression.* —**mean'ing•less•ly** *adv.*

meant |mĕnt|. Past tense and past participle of **mean.**

mean•time |mēn'tīm'| *n.* The time between one occurrence and another: *In the meantime, keep the horse in the garage.* —*adv.* Meanwhile.

mean•while |mēn'hwīl'| *or* |-wīl'| *adv.* **1.** During or in the intervening time: *Meanwhile, life goes on.* **2.** At the same time: *I washed up, and meanwhile, Mama put supper on the table.*

mea•sles |mē'zəlz| *n. (used with a singular verb).* **1.** A moderately severe, highly contagious virus disease that usually occurs in childhood. Its symptoms include coughing, fever, and numerous red spots that break out on the skin. **2.** Any of several milder diseases that have similar symptoms, especially German measles.

mea•sly |mē'zlē| *adj.* **mea•sli•er, mea•sli•est.** *Slang.* Contemptibly small; meager: *A measly old dime is all he gave me.*

meas•ure |mĕzh'ər| *n.* **1.** The size, amount, capacity, or degree of something, determined by comparison with a standard and expressed as a number or considered to exist as a number: *Name the measure of angle A. Do the line segments have equal measures?* **2.** Something used as a standard of comparison in determining measures: *The meter is a measure of length in the metric system.* **3.** A unit, usually derived from a standard, used in determining and expressing measures: *A pint is a measure of liquid capacity.* **4.** A system of such standards and units, such as the metric system. **5.** A device, such as a marked tape or graduated container, used in determining measures. **6.** The extent, amount, or degree of something: *With a good measure of curiosity, you*

mead¹·²

Mead¹ *was Old English* medu; *it is descended from prehistoric Indo-European* medhu, *"honey, honey wine."* **Mead²** *was Old English* mæd; *its original meaning was "a hayfield, a field of long grass for mowing," and it is related to* **mow¹**.

meal¹·²

Surprisingly enough, these two words are completely unrelated. **Meal¹** *was Old English* melu, *"flour, ground grain";* **meal²** *was Old English* mael, *"fixed time," hence "mealtime."*

mean¹·²·³

Mean¹ *was Old English* mænan, *"to intend, to signify, to tell."* **Mean²** *was Old English* gemǣne: *its original sense was "common, shared by all," later changing to "ordinary," and then to "inferior."* **Mean³** *is from Old French* meien, *which is from Latin* mediānus, *"middling, median."*

ă pat/ā pay/â care/ä father/ĕ pet/ ē be/ĭ pit/ī pie/î fierce/ŏ pot/ ō go/ô paw, for/oi oil/ŏŏ book/ ōō boot/ou out/ŭ cut/û fur/ *th* the/th thin/hw which/zh vision/ ə ago, item, pencil, atom, circus

could learn a lot. **7.** An evaluation or basis for comparison: *The scope of the project shouldn't be the measure of its appeal.* **8.** Limit; bounds: *His generosity knows no measure.* **9.** An action taken for a specified purpose or end: *The city takes many different measures to improve the flow of traffic.* **10.** A legislative bill or act. **11.** The notes and rests between two successive bars on a musical staff. *—v.* **meas•ured, meas•ur•ing. 1.** To find the size, amount, capacity, or degree of something. **2.** To serve as a measure of: *The inch measures length.* **3.** To have a measurement: *The paper measures 8 by 12 inches.* **4.** To estimate by comparison or evaluation; appraise: *measure the importance of a problem; measure his talent as an actor.* **5.** To choose with care; weigh: *She measured her words before telling the child the truth.* **6.** *Archaic.* To travel over: *We must measure 20 miles today.* ***—phrasal verbs.*** **measure off.** To mark or lay out by measuring: *The quarter notes are measured off into groups of two separated by a bar.* **measure out.** To distribute by or as if by measuring: *He measured out the animal's ration each day.* **measure up to. 1.** To be the equal of. **2.** To live up to certain standards: *He has not measured up to the demands of his position.* —**meas'ur•a•ble** *adj.* —**meas'ur•er** *n.*

Idioms. **for good measure.** In addition to the amount required. **in great (**or **large) measure.** To a great extent.

meas•ured |mĕzh'ərd| *adj.* **1.** Found out by measuring: *a measured distance of less than a mile.* **2.** Regular in rhythm and number: *a measured beat.* **3.** Careful; deliberate: *They took measured steps to finish the projects.* —**meas'ured•ly** *adv.*

meas•ure•ment |mĕzh'ər mənt| *n.* **1.** The act or process of measuring. **2.** A system of measuring: *measurement in inches, feet, and yards.* **3.** Size or dimensions found by measuring and expressed in units: *The dressmaker took Ann's waist and hip measurements.*

measuring worm. An inchworm.

meat |mēt| *n.* **1.** The flesh of an animal eaten as food, especially beef, pork, lamb, etc., as distinguished from fish or poultry. **2.** The firm or fleshy edible part of a nut, fruit, etc. **3.** *Archaic.* Food: *Meat and drink is the primary worry of many men.* **4.** The principal or essential part of something; the gist: *the meat of the story.* ***—modifier:*** *meat products.* ¶ *These sound alike* **meat, meet, mete.**

meat•ball |mēt'bôl'| *n.* A small ball of ground meat combined with various ingredients and cooked.

meat•y |mē'tē| *adj.* **meat•i•er, meat•i•est. 1.** Full of meat; fleshy: *a large, meaty hog.* **2.** Rich in substance; pithy: *a meaty book.* —**meat'i•ness** *n.*

mec•ca |mĕk'ə| *n.* A place regarded as a center of activity or interest: *His lab was the mecca of the world's chemists who came to learn his methods.*

Mec•ca |mĕk'ə|. A city in western Saudi Arabia; the birthplace of Mohammed and the spiritual center of Islam. Population, 367,000.

me•chan•ic |mə kăn'ĭk| *n.* A worker skilled in making, using, or repairing machines or tools. —**me•chan'ic** *adj.*

me•chan•i•cal |mə kăn'ĭ kəl| *adj.* **1.** Of or involving machines or tools. **2.** Operated, produced, or performed by machine. **3.** Suitable for performance by a machine: *dull, routine mechanical tasks.* **4.** Of, involving, or involved in the science of mechanics. **5.** Like a machine in operation; showing no emotion: *He spoke in a mechanical way, as if nothing had happened.* —**me•chan'i•cal•ly** *adv.*

mechanical advantage. The quotient of the force that is put out by a machine divided by the force that is put in, especially when power losses in the machine are neglected.

mechanical drawing. 1. A drawing on which measurements are given, as, for example, the plans of a house. **2.** The technique or art of making such drawings; drafting.

mechanical engineering. Engineering concerned with development, production, and use of machines and tools. —**mechanical engineer.**

me•chan•ics |mə kăn'ĭks| *n. (used with a singular verb).* **1.** The scientific study and analysis of the action of forces on matter and systems composed of matter. **2.** The development, production, operation, and use of machines and structures. **3.** *(used with a plural verb).* The technical aspects of an activity, sport, etc.: *The mechanics of football are learned with practice.*

mech•a•nism |mĕk'ə nĭz'əm| *n.* **1. a.** A machine or mechanical device. **b.** The arrangement of connected parts in a machine. **2.** Any system of parts that interact: *the mechanism of the solar system.* **3.** Any process or means by which something is done or is brought into being.

mech•a•nis•tic |mĕk'ə nĭs'tĭk| *adj.* Of or relating to mechanics as a branch of physics.

mech•a•nize |mĕk'ə nīz'| *v.* **mech•a•nized, mech•a•niz•ing.** To equip with machinery: *mechanize a factory.* —**mech'a•nized'** *adj.: a mechanized society.* —**mech'a•ni•za'tion** *n.*

med. medical; medicine.

med•al |mĕd'l| *n.* **1.** A small, flat piece of metal having a special shape and design, often awarded in honor of a great accomplishment or brave deed. **2.** A similar piece of metal with a religious figure or symbol on it. ¶ *These sound alike* **medal, meddle.** [SEE PICTURES]

me•dal•lion |mə dăl'yən| *n.* **1.** A large medal. **2.** A round or oval ornament, design, etc., resembling a large medal. [SEE PICTURE]

Medal of Honor. The highest U.S. military decoration, awarded for gallantry and bravery beyond the call of duty. Also called *Congressional Medal of Honor.*

med•dle |mĕd'l| *v.* **med•dled, med•dling. 1.** To handle something carelessly or ignorantly; tamper: *The owner was angry to see him meddling with the car engine.* **2.** To interfere in other people's business. ¶ *These sound alike* **meddle, medal.** —**med'dler** *n.*

med•dle•some |mĕd'l səm| *adj.* Inclined to interfere in other people's business. —**med'dle•some•ness** *n.*

me•di•a |mē'dē ə| *n.* A plural of **medium.**

me•di•ae•val |mē'dē ē'vəl| *or* |mĕd'ē-| *or* |mĭd'ē-| *or* |mĭ dē'vəl| *adj.* A form of the word **medieval.**

me•di•al |mē'dē əl| *adj.* **1.** Occurring in the middle: *the medial position in a row of seats.* **2.** Average or mean; ordinary. —**me'di•al•ly** *adv.*

medal
Above: Air Force Medal of Honor
Below: Religious medal with representation of the Holy Spirit

medallion
Sixth-century German

medicine man
Blackfoot Indian

Mediterranean

Mediterranean *is from Latin* mediterrāneus, *"in the middle of the land, surrounded by land":* medius, *"middle,"* + terra, *"land."*

medium

The word **media,** *in sense* **7.b.,** *is a collective plural. Television is* a mėdium, *the newspapers are* a medium; *all of the information systems together are* the media. *Three common mistakes are (1) to use* media *with a singular verb; (2) to refer to one system, such as television, as* a media; *and (3) to refer to several systems as* medias. *All three of these uses are overwhelmingly condemned by the American Heritage Usage Panel.*

ă **pat**/ā **pay**/â **care**/ä **father**/ĕ **pet**/ ē **be**/ĭ **pit**/ī **pie**/î **fierce**/ŏ **pot**/ ō **go**/ô **paw**, **for**/oi **oil**/ŏŏ **book**/ ōō **boot**/ou **out**/ŭ **cut**/û **fur**/ *th* **the**/th **thin**/hw **which**/zh **vision**/ ə **ago**, **item**, **pencil**, **atom**, **circus**

me•di•an |mē′dē ən| *n.* **1.** Something that lies halfway between two extremes; a medium. **2.** In a set of numbers, a number that has the property that half of the other numbers are greater than it and half less than it. **3.** A line joining a vertex of a triangle to the midpoint of the opposite side. **4.** A line that joins the midpoints of the non-parallel sides of a trapezoid. *—adj.* **1.** Located in the middle. **2.** Constituting the median of a set of numbers: *median score.*

me•di•ate |mē′dē āt′| *v.* **me•di•at•ed, me•di•at•ing. 1.** To help the opposing sides in a dispute come to an agreement, as by hearing their arguments and proposing a compromise. **2.** To settle (differences) by intervening in this way. **3.** To bring about (an agreement) by intervening in this way. —**me′di•a′tion** *n.*

me•di•a•tor |mē′dē ā′tər| *n.* A person or agency that mediates in a dispute.

med•ic |mĕd′ĭk| *n. Informal.* **1.** A physician or surgeon. **2.** A medical student or intern. **3.** A person in a medical corps of the armed services.

Med•i•caid, also **med•i•caid** |mĕd′ĭ kād′| *n.* A program, jointly sponsored by the federal government and the states, that provides medical aid for people who fall below a certain income level.

med•i•cal |mĕd′ĭ kəl| *adj.* **1.** Of, involving, or involved in the study or practice of medicine. **2.** Needing treatment other than surgery: *a medical problem. —n. Informal.* A thorough examination by a physician. —**med′i•cal•ly** *adv.*

me•dic•a•ment |mə dĭk′ə mənt| *or* |mĕd′ĭ kə-| *n.* A medicine; medication.

Med•i•care |mĕd′ĭ kâr′| *n.* A government-sponsored program that provides insurance to the aged for the payment of medical costs.

med•i•cate |mĕd′ĭ kāt′| *v.* **med•i•cat•ed, med•i•cat•ing.** To treat (a person, an injury, or a part of the body) with medicine. —**med′i•cat′ed** *adj.: a medicated hand lotion.*

med•i•ca•tion |mĕd′ĭ kā′shən| *n.* **1.** The act or process of medicating. **2.** A substance that helps to cure a disease or heal an injury; medicine.

me•dic•i•nal |mə dĭs′ə nəl| *adj.* Of or having the properties of medicine; capable of curing; healing. —**me•dic′i•nal•ly** *adv.*

med•i•cine |mĕd′ĭ sĭn| *n.* **1.** The scientific study of diseases and disorders of the body and the methods for diagnosing, treating, and preventing them. **2.** The branch of this science that deals with treatment by means other than surgery. **3.** The practice of this science as a profession. **4.** Any drug or other substance used to treat a disease of or injury to the body. **5.** Among North American Indians: **a.** Magical power. **b.** An object believed to have magical powers; a charm. *—**modifier:** a medicine dropper.*

medicine ball. A large, heavy, leather-covered ball used for exercise.

medicine man. 1. A member of a North American Indian tribe who presided at various ceremonies and practiced magic and folk medicine. **2.** A traveling peddler of medicines in 19th-century America. [SEE PICTURE]

me•di•e•val |mē′dē ē′vəl| *or* |mĕd′ē-| *or* |mĭd′ē-| *or* |mī dē′vəl| *adj.* Of or characteristic of the period in European history from the fall of the Roman Empire (about A.D. 500) to the rise of the Renaissance (about 1400).

Medieval Latin. Latin as used from about A.D. 700 to 1500.

Me•di•na |mə dē′nə|. A city of northwestern Saudi Arabia, about 250 miles north of Mecca. It is a sacred center of Islam. Population, 72,000.

me•di•o•cre |mē′dē ō′kər| *adj.* Neither good nor bad; ordinary; undistinguished.

me•di•oc•ri•ty |mē′dē ŏk′rĭ tē| *n., pl.* **me•di•oc•ri•ties. 1.** The fact or condition of being mediocre. **2.** An ordinary, undistinguished quality or performance: *impatient with mediocrity in his assistants.* **3.** A person of only average ability.

med•i•tate |mĕd′ĭ tāt′| *v.* **med•i•tat•ed, med•i•tat•ing. 1.** To think deeply and quietly; reflect: *retired to a quiet place in the country and meditated on the life of the spirit.* **2.** To consider at length; contemplate: *meditated a change of plans.* —**med′i•ta′tor** *n.*

med•i•ta•tion |mĕd′ĭ tā′shən| *n.* **1.** The process of meditating; contemplation: *sat by his window, lost in meditation.* **2.** An essay or speech containing religious or philosophical thoughts.

med•i•ta•tive |mĕd′ĭ tā′tĭv| *adj.* Devoted to or characterized by meditation; pensive. —**med′i•ta′tive•ly** *adv.* —**med′i•ta′tive•ness** *n.*

Med•i•ter•ra•ne•an |mĕd′ĭ tə rā′nē ən| *or* |-rān′yən| *adj.* Of the Mediterranean Sea or the countries bordering on it. *—n.* **the Mediterranean.** The **Mediterranean Sea.** [SEE NOTE]

Mediterranean Sea. The world's largest inland sea, dividing Europe from Africa.

me•di•um |mē′dē əm| *n.* **1.** *pl.* **me•di•ums.** A position, choice, or course of action midway between extremes; compromise: *a happy medium.* **2.** *pl.* **me•di•a** |mē′dē ə| or **mediums.** A substance in which something is kept, preserved, or mixed: *paint in a water medium.* **3.** *pl.* **media** or **mediums. a.** The substance in which an animal, plant, or other organism normally lives and thrives: *A fish in its medium is almost weightless.* **b.** An artificial substance in which bacteria or other microorganisms are grown for scientific purposes. **4.** *pl.* **media** or **mediums.** Something through which energy is transmitted, especially something necessary for transmission to take place: *Air is the medium of sound waves.* **5.** *pl.* **media** or **mediums.** A means by which something is accomplished or transferred: *money as a medium of exchange; speaking to a friend through the medium of the telephone.* **6.** *pl.* **mediums.** A person who claims to be able to communicate with the spirits of the dead. **7.** *pl.* **media** or **mediums. a.** A means for sending information to large numbers of people: *the billboard as an advertising medium.* **b. media.** The various means used to convey information in a society, including magazines, newspapers, radio, and television: *the mass media.* **8.** *pl.* **media** or **mediums. a.** An art or an art form: *Rodin achieved impressionistic effects through the medium of sculpture.* **b.** One of the techniques or means of expression available to an artist: *A composer has two primary media to choose from, the human voice and instruments.* **c.** A particular material used by a graphic artist: *the medium of oil paint. —adj.* Occurring midway between extremes; intermediate: *low, medium, and high speeds; of medium height.* [SEE NOTE]

medium frequency. Any radio-wave frequency

lying in the range between 300 and 3,000 kilohertz.

med•ley |mĕd′lē| *n., pl.* **med•leys. 1.** A mixture or variety, especially of sounds: *a medley of forest noises.* **2.** A musical arrangement that uses a series of melodies from different sources.

me•dul•la |mə dŭl′ə| *n., pl.* **me•dul•las** or **me•dul•lae** |mə dŭl′ē|. **1.** The inner core of certain structures of vertebrates, such as the marrow of bone. **2.** The **medulla oblongata.**

medulla ob•lon•ga•ta |ŏb′lông gä′tə| *or* |-lŏng-|. *pl.* **medulla ob•lon•ga•tas** or **medullae ob•lon•ga•tae** |ŏb′lông gä′tē| *or* |-lŏng-|. A mass of nerve tissue located at the top of the spinal cord and at the base of the brain. It controls breathing, circulation, and certain other bodily functions.

meed |mēd| *n.* A well-deserved reward: *She sang, got her meed of applause, and sat down.* ¶*These sound alike* **meed, mead.**

meek |mēk| *adj.* **meek•er, meek•est. 1.** Showing patience and humility; gentle; mild: *a meek and dignified manner.* **2.** Unresisting; peaceful; passive: *The swindler, made meek by the angry crowd, surrendered to the sheriff.* **—meek′ly** *adv.* **—meek′ness** *n.*

meer•schaum |mîr′shəm| *or* |-shôm′| *n.* **1.** A tough, compact, usually white mineral composed mainly of a silicate of magnesium, used as a building stone and for making tobacco pipes. **2.** A tobacco pipe with a meerschaum bowl.

meet[1] |mēt| *v.* **met** |mĕt|, **meet•ing. 1. a.** To come into contact; connect: *The scissor blades met and snipped the thread.* **b.** To connect with: *The Missouri River meets the Mississippi near St. Louis.* **2.** To come into each other's presence: *Penguins will bow to each other whenever they meet.* **3. a.** To come together by arrangement: *Let's meet at 4 o'clock.* **b.** To come together with (someone) by arrangement. **4. a.** To make the acquaintance of; be introduced to. **b.** To make each other's acquaintance; be introduced: *We first met in grade school.* **5.** To confer: *Parents will meet with the teachers on Monday.* **6.** To form a group; assemble: *Electors of the successful party meet in December and formally elect the President.* **7. a.** To come together as opponents; contend: *The two teams met on Tuesday to decide the championship.* **b.** To face in combat; confront: *He wanted to meet the count in a duel.* **8.** To come upon; encounter: *met three new words in the lesson.* **9.** To be present at the arrival of: *We went to the station to meet him.* **10.** To come to the notice of: *more here than meets the eye.* **11.** To experience; undergo: *met his death.* **12.** To deal or cope with: *running from her problems instead of meeting and overcoming them.* **13.** To fulfill; satisfy: *meeting his family's needs; a supply that doesn't meet the demand.* **14.** To pay: *helping to meet expenses; met the debt.* **—phrasal verb. meet with.** To experience; undergo: *dangers that the early settlers met with.* —*n.* A gathering of two or more teams for athletic competition. ¶*These sound alike* **meet, meat, mete.** [SEE NOTE]

meet[2] |mēt| *adj.* **meet•er, meet•est.** *Archaic.* Fitting; proper. ¶*These sound alike* **meet, meat, mete. —meet′ly** *adv.* [SEE NOTE]

meet•ing |mē′tĭng| *n.* **1.** A coming together by chance or arrangement; encounter. **2. a.** A gathering of people held at a fixed time and place, usually for a business, social, or religious purpose: *a meeting of the chess club; the Sunday Quaker meeting.* **b.** The people present at such a gathering: *Is there further business to come before the meeting?* **—modifier:** *a meeting place; a meeting ground.*

meet•ing•house, also **meet•ing-house** |mē′tĭng hous′| *n., pl.* **-hous•es** |-hou′zĭz|. A house of worship in certain Protestant denominations.

mega–. A word element meaning "one million": **megaton.** [SEE NOTE]

me•ga•cy•cle |mĕg′ə sī′kəl| *n.* **1.** One million cycles. **2.** Megahertz.

meg•a•hertz |mĕg′ə hûrts′| *n.* A unit of frequency of electromagnetic waves equal to one million cycles per second.

meg•a•lith |mĕg′ə lĭth′| *n.* A very large stone used in the building of prehistoric monuments, especially in western Europe from about 2000 B.C. to about 1000 B.C. [SEE PICTURE]

meg•a•lith•ic |mĕg′ə lĭth′ĭk| *adj.* **1.** Constructed of huge stones: *dolmens and other megalithic structures.* **2.** Of a prehistoric people who erected megaliths: *a megalithic culture.*

meg•a•lo•ma•ni•a |mĕg′ə lō mā′nē ə| *or* |-mān′yə| *n.* A mental disorder in which a person has fantasies of being very rich and powerful. **—meg′a•lo•ma′ni•ac′** *n.*

meg•a•lop•o•lis |mĕg′ə lŏp′ə lĭs| *n.* A region containing several large cities that are close enough together for their suburbs to merge and make the region one enormous city.

meg•a•phone |mĕg′ə fōn′| *n.* A funnel-shaped device that directs and projects the voice of someone who speaks or shouts into its smaller end.

meg•a•ton |mĕg′ə tŭn′| *n.* **1.** A unit of explosive force equal to the force with which one million (10^6) tons of TNT explodes. This unit is used mainly in expressing the force of nuclear explosions. **2.** One million tons.

meg•a•watt |mĕg′ə wŏt′| *n.* A unit of electrical power equal to one million watts.

mei•o•sis |mī ō′sĭs| *n., pl.* **mei•o•ses** |mī ō′sēz′|. The cell division that reduces the chromosomes of reproductive cells to half the normal number.

Meis•sen ware |mī′sən|. A delicate porcelain made in the city of Meissen, East Germany.

Me•kong |mā′kŏng′|. A river rising in Tibet and flowing through Southeast Asia into the South China Sea.

mel•an•cho•li•a |mĕl′ən kō′lē ə| *or* |-kōl′yə| *n.* A mental disorder in which a person suffers feelings of great sadness and depression and tends to withdraw from contact with others.

mel•an•chol•ic |mĕl′ən kŏl′ĭk| *adj.* Of, suffering from, or subject to melancholia. —*n.* A person suffering from melancholia.

mel•an•chol•y |mĕl′ən kŏl′ē| *n.* **1.** Low spirits; sadness. **2.** An atmosphere of sorrow or sadness; a pervasive gloom: *a somber country that oppresses the visitor with its rigor and melancholy.* —*adj.* **1.** Sad; gloomy. **2.** Making one feel sad; depressing: *the blank windows of a high melancholy square of empty buildings.*

Mel•a•ne•sia |mĕl′ə nē′zhə| *or* |-shə|. The small islands in the Pacific Ocean generally

meet[1-2]

Meet[1] *was Old English* mētan, *"to come together, assemble."* **Meet**[2] *was Old English* gemæte, *"fitting, suitable."*

mega–

This prefix, with its variant form megalo-, *is from Greek* megas, *"great"; it is related to Latin* magnus, *"great" (from which we have* **magnify***), and to* **much.**

megalith

south of the equator and west of the International Date Line. —**Mel'a•ne'sian** *adj. & n.*

mé•lange, also **me•lange** |mā **läNzh'**| *n.* A mixture.

mel•a•nin |**mĕl'**ə nĭn| *n.* A dark pigment found in the skin and hair.

mel•a•no•ma |mĕl'ə **nō'**mə| *n.* A dark-colored malignant tumor.

Mel•ba toast |**mĕl'**bə|. Crisp, thinly sliced toast.

Mel•bourne |**mĕl'**bərn|. The second-largest city in Australia. Population, 2,583,900.

meld[1] |mĕld| *v.* To combine; to blend: *The two coins were melded together by the heat.* —*n.* A combination; a blend. [SEE NOTE]

meld[2] |mĕld| *v.* To announce or show (a card or combination of cards) for a score in pinochle or similar games. —*n.* A combination of playing cards declared for a score. [SEE NOTE]

me•lee |**mā'**lā'| *or* |mā **lā'**| *n.* **1.** A confused fight among a number of people close together. **2.** A confused mingling of people or things.

mel•io•ra•tion |mēl'yə **rā'**shən| *or* |mē'lē ə-| *n.* **1.** The act or process of improving something. **2.** The linguistic process by which a word grows more elevated in meaning, more positive in connotation, etc. For example, the word *pretty* meant "sly" in Old English and came to mean "beautiful" in Modern English; this is an instance of melioration.

mel•lif•lu•ous |mə **lĭf'**lōō əs| *adj.* Like honey in smoothness or sweetness: *a mellifluous voice.* —**mel•lif'lu•ous•ly** *adv.* —**mel•lif'lu•ous•ness** *n.*

mel•low |**mĕl'**ō| *adj.* **mel•low•er, mel•low•est. 1. a.** Soft and sweet to the taste; fully ripened: *a mellow peach.* **b.** Rich and full in flavor; properly aged: *mellow wine.* **2. a.** Soft and resonant in sound: *mellow flute and cornet tones contrasting with the brassy brilliance of the trumpet.* **b.** Pleasingly free of harshness or sharp contrast; gentle on the eyes: *old, mellow furniture and wood paneling.* **3.** Moist and loamy: *indented the mellow soil with her hoe.* **4.** Conveying a feeling of comfort, harmony, and softness: *a perfect Indian summer day, warm and mellow.* **5.** Having or showing the gentleness and tolerance characteristic of mature age. **6.** Relaxed and good-humored; genial: *in a mellow mood.* —*v.* **1.** To make or become ripe, mature, or soft. **2.** To make or become milder; to moderate: *Time had mellowed the evangelist's fervor.* **3.** To make or become genial, kindly, or tolerant. —**mel'low•ly** *adv.* —**mel'low•ness** *n.*

me•lod•ic |mə **lŏd'**ĭk| *adj.* Of or containing melody. —**me•lod'i•cal•ly** *adv.*

me•lo•di•ous |mə **lō'**dē əs| *adj.* **1.** Containing a pleasing succession of sounds: *a melodious aria.* **2.** Full of or making pleasing sounds: *melodious birds.* **3.** Pleasant to listen to: *a melodious voice.* —**me•lo'di•ous•ly** *adv.* —**me•lo'di•ous•ness** *n.*

mel•o•dra•ma |**mĕl'**ə drä'mə| *or* |-drăm'ə| *n.* **1.** A play full of suspense, romance, and exciting scenes, with the heroes defeating the villains in the end. **2.** Plays of this kind in general. **3.** A situation or scene in real life resembling such a play, as in having heroes and villains engaged in an exciting struggle.

mel•o•dra•mat•ic |mĕl'ə drə **măt'**ĭk| *adj.* **1.** Of or suitable for melodrama: *melodramatic plays; melodramatic events.* **2.** Exaggerated or distorted to heighten sensation: *a melodramatic account of a boxing match.* **3.** Full of false or pretended emotion; sentimental. —**mel'o•dra•mat'i•cal•ly** *adv.*

mel•o•dy |**mĕl'**ə dē| *n., pl.* **mel•o•dies. 1. a.** A succession of musical tones. **b.** The structure of music considered with respect to successions of tones. **c.** A succession of musical tones associated with and organized by a particular rhythm. **d.** The main voice or part in a musical composition; tune; air. **2.** Musical quality: *a poem full of melody.*

mel•on |**mĕl'**ən| *n.* Any of several large fruits, such as a cantaloupe or watermelon, that grow on a vine and have a hard rind and juicy flesh.

melt |mĕlt| *v.* **1.** To change (a solid) to a liquid by or as a result of the action of heat or pressure. **2.** To dissolve: *Sugar melts in water.* **3.** To grow smaller, as if dissolving; diminish: *The crowd melted away.* **4.** To disappear; vanish: *struck swiftly and melted into the woods.* **5.** To merge gradually; blend: *stripes that melted into the background color.* **6.** To make or become gentler or milder; soften: *a look to melt the hardest heart.* —**melt'ed** *adj.: melted snow; melted wax.* —***phrasal verb.* melt down.** To melt (manufactured metal articles) in order to recover the metal as a raw material. —*n.* **1.** A mass of melted material. **2.** The amount melted: *the generous snow melt of the western slope.* —**melt'er** *n.*

melting point. The temperature at which a given solid becomes a liquid under normal atmospheric pressure.

melting pot. 1. A container in which a substance is melted; a crucible. **2.** A place where people of different cultures or races live together and influence each other.

Mel•ville |**mĕl'**vĭl|, **Herman.** 1819–1891. American novelist.

mem•ber |**mĕm'**bər| *n.* **1.** A part, organ, or limb of a human body or animal body. **2.** A person or thing that falls into a certain class, family, or category: *a member of the cat family; a member of the stringed group of instruments.* **3.** A person belonging to some group or organization: *club members; party members; a member of the United Nations.* **4. a.** Any element or item of a set. **b.** A mathematical expression connected to another such expression by an equal sign: *the left-hand member of an equation.* —***modifier:*** *member nations of the United Nations.*

mem•ber•ship |**mĕm'**bər shĭp'| *n.* **1.** The condition or status of being a member; participation in a group. **2.** The total number of members: *Unions increased their membership rapidly from 1937 to 1947.*

mem•brane |**mĕm'**brān'| *n.* **1.** A thin, flexible layer of tissue that covers surfaces or acts as the boundary between adjoining regions, structures, or organs in the body of an animal or plant. **2.** A thin sheet of natural or synthetic material through which dissolved substances can pass, as in osmosis. **3.** A thin sheet of a flexible, elastic material, such as rubber, plastic, parchment, etc.

mem•bra•nous |**mĕm'**brə nəs| *adj.* Of or like a membrane.

me•men•to |mə **mĕn'**tō| *n., pl.* **me•men•tos** or **me•men•toes.** A reminder of the past; a keep-

meld[1-2]

Meld[1], *apparently quite a new word, seems to be a blend of* **melt** *and* **weld. Meld**[2] *is from German* melden, *"to declare."*

ă pat/ā pay/â care/ä father/ĕ pet/ ē be/ĭ pit/ī pie/î fierce/ŏ pot/ ō go/ô paw, for/oi oil/ŏŏ book/ ōō boot/ou out/ŭ cut/û fur/ *th* the/th thin/hw which/zh vision/ ə ago, item, pencil, atom, circus

sake or souvenir: *a basement full of exotic mementos of his travels.*

mem•o |mĕm'ō| *n., pl.* **mem•os.** A memorandum.

mem•oir |mĕm'wär'| *or* |-wôr'| *n.* **1.** An account of experiences that the author has lived through. **2. memoirs.** An autobiography, especially one written by a famous person at the end of his career. **3.** A biography. **4. memoirs.** A record of the proceedings of a learned society.

mem•o•ra•bil•i•a |mĕm'ər ə bĭl'ē ə| *or* |-bĭl'yə| *pl.n.* Facts or things from the past that are worth remembering or keeping.

mem•o•ra•ble |mĕm'ər ə bəl| *adj.* **1.** Remarkable; unforgettable: *Memorable events are pictured on stamps.* **2.** Easy to remember: *Stephen Foster's songs are memorable and satisfying to sing.* —**mem'o•ra•ble•ness** *n.* —**mem'o•ra•bly** *adv.*

mem•o•ran•dum |mĕm'ə răn'dəm| *n., pl.* **mem•o•ran•dums** or **mem•o•ran•da** |mĕm'ə răn'də|. **1.** A short note written as a reminder. **2.** A written communication sent from one member or office of an organization to another or circulated generally. **3.** A short written statement outlining the terms of a legal or business agreement.

me•mo•ri•al |mə môr'ē əl| *or* |-mōr'-| *n.* **1.** A monument, shrine, or institution established to preserve the memory of a person or event. **2.** Anything kept or done in honor of a memory: *lit a candle every Sunday as a memorial to her father.* **3.** A petition addressed to a government or legislature. —*adj.* Serving to honor the memory of a person or event; commemorative: *memorial services; a memorial flame.*

Memorial Day. May 30, a holiday officially celebrated on the last Monday in May in honor of servicemen killed in war.

me•mo•ri•al•ize |mə môr'ē ə līz'| *or* |-mōr'-| *v.* **me•mo•ri•al•ized, me•mo•ri•al•iz•ing. 1.** To honor with a memorial; commemorate. **2.** To address a memorial to; petition.

mem•o•rize |mĕm'ə rīz'| *v.* **mem•o•rized, mem•o•riz•ing.** To commit to memory; learn by heart. —**mem'o•ri•za'tion** *n.*

mem•o•ry |mĕm'ə rē| *n., pl.* **mem•o•ries. 1.** The capability of storing past experiences in the mind and recalling them at will; the ability to remember. **2.** The exercise of this ability; the recalling of something in the past: *a sunset worthy of memory.* **3.** Something remembered; a thought of someone or something out of the past: *She had mixed memories of childhood.* **4.** The cherished thought of a past person, thing, or event: *His grandchildren kept his memory and brought offerings to his grave.* **5.** Honor and respect for someone or something in the past: *an arch built in memory of the emperor.* **6.** The period of time covered by such a stock of thoughts: *the heaviest gale in living memory.* **7.** A unit of a computer in which data is stored for later use; storage. —***modifier:*** *the memory bank of a computer.*

Mem•phis |mĕm'fĭs|. The largest city in Tennessee. Population, 620,000.

men |mĕn| *n.* Plural of **man.**

men•ace |mĕn'əs| *n.* **1.** A show of being ready to do harm; a threatening quality: *a voice full of menace.* **2.** Someone or something that threatens harm; a threat: *a reef that is a menace to passing ships.* **3.** A dangerous or annoying person. —*v.* **men•aced, men•ac•ing.** To threaten with harm; endanger: *an oil slick menacing the shoreline of California.* —**men'ac•ing** *adj.: a menacing look; menacing skies.*

mé•nage, also **me•nage** |mā näzh'| *n.* A household.

me•nag•er•ie |mə năj'ə rē| *or* |-näzh'-| *n.* **1.** A collection of wild animals kept in cages, pens, etc., so that people can come to see them. **2.** A place where such animals are kept.

mend |mĕnd| *v.* **1.** To repair; fix: *mend the rip in a jacket.* **2.** To correct; reform: *promised to mend his ways.* **3.** To get better; heal: *bones that break easily and mend slowly.* —*n.* The action of mending. —**mend'er** *n.* [SEE NOTE]

***Idiom.* on the mend.** Getting better; improving.

men•da•cious |mĕn dā'shəs| *adj.* **1.** Containing a lie or lies; untrue: *a mendacious explanation.* **2.** Given to telling lies; untruthful. —**men•da'cious•ly** *adv.* —**men•da'cious•ness** *n.*

men•dac•i•ty |mĕn dăs'ĭ tē| *n., pl.* **'men•dac•i•ties. 1.** Untruthfulness. **2.** A lie: *guilty of an occasional mendacity.*

men•de•le•vi•um |mĕn'dl ē'vē əm| *n.* Symbol **Md** One of the elements, a metal first produced by bombarding an einsteinium isotope with helium ions. It has two known isotopes with mass numbers 255 and 256, having half-lives of 30 minutes and 1.5 hours respectively. Atomic number 101.

Men•dels•sohn |mĕn'dl sən|, **Felix.** 1809–1847. German composer.

men•di•cant |mĕn'dĭ kənt| *adj.* Depending on alms for a living; practicing begging: *a mendicant order of friars.* —*n.* A beggar. —**men'di•can•cy** |mĕn'dĭ kən sē| *n.*

Men•e•la•us |mĕn'ə lā'əs|. In Greek mythology, a Spartan king who fought in the Trojan War for the return of his wife, Helen.

men•ha•den |mĕn hād'n| *n., pl.* **men•ha•den** or **men•ha•dens.** A fish of Atlantic waters, used chiefly as bait and as a source of oil or fertilizer.

me•ni•al |mē'nē əl| *or* |mēn'yəl| *adj.* **1.** Of or appropriate to a household servant: *We split the rent and shared the menial duties of the apartment.* **2.** Requiring little skill or responsibility; lowly: *They let me run errands and perform other menial tasks for them.* —*n.* **1.** A household servant. **2.** A person employed to perform simple, routine tasks. —**me'ni•al•ly** *adv.*

me•nin•ges |mĭ nĭn'jēz| *pl.n.* The less frequently used singular is **me•ninx** |mē'nĭngks|. The membranes that enclose the brain and spinal cord of vertebrates.

men•in•gi•tis |mĕn'ĭn jī'tĭs| *n.* Inflammation of any or all of the membranes that enclose the brain and spinal cord, usually resulting from a bacterial infection.

me•ninx |mē'nĭngks| *n.* Singular of **meninges.**

me•nis•cus |mə nĭs'kəs| *n., pl.* **me•nis•ci** |mə nĭs'ī'| or **me•nis•cus•es. 1.** An object that has the shape of a crescent. **2.** A lens that has a concave surface on one side and a convex surface on the other side. **3.** The curved upper surface of a liquid that stands in a container. The surface is concave if the liquid wets the container walls and convex if it does not.

mend, etc.
Latin mendum *meant "a fault, a physical defect"; from it was formed the verb* ēmendāre *(*ē-, *"out of"), "to eliminate the faults from, to improve or correct"; in Old French,* ēmendāre *became* amender, *which was borrowed into English as* **amend**; **mend** *is a shortening of* **amend**. *Also from Latin* mendum *was* mendīcus, *"cripple, beggar," and hence* mendicāre, *"to beg," with present participle* mendīcāns, *"begging"; this was borrowed into English as* **mendicant**. *Finally, related to Latin* mendum *was* mendāx, *"lying, a liar," from which we have* **mendacious**.

Me•nom•i•nee |mə **nŏm'**ə nē| *n., pl.* **Me•nom•i•nee** or **Me•nom•i•nees.** 1. A North American Indian tribe of Wisconsin. 2. A member of this tribe. 3. The Algonquian language of this tribe.

Men•non•ite |**mĕn'**ə nīt'| *n.* A member of an evangelical Protestant sect noted for its simplicity of living and dress and opposition to oath taking and military service.

men•o•pause |**mĕn'**ə pôz'| *n.* The time at which menstruation ceases to occur, usually between 45 and 50 years of age.

Me•no•rah |mə **nôr'**ə| *or* |**-nōr'**ə| *n.* A candlestick used in Jewish religious ceremonies, especially one with nine branches used in the celebration of Chanukah. [SEE PICTURE]

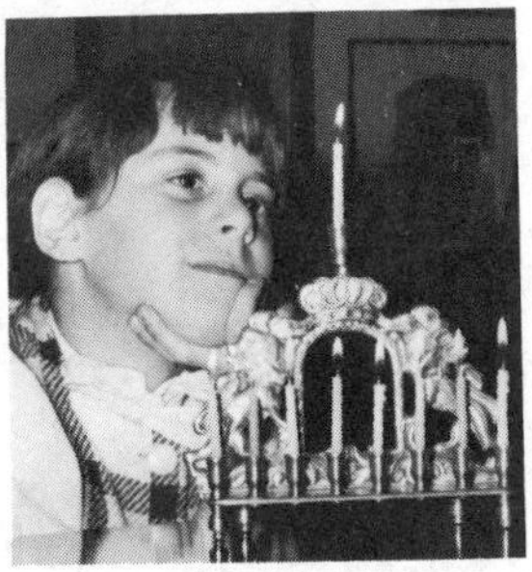

Menorah

men•ses |**mĕn'**sēz'| *pl.n.* The material discharged from the uterus in menstruation.

men•stru•al |**mĕn'**strōō əl| *or* |-strəl| *adj.* Of or involving menstruation.

men•stru•ate |**mĕn'**strōō āt'| *or* |-strāt'| *v.* **men•stru•at•ed, men•stru•at•ing.** To undergo menstruation.

men•stru•a•tion |mĕn'strōō **ā'**shən| *or* |mĕn **strā'-**| *n.* A process, occurring in women from puberty through middle age, in which blood and cell debris are discharged from the uterus through the reproductive tract if fertilization has not taken place. The process recurs at about 28-day intervals.

men•su•ra•tion |mĕn'sə **rā'**shən| *or* |-shə-| *n.* The act, process, or technique of measuring.

-ment. A suffix that forms nouns and means: 1. An action or process: **attachment; government.** 2. A condition: **amazement.** 3. The product, means, or result of an action: **entanglement.**

men•tal |**mĕn'**tl| *adj.* 1. Of or involving the mind: *mental capacity; a mental test.* 2. Occurring in or done by the mind: *a mental image.* 3. Of, suffering from, or for the care of mental diseases or disorders: *a mental patient; a mental hospital.* —**men'tal•ly** *adv.* [SEE NOTE]

mental/mind

Mental *is from Latin* mentālis, *"involving the mind," from* mens, ment-, *"mind." This is descended from the prehistoric Indo-European word* ment-, *"mind," which separately appears in Old English as* gemynd, *becoming* **mind** *in Modern English.*

mental age. A measure of mental development, as determined by intelligence tests, generally restricted to children.

mental deficiency. Mental ability or intelligence that is below normal, resulting from genetic causes or from brain damage due to disease or injury.

men•tal•i•ty |mĕn **tăl'**ĭ tē| *n., pl.* **men•tal•i•ties.** 1. The mental capacity or capability of a person; intelligence. 2. A habitual frame of mind; mental tendency: *the kind of cautious mentality that insists on punting on third down.*

mental retardation. **Mental deficiency.**

men•thol |**mĕn'**thôl'| *n.* A white crystalline organic compound having the formula $C_{10}H_{20}O$. It is obtained from peppermint oil and made synthetically and is used in perfumes, as a flavoring, and as a mild anesthetic.

men•tion |**mĕn'**shən| *v.* To speak or write about briefly, especially: 1. To refer to incidentally: *An index lists all the pages on which a subject is mentioned.* 2. To name; specify; itemize: *movie stars too numerous to mention.* 3. To call attention to; speak of: *made a point of mentioning the ache to his doctor.* —*n.* 1. a. The action of mentioning: *heroes worthy of mention.* b. The fact of being mentioned: *The very mention of spiders causes me to cringe.* 2. A reference: *searched the newspapers for a mention of the concert.* 3. A citation by name for good performance: *received an honorable mention in the contest.*

Idioms. **don't mention it.** Don't feel obligated by a favor: *"Thanks for lending me the power saw." "Don't mention it."* **not to mention.** In addition to; as well as: *Trees offer color and interesting outlines, not to mention shade and privacy.*

men•tor |**mĕn'**tôr'| *or* |-tər| *n.* A person depended upon for wise advice and guidance; a trusted counselor.

men•u |**mĕn'**yōō| *or* |**mā'**nyōō| *n.* 1. A list of foods and drinks available, as at a restaurant. 2. a. A list of dishes to be served in a meal or series of meals: *planned a diet menu for the week.* b. The dishes served.

me•ow |mē **ou'**| *or* |myou| *n.* The high-pitched, whining cry of a cat. —*v.* To make such a sound.

Meph•i•stoph•e•les |mĕf'ĭ **stŏf'**ə lēz'|. An evil spirit who appears in versions of the Faust legend as a tempter and buyer of human souls.

me•phit•ic |mə **fĭt'**ĭk| *adj.* Giving off an offensive odor: *Mephitic vapors rise from the swamp.*

mer•can•tile |**mûr'**kən tēl'| *or* |-tīl'| *or* |-tĭl| *adj.* 1. Of or relating to merchants or trade: *Coffee has been the foundation of Colombia's mercantile progress.* 2. Of mercantilism.

mer•can•til•ism |**mûr'**kən tē lĭz'əm| *or* |-tī-| *or* |-tĭ-| *n.* The national economic policies that prevailed in Europe after about 1500 and stressed profit from foreign trade, the founding of colonies and trade monopolies, and the storing of wealth in the form of gold and silver. —**mer'can•til'ist** *n.*

mer•ce•nar•y |**mûr'**sə nĕr'ē| *adj.* 1. Concerned only with making money; greedy for profit. 2. Hired for service in a foreign army. —*n., pl.* **mer•ce•nar•ies.** A professional soldier who is hired to serve in a foreign army.

mer•cer•ize |**mûr'**sə rīz'| *v.* **mer•cer•ized, mer•cer•iz•ing.** To treat (cotton thread) with sodium hydroxide, so as to shrink the fibers, give it a gloss, and make it hold dye better. —**mer'cer•i•za'tion** *n.*

mer•chan•dise |**mûr'**chən dīz'| *or* |-dīs'| *n.* 1. Things that may be bought or sold; commercial goods. 2. *Archaic.* The work of a merchant; trade. —*v.* |**mûr'**chən dīz'| **mer•chan•dised, mer•chan•dis•ing.** 1. To buy and sell (goods). 2. To promote the sale of by special displays, advertising, etc.: *Merchants have found that adding a pleasing scent helps to merchandise artificial flowers.* —**mer'chan•dis'er** *n.*

mer•chant |**mûr'**chənt| *n.* A person who buys and sells goods for profit. —*adj.* 1. Having to do with trade or commerce: *a merchant ship.* 2. Of the merchant marine.

mer•chant•man |**mûr'**chənt mən| *n., pl.* **-men** |-mən|. 1. A ship used in commerce. 2. *Archaic.* A merchant.

merchant marine. 1. A nation's ships that are engaged in commerce. 2. The personnel of such ships.

mer•ci•ful |**mûr'**sĭ fəl| *adj.* 1. Having mercy; compassionate; kindhearted. 2. Giving relief from pain or distress: *a death more swift and merciful than starvation.* —**mer'ci•ful•ly** *adv.* —**mer'ci•ful•ness** *n.*

mer•ci•less |mûr′sĭ lĭs| *adj.* Having or showing no mercy; cruel: *a merciless tyrant.* —**mer′ci•less•ly** *adv.* —**mer′ci•less•ness** *n.*

mer•cu•ri•al |mər kyo͝or′ē əl| *adj.* **1.** Clever, shrewd, and quick, like the Roman god Mercury. **2.** Changeable; fickle: *hard to predict her mercurial moods.* —**mer•cu′ri•al•ly** *adv.*

mer•cu•ric |mər kyo͝or′ĭk| *adj.* Of or containing mercury with a valence of +2.

Mer•cu•ro•chrome |mər kyo͝or′ə krōm′| *n.* A trademark for a complex green, crystalline organic compound that contains mercury, bromine, and sodium and is used in a bright-red water solution as an antiseptic.

mer•cu•rous |mər kyo͝or′əs| *or* |mûr′kyər-| *adj.* Of or containing mercury with a valence of +1.

mer•cu•ry |mûr′kyə rē| *n.* Symbol **Hg** One of the elements, a silvery-white, poisonous metal that is a liquid at room temperature. Atomic number 80; atomic weight 200.59; valences +1, +2; melting point −38.87°C; boiling point 356.58°C. —***modifier:*** *a mercury barometer.*

Mer•cu•ry[1] |mûr′kyə rē|. The Roman god who served as messenger to the other gods and presided over commerce, travel, and thievery.

Mer•cu•ry[2] |mûr′kyə rē| *n.* The planet of the solar system that is closest to the sun. Its diameter is roughly 3,000 miles, its average distance from the sun is about 36 million miles, and it takes about 88 days to complete an orbit around the sun.

mer•cy |mûr′sē| *n., pl.* **mer•cies. 1.** Kindness to a person in one's power or in distress; clemency: *fierce warriors who showed their captive no mercy.* **2.** A fortunate act or occurrence; a blessing: *It's a mercy no one was hurt.* —*interj.* A word used to express surprise, relief, or fear.

***Idiom.* at the mercy of.** In the power of: *The farmer is at the mercy of the weather.*

mere |mîr| *adj.* **1.** Being nothing more than what is specified: *a mere boy; a mere 50 cents an hour.* **2.** Considered apart from anything else; alone: *shocked by the mere idea; became a citizen by the mere fact of birth.*

mere•ly |mîr′lē| *adv.* Only; simply.

mer•est |mîr′ĭst| *adj.* Most small or insignificant; slightest: *The microphone could pick up the merest whisper in a far corner.*

mer•e•tri•cious |mĕr′ĭ trĭsh′əs| *adj.* Attracting attention by cheap or false means; showy; gaudy. —**mer′e•tri′cious•ly** *adv.* —**mer′e•tri′cious•ness** *n.*

mer•gan•ser |mər găn′sər| *n.* A duck with a narrow, slightly hooked bill and, usually, a crested head.

merge |mûrj| *v.* **merged, merg•ing. 1.** To bring or come together so as to form one; unite: *merged the two companies; rivers that run parallel before merging.* **2.** To pass gradually; change without a gap: *Spring merged into sultry summer.*

merg•er |mûr′jər| *n.* The action of merging, especially the union of two or more corporations or organizations.

me•rid•i•an |mə rĭd′ē ən| *n.* **1.** Any of the great semicircles of the earth that connect both of the geographic poles or both of a related set of poles: *a magnetic meridian.* **2.** A similar semicircle that joins the poles of a celestial body or the poles of the celestial sphere. **3.** The semicircle of this type that passes through a particular point on the earth's surface. **4.** A line drawn on a map to represent one of these semicircles. **5.** The meridian of the celestial sphere that passes through the point directly overhead; the zenith meridian. [SEE PICTURE]

me•ringue |mə răng′| *n.* **1.** A mixture of stiffly beaten egg whites and sugar, often used as a topping for cakes or pies. **2.** A small pastry shell made of meringue.

me•ri•no |mə rē′nō| *n., pl.* **me•ri•nos. 1.** A sheep of a breed having fine, soft wool. **2.** Cloth or yarn made from this wool.

mer•it |mĕr′ĭt| *n.* **1.** Superior value; excellence: *a painting of merit.* **2.** A praiseworthy feature or quality: *the merits and faults of country life.* **3. merits.** The actual facts of a legal case or other disputed issue. —***modifier:*** *a merit badge.* —*v.* To be worthy of; deserve.

mer•i•to•ri•ous |mĕr′ĭ tôr′ē əs| *or* |-tōr′-| *adj.* Having merit; deserving praise. —**mer′i•to′ri•ous•ly** *adv.*

merle |mûrl| *n.* A European blackbird with a clear, melodious song.

Mer•lin |mûr′lĭn|. In legends about King Arthur, a magician who served as the royal counselor.

mer•maid |mûr′mād′| *n.* A fabled sea creature with the head and upper body of a woman and the tail of a fish.

Mer•ri•mack |mĕr′ə măk′|. A warship captured from Union forces by the Confederacy during the Civil War, fitted with iron platings, and renamed the *Virginia.* It fought against the Union's *Monitor* at Hampton Roads, a waterway in Virginia, on March 9, 1862.

mer•ri•ment |mĕr′ĭ mənt| *n.* **1.** Amusement; mirthful delight: *Clowns performed for the merriment of the crowd.* **2.** Lighthearted celebration; festive gaiety: *a day given over to feasting and merriment.*

mer•ry |mĕr′ē| *adj.* **mer•ri•er, mer•ri•est.** Full of high-spirited gaiety; jolly: *a merry old man who loved to joke; a merry tune.* —**mer′ri•ly** *adv.*

***Idiom.* make merry.** To be jolly and gay; have fun.

mer•ry-go-round |mĕr′ē gō round′| *n.* **1.** A revolving circular platform having seats, usually in the form of horses, on which people ride for amusement. **2.** A series of events that follow in swift order: *Graduation week was a merry-go-round.*

mer•ry•mak•ing |mĕr′ē mā′kĭng| *n.* **1.** Fun and gaiety; festivity. **2.** A festive party or celebration. —**mer′ry•mak′er** *n.*

Mer•thi•o•late |mər thī′ə lāt′| *n.* A trademark for a crystalline organic compound that contains mercury, sodium, and sulfur and is used in the form of a bright red solution as an antiseptic for surface tissues of the body.

me•sa |mā′sə| *n.* A flat-topped hill or small plateau with steep sides, common in the southwestern United States. [SEE PICTURE]

mes•cal |mĕ skăl′| *n.* A cactus of southwestern North America, having buttonlike outgrowths that are the source of the drug mescaline.

mes•ca•line |mĕs′kə lēn′| *or* |-lĭn| *n.* An alkaloid drug, contained in mescal, that produces hallucinations and abnormal mental states.

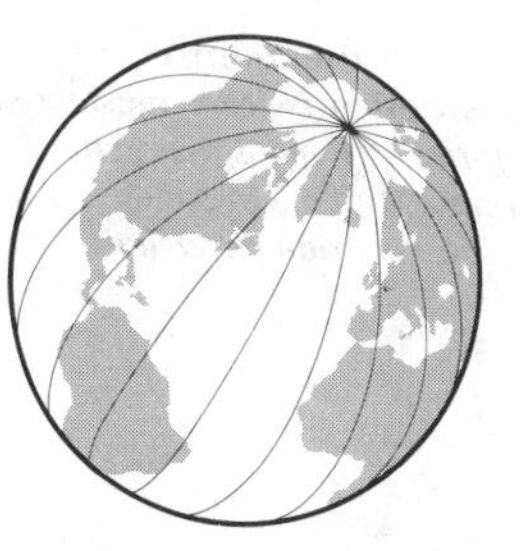

meridian
Earth encircled by meridians

mesa

Mes•dames |mā dăm'| *n.* **1.** Plural of **Madam.** **2.** Plural of **Madame.**

Mes•de•moi•selles |mā'də mə zĕl'| *or* |mād'-mwə-| *n.* Plural of **Mademoiselle.**

mes•en•ter•y |mĕs'ən tĕr'ē| *or* |mĕz'-| *n., pl.* **mes•en•ter•ies.** Any of several folds of tissue in the abdominal cavity that connect the intestines to the rear abdominal wall.

mesh |mĕsh| *n.* **1. a.** Any of the open spaces in a net, or sieve, or a wire screen. **b.** The size of these open spaces: *a fishnet of medium mesh.* **2.** Often **meshes.** The cords, threads, or wires forming a net or network. **3.** A knit or woven fabric with many small open spaces in it. **4.** **meshes.** An entanglement; a trap: *caught in the meshes of a long legal case.* **5.** The engagement of two sets of gear teeth. —*v.* **1.** To make by weaving or knotting threads together and leaving holes between them. **2.** To engage or interlock: *The teeth of the gears failed to mesh.* **3.** To fit together effectively: *The strategies of the allies meshed.* —**meshed'** *adj.: a meshed fabric.*
Idiom. **in mesh.** Properly engaged or fitted together.

mes•mer•ize |mĕz'mə rīz'| *or* |mĕs'-| *v.* **mes•mer•ized, mes•mer•iz•ing.** **1.** To hypnotize. **2.** To capture and charm; enthrall: *mesmerize an audience.* [SEE NOTE]

mesmerize
Mesmerize *is from* mesmerism, *a form of hypnosis practiced by Franz Anton* Mesmer *(1743–1815), Austrian physician.*

mes•o•derm |mĕz'ə dûrm'| *or* |mĕs'-| *n.* The middle of the three layers of cells found in an early embryo, developing in time into muscles, bones, and cartilage and the circulatory, excretory, and reproductive systems.

Mes•o•lith•ic |mĕz'ə lĭth'ĭk| *or* |mĕs'-| *n.* The period of human culture between the Paleolithic and Neolithic ages, marked by the appearance of the bow and of cutting tools. —*modifier: a Mesolithic ax.*

mes•on |mĕz'ŏn'| *or* |mĕs'-| *or* |mē'zŏn'| *or* |-sŏn'| *n.* Any of several subatomic particles having masses greater than that of an electron and less than that of a proton.

Mes•o•po•ta•mi•a |mĕs'ə pə tā'mē ə|. An ancient country between the Tigris and Euphrates rivers in present-day Iraq. —**Mes'o•po•ta'mi•an** *adj.* & *n.*

mes•o•sphere |mĕz'ə sfîr'| *or* |mĕs'-| *n.* The layer of the earth's atmosphere that extends from about 20 to 50 miles above the surface, decreasing in temperature from about 50°F to –135°F with increasing altitude.

Mes•o•zo•ic |mĕz'ə zō'ĭk| *or* |mĕs'-| *n.* Also **Mesozoic era.** The geologic era that began 230 million years ago and ended 63 million years ago, including the Triassic, Jurassic, and Cretaceous periods. Reptiles were the dominant form of life on the earth during this era. —*modifier: a Mesozoic fossil.*

mes•quite |mĕ skēt'| *or* |mĕs'kēt'| *n.* A thorny shrub or tree of southwestern North America, having feathery leaves and beanlike pods.

mess |mĕs| *n.* **1.** A disorderly gathering or scattering of things. **2.** A cluttered and untidy condition: *left his room in a mess.* **3.** A person, place, or thing in a dirty or untidy condition: *By the time the fudge was done, the kitchen was a mess.* **4.** A complicated or troublesome situation; a muddle: *Who got us into this mess?* **5.** A number of things acquired or gathered together: *fried a mess of fish.* **6.** An amount or portion of a soft, thick liquid: *a mess of oatmeal for breakfast.* **7.** Any unappetizing or disagreeable substance. **8. a.** A meal served to a group of soldiers, sailors, or campers: *shined his boots in time for morning mess.* **b.** A military group that takes its meals together: *members of the officers' mess.* **c.** A room or hall where such a group takes meals. —*modifier: a regimental mess hall; joined the mess line.* —*v.* **1.** To make untidy or disorderly; clutter: *messing up the playroom.* **2.** To make or leave a mess: *Don't mess in here.* **3.** *Informal.* To handle or manage badly; ruin; bungle: *his last chance and he messed it up.* **4.** To interfere; meddle: *afraid to mess with electrical fixtures.* **5.** To take a meal in a military group.
Idiom. **mess around** (or **about**). *Informal.* To pass time by playing or joking aimlessly; amuse oneself.

mes•sage |mĕs'ĭj| *n.* **1. a.** Spoken or written words or signals sent from one person or group to another. **b.** Any piece of information transmitted from one place to another: *The eye takes in light and relays the message to the brain.* **2.** A statement made or read before a gathering: *a Presidential message to Congress.* **3. a.** A basic theme or meaning: *the message of Buddhism.* **b.** A moral: *a movie with a tiresome message.*

mes•sen•ger |mĕs'ən jər| *n.* A person who carries messages or does similar tasks. —*modifier: a messenger boy.*

Mes•si•ah |mə sī'ə| *n.* **1.** The expected deliverer and king of the Jews, foretold by the prophets of the Old Testament. **2.** Christ, regarded by Christians as the fulfillment of this prophecy. **3.** **messiah.** Any person who is regarded as a savior or liberator of a people. [SEE NOTE]

Messiah
Messiah *is from Hebrew* māshiaḥ, *"he who is anointed." The Greek-speaking followers of Christ translated this into Greek as* khristos, *"anointed" (from* khriein, *"to anoint");* khristos *came into English as* **Christ.**

Mes•si•an•ic |mĕs'ē ăn'ĭk| *adj.* **1.** Of the Messiah. **2.** **messianic.** Of or suggesting the savior of a people or his coming: *a leader with a messianic quality; messianic hopes.*

Mes•sieurs |mĕs'ərz| *n.* Plural of **Monsieur.**

Messrs. **1.** Messieurs. **2.** Plural of **Mr.**

mess•y |mĕs'ē| *adj.* **mess•i•er, mess•i•est.** **1.** Disorderly; untidy; sloppy: *messy old clothes; a messy house.* **2.** Apt to cause a mess: *the messy job of squeezing lemons.* **3.** Difficult to solve or settle; complicated: *a messy business.*

mes•ti•zo |mĕ stē'zō| *n., pl.* **mes•ti•zos** or **mes•ti•zoes.** A person of mixed European and American Indian ancestry.

met |mĕt|. Past tense and past participle of **meet.**

meta–. A prefix borrowed from Greek *meta,* meaning "between, with, behind, after"; **method** is from Greek *methodos,* "a going after."

met•a•bol•ic |mĕt'ə bŏl'ĭk| *adj.* Of, involving, or carrying on metabolism. —**met'a•bol'i•cal•ly** *adv.*

me•tab•o•lism |mə tăb'ə lĭz'əm| *n.* **1.** The chemical and physical processes that living things carry on in order to maintain themselves; anabolism and catabolism. **2.** The use or functioning of a substance or class of substances within a living body: *carbohydrate metabolism.* **3.** *Informal.* **Basal metabolism.**

met•a•car•pal |mĕt'ə kär'pəl| *adj.* Of or involving the metacarpus. —*n.* Any of the bones of the metacarpus.

ă pat/ā pay/â care/ä father/ĕ pet/ ē be/ĭ pit/ī pie/î fierce/ŏ pot/ ō go/ô paw, for/oi oil/o͝o book/ o͞o boot/ou out/ŭ cut/û fur/ *th* the/th thin/hw which/zh vision/ ə ago, item, pencil, atom, circus

met•a•car•pus |mĕt′ə **kär′**pəs| *n.* The part of a hand or forefoot that contains the five bones extending from the bones of the fingers or toes to the wrist or ankle. [SEE PICTURE]

met•al |**mĕt′**l| *n.* **1.** Any of the elements that characteristically has a luster, conducts heat and electricity readily, forms chemical compounds by combining with nonmetals, and forms alloys by combining with other metals; for example, copper, iron, sodium, and mercury are metals. **2.** An alloy of two or more metals. **3.** An object made of metal. **4.** Strength of character; mettle: *The players were testing their metal on a bigger job.* —**modifier:** *a metal door.* ¶*These sound alike* **metal, mettle.**

me•tal•lic |mə **tăl′**ĭk| *adj.* **1.** Of or like metal: *metallic objects; a high metallic content.* **2.** Based on or containing a metal: *a metallic chemical compound.* **3. a.** Gleaming like polished metal: *a metallic blue glaze.* **b.** Harsh and abrupt in sound, like metal being struck: *an eerie metallic clanking.*

met•al•loid |**mĕt′**l oid′| *n.* An element that is not truly a metal but that has some of the properties of a metal, as the ability to form compounds with nonmetals or the ability to form alloys with metals; for example, arsenic and carbon are metalloids.

met•al•lur•gi•cal |mĕt′l **ûr′**jĭ kəl| *adj.* Of metallurgy.

met•al•lur•gist |**mĕt′**l ûr′jĭst| *n.* A person who specializes in metallurgy.

met•al•lur•gy |**mĕt′**l ûr′jē| *n.* The science and technology of extracting metals from their ores and making useful objects from the metals.

met•a•mor•phic |mĕt′ə **môr′**fĭk| *adj.* **1.** Of, involving, or changed by metamorphism: *metamorphic rock.* **2.** Of metamorphosis: *metamorphic stages of an insect.*

met•a•mor•phism |mĕt′ə **môr′**fĭz′əm| *n.* Any change in the composition, texture, or structure of rock produced by the action of great heat or pressure or by the action of water.

met•a•mor•phose |mĕt′ə **môr′**fōz′| *or* |-fōs′| *v.* **met•a•mor•phosed, met•a•mor•phos•ing. 1.** To undergo or cause to undergo metamorphism: *The crumbly rock called shale is metamorphosed into firm slate.* **2.** To change or be changed into a different stage of development by metamorphosis: *almost time for the tadpoles to metamorphose into frogs.* **3.** To transform completely, as by sorcery.

met•a•mor•pho•sis |mĕt′ə **môr′**fə sĭs| *n., pl.* **met•a•mor•pho•ses** |mĕt′ə **môr′**fə sēz′|. **1.** A complete, often sudden or dramatic change in appearance, character, or form. **2.** Changes in form and life function during natural development, as in the stages in which a caterpillar hatches from an egg and becomes a butterfly or a tadpole becomes a frog. [SEE PICTURES]

met•a•phase |**mĕt′**ə fāz′| *n.* The stage in mitosis during which the chromosomes group together toward the center of the cell and split lengthwise so as to double in number.

met•a•phor |**mĕt′**ə fôr′| *or* |-fər| *n.* A figure of speech in which something is named or described as if it were something quite different, to show the likeness between the two things; for example, *the evening of life, soaring hopes, the kingdom of the mind,* and *unleashing one's anger* are metaphors.

met•a•phor•i•cal |mĕt′ə **fôr′**ĭ kəl| *or* |**-fŏr′**-| or **met•a•phor•ic** |mĕt′ə **fôr′**ĭk| *or* |**-fŏr′**-| *adj.* **1.** Of or being a metaphor: *a metaphorical expression.* **2.** Full of metaphors: *highly metaphorical prose.* —**met′a•phor′i•cal•ly** *adv.*

met•a•phys•i•cal |mĕt′ə **fĭz′**ĭ kəl| *adj.* **1.** Of metaphysics. **2.** Dealing with beings, ideas, and forces that are not easily seen, proved, or understood; highly abstract: *a metaphysical explanation of life.* —**met′a•phys′i•cal•ly** *adv.*

met•a•phy•si•cian |mĕt′ə fĭ **zĭsh′**ən| *n.* A person skilled in metaphysics.

met•a•phys•ics |mĕt′ə **fĭz′**ĭks| *n.* *(used with a singular verb).* The branch of philosophy that deals with the ultimate nature or first causes of things.

me•tas•ta•sis |mə **tăs′**tə sĭs| *n., pl.* **me•tas•ta•ses** |mə **tăs′**tə sēz′|. The spread of a disease from its original location in the body to other locations, as in cancer or tuberculosis.

me•tas•ta•size |mə **tăs′**tə sīz′| *v.* **me•tas•ta•sized, me•tas•ta•siz•ing.** To spread from one part of the body to another, as do certain diseases.

met•a•tar•sal |mĕt′ə **tär′**səl| *adj.* Of or involving the metatarsus. —*n.* Any of the bones of the metatarsus.

met•a•tar•sus |mĕt′ə **tär′**səs| *n.* **1.** The part of the human foot that consists of five bones that extend from the toes to the ankle and that form the instep. **2.** A corresponding part of the foot of a bird or the hind foot of a four-legged animal.

mete |mēt| *v.* **met•ed, met•ing.** To give a proper share of; distribute; allot: *Zeus observed the mighty deeds of heroes and meted out rewards to them.* ¶*These sound alike* **mete, meat, meet.**

me•tem•psy•cho•sis |mə tĕm′sĭ **kō′**sĭs| *or* |mĕt′əm sī-| *n., pl.* **me•tem•psy•cho•ses** |mə-tĕm′sĭ **kō′**sēz′| *or* |mĕt′əm sī-|. The passing of the soul at death into the body of another person or animal.

me•te•or |**mē′**tē ər| *or* |-ôr′| *n.* **1.** The bright trail or streak seen in the sky when a fragment of solid material from space falls into the earth's atmosphere and burns. **2.** A solid fragment from space; a meteoroid.

me•te•or•ic |mē′tē **ôr′**ĭk| *or* |**-ŏr′**-| *adj.* **1.** Of or produced by a meteor or meteors: *a meteoric flash.* **2.** Like a meteor in speed, brilliance, or briefness: *his meteoric rise to fame; a meteoric career.*

me•te•or•ite |**mē′**tē ə rīt′| *n.* A part of a meteoroid, usually stony or metallic, that remains and strikes the earth after burning in the atmosphere.

me•te•or•oid |**mē′**tē ə roid′| *n.* Any of a large number of celestial bodies, ranging in size from specks of dust to bodies weighing thousands of tons, that appear as meteors when they enter the earth's atmosphere.

me•te•or•o•log•i•cal |mē′tē ər ə **lŏj′**ĭ kəl| *adj.* Of meteorology.

me•te•or•ol•o•gist |mē′tē ə **rŏl′**ə jĭst| *n.* A person who specializes in meteorology.

me•te•or•ol•o•gy |mē′tē ə **rŏl′**ə jē| *n.* The scientific study of the atmosphere and its effects,

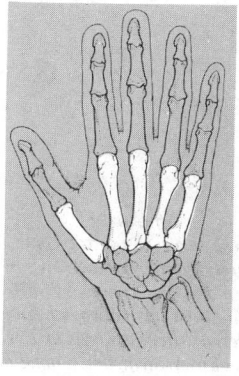

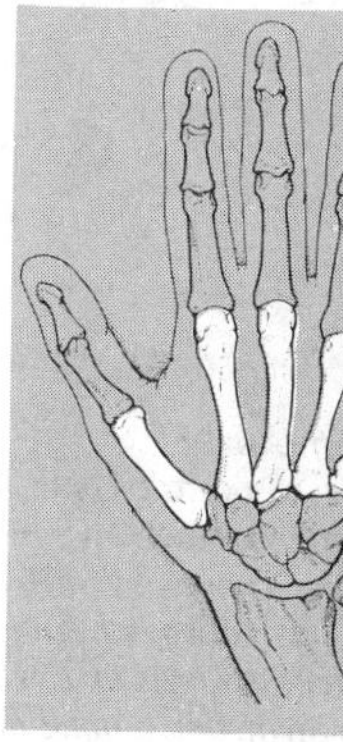

metacarpus

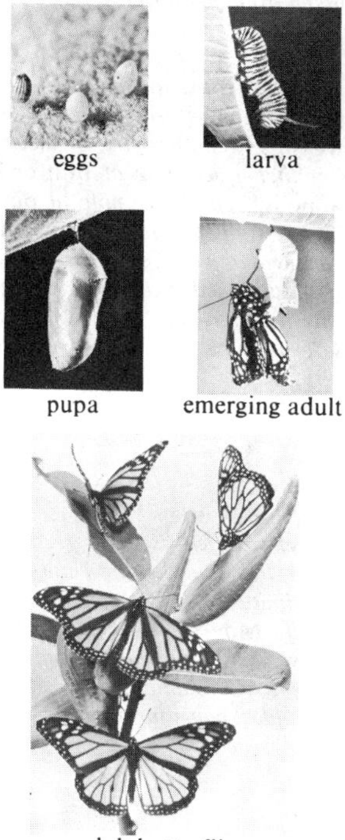

eggs larva pupa emerging adult adult butterflies

metamorphosis

Stages in metamorphosis of monarch butterfly

meter[1-2-3]
These three words all come ultimately from Greek metron, *"measure," but they came by different routes and have always been considered different words in English. Greek* metron *meant, among other things, "the measure of rhythm in poetry"; in this sense it was borrowed into Old English as* mēter, *becoming* **meter**[1] *in Modern English.* **Meter**[2] *is from French* mètre, *which was coined by the French Academy of Sciences after the French Revolution; it was taken directly from Greek* metron *in its basic sense of "measure." Greek* metron *was also the source of the suffix* **-meter**; **meter**[3] *is taken from this suffix.*

metropolis
Metropolis *is from Greek* mētropolis, *"mother-city":* mētēr, *"mother" (see note at* **matron**), + polis, *"city" (see note at* **policy**). *Originally, the Greek word was used of a city, such as Athens, that had founded colonies and was the "mother-city" to new cities; later it came to mean any capital city.*

mew[1-2]
Mew[1], *which is first recorded from the fourteenth century, is an imitative, or onomatopoeic, word.* **Mew**[2] *was Old English* mǣw, *and is descended from prehistoric Germanic* maiwa-; *it is our oldest name for a sea gull.*

ă pat/ā pay/â care/ä father/ĕ pet/ē be/ĭ pit/ī pie/î fierce/ŏ pot/ō go/ô paw, for/oi oil/o͝o book/o͞o boot/ou out/ŭ cut/û fur/*th* the/th thin/hw which/zh vision/ə ago, item, pencil, atom, circus

especially those effects that influence weather and weather conditions.

me•ter[1] |mē′tər| *n.* **1.** A rhythmic pattern used in verse, determined by the number and kinds of metric units in a typical line. See **foot**. **2. a.** The division of music into measures. **b.** Any particular grouping of beats that results from this, as indicated by a time signature. [SEE NOTE]

me•ter[2] |mē′tər| *n.* The basic unit of length in the metric system, equal to 39.37 inches. [SEE NOTE]

me•ter[3] |mē′tər| *n.* Any device designed to measure and indicate, record, or control the value of speed, temperature, distance, voltage, electric current, the rate of flow of a fluid, etc. —*v.* To measure or control with such a device. [SEE NOTE]

-meter. A word element meaning "a measuring device": **speedometer.**

meth•ane |mĕth′ān′| *n.* A colorless, ordorless gas that burns easily. It is composed of carbon and hydrogen and has the formula CH_4. It is obtained from natural gas and is used as a fuel and in the production of other organic compounds.

meth•a•nol |mĕth′ə nôl′| *or* |-nōl′| *n.* **Methyl alcohol.**

me•thinks |mĭ thĭngks′| *v. Archaic.* It seems to me: *"Methinks I see these things with parted eye, when every thing seems double."* (Shakespeare).

meth•od |mĕth′əd| *n.* **1.** A regular or deliberate way of doing something: *Three methods of purifying water are to filter it, to distill it, and to add chemicals to it.* **2.** Orderly arrangement; regularity. **3.** The established procedures used in a particular field: *the scientific method.*

me•thod•i•cal |mə thŏd′ĭ kəl| or **me•thod•ic** |mə thŏd′ĭk| *adj.* **1.** Arranged or done according to a clear plan; systematic: *a methodical inspection.* **2.** Orderly and systematic in one's habits or thinking: *The methodical Thomas Jefferson was annoyed by the lack of a standard money system in America.* —**me•thod′i•cal•ly** *adv.*

Meth•od•ism |mĕth′ə dĭz′əm| *n.* The beliefs and worship of the Methodists.

Meth•od•ist |mĕth′ə dĭst| *n.* A member of a Protestant denomination founded in 18th-century England on the teachings of John and Charles Wesley. —*adj.* Of or characteristic of this denomination.

Me•thu•se•lah |mə tho͞o′zə lə|. A Biblical patriarch said to have lived almost a thousand years.

meth•yl |mĕth′əl| *n.* The organic radical CH_3, derived from methane, having a valence of 1, and occurring in many important chemical compounds.

methyl alcohol. A colorless, flammable liquid compound of carbon, hydrogen, and oxygen, having the formula CH_4O. It is extremely poisonous and is used as an antifreeze, fuel, solvent, and to denature ethyl alcohol.

me•tic•u•lous |mə tĭk′yə ləs| *adj.* **1.** Very careful and precise: *kept meticulous records.* **2.** Taking great care with details; scrupulous: *a meticulous dresser.* —**me•tic′u•lous•ly** *adv.* —**me•tic′u•lous•ness** *n.*

me•tre |mē′tər| *n.* British form of the word **meter,** a unit, as in the metric system or in music or poetry.

met•ric |mĕt′rĭk| *adj.* **1.** Of, involving, or using the metric system. **2.** Of musical or poetic meter. **3.** Of or having to do with measurement.

met•ri•cal |mĕt′rĭ kəl| *adj.* **1.** Of musical or poetic meter. **2.** Composed in measures, especially regular measures: *metrical music.* **3.** Of or involving measurement. —**met′ri•cal•ly** *adv.*

met•ri•ca•tion |mĕt′rĭ kā′shən| *n.* Conversion to the metric system of weights and measures.

metric system. A decimal system of weights and measures based on the meter as a standard of length and the kilogram as a standard of mass or weight, with other units, as the liter for volume and the are for area, derived from these.

metric ton. A unit of mass or weight equal to 1,000 kilograms.

met•ri•fy |mĕt′rə fī′| *v.* **met•ri•fied, met•ri•fy•ing, met•ri•fies.** To convert to or adopt the metric system. —**met′ri•fi•ca′tion** *n.*

mét•ro or **Mét•ro** |mĕt′rō| *n., pl.* **mét•ros** or **Mét•ros.** The subway system in several cities, especially Paris and Montreal.

met•ro•nome |mĕt′rə nōm′| *n.* A device that makes a series of clicks separated by precise, adjustable intervals of time. It is used to provide a steady beat for practicing music.

me•trop•o•lis |mə trŏp′ə lĭs| *n., pl.* **me•trop•o•lis•es.** **1.** A large, busy city. **2.** The largest or most important city of a country, state, or region: *The town of Bend ranks as the metropolis of central Oregon.* [SEE NOTE]

met•ro•pol•i•tan |mĕt′rə pŏl′ĭ tən| *adj.* **1.** Of, from, or characteristic of a major city with its suburbs: *metropolitan daily newspapers.* **2.** Including a major city and the surrounding, heavily populated area: *Metropolitan Los Angeles has nearly three times the population of the city proper.* —*n.* **1.** A person from a major city. **2. a.** An archbishop of the Roman Catholic Church who has authority over bishops. **b.** A bishop of the Eastern Orthodox Church who presides over an ecclesiastical province.

met•tle |mĕt′l| *n.* **1.** Spirit; daring; pluck: *an old man who had had fire and mettle in his day.* **2.** A strength of character or purpose equal to a test: *The boatman proved his mettle in getting through the rapids.* ¶ *These sound alike* **mettle, metal.**

met•tle•some |mĕt′l səm| *adj.* High-spirited; plucky.

mew[1] |myo͞o| *n.* The high-pitched cry of a cat. —*v.* To make this sound. [SEE NOTE]

mew[2] |myo͞o| *n.* A gull of northern Europe and western North America. [SEE NOTE]

mewl |myo͞ol| *v.* To cry softly, as a baby does; whimper. —*n.* A weak cry or whimper. ¶ *These sound alike* **mewl, mule.**

mews |myo͞oz| *n. (used with a singular verb).* A small street behind a residential street, containing private stables or, in modern times, small apartments converted from stables. ¶ *These sound alike* **mews, muse.**

Mex. Mexican; Mexico.

Mex•i•can |mĕk′sĭ kən| *n.* A native or inhabitant of Mexico. —*adj.* Of Mexico, its inhabitants, or their language.

Mexican Spanish. Spanish as spoken in Mexico.

Mex•i•co |mĕk′sĭ kō′|. A country in North America, between the United States and Central

Weights and Measures

Length

U.S. Customary Unit	U.S. Equivalents	Metric Equivalents
inch	0.083 foot	2.54 centimeters
foot	⅓ yard. 12 inches	0.3048 meter
yard	3 feet. 36 inches	0.9144 meter
rod	5½ yards. 16½ feet	5.0292 meters
mile (statute, land)	1,760 yards. 5,280 feet	1.609 kilometers
mile (nautical, international)	1.151 statute miles	1.852 kilometers

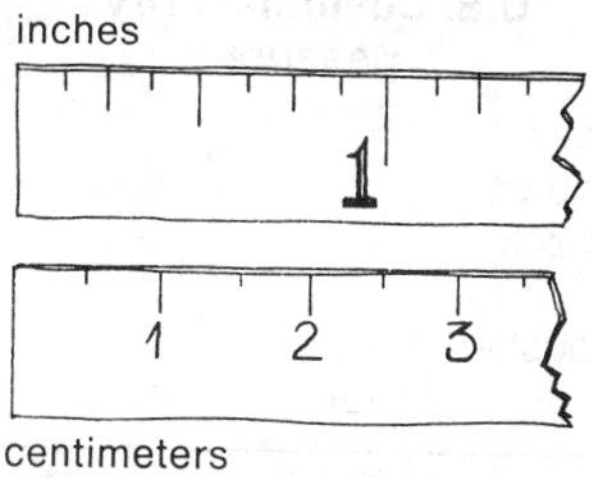

Area

U.S. Customary Unit	U.S. Equivalents	Metric Equivalents
square inch	0.007 square foot	6.4516 square centimeters
square foot	144 square inches	929.030 square centimeters
square yard	1,296 square inches. 9 square feet	0.836 square meter
acre	43,560 square feet. 4,840 square yards	4,047 square meters
square mile	640 acres	2.590 square kilometers

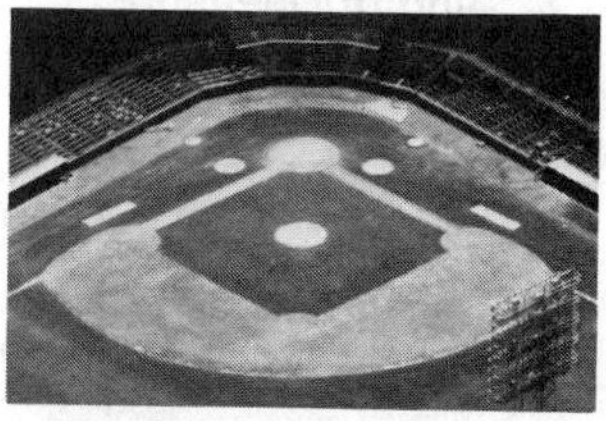

baseball diamond = 8100 square feet

Volume or Capacity

U.S. Customary Unit	U.S. Equivalents	Metric Equivalents
cubic inch	0.00058 cubic foot	16.387 cubic centimeters
cubic foot	1,728 cubic inches	0.028 cubic meter
cubic yard	27 cubic feet	0.765 cubic meter

17.6 cu. ft. refrigerator-freezer

U.S. Customary Liquid Measure	U.S. Equivalents	Metric Equivalents
fluid ounce	8 fluid drams. 1.804 cubic inches	29.573 milliliters
pint	16 fluid ounces. 28.875 cubic inches	0.473 liter
quart	2 pints. 57.75 cubic inches	0.946 liter
gallon	4 quarts. 231 cubic inches	3.785 liters
barrel	varies from 31 to 42 gallons, established by law or usage	

one gallon = 3.7 liter

Weights and Measures

U.S. Customary Dry Measure	U.S. Equivalents	Metric Equivalents
pint	½ quart. 33.6 cubic inches	0.551 liter
quart	2 pints. 67.2 cubic inches	1.101 liters
peck	8 quarts. 537.605 cubic inches	8.810 liters
bushel	4 pecks. 2,150.42 cubic inches	35.238 liters

bushel = 35.238 liters

British Imperial Liquid and Dry Measure	U.S. Customary Equivalents	Metric Equivalents
fluid ounce	0.961 U.S. fluid ounce. 1.734 cubic inches	28.412 milliliters
pint	1.032 U.S. dry pints. 1.201 U.S. liquid pints. 34.678 cubic inches	568.26 milliliters
quart	1.032 U.S. dry quarts. 1.201 U.S. liquid quarts. 69.354 cubic inches	1.136 liters
gallon	1.201 U.S. gallons. 277.420 cubic inches	4.546 liters
peck	554.84 cubic inches	0.009 cubic meter
bushel	1.032 U.S. bushels. 2,219.36 cubic inches	0.036 cubic meter

Weight

U.S. Customary Unit (Avoirdupois)	U.S. Equivalents	Metric Equivalents
grain	0.036 dram. 0.002285 ounce	64.79891 milligrams
dram	27.344 grains. 0.0625 ounce	1.772 grams
ounce	16 drams. 437.5 grains	28.350 grams
pound	16 ounces. 7,000 grains	453.59237 grams
ton (short)	2,000 pounds	0.907 metric ton (1,000 kilograms)
ton (long)	1.12 short tons. 2,240 pounds	1.016 metric tons

automobile = 3210 pounds

Apothecary Weight Unit	U.S. Customary Equivalents	Metric Equivalents
scruple	20 grains	1.296 grams
dram	60 grains	3.888 grams
ounce	480 grains. 1.097 avoirdupois ounces	31.103 grams
pound	5,760 grains. 0.823 avoirdupois pound	373.242 grams

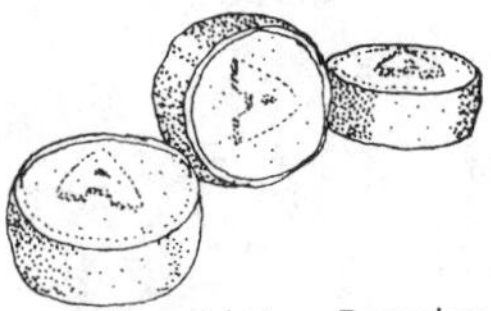

aspirin tablet = 5 grains

Picture Credits
aspirin tablet George Ulrich; **automobile** courtesy of Mercedes-Benz; **baseball diamond** courtesy of the Boston Red Sox; **boat** Michael Ryan; **bushel** Michael Ryan; **cubic inch/centimeter** George Ulrich; **cup/beaker** John Urban; **gallon** George Ulrich; **inch/centimeter** George Ulrich; **penny** George Ulrich; **snow scene** courtesy of the Vermont Development Agency; **thermometer** George Ulrich; **yard/meter stick** Michael Ryan.

Guide to the Metric System

Length

Unit	Number of Meters	Approximate U.S. Equivalent
myriameter	10,000	6.2 miles
kilometer	1,000	0.62 mile
hectometer	100	109.36 yards
dekameter	10	32.81 feet
meter	1	39.37 inches
decimeter	0.1	3.94 inches
centimeter	0.01	0.39 inch
millimeter	0.001	0.04 inch

yard = 36 inches

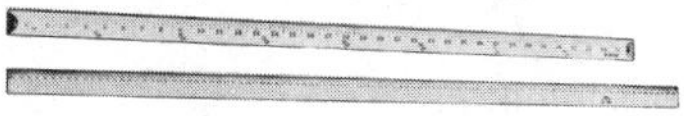

meter = 39.37 inches

Area

Unit	Number of Square Meters	Approximate U.S. Equivalent
square kilometer	1,000,000	0.3861 square mile
hectare	10,000	2.47 acres
are	100	119.60 square yards
centare	1	10.76 square feet
square centimeter	0.0001	0.155 square inch

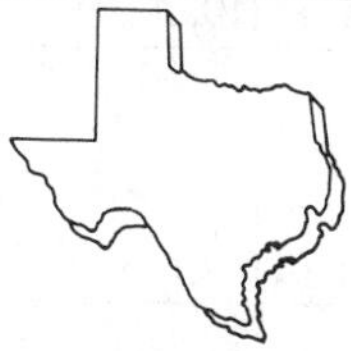

Texas = 695,081 square kilometers

Volume

Unit	Number of Cubic Meters	Approximate U.S. Equivalent
dekastere	10	13.10 cubic yards
stere	1	1.31 cubic yards
decistere	0.10	3.53 cubic feet
cubic centimeter	0.000001	0.061 cubic inch

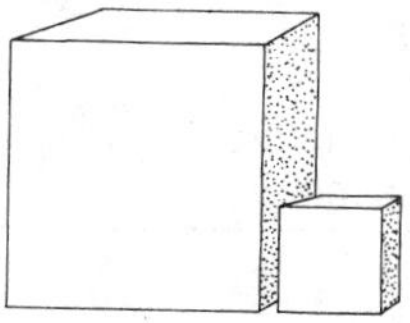

one cubic inch   one cubic centimeter

Capacity

Unit	Number of Liters	Approximate U.S. Equivalents: Cubic	Dry	Liquid
kiloliter	1,000	1.31 cubic yards		
hectoliter	100	3.53 cubic feet	2.84 bushels	
dekaliter	10	0.35 cubic foot	1.14 pecks	2.64 gallons
liter	1	61.02 cubic inches	0.908 quart	1.057 quarts
deciliter	0.10	6.1 cubic inches	0.18 pint	0.21 pint
centiliter	0.01	0.6 cubic inch		0.338 fluidounce
milliliter	0.001	0.06 cubic inch		0.27 fluidram

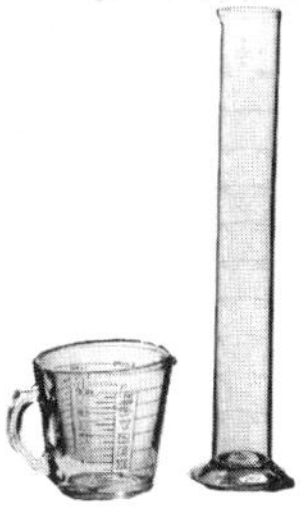

1 pint = 0.473 liter

Mass and Weight

Unit	Number of Grams	Approximate U.S. Equivalent
metric ton	1,000,000	1.1 tons
quintal	100,000	220.46 pounds
kilogram	1,000	2.2046 pounds
hectogram	100	3.527 ounces
dekagram	10	0.353 ounce
gram	1	0.035 ounce
decigram	0.10	1.543 grains
centigram	0.01	0.154 grain
milligram	0.001	0.015 grain

penny = 2.8 grams

Metric Conversion Chart – Approximations

When You Know	Multiply By	To Find
	Length	
millimeters	0.04	inches
centimeters	0.4	inches
meters	3.3	feet
meters	1.1	yards
kilometers	0.6	miles
	Area	
square centimeters	0.16	square inches
square meters	1.2	square yards
square kilometers	0.4	square miles
hectares (10,000m²)	2.5	acres
	Mass and Weight	
grams	0.035	ounce
kilograms	2.2	pounds
tons (1000kg)	1.1	short tons
	Volume	
milliliters	0.03	fluid ounces
liters	2.1	pints
liters	1.06	quarts
liters	0.26	gallons
cubic meters	35	cubic feet
cubic meters	1.3	cubic yards
	Temperature (exact)	
Celsius temp.	9/5, +32	Fahrenheit temp.
Fahrenheit temp.	−32, 5/9 x remainder	Celsius temp.
	Length	
inches	2.5	centimeters
feet	30	centimeters
yards	0.9	meters
miles	1.6	kilometers
	Area	
square inches	6.5	square centimeters
square feet	0.09	square meters
square yards	0.8	square meters
square miles	2.6	square kilometers
acres	0.4	hectares
	Mass and Weight	
ounces	28	grams
pounds	0.45	kilograms
short tons (2000 lb)	0.9	tons
	Volume	
fluid ounces	30	milliliters
pints	0.47	liters
quarts	0.95	liters
gallons	3.8	liters
cubic feet	0.03	cubic meters
cubic yards	0.76	cubic meters

30° Fahrenheit

30° Celsius

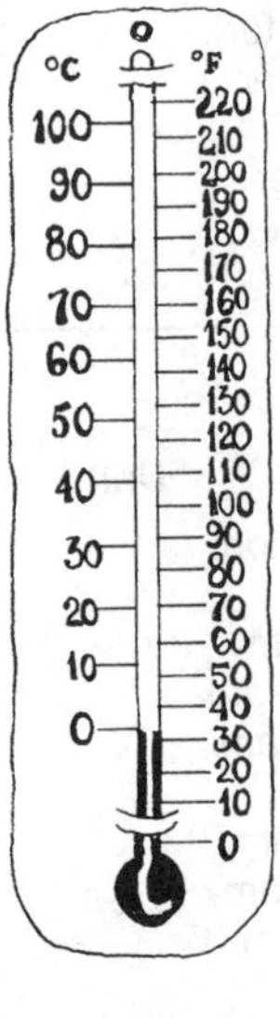

America. Population, 58,118,000. Capital, Mexico City.

Mexico, Gulf of. A part of the Atlantic Ocean south of the United States and east of Mexico.

Mexico City. The capital of Mexico. Population, 7,768,000.

me•zu•zah, also **me•zu•za** |mə zo͞oz′ə| *or* |-zo͞o′-zə| *n., pl.* **me•zu•zoth** |mə zo͞oz′ōth| or **me•zu•zahs.** A small piece of parchment inscribed with Biblical passages and a Hebrew word for God. The parchment is rolled up in a container and attached to a door frame as a sign that a Jewish family lives within, or is sometimes worn as an amulet. [SEE PICTURE]

mez•za•nine |mĕz′ə nēn′| *or* |mĕz′ə **nēn′**| *n.* **1.** A partial story between two main stories of a building. **2.** The lowest balcony in a theater or the first few rows of the balcony.

mez•zo |mĕt′sō| *or* |mĕd′zō| *or* |mĕz′ō|. In music: *adv.* Moderately: *a passage played mezzo forte.* —*n., pl.* **mez•zos.** A mezzo-soprano.

mez•zo-so•pran•o |mĕt′sō sə **prăn′ō**| *or* |-prä′-nō| *or* |mĕd′zō-| *or* |mĕz′ō-| *n., pl.* **mez•zo-so•pran•os. 1.** A woman's singing voice of medium range, lower than a soprano and higher than a contralto. **2.** A woman having such a voice. **3.** A part written in the range of this voice. ***—modifier:*** *a mezzo-soprano voice.*

mg milligram.

Mg The symbol for the element magnesium.

mho |mō| *n., pl.* **mhos.** A unit of electrical conductance. ¶ *These sound alike* **mho, mow**[1].

mi |mē| *n.* A syllable used in music to represent the third tone of a major scale or sometimes the tone E. ¶ *These sound alike* **mi, me.**

mi. mile.

Mi•am•i[1] |mī ăm′ē| *or* |-ăm′ə| *n., pl.* **Mi•am•i** or **Mi•am•is. 1.** A North American Indian tribe formerly living in Ohio, Indiana, Illinois, and Wisconsin. **2.** A member of this tribe. **3.** Algonquian language of this tribe.

Mi•am•i[2] |mī ăm′ē| *or* |-ăm′ə|. A resort city on the southeastern coast of Florida. Population, 346,931.

mi•as•ma |mī ăz′mə| *or* |mē-| *n., pl.* **mi•as•mas** or **mi•as•ma•ta** |mī ăz′mə tə| *or* |mē-|. **1.** A poisonous atmosphere formerly thought to rise from swamps and rotting matter and to cause disease. **2.** Any harmful atmosphere or influence. **—mi•as′mal** *adj.*

mi•ca |mī′kə| *n.* Any of a group of silicate minerals that are similar in physical structure and chemical composition and that split easily into thin transparent or translucent sheets. Mica is an excellent electrical insulator and is widely used for this purpose.

Mi•cah |mī′kə|. A Hebrew prophet of the eighth century B.C.

mice |mīs| *n.* Plural of **mouse.**

Mich. Michigan.

Mi•chael |mī′kəl|. In Christian tradition, one of the seven archangels and leader of the celestial armies.

Mich•ael•mas |mĭk′əl məs| *n.* A church festival celebrated on September 29 in honor of the archangel Michael.

Mi•chel•an•ge•lo |mī′kəl ăn′jə lō′| *or* |mĭk′əl-|. 1475–1564. Italian painter, sculptor, and architect.

Mich•i•gan |mĭsh′ĭ gən|. A Midwestern state of the United States. Population, 9,258,344. Capital, Lansing.

Michigan, Lake. One of the Great Lakes, the only one entirely within the United States, lying between the states of Michigan and Wisconsin.

Mic•mac |mĭk′măk′| *n., pl.* **Mic•mac** or **Mic•macs. 1.** A North American Indian tribe formerly living in Nova Scotia and New Brunswick. **2.** A member of this tribe. **3.** The Algonquian language of this tribe.

mi•cra |mī′krə| *n.* A plural of **micron.**

micro–. A word element meaning: **1.** Small or smaller: **microcosm. 2.** An instrument or technique for working with small things: **microscope. 3.** One-millionth: **microwave.**

mi•crobe |mī′krōb′| *n.* A living thing so small that it can be seen only through a microscope, especially one of the microorganisms that causes disease; a germ.

mi•cro•bi•o•log•i•cal |mī′krō bī′ə **lŏj′ĭ** kəl| *adj.* Of microbiology.

mi•cro•bi•ol•o•gist |mī′krō bī **ŏl′ə** jĭst| *n.* A scientist who specializes in microbiology.

mi•cro•bi•ol•o•gy |mī′krō bī **ŏl′ə** jē| *n.* The scientific study of microorganisms.

mi•cro•cir•cuit |**mī′**krō sûr′kĭt| *n.* An electronic circuit, especially an integrated circuit, made up of very tiny parts.

mi•cro•cosm |**mī′**krə kŏz′əm| *n.* **1.** A world or universe in miniature. **2.** Something or someone regarded as representing or closely resembling something else on a very small scale: *our student elections, a microcosm of democracy in action.*

mi•cro•far•ad |**mī′**krō făr′əd| *n.* A unit of capacitance equal to one-millionth (10^{-6}) of a farad.

mi•cro•film |**mī′**krə fĭlm′| *n.* **1.** A film on which written or printed material can be photographed in greatly reduced size. **2.** A reproduction made on microfilm. —*v.* To reproduce on microfilm.

Mi•cro•groove |**mī′**krə gro͞ov′| *n.* A trademark for a long-playing phonograph record.

mi•crom•e•ter |mī **krŏm′**ĭ tər| *n.* Any device used for measuring very small distances, especially by the use of a finely threaded screw.

mi•cro•mi•cro•far•ad |mī′krō **mī′**krō făr′əd| *n.* A picofarad.

mi•cron |**mī′**krŏn′| *n., pl.* **mi•crons** or **mi•cra** |**mī′**krə|. A unit of length equal to one-millionth (10^{-6}) of a meter.

Mi•cro•ne•sia |mī′krə **nē′**zhə| *or* |-shə|. The islands in the Pacific Ocean generally north of the equator and west of the International Date Line. **—Mi′cro•ne′sian** *adj. & n.*

mi•cro•or•gan•ism |mī′krō **ôr′**gə nĭz′əm| *n.* An organism, such as a bacterium or protozoa, so small that it can be seen only with the aid of a microscope.

mi•cro•phone |**mī′**krə fōn′| *n.* A device that converts sound waves into electric signals, as in recording or radio broadcasting. [SEE PICTURE]

mi•cro•pho•to•graph |mī′krō **fō′**tə grăf′| *or* |-gräf′| *n.* **1.** A photograph, as one on microfilm, that must be magnified in order to be seen clearly. **2.** A photomicrograph.

mi•cro•scope |**mī′**krə skōp′| *n.* An instrument in which the light reflected from or projected through a tiny object is passed through a combination of lenses so as to produce a magnified

mezuzah

microphone

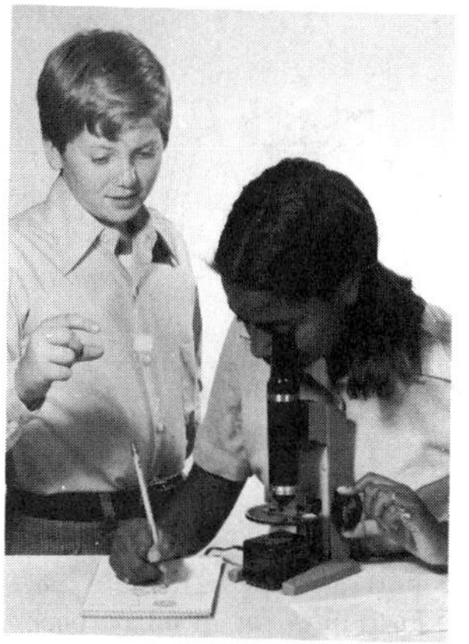

microscope

image that is large enough to be seen and studied. [SEE PICTURE on p. 563]

mi•cro•scop•ic |mī′krə skŏp′ĭk| *adj.* **1.** Too small to be seen by the eye alone but large enough to be seen through a microscope. **2.** Of, involving, or involved with a microscope or its use: *microscopic study of a specimen.* **3.** Like or used like a microscope; capable of making tiny objects visible. **4.** Very small; minute. —**mi′cro•scop′i•cal•ly** *adv.*

mi•cros•co•pist |mī krŏs′kə pĭst| *n.* Someone who specializes in microscopy.

mi•cros•co•py |mī krŏs′kə pē| *n.* **1.** The study of microscopes and their use. **2.** The use of microscopes.

mi•cro•sec•ond |mī′krō sĕk′ənd| *n.* A unit of time equal to one-millionth (10^{-6}) of a second.

mi•cro•volt |mī′krō vōlt′| *n.* A unit equal to one-millionth (10^{-6}) of a volt.

mi•cro•wave |mī′krō wāv′| *n.* Any electromagnetic wave having a wavelength in the range between about 300 millimeters and 1 millimeter.

mid¹ |mĭd| *adj.* Middle; central. [SEE NOTE]

mid² |mĭd| *prep.* Amid. Used chiefly in poetry. [SEE NOTE]

mid–. A word element meaning "a middle part, time, or location": **midway.** When *mid-* is followed by a capital letter, it appears with a hyphen: *mid-May.*

mid•air |mĭd âr′| *n.* A point or region in the middle of the air.

mid•day |mĭd′dā′| *n.* The middle of the day; noon. —***modifier:*** *a midday nap.*

mid•dle |mĭd′l| *n.* **1.** An area or point that is the same or approximately the same distance from extremes or outer limits; the center: *a skunk in the middle of the road; seated three abreast, with Janey in the middle.* **2.** Something placed or located between a beginning and an end; an intermediate part: *A story has a beginning, a middle, and an end.* **3.** A point in time, action, or experience halfway or approximately halfway between a beginning and an end: *by the middle of next year; in the middle of an assignment.* **4.** The waist of the human body: *a man with a bulging middle.* **5.** A position, with respect to belief or behavior, between extreme or contrary views: *staying safely in the middle, where controversial issues are concerned.* —*adj.* **1.** Equally distant from extremes or limits: *the middle finger of the left hand.* **2.** Coming between an earlier and a later period; intermediate in time or age: *the middle one of nine children.* **3.** Medium; moderate: *a dog of middle size.* [SEE NOTE]

middle age. The time of human life between youth and old age, usually reckoned as the years between 40 and 60.

mid•dle-aged |mĭd′l ājd′| *adj.* Of or characteristic of middle age.

Middle Ages. The period in European history from about A.D. 500 to about 1450.

Middle America. **1.** That part of the U.S. middle class thought of as being average in income and education and conservative in values and attitudes. **2.** The American heartland, thought of as being made up of small towns, small cities, and suburbs. —**Middle American.**

middle C. The musical tone whose pitch is indicated by the first ledger line below the treble clef and the first ledger line above the bass clef.

middle class. The people of a society who occupy a social and economic position between the laboring class and those who are wealthy in land or money or who, as in some countries, have the rank of nobility. —***modifier:* (middle-class):** *middle-class citizens.*

middle ear. The space between the tympanic membrane and the inner ear, containing three small bones that carry sound vibrations from the tympanic membrane to the inner ear; the tympanum.

Middle East. The area in Asia and Africa stretching from Libya on the west to Iraq and Saudi Arabia on the east and sometimes extended to include Turkey, Iran, Afghanistan, and Pakistan. —**Middle Eastern.** —**Middle Easterner.**

Middle English. English from about 1100 to 1500. The dialect of Middle English spoken around London became Modern English.

mid•dle•man |mĭd′l măn′| *n., pl.* **-men** |-mĕn′|. **1.** A trader who buys goods from producers for resale at a profit to retailers or consumers. **2.** An intermediary or go-between.

mid•dle•weight |mĭd′l wāt′| *n.* A boxer weighing between 147 and 160 pounds.

Middle West. A region of the United States extending from Ohio on the east to the Dakotas, Nebraska, and Kansas on the west. —**Middle Western.** —**Middle Westerner.**

mid•dling |mĭd′lĭng| *adj.* Of medium size, quality, etc.: *a man of middling intelligence.*

mid•dy |mĭd′ē| *n., pl.* **mid•dies. 1.** *Informal.* A midshipman. **2.** Also **middy blouse.** A loose blouse with a wide collar that is V-shaped in front with a square flap behind, worn by women and children.

Mid•east |mĭd′ēst′| *n.* The **Middle East.** —**Mid′east′, Mid′east′ern** *adj.*

midge |mĭj| *n.* A very small, gnatlike fly.

midg•et |mĭj′ĭt| *n.* **1.** A person who is of an abnormally small size but has a normally proportioned body. **2.** A very small or miniature type or kind: *Alongside his, our boat was just a midget.* —***modifier:*** *a midget computer.*

mid•land |mĭd′lənd| *n.* The middle or interior part of a country or region. —***modifier:*** *rich midland soil.*

mid•morn•ing |mĭd′môr′nĭng| *n.* The middle of the morning.

mid•most |mĭd′mōst′| *adj.* Situated in the exact middle or nearest the middle.

mid•night |mĭd′nīt′| *n.* The middle of the night; twelve o'clock at night. —*adj.* Of or at the middle of the night: *at the midnight point; a midnight supper.*

Idiom. **burn the midnight oil.** To work or study very late at night.

mid•point |mĭd′point′| *n.* **1.** A point in space or time that is halfway or approximately halfway between outer limits or between a beginning and an end: *a beam supported near midpoint; by midpoint of his first term as President.* **2.** The point of a line segment or arc that divides it into two equal lengths.

mid•rib |mĭd′rĭb′| *n.* The main, central vein of a leaf. [SEE PICTURE]

mid•riff |mĭd′rĭf′| *n.* **1.** The diaphragm, a part of the body. **2.** The part of the human body that

mid¹⁻², etc.
The adjective **mid¹** *was Old English* midd; *the preposition* **mid²** *is shortened from* **amid**; *the prefix* **mid-** *is from* **mid¹**. **Middle** *was* middel *in Old English. All these forms are descended from* medhyo-, *the prehistoric Indo-European word for "middle." This word appeared in Latin as* medius *(from which we have numerous words including* **medium** *and* **mean³**) *and in Greek as* mesos *(from which we have* meso- *in* **mesoderm**).

middle
Many languages are historically divided into old, middle, and modern periods. The dates vary considerably for each language; but the middle phase usually belongs to the late medieval period (roughly 1000–1500).

midrib

ă pat/ā pay/â care/ä father/ĕ pet/ ē be/ĭ pit/ī pie/î fierce/ŏ pot/ ō go/ô paw, for/oi oil/ŏŏ book/ ōō boot/ou out/ŭ cut/û fur/ *th* the/th thin/hw which/zh vision/ ə ago, item, pencil, atom, circus

extends from about the middle of the chest to the waist.

mid•sec•tion |mĭd′sĕk′shən| *n.* **1.** The middle region of the human body; the midriff. **2.** The middle part or section of anything.

mid•ship•man |mĭd′shĭp′mən| *or* |mĭd **shĭp′**-| *n., pl.* **-men** |-mən|. A student training to be an officer at a naval academy. [SEE PICTURE]

mid•ships |mĭd′shĭps′| *adv.* Amidships.

midst |mĭdst| *n.* **1.** The middle position or part; the center: *a tree in the midst of the garden.* **2.** A middle period in time or duration: *a lull in the midst of the storm.* **3.** The condition of being surrounded by or enveloped in something: *hardship in the midst of boom times.* **4.** A position or condition of being among members of a group: *introducing foreigners to our midst.* —*prep.* Among; amid.

mid•stream |mĭd′strēm′| *n.* **1.** The middle of a stream. **2.** The middle of a course of action or period of time.

mid•sum•mer |mĭd′sŭm′ər| *n.* **1.** The middle of the summer. **2.** The summer solstice, about June 21. —***modifier:*** *a midsummer afternoon.*

mid•term |mĭd′tûrm′| *n.* **1.** The middle of a school term or a political term of office. **2.** An examination given at the middle of a school term. —***modifier:*** *midterm examinations.*

mid•town |mĭd′toun′| *n.* The central part of a town or city. —***modifier:*** *heavy midtown traffic.*

mid•way |mĭd′wā′| *adv.* In the middle of a way or distance; halfway: *The line circling the earth midway between the poles is the equator.* —*adj.* In the middle of a way, distance, period of time, or succession of events: *at the midway point in the baseball season.* —*n.* |**mĭd′**wā′|. The area of a fair, carnival, or circus where side shows and other amusements are located.

mid•week |mĭd′wēk′| *n.* The middle of the week. —***modifier:*** *a midweek inspection.*

mid•week•ly |mĭd **wēk′**lē| *adj.* Occurring or performed in the middle of the week: *midweekly examinations.* —**mid′week′ly** *adv.*

Mid•west |mĭd′wĕst′| *n.* A region, the **Middle West.** —**Mid′west′, Mid′west′ern** *adj.* —**Mid′west′ern•er** *n.*

mid•wife |mĭd′wīf′| *n., pl.* **-wives** |-wīvz′|. A woman who assists women in childbirth.

mid•win•ter |mĭd′wĭn′tər| *n.* **1.** The middle of the winter. **2.** The winter solstice, about December 22. —***modifier:*** *midwinter holiday.*

mid•year |mĭd′yîr′| *n.* **1.** The middle of a year or school year. **2.** An examination given in the middle of a school year. —***modifier:*** *a midyear vacation.*

mien |mēn| *n.* A person's way of carrying or conducting himself; bearing; manner. ¶*These sound alike* **mien, mean.**

miff |mĭf| *v.* To cause (a person) to become offended or annoyed.

might¹ |mīt| *n.* **1.** Great power or force: *the ocean's might.* **2.** Physical or bodily strength: *threw a stone with all his might.* ¶*These sound alike* **might, mite.** [SEE NOTE]

might² |mīt| *v.* Past tense of **may** (auxiliary verb). —Used as an auxiliary to indicate: **1.** Conditional possibility: *Do as you are told, and we might let you go to the movies.* **2.** Probability: *The astronauts will need fewer supplies from Earth than one might think.* **3. a.** Request for permission. *Might* is used like *may* in this sense, except that it is felt to be less direct and thus more formal or polite: *Might I trouble you for another cup of tea?* **b.** Any request: *You might pay attention when I speak to you.* **4.** Complaint that a specified duty or act of politeness is being omitted: *He might at least call.* ¶*These sound alike* **might, mite.** [SEE NOTE]

might•n't |mīt′nt|. Might not.

might•y |mī′tē| *adj.* **might•i•er, might•i•est. 1.** Having or showing great power, strength, force, or skill: *a mighty army; a mighty hunter.* **2.** So great in size or scope as to cause awe or wonder: *mighty mountain peaks.* —*adv. Informal.* Very; extremely: *mighty juicy turnips.* —**might′i•ly** *adv.* —**might′i•ness** *n.* [SEE NOTE]

mi•gnon•ette |mĭn′yə **nĕt′**| *n.* A garden plant with clusters of small, fragrant, greenish flowers.

mi•graine |mī′grān′| *n.* A very severe headache, often accompanied by nausea, that usually affects just one side of the head and tends to recur.

mi•grant |mī′grənt| *n.* A person or animal that travels regularly from one region to another, especially as the season change. —*adj.* Traveling regularly from one region to another.

mi•grate |mī′grāt′| *v.* **mi•grat•ed, mi•grat•ing. 1.** To move from one country or region and settle in another. **2.** To move regularly to a different region, especially at a particular time of the year: *Many birds migrate to southern regions in the fall.* [SEE NOTE]

mi•gra•tion |mī **grā′**shən| *n.* **1.** The act of migrating. **2.** A group migrating together.

mi•gra•to•ry |mī′grə tôr′ē| *or* |-tōr′ē| *adj.* **1.** Migrating regularly: *migratory birds.* **2.** Of or having to do with migration: *long migratory flights.* **3.** Traveling from place to place; roving: *migratory workers.*

mi•ka•do |mĭ **kä′**dō| *n., pl.* **mi•ka•dos.** Often **Mikado.** The emperor of Japan.

mike |mīk| *n. Informal.* A microphone.

mil |mĭl| *n.* A unit of length equal to one-thousandth (10^{-3}) of an inch. ¶*These sound alike* **mil, mill.**

mi•la•dy |mĭ **lā′**dē| *n., pl.* **mi•la•dies.** My lady. A word used in speaking of or to a woman holding the rank of a lady.

Mi•lan |mĭ **lăn′**| *or* |**-län′**|. A city in northern Italy. Population, 1,725,000.

milch |mĭlch| *adj.* Giving milk: *a milch cow.*

mild |mīld| *adj.* **mild•er, mild•est. 1.** Gentle or kind in disposition, manner, or behavior: *a mild man.* **2.** Moderate in type, degree, force, or effect: *a mild reproach; mild winds; a mild soap.* **3.** Not very harmful; light: *suffered a mild stroke.* **4.** Not extreme in temperature; temperate: *this mild, damp climate.* **5.** Not sharp, bitter, or strong in taste or odor: *a mild curry powder; mild tobacco.* —**mild′ly** *adv.* —**mild′ness** *n.*

mil•dew |mĭl′dōō′| *or* |-dyōō′| *n.* **1.** A kind of fungus that forms a white or grayish coating on plant leaves, cloth, leather, etc., especially under damp, warm conditions. **2.** The coating thus formed. —*v.* To become covered or spotted with mildew.

mile |mīl| *n.* **1.** A unit of length equal to 5,280 feet, 1,760 yards, or 1,609.34 meters. **2.** A **nautical mile.**

midshipman

might¹·²

Might¹ *was* miht *in Old English; it is closely related to the verb* **might²** *(see note at* **may***).*

mighty

The use of **mighty** *as an adverb is very old; it is recorded as early as the fourteenth century. It has almost entirely died out in British English but has survived in informal usage in American English. An example of the old formal use occurs in a 1535 translation of the Bible: "(The Lord said) Tomorrow will I cause a mighty great hail to rain." (Exodus 9:18). A song by Frank Lebby Stanton (1857–1927) provides an example of the recent informal use:*

"Sweetest little feller—
Everybody knows;
Don't know what to call him,
But he's mighty lak a rose!"

*(*Lak *= like.)*

migrate

Migrate *is from Latin* migrāre, *"to go away, to move house."* **Emigrate** *is from Latin* ēmigrāre, *"to move out" (*ē-, *"out").* **Immigrate** *is from Latin* immigrāre, *"to move in" (*in-, *"in or into").*

milestone

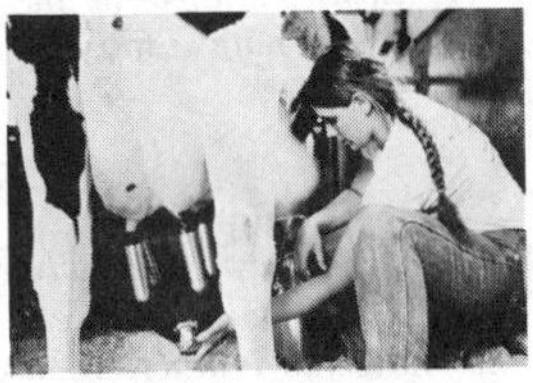

milk

mill¹·²

***Mill¹** was Old English* mylen, *which is an early Germanic borrowing from Latin* mola, *"millstone." (From* mola *was formed* molāris, *"tooth for grinding," which was borrowed into English as* **molar**.*)* **Mill²** *and* **mil** *are from Latin* millēsimus, *"thousandth," from* mille, *"thousand"; from* mille *we have also* **millennium** *("thousand years"),* **millipede** *("thousand feet"), and* **mile** *(a Roman mile was a thousand Roman paces).*

millibar

The **millibar** *is the unit of pressure that meteorologists most often use in expressing the pressure of the atmosphere. Normal atmospheric pressure, for example, is equal to 1,013 millibars, approximately 14.7 pounds per square inch.*

ă pat/ā pay/â care/ä father/ĕ pet/ ē be/ĭ pit/ī pie/î fierce/ŏ pot/ ō go/ô paw, for/oi oil/ŏŏ book/ ōō boot/ou out/ŭ cut/û fur/ *th* the/th thin/hw which/zh vision/ ə ago, item, pencil, atom, circus

mile•age |mī'lĭj| *n.* **1.** Length or distance as measured or expressed in miles. **2. a.** The amount of service, use, or wear measured by miles used or traveled: *a tire that gives long mileage.* **b.** The distance a motor vehicle travels per unit of fuel: *a mileage of 25 miles per gallon.* **3.** An allowance or expense, as for traveling a given number of miles or for the use of a car over a given number of miles.

mile•stone |mīl'stōn'| *n.* **1.** A stone marker set up on a roadside to indicate the distance in miles from a given point. **2.** An important event in history or in one's career: *The Magna Charta was a milestone in the history of human rights.* [SEE PICTURE]

mi•lieu |mēl yœ'| *n.* Environment or surroundings.

mil•i•tant |mĭl'ĭ tənt| *adj.* **1.** Fighting or making war: *militant tribes of New Guinea.* **2.** Prepared to fight or strive strenuously for the fulfillment of a cause; aggressive: *militant students.* —*n.* A person who is militant, especially in the advancement of a cause; an activist: *militants on our college campuses.* —**mil'i•tan•cy** *n.* —**mil'i•tant•ly** *adv.*

mil•i•ta•rism |mĭl'ĭ tə rĭz'əm| *n.* **1.** The practice of maintaining strong armed forces as a means of conducting a nation's affairs with other nations; a policy of aggressive preparedness. **2.** A system under which the armed forces of a nation control its government.

mil•i•ta•rist |mĭl'ĭ tər ĭst| *n.* A person who favors or supports militarism or warlike policies.

mil•i•ta•ris•tic |mĭl'ĭ tə rĭs'tĭk| *adj.* Of or devoted to militarism: *militaristic principles; a militaristic state.* —**mil'i•ta•ris'ti•cal•ly** *adv.*

mil•i•ta•rize |mĭl'ĭ tə rīz'| *v.* **mil•i•ta•rized, mil•i•ta•riz•ing. 1.** To equip or train for war; make military. **2.** To convert to militarism. —**mil'i•ta•ri•za'tion** *n.*

mil•i•tar•y |mĭl'ĭ tĕr'ē| *adj.* **1.** Of or by the armed forces: *a military base; military intervention.* **2.** Of or relating to war: *military conquest; military historians.* **3.** Characteristic of or appropriate to a soldier or to the armed forces: *a stiff military bearing.* —*n.* **the military.** Armed forces. —**mil'i•tar'i•ly** *adv.*

mil•i•tate |mĭl'ĭ tāt'| *v.* **mil•i•tat•ed, mil•i•tat•ing.** To operate or work: *His carelessness militated against his success.*

mi•li•tia |mĭ lĭsh'ə| *n.* A body of male citizens who receive military training outside the regular armed forces and who are on call for military service in times of emergency.

mi•li•tia•man |mĭ lĭsh'ə mən| *n., pl.* **-men** |-mən|. A member of a militia.

milk |mĭlk| *n.* **1. a.** A whitish liquid produced by specialized glands of female mammals for feeding their young. **b.** The milk of cows, used as food by human beings: *buy a quart of milk at the grocery store.* **2.** A liquid resembling milk: *coconut milk; milk of magnesia.* —**modifier:** *milk cattle; milk glands; milk products.* —*v.* **1.** To squeeze or draw milk from the teats or udder of: *milk a cow; spent all morning milking.* **2. a.** To subject (someone or something) to a process that extracts something by or as if by milking: *milked the snake of its venom.* **b.** To take or remove (something wanted or valuable) by or as if by milking: *ants that milk honeydew from aphids; milked venom from the snake.* [SEE PICTURE]

milk•maid |mĭlk'mād'| *n.* A girl or woman who milks cows.

milk•man |mĭlk'măn'| *n., pl.* **-men** |-mĕn'|. A man who sells or delivers milk.

milk shake. A beverage made of milk, flavoring, and usually ice cream, shaken or whipped until foamy.

milk snake. A nonpoisonous snake with brownish, gray, and black markings.

milk•sop |mĭlk'sŏp'| *n.* A boy or man who lacks courage or manliness; a weakling.

milk sugar. Lactose.

milk tooth. Any of the temporary teeth that first grow in the mouth of a young mammal.

milk•weed |mĭlk'wēd'| *n.* A plant with clusters of purplish flowers, milky juice, and large pods that split open to release downy seeds.

milk•y |mĭl'kē| *adj.* **milk•i•er, milk•i•est. 1.** Resembling milk, especially in color: *the milky sap of the rubber tree; a fair, milky complexion.* **2.** Of or containing milk or a milklike substance: *a milky pudding.* —**milk'i•ness** *n.*

Milky Way. The galaxy in which the solar system is located, visible as a bright band across the night sky.

mill¹ |mĭl| *n.* **1. a.** A machine that grinds or crushes something into powder or fine grains: *a coffee mill.* **b.** A building or establishment equipped with machines of this kind for grinding corn, wheat, etc., into flour or meal. **2.** A building or group of buildings equipped with machinery for processing a material of some kind: *a steel mill; a textile mill; a paper mill.* —*v.* **1.** To grind or crush (wheat, coffee, etc.) into powder or fine grains in a mill. **2.** To process or produce (steel, paper, etc.) in a mill. **3.** To cut or shape (metal) with a milling machine. **4.** To put ridges or grooves on the edge of (a coin). **5.** To move around in a confused or disorderly manner: *an angry crowd milling about in front of the theater.* ¶*These sound alike* **mill, mil.** [SEE NOTE]

mill² |mĭl| *n.* A unit of money equal to one-thousandth of a U.S. dollar, or one-tenth of a cent. ¶*These sound alike* **mill, mil.** [SEE NOTE]

mill•dam |mĭl'dăm'| *n.* A dam built across a stream to raise the water level so that the overflow will have enough force to turn a mill wheel.

mil•len•ni•um |mĭ lĕn'ē əm| *n., pl.* **mil•len•ni•ums** or **mil•len•ni•a** |mĭ lĕn'ē ə|. **1.** A span of one thousand years. **2.** A thousand-year reign of Christ on earth, expected by the early Christians. **3.** Any hoped-for epoch of joy, prosperity, and peace. —**mil•len'ni•al** *adj.*

mill•er |mĭl'ər| *n.* **1.** A person who works in, operates, or owns a mill for grinding grain. **2.** A moth having its wings and body covered with a whitish powder that resembles flour.

mil•let |mĭl'ĭt| *n.* **1.** A grass grown for its edible seeds and for use as hay. **2.** The white seeds of this plant, widely used as a food grain in Asia and Europe.

milli-. A word element meaning "one-thousandth": **millimeter.**

mil•li•bar |mĭl'ə bär'| *n.* A unit of pressure equal to a force of 100 newtons per square meter of surface. [SEE NOTE]

mil•li•gram |mĭl'ə grăm'| *n.* A unit of mass or

weight equal to one-thousandth of a gram.

mil•li•li•ter |mĭl′ə lē′tər| *n.* A unit of fluid volume or capacity equal to one-thousandth (10^{-3}) of a liter.

mil•li•me•ter |mĭl′ə mē′tər| *n.* A unit of length equal to one-thousandth (10^{-3}) of a meter.

mil•li•ner |mĭl′ə nər| *n.* A person who makes, trims, designs, or sells women's hats.

mil•li•ner•y |mĭl′ə nĕr′ē| *n.* **1.** Women's hats, including trimmings for hats. **2.** The business of making, designing, or selling women's hats.

mill•ing |mĭl′ĭng| *n.* **1.** The act or process of grinding, especially of grinding grain into flour or meal. **2.** The operation of cutting, shaping, or finishing metal or other products manufactured in a mill. **3.** The ridges cut on the edges of coins.

mil•lion |mĭl′yən| *n., pl.* **mil•lion** or **millions. 1.** A number, written 1,000,000 in Arabic numerals, that is equal to the sum of one thousand thousands. **2.** Often **millions.** *Informal.* An indefinitely large number: *There are millions of things that can go wrong with a car.* **—mil′lion** *adj. & pron.*

mil•lion•aire |mĭl′yə nâr′| *n.* A person whose wealth amounts to at least a million dollars, pounds, or other monetary units. ***—modifier:*** *a millionaire sportsman.*

mil•lionth |mĭl′yənth| *n.* **1.** In a set of items arranged to match the natural numbers in a one-to-one correspondence, the item that matches the number one million. **2.** One of one million equal parts of a unit; the fraction written $1/1{,}000{,}000$ or .000001, or 10^{-6}. **—mil′lionth** *adj. & adv.*

mil•li•pede |mĭl′ə pēd′| *n.* Any of a group of animals resembling the centipedes, having a body with many narrow segments, most of which have two pairs of legs. [SEE PICTURE]

mil•li•sec•ond |mĭl′ĭ sĕk′ənd| *n.* A unit of time equal to one-thousandth (10^{-3}) of a second.

mill•stone |mĭl′stōn′| *n.* **1.** One of a pair of large cylindrical stones used to grind grain. **2.** A heavy burden.

mill wheel. A wheel, usually driven by moving water, that supplies the power for a mill.

mi•lord |mĭ lôrd′| *n.* My lord. A word used in speaking of or to a man holding the rank of lord.

milque•toast |mĭlk′tōst′| *n.* A person who is meek or timid.

milt |mĭlt| *n.* The male reproductive cells of fishes, together with the liquid containing them, usually discharged into the water over the eggs laid by the female.

Mil•ton |mĭl′tən|, **John.** 1608–1674. English poet.

Mil•wau•kee |mĭl wô′kē|. The largest city in Wisconsin. Population 632,212.

mime |mīm| *n.* **1. a.** In ancient Greece and Rome, drama in which scenes and characters taken from real life were made fun of. **b.** An actor in such a play. **2. a.** Acting by means of gestures and movements without speech; pantomime. **b.** An actor in pantomime. *—v.* **mimed, mim•ing. 1.** To act out or play a part by movements of the face and body, usually without speaking. **2.** To imitate. [SEE PICTURE]

mim•e•o•graph |mĭm′ē ə grăf′| *or* |-gräf′| *n.* **1.** A machine that makes copies of material that is written, drawn, or typed on a stencil that is fitted around a drum covered with ink. **2.** A copy made by such a machine. *—v.* To copy with a mimeograph.

mim•ic |mĭm′ĭk| *v.* **mim•icked, mim•ick•ing. 1.** To copy or imitate closely, as in speech, expression, or gesture; ape. **2.** To copy or imitate so as to ridicule; mock: *American comics who mimicked President Kennedy's Boston accent.* *—n.* A person who imitates, especially a performer or comedian skilled in mimicking. *—adj.* **1.** Of or like mimicry; imitative: *the mimic antics of monkeys.* **2.** Make-believe; mock: *troop maneuvers culminating in a mimic invasion attempt.*

mim•ic•ry |mĭm′ĭk rē| *n.* **1.** The practice or art of mimicking. **2.** The resemblance of an animal, such as an insect or fish, to another kind of animal or to a leaf, stick, etc., as a means of hiding or protection from natural enemies.

mi•mo•sa |mĭ mō′sə| *or* |-zə| *n.* Any of several usually tropical trees or shrubs with featherlike leaves and ball-like clusters of small flowers.

min minute (unit of time).

min. minimum.

min•a•ret |mĭn′ə rĕt′| *n.* A tall, slender tower on a mosque from which a muezzin summons the people to prayer. [SEE PICTURE]

mince |mĭns| *v.* **minced, minc•ing. 1.** To cut or chop into very small pieces. **2.** To pronounce (words) in an affected way, as a show of refinement or elegance. **3.** To moderate or restrain (words) for the sake of politeness: *Jefferson minced no words, for the truth had to be told.* **4.** To walk in a prim or affected way, with very short steps: *members of the school band mincing along in a manner that is the reverse of military.* *—n.* Food that is finely chopped, especially mincemeat. ***—modifier:*** *mince pie.*

mince•meat |mĭns′mēt′| *n.* A mixture of finely chopped fruit, spices, suet, and sometimes meat, used especially as a pie filling.

mind |mīnd| *n.* **1.** That part of a human being which governs his thought, perception, feeling, will, memory, and imagination. **2.** The power to think and reason and to apply these processes constructively in one's actions; intellect and intelligence, distinguished from emotion or will. **3.** Center of attention: *keeping his mind on his job.* **4.** Time covered by remembrance; memory; recall: *the strangest coincidence within the mind of man.* **5.** Opinion or sentiment; position or point of view: *change one's mind.* **6.** Desire; purpose: *had half a mind not to go.* **7.** A healthy mental condition; sanity: *lose one's mind.* **8.** A person considered according to intellect or intelligence: *Newton, one of the greatest minds of science.* *—v.* **1.** To object to or dislike; care or be concerned: *The pony didn't mind the saddle. The wind howled, but I didn't mind.* **2.** To obey: *Mind your older brother. Good children always mind.* **3.** To take care or take charge of; look after: *She stayed home to mind the baby.* **4.** To attend to: *Mind your own affairs.* **5.** To make sure: *Mind you drive slowly.* **6.** To take notice; give heed: *This can change our lives, and change them, mind you, for the better.* **7.** To be careful about; take heed: *Mind how you swing that lance.* [SEE NOTE on p. 558]

Idioms. **in (one's) mind's eye.** As pictured in one's mind. **make up (one's) mind.** To reach a

millipede

mime
Marcel Marceau as his character Bip

minaret

mine[1-2]

Mine[1] is from Old French mine, *which is ultimately from a Celtic word meaning "ore."* **Mine[2]** *was Old English* mīn; **my** *is a reduced form of* mīn. *It is closely related to* mē, *which was* mē *or* me *in Old English and is descended from the prehistoric Indo-European pronoun* me-. *This pronoun appears with little change in all of the Indo-European languages, from Irish to Sanskrit.*

mini–/mini

The word **miniature** *did not originally mean "small." Its original meaning was "a painted book illustration"; since the illustrations in medieval books were usually very small and fine, the word* **miniature** *came to mean "a very small painting" (sense* **2.a.** *of the noun). It seems likely that the similarity of the word* **miniature** *to the unrelated words* **minimum, minute[2]**, *etc., helped* **miniature** *to take on the meaning "anything very small." And very probably the prefix* **mini-** *comes from both* **miniature** *and* **minimum**; *very recently the separate noun* **mini** *has appeared, referring to anything very small of its kind, from a skirt to a car.*

ă pat/ā pay/â care/ä father/ĕ pet/ ē be/ĭ pit/ī pie/î fierce/ŏ pot/ ō go/ô paw, for/oi oil/o͝o book/ o͞o boot/ou out/ŭ cut/û fur/ *th* the/th thin/hw which/zh vision/ ə ago, item, pencil, atom, circus

definite decision or opinion; decide. **never mind.** Disregard it; it doesn't matter. **on (one's) mind.** In one's thoughts. **out of (one's) mind. 1.** Insane. **2.** Frantic; wild. **piece of (one's) mind.** *Informal.* One's bluntly stated opinion, especially a strong rebuke. **put (one) in mind.** *Informal.* To remind one: *Her remark put me in mind of an experience I had.*

mind•ed |mīn'dĭd| *adj.* **1.** Having an intention; disposed; inclined: *He can speak like a book when so minded.* **2.** Having a specific kind of mind: *a strong-minded person.*

mind•ful |mīnd'fəl| *adj.* Attentive; aware; heedful: *always mindful of the danger of fire.*

mind•less |mīnd'lĭs| *adj.* **1.** Lacking intelligence or good sense; foolish. **2.** Giving or showing little attention or care: *going full-speed, mindless of the threat of ice.* —**mind'less•ly** *adv.*

mine[1] |mīn| *n.* **1. a.** A hole, tunnel, or passage dug in the earth in order to extract metals, coal, salt, or other minerals. **b.** The site of such an excavation, with its buildings, elevators, and associated equipment. **2.** An abundant supply or source of something valuable: *a mine of information.* **3. a.** A tunnel or excavation made under enemy positions or fortifications, usually in order to place explosives and destroy them. **b.** An explosive charge placed in such an excavation. **c.** A bomb or similar explosive device left floating or anchored in a body of water, capable of detecting the presence of a ship and exploding when one is nearby. **d.** A **land mine.** —*v.* **mined, min•ing. 1. a.** To extract (ores or minerals) from the earth. **b.** To dig or tunnel in the earth for this purpose. **2.** To place explosive mines in or under: *mine a harbor.* [SEE NOTE]

mine[2] |mīn| *pron.* A possessive form of **I. 1.** —Used to indicate that something or someone belongs or pertains to me; my own: *It can't be mine. You're no friend of mine.* **2.** —Used to indicate the one or ones belonging to me:, *a method different from mine.* **3.** *Archaic.* My: *mine honor; write mine epitaph.* —*Note*: In modern writing, *mine* is seldom used for *my* before a noun, as in the examples at 3. When it is used in this way, *mine* occurs directly before words beginning with *h* or a vowel. [SEE NOTE]

min•er |mī'nər| *n.* Someone who works in a mine and extracts minerals from the earth. ¶*These sound alike* **miner, minor.**

min•er•al |mĭn'ər əl| *n.* **1.** Any natural substance that has a definite chemical composition and characteristic physical structure. **2.** Any substance, such as granite or other rock, composed of a mixture of minerals. **3.** Any substance, such as coal or petroleum, that is organic in origin but has been changed into a form like that of a mineral. **4. a.** A metal, such as gold or silver, that is found uncombined in nature. **b.** An ore of a metal. **5.** Any substance that is not of plant or animal origin. —***modifier:*** *mineral deposits; mineral water.*

min•er•a•log•i•cal |mĭn'ər ə lŏj'ĭ kəl| *adj.* Of mineralogy. —**min'er•a•log'i•cal•ly** *adv.*

min•er•al•o•gist |mĭn'ə rŏl'ə jĭst| *or* |-răl'-| *n.* A scientist who specializes in mineralogy.

min•er•al•o•gy |mĭn'ə rŏl'ə jē| *or* |-răl'-| *n.* The scientific study of minerals and their distribution, identification, and properties.

mineral oil. Any of various light oils distilled from petroleum, especially a refined oil used in medicine as a laxative.

Mi•ner•va |mĭ nûr'və|. The Roman goddess of wisdom.

Ming |mĭng| *n.* A Chinese dynasty that ruled from 1368 to 1644, noted for its achievements in scholarship and the arts. —***modifier:*** *Ming emperors.*

min•gle |mĭng'gəl| *v.* **min•gled, min•gling. 1.** To mix or become mixed; unite; combine: *an expression that mingles grief and shame; chimes that mingled with the peal of the doorbell.* **2.** To become closely associated; join or take part with others: *people of all kinds mingling at the airport.*

mini–. A word element meaning "small": **miniskirt**; *minibus.* [SEE NOTE]

min•i |mĭn'ē| *n.* Anything that has a name beginning with *mini-*. [SEE NOTE]

min•i•a•ture |mĭn'ē ə chər| *or* |mĭn'ə-| *adj.* On a greatly reduced scale from the usual: *a miniature computer; miniature poodles.* —*n.* **1.** A copy or model that represents or reproduces something in greatly reduced size. **2. a.** A very small painting or portrait. **b.** A literary or musical work on a small scale.

min•i•a•tur•ize |mĭn'ē ə chə rīz'| *or* |mĭn'ə-| *v.* **min•i•a•tur•ized, min•i•a•tur•iz•ing** To plan or make on a greatly reduced scale.

min•im |mĭn'əm| *n.* A unit of fluid measure equal to $^1/_{60}$ of a fluid dram.

min•i•ma |mĭn'ə mə| *n.* A plural of **minimum.**

min•i•mal |mĭn'ə məl| *adj.* Smallest in amount or degree; least possible: *a task requiring minimal labor.* —**min'i•mal•ly** *adv.*

min•i•mize |mĭn'ə mīz'| *v.* **min•i•mized, min•i•miz•ing. 1.** To reduce to the smallest possible amount, extent, size, or degree: *keeping a finger in one ear to minimize the bell's clang.* **2.** To speak or write of as having the least degree of importance, value, or size; depreciate: *history books that minimize the contributions of minority groups.* —**min'i•mi•za'tion** *n.* —**min'i•miz'er** *n.*

min•i•mum |mĭn'ə məm| *n., pl.* **min•i•mums** or **min•i•ma** |mĭn'ə mə|. **1.** The smallest quantity or degree possible or allowable: *conveying ideas with a minimum of words.* **2.** The lowest quantity, degree, or number reached or recorded: *Yesterday's temperature minimum was only 75°.* —*adj.* **1.** Representing the least possible or allowed: *taking a minimum number of shirts.* **2.** Representing the lowest amount or degree reached or recorded: *statistics on minimum rainfall.*

minimum wage. The lowest wage, set by law or contract, that an employer may pay an employee for a specified job.

min•ing |mī'nĭng| *n.* **1.** The work, process, or business of extracting coal, minerals, ore, etc., from the earth. **2.** The process of placing explosive mines. —***modifier:*** *a mining engineer; mining machinery.*

min•ion |mĭn'yən| *n.* **1.** A person who is much loved or admired; a favorite. **2.** A person who follows or serves another in a slavish or servile manner.

min•i•skirt |mĭn'ē skûrt'| *n.* An extremely short skirt that extends to about the middle of the thigh or above. —**min'i•skirt'ed** *adj.*

min•is•ter |mĭn'ĭ stər| *n.* **1.** A clergyman; pastor of a church. **2.** A person in charge of a department of a country's government: *the minister of cultural affairs.* **3.** A person ranking below an ambassador who represents his government in diplomatic dealings in a foreign country. *—v.* To attend to the needs of others: *Nurses ministered to the wounded soldiers.* —**min'is·te'ri·al** |mĭn'ĭ stîr'ē əl| *adj.*

min·is·tra·tion |mĭn'ĭ strā'shən| *n.* **1. a.** The act or process of serving or aiding. **b.** The service or aid given. **2.** The act of performing the duties of a minister of religion.

min·is·try |mĭn'ĭ strē| *n., pl.* **min·is·tries. 1.** The position and duties of a minister of religion. **2.** Ministers of religion in general; the clergy. **3. a.** A department of government of which a minister has charge. **b.** The position, duties, and length of service of such a governmental minister. **c.** Governmental ministers in general. **4.** The act of serving or aiding.

mink |mĭngk| *n.* **1.** A weasellike animal with thick, soft brown fur. **2.** The fur of this animal, often used to make or trim clothing. *—**modifier:** a mink coat.* [SEE PICTURE]

Minn. Minnesota.

Min·ne·ap·o·lis |mĭn'ē ăp'ə lĭs|. The largest city in Minnesota. Population, 370,951.

Min·ne·so·ta |mĭn'ĭ sō'tə|. A north-central state of the United States. Population, 4,077,148. Capital, St. Paul. —**Min'ne·so'tan** *adj. & n.*

min·now |mĭn'ō| *n.* Any of several small freshwater fishes often used as bait.

Mi·no·an |mĭ nō'ən| *adj.* Of the Bronze Age culture that flourished in Crete from about 3000 to 1100 B.C.

mi·nor |mī'nər| *adj.* **1.** Smaller in amount, size, or extent: *minor expenses; a minor change.* **2.** Lesser in importance or rank: *a minor role; minor planets.* **3.** Lesser in seriousness or danger: *minor faults; a minor skirmish.* **4.** Not yet a legal adult: *minor children.* **5. a.** Of a minor scale. **b.** Smaller by a half step than the corresponding major interval: *a minor third; a minor sixth.* **c.** Containing a minor third: *a minor triad.* **d.** Based on a minor scale: *a minor key.* *—n.* **1.** A person who has not yet reached legal age. **2.** A subject to which a college student devotes fewer class hours than he spends on a major subject. **3.** A minor key, scale, interval or triad. **4. the minors.** The minor leagues of a sport in general. *—v.* To pursue studies in a minor academic field: *He is minoring in history.* ¶ *These sound alike* **minor, miner.**

Mi·nor·ca |mĭ nôr'kə|. One of the Balearic Islands.

mi·nor·i·ty |mĭ nôr'ĭ tē| *or* |-nŏr'-| *or* |mī-| *n., pl.* **mi·nor·i·ties. 1.** The smaller in number of two groups forming a whole. **2.** A group of people regarded as different from the larger population of which it is a part because of race, religion, politics, national origin, etc. **3.** The period before the attainment of the status of an adult: *an heir still in his minority.* *—**modifier:** minority groups; the minority view.*

minor league. In sports, a league that ranks below a major league in quality of play and usually in respect to the size of member cities; a subordinate league or group. *—**modifier:*** **(minor-league):** *a minor-league club.*

minor scale. A musical scale having whole tones between its first and second, third and fourth, and fourth and fifth steps, with a semitone between the second and third steps. It has several forms with different intervals above the fifth step.

Mi·nos |mī'nəs| *or* |-nŏs'|. In Greek mythology, a king of Crete.

Min·o·taur |mĭn'ə tôr'|. In Greek mythology, a monster, half bull and half human, slain in the Labyrinth by Theseus.

min·strel |mĭn'strəl| *n.* **1.** A medieval musician who traveled from place to place, singing and reciting poetry. **2.** A performer in a minstrel show.

minstrel show. A show, formerly popular in the United States, consisting of songs, dances, and jokes, given by performers some of whom were made up to play the part of Negroes.

min·strel·sy |mĭn'strəl sē| *n.* **1.** The art or profession of a minstrel. **2.** The songs or verses sung or recited by minstrels.

mint[1] |mĭnt| *n.* **1.** Any of several plants with leaves that have a strong, pleasant smell and taste and are the source of an oil used to flavor candy, chewing gum, etc. **2.** A candy with this flavor. [SEE NOTE]

mint[2] |mĭnt| *n.* **1.** A place where the coins of a country are made by authority of the government. **2.** *Informal.* A large amount, especially of money: *Jack's father left him a mint of money.* *—v.* **1.** To produce (money) by stamping metal; coin. **2.** To invent; make up: *a talent for minting funny expressions.* *—adj.* In original condition; freshly minted or made; unused: *dimes in mint condition.* [SEE NOTE]

mint·age |mĭn'tĭj| *n.* **1.** The act or process of minting coins. **2.** Money manufactured in a mint. **3.** The fee paid to a mint by a government for which coins have been made. **4.** The impression stamped on a coin.

mint julep. An iced drink made with whiskey, sugar, and crushed mint leaves, served in a tall frosted glass.

min·u·end |mĭn'yōō ĕnd'| *n.* A number from which another number is to be subtracted; for example, in the expression 8 = 5, 8 is the minuend.

min·u·et |mĭn'yōō ĕt'| *n.* **1.** A slow, stately dance that originated in 17th-century France. **2.** Music written to accompany or as if to accompany this dance.

mi·nus |mī'nəs| *prep.* **1.** Reduced by the subtraction of: *Seven minus four equals three.* **2.** *Informal.* Without; lacking: *arrived minus his wallet.* *—adj.* **1.** Less than zero; negative: *a minus value.* **2.** Slightly lower or less than: *a grade of A minus.* *—n.* **1.** Also **minus sign.** The sign (-) used to indicate subtraction or a negative number. **2.** A negative number or quantity.

min·us·cule |mĭn'ə skyōōl'| *or* |mĭ nŭs'kyōōl'| *n.* **1. a.** A style of writing having small letters, used in medieval manuscripts. **b.** A letter written in such a style. **2.** A lower-case letter. *—adj.* **1.** Of or written in minuscule. **2.** Very small; tiny: *minuscule screws.*

min·ute[1] |mĭn'ĭt| *n.* **1.** A unit of time equal to 1/60 of an hour or 60 seconds. **2.** A unit of angular measurement that is equal to 1/60 of a degree or

mink

mint[1-2]

Mint[1] *is ultimately from Greek* minthē, *"mint plant."* **Mint[2]** *is ultimately from Latin* monēta, *which meant both "the mint" and "money."* Monēta *was separately borrowed into Old French as* moneie, *and thence into English as* **money.**

60 seconds. **3.** Any short interval of time; a moment: *Wait a minute.* **4.** A specific point in time: *leaving this very minute.* **5. minutes.** An official record of the events or doings at a meeting of an organization. [SEE NOTE]

mi•nute[2] |mī no͞ot′| *or* |-nyo͞ot′| *or* |mĭ-| *adj.* **1.** Exceptionally small; tiny. **2.** Marked by close examination or careful study of small details: *a minute inspection of bacteria.* **—mi•nute′ly** *adv.* **—mi•nute′ness** *n.* [SEE NOTE]

min•ute•man, also **Min•ute•man** |mĭn′ĭt măn′| *n., pl.* **-men** |-mĕn′|. In the Revolutionary War, a member of the American militia or any armed civilian pledged to be ready to fight on a minute's notice.

mi•nu•ti•ae |mĭ no͞o′shē ē′| *or* |-nyo͞o′-| *pl.n.* The less frequently used singular is **mi•nu•ti•a** |mĭ no͞o′shē ə| *or* |-shə| *or* |-nyo͞o′-|. Details that are small or of little importance.

minx |mĭngks| *n.* A girl who is high-spirited, impudent, or flirtatious.

Mi•o•cene |mī′ə sēn′| *n.* Also **Miocene epoch.** A geologic epoch that began about 25 million years ago and ended about 13 million years ago, characterized by the appearance of whales, grazing animals, and primitive apes. ***—modifier:*** *a Miocene fossil.*

mir•a•cle |mĭr′ə kəl| *n.* **1.** An event believed to be an act of God or of a supernatural power because it appears impossible to explain by the laws of nature. **2.** A person, thing, or event that causes great admiration, awe, or wonder: *a miracle of money management; surgical miracles.*

miracle play. A religious drama of the Middle Ages based on the lives of saints or martyrs who performed miracles.

mi•rac•u•lous |mĭ răk′yə ləs| *adj.* **1.** Having the nature of a miracle: *a miraculous operation.* **2.** Having the power to work miracles: *a miraculous drug.* **—mi•rac′u•lous•ly** *adv.* **—mi•rac′u•lous•ness** *n.*

mi•rage |mĭ räzh′| *n.* An optical illusion in which nonexistent bodies of water and upside-down reflections of distant objects are seen. It is caused by distortions that occur as light passes between layers of air that are at different temperatures.

mire |mīr| *n.* **1.** An area of wet, muddy ground; a bog. **2.** Deep, slimy soil or mud. *—v.* **mired, mir•ing. 1.** To sink or become stuck in mire. **2.** To cause to sink or become stuck in mire.

mir•ror |mĭr′ər| *n.* **1.** Any surface that is capable of reflecting enough light without scattering it so that it shows an image of any object placed in front of it. **2.** A piece of reflecting glass that enables a person to see his own image. **3.** Anything that gives a general picture of something else: *The city is a mirror of the nation's progress.* *—v.* To reflect in or as if in a mirror: *The lake mirrored the sky and the clouds. Your voice often mirrors your personality.*

mirth |mûrth| *n.* Gaiety or merriment: *shouts of mirth.*

mirth•ful |mûrth′fəl| *adj.* Full of mirth; merry; gay. **—mirth′ful•ly** *adv.*

mis–. A prefix meaning: **1.** Error or wrongness: **misspell. 2.** Badness or impropriety: **misbehave. 3.** Opposite or lack of: **mistrust. 4.** Failure: **misfire.**

mis•ad•ven•ture |mĭs′əd vĕn′chər| *n.* An example of great misfortune; a disaster.

mis•an•thrope |mĭs′ən thrōp′| *or* |mĭz′-| *n.* A person who hates or distrusts mankind.

mis•an•throp•ic |mĭs′ən thrŏp′ĭk| *or* |mĭz′-| or **mis•an•throp•i•cal** |mĭs′ən thrŏp′ĭ kəl| *or* |mĭz′-| *adj.* Of or characteristic of a misanthrope.

mis•ap•ply |mĭs′ə plī′| *v.* **mis•ap•plied, mis•ap•ply•ing, mis•ap•plies.** To use or apply wrongly: *The word "horns" is often misapplied to include "antlers."* **—mis′ap•pli•ca′tion** *n.*

mis•ap•pre•hend |mĭs′ăp rĭ hĕnd′| *v.* To fail to interpret correctly; misunderstand: *misapprehend an order.*

mis•ap•pre•hen•sion |mĭs′ăp rĭ hĕn′shən| *n.* A failure to interpret correctly; a misunderstanding: *a misapprehension of one's intentions.*

mis•ap•pro•pri•ate |mĭs′ə prō′prē āt′| *v.* **mis•ap•pro•pri•at•ed, mis•ap•pro•pri•at•ing.** To take dishonestly for one's own use; embezzle: *misappropriate government funds.* **—mis′ap•pro′pri•a′tion** *n.*

mis•be•got•ten |mĭs′bĭ gŏt′n| *adj.* Born out of wedlock; illegitimate.

mis•be•have |mĭs′bĭ hāv′| *v.* **mis•be•haved, mis•be•hav•ing.** To behave badly. **—mis′be•hav′ior** *n.*

mis•cal•cu•late |mĭs kăl′kyə lāt′| *v.* **mis•cal•cu•lat•ed, mis•cal•cu•lat•ing. 1.** To calculate incorrectly; make a wrong estimate of: *I miscalculated the distance between the house and the river.* **2.** To make an error in judgment: *The coach seriously miscalculated the strength of the visiting team.* **—mis′cal•cu•la′tion** *n.*

mis•car•riage |mĭs kăr′ĭj| *n.* **1.** Failure to achieve the proper or desired result: *the miscarriage of a plan.* **2.** The birth of a fetus before it is developed enough to survive.

mis•car•ry |mĭs kăr′ē| *v.* **mis•car•ried, mis•car•ry•ing, mis•car•ries. 1.** To fail; go wrong: *The plan miscarried.* **2.** To bring forth a fetus too early; abort.

mis•cast |mĭs kăst′| *or* |-käst′| *v.* **mis•cast, mis•cast•ing.** To cast (a performer) in an unsuitable role.

mis•ce•ge•na•tion |mĭs′ĭ jə nā′shən| *or* |mĭ-sĕj′ə-| *n.* Breeding between persons who are considered to be of different races.

mis•cel•la•ne•ous |mĭs′ə lā′nē əs| *adj.* **1.** Made up of a variety of different elements or ingredients: *a miscellaneous assortment of chocolates.* **2.** Not falling into a particular category: *miscellaneous items in a budget.*

mis•cel•la•ny |mĭs′ə lā′nē| *n., pl.* **mis•cel•la•nies.** A collection of various items, parts, etc., especially of works of literature.

mis•chance |mĭs chăns′| *or* |-chäns′| *n.* An unfortunate occurrence caused by chance or luck: *If by some mischance I should be late, please substitute for me.*

mis•chief |mĭs′chĭf| *n.* **1. a.** Naughty or improper behavior. **b.** Trouble resulting from such behavior: *Hardly a day goes by that he doesn't get into some mischief.* **2.** A tendency to misbehave or cause trouble: *Little Johnny is full of mischief.* **3.** Harm or damage: *I hope you're proud of the mischief you've done!* [SEE NOTE]

mis•chie•vous |mĭs′chə vəs| *adj.* **1.** Full of

minute[1-2]

Minute[2] *is from Latin* minūtus, *"reduced, small," the past participle of* minuere, *"to make small, reduce." (The root* min-, *meaning "small," occurs also in* **minor** *and* **minimum**; *but see note at* **mini-**.*)* **Minute[1]** *is from Latin* minūta, *"small part," from* minūtus, *as above.*

mischief

"A little neglect may breed mischief: for want of a nail the shoe was lost; for want of a shoe the horse was lost; and for want of a horse the rider was lost." —*Benjamin Franklin.*

ă pat/ā pay/â care/ä father/ĕ pet/ē be/ĭ pit/ī pie/î fierce/ŏ pot/ō go/ô paw, for/oi oil/o͝o book/o͞o boot/ou out/ŭ cut/û fur/*th* the/th thin/hw which/zh vision/ə ago, item, pencil, atom, circus

mischief; naughty: *a mischievous child.* **2.** Showing a tendency to do mischief: *a mischievous look on one's face.* **3.** Causing harm or damage: *a mischievous act.* —**mis'chie•vous•ly** *adv.* —**mis'chie•vous•ness** *n.*

mis•ci•ble |mĭs'ə bəl| *adj.* Capable of being mixed in all proportions: *Water and alcohol are miscible.*

mis•con•ceive |mĭs'kən sēv'| *v.* **mis•con•ceived, mis•con•ceiv•ing.** To interpret incorrectly; misunderstand.

mis•con•cep•tion |mĭs'kən sĕp'shən| *n.* A mistaken idea; a delusion: *the misconception that wealth alone brings true happiness.*

mis•con•duct |mĭs kŏn'dŭkt| *n.* Improper conduct or behavior: *The judge was impeached for misconduct in office.*

mis•con•strue |mĭs'kən stro͞o'| *v.* **mis•con•strued, mis•con•stru•ing.** To mistake the meaning of; misinterpret; misunderstand: *misconstrue someone's words.*

mis•count |mĭs kount'| *v.* To count incorrectly. —*n.* |mĭs'kount'|. An inaccurate count.

mis•cre•ant |mĭs'krē ənt| *n.* An evil person; a villain.

mis•deal |mĭs dēl'| *v.* **mis•dealt** |mĭs dĕlt'|, **mis•deal•ing.** To deal (playing cards) incorrectly. —*n.* |mĭs'dēl'|. An incorrect dealing of playing cards.

mis•deed |mĭs dēd'| *n.* A wrong or improper act.

mis•de•mean•or |mĭs'dĭ mē'nər| *n.* In law, an offense less serious than a felony.

mis•di•rect |mĭs'dĭ rĕkt'| *or* |-dī-| *v.* **1.** To give incorrect or inaccurate instructions to: *misdirect a passer-by.* **2.** To put a wrong address on: *misdirect a letter.* **3.** To direct or channel toward an unworthy goal: *misdirect one's efforts.* —**mis'di•rec'tion** *n.*

mis•do•ing |mĭs do͞o'ĭng| *n.* Wrongdoing.

mi•ser |mī'zər| *n.* A stingy person, especially one who likes to hoard money.

mis•er•a•ble |mĭz'ər ə bəl| *or* |mĭz'rə-| *adj.* **1.** Very unhappy; wretched: *He has made her life miserable.* **2.** Bad; rotten; awful: *miserable weather.* **3.** Mean; shameful; disgraceful: *That was a miserable trick to play on her!* **4.** Wretchedly poor; squalid: *a miserable shack in the woods.* —**mis'er•a•bly** *adv.*

mi•ser•ly |mī'zər lē| *adj.* Like or typical of a miser; stingy: *too miserly to leave a tip.* —**mi'ser•li•ness** *n.*

mis•er•y |mĭz'ə rē| *n., pl.* **mis•er•ies. 1.** Prolonged suffering or distress: *Dad has been in misery for days with a pain in his shoulder.* **2.** Miserable conditions of life; dire poverty: *millions of people living in misery.* [SEE NOTE]

mis•fire |mĭs fīr'| *v.* **mis•fired, mis•fir•ing. 1.** To fail to fire or go off: *The gun misfired.* **2.** To fail to achieve the desired result; go awry: *His elaborate plan misfired.* —*n.* |mĭs'fīr'|. An example of misfiring.

mis•fit |mĭs'fĭt'| *or* |mĭs fĭt'| *n.* **1.** Something, especially a garment, that does not fit properly. **2.** A person who is badly adjusted to his work or is out of place among his associates or peers.

mis•for•tune |mĭs fôr'chən| *n.* **1.** Bad luck or fortune: *Be brave in times of misfortune.* **2.** An unfortunate occurrence: *The hurricane was a great misfortune for the fishermen of the area.*

mis•giv•ing |mĭs gĭv'ĭng| *n.* Often **misgivings.** A feeling of doubt or concern: *She has misgivings about lending him her new car.*

mis•gov•ern |mĭs gŭv'ərn| *v.* To govern or rule badly. —**mis•gov'ern•ment** *n.*

mis•guid•ed |mĭs gī'dĭd| *adj.* **1.** Mistaken; unrealistic: *a misguided faith in everyone's honesty.* **2.** Acting or done out of mistaken opinions or beliefs: *misguided efforts.* —**mis•guid'ed•ly** *adv.*

mis•han•dle |mĭs hăn'dl| *v.* **mis•han•dled, mis•han•dling. 1.** To handle roughly: *mishandle a parcel in the mail.* **2.** To manage badly: *mishandle money.*

mis•hap |mĭs'hăp'| *or* |mĭs hăp'| *n.* An unfortunate accident: *The trip was completed without mishap.*

mish•mash |mĭsh'măsh'| *or* |-mäsh'| *n.* A random mixture of unrelated things; a hodgepodge.

mis•in•form |mĭs'ĭn fôrm'| *v.* To give wrong or inaccurate information to: *She has misinformed you about her plans for her vacation.* —**mis'in•for•ma'tion** *n.*

mis•in•ter•pret |mĭs'ĭn tûr'prĭt| *v.* To draw the wrong conclusion from; interpret or understand incorrectly: *misinterpret someone's remarks.* —**mis'in•ter'pre•ta'tion** *n.*

mis•judge |mĭs jŭj'| *v.* **mis•judged, mis•judg•ing.** To judge, estimate, or evaluate incorrectly: *misjudge a person; misjudge a fly ball.* —**mis•judg'ment** *n.*

mis•lay |mĭs lā'| *v.* **mis•laid** |mĭs lād'|, **mis•lay•ing.** To lay or put down in a place one cannot remember: *I've mislaid my notebook.*

mis•lead |mĭs lēd'| *v.* **mis•led** |mĭs lĕd'|, **mis•lead•ing. 1.** To lead or guide in the wrong direction: *The sign at the traffic circle completely misled us.* **2.** To cause to gain a wrong impression: *misled by the false rumors.* **3.** To lead into wrongdoing: *Bad companions misled him and he lost his job.* —**mis•lead'ing** *adj.*: *misleading information.*

mis•man•age |mĭs măn'ĭj| *v.* **mis•man•aged, mis•man•ag•ing.** To manage badly or ineptly. —**mis•man'age•ment** *n.*

mis•match |mĭs măch'| *v.* To bring together or pair (people, teams, etc.) that are not right for each other. —*n.* |mĭs'măch'|. A bad match: *I think a marriage between them would be a terrible mismatch.*

mis•no•mer |mĭs nō'mər| *n.* A name that is wrongly applied: *To call a whale a "fish" would be to use a misnomer.*

mi•sog•y•nist |mĭ sŏj'ə nĭst| *n.* A person who hates women.

mis•place |mĭs plās'| *v.* **mis•placed, mis•plac•ing. 1.** To put in a wrong place. **2.** To mislay; lose: *misplace one's keys.* **3.** To place (trust, confidence, etc.) unwisely.

mis•print |mĭs'prĭnt'| *or* |mĭs prĭnt'| *n.* An error in printing.

mis•pro•nounce |mĭs'prə nouns'| *v.* **mis•pro•nounced, mis•pro•nounc•ing.** To pronounce incorrectly.

mis•quote |mĭs kwōt'| *v.* **mis•quot•ed, mis•quot•ing.** To quote incorrectly. —**mis'quo•ta'tion** *n.*

mis•read |mĭs rēd'| *v.* **mis•read** |mĭs rĕd'|, **mis•read•ing. 1.** To read incorrectly: *misread a sign.* **2.** To draw the wrong conclusion from; misin-

misery

"God doth not promise here
to man, that He
Will quickly free him
from his misery;
But in His own time,
and when He thinks fit,
Then He will give
a happy end to it."
—Robert Herrick (1647).

"Many of our miseries are merely comparative; we are often made unhappy, not by the presence of any real evil, but by the absence of some fictitious good."—Samuel Johnson (1753).

terpret: *I misread the nod of your head to mean "yes."*

mis•rep•re•sent |mĭs'rĕp'rĭ **zĕnt'**| *v.* To represent in a false or misleading manner: *The reporter's account of the meeting misrepresented the mayor's statements.* —**mis'rep•re•sen•ta'tion** *n.*

mis•rule |mĭs **rōōl'**| *n.* Incompetent or unjust rule: *The king was finally overthrown after twenty years of misrule.* —*v.* **mis•ruled, mis•rul•ing.** To rule incompetently or unjustly.

miss¹ |mĭs| *v.* **1.** To fail to hit or make contact with: *The shot missed the target. I fired three times but missed.* **2.** To fail to catch: *The first baseman missed the ball. I lunged for the ball but missed.* **3.** To fail to see or notice: *I missed the item in the newspaper. We missed the television special last night.* **4.** To fail to attend or be present for: *She missed three weeks of school.* **5.** To fail to meet: *We missed each other by seconds.* **6.** To fail to understand or grasp: *You're missing my point.* **7.** To fail to accomplish: *He just missed winning the race.* **8.** To be late for; not reach on time: *miss a school bus.* **9.** To fail to answer correctly; get wrong: *Of the twenty questions on the test I only missed two.* **10.** To let slip by: *miss one's turn.* **11.** To feel or regret the absence or loss of: *I miss my sister very much. I miss the friendliness of my home town.* **12.** To notice the absence or loss of: *It was only after we left the theater that I missed my wallet.* **13.** To avoid or escape: *That way you'll miss most of the traffic.* **14.** To lack: *The book is missing a few pages.* **15.** To fail to gain the benefit or pleasure of something: *I didn't want to miss out on any of the fun.* —*n.* A failure to hit, reach, touch, etc.: *a near miss; one bull's eye and two misses.* [SEE NOTE]

miss¹·²
Miss¹ *was Old English* missan; *its basic meaning was "to go wrong."* **Miss²** *is shortened from* **mistress.**

miss² |mĭs| *n.* **1.** An unmarried woman or girl: *a cute young miss.* **2. a. Miss.** A title of courtesy used before the last name of an unmarried woman or girl: *My teacher is Miss White.* **b.** A word used in speaking to an unmarried woman or girl, used without her name: *I beg your pardon, Miss.* **3. misses.** A range of sizes for girls' and women's clothes. [SEE NOTE & SEE NOTE on p. 586]

Miss. Mississippi.

mis•sal |**mĭs'**əl| *n.* A book containing all the prayers and responses necessary for celebrating the Roman Catholic Mass throughout the year. ¶*These sound alike* **missal, missile.**

mis•shap•en |mĭs **shā'**pən| *adj.* Shaped badly; deformed.

mis•sile |**mĭs'**əl| *or* |-īl'| *n.* **1.** Any object or weapon that is thrown, fired, dropped, or otherwise launched at a target. **2.** A **guided missile. 3.** A **ballistic missile.** —***modifier:*** *a missile launcher; a missile attack.* ¶*These sound alike* **missile, missal.**

miss•ing |**mĭs'**ĭng| *adj.* **1.** Lost: *the bureau of missing persons. He was listed as missing in action.* **2.** Absent: *Who is missing from class today?* **3.** Lacking: *Several pages are missing from the book.*

mis•sion |**mĭsh'**ən| *n.* **1.** An assignment that a person or group of persons is sent to carry out; a task: *a rescue mission; a goodwill mission.* **2.** A permanent diplomatic office in a foreign country: *the Norwegian mission to the United Nations.* **3.** A combat operation, especially a flight into a combat zone by military aircraft: *a bombing mission.* **4.** An establishment of missionaries in some territory or foreign country: *Los Angeles started as a small Spanish mission.* **5.** Something that a person assumes to be the main task of his life: *Her mission in life is helping the needy.*

mis•sion•ar•y |**mĭsh'**ə nĕr'ē| *n., pl.* **mis•sion•ar•ies.** A person sent to do religious or charitable work in some territory or foreign country. —***modifier:*** *missionary work.*

Mis•sis•sip•pi¹ |mĭs'ĭ **sĭp'**ē|. A Southern state of the United States. Population, 2,234,000. Capital, Jackson. —**Mis'sis•sip'pi•an** *adj. & n.*

Mis•sis•sip•pi² |mĭs'ĭ **sĭp'**ē|. A river in the central United States, rising in Minnesota and flowing south to the Gulf of Mexico.

Mis•sis•sip•pi•an |mĭs'ĭ **sĭp'**ē ən| *n.* Also **Mississippian period.** A geologic period that began about 345 million years ago and ended about 310 million years ago. —***modifier:*** *a Mississipian fossil.*

mis•sive |**mĭs'**ĭv| *n.* A letter or message.

Mis•sou•ri¹ |mĭ **zŏŏr'**ē| *or* |**-zŏŏr'**ə|. A Midwestern state of the United States. Population, 4,718,000. Capital, Jefferson City. —**Mis•sou'ri•an** *adj. & n.*

Mis•sou•ri² |mĭ **zŏŏr'**ē| *or* |**-zŏŏr'**ə|. A river rising in Montana and joining the Mississippi near St. Louis.

Mis•sou•ri³ |mĭ **zŏŏr'**ē| *or* |**-zŏŏr'**ə| *n., pl.* **Mis•sou•ri** or **Mis•sou•ris. 1.** A North American Indian tribe formerly living in Missouri. **2.** A member of this tribe. **3.** The Siouan language of this tribe.

mis•spell |mĭs **spĕl'**| *v.* **mis•spelled** or **mis•spelt** |mĭs **spĕlt'**|, **mis•spell•ing.** To spell incorrectly.

mis•spend |mĭs **spĕnd'**| *v.* **mis•spent** |mĭs-**spĕnt'**|, **mis•spend•ing.** To spend improperly, foolishly, or wastefully; squander.

mis•state |mĭs **stāt'**| *v.* **mis•stat•ed, mis•stat•ing.** To state wrongly or falsely; give a wrong account of. —**mis•state'ment** *n.*

mis•step |mĭs **stĕp'**| *n.* **1.** A misplaced or awkward step. **2.** A mistake in action or conduct.

miss•y |**mĭs'**ē| *n., pl.* **miss•ies.** Often **Missy.** A familiar form of the word **miss.**

mist |mĭst| *n.* **1.** A mass of tiny droplets of water in the air, close to or touching the earth. **2.** Water vapor that condenses on and clouds a surface: *mist on a windowpane.* **3.** A mass of tiny drops of any liquid, as perfume, sprayed into the air. **4.** Something that dims or obscures; a haze. —*v.* To rain in a fine shower: *It began to mist at four o'clock.*

mis•take |mĭ **stāk'**| *n.* An action, decision, assumption, computation, etc., that is wrong; an error: *a mistake in arithmetic; a mistake in judgment.* —*v.* **mis•took** |mĭ **stŏŏk'**|, **mis•tak•en** |mĭ **stā'**kən|, **mis•tak•ing. 1.** To understand incorrectly; misinterpret: *I mistook his statement to mean that he approved of the decision.* **2.** To recognize or identify incorrectly: *He mistook her for her sister.*

mis•tak•en |mĭ **stā'**kən| *adj.* Wrong; in error: *a mistaken idea. If I am not mistaken, you were last here about two years ago.* —**mis•tak'en•ly** *adv.*

mis•ter |**mĭs'**tər| *n.* **1. Mister.** A title of courtesy, usually written Mr., used before a man's last name: *Mr. Anderson.* **2.** A word used in speaking to a man, used without his name: *Could you give me a lift, mister?*

mis•tle•toe |mĭs'əl tō'| *n.* **1.** A plant that grows as a parasite on trees and has light-green leaves and white berries. **2.** A sprig of this plant, often used as a Christmas decoration. [SEE PICTURE]

mis•took |mĭ stŏŏk'|. Past tense of **mistake.**

mis•treat |mĭs trēt'| *v.* To treat badly or inconsiderately; abuse. —**mis•treat'ment** *n.*

mis•tress |mĭs'trĭs| *n.* **1.** A woman in a position of authority, control, or ownership, as the head of a household. **2.** The female owner of a dog, horse, or other animal. **3.** A man's female lover. **4. Mistress.** *Archaic.* Mrs.

mis•tri•al |mĭs trī'əl| *or* |-trīl'| *n.* **1.** A trial declared invalid because of a procedural problem or error. **2.** A trial in which the jurors fail to reach a verdict.

mis•trust |mĭs trŭst'| *n.* Lack of trust; suspicion; doubt. —*v.* To have no trust in; regard with suspicion: *mistrust strangers.*

mis•trust•ful |mĭs trŭst'fəl| *adj.* Feeling or showing mistrust: *mistrustful of everyone.* —**mis•trust'ful•ly** *adv.*

mist•y |mĭs'tē| *adj.* **mist•i•er, mist•i•est. 1.** Consisting of, filled with, or covered by mist: *a misty morning.* **2.** On the verge of shedding tears: *Her eyes grew misty as she read the letter.* **3.** Obscured by or as by mist; vague: *misty recollections.* —**mist'i•ly** *adv.* —**mist'i•ness** *n.*

mis•un•der•stand |mĭs'ŭn dər stănd'| *v.* **mis•un•der•stood** |mĭs'ŭn dər stŏŏd'|, **mis•un•der•stand•ing.** To understand incorrectly or imperfectly: *His remarks were misunderstood by many people.*

mis•un•der•stand•ing |mĭs'ŭn dər stăn'dĭng| *n.* **1.** A failure to understand. **2.** A quarrel or disagreement.

mis•use |mĭs yōōz'| *v.* **mis•used, mis•us•ing. 1.** To use wrongly or incorrectly: *misuse a word in a sentence.* **2.** To make improper use of; abuse: *misuse our natural resources.* —*n.* |mĭs yōōs'|. Wrong or improper use: *the misuse of language.*

mite¹ |mīt| *n.* Any of a group of very small animals related to the spiders. Mites often live as parasites on plants or other animals. ¶*These sound alike* **mite, might.** [SEE NOTE]

mite² |mīt| *n.* **1.** A small amount of money, especially one given as a contribution. **2.** A very small creature or object. ¶*These sound alike* **mite, might.** [SEE NOTE]

mi•ter |mī'tər| *n.* **1.** A tall, pointed hat worn by the pope, bishops, and abbots as a mark of office. **2.** Also **miter joint.** A kind of joint made by fitting together two beveled surfaces to form a right angle. —*v.* To join with a miter joint.

miter box. A device for guiding a handsaw, consisting of two upright sides joined at the bottom and having narrow slots for the saw.

mit•i•gate |mĭt'ĭ gāt'| *v.* **mit•i•gat•ed, mit•i•gat•ing.** To make less severe or intense; moderate: *The judge mitigated the sentence. Nothing could be done to mitigate her sorrow.* —**mit'i•ga'tion** *n.*

mi•to•chon•dri•a |mī'tə kŏn'drē ə| *pl.n.* The less frequently used singular is **mi•to•chon•dri•on** |mī'tə kŏn'drē ən|. Any of certain microscopic structures found in almost all living cells, containing enzymes that act in converting food to usable energy.

mi•to•sis |mī tō'sĭs| *n.* **1.** The process in which the chromosomes of a cell duplicate themselves and separate into two identical groups just before the cell divides. **2.** The entire sequence of processes involved in the division of a cell when both of the daughter cells have as many chromosomes as the original cell.

mi•tre |mī'tər| *n.* & *v.* **mi•tred, mi•tring.** British form of the word **miter.**

mitt |mĭt| *n.* **1.** A large, padded leather mitten or glove worn to protect the hand when catching a baseball. **2.** Any mitten. **3.** A **boxing glove. 4.** Often **mitts.** *Slang.* A hand or fist: *Put up your mitts and fight.* **5.** A woman's long glove that does not cover or fully cover the fingers. [SEE PICTURE]

mit•ten |mĭt'n| *n.* A covering that fits the hand, with a separate section for the thumb and one wide section for all four fingers.

mix |mĭks| *v.* **1.** To blend into a single mass, as by pouring or stirring: *mix flour, water, and eggs to form dough.* **2.** To be capable of being blended together: *Oil does not mix with water.* **3.** To make or create by combining different ingredients: *mix a cake; mix drinks.* **4.** To combine or join: *mix business with pleasure.* **5.** To bring together; bring into social contact: *mix boys with girls in the same classes.* **6.** To associate socially or mingle: *He never mixed much with the other members of the team.* —***phrasal verb.* mix up. 1.** To confuse: *Your directions only mixed us up even more.* **2.** To mistake (one thing, person, etc., for another): *I always mix up the words "principal" and "principle."* **3.** To throw into disorder; jumble: *The pieces of the jigsaw puzzle are all mixed up.* **4.** To involve, concern, or implicate: *He was mixed up in the robbery.* —*n.* Something formed by mixing; a mixture: *a cake mix.*

mixed |mĭkst| *adj.* **1.** Composed of various elements: *a mixed salad.* **2.** Composed of various, and often opposite, qualities: *a mixed reaction from the critics.* **3.** Composed of members of both sexes: *a mixed audience.* **4.** Involving different races or religions: *a mixed marriage.*

mixed fraction. A **mixed number.**

mixed metaphor. A succession of metaphors whose literal meanings contradict each other, thus producing an absurd effect; for example, *burning hatreds in a sea of discontent* is a mixed metaphor.

mixed number. A number, such as $7\frac{3}{8}$ or 6.295, that represents the sum of a whole number and a fraction.

mix•er |mĭk'sər| *n.* **1.** Any device that mixes or blends ingredients, especially by mechanical action: *a cement mixer.* **2.** *Informal.* A person who mixes or mingles easily with other people: *a good mixer.*

mix•ture |mĭks'chər| *n.* **1. a.** Any combination of different ingredients, things, kinds, etc.: *a mixture of flour or starch and water; a mixture of racial types.* **b.** Anything made up of substances that are not chemically combined: *Air is a mixture of several gases.* **2.** The act or process of mixing: *the mixture of flour, eggs, and water to make dough.* **3.** Any combination of diverse qualities, emotions, etc.: *greeted the news with a mixture of joy and sorrow.*

mix-up |mĭks'ŭp'| *n.* A confused situation, often resulting from a misunderstanding: *a mix-up over the starting time of the game.*

mistletoe

Mistletoe *was a sacred plant to the ancient Celts and Germans. It is still widely used as a Christmas decoration, although it is not supposed to be taken into a church. By tradition, a man may kiss a girl or woman who stands under a sprig of it. But according to* Brewer's Dictionary of Phrase and Fable, *"The correct procedure, now rarely observed, is that as the young man kisses a girl under the mistletoe he should pluck a berry, and that when the last berry is gone there should be no more kissing."*

mite¹·²

Mite¹ *was* mite *in Old English;* **mite²** *is borrowed from Dutch* mite. *The two words are related; the original meaning was "small biting insect," hence "small object, small coin."*

mitt

Baseball catcher's mitt

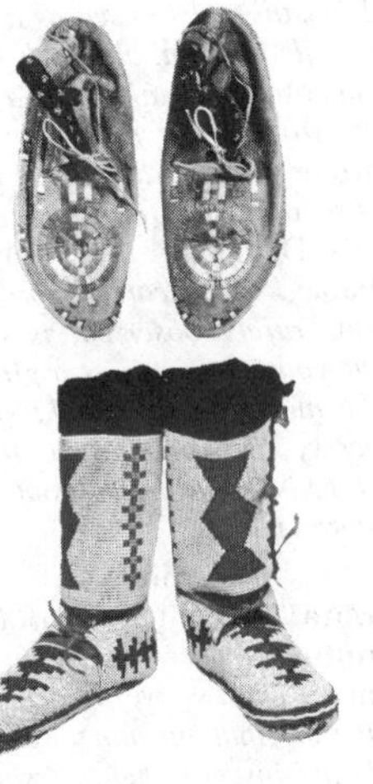
moccasin
Blackfoot Indian styles

mockingbird

miz•zen |mĭz′ən| *n.* A fore-and-aft sail set on the mizzenmast.
miz•zen•mast |mĭz′ən məst| *or* |-măst′| *or* |-mäst′| *n.* The third mast aft on sailing ships carrying three or more masts.
ml milliliter.
Mlle. Mademoiselle.
Mlles. Mesdemoiselles.
mm millimeter.
Mme. Madame.
Mmes. Mesdames.
Mn The symbol for the element manganese.
mne•mon•ic |nĭ mŏn′ĭk| *adj.* Designed to help someone to remember something: *a mnemonic device.* —*n.* Something, such as a formula or rhyme, that helps one to remember; for example, *i before e except after c* is a mnemonic device.
Mo The symbol for the element molybdenum.
Mo. Missouri.
mo•a |mō′ə| *n.* A large, extinct, ostrichlike bird of New Zealand.
moan |mōn| *n.* A low, drawn-out, mournful sound, usually of sorrow or pain. —*v.* **1.** To utter a moan or moans: *He became seasick immediately and lay moaning on the deck.* **2.** To make a sound resembling a moan: *The wind moaned in the chimney.* **3.** To utter with a moan or moans: *"We can't seem to win a game," moaned the coach.* ¶*These sound alike* **moan, mown.**
moat |mōt| *n.* A wide, deep ditch, usually filled with water, surrounding a medieval town or fortress. ¶*These sound alike* **moat, mote.**
mob |mŏb| *n.* **1.** A large, disorderly crowd, often one that commits violence: *The building was stormed by an angry mob.* **2. the mob.** The masses; the common people. **3.** An organized gang of criminals. —***modifier:*** *a mob scene; mob rule.* —*v.* **mobbed, mob•bing. 1.** To crowd around and jostle or annoy, especially in anger or enthusiasm: *Autograph seekers mobbed the stars.* **2.** To crowd into or jam (a place): *The department stores are mobbed this week.*
mo•bile |mō′bəl| *or* |-bēl′| *or* |-bīl′| *adj.* **1.** Capable of moving or being moved from place to place: *a mobile hospital.* **2.** Changing easily in expression or mood: *mobile features.* **3.** Allowing relatively easy movement from one social class to another: *a mobile society.* —*n.* |mō′bēl′|. A type of sculpture consisting of parts that sway in the breeze. —**mo•bil′i•ty** |mō bĭl′ĭ tē| *n.*
-mobile. A word element meaning "a specialized kind of vehicle": **bookmobile.**
mo•bi•lize |mō′bə līz′| *v.* **mo•bi•lized, mo•bi•liz•ing. 1.** To assemble or prepare for war or a similar emergency: *mobilize troops. The country mobilized.* **2.** To marshal or line up for a particular purpose: *mobilize public opinion to support the campaign.* —**mo′bi•li•za′tion** *n.*
Mö•bi•us strip |mœ′bē əs|. A mathematical surface having a single surface and a single edge. It can be represented as a model by taking a strip of paper, twisting one end through 180°, and attaching it to the other end.
mob•ster |mŏb′stər| *n. Slang.* A member of a criminal gang.
moc•ca•sin |mŏk′ə sĭn| *n.* **1. a.** A soft, heelless leather slipper, shoe, or boot, originally worn by North American Indians. **b.** A shoe resembling an Indian moccasin. **2.** A snake, the **water moccasin.** [SEE PICTURE]
moccasin flower. A North American wild orchid having a pink flower with a large, pouchlike part.
mo•cha |mō′kə| *n.* **1.** A rich Arabian coffee. **2.** A flavoring made of coffee, often mixed with chocolate.
mock |mŏk| *v.* **1.** To make fun of, often by imitating or depicting in an insulting way; ridicule: *mocking his way of speaking.* **2.** To treat with scorn or contempt; deride: *mock traditional values.* —*adj.* Simulated; false; sham: *a mock battle.*
mock•er•y |mŏk′ə rē| *n., pl.* **mock•er•ies. 1.** Ridicule; derision: *I sense mockery in your voice.* **2.** An object of ridicule. **3.** A ridiculous imitation of something; a travesty: *The trial was a mockery of justice.*
mock•ing•bird |mŏk′ĭng bûrd′| *n.* A gray and white bird that is common in the southern United States and that often imitates the songs of other birds. [SEE PICTURE]
mock•up or **mock-up** |mŏk′ŭp′| *n.* A full-sized model of a building, airplane, etc., used for demonstration, study, or testing.
mod |mŏd| *adj. Informal.* Stylishly up-to-date, especially in a modern unconventional way.
mo•dal |mōd′l| *adj.* **1.** Of or expressing the mood of a verb. **2.** Of, in, or characteristic of any of the ancient musical modes. —*n.* A **modal auxiliary.**
modal auxiliary. One of a set of English verbs, including *can, may, ought, should, will,* etc., that are used with other verbs to express mood or tense.
mode |mōd| *n.* **1.** A way, manner, or style of doing: *a mode of living; a mode of travel.* **2.** The current fashion or style in dress: *a dress in the latest mode.* **3.** Any of the musical scales produced by starting, in turn, on each of the tones of a major scale and proceeding through an octave. Modes were commonly used in plainsong and ancient church music. **4.** The value that occurs most frequently in a set of data. For example, if the weights of six persons are, in pounds, 125, 140, 172, 164, 140, and 110, 140 is the mode for that set of data.
mo•del |mŏd′l| *n.* **1.** A small-scale reproduction of something: *model of a sailing vessel.* **2.** A style or design of something: *This car is last year's model.* **3.** A person or thing serving as an ideal example of something: *a model of honesty. The farm is a model of efficient management.* **4.** A person hired to wear clothes in order to show them off, as in fashion shows or advertisements. **5.** A person who poses for an artist or photographer. **6.** In science, a description or concept of a system or set of observable events that accounts for all its known properties in a reasonable way. —*v.* **mod•eled** or **mod•elled, mod•el•ing** or **mod•el•ling. 1.** To make or construct out of clay, wax, or other material: *model animals in clay; bronze figures modeled from life.* **2.** To pattern after or in imitation of something: *The library was modeled after the Library of Congress in Washington.* **3.** To display (clothing) by wearing it, to show others how it looks: *She modeled her new dress.* **4.** To work as a fashion model:

ă pat/ā pay/â care/ä father/ĕ pet/ ē be/ĭ pit/ī pie/î fierce/ŏ pot/ ō go/ô paw, for/oi oil/ŏŏ book/ ōō boot/ou out/ŭ cut/û fur/ *th* the/th thin/hw which/zh vision/ ə ago, item, pencil, atom, circus

She models for a living. —*adj.* **1.** Constructed as a small-scale reproduction of something: *a model airplane.* **2.** Serving as a model: *a model home; a model farm.* **3.** Serving as a standard of excellence; perfect; exemplary: *a model child.* —**mod'el·er** *n.*

mod·er·ate |**mŏd'**ər ĭt| *adj.* **1.** Kept within reasonable limits; not excessive or extreme: *moderate speed; moderate prices.* **2.** Medium or average in amount or quality: *a moderate income.* **3.** Not severe; mild; temperate: *a moderate climate.* **4.** Avoiding political extremes: *moderate civil-rights leaders.* —*n.* In politics, someone who avoids extremes of either liberalism or conservatism. —*v.* |**mŏd'**ə rāt'| **mod·er·at·ed, mod·er·at·ing.** **1.** To make or become less extreme: *moderate one's demands. His views have moderated somewhat.* **2.** To preside over (a meeting or panel discussion): *Mr. Allen moderated the program. Who will moderate today?* —**mod'er·ate·ly** *adv.*

mod·er·a·tion |mŏd'ə **rā'**shən| *n.* **1.** The act of making more moderate: *moderation of one's demands.* **2.** The avoidance of extremes: *an advocate of political moderation.* **3.** Moderation in size, degree, etc.

Idiom. **in moderation.** Avoiding extremes or overindulgence: *After his heart attack he was advised to do everything in moderation.*

mod·e·ra·to |mŏd'ə **rä'**tō|. In music: *adj.* Moderate in tempo. —*adv.* In moderate tempo. —*n., pl.* **mod·e·ra·tos.** A section of a composition that is moderate in tempo.

mod·er·a·tor |**mŏd'**ə rā'tər| *n.* **1.** The person who presides over a meeting or panel discussion. **2.** A substance such as graphite or water placed in a nuclear reactor to slow neutrons down to speeds at which they are likely to cause additional nuclear fission.

mod·ern |**mŏd'**ərn| *adj.* **1.** Of or having to do with the present or recent past: *modern life; modern history; modern languages.* **2.** Up-to-date or advanced in style, equipment, or technology: *one of the most modern hospitals in the world; modern office buildings; modern methods of farming.* **3.** Of or having to do with the present style in the arts, marked by a break with tradition and bold new experimentation and originality: *modern art; modern dance.* —*n.* **1.** A person who lives in modern times. **2.** A person with modern ideas, tastes, or beliefs. [SEE NOTE]

mod·ern·ism |**mŏd'**ər nĭz'əm| *n.* **1.** Thought, practice, or behavior in agreement with modern ideas or standards. **2.** The theory and practice of modern art. —**mod'ern·ist** *n.*

mod·ern·i·ty |mō **dûr'**nĭ tē| *or* |mō-| *n.* The quality of being modern.

mod·ern·ize |**mŏd'**ər nīz'| *v.* **mod·ern·ized, mod·ern·iz·ing.** To make modern; alter or bring up-to-date so as to meet current needs: *modernize a kitchen.* —**mod'ern·i·za'tion** *n.*

mod·est |**mŏd'**ĭst| *adj.* **1.** Tending to minimize or play down one's own talents, abilities, or accomplishments. **2.** Retiring or reserved in manner; shy: *his quiet, modest demeanor.* **3.** Not elaborate or showy; unpretentious: *a modest house.* **4.** Moderate in size or amount; not large: *a modest salary.* —**mod'est·ly** *adv.*

mod·es·ty |**mŏd'**ĭ stē| *n.* **1.** Simplicity in form, appearance, etc. **2.** Reserve in behavior, dress, etc. **3.** Moderation in size, degree, etc.

mod·i·cum |**mŏd'**ĭ kəm| *n.* A small amount: *a subject in which I have only a modicum of interest.*

mod·i·fi·ca·tion |mŏd'ə fĭ **kā'**shən| *n.* **1.** The action or process of modifying: *The theory is still subject to some modification.* **2.** A result of modifying; a change or adaptation: *The design was approved with certain modifications.* **3.** Something resulting from a change or adaptation; a modified form or part: *Some insects have no stings or other modifications for self-protection.*

mod·i·fi·er |**mŏd'**ə fī'ər| *n.* **1.** Someone or something that modifies. **2.** A word, phrase, or clause that states or describes a quality of another word or phrase. A one-word modifier is usually an adjective, an adverb, or a noun.

mod·i·fy |**mŏd'**ə fī'| *v.* **mod·i·fied, mod·i·fy·ing, mod·i·fies.** **1. a.** To change; alter: *modify the terms of a deal.* **b.** To change in accordance with conditions or needs; adapt: *The inhabitants of Britain modified the Roman alphabet to suit their language.* **2.** In grammar, to qualify or limit the meaning of (a word, phrase, etc.).

mod·ish |**mō'**dĭsh| *adj.* Stylish; fashionable. —**mod'ish·ly** *adv.* —**mod'ish·ness** *n.*

mod·u·late |**mŏj'**o͞o lāt'| *or* |**mŏd'**yə-| *v.* **mod·u·lat·ed, mod·u·lat·ing.** **1.** To vary the amplitude, frequency, or some other characteristic of (a carrier wave) in a way that makes it correspond to a signal or information that is to be transmitted. **2.** To pass from one musical key or tonality to another by using a smooth chord progression or melodic phrase.

mod·u·la·tion |mŏj'o͞o **lā'**shən| *or* |mŏd'yə-| *n.* **1.** The process by which a characteristic of a carrier wave, such as its amplitude or frequency, is changed to make it correspond to a signal or information that is to be transmitted. **2. a.** The process by which music passes smoothly from one key or tonality to another. **b.** A passage of music that does this.

mod·ule |**mŏj'**o͞ol| *or* |**mŏd'**yo͞ol| *n.* **1.** A standard or unit of measurement. **2.** A standard element that is used over and over again in forming a building or structure. **3.** Any of a number of small systems, each individually housed or packaged, that are joined together to make a large, complex system: *the tuner module of a television set.* **4.** Any of the self-contained parts of a spacecraft, each of which is used for a particular job or set of jobs within the mission: *the command module; a lunar module.* —**mod'u·lar** *adj.*

Mog·a·dish·u |mŏg'ə **dĭsh'**o͞o|. The capital of Somalia. Population, 200,000.

mo·hair |**mō'**hâr'| *n.* **1.** The soft, silky hair of the Angora goat. **2.** Cloth made from this hair.

Mo·ham·med |mō **hăm'**ĭd| *or* |**-hä'**mĭd|. A.D. 570?–632. Arabian prophet; the founder of Islam.

Mo·ham·med·an |mō **hăm'**ĭ dən| *adj.* Of Islam, its believers, or its prophet Mohammed. —*n.* A believer in Islam.

Mo·ha·ve |mō **hä'**vē| *n., pl.* **Mo·ha·ve** or **Mo·ha·ves.** **1.** A North American Indian tribe formerly living in areas of the southwestern United States. **2.** A member of this tribe. **3.** The Yuman language of this tribe.

Mo·hawk |**mō'**hôk'| *n., pl.* **Mo·hawk** or **Mo·**

modern

The word **modern** *has a wide range of possible applications, according to context. It can refer to just the present and the past 10 years. More often, as in architecture, music, etc., it includes the past 50 years or so. In a larger sense, "modern history" is often defined as beginning around the year 1500; in technical linguistic contexts, as in the notes in this Dictionary, "Modern English" also begins in 1500 (before that it was "Middle English").*

mold[1-2-3]
Mold[1] *is from Old French* modle, *"small measure, model, shape."* **Mold**[2] *is ultimately from Old Norse* mugla, *"growth of mold."* **Mold**[3] *was Old English* molde, *"soft, crumbling earth."*

molder[1-2]
Molder[1] *is probably related to* **mold**[3]. **Molder**[2] *is from* **mold**[1].

mole[1-2-3]
Mole[1] *was Old English* māl, *"spot, blemish."* **Mole**[2] *is from Middle Dutch* mol, *an old Germanic name for the animal.* **Mole**[3] *is from German* mol, *shortened from* molekulargewicht, *"molecular weight."*

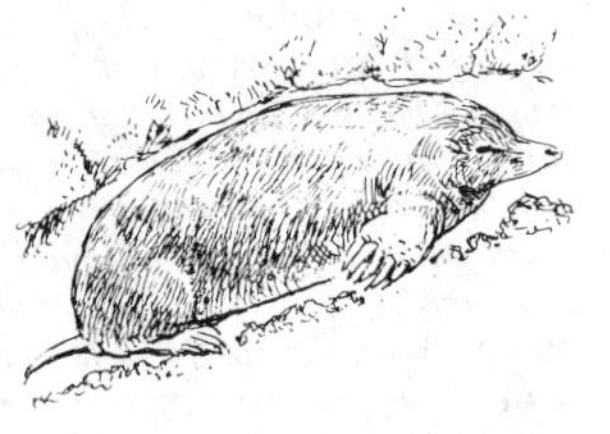

mole[2]

ă pat/ā pay/â care/ä father/ĕ pet/ ē be/ĭ pit/ī pie/î fierce/ŏ pot/ ō go/ô paw, for/oi oil/ŏŏ book/ ōō boot/ou out/ŭ cut/û fur/ *th* the/th thin/hw which/zh vision/ ə ago, item, pencil, atom, circus

hawks. 1. A North American Indian tribe of upper New York State. **2.** A member of this tribe. **3.** The Iroquoian language of this tribe.

Mo•he•gan |mō hē′gən| *n., pl.* **Mo•he•gan** or **Mo•he•gans. 1.** A North American Indian tribe formerly living in Connecticut. **2.** A member of this tribe. **3.** The Algonquian language of this tribe.

Mo•hi•can |mō hē′kən| *or* |mə-| *n., pl.* **Mo•hi•can** or **Mo•hi•cans.** A form of the word **Mahican.**

Mo•ho |mō′hō′| *n.* The **Mohorovičić discontinuity.**

Mo•ho•ro•vi•čić discontinuity |mō′hə rō′və-chĭch′|. The boundary between the earth's crust and the earth's mantle, ranging in depth from 6 to 8 miles under oceans and from 20 to 25 miles under continents.

Mohs scale |mōz|. A scale used to measure the relative hardness of a mineral by its resistance to scratching by 15 standard minerals ranging from talc, the softest, to diamond, the hardest.

moi•ré |mwä rā′| *or* |môr′ā| *or* |mōr′ā| *n.* **1.** A wavy or rippled pattern pressed on cloth by engraved rollers. **2.** Cloth, especially silk, that has a watery, wavy, rippled look.

moist |moist| *adj.* Slightly wet; damp: *a moist climate; moist air masses.* —**moist′ness** *n.*

mois•ten |moi′sən| *v.* To make slightly wet or damp: *The pitcher moistened his fingers on the rosin bag.*

mois•ture |mois′chər| *n.* **1.** Wetness, especially that caused by water present in the air as vapor or spread thinly over a surface or surfaces. **2.** Water, especially as collected from a diffuse source, such as vapor in the air or wet soil: *The roots of plants draw moisture from the ground.*

mo•lar |mō′lər| *n.* Any one of the teeth located toward the back of the jaws that have broad crowns for grinding food. Human beings have 12 molars.

mo•las•ses |mə lăs′ĭz| *n.* A thick syrup produced in refining sugar.

mold[1] |mōld| *n.* **1.** A hollow container of a particular shape, used for shaping liquid or semiliquid substances, such as gelatin, wax, plaster, or molten metal or glass: *pour the batter into a mold.* **2.** Something made or shaped from a mold: *a Jell-O mold.* **3.** General shape; form: *the square mold of his chin.* **4.** Distinctive character, kind, or type: *a man of serious mold.* —*v.* **1.** To shape in a mold. **2.** To determine the general character of; shape in a particular way: *mold a mass of undisciplined men into a tightly knit crew.* —**mold′a•ble** *adj.* [SEE NOTE]

mold[2] |mōld| *n.* **1.** A type of fungus that has fine threadlike stalks and that often forms a fuzzy coating on the surface of food and other plant or animal substances. **2.** The coating formed by such a fungus. —*v.* To become covered with such a coating. [SEE NOTE]

mold[3] |mōld| *n.* Loose soil that is rich in decayed plant and animal material. [SEE NOTE]

mold•er[1] |mōl′dər| *v.* To turn gradually to dust; crumble: *The old buildings are beginning to molder away.* [SEE NOTE]

mold•er[2] |mōl′dər| *n.* A person who molds: *a molder of metal.* [SEE NOTE]

mold•ing |mōl′dĭng| *n.* **1.** Anything that is molded. **2.** The process of shaping in a mold. **3.** An ornamental strip used to decorate a surface.

mold•y |mōl′dē| *adj.* **mold•i•er, mold•i•est. 1.** Covered with mold: *moldy bread.* **2.** Of or like mold: *spoiled food with a moldy taste.* **3.** Damp and musty: *a dark, moldy cupboard.* —**mold′i•ness** *n.*

mole[1] |mōl| *n.* A small growth on the human skin, existing from birth, usually dark and slightly raised and often covered with hair. [SEE NOTE]

mole[2] |mōl| *n.* A small, burrowing animal with tiny, underdeveloped eyes, a narrow snout, and short, silky fur. [SEE NOTE & PICTURE]

mole[3] |mōl| *n.* The amount of a substance that has a weight in grams numerically equal to the molecular weight of the substance. For example, carbon dioxide, CO_2, has a molecular weight of 44; therefore, one mole of it weighs 44 grams. [SEE NOTE]

mo•lec•u•lar |mə lĕk′yə lər| *adj.* Of, caused by, or existing between molecules. —**mo•lec′u•lar•ly** *adv.*

molecular weight. The sum of the atomic weights of the atoms contained in a molecule.

mol•e•cule |mŏl′ə kyōōl′| *n.* A stable, electrically neutral arrangement of atoms and electrons held together by electric and electromagnetic forces. It is the smallest and simplest unit that has the characteristic chemical and physical properties of a compound.

mole•hill |mōl′hĭl′| *n.* A small mound of earth dug up by a burrowing mole.
Idiom. **make a mountain out of a molehill.** To make a great deal of a trivial matter.

mole•skin |mōl′skĭn′| *n.* **1.** The short, soft, silky fur of the mole. **2.** A sturdy cotton cloth with a thick, fine nap on one side.

mo•lest |mə lĕst′| *v.* **1.** To annoy, bother, or disturb: *Few animals dare molest the lion or the elephant.* **2.** To make indecent advances to. —**mo•lest′er** *n.*

mol•li•fy |mŏl′ə fī′| *v.* **mol•li•fied, mol•li•fy•ing, mol•li•fies. 1.** To allay the anger of; placate: *a gesture designed to mollify his critics.* **2.** To make less intense; soften or soothe: *Her tender words mollified the child's distress.* —**mol′li•fi•ca′tion** *n.*

mol•lusk, also **mol•lusc** |mŏl′əsk| *n.* Any of a large group of soft-bodied animals usually living in water and having a hard outer shell. Snails, clams, and oysters are among the many mollusks with shells, but octopuses, squids, and slugs, which have no outer shell, are also mollusks.

mol•ly |mŏl′ē| *n., pl.* **mol•lies.** Any of several small, colorful tropical freshwater fish, often having a large, saillike back fin. Mollies are kept in home aquariums.

mol•ly•cod•dle |mŏl′ē kŏd′l| *n.* A man or boy of weak character who likes to be pampered and protected. —*v.* **mol•ly•cod•dled, mol•ly•cod•dling.** To be overprotective toward; spoil by pampering and coddling.

Mo•loch |mō′lŏk′| *or* |mŏl′ək|. In the Old Testament, a false god to whom children were sacrificed.

molt |mōlt| *v.* To shed (an outer covering such as skin or feathers) for replacement by a new growth: *molt feathers. Some snakes molt in spring.* —*n.* The act or process of molting.

mol•ten |mōl'tən| *adj.* Made liquid by heat; melted: *molten metal.*

mo•lyb•de•num |mə lĭb'də nəm| *n.* Symbol **Mo** One of the elements, a hard gray metal. Atomic number 42; atomic weight 95.94; valences +2, +3, +4, +5, +6; melting point 2,620°C; boiling point 4,800°C.

mom |mŏm| *n. Informal.* Mother.

mo•ment |mō'mənt| *n.* **1.** A very brief interval of time; an instant. **2.** A certain point in time: *the happiest moment of my life.* **3. the moment.** The present time: *Mr. Smith is busy at the moment.* **4.** Great significance or importance: *an event of great moment.*

mo•men•tar•i•ly |mō'mən târ'ĭ lē| *adv.* **1.** For an instant or moment: *I was momentarily at a loss for words.* **2.** At any moment; very soon: *Mr. Watson will see you momentarily.*

mo•men•tar•y |mō'mən tĕr'ē| *adj.* Lasting only an instant or moment: *I caught only a momentary glance of him as he flashed by.*

mo•men•tous |mō mĕn'təs| *adj.* Of the utmost importance or significance: *a momentous occasion; a momentous discovery.*

mo•men•tum |mō mĕn'təm| *n., pl.* **mo•men•ta** |mō mĕn'tə| or **mo•men•tums. 1.** The product of the mass and velocity of a moving body. **2.** Force or speed of motion; impetus: *The sled gained momentum as it raced down the hill.*

mom•my |mŏm'ē| *n., pl.* **mom•mies.** *Informal.* Mother.

Mon. Monday.

Mon•a•co |mŏn'ə kō'| *or* |mə nä'kō|. A tiny country on the Mediterranean coast in southeastern France. Population, 25,000. Capital, Monaco or Monaco-Ville. —**Mon'a•can** *adj. & n.*

mon•arch |mŏn'ərk| *n.* **1.** A ruler or sovereign, such as a king, queen, emperor, etc. **2.** A large orange and black butterfly. [SEE PICTURE]

mo•nar•chic |mə när'kĭk| or **mo•nar•chi•cal** |mə när'kĭ kəl| *adj.* Of or having to do with a monarch or monarchy.

mon•ar•chism |mŏn'ər kĭz'əm| *n.* **1.** A system of government headed by a single ruler or monarch. **2.** Belief in this system of government.

mon•ar•chist |mŏn'ər kĭst| *n.* A person who believes in or advocates monarchy.

mon•ar•chy |mŏn'ər kē| *n., pl.* **mon•ar•chies. 1.** Government by a monarch. **2.** A country ruled by a monarch.

mon•as•ter•y |mŏn'ə stĕr'ē| *n., pl.* **mon•as•ter•ies.** The place where a community of monks lives. —**mon'as•ter'i•al** |mŏn'ə stîr'ē əl| *or* |-stĕr'-| *adj.*

mo•nas•tic |mə năs'tĭk| *adj.* Of or having to do with monasteries, monks, or the secluded life within a monastery: *monastic vows.*

mon•a•tom•ic |mŏn'ə tŏm'ĭk| *adj.* Occurring as single atoms, as, for example, helium.

mon•au•ral |mŏn ôr'əl| *or* |mō nôr'-| *adj.* **1.** Of, for, or involving the reception of sound by one ear. **2.** Using a single channel to transmit or reproduce sound; monophonic.

mon•a•zite |mŏn'ə zīt'| *n.* A reddish-brown mineral composed of phosphates of rare earths and thorium.

Mon•day |mŭn'dē| *or* |-dā'| *n.* The second day of the week, after Sunday and before Tuesday. —***modifier:*** *a Monday evening.*

mon•e•tar•y |mŏn'ĭ tĕr'ē| *or* |mŭn'-| *adj.* **1.** Of or expressed in money: *monetary resources; monetary value of a painting.* **2.** Of a nation's currency or coinage: *a monetary system.* —**mon'e•tar'i•ly** *adv.*

mon•ey |mŭn'ē| *n., pl.* **mon•eys** or **mon•ies. 1.** Something, such as gold, silver, or beads, that is legally declared to have a fixed value and to be exchangeable for all goods and services. **2.** Official coins and printed bills issued by a government and used to buy or pay for things; currency: *counted out the money and paid the grocer.* **3.** A unit or form of currency: *a display of the various moneys of the world.* **4.** Wealth in any exchangeable form: *More money changes hands by check than by cash.* **5.** Often **moneys.** Sums of money collected or stored; funds: *distributing state tax moneys.* **6.** An amount of money sufficient for some purpose: *They lacked the money for a longer vacation.* **7.** An amount of money bet or risked: *put money on the favorite.*

***Idiom.* in** (or **out of**) **the money.** Among (or not among) the winners of prize money in a race.

mon•ey-back |mŭn'ē băk'| *adj.* Promising to return the customer's money if he is unsatisfied: *a money-back guarantee.*

mon•ey•bag |mŭn'ē băg'| *n.* **1.** A bag for holding money. **2. moneybags** *(used with a singular verb). Slang.* A rich and greedy person.

mon•eyed |mŭn'ēd| *adj.* **1.** Having much money; wealthy: *the great moneyed corporations.* **2.** Of or characteristic of the wealthier people: *the moneyed interests.*

money order. An order representing a sum of money that can be bought at a bank or post office, mailed, and cashed by the receiver.

Mon•gol |mŏng'gəl| *or* |-gōl'| *or* |mŏn'-| *n.* **1.** A native of Mongolia. **2.** A member of one of the nomadic tribes of Mongolia. **3.** The language of these people; Mongolian. **4.** Any Mongoloid person. —**Mon'gol** *adj.*

Mon•go•li•a |mŏng gō'lē ə| *or* |-gōl'yə| *or* |mŏn-|. **1.** Officially, Mongolian People's Republic. A country in Central Asia, between the Soviet Union and China. Population, 1,400,000. Capital, Ulan Bator. Also called *Outer Mongolia.* **2.** Officially, Inner Mongolian Autonomous Region. An administrative division of China. Also called *Inner Mongolia.*

mon•go•li•an |mŏng gō'lē ən| *or* |-gōl'yən| *or* |mŏn-| *adj.* Of or showing mongolism.

Mon•go•li•an |mŏng gō'lē ən| *or* |-gōl'yən| *or* |mŏn-| *n.* **1.** A native of Mongolia. **2.** Any of the languages of Mongolia, related to Turkish. **3.** A member of the Mongoloid division of the human species. —*adj.* Of Mongolia, the Mongolians, or their languages.

mon•gol•ism |mŏng'gə lĭz'əm| *or* |mŏn'-| *n.* A birth defect that results in idiocy and in which a child is born with a short, flattened skull, pronounced epicanthic folds, which make the eyes appear slanted, and other abnormalities.

mon•gol•oid |mŏng'gə loid'| *or* |mŏn'-| *adj.* Of or characterized by mongolism.

Mon•gol•oid |mŏng'gə loid'| *or* |mŏn'-| *adj.* **1.** Of or concerning a major division of the human species whose members characteristically have yellowish-brown to white skin, straight black hair, dark eyes with epicanthic folds, which make

monarch
Butterflies on milkweed pods

mongoose

monocle

monogram
Queen Anne
Queen of England (1702–14)
Albrecht Dürer
German painter (1471–1528)

ă pat/ā pay/â care/ä father/ĕ pet/
ē be/ĭ pit/ī pie/î fierce/ŏ pot/
ō go/ô paw, for/oi oil/ŏŏ book/
ōō boot/ou out/ŭ cut/û fur/
th the/th thin/hw which/zh vision/
ə ago, item, pencil, atom, circus

them appear slanted, and prominent cheekbones. This division is considered to include the Chinese, Japanese, and most other Asian peoples, and Eskimos and American Indians. **2.** Of the Mongols. *—n.* Someone who belongs to the Mongoloid division of the human species.

mon•goose |**mŏng′**gōōs′| *or* |**mŏn′**-| *n., pl.* **mon•goos•es.** Any of several weasellike animals of Asia and Africa, noted for their ability to kill poisonous snakes. [SEE PICTURE]

mon•grel |**mŭng′**grəl| *or* |**mŏng′**-| *or* |**mŏn′**-| *n.* An animal, especially a dog, of mixed breed.

mon•ies |**mŭn′**ēz| *n.* A plural of **money.**

mon•i•tor |**mŏn′**ĭ tər| *n.* **1.** A person who gives warnings, corrective advice, or instruction: *old enough to act as monitor for the younger children when Mother was shopping.* **2.** A student assigned to keep order in the school hallways, help take attendance, or perform similar duties. **3.** A device that can detect and give warning of what is approaching. **4.** Any device used in recording or controlling a process or activity: *a radiation monitor.* **5.** A screen in a television studio that shows the picture being broadcast or being picked up by a camera. **6.** Any of several large lizards of Asia, Africa, and Australia. *—v.* **1.** To keep watch over; supervise. **2.** To keep track of, especially with some technical means or device: *a graph that monitors a patient's heartbeats.* **3.** To record, test, or control (a process or activity) with special apparatus.

Mon•i•tor |**mŏn′**ĭ tər|. A Union ironclad warship that fought an inconclusive battle with the Confederate Merrimack on March 9, 1862.

mon•i•to•ry |**mŏn′**ĭ tôr′ē| *or* |-tōr′ē| *adj.* Giving a warning or reproof: *a monitory glance.*

monk |mŭngk| *n.* A member of a group of men living in a monastery and bound by vows to the rules and practices of a religious order.

mon•key |**mŭng′**kē| *n., pl.* **mon•keys. 1.** Any of many animals that belong to the same group as human beings and have hands with thumbs, especially one of the smaller, long-tailed kinds as distinguished from the larger apes. **2.** *Informal.* A playful or mischievous person. **3.** A person made to appear silly or foolish: *We made monkeys out of their varsity team.* *—v.* **mon•keyed, mon•key•ing, mon•keys. 1.** To behave in a silly or careless way: *told not to monkey around during the ceremony.* **2.** To tamper; meddle: *monkeyed with the gadget but couldn't get it to work.*

monkey bars. A **Jungle gym.**

monkey wrench. A hand tool with adjustable jaws for turning nuts and bolts of various sizes.

monk•ish |**mŭng′**kĭsh| *adj.* Of or like a monk or the monastic way of life.

mono–. A word element meaning "one, only, single": **monogamy.**

mon•o•chro•mat•ic |mŏn′ō krə **măt′**ĭk| *adj.* Of or having a single color: *monochromatic light.*

mon•o•cle |**mŏn′**ə kəl| *n.* An eyeglass, typically having a cord attached, worn in front of one eye. [SEE PICTURE]

mon•o•cot |**mŏn′**ə kŏt′| *n.* A monocotyledon.

mon•o•cot•y•le•don |mŏn′ə kŏt′l **ēd′**n| *n.* A flowering plant with a single cotyledon, or seed leaf.

mon•o•cot•y•le•don•ous |mŏn′ə kŏt′l **ēd′**-n əs| *adj.* Having a single cotyledon: *Grasses and lilies are monocotyledonous plants.*

mo•noc•u•lar |mə **nŏk′**yə lər| *adj.* **1.** Of or having a single eye. **2.** Designed for use with only one eye: *a monocular telescope.*

mo•nog•a•mous |mə **nŏg′**ə məs| *adj.* Of, involving, or practicing monogamy. **—mo•nog′a•mous•ly** *adv.*

mo•nog•a•my |mə **nŏg′**ə mē| *n.* **1.** The custom or condition of being married to only one person at a time. **2.** The condition of having just one mate for life.

mon•o•gram |**mŏn′**ə grăm′| *n.* A design made up of one or more letters, usually the initials of a name. *—v.* **mon•o•grammed, mon•o•gram•ming.** To mark with a monogram: *She monogrammed the sheets and towels.* **—mon′o•grammed** *adj.: monogrammed towels.* [SEE PICTURE]

mon•o•graph |**mŏn′**ə grăf′| *or* |-gräf′| *n.* A scholarly book or article on a specific and usually limited subject.

mon•o•lith |**mŏn′**ə lĭth′| *n.* A large, single block of stone.

mon•o•lith•ic |mŏn′ə **lĭth′**ĭk| *adj.* **1.** Consisting of a monolith: *a monolithic column.* **2.** Like a monolith in being massive, uniform, or unvarying: *a monolithic business empire.*

mon•o•logue |**mŏn′**ə lôg′| *or* |-lŏg′| *n.* **1.** A long speech delivered by an actor on the stage or a character in a story or poem. **2.** A series of jokes and stories told by a comedian on the stage alone. **3.** A long speech made by one person in a group: *Professor Smith had little regard for anyone else's views, his conversations mainly being monologues.*

mon•o•ma•ni•a |mŏn′ə **mā′**nē ə| *or* |**-mān′**yə| *n.* An intense preoccupation with one subject or idea. **—mon′o•ma′ni•ac′** |mŏn′ə **mā′**nē ăk′| *n.*

mo•no•mi•al |mŏ **nō′**mē əl| *or* |mə-| *or* |mō-| *n.* An algebraic expression consisting of a single term. *—adj.* Of a monomial or monomials.

mon•o•phon•ic |mŏn′ə **fŏn′**ĭk| *adj.* **1.** Consisting of only one melodic line or part. **2.** Using a single channel to record, store, or reproduce sound: *a monophonic phonograph; a monophonic recording.*

mon•o•plane |**mŏn′**ə plān′| *n.* An airplane having a single pair of wings.

mo•nop•o•list |mə **nŏp′**ə lĭst| *n.* A business leader who owns or promotes monopolies.

mo•nop•o•lis•tic |mə nŏp′ ə **lĭs′** tĭk| *adj.* **1.** Maintaining a monopoly: *archaic industries, monopolistic and inefficient.* **2.** Of or characteristic of a monopoly or a monopolist.

mo•nop•o•lize |mə **nŏp′**ə līz′| *v.* **mo•nop•o•lized, mo•nop•o•liz•ing. 1.** To gain and hold a monopoly over. **2.** To take all of; have all to oneself: *Power and privilege throughout the kingdom were monopolized by bishops and nobles.* **—mo•nop′o•li•za′tion** *n.* **—mo•nop′o•liz′er** *n.*

mo•nop•o•ly |mə **nŏp′**ə lē| *n., pl.* **mo•nop•o•lies. 1. a.** Complete control by one group of the means of producing or selling a product or service: *The early railroads had almost a monopoly on freight and passenger transportation.* **b.** A company having such complete control: *laws to limit the power of monopolies.* **c.** A product, service, or commercial activity completely controlled by one group: *Oil production was a monopoly of the government in Turkey.* **2.** Sole possession or control of anything: *the years of our monopoly on the atomic bomb.*

Mo•nop•o•ly |mə nŏp′ə lē| *n.* A trademark for a board game in which players use play money to buy and charge rent for squares that represent real estate.

mon•o•rail |mŏn′ə rāl′| *n.* **1.** A single rail on which a car or train of cars travels. **2.** A railway system using a track with such a rail.

mo•no•so•di•um glu•ta•mate |mŏn′ə sō′dē əm glōō′tə māt′|. **Sodium glutamate.**

mon•o•syl•lab•ic |mŏn′ō sĭ lăb′ĭk| *adj.* **1.** Having only one syllable. **2.** Consisting of or using many words of one syllable: *a monosyllabic language.*

mon•o•syl•la•ble |mŏn′ə sĭl′ə bəl| *n.* A word of one syllable.

mon•o•the•ism |mŏn′ō thē ĭz′əm| *n.* Belief in only one God. —**mon′o•the′ist** *n.*

mon•o•the•is•tic |mŏn′ō thē ĭs′tĭk| *adj.* Of or characterized by monotheism.

mon•o•tone |mŏn′ə tōn′| *n.* **1.** A succession of sounds or words uttered in a single tone of voice. **2. a.** The repeated singing of a single tone with different words and time values, as in chanting. **b.** A chant sung on a single tone. **3.** A tiresome lack of variety, as in sound, color, or style.

mo•not•o•nous |mə nŏt′n əs| *adj.* **1.** Uttered or sounded in one repeated tone; unvarying in pitch: *a monotonous drone that tires the listener and causes his attention to wander.* **2.** Never varied or enlivened; repetitiously dull: *a monotonous diet.* —**mo•not′o•nous•ly** *adv.*

mo•not•o•ny |mə nŏt′n ē| *n.* Tiresome lack of variety; dull sameness.

mon•ox•ide |mŏ nŏk′sīd′| *or* |mə-| *n.* An oxide in which each molecule contains a single atom of oxygen.

Mon•roe |mən rō′|, **James.** 1758–1831. Fifth President of the United States (1817–25).

Monroe Doctrine. A U.S. policy, set forth by President James Monroe in 1823, of opposing any attempt by a European power to extend its influence in the Western Hemisphere.

Mon•ro•vi•a |mən rō′vē ə|. The capital of Liberia. Population, 96,000.

Mon•sieur |mə syœ′| *n., pl.* **Mes•sieurs** |mĕs′ərz| *or* |mā syœ′|. A French word similar to Sir, used before the name of a man in speaking to or of him.

mon•soon |mŏn sōōn′| *n.* A system of winds that influences the climate of a large area and that changes direction with the seasons, especially the wind system that produces the wet and dry seasons in southern Asia.

mon•ster |mŏn′stər| *n.* **1.** An imaginary or legendary creature that is huge and frightening, especially one with body parts from various human or animal forms. **2.** A very large or grotesque animal, person, or thing: *Fish range from tiny animals to monsters 50 feet long.* **3.** An animal or plant that is abnormal in form and strange in appearance. **4.** A vicious or horrid creature: *The little monster bit my leg.* —***modifier:*** *a monster turtle; a monster rally.*

mon•stros•i•ty |mŏn strŏs′ĭ tē| *n., pl.* **mon•stros•i•ties. 1.** Someone or something that is monstrous. **2.** The condition or quality of being monstrous.

mon•strous |mŏn′strəs| *adj.* **1.** Of or like a monster: *monstrous birds called Harpies.* **2.** Deformed; grotesque: *gargoyles and other monstrous carvings.* **3.** Huge; enormous: *a monstrous iceberg.* **4.** Frightful; shocking: *monstrous behavior.* —**mon′strous•ly** *adv.* —**mon′strous•ness** *n.*

Mont. Montana.

mon•tage |mŏn täzh′| *n.* **1. a.** A picture made from many other pictures or designs placed next to or on top of one another. **b.** The art or process of making such pictures. **2. a.** A rapid succession of images or short scenes in a motion-picture film. **b.** This technique of film editing.

Mon•tan•a |mŏn tăn′ə|. A Northwestern state of the United States. Population, 700,000. Capital, Helena. —**Mon•tan′an** *adj. & n.*

mon•tane |mŏn′tān′| *adj.* Of or characteristic of mountain areas: *animals adapted to montane forests.*

Mont Blanc |môN bläN′|. The highest peak of the Alps, near the French-Italian border in Switzerland.

Mon•te Car•lo |mŏn′tē kär′lō|. A resort town in the principality of Monaco on the Mediterranean coast.

Mon•te•vi•de•o |mŏn′tə vĭ dā′ō| *or* |-vĭd′ē ō′|. The capital of Uruguay, at the mouth of the Río de la Plata. Population, 1,350,000.

Mont•gom•er•y |mŏnt gŭm′ə rē| *or* |-gŭm′rē|. The capital of Alabama. Population, 133,400.

month |mŭnth| *n.* **1. a.** Also **calendar month.** One of the twelve divisions of a year, lasting about 30 days. **b.** Any period of about 30 days. **2.** Also **lunar month.** The average time between successive full moons, equal to 29 days 7 hours 43 minutes. [SEE NOTE]

month•ly |mŭnth′lē| *adj.* **1.** Occurring, appearing, or payable every month: *a monthly meeting; monthly bills.* **2.** Covering a period of a month: *average monthly rainfall; a monthly sales quota.* —*adv.* Every month: *a magazine published monthly.* —*n., pl.* **month•lies.** A publication appearing once each month.

Mont•pe•lier |mŏnt pēl′yər|. The capital of Vermont. Population, 9,100.

Mon•tre•al |mŏn′trē ôl′| *or* |mŭn′-|. The largest city in Canada, located in Quebec Province at the head of the St. Lawrence Seaway. Population, 1,225,000.

mon•u•ment |mŏn′yə mənt| *n.* **1.** A structure, such as a tower, statue, or building, erected to honor a person, group, or event. **2.** Any structure preserved or admired for its historical importance. **3.** A place, area, or region preserved by a government for its special beauty or significance: *national parks and monuments.* **4.** Any outstanding or enduring work: **a.** One that honors or preserves a memory: *poems that are a matchless monument to his lady.* **b.** One serving as a model of its kind: *His book is a monument of careful scholarship.* **5.** An engraved stone, such as a tombstone, that marks an important spot: *Monuments placed by historical societies mark the Oregon Trail.*

mon•u•men•tal |mŏn′yə mĕn′tl| *adj.* **1.** Of, like, or serving as a monument: *a monumental arch.* **2.** Impressively large and sturdy: *monumental dams, tunnels, and viaducts.* **3.** Of endur-

month

No better method has been devised for remembering the number of days in each month than this old rhyme:

"Thirty days hath September,
April, June, and November;
All the rest have thirty-one,
Excepting February alone,
Which hath but twenty-eight in fine,
Till Leap Year gives it twenty-nine."

There are many variations of the rhyme; it goes back at least to the sixteenth century.

mood[1-2]
Mood[1] *was Old English* mōd, *"disposition, feeling."* **Mood[2]** *is a variant of* **mode,** *"way, style."*

moon
Moon *was* mōna *in Old English; it is descended from* mēn-, *the Indo-European word for "moon." From remote prehistoric times, men have counted days by the phases of the moon; Indo-European* mēn- *meant both "moon" and "month," and it is closely connected to a root meaning "to measure."*

moose

ă pat/ā pay/â care/ä father/ĕ pet/ē be/ĭ pit/ī pie/î fierce/ŏ pot/ō go/ô paw, for/oi oil/o͝o book/o͞o boot/ou out/ŭ cut/û fur/*th* the/th thin/hw which/zh vision/ə ago, item, pencil, atom, circus

ing importance; outstanding. **4.** Astounding; outrageous: *came to see his whole life as a monumental fraud.* —**mon'u•men'tal•ly** *adv.*

moo |mo͞o| *n.* The deep, long, throaty sound made by a cow. —*v.* **mooed, moo•ing.** To make such a sound.

mood[1] |mo͞od| *n.* **1.** A temporary state of mind or feeling: *He was in such a bad mood he boxed my ears for nothing.* **2.** An impression on the feelings or spirits of the listener, reader, etc.: *a movie that captures the mood of the book.* **3.** An atmosphere: *A gloomy mood prevailed throughout the old house.* [SEE NOTE]
Idioms. **in no mood.** Not inclined: *in no mood to argue.* **in the mood.** Inclined; willing.

mood[2] |mo͞od| *n.* A set of verb forms that tells how certain the speaker is of the action expressed. In English, the *indicative mood* is used for definite statements and questions; the *imperative mood* is used in giving commands; and the *subjunctive mood* is used, now only for the verb *be*, to suggest doubt or unlikelihood. [SEE NOTE]

mood•y |mo͞o'dē| *adj.* **mood•i•er, mood•i•est. 1.** Apt to change moods often, especially having spells of anger or gloom. **2.** Gloomy; morose; glum: *his moody silence.* —**mood'i•ly** *adv.* —**mood'i•ness** *n.*

moon |mo͞on| *n.* **1.** The natural satellite of the earth, visible by reflected sunlight and traveling around the earth in a slightly elliptical orbit at an average distance of about 237,000 miles. Its average diameter is 2,160 miles and its mass about 1/80 that of the earth. **2.** Any natural satellite of a planet: *the moons of Jupiter.* **3.** The moon as seen at a particular time in its cycle of phases: *a full moon; no moon tonight.* **4.** Moonlight. **5.** A month. **6.** A disk, ball, or crescent resembling the moon. —***modifier:*** *moon rocks.* —*v.* To drift or wander in a daze: *mooning around in love.* [SEE NOTE]

moon•beam |**mo͞on'**bēm'| *n.* A ray of moonlight.

moon•calf |**mo͞on'**kăf'| *or* |-käf'| *n., pl.* **moon•calves** |**mo͞on'**kăvz| *or* |-kävz|. A stupid, silly, or absent-minded person.

moon•light |**mo͞on'**līt'| *n.* The light that is reflected from the surface of the moon. —***modifier:*** *a moonlight stroll.* —*v.* **moon•light•ed, moon•light•ing.** To work at a second job, often at night, in addition to one's regular job. —**moon'light•er** *n.*

moon•scape |**mo͞on'**skāp'| *n.* A view or picture of the surface of the moon.

moon•shine |**mo͞on'**shīn'| *n.* **1.** Moonlight. **2.** *Slang.* Foolish talk or thinking; nonsense. **3.** *Slang.* Illegally distilled whiskey. —*v.* **moon•shined, moon•shin•ing.** *Slang.* To distill whiskey illegally.

moon•stone |**mo͞on'**stōn'| *n.* Any of several pearly, translucent forms of feldspar that are valued as gemstones.

moon•struck |**mo͞on'**strŭk'| *adj.* **1.** Mentally unbalanced; crazy: *moonstruck theorists.* **2.** Dazed with romantic love; infatuated.

moon•y |mo͞o'nē| *adj.* **moon•i•er, moon•i•est. 1.** Like the moon or moonlight: *a moony face; a moony luster.* **2.** Given to dreamy moods; absent-minded.

moor[1] |mo͝or| *v.* **1.** To make fast (a vessel or aircraft) by means of cables or anchors. **2.** To fix in place; secure: *a fish that moors itself to rocks.* **3.** To tie up a boat; anchor: *We moored out in the bay.* **4.** To be secured: *A sloop moored inside the cove.*

moor[2] |mo͝or| *n.* A broad stretch of open land, often with boggy areas and patches of low shrubs such as heather.

Moor |mo͝or| *n.* A member of a Moslem people now living in northern Africa. The Moors invaded Spain in the 8th century A.D.

moor•ing |**mo͝or'**ĭng| *n.* **1.** The action of securing a vessel or aircraft. **2.** A place at which a vessel or aircraft may be secured. **3.** Often **moorings.** Equipment, such as anchors, chains, or lines, for making fast a vessel or aircraft. **4.** A chain, anchored to the ground and buoyed at the surface, to which boats may be made fast: *untied the dory from its mooring.*

Moor•ish |**mo͝or'**ĭsh| *adj.* Of the Moors, especially those who invaded Spain in the 8th century A.D.: *the Moorish influence in Spanish music.*

moose |mo͞os| *n., pl.* **moose.** A large animal of northern regions, related to the deer and having broad antlers. —***modifier:*** *a moose head.* ¶*These sound alike* **moose, mousse.** [SEE PICTURE]

moot |mo͞ot| *adj.* Still open to debate; undecided: *a moot question.* —*v.* **1.** To bring up as a subject for debate. **2.** To discuss (an issue); debate.

mop |mŏp| *n.* **1.** A device for washing and drying floors, consisting of a sponge or a bundle of yarn or rags attached to a long handle. **2.** A cloth or other piece of absorbent material for wiping up liquids. **3.** A loosely tangled bunch or mass: *a mop of hair.* —*v.* **mopped, mop•ping.** To wash, scrub, or wipe with a mop. —***phrasal verb.*** **mop up. 1.** To finish (a nearly completed task). **2.** To clear (an area) of remaining enemy resistance after a military victory.

mope |mōp| *v.* **moped, mop•ing. 1.** To be gloomy or quietly resentful; sulk. **2.** To move or pass time aimlessly; dawdle. —*n.* **1.** A person who often has gloomy moods. **2. mopes.** Low spirits.

mop•pet |**mŏp'**ĭt| *n.* A young child.

mo•raine |mə **rān'**| *n.* A mass of boulders, stones, or other material that has been carried and deposited by a glacier.

mor•al |**môr'**əl| *or* |**mŏr'**-| *adj.* **1.** Of or concerned with the judgment of human life and behavior; dealing with how and why people should live: *the moral reflection that life is made up of sobs and smiles, with sobs predominating.* **2.** Of or concerned with the judgment of the goodness and badness of human action: *moral principles.* **3.** Teaching good or correct behavior: *a moral lesson.* **4.** Being or acting in accord with standards of what is good and just: *the old notion that whatever gives pleasure cannot be moral.* **5.** Arising from the inner sense of right and wrong: *a moral duty to help, but no legal obligation.* **6.** Psychological rather than physical or concrete: *a moral victory; moral support.* —*n.* **1.** The principle taught by a fable, story, or event. **2. morals.** Rules of good or correct conduct.

mo•rale |mə **răl'**| *n.* The state of a person's or group's spirits, as shown in confidence, cheerfulness, and willingness to work toward a goal: *The aim of the party was to heighten morale and increase the staff's will to work.*

mor•al•ist |môr'ə lĭst| *or* |mŏr'-| *n.* **1.** A person who is concerned with moral principles and questions: *Most novelists are moralists.* **2.** A person who wishes to regulate the behavior of others.

mor•al•is•tic |môr'ə lĭs'tĭk| *or* |mŏr'-| *adj.* **1.** Concerned with what is good and bad in human action. **2.** Concerned, often self-righteously, with the strict observance of rules of good conduct. —**mor'al•is'ti•cal•ly** *adv.*

mo•ral•i•ty |mə răl'ĭ tē| *or* |mô-| *n., pl.* **mo•ral•i•ties. 1.** A set of ideas about what is right and wrong in human conduct and relationships: *Christian morality.* **2.** The quality of being moral; goodness or rightness: *questioned the morality of selling firearms to the public.* **3.** Behavior that is in accord with approved codes and customs.

mor•al•ize |môr'ə līz'| *or* |mŏr'-| *v.* **mor•al•ized, mor•al•iz•ing. 1.** To view or explain in moral terms; consider the rights and wrongs of. **2.** To draw a lesson from: *an old schoolteacher who could moralize laughter itself.*

mor•al•ly |môr'ə lē| *or* |mŏr'-| *adv.* **1.** According to principles of right and wrong: *Is it ever morally permissible to kill?* **2.** According to accepted rules or conduct; virtuously. **3.** According to strong conviction or probability: *morally certain.*

mo•rass |mə răs'| *or* |mô-| *n.* **1.** An area of low, soggy ground; a bog or marsh. **2.** A situation that is hard to clarify or settle; entanglement: *applied for a permit but got caught in a morass of bureaucracy.*

mor•a•to•ri•um |môr'ə tôr'ē əm| *or* |-tōr'-| *or* |mŏr'-| *n., pl.* **mor•a•to•ri•ums** or **mor•a•to•ri•a** |môr'ə tôr'ē ə| *or* |-tōr'-| *or* |mŏr'-|. **1.** A stopping of some activity for the time being; a temporary ban or pause. **2.** A period of delay granted before a debt must be paid.

mo•ray |môr'ā| *or* |mōr'ā| *or* |mə rā'| *n.* Any of several tropical ocean eels that have sharp teeth and can be dangerous to swimmers.

mor•bid |môr'bĭd| *adj.* **1.** Of, caused by, or having to do with disease: *morbid changes in body tissues.* **2.** Abnormally intense or acute: *morbid curiosity.* **3.** Preoccupied with death, decay, or other unwholesome matters; gruesome: *a morbid chamber of horrors.* —**mor'bid•ly** *adv.* —**mor'bid•ness** *n.*

mor•bid•i•ty |môr bĭd'ĭ tē| *n., pl.* **mor•bid•i•ties. 1.** The condition of being morbid. **2.** The rate of occurrence of a disease.

mor•dant |môr'dnt| *adj.* **1. a.** Biting in thought or effect; keen; incisive. **b.** Bitter; sarcastic: *expressed resentment in mordant remarks.* **2.** Used to fix colors in dyeing. —*n.* **1.** A substance used to fix coloring matter in cloth, leather, or other materials. **2.** A substance, such as an acid, used to etch metal surfaces. —**mor'dan•cy** *n.* —**mor'dant•ly** *adv.*

more |môr| *or* |mōr| *adj.* Superlative **most** |mōst|. **1. a.** Greater in number. Comparative of **many:** *More people came to the show tonight than ever before.* Often used as a pronoun: *Go ahead and invite everybody you know—the more the merrier.* **b.** Greater in size, amount, extent, or degree. Comparative of **much:** *He does more work than anybody else.* Often used as a pronoun: *There is more than meets the eye in this caper.* **2.** Additional; extra: *We brought more food along, just in case.* —*n.* A greater or additional quantity, number, degree, or amount: *More of the same brand is being ordered. More of us are coming, so sit tight.* —*adv.* **1.** To or in a greater extent or degree. Used to form the comparative of many adjectives and adverbs: *more difficult; more intelligently.* **2.** In addition; again: *The conspirators stabbed him several times more and then fled.* [SEE NOTE]

Idioms. **more or less. 1.** Approximately; about: *The trip takes six hours more or less.* **2.** To some indefinite extent; somewhat: *Within a few years, the book was considered to be more or less a classic.* **(all) the more.** Even more: *Every delay in the negotiations made him all the more determined to drive a hard bargain.*

mo•rel |mə rĕl'| *or* |mô-| *n.* An edible mushroom with a brownish, spongelike cap. [SEE PICTURE]

more•o•ver |môr ō'vər| *or* |mōr-| *or* |môr'ō'-vər| *or* |mōr'-| *adv.* Beyond what has been said; further; besides: *We are, moreover, delighted to report that progress has been made.*

mo•res |môr'āz| *or* |-ēz| *or* |mōr'-| *pl.n.* **1.** The accepted customs and rules of behavior of a particular social group, generally regarded by that group as essential to survival and welfare and often having the force of law. **2.** Attitudes about proper behavior; moral conventions: *the manners and mores of suburban life.*

morgue |môrg| *n.* **1.** A place where the bodies of persons found dead are kept until identified or claimed. **2.** A file at a newspaper or magazine office for storing old issues and reference material.

mor•i•bund |môr'ə bŭnd'| *or* |mōr'-| *adj.* At the point of death; about to die.

Mor•mon |môr'mən| *n.* A member of the Church of Jesus Christ of Latter-day Saints, founded in 1830 by Joseph Smith. The church's main temple and historic center are in Salt Lake City, Utah. —*adj.* Of the Mormons.

Mor•mon•ism |môr'mə nĭz'əm| *n.* The beliefs and worship of the Mormons.

morn |môrn| *n.* The morning. ¶*These sound alike* **morn, mourn.**

morn•ing |môr'nĭng| *n.* **1.** The early part of the day, from midnight to noon or from sunrise to noon. **2.** The time of sunrise; dawn. —***modifier:*** *the morning sun.* ¶*These sound alike* **morning, mourning.**

mor•ning-glo•ry |môr'nĭng glôr'ē| *or* |-glōr'ē| *n., pl.* **-glo•ries.** Any of several twining vines with showy, funnel-shaped flowers that generally close in the afternoon. [SEE PICTURE]

morning star. A planet visible in the eastern sky before sunrise, especially Venus.

Mo•ro |môr'ō| *or* |mōr'ō| *n., pl.* **Mo•ros.** A member of any of the Moslem tribes of the southern Philippines. —*adj.* Of the Moros.

mo•roc•co |mə rŏk'ō| *n., pl.* **mo•roc•cos.** A soft, fine leather of goatskin, made originally in Morocco and used chiefly for binding books.

Mo•roc•co |mə rŏk'ō|. A country in northwestern Africa, bounded by the Mediterranean

more or **less**

There is more of **more** *and less of* **less.** *In the five million words on which this Dictionary is based,* **more** *occurs nearly 10,000 times and* **less** *occurs under 1,400 times. This fact is recorded merely as an idle curiosity; it is not suggested that it* means *anything.*

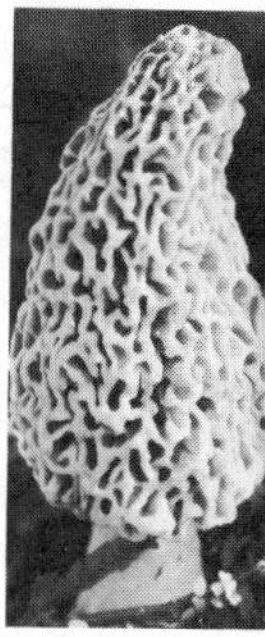

morel

morning-glory

A	•–	V	•••–
B	–•••	W	•––
C	–•–•	X	–••–
D	–••	Y	–•––
E	•	Z	––••
F	••–•	Á	•––•–
G	––•	Ä	•–•–
H	••••	É	••–••
I	••	Ñ	––•––
J	•–––	Ö	–––•
K	–•–	Ü	••––
L	•–••	1	•––––
M	––	2	••–––
N	–•	3	•••––
O	–––	4	••••–
P	•––•	5	•••••
Q	––•–	6	–••••
R	•–•	7	––•••
S	•••	8	–––••
T	–	9	––––•
U	••–	0	–––––
, (comma)	––••––		
. (period)	•–•–•–		
?	••––••		
;	–•–•–•		
:	–––•••		
/	–••–•		
- (hyphen)	–••••–		
apostrophe	•––––•		
parenthesis	–•––•–		
underline	••––•–		

Morse code

mosaic

Sea on the north and the Atlantic Ocean on the west. Population, 16,880,000. Capital, Rabat. —**Mo•roc'can** *adj. & n.*

mo•ron |môr'ŏn'| *or* |mōr'-| *n.* **1.** A mentally retarded person whose intelligence is equal to that of a child between 8 and 12 years of age. **2.** A very foolish or stupid person.

Mo•ro•ni |mə rō'nē|. The capital of Comoros. Population, 12,000.

mo•ron•ic |mə rŏn'ĭk| *or* |mô-| *adj.* Of or like a moron; feeble-minded; stupid.

mo•rose |mə rōs'| *or* |mô-| *adj.* Ill-humored; sullen; gloomy. —**mo•rose'ly** *adv.* —**mo•rose'ness** *n.*

mor•pheme |môr'fēm'| *n.* A unit of language that has meaning and that cannot be divided into smaller meaningful parts. For example, *fire* is a morpheme; the *-s* in *fires* is also a morpheme.

mor•phine |môr'fēn'| *n.* An addictive narcotic drug extracted from opium. Its soluble salts are used in medicine as an anesthetic and sedative.

mor•pho•log•i•cal |môr'fə lŏj'ĭ kəl| or **mor•pho•log•ic** |môr'fə lŏj'ĭk| *adj.* Of morphology.

mor•phol•o•gy |môr fŏl'ə jē| *n.* **1.** The biological study of the form and structure of living organisms. **2.** The form and structure of an organism, excluding its functions. **3.** In linguistics, the study of word formation, including the function of inflections and derivations.

mor•row |môr'ō| *or* |mŏr'ō| *n.* **1.** The following day; the next day: *stayed up late making plans for the morrow.* **2.** *Archaic.* The morning.

Morse |môrs|, **Samuel F(inley) B(reese).** 1791–1872. American inventor; developed the first telegraph.

Morse code. A communications code invented by Samuel Morse in which letters of the alphabet and numbers are represented by combinations of short and long sounds or beams of light, known as dots and dashes. [SEE PICTURE]

mor•sel |môr'səl| *n.* **1.** A small piece, especially of food; a bit: *begging for morsels of bread.* **2.** An inviting dish; a tasty tidbit.

mor•tal |môr'tl| *adj.* **1.** Subject to death: *All human beings are mortal and so will someday die.* **2.** Of or characteristic of human beings as imperfect creatures who must die: *mortal weaknesses.* **3.** Of this world; earthly: *mortal remains of a hero.* **4.** Causing or accompanying death: *a mortal wound.* **5.** Causing spiritual death in the view of the Roman Catholic Church: *Suicide is a mortal sin.* **6.** Fought to the death: *mortal battles.* **7.** Unrelenting; deadly: *a mortal enemy.* **8.** Extreme; dire: *in mortal fear.* —*n.* A human being, as a limited creature who must die: *dreaming dreams no mortal ever dared to dream before.* —**mor'tal•ly** *adv.*

mor•tal•i•ty |môr tăl'ĭ tē| *n., pl.* **mor•tal•i•ties. 1.** The condition of being subject to death. **2.** Death, especially of large numbers: *a war accompanied by widespread civilian mortality.* **3.** The proportion of a given group of people that dies in a given period of time; death rate.

mor•tar |môr'tər| *n.* **1.** A bowl used to hold substances while they are crushed or ground with a pestle. **2.** Any of various machines in which substances are ground or crushed. **3.** A building material made of sand, water, lime, and, often, cement, used to hold together bricks, stones, etc. **4.** A muzzle-loading cannon used to fire shells in a high arc. —***modifier:*** *a mortar attack.* —*v.* **1.** To plaster or join with mortar. **2.** To bombard with mortars.

mor•tar•board |môr'tər bôrd'| *or* |-bōrd'| *n.* **1.** A square board with a handle, used for holding and carrying mortar. **2.** An academic cap with a flat, square top and a tassel, worn at graduation and other ceremonies.

mort•gage |môr'gĭj| *n.* **1.** A legal pledge of property to a creditor as security for the payment of a loan or debt: *the mortgage of one's house to a bank.* **2.** A written agreement specifying the terms of such a pledge. **3.** The claim that the creditor has on property pledged in this way. —***modifier:*** *a mortgage loan; mortgage payments.* —*v.* **mort•gaged, mort•gag•ing. 1.** To pledge (property) as security for the payment of a debt. **2.** To put in jeopardy for some immediate benefit; to risk: *mortgaged his future.*

mor•tice |môr'tĭs| *n. & v.* **mor•ticed, mor•tic•ing.** A form of the word **mortise.**

mor•ti•cian |môr tĭsh'ən| *n.* A funeral director; an undertaker.

mor•ti•fi•ca•tion |môr'tə fĭ kā'shən| *n.* **1.** The action or practice of subduing one's body, impulses, desires, etc., by self-denial. **2.** Humiliation; embarrassment. **3.** Frustration. **4.** The death or decay of a part of a living body.

mor•ti•fy |môr'tə fī'| *v.* **mor•ti•fied, mor•ti•fy•ing, mor•ti•fies. 1.** To subject to pain or restraint; to discipline: *a chill air that mortified the flesh.* **2.** To subdue by practicing self-denial: *a saint who dressed in rags to mortify his pride.* **3.** To cause to feel shame or embarrassment; humiliate. **4.** To cause to feel annoyance; frustrate. **5.** To become gangrenous. —**mor'ti•fi'er** *n.*

mor•tise |môr'tĭs| *n.* A square hole in a piece of wood or other material, prepared to receive a tenon of another piece, so as to join the two. —*v.* **mor•tised, mor•tis•ing. 1.** To cut a mortise in. **2.** To join (two pieces) by means of a mortise and tenon.

mor•tu•ar•y |môr'chōō ĕr'ē| *n., pl.* **mor•tu•ar•ies.** A place where dead bodies are prepared or kept before burial or cremation.

mos. months.

mo•sa•ic |mō zā'ĭk| *n.* **1.** A picture or design made on a surface by fitting and cementing together small pieces of colored tile, glass, stone, etc. **2.** The art or process of making such pictures or designs. **3.** A virus disease of certain plants, such as tobacco or tomatoes, that causes the leaves to become spotted or wrinkled. —***modifier:*** *mosaic tile; a mosaic pavement.* [SEE PICTURE]

Mo•sa•ic |mō zā'ĭk| *adj.* Of Moses or his teachings: *the Mosaic Law.*

Mos•cow |mŏs'kou| *or* |-kō|. The capital and largest city of the Soviet Union, in the central part of European Russia. Population, 7,410,000.

Mo•ses |mō'zĭz| *or* |-zĭs|. The chief lawgiver of the Hebrews and leader of their exodus from Egypt.

mo•sey |mō'zē| *v.* **mo•seyed, mo•sey•ing, mo•seys.** *Informal.* **1.** To move slowly or leisurely; stroll. **2.** To get going; leave.

Mos•lem |mŏz'ləm| *or* |mŏs'-| *n.* A believer in Islam. —*adj.* Of Islam or its believers.

mosque |mŏsk| *n.* A Moslem house of worship.

ă pat/ā pay/â care/ä father/ĕ pet/ ē be/ĭ pit/ī pie/î fierce/ŏ pot/ ō go/ô paw, for/oi oil/ŏŏ book/ ōō boot/ou out/ŭ cut/û fur/ *th* the/th thin/hw which/zh vision/ ə ago, item, pencil, atom, circus

mos•qui•to |mə skē′tō| *n., pl.* **mos•qui•toes** or **mos•qui•tos.** Any of several winged insects of which the females bite and suck blood from animals and human beings. Some kinds transmit diseases such as malaria and yellow fever. [SEE PICTURE]

moss |môs| *or* |mŏs| *n.* **1.** Any of a group of small green plants that do not have flowers and that often form a dense, matlike growth on damp ground, rocks, or tree trunks. **2.** Any of several similar plants. See **club moss.**

moss•y |**mô′**sē| *or* |**mŏs′**ē| *adj.* **moss•i•er, moss•i•est.** Of, resembling, or covered with moss.

most |mōst| *adj.* **1. a.** Greatest in number or quantity. Superlative of **many:** *Our school has the most kids of any in the area. This is the most people I've ever seen in one place.* Often used as a pronoun: *Most came here by special bus.* **b.** Largest in amount, size, or degree. Superlative of **much:** *the most money.* Often used as a pronoun: *This is only part of the collection; most was lost in the war.* **2.** In the greatest number of instances: *Most fish have fins.* —*n.* **1.** The greatest amount, quantity, or degree; the largest part: *Most of this land is good.* **2.** The largest number; the majority: *Most of these stones are worthless.* **3. the most.** *Slang.* Someone or something extremely good or exciting: *That group is really the most.* —*adv.* **1.** In the highest degree, quantity, or extent. Used with many adjectives and adverbs to form the superlative: *most honest; most impatiently.* **2.** Very: *a most impressive piece of work.* **3.** *Informal.* Almost; just about: *Most everybody's here already.*

***Idioms.* at (the) most.** At the absolute limit: *She's in her late teens, 20 at the most.* **for the most part.** Mostly; mainly: *The settlers were, for the most part, farmers.* **make the most of.** To make the best use of: *making the most of a bad situation.*

-most. A suffix that forms the superlative degree of adjectives and adverbs: **innermost.**

most•ly |**mōst′**lē| *adv.* **1.** For the most part: *The strawberry plants we tended are mostly thriving.* **2.** Generally; usually: *We mostly try to get to bed before midnight.*

mote |mōt| *n.* A speck, especially of dust: *being bothered by a mote in one's eye.* ¶*These sound alike* **mote, moat.**

mo•tel |mō **tĕl′**| *n.* A hotel for motorists, usually opening directly on a parking area.

moth |môth| *or* |mŏth| *n., pl.* **moths** |mô*th*z| *or* |mŏ*th*z| *or* |môths| *or* |mŏths|. Any of a large number of insects related to the butterflies but often flying at night and generally having a stouter body and featherlike or slender, hairlike antennae.

moth•ball |**môth′**bôl′| *or* |**mŏth′**-| *n.* **1.** A marble-sized ball of camphor or naphthalene, stored with clothes to keep away moths. **2. mothballs.** A condition of long-term storage with protection against the weather: *a fleet of warships in mothballs.* —*adj.* In long-term storage: *the mothball fleet.*

moth-eat•en |**môth′**ēt′n| *or* |**mŏth′**-| *adj.* **1.** Eaten away by moths: *a moth-eaten bedspread.* **2.** Old and worn.

moth•er¹ |**mŭ*th*′**ər| *n.* **1.** A female parent or guardian. **2.** Source; cause: *Poverty is the mother of many ills.* —*adj.* **1.** Being a mother: *a mother hen.* **2.** Of a mother: *mother love.* **3.** Protecting or nourishing like a mother: *the mother church.* **4.** Native: *the mother tongue; one's mother country.* —*v.* **1.** To give birth to. **2.** To watch over or nourish. [SEE NOTE]

moth•er² |**mŭ*th*′**ər| *n.* A stringy slime, made up of yeast cells and bacteria, that forms on the surface of a fermenting liquid. It is often added to wine or cider to start production of vinegar. [SEE NOTE]

moth•er•hood |**mŭ*th*′**ər ho͝od′| *n.* **1.** The condition of being a mother. **2.** Mothers as a group or class.

moth•er-in-law |**mŭ*th*′**ər ĭn lô′| *n., pl.* **moth•ers-in-law.** The mother of one's wife or husband.

moth•er•land |**mŭ*th*′**ər lănd′| *n.* **1.** The country of one's birth. **2.** The native country of one's ancestors.

moth•er•less |**mŭ*th*′**ər lĭs| *adj.* Having lost one's mother.

moth•er•ly |**mŭ*th*′**ər lē| *adj.* **1.** Of a mother. **2.** Suited to or acting like a mother; loving and tender: *motherly affection; a motherly aunt.* —**moth′er•li•ness** *n.*

Mother of God. Mary, the mother of Christ.

moth•er-of-pearl |mŭ*th*′ər əv **pûrl′**| *n.* The hard, smooth, pearly layer on the inside of certain oyster shells and other seashells, used to make buttons, jewelry, etc. —***modifier:*** *mother-of-pearl cuff links.*

Mother's Day. A holiday celebrated on the second Sunday in May, in honor of mothers and motherhood.

mother superior. *pl.* **mothers superior.** A woman in charge of a convent or other female religious community.

mo•tif |mō **tēf′**| *n.* **1.** A repeated figure, shape, or color in a design, as of wallpaper or a building: *a necktie with a flower motif.* **2.** A short melodic fragment in a piece of music; the shortest bit of melody that can be recognized as belonging to a particular theme. **3.** An idea or symbol that recurs in various forms in a literary or artistic work.

mo•tion |**mō′**shən| *n.* **1. a.** The process of moving; change of position. **b.** An act of moving; a movement: *the darting motions of dragonflies.* **2.** The ability to move: *Early astronomers denied that the earth has motion.* **3.** A deliberate change in the position of an arm, head, or the whole body; a gesture: *the subtle motions of a dancer.* **4.** A movement necessary for some purpose: *Actors in silent pictures just went through the motions of talking.* **5.** Operation; activity: *put the engine in motion.* **6.** A sense of rapid movement; speed. **7.** A formal application or request: *No state by its own mere motion can get out of the Union.* **8.** A proposal put to a vote in a group following parliamentary procedure: *I moved to adjourn the meeting, and the motion passed by voice vote.* —*v.* **1.** To direct by a wave of the hand or another gesture; to signal: *The driver stopped short and motioned us to cross.* **2.** To make a gesture expressing one's wishes: *motioned for the child to sit beside her.*

mo•tion•less |**mō′**shən lĭs| *adj.* Not moving. —**mo′tion•less•ly** *adv.*

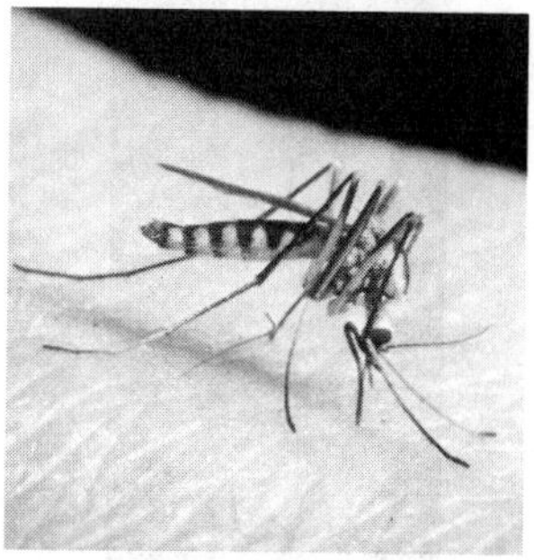

mosquito

mother¹⁻²

Mother¹ *was Old English* mōdor; *see note at* **matron. Mother²** *was originally called* mother of vinegar; *it was apparently thought that the slime was the original substance from which the vinegar was produced and was thus its "mother"; but this is uncertain.*

motion picture
Section of film showing a football being kicked toward the camera

mount[1-2]

Mount[2] *is from Old French* mont, *which is from Latin* mons, mont-, *"mountain." The adjective* montānus, *"belonging to mountains, living in mountains," was formed from* mons; *later* montānus *turned into a noun meaning "a mountain"; it became* montaigne *in Old French, and was borrowed into English as* **mountain**. *Also formed from Latin* mons *was the verb* montāre, *meaning "to go up a mountain, to climb"; this became Old French* monter, *and was borrowed into English as* **mount[1]**.

ă pat/ā pay/â care/ä father/ĕ pet/ ē be/ĭ pit/ī pie/î fierce/ŏ pot/ ō go/ô paw, for/oi oil/ŏŏ book/ ōō boot/ou out/ŭ cut/û fur/ *th* the/th thin/hw which/zh vision/ ə ago, item, pencil, atom, circus

motion picture. **1.** A series of pictures projected on a screen in rapid succession, creating the illusion that things in the pictures are moving as they would in life. **2.** A series of such pictures designed to tell a story or record a set of events. —***modifier:*** **(motion-picture):** *a motion-picture camera.* [SEE PICTURE]

motion sickness. Nausea, vomiting, and often dizziness caused by motion, as from riding in an automobile, airplane, or ship.

mo•ti•vate |mō′tə vāt′| *v.* **mo•ti•vat•ed, mo•ti•vat•ing. 1.** To provide with a motive; incite: *amateur pilots motivated by a curiosity about flying.* **2.** To instill with a desire to study or perform well; inspire: *a manager who charged the Dodgers with his spirit and motivated them with his leadership.* —**mo′ti•vat′ing** *adj.: a motivating force.*

mo•ti•va•tion |mō′tə **vā′**shən| *n.* **1.** The process of providing motives: *studied the motivation of human behavior.* **2.** The condition of having motives, especially to strive or perform well: *serious students with a high level of motivation.* **3.** A motive or set of motives; incentive.

mo•tive |**mō′**tĭv| *n.* **1.** A reason or an emotion that causes one to act in a certain way or causes an action to take place: *a crime with no apparent motive.* **2.** One of the deep impulses that determine a person's character or habitual behavior: *an insight into human motives.* **3.** A purpose: *drugs used with the motive of stimulating the heart.* **4.** |*also* mō **tēf′**|. A motif in music or design. —*adj.* Producing motion: *motive power supplied by a jet engine.*

mot•ley |**mŏt′**lē| *adj.* **1.** Made up of many different colors: *the motley suit of a clown.* **2.** Made up of an odd assortment of different types: *a motley crew of seamen.* —*n.* A costume of many colors worn by a clown or jester.

mo•tor |**mō′**tər| *n.* **1.** A device that changes electric power into mechanical power. **2.** A device that produces mechanical power from a fuel; an engine. **3.** Any device that produces or imparts motion: *the motor of a clock.* —*adj.* **1.** Propelled by an engine or motor: *a motor ski tow.* **2.** Of or involving vehicles propelled by engines: *motor accidents; a motor race.* **3.** Of, for, or involving motors or engines: *motor oil.* **4.** Of, involving, or controlling movements of the muscles. —*v.* To drive or travel in a motor vehicle.

mo•tor•boat |**mō′**tər bōt′| *n.* A boat powered by an internal-combustion engine.

mo•tor•car |**mō′**tər kär′| *n.* Also **motor car.** An automobile.

motor court. A motel.

mo•tor•cy•cle |**mō′**tər sī′kəl| *n.* A vehicle with two wheels, similar to a bicycle but larger and heavier, propelled by an internal-combustion engine. —*v.* **mo•tor•cy•cled, mo•tor•cy•cling.** To drive or ride on a motorcycle.

mo•tor•cy•clist |**mō′**tər sī′klĭst| *n.* A person who drives a motorcycle.

mo•tor•ist |**mō′**tər ĭst| *n.* A person who drives or rides in an automobile.

mo•tor•ize |**mō′**tə rīz′| *v.* **mo•tor•ized, mo•tor•iz•ing. 1.** To equip with a motor or motors. **2.** To supply with motor-driven vehicles: *eleven infantry divisions, of which seven are armored and motorized.*

mo•tor•man |**mō′**tər mən| *n., pl.* **-men** |-mən|. A man who drives a streetcar, locomotive, or subway train.

motor nerve. A nerve that is able to stimulate a muscle and cause motion.

motor scooter. A small vehicle that rides on two wheels and is propelled by an engine or motor.

motor vehicle. Any self-propelled vehicle that travels on wheels but does not run on rails.

mot•tle |**mŏt′**l| *v.* **mot•tled, mot•tling.** To cover (a surface) with spots or streaks of different colors: *Her back was mottled lightly with freckles.* —**mot′tled** *adj.: the mottled breast of a bird.* —*n.* **1.** One of many little spots or streaks. **2.** A pattern of such markings.

mot•to |**mŏt′**ō| *n., pl.* **mot•toes** or **mot•tos. 1.** A phrase expressing the character or ideal of a family, enterprise, state, or nation, inscribed on banners, documents, coins, etc.: *Canada's national coat of arms bears the motto "A mari usque ad mare" ("From Sea to Sea").* **2.** Any brief expression of a guiding principle; a slogan: *Robin Hood's motto was "take from the rich and give to the poor."*

mould |mōld| *n.* & *v.* A form of the word **mold.**

mould•ing |**mōl′**dĭng| *n.* A form of the word **molding.**

mould•y |**mōl′**dē| *adj.* A form of the word **moldy.**

mound |mound| *n.* **1.** A naturally formed area of high ground, such as a small hill. **2.** A pile of earth or rocks heaped up, as for protection or concealment: *the mound marking a woodchuck's hole; a burial mound.* **3.** A pile or mass of anything: *mounds of fluffy mashed potatoes.* **4.** A lump; a bulge on a surface: *The swelling extended around the scorpion bite in a hard mound.* **5.** The pitcher's area in the middle of a baseball diamond, raised about ten inches.

mount[1] |mount| *v.* **1.** To climb; ascend: *mounted the stairs; mounting to the top of the hill.* **2.** To go up; rise: *The rocket mounted to the sky and the space beyond.* **3.** To grow higher; increase: *The death toll mounted.* **4. a.** To get up on (a horse or other animal): *The knight mounted a fresh steed.* **b.** To provide with a riding horse. **5.** To plan and start to carry out: *The quarterback mounted a scoring drive against the opposing team.* **6.** To provide (a theatrical performance) with scenery and costumes; to stage. **7.** To put into place, especially: **a.** To fix on a raised structure: *mounted the weather vane on the chimney.* **b.** To set (guns) in position for firing. **c.** To place in a secure position for display or study: *a specimen mounted on a microscope slide.* **8.** To post (a guard): *mount sentries around the encampment.* —*n.* **1.** A horse or other animal for riding. **2. a.** A frame or background for holding something to be studied or displayed: *a picture mount.* **b.** A structure that secures and supports a machine or instrument: *the precision mounts of a telescope.* [SEE NOTE]

mount[2] |mount| *n.* A mountain. [SEE NOTE]

moun•tain |**moun′**tən| *n.* **1.** A raised portion of the earth's surface, generally massive and rising steeply to a great height. **2.** A large heap or quantity: *a mountain of paperwork.* —***modifier:*** *mountain scenery.*

mountain chain. A row or series of connected mountains.

Mountain Daylight-Saving Time. Daylight-saving time as observed in the region between the meridians at 97.5° and 112.5° west of Greenwich, England. The Rocky Mountain area of the United States is in this region. See **time zone.**

moun•tain•eer |moun'tə **nîr'**| *n.* **1.** A person who lives in a mountainous area: *ballads of the Appalachian mountaineers.* **2.** A person who climbs mountains for sport. —*v.* To climb mountains for sport.

mountain goat. A goatlike animal of the mountains of northwestern North America, having short black horns and thick white hair. [SEE PICTURE]

mountain laurel. A shrub with poisonous evergreen leaves and clusters of pink or white flowers.

mountain lion. A large, tawny wild cat of mountainous regions of western North America and South America.

moun•tain•ous |**moun'**tə nəs| *adj.* **1.** Having or characterized by many mountains: *a mountainous region.* **2.** Huge; massive: *mountainous snowdrifts.*

moun•tain•side |**moun'**tən sīd'| *n.* Any of the sloping sides of a mountain.

Mountain Standard Time. Standard time as reckoned in the region between the meridians at 97.5° and 112.5° west of Greenwich, England. The Rocky Mountain area of the United States is in this region. See **time zone.**

moun•tain•top |**moun'**tən tŏp'| *n.* The top of a mountain.

moun•te•bank |**moun'**tə băngk'| *n.* **1.** A roving peddler of quack medicines. **2.** Any swindler.

mount•ed |**moun'**tĭd| *adj.* **1.** Seated or riding on a horse: *a mounted guard.* **2.** Equipped with a horse or horses: *mounted policemen; a well-mounted cavalry.* **3. a.** Placed on a backing: *a mounted photograph.* **b.** Set on or in a supporting structure or framework: *a mounted gemstone.*

mount•ing |**moun'**tĭng| *adj.* **1.** Increasing; rising: *mounting tension.* **2.** Serving to support or hold something in place: *a mounting bracket for a shelf.* —*n.* A supporting structure or frame; a mount: *a globe that can be lifted from its mounting.*

Mount Ver•non |**vûr'**nən|. The home and burial place of George Washington, in Virginia, near Washington, D.C.

mourn |môrn| *or* |mōrn| *v.* **1.** To express or feel sorrow for (a death or loss); grieve: *a maiden mourning her fallen lover. She loved the old house and mourned over its loss.* **2.** To show public grief and honor for (someone who has died): *The President was mourned by the nation at various memorial services.* **3.** To regret sadly; lament: *mourning his unhappy lot.* ¶*These sound alike* **mourn, morn.** —**mourn'er** *n.*

mourn•ful |**môrn'**fəl| *or* |**mōrn'**-| *adj.* **1.** Feeling or showing grief. **2.** Suggesting grief in appearance or sound: *the mournful wail of a foghorn.* —**mourn'ful•ly** *adv.* —**mourn'ful•ness** *n.*

mourn•ing |**môr'**nĭng| *or* |**mōr'**-| *n.* **1.** The expression of grief and respect for a beloved person who has died: *The flag was flown at half-mast as a sign of mourning.* **2.** The condition of someone showing grief over a death or loss: *The entire tribe went into mourning.* **3.** Dark, plain clothes worn to show grief: *One can't weep and wear mourning forever.* —***modifier:*** *a mourning period.* ¶*These sound alike* **mourning, morning.**

mourning cloak. A butterfly having dark, brownish wings with a yellowish border.

mourning dove. A North American bird related to the pigeons, having a long tail and a hollow, mournful call.

mouse |mous| *n., pl.* **mice** |mīs|. Any of several small animals usually having a long, narrow, almost hairless tail. Some kinds live in or near the houses of human beings.

mous•er |**mou'**zər| *n.* An animal, especially a cat, that catches mice.

mouse•trap |**mous'**trăp'| *n.* A trap for catching mice.

mousse |mo͞os| *n.* **1.** A chilled dessert made with whipped cream or beaten egg whites, gelatin, and flavoring. **2.** A molded dish made from meat, fish, or shellfish and whipped cream. ¶*These sound alike* **mousse, moose.**

mous•tache |**mŭs'**tăsh'| *or* |mə **stăsh'**| *n.* Chiefly British form of the word **mustache.**

mous•y |**mou'**sē| *or* |-zē| *adj.* **mous•i•er, mous•i•est. 1.** Mouselike in color or appearance: *mousy hair.* **2.** Timid and unnoticeable: *a mousy person.* —**mous'i•ness** *n.*

mouth |mouth| *n., pl.* **mouths** |mou*th*z|. **1. a.** The opening of the body through which an animal takes in food. **b.** The group of organs associated with this opening and its function, including the teeth, lips, tongue, etc. **2.** The part of the lips that can be seen on a human face. **3.** A natural opening, such as the opening of a cave or canyon or the part of a river that empties into a larger body of water. **4.** An opening into a container or enclosure: *the mouth of a bottle; the mouth of a pipe.* —*v.* |mou*th*| **mouthed, mouth•ing. 1.** To utter mechanically, without conviction or understanding: *mouthing phrases.* **2.** To hold in or rub with the mouth: *The baby was mouthing her spoon.* [SEE PICTURE]

***Idiom.* down at the mouth.** *Informal.* Unhappy; depressed; crestfallen.

mouth•ful |**mouth'**fo͝ol'| *n., pl.* **mouth•fuls. 1.** An amount taken into the mouth at one time: *He ate a monstrous breakfast and felt his strength returning with each mouthful.* **2.** *Informal.* An utterance that is especially significant or truthful: *My friend, you just said a mouthful.* **3.** A word or phrase that is long and hard to pronounce.

mouth organ. Either of two musical instruments, a harmonica or a panpipe.

mouth•piece |**mouth'**pēs'| *n.* **1.** The part of a device that is in or near the mouth when the device is in use: *the mouthpiece of a telephone.* **2.** *Informal.* A person or journal used to express the viewpoint of another person or of a group.

mouth•wash |**mouth'**wôsh'| *or* |-wŏsh'| *n.* A liquid preparation used to cleanse the mouth and as a gargle.

mov•a•ble |**mo͞o'**və bəl| *adj.* **1.** Capable of being moved: *movable type; a movable platform.* **2.** Changing its date from year to year: *a movable holiday.* —*n.* Often **movables.** Furniture or other personal possessions that can be moved from place to place.

mountain goat

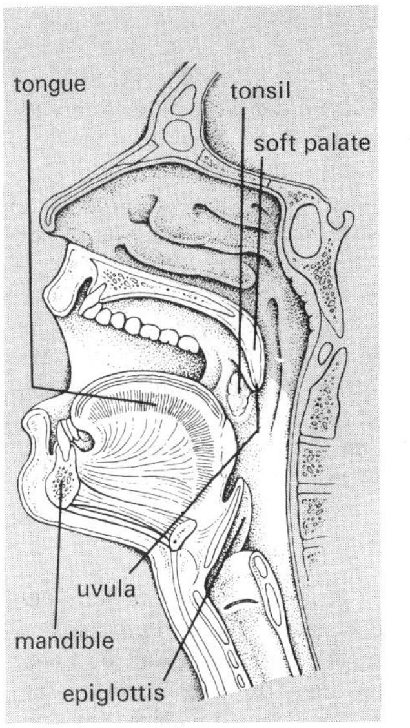

mouth

mow[1-2]
These two words are unrelated. **Mow[1]** *was* māwan *in Old English; its meaning has always been the same—"to cut grass or hay" —but of course the original process of using an iron sickle or scythe was utterly different from modern mechanized mowing.* **Mow[2]** *was Old English* mūwa, *"pile of hay."*

Mr./Mrs./Miss
In the school materials on which this Dictionary is based, **Mr.** *occurs 3,748 times,* **Mrs.** *occurs 1,619 times, and* **Miss** *occurs 1,056 times.*

Ms.
This abbreviation has recently been devised as an alternative to **Miss** *and* **Mrs.** *It is argued that since the masculine title* **Mr.** *is used for a man whether he is married or unmarried, there should be an equivalent feminine title. Like* **Miss** *and* **Mrs., Ms.** *can be derived from* **mistress.** *But* **Ms.** *has yet to find an agreed pronunciation: /mĭs/, /mĭz/, and simply* **/ĕm'ĕs'/** *seem to be the possibilities.*

ă pat/ā pay/â care/ä father/ĕ pet/ ē be/ĭ pit/ī pie/î fierce/ŏ pot/ ō go/ô paw, for/oi oil/o͝o book/ o͞o boot/ou out/ŭ cut/û fur/ *th* the/th thin/hw which/zh vision/ ə ago, item, pencil, atom, circus

move |mo͞ov| *v.* **moved, mov•ing. 1.** To change or cause to change in position from one place or point to another: *This rock won't move at all. Move your chair closer to the window.* **2.** To follow some specified course: *The earth moves in its orbit.* **3.** To change one's place of residence or business: *Our family has moved three times in the past year.* **4.** To advance; progress: *He felt that the work on the house was moving too slowly.* **5.** To rouse strong feelings in: *Her tears moved him deeply.* **6.** To persuade or motivate: *What moved him to enlist in the army?* **7. a.** To propose or suggest in a formal way, as at a meeting: *Betsy moved that the minutes of the previous meeting be approved.* **b.** To make a formal request or proposal: *move for a court adjournment.* **8.** In chess or checkers, to shift (a piece) to another position: *moved his king out of check. Hurry up and move.* **9.** To live or be active in a particular social setting: *He moves in the highest diplomatic circles.* **10.** *Informal.* To travel at a high speed: *Wow, this car is really moving!* **11.** To take action: *If the United Nations doesn't move fast, several species of whales will soon be extinct.* **12.** To empty (the bowels). —*n.* **1.** The act of moving: *He made no move to defend himself.* **2.** A calculated action to achieve an end: *The opponents, in a surprise move, changed their usual game plan.* **3.** In chess or checkers: **a.** A player's turn to move a piece: *It's your move.*

Idioms. **get a move on.** *Informal.* **1.** To get started. **2.** To hurry up. **move heaven and earth.** To make a gigantic effort. **move up in the world.** To rise in status. **on the move. 1.** Moving about; traveling: *As a union organizer, he's constantly on the move.* **2.** Making progress; advancing: *a nation on the move.*

move•a•ble |mo͞o'və bəl| *adj.* A form of the word **movable.**

move•ment |mo͞ov'mənt| *n.* **1. a.** The act or process of moving: *the movement of our eyes in dreaming slumber.* **b.** An example of this: *The shortstop snatched up the ball in a quick movement.* **2.** Action; activity: *Scotland Yard watched every movement of the spies.* **3.** A tendency; trend: *a movement toward greater freedom in the arts.* **4.** The activities of a group of people toward a specific goal: *the civil-rights movement.* **5.** A mass migration: *the westward movement of the American pioneers.* **6.** A military maneuver. **7.** An illusion of motion: *Countless vertical lines and pointed arches emphasized the vertical, upward movement of the cathedral.* **8.** The emptying of the bowels or the waste matter removed by this action. **9.** One of the large sections of a musical composition, usually having its own independent beginning and end. **10.** A mechanical device or system that produces or transmits motion: *the movement of a watch.*

mov•er |mo͞o'vər| *n.* **1.** Someone or something that moves: *The railroad became a prime mover of people and products in all directions.* **2.** A person or company that is hired to move furniture and other belongings from one place to another.

mov•ie |mo͞o'vē| *n. Informal.* **1.** A motion picture: *standing in line to see a movie.* **2.** A theater in which motion pictures are shown: *What's showing tonight at the movies?* **3. movies.** The motion-picture industry: *a big success in the movies.* —***modifier:*** *a movie house; a movie star.*

mov•ing |mo͞o'vĭng| *adj.* **1.** Changing or capable of changing position: *the moving parts of an engine.* **2.** Affecting the emotions: *a moving love story.* —*n.* The business of transporting furniture and other household belongings. —***modifier:*** *a moving van.*

mov•ing•ly |mo͞o'vĭng lē| *adv.* In a manner that affects the emotions: *The minister spoke movingly on Sunday.*

moving picture. A motion picture. —***modifier:*** **(moving-picture):** *a moving-picture director.*

mow[1] |mō| *v.* **mowed, mowed** or **mown** |mōn|, **mow•ing. 1.** To cut down (grass, grain, etc.) with a scythe, lawn mower, etc.: *Mow the grass before it gets too high. He went outside to mow.* **2.** To cut the grass, grain, etc., from: *mow the lawn; mow a field.* —***phrasal verb.*** **mow down.** To fell in great numbers, as in battle. ¶*These sound alike* **mow[1], mho.** [SEE NOTE]

mow[2] |mou| *n.* **1.** A pile of hay or grain, especially in a barn. **2.** The part of a barn where such a pile is stored. [SEE NOTE]

mow•er |mō'ər| *n.* **1.** A person who mows: *The mowers went out early to the fields.* **2.** A machine that mows: *a lawn mower.*

mown |mōn|. A part participle of **mow.** ¶*These sound alike* **mown, moan.**

Mo•zam•bique |mō'zăm bēk'|. A country on the southeastern coast of Africa. Population, 12,130,-000. Capital, Maputo. —**Mo'zam•bi'can** |mō'zəm-bē'kən| *adj. & n.*

Mo•zart |mōt'särt'|, **Wolfgang Amadeus.** 1756–1791. Austrian composer.

moz•za•rel•la |mŏt'sə rĕl'ə| *or* |mōt'-| *n.* A soft, white Italian cheese.

MP military police; military policeman.

M.P. 1. Member of Parliament. **2.** Military police; military policeman.

mpg, m.p.g. miles per gallon.

mph, m.p.h. miles per hour.

Mr. |mĭs'tər| *n., pl.* **Messrs.** |mĕs'ərz|. An abbreviation used as a title of courtesy before a man's last name. [SEE NOTE]

Mrs. |mĭs'ĭz| *n., pl.* **Mmes.** |mā däm'| *or* |-dăm'|. An abbreviation used as a title of courtesy before a married woman's last name. [SEE NOTE]

ms, ms., MS, MS. manuscript.

Ms. or **Ms** |mĭz|. An abbreviation used as a title of courtesy before a woman's last name or before her given name and last name, whether she is married or not. [SEE NOTE]

M.S. Master of Science.

MST, M.S.T. Mountain Standard Time.

mt., Mt. mount; mountain.

mu |myo͞o| *or* |mo͞o| *n.* The 12th letter of the Greek alphabet, written Μ, μ. In English it is represented as *M, m.*

much |mŭch| *adj.* **more** |môr| *or* |mōr|, **most** |mōst|. Great in quantity, degree, or extent: *much talk and little action.* —*n.* **1.** A large quantity or amount: *Did you get much done?* **2.** Anything remarkable or important: *She's never going to amount to much.* —*adv.* **more, most. 1.** To a large extent; greatly: *We are much impressed with the results of your research.* **2.** Just about; almost: *much the same. In old age she saw things much as she did when she was young.*

Idioms. **make much of.** To pay great attention

to: *We all made much of the baby when he started to talk.* **much as.** Even though; however much: *Much as I love skating, I'd rather go to the movies tonight.* **think much of.** To think highly of: *I don't really think much of this idea.*

mu•ci•lage |myōō′sə lĭj| *n.* An adhesive made from the natural gum of plants.

muck |mŭk| *n.* **1.** Moist animal dung mixed with rotting vegetable matter and used as fertilizer. **2.** Black earth containing rotting vegetable matter. **3.** A moist, sticky mixture, as of mud and filth.

muck•rake |mŭk′rāk′| *v.* **muck•raked, muck•rak•ing.** To search for and expose corruption in public affairs. **—muck′rak′er** *n.*

mu•cous |myōō′kəs| *adj.* **1.** Of or like mucus. **2.** Producing or secreting mucus. ¶*These sound alike* **mucous, mucus.**

mucous membrane. A membrane, covered with glands that secrete mucus, that lines all the passages of the body that connect with the outside. The alimentary canal and the respiratory system are lined with mucous membrane.

mu•cus |myōō′kəs| *n.* The sticky, slippery liquid material secreted by the glands of the mucous membrane as a protective, lubricating coating. ¶*These sound alike* **mucus, mucous.**

mud |mŭd| *n.* **1.** Wet, sticky, soft earth. **2.** Scandalous charges; slander: *sling mud at a political opponent.* **—modifier:** *a mud pie; a mud puddle.*

Idiom. **(one's) name is mud.** In bad favor.

mud•dle |mŭd′l| *v.* **mud•dled, mud•dling. 1.** To make a mess of: *muddle a task.* **2.** To confuse: *a report that muddles the issues.* **—phrasal verb. muddle through.** To avoid defeat or failure in spite of one's blunders. *—n.* A jumble; mess; confusion.

mud•dle-head•ed |mŭd′l hĕd′ĭd| *adj.* Mentally confused; stupid: *a muddle-headed decision.*

mud•dy |mŭd′ē| *adj.* **mud•di•er, mud•di•est. 1.** Covered or soiled with mud: *a muddy field; muddy shoes.* **2.** Cloudy or dull with or as if with mud: *a muddy creek; muddy coffee; muddy skies.* **3.** Confused; obscure: *a muddy style of writing.* *—v.* **mud•died, mud•dy•ing, mud•dies. 1.** To make soiled with mud: *He muddied his boots crossing the yard.* **2.** To make cloudy or dull with or as if with mud: *Soil erosion muddies the rivers.* **3.** To confuse: *His remarks only served to muddy the issue.* **—mud′di•ly** *adv.* **—mud′di•ness** *n.*

mud puppy. A salamander of lakes, ponds, and streams, having featherlike gills that remain in the adult form.

mud•sling•ing |mŭd′slĭng′ĭng| *n.* The practice of making malicious charges against an opponent, especially in a political campaign. **—mud′sling′er** *n.*

mu•ez•zin |myōō ĕz′ĭn| *or* |mōō-| *n.* A Moslem public crier who calls the faithful to prayer.

muff¹ |mŭf| *v.* **1.** To ruin or spoil through clumsiness or carelessness; bungle: *He muffed his only chance for the job.* **2.** To fail to catch (a ball): *The second baseman muffed the ball. The ball was thrown to him, and he muffed.* [SEE NOTE]

muff² |mŭf| *n.* A tubelike cover of fur or cloth with open ends into which the hands are put for warmth. [SEE NOTE & PICTURE]

muf•fin |mŭf′ĭn| *n.* A small, cup-shaped bread, often sweetened. **—modifier:** *a muffin pan.*

muf•fle |mŭf′əl| *v.* **muf•fled, muf•fling. 1.** To wrap up in order to keep warm, conceal, protect, etc.: *Mother muffled him up in a heavy coat and wool cap.* **2. a.** To make less loud or less distinct; deaden: *muffle sound.* **b.** To wrap up or pad in order to deaden the sound of: *muffle a drum.*

muf•fler |mŭf′lər| *n.* **1.** A scarf worn around the neck for warmth. **2.** A device that deadens noise, especially that of an automobile engine.

muf•ti |mŭf′tē| *n.* Civilian clothes worn by someone who is usually seen in uniform.

mug¹ |mŭg| *n.* A large, heavy drinking cup, usually having a handle. [SEE NOTE]

mug² |mŭg| *n.* *Slang.* A person's face. [SEE NOTE]

mug³ |mŭg| *v.* **mugged, mug•ging.** *Slang.* To assault with the intent of robbing. **—mug′ger** *n.* [SEE NOTE]

mug•gy |mŭg′ē| *adj.* **mug•gi•er, mug•gi•est.** Warm and humid, with little or no breeze: *a muggy day in August.* **—mug′gi•ness** *n.*

Mu•ham•mad |mōō hăm′ĭd| *or* |-hä′mĭd|. A form of the name **Mohammed.**

mu•lat•to |mə lăt′ō| *or* |-lä′tō| *or* |myōō′-| *n., pl.* **mu•lat•tos. 1.** A person having one Caucasoid parent and one Negroid parent. **2.** Any person of mixed Caucasoid and Negroid ancestry.

mul•ber•ry |mŭl′bĕr′ē| *n., pl.* **-ber•ries. 1. a.** A tree with irregularly shaped leaves and sweet, purplish or white fruit shaped like blackberries. **b.** The fruit of such a tree. **2.** A dull purplish red. *—adj.* Dull purplish red.

mulch |mŭlch| *n.* A covering of leaves, hay, etc., placed around growing plants as protection against cold or to keep the soil moist. *—v.* To cover with a mulch.

mule¹ |myōōl| *n.* **1.** A hybrid animal that is the offspring of a male donkey and a female horse. See **hinny. 2.** *Informal.* A stubborn person. **3.** A spinning machine that draws and twists fibers into yarn and winds the yarn at the same time. **—modifier:** *a mule driver; a mule train.* ¶*These sound alike* **mule, mewl.** [SEE PICTURE]

mule² |myōōl| *n.* An open lounging slipper that leaves the heel bare. ¶*These sound alike* **mule, mewl.**

mule•skin•ner |myōōl′skĭn′ər| *n.* A driver of mules.

mu•le•teer |myōō′lə tîr′| *n.* A driver of mules.

mul•ish |myōō′lĭsh| *adj.* Stubborn; unyielding: *mulish obstinacy; a mulish disposition.* **—mul′ish•ly** *adv.* **—mul′ish•ness** *n.*

mull¹ |mŭl| *v.* To heat and add sugar and spices to (wine, ale, cider, etc.). [SEE NOTE]

mull² |mŭl| *v.* To think about; ponder: *He mulled over the idea for days.* [SEE NOTE]

mul•lein |mŭl′ən| *n.* A tall plant having leaves covered with woolly down and long, tight clusters of yellow flowers.

mul•let |mŭl′ĭt| *n., pl.* **mul•let** or **mul•lets.** Any of several saltwater or freshwater fishes often used as food.

multi–. A word element meaning "many, much": **multicolored.**

mul•ti•col•ored |mŭl′tĭ kŭl′ərd| *adj.* Having many colors.

muff¹⁻²

Muff¹ *is of unknown origin.* **Muff²** *is related to* **muffle,** *which is from Old French* moufle, *"mitten."*

muff²

mug¹⁻²⁻³

Mug¹ *is of unknown origin, first occurring in the sixteenth century.* **Mug²** *first occurs in the eighteenth century; it is possible that it is from* **mug¹,** *since beer mugs were often made in the shape of faces.* **Mug³** *may originally have been a slang word meaning "to hit in the face," and thus have come from* **mug².** *It has to be admitted that none of these etymologies is very satisfactory.*

mule¹

mull¹⁻²

Mull¹ *is from Middle Dutch* mul, *"dust, powdered spice."* **Mull²** *originally meant "to grind"; it is related to* **mull¹.**

mum[1-2]

Mum[1], *like* **mumble**, *seems to have been formed in imitation of inarticulate sounds made with closed lips.* **Mum[2]** *is a shortening of* **chrysanthemum**.

mummy[1-2]

Mummy[1] *is ultimately from Arabic* mūmiyā, *"wax used for embalming corpses."* **Mummy[2]** *is a variant of* **mommy**.

mummy[1]

mul•ti•eth•nic |mŭl′tē **ĕth′**nĭk| *adj.* Of or including many ethnic groups: *a multiethnic city.*

mul•ti•far•i•ous |mŭl′tə **fâr′**ē əs| *adj.* Having much variety; of many kinds: *the multifarious occupations in a modern economy.*

mul•ti•me•di•a |mŭl′tĭ **mē′**dē ə| *adj.* Having to do with or using several media of communication, entertainment, or expression: *a multimedia advertising campaign.*

mul•ti•mil•lion•aire |mŭl′tə mĭl′yə **nâr′**| *n.* A person whose assets are worth many millions of dollars, pounds, etc.

mul•ti•ple |**mŭl′**tə pəl| *adj.* Of, having, or consisting of more than a single element, part, or individual: *a plan with multiple flaws.* —*n.* A number that has another number as one of its exact factors; for example, 4, 6, 8, and 12 are multiples of 2.

multiple sclerosis. A disease in which there is degeneration of the central nervous system, with hard patches of tissue formed throughout the brain or spinal cord.

mul•ti•pli•cand |mŭl′tə plĭ **kănd′**| *n.* A number that is considered to be multiplied by another number.

mul•ti•pli•ca•tion |mŭl′tə plĭ **kā′**shən| *n.* **1.** The act or process of multiplying. **2.** A mathematical operation performed on a pair of numbers in order to derive a third number called a product. It is sometimes convenient to consider multiplication as repeated addition in which one number indicates how many times the other is to be added together. For example, $3 \times 4 = 4 + 4 + 4 = 4 \times 3 = 3 + 3 + 3 + 3 = 12$.

multiplication sign. The sign (×) placed between a pair of numbers to show that multiplication is to be performed on them.

mul•ti•pli•ca•tive |**mŭl′**tə plĭ kā′tĭv| *or* |mŭl′tə **plĭk′**ə-| *adj.* Of or having to do with multiplication.

mul•ti•plic•i•ty |mŭl′tə **plĭs′**ĭ tē| *n., pl.* **mul•ti•plic•i•ties.** A great and varied number: *a multiplicity of courses to choose from.*

mul•ti•pli•er |**mŭl′**tə plī′ər| *n.* A number by which another number is considered to be multiplied.

mul•ti•ply |**mŭl′**tə plī′| *v.* **mul•ti•plied, mul•ti•ply•ing, mul•ti•plies. 1.** To increase in number or amount, by or as if by multiplication. **2.** To perform the mathematical operation of multiplication on (a pair of numbers).

mul•ti•ra•cial |mŭl′tə **rā′**shəl| *adj.* Composed of various races: *Hawaii is a good example of a multiracial society.*

mul•ti•stage |**mŭl′**tĭ stāj′| *adj.* Designed to perform a process or operation in two or more steps or stages: *a multistage rocket.*

mul•ti•tude |**mŭl′**tĭ to͞od′| *or* |-tyo͞od′| *n.* **1.** A large number: *Smoke drifted lazily from a multitude of quaint chimneys.* **2. the multitude.** The masses; the common people.

mul•ti•tu•di•nous |mŭl′tĭ **to͞od′**n əs| *or* |**-tyo͞od′-**| *adj.* Existing in great numbers; very numerous: *the multitudinous stars of our galaxy.*

mum[1] |mŭm| *adj.* Not talking; close-mouthed; silent: *Keep mum.* [SEE NOTE]

***Idiom.* mum's the word.** Don't talk.

mum[2] |mŭm| *n. Informal.* A chrysanthemum. [SEE NOTE]

mum•ble |**mŭm′**bəl| *v.* **mum•bled, mum•bling.** To speak or utter in an indistinct manner, as by lowering the voice and partially closing the mouth: *I can't understand you when you mumble. She mumbled a quick apology.* —*n.* A low, indistinct voice: *He answered the teacher in a mumble.*

mum•bo jum•bo |**mŭm′**bō **jŭm′**bō|. *Informal.* **1.** The ritual, incantations, etc., of a witch doctor. **2.** Speech or writing that is unnecessarily obscure.

mum•mi•fy |**mŭm′**ə fī′| *v.* **mum•mi•fied, mum•mi•fy•ing, mum•mi•fies. 1.** To make into a mummy. **2.** To shrivel up like a mummy. —**mum′mi•fi•ca′tion** *n.*

mum•my[1] |**mŭm′**ē| *n., pl.* **mum•mies. 1.** The body of a human being or animal embalmed after death, as practiced by the ancient Egyptians. **2.** Any dead body preserved by some accident of nature. [SEE NOTE & PICTURE]

mum•my[2] |**mŭm′**ē| *n., pl.* **mum•mies.** *Informal.* Mother. [SEE NOTE]

mumps |mŭmps| *n. (used with a singular verb).* A contagious virus disease that causes inflammation of the salivary glands, especially those at the back of the jaw, and sometimes of the pancreas and ovaries or testes.

munch |mŭnch| *v.* To chew (food) in a noisy, steady manner: *munch popcorn. They found our cow munching away in a neighbor's pasture.*

mun•dane |mŭn **dān′**| *or* |**mŭn′**dān′| *adj.* **1.** Worldly; not spiritual: *mundane interests.* **2.** Concerned with practical matters rather than ideals: *He decided to devote his life to the welfare of mankind, not to mundane commercial pursuits.*

Mu•nich |**myo͞o′**nĭk|. The capital of Bavaria, in southeastern West Germany. Population, 1,338,000.

mu•nic•i•pal |myo͞o **nĭs′**ə pəl| *adj.* Of or relating to a city or its government: *municipal politics; the municipal airport.*

mu•nic•i•pal•i•ty |myo͞o nĭs′ə **păl′**ĭ tē| *n., pl.* **mu•nic•i•pal•i•ties.** A city or town that is self-governing in local matters.

mu•nif•i•cent |myo͞o **nĭf′**ĭ sənt| *adj.* Very generous: *a munificent reward.* —**mu•nif′i•cence** *n.* —**mu•nif′i•cent•ly** *adv.*

mu•ni•tions |myo͞o **nĭsh′**ənz| *pl.n.* Supplies for warfare, especially guns and ammunition.

mu•ral |**myo͝or′**əl| *n.* A large picture or decoration applied directly to a wall or ceiling. —***modifier:*** *a mural painter.*

mur•der |**mûr′**dər| *n.* The unlawful and deliberate killing of one person by another. —*v.* **1.** To kill (a person or persons) unlawfully and with deliberate intent. **2.** *Informal.* To ruin; spoil: *a writer who murders the English language.*

mur•der•er |**mûr′**dər ər| *n.* A person who commits a murder; a killer.

mur•der•ous |**mûr′**dər əs| *adj.* **1.** Guilty of, capable of, or intent on murder: *A murderous mob gathered in front of the palace.* **2.** Angry or savage, as if intent on murder: *a murderous glance.* **3.** Of or relating to murder: *murderous acts; caught in a murderous ambush.*

mu•rex |**myo͝or′**ĕks′| *n.* Any of several sea mollusks with a rough or spiny spiral shell. One kind was used in ancient times as the source of a much-valued purplish dye.

murk |mûrk| *n.* Darkness; gloom: *groped his way*

ă pat/ā pay/â care/ä father/ĕ pet/ ē be/ĭ pit/ī pie/î fierce/ŏ pot/ ō go/ô paw, for/oi oil/o͝o book/ o͞o boot/ou out/ŭ cut/û fur/ *th* the/th thin/hw which/zh vision/ ə ago, item, pencil, atom, circus

through the murk of the moonless night.

murk•y |mûr′kē| *adj.* **murk•i•er, murk•i•est. 1.** Dark; gloomy: *a company that still conducts its business from murky cubbyholes.* **2.** Not clear; foggy; hazy: *a murky day.* **3.** Cloudy and dark with sediment: *Pools of murky water dotted the swampy shore.* —**murk′i•ly** *adv.* —**murk′i•ness** *n.*

mur•mur |mûr′mər| *n.* **1.** A low, continuous sound: *the murmur of the sea.* **2.** A complaint made in a low voice: *took his punishment without a murmur.* **3.** An abnormal sound made by the heart, lungs, or blood vessels. —*v.* **1.** To make a low, continuous sound: *The brook murmured through the forest.* **2.** To utter or say in a low, indistinct voice: *"Amen," the congregation murmured. The shy pupil murmured his answer.* **3.** To speak or complain in an undertone: *The students murmured among themselves about the new regulations.*

Mus•cat |mŭs′kăt′| *or* |-kət|. The capital of Oman. Population, 7,500.

mus•cle |mŭs′əl| *n.* **1.** A type of body tissue composed of fibers that are capable of contracting and relaxing to cause movement or exert force. **2.** Any one of the many structures of the body that are made of such tissue and cause bodily movement. **3.** Muscular strength; brawn: *He has plenty of muscle.* —*v.* **mus•cled, mus•cling.** To force one's way into a place or situation where one is not wanted: *muscle in on someone else's job.* ¶*These sound alike* **muscle, mussel.**

mus•cle-bound |mŭs′əl bound′| *adj.* Having muscles that are overly developed and stiff, usually as a result of incorrect exercise.

mus•co•vite |mŭs′kə vīt′| *n.* The most common form of mica, a mineral composed mostly of a silicate of potassium and aluminum.

mus•cu•lar |mŭs′kyə lər| *adj.* **1.** Of or consisting of muscle or muscles: *a muscular organ.* **2.** Done by the use of muscle or muscles: *a muscular feat.* **3.** Having strong, well-developed muscles: *a muscular fellow.* —**mus′cu•lar′i•ty** |mŭs′kyə lâr′ĭ-tē| *n.* —**mus′cu•lar•ly** *adv.*

muscular dys•tro•phy |dĭs′trə fē|. A chronic disease in which a person's muscles gradually and irreversibly deteriorate, causing weakness and finally complete disability. The disease is not contagious, and its cause is not known.

mus•cu•la•ture |mŭs′kyə lə chər| *n.* The system of muscles of an animal or of a body part.

muse |myo͞oz| *v.* **mused, mus•ing.** To consider at length; ponder; meditate: *He sat alone, musing over his chances in tomorrow's fight.* ¶*These sound alike* **muse, mews.**

Muse |myo͞oz| *n.* **1.** In Greek mythology, one of the nine sister goddesses who presided over the arts and sciences. **2. muse.** A source of inspiration, personified as a spirit. [SEE NOTE]

mu•se•um |myo͞o zē′əm| *n.* A building in which works of artistic, historical, or scientific interest are exhibited.

mush¹ |mŭsh| *n.* **1.** A porridge made of meal, especially corn meal, boiled in water or milk. **2.** Anything that resembles this in texture: *The thugs made a mush out of his face.* **3.** *Informal.* Extreme sentimentality: *Aw, that movie was just a lot of mush.* [SEE NOTE]

mush² |mŭsh| *interj.* A command to a team of sled dogs to start or go faster. [SEE NOTE]

mush•room |mŭsh′ro͞om′| *or* |-ro͝om′| *n.* **1.** A type of fungus having a stalk topped by a fleshy, umbrella-shaped cap. Some mushrooms are used as food, but many kinds are poisonous. **2.** Something resembling a mushroom in shape. —***modifier:*** *mushroom soup; a mushroom cloud.* —*v.* To grow, multiply, or spread quickly.

mush•y |mŭsh′ē| *adj.* **mush•i•er, mush•i•est. 1.** Resembling mush; soft and pulpy: *The apples were mushy and brown inside.* **2.** Sentimental to an extreme degree: *a mushy love story.* —**mush′i•ly** *adv.* —**mush′i•ness** *n.*

mu•sic |myo͞o′zĭk| *n.* **1.** The art of organizing sounds into combinations and sequences that will have meaning of some sort for a listener. **2.** Vocal or instrumental sounds that are characterized by rhythm, melody, harmony, or some combination of these. **3. a.** A musical composition. **b.** A group of such compositions that are related in some way: *Romantic music; the music of Bach.* **c.** A written or printed score or part for a musical composition: *Play from the music.* **d.** Such scores or parts in general. **4.** A group of musical performers: *entertainment with live music.* **5.** Any pleasing sound or combination of sounds. —***modifier:*** *a music teacher.*

***Idiom.* face the music.** To accept the consequences, especially of one's own actions.

mu•si•cal |myo͞o′zĭ kəl| *adj.* **1.** Of, involving, or used in producing music: *a musical instrument; musical training.* **2.** Accompanied by or set to music: *a musical play.* **3.** Devoted to or skilled in music. **4.** Pleasing to the ear; melodious: *a musical speaking voice.* —*n.* A musical comedy. —**mu′si•cal•ly** *adv.*

musical comedy. A play that uses spoken dialogue alternating with songs and dances.

mu•si•cale |myo͞o′zĭ kăl′| *n.* A musical program performed at a party or social gathering.

mu•si•cal•i•ty |myo͞o′ zĭ kăl′ĭ tē| *n.* **1.** Skill, artistry, and good taste as shown in a musical performance. **2.** Skill in, talent for, or capability to respond to music.

music box. An automatic mechanical device that produces musical sounds.

music drama. A type of opera in which the music and dramatic action go on without interruption rather than being divided into separate pieces such as arias, recitatives, duets, etc.

music hall. A theater for musical entertainment or vaudeville.

mu•si•cian |myo͞o zĭsh′ən| *n.* Someone who is skilled in performing or composing music, especially someone involved in music as a profession.

mu•si•cian•ship |myo͞o zĭsh′ən shĭp′| *n.* Skill, taste, and artistry in performing or composing music.

mu•si•col•o•gist |myo͞o′zĭ kŏl′ə jĭst| *n.* A person who specializes in musicology.

mu•si•col•o•gy |myo͞o′zĭ kŏl′ə jē| *n.* The historical and scientific study of music.

musk |mŭsk| *n.* **1.** A strong-smelling substance produced by special glands of the male **musk deer** of Asia and used in making perfume. **2.** A similar substance produced by other animals or made artificially. **3.** The odor of musk.

mus•kel•lunge |mŭs′kə lŭnj′| *n., pl.* **mus•kel•lunge** or **mus•kel•lung•es.** A large North Amer-

Muse

The names of the Muses and their departments are:

Calliope /kə **lī′**ə pē/: *heroic poetry*

Clio /**klī′**ō/: *history*

Erato /**ĕr′**ə tō′/: *love poetry*

Euterpe /yo͞o **tûr′**pē/: *flute music*

Melpomene /mĕl **pŏm′**ə nē/: *tragedy*

Polyhymnia /pŏl′ē **hĭm′**nē ə/: *singing*

Terpsichore /tûrp **sĭk′**ə rē/: *dance*

Thalia /thə **lī′**ə/ *or* /**thā′**lē ə/ *or* /**thāl′**yə/: *comedy*

Urania /yo͞o **rā′**nē ə/ *or* /yo͞o **rān′**yə/: *astronomy*

The Greek form of the word **Muse** *was* Mousa. Mousikē *meant "artistic and scientific activity in general"; this was borrowed into Latin as* mūsica *and later came to mean specifically "music"; it is the source of the word* **music.** Mouseion *meant "a home of the Muses, a place where* mousikē *is taught or cultivated"; this was borrowed into Latin as* mūsēum *and came to mean especially "a library or collection of art objects"; from this we have* **museum.**

mush¹·²

Mush¹ *is probably a variant of* **mash. Mush²** *is from Canadian French* mouche! *"run!"*

ican freshwater fish related to and resembling the pike.

mus•ket |mŭs′kĭt| *n.* An old type of long-barreled gun, used before the invention of the rifle.

mus•ket•eer |mŭs′kĭ tîr′| *n.* A soldier armed with a musket, especially a member of the French royal household bodyguard in the 17th and 18th centuries.

mus•ket•ry |mŭs′kĭ trē| *n.* **1.** Muskets or musket fire. **2.** The technique of firing small arms.

Mus•kho•ge•an |mŭs kō′gē ən| *n.* A family of North American Indian languages including Chickasaw, Choctaw, Creek, and Seminole. —**Mus•kho′ge•an** *adj.*

musk•mel•on |mŭsk′mĕl′ən| *n.* A cantaloupe or similar melon having a rough rind and flesh with a musky odor.

Mus•ko•ge•an |mŭs kō′gē ən| *n. & adj.* A form of the word **Muskhogean.**

musk ox

musk ox. A large animal of northern North America and Greenland, having dark, shaggy hair and curved horns. [SEE PICTURE]

musk•rat |mŭs′krăt′| *n.* **1.** A North American animal that lives in or near water and has thick brown fur and a narrow, flat, scaly tail. **2.** The fur of such an animal.

musk•y |mŭs′kē| *adj.* **musk•i•er, musk•i•est.** Having a heavy, sweetish odor like that of musk: *the musky smell of the wild boar.* —**musk′i•ness** *n.*

Mus•lim |mŭz′ləm| *or* |mŏŏs′-| *or* |mŏŏz′-| *n. & adj.* A form of the word **Moslem.**

mus•lin |mŭz′lĭn| *n.* A cotton cloth of plain weave, either coarse or sheer, used for sheets, curtains, dresses, etc. —***modifier:*** *muslin pillowcases.*

muss |mŭs| *v.* **1.** To make untidy or messy: *The wind mussed up her hair.* **2.** To ruin; spoil: *The weather mussed up our plans for the weekend.*

mus•sel |mŭs′əl| *n.* Any of several saltwater or freshwater mollusks having a pair of narrow, often dark-blue shells. ¶*These sound alike* **mussel, muscle.**

Mus•so•li•ni |mōō′sə lē′nē| *or* |mŏŏs′ə-|, **Benito.** 1883–1945. Fascist dictator of Italy (1922–43).

Mus•sul•man |mŭs′əl mən| *n., pl.* **-men** |-mən|. *Archaic.* A Moslem.

muss•y |mŭs′ē| *adj.* **muss•i•er, muss•i•est.** *Informal.* Disarranged; untidy: *Her hair is always mussy in the morning.* —**muss′i•ly** *adv.*

must |mŭst| *v.* —Used as an auxiliary to indicate: **1.** Necessity or obligation: *If you want to get high grades in school, you must read all your assignments.* **2.** Probability: *It must be about time for supper.* **3.** Certainty or inevitability: *All good things must come to an end.* **4.** Insistence: *I must repeat, she is an excellent swimmer and has earned her badge.* —*n. Informal.* An absolute requirement; something that should be seen, done, or otherwise acted on: *Catch that new movie; it's a must.*

mus•tache |mŭs′tăsh′| *or* |mə stăsh′| *n.* The hair growing on a man's upper lip, especially when it is not shaved off, but shaped and groomed.

mus•ta•chio |mə stăsh′ō| *or* |-stăsh′ē ō| *or* |-stä′shō| *or* |-shē ō′| *n., pl.* **mus•ta•chios.** Often **mustachios.** A mustache, especially one that is large and full.

mus•tang |mŭs′tăng′| *n.* A small, strong horse of the plains of western North America, especially a wild descendant of the horses brought to the New World by Spanish explorers.

mus•tard |mŭs′tərd| *n.* **1.** A plant with yellow flowers and small, sharp-tasting seeds. **2. a.** The powdered seeds of this plant. **b.** A spicy yellowish or brownish relish made by mixing this powder with vinegar, water, etc. **3.** A dark brownish yellow. —*adj.* Dark brownish yellow.

mustard plaster. A pastelike mixture of powdered mustard, flour, and water spread on a cloth and applied to a person's chest or back as a poultice.

mus•ter |mŭs′tər| *v.* **1.** To bring or come together; assemble: *mustered his platoon for inspection. The men mustered for roll call.* **2.** To call forth or bring forth: *He finally mustered enough courage to ask her for a date.* —***phrasal verbs.*** **muster in.** To enlist (someone) for military service. **muster out.** To discharge (someone) from military service. —*n.* **1.** A gathering, especially of troops, for inspection, roll call, etc. **2.** The official roll of men in a military unit.

must•n't |mŭs′ənt|. Must not.

must•y |mŭs′tē| *adj.* **must•i•er, must•i•est.** Stale or moldy: *a musty smell.* —**must′i•ness** *n.*

mu•ta•ble |myōō′tə bəl| *adj.* Able or likely to change: *All things in nature and society are mutable.* —**mu′ta•bil′i•ty** *n.*

mu•tant |myōōt′nt| *n.* A living thing that, as a result of mutation, has characteristics that are different from those of its parents. —*adj.* Changed as a result of mutation: *a mutant animal.*

mu•tate |myōō′tāt′| *or* |myōō tāt′| *v.* **mu•tat•ed, mu•tat•ing.** To undergo or cause to undergo change, especially by mutation.

mu•ta•tion |myōō tā′shən| *n.* **1. a.** Any change in the genes or chromosomes of a living thing that can be inherited by its offspring. **b.** A mutant. **2.** A change, as in form: *the soft, nasal mutations of the Welsh language.*

mute |myōōt| *adj.* **1.** Not having the power of speech. **2.** Refraining from speech; silent: *remained mute under questioning.* **3.** Unspoken: *The scorched leaves of the trees around the clearing bore mute testimony to the fire.* —*n.* **1.** A person incapable of speech, especially one both deaf and mute. **2.** Any of various attachments used to soften, muffle, or alter the tone of a musical instrument. —*v.* **mut•ed, mut•ing.** To muffle or soften the sound of: *When the wind muted its wild call, it made the world seem more bleak and icy than ever.* —**mute′ly** *adv.* —**mute′ness** *n.*

mu•ti•late |myōōt′l āt′| *v.* **mu•ti•lat•ed, mu•ti•lat•ing.** To damage by cutting off or mangling (a necessary part, limb, etc.). —**mu′ti•la′tion** *n.*

mu•ti•neer |myōōt′n îr′| *n.* A person, especially a soldier or sailor, who takes part in a mutiny.

mu•ti•nous |myōōt′n əs| *adj.* **1.** Engaged in or planning to engage in mutiny. **2.** Rebellious: *a mutinous child.* —**mu′ti•nous•ly** *adv.*

mu•ti•ny |myōōt′n ē| *n., pl.* **mu•ti•nies.** Open rebellion against authority, especially rebellion of soldiers or sailors. —*v.* **mu•ti•nied, mu•ti•ny•ing, mu•ti•nies.** To commit mutiny; rebel.

mutt |mŭt| *n. Slang.* A dog of mixed breed; a mongrel.

ă pat/ā pay/â care/ä father/ĕ pet/ ē be/ĭ pit/ī pie/î fierce/ŏ pot/ ō go/ô paw, for/oi oil/ŏŏ book/ ōō boot/ou out/ŭ cut/û fur/ *th* the/th thin/hw which/zh vision/ ə ago, item, pencil, atom, circus

mut•ter |mŭt′ər| *v.* **1.** To say or speak in a low, unclear tone: *She muttered to herself while she worked.* **2.** To complain or grumble: *The people muttered about the high price of food.* **3.** To make a low rumbling sound: *The forest fire muttered in the distance.* —*n.* A low, unclear sound.

mut•ton |mŭt′n| *n.* The meat of a full-grown sheep.

mu•tu•al |myo͞o′cho͞o əl| *adj.* **1.** Having the same relationship to each other: *mutual friends.* **2.** Possessed or shared in common: *mutual problems.* **3.** Given and received in equal amounts: *mutual concern; mutual feelings.* —**mu′tu•al•ly** *adv.*

mutual fund. A company that freely buys and sells its own shares and uses the pooled capital of its shareholders to invest in other companies.

muz•zle |mŭz′əl| *n.* **1.** The often projecting nose and jaws of certain animals, such as a dog or horse. **2.** A leather or wire device fitted over an animal's snout to prevent biting or eating. **3.** The front end of the barrel of a gun. —*v.* **muz•zled, muz•zling. 1.** To put a muzzle on (an animal). **2.** To prevent (someone) from expressing an opinion. [SEE PICTURE]

muz•zle•load•er |mŭz′əl lō′dər| *n.* A firearm loaded through the muzzle. —**muz′zle•load′ing** *adj.*

my |mī| *pron.* The possessive case of **I**, used before a noun as a modifier. **1.** Belonging or pertaining to me: *my pencil; my past failures.* **2.** Done by me: *my work.* **3.** Received by me, as an action: *my first defeat.* —*Note*: As a modifier, *my* is used in certain forms of polite address: *my lord; my dear Mrs. Fulton.* It is also used in expressions of surprise or dismay: *My word! My goodness!* —*interj.* A word used to express surprise or dismay: *Oh, my!*

my•ce•li•um |mī sē′lē əm| *n., pl.* **my•ce•li•a** |mī sē′lē ə|. A mass of threadlike, branching strands that form the main growing structure of a fungus.

my•col•o•gy |mī kŏl′ə jē| *n.* The scientific study of fungi.

my•na or **my•nah** |mī′nə| *n.* Any of several Asian birds related to the starlings. Some kinds can be taught to imitate human speech.

my•o•pi•a |mī ō′pē ə| *n.* A defect of the eye that makes distant objects appear blurred because their images are focused in front of the retina rather than on it; nearsightedness.

my•op•ic |mī ŏp′ĭk| *or* |-ō′pĭk| *adj.* Of or affected with myopia; nearsighted.

myr•i•ad |mĭr′ē əd| *adj.* Amounting to a very large, indefinite number: *the moon, sun, planets, and myriad stars.* —*n.* A vast number.

myrrh |mûr| *n.* A pleasant-smelling gummy substance obtained from certain African and Asian trees and shrubs and used in perfume and incense.

myr•tle |mûr′tl| *n.* **1.** A shrub with evergreen leaves, white or pinkish flowers, and blackish berries. **2.** A trailing vine with glossy, evergreen leaves and usually blue flowers; a periwinkle.

my•self |mī sĕlf′| *pron.* A special form of **me.** It is used: **1.** In place of *me*, serving as a direct object, indirect object, or object of a preposition, to show that the action of a reflexive verb refers back to the subject: *I injured myself* (direct object). *I gave myself a stern lecture* (indirect object). *I spent little of the money on myself* (object of a preposition). **2.** Following the pronoun *I*, to give emphasis: *I myself had to laugh. I found it amusing myself.* **3.** Following the pronoun *I*, to mean *my real, normal, or healthy self: After her death I was not myself.*

***Idiom.* by myself. 1.** Alone: *I went to the movie by myself.* **2.** Without help: *I made all the preparations by myself.*

mys•te•ri•ous |mĭ stîr′ē əs| *adj.* **1.** Of or implying a mystery: *Antarctica is a strange and mysterious land.* **2.** Difficult or impossible to understand or explain: *the mysterious disappearance of the books.* —**mys•te′ri•ous•ly** *adv.* —**mys•te′ri•ous•ness** *n.*

mys•te•ry |mĭs′tə rē| *n., pl.* **mys•te•ries. 1.** Anything that arouses curiosity because it is difficult to explain or is a secret: *Her whereabouts remains a mystery.* **2.** The quality associated with the unknown or unexplained: *The moon colors the world with magic and mystery.* **3.** A piece of fiction dealing with a puzzling matter, often a crime. —***modifier:*** *a mystery novel.*

mys•tic |mĭs′tĭk| *adj.* **1.** Of religious or supernatural rites and practices: *The tribe gathered for their mystic dance to welcome planting time.* **2.** Inspiring a quality of mystery; mysterious: *the mystic effects of a new moon.* **3.** Of mysticism. —*n.* Someone who practices or believes in mysticism.

mys•ti•cal |mĭs′tĭ kəl| *adj.* **1.** Of the mystics or mysticism and its practices: *the mystical books of the alchemists.* **2.** Based on spiritual insight or intuition: *the mystical spirituality of the East.* —**mys′ti•cal•ly** *adv.*

mys•ti•cism |mĭs′tĭ sĭz′əm| *n.* **1.** The belief that direct contact with the divine can be attained through deep meditation. **2.** The spiritual qualities or way of thinking of a person who believes in or practices mysticism. **3.** Confused and groundless thinking.

mys•ti•fy |mĭs′tə fī′| *v.* **mys•ti•fied, mys•ti•fy•ing, mys•ti•fies.** To perplex; bewilder: *Magicians sometimes perform tricks that mystify their audiences.* —**mys′ti•fi•ca′tion** *n.*

myth |mĭth| *n.* **1. a.** A traditional story dealing with ancestors, heroes, supernatural beings, etc., and usually making an attempt to explain some belief, practice, or natural phenomenon: *The myth told how thunder was made by the gods.* **b.** A body of such stories as told among a certain group: *Greek myth.* **c.** Such stories in general: *myth and legend.* **2.** A fictitious or imaginary story, person, thing, explanation, etc.: *the myth of a man-eating tree.* **3.** A fiction accepted as part of an ideology by an uncritical group: *the myth of Nordic supremacy.*

myth•i•cal |mĭth′ĭ kəl| *adj.* **1.** Of or existing only in myths: *a mythical beast such as Cyclops.* **2.** Imaginary; fancied: *a mythical account of a voyage through Africa.*

myth•o•log•i•cal |mĭth′ə lŏj′ĭ kəl| *adj.* **1.** Of or existing in myths: *a mythological animal.* **2.** Fabulous; imaginary; mythical.

my•thol•o•gy |mĭ thŏl′ə jē| *n., pl.* **my•thol•o•gies. 1.** A body of myths, especially one dealing with a specified cultural tradition: *Greek mythology.* **2.** The study of myths.

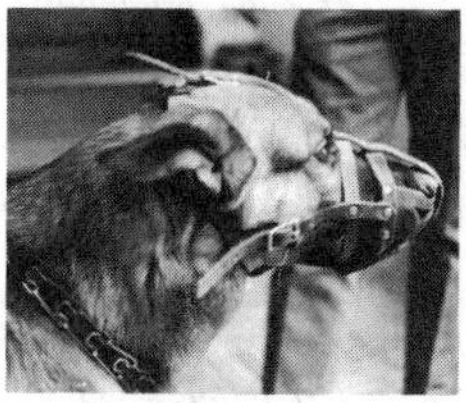

muzzle

Nn

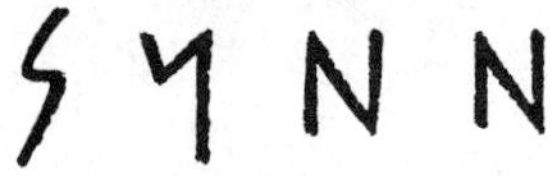

(1) (2) (3) (4)

The letter **N** *comes originally from the Phoenician letter* nūn *(1), which meant "fish" and stood for the consonant /n/. The Greeks borrowed it as* nu *(2), later making it symmetrical (3). The Romans borrowed it from the Greeks, and their version (4) is the basis of the modern letter.*

nag^1-2

Nag¹ *originally meant "to bite at" and is from Old Norse* gnaga, *which is related to* **gnaw**. **Nag²** *is from Middle Dutch* negghe, *"horse," which is related to* **neigh**.

nap^1-2

Nap¹ *is from Old English* hnappian, *"to doze."* **Nap²** *is from Middle Dutch* noppe.

ă pat/ā pay/â care/ä father/ĕ pet/ ē be/ĭ pit/ī pie/î fierce/ŏ pot/ ō go/ô paw, for/oi oil/ŏŏ book/ ōō boot/ou out/ŭ cut/û fur/ *th* the/th thin/hw which/zh vision/ ə ago, item, pencil, atom, circus

n, N |ĕn| *n., pl.* **n's** or **N's.** The 14th letter of the English alphabet. [SEE NOTE]

n 1. North; northern. **2.** *n* or *N* A mathematical symbol for an indefinite number, usually an integer.

N 1. North; northern. **2.** The symbol for the element nitrogen.

n. 1. n. or **N.** north; northern. **2.** noun.

Na The symbol for the element sodium.

N.A. North America.

NAACP, N.A.A.C.P. National Association for the Advancement of Colored People.

nab |năb| *v.* **nabbed, nab•bing.** *Slang.* **1.** To catch in the act; arrest: *The policeman nabbed the muggers.* **2.** To grab; snatch: *They nabbed all the tickets before we could get to the box office.*

na•celle |nə sĕl'| *n.* A streamlined enclosure, separate from the main fuselage, mounted on certain aircraft to house an engine, cargo, or the crew.

na•cre |nā'kər| *n.* Mother-of-pearl.

na•cre•ous |nā'krē əs| *adj.* Of or resembling mother-of-pearl; pearly.

na•dir |nā'dər| *or* |nā'dîr'| *n.* **1.** A point on the celestial sphere diametrically opposite the zenith. **2.** The place and time of deepest depression; the lowest point: *the nadir of misery.*

nag¹ |năg| *v.* **nagged, nag•ging.** To pester or annoy, as by complaining or scolding. *—n.* A person who nags. [SEE NOTE]

nag² |năg| *n.* A horse, especially an old or worn-out horse. [SEE NOTE]

Na•hua•tl |nä'wät'l| *n., pl.* **Na•hua•tl** or **Na•hua•tls. 1.** A group of Mexican and Central American Indian tribes. The Aztecs are members of this group. **2.** A member of any of these tribes. **3.** The Uto-Aztecan language of the Nahuatl. **—Na'hua'tl** *adj.*

nai•ad |nā'əd| *or* |-ăd'| *or* |nī'-| *n., pl.* **nai•a•des** |nā'ə dēz'| *or* |nī'-| or **nai•ads.** In Greek mythology, one of the nymphs living in or presiding over brooks, fountains, and streams.

nail |nāl| *n.* **1.** A slim, pointed piece of metal, often with a head, hammered into wood or other material as a fastener. **2. a.** A fingernail or toenail. **b.** A claw or talon. *—v.* **1.** To fasten, join, or attach with or as if with nails: *Nail the boards together.* **2.** *Informal.* To seize; catch: *nail a thief.* ***—phrasal verb.* nail down.** To settle; clinch: *nail down a contract.*

Nai•ro•bi |nī rō'bē|. The capital of Kenya. Population, 509,000.

na•ive or **na•ïve** |nä ēv'| *adj.* **1.** Simple and unaffected as a child; artless: *a naive girl.* **2.** Showing a lack of experience, judgment, etc.; unsophisticated: *naive remarks.* **—na•ive'ly** *adv.*

na•ive•té or **na•ïve•té** |nä'ēv tā'| *n.* The quality of being naive; natural simplicity.

na•ked |nā'kĭd| *adj.* **1.** Not wearing clothing or other covering on the body or on a specific part of the body; nude: *a naked boy; naked feet.* **2.** Stripped or bare: *trees with naked branches.* **3.** Not concealed or disguised: *the naked truth.* **—na'ked•ly** *adv.* **—na'ked•ness** *n.*

naked eye. The eye unaided by an optical instrument, such as a telescope.

name |nām| *n.* **1.** A word or words by which a person, thing, place, etc., is called, known, or designated. **2. a.** General reputation: *a bad name.* **b.** A distinguished reputation: *She has made a name for herself.* **3.** *Informal.* A famous person: *a big name in the movies.* *—v.* **named, nam•ing. 1. a.** To give a name to: *Have you named the baby?* **b.** To call by the name of: *They named the baby Mary.* **2.** To identify or cite by name: *Name the product of 3 × 12.* **3.** To specify, fix, or set: *name your price; name the day.* **4.** To nominate or appoint, as to a specific duty, honor, etc.: *He was named coach of the basketball team.* [SEE NOTE on p. 605]

***Idioms.* in the name of. 1.** For the sake of: *Let him answer the charges in the name of justice.* **2.** By the authority of: *Halt, in the name of the law.* **to (one's) name.** Among one's possessions.

name•less |nām'lĭs| *adj.* **1.** Having no name. **2.** Unknown by name; obscure: *the nameless dead.* **3.** Not designated by name; anonymous: *The donor shall remain nameless.* **4.** Too horrible or too difficult to describe or express: *a nameless crime.*

name•ly |nām'lē| *adv.* That is to say; specifically: *First-class mail includes written matter, namely letters and postcards.*

name•sake |nām'sāk'| *n.* Someone or something named after another.

Na•mi•bi•a |nə mĭb'ē ə|. A territory on the southwestern coast of Africa, administered by South Africa. Population, 690,000. Capital, Windhoek.

Nan•jing |nän'jĭng'| also **Nan•king** |năn'kĭng'|. A city in eastern China on the Yangtze River. Population, 2,000,000.

nan•ny |năn'ē| *n., pl.* **nan•nies.** A children's nurse.

nanny goat. A female goat.

nano–. A word element meaning "one-billionth": *nanosecond.*

nap¹ |năp| *n.* A brief sleep, usually during a period other than one's regular sleeping hours. *—v.* **napped, nap•ping. 1.** To doze or sleep for a brief period. **2.** To be unaware of danger or trouble soon to come. [SEE NOTE]

nap[2] |năp| *n.* A soft or fuzzy surface on certain kinds of cloth or leather, usually formed by raising fibers from the material underneath. *—v.* **napped, nap•ping.** To form or raise a nap on (cloth or leather). [SEE NOTE on p. 592]

na•palm |nā′päm′| *n.* A mixture of gasoline and chemicals that makes a flammable jelly for use in flame throwers and bombs.

nape |nāp| *n.* The back of the neck.

naph•tha |năf′thə| *or* |năp′-| *n.* Any of several flammable hydrocarbon liquids used as solvents, especially one derived from petroleum and used in making gasoline.

nap•kin |năp′kĭn| *n.* **1. a.** A piece of cloth or soft paper used while eating to protect the clothes or to wipe the mouth and fingers. **b.** Any similar cloth or towel. **2.** A **sanitary napkin.**

Na•ples |nā′pəlz|. A city and seaport of southwestern Italy. Population, 1,275,000.

na•po•le•on |nə pō′lē ən| *or* |-pōl′yən| *n.* An iced rectangular pastry with crisp, flaky layers separated by custard or cream.

Na•po•le•on I |nə pō′lē ən| *or* |-pōl′yən|. Full name, Napoleon Bonaparte. 1769–1821. French general; emperor of France (1804–15).

Na•po•le•on•ic |nə pō′lē ŏn′ĭk| *adj.* Of Napoleon I or his era: *the Napoleonic wars.*

nar•cis•si |när sĭs′ī′| *or* |-sĭs′ē| *n.* A plural of **narcissus.**

nar•cis•sism |när′sĭ sĭz′əm| *n.* Excessive admiration of oneself. *—***nar′cis•sist** *n.*

nar•cis•sus |när sĭs′əs| *n., pl.* **nar•cis•sus•es** or **nar•cis•si** |när sĭs′ī′| *or* |-sĭs′ē|. A garden plant related to the daffodil, having fragrant yellow or white flowers with a cup-shaped or trumpet-shaped central part. [SEE PICTURE]

nar•cot•ic |när kŏt′ĭk| *n.* Any drug, such as heroin or morphine, that dulls the senses, causes sleep, and tends to cause addiction when used regularly. *—adj.* **1.** Tending to cause sleep or stupor. **2.** Of narcotics.

Nar•ra•gan•set |năr′ə găn′sĭt| *n., pl.* **Nar•ra•gan•set** or **Nar•ra•gan•sets. 1.** A North American Indian tribe formerly living in Rhode Island. **2.** A member of this tribe. **3.** The Algonquian language of this tribe.

Nar•ra•gan•sett |năr′ə găn′sĭt| *n., pl.* **Nar•ra•gan•sett** or **Nar•ra•gan•setts.** A form of the word **Narraganset.**

nar•rate |năr′āt′| *or* |nă rāt′| *v.* **nar•rat•ed, nar•rat•ing. 1.** To give an oral or written account of; recite. **2.** To supply the running commentary for a motion picture or other performance. *—***nar′ra′tor** *n.*

nar•ra•tion |nă rā′shən| *n.* **1.** The act or an example of narrating. **2.** Something narrated; a narrative; an account or story.

nar•ra•tive |năr′ə tĭv| *n.* A story or description; a narrated account. *—adj.* Telling a story: *narrative poems.*

nar•row |năr′ō| *adj.* **nar•row•er, nar•row•est. 1.** Small or limited in width, especially in comparison with length: *a narrow face; a narrow ribbon.* **2.** Having little room: *narrow quarters.* **3.** Limited in scope, variety, etc.: *a narrow circle of friends.* **4.** Rigid in views and ideas; limited in outlook: *a man of narrow ideas.* **5.** Just barely successful; uncomfortably close: *a narrow escape.* *—v.* **1.** To make or become narrow or narrower: *He narrowed his eyes. The river narrows at that point.* **2.** To limit or restrict: *Narrow down your topic to something you can handle.* *—n.* **narrows.** A narrow body of water connecting two larger ones. *—***nar′row•ly** *adv.* *—***nar′row•ness** *n.*

nar•row-mind•ed |năr′ō mīn′dĭd| *adj.* Lacking in tolerance or sympathy; prejudiced. *—***nar′row-mind′ed•ly** *adv.* *—***nar′row-mind′ed•ness** *n.*

nar•whal |när′wəl| *n.* An animal of northern seas, related to the whales and having a single long, spirally twisted tusk. [SEE PICTURE]

nar•y |nâr′ē| *adj. Informal.* Not one; no: *Nary a bit of work has he done for the past six months.*

NASA |năs′ə|. National Aeronautics and Space Administration.

na•sal |nā′zəl| *adj.* **1.** Of or involving the nose: *nasal irritation.* **2. a.** Uttered so that most of the air passes through the nose rather than the mouth: *a nasal sound.* **b.** Resembling a sound uttered in such a way: *the nasal twang of a guitar.* *—n.* A nasal sound. *—***na′sal•ly** *adv.*

Nash•ville |năsh′vĭl′|. The capital of Tennessee. Population, 444,400.

Nas•sau |năs′ô′|. The capital of the Bahama Islands. Population, 101,000.

na•stur•tium |nə stûr′shəm| *or* |nă-| *n.* A garden plant with showy orange, yellow, or red flowers and rounded, strong-tasting leaves.

nas•ty |năs′tē| *adj.* **nas•ti•er, nas•ti•est. 1.** Filthy and disgusting: *the nasty gutter.* **2.** Morally offensive; indecent: *a nasty word.* **3.** Malicious; spiteful; mean: *a nasty old man.* **4.** Causing discomfort or trouble; unpleasant: *a nasty temper; nasty weather.* **5.** Painful and dangerous: *a nasty accident.* *—***nas′ti•ly** *adv.* *—***nas′ti•ness** *n.*

na•tal |nāt′l| *adj.* Of or accompanying birth: *natal injuries.* [SEE NOTE on p. 594]

Natch•ez |năch′ĭz| *n., pl.* **Natch•ez. 1.** A North American Indian tribe formerly living in Mississippi. **2.** A member of this tribe. **3.** The Muskhogean language of this tribe.

na•tion |nā′shən| *n.* **1.** A group of people organized under a single government; a country: *the new nations of Africa.* **2.** The territory occupied by a country: *All across the nation new industries are developing.* **3.** A federation or tribe, especially of North American Indians.

na•tion•al |năsh′ə nəl| *adj.* **1.** Of a nation as a whole: *national elections.* **2.** Peculiar to or symbolic of a nation: *The harp is the national symbol of Ireland.* **3.** Maintained or supported by the government of a nation: *national parks.* *—n.* A citizen of a particular nation. *—***na′tion•al•ly** *adv.*

National Guard. The military reserve units of each state of the United States.

na•tion•al•ism |năsh′ə nə lĭz′əm| *n.* **1.** Devotion to a particular nation. **2.** The belief that the independence and interests of one's own nation, rather than the interests of nations acting together, should come first in world affairs.

na•tion•al•ist |năsh′ə nə lĭst| *n.* Someone who believes in nationalism. *—adj.* Of or advocating nationalism: *a nationalist party.* *—***na′tion•al•is′tic** *adj.* *—***na′tion•al•is′ti•cal•ly** *adv.*

Nationalist China. The unofficial name for the Republic of China. See **Taiwan.**

na•tion•al•i•ty |năsh′ə năl′ĭ tē| *n., pl.* **na•tion•**

narcissus

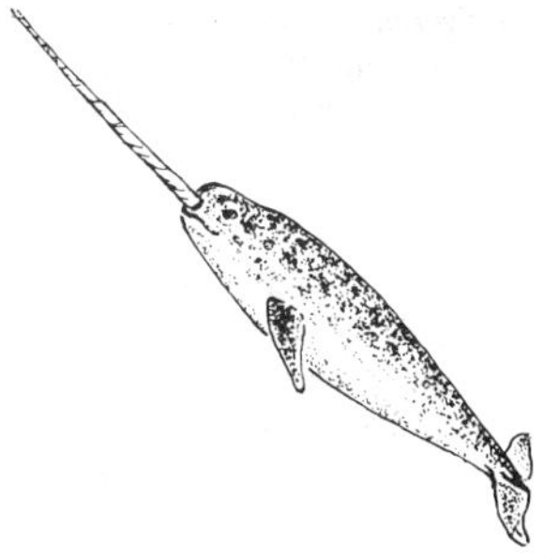

narwhal

al•i•ties. **1.** The status of belonging to a particular nation by reason of origin, birth, or naturalization: *American nationality.* **2.** A people having common origins or traditions: *Many nationalities have settled in America.*

na•tion•al•ize |năsh′ə nə līz′| *v.* **na•tion•al•ized, na•tion•al•iz•ing.** **1.** To change the control of (agriculture, an industry, etc.) from private to government ownership and control. **2.** To make into a nation. —**na′tion•al•i•za′tion** *n.*

National Socialism. Nazism.

na•tion•wide |nā′shən wīd′| *adj.* Throughout a whole nation: *a nationwide campaign.*

na•tive |nā′tĭv| *adj.* **1.** Belonging to one by nature; inborn; natural: *native ability.* **2.** Being such by birth or origin: *a native Englishman.* **3.** One's own because of the place of one's birth: *our native land; one's native language.* **4.** Originally living, growing, or produced in a particular place: *a plant native to Europe; the native handicrafts of Mexico.* **5.** Of or characteristic of the original inhabitants of a region, especially those whose culture is considered primitive: *a native custom.* **6.** Occurring in nature in pure or nearly pure form: *native copper.* —*n.* **1.** Someone associated with a place by birth: *a native of New York.* **2.** One of the original inhabitants of a region; an aborigine. **3.** The residents or inhabitants of a place as opposed to immigrants or visitors. **4.** Something, such as an animal or plant, that originated in a particular place. —**na′tive•ly** *adv.* [SEE NOTE]

native, natal, etc.
This group of words is from a group of Latin words based on the stem nāt-, *referring to various aspects of birth.* **Natal** *is from Latin* nātālis, *"relating to birth."* **Nation** *is from Latin* nātiō, *"a birth," hence "a breed, a family of people, a race."* **Native** *is from Latin* nātivus, *"born, beginning at birth."* **Nature** *is from Latin* nātūra, *"birth," hence "the world full of living things, the universe" and also "character with which an individual is born," etc.;* nātūra *had essentially the full spread of meanings that the English word has.*

Native American. An American Indian.

na•tiv•i•ty |nə tĭv′ĭ tē| *or* |nā-| *n., pl.* **na•tiv•i•ties.** **1.** Birth, especially the place, condition, or circumstances of one's birth. **2. the Nativity.** **a.** The birth of Christ. **b.** A representation, such as a painting, of Christ as an infant.

NATO |nā′tō|. North Atlantic Treaty Organization.

nat•ty |năt′ē| *adj.* **nat•ti•er, nat•ti•est.** Neat and trim; dapper: *a natty uniform.* —**nat′ti•ly** *adv.* —**nat′ti•ness** *n.*

nat•u•ral |năch′ər əl| *or* |năch′rəl| *adj.* **1.** Present in or produced by nature; not artificial or man-made: *The moon is a natural satellite of the earth.* **2.** Of the physical world and all objects, living things, and events that are part of it: *natural laws.* **3.** Expected or encountered in the course of nature: *a natural death; a natural enemy.* **4. a.** Having qualities or abilities that are or seem to be inborn: *a natural leader.* **b.** Present from birth; not acquired: *a natural curiosity.* **5.** Not artificial or affected; spontaneous: *a natural way of speaking.* **6.** In music, not having or using any sharps or flats. —*n.* **1.** In music: **a.** A tone that is not altered by a sharp or flat. **b.** A sign (♮) indicating that any sharps or flats that would otherwise affect a tone are to be canceled. **2.** *Informal.* Someone seeming to have the qualifications necessary for success: *She is a natural for the presidency.* —**nat′u•ral•ness** *n.*

nausea
Nausea *is from Greek* nausia, *"seasickness," literally "ship-disease," from* naus, *"ship."* Naus *is closely related to the Latin word for "ship,"* nāvis; *from* nāvis *we have* **navy** *and* **navigate**.

natural gas. A mixture of gaseous hydrocarbons, principally methane, that occurs with petroleum deposits. It is used as a fuel and in manufacturing organic compounds.

natural history. The study of living things and natural objects and happenings and of their origins and relationships.

nat•u•ral•ist |năch′ər ə lĭst| *or* |năch′rə-| *n.* A person who specializes in natural history, especially in the study of plants and animals in their natural surroundings.

nat•u•ral•ize |năch′ər ə līz′| *or* |năch′rə-| *v.* **nat•u•ral•ized, nat•u•ral•iz•ing.** **1.** To give full citizenship to (someone of foreign birth). **2.** To adopt (something foreign, as a word) into general use. **3.** To adapt or accustom (a plant or animal) to growing or living in new surroundings: *Dandelions are European plants that have been naturalized in North America.* —**nat′u•ral•i•za′tion** *n.*

nat•u•ral•ly |năch′ər ə lē| *or* |năch′rə-| *adv.* **1.** In a natural manner: *behave naturally.* **2.** By nature; inherently: *naturally blond hair.* **3.** Without a doubt; surely: *Naturally, the faster you grow, the more food you need.*

natural number. Any member of the set of positive integers; a whole number greater than zero.

natural resource. Something, as forests, mineral deposits, etc., that is the source of something necessary or useful to human beings.

natural science. A science, such as biology, chemistry, or physics, that is based chiefly on observations and measurements and hypotheses that explain them.

natural selection. The principle that in a given environment some members of a species have characteristics that aid survival. These tend to produce more offspring than the others, so that the proportion of the species having these characteristics increases with each generation.

na•ture |nā′chər| *n.* **1.** The world together with all living things and the objects and events that are normally part of it as distinguished from those that are artificial. **2.** The conditions, processes, etc., occurring in and typical of the world and all living things, regarded as an interrelated whole: *the laws of nature.* **3.** The world of living things and the outdoors; wildlife, natural scenery, etc.: *enjoying the beauties of nature.* **4.** Often **Nature.** A personification, often female, of the forces and processes of the physical world. **5.** The essential characteristics and qualities of a thing: *the mountainous nature of the region; the nature of the problem.* **6. a.** The fundamental character, instincts, disposition, or temperament of a person or animal: *It goes against her nature to be dishonest.* **b.** Kind; type: *The names were descriptive in nature.* —***modifier:*** *a nature lover; nature studies.*
Idiom. **in (**or **of) the nature of.** Belonging to the type or category of: *an association in the nature of a contract.*

na•tured |nā′chərd| *adj.* Having a certain kind of nature or temperament: *ill-natured; a good-natured man.*

naught |nôt| *pron.* Nothing: *There were no trees, no shrubs, no grasses, naught by a tremendous and terrible desolation.* —*n.* Zero; the digit 0.

naugh•ty |nô′tē| *adj.* **naugh•ti•er, naugh•ti•est.** Disobedient; mischievous: *a naughty boy.* —**naugh′ti•ly** *adv.* —**naugh′ti•ness** *n.*

nau•se•a |nô′zē ə| *or* |-zhə| *or* |-sē ə| *or* |-shə| *n.* **1.** A stomach disturbance that causes a feeling of the need to vomit. **2.** Strong disgust; repugnance. [SEE NOTE]

nau•se•ate |nô′zē āt′| *or* |-zhē-| *or* |-sē-| *or*

|-shē-| *v.* **nau•se•at•ed, nau•se•at•ing.** To cause (someone) to feel nausea.

nau•se•at•ed |nô′zē ā′tĭd| *or* |-zhē-| *or* |-sē-| *or* |-shē-| *adj.* Suffering from nausea.

nau•seous |nô′shəs| *or* |-zē əs| *adj.* **1.** Tending to cause nausea; sickening. **2.** Nauseated.

nau•ti•cal |nô′tĭ kəl| *adj.* Of ships, sailors, or navigation. —**nau′ti•cal•ly** *adv.*

nautical mile. A unit of length used in air and sea navigation, equal to 1,852 meters or about 6,076 feet.

nau•ti•lus |nôt′l əs| *n., pl.* **nau•ti•lus•es. 1.** Also **chambered nautilus** or **pearly nautilus.** A tropical sea mollusk related to the squids and octopuses, having a spiral shell divided into many partitions. **2.** Also **paper nautilus.** A related mollusk of which the female has a thin, papery shell. [SEE PICTURE]

Nav•a•ho |năv′ə hō′| *or* |nä′və-| *n., pl.* **Nav•a•ho** or **Nav•a•hos** or **Nav•a•hoes,** *& adj.* A form of the word **Navajo.**

Nav•a•jo |năv′ə hō′| *or* |nä′və-| *n., pl.* **Nav•a•jo** or **Nav•a•jos** or **Nav•a•joes. 1.** A group of North American Indians of New Mexico, Arizona, and Utah. **2.** A member of this group. **3.** The language of this group, which is the only North American Indian language growing in use. —**Nav′a•jo′** *adj.*

na•val |nā′vəl| *adj.* **1.** Of the personnel, equipment, or customs of a navy. **2.** Having a navy: *a great naval power.* ¶*These sound alike* **naval, navel.**

nave |nāv| *n.* The central part of a church flanked by the side aisles. ¶*These sound alike* **nave, knave.**

na•vel |nā′vəl| *n.* **1.** The mark left on the abdomen of mammals where the umbilical cord was attached before birth. **2.** A central point; the middle. ¶*These sound alike* **navel, naval.**

navel orange. A sweet, seedless orange having a navellike marking opposite the stem end.

nav•i•ga•ble |năv′ĭ gə bəl| *adj.* Deep enough or wide enough for navigation.

nav•i•gate |năv′ĭ gāt′| *v.* **nav•i•gat•ed, nav•i•gat•ing. 1.** To plot and control the course of (a ship or aircraft). **2.** *Informal.* To walk or get somewhere without assistance.

nav•i•ga•tion |năv′ĭ gā′shən| *n.* **1.** The theory and practice of navigating, especially the science of charting a course for a ship or aircraft. **2.** Travel or traffic by vessels, especially commercial shipping. —***modifier:*** *navigation charts.*

nav•i•ga•tor |năv′ĭ gā′tər| *n.* **1.** A crew member who plots the course of a ship or aircraft. **2.** A person who leads voyages of exploration: *the Phoenician navigators.* **3.** A device that directs the course of an aircraft or missile.

na•vy |nā′vē| *n., pl.* **na•vies. 1.** All of a nation's warships. **2.** Often **Navy.** A nation's entire organization for sea warfare, including vessels, personnel, and shore establishments. **3. Navy blue.** —***modifier:*** *a navy officer.* —*adj.* **Navy blue.**

navy bean. A small, whitish form of the kidney bean, used for making soup, baked beans, etc.

navy blue. A dark grayish blue. —*adj.* Dark grayish blue.

naw |nô| *adv. Informal.* No. ¶*These sound alike* **naw, gnaw.**

nay |nā| *adv.* **1.** No: *All but four Democrats voted nay to the treaty.* **2.** —Used to mark the introduction of a more precise or emphatic expression than the one first made: *If she came here in person she scarcely could outdo me. Nay, I will say more than that; I doubt if she could even equal me.* —*n.* **1.** A vote of "no." **2. the nays.** Those who vote no: *The nays carried it, and the treaty bill was defeated.* ¶*These sound alike* **nay, née, neigh.**

Naz•a•rene |năz′ə rēn′| *or* |năz′ə rēn′| *n.* **the Nazarene.** Christ.

Naz•a•reth |năz′ə rĭth|. A town in northern Israel where Christ spent his childhood.

Na•zi |nät′sē| *or* |năt′-| *n., pl.* **Na•zis.** A member of the National Socialist German Workers' Party founded in 1919 and brought to power by Hitler in 1933. —*adj.* Of, relating to, or typical of Nazis. [SEE NOTE]

Na•zism |nät′sĭz′əm| *or* |năt′-| *n.* The doctrines and practice of Nazis, especially their anti-Semitism and aggressive nationalism.

Nb The symbol for the element niobium.

n.b., N.B. note well. An abbreviation for the Latin phrase *nota bene.*

N.C. North Carolina.

NCO, N.C.O. noncommissioned officer.

Nd The symbol for the element neodymium.

N. Dak. North Dakota.

Ndja•me•na |ən jä′mə nə|. The capital of Chad. Population, 179,000.

Ne The symbol for the element neon.

NE northeast.

Ne•an•der•thal |nē ăn′dər thôl′| *or* |-tôl′| *or* |nā-än′dər täl′| *adj.* Of Neanderthal man, his life, and his culture: *Neanderthal finds made by archaeologists.*

Neanderthal man. An extinct species of prehistoric man that lived in caves and made and used stone tools. [SEE PICTURE]

neap tide |nēp|. A tide in which the level of water undergoes the smallest change, occurring when the sun and moon are about 90° apart.

near |nîr| *adv.* **near•er, near•est. 1.** To, at, or within a short distance or interval in space or time: *a house near the ocean.* **2.** Almost; nearly: *near exhausted by the heat.* —*adj.* **near•er, near•est. 1.** Close in space, time, position, or degree: *near neighbors; near equals.* **2.** Closely related by kinship or association; intimate: *near relatives.* **3. a.** Accomplished by a narrow margin; close: *a near escape.* **b.** Missed by a narrow margin: *a near tragedy.* **4.** Closer of two or more: *the near side of the house.* **5.** Short and direct: *Could you tell me the nearest route to the airport?* —*prep.* Close to, as in time, space, or degree: *We stayed at a little inn near London.* —*v.* To draw near or nearer; approach: *The holiday season nears.*

near•by |nîr′bī′| *adv.* Not far away; near at hand; close by: *A little brook ran nearby.* Also used prepositionally: *The forest began nearby our cabin.* —*adj.* Located a short distance away; adjacent: *a nearby trading post.*

Near East. A region including the countries of the eastern Mediterranean and the Arabian Peninsula.

near•ly |nîr′lē| *adv.* **1.** Almost but not quite: *That house cost nearly $100,000.* **2.** Closely or intimately: *nearly related.*

near•sight•ed |nîr′sī′tĭd| *adj.* Unable to see distant objects clearly; myopic. —**near′sight′ed•ness** *n.*

nautilus
Shell cut to show cross section

Nazi
In German "National Socialist" is Nationalsocialist. *The first two syllables of this are pronounced approximately* /**nät**′sē/; **Nazi** *is a respelled shortening of* Nationalsocialist.

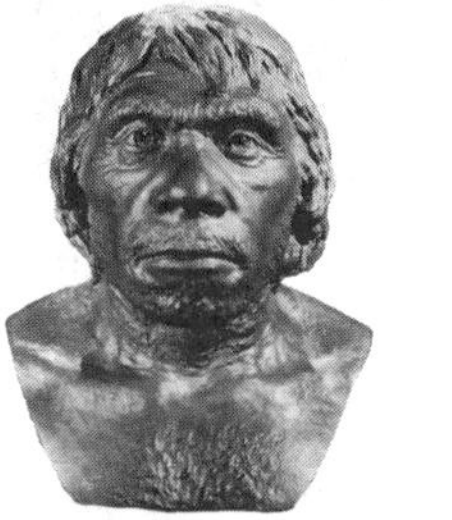

Neanderthal man
Reconstruction based on skulls

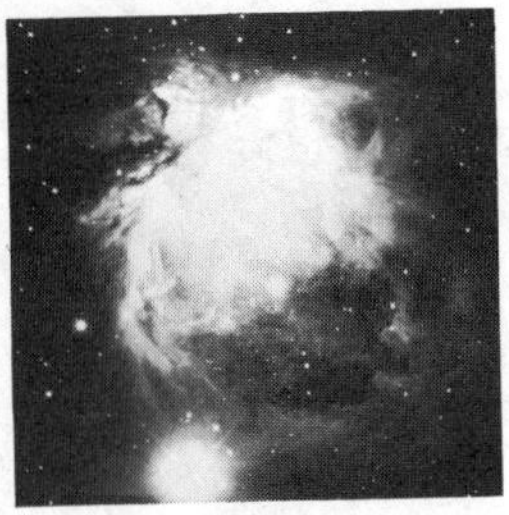

nebula
The Great Nebula in Orion

nectarine

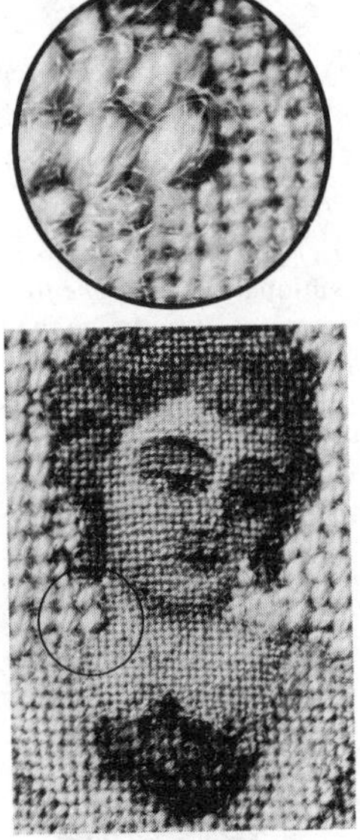

needlepoint
With enlargement of the circled area

ă pat/ā pay/â care/ä father/ĕ pet/ ē be/ĭ pit/ī pie/î fierce/ŏ pot/ ō go/ô paw, for/oi oil/o͝o book/ o͞o boot/ou out/ŭ cut/û fur/ *th* the/th thin/hw which/zh vision/ ə ago, item, pencil, atom, circus

neat |nēt| *adj.* **neat•er, neat•est. 1.** In good order or clean condition; tidy: *a neat room; neat handwriting.* **2.** Orderly, as in appearance; not careless or messy: *a neat person.* **3.** Performed with precision and skill: *a neat, graceful takeoff.* **4.** *Slang.* Wonderful; fine: *They have neat prizes at the fair.* **—neat'ly** *adv.* **—neat'ness** *n.*

neath or **'neath** |nēth| *prep.* Beneath. Used chiefly in poetry.

neat's-foot oil |**nēts'**fo͝ot'|. A pale-yellow oil made from the feet and leg bones of cattle and used mostly for processing leather.

Nebr. Nebraska.

Ne•bras•ka |nə **brăs'**kə|. A Midwestern state of the United States. Population, 1,497,000. Capital, Lincoln. **—Ne•bras'kan** *adj. & n.*

Neb•u•chad•nez•zar |nĕb'ə kəd **nĕz'**ər| *or* |nĕb'yo͞o-|. In the Bible, the king of Babylon who destroyed Jerusalem and carried off the Jews into captivity.

neb•u•la |**nĕb'**yə lə| *n., pl.* **neb•u•lae** |**nĕb'**yə lē'| *or* |-lī'| or **neb•u•las.** A thinly spread mass of interstellar gas or dust or both, appearing as a bright or dark patch in the sky depending on the way the light that strikes it is reflected, absorbed, or re-emitted. **—neb'u•lar** *adj.* [SEE PICTURE]

neb•u•lous |**nĕb'**yə ləs| *adj.* Lacking definite form; vague; unclear. **—neb'u•lous•ly** *adv.*

nec•es•sar•i•ly |nĕs'ĭ **sâr'**ə lē| *adv.* As a necessary result; inevitably: *A new quarterback does not necessarily mean that they'll win the game.*

nec•es•sa•ry |**nĕs'**ĭ sĕr'ē| *adj.* **1.** Needed to achieve a certain result or effect; essential; requisite: *Fill out the necessary forms.* **2.** Following as a certain result; inevitable: *the necessary consequence of overindulgence.* *—n., pl.* **nec•es•sa•ries.** Often **necessaries.** Something that is essential or needed.

ne•ces•si•tate |nə **sĕs'**ĭ tāt'| *v.* **ne•ces•si•tat•ed, ne•ces•si•tat•ing.** To make necessary or unavoidable.

ne•ces•si•ty |nə **sĕs'**ĭ tē| *n., pl.* **ne•ces•si•ties. 1.** Something needed for the existence, success, or functioning of something; a requirement: *The sun is a necessity to life on Earth.* **2.** The quality, condition, or fact of being necessary: *the necessity of sleep.* **3.** Something that must inevitably exist or occur: *the ugly necessities of war.* **4.** Pressing or urgent need, as that arising from poverty or misfortune.

neck |nĕk| *n.* **1.** The part of the body that joins the head to the trunk. **2.** The part of a garment that fits around the neck. **3.** Any relatively narrow part, projection, or connecting part: *a neck of land; the neck of a bottle.* **4.** The narrow part of a stringed instrument along which the strings extend to the pegs. ***—modifier:*** *neck muscles.* *—v. Slang.* To kiss and caress.

Idioms. **break (one's) neck.** *Slang.* To make a great effort to accomplish something. **neck of the woods.** *Informal.* An area or neighborhood. **stick (one's) neck out.** To act boldly despite risks of trouble or danger.

neck•er•chief |**nĕk'**ər chĭf| *n.* A kerchief worn around the neck.

neck•lace |**nĕk'**ləs| *n.* An ornament that goes around the neck, as a string of beads or jewels or a metal chain or band.

neck•line |**nĕk'**līn'| *n.* The outline formed by the edge of a garment at or below the neck: *a low neckline.*

neck•tie |**nĕk'**tī'| *n.* A narrow band of cloth worn around the neck beneath the collar and tied in front, either in a knot with hanging ends or in a small bow.

nec•tar |**nĕk'**tər| *n.* **1.** A sweet liquid in certain flowers, used by bees in making honey. **2.** In Greek mythology, the drink of the gods. **3.** Any delicious drink.

nec•tar•ine |nĕk'tə **rēn'**| *n.* A type of peach having a glossy skin. [SEE PICTURE]

nec•ta•ry |**nĕk'**tə rē| *n., pl.* **nec•ta•ries.** A flower part, usually at the base of the petals, in which nectar is secreted.

née, also **nee** |nā| *adj.* Born. Used when identifying a married woman by her maiden name. ¶*These sound alike* **née, nay, neigh.**

need |nēd| *n.* **1.** A condition or situation in which something is required or wanted: *crops in need of water. That boy is in need of a good haircut.* **2.** A wish for something that is lacking or desired: *She has a constant need for attention.* **3.** Something required or wanted: *a man of modest needs.* **4.** Necessity or obligation: *There wasn't any need for you to pay me back.* **5.** Extreme poverty or misfortune: *living in dire need.* *—v.* **1.** —Used as an auxiliary expressing necessity or obligation: *They needed to bring all their gear.* **2.** To require; have need of: *Let's collect everything that needs repairing.* **3.** To be in need or want: *I promised Mother that she would never need if she moved in with us.* ¶*These sound alike* **need, knead.**

Idiom. **if need be.** If necessary: *I'll send money or even go in person, if need be.*

need•ful |**nēd'**fəl| *adj.* Necessary; required: *provided with everything needful.* **—need'ful•ly** *adv.*

nee•dle |**nēd'**l| *n.* **1.** A small, slender sewing implement, made of polished steel, pointed at one end and having an eye at the other through which a length of thread is passed and held. **2. a.** A slender, pointed rod used in knitting. **b.** A similar implement with a hook at one end, used in crocheting. **3.** The stylus of a phonograph. **4.** The pointer or indicator of a gauge or compass. **5.** A **hypodermic needle. 6.** A sharp, pointed instrument used in engraving and etching. **7.** A stiff, narrow leaf, as of a pine or related tree. *—v.* **nee•dled, nee•dling.** *Informal.* To goad, provoke, or tease.

nee•dle•point |**nēd'**l point'| *n.* Embroidery on canvas done with even stitches to resemble a woven tapestry. [SEE PICTURE]

need•less |**nēd'**lĭs| *adj.* Not needed; unnecessary: *Pronouns help a writer avoid needless repetition.* **—need'less•ly** *adv.* **—need'less•ness** *n.*

nee•dle•work |**nēd'**l wûrk'| *n.* Work done with a needle, as embroidery, sewing, crocheting, knitting, etc.

need•n't |**nēd'**nt|. Need not.

need•y |**nē'**dē| *adj.* **need•i•er, need•i•est.** Being in need; poverty-stricken: *a needy family.*

ne'er |nâr| *adv.* Never. Used chiefly in poetry.

ne'er-do-well |**nâr'**do͞o wĕl'| *n.* An irresponsible person who never succeeds at anything; a good-for-nothing.

ne•far•i•ous |nə **fâr'**ē əs| *adj.* Evil; detestable: *a nefarious plot.*

ne•gate |nĭ gāt′| *v.* **ne•gat•ed, ne•gat•ing.** **1.** To make ineffective or invalid; nullify: *This new amendment negates the former bill.* **2.** To rule out; deny: *The new facts negate the testimony of the first witness.*

ne•ga•tion |nĭ gā′shən| *n.* **1.** The act or an example of negating; a denial. **2.** The opposite of something regarded as positive or affirmative: *His actions are a negation of his beliefs.*

neg•a•tive |nĕg′ə tĭv| *adj.* **1.** Expressing a denial or refusal: *a negative answer; a negative statement.* **2.** Not positive or affirmative; not constructive: *a negative approach to the problem; a negative personality.* **3.** Indicating opposition: *a negative response to the book.* **4.** Indicating that a suspected disease, disorder, or microorganism is not present: *a negative result of a test.* **5. a.** Less than zero. **b.** Of the sign (–) used to indicate a negative number or one that is to be subtracted. **6.** Of or having an electric charge that is like that of an electron and, therefore, tends to repel electrons. **7.** Of or showing resistance to, opposition to, or motion away from a stimulus: *a negative tropism.* *—n.* **1.** A denial or refusal. **2.** In grammar, a word or part of a word that expresses negation; for example, *no, not,* and *un-* are negatives. **3. the negative.** The side in a debate that contradicts or opposes the question being debated. **4. a.** An image in which the values of light and dark are reversed, the normally bright areas appearing dark and the normally dark areas appearing light. **b.** A film or photographic plate containing such an image. **5.** A negative number. **—neg′a•tive•ly** *adv.*

***Idiom.* in the negative.** In a sense or manner indicating a refusal or denial: *answered in the negative.*

negative electrode. A negatively charged electrode; cathode.

ne•glect |nĭ glĕkt′| *v.* **1.** To ignore or pay no attention to; disregard: *He neglected his family.* **2.** To fail to care for or give proper attention to: *He neglects his clothing.* **3.** To fail to do, as through carelessness: *He neglected to tell the committee about the extra expenses.* *—n.* **1.** The act or an example of neglecting: *his neglect of his work.* **2.** The condition of being neglected: *The garden has fallen into neglect.*

ne•glect•ful |nĭ glĕkt′fəl| *adj.* Marked by neglect; careless; heedless: *neglectful of his responsibility.* **—ne•glect′ful•ly** *adv.*

neg•li•gee, also **neg•li•gée** |nĕg′lĭ zhā′| *or* |nĕg′lĭ zhā′| *n.* A woman's loose dressing gown, often of soft, delicate material.

neg•li•gence |nĕg′lĭ jəns| *n.* **1.** A failure to act with care or concern. **2.** In law, neglect of any reasonable precaution, care, or action.

neg•li•gent |nĕg′lĭ jənt| *adj.* Guilty of neglect; lacking in proper care or concern: *a negligent worker.* **—neg′li•gent•ly** *adv.*

neg•li•gi•ble |nĕg′lĭ jə bəl| *adj.* Not worth considering; amounting to very little: *a negligible quantity.* **—neg′li•gi•bly** *adv.*

ne•go•tia•ble |nĭ gō′shə bəl| *or* |-shē ə-| *adj.* **1.** Capable of being negotiated: *a negotiable contract.* **2.** Capable of being legally transferred from one person to another: *This certificate is negotiable when signed.* **—ne•go′tia•bil′i•ty** *n.*

ne•go•ti•ate |nĭ gō′shē āt′| *v.* **ne•go•ti•at•ed, ne•go•ti•at•ing.** **1.** To confer or discuss (something) in order to come to terms or an agreement: *negotiate a peace treaty. The union is negotiating with the management.* **2.** To succeed in accomplishing or coping with: *The car negotiated several difficult turns.* **—ne•go′ti•a•tor** *n.*

ne•go•ti•a•tion |nĭ gō′shē ā′shən| *n.* Often **negotiations.** The act or process of negotiating: *secret negotiations between the two nations.*

Ne•gril•lo |nĭ grĭl′ō| *n., pl.* **Ne•gril•los** or **Ne•gril•loes.** Any member of a group of Negroid peoples of Africa, as the Pygmies, who are generally short in stature.

Ne•gri•to |nĭ grē′tō| *n., pl.* **Ne•gri•tos** or **Ne•gri•toes.** **1.** A Negrillo. **2.** Any member of several groups of Negroid peoples of short stature that live in parts of southeastern Asia and on various islands of the South Pacific.

Ne•gro |nē′grō| *n., pl.* **Ne•groes.** A Negroid person. *—adj.* **1.** Of or characteristic of Negroid persons. **2.** Negroid.

Ne•groid |nē′groid′| *adj.* Of a major division of the human species whose members characteristically have brown to black skin coloration and dark eyes and often have tightly curled hair and a relatively broad nose and thick lips. This division is considered to include the native inhabitants of central and southern Africa and their descendants in other parts of the world. *—n.* A Negroid person.

neigh |nā| *n.* The long, high-pitched, breathy sound made by a horse. *—v.* To make such a sound. ¶*These sound alike* **neigh, nay, née.**

neigh•bor |nā′bər| *n.* **1.** A person who lives next door to or near another. **2.** A person or thing adjacent to or near another: *Earth's nearest neighbor is the moon.* **3.** A fellow human being. [SEE NOTE]

neigh•bor•hood |nā′bər ho͝od′| *n.* **1.** A district or area with regard to its inhabitants or characteristics. **2.** The people who live in a particular area or district: *The shot disturbed the whole neighborhood.* **—modifier:** *the neighborhood children.*

***Idiom.* in the neighborhood of.** **1.** Near: *We left him in the neighborhood of that village.* **2.** Approximately: *inflation in the neighborhood of three per cent a year.*

neigh•bor•ing |nā′bər ĭng| *adj.* Living or located close by: *a neighboring tribe.*

neigh•bor•ly |nā′bər lē| *adj.* Appropriate to or showing the feelings of a friendly neighbor: *a neighborly act of kindness.* **—neigh′bor•li•ness** *n.*

nei•ther |nē′thər| *or* |nī′-| *adj.* Not either; not one nor the other: *Neither shoe fits comfortably.* *—pron.* Not either one; not the one nor the other: *Neither of them fits.* *—conj.* **1.** —Used with *nor* to mark two negative alternatives: *They had neither seen nor heard of us.* **2.** Nor: *So you don't have a job? Neither do I.* [SEE NOTE]

nel•son |nĕl′sən| *n.* A kind of hold in wrestling in which pressure is applied with the hand against the opponent's neck. See **full nelson, half nelson.**

nem•a•to•cyst |nĕm′ə tə sĭst′| *or* |nĭ măt′ə-| *n.* One of the stinging cells in the tentacles of a jellyfish, hydra, or related animal.

nem•a•tode |nĕm′ə tōd′| *n.* Any of a group of threadlike worms, many of which are parasites

neighbor

Neighbor *was Old English* nēahgebur, *"near-dweller, someone who lives nearby":* nēah, *"near, nigh,"* + gebur, *"dweller, one who lives."*

neither

Neither, *as adjective or pronoun, is limited to two persons or things. When more than two are involved,* **none** *is correct:* Painting, drawing, and sculpture are his interests, but he is expert in none of them.

neon
Neon *occurs in the atmosphere to the extent of 18 parts per million, and is obtained from liquid air. It glows reddish-orange in electric-discharge tubes, and is used extensively in illuminated signs and advertisements.*

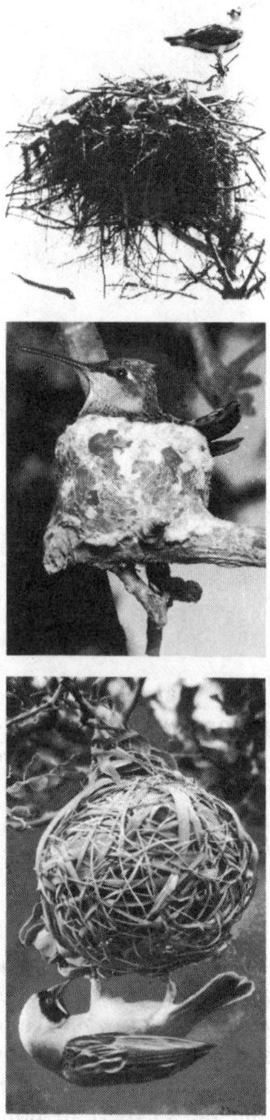

nest
osprey's nest
hummingbird's nest
hanging nest of
a weaverbird

ă pat/ā pay/â care/ä father/ĕ pet/ ē be/ĭ pit/ī pie/î fierce/ŏ pot/ ō go/ô paw, for/oi oil/ŏŏ book/ ōō boot/ou out/ŭ cut/û fur/ *th* the/th thin/hw which/zh vision/ ə ago, item, pencil, atom, circus

that cause disease or damage plants; a roundworm.

nem•e•sis |nĕm'ĭ sĭs| *n., pl.* **nem•e•ses** |nĕm'ĭ sēz'|. **1. a.** Someone or something that is the cause of just punishment. **b.** Just punishment for wrongdoing. **2.** An unbeatable rival: *He met his nemesis in the interstate tennis competition.*

neo–, also **Neo–.** A word element meaning "new or recent, especially a new form of something": **neologism.**

ne•o•dym•i•um |nē'ō dĭm'ē əm| *n.* Symbol **Nd** One of the elements, a bright, silvery rare-earth metal. Atomic number 60; atomic weight 144.24; valence +3; melting point 1,024°C; boiling point 3,027°C.

Ne•o•lith•ic |nē'ə lĭth'ĭk| *n.* The period of human culture that began around 10,000 B.C. in the Middle East, characterized by the introduction of farming and the making and use of fairly advanced stone tools and implements. *—modifier: a Neolithic weapon.*

ne•ol•o•gism |nē ŏl'ə jĭz'əm| *n.* A newly coined word, phrase, or expression or a new meaning for an existing word.

ne•on |nē'ŏn'| *n.* Symbol **Ne** One of the elements, a chemically inert gas. Atomic number 10; atomic weight 20.18; melting point –248.67°C; boiling point –245.92°C. [SEE NOTE]

ne•o•phyte |nē'ə fīt'| *n.* A beginner; novice.

ne•o•prene |nē'ə prēn'| *n.* A tough synthetic rubber that is resistant to the effects of oils, solvents, heat, and weather.

Ne•pal |nə pôl'| *or* |-päl'|. A country in the Himalayas between India and Tibet. Population, 12,321,000. Capital, Katmandu. **—Nep'al•ese'** |nĕp'ə lēz'| *or* |-lēs'| *adj. & n.*

neph•ew |nĕf'yōō| *n.* The son of one's brother or sister or one's spouse's brother or sister.

nep•o•tism |nĕp'ə tĭz'əm| *n.* Favoritism shown by persons in high office to relatives or close friends.

Nep•tune[1] |nĕp'tōōn'| *or* |-tyōōn'| *n.* The eighth planet of the solar system in order of increasing distance from the sun. Its diameter is about 28,000 miles, its average distance from the sun is about 2.8 billion miles, and it takes about 165 years to complete an orbit of the sun.

Nep•tune[2] |nĕp'tōōn'| *or* |-tyōōn'|. The Roman god of the sea.

nep•tu•ni•um |nĕp tōō'nē əm| *or* |-tyōō'-| *n.* Symbol **Np** One of the elements, a metal first produced by bombarding uranium with neutrons. It has thirteen isotopes with mass numbers ranging from 231 to 241 and half-lives ranging from 7.3 minutes to 2.2 million years. Atomic number 93.

nerve |nûrv| *n.* **1.** Any of the bundles of fibers that extend from the central nervous system to the various organs and parts of the body. They are capable of carrying impulses that represent stimuli to the central nervous system and of carrying impulses that activate muscles, glands, etc. **2. nerves.** Any of a group of symptoms, such as trembling, extreme restlessness, hysteria, etc., caused by the reaction of the nervous system to fear, anxiety, stress, etc.: *an attack of nerves.* **3.** Strong will; courage. **4.** *Informal.* Impudent boldness; audacity: *He has some nerve, saying that his team is better than ours.* *—modifier: nerve endings.* —*v.* **nerved, nerv•ing.** To give strength or courage to: *She tried to nerve herself to go down the spooky alley.*

Idiom. **get on (one's) nerves.** To irritate.

nerve cell. Any of the cells that make up the tissue of nerves and of the nervous system, consisting of a main portion that contains the nucleus and threadlike structures that extend from this portion, carrying impulses to and away from the cell; a neuron.

nerve fiber. Any of the threadlike structures that extend from the main body of a nerve cell; an axon or dendrite.

nerve impulse. The electrical and chemical disturbance that moves along a stimulated nerve fiber.

nerve•less |nûrv'lĭs| *adj.* **1.** Lacking strength or energy: *The pipe dropped from his nerveless fingers.* **2.** Not nervous; calm; poised: *nerveless in the face of competition.* **—nerve'less•ly** *adv.*

nerve-rack•ing, also **nerve-wrack•ing** |nûrv'răk'ĭng| *adj.* Intensely distressing or irritating to the nerves: *a nerve-racking scream.*

nerv•ous |nûr'vəs| *adj.* **1.** Of, affecting, or having to do with the nerves or the nervous system: *a nervous disorder; nervous exhaustion.* **2.** Having nerves easily affected; high-strung; jittery: *a nervous person.* **3.** Uneasy; anxious: *a nervous laugh.* **—nerv'ous•ly** *adv.* **—nerv'ous•ness** *n.*

nervous breakdown. Any severe or disabling mental or emotional disorder.

nervous system. A coordinating mechanism in most animals that consist of more than a single cell, serving to regulate internal functions and responses to stimuli. In vertebrates it includes the brain, spinal cord, nerves, and structures that are parts of the sense organs and the organs that perform the various actions of the organism.

nerv•y |nûr'vē| *adj.* **nerv•i•er, nerv•i•est.** *Informal.* Impudently bold or confident; rude: *a nervy answer.*

–ness. A suffix that forms nouns and means "a state, condition, or quality": **rudeness.**

nest |nĕst| *n.* **1. a.** A container or shelter made by birds for holding their eggs and young. **b.** A similar shelter, as of insects, fish, or animals such as mice or squirrels. **c.** A nest containing a number of birds, insects, etc.: *a nest of robins; a nest of hornets.* **2.** Any snug, warm, cozy place or shelter: *The runaway boy made himself a nest in the hay.* **3.** A place full of bad or dangerous persons or things: *a nest of robbers.* **4.** A set of objects of different sizes made so that each one fits into or under the one next above it in size: *a nest of tables.* —*v.* **1.** To build or stay in a nest: *Robins nested in the willow tree.* **2.** To place in or as if in a nest: *The diamond was nested in cotton fluff.* **3.** To fit snugly together or inside one another: *nest boxes for storage.* **—nest'ing** *adj.*: *nesting birds.* [SEE PICTURE]

nest egg. A sum of money saved for future use; savings.

nes•tle |nĕs'əl| *v.* **nes•tled, nes•tling. 1.** To settle down snugly and comfortably: *The children were nestled in their beds.* **2.** To press or snuggle close: *The child nestled up to his mother. The kitten nestled its chin on my lap.* **3.** To lie half-sheltered or partly hidden: *Farms nestle in the folds of the mountains.*

nest•ling |nĕs′lĭng| *n.* A bird too young to leave its nest.

net¹ |nĕt| *n.* **1.** An open fabric made of threads, cords, or ropes that are woven or knotted together with holes between them. **2.** A fine, lacelike, open fabric used for veils, curtains, etc. **3.** Any piece of net used for a special purpose: **a.** A device used to catch fish, birds, butterflies, etc., or to trap or snare other animals. **b.** A screen, shield, or covering used to protect a person or animal from insects such as mosquitoes, bees, or flies. **c.** Also **hair net.** A circular piece of mesh worn over the hair to hold it in place. **d.** A barrier strung between two posts to divide a tennis, badminton, or volleyball court, a Ping-Pong table, etc., in half. **e.** A bag with an open bottom, hung from a hoop and used as a target in basketball. **4.** Any trap or snare that can catch, trick, or trip up a victim. *—modifier: a net bag.* *—v.* **net•ted, net•ting. 1.** To make by weaving or knotting threads together, leaving holes between them: *net a veil.* **2.** To catch in or as if in a net: *He netted a rare butterfly. They found no fish large enough to be netted or hooked.* **3.** To cover with or as if with a net or network: *The sidewalk was netted with tiny cracks.* **—net′ted** *adj.: a netted fabric.* [SEE NOTE]

net² |nĕt| *adj.* **1.** Remaining after all necessary additions, subtractions, or adjustments have been made: *What was your net income after expenses?* **2.** Final; ultimate: *What was the net result?* *—n.* The net amount, as of profit, income, price, or weight. *—v.* **net•ted, net•ting. 1.** To bring in or yield: *The cargo of spices netted a huge profit.* **2.** To clear as profit: *They netted about $58,000 from $100,000 sales.* [SEE NOTE]

neth•er |nĕth′ər| *adj.* Located beneath or below; lower or under: *the nether regions of the earth.* [SEE NOTE]

Neth•er•lands, the |nĕth′ər ləndz|. A country in northwestern Europe, north of Belgium, on the North Sea. Population, 13,592,000. Constitutional capital, Amsterdam; de facto capital, The Hague. Also called *Holland.* **—Neth′er•land′er** *n.* [SEE NOTE]

Netherlands Antilles. A group of Dutch islands in the West Indies. Three are located east of Puerto Rico, and three off the northern coast of Venezuela.

neth•er•most |nĕth′ər mōst′| *adj.* Lowest.

net•ting |nĕt′ĭng| *n.* A fabric made with open spaces between crossing strands; net: *a tank under camouflage netting.*

net•tle |nĕt′l| *n.* Any of several plants having stems and leaves covered with hairs that sting when they are touched. *—v.* **net•tled, net•tling.** To annoy; irritate: *Nelly was nettled by the man's constant bragging.*

net•work |nĕt′wûrk′| *n.* **1.** An open fabric or structure in which cords, threads, wires, etc., cross at regular intervals: *a network of lace.* **2.** A system or pattern made up of a number of parts, passages, lines, or routes that cross, branch out, or interconnect: *a network of roads and railways; a network of veins.* **3.** A chain of interconnected radio or television broadcasting stations, usually sharing a large proportion of their programs. *—modifier: open network structures; network television programs.*

neu•ral |nŏŏr′əl| *or* |nyŏŏr′-| *adj.* Of the nerves or nervous system. **—neu′ral•ly** *adv.*

neu•ral•gia |nŏŏ răl′jə| *or* |nyŏŏ-| *n.* A fitful or spasmodic pain that occurs along a nerve.

neu•ri•tis |nŏŏ rī′tĭs| *or* |nyŏŏ-| *n.* Inflammation of a nerve, with symptoms such as pain, disturbances of sensation, paralysis, and loss of reflexes in the region affected by the nerve.

neu•ro•log•i•cal |nŏŏr′ə lŏj′ĭ kəl| *or* |nyŏŏr′-| *adj.* Of neurology.

neu•rol•o•gist |nŏŏ rŏl′ə jĭst| *or* |nyŏŏ-| *n.* A physician who specializes in neurology.

neu•rol•o•gy |nŏŏ rŏl′ə jē| *or* |nyŏŏ-| *n.* The scientific and medical study of the nervous system and its diseases and disorders.

neu•ron |nŏŏr′ŏn′| *or* |nyŏŏr′-| *n.* Any of the cells that make up the tissue of nerves and of the nervous system, consisting typically of a main portion that contains the nucleus and threadlike structures that extend from this portion, carrying impulses to and away from the cell; a nerve cell.

neu•ro•sis |nŏŏ rō′sĭs| *or* |nyŏŏ-| *n., pl.* **neu•ro•ses** |nŏŏ rō′sēz′| *or* |nyŏŏ-|. A disorder in which the function of the mind or emotions is disturbed with no apparent physical change in the nervous system, resulting in symptoms such as unreasonable fears, anxiety, depression, fits of anger, and abnormal behavior.

neu•rot•ic |nŏŏ rŏt′ĭk| *or* |nyŏŏ-| *adj.* **1.** Of, involving, or caused by a neurosis: *neurotic symptoms.* **2.** Suffering from or affected by neurosis: *a neurotic patient.* *—n.* A neurotic person. **—neu•rot′i•cal•ly** *adv.*

neu•ter |nŏŏ′tər| *or* |nyŏŏ′-| *adj.* **1.** In grammar, neither masculine nor feminine in gender; for example, *it* is a neuter pronoun. **2.** Lacking or having undeveloped sex glands or sex organs. *—n.* **1.** In grammar: **a.** The neuter gender. **b.** A neuter word. **2.** An animal or plant with undeveloped sex glands or organs, especially an undeveloped female insect, such as a worker in a colony of ants or bees.

neu•tral |nŏŏ′trəl| *or* |nyŏŏ′-| *adj.* **1. a.** Not allied with, supporting, or favoring any side in a war, dispute, contest, or struggle for power: *a neutral nation.* **b.** Not belonging to a warring country or opposing side: *neutral ships; neutral territory.* **2.** Of or indicating a color, such as gray, black, or white, that lacks hue; achromatic. **3.** Without definite or distinctive characteristics; colorless: *a man with a neutral personality.* **4.** Neither acid nor alkaline: *a neutral solution; a neutral salt.* **5.** Having positive electric charges exactly balanced by negative electric charges; having a net electric charge of zero: *a neutral atom; a neutral particle.* **6.** Of that arrangement of a set of gears in which no power can be transmitted: *the neutral position of the gear selector.* *—n.* **1.** A country, person, ship, etc., that does not take part or take sides in a war or other conflict: *Belligerents want to defeat their enemies and prevent neutrals from trading with them.* **2.** A neutral color. **3.** The arrangement of a set of gears in which no power can be transmitted: *Leave the car in neutral.* **—neu′tral•ly** *adv.*

neu•tral•i•ty |nŏŏ trăl′ĭ tē| *or* |nyŏŏ-| *n.* The condition, quality, or status of being neutral, especially a policy of taking no part or allying with no side in a war or dispute.

net¹⁻²

Net¹ was net *in Old English; it is related to Latin* nōdus, *"a knot," from which we have* **node. Net²** *originally meant "clear, plain"; it is borrowed from Old French* net, *"plain, simple, neat," from which we also have* **neat.**

nether/Netherlands

The word **nether,** *now quite rare, was* nithera, *"lower," in Old English.* **Netherlands** (Nederland *in Dutch) means "the Low Countries"; this region is literally the lowest part of western Europe, mostly consisting of flat country lying at or near sea level.*

neu•tral•ize |nōō'trə līz'| *or* |nyōō'-| *v.* **neu•tral•ized, neu•tral•iz•ing. 1.** To cancel or counteract the effect of: *neutralize a poison.* **2.** To counterbalance and reduce to zero: *neutralize an electric charge.* **3.** To declare (a country, area, etc.) neutral and immune from invasion, use, or control by any warring nation or competing power bloc: *A treaty neutralized Belgium in 1831.* **4.** To cause to be neither acid nor alkaline: *neutralize a solution.* —**neu'tral•i•za'tion** *n.* —**neu'tral•iz'er** *n.*

neu•tri•no |nōō trē'nō| *or* |nyōō-| *n., pl.* **neu•tri•nos.** Any of several electrically neutral subatomic particles that travel at the speed of light and, like photons, have a mass that would be zero if at rest.

neu•tron |nōō'trŏn'| *or* |nyōō'-| *n.* An electrically neutral subatomic particle having about the mass of a proton. It is stable when bound in an atomic nucleus, contributing to the mass of the nucleus without affecting atomic number or electric charge.

Nev. Nevada.

Ne•vad•a |nə văd'ə| *or* |-vä'də|. A Western state of the United States. Population, 799,184. Capital, Carson City. —**Ne•vad'an** *adj. & n.*

nev•er |nĕv'ər| *adj.* **1.** At no time; on no occasion; not ever: *I have never been here before.* **2.** Absolutely not; under no circumstances: *Steal? Never!* **3.** Not at all; in no way: *Never fear. Never mind.* **4.** Not so much as; not even: *Never a word of it passed his lips.*

nev•er•more |nĕv'ər môr'| *or* |-mōr'| *adv.* Never again.

nev•er•the•less |nĕv'ər *th*ə lĕs'| *adv.* All the same; anyway: *The plan may fail, but we must try it nevertheless.* —*conj.* In spite of that; still; however; but: *His speech was brief; nevertheless, it drew great applause.*

new |nōō| *or* |nyōō| *adj.* **new•er, new•est. 1. a.** Recently made, built, established, created, or formed: *a new skyscraper; a new nation; new roots.* **b.** Being or to be made, formed, or created: *cloth for a new dress.* **2.** Just found, discovered, or learned about; not known of before: *new information.* **3.** Recently obtained or acquired: *new political power.* **4.** Never used or worn; not old or secondhand: *a new bicycle.* **5.** Fresh: *a new coat of paint.* **6.** Recent; modern; up-to-date: *new styles; new techniques.* **7.** Additional: *Industry needed new sources of energy.* **8.** Coming after or taking the place of a previous one or ones: *a new edition of a book.* **9.** Starting over again in a cycle: *the new moon; the new year.* **10.** Unfamiliar; novel; strange: *words that are new to you.* **11.** Recently arrived or established in a place, position, or relationship: *new neighbors; the new salesgirl.* **12.** Inexperienced or untrained: *He is new at this work.* **13.** Not explored or settled before: *a wild, new country.* —*adv.* Freshly; newly; recently: *the smell of new-cut grass; new-found friends.* ¶ *These sound alike* **new, gnu, knew.** —**new'ness** *n.* [SEE NOTE]

new

New *was* nīwe *in Old English; it is descended from the prehistoric Indo-European word for "new," which was* newos. Newos *appears in Latin as* novus, *"new" (from which we have* **novel, innovate,** *etc.), and in Greek as* neos, *"new" (from which we have the prefix* **neo-***).*

Newfoundland[2]

New•ark |nōō'ərk| *or* |nyōō'-|. The largest city in New Jersey. Population, 329,248.

new•born |nōō'bôrn'| *or* |nyōō'-| *adj.* **1. a.** Just born: *newborn babies.* **b.** Recently founded, created, or brought into being: *The newborn United States was free of England.* **2.** Reborn or renewed: *newborn courage.* —*n., pl.* **new•born** or **new•borns.** A newborn child or animal.

New Bruns•wick |brŭnz'wĭk|. A Maritime Province of Canada, bordering Maine. Population, 688,926. Capital, Fredericton.

new•com•er |nōō'kŭm'ər| *or* |nyōō'-| *n.* A person, animal, or thing that has only recently arrived in a new place or situation.

New Deal. The programs and policies for economic recovery and reform introduced during the 1930's by President Franklin D. Roosevelt. —**New Dealer.**

New Del•hi |dĕl'ē|. The capital of India, in the north-central part of the country. Population, 301,801.

new•el |nōō'əl| *or* |nyōō'-| *n.* Also **newel post.** A post that supports a handrail at the bottom of a staircase or at one of the landings.

New Eng•land |ĭng'glənd|. The northeastern part of the United States, consisting of the states of Maine, New Hampshire, Vermont, Massachusetts, Connecticut, and Rhode Island. —**New Englander.**

new•fan•gled |nōō'făng'gəld| *or* |nyōō'-| *adj.* So new, recent, or modern as to be frowned on as unnecessary, undesirable, or too much of a novelty: *a newfangled gas engine; newfangled ideas.*

New•found•land[1] |nōō'fən lənd| *or* |-lănd'| *or* |nyōō'-| *or* |nōō **found'**lənd| *or* |nyōō-|. **1.** An island off the southeastern coast of Canada. **2.** A province of Canada, consisting of this island and Labrador. Population, 561,996. Capital, St. John's.

New•found•land[2] |nōō'fən lənd| *or* |nyōō'-| *n.* A large dog with a dark, thick coat. [SEE PICTURE]

New Guin•ea |gĭn'ē|. A large island in the Pacific Ocean north of Australia.

New Hamp•shire |hămp'shər| *or* |hăm'shər| *or* |-shîr'|. A New England state of the United States. Population, 920,610. Capital, Concord. —**New Hampshirite.**

New Ha•ven |hā'vən|. A city in southern Connecticut, the site of Yale University. Population, 126,109.

New Jer•sey |jûr'zē|. A Middle Atlantic state of the United States. Population, 7,364,158. Capital, Trenton. —**New Jerseyite.**

new•ly |nōō'lē| *or* |nyōō'-| *adv.* **1.** Recently; lately; just: *a newly acquired piece of property.* **2.** Freshly: *newly picked flowers.*

new•ly•wed |nōō'lē wĕd'| *or* |nyōō'-| *n.* A person recently married.

New Mex•i•co |mĕk'sĭ kō'|. A southwestern state of the United States. Population, 1,299,968. Capital, Santa Fe. —**New Mexican.**

new moon. 1. The phase of the moon that occurs as it passes between the sun and the earth and is invisible or visible only as a thin crescent at sunset. **2.** A crescent moon.

New Or•le•ans |ôr'lē ənz| *or* |-lənz| *or* |ôr **lēnz'**|. The largest city in Louisiana. Population, 557,482.

news |nōōz| *or* |nyōōz| *n. (used with a singular verb).* **1.** Information about one or more recent or current events, whether passed on from person to person or reported by newspapers, magazines, or radio and television broadcasts. **2.** Any fact,

ă pat/ā pay/â care/ä father/ĕ pet/ ē be/ĭ pit/ī pie/î fierce/ŏ pot/ ō go/ô paw, for/oi oil/ŏŏ book/ ōō boot/ou out/ŭ cut/û fur/ *th* the/th thin/hw which/zh vision/ ə ago, item, pencil, atom, circus

event, or happening that is interesting enough to be reported: *"When a dog bites a man that is not news, but when a man bites a dog that is news."* (Charles Anderson Dana).

news•cast |no͞oz′kăst| *or* |-kăst′| *or* |nyo͞oz′-| *n.* A radio or television program that broadcasts news reports. —**news′cast′er** *n.*

news•let•ter |no͞oz′lĕt′ər| *or* |nyo͞oz′-| *n.* A printed report, usually issued at regular intervals, giving news about or information of interest to a special group.

news•pa•per |no͞oz′pā′pər| *or* |nyo͞oz′-| *n.* **1.** A publication, usually issued daily or weekly, printed on loose sheets of paper that are folded together and containing current news, useful information, editorials, articles, advertisements, etc. **2.** The cheap, thin paper on which a newspaper is printed: *wadded pieces of newspaper.* —***modifier:*** *a newspaper reporter; a newspaper column.* [SEE NOTE]

news•pa•per•man |no͞oz′pā′pər măn′| *or* |nyo͞oz′-| *n., pl.* **-men** |-mĕn′|. **1.** A person who works for a newspaper as a reporter, writer, editor, etc. **2.** The owner or manager of a newspaper.

news•print |no͞oz′prĭnt′| *or* |nyo͞oz′-| *n.* The kind of cheap, thin paper, made from wood pulp, on which newspapers are printed.

news•reel |no͞oz′rēl| *or* |nyo͞oz′-| *n.* A short motion picture that gives a visual report of recent news events.

news•stand |no͞oz′stănd′| *or* |nyo͞oz′-| *n.* An open booth, shop, or stall where newspapers, magazines, etc., are sold.

news•y |no͞o′zē| *or* |nyo͞o′-| *adj.* **news•i•er, news•i•est.** *Informal.* Full of news; informative: *a newsy letter.*

newt |no͞ot| *or* |nyo͞ot| *n.* Any of several small salamanders that live both on land and in the water. [SEE PICTURE]

New Testament. The second of the two main divisions of the Christian Bible, containing records of the life, acts, and teachings of Christ and his followers.

new•ton |no͞ot′n| *or* |nyo͞ot′n| *n.* A unit of force equal to the force needed to accelerate a mass of one kilogram one meter per second per second.

New•ton |no͞ot′n| *or* |nyo͞ot′n|, **Sir Isaac.** 1642–1727. English mathematician, scientist, and philosopher; formulated laws of motion and gravitation.

New World. The Western Hemisphere; North and South America.

new year. 1. The year just beginning or about to begin: *resolutions for the new year.* **2. New Year. a.** The first day or days of any calendar year: *Happy New Year! When is the Chinese New Year?* **b.** The Jewish New Year, **Rosh Hashanah.**

New Year's Day. The first day of the year, falling on January 1.

New Year's Eve. The last day of the year, falling on December 31.

New York |yôrk|. **1.** A northeastern state of the United States. Population, 17,557,288. Capital, Albany. **2.** The largest city in the United States, located in southeastern New York State at the mouth of the Hudson River. Population, 7,071,-030. —**New Yorker.**

New Zea•land |zē′lənd|. A country consisting of two large islands and several smaller islands in the Pacific Ocean, located about 1,200 miles southeast of Australia. Population, 3,167,357. Capital, Wellington.

next |nĕkst| *adj.* **1.** Coming immediately after the present or previous one; directly following in time, order, or sequence: *next year. The next day was sunny.* **2. a.** Closest or nearest in space or position: *the next town.* **b.** Adjacent or adjoining: *the next room.* —*adv.* **1.** Following in order immediately after the present or previous thing or action: *What comes next?* **2.** On the first occasion after the present or previous one: *When will the hands of the clock be together next?* **3.** Closest in nature, rank, etc., to the one in question: *What is the next best way?* —*prep.* Close to; nearest: *I keep it next to my heart.*

next door. 1. In, to, or at the adjacent house, building, apartment, office, etc.: *He called to the man next door. Mike had just moved next door to Tom.* **2.** The adjacent house, building, etc.: *It's someone from next door.* —***modifier:*** **(next-door):** *her next-door neighbors.*

next to. 1. Beside or alongside: *someone sitting next to you.* **2.** Coming immediately before or after: *next to the last.* **3.** Nearly; practically; almost: *That's next to impossible.*

Nez Perce |nĕz′pûrs′| *pl.* **Nez Perce** or **Nez Perc•es** |nĕz′ pûr′sĭz|. **1.** A North American Indian tribe of the northwestern United States. **2.** A member of this tribe. **3.** The Sahaptin language of this tribe.

N.H. New Hampshire.

ni The symbol for the element nickel.

ni•a•cin |nī′ə sĭn| *n.* **Nicotinic acid.**

Ni•ag•a•ra |nī ăg′rə| *or* |-ăg′ər ə|. **1.** Also **Niagara River.** A river flowing from Lake Erie to Lake Ontario, dividing the United States and Canada. **2.** Also **Niagara Falls.** The twin waterfalls of this river, one in Canada and one in the United States.

Nia•mey |nyä mā′|. The capital of Niger. Population, 70,000.

nib |nĭb| *n.* **1.** The point of a pen. **2.** Any sharp point or tip. **3.** A bird's beak.

nib•ble |nĭb′əl| *v.* **nib•bled, nib•bling. 1. a.** To take small, quick, repeated bites: *You should nibble on raisins instead of potato chips. The rabbit's nose wiggled when he nibbled.* **b.** To eat with small, quick bites: *nibble cheese. Mice were nibbling in the pantry.* **2.** To bite at gently and repeatedly: *The fish nibbled the bait.* —*n.* **1.** A small or hesitant bite, such as a fish may take at bait. **2.** A small bite or morsel of food.

Nic•a•ra•gua |nĭk′ə rä′ gwə|. The largest country in Central America, located between Honduras and Costa Rica. Population, 2,084,000. Capital, Managua. —**Nic′a•ra′guan** *adj. & n.*

nice |nīs| *adj.* **nic•er, nic•est. 1.** Good; pleasant; agreeable: *a nice smell; a nice place to stay.* **2.** Enjoyable: *Have a nice time.* **3.** Especially good; choice: *Do you have any nice rib roasts?* **4.** Of good quality: *a nice pair of shoes.* **5.** Also **nice and.** Used as an intensive: *a nice big yard; stay nice and warm.* **6.** Attractive: *You look nice in your new outfit.* **7. a.** Kind and good; thoughtful; considerate: *It's very nice of you to help me.* **b.** Courteous and polite: *a nice child.* **8.** Morally upright; honorable; virtuous: *Don't associate*

newspaper

"A newspaper consists of just the same number of words, whether there be any news in it or not." —*Henry Fielding (1749).*

"The mass of every people must be barbarous where there is no printing . . . Knowledge is diffused among our people by the newspapers." —*Samuel Johnson (1772).*

"It is a newspaper's business to print the news, and raise hell." —*Wilbur F. Storey, editor of the Chicago* Times *(1861).*

newt

A newt *was originally* an ewt; ewt *is a variant of* **eft.**

night

Night *was* niht *in Old English; it is descended from the prehistoric Indo-European word for "night," which was* nekwt- *or* nokwt-. Nokwt- *appears in Latin as* noct-, nox, *which had the adjective* nocturnus, *"belonging to night"; this was borrowed into English as* **nocturnal**.

nightmare

The **nightmare** *has sometimes been thought of as a kind of ghostly horse, but in fact the word has no connection with* **mare**. *The* mare *in this case is not the female horse but an Old English dream demon or goblin called* maere.

nightshade

ă pat/ā pay/â care/ä father/ĕ pet/ ē be/ĭ pit/ī pie/î fierce/ŏ pot/ ō go/ô paw, for/oi oil/o͝o book/ o͞o boot/ou out/ŭ cut/û fur/ *th* the/th thin/hw which/zh vision/ ə ago, item, pencil, atom, circus

with boys who are not nice. **9.** Skillful; deft: *a nice bit of workmanship.* ¶*These sound alike* **nice, gneiss.** —**nice'ly** *adv.* —**nice'ness** *n.*

Ni•cene Creed |nī'sēn'|. A formal statement of doctrine of the Christian faith adopted at the Council of Nicaea in A.D. 325 and expanded in later councils.

ni•ce•ty |nī'sĭ tē| *n., pl.* **ni•ce•ties.** **1.** Precision or accuracy; exactness: *the nicety of the computer's calculations.* **2.** Often **niceties.** A fine point, small detail, or subtle distinction: *the niceties of word usage.* **3.** Often **niceties.** An elegant or refined feature: *the niceties of civilized life.*

niche |nĭch| *n.* **1.** A recess or alcove in a wall, as for holding a statue. **2.** A cranny, hollow, or crevice, as in rock.

Nich•o•las |nĭk'ə ləs|, **Saint.** Fourth-century bishop in Asia Minor; often identified with Santa Claus.

nick |nĭk| *n.* A small cut, notch, or chip in a surface or edge: *a plate with a nick in it.* —*v.* To make a small cut, notch, or chip in.
Idiom. **in the nick of time.** Just at the critical moment.

nick•el |nĭk'əl| *n.* **1.** Symbol **Ni** One of the elements, a hard, silvery metal. Atomic number 28; atomic weight 58.71; valences +1, +2, +3; melting point 1,453°C; boiling point 2,732°C. **2.** A U.S. or Canadian coin worth five cents, made of a nickel and copper alloy. **3.** A small sum of money; any money: *I haven't a nickel to my name.*

nick•name |nĭk'nām'| *n.* **1.** A descriptive name used instead of or along with the real name of a person, place, or thing: *He was a lanky youth, all arms and legs, and the nickname "Spider" fitted him perfectly.* **2. a.** A familiar or shortened form of a proper name: *Joseph's nickname was Joey.* **b.** An informal, unofficial, or affectionate name. —*v.* **nick•named, nick•nam•ing.** To call by a nickname.

Nic•o•si•a |nĭk'ə sē'ə|. The capital of Cyprus. Population, 118,000.

nic•o•tine |nĭk'ə tēn'| *n.* A poisonous alkaloid composed of carbon, hydrogen, and nitrogen in the proportions $C_{10}H_{14}N_2$. It is found in tobacco and is used in medicine and as an insect poison.

nic•o•tin•ic acid |nĭk'ə tĭn'ĭk|. A compound containing carbon, hydrogen, oxygen, and nitrogen in the proportions $C_6H_5O_2N$. It is a member of the vitamin B complex and is essential to living cells.

niece |nēs| *n.* A daughter of one's brother or sister or one's spouse's brother or sister.

nif•ty |nĭf'tē| *adj.* **nif•ti•er, nif•ti•est.** *Informal.* Stylish or first-rate: *a nifty new outfit.*

Ni•ger |nī'jər|. **1.** A country in western Africa, north of Nigeria. Population, 4,476,000. Capital, Niamey. **2.** A river in Africa, flowing through Mali, Niger, and Nigeria into the Atlantic.

Ni•ge•ri•a |nī jîr'ē ə|. The most populous country in Africa, in the west-central part of the continent. Population, 61,270,000. Capital, Lagos. —**Ni•ge'ri•an** *adj. & n.*

nig•gard |nĭg'ərd| *n.* A stingy person; a miser. —*adj.* Stingy; miserly.

nig•gard•ly |nĭg'ərd lē| *adj.* **1.** Unwilling to give, spend, or share; stingy; grudging. **2.** Small or meager: *a niggardly amount.* —*adv.* Stingily.

nigh |nī| *adv.* **nigh•er, nigh•est.** Near in time, space, or relationship: *I'd perch by her window as evening drew nigh.* —*adj.* Being near in time, place, or relationship; close: *I was sick and nigh to death.*

night |nīt| *n.* **1.** The period between sunset and sunrise, especially the hours of darkness. **2.** The part of the night devoted to sleep or rest: *He tossed and turned all night.* **3.** An evening or night devoted to some special purpose or event: *the opening night of a play.* **4.** Nightfall: *They worked from morning to night.* **5.** Darkness: *She ran out into the foggy night.* **6.** Any gloomy time of inactivity, sorrow, ignorance, or evil: *a long night of waiting before our dreams come true.* —**modifier:** *the night air; a night nurse.* ¶*These sound alike* **night, knight.** [SEE NOTE]

night blindness. Inability to see as well in dim light as a normal person does.

night•cap |nīt'kăp'| *n.* **1.** A cloth cap worn in bed. **2.** *Informal.* A drink taken just before bedtime.

night•clothes |nīt'klōz'| *or* |-klō*thz*'| *pl.n.* Clothes, such as nightgowns and pajamas, worn in bed.

night•club |nīt'klŭb'| *n.* An establishment that stays open late at night and provides food, drink, and entertainment.

night crawler. An earthworm that comes out of the ground at night.

night•fall |nīt'fôl'| *n.* The coming of darkness at the close of day.

night•gown |nīt'goun'| *n.* A loose gown worn to sleep in by a woman or child.

night•hawk |nīt'hôk'| *n.* **1.** A night-flying bird related to and resembling the whippoorwill. **2.** A person who habitually stays up late at night; a night owl.

night•in•gale |nīt'n gāl'| *or* |nī'tĭng gāl'| *n.* A brownish bird of Europe and Asia that has a melodious song and sings at night.

night•ly |nīt'lē| *adj.* Taking place, done, or used at night or every night: *secret nightly meetings; a watchman's nightly rounds.* —*adv.* Every night: *one to two hours of dreaming nightly.* ¶*These sound alike* **nightly, knightly.**

night•mare |nīt'mâr'| *n.* **1.** A bad dream that is very frightening. **2.** A terrible, frightening experience that is like a bad dream. [SEE NOTE]

night•mar•ish |nīt'mâr'ĭsh| *adj.* Like something in a bad dream; frightening; appalling: *a nightmarish experience.* —**night'mar'ish•ly** *adv.* —**night'mar'ish•ness** *n.*

night owl. A person who stays up late at night; a nighthawk.

night•shade |nīt'shād'| *n.* Any of several related plants with poisonous berries, as **black nightshade,** which has small white flowers and black berries, **deadly nightshade,** which is the source of the drug belladonna, or the purple-flowered kind often called bittersweet. [SEE PICTURE]

night•shirt |nīt'shûrt'| *n.* A kind of long, loose shirt worn to sleep in by a man or boy.

night•time |nīt'tīm'| *n.* The time between nightfall and dawn; night.

nil |nĭl| *n.* Nothing; zero.

Nile |nīl|. The longest river in Africa, rising in Lake Victoria and flowing north about 4,000 miles to the Mediterranean Sea.

nim•bi |nĭm′bī′| *n.* A plural of **nimbus.**

nim•ble |nĭm′bəl| *adj.* **nim•bler, nim•blest 1. a.** Moving or able to move quickly, lightly, and easily; agile: *nimble mountain goats; nimble fingers.* **b.** Quick, light, and easy: *nimble movements.* **2.** Quick and clever in thinking, understanding, or responding: *her nimble wit.* —**nim′ble•ness** *n.* —**nim′bly** *adv.*

nim•bo•stra•tus |nĭm′bō **strā′**təs| *or* |-**străt′**əs| *n.* A gray, often dark cloud found typically at a height of about one-fourth mile above the earth and usually dropping rain, sleet, or snow.

nim•bus |**nĭm′**bəs| *n., pl.* **nim•bus•es** or **nim•bi** |**nĭm′**bī′|. **1.** A halo or cloudy radiance glowing around the head of a god, goddess, saint, or monarch, as in a painting. **2.** A special atmosphere or aura, as of glory or romance, surrounding a person, place, or thing. **3.** Formerly, a rain cloud. [SEE PICTURE]

nin•com•poop |**nĭn′**kəm po͞op′| *or* |**nĭng′**-| *n.* A stupid or silly person; an idiot; fool.

nine |nīn| *n.* A number, written 9 in Arabic numerals, that is equal to the sum of 8 + 1. It is the positive integer that immediately follows 8. —**nine** *adj. & pron.*

nine•pins |**nīn′**pĭnz′| *n.* *(used with a singular verb).* A bowling game in which nine wooden pins are the target.

nine•teen |**nīn′tēn′**| *n.* A number, written 19 in Arabic numerals, that is equal to the sum of 18 + 1. It is the positive integer that immediately follows 18. —**nine′teen′** *adj. & pron.*

nine•teenth |**nīn′tēnth′**| *n.* **1.** In a set of items arranged to match the natural numbers in a one-to-one correspondence, the item that matches the number nineteen. **2.** One of nineteen equal parts of a unit, written $^1/_{19}$. —**nine′teenth′** *adj. & adv.*

nine•ti•eth |**nīn′**tē ĭth| *n.* **1.** In a set of items arranged to match the natural numbers in a one-to-one correspondence, the item that matches the number ninety. **2.** One of ninety equal parts of a unit, written $^1/_{90}$. —**nine′ti•eth** *adj. & adv.*

nine•ty |**nīn′**tē| *n., pl.* **nine•ties.** A number, written 90 in Arabic numerals, that is equal to the product of 9 × 10. It is the tenth positive integer after 80. —**nine′ty** *adj. & pron.*

nin•ny |**nĭn′**ē| *n., pl.* **nin•nies.** A fool; a simpleton.

ninth |nīnth| *n.* **1.** In a set of items arranged to match the natural numbers in a one-to-one correspondence, the item that matches the number nine. **2.** One of nine equal parts of a unit, written $^1/_9$. **3.** A musical interval equal to an octave plus a whole step or a half step. —**ninth** *adj. & adv.*

ni•o•bi•um |nī **ō′**bē əm| *n.* Symbol **Nb** One of the elements, a soft, silvery metal. Atomic number 41; atomic weight 92.91; valences +2, +3, +4, +5; melting point 2,468°C; boiling point 4,927°C.

nip[1] |nĭp| *v.* **nipped, nip•ping. 1. a.** To give a small, sharp bite or bites to: *One pony playfully nipped the other.* **b.** To pinch, press, or squeeze: *The lobster nipped my toe with its claw.* **2.** To remove by biting, pinching, or snipping: *The rabbit nipped off the plant leaf.* **3.** To sting or chill, as sharp, biting cold does: *The freezing weather nipped our ears.* **4.** To stop the further growth or development of; blight: *A spring frost may nip the young plants overnight.* **5.** *Slang.* In sports, to defeat (an opponent) or go over (a boundary) by a very small margin: *The baseball just nipped the outside corner for a strike.* **6.** *British Slang.* To move quickly; dart. —*n.* **1.** A small, sharp bite, pinch, or snip. **2.** Sharp, biting cold: *a nip in the autumn air.* **3.** A sharp, biting flavor; tang. [SEE NOTE]

***Idiom.* nip and tuck.** Very close; neck and neck: *The race was nip and tuck for a while.*

nip[2] |nĭp| *n.* A small drink, sip, or swallow of liquor. [SEE NOTE]

nip•per |**nĭp′**ər| *n.* **1.** Someone or something that nips. **2. nippers.** A tool, such as pliers or pincers, used for grasping or snipping. **3.** A pincerlike part, such as the large claw of a lobster. **4.** *British.* A boy. [SEE PICTURE]

nip•ple |**nĭp′**əl| *n.* **1. a.** A small projection near the center of the surface of a mammary gland, as of the human breast, containing in females the outlets of the milk ducts. **b.** A soft rubber cap made in imitation of this and used on a bottle from which a baby nurses. **2.** A short length of pipe with threads cut at both ends.

Nip•pon |nĭ **pŏn′**|. A Japanese name for Japan. —**Nip′pon•ese′** |nĭp′ə **nēz′**| *or* |-**nēs′**| *adj. & n.*

nip•py |**nĭp′**ē| *adj.* **nip•pi•er, nip•pi•est.** Sharp or biting, as because of frosty air or a tangy taste: *a nippy fall day; nippy apples in a salad.*

nir•va•na |nîr **vä′**nə| *or* |nər-| *n.* **1.** In Buddhism, the state of perfect bliss in which the self is freed from all suffering and desire and is united with the creator of the universe. **2.** Any ideal condition of rest, harmony, stability, or joy.

Ni•sei |**nē′**sā′| *n.* A person born in America of parents who emigrated from Japan.

nit |nĭt| *n.* The egg or young of a louse, especially of the kind that infests human hair. ¶*These sound alike* **nit, knit.**

ni•ter |**nī′**tər| *n.* A white, gray, or colorless mineral form of potassium nitrate.

ni•trate |**nī′**trāt′| *n.* **1.** A salt or ester of nitric acid. **2.** A fertilizer containing a salt of nitric acid. —*v.* **ni•trat•ed, ni•trat•ing.** To treat with nitric acid or a nitrate, as in causing nitration.

ni•tra•tion |nī **trā′**shən| *n.* A chemical reaction in which a nitro group, $-NO_2$, is substituted for a hydrogen atom or another univalent group, especially in an organic compound.

ni•tre |**nī′**tər| *n.* Chiefly British form of the word **niter.**

ni•tric |**nī′**trĭk| *adj.* Of, derived from, or containing nitrogen, especially in one of its higher valences.

nitric acid. A transparent, colorless to yellowish liquid composed of nitrogen, hydrogen, and oxygen and having the formula HNO_3. It is used in making fertilizers, explosives, and rocket fuels.

ni•tride |**nī′**trīd′| *n.* A compound of nitrogen and another element, in which the nitrogen gains electrons or shares them in a way that makes it the more negative of the two elements.

ni•tri•fi•ca•tion |nī′trə fĭ **kā′**shən| *n.* A process in which ammonia present in soil, as from the decomposition of protein matter, is oxidized by bacteria to form nitrites that are oxidized by other bacteria to form nitrates.

nimbus
Head of Christ in a painting by Titian

nip[1-2]
Nip[1] *is probably borrowed from Old Norse* hnippa, *"to pinch."* **Nip**[2] *is shortened from* nipperkin, *"a small measure of drink," which is probably related to Dutch* nippen, *"to sip."*

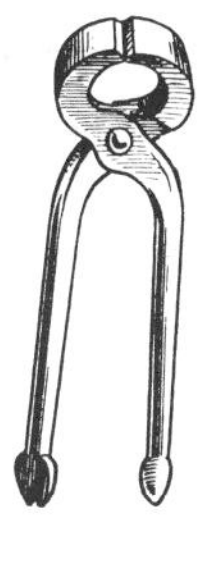

nippers

ni•tri•fy |nī′trə fī′| *v.* **ni•tri•fied, ni•tri•fy•ing, ni•tri•fies. 1.** To treat or combine with nitrogen or its compounds. **2.** To carry on nitrification.

ni•trite |nī′trīt′| *n.* A salt or ester of nitrous acid.

ni•tro•bac•te•ri•a |nī′trō băk tîr′ē ə| *pl.n.* Soil bacteria that perform nitrification.

ni•tro•cel•lu•lose |nī′trō sĕl′yə lōs′| *n.* A pulpy or cottonlike substance formed by nitrating cellulose. It is used in making explosives, rocket fuels, and plastics.

ni•tro•gen |nī′trə jən| *n.* Symbol **N** One of the elements, a colorless, odorless gas. Atomic number 7; atomic weight 14.01; valences −3, −2, −1, +1, +2, +3, +4, +5; melting point −209.86°C; boiling point −195.8°C. [SEE NOTE]

nitrogen cycle. The continuing process by which nitrogen in the atmosphere forms compounds that are deposited in the soil, transformed and assimilated by bacteria and living plants that are in turn eaten by animals, and returns to the atmosphere by the decomposition and metabolism of organic substances.

nitrogen fixation. 1. The conversion of atmospheric nitrogen into nitrogen compounds, either by natural means or by industrial processes. **2.** The conversion by certain algae and soil bacteria of inorganic nitrogen and nitrogen compounds into compounds that plants can assimilate.

ni•tro•gen-fix•ing bacteria |nī′trə jən fĭk′sĭng|. Bacteria that often form knoblike clusters on the roots of certain plants, such as clover, soybeans, or alfalfa, and that carry on the process of nitrogen fixation, thus increasing the fertility of the soil.

ni•trog•e•nous |nī trŏj′ə nəs| *adj.* Of, derived from, or containing nitrogen.

nitrogen oxides. A group of compounds, most of which are poisonous, that are formed of nitrogen and oxygen. They are produced in various combustion processes, as in engines and furnaces, and contribute to air pollution and the formation of smog.

ni•tro•glyc•er•in, also **ni•tro•glyc•er•ine** |nī′trō glĭs′ər ĭn| *n.* A thick, pale-yellow, dangerously explosive liquid formed by treating glycerin with nitric and sulfuric acids. It has the formula $C_3H_5(NO_3)_3$ and is used in making other explosives and in medicine as a drug that dilates the blood vessels.

ni•tro group |nī′trō|. The univalent radical that is composed of nitrogen and oxygen and has the formula $-NO_2$. It occurs in many important explosives and other organic compounds.

ni•trous |nī′trəs| *adj.* Of, derived from, or containing nitrogen, especially in one of its lower valences.

nitrous acid. A weak, unstable acid composed of nitrogen, hydrogen, and oxygen and having the formula HNO_2.

nitrous oxide. A colorless, sweet-smelling gas composed of nitrogen and oxygen and having the formula N_2O. It has an intoxicating effect and is used as a mild anesthetic.

nit•wit |nĭt′wĭt′| *n. Informal.* A stupid or silly person.

nix |nĭks|. *Slang. n.* Nothing. *—adv.* No: *Nix on that idea. —interj.* Stop! Watch out! *—v.* To say no to; reject; deny; veto: *The boss nixed my suggestion for the company's annual picnic.*

Nix•on |nĭk′sən|, **Richard Milhous.** Born 1913. Thirty-seventh President of the United States (1969–74); resigned.

N.J. New Jersey.

N. Mex. New Mexico.

no |nō| *adv.* **1.** Not so. Used to express refusal, denial, or disagreement: *Let's go! No, I'm not going.* **2.** Not at all. Used with the comparative: *no better; no more.* **3.** Not: *whether or no. —adj.* **1.** Not any: *There are no cookies left in the jar.* **2.** Not at all: *He is no fool. —n., pl.* **noes. 1.** A negative response; a denial or refusal: *Her suggestion met with a chorus of noes.* **2.** A negative vote or voter. ¶*These sound alike* **no, know.**

No The symbol for the element nobelium.

no., No. 1. north; northern. **2.** number.

No•ah |nō′ə|. In the Bible, the patriarch chosen by God to build the ark in which he, his family, and two of every kind of animal were saved from the Flood.

no•bel•i•um |nō bĕl′ē əm| *or* |-bē′lē-| *n.* Symbol **No** One of the elements, a metal first prepared by bombarding an isotope of curium with carbon nuclei. It has five isotopes with mass numbers ranging from 252 to 256 and half-lives ranging from 4.5 to 180 seconds. Atomic number 102.

No•bel Prize |nō bĕl′|. Any of five international prizes awarded annually for outstanding achievement in physics, chemistry, physiology or medicine, literature, and the promotion of peace. A sixth prize, in economics, has been awarded since 1969. [SEE NOTE]

no•bil•i•ty |nō bĭl′ĭ tē| *n., pl.* **no•bil•i•ties. 1.** A social class distinguished by hereditary rank or titles of rank and often wealth, power, and privilege; the class of nobles. **2.** Noble rank or status: *Congress may not grant titles of nobility.* **3.** Noble nature, character, or quality: *His music has qualities of nobility, loftiness, and grandeur.*

no•ble |nō′bəl| *adj.* **no•bler, no•blest. 1.** Of, in, or belonging to the nobility: *a noble family; a lady of noble birth.* **2.** Having or showing qualities of high moral character, as courage, generosity, self-sacrifice, etc.: *a noble spirit.* **3. a.** Excellent and admirable: *How noble a thing freedom is!* **b.** Worthy and virtuous: *a noble cause.* **c.** High; lofty; exalted: *a noble ideal.* **d.** Grand; stately; majestic: *noble mountain peaks.* **4.** Chemically inactive or inert. *—n.* A person of noble birth, rank, or title; a member of the nobility. **—no′ble•ness** *n.* **—no′bly** *adv.*

no•ble•man |nō′bəl mən| *n., pl.* **-men** |-mən|. A man of noble birth, rank, or title.

no•ble•wom•an |nō′bəl wo͝om′ən| *n., pl.* **-wom•en** |-wĭm′ĭn|. A woman of noble birth, rank, or title.

no•bod•y |nō′bŏd′ē| *or* |-bə dē| *pron.* No person; no one; not anybody: *Nobody was looking. Nobody else knew about it. —n., pl.* **no•bod•ies.** A person of no importance, influence, or position.

noc•tur•nal |nŏk tûr′nəl| *adj.* **1.** Of the night or occurring at night: *nocturnal stillness; a nocturnal breeze.* **2.** Active at night rather than by day: *Owls are nocturnal birds.* **—noc•tur′nal•ly** *adv.*

noc•turne |nŏk′tûrn′| *n.* A romantic musical composition intended to suggest or call forth thoughts and feelings of night.

nitrogen

Nitrogen *makes up 78 per cent of the atmosphere by volume and is obtained from liquid air. It is present in all proteins and is used to manufacture many important materials, including ammonia, explosives, and fertilizers.*

Nobel prize

These prizes were set up under the terms of the will of Alfred Nobel *(1833–1896), Swedish chemist and inventor of dynamite. The element* **nobelium,** *which was discovered in 1957 at the Nobel Institute, Stockholm, was named in honor of Nobel.*

nod |nŏd| *v.* **nod•ded, nod•ding. 1. a.** To move (the head) down and then up in a quick motion, as when saying yes, showing agreement or approval, giving a greeting or signal, or pointing something out: *She smiled and nodded her head.* **b.** To express or convey (approval, a greeting, etc.) by making such a motion of the head: *He nodded his approval.* **2.** To let the head droop and fall forward, as when getting sleepy or dozing: *He began to nod, and his eyes closed for a moment.* **3.** To droop, sway, or bend downward: *scarlet flowers nodding on long, frail stems.* —*n.* **1.** An act or gesture of nodding, as one used to give a greeting or signal, show approval, or point something out: *The stranger sat down without even a nod.* **2.** A nodding motion: *a nod of the head.*

***Idiom.* give** (or **get**) **the nod.** *Informal.* To give (or receive) approval or a favorable decision.

nod•al |**nōd'**l| *adj.* Of or of the nature of a node.

node |nōd| *n.* **1.** A mass of body tissue that has a clear outer boundary but few or no internal divisions or distinctions: *a lymph node.* **2.** An often knoblike marking on a plant stem at a point where a leaf or stem is attached; a joint. **3.** A point or region of a vibrating or oscillating system at which the amplitude of the vibration or oscillation is zero or at a minimum. **4. a.** Either of the two points at which the orbit of a planet intersects the ecliptic. **b.** Either of the two points at which the orbit of a satellite intersects the plane of orbit of its primary.

nod•ule |**nŏj'**o͞ol| *n.* **1. a.** A small node, as of body tissue. **b.** A swelling at a single, definite location in the body. **2.** A small, knoblike lump or outgrowth, such as one of those formed on the roots of clover, alfalfa, soybeans, etc. **3.** A small lump of a mineral or a mixture of minerals.

No•ël or **No•el** |nō **ĕl'**| *n.* **1.** Christmas. **2. no•ël** or **no•el.** A Christmas carol.

nog•gin |**nŏg'**ĭn| *n.* **1.** A small mug or cup. **2.** A small drink of liquor equal to one-fourth of a pint. **3.** *Informal.* The head.

noise |noiz| *n.* **1.** Sound or a sound that is loud, unpleasant, unexpected, or undesired: *You're making too much noise. I was awakened by a noise like a fire siren.* **2.** A loud, confused, or clashing combination of sounds: *the noise of city traffic.* **3.** Sound or a sound of any kind: *The only noise was the wind in the pines.* **4. a.** A fuss, stir, or commotion: *She made quite a noise about the lost luggage.* **b.** An effect or impact: *That small country makes a noise in the world far in excess of its dimensions.* —*v.* **noised, nois•ing.** To spread as a rumor or report: *He noised it about that his rival had cheated.* [SEE NOTE]

noise•less |**noiz'**lĭs| *adj.* Making little or no sound or noise; quiet or silent: *We slipped along the hedges, noiseless and swift.* —**noise'less•ly** *adv.*

noise•mak•er |**noiz'**mā'kər| *n.* **1.** Someone or something that makes noise. **2.** A device, such as a horn or rattle, used to make noise at a party.

noi•some |**noi'**səm| *adj.* **1.** Foul, offensive, or disgusting: *a noisome odor.* **2.** Harmful or injurious: *a noisome climate.* —**noi'some•ly** *adv.*

nois•y |**noi'**zē| *adj.* **nois•i•er, nois•i•est. 1.** Making a lot of noise: *a noisy crowd; a noisy engine.* **2.** Full of, characterized by, or accompanied by noise: *busy, crowded, noisy streets; a noisy telephone circuit.* —**nois'i•ly** *adv.* —**nois'i•ness** *n.*

no•mad |**nō'**măd'| *n.* **1.** A member of a group of people who have no permanent home, live mainly by keeping livestock, and move about from place to place seeking food, water, and grazing land. **2.** Any wanderer who roams about instead of settling in one place.

no•mad•ic |nō **măd'**ĭk| *adj.* **1.** Of nomads: *nomadic tribes.* **2.** Leading the life of a nomad or nomads: *nomadic herdsmen.*

nom de plume |nŏm' də **plo͞om'**|. A made-up name that a writer uses professionally instead of his real name; a pen name.

no•men•cla•ture |**nō'**mən klā'chər| *or* |nō**mĕn'**klə-| *n.* **1.** The act or practice of naming according to a special system or in a certain style: *The system of giving each plant or animal a scientific name of two parts is called binomial nomenclature.* **2.** The special system of names used in a particular science or art; terminology: *the nomenclature of anatomy.*

nom•i•nal |**nŏm'**ə nəl| *adj.* **1.** In name, but often in name only and not in actuality: *a premier with nominal powers but no real authority.* **2.** So small or low in relation to the real value as to be a mere token: *They charged a nominal sum for admission.* —**nom'i•nal•ly** *adv.* [SEE NOTE]

nom•i•nate |**nŏm'**ə nāt'| *v.* **nom•i•nat•ed, nom•i•nat•ing. 1.** To propose or select as a candidate, as in an election to fill an office. **2.** To appoint to a position, office, or honor, often subject to approval or confirmation: *The President nominated a new chief justice.* —**nom'i•nat'ing** *adj.: a nominating convention.*

nom•i•na•tion |nŏm'ə **nā'**shən| *n.* **1.** The act or process of nominating: *the nomination of a vice-presidential candidate.* **2.** Appointment to a position, office, or honor: *The President's nomination of an ambassador was confirmed by the Senate.* —***modifier:*** *a nomination speech.*

nom•i•na•tive |**nŏm'**ə nə tĭv| *adj.* Of or belonging to a grammatical case that indicates the subject of a verb and also words, such as a predicate, identified with the subject. The nominative case is the common case of nouns and one of the cases of personal pronouns. For example, in the sentences *These are the men* and *We leave at noon*, the words *men* and *We* are in the nominative case. —*n.* The nominative case.

nom•i•nee |nŏm'ə **nē'**| *n.* **1.** A person proposed or selected as a candidate for an office or award: *the party's Presidential nominee.* **2.** A person appointed to a position, office, or honor: *the President's nominee for chief justice.*

non–. A prefix meaning "not, absence of, or avoidance of": **nonviolence.** When *non-* is followed by a capital letter, it appears with a hyphen: *non-American.*

non•a•gon |**nŏn'**ə gŏn'| *or* |**nō'**nə-| *n.* A plane geometric figure bounded by nine line segments and containing nine angles. [SEE PICTURE]

non•al•co•hol•ic |nŏn'ăl'kə **hôl'**ĭk| *or* |**-hŏl'-**| *adj.* Containing no alcohol: *Ginger ale is a nonalcoholic beverage.*

non•a•ligned |nŏn'ə **līnd'**| *adj.* Not in alliance with any power bloc; neutral: *a nonaligned nation.*

nonce |nŏns| *n.* —**for the nonce.** For the present time or occasion; for the time being.

noise
Engineers have extended the meaning of **noise** *to refer to any disturbance that interferes with a communications system, especially a random or unpredictable disturbance. Such disturbance includes electrical signals that produce undesired sounds in radio and telephone receivers; it even includes "snow" seen on television screens and the background radiation that reaches the earth from space.*

nominal/name
The similarity between **name** *and* **nominal** *is not an accident; the words are cognates. The Indo-European word for "name" was* nomen-, *which appeared in: (1) Old English* nama, *becoming* **name** *in Modern English; and (2) Latin* nōmen, *"name," with the adjective* nōminālis, *"belonging to a name," which was borrowed into English as* **nominal**.

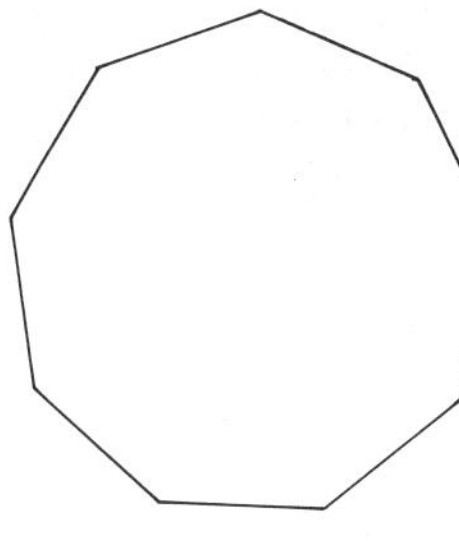

nonagon

nonce word. A word made up for use on one particular occasion. [SEE NOTE]

non•cha•lant |nŏn′shə **länt′**| *adj.* Cool, carefree, and casually unconcerned, or seeming so: *a nonchalant air.* —**non′cha•lance′** *n.* —**non′cha•lant′ly** *adv.*

non•com |**nŏn′**kŏm′| *n. Informal.* A noncommissioned officer.

non•com•bat•ant |nŏn′kəm **băt′**nt| *n.* **1.** A person serving in the armed forces whose duties exclude fighting, such as a chaplain or a member of the medical corps. **2.** A civilian in wartime.

non•com•mis•sioned officer |nŏn′kə **mĭsh′**-ənd|. An enlisted member of the armed forces appointed to a rank, such as sergeant or corporal, conferring leadership over other enlisted men. Noncommissioned officers rank below commissioned officers and warrant officers.

non•com•mit•tal |nŏn′kə **mĭt′**l| *adj.* Not indicating how one feels or what one thinks or plans to do: *She gave a noncommittal answer, "We shall see."*

non-com•mu•nist |nŏn **kŏm′**yə nĭst| *adj.* Not practicing or advocating a communist social, political, or economic system: *non-communist political parties.*

non-Com•mu•nist |nŏn **kŏm′**yə nĭst| *adj.* Not governed by or belonging to a Communist party: *non-Communist nations.* —*n.* A person who is not a Communist.

non•com•pli•ance |nŏn′kəm **plī′**əns| *n.* Failure or refusal to comply with something.

non com•pos men•tis |nŏn **kŏm′**pəs **mĕn′**tĭs|. Not of sound mind and hence not legally responsible. This was originally a Latin expression.

non•con•duc•tor |nŏn′kən **dŭk′**tər| *n.* A substance that does not conduct electricity, heat, sound, etc.; an insulator. —**non′con•duct′ing** *adj.*

non•con•form•ist |nŏn′kən **fôr′**mĭst| *n.* **1.** Someone who does not act in accordance with or feel bound to follow generally accepted customs, beliefs, or ways of doing things; an individualist. **2.** Often **Nonconformist.** A person who does not belong to a national or established church, especially an English Protestant who is outside the Church of England; a dissenter. —**non′con•form′i•ty** *n.*

non•de•nom•i•na•tion•al |nŏn′dĭ nŏm′ə **nā′**-shə nəl| *adj.* Not restricted to or associated with a particular religious denomination: *a nondenominational service.*

non•de•script |nŏn′dĭ **skrĭpt′**| *adj.* Lacking in distinctive qualities and thus difficult to describe: *a dull, nondescript piece of rock.*

none |nŭn| *pron.* **1.** Not any: *I went through all the pictures, but there were none of her.* **2.** Not one: *None dared to do it.* —*adv.* Not at all. Used with *too: Crops were none too plentiful that year.* ¶*These sound alike* **none, nun.** [SEE NOTE]

non•en•ti•ty |nŏn **ĕn′**tĭ tē| *n., pl.* **non•en•ti•ties.** A person or thing of no importance or significance; a nobody or a nothing.

non•es•sen•tial |nŏn′ĭ **sĕn′**shəl| *adj.* Not essential; not absolutely necessary; not basically important: *nonessential supplies.* —*n.* Something that is not essential: *Do not take any nonessentials on the hike.*

none•the•less |nŭn′*thə* **lĕs′**| *adv.* Also **none the less.** Nevertheless.

non-Eu•clid•e•an |nŏn′yōō **klĭd′**ē ən| *adj.* Of or having to do with any one of several forms of modern geometry that are based on postulates differing from those used by Euclid.

non•ex•ist•ent |nŏn′ĭg **zĭs′**tənt| *adj.* Not existing; absent, missing, or entirely lacking: *planets with poisonous or nonexistent atmospheres.* —**non′ex•ist′ence** *n.*

non•fat |**nŏn′făt′**| *adj.* Lacking fat solids, such as cream, or having had the fat content removed: *nonfat dry milk.*

non•fic•tion |nŏn **fĭk′**shən| *n.* **1.** The category of literature including writings that are not fiction, especially books of fact and general information, such as history books, biographies, essays, etc. **2.** Literary works of this category.

non•flam•ma•ble |nŏn **flăm′**ə bəl| *adj.* Not flammable; not tending to catch fire easily and burn rapidly. —**non•flam′ma•bil′i•ty** *n.*

non•in•ter•ven•tion |nŏn′ĭn tər **vĕn′**shən| *n.* Failure or refusal to intervene, especially a policy of refusing to interfere in the affairs of another nation.

non•liv•ing |nŏn **lĭv′**ĭng| *adj.* Not having life; not alive; inanimate: *nonliving things.*

non•met•al |nŏn **mĕt′**l| *n.* Any of the elements, such as oxygen or sulfur, that usually become more electrically negative in forming a compound, that have oxides that form acids, and that conduct heat and electricity poorly when in a solid state. —**non′me•tal′lic** |nŏn′mə **tăl′**ĭk| *adj.*

no-non•sense |nō **nŏn′**sĕns′| *or* |-səns| *adj.* Practical; businesslike: *a no-nonsense person.*

non•pa•reil |nŏn′pə **rĕl′**| *n.* Someone or something so excellent as to have no equal and to be beyond compare; a paragon. —*adj.* Having no equal; matchless; peerless.

non•par•ti•san |nŏn **pär′**tĭ zən| *adj.* Not limited to one political party or influenced by party membership: *a nonpartisan statesman.*

non•pay•ment |nŏn **pā′**mənt| *n.* Failure or refusal to pay: *nonpayment of debts.*

non•plus |nŏn **plŭs′**| *v.* **non•plused** or **non•plussed, non•plus•ing** or **non•plus•sing, non•plus•es** or **non•plus•ses.** To put at a loss so that one does not know what to think, say, or do; confuse; bewilder.

non•poi•son•ous |nŏn **poi′**zə nəs| *adj.* Not poisonous, especially: **1.** Not capable of harming or killing by means of poison or venom: *a nonpoisonous snake.* **2.** Containing no poison: *a nonpoisonous fluid.*

non•pro•duc•tive |nŏn′prə **dŭk′**tĭv| *adj.* **1.** Not yielding what was expected or wanted: *a nonproductive vineyard.* **2.** Not engaged in the direct production of goods: *productive factory workers and nonproductive clerical personnel.*

non•prof•it |nŏn **prŏf′**ĭt| *adj.* Not set up or managed for the purpose of making a profit: *a nonprofit organization.*

non•res•i•dent |nŏn **rĕz′**ĭ dənt| *adj.* Not making one's home at a particular place, especially not living where one works, attends school, owns property, or has official duties: *a nonresident taxpayer.* —*n.* A nonresident person.

non•re•stric•tive |nŏn′rĭ **strĭk′**tĭv| *adj.* In grammar, indicating a descriptive word, clause, or phrase that may be left out without changing the basic meaning of the sentence and that is set

nonce word

Some **nonce words** *are also nonsense words, made up to be ridiculous or amusing, for example, the* rhinostril *and the* hippoposthumous, *two otherwise unknown animals in a story by John Lennon.*

none

The pronoun **none** *comes from* no one, *and therefore it is by origin only singular:* None of my friends was there. *But it has come to be used in contexts where* no one *would not be a logical substitute:* None of the laundry is clean. *And it is also often used as a true plural:* None are more wretched than the victims of natural disasters. *Many people still prefer to keep* **none** *singular whenever it is logically possible, as in the first example above; they would disapprove of the construction* None of my friends were there. *This question is still being debated by the experts, but in practice the plural construction seems to be gaining headway.*

ă pat/ā pay/â care/ä father/ĕ pet/ ē be/ĭ pit/ī pie/î fierce/ŏ pot/ ō go/ô paw, for/oi oil/ŏŏ book/ ōō boot/ou out/ŭ cut/û fur/ *th* the/th thin/hw which/zh vision/ ə ago, item, pencil, atom, circus

off from the rest of the sentence by commas. For example, in the sentence *Mary, who has brown hair, is younger than Helen,* the nonrestrictive clause *who has brown hair* may be omitted.

non•sched•uled |nŏn **skĕj′**o͞old| *adj.* **1.** Not planned on a schedule: *a nonscheduled stop.* **2.** Not having a regular schedule of passenger or cargo flights, but operating in response to demand: *a nonscheduled airline.*

non•sec•tar•i•an |nŏn′sĕk **târ′**ē ən| *adj.* Not limited to or associated with a particular religious denomination: *a nonsectarian college.*

non•sense |**nŏn′**sĕns′| *or* |-səns| *n.* **1.** Foolish or senseless talk, writing, or behavior; foolishness: *She stood for no nonsense from the boys.* **2.** Something not true, serious, or sensible; a piece of foolishness, as a silly idea: *He called their theory nonsense.*

non•sen•si•cal |nŏn **sĕn′**sĭ kəl| *adj.* Foolish; ridiculous; silly; absurd: *a nonsensical objection.* —**non•sen′si•cal•ly** *adv.*

non se•qui•tur |nŏn **sĕk′**wĭ tər|. A conclusion that does not follow as the logical result of the premise or evidence that preceded it.

non•skid |**nŏn′skĭd′**| *adj.* Having a surface or tread designed to prevent or resist skidding: *a nonskid bath mat; nonskid tires.*

non•stan•dard |nŏn **stăn′**dərd| *adj.* **1.** Not standard. **2.** Of, on, or indicating a level of language usage that is usually avoided by educated speakers and writers. *She done it* and *You was wrong* are examples of nonstandard English.

non•stop |**nŏn′stŏp′**| *adv.* **1.** Without making any stops: *flying nonstop from New York to Paris.* **2.** Without a pause or break: *They talked nonstop.* —*adj.: a nonstop flight.*

non•un•ion |nŏn **yo͞on′**yən| *adj.* **1.** Not belonging to or following the rules of a labor union: *nonunion workers.* **2.** Not recognizing or dealing with a labor union or employing union members: *a nonunion shop.*

non•ver•bal |nŏn **vûr′**bəl| *adj.* Not using or relying on words; without words: *Gestures, signs, and symbols are forms of nonverbal communication.*

non•vi•o•lence |nŏn **vī′**ə ləns| *n.* The philosophy, policy, or practice of rejecting violence in favor of peaceful tactics as a means of gaining one's ends. —**non•vi′o•lent** *adj.*

non•white |nŏn **hwīt′**| *or* |**-wīt′**| *adj.* Not considered to be of the white race. —*n.* A nonwhite person.

noo•dle[1] |**no͞od′**l| *n.* A narrow, ribbonlike strip of dried dough, usually made of eggs, flour, and water. —*modifier: noodle soup.* [SEE NOTE]

noo•dle[2] |**no͞od′**l| *n.* **1.** *Slang.* The head. **2.** A silly person; a fool. [SEE NOTE]

nook |no͝ok| *n.* **1.** A corner, alcove, or recess, especially one that is part of a larger room: *a kitchen with a breakfast nook.* **2.** Any small, cozy, hidden, or secluded spot: *sea creatures snug in their nooks and sandy holes.*

noon |no͞on| *n.* The middle of the day; twelve o'clock in the daytime; midday. —*adj.* Of or at the middle of the day: *a noon meal.*

noon•day |**no͞on′**dā′| *adj.* Of or occurring at noon: *the noonday heat; a noonday meal.*

no one. No person; nobody: *No one answered, so I thought you were out.*

noon•tide |**no͞on′**tīd′| *n.* Noon.

noon•time |**no͞on′**tīm′| *n.* Noon.

noose |no͞os| *n.* **1.** A loop formed in a rope by means of a slipknot so that it binds tighter as the rope is pulled. **2.** A snare or trap: *fell into his noose.* [SEE PICTURE]

Noot•ka |**no͞ot′**kə| *or* |**no͞ot′**-| *n.* **1.** A North American Indian tribe of Vancouver Island and adjacent areas of Canada and the United States. **2.** A member of this tribe. **3.** The Wakashan language of this tribe.

nor |nôr| *or* |nər *when unstressed*| *conj.* And not; or not; not either. Used to give continuing negative force: *He has no experience, nor does he want any. He is neither able nor willing to do anything.*

Nor•dic |**nôr′**dĭk| *adj.* Of or belonging to the division of the Caucasoid group of the human species that is most predominant in Scandinavia, composed of people who typically are tall, long-headed, blond, and blue-eyed. —*n.* A Nordic person.

norm |nôrm| *n.* **1.** An average or a statistical mode. **2.** A standard or pattern that is considered to be typical of the members of a group.

nor•mal |**nôr′**məl| *adj.* **1.** Usual or ordinary; typical: *normal room temperature; one's normal weight.* **2.** Functioning or occurring in a natural, healthy way: *normal digestion; normal growth.* **3.** Not changed as a result of practice, training, experimentation, etc.: *Some athletes do what normal people cannot.* —*n.* The normal condition, level, measure, degree, etc.: *body temperature above normal.* —**nor′mal•ly** *adv.*

nor•mal•cy |**nôr′**məl sē| *n.* Normality.

nor•mal•i•ty |nôr **măl′**ĭ tē| *n.* The condition of being normal.

nor•mal•ize |**nôr′**mə līz′| *v.* **nor•mal•ized, nor•mal•iz•ing.** To make normal: *normalized relations with a foreign government.* —**nor′mal•i•za′tion** *n.*

normal school. A school that trains teachers, chiefly for the elementary grades.

Nor•man |**nôr′**mən| *n.* **1.** A member of a Scandinavian people who conquered Normandy in the tenth century. The descendants of these people invaded England in 1066. **2.** A native of Normandy. —**Nor′man** *adj.*

Norman Conquest. The conquest of England by the Normans under William the Conqueror in 1066.

Nor•man•dy |**nôr′**mən dē|. A region of northwestern France on the English Channel.

Norman French. **1.** The dialect of Old French used in medieval Normandy and England. **2.** The form of this dialect used in English court and legal circles from the Norman conquest until the 15th century.

Norse |nôrs| *adj.* Of ancient Scandinavia, its people, or their language. —*n.* **the Norse.** The people of ancient Scandinavia.

Norse•man |**nôrs′**mən| *n., pl.* **-men** |-mən|. A man who was a native of ancient Scandinavia.

north |nôrth| *n.* **1.** The direction along a meridian 90 degrees counterclockwise from east. **2.** Often **North.** A region or part of the earth in this direction: *Better farm lands lie in the north of the state.* **3. the North. a.** The Arctic region. **b.** The northern part of the United States, especially the

noodle[1·2]

Noodle[1] *is from German* nudel. **Noodle**[2] *was originally* noddle, *meaning "back of the head"; its further origin is unknown.*

noose
Figure-eight noose

states that supported the Union during the Civil War. *—adj.* **1.** Of, in, or toward the north: *the Bay of Biscay, north of Spain; the north shore of Long Island.* **2.** Often **North.** Forming or belonging to a region, country, etc., toward the north: *North Korea.* **3.** From the north: *a chill north wind.* *—adv.* In a direction to or toward the north: *We could not proceed north until we found a path free of icebergs.*

North America. The northern continent of the Western Hemisphere, including Canada, the United States, Mexico, and Central America. —**North American.**

North Car•o•li•na |kăr'ə lī'nə|. A Southern Atlantic state of the United States. Population, 5,874,429. Capital, Raleigh. —**North Carolinian.**

North Da•ko•ta |də kō'tə|. A north-central state of the United States. Population, 652,695. Capital, Bismarck. —**North Dakotan.**

north•east |nôrth ēst'| *n.* **1.** The direction that is 45 degrees counterclockwise from east and 45 degrees clockwise from north. **2.** An area or region lying in this direction. **3. the Northeast.** The part of the United States including New England, New York, and usually Pennsylvania and New Jersey: *The Northeast has traditionally favored high tariffs on imported goods.* *—adj.* **1.** Of, in, or toward the northeast. **2.** From the northeast: *northeast winds.* *—adv.* In a direction to or toward the northeast. —**north•east'ern** *adj.*

north•east•er |nôrth ē'stər| *or* |nôr ē'-| *n.* A storm or gale from the northeast.

north•east•er•ly |nôrth ē'stər lē| *or* |nôr ē'-| *adj.* **1.** In or toward the northeast: *Most tornadoes take a northeasterly path.* **2.** From the northeast: *bitter and chilling northeasterly gales.* *—adv.: a gale blowing northeasterly.*

north•east•ward |nôrth ēst'wərd| *adv.* Also **north•east•wards** |nôrth ēst'wərdz|. To or toward the northeast: *wandered northeastward.* *—adj.: a northeastward view.* *—n.* A direction or region to the northeast.

north•er |nôr'*th*ər| *n.* A sudden cold gale from the north, especially near the Gulf of Mexico.

north•er•ly |nôr'*th*ər lē| *adj.* **1.** In or toward the north: *The compass needle points in a northerly direction.* **2.** From the north: *The towering Alps protect Italy from northerly winds.* *—adv.: Lee's army advanced northerly.* *—n.* A storm or wind from the north.

north•ern |nôr'*th*ərn| *adj.* **1.** Of, in, or toward the north: *the northern border.* **2.** From the north: *northern winds.* **3.** Characteristic of or found in northern regions: *a northern climate; northern speech.* **4. Northern.** Of the North of the United States: *The Confederate Army lacked the means to seize the Northern capital.*

north•ern•er |nôr'*th*ər nər| *n.* Often **Northerner.** **1.** A person who lives in or comes from the north. **2.** A person from the north of the United States, especially during or before the Civil War: *The song "Dixie" was written by a Northerner.*

Northern Hemisphere. The half of the earth north of the equator.

Northern Ire•land |īr'lənd|. A component of the United Kingdom, in the northeastern part of the island of Ireland. Population, 1,500,000. Capital, Belfast.

northern lights. The **aurora borealis.**

north•ern•most |nôr'*th*ərn mōst'| *adj.* Farthest north.

Northern Spy. A yellowish-red apple.

north•ing |nôr'thĭng| *or* |-*th*ĭng| *n.* **1.** A difference in latitude between two positions as a result of northward movement. **2.** Northward movement.

North Korea. A country occupying the northern part of a peninsula in eastern Asia. Population, 17,914,000. Capital, Pyongyang.

north•land |nôrth'lănd'| *or* |-lənd| *n.* Often **Northland.** A region in the north, especially: **1.** Northern Canada and Alaska. **2.** Scandinavia.

North•man |nôrth'mən| *n., pl.* **-men** |-mən|. A Norseman.

North Pole. **1.** The northernmost point of the earth; the point in the north at which the earth's axis of rotation intersects the surface of the earth. **2.** The point, about one degree from the star Polaris, at which the earth's axis of rotation intersects the celestial sphere. **3. north pole.** The pole of a magnet that tends to point north when the magnet is free to move.

North Sea. A part of the Atlantic Ocean between Great Britain and northern Europe.

north-seek•ing pole |nôrth'sē'kĭng|. The pole of a magnet that is attracted to the north; the north pole.

North Star. Polaris.

North Vietnam. The former name for the northern part of **Vietnam.**

north•ward |nôrth'wərd| *adv.* Also **north•wards** |nôrth'wərdz|. To or toward the north: *turned the ship's prow northward.* *—adj.: northward progress.* *—n.* A direction or region to the north.

north•west |nôrth wĕst'| *n.* **1.** The direction that is 45 degrees counterclockwise from north and 45 degrees clockwise from west. **2.** An area or region lying in this direction. **3. the Northwest. a.** The northwestern part of the United States, especially the region including Washington, Oregon, and Idaho. **b.** The **Northwest Territory.** *—adj.* **1.** Of, in, or toward the northwest. **2.** From the northwest: *northwest winds.* *—adv.* In a direction to or toward the northwest. —**north•west'ern** *adj.*

north•west•er•ly |nôrth wĕst'ər lē| *or* |nôr wĕst'-| *adj.* **1.** In or toward the northwest: *a northwesterly course.* **2.** From the northwest: *northwesterly breezes.* *—adv.: a coastline extending northwesterly.*

Northwest Passage. A water route from the Atlantic Ocean to the Pacific Ocean through the islands of northern Canada. [SEE NOTE]

Northwest Territory. A former U.S. territory organized by Congress in 1787. It was later divided up into the present-day states of Ohio, Indiana, Michigan, Illinois, Wisconsin, and part of Minnesota.

north•west•ward |nôrth wĕst'wərd| *adv.* Also **north•west•wards** |nôrth wĕst'wərdz|. To or toward the northwest: *flying northwestward to Alaska.* *—adj.: northwestward migrations.* *—n.* A direction or region to the northwest.

Nor•way |nôr'wā'|. A country in northern Europe, in the western part of the Scandinavian peninsula. Population, 4,000,000. Capital, Oslo. [SEE NOTE]

Nor•we•gian |nôr wē'jən| *n.* **1.** A native or

Northwest Passage

From the beginning of European settlement in North America it was believed that it must be possible to sail from the Atlantic to the Pacific around the top of the continent. Attempts to find such a route have been made all through American history. The **Northwest Passage** *was first actually navigated in 1903–6, by the Norwegian explorer Roald Amundsen. The route is so icebound that it appeared to be useless for practical purposes; but recently a specially reinforced oil tanker made a successful voyage through some of the worst parts of the passage.*

Norway

The name **Norway** *was originally* Norweg *in English; it is borrowed from Old Norse* Norvegr, *"northern region":* northr, *"northern,"* + vegr, *"way, place."*

ă pat/ā pay/â care/ä father/ĕ pet/ ē be/ĭ pit/ī pie/î fierce/ŏ pot/ ō go/ô paw, for/oi oil/ŏŏ book/ ōō boot/ou out/ŭ cut/û fur/ *th* the/th thin/hw which/zh vision/ ə ago, item, pencil, atom, circus

inhabitant of Norway. **2.** The Germanic language of Norway. *—adj.* Of Norway, the Norwegians, or their language.

nos., Nos. numbers.

nose |nōz| *n.* **1.** In human beings and other animals, the structure, located on the face or the forward part of the head, that contains the nostrils and organs of smell and forms the beginning of the respiratory tract. **2.** The sense of smell: *The dog's nose told him dinner was ready.* **3.** The ability to detect things, as if by smell: *a nose for juicy gossip.* **4.** The forward end of an airplane, rocket, submarine, or other pointed structure. *—v.* **nosed, nos•ing. 1.** To smell: *nosed the wind and caught a scent.* **2.** To touch, push, or examine with the nose; nuzzle: *cats nosing around the garbage cans.* **3.** To pry curiously; meddle; snoop: *strangers nosing about the garden asking questions.* **4.** To steer (a vehicle or one's way) ahead cautiously: *The barge nosed its way past the sandbar. He saw a break in traffic and nosed into it.* ***—phrasal verbs.*** **nose down.** To descend or cause to descend steeply: *We nosed the submarine down into the deep undersea valley.* **nose out.** To defeat by a narrow margin. **nose over.** To turn over on the nose: *The plane nosed over on the runway.* [SEE PICTURE]

Idioms. **by a nose.** By a narrow margin. **follow (one's) nose.** To go straight ahead. **lead by the nose.** To dominate (someone) completely. **look down (one's) nose at.** To treat haughtily or disdainfully. **on the nose. 1.** Exactly; precisely: *predicted the amount on the nose.* **2.** Squarely: *hit the first pitch on the nose.* **pay through the nose.** To pay an unfairly high price. **turn up (one's) nose at.** To reject or ignore with contempt. **under (someone's) nose.** In plain view of: *robbed the bank right under the noses of the guards.*

nose•bleed |nōz′blēd′| *n.* Bleeding from the nostrils.

nose cone. The forwardmost and usually separable part of a rocket or missile, shaped for minimum air resistance and often covered with a heat-resistant material.

nose dive. 1. A very steep dive made by an airplane. **2.** A sudden drop or plunge: *The team's fortunes took a nose dive.*

nose-dive |nōz′dīv′| *v.* **-dived, -div•ing.** To perform a nose dive.

nose•gay |nōz′gā′| *n.* A small bunch of flowers.

nos•ey |nō′zē| *adj.* **nos•i•er, nos•i•est.** A form of the word **nosy.**

nos•tal•gi•a |nŏ stăl′jə| *or* |nə-| *n.* **1.** A bittersweet longing for the things of the past: *an old song that filled the room with nostalgia.* **2.** Homesickness.

nos•tal•gic |nŏ stăl′jĭk| *or* |nə-| *adj.* Full of nostalgia: *nostalgic memories.* **—nos•tal′gi•cal•ly** *adv.*

nos•tril |nŏs′trəl| *n.* Either of the external openings of the nose.

nos•trum |nŏs′trəm| *n.* **1.** A medicine with secret or doubtful ingredients; a quack remedy. **2.** A favorite but unproved remedy for problems or evils.

nos•y |nō′zē| *adj.* **nos•i•er, nos•i•est.** *Informal.* Intruding in other people's affairs; prying. **—nos′i•ly** *adv.* **—nos′i•ness** *n.*

not |nŏt| *adv.* In no way; to no degree. Used to express negation, denial, refusal, prohibition, etc.: *I will not go. You may not have any candy.* ¶*These sound alike* **not, knot.**

no•ta•ble |nō′tə bəl| *adj.* Worthy of notice; remarkable; striking: *a notable success.* *—n.* A well-known person; a prominent figure.

no•ta•bly |nō′tə blē| *adv.* **1.** Remarkably; strikingly: *Several of Lincoln's addresses were notably brief and eloquent.* **2.** Especially; particularly: *Much more dangerous to men are the large poisonous snakes, notably the king cobra.*

no•ta•rize |nō′tə rīz′| *v.* **no•ta•rized, no•ta•riz•ing.** To witness and authenticate (a document) as a notary public. **—no′ta•rized′** *adj.: a notarized deed.*

no•ta•ry |nō′tə rē| *n., pl.* **no•ta•ries.** A **notary public.**

notary public. *pl.* **notaries public.** A person legally empowered to witness the signing of documents and to authenticate them with his seal and signature.

no•tate |nō′tāt′| *v.* **no•tat•ed, no•tat•ing.** To put into notation, especially musical notation.

no•ta•tion |nō tā′shən| *n.* **1.** The use of standard symbols or figures to represent quantities, tones, or other values briefly and clearly: *musical notation.* **2.** A system of such symbols or figures used in a particular field, as in science. **3.** Something, especially a piece of music, written in such a system: *played the song without looking at the notation.* **4.** A note: *a blotter covered with notations.*

notch |nŏch| *n.* **1.** A V-shaped cut. **2.** A steep-sided gap in a ridge or mountain chain. **3.** *Informal.* A level; degree: *The defeat took him down a notch.* *—v.* **1.** To cut a notch in: *He first notched each tree that he intended to fell.* **2.** To record by making notches: *notched the days and weeks on a pole outside his hut.*

note |nōt| *n.* **1.** A short, informal letter or message. **2. a.** A brief record of what is heard, seen, or read, written down to aid the memory: *took notes during the lecture.* **b. notes.** A short sketch or outline touching the main points of a subject: *gave his speech from notes.* **3.** An explanation or comment on a passage in a text, usually printed at the bottom of a page or at the end of a chapter or book. **4. a.** A piece of paper money; a bill. **b.** A certificate representing an amount of money, issued by a government or bank. **c.** A promissory note. **5.** Importance; consequence: *gentlemen of note.* **6.** Notice; observation: *He peered out the window and took note of the weather.* **7. a.** A symbol used to represent a musical tone, indicating the pitch by its position on a staff and the relative length by its shape. **b.** A musical tone. **c.** A key, as of a piano or other instrument. **8.** The characteristic call or cry of a bird or other animal: *heard the clear note of a cardinal.* **9.** A sign or hint that reveals a certain quality: *ended his plea on a note of despair.* *—v.* **not•ed, not•ing. 1.** To observe; notice: *We noted the crocodile's slender head, which distinguishes it from the alligator.* **2.** To write down; make a brief record of: *went to the circus and noted it in his diary that night.* **3.** To make mention of; point out. [SEE PICTURE]

Idiom. **compare notes.** To exchange views or observations.

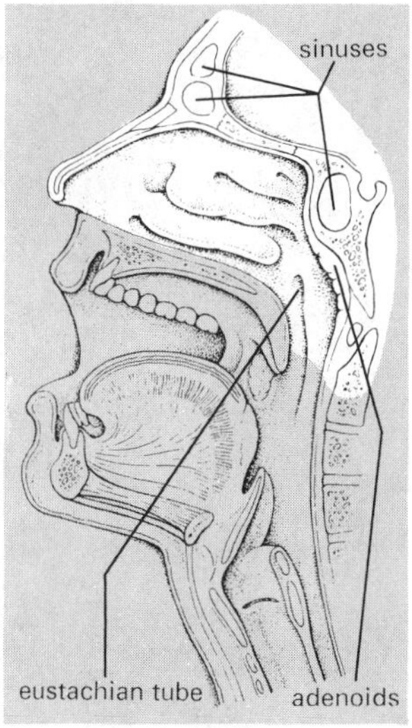

nose

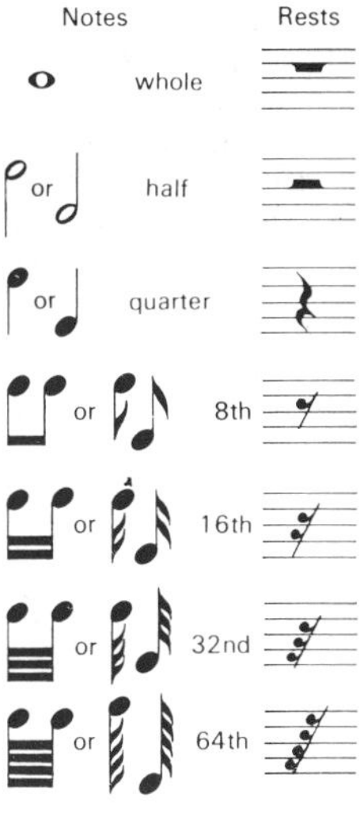

note

note•book |nōt′bo͝ok′| *n.* A book with blank pages for writing in.

not•ed |nō′tĭd| *adj.* Well-known; famous: *a noted film director; a noted beauty.*

note•wor•thy |nōt′wûr′*th*ē| *adj.* Deserving notice or attention; notable; significant. —**note′wor′thi•ly** *adv.* —**note′wor′thi•ness** *n.*

noth•ing |nŭth′ĭng| *pron.* Not anything: *I have nothing more to say.* —*n.* **1.** Zero; that which has no quantitative value: *Nothing plus nothing equals nothing.* **2.** A person of no importance: *She's just a nothing, you know.* **3.** A trifle, especially a trivial utterance: *sweet nothings.* —*adv.* Not at all: *He looks nothing like me.*

***Idioms.* for nothing.** **1.** Free of charge; gratis: *We got in for nothing at the theater.* **2.** In vain: *Our sacrifices were all for nothing.* **3.** For no reason: *It was not for nothing that I came here.* **nothing doing.** *Informal.* Certainly not: *You feel like a cigarette? Nothing doing, I'm trying to get in shape.*

noth•ing•ness |nŭth′ĭng nĭs| *n.* **1.** The condition or quality of being nothing; nonexistence. **2.** Space without things or features in it; emptiness: *The moon is vast and lonely, a great expanse of nothingness.*

no•tice |nō′tĭs| *v.* **no•ticed, no•tic•ing. 1.** To perceive with the senses; become aware of: *noticed a cloud of dust in the distance.* **2.** To perceive with the mind; take note of: *I could not help noticing a change in her behavior.* **3.** To observe and consider; appreciate: *Notice the artist's use of dark colors.* **4.** To pay attention to: *hoping that the girl would notice him.* —*n.* **1.** Perception; observation: *escaped notice by wearing a disguise.* **2.** Attention to another person or thing; consideration: *grateful for his notice.* **3.** A published or displayed announcement: *post a notice on the bulletin board.* **4.** An announcement of purpose, especially of one's intention to leave a job: *gave a week's notice to his employer.* **5.** A printed review, as of a play.

***Idiom.* take notice of.** To show interest or awareness; pay attention: *The public took little notice of the event.*

no•tice•a•ble |nō′tĭ sə bəl| *adj.* **1.** Easily observed; evident: *a noticeable difference in their ages.* **2.** Worth noting. —**no′tice•a•bly** *adv.*

no•ti•fi•ca•tion |nō′tə fĭ **kā′**shən| *n.* **1.** The action or an example of notifying. **2.** A letter or other form that makes something known: *a notification that he had left his job.*

no•ti•fy |nō′tə fī′| *v.* **no•ti•fied, no•ti•fy•ing, no•ti•fies. 1.** To let (someone) know; inform: *notify the police.* **2.** To direct or tell by a notice: *William was notified to appear before the court.* —**no′ti•fi′er** *n.*

no•tion |nō′shən| *n.* **1.** A mental picture of what something is or how it works; a general idea, belief, opinion, etc.: *the discarded notion of the planetary system with the earth at its center.* **2.** A vague understanding: *hadn't a notion of what it all meant.* **3.** A fanciful idea or impulse; a whim: *had a notion to climb the highest hill and shout for joy.* **4. notions.** Small useful items, such as needles, buttons, thread, ribbons, etc.

no•to•chord |nō′tə kôrd′| *n.* A cordlike strip of cartilage along the back of certain animals, such as the lancelets, belonging to the same group as the vertebrates. At some stage of embryonic development, all vertebrates have a similar notochord from which the spine develops.

no•to•ri•e•ty |nō′tə **rī′**ĭ tē| *n.* **1.** The condition of being notorious; a bad reputation. **2.** The condition of being the center of wide attention, interest, comment, etc.: *He hated politics and notoriety.*

no•to•ri•ous |nō **tôr′**ē əs| *or* |-**tōr′**-| *adj.* **1.** Known widely and regarded unfavorably; infamous: *a notorious swindler.* **2.** Well-known or famous for something, as a trait, a negative quality, etc.: *notorious for his consistency.* —**no•to′ri•ous•ly** *adv.* —**no•to′ri•ous•ness** *n.*

not•with•stand•ing |nŏt′wĭth **stăn′**dĭng| *or* |-wĭ*th*-| *prep.* In spite of: *Notwithstanding all the kind treatment he received, the little boy grew melancholy and pale.* —*adv.* All the same; nevertheless: *They were exhausted, but proceeded notwithstanding.*

Nouak•chott |nwăk′**shŏt′**|. The capital of Mauritania. Population, 70,000.

nou•gat |no͞o′gət| *n.* A candy made from nuts and honey or sugar.

nought |nôt| *pron., n., & adj.* A form of the word **naught.**

noun |noun| *n.* In grammar, a word used to name a person, place, thing, quality, or action. For example, in the sentence *The children found pieces of driftwood on the beach this morning, children, pieces, driftwood, beach,* and *morning* are nouns. Nouns can be singular (*driftwood, beach, morning*) or plural (*children, pieces*). A **common noun**, the kind given in the example above, names one or all of a whole class of persons or things. A **proper noun**, like *Willard* or *Chicago*, names a specific person or thing and is capitalized when written. —***modifier:*** *a noun suffix; the noun senses of a word.*

noun phrase. A phrase consisting of a noun and a word or words modifying it. For example, *a bluebird, the horse's mouth,* and *a cool night in September* are noun phrases, with *bluebird, mouth,* and *night* being the central nouns.

nour•ish |nûr′ĭsh| *or* |nŭr′-| *v.* **1.** To provide (a living thing) with the food or other substances it needs to grow and remain alive. **2.** To promote the growth or development of; sustain: *founded the business and nourished it with hard work during the lean years.* **3.** To keep alive; harbor: *She nourished evil intentions toward him in her heart.* —**nour′ish•ing** *adj.: a nourishing meal.*

nour•ish•ment |nûr′ĭsh mənt| *or* |nŭr′-| *n.* **1. a.** The act or process of nourishing. **b.** The condition of being nourished. **2.** Anything that a living thing uses to grow or maintain its life; food. **3.** Anything that feeds or sustains: *got his mental nourishment from listening to adults talk.*

Nov. November.

no•va |nō′və| *n., pl.* **no•vae** |nō′vē| or **no•vas.** A star that suddenly becomes brighter than normal, returning to its original brightness after a period of time. See **supernova.**

No•va Sco•tia |nō′və **skō′**shə|. A Maritime Province of Canada, consisting of a peninsula extending into the Atlantic Ocean and nearby islands. Population, 818,000. Capital, Halifax.

nov•el¹ |nŏv′əl| *n.* A book-length piece of writing that tells an invented story. [SEE NOTE]

novel¹⁻²

Novel² *is from Latin* novellus, *"new," an extended form of* novus, *"new" (see note at* **new**). *When short stories became popular, in the Renaissance period, they were called, in Italian,* storie novelle, *"new stories" (as opposed to traditional histories and romances). This was borrowed into English as* **novel¹**.

ă pat/ā pay/â care/ä father/ĕ pet/ē be/ĭ pit/ī pie/î fierce/ŏ pot/ō go/ô paw, for/oi oil/o͝o book/o͞o boot/ou out/ŭ cut/û fur/*th* the/th thin/hw which/zh vision/ə ago, item, pencil, atom, circus

nov•el[2] |nŏv′əl| *adj.* Strikingly new or different: *the novel method of painting with a string dipped in pigment.* [SEE NOTE on p. 610]

nov•el•ist |nŏv′ə lĭst| *n.* A writer of novels.

nov•el•ty |nŏv′əl tē| *n., pl.* **nov•el•ties.** **1.** The quality of being novel; refreshing newness: *We tried hopping backward until the novelty wore off.* **2.** Something new and unusual: *Edison's light bulb was at first merely an interesting novelty.* **3. novelties.** Small mass-produced articles for sale: *straw dolls, trinkets, key chains, and other novelties for tourists.* —***modifier:*** *a novelty act at the circus; a novelty shop.*

No•vem•ber |nō vĕm′bər| *n.* The 11th month of the year, after October and before December. It has 30 days. —***modifier:*** *a November storm.*

no•ve•na |nō vē′nə| *n.* In the Roman Catholic Church, prayers or devotions for something special, repeated on nine consecutive days.

nov•ice |nŏv′ĭs| *n.* **1.** A person new to a field or activity; a beginner. **2.** A person who has entered a religious order but has not yet taken the final vows. —***modifier:*** *a novice writer.*

no•vi•ti•ate |nō vĭsh′ē ĭt| *or* |-āt′| *n.* **1.** The period of being a beginner; apprenticeship. **2.** The period of training served by a novice in a religious order.

No•vo•cain |nō′və kān′| *n.* A trademark for a drug used in medicine and dentistry as a local anesthetic.

now |nou| *adv.* **1.** At the present time: *We do not now know whether life exists on other planets.* **2.** At once; immediately: *We'd better start now.* **3.** At this point in the series of events; then: *The ship now began to sink.* **4.** Nowadays: *You'll rarely see plowing with horses now.* **5.** —Used to express reproof, command attention, etc.: *Now, you wouldn't want your parents to know about this, would you? Now, I'd like to tell you a story.* **6.** —Used to introduce an idea, mark a transition, etc.: *Now, polar temperatures on Mars are pretty high by Earth standards.* —*conj.* Since; seeing that: *Now we're done eating, let's get out of here.* —*n.* The present: *She claimed she would prefer any circumstances to those of now.*

Idiom. **now and again** (or **then**). Occasionally: *I can be persuaded to play chess now and again. We've been healthy except for a cold now and then.*

now•a•days |nou′ə dāz′| *adv.* In the present times; in these days.

no•way |nō′wā′| *adv. Informal.* In no way; not at all: *This ranch is noway the place for me.*

no•where |nō′hwâr′| *or* |-wâr′| *adv.* **1.** Not anywhere: *The rifle was nowhere to be found.* **2.** To no place or result: *We were going nowhere, and everybody knew it.* —*n.* **1.** A remote or unknown place, especially a wilderness: *a cabin out in the middle of nowhere.* **2.** A state of not being known to exist or expected to appear: *Hundreds of mosquitoes came diving out of nowhere.*

no•wise |nō′wīz′| *adv.* In no way; not at all: *The band made a turn with its fine formation nowise disturbed.*

nox•ious |nŏk′shəs| *adj.* **1.** Harmful to the health of living things: *sulfur dioxide and other noxious agents in the city air.* **2.** Offensive to taste or morals; obnoxious. —**nox′ious•ly** *adv.*

noz•zle |nŏz′əl| *n.* A projecting opening, as at the end of a hose or the rear of a rocket, through which a liquid or gas is discharged under pressure.

Np The symbol for the element neptunium.

nth |ĕnth| *n.* In a set of items arranged to match the natural numbers in a one-to-one correspondence, the item that matches *n*, an indefinitely large whole number. —*adj.* **1.** Corresponding in order to *n*, an indefinitely large whole number. **2.** Highest; utmost: *delighted to the nth degree.*

nu |nōō| *or* |nyōō| *n.* The 13th letter of the Greek alphabet, written *N, ν*. In English it is represented as *N, n.*

nu•ance |nōō′äns′| *or* |nyōō′-| *or* |nōō äns′| *or* |nyōō-| *n.* A subtle variation, as in meaning, color, or tone; a delicate shading.

nub |nŭb| *n.* **1.** A lump or knob. **2.** The essence; the core: *the nub of the problem.*

nub•bin |nŭb′ĭn| *n.* **1.** A small, imperfectly developed ear of corn. **2.** A similar small thing or part.

nub•ble |nŭb′əl| *n.* A small lump or knob.

nub•bly |nŭb′lē| *adj.* **nub•bli•er, nub•bli•est.** Lumpy in texture: *a nubbly wool fabric.*

nub•by |nŭb′ē| *adj.* **nub•bi•er, nub•bi•est.** Lumpy; nubbly.

nu•cle•ar |nōō′klē ər| *or* |nyōō′-| *adj.* **1.** Of, forming, or having to do with a nucleus or nuclei. **2.** Of or using energy derived from the nuclei of atoms: *a nuclear power plant.* **3.** Having or using atomic or hydrogen bombs: *a nuclear attack; nuclear powers.*

nuclear energy. Energy that is released from an atomic nucleus, especially fission, fusion, or radioactive decay.

nuclear fission. See **fission.**

nuclear fusion. See **fusion.**

nuclear physics. The scientific study of the structure and reactions of atomic nuclei.

nuclear reaction. Any reaction that changes the energy, structure, or composition of an atomic nucleus.

nuclear reactor. A device in which a nuclear chain reaction is started and controlled, thus producing heat, which is usually used to generate electricity and a variety of radioactive isotopes.

nu•cle•i |nōō′klē ī′| *or* |nyōō′-| *n.* Plural of **nucleus.**

nu•cle•ic acid |nōō klē′ĭk| *or* |nyōō-|. Any member of two groups of complex chemical compounds that are found in living cells and are extremely important in their functioning. See **DNA, RNA.**

nu•cle•on•ics |nōō′klē ŏn′ĭks| *or* |nyōō′-| *n.* *(used with a singular verb).* The branch of science and engineering that deals with the practical application of nuclear energy.

nu•cle•us |nōō′klē əs| *or* |nyōō′-| *n., pl.* **nu•cle•i** |nōō′klē ī′| *or* |nyōō′-|. **1.** A central or essential part around which other parts are grouped; a core: *the nucleus of a city; the hitters who formed the nucleus of the team.* **2.** A basis for future growth; a starting point: *a small colony designed to be the nucleus for a future empire.* **3.** A complex, usually spherical structure contained within a living cell, controlling the metabolism, growth, reproduction, and heredity of the cell. **4.** The central, positively charged core of an atom, composed of protons and neutrons, and containing

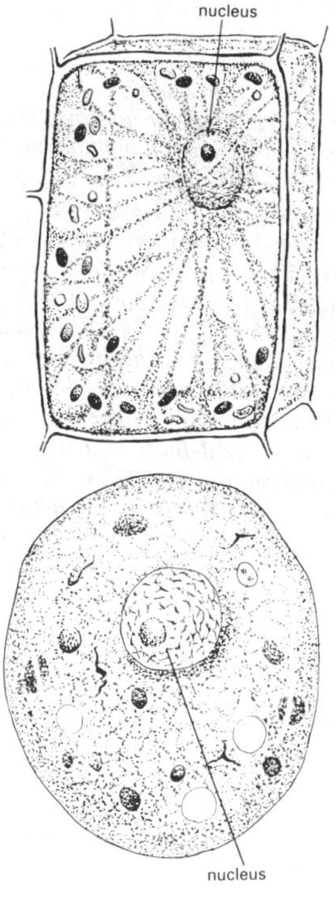

nucleus
Above: Nucleus of a plant cell
Below: Nucleus of an animal cell

number
From zero and the positive integers and the operation of addition, it is possible to define the negative integers, *those integers that can be added to positive integers and give a zero sum. Similarly, from multiplication and the integers it is possible to define* fractions, *which together with the integers make up the* rational numbers. *The operation of extracting roots leads to the definition of the* irrational numbers, *such as* $\sqrt{2}$, *that cannot be expressed as fractions. The set of* real numbers *includes the rational numbers and the irrational numbers. In order to define the square roots of negative numbers,* imaginary numbers *are introduced. The sum of a real number and an imaginary number is a* complex number. *Complex numbers, the most complete set of numbers normally used, include real and imaginary numbers as special cases.*

most of the mass of the atom. See **atomic number, mass number.** [SEE PICTURE on p. 611]

nude |no͞od| *or* |nyo͞od| *adj.* Without clothing; naked. —*n.* **1.** The unclothed human figure or a representation of it. **2.** The condition of being unclothed: *in the nude.* —**nude'ly** *adv.* —**nude'ness, nu'di•ty** |**no͞o'**dĭ tē| *or* |**nyo͞o'**-| *n.*

nudge |nŭj| *v.* **nudged, nudg•ing. 1.** To push or poke gently: *He nudged her with his elbow.* **2.** To maneuver with or as if with gentle pressure: *The liner was nudged into berth.* —*n.* A gentle push.

nud•ism |**no͞o'**dĭz'əm| *or* |**nyo͞o'**-| *n.* The belief in or practice of living in communities where people go without clothes. —**nud'ist** *n.*

nug•get |**nŭg'**ĭt| *n.* **1.** A hard lump of matter, especially of natural gold or another precious metal. **2.** A small but valuable unit or piece: *nuggets of information.*

nui•sance |**no͞o'**səns| *or* |**nyo͞o'**-| *n.* A source of inconvenience or annoyance; a bother.

null |nŭl| *adj.* **1.** Having no legal force; invalid: *a contract rendered null by a later agreement.* **2.** Having the quantity or value of zero; amounting to nothing. —*n.* Zero; nothing.

***Idiom.* null and void.** Having no legal force or effect; not binding.

nul•li•fy |**nŭl'**ə fī'| *v.* **nul•li•fied, nul•li•fy•ing, nul•li•fies. 1.** To deprive of legal force; annul; invalidate: *The Supreme Court has the right to nullify an act of Congress by finding it unconstitutional.* **2.** To reduce to nothing; negate: *nullified the impact of an idea by expressing it badly.* —**nul'li•fi•ca'tion** *n.* —**nul'li•fi'er** *n.*

null set. The set that contains no members; the empty set.

numb |nŭm| *adj.* **numb•er, numb•est. 1.** Deprived of the power to feel or move normally: *toes numb with cold.* **2.** Stunned or paralyzed, as from shock: *too numb with fear to cry out.* **3.** Slow in responding or understanding; stupid. —*v.* **1.** To deprive of the power to feel or move normally; stiffen: *a wind that numbed our hands and cheeks.* **2.** To stun; overwhelm: *a galaxy so large as to numb the imagination.* —**numbed'** *adj.*: *numbed ears.* —**numb'ing** *adj.*: *a numbing blow.* —**numb'ly** *adv.* —**numb'ness** *n.*

num•ber |**nŭm'**bər| *n.* **1. a.** Any member of the set of positive whole numbers or integers; one of a set of symbols that have unique meaning and that can be derived in a fixed order by counting. **b.** Any of the further set of mathematical objects, such as the negative integers and real numbers, that can be derived from the positive integers by various mathematical operations. **2. numbers.** Arithmetic: *good at numbers.* **3.** One of a series in numerical order: *What number are you in this line?* **4.** A numeral or series of numerals assigned to a person or thing for easy reference or identification: *my telephone number; Joe Namath's uniform number.* **5.** A quantity determined by adding up all units or members; a total; sum: *the number of feet in a mile.* **6.** Quantity: *The crowd was small in number.* **7.** Any of the selections in a program of music. **8. numbers.** Verses in meter; metrical poetry. **9.** In grammar, the indication of whether a word refers to one (singular) or more than one (plural): *The verb must agree in number with the subject.* **10. numbers.** A kind of lottery in which bets are made on what some unpredictable number, such as a daily stock-exchange figure, will turn out to be. —***modifier:*** *number two in order; a number series.* —*v.* **1.** To count: *numbering from one to ten in French.* **2.** To name one by one: *I'll number the reasons for you.* **3.** To amount to; to total: *an audience numbering close to a thousand.* **4.** To assign a number to: *Television channels are numbered.* **5.** To mark with a number or consecutive numbers: *Number your paper from 1 to 20.* **6.** To include in a certain category: *He was numbered among the better high jumpers.* **7.** To limit in number: *The days were numbered before cold weather would set in.* —**num'bered** *adj.*: *a numbered definition.* —**num'ber•ing** *adj.*: *the Arabic numbering system.* [SEE NOTE]

***Idioms.* a number of.** Quite a few; many: *used a number of sources for his report.* **any number of.** A large number; numerous: *Any number of people could do as well.* **without** (or **beyond**) **number.** Too many to be counted; countless.

num•ber•less |**nŭm'**bər lĭs| *adj.* **1.** Not marked with a number. **2.** Too many to be counted; countless.

number line. A line marked with a sequence of numbers at regularly spaced points along its length, especially a line whose points are considered to correspond with the real numbers in a one-to-one way.

number sentence. An equation in arithmetic.

numb•skull |**nŭm'**skŭl'| *n.* A form of the word **numskull.**

nu•mer•a•ble |**no͞o'**mər ə bəl| *or* |**nyo͞o'**-| *adj.* Capable of being counted; countable.

nu•mer•al |**no͞o'**mər əl| *or* |**nyo͞o'**-| *n.* **1.** A symbol or mark, or a group of symbols or marks, used to represent a number. See **Arabic numeral, Roman numeral. 2. numerals.** The last two digits of a student's year of graduation, used as a name or emblem of his class.

nu•mer•a•tion |no͞o'mə **rā'**shən| *or* |nyo͞o'-| *n.* **1.** The act or process of counting or numbering. **2.** The representation of numbers by means of numerals or other symbols: *Our decimal system of numeration is based on tens.* —***modifier:*** *a numeration system.*

nu•mer•a•tor |**no͞o'**mə rā'tər| *or* |**nyo͞o'**-| *n.* **1.** A number that tells how many of a number of equal subsets into which a whole set is divided are being compared with the whole set. In, for example, the fraction $2/7$ the 2 indicates that 2 of 7 equivalent subsets of the whole set are compared with the whole set itself. **2.** The number written above the line in a common fraction.

nu•mer•i•cal |no͞o **mĕr'**ĭ kəl| *or* |nyo͞o-| *adj.* **1.** Of a number or series of numbers: *numerical order.* **2.** Representing a number: *a numerical symbol.* **3.** Represented by or expressed as a number or numbers: *a numerical grade.* **4.** Measured in numbers: *the largest numerical group.* —**nu•mer'i•cal•ly** *adv.*

nu•mer•ous |**no͞o'**mər əs| *or* |**nyo͞o'**-| *adj.* **1.** Existing or occurring in large numbers; many: *numerous items for sale.* **2.** Consisting of many: *a numerous family.* —**nu'mer•ous•ly** *adv.*

nu•mis•ma•tic |no͞o'mĭz **măt'**ĭk| *or* |-mĭs-| *or* |nyo͞o'-| *adj.* Of numismatics: *a numismatic journal.*

nu•mis•ma•tics |no͞o'mĭz **măt'**ĭks| *or* |-mĭs-|

ă pat/ā pay/â care/ä father/ĕ pet/ē be/ĭ pit/ī pie/î fierce/ŏ pot/ō go/ô paw, for/oi oil/o͝o book/o͞o boot/ou out/ŭ cut/û fur/*th* the/th thin/hw which/zh vision/ə ago, item, pencil, atom, circus

or |nyōō′-| *n.* *(used with a singular verb).* **1.** The hobby of collecting coins. **2.** The study of coins, currency, and similar objects.

nu•mis•ma•tist |nōō **mĭz′**mə tĭst| *or* |**-mĭs′**-| *or* |nyōō-| *n.* **1.** A coin collector. **2.** A specialist in coins, currency, and similar objects.

num•skull |**nŭm′**skŭl′| *n.* A stupid person; a blockhead.

nun |nŭn| *n.* A woman who has devoted herself to a religious life in a church order. ¶*These sound alike* **nun, none.** [SEE PICTURE]

nun•ner•y |**nŭn′**ə rē| *n., pl.* **nun•ner•ies.** A place where a group of nuns live; a convent.

nup•tial |**nŭp′**shəl| *adj.* Relating to marriage or the wedding ceremony. —*n.* Often **nuptials.** A wedding ceremony.

nurse |nûrs| *n.* **1.** Someone trained to care for sick and disabled persons under the supervision of a physician. **2.** A woman employed to take care of another's children; a nursemaid. **3.** A woman employed to feed another's children at her breast. —*v.* **nursed, nurs•ing. 1.** To care for or tend (a sick person, invalid, infant, etc.). **2.** To do the work of a nurse, especially as a career. **3.** To feed (an infant) at the breast or mammary gland; suckle. **4.** To suck (milk) from the breast or mammary gland: *a calf nursing hungrily.* **5.** To clasp or hold carefully; fondle: *sat down and nursed the book in his lap.* **6.** To try to cure or treat: *She's nursed that cough for a week.* **7.** To keep alive or healthy with constant care: *nursed his orchard through the long winter.* **8.** To drink slowly, as if preserving: *nursed a Coke in the snack shop for an hour.* **9.** To keep up; harbor: *too busy to nurse regrets.*

nurse•maid |**nûrs′**mād′| *n.* A girl or woman employed to take care of infants or children.

nurs•er•y |**nûr′**sə rē| *or* |**nûrs′**rē| *n., pl.* **nurs•er•ies. 1.** A room set apart for the use of babies or children. **2.** A **nursery school. 3.** A place where plants are raised for sale, experimentation, etc. —***modifier:*** *nursery furniture.*

nur•ser•y•man |**nûr′**sə rē mən| *or* |**nûrs′**rē-| *n., pl.* **-men** |-mən|. A person who owns or works in a plant nursery.

nursery rhyme. A short poem for young children.

nursery school. A school for children who are not old enough to attend kindergarten.

nursing home. A place where old people and people who are recovering from illness are housed and cared for.

nurs•ling |**nûrs′**lĭng| *n.* An infant or young animal that is being suckled.

nur•ture |**nûr′**chər| *v.* **nur•tured, nur•tur•ing. 1.** To feed and protect; nourish: *carefully nurtured the plants in a greenhouse.* **2.** To help grow or develop; cultivate: *nurture a friendship.* —*n.* **1.** Nourishment; food. **2.** Upbringing; training.

nut |nŭt| *n.* **1. a.** A fruit or seed with a hard shell and usually a single kernel. **b.** The often edible kernel of such a fruit. **2.** *Slang.* **a.** A crazy or eccentric person. **b.** An enthusiast: *a movie nut.* **3.** A small block of metal or wood having a threaded hole in its center, designed to screw onto and hold a matching bolt, screw, threaded rod, etc. **4.** A device at the lower end of the bow of a stringed instrument, used to tighten or loosen the hairs.

nut•crack•er |**nŭt′**krăk′ər| *n.* **1.** An implement for cracking nuts, typically consisting of two hinged metal levers between which the nut is squeezed. **2.** A sharp-billed gray and white bird of the mountains of western North America, related to crows and magpies.

nut•hatch |**nŭt′**hăch′| *n.* A small, sharp-billed, grayish bird that climbs up and down tree trunks. [SEE PICTURE]

nut•meg |**nŭt′**mĕg′| *n.* **1.** The hard, egg-shaped, pleasant-smelling seed of a tropical tree, used as a spice when ground or grated. **2.** A tree that bears such seeds.

nu•tri•a |**nōō′**trē ə| *or* |**nyōō′**-| *n.* **1.** A beaverlike South American animal with thick, brownish fur. **2.** The fur of such an animal.

nu•tri•ent |**nōō′**trē ənt| *or* |**nyōō′**-| *n.* Something that nourishes, especially an ingredient in a food. —*adj.* Capable of nourishing; having nutritive value.

nu•tri•ment |**nōō′**trə mənt| *or* |**nyōō′**-| *n.* Nourishment; food.

nu•tri•tion |nōō **trĭsh′**ən| *or* |nyōō-| *n.* **1.** The process of nourishing or being nourished, especially the processes by which a living thing assimilates and uses food. **2.** Nourishment; diet: *Having good nutrition is important for good health.* **3.** The study of the foods people eat and need. —***modifier:*** *nutrition experts.*

nu•tri•tion•al |nōō **trĭsh′**ə nəl| *or* |nyōō-| *adj.* **1.** Of the processes of consuming and using food. **2.** Of or necessary to proper diet: *nutritional needs; a food with no nutritional value.* —**nu•tri′tion•al•ly** *adv.*

nu•tri•tious |nōō **trĭsh′**əs| *or* |nyōō-| *adj.* Capable of nourishing; tending to nourish; nutrient. —**nu•tri′tious•ly** *adv.* —**nu•tri′tious•ness** *n.*

nu•tri•tive |**nōō′**trĭ tĭv| *or* |**nyōō′**-| *adj.* Aiding nutrition; nutritious.

nuts |nŭts| *adj. Slang.* **1.** Crazy. **2.** Very enthusiastic: *nuts about comic strips.* —*interj. Slang.* A word used to express disappointment, contempt, or refusal.

nut•shell |**nŭt′**shĕl′| *n.* The shell enclosing the kernel of a nut.

Idiom. **in a nutshell.** In a few words; concisely: *That's my whole argument in a nutshell.*

nut•ty |**nŭt′**ē| *adj.* **nut•ti•er, nut•ti•est. 1.** Full of or tasting like nuts: *nutty cookies; a nutty flavor.* **2.** *Slang.* Crazy; silly. —**nut′ti•ness** *n.*

nuz•zle |**nŭz′**əl| *v.* **nuz•zled, nuz•zling.** To rub or push gently with the nose or snout: *The calf nuzzled its mother.*

NW northwest.

N.Y. New York.

N.Y.C. New York City.

ny•lon |**nī′**lŏn′| *n.* **1.** Any of various very strong, elastic synthetic resins. **2.** Cloth or yarn made from nylon. **3. nylons.** Women's stockings made of nylon. —***modifier:*** *nylon cord; nylon bristles; nylon stockings.*

nymph |nĭmf| *n.* **1.** In Greek and Roman mythology, one of the female spirits dwelling in woodlands and waters. **2.** A young, incompletely developed form of certain insects, such as the grasshopper or dragonfly, that go through a series of gradual changes before reaching the adult stage.

N.Z. New Zealand.

nun

nuthatch

Oo

The letter **O** *has always had its circular shape. Like the rest of the alphabet, it was invented by the Phoenicians, borrowed from them by the Greeks, and borrowed from the Greeks by the Romans.*

obelisk
Egyptian obelisks built about 1500 B.C.

obi

ă pat/ā pay/â care/ä father/ĕ pet/ē be/ĭ pit/ī pie/î fierce/ŏ pot/ō go/ô paw, for/oi oil/o͝o book/o͞o boot/ou out/ŭ cut/û fur/*th* the/th thin/hw which/zh vision/ə ago, item, pencil, atom, circus

o,O |ō| *n., pl.* **o's** or **O's. 1.** The 15th letter of the English alphabet. **2.** A zero. [SEE NOTE]

O¹ |ō| *interj.* **1.** A word used before the name of a person or thing being formally addressed: *Hear us, O Lord.* **2.** A word used to express surprise or strong emotion: *O my goodness!* ¶*These sound alike* **O, oh, owe.**

O² The symbol for the element oxygen.

o' |ə| *or* |ō| *prep.* Of.

oaf |ōf| *n., pl.* **oafs.** A clumsy or stupid person. —**oaf'ish** *adj.*

O•a•hu |ō ä'ho͞o|. An island of Hawaii; the site of Honolulu, the state capital.

oak |ōk| *n.* **1.** Any of several trees that bear acorns and often have leaves that are irregularly notched or lobed. **2.** The hard, strong wood of such a tree. —***modifier:*** *oak leaves; an oak table.*

oak apple. A rounded swelling on the twigs or leaves of oak trees, caused by the larva of a type of wasp.

oak•en |ō'kən| *adj.* Made of the wood of an oak: *oaken buckets.*

Oak•land |ōk'lənd|. A city in western California. Population, 358,000.

oa•kum |ō'kəm| *n.* Loose hemp or jute fiber used for caulking seams in wooden ships and packing pipe joints.

oar |ôr| *or* |ōr| *n.* **1.** A long, thin wooden pole with a blade at one end, used to row or steer a boat. **2.** A person using an oar; a rower. —*v.* To move by using oars: *oaring down the river.* ¶*These sound alike* **oar, o'er, or, ore.**

oar•lock |ôr'lŏk'| *or* |ōr'-| *n.* A U-shaped metal hoop used to hold an oar in place while rowing.

oars•man |ôrz'mən| *or* |ōrz'-| *n., pl.* **-men** |-mən|. A person who rows a boat; a rower.

OAS Organization of American States.

o•a•sis |ō ā'sĭs| *n., pl.* **o•a•ses** |ō ā'sēz'|. **1.** A fertile spot or area in a desert, watered by a spring, stream, or well. **2.** Any small place of beauty, refreshment, or comfort. —***modifier:*** *an oasis village.*

oat |ōt| *n.* **1.** Often **oats.** A grain-bearing grass with seeds used as food and as fodder for horses. **2. oats.** The seeds of this plant.

Idioms. **feel (one's) oats.** To be frisky or lively. **sow (one's) wild oats.** To lead a wild life when young.

oath |ōth| *n., pl.* **oaths** |ō*th*z| *or* |ōthz|. **1.** A declaration or promise to act in a certain way, made with God or some other sacred object as witness: *John Brown swore an oath to resist slavery for as long as he lived.* **2.** A formal statement that, when recited, binds the speaker on his honor to allegiance, obedience, or service: *the Presidential oath of office.* **3.** The act of calling upon a supernatural power for aid: *a wizard who excelled in trickery and oaths.* **4.** A word or phrase that irreverently uses the name of God or anything else sacred; profanity.

Idiom. **under (or on) oath.** Bound by an oath to tell the truth, as in a court of law.

oat•meal |ōt'mēl'| *or* |-mēl'| *n.* **1.** Meal made from ground oats or from oats that have been pressed flat by rollers. **2.** A porridge made from such meal. —***modifier:*** *oatmeal cookies.*

ob–. A prefix borrowed from Latin *ob,* meaning "toward, in front of, against"; **object** is from Latin *objicere,* to throw against, oppose. When *ob-* is followed by *c, f,* or *p,* it becomes *oc-, of-,* or *op-,* respectively. When it is followed by *m,* it is reduced to *o-.*

O•ba•di•ah |ō'bə **dī'**ə|. A Hebrew prophet of the sixth century B.C.

ob•bli•ga•to |ŏb'lĭ gä'tō|. In music: *adj.* Not to be left out; necessary. —*n., pl.* **ob•bli•ga•tos.** An obbligato accompaniment.

ob•du•ra•cy |ŏb **do͝or'**ə sē| *or* |**-dyo͝or'**-| *n.* The condition or quality of being obdurate.

ob•du•rate |**ŏb'**do͞o rĭt| *or* |-dyo͞o-| *adj.* **1.** Unmoved by pleas to be better, gentler, or kinder; hardhearted: *an obdurate judge.* **2.** Unmoved by persuasion; unyielding; stubborn: *obdurate in her refusal to practice the piano.* —**ob'du•rate•ly** *adv.*

o•be•di•ence |ō **bē'**dē əns| *n.* The action or practice of obeying rules, laws, or requests.

o•be•di•ent |ō **bē'**dē ənt| *adj.* Doing what is asked or required; willing to obey: *an obedient dog; obedient to the king.* —**o•be'di•ent•ly** *adv.*

o•bei•sance |ō **bā'**səns| *or* |ō **bē'**-| *n.* A bow, curtsy, or other gesture of submission or respect.

ob•e•lisk |**ŏb'**ə lĭsk'| *n.* A tall, four-sided shaft of stone, usually tapering to a pyramidal point. [SEE PICTURE]

o•bese |ō **bēs'**| *adj.* Extremely fat; corpulent. —**o•be'si•ty, o•bese'ness** *n.*

o•bey |ō **bā'**| *v.* **1.** To carry out or comply with (a request, order, or law): *obeying the traffic regulations; heard the instructions and obeyed.* **2.** To do what is commanded or requested by (a person or other authority): *respected and obeyed the captain.* **3.** To act or move in accordance with; follow: *Rockets obey the laws of physics.*

o•bi |**ō'**bē| *n.* A wide sash worn with a kimono by Japanese women. [SEE PICTURE]

o•bit•u•ar•y |ō **bĭch'**o͞o ĕr'ē| *n., pl.* **o•bit•u•ar•ies.** A printed notice of a person's death, often with a short biography. —***modifier:*** *the obituary page.*

obj. In grammar, object; objective.

ob•ject¹ |**ŏb'**jĭkt| *or* |-jĕkt'| *n.* **1.** A thing that has shape and can be seen or otherwise perceived; a material thing. **2.** A thing being viewed, studied, or handled: *Place the object directly beneath the microscope.* **3.** A person or thing toward which an emotion or effort is directed; a target: *an object of ridicule; an object of love.* **4.** A purpose; goal: *the object of the game; his object in requesting a secret meeting.* **5.** In grammar: **a.** A noun, pronoun, noun phrase, or noun clause that receives or is affected by the action of a verb. For example, in the sentence *I sent him a letter, a letter* is the direct object of the verb *sent,* and *him* is the indirect object. **b.** A noun, pronoun, noun phrase, or noun clause that follows a preposition. For example, in *against the tide, the tide* is the object of the preposition *against.* [SEE NOTE]

ob•ject² |əb **jĕkt'**| *v.* **1.** To express an opposing opinion or argument; protest: *Patrick Henry objected to the British tax on the colonies.* **2.** To be opposed: *He doesn't object to an occasional glass of wine.* **3.** To say in opposition or protest: *"Now see here," he objected.* [SEE NOTE]

ob•jec•tion |əb **jĕk'**shən| *n.* **1.** The expression of an opposing view or argument: *made no objection when the idea first came up.* **2.** A feeling of disapproval: *had no objection to the boy as his son-in-law.* **3.** A reason or cause for opposing or disapproving: *His only objection to buying the car was that it was too expensive.*

ob•jec•tion•a•ble |əb **jĕk'**shə nə bəl| *adj.* Causing or apt to cause objection; offensive; unpleasant: *objectionable odors; objectionable language.* —**ob•jec'tion•a•bly** *adv.*

ob•jec•tive |əb **jĕk'**tĭv| *adj.* **1.** Existing in a concrete or observable form; material: *Physics deals with objective phenomena.* **2.** Real; actual: *objective facts.* **3.** Not influenced by emotion or prejudice; impartial: *an objective account of a revolution.* **4.** In grammar, belonging to the objective case. —*n.* **1.** Something worked toward; a goal; purpose: *The prime objective of the Apollo program was to land a man on the moon.* **2.** In grammar, the **objective case. 3.** Also **objective lens.** In a telescope or microscope, the lens or system of lenses closest to the object under examination.

objective case. The case of a noun or pronoun that serves as the object of a verb or preposition.

objective complement. A noun, adjective, or pronoun that follows the direct object of certain verbs and is necessary to complete the meaning of the sentence. For example, in the sentence *We considered him our spokesman, our spokesman* is the objective complement.

ob•jec•tive•ly |əb **jĕk'**tĭv lē| *adv.* **1.** By some means or standard independent of human beings: *A lie detector is an apparatus that records emotional stress objectively.* **2.** Without emotional involvement or prejudice; impartially.

ob•jec•tiv•i•ty |ŏb'jĕk **tĭv'**ĭ tē| *n.* Lack of emotional involvement or prejudice; impartiality.

ob•jet d'art |ôb zhĕ **där'**| *or* |-zhā-|. *pl.* **ob•jets d'art** |ôb zhĕ **där'**| *or* |-zhā-|. An object valued for its artistic qualities.

ob•li•gate |**ŏb'**lĭ gāt'| *v.* **ob•li•gat•ed, ob•li•gat•ing.** To bind, compel, or constrain by a social, legal, or moral tie: *His growing fame obligated him to work harder than ever.*

ob•li•ga•tion |ŏb'lĭ **gā'**shən| *n.* **1.** A legal, social, or moral requirement, duty, or promise that has the power of binding one to a certain action: *an obligation to vote.* **2.** The binding power of a law, promise, contract, or sense of duty: *the obligation of friendship.* **3.** A debt owed in return for a special service or favor: *a social obligation.* **4.** A debt of money: *He settled all his obligations.*

o•blig•a•to•ry |ə **blĭg'**ə tôr'ē| *or* |-tōr'ē| *or* |**ŏb'**lĭ gə-| *adj.* Legally or morally binding; required or compulsory: *obligatory attendance.* —**o•blig'a•to'ri•ly** *adv.*

o•blige |ə **blīj'**| *v.* **o•bliged, o•blig•ing. 1.** To cause to comply by physical, legal, social, or moral means: *The weather obliged him to postpone his trip.* **2.** To make grateful or thankful: *They were obliged to him for his help.* **3.** To satisfy the wishes of; do a service or favor for; please: *The singer obliged the fans with another number.*

o•blig•ing |ə **blī'**jĭng| *adj.* Ready to do favors or to help others: *an obliging youth.* —**o•blig'ing•ly** *adv.* —**o•blig'ing•ness** *n.*

o•blique |ō **blēk'**| *adj.* **1. a.** Slanting or sloping, especially in direction. **b.** Neither parallel nor perpendicular. **2.** Indirect or evasive; not straightforward: *an oblique question.* —*n.* Something, such as a line, direction, etc., that is oblique. —**o•blique'ly** *adv.* —**o•blique'ness** *n.*

oblique angle. An acute angle or obtuse angle.

o•blit•er•ate |ə **blĭt'**ə rāt'| *v.* **o•blit•er•at•ed, o•blit•er•at•ing. 1.** To do away with completely; destroy: *The flood obliterated the miner's camp.* **2.** To cover or hide from view: *The sun obliterated the moon.* —**o•blit'er•a'tion** *n.*

o•bliv•i•on |ə **blĭv'**ē ən| *n.* **1.** The condition of being completely forgotten: *a great poet, now in oblivion.* **2.** The condition of being oblivious.

o•bliv•i•ous |ə **blĭv'**ē əs| *adj.* **1.** Lacking memory of something, as by being preoccupied; forgetful: *oblivious of past disappointments.* **2.** Unaware or unmindful: *oblivious to her surroundings.* —**o•bliv'i•ous•ly** *adv.* —**o•bliv'i•ous•ness** *n.*

ob•long |**ŏb'**lông'| *or* |-lŏng'| *adj.* Shaped like or resembling a rectangle or ellipse. —*n.* An oblong object or figure.

ob•lo•quy |**ŏb'**lə kwē| *n., pl.* **ob•lo•quies. 1.** Abusive language that is intended to discredit. **2.** The ill repute or discredit suffered because of such abuse.

ob•nox•ious |əb **nŏk'**shəs| *adj.* Extremely unpleasant or offensive. —**ob•nox'ious•ly** *adv.*

o•boe |**ō'**bō| *n.* A woodwind instrument having a high range and a piercing, rather nasal tone. It is basically conical in shape and is played with a double reed.

o•bo•ist |**ō'**bō ĭst| *n.* Someone who plays the oboe.

ob•scene |əb **sēn'**| *adj.* Offensive to accepted standards of decency or modesty: *obscene language.* —**ob•scene'ly** *adv.* —**ob•scene'ness** *n.*

ob•scen•i•ty |əb **sĕn'**ĭ tē| *n., pl.* **ob•scen•i•ties. 1.** Indecency or offensiveness in behavior, appearance, or expression. **2.** Something considered obscene, as a word or act.

ob•scure |əb **skyo͝or'**| *adj.* **ob•scur•er, ob•scur•est. 1.** Difficult to understand; vague: *an obscure reference to a past incident.* **2.** Unknown; humble: *an obscure professor.* **3.** Dark; gloomy: *the obscure room of the old house.* **4.** Not readily

object¹⁻²

Object¹ *is from Latin* objectum, *"something thrown in the way, something that is presented to the sight or to the mind," from* objicere, *"to present, to throw in the way":* ob-, *"in the way,"* + jacere, *"to throw." In meaning,* **object²** *is taken from* objicere, *"to throw (one's opinion) in the way"; it takes its form from* **object¹**.

perceived; indistinct: *obscure markings on a stone.* —*v.* **ob•scured, ob•scur•ing. 1.** To conceal from view; hide: *Clouds obscured the stars.* **2.** To make less clear; cause to be difficult to understand: *His vague speech obscured his real meaning.* —**ob•scure'ly** *adv.* —**ob•scure'ness** *n.*

ob•scu•ri•ty |əb skyŏŏr'ĭ tē| *n., pl.* **ob•scu•ri•ties. 1.** The condition of being unknown or inconspicuous: *a great movie star, now in obscurity.* **2.** The condition of being difficult to understand: *the obscurity of the text.* **3.** The lack of being distinct; indistinctness: *the obscurity of the print on the old newspaper.*

ob•se•qui•ous |əb sē'kwē əs| *adj.* Servile and fawning in obeying: *an obsequious person.* —**ob•se'qui•ous•ly** *adv.* —**ob•se'qui•ous•ness** *n.*

ob•se•quy |ŏb'sə kwē| *n., pl.* **ob•se•quies.** Often **obsequies.** A funeral rite or ceremony.

ob•serv•a•ble |əb zûr'və bəl| *adj.* **1.** Capable of being observed. **2.** Requiring special notice or observance: *an observable religious holiday.* —**ob•serv'a•bly** *adv.*

ob•ser•vance |əb zûr'vəns| *n.* **1.** The act of keeping or celebrating a holiday or religious festival: *the observance of Veterans Day.* **2.** The act of complying with a law, rule, or custom: *the observance of the rules of grammar.*

ob•ser•vant |əb zûr'vənt| *adj.* **1.** Quick to perceive; alert: *an observant student.* **2.** Following or observing a law, custom, or duty: *They are observant of the Sabbath.* —**ob•ser'vant•ly** *adv.*

ob•ser•va•tion |ŏb'zûr vā'shən| *n.* **1.** The act of observing, noticing, etc.: *a tower for the observation of the countryside.* **2.** The ability to pay attention and notice: *her great power of observation.* **3.** Something that has been observed: *writing his observations on current problems.* **4.** A comment or remark: *She made an observation about the weather.* —**modifier:** *an observation tower.* —**ob'ser•va'tion•al** *adj.*

ob•ser•va•to•ry |əb zûr'və tôr'ē| *or* |-tōr'ē| *n., pl.* **ob•ser•va•to•ries.** A place designed and equipped for making observations, as in astronomy or meteorology: *a weather observatory.* [SEE PICTURE]

ob•serve |əb zûrv'| *v.* **ob•served, ob•serv•ing. 1.** To perceive, notice, or watch attentively: *She observed a bird on the ledge. He observed carefully.* **2.** To make a comment or remark: *"It will soon be time for harvest," he observed.* **3.** To abide by (a law, duty, custom, etc.): *observed the speed limit.* **4.** To keep or celebrate (a holiday, rite, etc.): *observe the New Year.* —**ob•serv'er** *n.*

ob•sess |əb sĕs'| *v.* To recur to continually; occupy the mind of; haunt: *the vast search for perfection that obsessed them.*

ob•ses•sion |əb sĕsh'ən| *n.* **1.** Full, recurring attention to a fixed idea or emotion. **2.** An idea, thought, or emotion that occupies the mind continually: *Collecting rocks became an obsession.*

ob•ses•sive |əb sĕs'ĭv| *adj.* Of, like, or causing an obsession: *an obsessive fear of snakes.* —**ob•ses'sive•ly** *adv.* —**ob•ses'sive•ness** *n.*

ob•sid•i•an |ŏb sĭd'ē ən| *n.* A shiny, usually black or banded glass of volcanic origin.

ob•so•les•cent |ŏb'sə lĕs'ənt| *adj.* Passing out of use or usefulness; becoming obsolete. —**ob'so•les'cence** *n.* [SEE NOTE]

ob•so•lete |ŏb'sə lēt'| *or* |ŏb'sə lēt'| *adj.* No longer useful, in use, or in fashion: *an obsolete word; obsolete weapons.* —**ob'so•lete'ness** *n.* [SEE NOTE]

ob•sta•cle |ŏb'stə kəl| *n.* Something that opposes, retards, or stands in the way of progress toward a goal; a hindrance.

ob•stet•ric |ŏb stĕt'rĭk| or **ob•stet•ri•cal** |ŏb stĕt'rĭ kəl| *adj.* Of or having to do with obstetrics. —**ob•stet'ri•cal•ly** *adv.*

ob•ste•tri•cian |ŏb'stĭ trĭsh'ən| *n.* A physician who specializes in obstetrics.

ob•stet•rics |ŏb stĕt'rĭks| *n.* *(used with a singular verb).* The branch of medicine that deals with the care of women during pregnancy, childbirth, and the period following childbirth.

ob•sti•na•cy |ŏb'stə nə sē| *n.* The condition or quality of being obstinate; stubbornness.

ob•sti•nate |ŏb'stə nĭt| *adj.* Stubborn; resistant to argument or reason; inflexible: *an obstinate old man; an obstinate English class.* —**ob'sti•nate•ly** *adv.* —**ob'sti•nate•ness** *n.*

ob•strep•er•ous |əb strĕp'ər əs| *adj.* Noisily defiant; boisterous; unmanageable. —**ob•strep'er•ous•ly** *adv.* —**ob•strep'er•ous•ness** *n.*

ob•struct |əb strŭkt'| *v.* **1.** To make impassable with obstacles; block: *Fallen stone obstructed the mountain pass.* **2.** To interfere with so as to impede or retard; hinder or halt by interference: *obstructing justice.* **3.** To get in the way of so as to hide; cut off from view: *Buildings obstruct our view of the horizon.* —**ob•struc'tive** *adj.*

ob•struc•tion |əb strŭk'shən| *n.* **1.** Something that obstructs or gets in the way: *an obstruction in the road.* **2.** The act or action of obstructing: *the obstruction of justice.* **3.** The condition of being blocked: *an intestinal obstruction.*

ob•tain |əb tān'| *v.* **1.** To gain the possession of after planning or endeavor; get; acquire: *obtain an autograph.* **2.** To be established or accepted; be in use: *an ancient custom that still obtains.* —**ob•tain'a•ble** *adj.* —**ob•tain'er** *n.*

ob•trude |əb trōōd'| *v.* **ob•trud•ed, ob•trud•ing. 1.** To force (ideas, opinions, etc.) upon another without invitation: *He tries to obtrude his prejudices on others.* **2.** To force oneself upon another: *He would not obtrude upon their privacy.* **3.** To thrust out: *The clam obtruded its siphon.* —**ob•tru'sion** |əb trōō'zhən| *n.*

ob•tru•sive |əb trōō'sĭv| *or* |-zĭv| *adj.* **1.** Intruding and offensive: *obtrusive questions.* **2.** Unattractively noticeable: *obtrusive laughter.* —**ob•tru'sive•ly** *adv.* —**ob•tru'sive•ness** *n.*

ob•tuse |əb tōōs'| *or* |-tyōōs'| *adj.* **1.** Slow to perceive or apprehend; not discerning; dull: *an obtuse person.* **2.** Not sharp or pointed in form; blunt. —**ob•tuse'ly** *adv.* —**ob•tuse'ness** *n.*

obtuse angle. An angle that contains more than 90 degrees and less than 180 degrees.

obtuse triangle. A triangle that contains an obtuse angle.

ob•verse |ŏb vûrs'| *or* |ŏb'vûrs'| *adj.* Facing or turned toward the observer: *the obverse side of a clock.* —*n.* |ŏb'vûrs'| *or* |ŏb vûrs'|. The side or face of a coin, medal, etc., having the principal stamp or design. —**ob•verse'ly** *adv.*

ob•vi•ate |ŏb'vē āt'| *v.* **ob•vi•at•ed, ob•vi•at•ing.** To prevent by making unnecessary; preclude: *He tried to obviate the necessity of consulting the board of directors.* —**ob'vi•a'tion** *n.*

observatory
Dome housing the telescope at Mount Palomar Observatory, California

obsolescent/obsolete
The difference between **obsolescent** *and* **obsolete** *is the same as the difference between* **adolescent** *and* **adult**. *The* -escent *in both cases is the Latin suffix* -esc-, *which gives the meaning "beginning to," + the participial ending* -ent-, *which is equivalent to* **-ing**[1]. **Obsolete** *is from Latin* obsolētus, *"having gone out of use":* ob-, *"against, in the opposite direction,"* + sol-, *"to be in use,"* + -tus, *the participial ending equivalent to* **-ed**[1]. **Obsolescent** *is from Latin* obsolescens, *"beginning to go out of use," from the same basic elements but with the different ending.*

ă pat/ā pay/â care/ä father/ĕ pet/ ē be/ĭ pit/ī pie/î fierce/ŏ pot/ ō go/ô paw, for/oi oil/ŏŏ book/ ōō boot/ou out/ŭ cut/û fur/ *th* the/th thin/hw which/zh vision/ ə ago, item, pencil, atom, circus

ob•vi•ous |ŏb′vē əs| *adj.* Easily perceived or understood; evident: *her obvious pleasure; an obvious reason; an obvious advantage.* —**ob′vi•ous•ly** *adv.* —**ob′vi•ous•ness** *n.*

oc•a•ri•na |ŏk′ə **rē′**nə| *n.* A wind instrument having a roughly flutelike tone. It consists of an oval chamber equipped with a mouthpiece and with holes that are opened and closed by the player's fingers. [SEE PICTURE]

oc•ca•sion |ə **kā′**zhən| *n.* **1.** An event or happening: *enjoyable occasions.* **2.** A significant event or happening: *Thanksgiving dinner was quite an occasion.* **3.** The time of an event or happening; the moment when something occurs: *on the occasion of her first dance.* **4.** An opportunity; a chance: *He never missed any occasion of visiting the castle.* **5.** A reason or cause: *What was the occasion for all that laughter?* **6.** Necessity; need: *There was no occasion for a doctor.* —*v.* To be the reason for; cause; bring about: *The lack of cooperation occasions much grief.*

oc•ca•sion•al |ə **kā′**zhə nəl| *adj.* **1.** Occurring from time to time: *an occasional earthquake.* **2.** For use as the need arises: *occasional chairs for a reception.* **3.** Created for a special occasion: *an occasional song.*

oc•ca•sion•al•ly |ə **kā′**zhə nə lē| *adv.* From time to time; now and then.

Oc•ci•dent |**ŏk′**sĭ dənt| *n.* **1. occident.** The west; western lands or regions. **2.** The countries of Europe and the Western Hemisphere. [SEE NOTE on p. 628]

Oc•ci•den•tal |ŏk′sĭ **dĕn′**tl| *adj.* **1. occidental.** Western. **2.** Of the Occident or any of its peoples. —*n.* **1.** A native of the Occident. **2.** A person of Occidental descent.

oc•clude |ə **klōōd′**| *v.* **oc•clud•ed, oc•clud•ing. 1.** To close off or block off: *occlude a passageway.* **2.** To keep from passing: *occlude light.* **3.** To absorb or absorb large amounts of: *metal that occludes gases.* **4.** To force (air) upward from the surface of the earth, as a cold front does when it moves under a warm front. **5.** To bring (the upper and lower teeth) together in good alignment for chewing. **6.** To meet properly for chewing when brought together.

occluded front. The conditions that occur in the atmosphere when a warm front and cold front meet and occlusion occurs.

oc•clu•sion |ə **klōō′**zhən| *n.* The act or process of occluding, especially the manner in which the teeth fit when brought together.

oc•cult |ə **kŭlt′**| *or* |**ŏk′**ŭlt′| *adj.* **1.** Of or dealing with magic, astrology, supernatural powers, etc. **2.** Not readily explained; mysterious. —*n.* Occult practices or lore.

oc•cul•ta•tion |ŏk′ŭl **tā′**shən| *n.* A process in which a celestial object moves between an observer and a second celestial object, blocking the second object from the observer's view.

oc•cult•ism |ə **kŭl′**tĭz′əm| *or* |**ŏk′**ul-| *n.* A belief in or the study of occult powers and the supernatural. —**oc•cult′ist** *n.*

oc•cu•pan•cy |**ŏk′**yə pən sē| *n., pl.* **oc•cu•pan•cies. 1.** The act of taking or holding possession; the act of occupying. **2.** The period of someone's stay or use of certain premises or land.

oc•cu•pant |**ŏk′**yə pənt| *n.* Someone or something occupying a place or position: *the occupants of a building.*

oc•cu•pa•tion |ŏk′yə **pā′**shən| *n.* **1.** A means of making a living; a profession or job. **2.** Any activity that keeps one busy. **3.** The act or process of holding, possessing, or using a place: *prehistoric occupation of the cave.* **4.** The conquest and control of a nation or territory by a foreign military force: *the occupation of Germany after World War II.* —***modifier:*** *occupational accidents.*

oc•cu•py |**ŏk′**yə pī′| *v.* **oc•cu•pied, oc•cu•py•ing, oc•cu•pies. 1.** To take possession of and maintain control over by force: *The troops invaded and occupied the city.* **2.** To fill; take up: *Reading occupies his free time.* **3.** To dwell in; inhabit: *They occupy a small cabin.* **4.** To hold or control (an office or position): *He occupies the office of president.* **5.** To employ or busy the mind or time off. —**oc′cu•pied′** *adj.: an occupied table; occupied Germany.* —**oc′cu•pi′er** *n.*

oc•cur |ə **kûr′**| *v.* **oc•curred, oc•cur•ring. 1.** To take place; come about; happen: *Many accidents occur in the home.* **2.** To be found to exist; live, grow, appear, etc.: *minerals occurring in the earth's crust.* —***phrasal verb.*** **occur to.** To come to the mind of; suggest itself to.

oc•cur•rence |ə **kûr′**əns| *n.* **1.** The act or condition of occurring, taking place, appearing, etc.: *the occurrence of an accident.* **2.** Something that happens; an incident: *a strange occurrence.*

o•cean |**ō′**shən| *n.* **1.** The mass of salt water that covers about 72 per cent of the surface of the earth. **2.** Any of the principal divisions of this body of water, as the Atlantic, Pacific, Indian, and Arctic oceans. —***modifier:*** *the ocean floor; ocean winds.* [SEE NOTE]

O•ce•an•i•a |ō′shē **ăn′**ē ə| *or* |-**ā′**nē ə|. The islands of the central and southern Pacific Ocean, sometimes extended to include Australia, New Zealand, and Indonesia.

o•ce•an•ic |ō′shē **ăn′**ĭk| *adj.* **1.** Of or pertaining to the ocean. **2.** Living or found in the ocean, especially in the open sea rather than along coasts or shores.

o•ce•a•nog•ra•pher |ō′shē ə **nŏg′**rə fər| *or* |ō′-shə **nŏg′**-| *n.* A scientist who specializes in oceanography.

o•ce•a•nog•ra•phy |ō′shē ə **nŏg′**rə fē| *or* |ō′ shə-**nŏg′**-| *n.* A scientific study and exploration of the ocean.

oc•e•lot |**ŏs′**ə lŏt′| *or* |**ō′**sə-| *n.* A wild cat of Mexico, Central America, and South America, having a yellowish coat spotted with black. [SEE PICTURE]

o•cher |**ō′**kər| *n.* **1.** Any of several oxides of iron that occur as minerals. Their colors are yellow, brown, and red, and they are used as pigments. **2.** A yellowish or brownish orange. —*adj.* Yellowish or brownish orange.

o•chre |**ō′**kər| *n. & adj.* A form of the word **ocher.**

o'clock |ə **klŏk′**| *adv.* **1.** Of or according to the clock: *three o'clock.* **2.** According to a relative position on an imaginary clock dial, with the observer at the center and 12 o'clock considered as straight ahead horizontally or straight up vertically: *There are enemy planes approaching at 10 o'clock.*

o•co•ti•llo |ō′kə **tē′**yō| *or* |-**tēl′**-| *n., pl.* **o•co•ti•llos.** A prickly, cactuslike tree of desert regions of the southwestern United States and Mexico,

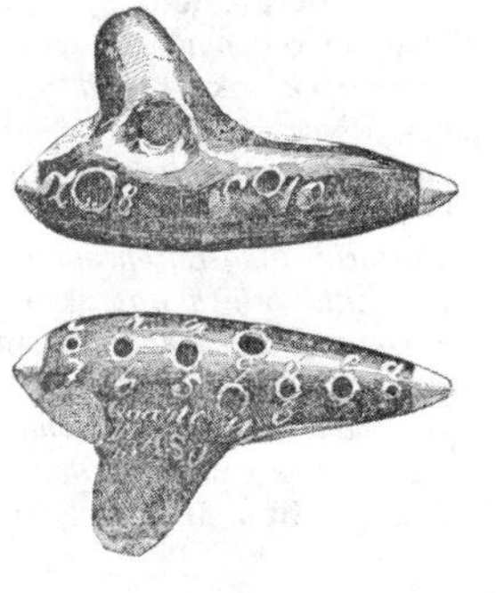

ocarina

ocean

"I do not know what I may appear to the world, but to myself I seem to have been only a boy playing on the sea-shore, and diverting myself in now and then finding a smoother pebble or a prettier shell than ordinary, whilst the great ocean of truth lay all undiscovered before me." —*Sir Isaac Newton.*

ocelot

octa-/octo-

These prefixes come, respectively, from Greek oktā- *and Latin* octō-, *which both mean "eight" and are obviously closely related. They are both descended from the prehistoric Indo-European word for "eight," which was* oktō. *In Germanic* oktō *changed to* ahtō, *because an Indo-European* k *always changed to a Germanic* h. Ahtō *became* eahta *in Old English and* **eight** *in Modern English.*

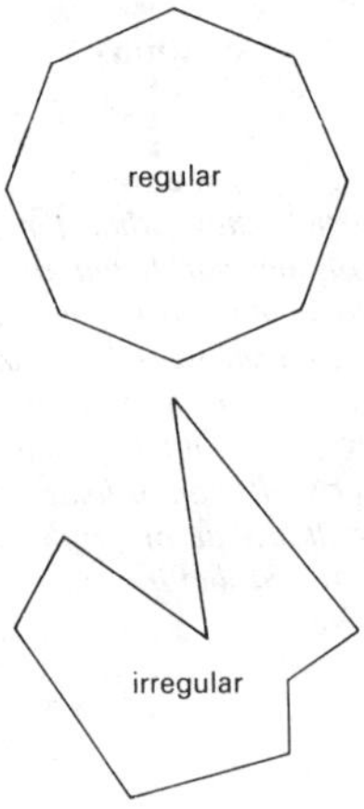

octagon

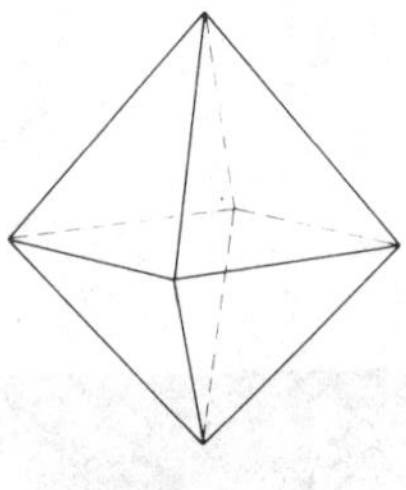

octahedron

ă pat/ā pay/â care/ä father/ĕ pet/ē be/ĭ pit/ī pie/î fierce/ŏ pot/ō go/ô paw, for/oi oil/o͝o book/o͞o boot/ou out/ŭ cut/û fur/*th* **the**/th **thin**/hw **which**/**zh** vision/ə ago, item, pencil, atom, circus

having clusters of tube-shaped red flowers.

Oct. October.

octa-. A word element meaning "eight": **octagon.** [SEE NOTE]

oc•ta•gon |ŏk'tə gŏn'| *n.* A plane geometric figure bounded by eight line segments and containing eight angles. [SEE PICTURE]

oc•tag•o•nal |ŏk tăg'ə nəl| *adj.* Shaped like or resembling an octagon; having eight sides.

oc•ta•he•dron |ŏk'tə hē'drən| *n., pl.* **oc•ta•he•drons** or **oc•ta•he•dra** |ŏk'tə hē'drə|. A solid geometric figure bounded by eight planes. [SEE PICTURE]

oc•tane |ŏk'tān'| *n.* Any of several hydrocarbon compounds having the formula C_8H_{18} and occurring in petroleum.

octane number. A number that measures the antiknock rating of gasoline, based on the percentage of a particular form of octane that is contained in the sample of gasoline.

oc•tant |ŏk'tənt| *n.* **1. a.** One-eighth of the arc of a circle; an arc of 45 degrees. **b.** One-eighth of the area of a circle; the area bounded by a pair of radii and an arc of 45 degrees that they intercept. **2.** A navigation instrument similar to a sextant but based on an arc of 45 degrees rather than 60 degrees.

oc•tave |ŏk'tĭv| *or* |-tāv'| *n.* **1.** The musical interval between two tones, one of which has twice as many vibrations per second as the other; an interval of eight diatonic scale degrees. **2.** Either of a pair of tones that are separated by this interval. **3.** A series of tones included in this interval: *the lowest octave of a flute.*

oc•ta•vo |ŏk tā'vō| *or* |-tä'-| *n., pl.* **oc•ta•vos.** **1.** The page size (from 5 × 8 inches to 6 × 9½ inches) of a book composed of printer's sheets folded into eight leaves. **2.** A book composed of pages of this size.

oc•tet |ŏk tĕt'| *n.* **1.** A musical composition for eight voices or instruments. **2.** Eight singers or instrumentalists. **3.** Any group of eight.

octo-. A word element meaning "eight": **octopus.** [SEE NOTE]

Oc•to•ber |ŏk tō'bər| *n.* The tenth month of the year, after September and before November. It has 31 days. ***—modifier:*** *October weather.*

oc•to•pus |ŏk'tə pəs| *n., pl.* **oc•to•pus•es** or **oc•to•pi** |ŏk'tə pī'|. A sea animal having a soft, saclike body and eight armlike tentacles studded along the undersides with suction disks used for grasping and holding.

oc•u•lar |ŏk'yə lər| *adj.* **1.** Of or having to do with the eye or the sense of vision. **2.** Seen by the eye; visual: *ocular evidence.* —*n.* The eyepiece of a microscope, telescope, etc.

oc•u•list |ŏk'yə lĭst| *n.* **1.** An ophthalmologist. **2.** An optometrist.

odd |ŏd| *adj.* **odd•er, odd•est.** **1.** Peculiar; unusual; strange: *an odd noise; an odd name.* **2. a.** Being one of an incomplete set or pair: *an odd spoon; an odd shoe.* **b.** Remaining after others are grouped: *They formed two teams, leaving one odd player.* **3.** Occasional: *an odd job.* **4.** Of or indicating whole numbers that do not contain 2 as a factor. **—odd'ly** *adv.* **—odd'ness** *n.*

odd•i•ty |ŏd'ĭ tē| *n., pl.* **odd•i•ties.** **1.** Someone or something that seems odd or strange: *a collector of seashells, fossils, old keys, and other oddities.* **2.** The condition of being odd; strangeness: *the oddity of human behavior.*

odd•ment |ŏd'mənt| *n.* Often **oddments.** Something left over; an item, fragment, remnant, etc.

odd number. A whole number that does not contain 2 as a factor.

odds |ŏdz| *pl.n.* **1.** The likelihood or probability that a given thing will happen: *The odds are that it will rain tomorrow.* **2.** A number or ratio that expresses this probability: *The odds are 2 to 1 that the champion will win.* **3.** The ratio of the amount a person risks in a bet to the amount that can be won: *He gave me odds of 4 to 1.* **4.** Advantages, as in a game or contest.

Idiom. **at odds.** In disagreement or conflict: *at odds about the housing project.*

odds and ends. Miscellaneous items.

ode |ōd| *n.* A poem that expresses in an exalted style the poet's feelings and thoughts.

O•din |ō'dĭn|. In Norse mythology, the ruler of the gods.

o•di•ous |ō'dē əs| *adj.* Exciting repugnance or aversion; abhorrent; hateful.

o•di•um |ō'dē əm| *n.* **1.** Intense dislike; hatred: *He returned after the trial to the odium of his town.* **2.** Disgrace that results from detestable conduct: *the odium of having lied to hurt others.*

o•dom•e•ter |ō dŏm'ĭ tər| *n.* A device that measures and indicates the total distance that a vehicle has traveled.

o•dor |ō'dər| *n.* Scent; smell.

o•dor•if•er•ous |ō'də rĭf'ər əs| *adj.* Having or giving off an odor, especially a pleasant one.

o•dor•less |ō'dər lĭs| *adj.* Having no odor.

o•dor•ous |ō'dər əs| *adj.* Having a distinct or characteristic odor that is usually but not necessarily unpleasant.

o•dour |ō'dər| *n.* British form of the word **odor.**

O•dys•se•us |ō dĭs'ē əs| *or* |-yo͞os'|. In Greek mythology, a leader of the Greeks during the Trojan War; hero of the "Odyssey."

od•ys•sey |ŏd'ĭ sē| *n., pl.* **od•ys•seys.** An extended, adventurous journey.

Od•ys•sey |ŏd'ĭ sē|. The ancient Greek epic poem, attributed to Homer, relating the wanderings of Odysseus after the fall of Troy.

Oed•i•pus |ĕd'ə pəs| *or* |ē'də-|. In Greek mythology, the king of Thebes who unwittingly killed his father and married his mother.

o'er |ôr| *or* |ōr| *prep. & adv.* Over: *o'er the land of the free and the home of the brave.* Used chiefly in poetry. ¶*These sound alike* **o'er, oar, or, ore.**

of |ŭv| *or* |ŏv| *or* |əv *when unstressed*| *prep.* **1.** Coming from: *men of the north.* **2.** Owing to: *He died of pneumonia.* **3.** So as to be separated or relieved from: *She was cured of cancer.* **4.** From the total or group making up: *two of my friends.* **5.** Composed or made from: *shoes of the finest leather.* **6.** Associated with or adhering to: *a person of his religion.* **7.** Belonging or connected to: *the rungs of a ladder.* **8.** Possessing; having: *a man of honor.* **9.** Containing or carrying: *a bag of groceries.* **10.** Named or called: *the busy city of Chicago.* **11.** Centering on or directed toward: *a deep love of humanity.* **12.** Produced by: *the fruits of our orchards.* **13.** Characterized by: *a year of famine.* **14.** Concerning; about: *We spoke of you last night.* **15.** Set aside for: *a day of rest.* **16.** Before; until: *five minutes of two.* **17.**

During: *Of recent years he has devoted himself to gardening.* [SEE NOTE]

off |ôf| *or* |ŏf| *adv.* **1.** At or to a distance from a nearer place: *driving off.* **2.** Distant in time: *a week off.* **3.** So as to be no longer on or connected: *The gas was off.* **4.** So as to be smaller, fewer, or less: *Business is dropping off these days.* **5.** So as to be away from work or duty: *taking the day off.* —*adj.* **1.** More distant or removed: *the off side of the barn.* **2.** Not on: *His shoes were off. The lights are off.* **3.** Not continuing, operating, or functioning: *The stove is off.* **4.** No longer effective; canceled: *The wedding is off.* **5.** Less or smaller: *Production is off this year.* **6.** Below standard: *His performance was somehow off.* **7.** In a specified condition: *well off; badly off.* **8.** In error: *off by several inches.* **9.** Away from work or duty: *I'm off tonight.* —*prep.* **1.** So as to be removed or distant from: *jumping off the edge.* **2.** Away or relieved from: *off duty.* **3.** By consuming or with the means provided by: *living off his pension.* **4.** Extending from: *a little alleyway off the main street.* **5.** Abstaining from: *staying off tobacco.* **6.** Seaward of: *a mile off Sandy Hook.* [SEE NOTE]

of•fal |ô'fəl| *or* |ŏf'əl| *n.* **1.** Waste parts, especially of a butchered animal. **2.** Refuse; rubbish. ¶*These sound alike* **offal, awful.**

off•beat |ôf'bēt'| *or* |ŏf'-| *n.* Any of the beats in a musical measure that are not normally accented. —*adj. Slang.* Not of an ordinary type; unconventional; different: *an offbeat film.*

off-col•or |ôf'kŭl'ər| *or* |ŏf'-| *adj.* **1.** Not of the usual or required color: *an off-color uniform.* **2.** Improper; in poor taste: *an off-color story.*

of•fence |ə fĕns'| *or* |ô'fĕns| *or* |ŏf'ĕns'| *n.* Chiefly British form of the word **offense.**

of•fend |ə fĕnd'| *v.* **1.** To cause anger, resentment, or annoyance in; insult or affront. **2.** To be displeasing to; be disagreeable to. **3.** To be the cause of displeasure: *odors that offend.* **4.** To break a moral or spiritual law or rule. —**of•fend'ed** *adj.: an offended guest.*

of•fend•er |ə fĕn'dər| *n.* Someone or something that offends, especially a violator of a law.

of•fense |ə fĕns'| *n.* **1.** The act of causing anger, resentment, displeasure, etc. **2.** A violation of a moral, legal, or social code; a transgression, sin, or crime. **3.** Something that offends: *The building was an offense to the eye.* **4.** |ô'fĕns| *or* |ŏf'ĕns'|. The act of attacking or assaulting. **5.** |ô'fĕns| *or* |ŏf'ĕns'|. In sports, the team in possession of the ball or puck.

Idioms. **give offense.** To cause anger, displeasure, resentment, etc. **take offense.** To become angered, displeased, resentful, etc.

of•fen•sive |ə fĕn'sĭv| *adj.* **1.** Offending the senses; unpleasant: *an offensive smell.* **2.** Causing anger, displeasure, resentment, etc.: *offensive language.* **3.** |ô'fĕn'sĭv| *or* |ŏf'ĕn'-|. Of an attack; aggressive; attacking: *an offensive play in football.* —*n.* **1.** An aggressive action; an attack: *their third major offensive of the war.* **2.** An attitude of attack: *take the offensive.* —**of•fen'sive•ly** *adv.* —**of•fen'sive•ness** *n.*

of•fer |ô'fər| *or* |ŏf'ər| *v.* **1.** To present for acceptance or refusal: *They offered him soup.* **2.** To put forward for consideration; propose: *offer advice.* **3.** To provide; afford: *His job offered many opportunities.* **4.** To show readiness to do; volunteer: *They offered their services.* **5.** To present as an act of worship: *offer a sacrifice.* **6.** To present for sale or rent: *The shop offers homemade articles.* **7.** To propose as payment: *offer a reward.* **8.** To produce; present to the public: *offered a program of music.* —*n.* **1.** Something offered, as a proposal, suggestion, etc.: *an offer to teach.* **2.** Something proposed as payment: *an offer for the house.* **3.** The act of offering: *the offer of his services.*

of•fer•ing |ô'fər ĭng| *or* |ŏf'ər-| *n.* **1.** The act of making an offer. **2.** Something offered, such as a contribution, gift, religious sacrifice, etc.

of•fer•to•ry |ô'fər tôr'ē| *or* |-tōr'ē| *or* |ŏf'ər-| *n., pl.* **of•fer•to•ries.** **1.** Often **Offertory.** The part of the Eucharist at which bread and wine are offered to God. **2. a.** A collection of offerings at a religious service. **b.** The music accompanying this collection.

off•hand |ôf'hănd'| *or* |ŏf'-| *adv.* Without preparation or forethought: *Can you say offhand when they'll call?* —*adj.: an offhand reply.*

of•fice |ô'fĭs| *or* |ŏf'ĭs| *n.* **1. a.** A place, such as a building, suite, or room, in which clerical and professional work is done: *the principal's office.* **b.** The staff working in such a place: *The office gave the boss a surprise party.* **2.** A special position of authority or trust, as in a government, corporation, club, etc.: *respectful of the office of President.* **3.** Employment as a public official; public position: *seek office.* **4.** A branch of the Federal government of the U.S. ranking just below a department. **5.** A duty, function, or role: *He did not shirk his office.* **6.** Often **offices.** Something performed for another; a service; a favor: *delighted by the kind offices of their friends.* **7.** A Christian religious ceremony, as a rite for the dead. —***modifier:*** *office buildings; office work.*

of•fi•cer |ô'fĭ sər| *or* |ŏf'ĭ-| *n.* **1.** A person holding authority or trust in a government, corporation, club, or other institution. **2. a.** A person holding a commission in the armed forces. **b.** A **noncommissioned officer.** **3.** The master or a mate of a ship in passenger service, the merchant marine, etc. **4.** A policeman. [SEE PICTURE]

of•fi•cial |ə fĭsh'əl| *adj.* **1.** Of an office or post of authority: *official duties.* **2. a.** Arising from authority: *an official document.* **b.** Designated as authorized: *the official language.* **3.** Authorized to perform a special duty or hold a certain office: *an official mediator.* **4.** Formal or ceremonious: *an official banquet.* —*n.* A person in a position of authority. —**of•fi'cial•ly** *adv.*

of•fi•ci•ate |ə fĭsh'ē āt'| *v.* **of•fi•ci•at•ed, of•fi•ci•at•ing.** To serve as a priest, minister, or rabbi at a religious service: *officiated at a wedding.*

of•fi•cious |ə fĭsh'əs| *adj.* Excessively forward in offering one's services or advice to others. —**of•fi'cious•ly** *adv.* —**of•fi'cious•ness** *n.*

off•ing |ô'fĭng| *or* |ŏf'ĭng| *n.* **1.** The part of the sea that is distant but visible from shore. **2.** The immediate future: *no such plans in the offing.*

off•ish |ô'fĭsh| *or* |ŏf'ĭsh| *adj.* Distant and reserved; aloof. —**off'ish•ly** *adv.* —**off'ish•ness** *n.*

off•set |ôf'sĕt'| *or* |ŏf'-| *n.* **1.** Something that balances, counteracts, or compensates: *A diver's weighted belt is an offset for the increased buoyancy of his body underwater.* **2. Offset printing.**

off/of

Off *and* **of** *are originally variants of one Old English preposition, which meant "away from." It is considered incorrect to use them together as in* I borrowed a dollar off of him. **Of** *is now the commonest of the prepositions and the second commonest of all English words. In the five million words on which this Dictionary is based,* **of** *occurs 146,000 times, or about 29 times in every 1,000 words.* **Off** *is much less common, occurring about 0.77 times in 1,000 words.*

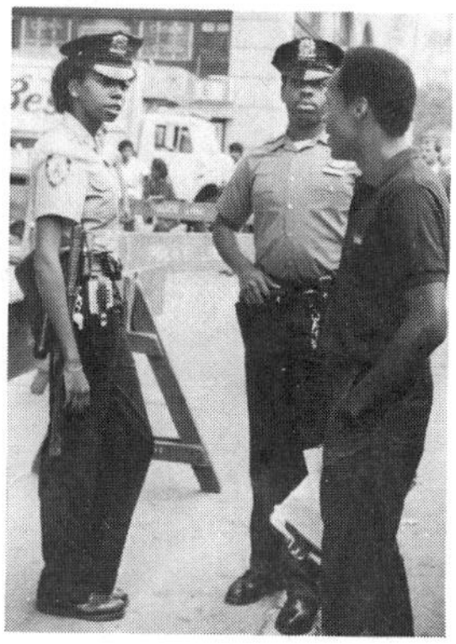

officer

O.K.
President Martin Van Buren, who was born at Kinderhook, New York, was nicknamed "Old Kinderhook." In 1840 a club of his supporters was founded in Boston, and called itself the O.K. *Club. Shortly after,* **O.K.** *became a slang expression meaning "Fine!" and subsequently it has become the most famous of all Americanisms, known in many other languages. American etymologists have done an enormous amount of research into the origins of* **O.K.** *The brief and rather mysterious story given above is true but is not really satisfactory. Many other theories have been put forward, including one that claims* **O.K.** *as an African word brought over by slaves from West Africa and only later popularized by the* O.K. *Club and others.*

okapi

ă pat/ā pay/â care/ä father/ĕ pet/ē be/ĭ pit/ī pie/î fierce/ŏ pot/ō go/ô paw, for/oi oil/ŏŏ book/ōō boot/ou out/ŭ cut/û fur/*th* the/th thin/hw which/zh vision/ə ago, item, pencil, atom, circus

—*v.* |ôf **sĕt'**| *or* |ŏf-| **off·set, off·set·ting.** To counterbalance or counteract; make up for: *His good passing should offset our weak defense.*

offset printing. A form of printing in which the image to be printed is transferred first to a surface, often that of a rotating cylinder, which in turn transfers it onto the surface to be printed.

off·shoot |**ôf'**shōōt'| *or* |**ŏf'**-| *n.* **1.** A shoot that branches out from the main stem of a plant. **2.** Something that branches out or originates from a main source.

off·shore |**ôf'shôr'**| *or* |**-shōr'**| *or* |**ŏf'**-| *adj.* **1.** Moving away from the shore: *an offshore breeze.* **2.** Distant from the shore: *offshore rocks.* **3.** Of or taking place in waters away from shore: *offshore fishing rights.* —*adv.* **1.** In a direction away from shore: *The breeze was blowing offshore.* **2.** At a distance from shore: *a sea lion swimming a half mile offshore.*

off·side |**ôf'sīd'**| *or* |**ŏf'**-| *adj.* **1.** In football, being ahead of the ball when it is put in play. **2.** In some other sports, being closer to the opposing team's goal than the rules permit. —*adv.: run offside.*

off·spring |**ôf'**sprĭng'| *or* |**ŏf'**-| *n., pl.* **off·spring. 1.** A child or children of a particular parent or parents. **2.** The young of an animal. **3.** Something that results from something else.

off·stage |**ôf'stāj'**| *or* |**ŏf'**-| *adv.* In or into the stage area not visible to the audience: *He walked offstage.* —*adj.: an offstage sound.*

off-white |**ôf'hwīt'**| *or* |**-wīt'**| *or* |**ŏf'**-| *n.* A grayish or yellowish white. —*adj.* Grayish or yellowish white.

oft |ôft| *or* |ŏft| *adv.* Often: *the President's oft-quoted peace formula.*

of·ten |**ô'**fən| *or* |**ŏf'**ən| *or* |**ôf'**tən| *or* |**ŏf'**-| *adv.* Frequently; repeatedly; many times.

of·ten·times |**ô'**fən tīmz'| *or* |**ŏf'**ən-| *or* |**ôf'**tən-| *or* |**ŏf'**-| *adv.* Often; frequently.

oft·times |**ôf'**tīmz'| *or* |**ŏf'**-| *or* |**ôft'**tīmz'| *or* |**ŏft'**-| *adv.* Often; oftentimes.

o·gle |**ō'**gəl| *or* |**ô'**gəl| *v.* **o·gled, o·gling.** To stare at (someone) in an impertinent or flirtatious manner: *ogling young girls on the street. The young girls ogled at the lifeguard.* —**o'gler** *n.*

o-grade form |ō **grād'**|. A linguistic form in which the vowel has changed from *e* to *o.*

o·gre |**ō'**gər| *n.* **1.** In folklore, one of a race of man-eating giants. **2.** Someone who is especially cruel or brutish.

oh |ō| *interj.* A word used to express emotion, such as surprise, anger, or pain. ¶*These sound alike* **oh, O, owe.**

O·hi·o¹ |ō **hī'**ō|. A Midwestern state of the United States. Population, 10,730,000. Capital, Columbus. —**O·hi'o·an** *adj. & n.*

O·hi·o² |ō **hī'**ō|. A river flowing from Pittsburgh, Pennsylvania, to the Mississippi in southern Illinois.

ohm |ōm| *n.* A unit of electrical resistance, equal to the resistance of a conductor through which a current of one ampere flows when a potential difference of one volt is applied to it.

ohm·me·ter |**ōm'**mē'tər| *n.* An instrument that measures and indicates the resistance of an electrical conductor in ohms, multiples of ohms, or fractions of an ohm.

Ohm's law. A law stating that the current, *I,* in an electric circuit is given by the equation $I = V/R$, where R is the effective resistance of the circuit and V is the voltage applied across that resistance.

-oid. A suffix that forms nouns and adjectives and means "like or resembling": **anthropoid.**

oil |oil| *n.* **1.** Any of a large class of substances, including animal and vegetable fats as well as substances of mineral or synthetic origin, that are characteristically thick, slippery, capable of being burned, liquid or easily melted, and incapable of mixing with water. **2. a.** Petroleum. **b.** A substance derived from petroleum, such as a substance for lubricating machinery. **3.** A liquid that resembles an oil. **4.** An **oil color. 5.** An **oil painting.** —***modifier:*** *oil glands; an oil lamp; oil companies.* —*v.* To lubricate, supply, cover, or polish with oil.

oil·cloth |**oil'**klôth'| *or* |**-**klŏth'| *n.* Cloth that has been coated with oil or paint to make it waterproof.

oil color. A color consisting of a pigment ground and mixed with linseed oil or a similar oil.

oil painting. 1. A painting done in oil colors. **2.** The art or process of painting with oil colors.

oil palm. An African palm tree with nutlike fruits that yield a yellowish oil, **palm oil,** used in making soaps, cosmetics, chocolate, etc.

oil shale. A dark-brown or black shale containing hydrocarbons that yield petroleum by distillation.

oil well. A hole dug or drilled in the earth or ocean floor in order to obtain petroleum.

oil·y |**oi'**lē| *adj.* **oil·i·er, oil·i·est. 1.** Of or like oil: *an oily liquid.* **2.** Covered with, soaked with, or containing much oil; greasy: *oily rags; an oily complexion.* **3.** Unpleasantly smooth, as in manner or behavior; unctuous: *his oily, insincere compliments.* —**oil'i·ness** *n.*

oint·ment |**oint'**mənt| *n.* A thick, often oily substance made to be rubbed on the skin as a medication or cosmetic; a salve.

O·jib·wa |ō **jĭb'**wā'| *or* |**-**wə| *n., pl.* **O·jib·wa** or **O·jib·was. 1.** A North American Indian tribe of the regions around Lake Superior. **2.** A member of this tribe. **3.** The Algonquian language of this tribe.

O·jib·way |ō **jĭb'**wā'| *n., pl.* **O·jib·way** or **O·jib·ways.** A form of the word **Ojibwa.**

O.K. or **OK** |**ō'kā'**| *or* |ō **kā'**|. *Informal. interj.* All right; very well: *O.K., fellows, let's go.* —*adj.* All right; acceptable; fine: *The plan is O.K. with me.* —*adv.* Well; acceptably: *He's doing O.K.* —*n., pl.* **O.K.'s** or **OK's.** Approval; acceptance; agreement: *Get your dad's O.K. before we start on the trip.* —*v.* **O.K.'d** or **OK'd, O.K.'ing** or **OK'ing, O.K.'s** or **OK's.** To approve; agree to: *The governor O.K.'d the plans for the construction of a new highway.* [SEE NOTE]

o·ka·pi |ō **kä'**pē| *n., pl.* **o·ka·pis.** An African animal related to the giraffe, but having a shorter neck and a dark coat with white stripes on the legs and hindquarters. [SEE PICTURE]

o·kay |**ō'kā'**| *or* |ō **kā'**| *interj., adj., adv., n., & v.* A form of the word **O.K.**

O·kie |**ō'**kē| *n. Informal.* A poor farm worker who travels from place to place, especially one forced to leave a farm in Oklahoma during the depression of the 1930's.

Okla. Oklahoma.

O•kla•ho•ma |ō′klə hō′mə|. A Southwestern state of the United States. Population 3,025,266. Capital, Oklahoma City. —**O′kla•ho′man** *adj. & n.*

O•kla•ho•ma City |ō′klə hō′mə|. The capital and largest city of Oklahoma, in the central part of the state. Population, 403,213.

ok•ra |ō′krə| *n.* **1.** A tall plant with narrow, sticky seed pods. **2.** The pods of this plant, usually used in soups or stews. [SEE PICTURE]

old |ōld| *adj.* **old•er** or **eld•er** |ĕl′dər|, **old•est** or **eld•est** |ĕl′dĭst|. **1. a.** Having lived for a long time; of great age or advanced years: *an old man with white whiskers; a gnarled old pine tree.* **b.** Relatively advanced in age: *her older brothers and sisters.* **2.** Of a certain age: *a ten-year-old girl.* **3.** In existence for a long time; made or known long ago; not new: *an old part of the city; a collection of old dolls.* **4.** Worn, run-down, etc., as from age, use, or neglect: *an old haunted house.* **5.** Seeming or acting like an aged person: *His life had been so hard that he grew old much sooner than most people.* **6.** Having the maturity or wisdom of age: *I never knew so young a person with so old a head.* **7.** Of, belonging to, or associated with an earlier time or period of existence: *visiting his old neighborhood; seeing all her old friends.* **8.** Often **Old.** Being the earlier or earliest of two or more related things, forms, etc.: *the Old Testament; Old English.* **9.** Former; original: *He seems to be his old self again.* **10.** Established by time or tradition: *old customs.* **11.** Skilled through long experience: *an old hand at sailing.* **12.** *Informal.* Known for a long time and well-liked; dear: *good old Harry.* **13.** *Informal.* Used as an intensive: *I can fight you any old time.* —*n.* **1.** Former times; yore: *in days of old.* **2.** Someone or something of a certain age: *She is mature for a nine-year-old. That horse is a three-year-old.*

old•en |ōl′dən| *adj.* Of an earlier time when things were quite different from the way they are now: *in olden days.*

Old English. The English language from about A.D. 705 to 1150; Anglo-Saxon. [SEE NOTE]

old-fash•ioned |ōld′făsh′ənd| *adj.* **1.** Belonging to or typical of an earlier time and no longer in style: *old-fashioned clothes.* **2.** Sticking to, preferring, or in keeping with ways or ideas of an earlier time: *strict, old-fashioned grandparents.*

Old French. The French language from about A.D. 800 to 1500. [SEE NOTE]

Old Glory. A nickname for the flag of the United States.

Old High German. The language of southern Germany from about A.D. 850 to 1100.

old maid. **1.** *Informal.* A woman, especially an older woman, who is not married. **2.** *Informal.* A person who is prim or fussy. **3.** A card game.

old master. **1.** An outstanding European artist, especially a painter, chiefly of the period from around 1500 to the early 1700's. **2.** A work by such an artist.

Old Nick |nĭk|. *Informal.* The devil; Satan.

Old Norse. The Germanic language from which the Scandinavian languages are descended.

old•ster |ōld′stər| *n. Informal.* An old, older, or elderly person.

Old Testament. The first of the two main divisions of the Christian Bible, relating to God's covenant with the Hebrews and containing much of their history, laws, etc.; the **Hebrew Scriptures.**

old-time |ōld′tīm′| *adj.* Of, belonging to, or typical of a time in the past: *an old-time whaling ship; old-time tunes; an old-time Christmas.*

old-tim•er |ōld′tī′mər| *n. Informal.* A person who has lived in a place, belonged to a group, or engaged in a certain kind of work or activity for a long time.

Old World. The Eastern Hemisphere; Europe, Asia, and Africa, especially Europe.

old-world, also **Old-World** |ōld′wûrld′| *adj.* Of or typical of the Old World, especially in earlier times: *the old-world charm of the little Spanish town.*

o•le•ag•i•nous |ō′lē ăj′ə nəs| *adj.* **1.** Containing or consisting of oil: *an oleaginous substance.* **2.** Unpleasantly smooth or insinuating; oily. —**o′le•ag′i•nous•ly** *adv.* —**o′le•ag′i•nous•ness** *n.*

o•le•an•der |ō′lē ăn′dər| *or* |ō′lē ăn′-| *n.* A poisonous shrub of warm regions, having evergreen leaves and showy clusters of fragrant white or reddish flowers.

o•le•fin |ō′lə fĭn| *n.* Any of a class of hydrocarbon compounds, such as ethylene, that contain two atoms of hydrogen for each atom of carbon. They are unsaturated and have relatively high chemical activity.

o•le•o |ō′lē ō| *n.* Oleomargarine.

o•le•o•mar•ga•rine |ō′lē ō mär′jər ĭn| *or* |-jə-rēn′| *n.* Margarine.

o•le•o•res•in |ō′lē ō rĕz′ĭn| *n.* A naturally occurring mixture of an oil and a resin, such as the substance exuded by pine trees.

ol•fac•to•ry |ŏl făk′tə rē| *or* |-trē| *or* |ōl-| *adj.* Of, pertaining to, or contributing to the sense of smell: *olfactory organs.*

ol•i•gar•chic |ŏl′ĭ gär′kĭk| or **ol•i•gar•chi•cal** |ŏl′ĭ gär′kĭ kəl| *adj.* Of an oligarchy.

ol•i•gar•chy |ŏl′ĭ gär′kē| *n., pl.* **ol•i•gar•chies. 1.** A form of government in which power is exercised by a small group of people. **2.** The people forming such a group. **3.** A country, community, etc., governed by such a group. —**ol′i•gar′chic, ol′i•gar′chi•cal** *adj.*

Ol•i•go•cene |ŏl′ĭ gō sēn′| *n.* Also **Ol•i•go•cene epoch.** The geologic epoch of the Cenozoic era that began about 36 million years ago and ended about 25 million years ago. —***modifier:*** *an Oligocene rock.*

ol•ive |ŏl′ĭv| *n.* **1. a.** The small, oval, greenish or blackish fruit of a tree native to the Mediterranean region. Olives are eaten as a relish or pressed to extract **olive oil,** a yellowish oil used for cooking, in salad dressings, for making soap, etc. **b.** A tree that bears olives. **2.** A dull yellowish green. —***modifier:*** *an olive grove; olive pits.* —*adj.* **1.** Dull yellowish green. **2.** Having a slight tinge of this color: *an olive complexion.* [SEE PICTURE]

olive branch. **1.** A branch of an olive tree, regarded as a symbol of peace. **2.** An action, sign, etc., intended as an offer of peace.

olive drab. **1.** A dull brownish or grayish green. **2.** Cloth of this color, often used for military uniforms.

Ol•mec |ōl′mĕk′| *n., pl.* **Ol•mec** or **Ol•mecs.** A member of an ancient people of southeastern Mexico who created the earliest civilization in

okra
Okra pods

Old English, Old French, etc. *Many languages are divided into old, middle, and modern periods. These periods are different for different languages. The old period begins with the earliest written records in the particular language;* **Old English** *begins in the eighth century,* **Old French** *in the ninth. The middle stage of a language often corresponds to the medieval period of European history;* **Middle English** *runs from the Norman Conquest to 1500. The modern stage, as with English, generally begins around the time of the Renaissance. (See also note at* **proto-**.*)*

olive

omnibus
In 1825 the first successful system of cheap public transportation was set up in Paris. The carriages used were given the name of voitures omnibus. Voitures *is French for "carriages, vehicles."* Omnibus *is the dative plural of the Latin adjective* omnis, *"all"; the dative case gives the meaning "for," so* omnibus *means "for all (people)."* Voitures omnibus *thus means "vehicles for all," but it is an extremely strange and pedantic way of saying it (why not simply* voitures pour tout *or* voitures publiques, *"public vehicles"?). Anyway, the name stuck, was immediately borrowed into English, and by 1832 was being shortened to* **bus**. *Thus a Latin inflectional ending turned into a very common modern noun. At the same time,* **omnibus** *was extended to mean also "something all-purpose" (see sense* **2** *and the adjective).*

ă pat/ā pay/â care/ä father/ĕ pet/ ē be/ĭ pit/ī pie/î fierce/ŏ pot/ ō go/ô paw, for/oi oil/ŏŏ book/ ōō boot/ou out/ŭ cut/û fur/ *th* the/th thin/hw which/zh vision/ ə ago, item, pencil, atom, circus

the Americas. —*adj.* Of the Olmecs.

O•lym•pi•a |ō lĭm′pē ə|. **1.** A plain in ancient Greece where the Olympic games were held. **2.** The capital of the state of Washington. Population, 22,400.

O•lym•pi•an |ō lĭm′pē ən| *adj.* **1.** Of Mount Olympus or the gods of ancient Greece who were believed to have lived on Mount Olympus: *the Olympian abode of the gods.* **2.** Godlike, majestic, or lofty in manner: *Olympian pronouncements from the royal palace.* —*n.* One of the gods of ancient Greece who were believed to have lived on Mount Olympus.

O•lym•pic |ō lĭm′pĭk| *adj.* Of or relating to the festival of contests held in Olympia in ancient Greece, or especially the modern international contests based on them: *Wilma Rudolph made Olympic history as the first American woman to win three gold medals in track.* —*n.* **Olympics.** The Olympic games of modern times.

Olympic games. **1.** An ancient Greek festival of athletic competitions and contests in poetry and dancing, held every four years in Olympia in honor of the god Zeus. **2.** A modern international athletic competition held every four years in a different part of the world.

O•lym•pus |ō lĭm′pəs|, **Mount.** The highest mountain of Greece, believed by the ancient Greeks to be the home of the chief gods and goddesses.

O•ma•ha |ō′mə hô′| *or* |-hä′|. The largest city in Nebraska. Population, 371,000.

O•man |ō män′|. A country of eastern Arabia. Population, 750,000. Capital, Muscat.

om•buds•man |ŏm′bŭdz′mən| *or* |-bo͝odz′-| *n., pl.* **-men** |-mən|. A government official, originally in Scandinavian countries, who handles citizens' complaints against the government.

o•me•ga |ō mē′gə| *or* |-mā′-| *or* |ō mĕg′ə| *n.* **1.** The 24th and last letter of the Greek alphabet, written Ω. In English it is represented as long *o.* **2.** The last of anything; the ending.

om•e•let, also **om•e•lette** |ŏm′ə lĭt| *or* |ŏm′lĭt| *n.* A dish of beaten eggs, cooked and often folded around a filling of jelly, cheese, etc.

o•men |ō′mən| *n.* A thing or event regarded as a sign of future good or bad luck.

om•i•cron |ŏm′ĭ krŏn′| *or* |ō′mĭ-| *n.* The 15th letter of the Greek alphabet, written O, o. In English it is represented as *O, o.*

om•i•nous |ŏm′ə nəs| *adj.* Seeming to foretell or be a sign of trouble, danger, or disaster; threatening: *ominous clouds.* —**om′i•nous•ly** *adv.* —**om′i•nous•ness** *n.*

o•mis•sion |ō mĭsh′ən| *n.* **1.** The act or fact of omitting something or having been omitted: *the omission of several letters from a word.* **2.** Something that has been omitted: *several omissions in the guest list.*

o•mit |ō mĭt′| *v.* **o•mit•ted, o•mit•ting.** **1.** To leave out; not include: *Omit unnecessary words and ideas.* **2.** To fail to include, do, take advantage of, etc.; skip; neglect: *She omitted no opportunity to tell him how silly she thought he was.*

omni-. A word element meaning "all": **omnipotent.**

om•ni•bus |ŏm′nə bŭs′| *n., pl.* **om•ni•bus•es.** **1.** A bus. **2.** A printed collection of the works of one author or of writings on related subjects: *a Mark Twain omnibus; an omnibus of ghost stories.* —*adj.* Including many different things, matters, items, etc.: *an omnibus bill passed by Congress.* [SEE NOTE]

om•nip•o•tent |ŏm nĭp′ə tənt| *adj.* Having unlimited or universal power, authority, or force; all-powerful. —*n.* **the Omnipotent.** God. —**om•nip′o•tence** *n.*

om•ni•pres•ent |ŏm′nə prĕz′ənt| *adj.* Present or seeming to be present everywhere. —**om′ni•pres′ence** *n.*

om•nis•cient |ŏm nĭsh′ənt| *adj.* Having unbounded knowledge; knowing everything. —**om•nis′cience** *n.*

om•ni•vore |ŏm′nə vôr′| *or* |-vōr′| *n.* An animal that eats both plant and animal food.

om•niv•o•rous |ŏm nĭv′ər əs| *adj.* **1.** Eating both plant and animal substances or products as food; eating all kinds of food: *Rats and human beings are omnivorous.* **2.** Taking in everything one can, as with the mind: *an omnivorous reader.* —**om•niv′o•rous•ly** *adv.* —**om•niv′o•rous•ness** *n.*

on |ŏn| *or* |ôn| *prep.* **1.** —Used to indicate: **a.** Position upon: *a plate on the table.* **b.** Contact with: *a picture on the wall.* **c.** Location at: *a house on the beach.* **d.** Nearness to: *a city on the frontier.* **e.** Attachment to or suspension from: *beads on a string.* **2.** —Used to indicate motion or direction toward or against: *throwing the books on the floor; marching on Washington.* **3.** —Used to indicate: **a.** Occurrence during: *on Tuesday.* **b.** The occasion of what is stated: *On seeing him, she fainted.* **4.** —Used to indicate: **a.** The object affected by an action: *The spotlight fell on the actress.* **b.** The cause of a specified action: *cut his foot on a piece of broken glass.* **c.** Something used to perform a stated action: *talking on the phone.* **5.** —Used to indicate an originating or sustaining source or cause: *making money on the horses.* **6.** —Used to indicate: **a.** The state, condition, or process of: *on leave; on fire.* **b.** The purpose of: *traveling on business.* **c.** A means of conveyance: *riding on a train.* **d.** Availability by means of: *beer on tap.* **e.** Association with: *a doctor on the staff.* **f.** The basis for: *on principle.* **g.** Addition or repetition: *error on error.* **7.** Concerning; about: *a book on carpentry.* **8.** In one's possession: *I don't have a cent on me.* **9.** At the expense of: *drinks on the house. This meal is on me.* —*adv.* **1.** In or into a position of being attached to or covering something: *He pulled his coat on.* **2.** In the direction of something: *He was looking on when the ship came in.* **3.** Forward or ahead: *moving on to the next town.* **4.** In a continuous course: *going on and on until they reached the sea.* **5.** In or into action or operation: *turning the television on.* **6.** In or at the present position: *staying on.*

once |wŭns| *adj.* **1.** One time only: *once a day.* **2.** Formerly: *I was a little kid once too.* **3.** At any time; ever: *In this country, if it once starts raining it won't stop.* —*n.* One single time or occurrence: *Let me go out just this once.* —*conj.* As soon as; if ever; when: *Once we get started, I'll show you what to do.* —*adj.* Having been formerly; former: *the once kingdom of Aragon.*

Idioms. **all at once.** **1.** All at the same time. **2.** Suddenly. **at once.** **1.** All together; simultaneously. **2.** Immediately. **once and for all.** Finally; conclusively. **once in a while.** Now and then. **once upon a time.** At some indefinite time long ago.

once-o•ver |wŭns′ō′vər| *n. Informal.* A quick but thorough look or going over.

on•com•ing |ŏn′kŭm′ĭng| *or* |ôn′-| *adj.* Coming nearer or toward someone or something; approaching: *the oncoming storm.*

one |wŭn| *adj.* **1.** Being a single entity, unit, or object; single; individual: *one dog and three cats.* **2.** Characterized by unity; undivided: *We are of one mind on this question. With one accord the audience rose and sang the national anthem.* **3.** —Used to designate a person or thing that is contrasted with another or others: *He was at one end of the hall and I was at the other.* **4.** —Used to designate a certain person, especially someone not previously known or mentioned: *One Bob Johnson is directing the Institute's research program.* **5.** *Informal.* —Used intensively for the indefinite article: *That is one fine mess you've gotten us into!* **6.** Single in kind; alike or the same: *This all happened on one and the same day.* —*n.* **1.** A number, written 1 in Arabic numerals, that leaves any other number unchanged when multiplied with it. If *n* stands for any number at all, then $n \times 1 = 1 \times n = n$. It can be proved that 1 is the smallest of the positive integers. **2.** A single person or unit: *I'd like a dozen apples, but please don't give me any green ones.* —*pron.* **1.** Someone or something, especially as among persons or things already known or mentioned: *one of my teammates.* **2.** Any person; a person: *One doesn't act like that, my dear. One should always do one's best in class.* ¶*These sound alike* **one, won**[2].

Idioms. **all one.** Of equal importance; all the same: *Maybe she's coming and maybe not—it's all one to me.* **at one.** In accord or agreement: *We found ourselves at one on the whole treaty issue.* **one and all.** Everyone: *We had a good time one and all.* **one another.** Each other: *loving one another.* **one by one.** Individually and in succession.

O•nei•da |ō nī′də| *n., pl.* **O•nei•da** or **O•nei•das. 1.** A North American Indian tribe of central New York State. **2.** A member of this tribe. **3.** The Iroquoian language of this tribe.

O'Neill |ō nēl′|, **Eugene.** 1888–1953. American dramatist.

one•ness |wŭn′nĭs| *n.* **1.** The condition of being one and the same. **2.** Agreement; unity: *oneness of mind and purpose.*

one•self |wŭn sĕlf′| *pron.* A form of the third person singular pronoun **one**. It is used: **1.** As a reflexive pronoun, forming the direct or indirect object of a verb or the object of a preposition: *There is nothing like losing oneself in a good adventure story. He said some things about newfangled ideas and getting above oneself only leading to trouble.* **2.** For emphasis, after *one: What's the good of thinking about misery when one is already miserable oneself?*

one's self. A form of the word **oneself**.

one-sid•ed |wŭn′sī′dĭd| *adj.* **1.** Favoring one side or group; partial; biased: *a one-sided version of the disagreement.* **2.** Unbalanced, so that one side is more prominent, active, etc.: *a one-sided partnership.*

one-time, also **one•time** |wŭn′tīm′| *adj.* At or of some time in the past; former: *one-time boxing champion.*

one-to-one |wŭn′tə wŭn′| *adj.* Of a mathematical rule of correspondence that matches each member of a set with one and only one member of the same set or another set.

one-track |wŭn′trăk′| *adj.* Narrowly limited to a single idea or way of thinking: *a one-track mind.*

one-way |wŭn′wā′| *adj.* Moving or permitting movement, travel, or use in one direction only: *a one-way street; a one-way ticket to Boston.*

on•go•ing |ŏn′gō′ĭng| *or* |ôn′-| *adj.* Going onward; continuing or progressing: *the ongoing rate of pollution.*

on•ion |ŭn′yən| *n.* **1.** The rounded, strong-smelling, strong-tasting bulb of a plant widely grown as a vegetable. **2.** A plant that grows from such a bulb, having long, narrow, grasslike leaves. —***modifier:*** *onion soup.* [SEE PICTURE]

on•ion•skin |ŭn′yən skĭn′| *n.* A thin, strong, translucent paper.

on•look•er |ŏn′lo͝ok′ər| *or* |ôn′-| *n.* Someone who watches or looks on; a spectator.

on•ly |ōn′lē| *adj.* **1.** Alone in kind or class; sole: *our only reason for going; their only child.* **2.** Most suitable or fit of all: *the only contenders of the football season.* —*adv.* **1.** Without anyone or anything else; alone: *Only three survived.* **2.** Merely; just: *I only followed orders.* **3.** Exclusively; solely: *I fill only written orders.* —*conj.* But: *Go ahead and quit school, only don't come complaining when you can't get a job.*

Idiom. **only too.** Eagerly; readily: *I'm only too delighted to help.*

on•o•mat•o•poe•ia |ŏn′ə măt′ə pē′ə| *n.* The use or sound of a word that imitates or resembles what it stands for or describes. —**on′o•mat′o•poe′ic** *adj.* [SEE NOTE]

On•on•da•ga |ŏn′ən dô′gə| *or* |-dä′-| *n., pl.* **On•on•da•ga** or **On•on•da•gas. 1.** A North American Indian tribe of central New York State. **2.** A member of this tribe. **3.** The Iroquoian language of this tribe.

on•rush |ŏn′rŭsh′| *or* |ôn′-| *n.* A forward or onward rush or flow.

on•rush•ing |ŏn′rŭsh′ĭng| *or* |ôn′-| *adj.* Rushing or surging onward or forward: *the onrushing tide.*

on•set |ŏn′sĕt′| *or* |ôn′-| *n.* **1.** A beginning; start: *the onset of a disease.* **2.** An attack or rushing charge, or something resembling this: *the onset of the hurricane.*

on•shore |ŏn′shôr′| *or* |-shōr′| *or* |ôn′-| *adj.* **1.** Moving or directed toward the shore: *an onshore breeze.* **2.** Located or operating on the shore: *an onshore patrol.* —*adv.: The wind shifted onshore.*

on•slaught |ŏn′slôt′| *or* |ôn′-| *n.* A violent attack or charge: *the enemy onslaught.*

on•stage |ŏn′stāj′| *or* |ôn′-| *adv.* On or onto the stage, as in a theatrical performance: *tripped as he walked onstage.* —*adj.: applauded all the onstage actors.*

On•tar•i•o[1] |ŏn târ′ē ō|. A province of Canada. Population, 8,264,465. Capital, Toronto.

On•tar•i•o[2] |ŏn târ′ē ō|, **Lake.** One of the Great Lakes, lying between New York State and Ontario, Canada.

on•to |ŏn′to͞o′| *or* |ôn′-| *or* |ŏn′tə *when unstressed*| *or* |ôn′-| *prep.* **1.** To a position on or upon: *A crowd is getting onto the airplane.* **2.** *Informal.*

onion

onomatopoeia

Onomatopoeia *is from Greek* onomatopoiia, *"the making of words (in imitation of sounds)":* onoma, *"name, word,"* + -poiia, *"a making." (In this Dictionary, the term* **imitative** *is usually used in preference to* **onomatopoeic**.*)*

ooze[1-2]/oozy[1-2]
Ooze[1] *was* wosen *in Middle English and meant "to exude like sap from a tree"; it is from* wos, *"juice, sap."* **Ooze[2]** *was Old English* wāse, *"mud," and is not related to* **ooze[1]**. **Oozy[1]** *belongs with* **ooze[1]** *and* **oozy[2]** *with* **ooze[2]**; *but in practice it is sometimes impossible to tell the two adjectives apart.*

openwork

opera[1-2]
Latin opus, *"work," was a neuter noun whose plural was* opera; *this is the source of English* **opus** *with its plural* **opera[2]**. *Closely related to* opus *was a separate feminine noun,* opera, *also meaning "work" in slightly different senses; this passed into Italian as* opera *and became the special term for a musical drama; it was borrowed into English as* **opera[1]**.

ă pat/ā pay/â care/ä father/ĕ pet/ē be/ĭ pit/ī pie/î fierce/ŏ pot/ō go/ô paw, for/oi oil/o͝o book/o͞o boot/ou out/ŭ cut/û fur/*th* the/th thin/hw which/zh vision/ə ago, item, pencil, atom, circus

In or into a state of knowing about: *Miss Smith is onto us, so we'd better not cut this class.*

o•nus |ō'nəs| *n.* A heavy or burdensome necessity, responsibility, obligation, etc.

on•ward |ŏn'wərd| *or* |ôn'-| *adv.* Also **on•wards** |ŏn'wərdz| *or* |ôn'-|. In a direction or toward a position that is ahead in space or time; forward: *plodding onward through the storm.* —*adj.: their onward progress.*

-onym. A word element meaning "name, word": **antonym.**

on•yx |ŏn'ĭks| *n.* A type of quartz that occurs in bands of different colors, often black and white.

oo•dles |o͞od'lz| *pl.n. Informal.* A great amount or large number; lots.

ooh or **oo** |o͞o| *interj.* Often **oooh, ooo,** etc. Used to express excitement, surprise, pain, fear, etc.

oo•mi•ak |o͞o'mē ăk'| *n.* A form of the word **umiak.**

oops |o͝ops| *or* |o͞ops| *interj.* Used to express surprise or dismay.

ooze[1] |o͞oz| *v.* **oozed, ooz•ing. 1.** To flow, drip, or leak slowly or in small amounts; seep: *Blood oozed from the cut on his finger.* **2.** To give off by or as if by dripping or flowing thickly: *trees oozing sticky sap. He oozes insincere flattery.* **3.** To disappear as if by slowly leaking or draining: *His courage oozed away.* [SEE NOTE]

ooze[2] |o͞oz| *n.* Soft, thin mud or a similar substance, such as that covering the bottoms of oceans and lakes, formed mainly of the remains of microscopic animals. [SEE NOTE]

ooz•y[1] |o͞o'zē| *adj.* **ooz•i•er, ooz•i•est.** Tending to ooze: *an oozy package of ice cream.* [SEE NOTE]

ooz•y[2] |o͞o'zē| *adj.* **ooz•i•er, ooz•i•est.** Of or like ooze; wet and sticky: *oozy mud.* [SEE NOTE]

Op., op. opus.

o•pac•i•ty |ō păs'ĭ tē| *n.* The condition or property of being opaque.

o•pal |ō'pəl| *n.* A translucent mineral composed of a form of silica, having rainbowlike, iridescent colors and often used as a gem.

o•pal•es•cent |ōp'ə lĕs'ənt| *adj.* Having the rainbowlike, iridescent colors of an opal. —**o'pal•es'cence** *n.*

o•paque |ō pāk'| *adj.* **1.** Not capable of letting light pass through; neither transparent nor translucent: *Metals and some minerals are opaque.* **2.** Not reflecting light; not shiny; dull: *an opaque finish on a surface.* **3.** Hard to understand; obscure. —**o•paque'ly** *adv.* —**o•paque'ness** *n.*

op. cit. In the book or work already referred to. An abbreviation for the Latin phrase *opere citato.*

ope |ōp| *v.* **oped, op•ing.** To open. Used chiefly in poetry.

OPEC |ō'pĕk'|. Organization of Petroleum Exporting Countries.

o•pen |ō'pən| *adj.* **1. a.** Providing entrance and exit: *an open door.* **b.** Not shut, closed, fastened, or sealed: *an open book; an open lock.* **2.** Providing free passage or view; not blocked or enclosed: *open country.* **3.** Having no protecting or concealing cover; exposed: *cooking over open fires.* **4.** Unprotected; vulnerable: *laid himself open to trouble.* **5.** Having spaces, gaps, or intervals: *a coarse, open weave.* **6. a.** Available or accessible; not restricted: *lands open to licensed hunters.* **b.** Available or obtainable; not closed or decided: *a job still open.* **7.** Ready to transact business; operating: *the only restaurant open.* **8.** Free from pretense or reserve: *She comes on warm, open, friendly, and real.* **9.** Free from prejudice or settled belief: *keeping an open mind.* **10.** Not hidden, concealed, or secret: *showing open defiance.* —*v.* **1.** To make or become no longer shut, fastened, sealed, or enclosed: *opened the envelope. The door opened suddenly.* **2.** To spread apart; unfold: *opened the treasure map; when the buds open in spring.* **3.** To begin; commence: *the topic that opens this chapter; a meeting that opened with high hopes.* **4.** To begin the operation of; begin business or operation: *plans for opening a taxi stand; stores that open at noon.* **5.** To make or become available for use: *Japan opened her ports to western trade.* **6.** To make or become receptive, understanding, or sympathetic: *open one's heart; minds that open wide to new ideas.* **7.** To give access or view: *doors opening into the ship's hold.* —*n.* **the open. 1.** An area of land or water that is not covered or concealed; an opening or clearing: *a wounded man crawling into the open.* **2.** The outdoors: *used to living in the open.* **3.** A condition free of secrecy, concealment, or disguise: *bring the facts into the open.* —**o'pen•ly** *adv.* —**o'pen•ness** *n.*

open air. The outdoors. —*modifier:* **(open-air):** *an open-air market.*

o•pen•er |ō'pə nər| *n.* Something or someone that opens, especially: **1.** An instrument used to cut open cans or pry off bottle caps. **2.** The first act, number, or game in a show, series, etc.

o•pen-eyed |ō'pən īd'| *adj.* **1.** Having the eyes wide open, as in surprise. **2.** Watchful and alert.

o•pen•hand•ed |ō'pən hăn'dĭd| *adj.* Giving freely; generous. —**o'pen•hand'ed•ly** *adv.* —**o'pen•hand'ed•ness** *n.*

o•pen-heart |ō'pən härt'| *adj.* Of or having to do with surgery that is performed on the heart while it is stopped and its functions are being performed by external devices.

open house. 1. A social event that may be attended by all who wish to do so. **2.** An occasion in which a school or other institution is open for visiting and inspection.

o•pen•ing |ō'pə nĭng| *n.* **1.** The act of becoming open or being made to open: *the opening of the West.* **2.** An open space or clearing: *an opening in the woods.* **3.** The first period or stage of something: *at the opening of the story.* **4.** The first occasion of something, especially of a play. **5.** A favorable opportunity: *boxers sparring for an opening.* **6.** An unfilled job or position; a vacancy: *an opening on the teaching staff.* —*modifier: an opening statement.*

o•pen-mind•ed |ō'pən mīn'dĭd| *adj.* Having a mind willing to consider new ideas; unprejudiced. —**o'pen-mind'ed•ly** *adv.* —**o'pen-mind'ed•ness** *n.*

open shop. A business establishment or factory in which membership in a labor union is not a requirement for getting or holding employment.

o•pen•work |ō'pən wûrk'| *n.* Anything made with a pattern of holes or open spaces in it, as lacy ironwork or fabric. [SEE PICTURE]

op•er•a[1] |ŏp'ər ə| *or* |ŏp'rə| *n.* A musical and dramatic work consisting of a play with stage action and the words sung to music, usually with orchestral accompaniment. [SEE NOTE]

o•pe•ra² |ō′pər ə| *or* |ŏp′ər ə| *n.* A plural of **opus.** [SEE NOTE on p. 624]

op•er•a•ble |ŏp′ər ə bəl| *adj.* **1.** Capable of being used or operated: *a broken-down but operable aircraft.* **2.** Capable of being put into practice; practicable: *an operable plan.* **3.** Capable of being treated by surgery: *an operable tumor.*

opera glasses. Small, low-powered binoculars, used especially in a theater.

opera house. A theater designed chiefly for operas.

op•er•ate |ŏp′ə rāt′| *v.* **op•er•at•ed, op•er•at•ing. 1.** To function in an effective way; work: *a machine that operates well.* **2.** To control the running or functioning of: *operate an aircraft; operate a cleaning plant.* **3.** To perform surgery.

op•er•at•ic |ŏp′ə **răt′**ĭk| *adj.* Of, related to, or like an opera: *an operatic aria.*

op•er•a•tion |ŏp′ə **rā′**shən| *n.* **1.** The act, process, or way of operating. **2.** The condition of being capable of operating or functioning: *a machine no longer in operation.* **3.** Any process for curing a disease, disorder, injury, etc., in a living body, especially a process in which surgical instruments are used. **4.** The use of a known rule or procedure to establish correspondence between pairs of elements of a set and single members of that set, or between single elements of two different sets: *Addition is a mathematical operation.* **5.** A military or naval action or series of actions. [SEE NOTE]

op•er•a•tion•al |ŏp′ə **rā′**shə nəl| *adj.* **1.** Of an operation or series of operations. **2.** Capable of operating properly: *an operational aircraft.*

op•er•a•tive |ŏp′ər ə tĭv| *or* |ŏp′rə-| *or* |-ə rā′-| *adj.* **1.** Working correctly; functioning; efficient: *operative equipment.* **2.** Of or having to do with a surgical operation. —*n.* **1.** A skilled worker. **2.** A secret agent or private detective. —**op′er•a•tive•ly** *adv.*

op•er•a•tor |ŏp′ə rā′tər| *n.* **1.** Someone who operates a machine or device: *a telephone operator.* **2.** Someone who owns or operates a business, industrial concern, etc.: *a mine operator.* **3.** A symbol, such as + for addition, that represents a mathematical operation. **4.** *Informal.* Someone who gets what he wants by shrewd and often unfair methods. [SEE PICTURE]

op•e•ret•ta |ŏp′ə **rĕt′**ə| *n.* A musical and dramatic work that is similar to an opera but is lighter and more popular in subject and style and contains spoken dialogue.

oph•thal•mol•o•gist |ŏf′thăl **mŏl′**ə jĭst| *or* |ŏp′-| *n.* A physician who specializes in ophthalmology; an eye doctor.

oph•thal•mol•o•gy |ŏf′thăl **mŏl′**ə jē| *or* |ŏp′-| *n.* The scientific and medical study of the eye, its structure and functioning, its diseases and disorders, and its treatment.

o•pi•ate |ō′pē ĭt| *or* |-āt′| *n.* **1.** A drug containing opium. **2.** Any sedative or narcotic drug. —***modifier:*** *an opiate drug.*

o•pine |ō **pīn′**| *v.* **o•pined, o•pin•ing.** To hold or state as an opinion; think.

o•pin•ion |ō **pĭn′**yən| *n.* **1.** A belief or conclusion held with confidence but not supported by positive knowledge or proof. **2.** An evaluation or judgment based on special knowledge and given by an expert. **3.** A judgment or estimate of the worth or value of a person or thing: *his low opinion of us.* **4.** The common or prevailing feeling or sentiment among a group: *public opinion.*

o•pin•ion•at•ed |ō **pĭn′**yə nā′tĭd| *adj.* Holding stubbornly to one's own opinions or showing the strong influence of one's opinions: *an opinionated critic.*

o•pi•um |ō′pē əm| *n.* A bitter yellowish-brown drug prepared from the pods of a certain variety of poppy, and from which codeine, morphine, heroin, and other alkaloid drugs are derived.

o•pos•sum |ə **pŏs′**əm| *or* |**pŏs′**əm| *n.* A furry animal that lives mostly in trees and carries its young in a pouch. Also called *possum.* [SEE PICTURE]

op•po•nent |ə **pō′**nənt| *n.* A person or group that opposes another in a battle, contest, controversy, or debate. —*adj.* Opposing: *opponent armies.*

op•por•tune |ŏp′ər **to͞on′**| *or* |**-tyo͞on′**| *adj.* **1.** Suited for a particular purpose: *an opportune suggestion.* **2.** Occurring at a time that is advantageous: *an opportune moment.*

op•por•tun•ism |ŏp′ər **to͞o′**nĭz′əm| *or* |**-tyo͞o′**-| *n.* The practice of using any opportunity available to achieve one's purpose or desire, usually with little or no regard for the principles of right and wrong. —**op′por•tun′ist** *n.*

op•por•tu•ni•ty |ŏp′ər **to͞o′**nĭ tē| *or* |**-tyo͞o′**-| *n.* A time or occasion that is suitable for a certain purpose; a favorable combination of circumstances: *opportunities for glory.*

op•pose |ə **pōz′**| *v.* **op•posed, op•pos•ing. 1.** To offer resistance to or contend against: *oppose the enemy; oppose a plan.* **2.** To place in opposition or be in opposition to; contrast or counterbalance: *oppose one football team to another.* —**op•pos′ing** *adj.: opposing points of view; opposing teams.* —**op•pos′er** *n.*

op•po•site |ŏp′ə zĭt| *or* |-sĭt| *adj.* **1.** Placed or located directly across from something else or from each other: *the opposite sides of a house.* **2.** Moving or tending away from each other: *They went off in opposite directions.* **3.** Contrary in nature or tendency; altogether different: *opposite personalities.* —*n.* Someone or something that is contrary to another: *What you're saying today is the exact opposite of what you were saying yesterday.* —*adv.* In an opposite position or positions: *They sat down opposite to each other.* —*prep.* **1.** Across from or facing: *Park your car opposite the school.* **2.** In a complementary dramatic role to: *She played opposite him.* —**op′po•site•ly** *adv.* —**op′po•site•ness** *n.*

op•po•si•tion |ŏp′ə **zĭsh′**ən| *n.* **1.** The act or condition of opposing or of being in conflict; resistance or antagonism: *joined in opposition to the President's program.* **2.** Something that serves as an opposing force or obstacle: *their offense met with fierce opposition from our team.* **3.** A position or location opposite or opposed to another. **4.** Sometimes **Opposition.** A political party or organization opposed to the group, party, or government in power: *the opposition's demand for a general election.* **5.** An arrangement in which the earth lies along a line segment that extends between the sun and another planet. —***modifier:*** *new opposition parties.*

op•press |ə **prĕs′**| *v.* **1.** To persecute or subject

operation

Addition as an **operation** *(in sense* **4***) forms correspondences of which the following are examples: (5, 3) 8; (5, 1) 6; (2, 3) 5. These have been written in this way rather than in the usual way in order to show that addition matches pairs of the set of whole numbers with single whole numbers. Similarly, the correspondences 1 —1; 5 —5; x —x are characteristic of an operation we may call* negation, *which matches each member of the set of positive real numbers with exactly one of the negative real numbers.*

operator

opossum

opus
Opus *numbers are assigned to musical compositions to keep track of the order in which they were written.*

orange

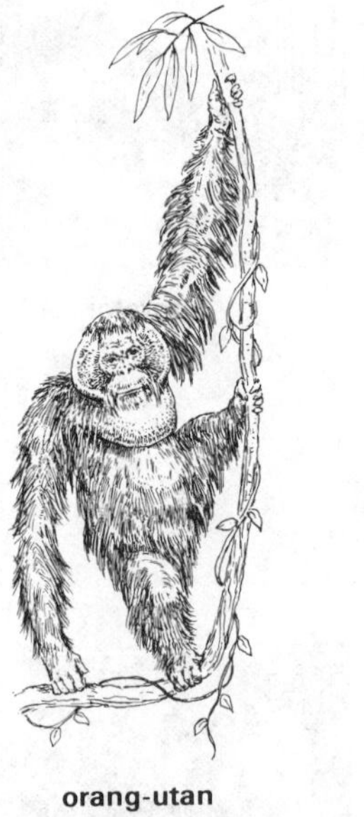
orang-utan

ă pat/ā pay/â care/ä father/ĕ pet/ ē be/ĭ pit/ī pie/î fierce/ŏ pot/ ō go/ô paw, for/oi oil/ŏŏ book/ ōō boot/ou out/ŭ cut/û fur/ *th* the/th thin/hw which/zh vision/ ə ago, item, pencil, atom, circus

to harsh treatment; treat as conquered people: *Foreign invaders long oppressed their people.* **2.** To weigh heavily upon so as to depress the mind or spirit: *Grief oppressed her.*

op•pres•sion |ə **prĕsh**′ən| *n.* **1.** The act of oppressing or the condition of being oppressed: *oppression of the slaves; a prison that was a symbol of their oppression.* **2.** Something that oppresses: *a statement of their grievances and oppressions.*

op•pres•sive |ə **prĕs**′ĭv| *adj.* **1.** Difficult to bear; harsh; tyrannical: *Their kings became steadily more oppressive.* **2.** Causing physical or mental distress: *oppressive effects of bad weather; an oppressive silence.* **—op•pres′sive•ly** *adv.* **—op•pres′sive•ness** *n.*

op•pres•sor |ə **prĕs**′ər| *n.* A person who persecutes or oppresses; a tyrant.

op•pro•bri•ous |ə **prō**′brē əs| *adj.* **1.** Expressing or carrying a sense of disgrace or scorn: *an opprobrious remark.* **2.** Shameful; unworthy: *opprobrious behavior.* **—op•pro′bri•ous•ly** *adv.*

op•pro•bri•um |ə **prō**′brē əm| *n.* **1.** Disgrace arising from shameful conduct. **2.** A cause of shame or disgrace.

opt |ŏpt| *v.* To make a choice.

op•tic |**ŏp**′tĭk| *adj.* Of or having to do with vision or the eye.

op•ti•cal |**ŏp**′tĭ kəl| *adj.* **1.** Of or having to do with sight: *an optical illusion.* **2.** Designed to assist sight: *optical instruments.* **3.** Of the science of optics. **—op′ti•cal•ly** *adv.*

op•ti•cian |ŏp **tĭsh**′ən| *n.* Someone who makes or sells lenses, eyeglasses, or other optical equipment.

optic nerve. Either of the two nerves that connect the retinas of the eyes to the brain.

op•tics |**ŏp**′tĭks| *n.* *(used with a singular verb).* The scientific study of light and vision.

op•ti•ma |**ŏp**′tə mə| *n.* A plural of **optimum.**

op•ti•mism |**ŏp**′tə mĭz′əm| *n.* **1.** A tendency to take a hopeful view of a situation, or to expect the best possible outcome. **2.** The belief that our world is the best of all possible worlds. **3.** The belief that good will ultimately overcome evil. **—op′ti•mist** *n.*

op•ti•mis•tic |ŏp′tə **mĭs**′tĭk| *adj.* **1.** Inclined to or showing optimism. **2.** Of optimism. **—op′ti•mis′ti•cal•ly** *adv.*

op•ti•mum |**ŏp**′tə mŭm| *n., pl.* **op•ti•ma** |**ŏp**′tə mə| or **op•ti•mums.** The best or most favorable condition, degree, or amount for a particular situation. *—adj.* Most favorable; best: *optimum conditions for long-range investments.*

op•tion |**ŏp**′shən| *n.* **1.** The act of choosing; choice: *refused to disclose his option.* **2.** The power or right of choosing; freedom to choose: *having no option but to comply.* **3.** Something chosen or available as a choice: *a headlight system that is an option on some new cars.* **4.** The exclusive right to buy or sell property within a specified time and at a specified price.

op•tion•al |**ŏp**′shə nəl| *adj.* Left to choice; not required or automatic: *an optional ingredient of the recipe; electives, which are optional courses.* **—op′tion•al•ly** *adv.*

op•tom•e•trist |ŏp **tŏm**′ĭ trĭst| *n.* A person who specializes in optometry.

op•tom•e•try |ŏp **tŏm**′ĭ trē| *n.* The profession of examining, measuring, and treating certain visual defects by means of corrective lenses or other methods in which the services of a physician are not needed.

op•u•lence |**ŏp**′yə ləns| *n.* **1.** Great wealth. **2.** A great amount or supply; abundance.

op•u•lent |**ŏp**′yə lənt| *adj.* **1.** Having or showing great wealth; rich: *an opulent society.* **2.** Abundant; plentiful; lavish: *opulent vegetation.* **3.** Marked by fullness and vitality: *an opulent figure.* **—op′u•lent•ly** *adv.*

o•pus |**ō**′pəs| *n., pl.* **o•per•a** |**ō**′pər ə| *or* |**ŏp**′ər ə| or **o•pus•es.** An artistic work, especially a musical composition or group of compositions. [SEE NOTE]

or |ôr| *or* |ər *when unstressed*| *conj.* **1.** —Used to indicate: **a.** An alternative: *hot or cold.* **b.** The second of two alternatives, the first being preceded by *either* or *whether: Either he's stupid, or I'm wrong and he's very sly indeed. I don't know whether to laugh or to cry.* **c.** A synonymous or equivalent expression: *catarrh, or sore throat.* **d.** Uncertainty or indefiniteness: *He's called here three or four times already.* **2.** Otherwise: *Get out of here or I'll break your neck.* ¶*These sound alike* **or, oar, o'er, ore.**

-or[1]. A suffix that forms nouns from verbs: **percolator.**

-or[2]. A suffix that forms nouns and means "condition or activity": **behavior.**

or•a•cle |**ôr**′ə kəl| *or* |**ŏr**′-| *n.* **1.** In ancient Greece, a shrine for the worship and consultation of a god who revealed knowledge or disclosed the future. **2.** The priest or other person who passed on the prophecies or messages from such a god to visitors at the shrine. **3.** A prophecy or message made known at such a shrine. **4.** Any person or agency considered to be a source of wise counsel or prophetic opinion; an authority or judge. ¶*These sound alike* **oracle, auricle.**

o•rac•u•lar |ô **răk**′yə lər| *or* |ō **răk**′-| *adj.* **1.** Of an oracle: *oracular sites in ancient Greece and Rome.* **2.** Resembling an oracle, especially: **a.** Solemnly prophetic; wise: *words in a deep oracular tone.* **b.** Brief but open to doubt as to exact meaning; deep; mysterious: *Because of its laconic and oracular style, the Constitution lends itself to various interpretations.* **—o•rac′u•lar•ly** *adv.*

o•ral |**ôr**′əl| *or* |**ōr**′-| *adj.* **1.** Spoken rather than written: *an oral examination.* **2.** Of the mouth: *oral hygiene.* **3.** Used in or taken through the mouth: *an oral thermometer; oral medication.* ¶*These sound alike* **oral, aural.** **—o′ral•ly** *adv.*

or•ange |**ôr**′ĭnj| *or* |**ŏr**′-| *n.* **1.** A round fruit related to the grapefruit, lemon, and lime, having a reddish-yellow rind and juicy pulp divided into sections. **2.** A tree that bears such fruit, having evergreen leaves and fragrant white flowers. **3.** The color of the rind of this fruit, between yellow and red. *—modifier: orange juice. —adj.* Of the color orange. [SEE PICTURE]

or•ange•ade |ôr′ĭn **jād**′| *or* |ŏr′-| *n.* A drink consisting of orange juice, sugar, and water.

o•rang-ou•tang |ō **răng**′ə tăng′| *or* |ə **răng**′-| *n.* A form of the word **orang-utan.**

o•rang-u•tan or **o•rang•u•tan** |ō **răng**′ə tăn′| *or* |ə **răng**′-| *n.* A large ape of the islands of Borneo and Sumatra, having long arms and reddish brown hair. [SEE PICTURE]

o•rate |ô rāt′| *or* |ō rāt′| *or* |ôr′āt′| *or* |ōr′-| *v.* **o•rat•ed, o•rat•ing.** To speak publicly in a formal, lofty, or pompous manner.

o•ra•tion |ô rā′shən| *or* |ō rā′-| *n.* A formal address or speech, usually given on a special occasion.

or•a•tor |ôr′ə tər| *or* |ŏr′-| *n.* **1.** A person who delivers an oration. **2.** A person skilled in public speaking.

or•a•tor•i•cal |ôr′ə tôr′ĭ kəl| *or* |ŏr′ə tŏr′-| *adj.* Of or appropriate to an orator or oratory: *oratorical contests.* **—or′a•tor′i•cal•ly** *adv.*

or•a•to•ri•o |ôr′ə tôr′ē ō| *or* |-tōr′-| *or* |ŏr′-| *n., pl.* **or•a•to•ri•os.** A large musical composition that is somewhat like an opera, except that the subject is usually religious and that it is performed without costumes, scenery, or dramatic action.

or•a•to•ry[1] |ôr′ə tôr′ē| *or* |-tōr′-| *or* |ŏr′-| *n.* **1.** The art of public speaking. **2.** Skill or style in public speaking. [SEE NOTE]

or•a•to•ry[2] |ôr′ə tôr′ē| *or* |-tōr′-| *or* |ŏr′-| *n., pl.* **or•a•to•ries.** A place for prayer, as a small private chapel. [SEE NOTE]

orb |ôrb| *n.* **1.** A sphere; a globe. **2.** Any of a series of spheres that early astronomers thought revolved around the earth supporting the moon, planets, and stars. **3.** A sphere decorated with jewels and surmounted by a cross, part of the ceremonial emblems of an emperor or other ruler. **4.** Also **orb web.** The wheel-shaped web made by certain kinds of spiders.

or•bit |ôr′bĭt| *n.* **1.** The path of a celestial body or artificial satellite in space, especially a closed path about another body. **2.** The path of any body in a field of force, especially a path that surrounds another body: *the orbit of an electron.* **3.** Either of the pair of bony depressions in the skull into which the eyes and their associated structures fit. **4.** A range of activity, influence, or control: *within the Soviet orbit.* —*v.* **1.** To put into or cause to move in an orbit: *orbit a satellite; a spacecraft orbiting for four days.* **2.** To move in an orbit around: *The moon orbits the earth.* **—or′bit•al** *adj.*

or•chard |ôr′chərd| *n.* **1.** A piece of land on which trees are grown for their fruit. **2.** A group of such trees.

or•ches•tra |ôr′kĭ strə| *n.* **1. a.** A group, usually fairly large, of musicians who play together on various instruments, generally including string, woodwind, brass, and percussion instruments. **b.** The instruments played by such a group of musicians. **2.** In a theater, the area where the musicians sit, in front of and below the stage. **3. a.** The main floor of a theater. **b.** The seats in the front part of the main floor of a theater. **—or•ches′tral** |ôr kĕs′trəl| *adj.*

or•ches•trate |ôr′kĭ strāt′| *v.* **or•ches•trat•ed, or•ches•trat•ing.** To prepare or arrange (music) for performance by an orchestra. **—or′ches•tra′tion** *n.*

or•chid |ôr′kĭd| *n.* **1. a.** Any of many related plants with irregularly shaped, often large and brightly colored flowers. **b.** The flower of such a plant. **2.** A light reddish purple. —*adj.* Light reddish purple. [SEE PICTURE]

or•dain |ôr dān′| *v.* **1.** To install as a minister, priest, or rabbi; confer holy orders upon. **2.** To order by means of superior authority; decree. **3.** To arrange or determine beforehand; predestine: *proclaiming that divine providence had ordained that their nation was to rule the world.* **—or•dain′ment** *n.*

or•deal |ôr dēl′| *n.* A very difficult or painful experience, especially one that tests a person's character or endurance.

or•der |ôr′dər| *n.* **1.** A condition or arrangement of parts or elements that permits proper functioning, appearance, etc.: *a machine a trifle out of order; put the captain's room in order.* **2. a.** A sequence or arrangement of things one after the other: *alphabetical order.* **b.** The established sequence or arrangement; proper or customary procedure: *the team's batting order.* **3.** A condition in society marked by rule of law or custom; peaceful observance of prescribed regulations: *when law and order came to the frontier.* **4.** A command or direction: *a court order.* **5. a.** A commission or direction to buy, sell, or supply something: *a government order for 10,000 blankets.* **b.** The thing supplied, bought, or sold: *unwilling to ship orders C.O.D.* **6.** A portion of food in a restaurant: *an order of fried potatoes.* **7. orders. a.** The position and rank of an ordained minister or priest. **b.** The ceremony of admission into the priesthood or ministry. **8. Order.** A monastic organization or institution: *the Order of St. Benedict.* **9.** A social organization or club: *the Benevolent and Protective Order of Elks.* **10.** Often **Order.** A group of persons upon whom a government has conferred honor for unusual service or merit, or an emblem of such honor: *the Order of the Garter.* **11.** Degree of quality or importance; rank; distinction: *work of the highest order.* **12.** Any of several styles of ancient Greek and Roman architecture distinguished by the type of column employed: *Corinthian order.* **13.** A group of animals or plants that are similar in many ways, ranking between a class and a family. Rodents such as rats, mice, hamsters, and beavers belong to the same order. —*v.* **1.** To issue a command or an instruction to: *ordered the company to attention.* **2.** To command or direct that something be done: *ordered a review of the budget.* **3.** To give an order for; request to be supplied with: *order groceries for the week.* **4.** To arrange in a sequence; put into an order: *order books according to library procedure.* **5.** To manage, direct, or regulate: *order one's affairs.*

***Idioms.* in order to.** For the purpose of; so that. **in short order.** Quickly; without delay. **on order.** Requested or purchased but not yet delivered: *a case of nails on order.* **on the order of.** Similar to; like; resembling: *on the order of a light opera.* **out of order.** Not according to rule or acceptable procedure: *a parliamentary motion that was out of order.* **to order.** According to the buyer's specifications: *a suit made to order.*

ordered pair. A pair of numbers, one of which is considered to be the first and the other the second, that may not be interchanged.

or•der•ly |ôr′dər lē| *adj.* **1.** Well arranged or managed; neat; efficient: *an orderly kitchen; an orderly disposition of his legal affairs.* **2.** Without violence or disruption; peaceful: *our right to assemble and protest in an orderly manner.* —*n.*,

oratory[1-2]

Latin ōrāre, *"to speak," had two distinct meanings: (1) "to speak in public, to address a crowd," and (2) "to pray." In sense (1) it formed* ōrātiō, *"speech,"* ōrātor, *"speaker," and* (ars) ōrātōria, *"(the art of) public speaking"; from these we have* **oration, orator,** *and* **oratory**[1]. *In sense (2) it formed* ōrātōrium, *"a place for praying," from which we have* **oratory**[2].

orchid

Above: Showy tropical orchid
Below: Wild North American orchid

organ

organism
For a long time, scientists divided **organisms** *into only two kinds, the plants and the animals. More recently, they have added another group, the protists, which includes many single-celled organisms, such as the protozoans or bacteria, that cannot readily be classified as plants or animals.*

Orient/Occident
Orient *is from Latin* oriēns, *"rising sun," from the present participle of* orīrī, *"to rise."* **Occident** *is from Latin* occidēns, *"setting sun," from the present participle of* occidere, *"to set, to go down."*

ă pat/ā pay/â care/ä father/ĕ pet/ē be/ĭ pit/ī pie/î fierce/ŏ pot/ō go/ô paw, for/oi oil/ŏŏ book/ōō boot/ou out/ŭ cut/û fur/*th* the/th thin/hw which/zh vision/ə ago, item, pencil, atom, circus

pl. **or•der•lies. 1.** A male attendant in a hospital. **2.** A soldier assigned to a superior officer to carry orders or messages. **—or'der•li•ness** *n.*

Order of the Garter. In Great Britain, the highest order of knighthood.

or•di•nal |ôr'dn əl| *adj.* Corresponding in order to a particular one of the natural numbers: *an ordinal rank of seventh.* **—n.** An **ordinal number.**

ordinal number. A number whose most important property is that it corresponds in order to one of the natural numbers. For example, *first, sixth,* etc., are ordinal numbers.

or•di•nance |ôr'dn əns| *n.* A municipal statute or regulation.

or•di•nar•i•ly |ôr'dn âr'ə lē| *or* |ôr'dn ĕr'-| *adv.* As a general rule; usually: *Milk is ordinarily gotten from cows.*

or•di•nar•y |ôr'dn ĕr'ē| *adj.* **1.** Commonly encountered; usual; normal: *when the creek drained back to its ordinary size.* **2.** Average in rank or merit; of no exceptional degree or quality; commonplace: *The child of quite ordinary parents may be a genius.*

ordinary seaman. A seaman of the lowest grade in the merchant marine.

or•di•nate |ôr'dn ĭt| *or* |-āt'| *n.* In a system of plane Cartesian coordinates, the second coordinate, that is, the number that is the measure of the distance, measured parallel to the y-axis, between a point and the x-axis.

or•di•na•tion |ôr'dn ā'shən| *n.* **1.** The ceremony by which a person is admitted to the ministry of a church. **2.** The act of installing in the ministry.

ord•nance |ôrd'nəns| *n.* Military supplies, including weapons, ammunition, and maintenance equipment.

Or•do•vi•cian |ôr'də vĭsh'ən| *n.* Also **Ordovician period.** A geologic period that began about 500 million years ago and ended about 400 million years ago, characterized by the appearance of primitive fishes. **—modifier:** *an Ordovician sedimentary deposit.*

ore |ôr| *or* |ōr| *n.* A mineral or rock from which a valuable substance, especially a metal, can be extracted at a reasonable cost. ¶*These sound alike* **ore, oar, o'er, or.**

Oreg. Oregon.

o•reg•a•no |ə rĕg'ə nō'| *or* |ô rĕg'-| *n.* An herb similar to marjoram, having spicy, rather strong-tasting leaves used as flavoring for food.

Or•e•gon |ôr'ə gən| *or* |-gŏn'| *or* |ŏr'-|. A Pacific Northwestern state of the United States. Population, 2,225,000. Capital, Salem. **—Or'e•go'ni•an** |ôr'ə gō'nē ən| *or* |ŏr'-| *adj.* & *n.*

Oregon Trail. The main wagon route to the Oregon country for settlers from the East in the 1840's.

or•gan |ôr'gən| *n.* **1.** A musical instrument consisting of a number of pipes that sound the tones of a musical scale when supplied with air, and a keyboard that operates a mechanism controlling the flow of air to the pipes. **2.** Any of various instruments that are like or designed to imitate the organ, either in tone or mechanism: *an electronic organ.* **3.** A distinct part of a living thing, adapted for a particular function: *the stomach and other organs of digestion.* **4.** A body or agency that is part of a larger organization: *The General Assembly is one of the six major organs of the United Nations.* **5.** A periodical published by a political party, business firm, etc. **—modifier:** *organ music.* [SEE PICTURE]

or•gan•dy, also **or•gan•die** |ôr'gən dē| *n., pl.* **or•gan•dies.** A light, sheer, crisp cotton cloth used for dresses, curtains, trimmings, etc.

or•gan•ic |ôr găn'ĭk| *adj.* **1.** Of or affecting an organ or organs of a living thing. **2.** Of or derived from living things: *decaying organic matter.* **3.** Of, involving, or indicating compounds of carbon. **4.** Of, grown by, involving, or indicating methods of gardening or farming and food processing in which artificial chemical fertilizers, insect poisons, and food additives are not used. **—or•gan'i•cal•ly** *adv.*

organic chemistry. The chemistry of carbon compounds.

or•gan•ism |ôr'gə nĭz'əm| *n.* Any living thing; a plant or animal. [SEE NOTE]

or•gan•ist |ôr'gə nĭst| *n.* A person who plays the organ.

or•gan•i•za•tion |ôr'gə nĭ zā'shən| *n.* **1.** The act of organizing: *planning the organization of a rally.* **2.** The condition of being organized: *a high degree of organization.* **3.** The way in which something is organized: *studying the organization of American business corporations.* **4.** A number of people, groups, nations, etc., united for some purpose or work: *a political organization.*

or•gan•ize |ôr'gə nīz'| *v.* **or•gan•ized, or•gan•iz•ing. 1.** To put together or arrange in an orderly, systematic way: *organize one's thoughts before speaking.* **2.** To form a group in order to work together for a particular purpose: *organize a club; organize a football team. We'll never get anywhere unless we organize.* **3. a.** To cause (employees) to form or join a labor union: *organize farm workers.* **b.** To cause the employees of (a factory or industry) to form or join a labor union: *organize the shoe industry.* **—or'gan•ized'** *adj.: organized labor.* **—or'gan•iz'er** *n.*

or•gan•za |ôr găn'zə| *n.* A sheer, stiff fabric used for evening dresses, trimmings, etc.

or•gasm |ôr'găz'əm| *n.* The climax of sexual excitement.

or•gy |ôr'jē| *n., pl.* **or•gies.** A wild, drunken, and often indecent party or celebration.

o•ri•ent |ôr'ē ĕnt'| *or* |ōr'-| *v.* **1.** To set or arrange in a position relative to the points of the compass: *orient the swimming pool north and south.* **2.** To familiarize (someone) with a new or unfamiliar situation: *a book designed to help orient new students.*

O•ri•ent |ôr'ē ənt| *or* |-ĕnt'| *or* |ōr'-| *n.* **1. orient.** The east; eastern lands. **2.** The countries of eastern Asia; the Far East. [SEE NOTE]

O•ri•en•tal |ôr'ē ĕn'tl| *or* |ōr'-| *adj.* **1. oriental.** Eastern. **2.** Of the Orient or any of its peoples. **—n. 1.** A native of the Orient. **2.** A person of Oriental descent.

or•i•en•tate |ôr'ē ĕn tāt'| *or* |-ən-| *or* |ōr'-| *v.* **or•i•en•tat•ed, or•i•en•tat•ing.** To orient.

o•ri•en•ta•tion |ôr'ē ĕn tā'shən| *or* |-ən-| *or* |ōr'-| *n.* **1.** Location or position with respect to the points of the compass or some system of coordinates: *the orientation of a rocket in space.* **2.** A person's awareness of the outside world in relation to himself. **3.** Introductory instruction for people in a new place or situation: *orientation for incoming freshmen.* —**modifier:** *an orientation session for freshmen.*

or•i•fice |ôr'ə fĭs'| *or* |ŏr'-| *n.* A mouth or vent; an opening into a cavity.

or•i•gin |ôr'ə jĭn| *or* |ŏr'-| *n.* **1.** The beginning or coming into being of something: *the origin of life; the origin of a word.* **2.** The original source or cause of something: *the origin of a fire.* **3.** Parentage or ancestry: *people of Swedish origin.* **4.** That one of the two points of attachment of a muscle at which there is the least motion. **5.** The point at which the axes of a coordinate system intersect.

o•rig•i•nal |ə rĭj'ə nəl| *adj.* **1.** Existing from the beginning: *the original thirteen states of the Union.* **2.** Fresh and newly created; not copied or based on something else: *an original screenplay.* **3.** Frequently producing new ideas: *an original thinker.* **4.** Being that from which a copy or translation is made: *an original painting by a great master; a book in the original German.* —*n.* The first form of anything from which varieties arise or are made: *Later models retained many features of the original.*

o•rig•i•nal•i•ty |ə rĭj'ə **năl'**ĭ tē| *n.* Freshness or creativity: *a work of great originality.*

o•rig•i•nal•ly |ə **rĭj'**ə nə lē| *adv.* **1.** At first; in the beginning: *This dress was originally priced at $25.* **2.** By origin: *I am originally from Oklahoma.*

o•rig•i•nate |ə **rĭj'**ə nāt'| *v.* **o•rig•i•nat•ed, o•rig•i•nat•ing.** To bring or come into being: *The ancient Greeks originated the cymbal. The idea of mass production originated in America.* —**o•rig'i•na'tor** *n.*

O•ri•no•co |ôr'ə **nō'**kō| *or* |ōr'-|. A river in Venezuela flowing into the Atlantic Ocean.

o•ri•ole |ôr'ē ōl'| *or* |ōr'-| *n.* Any of several songbirds that have black and yellow or black and orange feathers and that often build hanging nests. [SEE PICTURE]

O•ri•on |ō **rī'**ən| *n.* A constellation near the celestial equator containing several bright stars.

Ork•ney Islands |**ôrk'**nē|. A group of islands off the northern coast of Scotland.

Or•lon |**ôr'**lŏn'| *n.* A trademark for a synthetic fiber that is used in a variety of fabrics.

or•na•ment |**ôr'**nə mənt| *n.* Something that adorns or makes more attractive or beautiful; a decoration. —*v.* |**ôr'**nə mənt'|. To supply or furnish with ornaments; decorate: *ornament a carriage with gold.*

or•na•men•tal |ôr'nə **mĕn'**tl| *adj.* Serving to adorn or ornament: *ornamental jewelry; ornamental plants.*

or•na•men•ta•tion |ôr'nə mĕn **tā'**shən| *n.* **1.** The act of ornamenting. **2.** Something that ornaments or adorns; a decoration.

or•nate |ôr **nāt'**| *adj.* Made with lavish or elaborate decorations: *an ornate palace.* —**or•nate'ly** *adv.* —**or•nate'ness** *n.*

or•ner•y |**ôr'**nə rē| *adj.* **or•ner•i•er, or•ner•i•est.** *Informal.* Mean and stubborn: *an ornery child.*

or•ni•thol•o•gist |ôr'nə **thŏl'**ə jĭst| *n.* A scientist who specializes in ornithology.

or•ni•thol•o•gy |ôr' nə **thŏl'**ə jē| *n.* The scientific study of birds.

o•ro•tund |**ôr'**ə tŭnd'| *or* |**ōr'**-| *adj.* **1.** Full, clear, and strong: *an orotund voice.* **2.** High-sounding; pompous: *orotund talk.*

or•phan |**ôr'**fən| *n.* A child whose parents are dead or, less often, one of whose parents is dead. —**modifier:** *an orphan child; an orphan home.* —*v.* To make (a child) an orphan: *The fire orphaned my best friend.*

or•phan•age |**ôr'**fə nĭj| *n.* A public institution for the care and protection of orphans and abandoned children.

Or•phe•us |**ôr'**fē əs| *or* |-fyōōs'|. In Greek mythology, a poet and musician who tried to bring his wife back from the underworld but lost her by looking back at her shadow.

or•ris•root |**ôr'**ĭs rōōt'| *or* |-rŏŏt'| *or* |**ŏr'**-| *n.* The fragrant root of a kind of iris, used in dried, powdered form for making perfume, sachets, etc.

or•thi•con |**ôr'**thĭ kŏn'| *n.* A type of television camera tube in which a beam of low-velocity electrons is swept over a light-sensitive surface.

or•tho•clase |**ôr'**thə klās'| *or* |-klāz'| *n.* A type of feldspar found in igneous rock.

or•tho•don•tia |ôr'thə **dŏn'**shə| *n.* The dental practice of correcting abnormal position or alignment of the teeth. [SEE NOTE]

or•tho•don•tics |(ôr'thə **dŏn'**tĭks)| *n.* (*used with a singular verb*). Orthodontia.

or•tho•don•tist |ôr'thə **dŏn'**tĭst| *n.* A dentist who specializes in orthodontia.

or•tho•dox |**ôr'**thə dŏks'| *adj.* **1.** Adhering to basic and officially approved doctrines or beliefs: *orthodox theology.* **2.** Following conventional or traditional practice or custom: *orthodox ideas.* **3. Orthodox. a.** Of the Eastern Orthodox Church. **b.** Of that branch of Judaism that adheres strictly to traditional custom.

or•tho•dox•y |**ôr'**thə dŏk'sē| *n.* Adherence to traditional practice, custom, or belief.

or•thog•o•nal |ôr **thŏg'**ə nəl| *adj.* Of, containing, or forming right angles: *orthogonal lines.*

or•tho•graph•ic |ôr'thə **grăf'**ĭk| *adj.* Having to do with the way a word is spelled. —**or'tho•graph'i•cal•ly** *adv.*

or•thog•ra•phy |ôr **thŏg'**rə fē| *n.* **1.** Correct spelling. **2.** The study of spelling.

or•tho•pe•dics |ôr'thə **pē'**dĭks| *n.* (*used with a singular verb*). The correction or treatment, by surgery or manipulation, of disorders or injuries of the bones, joints, and associated muscles.

or•tho•ped•ist |ôr'thə **pē'**dĭst| *n.* A physician who specializes in orthopedics.

-ory[1]. A suffix that forms nouns and means "a place of or for": **reformatory.**

-ory[2]. A suffix that forms adjectives and means "of, involving, or tending toward": **compensatory.**

or•yx |**ôr'**ĭks| *or* |**ōr'**-| *n.* An antelope of Africa and southwestern Asia, having long, sharp, backward-slanting horns.

Os The symbol for the element osmium.

O•sage |**ō'**sāj'| *or* |ō **sāj'**| *n., pl.* **O•sage** or **O•sag•es. 1.** A North American Indian tribe formerly living in the region between the Missouri and Arkansas rivers. **2.** A member of this tribe. **3.** The Siouan language of this tribe.

O•sa•ka |ō **sä'**kə|. The second-largest city in Japan. Population, 2,889,000.

os•cil•late |**ŏs'**ə lāt'| *v.* **os•cil•lat•ed, os•cil•lat•ing.** To move or vary back and forth about a central or average position or value: *a pendulum that oscillates.*

oriole

orthodontia, etc.
The prefix ortho- *is from Greek* orthos, *"right, correct, straight";* **orthodontia** *is the straightening of teeth,* **orthodox** *is following the right doctrine,* **orthogonal** *pertains to right (or upright) angles,* **orthography** *is correct spelling, and* **orthopedics** *is corrective therapy.*

ostrich

otter

ounce[1·2]
Ounce[1] *is from Old French* unce, *which is from Latin* uncia, *"unit, one-twelfth part," from* ūnus, *"one."* Uncia *meant both "one twelfth of a pound" and "one twelfth of a foot"; in the latter meaning it was separately borrowed into Old English as* ince, *becoming Modern English* **inch**. **Ounce[2]** *is from Old French* once; *this word was originally* lonce, *but the* l *was mistaken for the definite article* le, *as if* lonce *were* l'once *(for an equivalent in English, see note at* **apron**); lonce *is from Latin* lynx, *"lynx."*

ă pat/ā pay/â care/ä father/ĕ pet/ ē be/ĭ pit/ī pie/î fierce/ŏ pot/ ō go/ô paw, for/oi oil/ŏŏ book/ ōō boot/ou out/ŭ cut/û fur/ *th* the/th thin/hw which/zh vision/ ə ago, item, pencil, atom, circus

os•cil•la•tion |ŏs'ə **lā'**shən| *n.* **1.** The act, process, or condition of oscillating. **2.** A single cycle of motion or variation about a central position. **3.** A wave, especially an electromagnetic wave: *oscillations that are visible in the form of light.*

os•cil•la•tor |**ŏs'**ə lā'tər| *n.* Something that oscillates, especially a device that produces electromagnetic waves or an alternating current.

os•cil•lo•scope |ə **sĭl'**ə skōp'| *n.* An electronic instrument that produces on a cathode-ray tube a visual display representing an oscillation or electric current.

–ose. A suffix that forms adjectives and means "having or similar to": **grandiose.**

o•sier |**ō'**zhər| *n.* **1.** A willow with long, slender, flexible twigs used in making baskets, wicker furniture, etc. **2.** A twig of such a willow.

O•si•ris |ō **sī'**rĭs|. The ancient Egyptian god of death and resurrection.

–osis. A suffix that forms nouns and means: **1.** Action or process: **osmosis. 2.** Diseased condition: **tuberculosis.**

Os•lo |**ŏz'**lō| *or* |**ŏs'**-|. The capital of Norway. Population, 488,000.

os•mi•um |**ŏz'**mē əm| *n.* Symbol **Os** One of the elements, a hard, bluish-white metal. Atomic number 76; atomic weight 190.2; valences +2, +3, +4, +8; melting point 3,000°C; boiling point 5,000°C.

os•mo•sis |ŏz **mō'**sĭs| *or* |ŏs-| *n.* **1.** A process in which fluids and substances dissolved in liquids pass through a membrane until all substances involved are present in equal concentrations on both sides of the membrane. **2.** The tendency of fluids to carry on this process.

os•mot•ic |ŏz **mŏt'**ĭk| *or* |ŏs-| *adj.* Of or involving osmosis. **—os•mot'i•cal•ly** *adv.*

os•prey |**ŏs'**prē| *n., pl.* **os•preys.** A large, fish-eating hawk with blackish and white feathers.

os•si•fy |**ŏs'**ə fī'| *v.* **os•si•fied, os•si•fy•ing, os•si•fies.** To change into bone; make or become bony or bonelike. **—os'si•fi•ca'tion** *n.*

os•ten•si•ble |ə **stĕn'**sə bəl| *adj.* Seeming or stated to be such, but often not actually so; pretended: *His ostensible purpose was charity, his real goal popularity.* **—os•ten'si•bly** *adv.*

os•ten•ta•tion |ŏs'tĕn **tā'**shən| *or* |-tən-| *n.* Showy, unnecessary display of wealth meant to impress others.

os•ten•ta•tious |ŏs'tĕn **tā'**shəs| *or* |-tən-| *adj.* Elaborately showy so as to impress others: *an ostentatious party.* **—os'ten•ta'tious•ly** *adv.*

os•te•o•path |**ŏs'**tē ə păth'| *n.* A physician who practices osteopathy.

os•te•op•a•thy |ŏs'tē **ŏp'**ə thē| *n.* A form of medical practice that stresses the use of manipulation in correcting body abnormalities that are thought to cause disease and slow recovery.

ost•mark |**ôst'**märk'| *or* |**ŏst'**-| *n., pl.* **ost•marks.** The basic unit of money of the German Democratic Republic.

os•tra•cism |**ŏs'**trə sĭz'əm| *n.* Banishment or exclusion from a group, organization, or society in general.

os•tra•cize |**ŏs'**trə sīz'| *v.* **os•tra•cized, os•tra•ciz•ing.** To banish or exclude from a group or from society.

os•trich |**ŏs'**trĭch| *or* |**ô'**strĭch| *n.* A very large, long-legged, long-necked African bird that cannot fly but can run very fast. Its long, soft plumes are used for decoration or for making fans, feather dusters, etc. [SEE PICTURE]

oth•er |**ŭth'**ər| *adj.* **1. a.** Being the remaining one of two or more: *Let me look at the other shoe.* **b.** Being the remaining ones of several: *My other friends are away on vacation.* **2.** Different: *Call me some other time. Any other kid would have run away.* **3.** Just recent or past: *the other day.* **4.** Additional; extra: *I have no other clothes than what I'm wearing.* **5.** Opposite or reverse: *Turn the sheet over and look at the other side.* **6.** Alternate; second: *We play tennis every other day.* —*n.* **1. a.** The remaining one of two or more: *One took a taxi, a second took the subway, and the other walked home.* **b. others.** The remaining ones of several: *How are the others doing now that I'm gone?* **2. a.** A different person or thing: *one hurricane after the other.* **b.** An additional person or thing: *If these are only a few of the guests, how many others are you expecting?* —*pron.* Another person or thing: *The mayor's out at the airport welcoming some V.I.P. or other.* —*adv.* Otherwise: *He soon found that he would never succeed other than by work.*

oth•er•wise |**ŭth'**ər wīz'| *adv.* **1.** In another way; differently: *She could not behave otherwise.* **2.** Under other circumstances, especially without some specified action or condition: *Experiments make clear some things which you might not understand otherwise.* **3.** In other respects: *A light shone in one window, but otherwise that side of the house was dark.* —*adj.* Other than supposed; different: *The truth of the matter was otherwise.*

Ot•ta•wa[1] |**ŏt'**ə wə| *or* |-wä'| *or* |-wô'|. The capital of Canada. Population, 290,000.

Ot•ta•wa[2] |**ŏt'**ə wə| *or* |-wä'| *or* |-wô'| *n., pl.* **Ot•ta•wa** or **Ot•ta•was. 1.** A North American Indian tribe of Ontario. **2.** A member of this tribe. **3.** The Algonquian language of this tribe.

ot•ter |**ŏt'**ər| *n.* **1.** A weasellike animal that lives in or near water and has webbed feet and thick, dark-brown fur. **2.** The fur of such an animal. [SEE PICTURE]

ot•to•man |**ŏt'**ə mən| *n.* **1.** A low, backless, armless seat or sofa. **2.** A cushioned footstool. **3.** A heavy fabric with a distinct crosswise rib. **4. Ottoman.** A Turk. —*adj.* **Ottoman.** Turkish.

Oua•ga•dou•gou |wä'gə **dōō'**gōō|. The capital of Upper Volta. Population, 115,000.

ouch |ouch| *interj.* A word used to express sudden pain.

ought |ôt| *v.* —Used as an auxiliary to indicate: **1.** Obligation or duty: *We ought to feed her.* **2. a.** Expediency: *Maybe we ought to try something else for bait.* **b.** Prudence: *The doctor said he ought to get plenty of rest.* **3.** Reasonable expectation: *a cashier who knew how much ought to be in the register.* **4.** Desirability: *We ought to go swimming every day!* **5.** Probability; likelihood: *Tonight ought to be a good night for looking at the stars.* ¶*These sound alike* **ought, aught.**

ounce[1] |ouns| *n.* **1. a.** A unit of avoirdupois weight equal to $^1/_{16}$ pound and containing 16 drams or 437.5 grains. **b.** A unit of apothecary weight equal to 1.097 avoirdupois ounces. **2.** A unit of volume or capacity used to measure liquids, equal to $^1/_{16}$ pint and containing 8 fluid drams or 1.804 cubic inches. [SEE NOTE]

ounce² |ouns| *n.* The **snow leopard.** [SEE NOTE on p. 630]

our |our| *pron.* A possessive form of **we,** used before a noun as a modifier. **1.** Of or belonging to us: *our problems; our automobile.* **2.** Done or performed by us: *our homework.* **3.** Received by us as an action: *our greatest setback.* ¶ *These sound alike* **our, hour.**

ours |ourz| *pron.* A possessive form of **we. 1.** —Used to indicate that someone or something belongs or pertains to us: *He is an acquaintance of ours. This responsibility is ours.* **2.** —Used to indicate the one or ones belonging to us: *Ours was the only town damaged by the flood.* —*Note: Ours* and *our* both show possession or ownership. They differ in that *our* is always used before a noun as a modifier; *ours* is never so used, but takes the place of a noun or pronoun.

our•selves |our sĕlvz'| *or* |är-| *pron.* A special form of **us.** It is used: **1.** In place of *us,* serving as a direct object, indirect object, or object of a preposition, to show that the action of a reflexive verb refers back to the subject: *We disgraced ourselves* (direct object). *We caused ourselves* (indirect object) *much trouble. Let's keep it to ourselves* (object of a preposition). **2.** Following or referring to a noun or the pronoun *we,* to give emphasis: *We made the cake ourselves. We ourselves can help.* **3.** Referring to the subject, to mean *our real, normal, or healthy selves: We thought we would never be ourselves again after the trouble.*

***Idiom.* by ourselves. 1.** Alone: *We're going by ourselves.* **2.** Without help: *We'll make that decision by ourselves.*

-ous. A suffix that forms adjectives and means "full of or having": **joyous.**

oust |oust| *v.* To eject; force out: *oust an official from office.*

oust•er |ous'tər| *n.* An example of ousting or being ousted: *The king attributed his ouster to a small revolutionary group.*

out |out| *adv.* **1.** Away or forth from inside: *going out of the house.* **2.** Away from the center or middle: *The searchers spread out.* **3.** Away from a usual place: *She's stepped out for a minute.* **4.** To depletion or extinction: *Supplies ran out.* **5.** Into being or view: *The moon came out.* **6.** Without inhibition; boldly: *Speak out.* **7.** Into disuse or an unfashionable status: *Bloomers went out a long time ago.* **8.** So as to be retired in baseball: *He was struck out.* —*adj.* **1.** In disrepair: *The road is out beyond this point.* **2.** Not available; not to be considered: *A taxi is out because we're broke.* **3.** Bare or threadbare: *His jacket is out at the elbow.* **4.** In baseball, retired from play. —*prep.* **1.** Through; forth from: *falling out the window.* **2.** Beyond or outside of: *Out this door is the garage.* —*n.* **1.** Often **outs.** Those having no power or inside influence: *the outs versus the ins.* **2.** A means of escaping from something: *His lawyer discovered an ingenious out for him.* **3.** Any play in which a batter or base runner is retired in baseball.

out-. A prefix meaning: **1.** To a superior degree: **outwit. 2.** Located outside: **outdoors.**

out-and-out |out'n out'| *adj.* Complete; utter: *an out-and-out liar.*

out•bid |out bĭd'| *v.* **-bid, -bid•den** |-bĭd'n| or **bid.** To bid higher than: *He outbid his opponents.*

out-board motor |out'bôrd'| *or* |-bōrd'|. A removable propulsion unit mounted at the stern of a boat, consisting of a gasoline engine linked to a propeller. [SEE PICTURE]

out•bound |out'bound'| *adj.* Outward bound; headed away: *the outbound train.*

out•break |out'brāk'| *n.* A sudden eruption: *an outbreak of violence; an outbreak of disease.*

out•build•ing |out'bĭl'dĭng| *n.* A building that is separate from a main building.

out•burst |out'bûrst'| *n.* A sudden, violent display, as of activity or emotion; flare-up: *an outburst of laughter.*

out•cast |out'kăst'| *or* |-käst'| *n.* A person who has been excluded from a society or system. —*adj.* Cast out; driven out; rejected.

out•class |out klăs'| *or* |-kläs'| *v.* To surpass or excel to such a degree as to be clearly of a different class: *He completely outclassed his opponents.*

out•come |out'kŭm'| *n.* A final result: *the outcome of an election.*

out•crop |out'krŏp'| *n.* A piece of bedrock or other rock from a lower stratum that extends up above the level of the soil.

out•cry |out'krī'| *n., pl.* **out•cries. 1.** A loud cry or clamor. **2.** A strong protest: *The rise in prices provoked a loud public outcry.*

out•dat•ed |out dā'tĭd| *adj.* Out-of-date; no longer used or applicable to the present time: *outdated methods of farming.*

out•dis•tance |out dĭs'təns| *v.* **-dis•tanced, -dis•tanc•ing. 1.** To outrun, as in a long-distance race. **2.** To surpass by a wide margin.

out•do |out dō'| *v.* **-did** |-dĭd'|, **-done** |-dŭn'|, **-do•ing.** To surpass in performance; do better than: *a man not to be outdone by anyone.*

out•door |out'dôr'| *or* |-dōr'| *adj.* **1.** Located in, done in, or suitable for the outdoors: *outdoor clothing; an outdoor fireplace.* **2.** Fond of the outdoors: *She was never the outdoor type.*

out•doors |out dôrz'| *or* |-dōrz'| *adv.* In or into the open air; outside a house or building: *eat outdoors.* —*n.* Any area outside a house or building in the open air.

out•er |out'ər| *adj.* **1.** Located on the outside; external: *outer garments; the outer wall of a fortress.* **2.** Farther from the center: *the outer limits of the universe.*

outer ear. The external part of the ear, consisting of the structure that projects from the side of the head and the canal that leads to the middle ear.

out•er•most |out'ər mōst'| *adj.* Most distant from the center.

outer space. Space beyond the limits of a celestial body or system.

out•field |out'fēld'| *n.* **1.** The grass-covered playing area extending outward from a baseball diamond, divided into right, center, and left fields. **2.** The members of a baseball team playing in the outfield. —**out'field'er** *n.*

out•fit |out'fĭt'| *n.* **1.** A set of equipment for a particular purpose: *a diving outfit.* **2.** A set of clothing and accessories that go together: *She wore a pretty tweed outfit.* **3.** A military unit, business organization, or other association: *an infantry outfit. That team is a pretty tough outfit.* —*v.* **-fit•ted, -fit•ting.** To furnish with the nec-

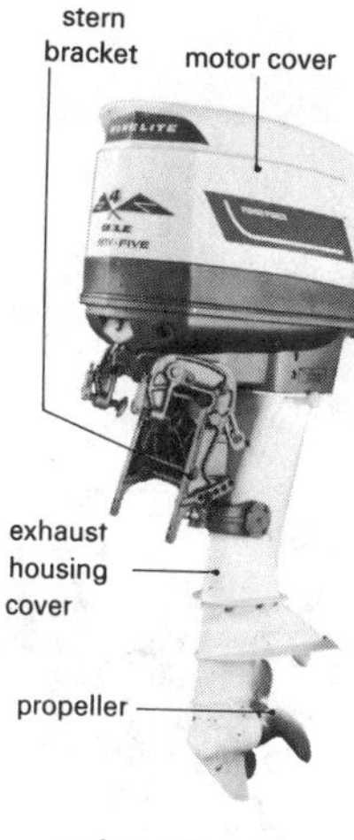

outboard motor

outlaw
In early Anglo-Saxon law, when a person was declared "outside the law" he lost all legal standing; he no longer had the right to own property, and if anyone killed him it was not considered to be murder.

outrigger
The **outrigger** seems to have been invented by the seagoing peoples of the Pacific islands; the picture shows a Tahitian canoe.

ă pat/ā pay/â care/ä father/ĕ pet/ ē be/ĭ pit/ī pie/î fierce/ŏ pot/ ō go/ô paw, for/oi oil/ŏŏ book/ ōō boot/ou out/ŭ cut/û fur/ *th* the/th thin/hw which/zh vision/ ə ago, item, pencil, atom, circus

essary equipment or clothing: *outfit a ship for an expedition.* —**out'fit'ter** *n.*

out•go |**out'**gō'| *n.* Something that goes out, especially money spent.

out•go•ing |**out'**gō'ĭng| *adj.* **1.** Leaving; departing: *an outgoing steamship.* **2.** To be taken out: *an outgoing order.* **3.** Friendly; sociable: *an outgoing person.*

out•grow |out **grō'**| *v.* **-grew** |-**grōō'**|, **-grown** |-**grōn'**|, **-grow•ing. 1.** To grow too large for: *He outgrew his shoes.* **2.** To discard in the course of growing up or maturing: *She outgrew dolls.* **3.** To grow larger than: *He outgrew his father.*

out•growth |**out'**grōth'| *n.* **1.** Something that grows out of something else: *an outgrowth on a tree branch.* **2.** A result or effect: *Our current musicals are an outgrowth of the early operettas.*

out•guess |out **gĕs'**| *v.* To guess or anticipate correctly and thus outwit or gain an advantage.

out•house |**out'**hous'| *n., pl.* **-hous•es** |-hou'zĭz|. A toilet in a small structure separate from a main building.

out•ing |**ou'**tĭng| *n.* An excursion or walk outdoors for pleasure.

out•land•ish |out **lăn'**dĭsh| *adj.* Unconventionally strange in appearance or manner: *outlandish clothes.*

out•last |out **lăst'**| *or* |-**läst'**| *v.* To exist, endure, or last longer than.

out•law |**out'**lô'| *n.* **1.** A person who defies the law; a declared criminal. **2.** A person who is excluded from normal legal protection. —*v.* **1.** To declare illegal. **2.** To deprive of the protection of the law. [SEE NOTE]

out•lay |**out'**lā'| *n.* **1.** The act of spending money. **2.** The total amount spent: *The total outlay was $50.*

out•let |**out'**lĕt'| *or* |-lĭt| *n.* **1.** A passage or opening for letting something out; a vent. **2.** A means of reaching the outside: *The city lacks an outlet to the sea.* **3.** A means of releasing energies, desires, etc.: *Music was an outlet for her talent.* **4.** A store or other commercial enterprise through which a manufacturer sells his goods: *a retail outlet.* **5.** An electric receptacle, especially one that is mounted in a wall, connected to a power line, and equipped with a socket for a plug.

out•line |**out'**līn'| *n.* **1.** A line forming the outer edge, limit, or boundary of something. **2.** A drawing that consists of only the outer edge of an object: *Trace an outline of California from the map.* **3.** A short summary, description, or account, usually arranged point by point: *an outline for a composition.* **4. outlines.** The general features of a given subject: *the broad outlines of the contract.* —***modifier:*** *an outline map.* —*v.* **-lined, -lin•ing. 1.** To draw the outline of: *outline a picture before drawing in the details.* **2.** To give the main points of; summarize: *outline a plan.*

out•live |out **lĭv'**| *v.* **-lived, -liv•ing.** To live or last longer than.

out•look |**out'**lŏŏk'| *n.* **1.** A place from which something can be viewed: *a photograph taken from an outlook high in the mountains.* **2.** A point of view or mental attitude: *a happy outlook on life.* **3.** The probable situation or result; the prospects: *the weather outlook for tomorrow.*

out•ly•ing |**out'**lī'ĭng| *adj.* Lying outside the limits or boundaries of a certain area: *factories being built in the outlying suburbs.*

out•mod•ed |out **mō'**dĭd| *adj.* **1.** No longer in fashion: *an outmoded style of dress.* **2.** No longer practical: *outmoded methods of production.*

out•num•ber |out **nŭm'**bər| *v.* To be more numerous than; exceed in number.

out-of-date |**out'**əv **dāt'**| *adj.* Outmoded; old-fashioned.

out-of-door |**out'**əv **dôr'**| *or* |-**dōr'**| *adj.* Outdoor.

out-of-doors |**out'**əv **dôrz'**| *or* |-**dōrz'**| *n.* Outdoors.

out-of-the-way |**out'**əv *thə* **wā'**| *adj.* Away from areas normally or frequently visited; remote: *an out-of-the-way place.*

out•pa•tient |**out'**pā'shənt| *n.* Someone who receives treatment at a hospital or clinic without being confined there. —***modifier:*** *an outpatient clinic.*

out•post |**out'**pōst'| *n.* **1.** A detachment of troops stationed at a distance from the main unit to warn of or prevent a surprise attack. **2.** A remote settlement: *an outpost in the wilderness.*

out•put |**out'**pŏŏt'| *n.* **1.** An amount of something produced, especially during a given period of time: *the output of a mine.* **2. a.** The energy, power, signal, work, etc., produced by a system or device: *the output of an engine; the output of a loudspeaker.* **b.** The point or place in the system from which this is taken: *the energy that appears at the output.* **3.** The information that a computer produces by processing a given collection of data.

out•rage |**out'**rāj'| *n.* **1.** An extremely vicious or wicked act. **2.** Great anger aroused by such an act: *public outrage over the incident.* —*v.* **out•raged, out•rag•ing. 1.** To give offense to: *Such an act outrages everyone's sense of justice.* **2.** To make extremely angry or resentful: *Everyone was outraged by his behavior.*

out•ra•geous |out **rā'**jəs| *adj.* Exceeding all bounds of what is right or proper; shocking; monstrous: *an outrageous crime; outrageous prices.* —**out•ra'geous•ly** *adv.*

out•rank |out **răngk'**| *v.* To rank above: *A colonel outranks a major.*

out•rig•ger |**out'**rĭg'ər| *n.* A long, thin float attached parallel to a seagoing canoe by projecting spars as a means of preventing it from capsizing. [SEE PICTURE]

out•right |**out'**rīt'| *adj.* Complete; unconditional; out-and-out: *an outright gift; an outright lie.* —*adv.* |**out'rīt'**| *or* |-rīt'|. **1.** Completely; unconditionally: *accepted his offer outright.* **2.** Openly; straight to one's face: *I decided to tell him the news outright.* **3.** Without delay; on the spot: *kill someone outright.*

out•run |out **rŭn'**| *v.* **-ran** |-**răn'**|, **-run, -run•ning. 1.** To run faster than: *He outran all his opponents.* **2.** To escape from; elude: *He outran three pursuing policemen.* **3.** To go beyond; exceed: *Expenses are outrunning those of last year.*

out•sell |out **sĕl'**| *v.* **-sold** |-**sōld'**|, **-sell•ing. 1.** To sell more than: *That store consistently outsells the others.* **2.** To sell faster or better than: *a new model car that has outsold all competition.*

out•set |**out'**sĕt'| *n.* The beginning; start.

out•shine |out **shīn'**| *v.* **-shone** |-**shōn'**|, **-shin•**

ing. 1. To shine brighter than. **2.** To be or appear better than: *He outshines his opponents.*

out•side |out **sīd′**| *or* |**out′**sīd′| *n.* **1.** The outer surface; exterior: *the outside of a house.* **2.** The external or surface aspect: *On the outside, it's very attractive.* —*adj.* **1.** Coming from without: *outside agitators.* **2.** External: *an outside door.* **3.** Apart from one's regular occupation: *outside free-lancing.* **4.** Maximum: *$5,000 is an outside estimate on that car.* **5.** Slight; remote: *an outside possibility.* —*adv.* On or to the outside: *going outside.* —*prep.* **1.** On or to the outer side of: *going outside the house.* **2.** Beyond the limits of: *going outside the country.* **3.** Except: *no information outside the figures already given.*

***Idioms.* at the outside.** At the most: *We'll be gone a week at the outside.* **outside of.** Outside: *He cared for nothing outside of his music.*

out•sid•er |out **sī′**dər| *n.* A person who is not part of a certain group or activity: *a gate to prevent outsiders from entering.*

out•skirts |**out′**skûrts′| *pl.n.* The regions away from a central district; the surrounding areas: *on the outskirts of town.*

out•spo•ken |out **spō′**kən| *adj.* **1.** Spoken without reserve: *outspoken remarks.* **2.** Frank and bold in speech: *an outspoken politician.* —**out•spo′ken•ly** *adv.* —**out•spo′ken•ness** *n.*

out•spread |**out′spred′**| *adj.* Spread out; extended.

out•stand•ing |out **stăn′**dĭng| *or* |**out′**stăn′-| *adj.* **1.** Standing out among others; prominent; distinguished: *one of the outstanding men of our age.* **2.** Exceptional; extraordinary: *a medal awarded for outstanding heroism on the battlefield.* **3.** Not settled or resolved: *outstanding debts.* —**out•stand′ing•ly** *adv.*

out•stretched |**out′strĕcht′**| *adj.* Spread or stretched out: *an outstretched hand.*

out•strip |out **strĭp′**| *v.* **-stripped, -strip•ping. 1.** To leave behind; outrun. **2.** To surpass: *Grain came to outstrip cattle in economic importance.*

out•ward |**out′**wərd| *adv.* Also **out•wards** |**out′**wərdz|. Away from the center. —*adj.* **1.** Toward the outside or exterior: *an outward flow of gold.* **2.** Visible on the surface: *an outward appearance of calm.* —**out′ward•ly** *adv.*

out•wear |out **wâr′**| *v.* **-wore** |**-wôr′**| *or* |**-wōr′**|, **-worn** |**-wôrn′**| *or* |**-wōrn′**|, **-wear•ing.** To wear or last longer than: *These shoes will outwear all others.*

out•weigh |out **wā′**| *v.* **1.** To weigh more than: *He outweighs everyone on the team.* **2.** To be of greater importance or significance than: *an objection that outweighs all others.*

out•wit |out **wĭt′**| *v.* **out•wit•ted, out•wit•ting.** To get the better of with cleverness or cunning.

ou•zel |**o͞o′**zəl| *n.* **1.** A European blackbird. **2.** See **water ouzel.**

o•va |**ō′**və| *n.* Plural of **ovum.**

o•val |**ō′**vəl| *adj.* **1.** Resembling an egg in shape: *an oval dish; an oval face.* **2.** Resembling an ellipse in shape. —*n.* An oval figure, form, structure, etc. [SEE PICTURE]

oval window. An oval-shaped opening that leads from the middle ear to the vestibule of the inner ear, normally filled by the base of the stirrup bone.

o•va•ry |**ō′**və rē| *n., pl.* **o•va•ries. 1.** Either of the reproductive glands of female animals, producing egg cells and various hormones. **2.** A plant part at the base of the pistil of a flower, in which the seeds are formed. [SEE PICTURE]

o•va•tion |ō **vā′**shən| *n.* A loud and enthusiastic display of approval, usually in the form of shouting or hearty applause.

ov•en |**ŭv′**ən| *n.* An enclosed chamber used for baking, heating, or drying objects.

ov•en•bird |**ŭv′**ən bûrd′| *n.* A small, brownish North American bird that has a noisy, repeated call and builds a dome-shaped nest on the ground.

o•ver |**ō′**vər| *prep.* **1.** Above: *a sign over the door.* **2.** On or above and across: *hop over the fence.* **3.** On the other side of: *a town over the border.* **4.** Upon: *a coat of varnish over the woodwork.* **5.** Throughout or during: *over the years.* **6.** Along the length of: *traveling over the same road.* **7.** In excess of; more than: *over ten miles.* **8.** While engaged in or partaking of: *a chat over coffee.* **9.** On account of or with reference to: *an argument over methods.* —*adv.* **1.** Above: *A plane flew over.* **2. a.** Across to another or opposite side: *flying over to Europe.* **b.** Across the edge or brim: *The coffee spilled over.* **3.** To a different opinion or allegiance: *winning over converts. Many came over.* **4.** To a different person, condition, or title: *signing land over to a bank.* **5.** So as to be completely covered: *The river froze over.* **6.** Through or thoroughly: *thinking it over.* **7. a.** From an upright position: *The ship keeled over.* **b.** From an upward to an inverted or reversed position: *Turn the book over.* **8. a.** Again: *He had to do his homework over.* **b.** In repetition: *He sang the same song ten times over.* **9.** In addition or excess: *staying a week over. I have a dollar left over.* —*adj.* **1.** Finished: *The movie is over.* **2.** In excess: *My guess was $50 over.* —*interj.* A word used in radio conversations to mark the end of a transmission.

over–. A prefix meaning: **1.** Superiority of rank: **overseer. 2.** Above or across: **overhead. 3.** Beyond a limit or boundary: **overestimate. 4.** To a lower or inferior position: **overturn.**

o•ver•a•chieve |ō′vər ə **chēv′**| *v.* **-a•chieved, -a•chiev•ing.** To perform better than expected, especially in schoolwork. —**o′ver•a•chiev′er** *n.*

o•ver•all |**ō′**vər ôl′| *adj.* **1.** Including everything; total: *the overall cost of the project.* **2.** Viewed as a whole; general: *The overall effect is very pleasing.*

o•ver•alls |**ō′**vər ôlz′| *pl.n.* Coarse, loose-fitting trousers with a top part that covers the chest, often worn over regular clothes to protect them from dirt. [SEE PICTURE]

o•ver•arm |**ō′**vər ärm′| *adj. & adv.* Performed or executed with the arm raised above the shoulder; overhand: *an overarm throw; throw overarm.*

o•ver•awe |ō′vər **ô′**| *v.* **-awed, -aw•ing.** To overcome with awe.

o•ver•bear•ing |ō′vər **bâr′**ĭng| *adj.* Arrogant and domineering in manner: *an overbearing person.*

o•ver•board |**ō′**vər bôrd′| *or* |-bōrd′| *adv.* Over the side of a boat: *He fell overboard.*

***Idiom.* go overboard.** *Informal.* To show much enthusiasm.

o•ver•bur•den |ō′vər **bûr′**dn| *v.* **1.** To burden with excess weight. **2.** To burden with too much work, care, or responsibility.

oval

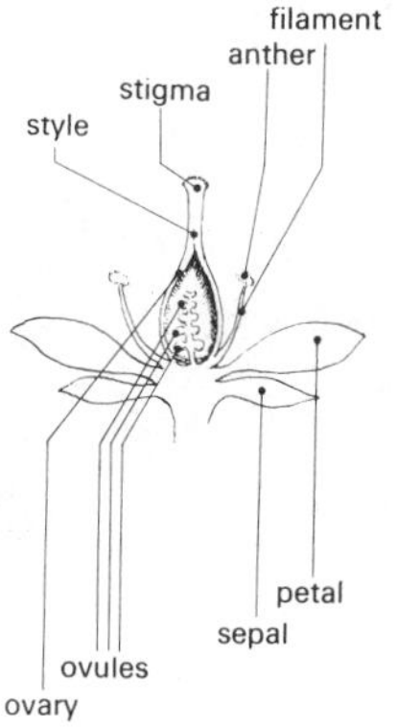

ovary
Section of a flower ovary showing the ovules

overalls

overcome
The song We Shall Overcome *was first published in 1962. It was written in its original form by Zilphia Horton in the late 1940's and grew and changed as folk songs often do. Major contributions were made by the folk singers Pete Seeger, Frank Hamilton, and Guy Carawan.*

ă pat/ā pay/â care/ä father/ĕ pet/ ē be/ĭ pit/ī pie/î fierce/ŏ pot/ ō go/ô paw, for/oi oil/ŏŏ book/ ōō boot/ou out/ŭ cut/û fur/ *th* the/th thin/hw which/zh vision/ ə ago, item, pencil, atom, circus

o•ver•cast |ō′vər kăst′| *or* |-kăst′| *or* |ō′vər-**kăst′**| *or* |**-käst′**| *adj.* **1.** Covered over, as with clouds or mist; cloudy. **2.** Gloomy; dark. —*n.* |**ō′**vər kăst′| *or* |-käst′|. **1.** A covering, as of mist or clouds. **2.** A sewing stitch in which the thread goes back and forth over the edge of the cloth. —***modifier:*** *an overcast stitch.* —*v.* |ō′vər-**kăst′**| *or* |**-käst′**|. To sew (a cloth edge) with long stitches that go over the edge to prevent raveling.

o•ver•charge |ō′vər **chärj′**| *v.* **-charged, -charg•ing. 1.** To charge too high a price. **2.** To fill too full; overload. —*n.* |**ō′**vər chärj′|. An excessive price or charge.

o•ver•coat |**ō′**vər kōt′| *n.* A long, heavy outdoor coat worn over a suit or other clothing.

o•ver•come |ō′vər **kŭm′**| *v.* **-came** |**-kām′**|, **-com•ing. 1.** To get the better of; surmount: *overcome the problem of returning to the earth's atmosphere safely.* **2.** To get the better of in a struggle, contest, etc.; defeat: *overcome a powerful team.* **3.** To upset emotionally; overpower: *Fear overcame him.* [SEE NOTE]

o•ver•do |ō′vər **dōō′**| *v.* **-did** |**-dĭd′**|, **-done** |**-dŭn′**|, **-do•ing, -does** |**-dŭz′**|. **1.** To do or use to excess; carry too far: *Don't overdo the thanks or your letter will sound insincere.* **2.** To tire oneself completely: *When you are recuperating, you must not overdo.* **3.** To cook too long or too much. ¶*These sound alike* **overdo, overdue.**

o•ver•dose |**ō′**vər dōs′| *n.* An excessively large dose, as of medicine or a drug.

o•ver•draw |ō′vər **drô′**| *v.* **-drew** |**-drōō′**|, **-drawn** |**-drôn′**|, **-draw•ing.** To withdraw more from (an account) than one has credit for.

o•ver•dress |ō′vər **drĕs′**| *v.* To dress up in too formal or fancy a way for the occasion.

o•ver•due |ō′vər **dōō′**| *or* |**-dyōō′**| *adj.* **1.** Unpaid after being due. **2.** Later than scheduled or expected: *an overdue train; long overdue changes.* ¶*These sound alike* **overdue, overdo.**

o•ver•eat |ō′vər **ēt′**| *v.* **-ate** |**-āt′**|, **-eat•en** |**-ēt′**n|, **-eat•ing.** To eat too much at one time.

o•ver•es•ti•mate |ō′vər **ĕs′**tə māt′| *v.* **-es•ti•mat•ed, -es•ti•mat•ing. 1.** To rate or estimate too highly. **2.** To value or esteem too highly. —*n.* |ō′vər **ĕs′**tə mĭt|. An estimate that is or proves to be too high.

o•ver•ex•pose |ō′vər ĭk **spōz′**| *v.* **-ex•posed, ex•pos•ing.** To expose too long or too much: *overexpose a picture; overexpose oneself to the sun.* —**o′ver•ex•po′sure** *n.*

o•ver•flow |ō′vər **flō′**| *v.* **1.** To flow over (the top, brim, or banks): *The Nile overflows its banks every year. The heavy rains caused the river to overflow.* **2.** To fill beyond capacity and spread further: *The people overflowed from the stands onto the playing field.* —*n.* |**ō′**vər flō′|. **1.** The act or an example of overflowing. **2.** The amount or excess that overflows.

o•ver•grow |ō′vər **grō′**| *v.* **-grew** |**-grōō′**|, **-grown** |**-grōn′**|, **grow•ing. 1.** To cover over with growth: *The bushes overgrew the pathway.* **2.** To grow too much or larger than normal.

o•ver•hand |**ō′**vər hănd′| *adj.* In sports, performed with the hand moving above the level of the shoulder: *an overhand pitch.* —*adv.: He throws overhand.*

o•ver•hang |ō′vər **hăng′**| *v.* **-hung** |**-hŭng′**|, **-hang•ing.** To project, extend, or jut out over: *A ledge overhangs the house.* —*n.* |**ō′**vər hăng′|. Something that overhangs; a projection.

o•ver•haul |ō′vər **hôl′**| *or* |**ō′**vər hôl′| *v.* **1.** To inspect, examine, or review in order to repair or make changes: *overhaul a car.* **2.** To gain upon in a chase; overtake. —*n.* |**ō′**vər hôl′|. The act or an example of overhauling.

o•ver•head |ō′vər **hĕd′**| *adv.* Above one's head: *birds darting overhead.* —*adj.* |**ō′**vər hĕd′|. Located above the level of the head: *an overhead light.* —*n.* |**ō′**vər hĕd′|. The operating expenses of a business, such as rent, insurance, taxes, lighting, etc., that cannot be charged to labor or materials.

o•ver•hear |ō′vər **hîr′**| *v.* **-heard** |**-hûrd′**|, **-hear•ing.** To hear without being addressed by the speaker; hear accidentally.

o•ver•heat |ō′vər **hēt′**| *v.* To make or become excessively hot: *The furnace overheated the room. The engine overheated.*

o•ver•in•dulge |ō′vər ĭn **dŭlj′**| *v.* **-in•dulged, -in•dulg•ing.** To gratify or spoil to excess. —**o′ver•in•dulg′ence** *n.*

o•ver•joyed |ō′vər **joid′**| *adj.* Extremely happy or delighted.

o•ver•kill |**ō′**vər kĭl′| *n.* **1.** Nuclear destructive capacity exceeding the amount needed to destroy an enemy. **2.** Any excessive action: *police overkill in dealing with demonstrators.*

o•ver•land |**ō′**vər lănd′| *or* |-lənd| *adj.* Over or across land: *an overland journey.* —*adv.: He traveled overland.*

o•ver•lap |ō′vər **lăp′**| *v.* **o•ver•lapped, o•ver•lap•ping. 1.** To lie or extend over and cover part of another thing: *The scales of a fish overlap, forming a protective covering.* **2.** To have some part in common with something; coincide partly: *Our vacations overlap.* —*n.* |**ō′**vər lăp′|. **1.** A part that overlaps. **2.** The amount that overlaps. **3.** An example of overlapping.

o•ver•lay |ō′vər **lā′**| *v.* **-laid** |**-lād′**|, **-lay•ing.** To cover or decorate with a surface layer: *He overlaid the wood with silver.* —*n.* |**ō′**vər lā′|. **1.** Anything laid over something else to cover it. **2.** A layer or decoration, such as gold leaf or wood veneer, applied to a surface.

o•ver•load |ō′vər **lōd′**| *v.* **1.** To put too large a load in or on: *overload a bridge.* **2.** To cause (an electric device, circuit, or system) to work beyond its capacity, especially by drawing too much current from it. —*n.* |**ō′**vər lōd′|. **1.** An excessively large load. **2.** An electric current that is too large for a circuit, device, or system.

o•ver•look |ō′vər **lŏŏk′**| *v.* **1. a.** To look over from a higher place: *The porch overlooks the sea.* **b.** To afford a view of: *The restaurant overlooks San Francisco Bay.* **2.** To fail to notice or consider: *overlook an important detail.* **3.** To ignore deliberately; disregard: *We must not allow ourselves to overlook injustice.* —*n.* |**ō′**vər lŏŏk′|. A place that overlooks and especially affords a view of something.

o•ver•ly |**ō′**vər lē| *adv.* Excessively; unduly; too: *an overly sharp knife; an overly long movie.*

o•ver•night |**ō′**vər nīt′| *adj.* **1.** Lasting for a night: *an overnight trip.* **2.** For use over a single night: *an overnight bag.* **3.** Happening as if in a single night; sudden: *an overnight success.* —*adv.*

|ō′vər **nīt′**|. **1.** During or for the length of a night: *Soak the beans overnight.* **2.** As if in the course of a night; suddenly: *The fashion spread like wildfire overnight through the campus.*

o•ver•pass |**ō′**vər păs′| *or* |-päs′| *n.* A roadway or bridge that crosses above another roadway or thoroughfare. [SEE PICTURE]

o•ver•pow•er |ō′vər **pou′**ər| *v.* **1.** To get the better of or conquer by superior force: *The Yankee hitters overpowered the Dodgers.* **2.** To affect strongly; overwhelm: *The heat overpowered everyone and they had to leave the beach.* **—o′ver•pow′er•ing** *adj.*: *an overpowering impulse to cry.*

o•ver•pro•duce |ō′vər prə **dōōs′**| *or* |**-dyōōs′**| *v.* **-pro•duced, -pro•duc•ing.** To produce too much or too many of. **—o′ver•pro•duc′tion** |ō′vər-prə **dŭk′**shən| *n.*

o•ver•rate |ō′vər **rāt′**| *v.* **-rat•ed, -rat•ing.** To rate too highly.

o•ver•reach |ō′vər **rēch′**| *v.* **1.** To extend or reach over or beyond. **2.** To miss by reaching too far or attempting too much: *overreach a goal.* **3.** To defeat (oneself) by going too far or doing too much.

o•ver•ride |ō′vər **rīd′**| *v.* **-rode** |**-rōd′**|, **-rid•den** |**-rĭd′**n|, **-rid•ing. 1.** To trample upon; ride over. **2.** To prevail over; dominate: *His fear of the cold overrides all other considerations.* **3.** To declare null and void; set aside: *The President's veto was overridden by Congress.*

o•ver•rule |ō′vər **rōōl′**| *v.* **-ruled, -rul•ing. 1.** To rule against. **2.** To declare null and void; invalidate. **3.** To prevail over so as to change an opinion or action; influence.

o•ver•run |ō′vər **rŭn′**| *v.* **-ran** |**-răn′**|, **-run, -run•ning. 1.** To spread or swarm over in great numbers: *Weeds overran the garden.* **2.** To run or extend beyond; exceed: *The plane overran the runway.*

o•ver•seas |ō′vər **sēz′**| *or* |**ō′**vər sēz′| *adv.* Across the sea; abroad: *He was sent overseas.* *—adj.* Of, from, or situated across the sea: *an overseas flight.*

o•ver•see |ō′vər **sē′**| *v.* **-saw** |**-sô′**|, **-seen** |**-sēn′**|, **-see•ing.** To watch over and direct; supervise.

o•ver•se•er |**ō′**vər sē′ər| *n.* A person who watches over and directs workers.

o•ver•sha•dow |ō′vər **shăd′**ō| *v.* **1.** To cast a shadow over. **2.** To make insignificant in comparison.

o•ver•shoe |**ō′**vər shōō′| *n.* A shoe or boot, often of rubber or plastic, worn over an ordinary shoe for added protection in wet or cold weather.

o•ver•shoot |ō′vər **shōōt′**| *v.* **-shot** |**-shŏt′**|, **-shoot•ing.** To exceed or pass beyond a location, value, limit, etc.: *overshoot a target. The plane overshot the runway.*

o•ver•shot |**ō′**vər shŏt′| *adj.* **1.** Having an upper part that extends out past the lower part: *an overshot jaw.* **2.** Operated or turned by a stream of water that passes over its top: *an overshot water wheel.* [SEE PICTURE]

o•ver•sight |**ō′**vər sīt′| *n.* An omission or mistake that is not made on purpose; an unintentional error.

o•ver•size |ō′vər **sīz′**| *adj.* Larger than the usual, expected, or required size: *an oversize sofa.*

o•ver•sized |ō′vər **sīzd′**| *adj.* Oversize.

o•ver•sleep |ō′vər **slēp′**| *v.* **-slept** |**-slĕpt′**|, **-sleep•ing.** To sleep longer than planned.

o•ver•state |ō′vər **stāt′**| *v.* **-stat•ed, -stat•ing.** To emphasize unduly; exaggerate. **—o′ver•state′ment** *n.*

o•ver•stay |ō′vər **stā′**| *v.* To stay past an expected duration of: *He overstayed his welcome.*

o•ver•step |ō′vər **stĕp′**| *v.* **-stepped, step•ping.** To go beyond (a limit or bound): *She overstepped the rules.*

o•ver•stuffed |**ō′**vər stŭft′| *adj.* Filled with too much stuffing: *an overstuffed pillow.*

o•vert |ō **vûrt′**| *adj.* Not concealed or hidden; open: *an overt act of war.*

o•ver•take |ō′vər **tāk′**| *v.* **-took** |**-tŏŏk′**|, **-tak•en** |**-tā′**kən|, **-tak•ing. 1.** To catch up with: *A strange man on horseback overtook him on the mountain road.* **2.** To pass after catching up with: *The car overtook him in the race.* **3.** To come upon unexpectedly: *A violent storm overtook him on the road to Cambridge.*

o•ver•throw |ō′vər **thrō′**| *v.* **-threw** |**-thrōō′**|, **-thrown** |**-thrōn′**|, **-throw•ing. 1.** To throw over; overturn: *overthrow a table.* **2.** To bring about the downfall or destruction of: *overthrow the government.* **3.** To throw a ball beyond an intended mark: *She overthrew first base.* *—n.* |**ō′**vər thrō′|. **1.** The downfall or destruction, as of a government. **2.** The act of throwing a ball beyond an intended mark.

o•ver•time |**ō′**vər tīm′| *n.* Time beyond an established limit: *The game went into overtime.* *—adv.* Beyond an established time limit, such as working hours: *work overtime.* *—adj.* Of or for overtime: *overtime pay.*

o•ver•tone |**ō′**vər tōn′| *n.* **1.** Any of the pure tones that sound along with a basic tone and give it its characteristic timbre. **2.** An accompanying effect; a suggestion or implication: *Words often have strong emotional overtones.*

o•ver•ture |**ō′**vər chər| *n.* **1. a.** An instrumental composition of moderate length written as an introduction to an opera, oratorio, or suite. **b.** An independent instrumental composition that resembles this. **2.** An offer or proposal indicating readiness to negotiate or establish something: *making peace overtures.*

o•ver•turn |ō′vər **tûrn′**| *v.* **1.** To turn over or capsize; upset: *overturn a glass of water.* **2.** To overthrow; defeat.

o•ver•use |ō′vər **yōōz′**| *v.* **-used, -us•ing.** To use to excess. *—n.* |ō′vər **yōōs′**|. Too much or excessive use.

o•ver•view |**ō′**vər vyōō′| *n.* A broad, comprehensive view; an overall survey.

o•ver•ween•ing |ō′vər **wē′**nĭng| *adj.* Presumptuously arrogant; overbearing.

o•ver•weight |ō′vər **wāt′**| *adj.* Weighing more than is normal or required. *—n.* |**ō′**vər wāt′|. Weight that is above normal or usual.

o•ver•whelm |ō′vər **hwĕlm′**| *or* |**-wĕlm′**| *v.* **1.** To surge over and submerge; engulf: *Loneliness overwhelmed her.* **2.** To overcome completely; overpower. **—o′ver•whelm′ing** *adj.*: *an overwhelming majority.*

o•ver•work |ō′vər **wûrk′**| *v.* To work or cause to work too hard: *She overworks terribly. The manager overworks her.* *—n.* |**ō′**vər wûrk′|. Too much work.

overpass

overshot

owl
Above: Barn owl
Below: Great horned owl

oxygen
Oxygen *is the third most abundant element in the universe and forms 21 per cent of the volume of the earth's atmosphere. It is required for most forms of combustion and is essential for the respiration of nearly all animals and plants. Oxygen is highly reactive chemically and occurs in hundreds of thousands of compounds.*

ă pat/ā pay/â care/ä father/ĕ pet/ ē be/ĭ pit/ī pie/î fierce/ŏ pot/ ō go/ô paw, for/oi **oi**l/o͝o b**oo**k/ o͞o b**oo**t/ou **ou**t/ŭ c**u**t/û f**ur**/ *th* **th**e/th **th**in/hw **wh**ich/zh vi**si**on/ ə **a**go, it**e**m, penc**i**l, at**o**m, circ**u**s

o•ver•wrought |ō′vər **rôt′**| *adj.* Nervous or excited; very agitated.

o•vi•duct |**ō′**vĭ dŭkt′| *n.* In animals, a tube through which eggs or egg cells travel from an ovary to the outside of the body, or, in mammals, to the uterus.

o•vip•a•rous |ō **vĭp′**ər əs| *adj.* Producing eggs that hatch outside the body, as birds do.

o•vi•pos•i•tor |ō′və **pŏz′**ĭ tər| *n.* A tubelike part that extends from the end of the abdomen in certain insects, such as grasshoppers or wasps, and is used to lay eggs.

o•void |**ō′**void′| *adj.* Having the shape of an egg: *an ovoid face.* —*n.* Something having this shape.

o•vo•vi•vip•a•rous |ō′vō vī **vĭp′**ər əs| *adj.* Producing eggs that hatch within the female's body, as certain fish and reptiles do.

o•vu•late |**ō′**vyə lāt′| *v.* **o•vu•lat•ed, o•vu•lat•ing.** To produce or discharge an egg cell. —**o′vu•la′tion** *n.*

o•vule |**ō′**vyo͞ol| *n.* **1.** A small part in a plant ovary that becomes a seed after it has been fertilized by a male cell. **2.** An immature ovum.

o•vum |**ō′**vəm| *n., pl.* **o•va** |**ō′**və|. A female reproductive cell; an egg.

owe |ō| *v.* **owed, ow•ing. 1. a.** To be indebted in the sum of: *He owes the store $10.* **b.** To be indebted for: *We owe rent for six months.* **2.** To be under obligation to give: *owe an apology.* **3.** To have or possess as something derived from or bestowed by; be obliged for: *Western civilization owes much to the ancient Greeks.* ¶*These sound alike* **owe, O, oh.**

ow•ing |**ō′**ĭng| *adj.* Still to be paid; owed: *a sum that was owing.*

Idiom. **owing to.** Because of; on account of.

owl |oul| *n.* Any of several birds of prey that usually fly at night and that have a large head, a short, hooked bill, and a flat, disklike face. [SEE PICTURE]

owl•et |**ou′**lĭt| *n.* A young or small owl.

own |ōn| *adj.* **1.** Of or belonging to oneself or itself: *Jim's own book; my own home.* **2.** Used as an intensive: *I'll do my own homework, thank you.* —*v.* **1.** To have or possess: *own a car.* **2.** To acknowledge or admit: *I own that I've made a mistake.* —***phrasal verb.*** **own up.** To confess fully and openly: *The detectives assured him that he would feel better if he owned up.*

Idioms. **come into (one's) own.** To obtain deserved recognition and prosperity: *Jazz really came into its own after World War II.* **hold (one's) own.** To maintain one's position successfully in spite of attack, criticism, etc. **on (one's) own.** Completely independent: *If you quit school, you're on your own.*

own•er |**ō′**nər| *n.* Someone who owns something, especially someone who has legal title to something.

own•er•ship |**ō′**nər shĭp′| *n.* The condition of being an owner; legal title.

ox |ŏks| *n., pl.* **ox•en** |**ŏk′**sən|. **1.** A castrated adult male of domestic cattle. **2.** Any of several animals, such as the musk ox, related to domestic cattle.

ox•a•lic acid |ŏk **săl′**ĭk|. A poisonous acid composed of carbon, hydrogen, and oxygen and having the formula $C_2H_2O_4$. It is used as a general cleanser and bleach.

ox•blood |**ŏks′**blŭd′| *n.* A deep red or reddish brown. —*adj.* Deep red or reddish brown.

ox•bow |**ŏks′**bō′| *n.* **1.** A U-shaped piece of wood that fits under the neck of an ox, with its upper ends attached to the bar of the yoke. **2.** A U-shaped bend in a river.

ox•cart |**ŏks′**kärt′| *n.* A cart drawn by oxen.

ox•en |**ŏk′**sən| *n.* Plural of **ox.**

ox•eye daisy |**ŏks′**ī′|. The common daisy of North America, having flowers with a yellow center surrounded by white petallike rays.

ox•ford |**ŏks′**fərd| *n.* **1.** A low shoe that laces over the instep. **2.** A cotton or rayon cloth used for men's shirts and women's sports clothes.

Ox•ford |**ŏks′**fərd|. A city located about 50 miles northwest of London, England; the site of Oxford University. Population, 110,000.

ox•i•da•tion |ŏk′sĭ **dā′**shən| *n.* **1.** The chemical combination of a substance with oxygen. **2.** A chemical reaction in which the atoms of an element lose electrons or have them moved to more distant positions, thus undergoing an increase in valence.

ox•ide |**ŏk′**sīd′| *n.* A compound of oxygen and another element or a radical.

ox•i•dize |**ŏk′**sĭ dīz′| *v.* **ox•i•dized, ox•i•diz•ing. 1.** To combine with oxygen; make into or become an oxide. **2.** To coat with oxide: *Air oxidizes the surface of aluminum.* **3.** To subject to oxidation.

ox•i•diz•er |ŏk′sĭ **dī′**zər| *n.* **1.** An **oxidizing agent. 2.** A substance that reacts with a rocket fuel to produce the hot gas used for propulsion.

oxidizing agent. A substance that oxidizes another substance or causes it to oxidize.

ox•tail |**ŏks′**tāl′| *n.* The tail of an ox, especially one used in soup or stew.

ox•y•a•cet•y•lene |ŏk′sē ə **sĕt′**l ĭn| *or* |-ēn′| *adj.* Using a mixture of oxygen and acetylene: *an oxyacetylene welding torch.*

ox•y•gen |**ŏk′**sĭ jən| *n.* Symbol **O** One of the elements, a colorless, odorless, tasteless gas. Atomic number 8; atomic weight 16.00; valence –2; melting point –218.4°C; boiling point –183°C. [SEE NOTE]

ox•y•gen•ate |**ŏk′**sĭ jə nāt′| *v.* **ox•y•gen•at•ed, ox•y•gen•at•ing.** To combine, treat, or mix with oxygen. —**ox′y•gen•a′tion** *n.*

oxygen mask. A covering that fits closely over the mouth and nose and is connected by a hose to a supply of oxygen.

oxygen tent. An enclosure, supplied with oxygen, that is placed over the head and shoulders of a patient who is having difficulty breathing.

o•yez |**ō′**yĕs′| *or* |**ō′**yĕz′| *or* |ō **yā′**| *interj.* A word used three times in a row to introduce the opening of a law court.

oy•ster |**oi′**stər| *n.* A soft-bodied sea animal of shallow waters, having a rough, irregularly shaped, double-hinged shell. Many kinds of oysters are used as food, and some kinds produce pearls inside their shells.

oz ounce (unit of weight).

O•zark Mountains |**ō′**zärk′|. Also **Ozarks.** A mountain range covering parts of Missouri, Arkansas, and Oklahoma.

o•zone |**ō′**zōn′| *n.* A poisonous, blue, unstable gaseous form of oxygen that has three atoms per molecule rather than the usual two.

Pp

p, P |pē| *n., pl.* **p's** or **P's.** The 16th letter of the English alphabet. [SEE NOTE]
p, p. In music, piano (a direction).
P The symbol for the element phosphorus.
p. 1. page. **2.** participle. **3.** pint.
pa |pä| *n. Informal.* Father.
Pa The symbol for the element protactinium.
PA public-address system.
Pa. Pennsylvania.
pace |pās| *n.* **1. a.** A step made in walking; a stride. **b.** The distance spanned by such a step, specifically a unit of length equal to 30 inches. **2. a.** The rate of speed at which a person, animal, or group walks or runs. **b.** The speed at which any activity proceeds: *the fast pace of Manhattan living.* **3.** A gait of a horse in which both feet on one side leave and return to the ground together. —*v.* **paced, pac•ing. 1.** To walk up and down or back and forth across: *The tiger paced nervously in his cage. He paced the floor impatiently.* **2.** To measure by paces. **3.** To set or regulate the pace of. —**pac'er** *n.*

Idioms. **keep pace with.** To match the progress of. **put (one) through (one's) paces.** To test one's abilities or skills. **set the pace. 1.** To set a speed to be followed by competitors. **2.** To set an example for others to follow.
pach•y•derm |păk′ĭ dûrm′| *n.* A large, thick-skinned animal such as an elephant, rhinoceros, or hippopotamus.
pa•cif•ic |pə sĭf′ĭk| —*adj.* **1.** Loving peace; peaceful: *a pacific people.* **2.** Peaceful in nature; serene. —**pa•cif'i•cal•ly** *adv.* [SEE NOTE]
Pa•cif•ic Daylight-Saving Time |pə sĭf′ĭk|. Daylight-saving time as reckoned in the region between the meridians at 112.5° and 127.5° west of Greenwich, England. The west coast of the United States is in this region. See **time zone.**
Pacific Ocean. The largest of the oceans, extending from the Arctic to the Antarctic and from the Americas to Asia and Australia.
Pacific Standard Time. Standard time as reckoned in the region between the meridians at 112.5° and 127.5° west of Greenwich, England. The west coast of the United States is in this region. See **time zone.**
pac•i•fi•er |păs′ə fī′ər| *n.* **1.** Someone or something that pacifies. **2.** A rubber or plastic nipple or teething ring for a baby to suck or chew on.
pac•i•fism |păs′ə fĭz′əm| *n.* **1.** The belief that disputes between nations must be settled exclusively by peaceful means; opposition to war of any kind. **2.** Opposition to particular wars believed to be unjust. —**pac'i•fist** *n.* —**pac'i•fis'tic** *adj.* —**pac'i•fis'ti•cal•ly** *adv.*
pac•i•fy |păs′ə fī′| *v.* **pac•i•fied, pac•i•fy•ing, pac•i•fies. 1.** To quiet; calm: *pacify a baby.* **2.** To establish peace in: *pacify the frontier.* —**pac'i•fi•ca'tion** *n.*
pack |păk| *n.* **1.** A collection of items tied up or wrapped together; a bundle. **2. a.** A small package containing a standard number of identical or similar items: *a pack of matches.* **b.** A set of related items: *a pack of cards.* **3.** A group of animals or people: *a pack of wolves; a pack of thieves.* **4.** A large amount: *a pack of trouble; a pack of lies.* **5.** Something applied to a part of the body or inserted into a wound or opening of the body as treatment for an injury or disorder. —*v.* **1.** To put into a bag, box, or other container for storage, preserving, selling, etc.: *pack groceries; pack clothes.* **2.** To fill with items: *pack a suitcase.* **3.** To be capable of being stored compactly: *Sweaters pack well.* **4.** To press or become pressed together: *He packed his tobacco into his pipe. Certain kinds of flour pack well for measuring.* **5. a.** To crowd together: *The ushers packed the theatergoers into the hall.* **b.** To fill up tight; cram: *The crowd packed the stadium.* **c.** To include in: *A lot of information is packed into a dictionary.* **6.** To treat medically with a pack: *pack a wound.* **7.** *Informal.* To have ready for action: *pack a pistol.* **8.** To rig (a jury, panel, etc.) so as to be fraudently favorable: *pack a jury.* **9.** To cause to go, leave, etc.: *pack the kids off to camp.* —*adj.* Used for carrying a pack: *a pack animal.*

Idiom. **send packing.** To dismiss (someone) abruptly.
pack•age |păk′ĭj| *n.* **1.** A wrapped or boxed parcel containing one or more objects. **2.** A container meant to hold something for storage or transporting. **3.** A proposition or offer made up of several items, each of which must be accepted. —*v.* **pack•aged, pack•ag•ing.** To place in a package or make a package of.
package store. A store that sells sealed bottles of alcoholic beverages for consumption away from its premises.
pack•er |păk′ər| *n.* A person who packs goods, especially meat products, for transportation and sale.
pack•et |păk′ĭt| *n.* **1.** A small package or bundle, as of mail. **2.** A ship that sails on a regular route, carrying freight, passengers, and mail.
pack rat. A North American rat that carries off objects and collects them in its nesting place.
pack•sack |păk′săk′| *n.* A canvas or leather pack carried strapped to the shoulders.
pact |păkt| *n.* **1.** A formal agreement, as between nations; a treaty. **2.** A compact; bargain.

(1) (2) (3)

The letter **P** *comes originally from the Phoenician letter* pē *(1), which meant "mouth" and stood for /p/. The Greeks borrowed it from the Phoenicians, turning it to face in the opposite direction (2) and renaming it* pi. *The Romans borrowed it from the Greeks, closing up the curve to make a complete loop (3). The Roman shape is the basis of our modern letter* **P**.

pacific
The word **pacific** *is from Latin* pācificus, *"peacemaking, peaceable":* pāx, pāc-, *"peace,"* + -ficus, *"-making." The* **Pacific Ocean** *was named by Ferdinand Magellan, the first European to reach it; after his extremely dangerous stormy passage of the Strait of Magellan in 1520, he found calm and "pacific" weather in the new ocean.*

pad[1-2]
Pad[1] *originally meant "straw mattress"; its origin is obscure.* **Pad[2]** *is probably from Middle Dutch* padden, *"to walk along a path"; it is related to* **path**.

paddle[1-2]
Both **paddle[1]** *and* **paddle[2]** *are of unknown origin.*

paddle wheel

page[1-2]
Page[1] *is from Latin* pāgina, *"a sheet of writing."* **Page[2]** *is from Italian* paggio, *which is from Greek* paidion, *"boy."*

ă pat/ā pay/â care/ä father/ĕ pet/ ē be/ĭ pit/ī pie/î fierce/ŏ pot/ ō go/ô paw, for/oi oil/ŏŏ book/ ōō boot/ou out/ŭ cut/û fur/ *th* the/th thin/hw which/zh vision/ ə ago, item, pencil, atom, circus

pad[1] |păd| *n.* **1.** A cushion or mass of soft, firmly packed material used for stuffing, lining, or protection against injury: *chair pads; shoulder pads.* **2. a.** Any small wad of material: *a steel-wool pad for scouring.* **b.** A piece of absorbent material placed in a container and used to hold ink for stamping: *an ink pad.* **3.** A number of sheets of paper of the same size stacked one on top of the other and glued together at one end: *a memo pad.* **4.** A broad, floating leaf of a water lily or similar plant. **5. a.** The cushionlike flesh on the under-part of the toes and feet of many animals. **b.** The fleshy tissue at the end of a finger or toe on the side opposite the nail. **6.** A **launch pad. 7.** *Slang.* An apartment or room. *—v.* **pad•ded, pad•ding. 1.** To line, stuff, or cover with soft, firmly packed material: *pad a sleeve.* **2.** To lengthen with unnecessary material: *pad a term paper.* **3.** To add fictitious expenses or costs to: *pad an expense account.* **—pad'ded** *adj.: a padded bench.* [SEE NOTE]

pad[2] |păd| *v.* **pad•ded, pad•ding.** To go on foot, especially with a soft, almost inaudible, step: *The boys like to pad about the house barefooted. —n.* A muffled sound resembling that of soft footsteps: *the soft pad of feet.* [SEE NOTE]

pad•ding |păd'ĭng| *n.* **1.** Soft material used to stuff, fill, protect, or line something. **2.** Unnecessary material added to a speech or written work to lengthen it.

pad•dle[1] |păd'l| *n.* **1.** A short wooden implement with a flat blade at one end, used without an oarlock to propel a canoe, raft, etc. **2.** Any of various implements with a similar shape, as a tool for stirring molten ore, a racket used in Ping-Pong, etc. *—v.* **pad•dled, pad•dling. 1.** To propel (a canoe, raft, etc.) with a paddle or paddles: *Paddle your own canoe. They paddled against the current.* **2.** To beat or spank with or as if with a paddle. **—pad'dler** *n.* [SEE NOTE]

pad•dle[2] |păd'l| *v.* **pad•dled, pad•dling.** To splash gently or playfully in shallow water. [SEE NOTE]

pad•dle•fish |păd'l fĭsh'| *n., pl.* **-fish** or **-fish•es.** A large fish of the Mississippi River and its branches, having a long, paddle-shaped snout.

paddle wheel. A steam-driven wheel with boards or paddles around its rim, used to propel a ship. **—*modifier:* (paddle-wheel):** *a paddle-wheel steamboat.* [SEE PICTURE]

pad•dock |păd'ək| *n.* A fenced field or area, usually near a stable, in which horses are kept, for grazing, for exercising, or for being saddled and paraded before a race.

pad•dy |păd'ē| *n., pl.* **pad•dies.** A marshy, flooded, or specially watered field in which rice is grown.

pad•lock |păd'lŏk'| *n.* A detachable lock with a U-shaped bar hinged at one end, designed to be passed through a staple, link, or ring and then snapped into a hole in the body of the lock. *—v.* To lock up with or as if with a padlock.

pa•dre |pä'drā| *or* |-drē| *n.* **1.** A priest in Italy, Spain, Portugal, and Latin America. **2.** A title used for a priest in those countries.

pae•an |pē'ən| *n.* **1.** A fervent expression of joy or praise. **2.** A hymn of thanksgiving to a god.

pa•gan |pā'gən| *n.* **1.** A person who is not a Christian, Moslem, or Jew; a heathen. **2.** A person who has no religion. *—adj.* Of pagans or paganism: *a pagan ceremony; pagan gods.*

pa•gan•ism |pā'gə nĭz'əm| *n.* **1.** Pagan beliefs or practices. **2.** The condition of being a pagan.

page[1] |pāj| *n.* **1. a.** One side of a leaf of a book, letter, newspaper, etc. **b.** The writing or printing on one side of a leaf. **2.** A memorable event: *a new page in the course of human history.* **—*modifier:*** *a page number. —v.* **paged, pag•ing.** To number the pages of. [SEE NOTE]

page[2] |pāj| *n.* **1.** A boy who attended a medieval knight as a first stage of training for knighthood. **2.** Someone employed to run errands, carry messages, or act as a guide, as in a hotel, club, legislative body, etc. *—v.* **paged, pag•ing.** To summon or call (a person) by name, as over a loudspeaker. [SEE NOTE]

pag•eant |păj'ənt| *n.* **1.** A play or dramatic spectacle usually based on an event in history. **2.** A procession or celebration.

pag•eant•ry |păj'ən trē| *n.* **1.** Pageants and their presentation. **2.** Grand or showy display.

pa•go•da |pə gō'də| *n.* A many-storied Buddhist tower, usually built as a memorial or shrine.

Pa•go Pa•go |păng'ō păng'ō|. The capital of American Samoa. Population, 3,058.

paid |pād|. Past tense and past participle of **pay**.

pail |pāl| *n.* **1.** A cylindrical container, open at the top and fitted with a handle, used for carrying water, sand, etc.; a bucket. **2. a.** A pail with something in it: *carry a pail of water.* **b.** The amount that a pail holds: *pour out a pail of sand.* **3.** Any metal container with a handle: *a lunch pail* ¶ *These sound alike* **pail, pale.**

pain |pān| *n.* **1.** An unpleasant feeling or hurt, as a result of injury, disease, etc., usually localized in some part of the body. **2.** Mental or emotional suffering; distress. **3. pains.** Trouble, care, or effort: *take great pains to do something right. —v.* **1.** To cause pain to (a person or animal); hurt. **2.** To cause to suffer; distress: *It pained her to see him so unhappy.* **—pained'** *adj.: a pained look.* ¶ *These sound alike* **pain, pane.**

***Idiom.* on (or upon or under) pain of.** Subject to the penalty of some specified punishment: *You will answer on pain of death.*

Paine |pān|, **Thomas.** 1737–1809. American Revolutionary author and pamphleteer.

pain•ful |pān'fəl| *adj.* **1.** Causing or full of pain; hurtful: *a painful injury.* **2.** Causing suffering or anxiety; distressing: *a painful decision.* **—pain'ful•ly** *adv.* **—pain'ful•ness** *n.*

pain•kill•er |pān'kĭl'ər| *n.* Something, such as a drug, that relieves pain.

pain•less |pān'lĭs| *adj.* Not painful; causing no unpleasant sensations: *a painless operation.* **—pain'less•ly** *adv.* **—pain'less•ness** *n.*

pains•tak•ing |pānz'tā'kĭng| *adj.* Involving or showing great care, thoroughness, etc.; careful: *painstaking research.* **—pains'tak'ing•ly** *adv.*

paint |pānt| *n.* **1. a.** A liquid mixture, usually of a finely ground solid pigment and a liquid, applied to surfaces as a protective or decorative coating. **b.** The thin film formed, as on a surface, when the liquid in such a mixture dries and reacts with the air. **c.** The solid pigment before it is mixed with the liquid. **2.** A cosmetic, such as rouge or lipstick, that colors. **3.** A spotted horse; a pinto. **—*modifier:*** *a paint can. —v.* **1.** To coat or decorate with paint: *paint a house.* **2.** To make (a picture) with paints: *He painted four pictures. She paints for a living.* **3. a.** To represent in a painting: *She painted a horse.* **b.** To describe vividly in words: *paint a picture of their trip through Africa.* **4.** To cover the surface of with a liquid medicine; swab: *paint a wound.* **—paint'ed** *adj.: a brightly painted cabinet.*

paint•brush |pānt'brŭsh'| *n.* A brush for applying paint.

paint•er[1] |pān'tər| *n.* A person who paints, either as an artist or as a workman. [SEE NOTE]

pain•ter[2] |pān'tər| *n.* A rope attached to the bow of a boat, used for tying up. [SEE NOTE]

pain•ter[3] |pān'tər| *n.* A mountain lion or other North American wild cat. [SEE NOTE]

paint•ing |pān'tĭng| *n.* **1.** The art, process, or occupation of working with paints. **2.** A picture or design in paint.

pair |pâr| *n.* **1.** A set that contains exactly two members, especially if they are somehow matched or associated in function or form: *a pair of boots.* **2.** One object consisting of two joined or similar parts dependent upon each other: *a pair of binoculars; a pair of trousers.* **3. a.** Two persons joined together in marriage or engagement. **b.** Two persons, animals, or things having something in common and considered together: *a pair of scientists; a pair of oxen.* **c.** Two mated animals. *—v.* **1.** To arrange in sets of two; couple: *Pair the synonyms in the two columns.* **2.** To provide a partner for: *She paired John with Alice.* ***—phrasal verb.*** **pair off.** To form a pair or pairs: *The young couples paired off for the waltz.* ¶*These sound alike* **pair, pare, pear.**

pais•ley |pāz'lē| *adj.* Having a colorful pattern of curved shapes and swirls: *a paisley dress.* [SEE PICTURE]

Pai•ute |pī'yo͞ot'| *or* |pī yo͞ot'| *n., pl.* **Pai•ute** or **Pai•utes. 1.** A North American Indian tribe of the southwestern United States. **2.** A member of this tribe. **3.** Their Uto-Aztecan language.

pa•ja•mas |pə jä'məz| *or* |-jăm'əz| *pl.n.* A loose-fitting outfit of jacket and trousers worn to sleep in or for lounging. ***—modifier:*** **(pajama):** *pajama bottoms.*

Pak•i•stan |păk'ĭ stăn'| *or* |pä' kĭ stän'|. Officially, Islamic Republic of Pakistan. A country in southern Asia. Population, 68,214,000. Capital, Islamabad. **—Pa'ki•sta'ni** |pä'kĭ stä'nē| *n. & adj.*

pal |păl|. *Informal. n.* A friend; chum. *—v.* **palled, pal•ling.** To associate as friends.

pal•ace |păl'ĭs| *n* **1.** The official residence of a royal person. **2.** Any splendid residence. ***—modifier:*** *palace gardens.*

pal•at•a•ble |păl'ə tə bəl| *adj.* **1.** Acceptable to the taste; agreeable enough in flavor to be eaten: *palatable food.* **2.** Acceptable to the mind or sensibilities; agreeable: *a palatable way of handling the problem.* **—pal'at•a•bil'i•ty** *n.*

pal•ate |păl'ĭt| *n.* **1.** The roof of the mouth in vertebrates, forming a complete or partial separation between the mouth cavity and the passages of the nose. See **hard palate, soft palate. 2.** The sense of taste. ¶*These sound alike* **palate, palette, pallet.**

pa•la•tial |pə lā'shəl| *adj.* Of or like a palace; spacious and magnificent: *a palatial hotel.*

pa•lav•er |pə lăv'ər| *or* |-lä'vər| *n.* **1.** Idle chatter, especially that meant to flatter or deceive. **2.** A parley between two groups, especially a parley formerly held between European explorers and representatives of local populations in Africa. *—v.* To chatter idly.

pale[1] |pāl| *n.* **1.** A stake or pointed stick; a picket. **2.** A limit or boundary. *—v.* **paled, pal•ing.** To enclose with pales; fence in. ¶*These sound alike* **pale, pail.** [SEE NOTE]

Idiom. **beyond the pale.** Beyond the limits of good taste, reason, etc.

pale[2] |pāl| *adj.* **pal•er, pal•est. 1.** Whitish or lighter than normal in complexion, often because of a poor supply of blood to the skin, as in weakness or some illnesses. **2.** Containing a large proportion of white; not intense; light: *a pale blue.* **3.** Not bright; dim; faint: *a pale moon.* *—v.* **paled, pal•ing. 1.** To lose normal skin coloration; turn pale. **2.** To become pale: *The sky crimsoned, then paled.* ¶*These sound alike* **pale, pail.** [SEE NOTE]

pale•face |pāl'fās'| *n.* A white person. The word "paleface" is thought to have been first used by North American Indians.

Pa•le•o•cene |pā'lē ə sēn'| *n.* Also **Paleocene epoch.** A geologic epoch that began about 63 million years ago and ended about 58 million years ago, characterized by the appearance of more advanced mammals. ***—modifier:*** *a Paleocene fossil.*

Pa•le•o•lith•ic |pā'lē ə lĭth'ĭk| *n.* The period of human culture that began about 750,000 years ago and ended about 15,000 years ago, marked by the earliest use of tools made of chipped stone. ***—modifier:*** *a Paleolithic tool.*

pa•le•on•tol•o•gist |pā'lē ən tŏl'ə jĭst| *n.* A scientist who specializes in paleontology.

pa•le•on•tol•o•gy |pā'lē ən tŏl'ə jē| *n.* The scientific study of fossils and ancient forms of life.

Pa•le•o•zo•ic |pā'lē ə zō'ĭk| *n.* Also **Paleozoic era.** A geologic era that began about 600 million years ago and ended about 230 million years ago, characterized by the appearance of invertebrate sea life, primitive fishes and reptiles, and land plants. ***—modifier:*** *a Paleozoic rock.*

Pal•es•tine |păl'ĭ stīn'|. The land between the Mediterranean Sea and the Jordan River, the scene of most of the events in the Bible.

pal•ette |păl'ĭt| *n.* A thin board, often with a hole for the thumb, upon which an artist mixes colors. ¶*These sound alike* **palette, palate, pallet.**

pal•frey |pôl'frē| *n., pl.* **pal•freys.** *Archaic.* A horse used for riding, especially by a woman.

pal•ing |pā'lĭng| *n.* **1.** One or more of the pales or pickets forming a fence. **2.** A fence made of pales or pickets.

pal•i•sade |păl'ĭ sād'| *n.* **1.** A fence of stakes forming a fortification. **2. palisades.** A line of high cliffs, usually along a river.

pall[1] |pôl| *n.* **1.** A cloth covering, often of black velvet, for a coffin or tomb. **2.** A coffin being borne to a grave. **3.** A dark, gloomy covering: *a pall of smog over the city.* **4.** A gloomy atmosphere: *The bad news cast a pall over the household.* ¶*These sound alike* **pall, pawl.** [SEE NOTE]

pall[2] |pôl| *v.* To grow dull or tiresome: *a clever idea that begins to pall by the end of the movie.* ¶*These sound alike* **pall, pawl.** [SEE NOTE]

painter[1-2-3]
Painter[1], *obviously, is from* **paint. Painter[2]** *probably comes from Old French* pentoir, *"clothesline, hanging rope," from* pendre, *"to hang."* **Painter[3]**, *an Americanism first occurring in the late colonial period, is a variant of* **panther.**

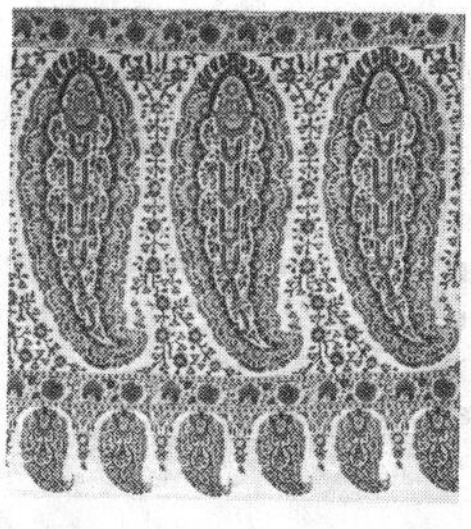

paisley
The **paisley** pattern is so called because it was popular in shawls that were mass-produced in *Paisley,* a textile-manufacturing city in Scotland.

pale[1-2]
Pale[1] *is from Latin* pālus, *"pointed stick"; it is related to* **palisade** *and to* **pole[2]. Pale[2]** *is from Latin* pallidus, *"pallid."*

pall[1-2]
Pall[1] *was Old English* pæll, *which was borrowed from Latin* pallium, *"cloak."* **Pall[2]** *is shortened from* **appall.**

pal•la•di•um |pə lā′dē əm| *n.* Symbol **Pd** One of the elements, a soft, white, tarnish-resistant metal. Atomic number 46; atomic weight 106.4; valences +2, +3, +4; melting point 1,552°C; boiling point 2,927°C.

Pal•las Athena |păl′əs|. The Greek goddess Athena.

pall•bear•er |pôl′bâr′ər| *n.* One of the persons who carry the coffin at a funeral.

pal•let |păl′ĭt| *n.* A narrow, hard bed or straw-filled mattress. ¶*These sound alike* **pallet, palate, palette.**

pal•li•ate |păl′ē āt′| *v.* **pal•li•at•ed, pal•li•at•ing. 1.** To make (an offense or fault) seem less serious; help to excuse. **2.** To ease the pain or force of, without curing; moderate: *took aspirin to palliate his cold symptoms.* —**pal′li•a′tion** *n.*

pal•li•a•tive |păl′ē ə tĭv| *adj.* Serving to palliate; helpful but not curing: *a palliative drug.* —*n.* Something that palliates.

pal•lid |păl′ĭd| *adj.* Lacking healthy color; pale. —**pal′lid•ly** *adv.* —**pal′lid•ness** *n.*

pal•lor |păl′ər| *n.* Unhealthy paleness.

palm¹ |päm| *n.* **1. a.** The inside surface of the hand between the wrist and the base of the fingers. **b.** A similar part of the forefoot of an animal. **2.** A unit of length equal to the width of the hand, or about three inches. —*v.* **1.** To conceal (an object) in the palm of the hand. **2.** To pick up secretly. —***phrasal verb.* palm off.** To get rid of by deception: *palmed off a broken tennis racket on his neighbor.* [SEE NOTE]

palm² |päm| *n.* **1.** Any of many related trees of the tropics or warm regions, usually having an unbranched trunk with a crown of large featherlike or fanlike leaves. **2.** A leaf or frond of such a tree, used as a symbol of victory, success, or joy. —***modifier:*** *palm nuts.* [SEE NOTE]

palm¹⁻²
Palm¹ *and* **palm²** *are separate borrowings from Latin* palma, *which meant "palm of the hand" and hence "palm tree" (since the leaflets of a palm leaf are like the fingers of an outstretched hand).*

pal•met•to | |păl mĕt′ō| *or* |päl-| *n., pl.* **pal•met•tos** or **pal•met•toes.** Any of several often small palm trees with fan-shaped leaves.

Palm Sunday. A church festival celebrated on the Sunday before Easter in memory of Christ's triumphant entry into Jerusalem.

pal•o•mi•no |păl′ə mē′nō| *n., pl.* **pal•o•mi•nos.** A horse with a light tan coat and a whitish mane and tail. [SEE PICTURE]

palp |pălp| *n.* A sense organ in or near the mouth of an insect, crustacean, etc.

pal•pa•ble |păl′pə bəl| *adj.* **1.** Capable of being touched or felt. **2.** Easily perceived; obvious. —**pal′pa•bil′i•ty** *n.* —**pal′pa•bly** *adv.*

pal•pi |păl′pī′| *n.* Plural of **palpus.**

pal•pi•tate |păl′pĭ tāt′| *v.* **pal•pi•tat•ed, pal•pi•tat•ing. 1.** To shake; quiver. **2.** To beat rapidly and loudly; throb. —**pal′pi•ta′tion** *n.*

pal•pus |păl′pəs| *n., pl.* **pal•pi** |păl′pī′|. A palp.

pal•sy |pôl′zē| *n., pl.* **pal•sies. 1.** Paralysis. **2.** A disorder or disease in which movement in some part of the body cannot be felt or controlled. —*v.* **pal•sied, pal•sy•ing, pal•sies.** To paralyze.

pal•try |pôl′trē| *adj.* **pal•tri•er, pal•tri•est. 1.** Meager; insignificant: *Jack sold the cow for a few paltry beans.* **2.** Lowly; contemptible: *paltry cowards.* —**pal′tri•ness** *n.*

pam•pa |păm′pə| *n.* Often **pampas.** The grassy plains that cover most of central Argentina and Uruguay.

pam•per |păm′pər| *v.* To treat with extreme indulgence or kindness; coddle: *pampered the robins with sunflower seed, the filet mignon of bird food.* —**pam′pered** *adj.: a pampered only child.*

pam•phlet |păm′flĭt| *n.* A short book or printed essay with a paper cover and no binding.

pam•phlet•eer |păm′flĭ tîr′| *n.* A writer of pamphlets, especially on political subjects.

pan¹ |păn| *n.* **1.** A wide, shallow, open container for holding liquids, for cooking, and for other household purposes. **2.** Any similar flat, shallow container, such as one used to separate gold from earth or gravel by washing. —*v.* **panned, pan•ning. 1.** To place or cook in a pan. **2.** To wash (earth or gravel) in a pan in search of gold: *panned the debris carefully; panning for gold in the high Sierras.* **3.** *Informal.* To review unfavorably: *The critics panned the musical.* —***phrasal verb.* pan out.** *Informal.* To turn out well; succeed: *had another plan if that one didn't pan out.* [SEE NOTE]

pan² |păn| *v.* **panned, pan•ning.** To turn (a motion-picture or television camera) to follow a moving object or scan a scene. [SEE NOTE]

pan¹⁻²
Pan¹ *was Old English* panne. **Pan²** *is shortened from* **panorama.** *The element* **pan-** *is from Greek* pan-, pas, *"all."*

Pan |păn|. The Greek god of woodlands, fields, and flocks.

pan–. A word element meaning "all": **panorama.** When *pan-* is followed by a capital letter, it appears with a hyphen: **Pan-American.**

pan•a•ce•a |păn′ə sē′ə| *n.* A remedy for all diseases or woes; a cure-all.

Pan•a•ma |păn′ə mä′|. **1.** A country in southeastern Central America, bordering Colombia, South America. Population, 1,631,000. **2.** Also **Panama City.** The capital of this country. Population, 455,000. —**Pan′a•ma′ni•an** |păn′ə mā′nē ən| *n. & adj.*

Panama Canal. A canal across Panama, connecting the Caribbean Sea with the Pacific Ocean.

Panama hat. A natural-colored, hand-plaited hat made from the leaves of a palmlike tropical American plant.

Pan-A•mer•i•can |păn′ə mĕr′ĭ kən| *adj.* Of or including the countries of North, Central, and South America: *Pan-American conferences.*

pan•cake |păn′kāk′| *n.* A thin, flat cake of batter, cooked on a hot, greased griddle or skillet. —***modifier:*** *pancake flour.*

pan•chro•mat•ic |păn′krə măt′ĭk| *adj.* Sensitive to light of all colors.

pan•cre•as |păng′krē əs| *or* |păn′-| *n.* A long, soft, irregularly shaped gland located behind the stomach. It secretes digestive juices.

pan•cre•at•ic |păng′krē ăt′ĭk| *or* |păn′-| *adj.* Of or secreted by the pancreas: *pancreatic juice.*

pan•da |păn′də| *n.* **1.** Also **giant panda.** A bearlike animal of the mountains of China and Tibet, having woolly fur with black and white markings. **2.** Often **lesser panda.** A small raccoonlike animal of northeastern Asia, having reddish fur and a long, ringed tail. [SEE PICTURE]

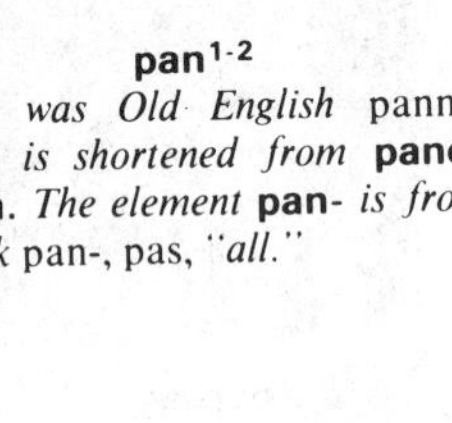

panda

pan•da•nus |păn dā′nəs| *n., pl.* **pan•da•nus•es.** A palmlike tropical tree with large prop roots and narrow leaves that yield a fiber used in weaving mats and other articles.

pan•dem•ic |păn dĕm′ĭk| *adj.* Occurring as an epidemic through a very wide area: *diseases that are pandemic in tropical areas.* —*n.* A pandemic disease.

ă pat/ā pay/â care/ä father/ĕ pet/ ē be/ĭ pit/ī pie/î fierce/ŏ pot/ ō go/ô paw, for/oi oil/ŏŏ book/ ōō boot/ou out/ŭ cut/û fur/ *th* the/th thin/hw which/zh vision/ ə ago, item, pencil, atom, circus

pan•de•mo•ni•um |păn′də mō′nē əm| *n.* Wild confusion and noise; uproar.

pan•der |păn′dər| *n.* Someone who profits by exploiting the needs and weaknesses of others. —*v.* To act as a pander: *His work panders to popular tastes.* —**pan′der•er** *n.*

pane |pān| *n.* **1.** A sheet of glass, especially one in a window or door. **2.** One of the divisions of a window or door, including the glass and its frame. ¶*These sound alike* **pane, pain.**

pan•el |păn′əl| *n.* **1.** A flat piece, such as a wooden board, forming part of a surface or overlaying it: *a great door with gold-inlaid panels.* **2.** A piece of cloth sewn lengthwise into or onto a skirt or dress. **3.** A framed section in a wall or other surface: *a large fish tank with viewing panels on the side.* **4.** A sliding door, hatch, or partition: *a secret panel leading to the roof.* **5.** A board with instruments or controls. **6.** A thin wooden board used as a surface for oil painting. **7.** A picture in a rectangular frame or boundary. **8. a.** A list or group of persons chosen for jury duty. **b.** A jury. **9.** A group of persons gathered together to discuss or decide something: *a panel of medical and legal experts.* —***modifier:*** *panel members; a panel discussion.* —*v.* **pan•eled** or **pan•elled, pan•el•ing** or **pan•el•ling.** To cover or decorate with panels.

pan•el•ing |păn′ə lĭng| *n.* **1.** A set of wooden panels covering a wall or other surface. **2.** Wood or other material used for covering walls.

pan•el•ist |păn′ə lĭst| *n.* A member of a panel.

panel truck. A small delivery truck with a closed top and back.

pang |păng| *n.* **1.** A brief, sharp sensation, as of pain; a spasm: *hunger pangs.* **2.** A brief, sharp feeling of strong emotion: *a pang of remorse.*

pan•go•lin |păng gō′lĭn| *n.* A long-tailed African or Asian animal having a body covered with overlapping scales and a sticky tongue with which it catches ants. [SEE PICTURE]

pan•han•dle |păn′hăn′dl| *n.* **1.** The handle of a pan. **2.** Often **Panhandle.** A narrow strip of territory extending like the handle of a pan from a broader area: *the Oklahoma Panhandle.* —*v.* **pan•han•dled, pan•han•dling.** *Slang.* To beg for money on the streets. —**pan′han′dler** *n.*

pan•ic |păn′ĭk| *n.* **1.** A sudden, overwhelming terror. **2.** A sudden fear of financial loss among investors. —*adj.* Of panic: *a panic reaction.* —*v.* **pan•icked, pan•ick•ing, pan•ics. 1.** To be stricken with panic: *The troops panicked and retreated in disorder.* **2.** To cause panic in: *Gunshots panicked the cattle.*

pan•ick•y |păn′ĭ kē| *adj.* Full of or showing signs of panic: *a panicky voice.*

pan•nier |păn′yər| *or* |păn′ē ər| *n.* One of a pair of baskets carried on either side of a pack animal.

pan•o•ply |păn′ə plē| *n., pl.* **pan•o•plies. 1.** The complete arms and armor of a warrior. **2.** Something that covers or protects like armor: *a panoply of Air Force bases.* **3.** Magnificent display.

pan•o•ram•a |păn′ə răm′ə| *or* |-rä′mə| *n.* **1.** A view or picture of everything visible over a wide area: *a vast panorama of mountain scenery.* **2.** A view or picture of a long series of events, stages, or things: *a book that presents a panorama of man's ascent from savagery to civilization.* **3.** A wide picture depicting a scene or story that is unrolled a part at a time before spectators.

pan•o•ram•ic |păn′ə răm′ĭk| *adj.* Of or like a panorama: *panoramic views; a panoramic photograph.* —**pan′o•ram′i•cal•ly** *adv.*

pan•pipe |păn′pīp′| *n.* A musical instrument consisting of a set of tubes or reeds of graduated lengths bound together, played by blowing air across the tops of the tubes.

pan•sy |păn′zē| *n., pl.* **pan•sies. 1.** A garden plant having variously colored, often purple and yellow flowers with rounded, velvety petals. **2.** A flower of this plant. [SEE PICTURE]

pant |pănt| *v.* **1.** To breathe in short, quick gasps. **2.** To yearn desperately: *panted for the light of dawn to come.* **3.** To utter breathlessly: *"Are we nearly there?" Alice managed to pant out.* —*n.* A short, quick gasp.

pan•ta•lets, also **pan•ta•lettes** |păn′tl ĕts′| *pl.n.* Long underpants with frills or ruffles showing below the skirt, worn by girls and women in the mid-19th century.

pan•ta•loon |păn′tl o͞on′| *n.* **1. Pantaloon.** A comic pantomime character usually appearing as a foolish old man. **2. pantaloons.** Trousers, especially loose, baggy ones.

pan•the•ism |păn′thē ĭz′əm| *n.* **1.** The belief that God and nature are one. **2.** The worship of many or all gods. —**pan′the•ist** *n.* —**pan′the•is′tic** *adj.*

pan•the•on |păn′thē ŏn′| *n.* **1.** A temple dedicated to all of the gods. **2.** A public building commemorating the great men of a nation. **3.** All the gods of a people.

pan•ther |păn′thər| *n.* A large wild cat, especially the leopard in its black, unspotted form or the mountain lion. [SEE PICTURE]

pant•ies |păn′tēz| *pl.n. Informal.* Short underpants for women or children.

pan•to•mime |păn′tə mīm′| *n.* **1. a.** Acting that consists mostly of gestures and other body movement without speech. **b.** A play or entertainment acted in this way. **2.** Movements of the face and body used in place of words to express a message or meaning. —*v.* **pan•to•mimed, pan•to•mim•ing.** To perform or represent by gestures without speech. —**pan′to•mim′ist** *n.*

pan•try |păn′trē| *n., pl.* **pan•tries.** A small room or closet, usually next to a kitchen, where food, china, silver, linens, etc., are stored.

pants |pănts| *pl.n.* **1.** Trousers. **2.** Underpants.

pant•suit |pănt′so͞ot′| *n.* Also **pants suit.** A woman's suit having trousers instead of a skirt.

pant•y hose |păn′tē|. A garment consisting of stockings and underpants in one piece.

pap |păp| *n.* **1.** Soft, easily digestible food for infants or invalids. **2.** Matter designed to satisfy or entertain but lacking real value or substance: *the pap given to daytime television viewers.*

pa•pa |pä′pə| *or* |pə pä′| *n.* Father. Used chiefly by children.

pa•pa•cy |pā′pə sē| *n., pl.* **pa•pa•cies. 1.** The office or authority of the pope. **2.** Often **Papacy.** The system of church government headed by the pope: *Rome, the seat of the Papacy.* **3.** All of the popes or a series of popes: *the medieval papacy.* **4.** The period during which a pope is in office.

pa•pal |pā′pəl| *adj.* Of the pope or his office: *papal rule; papal history.* —**pa′pal•ly** *adv.*

pangolin

pansy

panther

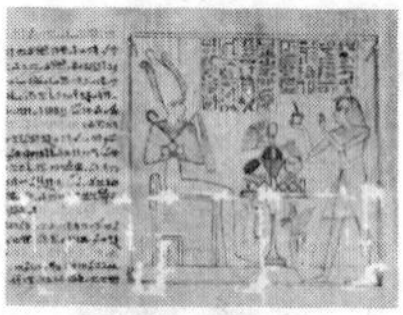

papyrus
Above: The plant
Below: Ancient Egyptian manuscript
The word **paper** is ultimately from Greek *papuros,* "papyrus."

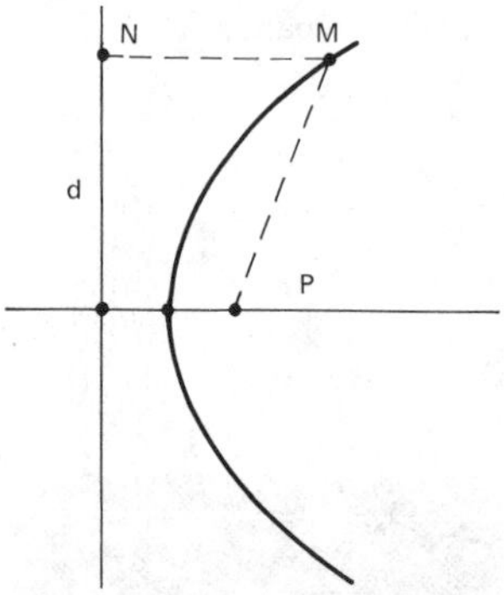

parabola
Any given point on the parabola, M for example, is equidistant from the line d and the point P

ă pat/ā pay/â care/ä father/ĕ pet/ ē be/ĭ pit/ī pie/î fierce/ŏ pot/ ō go/ô paw, for/oi oil/ŏŏ book/ ōō boot/ou out/ŭ cut/û fur/ *th* the/th thin/hw which/zh vision/ ə ago, item, pencil, atom, circus

pa•paw |pô′pô′| *or* |pə pô′| *n.* **1.** A North American tree with fleshy, sweet-tasting fruit. **2.** The fruit of this tree.

pa•pa•ya |pə pä′yə| *n.* **1.** The large, yellow, melonlike fruit of a tropical American tree. **2.** A tree that bears such fruit.

pa•per |pā′pər| *n.* **1. a.** A material produced, usually in thin sheets, from cellulose pulp derived mainly from wood, rags, and certain grasses. It is used for writing, printing, drawing, wrapping, and covering walls. **b.** A single sheet of this material. **c.** A sheet of this material with writing or printing on it. **2. a.** A document: *legal papers.* **b. papers.** Documents that establish identity or give other information about the bearer. **3. papers.** A collection of letters, memoranda, and other personal writings. **4.** A newspaper. **5. a.** A report or essay assigned in school. **b.** A scholarly essay: *"The Federalist" is a series of papers about the U.S. Constitution.* —**modifier:** *a paper cup; paper clips; a paper mill.* —*v.* **1.** To cover or wrap in paper: *Photos of old movie stars papered the mirror.* **2.** To cover with wallpaper. —**pa′per•y** *adj.*

pa•per•back |pā′pər băk′| *n.* A book with a flexible paper binding. —**modifier:** *a paperback edition.*

pa•per•weight |pā′pər wāt′| *n.* A small, heavy object for holding down loose papers.

pa•pier-mâ•ché |pā′pər mə shā′| *n.* A material made from paper pulp mixed with glue or paste, that can be molded into various shapes when wet. —**modifier:** *a papier-mâché dragon.*

pa•pil•la |pə pĭl′ə| *n., pl.* **pa•pil•lae** |pə pĭl′ē|. Any small, nipplelike part that projects from a body surface, as one of the tiny projections on the top of the tongue.

pa•pist |pā′pĭst| *n.* A **Roman Catholic.** —*adj.* **Roman Catholic.** The word "papist" is used contemptuously by non-Catholics.

pa•poose |pă pōōs′| *n.* A North American Indian baby: *squaws traveling with papooses on their backs.*

pap•ri•ka |pă prē′kə| *or* |păp′rĭ kə| *n.* A mild-tasting powdered seasoning made from sweet red peppers.

Pap•u•a New Guin•ea |păp′yōō ə, gĭn′ē|. A country located on the eastern half of the island of New Guinea. Population, 2,650,000. Capital, Port Moresby.

pa•py•rus |pə pī′rəs| *n.* **1.** A tall, reedlike water plant of northern Africa and nearby regions. **2.** A kind of paper made from the stems and pith of this plant by the ancient Egyptians. **3.** *pl.* **pa•py•ri** |pə pī′rī′| or **pa•py•rus•es.** A document written on this material. [See Picture]

par |pär| *n.* **1.** An accepted or normal average: *below par in physical condition.* **2.** A level of equality; equal footing: *good wine, but not on a par with imported kinds.* **3.** The number of golf strokes regarded as necessary to complete a given hole or course in expert play. **4.** The value printed on the face of a stock or bond as distinguished from the current market value. —**modifier:** *the par value.* —*adj.* Equal to the standard; normal: *a par performance.*

para–[1]. A prefix meaning: **1.** Alongside; near: **parathyroid gland.** **2.** Closely resembling: **paratyphoid fever.**

para–[2]. A word element meaning "parachute": **paratrooper.**

par•a•ble |păr′ə bəl| *n.* A simple, realistic story illustrating a moral or religious lesson.

pa•rab•o•la |pə răb′ə lə| *n.* The curve formed by the set of points in a plane that are all equally distant from a given line and a given point not on the line. [See Picture]

par•a•bol•ic |păr′ə bŏl′ĭk| *adj.* Of or shaped like a parabola. —**par′a•bol′i•cal•ly** *adv.*

par•a•chute |păr′ə shōōt′| *n.* **1.** A foldable umbrella-shaped device used to slow the fall of persons or objects from great heights. **2.** A similar device used to slow speeding vehicles. —*v.* **par•a•chut•ed, par•a•chut•ing.** **1.** To descend by parachute. **2.** To drop (supplies, weapons, etc.) by parachute. —**par′a•chut′ist** *n.*

pa•rade |pə răd′| *n.* **1.** A festive public event in which assembled people or vehicles pass by spectators, often with music, costumes, and colorful display. **2. a.** A formal review of marching soldiers or sailors. **b.** Also **parade ground.** The grounds on which such reviews are held. **3.** The group participating in such a public event or military review. **4.** Any large number of people walking by, as if on public display: *the parade of Sunday strollers.* **5.** A long line or succession: *The cars on the highway began to resemble a parade of ants.* **6.** An elaborate or vulgar display: *making a parade of his wealth.* —**modifier:** *parade banners.* —*v.* **pa•rad•ed, pa•rad•ing.** **1.** To take part in a parade: *A company of firemen paraded in uniform.* **2.** To assemble and guide (troops, famous persons, etc.) in a parade. **3.** To display oneself proudly or vainly: *a peacock parading before his mate.* **4.** To exhibit proudly or vainly: *paraded his nine children before the guests.* —**pa•rad′er** *n.*

par•a•digm |păr′ə dīm′| *n.* **1.** A list of the inflectional forms of a word, considered as a model for determining the forms of other words like it. **2.** Any example of how something should be done or treated; a model.

par•a•dise |păr′ə dīs′| *or* |-dīz′| *n.* **1.** Heaven. **2.** Often **Paradise.** Eden. **3.** A place or condition of perfect happiness or beauty. **4.** A perfect or ideal place: *a paradise for fishermen.*

par•a•dox |păr′ə dŏks′| *n.* **1.** A statement that contains or implies its own contradiction and therefore has an uncertain meaning or no meaning; for example, *"We destroyed the town in order to save it"* is a paradox. **2.** A statement that appears to contradict itself or to be untrue but that may be true; for example, "Light consists both of waves and of particles" is a paradox that can be demonstrated in simple experiments. **3.** A group of facts, qualities, or circumstances that seem to contradict each other.

par•a•dox•i•cal |păr′ə dŏk′sĭ kəl| *adj.* Containing a paradox; apparently contradictory. —**par′a•dox′i•cal•ly** *adv.*

par•af•fin |păr′ə fĭn| *n.* A waxy, white or colorless, solid hydrocarbon mixture used in making candles, wax paper, lubricating materials, and sealing materials. —*v.* To treat, coat, or seal with paraffin.

paraffin series. A family of related hydrocarbon compounds composed so that if *n* is the number of carbon atoms contained, $2n + 2$ is the number of hydrogen atoms contained.

par•a•gon |păr′ə gŏn′| *n.* A model of excellence; a perfect example: *a paragon of honesty.*

par•a•graph |păr′ə grăf′| *or* |-gräf′| *n.* **1.** A division of a piece of writing that begins on a new, usually indented line and that consists of one or more sentences on a single idea or aspect of the subject. **2.** A mark, ¶, used to indicate where a new paragraph should begin. —*v.* To divide (a written work) into paragraphs. —**par′a•graph′ic, par′a•graph′i•cal** *adj.*

Par•a•guay |păr′ə gwā′|. A country in central South America. Population, 2,572,000. Capital, Asunción. —**Par′a•guay′an** *n. & adj.*

par•a•keet |păr′ə kēt′| *n.* Any of several small parrots usually having a long, pointed tail. [SEE PICTURE]

par•al•lax |păr′ə lăks′| *n.* An apparent change in the position of an object caused by a change in the observer's position.

par•al•lel |păr′ə lĕl′| *adj.* **1.** Lying in the same plane and not intersecting: *parallel lines.* **2.** Not intersecting: *parallel planes.* **3.** Having corresponding points always separated by the same distance: *parallel curves; parallel to the river.* **4.** Matching feature for feature; corresponding: *parallel economic developments in other countries.* **5.** Of, consisting of, or containing electric devices connected so that the same source of voltage appears across each. —*adv.* In a parallel course or direction: *a reef running parallel to the shore.* —*n.* **1.** Any of a set of parallel geometric figures, especially lines. **2.** Something closely resembling something else; a corresponding case or instance. **3.** A comparison showing close resemblance; an analogy: *a chilling parallel between our times and the decline of Rome.* **4.** Any of the lines considered to encircle the earth parallel to the plane of the equator, used to represent degrees of latitude. —*v.* **1.** To make or place parallel: *paralleled the two edges of the fabric.* **2.** To be or extend parallel to: *The town's main street paralleled a ship canal.* **3.** To correspond to; follow closely.

par•al•lel•e•pi•ped |păr′ə lĕl′ə **pī′**pĭd| *n.* A solid geometric figure having six faces, each one a parallelogram.

par•al•lel•ism |păr′ə lĕl ĭz′əm| *n.* **1.** The condition, position, or relationship of being parallel. **2.** Similarity; correspondence.

par•al•lel•o•gram |păr′ə **lĕl′**ə grăm′| *n.* A plane, four-sided geometric figure in which each pair of opposite sides is parallel.

pa•ral•y•sis |pə **răl′**ĭ sĭs| *n.* **1.** Partial or complete loss of the ability to feel sensations in or move a part of the body, resulting from disease or injury that damages the nerves going to and from the part. **2.** An inability to act or move normally.

par•a•lyt•ic |păr′ə **lĭt′**ĭk| *adj.* Of, causing, or affected with paralysis. —*n.* Someone affected with paralysis.

par•a•lyze |păr′ə līz′| *v.* **par•a•lyzed, par•a•lyz•ing. 1.** To affect with paralysis; make unable to feel or move. **2. a.** To make helpless or motionless: *paralyzed by fear.* **b.** To block the normal functioning of; bring to a standstill: *The blizzard paralyzed large sections of the city.*

Par•a•mar•i•bo |păr′ə **măr′**ə bō′|. The capital of Surinam. Population, 103,000.

par•a•me•ci•um |păr′ə **mē′**shē əm| *or* |-sē-| *n., pl.* **par•a•me•ci•a** |păr′ə **mē′**shē ə| *or* |-sē-| or **par•a•me•ci•ums.** A very small one-celled organism that is usually slipperlike or oval in shape and that moves by means of tiny, hairlike projections called cilia. [SEE PICTURE]

par•a•med•ic |păr′ə **mĕd′**ĭk| *n.* A person who assists a highly trained medical professional, as a laboratory technician, nurse, or the like.

par•a•med•i•cal |păr′ə **mĕd′**ĭ kəl| *adj.* Of or designating the work of paramedics.

pa•ram•e•ter |pə **răm′**ə tər| *n.* **1.** A variable or an arbitrary constant appearing in a mathematical expression, each value of which restricts or determines the specific form of the expression. **2.** *Informal.* A fixed limit or boundary: *Stay within the parameters of the present budget.*

par•a•mil•i•tar•y |păr′ə **mĭl′**ĭ tĕr′ē| *adj.* Organized or functioning like a military unit but outside of the regular military forces.

par•a•mount |păr′ə mount′| *adj.* **1.** Supreme in rank or position; leading. **2.** Of greatest importance or concern; primary.

par•a•noi•a |păr′ə **noi′**ə| *n.* **1.** A serious mental disorder in which a person imagines himself to be persecuted and often has an exaggerated idea of his own importance. **2.** Irrational fear for one's security.

par•a•noi•ac |păr′ə **noi′**ăk′| *n.* Someone who is affected with paranoia. —*adj.* Of or resembling paranoia.

par•a•noid |păr′ə noid′| *adj.* Of, affected with, or characteristic of paranoia. —*n.* Someone affected with paranoia; a paranoiac.

par•a•pet |păr′ə pĭt| *or* |-pĕt′| *n.* **1.** A low wall or railing along the edge of a roof or balcony. **2.** An embankment protecting soldiers from enemy fire.

par•a•pher•na•lia |păr′ə fə **nāl′**yə| *n. (used with a singular or plural verb).* **1.** One's personal belongings. **2.** The equipment used in or associated with some activity; gear.

par•a•phrase |păr′ə frāz′| *v.* **par•a•phrased, par•a•phras•ing.** To express the meaning of in a different form; restate in other words: *paraphrasing a Biblical passage to clarify its meaning.* —*n.* A restatement in other words.

par•a•ple•gi•a |păr′ə **plē′**jē ə| *n.* Paralysis of the entire lower part of the body, caused by injury or disease of the spinal cord.

par•a•ple•gic |păr′ə **plē′**jĭk| *adj.* Of or affected by paraplegia. —*n.* Someone with paraplegia.

par•a•site |păr′ə sīt′| *n.* **1.** An organism that lives in or on a different kind of organism from which it gets its nourishment and to which it is sometimes harmful. **2.** A person who depends on someone else for a living without making any useful return.

par•a•sit•ic |păr′ə **sĭt′**ĭk| *adj.* **1.** Of or caused by a parasite: *a parasitic disease.* **2.** Living as a parasite: *Mistletoe is a parasitic plant.*

par•a•sit•ize |păr′ə sĭ tīz′| *v.* **par•a•sit•ized, par•a•sit•iz•ing.** To live on (another organism) as a parasite.

par•a•sol |păr′ə sôl′| *or* |-sŏl′| *n.* A small, light umbrella used, especially by women, as a protection against the sun. [SEE PICTURE]

par•a•thy•roid gland |păr′ə **thī′**roid′|. Any of four small kidney-shaped glands that lie in pairs

parakeet

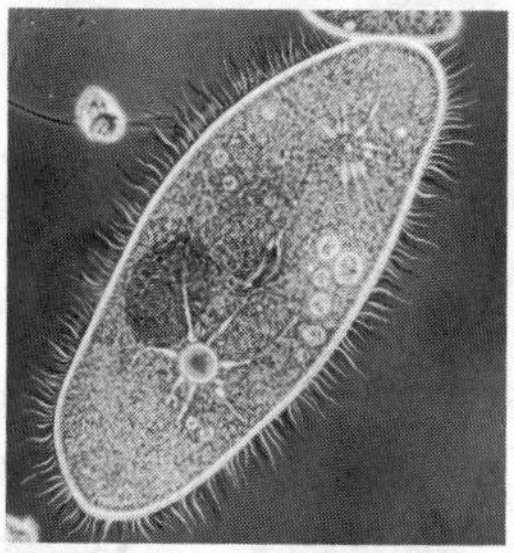

paramecium

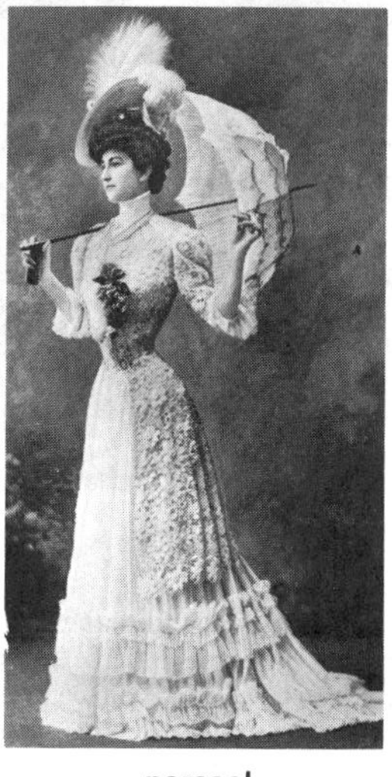

parasol

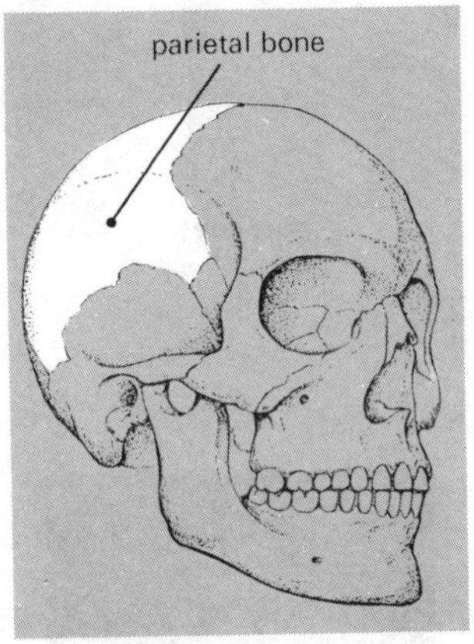

parietal bone

parka

ă pat/ā pay/â care/ä father/ĕ pet/ ē be/ĭ pit/ī pie/î fierce/ŏ pot/ ō go/ô paw, for/oi oil/ŏŏ book/ ōō boot/ou out/ŭ cut/û fur/ *th* the/th thin/hw which/zh vision/ ə ago, item, pencil, atom, circus

at the sides of the thyroid gland. They secrete a hormone that controls the metabolism of calcium and phosphorus.

par•a•troop•er |păr′ə trōō′pər| *n.* A member of an infantry unit trained and equipped to parachute from airplanes.

par•a•ty•phoid fever |păr′ə tī′foid′|. An intestinal disease that is similar to typhoid fever but less severe, caused by bacteria.

par•boil |pär′boil′| *v.* To boil (food) briefly.

par•cel |pär′səl| *n.* **1.** Something wrapped up in a bundle; a package. **2.** A section or division of land; a plot. **3.** A group; bunch: *a parcel of chattering assistants.* —*v.* To divide into parts and distribute; allot: *parcel out work.*

parcel post. The branch of the postal service that handles parcels.

parch |pärch| *v.* **1.** To make or become very dry, especially with intense heat: *A constant south wind parched the topsoil. The skin wrinkles and parches with age.* **2.** To dry or roast (corn, peanuts, etc.) by heating.

parch•ment |pärch′mənt| *n.* **1.** The skin of a sheep or goat, prepared as a material to write on. **2.** A piece of writing on a sheet or roll of parchment. **3.** A diploma. **4.** Heavy paper that looks like parchment.

par•don |pär′dn| *v.* **1.** To release (a person) from punishment or disfavor. **2.** To pass over (an offense or fault) without punishment or disfavor. **3.** To accept or hear without taking offense; tolerate: *Will you pardon a few more questions? Pardon me for asking.* —*n.* **1.** The act of pardoning; forgiveness: *imploring your pardon.* **2.** Exemption from punishment granted by an official with authority over a legal case. **3.** Polite forgiveness, as for a discourtesy, interruption, or failure to hear: *begged her pardon for being late.*

par•don•a•ble |pär′dn ə bəl| *adj.* Easily pardoned; excusable: *displayed her gold medal with pardonable pride.* —**par′don•a•bly** *adv.*

pare |pâr| *v.* **pared, par•ing. 1.** To remove the skin or other surface part of with a knife: *pare potatoes.* **2.** To remove (a surface part) with a knife; trim off: *held the avocado firmly and pared away the rind.* **3.** To make smaller by or as if by cutting: *pared the budget to a bare minimum.* ¶*These sound alike* **pare, pair, pear.**

par•en•chy•ma |pə rĕng′kə mə| *n.* Tissue that is characteristic of an organ as distinguished from connective tissue that holds it in place.

par•ent |pâr′ənt| *or* |păr′-| *n.* **1.** A father or mother. **2.** A guardian; protector. **3.** Any living thing that produces or generates another. **4.** The source or cause from which something comes.

par•ent•age |pâr′ən tĭj| *or* |păr′-| *n.* Descent from parents or ancestors; lineage; origin.

pa•ren•tal |pə rĕn′tl| *adj.* **1.** Of a parent: *parental control of a child's money.* **2.** Like or suited to a parent; fatherly or motherly: *He took a parental interest in her career.* —**pa•ren′tal•ly** *adv.*

pa•ren•the•sis |pə rĕn′thĭ sĭs| *n., pl.* **pa•ren•the•ses** |pə rĕn′thĭ sēz′|. **1.** Either or both of the upright curved lines, ( ), used to mark off additional remarks in printing or writing. **2.** An additional phrase, explanation, etc., enclosed within such marks. **3.** A qualifying phrase placed within a sentence in such a way that the sentence is grammatically complete without it. **4.** Any comment departing from the main topic.

par•en•thet•i•cal |păr′ən thĕt′ĭ kəl| or **par•en•thet•ic** |păr′ən thĕt′ĭk| *adj.* **1.** Contained or grammatically capable of being contained within parentheses: *a parenthetical construction at the end of a sentence.* **2.** Forming a brief explanation or digression: *a parenthetical aside during a speech.* —**par′en•thet′i•cal•ly** *adv.*

par•ent•hood |pâr′ənt hŏŏd′| *or* |păr′-| *n.* The condition of being a parent.

pa•re•sis |pə rē′sĭs| *or* |păr′ĭ sĭs| *n.* Slight or partial paralysis.

par•fait |pär fā′| *n.* **1.** A sweet frozen dessert of cream, eggs, and flavoring, served in a tall glass. **2.** A dessert of layers, often of ice cream with various toppings, served in a tall glass.

pa•ri•ah |pə rī′ə| *n.* A person who has been excluded from society; an outcast.

pa•ri•e•tal bone |pə rī′ĭ təl|. Either of the two bones that form the top and sides of the skull. [SEE PICTURE]

par•i-mu•tu•el |păr′ĭ myōō′chōō əl| *n., pl.* **par•i-mu•tu•els. 1.** A system of betting on races in which the winners divide the total amount bet in proportion to the amounts they bet individually. **2.** Also **pari-mutuel machine.** A machine for recording and totaling bets made under this system. —***modifier:*** *pari-mutuel wagering.*

Par•is[1] |păr′ĭs|. The capital and largest city of France. Population, 2,500,000.

Par•is[2] |păr′ĭs|. In Greek mythology, the Trojan prince whose abduction of Helen caused the Trojan War.

par•ish |păr′ĭsh| *n.* **1. a.** A division of an Anglican or Roman Catholic diocese consisting of an area with its own church. **b.** The members of such a district. **2.** An administrative district in Louisiana corresponding to a county in other states. —***modifier:*** *a parish priest.*

pa•rish•ion•er |pə rĭsh′ə nər| *n.* A member or resident of a parish.

par•i•ty |păr′ĭ tē| *n.* **1.** Equality, as in amount, status, value, or price: *firemen striking for parity of pay with policemen.* **2.** A fixed relative value between two different kinds of money: *the problem of maintaining the parity between gold coins and paper currency.* **3.** A level of prices paid to farmers for their products that gives the farmers the same purchasing power they had during a chosen earlier period.

park |pärk| *n.* **1.** A tract of land enclosed for recreational use inside a town or city. **2.** A tract of land kept in its natural state for recreational use. **3.** Any fairly large or open area used for recreation or entertainment: *an amusement park.* **4.** A stadium or enclosed playing field: *a ball park.* **5.** A place for storing or leaving vehicles: *a trailer park; a car park.* —*v.* **1.** To stop or leave (a vehicle) for a time in a certain place away from traffic: *park a car; parked along the roadside and ate lunch.* **2.** *Informal.* To place or leave at a certain location: *parked himself under the basket and waited for a high pass; parked the baby with a neighbor for the evening.* —**parked′** *adj.: parked cars.*

par•ka |pär′kə| *n.* A warm fur or cloth jacket with a hood. [SEE PICTURE]

Par•kin•son's disease |pär′kĭn sənz|. A progressive disease of the nervous system that occurs mainly in older people. Its symptoms include weakness, muscular tremors, slowing of movement, and partial paralysis of the face.

park•way |pärk'wā'| *n.* **1.** A broad landscaped highway. **2.** A grassy or tree-lined public walk.

par•lance |pär'ləns| *n.* A special kind or style of language: *in the parlance of lawyers.*

par•lay |pär'lā'| *or* |-lē| *n.* A bet on two or more successive events at once, with the winnings of one, plus the original stake, to be automatically risked on the next. —*v.* **1.** To bet (money) in a parlay. **2.** To increase (money) to a much larger amount by repeated investments: *parlayed his small capital into a fortune.* **3.** To use to great advantage or profit: *parlayed a knack for mimicry into a career as an entertainer.*

par•ley |pär'lē| *n., pl.* **par•leys. 1.** A conference, especially between enemies or opponents. **2.** Discussion; conversation: *no time for parley.* —*v.* To hold a parley; confer.

par•lia•ment |pär'lə mənt| *n.* **1.** An assembly of persons that makes the laws for a nation. **2. Parliament.** The national legislature of the United Kingdom, made up of the House of Commons and the House of Lords.

par•lia•men•tar•i•an |pär'lə mĕn târ'ē ən| *n.* An expert in parliamentary rules and procedures.

par•lia•men•ta•ry |pär'lə mĕn'tə rē| *or* |-trē| *adj.* **1.** Of a parliament. **2.** Observing, following, or directing the rules of procedure of a parliament or similar body: *parliamentary debate.* **3.** Having a parliament: *parliamentary government.*

par•lor |pär'lər| *n.* **1.** A room for entertaining visitors. **2.** A room designed for some special use or business: *a beauty parlor; a billiard parlor.* —***modifier:*** *parlor games.*

par•lour |pär'lər| *n.* A British form of the word **parlor.**

Par•me•san |pär'mĭ zän'| *or* |-zăn'| *or* |-zən| *n.* A hard, dry Italian cheese, usually served grated.

pa•ro•chi•al |pə rō'kē əl| *adj.* **1.** Of a church parish: *a parochial priest.* **2.** Limited in range or understanding; narrow: *a parochial mind.*

parochial school. A school supported by a church parish.

pa•ro•chi•al•ism |pə rō'kē ə lĭz'əm| *n.* **1.** Narrowness of range or understanding. **2.** A parochial attitude or opinion.

par•o•dy |păr'ə dē| *n., pl.* **par•o•dies.** A comic imitation, as of a person, literary work, style, etc., that exaggerates the characteristics of the original to make it seem ridiculous. —*v.* **par•o•died, par•o•dy•ing, par•o•dies.** To present, perform, or be a parody of: *parodied the pompous style of editorial writers.*

pa•role |pə rōl'| *n.* The early release of a prisoner on condition of good behavior. —*v.* **pa•roled, pa•rol•ing.** To release on parole.

par•ox•ysm |păr'ək sĭz'əm| *n.* **1.** A spasm or fit; a convulsion. **2.** A sudden outburst of strong emotion: *turned on him in a paroxysm of rage.*

par•quet |pär kā'| *n.* **1.** A floor made of inlaid pieces of wood that are fitted together into a design. **2.** The main floor of a theater. —***modifier:*** *a parquet floor.* [SEE PICTURE]

par•ri•cide |păr'ĭ sīd'| *n.* **1.** A person who murders his father or mother or other near relative. **2.** The act of committing such a murder. —**par'ri•cid'al** *adj.*

par•rot |păr'ət| *n.* **1.** Any of several tropical birds with a short, hooked bill and usually brightly colored feathers. Some kinds are kept as pets and can be taught to imitate spoken words. **2.** A person who repeats or imitates something without understanding it. —*v.* To repeat or imitate (another's words or another person) without understanding. [SEE PICTURE]

par•ry |păr'ē| *v.* **par•ried, par•ry•ing, par•ries. 1.** To turn aside; deflect: *parry a thrust in fencing.* **2.** To avoid skillfully; evade: *parried questions of the reporters.* —*n., pl.* **par•ries. 1.** The act or maneuver of deflecting a blow, especially in fencing. **2.** An evasive action or answer: *met the accusation with a deft parry.*

parse |pärs| *v.* **parsed, pars•ing. 1.** To break (a sentence or phrase) down into its parts of speech with an explanation of the form and function of each word. **2.** To indicate the part of speech, form, and function of (a word in a sentence or phrase). **3.** To be clearly divisible into parts of speech: *a sentence that doesn't parse.*

par•sec |pär'sĕk'| *n.* A unit of astronomical distance equal to 3.258 light years.

Par•see |pär'sē'| *n.* A member of the surviving sect of Zoroastrianism in India.

par•si•mo•ni•ous |pär'sə mō'nē əs| *adj.* Marked by parsimony; ungenerous; stingy. —**par'si•mo'ni•ous•ly** *adv.*

par•si•mo•ny |pär'sə mō'nē| *n.* **1.** Extreme or excessive reluctance to spend money or use resources; stinginess. **2.** The use of as few assumptions as possible in logical thinking.

pars•ley |pär'slē| *n.* A plant with feathery, often curled leaves used to flavor or decorate food.

pars•nip |pär'snĭp| *n.* **1.** A plant with a long, whitish, rather strong-tasting root. **2.** The root of this plant, eaten as a vegetable.

par•son |pär'sən| *n.* **1.** A clergyman in charge of a parish, especially in the Anglican Church. **2.** Any clergyman.

par•son•age |pär'sə nĭj| *n.* The official residence of a parson, as provided by his church.

part |pärt| *n.* **1.** Something that along with other things makes a whole; a portion or division of a larger thing: *arrived late and missed part of the movie; gave her brother a part of the candy bar.* **2. a.** One of several equal portions that when combined make up a whole: *For the dressing we mixed two parts of olive oil with one part of vinegar.* **b.** A fraction: *What part of a quart is a pint?* **3.** Something or someone that is not distinct or separable from something else: *She was treated as part of the family.* **4.** An organ, limb, or other division of an animal or plant. **5.** A piece in a machine or assemblage that can be removed or replaced; a component. **6.** One of the functions or tasks that must be performed in a common effort; a share of the work: *doing one's part.* **7.** A role: *a small part in the class play.* **8. a.** Any of the individual melodic lines that go together to make up music: *singing the soprano part.* **b.** A written representation of such a melodic line, read by the person who sings or plays it. **9.** A side in a dispute or controversy: *We saw a small boy being bullied and took his part.* **10. parts.** Regions; lands; areas: *relatives scattered in re-*

parquet
Section of a nineteenth-century parquet floor

parrot

mote parts. **11. parts.** Natural abilities; talents: *a gentleman of parts.* **12.** A line on either side of which one combs his hair in different directions. —*v.* **1.** To divide into two or more parts; split: *parted the log with his ax; a tree trunk that parted into branches higher up.* **2.** To move away from each other: *His lips parted in expectation. She parted the curtains.* **3.** To make a gap or space through: *Moses parted the waters.* **4.** To leave one another; separate: *They reached the corner where they usually parted.* **5.** To put or keep apart; come between: *They were good friends until a silly quarrel parted them.* **6.** To go away; depart: *didn't part from his bedside until almost midnight.* —***phrasal verb.* part with.** To give up; yield: *hated to part with a penny.* —*adj.* Not full; partial: *owned a part interest in a lemonade stand; a part owner.* —*adv.* In part; partially: *Her dog is part collie, part German shepherd.*

***Idioms.* for (one's) part.** As far as one is concerned: *For my part, I have no objection.* **for the most part.** In most cases; chiefly. **in good part. 1.** With good grace; good-humoredly: *accepted the reproach in good part.* **2.** Largely; chiefly. **in large part.** Largely; chiefly. **in part.** To a certain extent; partly. **part and parcel.** An inseparable part: *The house furnishings were part and parcel of the deal.* **part company. 1.** To go different ways; separate. **2.** To end a relationship or alliance: *friends who parted company on the issue of slavery.* **take part.** To be active; participate.

part. participle.

par•take |pär tāk′| *v.* **par•took** |pär to͝ok′|, **par•tak•en** |pär tā′kən|, **par•tak•ing. 1.** To take part; participate: *partake in the festivities.* **2.** To take a portion; eat or drink a helping: *invited to partake of their dinner.* **3.** To share some of the properties of something else: *mirthless laughter that partook of the grimness of death.* —**par•tak′er** *n.*

Par•the•non |pär′thə nŏn′|. The temple of Athena built on the Acropolis in Athens in the fifth century B.C.

par•tial |pär′shəl| *adj.* **1.** Not total; incomplete: *partial success.* **2.** Favoring one side; biased. **3.** Especially attracted or inclined: *She's partial to boys with long hair.* [SEE NOTE]

par•ti•al•i•ty |pär′shē ăl′ĭ tē| *n., pl.* **par•ti•al•i•ties. 1.** An inclination to favor one side over another or others; bias: *trying to judge without partiality.* **2.** A strong preference; a special fondness: *a partiality for old clothes and shoes.*

par•tial•ly |pär′shə lē| *adv.* To a certain degree or extent; incompletely: *partially thawed food.*

partial product. A product formed by multiplying the multiplicand by one digit of the multiplier when the multiplier has more than one digit in its numeral. For example, the product of 67 multiplied by 12 is 134 + 670 = 804. In this example 134 and 670 are partial products.

partial quotient. A quotient that appears after any stage of a division problem requiring two or more stages and that is added to the others to give the final quotient. For example, in the problem 248 ÷ 4 = 60 + 2 = 62, 60 and 2 are partial quotients.

par•tic•i•pant |pär tĭs′ə pənt| *n.* Someone who participates: *participants in a card game.*

par•tic•i•pate |pär tĭs′ə pāt′| *v.* **par•tic•i•pat•ed, par•tic•i•pat•ing.** To join with others in being active; take part: *She participated in a church discussion group.* —**par•tic′i•pa′tion** *n.*

par•tic•i•pa•to•ry |pär tĭs′ə pə tôr′ē| *or* |-tōr′ē| *adj.* Involving the active participation of many: *participatory democracy.*

par•ti•cip•i•al |pär′tĭ sĭp′ē əl| *adj.* Based on, forming, or formed from a participle: *a participial phrase; a participial adjective.*

par•ti•ci•ple |pär′tĭ sĭp′əl| *n.* Either of two verb forms that are used with auxiliary verbs to indicate certain tenses and that can also function in certain cases as adjectives or nouns. See **past participle, present participle.**

par•ti•cle |pär′tĭ kəl| *n.* **1.** A very small piece of solid matter; a speck: *particles of dust.* **2.** An **elementary particle. 3. a.** The smallest possible unit or portion: *applying every particle of strength she had left.* **b.** The least bit or degree: *hardly a particle of difference between the twins.* **4.** In grammar, any of a class of words, including many prepositions and conjunctions, that have little meaning by themselves but help to specify, connect, or limit the meanings of other words.

par•tic•u•lar |pər tĭk′yə lər| *adj.* **1.** Of or for a single person, group, or thing: *Each camper did his particular job.* **2.** Unmistakably connected with or expressive of a certain person or thing; peculiar; unique: *the particular tone of hunger in the dog's howl.* **3.** Distinct from others; specific; certain: *at that particular time of year.* **4.** Exceptional; special: *paying particular attention.* **5.** Providing full details: *a particular account.* **6.** Giving or demanding close attention to details; fussy: *She's very particular about how her meat is cooked.* —*n.* **1.** A single item, fact, or detail: *correct in every particular.* **2. particulars.** Items of information; detailed news: *reported the particulars of their voyage to the king.*

***Idiom.* in particular.** Specifically; particularly.

par•tic•u•lar•i•ty |pər tĭk′yə lăr′ĭ tē| *n., pl.* **par•tic•u•lar•i•ties. 1.** The quality of being particular rather than general or universal: *the particularity of a proper noun, which names only one thing or person.* **2.** The quality of including or providing details: *the particularity of a newspaper story.* **3.** A detail; a particular. **4.** Close attention to details; fussiness.

par•tic•u•lar•ize |pər tĭk′yə lə rīz′| *v.* **par•tic•u•lar•ized, par•tic•u•lar•iz•ing. 1.** To name one by one; itemize: *an indictment that particularized the charges against him.* **2.** To provide or support with full details: *particularizing a story by adding a subplot and minor characters.* **3.** To make separate or distinctive; individualize: *She began with mere stick figures, then particularized them by drawing in capes, dresses, and hats.* —**par•tic′u•lar•i•za′tion** *n.*

par•tic•u•lar•ly |pər tĭk′yə lər lē| *adv.* **1.** As one specific case; specifically: *observing the constellations, particularly the Big Dipper.* **2.** To a great degree; especially: *a particularly good play.* **3.** With attention to particulars; in detail: *spread out the chart and studied it particularly.*

part•ing |pär′tĭng| *n.* **1.** A separation into two or more parts: *a parting in the trail.* **2.** A departure or leave-taking. **3.** Someone's death. —***modifier:*** *a parting gift; parting words.* —*adj.* Leaving; departing: *a parting friend.*

par•ti•san |pär′tĭ zən| *n.* **1.** A strong supporter,

partial, etc.
All of the words from **part** *to* **partnership,** *and many others besides, are based on the Latin word* pars, part-, *"a piece, bit, share, section, group of people."* **Participate** *is from Latin* participāre, *"to take part, to share" (*part- + cip-, *"take").* **Participle** *is from the same word (since a participle shares or* participates *in the functions of both verb and adjective).* **Particle** *is from Latin* particula, *"small part," a diminutive noun from* pars, part-; *and* **particular** *is also from* particula *—its original meaning was "concerned with small details or particles."*

ă pat/ā pay/â care/ä father/ĕ pet/ ē be/ĭ pit/ī pie/î fierce/ŏ pot/ ō go/ô paw, for/oi oil/o͝o book/ o͞o boot/ou out/ŭ cut/û fur/ *th* the/th thin/hw which/zh vision/ ə ago, item, pencil, atom, circus

as of a party, cause, team, or person: *the President and his partisans in Congress.* **2.** A member of a loosely organized body of fighters who attack an enemy within occupied territory. —*adj.* **1.** Having or showing a strong preference or bias: *too partisan to give a fair account of the battle.* **2.** Of or marked by conflicting parties or factions: *partisan politics.* **3.** Of or carried on by military partisans: *partisan attacks.*

par•ti•tion |pär **tĭsh'**ən| *n.* **1.** A usually thin structure, such as a panel or screen, that divides up a room or other enclosure. **2.** Any structure that divides a space. **3. a.** The division of something into parts: *European powers arranged the partition of Africa into colonies.* **b.** The condition of being divided into parts. **4. a.** A representation of a positive whole number as a sum of positive whole numbers. **b.** The division of a set into a number of subsets that have no elements in common. —*v.* **1.** To divide into separate spaces, parts, or sections: *partitioned the room with a curtain.* **2.** To form into a separate space by means of a partition: *partitioned off the dining area from the kitchen.*

part•ly |**pärt'**lē| *adv.* To some extent; in part: *a journey partly by boat and partly on foot.*

part•ner |**pärt'**nər| *n.* **1.** One of two or more persons associated in some common activity: **a.** A member of a business partnership. **b.** A friend with whom one lives, travels, or works: *the cowboy and his partner.* **c.** A spouse or mate. **d.** Either of two persons dancing together. **e.** Either of two persons playing a game together. **2.** An ally: *Athens and her partners controlled the Aegean Sea.* **3.** An active participant: *Every citizen of a republic is a partner in planning the future of the nation.* **4.** *Informal.* Friend. A word used in speaking cordially to someone: *Sit down and rest yourself, partner.*

part•ner•ship |**pärt'**nər shĭp'| *n.* **1.** The condition of being partners: *built the tree house in partnership with two friends.* **2.** A business contract or relationship between two or more persons in which each agrees to work for a common enterprise and to share the profits or losses. **3.** Any close relationship in which each member helps or cooperates with the other: *the partnership of science and industry.*

part of speech. Any of the grammatical classes into which words are placed according to how they function in a given context. Traditionally, the parts of speech in English are *noun, pronoun, verb, adjective, adverb, preposition, conjunction,* and *interjection.* Sometimes *article* is considered a separate part of speech.

par•took |pär **to͝ok'**|. Past tense of **partake.**

par•tridge |**pär'**trĭj| *n.* Any of several plump-bodied birds with brownish feathers, often hunted as game. [SEE PICTURE]

part-time |**pärt'**tīm'| *adj.* For or during only part of the usual or standard working time: *a part-time job.* —*adv.* |**pärt'tīm'**|: *work part-time.*

par•tu•ri•tion |pär'cho͞o **rĭsh'**ən| *n.* The act or process of giving birth; childbirth.

part•way |**pärt'wā'**| *adv.* To a part of the way; partly: *pushed a thumbtack partway into the wood.*

par•ty |**pär'**tē| *n., pl.* **par•ties.** **1.** A group of persons participating together in some activity: *a search party.* **2.** An event in which a group is gathered together for pleasure or entertainment: *a birthday party.* **3.** A group organized to advance its political views and usually to nominate and support candidates for public office. **4. a.** A person or group involved in a legal proceeding: *the two parties in a lawsuit.* **b.** A person or group taking part in some action or matter; a participant: *She refused to be a party to the dispute.* —**modifier:** *a party dress; a party convention.*

pas•chal |**păs'**kəl| *adj.* Of Passover or Easter.

pa•sha |**pä'**shə| *or* |**păsh'**ə| *n.* A former Turkish title of honor placed after a name.

pasque•flow•er |**păsk'**flou'ər| *n.* An anemone with seeds with silky, featherlike tufts and large purplish or white flowers.

pass |păs| *or* |päs| *v.* **1. a.** To go from one place or position to another: *people passing from shop to shop on the busy streets.* **b.** To cause to go or move: *passed her hand over her brow.* **2. a.** To go over or through (an obstacle, barrier, etc.): *We managed to pass the reef safely. The gatekeeper wouldn't let us pass.* **b.** To cause to go over or through something: *pass water through a filter.* **3.** To extend: *A diameter passes through the center of a circle.* **4.** To go by without stopping: *passed old farmhouses along the highway; counted the railroad cars as they passed.* **5.** To catch up with and go by (a vehicle, runner, etc.): *The truck slowed down to let us pass. It is unwise to pass a car on a bend.* **6.** To go beyond; exceed: *peace that passes understanding.* **7. a.** To go by in time: *Fishermen sing to make the hours pass faster.* **b.** To spend (time): *passed her vacation in the country.* **8.** To come to an end: *waiting for the bad weather to pass.* **9. a.** To hand over: *passed his plate for more turkey.* **b.** To be transferred: *a territory that passed into the hands of the British.* **10.** To send or be sent; circulate: *rumors that pass quickly among journalists.* **11.** To change into something different: *spring passing gradually into summer.* **12.** To be accepted as something different: *spoke French so well that she passed as a native.* **13.** To come out of; issue from: *Not a sound passed his lips.* **14.** To discharge (bodily wastes). **15.** To take place; happen: *missed nothing that passed.* **16.** To happen without notice or offense; go unchallenged: *letting the insult pass.* **17. a.** To undergo (a test, trial, inspection, etc.) with adequate results: *I passed the exam. Did you pass?* **b.** To give an acceptable grade to: *The teacher passed him reluctantly.* **18. a.** To enact or be enacted: *Congress passed the bill despite the President's veto. The measure passed by one vote.* **b.** To be enacted by: *The amendment passed the Senate, but was blocked in the House.* **19. a.** To come to or announce a decision, opinion, or sentence: *A panel of judges passed on the quality of the essays.* **b.** To pronounce: *pass judgment.* **20.** To propel (a ball or puck) to a teammate, especially to throw (a football) overhand to a teammate in front of one. **21.** To let one's turn to play or bid, as in a card game, go by. —***phrasal verbs.*** **pass away.** **1.** To recede or cease: *The sound of the blast took a few seconds to pass away.* **2.** To die. **pass on.** To give by or as if by inheritance: *Parents pass on their characteristics to their young.* **pass out.** **1.** To distribute: *passing out free tickets to the circus.* **2.** To faint. **pass over.** **1.** To omit or overlook: *noticing things that other*

partridge

passenger pigeon

passionflower

ă pat/ā pay/â care/ä father/ĕ pet/ ē be/ĭ pit/ī pie/î fierce/ŏ pot/ ō go/ô paw, for/oi oil/o͝o book/ o͞o boot/ou out/ŭ cut/û fur/ *th* the/th thin/hw which/zh vision/ ə ago, item, pencil, atom, circus

people pass over. **2.** To treat lightly or briefly. **pass up.** *Informal.* To turn down; refuse: *unwilling to pass up a free meal.* —*n.* **1.** An act of passing, especially a transfer of something into another's hands. **2.** A motion with the hand or something held in the hand: *made a few more passes with the sponge over the tablecloth to clean it.* **3.** A route of travel through land that presents an obstacle, especially a gap in a mountain range or ridge. **4. a.** A permit granting the bearer the right to go through a restricted area. **b.** Any document that grants special rights of movement or access. **c.** A written leave of absence from a military post or assignment for a brief period. **d.** A ticket granting free entrance or transportation. **5. a.** An act of passing a ball or puck to a teammate. **b.** The ball or puck passed: *caught the pass and ran 70 yards for a touchdown.* **6.** A run by a military aircraft over a target area. **7.** An attempt; effort: *made a pass at a few ballads with his guitar.* **8.** A situation, especially a difficult or threatening one: *His own folly had brought him to this pass.*

Idioms. **bring to pass.** To cause to happen; bring about. **come to pass.** To happen.

pass•a•ble |păs′ə bəl| *or* |pä′sə-| *adj.* **1.** Capable of being passed or crossed: *a passable road.* **2.** Satisfactory but not outstanding; adequate: *a passable job of acting.* —**pass′a•bly** *adv.*

pas•sage |păs′ĭj| *n.* **1.** The act or process of passing: *The channel is deep enough for safe passage. They opened the vents to allow the passage of air.* **2.** A journey, especially by water: *a rough passage across the Atlantic.* **3.** The right to travel on something, especially a ship: *We booked passage to London.* **4.** A narrow path or way between two points: *an underground passage.* **5.** A channel, duct, path, etc., through or along which something may pass: *the nasal passages.* **6.** Approval of a legislative measure: *Passage of the bill seems assured.* **7.** A sentence or paragraph from a literary work: *a Biblical passage.* **8.** A section of a musical composition: *a passage for solo violin.*

pas•sage•way |păs′ĭj wā′| *n.* A corridor or hallway.

pass•book |păs′bo͝ok′| *or* |päs′-| *n.* A bankbook.

pas•sé |pă sā′| *adj.* No longer in fashion.

pas•sen•ger |păs′ən jər| *n.* A person riding in, but not driving, a train, airplane, ship, bus, car, or other vehicle. —***modifier:*** *a passenger list.*

passenger pigeon. A pigeon that used to be common in North America but has been extinct since the late 19th century. [SEE PICTURE]

pass•er-by |păs′ər bī′| *or* |-bī′| *or* |pä′sər-| *n., pl.* **pass•ers-by.** A person who happens to be passing by at a certain time.

pass•ing |păs′ĭng| *or* |pä′sĭng| *adj.* **1.** Going by: *a passing car.* **2.** Not lasting long; temporary: *a passing fad.* **3.** Superficial; casual: *a passing glance; a passing remark.* **4.** Satisfactory: *a passing grade.* —*n.* **1.** The act of going by or past. **2.** The end of something; death: *the passing of a year. We mourned his passing.*

pas•sion |păsh′ən| *n.* **1.** A powerful feeling or desire, as love, joy, hatred, lust, etc. **2. a.** Great enthusiasm for a certain activity, subject, etc.: *a passion for music.* **b.** The object of such enthusiasm or devotion: *Golf is his passion.* **3. Passion. a.** The sufferings of Christ on the cross. **b.** A narrative of this, as in the Gospels. **c.** A musical setting of such a narrative.

pas•sion•ate |păsh′ə nĭt| *adj.* **1.** Full of passion; intense; ardent: *a passionate attachment to one's country.* **2.** Having strong or intense feelings. —**pas′sion•ate•ly** *adv.*

pas•sion•flow•er |păsh′ən flou′ər| *n.* Any of several chiefly tropical vines with large, showy flowers. Some kinds have sweet, edible fruit called **passion fruit.** [SEE PICTURE]

pas•sive |păs′ĭv| *adj.* **1.** Not participating; not active: *a passive role.* **2.** Offering no resistance; submissive: *a passive acceptance of one's fate.* **3.** In grammar, showing or expressing the effect of an action: *a passive verb.* See **passive voice.** —*n.* The passive voice in grammar. —**pas′sive•ly** *adv.* —**pas′sive•ness** *n.*

passive voice. In grammar, a form of a transitive verb or phrasal verb that shows that the subject of the sentence is the object or recipient of the action expressed by the verb. In the sentence *The money was stolen, was stolen* is in the passive voice. See **active voice.**

pas•siv•i•ty |pă sĭv′ĭ tē| *n.* The condition or quality of being passive; submissiveness.

pass•key |păs′kē′| *or* |päs′-| *n.* A master key or skeleton key.

Pass•o•ver |păs′ō′vər| *or* |päs′-| *n.* A Jewish festival lasting eight days in the spring. It commemorates the escape of the Jews from Egypt and their bondage there.

pass•port |păs′pôrt′| *or* |-pōrt′| *or* |päs′-| *n.* **1.** An official document, generally in booklet form, that identifies a person as a citizen of a country and grants him permission to travel abroad under his government's protection. **2.** Anything that assures the achievement of something: *Talent is often a passport to success.*

pass•word |păs′wûrd′| *or* |päs′-| *n.* A secret word or phrase spoken to a guard or sentry in order to gain admission.

past |păst| *or* |päst| *adj.* **1.** Gone by; over: *That day is past.* **2.** Having existed or occurred at an earlier time; bygone: *past events.* **3.** Just ended; just over: *in the past week.* **4.** Having formerly been or served as: *a past vice president.* **5.** In grammar, of or denoting a verb tense or form used to express an action or condition prior to the time it is expressed. —*n.* **1. the past.** The indefinite period of time that has gone by: *memories of the past.* **2.** A person's history, background, or former activities: *His past returned to haunt him.* **3.** The **past tense.** —*prep.* **1.** Alongside and beyond: *The Mississippi flows past St. Louis.* **2.** Beyond in position: *How did you get past the guard?* **3.** Beyond in time: *He is past fifty. It is well past midnight.* **4.** Beyond the power or scope of: *His behavior is past all explanation.* —*adv.* To and beyond a point near at hand; by: *He tooted the horn as he drove past.*

pas•ta |pä′stə| *n.* **1.** Dough made from flour and water. **2.** A prepared dish of pasta.

paste |pāst| *n.* **1.** A smooth, sticky substance, as that made of flour and water or starch and water, used to fasten things together. **2.** A dough of flour, water, and shortening, used in making pastry. **3.** A food that has been made soft and creamy by pounding or grinding: *almond paste.* **4.** A hard, brilliant glass used in making artificial gems. *—v.* **past•ed, past•ing. 1.** To fasten or attach with paste: *paste the broken pieces together.* **2.** To cover with something to which paste has been applied: *paste the wall with posters.* **3.** *Slang.* To punch or smack.

paste•board |pāst'bôrd'| *or* |-bōrd'| *n.* A thin, firm board made of pressed wood pulp or sheets of paper pasted together. *—modifier: a pasteboard box.*

pas•tel |pă stĕl'| *n.* **1.** A chalklike crayon used in drawing or marking. **2.** A picture drawn or painted with such crayons. **3.** A soft, delicate color or hue. *—modifier: a pastel drawing.*

pas•tern |păs'tərn| *n.* The part of the leg of a horse or similar hoofed animal that is between the fetlock and the hoof.

Pas•teur |pă stûr'|, **Louis.** 1822–1895. French chemist; the founder of modern bacteriology.

pas•teur•i•za•tion |păs'chə rĭ zā'shən| *n.* A process in which milk, beer, and other liquids are heated to about 155°F for about 30 minutes and then chilled to 50°F in order to kill harmful germs or prevent further fermentation.

pas•teur•ize |păs'chə rīz'| *v.* **pas•teur•ized, pas•teur•iz•ing.** To treat (a liquid) by pasteurization.

pas•time |păs'tīm'| *n.* An activity that occupies one's time pleasantly.

pas•tor |păs'tər| *n.* A Christian minister who is the leader of a congregation.

pas•tor•al |păs'tər əl| *adj.* **1.** Of or portraying shepherds or the simple quality of country life: *a pastoral scene.* **2.** Of or having to do with a pastor: *pastoral duties.*

pas•tor•ate |păs'tər ĭt| *n.* **1.** The office or term of office of a pastor. **2.** Pastors in general.

past participle. A participle that expresses past condition or state or past or completed action. It is used as an adjective, as in the phrase *guided missile,* and also to form the passive voice and the perfect tenses.

past perfect tense. A verb tense expressing action completed before a specified or implied time in the past. It is formed in English by combining *had* with a past participle. In the sentence *By the time he was twelve, he had already read all the works of Mark Twain, had . . . read* is in the past perfect tense.

pas•tra•mi |pə strä'mē| *n.* A seasoned, smoked cut of beef, usually from the shoulder.

pas•try |pā'strē| *n., pl.* **pas•tries. 1.** Dough of flour, water, and shortening, used for the crusts of pies, tarts, etc. **2.** Baked food, such as tarts, made with such dough. *—modifier: a pastry shop.*

past tense. A verb tense used to express an action or condition that occurred in or during the past. In the sentence *I picked the winner,* the verb *picked* is in the past tense.

pas•tur•age |păs'chər ĭj| *or* |päs'-| *n.* Grass and other plants eaten by grazing animals.

pas•ture |păs'chər| *or* |päs'-| *n.* **1.** A piece of land covered with grass and other plants eaten by grazing animals such as cattle, horses, or sheep. **2.** Grass and other plants eaten by grazing animals. *—v.* **pas•tured, pas•tur•ing. 1.** To put (animals) in a pasture to graze. **2.** To graze in a pasture.

past•y[1] |pā'stē| *adj.* **past•i•er, past•i•est.** Resembling paste in color or texture. *—***past'i•ness** *n.* [SEE NOTE]

pas•ty[2] |păs'tē| *or* |pä'stē| *n., pl.* **pas•ties.** *British.* A seasoned meat pie. [SEE NOTE]

pat |păt| *v.* **pat•ted, pat•ting. 1.** To stroke gently or affectionately with the open hand. **2.** To flatten or shape by patting: *pat down the curls.* *—n.* **1. a.** A light stroke or tap. **b.** The sound made by such a stroke or tap or by light footsteps. **2.** A small piece or lump: *a pat of butter.* *—adj.* Of a set form or pattern and ready for immediate use: *a pat answer for everything.*

Idioms. **have down pat.** To know thoroughly or by heart. **stand pat.** To stick firmly to one's position or policy.

pat. patent.

patch |păch| *n.* **1.** A small piece of material used to cover a hole, rip, or worn place. **2.** A protective pad, dressing, or bandage worn over a wound or an injured eye. **3.** A small piece of land, usually with plants growing on it: *a berry patch.* **4.** A small area on a surface that differs from or contrasts with what surrounds it: *a patch of blue sky.* *—v.* **1.** To cover or mend with a patch or patches. **2.** To make by sewing scraps of material together: *patch a quilt.* ***—phrasal verb.*** **patch up.** To settle or smooth over: *They patched up their quarrel.*

patch•work |păch'wûrk'| *n.* **1. a.** Pieces of cloth of various colors, shapes, and sizes sewn together in a pattern to make a covering. **b.** This type of needlework. **2.** A mixture of many diverse elements; a jumble: *The wallpaper is a patchwork of many colors.* *—modifier: a patchwork quilt.* [SEE PICTURE]

pate |pāt| *n.* The head, especially the top of the head: *a bald pate.*

pâ•té |pä tā'| *n.* A meat paste.

pa•tel•la |pə tĕl'ə| *n.* A flat, triangular bone at the front of the knee joint; the kneecap.

pat•ent |păt'nt| *n.* A grant made by a government to an inventor, assuring him the exclusive right to manufacture, use, and sell his invention for a stated period of time. *—modifier: a patent attorney.* *—v.* **1.** To obtain a patent on. **2.** To grant a patent to. *—adj.* |*also* pāt'nt|. Obvious; plain: *a patent falsehood.* — **pat'ent•ly** *adv.*

patent leather. Leather with a smooth, hard, shiny surface, used for shoes, belts, pocketbooks, etc. *—modifier:* **(patent-leather):** *a patent-leather purse.*

patent medicine. A drug or medicinal preparation that is sold under a protected trademark and is available without prescription.

pa•ter•nal |pə tûr'nəl| *adj.* **1.** Of a father; fatherly. **2.** Received from a father: *a paternal trait in his make-up.* **3.** Related to through one's father. *—***pa•ter'nal•ly** *adv.* [SEE NOTE]

pa•ter•nal•ism |pə tûr'nə lĭz'əm| *n.* The policy or practice of treating or governing people in a fatherly manner by providing for their needs without giving them responsibility. *—***pa•ter'nal•is'tic** *adj.*

pa•ter•ni•ty |pə tûr'nĭ tē| *n.* **1.** The fact or condition of being a father. **2.** Ancestry or descent on a father's side.

pa•ter•nos•ter |pā'tər nŏs'tər| *or* |păt'ər-| *n.* The **Lord's Prayer.**

path |păth| *or* |päth| *n., pl.* **paths** |păthz| *or*

pasty[1-2]
Pasty[1] *is from* **paste. Pasty[2]** *is from Old French* pastee, *from* paste, *"pastry"; in Modern French* pastee *became* pâté *(a circumflex accent is often the sign that an old* s *has dropped out); this was reborrowed into Modern English as* **pâté.**

patchwork
Early nineteenth-century American patchwork coverlet

paternal
Paternal *is from Latin* paternālis, *from* pater, *"father."* Pater *is descended from the prehistoric Indo-European word for "father," which was* pətēr. *In Germanic,* pətēr *became* fadar *(an Indo-European* p *always remained unchanged in Latin but changed to* f *in Germanic);* fadar *became* fæder *in Old English and* **father** *in Modern English.*

|päthz| *or* |pāths| *or* |päths|. **1.** A track or way made by footsteps: *a path in the woods.* **2.** A way made for walking: *shovel a path through the snow.* **3.** The route or course along which something moves: *the path of a hurricane.* **4.** A manner of conduct: *the path of righteousness.*

pa•thet•ic |pə thĕt'ĭk| *adj.* **1.** Arousing pity, sympathy, or sorrow; sad; pitiful. **2.** Distressing and inadequate: *a pathetic effort at humor.* —**pa•thet'i•cal•ly** *adv.*

path•o•gen |păth'ə jən| *n.* Anything, especially a virus or microorganism, that causes disease.

path•o•gen•ic |păth'ə jĕn'ĭk| *adj.* Capable of causing disease: *pathogenic bacteria.*

path•o•log•i•cal |păth'ə lŏj'ĭ kəl| *adj.* **1.** Of, caused by, or affected with physical or mental disease: *pathological symptoms; a pathological liar.* **2.** Of pathology. —**path'o•log'i•cal•ly** *adv.*

pa•thol•o•gist |pə thŏl'ə jĭst| *n.* A physician who specializes in pathology.

pa•thol•o•gy |pə thŏl'ə jē| *n.* **1.** The scientific and medical study of disease, its causes, its processes, and its effects. **2.** The physical changes in the body and its functioning as a result of a disease or disorder.

pa•thos |pā'thŏs'| *n.* A quality in something or someone that arouses feelings of pity, sympathy, tenderness, or sorrow in another.

path•way |păth'wā'| *or* |päth'-| *n.* A path.

pa•tience |pā'shəns| *n.* Calm endurance of a trying, tedious, or annoying situation.

pa•tient |pā'shənt| *adj.* **1.** Enduring trouble, hardship, annoyance, delay, etc., without complaint or anger: *Please be patient.* **2.** Requiring patience: *the patient piecing together of evidence.* **3.** Showing or expressing patience: *a patient look.* —*n.* Someone under medical treatment: *a hospital patient.* —**pa'tient•ly** *adv.*

pat•i•o |păt'ē ō'| *n., pl.* **pat•i•os. 1.** An inner courtyard open to the sky. **2.** A space for dining or recreation, next to a house or apartment.

pat•ois |pă twä'| *n., pl.* **pat•ois** |pă twäz'|. A regional dialect of a language.

pat. pend. patent pending.

pa•tri•arch |pā'trē ärk'| *n.* **1.** The male leader of a family, clan, or tribe, often the father, grandfather, etc., of most or all of its members. **2.** In certain churches, a title held by high-ranking bishops. **3.** A very old and respected man. —**pa'tri•ar'chal** *adj.*

pa•tri•cian |pə trĭsh'ən| *n.* **1.** In ancient Rome, a member of the nobility. **2.** A member of an aristocracy. **3.** A person of refined upbringing, manners, and tastes.

pat•ri•cide |păt'rĭ sīd'| *or* |pā'trĭ-| *n.* **1.** The act of murdering one's father. **2.** A person who murders his father. —**pat'ri•cid'al** *adj.*

Pat•rick |păt'rĭk|, **Saint.** 389?–461? Christian missionary; the patron saint of Ireland.

pat•ri•mo•ny |păt'rə mō'nē| *n., pl.* **pat•ri•mo•nies. 1.** Property inherited from a father or other ancestor. **2.** Anything inherited; heritage. **3.** Funds or property belonging to a church. —**pat'ri•mo'ni•al** *adj.*

pa•tri•ot |pā'trē ət| *or* |-ŏt'| *n.* A person who loves, supports, and defends his country.

pa•tri•ot•ic |pā'trē ŏt'ĭk| *adj.* Feeling or expressing love for one's country: *a patriotic song.* —**pa'tri•ot'i•cal•ly** *adv.*

pa•tri•ot•ism |pā'trē ə tĭz'əm| *n.* Love of and devotion to one's country.

pa•trol |pə trōl'| *v.* **pa•trolled, pa•trol•ling.** To walk or travel through (an area) checking for possible trouble. —*n.* **1.** The act of patrolling: *The soldiers are out on patrol.* **2.** A group of persons, vehicles, ships, or aircraft that performs such a mission: *the highway patrol.* **3.** A group of eight Boy Scouts, a division of a troop. —***modifier:*** *a patrol boat.*

patrol car. A **squad car.**

pa•trol•man |pə trōl'mən| *n., pl.* **-men** |-mən|. A policeman or guard who patrols an area.

patrol wagon. A police truck used to convey prisoners.

pa•tron |pā'trən| *n.* **1.** A person who supports or champions an activity, institution, etc.; a benefactor: *a patron of the arts.* **2.** A regular customer of a store, restaurant, etc.

pa•tron•age |pā'trə nĭj| *n.* **1.** Support or encouragement from a patron: *dependent upon the patronage of the rich.* **2.** The trade given to a store or restaurant by its customers. **3.** Customers; clientele: *The hotel has a very exclusive patronage.* **4.** The power of appointing people to governmental or political positions.

pa•tron•ize |pā'trə nīz'| *v.* **pa•tron•ized, pa•tron•iz•ing. 1.** To act as a patron to; support: *patronize the arts.* **2.** To go to regularly as a customer: *patronize a store.* **3.** To treat (someone) in a condescending way; talk down to. —**pa'tron•iz'ing** *adj.: a patronizing attitude.*

patron saint. A saint regarded as the special guardian of a country, place, person, trade, etc.

pa•troon |pə trōōn'| *n.* Under Dutch colonial rule, a landholder in New York and New Jersey who was granted certain feudal powers.

pat•ter¹ |păt'ər| *v.* **1.** To make a series of quick, light taps: *Rain pattered on the roof.* **2.** To walk or move softly and quickly. —*n.* A series of quick, light tapping sounds: *the patter of feet.* [SEE NOTE]

pat•ter² |păt'ər| *n.* Glib, rapid-fire speech, such as that used by a salesman or comedian. [SEE NOTE]

> **patter¹·²**
> **Patter¹** *is an extended form of* **pat. Patter²** *originally meant "to recite prayers rapidly"; it is shortened from* **paternoster,** *"the Lord's Prayer."*

pat•tern |păt'ərn| *n.* **1.** An artistic or decorative design: *a floral pattern.* **2.** A diagram used in cutting out garments to be made, consisting of separate pieces, usually of paper, cut to a certain size and style. **3.** A combination of elements, qualities, actions, or events that form a generally regular or consistent arrangement: *sentence patterns, weather patterns.* —*v.* To form or design according to a certain model: *The country's constitution is patterned after our own.*

pat•ty |păt'ē| *n., pl.* **pat•ties.** A small, flat, oval mass of ground or minced food.

pau•ci•ty |pô'sĭ tē| *n.* Short supply; scarcity; dearth: *a paucity of natural resources.*

Paul |pôl|, **Saint.** 5?–67? A.D. One of the Apostles; author of several New Testament epistles.

paunch |pônch| *n.* The belly, especially a pot-belly.

pau•per |pô'pər| *n.* A very poor person, often one who lives on charity.

pause |pôz| *n.* **1.** A brief stop or break in action, speech, etc. **2.** In music, a hold. —*v.* **paused, paus•ing.** To stop briefly in the midst of an action or while speaking.

***Idiom.* give (one) pause.** To cause to hesitate or wonder.

pa•van, also **pa•vane** |pə vän′| *or* |-văn′| *n.* **1.** A slow, stately court dance of the 16th century. **2.** Music written to accompany or as if to accompany this dance.

pave |pāv| *v.* **paved, pav•ing.** To cover (a road, sidewalk, etc.) with a hard surface of concrete, asphalt, etc. **—paved′** *adj.: a paved highway.*

***Idiom.* pave the way.** To make progress or development easier: *His experiments paved the way for important new discoveries.*

pave•ment |pāv′mənt| *n.* A hard, paved surface, especially of a road or sidewalk.

pa•vil•ion |pə vĭl′yən| *n.* **1.** An ornate tent. **2.** An open structure with a roof, used at parks or fairs for amusement or shelter. **3.** One of a group of buildings that make up a hospital.

pav•ing |pā′vĭng| *n.* **1.** Pavement. **2.** Asphalt, cement, and other materials used in making a pavement. ***—modifier:*** *a paving stone.*

paw |pô| *n.* The foot of an animal, especially of an animal that has claws. *—v.* **1. a.** To touch or strike with a paw. **b.** To scrape with a front foot. **2.** To handle in a clumsy or rude way.

pawl |pôl| *n.* A hinged or pivoted device that fits into a notch of a ratchet wheel, either to drive it forward or to prevent backward motion. ¶*These sound alike* **pawl, pall.** [SEE PICTURE]

pawn¹ |pôn| *v.* To give or leave as security for the payment of money borrowed: *pawn jewels.* *—n.* Something given as security for a loan. [SEE NOTE]

pawn² |pôn| *n.* **1.** A chessman of the lowest value. It can move forward one square at a time (or two squares on its first move) and capture on either of the two squares diagonally forward. **2.** A person used or controlled by others. [SEE NOTE]

pawn•bro•ker |pôn′brō′kər| *n.* A person who lends money at interest in exchange for personal property left in his keeping as security.

Paw•nee |pô nē′| *n., pl.* **Paw•nee** or **Paw•nees.** **1.** A confederation of four Caddoan-speaking tribes of Plains Indians now living in Oklahoma. **2.** A member of any of these tribes.

pawn•shop |pôn′shŏp′| *n.* The shop of a pawnbroker.

paw•paw |pô′pô′| *n.* A form of the word **papaw.**

pay |pā| *v.* **paid** |pād|, **pay•ing. 1.** To give (money) in exchange for goods or services: *How much did you pay for the tickets? He refuses to pay.* **2.** To give the required amount of; discharge (a debt or obligation): *pay the rent; pay taxes.* **3.** To yield as return: *The job pays fifty dollars a week.* **4.** To bear the cost of: *The company paid my way.* **5.** To be profitable or worthwhile; be worth the effort: *It pays to notice things.* **6.** To give, render, or express: *pay attention; pay a compliment.* ***—modifier:*** *a pay telephone.* ***—phrasal verbs.* pay back.** To retaliate upon; get even with: *I paid him back for his insults.* **pay for.** To suffer the consequences of: *pay for one's mistakes.* *—n.* **1.** Money given in return for work done; wages or salary: *equal work for equal pay. The pay is very good.* **2.** Employ: *in the pay of the CIA.* ***—modifier:*** *a pay raise.* **—pay′er** *n.*

pay•a•ble |pā′ə bəl| *adj.* **1.** Requiring payment on a certain date; due: *a note payable on demand.* **2.** Specifying payment to a particular person: *Make the check payable to me.*

pay•check |pā′chĕk′| *n.* **1.** A check issued to an employee in payment of his salary or wages. **2.** Salary: *a larger paycheck.*

pay•ee |pā ē′| *n.* A person to whom money is or is to be paid.

pay•load |pā′lōd′| *n.* **1.** The part of a cargo producing revenue as distinguished from the weight of the vehicle. **2. a.** The total weight of passengers and cargo that an aircraft carries or can carry. **b.** The total weight of the warhead or instruments, crew, and life-support systems that a rocket can carry.

pay•mas•ter |pā′măs′tər| *or* |-mä′stər| *n.* A person in charge of paying wages and salaries.

pay•ment |pā′mənt| *n.* **1.** The act of paying: *Prompt payment of the bill will be appreciated.* **2.** Something that is paid: *The balance is due in monthly payments.* **3.** Reward or compensation: *To see the child healthy again is payment enough for my services.*

pay•roll |pā′rōl′| *n.* **1.** A list of employees and wages due to each. **2.** The total amount of money paid to employees at a given time.

Pb The symbol for the element lead.

pct. per cent.

pd. paid.

Pd The symbol for the element palladium.

P.D. Police Department.

pea |pē| *n.* **1.** A vine that has round, edible green seeds enclosed in long green pods. **2.** The seed of such a plant, eaten as a vegetable. ***—modifier:*** *pea soup.*

peace |pēs| *n.* **1.** The absence of war or other hostilities. **2.** A treaty ending a war: *peace was signed in 1918.* **3.** Calm; tranquillity: *a little peace and quiet.* **4.** Freedom from anxiety, annoyance, etc.; inner calm: *peace of mind.* **5.** Public security; law and order: *He was arrested for disturbing the peace.* ***—modifier:*** *a peace treaty; peace talks.* ¶*These sound alike* **peace, piece.**

***Idioms.* at peace. 1.** In a tranquil state; calm. **2.** Free from strife, war, etc. **hold** (or **keep**) **(one's) peace.** To be silent; refrain from speaking.

peace•a•ble |pē′sə bəl| *adj.* **1.** Not quarrelsome, rebellious, or unruly: *a peaceable disposition.* **2.** Without or avoiding war; peaceful: *a peaceable solution.* **—peace′a•bly** *adv.*

peace•ful |pēs′fəl| *adj.* **1.** Not disposed to, marked by, or involving war: *a peaceful nation; peaceful uses of atomic energy.* **2.** Calm; serene; tranquil. **—peace′ful•ly** *adv.*

peace•mak•er |pēs′mā′kər| *n.* Someone who makes peace, especially by settling the disputes of others.

peace pipe. A calumet.

peace•time |pēs′tīm′| *n.* A time without war.

peach |pēch| *n.* **1. a.** A sweet, round, juicy fruit with downy yellowish or reddish skin and a hard-shelled pit. **b.** A tree that bears such fruit. **2.** A light yellowish pink. **3.** *Informal.* An outstandingly excellent or especially likeable person or thing. ***—modifier:*** *a peach pie; peach blossoms.* *—adj.* Light yellowish pink. [SEE PICTURE]

pea•cock |pē′kŏk′| *n.* **1.** The male of the peafowl, having brilliant blue or green feathers and very long tail feathers that are marked with eyelike spots and can be spread out like a

pawl
Ratchet wheel with pawl

pawn¹⁻²
Pawn¹ *is from Old French* pan, *"a pledge"; this originally meant "a piece of cloth, a garment" (garments have often been used for pawning purposes).* **Pawn²** *is from Old French* peon, *"chess pawn," from Medieval Latin* pedō, *"foot soldier, soldier of lowest rank."* Pedo *in Spanish became* peon, *which was separately borrowed into English as* **peon.**

peach

peacock

peaked[1-2]
Peaked[1] *is from* **peak. Peaked**[2] *is from obsolete* peak, *an old word meaning "to become sickly."*

peccary

peck[1-2]
Peck[1] *was originally* piken, *and it is related to* **pike**[4]. **Peck**[2] *is from Norman French* pek.

ă pat/ā pay/â care/ä father/ĕ pet/ ē be/ĭ pit/ī pie/î fierce/ŏ pot/ ō go/ô paw, for/oi oil/ŏŏ book/ ōō boot/ou out/ŭ cut/û fur/ *th* the/th thin/hw which/zh vision/ ə ago, item, pencil, atom, circus

large fan. **2.** A person who is very vain about his clothes and appearance. [SEE PICTURE]

pea•fowl |pē′foul′| *n., pl.* **-fowl** or **-fowls.** A large Asian bird related to the pheasants.

pea•hen |pē′hĕn′| *n.* The female of the peafowl, lacking the brilliant coloring of the male.

peak |pēk| *n.* **1. a.** The pointed or narrow top of a mountain. **b.** The mountain itself. **2.** Any tapering point that projects upward: *the peak of a pyramid.* **3.** The point of greatest development, value, height, or intensity: *The maple sugar season reaches its peak in March.* —*v.* **1.** To be formed into a peak or peaks. **2.** To achieve the point of greatest development, intensity, etc.: *The temperature peaked at noon.* ¶*These sound alike* **peak, peek, pique.**

peaked[1] |pēkt| *adj.* Ending in a peak; pointed: *a peaked cap.* [SEE NOTE]

peak•ed[2] |pē′kĭd| *adj.* Sickly or pale in appearance; drawn: *a peaked face.* [SEE NOTE]

peal |pēl| *n.* **1.** A ringing of a set of bells. **2.** A set of bells tuned to each other; carillon. **3.** A loud burst of noise or series of noises: *peals of laughter.* —*v.* To sound loudly; ring: *The bells pealed joyfully.* ¶*These sound alike* **peal, peel.**

pea•nut |pē′nŭt′| *or* |-nət| *n.* **1.** A pealike vine that grows in warm regions and bears nutlike seeds enclosed in brittle-shelled light-brown pods that ripen underground. **2.** The oily, edible seed of this plant. **3.** The nutlike seed pod of this plant. —***modifier:*** *peanut brittle.*

peanut butter. A spread made from roasted ground peanuts.

pear |pâr| *n.* **1.** A fruit with a rounded base and a tapering stem end. **2.** A tree that bears such fruit. ¶*These sound alike* **pear, pair, pare.**

pearl |pûrl| *n.* **1.** A smooth, slightly iridescent white or grayish rounded growth formed inside the shells of some kinds of oysters and valued as a gem. **2.** Mother-of-pearl. **3.** Something resembling a pearl: *pearls of dew.* **4.** Someone or something that is very highly thought of: *a pearl among women.* —***modifier:*** *a pearl pendant.* ¶*These sound alike* **pearl, purl.**

Pearl Harbor. A harbor near Honolulu, Hawaii, the site of the U.S. naval base attacked by Japan on December 7, 1941.

pearl•y |pûr′lē| *adj.* **pearl•i•er, pearl•i•est.** Resembling pearls, as in whiteness, size, etc.: *pearly teeth.*

peas•ant |pĕz′ənt| *n.* A member of the class of small farmers and farm laborers of Europe.

peas•ant•ry |pĕz′ən trē| *n.* The social class made up of peasants.

pease |pēz| *n.* **1.** *Archaic.* A plural of **pea. 2.** *Archaic.* A pea.

peat |pēt| *n.* Vegetable matter, found in bogs, that has been partially converted to carbon. It is used as a fuel and as a fertilizer.

peb•ble |pĕb′əl| *n.* A small stone worn smooth by erosion. —*v.* **peb•bled, peb•bling. 1.** To pave or cover with pebbles. **2.** To produce an irregular, rough surface, as on leather or paper.

peb•bly |pĕb′lē| *adj.* Covered with, resembling, or containing pebbles.

pe•can |pĭ kän′| *or* |-kăn′| *or* |pē′kăn′| *n.* **1.** An edible nut with a smooth, oval shell. **2.** A tree that bears such nuts. —***modifier:*** *pecan pie.*

pec•ca•dil•lo |pĕk′ə dĭl′ō| *n., pl.* **pec•ca•dil•loes** or **pec•ca•dil•los.** A small sin or fault.

pec•ca•ry |pĕk′ə rē| *n., pl.* **pec•ca•ries.** A piglike tropical American animal with long, dark bristles. [SEE PICTURE]

peck[1] |pĕk| *v.* **1. a.** To strike with a beak or sharp-pointed instrument. **b.** To tap or strike repeatedly: *peck at a typewriter.* **2.** To cut, make a hole in, or open by striking repeatedly with or as if with a beak. **3.** To pick up (grain, feed, etc.) with a beak. —***phrasal verb.*** **peck at.** To eat in small bits; nibble. —*n.* **1. a.** A stroke or light blow with the beak. **b.** A hole or mark made by such a blow. **2.** *Informal.* A light, quick kiss. [SEE NOTE]

peck[2] |pĕk| *n.* **1.** A unit of volume or capacity equal to 8 quarts. **2.** A container holding or measuring this amount. **3.** *Informal.* A great deal: *a peck of trouble.* [SEE NOTE]

pec•tin |pĕk′tĭn| *n.* Any of a group of colloidal substances found in ripe fruits, such as apples, that can be made to form gels, used in preparing jellies and in certain medicines and cosmetics.

pec•to•ral |pĕk′tər əl| *adj.* Of or located in the chest or breast: *a pectoral muscle.* —*n.* A muscle or organ of the chest.

pe•cu•liar |pĭ kyōōl′yər| *adj.* **1.** Unusual or eccentric; strange. **2.** Belonging distinctively to a person, place, etc.; characteristic of: *music peculiar to the Middle East.* —**pe•cu′liar•ly** *adv.*

pe•cu•li•ar•i•ty |pĭ kyōō′lē ăr′ĭ tē| *n., pl.* **pe•cu•li•ar•i•ties. 1.** The quality or condition of being strange or peculiar. **2.** A notable or distinctive feature or characteristic: *the peculiarities of a New York accent.* **3.** Something odd or eccentric; a quirk: *his peculiarities about money.*

pe•cu•ni•ar•y |pĭ kyōō′nē ĕr′ē| *adj.* Of money or financial matters: *a pecuniary loss.*

ped•a•gog•ic |pĕd′ə gŏj′ĭk| or **ped•a•gog•ic•al** |pĕd′ə gŏj′ĭ kəl| *adj.* Of teaching: *pedagogic techniques.*

ped•a•gogue |pĕd′ə gŏg′| *n.* **1.** A schoolteacher; an educator. **2.** A person who teaches in a narrow-minded, dogmatic manner.

ped•a•go•gy |pĕd′ə gō′jē| *or* |-gŏj′ē| *n.* The art or profession of teaching.

ped•al |pĕd′l| *n.* A lever operated by the foot, as on a machine such as an automobile or bicycle or on a musical instrument such as a piano or organ. —*v.* **1.** To use or operate the pedal or pedals of. **2.** To ride a bicycle. ¶*These sound alike* **pedal, peddle.**

ped•ant |pĕd′nt| *n.* **1.** A person who pays too much attention to book learning and formal rules. **2.** A person who makes a great show of his learning or scholarship.

pe•dan•tic |pə dăn′tĭk| *adj.* Narrowly academic: *a pedantic mind.* —**pe•dan′ti•cal•ly** *adv.*

ped•ant•ry |pĕd′n trē| *n.* Pedantic attention to detail or rules.

ped•dle |pĕd′l| *v.* **ped•dled, ped•dling. 1.** To travel about selling (goods): *peddle magazines; peddle for a living.* **2.** To spread or deal out: *Don't peddle lies.* ¶*These sound alike* **peddle, pedal.**

ped•dler |pĕd′lər| *n.* A person who peddles.

ped•es•tal |pĕd′ĭ stəl| *n.* **1.** A support or base, as for a column or statue. **2.** A position of adoration or esteem: *Putting people on pedestals can lead to disappointment.*

pe•des•tri•an |pə dĕs'trē ən| *n.* A person traveling on foot, especially on city streets. —*adj.* **1.** Of or for pedestrians: *a pedestrian crossing.* **2.** Commonplace; ordinary: *pedestrian writing.*
pe•di•a•tri•cian |pē'dē ə trĭsh'ən| *n.* A physician who specializes in pediatrics.
pe•di•at•rics |pē'dē ăt'rĭks| *n.* *(used with a singular verb).* The branch of medicine that deals with the care of infants and children and the treatment of their diseases.
ped•i•cure |pĕd'ĭ kyo͝or'| *n.* A cosmetic treatment of the feet and toenails. —*v.* **ped•i•cured, ped•i•cur•ing.** To give a pedicure to.
ped•i•gree |pĕd'ĭ grē'| *n.* **1.** A line of ancestors; ancestry. **2.** A list of ancestors. **3.** A list or record of the ancestors of a purebred animal.
ped•i•greed |pĕd'ĭ grēd'| *adj.* Having a line of purebred ancestors: *pedigreed cattle.*
ped•i•ment |pĕd'ə mənt| *n.* **1.** A wide triangular gable over the façade of some buildings in Greek architectural style. **2.** A similar piece used widely in architecture and decoration.
ped•lar |pĕd'lər| *n.* A form of the word **peddler.**
pe•dom•e•ter |pə dŏm'ĭ tər| *n.* An instrument that measures and indicates the approximate distance a person travels on foot by keeping track of the number of steps taken.
peek |pēk| *v.* To look, peer, glance, or show briefly, as from a place of concealment. —*n.* A quick, sly glance or look. ¶ *These sound alike* **peek, peak, pique.**
peel |pēl| *n.* The skin or rind of certain fruits, such as an orange or banana. —*v.* **1.** To remove the skin or rind from: *peel a banana.* **2.** To strip away; pull off (an outer covering): *peel the bark off a tree.* **3.** To come off in thin strips or layers, as skin, paint, etc. **4.** To lose or shed skin or other covering: *peel after a day in the sun.* ¶ *These sound alike* **peel, peal.**
Idiom. **keep (one's) eyes peeled.** *Informal.* To be on the alert.
peen |pēn| *n.* The end of a hammerhead opposite the flat striking surface, often wedge-shaped or ball-shaped and used for bending, indenting, or cutting. —*v.* To hammer, bend, or shape with a peen.
peep¹ |pēp| *n.* A weak, high-pitched chirping sound, like that made by a young bird. —*v.* To make such a sound. [SEE NOTE]
peep² |pēp| *v.* To look, glance, or show from a concealed place; peek. —*n.* A quick look or glance; a peek. [SEE NOTE]
peep•er |pē'pər| *n.* **1.** Often **spring peeper.** A small tree frog with a high, chirping call heard in early spring. **2.** Any creature that peeps, as a baby chicken.
peeping Tom A person who gets pleasure from secretly watching the actions of others.
peer¹ |pîr| *v.* **1.** To look intently, searchingly, or with difficulty. **2.** To be partially visible; show: *The moon peered from behind a cloud.* ¶ *These sound alike* **peer, pier.** [SEE NOTE]
peer² |pîr| *n.* **1.** A member of the British peerage; a duke, marquis, earl, viscount, or baron. **2.** Someone who has equal standing with another, as in rank, class, age, etc. ¶ *These sound alike* **peer, pier.** [SEE NOTE]
peer•age |pîr'ĭj| *n.* **1.** Peers in general. **2.** The rank or title of a peer. **3.** A book listing the peers and the members of their families.
peer•ess |pîr'ĭs| *n.* **1.** The wife of a peer. **2.** A woman who is a member of the peerage in her own right.
peer•less |pîr'lĭs| *adj.* Without equal; unmatched: *the peerless playing of the string quartet.* —**peer'less•ly** *adv.* —**peer'less•ness** *n.*
peeve |pēv| *v.* **peeved, peev•ing.** To annoy or make irritable. —*n.* Something that annoys: *Her biggest peeve is students who chatter.*
peev•ish |pē'vĭsh| *adj.* Annoyed; irritable; fretful. —**peev'ish•ly** *adv.* —**peev'ish•ness** *n.*
peg |pĕg| *n.* **1.** A cylindrical or conical pin, often of wood, used to fasten things or to plug a hole. **2.** One of the pins to which the strings of a musical instrument are attached. The pins can be turned to loosen or tighten the strings so as to regulate their pitch. **3.** A degree in estimation, pride, etc. —*v.* **pegged, peg•ging. 1.** To fasten or plug with a peg. **2.** To set or fix: *peg exchange rates to the price of gold.*
Idioms. **peg away (at).** To work steadily; persist. **take down a peg.** To reduce the pride of; humble.
peg leg. *Informal.* An artificial leg, especially a wooden one.
peg•ma•tite |pĕg'mə tīt'| *n.* A coarse-grained igneous rock, largely granite, that is a source of tantalum, tungsten, and uranium.
Pe•kin•ese |pē'kĭ nēz'| *or* |-nēs'| *n.* A form of the word **Pekingese.**
Pe•king |pē'kĭng'|. The former name for **Beijing.**
Pe•king•ese |pē'kĭ nēz'| *or* |-nēs'| *or* |-kĭng ēz'| *or* |-kĭng ēs'| *n., pl.* **Pe•king•ese. 1.** A native or inhabitant of Peking. **2.** The dialect of Chinese spoken in and around Peking. **3.** |pē'kĭ nēz'| *or* |-nēs'|. A small, short-legged dog with long hair and a flat nose, originally raised in China.
pe•koe |pē'kō'| *n.* A type of black tea, of which the best-known kind is **orange pekoe,** consisting of small leaves and sometimes leaf buds. ¶ *These sound alike* **pekoe, picot.**
pelf |pĕlf| *n.* Wealth or riches, especially when dishonestly acquired.
pel•i•can |pĕl'ĭ kən| *n.* A large, long-billed, web-footed bird of warm regions, having under its lower bill a large pouch used for holding the fish it has caught. [SEE PICTURE]
pel•lag•ra |pə lăg'rə| *or* |-lā'grə| *n.* A disease caused by a lack of niacin. Its symptoms include skin eruptions, nervous and digestive disorders, and eventual loss of mental powers.
pel•let |pĕl'ĭt| *n.* **1.** A small, densely packed ball, as of bread, wax, medicine, etc. **2.** A small bullet or shot.
pell-mell, also **pell•mell** |pĕl'mĕl'| *adv.* In a jumbled and confused manner; helter-skelter: *The crowd rushed on pell-mell.*
pel•lu•cid |pə lo͞o'sĭd| *adj.* **1.** Admitting the passage of light; transparent. **2.** Easy to understand; clear: *pellucid prose.*
Pel•o•pon•ne•sus |pĕl'ə pə nē'səs|. A peninsula forming the southern part of Greece. —**Pel'o•pon•ne'sian** *adj. & n.*
pelt¹ |pĕlt| *n.* An animal skin, especially with the hair or fur still on it.
pelt² |pĕlt| *v.* **1.** To strike repeatedly with or as if with blows or missiles; bombard: *schoolboys pelt-*

peep¹⁻²
Peep¹ *is an imitative word.* **Peep²** *is a variant of* **peek.**

peer¹⁻²
The original meaning of **peer¹** *was "to be partially visible" (now sense* **2***). It has been suggested that the word is a shortening of* **appear,** *but this is no more than a guess.* **Peer²** *in medieval law meant "an equal"; the feudal lords of the highest ranks were especially referred to as* equals *(to each other and nobody else). The word is from Old French* per, *from Latin* par, *"equal."*

pelican

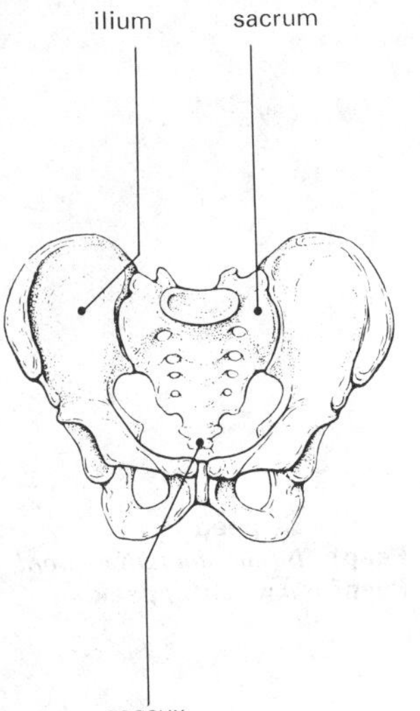

pelvis
Pelvis of a man

pen^1·2·3
Pen[1] *is from Old French* penne, *which is from Latin* penna, *"feather, quill pen."* **Pen**[2] *was Old English* penn, *"enclosure for animals."* **Pen**[3] *is a shortening of* **penitentiary.**

penguin

ă pat/ā pay/â care/ä father/ĕ pet/ ē be/ĭ pit/ī pie/î fierce/ŏ pot/ ō go/ô paw, for/oi oil/o͝o book/ o͞o boot/ou out/ŭ cut/û fur/ *th* the/th thin/hw which/zh vision/ ə ago, item, pencil, atom, circus

ing their friends with snowballs. The rain pelted down for an hour. **2.** To cast, hurl, or throw (missiles): *pelting stones at the windows.* —*n.* A sharp blow; whack.

pel•ves |pĕl′vēz′| *n.* A plural of **pelvis.**

pel•vic |pĕl′vĭk| *adj.* Of, in, or near the pelvis.

pel•vis |pĕl′vĭs| *n., pl.* **pel•vis•es** or **pel•ves** |pĕl′-vēz′|. A basin-shaped structure, formed of several different bones, that rests on the lower limbs and supports the lower end of the spine. [SEE PICTURE]

pem•mi•can |pĕm′ĭ kən| *n.* A food made by North American Indians from a paste of lean meat mixed with fat and berries.

pen[1] |pĕn| *n.* An instrument for writing with ink, formerly made from a large quill, now having a metal point and often a supply of ink in the holder. —*v.* **penned, pen•ning.** To write or compose with a pen. [SEE NOTE]

pen[2] |pĕn| *n.* A small, fenced-in area, especially one in which animals are kept. —*v.* **penned** or **pent** |pĕnt|, **pen•ning.** To confine in or as if in a pen. [SEE NOTE]

pen[3] |pĕn| *n. Slang.* A penitentiary. [SEE NOTE]

pe•nal |pē′nəl| *adj.* **1.** Of or prescribing punishment, as for breaking the law: *a penal code.* **2.** Subject to punishment: *a penal offense.*

pe•nal•ize |pē′nə līz′| *v.* **pe•nal•ized, pe•nal•iz•ing.** To subject to a penalty, as for an offense or an infringement of a rule.

pen•al•ty |pĕn′əl tē| *n., pl.* **pen•al•tiies. 1.** A punishment established by law or authority for a crime: *death penalty.* **2.** Something, such as a sum of money, loss of position, etc., that must be sacrificed for an offense.

pen•ance |pĕn′əns| *n.* **1.** An act of self-mortification or devotion performed voluntarily to show sorrow for a sin or other wrongdoing. **2.** In some Christian churches, a sacrament that includes contrition, confession to a priest, acceptance of punishment, and absolution.

pence |pĕns| *n. British.* A plural of **penny.**

pen•chant |pĕn′chənt| *n.* A strong inclination; a definite tendency: *a penchant for swimming.*

pen•cil |pĕn′səl| *n.* **1.** A thin stick of graphite encased in wood, used for writing. **2.** Something shaped or used like a pencil: *a styptic pencil; an eyebrow pencil.* —***modifier:*** *a pencil drawing.* —*v.* **pen•ciled** or **pen•cilled, pen•cil•ing** or **pen•cil•ling.** To write or mark with a pencil.

pen•dant |pĕn′dənt| *n.* A hanging ornament, as one worn dangling from a necklace or from the ear. ¶ *These sound alike* **pendant, pendent.**

pen•dent |pĕn′dənt| *adj.* **1.** Hanging down; dangling: *pendent vines.* **2.** Jutting; overhanging: *pendent cliffs.* **3.** Awaiting settlement; pending. ¶ *These sound alike* **pendent, pendant.**

pend•ing |pĕn′dĭng| *adj.* Not yet decided or settled; awaiting action: *legislation pending before Congress.* —*prep.* While awaiting; until: *The swimming pool is closed pending an investigation of the accident.*

pen•du•lum |pĕn′jə ləm| *or* |-dyə-| *n.* **1.** A mass hung by a relatively light cord so that it is able to swing freely. **2.** An apparatus of this kind used to regulate the action of some device, especially a clock.

pe•ne•plain, also **pe•ne•plane** |pē′nə plān′| *n.* A large, nearly flat eroded land surface.

pe•nes |pē′nēz′| *n.* A plural of **penis.**

pen•e•tra•ble |pĕn′ĭ trə bəl| *adj.* Capable of being penetrated: *dense jungle penetrable only by boat.* —**pen′e•tra•bil′i•ty** *n.*

pen•e•trate |pĕn′ĭ trāt′| *v.* **pen•e•trat•ed, pen•e•trat•ing. 1.** To go or enter into or through; pierce: *little light penetrating the forest; an unexplored region too difficult to penetrate.* **2.** To enter into and permeate: *Cold penetrated my bones.* **3.** To observe and study; understand: *penetrating deeper into the cell as the power of the microscope grows.* —**pen′e•tra′ting** *adj.: penetrating cold; a penetrating mind.*

pen•e•tra•tion |pĕn′ĭ trā′shən| *n.* **1.** The act or process of penetrating. **2.** The power or ability to penetrate: *The greater the strength of the drill, the greater the penetration.* **3.** The ability to understand; insight: *He captures with remarkable penetration the personalities of his subjects.*

pen•guin |pĕng′gwĭn| *n.* Any of several sea birds that live mostly in or near Antarctica, have narrow, flipperlike wings and webbed feet, and are unable to fly. [SEE PICTURE]

pen•i•cil•lin |pĕn′ĭ sĭl′ən| *n.* Any of a group of related antibiotic compounds obtained from molds and used to treat various diseases and infections.

pen•in•su•la |pə nĭn′sə lə| *or* |-nĭns′yə-| *n.* A portion of land nearly surrounded by water and connected with a larger land mass.

pen•in•su•lar |pə nĭn′sə lər| *or* |-nĭns′yə-| *adj.* Of or located on a peninsula: *peninsular wars.*

pe•nis |pē′nĭs| *n., pl.* **pe•nis•es** or **pe•nes** |pē′nēz′|. **1.** The organ by means of which the males of the higher vertebrates pass sperm cells to the females, also used by most male mammals for urination. **2.** Any similar organ found in the males of lower animals.

pen•i•tent |pĕn′ĭ tənt| *adj.* Feeling or showing sorrow for one's misdeeds or sins. —*n.* Someone who is penitent. —**pen′i•tence** *n.*

pen•i•ten•tia•ry |pĕn′ĭ tĕn′shə rē| *n., pl.* **pen•i•ten•tia•ries.** A prison for those convicted of serious crimes.

pen•knife |pĕn′nīf′| *n., pl.* **-knives** |-nīvz′|. A small pocketknife.

pen•man |pĕn′mən| *n., pl.* **-men** |-mən|. **1.** An expert in penmanship. **2.** An author; writer.

pen•man•ship |pĕn′mən shĭp′| *n.* The art, skill, style, or manner of handwriting.

Penn |pĕn|, **William.** 1644–1718. English Quaker leader; the founder of Pennsylvania.

pen name. A fictitious name assumed by an author.

pen•nant |pĕn′ənt| *n.* **1.** A long, tapering flag, used on ships for signaling or identification. **2. a.** A flag that serves as the emblem of the championship in professional baseball. **b.** The yearly championship in professional baseball.

pen•ni•less |pĕn′ē lĭs| *adj.* Wtihout money; very poor. —**pen′ni•less•ness** *n.*

pen•non |pĕn′ən| *n.* **1.** A long, narrow banner borne upon a lance. **2.** Any banner or flag.

Penn•syl•va•nia |pĕn′səl vān′yə| *or* |-vā′nē ə|. An Eastern state of the United States. Population, 11,884,000. Capital, Harrisburg. —**Penn′syl•va′nian** *adj. & n.*

Pennsylvania Dutch. 1. The descendants of German and Swiss immigrants who settled in

Pennsylvania in the 17th and 18th centuries. **2.** The dialect of German spoken by this group.

Penn•syl•va•ni•an |pĕn'səl **vān'**yən| *or* |-**vā'**-nē ən| *n.* Also **Pennsylvanian period.** A geologic period that began about 310 million years ago and ended about 280 million years ago, characterized by the development of coal-bearing rocks. —*modifier: a Pennsylvanian rock.*

pen•ny |**pĕn'**ē| *n.* **1.** *pl.* **pen•nies.** A U.S. or Canadian coin worth $^1/_{100}$ of a dollar; a cent. **2.** *pl.* **pence** |pĕns| or **pen•nies. a.** A British coin worth $^1/_{100}$ of a pound. Before 1971, it was worth $^1/_{240}$ of a pound. **b.** A subdivision of the pound of Gambia, the Republic of Ireland, Jamaica, Malawi, Malta, Nigeria, Rhodesia, and various dependent territories of the United Kingdom. **3.** A small sum of money; any money: *I haven't a penny to my name.* —*modifier: penny candy.*
Idiom. a pretty penny. *Informal.* A lot of money: *That will cost a pretty penny.*

pen•ny•roy•al |pĕn'ē **roi'**əl| *n.* A strong-smelling plant with hairy leaves and small bluish flowers.

pen•ny•weight |**pĕn'**ē wāt'| *n.* A unit of troy weight equal to 24 grains or $^1/_{20}$ of a troy ounce.

pen•ny-wise |**pĕn'**ē wīz'| *adj.* —**penny-wise and pound-foolish.** Careful with small sums or minor matters but careless when handling large sums or important matters.

pen•ny•worth |**pĕn'**ē wûrth'| *n.* **1.** As much as a penny will buy. **2.** A small or trifling amount. **3.** A bargain.

pe•nol•o•gy |pĭ **nŏl'**ə jē| *n.* The theory and practice of prison management.

pen•sion[1] |**pĕn'**shən| *n.* A sum of money paid regularly as a retirement benefit or by way of patronage. —*modifier: pension funds; a pension plan.* —*v.* **1.** To give a pension to. **2.** To retire or dismiss with a pension: *The old man did not want to be pensioned off.* [SEE NOTE]

pen•sion[2] |päN **syôN'**| *n.* A small boarding house or hotel in Europe. [SEE NOTE]

pen•sion•er |**pĕn'**shə nər| *n.* Someone who receives a pension.

pen•sive |**pĕn'**sĭv| *adj.* Showing or engaged in deep, often melancholy, thoughtfulness: *pensive eyes.* —**pen'sive•ly** *adv.* —**pen'sive•ness** *n.*

pen•stock |**pĕn'**stŏk'| *n.* **1.** A sluice or gate used to control a flow of water. **2.** A pipe used to carry water, as to a water wheel.

pent |pĕnt|. A past tense and past participle of **pen** (to confine).

penta–. A word element meaning "five": **pentagon.**

pen•ta•gon |**pĕn'**tə gŏn'| *n.* **1.** A plane geometric figure bounded by five line segments and containing five angles. **2. the Pentagon. a.** A five-sided building near Washington, D.C., containing the U.S. Department of Defense and the offices of the U.S. Armed Forces. **b.** The U.S. Department of Defense. [SEE PICTURE]

pen•tag•o•nal |pĕn **tăg'**ə nəl| *adj.* Having the form of a pentagon; five-sided.

pen•tam•e•ter |pĕn **tăm'**ĭ tər| *n.* A line of verse composed of five metrical feet.

Pen•ta•teuch |**pĕn'**tə to͞ok'| *or* |-tyo͞ok'| *n.* The first five books of the Old Testament.

pen•tath•lon |pĕn **tăth'**lən| *n.* An athletic contest in which each participant enters five events.

Pen•te•cost |**pĕn'**tĭ kôst'| *or* |-kŏst'| *n.* **1.** A Christian festival celebrated on the seventh Sunday after Easter in memory of the descent of the Holy Ghost upon the disciples; Whitsunday. **2.** Shavuot. —**Pen'te•cos'tal** *adj.*

pent•house |**pĕnt'**hous'| *n., pl.* **-hous•es** |-hou'-zĭz|. An apartment or dwelling, usually with a terrace, located on the roof of a building.

pent-up |**pĕnt'ŭp'**| *adj.* Not given expression; repressed: *pent-up anger at her lack of propriety.*

pe•nult |**pē'**nŭlt'| *n.* The next to the last syllable in a word.

pe•nul•ti•mate |pĭ **nŭl'**tə mĭt| *adj.* Next to last: *the penultimate chapter of the book.*

pe•num•bra |pĭ **nŭm'**brə| *n., pl.* **pe•num•brae** |pĭ **nŭm'**brē| or **pe•num•bras. 1.** A region of partial shadow between regions of complete shadow and complete illumination, especially when the shadow is that of a celestial body involved in an eclipse. **2.** The partly darkened fringe that surrounds a sunspot.

pe•nu•ri•ous |pĭ **no͝or'**ē əs| *or* |**-nyo͝or'**-| *adj.* **1.** Miserly; stingy: *a penurious woman who shares with nobody.* **2.** Extremely needy; poverty-stricken. —**pe•nu'ri•ous•ly** *adv.* —**pe•nu'ri•ous•ness** *n.*

pen•u•ry |**pĕn'**yə rē| *n.* Extreme poverty.

Pe•nu•ti•an |pə **no͞o'**tē ən| *or* |-shən| *n.* A family of North American Indian languages of Pacific coastal areas.

pe•on |**pē'**ŏn'| *or* |-ən| *n.* **1.** An unskilled laborer or farm worker in Latin America. **2.** A person once held in a state of servitude to a creditor in Mexico and the southwestern United States.

pe•o•ny |**pē'**ə nē| *n., pl.* **pe•o•nies. 1.** A garden plant with large pink, red, or white flowers. **2.** The flower of such a plant. [SEE PICTURE]

peo•ple |**pē'**pəl| *n., pl.* **peo•ple. 1.** Human beings as distinct from other creatures. **2.** A body of persons living in the same country under one national government: *the American people.* **3.** *pl.* **peo•ples.** An ethnic group sharing a common religion, culture, language, etc.: *primitive peoples.* **4. the people.** The mass of ordinary persons; the populace: *the rights of the people.* **5.** Family, relatives, or ancestors: *Her people are farmers.* —*v.* **peo•pled, peo•pling.** To furnish with a population; populate: *Thousands of tiny creatures peopled the mysterious place.*

People's Republic of China. The official name of China. See **China.**

pep |pĕp|. *Informal. n.* Energy; high spirits. —*v.* —**pep up.** To bring energy or liveliness to.

pep•per |**pĕp'**ər| *n.* **1.** A sharp-tasting seasoning made from the dried, blackish berries of a vine of the East Indies. **Black pepper** is made from the whole ground berries, and **white pepper**, from the ground seeds with the dark outer covering removed. **2.** The fruit of a bushy plant, used as seasoning or as a vegetable. **Hot pepper** and **red pepper** are sharp-tasting seasonings made from the ground pods of one variety of this plant, and the crisp, hollow **bell pepper**, or **sweet pepper**, which is usually eaten green but turns red when ripe, is the mild-flavored fruit of another variety of this plant. —*v.* **1.** To season with pepper. **2.** To sprinkle or spray with many small objects.

pep•per•corn |**pĕp'**ər kôrn'| *n.* A dried, blackish berry of the pepper vine.

pension[1-2]

Pension[1] *is from Old French* pension, *which is from Latin* pensiō, *"payment," from* pendere, *"to pay." In later French,* pension *came to mean "payment for lodging at a school" and later "lodgings, boarding house"; in this sense, it was reborrowed into Modern English as* **pension[2]**.

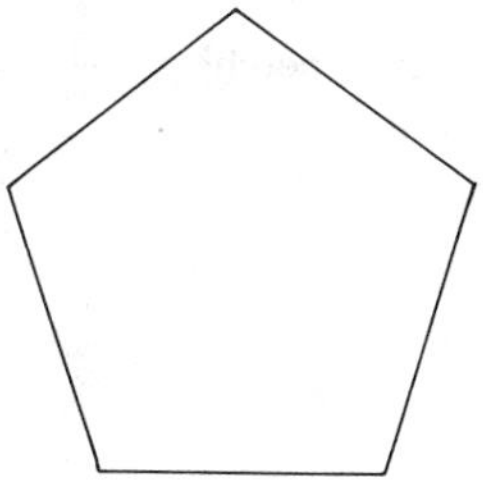

pentagon

peony

perch[1-2]
Perch[1] *is from Old French* perche, *which is from Latin* pertica, *"a pole or stick."* **Perch[2]** *is from another Old French word spelled* perche; *this is from Latin* perca, *which is from Greek* perkē, *"freshwater perch."*

perch[2]

peregrine falcon

ă pat/ā pay/â care/ä father/ĕ pet/ ē be/ĭ pit/ī pie/î fierce/ŏ pot/ ō go/ô paw, for/oi oil/ŏŏ book/ ōō boot/ou out/ŭ cut/û fur/ *th* the/th thin/hw which/zh vision/ ə ago, item, pencil, atom, circus

pep•per•mint |pĕp′ər mĭnt′| *n.* **1.** A plant with a strong, pleasant taste and smell. **2.** An oil or flavoring from this plant. **3.** A candy with this flavoring. —***modifier:*** *peppermint candy.*

pep•per•y |pĕp′ə rē| *adj.* **1.** Of or containing pepper; hot and spicy: *a peppery stew.* **2.** Sharp-tempered in disposition and manner.

pep•sin |pĕp′sĭn| *n.* **1.** An enzyme, produced in the stomach, that acts as a catalyst in one stage of the digestion of protein. **2.** A substance containing this enzyme, obtained from the stomach of hogs and used to aid digestion.

pep talk. *Informal.* A speech of encouragement, as one given by a coach to his team.

pep•tic |pĕp′tĭk| *adj.* **1. a.** Of or assisting digestion: *a peptic secretion.* **b.** Caused by or associated with the action of digestive juices: *a peptic ulcer.* **2.** Of pepsin.

Pe•quot |pē′kwŏt′| *n., pl.* **Pe•quot** or **Pe•quots. 1.** A North American Indian tribe formerly of southern New England. **2.** A member of this tribe. **3.** The Algonquian language of this tribe.

per |pûr| *prep.* **1.** For or to; for every: *40 cents per gallon.* **2.** According to: *per instructions.* **3.** By means of; through: *per bearer.*

per•am•bu•late |pə răm′byə lāt′| *v.* **per•am•bu•lat•ed, per•am•bu•lat•ing. 1.** To inspect by walking through: *perambulate the plant site.* **2.** To walk about; stroll. —**per•am′bu•la′tion** *n.*

per•am•bu•la•tor |pə răm′byə lā′tər| *n. British.* A baby carriage; a pram.

per•cale |pər kāl′| *n.* A strong, smooth, closely woven cotton cloth used to make sheets and clothing. —***modifier:*** *a percale pillowcase.*

per cap•i•ta |pər kăp′ĭ tə|. Per person; of, for, or by each individual: *per capita income.* This was originally a Latin expression.

per•ceive |pər sēv′| *v.* **per•ceived, per•ceiv•ing. 1.** To become aware of through any of the senses, especially to see or hear. **2.** To achieve understanding of: *Try to perceive the meaning of these sentences.* —**per•ceiv′er** *n.*

per cent. Per hundred; for or out of each hundred: *Twenty-five per cent of the members voted.*

per•cent |pər sĕnt′| *n.* A form of the phrase **per cent.**

per•cent•age |pər sĕn′tĭj| *n.* **1.** A fraction that is understood to have 100 as its denominator; a fraction expressed by using the phrase *per cent.* **2.** A portion or share in relation to the whole. **3. percentages.** Odds; probability: *Percentages favor a left-handed batter when the pitcher is right-handed.*

per•cen•tile |pər sĕn′tīl′| *n.* Any of the smaller numerical ranges formed by dividing the total range of a variable into 100 equal parts that do not overlap. The percentile into which a value of this variable falls is determined by the percentage of the other values that it exceeds. For example, an examination score that exceeds 95 per cent of the other scores is in the 95th percentile.

per•cep•ti•ble |pər sĕp′tə bəl| *adj.* Capable of being perceived; noticeable: *a perceptible improvement in the patient's condition.* —**per•cep′ti•bil′i•ty** *n.* —**per•cep′ti•bly** *adv.*

per•cep•tion |pər sĕp′shən| *n.* **1.** The act or process of perceiving. **2.** The faculty of perceiving or the ability to perceive: *depth perception.* **3.** Something perceived; an insight.

per•cep•tive |pər sĕp′tĭv| *adj.* **1.** Having the ability to perceive; keen; knowing: *a perceptive woman.* **2.** Marked by understanding and insight: *a perceptive thought.* —**per•cep′tive•ly** *adv.*

perch[1] |pûrch| *n.* **1.** A branch or rod that a bird grasps with its claws while at rest. **2.** Any resting place or vantage point: *Jed slid down from his perch on a haystack.* —*v.* **1.** To alight or rest on or as if on a perch. **2.** To occupy an elevated position: *villages that perch on the hillsides.* **3.** To place on or as if on a perch: *She perched the straw hat on her head.* [SEE NOTE]

perch[2] |pûrch| *n., pl.* **perch** or **perch•es.** Any of several mostly freshwater fishes often used as food. [SEE NOTE & PICTURE]

per•chance |pər chăns′| *or* |-chäns′| *adv.* Perhaps; possibly.

per•co•late |pûr′kə lāt′| *v.* **per•co•lat•ed, per•co•lat•ing. 1.** To pass or cause (a liquid) to pass through small holes or through a porous substance: *rain percolating into the dry soil; percolate oil through a filter.* **2.** To pass a liquid through (a porous substance): *percolate sand with water.* **3.** *Informal.* To become lively or active: *Her mind began to percolate.* —**per′co•la′tion** *n.*

per•co•la•tor |pûr′kə lā′tər| *n.* A type of coffeepot in which boiling water is forced repeatedly to pass up through a center tube and filter through a basket of ground coffee.

per•cus•sion |pər kŭsh′ən| *n.* **1. a.** The striking together of two bodies, especially when it creates noise. **b.** A sound, vibration, or shock produced in this way. **2.** A method of medical examination in which a physician taps areas of the body and draws conclusions about internal conditions on the basis of the sounds produced. **3.** Percussion instruments as a group. —***modifier:*** *the percussion section of the band.*

percussion cap. A metal cap containing a detonator that explodes on being struck.

percussion instrument. A musical instrument, such as a drum, xylophone, or piano, in which sound is produced by striking.

per di•em |pər dē′əm|. Per day. This was originally a Latin expression.

per•di•tion |pər dĭsh′ən| *n.* **1. a.** The loss of the soul; eternal damnation. **b.** Hell. **2.** *Archaic.* Utter loss or ruin.

per•e•grine falcon |pĕr′ə grĭn|. A swift-flying hawk often trained, especially in earlier times, to hunt for and catch small animals and birds. [SEE PICTURE]

per•emp•to•ry |pə rĕmp′tə rē| *adj.* **1.** Admitting no contradiction; imperative: *a peremptory order.* **2.** Offensively self-assured; dictatorial: *his peremptory manner.* —**per•emp′to•ri•ly** *adv.*

per•en•ni•al |pə rĕn′ē əl| *adj.* **1.** Living, growing, and flowering and producing seeds for several or many years. **2.** Lasting indefinitely; perpetual: *perennial happiness.* **3.** Repeated regularly; appearing again and again: *perennial fiscal problems.* —*n.* A plant that continues to live, grow, flower, and produce seeds for several or many years. —**per•en′ni•al•ly** *adv.*

per•fect |pûr′fĭkt| *adj.* **1. a.** Lacking nothing essential to the whole; satisfying all requirements: *There is no perfect food that contains all necessary nutrients.* **b.** Completely accurate; exact: *a per-*

fect copy. **2.** Without faults, flaws, or defects: *a perfect piece of marble.* **3.** Completely qualified in a certain field or area: *a perfect actor for the part.* **4.** Excellent and delightful in all respects: *perfect weather.* **5.** Pure; undiluted: *the perfect redness of the apple.* **6.** Complete; thorough; utter: *a perfect fool.* **7.** Having a root that is a whole number; formed by raising an integer to an integral power; for example, 25 is a perfect square, and 27 is a perfect cube. **8.** In grammar, of a verb form that expresses an action completed prior to a fixed point in time; for example, *he has played* is in the present perfect tense, *he had played* is in the past perfect tense, and *he will have played* is in the future perfect tense. *—n.* **1.** The perfect tense. **2.** A verb form in the perfect tense. *—v.* |pər **fĕkt′**|. To bring to perfection or completion.

per•fec•tion |pər **fĕk′**shən| *n.* **1.** The act or process of perfecting. **2.** The quality or condition of being perfect. **3.** Something or someone considered to be a perfect example of excellence.

per•fec•tion•ism |pər **fĕk′**shə nĭz′əm| *n.* **1.** A tendency to set extremely high standards and to be dissatisfied with anything less. **2.** A belief that man can achieve moral or spiritual perfection. **—per•fec′tion•ist** *n.*

per•fect•ly |**pûr′**fĭkt lē| *adv.* **1. a.** In a perfect or flawless manner: *The boy played the violin perfectly.* **b.** To a perfect degree; precisely: *This circle is perfectly round.* **2. a.** Completely; wholly: *Some mushrooms are perfectly safe to eat.* **b.** Adequately: *He speaks perfectly good English.*

perfect number. A positive integer, such as 6 or 28, that equals the sum of all of its divisors other than itself. For example, the divisors of 6, not counting 6 itself, are 1, 2, and 3. Their sum is 6.

per•fid•i•ous |pər **fĭd′**ē əs| *adj.* Disloyal; treacherous. **—per•fid′i•ous•ly** *adv.*

per•fi•dy |**pûr′**fĭ dē| *n., pl.* **per•fi•dies.** Deliberate breach of faith; treachery.

per•fo•rate |**pûr′**fə rāt′| *v.* **per•fo•rat•ed, per•fo•rat•ing.** **1.** To punch or bore a hole or holes in; pierce: *Perforate the top of the pie so as to let the steam escape.* **2.** To pierce or stamp with rows of holes to allow easy separation. **—per′fo•rat′ed** *adj.*: *a perforated spoon.*

per•fo•ra•tion |pûr′fə **rā′**shən| *n.* **1.** The act of perforating. **2.** A hole or series of holes, as those between postage stamps.

per•force |pər **fôrs′**| *or* |-**fōrs′**| *adv.* By force of circumstance; of necessity: *Mountain folk must perforce live in sturdy, wind-resistant houses.*

per•form |pər **fôrm′**| *v.* **1.** To begin and carry through to completion; do; execute: *perform an experiment; perform a somersault.* **2.** To carry out or fulfill (a promise, duty, task, etc.). **3.** To act or function in a specified manner: *The car performs well on curves.* **4.** To present or enact (a musical work, dramatic role, feat, etc.) before an audience: *perform a symphony; perform for food.* **—per•form′ing** *adj.*: *a performing elephant.*

per•form•ance |pər **fôr′**məns| *n.* **1.** The act, process, or manner of performing. **2.** The way in which someone or something functions: *Look for good, steady performance when buying an automobile.* **3.** A public presentation of something, such as a musical or dramatic work, a feat, etc. **4.** Something performed; an accomplishment.

per•form•er |pər **fôr′**mər| *n.* Someone or something that performs, especially an entertainer.

per•fume |**pûr′**fyōōm′| *or* |pər **fyōōm′**| *n.* **1.** A fragrant liquid distilled from flowers or prepared by synthetic means. **2.** A pleasing scent or odor. *—v.* |pər **fyōōm′**|. To apply or fill with a fragrance.

per•func•to•ry |pər **fŭngk′**tə rē| *adj.* Done or acting routinely and with little interest or care: *She gave him a perfunctory wave and walked away.* **—per•func′to•ri•ly** *adv.*

per•haps |pər **hăps′**| *adv.* Maybe; possibly: *Perhaps he'll come with us.*

peri–. A prefix meaning "around, about, or enclosing": **perihelion.** [SEE NOTE]

per•i•car•di•um |pĕr′ĭ **kär′**dē əm| *n., pl.* **per•i•car•di•a** |pĕr′ĭ **kär′**dē ə|. The sac composed of membrane that encloses the heart.

Per•i•cles |**pĕr′**ĭ klēz′|. 495?–429 B.C. Athenian statesman, orator, and general.

per•i•gee |**pĕr′**ə jē′| *n.* The point in the orbit of a natural or artificial satellite of the earth at which it is closest to the earth.

per•i•he•lion |pĕr′ə **hēl′**yən| *n., pl.* **per•i•he•lia** |pĕr′ə **hēl′**yə|. The point in the orbit of a planet or other body that travels around the sun at which it is closest to the sun.

per•il |**pĕr′**əl| *n.* **1.** The condition of present danger; exposure to the risk of harm or loss: *His life will be in peril if the oxygen tank does not work properly.* **2.** Something dangerous; a serious risk: *the perils of a journey in a covered wagon.*

per•il•ous |**pĕr′**ə ləs| *adj.* Full of peril; hazardous. **—per′il•ous•ly** *adv.*

pe•rim•e•ter |pə **rĭm′**ĭ tər| *n.* **1. a.** The sum of the lengths of the segments that form the sides of a polygon. **b.** The total length of any closed curve, such as a circle or ellipse. **2.** A fortified strip or boundary protecting a military position.

pe•ri•od |**pîr′**ē əd| *n.* **1.** An interval of time having a specified length or characterized by certain conditions or events: *a period of 12 months; a dormant period.* **2.** A span of time during which a specified culture, set of beliefs, technology, etc., was predominant; a historical era: *the Baroque period.* **3.** Any of various intervals of time, as the divisions of the academic day or of playing time in a game. **4.** A unit of geologic time, longer than an epoch and shorter than an era. **5.** The interval of time between corresponding points in successive occurrences of an action or event that repeats; cycle. **6.** An instance or occurrence of menstruation. **7. a.** A punctuation mark (.) used at the end of certain sentences and after many abbreviations. **b.** A **decimal point.** *—adj.* Of a certain historical age or time: *period furniture.*

pe•ri•od•ic |pîr′ē **ŏd′**ĭk| *adj.* **1.** Happening or repeating at regular intervals; cyclic: *the periodic motion of a pendulum.* **2.** Taking place from time to time; intermittent: *the periodic invasions of the barbarians across Europe.* **—pe′ri•od′i•cal•ly** *adv.*

pe•ri•od•i•cal |pîr′ē **ŏd′**ĭ kəl| *adj.* **1.** Periodic. **2.** Of a publication that appears at regular intervals of more than one day. *—n.* A publication, especially a magazine, that appears at regular intervals of more than one day.

periodic law. The law that elements having similar properties occur at regular intervals when

peri–

The prefix **peri-** *comes from Greek* peri, *"around, about," also "near." The* **pericardium** *is* around *the heart;* **perigee** *and* **perihelion** *are* near *points in orbits;* **perimeter** *is the measurement of distance* around *an area;* **periosteum** *is* around *the bone;* **periphery** *is the region* around *an area; a* **periscope** *looks* around *corners.*

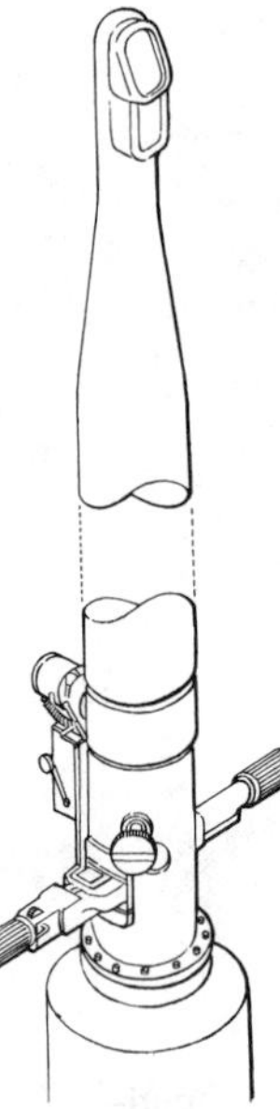

periscope
Periscope of a submarine

periwinkle[1-2]
Periwinkle[1] *is an alteration of Old English* pīnewincle, *"mussel shell"*: pīne-, *"mussel,"* + wincle, *"shell."* **Periwinkle[2]** *is an alteration of Latin* pervinca, *the name of a plant. Apparently the two words have influenced each other.*

periwinkle[1]

ă pat/ā pay/â care/ä father/ĕ pet/ ē be/ĭ pit/ī pie/î fierce/ŏ pot/ ō go/ô paw, for/oi oil/o͝o book/ o͞o boot/ou out/ŭ cut/û fur/ *th* the/th thin/hw which/zh vision/ ə ago, item, pencil, atom, circus

all of the elements are arranged in order of increasing atomic number.

periodic table. A table in which the elements are presented in order of increasing atomic number, elements that have similar properties usually being arranged in columns.

per•i•pa•tet•ic |pĕr′ĭ pə **tĕt′**ĭk| *adj.* **1.** Walking or traveling about from place to place: *peripatetic political candidates.* **2.** Carried on while walking about from place to place: *a peripatetic conversation.*

pe•riph•er•al |pə **rĭf′**ər əl| *adj.* Of or located on the periphery: *the peripheral regions of the state.* —**pe•riph′er•al•ly** *adv.*

pe•riph•er•y |pə **rĭf′**ə rē| *n., pl.* **pe•riph•er•ies. 1.** The outermost part within a boundary. **2.** A region immediately beyond a boundary.

per•i•scope |**pĕr′**ĭ skōp′| *n.* Any of several instruments in which mirrors or prisms allow observation of objects that are not in a direct line of sight. [SEE PICTURE]

per•ish |**pĕr′**ĭsh| *v.* **1.** To die, especially in a violent manner: *Ten people perished in the accident.* **2.** To pass from existence; disappear gradually: *The dinosaur perished from the earth.*

per•ish•a•ble |**pĕr′**ĭ shə bəl| *adj.* Liable to decay or spoil easily: *perishable fruits and vegetables.* —*n.* **perishables.** Things, such as foods, that spoil or decay easily.

per•i•stal•sis |pĕr′ĭ **stăl′**sĭs| *or* |**-stôl′-**| *n.* A wavelike contraction of muscles in a tubular organ, such as an intestine, that moves the material contained in it along its length.

per•i•to•ne•um |pĕr′ĭ tə **nē′**əm| *n., pl.* **per•i•to•ne•a** |pĕr′ĭ tə **nē′**ə|. The membrane that lines the inside of the abdomen and encloses the abdominal organs.

per•i•to•ni•tis |pĕr′ĭ tə **nī′**tĭs| *n.* Inflammation of the peritoneum.

per•i•wig |**pĕr′**ĭ wĭg′| *n.* A wig, especially a large powdered wig worn by men in the 17th and 18th centuries.

per•i•win•kle[1] |**pĕr′**ĭ wĭng′kəl| *n.* A small sea snail with a broad, tapering shell, sometimes eaten as food. [SEE NOTE & PICTURE]

per•i•win•kle[2] |**pĕr′**ĭ wĭng′kəl| *n.* A trailing vine with evergreen leaves and usually blue flowers; myrtle. [SEE NOTE]

per•jure |**pûr′**jər| *v.* **per•jured, per•jur•ing.** To make (oneself) guilty of perjury: *The witness perjured himself.* —**per′jur•er** *n.*

per•ju•ry |**pûr′**jə rē| *n., pl.* **per•ju•ries.** In law, the deliberate giving of false or misleading testimony while under oath.

perk |pûrk| *v.* To raise or stick up in a jaunty way, as a dog's ear. —***phrasal verb.*** **perk up. 1.** To regain or cause to regain one's good spirits or liveliness: *She perked up at the news. The hot soup perked him up.* **2.** To add to the appearance of; spruce up: *She perked up the blouse with embroidered flowers.*

perk•y |**pûr′**kē| *adj.* **perk•i•er, perk•i•est.** Cheerful and brisk; chipper; jaunty. —**perk′i•ly** *adv.*

per•ma•nence |**pûr′**mə nəns| *n.* The quality or condition of being permanent.

per•ma•nen•cy |**pûr′**mə nən sē| *n.* A form of the word **permanence.**

per•ma•nent |**pûr′**mə nənt| *adj.* Lasting or meant to last indefinitely; enduring. —*n.* A permanent wave. —**per′ma•nent•ly** *adv.*

per•ma•nent-press |**pûr′**mə nənt **prĕs′**| *adj.* Requiring little or no ironing.

permanent wave. An arrangement of the hair into artificial waves or curls that are set in by chemicals and last for several months.

per•man•ga•nate |pər **măng′**gə nāt′| *n.* Any of the salts of permanganic acid, all of which are strong oxidizing agents.

per•man•gan•ic acid |pûr′măng **găn′**ĭk|. An unstable acid composed of hydrogen, manganese, and oxygen and having the formula $HMnO_4$.

per•me•a•ble |**pûr′**mē ə bəl| *adj.* Capable of being passed through or permeated. —**per′me•a•bil′i•ty** *n.* —**per′me•a•bly** *adv.*

per•me•ate |**pûr′**mē āt′| *v.* **per•me•at•ed, per•me•at•ing. 1.** To spread or flow throughout: *The odor permeated the factory.* **2.** To pass through the tiny openings of.

Per•mi•an |**pûr′**mē ən| *n.* Also **Permian period.** A geologic period that began about 280 million years ago and ended about 230 million years ago; the final period of the Paleozoic era. —***modifier:*** *a Permian fossil.*

per•mis•si•ble |pər **mĭs′**ə bəl| *adj.* Such as can be permitted; admissible; allowable: *a permissible error.* —**per•mis′si•bly** *adv.*

per•mis•sion |pər **mĭsh′**ən| *n.* Consent, especially formal consent; authorization.

per•mis•sive |pər **mĭs′**ĭv| *adj.* **1.** Granting permission; allowing: *a permissive statute.* **2.** Allowing freedom; lenient: *permissive parents.* —**per•mis′sive•ly** *adv.* —**per•mis′sive•ness** *n.*

per•mit |pər **mĭt′**| *v.* **per•mit•ted, per•mit•ting. 1.** To give consent or permission to; allow; authorize: *permit access to their files; permit smoking.* **2. a.** To afford opportunity to; make possible: *The assembly line permitted mass production.* **b.** To afford opportunity; allow: *If weather permits, we will fly.* —*n.* |**pûr′**mĭt| *or* |pər **mĭt′**|. A document or certificate giving permission to do something; a license.

per•mu•ta•tion |pûr′myo͞o **tā′**shən| *n.* **1.** A complete change; transformation: *Notice the permutations that certain spices undergo when cooked.* **2. a.** Any of the ordered subsets that can be formed from the elements of a set. For example, the permutations of the set composed of *x, y,* and *z* are *x, y, z, xy, xz, yx, yz, zx, zy, xyz, xzy, yxz, yzx, zxy, zyx.* **b.** The act or process of forming such a subset of another set.

per•mute |pər **myo͞ot′**| *v.* **per•mut•ed, per•mut•ing.** To subject (a set) to permutation.

per•ni•cious |pər **nĭsh′**əs| *adj.* **1.** Tending to cause death or serious injury; deadly: *a pernicious disease.* **2.** Causing great harm; evil; destructive: *a pernicious habit.* —**per•ni′cious•ly** *adv.* —**per•ni′cious•ness** *n.*

per•ox•ide |pə **rŏk′**sīd′| *n.* **1. Hydrogen peroxide. 2.** Any compound containing oxygen that yields hydrogen peroxide when treated with an acid. —*v.* **per•ox•id•ed, per•ox•id•ing.** To bleach (hair) with hydrogen peroxide.

per•pen•dic•u•lar |pûr′pən **dĭk′**yə lər| *adj.* **1.** Intersecting at or forming a right angle or right angles: *perpendicular lines.* **2.** At right angles to the plane of the horizon; vertical. —*n.* A line or plane that intersects another line or plane at right angles. —**per'pen•dic'u•lar•ly** *adv.*

per•pe•trate |pûr'pĭ trāt'| *v.* **per•pe•trat•ed, per•pe•trat•ing.** To be guilty of; commit: *perpetrate a crime.* —**per'pe•tra'tion** *n.* —**per'pe•tra'tor** *n.*

per•pet•u•al |pər pĕch'o͞o əl| *adj.* **1.** Lasting forever or for an indefinitely long time: *the perpetual ice and snow of the polar regions; vows of perpetual friendship.* **2.** Ceaselessly repeated or continuing without interruption: *perpetual nagging.* —**per•pet'u•al•ly** *adv.* —**per•pet'u•al•ness** *n.*

per•pet•u•ate |pər pĕch'o͞o āt'| *v.* **per•pet•u•at•ed, per•pet•u•at•ing.** To prolong the existence of; cause to be remembered for a long time: *perpetuate a legend.* —**per•pet'u•a'tion** *n.*

per•pe•tu•i•ty |pûr'pĭ to͞o'ĭ tē| *or* |-tyo͞o'-| *n.* The quality or condition of being eternal.
Idiom. **in perpetuity.** Forever; eternally.

per•plex |pər plĕks'| *v.* To confuse or puzzle; bewilder. —**per•plexed'** *adj.*: *a perplexed look.* —**per•plex'ing** *adj.*: *perplexing problems.*

per•plex•i•ty |pər plĕk'sĭ tē| *n., pl.* **per•plex•i•ties. 1.** The condition of being perplexed; bewilderment. **2.** Something that perplexes.

per se |pər sā'|. In or by itself; intrinsically. This was originally a Latin expression.

per•se•cute |pûr'sĭ kyo͞ot'| *v.* **per•se•cut•ed, per•se•cut•ing. 1.** To cause to suffer, especially on account of politics, religion, etc.; oppress: *The Nazis persecuted the Jews.* **2.** To annoy persistently; bother: *She persecutes people with her pettiness.* —**per'se•cu'tion** *n.* —**per'se•cu'tor** *n.*

per•se•ver•ance |pûr'sə vîr'əns| *n.* The act or quality of holding to a course, belief, purpose, etc., without giving way; steadfastness: *It took great perseverance for the Wright Brothers to continue trying to build an airplane.*

per•se•vere |pûr'sə vîr'| *v.* **per•se•vered, per•se•ver•ing.** To hold to or persist in a course, belief, purpose, etc., in spite of opposition or discouragement: *Many religions have persevered even under the most serious persecution.*

Per•shing |pûr'shĭng|, **John Joseph.** 1860–1948. American General of the Armies; commander in chief of Allied forces in World War I.

Per•sia |pûr'zhə|. **1.** The former name of Iran. **2.** An ancient empire located in western and southwestern Asia.

Per•sian |pûr'zhən| *n.* **1.** A native or inhabitant of ancient Persia or modern Iran. **2.** The Indo-European language of Iran. **3.** Also **Persian cat.** A cat with long, silky fur, often kept as a pet. —*adj.* Of Iran, the Iranians, or their language. [SEE PICTURE]

Persian Gulf. A gulf between the peninsula of Arabia and Iran.

Persian lamb. The glossy, tightly curled fur of a young lamb of the karakul sheep.

per•sim•mon |pər sĭm'ən| *n.* **1.** An orange-red fruit with pulp that is sweet and edible only when fully ripe. **2.** A tree that bears such fruit. [SEE PICTURE]

per•sist |pər sĭst'| *v.* **1.** To insist or repeat obstinately; be tenacious: *She persisted in denying her guilt.* **2.** To continue in existence; last: *Elk persisted in Pennsylvania until 1867.*

per•sist•ence |pər sĭs'təns| *n.* **1.** The act of persisting. **2.** The quality of being persistent; perseverance. **3.** The continuance of an effect after the cause is removed: *persistence of vision.*

per•sis•ten•cy |pər sĭs'tən sē| *n.* A form of the word **persistence.**

per•sist•ent |pər sĭs'tənt| *adj.* **1.** Refusing to give up or let go; undaunted: *a persistent salesman.* **2.** Lasting; unceasing: *a persistent cough.* **3.** Existing or continuing for a long period of time; enduring: *The persistent goal of alchemy was to change common metals into gold or silver.* —**per•sist'ent•ly** *adv.*

per•snick•e•ty |pər snĭk'ĭ tē| *adj. Informal.* Excessively attentive to detail; fastidious.

per•son |pûr'sən| *n.* **1.** A living human being; an individual. **2.** The living body of a human being: *He had two guns on his person.* **3.** In grammar, any of three groups of pronoun forms with corresponding verb forms that refer to the speaker (first person), the individual addressed (second person), or the individual or thing spoken of (third person). For example, in the sentence *I spoke to you about her, I* is in the first person, *you* is in the second person, and *her* is in the third person.
Idioms. **in person.** Physically present.

per•son•a•ble |pûr'sə nə bəl| *adj.* Pleasing in appearance or personality; attractive.

per•son•age |pûr'sə nĭj| *n.* **1.** A character in a literary work. **2. a.** A person. **b.** A person of rank or distinction.

per•son•al |pûr'sə nəl| *adj.* **1.** Of a particular person; private; one's own: *a personal experience.* **2.** Of a particular person and his private life; intimate: *a personal matter.* **3. a.** Aimed at some aspect of a person, especially in a critical or unfriendly manner: *a highly personal remark.* **b.** Tending to make remarks about or pry into another's affairs: *He always becomes personal in an argument.* **4. a.** Done or made in person: *a personal appearance.* **b.** For a particular person: *a personal favor.* **5.** Of the body or physical being: *personal cleanliness.* **6.** In law, of a person's movable belongings: *personal property.* —*n.* A personal item or notice in a newspaper.

per•son•al•i•ty |pûr'sə năl'ĭ tē| *n., pl.* **per•son•al•i•ties. 1. a.** The totality of qualities and traits, as of character, behavior, etc., that are peculiar to each person: *a pleasing personality.* **b.** A person regarded as having distinctive traits. **2.** The distinctive qualities that make someone socially appealing: *Candidates often win more on personality than on capability.* **3.** A person of importance or renown: *television personalities.* **4.** The characteristics of a place or situation that give it distinctive character: *Colors give a room personality.* —***modifier:*** *personality traits.*

per•son•al•ize |pûr'sə nə līz'| *v.* **per•son•al•ized, per•son•al•iz•ing.** To make personal, especially by marking as personal property.

per•son•al•ly |pûr'sə nə lē| *adv.* **1.** In person or by oneself; without the help of another: *I thanked her personally.* **2.** As far as oneself is concerned: *Personally, I can't stand her.* **3.** As a person: *I don't know him personally.* **4.** In a personal manner: *Don't take it personally.*

personal pronoun. In grammar, a pronoun that indicates the person speaking *(I, me, we, us),* the person spoken to *(you),* or the person or thing spoken about *(he, she, it, they, him, her, them).*

per•so•na non gra•ta |pər sō'nə nŏn grä'tə|. An unwelcome person, especially a diplomat

Persian cat

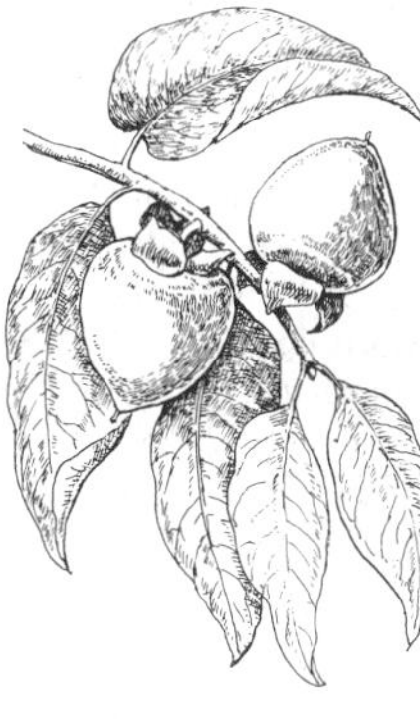

persimmon

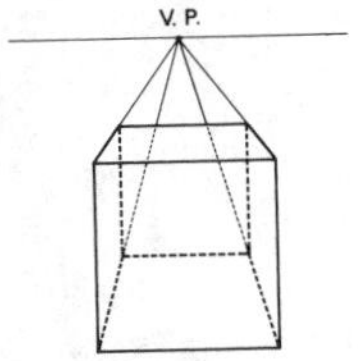

perspective referred to one vanishing point (V.P.)

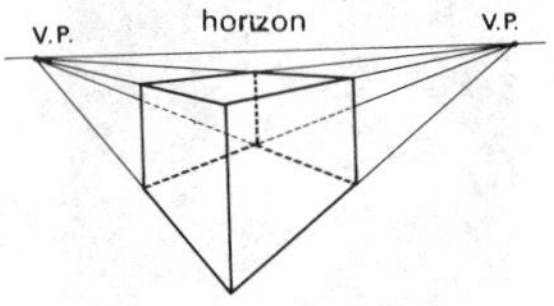

perspective referred to two vanishing points (V.P.)

perspective
Two perspective views of a cube

peruke
Two of the many styles of **peruke** *or* **periwig**. *For more than a century (from about 1660 to 1780), decorative wigs were almost universally worn by fashionable men and women in Europe. The general term for "wig" began with Italian* perruca, *which originally meant "bushy head of hair" and later "wig."* Perruca *was borrowed into French as* perruque; perruque *was borrowed into English in the two forms (1)* **peruke** *and (2)* perwike, *which changed to* **periwig**. *Finally,* **periwig** *was shortened to* **wig**, *which is now the only form in common usage.*

ă pat/ā pay/â care/ä father/ĕ pet/ ē be/ĭ pit/ī pie/î fierce/ŏ pot/ ō go/ô paw, for/oi oil/ŏŏ book/ ōō boot/ou out/ŭ cut/û fur/ *th* the/th thin/hw which/zh vision/ ə ago, item, pencil, atom, circus

who is unacceptable to a foreign government. This was originally a Latin expression.

per•son•i•fi•ca•tion |pər sŏn′ə fĭ **kā′**shən| *n.* **1. a.** The act of personifying. **b.** Something that personifies. **2.** Someone or something that typifies a certain quality or idea; an embodiment: *He is the personification of evil.*

per•son•i•fy |pər **sŏn′**ə fī′| *v.* **per•son•i•fied, per•son•i•fy•ing, per•son•i•fies. 1.** To think of or represent ideas or inanimate objects as having human qualities or human form: *personifying justice as a blindfolded woman.* **2.** To be the embodiment or perfect example of a certain quality or idea: *His life personifies the paradox and promise of the American dream.*

per•son•nel |pûr′sə **nĕl′**| *n.* **1.** The body of persons employed by or active in an organization, business, or service. **2.** The division of a company or other organization concerned with the selection, placement, training, etc., of employees. **—modifier:** *a personnel manager.*

per•spec•tive |pər **spĕk′**tĭv| *n.* **1.** The technique of representing objects on a flat surface so that they have the three-dimensional quality they have when seen with the eye. **2.** A picture drawn in perspective. **3.** A view or vista: *the perspective of the city as seen from the rooftops.* **4.** A mental view of the relationships of the aspects of a subject to each other and to a whole: *a narrow perspective of the situation.* **5.** An idea of the relative importance of something; a viewpoint: *Try to get a new perspective on the negotiations.* [SEE PICTURE]

per•spi•ca•cious |pûr′spĭ **kā′**shəs| *adj.* Able to perceive, discern, or understand clearly: *a perspicacious student.* **—per′spi•ca′cious•ly** *adv.*

per•spi•cac•i•ty |pûr′spĭ **kăs′**ĭ tē| *n.* The ability to perceive, discern, or understand clearly.

per•spi•ra•tion |pûr′spə **rā′**shən| *n.* **1.** The salty moisture excreted through the skin by the sweat glands; sweat. **2.** The act or process of perspiring.

per•spire |pər **spīr′**| *v.* **per•spired, per•spir•ing.** To give off perspiration from the pores of the skin.

per•suade |pər **swād′**| *v.* **per•suad•ed, per•suad•ing.** To cause (someone) to do or believe something by arguing, pleading, or reasoning; convince: *He tried to persuade them to come with us.* **—per•suad′er** *n.*

per•sua•sion |pər **swā′**zhən| *n.* **1.** The act or process of persuading. **2. a.** A strong belief: *of a certain political persuasion.* **b.** Religious belief; a religion: *people of all persuasions.*

per•sua•sive |pər **swā′**sĭv| *or* |-zĭv| *adj.* Tending to or having the power to persuade. **—per•sua′sive•ly** *adv.* **—per•sua′sive•ness** *n.*

pert |pûrt| *adj.* **1.** Impudently bold or saucy: *a pert answer.* **2.** Trim and chic: *a pert dress.* **3.** High-spirited; lively: *a pert little dog.* **—pert′ly** *adv.* **—pert′ness** *n.*

per•tain |pər **tān′**| *v.* **1.** To have reference; relate: *a discussion pertaining to art.* **2.** To belong to as a part or accessory of: *engineering skills pertaining to aeronautics.*

per•ti•na•cious |pûr′tn **ā′**shəs| *adj.* Holding firmly to some belief, purpose, or opinion; stubbornly persistent: *a pertinacious bill collector.* **—per′ti•na′cious•ly** *adv.* **—per′ti•na′cious•ness** *n.*

per•ti•nac•i•ty |pûr′tn **ăs′**ĭ tē| *n.* The quality of being pertinacious.

per•ti•nent |**pûr′**tn ənt| *adj.* Related to a specific matter; relevant: *discussing pertinent topics.* **—per′ti•nence** *n.*

per•turb |pər **tûrb′**| *v.* To make uneasy or anxious; disturb; upset: *He was easily perturbed over small matters.* **—per′tur•ba′tion** *n.*

Pe•ru |pə **rōō′**|. A country on the Pacific coast of South America. Population, 15,383,000. Capital, Lima.

pe•ruke |pə **rōōk′**| *n.* A periwig. [SEE NOTE & PICTURE]

pe•rus•al |pə **rōō′**zəl| *n.* The action of perusing; a thorough reading.

pe•ruse |pə **rōōz′**| *v.* **pe•rused, pe•rus•ing.** To look through, read, or examine, especially with great care.

Pe•ru•vi•an |pə **rōō′**vē ən| *n.* A native or inhabitant of Peru. *—adj.* Of Peru or the Peruvians.

per•vade |pər **vād′**| *v.* **per•vad•ed, per•vad•ing.** To spread or be present throughout; permeate: *The strong scent of gardenias pervaded the whole house.*

per•va•sive |pər **vā′**sĭv| *or* |-zĭv| *adj.* Tending to pervade: *a pervasive aroma.* **—per•va′sive•ly** *adv.* **—per•va′sive•ness** *n.*

per•verse |pər **vûrs′**| *adj.* **1.** Contrary to what is considered the right course of action: *perverse behavior.* **2.** Stubbornly opposed to something; willful; obstinate: *a perverse child.* **—per•verse′ly** *adv.* **—per•verse′ness** *n.*

per•ver•sion |pər **vûr′**zhən| *n.* **1.** The act of perverting or the condition of being perverted. **2.** Any form of sexual behavior that is considered abnormal or unnatural.

per•ver•si•ty |pər **vûr′**sĭ tē| *n., pl.* **per•ver•si•ties. 1.** The quality of being perverse. **2.** An example of being perverse.

per•vert |pər **vûrt′**| *v.* **1.** To cause to turn from what is considered the right course of action: *pervert the course of justice.* **2.** To use wrongly or improperly: *pervert the value of the instruction by misguiding the students.* **3.** To interpret wrongly: *He perverted the meaning of the poem.* **—per•vert′ed** *adj.: a perverted notion of the truth.* **—***n.* |**pûr′**vûrt′|. Someone whose sexual behavior is considered abnormal or criminal.

Pe•sach |**pä′**säKH′| *n.* Passover.

pe•se•ta |pə **sā′**tə| *n., pl.* **pe•se•tas.** The basic unit of money of Spain.

pes•ky |**pĕs′**kē| *adj.* **pes•ki•er, pes•ki•est.** *Informal.* Troublesome; annoying: *a pesky swarm of gnats.* **—pes′ki•ly** *adv.* **—pes′ki•ness** *n.*

pe•so |**pā′**sō| *n., pl.* **pe•sos.** The basic unit of money of Argentina, Bolivia, Colombia, Cuba, the Dominican Republic, Mexico, the Philippines, and Uruguay.

pes•si•mism |**pĕs′**ə mĭz′əm| *n.* **1.** A tendency to take the gloomiest possible view of a situation or of the world. **2.** The belief that the evil in the world outweighs the good. **—pes′si•mist** *n.*

pes•si•mis•tic |pĕs′ə **mĭs′**tĭk| *adj.* Of or marked by pessimism: *a pessimistic person.* **—pes′si•mis′ti•cal•ly** *adv.*

pest |pĕst| *n.* **1.** An annoying person: *My kid sister is a real pest.* **2.** A harmful or annoying animal, such as an insect or a rat, or a troublesome plant, such as a rapidly spreading weed.

pes•ter |pĕs′tər| *v.* To annoy or bother: *a hound that pestered folks out of their wits.*

pes•ti•cide |pĕs′tĭ sīd′| *n.* Any chemical used to kill harmful animals or plants, especially insects and rodents.

pes•tif•er•ous |pĕ stĭf′ər əs| *adj.* Breeding or spreading disease: *pestiferous swamplands.*

pes•ti•lence |pĕs′tə ləns| *n.* **1.** A deadly epidemic disease, especially bubonic plague. **2.** An epidemic of such a disease.

pes•ti•lent |pĕs′tə lənt| *adj.* **1.** Tending to cause death; deadly; fatal: *a pestilential disease.* **2.** Harmful to law and order, morals, society, etc.: *the pestilent threat of drug peddling.*

pes•ti•len•tial |pĕs′tə lĕn′shəl| *adj.* A form of the word **pestilent.**

pes•tle |pĕs′əl| *or* |pĕs′təl| *n.* A tool, often with a heavy, rounded end, used for crushing or mashing substances, as in a mortar.

pet |pĕt| *n.* **1.** An animal kept for companionship or amusement. **2.** Someone or something of which one is especially fond; a favorite. ***—modifier:*** *a pet cat; the scientist's pet project.* —*v.* **pet•ted, pet•ting.** To stroke or pat gently; caress.

pet•al |pĕt′l| *n.* One of the usually brightly or delicately colored leaflike parts of a flower.

pe•tard |pə tärd′| *n.* A small bell-shaped bomb, formerly used to blow apart a gate or wall. ***Idiom.* hoist with** (or **by**) **(one's) own petard.** Harmed or foiled by one's own cleverness; caught in one's own trap.

pet•cock |pĕt′kŏk′| *n.* A small valve or faucet used in draining excess water from pipes, radiators, boilers, etc.

pe•ter |pē′tər| *v.* ***—phrasal verb.* peter out. 1.** To come to an end; disappear: *Our supplies petered out.* **2.** To cease to be productive; become worked out: *The mine petered out.* **3.** To become exhausted: *I'm all petered out from the day's work.*

Pe•ter |pē′tər|, **Saint.** Died A.D. 67? One of the twelve Apostles, considered the first pope and founder of the Christian Church.

pet•i•ole |pĕt′ē ōl′| *n.* The stalk by which a leaf is attached to a stem; a leafstalk.

pet•it |pĕt′ē| *adj.* In law, lesser; minor: *petit jury; petit larceny.*

pe•tite |pə tēt′| *adj.* Small and slender; dainty.

pe•ti•tion |pə tĭsh′ən| *n.* **1.** An entreaty, especially to a person or group in authority: *a petition for an audience.* **2.** A formal written document requesting a right or benefit from authority: *collect signatures on a petition for a new school.* —*v.* **1.** To address a petition to; entreat: *Hawaii first petitioned Congress for statehood in 1902.* **2.** To make a formal request: *His lawyer petitioned for a retrial.* **—pe•ti′tion•er** *n.*

pet•it point |pĕt′ē|. Decorative needlework, as done on canvas, using a small, diagonal stitch.

pet•rel |pĕt′rəl| *n.* Any of several sea birds that are usually small and dark-colored and that fly over the open ocean far from land. ¶*These sound alike* **petrel, petrol.** [SEE PICTURE]

pet•ri•fy |pĕt′rə fī′| *v.* **pet•ri•fied, pet•ri•fy•ing, pet•ri•fies. 1.** To turn (wood or other organic material) into a stony mass by causing minerals to fill and finally replace its internal structure. **2.** To stun or paralyze, as with fear or astonishment. **—pet′ri•fac′tion** |pĕt′rə făk′shən| *n.*

pe•trog•ra•phy |pə trŏg′rə fē| *n.* The scientific description and classification of rocks.

pet•rol |pĕt′rəl| *n. British.* Gasoline. ¶*These sound alike* **petrol, petrel.**

pet•ro•la•tum |pĕt′rə lā′təm| *n.* A jellylike, usually colorless mixture of hydrocarbons obtained from petroleum, used in making ointments and lubricants.

pe•tro•le•um |pə trō′lē əm| *n.* A thick, yellowish-black, flammable liquid mixture of hydrocarbons that occurs naturally, mainly below the surface of the earth.

pe•trol•o•gy |pə trŏl′ə jē| *n.* The science of the origin, composition, and structure of rocks.

pet•ti•coat |pĕt′ē kōt′| *n.* A skirt or slip worn by girls and women as an undergarment.

pet•tish |pĕt′ĭsh| *adj.* Ill-tempered; peevish: *The baby has been in a pettish mood all day.* **—pet′tish•ly** *adv.* **—pet′tish•ness** *n.*

pet•ty[1] |pĕt′ē| *adj.* **pet•ti•er, pet•ti•est. 1.** Small or trivial: *petty annoyances.* **2.** Narrow-minded; selfish: *petty partisanship.* **3.** *Informal.* Spiteful; mean: *He scolded her in a very petty way.* **—pet′ti•ly** *adv.* **—pet′ti•ness** *n.*

pet•ty[2] |pĕt′ē| *adj.* A form of the word **petit.**

petty cash. A small amount of money kept in an office for incidental expenses.

petty larceny. The theft of objects having a relatively small value.

petty officer. A noncommissioned officer in the navy.

pet•u•lant |pĕch′ōō lənt| *adj.* Ill-tempered; peevish. **—pet′u•lance** *n.* **—pet′u•lant•ly** *adv.*

pe•tu•nia |pə tōō′nyə| *or* |-tyōō′-| *n.* A garden plant with funnel-shaped white, reddish, or purple flowers. [SEE PICTURE]

pew |pyōō| *n.* A bench for the congregation in a church.

pe•wee |pē′wē| *n.* A small, brownish North American bird with a call that sounds like its name.

pew•ter |pyōō′tər| *n.* **1.** Any of a number of alloys of tin with varying amounts of antimony, copper, and lead, formerly used for making kitchen utensils and tableware. **2.** Pewter articles in general. ***—modifier:*** *a pewter dish.*

Pfc, Pfc. private first class.

PG |pē′jē′| *adj.* Indicating a rating given a motion picture deemed appropriate for persons of all ages but suggesting parental guidance in the case of children.

pH A numerical measure of the acidity or alkalinity of a solution, equal to 7 for neutral solutions, less than 7 for acid solutions, and more than 7 for alkaline solutions.

pha•lanx |fā′lăngks′| *n., pl.* **pha•lanx•es** or **pha•lan•ges** |fə lăn′jēz| *or* |fā-|. **1.** In ancient Greece, a formation of infantry carrying overlapping shields and long spears. **2.** Any compact gathering of persons: *a solid phalanx of demonstrators on the capitol steps.* **3.** *pl.* **phalanges.** Any of the bones of a finger or toe. [SEE PICTURE]

phan•tasm |făn′tăz′əm| *n.* **1.** A ghost. **2.** An unreal mental image. **—phan•tas′mal** *adj.*

phan•ta•sy |făn′tə sē| *or* |-zē| *n., pl.* **phan•ta•sies.** A form of the word **fantasy.**

phan•tom |făn′təm| *n.* **1.** A ghost; apparition. **2.** An unreal mental image.

petrel

petunia

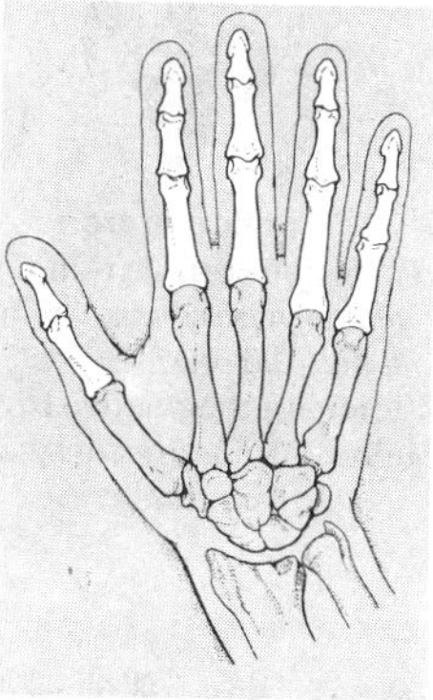

phalanx
Phalanges of the hand

pheasant

philodendron

Philodendron is from Greek *philodendros,* "tree-loving": *philos,* "loving," + *dendron,* "tree." In their native tropics, philodendrons are conspicuous tree-climbers.

ă pat/ā pay/â care/ä father/ĕ pet/ ē be/ĭ pit/ī pie/î fierce/ŏ pot/ ō go/ô paw, for/oi oil/ŏŏ book/ ōō boot/ou out/ŭ cut/û fur/ *th* the/th thin/hw which/zh vision/ ə ago, item, pencil, atom, circus

Phar•aoh, also **phar•aoh** |fâr'ō| *or* |fā'rō| *n.* A king of ancient Egypt.

phar•i•see |făr'ĭ sē'| *n.* **1. Pharisee.** In Biblical times, a member of a Jewish sect that believed in strict observance of the Mosaic Law. **2.** A smug hypocrite.

phar•ma•ceu•ti•cal |fär'mə sōō'tĭ kəl| or **phar•ma•ceu•tic** |fär'mə sōō'tĭk| *adj.* Of pharmacy or pharmacists. —*n.* A pharmaceutical drug, preparation, or product.

phar•ma•ceu•tics |fär'mə sōō'tĭks| *n. (used with a singular verb).* The science and techniques of preparing and dispensing drugs.

phar•ma•cist |fär'mə sĭst| *n.* Someone who specializes in pharmacy; a druggist.

phar•ma•col•o•gy |fär'mə kŏl'ə jē| *n.* The scientific study of drugs and their uses, effects, and composition.

phar•ma•cy |fär'mə sē| *n., pl.* **phar•ma•cies. 1.** The methods and techniques of preparing and dispensing drugs. **2.** A place where drugs are sold; a drugstore.

pha•ryn•ge•al |fə rĭn'jē əl| *or* |-jəl| *or* |făr'ĭn jē'əl| *adj.* Of, in, or from the pharynx.

phar•ynx |făr'ĭngks| *n., pl.* **pha•ryn•ges** |fə rĭn'jēz| or **phar•ynx•es.** The part of the digestive tract that extends from the cavities of the nose to the larnyx, there joining with the esophagus.

phase |fāz| *n.* **1.** A distinct stage of development: *the next phase of our space program.* **2.** An aspect; part: *considering every phase of the problem.* **3.** Any of the forms, recurring in cycles, in which the moon or a planet appears. **4.** A part of a physical system that is uniform, apart from atomic or molecular structure, distinct from the rest, and separable from the rest: *Steam and ice are phases of water.* —*v.* **phased, phas•ing.** To plan or carry out so as to progress in stages: *The highway construction program was carefully phased.* —***phrasal verbs.*** **phase in.** To introduce in stages. **phase out.** To eliminate in stages. ¶ *These sound alike* **phase, faze.**

Ph.D. Doctor of Philosophy.

pheas•ant |fĕz'ənt| *n.* Any of several longtailed, often brightly colored birds, frequently hunted as game. [SEE PICTURE]

phe•no•bar•bi•tal |fē'nō bär'bĭ tôl'| *n.* A white, shiny, crystalline compound used in medicine as a sedative and hypnotic drug.

phe•nol |fē'nôl'| *or* |-nōl'| *n.* **1.** A poisonous, irritating, white crystalline compound having the formula C_6H_6O. It is used as a disinfectant and in making plastics and drugs. **2.** Any of various related chemical compounds.

phe•nol•phthal•ein |fē'nōl thăl'ēn'| *or* |-ē ĭn| *or* |-thā'lēn'| *or* |-lē ĭn| *n.* A crystalline powder used as an indicator for acid and basic solutions, in making dyes, and as a laxative.

phe•nom•e•na |fĭ nŏm'ə nə| *n.* A plural of **phenomenon.**

phe•nom•e•nal |fĭ nŏm'ə nəl| *adj.* Extraordinary; remarkable: *a phenomenal memory; a phenomenal score.* —**phe•nom'e•nal•ly** *adv.*

phe•nom•e•non |fĭ nŏm'ə nŏn| *n., pl.* **phe•nom•e•na** |fĭ nŏm'ə nə| or **phe•nom•e•nons. 1.** Any occurrence or fact that can be perceived by the senses: *Floods are natural phenomena.* **2.** Someone or something that is unusual or noteworthy: *He's considered quite a phenomenon by the sports writers and his teammates.*

phi |fī| *n.* The 21st letter of the Greek alphabet, written Φ, φ. In English it is represented as *ph.*

phi•al |fī'əl| *n.* A form of the word **vial.**

Phil•a•del•phi•a |fĭl'ə dĕl'fē ə|. The largest city in Pennsylvania. Population, 1,881,000. —**Phil'a•del'phi•an** *adj. & n.*

phil•an•throp•ic |fĭl'ən thrŏp'ĭk| *adj.* Of or engaged in philanthropy; charitable. —**phil'an•throp'i•cal•ly** *adv.*

phi•lan•thro•pist |fĭ lăn'thrə pĭst| *n.* A person who is involved in promoting human welfare, as by making charitable donations.

phi•lan•thro•py |fĭ lăn'thrə pē| *n., pl.* **phi•lan•thro•pies. 1. a.** The desire or effort to help mankind, as by charitable donations. **b.** The act of making a charitable gift or donation. **2.** An institution, cause, etc., designed to promote human welfare.

phil•a•tel•ic |fĭl'ə tĕl'ĭk| *adj.* Of or concerned with philately: *a philatelic club.*

phi•lat•e•list |fĭ lăt'l ĭst| *n.* A person who collects and studies postage stamps.

phi•lat•e•ly |fĭ lăt'l ē| *n.* The collection and study of postage stamps.

phil•har•mon•ic or **Phil•har•mon•ic** |fĭl'här mŏn'ĭk| *or* |fĭl'ər-| *n.* A symphony orchestra or the group of people that supports it.

phi•lip•pic |fĭ lĭp'ĭk| *n.* A passionate speech intended to arouse opposition; tirade.

Phil•ip•pines |fĭl'ə pēnz'|. A country consisting of the Philippine Islands, a group of islands in the western Pacific. Population, 47,914,000. Constitutional capital, Quezon City; de facto capital, Manila. —**Phil'ip•pine'** *adj.*

Phi•lis•tine |fĭl'ĭ stēn'| *or* |fə lĭs'tĭn| *or* |-tēn'| *n.* **1.** A member of an ancient people in Palestine who were enemies of the Hebrews. **2.** Also **philistine.** A person with conventional ideas, regarded as narrow-minded and hypocritical. —*adj.* **1.** Of the ancient Philistines. **2.** Also **philistine.** Conventional and narrow-minded: *a philistine urge to remain ignorant.*

phil•o•den•dron |fĭl'ə dĕn'drən| *n.* Any of several climbing plants with evergreen leaves, often grown as house plants. [SEE PICTURE]

phi•lol•o•gist |fĭ lŏl'ə jĭst| *n.* An expert in philology.

phi•lol•o•gy |fĭ lŏl'ə jē| *n.* The study of the chronological development of languages.

phi•los•o•pher |fĭ lŏs'ə fər| *n.* **1.** A student of or expert in philosophy. **2.** A person who develops and expounds a philosophic system. **3.** A calm, self-assured, and patient person.

philosopher's stone. In medieval alchemy, the substance that was supposed to transmute base metals into gold.

phil•o•soph•i•cal |fĭl'ə sŏf'ĭ kəl| or **phil•o•soph•ic** |fĭl'ə sŏf'ĭk| *adj.* **1.** Of philosophy: *philosophic theories.* **2.** Calm; serene: *He accepted his fate with philosophical resignation.* —**phil'o•soph'i•cal•ly** *adv.*

phi•los•o•phize |fĭ lŏs'ə fīz'| *v.* **phi•los•o•phized, phi•los•o•phiz•ing. 1.** To reason or think as a philosopher. **2.** To express one's opinions, ideas, etc., in a manner considered suitable for a philosopher. —**phi•los'o•phiz'er** *n.*

phi•los•o•phy |fĭ lŏs'ə fē| *n., pl.* **phi•los•o•phies. 1. a.** The study by logical reasoning of the basic truths and laws governing the universe, nature, life, morals, etc. **b.** A formal system of ideas based upon such study: *the philosophy of Aristotle.* **2.** A personal set of opinions about life, the world, etc.: *"Might makes right" was the tyrant's philosophy.* **3.** A basic practical rule or set of rules: *Vince Lombardi's philosophy of coaching.* —**modifier:** *a philosophy professor.*

phil•ter, also **phil•tre** |fĭl′tər| *n.* A magic potion, especially a love potion. ¶*These sound alike* **philter, filter.**

phlegm |flĕm| *n.* Mucus produced by the mucous membranes of the respiratory tract.

phleg•mat•ic |flĕg măt′ĭk| *adj.* **1.** Of or like phlegm. **2.** Having or suggesting a calm, sluggish temperament; unemotional: *a properly phlegmatic English lord.* —**phleg•mat′i•cal•ly** *adv.*

phlo•em |flō′ĕm′| *n.* Plant tissue consisting mainly of long, tubular cells through which food is conducted from the leaves to plant parts.

phlox |flŏks| *n.* A plant with clusters of reddish, purple, or white flowers. [SEE PICTURE]

Phnom Penh |pə nôm′ pĕn′|. The capital of Cambodia. Population, 403,000.

pho•bi•a |fō′bē ə| *n.* A lasting, abnormal, or unreasonable fear of a thing or a situation: *She had a phobia about riding in elevators.*

phoe•be |fē′bē| *n.* A small, grayish North American bird with a call that sounds like its name.

Phoe•ni•cia |fə nē′shə| *or* |-nĭsh′ə|. An ancient country at the eastern end of the Mediterranean Sea.

Phoe•ni•cian |fə nē′shən| *or* |-nĭsh′ən| *n.* **1.** A native or inhabitant of ancient Phoenicia. **2.** The Semitic language of the Phoenicians. —**Phoe•ni′cian** *adj.*

phoe•nix |fē′nĭks| *n.* A fabled bird of Arabia said to consume itself by fire every 500 years and to rise renewed from its own ashes.

Phoe•nix |fē′nĭks|. The capital of Arizona. Population, 780,000.

phone |fōn|. *Informal. n.* A telephone. —*v.* **phoned, phon•ing. 1.** To call by telephone: *He phoned her to ask for a date.* **2.** To transmit by telephone: *The reporter phoned in his story from the scene of the accident.* —**modifier:** *a phone call.*

-phone. A word element that forms nouns and means "sound, voice": **earphone.**

pho•neme |fō′nēm′| *n.* In linguistics, the smallest unit of sound that can distinguish one word from another. For example, the *m* of *mat* and the *b* of *bat* are phonemes.

pho•ne•mic |fə nē′mĭk| *adj.* Of or indicating a phoneme or phonemes: *a phonemic sound.*

pho•net•ic |fə nĕt′ĭk| *adj.* **1.** Of phonetics. **2.** Representing the sounds of speech with a set of symbols, each denoting a single sound: *phonetic spelling.* —**pho•net′i•cal•ly** *adv.*

pho•net•ics |fə nĕt′ĭks| *n. (used with a singular verb).* The study of the sounds of speech and of their representation by symbols. —**pho′ne•ti′cian** |fō′nĭ tĭsh′ən| *n.*

pho•ney |fō′nē| *n., pl.* **pho•nies,** & *adj.* **pho•ni•er, pho•ni•est.** A form of the word **phony.**

phon•ic |fŏn′ĭk| *adj.* Of or involving sound, especially in speech. —**phon′i•cal•ly** *adv.*

phon•ics |fŏn′ĭks| *n. (used with a singular verb).* The scientific study of sound; acoustics.

phono–. A word element meaning "sound, voice, or speech": **phonograph.**

pho•no•graph |fō′nə grăf′| *or* |-gräf′| *n.* A device that reproduces sound from a groove cut into a disk. —**modifier:** *a phonograph record.*

pho•ny |fō′nē|. *Informal. adj.* **pho•ni•er, pho•ni•est. 1.** Not genuine; fake: *a phony diamond.* **2.** Insincere; hypocritical; deceitful: *He flashed her a phony smile.* —*n., pl.* **pho•nies.** A person who is insincere or hypocritical; a fake or impostor. —**pho′ni•ly** *adv.* —**pho′ni•ness** *n.*

phoo•ey |fo͞o′ē| *interj.* A word used to express disappointment or contempt.

phos•phate |fŏs′fāt′| *n.* **1.** A salt or ester of phosphoric acid. **2.** A fertilizer containing compounds of phosphorus.

phos•phor |fŏs′fər| *n.* **1.** A substance that can emit light after absorbing some form of radiation. **2.** Something that shows phosphorescence.

phos•pho•res•cence |fŏs′fə rĕs′əns| *n.* **1.** The process or phenomenon by which a body emits light as a result of and for some time after being exposed to radiation. **2.** The generation of light by a living thing; bioluminescence. **3.** The light that results from either of these.

phos•pho•res•cent |fŏs′fə rĕs′ənt| *adj.* Having or showing the property of phosphorescence.

phos•phor•ic |fŏs fôr′ĭk| *or* |-fŏr′-| *adj.* Of or containing phosphorus, especially with a valence of 5.

phosphoric acid. Any of the three acids that are formed when the oxide of phosphorus that has the formula P_2O_5 reacts with water. The most important of these has the formula H_3PO_4 and is widely used in manufacturing.

phos•pho•rous |fŏs′fər əs| *adj.* Of or containing phosphorus, especially with a valence of 3.

phos•pho•rus |fŏs′fər əs| *n.* Symbol **P** One of the elements, a highly reactive, poisonous solid, occurring in white (sometimes yellow), red, and black forms. Atomic number 15; atomic weight 30.97; valences −3, +3, +5; melting point of white phosphorus 44.1°C; boiling point of white phosphorus 280°C. [SEE NOTE]

pho•to |fō′tō| *n., pl.* **pho•tos.** *Informal.* A photograph.

photo–. A word element meaning: **1.** Light: **photoelectric. 2.** Photographic: **photocopy.**

pho•to•cell |fō′tō sĕl′| *n.* A **photoelectric cell.**

pho•to•cop•i•er |fō′tō kŏp′ē ər| *n.* A device for photocopying graphic material.

pho•to•cop•y |fō′tō kŏp′ē| *v.* **-cop•ied, -cop•y•ing, -cop•ies.** To make a photographic reproduction of (printed, written, or pictorial material). —*n., pl.* **-cop•ies.** A photographic reproduction.

pho•to•e•lec•tric |fō′tō ĭ lĕk′trĭk| *adj.* Of or having to do with electrical effects that result from or depend on the presence of light. —**pho′to•e•lec′tri•cal•ly** *adv.*

photoelectric cell. An electronic device having an electrical output that varies in response to the intensity of the light striking it.

pho•to•gen•ic |fō′tə jĕn′ĭk| *adj.* Attractive as a subject for photography: *She has a very photogenic smile.* —**pho′to•gen′i•cal•ly** *adv.*

pho•to•graph |fō′tə grăf′| *or* |-gräf′| *n.* An image formed on a light-sensitive surface by a camera and developed by chemical means to

phlox

phosphorus

White **phosphorus** *will catch fire and burn spontaneously in air. Red phosphorus is more stable and is used to make safety matches, fireworks, smoke bombs, and a variety of incendiary devices. Phosphorus is an essential ingredient of all protoplasm, and phosphorus compounds have been widely used in detergents and fertilizers.*

produce a positive print. —*v.* **1.** To make a photograph of. **2.** To be a subject for photographs: *Some models photograph better than others.*

pho•tog•ra•pher |fə tŏg′rə fər| *n.* Someone who takes photographs, especially as a profession.

pho•to•graph•ic |fō′tə grăf′ĭk| *adj.* **1.** Of or used in photography or a photograph: *a photographic lens.* **2.** Resembling a photograph, as in accuracy and detail: *a photographic memory.* —**pho′to•graph′i•cal•ly** *adv.*

pho•tog•ra•phy |fə tŏg′rə fē| *n.* **1.** The process or technique of creating images on light-sensitive surfaces. **2.** The art, practice, or profession of making photographs. **3.** A collection of photographs or photographic works.

pho•tom•e•ter |fō tŏm′ĭ tər| *n.* An instrument used to measure and indicate some property of light, especially its intensity.

pho•tom•e•try |fō tŏm′ĭ trē| *n.* The measurement of the intensity, brightness, or other properties of light.

pho•ton |fō′tŏn′| *n.* The quantum of light or other electromagnetic energy, considered to be a stable particle that travels at the speed of light and to have a mass of zero.

pho•to•re•cep•tor |fō′tō rĭ sĕp′tər| *n.* A part of an animal that is specially adapted for sensitivity to light.

pho•to•sen•si•tive |fō′tō sĕn′sĭ tĭv| *adj.* Undergoing or capable of undergoing some chemical or physical change as a result of exposure to light. —**pho′to•sen′si•tiv′i•ty** *n.*

pho•to•sphere |fō′tə sfîr′| *n.* The layer of a star, such as the sun, that emits directly observable light or other radiation.

Pho•to•stat |fō′tə stăt′| *n.* **1.** A trademark for a device used to make quick copies of written or printed material. **2.** A copy made by Photostat. —*v.* To make a copy of by Photostat.

pho•to•syn•the•sis |fō′tō sĭn′thĭ sĭs| *n.* The chemical process by which plants that contain chlorophyll, such as green plants, use light to convert carbon dioxide and water to carbohydrates, releasing oxygen as a by-product.

pho•to•tax•is |fō′tə tăk′sĭs| *n.* The movement of a living thing in response to light.

pho•tot•ro•pism |fō tŏt′rə pĭz′əm| *n.* The movement or growth of a living organism in response to light.

phrase |frāz| *n.* **1.** In grammar, a sequence of words that is meaningful but lacks the subject and predicate of a complete sentence. For example, *on the table* is a phrase. **2.** A brief, cogent expression. For example, *from the frying pan into the fire* is a phrase. **3.** A short section of a musical composition, typically consisting of from four to eight measures. —*v.* **phrased, phras•ing. 1.** To express in spoken or written words: *He phrased his answer carefully.* **2. a.** To divide (a musical passage) into phrases. **b.** To combine (notes or measures) into phrases. —**phras′al** *adj.*

phra•se•ol•o•gy |frā′zē ŏl′ə jē| *n., pl.* **phra•se•ol•o•gies. 1.** A manner or style of speaking or writing: *flowery phraseology.* **2.** A set of expressions used by a particular person or group: *nautical phraseology.*

phre•nol•o•gy |frə nŏl′ə jē| *n.* A method of attempting to determine intelligence and character by studying the shape of a person's skull.

phy•lum |fī′ləm| *n., pl.* **phy•la** |fī′lə|. One of the larger groups into which living organisms are divided, ranking between a kingdom and a class and including animals and plants with certain basic similarities. Insects, lobsters, spiders, and other invertebrate animals with jointed legs belong to the same phylum. [SEE NOTE]

phys•ic |fĭz′ĭk| *n.* A medicine or drug, especially a laxative.

phys•i•cal |fĭz′ĭ kəl| *adj.* **1.** Of the body rather than the mind or emotions: *physical fitness.* **2.** Solid; material: *a physical object.* **3.** Of nonliving matter and energy as distinguished from living phenomena: *the physical sciences.* **4.** Of the natural rather than man-made phenomena of the earth's surface: *a physical map.* —*n.* A **physical examination.** —**phys′i•cal•ly** *adv.*

physical education. 1. The branch of educational science concerned with the training and care of the human body, especially through sports. **2.** A course in school consisting of calisthenics, sports, and hygiene.

physical science. Any science, such as physics, chemistry, astronomy, or geology, that deals mainly with matter and energy. [SEE NOTE]

physical therapy. The treatment of injury or disease by such means as exercise, massage, baths, or application of heat or cold.

phy•si•cian |fĭ zĭsh′ən| *n.* A person licensed to practice medicine; a doctor.

phys•i•cist |fĭz′ĭ sĭst| *n.* A scientist who specializes in physics.

phy•sics |fĭz′ĭks| *n.* *(used with a singular verb).* **1.** The science of matter and energy and the relations between them. **2.** Physical study, analysis, properties, laws, etc.: *the physics of space travel.* —***modifier:*** *a physics teacher.*

phys•i•og•no•my |fĭz′ē ŏg′nə mē| *n., pl.* **phys•i•og•no•mies. 1.** Facial features, regarded as revealing character. **2.** The external aspect of something; contour: *the rugged physiognomy of Colorado as seen from an airplane.*

phys•i•o•log•i•cal |fĭz′ē ə lŏj′ĭ kəl| *adj.* **1.** Of physiology. **2.** Of, involving, or affecting the processes or functioning of a living thing. —**phys′i•o•log′i•cal•ly** *adv.*

phys•i•ol•o•gy |fĭz′ē ŏl′ə jē| *n.* **1.** The scientific study of the processes, activities, and functions essential to and characteristic of life. **2.** The vital processes and functions of a living thing.

phys•i•o•ther•a•py |fĭz′ē ō thĕr′ə pē| *n.* **Physical therapy.**

phy•sique |fĭ zēk′| *n.* The body, considered in terms of its proportions, muscle development, and appearance: *the physique of an athlete.*

pi |pī| *n., pl.* **pis. 1.** The 16th letter of the Greek alphabet, written Π, π. In English it is represented as *P, p.* **2.** Symbol π A transcendental number equal to the quotient of the circumference of a circle divided by its diameter, or approximately 3.14159. ¶*These sound alike* **pi, pie.**

pi•a ma•ter |pī′ə mā′tər|. The fine, cobweblike membrane that is the innermost covering of the brain and spinal cord.

pi•a•nis•si•mo |pē′ə nĭs′ə mō′|. In music: *adj.* Very quiet or soft. —*adv.* Very quietly or softly. —*n., pl.* **pi•a•nis•si•mos.** Something that is per-

phylum
Botanists often prefer the word **division** *for a group of plants corresponding to a* **phylum**.

physical science
It might have been correct at one time to say that the **physical sciences** *are concerned with matter and energy rather than with the behavior of living things. It is no longer true. Living things are, of course, composed of matter and energy. To the extent that the matter and energy of living things are subject to the same laws as other matter and energy, they are the concern of physical scientists. Biochemistry and biophysics are specifically concerned with the matter and energy of living things.*

ă pat/ā pay/â care/ä father/ĕ pet/ ē be/ĭ pit/ī pie/î fierce/ŏ pot/ ō go/ô paw, for/oi oil/ŏŏ book/ ōō boot/ou out/ŭ cut/û fur/ *th* the/th thin/hw which/zh vision/ ə ago, item, pencil, atom, circus

formed or to be performed very softly or quietly.

pi•an•ist |pē ăn′ĭst| *or* |pē′ə nĭst| *n.* Someone who plays the piano.

pi•an•o¹ |pē ăn′ō| *n., pl.* **pi•an•os.** A keyboard musical instrument in which the movement of a key by the player's finger actuates a felt-covered hammer that strikes a metal string and produces a tone. —***modifier:*** *a piano score.* [SEE NOTE]

pi•an•o² |pē än′ō| *or* |-ä′nō|. In music: *adj.* Soft or quiet. —*adv.* Softly or quietly. —*n., pl.* **pi•an•os.** Something that is performed or to be performed quietly or softly. [SEE NOTE]

pi•an•o•for•te |pē ăn′ə fôr′tē| *or* |-fōr′-| *n.* A piano, a musical instrument.

pi•az•za |pē ăz′ə| *or* |-ä′zə| *n.* **1.** A public square in an Italian town. **2.** A porch.

pi•ca |pī′kə| *n.* **1.** A printer's type size equal to 12 points. **2.** The height of this type, about 1/6 inch, used as a unit of measure. **3.** A type size for typewriters. ¶ *These sound alike* **pica, pika.**

pic•a•resque |pĭk′ə rĕsk′| *adj.* Of or involving clever rogues or adventurers.

Pi•cas•so |pĭ kä′sō|, **Pablo.** 1881–1973. Spanish-born painter and sculptor.

pic•a•yune |pĭk′ē yo͞on′| *adj.* **1.** Trivial; paltry: *a picayune amount.* **2.** Concerned with or spiteful about trivial matters; petty: *Don't be so picayune about everything!*

pic•ca•lil•li |pĭk′ə lĭl′ē| *n.* A pickled relish of chopped vegetables.

pic•co•lo |pĭk′ə lō′| *n., pl.* **pic•co•los.** A small flute with a hard, brilliant tone and a range about an octave above that of an ordinary flute. —**pic′co•lo′ist** *n.*

pick¹ |pĭk| *v.* **1.** To choose or select: *pick the right man for the job.* **2.** To gather by or as if by plucking off or out with the fingers: *pick flowers; pick cotton.* **3.** To leave bare by removing something, as feathers or shreds of flesh, that covers or clings: *pick the bones clean.* **4.** To dig at (with a toothpick, one's finger, etc.): *pick one's teeth.* **5.** To cause deliberately; provoke: *Are you trying to pick a fight with me?* **6.** To gain the knowledge contained in: *pick someone's brains.* **7.** To open without using a key, as with a piece of wire: *pick a lock.* **8.** To steal the contents of: *pick someone's pocket.* **9. a.** To pluck (the strings) of a musical instrument. **b.** To play (a tune or melody) in this way: *He picked a tune on his guitar.* —***phrasal verbs.*** **pick at. 1.** To eat in small bites, without much appetite. **2.** To criticize (someone) repeatedly in small ways. **pick on.** *Informal.* To bully or tease: *Stop picking on me.* **pick out. 1.** To choose or select: *A decorator helped Mrs. Johnson pick out some pretty floral wallpaper.* **2.** To play (a tune or melody) in an uncertain, hesitating way: *pick out a tune on the piano.* **pick up. 1.** To lift up or take up: *He picked up his suitcase and began walking toward the train.* **2.** To take on (passengers, freight, etc.): *The truck stopped to pick up a hitchhiker.* **3.** To acquire by the way: *pick up a suit from the cleaners.* **4.** To accelerate: *picked up speed.* **5.** To change for the better; improve: *Business will pick up next year.* **6.** To take into custody; arrest: *The police picked him up only a few blocks from the scene of the crime.* **7.** To receive or intercept: *He picked up radio signals from a ship in distress.* **8.** To learn without great effort: *He picked up several foreign languages during his years abroad.* **9.** To set (things) back in order; clean up: *Mother was getting tired of picking up after the twins.* —*n.* **1.** A choice or selection: *She took her pick of the tomatoes.* **2.** The best or choicest one or part: *This puppy is the pick of the litter.* —**pick′er** *n.* [SEE NOTE]

Idioms. **pick and choose.** To choose or select with care. **pick holes in.** To find flaws in.

pick² |pĭk| *n.* **1.** A tool for loosening or breaking up soil, consisting of a slightly curved bar sharpened at both ends and fitted onto a long handle. **2.** Any pointed tool used for piercing, breaking, or picking, as an ice pick or a toothpick. **3.** A small flat piece of plastic, bone, etc., used to pluck the strings of an instrument; a plectrum. [SEE NOTE]

pick•a•back |pĭk′ə băk′| *adv.* A form of the word **piggyback.**

pick•ax or **pick•axe** |pĭk′ăks′| *n.* A pick with one end of the head pointed and the other with a chisellike edge.

pick•er•el |pĭk′ər əl| *n., pl.* **pick•er•el** or **pick•er•els.** A North American freshwater fish related to and resembling the pike but generally smaller.

pick•et |pĭk′ĭt| *n.* **1.** A pointed stake or spike, as one driven into the ground to support a fence, secure a tent, or tether an animal. **2.** A detachment of one or more soldiers placed in a position to give warning of enemy approach. **3.** Someone stationed outside a building to express grievance or protest, as during a strike. —*v.* **1.** To enclose, secure, tether, etc., with a picket. **2.** To demonstrate against, as during a strike. —***modifier:*** *a picket line; a picket sign.*

picket fence. A fence of upright pickets.

pick•ing |pĭk′ĭng| *n.* **1.** The act of gathering, harvesting, etc.: *cotton picking.* **2. pickings. a.** Leftovers or scraps: *We arrived at the picnic only in time for the pickings.* **b.** The amount obtained; the yield: *When easy pickings were all taken in one place, the prospectors moved on.*

pick•le |pĭk′əl| *n.* **1.** Any food, such as a cucumber, that has been preserved and flavored in vinegar or a brine. **2.** A preparation of vinegar or brine for preserving food. **3.** An acid or other chemical bath used to clean the surface of a metal. **4.** *Informal.* A troublesome or difficult situation. —***modifier:*** *a pickle jar; pickle slices.* —*v.* **pick•led, pick•ling.** To preserve or flavor in vinegar or a brine solution. —**pick′led** *adj.*: *pickled onions; pickled beets.*

pick•pock•et |pĭk′pŏk′ĭt| *n.* A thief who stealthily steals from his victim's pockets.

pick•up |pĭk′ŭp′| *n.* **1.** The act or process of picking up packages, work, passengers, freight, etc.: *The truck made a pickup at 4:00.* **2.** Someone or something that is picked up. **3.** *Informal.* An improvement: *a pickup in attendance.* **4.** Ability to accelerate rapidly: *a car with good pickup.* **5.** The part of a phonograph that changes the variations of the record groove into an electrical signal to be amplified as it is fed to a loudspeaker. **6.** A **pickup truck.**

pickup truck. A small, light truck with an open body and low sides.

pick•y |pĭk′ē| *adj.* **pick•i•er, pick•i•est.** *Informal.* Excessively concerned with details.

pic•nic |pĭk′nĭk| *n.* A meal eaten outdoors. —*v.* **pic•nicked, pic•nick•ing, pic•nics.** To have a pic-

piano¹·²

Piano² *is from Italian* piano, *"soft," which is descended from Latin* plānus, *"smooth."* **Piano¹** *is shortened from* **pianoforte,** *which is from Italian* pianoforte, *"soft-loud":* piano, *"soft,"* + forte, *"loud." The piano, invented in the early eighteenth century, was the first keyboard instrument to have pedals that soften or sustain sound.*

pick¹·²

Pick¹ *is probably from Old French* piquer, *"to prick or pierce."* **Pick²** *was Old English* pic, *"sharp object."*

piebald

Pie is the original name of the **magpie**. **Bald** *used to mean "streaked with white." So* **piebald,** *which is first recorded from the sixteenth century, means "streaked with white like a magpie."*

ă pat/ā pay/â care/ä father/ĕ pet/ ē be/ĭ pit/ī pie/î fierce/ŏ pot/ ō go/ô paw, for/oi oil/ŏŏ book/ ōō boot/ou out/ŭ cut/û fur/ *th* the/th thin/hw which/zh vision/ ə ago, item, pencil, atom, circus

nic. *—**modifier:** a picnic table.* **—pic'nick•er** *n.*

pico–. A word element meaning "a trillionth": **picofarad.**

pi•co•far•ad |pī'kō făr'əd| *n.* A unit of capacitance equal to one trillionth, 10^{-12}, of a farad.

pi•cot |pē'kō| *n.* One of a series of small loops that form a fancy edging, as on ribbon or lace. ¶*These sound alike* **picot, pekoe.**

pic•to•gram |pĭk'tə grăm'| *n.* A diagram that represents numerical data or relationships.

pic•to•graph |pĭk'tə grăf'| *or* |-gräf'| *n.* **1.** A picture that represents a word or idea. **2.** Something, such as a diagram or chart, using such pictures. **—pic•tog'ra•phy** |pĭk tŏg'rə fē| *n.*

pic•to•ri•al |pĭk tôr'ē əl| *or* |-tōr'-| *adj.* **1.** Of pictures: *pictorial materials.* **2.** Represented as if in pictures; descriptive: *pictorial imagery.* **3.** Composed of or illustrated by pictures: *pictorial representations of the planets.* **—pic•to'ri•al•ly** *adv.*

pic•ture |pĭk'chər| *n.* **1.** A painting, drawing, photograph, or similar visual representation or image. **2.** A vivid verbal description; an image in words. **3.** Someone or something that closely resembles another: *He is the picture of his father.* **4.** Someone or something that is a good example of a certain emotion, mood, etc.: *The dog was the picture of eagerness.* **5.** A combination of circumstances; the situation: *How did a doll figure in the picture?* **6.** An image or series of images on a television or movie screen. **7.** A **motion picture.** *—**modifier:** a picture book.* *—v.* **pic•tured, pic•tur•ing. 1.** To make a representation or picture of: *A graph is a good way to picture data.* **2.** To form a mental image of; visualize; imagine: *He pictured huge dogs attacking the intruders.* **3.** To describe vividly; make a verbal image of.

pic•tur•esque |pĭk'chə rĕsk'| *adj.* **1.** Of or suggesting a picture; striking or interesting; unusually or quaintly attractive: *picturesque Alpine villages.* **2.** Strikingly expressive; vivid: *picturesque slang in a sports column.* **—pic'tur•esque'ly** *adv.* **—pic'tur•esque'ness** *n.*

picture tube. The cathode-ray tube of a television receiver, on which the visual portion of a telecast is shown.

pid•dling |pĭd'lĭng| *adj.* Unimportant; trivial.

pidg•in |pĭj'ĭn| *n.* A simple form of speech based on a mixture of two or more languages and used for communication between groups speaking different languages. ¶*These sound alike* **pidgin, pigeon.**

Pidgin English. A pidgin based on English and used as a trade language in the Far East.

pie |pī| *n.* A food consisting of a filling, such as fruit, meat, etc., baked in a pastry shell and often covered with a crust or meringue. *—**modifier:** a pie pan.* ¶*These sound alike* **pie, pi.**

pie•bald |pī'bôld'| *adj.* Marked with spots or patches, especially of black and white: *a piebald horse.* *—n.* A piebald horse. [SEE NOTE]

piece |pēs| *n.* **1.** Something considered as a part of a larger quantity or group; a portion: *a piece of wood; a piece of land.* **2.** A portion or part that has been separated from a whole: *a piece of pie.* **3.** A part of a set: *sixty pieces in a set of china.* **4.** An artistic, musical, or literary work: *play a piece on the piano; say a piece in front of the class.* **5.** An instance; a specimen; an example: *What a fine piece of work!* **6.** A coin: *a gold piece; a 50-cent piece.* **7.** A fully expressed opinion: *She spoke her piece and stomped out of the room.* **8.** In certain board games, one of the small objects used in playing. **9.** In chess, any chessman other than a pawn; a king, queen, bishop, knight, or rook. **10.** A firearm. *—v.* **pieced, piec•ing. 1.** To join or unite the parts of: *pieced the puzzle together.* **2.** To mend by adding a fragment or part to: *She pieced his ragged trousers.* ¶*These sound alike* **piece, peace. —piec'er** *n.*

Idioms. **a piece of (one's) mind.** *Informal.* Vehement, frank criticism or censure, often based on one's own attitude or opinions: *He gave her a piece of his mind.* **go to pieces. 1.** To break into small bits or fragments; fall apart. **2.** *Informal.* To lose self-control; break down. **of a piece.** Of the same kind, type, or group.

pièce de ré•sis•tance |pyĕs' də rā zē stäɴs'|. *French.* **1.** The principal dish of a meal. **2.** An outstanding item, accomplishment, etc.

piece•meal |pēs'mēl'| *adv.* **1.** Piece by piece; gradually: *built up the collection piecemeal.* **2.** In pieces; apart: *The puzzle lay piecemeal on the floor.* *—adj.* Done or made piece by piece; gradually: *a piecemeal accumulation.*

piece of eight. An obsolete Spanish silver coin.

piece•work |pēs'wûrk'| *n.* Work paid for by the number of products produced. **—piece'work'er** *n.*

pied |pīd| *adj.* Having patches of color; piebald: *a pied flower.*

Pied•mont |pēd'mŏnt'|. **1.** A plateau lying east of the Appalachian Mountains, extending from Virginia to Alabama. **2.** A region in northwestern Italy.

Pied Piper. 1. In German folk legend, a piper dressed in pied clothing who rid the town of Hamelin of its rats by piping. Refused payment, he led away the children of the town. **2.** Someone who misleads.

pier |pîr| *n.* **1.** A platform extending from a shore over water, used to secure, protect, and provide access to ships or boats. **2.** A structure that supports a bridge at the points where its various spans join. **3.** Any of various other supporting structures, such as a pillar, a buttress, or the part of a wall between two windows. ¶*These sound alike* **pier, peer.**

pierce |pîrs| *v.* **pierced, pierc•ing. 1. a.** To pass into or through (something) with or as with a sharp instrument: *Arrows pierced his body.* **b.** To penetrate suddenly, as if by stabbing: *A cry pierced the air.* **2.** To make a hole or opening in: *A nail pierced the tire.* **3.** To make a way through: *explorers piercing the wilderness.* **4.** To move the emotions of; affect deeply: *Their friendship pierced her customary gloom.* **5.** To discern or understand: *pierce the mystery.*

Pierce |pîrs|, **Franklin.** 1804–1869. Fourteenth President of the United States (1853–57).

pierc•ing |pîr'sĭng| *adj.* Sharp; penetrating: *piercing cold; piercing eyes.* **—pierc'ing•ly** *adv.*

Pierre |pîr|. The capital of South Dakota. Population, 9,700.

pi•e•ty |pī'ĭ tē| *n., pl.* **pi•e•ties. 1.** Religious devotion and reverence. **2.** Devotion and reverence to one's family, homeland, ideals, etc. **3.** A pious act or thought.

pi•e•zo•e•lec•tric |pī ē'zō ĭ lĕk'trĭk| *adj.* Of or exhibiting piezoelectricity.

pi•e•zo•e•lec•tric•i•ty |pī ē′zō ĭ lĕk′**trĭs**′ĭ tē| *or* |-ē′lĕk-| *n.* A property of certain nonconducting crystals that results in voltages being generated across them when they are subjected to mechanical stress and that causes them to change slightly in shape when voltages are applied across them.

pig |pĭg| *n.* **1.** A hoofed animal with short legs, bristly hair, and a blunt snout used for digging. Pigs are often raised for meat and other products. **2.** A greedy, messy, or dirty person. **3. a.** An oblong block of metal, usually iron or lead, cast from a smelting furnace. **b.** A mold in which such a block is cast. —***modifier:*** *a pig crate.* [SEE PICTURE]

pi•geon |**pĭj**′ĭn| *n.* Any of several birds with short legs, a rounded chest, and a small head, especially a kind common in cities and often raised for food or trained to carry messages. ¶*These sound alike* **pigeon, pidgin.**

pi•geon•hole |**pĭj**′ĭn hōl′| *n.* **1.** A small hole in which pigeons may nest. **2.** A small compartment, as in a desk, for holding letters or other papers. —*v.* **pi•geon•holed, pi•geon•hol•ing. 1.** To place in or as if in a small compartment. **2.** To classify into a group; categorize: *a tendency to pigeonhole his colleagues.*

pi•geon-toed |**pĭj**′ĭn tōd′| *adj.* Having the feet turned inward so that the toes tend to meet.

pig•gish |**pĭg**′ĭsh| *adj.* Greedy or dirty. —**pig′gish•ly** *adv.* —**pig′gish•ness** *n.*

pig•gy•back |**pĭg**′ē băk′| *adv.* **1.** On the shoulders or back of another: *ride piggyback.* **2.** In or by means of truck trailers carried on railroad cars: *goods shipped piggyback.* —***modifier:*** *a piggyback system of transportation.*

piggy bank. A child's bank for saving coins, made in the shape of a pig.

pig•head•ed |**pĭg**′hĕd′ĭd| *adj.* Stupidly obstinate or stubborn. —**pig′head′ed•ly** *adv.* —**pig′head′ed•ness** *n.*

pig iron. Impure iron as it is drawn from a blast furnace, usually cast in oblong blocks.

pig•let |**pĭg**′lĭt| *n.* A young, small pig.

pig•ment |**pĭg**′mənt| *n.* **1.** A substance or material used to give color to something: *the pigments used in a paint.* **2.** A substance, such as chlorophyll or hemoglobin, that gives a characteristic color to plant or animal tissues.

pig•men•ta•tion |pĭg′mən **tā**′shən| *n.* Coloring of animal or plant tissues by pigments.

pig•my |**pĭg**′mē| *adj. & n., pl.* **pig•mies.** A form of the word **pygmy.**

pig•nut |**pĭg**′nŭt′| *n.* **1.** An edible, nutlike plant tuber, seed pod, etc., that grows underground. **2.** The hard, bitter nut of a tree related to the hickories.

pig•pen |**pĭg**′pĕn′| *n.* **1.** A fenced area where pigs are kept. **2.** A dirty or untidy place.

pig•skin |**pĭg**′skĭn′| *n.* **1.** The skin of a pig. **2.** Leather made from this. **3.** *Informal.* A football. —***modifier:*** *pigskin gloves.*

pig•sty |**pĭg**′stī′| *n., pl.* **-sties. 1.** A place where pigs are kept. **2.** A dirty or untidy place.

pig•tail |**pĭg**′tāl′| *n.* A braid of hair at the back of the head.

pi•ka |**pī**′kə| *n.* A small, rabbitlike animal of the mountains of western North America and Asia, having rounded ears and no visible tail. ¶*These sound alike* **pika, pica.** [SEE PICTURE]

pike¹ |pīk| *n., pl.* **pike** or **pikes.** A large freshwater fish with a narrow body and a long snout, often caught for sport.

pike² |pīk| *n.* A long spear formerly used by infantry.

pike³ |pīk| *n.* A turnpike.

pike⁴ |pīk| *n.* A spike or sharp point.

Pikes Peak |pīks|. A peak of the Rocky Mountains, in central Colorado.

pike•staff |**pīk**′stăf′| *or* |-stäf′| *n., pl.* **-staves** |-stāvz′|. **1.** The long handle of a pike. **2.** A walking stick with a sharp metal point.

pi•laf, also **pi•laff** |pĭ **läf**′| *or* |pē-| *n.* A spiced dish of steamed rice, often with meat or vegetables.

pi•las•ter |pĭ **lăs**′tər| *n.* A vertical column projecting slightly from a wall.

Pi•late |**pī**′lĭt|, **Pontius.** Roman governor of Judea (A.D. 26?–36?); assumed to have authorized the execution of Christ.

pil•chard |**pĭl**′chərd| *n.* A small ocean fish related to the herrings.

pile¹ |pīl| *n.* **1.** A mass of things heaped or stacked together; a heap: *a pile of sawdust; a pile of firewood.* **2.** *Informal.* A large amount or quantity: *piles of places to visit.* **3.** *Slang.* A large sum of money; a fortune: *He made his pile and retired to Florida.* **4.** A **nuclear reactor.** —*v.* **piled, pil•ing. 1.** To place or stack in or as if in a heap: *They piled the dishes in the sink.* **2.** To place or heap in abundance: *piled honors on him.* **3.** To load or fill with or as if with a pile: *piled a tray with apples.* **4.** To move, often in haste, in a disorderly group or mass: *Baseball fans piled out of the stadium.* **5.** To form or accumulate into or as if into a mass or heap: *During the windstorm sand piled high against the fence.* [SEE NOTE]

pile² |pīl| *n.* A heavy beam of timber, concrete, or steel, driven into the ground as a foundation or support for a structure. [SEE NOTE]

pile³ |pīl| *n.* **1.** Cut or uncut loops of yarn forming the surface of certain carpets or of fabrics such as velvet and plush. **2.** Soft, fine hair, fur, or wool. [SEE NOTE]

piles |pīlz| *pl.n.* Hemorrhoids. [SEE NOTE]

pil•fer |**pĭl**′fər| *v.* To steal (small sums of money or things of little value): *He pilfered some blackberry jam, three biscuits, and a jug of cider. He pilfered from his aunt's pantry.* —**pil′fer•er** *n.*

pil•grim |**pĭl**′grĭm| *n.* **1.** Someone who travels to a religious shrine or sacred place. **2.** Someone who makes a long, sacred or otherwise important journey. **3. Pilgrim.** One of the English Puritans who founded Plymouth Colony in New England in 1620.

pil•grim•age |**pĭl**′grə mĭj| *n.* **1.** A journey to a sacred place. **2.** A long journey with a meaningful purpose.

pil•ing |**pī**′lĭng| *n.* A structure composed of a number of piles driven into the earth.

pill |pĭl| *n.* **1.** A small lump or tablet of medicine, often coated, to be taken by mouth. **2.** *Slang.* Something distasteful or unpleasant that must be accepted: *swallow the bitter pill of failure.* **3.** *Slang.* A boring or disagreeable person.

pil•lage |**pĭl**′ĭj| *v.* **pil•laged, pil•lag•ing.** To rob of goods by force; plunder: *Barbarian hordes pillaged the countryside. The pirates pillaged along*

pig

pika

pile¹⁻²⁻³/piles

Pile¹ *is from Old French* pile, *"heap of stone"; it is related to* **pillar. Pile²** *was Old English* pīl, *"pointed stake of wood," from Latin* pīlum, *"heavy javelin."* **Pile³** *is from Latin* pilus, *"hair."* **Piles** *is from Latin* pila, *"ball."*

the coast. —*n.* The act of pillaging: *the pillage of the city.* —**pil′lag•er** *n.*

pil•lar |pĭl′ər| *n.* **1. a.** A vertical structure, often cylindrical in shape, used as a support or decoration for a building; a column. **b.** Such a structure standing alone and serving as a monument. **2.** Something that resembles a pillar in size or shape: *a pillar of flame from the volcano.* **3.** Someone or something occupying a central position; a mainstay: *a pillar of the community.* —*v.* To support or brace with pillars.

***Idiom.* from pillar to post.** From one place or situation to another.

pill•box |pĭl′bŏks′| *n.* **1.** A small box for pills. **2.** A small emplacement of reinforced concrete for a machine gun or other weapon. **3.** A woman's small, round hat.

pillory

pil•lo•ry |pĭl′ə rē| *n., pl.* **pil•lo•ries.** A wooden framework on a post, with holes for the head and hands. Formerly, offenders were locked in this framework and subjected to public scorn as punishment. —*v.* **pil•lo•ried, pil•lo•ry•ing, pil•lo•ries. 1.** To put in a pillory as punishment. **2.** To expose to ridicule and scorn: *He pilloried his former friends in novels.* [SEE PICTURE]

pil•low |pĭl′ō| *n.* Something used as a support for the head while relaxing or sleeping, especially a cloth case stuffed with soft material, such as down, feathers, or foam rubber. —*v.* **1.** To rest (one's head) on or as if on a pillow: *She pillowed her head on her arms.* **2.** To serve as a pillow for: *The mother's lap pillowed the child's head.*

pil•low•case |pĭl′ō kās′| *n.* A cloth cover with an open end, shaped to fit over a pillow.

pillow slip. A pillowcase.

pi•lot |pī′lət| *n.* **1.** Someone who operates an aircraft or spacecraft. **2.** A licensed specialist who steers large ships in and out of port or through dangerous waters. **3.** A ship's helmsman. **4.** Someone who guides others as a leader. **5.** A small-scale experimental model. **6.** A **pilot light.** —*adj.* Serving as a small-scale model for future work: *a pilot project.* —*v.* **pi•lot•ed, pi•lot•ing. 1.** To operate and set the course of (a plane, ship, or vehicle). **2.** To direct or lead, as through difficulties.

pilot fish. A small ocean fish that often swims along with sharks.

pi•lot•house |pī′lət hous′| *n., pl.* **-hous•es** |-hou′zĭz|. An enclosed section on a bridge of a vessel from which the vessel is steered.

pilot light. 1. A small jet of gas kept burning to ignite a gas burner, as in a stove or water heater. **2.** A small lamp, usually red, to show that an appliance, machine, etc., is turned on.

Pi•ma |pē′mə| *n., pl.* **Pi•ma** or **Pi•mas. 1.** A North American Indian tribe of southern Arizona and northern Mexico. **2.** A member of this tribe. **3.** The Uto-Aztecan language of this tribe.

pi•men•to |pĭ mĕn′tō| *n., pl.* **pi•men•tos.** A mild-flavored red pepper; a pimiento.

pi•mien•to |pĭ mĕn′tō| *n., pl.* **pi•mien•tos.** A mild-flavored red pepper, often used as flavoring, for stuffing olives, or as a colorful garnish.

pim•per•nel |pĭm′pər nĕl′| *n.* A low-growing plant with small red, pink, or purplish flowers that close in cloudy weather.

pim•ple |pĭm′pəl| *n.* A small swelling on the skin, sometimes containing pus.

pim•ply |pĭm′plē| *adj.* **pim•pli•er, pim•pli•est.** Full of or covered with pimples.

pin |pĭn| *n.* **1.** A short, straight, stiff piece of wire with a round head and a sharp point, used to fasten one thing to another. **2.** Anything like a pin in shape or use, as a hairpin, clothespin, or safety pin. **3.** An ornament or badge fastened to the clothing with a pin, clasp, or catch. **4.** A bar or rod, made of wood or metal, that supports or fastens things, especially by passing through or into a series of prepared holes. **5.** On a golf course, a long metal or wooden rod with a small flag at one end, inserted into a cup to indicate its location. **6.** One of the wooden clubs at which the ball is aimed in bowling. —*v.* **pinned, pin•ning. 1.** To fasten or secure with a pin or pins: *pinned the flower to her coat.* **2.** To make completely dependent on someone or something: *We pinned our hopes on him.* **3.** To win a fall from in wrestling: *Joe's teammates wanted him to pin the champ.* **4.** To cause to be unable to move; hold fast; immobilize: *The tree fell and pinned him against the ground.* **5.** To regard or designate as the cause of (a wrongdoing or crime): *They tried to pin the theft on him.* —***phrasal verb.* pin down. 1. a.** To fix or establish clearly: *pin down the age of a fossil.* **b.** To decide or determine the meaning, significance, or cause of: *pin down a lie.* **2.** To cause (someone) to make a response or commitment: *We cannot pin him down on that issue.*

***Idiom.* on pins and needles.** In a state of suspense or anxiety.

pin•a•fore |pĭn′ə fôr′| *or* |-fōr′| *n.* A sleeveless garment like an apron, especially one worn over a little girl's dress.

pi•ña•ta |pĭn yä′tə| *n.* A colorfully decorated container filled with sweetmeats and toys and suspended from the ceiling. As part of the traditional Christmas celebration in certain Latin American countries, a blindfolded child tries to break the piñata with a stick.

pin•cers |pĭn′sərz| *n.* *(used with a plural verb).* **1.** A tool having a pair of jaws and handles pivoted together, used in gripping things, pulling nails, etc. **2.** A jointed, clawlike grasping part, as of a lobster or crab.

pinch |pĭnch| *v.* **1.** To squeeze between the thumb and a finger, pincers, or other edges. **2.** To squeeze or compress so as to cause pain or discomfort: *The shoes pinched her feet.* **3.** To make drawn, shriveled, or withered: *a face pinched by fear and fatigue.* **4.** To be thrifty or frugal; economize: *We had to pinch and scrape to pay the bills.* **5.** *Slang.* To steal: *He pinched some doughnuts from the tray.* **6.** *Slang.* To arrest. —*n.* **1.** A squeeze or other pressure caused by pressing between the thumb and a finger, pincers, or other edges: *The crab gave him a pinch on the toe.* **2.** The amount that can be held between the thumb and forefinger: *a pinch of salt.* **3.** Pressure; stress; strain: *the pinch of wartime.* **4.** A time of trouble or difficulty; an emergency: *In a pinch Johnny can take over the work.* **5.** *Slang.* A theft. **6.** *Slang.* An arrest. —**pinch′er** *n.*

***Idiom.* pinch pennies.** To be thrifty or frugal.

pinch-hit |pĭnch′hĭt′| *v.* **-hit, -hit•ting. 1.** In baseball, to bat as a substitute. **2.** *Informal.* To substitute for another: *I'm pinch-hitting for the mechanic today.* —**pinch hit.** —**pinch hitter.**

pin•cush•ion |pĭn'ko͝osh'ən| *n.* A small, firm cushion in which pins and needles are stuck when not in use.

pine[1] |pīn| *n.* **1.** Any of several evergreen trees that bear cones and have clusters of needle-shaped leaves. **2.** The wood of such a tree. *—**modifier:** pine cones.* [SEE NOTE]

pine[2] |pīn| *v.* **pined, pin•ing.** To lose health or waste away from longing or grief. [SEE NOTE]

pin•e•al body |pĭn'ē əl|. A small mass of poorly developed glandular tissue found in the brain. Its function is not known.

pine•ap•ple |pīn'ăp'əl| *n.* **1.** A large, fleshy tropical fruit with a rough, spiny skin and a tuft of narrow, prickly leaves at the top. **2.** A plant that bears such fruit. *—**modifier:** pineapple juice.*

pine•y |pī'nē| *adj.* A form of the word **piny.**

pin•feath•er |pĭn'fĕth'ər| *n.* A feather still enclosed in a narrow horny covering and just beginning to grow out from the skin.

Ping-Pong |pĭng'pông'| *or* |-pŏng'| *n.* A trademark for table-tennis equipment. Often applied to the game of table tennis.

pin•hole |pĭn'hōl'| *n.* A tiny hole, such as one made by a pin.

pin•ion[1] |pĭn'yən| *n.* A bird's wing. *—v.* **1. a.** To clip or tie (the wings) of a bird to prevent it from flying. **b.** To prevent (a bird) from flying by doing this. **2.** To hold or fasten (a person's arms, legs, etc.) to prevent movement. ¶*These sound alike* **pinion, piñon.** [SEE NOTE]

pin•ion[2] |pĭn'yən| *n.* A small gearwheel that engages a larger gearwheel or a rack. ¶*These sound alike* **pinion, piñon.** [SEE NOTE]

pink[1] |pĭngk| *n.* **1.** A light or pale red. **2.** Any of several plants related to the carnation, grown for their fragrant flowers. **3.** The highest degree; the best: *the pink of perfection.* *—adj.* **pink•er, pink•est.** Light or pale red. [SEE NOTE]

pink[2] |pĭngk| *v.* **1.** To cut the edge of (cloth) into notches or scallops for decoration or to prevent raveling. **2.** To decorate with a pattern of small holes. **3.** To stab lightly or prick with a pointed weapon. [SEE NOTE]

pink•eye |pĭngk'ī'| *n.* Also **pink eye.** A severe, highly contagious inflammation of the mucous membrane of the eyelids and eyeballs that makes the eyes appear pink.

pink•ie |pĭng'kē| *n.* The fifth, or little, finger.

pink•ish |pĭng'kĭsh| *adj.* Somewhat pink.

pin money. Money for small expenses.

pin•na•cle |pĭn'ə kəl| *n.* **1.** A tall, pointed formation, as a mountain peak. **2.** The peak or summit of anything: *at the pinnacle of his fame.* **3.** A small turret or spire on a roof.

pin•nate |pĭn'āt'| *adj.* Having parts or divisions, such as leaflets, in a close arrangement along each side of a stalk. *—**pin'nate'ly** adv.*

pi•noch•le |pē'nŭk'əl| *or* |-nŏk'-| *n.* A card game played with a deck of 48 cards having no card below a nine.

pi•ñon |pĭn'yən| *or* |-yōn'| *n.* A pine tree of western North and South America, bearing edible seeds. ¶*These sound alike* **piñon, pinion.**

pin•point |pĭn'point'| *n.* **1.** The point of a pin. **2.** Something extremely small: *bright pinpoints of flame.* *—v.* To locate and identify precisely: *an attempt to pinpoint the targets; pinpoint the reason for the change.* *—adj.* **1.** Showing care and precision: *pinpoint accuracy.* **2.** Very small; minute: *the pinpoint organisms in the sea.*

pin•scher |pĭn'shər| *n.* See **Doberman pinscher.**

pin•stripe |pĭn'strīp'| *n.* **1.** A thin, narrow stripe on a fabric. **2.** A fabric with thin stripes. *—**modifier:** a pinstripe suit.*

pint |pīnt| *n.* **1.** A unit of volume or capacity used in liquid measure, equal to 16 fluid ounces or 28.875 cubic inches. **2.** A unit of volume or capacity used in dry measure, equal to ½ quart or 33.6 cubic inches. *—**modifier:** a pint bottle.*

pin•to |pĭn'tō| *n., pl.* **pin•tos.** A horse with irregular spots or markings. *—adj.* Having irregular spots or markings: *a pinto horse.*

pin-up |pĭn'ŭp'| *n.* A picture to be pinned on a wall, especially a picture of a pretty girl.

pin•wheel |pĭn'hwēl'| *or* |-wēl'| *n.* **1.** A toy consisting of blades of colored paper or plastic pinned to the end of a stick so as to revolve in the wind. **2.** A firework that forms a rotating wheel of colored flames.

pin•worm |pĭn'wûrm'| *n.* A small parasitic worm that infests the lower part of the intestine and the rectum in human beings.

pin•y |pī'nē| *adj.* **pin•i•er, pin•i•est. 1.** Covered with or consisting of pines: *piny woods.* **2.** Of or like pines, especially in odor: *a fresh, piny smell.*

pin•yon |pĭn'yən| *or* |-yōn'| *n.* A form of the word **piñon.**

pi•o•neer |pī'ə nîr'| *n.* **1.** A person who first enters or settles a region, opening it up for others. **2.** A person who leads the way in a field of science, research, etc. **3.** A plant or animal that is the first kind to grow or live in an environment where there have been no living things. *—**modifier:** the hardships of pioneer life; a pioneer plant.* *—v.* **1. a.** To explore or open up (a region): *His great-grandfather pioneered those mountains.* **b.** To settle: *His family pioneered North Dakota. They pioneered in a river valley.* **2.** To take part in the development of: *pioneered a manned spacecraft to the moon.* **3.** To lead the way in a certain field: *He pioneered in the use of antiseptics in surgery.* *—**pi'o•neer'ing** adj.: a pioneering thinker; a pioneering invention.*

pi•ous |pī'əs| *adj.* **1.** Reverently and earnestly religious; devout: *a simple, pious people.* **2.** Marked by noticeable devoutness: *a pious silence.* **3.** Falsely and ostentatiously devout: *a pious speech to impress the ladies.* *—**pi'ous•ly** adv.*

pip[1] |pĭp| *n.* A small fruit seed, as of an orange or an apple. [SEE NOTE]

pip[2] |pĭp| *n.* A disease of birds. [SEE NOTE]

pip[3] |pĭp| *v.* **pipped, pip•ping.** To break through (an eggshell) in hatching. [SEE NOTE]

pip[4] |pĭp| *n.* **1.** Any of the dots on dice or dominoes. **2.** A reflected signal, as shown on a radar screen; a blip. [SEE NOTE]

pipe |pīp| *n.* **1. a.** A tube or hollow cylinder through which a liquid or gas can be made to flow. **b.** A section of such a tube. **2. a.** An object used for smoking, consisting of a hollow tube with a mouthpiece at one end and a small bowl at the other. **b.** The amount of tobacco needed to fill the bowl of such a pipe: *He smoked a pipe of tobacco.* **3.** A tubelike part or organ of the body. **4. a.** A tubular musical instrument, especially a simple or primitive one, similar to a flute, clarinet, or oboe. **b.** Any of the tubes used

pine[1-2]

Pine[1] *was* pīn *in Old English, and was borrowed from Latin* pīnus, *"pine tree."* **Pine**[2] *was Old English* pīnian; *it originally meant "to torment," hence later "to be tormented, to suffer"; it was borrowed from Latin* poena, *"punishment, torture."*

pinion[1-2]

Pinion[1] *is from Old French* pignon, *ultimately from Latin* pinna *or* penna, *"feather, wing" (which is also the source of* **pen**[1]*).* **Pinion**[2] *is from Old French* peignon, *from* peigne, *"comb."*

pink[1-2]

The origin of **pink**[1] *is mysterious; it is first recorded in sense* **2** *and shortly afterward in sense* **3** *("I am the very pink of courtesy"—Shakespeare). The word was not used for the color (sense* **1***) until the eighteenth century.* **Pink**[2] *is probably from Low German* pinken, *"to peck."*

pip[1-2-3-4]

Pip[1] *is a shortening of* **pippin,** *which originally meant "seed."* **Pip**[2] *is from Middle Dutch* pippe, *"mucus."* **Pip**[3] *is a variant of* **peep**[1]. **Pip**[4] *is of obscure origin.*

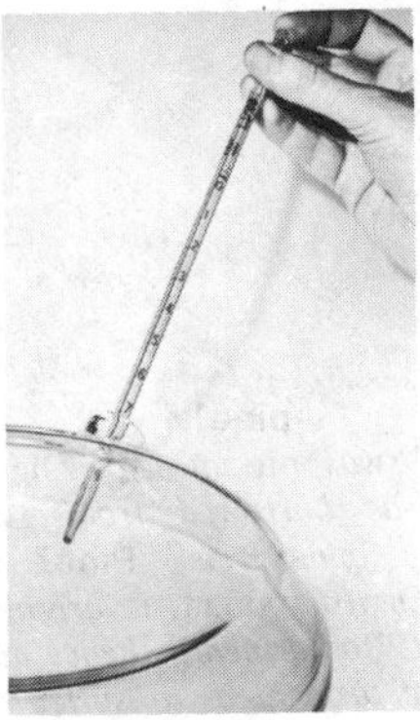

pipette

pistil

pit¹⁻²

Pit¹ *was Old English* pytt, *which was borrowed from Latin* puteus, *"a well."* **Pit²** *is from Middle Dutch* pitte; *it is related to* **pith.**

pitch¹⁻²

Pitch¹ *was Old English* pic, *which was borrowed from Latin* pix, pic-, *"pitch."* **Pitch²** *was* picchen *in Middle English and originally meant "to fix or set."*

ă pat/ā pay/â care/ä father/ĕ pet/ ē be/ĭ pit/ī pie/î fierce/ŏ pot/ ō go/ô paw, for/oi oil/o͝o book/ o͞o boot/ou out/ŭ cut/û fur/ *th* the/th thin/hw which/zh vision/ ə ago, item, pencil, atom, circus

in an organ to produce musical tones. **c. pipes.** A small wind instrument consisting of a number of tuned tubes bound together. —*modifier: a pipe rack; pipe tobacco.* —*v.* **piped, pip•ing. 1.** To transport or transmit by means of a pipe or pipes. **2.** To play (music) on a pipe or pipes: *Piper piped a song about a lamb. So he piped with merry cheer.* **3.** To speak or sing in a shrill tone: *The child piped a question.* —*phrasal verb.* **pipe up.** To begin speaking in a small, shrill voice: *"Maybe I can help," the child piped up timidly.* [SEE NOTE on p. 344]

Idiom. **pipe down.** *Slang.* To stop talking; be quiet.

pipe•line |pīp′līn′| *n.* **1.** A channel or pipe used to carry water, petroleum, natural gas, etc., over great distances. **2.** A line of communication or route of supply. —*v.* **-lined, -lin•ing.** To transport by means of a pipeline.

pipe organ. The organ, a musical instrument.

pip•er |pī′pər| *n.* Someone who plays music on a bagpipe or another type of pipe.

pi•pette |pī pĕt′| *n.* Any of a number of variously shaped glass tubes, open at both ends and often graduated, used for transferring liquids in a laboratory. [SEE PICTURE]

pip•ing |pī′pĭng| *n.* **1.** A system of pipes, such as one used to carry water. **2.** The act of playing music on a pipe. **3.** A shrill, high-pitched sound, such as that of music played on a pipe. **4.** A narrow band or fold of material, used as a trimming on edges or seams. —*adj.* Thin, clear, high-pitched, and shrill: *the high, piping notes of the flute.* —*adv.* Extremely: *piping hot biscuits.*

pip•it |pĭp′ĭt| *n.* Any of several small songbirds with brownish feathers.

pip•pin |pĭp′ĭn| *n.* Any of several varieties of apple, used mainly in cooking.

pip•squeak |pĭp′skwēk′| *n.* A small or unimportant person.

pi•quant |pē′kənt| *or* |-känt′| *adj.* **1.** Pleasantly pungent; sharp and spicy: *a piquant odor.* **2.** Pleasantly disturbing, provocative, or stimulating: *piquant prose.* —**pi′quan•cy, pi′quant•ness** *n.* —**pi′quant•ly** *adv.*

pique |pēk| *n.* A resentful feeling or vexation caused by wounded pride or feelings. —*v.* **piqued, piqu•ing. 1.** To cause to feel resentment or vexation: *Her arrogant manner piqued her neighbors.* **2.** To stimulate; arouse; stir: *The unusual objects piqued his curiosity.* ¶*These sound alike* **pique, peak, peek.**

pi•qué |pĭ kā′| *or* |pē-| *n.* A firm cloth, usually cotton, woven with lengthwise ribs or with a diamond, honeycomb, or waffle pattern. —*modifier: a piqué dress.*

pi•ra•cy |pī′rə sē| *n., pl.* **pi•ra•cies. 1.** Armed robbery on the high seas or using the sea as a basis of operations. **2.** Unauthorized use of another's invention or creation.

pi•ra•nha |pĭ rän′yə| *n.* A tropical American freshwater fish with very sharp teeth. Although piranhas are comparatively small in size, they school together and attack and often destroy human beings and large animals.

pi•rate |pī′rĭt| *n.* A person who robs ships at sea or plunders the land from the sea. —*modifier: a pirate ship; the pirate treasure.* —*v.* **pi•rat•ed, pi•rat•ing. 1.** To attack and rob at sea. **2.** To publish or reproduce (another's invention or creation) without permission.

pi•rat•i•cal |pī răt′ĭ kəl| *adj.* Of or like piracy or pirates. —**pi•rat′i•cal•ly** *adv.*

pi•rogue |pĭ rōg′| *n.* A canoe made from a hollowed tree trunk.

pir•ou•ette |pîr′o͞o ĕt′| *n.* In dancing, a full turn of the body on the tip of the toe or the ball of the foot. —*v.* **pir•ou•et•ted, pir•ou•et•ting.** To perform a pirouette.

Pi•sces |pī′sēz|. The 12th sign of the zodiac.

pis•ta•chi•o |pĭ stăsh′ē ō′| *n., pl.* **pis•ta•chi•os. 1.** A tree of the Mediterranean region and western Asia, bearing small, hard-shelled nuts with a sweet green kernel. **2.** Also **pistachio nut.** The nut of such a tree. **3.** Often **pistachio green.** A light yellowish green. —*modifier: pistachio ice cream.* —*adj.* A light yellowish green.

pis•til |pĭs′təl| *n.* The female reproductive organ of a flower, containing parts that receive pollen and in which the seeds develop. ¶*These sound alike* **pistil, pistol.** [SEE PICTURE]

pis•tol |pĭs′təl| *n.* A small gun designed to be held and fired with one hand. —*modifier: pistol shots.* ¶*These sound alike* **pistol, pistil.**

pis•ton |pĭs′tən| *n.* **1.** A cylinder or disk that fits snugly into a hollow cylinder and moves back and forth under the pressure of a fluid, as in many engines, or moves or compresses a fluid, as in a pump or compressor. **2.** A valve mechanism in brass instruments, used for changing pitch.

pit¹ |pĭt| *n.* **1.** A relatively deep hole in the ground, either natural or man-made. **2.** A relatively shallow man-made hole: *a barbecue pit.* **3. a.** A natural depression in the surface of a body, organ, or part: *the pit of the stomach.* **b.** A small depression in the skin left by a disease or injury; a pockmark. **4.** An abyss, especially the abyss in which hell is said to be located. **5.** The area directly in front of the stage of a theater, in which the musicians sit. **6.** A sunken area in a garage where mechanics can work underneath automobiles. **7.** An enclosed space in which animals are kept or are set to fight: *a snake pit.* —*v.* **pit•ted, pit•ting. 1.** To make holes, craters, or depressions in: *The moon may have been pitted by meteoroid impacts.* **2.** To mark with small scars: *Smallpox pitted his face during childhood.* **3.** To set in competition; match: *a tournament that pits one school against another.* [SEE NOTE]

pit² |pĭt| *n.* The single, hard-shelled seed of certain fruits, such as a peach or cherry; stone. —*v.* **pit•ted, pit•ting.** To remove the pits from. [SEE NOTE]

pi•ta |pē′tə| *n.* Round, flat bread that is hollow inside and forms a pocket when cut.

pitch¹ |pĭch| *n.* **1.** Any of various sticky, dark, thick substances obtained from coal tar, wood tar, or petroleum and used for roofing, waterproofing, and paving. **2.** Any of various natural bitumens, such as asphalt, having similar uses. **3.** A resin derived from sap of a pine tree or a similar tree that bears cones. —*v.* To cover with pitch. [SEE NOTE]

pitch² |pĭch| *v.* **1.** To throw in a specific direction: *pitching horseshoes.* **2.** In baseball: **a.** To throw the ball from the mound to the batter: *The fans held their breath as he wound up to pitch.* **b.** To play (a game or part of it) in the position of pitcher: *pitched the final game of the Series.* **3.** To put up or establish: *pitch a tent; pitch camp.* **4.** To fall forward; plunge: *He pitched headlong from the cliff to his doom.* **5.** To plunge forward and backward alternately: *Heavy storms made the ship pitch and toss.* **6.** To set at or as if at a given level, musical key, etc.: *He pitched his voice so it would cut through the noise. He pitched his hopes too high.* —**phrasal verb. pitch in. 1.** To set to work vigorously, especially in cooperation with others: *The neighbors pitched in to help him build his cabin.* **2.** *Informal.* To donate money to a common fund: *They all pitched in to buy a wedding gift.* —*n.* **1.** An act or an example of pitching: *My pitch missed the wastebasket by a mile. The pitch of the boat turned the passengers green.* **2.** In baseball: **a.** A throw of the ball by a pitcher to a batter: *On the next pitch, the batter struck out.* **b.** A ball so thrown: *Babe knocked the next pitch out of the park.* **c.** A manner of so throwing: *the screwball and other fancy pitches.* **3.** A degree or level of intensity: *The dispute reached a feverish pitch.* **4.** A steep slant, as that of some roofs. **5. a.** The quality of a musical tone or other complex sound by which someone can judge it to be high or low, determined mostly by the frequency of the sound. **b.** The relative position of a tone in a scale, as determined by this property. **c.** Any of several standards that establish the frequency of each musical tone: *Pitch is higher now than in the time of Mozart.* **6.** The distance between corresponding points on adjoining screw threads or gear teeth. **7.** The distance a propeller would travel in one complete revolution through an ideal medium. **8.** *Slang.* A line of talk designed to persuade: *a salesman's pitch.* [SEE NOTE on p. 670]

pitch-black |**pĭch'blăk'**| *adj.* Extremely black.

pitch•blende |**pĭch'**blĕnd'| *n.* A brownish-black, often crusty mineral that is the principal ore of uranium.

pitch-dark |**pĭch'därk'**| *adj.* Very dark.

pitch•er[1] |**pĭch'**ər| *n.* The baseball player who pitches the ball to the batter. [SEE NOTE]

pitch•er[2] |**pĭch'**ər| *n.* **1.** A container used to hold and pour out liquids, having a handle on one side and a lip or spout on the other. **2. a.** A pitcher with something in it: *a pitcher of milk.* **b.** The amount that a pitcher holds. [SEE NOTE & PICTURE]

pitcher plant. Any of several plants with pitcher-shaped leaves containing a liquid in which insects are trapped. [SEE PICTURE]

pitch•fork |**pĭch'**fôrk'| *n.* A large fork with sharp, widely spaced prongs, used to pitch hay.

pitch pipe. A small pipe that, when sounded, gives the standard pitch for a piece of music or for tuning an instrument.

pit•e•ous |**pĭt'**ē əs| *adj.* Arousing pity: *the piteous mewing of a lost kitten.* —**pit'e•ous•ly** *adv.*

pit•fall |**pĭt'**fôl'| *n.* **1.** A concealed pit used for trapping animals. **2.** A hidden danger or unexpected difficulty: *Life is full of pitfalls.*

pith |pĭth| *n.* **1.** The soft, spongelike substance in the center of the stems of many plants. **2.** The central or essential part; the essence; gist: *the pith of his lengthy discussion.*

pith•e•can•thro•pus |pĭth'ĭ **kăn'**thrə pəs| *or* |-kăn **thrō'**-| *n.* An extinct early race of man.

pith helmet. A light, hard sun hat made of dried pith.

pith•y |**pĭth'**ē| *adj.* **pith•i•er, pith•i•est. 1.** Full of or resembling pith: *the pithy stem of a plant.* **2.** Terse and meaningful: *a pithy sentence.* —**pith'i•ly** *adv.* —**pith'i•ness** *n.*

pit•i•a•ble |**pĭt'**ē ə bəl| *adj.* Arousing pity: *The child was a pitiable figure.* —**pit'i•a•bly** *adv.*

pit•i•ful |**pĭt'**ĭ fəl| *adj.* **1.** Arousing pity: *The puppy, cold and hungry, was a pitiful sight.* **2.** Paltry or contemptible: *a pitiful excuse.* —**pit'i•ful•ly** *adv.* —**pit'i•ful•ness** *n.*

pit•i•less |**pĭt'**ĭ lĭs| *adj.* **1.** Without pity; merciless: *a pitiless massacre.* **2.** Relentless, as if without pity: *pitiless Arctic winds.* —**pit'i•less•ly** *adv.* —**pit'i•less•ness** *n.*

pit•tance |**pĭt'**ns| *n.* **1.** A small allowance of money: *The widow lived on a mere pittance.* **2.** A small amount: *a pittance of bread.*

pit•ted |**pĭt'**ĭd| *adj.* **1.** Containing pits; having pits in the surface: *the pitted surface of the moon.* **2.** Pockmarked: *the pitted and tattooed face of a savage warrior.*

pit•ter-pat•ter |**pĭt'**ər **păt'**ər| *n.* A rapid, light, tapping sound: *the pitter-patter of little feet.*

Pitts•burgh |**pĭts'**bûrg'|. An industrial city in western Pennsylvania. Population, 513,000.

pi•tu•i•tar•y |pĭ **tōō'**ĭ tĕr'ē| *or* |-**tyōō'**-| *n.* **1.** The **pituitary gland. 2.** Any of various extracts derived from the pituitary glands of domestic animals and used in medicine. —*adj.* Of the pituitary gland.

pituitary gland. A small, oval endocrine gland attached to the base of the brain in vertebrates. Its secretions control the other endocrine glands and influence growth and metabolism.

pit viper. A poisonous snake, such as a rattlesnake or copperhead, having a small pit, or indentation, on each side of the head.

pit•y |**pĭt'**ē| *n., pl.* **pit•ies. 1.** A feeling of sorrow for another's suffering. **2.** A cause for sorrow or regret: *It's a pity that she cut her hair.* —*v.* **pit•ied, pit•y•ing.** To feel sorry for.

Idiom. **have** (or **take**) **pity on.** To show pity for (another) by helping or forgiving.

piv•ot |**pĭv'**ət| *n.* **1.** A short rod or shaft about which a related part rotates or swings. **2.** A wheeling movement made as if on a pivot: *a quick pivot placed him under the basket, ready for a shot.* —*v.* **1.** To swing or turn on or as if on a pivot: *The needle pivots on a jeweled bearing.* **2.** To depend on: *The whole project pivots on his ability as a fund raiser.*

piv•ot•al |**pĭv'**ə təl| *adj.* **1.** Of or used as a pivot. **2.** Of central importance: *pivotal decisions.*

pix•ie |**pĭk'**sē| *n.* A form of the word **pixy.**

pix•y |**pĭk'**sē| *n., pl.* **pix•ies. 1.** In Celtic folklore, an elfin creature. **2.** A mischievous, playful young girl.

Pi•zar•ro |pĭ **zär'**ō|, **Francisco.** 1470?–1541. Spanish conqueror of Peru.

piz•za |**pēt'**sə| *n.* A baked dish, Italian in origin, consisting of a shallow, pielike crust covered with various spiced mixtures, as of tomatoes, cheese, sausage, etc.

piz•zi•ca•to |pĭt'sĭ **kä'**tō|. In music: *adj.* Played by plucking rather than bowing the strings of an instrument. —*adv.* By plucking rather than bowing the strings of an instrument.

pitcher[1-2]

Pitcher[1], *obviously, is from* **pitch**[2]. **Pitcher**[2] *is from Old French* pichier *or* bichier; *it is related to* **beaker.**

pitcher[2]
Early eighteenth-century American

pitcher plant

plague
The word **plague** *was formerly much used in imprecations like* Plague take it! *or* A plague on you! *The most famous example of this is in Shakespeare's* Romeo and Juliet*; Mercutio, fatally wounded in a fight caused by hatred between the houses (or families) of Capulet and Montagu, says, "A plague on both your houses!"*

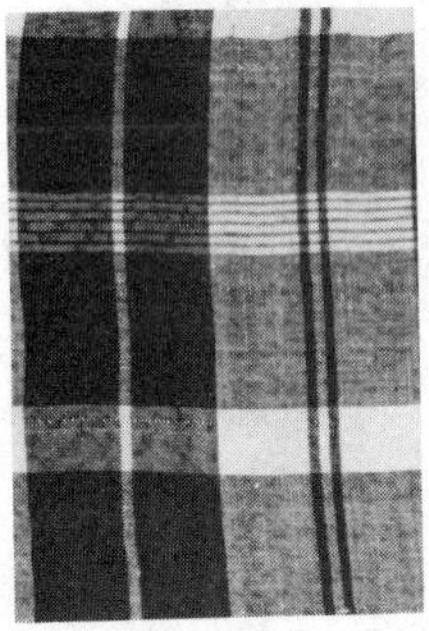

plaid
In Scotland, the cloth and pattern defined in senses **1** *and* **2** *are never called* **plaid,** *but only* **tartan**; **plaid** *refers only to the Scottish garment (sense* **3***), which is not necessarily made of tartan cloth (it can be plain tweed). Furthermore, the pronunciation /plăd/ seems to have arisen in England; in Scotland the word is pronounced /plād/, as one would expect from the spelling.*

ă pat/ā pay/â care/ä father/ĕ pet/ ē be/ĭ pit/ī pie/î fierce/ŏ pot/ ō go/ô paw, for/oi oil/ŏŏ book/ ōō boot/ou out/ŭ cut/û fur/ *th* the/th thin/hw which/zh vision/ ə ago, item, pencil, atom, circus

—*n., pl.* **piz•zi•ca•tos.** Something played pizzicato.

pl. plural.

plac•ard |plăk'ärd'| *or* |-ərd| *n.* A notice to be publicly displayed, especially a poster. —*v.* To post placards on, in, or throughout: *placard a wall.*

pla•cate |plā'kāt'| *or* |plăk'āt'| *v.* **pla•cat•ed, pla•cat•ing.** To calm the anger of; soothe; appease: *placated the child with a lollipop.* —**pla'cat•er** *n.* —**pla•ca'tion** *n.*

place |plās| *n.* **1.** A particular area or spot. **2.** A city or other locality: *What place were you born in?* **3.** A dwelling; residence: *Come over to my place for supper.* **4. Place.** A public square or a short city street: *She lives on Butler Place.* **5.** A building or area set aside for a definite purpose: *a place of worship; a place of learning.* **6. a.** A space for one person to sit or stand: *two empty places near the back of the theater.* **b.** A table setting for one person: *Set an extra place for supper.* **7.** A position or job: *She found a place as a teacher.* **8.** A duty or right: *It's not my place to tell you how to do your job.* **9.** The position of a digit in relation to the other digits of a numeral. **10.** Position or rank: *Aunt Eva's jam won first place at the fair.* **11.** The position of a person or thing as occupied by a substitute; stead: *I'm glad I'm not in his place.* **12.** Proper or usual position, order, context, time, etc.: *She felt out of place with the older girls.* **13.** The point to which one has read in a book: *mark one's place with a bookmark.* —*v.* **placed, plac•ing. 1.** To put in a particular spot, position, or order: *place an astronaut on the moon; place cups and saucers on the table; place words in alphabetical order.* **2.** To remember where or how (someone or something) was first encountered: *His face looks familiar, but I can't place him.* **3.** To put; let reside: *place one's trust in the government.* **4.** To finish a contest in a particular rank: *The horse we bet on placed third.* **5.** To make: *place a telephone call.* ¶*These sound alike* **place, plaice.**

Idioms. **go places.** *Informal.* To become successful. **in place of.** Instead of. **in the first place.** In the beginning. **take place. 1.** To happen; occur: *Sometimes, changes in a person take place very slowly.* **2.** To be set in (a particular time, region, etc.): *a story that takes place in 17th-century England.* **take the place of.** To be a substitute for. **the place to go.** A popular meeting place.

pla•ce•bo |plə sē'bō| *n., pl.* **pla•ce•bos** or **pla•ce•boes. 1.** A preparation that appears to contain medicine but actually does not, given to humor a troublesome patient. **2.** A similar substance used as the control in an experiment to test the effectiveness of a drug.

place kick. In football, a kick made while the ball is propped up on the ground.

place-kick |plās'kĭk'| *v.* **-kicked, -kick•ing.** To kick (a football) propped up on the ground.

place•ment |plās'mənt| *n.* **1.** The act of placing, especially the business or function of finding jobs, housing, etc., for applicants. **2.** A particular arrangement or distribution: *a different placement of the pictures on the museum walls.* —***modifier:*** *a placement office; a placement test.*

pla•cen•ta |plə sĕn'tə| *n., pl.* **pla•cen•tas** or **pla•cen•tae** |plə sĕn'tē|. **1.** A spongy, membranous organ that develops in the uterus of a female mammal during pregnancy, lining the uterus and partially surrounding the fetus, to which it is attached by the umbilical cord. It supplies the fetus with nourishment and is expelled after birth. **2.** A similar organ in other animals, such as certain sharks and reptiles.

plac•er |plăs'ər| *n.* A deposit left by a river or glacier, containing particles of valuable minerals.

plac•id |plăs'ĭd| *adj.* Calm; peaceful. —**plac'id•ly** *adv.* —**plac'id•ness** *n.*

pla•cid•i•ty |plə sĭd'ĭ tē| *n.* Calmness; peacefulness.

plack•et |plăk'ĭt| *n.* A slit in a garment to make it easy to put on or take off, especially an opening closed by a zipper.

pla•gia•rism |plā'jə rĭz'əm| *n.* **1.** The act of plagiarizing: *The producers of the show were guilty of plagiarism.* **2.** The ideas, words, etc., that are plagiarized: *His poem was a complete plagiarism from a little-known magazine.* —**pla'gia•rist** *n.*

pla•gia•rize |plā'jə rīz'| *v.* **pla•gia•rized, pla•gia•riz•ing. 1.** To take and use (the ideas or writings of another) as one's own: *a writer that plagiarized from many sources.* **2.** To take ideas or written passages from (another) and use them as one's own: *accused of plagiarizing Shakespeare.* —**pla'gia•riz'er** *n.*

plague |plāg| *n.* **1.** A calamity or affliction, especially when regarded as a punishment from God: *And the Lord sent down a plague upon Pharaoh's people.* **2.** A very contagious, usually fatal, epidemic disease, especially bubonic plague or a closely related disease. **3.** A sudden influx or increase, as of anything evil. **4.** *Informal.* A cause of annoyance; a nuisance: *Dennis was the plague of Miss Austin's third grade.* —*v.* **plagued, pla•guing. 1.** To cause misery or trouble in or for: *Sleeping sickness has plagued Africa for many centuries.* **2.** To annoy; pester; harass: *Stop plaguing me with your petty complaints.* [SEE NOTE]

plaice |plās| *n., pl.* **plaice** or **plaic•es.** A large flatfish related to the flounders, used as food, especially in Europe. ¶*These sound alike* **plaice, place.**

plaid |plăd| *n.* **1.** A pattern of squares formed by stripes of different widths and colors crossing at right angles; a tartan. **2.** A fabric with such a pattern. **3.** A long, woolen scarf with such a pattern, worn over one shoulder by Scottish Highlanders. —***modifier:*** *a plaid skirt.* [SEE NOTE & PICTURE]

plain |plān| *adj.* **plain•er, plain•est. 1.** Easy to understand; perfectly clear: *His meaning was quite plain.* **2.** Open to view; clear; distinct: *The mountain stood out plain against the sky.* **3.** Not fancy; simple: *a plain dress; plain food.* **4.** Ordinary; average: *My dog is a plain old mutt.* **5.** Not beautiful or handsome: *a plain face.* **6.** Not pretentious; unaffected: *the plain folks back home.* **7.** Frank; candid; down-to-earth: *plain talk.* **8.** Pure; unadulterated; natural: *plain water instead of soda water.* —*adv.* **1.** Clearly; without obstruction: *He could see the target plain.* **2.** Bluntly and honestly: *He spoke plain to me.* **3.** Utterly; completely: *It was just plain silly.* —*n.* A large, flat, treeless area of land. ¶*These* *sound alike* **plain, plane.** —**plain'ly** *adv.* —**plain'ness** *n.* [SEE NOTE]

plain•chant |**plān'**chănt'| *or* |-chänt'| *n.* Plainsong, a form of early music.

plain•clothes man |**plān'klōz'**|. A member of a police force who wears civilian clothes on duty.

Plains Indian. A member of any of the North American Indian tribes that once lived on the plains of the central United States.

plain•song |**plān'**sông'| *or* |-sŏng'| *n.* **1. Gregorian chant. 2.** Any of the unaccompanied church music of the Middle Ages.

plain-spo•ken |**plān'spō'**kən| *adj.* Frank; straightforward: *a plain-spoken critic.*

plaint |plānt| *n.* A complaint.

plain•tiff |**plān'**tĭf| *n.* The party that institutes a suit in a court of law.

plain•tive |**plān'**tĭv| *adj.* Sad; mournful: *a plaintive song.* —**plain'tive•ly** *adv.* —**plain'tive•ness** *n.*

plait |plāt| *or* |plăt| *n.* **1.** A braid, especially of hair. **2.** A pleat. —*v.* **1.** To braid: *She plaited her hair.* **2.** To pleat. ¶*These sound alike* **plait, plate.**

plan |plăn| *n.* **1.** An idea of what to do or how to do it, thought out ahead of time: *What are your plans for the evening? Always follow the game plan.* **2.** A drawing or diagram showing how to build or assemble something: *plans for a new jet fighter.* —*v.* **planned, plan•ning. 1.** To think out (what to do or how to do it) ahead of time: *plan one's vacation; plan carefully.* **2.** To have in mind; intend: *She plans to go to Europe this summer.* **3.** To design (something to be built or made): *plan a new school.* —**plan'ner** *n.*

pla•nar•i•a |plə **nâr'**ē ə| *n.* A planarian.

pla•nar•i•an |plə **nâr'**ē ən| *n.* A nonparasitic freshwater flatworm with a broad body.

plane[1] |plān| *n.* **1.** A geometric surface that contains all the straight lines required to connect every pair of points lying on the surface. **2.** Any flat or level surface. **3.** A level or stage of existence or development: *a high moral plane.* **4.** An airplane or hydroplane. —*adj.* Lying in a plane: *a plane curve; a plane figure.* ¶*These sound alike* **plane, plain.** [SEE NOTE]

plane[2] |plān| *n.* A tool with an adjustable blade for smoothing and leveling wood. —*v.* **planed, plan•ing.** To smooth or finish with a plane. ¶*These sound alike* **plane, plain.** [SEE NOTE]

plane[3] |plān| *n.* A sycamore or related tree, having leaves resembling those of the maple and ball-shaped seed clusters. ¶*These sound alike* **plane, plain.** [SEE NOTE & PICTURE]

plane geometry. The geometry of plane figures.

plan•er |**plā'**nər| *n.* **1.** Someone or something that planes. **2.** A machine tool for planing the surface of wood or metal.

plan•et |**plăn'**ĭt| *n.* **1.** A celestial body, incapable of shining by itself, illuminated by light from a star, about which it moves in an orbit. **2.** Any of the nine largest such bodies that orbit the sun, including the earth.

plan•e•tar•i•um |plăn'ĭ **târ'**ē əm| *n., pl.* **plan•e•tar•i•ums** or **plan•e•tar•i•a** |plăn'ĭ **târ'**ē ə|. **1.** An optical device for projecting images of celestial bodies in their courses onto the ceiling of a dome. **2.** A building in which such a device is housed, or the room in which it is operated. **3.** A mechanical model of the solar system.

plan•e•tar•y |**plăn'**ĭ tĕr'ē| *adj.* Of or resembling a planet or the characteristics of a planet.

plan•e•toid |**plăn'**ĭ toid'| *n.* An asteroid.

plank |plăngk| *n.* **1.** A thick, wide, long piece of lumber. **2.** One of the principles of a political platform. **3.** The gangplank of a ship. —*v.* **planked, plank•ing. 1.** To furnish or cover with planks: *plank a boat.* **2.** To bake or broil and serve on a board: *plank a steak.*

***Idiom.* walk the plank.** To be forced to walk the length of a plank extending from the side of a ship, thus falling into the sea and drowning.

plank•ton |**plăngk'**tən| *n.* Plants and animals, usually of very small size, that float or drift in great numbers in bodies of salt or fresh water.

plant |plănt| *or* |plänt| *n.* **1.** A living thing that generally differs from an animal by being able to manufacture its own food, by being unable to move by itself from place to place, and by having cells with walls made of cellulose. **2.** A plant having no permanent woody stem, as distinguished from a tree or shrub. **3.** A factory or similar place where something is produced or processed. **4.** The buildings and equipment of an institution. —***modifier:*** *plant seeds.* —*v.* **1. a.** To place (seeds, seedlings, cuttings, etc.) in the ground or in soil for growing. **b.** To cause (a plant, crop, etc.) to start to grow: *plant cotton.* **2.** To sow or supply (ground) with seeds, seedlings, etc., for growing: *plant a field with corn.* **3.** To fix or set firmly: *plant one's feet on the ground.* **4.** To start; establish: *plant new colonies in a distant land.* **5.** To cause to take hold or develop; introduce: *plant new ideas in their minds.* **6.** To place as a means of trapping or deceiving someone: *plant spies in an organization.*

plan•tain[1] |**plăn'**tən| *n.* A weedy plant with a dense, narrow cluster of small green or whitish flowers. [SEE NOTE]

plan•tain[2] |**plăn'**tən| *n.* **1.** A treelike tropical plant related to the banana, bearing similar fruit, but not as sweet. **2.** The fruit of this plant, used as a food in tropical regions. [SEE NOTE]

plan•ta•tion |plăn **tā'**shən| *n.* **1.** A large farm or estate on which crops such as cotton, sugar, or rubber are tended and gathered by workers who often live on the same property. **2.** A group of cultivated plants or trees or the ground on which they grow.

plant•er |**plăn'**tər| *or* |**plän'**-| *n.* **1.** Someone or something that plants, especially a tool or machine for planting or sowing seeds. **2.** The owner of a plantation. **3.** A decorative container for growing plants.

plaque |plăk| *n.* An ornamented or engraved plate, slab, or disk, used for decoration or to carry an inscription on a monument.

plas•ma |**plăz'**mə| *n.* **1.** The clear, yellowish liquid part of blood, lymph, etc., in which cells are suspended. **2.** Protoplasm or cytoplasm. **3.** An electrically neutral, usually hot gas containing positively charged and negatively charged particles and some neutral particles.

plas•mo•di•um |plăz **mō'**dē əm| *n., pl.* **plas•mo•di•a** |plăz **mō'**dē ə|. **1.** A protozoan of the kind that causes malaria. **2.** A mass of protoplasm forming one of the stages in the life cycle of a slime mold.

plas•ter |**plăs'**tər| *or* |**plä'**stər| *n.* **1.** A mixture

plane[1-2]/plain

Latin plānus, *"flat, smooth," became Old French* plain, *which was borrowed into English as* **plain.** Plānus *also formed two nouns: (1)* plānum, *"a flat surface," which was borrowed into English as* **plane[1]**; *(2)* plāna, *"a smoothing tool," borrowed into English as* **plane[2]**. *(In Italian,* plānus *became* piano, *"soft"; see note at* **piano.**

plane[3]

plantain[1-2]/plane[3]

Plantain[1] *is from Latin* plantāgō, *which is related to* **plant. Plaintain[2]** *is from Spanish* plantano *or* platano, *"plane tree," from Latin* platanus, *"plane tree."* **Plane[3]** *is from Old French* plane, *which is also from Latin* platanus.

plastic
The adjective **plastic** *is from Greek* plastikos, *"molded, moldable," from* plassein, *"to mold."* (**Plastic surgery** *is surgery that* molds *or* reshapes *damaged or ugly tissue; it has nothing to do with the substance* **plastic.**)

platinum
Platinum *occurs in minerals mixed with other metals, especially nickel. It can be rolled into sheets or drawn to form wire, and it does not tarnish in air. Platinum is used as a chemical catalyst and in jewelry, dentistry, and electrical parts.*

platypus

ă pat/ā pay/â care/ä father/ĕ pet/ ē be/ĭ pit/ī pie/î fierce/ŏ pot/ ō go/ô paw, for/oi oil/ŏŏ book/ ōō boot/ou out/ŭ cut/û fur/ *th* the/th thin/hw which/zh vision/ ə ago, item, pencil, atom, circus

of sand, lime, and water, sometimes with a fibrous material added, that hardens to form a smooth solid surface, used for covering walls and ceilings. **2.** **Plaster of Paris.** **3.** A pastelike mixture applied to a part of the body, either as a remedy or as a cosmetic. —*v.* **1.** To cover (a wall, ceiling, etc.) with plaster: *plaster cracks in the ceiling.* **2.** To cover as if with plaster: *The students plastered campaign posters all over town.* —**plas′ter•er** *n.*

plaster of Paris. Any of a group of cements made by heating gypsum to drive off part of its water of crystallization, forming, when mixed with water, a paste that hardens into a solid.

plas•tic |plăs′tĭk| *n.* Any of numerous organic chemical compounds formed by repeatedly linking simple units into what is, in effect, a giant molecule. Plastics can be formed into films and objects of practically any shape, or drawn into fibers for use in textiles. —*adj.* **1.** Capable of being shaped or molded: *Clay is a plastic material.* **2.** Concerned with the shaping or molding of materials as a means of expression: *Sculpture is one of the plastic arts.* **3.** Made of plastic: *a plastic cup.* —**plas•tic′i•ty** *n.* [SEE NOTE]

plastic surgery. Surgery to repair or restore injured or defective body tissue or parts.

plas•tid |plăs′tĭd| *n.* One of several kinds of tiny structures in the protoplasm of plant cells, sometimes containing coloring or starch.

plat |plăt| *n.* & *v.* **plat•ted, plat•ting.** A form of the word **plait** (braid).

plate |plāt| *n.* **1.** A shallow dish, usually circular, from which food is eaten. **2.** The contents of such a dish: *Finish your plate.* **3.** Food and service for one person at a meal: *supper at a dollar a plate.* **4.** A thin, flat sheet or piece of metal or other material. **5.** A piece of flat metal on which something is engraved, as a license plate, name plate, etc. **6.** A print of a woodcut or lithograph, especially when reproduced in a book. **7.** A full-page book illustration, often in color and printed on special paper. **8.** A sheet of light-sensitive glass or metal upon which a photographic image can be recorded. **9.** A piece of metal or plastic fitted to the gums to hold false teeth in place. **10. the plate.** In baseball, home plate. **11.** Dishes and other household articles made of or plated with gold or silver. **12.** A thin cut of beef from the brisket. **13. a.** An electrode, as in a storage battery or capacitor. **b.** The positive electrode of an electron tube. —*v.* **plat•ed, plat•ing.** To coat or cover with a thin layer of metal. ¶*These sound alike* **plate, plait.**

pla•teau |plă tō′| *n.* **1.** A relatively level area that is at a higher elevation than the land around it. **2. a.** A level or stage of growth or development: *The Japanese economy has reached a new plateau.* **b.** A period of little apparent progress following a period of rapid progress, as in the acquisition of a skill.

plate•ful |plāt′fŏŏl′| *n., pl.* **plate•fuls.** The amount, especially of food, that a plate will hold.

plate glass. Glass made in the form of strong, polished sheets containing few defects, used for making large windows and mirrors.

plate•let |plāt′lĭt| *n.* Any of the numerous cell-like bodies, shaped like irregular disks and lacking nuclei, that are found in the blood of vertebrates. They are thought to function in the clotting of blood.

plat•en |plăt′n| *n.* The roller of a typewriter against which the paper is held.

plat•form |plăt′fôrm′| *n.* **1.** Any floor or horizontal surface higher than an adjoining area: *a speakers' platform; a railroad station platform.* **2.** A formal declaration of principles, as by a political party or candidate.

plat•i•num |plăt′n əm| *n.* Symbol **Pt** One of the elements, a silver-white metal. Atomic number 78; atomic weight 195.09; valences +1, +2, +3, +4; melting point 1,769°C; boiling point 3,827°C. [SEE NOTE]

plat•i•tude |plăt′ĭ tōōd′| *or* |-tyōōd′| *n.* A commonplace and shallow idea or remark. For example, "Money is the root of all evil" is a platitude.

plat•i•tu•di•nous |plăt′ĭ **tōōd′**n əs| *or* |**-tyōōd′-**| *adj.* **1.** Commonplace; trite: *a platitudinous remark.* **2.** Full of or inclined to use platitudes: *a platitudinous sermon; a platitudinous writer.*

Pla•to |plā′tō|. 427?–347 B.C. Greek philosopher.

Pla•ton•ic |plə **tŏn′**ĭk| *adj.* **1.** Of Plato, his writings, or his philosophy. **2. platonic.** Not involving physical passion; purely intellectual or spiritual: *a platonic friendship.*

Pla•to•nism |plā′tn ĭz′əm| *n.* The philosophy of Plato, especially the idea that the world is a shadow or reflection of a higher reality.

pla•toon |plə **tōōn′**| *n.* **1.** A unit of soldiers smaller than a company but larger than a squad, normally commanded by a lieutenant. **2.** A similar unit, as of police or firemen. **3.** In a football team, a group of players that are specially trained for offense or defense and that are sent in or withdrawn from a game as a unit.

plat•ter |plăt′ər| *n.* **1.** A large, shallow dish or plate for serving food. **2.** The amount contained in such a dish or plate: *a platter of fried fish.* **3.** *Slang.* A phonograph record.

plat•y |plăt′ē| *n., pl.* **plat•ys** or **plat•ies.** A small, brightly colored tropical freshwater fish, often kept in home aquariums.

plat•y•pus |plăt′ə pəs| *n., pl.* **plat•y•pus•es.** Also **duckbilled platypus.** A furry, egg-laying Australian mammal having webbed feet and a snout resembling a duck's bill, and living in or near water. [SEE PICTURE]

plau•dit |plô′dĭt| *n.* A strong expression of praise or approval, such as a cheer, a round of applause, etc.: *the plaudits of the critics.*

plau•si•ble |plô′zə bəl| *adj.* Appearing true or reasonable: *a plausible excuse.* —**plau′si•bly** *adv.* —**plau′si•bil′i•ty** *n.*

play |plā| *v.* **played, play•ing.** **1.** To have fun; amuse oneself: *The children went outdoors to play. Susan likes to play with dolls.* **2.** To take part in (a game): *play baseball. The Jets play in Atlanta next week.* **3.** To compete against in a game: *The Giants played the Dodgers last night.* **4.** To occupy the position of in a game: *Tom played quarterback.* **5.** To use in a game: *The coach promised to play him in the next game. He played the ace of spades.* **6. a.** To act in a drama: *He played in "Hamlet."* **b.** To act the role of, in or as if in a drama: *He played Hamlet.* **c.** To perform (a role or part) in a process: *The stom-*

ach plays a crucial part in digestion. **7.** To be presented for an audience: *"Gunsmoke" is playing on TV tonight.* **8.** To pretend to be: *play sick; play cowboys and Indians.* **9.** To act in a particular way: *You're not playing fair.* **10.** To give forth or produce sound, especially musical sound: *The orchestra will play next. The radio plays badly.* **11. a.** To perform on (a musical instrument): *play a trumpet.* **b.** To perform (music) on an instrument or instruments: *The band played a march.* **12. a.** To cause (a record, phonograph, radio, etc.) to produce sounds that have been recorded or broadcast. **b.** To cause to sound on a radio, phonograph, etc.: *play some popular music.* **13.** To bring about; cause: *play havoc.* **14.** To trifle or toy: *He played with her feelings.* **15.** To bet on: *play the horses.* **16.** To move or cause to move rapidly, lightly, or irregularly: *A noisy March wind played over the island. The guards played the searchlight over the courtyard.* —***phrasal verbs.*** **play along.** To cooperate or pretend to cooperate: *He played along with the robbers.* **play down.** To minimize the importance of, as by giving little publicity to: *The newspapers played down the scandal.* **play on** (or **upon**). To take advantage of (another's feelings or hopes) for one's own purposes. **play out.** **1.** To play (a game) to the finish. **2.** To let out (a rope, line, etc.) little by little. **play up.** To emphasize or publicize, often with some exaggeration: *The newspapers of the time played up Buffalo Bill's exploits.* **play up to.** To try to win the favor of (someone) by flattery. —*n.* **1. a.** A literary work written for the stage: *a play by Shakespeare.* **b.** The performance of such a work: *We went to a play last night.* **2.** Activity engaged in for pleasure; recreation: *All work and no play make Jack a dull boy.* **3.** A manner of playing a game. **4.** A manner of dealing with people: *He believes in fair play.* **5.** A move or action in a game: *a hit-and-run play.* **6.** The act of playing a game: *Play begins with the kickoff.* **7.** Movement or freedom of movement: *the play of colored lights across a stage; loosened his jacket to give his arms more play.* **8.** Action; use: *brought his influence into full play.* —***modifier:*** *play clothes.* [SEE NOTE]

Idioms. **in play.** In legitimate motion or use, as defined by official game rules: *The ball is in play.* **out of play.** Not in legitimate motion or use, as defined by official game rules; dead. **play ball.** To cooperate: *He refused to play ball with the mobsters.* **play both ends against the middle.** To maneuver between two antagonists to get what one wants. **play into the hands of.** To act or react so as to give an advantage to an opponent. **play on words.** **1.** A pun. **2.** An act of punning.

pla•ya |plī′ə| *n.* An almost level area at the bottom of a desert basin, sometimes covered with water for a time.

play•bill |plā′bĭl′| *n.* **1.** A program for a theatrical performance. **2.** A poster announcing a theatrical performance.

play•er |plā′ər| *n.* **1.** A person who takes part in a game or sport. **2.** An actor. **3.** A person who plays a musical instrument. **4.** A phonograph or tape recorder.

player piano. A mechanical piano that uses a punched paper roll to control the keys.

play•fel•low |plā′fĕl′ō| *n.* A playmate.

play•ful |plā′fəl| *adj.* **1.** Full of fun and high spirits; frolicsome: *a playful cat.* **2.** Humorous; jesting: *a playful discussion.* —**play′ful•ly** *adv.* —**play′ful•ness** *n.*

play•ground |plā′ground′| *n.* An outdoor area for recreation and play. —***modifier:*** *playground equipment.* [SEE PICTURE]

play•house |plā′hous′| *n., pl.* **-hous•es** |-hou′zĭz|. **1.** A theater. **2.** A small house for children to play in. **3.** A child's toy house; a doll house.

playing card. Any of the cards, usually in a deck of 52, used to play a wide variety of games. Each card has one of 4 suits and one of 13 ranks.

play•mate |plā′māt′| *n.* A companion in play.

play-off |plā′ôf′| *or* |-ŏf′| *n.* A final game or series of games played to determine a winner or championship. —***modifier:*** *a play-off game.*

play•pen |plā′pĕn′| *n.* A portable enclosure in which a baby or young child can be left to play.

play•thing |plā′thĭng′| *n.* A thing to play with; a toy.

play•wright |plā′rīt′| *n.* A person who writes plays; a dramatist.

pla•za |plăz′ə| *or* |plä′zə| *n.* A public square or similar open area in a town or city.

plea |plē| *n.* **1.** An appeal or urgent request; an entreaty: *a plea for help.* **2.** An excuse; a pretext. **3.** In law, the answer of the accused to the charges against him.

plead |plēd| *v.* **plead•ed** or **pled** |plĕd|, **plead•ing.** **1.** To appeal or beg fervently; implore; entreat: *They were pleading with him to return.* **2.** To put forward a plea in a court of law: *He pleaded guilty.* **3.** To argue (a case) in a court of law. **4.** To put forward as a defense: *plead the Fifth Amendment.* **5.** To give as an excuse: *He pleaded insanity to escape punishment.* —**plead′er** *n.*

pleas•ant |plĕz′ənt| *adj.* **pleas•ant•er, pleas•ant•est.** **1.** Pleasing; agreeable; delightful: *a pleasant climate; a pleasant aroma.* **2.** Pleasing or favorable in manner; amiable; good-natured: *a pleasant person; a pleasant disposition.* —**pleas′ant•ly** *adv.* —**pleas′ant•ness** *n.*

pleas•ant•ry |plĕz′ən trē| *n., pl.* **pleas•ant•ries.** **1.** A jesting or humorous remark or action. **2.** Pleasant playfulness in conversation.

please |plēz| *v.* **pleased, pleas•ing.** **1.** To give (someone or something) pleasure or satisfaction: *The island pleased the settlers. John is eager to please.* **2.** To be willing to; be so kind as to. Used in the imperative to introduce a request or as an exclamation showing wish or protest: *Please tell us a story. Attention, please!* **3.** To have the will or desire; wish; prefer: *do exactly as they please.* **4.** To be the will or desire of: *May it please the court to admit this evidence.*

Idiom. **if you please.** If it is your will or pleasure.

pleas•ing |plē′zĭng| *adj.* Giving pleasure or satisfaction; agreeable; gratifying: *a pleasing effect; a pleasing scent.* —**pleas′ing•ly** *adv.*

pleas•ur•a•ble |plĕzh′ər ə bəl| *adj.* Satisfying; agreeable; gratifying: *a pleasurable experience.* —**pleas′ur•a•ble•ness** *n.* —**pleas′ur•a•bly** *adv.*

pleas•ure |plĕzh′ər| *n.* **1.** A pleasant sensation, emotion, or occurrence; satisfaction; delight: *She smiled with pleasure.* **2.** A source of enjoyment, satisfaction, or delight: *Reading is his chief*

play
"Work consists of whatever a body is obliged *to do . . . Play consists of whatever a body is not obliged to do."* — *Mark Twain.*

playground

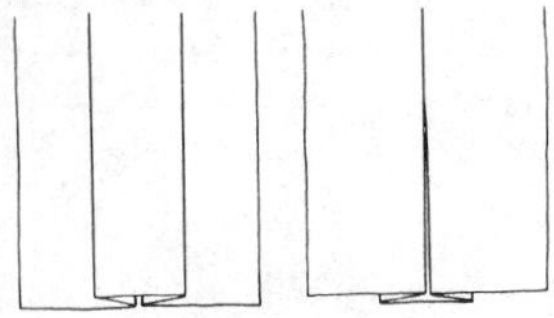

pleat

Pleistocene, etc.
The **Cenozoic** *era is divided into the following epochs:* **Paleocene, Eocene, Oligocene, Miocene, Pliocene,** *and* **Pleistocene**. *The ending* -cene *is from Greek* kainos, *"new, recent"; the geologic terms refer to the quantities of fossil remains of* recent *species found in the different strata.* **Paleocene** *means "ancient-recent";* **Eocene** *means "dawn-of-recent";* **Oligocene** *means "a-few-of-recent";* **Miocene** *means "minor-recent";* **Pliocene** *means "major-recent";* **Pleistocene** *means "maximum-recent." A more confusing and illogical system of names could hardly be devised; almost anyone could invent much better ones that would be easy to remember. The terms were invented by the great English geologist Charles Lyell (1797–1875). Fowler's* Modern English Usage *(1926) indignantly condemns them as "barbarisms," but we are probably stuck with them.*

plight[1-2]
Plight[1] *originally meant "a fold, a twist" and later came to mean "situation"; it is from Old French* pleit *and is related to* **pleat**. **Plight**[2] *in* **plight one's troth** *originally meant "to risk" and later "to offer as a pledge"; it is from Old English* pliht, *"danger."*

ă pat/ā pay/â care/ä father/ĕ pet/ē be/ĭ pit/ī pie/î fierce/ŏ pot/ō go/ô paw, for/oi oil/ŏŏ book/ōō boot/ou out/ŭ cut/û fur/*th* the/th thin/hw which/zh vision/ə ago, item, pencil, atom, circus

pleasure. **3.** Amusement; diversion: *He grew tired of living for pleasure.* **4.** The preference or desire; the wish, choice, or will: *obliged to suffer the pleasure of the king.* —***modifier:*** *a pleasure trip; a pleasure boat.* —*v.* **pleas•ured, pleas•ur•ing.** To please; delight: *It pleasures us to welcome you.*

pleat |plēt| *n.* A flat fold in cloth or other material, made by doubling the material on itself and pressing or sewing it in place. —*v.* To form pleats in; arrange in pleats: *pleat a ruffle.* —**pleat'ed** *adj.: a pleated skirt.* [SEE PICTURE]

plebe |plēb| *n.* A freshman at the U.S. Military Academy or the U.S. Naval Academy.

ple•be•ian |plĭ bē'ən| *adj.* **1.** Of the common people, especially those of ancient Rome; not patrician. **2.** Of anything considered crude or vulgar: *plebeian tastes.* —*n.* **1.** A member of the common people, especially of ancient Rome. **2.** A person considered coarse or vulgar.

pleb•i•scite |plĕb'ĭ sīt'| *n.* A direct vote by an entire people on an important issue.

plec•trum |plĕk'trəm| *n., pl.* **plec•trums** or **plec•tra** |plĕk'trə|. A small, thin, flexible piece of metal, plastic, bone, etc., used to pluck the strings of a musical instrument; a pick.

pled |plĕd|. A past tense and past participle of **plead.**

pledge |plĕj| *n.* **1.** A formal vow; a solemn promise: *made a pledge to do their duty.* **2.** The words or text of a formal vow, oath, or promise: *The child memorized the pledge.* **3. a.** Something considered as security to guarantee payment of a debt or an obligation: *a necklace left as a pledge for a loan.* **b.** The condition of something considered as such security: *Her jewels were left in pledge.* **4.** A token or sign: *They exchanged rings as a pledge of devotion.* **5.** A toast to someone. **6.** Someone who has been accepted for membership in a fraternity or similar organization but has not yet been initiated. —*v.* **pledged, pledg•ing. 1.** To make (a commitment) by a solemn promise or vow: *pledged their support.* **2.** To bind (someone or something) by a solemn promise or vow: *They were pledged to secrecy.* **3.** To promise as security: *He pledged future crops.* **4. a.** To promise to join (a fraternity or similar organization). **b.** To accept as a member of such an organization.

Pleis•to•cene |plī'stə sēn'| *n.* Also **Pleistocene epoch.** The epoch of geologic time that began between 500,000 and 2,000,000 years ago and ended about 11,000 years ago, characterized by the alternate appearance and recession of glaciers in the Northern Hemisphere and by the appearance of the ancestors of modern man. —***modifier:*** *a Pleistocene fossil.* [SEE NOTE]

ple•na |plē'nə| *n.* A plural of **plenum.**

ple•na•ry |plē'nə rē| *or* |plĕn'ə-| *adj.* **1.** Complete in all aspects; full; absolute: *plenary powers.* **2.** Fully attended by all qualified members: *a plenary meeting of the council.*

plen•i•po•ten•ti•ar•y |plĕn'ə pə tĕn'shē ĕr'ē| *adj.* Invested with full powers. —*n., pl.* **plen•i•po•ten•ti•ar•ies.** A diplomatic agent having full powers to represent his government.

plen•i•tude |plĕn'ĭ tōōd'| *or* |-tyōōd'| *n.* Abundance; fullness.

plen•te•ous |plĕn'tē əs| *adj.* Abundant; plentiful. —**plen'te•ous•ly** *adv.* —**plen'te•ous•ness** *n.*

plen•ti•ful |plĕn'tĭ fəl| *adj.* **1.** In abundant supply; ample: *plentiful food; plentiful rainfall.* **2.** Producing or yielding in abundance: *a plentiful land.* —**plen'ti•ful•ly** *adv.* —**plen'ti•ful•ness** *n.*

plen•ty |plĕn'tē| *n.* **1.** An ample amount or supply; as much as is needed: *plenty of exercise; plenty of time.* **2.** A large amount or number; a lot: *plenty of work to do; in plenty of trouble.* **3.** General abundance or prosperity: *a time of plenty.* —*adj.* Ample; more than enough: *There's plenty room here.* —*adv. Informal.* Excessively; very: *The wound hurt plenty. They were plenty hungry.*

ple•num |plē'nəm| *n., pl.* **ple•nums** or **ple•na** |plē'nə|. An enclosure in which air or other gas is kept at a pressure greater than that outside.

ple•si•o•saur |plē'sē ə sôr'| *or* |-zē-| *n.* A large, extinct water reptile with a long neck and four paddlelike flippers. Plesiosaurs lived millions of years ago, at about the same time as the dinosaurs.

ple•si•o•saur•us |plē'sē ə sôr'əs| *or* |-zē-| *n.* A plesiosaur.

pleu•ra |plŏŏr'ə| *n., pl.* **pleu•rae** |plŏŏr'ē'|. Either of the membranous sacs lining one side of the chest cavity and enveloping the lung on that side. —**pleu'ral** *adj.*

pleu•ri•sy |plŏŏr'ĭ sē| *n.* Inflammation of the pleura.

Plex•i•glas |plĕk'sĭ glăs'| *or* |-gläs'| *n.* A trademark for a light, strong, transparent plastic.

plex•us |plĕk'səs| *n., pl.* **plex•us** or **plex•us•es** A network, as of nerves, blood vessels, etc., in the body: *the solar plexus.*

pli•a•ble |plī'ə bəl| *adj.* **1.** Easily bent or shaped without breaking; flexible; pliant: *pliable strips of wood.* **2.** Tending to be easily influenced or dominated: *a pliable mind.* —**pli'a•bil'i•ty, pli'a•ble•ness** *n.* —**pli'a•bly** *adv.*

pli•ant |plī'ənt| *adj.* **1.** Easily bent or shaped; pliable: *pliant materials.* **2.** Readily changing to fit conditions or to suit others: *a pliant personality.* —**pli'an•cy** *n.* —**pli'ant•ly** *adv.*

pli•ers |plī'ərz| *n. (used with a plural verb).* A tool with two parts attached together as in a pair of scissors, used for holding, bending, or cutting.

plies |plīz|. **1.** Plural of the noun **ply. 2.** Third person singular present tense of the verb **ply.**

plight[1] |plīt| *n.* A serious condition or a situation of difficulty or peril. [SEE NOTE]

plight[2] |plīt| *v.* To promise or bind by solemn pledge. [SEE NOTE]
Idiom. **plight one's troth.** To give one's solemn promise to marry.

plinth |plĭnth| *n.* A block or slab upon which a pedestal, column, or statue is placed.

Pli•o•cene |plī'ə sēn'| *n.* Also **Pliocene epoch.** The epoch of geologic time that began about 13 million years ago and ended about 2 million years ago, characterized by the appearance of distinctly modern plants and animals. —***modifier:*** *a Pliocene rock.*

plod |plŏd| *v.* **plod•ded, plod•ding. 1.** To walk heavily or with great effort: *They plodded wearily home through the twilight.* **2.** To work or act slowly and wearily: *She plodded through her lessons.* —**plod'ding** *adj.: a plodding donkey.*

plop |plŏp| *v.* **plopped, plop•ping. 1. a.** To fall or move with a sound like that of an object falling into water: *He let the dough plop down into the sink.* **b.** To place or drop something so as to make such a sound: *She plopped the tomatoes onto the plate.* **2.** To drop or sink heavily or wearily: *He plopped into the chair.* —*n.* A dull sound suggesting that of an object falling into water or a movement associated with such a sound: *The pebble fell with a plop into the pool.* —*adv.* With the sound of a plop: *He heard the frog jump plop into the creek.*

plot |plŏt| *n.* **1. a.** A small piece of ground: *a plot of good land.* **b.** A measured area of land; a lot: *a family plot at the cemetery.* **2.** The series of actions or events in a novel, play, etc. **3.** A secret plan to accomplish an often illegal purpose: *a plot against the king.* —*v.* **plot•ted, plot•ting. 1.** To mark, note, or represent, as on a chart or map. **2.** To plan or scheme secretly or deviously: *plot revenge.* —**plot'ter** *n.*

plough |plou| *n.* & *v.* British form of the word **plow.**

plov•er |**plŭv'**ər| *or* |**plō'**vər| *n.* Any of several small, short-billed, short-tailed shore birds.

plow |plou| *n.* **1.** A farm implement drawn either by animal or motor vehicle, used for breaking up soil and cutting furrows in preparation for sowing. **2.** Any device or vehicle of similar function, as a snowplow. —***modifier:*** *a plow horse.* —*v.* **1.** To break and turn over (soil) with a plow; till with a plow: *plowed the field; plowed around the hill.* **2. a.** To advance or progress steadily and with effort: *plow through the waves.* **b.** To make (one's way) steadily and with effort: *plowed his way through the deep snow.* **3.** To remove snow from with a snowplow: *plowed the streets after the blizzard.* —***phrasal verbs.*** **plow back.** To reinvest (earnings or profits) in one's business. **plow into.** *Informal.* **1.** To run into with force: *The truck plowed into the stalled cars.* **2.** To undertake with enthusiasm or energy. **plow under.** To turn (something) under the soil by using a plow: *plow under clover.* [SEE PICTURE]

plow•man |**plou'**mən| *n., pl.* **-men** |-mən|. A man who operates a plow.

plow•share |**plou'**shâr'| *n.* The cutting blade of a plow.

ploy |ploi| *n.* A cunning tactic, stratagem, or artifice to obtain advantage over an opponent.

pluck |plŭk| *v.* **1.** To detach by pulling with the fingers; pick: *pluck a flower.* **2.** To pull out the feathers or hair of: *pluck a chicken.* **3.** To shape by pulling out some hairs: *plucked her eyebrows.* **4.** To pull; tug: *pluck a sleeve; pluck aimlessly at the grass.* **5.** To sound (a string or strings of an instrument) by stretching and releasing, as with the fingers or a plectrum. —*n.* **1.** A tug; a pull. **2.** Courage and daring; spirit.

pluck•y |**plŭk'**ē| *adj.* **pluck•i•er, pluck•i•est.** Showing spirit and courage in the face of great odds.

plug |plŭg| *n.* **1.** A piece of wood, cork, or other material, used to stop a hole, leak, etc. **2.** An electrical device connected to the end of a wire or cable, capable of fitting into a matching socket to make an electrical connection. **3.** A **spark plug. 4.** A fireplug. **5.** A flat cake of pressed or twisted chewing tobacco. **6.** *Slang.* Something considered inferior or defective, as an old horse. **7.** *Informal.* A favorable public mention of something, especially on television or radio. —*v.* **plugged, plug•ging. 1.** To fill (a hole, gap, leak, etc.) with or as if with a plug or stopper; stop up. **2. a.** To connect (an electrical appliance or device) into a socket by means of a plug: *plug in a lamp.* **b.** To connect into the socket of an electrical device: *This gadget plugs into the stereo.* **3.** *Informal.* To mention favorably; advertise: *plug a new brand of soap.* **4.** *Informal.* To work doggedly and persistently: *plug away at a job.* —**plug'ger** *n.*

plum |plŭm| *n.* **1. a.** A fruit with smooth skin, juicy flesh, and a hard-shelled pit. **b.** A tree that bears such fruit. **2.** A raisin in a pudding or pie. **3.** A dark reddish purple. **4.** Something very much wanted or envied, such as a job that pays well or is considered an honor to hold. —***modifier:*** *plum jam.* —*adj.* Dark reddish purple. ¶*These sound alike* **plum, plumb.**

plum•age |**plōō'**mĭj| *n.* The feathers of a bird.

plumb |plŭm| *n.* A weight hung from the end of a cord, used to measure depth or test vertical alignment. —*adj.* **1.** Exactly vertical: *a plumb wall.* **2.** *Informal.* Utter; sheer: *a plumb fool.* —*adv.* **1.** Vertically; straight up and down: *a post that stands plumb.* **2.** *Informal.* Completely; utterly: *plumb wrong.* —*v.* To test the depth or alignment of with or as if with a plumb. —***phrasal verb.*** **plumb up.** To make vertical; adjust until vertical: *plumb up a post.* ¶*These sound alike* **plumb, plum.**

plumb•er |**plŭm'**ər| *n.* A person who installs and repairs pipes and plumbing.

plumb•ing |**plŭm'**ĭng| *n.* **1.** The work or occupation of a plumber. **2.** The pipes, fixtures, and other equipment used in a system through which a liquid or gas flows.

plume |plōōm| *n.* **1.** A feather, especially a large or showy one used for decoration. **2.** Something resembling a large feather: *A plume of smoke rose from the chimney.* —*v.* **plumed, plum•ing.** To decorate with or as if with plumes. —**plumed'** *adj.: a plumed helmet.*

plum•met |**plŭm'**ĭt| *v.* To drop straight down; plunge: *A rock plummeted down from the cliff.*

plump[1] |plŭmp| *adj.* **plump•er, plump•est.** Rounded and full in form: *a plump figure; a plump peach.* —*v.* To make or become rounded and full: *He plumped up the pillow. The child plumped out as she grew.* —**plump'ly** *adv.* —**plump'ness** *n.* [SEE NOTE]

plump[2] |plŭmp| *v.* **1.** To drop heavily or wearily; plop: *She plumped down on the grass.* **2.** To place or throw heavily or abruptly: *plumped the napkins into the washing machine.* —*n.* **1.** A heavy, abrupt fall or impact. **2.** The dull sound of a heavy, abrupt fall. —*adv.* Heavily or suddenly: *He fell down plump on the ground.* [SEE NOTE]

plum pudding. A sweet spiced pudding made with flour, suet, raisins, and currants.

plun•der |**plŭn'**dər| *v.* To take booty or valuables from; pillage; rob: *Pirates plundered the coastal city.* —*n.* **1.** Property stolen by force or by fraud; booty: *digging to hide their plunder.* **2.** The taking of property by force.

plunge |plŭnj| *v.* **plunged, plung•ing. 1.** To throw oneself suddenly or energetically into a

plow
Above: Plow drawn by horses
Below: Mechanized plow

plump[1·2]
Plump[1] *is from Low German* plomp, *"thick, blunt."* **Plump[2]** *is from Low German* plumpen, *"to fall into water." It seems possible that the two Low German words are related, but it is hard to see just how.*

body of water, place, etc.: *He plunged into the sea. She plunged into her work.* **2.** To thrust, throw, or place forcefully or suddenly into something: *plunged the pitchfork into the hay.* **3.** To cause to enter or enter suddenly or violently into a situation or activity: *events that plunged the world into war. The country plunged into debt.* **4.** To descend steeply or sharply; fall: *The river plunged into the gorge. Her temperature plunged lower than normal.* **5.** To rush or move forward into or toward something quickly and rapidly: *animals plunging through the undergrowth.* —*n.* **1.** The act of plunging: *a plunge into work.* **2.** A swim: *an early morning plunge.*

plung•er |**plŭn**′jər| *n.* **1.** The part of a device that operates with a repeated thrusting or plunging movement, as a piston. **2.** A device consisting of a suction cup attached to the end of a stick, used to clean out clogged drains and pipes.

plunk |plŭngk|. *Informal. v.* **1.** To throw or place heavily or abruptly: *He plunked the nickel on the table.* **2.** To drop or sink heavily or wearily; plop: *They plunked down on a bench.* **3.** To strum or pluck (the strings of a musical instrument). **4.** To make a short, hollow, twanging sound. —*n.* **1.** A short, hollow, twanging sound. **2.** A heavy blow or hit.

plu•per•fect |plo͞o **pûr**′fĭkt| *adj.* Of the past perfect tense. —*n.* The **past perfect tense.**

plu•ral |**plo͝or**′əl| *adj.* **1.** Of or composed of more than one. **2.** In grammar, of the form of a word that designates more than one. —*n.* The plural form of a word. For example, *birds* is the plural of *bird*, and *children* is the plural of *child.* —**plu′ral•ly** *adv.*

plu•ral•i•ty |plo͞o **răl**′ĭ tē| *n., pl.* **plu•ral•i•ties. 1.** The condition of being plural. **2. a.** In a contest of more than two candidates, the number of votes cast for the winner if this number is less than half of the total votes cast. **b.** The number by which the vote of a winning candidate is more than that of his closest opponent.

plus |plŭs| *prep.* **1.** Added to: *Two plus three equals five.* **2.** Increased by; along with: *wages plus bonuses.* —*adj.* **1.** Of addition: *a plus sign.* **2.** Greater than zero; positive. **3.** Of or indicating an electric charge that is like that of a proton and unlike that of an electron. **4.** Added or extra: *a plus benefit.* **5.** Slightly more than: *a grade of B plus.* —*n.* **1.** Also **plus sign.** The sign (+), used to show addition or a positive number. **2.** A positive number. **3.** A favorable factor or trait. [SEE NOTE]

plush |plŭsh| *n.* A fabric resembling velvet but having a thicker, deeper pile. —*modifier: a plush sofa.* —*adj.* **plush•er, plush•est.** *Informal.* Expensive; luxurious; elegant: *a plush restaurant.*

Plu•to[1] |**plo͞o**′tō|. The Roman god of the underworld.

Plu•to[2] |**plo͞o**′tō| *n.* The ninth planet of the solar system in order of increasing distance from the sun. Its diameter is about one-half that of the earth, its average distance from the sun is about 3,666 million miles, and it takes about 249 years to complete a single orbit around the sun.

plu•toc•ra•cy |plo͞o **tŏk**′rə sē| *n., pl.* **plu•toc•ra•cies. 1.** Government by the wealthy. **2.** A wealthy class that controls a government.

plu•to•crat |**plo͞o**′tə krăt′| *n.* Someone having political power because of wealth. —**plu′to•crat′ic** *adj.*

plu•to•ni•um |plo͞o **tō**′nē əm| *n.* Symbol **Pu** One of the elements, a naturally radioactive, silvery metal that occurs in trace quantities in uranium ores. It has 15 isotopes with mass numbers ranging from 232 to 246 and half-lives from 20 minutes to 76 million years. Atomic number 94; valences +3, +4, +5, +6; melting point 639.5°C; boiling point 3,235°C.

ply[1] |plī| *n., pl.* **plies. 1.** A layer or thickness, as of folded cloth or of wood. **2.** One of the strands twisted together to make yarn, rope, or thread having a certain number of strands, twists, or folds: *three-ply yarn.* [SEE NOTE]

ply[2] |plī| *v.* **plied, ply•ing, plies. 1.** To traverse (a route or course) regularly: *Convoys plied the seas. Steamers plied to and from London.* **2.** To keep supplying or offering to: *plying her with candy; plying him with questions.* **3.** To engage in (a trade or task); perform regularly: *ply the baker's trade.* **4.** To use or handle (a tool); wield: *ply a broom in sweeping.* [SEE NOTE]

Plym•outh |**plĭm**′əth|. A town in Massachusetts where the Pilgrims landed in 1620.

Plymouth Colony. A New England settlement established in December, 1620, by the Pilgrims.

Plymouth Rock. 1. A boulder on the Massachusetts coast, traditionally regarded as the landing place of the Pilgrims. **2.** One of a breed of chickens raised for eggs and meat.

ply•wood |**plī**′wo͝od′| *n.* A building material made of layers of wood glued together, usually with the grains of adjoining layers at right angles.

p.m., P.M. after noon.

Pm The symbol for the element promethium.

pneu•mat•ic |no͞o **măt**′ĭk| *or* |nyo͞o-| *adj.* **1.** Of air or another gas: *pneumatic pressure.* **2.** Filled with or operated by compressed air.

pneu•mo•nia |no͞o **mōn**′yə| *or* |nyo͞o-| *n.* Any of several usually serious diseases, caused by bacteria, viruses, chemicals, or irritation, in which the lungs become inflamed.

Po The symbol for the element polonium.

P.O. post office.

poach[1] |pōch| *v.* To cook (eggs, fish, etc.) in a liquid that is gently boiling or simmering. —**poached′** *adj.: a poached egg.* —**poach′er** *n.* [SEE NOTE]

poach[2] |pōch| *v.* **1.** To trespass on (a wildlife preserve or private property) in order to hunt or fish. **2.** To take (fish or game) from a wildlife preserve or private property. —**poach′er** *n.* [SEE NOTE]

Po•ca•hon•tas |pō′kə **hŏn**′təs|. 1595?–1617. American Indian princess who allegedly saved the life of John Smith.

pock |pŏk| *n.* **1.** A pus-filled swelling of the skin caused by smallpox or a similar disease. **2.** A pockmark.

pock•et |**pŏk**′ĭt| *n.* **1.** A small pouch, open at the top, sewn into or onto a garment and used to hold things. **2.** Any receptacle, cavity, container, or pouch that resembles a pocket in appearance or function. **3.** A mass or accumulation of a substance surrounded by another substance from which it is more or less distinct: *a pocket of air in the ice.* **4.** A small, isolated or protected area or group: *pockets of civilization.* —*adj.* **1.**

plus

Plus *has started to be used as a conjunction meaning "and furthermore" in such sentences as "He's a fast tackle, plus he has stamina and experience." This is not accepted in formal usage; many people would condemn it completely, even in informal speech.*

ply[1-2]

Ply[1] *is from Old French* pli, *"a fold," from* plier, *"to fold," from Latin* plicāre, *"to fold."* **Ply**[2] *originally meant "to work away at" (as in senses* **3** *and* **4**)*; it is a shortening of* **apply**.

poach[1-2]

Poach[1] *is from Old French* pocher, *"to put into a bag" (referring to the shape of a poached egg), from* poche, *"bag, pocket"; it is related to* **pocket** *and to* **pouch**. **Poach**[2] *is from Old French* pochier, *"to trample, encroach on private land."*

ă pat/ā pay/â care/ä father/ĕ pet/ ē be/ĭ pit/ī pie/î fierce/ŏ pot/ ō go/ô paw, for/oi oil/o͝o book/ o͞o boot/ou out/ŭ cut/û fur/ *th* the/th thin/hw which/zh vision/ ə ago, item, pencil, atom, circus

Suitable for being carried in one's pocket: *a pocket watch; a pocket handkerchief.* **2.** Small enough to be carried in one's pocket; relatively small: *a pocket edition of a book.* —*v.* **1.** To place in or as if in a pocket: *pocket a dime; pocket one's pride.* **2.** To take possession of dishonestly: *pocket the petty cash.*

Idioms. **in (one's) pocket.** In one's control or possession: *kept the legislature in his pocket.* **line (one's) pocket.** To make extra money, especially by illegal means.

pock•et•book |pŏk′ĭt bo͝ok′| *n.* **1.** A container used to hold money, papers, cosmetics, and other small articles; a handbag. **2.** A container for paper money or coins that is small enough to fit into a pocket or handbag. **3.** Supply of money: *too expensive for our pocketbook.* **4.** A small, usually paperbound book.

pock•et•knife |pŏk′ĭt nīf′| *n., pl.* **-knives** |-nīvz′|. A small knife with a blade or blades that fold into the handle. [See Picture]

pock•mark |pŏk′märk′| *n.* A pitlike scar left on the skin as a result of smallpox or a similar disease. —**pock′marked′** *adj.*

pod |pŏd| *n.* A seed case as of a pea, bean, or certain other plants, that splits open to release the enclosed seeds. [See Picture]

-pod. A word element meaning "a number or kind of feet": **pseudopod.**

po•di•a |pō′dē ə| *n.* A plural of **podium.**

po•di•a•try |pə dī′ə trē| *n.* The study and treatment of foot ailments. —**po•di′a•trist** *n.*

po•di•um |pō′dē əm| *n., pl.* **po•di•a** |pō′dē ə| or **po•di•ums.** An elevated platform on which an orchestra conductor, lecturer, etc., stands.

Poe |pō|, **Edgar Allan.** 1809–1849. American short-story writer, poet, and journalist.

po•em |pō′əm| *n.* **1.** A work of poetry; a composition, usually in verse, with language especially chosen for its sound, beauty, and power to convey a vivid and imaginative sense of experience. **2.** Anything thought to have the beauty or perfection of form of poetry.

po•e•sy |pō′ĭ zē| *or* |-sē| *n. Archaic.* Poetry.

po•et |pō′ĭt| *n.* A writer of poems.

po•et•ess |pō′ĭ tĭs| *n.* A female poet.

po•et•ic |pō ĕt′ĭk| *adj.* **1.** Of poetry: *poetic works.* **2.** Having a quality or style characteristic of poetry: *poetic language.* **3.** Of or befitting a poet: *poetic thoughts.* **4.** Written in verse form: *a poetic drama.* **5.** Suitable as a subject of poetry.

po•et•i•cal |pō ĕt′ĭ kəl| *adj.* **1.** Poetic. **2.** Highly fanciful or idealized: *poetical notions about pioneer life.* —**po•et′i•cal•ly** *adv.*

poetic justice. The justice that is achieved when those who plan mischief or evil suffer from their own plans.

poet laureate. *pl.* **poets laureate** or **poet laureates.** A poet appointed by the British sovereign as chief poet of the kingdom for life.

po•et•ry |pō′ĭ trē| *n.* **1.** The art or work of a poet. **2.** Poems regarded as a division of literature: *Our class will be reading poetry for the next two weeks.* **3.** The poems of an author, country, etc.: *Milton's poetry.* **4.** A quality that pleases or stirs the imagination; beauty. —***modifier:*** *a poetry book; a poetry class.*

po•go stick |pō′gō|. A strong stick with footrests and a heavy spring set into the bottom end, propelled along the ground by hopping. [See Picture]

po•grom |pə grŭm′| *or* |-grŏm′| *or* |pō′grəm| *n.* An organized and often officially sanctioned massacre or persecution of a minority group.

poi |poi| *or* |pō′ē| *n.* A Hawaiian food consisting of a starchy, fermented paste made from cooked taro root.

poign•ant |poin′yənt| *adj.* **1.** Keenly distressing or painful: *poignant grief.* **2.** Affecting the emotions; appealing; touching: *poignant memories.* **3.** Piercing; penetrating: *poignant criticism.* —**poign′an•cy** *n.* —**poign′ant•ly** *adv.*

poin•set•ti•a |poin sĕt′ē ə| *n.* A tropical plant with small, yellowish flowers surrounded by showy, usually bright-red petallike leaves.

point |point| *n.* **1.** The sharp or tapered end of something: *the point of a pencil.* **2.** A tapering piece of land that extends into a body of water. **3.** A dot or period, as one used to separate the fractional and integral parts of a numeral. **4.** A geometric object having no dimensions and no property other than its location. **5.** Any of the 32 directions indicated on a mariner's compass. **6.** A position or place: *the highest point in the county.* **7.** A specified degree or condition: *the boiling point; the point of no return.* **8.** A specific moment in time: *At that point he noticed someone running away.* **9.** An important or essential factor, part, or idea: *the point of a story.* **10.** A purpose, goal, or reason: *He came to the point of his visit.* **11.** A separate item or element: *the major points in the speech.* **12.** A distinctive quality or characteristic: *made the most of their good points.* **13.** A score of 1 in a game, contest, or test. **14.** In printing, a unit of type size equal to about 1/72 of an inch. **15.** A unit equal to one dollar and used to state the current prices of stocks, commodities, etc. —*v.* **1.** To direct or aim: *pointed the flashlight down the road.* **2.** To direct attention toward something with or as if with the finger: *He pointed to the tree.* **3.** To be turned or directed, as in a given direction: *The compass needle pointed north.* **4.** To indicate (a direction, position, etc.): *She pointed the way to the settlement.* **5.** To provide with a point; sharpen: *He pointed the pole to use as a spear.* **6.** To emphasize; stress: *His comment pointed up his anger.* **7.** To show the location of animals hunted as game by standing still and facing in that direction, as a hunting dog does. —***phrasal verbs.*** **point off.** To supply (a numeral) with a decimal point or similar mark. **point out.** To make known, as by showing: *The librarian pointed out the merits of the new book.* **beside the point.** Not pertaining to the matter at hand; irrelevant. **in point.** Being considered: *three cases in point.* **make a point of.** To stick to a course of action, ideal, etc.: *make a point of being on time.* **stretch** (or **strain**) **a point. 1.** To make an exception. **2.** To exaggerate.

point•blank |point′blăngk′| *adj.* **1.** Aimed straight at a mark or target: *a pointblank shot.* **2.** Very close to a mark or target: *at pointblank range.* **3.** Straightforward; blunt: *a pointblank answer.* —*adv.* **1.** With a direct aim; straight: *He fired pointblank.* **2.** Without hesitating; bluntly: *answered pointblank.*

point•ed |poin′tĭd| *adj.* **1.** Having a sharp or tapered end or part: *pointed leaves.* **2.** Cutting;

pocketknife

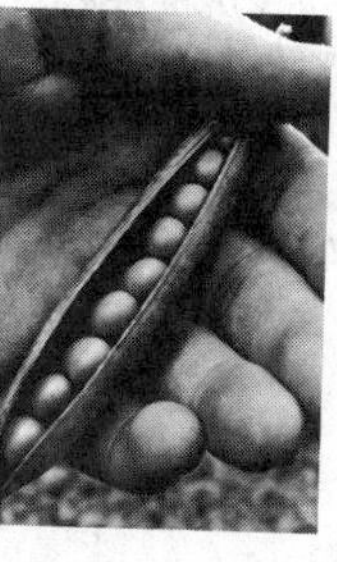
pod
pea pod

pogo stick

poison ivy

poke[1-2-3-4]
Poke[1] *is from Middle Dutch* poken, *"to strike, to thrust."* **Poke[2]** *in* **poke bonnet** *originally meant "projecting, sticking out" (referring to the brim of the bonnet); it is from* **poke[1]**. **Poke[3]** *is from Old French* poque, *a variant of* poche, *"bag, pocket"; see note at* **poach**. **Poke[4]** *is from Algonquian* pakon, *"bloody" (referring to the color of the berries).*

polar bear

pole[1-2]
Pole[1] *is from Greek* polos, *"turning point, pivot."* **Pole[2]** *was Old English* pāl, *which was borrowed from Latin* pālus, *"pointed stick"; see note at* **pale**.

ă pat/ā pay/â care/ä father/ĕ pet/ē be/ĭ pit/ī pie/î fierce/ŏ pot/ō go/ô paw, for/oi oil/ŏŏ book/ōō boot/ou out/ŭ cut/û fur/*th* the/th thin/hw which/zh vision/ə ago, item, pencil, atom, circus

piercing: *a pointed manner.* **3.** Clearly directed or aimed, as at a particular person: *a pointed remark.* **—point'ed•ly** *adv.* **—point'ed•ness** *n.*

point•er |**poin'**tər| *n.* **1.** Something that directs, indicates, or points. **2.** A marker, movable bar, etc., that indicates a number on a scale, as in a clock or meter. **3.** A long stick used for indicating something on a map, blackboard, etc. **4.** A dog with a short, smooth coat, often trained to hunt for and show the location of game by standing still and facing toward it. **5.** Information; advice: *pointers on buying rare stamps.*

point•less |**point'**lĭs| *adj.* **1.** Having no point. **2.** Having no purpose, sense, meaning, etc.: *a pointless question; a pointless regulation.*

point of view. **1.** The position from which something is observed or considered: *The story has more than one point of view.* **2.** The manner of viewing things; attitude: *a liberal point of view.*

poise |poiz| *v.* **poised, pois•ing.** **1.** To balance or be balanced: *He poised the flashlight on the edge of the table. She poised on the edge of the cliff.* **2.** To remain in one spot as if suspended: *A hummingbird poises over a flower.* —*n.* **1.** Balance; stability; equilibrium. **2.** Dignity and self-possession of manner; composure.

poi•son |**poi'**zən| *n.* **1.** Any substance that causes injury, sickness, or death, especially by chemical means. **2.** Anything that causes harm or destruction. —*v.* **1.** To kill or harm with poison. **2.** To put poison on or in. **3.** To have a harmful or destructive influence on: *poisoned their minds.* **—poi'soned** *adj.*: *a poisoned arrow.* —*adj.* Poisonous. **—poi'son•er** *n.*

poison ivy. A shrubby or climbing plant that has small, greenish berries and leaflets in groups of three and that can cause a severe, itching skin rash if touched. [SEE PICTURE]

poison oak. A plant related to and resembling poison ivy and causing a similar skin rash.

poi•son•ous |**poi'**zə nəs| *adj.* **1.** Capable of harming or killing, by or as if by poison. **2.** Containing poison. **3.** Full of ill will or enmity; malicious; malevolent: *poisonous remarks.* **—poi'son•ous•ly** *adv.*

poke[1] |pōk| *v.* **poked, pok•ing.** **1.** To give (someone) a sudden sharp jab, as with a finger or elbow: *poke someone in the ribs.* **2.** To thrust forward; push: *poked his head out the window. The otter's head poked out of the water.* **3.** To make repeated thrusting or jabbing motions: *The hungry bear poked at the empty barrel.* **4.** To make by thrusting or jabbing: *poke a hole in the canvas.* **5.** To stir with a poker or stick: *poke a fire.* **6.** To look or search in a leisurely manner: *I was just poking around the attic and came across this photograph.* **7.** To proceed in a slow or lazy manner: *The old jalopy is still poking along.* —*n.* A sudden sharp jab, especially with the finger or elbow. [SEE NOTE]
Idioms. **poke fun at.** To make fun of; kid. **poke (one's) nose into.** To pry or meddle in.

poke[2] |pōk| *n.* Also **poke bonnet.** A large bonnet with a rounded brim in front. [SEE NOTE]

poke[3] |pōk| *n.* A sack or bag. [SEE NOTE]
Idiom. **a pig in a poke.** Something offered for sale sight unseen.

poke[4] |pōk| *n.* Pokeweed. [SEE NOTE]

poke•ber•ry |**pōk'**bĕr'ē| *n., pl.* **-ber•ries.** **1.** The blackish-red berry of the pokeweed. **2.** The pokeweed plant itself.

pok•er[1] |**pō'**kər| *n.* A metal rod used to stir a fire.

pok•er[2] |**pō'**kər| *n.* A card game played by two or more persons who bet on the value of their hands in order to win a pool.

poke•weed |**pōk'**wēd'| *n.* A bushy plant with long clusters of small white flowers, blackish-red berries, and a poisonous root. The young shoots are sometimes eaten as greens.

pok•ey |**pō'**kē| *n., pl.* **pok•eys.** *Slang.* A jail.

pok•y or **pok•ey** |**pō'**kē| *adj.* **pok•i•er, pok•i•est.** **1.** Not lively; dull; slow: *a poky little town.* **2.** Small and crowded: *a poky apartment.*

Po•land |**pō'**lənd|. A country in central Europe. Population, 33,869,000. Capital, Warsaw.

po•lar |**pō'**lər| *adj.* **1.** Of, indicating, or measured in relation to a pole: *the polar region of a magnet.* **2.** Of or near the North Pole or the South Pole: *polar regions; a polar expedition.*

polar bear. A large white bear of far northern regions. [SEE PICTURE]

polar cap. **1.** Either of the masses of ice found in the polar regions of the earth. **2.** A polar region of a planet with a different appearance from the rest of the planet.

polar circle. **1.** The **Arctic Circle.** **2.** The **Antarctic Circle.**

Po•lar•is |pō **lăr'**ĭs| *or* |-**lâr'**-| *n.* A bright star near the North Pole of the celestial sphere.

po•lar•i•ty |pō **lăr'**ĭ tē| *or* |-**lâr'**-| *n., pl.* **po•lar•i•ties.** **1.** A basic division or separation into opposing or contrary types, as of a physical property: *electric polarity; magnetic polarity.* **2.** Either of a pair of opposite or contrary types or natures: *a negative electric polarity.*

po•lar•ize |**pō'**lə rīz'| *v.* **po•lar•ized, po•lar•iz•ing.** **1.** To cause polarity in; make polar. **2.** To cause the positive and negative electric charges in (a physical body or system) to become separated, either wholly or in part. **3.** To operate on light or other electromagnetic radiation so that the directions of its electric and magnetic effects can be predicted at any point. **4.** To set at opposite extremes, leaving no middle ground: *polarize public opinion.* **—po'lar•i•za'tion** *n.*

pole[1] |pōl| *n.* **1.** Either of the points at which an axis that passes through the center of a sphere intersects the surface of the sphere. **2.** Either of the points at which the earth's axis of rotation intersects the earth's surface; the North Pole or South Pole. **3.** A **celestial pole.** **4.** A **magnetic pole.** **5.** Either of a pair of oppositely charged electric terminals. **6.** A region at either extreme of a nucleus, cell, or organism that is distinct in form, structure, or function from the regions around it. **7.** The fixed point used as a reference in a system of polar coordinates. ¶*These sound alike* **pole, poll.** [SEE NOTE]

pole[2] |pōl| *n.* **1.** A long slender rod: *a fishing pole.* **2.** An upright post: *a telephone pole; a totem pole.* —*v.* **poled, pol•ing.** To push or move along by using a pole: *pole a boat down the river.* ¶*These sound alike* **pole, poll.** [SEE NOTE]

Pole |pōl| *n.* A native or inhabitant of Poland.

pole•ax or **pole•axe** |**pōl'**ăks'| *n.* A weapon, used in the Middle Ages, consisting of an ax and hammer combination mounted on a long pole.

pole•cat |pōl'kăt'| *n.* **1.** A weasellike animal of Europe, Asia, and northern Africa, having dark-brown fur. **2.** A skunk.

po•lem•ic |pə lĕm'ĭk| *n.* **1.** A controversial argument, especially an attack on a certain widely accepted doctrine or belief. **2. polemics** *(used with a singular verb).* The art or practice of arguing or debating controversial subjects. *—adj.* **1.** Likely to cause an argument; controversial: *polemic writings.* **2.** Inclined to argue; argumentative: *his polemic nature.*

pole•star |pōl'stär'| *n.* The star Polaris.

pole vault. An athletic contest in which each participant attempts to leap over a high crossbar using a long pole. [SEE PICTURE]

pole-vault |pōl'vôlt'| *v.* To perform or complete a pole vault. —**pole'-vault'er** *n.*

po•lice |pə lēs'| *n., pl.* **po•lice. 1.** The department of government established to maintain order, enforce the law, and prevent and detect crime. **2.** *(used with a plural verb).* The members of this department; policemen. —***modifier:*** *a police district; a police escort.* —*v.* **po•liced, po•lic•ing. 1.** To guard or patrol in order to maintain order. **2.** To clean or tidy up.

po•lice•man |pə lēs'mən| *n., pl.* **-men** |-mən|. A member of a police force.

pol•i•cy¹ |pŏl'ĭ sē| *n., pl.* **pol•i•cies.** A general plan, principle, outlook, or course of action followed by a government, individual, etc. [SEE NOTE]

pol•i•cy² |pŏl'ĭ sē| *n., pl.* **pol•i•cies.** A written contract of insurance between a company and an individual, specifying the premiums to be paid and the money awarded in the event of damage, injury, or death. [SEE NOTE]

po•li•o |pō'lē ō'| *n.* Poliomyelitis.

po•li•o•my•e•li•tis |pō'lē ō mī'ə lī'tĭs| *n.* A contagious virus disease that occurs mainly in children, causing, in its more severe forms, damage to the central system that results in paralysis, loss of muscle tissue, deformity, and often death.

pol•ish |pŏl'ĭsh| *v.* **1.** To make or become smooth and shiny, as by abrasion, chemical action, or both: *polish silver; a wood that polishes easily.* **2.** To refine or perfect to a high degree: *polish one's style of writing.* —**pol'ished** *adj.: polished manners; a polished performance.* —***phrasal verb.*** **polish off.** *Informal.* To finish or dispose of quickly and easily: *polish off a meal.* *—n.* **1.** A substance containing chemicals or an abrasive material for smoothing or shining a surface. **2.** Smoothness and shininess of a surface or finish. **3.** A high degree of refinement: *His performance lacks polish.* —**pol'ish•er** *n.*

Po•lish |pō'lĭsh| *n.* The Slavic language of Poland. *—adj.* Of Poland, the Poles, or their language.

po•lite |pə līt'| *adj.* **po•lit•er, po•lit•est. 1.** Having or showing good manners; courteous: *a polite girl; a polite note.* **2.** Refined: *polite society.* —**po•lite'ly** *adv.* —**po•lite'ness** *n.* [SEE NOTE]

pol•i•tic |pŏl'ĭ tĭk| *adj.* Showing good judgment; prudent; judicious: *a politic decision.*

po•lit•i•cal |pə lĭt'ĭ kəl| *adj.* **1.** Of or having to do with the structure or affairs of government: *a political system.* **2.** Of or having to do with politics or politicians: *a political party; a political campaign.* —**po•lit'i•cal•ly** *adv.* [SEE NOTE]

political science. The study of government and political institutions.

pol•i•ti•cian |pŏl'ĭ tĭsh'ən| *n.* **1.** A person active in politics, especially one holding a political office. **2.** A person who uses cunning and guile to achieve power or success.

pol•i•tics |pŏl'ĭ tĭks| *n.* **1.** *(used with a singular verb).* The art or science of government; political science. **2.** *(used with a singular verb).* The activities or affairs of a government, politician, or political party: *They never discuss politics at home.* **3.** *(used with a plural verb).* Intrigue or maneuvering within a group: *office politics.* **4.** *(used with a plural verb).* A person's general position or attitude on political subjects: *His politics are conservative.*

pol•i•ty |pŏl'ĭ tē| *n., pl.* **pol•i•ties. 1.** The form of government of a nation or state. **2.** A community or society living under a certain form of government.

Polk |pōk|, **James Knox.** 1795–1849. Eleventh President of the United States (1845–49).

pol•ka |pōl'kə| *or* |pō'kə| *n.* **1.** A lively round dance of central European origin, performed by couples. **2.** Music written to accompany or as if to accompany this dance. *—v.* **pol•kaed, pol•ka•ing.** To dance the polka.

pol•ka dot |pō'kə|. **1.** One of many round dots that are evenly spaced to form a pattern. **2.** A pattern or fabric with such dots.

poll |pōl| *n.* **1.** The casting and registering of votes in an election. **2. polls.** The place where votes are cast and counted. **3.** A survey made to determine public opinion on a particular question. **4.** The top of the head. *—v.* **1.** To receive (a given number of votes). **2.** To sample and record the opinions of: *polled the voters.* **3.** To cut the horns, upper branches, etc., from. ¶*These sound alike* **poll, pole.**

pol•len |pŏl'ən| *n.* Powderlike grains that contain the male reproductive cells of flowering plants and that unite with female reproductive cells, or egg cells, in the process of fertilization.

pol•li•nate |pŏl'ə nāt'| *v.* **pol•li•nat•ed, pol•li•nat•ing.** To fertilize by carrying or transferring pollen to the female part of (a flower or plant). —**pol'li•na'tion** *n.* —**pol'li•na'tor** *n.*

pol•li•wog |pŏl'ē wŏg'| *or* |-wôg'| *n.* A tadpole.

poll•ster |pōl'stər| *n.* A person who takes public-opinion surveys.

pol•lu•tant |pə lo͞ot'nt| *n.* Anything that pollutes, especially a waste material that makes the environment less suitable for living things.

pol•lute |pə lo͞ot'| *v.* **pol•lu•ted, pol•lu•ting.** To make unfit for or harmful to living things, especially by the addition of waste matter: *Sewage pollutes rivers.* —**pol•lut'er** *n.*

pol•lu•tion |pə lo͞o'shən| *n.* The contamination of air, water, etc., by harmful substances. —***modifier:*** *growing pollution problems.*

pol•ly•wog |pŏl'ē wŏg'| *or* |-wôg'| *n.* A form of the word **polliwog.**

po•lo |pō'lō| *n.* A sport played on a large field in which horseback riders use long-handled mallets to maneuver a ball, with the object of hitting the ball into the opposing team's goal.

Po•lo |pō'lō|, **Marco.** 1254?–1324? Venetian traveler who visited China.

pol•o•naise |pŏl'ə nāz'| *or* |pō'lə-| *n.* **1.** A

pole vault

policy¹·²

Policy¹ *is from Greek* politeia, *"government, constitution," from* polis, *"city."* **Polity** *is also from Greek* politeia, *and so is* **police,** *which originally meant "civil administration, enforcement of laws."* **Policy²** *was originally* policy of assurance, *meaning "document of insurance"; it is from Italian* polizza, *"document, proof," from Greek* apodeixis, *"demonstration, proof."*

polite/political

Polite *is from Latin* polītus, *"polished, refined," from* polīre, *"to polish."* **Political** *is from Greek* politikos, *"civic, concerned with citizenship and government," from* politēs, *"citizen," from* polis, *"city." See also note at* **policy.**

polygraph
The use of a polygraph as a "lie detector" depends on the observation that a person tends to breathe slightly faster, have higher blood pressure, perspire more, and have a higher pulse rate when he is lying than when he is telling the truth. Thus, by observing these responses and asking careful questions, a skillful investigator can often determine when someone is lying. The test is not, however, foolproof.

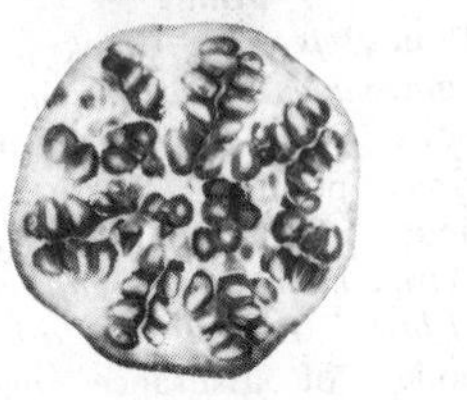

pomegranate
fruit
transverse section

poncho
Quechua Indian of Peru

ă pat/ā pay/â care/ä father/ĕ pet/ ē be/ĭ pit/ī pie/î fierce/ŏ pot/ ō go/ô paw, for/oi oil/o͝o book/ o͞o boot/ou out/ŭ cut/û fur/ *th* the/th thin/hw which/zh vision/ ə ago, item, pencil, atom, circus

stately, marchlike dance of Polish origin, consisting mainly of a promenade of couples. **2.** Music written to accompany or as if to accompany this dance.

po•lo•ni•um |pə lō′nē əm| *n.* Symbol **Po** One of the elements, a naturally radioactive metal produced by the disintegration of radium. It has 27 isotopes with mass numbers ranging from 192 to 218, of which the isotope Po 210, with a half-life of 138 days, is the most readily available. Atomic number 84; valences −2, +2, +4, +6; melting point 254°C; boiling point 962°C.

pol•troon |pŏl tro͞on′| *n.* An utter coward.

poly–. A word element meaning "more than one, many": **polygon.**

pol•y•es•ter |pŏl′ē ĕs′tər| *n.* Any of various light, strong, weather-resistant synthetic resins.

po•lyg•a•mist |pə lĭg′ə mĭst| *n.* Someone who practices polygamy.

po•lyg•a•my |pə lĭg′ə mē| *n.* The practice or condition of having more than one husband, wife, or mate at one time. —**po•lyg′a•mous** *adj.*

pol•y•glot |pŏl′ē glŏt′| *adj.* Knowing or speaking many languages. —*n.* A person who speaks many languages.

pol•y•gon |pŏl′ē gŏn′| *n.* A flat, closed geometric figure bounded by three or more line segments.

pol•y•graph |pŏl′ē grăf′| *or* |-gräf′| *n.* An instrument that simultaneously records changes in several body actions, such as blood pressure, pulse rate, and breathing rate, sometimes used to determine if a person is lying. [SEE NOTE]

pol•y•he•dron |pŏl′ē hē′drən| *n., pl.* **pol•y•he•drons** or **pol•y•he•dra** |pŏl′ē hē′drə|. A solid geometric figure bounded by polygons.

pol•y•mer |pŏl′ə mər| *n.* Any of a large number of natural or synthetic chemical compounds of extremely high molecular weight, formed of simple structural units, actually simple molecules, that are linked together into giant molecules.

pol•y•mer•ic |pŏl′ə mĕr′ĭk| *adj.* Of or consisting of a polymer or polymers.

po•lym•er•ize |pə lĭm′ə rīz′| *or* |pŏl′ə mə-| *v.* **po•lym•er•ized, po•lym•er•iz•ing.** To make or combine into a polymer. —**po•lym′er•i•za′tion** *n.*

Pol•y•ne•sia |pŏl′ə nē′zhə| *or* |-shə|. The islands in the Pacific Ocean generally east of the International Date Line.

Pol•y•ne•sian |pŏl′ə nē′zhən| *or* |-shən| *n.* **1.** A native of Polynesia. **2.** Any of the languages of Polynesia. —*adj.* Of Polynesia, the Polynesians, or their languages.

pol•y•no•mi•al |pŏl′ē nō′mē əl| *n.* **1.** An algebraic expression that is represented as the sum of two or more terms. **2.** An algebraic expression of the form $a_0x^n + a_1x^{n-1} + \ldots + a_{n-1}x + a_n$, where x is a real variable, a_0, a_1, etc., are a set of real coefficients in which $a_0 \neq 0$, and n is a positive integer called the degree of the polynomial. —***modifier:*** *a polynomial expression.*

pol•yp |pŏl′ĭp| *n.* **1.** A water animal, such as a coral, hydra, or sea anemone, having a hollow, tube-shaped body and a mouth opening surrounded by tentacles. **2.** An abnormal growth extending from the mucous membrane that lines an organ, such as the nose.

po•lyph•o•ny |pə lĭf′ə nē| *n.* The simultaneous combination of two or more independent melodic parts. —**pol′y•phon′ic** *adj.*

pol•y•sty•rene |pŏl′ē stī′rēn′| *n.* A clear, hard, rigid plastic resin that is easily colored and has a wide variety of uses. It is commonly used in the form of a solid foam as an insulator.

pol•y•syl•lab•ic |pŏl′ē sĭ lăb′ĭk| *adj.* Having more than three syllables: *a polysyllabic word.*

pol•y•tech•nic |pŏl′ē tĕk′nĭk| *adj.* Dealing with or instructing in many technical subjects.

pol•y•the•ism |pŏl′ē thē ĭz′əm| *n.* Belief in more than one god. —**pol′y•the′ist** *n.*

pol•y•un•sat•u•rat•ed |pŏl′ē ŭn săch′ə rā′tĭd| *adj.* Of organic compounds, especially fats, in which more than one pair of carbon atoms are joined by two or more bonds.

pol•y•ur•e•thane |pŏl′ē yo͝or′ə thān′| *n.* Any of various plastic resins used in making tough, resistant coatings, adhesives, and electrical insulation. —***modifier:*** *polyurethane varnish.*

po•made |pə măd′| *or* |-mäd′| *or* |pō-| *n.* A perfumed ointment for the hair.

pome•gran•ate |pŏm′grăn′ĭt| *or* |pŭm′-| *n.* **1.** A fruit with a tough, reddish rind and many small seeds, each enclosed in juicy red flesh with a pleasant, slightly sour taste. **2.** A tree that bears such fruit. —***modifier:*** *pomegranate seeds.* [SEE PICTURE]

Pom•er•a•ni•an |pŏm′ə rā′nē ən| *or* |-rān′yən| *n.* A small dog with long, silky hair.

pom•mel |pŭm′əl| *or* |pŏm′-| *n.* **1.** A knob on the handle of a sword. **2.** The raised part at the front of a saddle. —*v.* **pom•meled** or **pom•melled, pom•mel•ing** or **pom•mel•ling.** To beat severely.

pomp |pŏmp| *n.* Showy or stately display.

pom•pa•dour |pŏm′pə dôr′| *or* |-dōr′| *n.* A puffed-up hair style in which the hair is brushed straight up from the forehead.

pom•pa•no |pŏm′pə nō′| *or* |pŭm′-| *n., pl.* **pom•pa•no** or **pom•pa•nos.** A fish of warm Atlantic waters, having a flattened, silvery body and much valued as food.

pom•pom |pŏm′pŏm′| *n.* A form of the word **pompon.**

pom•pon |pŏm′pŏn′| *n.* **1.** A tuft or ball of wool, feathers, ribbon, etc., worn as a decoration, especially on a hat. **2.** A small, buttonlike chrysanthemum.

pom•pous |pŏm′pəs| *adj.* **1.** Acting with an air of great dignity and self-importance. **2.** Full of high-sounding words and phrases. —**pom′pous•ly** *adv.* —**pom•pos′i•ty** |pŏm pŏs′ĭ tē|, **pom′pous•ness** *n.*

Ponce de Le•ón |pŏns′ də lē′ən|, **Juan.** 1460?–1521. Spanish explorer; discoverer of Florida.

pon•cho |pŏn′chō| *n., pl.* **pon•chos.** **1.** A blanketlike cloak with a hole in the center for the head, worn in South America. **2.** A similar garment used as a raincoat. [SEE PICTURE]

pond |pŏnd| *n.* A still body of water, smaller than a lake.

pon•der |pŏn′dər| *v.* To think or consider carefully and at length: *She pondered the meaning of her dream. He pondered over the decision.*

pon•der•o•sa pine |pŏn′də rō′sə|. A tall pine tree of western North America, having heavy wood valued as lumber.

pon•der•ous |pŏn′dər əs| *adj.* **1.** Heavy, massive, and often clumsy: *In prehistoric times pon-*

derous creatures walked the earth. **2.** Long, detailed, and difficult to read or understand: *a ponderous history of the Middle Ages.* **—pon'der•ous•ly** *adv.* **—pon'der•ous•ness** *n.*

pon•iard |pŏn'yərd| *n.* A dagger.

pon•tiff |pŏn'tĭf'| *n.* **1.** A bishop. **2.** The pope.

pon•tif•i•cal |pŏn tĭf'ĭ kəl| *adj.* Of or having to do with a pope or bishop.

pon•tif•i•cate |pŏn tĭf'ĭ kāt'| *v.* **pon•tif•i•cat•ed, pon•tif•i•cat•ing.** To speak in a pompous way.

pon•toon |pŏn to͞on'| *n.* **1. a.** A flat-bottomed boat or other floating structure used to support a bridge. **b.** A floating structure that serves as a dock. **2.** One of the floats that supports a seaplane on water.

po•ny |pō'nē| *n., pl.* **po•nies. 1.** Any of several types or breeds of horses that are small in size when full-grown. **2.** *Informal.* A translation used in preparing foreign-language lessons.

pony express. A former system of carrying mail by relays of ponies, used between the Midwest and the Pacific coast.

pony tail. A hair style in which the hair is drawn back and fastened with a clip or band so that it hangs down like a horse's tail.

poo•dle |po͞od'l| *n.* A dog of a breed having thick, curly hair and ranging in size from the rather large standard poodle to the very small toy poodle. [SEE PICTURE]

pooh |po͞o| *interj.* A word used to express annoyance or disapproval.

pooh-pooh |po͞o'po͞o'| *v. Informal.* To dismiss as having no value: *He pooh-poohed the idea.*

pool[1] |po͞ol| *n.* **1.** A small, still body of water. **2.** A small collection of a liquid; a puddle: *a pool of molten steel.* **3.** A deep place in a river or stream. **4.** A **swimming pool.** [SEE NOTE]

pool[2] |po͞ol| *n.* **1.** A game played on a table that has pockets on the sides and corners, the object being to make a white ball strike one or more variously colored balls so they drop into the pockets. **2. a.** A game of chance, resembling a lottery, in which the contestants put money into a common fund that is later paid to the winner or winners. **b.** The fund containing the bets made in a game of chance or on a horse race. **3.** An arrangement for sharing the use of a number of persons, vehicles, etc.: *a car pool.* **—modifier:** *a pool table.* —*v.* To put into a common fund for use by all: *Several nations agreed to pool their iron resources.* [SEE NOTE]

poop[1] |po͞op| *n.* A raised structure in the stern of a ship. [SEE NOTE]

poop[2] |po͞op| *v. Slang.* To exhaust. [SEE NOTE]

poor |po͝or| *adj.* **poor•er, poor•est. 1.** Having little or no money or wealth; needy. **2.** Inferior; not up to standard; not up to expectations. **3.** Deserving of sympathy or pity; unfortunate.

poor•house |po͝or'hous'| *n., pl.* **-hous•es** |-hou'zĭz|. A place where poor people are maintained at public expense.

poor•ly |po͝or'lē| *adv.* In a poor way; badly.

pop[1] |pŏp| *n.* **1.** A sudden sharp, explosive sound: *The balloon burst with a pop.* **2.** A carbonated beverage: *soda pop.* **3.** A **pop fly. —modifier:** *a pop bottle.* —*v.* **popped, pop•ping. 1.** To make or cause to make a sound like a pop: *The children were popping corn. The fire crackled and popped.* **2.** To burst or cause to burst with a pop: *Be careful not to pop the balloon. Flash bulbs were popping all around.* **3.** To put quickly or suddenly: *pop the dinner into the oven.* **4.** To appear suddenly or unexpectedly: *I just popped in to say hello.* **5.** To open wide suddenly: *The magician had everyone's eyes popping.* **6.** In baseball, to hit a pop fly: *He popped out to the third baseman.* [SEE NOTE]

Idiom. **pop the question.** To propose marriage.

pop[2] |pŏp| *n. Informal.* Father. [SEE NOTE]

pop[3] |pŏp| *adj. Informal.* Popular: *pop music.* [SEE NOTE]

pop. population.

pop•corn |pŏp'kôrn'| *n.* **1.** A type of corn with hard kernels that burst when heated to form white, irregularly shaped puffs. **2.** The puffed kernels of this corn after heating.

pope |pōp| *n.* Often **Pope.** The bishop of Rome and head of the Roman Catholic Church.

pop fly. In baseball, a short high fly ball.

pop•gun |pŏp'gŭn'| *n.* A toy gun that shoots small corks with a popping noise.

pop•in•jay |pŏp'ən jā'| *n.* A vain, talkative, conceited person.

pop•lar |pŏp'lər| *n.* **1.** Any of several trees with triangular leaves and soft, light-colored wood. **2.** The wood of such a tree.

pop•lin |pŏp'lĭn| *n.* A strong fabric of silk, rayon, wool, or cotton with fine crosswise ridges. **—modifier:** *a poplin dress.*

pop•o•ver |pŏp'ō'vər| *n.* A light, puffy, hollow muffin. While baking, it expands and pops up over the rim of the pan.

pop•pa |pŏp'ə| *n. Informal.* Father.

pop•py |pŏp'ē| *n., pl.* **pop•pies. 1.** Any of several plants with showy, often bright-red flowers and milky juice. The small dark seeds of some kinds are used in cooking and baking. The **opium poppy** of Asia often has whitish flowers, and its juice is the source of opium, heroin, and other narcotic drugs. **2.** The flower of any of these plants.

pop•py•cock |pŏp'ē kŏk'| *n. Informal.* Foolish talk; nonsense.

pop•u•lace |pŏp'yə ləs| *n.* The common people; the masses. ¶*These sound alike* **populace, populous.**

pop•u•lar |pŏp'yə lər| *adj.* **1.** Well-liked; having many friends or admirers: *a popular teacher.* **2.** Of or representing the common people or the people at large: *the popular vote.* **2.** Enjoyed by many or most people: *a popular pastime.* **4.** Accepted or held by many people; widespread: *a popular notion.*

pop•u•lar•i•ty |pŏp'yə lăr'ĭ tē| *n.* The quality of being liked by many people.

pop•u•lar•ize |pŏp'yə lə rīz'| *v.* **pop•u•lar•ized, pop•u•lar•iz•ing.** To make popular; make known or understandable to the general public. **—pop'u•lar•i•za'tion** *n.*

pop•u•lar•ly |pŏp'yə lər lē| *adv.* Commonly; generally; by most people: *President Eisenhower was popularly known as "Ike."*

pop•u•late |pŏp'yə lāt'| *v.* **pop•u•lat•ed, pop•u•lat•ing. 1.** To supply with inhabitants: *populate a remote region.* **2.** To live in; inhabit.

pop•u•la•tion |pŏp'yə lā'shən| *n.* **1. a.** All of the people who live in a specified area. **b.** The total number of such people. **2.** The set of individuals, items, or data from which a statistical sample is

poodle

pool[1-2]

Pool[1] *was Old English* pōl, *"pond."* **Pool[2]** *is from French* poule, *"hen," also "collection of bets in a betting game"; it apparently comes from an old game called* jeu de la poule, *"game of the hen," in which the prize was a chicken.*

poop[1-2]

Poop[1] *is from Old French* poupe, *from Latin* puppis, *"stern of a ship."* **Poop[2]** *is of unknown origin.*

pop[1-2-3]

Pop[1] *is an imitative word.* **Pop[2]** *is a variant of* **papa. Pop[3]** *is shortened from* **popular.**

porcupine

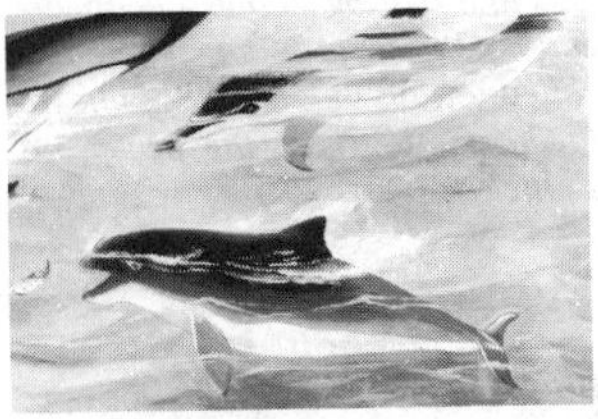

porpoise

port¹·²·³·⁴

Port¹ *is from Latin* portus, *"entrance, harbor."* **Port²** *dates only from the seventeenth century, while* **starboard** *is Old English; the original term for "left side of a ship" was* **larboard**, *but because this sounds so much like* **starboard** *it was abandoned in favor of* **port²**. *It is uncertain where the word* **port²** *comes from; it may be connected with* **port¹** *in some way.* **Port³** *is from Latin* porta, *"door," which is closely related to* portus, *"entrance."* **Port⁴** *is shortened from* Oporto *wine, "wine imported from Oporto, Portugal"; the name* Oporto *means "the port" in Portuguese, and is descended from Latin* portus, *"entrance, harbor."*

ă pat/ā pay/â care/ä father/ĕ pet/ ē be/ĭ pit/ī pie/î fierce/ŏ pot/ ō go/ô paw, for/oi oil/ŏŏ book/ ōō boot/ou out/ŭ cut/û fur/ *th* the/th thin/hw which/zh vision/ ə ago, item, pencil, atom, circus

taken. **3.** All the plants or animals of the same kind living in a particular region. —***modifier:*** *population density.*

pop·u·lous |pŏp′yə ləs| *adj.* Heavily populated; having many inhabitants. ¶*These sound alike* **populous, populace.**

por·ce·lain |pôr′sə lĭn| *or* |pōr′-| *n.* **1.** A hard, white, translucent material made by baking a fine clay at a high temperature and glazing it with one of several variously colored materials. **2.** An object or objects made of this material. —***modifier:*** *a porcelain figure; a porcelain inlay.*

porch |pôrch| *or* |pōrch| *n.* **1.** A roofed platform at the entrance to a house. **2.** A gallery or room attached to the outside of a building.

por·cine |pôr′sīn′| *adj.* Of, resembling, or typical of a pig or pigs: *a porcine snout.*

por·cu·pine |pôr′kyə pīn′| *n.* An animal, related to the rats and squirrels, having the back and sides covered with long, sharp spines, or quills, that serve as protection. [SEE PICTURE]

pore¹ |pôr| *or* |pōr| *n.* A tiny opening, as one of those in an animal's skin, through which perspiration passes or, on the surface of a leaf, through which water vapor, carbon dioxide, and oxygen pass. ¶*These sound alike* **pore, pour.**

pore² |pôr| *or* |pōr| *v.* **pored, por·ing.** To examine with great care and attention: *poring over old documents.* ¶*These sound alike* **pore, pour.**

por·gy |pôr′gē| *n., pl.* **por·gies** or **por·gy.** Any of several saltwater fishes used as food.

pork |pôrk| *or* |pōrk| *n.* The meat of a pig or hog used as food. —***modifier:*** *pork chops.*

pork·er |pôr′kər| *or* |pōr′-| *n.* A pig raised or fattened for use as food.

por·nog·ra·phy |pôr nŏg′rə fē| *n.* Indecent writing or pictures. —**por′no·graph′ic** *adj.*

po·ros·i·ty |pə rŏs′ĭ tē| *or* |pô-| *or* |pō-| *n., pl.* **po·ros·i·ties.** **1.** The condition or property of being porous. **2.** The degree to which something is porous: *a material of high porosity.*

po·rous |pôr′əs| *or* |pōr′-| *adj.* **1.** Full of or having pores. **2.** Full of small openings into or through which a liquid or gas can pass. —**po′rous·ly** *adv.* —**po′rous·ness** *n.*

por·phy·ry |pôr′fə rē| *n., pl.* **por·phy·ries.** A fine-grained igneous rock containing relatively large crystals, especially of feldspar or quartz.

por·poise |pôr′pəs| *n.* A sea animal related to the whales but smaller and usually having a short, blunt snout. [SEE PICTURE]

por·ridge |pôr′ĭj| *or* |pŏr′-| *n.* Oatmeal or other meal boiled in water or milk until thick.

por·rin·ger |pôr′ĭn jər| *or* |pŏr′-| A shallow cup or bowl with a handle.

port¹ |pôrt| *or* |pōrt| *n.* **1.** A harbor town where ships may dock. **2.** A place on a waterway or along a coast that provides a harbor or shelter for ships; a haven. [SEE NOTE]

port² |pôrt| *or* |pōrt| *n.* The left side of a ship or aircraft facing forward. —*adj.* On this side of a ship or aircraft: *a port cabin.* [SEE NOTE]

port³ |pôrt| *or* |pōrt| *n.* **1.** An opening in the side of a ship to let in air and light; a porthole. **2.** A slit or opening through which a gun may be fired. [SEE NOTE]

port⁴ |pôrt| *or* |pōrt| *n.* A sweet fortified wine. [SEE NOTE]

port·a·ble |pôr′tə bəl| *or* |pōr′-| *adj.* Easily or conveniently carried: *a portable radio.*

port·age |pôr′tĭj| *or* |pōr′-| *n.* **1.** The carrying of boats and supplies overland between waterways. **2.** The cost of doing this. **3.** A route by which this is done. —*v.* **port·aged, port·ag·ing. 1.** To transport by portage. **2.** To make a portage.

por·tal |pôrt′l| *or* |pōr′-| *n.* A doorway or entrance, especially a large, imposing one.

Port-au-Prince |pôrt′ō prĭns′| *or* |pōrt′-|. The capital of Haiti. Population, 300,000.

port·cul·lis |pôrt kŭl′ĭs| *or* |pōrt-| *n.* A grating suspended in the gateway of a fortified place so that it can be lowered quickly in case of attack.

por·tend |pôr tĕnd′| *or* |pōr-| *v.* To serve as an advance indication of; presage: *an incident that portends further trouble.*

por·tent |pôr′tĕnt′| *or* |pōr′-| *n.* **1.** An indication of something that is about to occur. **2.** Great or ominous significance: *a vision of dire portent.*

por·ten·tous |pôr tĕn′təs| *or* |pōr-| *adj.* **1.** Indicating trouble or calamity: *a portentous silence.* **2.** Of great significance: *a portentous event.* —**por·ten′tous·ly** *adv.*

por·ter |pôr′tər| *or* |pōr′-| *n.* **1.** A person hired to carry baggage at a station, airport, or hotel. **2.** An attendant who waits on passengers in a sleeping car or other railroad car. **3.** A person hired to do cleaning and other menial tasks in a store, office building, school, factory, etc.

por·ter·house |pôr′tər hous′| *or* |pōr′-| *n., pl.* **-hous·es** |-hou′zĭz|. A cut of beef taken from the loin, with a T-shaped bone and a sizable tenderloin.

port·fo·li·o |pôrt fō′lē ō′| *or* |pōrt-| *n., pl.* **port·fo·li·os. 1.** A portable case for holding loose papers, documents, etc. **2.** The office or post of a cabinet member or minister of state. **3.** The stocks, bonds, or other securities held by an investor or financial institution.

port·hole |pôrt′hōl′| *or* |pōrt′-| *n.* A small circular window in a ship's side.

por·ti·co |pôr′tĭ kō′| *or* |pōr′-| *n., pl.* **por·ti·coes** or **por·ti·cos.** A porch or walkway with a roof supported by columns.

por·tion |pôr′shən| *or* |pōr′-| *n.* **1.** A part of a whole; a section or quantity of a larger thing: *the solid portion of a design. A portion of your paycheck is withheld to pay taxes.* **2.** A single helping of food: *a portion of mashed potatoes.* —*v.* To distribute in portions; parcel out.

Port·land |pôrt′lənd| *or* |pōrt′-|. **1.** The largest city in Oregon. Population, 366,383. **2.** The largest city in Maine. Population, 61,572.

Portland cement. A cement that hardens after being mixed with water, made by roasting a mixture of minerals and other material that contains calcium, and used in making concrete.

Port Lou·is |lōō′ĭs| *or* |lōō′ē|. The capital of Mauritius. Population, 142,000.

port·ly |pôrt′lē| *or* |pōrt′-| *adj.* **port·li·er, port·li·est.** Fat or stout, especially in a dignified or imposing way: *a portly senator.* —**port′li·ness** *n.*

Port Mores·by |môrz′bē| *or* |mōrz′-|. The capital of Papua New Guinea, on the southeastern coast of New Guinea. Population, 50,000.

Port of Spain. The capital of Trinidad and Tobago. Population, 63,000.

Por·to-No·vo |pôr′tō nō′vō|. The capital of Benin. Population, 80,000.

por•trait |pôr′trĭt′| *or* |-trāt′| *or* |pōr′-| *n.* A painting, photograph, or other likeness of a person, especially one showing the face. —*modifier: a portrait painter.*

por•trai•ture |pôr′trĭ chər| *or* |pōr′-| *n.* The art of making portraits.

por•tray |pôr trā′| *or* |pōr-| *v.* **1.** To show by means of a picture: *an attempt to portray a mother's sorrow.* **2.** To describe or picture through the use of words: *The novel portrays colonial life.* **3.** To play on stage or on the screen: *portray a role; portray Lincoln.*

por•tray•al |pôr trā′əl| *or* |pōr-| *n.* The act of portraying, representing, or acting: *a brilliant portrayal of the leading role.*

Por•tu•gal |pôr′chə gəl| *or* |pōr′-|. A country in southwestern Europe, in the western part of the Iberian Peninsula. Population, 9,000,000. Capital, Lisbon.

Por•tu•guese |pôr′chə gēz′| *or* |-gēs′| *or* |pōr′-| *n., pl.* **Por•tu•guese. 1.** A native or inhabitant of Portugal. **2.** The Romance language of Portugal and Brazil. —*adj.* Of Portugal, the Portuguese, or their language.

Portuguese man-of-war. A tropical sea organism having a bluish, balloonlike floating part and many long, stinging tentacles that can cause serious injury. [SEE PICTURE]

pose |pōz| *v.* **posed, pos•ing. 1.** To assume or place in a certain position, as for a portrait or photograph: *The children posed in front of the fireplace.* **2.** To make oneself out to be someone or something that one is not: *caught posing as a detective.* **3.** To present, raise, or put forward: *pose a threat; pose a question.* —*n.* **1.** A position assumed or taken, as for a portrait or photograph. **2.** A false appearance or attitude; a pretense: *His outer cheerfulness is only a pose.*

Po•sei•don |pō sīd′n|. The Greek god of the sea.

posh |pŏsh| *adj.* Smart and fashionable.

pos•it |pŏz′ĭt| *v.* To put forward as a fact or assumption; postulate.

po•si•tion |pə zĭsh′ən| *n.* **1.** The place where someone or something is located: *the position of the sun in the sky.* **2.** The right or proper place of a person or thing: *The guns are in position.* **2.** The way in which something or someone is placed or arranged: *Try not to sit in one position too long.* **4.** An advantageous place or location: *jockeys maneuvering for position.* **5.** A situation as it relates to the surrounding circumstances: *You've put me in an awkward position.* **6.** A point of view or attitude on a certain question: *What is your position on the issue of gun control?* **7.** A post of employment; a job: *an important position in the government.* **8.** In sports, the area or station assigned to each member of a team: *defensive positions.* —*v.* To place in proper position: *position a gun for firing.*

pos•i•tive |pŏz′ĭ tĭv| *adj.* **1.** Expressing affirmation or approval; favorable: *a positive answer; a positive statement.* **2.** Affirmative; constructive: *a positive approach to the problem.* **3.** Indicating agreement or acceptance: *a positive response.* **4. a.** Absolutely certain: *I'm positive about that.* **b.** Leaving no room for doubt or question: *positive proof.* **5.** Indicating that a suspected disease, disorder, or microorganism is present. **6. a.** Greater than zero: *a positive integer.* **b.** Of the sign (+) used to indicate a positive number or one that is to be added. **7.** Of or having an electric charge capable of neutralizing a charge like that carried by an electron and, therefore, tending to attract electrons. **8.** Indicating a response in which a living thing moves toward a stimulus: *a positive reaction to light.* **9.** Of the simple, uncompared degree of an adjective or adverb as distinguished from the comparative or superlative degree. —*n.* **1.** A positive answer. **2.** In grammar: **a.** A word or part of a word that expresses affirmation; for example, *yes* and *pro-* are positives. **b.** The positive degree of an adjective or adverb. **3. the positive.** The side in a debate that agrees with the statement being debated. **4. a.** A photographic image in which the light and dark areas are arranged as they normally occur. **b.** A film or photographic plate containing such an image. **5.** A positive number. —**pos′i•tive•ness** *n.*

Idiom. **in the positive.** In a sense or manner indicating affirmation: *answered in the positive.*

positive electrode. A positively charged electrode; anode.

pos•i•tive•ly |pŏz′ĭ tĭv lē| *adv.* **1.** In a positive manner: *think positively. Protons are positively charged.* **2.** |*also* pŏz′ĭ tĭv′lē|. Absolutely: *It's positively driving me crazy.*

pos•i•tron |pŏz′ĭ trŏn′| *n.* The antiparticle that corresponds to the electron.

pos•se |pŏs′ē| *n.* A body of men summoned by a sheriff to aid in maintaining the peace.

pos•sess |pə zĕs′| *v.* **1.** To have or own. **2.** To gain control over; dominate the mind or thoughts of: *Fury possessed him.* —**pos•ses′sor** *n.*

pos•sessed |pə zĕst′| *adj.* **1.** Having or owning: *possessed of almost superhuman strength.* **2.** Seized by a very powerful emotion or as if by an evil spirit: *behaving like a man possessed.*

pos•ses•sion |pə zĕsh′ən| *n.* **1.** The fact or condition of having or possessing something: *Both teams fought for possession of the ball. An apostrophe is used to show possession.* **2.** Something that is owned or possessed: *leaving most of their possessions behind.* **3.** A territory ruled by an outside power: *The Philippine Islands were once a possession of the United States.*

pos•ses•sive |pə zĕs′ĭv| *adj.* **1.** Having a desire to dominate, own, or control: *a possessive mother.* **2.** Of or indicating possession: *a possessive adjective.* —*n.* **1.** The **possessive case. 2.** A word in the possessive case. —**pos•ses′sive•ly** *adv.* —**pos•ses′sive•ness** *n.*

possessive adjective. A term applied to a personal or relative pronoun in the possessive case in constructions in which the thing possessed is expressed. In the sentences *This is my duty* and *The girl whose dress was red left early,* the possessive adjectives are *my* and *whose.*

possessive case. In grammar, the form of a noun or pronoun that indicates possession. In the sentences *Bill's car was being repaired* and *Mary gave John her books, Bill's* and *her* are in the possessive case.

possessive pronoun. One of several pronouns denoting possession and capable of substituting for noun phrases. The possessive pronouns are *mine, his, hers, its, ours, yours, theirs,* and *whose.*

Portuguese man-of-war
The **Portuguese man-of-war** is not strictly a single animal but a colony of several different kinds of small organisms, each having its own function.

post[1-2-3]

Post[1] *was Old English* post, *which was borrowed from Latin* postis, *"post, door post."* **Post[2]** *is from Italian* posto, *from Latin* positum, *"station, position."* **Post[3]** *originally meant "relay station for mail" (now sense* **2***); it is from Italian* posta, *which is from Latin* posita, *"station." Both* positum *and* posita *basically meant "something placed or positioned, a fixed station," and both are from* positus, *the past participle of* pōnere, *"to place." (The prefix* **post-** *is from Latin* post, *"after.")*

postage stamp
U.S. two-cent stamp (1928)

ă pat/ā pay/â care/ä father/ĕ pet/ ē be/ĭ pit/ī pie/î fierce/ŏ pot/ ō go/ô paw, fôr/oi oil/o͝o book/ o͞o boot/ou out/ŭ cut/û fur/ *th* the/th thin/hw which/zh vision/ ə ago, item, pencil, atom, circus

pos•si•bil•i•ty |pŏs′ə **bĭl′**ĭ tē| *n., pl.* **pos•si•bil•i•ties. 1.** The fact or condition of being possible: *the possibility of life on Mars.* **2.** Something that is possible: *His promotion now seems a possibility.* **3.** Someone or something that is capable of being chosen or winning a contest: *an outside possibility in the pennant race.* **4. possibilities.** Potentially favorable results: *The idea has tremendous possibilities.*

pos•si•ble |**pŏs′**ə bəl| *adj.* **1.** Capable of happening, existing, or being accomplished: *prepared for all possible occurrences. It may be possible to get there by helicopter.* **2.** Capable of being used for a certain purpose: *a possible site for the new capital.*

pos•si•bly |**pŏs′**ə blē| *adv.* **1.** Perhaps: *He hesitated for a moment, possibly remembering his sad experience the last time.* **2.** Conceivably: *Could they possibly be here already?* **3.** Under any circumstances: *I can't possibly do it.*

pos•sum |**pŏs′**əm| *n.* An animal, the opossum. ***Idiom.* play possum.** To pretend to be dead or unconscious, as an opossum does when frightened or in danger.

post[1] |pōst| *n.* **1.** A piece of wood or other material set upright in the ground to serve as a marker or support. **2.** The starting gate at a race-track. **3.** A small projecting metal rod around which a wire is wrapped to make an electrical connection, often threaded to accept a nut that holds the connection tight, as on a dry cell. *—v.* To put up in a prominent place for everyone to see: *The winners' names will be posted on the bulletin board.* [SEE NOTE]

post[2] |pōst| *n.* **1.** A military base at which troops are stationed: *an army post.* **2.** A local organization of military veterans: *an American Legion post.* **3.** An assigned position or station, as of a guard or sentry: *a lookout post.* **4.** A position of employment, especially an appointed public office: *a high post in the government.* **5.** A place to which a person is assigned for duty: *an overseas post.* ***—modifier:*** *the post hospital. —v.* **1.** To assign to a post or station: *post a sentry. The ambassador was posted to Tokyo.* **2.** To put forward; present: *post bail.* [SEE NOTE]

post[3] |pōst| *n.* **1.** *Chiefly British.* **a.** The transportation and delivery of mail: *letters sent by post.* **b.** The mail delivered: *the morning post.* **2.** In former times, one of a series of stations along a mail route, furnishing fresh horses and riders. *—v.* **1.** *Chiefly British.* To mail (a letter). **2.** To inform of the latest news: *I try to keep posted on current events.* **3.** In bookkeeping, to transfer (figures) to a ledger. [SEE NOTE]

post–. A prefix meaning: **1.** After in time; later: **postoperative. 2.** After in position; behind: **postscript.**

post•age |**pō′**stĭj| *n.* The charge for sending something by mail.

postage stamp. A small engraved piece of paper, usually with an adhesive on the back, that is issued by a government for an amount indicated on the front. It is placed on a letter, package, etc., as a means of paying the charge for mailing the item. [SEE PICTURE]

post•al |**pō′**stəl| *adj.* Of the post office or mail service: *postal rates; postal service.*

postal card. A card printed with a postage stamp, used for sending messages through the mail at a rate less than that charged for a letter.

post•card |**pōst′**kärd′| *n.* Also **post card. 1.** A **postal card. 2.** A card used for sending short messages through the mail, usually containing a picture on one side, with space on the other side for a postage stamp, an address, and a short message.

post•date |pōst **dāt′**| *v.* **-dat•ed, -dat•ing.** To put a date on (a check, letter, or document) that is later than the actual date.

post•er |**pō′**stər| *n.* A large printed notice or announcement, often illustrated, posted to advertise or publicize something.

pos•te•ri•or |pŏ **stîr′**ē ər| *adj.* **1. a.** Of, in, or near the side of the human body in which the spine is located. **b.** Of, in, or near the part of an animal body that is close to the tail. **2.** Following in time; later; subsequent. *—n.* The buttocks.

pos•ter•i•ty |pŏ **stĕr′**ĭ tē| *n.* **1.** Future generations: *He left a rich body of literature to posterity.* **2.** A person's descendants.

pos•tern |**pō′**stərn| *or* |**pŏs′**tərn| *n.* A small rear gate, especially in a fort or castle.

post exchange. A store on a military base for the sale of merchandise to military personnel and their families at reduced prices.

post•grad•u•ate |pōst **grăj′**o͞o ĭt| *or* |-āt′| *adj.* Of or taking courses beyond the level of a bachelor's degree: *postgraduate courses. —n.* A person taking such courses.

post•haste |**pōst′hāst′**| *adv.* With great speed; hastily; rapidly.

post•hu•mous |**pŏs′**chə məs| *or* |-cho͞o-| *adj.* **1.** Occurring or continuing after one's death: *a posthumous award.* **2.** Published after the author's death: *a posthumous book.* **3.** Born after the death of the father: *a posthumous child.* **—post′hu•mous•ly** *adv.*

post•man |**pōst′**mən| *n., pl.* **-men** |-mən|. A mailman.

post•mark |**pōst′**märk′| *n.* A mark stamped on a piece of mail that cancels the stamp and records the date and place of mailing. *—v.* To stamp with a postmark.

post•mas•ter |**pōst′**măs′tər| *or* |-mä′stər| *n.* A man in charge of a post office.

post-mor•tem |pōst **môr′**təm| *adj.* **1.** Occurring or done after death. **2.** Of a post-mortem examination. *—n.* **1.** A **post-mortem examination. 2.** An analysis or review of an event that has just taken place.

post-mortem examination. A medical or scientific investigation, especially an autopsy, of a corpse.

post•na•sal |pōst **nā′**zəl| *adj.* Of, in, or from the part of the respiratory system that is located in back of the nose.

post•na•tal |pōst **nāt′**l| *adj.* Of, happening, or done in the time immediately after birth: *postnatal care.*

post office. 1. The public department responsible for the transportation and delivery of the mails. **2.** A local office where mail is sorted, stamps are sold, etc.

post•op•er•a•tive |pōst **ŏp′**ər ə tĭv| *or* |**-ŏp′**rə-| *or* |**-ŏp′**ə rā′-| *adj.* Happening or done after a surgical operation: *postoperative care.*

post•paid |pōst′pād′| *adj.* With the postage paid in advance: *a postpaid reply card.* [SEE NOTE]

post•pone |pōst **pōn′**| *v.* **post•poned, post•pon•ing.** To put off until a later time: *It may be wise to postpone your visit.* —**post•pone′ment** *n.*

post•script |**pōst′**skrĭpt′| *n.* **1.** A message added at the end of a letter, after the writer's signature. **2.** Something added to a book, article, etc.

pos•tu•late |**pŏs′**chə lāt′| *v.* **pos•tu•lat•ed, pos•tu•lat•ing.** To assume the truth or existence of (something) without proof, especially as a basis for study or discussion; accept as an axiom; take for granted: *Aristotle postulated an "Unmoved Mover" working endlessly to keep the planets in motion.* —*n.* |**pŏs′**chə lĭt| *or* |-lāt′|. Something, such as a theory or statement, assumed to be true without proof, especially a secondary axiom.

pos•ture |**pŏs′**chər| *n.* **1.** The way in which a person holds or carries his body; carriage: *a person who has good posture.* **2.** A position or arrangement of the body or its parts: *a kneeling posture.* **3.** An intellectual attitude, tendency, or position; stance: *a defensive posture.* —*v.* **pos•tured, pos•tur•ing.** To assume a pose or attitude, especially an exaggerated or unnatural one: *The puppets danced and postured on their strings.*

post•war |**pōst′wôr′**| *adj.* After a certain war: *World War I and the postwar period.*

po•sy |**pō′**zē| *n., pl.* **po•sies.** A flower or bunch of flowers.

pot |pŏt| *n.* **1.** A deep, rounded container made of metal, earthenware, etc., and used for cooking, holding food or liquid, and many other purposes: **a.** One in which plants are grown, often made of baked clay or plastic material. **b.** One used for making and serving coffee or tea. **c.** Also **chamber pot.** A portable one used as a toilet. **d.** A decorative ceramic one of any size or shape. **2. a.** A pot with something in it: *a pot of soup; a pot of geraniums.* **b.** The amount that a pot holds: *make a pot of coffee.* **3.** A trap for lobsters, fish, or eels, consisting of a wooden, wire, or wicker cage or basket: *a lobster pot.* **4.** In poker and other card games, the total amount of money bet by all the players on the outcome of a hand: *Who won the pot?* **5.** *Informal.* A fund to which the members of a group contribute for their common use. **6.** *Slang.* Marijuana. —*v.* **pot•ted, pot•ting. 1.** To plant or put in a pot: *She potted the tulip bulbs.* **2.** To preserve (meat, fish, etc.) in a pot, jar, or can. **3.** To shoot (a game animal or bird) at rest, especially for use as food: *He potted a sitting duck.* —**pot′ted** *adj.: a potted plant; potted meat.*

***Idiom.* go to pot.** To become bad; go to ruin; deteriorate.

po•ta•ble |**pō′**tə bəl| *adj.* Fit to drink: *potable water.* —*n.* **potables.** Liquids that are fit for drinking; drinks; beverages.

pot•ash |**pŏt′**ăsh′| *n.* Any of several chemical compounds that contain potassium, especially a strongly alkaline material obtained from wood ashes.

po•tas•si•um |pə **tăs′**ē əm| *n.* Symbol **K** One of the elements, a soft, lightweight, highly reactive, silver-white metal. Atomic number 19; atomic weight 39.10; valence +1; melting point 63.65°C; boiling point 774°C.

potassium bi•tar•trate |bī **tär′**trāt′|. A white powder that has the formula $KHC_4H_4O_6$, used in baking powder and in laxatives.

potassium carbonate. A strongly alkaline white powder that has the formula K_2CO_3. It is used in making glass, pigments, and soaps.

potassium hydroxide. A corrosive solid that is a strong alkali and has the formula KOH. It is used in bleaching and in making soaps and detergents.

po•ta•to |pə **tā′**tō| *n., pl.* **po•ta•toes. 1.** Also **white potato** or **Irish potato.** The starchy tuber, or enlarged underground stem, of a widely grown plant, eaten as a vegetable. **2.** A plant that bears such tubers. **3.** See **sweet potato.** —***modifier:*** *potato salad.* [SEE NOTE & PICTURE]

potato chip. A thin slice of potato fried until crisp and then salted.

Pot•a•wat•o•mi |pŏt′ə **wŏt′**ə mē| *n., pl.* **Pot•a•wat•o•mi** or **Pot•a•wat•o•mis. 1.** A North American Indian tribe of Michigan. **2.** A member of this tribe. **3.** The Algonquian language of this tribe.

pot•bel•ly |**pŏt′**bĕl′ē| *n., pl.* **-bel•lies.** An abdomen that sags or sticks out.

po•tent |**pōt′**nt| *adj.* **1.** Strong, powerful, or forceful; mighty: *a potent ruler.* **2.** Having a powerful influence on the mind or feelings; highly effective: *The narratives of former slaves became a potent weapon in the battle against slavery.* **3.** Having or capable of having strong effects on a living organism: *a potent drug; a potent poison.* —**po′ten•cy** |**pōt′**n sē| *n.*

po•ten•tate |**pōt′**n tāt′| *n.* A person who has the power and position to rule over others; a monarch; ruler.

po•ten•tial |pə **tĕn′**shəl| *adj.* **1.** Possible or future, though not yet actual, definite, or real: *potential buyers; potential problems.* **2.** Capable of being developed, realized, or used: *the sea as a potential source of minerals.* —*n.* **1.** Capacity for further growth, development, or progress; promise: *a program to encourage students high in potential but low in hope.* **2.** The potential energy of a unit electric charge at any point in an electric circuit or field, measured with respect to a given reference point in the circuit or field. —**po•ten′tial•ly** *adv.*

potential energy. 1. The energy that a particle or system of particles derives from position in a field of force rather than from motion. See **kinetic energy. 2.** Energy that is stored as an unrelieved strain in a material object, such as a coiled spring, that is stored in chemical bonds or that is stored in some form in which it can remain for an indefinite time with no motion involved.

po•ten•ti•al•i•ty |pə tĕn′shē **ăl′**ĭ tē| *n., pl.* **po•ten•ti•al•i•ties. 1.** Capacity for growth, development, or progress: *estimating a student's potentiality.* **2.** An ability, quality, tendency, or talent that can be developed: *choosing applicants according to their qualifications and potentialities.*

po•ten•ti•om•e•ter |pə tĕn′shē **ŏm′**ĭ tər| *n.* **1.** An electrical device consisting of a resistor provided with a movable tap that can be located so that the ratio of the resistance of the two parts into which the resistor is divided has any desired value. Devices of this kind are used in radios and

postpaid

Postpaid *is not, as is sometimes thought, the opposite of* **prepaid.** *The post- in* **postpaid** *is not the prefix* **post-** *but the noun* **post[3]**. *Thus a* **postpaid** *package is one on which the postage has been paid in advance.*

potato

Potato plant showing root system with tubers and *(above)* flowers

In the early sixteenth century the Spanish found a plant with edible roots growing in Haiti; the Taino people there called it *batata,* which in English became **potato**. Later in the same century the Spanish found another (unrelated) root plant cultivated on the east coast of South America; when the English obtained this plant they at first called it the *bastard potato* but later simply the **potato**; and the original *batata* was renamed the **sweet potato**.

potlatch
Potlatch *is a Chinook Indian word, coming from the Nootka word* patshatl, *"giving" or "gift."*

potter's wheel

pound1-2-3
Pound1 *was Old English* pund, *"weight," which was borrowed from Latin* pondo, *"weight."* **Pound**2 *was Old English* pūnian, *"to crush."* **Pound**3 *was Old English* pund-, *"enclosure."*

ă pat/ā pay/â care/ä father/ĕ pet/ ē be/ĭ pit/ī pie/î fierce/ŏ pot/ ō go/ô paw, for/oi oil/o͝o book/ o͞o boot/ou out/ŭ cut/û fur/ *th* the/th thin/hw which/zh vision/ ə ago, item, pencil, atom, circus

television sets as volume controls, brightness controls, etc. **2.** A specially calibrated device of this type used to compare an unknown voltage to a standard voltage.

po•tion |pō′shən| *n.* A drink or dose of liquid used to cure, kill, bring on sleep, or cast a magic spell: *a sleeping potion; a love potion.*

pot•latch |pŏt′lăch′| *n.* A ceremonial feast among Indian tribes living on the northwest Pacific coast, in which the host gives valuables away or destroys them to show how rich he is and to gain social prestige. [SEE NOTE]

pot•luck |pŏt′lŭk′| *n.* Whatever food happens to be available for a meal, especially when offered to a guest invited at the last minute.

Po•to•mac River |pə tō′mək|. A river flowing into Chesapeake Bay, forming the boundary between Maryland and Virginia.

pot•pie |pŏt′pī′| *n.* A mixture of meat and vegetables covered with a crust of pastry and baked in a deep dish.

pot•pour•ri |pō′po͞o rē′| *n.* **1.** A fragrant mixture of dried flower petals and spices in a jar or box. **2.** A miscellaneous collection or assortment; a medley: *The book was a potpourri of poems, legends, songs, and sayings.*

pot shot. **1.** A shot fired without taking careful aim or fired at a target within easy range. **2.** A criticism made without careful thought and aimed at a handy target for attack: *disgruntled citizens taking pot shots at the mayor.*

pot•tage |pŏt′ĭj| *n.* A thick soup or stew.

pot•ter1 |pŏt′ər| *n.* A person who makes pots, dishes, or other objects from clay.

pot•ter2 |pŏt′ər| *v.* To keep oneself busy with aimless activity or trivial tasks; putter: *pottering around with some minor chores.*

potter's field. A piece of ground in which poor or unknown persons and sometimes criminals are buried.

potter's wheel. A disk or turntable on which a mass of clay is spun as a potter shapes it by hand or with hand tools.

pot•ter•y |pŏt′ə rē| *n., pl.* **pot•ter•ies.** **1.** Objects, such as pots, vases, or dishes, shaped from moist clay and hardened by heat. **2.** The art, craft, or work of a potter. **3.** The place where a potter works. ***—modifier:*** *a pottery dish.*

pouch |pouch| *n.* **1.** A small or medium-sized bag of flexible material, such as cloth or leather, used for holding or carrying various things: *a mail pouch; a tobacco pouch; a cartridge pouch.* **2.** A baglike or pocketlike body part, such as the one in which a kangaroo, opossum, or other marsupial carries its young or the one in which a pelican catches and holds fish. **3.** A baglike or puffy part, such as a fold of flesh: *He had pouches under his eyes.*

poul•tice |pōl′tĭs| *n.* A soft, moist, sticky mixture, usually heated, spread on cloth and applied to an aching or inflamed part of the body.

poul•try |pōl′trē| *n.* **1.** Chickens, turkeys, ducks, geese, or similar birds raised for their eggs or meat. **2.** The flesh of such birds, eaten as food. ***—modifier:*** *a poultry farm.*

pounce |pouns| *v.* **pounced, pounc•ing.** To spring or swoop suddenly so as to seize something, as a cat or hawk does in catching its prey: *The playful kitten pounced on the bouncing rubber ball. The salesman pounced at the prospective buyer.* —*n.* The action of pouncing.

pound1 |pound| *n., pl.* **pounds** or **pound.** **1. a.** A unit of avoirdupois weight equal to 16 ounces or 7,000 grains. **b.** A unit of apothecary weight equal to 5,760 grains or 0.823 avoirdupois pound. **2.** A unit of force equal to the downward force exerted by a one-pound weight where the acceleration of gravity is 32.174 feet per second per second, equivalent to a force of 4.448 newtons. **3.** Also **pound sterling. a.** The basic unit of money of the United Kingdom. **b.** The basic unit of money of Ireland, Malta, and various dependent territories of the United Kingdom. **4.** The basic unit of money of Cyprus, Israel, Lebanon, Sudan, Syria, and Egypt. [SEE NOTE]

pound2 |pound| *v.* **1.** To hit, strike, beat, or knock forcefully, often repeatedly: *Pound the nail into the board. The surf pounded against the rocks.* **2.** To beat, throb, or thump rapidly or violently: *Her heart was pounding with excitement.* **3.** To move or move over with a thudding, thumping, or rumbling sound: *Jack heard the giant pounding down the hall. The feet of the cattle pounded the ground.* **4.** To crush to a powder or pulp: *pounding corn into meal.* **—pound′ing** *adj.: the thunder of pounding hoofs.* —*n.* **1.** A heavy blow. **2.** The sound of a heavy blow. [SEE NOTE]

pound3 |pound| *n.* An enclosed place, such as a pen, kennel, or corral, used for confining stray animals or livestock or for trapping wild animals or fish: *the city dog pound.* [SEE NOTE]

pound-fool•ish |pound′fo͞o′lĭsh| *adj.* See **penny-wise.**

pour |pôr| *or* |pōr| *v.* **1. a.** To cause (a fluid or loose particles) to flow in a steady stream: *When you pour the milk, pour slowly.* **b.** To serve (a drink or drinks) by letting liquid flow from a larger container into a glass, cup, etc.: *Mary poured herself a glass of lemonade. Janet's sister poured during the tea.* **c.** To empty or drain by pouring: *The workmen poured the last bucket of concrete. Pour off the excess grease.* **2. a.** To flow or run freely: *Salt pours easily.* **b.** To stream or gush in or as if in a flood: *The rain poured down in torrents.* **c.** To rain hard: *It isn't sprinkling, it's pouring.* **3.** To come or go in large numbers or amounts; swarm or flood: *Immigrants continued to pour into the cities.* **4.** To supply or send forth abundantly: *They poured money into the project.* **5.** To express or utter freely and fully: *He poured out his story. The victim's mother poured forth lamentations.* **—pour′ing** *adj.: a kettle with a pouring spout; a pouring rain.* ¶*These sound alike* **pour, pore.**

pout |pout| *v.* **1.** To push out the lips, especially as a sign of sullen annoyance. **2.** To show disappointment or resentment by sulking. —*n.* A sulky or sullen expression made by pushing out the lips.

pout•er |pou′tər| *n.* Also **pouter pigeon.** One of a breed of pigeons that can swell a pouchlike part of its digestive tract so that its breast becomes puffed out.

pov•er•ty |pŏv′ər tē| *n.* **1.** The condition of being poor and in need; lack of sufficient money, food, shelter, etc. **2.** A lack of or deficiency in anything needed or desired: *a poverty of imagi-*

nation. **3.** The condition of being of poor quality: *the poverty of the rocky soil.*

POW, P.O.W. prisoner of war.

pow•der |pou′dər| *n.* **1. a.** A substance in the form of a great number of very fine particles; dust. **b.** Something prepared in this form, as a medicine, cosmetic, cleaning agent, etc.: *face powder; soap powder.* **2.** Gunpowder or a similar explosive mixture. **3.** Light, loose, dry snow. —*v.* **1.** To turn into powder, as by pulverizing, crumbling, or dehydrating: *They powdered the milk by evaporating 95 per cent of its moisture. Chalk powders easily.* **2.** To cover, dust, or sprinkle with or as if with powder: *powder cookies with sugar.* **3.** To put powder on (the face, body, or hair) as a cosmetic: *She powdered her nose. They powdered and dressed.* —**pow′dered** *adj.*: *powdered milk; powdered hair.*

powder horn. A container for gunpowder, consisting of an animal's horn with a cap or stopper at the open end. [SEE PICTURE]

pow•der•y |pou′də rē| *adj.* **1.** Of, like, or in the form of powder: *powdery dust; powdery snow.* **2.** Covered or dusted with or as if with powder: *a lily powdery with pollen.* **3.** Easily made into powder; crumbly: *a soft, powdery rock.*

pow•er |pou′ər| *n.* **1. a.** Force or strength: *the pulling power of oxen.* **b.** Military might: *a nation's air power.* **2.** Forcefulness; effectiveness; impact: *a book of unusual power.* **3.** The ability to do or accomplish something: *His paralyzed leg had no power of movement. We now have it in our power to preserve the environment.* **4. powers. a.** Mental or physical abilities, capabilities, or skills: *The boy longed for a chance to test his powers in the race.* **b.** Properties or virtues: *the chemical powers of chlorophyll.* **5.** The right to decide or command; authority over others: *The emperor ruled with absolute power.* **6.** Control or leadership, especially of a government: *the party in power; a dictator seizing power.* **7.** Dominance or ascendancy over others in strength, achievement, influence, or prestige: *a civilization at the height of its power.* **8.** A source of authority or influence, especially a strong and influential nation: *a world power.* **9. a.** The rate at which work is done with respect to time, measured in units such as the watt or horsepower. **b.** The rate, with respect to time, at which electricity does work or creates its equivalent in heat. **c.** Relative capability for doing work in a given time: *an engine with lots of power.* **10. a.** Energy that can be used for doing work, derived from such sources as wind, water, fuel, electricity, etc.: *water power; atomic power.* **b.** Electricity: *The power failed during the storm.* **11.** The number of times a number or expression is indicated as a factor, as by an exponent: *ten to the sixth power.* **12.** A number that represents the magnification of an optical instrument, such as a microscope or telescope. —***modifier:*** *power machinery; a power company.* —*v.* To supply with power, especially mechanical power: *The truck is powered by a gasoline engine.* [SEE NOTE]

***Idiom.* the powers that be.** The individuals or forces in authority or control.

pow•er•boat |pou′ər bōt′| *n.* A motorboat.

pow•er•ful |pou′ər fəl| *adj.* **1. a.** Having or capable of exerting great power: *powerful machines; a powerful nation; powerful muscles.* **b.** Strong or forceful: *a powerful push.* **2.** Highly effective; potent: *a powerful poison.* **3.** Having authority, influence, or high position: *rich and powerful people.* —**pow′er•ful•ly** *adv.*

pow•er•house |pou′ər hous′| *n., pl.* **-hous•es** |-hou′zĭz|. **1.** A place where equipment for generating electric power is located and operated. **2. a.** A strong, powerful team or group. **b.** A forceful, energetic person.

pow•er•less |pou′ər lĭs| *adj.* Lacking strength, power, or authority to act or resist, especially: **1.** Helpless: *They were powerless and at the mercy of their enemies.* **2.** Unable: *We were powerless to stop them.* —**pow′er•less•ly** *adv.*

power of attorney. 1. A written document giving someone legal authority to act for or represent another, as in handling business affairs. **2.** The authority conferred by such a document.

power tool. A tool, such as a drill or saw, that is driven by an electric motor or sometimes by a small gasoline engine.

Pow•ha•tan¹ |pou′hə tăn′|. 1550?–1618. American Indian chief; father of Pocahontas.

Pow•ha•tan² |pou′hə tăn′| *n., pl.* **Pow•ha•tan** or **Pow•ha•tans. 1.** A confederation of Algonquian-speaking tribes of North American Indians formerly living in eastern Virginia. **2.** A member of any of these tribes.

pow•wow |pou′wou′| *n.* **1.** Among North American Indians, a ceremony in which charms, spells, and dances are used to call down divine help in hunting, fighting, or healing. **2.** A conference or meeting with or of North American Indians. **3.** *Informal.* Any gathering, meeting, or conference, especially one full of noisy confusion. —*v.* To hold a conference or powwow.

pox |pŏks| *n.* **1.** A disease, such as chicken pox or smallpox, characterized by pus-filled eruptions of the skin. **2.** Syphilis.

pp. pages.

p.p. past participle.

pr. pair.

Pr The symbol for the element praseodymium.

prac•ti•ca•ble |prăk′tĭ kə bəl| *adj.* **1.** Capable of being done, carried out, or put into effect; possible: *a practicable solution to the problem.* **2.** Capable of being used for a certain purpose: *a practicable ski slope.* —**prac′ti•ca•bil′i•ty** *n.* —**prac′ti•ca•bly** *adv.*

prac•ti•cal |prăk′tĭ kəl| *adj.* **1. a.** Serving or capable of serving a useful purpose; useful, workable, effective, or efficient: *The inventor turned the idea into a practical machine.* **b.** Filling a need or requirement: *No practical purpose would be served by that course of action.* **2.** Coming from or involving experience, practice, or use rather than theory, study, or speculation: *practical knowledge as opposed to book learning.* **3.** Concerned with useful, down-to-earth matters; realistic rather than idealistic: *a practical man.* **4.** Having or showing good judgment; sensible: *Was he practical when he stuffed himself with too many hot dogs?* **5.** Being actually so, though not officially or admittedly so; virtual: *a practical disaster.* —**prac′ti•cal′i•ty** *n.*

practical joke. A mischievous trick or prank played on a person to make him look or feel foolish.

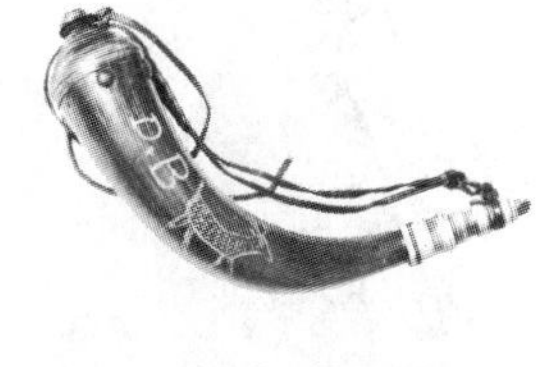

powder horn
Daniel Boone's powder horn

power
The watt is a particularly convenient unit for measuring electric power. If current is expressed in amperes and voltage is expressed in volts, the power represented as the product of a particular current and voltage is automatically expressed in watts.

prac•ti•cal•ly |prăk′tĭk lē| *adv.* **1.** Almost but not quite; nearly: *The boy's leg was practically torn off.* **2.** To all intents and purposes; in effect; virtually: *The weather was practically perfect.* **3.** In a practical way: *They dressed practically for the long hike.*

practical nurse. A professional nurse who has experience but who is not a graduate of a school of nursing.

prac•tice |prăk′tĭs| *v.* **prac•ticed, prac•tic•ing. 1. a.** To do or work on over and over in order to learn or master: *practiced a jump shot; practice the piano.* **b.** To exercise, drill, or rehearse in order to gain, maintain, or improve a skill: *The athletes practice every day.* **2. a.** To carry out in action or put into effect: *You should practice what you preach.* **b.** To make a habit of; use, perform, or employ regularly: *Learn to practice self-control.* **3.** To work at or follow (a profession or calling) actively: *practice medicine; a Greek physician who practiced in Rome.* —*n.* **1. a.** Experience, exercise, or drill in doing something that develops, maintains, or improves one's skill: *He had once fancied himself a good dancer, but in later years he got no practice.* **b.** Skill gained or maintained through repeated exercise: *He was out of practice.* **c.** A training period or session devoted to exercise or drill in some activity: *football practice; batting practice.* **2. a.** A custom or habit: *the practice of reading from left to right.* **b.** A way of doing things; method or technique: *unfair business practices.* **3.** Action, performance, use, or effect: *Put into practice what you have learned.* **4. a.** The exercise of a profession or occupation: *the practice of law.* **b.** The business built up by a professional person, especially a doctor's group of patients or a lawyer's clients: *The young doctor inherited a large practice from his predecessor.* —*modifier: practice sessions; practice exercises.*

prairie dog
Prairie dogs are not true dogs but are rodents related to the woodchucks and ground squirrels.

prac•ticed |prăk′tĭst| *adj.* Experienced; expert: *a practiced archer.*

prac•tise |prăk′tĭs| *n.* & *v.* **prac•tised, prac•tis•ing.** Chiefly British form of the word **practice.**

prac•ti•tion•er |prăk **tĭsh′**ə nər| *n.* A person who practices a certain profession, technique, art, etc.

prae•tor |prē′tər| *n.* An elected magistrate of the ancient Roman republic, ranking below a consul and serving as a judge.

prae•to•ri•an |prē **tôr′**ē ən| *or* |-**tōr′**-| *adj.* **1.** Of or concerning a praetor. **2. Praetorian.** Of, making up, or belonging to the bodyguard of a Roman emperor. —*n.* **1.** A person holding the rank of a praetor. **2. Praetorian.** A member of the bodyguard of a Roman emperor.

prairie schooner

prag•mat•ic |prăg **măt′**ĭk| *adj.* **1.** Concerned with causes and effects or with needs and results rather than with ideas or theories; practical: *a pragmatic approach to solving problems.* **2.** Of or following the theory or methods of pragmatism.

prag•ma•tism |prăg′mə tĭz′əm| *n.* **1.** The philosophical theory that an idea, belief, or course of action is to be judged by its practical results. **2.** A method of conducting political affairs by using practical means to meet immediate needs. —**prag′ma•tist** *n.*

Prague |präg|. The capital of Czechoslovakia. Population, 1,083,000.

prai•rie |prâr′ē| *n.* A wide area of flat or rolling country covered with tall grass, as in the central United States.

prairie chicken. A brownish bird of western North America, related to the grouse.

prairie dog. A burrowing animal of the plains of central North America, having a barklike call and living in large colonies. [SEE PICTURE]

prairie schooner. A **covered wagon.** [SEE PICTURE]

praise |prāz| *n.* **1. a.** Approval, admiration, commendation, or acclaim: *words of praise.* **b.** An expression of warm approval: *Praise from the coach meant a lot to him.* **2.** Glory, honor, and adoration, especially that given to God in worship: *They sang a hymn of praise.* **3.** The act of acclaiming, honoring, or exalting: *the praise of freedom.* —*v.* **praised, prais•ing. 1.** To express approval of or admiration for; applaud; commend: *Everyone praised her good sense and learning.* **2.** To give glory to; glorify; honor; exalt: *Praise God!* **3.** To express or utter praise: *He often criticized but seldom praised.*

praise•wor•thy |prāz′wûr′*th*ē| *adj.* Deserving praise; admirable; commendable: *a praiseworthy devotion to duty.*

pram |prăm| *n. British.* A baby carriage.

prance |prăns| *v.* **pranced, pranc•ing. 1. a.** To rise on the hind legs and spring forward, as a spirited horse does. **b.** To move by making such springs or bounds. **2.** To run, leap, or dance about playfully; caper: *a carnival where clowns skip and prance.* **3.** To move in a proud, bold, self-important way; strut: *A dancer pranced out onstage.* —**pranc′ing** *adj.: a prancing horse.* —*n.* An act of prancing or a prancing movement.

prank |prăngk| *n.* A playful, often mischievous trick, joke, or caper.

prank•ster |prăngk′stər| *n.* A person who plays tricks or pranks.

pra•se•o•dym•i•um |prā′zē ō **dĭm′**ē əm| *or* |-sē-| *n.* Symbol **Pr** One of the elements, a soft, silvery rare-earth metal. Atomic number 59; atomic weight 140.91; valences +3, +4; melting point 935°C; boiling point 3,127°C.

prate |prāt| *v.* **prat•ed, prat•ing.** To talk on and on about silly or childish things; chatter.

prat•tle |prăt′l| *v.* **prat•tled, prat•tling. 1.** To talk or chatter foolishly: *prattling about how much things cost.* **2.** To say in childish tones. —*n.* Childish talk or foolish chatter.

prawn |prôn| *n.* A water animal related to and resembling the shrimps, eaten as food.

pray |prā| *v.* **1. a.** To say (a prayer or prayers) to God or a god, as when asking or giving thanks for help, protection, guidance, etc.: *They all knelt and prayed. Each one prayed a private prayer.* **b.** To address a prayer or prayers: *Pray to God.* **c.** To ask in a prayer or appeal: *I pray the Lord my soul to keep. Pray for help.* **2.** To beg earnestly; beseech: *I pray you give me leave to go from hence.* **3.** To hope very hard; wish fervently: *I hope and pray that the teacher won't call on me today.* **4. a.** To be so obliging as to; please. Used to introduce a request or invitation: *Pray excuse me. Pray be seated.* **b.** To be so good as to tell or reveal. Used in asking a question: *Pray, how did you manage to do it?* **c.** To ask: *What's the matter, I pray?* ¶*These sound alike* **pray, prey.**

prayer |prâr| *n.* **1.** An expression of human

thoughts, hopes, or needs directed to God or a god, as when asking or giving thanks for divine help, favor, or forgiveness. **2.** A special formula of words used in speaking or appealing to God: *the Lord's Prayer.* **3.** The act of praying: *He clasped his hands in prayer.* **4.** Often **prayers.** A worship service for the saying of prayers: *morning prayer; family prayers.* **5.** An earnest appeal, request, or plea: *a prayer for mercy.* **6.** The slightest chance or hope, as for survival or success: *I fear the lost explorers don't have a prayer.*

praying mantis. See **mantis.**

pre–. A prefix meaning "before": **precaution.** When *pre-* is followed by a vowel, it may appear with a hyphen: **pre-empt, preempt.** When it is followed by a capital letter, it always appears with a hyphen: *pre-Christian.*

preach |prēch| *v.* **1.** To deliver (a sermon or sermons) giving religious or moral instruction: *The minister preached the morning sermon. He preached on Sundays.* **2.** To teach or advocate and urge others to accept or follow: *The leaders preach economy. Practice what you preach.* **3.** To point out a moral or offer advice, often in a long-winded or self-righteous way: *a writer with an unfortunate tendency to preach.*

preach•er |**prē**'chər| *n.* A person who preaches, especially a minister or clergyman.

pre•am•ble |**prē**'ăm'bəl| *n.* An introduction to a formal document, statute, or proclamation, explaining its purpose or the reasons behind it. [SEE NOTE]

pre•am•pli•fi•er |prē **ăm**'plə fī'ər| *n.* An electronic circuit or device designed to amplify and often otherwise process very weak signals before they are further amplified.

Pre•cam•bri•an or **Pre-Cam•bri•an** |prē-**kăm**'brē ən| *n.* Also **Precambrian era** or **Pre-Cambrian era.** The era that represents the oldest and largest division of geologic time, ending about 600 million years ago and characterized by the appearance of primitive forms of life. *—modifier: Precambrian rocks.*

pre•car•i•ous |prĭ **kâr**'ē əs| *adj.* Dangerously insecure, unsafe, or uncertain: *dangling in a precarious position.* —**pre•car'i•ous•ly** *adv.*

pre•cau•tion |prĭ **kô**'shən| *n.* **1.** An action or step taken in advance to guard against possible danger, error, or accident: *take safety precautions.* **2.** Care taken or caution shown in advance: *a need for precaution.*

pre•cede |prĭ **sēd**'| *v.* **pre•ced•ed, pre•ced•ing.** To go or come before in time, order, position, rank, etc.: *A small surge of water precedes all geyser eruptions. The word "very" may precede an adjective.* —**pre•ced'ing** *adj.: the preceding winter; the preceding page.*

pre•ced•ence |**prĕs**'ĭ dəns| *or* |prĭ **sēd**'ns| *n.* **1.** The right to go before or to be considered before, as because of rank or importance: *A duke has precedence over an earl. Business takes precedence over pleasure.* **2.** The act of preceding, as in time or position.

prec•e•dent |**prĕs**'ĭ dnt| *n.* **1.** A previous case, instance, or decision that can serve as an example or rule to be followed later in similar cases. **2.** A model or example that may be followed or referred to later: *The case set a precedent for other judicial decisions.*

pre•cept |**prē**'sĕpt'| *n.* A rule of conduct or procedure.

pre•cep•tor |prĭ **sĕp**'tər| *or* |**prē**'sĕp'-| *n.* An instructor; teacher.

pre•ces•sion |prĭ **sĕsh**'ən| *n.* **1.** A movement of the axis of rotation of a spinning body that arises when an external force, or torque, tends to displace the axis. If the rotating body is symmetrical and rotates with a constant speed, and if the torque tending to move the axis is constant, the body moves so that its axis traces a cone in space. **2. a.** A movement of this kind made by the earth in space. **b.** Also **precession of the equinoxes.** A gradual westward shift of the equinoxes along the plane of the ecliptic as a result of this motion.

pre•cinct |**prē**'sĭngkt| *n.* **1.** An election district of a city or town: *a canvass of the voters in his precinct.* **2.** A district of a city patrolled by a unit of the police force. **3.** Often **precincts.** An area or enclosure with definite boundaries: *within the precincts of the university.* **4. precincts.** A neighboring region; environs.

pre•cious |**prĕsh**'əs| *adj.* **1.** Of high price; valuable: *precious metals.* **2.** Highly prized or esteemed; cherished: *thanked the old man for his precious advice.* **3.** Dear; beloved: *kissed her precious little face.* **4.** Used as an intensive: *A precious lot you know about dogs!* —**pre'cious•ly** *adv.* —**pre'cious•ness** *n.* [SEE NOTE]

prec•i•pice |**prĕs**'ə pĭs| *n.* **1.** A very steep or overhanging mass of rock, such as the face of a cliff. **2.** The point of decision before a disaster or great folly: *He was tempted to try hard drugs, but halted at the precipice.*

pre•cip•i•tate |prĭ **sĭp**'ĭ tāt'| *v.* **pre•cip•i•tat•ed, pre•cip•i•tat•ing.** **1.** To throw from a height; cast down. **2.** To cause to happen; bring on: *a vibration on the mountain slope that precipitated an avalanche.* **3.** To cause (water vapor) to condense from the atmosphere and fall as rain, snow, etc. **4.** To condense and fall to the earth as rain, snow, etc. **5.** To drop; deposit: *The river precipitates sediments where the current is slow.* **6.** To separate chemically from a solution in the form of a solid: *We precipitated the minerals from the water by adding borax.* —*adj.* |prĭ **sĭp**'ĭ tĭt| *or* |-tāt'|. **1.** Moving rapidly and forcefully; speeding headlong: *the precipitate course of a tornado.* **2.** Acting or made hastily or impulsively; rash: *a precipitate decision, made on the spot.* **3.** Sudden and sharp; abrupt: *a precipitate drop in prices.* —*n.* |prĭ **sĭp**'ĭ tāt'| *or* |-tĭt|. A solid material separated from a solution by chemical means.

pre•cip•i•ta•tion |prĭ sĭp'ĭ **tā**'shən| *n.* **1.** The act or process of precipitating. **2.** Great haste. **3.** Lack of forethought; rashness; impulsiveness. **4. a.** Any form of water that condenses from the atmosphere and passes to the surface of the earth; rain, snow, sleet, etc. **b.** The amount of this in a given area during a given period of time: *The average annual precipitation for the United States is about 29 inches.* **5.** The production of a precipitate, as in a chemical reaction.

pre•cise |prĭ **sīs**'| *adj.* **1.** Definite; not vague: *Tell me how to get there, and please be precise.* **2.** Distinct from others; particular: *on this precise spot.* **3.** Limited in meaning or application: *"Lane," "avenue," and "boulevard" are more pre-*

preamble

Preamble *is from Medieval Latin* preambulum, *"something that goes in front, an introduction":* pre-, *"in front, before,"* + ambulāre, *"to go, walk, amble."*

precious/price

Precious *is from Latin* pretiōsus, *"high-priced, expensive, valuable," from* pretium, *"price, value." In Old French,* pretium *became* pris, *which was borrowed into English as* **price.** *See also note at* **prize.**

cise words for "street." **4.** Done, made, or capable of operating within very small limits of error or variation: *a precise measurement.* **5.** Exactly corresponding to what is called for: *measured out the precise amount of yeast with a teaspoon.* **6.** Clear and correct: *precise speech.* **7.** Strictly observing established forms and procedures: *a precise old gentleman who breakfasted at 7:15 sharp each morning.* —**pre•cise'ly** *adv.* —**pre•cise'ness** *n.*

pre•cis•ion |prĭ **sĭzh'**ən| *n.* The condition, property, or quality of being precise: *the precision of a chemist's scales.* —**modifier:** *precision instruments.*

pre•clude |prĭ **klo͞od'**| *v.* **pre•clud•ed, pre•clud•ing.** To make impossible or unlikely by consequence: *High temperatures on the surface of Venus preclude any chance of life as we know it.*

pre•co•cious |prĭ **kō'**shəs| *adj.* Showing skills or abilities at an earlier age than is normal: *a precocious child.* —**pre•co'cious•ly** *adv.* —**pre•co'cious•ness, pre•coc'i•ty** |prĭ **kŏs'**ĭ tē| *n.*

pre-Co•lum•bi•an |prē'kə **lŭm'**bē ən| *adj.* Of the period in the Americas before Columbus's voyage in 1492: *pre-Columbian empires.*

pre•con•ceive |prē'kən **sēv'**| *v.* **-con•ceived, -con•ceiv•ing.** To form (an opinion, idea, etc.) before full or adequate knowledge is available; have as a prejudice. —**pre'con•ceived'** *adj.: preconceived notions.*

pre•con•cep•tion |prē'kən **sĕp'**shən| *n.* An idea or opinion formed before full knowledge is available; a prejudice.

pre•cur•sor |prĭ **kûr'**sər| *or* |**prē'**kûr'-| *n.* **1.** An indicator of someone or something to come; a forerunner: *a heavy stillness that was a precursor of the downpour.* **2.** An early stage or example: an ancestor; predecessor: *portable sundials, precursors of the pocket watch.*

pred. predicate.

pre•date |prē **dāt'**| *v.* **-dat•ed, -dat•ing.** **1.** To come before (another event) in time; antedate: *The American Revolution predates the French Revolution by about 13 years.* **2.** To mark with a date earlier than the actual one: *predate a check.*

pred•a•tor |**prĕd'**ə tər| *or* |-tôr'| *n.* **1.** An animal that lives by capturing and feeding on other animals; a preying animal. **2.** Someone who plunders or abuses other people for his own profit.

pred•a•to•ry |**prĕd'**ə tôr'ē| *or* |-tōr'ē| *adj.* **1.** Preying on other animals: *a predatory animal.* **2.** Plundering or destroying others for one's own gain: *predatory businessmen.* [SEE NOTE]

predatory/prey
Predatory *is from Latin* praedātōrius, *"plundering, rapacious," from* praeda, *"plunder, loot," also "animal that is hunted, prey." In Old French,* praeda *became* preie, which was borrowed into English as **prey**.

pred•e•ces•sor |**prĕd'**ĭ sĕs'ər| *or* |**prē'**dĭ-| *n.* **1.** Someone or something that precedes another in time, especially in an office or function: *the catapult, predecessor of the modern rocket launcher.* **2.** An ancestor: *The extravagance of his predecessors had impaired the family fortune.*

pre•des•ti•na•tion |prē dĕs'tə **nā'**shən| *n.* **1. a.** The religious doctrine that all events have been planned and ordered in advance by God. **b.** The religious doctrine that the soul of every person has been assigned from the beginning to salvation or damnation. **2.** Fate; destiny.

pre•des•tine |prē **dĕs'**tĭn| *v.* **-des•tined, -des•tin•ing.** To decide or appoint unalterably in advance; fix beforehand, as by divine decree: *The Greeks believed that the gods predestined the early death of heroes.*

pre•de•ter•mine |prē'dĭ **tûr'**mĭn| *v.* **-de•ter•mined, -de•ter•min•ing.** To determine in advance: *Climate predetermines the kinds of animals that can live in a region.* —**pre'de•ter'mined** *adj.: a predetermined goal.* —**pre'de•ter'mi•na'tion** *n.*

pre•dic•a•ment |prĭ **dĭk'**ə mənt| *n.* A difficult or embarrassing situation.

pred•i•cate |**prĕd'**ĭ kĭt| *n.* The part of a sentence that tells something about the subject. It consists of a verb and may include an object, an objective or subjective complement, and modifiers. In the sentences *Buttermilk tastes good, My brother and I have sworn to be loyal forever,* and *Faster and faster rode the messenger,* the predicates are *tastes good, have sworn to be loyal forever,* and *faster and faster rode.* —*v.* |**prĕd'**ĭ kāt'| **pred•i•cat•ed, pred•i•cat•ing.** **1.** To declare; assert. **2.** To base; establish: *the moral attitudes on which human conduct is predicated.*

predicate adjective. An adjective that follows a linking verb and modifies the subject of the sentence. For example, in the sentences *The weather was lovely* and *You look sleepy* the words *lovely* and *sleepy* are predicate adjectives.

predicate nominative. A noun or pronoun that follows a linking verb and refers to the same person or thing as the subject. For example, in the sentences *Roosevelt became President* and *This is he,* the words *President* and *he* are predicate nominatives.

predicate noun. A noun that is a predicate nominative.

pre•dict |prĭ **dĭkt'**| *v.* To tell about or make known in advance, especially on the basis of present knowledge; foretell: *predicted showers for this evening.* —**pre•dict'a•ble** *adj.*

pre•dic•tion |prĭ **dĭk'**shən| *n.* **1.** The act of predicting. **2.** Something that is predicted: *Her worst predictions came true.*

pre•di•lec•tion |prĕd'ə **lĕk'**shən| *or* |prē'də-| *n.* A natural or habitual preference.

pre•dis•pose |prē'dĭ **spōz'**| *v.* **-dis•posed, -dis•pos•ing.** **1.** To make susceptible: *conditions that predispose miners to lung disease.* **2.** To incline or influence beforehand: *Her sense of humor predisposed me in her favor.*

pre•dis•po•si•tion |prē'dĭs pə **zĭsh'**ən| *n.* **1.** A tendency to be subject to something; susceptibility: *a predisposition to allergies.* **2.** A prior inclination to like or dislike; a prejudice.

pre•dom•i•nant |prĭ **dŏm'**ə nənt| *adj.* **1.** Greater than all others in strength, authority, or importance; dominant: *the predominant nation of the Middle East.* **2.** Most common, numerous, or noticeable: *the predominant color in a design.* —**pre•dom'i•nance** *n.* —**pre•dom'i•nant•ly** *adv.*

pre•dom•i•nate |prĭ **dŏm'**ə nāt'| *v.* **-dom•i•nat•ed, -dom•i•nat•ing.** **1.** To be greater than others in strength, number, importance, or prominence: *Red and yellow predominate in this plaid.* **2.** To have power or controlling influence; prevail.

pre-em•i•nent or **pre•em•i•nent** |prē **ĕm'**ə nənt| *adj.* Superior to all others in importance, prominence, or excellence; outstanding: *the preeminent artist of the movement.* —**pre-em'i•nence** *n.* —**pre-em'i•nent•ly** *adv.*

pre-empt or **pre•empt** |prē **ĕmpt'**| *v.* To take

ă pat/ā pay/â care/ä father/ĕ pet/ē be/ĭ pit/ī pie/î fierce/ŏ pot/ō go/ô paw, for/oi oil/o͝o book/o͞o boot/ou out/ŭ cut/û fur/*th* the/th thin/hw which/zh vision/ə ago, item, pencil, atom, circus

possession of before anyone else can: *got to the market early and pre-empted the bargains.*

preen |prēn| *v.* **1.** To smooth or clean (the feathers) with the beak: *The parrot preened its feathers. Ducks preened and dipped in the pond.* **2.** To dress or groom (oneself) with elaborate care; primp. **3.** To take self-satisfied pride in (oneself): *Mr. Holmes preened himself on his success as a writer.*

pre•fab |**prē′**făb′| *n.* A prefabricated house or other structure. *—adj.* Prefabricated.

pre•fab•ri•cate |prē **făb′**rĭ kāt′| *v.* **-fab•ri•cat•ed, -fab•ri•cat•ing. 1.** To build or manufacture in advance. **2.** To manufacture in sections that can be easily shipped and assembled. **—pre•fab′ri•cat′ed** *adj.: a prefabricated house.*

pref•ace |**prĕf′**ĭs| *n.* **1.** An introductory essay, usually by the author, placed at the beginning of a book. **2.** A statement or series of remarks that introduces or explains what is to come: *a preface to a speech.* *—v.* **pref•aced, pref•ac•ing. 1.** To introduce or provide with a preface: *prefaced his lecture with a joke.* **2.** To serve as an introduction to: *the Scriptural reading that prefaced the sermon.* **—pref′ac•er** *n.*

pref•a•to•ry |**prĕf′**ə tôr′ē| *or* |-tōr′ē| *adj.* Serving as an introduction; preliminary: *prefatory remarks.*

pre•fect |**prē′**fĕkt′| *n.* **1.** Any of various ancient Roman officials of high rank. **2.** Any of various modern administrative officials, such as a chief of police in France.

pre•fer |prĭ **fûr′**| *v.* **pre•ferred, pre•fer•ring. 1.** To choose as more desirable; like better: *I prefer to stay at home tonight. Younger people in Japan prefer Western music.* **2.** To file or present for consideration before a legal authority: *preferred charges against the captured burglar.* **—pre•ferred′** *adj.: a preferred spelling.*

pref•er•a•ble |**prĕf′**ər ə bəl| *adj.* More desirable; preferred. **—pref′er•a•bly** *adv.*

pref•er•ence |**prĕf′**ər əns| *n.* **1.** The act of preferring; the exercise of choice: *She dressed simply, not because she had to, but by preference.* **2.** A liking for someone or something over another or others: *He expressed a preference for old shoes.* **3.** Someone or something preferred; one's choice: *asked for a window seat, but did not obtain his preference.*

pref•er•en•tial |prĕf′ə **rĕn′**shəl| *adj.* Showing preference; favoring one over others: *Her friends always received preferential treatment.* **—pref′er•en′tial•ly** *adv.*

pre•fer•ment |prĭ **fûr′**mənt| *n.* **1. a.** The act of singling someone out for promotion or favored treatment: *We resented the boss's preferment of his son to an executive position.* **b.** The condition or fact of being thus singled out: *a violinist proud of his preferment to the first chair.* **2.** The action of filing or presenting: *the preferment of a legal suit.*

pre•fix |**prē′**fĭks′| *n.* **1.** A form that cannot stand alone but when placed at the beginning of words changes their meaning. For example, *un-* in *unable, pre-* in *preheat,* and *re-* in *replay* are prefixes. **2.** A title placed before a person's name. *—v.* |prē **fĭks′**|. To add at the beginning or front: *prefixed the title "Dr." to his name.*

preg•nan•cy |**prĕg′**nən sē| *n., pl.* **preg•nan•cies. 1.** The condition of being pregnant. **2.** The time during which the uterus contains a developing fetus.

preg•nant |**prĕg′**nənt| *adj.* **1.** Carrying a developing fetus within the uterus. **2.** Heavy with significance; full of meaning: *a pregnant pause; a pregnant stillness.* **3.** Full of something specified; laden: *a situation pregnant with danger.*

pre•hen•sile |prĭ **hĕn′**sĭl| *or* |-sīl′| *adj.* Used or suited for grasping or holding, especially by wrapping around something: *a monkey's prehensile tail.*

pre•his•tor•ic |prē′hĭ **stôr′**ĭk| *or* |**-stŏr′**-| *adj.* Of or belonging to the time before history or events were recorded in writing: *a prehistoric animal.* **—pre′his•tor′i•cal•ly** *adv.*

prej•u•dice |**prĕj′**ə dĭs| *n.* **1.** A strong feeling about some subject, formed unfairly or before one knows the facts; a bias: *a prejudice in favor of his home town; a prejudice against unfamiliar foods.* **2.** Hostility toward members of races, religions, or nationalities other than one's own. **3.** Harm; injury: *settled the matter without prejudice to anyone's rights or interests.* *—v.* **prej•u•diced, prej•u•dic•ing. 1.** To fill with prejudice; bias: *an experience that prejudiced her against dogs.* **2.** To harm in the estimation of another or others: *testimony that prejudiced the defendant in the eyes of the jury.* **3.** To do harm to; injure: *prejudice a cause.* **—prej′u•diced** *adj.: a prejudiced decision; prejudiced thinking.* [SEE NOTE]

prej•u•di•cial |prĕj′ə **dĭsh′**əl| *adj.* Harmful; detrimental. **—prej′u•di′cial•ly** *adv.*

prel•ate |**prĕl′**ĭt| *n.* A high-ranking clergyman, as an archbishop or cardinal.

pre•lim•i•nar•y |prĭ **lĭm′**ə nĕr′ē| *adj.* Leading to or preparing for the main event, action, or business: *preliminary sketches for a building.* *—n., pl.* **pre•lim•i•nar•ies.** Something that leads to or serves as preparation for a main event, action, or business: *Without preliminaries, she walked to the edge of the pool and dived in.*

prel•ude |**prĕl′**yo͞od′| *or* |**prā′**lo͞od′| *n.* **1.** An event or action that precedes or leads to a more important one; a preliminary. **2. a.** A piece or movement of music that acts as introduction to a larger work. **b.** A fairly short composition in a free style, usually for piano or orchestra. *—v.* **prel•ud•ed, prel•ud•ing.** To serve as a prelude to.

pre•ma•ture |prē′mə **to͝or′**| *or* |**-tyo͝or′**| *or* |**-cho͝or′**| *adj.* **1.** Appearing or occurring before the usual time; unexpectedly early: *a premature death; premature gray hair.* **2.** Done or happening too soon; too hasty: *a premature judgment.* **3.** Born after too short a period of development in the uterus: *a premature baby.* **—pre′ma•ture′ly** *adv.*

pre•med |**prē′mĕd′**|. *Informal. adj.* Premedical. *—n.* **1.** A premedical student. **2.** Premedical studies.

pre•med•i•cal |prē′**mĕd′**ĭ kəl| *adj.* In preparation for the study of medicine.

pre•med•i•tate |prĭ **mĕd′**ĭ tāt′| *v.* **-med•i•tat•ed, -med•i•tat•ing.** To plan or think out in advance. **—pre•med′i•ta′tion** *n.*

pre•mier |**prē′**mē ər| *or* |prĭ **mîr′**| *adj.* **1.** First in importance; chief. **2.** Earliest. *—n.* |prĭ**mîr′**|. The chief minister or chief executive of a government; a prime minister. [SEE NOTE]

pre•mière |prĭ **mîr′**| *or* |**-myâr′**| *n.* The first

prejudice

Prejudice *comes from Latin* praejūdicium, *"previous judgment": prae-, "before," +* jūdicium, *"judgment." It is obvious that people constantly have to make judgments and decisions without considering all the available evidence. Doing this does not necessarily involve unfairness, and so it is not usually called prejudice. But the modern senses* **2** *and* **3** *of the word come from a specific meaning in legal terminology, where prejudice is "harm caused to a person by a* previous legal action *(or judgment) in which his rights were disregarded."*

premier, etc.

The adjective **premier** *is from French* premier, *from Latin* prīmārius, *"of the first rank," from* prīmus, *"first." From* prīmārius *we also have* **primary,** *and from* prīmus *we have* **prime. Prime minister** *was originally the title of the "first servant" of a monarch, the "chief official" of a court; as the powers of kings declined, their officers took over and became chief executives, as in Great Britain. The noun* **premier** *is shortened from the equivalent French phrase* premier ministre.

public performance of a play, motion picture, or other theatrical work.

prem•ise |prĕm′ĭs| *n.* **1.** A statement upon which an argument is based or from which a conclusion is drawn. **2.** An idea or theory that forms a basis for action; a working assumption: *He started his business on the premise that people wanted durable, well-made clothes.* **3. premises.** Property under a single ownership; someone's land or building: *The playground is part of the school premises.* —*v.* **prem•ised, prem•is•ing.** To state in advance as a proposition or assumption.

pre•mi•um |prē′mē əm| *n.* **1.** A prize awarded for quality or performance. **2.** An extra or unexpected benefit; a bonus: *The store gave out gifts as premiums to the first-day customers.* **3. a.** An amount charged in addition to the standard or usual price: *had to pay a premium for ringside seats at the boxing match.* **b.** An amount added to the face value of a security, stock, etc. **4.** An unusually high value: *Some high-school coaches place an undue premium on winning.* **5.** An amount paid for an insurance policy, especially one of a series of payments that fall due at specified times: *an annual life-insurance premium.* —***modifier:*** *premium gifts.* —*adj.* Of especially high quality or price: *premium gasoline.*

***Idiom.* at a premium.** Especially valuable or hard to obtain.

pre•mo•lar |prē mō′lər| *n.* Any of eight bicuspid teeth arranged in pairs on both sides of the upper and lower jaws between the canines and molars. —***modifier:*** *premolar teeth.*

pre•mo•ni•tion |prē′mə nĭsh′ən| *or* |prĕm′ə-| *n.* **1.** An advance warning: *gave no premonition of her plans.* **2.** A feeling that something is going to happen; a presentiment: *felt a sudden premonition of disaster.*

pre•na•tal |prē nāt′l| *adj.* Of, happening in, or done in the time before birth.

pre•oc•cu•pied |prē ŏk′yə pīd′| *adj.* **1.** Deep in thought; engrossed: *sat quietly all through dinner, frowning and preoccupied.* **2.** Attentive to what one is doing; busy: *children too preoccupied with their games to notice the time.*

pre•oc•cu•py |prē ŏk′yə pī′| *v.* **pre•oc•cu•pied, pre•oc•cu•py•ing, pre•oc•cu•pies.** To hold the attention or interest of; engage deeply or completely: *questions that have preoccupied scientists for centuries.* —**pre•oc′cu•pa′tion** *n.*

prep |prĕp|. *Informal. adj.* Preparatory. —*n.* A preparatory school.

prep. preposition.

pre•paid |prē′pād′| *adj.* Paid or paid for in advance: *a prepaid vacation tour.*

prep•a•ra•tion |prĕp′ə rā′shən| *n.* **1. a.** The action of preparing: *the preparation of dinner for six persons.* **b.** The condition of being prepared; readiness: *a ship in good preparation for a voyage.* **2.** An action necessary in getting ready for something: *final preparations for a rocket launch.* **3.** A substance or mixture prepared for a certain use: *a preparation of herbs for seasoning vegetables.*

pre•par•a•to•ry |prĭ păr′ə tôr′ē| *or* |-tōr′ē| *or* |-pâr′-| *adj.* Of preparation; serving to make ready: *preparatory exercises before a race.*

***Idiom.* preparatory to.** In preparation for: *classes preparatory to entering a college.*

preparatory school. A private school for training students for college.

pre•pare |prĭ pâr′| *v.* **pre•pared, pre•par•ing. 1.** To make ready for some purpose, task, or event: *Prepare yourself for a shock. Prepare the wood surface by cleaning and smoothing it.* **2.** To make ready for presentation; plan and make: *prepare a book report; prepare an announcement for the press.* **3.** To put together and make from various ingredients: *foods that are easy to prepare.* **4.** To put things or oneself in readiness; get ready: *preparing to leave town.*

pre•pay |prē pā′| *v.* **-paid, -pay•ing.** To pay or pay for beforehand: *She prepaid the rent.* —**pre•pay′ment** *n.*

pre•pon•der•ance |prĭ pŏn′dər əns| *n.* A clear superiority in weight, number, importance, etc.

pre•pon•der•ant |prĭ pŏn′dər ənt| *adj.* Greater in weight, number, importance, etc.: *A preponderant number of people are right-handed.* —**pre•pon′der•ant•ly** *adv.*

prep•o•si•tion |prĕp′ə zĭsh′ən| *n.* **1.** A word used with a noun, pronoun, or noun equivalent (called the object of a preposition) to indicate the relationship between that object and something or someone else. For example, the preposition *on* in *the store on the street corner* shows the relationship between *street corner* and *store.* Some other common prepositions are *at, by, from, in, to,* and *with.* **2.** A phrase, such as *instead of* or *in regard to,* that functions as a preposition. —**prep′o•si′tion•al** *adj.* —**prep′o•si′tion•al•ly** *adv.*

prepositional phrase. A phrase consisting of a preposition and its object.

pre•pos•sess•ing |prē′pə zĕs′ĭng| *adj.* Pleasing; attractive. —**pre′pos•sess′ing•ly** *adv.*

pre•pos•ter•ous |prĭ pŏs′tər əs| *adj.* **1.** Completely unreasonable or incredible; nonsensical; absurd: *the preposterous idea of painting the roses blue.* **2.** Ridiculous in appearance; grotesque: *a preposterous hat.* —**pre•pos′ter•ous•ly** *adv.*

prep school. *Informal.* A **preparatory school.**

pre•puce |prē′pyo͞os′| *n.* **1.** The loose fold of skin that covers the tip of the penis. **2.** A similar fold at the tip of the clitoris.

pre•req•ui•site |prĭ rĕk′wĭ zĭt| *adj.* Required as a condition for something else; necessary: *a course that is prerequisite to more advanced studies.* —*n.* Something that is prerequisite.

pre•rog•a•tive |prĭ rŏg′ə tĭv| *n.* A right or privilege, especially one that accompanies the rank, status, or job of an individual or group.

pres. present.

Pres. president.

pres•age |prĕs′ĭj| *n.* **1.** A sign or warning of what is going to happen; an omen. **2.** A feeling about what is going to happen; a premonition. —*v.* **pre•sage** |prĭ sāj′| *or* |prĕs′ĭj|, **pre•saged, pre•sag•ing. 1.** To be a presage of; indicate as something that will happen; portend: *He believed that recent wars and disasters presaged the coming end of the world.* **2.** To foretell; prophesy: *gloomy writers who always presage doom.*

pres•by•ter |prĕz′bĭ tər| *or* |prĕs′-| *n.* **1.** An officer of a Presbyterian Church congregation; an elder. **2.** An official in various other churches, as a priest in the Anglican Church. [SEE NOTE]

Pres•by•te•ri•an |prĕz′bĭ tîr′ē ən| *or* |prĕs′-| *n.*

presbyter, etc.
The earliest Christian churches, set up by St. Paul, were run by councils of "elders." "Elder" in Greek was presbuteros, *becoming* presbyter *in Latin. This word was borrowed into Old English as* prēost, *becoming* **priest** *in Modern English. In the sixteenth century, the Protestant Church of Scotland revived the early system of church government by "elders," and they also revived the old word* **presbyter,** *from which the* **Presbyterian Church** *is named. Later, the Scots tried to make the English join the Presbyterian Church; the English poet and politician John Milton, who was good at etymology, wrote sarcastically, "New Presbyter is but old Priest writ large."*

ă pat/ā pay/â care/ä father/ĕ pet/ē be/ĭ pit/ī pie/î fierce/ŏ pot/ō go/ô paw, for/oi oil/o͝o book/o͞o boot/ou out/ŭ cut/û fur/*th* the/th thin/hw which/zh vision/ə ago, item, pencil, atom, circus

A member of a Presbyterian Church. —*adj.* Of the Presbyterian Church or Presbyterianism.

Presbyterian Church. Any of various Protestant churches that are governed according to a system in which congregations choose elders to represent them.

Pres•by•te•ri•an•ism |prĕz'bĭ tîr'ē ə nĭz'əm| *or* |prĕs'-| *n.* The beliefs, worship, or system of church government of Presbyterians.

pre•school |**prē'sko͞ol'**| *adj.* Of or intended for a child before he enters elementary school.

pre•sci•ence |**prē'**shē əns| *or* |**prĕsh'**ē-| *n.* Accurate calculation of what the future will bring. —**pre'sci•ent** *adj.*

pre•scribe |prĭ **skrīb'**| *v.* **pre•scribed, pre•scrib•ing. 1.** To order or recommend the use of (a drug, diet, remedy, etc.): *The doctor prescribed bed rest and lots of liquids.* **2.** To set down as a rule or guide; impose or direct: *The government prescribes standards for the purity of food. Convention prescribes that we thank the host.* **3.** To state or indicate specifically; specify: *a program that prescribes the order of events.* —**pre•scribed'** *adj.: a prescribed dose; a prescribed temperature.*

pre•scrip•tion |prĭ **skrĭp'**shən| *n.* **1.** The act or process of prescribing. **2.** Something that is prescribed; a recommendation or rule: *prescriptions for correct usage in an English textbook.* **3. a.** A written instruction from a physician indicating what treatment or medication a patient is to receive. **b.** A medicine ordered by prescription. **c.** Specifications for a set of corrective lenses for eyeglasses, written by an ophthalmologist.

pre•scrip•tive |prĭ **skrĭp'**tĭv| *adj.* Laying down rules to be followed; giving instructions on what to do or how to do it: *a prescriptive grammar.* —**pre•scrip'tive•ly** *adv.*

pres•ence |**prĕz'**əns| *n.* **1.** The fact or condition of being present: *Your presence is not required at the meeting.* **2.** The immediate nearness of someone or something: *Slow oxidation of the metal in the presence of moisture causes rust.* **3.** An influence felt to be nearby: *A mysterious presence frightened them away.* **4.** A person's manner of carrying himself; bearing: *She has great presence on the stage.*

pres•ent[1] |**prĕz'**ənt| *n.* **1.** A moment or period of time that is intermediate between past and future; now. **2.** In grammar: **a.** The **present tense. b.** A verb form in the present tense. —*adj.* **1.** Being or occurring in the time considered as the present: *the present time; present research into space; his present difficulties.* **2.** Being in view or at hand; being in the same place as someone or something: *The people present broke into loud applause. A Geiger counter signals when uranium is present.* **3.** Being a verb form in the present tense.

***Idioms.* at present.** At the present time; right now. **for the present.** For the time being; temporarily.

pre•sent[2] |prĭ **zĕnt'**| *v.* **1. a.** To make a gift or award of: *She presented the pennant to the winners.* **b.** To make a gift or award to: *present the sheriff with two horses.* **2. a.** To introduce (a person) to another or others: *She was presented at the debutante's ball.* **b.** To put (oneself) before a person, at a place, etc.: *She presented herself to the committee.* **3.** To bring before the public; display; exhibit: *present a skit for parents; present historical material in chronological order.* **4.** To offer for consideration: *Teaching presents many difficult problems.* —*n.* **pres•ent** |**prĕz'**ənt|. Something presented; a gift.

pre•sent•a•ble |prĭ **zĕn'**tə bəl| *adj.* Fit for introduction to others: *He did what he could to make himself presentable.* —**pre•sent'a•bil'i•ty** *n.*

pres•en•ta•tion |prĕz'ən **tā'**shən| *or* |prē'zĕn-| *n.* **1.** The act of presenting, especially for acceptance or approval. **2.** Something presented, especially for public viewing.

pres•ent-day |**prĕz'**ənt **dā'**| *adj.* Existing or occurring now; current: *present-day living.*

pre•sen•ti•ment |prĭ **zĕn'**tə mənt| *n.* A sense of something about to occur.

pres•ent•ly |**prĕz'**ənt lē| *adv.* **1.** In a short time; soon: *Presently she heard a dog bark.* **2.** At this time or period; now: *An expedition is presently exploring the area.*

present participle. A participle that expresses present action, condition, or state. It is formed in English by adding *-ing* to the infinitive, as in *he is playing*, and is sometimes used as an adjective, as in *an appalling amount.*

present perfect tense. A verb tense used to express action or state completed at the time of speaking. It is formed in English by combining the present tense of *have* with the past participle. For example, in the sentence *He has spoken,* the verb *has spoken* is in the present perfect tense.

present tense. A verb tense used to express action, condition, or state in the present. For example, in the sentences *She hits the ball* and *I am happy*, the verbs *hits* and *am* are in the present tense.

pres•er•va•tion |prĕz'ər **vā'**shən| *n.* The act of preserving or the state of being preserved.

pre•serv•a•tive |prĭ **zûr'**və tĭv| *adj.* Tending to preserve or capable of preserving. —*n.* Something used to preserve, especially a chemical added to a food to retard spoilage.

pre•serve |prĭ **zûrv'**| *v.* **pre•served, pre•serv•ing. 1.** To protect, as from injury or peril; maintain in safety: *concerned with preserving his life in the wilderness.* **2.** To keep in perfect or unchanged condition or form; maintain intact: *Any sound can be recorded and preserved on tape.* **3.** To protect (food) from spoilage and prepare it for future use, as by freezing, canning, etc. —*n.* **1.** Often **preserves.** Fruit cooked with sugar to protect against decay or fermentation. **2.** An area maintained for the protection of wildlife or natural resources. —**pre•serv'er** *n.*

pre•side |prĭ **zīd'**| *v.* **pre•sid•ed, pre•sid•ing. 1.** To hold the position of authority, as at a meeting; act as a chairman: *presided over a meeting.* **2.** To possess, seem to possess, or exercise authority or control: *Mother presides at the dinner table.* —**pre•sid'ing** *adj.: a presiding judge.*

pres•i•den•cy |**prĕz'**ĭ dən sē| *n., pl.* **pres•i•den•cies.** Often **Presidency.** The office of a president or the period during which a president is in office.

pres•i•dent |**prĕz'**ĭ dənt| *n.* **1.** Often **President.** The chief executive of a republic, such as the United States. **2.** The chief officer of an organization or institution, such as a club, corporation, or university. [SEE NOTE]

president

"No man will ever bring out of the Presidency the reputation which carries him into it." —*Thomas Jefferson (1796).*

"No man who ever held the office of President would congratulate a friend on obtaining it." —*John Adams (1824) (his son, John Quincy Adams, had just been elected President).*

press[1-2]

Press[1] *is from Latin* pressāre, *"to press, squeeze."* **Press**[2] *is not related; it was originally* prest *and meant "money paid to a man to enlist in the army," from Old French* prester, *"to lend, to pay in advance." The old system of getting a man into the army or navy was to persuade him to accept a* prest, *a small amount of money as a down payment against wages; if he took it he was automatically signed up. Later, men were simply kidnaped forcibly by* prest gangs, *and by influence of the word* **press**[1], prest *changed to* **press**[2].

pressure suit

ă pat/ā pay/â care/ä father/ĕ pet/ ē be/ĭ pit/ī pie/î fierce/ŏ pot/ ō go/ô paw, for/oi oil/ŏŏ book/ ōō boot/ou out/ŭ cut/û fur/ *th* the/th thin/hw which/zh vision/ ə ago, item, pencil, atom, circus

pres•i•den•tial |prĕz′ĭ **dĕn′**shəl| *adj.* Often **Presidential.** Of a president or presidency: *a presidential election.*

press[1] |prĕs| *v.* **1. a.** To exert force or pressure against; bear down on: *Press the button.* **b.** To exert force or pressure: *Does compressed air press with more or less force than the air around you?* **c.** To make compact, form into a desired shape, flatten, etc., by exerting pressure: *Giant crushers press useless cars into small blocks.* **2. a.** To squeeze the juice or other contents from: *press grapes to make wine.* **b.** To extract (juice or other contents) by squeezing: *press juice from oranges.* **3.** To smooth (clothes, fabric, etc.) by applying heat and pressure; iron: *The dry cleaner pressed the trousers.* **4.** To clasp or embrace, as with affection: *Michael pressed her hand with gratitude.* **5.** To try hard to persuade; ask or entreat insistently: *Joy pressed her aunt to stay for the holiday.* **6.** To urge on or push forward: *pressing the driver to go faster.* **7.** To carry on or attack vigorously: *Critics charged that the Confederates should have pressed on and taken Washington.* **8.** To crowd or push together or in a certain direction; mass: *The police pressed the crowds back. Shouting crowds pressed against the walls.* **9.** To weigh heavily, as on the mind: *A feeling of doom pressed down on him.* **10.** To require haste: *Time presses and we must part.* —*n.* **1.** Any of various machines or devices used to squeeze or exert pressure on something. **2.** A **printing press.** **3. a.** Printed matter as a whole, especially newspapers and magazines. **b.** The people, as editors and reporters, involved in such publications. **4.** A throng: *a press of people in the square.* **5.** Pressure, haste, or urgency: *The press of business weighs heavily on her time.* **6.** The shape or set of proper creases in a garment or fabric, formed by ironing: *These slacks will keep their press.* —**press′er** *n.* [SEE NOTE]

Idioms. **be (hard) pressed for.** To be lacking in: *be hard pressed for time.* **press (one's) luck.** To push for something in spite of odds against it.

press[2] |prĕs| *v.* To force into service in the army or navy. [SEE NOTE]

press agent. A person hired to gain favorable public attention for an employer or for his activities, chiefly through articles and pictures in newspapers or other publications.

press•ing |**prĕs′**ĭng| *adj.* Demanding immediate attention; critical: *the pressing problems of the world.*

pres•sure |**prĕsh′**ər| *n.* **1.** The act of pressing or the condition of being pressed. **2.** The application of a continuous force on one body by another with which it is in contact. **3.** The amount of force applied per unit of area of a surface. **4.** A physical or mental burden that causes distress: *The pressure of getting into college is very hard for some students.* **5.** Urgent claim or demand: *She has many pressures on her time.* **6.** A force or influence, as on the mind or will: *political pressure.* —***modifier:*** *a pressure point.* —*v.* **pres•sured, pres•sur•ing.** To force, as by influencing or persuading: *The studio tried to pressure her into making public appearances.*

pressure cooker. An airtight metal pot for quick cooking by means of steam maintained under pressure.

pressure suit. An airtight suit worn by crews of spacecraft and high-altitude aircraft to keep the body surrounded by pressure close to the normal atmospheric pressure. [SEE PICTURE]

pres•sur•ize |**prĕsh′**ə rīz′| *v.* **pres•sur•ized, pres•sur•iz•ing. 1.** To subject to a greater pressure than normal. **2.** To keep (a compartment, as in an aircraft) at normal atmospheric pressure. —**pres′sur•ized′** *adj.: a pressurized cabin.* —**pres′sur•i•za′tion** *n.*

pres•ti•dig•i•ta•tion |prĕs′tĭ dĭj′ĭ **tā′**shən| *n.* Skill with one's hands, as in juggling or performing tricks. —**pres′ti•dig′i•ta′tor** *n.*

pres•tige |prĕ **stēzh′**| *or* |**-stēj′**| *n.* Prominence or status in the eyes of others, achieved through success, fame, or wealth.

pres•tig•ious |prĕ **stĭj′**əs| *or* |**-stē′**jəs| *adj.* Generally regarded as full of prestige: *a prestigious occupation.* —**pres•tig′ious•ly** *adv.* —**pres•tig′ious•ness** *n.*

pres•tis•si•mo |prĕ **stĭs′**ə mō′|. In music: *adj.* To be performed at as fast a tempo as possible. —*adv.* At as fast a tempo as possible. —*n., pl.* **pres•tis•si•mos.** A passage, movement, chord, etc., that is or is to be performed as fast as possible.

pres•to |**prĕs′**tō| *adj.* In music, very fast. —*adv.* **1.** In music, very quickly. **2.** Suddenly; at once. —*n., pl.* **pres•tos.** A musical passage, chord, etc., that is or is to be performed very quickly.

pre•sum•a•ble |prĭ **zōō′**mə bəl| *adj.* Able to be presumed or taken for granted; reasonably supposed: *a presumable result.* —**pre•sum′a•bly** *adv.*

pre•sume |prĭ **zōōm′**| *v.* **pre•sumed, pre•sum•ing. 1.** To assume to be true in the absence of anything to the contrary; take for granted: *I presume that she will accept the job.* **2.** To act without authority or permission; take liberties: *He presumed to make the wedding arrangements without her knowledge.* —***phrasal verb.*** **presume on** (or **upon**). To take uncalled-for advantage of: *She presumed on his good nature.*

pre•sump•tion |prĭ **zŭmp′**shən| *n.* **1.** Behavior or language that is arrogant or offensive. **2.** The act of presuming or accepting as true: *a presumption of innocence.* **3.** Acceptance or belief based on reasonable evidence.

pre•sump•tu•ous |prĭ **zŭmp′**chōō əs| *adj.* Excessively forward, confident, or arrogant in behavior: *a presumptuous attitude.*

pre•sup•pose |prē′sə **pōz′**| *v.* **pre•sup•posed, pre•sup•pos•ing. 1.** To assume or suppose in advance; take for granted: *The chemistry teacher presupposed that the students had taken math.* **2.** To require as a necessary prior condition: *an effect that presupposes a cause.* —**pre′sup•po•si′tion** |prē′sŭp ə **zĭsh′**ən| *n.*

pre•tend |prĭ **tĕnd′**| *v.* **1.** To put on a false show of: *pretend illness.* **2.** To make believe: *Pretend you are a sponge soaking up all the sounds you hear.* **3.** To put forward a claim or allege falsely: *The quack pretended to have scientific knowledge.* —**pre•tend′ed** *adj.: his pretended loyalty.*

pre•tend•er |prĭ **tĕn′**dər| *n.* **1.** Someone who pretends or alleges falsely. **2.** Someone who sets forth a claim to a throne.

pre•tense |**prē′**tĕns′| *or* |prĭ **tĕns′**| *n.* **1.** A false appearance or action intended to mislead. **2.** A false show; an affectation: *He made no pretense* *of grief.* **3.** A false reason, intention, purpose, etc.: *He came to the meeting under false pretenses.* **4.** A claim not based on reality: *There was not even a pretense of justice.* **5.** Something make-believe or pretended.

pre•ten•sion |prĭ tĕn′shən| *n.* **1.** A doubtful claim. **2.** Pretentious or showy behavior.

pre•ten•tious |prĭ tĕn′shəs| *adj.* **1.** Making false or unjustified claims or demands. **2.** Extravagantly showy: *a pretentious house.* —**pre•ten′tious•ly** *adv.* —**pre•ten′tious•ness** *n.*

pret•er•it |prĕt′ər ĭt| *n.* **1.** A verb tense used to express past or completed action or condition. **2.** A verb form in this tense. —*adj.* Being a verb form in the preterit.

pre•text |prē′tĕkst′| *n.* A purpose or excuse given to hide the real reason for something.

Pre•to•ri•a |prĭ tôr′ē ə| *or* |-tōr′-|. The administrative capital of South Africa. Population, 545,000.

pret•ty |prĭt′ē| *adj.* **pret•ti•er, pret•ti•est. 1.** Pleasing or appealing in a delicate way: *a pretty girl; a pretty shell.* **2.** Excellent; fine. Often used ironically: *This is a pretty time to tell us.* **3.** *Informal.* Large in size or extent: *a pretty fortune.* —*adv.* To a fair degree; somewhat: *We are in pretty bad shape. We will leave pretty soon.* —*v.* **pret•tied, pret•ty•ing, pret•ties.** *Informal.* To make pretty: *We can pretty up the spare room for you.* —**pret′ti•ly** *adv.* —**pret′ti•ness** *n.*

Idiom. **sitting pretty.** *Informal.* In a favorable condition or position.

pret•zel |prĕt′səl| *n.* A thin roll of dough, often salted on the outside, baked in the form of a loose knot or a stick. [SEE PICTURE]

pre•vail |prĭ vāl′| *v.* **1.** To be greater in strength and influence; triumph: *"The wrong shall fail, the right prevail"* (Longfellow). **2.** To be most common or frequent; be predominant: *Similar climatic conditions prevail above the timberline.* **3.** To be in force or use; be current: *an attitude that prevailed in the 1950's.* —**pre•vail′ing** *adj.*: *the prevailing attitude; prevailing winds.* —***phrasal verb.*** **prevail on** (or **upon**). To persuade successfully: *The cowboy at last prevailed on his horse to stand steady.*

prev•a•lent |prĕv′ə lənt| *adj.* Widely existing or commonly occurring: *Sickness is not as prevalent in dry, cool areas as it is in hot, humid areas.* —**prev′a•lence** *n.* —**prev′a•lent•ly** *adv.*

pre•var•i•cate |prĭ văr′ĭ kāt′| *v.* **pre•var•i•cat•ed, pre•var•i•cat•ing.** To stray from the truth; speak evasively. —**pre•var′i•ca′tion** *n.* —**pre•var′i•ca′tor** *n.*

pre•vent |prĭ vĕnt′| *v.* **1.** To keep from happening; avert: *prevent illness.* **2.** To deprive (someone) of success in doing something; hinder or impede: *His snoring prevents me from sleeping.* —**pre•vent′a•ble, pre•vent′i•ble** *adj.*

pre•ven•ta•tive |prĭ vĕn′tə tĭv| *adj., n.* Preventive.

pre•ven•tion |prĭ vĕn′shən| *n.* **1.** The act or an example of preventing: *the prevention of illness.* **2.** Something that prevents; a hindrance: *Vitamin C is believed to be a prevention against colds.*

pre•ven•tive |prĭ vĕn′tĭv| *adj.* Designed to prevent or hinder: *preventive steps against accidents.* —*n.* Something that is preventive.

pre•view |prē′vyōō′| *n.* **1.** An advance showing of a motion picture, art exhibition, play, etc., to an invited audience, prior to presentation to the general public. **2.** An advance viewing, especially of several scenes of a forthcoming motion picture. —*v.* To view or exhibit in advance.

pre•vi•ous |prē′vē əs| *adj.* Existing or occurring prior to something else: *in the previous chapter.* —**pre′vi•ous•ly** *adv.*

Idiom. **previous to.** Prior to; before.

pre•war |prē′wôr′| *adj.* Before a certain war.

prey |prā| *n.* **1.** An animal or animals hunted or seized by another for food. **2.** Someone or something helpless against attack, trouble, etc.; a victim: *The Mayas fell prey to the invading Spaniards.* —*v.* —**prey on** (or **upon**). **1.** To feed by or as if by seizing as prey: *Owls prey on mice.* **2.** To take unfair advantage of, as by swindling; victimize. **3.** To have a harmful or troublesome effect: *Worry preyed on his mind.* ¶*These sound alike* **prey, pray.** [SEE NOTE on p. 692]

Idiom. **of prey.** Living by seizing other animals as prey: *Owls are birds of prey.*

price |prīs| *n.* **1.** The amount of money asked or given for something: *The price is $5.99.* **2.** The cost, as in suffering, at which something is obtained: *The price of his independence was poverty.* **3.** The cost of bribing someone: *Every man has his price.* **4.** An amount offered as a reward for the capture or killing of a person: *a price on his head.* —***modifier:*** *price tags.* —*v.* **priced, pric•ing. 1.** To establish a price for: *priced squash at 29¢ a pound.* **2.** To find out the price of: *Let's go in and price the painting.* [SEE NOTE on p. 691]

price•less |prīs′lĭs| *adj.* **1.** Having great worth; invaluable: *priceless treasures.* **2.** Very amusing or odd: *Children often say priceless things.*

prick |prĭk| *n.* **1.** The act of piercing or puncturing. **2.** The sensation of being pierced. **3.** A hole or mark left by piercing. —*v.* **1.** To pierce or puncture lightly with or as if with a pointed object: *The straw poked out of the mattress and pricked her. Fireflies prick the darkness.* **2.** To sting with emotional pain: *My conscience pricks me at the thought of the deed.*

Idiom. **prick up (one's) ears.** To listen with interest.

prick•le |prĭk′əl| *n.* **1.** A small, sharp point, such as a spine or thorn. **2.** A tingling sensation. —*v.* **prick•led, prick•ling.** To feel or cause tingling sensations: *This lotion will prickle your face. The thought of a haircut makes my scalp prickle.*

prick•ly |prĭk′lē| *adj.* **prick•li•er, prick•li•est. 1.** Having prickles: *a prickly cactus.* **2.** Tingling: *a prickly feeling.* **3.** Easily irritated: *She is quite prickly today.* —**prick′li•ness** *n.*

prickly pear. 1. A cactus with flat, spiny stems, showy, usually yellow flowers, and egg-shaped, bristly, but often edible fruit. **2.** The fruit of such a cactus. [SEE PICTURE]

pride |prīd| *n.* **1.** A sense of one's own proper dignity or worth; self-respect. **2.** Pleasure or satisfaction in one's accomplishments or possessions: *My aunt takes a great deal of pride in her furniture.* **3.** Someone or something that is a source or cause of pride: *The painting was the pride of his collection.* **4.** An excessively high opinion of oneself; conceit: *Pride is one of the seven deadly sins.* **5.** A group of lions. —*v.* **prid•ed, prid•ing.** —**pride (oneself) on.** To be proud of: *She prided herself on her eloquence.*

pretzel

prickly pear

priest |prēst| *n.* **1.** In certain Christian churches, a member of the clergy having the authority to give absolution and administer all the sacraments except ordination. **2.** In a non-Christian religion, a man having a role comparable to that of a priest.

priest•ess |prē′stĭs| *n.* A female priest, especially of a pagan religion.

priest•hood |prēst′ho͝od′| *n.* **1.** The office or functions of a priest. **2.** Priests in general.

priest•ly |prēst′lē| *adj.* Of or befitting a priest: *priestly garb.*

prig |prĭg| *n.* An arrogant, smug, or narrow-minded person; a prude. **—prig′gish** *adj.*

prim |prĭm| *adj.* **prim•mer, prim•mest.** Stiffly formal or precise in manner or appearance. **—prim′ly** *adv.* **—prim′ness** *n.*

pri•ma•cy |prī′mə sē| *n., pl.* **pri•ma•cies. 1.** The condition of being first or foremost; superiority: *the lion's primacy among beasts.* **2.** The office or functions of an ecclesiastical primate.

pri•ma don•na |prē′mə dŏn′ə| *or* |prĭm′ə|. **1.** The principal female soloist of an opera company. **2.** A self-centered, temperamental person.

pri•mal |prī′məl| *adj.* **1.** Being first in time; original: *the primal innocence of the natives.* **2.** Of first importance; primary: *a primal necessity.*

pri•ma•ri•ly |prī mĕr′ĭ lē| *or* |-mâr′-| *adv.* In the first place; chiefly: *Europeans were primarily responsible for the settlement of our land.*

pri•ma•ry |prī′mĕr′ē| *or* |-mə rē| *adj.* **1.** First in time or sequence; original: *the primary stages of the project.* **2.** First in importance, degree, or quality; chief: *The primary function of furniture is comfort.* **3.** Being a fundamental part; basic: *the primary needs of man.* **4.** Of a primary school. **5.** Of a primary color. **6.** Of the part of a transformer or similar device to which electricity is supplied. **7.** Of a primary election. *—n., pl.* **pri•ma•ries. 1.** Something that is primary. **2.** A **primary election. 3.** The circuit, coil, or winding of a transformer into which electricity is fed.

primary accent. 1. The strongest degree of stress, placed on that syllable of a word that is spoken loudest. **2.** Also **primary stress.** The mark (′) used to indicate which syllable of a word receives the strongest degree of stress.

primary color. 1. Any of the three colors of light, red, green, and blue, from which light of any color can be made by mixing. **2.** Any of the three colors of pigment, purplish red, greenish blue, and yellow, from which pigment of any color can be made by mixing. **3.** Any of the colors, red, yellow, green, and blue, and black and white, into which any color can be mentally broken down. [SEE NOTE]

primary color
The **primary colors** *of sense* **1** *are sometimes called* light primaries, *those of sense* **2** pigment primaries, *and those of sense* **3** psychological primaries.

primary election. A preliminary election in which registered voters, usually the voters of each party, nominate candidates for office.

primary school. A school including the first three or four grades and sometimes kindergarten.

pri•mate |prī′māt′| *n.* **1.** Any member of the group of mammals that includes the lemurs, monkeys, apes, and human beings. Primates have a very highly developed brain and hands that have thumbs and are especially adapted for holding and grasping **2.** |prī′mĭt| *or* |-māt′|. A bishop of the highest rank in a province or country.

prime |prīm| *adj.* **1.** First in importance, degree, value, significance, etc.; *his prime concern; her prime accomplishments.* **2.** Graded by U.S. Government standards as the highest in quality, above both good and choice: *prime cuts of meat.* **3.** Of or indicating a prime number. *—n.* **1.** The stage of ideal physical perfection or intellectual vigor in a person's life. **2. a.** A mark (′) placed above and to the right of a letter to distinguish it from the same letter already in use: *Compare the angles b and b′.* **b.** The same mark used to represent the units feet, minutes of arc, or minutes of time: *a 10′ board; an angle of 27°13′.* **3.** A **prime number.** *—v.* **primed, prim•ing. 1.** To prepare (a pump or similar device) for operation by or as if by filling it with liquid. **2.** To prepare (a surface) for painting or finishing by covering with size, primer, or an undercoat. **3.** To make ready; prepare, as with information: *primed him for the contest.*

prime factor. Any prime number that when multiplied by an integer gives a product equal to a given integer.

prime meridian. The meridian whose position is indicated as 0°, used as a reference line from which longitude is measured. It passes through Greenwich, England.

prime minister. 1. A chief governmental minister appointed by a ruler. **2.** In some countries, a government official who is head of the cabinet and often chief executive.

prime number. An integer whose only factors that are also integers are itself and 1. For example, 7, 13, and 19 are prime numbers.

prim•er¹ |prĭm′ər| *n.* **1.** An elementary reading textbook. **2.** A book that covers the basic elements of any subject.

prim•er² |prī′mər| *n.* **1.** A coat of paint or similar material applied to a surface to prepare it for further painting or finishing. **2.** A device for setting off an explosive charge.

prime time. In radio or television, the hours, usually during the evening, when the largest audience is available.

pri•me•val |prī mē′vəl| *adj.* Of the earliest ages of the world; primitive. **—pri•me′val•ly** *adv.*

prim•ing |prī′mĭng| *n.* **1. a.** The preparation of a surface for painting or finishing by application of a primer. **b.** The substance used to do this; a primer. **2.** The explosive used to ignite a charge.

prim•i•tive |prĭm′ĭ tĭv| *adj.* **1.** Of or in an early stage of development: *a primitive form of life.* **2.** Of or in an early stage in the development of human culture: *a primitive tribe.* **3.** Simple or crude; not sophisticated: *a primitive form of rocket.* *—n.* A member of a primitive tribe, society, etc. **—prim′i•tive•ly** *adv.* **—prim′i•tive•ness** *n.*

pri•mo•gen•i•ture |prī′mə jĕn′ə chər| *n.* **1.** The condition of being the first-born child. **2.** In law, the right of the eldest son to inherit all of his parents' estates.

primp |prĭmp| *v.* To neaten (one's appearance) with considerable attention to detail: *She primped her hair. He primped for hours.*

primrose

prim•rose |prĭm′rōz′| *n.* **1.** Any of several plants often grown for their clusters of variously colored flowers. **2.** Also **evening primrose.** A plant with four-petaled yellow flowers that open in the evening and close during the day. [SEE

PICTURE]

prince |prĭns| *n.* **1.** *Archaic.* A king. **2.** The male ruler of a principality. **3.** A male member of a royal family other than a king. **4.** A nobleman of varying rank in different countries. **5.** An outstanding member of any group or class: *a prince of tricksters.* [SEE NOTE]

prince consort. The husband of a sovereign queen.

Prince Edward Island. An island in the Gulf of St. Lawrence, one of the Maritime Provinces of Canada. Population, 118,229. Capital, Charlottetown.

prince•ly |**prĭns**′lē| *adj.* Of or befitting a prince: *a princely act.*

prin•cess |**prĭn**′sĭs| *or* |-sĕs′| *or* |prĭn **sĕs**′| *n.* **1.** *Archaic.* A queen. **2.** The female ruler of a principality. **3.** A female member of a royal family other than the monarch. **4.** A noblewoman of varying rank in different countries. **5.** The wife of a prince. —*adj.* Describing a garment designed to hang in smooth, close-fitting, unbroken lines from the shoulder to the flared hem of the skirt: *a dress cut princess style.*

prin•ci•pal |**prĭn**′sə pəl| *adj.* First or foremost in rank, degree, importance, etc.; chief: *the principal character in the story; the principal reason for going.* —*n.* **1.** A person who holds a leading position, especially the head of an elementary, junior high, or high school. **2.** A main participant, as in a business deal or a play. **3. a.** A financial holding as distinguished from the interest or revenue earned from it. **b.** A sum of money owed as a debt, on which interest is calculated. ¶*These sound alike* **principal, principle.** —**prin′ci•pal•ly** *adv.* [SEE NOTE]

prin•ci•pal•i•ty |prĭn′sə **păl**′ĭ tē| *n., pl.* **prin•ci•pal•i•ties.** The territory ruled by a prince or from which a prince derives his title.

principal parts. In inflected languages, the main forms of the verb from which all other forms are derived. In English, the principal parts are considered to be the present infinitive (*walk, take*), the past tense (*walked, took*), the past participle (*walked, taken*), and the present participle (*walking, taking*).

prin•ci•ple |**prĭn**′sə pəl| *n.* **1.** A basic or fundamental truth or law: *the principles of Christianity.* **2. a.** A rule or standard of behavior: *a woman of dedicated political principles.* **b.** Moral standards in general: *a man of principle.* **3.** An underlying policy or quality that determines behavior: *the principles of self-preservation.* **4.** A statement or set of statements describing the way something acts or operates; a scientific law: *the principle of conservation of energy.* ¶*These sound alike* **principle, principal.** [SEE NOTE]

***Idioms.* in principle.** With respect to basic elements but not with respect to details: *The idea sounds good in principle, but will it work?* **on principle.** Because of one's standard of conduct: *I object to it on principle.*

print |prĭnt| *n.* **1.** A mark or impression made in or upon a surface by pressure, especially a fingerprint or footprint. **2. a.** Lettering produced by printing or a similar method. **b.** Matter, such as newsprint, so produced. **3.** A design or picture transferred from an engraved plate, wood block, etc. **4. a.** Cloth stamped with a dyed pattern or design: *a cotton print.* **b.** The pattern or design stamped on such cloth: *a paisley print.* **c.** A dress made from such cloth: *She wore a print.* **5.** The positive image of a photograph. —***modifier:*** *a print dress.* —*v.* **1.** To press (a stamp, mark, design, etc.) onto or into a surface. **2.** To produce (letters, newspapers, books, etc.) on a printing press: *The government prints money. The press prints very fast.* **3.** To offer in printed form; publish: *The newspaper refused to print the letter.* **4. a.** To write (something) in block letters similar to those commonly used in printed matter: *Print your name on the dotted line.* **b.** To write such letters: *She prints well.* **5.** To produce (a photographic print) by passing light through a negative onto a sensitized surface. —**print′ed** *adj.: a printed fabric; printed matter.* —***phrasal verb.* print out.** To print (a message, statement, instruction, etc.) automatically, as a computer or teletypewriter does.

***Idioms.* in print. 1.** In printed or published form: *The editor replied in print.* **2.** Still offered for sale by a publisher: *books in print.* **out of print.** No longer offered for sale by a publisher.

print•er |**prĭn**′tər| *n.* **1.** A person whose job or business is printing. **2.** Something that prints.

print•ing |**prĭn**′tĭng| *n.* **1.** The art, process, or business of producing printed matter on a printing press or by similar means. **2. a.** Printed matter. **b.** All the copies of something, such as a book, printed at one time: *the first printing of the dictionary.* **3.** Letters written in a style similar to the one commonly used in print.

printing press. A machine that transfers images, especially of printed matter, onto sheets of paper or similar material by contact with an inked surface.

print-out |**prĭnt**′out′| *n.* Printed material produced by a computer, teletypewriter, etc.

pri•or¹ |**prī**′ər| *adj.* **1.** Preceding in time or order: *his prior employment.* **2.** Preceding in importance or value: *a prior consideration.*

***Idiom.* prior to.** Before: *Prior to that time, no inspection was made.*

pri•or² |**prī**′ər| *n.* The monk in charge of a monastery, ranking below an abbot.

pri•or•ess |**prī**′ə rĭs| *n.* The nun in charge of a convent, ranking next below an abbess.

pri•or•i•ty |prī **ôr**′ĭ tē| *or* |-**ŏr**′-| *n., pl.* **pri•or•i•ties.** **1.** Precedence in importance or urgency: *Safety is given high priority in factories.* **2.** Something more important than other considerations: *Her major priority is getting out of debt.*

pri•or•y |**prī**′ə rē| *n., pl.* **pri•or•ies.** A monastery or convent governed by a prior or prioress.

prism |**prĭz**′əm| *n.* **1.** A geometric solid or polyhedron having congruent polygons lying in parallel planes as its bases and parallelograms as its sides. **2.** A solid of this type, usually with triangular bases and rectangular sides, made of a transparent material and used to refract light or break it up into a spectrum. [SEE PICTURE]

pris•mat•ic |prĭz **măt**′ĭk| *adj.* **1.** Of or like a prism. **2.** Refracting light as a prism does. **3.** Sparkling with colors, as from refracted light.

pris•on |**prĭz**′ən| *n.* **1.** A place of confinement for persons convicted or accused of crimes. **2.** Any place or condition of confinement: *His job seemed a prison to him.* —***modifier:*** *a prison cell.*

prince/principal/principle

Prince *is from Latin* princeps, *"chief, head, leader" (used as a title).* Princeps *had two derivatives: (1) the adjective* principālis, *"leading, first, chief," which is the source of* **principal**; *and (2) the abstract noun* principium, *"beginning, origin, foundation, basic element"; this became Old French* principe, *which was borrowed into English as* **principle** *(the change to an ending in* -le *is irregular).*

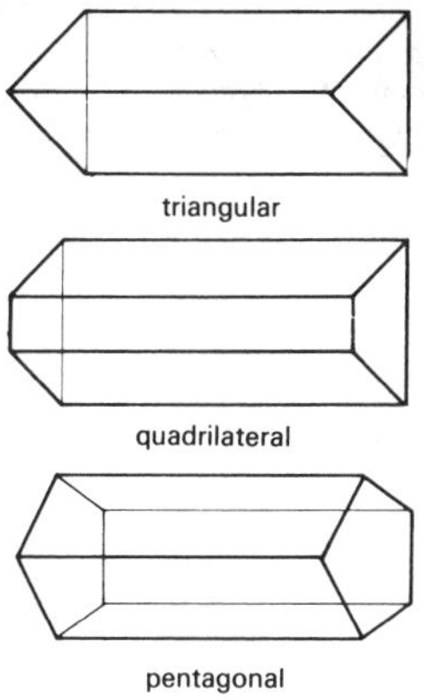

prism
Geometric prisms

private
The noun **private** *for a soldier of the lowest grade developed in the sixteenth century from sense* **5** *of the adjective; as a* private citizen *is a person who holds no public office, so a* private soldier *is a soldier who holds no special rank.*

prize¹·²·³
Prize¹ *is a variant of* **price** *(see note at* **precious***).* **Prize²** *is from Old French* prise, *"something seized," from Latin* prensus, *"taken."* **Prize³** *originally meant "a lever or crowbar"; it is also from Old French* prise, *in the sense "a seizing or grasping," and is thus a doublet of* **prize²**.

ă pat/ā pay/â care/ä father/ĕ pet/ ē be/ĭ pit/ī pie/î fierce/ŏ pot/ ō go/ô paw, for/oi oil/ŏŏ book/ ōō boot/ou out/ŭ cut/û fur/ *th* the/th thin/hw which/zh vision/ ə ago, item, pencil, atom, circus

pris•on•er |prĭz'ə nər| *or* |prĭz'nər| *n.* **1.** A person held in custody, especially in a prison. **2.** A person deprived of freedom of action or expression: *a prisoner of his fears.*

prisoner of war. A person taken by or surrendering to the enemy in wartime.

pris•tine |prĭs'tēn'| *or* |prĭ stēn'| *adj.* **1.** Of the earliest time or condition; primitive; original: *a pristine form of life.* **2.** Remaining in a pure state; untouched or uncorrupted, as by man: *the pristine beauty of snow-covered peaks.*

prith•ee |prĭth'ē| *or* |prĭth'ē| *interj. Archaic.* Please; I pray thee.

pri•va•cy |prī'və sē| *n., pl.* **pri•va•cies. 1.** The condition of being apart or secluded from others: *Her privacy is important to her.* **2.** Isolation, seclusion, or secrecy: *the right of privacy.*

pri•vate |prī'vĭt| *adj.* **1. a.** Of or confined to one person: *private opinion.* **b.** Intimate; secret: *a private thought.* **2.** Owned by a person or group of persons rather than the public or government: *a private house; private property.* **3.** Not available for public use or participation: *a private party.* **4.** Not known publicly; secret: *private negotiations.* **5.** Not holding public office: *a private citizen.* **6.** Secluded; isolated: *a private corner.* —*n.* An enlisted man of the lowest rank in the Army or Marine Corps. A **private first class** ranks above a private. —**pri'vate•ly** *adv.* [SEE NOTE]
***Idiom.* in private.** Secretly; confidentially.

pri•va•teer |prī'və tîr'| *n.* **1.** A ship, privately owned and manned, that is authorized by a government to attack and capture enemy vessels during wartime. **2.** The master or a crew member of such a ship. —*v.* To sail as a privateer.

private school. A school operated and supported by a private individual or group.

pri•va•tion |prī vā'shən| *n.* A condition of deprivation resulting from a lack of the basic necessities of life.

priv•et |prĭv'ĭt| *n.* A shrub with small dark-green leaves and clusters of small white flowers, often used for hedges.

priv•i•lege |prĭv'ə lĭj| *n.* A special right, immunity, benefit, permission, etc., granted to or enjoyed by an individual, class, group, or caste.

priv•i•leged |prĭv'ə lĭjd| *adj.* Enjoying or having privileges: *the privileged classes.*

priv•y |prĭv'ē| *adj.* Belonging to a person, such as the British sovereign, in his private rather than his official capacity: *Privy Council.* —*n., pl.* **priv•ies.** A latrine or outhouse.
***Idiom.* privy to.** Participating in a secret: *privy to the plan.*

prize¹ |prīz| *n.* **1.** Something offered or won as an award for excellence in a competition, winning a game, superiority in a contest, etc. **2.** Something worth having or striving for: *These tomatoes are the prize of the crop.* —*adj.* **1.** Offered or given as a prize: *prize money.* **2.** Given or likely to win a prize: *a prize Siamese cat.* **3.** Worthy of some prize or recognition. Often used ironically: *a prize mistake.* —*v.* **prized, priz•ing.** To value highly; esteem: *The Chinese prize jade.* [SEE NOTE]

prize² |prīz| *n.* Something seized by force in wartime, especially an enemy ship and its cargo captured at sea. [SEE NOTE]

prize³ |prīz| *v.* To move or force with or as if with a lever; pry: *prize a fungus off a tree trunk.* [SEE NOTE]

prize fight. A match fought between professional boxers for money. —**prize fighter.** —**prize fighting.**

pro¹ |prō| *n., pl.* **pros.** An argument in favor of something: *discussed the pros and cons.* —*adv.* In favor of: *argue pro and con.* —*adj.: the arguments pro and con.*

pro² |prō|. *Informal. n., pl.* **pros.** A professional, especially in sports. —*adj.* Professional: *pro football.*

pro–¹. A prefix meaning: **1.** Favor or support: *prorevolutionary.* **2.** Acting as; substituting for: **pronoun.** When *pro-* is followed by a capital letter, it appears with a hyphen: *pro-American.*

pro–². A prefix borrowed from Greek *pro,* meaning "before, in front of"; **prologue** is from Greek *prologos,* introduction.

prob•a•bil•i•ty |prŏb'ə bĭl'ĭ tē| *n., pl.* **prob•a•bil•i•ties. 1.** The condition of being probable; likelihood. **2.** Something, such as a situation or event, that is probable. **3.** A number expressing the likelihood of the occurrence of a given event, especially a fraction expressing how many times the event will happen in a given number of trials.

prob•a•ble |prŏb'ə bəl| *adj.* **1.** Likely to happen or be true: *the probable cost of the expedition.* **2.** Relatively likely but not certain; plausible: *a probable explanation.* —**prob'a•bly** *adv.*

pro•bate |prō'bāt'| *n.* Legal establishment of the validity of a will. —*v.* **pro•bat•ed, pro•bat•ing.** To establish the legal validity of (a will). —*adj.* Of probate: *probate court.*

pro•ba•tion |prō bā'shən| *n.* **1.** A trial period for testing a person's ability, behavior, willingness to work, etc. **2. a.** The release of a convicted offender on condition of good behavior. **b.** The period during which an offender is released on condition of good behavior. —***modifier:*** *probation officer.*

pro•ba•tion•er |prō bā'shə nər| *n.* A person on probation.

probe |prōb| *n.* **1.** An object introduced into a place, region, etc., for purposes of research or investigation: *a space probe.* **2.** Any of various long, slender tools used to reach into or touch something in order to examine it, especially an instrument used to explore a wound or body cavity. **3.** An examination or study with or as if with a probe. —*v.* **probed, prob•ing. 1.** To explore or examine (something) with or as if with a probe. **2.** To investigate or explore: *The committee is probing the causes of the strike.*

pro•bi•ty |prō'bĭ tē| *n.* Complete integrity; uprightness.

prob•lem |prŏb'ləm| *n.* **1.** A question or situation that presents uncertainty, confusion, difficulty, etc.: *traffic problems.* **2.** Someone who is difficult to deal with: *My boss is a real problem.* **3.** A question meant to be solved by mathematical means. —*adj.* Difficult to deal with: *a problem child.*

prob•lem•at i•cal |prŏb'lə măt'ĭ kəl| or **prob•lem•at•ic** |prŏb'lə măt'ĭk| *adj.* Posing a problem or question: *a problematical situation.*

pro•bos•cis |prō bŏs'ĭs| *n., pl.* **pro•bos•cis•es** or **pro•bos•ci•des** |prō bŏs'ĭ dēz'|. **1.** A long, movable snout, as an elephant's trunk. **2.** A long, tubelike mouth part of certain insects, used for sucking food. **3.** An unusually large nose.

pro•ce•dure |prə sē'jər| *n.* A manner of proceeding; a way of doing something or going about getting something done: *parliamentary procedure.* —**pro•ce'dur•al** *adj.*

pro•ceed |prə sēd'| *v.* **1.** To go forward or onward, especially after an interruption: *Proceed with caution.* **2.** To carry on some action or process; continue: *She proceeded to talk about the film.* —***phrasal verb.*** **proceed from.** To issue from; arise; result: *diseases that proceed from lack of proper foods.*

pro•ceed•ing |prə sē'dĭng| *n.* **1.** A course of action: *a reckless proceeding.* **2. proceedings. a.** The formal actions or activities of a court of law, legislative body, business organization, etc. **b.** The minutes or records of such actions or activities.

pro•ceeds |prō'sēdz'| *pl.n.* The amount of money derived from a fund-raising venture; profits.

proc•ess |prŏs'ĕs'| *or* |prō'sĕs'| *n.* **1.** A series of steps, actions, or operations used in making something or bringing about a desired result: *a manufacturing process; a cleaning process.* **2.** A series of actions, changes, etc., by which something passes from one condition to another: *a lake in the process of drying up.* **3.** Course of events or passage of time: *He started working hard, and in the process he lost ten pounds.* **4. a.** A summons or writ to appear in court. **b.** The entire course of a legal action. **5.** A part that extends or projects from the body or one of its organs: *The nose is a process that extends from the face.* —*v.* **1.** To put through a given series of steps: *process an application.* **2.** To prepare, treat, or convert by means of some process. —**proc'ess'ing** *adj.*: *a processing plant.*

pro•ces•sion |prə sĕsh'ən| *n.* **1.** The act of proceeding, especially in an orderly, regulated way: *Man has watched the stately processions of the heavenly bodies for many centuries.* **2.** A group of persons, vehicles, objects, etc., moving along in an orderly line: *a funeral procession.*

pro•ces•sion•al |prə sĕsh'ə nəl| *adj.* Used for or suitable for accompanying a procession: *a processional march.* —*n.* A musical piece used to accompany a procession.

pro•claim |prō klām'| *or* |prə-| *v.* **1.** To announce officially and publicly; declare: *proclaim a holiday.* **2.** To indicate unmistakably; make plain: *His behavior proclaims him incapable of holding any position of leadership.*

proc•la•ma•tion |prŏk'lə mā'shən| *n.* **1.** The act of proclaiming. **2.** Something proclaimed, especially an official public announcement.

pro•cliv•i•ty |prō klĭv'ĭ tē| *n., pl.* **pro•cliv•i•ties.** A natural inclination; predisposition: *a proclivity for the arts.*

pro•con•sul |prō kŏn'səl| *n.* In ancient Rome, a provincial administrator.

pro•cras•ti•nate |prə krăs'tə nāt'| *v.* **pro•cras•ti•nat•ed, pro•cras•ti•nat•ing.** To put off, postpone, or delay needlessly: *When it comes to work, he always procrastinates.* —**pro•cras'ti•na'tion** *n.* —**pro•cras'ti•na'tor** *n.* [SEE NOTE]

pro•cre•ate |prō'krē āt'| *v.* **pro•cre•at•ed, pro•cre•at•ing.** To produce (offspring), as a living thing does. —**pro'cre•a'tion** *n.*

proc•tor |prŏk'tər| *n.* In a college or university, a person appointed to supervise students during examinations. —*v.* To supervise (an examination).

pro•cure |prō kyŏŏr'| *v.* **pro•cured, pro•cur•ing.** **1.** To obtain; acquire: *procured tickets for the circus.* **2.** To bring about; effect: *striving to procure a solution to the problem.* —**pro•cure'ment** *n.*

prod |prŏd| *v.* **prod•ded, prod•ding.** **1.** To jab or poke, as with a pointed instrument: *She prodded the cattle along.* **2.** To incite to action; urge: *She continually prodded him to do his homework.* —*n.* Anything pointed used to prod: *a cattle prod.* —**prod'der** *n.*

prod•i•gal |prŏd'ĭ gəl| *adj.* **1.** Recklessly or extravagantly wasteful: *our prodigal waste of natural resources.* **2.** Extravagantly generous or abundant: *prodigal praise.* —*n.* An extravagant person; a spendthrift. —**prod'i•gal'i•ty** *n.* —**prod'i•gal•ly** *adv.* [SEE NOTE]

pro•di•gious |prə dĭj'əs| *adj.* **1.** Impressively large in size, force, or extent: *a prodigious sea monster.* **2.** Extraordinary: *a prodigious memory.* —**pro•di'gious•ly** *adv.* [SEE NOTE]

prod•i•gy |prŏd'ə jē| *n., pl.* **prod•i•gies.** **1.** A person with exceptional talents or powers: *a child prodigy.* **2.** Something extraordinary or rare; a marvel: *geysers and rock formations that are prodigies of nature.* [SEE NOTE]

pro•duce |prə dōōs'| *or* |-dyōōs'| *v.* **pro•duced, pro•duc•ing.** **1.** To bring forth (something); yield: *Seeds grow up to produce plants. The oil well produces at a rapid rate.* **2.** To give form or shape to; manufacture: *produce parts for machines.* **3.** To cause to exist; give rise to: *Industrial growth produced a new kind of business organization.* **4.** To bring forward; show; exhibit: *The little boy produced a snake from his pocket.* **5.** To sponsor and present publicly: *produce a movie.* —*n.* |prŏd'ōōs| *or* |-yōōs| *or* |prō'dōōs| *or* |-dyōōs|. Farm products, such as fruits or vegetables, raised for selling.

pro•duc•er |prə dōō'sər| *or* |-dyōō'-| *n.* **1.** A person or thing that produces: **a.** A person or organization that makes something: *a leading producer of cast iron.* **b.** A thing that yields something: *an oil well that is a good producer.* **2.** A person who supervises and manages the business details of the production of a play, motion picture, television show, or other entertainment.

prod•uct |prŏd'əkt| *n.* **1.** Something produced, as by nature, manufacturing, etc.: *industrial products. The rumor was a product of her imagination.* **2.** A direct result: *His lack of discipline is the product of a permissive education.* **3.** The result obtained when multiplication is performed.

pro•duc•tion |prə dŭk'shən| *n.* **1.** The act or process of producing: *automobile production.* **2.** Something produced, especially a motion picture, play, etc.: *This is the company's finest production to date.* **3.** The output or yield of producing: *Production is down this week.*

pro•duc•tive |prə dŭk'tĭv| *adj.* **1.** Producing or capable of producing: *an economically productive business.* **2.** Producing abundantly; fertile: *productive farmlands.* **3.** Producing favorable results or conditions; constructive: *a productive life.* —**pro•duc'tive•ly** *adv.* —**pro'duc•tiv'i•ty** |prō'dŭk-

procrastinate

Procrastinate *comes from Latin* prōcrastināre, *"to put off until tomorrow":* prō-, *"forward,"* + crās, *"tomorrow."*

prodigy/prodigious/prodigal

Prodigy *is from Latin* prōdigium, *"miraculous occurrence foretelling the future, omen, marvel."* **Prodigious** *is the adjective of* **prodigy. Prodigal** *is not related; it is from Latin* prōdigus, *"wasteful, lavish," from* prōdigere, *"to waste, spend."*

profess/profession/professor
Profess *is from Latin* profess-, *stem of* profitērī, *"to declare publicly, to claim to be (something)":* pro-, *"in public,"* + fatērī, *"to declare, claim." The meaning "to claim to be an expert teacher of (a subject)" had already developed in classical Latin and gave rise to the nouns* professiō, *"a special subject or pursuit," and* professor, *"a publicly recognized teacher." In the medieval universities of Europe,* professor *became the official title of teachers of the highest rank;* **profession** *and* **professor** *both became common in English from the sixteenth century.*

profile

ă pat/ā pay/â care/ä father/ĕ pet/ē be/ĭ pit/ī pie/î fierce/ŏ pot/ō go/ô paw, for/oi oil/o͝o book/o͞o boot/ou out/ŭ cut/û fur/*th* the/th thin/hw which/zh vision/ə ago, item, pencil, atom, circus

tĭv'ĭ tē| *or* |prŏd'ək-|, **pro•duc'tive•ness** *n.*

prof., Prof. professor.

prof•a•na•tion |prŏf'ə **nā'**shən| *n.* **1.** The act of profaning or the condition of being profaned; desecration: *hid the altar to save it from profanation by the invaders.* **2.** A particular act of profaning.

pro•fane |prə **fān'**| *or* |prō-| *adj.* **1.** Not religious in nature or use; secular: *sacred and profane music.* **2.** Showing contempt for God or sacred things; irreverent: *the profane use of God's name.* **3.** Using or containing irreverent, coarse, or vulgar language: *a fiery, profane man who cursed like a trooper.* —*v.* **pro•faned, pro•fan•ing. 1.** To treat or use (something sacred) in a way that shows contempt or irreverence: *profaning the names of the saints in oaths.* **2.** To put to an unworthy or degrading use; misuse: *profaning lovely French words by mispronunciation.* —**pro•fane'ly** *adv.* —**pro•fane'ness** *n.*

pro•fan•i•ty |prə **făn'**ĭ tē| *or* |prō-| *n., pl.* **pro•fan•i•ties. 1.** The quality of being profane; irreverence or vulgarity. **2. a.** The use of profane language. **b.** Language or an oath or word that is profane.

pro•fess |prə **fĕs'**| *v.* **1.** To declare openly; admit: *professed an interest in flying saucers.* **2.** To make a show of; pretend: *professing a sympathy that he did not really feel.* **3. a.** To claim knowledge of: *a critic who professes all the arts.* **b.** To practice (a profession or trade): *profess medicine.* **4.** To be an adherent of: *Most of the population professes Christianity.* [SEE NOTE]

pro•fessed |prə **fĕst'**| *adj.* **1.** Openly declared; avowed: *a professed enemy of tyranny in every form.* **2.** Declared with the purpose of deceiving; pretended: *his professed honesty.* —**pro•fess'ed•ly** *adv.*

pro•fes•sion |prə **fĕsh'**ən| *n.* **1.** The act of professing; an open declaration: *a profession of faith.* **2. a.** A kind of regular work, especially an occupation that requires training and specialized study: *the profession of medicine.* **b.** The group of qualified persons practicing such an occupation: *the teaching profession.* [SEE NOTE]

pro•fes•sion•al |prə **fĕsh'**ə nəl| *adj.* **1.** Of or for a profession: *professional schools of engineering and architecture; professional training.* **2.** Engaged in or trained for a profession: *lawyers, doctors, and other professional people.* **3.** Made or performed by a trained and qualified specialist: *Women with straight hair may acquire curls by either professional or home permanents.* **4.** Showing specialized skill or fine workmanship: *Sewing with a machine will give your garments a more professional appearance.* **5.** Doing a specified kind of work for a living or as a career: *a professional writer.* **6.** Performed by or consisting of persons receiving pay; not amateur: *professional football.* —*n.* **1.** A person who follows a profession. **2.** A person, especially an athlete, who performs or works for pay. **3.** A person who is skilled or experienced in a certain field; a qualified expert. —**pro•fes'sion•al•ly** *adv.*

pro•fes•sor |prə **fĕs'**ər| *n.* **1.** A teacher of the highest rank in a college or university. **2.** Any teacher or instructor. [SEE NOTE]

pro•fes•so•ri•al |prō'fĭ **sôr'**ē əl| *or* |-**sōr'**-| *or* |prŏf'ĭ-| *adj.* Of, like, relating to, or characteristic of a professor. —**pro'fes•so'ri•al•ly** *adv.*

pro•fes•sor•ship |prə **fĕs'**ər shĭp'| *n.* The rank or position of a professor.

prof•fer |**prŏf'**ər| *v.* To present for acceptance; offer: *proffered her services to a blind man at a street corner.* —*n.* An offer: *the proffer of help.*

pro•fi•cient |prə **fĭsh'**ənt| *adj.* Performing correctly and skillfully; competent through training or practice; adept: *proficient at playing the harmonica.* —**pro•fi'cien•cy** *n.* —**pro•fi'cient•ly** *adv.*

pro•file |**prō'**fīl'| *n.* **1. a.** A side view of an object, especially of the human head. **b.** A representation of a human head or other object seen from the side: *the profile of Lincoln on the penny.* **2.** The outline of something: *the jagged profile of the city; mapping a profile of the ocean floor.* **3. a.** The succession of layers that compose a soil, from rock up to the land surface. **b.** A representation and description of these layers. **4.** A piece of writing or reporting, especially a biographical sketch. [SEE PICTURE]

prof•it |**prŏf'**ĭt| *n.* **1.** An advantage gained from doing something; a benefit: *decided there was little profit in complaining.* **2.** The money made in a business venture, sale, or investment after all expenses have been met: *made a profit of five cents on every paper he sold.* —*v.* **1.** To gain an advantage; benefit: *profiting from the experience of others.* **2.** To be an advantage to; help advance or improve: *It would profit you to pay closer attention.* ¶*These sound alike* **profit, prophet.** —**prof'it•less** *adj.*

prof•it•a•ble |**prŏf'**ĭ tə bəl| *adj.* **1.** Yielding a profit; money-making: *a profitable fur trade with the Indians.* **2.** Yielding benefits; rewarding; worthwhile: *learned much during his lean years that was profitable to him later.* —**prof'it•a•bly** *adv.*

prof•i•teer |prŏf'ĭ **tîr'**| *n.* A person who makes excessive profits on the goods he sells, especially in a time of short supply. —*v.* To act as a profiteer.

prof•li•gate |**prŏf'**lĭ gĭt| *or* |-gāt'| *adj.* **1.** Recklessly wasteful of money or resources; wildly extravagant. **2.** Completely given over to self-indulgence and vice; dissolute. —*n.* A very wasteful or dissolute person. —**prof'li•ga•cy** *n.*

pro•found |prə **found'**| *adj.* **pro•found•er, pro•found•est. 1.** Extending to or coming from a great depth; deep: *a tradition with profound roots in Eastern culture.* **2.** Far-reaching; thoroughgoing: *a profound influence.* **3.** Penetrating well beyond what is apparent or superficial; wise and full of insight: *a profound knowledge of music; a profound mind.* **4.** Coming as if from the depths of one's being; deeply felt or held: *profound grief.* **5.** Total: *a profound silence.* —**pro•found'ly** *adv.* —**pro•found'ness** *n.*

pro•fun•di•ty |prə **fŭn'**dĭ tē| *n., pl.* **pro•fun•di•ties. 1.** The quality of being profound; great depth. **2.** Depth of intellect; wisdom: *serving up generalizations that often passed for profundity.* **3.** An idea, problem, or subject requiring deep and careful thought.

pro•fuse |prə **fyo͞os'**| *adj.* **1.** Abundant; plentiful: *a profuse variety of foods.* **2.** Given or giving generously; extravagant; lavish: *profuse praise.* —**pro•fuse'ly** *adv.* —**pro•fuse'ness** *n.*

pro•fu•sion |prə **fyo͞o'**zhən| *n.* Great quantity or amount: *A profusion of old chairs, books,* *suitcases, crates, and picture frames filled the attic.*

pro•gen•i•tor |prō jĕn′ĭ tər| *n.* **1.** A direct ancestor. **2.** A person or thing that originates or sets a pattern for something.

prog•e•ny |prŏj′ə nē| *n., pl.* **prog•e•nies.** Children or descendants; offspring.

prog•no•sis |prŏg nō′sĭs| *n., pl.* **prog•no•ses** |prŏg nō′sēz′|. **1. a.** A prediction of the likely course and outcome of a disease. **b.** The likelihood of recovering from a disease. **2.** Any prediction or forecast.

prog•nos•tic |prŏg nŏs′tĭk| *adj.* Of prognosis; predictive: *prognostic powers.* —*n.* **1.** A prognosis; prediction. **2.** A sign of future events; a portent.

prog•nos•ti•cate |prŏg nŏs′tĭ kāt′| *v.* **prog•nos•ti•cat•ed, prog•nos•ti•cat•ing.** To predict on the basis of present signs or symptoms: *prognosticate a poor year for farm crops.* —**prog•nos′ti•ca′tion** *n.* —**prog•nos′ti•ca′tor** *n.*

pro•gram |prō′grăm| *or* |-grəm| *n.* **1.** A list of the order of events and other information for some public performance, presentation, entertainment, etc.: *a printed program at a concert.* **2.** Such a performance, presentation, or entertainment; a show before an audience: *The senior class planned and gave a program of folk music.* **3.** A radio or television show. **4.** A list of activities, courses, or procedures; a schedule: *arranged her program for the fall semester so that she could work part-time.* **5.** An organized series of activities, courses, or events: *the school athletic program.* **6.** An organized, usually large-scale effort to achieve a goal by stages; a project: *the space program.* **7.** A plan or set of plans for future action: *The President presented his legislative program to Congress.* **8. a.** The set of steps necessary to collect the data needed for solving a problem, to solve the problem, and to present the answer. **b.** The set of instructions that a digital computer must execute in carrying out these steps. —*v.* **pro•grammed** or **pro•gramed, pro•gram•ming** or **pro•gram•ing. 1.** To include in a program of events, offerings, or activities; schedule. **2.** To plan or schedule radio or television programs. **3.** To provide (a computer) with a program. **4.** To train or regulate (the mind, senses, etc.) to perform in a certain way: *Our eyes have been programmed to overlook unimportant details.* [SEE NOTE]

pro•gram•er |prō′grăm′ər| *n.* A form of the word **programmer.**

pro•gram•mer |prō′grăm ər| *n.* Someone who prepares programs for computers.

prog•ress |prŏg′rĕs′| *or* |-rĭs| *n.* **1.** Onward movement; advance: *made slow progress through traffic.* **2.** Steady improvement, as in a civilization or individual: *Japan's progress since the war; a baby who was making progress in learning how to talk.* —*v.* **pro•gress** |prə grĕs′|. **1.** To move along; advance; proceed: *Make your sentences progress from general information to more specific information.* **2.** To make steady or regular improvements: *She had progressed to the point where she no longer needed a piano teacher.* [SEE NOTE]

***Idiom.* in progress.** Taking place; going on.

pro•gres•sion |prə grĕsh′ən| *n.* **1.** Movement; progress: *limbs adapted for progression on land.* **2.** Advancement to a higher or different stage: *the hero's progression from boy to man.* **3.** A series of things or events; sequence: *the formal dinner with its progression of great dishes and fine wines.* **4.** A sequence of numbers, each derived from the one before by some regular rule. See **arithmetic progression, geometric progression.**

pro•gres•sive |prə grĕs′ĭv| *adj.* **1.** Moving or advancing steadily or step by step: *the progressive erosion of a cliff over the years.* **2.** Spreading or growing continuously worse, as certain diseases do: *progressive paralysis.* **3.** Working for or favoring the changes necessary for progress or steady improvement: *an industrious, progressive people.* **4.** Working for or favoring reforms, as in government, the social system, or education; liberal. **5.** Of a system of taxation in which the rate of tax increases as the taxable amount increases: *The federal income tax is progressive, but sales taxes are not.* **6.** Of a verb tense or form used to express an action or condition that is in progress at the time spoken of. The progressive tense is formed in English with a present participle preceded by a form of the auxiliary verb *be.* For example, the following sentences are in the progressive tense: *I am growing. He had been growing. She will be growing.* —*n.* A person who works for or favors steady improvements or reforms. —**pro•gres′sive•ly** *adv.* —**pro•gres′sive•ness** *n.*

pro•hib•it |prō hĭb′ĭt| *v.* **1.** To make unlawful; forbid by law or authority: *Stock-car racing rules prohibit the use of more than one carburetor.* **2.** To prevent from doing something by law or authority: *Laws prohibit employers from discriminating against union members.*

pro•hi•bi•tion |prō′ə bĭsh′ən| *n.* **1.** The act of prohibiting or the condition of being prohibited: *the prohibition of firecrackers.* **2.** A law or an order that prohibits something: *a prohibition on smoking.* **3. Prohibition.** In the United States, the ban on the manufacture and sale of alcoholic beverages in the period from 1920 to 1933.

proj•ect |prŏj′ĕkt′| *or* |-ĭkt| *n.* **1.** An undertaking, plan, enterprise, etc., especially one requiring systematic planning and work: *the secret atom-bomb project; a land-irrigation project.* **2.** A special study or experiment undertaken by a student or group of students: *For her science project she decided to build an ant colony.* **3.** The product of a task or special study; a piece of work in progress or completed: *We mounted and displayed our art projects.* **4.** Also **housing project.** A group of houses or apartment buildings planned and built as a unit, usually with government financial support. —*v.* **pro•ject** |prə jĕkt′|. **1.** To extend forward or outward; jut: *Two horns projected from the boar's snout.* **2.** To shoot or throw forward or upward; hurl: *A stream of water projected from the fountain. An automatic triggering device projected the missile toward its target.* **3.** To convey; transmit: *Swedish folk songs project a mood of restrained sadness.* **4.** To cause a beam of light to direct an image of (a picture, a shadow, etc.) onto a surface: *projecting color slides onto a wall.* **5.** To imagine (something) in another time, place, situation, etc.: *a science-fiction story that projects the reader into the future; project the population of*

program

The British spelling of **program** *is* programme. *The word was first borrowed in the seventeenth century from Greek* programma, *"a public notice": pro-, "in public," + gramma, "something written." The original spelling, even in British English, was always* **program.** *But in the nineteenth century the word was reintroduced from its French equivalent, which is spelled* programme; *since then the British have gradually eliminated the older spelling, but many would admit that the Americans have been more reasonable in retaining it. (There is no variant British spelling for any of the other words, such as* **telegram** *or* **epigram,** *ending in* -gram.*)*

progress

"As natural selection works solely by and for the good of each being, all corporeal and mental endowments will tend to progress toward perfection." —Charles Darwin (1859).

"The reasonable man adapts himself to the world: the unreasonable one persists in trying to adapt the world to himself. Therefore all progress depends on the unreasonable man." —George Bernard Shaw (1903).

metropolitan Tokyo at 9,500,000 in 1990.* **6.** To imagine that (one's feelings or thoughts) are being expressed in the behavior of another. **7.** To plan; intend: *projecting a new superhighway.*

pro·jec·tile |prə **jĕk'**təl| *or* |-tīl'| *n.* **1.** An object, such as a bullet or arrow, that is thrown, fired, or otherwise launched through space. **2.** A self-propelling missile, rocket, etc.

pro·jec·tion |prə **jĕk'**shən| *n.* **1.** The act or process of projecting. **2.** Something that thrusts or juts outward: *an insect with spiny projections on its back.* **3.** An image produced by a pattern of light falling on a surface. **4.** An estimate of what something will be in the future, based on the present trend or rate of change: *Projections indicate that sales of new cars will be approaching record levels by 1986.*

pro·jec·tion·ist |prə **jĕk'**shə nĭst| *n.* A person who operates a motion-picture projector.

pro·jec·tor |prə **jĕk'**tər| *n.* A machine that uses lenses and a source of light to project images, as of motion pictures, onto a surface.

pro·le·tar·i·an |prō'lĭ **târ'**ē ən| *adj.* Of, connected with, or characteristic of the working class: *a proletarian revolution.* —*n.* A member of the working class. [SEE NOTE]

pro·le·tar·i·at |prō'lĭ **târ'**ē ət| *n.* The class of people who live by selling their labor for wages; the working class.

pro·lif·er·ate |prə **lĭf'**ə rāt'| *v.* **pro·lif·er·at·ed, pro·lif·er·at·ing. 1.** To produce new growth or offspring rapidly and repeatedly; multiply at a fast rate: *Viruses proliferate in living tissue.* **2.** To increase or spread rapidly: *The branches of physics have proliferated during this century.* —**pro·lif'·er·a'tion** *n.*

pro·lif·ic |prə **lĭf'**ĭk| *adj.* **1.** Producing offspring or fruit in great numbers: *prolific animals.* **2.** Causing or sustaining abundant growth: *the prolific tropical sun; a soil prolific of short, nutritious grasses.* **3.** Producing numerous works: *a prolific author.* —**pro·lif'i·cal·ly** *adv.* [SEE NOTE]

pro·lix |prō **lĭks'**| *or* |**prō'**lĭks'| *adj.* Wordy and tiresome; verbose. —**pro·lix'i·ty** *n.* —**pro·lix'ly** *adv.*

pro·logue |**prō'**lôg'| *or* |-lŏg'| *n.* **1.** A beginning section of a play, opera, or literary work that introduces or explains what follows. **2.** An introductory act or event.

pro·long |prə **lông**| *or* |**-lŏng'**| *v.* **1.** To lengthen in duration; protract: *a special diet for prolonging one's life.* **2.** To lengthen in extent or space: *no need to prolong a business letter.*

pro·lon·ga·tion |prō'lông **gā'**shən| *or* |-lŏng-| *n.* **1.** The act of prolonging in time or extent: *the prolongation of a waiting period.* **2. a.** An extension in time; a continuation or delay. **b.** An extension in space; a projecting part: *fish with fleshy prolongations that look like tails.*

prom |prŏm| *n.* A formal dance held for a school class.

prom·e·nade |prŏm'ə **näd'**| *or* |**-näd'**| *n.* **1.** A leisurely walk in a public place. **2.** A public place for strolling, as a park mall or an upper deck of a passenger ship. **3.** A formal dance. **4.** A march performed by the couples at the beginning of or between the figures of a square dance. —***modifier:*** *a promenade deck.* —*v.* **prom·e·nad·ed, prom·e·nad·ing. 1.** To go on a leisurely walk; stroll. **2.** To escort in or perform a square-dancing promenade: *Promenade your partner. Swing your partner and promenade to your seats.*

pro·me·thi·um |prə **mē'**thē əm| *n.* Symbol **Pm** One of the elements, a radioactive rare-earth metal. It has 14 isotopes with masses ranging between 141 and 154. Atomic number 61; valence +3; melting point 1,035°C; boiling point 2,730°C. [SEE NOTE]

prom·i·nence |**prŏm'**ə nəns| *n.* **1.** The quality or condition of being prominent; eminence or importance: *rose to a position of prominence in government.* **2.** Something that rises sharply upward or outward from its surroundings: *climbed the nearest prominence for a view of the terrain.* **3.** A slender, wavy cloud of shining gas that rises from the surface of the sun. [SEE PICTURE]

prom·i·nent |**prŏm'**ə nənt| *adj.* **1.** Projecting outward; bulging or jutting: *prominent brows.* **2.** Highly noticeable; readily evident; conspicuous: *You will find the card catalog in a prominent place in your library.* **3.** Well-known; leading; eminent: *a prominent politician; a prominent career in public service.* —**prom'i·nent·ly** *adv.*

pro·mis·cu·ous |prə **mĭs'**kyōō əs| *adj.* **1.** Careless in the choice of sexual partners; having sexual relations with many persons. **2.** Showing a lack of careful choice; indiscriminate: *a gallery with a promiscuous assortment of good and bad paintings.* —**prom'is·cu'i·ty** |prŏm'ĭ **skyōō'**ĭ tē| *or* |prō'mĭ-|, **pro·mis'cu·ous·ness** *n.* —**pro·mis'cu·ous·ly** *adv.*

prom·ise |**prŏm'**ĭs| *n.* **1.** A declaration that one will or will not do a certain thing; a vow: *kept her promise to write home once a week.* **2. a.** Indication of something forthcoming; grounds for expectation: *the promise of snow in the chill wind.* **b.** Indication of future success or profit: *a rookie pitcher who shows promise.* —*v.* **prom·ised, prom·is·ing. 1.** To make a promise; offer assurance: *promised to come home early.* **2.** To give one's word that one will provide or bring about: *promised her a special treat; promised full employment to the workers.* **3.** To give grounds for expecting: *clouds that promised rain.*

Promised Land. 1. In the Bible, the land of Canaan, promised by God to Abraham and his descendants. **2. promised land.** Any place of expected or longed-for happiness: *America was viewed as a promised land by many immigrants.*

prom·is·ing |**prŏm'**ĭ sĭng| *adj.* Giving hope of future success or profit: *a promising career.* —**prom'is·ing·ly** *adv.*

prom·is·so·ry note |**prŏm'**ĭ sôr'ē| *or* |-sōr'ē|. A written promise to pay a certain sum of money at a stated time or on demand.

pro·mon·to·ry |**prŏm'**ən tôr'ē| *or* |-tōr'ē| *n., pl.* **pro·mon·to·ries.** A high ridge of land or rock jutting out into a body of water.

pro·mote |prə **mōt'**| *v.* **pro·mot·ed, pro·mot·ing. 1.** To aid the progress or growth of; advance; further: *promoting the general welfare.* **2.** To urge the adoption or use of; advocate: *promote a measure in Congress.* **3.** To try to sell or make popular, as by advertising; publicize: *promoting a new line of products.* **4.** To raise to a higher rank, position, or class.

pro·mot·er |prə **mō'**tər| *n.* **1.** An active sup-

prolific/proletarian

Prolific *is from Medieval Latin* prōlificus, *"offspring-producing":* prōlēs, *"offspring, children,"* + -ficus, *"-making,"* **-fic. Proletarian** *is from the ancient Latin legal term* prōlētārius, *"free citizen of the lowest class." In the earliest Roman law, citizens were classed either as taxpaying property owners or as landless* prōlētāriī, *"offspring-people" (also from* prōlēs, *"offspring"), whose only contribution to the state was the breeding of children.*

promethium

Promethium *apparently does not occur in the earth's crust. It is obtained entirely by nuclear transmutation of other elements. Promethium has been used experimentally in long-lived batteries and portable x-ray units.*

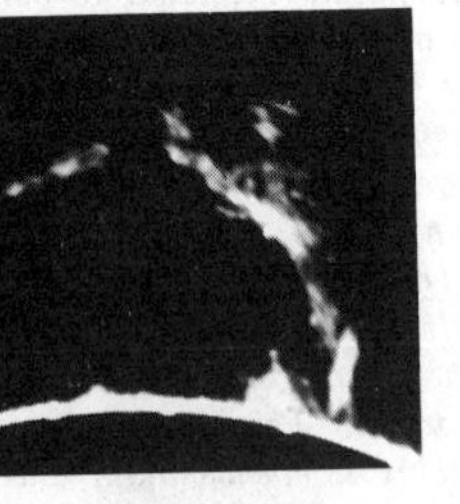

prominence
Solar prominence estimated to be 205,000 miles high

ă pat/ā pay/â care/ä father/ĕ pet/ ē be/ĭ pit/ī pie/î fierce/ŏ pot/ ō go/ô paw, for/oi oil/ŏŏ book/ ōō boot/ou out/ŭ cut/û fur/ *th* the/th thin/hw which/zh vision/ ə ago, item, pencil, atom, circus

porter; an advocate: *promoters of a larger defense budget.* **2. a.** A person in charge of finance and publicity for a business venture. **b.** A businessman who organizes and finances sporting matches, exhibitions, and other public events.

pro•mo•tion |prə **mō′**shən| *n.* **1.** Encouragement; furtherance: *societies for the promotion of knowledge.* **2.** Publicity, as for a product on sale or a business venture. **3.** An advancement to a higher rank, position, or class.

prompt |prŏmpt| *adj.* **prompt•er, prompt•est.** **1.** On time; punctual: *She was usually prompt in meeting deadlines.* **2.** Done, performed, or sent without delay; immediate: *a prompt reply.* **3.** Acting quickly and firmly; responding swiftly: *prompt to avenge any slight to his honor.* —*v.* **1.** To urge (someone) to some action; stimulate: *a news report that prompted her to write her family.* **2.** To inspire or encourage: *relying on the threat of the draft to prompt enlistments.* **3.** To assist by supplying a forgotten word, a cue, or another reminder: *prompt an actor.* —**prompt′ly** *adv.* —**prompt′ness** *n.*

prompt•er |**prŏmp′**tər| *n.* A person who prompts, especially a person not seen by the audience who gives reminders to actors or singers when they forget what to say or sing during a theatrical performance.

prom•ul•gate |**prŏm′**əl gāt′| *or* |prō **mŭl′**-| *v.* **prom•ul•gat•ed, prom•ul•gat•ing.** To announce publicly and officially; proclaim: *promulgate a new constitution.* —**prom′ul•ga′tion** *n.*

pron. **1.** pronoun. **2.** pronunciation.

prone |prōn| *adj.* **1.** Lying with the front or face downward. **2.** Tending; inclined: *prone to make hasty judgments.* —**prone′ly** *adv.* —**prone′ness** *n.*

prong |prông| *or* |prŏng| *n.* One of the sharply pointed ends of a fork or other implement.

pronged |prôngd| *or* |prŏngd| *adj.* Having prongs of a certain number or kind: *a three-pronged electrical plug.*

prong•horn |**prông′**hôrn′| *or* |**prŏng′**-| *n.* Also **pronghorn antelope.** A swift-running hoofed animal of western North America, having short, forked horns. [SEE PICTURE]

pro•nom•i•nal |prō **nŏm′**ə nəl| *adj.* Of, resembling, or functioning as a pronoun.

pro•noun |**prō′**noun′| *n.* In grammar, any of a class of words used as substitutes for nouns or noun phrases. [SEE NOTE]

pro•nounce |prə **nouns′**| *v.* **pro•nounced, pro•nounc•ing.** **1. a.** To articulate or produce (a word or speech sound); utter in a proper or specified manner: *used the dictionary to find out how to pronounce unfamiliar words.* **b.** To represent (a word) in phonetic symbols. **2.** To give utterance to; deliver formally: *pronounced a speech.* **3.** To declare: *pronounced them man and wife.* —**pro•nounce′a•ble** *adj.*

pro•nounced |prə **nounst′**| *adj.* Distinct; marked; unmistakable: *a pronounced limp; a pronounced bias.*

pro•nounce•ment |prə **nouns′**mənt| *n.* **1.** A formal declaration; an edict: *The king governed by issuing pronouncements from the palace.* **2.** An authoritative statement or judgment.

pron•to |**prŏn′**tō| *adv. Informal.* Right away; immediately.

pro•nun•ci•a•tion |prə nŭn′sē **ā′**shən| *n.* **1.** The act or manner of pronouncing words. **2.** A phonetic representation of a word, showing how it is pronounced. —***modifier:*** *a pronunciation key.*

proof |prōōf| *n.* **1.** Evidence or demonstration of the truth or validity of something: *The police suspected him but had no proof of his guilt. Accident figures offer us undeniable proof of the value of using safety belts.* **2.** A demonstration of the truth of a mathematical or logical statement, based on axioms and theorems derived from these axioms. **3.** The act of testing the truth or validity of something by experiment or trial: *the burden of proof is on the prosecution.* **4. a.** Also **proof sheet.** A trial sheet of printed material, checked against the original manuscript for errors. **b.** A trial impression of an engraved plate, stone, or block. **c.** A trial print of a photograph. **5.** The alcoholic content of a liquor, expressed in the United States as a given number of parts of alcohol per 200 parts of liquor. Liquor marked 100 proof is 50 per cent alcohol. —*adj.* Fully resistant; impervious: *a wood lacquer that is proof against termites.* —*v.* **1.** To proofread. **2.** To make resistant or impervious: *a chamber that has been proofed against outside noises.*

-proof. A word element meaning "safe from, resistant to": **waterproof.**

proof•read |**prōōf′**rēd′| *v.* **proof•read** |**prōōf′**-rĕd′|, **proof•read•ing.** To read and mark corrections in (printed, typed, or written material). —**proof′read′er** *n.*

prop[1] |prŏp| *v.* **propped, prop•ping.** **1.** To keep from falling; support: *propped up the overloaded shelf with a two-by-four.* **2.** To keep from declining or failing; sustain temporarily or artificially: *propping up the economy.* **3.** To place in a leaning or resting position: *propped her chin in her hands and listened.* —*n.* **1.** A vertical support used to keep something from falling. **2.** Someone or something depended on for support or assistance. [SEE NOTE]

prop[2] |prŏp| *n.* A stage property: *Chaplin's props were a bowler and an umbrella.* [SEE NOTE]

prop[3] |prŏp| *n. Informal.* A propeller. —***modifier:*** *a prop plane.* [SEE NOTE]

prop. proprietor.

prop•a•gan•da |prŏp′ə **găn′**də| *n.* **1.** The communication of a given doctrine to large numbers of people, especially by constantly repeating the doctrine and only giving information that supports it: *Government-controlled radio can be an instrument of propaganda.* **2.** Ideas, information, or other material distributed for the purpose of winning people over to a given doctrine, often without regard to truth or fairness.

prop•a•gan•dist |prŏp′ə **găn′**dĭst| *n.* A person engaged in spreading propaganda.

prop•a•gan•dize |prŏp′ə **găn′**dīz′| *v.* **prop•a•gan•dized, prop•a•gan•diz•ing.** **1.** To spread propaganda. **2.** To influence or subject to by propaganda: *television programs that propagandize children into accepting the world as it is.*

prop•a•gate |**prŏp′**ə gāt′| *v.* **prop•a•gat•ed, prop•a•gat•ing.** **1.** To produce or cause to produce offspring or new individuals; breed; reproduce: *insects that propagate in huge numbers; propagate plants from cuttings.* **2.** To transmit (heat, light, etc.) through space or a medium. **3.** To make known or accepted among many

pronghorn

pronoun/noun

Noun *is from Norman French* noun, *which is from Latin* nōmen, *"a name," hence also "a noun."* **Pronoun** *is formed by analogy directly from Latin* prōnōmen, *"word acting for a noun, pronoun." The adjective of* nōmen *was* nōminālis, *from which we have* **nominal,** *and likewise the adjective of* prōnōmen *was* prōnōminālis, *which was borrowed as* **pronominal.**

prop[1-2-3]

Prop[1] *is probably from Middle Dutch* proppe, *"support for vines."* **Prop**[2] *is a shortening of* **property,** *and* **prop**[3] *of* **propeller.**

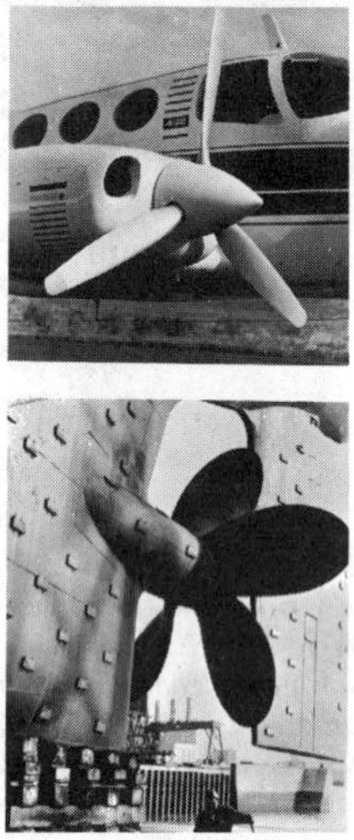

propeller
Above: Aircraft propeller
Below: Ship's propeller

ă pat/ā pay/â care/ä father/ĕ pet/ ē be/ĭ pit/ī pie/î fierce/ŏ pot/ ō go/ô paw, for/oi oil/ŏŏ book/ ōō boot/ou out/ŭ cut/û fur/ *th* the/th thin/hw which/zh vision/ ə ago, item, pencil, atom, circus

people; spread information about: *propagate a new industrial technique.* —**prop'a·ga'tion** *n.*

pro·pane |prō'pān'| *n.* A colorless, gaseous hydrocarbon that has the formula C_3H_8. It is found in petroleum and natural gas and is widely used as a fuel.

pro·pel |prə pĕl'| *v.* **pro·pelled, pro·pel·ling. 1.** To cause (a vehicle, rocket, body, etc.) to move or continue in motion: *the rearward thrust that propels a jet airplane.* **2.** To throw or launch forcefully; hurl: *The sailor leaned back and propelled the harpoon.* **3.** To urge on; inspire: *Spanish explorers were propelled by visions of golden cities in the New World.*

pro·pel·lant, also **pro·pel·lent** |prə pĕl'ənt| *n.* **1.** A fuel or explosive charge used to propel something, especially a rocket or projectile. **2.** The compressed gas used in an aerosol container or similar device to force out the contents.

pro·pel·ler |prə pĕl'ər| *n.* A rotary, fanlike device, usually driven by an engine or motor, used to propel an aircraft or boat. [SEE PICTURE]

pro·pen·si·ty |prə pĕn'sĭ tē| *n., pl.* **pro·pen·si·ties.** A natural or strong tendency; an inclination: *her propensity to gambling.*

prop·er |prŏp'ər| *adj.* **1.** Suitable; appropriate: *the proper tools for mending a leaky roof.* **2.** Normally or characteristically belonging to the person or thing in question: *regained his proper frame of mind; restored to her proper shape by the magician.* **3.** Called for by rules or conventions; correct because of effectiveness: *the proper way to hold a fork; the proper form for a business letter.* **4.** Strictly following rules or conventions, especially in social behavior; seemly: *a proper lady; not a proper activity for the Sabbath.* **5.** In the strict sense of the term: *We drove through the suburbs and entered the city proper.* —**prop'er·ly** *adv.* —**prop'er·ness** *n.*

proper fraction. A common fraction in which the numerator is less than the denominator.

proper noun. A noun that is the name of a particular person, place, or thing. See **noun.**

proper subset. A subset that does not contain all of the elements contained in the set from which it is derived.

prop·er·ty |prŏp'ər tē| *n., pl.* **prop·er·ties. 1.** Something or a number of things owned by someone; a possession or stock of possessions: *A post office is the property of the federal government. He could put all his property, except his bicycle, into two suitcases.* **2.** Land owned by someone: *a stream on the border of our property.* **3.** Something that one has the right to use: *A contribution of one scientist becomes the property of scientists to follow.* **4.** A quality or attribute, especially one that serves to define or describe something: *the chemical properties of a metal.* **5.** Any movable object, except costumes and scenery, that appears on the stage during a dramatic performance.

pro·phase |prō'fāz'| *n.* The first stage through which a living cell passes in mitosis, during which chromosomes form from the chromatin in the nucleus.

proph·e·cy |prŏf'ĭ sē| *n., pl.* **proph·e·cies. 1.** Something said by a prophet that reveals the divine will. **2.** A declaration or warning of something to come; a vivid, pointed, or solemn prediction: *prophecies of financial disaster that were fulfilled many years later.*

proph·e·sy |prŏf'ĭ sī'| *v.* **proph·e·sied, proph·e·sy·ing, proph·e·sies. 1.** To reveal (the will or message of God) by divine inspiration: *The soothsayer prophesied that a calf must be sacrificed on the altar.* **2.** To predict (what is to happen) solemnly or confidently.

proph·et |prŏf'ĭt| *n.* **1. a.** A religious leader who is inspired by God and acts as His spokesman among a people. **b. the Prophet.** Mohammed. **2.** The chief spokesman of a movement or cause: *the prophet of nonviolence and brotherhood.* **3.** A person who can foretell the future and give wise or inspired advice; a soothsayer. **4.** A predictor: *The election results confounded the newspaper prophets.* ¶*These sound alike* **prophet, profit.**

pro·phet·ic |prə fĕt'ĭk| *adj.* **1.** Of or characteristic of a prophet: *prophetic writings of the Old Testament.* **2.** Having or showing the ability to predict the future: *a warning that proved prophetic.* —**pro·phet'i·cal·ly** *adv.*

pro·phy·lac·tic |prō'fə lăk'tĭk| *or* |prŏf'ə-| *adj.* Acting to protect or defend against something, especially disease. —*n.* A prophylactic medicine, device, or action.

pro·pi·ti·ate |prō pĭsh'ē āt'| *v.* **pro·pi·ti·at·ed, pro·pi·ti·at·ing.** To soothe and win over (someone angry or offended); conciliate; appease: *propitiate a god with offerings.* —**pro·pi'ti·a'tion** *n.*

pro·pi·tious |prō pĭsh'əs| *adj.* Favorable; suitable: *a propitious time to ask his father for a loan; a climate propitious to the growth of mosses.* —**pro·pi'tious·ly** *adv.* —**pro·pi'tious·ness** *n.*

pro·po·nent |prə pō'nənt| *n.* A person who argues in support of something; advocate: *They are proponents of socialized medicine.*

pro·por·tion |prə pôr'shən| *or* |-pōr'-| *n.* **1.** The amount of a part compared with the total amount; a fraction of a whole: *the proportion of gold in an alloy.* **2.** The size, amount, or extent of one thing compared with that of another thing: *getting the proportions of the head, arms, and legs right in a figure drawing.* **3.** A mathematical statement that a pair of fractions are equal. For example, the statement $a/b = c/d$ is a proportion. **4. a.** A pleasing or desirable relationship between the various parts of a whole: *a face swollen out of all proportion.* **b.** Balance; symmetry: *the splendid proportion of a monument.* **5.** Often **proportions.** Size; dimensions: *a disease that reached epidemic proportions.* —*v.* **1.** To adjust the size or dimensions of (something) to something else; fit: *proportion the lettuce to the size of the sandwich.* **2.** To measure the relative amounts of: *proportion the ingredients of a cake.* **3.** To make the parts of harmonious or pleasing: *proportioned the figure nicely.*

pro·por·tion·al |prə pôr'shə nəl| *or* |-pōr-| *adj.* **1.** Corresponding in size, amount, or degree; in proportion: *the effects of the drug were proportional to the dose.* **2.** Related by a constant factor. For example, if $y = 6x$, x and y are proportional. **3.** Determined or calculated by means of fixed proportions: *a proportional share of the profits.* **4.** Used in determining proportions: *a draftsman's proportional compass.* —**pro·por'tion·al·ly** *adv.*

pro·por·tion·ate |prə pôr'shə nĭt| *or* |-pōr'-| *adj.* Being in proportion; corresponding: *a pro-*

motion with a proportionate increase in responsibility. —**pro•por'tion•ate•ly** *adv.*

pro•pos•al |prə **pō'**zəl| *n.* **1.** The act of proposing; an offer: *a shy proposal of friendship.* **2.** Something proposed; a plan or scheme offered for consideration. **3.** An offer of marriage. [SEE NOTE]

pro•pose |prə **pōz'**| *v.* **pro•posed, pro•pos•ing. 1.** To put forward for consideration or acceptance; suggest: *propose a new law.* **2.** To suggest (a person) for a position, mission, or membership; nominate. **3.** To declare an intention; intend: *He proposed to beat me at my own game.* **4.** To make an offer of marriage: *He proposed the day after he met her.* —**pro•posed'** *adj.: proposed changes.*

prop•o•si•tion |prŏp'ĭ **zĭsh'**ən| *n.* **1.** An offer; proposal: *The stranger said he had a business proposition to make to us.* **2.** A plan or scheme offered for consideration: *the proposition to extend daylight-saving time.* **3.** A statement or idea advanced tentatively or against opposition; a hypothesis: *"dedicated to the proposition that all men are created equal"* (Gettysburg Address). **4. a.** A mathematical statement, as the statement of a theorem. **b.** A statement in logic, especially one that satisfies certain rules or is constructed in a certain form. **5.** A matter to be handled or dealt with; an undertaking: *Maintaining rail lines is a difficult proposition in a land of mountains.* —*v.* To propose a bargain to (someone), especially a secret or immoral bargain. [SEE NOTE]

pro•pound |prə **pound'**| *v.* To set forth; propose or recommend: *propound a theory.*

pro•pri•e•tar•y |prə **prī'**ĭ tĕr'ē| *adj.* **1.** Of an owner or ownership: *proprietary rights; a proprietary interest in a business.* **2.** Characteristic of an owner: *a proprietary feeling about the view from his window.* **3.** Made and sold by a firm having the exclusive right to do so: *proprietary medicines.* **4.** Administered by a person or group appointed by the English Crown with full rights of government: *a proprietary colony.* —*n., pl.* **pro•pri•e•tar•ies. 1.** An owner; proprietor. **2.** A proprietary medicine. —**pro•pri'e•tar'i•ly** *adv.*

pro•pri•e•tor |prə **prī'**ĭ tər| *n.* **1. a.** A person who owns or has legal title to something: *the proprietor of an apartment building.* **b.** The owner or owner-manager of a business: *liked to patronize the stationery store because the proprietor was so friendly.* **2.** A person to whom a proprietary colony is granted.

pro•pri•e•tor•ship |prə **prī'**ĭ tər shĭp'| *n.* Ownership.

pro•pri•e•ty |prə **prī'**ĭ tē| *n., pl.* **pro•pri•e•ties. 1.** The quality of being proper; suitability; appropriateness. **2.** Conformity to rules and conventions, especially in social conduct; seemliness: *She insisted on strict propriety at her dinner parties.* **3. the proprieties.** The rules and conventions of polite social behavior.

pro•pul•sion |prə **pŭl'**shən| *n.* **1.** The act or process of propelling. **2.** Anything that acts to propel. —***modifier:*** *the propulsion system of a ship.*

prop•wash |**prŏp'**wŏsh'| *or* |-wôsh'| *n.* Also **prop wash.** The stream of air directed backward by the propeller of an aircraft.

pro•rate |prō **rāt'**| *or* |**prō'**rāt'| *v.* **pro•rat•ed, pro•rat•ing.** To divide (an amount, expense, tax, etc.) proportionately: *prorating the phone bills among the roommates.*

pro•sa•ic |prō **zā'**ĭk| *adj.* **1.** Like prose rather than poetry, as in being straightforward and factual: *a prosaic description of events.* **2.** Commonplace; everyday; ordinary: *prosaic household tasks.* **3.** Lacking in imagination or powers of fantasy: *Most children nowadays are too prosaic to believe in fairies and goblins.* —**pro•sa'i•cal•ly** *adv.* —**pro•sa'ic•ness** *n.*

pro•scribe |prō **skrīb'**| *v.* **pro•scribed, pro•scrib•ing. 1.** To make unlawful; prohibit. **2.** To banish; outlaw: *The king proscribed those of his enemies who managed to escape.* —**pro•scrib'er** *n.*

pro•scrip•tion |prō **skrĭp'**shən| *n.* The act of proscribing or the condition of being proscribed.

prose |prōz| *n.* Ordinary speech or writing as distinguished from verse or poetry. —***modifier:*** *a prose narrative.*

pros•e•cute |**prŏs'**ĭ kyōōt'| *v.* **pros•e•cut•ed, pros•e•cut•ing. 1. a.** To initiate or conduct a legal action against (someone): *charged with prosecuting people who break federal laws. The victim decided not to prosecute.* **b.** To present (a case, crime, suit, etc.) before a court of law for punishment or settlement. **2.** To press to completion; pursue determinedly: *prosecuting a war.* **3.** To engage in; perform or practice: *prosecuting his occupation.*

pros•e•cu•tion |prŏs'ĭ **kyōō'**shən| *n.* **1. a.** The act of prosecuting a person or case in a court of law. **b.** The condition of being thus prosecuted: *risked prosecution by breaking the law.* **2. the prosecution.** The party, usually a government, that brings legal action against a person accused of a crime: *a witness for the prosecution.* **3.** The act of pursuing or performing: *the prosecution of her duties.*

pros•e•cu•tor |**prŏs'**ĭ kyōō'tər| *n.* The person who initiates a legal action, especially the public official who represents the state and the people in court.

pros•e•lyte |**prŏs'**ə līt'| *n.* A person who has been won over to a religion, party, doctrine, etc.; a convert. —*v.* **pros•e•lyt•ed, pros•e•lyt•ing.** To proselytize. [SEE NOTE]

pros•e•ly•tize |**prŏs'**ə lĭ tīz'| *v.* **pros•e•ly•tized, pros•e•ly•tiz•ing. 1.** To convert (a person) from one religion, party, doctrine, etc., to another. **2.** To make or seek converts.

pros•o•dy |**prŏs'**ə dē| *n., pl.* **pros•o•dies. 1.** The study of the form of verse, especially of its meter. **2.** A particular system of form or structure in verse.

pros•pect |**prŏs'**pĕkt'| *n.* **1.** Something presented to the eye; a scene; view: *a lovely prospect from the tower.* **2.** Something expected or foreseen; an expectation: *hurried home with the prospect of a good dinner.* **3. prospects.** Chances for success: *a young man with prospects.* **4.** A possible customer. **5.** A possible candidate, as for a team or position: *a football scout who looked over the college prospects.* —*v.* **1.** To search about; explore: *prospecting for a place to build his house.* **2.** To explore (a region) in search of gold or other mineral deposits: *prospecting the Sierras; prospecting for uranium ore.*

pro•spec•tive |prə **spĕk'**tĭv| *adj.* **1.** Expected to be or occur; forthcoming; future: *prospective*

proposal/proposition

By origin and formation, these two nouns should have essentially the same meaning, but they have developed considerable contrast. While senses **1** *and* **2** *of each differ only in emphasis, sense* **3** *of* **proposal** *does not exist for* **proposition,** *and senses* **3, 4,** *and* **5** *of* **proposition** *do not exist for* **proposal.** *It is probable that any such pair of closely parallel words will inevitably tend to diverge in this way.*

proselyte/prostitute

Proselyte *is from Greek* prosēlutos, *"a newcomer, someone who arrives at a place," hence "a religious convert":* pros-, *"to, toward, at,"* + ēlut-, *"to come."* **Prostitute** *is from Latin* prōstitūtus, *"someone offered for sale":* prō-, *"in public,"* + stitu-, *"to set up, offer."*

protean
The word **protean** *comes from Greek* Prōteus, *the name of a sea god who could change his shape at will. Proteus was very wise, but mortals who wanted to ask him a question had first to tie him down securely. Then he would change into a wild boar or a tiger, and then into a rush of water and a raging fire. If the questioner held fast through all this, Proteus would return to his original shape and give an answer.*

protest/Protestant
The original meaning of the verb **protest** *was "to declare publicly," especially "to state one's rejection of something." It comes from Latin* prōtestārī, *"to make a public statement":* prō-, *"in public,"* + testārī, *"to state, to bear witness." In 1529 certain German princes and cities publicly declared ("protested") their defiance of the Catholic church, which had condemned Luther and the Reformation; those who made this public declaration called themselves the* **Protestants.**

ă pat/ā pay/â care/ä father/ĕ pet/ ē be/ĭ pit/ī pie/î fierce/ŏ pot/ ō go/ô paw, for/oi oil/ŏŏ book/ ōō boot/ou out/ŭ cut/û fur/ *th* the/th thin/hw which/zh vision/ ə ago, item, pencil, atom, circus

budget cuts; a prospective bride. **2.** Possible: *prospective customers.* **—pro•spec'tive•ly** *adv.*

pros•pec•tor |prŏs'pĕk'tər| *n.* Someone who explores an area for gold or other valuable mineral deposits.

pro•spec•tus |prə spĕk'təs| *n.* A printed description of a proposed business or other venture, sent out to gain interest or support for the venture.

pros•per |prŏs'pər| *v.* To be successful; thrive. **—pros'per•ing** *adj.: a prospering community.*

pros•per•i•ty |prŏ spĕr'ĭ tē| *n.* The condition of being prosperous; success, especially economic success.

pros•per•ous |prŏs'pər əs| *adj.* **1.** Vigorous and healthy; thriving: *a prosperous garden.* **2.** Economically successful; enjoying wealth or profit: *prosperous cities; a prosperous business.* **—pros'per•ous•ly** *adv.*

pros•tate |prŏs'tāt'| *n.* An organ composed partly of glandular tissue and partly of muscle tissue, found surrounding the urethra of male mammals at the point where it joins the bladder.

pros•ti•tute |prŏs'tĭ to͞ot'| *or* |-tyo͞ot'| *n.* **1.** Someone who performs sexual acts with others for pay. **2.** Someone who debases himself or his abilities for money or an unworthy motive. *—v.* **pros•ti•tut•ed, pros•ti•tut•ing. 1.** To offer (oneself or someone else) for sexual acts in return for pay. **2.** To sell (oneself or one's abilities) to some unworthy cause; debase. [SEE NOTE on p. 707]

pros•ti•tu•tion |prŏs'tĭ to͞o'shən| *or* |-tyo͞o'-| *n.* **1.** The practice or work of a prostitute. **2.** The act of prostituting; debasement: *the prostitution of an artist's talents.*

pros•trate |prŏs'trāt'| *adj.* **1.** Lying flat: *a sleeper prostrate on the floor.* **2.** Kneeling or lying face down, as in submission: *He fell prostrate before the throne.* **3.** Exhausted or overcome physically, emotionally, etc.; helpless: *prostrate with fear.* *—v.* **pros•trat•ed, pros•trat•ing. 1.** To throw down flat. **2.** To put (oneself) in a prostrate position. **3.** To exhaust or overcome physically, emotionally, etc.; render helpless: *a disease that prostrates its victims.*

pros•tra•tion |prŏ strā'shən| *n.* **1. a.** The act or process of prostrating. **b.** The condition of being prostrate. **2.** Complete mental or physical exhaustion.

Prot. Protestant.

pro•tac•tin•i•um |prō'tăk tĭn'ē əm| *n.* Symbol **Pa** One of the elements, a rare radioactive metal, chemically similar to uranium. It has 12 isotopes, the most common of which is Pa 231, with a half-life of 32,480 years. Atomic number 91; valences +4, +5; melting point 1,230°C.

pro•tag•o•nist |prō tăg'ə nĭst| *n.* The main character in a drama or literary work.

pro•te•an |prō'tē ən| *or* |prō tē'-| *adj.* Taking on many different shapes or forms; highly variable: *a protean talent; the protean colors of a psychedelic light show.* [SEE NOTE]

pro•tect |prə tĕkt'| *v.* **1.** To keep from harm, attack, or injury; guard: *wore sunglasses to protect her eyes from the glare; inoculations that protect against disease.* **2.** To prevent the destruction or misuse of; preserve: *game laws that protect certain species of bird.*

pro•tec•tion |prə tĕk'shən| *n.* **1. a.** The condition of being protected: *a hedge for protection against the wind.* **b.** The act of protecting. **2.** Someone or something that protects: *a dog that was both a companion and a protection.*

pro•tec•tive |prə tĕk'tĭv| *adj.* Serving to protect: *a protective coat of shellac; a protective moat.* **—pro•tec'tive•ly** *adv.* **—pro•tec'tive•ness** *n.*

pro•tec•tor |prə tĕk'tər| *n.* **1.** Someone or something that protects; a defender or guardian: *She decided to become the protector of the orphan colt. The catcher wore a cushioned chest protector.* **2.** A person appointed to rule a kingdom during the absence or childhood of the monarch.

pro•tec•tor•ate |prə tĕk'tər ĭt| *n.* **1. a.** A relationship of protection and partial control assumed by a strong nation over a dependent foreign country. **b.** A dependent country or region in such a relationship. **2.** The rule or office of a protector, as of a kingdom, or the period during which a protector is in power.

pro•té•gé |prō'tə zhā'| *n.* A person guided in his career by another, more influential or experienced person.

pro•tein |prō'tēn'| *n.* A member of a large class of organic chemical compounds that contain nitrogen, have very high molecular weights, and are complex in structure. They occur in and form the basis of living tissues. *—**modifier:** a protein molecule.*

Prot•er•o•zo•ic |prŏt'ər ə zō'ĭk| *or* |prō'tər-| *n.* Also **Proterozoic era.** A geologic era extending from the middle of the Precambrian era to the beginning of the Paleozoic era, ending about 600 million years ago. *—**modifier:** a Proterozoic fossil.*

pro•test |prō'tĕst'| *n.* **1.** A formal statement expressing disapproval or objection: *sent a protest to the mayor's office.* **2. a.** An expression of disapproval or objection: *refused to buy tea in protest against the new tax.* **b.** A public gathering called to express opposition; a demonstration: *a student protest against the war.* *—**modifier:** a protest movement; protest songs.* *—v.* |prə tĕst'| *or* |prō-|. **1.** To express strong objections to (something), as in a formal statement or public demonstration: *opposed the new law and protested to the governor.* **2.** To say or claim in protest: *protested that he had been given too little cake.* **3.** To declare earnestly; affirm: *protested his innocence.* **—pro•test'er** *n.* [SEE NOTE]

Idiom. **under protest.** After making known one's objections: *He went to the tea party only under protest.*

Prot•es•tant |prŏt'ĭ stənt| *n.* Any Christian belonging to a sect descending from those that broke away from the Roman Catholic Church in the 16th century. *—adj.* Of or adhering to Protestantism: *the Protestant Bible.* [SEE NOTE]

Protestant Episcopal Church. A church in the United States that was originally a branch of the Church of England and that became an independent body in 1789. Also called *Episcopal Church.*

Prot•es•tant•ism |prŏt'ĭ stən tĭz'əm| *n.* **1.** The beliefs and practices of Protestants. **2.** Protestant churches or their membership in general.

prot•es•ta•tion |prŏt'ĭ stā'shən| *or* |prō'tĭ-| *n.* An earnest declaration; avowal.

pro•tist |prō'tĭst| *n.* Any of a large group of

usually one-celled organisms, considered by many scientists to be neither animals nor plants, and including the protozoans, bacteria, certain algae, and the slime molds. The protists are regarded as forming a separate kingdom.

pro•ti•um |prō′tē əm| *or* |-shē-| *n.* The most abundant isotope of hydrogen, having an atomic mass of 1.

proto–. A word element meaning: **1.** The earliest or first form: **prototype. 2.** The earliest stage of a language as reconstructed by linguists: *Proto-Indo-European.* [SEE NOTE]

pro•to•col |**prō′**tə kôl′| *or* |-kōl′| *or* |-kŏl′| *n.* **1.** The forms of ceremony and social etiquette observed by diplomats and heads of state. **2.** A record or memorandum of an agreement, especially one used as the basis for a later, formal document: *the protocol of an international treaty.*

pro•ton |**prō′**tŏn′| *n.* A stable subatomic particle having a positive charge equal in magnitude to that of an electron and a mass equal to 1,836 times that of an electron.

pro•to•plasm |**prō′**tə plăz′əm| *n.* A jellylike substance that forms the living matter in all plant and animal cells.

pro•to•type |**prō′**tə tīp′| *n.* **1.** A first or early example of something, on which later examples are based or judged: *Edison's invention factory was the prototype of modern engineering laboratories.* **2.** The first full-scale model to be constructed of a new type of vehicle, machine, device, etc.: *the prototype of a new jet airplane.* —***modifier:*** *a prototype nuclear reactor.*

pro•to•zo•an |prō′tə **zō′**ən| *n., pl.* **pro•to•zo•ans** or **pro•to•zo•a** |prō′tə **zō′**ə|. Any of a large group of very small one-celled organisms considered to be the simplest forms of animal life. Protozoans are usually too small to be seen without a microscope and include, among others, the amebas, paramecia, and some of the microorganisms that cause disease.

pro•tract |prō **trăkt′**| *v.* To draw out in time; lengthen; prolong. —**pro•tract′ed** *adj.: a protracted conversation.* —**pro•trac′tion** *n.*

pro•trac•tor |prō **trăk′**tər| *n.* A semicircular instrument marked off in degrees, used for measuring and drawing angles. [SEE PICTURE]

pro•trude |prō **trōōd′**| *v.* **pro•trud•ed, pro•trud•ing.** To stick out from a surface; project: *Curly hair protruded from the edges of his cap. The cat protruded its nose into the hole in the wall.* —**pro•trud′ing** *adj.: protruding ears.*

pro•tru•sion |prō **trōō′**zhən| *n.* **1.** The act of protruding or the condition of being protruded. **2.** A part or object that protrudes; a projection.

pro•tu•ber•ance |prō **tōō′**bər əns| *or* |**-tyōō′-**| *n.* **1.** The condition of being protuberant. **2.** A protuberant part or object; a bulge or knob.

pro•tu•ber•ant |prō **tōō′**bər ənt| *or* |**-tyōō′-**| *adj.* Bulging or swelling outward from a surface: *slightly protuberant eyes.* —**pro•tu′ber•ant•ly** *adv.*

proud |proud| *adj.* **proud•er, proud•est. 1. a.** Feeling pleasure and satisfaction over something one owns, makes, does, or is a part of: *proud of his black skin; proud to be named to the Olympic team.* **b.** Arousing or marked by such a feeling; gratifying: *his proudest possessions; a proud moment.* **2.** Full of self-respect and independence of spirit: *too proud to ask for help; a proud and rugged Indian people.* **3.** Highly respected; honored: *a proud name; a proud heritage.* **4.** Dignified; stately; majestic: *the proud carriage of a queen.* **5.** Overconscious of one's high rank or great beauty; haughty; overbearing and arrogant: *a nobleman too proud to speak to commoners.* —**proud′ly** *adv.*

prove |prōōv| *v.* **proved, proved** or **prov•en** |**prōō′**vən|, **prov•ing. 1.** To show beyond doubt; demonstrate convincingly: *He proved that he could lift 400 pounds.* **2.** To show to be true or valid by giving evidence or arguments: *proved the charge of murder at the trial.* **3.** To find out by testing: *proving who could run faster.* **4. a.** To test; try out: *proving a new car on the open road.* **b.** To test with good results; show the worth of: *He resolved not to come back until he had proved himself in battle.* **5.** To turn out: *an estimate that proved too low.* —**prov′a•ble** *adj.*

Pro•ven•çal |prō′vən **säl′**| *or* |prŏv′ən-| *n.* **1.** A native or inhabitant of Provence. **2.** The Romance language of Provence. —*adj.* Of Provence, the Provençals, or their language.

Pro•vence |prô **väns′**| *or* |prə-|. A region of southeastern France.

prov•en•der |**prŏv′**ən dər| *n.* Dry food, such as hay, for livestock; feed.

prov•erb |**prŏv′**ərb| *n.* A short, common saying that illustrates a truth. [SEE NOTE]

pro•ver•bi•al |prə **vûr′**bē əl| *adj.* **1.** Of the nature of a proverb or proverbs: *proverbial sayings.* **2.** Referred to in a proverb or other well-known saying: *slept like the proverbial baby.* **3.** Widely known and spoken of; famous: *Her skill at cards is proverbial.* —**pro•ver′bi•al•ly** *adv.*

pro•vide |prə **vīd′**| *v.* **pro•vid•ed, pro•vid•ing. 1.** To give (something needed or useful); supply: *generators that provide electrical energy.* **2.** To furnish with something needed or useful; equip: *provided him with enough money for the trip.* **3.** To serve as; constitute: *a river that provides a means of safe transport.* **4.** To make available; have or offer for the use of others: *a filling station that provides rest rooms.* **5.** To supply means of subsistence or maintenance: *He worked hard to provide for his large family.* **6.** To make ready; prepare: *We provided against emergencies by taking extra money and clothing.* **7.** To set down an instruction, rule, or condition: *He provided for a scholarship fund in his will.* —**pro•vid′er** *n.*

pro•vid•ed |prə **vī′**dĭd| *conj.* On the condition; if: *You may go provided your work is done.*

prov•i•dence |**prŏv′**ĭ dəns| *n.* **1.** The quality of being provident; careful preparation for future needs. **2.** The control and protection of God; divine direction. **3. Providence.** God.

Prov•i•dence |**prŏv′**ĭ dəns| *or* |-dĕns′|. The capital of Rhode Island. Population, 177,000.

prov•i•dent |**prŏv′**ĭ dənt| *adj.* **1.** Providing for the future; showing prudent forethought. **2.** Frugal; thrifty. —**prov′i•dent•ly** *adv.*

prov•i•den•tial |prŏv′ĭ **dĕn′**shəl| *adj.* **1.** Of or resulting from divine guidance or control: *the providential mission of a prophet.* **2.** Happening as if through divine intervention; very fortunate: *The providential arrival of reinforcements saved the day.* —**prov′i•den′tial•ly** *adv.*

prov•ince |**prŏv′**ĭns| *n.* **1.** A part; division; region: *The brain is a little-explored province of*

proto–

In favorable circumstances, linguists can deduce many details of what a language was like before it was recorded in writing. A prehistoric reconstruction of this kind is called a proto-language *(***proto-** *is from Greek* prōtos, *"first, earliest"). Examples:* Proto-Algonquian *(spoken by Algonquian Indians in eastern North America long before the coming of European settlers);* Proto-Indo-European *(see note at* **Indo-European***);* Proto-Semitic *(the language ancestral to Arabic and Hebrew, spoken more than five thousand years ago).*

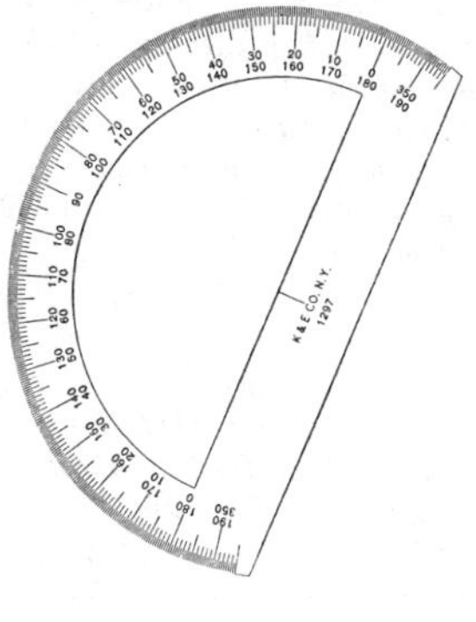

protractor

proverb

A selection of English proverbs, all recorded from the eighteenth century or earlier:
"Oaks may fall when reeds stand the storm." "A penny saved is a penny gained." "A bad workman blames his tools." "April showers bring May flowers." "He was a bold man that first ate an oyster." "A cat in gloves catches no mice." "Fine words butter no parsnips." "Empty vessels make the greatest sounds." "Money burns a hole in your pocket." "Love me, love my dog." "Marry in haste, repent at leisure." "No news is good news."

prune[1-2]
Prune[1] *and* **plum** *are doublets, coming by separate routes from Latin* prūnum, *"a plum."* Prūnum *was borrowed into Old English as* plūme, *becoming* **plum** *in Modern English. In Old French,* prūnum *became* prune, *which was borrowed into English as* **prune**, *at first meaning simply "a plum" but later "dried plum imported from France."* **Prune**[2] *is from Old French* proignier, *which is descended from an unattested Latin word,* prō-rotundiāre, *meaning "to cut around":* prō-, *"in front, off,"* + rotundus, *"round."*

pry[1-2]
Pry[2], *first recorded from the fourteenth century, is of obscure origin.* **Pry**[1] *is a kind of back-formation from* **prize**[3]; *apparently* prize *was understood as* (he) pries, *the third person singular present tense of a verb, which could only be* **pry**[2].

ă pat/ā pay/â care/ä father/ĕ pet/ ē be/ĭ pit/ī pie/î fierce/ŏ pot/ ō go/ô paw, for/oi oil/o͝o book/ o͞o boot/ou out/ŭ cut/û fur/ *th* the/th thin/hw which/zh vision/ ə ago, item, pencil, atom, circus

the body. **2.** A political subdivision of a country: *Ontario and Quebec are the leading industrial provinces of Canada.* **3. the provinces.** The outlying areas of a country, away from the capital. **4.** The range of one's proper knowledge, functions, or responsibility; scope.

pro•vin•cial |prə vĭn'shəl| *adj.* **1.** Of a province: *a provincial capital.* **2.** Of areas away from the capital of a country: *French provincial life.* **3.** Characteristic of people or things away from the capital of a country: *a provincial simplicity of speech and dress.* **4.** Limited in range or perspective; narrow; ill-informed: *provincial attitudes.* —*n.* Someone from the provinces. —**pro•vin'ci•al'i•ty** *n.* —**pro•vin'cial•ly** *adv.*

pro•vin•cial•ism |prə vĭn'shə lĭz'əm| *n.* **1.** Narrowness of outlook, attitudes, or loyalties. **2.** A word or phrase peculiar to the speech of people from a certain limited area.

pro•vi•sion |prə vĭzh'ən| *n.* **1.** The act of providing or supplying: *the provision of mosquito nets for the safari.* **2.** Something that is provided for one's benefit: *A fire escape is an important safety provision in a tall building.* **3. provisions.** Stocks of food and other necessary supplies. **4.** A measure taken in preparation: *making provisions for her wedding.* **5.** A section of a contract, will, or other document that covers a certain subject; a stipulation: *a provision of a peace treaty forbidding rearmament.* —*v.* To supply with provisions.

pro•vi•sion•al |prə vĭzh'ə nəl| *adj.* Serving for the time being; temporary: *a provisional government; a provisional theory.* —**pro•vi'sion•al•ly** *adv.*

prov•o•ca•tion |prŏv'ə kā'shən| *n.* **1.** The act of provoking; incitement. **2.** An action that provokes anger or aggression: *Sharks will sometimes attack men without provocation.*

pro•voc•a•tive |prə vŏk'ə tĭv| *adj.* **1.** Tending to arouse curiosity or interest; stimulating: *a provocative new theory.* **2.** Tending to irritate or arouse resentment: *his provocative boastfulness.* —**pro•voc'a•tive•ly** *adv.* —**pro•voc'a•tive•ness** *n.*

pro•voke |prə vōk'| *v.* **pro•voked, pro•vok•ing.** **1.** To bring on; arouse: *The comedian provoked steady laughter.* **2.** To stir to action; incite: *Conscience provoked them to speak out.* **3.** To arouse the anger or resentment of: *goaded and provoked the bear to attack.*

pro•vost |prō'vōst'| *or* |prŏv'əst| *or* |prō'vəst| *n.* **1.** A high-ranking administrative officer at certain colleges and universities. **2.** Any of various presiding officials: **a.** A clergyman in charge of a cathedral. **b.** The mayor of a Scottish city.

prow |prou| *n.* **1.** The forward part of a ship's hull; bow. **2.** Any similar projecting front part, such as the nose of an aircraft.

prow•ess |prou'ĭs| *n.* **1.** Bravery and resourcefulness, especially in battle: *proved his prowess by outrunning his enemies.* **2.** Exceptional skill; excellence: *showed prowess as a carpenter.*

prowl |proul| *v.* To roam stealthily, as if in search of prey: *City cats prowl through alleys at night. Solitary trappers and hunters prowled the wilderness.* —*n.* An act of prowling: *took a prowl through the antique shops.* —**prowl'er** *n.*

prowl car. A police patrol car; a squad car.

prox•im•i•ty |prŏk sĭm'ĭ tē| *n.* The quality or fact of being near; closeness.

prox•y |prŏk'sē| *n., pl.* **prox•ies.** **1.** A person authorized to act for another. **2.** The authority to substitute or act of substituting for another: *vote by proxy.*

prude |pro͞od| *n.* A person who is too concerned with being proper and virtuous and who is easily offended by sexual references.

pru•dence |pro͞od'ns| *n.* The quality of being prudent, especially: **1.** Sound and considered judgment. **2.** Caution; forethought; discretion. **3.** Careful management of resources; frugality.

pru•dent |pro͞od'nt| *adj.* **1.** Having or showing good judgment; well-advised; sensible: *a prudent man; a prudent decision.* **2.** Careful of one's resources; frugal; thrifty. —**pru'dent•ly** *adv.*

pru•den•tial |pro͞o dĕn'shəl| *adj.* Prudent. —**pru•den'tial•ly** *adv.*

prud•er•y |pro͞o'də rē| *n., pl.* **prud•er•ies.** **1.** The quality of being prudish; excessive concern for being proper and virtuous. **2.** An example of prudish behavior or speech.

prud•ish |pro͞o'dĭsh| *adj.* Characteristic of or being a prude; excessively proper and virtuous: *a prudish distaste for kissing games.* —**prud'ish•ly** *adv.* —**prud'ish•ness** *n.*

prune[1] |pro͞on| *n.* A dried plum. [SEE NOTE]

prune[2] |pro͞on| *v.* **pruned, prun•ing.** **1. a.** To cut or trim branches, stems, etc., from (a tree or plant) to improve its growth or shape. **b.** To cut or trim (branches, stems, etc.) for this purpose. **2. a.** To shorten or improve by removing unnecessary parts: *prune a long composition.* **b.** To remove (unwanted or undesirable parts or elements): *prune unnecessary expenses.* [SEE NOTE]

Prus•sia |prŭsh'ə|. A former country occupying most of present-day Germany. —**Prus'sian** *n.* & *adj.*

pry[1] |prī| *v.* **pried, pry•ing, pries.** **1.** To raise, move, or force open with or as with a lever: *pry the lid off a box.* **2.** To obtain or extract with difficulty: *pried answers from the child.* —*n., pl.* **pries.** Something used as a lever. [SEE NOTE]

pry[2] |prī| *v.* **pried, pry•ing, pries.** To look or investigate closely or curiously, often in a secret or furtive manner: *prying into his past.* —**pry'ing** *adj.*: *a prying person; prying eyes.* [SEE NOTE]

P.S. **1.** postscript. **2.** public school.

psalm |säm| *n.* A sacred song or hymn.

psalm•ist |sä'mĭst| *n.* A writer of psalms.

Psalms |sämz| *n.* *(used with a singular verb).* A book of the Old Testament containing 150 sacred songs.

Psal•ter |sôl'tər| *n.* A book containing the Psalms.

psal•ter•y |sôl'tə rē| *n., pl.* **psal•ter•ies.** An ancient stringed instrument played by plucking the strings with the fingers or a plectrum.

pseu•do |so͞o'dō| *adj.* Fake; counterfeit; false.

pseudo–. A word element meaning: **1.** Inauthentic; fake: **pseudonym.** **2.** Deceptively similar: **pseudopod.**

pseu•do•nym |so͞od'n ĭm| *n.* A fictitious name, especially one assumed by an author.

pseu•do•pod |so͞o'də pŏd'| *n.* An irregularly shaped temporary extension of the protoplasm of a one-celled organism such as the ameba, used for moving about and for surrounding and taking in food. [SEE PICTURE]

pshaw |shô| *interj.* A word used to indicate

impatience, irritation, or disbelief.

psi |sī| *or* |psī| *n.* The 23rd letter of the Greek alphabet, written Ψ, ψ. In English it is represented as *ps.*

psit•ta•co•sis |sĭt′ə **kō′**sĭs| *n.* A virus disease of parrots and related birds, which can be communicated to human beings, producing high fever and complications that are like pneumonia.

pso•ri•a•sis |sə **rī′**ə sĭs| *n.* A chronic, noncontagious disease of the skin. It causes inflammation and white, scaly patches on the skin.

PST, P.S.T. Pacific Standard Time.

psych |sīk| *n. Informal.* Psychology. *—v.* **psyched, psych•ing, psychs.** *Informal.* **1.** To put into the right frame of mind: *She psyched herself for the game by watching the earlier matches.* **2.** To undermine the confidence of by using psychology: *psych out an opponent.*

psy•che |**sī′**kē| *n.* **1.** The soul or spirit as distinguished from the body. **2.** The mind considered as the source and center of thought, feeling, and behavior.

psych•e•del•ic |sī′kĭ **dĕl′**ĭk| *adj.* Of or causing hallucinations, distortions of perception, and sometimes mental states that resemble psychosis: *psychedelic drugs.*

psy•chi•at•ric |sī′kē **ăt′**rĭk| *adj.* Of psychiatry. **—psy′chi•at′ri•cal•ly** *adv.*

psy•chi•a•trist |sĭ **kī′**ə trĭst| *or* |sī-| *n.* A physician who specializes in psychiatry.

psy•chi•a•try |sĭ **kī′**ə trē| *or* |sī-| *n.* The medical study, diagnosis, treatment, and prevention of mental illness. [SEE NOTE]

psy•chic |**sī′**kĭk| *adj.* **1.** Of the human mind or psyche. **2. a.** Of extraordinary or apparently supernatural processes, such as extrasensory perception or mental telepathy. **b.** Of, produced by, or affected by such processes. *—n.* A person who is apparently responsive to supernatural phenomena.

psy•chi•cal |**sī′**kĭ kəl| *adj.* Psychic. **—psy′chi•cal•ly** *adv.*

psycho–. A word element meaning "the mind or mental processes": **psychoanalysis.**

psy•cho•a•nal•y•sis |sī′kō ə **năl′**ĭ sĭs| *n.* **1.** A system of psychotherapy that uses free association, interpretation of dreams, and analysis of the patient's actions and behavior to investigate mental processes and relieve psychic problems. **2.** A theory of human psychology based on discoveries made in psychotherapy of this type, especially discoveries made by Sigmund Freud and his followers.

psy•cho•an•a•lyst |sī′kō **ăn′**ə lĭst| *n.* Someone who practices psychoanalysis.

psy•cho•an•a•lyt•ic |sī′kō ăn′ə **lĭt′**ĭk| *adj.* Of or having to do with psychoanalysis. **—psy′cho•an′a•lyt′i•cal•ly** *adv.*

psy•cho•an•a•lyze |sī′kō **ăn′**ə līz′| *v.* **psy•cho•an•a•lyzed, psy•cho•an•a•lyz•ing.** To treat (a patient) by psychoanalysis.

psy•cho•log•i•cal |sī′kə **lŏj′**ĭ kəl| *adj.* **1.** Of psychology. **2.** Of or derived from the mind or emotions. **3.** Capable of influencing the mind or emotions: *psychological persuasion.* **—psy′cho•log′i•cal•ly** *adv.*

psy•chol•o•gist |sī **kŏl′**ə jĭst| *n.* **1.** A scientist who specializes in psychology. **2.** A psychotherapist.

psy•chol•o•gy |sī **kŏl′**ə jē| *n., pl.* **psy•chol•o•gies. 1.** The scientific study of mental processes and behavior. **2.** The emotional characteristics and behavior associated with an individual, group, or activity: *the psychology of war.* **3.** Action or behavior, often subtle, intended to persuade or manipulate: *He used poor psychology in showing his anger.* [SEE NOTE]

psy•cho•path |**sī′**kə păth′| *n.* A person who has a severe personality disorder, especially one that is shown in aggressive and destructive behavior.

psy•cho•sis |sī **kō′**sĭs| *n., pl.* **psy•cho•ses** |sī-**kō′**sēz′|. Any of a class of serious mental disorders in which the mind cannot function normally and the ability to deal with reality is impaired or lost.

psy•cho•so•mat•ic |sī′kō sə **măt′**ĭk| *adj.* **1.** Of functions or disorders that involve both the mind and the body. **2.** Originating in the mind.

psy•cho•ther•a•py |sī′kō **thĕr′**ə pē| *n., pl.* **psy•cho•ther•a•pies.** The treatment of mental, emotional, and nervous disorders, especially without the use of drugs or surgery.

psy•chot•ic |sī **kŏt′**ĭk| *adj.* Of, affected with, or caused by psychosis. *—n.* Someone who is affected with psychosis.

Pt The symbol for the element platinum.

pt. 1. pint. **2.** point.

PTA, P.T.A. Parent-Teachers Association.

ptar•mi•gan |**tär′**mĭ gən| *n., pl.* **ptar•mi•gan** or **ptar•mi•gans.** A grouselike bird of northern regions, having feathers that are brownish in summer and white in winter and feathered "leggings" covering the legs and feet.

PT boat. A fast, maneuverable vessel used to torpedo enemy ships.

pte•rid•o•phyte |tə **rĭd′**ə fīt′| *or* |**tĕr′**ĭ dō-| *n.* Any member of a large group of plants that includes the ferns and club mosses.

pter•o•dac•tyl |tĕr′ə **dăk′**təl| *n.* An extinct flying lizard that had wings formed by a flap of skin extending from a long, fingerlike toe on each front leg. [SEE PICTURE]

pter•o•saur |**tĕr′**ə sôr′| *n.* An extinct flying lizard of the group to which the pterodactyls belonged.

Ptol•e•ma•ic system |tŏl′ə **mā′**ĭk|. A description or model of the universe in which the earth is considered to be the center, with all other bodies revolving around it.

Ptol•e•my |**tŏl′**ə mē|. Greek astronomer and mathematician of the second century A.D.

pto•maine |**tō′**mān′| *or* |tō **mān′**| *n.* Any of a class of nitrogen-containing substances, some poisonous, that form when proteins decay and decompose.

pty•a•lin |**tī′**ə lən| *n.* A salivary enzyme that acts on starches, turning them into sugars.

Pu The symbol for the element plutonium.

pub |pŭb| *n.* A tavern; an inn.

pu•ber•ty |**pyōō′**bər tē| *n.* The stage in the development of an individual at which the reproductive organs become fully capable of functioning, occurring between ages 13 and 16 in boys and between 12 and 14 in girls.

pu•bes |**pyōō′**bēz′| *n.* Plural of **pubis.**

pu•bic |**pyōō′**bĭk| *adj.* Of or in the region of the lower part of the abdomen.

pu•bis |**pyōō′**bĭs| *n., pl.* **pu•bes** |**pyōō′**bēz′|. The

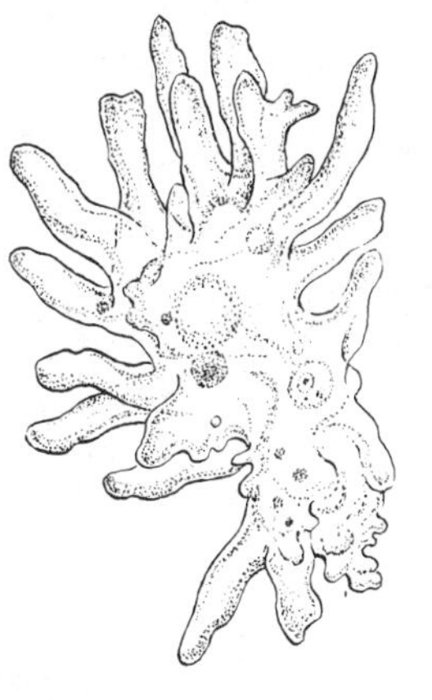

pseudopod

psychology/psychiatry

Psychology *is the general study of the mind (from Greek* -logia, *"study"). **Psychiatry** is the healing or therapy of the mind (from Greek* iatros, *"physician"). A psychiatrist must also be a psychologist, but most psychologists do not specialize in psychiatry.*

pterodactyl

forward portion of either of the hipbones, joining to form the front arch of the pelvis.

pub•lic |pŭb′lĭk| *adj.* **1.** Of or affecting the people or community: *public opinion; public safety.* **2.** Supported by, used by, or open to the people or community; not private: *the public library; a public telephone.* **3.** Serving or acting on behalf of the people or community: *a public official.* **4.** Presented in the presence of people: *made a public address.* **5.** Open to the knowledge or awareness of everybody: *made the testimony public.* **6.** Participated in by the people or community: *a public occasion.* —*n.* **1.** The people as a whole: *a building open to the public.* **2.** A group of people with a common interest: *the theater-going public.*

***Idiom.* in public.** In the presence of the people; not private; openly: *how to act in public.*

pub•lic-ad•dress system |pŭb′lĭk ə drĕs′|. An electronic system using amplifiers, loudspeakers, and other equipment to project sound throughout a given area or set of areas.

pub•li•can |pŭb′lĭ kən| *n.* **1.** A collector of taxes in the ancient Roman Empire. **2.** *Chiefly British.* The keeper of a public house.

pub•li•ca•tion |pŭb′lĭ kā′shən| *n.* **1.** The act of publishing printed matter. **2.** Printed matter, such as a magazine or newspaper, offered for sale or distribution. **3.** The act of making something known to the public.

pueblo

public house. *British.* A tavern, bar, or similar place licensed to sell alcoholic beverages.

pub•li•cist |pŭb′lĭ sĭst| *n.* A person who brings someone or something to public attention; a press agent.

pub•lic•i•ty |pŭ blĭs′ĭ tē| *n.* **1.** Information given out, as to the press, as a means of attracting public notice to a person or thing. **2.** Public notice directed toward someone or something. **3.** The work of a person hired to bring someone or something to public notice. —***modifier:*** *a publicity photograph; a publicity director.*

pub•li•cize |pŭb′lĭ sīz′| *v.* **pub•li•cized, pub•li•ciz•ing.** To bring to public attention; advertise. —**pub′li•cized′** *adj.: a publicized exploit.*

pub•lic•ly |pŭb′lĭk lē| *adv.* **1.** In public; not privately; openly: *They publicly acknowledged the partnership.* **2.** By the public: *a publicly owned water system.*

public relations. **1.** *(used with a plural verb).* The relationship between a person or organization and the public; the feeling, good or bad, that the public has for someone or something: *The company's public relations need improvement.* **2. a.** *(used with a singular verb).* The methods or means by which a person or organization seeks to bring about a favorable relationship with the public: *Good public relations involves good deeds.* **b.** *(used with a singular verb).* The work of a person hired to bring about such a favorable relationship.

public school. **1.** A school supported by taxes and providing free education for the children of a community. **2.** *British.* A private boarding school for study before entering a university.

public servant. A person who holds a government position.

pub•lic-spir•it•ed |pŭb′lĭk spĭr′ĭ tĭd| *adj.* Dedicated to promoting the well-being of the general public: *public-spirited people in high offices.*

public utility. A private company that is subject to governmental regulation because it provides an essential service or commodity, such as water, electricity, or communication.

pub•lish |pŭb′lĭsh| *v.* **1.** To prepare and issue (printed matter) for distribution or sale to the public. **2.** To bring to public attention; announce. —**pub′lished** *adj.: a published account.* —**pub′lish•ing** *adj.: the publishing business; a publishing company.*

pub•lish•er |pŭb′lĭ shər| *n.* A person or company that produces and distributes printed matter, such as books, magazines, or newspapers.

puce |pyo͞os| *n.* A deep, grayish red or purple. —*adj.* Deep, grayish red or purple.

puck |pŭk| *n.* A hard rubber disk used in ice hockey.

Puck |pŭk|. In English folklore, a mischievous sprite.

puck•er |pŭk′ər| *v.* To draw up into small wrinkles, furrows, or folds: *She gathered the cloth to pucker it. Damp cloth sometimes puckers.* —***phrasal verb.* pucker up.** To draw the lips together and stick them out, as for a kiss: *pucker up and whistle.* —*n.* A small wrinkle or wrinkled part, as in tightly stitched cloth.

pud•ding |po͝od′ĭng| *n.* **1.** A sweet custardlike or cakelike dessert, usually containing a starch or a cereal. **2.** Any of various unsweetened dishes, such as Yorkshire pudding, that are boiled or baked. —***modifier:*** *a pudding mix.*

pud•dle |pŭd′l| *n.* **1.** A small pool of dirty or muddy water. **2.** A small pool of any liquid.

pudg•y |pŭj′ē| *adj.* **pudg•i•er, pudg•i•est.** Short and stocky; thickset; chubby. —**pudg′i•ness** *n.*

pueb•lo |pwĕb′lō| *n., pl.* **pueb•los.** **1.** A flat-roofed community dwelling, up to five stories high, used by certain North American Indian tribes of the Southwest. **2. Pueblo.** A member of a tribe, such as the Hopi, inhabiting such dwellings. **3.** An Indian village of the southwestern United States. [SEE PICTURE]

puer•ile |pyo͝or′ĭl| *or* |-īl′| *adj.* Immature; childish; juvenile.

Puer•to Ri•co |pwĕr′tō rē′kō| *or* |pôr′-| *or* |pōr′-|. An island commonwealth associated with the United States, in the West Indies east of Hispaniola. Population, 3,187,570. Capital, San Juan. —**Puerto Rican.**

puff |pŭf| *n.* **1. a.** A short, forceful discharge or gust, as of air, smoke, or vapor. **b.** A short, abrupt sound produced by such a discharge or gust. **2.** An act of drawing in and breathing out, as in smoking tobacco. **3.** Something that looks light and fluffy: *little puffs of white clouds.* **4.** A soft pad for applying cosmetic powder. **5.** A light, flaky pastry, often filled with custard or cream. **6.** A soft roll of hair forming part of a hairdo. **7.** A section of full, gathered fabric that balloons out as though filled with air. —***modifier:*** *puff sleeves.* —*v.* **1.** To blow in short, forceful gusts, as the wind does. **2.** To come forth in a puff or puffs: *Spurts of smoke puffed from the steamboat.* **3.** To breathe heavily and rapidly, as from fatigue: *She began to puff from the hard climb to the fifth floor.* **4.** To emit short discharges of air, smoke, vapor, etc., often with accompanying short, abrupt sounds: *A steam locomotive puffed along the track.* **5. a.** To smoke (a pipe, cigarette, cigar, etc.):

He puffed an old, odorous corncob pipe. **b.** To take puffs while smoking: *puffed slowly on the pipe.* **6.** To swell or seem to swell, as with air or pride: *Her feet puffed up from the long walk. He puffed up over his victory.* **7.** To fill with or as if with air or padding so as to make or become full and rounded: *The bustle puffed out her skirt. His cheeks puffed out as he held his breath.* **8.** To extinguish by blowing: *puff out the candle.*

puff•ball |**pŭf**′bôl′| *n.* **1.** A ball-shaped fungus that lets out a puff of dustlike spores when broken open. **2.** The fluffy head of a dandelion that has gone to seed. [SEE PICTURE]

puf•fin |**pŭf**′ĭn| *n.* A chunky black and white northern sea bird with a short, flattened, brightly colored bill. [SEE PICTURE]

puff•y |**pŭf**′ē| *adj.* **puff•i•er, puff•i•est.** **1.** Swollen: *the puffy eyes of a crying child.* **2.** Full and rounded, like a balloon filled with air: *puffy sleeves.* **3.** Coming in puffs: *short, puffy breaths.* —**puff′i•ness** *n.*

pug |pŭg| *n.* A small, short-haired dog with a short, flattened nose, a wrinkled face, and a curled tail.

pu•gi•lism |**pyo͞o**′jə lĭz′əm| *n.* Boxing.

pu•gi•list |**pyo͞o**′jə lĭst| *n.* A professional boxer.

pug•na•cious |pŭg **nā**′shəs| *adj.* Eager to fight; having a quarrelsome or aggressive disposition. —**pug•na′cious•ly** *adj.* —**pug•nac′i•ty** |pŭg **năs**′ĭ tē|, **pug•na′cious•ness** *n.*

pug nose. A short nose that is somewhat flattened and turned up at the end.

puke |pyo͞ok| *v.* **puked, puk•ing.** To vomit (something) up. —*n.* **1.** Vomit. **2.** The act of vomiting. The word "puke" is sometimes considered offensive.

pull |po͝ol| *v.* **1. a.** To apply force to (something), especially so as to cause motion toward the source of the force: *pull the plow; pull on the rope.* **b.** To cause (something) to move or tend to move toward a point or center, as by exerting a force; attract: *Gravity pulls things toward the center of the earth.* **2.** To take from a fixed position or place; remove: *pull weeds; pull off bark.* **3.** To move: *A truck pulled off the road. The driver pulled the car off the road.* **4.** To tug at; jerk: *pulled her hair.* **5.** To draw apart; tear or break: *The puppy pulled the towel into bits.* **6.** To stretch (taffy, for example) repeatedly into long strips. **7.** To injure (a muscle) by stretching or straining it too much. **8.** To put on (an article of clothing): *pull on overalls; pull on a glove.* **9.** *Informal.* To attract the notice or attendance of; draw: *The play pulls large crowds.* **10.** *Informal.* To perform: *pull a stunt.* **11.** *Slang.* To draw out (a knife or gun). **12.** To force: *He pulled his mind away from dreamy thoughts.* **13.** To drink or inhale deeply. —***phrasal verbs.*** **pull down.** **1.** To tear down; raze: *pull down a building.* **2.** To earn (a salary, for example). **pull for.** To work or hope for the success of: *We are pulling for you.* **pull in.** To arrive: *The train pulled in at five o'clock.* **pull off.** To do or accomplish (something) in spite of difficulties: *He managed to pull the deal off.* **pull out.** To leave; depart: *They pulled out before winter.* **pull over.** To stop a vehicle on the side of a road: *The patrolman told us to pull over.* **pull through.** To come or bring successfully through difficulty: *He'll pull through with your help. The doctor pulled her through the illness.* **pull up.** To come to a stop: *The truck pulled up in front of the building.* —*n.* **1.** The act or process of pulling. **2.** The force used in pulling: *a rope that will stand a 200-pound pull.* **3.** A force that attracts or draws: *magnetic pull.* **4.** The pressure resulting from pulling: *the pull of the bit in the horse's mouth.* **5.** A prolonged effort: *a steady pull to reach camp by night.* **6.** Something used in pulling, such as a knob on a rope for drawing a curtain. **7.** An act of inhaling or drinking deeply. **8.** *Slang.* Special influence: *He has a lot of pull in that town.* —**pull′er** *n.*

Idioms. **pull (oneself) together.** To regain one's composure or self-control. **pull together.** To cooperate.

pul•let |**po͝ol**′ĭt| *n.* A young hen, especially one less than a year old.

pul•ley |**po͝ol**′ē| *n., pl.* **pul•leys.** **1.** A device consisting of a freely turning wheel with a groove around its edge through which a rope, chain, cable, etc., runs. It acts to change the direction of the force exerted on the rope or chain. **2.** A similar wheel that drives or is driven by a belt passing around its edge.

Pull•man |**po͝ol**′mən| *n.* Often **Pullman car.** A railroad car having private sleeping compartments or parlors.

pull•out |**po͝ol**′out′| *n.* **1.** A withdrawal, especially of troops. **2.** An aircraft's change from a dive to level flight.

pull•o•ver |**po͝ol**′ō′vər| *n.* A garment, such as a sweater, that must be put on by being drawn over the head. —***modifier:*** *a pullover shirt.*

pul•mo•nar•y |**po͝ol**′mə nĕr′ē| *adj.* Of or affecting the lungs: *a pulmonary infection.*

pulp |pŭlp| *n.* **1. a.** A soft, moist substance. **b.** A shapeless mass of such material. **2.** The soft, juicy or fleshy part of fruit or of certain vegetables. **3.** A moist mixture of ground wood, rags, etc., used to make paper. **4.** The soft inner part of a tooth, containing blood vessels and nerve tissue. **5.** A magazine containing sensational subject matter and usually printed on rough, coarse paper. —***modifier:*** *pulp mills; a pulp magazine.* —*v.* To reduce to pulp.

pul•pit |**po͝ol**′pĭt| *or* |**pŭl**′-| *n.* **1.** An elevated platform with a lectern used by the clergy of some churches in speaking to the congregation. **2. a. the pulpit.** Clergymen as a group. **b.** The ministry as a profession: *He chose the pulpit rather than the military life.*

pulp•wood |**pŭlp**′wo͝od′| *n.* Wood, such as pine, spruce, or aspen, used in making paper. —***modifier:*** *the pulpwood industry.*

pulp•y |**pŭl**′pē| *adj.* **pulp•i•er, pulp•i•est.** Of, containing, or resembling pulp: *a pulpy fruit.*

pul•sar |**pŭl**′sär′| *n.* Any of a class of celestial objects that emit radio waves, varying the intensity of radiation at short intervals of precise length.

pul•sate |**pŭl**′sāt′| *v.* **pul•sat•ed, pul•sat•ing.** **1.** To expand and contract rhythmically, as the heart does. **2.** To move or occur in a regular, rhythmical way: *electricity pulsating through a wire.* —**pul′sat′ing** *adj.:* *a pulsating movement; a pulsating heart.*

pul•sa•tion |pŭl **sā**′shən| *n.* **1.** The act or proc-

puffball
Head of a dandelion

puffin

ess of pulsating. **2.** A single beat, throb, vibration, etc.

pulse[1] |pŭls| *n.* **1.** The rhythmical expansion and contraction of the arteries as blood is pushed through them by the beating of the heart. **2.** Any regular or rhythmical beating: *the pulse of the drums.* **3.** A single beat or throb; pulsation. **4.** A short, sudden, and temporary change in some characteristic of a physical system, especially a short burst of electrical energy or wave energy: *A telegraph message is sent as a series of electrical pulses.* —*modifier: the pulse rate; a pulse beat.* —*v.* **pulsed, puls•ing.** To pulsate. [SEE NOTE]

pulse[2] |pŭls| *n.* **1.** The edible seeds of certain plants, such as peas, beans, or lentils. **2.** Plants bearing such seeds. [SEE NOTE]

pul•ver•ize |pŭl′və rīz′| *v.* **pul•ver•ized, pul•ver•iz•ing. 1.** To pound, crush, or grind into tiny particles; reduce to powder or dust. **2.** To become powder or dust. —**pul′ver•i•za′tion** *n.*

pu•ma |pyōō′mə| *n.* The **mountain lion.**

pum•ice |pŭm′ĭs| *n.* A lightweight rock of volcanic origin, used as an abrasive. —*v.* **pum•iced, pum•ic•ing.** To clean with pumice.

pum•mel |pŭm′əl| *v.* **pum•meled** or **pum•melled, pum•mel•ing** or **pum•mel•ling.** To pommel.

pump[1] |pŭmp| *n.* **1.** A device used to move something, as a liquid or gas, from one place or container to another. **2.** An act of moving up and down or back and forth: *He gave my hand a quick pump.* —*modifier: a pump handle.* —*v.* **1.** To raise or move (a liquid or gas) by means of a pump. **2.** To fill with gas by means of a pump: *pump up a tire.* **3.** To empty of liquid or gas by means of a pump: *pump out a flooded cellar.* **4.** To move up and down or back and forth, in the manner of a pump handle or piston. **5.** To put forth or force in the manner of a pump: *pumped bullets into a target.* **6. a.** To question closely: *pumped him for information.* **b.** To obtain by questioning closely: *pumped information from the witness.* —**pump′ing** *adj.: a pumping system.* —**pump′er** *n.* [SEE NOTE]

pump[2] |pŭmp| *n.* A low-cut shoe without laces, straps, or other fasteners. [SEE NOTE]

pum•per•nick•el |pŭm′pər nĭk′əl| *n.* A dark bread made from coarsely ground rye.

pump•kin |pŭmp′kĭn| *or* |pŭm′-| *or* |pŭng′-| *n.* **1.** A large, round fruit with a thick orange rind and pulp often used for making pies. **2.** The coarse trailing vine that bears such fruit. —*modifier: pumpkin pie.*

pun |pŭn| *n.* A play on words that involves different senses of the same word or the similar sense or sound of different words. —*v.* To make a pun. —**pun′ner** *n.* [SEE NOTE]

punch[1] |pŭnch| *v.* **1.** To make (a hole, mark, or design) by or as if by piercing, perforating, etc. **2.** To make a hole or holes in; perforate: *punching cards.* **3.** To remove (something separated by perforations) by or as if by pushing with the fingers: *punching out paper dolls.* **4.** To push through a material: *He punched the awl through the leather.* —*n.* **1.** A tool for piercing, perforating, etc. **2.** A tool for forcing a pin, rivet, etc., in or out of a hole. [SEE NOTE]

punch[2] |pŭnch| *v.* **1.** To hit with or as if with the fist: *He punched the bus driver. The boxer punched with his left.* **2.** In the western U.S. and Canada, to herd (cattle). **3.** To press in order to cause to operate: *He punched the clock when he got to the factory.* —*n.* **1.** A blow with or as with the fist. **2.** Vigor; drive: *They were full of punch.* —**punch′er** *n.* [SEE NOTE]

Idiom. **punch in** (or **out**). To check in (or out) formally at a job before (or after) a day's work: *punched in at 8:00 a.m.; punched out at 5:00 p.m.*

punch[3] |pŭnch| *n.* A sweet beverage of fruit juices, often with wine or liquor and spices. —*modifier: a punch bowl.* [SEE NOTE]

pun•cheon[1] |pŭn′chən| *n.* **1.** A roughly dressed, heavy timber, with one face finished flat. **2.** A tool used for punching, perforating, or stamping.

pun•cheon[2] |pŭn′chən| *n.* **1.** A cask that can hold 84 U.S. gallons. **2.** The amount a puncheon holds.

punching bag. A stuffed or inflated bag, usually suspended so that it can be punched with the fists for exercise.

punch line. The climax of a joke or humorous story.

punc•til•i•o |pŭngk tĭl′ē ō′| *n., pl.* **punc•til•i•os.** A fine point of etiquette.

punc•til•i•ous |pŭngk tĭl′ē əs| *adj.* **1.** Attentive to the details of etiquette. **2.** Conscientious and exacting; precise. —**punc•til′i•ous•ly** *adv.*

punc•tu•al |pŭngk′chōō əl| *adj.* Acting or arriving on time; prompt. —**punc′tu•al′i•ty** *n.* —**punc′tu•al•ly** *adv.*

punc•tu•ate |pŭngk′chōō āt′| *v.* **punc•tu•at•ed, punc•tu•at•ing. 1.** To provide (written or printed material) with punctuation: *punctuate the sentence; punctuate carefully.* **2.** To interrupt repeatedly: *the constant din of traffic punctuated by the shrill sounds of sirens.* **3.** To emphasize; stress: *punctuating their cheers with rhythmical clapping.*

punc•tu•a•tion |pŭngk′chōō ā′shən| *n.* **1.** The use of standard marks in writing and printing to separate sentences and parts of sentences in order to make the meaning clear. **2.** A mark or the marks so used.

punctuation mark. One of the marks used in punctuating written or printed material. For example, the comma (,), the semicolon (;), and the period (.) are punctuation marks.

punc•ture |pŭngk′chər| *v.* **punc•tured, punc•tur•ing. 1.** To pierce with something sharp: *The snake's fangs punctured the skin of her arm.* **2.** To cause to collapse or deflate by or as if by piercing with something sharp: *punctured her ego.* —*n.* **1.** A hole, wound, etc., made by something sharp, especially such a hole in a pneumatic tire. **2.** An act or an example of puncturing.

pun•dit |pŭn′dĭt| *n.* A learned person, especially an expert or authority: *newspapermen and political pundits.*

pun•gent |pŭn′jənt| *adj.* **1.** Sharp or acrid to the taste or smell: *a pungent sauce; pungent smoke.* **2.** Penetrating; biting; caustic: *pungent remarks.* —**pun′gen•cy** *n.* —**pun′gent•ly** *adv.*

pun•ish |pŭn′ĭsh| *v.* **1.** To cause (a person or animal) to undergo penalty for a crime, fault, or misbehavior: *punished a child; punished severely.* **2.** To inflict a penalty for: *punish cruelty.* **3.** To treat roughly or harshly: *Heavy surf and strong*

pulse[1-2]
These two words are not related. **Pulse[1]** *is from Latin* pulsus, *"a beating, a striking."* **Pulse[2]** *is from Latin* puls, *"bean curd, porridge made from peas and beans."*

pump[1-2]
Pump[1] *is from Middle Dutch* pompe. **Pump[2]** *is of unknown origin.*

pun
"When I am dead, I hope it may be said: 'His sins were scarlet, but his books were read.'"—Hilaire Belloc (1870–1953).

punch[1-2-3]
Punch[1] *and* **punch[2]** *have separate histories, but they are both ultimately related to* **puncture**. **Punch[3]** *is supposed to have originated in India in the seventeenth century and to have been made of five ingredients—liquor, sugar, lime juice, spices, and water; the word is said to be from Hindi* pānch, *"five." But this etymology, plausible though it is, has been strongly criticized on various grounds; it must be considered to be only a possibility.*

ă pat/ā pay/â care/ä father/ĕ pet/ ē be/ĭ pit/ī pie/î fierce/ŏ pot/ ō go/ô paw, for/oi oil/ŏŏ book/ ōō boot/ou out/ŭ cut/û fur/ *th* the/th thin/hw which/zh vision/ ə ago, item, pencil, atom, circus

winds punished the small craft. —**pun'ish•er** *n.*

pun•ish•a•ble |pŭn'ĭ shə bəl| *adj.* Liable to punishment: *a crime punishable by imprisonment.*

pun•ish•ment |pŭn'ĭsh mənt| *n.* **1.** A penalty for a crime or wrongdoing: *What punishment was he given?* **2. a.** An act of punishing: *the punishment of wrongdoers.* **b.** The condition of being punished: *learned to take punishment.* **3.** *Informal.* Rough or harsh handling or treatment: *These shoes have had a lot of punishment.*

pu•ni•tive |pyōō'nĭ tĭv| *adj.* Inflicting or intending to inflict punishment: *a punitive decree.* —**pu'ni•tive•ly** *adv.* —**pu'ni•tive•ness** *n.*

punk[1] |pŭngk| *n.* A light, dry, easily burned substance, such as decayed wood, used to light fires. [SEE NOTE]

punk[2] |pŭngk|. *Slang. n.* A hoodlum; a tough. —*adj.* Of poor quality; inferior. [SEE NOTE]

pun•ster |pŭn'stər| *n.* Someone who makes puns.

punt[1] |pŭnt| *n.* A long flat-bottomed boat with squared ends for use in shoal waters, propelled with a long pole. —*v.* **1.** To propel (a boat) with a pole. **2.** To carry in a punt. —**punt'er** *n.* [SEE NOTE]

punt[2] |pŭnt| *n.* In football, a kick in which the ball is dropped from the hands and kicked before it touches the ground. —*v.* To kick (a ball) by means of a punt. —**punt'er** *n.* [SEE NOTE]

pu•ny |pyōō'nē| *adj.* **pu•ni•er, pu•ni•est.** Small or inferior in size, strength, or worth; weak. —**pu'ni•ly** *adv.* —**pu'ni•ness** *n.*

pup |pŭp| *n.* **1.** A young dog; a puppy. **2.** The young of certain other animals, such as a coyote, fox, or seal.

pu•pa |pyōō'pə| *n., pl.* **pu•pae** |pyōō'pē'| or **pu•pas.** The inactive stage in the life cycle of many insects, between the larva and the adult form. A pupa is often enclosed in a protective covering such as a cocoon.

pu•pal |pyōō'pəl| *adj.* **1.** Of a pupa or pupae: *A cocoon is a pupal case.* **2.** Existing as or having the form of a pupa: *the pupal stage.* ¶*These sound alike* **pupal, pupil.**

pu•pate |pyōō'pāt'| *v.* **pu•pat•ed, pu•pat•ing.** To become or exist as a pupa. —**pu•pa'tion** *n.*

pu•pil[1] |pyōō'pəl| *n.* A student receiving instruction from a teacher. ¶*These sound alike* **pupil, pupal.** [SEE NOTE]

pu•pil[2] |pyōō'pəl| *n.* The opening in the center of the iris by which light enters the eye. ¶*These sound alike* **pupil, pupal.** [SEE NOTE]

pup•pet |pŭp'ĭt| *n.* **1.** A small figure resembling a person or animal and fitting over the hand or fitted with strings that are moved from above. **2.** A person, group, or government whose behavior is controlled by another. —***modifier:*** *a puppet show; a puppet government.* [SEE PICTURE]

pup•pet•eer |pŭp'ĭ tîr'| *n.* A person who operates puppets to entertain.

pup•pet•ry |pŭp'ĭ trē| *n., pl.* **pup•pet•ries.** **1.** The art of making puppets and operating them. **2.** The actions of puppets. **3.** Stilted behavior.

pup•py |pŭp'ē| *n., pl.* **pup•pies.** A young dog.

pup tent. A small tent of waterproof material.

pur•blind |pûr'blīnd'| *adj.* **1.** Having poor vision. **2.** Slow in understanding or discerning; dull. —**pur'blind'ly** *adv.* —**pur'blind'ness** *n.*

pur•chase |pûr'chĭs| *v.* **pur•chased, pur•chas•ing.** To obtain (something) by paying money or its equivalent; buy. —*n.* **1.** Something that is bought: *The car was a wise purchase.* **2.** The act of buying: *the purchase of land.* **3.** A secure position, grasp, or hold: *Using the narrow ledge for a purchase he paused in the climb.* —**pur'chas•a•ble** *adj.* —**pur'chas•er** *n.*

pure |pyŏŏr| *adj.* **pur•er, pur•est.** **1.** Free from foreign elements, impurities, etc.; not mixed; clean or clear: *pure oxygen; pure water.* **2.** Complete; utter: *pure happiness; pure ignorance.* **3.** Without fault or evil; sinless: *a pure heart.* **4.** Chaste; virgin. **5.** Of unmixed blood or ancestry; purebred. **6.** Not concerned with or directed toward practical application; theoretical: *pure mathematics.* —**pure'ness** *n.*

pure•bred |pyŏŏr'brĕd'| *adj.* Having many generations of ancestors of the same breed or kind: *a purebred dog.* —*n.* A purebred animal.

pu•rée |pyŏŏ rā'| *or* |pyŏŏr'ā| *v.* To put (food) through a strainer or sieve so that it becomes a mushy pulp. —*n.* Food prepared in this way.

pure•ly |pyŏŏr'lē| *adv.* **1.** Entirely; completely; totally: *a purely factual account.* **2.** Merely; simply: *purely by accident.* **3.** Innocently; chastely. **4.** In a pure manner: *a purely bred dog.*

pur•ga•tive |pûr'gə tĭv| *adj.* Tending to cleanse or purge, especially tending to cause the bowels to empty. —*n.* A purgative medicine or drug; a strong laxative.

pur•ga•to•ry |pûr'gə tôr'ē| *or* |-tōr'ē| *n.* In some Christian beliefs, a place or condition of temporary punishment in or through which souls who have died in grace are purged of their sins.

purge |pûrj| *v.* **purged, purg•ing.** **1. a.** To cause (the bowels) to empty. **b.** To cause the bowels of to empty. **2.** To rid of what is considered undesirable or harmful: *purge society of every possible evil.* **3.** To rid (a nation, political party, etc.) of persons considered undesirable, especially by harsh methods. —*n.* **1.** The act or process of purging. **2.** A medicine or drug used to empty the bowels; a purgative.

pu•ri•fy |pyŏŏr'ə fī'| *v.* **pu•ri•fied, pu•ri•fy•ing, pu•ri•fies.** **1.** To free from anything harmful or undesirable; cleanse; make pure: *purify water.* **2.** To become pure: *The air gradually purified.* **3.** To free from sin, guilt, etc.: *purify the soul.* —**pu'ri•fi•ca'tion** *n.* —**pu'ri•fi'er** *n.*

Pu•rim |pŏŏr'ĭm| *n.* A Jewish holiday celebrating the rescue of the ancient Jews by Esther from a plot to massacre them.

Pu•ri•tan |pyŏŏr'ĭ tən| *n.* **1.** A member of a group of Protestants in England and the American Colonies in the 16th and 17th centuries who advocated reform of the Church of England and a strict morality. **2. puritan.** A person who is strict or overstrict in morals and religion.

pu•ri•tan•i•cal |pyŏŏr'ĭ tăn'ĭ kəl| *adj.* **1. a.** Strict in matters of religious or moral conduct: *a puritanical education.* **b.** Enforcing a strict morality: *puritanical liquor laws.* **2. Puritanical.** Of the Puritans.

Pu•ri•tan•ism |pyŏŏr'ĭ tə nĭz'əm| *n.* **1.** The Puritan movement or its doctrines. **2. puritanism.** Moral strictness, especially in regard to sensual pleasures.

pu•ri•ty |pyŏŏr'ĭ tē| *n., pl.* **pu•ri•ties.** **1.** The condition or quality of being pure: *the purity of*

punk[1-2]
Both of these words are of unknown origin.

punt[1-2]
Punt[1] *is related to* **pontoon. Punt[2]** *is of obscure origin.*

pupil[1-2]
Pupil[1] *is from Latin* pūpillus, *"little boy."* **Pupil[2]** *is from Latin* pūpilla, *"little girl." When you look closely into the pupil of someone's eye, you see a tiny reflection of yourself; the Romans called this image "the little girl,"* pūpilla.

puppet
Two of Jim Henson's "Muppets" from *Sesame Street*

mountain air. **2.** The degree to which something is pure: *golf of high purity.* **3.** Freedom from sin; goodness: *She led a life of great purity.*

purl[1] |pûrl| *v.* To flow in ripples or with a low murmur, as a brook does. *—n.* The sound made by rippling water. ¶ *These sound alike* **purl, pearl.** [SEE NOTE]

purl[2] |pûrl| *n.* Also **purl stitch.** A knitting stitch made backward, often alternated with the plain stitch to produce a ribbed effect. *—v.* To knit with a backward stitch. ¶ *These sound alike* **purl, pearl.** [SEE NOTE]

purl[1-2]
Purl[1] *is from Norwegian* purla, *"to bubble up."* **Purl[2]** *is of unknown origin.*

pur•loin |pər **loin'**| *or* |**pûr'**loin'| *v.* To steal; filch. **—pur•loin'er** *n.*

pur•ple |**pûr'**pəl| *n.* **1.** A color like that of grape juice or an amethyst, produced by mixing red and blue pigments or dyes. **2.** Cloth or clothing of this color, worn in former times as a symbol of royalty or high rank. *—adj.* **1.** Of the color purple. **2.** Showy and high-flown; flowery: *the purple prose of a third-rate writer.*

pur•plish |**pûr'**plĭsh| *adj.* Somewhat purple.

pur•port |pər **pôrt'**| *or* |**-pōrt'**| *v.* To claim (to do or be something), especially falsely: *a rumor purported to have come from headquarters.* *—n.* |**pûr'**pôrt'| *or* |-pōrt'|. Meaning; significance: *the purport of a story.* **—pur•port'ed•ly** *adv.*

pur•pose |**pûr'**pəs| *n.* **1.** The intended or desired result; a goal; aim; intent: *The yacht club's sole purpose is to promote the sport of sailing.* **2.** Determination; resolve: *a man of purpose.* *—v.* **pur•posed, pur•pos•ing.** To resolve on; intend: *They purposed to form a further expedition.*

Idioms. **for all practical purposes.** Effectively; in fact if not in name: *For all practical purposes, Russia has gone capitalist again.* **on purpose.** Intentionally; deliberately. **to good purpose.** With good results. **to little (or no) purpose.** With a few (or no) results.

pur•pose•ful |**pûr'**pəs fəl| *adj.* **1.** Having a purpose; intentional: *a purposeful snub.* **2.** Bursting with purpose; determined: *His stride was sure and purposeful.* **—pur'pose•ful•ly** *adv.* **—pur'pose•ful•ness** *n.*

pur•pose•ly |**pûr'**pəs lē| *adv.* With a specific purpose; deliberately.

purr |pûr| *n.* **1.** The low vibrant sound made by a cat when it seems to be pleased. **2.** Any similar sound: *the soft purr of the radiator.* *—v.* **1.** To make a purr. **2.** To express by a purr.

purse |pûrs| *n.* **1.** A small bag or pouch, used to carry money. **2.** A woman's handbag or pocketbook. **3.** Money; funds; means; resources: *the family purse.* **4.** A sum of money given as a gift or prize: *a wrestling match with a purse of $1,000.* *—v.* **pursed, purs•ing.** To pucker or wrinkle: *purse one's lips; purse one's brow.*

purs•er |**pûr'**sər| *n.* The officer in charge of money matters on board a ship.

pur•su•ance |pər **so͞o'**əns| *n.* The act of putting something into effect: *In pursuance of his plans, the coach called a practice session for Monday.*

pur•su•ant |pər **so͞o'**ənt| *adj.* In accordance with: *Pursuant to the new treaty, the Indians once again moved westward.*

pur•sue |pər **so͞o'**| *v.* **pur•sued, pur•su•ing. 1.** To chase in order to catch: *The posse pursued the outlaws.* **2.** To hunt as game or prey: *The white man pursued the buffalo to the brink of extinction. Jaguars will pursue almost any kind of animal.* **3.** To engage in or keep at (an activity): *pursue one's studies.* **4.** To strive to achieve, gain, etc.: *Should she pursue her ambition to be a nurse?* **5.** To follow (a course of action): *He is pursuing the wrong tactics.* **—pur•su'er** *n.*

pur•suit |pər **so͞ot'**| *n.* **1.** The act of pursuing, as to kill or capture: *the howl of the dogs in the frenzy of pursuit.* **2.** The act of striving to achieve, gain, etc.: *in the pursuit of happiness.* **3.** An activity of work or play: *the pastoral pursuits of primitive man.*

pur•vey |pər **vā'**| *v.* To supply or furnish: *purvey provisions for an army.*

pur•vey•ance |pər **vā'**əns| *n.* The act of purveying.

pur•vey•or |pər **vā'**ər| *n.* A person who purveys something: *a purveyor of food.*

pus |pŭs| *n.* A thick, yellowish-white liquid that forms in infected body tissues and consists mostly of white blood cells.

push |po͝osh| *v.* **1.** To exert force on (an object) to move it away: *He pushed the rock, but it wouldn't budge. He pushed in vain.* **2.** To move (an object) by exerting force in this way: *push a stalled car out of the intersection. They pushed until the desk was against the wall.* **3.** To exert force outward or away: *A gas pushes on the walls of its container.* **4.** To exert force on an object with (a part of the body, a tool, etc.): *The policeman pushed his shoulder against the door.* **5.** To be moved by pushing: *The door is stuck and won't push.* **6.** To force one's way: *He pushed through the crowd.* **7.** To pressure (someone) to do something: *They pushed Kim to try out for the football team.* **8.** To make a vigorous effort: *He really pushed to finish his quota on time.* **9.** To extend: *Hardy pioneers pushed the plowed fields westward.* **10.** To press with one's finger: *push a button.* **11.** To promote or try to sell: *push a new brand of toothpaste.* **12.** *Slang.* To sell (narcotics) illegally. ***—phrasal verbs.*** **push around.** To subject to harassment or unfair treatment. **push off.** *Informal.* To set out; depart. **push on.** To proceed; continue. *—n.* **1.** The act of pushing; a shove: *His car needed a push to get started.* **2.** A force that is directed outward or away: *the push of the wind on a structure.* **3. a.** A vigorous effort: *a real push to finish the project on time.* **b.** A period in which such an effort is required: *The push is on.* **4.** An attack; onslaught. **5.** *Informal.* Energy; drive; enterprise: *a salesman with plenty of push.*

Idiom. **push (one's) luck.** To behave recklessly.

push•cart |**po͝osh'**kärt'| *n.* A light cart pushed by hand.

push•er |**po͝osh'**ər| *n.* **1.** A person or thing that pushes. **2.** *Slang.* A person who sells drugs illegally.

push•o•ver |**po͝osh'**ō'vər| *n.* **1.** Anything easily done: *an exam that was a pushover.* **2.** A person or group easily defeated or taken advantage of: *The team we played last week was a pushover.*

push•up |**po͝osh'**ŭp'| *n.* An exercise for strengthening arm muscles, done by lying with one's face to the floor and pushing one's body up and down with the arms. [SEE PICTURE]

pushup

push•y |**po͝osh'**ē| *adj.* **push•i•er, push•i•est.** *Informal.* Forward or aggressive in a disagreeable manner: *a pushy salesman.* **—push'i•ly** *adv.*

ă pat/ā pay/â care/ä father/ĕ pet/ ē be/ĭ pit/ī pie/î fierce/ŏ pot/ ō go/ô paw, for/oi oil/o͝o book/ o͞o boot/ou out/ŭ cut/û fur/ *th* the/th thin/hw which/zh vision/ ə ago, item, pencil, atom, circus

pu•sil•lan•i•mous |pyo͞o'sə **lăn**'ə məs| *adj.* Cowardly; faint-hearted: *Britain's pusillanimous appeasement of Hitler at Munich.* —**pu'sil•lan'i•mous•ly** *adv.* —**pu'sil•lan'i•mous•ness** *n.*

puss[1] |po͝os| *n. Informal.* A cat. [SEE NOTE]

puss[2] |po͝os| *n. Slang.* **1.** The mouth. **2.** The face. [SEE NOTE]

puss•y |**po͝os**'ē| *n., pl.* **puss•ies.** *Informal.* A cat.

puss•y•foot |**po͝os**'ē fo͝ot'| *v.* To fail to take a stand; avoid getting involved: *Stop pussyfooting around!* —**puss'y•foot'er** *n.*

pussy willow. A shrub or small tree that has small, dense, silky, silvery flower clusters, or catkins, in early spring. [SEE PICTURE]

pus•tule |**pŭs**'cho͞ol| *or* |-tyo͞ol| *n.* **1.** A small, inflamed bump on the skin filled with pus. **2.** Any small swelling that is like a blister or pimple.

put |po͝ot| *v.* **put, putting. 1.** To place in a specified location; set. **2.** To cause to undergo something: *He put me through a lot of trouble.* **3.** To attribute or assign: *put a high value on material wealth.* **4.** To impose or levy: *put a tax on tobacco.* **5.** To bet: *putting $5 on a horse.* **6.** To express or state: *putting it bluntly.* **7.** To apply: *We must put our minds to it.* **8.** To proceed; go: *The ship put into New York harbor.* —***phrasal verbs.*** **put across. 1.** To communicate (something) convincingly: *couldn't put across an idea.* **2.** To carry out by cheating or deceit: *always trying to put across some trick.* **put aside. 1.** To discard: *put aside old habits.* **2.** To save: *putting aside some money.* **put away. 1.** To put in prison or in an asylum. **2.** To abandon; renounce: *put away childish things.* **3.** *Informal.* To kill: *The cat had to be put away.* **4.** To eat or drink: *He really puts it away.* **put by.** To save: *put by some money for a rainy day.* **put down. 1.** To set (one's work) aside: *Put down what you're doing.* **2.** To suppress: *put down an uprising.* **3.** *Slang.* To criticize or reject. **4.** To set down in writing: *putting it all down in black and white.* **put forth. 1.** To sprout: *branches putting forth buds.* **2.** To exert: *Put forth all the strength you've got.* **3.** To advance or propose. **4.** To issue: *put forth a new set of guidelines.* **5.** To set forth or embark: *putting forth to sea.* **put forward.** To suggest; advance: *He put forward an alternate plan.* **put in. 1.** To enter: *putting in an insurance claim.* **2.** To do: *putting in a hard day's work.* **3.** To make a stop at a port: *They put in at Pearl Harbor for repairs.* **4.** To say; insert: *put in a good word for me.* **put off. 1.** *Informal.* To repel (someone): *Her behavior puts me off.* **2.** *Informal.* To evade: *He keeps putting me off with promises.* **3.** To postpone: *Don't put off until tomorrow what you can do today.* **put on. 1.** To clothe oneself with; don: *putting on hat and coat.* **2.** To set on the stove or fire: *put on the kettle for tea.* **3.** To apply or activate: *put on the brake.* **4.** To assume or pretend to have: *putting on an air of kindliness.* **5.** *Slang.* To mock or fool (someone): *He's always putting somebody on.* **6.** To present (a play). **7.** To add: *putting on weight.* **put out. 1.** To extinguish: *put out a cigar.* **2.** *Informal.* To worry, annoy, or anger: *put out by her lateness.* **3.** To put (oneself) to some trouble or inconvenience for another. **4.** In baseball, to cause (a batter or runner) to be out. **put through. 1.** To complete successfully: *That deal shouldn't be hard to put through.* **2.** To connect by phone: *Please put me through to the hospital.* **put up. 1.** To raise: *put up your hands.* **2.** To build: *putting up a new barn.* **3.** To provide or contribute: *putting up $10 apiece.* **4.** To offer, as for sale: *putting the house up for sale.* **5.** To prepare: *putting up plum jelly.* **6.** To accommodate: *He put us up for the night.* **7.** *Informal.* To endure: *That's more than I can put up with.* —*n.* A heave of the shot in shotput.

Idioms. **be hard put.** To have difficulty doing, finding, or getting something: *hard put for an excuse.* **put in for.** To apply for: *putting in for a different job.* **put up with.** To endure; tolerate.

put-down |**po͝ot**'doun'| *n. Slang.* A criticism insult, or slight: *She interpreted his remarks about her as a put-down.*

put-on |**po͝ot**'ŏn'| *adj.* Feigned; pretended: *a put-on air of friendliness.* —*n. Slang.* Something intended to deceive, often as a joke: *His wild answers to the interviewer were only a put-on.*

pu•tre•fy |**pyo͞o**'trə fī'| *v.* **pu•tre•fied, pu•tre•fy•ing, pu•tre•fies. 1. a.** To cause to undergo decay or decomposition, especially by the action of microorganisms. **b.** To undergo such decomposition or decay. **2.** To make or become gangrenous. —**pu'tre•fac'tion** |pyo͞o'trə **făk**'shən| *n.*

pu•trid |**pyo͞o**'trĭd| *adj.* **1.** Partially decayed or decomposed and having a foul smell; rotting: *The lion's claws were coated with putrid meat from his kills.* **2.** Of, showing, or caused by putrefaction: *a putrid smell.*

putt |pŭt| *n.* In golf, a light stroke made on the green to get the ball into the hole. —*v.* To hit a ball with such a stroke.

put•tee |pŭ **tē**'| *or* |**pŭt**'ē| *n.* **1.** A strip of cloth wound spirally around the lower leg from the knee to the ankle, worn by soldiers and sportsmen. **2.** A gaiter covering the lower leg.

put•ter[1] |**pŭt**'ər| *n.* **1.** A golf club used to putt. **2.** A golfer who is putting: *a good putter.*

put•ter[2] |**pŭt**'ər| *v.* To busy oneself without really accomplishing much: *puttering around the garden.* —**put'ter•er** *n.*

putting green. In golf, the area of smooth grass that surrounds a hole.

put•ty |**pŭt**'ē| *n., pl.* **put•ties.** A doughlike cement made by mixing whiting and linseed oil, used to fill holes in woodwork, hold panes of glass in place, etc. —***modifier:*** *a putty knife.* —*v.* **put•tied, put•ty•ing, put•ties.** To fill, cover, or fasten with putty.

put-u•pon |**po͝ot**'ə pŏn'| *or* |-pôn'| *adj.* Imposed on; taken advantage of: *feeling put-upon by his friends.*

puz•zle |**pŭz**'əl| *n.* **1.** Something that confuses or perplexes; a problem, enigma, etc.: *It's a puzzle to me how she can finish her homework so quickly.* **2.** A toy or game that presents one with a perplexing problem or task: *a jigsaw puzzle; a crossword puzzle.* —*v.* **1.** To confuse or perplex: *Sally's rude conduct puzzled the teacher.* **2.** To ponder laboriously: *Mary puzzled over her algebra assignment.* —**puz'zled** *adj.: a puzzled look.* [SEE NOTE]

puz•zle•ment |**pŭz**'əl mənt| *n.* The condition of being puzzled: *expressed his hopeless puzzlement by a sheepish grin.*

pvt., Pvt. private.

PX post exchange; Post Exchange.

pyg•my |**pĭg**'mē| *n., pl.* **pyg•mies. 1. Pygmy.** A

puss[1-2]

Puss[1] *may be from Old English* pusa, *"soft object."* **Puss**[2] *is from Irish* bus, *"lip, mouth."*

pussy willow

puzzle

The word **puzzle** *is first recorded from the sixteenth century. Its origin is, appropriately, unknown.*

member of any of several African or Asian peoples whose height ranges between about four feet and five feet. **2.** An individual of unusually small size. *—adj.* **1.** Much smaller than the usual or typical kind: *a pygmy hippopotamus.* **2.** Very small; tiny.

py•ja•mas |pə jä′məz| *or* |**-jăm′**əz| *pl.n.* Chiefly British form of the word **pajamas.**

py•lon |**pī′**lŏn′| *n.* **1.** A monumental gateway to an Egyptian temple, formed by a pair of flat-topped pyramids. **2.** A tower marking a turning point in an air race. **3.** A steel tower that supports high-tension electric wires or cables. **4.** Something that gives support: *The one secular pylon of strength that has held society together is the family.*

py•lo•rus |pī **lôr′**əs| *or* |**-lōr′-**| *n.* The passage that connects the stomach to the beginning of the small intestine.

pyramid
Above: Egyptian
Below: Mayan

Pyong•yang |**pyŭng′yăng′**|. The capital of North Korea. Population, 1,500,000.

py•or•rhe•a |pī′ə **rē′**ə| *n.* An inflammation of the gums and tooth sockets that causes the teeth to become loose.

pyr•a•mid |**pĭr′**ə mĭd| *n.* **1.** A solid geometric figure having a polygon as its base and triangular faces that meet at a common vertex. **2.** A massive monument found especially in Egypt, having a rectangular base and four triangular faces with a single apex and serving as a tomb or temple. [SEE PICTURE]

py•ram•i•dal |pĭ **răm′**ĭ dəl| *adj.* Having the shape of a pyramid. **—py•ram′i•dal•ly** *adv.*

pyre |pīr| *n.* A pile of wood for burning a corpse as part of a funeral rite.

Pyr•e•nees |**pîr′**ə nēz′|. A mountain range along the border between France and Spain.

py•re•thrum |pī **rē′**thrəm| *or* |**-rĕth′**rəm| *n.* **1.** A plant related to the chrysanthemums and daisies. Its flowers are poisonous to insects and are used in powdered form as an insecticide. **2.** The powdered flowers of this plant.

Py•rex |**pī′**rĕks′| *n.* A trademark for any of several types of glass that resists heat and chemicals.

py•rite |**pī′**rīt′| *n.* **1.** A yellow to brown mineral composed chiefly of a sulfide of iron, used as an iron ore and in making sulfur dioxide. Also called *fool's gold.* **2.** Any of a group of minerals that are composed chiefly of metallic sulfides, especially of iron.

py•ro•ma•ni•a |pī′rō **mā′**nē ə| *n.* A mental disorder in which there is an uncontrollable urge to start fires. **—py′ro•ma′ni•ac′** *adj.& n.*

py•ro•tech•nic |pī′rō **tĕk′**nĭk| *adj.* Of or resembling fireworks: *a pyrotechnic display.*

py•ro•tech•nics |pī′rō **tĕk′**nĭks| *n.* *(used with a singular or plural verb).* **1.** A fireworks display. **2.** Any brilliant display: *The pyrotechnics of his speech awed the audience.*

Pyr•rhic victory |**pîr′**ĭk|. A victory won with staggering losses. It was so named after **Pyr•rhus** |**pîr′**əs|, a king of ancient times whose victory over the Romans in 279 B.C. was ruinous to him.

Py•thag•o•re•an theorem |pĭ thăg′ə **rē′**ən|. A theorem stating the square of the length of the longest side of a right triangle is equal to the sum of the squares of the lengths of the other sides Suppose that in a right triangle the longest side measures c and the other sides measure a and b. This theorem assures that $c^2 = a^2 + b^2$.

py•thon |**pī′**thŏn′| *n.* A very large nonpoisonous snake of Africa, Asia, and Australia, which coils around and crushes its prey. [SEE PICTURE]

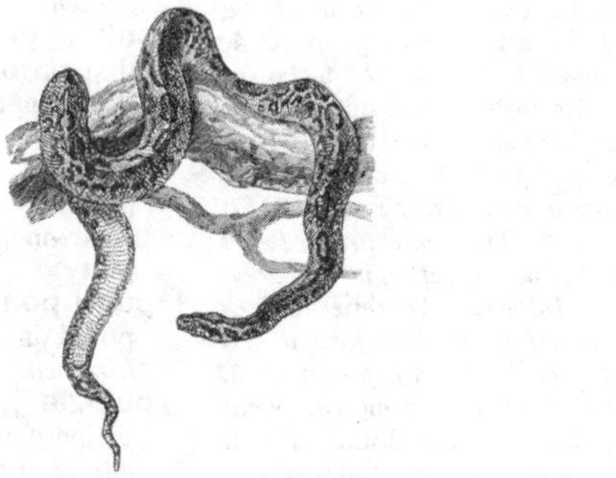

python

ă **pat**/ā **pay**/â **care**/ä **father**/ĕ **pet**/
ē **be**/ĭ **pit**/ī **pie**/î **fierce**/ŏ **pot**/
ō **go**/ô **paw**, **for**/oi **oil**/ŏŏ **book**/
ōō **boot**/ou **out**/ŭ **cut**/û **fur**/
th **the**/th **thin**/hw **which**/zh **vision**/
ə **ago**, **item**, **pencil**, **atom**, **circus**

Qq

q, Q |kyōō| *n., pl.* **q's** or **Q's** The 17th letter of the English alphabet. [SEE NOTE]

q. quart.

Qa•tar |**kä**'tär'|. A country of southwestern Asia on a peninsula in the Persian Gulf. Population, 220,000. Capital, Doha.

Q.E.D. which was to be demonstrated or proved. An abbreviation for the Latin phrase *quod erat demonstrandum.*

qt, qt. quart (unit of volume).

quack¹ |kwăk| *n.* The hoarse sound made by a duck. —*v.* To make such a sound.

quack² |kwăk| *n.* Someone who pretends to have knowledge, especially medical knowledge, that he does not have; a charlatan. —***modifier:*** *a quack cure; a quack healer.*

quack•er•y |**kwăk**'ə rē| *n., pl.* **quack•er•ies.** The practices, claims, etc., of a quack.

quad |kwŏd| *n. Informal.* A quadrangle.

quad•ran•gle |**kwŏd**'răng'gəl| *n.* **1.** A plane geometric figure consisting of four points, no three of which lie on the same straight line, connected by straight lines; a quadrilateral. **2. a.** A rectangular area bordered by buildings. **b.** The buildings surrounding such an area.

quad•rant |**kwŏd**'rənt| *n.* **1. a.** An arc equal to one-quarter of the circumference of a circle; an arc of 90°. **b.** The region of a plane bounded by such an arc and the pair of radii that extend from its endpoints to the center of the circle of which it is a part. **c.** Any of the four regions into which a plane is divided by the axes of a Cartesian coordinate system. **2.** An object, such as a machine part, shaped like one-quarter of a circle. **3.** An instrument, similar to a sextant but based on an arc of 90°, used to measure angles, as between an object and the horizon.

quad•ra•phon•ic |kwŏd'rə **fŏn**'ĭk| *adj.* Of or used in a stereophonic sound-reproduction system that uses two additional channels.

quad•rat•ic |kwŏ **drăt**'ĭk| *adj.* Of or containing mathematical terms or expressions that are of the second degree and no higher.

quadratic equation. An equation of the general form $ax^2 + bx + c = 0$, where x is the independent variable, a, b, and c are constants, and $a \neq 0$.

quad•ren•ni•al |kwŏ **drĕn**'ē əl| *adj.* **1.** Happening once in four years: *the quadrennial Olympic games.* **2.** Lasting for four years. —**quad•ren'ni•al•ly** *adv.*

quad•ri•ceps |**kwŏd**'rĭ sĕps'| *n.* The large four-part muscle at the front of the thigh that acts to extend the leg.

quad•ri•lat•er•al |kwŏd'rĭ **lăt**'ər əl| *n.* Any polygon that has four sides. —*adj.* Having four sides.

qua•drille |kwŏ **drĭl**'| or |kwə-| *n.* **1.** A square dance of French origin, performed by four couples. **2.** Music written to accompany or as if to accompany this dance.

quad•ril•lion |kwŏ **drĭl**'yən| *n.* **1.** In the United States, one thousand trillion; 1,000,000,000,000,000 or 10^{15}. **2.** In Great Britain, one trillion trillion, written as 1 followed by 24 zeros or as 10^{24}.

quad•ru•ped |**kwŏd**'rōō pĕd'| *n.* A four-footed animal.

quad•ru•ple |kwŏ **drōō**'pəl| or |-**drŭp**'əl| or |**kwŏd**'rōō pəl| *adj.* **1.** Having four parts. **2.** Multiplied by four: *a quadruple penalty.* —*n.* A number or amount four times as many or as much as another. —*v.* **quad•ru•pled, quad•ru•pling.** To make or become four times as great: *Sam quadrupled his salary. The population of the town quadrupled.*

quad•ru•plet |kwŏ **drŭp**'lĭt| or |-**drōō**'plĭt| or |**kwŏd**'rōō plĭt| *n.* **1.** One of four children born in a single birth. **2.** A group or combination of four things of one kind.

quaff |kwŏf| or |kwăf| or |kwôf| *v.* **quaffed, quaff•ing.** To drink (something) heartily: *He quaffed a mug of ale. We quaffed at the tavern all evening.*

quag•mire |**kwăg**'mīr'| or |**kwŏg**'-| *n.* **1.** A bog whose surface gives way when stepped on. **2.** A difficult situation.

qua•hog |**kwô**'hôg'| or |-hŏg'| or |**kwō**'-| *n.* A clam of the Atlantic coast of North America, having a hard, rounded shell. The quahog is much used as food, and its shell was used by Indians to make wampum.

quail¹ |kwāl| *n., pl.* **quail** or **quails.** Any of several rather small, plump, short-tailed birds with brownish feathers. [SEE NOTE]

quail² |kwāl| *v.* To lose courage; cower: *Harvey's dog looks ferocious, but he quails at the sight of a stranger.* [SEE NOTE]

quaint |kwānt| *adj.* **quaint•er, quaint•est. 1.** Old-fashioned, especially in a pleasing way: *a quaint village.* **2.** Unfamiliar or unusual; curious: *a land full of sloths, kangaroos, and other quaint animals.* —**quaint'ly** *adv.* —**quaint'ness** *n.*

quake |kwāk| *v.* **quaked, quak•ing. 1.** To shake or vibrate, as from a shock or lack of balance: *The ground quaked as the stampede passed.* **2.** To shiver or tremble, as from fear or cold: *A ghastly stage fright seized him, and his legs quaked under him.* —*n.* **1.** An example of shaking or quivering: *a quake in one's voice.* **2.** An earthquake.

(1) (2) (3)

The letter **Q** *comes originally from the Phoenician letter* qōph *(1), which meant "monkey" and stood for a sound that was similar to, but distinct from, /k/. The Greeks borrowed it as* qoppa *(2), but it had no useful role in Greek and was dropped. The Romans took it over (3) and used it with* U *for the sound /kw/. This is the basis of our modern letter* **Q.**

quail¹⁻²

Quail¹ *is from Old French* quaille; *the name occurs first, in the dialect of Latin that was spoken in the Roman province of Gaul, as* coaccula, *later* quaccula, *originally a word imitative of the bird's cry.* **Quail²** *is of obscure origin.*

quality/quantity
Quality *is from Latin* quālitās, *from* quālis, *"of what kind."* **Quantity** *is from Latin* quantitās, *from* quantus, *"how much, how large." Both* quālis *and* quantus *are formed from the Indo-European root* kwo-, *which meant "what," "who," "how," etc.*

Quak•er |kwā′kər| *n.* A member of the Society of Friends. The word "Quaker" is not used officially by the Friends. **—modifier:** *Quaker garb.* **—Quak′er•ism′** *n.*

qual•i•fi•ca•tion |kwŏl′ə fĭ kā′shən| *n.* **1.** The act of qualifying or condition of being qualified: *His qualification as a surgeon took years of hard work.* **2.** A skill or other quality that suits a person for a particular job or task: *What are the qualifications for an airline pilot?* **3.** Something that limits or restricts: *The group accepted her proposal without qualification.*

qual•i•fied |kwŏl′ə fīd′| *adj.* **1.** Competent or meeting the formal requirements, as for a job: *a fully qualified doctor.* **2.** Limited; restricted: *an attitude of qualified optimism.* **—qual′i•fied′ly** |kwŏl′ə fīd′lē| *or* |-fī′ĭd lē| *adv.*

qual•i•fi•er |kwŏl′ə fī′ər| *n.* **1.** Someone or something that qualifies. **2.** In grammar, a word or phrase that limits or modifies the meaning of another word or phrase; for example, an adjective is a qualifier.

qual•i•fy |kwŏl′ə fī′| *v.* **qual•i•fied, qual•i•fy•ing, qual•i•fies. 1.** To make, be, or become eligible or qualified, as for a position, task, etc.: *Her grades qualify her for the Honor Society. To qualify for the Air Scouts, a boy must be at least 12 years old.* **2.** To make less harsh or extreme; moderate: *He qualified his remarks to avoid offending anyone.* **3.** To limit the meaning of; modify: *Adjectives qualify other words.*

qual•i•ta•tive |kwŏl′ə tā′tĭv| *adj.* Of quality or kind as distinguished from quantity or amount: *qualitative differences between forms of energy.* **—qual′i•ta′tive•ly** *adv.*

qual•i•ty |kwŏl′ĭ tē| *n., pl.* **qual•i•ties. 1.** Any property or feature that makes something what it is: *the sour quality of vinegar.* **2.** A personal trait, especially a character trait: *She has many good qualities.* **3.** The characteristic effect of something, as on the senses or emotions: *capture with water colors the quality of a Caribbean sunset.* **4.** Excellence; superiority: *a store that only sells clothes of quality.* **5.** Degree or grade of merit: *meat of poor quality.* **6.** High social position: *a lady of quality.* [SEE NOTE]

qualm |kwäm| *or* |kwôm| *n.* **1.** A feeling of doubt or misgiving; uneasiness: *I had some qualms about flying in an airplane.* **2.** A pang of conscience: *He had no qualms about telling lies.* **3.** A sudden feeling of faintness, nausea, etc.

qualm•ish |kwä′mĭsh| *or* |kwô′-| *adj.* **1.** Having or feeling qualms: *She was qualmish about marrying him.* **2.** Of or producing qualms: *a qualmish feeling in the stomach.* **—qualm′ish•ly** *adv.* **—qualm′ish•ness** *n.*

quan•da•ry |kwŏn′drē| *or* |-də rē| *n., pl.* **quan•da•ries.** A condition of uncertainty or doubt; a dilemma: *in a quandary over what to do next.*

quan•ta |kwŏn′tə| *n.* Plural of **quantum.**

quan•ti•ta•tive |kwŏn′tĭ tā′tĭv| *adj.* Of quantity, measure, or amount: *experiments that give quantitative proof of a theory.* **—quan′ti•ta′tive•ly** *adv.*

quan•ti•ty |kwŏn′tĭ tē| *n., pl.* **quan•ti•ties. 1.** An amount or number of a thing or things: *The elements are found in nature in various quantities.* **2.** A considerable amount or number: *Pennsylvania was the first state to produce oil in quantity.* **3.** Something, such as a number or a symbol that represents a number, on which a mathematical operation is performed. [SEE NOTE]

quan•tum |kwŏn′təm| *n., pl.* **quan•ta** |kwŏn′tə|. An indivisible unit of energy, as a photon.

quantum theory. A theory of physics based on a complex use of mathematics and proposed to explain the interactions of matter and energy at the atomic and subatomic levels. Its essential features include the idea that energy occurs in quanta and that particles and waves have certain properties in common.

quar•an•tine |kwôr′ən tēn′| *or* |kwŏr′-| *n.* **1. a.** A period of time during which a person, a vehicle, goods, etc., thought to carry a contagious disease can be held at a port of entry and kept in isolation. **b.** A place where such persons, vehicles, goods, etc., are held. **2.** Any enforced confinement or isolation, especially one meant to keep a contagious disease from spreading. **—*v.*** **quar•an•tined, quar•an•tin•ing.** To keep confined or isolated, especially to keep a disease from spreading; place in quarantine.

quar•rel |kwôr′əl| *or* |kwŏr′-| *n.* **1.** An angry argument or dispute: *Betsy and Sally had a quarrel over Tom.* **2.** A reason for argument or dispute: *I have no quarrel with what you say.* **—*v.*** **quar•reled** or **quar•relled, quar•rel•ing** or **quar•rel•ling. 1.** To engage in a quarrel; argue or dispute angrily: *The boys quarreled over the use of the tennis court.* **2.** To find fault: *quarrel with a court decision.* **—quar′rel•er, quar′rel•ler** *n.*

quar•rel•some |kwôr′əl səm| *or* |kwŏr′-| *adj.* Tending to quarrel: *Ours is a quarrelsome family.*

quar•ry[1] |kwôr′ē| *or* |kwŏr′-| *n., pl.* **quar•ries.** An open excavation from which stone is obtained by digging, cutting, or blasting. **—*v.*** **quar•ried, quar•ry•ing, quar•ries. 1.** To obtain from a quarry. **2.** To make a quarry in: *quarry a mountain for its marble.* [SEE NOTE]

quar•ry[2] |kwôr′ē| *or* |kwŏr′ē| *n., pl.* **quar•ries. 1.** An animal hunted or chased. **2.** Anything pursued in a similar manner. [SEE NOTE]

quarry[1·2]
Quarry[1] *is from Old French* quarriere, *"place for cutting blocks of stone," from Latin* quadrātum, *"squared block of stone."* **Quarry**[2] *originally meant "the parts of a deer that were given to the hounds"; it is from Old French* cuiree, *from Late Latin* corāta, *"entrails," from* cor, *"heart."*

quart |kwôrt| *n.* **1. a.** A unit of volume or capacity used for measuring liquids, equal to two pints or 57.75 cubic inches. **b.** A unit of volume or capacity used for measuring dry substances, equal to two pints or 67.2 cubic inches. **2. a.** A container having a capacity of one quart. **b.** A quart with something in it: *pick up a quart of milk at the store.* **—modifier:** *a quart jar.*

quar•ter |kwôr′tər| *n.* **1.** Any of four equal parts into which a unit, amount, object, etc., is divided. **2.** One-fourth of the period of the moon's revolution about the earth. **3.** A period of three months; one-fourth of a year: *Sales picked up in the last quarter.* **4. a.** A period of 15 minutes; one-fourth of an hour. **b.** The moment when such a period begins or ends: *The clock strikes on the quarter.* **5.** A U.S. or Canadian coin worth twenty-five cents. **6.** In football and other sports, any of the four time periods that make up a game. **7.** A school or college term lasting about three months. **8.** One leg of a four-legged animal, including the adjacent parts: *a quarter of beef.* **9. a.** Any of the four main points of the compass or divisions of the horizon. **b.** Any region or place: *Men from every quarter came forward to defend the Union.* **10.** A district or section, as of a city: *the Arab quarter.* **11. quar-**

ters. a. A place to which one is assigned to sleep or reside: *the officers' quarters on a ship; the family quarters in the White House.* **b.** A place where a business or other activity is conducted: *moved his office to new quarters.* **c.** An assigned post or station, as on a ship: *a call to quarters.* **12.** An unspecified person or group of persons: *Help arrived from an unexpected quarter.* **13.** Mercy, especially when granted to a foe: *The Tatars gave no quarter to their enemies.* —*v.* **1.** To cut or divide into four equal parts: *Mother quartered an orange for us.* **2.** To furnish with lodgings: *The general quartered his troops among the townspeople.* —*adj.* **1.** Being one of four equal parts: *received a quarter share of the inheritance.* **2.** Being equal to one-fourth of a particular unit of measure: *a quarter cup of flour.*

***Idiom.* at close quarters.** At close range.

quar•ter•back |kwôr′tər băk′| *n.* In football, the player who directs the offense and usually does the passing.

quar•ter•deck |kwôr′tər dĕk′| *n.* The after part of the upper deck of a sailing ship, usually reserved for officers.

quar•ter•ly |kwôr′tər lē| *adj.* Issued, due, etc., at three-month intervals: *a quarterly magazine; a quarterly payment.* —*adv.* At three-month intervals: *receive dividends quarterly.* —*n., pl.* **quar•ter•lies.** A magazine published at three-month intervals.

quar•ter•mas•ter |kwôr′tər măs′tər| *or* |-mä′stər|. *n.* **1.** A military officer responsible for the food, clothing, and equipment of troops. **2.** A naval petty officer responsible for the navigation of a ship.

quarter note. A musical note that has one-fourth the time value of a whole note.

quar•ter•staff |kwôr′tər stăf′| *or* |-stäf′| *n., pl.* **-staves** |-stāvz′|. A long wooden pole with an iron tip, formerly used as a weapon.

quar•tet |kwôr tĕt′| *n.* **1. a.** A musical composition that requires four performers, especially a composition for two violins, a viola, and a cello. **b.** A group of four musicians who perform a quartet or quartets. **2.** A group of four people or things. [SEE PICTURE]

quar•to |kwôr′tō| *n., pl.* **quar•tos. 1.** The page size obtained by folding a sheet of paper into four leaves. **2.** A book printed on pages of this size or folded in this way.

quartz |kwôrts| *n.* A clear, hard, transparent mineral composed of silicon dioxide. It occurs as a component of rocks and in pure crystalline forms, many of which are considered gemstones. [SEE PICTURE]

quartz glass. A type of glass made of pure silica. Quartz glass is highly transparent to ultraviolet light.

quartz•ite |kwôrt′sīt′| *n.* A metamorphic rock formed by the compression of sandstone.

qua•sar |kwā′sär′| *or* |-sär′| *n.* A **quasi-stellar object.**

quash[1] |kwŏsh| *v.* To put down or suppress by or as if by force: *quash a rebellion.*

quash[2] |kwŏsh| *v.* In law, to set aside or annul: *The judge quashed the indictment.*

qua•si |kwā′zī′| *or* |-sī′| *or* |kwä′zē| *or* |-sē| *adv.* To some degree; almost or somewhat: *a quasi-public high school.* —*adj.* Resembling but not being: *Phrenology is a quasi science.*

qua•si-stel•lar object |kwā′zī′stĕl′ər| *or* |-sī′-| *or* |kwä′zē-| *or* |-sē-|. Any of various celestial objects that emit light having a very large red shift and that usually also emit radio waves. These objects are thought to be at immense distances from the earth and to have immense speeds and energies.

Qua•ter•nar•y |kwŏt′ər nĕr′ē| *or* |kwə tûr′nə rē| *n.* Also **Quaternary period.** A geologic period that began 2,000,000 to 500,000 years ago and extends to the present, characterized by the appearance and development of human beings. —***modifier:*** *a Quaternary rock.*

quat•rain |kwŏt′rān′| *or* |kwŏ trān′| *n.* A stanza of four lines in a poem.

qua•ver |kwā′vər| *v.* To shake, as from fear; tremble; quiver. —*n.* A quavering sound.

quay |kē| *n.* A stone wharf or reinforced bank where ships are loaded or unloaded. ¶ *These sound alike* **quay, key.**

quea•sy |kwē′zē| *adj.* **queas•i•er, queas•i•est. 1.** Sick to one's stomach; nauseated. **2.** Easily nauseated. **3.** Causing nausea; sickening. **4.** Easily troubled; squeamish. —**quea′si•ly** *adv.* —**quea′si•ness** *n.*

Que•bec |kwĭ bĕk′|. **1.** A province of eastern Canada. Population, 6,234,445. **2.** The capital of this province. Population, 177,082.

Quech•ua |kĕch′wə| *or* |-wä′| *n.* **1.** A member of a South American Indian people that originally made up the ruling class of the Empire of the Incas. **2.** The language of this people, still spoken in Peru, Bolivia, and Ecuador. —**Quech′uan** *adj.*

queen |kwēn| *n.* **1. a.** A female monarch. **b.** The wife of a king. **2.** A woman who is chosen or considered as the most outstanding in some way: *a beauty queen.* **3.** A playing card bearing the figure of a queen. It ranks above a jack and below a king. **4.** In chess, a player's most powerful piece, able to move in any direction across any number of unoccupied squares. **5.** In a colony of bees, ants, or termites, a large, specially developed female who is able to lay eggs and produce offspring and is usually the only one of this kind in the colony. —*v.* In chess, to raise (a pawn) to queen when it has reached the opponent's end of the board. [SEE NOTE]

Queen Anne's lace |ănz|. A plant with feathery leaves and flat clusters of small white flowers. It is a wild form of the carrot. [SEE PICTURE]

queen consort. The wife of a sovereign king.

queen•ly |kwēn′lē| *adj.* **queen•li•er, queen•li•est. 1.** Of a queen: *queenly duties.* **2.** Resembling or befitting a queen: *her queenly manner.* —**queen′li•ness** *n.*

queen mother. A dowager queen who is the mother of the reigning monarch.

queer |kwîr| *adj.* **queer•er, queer•est.** Unusual; odd; strange; peculiar: *a queer expression on his face.* —**queer′ly** *adv.* —**queer′ness** *n.*

quell |kwĕl| *v.* **1.** To put down; suppress: *quell a revolt.* **2.** To allay; calm: *quell one's fears.*

quench |kwĕnch| *v.* **1.** To put out or extinguish (a fire, flame, etc.). **2.** To satisfy; appease: *quenched his thirst with a can of soda.*

quer•u•lous |kwĕr′ə ləs| *or* |kwĕr′yə-| *adj.* **1.** Given to complaining or fretting; peevish: *a*

quartet

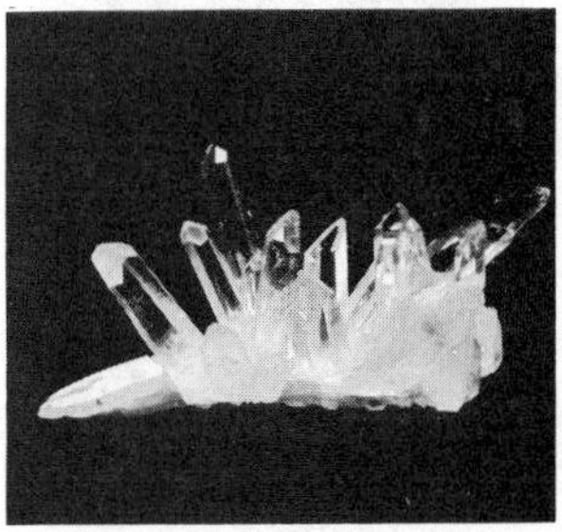

quartz
Rock quartz

queen
Queen *was* cwēn *in Old English and originally meant "woman, wife," hence "queen." It is descended from prehistoric Germanic* kwēn-, *which in turn is from Indo-European* gwēn-, *or* gwen-, *"woman."* Gwen- *also appears in Greek as* gunē, *"woman," which has been borrowed into English to form the word* **gynecology**.

Queen Anne's lace

quetzal
The name **quetzal** is from Aztec *quetzall,* "large, brilliant tail feather."

queue
Queue *is from French* queue, *"tail," also "pigtail, line of people," from Latin* cauda, *"tail."*

quid[1-2]
Quid[1] *was Middle English* quide, *originally Old English* cwidu *or* cudu, *"cud, thing for chewing."* Cudu *separately became* **cud** *in Modern English, so* **quid**[1] *is a doublet of* **cud**. **Quid**[2] *is of obscure origin.*

quill
A flight feather

ă pat/ā pay/â care/ä father/ĕ pet/ ē be/ĭ pit/ī pie/î fierce/ŏ pot/ ō go/ô paw, for/oi oil/ŏŏ book/ ōō boot/ou out/ŭ cut/û fur/ *th* the/th thin/hw which/zh vision/ ə ago, item, pencil, atom, circus

querulous person. **2.** Showing or uttering complaints or criticism: *the querulous tone of his voice.* —**quer'u•lous•ly** *adv.* —**quer'u•lous•ness** *n.*

que•ry |kwîr'ē| *n., pl.* **que•ries.** A question; an inquiry. —*v.* **que•ried, que•ry•ing, que•ries. 1.** To ask questions of: *The police queried the suspect about his recent activities.* **2.** To express doubt about; question: *querying the wisdom of his decision.*

quest |kwĕst| *n.* **1.** A search for something held valuable or precious: *Space exploration represent's man's latest quest for knowledge of the universe.* **2.** In stories of the Middle Ages, an expedition undertaken by a knight in order to find something or achieve a lofty purpose: *the quest for the Grail.*

ques•tion |kwĕs'chən| *n.* **1.** Something that is asked in order to obtain information in reply. **2.** A subject or point open to debate; an unsettled issue: *Your point raises broad constitutional questions.* **3.** A subject that is being debated: *The chairman called for a vote on the question of building a new library.* **4.** A matter of uncertainty about something; problem: *It is only a question of money.* **5.** Uncertainty; doubt: *There is no question about his ability to do the job.* —*v.* **1.** To ask questions of; interrogate: *Dad questioned me about the party last night.* **2.** To express doubt about; dispute: *No one questions his decisions.* —**ques'tion•er** *n.*

Idioms. **in question.** Under discussion; concerned: *the individual in question.* **out of the question.** Not to be considered; unthinkable.

ques•tion•a•ble |kwĕs'chə nə bəl| *adj.* Open to doubt or suspicion; uncertain: *a questionable assumption; remedies of questionable value.* —**ques'tion•a•bly** *adv.*

question mark. A punctuation mark (?) written at the end of a sentence or phrase to show that a question is being asked.

ques•tion•naire |kwĕs'chə **nâr'**| *n.* A printed form with a series of questions, often used to obtain statistical information or to sample public opinion on a certain subject.

quet•zal |kĕt **säl'**| *n.* **1.** A brilliant green and red Central American bird of which the male has very long tail feathers. **2.** The basic unit of money of Guatemala. [SEE PICTURE]

Quet•zal•co•a•tl |kĕt säl'kō **ät'**l|. The plumed serpent god of the Aztecs.

queue |kyōō| *n.* **1.** A line of people awaiting their turn, as at a ticket window. **2.** A long braid of hair that hangs down the back; a pigtail. —*v.* *Chiefly British.* To get in line; wait in a queue: *We'll have to queue up for tickets.* ¶*These sound alike* **queue, cue.** [SEE NOTE]

Que•zon City |kā'sôn'|. The constitutional capital of the Philippines. Population, 545,000.

quib•ble |kwĭb'əl| *n.* **1.** The skillful use of trivial arguments or vague language in discussing something. **2.** A minor criticism or objection. —*v.* **quib•bled, quib•bling.** To raise trivial points and objections; argue over minor matters: *quibble over petty details.*

quick |kwĭk| *adj.* **quick•er, quick•est. 1.** Moving or acting with speed; fast: *quick on one's feet. He was quick to sense that something was wrong.* **2.** Done or accomplished in a brief space of time: *quick action; a quick trip; a quick recovery.* **3.** Prompt to understand, think, or learn; bright; alert: *a quick mind.* **4.** Easily stirred up or aroused: *a quick temper.* —*adv.* Quickly; promptly: *Come quick! He'll find out quick enough.* —*n.* The sensitive, tender flesh under the fingernails. —**quick'ly** *adv.* —**quick'ness** *n.*

Idiom. **cut to the quick.** To wound or offend deeply.

quick•en |kwĭk'ən| *v.* **1.** To make or become more rapid; accelerate: *quicken one's steps. The pace of history quickens as technology becomes more advanced.* **2.** To make or become keener, livelier, or more intense; stir: *Such stories quicken the imagination. Interest in the elections quickened rapidly.*

quick-freeze |kwĭk'frēz'| *v.* **-froze** |-frōz'|, **-fro•zen** |-frō'zən|, **-freez•ing.** To freeze (food) quickly enough so that it keeps its natural flavor, nutritional value, appearance, etc.

quick•lime |kwĭk'līm'| *n.* **Calcium oxide.**

quick•sand |kwĭk'sănd'| *n.* A bed of loose sand mixed with water, forming a soft, shifting mass that yields easily to pressure and tends to suck down any object resting on its surface.

quick•sil•ver |kwĭk'sĭl'vər| *n.* The element mercury.

quick-tem•pered |kwĭk'tĕm'pərd| *adj.* Easily angered.

quick-wit•ted |kwĭk'wĭt'ĭd| *adj.* Quick to think and act; mentally alert.

quid[1] |kwĭd| *n.* A piece of something to be chewed, as tobacco. [SEE NOTE]

quid[2] |kwĭd| *n., pl.* **quid** or **quids.** *British Slang.* A pound (unit of money). [SEE NOTE]

qui•es•cent |kwī ĕs'ənt| *or* |kwē-| *adj.* Inactive; quiet; dormant. —**qui•es'cence** *n.*

qui•et |kwī'ĭt| *adj.* **qui•et•er, qui•et•est. 1.** Making little or no noise; silent or almost silent: *quiet neighbors; a quiet engine.* **2.** Free of noise; hushed: *a quiet street.* **3.** Not loud: *He spoke in a quiet voice.* **4.** Not moving; still; calm: *The sea is quiet after the storm.* **5.** Tranquil; peaceful; serene: *a quiet evening at home; a quiet place in the country.* **6.** Not showy or bright; subdued: *quiet colors.* —*n.* **1.** Freedom from noise; silence: *The speaker asked for quiet.* **2.** Freedom from disturbance; tranquillity: *He retired to the quiet of his country estate.* —*v.* To make or become quiet: *The teacher quieted the class. It was several minutes before the audience quieted down.* —**qui'et•ly** *adv.*

qui•e•tude |kwī'ĭ tōōd'| *or* |-tyōōd'| *n.* Calm; tranquillity.

quill |kwĭl| *n.* **1. a.** A long, stiff feather, usually from the tail or wing of a bird. **b.** The hollow, stemlike central part of a feather. **2.** Also **quill pen.** A writing pen made from a long, stiff feather. **3.** One of the hollow spines of a porcupine. **4.** A stiff, picklike device, usually made of leather, that plucks a string of a harpsichord when a key is pressed. [SEE PICTURE]

quilt |kwĭlt| *n.* A padded bed covering made of two layers of cloth with a layer of cotton, wool, down, or feathers in between, all stitched firmly together, usually in a crisscross design. —*v.* **1.** To work on or make a quilt or quilts: *They quilted together once a week.* **2.** To make like a quilt, with an inner layer of padding: *quilt a skirt.* —**quilt'ed** *adj.: a quilted robe.*

quilt•ing |kwĭl′tĭng| *n.* **1.** The act of doing quilted work. **2.** Material used to make quilts. **3.** Quilted material.

quince |kwĭns| *n.* **1.** A hard, pleasant-smelling, applelike fruit used chiefly for making jam or jelly. **2.** A tree that bears such fruit. —***modifier:*** *quince jelly.*

qui•nine |**kwī′**nīn′| *n.* **1.** A bitter, colorless drug derived from certain cinchona barks and used to treat malaria. **2.** Any of various drugs or chemicals derived from quinine.

quinine water. Carbonated water flavored with quinine and sugar.

quin•sy |**kwĭn′**zē| *n.* A severe inflammation of the tonsils and throat, often leading to the formation of an abscess.

quin•tes•sence |kwĭn **tĕs′**əns| *n.* **1.** The essence or basic element of something: *The quintessence of democracy is freedom of choice.* **2.** The purest or most typical example of something: *He is the quintessence of the new generation of folk singers.*

quin•tet |kwĭn **tĕt′**| *n.* **1. a.** A musical composition that requires five performers. **b.** A group of five musicians who perform a quintet or quintets. **2.** A group of five people or things.

quin•tu•ple |kwĭn **tōō′**pəl| *or* |**-tyōō′-**| *or* |**-tŭp′**əl| *or* |**kwĭn′**tōō pəl| *adj.* **1.** Having five parts. **2.** Multiplied by five: *a quintuple increase.* —*n.* A number or amount five times as many or as much as another. —*v.* **quin•tu•pled, quin•tu•pling.** To make or become five times as great.

quin•tu•plet |kwĭn **tŭp′**lĭt| *or* |**-tōō′**plĭt| *or* |**-tyōō′-**| *or* |**kwĭn′**tōō plĭt| *n.* **1.** One of five children born in a single birth. **2.** A group or combination of five related things.

quip |kwĭp| *n.* A clever or witty remark. —*v.* **quipped, quip•ping.** To make a quip or quips.

qui•pu |**kē′**pōō| *n.* A device used by the ancient Incas of Peru for making computations and recording important facts and events. It consisted of variously colored and knotted cords attached to a base rope.

quire |kwīr| *n.* A unit consisting of 24 or sometimes 25 sheets of paper of the same size and stock; $^{1}/_{20}$ of a ream. ¶*These sound alike* **quire, choir.**

quirk |kwûrk| *n.* **1.** A peculiarity of behavior: *Everyone has his quirks.* **2.** An unpredictable twist or turn: *a quirk of fate.*

quirt |kwûrt| *n.* A riding whip with a short handle and a braided leather lash.

quit |kwĭt| *v.* **quit, quit•ting. 1.** To discontinue; stop; cease: *quit smoking. Quit bothering me!* **2.** To give up; abandon or resign: *quit school; quit one's job.* **3.** To leave; depart from: *They decided to quit the city for the country.* **4.** To cease functioning: *The motor quit when we were a few miles from home.* **5.** To give up, as in defeat.

quit•claim |**kwĭt′**klām′| *n.* The legal release of a claim or right to another. —*v.* To release a claim or right to another legally.

quite |kwīt| *adv.* **1.** Completely; altogether: *Plant cells are not quite the same as animal cells.* **2.** Somewhat; rather: *Our own group of planets is quite small.* **3.** Really; actually; truly: *a quite considerable number of errors.*

Idioms. **quite a.** Outstanding, unusual, remarkable, etc.: *quite a large crowd; quite a football player.* **quite a few.** A large number; many.

Qui•to |**kē′**tō|. The capital of Ecuador. Population, 551,000.

quits |kwĭts| *adj.* —**be quits with.** To be even with as a result of repayment or revenge. —**call it quits.** To call a halt to something; stop what one is doing.

quit•ter |**kwĭt′**ər| *n.* A person who gives up easily.

quiv•er¹ |**kwĭv′**ər| *v.* To shake with a slight vibrating motion; tremble: *His lips quivered with excitement. Her voice quivered as she spoke.* —*n.* A slight vibrating motion. [SEE NOTE]

quiv•er² |**kwĭv′**ər| *n.* A case for holding and carrying arrows. [SEE NOTE & PICTURE]

quix•ot•ic |kwĭk **sŏt′**ĭk| *adj.* Full of romantic or impractical ideas. —**quix•ot′i•cal•ly** *adv.*

quiz |kwĭz| *n., pl.* **quiz•zes.** A short oral or written examination. —*v.* **quizzed, quiz•zing. 1.** To question closely; interrogate. **2.** To test the knowledge of by asking questions.

quiz•zi•cal |**kwĭz′**ĭ kəl| *adj.* Showing puzzlement; perplexed: *a quizzical look on his face.* —**quiz′zi•cal•ly** *adv.*

quoin |koin| *or* |kwoin| *n.* **1. a.** An outside corner of a wall. **b.** A stone forming such a corner. **2.** A keystone. **3.** A wedge-shaped block used by printers to lock type into a galley. ¶*These sound alike* **quoin, coin.**

quoit |kwoit| *or* |koit| *n.* **1. quoits** *(used with a singular verb).* A game in which players try to toss rings of iron or rope onto a peg. **2.** One of the rings used in this game.

Quon•set hut |**kwŏn′**sĭt|. A trademark for a prefabricated hut having a semicircular roof of corrugated metal that curves down to form walls.

quo•rum |**kwôr′**əm| *or* |**kwōr′-**| *n.* The minimum number of members of a committee or organization that must be present for the valid transaction of business.

quo•ta |**kwō′**tə| *n.* **1.** An amount of something assigned to be done, made, sold, etc.: *a production quota.* **2.** The maximum number or proportion of persons or things that may be admitted, as to a country, group, institution, etc.: *an immigration quota; an import quota.*

quo•ta•tion |kwō **tā′**shən| *n.* **1.** The act of quoting: *These remarks are not for direct quotation.* **2.** A passage that is quoted: *a quotation from Shakespeare.* **3.** A statement of the price of a security or the price itself: *the latest stock-market quotations.*

quotation mark. Either of a pair of punctuation marks (" ") used to mark the beginning (") and end (") of a passage attributed to another and repeated exactly. Single quotation marks (' ') usually indicate a quotation within a quotation.

quote |kwōt| *v.* **quot•ed, quot•ing. 1. a.** To repeat or cite (a sentence, paragraph, etc.): *quote a familiar proverb.* **b.** To repeat a passage in or statement by: *quote the Bible; quote the mayor.* **2.** To state (a price) for securities, goods, or services. —*n.* **1.** A quotation. **2.** A **quotation mark.** —**quot′a•ble** *adj.*

quoth |kwōth| *v. Archaic.* Said; spoke.

quo•tient |**kwō′**shənt| *n.* The number that results when one number is divided by another.

q.v. which see. An abbreviation for the Latin expression *quod vide.*

quiver¹·²

Quiver¹ *is from Old English* cwifer-, *"nimble," which is probably related to* **quick. Quiver²** *is from Old French* cuivre, *which is ultimately from Mongolian* kökür, *"a quiver"; the word seems to have been brought to Europe by the Huns.*

quiver ²

Rr

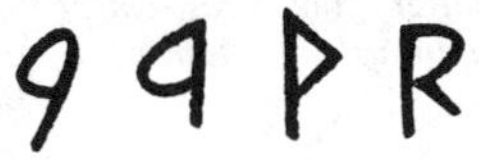
(1) (2) (3) (4)

The letter **R** *comes originally from the Phoenician letter* rēsh *(1), which meant "head" and stood for /r/. The Greeks borrowed it as* rhō *(2), later turning it around to face in the opposite direction (3). The Romans borrowed it from the Greeks and added a tail (4) to distinguish it from their letter* P. *The Roman letter is the basis of our modern letter* **R**.

race[1-2]
Race[1] *is from Old Norse* rās, *"a running, a fast current of water."* **Race**[2] *is from Old French* race, *"group of people"; its further origin is obscure.*

racket[1-2]
Racket[1] *is from Old French* rachette *or* raquette, *"palm of the hand," also "snowshoe, tennis racket."* **Racket**[2] *is of obscure origin.*

ă pat/ā pay/â care/ä father/ĕ pet/ ē be/ĭ pit/ī pie/î fierce/ŏ pot/ ō go/ô paw, for/oi oil/o͝o book/ o͞o boot/ou out/ŭ cut/û fur/ *th* the/th thin/hw which/zh vision/ ə ago, item, pencil, atom, circus

r, R |är| *n., pl.* **r's** or **R's.** The 18th letter of the English alphabet. [SEE NOTE]

r, R 1. radius **2.** resistance, as in an electric circuit.

r., R. 1. right. **2.** river.

R roentgen.

R |är| *adj.* Indicating a rating given a motion picture deemed unsuitable for persons under a certain age (17) unless accompanied by a parent or guardian.

Ra The symbol for the element radium.

Ra•bat |rä **bät′**|. The capital of Morocco. Population, 436,000.

rab•bi |**răb′**ī′| *n.* **1.** The spiritual leader of a Jewish congregation. **2.** In former times, a scholar who interpreted Jewish law.

rab•bin•i•cal |rə **bĭn′**ĭ kəl| *adj.* Of or characteristic of rabbis.

rab•bit |**răb′**ĭt| *n.* **1.** A burrowing animal with long ears, soft fur, and a short, furry tail. **2.** The fur of such an animal. ***—modifier:*** *a rabbit hutch.*

rabbit ears. An indoor television antenna consisting of two adjustable rods connected to a base and swiveling apart at a V-shaped angle.

rab•ble |**răb′**əl| *n.* **1.** A noisy, unruly crowd or mob. **2. the rabble.** The common people, often regarded with contempt.

rab•ble-rous•er |**răb′**əl rou′zər| *n.* A person who appeals to the emotions and prejudices of the public; a demagogue.

rab•id |**răb′**ĭd| *adj.* **1.** Of or affected with rabies. **2.** Overzealous; fanatical: *a rabid baseball fan.*

ra•bies |**rā′**bēz| *n.* An infectious virus disease that can affect any mammal, attacks the central nervous system, and practically always causes death. It is transmitted by the bite of an infected animal.

rac•coon |ră **ko͞on′**| *n.* **1.** A North American animal with grayish-brown fur, black, masklike face markings, and a bushy, black-ringed tail. **2.** The fur of such an animal.

race[1] |rās| *n.* **1. a.** A contest of speed, as in running or riding: *a horse race.* **b. races.** A series of such competitions, especially horse races: *win at the races.* **2.** Any contest for supremacy: *the arms race.* —*v.* **raced, rac•ing. 1.** To take part in or compete against in a race: *I'll race you to the house. The horse hasn't raced in months.* **2.** To enter in a race or races: *He races horses for a living.* **3.** To rush at top speed; dash: *raced home.* **4.** To run or cause to run at high speed: *race an engine.* [SEE NOTE]

race[2] |rās| *n.* **1. a.** A group of people considered to be more or less distinct on the basis of physical characteristics that are transmitted by genes. **b.** The fact of belonging to a certain race: *people classified by race.* **2.** Mankind as a whole. **3.** A group of plants or animals that have inherited similar characteristics and form a distinct type within a species or breed. ***—modifier:*** *race relations.* [SEE NOTE]

race•horse |**rās′**hôrs′| *n.* A horse bred and trained for racing.

ra•ceme |**rā′**sēm′| *n.* A flower cluster with stalked flowers arranged singly along a stem.

rac•er |**rā′**sər| *n.* **1.** A person or thing that competes in a race or in races. **2.** Any of several fast-moving North American snakes.

race•track |**rās′**trăk′| *n.* A course laid out for racing.

ra•cial |**rā′**shəl| *adj.* Of or based on race or a race: *racial characteristics.* **—ra′cial•ly** *adv.*

rac•ism |**rā′**sĭz′əm| *n.* Racial prejudice or discrimination.

rac•ist |**rā′**sĭst| *n.* A person who advocates or practices racism. ***—modifier:*** *racist policies.*

rack |răk| *n.* **1. a.** A stand or bar on which to hang certain articles: *a coat rack.* **b.** A shelf or series of shelves for holding certain articles: *a book rack.* **c.** A frame, often with upright partitions, for standing a number of similar articles: *a magazine rack.* **2.** A triangular frame for arranging billiard balls at the start of a game. **3.** A frame for holding bombs in an airplane. **4.** A metal bar having teeth that mesh with those of a pinion or gearwheel. **5.** An old instrument of torture on which the victim's legs were stretched and broken. —*v.* **1.** To place in or on a rack. **2.** To torment or afflict: *Pain racked his entire body.* ***—phrasal verb.*** **rack up.** *Slang.* To score; achieve: *rack up a victory.* ¶*These sound alike* **rack, wrack.**

rack•et[1] |**răk′**ĭt| *n.* In sports, a device used to strike a ball or shuttlecock, consisting of a frame with tight interlaced strings and a handle. ¶*These sound alike* **racket, racquet.** [SEE NOTE]

rack•et[2] |**răk′**ĭt| *n.* **1.** A loud, continuing, unpleasant noise or sound. **2.** A business that uses illegal methods, threats, or violence. ¶*These sound alike* **racket, racquet.** [SEE NOTE]

rack•et•eer |răk′ĭ **tîr′**| *n.* A person who runs or works in a criminal racket.

ra•coon |ră **ko͞on′**| *n.* A form of the word **raccoon.**

rac•quet |**răk′**ĭt| *n.* **1.** A form of the word **racket** (the term in sports). **2. racquets** *(used with a singular verb).* A game similar to tennis but played on a court with no net and enclosed by four walls. ¶*These sound alike* **racquet, racket.**

rac•y |**rā′**sē| *adj.* **rac•i•er, rac•i•est. 1.** Lively;

sprightly. **2.** Slightly improper or indecent. —**rac'i•ly** *adv.* —**rac'i•ness** *n.*

ra•dar |rā'där'| *n.* **1.** A method of detecting distant objects and determining their position, speed, size, etc., by causing radio waves to be reflected from them and analyzing the reflected waves. **2.** The equipment used in doing this. —***modifier:*** *a radar station.*

ra•di•al |rā'dē əl| *adj.* **1.** Of, arranged like, or directed along a radius or radii. **2.** Of or having parts that are arranged like radii: *the radial body of a starfish.* —**ra'di•al•ly** *adv.*

radial symmetry. A pattern in which forms or features that are opposite each other at equal distances from a central point are identical. [SEE PICTURE]

ra•di•ance |rā'dē əns| *n.* **1.** Vivid brightness. **2.** Cheerfulness or warmth.

ra•di•ant |rā'dē ənt| *adj.* **1.** Sending forth light, heat, or other radiation: *a radiant star.* **2.** Consisting of or transmitted as radiation: *radiant energy.* **3.** Filled with brightness and happiness; beaming: *a radiant smile.* —**ra'di•ant•ly** *adv.*

ra•di•ate |rā'dē āt'| *v.* **ra•di•at•ed, ra•di•at•ing.** **1.** To send forth (heat, light, or other energy), especially in the form of waves. **2.** To be sent forth as radiation: *light that radiates from a star.* **3.** To spread out from a center. **4.** To exude; project: *radiate confidence.*

ra•di•a•tion |rā'dē ā'shən| *n.* **1.** The act or process of radiating. **2. a.** The emission and movement of waves, atomic particles, etc., through space or other media. **b.** The waves or particles that are emitted and caused to travel.

ra•di•a•tor |rā'dē ā'tər| *n.* **1.** A heating device for the circulation of steam or hot water. **2.** A cooling device, as in automotive engines.

rad•i•cal |răd'ĭ kəl| *adj.* **1.** Going to the root or source; fundamental; drastic; sweeping: *radical changes.* **2.** Advocating extreme or revolutionary changes, especially in politics or government. —*n.* **1.** A militant reformer. **2.** A revolutionary. **3.** A root, such as $\sqrt{x}$ or $\sqrt[3]{2}$, especially as indicated by a radical sign. **4.** A group of atoms that behaves as a unit in chemical reactions and is not stable except as a part of a compound. —**rad'i•cal•ly** *adv.*

rad•i•cal•ism |răd'ĭ kə lĭz'əm| *n.* The advocacy of revolutionary changes in government and politics, often by violent means.

radical sign. The sign $\sqrt{\ }$ placed around a number, as in $\sqrt[3]{9}$, to show that a root of the enclosed number is to be taken.

rad•i•cand |răd'ĭ kănd'| *n.* The number or expression written inside a radical sign, as the 3 in $\sqrt{3}$ or $x - 5$ in $\sqrt{x-5}$.

rad•i•ces |răd'ĭ sēz'| *n.* A plural of **radix.**

ra•di•i |rā'dē ī'| *n.* Plural of **radius.**

ra•di•o |rā'dē ō'| *n., pl.* **ra•di•os.** **1.** The use of electromagnetic waves lying between about 10 kilohertz and 300,000 megahertz to carry messages or information between points without the use of wires. **2. a.** The equipment used to generate such electromagnetic waves and alter them so that they carry information; a transmitter. **b.** The equipment used to receive such waves; a receiver. **3.** The sending forth of programs of entertainment, news, information, etc., in this way, especially as a business; broadcasting. —***modifier:*** *a radio wave; a radio broadcast.* —*v.* **ra•di•oed, ra•di•o•ing, ra•di•os.** **1.** To send (messages, information, etc.) by radio. **2.** To signal or communicate with by radio.

radio–. A word element meaning "radiation": **radiograph.**

ra•di•o•ac•tive |rā'dē ō ăk'tĭv| *adj.* Of or showing radioactivity: *a radioactive element.*

ra•di•o•ac•tiv•i•ty |rā'dē ō ăk tĭv'ĭ tē| *n.* **1.** The process or property by which atomic nuclei emit radiation. **2.** The radiation released.

radio astronomy. The scientific study of celestial objects and phenomena by observation of radio waves that reach the earth.

radio beam. A beam of radio signals transmitted by a beacon to guide aircraft or ships.

ra•di•o•car•bon |rā'dē ō kär'bən| *n.* Any radioactive isotope of carbon, especially carbon 14.

ra•di•o•gram |rā'dē ō grăm'| *n.* A message sent by wireless telegraphy.

ra•di•o•graph |rā'dē ō grăf'| *or* |-gräf'| *n.* An image produced, as on photographic film, by radiation other than light, especially by x-rays. —*v.* To make a radiograph of.

ra•di•o•i•so•tope |rā'dē ō ī'sə tōp'| *n.* A radioactive isotope of one of the elements.

ra•di•ol•o•gist |rā'dē ŏl'ə jĭst| *n.* A physician who specializes in radiology.

ra•di•ol•o•gy |rā'dē ŏl'ə jē| *n.* **1.** The use of x-rays and other ionizing radiation in medical diagnosis and treatment. **2.** The use of radiation to examine physical objects and structures.

ra•di•om•e•ter |rā'dē ŏm'ĭ tər| *n.* A device used to detect and measure radiation, consisting of a glass bulb containing a partial vacuum in which a set of vanes, each darkened on one side and shiny on the other, spin about a central axis when radiation strikes them.

radio telescope. A very sensitive radio receiver, typically equipped with a large, dishlike reflecting antenna, used to detect radio waves that reach the earth from space.

radio wave. An electromagnetic wave having a frequency in the range used for radio, radar, etc.

rad•ish |răd'ĭsh| *n.* **1.** A plant grown for its strong-tasting red-skinned or white root. **2.** The root of this plant, eaten raw.

ra•di•um |rā'dē əm| *n.* Symbol **Ra** One of the elements, a rare, white, highly radioactive metal. It has 13 isotopes with mass numbers ranging from 213 to 230, of which Ra 226, with a half-life of 1,622 years, is the most common. Atomic number 88; valence +2; melting point 700°C; boiling point 1,737°C. [SEE NOTE]

ra•di•us |rā'dē əs| *n., pl.* **ra•di•i** |rā'dē ī'|. **1. a.** Any line segment that joins the center of a circle with any point on its circumference. **b.** Any line segment that joins the center of a sphere with any point on its surface. **2.** The length of such a line segment. **3.** Such a line segment used as a measure of circular area. **4.** The shorter and thicker of the two bones that make up the forearm.

ra•dix |rā'dĭks| *n., pl.* **rad•i•ces** |răd'ĭ sēz'| or **ra•dix•es.** The base of a system of numeration; the number written 10 in that system of numeration, such as 2 (base 10) in the binary system or 10 (base 10) in the decimal system.

ra•don |rā'dŏn'| *n.* Symbol **Rn** One of the

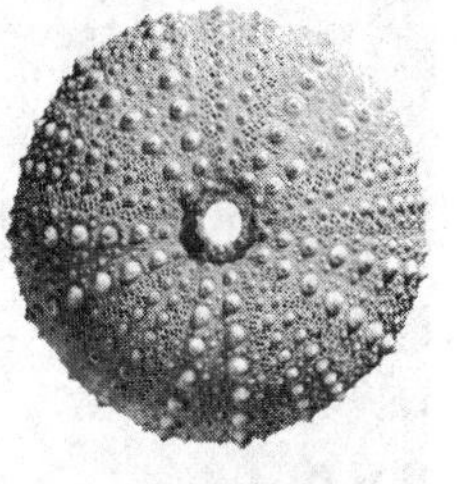

radial symmetry
Shell of sea urchin showing radial symmetry

radium/radon
The word **radium** *is from Latin* radius, *"ray" (referring to its luminescence). Radium is obtained chiefly from pitchblende, although it occurs in all uranium ores. It is used in radiotherapy, in the production of luminescent paints, and as a source of neutrons. The word* **radon** *is from* **radium,** *since radon is produced by the radioactive decay of radium. Radon is used as a source of radiation for treating cancer and as a source of neutrons.*

ragweed
Giant ragweed

rake[1-2-3]
Rake[1] *was* raca *in Old English.* **Rake[2]** *is a shortening of the obsolete word* rakehell, *"a totally depraved man"; the verb* **rake[1]** *used to mean "to go through something with a rake, to comb," and was used in the proverbial expression "You'd need to rake through hell to find a man as bad as him."* **Rake[3]** *is of unknown origin.*

rake[1]

ă pat/ā pay/â care/ä father/ĕ pet/ ē be/ĭ pit/ī pie/î fierce/ŏ pot/ ō go/ô paw, for/oi oil/ŏŏ book/ ōō boot/ou out/ŭ cut/û fur/ *th* the/th thin/hw which/zh vision/ ə ago, item, pencil, atom, circus

elements, a colorless, radioactive, inert gas. Atomic number 86; atomic weight 222; valence 0; melting point -71°C; boiling point -68.1°C. [SEE NOTE on p. 725]

raf•fi•a |răf'ē ə| *n.* Fiber from the leaves of an African palm tree, used for baskets, mats, etc.

raf•fle |răf'əl| *n.* A method of raising money, often for charity, in which many chances are sold and a drawing is held to determine the winner or winners. —*v.* **raf•fled, raf•fling.** To offer as a prize in a lottery: *raffle off a car.*

raft[1] |răft| *or* |räft| *n.* A floating platform made of planks, logs, or other buoyant materials.

raft[2] |răft| *or* |räft| *n. Informal.* A great number or amount.

raft•er |răf'tər| *or* |räf'-| *n.* One of the beams that support a pitched roof.

rag |răg| *n.* **1.** A scrap of torn, frayed, or leftover cloth. **2. rags.** Shabby, torn, or tattered clothing: *a tramp in rags.*

rag•a•muf•fin |răg'ə mŭf'ĭn| *n.* A dirty, ragged child.

rage |rāj| *n.* **1.** Violent anger or a fit of such anger: *livid with rage; flying into a rage.* **2.** *Informal.* A fad or craze: *Boogie-woogie became the rage during the 1930's.* —*v.* **raged, rag•ing. 1.** To show violent anger. **2.** To continue with great violence: *The storm raged outside.*

rag•ged |răg'ĭd| *adj.* **1.** Torn, frayed, or tattered: *ragged clothes.* **2.** Dressed in shabby, torn, or tattered clothes: *a ragged tramp.* **3.** Rough; jagged; uneven: *a ragged edge.* **4.** Imperfect; sloppy: *The actor gave a ragged performance.* —**rag'ged•ly** *adv.* —**rag'ged•ness** *n.*

rag•time |răg'tīm'| *n.* A form of jazz in which a highly syncopated melody is played against a steadily accented accompaniment.

rag•weed |răg'wēd'| *n.* A weedy plant with narrow clusters of small greenish flowers whose pollen is one of the chief causes of hay fever. [SEE PICTURE]

raid |rād| *n.* **1.** A sudden attack, as one made by soldiers or a group of aircraft: *an air raid.* **2.** A sudden and forcible entry of a place by police in order to make arrests and seize illegal items. —*v.* To carry out a raid on. —**raid'er** *n.*

rail[1] |rāl| *n.* **1.** A horizontal bar or timber supported at both ends or at close intervals, as in a fence. **2.** A low fence or barrier along the side of a road, bridge, etc. **3.** A steel bar used, usually as one of a pair, to form a path for railroad cars, engines, etc. **4.** Railroads as a means of transportation: *travel by rail.* —***modifier:*** *a rail fence.* —*v.* To enclose or supply with a rail or rails.

rail[2] |rāl| *v.* To use strong or emphatic language; complain loudly and bitterly.

rail[3] |rāl| *n.* A brownish, short-winged marsh bird.

rail•ing |rā'lĭng| *n.* **1.** A fence made of rails. **2.** A banister or handrail.

rail•ler•y |rā'lə rē| *n.* Good-natured teasing or ridicule.

rail•road |rāl'rōd'| *n.* **1.** A pathway built of steel rails, usually arranged in parallel pairs and supported by ties, used by trains, locomotives, etc. **2.** A system of transportation using such pathways, together with the stations, land, trains, and other property needed for its operation. —***modifier:*** *a railroad train.* —*v.* **1.** To work for a railroad company. **2.** *Informal.* To rush or push through without adequate consideration: *railroad a bill through the legislature.* **3.** *Slang.* To convict and send to prison without a fair trial or on false evidence.

rail•way |rāl'wā'| *n.* **1.** A railroad, especially one operated over a limited area. **2.** A track that acts as a pathway for equipment with wheels.

rai•ment |rā'mənt| *n. Archaic.* Clothing.

rain |rān| *n.* **1. a.** Water that condenses from vapor in the atmosphere and falls to the earth as drops. **b.** A fall of such water; a rainstorm or shower. **2.** Often **rains.** A season or time of rainy weather. —***modifier:*** *a rain cloud.* —*v.* **1.** To fall in drops of water from the clouds: *It may rain tomorrow.* **2.** To release rain: *clouds that rain on the land.* **3.** To send down or fall like rain: *bombs raining destruction on the hapless villages. Ticker tape rained down on the passing motorcade.* **4.** To give or offer in great amounts: *rain favors on someone.* —***phrasal verb.* rain out.** To force the postponement of (an outdoor event) because of rain. ¶ *These sound alike* **rain, reign, rein.**

rain•bow |rān'bō'| *n.* **1.** An arc-shaped spectrum of color seen in the sky opposite the sun, especially after rain, caused by sunlight refracted by droplets of water. **2.** Any similar spectrum, as one seen in the mist of a waterfall.

rain•coat |rān'kōt'| *n.* A waterproof or water-resistant coat worn over other clothes.

rain•fall |rān'fôl'| *n.* **1.** A fall of rain; shower. **2.** The amount of water, usually measured in inches, that falls over a given area during a given time in the form of rain, snow, etc.

rain forest. A dense evergreen forest occupying a tropical region with an annual rainfall of at least 100 inches.

rain•y |rā'nē| *adj.* **rain•i•er, rain•i•est.** Marked by much rain: *a rainy afternoon; rainy weather.* —**rain'i•ness** *n.*

***Idiom.* rainy day.** A possible future time of need: *put money aside for a rainy day.*

raise |rāz| *v.* **raised, rais•ing. 1.** To move to a higher position; lift: *raise the window slightly.* **2.** To increase in amount; make higher: *raise prices.* **3.** To bring up; rear: *raise children; born and raised in Philadelphia.* **4.** To grow or breed: *raise corn; raise livestock.* **5.** To increase in volume; make louder: *Don't raise your voice at me.* **6.** To gather together; collect: *raise money.* **7.** To bring about; cause; evoke: *raise doubts.* **8.** To bring up; put forward: *raise a question.* **9.** To build; erect: *raise a barn.* **10.** To start; create; set in motion: *raise a fuss.* —*n.* An increase in wages: *ask for a raise.* ¶ *These sound alike* **raise, raze.** —**rais'er** *n.*

***Idiom.* raise to a power. 1.** To indicate, as by an exponent, that a number or mathematical quantity is to be used a given number of times as a factor. **2. a.** To calculate the value of (a number, such as 9^4, to which an exponent has been applied). **b.** To write an (algebraic expression affected by an exponent, such as $[a + b]^2$) in expanded form, such as $a^2 + 2ab + b^2$.

rai•sin |rā'zən| *n.* A sweet dried grape.

ra•jah or **ra•ja** |rä'jə| *n.* A prince or ruler in India or the East Indies.

rake[1] |rāk| *n.* A long-handled tool with teeth or prongs at one end, used to gather leaves, stones, etc., or to loosen or smooth earth. —*v.* **raked, rak•ing. 1.** To gather or smooth with a rake:

rake leaves; rake the lawn. **2.** To unearth; bring to light: *rake up old gossip.* **3.** To direct gunfire along the length of: *rake the trenches with machine-gun fire.* **4.** To run through or along the surface of something: *He raked his fingers through his hair.* [SEE NOTE & PICTURE on p. 726]

***Idiom.* rake over the coals.** To subject to severe criticism.

rake[2] |rāk| *n.* A person who leads a loose or dissolute life. [SEE NOTE on p. 726]

rake[3] |rāk| *n.* Inclination from the vertical, as of a ship's mast. [SEE NOTE on p. 726]

rak•ish |rā'kĭsh| *adj.* Gay and careless in appearance. —**rak'ish•ly** *adv.*

Ra•leigh |rô'lē| *or* |rä'-|. The capital of North Carolina. Population, 149,771.

Ra•leigh |rô'lē| *or* |rä'-|, **Sir Walter.** 1552?–1618. English navigator, colonizer, and poet.

ral•ly |răl'ē| *v.* **ral•lied, ral•ly•ing, ral•lies. 1.** To reassemble for further action: *The general rallied his men. The troops rallied.* **2.** To gather or join together in support of a common cause: *trying to rally the public behind his program. Many people rallied to his defense.* **3.** To rouse or revive: *rally the team's confidence.* **4.** To show a sudden improvement in health or mental condition: *The patient rallied after four days of fever.* **5.** To recover or snap back from a disadvantageous position: *The stock market rallied in the final hour of trading.* —*n., pl.* **ral•lies. 1.** A mass meeting organized in support of a cause: *a political rally; a football rally.* **2.** A sudden improvement in health, mental condition, etc.

ram |răm| *n.* **1.** A male sheep. **2.** A battering ram. —*v.* **rammed, ram•ming. 1.** To force into a narrow space; jam: *ram food down a patient's throat.* **2.** To crash or smash into: *An iceberg rammed the ship and sank it. A tugboat rammed into the ferry.* [SEE PICTURE]

Ram•a•dan |răm'ə **dän'**| *n.* The ninth month of the Moslem year, observed with fasting from sunrise to sunset.

ram•ble |răm'bəl| *v.* **ram•bled, ram•bling. 1.** To wander aimlessly; stroll or roam: *The children rambled in the woods.* **2.** To follow a winding course; meander: *The highway rambles through the countryside.* **3.** To speak or write in an aimless manner, often wandering off the subject: *He rambled on endlessly about his recent illness.* —*n.* A leisurely stroll: *an early morning ramble.*

ram•bler |răm'blər| *n.* **1.** Someone or something that rambles. **2.** A climbing rose with many small flowers.

ram•bling |răm'blĭng| *adj.* **1.** Wandering; roving: *a rambling herd of buffalo.* **2.** Following a winding or irregular course: *a rambling stream.* **3.** Extending out in an irregular pattern: *a rambling old mansion.* **4.** Following no consistent pattern: *a rambling speech.*

ram•bunc•tious |răm **bŭngk'**shəs| *adj. Informal.* Wild; boisterous; unruly.

ram•i•fi•ca•tion |răm'ə fĭ **kā'**shən| *n.* **1.** The process of branching out. **2.** A branch or an arrangement of branching parts extending from a main body. **3.** A resulting development; consequence.

ram•i•fy |răm'ə fī'| *v.* **ram•i•fied, ram•i•fy•ing, ram•i•fies.** To extend in branches or divisions; branch out.

ramp |rămp| *n.* **1.** A sloping passage or roadway that leads from one level to another. **2.** A movable stairway used for entering and leaving an airplane.

ram•page |răm'pāj'| *n.* A course or period of violent, destructive, or unrestrained action. —*v.* |răm **pāj'**| **ram•paged, ram•pag•ing.** To race about wildly or destructively; rage: *a mob rampaging through the streets.*

ram•pant |răm'pənt| *adj.* **1.** Growing or extending unchecked: *a rampant growth of weeds; rampant corruption.* **2.** Rearing up on the hind legs with the forelegs raised: *a rampant lion on a coat of arms.* —**ram'pant•ly** *adv.*

ram•part |răm'pärt'| *or* |-pərt| *n.* **1.** A wall or bank raised around a fort, city, or other area for protection against attack. **2.** Any protective barrier. **3.** Any large, imposing mass.

ram•rod |răm'rŏd'| *n.* **1.** A metal rod used to force the charge into the muzzle of a gun. **2.** A rod used to clean the barrel of a gun.

ram•shack•le |răm'shăk'əl| *adj.* Close to falling apart; broken-down; shaky: *a ramshackle hut.*

ran |răn|. Past tense of **run.**

ranch |rănch| *n.* A large farm in western North America, especially one on which cattle, sheep, or horses are raised. —***modifier:*** *ranch land.* —*v.* To work on or own a ranch. [SEE NOTE]

ranch•er |răn'chər| *n.* A person who owns or manages a ranch.

ran•che•ro |răn **châr'**ō| *n., pl.* **ran•che•ros.** In the southwestern United States, a rancher.

ran•cid |răn'sĭd| *adj.* Having the unpleasant smell or taste of decomposed oils or fats.

ran•cor |răng'kər| *n.* Bitter resentment; deep-seated ill will. —**ran'cor•ous** *adj.*

rand |rănd| *or* |ränd| *n.* The basic unit of money of the Republic of South Africa.

ran•dom |răn'dəm| *adj.* **1.** Having no particular pattern, purpose, organization, or structure: *random noise; a random set.* **2.** Included in or making up a random set: *random numbers.*

***Idiom.* at random.** Without a definite purpose or method; by chance: *picked a book at random.*

rang |răng|. Past tense of **ring.**

range |rānj| *n.* **1.** An extent or region within which something can vary: *a wide range of prices.* **2.** An extent of perception, knowledge, or understanding: *within viewing range; a mind of limited range.* **3.** An area treated or considered; scope: *A partial list of the contents suggests the range of the book.* **4.** The set of values that the dependent variable of a mathematical function can take. See **domain. 5.** The maximum or effective distance that a sound, radio signal, missile, etc., can travel: *a cannon with a range of 20 miles.* **6.** The maximum distance that a ship, aircraft, or other vehicle can travel before using up its fuel. **7.** The distance to an object being viewed or aimed at: *observing the reptiles at close range in a zoo.* **8.** A place for shooting at targets. **9.** A testing area in which rockets and missiles are fired and flown. **10.** A number or extent of various things; variety: *A wide range of courses is offered.* **11.** The area in which a kind of animal or plant normally lives or grows. **12.** A large expanse of open land on which cattle, horses, etc., wander and graze. **13.** A large stove with spaces for cooking a number of things at the same time: *a new electric range.* **14.** An

ram

ranch/range

Ranch *is from Mexican Spanish* rancho, *which is ultimately from Old French* range, *"range, line." The English word* range *is borrowed directly from Old French* range, *which in turn is from* renc, *"line, row, rank," originally "a place marked out for a meeting." See note at* **rink.**

rank[1-2]

Rank[1] *is from Old French* renc, *"line, row, rank" (see note at* **ranch***).* **Rank[2]** *was Old English* renc, *"full-grown, overbearing."*

rape[1-2]

Rape[1] *is from Latin* rapere, *"to seize." Sense* **2** *is the original meaning of the Latin word and refers to a very ancient legal form of marriage that has existed among various peoples; the man abducts the woman with a ritual show of force, and she becomes his legal wife without the consent of her family.* **Rape[2]** *is from Latin* rapa, *"turnip."*

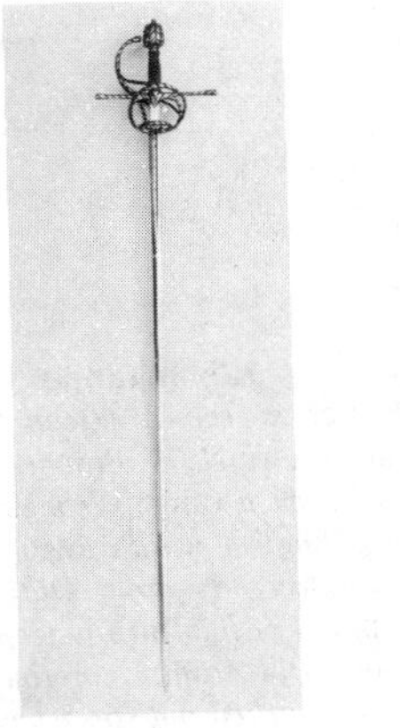

rapier
Sixteenth-century Spanish

rare[1-2]

Rare[1] *is from Latin* rārus, *"thin, scarce."* **Rare[2]**, *which was Old English* hrēr, *"undercooked," originally referred also to eggs and meant "soft-boiled."*

ă pat/ā pay/â care/ä father/ĕ pet/ ē be/ĭ pit/ī pie/î fierce/ŏ pot/ ō go/ô paw, for/oi oil/ŏŏ book/ ōō boot/ou out/ŭ cut/û fur/ *th* the/th thin/hw which/zh vision/ ə ago, item, pencil, atom, circus

extended group or series, especially of mountains. —*v.* **ranged, rang•ing. 1.** To vary or move between specified limits: *children whose ages ranged from four to ten.* **2.** To travel or roam about over (a wide area), as in exploration: *ranged the plateau in search of a safe campsite.* **3.** To wander and graze over (an area): *when buffaloes ranged the plains.* **4.** To live or grow over a certain region. **5.** To extend in a certain direction: *a ridge ranging westward from the peak.* **6.** To place in a particular order, especially in a row: *ranged the cups on hooks along the wall.* **7.** To place in a group or category; classify: *Able thinkers were ranged on opposite sides of the controversy.* [SEE NOTE on p. 727]

rang•er |rān'jər| *n.* **1.** A wanderer. **2.** A person employed to patrol a government-owned forest or park. **3.** One of an armed troop that patrols a specific region. —***modifier:*** *a ranger station.*

Ran•goon |răng gōōn'|. The capital of Burma. Population, 1,700,000.

rang•y |rān'jē| *adj.* **rang•i•er, rang•i•est.** Long-legged and thin: *a tall, rangy young man.*

rank[1] |răngk| *n.* **1.** A relative position on a scale of performance, production, value, quality, etc.: *in the middle rank of his class.* **2.** High position in society; eminence: *gentlemen of rank.* **3.** An official position or grade: *an adviser with cabinet rank.* **4.** A row or line, especially of people or things side by side: *The soldiers formed ranks for inspection.* **5. ranks. a.** The **armed forces. b.** The enlisted men of a military force, as distinguished from the officers. **c.** The people in any organization who follow orders rather than give them: *He was promoted from the ranks to become a factory foreman.* **6. ranks.** A body of people classed together; numbers: *joined the ranks of the unemployed.* —*v.* **1.** To hold a certain rank: *ranked eighth in a class of 160.* **2.** To assign a rank to; evaluate in a certain way: *Sports writers rank the team second in the nation.* **3.** To arrange in a row or on a scale: *ranked the children according to height.* [SEE NOTE]

rank[2] |răngk| *adj.* **rank•er, rank•est. 1.** Growing thickly and without control: *rank weeds.* **2.** Strong and unpleasant in odor or taste: *a rank cigar.* **3.** Complete; out-and-out: *a rank amateur.* [SEE NOTE]

rank and file. 1. The troops of an army. **2.** The ordinary members of a group or organization, as distinguished from the leaders and officers.

rank•ing |răng'kĭng| *adj.* Having a high or the highest rank; senior: *the ranking officer.*

ran•kle |răng'kəl| *v.* **ran•kled, ran•kling.** To fill (someone) with a nagging resentment; annoy.

ran•sack |răn'săk'| *v.* **1.** To search thoroughly and often roughly. **2.** To rob of valuables and leave in disarray; pillage. —**ran'sack'er** *n.*

ran•som |răn'səm| *n.* **1.** The release of someone held captive in return for the payment of a demanded price. **2.** The price or payment demanded. —*v.* **1.** To obtain the release of (someone held captive) by paying a demanded price. **2.** To release after receiving such a payment.

rant |rănt| *v.* To speak loudly, violently, and at length; rave: *ranted against high taxes.* —*n.* A loud, violent speech; a tirade. —**rant'er** *n.*

rap |răp| *v.* **rapped, rap•ping. 1.** To hit (a surface) sharply; strike: *rapped the table with his fist.* **2.** To strike a surface with (an object); knock: *The judge rapped his gavel to call for order. He rapped on the door with his cane.* **3.** To communicate or utter with sharp, loud sounds: *rap out a message on the telegraph.* **4.** *Slang.* To talk; converse. **5.** *Informal.* To criticize adversely; reprimand. —*n.* **1.** A sharp, swift blow; a knock. **2.** A knocking or tapping sound. **3.** *Slang.* A talk or discussion. **4.** *Informal.* A reprimand; rebuke. **5.** *Slang.* **a.** A criminal charge: *a burglary rap.* **b.** A prison sentence. **c.** Blame or responsibility: *took the rap for his friends.* ¶*These sound alike* **rap, wrap.**

ra•pa•cious |rə pā'shəs| *adj.* Seizing what belongs to others without mercy; fierce and greedy: *rapacious pirates.* —**ra•pa'cious•ly** *adv.* —**ra•pac'i•ty** |rə păs'ĭ tē|, **ra•pa'cious•ness** *n.*

rape[1] |rāp| *n.* **1.** The act or crime of forcing a woman to submit to sexual intercourse. **2.** *Archaic.* The act of seizing and carrying off a woman by force. —*v.* **raped, rap•ing. 1.** To force (a woman) to submit to sexual intercouse. **2.** *Archaic.* To seize and carry off (a woman) by force. **3.** To plunder. [SEE NOTE]

rape[2] |rāp| *n.* A plant with small seeds used as a source of oil and animal feed. [SEE NOTE]

rap•id |răp'ĭd| *adj.* Fast; swift: *rapid progress; walking with rapid strides.* —*n.* **rapids.** A place in a river where the water flows very fast because of a steep slope in the riverbed. —**ra•pid'i•ty, rap'id•ness** *n.* —**rap'id•ly** *adv.*

ra•pi•er |rā'pē ər| *n.* A sword with a double-edged blade, used for thrusting. [SEE PICTURE]

rap•ine |răp'ĭn| *n.* The seizure of property by force; plunder.

rap•ist |rā'pĭst| *n.* Someone who commits rape.

rap•port |ră pôr'| *or* |-pōr'| *n.* A relationship of mutual trust and understanding.

rap•scal•lion |răp skăl'yən| *n.* A rascal.

rapt |răpt| *adj.* **1.** Deeply moved or delighted; enchanted: *The children were listening with rapt admiration.* **2.** Deeply absorbed; preoccupied: *The painter stood at his easel, rapt.* ¶*These sound alike* **rapt, wrapt.**

rap•ture |răp'chər| *n.* Overwhelming delight; joy that carries one away; bliss.

rap•tur•ous |răp'chər əs| *adj.* Feeling or expressing rapture; joyful. —**rap'tur•ous•ly** *adv.*

rare[1] |râr| *adj.* **rar•er, rar•est. 1.** Occurring or found infrequently: *a rare disease.* **2.** Highly valued; special: *a rare gift for carving.* **3.** Of low density: *rare gases in the earth's upper atmosphere.* —**rare'ness** *n.* [SEE NOTE]

rare[2] |râr| *adj.* **rar•er, rar•est.** Cooked a short time: *rare meat.* —**rare'ness** *n.* [SEE NOTE]

rare•bit |râr'bĭt| *n.* **Welsh rabbit.**

rare earth. 1. An oxide of a rare-earth element. **2.** A **rare-earth element.**

rare-earth element |râr'ûrth'|. Any of the metallic elements with atomic numbers ranging from 57 to 71.

rare•ly |râr'lē| *adv.* Infrequently; seldom.

rar•i•ty |răr'ĭ tē| *n., pl.* **rar•i•ties. 1.** The quality or condition of being rare; infrequency of occurrence: *the rarity of four-leaf clovers.* **2.** Something that is rare: *Snow is a rarity in Florida.*

ras•cal |răs'kəl| *n.* **1.** A dishonest person; a scoundrel; villain. **2.** A person, especially a child, who playfully misbehaves.

rash[1] |răsh| *adj.* **rash•er, rash•est.** Too bold or hasty; reckless. —**rash'ly** *adv.* —**rash'ness** *n.* [SEE NOTE]

rash[2] |răsh| *n.* **1.** Any abnormal eruption of the skin. **2.** An outbreak of many occurrences within a brief period: *a rash of burglaries in the building.* [SEE NOTE]

rasp |răsp| *or* |räsp| *n.* **1.** A coarse file with sharp raised points on its surface instead of ridges. **2.** A harsh, grating sound. —*v.* **1.** To scrape or file with a rasp. **2.** To make a harsh, grating sound. —**rasp'ing** *adj.*: *a rasping voice.*

rasp•ber•ry |răz'bĕr'ē| *or* |räz'-| *n., pl.* **-ber•ries.** **1. a.** A sweet, many-seeded berry that grows on a prickly plant with long, woody stems. **b.** A plant or shrub that bears such berries. **2.** A dull purplish red or deep rose. **3.** *Slang.* A jeering sound made by vibrating the tongue between the lips. —***modifier:*** *raspberry jam.* —*adj.* Dull purplish red or deep rose. [SEE PICTURE]

rasp•y |răs'pē| *adj.* **rasp•i•er, rasp•i•est.** Grating; rough.

rat |răt| *n.* **1.** A long-tailed gnawing animal related to and resembling the mouse but larger. **2.** A hateful, sneaky, or untrustworthy person. —*v.* **rat•ted, rat•ting.** **1.** To hunt for or catch rats. **2.** *Slang.* To betray one's comrades by giving information; squeal. —**rat'ter** *n.* [SEE PICTURE]

rat cheese *n.* Cheddar.

ratch•et |răch'ĭt| *n.* **1.** A mechanism made up of a pawl, or hinged catch, that fits into the sloping teeth of a wheel or bar, allowing motion in one direction only. **2.** The pawl, wheel, or bar of such a mechanism. —***modifier:*** *a ratchet wheel; a ratchet jack.*

rate |rāt| *n.* **1. a.** A quantity measured with respect to another measured quantity. For example, the distance that is or could be traveled during a given unit of time is called a rate of speed. **b.** Progress; pace: *Light and heavy objects fall at the same rate.* **2.** A measure of a part with respect to a whole; proportion: *a national unemployment rate of 4.8 per cent.* **3.** The cost or price charged per unit of a commodity or service: *postal rates.* **4.** A level of quality; grade: *a jewel of no common rate.* —*v.* **rat•ed, rat•ing.** **1.** To place in a particular grade on a scale; rank: *rated her third in her class.* **2.** To estimate the quality of; evaluate: *How do you rate this restaurant?* **3.** To consider; regard: *stocks that are rated a bad risk.* **4.** To hold a certain rank; be valued or placed: *Such hypocrites rate low in my estimation.* **5.** To be worthy of; deserve: *We thought we rated better treatment.*
Idiom. **at any rate.** **1.** Whatever happens; in any case. **2.** At least.

rath•er |răth'ər| *or* |rä'thər| *adv.* **1.** To a certain extent; somewhat: *feeling rather sleepy.* **2.** Preferably; more willingly: *I'd rather stay home tonight.* **3.** More exactly; more accurately: *He is a businessman or, rather, a banker.* **4.** Instead; to the contrary: *The photograph did not show the whole family, but rather all the boys.*

rat•i•fy |răt'ə fī'| *v.* **rat•i•fied, rat•i•fy•ing, rat•i•fies.** To approve and thus make officially valid; confirm: *ratify an amendment to the Constitution.* —**rat'i•fi•ca'tion** *n.*

rat•ing |rā'tĭng| *n.* **1.** A classification assigned according to quality, performance, skill, etc.: *beef marked with a "choice" rating.* **2.** An estimate of someone's financial status and ability to pay back debts: *a high credit rating.* **3.** An estimate of the popularity of a television or radio program, made by polling the audience.

ra•tio |rā'shō| *or* |-shē ō'| *n., pl.* **ra•tios.** **1.** An indicated quotient of a pair of numbers, often used as a means of comparing them. **2.** A relationship between the amounts or sizes of two things, expressed as such a quotient; proportion: *mixed flour and water in the ratio of five to two.*

ra•tion |răsh'ən| *or* |rā'shən| *n.* **1.** A fixed amount, especially of food, allotted periodically: *a horse's daily ration of oats.* **2.** **rations.** Food issued or available to members of a group: *a soldier's rations.* —*v.* **1.** To give out or make available in fixed, limited amounts during a period of scarcity: *a drought that made it necessary to ration water.* **2.** To supply with allotments of food; give rations to.

ra•tion•al |răsh'ə nəl| *adj.* **1.** Having or using the ability to reason: *man, the rational animal.* **2.** Consistent with or based on reason; logical: *rational behavior.* **3.** Of a rational number. —*n.* A **rational number.** —**ra'tion•al•ly** *adv.*

ra•tion•al•ize |răsh'ə nə līz'| *v.* **ra•tion•al•ized, ra•tion•al•iz•ing.** **1.** To cause to obey logical rules; make rational: *Attempts to rationalize English spelling have failed.* **2.** To invent explanations for (one's behavior) that seem satisfactory although they are probably false: *He rationalized his miserliness by calling it thrift.* —**ra'tion•al•i•za'tion** *n.*

rational number. Any number that can be expressed as an integer or a quotient of integers.

rat•line |răt'lĭn| *n.* Any of the rope ladders rigged between the shrouds of a sailing ship.

rat•tan |ră tăn'| *n.* The stems of a climbing tropical palm tree, used for furniture, canes, etc.

rat•tle |răt'l| *v.* **rat•tled, rat•tling.** **1. a.** To make or cause to make a quick succession of short, sharp sounds: *so frightened that his teeth rattled; a gale that rattled the windows.* **b.** To move with such sounds: *an old tractor that rattled along the road.* **2.** To shake noisily: *rattled the coins in his pocket.* **3.** To talk or utter rapidly and without pausing: *rattled on about his relatives.* **4.** *Informal.* To disturb the composure or confidence of; unnerve. —*n.* **1.** A quick succession of short, sharp sounds: *the rattle of the rain on the roof.* **2.** A device that rattles when shaken: *a baby's rattle.* **3. a.** The dry, horny rings at the end of a rattlesnake's tail, making a rattling or buzzing sound when shaken. **b.** One of these rings.

rat•tler |răt'lər| *n.* **1.** Someone or something that rattles. **2.** A rattlesnake.

rat•tle•snake |răt'l snāk'| *n.* Any of several poisonous American snakes having at the end of the tail several dry, horny rings that can be shaken rapidly to make a rattling or buzzing sound. [SEE PICTURE]

rau•cous |rô'kəs| *adj.* **1.** Loud and harsh: *raucous cries.* **2.** Boisterous; disorderly: *a raucous party.* —**rau'cous•ly** *adv.* —**rau'cous•ness** *n.*

rav•age |răv'ĭj| *v.* **rav•aged, rav•ag•ing.** To bring heavy destruction upon; devastate: *a hurricane ravaging the coast.* —*n.* **1.** The act of ravaging; heavy destruction. **2.** Often **ravages.** Severe damage; destructive effect: *the ravages of smallpox.*

rave |rāv| *v.* **raved, rav•ing.** **1.** To speak or shout in a wild, uncontrolled way without making any sense: *ranting and raving against the younger*

rash[1-2]
Rash[1] *is from Middle Dutch* rasch, *"nimble, quick."* **Rash[2]** *is probably from French* rache, *"eruption of the skin."*

raspberry

rat

rattlesnake

generation. **2.** To speak with wild enthusiasm or praise: *raving about his mother's cooking.* **3.** To move violently and loudly; roar: *the din of a river that races and raves.* —*n.* **1.** An act of raving. **2.** *Informal.* An opinion, description, or review full of enthusiastic praise. —**modifier:** *rave reviews.*

raven
Painting by
John James Audubon

rav•el |răv′əl| *v.* **rav•eled** or **rav•elled, rav•el•ing** or **rav•el•ling.** To separate into single, loose threads; fray: *raveled the edge of cloth. The rug raveled.* —*n.* A loose thread that has become separated from woven or knitted material.

ra•ven |rā′vən| *n.* A large, crowlike black bird with a croaking cry. [SEE PICTURE]

rav•en•ing |răv′ə nĭng| *adj.* Greedily seeking and seizing prey; predatory.

rav•en•ous |răv′ə nəs| *adj.* **1.** Greedily eager for food; extremely hungry: *a ravenous appetite.* **2.** Urgently demanding satisfaction or gratification: *ravenous desires.* —**rav′en•ous•ly** *adv.*

ra•vine |rə vēn′| *n.* A deep, narrow cut, similar to a canyon or gorge, in the earth's surface.

rav•ing |rā′vĭng| *adj.* **1.** Talking in a wild, uncontrolled way: *a raving maniac.* **2.** *Informal.* Worthy of extravagant praise; splendid: *a raving beauty.* —*n.* Wild, uncontrolled speech.

rav•ish |răv′ĭsh| *v.* **1.** To seize and take by force. **2.** To rape. **3.** To ruin; despoil. **4.** To carry (someone) away with delight or other strong emotion; enrapture. —**rav′ish•ment** *n.*

ray[1-2]

Ray[1] *is from Old French* rai, *which is from Latin* radius, *"spoke of a wheel," hence "radius," also "ray of light."* **Ray[2]** *is from Old French* raie, *which is from Latin* raia, *"ray" (the fish).*

rav•ish•ing |răv′ĭ shĭng| *adj.* Filling one with delight or admiration; enchanting: *a ravishing symphony.* —**rav′ish•ing•ly** *adv.*

raw |rô| *adj.* **raw•er, raw•est. 1. a.** In a natural condition; not processed or refined: *raw wool.* **b.** To be further processed or refined: *raw metal.* **2.** Uncooked: *raw meat.* **3.** Not finished, covered, or coated: *furniture sanded down to raw wood.* **4.** Not moderated or softened; crude: *raw power.* **5.** Inexperienced; unskilled: *raw recruits.* **6.** Having tissue below the skin exposed: *a raw, open wound.* **7.** Badly irritated; inflamed; sore: *a patch of raw skin on her knee.* **8.** Unpleasantly damp and chilly: *raw weather.*

Idiom. in the raw. 1. In a natural or unrefined condition. **2.** *Informal.* Naked.

raw•hide |rô′hīd′| *n.* **1.** The hide of cattle before it has been tanned. **2.** A whip or rope made of such hide. —**modifier:** *rawhide boots.*

ray[2]

raw material. 1. Any product or material that is converted into another product or material by processing or manufacturing. **2.** Any material from which something is made or built.

ray[1] |rā| *n.* **1.** A thin line or narrow beam of light or other radiation. **2.** A small amount; a trace; hint: *a ray of hope.* **3.** One of several lines or parts extending from a common center. **4.** Also **ray flower.** One of the narrow, petallike flowers surrounding the dense, buttonlike or disklike central flower cluster of a daisy, aster, sunflower, etc. ¶*These sound alike* **ray, re.** [SEE NOTE]

ray[2] |rā| *n.* Any of several ocean fishes having a flattened body, often with the fins forming winglike extensions, and a long, narrow tail. ¶*These sound alike* **ray, re.** [SEE NOTE & PICTURE]

ray•on |rā′ŏn′| *n.* **1.** Any of several types of synthetic fibers made from cellulose. **2.** Cloth or yarn made from rayon. —**modifier:** *rayon pajamas.*

ă pat/ā pay/â care/ä father/ĕ pet/
ē be/ĭ pit/ī pie/î fierce/ŏ pot/
ō go/ô paw, for/oi oil/ŏŏ book/
ōō boot/ou out/ŭ cut/û fur/
th the/th thin/hw which/zh vision/
ə ago, item, pencil, atom, circus

raze |rāz| *v.* **razed, raz•ing.** To destroy or tear down completely; level: *razed old tenements.* ¶*These sound alike* **raze, raise.**

ra•zor |rā′zər| *n.* A sharp cutting instrument, sometimes electrically driven, used primarily for shaving the face. —**modifier:** *a razor blade.*

razz |răz| *v. Slang.* To ridicule; heckle.

Rb The symbol for the element rubidium.

Rd. road.

re[1] |rā| *n.* A syllable used in music to represent the second tone of a major scale or sometimes the tone D. ¶*These sound alike* **re, ray.**

re[2] |rā| *or* |rē| *prep.* Concerning; in reference to. ¶*These sound alike* **re, ray.**

Re The symbol for the element rhenium.

re–. A prefix meaning: **1.** Again; anew: **reassemble. 2.** Back; backward: **recall.** When *re-* is followed by *e,* it may appear with a hyphen: **re-entry; reentry.**

reach |rēch| *v.* **1.** To go or extend as far as; get to: *the first to reach the moon; before news of his death had reached us.* **2.** To stretch out; extend: *Nerves reach out to every part of the body.* **3.** To extend to a desired distance: *an electrical cord that doesn't quite reach.* **4.** To extend an arm or other bodily part: *reached for a pad of paper; reached up to pick an apple.* **5.** To pursue a goal; strive eagerly: *a writer who reaches too far for originality.* **6.** To touch or grasp by stretching out an arm or other bodily part: *couldn't reach the bread from where I was sitting.* **7.** To attain; achieve: *jets that reach supersonic speeds; reaching old age.* **8.** To form by a process of reasoning or deliberation: *reaching a conclusion.* **9.** To succeed in communicating with; get in touch with: *reached the fire department in time to save the building.* —*n.* **1.** An act of stretching out an arm or other bodily part: *The frog seized the butterfly with a sudden reach of its tongue.* **2.** The distance to which one can extend an arm: *a boxer with a short reach.* **3.** The distance or range within which one can touch or seize things: *held the biscuit just out of the dog's reach.*

re•act |rē ăkt′| *v.* **1.** To act in response to a stimulus or prompting: *The eye reacts to light.* **2.** To act in opposition to some former condition or act: *composers who reacted against romanticism.* **3.** To take part in or undergo chemical change.

re•ac•tion |rē ăk′shən| *n.* **1.** An effect or action that arises from another action, generally opposing it in some way: *the body's reaction to a drug.* **2.** An action, feeling, or attitude aroused by something: *Her first reaction was to cry.* **3.** The response of a living thing to a stimulus: *Age had slowed his reactions.* **4. a.** The process or condition of taking part in a chemical change. **b.** A chemical change. **5. a.** Opposition to something new or proposed. **b.** Political opposition to progress, reform, or change.

re•ac•tion•ar•y |rē ăk′shə nĕr′ē| *adj.* Opposing progress, reform, or change: *a reactionary politician.* —*n., pl.* **re•ac•tion•ar•ies.** A person who is reactionary.

re•ac•tor |rē ăk′tər| *n.* **1.** Someone or something that reacts. **2.** A capacitor or inductor connected into an electric circuit to introduce reactance. **3.** A **nuclear reactor.**

read |rēd| *v.* **read** |rĕd|, **read•ing. 1.** To look through and take in the meaning of (written or printed words or symbols): *reading books; reading quickly through her mail.* **2.** To speak aloud the words of (something written or printed): *She read the poem while we listened. He read to his children every night.* **3.** To know (a language) well enough to understand written and printed matter. **4.** To become informed or learn through written or printed matter: *reading about the Seneca Indians.* **5.** To take in the meaning of (something symbolic, graphic, hidden, or in code); interpret: *reading a blueprint.* **6.** To detect by observing closely: *read disappointment in her eyes.* **7.** To have or bear a certain wording: *The sign read "Keep Out."* **8.** To have a certain character evident to the reader; sound in the mind's ear: *Chaucer's English reads very differently from Shakespeare's.* **9.** To indicate or register: *The speedometer read 50 miles per hour.* ¶*These sound alike* **read, reed.** [SEE NOTE]

Idioms. **read between the lines.** To find an implicit or hidden meaning that is not actually expressed. **read up on.** To gain information about by reading.

read•a•ble |rē′də bəl| *adj.* **1.** Capable of being read easily. **2.** Holding the reader's interest. —**read′a•bil′i•ty, read′a•ble•ness** *n.*

read•er |rē′dər| *n.* **1.** A person who reads. **2.** A textbook with passages for practice in reading.

read•i•ly |rĕd′l ē| *adv.* **1.** Without hesitation; willingly and promptly: *advice that was readily accepted.* **2.** Without difficulty; easily: *paints that are readily available at a hardware store.*

read•i•ness |rĕd′ē nĭs| *n.* **1.** The condition of being ready; preparedness for a future event: *a pitcher held in readiness for the big game.* **2.** Favorable disposition; willingness: *readiness to help.* **3.** Ease and promptness; facility.

read•ing |rē′dĭng| *n.* **1.** The activity of gaining pleasure and knowledge from books and other written material. **2. a.** Books and other material to be read. **b.** A passage or selection to be read. **3.** A public recitation of a document, a passage from a book, or other written material. **4.** An interpretation of a word or passage in a text. **5.** The data or information shown by an instrument, gauge, etc. [SEE NOTE]

re•ad•just |rē′ə jŭst′| *v.* **1.** To adjust again; rearrange or reset: *readjust a machine.* **2.** To adapt oneself again: *had trouble readjusting to school after the long vacation.* —**re′ad•just′ment** *n.*

read•y |rĕd′ē| *adj.* **read•i•er, read•i•est. 1.** Prepared for action or use: *getting ready for school; ground ready for planting.* **2.** Inclined; willing: *ready to accept any reasonable offer.* **3.** About to do something; liable: *seemed ready to cry.* **4.** Quick in understanding or responding; alert and prompt: *a ready wit.* **5.** Conveniently available; close at hand: *ready cash; a ready means of transportation.* —*v.* **read•ied, read•y•ing, read•ies.** To make ready; prepare.

read•y-made |rĕd′ē mād′| *adj.* **1.** Already made, prepared, or available for use: *a ready-made dinner.* **2.** Thought up by someone else; preconceived: *ready-made opinions.*

Rea•gan |rā′gən|, **Ronald Wilson.** Born 1911. Fortieth President of the United States (1981–1989).

re•a•gent |rē ā′jənt| *n.* Any substance used in a chemical reaction to detect, measure, or produce another substance.

re•al |rē′əl| *or* |rēl| *adj.* **1.** Not imaginary, fictional, or pretended; actual: *a story about real people; concealed his real purpose and identity.* **2.** Not artificial; authentic or genuine: *a real cat sitting next to a picture of one.* **3.** Essential; basic: *The real subject is people.* **4.** Being no less than what is stated; worthy of the name: *a real friend.* **5.** Serious; not to be taken lightly: *in real trouble.* **6.** Of or being land, buildings, or other property that cannot be moved by the owner: *a tax on his real property.* **7.** Of or indicating an image formed by light rays that converge in space. See **virtual image. 8.** Of a real number. —*adv. Informal.* Very: *got real angry.*

real estate. Land and anything on it, as buildings and other property. —***modifier:*** **(real-estate):** *a real-estate agency.*

re•al•ism |rē′ə lĭz′əm| *n.* **1.** Conformity to reality; authenticity: *imitated the birdcalls with great realism.* **2.** Concern with facts and things as they actually are rather than with ideals and dreams. **3.** The depiction of reality, as in painting, sculpture, literature, etc. —**re′al•ist** *n.*

re•al•is•tic |rē′ə lĭs′tĭk| *adj.* **1.** Closely resembling what is imitated or depicted; accurately represented: *realistic characters in a play.* **2.** Showing an awareness of facts and things as they actually are; practical: *a realistic admission of defeat.* **3.** Of or marked by artistic or literary realism. —**re′al•is′ti•cal•ly** *adv.*

re•al•i•ty |rē ăl′ĭ tē| *n., pl.* **re•al•i•ties. 1.** The condition or quality of being real; actual existence: *an author who creates belief in the reality of his characters.* **2.** The sum total of things that actually exist; the real world: *losing one's grip on reality.* **3.** Someone or something that is real: *seeing their dreams become realities.*

re•al•i•za•tion |rē′ə lĭ zā′shən| *n.* **1.** The act or fact of realizing: *shocked by the realization that they had run out of money.* **2.** Attainment of something planned, hoped for, or expected: *turned his efforts toward the realization of his hopes.* **3.** Something realized: *The house was perfect, the realization of our dreams.*

re•al•ize |rē′ə līz′| *v.* **re•al•ized, re•al•iz•ing. 1.** To be fully aware of; accept as a fact or reality; grasp: *realized that the world was larger than she had thought.* **2.** To make real; achieve: *realized his ambition to succeed.* **3.** To obtain or bring in as profit: *realized a large sum on the investment.*

re•al•ly |rē′ə lē| *or* |rē′lē| *adv.* **1.** In actual truth or fact: *The horseshoe crab isn't really a crab at all.* **2.** Truly: *a really beautiful morning.* **3.** *Informal.* Used as an intensive: *Suddenly I saw this really beautiful girl coming out the door.* **4.** Indeed: *Really, you shouldn't have done it.*

realm |rĕlm| *n.* **1.** A kingdom. **2.** An area in which something prevails or has influence or prominence: *studying the realm of insects with a microscope.* **3.** Any field of activity, interest, or achievement: *the realm of piano music.*

real number. Any member of the set of rational numbers or irrational numbers.

re•al•tor |rē′əl tər| *n.* A person who buys and sells real estate for a living.

re•al•ty |rē′əl tē| *n., pl.* **re•al•ties.** Land and the property on it; real estate.

read/reading

"Reading is to the mind what exercise is to the body."—Sir Richard Steele (1672–1729). "A young man should read five hours in a day, and so may acquire a great deal of knowledge."—Samuel Johnson.

ream[1-2]

Ream[1] *is from Old French* remme, *which is from Arabic* rizmah, *"bundle."* **Ream**[2] *is probably from Old English* rȳman, *"to widen, to make room," which is related to* **room.**

reaper

Horse-drawn reaper in Kansas, 1937

rear[1-2]

Rear[1] *is shortened from* **arrear,** *which is from Old French* arrere, *from Latin* ad retro, *"backward."* **Rear**[2] *was Old English* rǣran, *"to raise, lift up."*

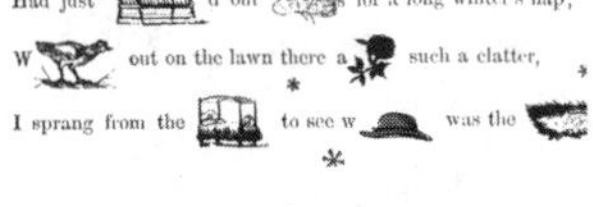

rebus

ă pat/ā pay/â care/ä father/ĕ pet/ ē be/ĭ pit/ī pie/î fierce/ŏ pot/ ō go/ô paw, for/oi oil/ŏŏ book/ ōō boot/ou out/ŭ cut/û fur/ *th* the/th thin/hw which/zh vision/ ə ago, item, pencil, atom, circus

ream[1] |rēm| *n.* **1.** A quantity of paper of the same size and stock. **2. reams.** A large amount of written matter: *reams of documents to fill out.* [SEE NOTE]

ream[2] |rēm| *v.* To shape, enlarge, or clean out (a hole, tube, gun barrel, etc.) with a pointed tool: *reamed the hole in the wall after drilling it.* [SEE NOTE]

ream•er |**rē′**mər| *n.* **1.** A tool for shaping, enlarging, or cleaning out holes. **2.** A kitchen utensil consisting of a ridged projection on a bowl, used for extracting juice from citrus fruits.

reap |rēp| *v.* **1.** To cut down and gather (grain or a similar crop): *reap wheat. Farmers sow seed in the spring and reap in the fall.* **2.** To gather a crop from: *reap a field.* **3.** To gain as a benefit or as a result of effort: *Edison reaped fame and profit from his many inventions.*

reap•er |**rē′**pər| *n.* **1.** Someone who cuts down and gathers grain or a similar crop. **2.** A machine for harvesting. [SEE PICTURE]

re•ap•pear |rē′ə **pîr′**| *v.* **1.** To come into view again: *Halley's comet will reappear in 1986.* **2.** To be presented or published again: *The story reappeared in an anthology.* —**re′ap•pear′ance** *n.*

rear[1] |rîr| *n.* **1.** The part of something that is at or closest to the back and farthest from the front: *the rear of the head.* **2.** *Informal.* The buttocks. **3.** The area or direction behind something or someone: *a garden at the rear of the house.* **4.** The part of an army or arrangement of troops or ships that is farthest from the fighting. —*adj.* Of, at, or located in the rear: *a rear entrance.* [SEE NOTE]

Idiom. **bring up the rear.** To be last in line.

rear[2] |rîr| *v.* **1.** To care for during the early years of growth and learning; bring up. **2.** To raise; breed: *rearing sheep for meat and wool.* **3.** To build; erect: *rear a skyscraper.* **4.** To rise on the hind legs: *The frightened horse reared and neighed.* [SEE NOTE]

rear admiral. See **admiral.**

re•ar•range |rē′ə **rānj′**| *v.* **re•ar•ranged, re•ar•rang•ing.** To arrange in a different way or order. —**re′ar•range′ment** *n.*

rea•son |**rē′**zən| *n.* **1.** A motive for acting, thinking, or feeling in a certain way; a rational or practical purpose. **2.** A fact or cause that explains why something exists or occurs: *reasons for being late.* **3.** A statement or fact that justifies or establishes the truth of a conclusion, statement, etc.: *I have reason to believe that he is wrong.* **4.** The ability to think, understand, and make decisions clearly and sensibly; mental balance; sanity: *an appeal to reason; lost his reason.* **5.** Sound judgment; good sense: *a man of reason.* —*v.* **1.** To use the ability to think clearly and sensibly: *reason about the world.* **2.** To conclude: *He reasoned that she was guilty as charged.* **3.** To argue logically and persuasively: *tried to reason with the angry crowd.*

Idioms. **by reason of.** Because of. **stand to reason.** To be logical or predictable: *It stands to reason that a building so tall will have an elevator.* **with reason.** With good reasons; justifiably: *angry, and with reason.*

rea•son•a•ble |**rē′**zə nə bəl| *adj.* **1.** Using or capable of using reason to settle problems or disputes; rational: *a reasonable man.* **2.** In accordance with reason; fair or logical: *a reasonable solution.* **3.** Not excessive or extreme; moderate: *a reasonable price.* —**rea′son•a•ble•ness** *n.* —**rea′son•a•bly** *adv.*

rea•son•ing |**rē′**zə nĭng| *n.* **1.** The process of thinking in an orderly way to form conclusions, judgments, etc.; the use of reason. **2.** A particular process or course of thought leading to a conclusion. —***modifier:*** *reasoning ability.*

re•as•sem•ble |rē′ə **sĕm′**bəl| *v.* **re•as•sem•bled, re•as•sem•bling.** **1.** To put together again. **2.** To bring or come together again.

re•as•sure |rē′ə **shŏŏr′**| *v.* **re•as•sured, re•as•sur•ing.** To assure again; restore confidence to. —**re′as•sur′ance** *n.*

re•bate |**rē′**bāt′| *n.* A return of part of an amount of money given in payment or a reduction in an amount to be paid; a refund or discount. —*v.* **re•bat•ed, re•bat•ing.** To return (part of an amount paid) or make a reduction in (an amount due).

re•bel |rĭ **bĕl′**| *v.* **re•belled, re•bel•ling.** **1.** To refuse loyalty to an established government or ruling authority or to oppose it by force. **2.** To resist or oppose openly any authority based on law, custom, or convention: *The boys rebelled against the tyranny of wearing ties in summer.* —*n.* **reb•el** |**rĕb′**əl|. A person who rebels or is in rebellion. —***modifier:*** *a rebel attack; the rebel leader.*

re•bel•lion |rĭ **bĕl′**yən| *n.* **1.** An uprising intended to change or overthrow an existing government or ruling authority by means of force; a revolt. **2.** An act or show of defiance or strong opposition toward any authority.

re•bel•lious |rĭ **bĕl′**yəs| *adj.* **1.** In open revolt against a government or ruling authority. **2.** Marked by or showing open resistance to established authority: *in these rebellious times.* **3.** Not manageable; unruly: *a rebellious donkey.* —**re•bel′lious•ly** *adv.* —**re•bel′lious•ness** *n.*

re•birth |rē **bûrth′**| *or* |**rē′**bûrth′| *n.* A return to life or activity after a period of quiet or neglect; revival: *the rebirth of classical learning.*

re•born |rē **bôrn′**| *adj.* Born again.

re•bound |rĭ **bound′**| *v.* **1.** To spring back or bounce away, often as if reflected, after hitting or colliding with an object. **2.** To cause to rebound. —*n.* |**rē′**bound′|. The act or process of rebounding.

re•buff |rĭ **bŭf′**| *n.* An unfriendly reply or response to an offer or proposal of a course of action; a blunt refusal, snub, or repulse. —*v.* To refuse bluntly; repel.

re•build |rē **bĭld′**| *v.* **re•built** |rē **bĭlt′**|, **re•build•ing.** To build again; reconstruct: *rebuild a church.*

re•buke |rĭ **byŏŏk′**| *v.* **re•buked, re•buk•ing.** To criticize sharply; upbraid. —*n.* Words or actions expressing strong disapproval; severe criticism.

re•bus |**rē′**bəs| *n., pl.* **re•bus•es.** A puzzle composed of words or syllables that appear in the form of pictures. [SEE PICTURE]

re•but |rĭ **bŭt′**| *v.* **re•but•ted, re•but•ting.** To prove (something) false by presenting opposing evidence or arguments.

re•but•tal |rĭ **bŭt′**l| *n.* **1.** The act of rebutting. **2.** The statement made in such an act.

re•cal•ci•trant |rĭ **kăl′**sĭ trənt| *adj.* Stubbornly

opposed to being ruled or guided: *a recalcitrant child.* —**re·cal'ci·trance** *n.*

re·call |rĭ **kôl'**| *v.* **1.** To call back; ask or order to return: *The government in London recalled the ambassador.* **2.** To bring back to memory; remember or recollect: *recalling his boyhood love of horses.* **3.** To cancel, take back, or revoke: *recalled her driver's license.* —*n.* |rĭ **kôl'**| *or* |**rē'**-kôl'|. **1.** The act of recalling or summoning back; an official order to return or be returned. **2.** The ability to remember information or experiences; recollection; remembrance. **3.** The act of removing a public official from office by popular vote.

re·cant |rĭ **kănt'**| *v.* **1.** To deny formally or withdraw support of; give up as untrue: *recanted his position on civil rights.* **2.** To make a formal denial or disavowal of an earlier statement or belief. —**re'can·ta'tion** *n.*

re·ca·pit·u·late |rē'kə **pĭch'**ə lāt'| *v.* **re·ca·pit·u·lat·ed, re·ca·pit·u·lat·ing.** To repeat in shorter form by stating again main points or themes; summarize or sum up. —**re'ca·pit'u·la'tion** *n.*

re·cap·ture |rē **kăp'**chər| *v.* **re·cap·tured, re·cap·tur·ing.** **1.** To capture again: *recapture a city.* **2.** To recollect or recall vividly. —*n.* The act of taking or discovering again.

re·cast |rē **kăst'**| *or* |-**kăst'**| *v.* **re·cast, re·cast·ing.** **1.** To mold again: *recast the statue.* **2.** To change so as to give a new wording, form, plan, or arrangement: *recast a question.*

re·cede |rĭ **sēd'**| *v.* **re·ced·ed, re·ced·ing.** **1.** To move back or away from a limit, point, or mark: *after the flood had receded.* **2.** To slope backward: *observed that the human forehead recedes.*

re·ceipt |rĭ **sēt'**| *n.* **1.** The fact of receiving something: *at receipt of word from you.* **2. receipts.** The quantity or amount received: *box-office receipts.* **3.** A written acknowledgment that a sum of money has been paid or received or that a certain article or delivery of merchandise has been received. —*v.* To mark (a bill) as having been paid.

re·ceiv·a·ble |rĭ **sē'**və bəl| *adj.* Awaiting or requiring payment: *accounts receivable.*

re·ceive |rĭ **sēv'**| *v.* **re·ceived, re·ceiv·ing.** **1.** To get or acquire (something given, offered, or transmitted): *receive payment.* **2.** To acquire knowledge of: *received word of his friend's illness.* **3.** To take the force or impact of: *received the full fury of the gale.* **4.** To bear; support: *girders sunk deep to receive the weight of the building.* **5.** To greet or welcome: *received us as if we were royalty.* **6.** To accept and demodulate electromagnetic or electrical signals, as in radio or telegraphy. [SEE NOTE]

re·ceiv·er |rĭ **sē'**vər| *n.* **1.** Someone or something that receives; a recipient. **2.** The unit of a communications system, such as radio, telephone, television, etc., that receives an incoming signal and converts it into the form, such as a sound or picture, in which it is to be used. **3.** A person appointed by a court to hold the funds or property of another while a court case is being decided.

re·ceiv·er·ship |rĭ **sē'**vər shĭp'| *n.* In law: **1.** The office or function of a receiver. **2.** The condition of being held by a receiver.

re·cent |**rē'**sənt| *adj.* **1.** Of a time immediately before the present. **2. Recent.** Of, belonging to, or indicating the Holocene epoch. —**re'cent·ly** *adv.* —**re'cent·ness** *n.*

re·cep·ta·cle |rĭ **sĕp'**tə kəl| *n.* Something that holds or contains; a container.

re·cep·tion |rĭ **sĕp'**shən| *n.* **1.** The act or process of receiving something. **2.** A social gathering or entertainment honoring or introducing someone: *a wedding reception.* **3. a.** The act or process of receiving electrical or electromagnetic signals. **b.** The condition or quality of the signals received. [SEE NOTE]

re·cep·tion·ist |rĭ **sĕp'**shə nĭst| *n.* A person employed in an office to receive callers and answer the telephone.

re·cep·tive |rĭ **sĕp'**tĭv| *adj.* Ready or willing to receive something favorably: *receptive to change.*

re·cess |rĭ **sĕs'**| *or* |**rē'**sĕs'| *n.* **1. a.** A temporary halt in or stoppage of customary activity: *a court recess ordered by the judge.* **b.** The period of time of such a halt: *played games during recess at school.* **2.** Often **recesses.** A remote, secret, or hidden place: *the inmost recesses of her desk.* **3.** A small hollow place; an indentation or notch. —*v.* **1.** To put in a hollow, indentation, or notch. **2.** To make a hollow place or indentation in: *recessed the wall to provide room for shelves.* **3.** To stop (customary activity) temporarily; suspend or adjourn.

re·ces·sion |rĭ **sĕsh'**ən| *n.* **1.** The act of withdrawing or going back. **2.** A moderate and temporary decline in economic activity.

re·ces·sion·al |rĭ **sĕsh'**ə nəl| *n.* A hymn or other music played at the close of a church service.

re·ces·sive |rĭ **sĕs'**ĭv| *adj.* **1.** Tending to recede or go backward. **2.** Of or indicating a gene whose action is not apparent in the physical characteristics of an organism when it is paired with an unlike gene for the same characteristic. —*n.* A recessive gene.

rec·i·pe |**rĕs'**ə pē| *n.* **1.** A set of directions for making or preparing something, especially food. **2.** A formula for accomplishing a certain thing: *a recipe for a happy marriage.* [SEE NOTE]

re·cip·i·ent |rĭ **sĭp'**ē ənt| *n.* Someone or something that receives. —*adj.* Receiving or able to receive.

re·cip·ro·cal |rĭ **sĭp'**rə kəl| *adj.* **1.** Given or shown in return: *a system of reciprocal trade concessions.* **2.** Felt or shown by both of two; existing on both sides; mutual: *reciprocal respect as a basis for true partnership.* **3.** Of or indicating either or both of a pair of numbers whose product is 1. —*n.* Either of a pair of numbers whose product is 1; for example, the number *a* is the reciprocal of 1/*a*. —**re·cip'ro·cal·ly** *adv.*

re·cip·ro·cate |rĭ **sĭp'**rə kāt'| *v.* **re·cip·ro·cat·ed, re·cip·ro·cat·ing.** **1.** To give or take mutually: *reciprocating favors.* **2.** To make a return for something given or done. **3.** To show or feel in return: *reciprocated her love.* **4.** To move back and forth alternately, as a machine part. —**re·cip'ro·ca'tion** *n.*

rec·i·proc·i·ty |rĕs'ə **prŏs'**ĭ tē| *n.* **1.** A reciprocal condition or relationship. **2.** A mutual exchange or interchange, especially the exchange of rights or privileges of trade between nations.

re·cit·al |rĭ **sīt'**l| *n.* **1.** A very detailed account

receive/reception, etc.

The Latin verb capere, *"to take," had several important compounds in which* capere *changed to* -cipere. *Three of these were* dēcipere, *"to take (someone) falsely, to cheat,"* percipere, *"to take hold of (something), to grasp with the mind, to understand," and* recipere, *"to take back, to accept." When these verbs passed into Old French, they all underwent identical changes, becoming, respectively,* deceivre, perceivre, *and* receivre; *all three of the French forms were borrowed into English, becoming* **deceive, perceive,** *and* **receive.** *Latin* capere *formed the abstract noun* captiō, *"act of taking"; each of the compound verbs formed similar abstract nouns in* -ceptiō: dēceptiō, *"act of taking falsely or cheating,"* perceptiō, *"act of taking hold or understanding," and* receptiō, *"act of taking back or accepting." These appear in English as* **deception, perception,** *and* **reception,** *respectively.*

recipe

Recipe *originally meant "a medical prescription" and only later came to mean "a formula used in cooking." The word is Latin for "Take!" the imperative form of* recipere, *"to take, to receive." In Medieval Latin,* Recipe *was the usual first word of medical prescriptions beginning "Take an ounce of. . . ." In writing it was often abbreviated to* R., *with a small slash through the tail; this is the origin of the pharmacists' symbol* ℞.

or report of something: *father's recital of his experiences.* **2.** A performance of music or dance, especially one by a solo performer.

rec•i•ta•tion |rĕs′ĭ **tā′**shən| *n.* **1.** The act of reciting something memorized, as a poem or an oration, in a public performance. **2.** A spoken presentation or report of prepared lessons by a student in school.

rec•i•ta•tive |rĕs′ĭ tə **tēv′**| *n.* **1.** A musical style, used in opera and oratorio, in which the text is declaimed in the rhythm of natural speech with slight melodic variation. **2.** A musical passage in this style.

re•cite |rĭ **sīt′**| *v.* **re•cit•ed, re•cit•ing.** **1.** To repeat from memory, especially before an audience. **2.** To repeat in detail after memorizing or preparing, especially in school. **3.** To tell in detail: *recited his difficulties.*

reck•less |**rĕk′**lĭs| *adj.* Without care or caution; careless: *reckless driving.* —**reck′less•ly** *adv.* [SEE NOTE]

reck•on |**rĕk′**ən| *v.* **1.** To count or calculate; figure: *reckon time; a child who learned to reckon before he could talk.* **2.** To consider as being; regard as: *reckoned him a savage.* **3.** *Informal.* To think or assume: *Do you reckon we'll be through in time?* —***phrasal verb.*** **reckon with.** To come to terms or settle accounts with.

reck•on•ing |**rĕk′**ə nĭng| *n.* **1.** The act or process of counting or computing. **2.** The determination of the position of a ship, aircraft, etc., by calculation. **3.** A statement of an amount due.

re•claim |rĭ **klām′**| *v.* **1.** To make (land, soil, etc.) usable for growing crops or living on, as by draining, irrigating, or fertilizing. **2.** To extract (useful substances) from garbage or other waste products. **3.** To turn (a person) from error or evil; convert to something better; reform: *reclaimed him from his wicked life.* —**re•claim′a•ble** *adj.* —**rec′la•ma′tion** |rĕk′lə **mā′**shən| *n.*

re•cline |rĭ **klīn′**| *v.* **re•clined, re•clin•ing.** To lie back or down: *The king reclined on his couch.*

rec•luse |**rĕk′**lo͞os′| *or* |rĭ **klo͞os′**| *n.* A person who withdraws from the world to live alone. —*adj.* Withdrawn from the world; solitary.

rec•og•ni•tion |rĕk′əg **nĭsh′**ən| *n.* **1.** The act of recognizing or the condition of being recognized. **2.** The act of acknowledging or accepting the status, position, or claim to rank of someone or something. **3.** Attention or favorable notice; praise: *world recognition for his work in physics.*

rec•og•niz•a•ble |**rĕk′**əg nī′zə bəl| *adj.* Capable of being recognized. —**rec′og•niz′a•bly** *adv.*

rec•og•nize |**rĕk′**əg nīz′| *v.* **rec•og•nized, rec•og•niz•ing.** **1.** To know or identify from past experience or knowledge: *recognized him by his face and voice.* **2.** To know, understand, or realize: *recognize the value of virtue.* **3.** To acknowledge or accept: *recognized his right to vote.* **4.** To acknowledge or accept the status or position of: *recognize and deal with unions.* **5.** To admit the acquaintance of; greet: *scarcely recognized me.* **6.** To acknowledge as a speaker in a formally conducted meeting.

re•coil |rĭ **koil′**| *v.* **1.** To move or jerk backward, as a gun upon firing. **2.** To shrink back in fear or dislike. **3.** To fall back; return: *the day of judgment, when our every evil deed recoils on us.* —*n.* |**rē′**koil′| *or* |rĭ **koil′**|. The act of recoiling.

re-col•lect |rē′kə **lĕkt′**| *v.* **1.** To collect again. **2.** To calm or control (oneself).

rec•ol•lect |rĕk′ə **lĕkt′**| *v.* To remember.

rec•ol•lec•tion |rĕk′ə **lĕk′**shən| *n.* **1.** The act or power of recollecting. **2.** Something recollected.

rec•om•mend |rĕk′ə **mĕnd′**| *v.* **1.** To praise or commend to another or others as being worthy or desirable: *recommend a man for the job.* **2.** To advise or counsel (a course of action). **3.** To make attractive or acceptable: *lack of discipline that did not recommend him.*

rec•om•men•da•tion |rĕk′ə mĕn **dā′**shən| *n.* **1.** The act of recommending. **2.** Something that recommends, as a letter or a favorable statement about the qualifications or character of someone.

rec•om•pense |**rĕk′**əm pĕns′| *v.* **rec•om•pensed, rec•om•pens•ing.** **1.** To pay or reward: *recompensed him for his services.* **2.** To make up for: *recompense losses.* —*n.* **1.** Amends made for something, such as damage or loss. **2.** Payment in return for something given or done.

rec•on•cile |**rĕk′**ən sīl′| *v.* **rec•on•ciled, rec•on•cil•ing.** **1.** To restore friendship between; make friendly again: *reconcile old enemies.* **2.** To bring (oneself) to accept: *reconciling herself to the loss of a ring.* **3.** To bring into harmony or agreement: *reconcile different points of view.* —**rec′on•cil′i•a′tion** *n.*

re•con•nais•sance |rĭ **kŏn′**ə səns| *or* |-zəns| *n.* An inspection or exploration of an area, especially one made to gather information about the presence, arrangement, or activity of military forces. —***modifier:*** *reconnaissance flights.*

re•con•noi•ter |rē′kə **noi′**tər| *or* |rĕk′ə-| *v.* **1.** To make a survey or inspection of, as in preparation for something. **2.** To make a reconnaissance.

re•con•sid•er |rē′kən **sĭd′**ər| *v.* To consider again, especially with the possibility of making a change. —**re′con•sid′er•a′tion** *n.*

re•con•struct |rē′kən **strŭkt′**| *v.* **1.** To construct or build again; restore. **2.** To determine or trace from information or clues: *reconstruct the events that preceded the accident.*

re•con•struc•tion |rē′kən **strŭk′**shən| *n.* **1.** The act or result of reconstructing. **2.** Often **Reconstruction.** The period (1865–77) during which the states of the Southern Confederacy were controlled by the Federal government and forced to change their laws and customs before being given full return to the Union.

rec•ord |**rĕk′**ərd| *n.* **1.** Information, facts, etc., usually set down in writing as a means of preserving knowledge: *a record of what happened at club meetings; police records.* **2.** The known history of performance or achievement: *your high-school record.* **3. a.** The best performance known, as in a sport: *the world record in the mile run.* **b.** The highest or lowest statistical mark known, as in weather readings: *the record for least rainfall in a year.* **4.** A disk designed to be played on a phonograph. —***modifier:*** *a record altitude; record dealers.* —*v.* **re•cord** |rĭ **kôrd′**|. **1.** To set down for preservation in writing or other permanent form: *Record the time you spent on each job.* **2.** To register or indicate, especially in permanent form: *A thermometer records temperature.* **3.** To store (sound) in some permanent form, such as a trace cut in a surface of a disk or

reckless

The reck *of* **reckless**, *still sometimes in use, means "to take care"; it was Old English* reccan, *"to pay attention."*

ă pat/ā pay/â care/ä father/ĕ pet/ē be/ĭ pit/ī pie/î fierce/ŏ pot/ō go/ô paw, for/oi oil/o͝o book/o͞o boot/ou out/ŭ cut/û fur/*th* the/th thin/hw which/zh vision/ə ago, item, pencil, atom, circus

a series of variations in the magnetization of a tape.

Idioms. **off the record.** Not for publication, as in a news report. **on record.** Known to have taken or stated a certain position: *two Congressmen on record as favoring the appointment.*

re•cord•er |rĭ **kôr′**dər| *n.* **1.** Someone or something that records. **2.** A flute with a whistlelike mouthpiece and eight holes. [SEE PICTURE]

re•cord•ing |rĭ **kôr′**dĭng| *n.* **1.** Something on which sound is recorded, as a magnetic tape or a phonograph record. **2.** The sound recorded in this way. *—modifier: a recording session.*

re•count |rĭ **kount′**| *v.* To tell in detail; narrate the particulars of: *The "Iliad" recounts the siege of Troy.*

re•coup |rĭ **ko͞op′**| *v.* **1.** To receive the equivalent of (something lost); make up for: *recouped his fortune; losses that can never be recouped.* **2.** To pay back; compensate: *recouped his tenants for damages.*

re•course |**rē′**kôrs′| *or* |-kōrs′| *or* |rĭ **kôrs′**| *or* |-**kōrs′**| *n.* **1.** A turning or applying to a person or thing for aid, support, or protection: *have recourse to the courts.* **2.** Someone or something to turn to for help or as a solution.

re•cov•er |rĭ **kŭv′**ər| *v.* **1.** To get back; regain: *a Crusade to recover the Holy Land.* **2. a.** To return to a normal condition, as of physical or mental health: *recover after a long illness.* **b.** To regain control over (oneself): *recovered himself sufficiently to speak in public.* **3.** To make up for; compensate for. **—re•cov′er•a•ble** *adj.*

re•cov•er•y |rĭ **kŭv′**ə rē| *n., pl.* **re•cov•er•ies. 1.** A return to a normal condition, as of health. **2.** The act of getting back or regaining.

rec•re•ant |**rĕk′**rē ənt| *adj.* **1.** Unfaithful or disloyal. **2.** Cowardly. *—n.* **1.** An unfaithful or disloyal person. **2.** A coward.

re-cre•ate |rē′krē **āt′**| *v.* **re-cre•at•ed, re-cre•at•ing.** To create again or anew.

rec•re•a•tion |rĕk′rē **ā′**shən| *n.* Refreshment of one's mind or body after work through some activity, such as sports and games, that amuses or stimulates. *—modifier: a recreation center.*

re•crim•i•nate |rĭ **krĭm′**ə nāt′| *v.* **re•crim•i•nat•ed, re•crim•i•nat•ing.** To accuse (a person) in return. **—re•crim′i•na′tion** *n.*

re•cru•desce |rē′kro͞o **dĕs′**| *v.* **re•cru•desced, re•cru•desc•ing.** To break out anew after an inactive period, as a disease. **—re′cru•des′cence** *n.* **—re′cru•des′cent** *adj.*

re•cruit |rĭ **kro͞ot′**| *v.* **1. a.** To enroll or enlist (persons) in military service. **b.** To raise (an armed force) by enlistment: *recruit a new army.* **2.** To secure the support or services of for a particular activity: *a university program for recruiting athletes.* *—n.* **1.** A newly enlisted member of the armed forces. **2.** A new member of any organization or body of persons. **—re•cruit′er** *n.* **—re•cruit′ment** *n.*

rec•tal |**rĕk′**təl| *adj.* Of or near the rectum.

rec•tan•gle |**rĕk′**tăng′gəl| *n.* A parallelogram that contains an angle of 90 degrees.

rec•tan•gu•lar |rĕk **tăng′**gyə lər| *adj.* **1.** Having the shape of a rectangle. **2.** Of or indicating a system of coordinates using axes that meet at right angles.

rec•ti•fy |**rĕk′**tə fī′| *v.* **rec•ti•fied, rec•ti•fy•ing, rec•ti•fies. 1.** To set right; correct. **2.** To refine or purify, especially by distillation.

rec•ti•tude |**rĕk′**tĭ to͞od′| *or* |-tyo͞od′| *n.* Moral goodness.

rec•tor |**rĕk′**tər| *n.* **1.** In the Protestant Episcopal and Anglican churches, a clergyman in charge of a parish. **2.** In the Roman Catholic Church, a priest in a church, seminary, or university who is both its spiritual head and manager of its affairs. **3.** The principal of certain schools, colleges, or universities.

rec•to•ry |**rĕk′**tə rē| *n., pl.* **rec•to•ries.** The house in which a rector lives.

rec•tum |**rĕk′**təm| *n.* The lower end of the alimentary canal, extending from the colon to the anus.

re•cum•bent |rĭ **kŭm′**bənt| *adj.* Lying down; reclining.

re•cu•per•ate |rĭ **ko͞o′**pə rāt′| *v.* **re•cu•per•at•ed, re•cu•per•at•ing. 1.** To return to normal health or strength; recover. **2.** To recover from a loss. **—re•cu′per•a′tion** *n.* **—re•cu′per•a′tive** *adj.*

re•cur |rĭ **kûr′**| *v.* **re•curred, re•cur•ring.** To happen, come up, or show up again or repeatedly; return: *an area where earthquakes recur.*

re•cur•rent |rĭ **kûr′**ənt| *or* |-**kŭr′**-| *adj.* Occurring or appearing again or repeatedly; returning regularly. **—re•cur′rence** *n.*

re•cy•cle |rē **sī′**kəl| *v.* **re•cy•cled, re•cy•cling. 1.** To extract useful materials from (garbage, waste, etc.) and reuse them. **2.** To extract and reuse (useful substances found in garbage, waste, etc.)

red |rĕd| *n.* **1.** The color of blood or of a ripe strawberry. **2.** Often **Red.** A revolutionary, especially a Communist. *—adj.* **red•der, red•dest. 1.** Of the color red. **2.** Often **Red.** Of, directed by, or favoring Communists: *Red China; red sympathizers.* **—red′ness** *n.* [SEE NOTE]

Idiom. **in the red.** Operating at a loss; in debt.

red blood cell. Any of the cells in the blood, disk-shaped and lacking nuclei, that contain hemoglobin and give the blood its red color.

red•breast |**rĕd′**brĕst′| *n.* A bird with a red or reddish breast, especially a robin.

red•coat |**rĕd′**kōt′| *n.* A British soldier during the American Revolution and the War of 1812.

Red Cross. An international organization established to care for the victims of war, floods, earthquakes, etc.

red deer. A European deer with a reddish-brown coat and branching antlers.

red•den |**rĕd′**n| *v.* To make or become red.

red•dish |**rĕd′**ĭsh| *adj.* Somewhat red.

re•deem |rĭ **dēm′**| *v.* **1.** To recover ownership of by paying a specified sum: *redeemed his ring from the pawnbroker.* **2.** To pay off, as a promissory note. **3.** To turn in (coupons, trading stamps, etc.) and receive something in exchange. **4. a.** To set free; rescue. **b.** To save from sin. **5.** To make up for: *a deed that redeemed his earlier mistake.* **—re•deem′a•ble** *adj.*

re•deem•er |rĭ **dē′**mər| *n.* **1.** A person who redeems. **2. the Redeemer.** Christ.

re•demp•tion |rĭ **dĕmp′**shən| *n.* **1.** The act of redeeming: *redemption of a promissory note.* **2.** A recovery of something pawned or mortgaged; a repurchase. **3.** The act of rescuing, as by payment of ransom or by complying with demands: *redemption of hostages held by the guerrillas.* **4.**

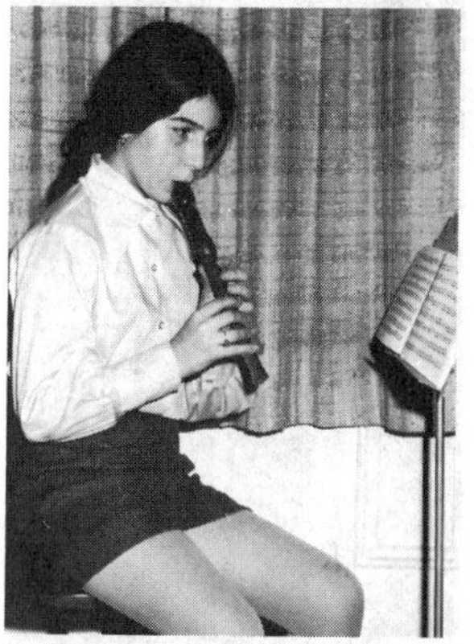

recorder

The verb **record** once meant "to practice a tune" and also (chiefly of birds) "to sing or whistle." It is from this sense that the instrument is called a **recorder.**

red

Red *seems to be the most frequently used color word (if white, black, and gray are not counted as colors). In the materials on which this Dictionary is based,* **red** *occurs 282 times per million words; then come* **green** *with 222 occurrences per million,* **blue** *with 194,* **brown** *with 148, and* **yellow** *with 111.*

redwood

reef[1-2]
Reef[1] *was originally* riff, *and was borrowed from Middle Dutch* rif, *"ridge, ledge of rock."* **Reef[2]** *is from Old Norse* rif, *"a rib," hence also "reef in a sail"; it is probably related to* **reef[1]**.

reel[1-2-3]
Reel[1] *was Old English* hrēol, *"spool."* **Reel[2]** *was Middle English* relen, *"to whirl around, stagger"; it is probably from* **reel[1]**. **Reel[3]**, *which first occurs in the sixteenth century, is probably also from* **reel[1]** *or from* **reel[2]**, *since the dance involves much fast turning.*

reel[1]
Bait-casting reel

ă **pat**/ā **pay**/â **care**/ä **father**/ĕ **pet**/ē **be**/ĭ **pit**/ī **pie**/î **fierce**/ŏ **pot**/ō **go**/ô **paw**, **for**/oi **oil**/o͝o **book**/o͞o **boot**/ou **out**/ŭ **cut**/û **fur**/*th* **the**/th **thin**/hw **which**/**zh** vision/ə **ago**, item, pencil, atom, circus

Salvation from sin through Christ's sacrifice.

red-hand•ed |**rĕd'hăn'**dĭd| *adv.* In the act of committing, or having just committed, a crime: *The thief was caught red-handed with the loot.*

red•head |**rĕd'**hĕd'| *n.* A person with red hair.

red•head•ed |**rĕd'**hĕd'ĭd| *adj.* Having red hair: *a redheaded boy.*

red herring. 1. A smoked herring having a reddish color. **2.** Something used to draw attention away from the subject under notice or discussion.

red-hot |**rĕd'hŏt'**| *adj.* **1.** Hot enough to glow red: *a red-hot bar of steel.* **2.** Heated, as with excitement or anger. **3.** *Informal.* New; very recent: *red-hot information.*

red-let•ter |**rĕd'**lĕt'ər| *adj.* Memorably happy; important: *a red-letter day.*

red light *n.* **1.** A red traffic or danger signal indicating stop. **2.** A sign of caution; deterrent.

red•line |**rĕd'**līn'| *v.* To discriminate against (an area or neighborhood) by refusing to grant fair loans, mortgages, or insurance policies.

red•o•lent |**rĕd'**l ənt| *adj.* **1.** Having or giving off a pleasant odor; scented: *redolent clusters of honeysuckle.* **2.** Reminiscent: *a campaign redolent of machine politics.* —**red'o•lence** *n.*

re•dou•ble |rē **dŭb'**əl| *v.* **re•dou•bled, re•dou•bling.** To make or become twice as great.

re•doubt•a•ble |rĭ **dou'**tə bəl| *adj.* **1.** Causing awe or fear. **2.** Worthy of respect or honor.

re•dound |rĭ **dound'**| *v.* To have an effect or consequence, especially by bringing or reflecting credit or discredit.

red pepper. Cayenne pepper or a similar sharp-tasting seasoning. See **pepper.**

re•dress |rĭ **drĕs'**| *v.* To set right; remedy or rectify (something considered wrong or unjust). —*n.* |**rē'**drĕs'| *or* |rĭ **drĕs'**|. **1.** The act of setting right; correction; remedy: *a redress of a wrong.* **2.** Satisfaction or amends for wrong done.

Red Sea. A sea between Africa and Arabia, connected with the Mediterranean Sea by the Suez Canal.

red•skin |**rĕd'**skĭn'| *n. Informal.* A North American Indian.

red•start |**rĕd'**stärt'| *n.* A small bird with black feathers and orange patches on the wings and tail.

red tape. Procedures or practices, especially those connected with the official business of a government, that require great attention to detail and often result in delay or inaction.

red tide. Ocean waters colored by the proliferation of red, one-celled plantlike animals in sufficient numbers to kill fish.

re•duce |rĭ **do͞os'**| *or* |**-dyo͞os'**| *v.* **re•duced, re•duc•ing. 1.** To make or become less in amount, degree, size, rank, etc.; diminish: *reduced their demands for wage increases; as the volume of noise gradually reduces.* **2.** To gain control of; conquer: *a design to reduce them under absolute despotism.* **3.** To bring into a given condition or state: *reduce marble to dust; reduce life to a dull routine.* **4. a.** To lower the valence of (an atom or element). **b.** To remove oxygen from chemical combination with or in (an element or compound). **c.** To change to a pure metallic state; smelt. **5.** To change (a mathematical expression) into a simpler form without affecting its value or meaning. **6.** To lose body weight, as by dieting.

re•duc•tion |rĭ **dŭk'**shən| *n.* **1.** The act or process of reducing. **2.** The amount by which something is made smaller or less. **3.** The first cell division in meiosis, in which the number of chromosomes in the cell is reduced. **4.** The changing of a fraction into a simpler form, especially by dividing the numerator and denominator by any integral factors that they have in common.

re•dun•dan•cy |rĭ **dŭn'**dən sē| *n., pl.* **re•dun•dan•cies. 1.** The condition of being redundant. **2.** A word or expression that unnecessarily repeats an idea or meaning. For example, in the sentence *He did not know the answer, but he raised his hand, however,* the word "however" is a redundancy.

re•dun•dant |rĭ **dŭn'**dənt| *adj.* **1.** Composed of or containing more words than necessary; verbose; repetitive: *a redundant message.* **2.** In excess of the minimum necessary; extra: *redundant machine parts.* —**re•dun'dant•ly** *adv.*

red-winged blackbird |**rĕd'**wĭngd'|. A blackbird with bright-red patches on the wings.

red•wood |**rĕd'**wo͝od'| *n.* **1.** A very tall cone-bearing evergreen tree of northwestern California. It is the tallest kind of tree in the world, sometimes growing to a height of over 300 feet. See **sequoia. 2.** The soft but strong reddish-brown wood of such a tree. —***modifier:*** *a redwood forest; redwood picnic tables.* [SEE PICTURE]

reed |rēd| *n.* **1.** Any of several tall, hollow-stemmed grasses or similar plants that grow in wet places. **2. a.** A springy strip of cane or metal used in the mouthpiece of certain wind instruments. It vibrates when air passes over it and causes the air in the instrument to vibrate. **b.** A similar strip of metal that causes the air in an organ pipe to vibrate. **c.** A woodwind instrument, such as an oboe or clarinet, played with a reed. **d.** An organ stop using pipes that have reeds. —***modifier:*** *a reed basket; the reed instruments of a band.* ¶ *These sound alike* **reed, read.**

reed•y |**rē'**dē| *adj.* **reed•i•er, reed•i•est. 1.** Full of reeds: *a reedy marsh.* **2.** Resembling a reed: *a slim, reedy girl.* **3.** Having the high, shrill, or breathy sound of a reed instrument: *the oboe's reedy tone.* —**reed'i•ness** *n.*

reef[1] |rēf| *n.* A strip or ridge of rock, sand, or coral that rises to or close to the surface of a body of water. [SEE NOTE]

reef[2] |rēf| *n.* A portion of a sail tucked in and tied down so as to decrease the area of the sail that is exposed to the wind. —*v.* To reduce the size of (a sail) by tying a reef. [SEE NOTE]

reek |rēk| *v.* To give off a strong or unpleasant odor: *a salad reeking of garlic.* —*n.* A strong, unpleasant odor: *the musty reek of a mountain lion.* ¶ *These sound alike* **reek, wreak.**

reel[1] |rēl| *n.* **1.** A spoollike device that turns on a central bar, used for winding a hose, rope, film, tape, fishing line, etc. **2.** The amount held by a reel. —*v.* **1.** To wind onto a reel. **2.** To pull in (a fish) by winding on a reel: *reel in a marlin.* —***phrasal verb.*** **reel off.** To recite fluently. [SEE NOTE & PICTURE]

reel[2] |rēl| *v.* **1.** To stagger: *reeling out of the smoky room, half-suffocated.* **2.** To go round and round in a whirling motion: *The events of the day reeled in his mind.* [SEE NOTE]

reel[3] |rēl| *n.* **1.** Any of several fast, lively folk dances. **2.** Music written to accompany or as if to accompany any of these dances. [SEE NOTE]

re•e•lect or **re-e•lect** |rē'ĭ lĕkt'| *v.* To elect again. —**re'e•lec'tion, re'-e•lec'tion** *n.*

re-en•ter or **re•en•ter** |rē ĕn'tər| *v.* **1.** To come in or enter again. **2.** To record again on a list or ledger. —**re-en'trance, re•en'trance** *n.*

re-en•try or **re•en•try** |rē ĕn'trē| *n., pl.* **re-en•tries** or **re•en•tries. 1.** The act of re-entering; a second or subsequent entry. **2.** The return of a missile or spacecraft to the earth's atmosphere.

re-es•tab•lish or **re•es•tab•lish** |rē'ĭ stăb'lĭsh| *v.* To establish again; restore. —**re'-es•tab'lish•ment, re'es•tab'lish•ment** *n.*

re•fec•to•ry |rĭ fĕk'tə rē| *n., pl.* **re•fec•to•ries.** A room where meals are served.

re•fer |rĭ fûr'| *v.* **re•ferred, re•fer•ring. 1.** To direct to a person or thing for help or information: *refer a patient to a heart specialist.* **2.** To turn to, as for information or authority: *refer to the chart on the page opposite the text.* **3.** To submit (something) to a person or group for examination or action: *refer a proposed bill to a committee.* **4.** To pertain; apply: *exercises that refer to today's lecture.* **5.** To allude or make reference: *referring to Connecticut as the "Nutmeg State."*

ref•e•ree |rĕf'ə rē'| *n.* **1.** In sports competitions, a person in charge of play; an official who enforces the rules. **2.** In law, someone to whom something is referred for consideration; an arbitrator or arbiter. —*v.* **ref•e•reed, ref•e•ree•ing.** To judge or act as a referee.

ref•er•ence |rĕf'ər əns| *or* |rĕf'rəns| *n.* **1.** The act of referring. **2.** Relation; regard; respect: *a reply in reference to your query.* **3.** An allusion or mention: *frequent references to his trip to Europe.* **4.** A note in a book or other publication that directs the reader to another part of the book or to another source of information. **5. a.** A person who has knowledge of another and is therefore in a position to recommend him or to vouch for his fitness, as for a job. **b.** A statement about a person's character or qualifications for something.

reference book. A book, such as a dictionary, encyclopedia, etc., that provides specific information arranged according to a plan or system.

ref•er•en•dum |rĕf'ə rĕn'dəm| *n., pl.* **ref•er•en•dums. 1.** The practice of placing a measure directly before the voters rather than deciding it through a legislative body. **2.** Such a vote: *Our town had a referendum on the school bond issue.*

re•fill |rē fĭl'| *v.* To fill again: *He used all the ice cubes and forgot to refill the tray.* —*n.* |rē'fĭl'|. **1.** A second or subsequent filling: *held out his glass for a refill.* **2.** A replacement for something used up.

re•fine |rĭ fīn'| *v.* **re•fined, re•fin•ing. 1.** To remove unwanted matter from; make pure: *refine oil; refine sugar.* **2.** To make polished or elegant: *refine one's table manners.* —**re•fin'er** *n.*

re•fined |rĭ fīnd'| *adj.* **1.** Made pure, as through an industrial refining process: *refined uranium.* **2.** Cultivated; elegant: *a refined young lady.*

re•fine•ment |rĭ fīn'mənt| *n.* **1.** The act or process of refining: *the continual refinement of the English language.* **2.** A small change or addition intended to improve something: *Our new Buick has a full set of instruments and other refinements.* **3.** Elegance; cultivation: *ladies of refinement.*

re•fin•er•y |rĭ fī'nə rē| *n., pl.* **re•fin•er•ies.** A factory for purifying and processing a crude substance, such as petroleum, sugar, fat, or ore.

re•flect |rĭ flĕkt'| *v.* **1.** To send back or turn back (radiation, particles, etc.) that strike a surface, especially so that the incoming and outgoing paths make equal angles with a perpendicular: *a surface that reflects light.* **2.** To be sent or turned back in this way: *light that reflects from the ceiling.* **3.** To form an image of by or as if by turning back light in this way: *The mirror reflected his face—tired and grim-looking.* **4.** To reveal as if through a mirror: *Dogs reflect their masters' habits.* **5.** To be influenced or determined by: *Prices reflect a store's overhead costs.* **6.** To think seriously; contemplate: *reflected before deciding.* —*phrasal verb.* **reflect on** (or **upon**). To bring blame or discredit on.

reflecting telescope. An optical telescope in which the main light-gathering element is a concave mirror.

re•flec•tion |rĭ flĕk'shən| *n.* **1.** The act or process of reflecting: *the reflection of light by a mirror.* **2.** Something reflected, as sound, electromagnetic waves, etc. **3.** An image formed by reflected light: *She gazed at her reflection in the forest pool.* **4. a.** Serious thought; meditation: *After long reflection, he decided not to drop out of school.* **b.** An idea, remark, or piece of writing resulting from this.

re•flec•tive |rĭ flĕk'tĭv| *adj.* **1. a.** Of, produced by, or resulting from reflection: *the reflective properties of glass.* **b.** Tending to reflect: *a polished, highly reflective surface.* **2.** Thoughtful; pensive: *He's in a reflective mood.*

re•flex |rē'flĕks'| *n.* **1.** An involuntary response to a stimulus. **2.** An instinctive or unlearned response to a stimulus. **3.** A reflection or an image produced by reflection.

re•flex•ive |rĭ flĕk'sĭv| *adj.* **1.** Of a reflex: *a reflexive twitch.* **2.** Describing a verb that has an identical subject and direct object. For example, in the sentence *She dressed herself, dressed* is a reflexive verb. **3.** Describing a pronoun used as direct object of a reflexive verb. For example, in the sentence *He blames himself, himself* is a reflexive pronoun. —*n.* A reflexive verb or pronoun. —**re•flex'ive•ly** *adv.*

re•form |rĭ fôrm'| *v.* **1.** To correct errors, abuses, etc., in; make more just or humane: *young idealists who set out to reform society.* **2.** To improve in form, style, method, etc.: *a plan to reform English spelling.* **3.** To cause to give up or give up evil ways: *work designed to reform criminals. Sammy promised his father he would reform.* —*n.* **1.** An act, process, or example of making something better; an improvement: *the reform of city government.* **2.** A movement or policy that aims at this: *prison reform; land reform.*

ref•or•ma•tion |rĕf'ər mā'shən| *n.* **1.** The act of reforming or condition of being reformed: *dreamed of a total reformation of the public school system.* **2. Reformation.** The political and religious rebellion in 16th-century Europe against the Roman Catholic Church.

re•for•ma•to•ry |rĭ fôr'mə tôr'ē| *or* |-tōr'ē| *n., pl.* **re•for•ma•to•ries.** An institution, partly a prison and partly a school, for young lawbreakers.

re•form•er |rĭ fôr'mər| *n.* A person who tries to

bring about change, especially social or political change, by reform.

reform school. A reformatory.

re•fract |rĭ **frăkt′**| *v.* To cause the path of (light or other radiation) to bend or deflect by refraction.

refracting telescope. A telescope that gathers light and produces an image by means of lenses only.

re•frac•tion |rĭ **frăk′**shən| *n.* **1.** The bending or deflection of the path of a wave, as of light or sound, as it passes between mediums in which its velocity is different, with its original path meeting the boundary between the mediums at an oblique angle. **2.** The amount by which the apparent position of a celestial body is displaced by such bending of light as it enters the earth's atmosphere.

re•frac•to•ry |rĭ **frăk′**tə rē| *adj.* **1. a.** Difficult to melt, refine, shape, or work: *a refractory ore.* **b.** Resistant to heat or high temperatures: *refractory bricks.* **2.** Not responsive to medical treatment: *a refractory disease.* **3.** Stubborn; unmanageable: *a refractory child.*

re•frain¹ |rĭ **frān′**| *v.* To hold oneself back; forbear: *refrain from talking.* [SEE NOTE]

re•frain² |rĭ **frān′**| *n.* **1.** A phrase or verse repeated several times throughout the course of a song or poem, especially at the end of each stanza. **2.** The music for this. [SEE NOTE]

re•fresh |rĭ **frĕsh′**| *v.* **1.** To make fresh again with or as if with food, drink, or rest: *Mother refreshed herself with an afternoon nap.* **2.** To make cool, clean, or damp; freshen: *An afternoon shower refreshed the sidewalks.* **3.** To rouse; stimulate: *refresh one's memory.* —**re•fresh′er** *n.*

re•fresh•ing |rĭ **frĕsh′**ĭng| *adj.* **1.** Serving to refresh: *a refreshing soft drink; a refreshing breeze.* **2.** New and different in a pleasant way: *a refreshing viewpoint on art.* —**re•fresh′ing•ly** *adv.*

re•fresh•ment |rĭ **frĕsh′**mənt| *n.* **1.** The act of refreshing. **2.** Something that refreshes. **3. refreshments.** A light meal or snack.

re•frig•er•ant |rĭ **frĭj′**ər ənt| *n.* A substance used to cool something by absorbing heat from it, either directly or in a repeating cycle, as in a refrigerator.

re•frig•er•ate |rĭ **frĭj′**ə rāt′| *v.* **re•frig•er•at•ed, re•frig•er•at•ing.** **1.** To make or keep cool or cold. **2.** To preserve (food) by storing at a low temperature. —**re•frig′er•a′tion** *n.*

re•frig•er•a•tor |rĭ **frĭj′**ə rā′tər| *n.* A box, cabinet, etc., in which something perishable, such as food, is kept at a low temperature.

ref•uge |**rĕf′**yo͞oj| *n.* **1.** Protection; shelter: *seeking refuge in the castle.* **2.** A place of protection or shelter: *a wildlife refuge.*

ref•u•gee |rĕf′yo͞o **jē′**| *n.* A person who flees, especially from his country, to find refuge from oppression, persecution, etc.

re•ful•gent |rĭ **fŭl′**jənt| *adj.* Shining radiantly; brilliant: *a diadem refulgent with gems.*

re•fund |rĭ **fŭnd′**| *v.* To pay back (money): *The store refunded the full price of the television set.* —*n.* |**rē′**fŭnd′|. **1.** A repayment of funds: *She demanded a refund.* **2.** The amount repaid: *How much was your refund?* —**re•fund′a•ble** *adj.*

re•fur•bish |rē **fûr′**bĭsh| *v.* To brighten or freshen up; renovate: *refurbish a house.*

re•fus•al |rĭ **fyo͞o′**zəl| *n.* The act of refusing: *His proposal of marriage met with a stout refusal.*

re•fuse¹ |rĭ **fyo͞oz′**| *v.* **re•fused, re•fus•ing.** **1.** To decline to do (something). **2.** To decline to accept; turn down: *refuse an offer.* **3.** To decline to give: *refused permission.* [SEE NOTE]

ref•use² |**rĕf′**yo͞os| *n.* Worthless matter; waste. [SEE NOTE]

re•fute |rĭ **fyo͞ot′**| *v.* **re•fut•ed, re•fut•ing.** To prove (a person, idea, etc.) to be wrong: *refuted their statements.* —**ref′u•ta′tion** *n.* —**re•fut′er** *n.*

re•gain |rĭ **gān′**| *v.* **1.** To recover: *regain one's health.* **2.** To manage to reach again: *regain shore.*

re•gal |**rē′**gəl| *adj.* **1.** Of a king; royal: *regal power.* **2.** Befitting a king: *a regal bearing.*

re•gale |rĭ **gāl′**| *v.* **re•galed, re•gal•ing.** To entertain, by or as if by providing with a feast.

re•ga•lia |rĭ **gāl′**yə| *n.* **1.** The emblems and symbols of royalty, as the crown and scepter. **2.** The special symbols and costume that distinguish a certain rank, office, fraternal order, etc. **3.** Fine or fancy clothes; finery.

re•gard |rĭ **gärd′**| *v.* **1.** To look at; observe: *The farmer regarded the trespassers with a fixed stare.* **2.** To consider in a particular way: *regarded her with favor.* **3.** To hold in affection or esteem: *She regards her teachers highly.* **4.** To relate to; concern: *a decision that regards one's future.* —*n.* **1.** A look or gaze: *a judge's cold regard.* **2.** Esteem or affection: *showing regard for his parents.* **3. regards.** Good wishes; greetings: *Send her my regards, will you?* **4.** Relation: *replying in regard to your ad.* **5.** A particular point or matter: *I can't help you in that regard.*

re•gard•ful |rĭ **gärd′**fəl| *adj.* **1.** Attentive; mindful: *regardful of the feelings of other people.* **2.** Respectful: *addressing her in a regardful voice.*

re•gard•ing |rĭ **gär′**dĭng| *prep.* In reference to; concerning: *laws regarding sanitation.*

re•gard•less |rĭ **gärd′**lĭs| *adj.* Heedless; unmindful: *I'll take the job, regardless of the pay.* —*adv.* In spite of everything; anyway: *She still loved him, regardless.*

re•gat•ta |rĭ **gă′**tə| *or* |**-găt′**ə| *n.* A boat race or races, organized as a sporting event.

re•gen•cy |**rē′**jən sē| *n., pl.* **re•gen•cies.** **1.** A group of regents appointed to rule a kingdom jointly. **2.** The government or period of rule of a regent. **3. Regency.** The period of such rule in England from 1811 to 1820.

re•gen•er•ate |rĭ **jĕn′**ə rāt′| *v.* **re•gen•er•at•ed, re•gen•er•at•ing.** **1.** To give new life to; revive: *The reforms were intended to regenerate the nation's economic life.* **2.** To replace (a damaged or lost part or organ) by growing new tissue: *A starfish that has lost an arm will regenerate a new one.* —**re•gen′er•a′tion** *n.* —**re•gen′er•a′tive** *adj.*

re•gent |**rē′**jənt| *n.* **1.** A person appointed to rule during the period a sovereign is too young or unable to rule. **2.** A member of the governing board of a state university or a state system of schools.

re•gime |rĭ **zhēm′**| *or* |rā-| *n.* **1.** A system of government: *a democratic regime.* **2.** The administration or rule of a particular leader, faction, party, etc. **3.** A form of the word **regimen.**

reg•i•men |**rĕj′**ə mən| *or* |**-mĕn′**| *n.* A system or method of treatment or cure.

refrain¹·²

Refrain¹ *is from Old French* refrener, *which is from Latin* refrēnāre, *"to pull back (a horse) by the bridle," hence "to curb, to check":* re-, *"back,"* + frēnum, *"bridle."* **Refrain²** *is from Old French* refrain, *which is from* refraindre, *"to break off" (since a musical refrain* breaks off *the main song).*

refuse¹·²

These are separate words but are closely related. **Refuse¹** *is from Old French* refuser, *which is from Latin* refūs-, *"to pour back, to get rid of":* re-, *"back,"* + fūs-, fund-, *"pour."* **Refuse²** *is from Old French* refus, *"refusal, something refused or rejected," from* refuser *(as above).*

ă pat/ā pay/â care/ä father/ĕ pet/ ē be/ĭ pit/ī pie/î fierce/ŏ pot/ ō go/ô paw, for/oi oil/o͝o book/ o͞o boot/ou out/ŭ cut/û fur/ *th* the/th thin/hw which/zh vision/ ə ago, item, pencil, atom, circus

reg•i•ment |rĕj′ə mənt| *n.* A unit of soldiers, composed of two or more battalions. —*v.* To force to conform to a single pattern, as by rigid discipline: *regiment students.*

reg•i•men•tal |rĕj′ə **mĕn′**tl| *adj.* Of or belonging to a regiment: *the regimental colors.* —*n.* **regimentals.** The uniform and insignia of a particular regiment.

reg•i•men•ta•tion |rĕj′ə mĕn **tā′**shən| *n.* The act of regimenting or condition of being regimented: *the regimentation of army recruits.*

Re•gi•na |rĭ **jī′**nə|. The capital of Saskatchewan, Canada. Population, 149,593.

re•gion |**rē′**jən| *n.* **1.** An area of the earth's surface, especially a large area: *the polar regions.* **2.** A section or area of the body: *the abdominal region.* **3.** Any area, volume, realm, etc.: *the uncharted regions of outer space.* **4.** A part of a plane or space, separated from the rest of the plane or space by a boundary.

re•gion•al |**rē′**jə nəl| *adj.* **1.** Of an entire region rather than a locality: *the regional play-offs.* **2.** Of a particular region: *a regional accent.* —**re′gion•al•ly** *adv.*

reg•is•ter |**rĕj′**ĭ stər| *n.* **1. a.** An official record of items, names, transactions, etc.: *a register of all real-estate properties.* **b.** A book in which such a record is kept. **c.** An entry in such a book. **2.** A person who registers: *a register of deeds.* **3.** A device that automatically records or displays a number or quantity. **4.** A grill-like device that can be adjusted to control a flow of air, as into or out of a room. **5. a.** The range of a voice or musical instrument. **b.** A part of such a range: *the low register of a contralto.* —*v.* **1.** To record officially, in or as if in a register: *register a birth.* **2.** To make known for the record; file: *register a complaint.* **3.** To indicate or be indicated, as on a scale or device. **4.** To enroll or help (students) to enroll in classes. **5.** To place or cause (one's name) to be placed on a list of eligible voters. **6.** To reveal; show: *His face registered no emotion.* **7.** To create an impression: *Her name doesn't register in my memory.* **8.** To cause (mail) to be officially recorded by the post office. [SEE PICTURE]

registered nurse. A nurse who has graduated from a school of nursing and passed a registration examination given by the state.

reg•is•trar |**rĕj′**ĭ strär′| *or* |rĕj′ĭ **strär′**| *n.* An official of a college, corporation, etc., who is responsible for keeping records.

reg•is•tra•tion |rĕj′ĭ **strā′**shən| *n.* **1.** The act or process of registering, as of voters, students, etc. **2.** The number of people or things registered: *Voter registration in our county is 11,000.* **3.** An entry in a register. **4.** A card, paper, etc., carried as proof of registration. **5.** The condition or fact of registration: *a certificate of registration.* —***modifier:*** *a registration form.*

reg•is•try |**rĕj′**ĭ strē| *n.* **1.** The act of registering; registration. **2.** A ship's registered nationality; flag: *The tanker has a Liberian registry.* **3.** An official record of births, deaths, etc.: *entered her name in the registry.* **4.** A place where such records are kept.

re•gress |rĭ **grĕs′**| *v.* To go back to a previous condition: *Under hypnosis, the patient regressed to her early childhood.* —*n.* |**rē′**grĕs′|. A way of going back or returning: *a situation that offers no regress.* —**re•gres′sion** *n.*

re•gret |rĭ **grĕt′**| *v.* **re•gret•ted, re•gret•ting. 1.** To feel sorry about: *regret an error.* **2.** To feel a sense of loss over; mourn: *regretted leaving her classmates.* —*n.* **1.** A sense of distress over a past event or deed. **2.** A sense of reluctance over something one must do. **3.** Sadness; disappointment: *deep regret.* **4. regrets.** A polite reply turning down an invitation: *send one's regrets.* —**re•gret′ta•ble** *adj.* [SEE NOTE]

re•gret•ful |rĭ **grĕt′**fəl| *adj.* Full of regret: *Excited but regretful, Tommy left home for the big city.* —**re•gret′ful•ly** *adv.* —**re•gret′ful•ness** *n.*

reg•u•lar |**rĕg′**yə lər| *adj.* **1.** Usual; normal; standard: *selling radios at 25 per cent off the regular price.* **2.** Ordinary; not of a special type: *regular movies as well as cartoons.* **3.** Steady; habitual: *a regular patron.* **4.** Occurring again and again at a fixed time: *regular meals.* **5.** Well-balanced; symmetrical: *Her face has regular features.* **6.** Smooth; even: *a regular coastline.* **7.** Evenly spaced: *at regular intervals.* **8.** *Informal.* Likable; swell: *He's a regular guy.* **9.** Informal. Complete; thorough: *He's a regular little devil, isn't he?* **10.** Belonging to or constituting the permanent army of a country. **11.** Having all sides equal and all angles equal: *a regular polyhedron.* **12.** In grammar, belonging to a standard mode of inflection or conjugation: *a regular verb.* —*n.* **1.** A soldier belonging to a regular army. **2.** *Informal.* A steady customer: *The waitress recognized him as one of the regulars.* —**reg′u•lar′i•ty** *n.* —**reg′u•lar•ly** *adv.*

reg•u•late |**rĕg′**yə lāt′| *v.* **reg•u•lat•ed, reg•u•lat•ing. 1.** To control or direct according to a rule or rules: *power to regulate commerce.* **2.** To adjust (a device, machine, system, etc.) so that it works properly. **3.** To adjust or control (a flow, rate, output, etc.) so that it remains within certain limits: *regulate the movement of traffic.* —**reg′u•la′tor** *n.* —**reg′u•la•to′ry** |**rĕg′**yə lə tôr′ē| *or* |-tōr′ē| *adj.*

reg•u•la•tion |rĕg′yə **lā′**shən| *n.* **1.** The act or process of regulating. **2.** The condition of being regulated: *freedom from government regulation.* **3.** A rule, order, or law by which something is regulated: *traffic regulations.* —*adj.* Conforming to a regular method, style, rule, etc.: *a regulation uniform.*

re•gur•gi•tate |rĭ **gûr′**jĭ tāt′| *v.* **re•gur•gi•tat•ed, re•gur•gi•tat•ing. 1.** To pour back (partially digested food) from the stomach through the mouth; vomit. **2.** To give forth, as if by vomiting. —**re•gur′gi•ta′tion** *n.*

re•ha•bil•i•tate |rē′hə **bĭl′**ĭ tāt′| *v.* **re•ha•bil•i•tat•ed, re•ha•bil•i•tat•ing. 1.** To restore to useful life, as through training, therapy, etc.: *a program to rehabilitate blinded veterans.* **2.** To restore the good name or former rank of; reinstate. —**re′ha•bil′i•ta′tion** *n.*

re•hash |rē **hăsh′**| *v.* To work up again or go over again, without anything new resulting: *John and Susan rehashed their disagreement.* —*n.* |**rē′**-hăsh′|. **1.** The act or process of reworking, repeating, etc. **2.** Something that is reworked, repeated, etc., in an uncreative way: *His book is a rehash of some old folk tales.*

re•hears•al |rĭ **hûr′**səl| *n.* **1.** The act or process

register

regret
"I only regret that I have but one life to lose for my country." Nathan Hale (prior to his execution, September 22, 1776).

reign

Reign *is from Old French* reigne, *which is from Latin* rēgnum, *"kingdom, rule of a king," from* rēg-, rēx, *"king."* Rēx *is descended from* rēg-, *the prehistoric Indo-European title of the tribal king.* (Rēg- *also appears in Sanskrit as* rājan, *"king," which in Hindi became* rājā *and was borrowed into English as* **rajah**.)

rein

Rein *is from Old French* rene, *which is from an unattested Latin word,* retina, *"a rein or curb," from* retinēre, *"to hold back, retain."*

reindeer

Reindeer is from Old Norse *hreindȳri*. The word *hreinn* itself means "reindeer" (it is related to **horn**); the *dȳri* means "deer" (and so is strictly speaking unnecessary). Reindeer are considered to be identical to the caribou of arctic North America, although the caribou has never been domesticated.

ă pat/ā pay/â care/ä father/ĕ pet/ ē be/ĭ pit/ī pie/î fierce/ŏ pot/ ō go/ô paw, for/oi oil/ŏŏ book/ ōō boot/ou out/ŭ cut/û fur/ *th* the/th thin/hw which/zh vision/ ə ago, item, pencil, atom, circus

of practicing in preparation for a performance, ceremony, etc. **2.** A session devoted to such practice: *a wedding rehearsal; a play rehearsal.*

re•hearse |rĭ hûrs'| *v.* **re•hearsed, re•hears•ing. 1.** To practice (all or part of a program) in preparation for a performance: *The boys rehearsed their skit. The actors rehearsed five hours a day.* **2.** To train by rehearsal: *rehearse a choir.*

reign |rān| *n.* **1. a.** The exercise of real or symbolic political power by a monarch. **b.** The period of such a rule. **2.** Dominant influence or effect; sway: *the reign of theology in the Middle Ages.* —*v.* **1.** To exercise the real or symbolic power of a monarch. **2.** To be predominant or pervasive: *A stillness reigned throughout the schoolroom all morning.* ¶ *These sound alike* **reign, rain, rein.** [SEE NOTE]

re•im•burse |rē'ĭm bûrs'| *v.* **re•im•bursed, re•im•burs•ing.** To pay back; compensate. —**re'im•burs'a•ble** *adj.* —**re'im•burse'ment** *n.*

rein |rān| *n.* Often **reins. 1.** A long, narrow leather strap attached to the bit in a horse's mouth and held by the rider or driver to control the horse. **2.** Any means of restraint, guidance, etc.: *the reins of government.* —*v.* To check or hold back, by or as if by exerting pressure on the reins: *The scouts reined their horses. John carefully reined his anger.* —***phrasal verb.*** **rein up** (or **in**). To stop (one's horse) by pulling on the reins. ¶ *These sound alike* **rein, rain, reign.** [SEE NOTE]

Idiom. **give (free) rein to.** To release from restraints.

re•in•car•na•tion |rē'ĭn kär **nā'**shən| *n.* Transmigration of the soul at death, especially from one human body to another.

rein•deer |**rān'**dîr'| *n., pl.* **rein•deer.** A deer of arctic regions of Europe and Greenland, having large, spreading antlers in both the males and females. [SEE PICTURE]

re•in•force |rē'ĭn **fôrs'**| *or* |**-fōrs'**| *v.* **re•in•forced, re•in•forc•ing.** To make stronger by or as if by adding extra support to; strengthen: *reinforce a bridge; troops sent to reinforce the local militia.* —**re'in•forc'a•ble** *adj.*

re•in•force•ment |rē'ĭn **fôrs'**mənt| *or* |**-fōrs'-**| *n.* **1.** The act or process of reinforcing. **2.** Something that reinforces. **3. reinforcements.** Military units sent to reinforce units already sent.

re•in•state |rē'ĭn **stāt'**| *v.* **re•in•stat•ed, re•in•stat•ing.** To restore to a previous condition or position: *Miss Brown was reinstated in her teaching job.* —**re'in•state'ment** *n.*

re•it•er•ate |rē **ĭt'**ə rāt'| *v.* **re•it•er•at•ed, re•it•er•at•ing.** To say over again; repeat: *The doctor reiterated his warning.* —**re'it•er•a'tion** *n.*

re•ject |rĭ **jĕkt'**| *v.* **1.** To refuse to accept, use, grant, consider, etc.: *Dad rejected my plea for a bigger allowance.* **2.** To fail to give affection or love to: *Johnny feels that his parents rejected him as a child but accept him wholeheartedly now.* **3.** To throw out; discard. —*n.* |**rē'**jĕkt'|. **1.** Something, especially a product, that is rejected as not meeting minimum standards. **2.** A person that is rejected as unfit, especially for military service.

re•jec•tion |rĭ **jĕk'**shən| *n.* **1.** The act or process of rejecting. **2.** The condition of being rejected: *years of persecution and rejection.* **3.** A rebuff: *As a young writer, Jack London received rejection after rejection from publishers.*

re•joice |rĭ **jois'**| *v.* To feel or express joy: *"Be not too hasty to rejoice," said the grandmother.*

re•join[1] |rē **join'**| *v.* **1.** To join together again. **2.** To go back to; return to; reunite with: *The prisoner was released to rejoin his family.*

re•join[2] |rĭ **join'**| *v.* To answer; reply; respond: *"I'll do whatever I please!" Sammy angrily rejoined.*

re•join•der |rĭ **join'**dər| *n.* An answer, as in response to another's answer: *His torrent of abuse met with no rejoinder.*

re•ju•ve•nate |rĭ **jōō'**və nāt'| *v.* **re•ju•ve•nat•ed, re•ju•ve•nat•ing.** To restore youthfulness or youthful vigor to: *His vacation completely rejuvenated him.* —**re•ju've•na'tion** *n.*

re•lapse |rĭ **lăps'**| *v.* **re•lapsed, re•laps•ing. 1.** To fall back into a previous condition, mode of behavior, etc.: *Their lives relapsed into the old routine.* **2.** To become sick again after a partial recovery: *The patient relapsed during the night.* —*n.* |*also* **rē'**lăps'|. The act or result of relapsing, especially a return to illness.

re•late |rĭ **lāt'**| *v.* **re•lat•ed, re•lat•ing. 1.** To tell or narrate: *relate a story.* **2.** To have a relation or connection to: *Every sentence in a paragraph should relate closely to the topic sentence.* **3.** *Informal.* To interact with other persons in a meaningful way: *Sally relates poorly to her classmates.*

re•lat•ed |rĭ **lā'**tĭd| *adj.* **1.** Connected; associated: *"Probability" and "statistics" are closely related topics.* **2.** Connected by kinship, marriage, or common origin: *Aunt Ethel is related to me on my mother's side.*

re•la•tion |rĭ **lā'**shən| *n.* **1.** A connection or association between two or more things; the bearing of one thing on another: *the relation of good grades and hard work.* **2.** The connection of persons by blood or marriage. **3.** A relative. **4. relations.** Dealings or associations with others: *a country's foreign relations.* **5.** The act of telling; an account: *his relation of his experiences in Alaska.*

re•la•tion•ship |rĭ **lā'**shən shĭp'| *n.* **1.** A connection between things, processes, facts, etc.: *the relationship between the moon and the tides.* **2.** A connection or tie between persons: *a strictly business relationship.* **3.** Kinship: *He claimed relationship to the deceased.*

rel•a•tive |**rĕl'**ə tĭv| *adj.* **1.** Related or relating: *your comment relative to my work.* **2.** Considered in comparison with something else: *the relative value of action and mere words.* **3.** Dependent on something else for meaning; not absolute: *"Expensive" is a relative word; its meaning depends on one's income.* **4.** In grammar, referring to an antecedent. —*n.* **1.** A person related by blood or marriage. **2.** In grammar, a relative term, especially a relative pronoun.

relative clause. A dependent clause introduced by a relative pronoun. For example, in the sentence *He who hesitates is lost,* the relative clause is *who hesitates.*

relative humidity. The quotient of the amount of water vapor contained in the air at a given temperature divided by the maximum that the air could contain at that temperature.

rel•a•tive•ly |**rĕl'**ə tĭv lē| *adv.* In comparison with other persons or things: *Africa is a relatively underpopulated continent.*

relative pitch. **1.** The pitch of a tone as determined by its position in a scale. **2.** The ability to judge the relation between any pair of musical tones. See **absolute pitch.**

relative pronoun. A pronoun that refers back to antecedent. For example, in the sentence *He who hesitates is lost,* the relative pronoun is *who* referring back to *he.*

rel•a•tiv•i•ty |rĕl'ə tĭv'ĭ tē| *n.* **1.** The condition of being relative: *the relativity of means to ends.* **2.** **General relativity** or **special relativity,** theories formulated by Albert Einstein.

re•lax |rĭ lăks'| *v.* **1.** To make or become less tight or tense: *relax one's muscles. The coach's grip on Jerry's arm relaxed.* **2.** To make or become less severe or strict: *relax classroom discipline. Army regulations have relaxed greatly in recent years.* **3.** To take one's ease: *Nancy relaxed in a bubble bath.* **4.** To make or become less worried, anxious, etc.: *Listening to jazz relaxes me. He enjoyed relaxing with a good detective story.* —**re•laxed'** *adj.: a relaxed posture; a relaxed evening meal.*

re•lax•a•tion |rē'lăk sā'shən| *n.* **1.** The act or process of relaxing: *a relaxation of the muscles.* **2.** The condition of being relaxed: *She lay in the hammock in perfect relaxation.* **3.** Refreshment of body or mind; fun; diversion.

re•lay |rē'lā'| *n.* **1.** A fresh animal or team of animals, as for a stagecoach. **2.** A crew of laborers who relieve another crew; a shift. **3.** A **relay race.** **4.** A switch that is operated by an electric current rather than by hand. —***modifier:*** *a relay post; a relay tower.* —*v.* |*also* rĭ lā'|. To pass or send along by or as if by relay: *relay live television communications across the Atlantic.*

relay race. A swimming or running race between two groups, in which each member of a group goes only a part of the total distance.

re•lease |rĭ lēs'| *v.* **re•leased, re•leas•ing.** **1.** To set free; liberate: *release prisoners from an internment camp.* **2.** To let fall, let fly, etc.: *The archer released the arrow.* **3.** To relieve, as from an obligation: *an order that released Private Davis from active duty.* **4.** To make available, as to the public: *release a film.* —*n.* **1.** The act of releasing: *the release of a lion from its cage.* **2.** An instance of being released: *his release from the hospital.* **3.** Something that is issued to the public: *a press release.* **4.** A document or order granting freedom from prison or from an obligation: *The prisoner's release finally arrived.* **5.** A level, control, or device that causes something that is normally held fast to be freed.

rel•e•gate |rĕl'ĭ gāt'| *v.* **rel•e•gat•ed, rel•e•gat•ing.** **1.** To send or consign, especially to a place, position, or condition of less importance or prestige: *relegated him to the ranks.* **2.** To refer or assign (a task, duty, or chore) to someone else. —**rel'e•ga'tion** *n.*

re•lent |rĭ lĕnt'| *v.* To become softened or gentler in attitude, temper, or determination. —**re•lent'ing•ly** *adv.*

re•lent•less |rĭ lĕnt'lĭs| *adj.* **1.** Mercilessly harsh; unyielding; pitiless: *a relentless killer.* **2.** Steady and persistent; incessant; unremitting: *relentless heat.* —**re•lent'less•ly** *adv.*

rel•e•vant |rĕl'ə vənt| *adj.* Related to the matter at hand; pertinent: *relevant questions.* —**rel'e•vance, rel'e•van•cy** *n.* —**rel'e•vant•ly** *adv.*

re•li•a•ble |rĭ lī'ə bəl| *adj.* Capable of being relied upon; dependable. —**re•li'a•bil'i•ty, re•li'a•ble•ness** *n.* —**re•li'a•bly** *adv.*

re•li•ance |rĭ lī'əns| *n.* **1.** The condition or act of relying; dependence: *a reliance on industry.* **2.** Confidence; trust: *complete reliance in their friends.* **3.** Someone or something depended on; a mainstay: *His main reliance was the boat.*

re•li•ant |rĭ lī'ənt| *adj.* Having or showing reliance. —**re•li'ant•ly** *adv.*

rel•ic |rĕl'ĭk| *n.* **1.** An object or custom surviving from a culture or period that has disappeared: *relics of an ancient civilization.* **2.** Something that is treasured for its age or for its association with a person, place, or event: *Civil War relics.* **3.** An object of religious significance, especially something thought to be associated with a saint or martyr. **4. relics.** A corpse. [SEE NOTE]

re•lief |rĭ lēf'| *n.* **1.** Ease from or lessening of pain, discomfort, anxiety, etc.: *relief from a cold; relief from the day's labors.* **2.** Anything that lessens pain, discomfort, anxiety, etc.: *the relief of tears.* **3.** Assistance and help, as in the form of food or money, given to the needy, aged, or disaster victims. **4. a.** A release from a job, post of duty, etc. **b.** A person or persons taking over the duties of another: *a sentry waiting for his relief.* **5. a.** The projection of a sculptured figure from a flat background. **b.** The apparent projection of a figure in a painting or drawing, as achieved by shading, coloring, etc. **6.** The variations in elevation of any area of the earth's surface: *a map that shows relief.* **7.** Sharpness of outline resulting from contrast: *a white sail in relief against the dark blue of sea and sky.* —***modifier:*** *a relief carving.* [SEE PICTURE]

Idioms. **in relief.** Carved, drawn, etc., so as to project or seem to project from a flat background. **on relief.** Receiving assistance from the government because of need or poverty.

relief map. A map that shows the physical features of land, as by using lines, colors, or shading.

re•lieve |rĭ lēv'| *v.* **re•lieved, re•liev•ing.** **1.** To lessen or reduce (pain, discomfort, anxiety, etc.); ease. **2.** To free from pain, discomfort, anxiety, etc.: *relieve them of worries.* **3.** To take something from the possession of: *relieved him of his gun.* **4.** To release from a duty, position, etc., by being or providing a substitute: *He was relieved of his duties because of illness.* **5.** To give assistance or aid to: *relieve the victims of the flood.* **6.** To make less unpleasant, tiresome, boring, etc.: *We sang songs to relieve the monotony of the work.* —**re•liev'a•ble** *adj.* —**re•liev'er** *n.*

re•lig•ion |rĭ lĭj'ən| *n.* **1.** Belief in and reverence for a supreme, supernatural being or beings, often expressed by worship, ritual, and a certain way of life. **2.** A particular organized system of such belief: *the Hindu religion.* **3.** Anything considered of immense value to one's personal life: *Politics is his religion.* [SEE NOTE]

re•lig•ious |rĭ lĭj'əs| *adj.* **1.** Of religion: *religious services; religious freedom.* **2.** Adhering to religion; pious; devout: *a religious family.* **3.** Very faithful; conscientious: *a religious attention to detail.* **4.** Of or belonging to a monastic order. —*n.* A member of a monastic order. —**re•lig'ious•ly** *adv.* —**re•lig'ious•ness** *n.*

relic/relinquish

Relic *is from Old French* relique, *which is from Latin* reliquiae, *"remains, relics," from* relinquere, *"to leave behind":* re-, *"back, behind,"* + linquere, *"to leave."* Relinquere *became Old French* relinquir, relinquiss-, *which was borrowed into English as* **relinquish.**

relief

religion

"The world is my country, all mankind are my brethren, and to do good is my religion."—Thomas Paine (1794).

reluctant

Reluctant *comes from Latin* re-luctāns, *"struggling against," the present participle of* reluctārī, *"to struggle against, resist, be reluctant":* re-, *"against, back,"* + luctārī, *"to struggle."*

re•lin•quish |rĭ lĭng′kwĭsh| *v.* **1.** To leave; abandon: *He relinquished his place in line.* **2.** To give up, put aside, or surrender: *relinquish claim to the land; relinquish an idea.* **3.** To let go; release: *relinquished her grasp on the fishing pole.* —**re•lin′quish•ment** *n.* [SEE NOTE on p. 741]

rel•ish |rĕl′ĭsh| *n.* **1.** An appetite for something; an appreciation or liking: *I have no relish for that game.* **2. a.** Great enjoyment; pleasure; zest: *He began the task with relish.* **b.** Something that adds zest or pleasure: *His wit gave relish to the discussion.* **3.** A spicy condiment, such as chopped pickles, served with food. —*v.* To take pleasure in; enjoy: *He relished her insistent curiosity.*

re•live |rē lĭv′| *v.* **re•lived, re•liv•ing.** **1.** To undergo again; live through another time: *relive a momentous occasion.* **2.** To live again: *Old heroes relive in the stories written about them.*

re•lo•cate |rē lō′kāt′| *v.* **re•lo•cat•ed, re•lo•cat•ing.** To establish or become established in a new place. —**re′lo•ca′tion** *n.*

re•luc•tant |rĭ lŭk′tənt| *adj.* **1.** Unwilling; averse: *reluctant to leave.* **2.** Marked by unwillingness: *a reluctant confession.* —**re•luc′tance** *n.* —**re•luc′tant•ly** *adv.* [SEE NOTE]

re•ly |rĭ lī′| *v.* **re•lied, re•ly•ing, re•lies.** —**rely on** (or **upon**). To depend on; trust confidently: *They don't rely on magic. We rely upon his judgment.*

re•main |rĭ mān′| *v.* **1.** To continue to be; go on being: *Things at rest tend to remain at rest.* **2.** To be left as still to be dealt with: *The solution to the problem remains to be seen.* **3.** To stay in the same place or behind: *The children remained after their mother left.* **4.** To be left over after the loss, removal, destruction, etc., of others: *A few stone columns remained.*

re•main•der |rĭ mān′dər| *n.* **1.** The remaining part; the rest: *the remainder of the year.* **2. a.** In division, the difference between the dividend and the product of the quotient and divisor. **b.** In subtraction, a difference.

re•mains |rĭ mānz′| *pl.n.* **1.** All that remains after the loss, removal, destruction, etc., of other parts: *the remains of last night's supper.* **2.** A corpse. **3.** Ancient ruins or fossils.

re•mand |rĭ mănd′| *or* |-mänd′| *v.* **1.** To send back (a prisoner) to another prison, another court, or another agency for further proceedings. **2.** To send back (a legal case) to a lower court for further proceedings. —*n.* **1.** The act of remanding. **2.** The condition of being remanded: *a prisoner on remand.* —**re•mand′ment** *n.*

re•mark |rĭ märk′| *n.* **1.** A casual statement; a comment: *a remark about the weather.* **2.** The act of noticing or observing; mention: *a score worthy of remark.* —*v.* **1.** To say or write (a comment or comments) casually: *"The flowers are pretty," she remarked. He remarked about the freshness of the flowers.* **2.** To notice; observe: *They remarked several changes in the town.*

re•mark•a•ble |rĭ mär′kə bəl| *adj.* Worthy of notice; extraordinary; uncommon: *a remarkable achievement.* —**re•mark′a•bly** *adv.*

re•me•di•al |rĭ mē′dē əl| *adj.* **1.** Supplying a remedy: *a remedial operation.* **2.** Intended to correct something, especially faulty study habits, reading skills, etc.: *remedial reading; remedial training.* —**re•me′di•al•ly** *adv.*

rem•e•dy |rĕm′ĭ dē| *n., pl.* **rem•e•dies.** **1.** Something, such as a medicine or treatment, used or given to relieve pain, cure disease, or correct disorders. **2.** Something that corrects a fault, error, etc.: *a remedy for inflation.* —*v.* **rem•e•died, rem•e•dy•ing, rem•e•dies.** To relieve, cure, or correct (a pain, disease, etc.).

re•mem•ber |rĭ mĕm′bər| *v.* **1.** To recall to the mind; think of again: *She could not remember how to stop the machine.* **2.** To keep carefully in memory: *remembered songs of their homeland.* **3.** To give (someone) a gift, tip, etc.: *remembered her nieces at Christmas.* **4.** To mention (someone) to another as sending greetings: *Remember me to your parents.*

re•mem•brance |rĭ mĕm′brəns| *n.* **1.** The act of remembering: *the remembrance of things past.* **2.** The condition of remembering. **3.** Something that serves to remind; a memento or souvenir. **4. remembrances.** Greetings.

re•mind |rĭ mīnd′| *v.* To cause (someone) to remember or think of something: *Remind her to water the plants.* —**re•mind′er** *n.*

rem•i•nisce |rĕm′ə nĭs′| *v.* **rem•i•nisced, rem•i•nisc•ing.** To remember and tell of past experiences or events.

rem•i•nis•cence |rĕm′ə nĭs′əns| *n.* **1.** The act or process of recalling the past: *the reminiscence of childhood.* **2.** Something remembered; a memory: *pleasant reminiscences of the summer.* **3.** Often **reminiscences.** A book or other narration of past experiences or events.

rem•i•nis•cent |rĕm′ə nĭs′ənt| *adj.* Recalling to the mind; suggestive: *a melody reminiscent of a folk song.*

re•miss |rĭ mĭs′| *adj.* Careless in attending to duty; negligent: *She's very remiss in answering letters.* —**re•miss′ness** *n.*

re•mis•sion |rĭ mĭsh′ən| *n.* **1.** Pardon or forgiveness: *the remission of sin.* **2.** Release from a debt, obligation, etc. **3.** A temporary lessening of the intensity, seriousness, or destructive effect of a pain, disease, or disorder.

re•mit |rĭ mĭt′| *v.* **re•mit•ted, re•mit•ting.** **1.** To send (money); transmit. **2.** To cancel (a punishment, penalty, etc.): *remitted his fine.* **3.** To pardon; forgive. **4.** To relax; slacken: *remitted his search.* —**re•mit′ter** *n.*

re•mit•tance |rĭ mĭt′ns| *n.* **1.** Money or credit sent to someone. **2.** The act of sending money or credit.

rem•nant |rĕm′nənt| *adj.* **1.** A portion or quantity left over; a remainder: *remnants of an old document.* **2.** A surviving trace or vestige: *the last remnants of an ancient empire.* **3.** A leftover piece of cloth remaining after the rest of the bolt has been sold. —***modifier:*** *a remnant sale.*

re•mod•el |rē mŏd′l| *v.* **-mod•eled** or **-mod•elled, -mod•el•ing** or **-mod•el•ling.** To rebuild or redesign in order to improve; renovate: *remodel a house.* —**re•mod′el•er** *n.*

re•mon•strance |rĭ mŏn′strəns| *n.* A strong protest or objection.

re•mon•strate |rĭ mŏn′strāt′| *v.* **re•mon•strat•ed, re•mon•strat•ing.** To argue or plead in protest against or objection to something.

rem•o•ra |rĕm′ər ə| *n.* A fish having on the top of its head a sucking disk with which it attaches itself to sharks, whales, etc. [SEE PICTURE]

remora

ă pat/ā pay/â care/ä father/ĕ pet/ ē be/ĭ pit/ī pie/î fierce/ŏ pot/ ō go/ô paw, for/oi oil/ŏŏ book/ ōō boot/ou out/ŭ cut/û fur/ *th* the/th thin/hw which/zh vision/ ə ago, item, pencil, atom, circus

re•morse |rĭ **môrs'**| *n.* Bitter regret or guilt for having done something harmful or unjust. [SEE NOTE]

re•morse•ful |rĭ **môrs'**fəl| *adj.* Having or showing remorse: *a remorseful child; a remorseful sob.* **—re•morse'ful•ly** *adv.*

re•mote |rĭ **mōt'**| *adj.* **re•mot•er, re•mot•est. 1.** Located far away: *a remote Arctic island.* **2.** Distant in time, relationship, etc.: *the remote past; ideas remote from reality.* **3.** Barely perceptible; slight: *I haven't even a remote idea of what you are talking about.* **4.** Being distantly related by blood or marriage: *a remote cousin.* **5.** Distant in manner; aloof. **—re•mote'ly** *adv.*

remote control. Control of an activity, process, machine, etc., from a distance, especially by radio or by electricity. ***—modifier:*** **(remote-control):** *a remote-control device.*

re•mov•al |rĭ **mōō'**vəl| *n.* **1.** The act of removing: *ordered the removal of troops from the region.* **2.** Relocation: *the removal of the business to New Jersey.* **3.** Dismissal, as from office or duties: *the removal of an adviser.*

re•move |rĭ **mōōv'**| *v.* **re•moved, re•mov•ing. 1.** To move or convey from a position or place: *remove the pie from the oven.* **2.** To take off or away: *removed his coat; remove stains.* **3.** To do away with; eliminate: *remove fears.* **4.** To dismiss from office. *—n.* A distance or degree that separates: *quite a remove from his former home.* **—re•mov'a•ble** *adj.*

re•mu•ner•ate |rĭ **myōō'**nə rāt'| *v.* **re•mu•ner•at•ed, re•mu•ner•at•ing.** To pay (a person) for goods, services, etc.

re•mu•ner•a•tion |rĭ myōō'nə **rā'**shən| *n.* **1.** An act of remunerating. **2.** A recompense or compensation; a payment or reward.

re•mu•ner•a•tive |rĭ **myōō'**nə rā'tĭv| *or* |-nər ə-| *adj.* Likely to be remunerated; profitable.

ren•ais•sance |rĕn'ĭ **säns'**| *or* |**-zäns'**| *or* |rĭ **nā'**səns| *n.* **1.** A rebirth; a revival: *an intellectual renaissance in the community.* **2. Renaissance. a.** The humanistic revival of classical art, literature, and learning in Europe. **b.** The period of this revival, roughly from the 14th through the 16th century. *—adj.* **Renaissance.** Of the Renaissance or its artistic works or styles.

re•nas•cence |rĭ **năs'**əns| *or* |**-nā'**səns| *n.* **1.** A renaissance; a rebirth. **2. Renascence.** The Renaissance.

rend |rĕnd| *v.* **rent** |rĕnt| or **rend•ed, rend•ing. 1.** To tear, pull, or wrench apart violently: *"And Jacob rent his clothes . . . and mourned for his son many days"* (Genesis 37:34). **2.** To remove with force; wrest: *rending the torch from his hand.*

ren•der |**rĕn'**dər| *v.* **1.** To cause to become: *The hailstorm rendered the crop worthless.* **2.** To give, bestow, or make available: *render service.* **3.** To give in return: *render thanks for her thoughtfulness.* **4.** To pronounce; hand down: *render a judgment.* **5.** To represent in words or in art: *render a leaf in detail.* **6.** To translate: *render a Latin text into English.* **7.** To perform (a musical composition, dramatic work, etc.). **8.** To melt down or process (fat) by heating.

ren•dez•vous |**rän'**dā vōō'| *or* |-də-| *n., pl.* **ren•dez•vous** |**rän'**dā vōōz'| *or* |-də-|. **1.** A prearranged meeting: *a rendezvous of the explorers in the wilderness.* **2.** A designated place for a meeting. *—v.* **ren•dez•voused** |**rän'**dā vōōd'| *or* |-də-|, **ren•dez•vous•ing** |**rän'**dā vōō'ĭng| *or* |-də-|, **ren•dez•vous** |**rän'**dā vōōz'| *or* |-də-|. To meet together or cause to meet together at a certain time and place. [SEE NOTE]

ren•di•tion |rĕn **dĭsh'**ən| *n.* **1.** The act of rendering: *the rendition of a decision.* **2.** A translation: *an English rendition of a German phrase.* **3.** An interpretation or performance of a musical composition, dramatic work, etc.

ren•e•gade |**rĕn'**ĭ găd'| *n.* **1.** Someone who rejects a cause, allegiance, group, etc., in preference for another; a deserter; a traitor. **2.** An outlaw. ***—modifier:*** *a renegade leader.*

re•nege |rĭ **nĭg'**| *or* |**-nĕg'**| *v.* **re•neged, re•neg•ing. 1.** To fail to carry out a promise or duty: *renege on a commitment.* **2.** In card games, to fail to follow suit when possible and when required by the rules.

re•new |rĭ **nōō'**| *or* |**-nyōō'**| *v.* **1.** To make new or as if new again; restore: *renew an old building.* **2.** To take up again; revive: *renewed the association; renewed her study of the subject.* **3.** To arrange for an extension of: *renew a prescription.* **4.** To refill the supply of; replace: *renew supplies.* **—re•newed'** *adj.: a renewed faith; renewed stock.* **—re•new'a•ble** *adj.* **—re•new'al** *n.*

ren•net |**rĕn'**ĭt| *n.* **1.** The inner lining of the fourth stomach of calves or the young of related animals. **2.** A dried extract prepared from this lining, used to curdle milk and to make cheese and junket. **3.** Rennin.

ren•nin |**rĕn'**ĭn| *n.* An enzyme that causes milk to curdle, extracted from rennet and used in making cheeses and junkets.

re•nounce |rĭ **nouns'**| *v.* **re•nounced, re•nounc•ing. 1.** To give up or turn down, especially by formal announcement: *renounce her title.* **2.** To reject; disown: *renounced their children.* **—re•nounce'ment** *n.* **—re•nounc'er** *n.*

ren•o•vate |**rĕn'**ə vāt'| *v.* **ren•o•vat•ed, ren•o•vat•ing.** To renew; repair: *renovate an old cottage.* **—ren'o•va'tion** *n.* **—ren'o•va'tor** *n.*

re•nown |rĭ **noun'**| *n.* Widespread honor and fame.

re•nowned |rĭ **nound'**| *adj.* Having renown; honored and famous: *a renowned orator.*

rent¹ |rĕnt| *n.* A contracted payment made at regular intervals for the use of the property of another: *pay the monthly rent.* *—v.* **1.** To occupy or use (another's property) in return for regular payment: *rent an apartment; rent a bicycle.* **2.** To grant the use of (one's own property) in return for regular payments. **3.** To be for rent: *Rooms rent for ten dollars a day.* **—rent'ed** *adj.: a rented boat; a rented car.* **—rent'er** *n.* [SEE NOTE]

Idiom. **for rent.** Available for use in return for regular payment: *rooms for rent.*

rent² |rĕnt|. A past tense and past participle of **rend.** *—n.* **1.** An opening made by or as if by rending: *a rent in the garment; a sound making a rent in the silence.* **2.** A breach, as in a group; a split: *a rent in the family.* [SEE NOTE]

rent•al |**rĕn'**tl| *n.* **1.** An amount paid or received as rent: *a high rental.* **2.** The act of renting: *the rental of a car.* **3.** Property for rent. ***—modifier:*** *a rental agent; rental money.*

re•nun•ci•a•tion |rĭ nŭn'sē **ā'**shən| *n.* The act of renouncing: *the renunciation of a belief.*

remorse

Remorse *is from Old French* remors, *which is from Medieval Latin* remorsus conscientiae, *"torment of the conscience"*; remorsus *is from Latin* remordēre, *"to bite back, to gnaw at, to torment":* re-, *"back,"* + mordēre, *"to bite."*

rendezvous

Rendezvous *is from French* rendezvous, *a noun formed from the phrase* rendez vous, *"present yourselves." This was originally a command to soldiers, and the English word, which was first borrowed in the sixteenth century, remains in technical military use, both as a noun and as a verb, up to the present day.*

rent¹·²

Rent¹ *is from Old French* rente, *"payment, income from real estate"; this is from an unattested Latin word,* rendita, *"money paid," from* rendere *or* reddere, *"to give back, to give in exchange, to pay":* re-, *"back,"* + dare, *"to pay."* (Rendere *became Old French* rendre, *which was borrowed into English as* **render.**) **Rent²** *is from* **rend,** *which was Old English* rendan, *"to tear."*

re•o•pen |rē ō'pən| *v.* **1.** To open or become open again: *They reopened a trail. The clams slowly reopened.* **2.** To take up again; resume: *reopen hostilities.*

re•or•gan•ize |rē ôr'gə nīz'| *v.* **-or•gan•ized, -or•gan•iz•ing.** To organize or become organized again or differently: *She reorganized her ideas. The group will reorganize by autumn.* —**re•or'gan•i•za'tion** *n.* —**re•or'gan•iz'er** *n.*

Rep. **1.** Representative. **2.** Republican.

re•pair¹ |rĭ pâr'| *v.* **1.** To restore to proper or useful condition, as after damage, injury, or wear; fix: *repair an automobile.* **2.** To set right; remedy: *repair the damage.* —*n.* **1.** The work, act, or process of repairing: *cars in need of repair.* **2.** General operating condition, as of a machine or system: *a truck kept in good repair.* **3.** Often **repairs.** An instance in which repairing is done. —**modifier:** *a repair shop; a repair kit.* —**re•pair'a•ble** *adj.* —**re•pair'er** *n.* [SEE NOTE]

re•pair² |rĭ pâr'| *v.* To go: *The guests repaired to the drawing room.* [SEE NOTE]

repair¹·²

Repair¹ *is from Old French* reparer, *from Latin* reparāre, *"to restore, to repair":* re-, *"back"* + parāre, *"to set in order."* **Repair²** *is from Old French* repairer, *from Latin* repatriāre, *"to go back to one's own country,"* *later simply "to return":* re-, *"back,"* + patria, *"fatherland, country."* Repatriāre *was later reborrowed in a transitive sense as* **repatriate.**

rep•a•ra•tion |rĕp'ə rā'shən| *n.* **1.** The act or process of making amends for a wrong or injury. **2.** Something done to make amends; a compensation. **3. reparations.** Compensation required from a defeated nation for damage or injury during a war.

rep•ar•tee |rĕp'ər tē'| *or* |-tā'| *n.* **1.** A quick, witty reply; a spirited, clever retort. **2.** Spirited exchange of wit in conversation. **3.** Skill in making witty retorts and conversation.

re•past |rĭ păst'| *or* |-päst'| *n.* A meal or the food served or eaten at a meal.

re•pa•tri•ate |rē pā'trē āt'| *v.* **re•pa•tri•at•ed, re•pa•tri•at•ing.** To cause to return to the country of one's birth or citizenship: *repatriated the refugees.* —**re•pa'tri•a'tion** *n.*

re•pay |rĭ pā'| *v.* **re•paid** |rĭ pād'|, **re•pay•ing.** **1.** To pay back. **2.** To give compensation for; make a return for: *repay a kindness with kindness.* **3.** To make or do in return: *repay a visit.* —**re•pay'a•ble** *adj.* —**re•pay'ment** *n.*

re•peal |rĭ pēl'| *v.* To withdraw or annul officially; revoke: *repeal a law.* —*n.* The act or process of repealing: *the repeal of an amendment.*

re•peat |rĭ pēt'| *v.* **1.** To say, state, do, or go through again: *repeat a question; repeat a grade.* **2.** To say in duplication of what another has said: *repeat the phrase after the teacher.* **3.** To recite from memory: *repeat a poem.* **4.** —**repeat oneself.** To manifest or express in the same way or words: *She repeats herself in conversation.* **5.** To tell to someone else: *repeat gossip.* —*n.* **1.** The act of repeating: *the repeat of a performance.* **2.** Something repeated: *This television program is a repeat.* **3. a.** A section of a musical composition that is repeated or to be repeated. **b.** A sign consisting of a pair of dots arranged in a vertical line, used to mark the beginning and end of such a passage. —**modifier:** *a repeat program.* —**re•peat'er** *n.* [SEE PICTURE]

repeat

repeating decimal. A decimal whose numeral consists of or contains a pattern of digits that is repeated endlessly, as .145145145 . . .

re•pel |rĭ pĕl'| *v.* **re•pelled, re•pel•ling.** **1.** To drive off, force back, or keep away: *repel an enemy attack.* **2.** To cause aversion in: *The loud, shrill voice repelled them.* **3.** To be resistant to: *a fabric that repels water.* **4.** To refuse; reject: *repelled her offer of help.* [SEE NOTE]

repel/repulse

Repel *is from Latin* repellere, *"to push back, to reject, to drive off":* re-, *"back,"* + pellere, *"to push, to drive." The past participle of* repellere *was* repulsus; *English often takes verb forms from Latin past participles, and* repulsus *was borrowed as* **repulse,** *with the same basic meaning as* **repel.** *But now the two verbs are only partly synonymous; sense* **1** *of each is still the same, but other meanings and uses have developed separately. It is similar with the derivative adjectives* **repellent** *and* **repulsive.**

re•pel•lent |rĭ pĕl'ənt| *adj.* **1.** Acting or tending to repel; capable of repelling: *an odor that is repellent to dogs.* **2.** Resistant or impervious to a specified substance or influence: *The jacket was made from a water-repellent cloth.* **3.** Causing aversion or disgust: *a repellent manner.* —*n.* **1.** A substance used to drive off a pest or pests: *an insect repellent.* **2.** A substance used to treat something to make it repellent, as a substance that makes cloth resistant to water.

re•pent |rĭ pĕnt'| *v.* **1.** To feel remorse or regret for (what one has done or failed to do): *She repented her anger. She repented later.* **2.** To regret and change one's mind about (past conduct): *He repented of his boasting.* —**re•pent'er** *n.*

re•pen•tance |rĭ pĕn'tns| *n.* Remorse or contrition for past conduct or sin.

re•pen•tant |rĭ pĕn'tnt| *adj.* Feeling or showing repentance; penitent: *a repentant heart.*

re•per•cus•sion |rē'pər kŭsh'ən| *n.* **1.** An indirect effect or result produced by an event or action: *His decision may have alarming repercussions.* **2.** A reflection or echo.

rep•er•toire |rĕp'ər twär'| *or* |-twôr'| *n.* All of the songs, plays, operas, or other works that a person or company is prepared to perform.

rep•er•to•ry |rĕp'ər tôr'ē| *or* |-tōr'ē| *n., pl.* **rep•er•to•ries.** **1.** A repertoire. **2.** A collection, as of information. —**modifier:** *a repertory company.*

rep•e•ti•tion |rĕp'ĭ tĭsh'ən| *n.* **1.** The act or process of repeating: *the repetition of a word.* **2.** Something repeated or produced by repeating: *an exact repetition of a design.*

rep•e•ti•tious |rĕp'ĭ tĭsh'əs| *adj.* Characterized by or filled with much repetition, especially tedious repetition: *repetitious arguments.* —**rep'e•ti'tious•ly** *adv.* —**rep'e•ti'tious•ness** *n.*

re•place |rĭ plās'| *v.* **re•placed, re•plac•ing.** **1.** To take or fill the place of: *automobiles replaced horses.* **2.** To provide a substitute for: *replace a broken window.* **3.** To put back in place: *replaced the dish in the cabinet.* **4.** To pay back or return; refund. —**re•place'a•ble** *adj.*

re•place•ment |rĭ plās'mənt| *n.* **1.** The act or process of replacing: *the replacement of funds.* **2.** Someone or something that replaces: *Stay until your replacement arrives.*

re•plen•ish |rĭ plĕn'ĭsh| *v.* To add a new stock or supply to; fill again: *replenish the water in the tank.* —**re•plen'ish•er** *n.* —**re•plen'ish•ment** *n.*

re•plete |rĭ plēt'| *adj.* **1.** Plentifully supplied; abounding: *a land replete with streams and forests.* **2.** Filled; gorged: *After finishing the pumpkin pie, he felt replete.* —**re•ple'tion** *n.*

rep•li•ca |rĕp'lĭ kə| *n.* **1.** A copy or reproduction of a work of art by the original artist. **2.** Any copy or close reproduction: *a replica of an early telephone.*

re•ply |rĭ plī'| *v.* **re•plied, re•ply•ing, re•plies.** To say or give (an answer): *He replied kindly. He replied that he would go.* —*n., pl.* **re•plies.** An answer or response. —**re•pli'er** *n.*

re•port |rĭ pôrt'| *or* |-pōrt'| *n.* **1.** An oral or written account containing information, often prepared or delivered in organized form: *a weather report; a news report.* **2.** Rumor; talk: *There are reports in the paper of strange happenings in town.* **3.** An ex-

ă pat/ā pay/â care/ä father/ĕ pet/ ē be/ĭ pit/ī pie/î fierce/ŏ pot/ ō go/ô paw, for/oi oil/ŏŏ book/ ōō boot/ou out/ŭ cut/û fur/ *th* the/th thin/hw which/zh vision/ ə ago, item, pencil, atom, circus

plosive sound, as of a firearm being discharged. **4.** Reputation: *someone of good report.* —*v.* **1.** To make or present an account of (something), often formally or in organized form: *report the performance of the flight; report on a book.* **2.** To provide (an account) for publication or broadcast: *report the news; report for a radio show.* **3.** To carry back and repeat to another: *reported a message.* **4.** To present oneself: *report for duty.* **5.** To denounce: *report them to the police.*

report card. A report of a student's achievement presented at regular intervals to a parent or guardian.

re•port•er |rĭ **pôr′**tər| *or* |-**pōr′**-| *n.* **1.** A person who reports. **2.** A person who gathers information for news stories that are written or broadcast. **3.** A person who writes down the official account of the proceedings in a courtroom.

re•pose¹ |rĭ **pōz′**| *n.* **1.** Rest or relaxation. **2.** Peace of mind; freedom from anxiety: *seeking security and repose.* **3.** Calmness; tranquillity: *a feeling of repose in the forest.* —*v.* **re•posed, re•pos•ing. 1.** To lay (oneself) down to rest. **2.** To lie at rest; relax or sleep: *workers reposing at the end of day.* **3.** To lie supported by something: *a dish reposing on the table.* [SEE NOTE]

re•pose² |rĭ **pōz′**| *v.* **re•posed, re•pos•ing.** To place (faith, trust, etc.): *They repose their hopes in him.* [SEE NOTE]

re•pos•i•to•ry |rĭ **pŏz′**ĭ tôr′ē| *or* |-tōr′ē| *n., pl.* **re•pos•i•to•ries.** A place where things are placed for safekeeping.

re•pos•sess |rē′pə **zĕs′**| *v.* To retake or regain possession of: *repossess an appliance bought on credit.* —**re′pos•ses′sion** *n.*

rep•re•hend |rĕp′rĭ **hĕnd′**| *v.* To show disapproval of; reprove; censure: *reprehend their actions.* —**rep′re•hen′sion** *n.*

rep•re•hen•si•ble |rĕp′rĭ **hĕn′**sə bəl| *adj.* Deserving rebuke or censure; worthy of blame: *a reprehensible deed.* —**rep′re•hen′si•bil′i•ty** *n.* —**rep′re•hen′si•bly** *adv.*

rep•re•sent |rĕp′rĭ **zĕnt′**| *v.* **1.** To stand for; symbolize: *The Romans used the letter C to represent 100.* **2.** To portray, as in a picture; depict: *a king represented in full regalia.* **3.** To describe (something) as having certain characteristics: *represented a product's value falsely.* **4.** To serve as an example of; typify: *Her feelings represent those of the majority.* **5.** To be the equivalent of; constitute: *The amount you eat plus the amount you drink represents your total intake.* **6.** To act as a spokesman for, especially in a legislative body.

rep•re•sen•ta•tion |rĕp′rĭ zĕn **tā′**shən| *or* |-zən-| *n.* **1.** The act of representing or the condition of being represented. **2.** Something that represents, such as a picture, symbol, etc. **3.** The right or privilege of being represented in a governmental body: *no taxation without representation.* **4.** An account or statement of facts, conditions, or arguments: *improper representations of a product.*

rep•re•sen•ta•tive |rĕp′rĭ **zĕn′**tə tĭv| *n.* **1.** A person or thing serving as an example or type for others of the same class; someone or something that is typical. **2.** A person chosen to act and speak for a group in a given matter. **3. Representative.** In the United States, a member of the House of Representatives or of a state legislature. —*adj.* **1.** Representing a group or class. **2.** Having power granted by a group of persons and answerable to them: *representative government.* **3.** Serving as a typical example.

re•press |rĭ **prĕs′**| *v.* **1.** To keep down or hold back; restrain: *trying to repress his laughter.* **2.** To suppress; quell: *repress an uprising.* **3.** To force (memories, fears, thoughts, etc.) into the subconscious and out of the conscious mind.

re•pres•sion |rĭ **prĕsh′**ən| *n.* **1.** The action of repressing or the condition of being repressed. **2.** The exclusion of painful memories, desires, impulses, fears, etc., from the conscious mind.

re•pres•sive |rĭ **prĕs′**ĭv| *adj.* Of or tending to cause repression: *repressive measures.* —**re•pres′sive•ly** *adv.*

re•prieve |rĭ **prēv′**| *n.* **1.** The postponement of a punishment. **2.** Temporary relief, as from danger. —*v.* **re•prieved, re•priev•ing.** To postpone the punishment of.

rep•ri•mand |**rĕp′**rĭ mănd′| *or* |-mänd′| *n.* A severe scolding or official rebuke. —*v.* To rebuke severely or officially.

re•pri•sal |rĭ **prī′**zəl| *n.* Retaliation for injury or damage inflicted, often by one nation against another.

re•proach |rĭ **prōch′**| *v.* To rebuke severely or sternly; blame. —*n.* **1.** Blame; disapproval: *a term of reproach.* **2.** A rebuke or scolding: *a stern reproach from his teacher.* **3.** A source of shame.

re•proach•ful |rĭ **prōch′**fəl| *adj.* Expressing blame or reproach: *a reproachful glance.* —**re•proach′ful•ly** *adv.*

rep•ro•bate |**rĕp′**rə bāt′| *n.* A wicked, immoral person. —*adj.* Immoral; depraved; corrupt.

re•pro•ba•tion |rĕp′rə **bā′**shən| *n.* Strong disapproval; condemnation.

re•pro•duce |rē′prə **dōōs′**| *or* |-**dyōōs′**| *v.* **-pro•duced, -pro•duc•ing. 1.** To make an image, copy, etc., of: *reproduce a photograph. A phonograph reproduces music.* **2.** To be duplicated or copied in this way: *Black-and-white photographs reproduce more easily than color ones do.* **3.** To generate or give rise to (offspring), as a living thing.

re•pro•duc•tion |rē′prə **dŭk′**shən| *n.* **1.** The act or process of reproducing: *the reproduction of sound.* **2.** Something that is reproduced; a copy: *a reproduction of a painting.* **3.** The process by which living things produce other living things of the same kind: *sexual reproduction.*

re•pro•duc•tive |rē′prə **dŭk′**tĭv| *adj.* **1.** Of reproduction, especially by living things. **2.** Capable of reproducing or tending to reproduce, especially as living things do.

re•proof |rĭ **prōōf′**| *n.* **1.** Blame or censure for a misdeed. **2.** A mild rebuke or scolding.

re•prove |rĭ **prōōv′**| *v.* **re•proved, re•prov•ing.** To rebuke; scold.

rep•tile |**rĕp′**tīl′| *n.* Any of a group of cold-blooded animals that have a backbone and are covered with scales or horny plates, such as a snake, turtle, or dinosaur. [SEE NOTE]

rep•til•i•an |rĕp **tĭl′**ē ən| *or* |-**tĭl′**yən| *adj.* **1.** Of or belonging to reptiles: *reptilian eggs.* **2.** Resembling or typical of a reptile, especially in an unpleasant way: *his cold, reptilian eyes.* —*n.* A reptile.

re•pub•lic |rĭ **pŭb′**lĭk| *n.* A country governed by

repose¹⁻²

Repose¹ *is from Old French* reposer, *from Late Latin* repausāre, *"to rest again":* re-, *"again,"* + pausāre, *"to rest, pause."* **Repose²** *was formed in English from* **re-** + **pose,** *"to put."*

reptile

Reptile *is from Late Latin* reptile, *used in the Latin Bible to mean "a creeping animal," from* repere, *"to creep."*

republic

Republic *is from Latin* rēspublica, *a compound noun meaning "public affairs, the state":* rēs, *"affairs, business,"* + publica, *"public." The Roman idea of the state is effectively summed up by the word* rēspublica; *the Romans regarded government as being "the public concern, the business of the whole community." The Romans were never truly democratic like some of the Greeks, but they strongly believed that it was everyone's duty to serve "the common good, the commonwealth." After a long history their republic was subverted by emperors, but their republican concept survived to be highly influential in modern European and American history.*

the elected representatives of the people. [SEE NOTE on p. 745]

re•pub•li•can |rĭ **pŭb**′lĭ kən| *adj.* **1.** Of, like, or advocating a republic: *a republican form of government.* **2. Republican.** Of or belonging to the Republican Party. —*n.* **1.** A person who advocates a republican form of government. **2. Republican.** A member or a supporter of the Republican Party.

Republican Party. One of the two major political parties of the United States, dating from 1854. [SEE PICTURE]

Republican Party
Symbol of the party

re•pu•di•ate |rĭ **pyōō**′dē āt′| *v.* **re•pu•di•at•ed, re•pu•di•at•ing. 1.** To declare to have no force or validity; renounce; disavow: *repudiate an agreement.* **2.** To reject as untrue; persuasively deny: *repudiate an accusation.* **3.** To reject with disapproval: *The voters repudiated the President's new philosophy of government.* —**re•pu′di•a′tion** *n.* —**re•pu′di•a′tive** *adj.*

re•pug•nance |rĭ **pŭg**′nəns| *n.* Extreme dislike or aversion.

re•pug•nant |rĭ **pŭg**′nənt| *adj.* Arousing extreme disgust or aversion; offensive; repulsive: *a repugnant odor; repugnant tasks.*

re•pulse |rĭ **pŭls**′| *v.* **re•pulsed, re•puls•ing. 1.** To drive back; repel: *repulse the enemy attackers.* **2.** To rebuff or reject firmly, coldly, or abruptly: *She repulsed his efforts to be friendly.* —*n.* **1.** An instance of repelling or driving back. **2.** A firm rejection. [SEE NOTE on p. 744]

re•pul•sion |rĭ **pŭl**′shən| *n.* **1.** The act or process of repulsing or repelling: *the repulsion of a surprise attack.* **2.** A feeling of strong dislike or aversion; revulsion.

re•pul•sive |rĭ **pŭl**′sĭv| *adj.* **1.** Of or tending to cause repulsion: *repulsive forces.* **2.** Arousing a feeling of strong dislike or aversion; disgusting: *a repulsive person; a repulsive odor.*

rep•u•ta•ble |**rĕp**′yə tə bəl| *adj.* Having a good reputation; honorable: *a reputable car dealer.*

rep•u•ta•tion |rĕp′yə **tā**′shən| *n.* **1.** The general esteem in which a person is held by others or by the general public. **2.** Public recognition. *The novel established his reputation as a writer.* **3.** A particular characteristic for which someone or something is noted: *a reputation for honesty.*

re•pute |rĭ **pyōōt**′| *n.* Reputation or esteem: *a man held in high repute by his colleagues.* —*v.* **re•put•ed, re•put•ing.** To think of in a certain way; ascribe a certain fact or characteristic to.

re•put•ed |rĭ **pyōō**′tĭd| *adj.* Supposed, assumed, or thought to be: *the reputed leader of the movement.* —**re•put′ed•ly** *adv.*

re•quest |rĭ **kwĕst**′| *v.* **1.** To ask for: *a letter requesting information.* **2.** To ask (a person or persons) to do something: *I requested him to leave.* —*n.* **1.** The act of asking for something: *Other sizes are available on request.* **2.** Something that is asked for: *We have received numerous requests for extra copies of the article.*

req•ui•em |**rĕk**′wē əm| *or* |**rē**′kwē-| *n.* **1.** A mass sung for a person or persons who have died. **2.** A musical setting for the words of certain sections of such a mass. [SEE NOTE]

requiem
The purpose of a requiem is to pray that the dead may have rest; the word **requiem** *is the first word of a Latin phrase that is said or sung at the service:* Requiem aeternam dona eis, Domine *("Rest eternal give to them, Lord").* Requiem *is from* requiēs, *"rest," which is related to* **quiet**.

re•quire |rĭ **kwīr**′| *v.* **re•quired, re•quir•ing. 1.** To need; demand; call for: *Tightrope walking requires considerable practice.* **2.** To impose an obligation upon: *The regulation requires all students to take at least one year of mathematics.*

re•quire•ment |rĭ **kwīr**′mənt| *n.* **1.** Something that is needed: *A person's daily food requirement.* **2.** Something that is established as a necessary condition to something else.

req•ui•site |**rĕk**′wĭ zĭt| *adj.* Necessary to fulfill a certain requirement or quota: *The requisite number of teachers for a faculty.* —*n.* Something that is essential; a necessity.

req•ui•si•tion |rĕk′wĭ **zĭsh**′ən| *n.* **1.** A formal written request for something that is needed. **2.** A demand made by military authorities for supplies, personnel, shelter, etc. —*v.* To put in a written order for: *requisition new desks.*

re•run |rē **rŭn**′| *v.* **re•ran** |rē **răn**′|, **re•run, re•run•ning. 1.** To run again: *rerun a race.* **2.** To show or exhibit again: *rerun an old motion picture.* —*n.* |**rē**′rŭn′|. **1.** A reshowing of a motion picture or television program. **2.** The picture or program that is reshown.

re•sale |**rē**′sāl′| *or* |rē **sāl**′| *n.* The selling of something one has bought to someone else.

res•cue |**rĕs**′kyōō| *v.* **res•cued, res•cu•ing.** To save from danger, harm, capture, evil, etc.: *rescue a drowning man.* —*n.* An act of rescuing or saving: *A passer-by came to our rescue.* —**modifier:** *rescue work; a rescue ship; a rescue team.* —**res′cu•er** *n.*

re•search |rĭ **sûrch**′| *or* |**rē**′sûrch′| *n.* Systematic study of a given subject, field, or problem: *scientific research; medical research.* —**modifier:** *research work; a research institute.* —*v.* To do research on. —**re•search′er** *n.*

re•sem•blance |rĭ **zĕm**′bləns| *n.* Similarity in appearance; likeness: *He bears a certain resemblance to your brother.*

re•sem•ble |rĭ **zĕm**′bəl| *v.* **re•sem•bled, re•sem•bling.** To have a similarity to; be like.

re•sent |rĭ **zĕnt**′| *v.* To feel angry or bitter about: *resent a remark.*

re•sent•ful |rĭ **zĕnt**′fəl| *adj.* Feeling or showing resentment. —**re•sent′ful•ly** *adv.*

re•sent•ment |rĭ **zĕnt**′mənt| *n.* Bitterness or indignation over something that is thought to be uncalled-for or unfair.

res•er•va•tion |rĕz′ər **vā**′shən| *n.* **1.** An arrangement by which space, as in a hotel or restaurant or on an airplane, is secured in advance. **2.** Something that limits, restricts, or makes less than complete: *He has certain reservations about the proposal.* **3.** A tract of land set apart by the Federal government for a certain purpose: *an Indian reservation.*

re•serve |rĭ **zûrv**′| *v.* **re•served, re•serv•ing. 1.** To hold aside for a particular purpose or for later use: *reserve a tablecloth for special occasions.* **2.** To order or book in advance for a specified time or date: *reserve a table in a restaurant.* **3.** To keep or retain for oneself: *I reserve the right to reply at a later date.* **4.** To put off; postpone: *reserve judgment on a certain matter.* —*n.* **1.** A supply of something available for use when needed: *a fuel reserve.* **2.** The condition of being set aside or available when needed: *funds held in reserve.* **3.** A qualification or reservation. **4.** A tendency to talk little and keep one's feelings to oneself. **5.** A member of a team who plays only as a substitute for another player. **6.** Often **reserves.** The part of a country's armed forces not on active duty but subject to immediate call in the event of an

ă **pat**/ā **pay**/â **care**/ä **father**/ĕ **pet**/ē **be**/ĭ **pit**/ī **pie**/î **fierce**/ŏ **pot**/ō **go**/ô **paw**, **for**/oi **oil**/ŏŏ **book**/ōō **boot**/ou **out**/ŭ **cut**/û **fur**/*th* **the**/th **thin**/hw **which**/zh **vision**/ə **ago**, **item**, **pencil**, **atom**, **circus** emergency. —*modifier:* *a reserve supply of food; a reserve officer.*

re•served |rĭ zûrvd'| *adj.* **1.** Ordered in advance and held for a particular person or persons: *a reserved seat.* **2.** Quiet and withdrawn in manner; keeping one's feelings to oneself. —**re•serv'ed•ly** |rĭ zûr'vĭd lē| *adv.*

re•serv•ist |rĭ zûr'vĭst| *n.* A member of a military reserve.

res•er•voir |rĕz'ər vwär'| *n.* **1.** A natural or artificial lake used as a storage place for water. **2.** A chamber or container used for storing a fluid: *the reservoir of a fountain pen.* **3.** A large supply of something built up over a long period of time: *a reservoir of good will.*

re•side |rĭ zīd'| *v.* **re•sid•ed, re•sid•ing. 1.** To live or dwell; make one's home: *He resides in Boston.* **2.** To lie or be contained: *the spirit of fellowship that resides within us.*

res•i•dence |rĕz'ĭ dəns| *n.* **1.** The house or other building in which a person lives. **2.** The act or fact of residing somewhere: *Chicago is my place of residence. He learned Spanish during his residence in Mexico.* **3.** Residency.

res•i•den•cy |rĕz'ĭ dən sē| *n., pl.* **res•i•den•cies.** The period during which a physician is attached to the staff of a hospital for specialized clinical training.

res•i•dent |rĕz'ĭ dənt| *n.* **1.** A person who makes his home in a particular place. **2.** A physician who is serving his period of residency. —*adj.* **1.** Living in a particular place: *a resident New Yorker.* **2.** Living somewhere in connection with one's work: *a resident physician.*

res•i•den•tial |rĕz'ĭ dĕn'shəl| *adj.* **1.** Containing or suitable for homes: *a residential neighborhood.* **2.** Of or having to do with residence: *a residential requirement for voting.*

re•sid•u•al |rĭ zĭj'o͞o əl| *adj.* Of, characteristic of, or remaining as a residue: *the residual solids left when a liquid evaporates.* —*n.* Something left over, as at the end of a process; a remainder; residue. —**re•sid'u•al•ly** *adv.*

res•i•due |rĕz'ĭ do͞o'| *or* |-dyo͞o'| *n.* The part or fraction left after something is removed, as by means of some process; the remainder.

re•sign |rĭ zīn'| *v.* To give up or quit (a position). [SEE NOTE]

Idiom. **resign (oneself) to.** To submit passively to; accept as inevitable.

res•ig•na•tion |rĕz'ĭg nā'shən| *n.* **1.** The act of giving up, leaving, or retiring from a position: *The commissioner announced his resignation.* **2.** Passive acceptance of or submission to an unpleasant fate: *a tone of resignation in his voice.*

re•signed |rĭ zīnd'| *adj.* Feeling or showing resignation: *a resigned look on his face.* —**re•sign'ed•ly** *adv.*

re•sil•ient |rĭ zĭl'yənt| *adj.* **1.** Springing back to its original shape or position after being stretched, bent, or compressed; elastic. **2.** Snapping back quickly from illness, misfortune, etc. —**re•sil'ience** *n.*

res•in |rĕz'ĭn| *n.* **1.** Any of several clear or translucent yellowish or brownish substances that ooze from certain trees and plants and are used in liquid or hardened form in varnishes, lacquers, and for many other purposes. **2.** Any of various artificial substances that have similar properties and are used in making plastics.

res•in•ous |rĕz'ə nəs| *adj.* Of, containing, or resembling resin: *a resinous substance.*

re•sist |rĭ zĭst'| *v.* **1.** To work against; try to stop; oppose (an enemy, attack, etc.): *resist an attack. The people resisted with all their might.* **2.** To undergo little or no change as a result of the action of; withstand: *a material that resists heat.* **3.** To keep from giving in or yielding to: *resist pressure; resist temptation.* —*n.* A substance used to cover and protect a surface, as against corrosion.

re•sis•tance |rĭ zĭs'təns| *n.* **1.** The act, process, or capability of resisting: *The enemy offered little resistance.* **2.** Any force that tends to oppose or retard motion: *an automobile body shaped to lessen wind resistance.* **3. a.** The opposition that a material body offers to the passage of an electric current resulting from work that the current is made to perform, as, for example, in heating the body. **b.** An electric circuit element that has only resistance; an ideal resistor. **4.** Often **Resistance.** An underground organization leading the struggle for national liberation in a country under military occupation.

re•sis•tant |rĭ zĭs'tənt| *adj.* Capable of resisting: *Formica is resistant to heat and stains.*

re•sis•tor |rĭ zĭs'tər| *n.* An electric circuit element having two terminals between which a given value of resistance appears, used to provide resistance in a circuit.

res•o•lute |rĕz'ə lo͞ot'| *adj.* Having or showing strong will and determination: *a resolute voice.* —**res'o•lute'ly** *adv.* —**res'o•lute'ness** *n.*

res•o•lu•tion |rĕz'ə lo͞o'shən| *n.* **1.** The quality of being resolute; determination: *face the future with courage and resolution.* **2.** A formal statement or expression of opinion adopted by an assembly, legislature, or other organization. **3.** The act of solving or resolving something: *the resolution of a problem.* **4.** A solution or explanation; an answer. **5.** A vow or pledge to do something or refrain from doing something: *a New Year's resolution to stop smoking.* **6. a.** A correct musical progression of a dissonant tone or chord to another, usually consonant, tone or chord. **b.** The tone or chord to which such a dissonant tone or chord passes.

re•solve |rĭ zŏlv'| *v.* **re•solved, re•solv•ing. 1.** To make a firm decision: *He resolved to work harder.* **2.** To state formally in a resolution: *"We here highly resolve that these dead shall not have died in vain"* (Gettysburg Address). **3.** To find a solution to; solve: *resolve a problem; resolve a conflict.* **4.** To change or transform: *The issue resolved itself to a single question.* **5.** To cause (a dissonant tone or chord) to pass to another tone or chord by a correct musical progression. —*n.* **1.** A decision or resolution: *a resolve to try harder.* **2.** Firmness of purpose; resoluteness; determination: *work together with resolve.*

res•o•nance |rĕz'ə nəns| *n.* **1.** The condition or property of being resonant: *the resonance of a speaker's voice.* **2. a.** The increased response of a physical body or system to an oscillating driving force when the force oscillates at a frequency at which the body or system tends to oscillate naturally. **b.** A frequency at which such a body or system tends to oscillate naturally. **c.** A re-

resign

Etymologically, to **resign** *is not "to sign off," although it is related to the word* **sign.** *It is from Latin* resignāre, *"to unseal," hence "to cancel, to annul an agreement":* re-, *"back,"* **un-**[2], + signāre, *"to seal" (see note at* **sign**).

resonance

Resonance is often considered to be a pleasing property in a concert hall. This is true when the resonances, the frequencies at which the air in the hall tends to vibrate, lie so close together that the response of the hall is relatively even for all musical pitches. But when they are not arranged in this way, the resonances of a building cause some tones to sound too loud or for too long, which can be quite annoying.

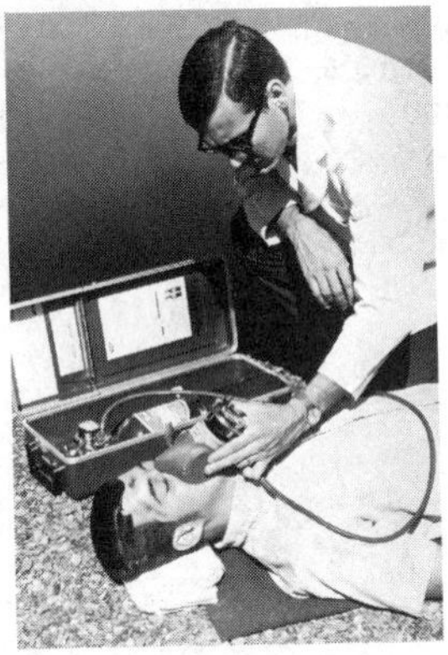

respirator

rest[1-2]

Rest[1] *was Old English* reste *or* ræste, *"relaxation by sleep or quiet."* **Rest[2]** *is from Old French* reste, *"remainder," from* rester, *"to remain"; this is from Latin* restāre, *"to stay back, to be left, to remain":* re-, *"back,"* + stāre, *"to stand."*

ă pat/ā pay/â care/ä father/ĕ pet/ē be/ĭ pit/ī pie/î fierce/ŏ pot/ō go/ô paw, for/oi oil/o͝o book/o͞o boot/ou out/ŭ cut/û fur/*th* the/th thin/hw which/zh vision/ə ago, item, pencil, atom, circus

inforcement or lengthening of sounds, especially musical tones, as a result of resonances in the room or concert hall in which they are produced. [SEE NOTE]

res•o•nant |**rĕz'**ə nənt| *adj.* **1.** Of or showing resonance. **2.** Having a full, pleasing sound: *a deep, resonant voice.* —**res'o•nant•ly** *adv.*

re•sort |rĭ **zôrt'**| *v.* To go or turn for help or as a means of achieving something: *resort to violence.* —*n.* **1.** A place where people go for relaxation or recreation: *a ski resort.* **2.** A person or thing to which one turns for help: *I would ask him only as a last resort.* **3.** The act of turning for help in a certain situation: *raising money without resort to borrowing.* —***modifier:*** *a resort hotel.*

re•sound |rĭ **zound'**| *v.* **1.** To be filled with sound: *The stadium resounded with cheers.* **2.** To make a loud sound: *The music resounded through the hall.*

re•source |rĭ **sôrs'**| *or* |-**sōrs'**| *or* |**rē'**sôrs'| *or* |-sōrs'| *n.* **1.** Something that can be turned to for support or help: *We have exhausted every resource at our disposal.* **2. resources.** Money that is available or on hand; assets: *We pooled our resources and bought a trailer.* **3.** Something that is a source of wealth to a country.

re•source•ful |rĭ **sôrs'**fəl| *or* |-**sōrs'**-| *adj.* Clever and imaginative, especially in finding ways to deal with a difficult situation. —**re•source'ful•ly** *adv.* —**re•source'ful•ness** *n.*

re•spect |rĭ **spĕkt'**| *n.* **1.** A feeling of honor or esteem: *respect for one's elders.* **2.** Regard or consideration: *respect for the law.* **3.** The condition of being regarded with honor or esteem: *He is held in respect by his colleagues.* **4. respects.** Polite expressions of consideration or regard: *pay one's respects to the widow of the deceased.* **5.** A particular aspect or feature: *The two plans differ in one major respect.* —*v.* To have or show respect for: *I respect your opinion even if I do not agree with it.* —**re•spect'ed** *adj.:* *a respected member of the community.*

re•spect•a•ble |rĭ **spĕk'**tə bəl| *adj.* **1.** Proper in behavior, character, or appearance: *respectable people.* **2.** Good enough that one need not feel embarrassed or ashamed: *a respectable showing even though we lost.* —**re•spect'a•bil'i•ty** *n.* —**re•spect'a•bly** *adv.*

re•spect•ful |rĭ **spĕkt'**fəl| *adj.* Showing proper respect: *I replied to his questions in a respectful tone of voice.* —**re•spect'ful•ly** *adv.*

re•spect•ing |rĭ **spĕk'**tĭng| *prep.* With respect to; concerning: *laws respecting personal property.*

re•spec•tive |rĭ **spĕk'**tĭv| *adj.* Pertaining to each of two or more persons or things; particular: *Each delegate to the conference is an expert in his respective field.*

re•spec•tive•ly |rĭ **spĕk'**tĭv lē| *adv.* Each in the order named: *Albany, Augusta, and Atlanta are, respectively, the capitals of New York, Maine, and Georgia.*

res•pi•ra•tion |rĕs'pə **rā'**shən| *n.* **1.** The act or process of inhaling and exhaling; breathing. **2.** A process of metabolism by which a living thing takes in oxygen and oxidizes nutrients to produce energy, usually releasing carbon dioxide and other products.

res•pi•ra•tor |**rĕs'**pə rā'tər| *n.* **1.** A device, usually having a mask that fits over a victim's nose and mouth, for giving artificial respiration. **2.** A filter worn over the mouth or nose, or both, to protect the respiratory system. [SEE PICTURE]

res•pi•ra•to•ry |**rĕs'**pər ə tôr'ē| *or* |-tōr'ē| *or* |rĭ **spīr'**-| *adj.* Of or affecting respiration.

respiratory system. Also **respiratory tract.** The system of air passages through which a living thing breathes, especially, in land vertebrates, the passages beginning with the nose and mouth and leading to the air sacs of the lungs.

re•spire |rĭ **spīr'**| *v.* **re•spired, re•spir•ing. 1.** To inhale and exhale; breathe. **2.** To carry on the metabolic process of respiration.

res•pite |**rĕs'**pĭt| *n.* **1.** A short interval of rest or relief. **2.** A postponement or delay, especially of the carrying out of a death sentence.

re•splen•dent |rĭ **splĕn'**dənt| *adj.* Shining with brilliance and splendor; dazzling: *She was resplendent in her jeweled gown.* —**re•splen'dence** *n.*

re•spond |rĭ **spŏnd'**| *v.* **1.** To make a reply; answer: *Animals respond more readily to a voice they know.* **2.** To act in return or in answer: *respond to a challenge.* **3.** To react in a particular or desired way to a stimulus or action: *The patient failed to respond to treatment.*

re•sponse |rĭ **spŏns'**| *n.* **1.** An answer or reply: *The response to our appeal has been most heartening.* **2.** A reaction, as that of a living thing or mechanism to a stimulus or action.

re•spon•si•bil•i•ty |rĭ spŏn'sə **bĭl'**ĭ tē| *n., pl.* **re•spon•si•bil•i•ties. 1.** The quality or fact of being responsible: *a sense of responsibility. The job carries a lot of responsibility.* **2.** Something that one is responsible for; a duty or obligation.

re•spon•si•ble |rĭ **spŏn'**sə bəl| *adj.* **1.** Liable to blame for anything that happens or goes wrong: *Each person is responsible for his own belongings.* **2.** Having a certain duty or obligation: *The President is responsible for the conduct of foreign affairs.* **3.** Having to account for one's actions; accountable: *a government responsible to the people.* **4.** Being the cause or source of something: *Viruses are responsible for many diseases.* **5.** Dependable; reliable; trustworthy: *a mature and responsible man.* **6.** Involving important duties or obligations: *a responsible job.*

re•spon•sive |rĭ **spŏn'**sĭv| *adj.* **1.** Responding warmly and sympathetically: *a responsive audience.* **2.** Marked by alternation between leader and group: *a responsive reading.* —**re•spon'sive•ly** *adv.* —**re•spon'sive•ness** *n.*

rest[1] |rĕst| *n.* **1.** A period of inactivity, relaxation, or sleep: *The hikers stopped for a brief rest.* **2.** Ease or relaxation resulting from this: *Be sure to get plenty of rest.* **3.** An absence or ending of motion: *The car slowed and came to rest.* **4.** Something that serves as a support: *a footrest.* **5.** Death: *go to one's eternal rest.* **6. a.** A musical symbol indicating that a performer or group of performers is to be silent for a time equal to the length of a given note. **b.** The interval of silence corresponding to such a symbol or a series of such symbols. —***modifier:*** *a rest period; a rest home.* —*v.* **1.** To stop working, relax, lie down, or sleep in order to regain one's strength or vitality: *rest before dinner.* **2.** To allow to cease motion, work, or activity: *rest one's weary feet.* **3.** To place, lay, or lean on something for support: *Rest the suitcase on the ground.* **4.** To lie or lean on a support: *His head rested on the pillow.* **5.** To fall or land: *His gaze rested on her.* **6.** To be, belong, or lie: *The responsibility rests on him.* **7.** To be based: *The whole theory rests on one basic assumption.* **8.** To conclude the presentation of evidence in (a case). ¶*These sound alike* **rest, wrest.** [SEE NOTE on p. 748]

***Idioms.* at rest.** Not moving; stationary. **lay to rest.** To bury.

rest² |rĕst| *n.* **1.** The part that is left over after something has been taken away; the remainder: *pay the rest on credit.* **2.** *(used with a plural verb).* Those people remaining; the others: *He is staying, but the rest are going.* ¶*These sound alike* **rest, wrest.** [SEE NOTE on p. 748]

res•tau•rant |rĕs'tər ənt| *or* |-tə rănt'| *n.* A place where meals are served to the public. [SEE NOTE]

res•tau•ra•teur |rĕs'tər ə tûr'| *n.* The manager or owner of a restaurant.

rest•ful |rĕst'fəl| *adj.* **1.** Offering or full of rest: *a restful day; a restful vacation.* **2.** Having a pleasant or soothing effect: *restful colors.*

res•ti•tu•tion |rĕs'tĭ to͞o'shən| *or* |-tyo͞o'-| *n.* **1.** The act of restoring something to its rightful owner. **2.** The act of making good or compensating for damage, loss, or injury.

rest•ive |rĕs'tĭv| *adj.* **1.** Impatient or restless under restriction, pressure, or delay: *The crowd gradually became restive.* **2.** Hard to handle; unruly; balky: *a restive horse.* **—rest'ive•ly** *adv.*

rest•less |rĕst'lĭs| *adj.* **1.** Without rest or sleep: *a restless night.* **2.** Unable to rest, relax, or be still: *a restless child.* **—rest'less•ly** *adv.* **—rest'less•ness** *n.*

res•to•ra•tion |rĕs'tə rā'shən| *n.* **1. a.** The action of restoring: *The damage was too great for restoration.* **b.** A particular act of restoring: *The restoration of the damaged sculptures was expensive.* **2.** Something restored: *Williamsburg, Virginia, is a restoration.* **3. the Restoration. a.** The return of Charles II to the British throne in 1660. **b.** The period between his return and the Revolution of 1688.

re•store |rĭ stôr'| *or* |-stōr'| *v.* **re•stored, re•stor•ing. 1.** To bring back into existence: *Such stories restore my faith in humanity.* **2.** To bring back to an original condition: *restore an old building. Patient care restored the child to health.* **3.** To bring back to a prior position: *restore an emperor to the throne.* [SEE NOTE]

re•strain |rĭ strān'| *v.* **1.** To hold back by physical force. **2.** To check; suppress; hold back.

re•straint |rĭ strānt'| *n.* **1.** The act of restraining. **2.** The condition of being restrained: *He had to be held in restraint.* **3.** Something that holds back or restrains: *a program of wage restraints.* **4.** Reserve or moderation in actions.

re•strict |rĭ strĭkt'| *v.* To keep within certain limits; confine.

re•strict•ed |rĭ strĭk'tĭd| *adj.* **1.** Kept within certain limits: *a restricted number of students.* **2.** Closed to members of minority groups: *a restricted neighborhood.*

re•stric•tion |rĭ strĭk'shən| *n.* **1.** The act of limiting or restricting: *restriction of immigration.* **2.** Something that limits or restricts: *The students were subjected to severe restrictions.*

re•stric•tive |rĭ strĭk'tĭv| *adj.* **1.** Tending or serving to restrict: *restrictive legislation.* **2.** In grammar, indicating a descriptive word, clause, or phrase that limits the scope of a word or words that it modifies. For example, in the sentence *People who read a great deal have large vocabularies,* the words *who read a great deal* are a restrictive clause.

rest room. A public lavatory.

re•sult |rĭ zŭlt'| *n.* The consequence of a particular action, operation, or course; outcome: *The book is the result of years of hard work.* —*v.* **1.** To come about as a result of something: *Nothing resulted from his efforts.* **2.** To lead to a certain result.

re•sult•ant |rĭ zŭl'tənt| *adj.* Resulting: *war, revolution, and the resultant chaos.*

re•sume |rĭ zo͞om'| *v.* **re•sumed, re•sum•ing. 1.** To begin again or continue after a break. **2.** To assume or take again: *The former prime minister resumed power.* [SEE NOTE]

rés•u•mé |rĕz'o͝o mā'| *or* |rĕz'o͝o mā'| *n.* **1.** A summary: *a brief résumé of the week's events.* **2.** An outline of one's personal history and experience, submitted when applying for a job.

re•sump•tion |rĭ zŭmp'shən| *n.* The act of resuming: *a resumption of diplomatic relations.* [SEE NOTE]

re•sur•gence |rĭ sûr'jəns| *n.* A sudden rise or increase in something: *a resurgence of interest in astrology.* **—re•sur'gent** *adj.*

res•ur•rect |rĕz'ə rĕkt'| *v.* **1.** To bring back to life; raise from the dead. **2.** To bring back into practice, notice, or use: *resurrect an old custom.*

res•ur•rec•tion |rĕz'ə rĕk'shən| *n.* **1.** The act of rising from the dead or returning to life. **2.** The act of bringing back into use; revival: *the resurrection of an ancient religious practice.* **3. the Resurrection.** The rising of Christ from the dead on the third day after his burial.

re•sus•ci•tate |rĭ sŭs'ĭ tāt'| *v.* **re•sus•ci•tat•ed, re•sus•ci•tat•ing.** To return to life or consciousness; revive. **—re•sus'ci•ta'tion** *n.*

re•tail |rē'tāl'| *n.* The sale of commodities to the general public. ***—modifier:*** *a retail store; retail prices.* —*adv.* At a retail price: *The radio costs $20 more retail than wholesale.* —*v.* To sell at a retail price. **—re'tail'er** *n.*

re•tain |rĭ tān'| *v.* **1.** To keep possession of; continue to have: *The new premier retained his post as minister of finance.* **2.** To keep or hold in a particular place, condition, or position: *Certain plants retain moisture.* **3.** To keep in mind; remember: *Be sure to take notes since you can't possibly retain everything he says.* **4.** To hire by the payment of a fee: *retain a lawyer.*

re•tain•er |rĭ tā'nər| *n.* **1.** In medieval times, an attendant who ranked higher than a servant. **2.** The fee paid to engage the services of a lawyer or other professional person.

re•tal•i•ate |rĭ tăl'ē āt'| *v.* **re•tal•i•at•ed, re•tal•i•at•ing.** To reply to or pay back an unfriendly act with a similar one: *retaliate against an enemy attack.* **—re•tal'i•a'tion** *n.* **—re•tal'i•a•to'ry** |rĭ tăl'ē ə tôr'ē| *or* |-tōr'ē| *adj.*

re•tard |rĭ tärd'| *v.* To slow the progress of; delay; hold back.

re•tar•da•tion |rē'tär dā'shən| *n.* **1.** The act or process of retarding: *retardation of growth.* **2. Mental deficiency.**

restore/restaurant

Restore *is from Latin* restaurāre, *"to renew, to rebuild":* re-, *"again,"* + -staurāre, *"to set up." In French* restaurāre *became* restaurer, *which took on the special sense "to restore one's strength by eating"; from this was formed the word* restaurant, *"restoring place." The first* **restaurants** *are supposed to have been opened in Paris in the mid-eighteenth century (before that, only inns and hotels served full meals to the public). An early Parisian restaurateur took as his motto: "Come to me, all you who labor in the stomach, and I will restore you."*

resume/resumption, etc.

The Latin verb sūmere, *"to take hold of," had the abstract noun* sumptiō, *"a taking hold." From* sūmere *were formed four compound verbs that have been borrowed into English:* assūmere, *"to take to oneself, take for granted,"* consūmere, *"to take completely, use up, eat, destroy,"* praesūmere, *"to take before, take something as true before seeing it," and* resūmere, *"to take up again." All four verbs had regular abstract nouns ending in* -sumptiō. *These are the origins, respectively, of English* **assume, consume, presume,** *and* **resume,** *with their corresponding nouns* **assumption, consumption, presumption,** *and* **resumption.**

retriever

re•tard•ed |rĭ tär′dĭd| *adj.* Abnormally slow in mental or emotional development.

retch |rĕch| *v.* To strain or make an effort to vomit; heave.

re•ten•tion |rĭ tĕn′shən| *n.* **1.** The act or process of retaining something: *retention of moisture in the soil.* **2.** The ability to retain or remember things: *remarkable powers of retention.*

re•ten•tive |rĭ tĕn′tĭv| *adj.* Having the ability to retain: *a retentive memory.* —**re•ten′tive•ness** *n.*

ret•i•cent |rĕt′ĭ sənt| *adj.* Hesitant or disinclined to speak out; quiet; reserved: *a reticent child.* —**ret′i•cence** *n.*

ret•i•na |rĕt′n ə| *or* |rĕt′nə| *n., pl.* **ret•i•nas** or **ret•i•nae** |rĕt′n ē′|. A delicate, light-sensitive membrane that lines the inside of the eyeball and is connected to the brain by the optic nerve.

ret•i•nue |rĕt′n o͞o′| *or* |-yo͞o′| *n.* A group of servants or attendants accompanying a person of rank.

re•tire |rĭ tīr′| *v.* **re•tired, re•tir•ing. 1. a.** To give up one's work, business, or career, usually because of advancing age: *retire from baseball.* **b.** To cause or force (a person) to do this: *The company retired him after 30 years of service.* **2.** To withdraw; go away; disappear: *The judge retired to his study.* **3.** To go to bed: *retire for the night.* **4.** To remove from circulation: *retire old dollar bills.* **5.** In baseball, to put out (a batter or batters). —**re•tired′** *adj.: a retired army officer.* —**re•tire′ment** *n.*

re•tir•ing |rĭ tī′rĭng| *adj.* Shy and reserved; seeking to avoid attention or notice: *Deer are shy, retiring animals.*

re•tort |rĭ tôrt′| *v.* To make a quick, clever, or angry reply: *"Over my dead body," Jim retorted.* —*n.* Such a reply.

re•touch |rē tŭch′| *v.* **1.** To make minor changes in, in order to improve; touch up: *retouch a painting.* **2.** To alter (a photographic negative or print), as by removing flaws or unwanted material.

re•trace |rē trās′| *v.* **re•traced, re•trac•ing.** To go back over: *retrace one's steps.*

re•tract |rĭ trăkt′| *v.* **1.** To pull back or in: *The airplane retracted its landing gear.* **2.** To take back; disavow: *He refused to retract his statement.* —**re•tract′a•ble** *adj.* —**re•trac′tion** *n.*

re•treat |rĭ trēt′| *v.* **1.** To fall back or withdraw in the face of an enemy attack: *The soldiers retreated into the hills.* **2.** To retire to a quiet, secluded place. —*n.* **1.** The withdrawal of a military force when endangered by an enemy attack: *a hasty retreat at dawn.* **2.** The signal for such a withdrawal, made on a drum or trumpet. **3.** A bugle call sounded during the lowering of the flag at sunset. **4.** A quiet, secluded place.

re•trench |rĭ trĕnch′| *v.* **1.** To cut down; reduce; curtail: *retrench expenses.* **2.** To reduce or scale down the scope of one's operations.

ret•ri•bu•tion |rĕt′rə byo͞o′shən| *n.* Deserved punishment for evil or wrongdoing.

re•trieve |rĭ trēv′| *v.* **re•trieved, re•triev•ing. 1.** To get back; recover: *retrieved the ball in the end zone.* **2.** To locate (data or information) in a file, library, storage, etc., and make it available for use, especially by means of a computer. **3.** To find and bring back (birds or animals that have been shot), as a hunting dog does.

re•triev•er |rĭ trē′vər| *n.* A dog of a breed trained to find and bring back birds or animals shot by hunters. [See Picture]

retro–. A prefix meaning "back, backward": **retrograde.**

ret•ro•ac•tive |rĕt′rō ăk′tĭv| *adj.* Reverting to a period prior to enactment: *a retroactive pay increase.* —**ret′ro•ac′tive•ly** *adv.*

ret•ro•grade |rĕt′rə grād′| *adj.* Backward or reversed: *retrograde motion; retrograde order.*

ret•ro•rock•et |rĕt′rō rŏk′ĭt| *n.* A rocket engine used to slow, stop, or reverse the motion of an aircraft, spacecraft, missile, or other vehicle.

ret•ro•spect |rĕt′rə spĕkt′| *n.* A review, survey, or contemplation of the past.

ret•ro•spec•tive |rĕt′rə spĕk′tĭv| *adj.* Of, looking back on, or contemplating the past: *a retrospective examination of his career.*

re•turn |rĭ tûrn′| *v.* **1.** To go, come, or send back to a former condition, position, or place: *return home. Spring returned.* **2.** To come, give, or send back, as to a former or rightful owner: *returned her wallet. Return to sender.* **3.** To give back, as in exchange for or response to something: *return his affection; return merchandise.* **4.** To answer; respond: *"I don't care," returned Susan.* **5.** To produce (as interest or profit): *Selling hot dogs returned him about 10 per cent on his investment.* **6.** To deliver (an indictment or verdict). —*n.* **1.** The act of coming, going, bringing, or sending back to a former condition, place, or position: *a return home; the return of winter.* **2.** Something returned. **3.** The profit or interest earned, as on an investment: *a 5 per cent return.* **4.** An official report, list, or set of statistics: *an income-tax return.* **5. returns.** A report on the vote in an election. —***modifier:*** *a return address; a return trip.* —**re•turn′a•ble** *adj.*

re•un•ion |rē yo͞on′yən| *n.* **1.** The act or an example of reuniting: *the reunion of chromosomes.* **2.** A gathering of the members of a group who have been separated: *a yearly family reunion.*

re•u•nite |rē′yo͞o nīt′| *v.* **-u•nit•ed, -u•nit•ing.** To bring or come together.

rev |rĕv|. *Informal. n.* A revolution, as of an engine or motor: *an engine screaming at 7,500 revs a minute.* —*v.* **revved, rev•ving.** To increase the speed of (an engine or motor).

Rev. reverend.

re•vamp |rē vămp′| *v.* To patch up, revise, restore, or reconstruct: *revamp a magazine's layout.* [See Note]

re•veal |rĭ vēl′| *v.* **1.** To make known; disclose: *reveal a secret.* **2.** To bring to view; show: *The anecdote revealed much about his character.*

rev•eil•le |rĕv′ə lē| *n.* The sounding of a bugle early in the morning to awaken persons in a camp or garrison.

rev•el |rĕv′əl| *v.* **rev•eled** or **rev•elled, rev•el•ing** or **rev•el•ling. 1.** To take great pleasure or delight: *He revels in making fun of others.* **2.** To be festive in a riotous way: *The dancers reveled for an entire weekend.* —*n.* A noisy festivity. —**rev′el•er, rev′el•ler** *n.*

rev•e•la•tion |rĕv′ə lā′shən| *n.* **1.** Something revealed, especially something surprising. **2.** The act of revealing. **3.** In theology, a manifestation of divine will or truth. **4. Revelation.** The last book of the New Testament, containing

revamp

Revamp *originally meant "to put a new vamp on a shoe." See* **vamp.**

ă pat/ā pay/â care/ä father/ĕ pet/ ē be/ĭ pit/ī pie/î fierce/ŏ pot/ ō go/ô paw, for/oi oil/o͝o book/ o͞o boot/ou out/ŭ cut/û fur/ *th* the/th thin/hw which/zh vision/ ə ago, item, pencil, atom, circus

symbolic prophecies of the fall of Rome and end of the world.

rev•el•ry |rĕv'əl rē| *n., pl.* **rev•el•ries.** Boisterous merrymaking.

re•venge |rĭ vĕnj'| *v.* **re•venged, re•veng•ing.** To inflict punishment in return for (an injury or insult): *The boys had to revenge their father's death.* —*n.* The act or an example of revenging.

rev•e•nue |rĕv'ə no͞o'| *or* |-nyo͞o'| *n.* **1.** The income of a government collected for payment of public expenses. **2.** Yield from property or investment; income. —*modifier: revenue bureau.*

re•ver•ber•ate |rĭ vûr'bə rāt'| *v.* **re•ver•ber•at•ed, re•ver•ber•at•ing.** To echo back; resound: *The boom of a bell reverberated throughout the town.* —**re•ver'ber•a'tion** *n.*

Re•vere |rĭ vîr'|, **Paul.** 1735–1818. American silversmith and Revolutionary patriot.

re•vere |rĭ vîr'| *v.* **re•vered, re•ver•ing.** To regard with great awe, affection, respect, or devotion. [SEE NOTE]

rev•er•ence |rĕv'ər əns| *n.* **1.** A feeling of awe and respect and often of love. **2.** A bow or curtsy. **3. Reverence.** A title of respect used in speaking to or of a high-ranking clergyman: *his Reverence; your Reverence.*

rev•er•end |rĕv'ər ənd| *adj.* **1.** Worthy of or inspiring reverence: *a reverend man.* **2.** Feeling or showing reverence: *reverend awe.* —*n. Informal.* A cleric or minister. [SEE NOTES]

rev•er•ent |rĕv'ər ənt| *adj.* Feeling or showing reverence: *a reverent hymn.* —**rev'er•ent•ly** *adv.* [SEE NOTE]

rev•er•ie |rĕv'ə rē| *n.* **1.** Abstracted thought; daydreaming: *lost in reverie.* **2.** A daydream.

re•ver•sal |rĭ vûr'səl| *n.* **1.** The act or an example of reversing. **2.** A change for the worse.

re•verse |rĭ vûrs'| *adj.* **1.** Turned backward or over: *in reverse order; the reverse side of the page.* **2.** Causing backward movement: *reverse gear.* —*n.* **1.** The opposite or contrary of something: *the exact reverse of my opinion.* **2.** The back or rear of something: *the reverse of a page.* **3.** A mechanism for moving backward, as a gear in an automobile. **4.** A change for the worse; a setback: *the many reverses in her long career.* —*v.* **re•versed, re•vers•ing. 1.** To turn to or move in the opposite direction or tendency: *reverse one's opinions. The skater has to reverse several times in each figure.* **2.** To turn inside out or upside down: *reverse the page.* **3.** To exchange the positions of: *reverse the order of the numbers.* **4.** To annul (a decision or decree): *The court reversed the decision.* —**re•verse'ly** *adv.* —**re•vers'er** *n.*

***Idiom.* in reverse. 1.** In an opposite manner or direction. **2.** In reverse gear.

re•vers•i•ble |rĭ vûr'sə bəl| *adj.* **1.** Capable of being reversed. **2.** Capable of being worn or used with either side out, often having a different color, pattern, or fabric on the opposite side.

re•ver•sion |rĭ vûr'zhən| *n.* **1.** The act or an example of reverting, as to a former belief, condition, interest, etc. **2.** A turning away or in the opposite direction.

re•vert |rĭ vûrt'| *v.* **1.** To return or go back to a former condition, belief, interest, thought, etc. **2.** In law, to return (an estate) to the former owner or his heirs.

re•view |rĭ vyo͞o'| *v.* **1.** To look over; examine again: *Review Chapter 5.* **2.** To look back on; think over. **3.** To write or give a critical report on (a new book or play, for example). **4.** To inspect formally (a group of soldiers or other military personnel). —**re•view'ing** *adj.: a reviewing stand.* —*n.* **1.** A re-examination or reconsideration. **2.** An inspection or examination. **3.** A period of going over or studying again something covered earlier in school. **4.** A report or essay that discusses something and attempts to judge its worth: *a book review; a review of a concert.* **5.** A formal military inspection. —*modifier: a review lesson.* ¶*These sound alike* **review, revue.** —**re•view'er** *n.*

re•vile |rĭ vīl'| *v.* **re•viled, re•vil•ing.** To denounce with abusive language.

re•vise |rĭ vīz'| *v.* **re•vised, re•vis•ing. 1.** To edit in order to improve or bring up to date: *revise a paragraph.* **2.** To change or modify.

re•vi•sion |rĭ vĭzh'ən| *n.* **1.** The act or process of revising. **2.** Something revised; a new or corrected version.

re•viv•al |rĭ vī'vəl| *n.* **1. a.** The act or process of reviving. **b.** The condition of being revived. **2.** A new presentation of an old motion picture or play. **3.** A renewal of interest in religion. **4.** Also **revival meeting.** A meeting or meetings promoting such a religious renewal and often characterized by emotional preaching and excitement.

re•vive |rĭ vīv'| *v.* **re•vived, re•viv•ing. 1.** To bring back or return to life or consciousness: *revive a drowning boy. The victim revived after a heart massage.* **2.** To bring back or give vigor or strength to (something): *The music revived my spirits. His hopes revived last week.* **3.** To restore or return to use: *Congress revived the rank of full general to honor Grant.* —**re•viv'er** *n.*

re•voke |rĭ vōk'| *v.* **re•voked, re•vok•ing.** To make void, as by reversing or withdrawing; cancel: *revoke an edict; revoke a license.* —**rev'o•ca'tion** |rĕv'ə kā'shən| *n.*

re•volt |rĭ vōlt'| *v.* **1.** To begin or take part in a rebellion against authority, especially state authority. **2.** To fill with disgust; repel. —*n.* An act of rebellion against authority; an uprising.

re•volt•ing |rĭ vōl'tĭng| *adj.* Causing disgust; offensive: *a revolting display of bad manners.*

rev•o•lu•tion |rĕv'ə lo͞o'shən| *n.* **1.** A sudden political overthrow from within a given system. **2.** Any sudden or momentous change: *the industrial revolution.* **3. a.** Movement around a point in a closed path, especially as distinguished from rotation on an axis. **b.** A spinning or rotation about an axis. **c.** A single complete cycle of motion about a point in a closed path.

rev•o•lu•tion•ar•y |rĕv'ə lo͞o'shə nĕr'ē| *adj.* **1.** Of or tending to promote political revolution: *revolutionary groups.* **2.** Characterized by radical change: *a revolutionary new teaching idea.* —*n.* Someone who is engaged in or favors revolution.

Revolutionary War. The **American Revolution.**

rev•o•lu•tion•ist |rĕv'ə lo͞o'shə nĭst| *n.* A revolutionary.

rev•o•lu•tion•ize |rĕv'ə lo͞o'shə nīz'| *v.* **rev•o•lu•tion•ized, rev•o•lu•tion•iz•ing.** To bring about a radical change in; alter drastically.

re•volve |rĭ vŏlv'| *v.* **re•volved, re•volv•ing. 1.** To move in an orbit: *The earth revolves around the*

revere/reverend/reverent

Revere *is from Latin* reverērī, *"to feel deep respect for":* re-, *"again,"* + verērī, *"to respect, to fear."* **Reverend** *and* **reverent** *come from two different parts of* reverērī. *The "gerundive" form of a Latin verb gives the meaning "fit to be," rather like the meaning of English* **-able**; *the gerundive of* reverērī *was* reverendus, *"fit to be revered," which was borrowed as* **reverend.** *The present participle gives the same meaning as English* **-ing**[1]; *the present participle of* reverērī *was* reverent-, *borrowed as* **reverent.**

Reverend

The most proper use of this title is with the *and the full name of the clergyman:* the Reverend Joseph Hames. *In writing,* Reverend *may be abbreviated as* Rev. *Another correct form is* the Reverend Mr. Hames. *Such forms as* Reverend Hames *and the use of* Reverend *as a noun or as a form of direct address* ("Good morning, Reverend") *have long been widespread in the United States and probably still are; but many authorities, including many clergymen, consider these forms improper and unacceptable.*

revolver

rhinoceros
The word **rhinoceros** is from Greek *rhinokeros,* "nose-horned": *rhis, rhin-,* "nose," + *keras,* "horn."

rhododendron
The word **rhododendron** is from Greek *rhododendron,* "rose tree": *rhodon,* "rose," + *dendron,* "tree."

ă pat/ā pay/â care/ä father/ĕ pet/ ē be/ĭ pit/ī pie/î fierce/ŏ pot/ ō go/ô paw, for/oi oil/ŏŏ book/ ōō boot/ou out/ŭ cut/û fur/ *th* the/th thin/hw which/zh vision/ ə ago, item, pencil, atom, circus

sun. **2.** To turn or cause to turn on an axis; rotate. —**re•volv'ing** *adj: a revolving door.*

re•volv•er |rĭ vŏl'vər| *n.* A pistol with a revolving cylinder that places the cartridges one at a time in a position to be fired. [SEE PICTURE]

re•vue |rĭ vyōō'| *n.* A musical show consisting of a series of songs and skits that often have the same theme or idea but are not joined to tell a story. ¶ *These sound alike* **revue, review.**

re•vul•sion |rĭ vŭl'shən| *n.* **1.** A feeling of strong disgust or loathing. **2.** A turning away or withdrawal from something: *revulsion of public opinion from support of the war.*

re•ward |rĭ wôrd'| *n.* **1.** Something given or received in turn for some act, service, or accomplishment. **2.** Money offered for a special service, such as the capture of a criminal. **3.** A satisfying return or result: *Farmers often work for little reward.* —*v.* To give a reward to: *reward her for bravery.* —**re•ward'ing** *adj.: a rewarding experience.*

Rey•kja•vík |rā'kyə vēk'|. The capital of Iceland. Population, 82,000.

RFD, R.F.D. rural free delivery.

Rh The symbol for the element rhodium.

rhap•so•dy |răp'sə dē| *n., pl.* **rhap•so•dies. 1.** Excessively enthusiastic expression of feeling in speech or writing. **2.** A musical composition with a free or irregular form, typically written in a romantic style.

rhe•a |rē'ə| *n.* A South American bird related to and resembling but smaller than the ostrich.

rhe•ni•um |rē'nē əm| *n.* Symbol **Re** One of the elements, a rare dense silvery-white metal with a very high melting point. Atomic number 75; atomic weight 186.2; valences −1, +2, +3, +4, +5, +6, +7; melting point 3,180°C; boiling point 5,627°C.

rhe•o•stat |rē'ə stăt'| *n.* A resistor whose value can be continuously varied between two extremes, used to control the flow of current in an electric circuit.

rhe•sus monkey |rē'səs|. A brownish monkey of India, much used in biological experiments.

rhet•o•ric |rĕt'ə rĭk| *n.* **1.** The study of the elements of writing or public speaking, such as style and content. **2.** Affected or exaggerated writing or speech.

rhe•tor•i•cal |rə tôr'ĭ kəl| *or* |-tŏr'-| *adj.* **1.** Concerned primarily with effect; showy. **2.** Of rhetoric. —**rhe•tor'i•cal•ly** *adv.*

rheum |rōōm| *n.* A thin or watery discharge of mucus from the nose or eyes. ¶ *These sound alike* **rheum, room.**

rheu•mat•ic |rōō măt'ĭk| *adj.* Of or affected with rheumatism. —*n.* A person affected with rheumatism.

rheumatic fever. A severe infectious disease, chiefly of children. Its symptoms include fever and painful inflammation of the joints, and it often causes permanent damage to the heart.

rheu•ma•tism |rōō'mə tĭz'əm| *n.* Any of several diseased conditions that affect the muscles, tendons, bones, joints, or nerves, causing pain and disability.

Rh factor. Any of several antigens present in the red blood cells of most people. Those having these antigens are termed **Rh positive;** those lacking them are termed **Rh negative.**

Rhine |rīn|. A river rising in Switzerland and flowing through Germany and the Netherlands to the North Sea.

rhine•stone |rīn'stōn'| *n.* A colorless artificial gem of glass or paste, cut in imitation of a diamond. —***modifier:*** *rhinestone earrings.*

rhi•no |rī'nō| *n., pl.* **rhi•nos.** A rhinoceros.

rhi•noc•er•os |rī nŏs'ər əs| *n.* A large African or Asian animal with short legs, thick, tough skin, and one or two upright horns on the snout. [SEE PICTURE]

rhi•zoid |rī'zoid| *n.* One of the slender, rootlike strands by means of which a moss, lichen, or similar plant is attached to the soil or rock surface on which it grows.

rhi•zome |rī'zōm'| *n.* A rootlike plant stem that grows under or along the ground and that sends out roots from its lower surface and leaves or stalks from its upper surface.

rho |rō| *n.* The 17th letter of the Greek alphabet, written Ρ, ρ. In English it is represented as *r* or *rh.* ¶ *These sound alike* **rho, roe, row[1], row[2].**

Rhode Island |rōd|. The smallest of the United States, located in New England. Population, 950,000. Capital, Providence. —**Rhode Islander.**

Rho•de•sia |rō dē'zhə|. The former name for **Zimbabwe.** —**Rho•de'sian** *adj. & n.*

rho•di•um |rō'dē əm| *n.* Symbol **Rh** One of the elements, a hard, durable, silvery-white metal. Atomic number 45; atomic weight 102.905; valences +2, +3, +4, +5; melting point 1,966°C; boiling point 3,727°C.

rho•do•den•dron |rō'də dĕn'drən| *n.* A shrub with evergreen leaves and clusters of white, pinkish, or purplish flowers. [SEE PICTURE]

rhom•bus |rŏm'bəs| *n., pl.* **rhom•bus•es** or **rhom•bi** |rŏm'bī'|. A parallelogram that has four equal sides.

Rhone, also **Rhône** |rōn|. A river rising in southwestern Switzerland and flowing through France into the Mediterranean.

rhu•barb |rōō'bärb'| *n.* **1. a.** A plant having large leaves, with long, fleshy reddish or green stalks. **b.** The stalks of this plant, used, when sweetened and cooked, as a dessert, pie filling, etc. **2.** *Slang.* A noisy argument or quarrel.

rhyme |rīm| *n.* **1.** Correspondence or repetition of sounds of two or more words, syllables, or the ends of lines of verse. **2.** A poem having a regular repitition of sounds at the ends of lines. —*v.* **rhymed, rhym•ing. 1.** To correspond in sound: *Hour rhymes with power.* **2.** To make use of or have rhymes: *Not all poetry rhymes.* ¶ *These sound alike* **rhyme, rime.** —**rhym'er** *n.*

rhythm |rĭ*th*'əm| *n.* **1.** A movement, action, or condition that recurs alternately or in regular sequence: *the rhythm of the tides.* **2. a.** A musical pattern formed by a series of notes or beats that are of different lengths and have different stresses. **b.** A particular pattern of this type: *a waltz rhythm.* **c.** The structure of music as seen in terms of the arrangement and interactions of such patterns.

rhyth•mic |rĭ*th*'mĭk| or **rhyth•mi•cal** |rĭ*th*'mĭ-kəl| *adj.* Of or having rhythm. —**rhyth'mi•cal•ly** *adv.*

R.I. Rhode Island.

ri•al |rē ôl'| *or* |-äl'| *n.* The basic unit of money of Iran.

rib |rĭb| *n.* **1. a.** Any of a series of long curved bones, occurring in 12 pairs in human beings, extending from the spine to or toward the breastbone and enclosing the chest cavity. **b.** A similar bone found in most vertebrates. **2.** A curved structural part similar in function to a rib of the body: *a rib of an umbrella.* **3.** A cut of meat containing one or more ribs. **4.** One of the main veins of a leaf. **5.** A raised ridge in woven cloth or knitted material. *—v.* **ribbed, rib•bing. 1.** To support, shape, or provide with a rib or ribs. **2.** *Slang.* To make fun of; tease. **—ribbed'** *adj.: a ribbed fabric.* [SEE PICTURE]

rib•ald |rĭb'əld| *adj.* Of or indulging in vulgar, lewd humor: *a ribald story; a ribald person.* **—rib'ald•ry** *n.*

rib•bon |rĭb'ən| *n.* **1.** A narrow strip or band of fine fabric, such as satin or velvet, used for decorating or tying things. **2. ribbons.** Tattered or ragged strips: *torn to ribbons.* **3.** A strip of cloth treated with ink and wound on a reel for use in a typewriter. **4.** A strip or band of colored cloth worn or displayed as the symbol of a prize, medal, etc.: *win a blue ribbon; a soldier's campaign ribbon.* ***—modifier:*** *a ribbon bow.*

ri•bo•fla•vin |rī'bō flā'vĭn| *n.* **Vitamin** B_2**.**

ri•bo•nu•cle•ic acid |rī'bō no͞o klē'ĭk| *or* |-nyo͞o-|. RNA, a compound found in all living cells.

ri•bo•some |rī'bə sōm'| *n.* A small spherical particle occurring in the cytoplasm of living cells.

rice |rīs| *n.* **1.** A grain-bearing grass much grown in warm regions as a source of food. **2.** The starchy seeds of such a plant. ***—modifier:*** *a rice field; rice pudding.* *—v.* **riced, ric•ing.** To sieve (food) so that it resembles rice.

rich |rĭch| *adj.* **rich•er, rich•est. 1.** Having great wealth: *a rich man; a rich industrial nation.* **2.** Made of rare or costly materials and often with fine craftsmanship: *a rich brocade.* **3.** Abundantly supplied; plentiful: *Milk is rich in protein.* **4. a.** Abundant in natural resources: *rich land.* **b.** Producing abundantly; fertile: *rich soil.* **5.** Yielding much: *a rich harvest.* **6.** Containing a large proportion of tasty, especially fatty, ingredients: *Chocolate is richer than cocoa.* **7.** Pleasing to the senses: *a rich color; a rich voice.* **8.** *Informal.* Satisfyingly funny: *a rich joke.* **—rich'ly** *adv.* **—rich'ness** *n.*

Rich•ard I |rĭch'ərd|. Called "the Lion-Hearted." 1157–1199. King of England (1189–99).

Ri•che•lieu |rĭsh'ə lo͞o'|, **Duc de.** 1585–1642. French cardinal and statesman.

rich•es |rĭch'ĭz| *pl.n.* **1.** Great wealth. **2.** Valuable possessions.

Rich•mond |rĭch'mənd|. The capital of Virginia. Population, 248,000.

Rich•ter scale |rĭk'tər|. A logarithmic scale ranging from 1 to 10, used to express the magnitude or total energy of an earthquake.

rick•ets |rĭk'ĭts| *n.* A disease, found mostly in children and young mammals, that results from a lack of exposure to sunlight and a lack of vitamin D in the diet. It results in defective or deformed growth of the bones.

rick•et•y |rĭk'ĭ tē| *adj.* **rick•et•i•er, rick•et•i•est. 1.** Likely to fall apart or break; shaky: *a rickety old car.* **2.** Of, like, or suffering from rickets.

rick•sha or **rick•shaw** |rĭk'shô'| *n.* A jinriksha.

ric•o•chet |rĭk'ə shā'| *v.* **ric•o•cheted** |rĭk'ə shād'| or **ric•o•chet•ted** |rĭk'ə shĕt'ĭd|, **ric•o•chet•ing** |rĭk'ə shā'ĭng| or **ric•o•chet•ting** |rĭk'ə shĕt'ĭng|. To rebound at least once from a surface or surfaces: *a bullet that struck a rock and ricocheted.* *—n.* An example of such a rebound.

rid |rĭd| *v.* **rid** or **rid•ded, rid•ding.** To free from something objectionable or unwanted.

rid•dance |rĭd'ns| *n.* A removal of or deliverance from something.

rid•den |rĭd'n|. Past participle of **ride.**

rid•dle[1] |rĭd'l| *v.* **rid•dled, rid•dling. 1.** To pierce with numerous holes: *riddle with bullets.* **2.** To permeate thoroughly; debase: *a government riddled with corruption.* *—n.* A coarse sieve. [SEE NOTE]

rid•dle[2] |rĭd'l| *n.* **1.** A question or statement requiring thought to answer or understand. **2.** Anything that is difficult to understand: *It is a riddle to me why she is so upset.* [SEE NOTE]

ride |rīd| *v.* **rode** |rōd|, **rid•den** |rĭd'n|, **rid•ing. 1.** To sit on and control or drive (an animal or machine): *ride a tricycle; cowboys riding on the range.* **2.** To travel or be conveyed in a vehicle: *ride in a car.* **3.** To be supported or carried upon: *surfers riding the waves.* **4.** To lie on or rest on; overlap: *The spring rides on the bar of metal below it.* **5.** To carry a rider or move in a particular manner: *The car rides well.* **6.** To float or move on or as if on water or in or as if in space: *the sun riding high in the sky.* **7.** To take part in by sitting on and controlling a horse: *ride the fourth race.* **8.** To cause to leave, especially on horseback: *ride the thief out of town.* **9.** To allow to continue: *let the problem ride.* **10.** *Informal.* To tease or ridicule. ***—phrasal verbs.*** **ride on.** To depend on: *The outcome rides on her popularity with the voters.* **ride out.** To survive successfully: *ride out the storm.* *—n.* **1.** A journey or trip on an animal, in a vehicle, or by other means. **2.** Any of various structures on or in which people ride for pleasure, as at amusement parks.

Idioms. **ride for a fall.** To court danger or disaster. **ride roughshod over.** To do something with no regard for the well-being of others. **take for a ride.** *Slang.* **1.** To transport to a place and kill (someone). **2.** To deceive or swindle.

rid•er |rī'dər| *n.* **1.** Someone or something that rides. **2.** A clause, usually having little relevance to the main issue, added to a legislative bill.

ridge |rĭj| *n.* **1.** A long, narrow peak or crest of something: *the ridge of a wave; the ridge of a roof.* **2.** A long, narrow formation of raised land; a long hill or chain of mountains. **3.** Any narrow raised strip, as in cloth or on plowed ground. *—v.* **ridged, ridg•ing.** To mark with, form into, or provide with a ridge or ridges.

rid•i•cule |rĭd'ĭ kyo͞ol'| *n.* Words or actions intended to cause laughter at or mocking of someone or something. *—v.* To laugh at; mock.

ri•dic•u•lous |rĭ dĭk'yə ləs| *adj.* Deserving or inspiring ridicule: *a ridiculous idea.* **—ri•dic'u•lous•ly** *adv.* **—ri•dic'u•lous•ness** *n.*

rife |rīf| *adj.* **rif•er, rif•est. 1.** Frequent; widespread: *Rumors of impending disaster were rife throughout the town.* **2.** Abounding; full: *rife with graft and corruption.*

riff•raff |rĭf'răf'| *n.* Disreputable persons.

ri•fle[1] |rī'fəl| *n.* A gun with a long barrel con-

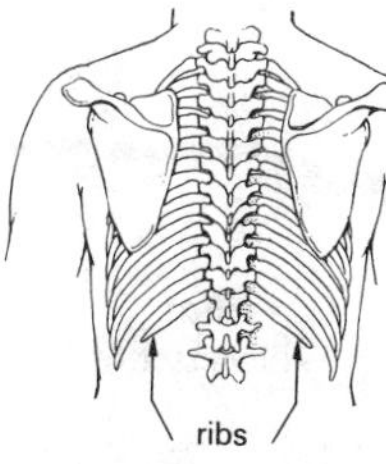

rib
The human ribs viewed from behind

Richter scale
This scale was devised in 1935 by the American seismologist Charles F. Richter. An earthquake whose magnitude is greater than about 4.5 on this scale can cause damage; severe earthquakes have magnitudes greater than 7. The Alaska earthquake of 1964 was 8.4 on the Richter scale, and the famous San Francisco earthquake of 1906 was 7.8.

riddle[1-2]
Riddle[1] *originally meant "to sift something through a sieve" and only recently came to mean "to fill with holes." It comes from Old English* hriddel, *"sieve."* **Riddle[2]** *was Old English* rædels, *"opinion, attempt to answer a riddle," also "the riddle itself."*

rifle¹⁻²
These two words are closely related. **Rifle¹** *originally meant "spiral groove" (rifled guns came in in the eighteenth century); the word is from Old French* rifler, *"to file, to cut grooves in metal."* **Rifle²** *is a separate borrowing from Old French* rifler, *which also meant "to scratch" and "to plunder."*

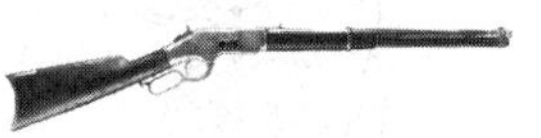

rifle¹
Winchester 66

Right
Sense **2** *of* **right** *goes back to the beginning of the French Revolution. In the French National Assembly of 1789, the nobles chose to sit on the president's right, and the commoners sat on the left. Ever since, the equivalent seating has been traditional in the French Parliament; hence, in most countries, the generally conservative political side has come to be called the right, and the other side the left.*

right

ă pat/ā pay/â care/ä father/ĕ pet/ ē be/ĭ pit/ī pie/î fierce/ŏ pot/ ō go/ô paw, for/oi oil/o͝o book/ o͞o boot/ou out/ŭ cut/û fur/ *th* the/th thin/hw which/zh vision/ ə ago, item, pencil, atom, circus

taining spiral grooves to give the bullet spin, and thus greater accuracy, when fired. [SEE NOTE & PICTURE]

ri•fle² |rī′fəl| *v.* **ri•fled, ri•fling.** To rob; plunder. [SEE NOTE]

rift |rĭft| *n.* **1. a.** A fault, as in a system of rock. **b.** A narrow break or crack in a rock. **c.** Any narrow opening: *a rift in a cloud bank.* **2.** A break in friendly relations. *—v.* To break or cause to break apart; split.

rig |rĭg| *v.* **rigged, rig•ging. 1.** To fit out or equip; prepare: *rig up a temporary harness; rig out the barn for the storm.* **2. a.** To equip (a ship) with sails, shrouds, and yards. **b.** To fit (sails, shrouds, etc.) to masts and yards. **3.** To manipulate dishonestly: *rig a prize fight.* **4.** *Informal.* To dress or clothe: *rigged out in her best dress.* *—n.* **1.** The arrangement of masts, spars, and sails on a sailing vessel: *a fore-and-aft rig.* **2.** Any special equipment or gear: *a drilling rig.* **3.** A vehicle with one or more horses harnessed to it. **4.** *Informal.* An outfit: *a curious rig.*

rig•ging |rĭg′ĭng| *n.* **1.** The system of ropes, chains, and tackle used to support and control the masts, sails, and yards of a sailing vessel. **2.** Gear for a specific task, such as drilling for oil or construction work.

right |rīt| *n.* **1. a.** The side opposite the left: *The number 3 is on the right of the face of a clock.* **b.** The direction of this side: *Read the column from left to right.* **2.** Often **the Right.** The political parties and spokesmen that tend toward conservative or reactionary policies. **3.** That which is morally and ethically proper, fitting, or good: *People must be taught the difference between right and wrong.* **4.** A just moral or legal claim: *women's rights; patent rights.* **5.** A right-handed blow in boxing. **6.** A turn to the right, especially one made in an automobile. *—adj.* **1. a.** Of or located on the side opposite the left: *the right hand; the right side of the street.* **b.** Toward this side: *a right turn.* **2.** Often **Right.** Of the political right; of the right wing: *Rural communities tend to be more right than left.* **3.** Intended to be worn facing outward: *the right side of the dress.* **4.** In accordance with fact, reason, or truth; correct: *the right answer.* **5.** Morally correct or justifiable: *the right thing to do.* **6.** Advantageous, desirable, or favorable: *in the right place at the right time.* **7.** Suitable, fitting, or proper: *just right for the part.* *—adv.* **1.** To or on the right: *turning right.* **2.** In a straight line; directly: *came right by the door.* **3.** In a correct manner; properly: *doing it right; working right.* **4.** Exactly; just: *right where he was standing.* **5.** Immediately: *right after breakfast; right then.* **6.** Very: *the Right Reverend Mr. Smith.* **7.** —Used as an intensive: *Keep right on going.* *—v.* **1.** To put into, restore to, or regain an upright or proper position: *She righted the kayak. The car rolled over twice and then righted.* **2.** To make reparation for: *right a wrong.* ¶*These sound alike* **right, rite, write.** **—right′ness** *n.* [SEE NOTE & PICTURE]

right angle. An angle formed by two perpendicular rays or line segments; an angle of 90 degrees.

right•eous |rī′chəs| *adj.* Morally right; just: *a righteous cause; a righteous person.* **—right′eous•ly** *adv.* **—right′eous•ness** *n.*

right field. 1. In baseball, the part of the outfield that is to the right as viewed from home plate. **2.** The position played by the right fielder. *—modifier:* **(right-field):** *the right-field line.*

right fielder. The baseball player who defends right field.

right•ful |rīt′fəl| *adj.* **1.** Right; just: *a rightful position of honor.* **2.** Having a just, proper, or legal claim: *the car's rightful owner.* **3.** Owned by a just or proper claim: *a rightful share of the money.* **—right′ful•ly** *adv.* **—right′ful•ness** *n.*

right-hand |rīt′hănd′| *adj.* **1.** Located on the right: *the right-hand margin.* **2.** Directed toward the right side: *a right-hand turn.* **3.** Of or done with the right hand: *a right-hand throw.* **4.** Helpful; reliable: *her right-hand man.*

right-hand•ed |rīt′hăn′dĭd| *adj.* **1.** Using the right hand more skillfully than the left: *a right-handed woman.* **2.** Done with the right hand: *a right-handed throw.* **3.** Made to be used by the right hand: *a right-handed glove.* **4.** Turning or spiraling from left to right; clockwise: *a screw with a right-handed thread.* *—adv.* With the right hand: *bat right-handed.* **—right′-hand′ed•ly** *adv.*

right•ist |rī′tĭst| *n.* A political conservative or reactionary. *—modifier: rightist political views.*

right•ly |rīt′lē| *adv.* **1.** In a right or proper manner: *act rightly.* **2.** With honesty; justly: *Rightly or wrongly, I think he should be punished.* **3.** *Informal.* Really: *I don't rightly know.*

right on. *interj. Slang.* An expression used to indicate encouragement, support, etc.

right triangle. A triangle that contains a right angle.

right wing. The conservative elements or groups within a political sphere; the right. *—modifier:* **(right-wing):** *a right-wing party.*

rig•id |rĭj′ĭd| *adj.* **1.** Not changing shape or bending; stiff; inflexible: *a rigid iron frame.* **2.** Harsh and exacting; rigorous: *a rigid examination.* **3.** Strict; undeviating: *a rigid social structure.* **—rig′id•ly** *adv.* **—rig′id•ness** *n.*

ri•gid•i•ty |rĭ jĭd′ĭ tē| *n., pl.* **ri•gid•i•ties. 1.** The condition or quality of being rigid; stiffness; inflexibility. **2.** An example of being rigid.

rig•ma•role |rĭg′mə rōl′| *n.* **1.** Confused and rambling speech; nonsense. **2.** A complicated and petty set of procedures.

rig•or |rĭg′ər| *n.* **1.** Strictness; severity: *the rigor with which she pursued her goals.* **2.** A harsh or trying condition or circumstance; hardship.

rig•or•ous |rĭg′ər əs| *adj.* **1.** Full of rigors; harsh: *the rigorous physical training of the astronauts.* **2.** Precisely accurate; strict: *a rigorous examination of policy.* **—rig′or•ous•ly** *adv.*

rile |rīl| *v.* **riled, ril•ing.** To anger or irritate; vex.

rill |rĭl| *n.* **1.** A small brook. **2.** Any of various straight depressions in the surface of the moon.

rim |rĭm| *n.* **1.** The border, edge, or margin of something: *the rim of the cup.* **2.** The outer part of a wheel around which the tire is fitted. *—v.* **rimmed, rim•ming. 1.** To furnish with a rim; put a rim around; border. **2.** To circle the rim of (a basket, hole, cup, etc.): *The ball rimmed the basket several times before falling in.*

rime¹ |rīm| *n.* A frost or coating of grains of ice, as on grass or trees; hoarfrost. *—v.* **rimed, rim•ing.** To cover with or as if with rime. ¶*These sound alike* **rime, rhyme.**

rime² |rīm| *n.* & *v.* **rimed, rim•ing.** A form of the word **rhyme.**

rind |rīnd| *n.* A tough outer covering, skin, or coating, as of certain fruits, such as a melon or lemon, or of some cheeses.

ring¹ |rĭng| *n.* **1. a.** A circle with a vacant center: *a ring of fire; a smoke ring. Hold hands and form a ring.* **b.** Anything circular meant to carry, encircle, or hold something: *a napkin ring. Draw a ring around the correct answer.* **c.** Any circular part, marking, etc. **2.** A small circular band, often of precious metal, worn on a finger. **3.** An enclosed, usually circular, area in which exhibitions, sports, or contests take place: *the circus ring.* **4. a.** A rectangular arena, set off by ropes, in which boxing matches are held. **b. the ring.** Boxing. **5.** A group of persons acting privately or illegally for their own gain: *a ring of thieves.* **6.** A group of atoms bound together chemically in an arrangement that can be represented as a closed geometric figure: *a benzene ring.* —*v.* **1.** To surround with a ring; encircle: *Let's ring the potato patch with clover.* **2.** To ornament or fit with a ring or rings: *The raccoon's tail is ringed around.* **3.** To hem in (cattle or other animals) by riding in a circle around them. ¶*These sound alike* **ring, wring.** [SEE NOTE]

ring² |rĭng| *v.* **rang** |răng|, **rung** |rŭng|, **ring•ing. 1.** To give forth or cause to give forth a clear piercing sound, as that of a bell when struck: *The doorbell rang. Ring the bell.* **2.** To sound a bell in order to summon someone. **3.** To hear a persistent buzzing or humming: *ears ringing from the blast.* **4.** To be filled with; resound: *The whole world rings with stories of your wisdom.* **5.** To appear to be; seem: *That story rings true.* **6.** To telephone: *Ring him up before breakfast.* —***phrasal verbs.* ring for.** To summon: *ring for the servant.* **ring up.** To record: *ring up a sale.* —*n.* **1.** The sound made by a bell or other metallic object. **2.** Any loud sound that is continued or repeated: *the ring of the whistling wind.* **3.** A telephone call. **4.** A suggestion of a particular quality: *Her words have the ring of poetry.* ¶*These sound alike* **ring, wring.** [SEE NOTE]

ring•let |**rĭng**′lĭt| *n.* A long curl of hair.

ring•side |**rĭng**′sīd′| *n.* A place providing a close view of a spectacle, especially the area immediately outside the ring at a prize fight.

ring•worm |**rĭng**′wûrm′| *n.* A contagious skin disease caused by a fungus and resulting in ring-shaped, scaly, itching patches on the skin.

rink |rĭngk| *n.* **1.** An area surfaced with smooth ice for skating. **2.** A smooth floor suited for roller-skating. [SEE NOTE]

rinse |rĭns| *v.* **rinsed, rins•ing. 1.** To wash lightly with water: *Rinse the dishes before putting them in the dishwasher.* **2.** To remove soap, dirt, etc., from with water or another solution: *Rinse out your mouth.* —*n.* **1.** The act or an example of rinsing. **2.** The water or other solution used in rinsing. **3.** A cosmetic solution used in conditioning or coloring the hair.

Ri•o de Ja•nei•ro |rē′ō dē jə **nâr**′ō| *or* |zhə-**nâr**′ō|. A major city and former capital of Brazil. Population, 5,517,000.

Ri•o de la Pla•ta |rē′ō də lə **plä**′tə|. An estuary between Argentina and Uruguay.

Ri•o Grande |rē′ō **grănd**′|. A river rising in southern Colorado and forming the entire boundary between Texas and Mexico.

ri•ot |**rī**′ət| *n.* **1.** A wild disturbance created by a large number of people. **2.** In law, a violent disturbance of the peace by three or more persons assembled for a common purpose. **3.** A profuse display, as of colors. **4.** *Slang.* Someone or something extremely funny. —*v.* **1.** To take part in a riot. **2.** To indulge in unrestrained and boisterous merrymaking. —**ri′ot•er** *n.*

***Idioms.* read (someone) the riot act.** To reprimand harshly. **run riot. 1.** To move or act wildly. **2.** To grow luxuriantly or abundantly.

ri•ot•ous |**rī**′ə təs| *adj.* **1.** Of or taking part in a riot: *riotous mobs.* **2.** Boisterous or unrestrained: *riotous laughter.* —**ri′ot•ous•ly** *adv.*

rip¹ |rĭp| *v.* **ripped, rip•ping. 1.** To tear open or split apart: *The cat's claws ripped the curtain. The sleeve ripped along the seam.* **2.** To remove by pulling or tearing roughly: *She ripped out the seams in the dress.* **3.** To split or saw (wood) along its grain. —***phrasal verb.* rip into.** To attack vehemently. **rip off.** *Slang.* **1.** To steal from; rob: *Shoplifters ripped off the store.* **2.** To steal: *rip off merchandise.* **3.** To exploit or swindle. —*n.* **1.** A torn or split place: *Sew up the rip.* **2.** The act of ripping: *With a rip, she tore the rag in two.* [SEE NOTE]

rip² |rĭp| *n.* A stretch of rough water in a river, channel, or estuary. [SEE NOTE]

rip•cord |**rĭp**′kôrd′| *n.* A cord pulled to release a parachute from its pack.

ripe |rīp| *adj.* **rip•er, rip•est. 1.** Fully grown and developed: *ripe peaches; ripe grain; ripe seeds.* **2.** Aged and ready for use: *a ripe cheese.* **3.** Advanced in years: *the ripe age of 85.* **4.** Fully prepared; ready: *a team ripe for its first victory.* **5.** Thoroughly matured; seasoned: *ripe judgment.* —**ripe′ness** *n.*

rip•en |**rī**′pən| *v.* To become or make ripe.

rip-off |**rĭp**′ôf′| *or* |-ŏf′| *n. Slang.* **1.** A theft. **2.** A thief. **3.** An act of exploitation.

rip•ple |**rĭp**′əl| *n.* **1.** A small wave or wavelike ridge, such as one formed on the surface of water when it is disturbed. **2.** A wavelike motion; undulation: *the ripple of the smooth muscles as the horse passed by.* **3.** A faint, vibrating sound: *a ripple of laughter in the audience.* **4.** A small rapid in a river. —*v.* **rip•pled, rip•pling.** To form or cause to form ripples: *The velvet curtain rippled in the wind. A breeze rippled the prairie grass.* —**rip′pling** *adj.: rippling water; rippling muscles.*

rip-roar•ing |**rĭp**′rôr′ĭng| *or* |-rōr′-| *adj. Informal.* Full of noise and excitement; boisterous.

rip•saw |**rĭp**′sô′| *n.* A saw with coarse teeth, used for cutting wood along the grain.

rise |rīz| *v.* **rose** |rōz|, **ris•en** |**rĭz**′ən|, **ris•ing. 1.** To move from a lower to a higher position; go up; ascend: *Hot air rises. The kite rose quickly.* **2.** To get up from a sitting or lying position; stand up. **3.** To exert oneself to deal with a matter: *The boy was willing to rise to the challenge of an adventure.* **4.** To get out of bed. **5.** To increase to a higher surface level or elevation: *The Mississippi rises every spring.* **6.** To increase in number, amount, price, or value: *The temperature that day rose to 101°F. Membership is rising.* **7.** To increase in intensity, force, or speed: *Nationalistic feeling was rising. The wind has risen.*

ring¹⁻²

Ring¹ *was Old English* hring. **Ring²** *was Old English* hringan. *They are not related.*

rink

Rink *was originally a Scottish word meaning "area marked out for a game," hence especially "area of ice cleared for the game of curling or for skating." It was borrowed from Old French* renc, *"line, row, rank," originally "a place marked out for a meeting"; this in turn is from Frankish* hring-, *"circle, ring."*

rip¹⁻²

Rip¹ *is probably from Flemish* rippen, *"to strip off roughly."* **Rip²** *is of obscure origin.*

ritzy
The word **ritzy** *comes from the various celebrated hotels called* Ritz, *some of which have long been at the highest level of opulent elegance; perhaps the leading examples are the* Hotel Ritz *in Paris, the* Ritz Hotel *in London, and the* Ritz-Carlton Hotel *in New York. They were founded by the Swiss hotel owner César* Ritz *(1850–1918).*

roadrunner

ă pat/ā pay/â care/ä father/ĕ pet/ē be/ĭ pit/ī pie/î fierce/ŏ pot/ō go/ô paw, for/oi oil/ŏŏ book/ōō boot/ou out/ŭ cut/û fur/*th* the/th thin/hw which/zh vision/ə ago, item, pencil, atom, circus

8. To increase in pitch or volume: *The sound of the subway beneath them rose and faded.* **9.** To advance in status, rank, or condition: *He wants very much to rise in the world.* **10.** To slope or extend upward: *Mt. McKinley rises to 20,320 feet.* **11.** To become visible above the horizon: *The sun rises a little later each morning in the fall.* **12.** To come out of the sea, the earth, or another enclosure; emerge: *Whales must rise periodically to take in air.* **13.** To appear or become felt out of a depth or inner place: *A terrible image suddenly rose out of his subconscious mind.* **14.** To come back to life: *The phoenix is said to rise from its own ashes.* **15.** To come into existence; spring up: *Many streams rise in the snow-capped Andes.* **16.** To be erected: *Hideous office buildings are rising all around us.* **17.** To puff up; expand: *Bread dough rises.* **18.** To vanish; dissipate: *The fog rose quickly.* —**ris'ing** *adj.*: *rising steam; a rising population; a rising young executive.* —*n.* **1.** An act of rising; upward movement. **2.** An increase in surface level or height: *the slow rise of the water as the tide comes in.* **3.** An increase in number, amount, value, pitch, intensity, etc.: *a rise in prices.* **4.** An improvement in status, rank, or condition: *her rise to stardom.* **5.** An origin; beginning: *the rise of a river.* **6.** A gently sloping hill.

***Idiom.* give rise to.** To be the cause or occasion of; lead to: *Shipbuilding in colonial times gave rise to other industries.*

ris•er |rī'zər| *n.* **1.** A person who rises, especially from sleep in the morning: *a late riser.* **2.** The vertical part of a stair step.

risk |rĭsk| *n.* **1.** The possibility of suffering harm or loss; danger. **2.** A situation, factor, or course of action that exposes one to harm or loss. **3.** A person or thing in reference to a chance of loss: *A man who pays his bills is a good credit risk.* —*v.* **1.** To expose to a chance of harm or loss; hazard: *risked her life.* **2.** To incur the possibility of; subject oneself to the chance of: *risking an accident.*

risk•y |rĭs'kē| *adj.* **risk•i•er, risk•i•est.** Involving a risk; dangerous. —**risk'i•ness** *n.*

ris•qué |rĭ skā'| *adj.* Bordering on indelicacy or indecency: *risqué stories about his wild youth.*

rite |rīt| *n.* **1.** Often **rites.** A ceremony or other formal or solemn procedure: *the burial rite; performed the marriage rites.* **2.** The form prescribed by custom or law for conducting a religious ceremony: *introducing new features into the rite of confirmation.* **3.** Often **Rite.** A branch of the Christian church distinguished by its own forms of worship: *Catholics of the Latin Rite.* ¶*These sound alike* **rite, right, write.**

rit•u•al |rĭch'ōō əl| *n.* **1.** The form or order of events followed during a religious or other ceremony. **2.** The group of ceremonies used by a church, religion, tribe, fraternal organization, etc.: *Hindu ritual; Masonic ritual.* **3.** Any procedure faithfully and regularly followed: *An exercise period was part of her morning ritual.* —*adj.* Of or in accordance with rituals: *ritual dances.* —**rit'u•al•ly** *adv.*

ritz•y |rĭt'sē| *adj.* **ritz•i•er, ritz•i•est.** *Slang.* Fashionable; fancy: *ritzy hotels.* [SEE NOTE]

ri•val |rī'vəl| *n.* **1.** Someone who competes with or tries to outdo another; a competitor. **2.** Someone or something that equals or almost equals another; a match: *a performance without rival.* —*adj.* Being a rival or rivals; competing: *rival nations.* —*v.* **ri•valed** or **ri•valled, ri•val•ing** or **ri•val•ling. 1.** To compete with: *When he ran for reelection, no one presumed to rival him.* **2.** To be the equal of; match in excellence: *a woman whose talents rival her beauty.*

ri•val•ry |rī'vəl rē| *n., pl.* **ri•val•ries.** The effort of striving to equal or outdo another; competition.

riv•er |rĭv'ər| *n.* **1.** A large natural stream of water that flows into an ocean, lake, etc., usually receiving water from smaller streams that flow into it. **2.** A stream or flow of liquid resembling a river. —***modifier:*** *a river valley; a river barge.*

river basin. The land area drained by a river and its tributaries.

riv•et |rĭv'ĭt| *n.* A metal bolt or pin with a head on one end, used to join metal plates or other objects by being set through a hole in each piece and having the headless end hammered or compressed to form another head. —*v.* **1.** To fasten with a rivet: *rivet leather straps onto the ends of a trunk.* **2.** To fix rigidly in place: *He stood riveted to the spot.* **3.** To attract and hold unwaveringly: *a knock that riveted our attention on the door.*

Riv•i•er•a |rĭv'ē âr'ə|. A resort area along the Mediterranean Sea in France and Italy.

riv•u•let |rĭv'yə lĭt| *n.* A small stream; brook.

Ri•yadh |rē yäd'|. The capital of Saudi Arabia. Population, 400,000.

ri•yal |rē ôl'| *or* |-äl'| *n.* The basic unit of money of Qatar, Saudi Arabia, and Yemen.

Rn The symbol for the element radon.

RNA A nucleic acid having a very complicated structure, found in the nucleus, cytoplasm, and ribosomes of all living cells and functioning mainly in the synthesis of proteins; ribonucleic acid.

roach |rōch| *n.* A cockroach.

road |rōd| *n.* **1.** An open way for the passage of vehicles, persons, and animals. **2.** Any path or course: *the road to enlightenment.* **3.** A railroad. **4. roads.** An offshore anchorage area for ships; a roadstead: *ships lying in the roads.* —***modifier:*** *road signs.* ¶*These sound alike* **road, rode.**

***Idiom.* on the road. 1.** On tour. **2.** Wandering or traveling, as a salesman or a vagabond.

road•block |rōd'blŏk'| *n.* An obstruction in a road, especially a barricade.

road•run•ner |rōd'rŭn'ər| *n.* A long-tailed, swift-running bird of southwestern North America, having brownish, streaked feathers and a crested head. [SEE PICTURE]

road•stead |rōd'stĕd'| *n.* An offshore anchorage area for ships.

roam |rōm| *v.* To travel over or through (an area) without a fixed goal; wander: *At night the coyotes roam the forest, howling for food. She loved to roam about a strange city.* —**roam'er** *n.*

roan |rōn| *adj.* Brownish or blackish and thickly sprinkled with white or gray hairs: *a roan horse.* —*n.* **1.** The coloring of a roan horse or other animal. **2.** A roan horse or other animal.

roar |rôr| *or* |rōr| *n.* **1.** A loud, deep sound such as that made by a lion or certain other large animals. **2.** A loud, deep cry of rage or anger. **3.** Any loud, deep sound or noise: *the roar of a rocket engine.* —*v.* **1.** To make a loud, deep sound like that of a lion, tiger, etc. **2.** To make or produce a loud, deep sound or noise: *The engines roared. The crowd roared.* **3.** To move with or as if with such a noise: *The train roared into the station.* **4.** To express with such a noise: *We roared our approval.* —**roar'ing** *adj.*: *a roaring fire.*

roast |rōst| *v.* **1.** To cook with dry heat, as in an oven or in hot ashes. **2.** To dry or brown by heating: *they roasted coffee beans.* —**roast'ed** *adj.*: *roasted pigeons; roasted peanuts.* —*n.* **1.** A cut of meat for roasting. **2.** Something roasted. —***modifier:*** *roast beef; roast lamb.*

roast•er |rō'stər| *n.* **1.** A pan or other utensil for roasting. **2.** A chicken or other animal suitable for roasting.

rob |rŏb| *v.* **robbed, rob•bing. 1.** To take property or valuables from (a person or place) unlawfully and by force. **2.** To take (property or valuables) unlawfully; steal: *rob money from a safe.* **3.** To deprive harmfully or unfairly: *billboards that rob the countryside of its beauty.* —**rob'ber** *n.*

rob•ber•y |rŏb'ə rē| *n., pl.* **rob•ber•ies.** The act or crime of unlawfully taking the property of another by force.

robe |rōb| *n.* **1.** A long, loose, flowing outer garment. **2.** Often **robes.** A long, loose garment worn over other clothes on formal occasions: *a judge's robe.* **3.** A bathrobe or dressing gown. **4.** A blanket or covering, especially one for the lap and legs: *a lap robe.* —*v.* **robed, rob•ing.** To dress in a robe or robes.

rob•in |rŏb'ĭn| *n.* **1.** A North American songbird with a rust-red breast and a dark gray back. **2.** A small European bird with an orange breast and a brown back. [SEE NOTE & PICTURE]

Rob•in Hood |rŏb'ĭn hood'|. A legendary English outlaw of the 12th century, whose followers robbed from the rich to give to the poor.

ro•bot |rō'bət| *or* |-bŏt'| *n.* **1.** A machine having the appearance of a human being and the ability to perform human tasks or to imitate human actions. **2.** A person who works or follows orders mechanically. **3.** A machine that operates automatically or by remote control. [SEE NOTE]

ro•bust |rō bŭst'| *or* |rō'bŭst'| *adj.* Full of health and strength; vigorous: *a robust breed of Yankee sea captains.*

roc |rŏk| *n.* A legendary bird of prey of enormous size, capable of carrying off elephants in its talons. ¶ *These sound alike* **roc, rock.**

rock¹ |rŏk| *n.* **1. a.** Any relatively hard naturally occurring material that is of mineral origin. **b.** A fairly small piece of such material; a stone. **c.** A large mass of such material, as a cliff or peak. **2.** Any naturally formed mineral matter that makes up a significant part of the earth's crust. **3.** Someone or something that is very firm, stable, or dependable. —***modifier:*** *a rock formation.* ¶ *These sound alike* **rock, roc.** [SEE NOTE]

Idiom. **on the rocks. 1.** About to fail or come to ruin. **2.** Served without water and over ice cubes: *a whiskey on the rocks.*

rock² |rŏk| *v.* **1. a.** To move back and forth or from side to side in a rhythmic motion: *A breeze rocked the hammock. The boat rocked in the waves.* **b.** To move back and forth gently and soothingly, as in a cradle or chair: *She rocked the baby to sleep. Grandpa rocked thoughtfully on the porch.* **2.** To shake violently, as from a shock or blow: *The earthquake rocked nearby villages. The house rocked from the explosion.* **3.** To stun; shock: *a scandal that rocked the industry.* —*n.* **1.** An act of rocking. **2.** A rhythmic, swaying motion. **3. Rock 'n' roll.** —***modifier:*** *rock music.* ¶ *These sound alike* **rock, roc.** [SEE NOTE]

Idiom. **rock the boat.** *Slang.* To disrupt the plans or progress of one's group.

rock-and-roll |rŏk'ən rōl'| *n.* A form of the phrase **rock 'n' roll.**

rock crystal. Transparent quartz, especially when colorless.

rock•er |rŏk'ər| *n.* **1.** Someone or something that rocks. **2.** A **rocking chair. 3.** A **rocking horse. 4.** One of the two curved pieces on which a cradle, rocking chair, etc., sways from side to side. **5.** A machine part, especially a pivoted lever, that has a rocking motion.

Idiom. **off (one's) rocker.** *Slang.* Out of one's mind; crazy.

rock•et |rŏk'ĭt| *n.* **1. a.** Any device propelled by a force or thrust that is developed by ejecting matter, especially a high-velocity stream of gas produced by burning fuel with oxygen or an oxidizer carried in the device. **b.** An engine that produces a thrust in this way. **2.** A weapon consisting of an explosive charge or other warhead and propelled by a small rocket engine. **3.** A firework that is shot up into the sky. —***modifier:*** *rocket fuel.* —*v.* **1.** To travel in or by means of a rocket: *rocketing to the moon.* **2.** To move with great speed: *a train that went rocketing by.* **3.** To transport or propel by rocket: *rocketing a satellite into orbit.*

rock•et•ry |rŏk'ĭ trē| *n.* The science and technology of designing, building, and flying rockets.

Rock•ies |rŏk'ēz|. The **Rocky Mountains.**

rocking chair. A chair mounted on rockers.

rocking horse. A toy horse large enough for a child to ride, mounted on rockers or springs.

rock 'n' roll. A form of popular music characterized by a strongly accented beat and combining elements of blues and certain types of folk music.

rock-ribbed |rŏk'rĭbd'| *adj.* **1.** Rocky. **2.** Stern and unyielding.

rock salt. Common salt, mainly sodium chloride, occurring in large solid masses.

rock•y |rŏk'ē| *adj.* **rock•i•er, rock•i•est. 1.** Consisting of or full of rocks: *a rocky cliff; rocky soil.* **2.** Full of obstacles or difficulties: *a rocky career.*

Rocky Mountains. The major mountain system of North America, extending from Alaska to Mexico.

Rocky Mountain spotted fever. A severe infectious disease having symptoms that include muscle pains, high fever, and skin eruptions. It is caused by microorganisms and transmitted by the bite of infected ticks.

ro•co•co |rə kō'kō| *or* |rō'kə kō'| *n.* Often **Rococo.** The florid and ornate style of art, architecture, furniture, and music that prevailed in Europe from about 1730 to 1775. —*adj.* Of or in the style of rococo: *a rococo painting.*

rod |rŏd| *n.* **1.** A slender, stiff, straight piece of metal, wood, or other material; a stick or bar: *a steel curtain rod; a fishing rod.* **2.** A branch or a stick used to punish people by whipping or thrashing. **3.** Punishment by whipping or thrashing: *studied his lessons under the threat of*

robin

The European robin *(above)* was originally called *Robin redbreast* (*Robin* being simply a use of the given name *Robin*). This very small bird does not exist in America; the English settlers transferred the name to the much larger American robin *(below)* because of its similar marking.

robot

The word **robot** *was invented by the Czech author Karel Čapek (1890–1938) in his play called* R.U.R. *(standing for* Rossum's Universal Robots*); he took the word from Czech* robota, *"forced labor, drudgery." It is perhaps significant that although no practical, humanlike robot has ever yet been produced, science-fiction writers often picture robots as eventually rebelling and attacking human beings.*

rock¹·²

Rock¹ *is from Old French* roque *or* roche, *"stone."* **Rock²** *was Old English* roccian, *"to sway to and fro."*

rodent
Rodent *is from Latin* rōdens, rōdent-, *"gnawing," the present participle of* rōdere, *"to gnaw."*

roe[1-2]
Roe[1] *is from Middle Dutch* roge, *"fish eggs."* **Roe**[2] *was Old English* rā, *originally meaning "speckled deer."*

roller coaster

ă pat/ā pay/â care/ä father/ĕ pet/ ē be/ĭ pit/ī pie/î fierce/ŏ pot/ ō go/ô paw, for/oi oil/ŏŏ book/ ōō boot/ou out/ŭ cut/û fur/ *th* the/th thin/hw which/zh vision/ ə ago, item, pencil, atom, circus

the rod. **4.** A measuring stick. **5.** A unit of length equal to 16.5 feet. **6.** Any of the elongated cells in the retina of the eye that are sensitive to dim light and incapable of distinguishing colors. **7.** *Slang.* A pistol.

rode |rōd|. Past tense of **ride.** ¶*These sound alike* **rode, road.**

ro•dent |**rōd'**nt| *n.* Any of several related animals, such as a mouse, rat, squirrel, or beaver, having large front teeth used for gnawing. [SEE NOTE]

ro•de•o |**rō'**dē ō'| *or* |rō **dā'**ō| *n., pl.* **ro•de•os.** A public show in which cowboys parade, display horsemanship, and compete in riding bucking broncos, roping calves, etc.

roe[1] |rō| *n.* The eggs of a fish, often together with the membrane of the ovary in which they are held. ¶*These sound alike* **roe, rho, row**[1], **row**[2]. [SEE NOTE]

roe[2] |rō| *n.* Often **roe deer.** A small deer of Europe and Asia, having short, branched antlers. ¶*These sound alike* **roe, rho, row**[1], **row**[2]. [SEE NOTE]

roe•buck |**rō'**bŭk'| *n.* A male roe deer.

roent•gen |**rĕnt'**gən| *or* |**rŭnt'**-| *n.* An obsolete unit used to measure the intensity of exposure to x-rays, gamma rays, and similar ionizing radiation.

Rog•er, also **rog•er** |**rŏj'**ər| *interj.* A word used in radio communications to indicate message received.

rogue |rōg| *n.* **1.** A person who tricks or cheats others; a scoundrel; rascal. **2.** A mischievous person; a scamp. **3.** An animal, especially an elephant, that lives by itself rather than with its herd and that has become wild and dangerous.

ro•guish |**rō'**gĭsh| *adj.* **1.** Dishonest; unprincipled. **2.** Playfully teasing; mischievous. —**ro'•guish•ly** *adv.*

roil |roil| *v.* **1.** To make (a liquid) cloudy by stirring up sediment. **2.** To disturb; vex.

role |rōl| *n.* **1.** A character played by an actor in a dramatic performance; a part. **2.** The usual or proper function of a person, thing, etc.: *happy in the role of spectator; disagreeing about the role of government.* ¶*These sound alike* **role, roll.**

roll |rōl| *v.* **1. a.** To move or travel along a surface while rotating and remaining in contact with the surface: *He watched helplessly as the coin rolled across the sidewalk and through the grating.* **b.** To push or keep in such rotating motion: *I found a huge truck tire and rolled it home.* **2.** To move along on wheels, on rollers, or in a wheeled vehicle: *The car rolled to a stop. Roll the wheelbarrow to the tool shed.* **3. a.** To turn on or as if on an axis: *He rolled over onto his side sleepily.* **b.** To turn over and over: *Pigs like to roll in mud to keep cool.* **4.** To rotate in the eye sockets: *She has a way of rolling her eyes to express impatience.* **5.** To wrap or wind (something) round and round upon itself or over something else: *roll up a scroll. She rolled up her hair on curlers.* **6.** To flatten or shape (a substance) by or as if by passing a roller over it: *rolling dough for the pie crust.* **7.** To move with steady or increasing momentum: *A thick fog was rolling in from the ocean.* **8.** To pass steadily; go by smoothly: *The years rolled by.* **9.** To sway or cause to sway from side to side: *The little sailboat rolled and pitched in the storm.* **10.** To make or send forth a prolonged, deep sound: *The clouds rolled with thunder.* **11.** To beat (a drum) with a rapid series of strokes. **12.** To pronounce with a trill: *Scottish people roll their "r's."* —*n.* **1.** A rolling movement or a particular act of rolling: *watched the roll of the golf ball toward the cup.* **2. a.** A tilt or sway to the side: *With a roll to his left he evaded the punch.* **b.** A tilting or swaying motion: *the comforting roll of the ship beneath him.* **3.** A gentle rise and fall in a surface: *the roll of the plains.* **4.** Anything rolled up in the form of a cylinder or tube: *a roll of cloth.* **5.** A long piece of paper suitable for rolling up; a scroll. **6. a.** A list, especially of the names of the members of a group: *The roll is called before a council meeting begins.* **b.** Attendance: *The teacher took roll.* **c.** Often **rolls.** An official register. **7. a.** A small, soft, rounded portion of bread. **b.** Any portion of food shaped like a tube with a filling: *an egg roll.* **8.** A deep rumble: *a roll of thunder.* **9.** A continuous or apparently continuous sound made by beating a drum rapidly. ¶*These sound alike* **roll, role.**

Idioms. **roll in. 1.** To arrive in large numbers; pour in: *Contributions are rolling in.* **2.** *Informal.* To enjoy ample amounts of; abound in: *rolling in money.* **roll up.** To acquire; amass: *rolled up a huge stamp collection over the years.*

roll call. The procedure of reading aloud a list of names to determine who is present.

roll•er |**rō'**lər| *n.* **1.** A small wheel, as on a roller skate, or ball, as a caster. **2.** A cylinder around which something is wound: *a window-shade roller.* **3.** A small cylinder, as of wire mesh, upon which hair is wound to produce a soft curl or wave. **4.** Any of various cylinders used to flatten, crush, or squeeze things. **5.** A cylinder for applying paint, ink, etc., onto a surface. **6.** A large, heavy wave that breaks along a coastline.

roller coaster. An elevated railway in an amusement park, with steep inclines and sharp turns. [SEE PICTURE]

roller skate. A skate with four small wheels, worn for skating on pavement and hard floors. It may be a boot on wheels or a separate metal frame that is fastened to the sole of a shoe.

rol•ler-skate |**rō'**lər skāt'| *v.* **-skat•ed, -skat•ing.** To skate on roller skates. —**roller skater.**

rol•lick•ing |**rŏl'**ĭ kĭng| *adj.* High-spirited and full of fun; boisterous: *a rollicking cowboy song.*

rolling mill. 1. A factory in which metal is rolled into sheets, bars, or other forms. **2.** A machine in which metal is rolled in this way.

rolling pin. A cylinder, often of wood, with a handle at each end, used for rolling out dough.

ro•ly-po•ly |**rō'**lē **pō'**lē| *adj.* Short and plump; roundish in shape: *Baby chicks are so roly-poly that their necks and tails barely show.* —*n., pl.* **ro•ly-po•lies.** A roly-poly creature.

Rom. 1. Roman. **2.** Romance (language).

ro•maine |rō **mān'**| *n.* A type of lettuce with long, crisp leaves forming a narrow head.

ro•man, also **Ro•man** |**rō'**mən| *n.* The most common style of type, characterized by upright letters. This definition is printed in roman. —*adj.* Printed in roman.

Ro•man |**rō'**mən| *adj.* **1.** Of Rome and its people, especially ancient Rome. **2.** Latin: *the Roman language; the Roman alphabet.* **3.** Of the

Roman Catholic Church. *—n.* **1.** A native or inhabitant of Rome, especially ancient Rome. **2.** Latin.

Roman Catholic. **1.** A member of the Roman Catholic Church. **2.** Of the Roman Catholic Church.

Roman Catholic Church. The Christian church that is organized in a hierarchical structure of bishops and priests with the pope in Rome at its head.

Roman Catholicism. The faith and doctrines of the Roman Catholic Church.

ro•mance |rō **măns′**| *or* |**rō′**măns| *n.* **1. a.** A long verse or prose story about the adventures of heroes, often with exotic settings and extraordinary events: *the medieval romance of King Arthur.* **b.** The class of literature composed of such stories: *writers of historical romance.* **2.** A quality that suggests the adventure and heroic deeds found in such stories: *an appealing air of romance about the old castle.* **3.** A spirit or quality favorable to love: *Candlelight adds romance to a dinner for two.* **4.** A love affair. **5.** A fanciful notion or explanation. *—v.* |rō **măns′**| **ro•manced, ro•manc•ing.** **1.** To invent fanciful stories. **2.** *Informal.* To carry on a love affair or courtship with (someone).

Romance languages. A group of languages that developed from Vulgar Latin, the principal ones being French, Italian, Portuguese, Rumanian, and Spanish.

Roman Empire. The empire of the ancient Romans, which was founded in 27 B.C. and spread to include most of Europe, northern Africa, and Asia Minor. It lasted until A.D. 395, when it split into eastern and western divisions and went into decline.

Ro•man•esque |rō′mə **nĕsk′**| *adj.* Of or belonging to a style of architecture that prevailed in Europe from the 9th to the 12th century. *—n.* The Romanesque style of architecture.

Ro•ma•ni•a |rō **mā′**nē ə| *or* |**-mān′**yə|. A form of the word **Rumania.**

Ro•ma•ni•an |rō **mā′**nē ən| *or* |**-mān′**yən| *n. & adj.* A form of the word **Rumanian.**

Roman numeral. Any of the numerals formed with the characters I, V, X, L, C, D, and M in the system of numeration used by the ancient Romans. [SEE PICTURE]

ro•man•tic |rō **măn′**tĭk| *adj.* **1.** Of or characteristic of the stories of romance: *a romantic hero.* **2.** Full of the quality or spirit of romance; suggesting adventure, heroism, or love: *the romantic occupation of lumbering; a soft romantic light.* **3.** Inclined to dream of adventure, heroism, or love. **4.** Of love or a love affair: *a romantic involvement.* **5.** Of romanticism in the arts or literature: *a romantic composer; romantic dramas.* *—n.* **1.** A romantic person. **2.** A romanticist. **—ro•man′ti•cal•ly** *adv.*

ro•man•ti•cism |rō **măn′**tĭ sĭz′əm| *n.* **1.** An artistic and intellectual movement that originated in Europe in the late 18th century. It stressed the importance of strong emotion, a rich and exotic imagination, freedom from classical correctness in art forms, and rebellion against social conventions. **2.** The spirit and attitudes characteristic of this movement. **—ro•man′ti•cist** *n.*

Rom•a•ny |**rŏm′**ə nē| *or* |**rō′**mə-| *n., pl.* **Rom•a•ny** or **Rom•a•nies.** **1.** A Gypsy. **2.** The language of the Gypsies; Gypsy. *—adj.* Of the Gypsies or their language.

Rome |rōm|. **1.** The capital of Italy. Population, 2,800,000. **2.** The ancient Roman kingdom, republic, or empire.

Ro•me•o |**rō′**mē ō|. The hero and lover of Juliet in Shakespeare's *Romeo and Juliet.*

romp |rŏmp| *v.* To race about playfully; frolic: *dogs romping in a vacant lot.* *—n.* Lively, high-spirited play. **—romp′er** *n.*

romp•ers |**rŏm′**pərz| *pl.n.* A child's loose-fitting one-piece play suit with legs like short bloomers.

ron•do |**rŏn′**dō| *or* |rŏn **dō′**| *n., pl.* **ron•dos.** A musical composition in which a refrain occurs at least three times in its original key between contrasting themes.

rood |ro͞od| *n.* **1.** A cross or crucifix. **2.** A measure of land area equal to ¼ acre. ¶*These sound alike* **rood, rude.**

roof |ro͞of| *or* |ro͝of| *n.* **1.** The outside top covering of a building. **2.** The top covering of anything: *the roof of a car.* **3.** The upper part of the mouth. *—v.* To cover with a roof. **—roofed′** *adj.: a roofed porch.*

roof•ing |**ro͞o′**fĭng| *or* |**ro͝of′**ĭng| *n.* Material used in building a roof. **—modifier:** *roofing tiles.*

rook[1] |ro͝ok| *n.* A crowlike European bird that roosts and nests in large colonies. *—v. Informal.* To cheat; swindle: *The sly crook rooked Aunt Jenny of a hundred dollars.* [SEE NOTE]

rook[2] |ro͝ok| *n.* A chess piece that can move horizontally or vertically across any number of unoccupied squares. [SEE NOTE]

rook•er•y |**ro͝ok′**ə rē| *n., pl.* **rook•er•ies.** **1.** A place where rooks roost or nest. **2.** A place where certain other birds or animals, such as penguins or seals, gather to breed.

rook•ie |**ro͝ok′**ē| *n.* **1.** A player in his first year, as in major-league baseball or football. **2.** *Informal.* A beginner; novice. **—modifier:** *a rookie infielder.*

room |ro͞om| *or* |ro͝om| *n.* **1.** Space: *This desk takes up too much room.* **2. a.** An area of a building set off by walls or partitions. **b.** The people present in a room: *The whole room laughed.* **3. rooms.** Living quarters. **4.** The capacity to receive, accept, or allow something: *no room for error.* *—v.* To occupy a rented room as a lodger: *rooming with a private family.* ¶*These sound alike* **room, rheum.**

room•er |**ro͞o′**mər| *or* |**ro͝om′**ər| *n.* A person who rents a room; a lodger. ¶*These sound alike* **roomer, rumor.**

rooming house. A house where lodgers can rent rooms.

room•mate |**ro͞om′**māt′| *or* |**ro͝om′**-| *n.* A person with whom one shares a room or apartment.

room•y |**ro͞o′**mē| *or* |**ro͝om′**ē| *adj.* **room•i•er, room•i•est.** Having plenty of room; spacious: *roomy closets; roomy boots.* **—room′i•ness** *n.*

Roo•se•velt |**rō′**zə vĕlt′| *or* |-vəlt| *or* |**ro͞o′**-|. **1. Theodore.** 1858–1919. Twenty-sixth President of the United States (1901–09). **2. Franklin Delano.** 1882–1945. Thirty-second President of the United States (1933–45); died in office.

roost |ro͞ost| *n.* **1.** A branch, rod, or similar resting place on which birds perch or settle for the night. **2.** A place where birds perch or settle

I	1
II	2
III	3
IV	4
V	5
VI	6
VII	7
VIII	8
IX	9
X	10
XI	11
XII	12
XIII	13
XIV	14
XV	15
XVI	16
XVII	17
XVIII	18
XIX	19
XX	20
XXI	21
XXIX	29
XXX	30
XL	40
XLVIII	48
IL	49
L	50
LX	60
XC	90
XCVIII	98
IC	99
C	100
CI	101
CC	200
D	500
DC	600
CM	900
M	1,000
MDCLXVI	1666
MCMLXX	1970
MCMLXXII	1972

Roman numeral

rook[1-2]

Rook[1] *was Old English* hrōc. **Rook**[2] *is ultimately from Persian* rukh.

root[1-2-3]
Root[1] *was Old English* rōt. **Root**[2] *was Old English* wrōtan. *The two are not related, but* **root**[2] *may have been helped to lose its original* w- *by its resemblance to* **root**[1]. **Root**[3] *is of obscure origin.*

rose[1]
Above: Wild rose
Below: Cultivated rose

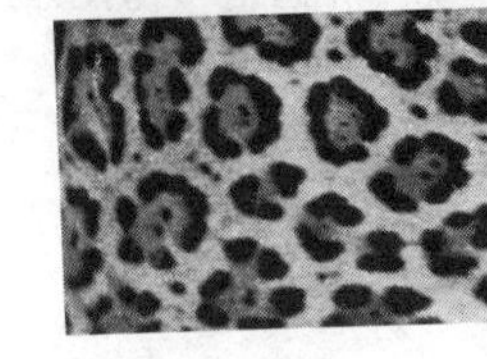

rosette
Above: Mullein leaves
Below: Leopard's fur

ă pat/ā pay/â care/ä father/ĕ pet/ ē be/ĭ pit/ī pie/î fierce/ŏ pot/ ō go/ô paw, for/oi oil/ŏŏ book/ ōō boot/ou out/ŭ cut/û fur/ *th* the/th thin/hw which/zh vision/ ə ago, item, pencil, atom, circus

for the night. —*v.* To perch, rest, or settle for the night as a bird does.

roost•er |rōō′stər| *n.* A full-grown male chicken.

root[1] |rōōt| *or* |rŏŏt| *n.* **1.** The often branching part of a plant that usually grows down into the ground and that absorbs water and minerals from the soil, stores food, and keeps the plant securely in place. **2.** A usually underground plant part similar to a root, as a tuber or rhizome. **3.** The part of an organ or body structure, as a hair or tooth, that is embedded in other tissue. **4.** The bottom or supporting part of anything; base. **5.** A source; origin: *superstitions that have their roots in ancient history.* **6.** The essential part; core; heart: *the root of the matter.* **7. roots.** Relationships and feelings of loyalty that make one belong to a place, group, tradition, etc.; ties: *We've lived here too short a time to have any roots.* **8.** A word or word element from which other words are formed, as by adding affixes. **9. a.** A number that when used as a factor in multiplication a given number of times produces a specified product. For example, since $2 \times 2 \times 2 \times 2 = 16$, 2 is a fourth root of 16. **b.** A number that changes an equation to an identity if it is substituted for a variable in that equation; a solution. —***modifier:*** *root tips; root words.* —*v.* **1.** To send forth or start the growth of a root or roots: *Carrot tops will root in water. Root the plant cuttings in damp sand.* **2.** To plant or fix in place by or as if by roots: *Our determination not to be afraid rooted us to the ground.* **3.** To pull up or remove by or as if by the roots: *rooting out tree stumps with a tractor.* —**root′ed** *adj.: a deeply rooted prejudice.* ¶*These sound alike* **root, route.** —**root′less** *adj.* [SEE NOTE]

***Idiom.* take root. 1.** to send forth roots and begin to grow. **2.** To become firmly fixed.

root[2] |rōōt| *or* |rŏŏt| *v.* **1.** To dig or dig up with the snout or nose: *pigs rooting in the mud; rooting peanuts from the ground.* **2.** To rummage for something: *rooting in his desk drawer for an eraser.* ¶*These sound alike* **root, route.** —**root′er** *n.* [SEE NOTE]

root[3] |rōōt| *or* |rŏŏt| *v.* To give encouragement by or as if by cheering: *rooting for the home team.* ¶*These sound alike* **root, route.** —**root′er** *nn.* [SEE NOTE]

root beer. A carbonated soft drink made from extracts of certain plant roots.

root•stock |rōōt′stŏk′| *or* |rŏŏt′-| *n.* A rootlike plant stem; a rhizome.

rope |rōp| *n.* **1. a.** A heavy cord made of twisted strands of fiber. **b.** A heavy, strong cord made of some other material: *wire rope.* **2. a.** A lasso or lariat. **b.** A noose for hanging a person. **3.** A braided or twisted length, as of hair: *made a rope of the horse's tail.* **4.** A string of things attached or entwined together: *a rope of onions.* **5. ropes.** *Informal.* The techniques and procedures involved in a certain task or job: *learning the ropes.* —*v.* **roped, rop•ing. 1.** To tie or fasten with a rope. **2.** To catch with a throw of a lasso: *rope a calf.* **3.** To enclose or mark (an area) with ropes: *roped off the playing field to keep the crowd away.* —***phrasal verb.* rope in.** *Informal.* To deceive; take in: *swindlers who rope in tourists.*

Roque•fort cheese |rōk′fərt|. A tangy French cheese containing a blue mold.

ro•sa•ry |rō′zə rē| *n., pl.* **ro•sa•ries. 1.** A series of prayers. **2.** A string of beads on which prayers may be counted off while they are being said.

rose[1] |rōz| *n.* **1. a.** Any of several usually prickly shrubs or vines with showy, often very fragrant flowers. **b.** The flower of such a plant, often red or pink in color but also white or yellow. **2.** A deep pink. —***modifier:*** *rose petals.* —*adj.* Deep pink. [SEE PICTURE]

rose[2] |rōz|. Past tense of **rise.**

ro•se•ate |rō′zē ĭt| *or* |-āt′| *adj.* Rose-colored.

Ro•seau |rō zō′|. The capital of Dominica. Population, 10,000.

rose•bud |rōz′bŭd′| *n.* The bud of a rose.

rose•bush |rōz′bŏŏsh′| *n.* A shrub or vine that bears roses.

rose fever *n.* A type of hay faver that occurs in spring or early summer.

rose•mar•y |rōz′mâr′ē| *n.* **1.** A shrub with small, spicy-smelling, grayish-green leaves. **2.** The leaves of this plant, used as seasoning in cooking.

ro•sette |rō zĕt′| *n.* **1.** An ornament or badge made of ribbon or silk gathered and shaped to resemble a rose. **2.** Something shaped like a rose, as a rounded cluster of leaves or the clusters of spots on a leopard's fur. [SEE PICTURE]

rose•wood |rōz′wŏŏd′| *n.* **1.** The hard, often fragrant wood of any of several tropical trees. It has dark or reddish markings and is used for furniture and other fine woodwork. **2.** A tree having such wood.

Rosh Ha•sha•nah, also **Rosh Ha•sha•na** |rŏsh hə shä′nə| *or* |rōsh′|. The Jewish New Year, celebrated in September or October.

ros•in |rŏz′ĭn| *n.* A translucent yellowish or brownish substance obtained from the sap of pine trees. It is used to prevent slipping on the bows of violins and other stringed instruments and on dancers' shoes; it is also used as an ingredient in varnish, solder, and other products. —*v.* To rub or coat with rosin.

ros•ter |rŏs′tər| *n.* **1.** A list of names or other items. **2.** A list of the names of personnel available for duty: *a team's roster.*

ros•trum |rŏs′trəm| *n.* A dais, platform, or similar raised place for public speaking.

ros•y |rō′zē| *adj.* **ros•i•er, ros•i•est. 1.** Having a reddish or deep pink color: *round, rosy cheeks; rosy sunset clouds.* **2.** Bright and cheerful; optimistic: *The future looks rosy.* —**ros′i•ly** *adv.* —**ros′i•ness** *n.*

rot |rŏt| *v.* **rot•ted, rot•ting. 1.** To spoil or decay by the breaking down of plant or animal substances: *Meat may rot if it is not refrigerated. Disease and bad weather had rotted the grain crop.* **2.** To fall or come apart from decay: *The roof of the old house had rotted away.* —*n.* **1.** The process of rotting or the result of being rotted; decay. **2.** A destructive plant disease caused by fungi, bacteria, etc. **3.** *Informal.* Foolish or pointless talk, writing, etc.; nonsense.

ro•ta•ry |rō′tə rē| *adj.* Of, causing, or characterized by rotation: *rotary motion; a rotary water sprinkler.* —*n., pl.* **ro•ta•ries. 1.** A device or machine part that rotates. **2.** A **traffic circle.**

ro•tate |rō′tāt′| *v.* **ro•tat•ed, ro•tat•ing. 1.** To turn or spin on an axis; undergo or cause to undergo rotation. **2.** To proceed in sequence from one task or position to another in a recurring order: *After* *every inning, each player rotates to a new position.* **3.** To vary (crops) so that a different one is planted in a field each year.

ro•ta•tion |rō tā'shən| *n.* **1. a.** A motion in which the path of each point in the moving object is a circle or an arc of a circle with the center of all the circles the same or lying on the same straight line; spin: *the rotation of the earth.* **b.** A complete turning about as a result of such motion. **2.** Passage from one person, task, or position to another in a recurring order: *the rotation of duties in a military unit.* **3.** Variation of the crops planted in a field to keep the soil from being depleted.

ROTC, R.O.T.C. Reserve Officers' Training Corps.

rote |rōt| *n.* **1.** A process of memorizing by repetition, without full understanding: *She learned the French song by rote.* **2.** Mechanical routine. —***modifier:*** *rote learning.* ¶*These sound alike* **rote, wrote.**

ro•ti•fer |rō'tə fər| *n.* A very small water animal having at the front end a wheellike ring of tiny hairs, or cilia, with which it moves and takes in food.

ro•tis•se•rie |rō tĭs'ə rē| *n.* A broiler with a rotating spit for roasting meat. [SEE PICTURE]

ro•tor |rō'tər| *n.* **1.** A rotating part of a machine or device such as an electric motor. **2.** An assembly of airfoils that rotates, as in a helicopter.

rot•ten |rŏt'n| *adj.* **rot•ten•er, rot•ten•est. 1.** Decayed or decomposed: *rotten wood; rotten meat.* **2.** Having a foul odor that results from or suggests the presence of rot. **3. a.** Not honest, honorable, or decent; corrupt. **b.** Mean; nasty: *a rotten thing to do.* **4.** *Informal.* Very bad; terrible: *rotten weather; rotten luck.* —**rot'ten•ly** *adv.* —**rot'ten•ness** *n.*

Rot•ter•dam |rŏt'ər dăm'|. A city in the Netherlands. Population, 700,000.

ro•tund |rō tŭnd'| *adj.* **1.** Rounded in shape or figure; plump. **2.** Full and sonorous: *a rotund voice.* —**ro•tun'di•ty** *n.* —**ro•tund'ly** *adv.*

ro•tun•da |rō tŭn'də| *n.* **1.** A circular building or hall, especially one with a dome. **2.** A large room with a high ceiling.

rou•ble |ro͞o'bəl| *n.* The basic unit of money of the Soviet Union.

rouge |ro͞ozh| *n.* **1.** A pink or red cosmetic for coloring the cheeks or lips. **2.** A fine reddish powder, chiefly an oxide of iron, used in polishing metal and glass. —*v.* **rouged, roug•ing.** To color with rouge.

rough |rŭf| *adj.* **rough•er, rough•est. 1. a.** Having an irregular surface; not smooth or even: *a rough, bumpy road.* **b.** Coarse to the touch: *rough wool.* **c.** Harsh to the ear: *the rough, reedy sound of bagpipes.* **2.** Not finely made or fitted; crude: *rough, homespun clothing.* **3.** Not finished, refined, or perfected: *a rough gem.* **4.** Not gentle, restrained, or careful: *a rough push.* **5.** Rude; uncivil: *rough manners.* **6.** Ready to give and take blows; disposed to fight or use force: *a rough and tough lawman.* **7.** Marked by vigorous physical exertion or competition: *Rugby is a rough team game something like football.* **8.** Stormy: *rough weather ahead.* **9.** *Informal.* Difficult to endure or do; taxing: *the roughest test we ever took.* **10.** Not precise; approximate: *rough measurements.* **11.** Not complete or fully detailed; tentative: *a rough draft.* —*v.* **1.** To make rough; roughen. **2.** To treat (an opponent) with unnecessary physical violence, especially in football: *penalized for roughing the passer.* —***phrasal verbs.*** **rough in.** To build or install without performing the final or finishing operations: *rough in a fireplace.* **rough up. 1.** To damage or injure; harm: *The car was roughed up badly in the accident.* **2.** To beat up. —*n.* **1.** Rugged, overgrown ground. **2.** The unmowed, uncleared part of a golf course that borders the open fairways and greens. ¶*These sound alike* **rough, ruff.** —**rough'ly** *adv.* —**rough'ness** *n.*

Idioms. **in the rough.** In a natural or unrefined condition: *a diamond in the rough.* **rough it.** To go without the usual comforts, as in traveling or camping.

rough•age |rŭf'ĭj| *n.* **1.** The coarse, indigestible part of certain foods, containing cellulose and stimulating the muscles of the intestinal walls. **2.** Any rough, coarse, or unprocessed material.

rough•en |rŭf'ən| *v.* To make or become rough, especially in texture.

rough-hew |rŭf'hyo͞o'| *v.* **-hewed, -hewed** or **-hewn** |-hyo͞on'|, **-hew•ing. 1.** To hew or cut (timber or stone) roughly, without smoothing the sides. **2.** To make in a rough form; fashion crudely. —**rough'-hewn'** *adj.:* *rough-hewn timbers.*

rough•neck |rŭf'nĕk'| *n.* A rowdy or unruly person.

rough•shod |rŭf'shŏd'| *adj.* Shod with horseshoes having projecting nails or points to prevent slipping.

Idiom. **ride roughshod over.** To treat in a rude, bullying, or overbearing way.

rou•lette |ro͞o lĕt'| *n.* **1.** A gambling game in which players bet on where on a rotating disk a ball will come to rest. **2.** A hand tool with a rotating toothed disk for making rows of slits or perforations.

Rou•ma•ni•a |ro͞o mā'nē ə| *or* |-mān'yə|. A form of the word **Rumania.**

Rou•ma•ni•an |ro͞o mā'nē ən| *or* |-mān'yən| *n.* & *adj.* A form of the word **Rumanian.**

round |round| *adj.* **round•er, round•est. 1. a.** Having a shape that is spherical or nearly spherical; ball-shaped. **b.** Having a cross section that is circular or nearly circular, as a cylinder or cone. **c.** Having a curved surface: *an old man's round back.* **2.** Full; complete: *added one to make a round dozen.* **3.** Made with full force: *a round denunciation.* **4.** Full in sound or articulation: *round tones.* **5.** Formed with the lips assuming an oval shape: *a round vowel.* **6.** Adjusted so as to have less precision; approximate: *lengths expressed in round numbers.* —*n.* **1.** The condition or property of being round. **2.** Something round: *a round of bread.* **3.** A rung of a ladder or chair. **4.** Movement in or as if in a circle; circuit: *the sun's round.* **5.** Often **rounds.** A customary course of places visited or duties performed: *a watchman on his round.* **6.** A series of similar events or acts that covers a whole range once: *a round of parties.* **7. a.** A single shot or volley from a firearm or firearms. **b.** Ammunition for a single shot. **8.** A period of struggle or competition: *In the next round, the union hopes to win its demands.* **9.** A **round dance.**

rotisserie

Roundhead
At the time of the English Civil War, it was high fashion for men to wear their hair very long and flowing. Many of the Royalists, including the king, followed this style. Many of the other side, the supporters of the Parliament, were Puritans by religion and preferred plain dress and short haircuts. The Royalists contemptuously called them **Roundheads,** *and at least one distinguished member of Parliament retorted by calling the Royalists "long-haired rattleheads." The use of hair style to symbolize life-style has a familiar modern ring.*

rout[1-2]/route
Rout[1] *is from Old French* route, *"broken or defeated troop," from Latin* ruptus, *"broken."* **Rout[2]** *is a variant of* **root[2]**. **Route** *is from Old French* rute, *which originally meant "beaten path, track broken through forest or wilderness"; it is also from Latin* ruptus, *"broken," and is thus closely related to* **rout[1]**.

row[1-2-3]
Row[1] *was Old English* rāw, *"line."* **Row[2]** *was Old English* rōwan, *"to row with an oar"; it is related to* **rudder**, *which was Old English* rōther *and originally meant "oar with which one steers."* **Row[3]** *is of unknown origin.*

ă pat/ā pay/â care/ä father/ĕ pet/ ē be/ĭ pit/ī pie/î fierce/ŏ pot/ ō go/ô paw, for/oi oil/ŏŏ book/ ōō boot/ou out/ŭ cut/û fur/ *th* the/th thin/hw which/zh vision/ ə ago, item, pencil, atom, circus

10. A musical composition for two or more voices in which each voice enters at a different time with the same melody at the same pitch. **11.** The part of a hind leg of beef between the rump and the shank. —*v.* **1.** To make or become round. **2.** To make a turn to or on the other side of: *The car rounded a bend in the road.* **3.** To go completely around: *rounding the bases.* **4.** To make less angular or jagged: *rounding one's fingernails.* **5.** To make full, complete, or properly balanced: *a description rounded out with details.* **6.** To adjust (a number) to a lower order of precision, as in representing 514 as 510 or 516 as 520. —**round'ed** *adj.: a rounded edge; a rounded number.* —***phrasal verb.*** **round up. 1.** To herd (cattle, sheep, etc.) together. **2.** To seek out and bring together; gather: *rounding up the children for lunch.* —*adv.* Around: *a wheel spinning round and round.* —*prep.* Around: *flung her arms round his neck.* —**round'ness** *n.*

round•a•bout |round'ə bout'| *adj.* Not going straight to the goal or conclusion; indirect: *The travelers chose a roundabout course that avoided the heavy traffic.*

round dance. A dance, especially a folk dance, performed with the dancers arranged in a circle.

Round•head |round'hĕd'| *n.* A supporter of Parliament during the English Civil War (1642–52). [SEE NOTE]

round•ish |roun'dĭsh| *adj.* Somewhat round.

round•ly |round'lē| *adv.* **1.** In the form of a circle, sphere, or curve. **2.** With full force or vigor; severely or thoroughly: *roundly applauded.* **3.** Bluntly; frankly: *speaking roundly.*

round-shoul•dered |round'shōl'dərd| *adj.* Having the shoulders and upper back bent forward; stooped.

Round Table. 1. a. King Arthur and his knights as a group. **b.** The circular table at which King Arthur and his knights conferred. **2. round table.** A conference at which a number of people sit around a table and discuss a given topic. —***modifier:*** **(round-table):** *a round-table discussion.*

round trip. A trip to a place and then back again; a two-way trip. —***modifier:*** **(round-trip):** *a round-trip ticket.*

round•up |round'ŭp'| *n.* **1. a.** The act of herding cattle or other animals together for inspection, branding, or shipping. **b.** The cowboys and horses that take part in such an act. **2.** Any similar gathering up of persons or things: *a roundup of suspects conducted by the police.*

round•worm |round'wûrm'| *n.* Any of a group of threadlike worms that are often parasites and cause disease in animals and human beings; a nematode.

rouse |rouz| *v.* **roused, rous•ing. 1.** To wake up; awaken. **2.** To cause to become active, attentive, or excited: *a sight that roused her curiosity.*

rous•ing |rou'zĭng| *adj.* **1.** Stirring; inspiring: *a rousing call to action.* **2.** Energetic; vigorous: *a rousing dance tune.*

Rous•seau |rōō sō'|, **Jean Jacques.** 1712–1778. French philosopher and social reformer.

roust•a•bout |rous'tə bout'| *n.* An unskilled laborer who moves from job to job, especially on docks or ships or in circuses or oil fields.

rout[1] |rout| *n.* **1.** An overwhelming defeat. **2.** A disorderly flight after a defeat: *put all the enemy forces to rout.* **3.** A disorderly gathering or crowd; a mob. —*v.* **1.** To defeat overwhelmingly; crush: *routed the opposing team.* **2.** To put to disorderly flight; scatter. [SEE NOTE]

rout[2] |rout| *v.* **1.** To drive or force from a resting or hiding place: *routing the cattle from the barn.* **2.** To dig up or uncover; root: *routing potatoes from the hard earth.* [SEE NOTE]

route |rōōt| *or* |rout| *n.* **1.** A road or course for traveling from one place to another. **2.** A highway: *Route 66.* **3.** A customary or regularly used line of travel: *a pony-express route.* **4.** A series of places or customers visited regularly by a salesman or deliveryman: *a newspaper route.* **5.** A means: *the route to fame and power.* —*v.* **rout•ed, rout•ing. 1.** To send or pass on by a certain route. **2.** To assign a route to. ¶*These sound alike* **route, root.** [SEE NOTE]

rou•tine |rōō tēn'| *n.* **1.** A series of activities performed regularly; standard or usual procedure. **2.** A program or piece of entertainment designed to be performed regularly. —*adj.* **1.** In accordance with or part of standard procedure: *a routine check of passports.* **2.** Not special; ordinary: *a routine day.* —**rou•tine'ly** *adv.*

rove |rōv| *v.* **roved, rov•ing.** To wander or roam, especially over a wide area: *Nomads roved about the desert with their herds.* —**rov'ing** *adj.: a roving minstrel.*

rov•er |rō'vər| *n.* **1.** A person or animal that roves; a wanderer. **2.** A pirate.

row[1] |rō| *n.* **1.** A series of persons or things placed next to each other, usually in a straight line: *a row of poplar trees.* **2.** A line of adjacent seats running across a theater, classroom, etc. **3.** A line of numbers, words, etc., that runs across a page. **4.** A succession without a break or gap in time: *won the title for three years in a row.* **5. a.** A continuous line of buildings along a street. **b.** A street with such buildings. ¶*These sound alike* **row[1], rho, roe, row[2].** [SEE NOTE]

row[2] |rō| *v.* **1.** To propel (a boat) with oars. **2.** To carry in a boat propelled by oars. —*n.* **1.** A shift at the oars of a rowboat. **2.** A trip in a rowboat. ¶*These sound alike* **row[2], rho, roe, row[1].** —**row'er** *n.* [SEE NOTE]

row[3] |rou| *n.* **1.** A noisy quarrel or fight; a brawl. **2.** A loud noise; clamor; racket. —*v.* To quarrel noisily. [SEE NOTE]

row•boat |rō'bōt'| *n.* A small boat propelled by oars.

row•dy |rou'dē| *adj.* **row•di•er, row•di•est.** Noisy and disorderly. —*n., pl.* **row•dies.** A disorderly person. —**row'di•ness** *n.*

roy•al |roi'əl| *adj.* **1. a.** Of a king or queen. **b.** Belonging to royalty: *princes of the blood royal.* **2.** Like or fit for a king: *a royal banquet.* **3.** Of the government of a king or queen. **4.** Often **Royal.** Founded or authorized by a king or queen: *the Royal Society.* —**roy'al•ly** *adv.*

roy•al•ist |roi'ə lĭst| *n.* **1.** A supporter of government by a king or queen; a monarchist. **2. Royalist. a.** A Cavalier. **b.** An American loyal to British rule during the American Revolution; a Tory. —*adj.* Of royalists.

roy•al•ty |roi'əl tē| *n., pl.* **roy•al•ties. 1.** A king, queen, or other member of a royal family. **2.** Kings, queens, and their relatives in general.

3. The rank or power of a sovereign. **4.** Often **royalties.** A share paid to an author, composer, or inventor out of the profits resulting from the sale or use of his work.

r.p.m. revolutions per minute.

R.R. railroad.

r.s.v.p., R.S.V.P. please reply. An abbreviation for the French phrase *répondez s'il vous plaît.*

Ru The symbol for the element ruthenium.

rub |rŭb| *v.* **rubbed, rub•bing. 1.** To press something against (a surface) and move it back and forth: *rub a window with a piece of cloth.* **2.** To press (something) against a surface and move it back and forth: *rub a cloth against a window pane.* **3.** To clean, polish, shape, or remove by rubbing. **4.** To move along in contact with a surface; scrape: *He fell, and his knee rubbed on the ground.* **5.** To make contact or remain in contact while moving: *machine parts that rub together.* **6.** To apply (a substance) to a surface by rubbing: *rub a salve onto inflamed skin.* **7.** To be removed or transferred by or as if by rubbing: *The price tag rubs off easily. Her cheerful mood rubbed off on the rest of the group.* **—phrasal verb. rub down.** To massage. *—n.* **1.** An act or gesture of rubbing. **2.** An act or remark that hurts someone's feelings. **3.** A difficulty; a catch: *You may have all the pie that you can eat, but the rub is that you can't use your hands.*

***Idioms.* rub it in.** To remind someone repeatedly of his mistake, failure, bad luck, etc. **rub (someone) the wrong way.** To impress unfavorably; arouse dislike in.

rub•ber[1] |rŭb'ər| *n.* **1. a.** An elastic or plastic substance prepared from the milky sap of a tropical tree, the **rubber tree,** and certain other tropical plants and used, after processing and treatment with additives, in a great variety of products, including electric insulation, tires, and containers. **b.** Any of various synthetic materials having properties that are similar to those of this substance. **2.** Often **rubbers.** A low overshoe made of rubber. **3.** An eraser. **—*modifier:*** *rubber gloves.* [SEE NOTE]

rub•ber[2] |rŭb'ər| *n.* **1.** A series of three games, as in bridge, two of which must be won to end play. **2.** The deciding game in such a series. [SEE NOTE]

rubber band. An elastic loop of rubber, used to hold objects together.

rub•ber•ize |rŭb'ə rīz'| *v.* **rub•ber•ized, rub•ber•iz•ing.** To coat, treat, or impregnate with rubber.

rub•ber•neck |rŭb'ər nĕk'| *n. Slang.* A tourist who gawks at the sights.

rubber stamp. 1. A stamp made of rubber, used to print names, dates, addresses, standard messages, etc. **2.** A person or group that gives quick approval to a program or policy without seriously considering its merits. **—*modifier:* (rubber-stamp):** *a rubber-stamp parliament.*

rub•ber•y |rŭb'ə rē| *adj.* **rub•ber•i•er, rub•ber•i•est.** Of or like rubber; elastic or pliable.

rub•bish |rŭb'ĭsh| *n.* **1.** Discarded or worthless material; junk; trash. **2.** Nonsense.

rub•ble |rŭb'əl| *n.* **1.** Irregular, broken pieces of rock. **2.** Fragments of stone or other material left after the destruction or decay of a building: *a cannon shot that reduced the tower to rubble.*

ru•bel•la |ro͞o bĕl'ə| *n.* **German measles.**

ru•bi•cund |ro͞o'bĭ kənd| *adj.* Reddish in complexion; ruddy.

ru•bid•i•um |ro͞o bĭd'ē əm| *n.* Symbol **Rb** One of the elements, a soft silvery metal with chemical properties that are similar to those of potassium and sodium. Atomic number 37; atomic weight 85.47; valences +1, +2, +3, +4; melting point 39.89°C; boiling point 688°C.

ru•ble |ro͞o'bəl| *n.* A form of the word **rouble.**

ru•by |ro͞o'bē| *n., pl.* **ru•bies. 1.** A deep-red, translucent form of corundum that is greatly valued as a precious stone. **2.** A deep red. **—*modifier:*** *ruby earrings. —adj.* Deep red.

ruck•sack |rŭk'săk'| *or* |ro͝ok'-| *n.* A knapsack.

ruck•us |rŭk'əs| *n. Informal.* A noisy disturbance; a commotion.

rud•der |rŭd'ər| *n.* **1.** A vertically hinged plate of metal or wood mounted at the stern of a vessel for directing its course. **2.** A similar surface in the tail of an aircraft, used for making horizontal changes of course. [SEE PICTURE]

rud•dy |rŭd'ē| *adj.* **rud•di•er, rud•di•est.** Having a healthy pink or reddish color.

rude |ro͞od| *adj.* **rud•er, rud•est. 1.** Not finely or skillfully made; crude: *fashioning rude images.* **2.** Uncivilized; primitive: *a rude people.* **3.** Offensive to the feelings of others; ill-mannered: *apologizing for being rude.* **4.** Sudden and jarring: *a rude shock.* ¶*These sound alike* **rude, rood. —rude'ly** *adv.* **—rude'ness** *n.*

ru•di•ment |ro͞o'də mənt| *n.* **1. rudiments.** The basic principles or skills of a given field of learning: *learning the rudiments of grammar.* **2.** An imperfectly or incompletely developed organ or part: *The wings of the kiwi are mere rudiments.*

ru•di•men•ta•ry |ro͞o'də mĕn'tə rē| *adj.* **1.** Of basic principles or skills; elementary: *a rudimentary knowledge of economics.* **2.** Grown or developed in an imperfect or incomplete way: *the rudimentary tail of a Manx cat.*

rue[1] |ro͞o| *v.* **rued, ru•ing.** To feel shame or sorrow for. *—n. Archaic.* Regret. [SEE NOTE]

rue[2] |ro͞o| *n.* A plant with strong-smelling, bitter leaves whose juice or oil was used in former times as medicine. [SEE NOTE]

rue•ful |ro͞o'fəl| *adj.* **1.** Full of sorrow or shame; regretful: *a rueful admission of guilt.* **2.** Inspiring pity or compassion: *cutting a rueful figure.* **—rue'ful•ly** *adv.* **—rue'ful•ness** *n.*

ruff |rŭf| *n.* **1.** A wide, round, stiffly starched, frilled or pleated collar worn by men and women in the 16th and 17th centuries. **2.** A collarlike, projecting growth of fur or feathers around the neck of an animal or bird. ¶*These sound alike* **ruff, rough.**

ruffed grouse. A chickenlike North American bird with brownish feathers.

ruf•fi•an |rŭf'ē ən| *or* |rŭf'yən| *n.* A tough or rowdy fellow.

ruf•fle |rŭf'əl| *n.* **1.** A strip of gathered or pleated cloth, lace, ribbon, etc., attached to fabric by one edge and used as a trimming. **2.** A ruff. *—v.* **ruf•fled, ruf•fling. 1.** To disturb the smoothness or evenness of: *ruffled the boy's hair affectionately.* **2.** To upset; fluster: *ruffled his dignity.* **3.** To cause (feathers) to stand up in tufts or projections. **4.** To draw into pleats, folds, or gathers: *ruffle a strip of satin.* **—ruf'fled** *adj.: a ruffled dress.*

rubber[1-2]
Rubber[1] *is from* **rub.** *The substance was introduced into Europe in the late eighteenth century, and one of its first uses was erasing pencil marks from paper.* **Rubber[2]** *is of unknown origin.*

rudder

rue[1-2]
Rue[1] *was Old English* hrēowan *and originally meant "to distress" rather than "to be distressed."* **Rue[2]** *is from Latin* rūta, *"bitter herb."*

rugby
Rugby *was invented at* Rugby School, *England, in the early nineteenth century. In England the game is often informally called* rugger *(compare note at* **soccer***).*

ruminant/ruminate
The Latin word rūmen, "throat," *was used to mean "the part of the throat from which a cow brings up her cud." (It is now known that it is not in fact part of the throat, but the first compartment of the stomach.) From* rūmen *was formed the verb* rūminārī, *"to chew the cud," and this also meant "to chew (anything) over, to think over, to ponder"; it was borrowed into English as* **ruminate**, *from which* **ruminant** *was later formed.*

rug |rŭg| *n.* **1.** A piece of thick, heavy fabric used to cover part or all of a floor. **2.** An animal skin used as a floor covering: *a bear rug.* **3.** *British.* A piece of thick, warm fabric or fur used as a blanket or lap robe.

rug•by |rŭg'bē| *n.* Also **Rugby football.** A British form of football in which players may kick, dribble, or run with the ball and play is continuous. [SEE NOTE]

rug•ged |rŭg'ĭd| *adj.* **1.** Having an uneven surface or a jagged outline: *rugged terrain.* **2.** Strongly marked: *a rugged face.* **3.** Full of endurance; sturdy; hardy: *a rugged people.* **4.** Resistant to wear or decay; durable: *a rugged car.* —**rug'ged•ly** *adv.* —**rug'ged•ness** *n.*

Ruhr |ro͝or|. **1.** A river in West Germany, flowing into the Rhine. **2.** The major coal-mining and industrial region of West Germany.

ru•in |ro͞o'ĭn| *n.* **1.** Severe destruction or damage, making something useless or worthless. **2.** Total loss of one's fortune, position, or honor. **3.** The cause of such destruction or loss: *Gambling was his ruin.* **4.** Often **ruins.** The remains of a structure or group of structures that has been destroyed or has fallen into pieces from age: *Aztec ruins.* —*v.* **1.** To harm irreparably; make useless or worthless. **2.** To reduce to poverty, bankruptcy, or hopelessness: *The venture failed and ruined us.* —**ru'ined** *adj.*: *ruined mansions.*

ru•in•a•tion |ro͞o'ə nā'shən| *n.* Destruction.

ru•in•ous |ro͞o'ə nəs| *adj.* **1.** Causing or likely to cause ruin; disastrous: *ruinous consequences.* **2.** In ruins. —**ru'in•ous•ly** *adv.*

rule |ro͞ol| *n.* **1.** A statement that tells how to do something or what may or may not be done: *the rules of a ball game.* **2.** A statement that tells what happens, exists, or is true in most or all cases: *Most mammals are covered with fur, but human beings are an exception to this rule.* **3.** A usual or customary course of action. **4. a.** The act or power of governing or controlling: *rule by the people.* **b.** A period of government: *during the rule of King George III.* **c.** The condition of being governed or controlled; authority: *America under colonial rule.* **5. a.** A straightedge; ruler. **b.** A line drawn with a straightedge. **c.** A thin metal strip used by printers to print borders or lines. —*v.* **ruled, rul•ing. 1.** To have political control or authority over (a country, people, etc.); govern. **2.** To dominate: *allowed his passions to rule his judgment.* **3.** To declare or decide judicially: *The Supreme Court ruled that the law was unconstitutional.* **4.** To mark (paper or another surface) with straight, parallel lines. —**ruled'** *adj.*: *ruled stationery.* —***phrasal verb.*** **rule out.** To remove from consideration; exclude.

Idiom. **as a rule.** In most cases; generally.

rul•er |ro͞o'lər| *n.* **1.** A person, such as a king, who governs a country. **2.** A straightedge.

rul•ing |ro͞o'lĭng| *adj.* **1.** Having control, especially political control; governing: *a ruling body; the ruling classes.* **2.** Prevailing; dominant: *a ruling passion.* —*n.* An official decision, especially the decision of a court of law.

rum |rŭm| *n.* An alcoholic liquor distilled from sugar cane molasses or syrup.

Ru•ma•ni•a |ro͞o mā'nē ə| *or* |-mān'yə|. A country in southeastern Europe. Population, 21,030,000. Capital, Bucharest.

Ru•ma•ni•an |ro͞o mā'nē ən| *or* |-mān'yən| *n.* **1.** A native or inhabitant of Rumania. **2.** The Romance language of Rumania. —*adj.* Of Rumania, the Rumanians, or their language.

rum•ble |rŭm'bəl| *v.* **rum•bled, rum•bling. 1.** To make a deep, long, rolling sound, as thunder does. **2.** To move with such a sound: *A heavy truck rumbled over the wooden bridge.* —*n.* **1.** A deep, long, rolling sound. **2.** *Slang.* A gang fight.

ru•mi•nant |ro͞o'mə nənt| *n.* Any of a group of animals, such as cattle, sheep, goats, and deer, that have a stomach divided into four sections and that chew a cud consisting of partly digested food that has been brought up to the mouth from the first stomach division. [SEE NOTE]

ru•mi•nate |ro͞o'mə nāt'| *v.* **ru•mi•nat•ed, ru•mi•nat•ing. 1.** To chew a cud, as a cow or sheep does. **2.** To spend time in thought; ponder; meditate. —**ru'mi•na'tion** *n.* [SEE NOTE]

rum•mage |rŭm'ĭj| *v.* **rum•maged, rum•mag•ing. 1.** To search thoroughly by turning over or disarranging things. **2.** To find after a thorough search: *rummaged up an old photograph.* —*n.* A search through a confusion of things.

rum•my |rŭm'ē| *n.* Any of various card games in which the players try to obtain sets of three or more cards of the same rank or suit.

ru•mor |ro͞o'mər| *n.* **1.** A report of uncertain origin and truthfulness, spread by word of mouth; a doubtful piece of information. **2.** Information by word of mouth; hearsay. —*v.* To suggest or report by rumor. ¶*These sound alike* **rumor, roomer.**

rump |rŭmp| *n.* **1. a.** The fleshy part above the hind legs of a four-footed animal. **b.** A cut of meat from this part. **2.** The human buttocks.

rum•ple |rŭm'pəl| *v.* **rum•pled, rum•pling. 1.** To wrinkle or crease: *Don't rumple the suit. Pack the clothes so they won't rumple.* **2.** To muss up; tousle: *He rumpled the boy's hair.* —*n.* A wrinkle or an untidy crease.

rum•pus |rŭm'pəs| *n.* A noisy disturbance or dispute.

run |rŭn| *v.* **ran** |răn|, **run, run•ning. 1. a.** To move on foot at a pace faster than a walk and with both feet leaving the ground during each stride: *The boy runs like a deer.* **b.** To cover (a specified distance) at this pace: *We ran a mile.* **c.** To cause to move at this pace: *running his horse.* **d.** To carry or convey at or as if at this pace: *The halfback ran the ball six yards.* **2.** To travel quickly on wheels, on foot, or in a vehicle: *ran down to the docks on his bicycle.* **3.** To move about or roam freely: *We let the dog run in the yard.* **4.** To leave hastily; flee: *I only have time to eat and run.* **5.** To go from stop to stop on a regular route or schedule: *The trains are running slow today.* **6.** To travel in large numbers, as fish do when they go upstream or inshore to spawn. **7.** To drive; chase: *running the swindler out of town.* **8.** To become in the course of time or use: *I'll love you till the seas run dry.* **9.** To take part in (a foot race or other contest): *running in the sweepstakes.* **10.** To present as a candidate or contestant: *running the senator for President.* **11.** To compete for elected office: *running for mayor.* **12.** To finish a race, contest, or election in a specified position: *running last in a field of 12.* **13.** To move or pass quickly: *An ice-cold shiver ran through her*

ă pat/ā pay/â care/ä father/ĕ pet/ ē be/ĭ pit/ī pie/î fierce/ŏ pot/ ō go/ô paw, for/oi oil/o͝o book/ o͞o boot/ou out/ŭ cut/û fur/ *th* the/th thin/hw which/zh vision/ ə ago, item, pencil, atom, circus

body. **14.** To pass smoothly through, over, or along a surface: *He stopped to run his toes through the grass.* **15.** To thrust: *Don Quixote rushed forward to run his lance into the windmill.* **16.** To pass through despite opposition or danger: *running a blockade.* **17.** To subject oneself to: *running a risk.* **18.** To do or accomplish by proceeding quickly: *run errands.* **19. a.** To move in a steady stream, as a fluid does; flow: *Melted wax ran over the candlestick.* **b.** To cause to flow: *ran water over the dishes.* **20.** To discharge a fluid: *The smog made our eyes run.* **21.** To spread beyond proper or intended limits: *The India ink ran and made fuzzy lines.* **22.** To have as a symptom: *running a fever.* **23.** To extend in space; stretch: *lines running parallel to the equator.* **24.** To extend in time; continue: *The guarantee runs for six years.* **25.** To range; vary: *colors that run from pale tints to the deepest black.* **26.** To incline; tend: *His taste runs to the sensational.* **27.** To function or cause to function: *an engine that runs well in cold weather. Water runs the turbines in hydroelectric power plants.* **28.** To manage; direct: *the leaders who run the country.* **29.** To print or publish: *ran the ad on the back page.* **30.** To sew with an even, unbroken line of stitches: *run a seam.* **31.** To tear or unravel along a line: *Her nylon stocking ran.* —***phrasal verbs.*** **run across.** To find by chance; come upon. **run after.** To pursue; chase. **run along.** To go away; leave. **run around.** *Informal.* To be companions; keep company: *I wish Prince wouldn't run around with stray dogs.* **run away.** To flee or escape from a home, group, herd, etc. **run down. 1.** To slow down and stop: *A good story should not run down like an unwound clock.* **2.** To tire out; exhaust. **3.** To knock down with a moving vehicle. **4.** To chase and capture; overtake. **5.** To speak ill of; disparage. **run into. 1.** To meet or find by chance: *ran into an old friend.* **2.** To encounter: *ran into trouble.* **3.** To collide with. **run off. 1.** To print or duplicate, usually in large numbers: *run off 20 copies of the notice.* **2.** To spill over. **run on.** To continue without a pause or break. **run out. 1.** To become used up; be exhausted: *My money has run out.* **2.** To exhaust the supply: *running out of gas.* **run over. 1.** To ride over in a vehicle. **2.** To read or review quickly. **run up. 1.** To raise or hoist, as on a pole or mast: *run up the flag.* **2.** To allow to become higher and higher: *running up a bill.* **3.** To make quickly: *She ran up a skirt on her sewing machine.* —*n.* **1.** A pace faster than a walk. **2. a.** An act or period of running. **b.** A distance covered or to be covered by running. **3. a.** A journey, especially one on a regular or scheduled route. **b.** The distance covered during such a journey: *The ship's run averaged 300 knots a day.* **4.** A course or track along or down which something can travel: *the beginners' run on a ski slope.* **5.** Any swift passage or transit: *The plane made several runs over our raft, but the pilot didn't see us.* **6.** A trail or way used by wild animals. **7.** An enclosure in which domestic animals feed and exercise: *a chicken run.* **8.** Freedom to move about or use a place without restrictions: *The old caretaker gave us the run of the castle.* **9.** A flow, as of liquid or loose particles. **10.** A narrow, fast-flowing stream or brook. **11.** A large migration of fish, especially upstream or inshore to spawn: *fish swimming up rapids during the salmon run.* **12. a.** A continuous period of operation by a machine, factory, etc.: *a trial run of a new engine.* **b.** The amount printed, produced, processed, etc., during such a period: *a run of 5,000 copies of the book.* **13.** A continuous length of something: *a long run of wire.* **14.** A length of unraveled or torn stitches in a knitted fabric: *a run in her stocking.* **15.** An unbroken series or sequence: *a run of victories.* **16.** A rapid sequence of musical tones. **17.** A number of consecutive performances: *a musical about to end a long run on Broadway.* **18.** A series of unexpected demands by depositors or customers: *a run on a bank.* **19.** A score made in baseball by advancing around the bases and reaching home plate safely. **20.** The common or average kind: *a book that is better than the run of best-sellers.* **21.** A direction or tendency: *the run of the stock market.* [SEE NOTE]

Idioms. **a run for (one's) money.** Hard competition. **in the long run.** Eventually; ultimately. **on the run. 1.** While running or hurrying from place to place. **2.** Very busy. **3.** Running away, as from pursuers. **4.** Retreating. **run away with.** To win (a prize or competition) by a wide margin. **run for it.** To try to escape by running.

run·a·way |rŭn′ə wā′| *n.* **1.** A person who has run away, as from home or from slavery. **2.** Something that has escaped from control or proper confinement. **3.** *Informal.* An easy victory. —*adj.* **1.** Having run away: *a runaway slave.* **2.** Out of control or proper confinement: *a runaway car rolling down the hill.* **3.** *Informal.* Easily won: *a runaway victory.*

run-down |rŭn′doun′| *adj.* **1.** Old and decayed: *run-down tenements.* **2.** Exhausted of energy; tired or listless: *feeling run-down.* **3.** Unwound and not running: *a run-down clock.* —*n.* A summary: *a run-down of the day's news.*

rune |ro͞on| *n.* **1.** Any of the letters of an alphabet used by ancient Germanic peoples, especially by the priests of the ancient Scandinavians and Anglo-Saxons. **2.** Any mark, symbol, or formula thought to have magical power. —**ru′nic** *adj.* [SEE PICTURE]

rung¹ |rŭng| *n.* **1.** A rod or bar forming a step of a ladder. **2.** A crosspiece supporting the legs or back of a chair. ¶*These sound alike* **rung, wrung.**

rung² |rŭng|. Past participle of **ring** (sound a bell). ¶*These sound alike* **rung, wrung.**

run-in |rŭn′ĭn′| *n. Informal.* A quarrel; fight.

run·ner |rŭn′ər| *n.* **1.** Someone or something that runs. **2.** A messenger. **3.** A part on or in which something moves: **a.** One of the parallel blades on which a sled or sleigh moves. **b.** The blade of an ice skate. **4.** A creeping plant stem that puts forth roots at intervals along its length, thus producing new plants. **5.** A long narrow carpet, as one for a hall or stairway.

run·ner-up |rŭn′ər ŭp′| *n.* A contestant that finishes a competition in second place.

run·ning |rŭn′ĭng| *n.* Competition: *Three students were in the running for class president.* —*adj.* Continuous: *a running commentary on the action.* —*adv.* Consecutively: *for four years running.*

running mate. A candidate for a less important office who is paired with the candidate for the higher office on a party ticket.

run
The word **run** *was Old English* rinnan, *descending from prehistoric Germanic* rinwan, *"to run" (which appears in Modern German as* rinnen, *"to run").*

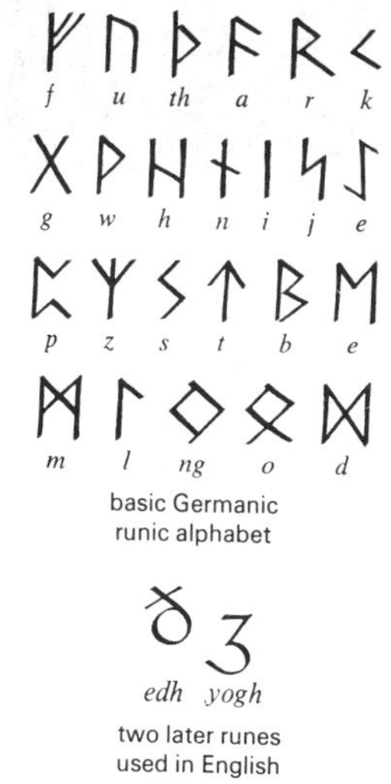

rune
The basic runic alphabet
Old English *rūn* meant both "mystery" and "runic letter."

rut[1-2]
Rut[1] *is from Old French* rote *or* rute, *"beaten path" (see note at* **route**). **Rut[2]** *is from Old French* ruit, *"roar, the bellowing of stags in rut."*

rye

run-off |rŭn′ôf′| *or* |-ŏf′| *n.* **1.** Rainfall that is not absorbed by the soil, finally reaching streams and rivers and draining away. **2.** An extra contest held to break a tie or decide the winner. *—modifier: a run-off election.*

run-on |rŭn′ŏn′| *or* |-ôn′| *n.* Printed matter that is added to the main body of print without beginning a new paragraph, item, or section. For example, in dictionaries, a word derived from an entry word by the addition of a suffix is often printed at or near the end of the entry as a run-on. The meaning of such a word can be readily understood from the definitions above it.

runt |rŭnt| *n.* **1.** An undersized animal, especially the smallest in a litter. **2.** An unusually small person, especially one regarded with scorn.

runt•y |rŭn′tē| *adj.* **runt•i•er, runt•i•est.** Unusually small; undersized: *a runty pig.*

run•way |rŭn′wā′| *n.* **1.** A path, track, or channel over which something runs or passes. **2.** A strip of level ground, usually paved, on which aircraft take off and land.

ru•pee |ro͞o pē′| *or* |ro͞o′pē| *n.* The basic unit of money of India, Pakistan, Maldive Islands, Mauritius, Nepal, and Sri Lanka.

ru•pi•ah |ro͞o pē′ä| *n.* The basic unit of money of Indonesia.

rup•ture |rŭp′chər| *n.* **1.** The act or process of breaking open or bursting. **2.** A break; a split: *a rupture in diplomatic relations.* **3.** A crack; fissure: *A spring bubbled out of a rupture in the stone.* **4. a.** A hernia, especially in the groin or intestinal region. **b.** A tear in a tissue of the body. *—v.* **rup•tured, rup•tur•ing. 1.** To break; burst. **2.** To break off; discontinue: *rupture an alliance between nations.*

ru•ral |ro͝or′əl| *adj.* **1.** Of or in the country: *rural areas.* **2.** Characteristic of the country or country people; rustic: *a rural accent.* **—ru′ral•ly** *adv.*

ruse |ro͞oz| *n.* An action meant to confuse or mislead an opponent; a deception.

rush[1] |rŭsh| *v.* **1.** To move or act swiftly or hastily; hurry: *Fire engines rushed past us. He rushed to the rescue.* **2.** To force or persuade to move hastily: *Don't rush me.* **3.** To do or perform hastily: *rushed the throw and made an error.* **4.** To carry or transport hastily: *rushed supplies to the front.* **5.** To flow or surge rapidly and often with a continuous noise: *Tons of water rushed over the falls.* **6.** To attack suddenly; charge: *rushing the barricades.* **7.** In football, to advance the ball by running rather than passing. *—n.* **1.** The act of rushing; a swift movement. **2.** A rapid and eager movement to or from a place in large numbers: *After the Civil War a new rush westward began.* **3.** A flurry of hasty activity; a great hurry: *left in such a rush that she forgot her purse.* **4.** A rapid, often noisy flow or passage: *a rush of air; a rush of words.* **5.** A sudden attack; a charge. **6.** Often **rushes.** The first, unedited print of a motion-picture scene. *—adj.* Requiring or done with haste: *a rush job.*

rush[2] |rŭsh| *n.* Any of several tall plants that grow in wet places and have hollow or pithy stems used to make chair seats, mats, etc.

Russ. Russia; Russian.

rus•set |rŭs′ĭt| *n.* **1.** A reddish brown. **2.** A type of apple with reddish-brown skin. *—adj.* Reddish brown.

Rus•sia |rŭsh′ə|. The name commonly applied to the **Union of Soviet Socialist Republics.**

Rus•sian |rŭsh′ən| *n.* **1.** A native or inhabitant of Russia. **2.** The Slavic language of Russia. *—adj.* Of Russia, the Russians, or their language.

Russian Orthodox Church. An independent branch of the Eastern Orthodox Church in the Soviet Union.

rust |rŭst| *n.* **1.** Any of the various reddish-brown oxides of iron that form on iron and many of its alloys when they are exposed to oxygen in the presence of moisture at ordinary temperatures. **2.** Any of several plant diseases caused by parasitic fungi, which produce reddish or brownish spots on leaves, stems, etc. **3.** A reddish brown. *—modifier: a rust remover; a rust preventative.* *—v.* To make or become corroded or oxidized. *—adj.* Reddish brown.

rus•tic |rŭs′tĭk| *adj.* **1.** Of or typical of the country: *cheeks glowing with rustic health.* **2.** Plain and unsophisticated: *figures carved with a rustic charm.* *—n.* **1.** A person from the country. **2.** A crude, coarse, or simple-minded person.

rus•tle |rŭs′əl| *v.* **rus•tled, rus•tling. 1. a.** To make or cause to make a soft, fluttering or crackling sound: *leaves rustled in the wind. A draft rustled the pages of the wall calendar.* **b.** To move with such a sound: *a sleigh rustling through the deep snow.* **2.** *Informal.* To make, prepare, or get quickly or briskly: *rustle up a dinner.* **3.** To steal (cattle). *—n.* A soft, fluttering or crackling sound: *a rustle of papers.*

rus•tler |rŭs′lər| *n.* A person who steals cattle.

rust•y |rŭs′tē| *adj.* **rust•i•er, rust•i•est. 1.** Covered or coated with rust; corroded. **2.** Rust-colored. **3.** Weakened or imperfect because of lack of use or practice. **—rust′i•ness** *n.*

rut[1] |rŭt| *n.* **1.** A track, as in a dirt road, made by the passage of wheeled vehicles. **2.** A habitual, unvaried way of acting or living. *—v.* **rut•ted, rut•ting.** To make ruts in. [SEE NOTE]

rut[2] |rŭt| *n.* The sexually active condition of a male deer or other male animal ready to mate during the breeding season. *—v.* **rut•ted, rut•ting.** To be in this condition. [SEE NOTE]

ru•ta•ba•ga |ro͞o′tə bā′gə| *n.* **1.** A turniplike plant with a yellowish root used as food and as animal feed. **2.** The root of such a plant.

Ruth |ro͞oth|. In the Bible, a widow who left her homeland and accompanied her mother-in-law to Bethlehem. Ruth was the great-grandmother of David.

ru•the•ni•um |ro͞o thē′nē əm| *n.* Symbol **Ru** One of the elements, a hard white metal that resists attack by acids. Atomic number 44; atomic weight 101.07; valences 0, +1, +2, +3, +4, +5, +6, +7, +8; melting point 2,250°C; boiling point 3,900°C.

ruth•less |ro͞oth′lĭs| *adj.* Showing no pity; cruel. **—ruth′less•ly** *adv.* **—ruth′less•ness** *n.*

Rwan•da |ro͞o än′də|. A small country in east-central Africa, north of Burundi. Population, 4,123,000. Capital, Kigali.

rye |rī| *n.* **1.** A grain-bearing grass with seeds used for making flour and whiskey. **2.** The seeds of this plant. **3.** Whiskey made from this grain. *—modifier: rye bread.* ¶*These sound alike* **rye, wry.** [SEE PICTURE]

ă pat/ā pay/â care/ä father/ĕ pet/ ē be/ĭ pit/ī pie/î fierce/ŏ pot/ ō go/ô paw, for/oi oil/o͝o book/ o͞o boot/ou out/ŭ cut/û fur/ *th* the/th thin/hw which/zh vision/ ə ago, item, pencil, atom, circus

Ss

S, S |ĕs| *n., pl.* **s's** or **S's.** The 19th letter of the English alphabet. [SEE NOTE]

s second (unit of time).

S **1.** **S** or **s** south; southern. **2.** The symbol for the element sulfur.

s. **1.** singular. **2.** **s.** or **S.** south; southern. **3.** shilling (British currency).

–s[1]**.** A suffix that forms the plural of most nouns not ending in *-s, -z, -ch, -sh,* and of some not ending in *-y* or *-f: girls.* See **-es**[1]**.**

–s[2]**.** A suffix that forms the third person singular present indicative of most verbs not ending in *-s, -z, -ch, -sh,* and of some not ending in *-y* or *-f: talks.* See **-es**[2]**.**

–'s[1]**.** A suffix that forms the possessive of most nouns: *women's.*

–'s[2]**.** A shortened form of: **1.** Is: *She's unhappy.* **2.** Has: *He's been away.* **3.** Us: *Let's go to lunch.*

S.A. South America.

Saar |sär|. **1.** A river rising in northeastern France and flowing north to West Germany. **2.** A coal-mining region of West Germany, bordering France and Luxembourg.

Sab•bath |săb'əth| *n.* Also **Sabbath Day.** **1.** The seventh day of the week, Saturday, observed as a day of rest and worship by Jews and some Christians. **2.** The first day of the week, Sunday, observed as a day of rest and worship by most Christian churches.

sab•bat•i•cal |sə băt'ĭ kəl| *adj.* Of or like the Sabbath. *—n.* A time off from work, especially the leave of absence with pay given to some college professors every seven years.

sa•ber |sā'bər| *n.* **1.** A heavy cavalry sword with a single-edged, slightly curved blade. **2.** A light, double-edged sword used in fencing. *—v.* To strike, cut, or kill with a saber.

sa•ber-toothed tiger |sā'bər to͞otht'|. Any of several large, extinct catlike animals of prehistoric times, having long, sharp upper canine teeth. [SEE PICTURE]

Sa•bin vacccine |sā'bĭn|. An oral vaccine against poliomyelitis that contains weakened but live viruses.

sa•ble |sā'bəl| *n.* **1. a.** An animal of northern Europe and Asia that is related to the mink and weasel and has soft, dark fur. **b.** The highly valued fur of this animal. **2. a.** The color black. **b.** **sables.** Black garments worn in mourning. ***—modifier:*** *a sable coat. —adj.* Black.

sa•bot |să bō'| *or* |săb'ō| *n.* **1.** A shoe carved from a single piece of wood, worn by peasants in France, Belgium, the Netherlands, etc. **2.** A shoe with a wooden sole and a leather band across the instep.

sab•o•tage |săb'ə täzh'| *n.* The deliberate destruction of property or disruption of work by enemy agents, resistance fighters in wartime, or by protesting or striking workers. *—v.* **sab•o•taged, sab•o•tag•ing.** To damage, destroy, or defeat by sabotage.

sab•o•teur |săb'ə tûr'| *n.* A person who commits sabotage.

sa•bre |sā'bər| *n. & v.* The British form of the word **saber.**

sac |săk| *n.* A baglike or pouchlike part of an animal or plant. ¶*These sound alike* **sac, sack.**

sac•cha•rin |săk'ər ĭn| *n.* A white, crystalline powder composed of carbon, hydrogen, nitrogen, oxygen, and sulfur and having the formula $C_7H_5NO_3S$. It tastes about 500 times sweeter than sugar and is used as a calorie-free sweetener. ¶*These sound alike* **saccharin, saccharine.**

sac•cha•rine |săk'ər ĭn| *or* |-ə rīn'| *adj.* **1.** Of or like sugar; sweet. **2.** Insincerely or sickeningly sweet; sugary: *a saccharine smile.* ¶*These sound alike* **saccharine, saccharin.**

sac•er•do•tal |săs'ər dōt'l| *or* |săk'-| *adj.* Of or relating to priests or the priesthood.

sa•chem |sā'chəm| *n.* The chief of a tribe or confederation among some North American Indians.

sa•chet |să shā'| *n.* A small, sealed bag or packet filled with a sweet-smelling substance and used to scent clothes and linens in closets, drawers, etc. ¶*These sound alike* **sachet, sashay.**

sack[1] |săk| *n.* **1. a.** A large bag of strong, coarse material used or designed for holding various things: *a flour sack.* **b.** A smaller bag of paper, cloth, or plastic: *a brown paper sack.* **2. a.** A sack with something in it: *a sack of mail.* **b.** The amount that a sack holds: *use a sack of sugar.* **3.** A thing or part resembling a bag. **4.** A loose-fitting dress, jacket, or short coat. **5.** *Slang.* A bed, mattress, or sleeping bag. **6.** **the sack.** *Slang.* Dismissal from a job or position: *His boss gave him the sack. —v.* **1.** To put into a sack. **2.** *Slang.* To fire from a job: *His boss sacked him.* ¶*These sound alike* **sack, sac.** [SEE NOTE]

Idiom. **hit the sack.** *Slang.* To go to bed.

sack[2] |săk| *v.* To rob (a captured city, fortress, etc.) of its valuables in a violent, destructive way; loot or plunder. *—n.* The robbing, looting, or plundering of a place captured by the enemy. ¶*These sound alike* **sack, sac.** [SEE NOTE]

sack[3] |săk| *n.* A strong, light-colored Spanish wine, popular in England in Shakespeare's time. ¶*These sound alike* **sack, sac.** [SEE NOTE]

sack•cloth |săk'klôth'| *or* |-klŏth'| *n.* **1.** Rough, coarse cloth of the type used for making

(1) (2) (3) (4)

The letter **S** *comes originally from the Phoenician letter* shin *(1), which meant "tooth" and stood for the sound /sh/. The Greeks borrowed it from the Phoenicians, changing the shape (2) and using it to stand for /s/. When the Romans borrowed it from the Greeks, they at first kept its angular shape (3) but later gave it the rounded form (4) that is the basis of our modern letter* **S.**

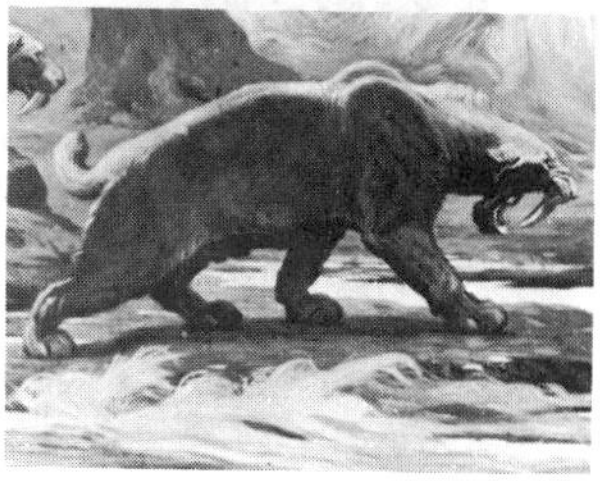

saber-toothed tiger

sack[1-2-3]

Sack[1] *is from Greek* sakkos, *which is from Hebrew* saq, *"sackcloth."* **Sack**[2] *probably originated from the verb* **sack**[1]**,** *in the sense "to put (loot) into a sack," hence "to plunder."* **Sack**[3] *is from Old French* (vin) sec, *"dry (wine)."*

sacks. **2.** Garments made of such cloth, worn as a symbol of sorrow or repentance.

sack•ing |săk′ĭng| *n.* Coarse cloth, such as burlap, used for making sacks.

sa•cra |sā′krə| *n.* Plural of **sacrum.**

sac•ra•ment |săk′rə mənt| *n.* In Christian churches, one of the sacred rites or ceremonies that are considered to have been instituted by Christ, as Holy Communion or baptism. —**sac′ra•men′tal** |săk′rə mĕn′tl| *adj.*

Sac•ra•men•to |săk′rə mĕn′tō|. The capital of California. Population, 257,800.

sa•cred |sā′krĭd| *adj.* **1.** Regarded or treated with special reverence as belonging to, coming from, or being associated with God or a divine being or power; holy: *a sacred place; a sacred book.* **2.** Dedicated or devoted to a religious use or purpose: *sacred and secular music.* —**sa′cred•ly** *adv.* —**sa′cred•ness** *n.*

sac•ri•fice |săk′rə fīs′| *n.* **1. a.** The act of offering something, such as a person's or animal's life, to God or a god in order to show respect, appease anger, or win favor or forgiveness. **b.** Something, such as a victim, offered as a sacrifice: *a human sacrifice.* **2. a.** The act of giving up some valuable thing or benefit for the sake of serving another purpose, interest, or cause. **b.** A thing or benefit given up in this way. **3.** A loss of profit suffered by selling something at less than its value or cost: *forced to sell at a sacrifice.* **4.** In baseball, a bunt, called a **sacrifice hit,** or a fly ball, called a **sacrifice fly,** that puts the batter out but allows a runner on base to advance or score. —*v.* **sac•ri•ficed, sac•ri•fic•ing. 1.** To offer (a person, animal, etc.) as a sacrifice to God or a god. **2.** To give up (something valuable) for the sake of serving another purpose, interest, or cause. **3.** To make a sacrifice or sacrifices: *parents willing to sacrifice for their children's education.* **4.** In baseball, to advance (a base runner) by means of a sacrifice. **5.** To sell at a loss. —**sac′ri•fi′cial** |săk′rə fĭsh′əl| *adj.*

sac•ri•lege |săk′rə lĭj| *n.* An act of disrespect or violence toward something sacred. —**sac′ri•le′gious** |săk′rə lĭj′əs| *or* |-lē′jəs| *adj.*

sac•ris•ty |săk′rĭ stē| *n., pl.* **sac•ris•ties.** A room in a church where vestments and sacred articles are kept; a vestry.

sac•ro•il•i•ac |săk′rō ĭl′ē ăk′| *adj.* Of or affecting the sacrum and ilium, the joint between them, or the ligaments associated with them. —*n.* The sacroiliac region or cartilage.

sac•ro•sanct |săk′rō săngkt′| *adj.* Extremely sacred and not to be violated: *the sacrosanct precincts of the temple.*

sa•crum |sā′krəm| *n., pl.* **sa•cra** |sā′krə|. A triangular bone, made up of five fused vertebrae, that forms the rear section of the pelvis.

sad |săd| *adj.* **sad•der, sad•dest. 1.** Showing, filled with, or expressing sorrow or regret: *a long, sad face.* **2.** Causing sorrow, gloom, or regret: *sad memories.* **3.** Unfortunate; regrettable: *It would be sad to be so near the ocean and not see it.* **4.** Sorry; deplorable: *This place is in sad shape.* —**sad′ly** *adv.* —**sad′ness** *n.*

sad•den |săd′n| *v.* To make or become sad.

sad•dle |săd′l| *n.* **1. a.** A padded leather seat strapped onto the back of a horse or other animal to hold a rider. **b.** Any similar pad or padded part that fits over an animal's back, as to support a pack or load or to form part of a harness. **2.** The seat of a bicycle, motorcycle, or similar vehicle. **3.** A cut of meat, such as lamb, mutton, venison, etc., containing part of the backbone and both loins: *a saddle of veal.* —*modifier: saddle leather.* —*v.* **sad•dled, sad•dling. 1.** To put a saddle on: *saddle a pony.* **2.** To load down or burden: *She was saddled with all the responsibility.* [SEE PICTURE]

sad•dle•bag |săd′l băg′| *n.* A sturdy bag or pouch, especially one of a connected pair, hung from a saddle to hold supplies, mail, etc. [SEE PICTURE]

saddle soap. A mild soap containing a special oil, used for cleaning and softening leather.

sa•dism |sā′dĭz′əm| *or* |săd′ĭz′-| *n.* **1.** An emotional disorder in which a person gets pleasure from causing pain to others. **2.** Enjoyment of cruelty or abuse inflicted on others. —**sa′dist** *n.*

sa•dis•tic |sə dĭs′tĭk| *adj.* Displaying or characterized by sadism; deliberately cruel or abusive. —**sa•dis′ti•cal•ly** *adv.*

sa•fa•ri |sə fä′rē| *or* |-făr′ē| *n.* A hunting trip or journey of exploration in Africa.

safe |sāf| *adj.* **saf•er, saf•est. 1.** Free from danger, risk, or threat of harm. **2.** Providing protection or security: *a safe refuge.* **3.** Not likely to do any harm; not dangerous: *driving at a safe speed.* **4. a.** Reliable; trustworthy; dependable: *a safe car.* **b.** Showing care and caution: *a safe driver.* **5.** Certain to succeed; not risky; sure: *a safe bet.* **6.** Not likely to be disputed: *It seems safe to say that we'll never see a live dinosaur.* **7.** In baseball, having reached a base successfully without being put out: *He was safe on third.* —*adv.* **1.** So as to cause or suffer no harm: *You'd better play safe.* **2.** In baseball, so as not to be put out: *He ran from third to home and got in safe.* —*n.* A strong metal container in which valuables, such as money and jewels, are kept for protection. —**safe′ly** *adv.*

safe•guard |sāf′gärd′| *v.* To protect from danger, challenge, or attack; keep safe and secure; guard: *laws to safeguard individual rights.* —*n.* A means of protection or defense, as a safety precaution or a protective device.

safe•keep•ing |sāf′kē′pĭng| *n.* The act of keeping or the condition of being kept safe.

safe•ty |sāf′tē| *n., pl.* **safe•ties. 1. a.** The condition of being or remaining safe; freedom from danger, accident, injury, or threat of harm: *operating in safety beneath the sea.* **b.** The purpose of keeping safe; protection; security; defense: *The rabbit ran into a hollow log for safety.* **2.** A device designed to prevent accidents, especially a lock on a gun to keep it from firing accidentally. **3.** In football: **a.** A score of two points for the defensive team made by tackling the opponent who is carrying the ball when he is behind his own goal line. **b.** Also **safety man.** A member of a team's defensive backfield playing closest to his team's goal line. —*modifier: safety rules.*

safety belt. 1. A **seat belt. 2.** A strap or harness used to support someone working at a dangerous height.

safety match. A match that will light only when it is struck on a specially prepared surface.

safety pin. A pin made in the form of a clasp

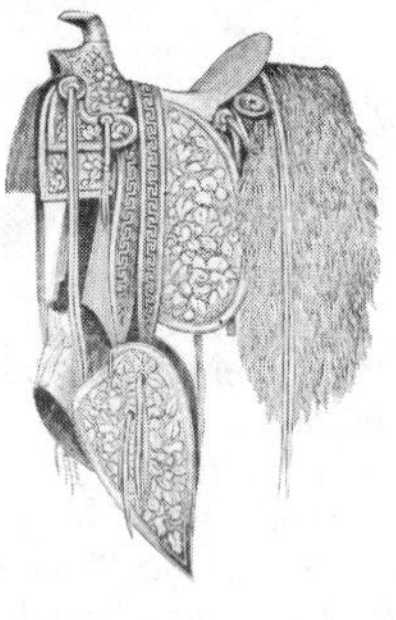

saddle

saddlebag

ă pat/ā pay/â care/ä father/ĕ pet/ ē be/ĭ pit/ī pie/î fierce/ŏ pot/ ō go/ô paw, for/oi oil/ŏŏ book/ ōō boot/ou out/ŭ cut/û fur/ *th* the/th thin/hw which/zh vision/ ə ago, item, pencil, atom, circus

with a guard covering the point so that it will not prick the wearer or become unfastened.

safety valve. **1.** A valve used on a container, such as a steam boiler, that holds a fluid under pressure. It allows some of the steam to escape if the pressure approaches a dangerous level. **2.** Any safe outlet for the release of bottled-up energy or emotion.

saf•flow•er |săf′lou′ər| *n.* A plant with orange flowers used for making dye and seeds that yield an oil used in cooking, medicine, etc.

saf•fron |săf′rən| *n.* **1.** The dried orange-yellow stigmas from the flowers of a kind of crocus, used to flavor food and in making dye. **2.** An orange-yellow color. —*adj.* Orange yellow.

sag |săg| *v.* **sagged, sag•ging. 1.** To curve, sink, or slope downward in the center, as from pressure or warping: *His weight made the net sag.* **2.** To be weighted down so as to droop: *The trees in the orchard sagged with fruit.* **3.** To hang loosely or unevenly: *Her skirt sagged.* **4.** To droop, slump, or slacken, as from tiredness or discouragement: *His broad shoulders sagged.* **5.** To decline in amount or value: *Profits sagged.* —*n.* **1.** The act, fact, or extent of sagging or drooping: *the sag of the roof.* **2.** A sagging or sunken place: *a sag in the ceiling.*

sa•ga |sä′gə| *n.* **1.** A long Scandinavian adventure story of the Middle Ages, telling about historical or legendary heroes, families, deeds, and events. **2.** Any long history or tale.

sa•ga•cious |sə gā′shəs| *adj.* Shrewd and wise. —**sa•gac′i•ty** |sə găs′ĭ tē| *n.*

sage¹ |sāj| *n.* A very wise person, usually old and highly respected. —*adj.* **sag•er, sag•est.** Full of, showing, or noted for wisdom and sound judgment. —**sage′ly** *adv.* [SEE NOTE]

sage² |sāj| *n.* **1.** A plant with grayish-green, spicy-smelling leaves used as flavoring in cooking. **2.** Sagebrush. [SEE NOTE]

sage•brush |sāj′brŭsh′| *n.* A shrub of dry regions of western North America, having strong-smelling silver-green leaves and clusters of small white flowers.

Sag•it•ta•ri•us |săj′ĭ târ′ē əs| *n.* The ninth sign of the zodiac.

sa•go |sā′gō| *n.* A powdery starch obtained from the pith of various Asian palm trees and used to thicken foods such as puddings.

sa•gua•ro |sə gwär′ō| *or* |-wär′ō| *n., pl.* **sa•gua•ros.** A very large cactus of the southwestern United States and Mexico, having upward-curving branches, white flowers, and edible red fruit. [SEE PICTURE]

Sa•hap•tin |sä hăp′tən| *n.* A family of American Indian languages of Idaho, Oregon, and Washington.

Sa•har•a |sə hâr′ə| *or* |-hăr′ə| *or* |-här′ə|. The largest desert in the world, covering much of northern Africa. —**Sa•har′an** *adj.*

sa•hib |sä′ĭb| *or* |-ēb| *n.* A title of respect equivalent to "master," "Mr.," or "sir," formerly used by the people of colonial India in speaking of or to Europeans.

said |sĕd|. Past tense and past participle of **say.** —*adj.* In legal use, previously named or mentioned: *The said tenant violated the lease.*

Sai•gon |sī gŏn′|. The former name for **Ho Chi Minh City.**

sail |sāl| *n.* **1.** A piece of strong material attached to a ship, boat, etc., in such a way as to stretch out, catch the wind, and cause the craft to move. **2. a.** Sails: *The yacht carried 7,500 feet of working sail.* **b.** *pl.* **sail.** A ship or boat propelled by sails: *a fleet of 50 sail.* **3.** A trip in a ship or boat, especially a sailboat: *We went for a sail on the lake.* **4.** Something that looks like or catches the wind like a sail, as the blade of a windmill or the winglike part of a maple seed. —*v.* **1.** To travel by ship or boat: *sail around the world.* **2.** To travel on, over, or across (water): *sail the Atlantic.* **3.** To operate, guide, or steer (a ship or boat, especially one moved by a sail or sails): *learn how to sail.* **4.** To start out on a voyage across a body of water: *The ship will sail tomorrow.* **5.** To go, move, or travel as if on a boat: *The elves sailed over the stream on a leaf.* **6.** To move swiftly, smoothly, or effortlessly, as when gliding, soaring, or flying: *The skaters sailed along the ice.* —**sail′ing** *adj.*: *a sailing ship.* —***phrasal verb.*** **sail into. 1.** To begin with vigor or energy; launch into energetically: *She sailed into the work.* **2.** To attack, criticize, or scold forcefully; light into; assail: *He sailed into us for loafing on the job.* ¶ *These sound alike* **sail, sale.**

Idiom. **set sail.** To leave on or as a ship headed for a destination; start out on a voyage: *The men set sail for home.*

Sail•board |sāl′bôrd′| *or* |-bōrd′| *n.* A trademark for a small light sailboat with a flat hull.

sail•boat |sāl′bōt′| *n.* A boat that has a sail or sails so that it can be propelled by the wind.

sail•fish |sāl′fĭsh′| *n., pl.* **-fish** or **-fish•es.** A large ocean fish with a high, saillike fin along its back and the upper jaw projecting to form a bony, spearlike snout. [SEE PICTURE]

sail•ing |sā′lĭng| *n.* **1.** The activity, craft, or sport of operating a ship or boat, especially one moved by a sail or sails. **2.** The departure or time of departure of a ship: *The sailing is at 2:00 in the afternoon.* —***modifier:*** *sailing lessons.*

sail•or |sā′lər| *n.* **1.** Someone who works as a member of a ship's crew or who serves in a navy as an enlisted man. **2.** Someone who sails or navigates a ship or boat. **3.** Also **sailor hat.** A straw hat with a low, flat crown and a straight brim.

saint |sānt| *n.* **1. a.** Often **Saint.** A very good and holy person, especially one who has been canonized by a church after death as being worthy of special reverence. **b.** Any person honored by a particular religion as a hero, martyr, or example of virtue. **2.** A person who is very patient, unselfish, virtuous, etc.

saint•ly |sānt′lē| *adj.* **saint•li•er, saint•li•est. 1.** Holy and pious; saintlike. **2.** Of or fit for a saint or saints. —**saint′li•ness** *n.*

Saint Pat•rick's Day |păt′rĭks|. March 17, the day set aside to honor Saint Patrick, the patron saint of Ireland.

Saint Val•en•tine's Day |văl′ən tīnz′|. February 14, the day set aside to honor Saint Valentine and celebrated by exchanging valentines.

sake¹ |sāk| *n.* **1.** Reason; purpose; motive: *Do not conform just for the sake of conforming.* **2.** Benefit; interest; welfare; well-being: *for the sake of those whose safety depended upon me.* **3.** Good; advantage: *He moved for the sake of his health.*

sage¹⁻²
Sage¹ *is from Old French* sage, *"wise," which is indirectly from Latin* sapere, *"to be wise."* **Sage²** *is from Old French* sauge, *which is from Latin* salvia, *"the healing herb," from* salvus, *"healthy."*

saguaro

sailfish

salamander

Salk vaccine
This was introduced by Jonas E. Salk *(born 1914), American microbiologist.*

salmon
Salmon *are hatched in rivers, and when young they swim downstream to spend most of their lives in the ocean. In order to breed, each salmon finds its way back to the same river where it was hatched, often covering very long distances.*

sa•ke² |sä'kē| *n.* A Japanese liquor made from fermented rice.

sal |săl| *n.* Salt.

sal•a•ble |sā'lə bəl| *adj.* Fit and suitable to sell or capable of attracting buyers.

sal•ad |săl'əd| *n.* Any of various dishes made up of vegetables, such as lettuce, tomatoes, potatoes, etc., sometimes with meat, cheese, etc., and served with a dressing. —***modifier:*** *a salad fork.*

sal•a•man•der |săl'ə măn'dər| *n.* **1.** Any of several animals that somewhat resemble lizards but have smooth, moist skin. **2.** In mythology, a lizardlike creature believed to be capable of living in fire. [SEE PICTURE]

sa•la•mi |sə lä'mē| *n.* A highly spiced and salted sausage of pork or beef or of both these meats. —***modifier:*** *a salami sandwich.*

sal am•mo•ni•ac |ə mō'nē ăk'|. **Ammonium chloride.**

sal•a•ried |săl'ə rēd| *adj.* **1.** Getting a salary, as an employee does: *salaried staff members.* **2.** Paying a salary, as a job does: *a salaried position.*

sal•a•ry |săl'ə rē| *n., pl.* **sal•a•ries.** A set sum of money or other compensation paid to a person on a regular basis for doing a job.

sale |sāl| *n.* **1. a.** The act of selling: *the sale of the tickets.* **b.** A particular act or instance of selling something to a buyer: *a commission on the sale.* **2.** An occasion on which goods, services, or pieces of property are offered for purchase or are sold at reduced prices: *a half-price sale at the store.* **3. sales. a.** The business of advertising and selling goods or services. **b.** The amount of goods sold or of money brought in by selling goods. —***modifier:*** *a sale price; a sales department.* ¶*These sound alike* **sale, sail.**

Idiom. **for sale.** Offered or available for purchase; on the market: *This house is not for sale.*

Sa•lem |sā'ləm|. **1.** The capital of Oregon. Population, 68,300. **2.** A seaport in Massachusetts where witch trials were held in the 17th century. Population, 40,000.

sales•clerk |sālz'klûrk'| *n.* A person who sells goods in a store.

sales•man |sālz'mən| *n., pl.* **-men** |-mən|. A man who works at selling goods or services.

sales•man•ship |sālz'mən shĭp'| *n.* Skill, ability, or persuasiveness in selling.

sales•per•son |sālz'pûr'sən| *n.* A salesclerk.

sales tax. A tax on the sale of goods or services, representing a fixed percentage of the purchase price and usually collected by the seller.

sales•wom•an |sālz'wo͝om'ən| *n., pl.* **-wom•en** |-wĭm'ĭn|. A woman who works at selling goods or services.

sa•li•ent |sā'lē ənt| *or* |sāl'yənt| *adj.* Standing out and attracting attention; notable; striking; conspicuous: *the salient points of a plan.* —*n.* A projecting angle or part, especially a place where a battle line or fortification projects farthest outward toward the enemy.

sa•line |sā'lēn'| *or* |-līn'| *adj.* Of, like, or containing salt; salty.

sa•lin•i•ty |sə lĭn'ĭ tē| *n.* **1.** The condition or property of being saline; saltiness. **2.** The degree to which something is saline or salty.

Salis•bur•y |sôlz'bĕr'ē|. The capital of Zimbabwe. Population, 118,000.

Sa•lish |sā'lĭsh| *n.* A family of American Indian languages of the northwestern United States and British Columbia.

sa•li•va |sə lī'və| *n.* The watery, tasteless fluid that is secreted into the mouth by various glands, serving to moisten food as it is chewed and to begin the digestion of starches.

sal•i•var•y |săl'ə vĕr'ē| *adj.* Of or producing saliva.

salivary gland. A gland that secretes saliva, especially one of three pairs of large glands that secrete saliva into the mouth.

sal•i•vate |săl'ə vāt'| *v.* **sal•i•vat•ed, sal•i•vat•ing.** To produce or secrete saliva. —**sal'i•va'tion** *n.*

Salk vaccine |sôlk| *or* |sôk|. A vaccine against poliomyelitis, containing killed viruses. [SEE NOTE]

sal•low |săl'ō| *adj.* **sal•low•er, sal•low•est.** Of a sickly yellowish color or complexion.

sal•ly |săl'ē| *v.* **sal•lied, sal•ly•ing, sal•lies.** —**sally forth** (or **out**). **1.** To rush forth or come out suddenly or abruptly. **2.** To set out for a destination in a spirited, energetic way: *He sallied forth to seek his fortune.* —*n., pl.* **sal•lies. 1.** A sudden rush forward. **2.** A quick, clever or witty remark; a joke or quip. **3.** A short trip or outing; a jaunt.

salm•on |săm'ən| *n., pl.* **salm•on. 1.** Any of several large fish of northern waters, having usually pinkish flesh and valued as food. **2.** A yellowish pink or pinkish orange color. —***modifier:*** *a salmon salad.* —*adj.* Yellowish pink or pinkish orange. [SEE NOTE]

Sa•lo•me |sə lō'mē| *or* |săl'ə mā'|. A Hebrew princess who demanded the head of John the Baptist in return for dancing. (The Bible, Matthew 14:6–11.)

sa•lon |sə lŏn'| *or* |să lôN'| *n.* **1.** A large, elegant room or hall for receiving and entertaining guests. **2.** A regular gathering of prominent persons, such as artists, writers, socialites, or politicians, customarily held at the home of a distinguished hostess. **3.** A hall or gallery in which works of art are exhibited.

sa•loon |sə lo͞on'| *n.* **1.** A place where alcoholic drinks are sold and drunk; a bar; tavern. **2.** A large room or hall for social gatherings, as a drawing room, ballroom, banquet room, etc.

sal soda. Sodium carbonate when used as a cleanser.

salt |sôlt| *n.* **1.** A colorless or white crystalline solid, chiefly sodium chloride, widely used as a seasoning and preservative for food. **2.** Any of a large class of chemical compounds formed when one or more hydrogen ions of an acid are replaced by metallic ions. **3. salts.** Any of various salts of inorganic acids used as laxatives or cathartics or for bathing. **4. salts. a. Smelling salts. b. Epsom salts. 5.** Anything that is like salt in adding flavor or zest to something. **6.** *Informal.* A sailor: *a crusty old salt.* —*adj.* **1.** Of or containing salt: *salt crystals; a salt mine.* **2.** Having the taste or smell of salt. **3.** Preserved in salt or brine: *salt pork.* —*v.* **1.** To season or sprinkle with or as if with salt: *Salt the stew.* **2.** To preserve (meat, fish, etc.) by treating it with salt. —**salt'ed** *adj.*: *salted peanuts; salted fish.* —***phrasal verb.*** **salt away** (or **down**). **1.** To preserve in or with salt: *salt down meat.* **2.** *Informal.* To put aside and save, as money.

ă **pat**/ā **pay**/â **care**/ä **father**/ĕ **pet**/ē **be**/ĭ **pit**/ī **pie**/î **fierce**/ŏ **pot**/ō **go**/ô **paw**, **for**/oi **oil**/o͝o **book**/o͞o **boot**/ou **out**/ŭ **cut**/û **fur**/*th* **the**/th **thin**/hw **which**/zh **vision**/ə **ago**, **item**, **pencil**, **atom**, **circus**

***Idiom.* with a grain of salt.** With some doubt about the truth or reliability of something.

salt•cel•lar |sôlt′sĕl′ər| *n.* A small dish or shaker for dispensing salt.

Salt Lake City. The capital of Utah. Population, 177,000.

salt lick. A natural deposit or block of salt that animals lick.

salt•pe•ter, also **salt•pe•tre** |sôlt′pē′tər| *n.* **1.** Potassium nitrate or sodium nitrate. **2.** Niter.

salt•shak•er |sôlt′shā′kər| *n.* A container for holding and sprinkling salt, having a top with small holes in it.

salt water. **1.** Water that contains a large amount of dissolved salt, especially sodium choloride. **2.** The water of a sea or ocean; brine. —***modifier:*** **(salt-water):** *a salt-water pond.*

salt•y |sôl′tē| *adj.* **salt•i•er, salt•i•est. 1.** Of, containing, tasting of, or full of salt: *salty food.* **2.** Of the sea: *By what salty ways did the shipwrecked man come to the island?* **3.** Sharp, seasoned, and spicy in nature or temper: *salty humor.* —**salt′i•ness** *n.*

sa•lu•bri•ous |sə lo͞o′brē əs| *adj.* Good for the health; healthful; wholesome.

sal•u•tar•y |săl′yə tĕr′ē| *adj.* **1.** Helpful; beneficial: *salutary advice.* **2.** Good for the health; healthful: *a salutary climate.*

sal•u•ta•tion |săl′yə tā′shən| *n.* **1.** An expression or gesture of greeting or respect: *He bowed in salutation.* **2.** The words of greeting used at the beginning of a letter or speech; for example, *Dear Sir is a salutation.*

sa•lu•ta•to•ri•an |sə lo͞o′tə tôr′ē ən| *or* |-tōr′-| *n.* In some schools and colleges, the student ranking second in the graduating class, who gives the opening address at commencement.

sa•lu•ta•to•ry |sə lo͞o′tə tôr′ē| *or* |-tōr′ē| *n., pl.* **sa•lu•ta•to•ries.** An opening address, especially one delivered at commencement exercises by a salutatorian. —*adj.* Having to do with or expressing a greeting or welcome.

sa•lute |sə lo͞ot′| *v.* **sa•lut•ed, sa•lut•ing. 1.** To make a formal gesture of respect for (someone or something), as by raising the right hand stiffly to the forehead, by firing cannons, etc. **2.** To pay respect or tribute to; praise. **3.** To greet with a polite, respectful, or friendly gesture: *He saluted his dancing partner with a bow.* —*n.* **1.** A formal act, gesture, or display of respect, made by raising the hand, firing cannons, etc. **2.** The act of saluting: *raise a hand in salute.* **3.** A sign of greeting or recognition, as a bow, wave, or nod. [SEE PICTURE]

sal•vage |săl′vĭj| *v.* **sal•vaged, sal•vag•ing. 1.** To save (a wrecked, damaged, or sunken ship or its cargo or parts) from total loss or ruin. **2.** To save or rescue (anything of use or value) that would otherwise be lost, discarded, damaged, or destroyed. —*n.* **1.** The rescue of a wrecked, damaged, or sunken ship or of its cargo or parts. **2.** The act of saving endangered property from total loss. **3.** Goods or property saved from a general destruction or disaster. —***modifier:*** *a salvage job; salvage workers.*

sal•va•tion |săl vā′shən| *n.* **1.** The act of saving or condition of being saved, as from loss, danger, or destruction; rescue. **2.** In the Christian religion, the saving of the soul from sin and death; redemption. **3.** Someone or something that saves, rescues, or preserves: *The emergency supplies were our salvation when we were snowbound.*

Salvation Army. An international Christian organization set up along military lines to spread religious teachings and do charitable work.

salve |săv| *or* |säv| *n.* **1.** A soothing ointment applied to wounds, burns, sores, etc., to heal them or relieve pain. **2.** Anything that soothes or comforts; a balm: *The compliment was a salve to her wounded pride.* —*v.* **salved, salv•ing.** To soothe as if with salve: *Your praise salved their hurt feelings.*

sal•ver |săl′vər| *n.* A serving tray.

sal•vo |săl′vō| *n., pl.* **sal•vos** or **sal•voes. 1.** The firing of a number of weapons or the dropping of a number of bombs at the same time or one after another. **2.** Any sudden outburst, as of cheers.

sam•a•ra |săm′ər ə| *or* |sə mâr′ə| *n.* A fruit, such as that of the maple, ash, or elm, having a thin, winglike covering that extends from it.

Sa•mar•i•tan |sə măr′ĭ tən| *n.* A **Good Samaritan.**

sa•mar•i•um |sə mâr′ē əm| *n.* Symbol **Sm** One of the rare-earth elements, a silvery or pale-gray metal. Atomic number 62; atomic weight 150.35; valences +2, +3; melting point 1,072°C; boiling point 1,900°C.

same |sām| *adj.* **1.** Being exactly alike or equal; identical: *These books are the same size.* **2.** Being the very one or ones and not another or others: *This is the same seat I had yesterday.* **3.** Not changed or different in any way: *Despite his fame, he's the same person as ever.* —*pron.* The very person or thing just mentioned or described: *Is she the one you mean? The same.* —*adv.* **the same.** In the same way: *The words "sail" and "sale" are pronounced the same.*

same•ness |sām′nĭs| *n.* **1.** The condition of being alike or equal; identity: *a sameness in size.* **2.** Lack of variety or change; monotony.

Sa•mo•a |sə mō′ə|. A group of islands in the South Pacific Ocean east-northeast of Fiji, divided into **American Samoa** and **Western Samoa.** —**Sa•mo′an** *adj. & n.*

sam•o•var |săm′ə vär′| *or* |săm′ə vär′| *n.* A metal urn with a spigot, used chiefly in Russia to boil water for tea. [SEE PICTURE]

sam•pan |săm′păn′| *n.* A small, flat-bottomed boat used on the waterways of the Orient, propelled by an oar or oars at the stern and sometimes having a sail. [SEE PICTURE]

sam•ple |săm′pəl| *or* |säm′-| *n.* **1. a.** A part, piece, amount, or selection that is considered to represent or to be typical of the whole; specimen: *samples of moon rock and soil.* **b.** A subset chosen from a larger set and used as a basis for estimating the statistical properties of the larger set. **2.** An example, illustration, or typical instance: *That story will give you a sample of Mark Twain's wit.* **3.** An item of merchandise used for display or for introducing or demonstrating a product. —***modifier:*** *sample sentences; a salesman's sample case.* —*v.* **sam•pled, sam•pling. 1.** To take a sample or samples of, as for study. **2.** To test by trying a little of, as in tasting.

sam•pler |săm′plər| *or* |säm′-| *n.* **1.** A person who samples. **2.** A piece of cloth embroidered with designs, mottoes, etc., as a display of fancy

salute

samovar

sampan

sand dollar

sandpiper

sandwich

Sandwich *is a small and ancient town in Kent, England. Its name in Old English means "sand town," that is, "town built on sandy soil." The noble family of Montague became Earls of Sandwich in the seventeenth century. The fourth Earl (1718–92) was a diplomat and politician; he was also a keen gambler, who is said to have stayed at the card table for twenty-four hours at a time with no food but cold beef slices and bread; hence the word* **sandwich.**

ă **pat**/ā **pay**/â **care**/ä **father**/ĕ **pet**/ ē **be**/ĭ **pit**/ī **pie**/î **fierce**/ŏ **pot**/ ō **go**/ô **paw**, **for**/oi **oil**/o͝o **book**/ o͞o **boot**/ou **out**/ŭ **cut**/û **fur**/ *th* **the**/th **thin**/hw **which**/zh **vision**/ ə **ago**, **item**, **pencil**, **atom**, **circus**

stitching or needlework. **3.** Anything containing a representative selection of something: *a sampler full of chocolate candies.*

Sam•son |săm′sən|. **1.** In the Bible, an Israelite judge who lost his great strength when his hair was cut. **2.** Any very strong man.

Sam•u•el |săm′yo͞o əl|. A Hebrew judge and prophet of the 11th century B.C.

sam•u•rai |săm′o͞o rī′| *n., pl.* **sam•u•rai** or **sam•u•rais. 1.** The military aristocracy of feudal Japan. **2.** A warrior belonging to this social category. —***modifier:*** *a samurai sword.*

San•a |sä nä′| *or* |săn′ä|. The capital of Yemen. Population, 135,000.

San An•to•ni•o |săn′ ăn tō′nē ō′|. A city in south-central Texas. Population, 650,000.

san•a•to•ri•um |săn′ə tôr′ē əm| *or* |-tōr′-| *n., pl.* **san•a•to•ri•ums** or **san•a•to•ri•a** |săn′ə tôr′ē ə| *or* |-tōr′-|. **1.** An institution for the treatment of chronic diseases. **2.** A health resort; a sanitarium.

sanc•ta |săngk′tə| *n.* A plural of **sanctum.**

sanc•ti•fy |săngk′tə fī′| *v.* **sanc•ti•fied, sanc•ti•fy•ing, sanc•ti•fies. 1.** To make holy or sacred: *sanctify the day of his birth.* **2.** To give religious sanction to: *sanctify a marriage.*

sanc•ti•mo•ni•ous |săngk′tə mō′nē əs| *adj.* Pretentiously pious or righteous. —**sanc′ti•mo′ni•ous•ly** *adv.* —**sanc′ti•mo′ni•ous•ness** *n.*

sanc•tion |săngk′shən| *n.* **1.** Authoritative permission or approval. **2.** A measure or measures adopted by several nations taking action against a nation considered to have violated international law. —*v.* To give approval to; authorize.

sanc•ti•ty |săngk′tĭ tē| *n.* **1.** Saintliness; godliness. **2.** The quality of being holy or sacred; sacredness.

sanc•tu•ar•y |săngk′cho͞o ĕr′ē| *n., pl.* **sanc•tu•ar•ies. 1.** A consecrated place, such as a house of worship. **2.** A place of refuge, asylum, or protection. **3.** Asylum or protection: *He asked for sanctuary.* **4.** Any area where wildlife is protected by law: *a bird sanctuary.*

sanc•tum |săngk′təm| *n., pl.* **sanc•tums** or **sanc•ta** |săngk′tə|. A private room or study.

sanctum sanc•to•rum |săngk tôr′əm| *or* |-tōr′-|. **1.** A holy place. **2.** A sanctum.

sand |sănd| *n.* **1.** Loose grains or particles of disintegrated rock, finer than gravel and coarser than dust. **2.** Usually **sands.** Land, such as a beach or desert, covered with this material. —***modifier:*** *a sand castle.* —*v.* **1.** To sprinkle or cover with sand or similar material: *sand an icy sidewalk.* **2.** To rub with sand or sandpaper.

san•dal |săn′dl| *n.* **1.** A shoe made of a sole and thongs or straps used to fasten it to the foot. **2.** Any low-cut shoe with openings or cut-out places in the upper part.

san•dal•wood |săn′dl wo͝od′| *n.* **1.** The pleasant-smelling wood of a tropical tree, used for carving decorative objects and for making perfume. **2.** A tree having such wood. —***modifier:*** *A sandalwood box.*

sand•bag |sănd′băg′| *n.* A bag or sack filled with sand, often used in protective walls, dikes, etc. —*v.* **-bagged, -bag•ging.** To put sandbags in or around, as for protection.

sand•bar |sănd′bär′| *n.* Also **sand bar.** A mass of sand built up in the water near a shore, beach, etc., by the action of waves or currents.

sand•box |sănd′bŏks′| *n.* An enclosed area filled with sand for children to play in.

sand dollar. A thin, flat, circular sea animal related to the sea urchins, living along sandy shores. [SEE PICTURE]

sand•er |săn′dər| *n.* **1.** Someone or something that spreads sand, as on a road covered with ice. **2.** A machine with a disk or belt of sandpaper, used for smoothing, polishing, or refinishing.

San Di•e•go |săn′ dē ā′gō|. A city in southern California, on the Pacific coast. Population, 771,000.

sand•pa•per |sănd′pā′pər| *n.* Heavy paper coated on one side with sand or other abrasive material, used for smoothing or cleaning surfaces. —*v.* To smooth, polish, clean, etc., by rubbing with sandpaper.

sand•pi•per |sănd′pī′pər| *n.* Any of several small shore birds with a slender, pointed bill. [SEE PICTURE]

sand•stone |sănd′stōn′| *n.* A type of sedimentary rock that occurs in a variety of colors, formed of sandlike grains of quartz held together by lime or other materials.

sand•wich |sănd′wĭch| *or* |săn′-| *n.* **1.** Two or more slices of bread with a filling of meat, cheese, etc., placed between them. **2.** One slice of bread spread with a filling: *an open-faced sandwich.* —*v.* **1.** To arrange in tight alternating layers. **2.** To fit between two other things that allow little room, time, etc. [SEE NOTE]

sand•y |săn′dē| *adj.* **sand•i•er, sand•i•est. 1.** Of, full of, or covered with sand. **2.** Of the color of sand; yellowish red. —**sand′i•ness** *n.*

sane |sān| *adj.* **san•er, san•est. 1.** Of sound mind; mentally healthy: *a sane person.* **2.** Showing good judgment; logical: *a sane approach to the problem.* ¶*These sound alike* **sane, seine.** —**sane′ly** *adv.* —**sane′ness** *n.*

San•for•ized |săn′fə rīzd′| *adj.* Being or bearing a trademark for cloth that has been shrunk in advance by a special process to keep it from shrinking more later: *a Sanforized garment.*

San Fran•cis•co |săn′ frən sĭs′kō| *or* |frăn-|. A city on the coast of central California. Population, 677,000.

sang |săng|. A past tense of **sing.**

san•guine |săng′gwĭn| *adj.* **1. a.** Of the color of blood; red. **b.** Ruddy: *a sanguine complexion.* **2.** Eagerly optimistic; cheerful. —**san′guine•ly** *adv.* —**san•guin′i•ty** *n.*

san•i•tar•i•um |săn′ĭ târ′ē əm| *n.* **1.** A health resort. **2.** A sanatorium.

san•i•tar•y |săn′ĭ tĕr′ē| *adj.* **1.** Of or used for the preservation of health. **2.** Free of germs; clean; hygienic. —**san′i•tar′i•ly** *adv.*

sanitary napkin. A disposable pad of absorbent material worn to absorb menstrual flow.

san•i•ta•tion |săn′ĭ tā′shən| *n.* **1.** The study and application of procedures and regulations that are meant to protect public health. **2.** The disposal of sewage and wastes. —***modifier:*** *a sanitation worker.*

san•i•ty |săn′ĭ tē| *n.* **1.** Soundness of mind; good mental health. **2.** The ability to make sound or reasonable judgments.

San Jo•sé |săn′ hō zā′| . The capital of Costa Rica. Population, 211,000.

San Juan |săn' **hwän'**| *or* |**wän'**| *or* |săn'-**hwän'**|. The capital of Puerto Rico. Population, 455,000.

sank |săngk|. Past tense of **sink.**

San Sal•va•dor |săn **săl'**və dôr'|. The capital of El Salvador. Population, 337,000.

San•skrit |**săn'**skrĭt'| *n.* An ancient Indo-European language of India. Sanskrit is the language of Hinduism and is now used in sacred and scholarly writings. —**San'skrit'** *adj.*

San•ta Claus |**săn'**tə klôz'|. The personification of the spirit of Christmas, said to bring gifts to children on Christmas Eve. [SEE NOTE]

San•ta Fe |**săn'**tə **fā'**|. The capital of New Mexico. Population, 39,000.

San•ti•a•go |săn' tē **ä'**gō|. The capital of Chile. Population, 2,586,000.

San•to Do•min•go |**săn'**tō dō **mĭng'**gō|. The capital of the Dominican Republic. Population, 671,000.

São Pau•lo |souN' **pou'**lo͞o|. The largest city of Brazil. Population, 7,195,000.

São To•mé e Prín•ci•pe |souN to͞o **mĕ'**ē **prēn'**sē pĭ|. A country consisting of two islands, located off the western coast of Africa. Population, 78,000. Capital, São Tomé.

sap[1] |săp| *n.* **1.** The liquid that circulates through plant tissues, carrying dissolved minerals and other food substances to the various plant parts. **2.** A substance or quality that seems to be the source of health, energy, or vigor. **3.** *Slang.* A foolish person. [SEE NOTE]

sap[2] |săp| *v.* **sapped, sap•ping.** To deplete or weaken gradually: *heat sapping one's strength.* [SEE NOTE]

sap•ling |**săp'**lĭng| *n.* A young tree.

sap•o•dil•la |săp'ə **dĭl'**ə| *n.* A tropical American tree whose milky juice is the source of chicle, the main ingredient in chewing gum.

sap•phire |**săf'**īr'| *n.* **1.** Any of several fairly pure forms of corundum, especially a blue form valued as a gem. **2.** A gem of this type. —***modifier:*** *a sapphire ring.*

sap•py |**săp'**ē| *adj.* **sap•pi•er, sap•pi•est. 1.** Full of sap, juice, or vigor. **2.** *Slang.* Foolish; silly.

sap•ro•phyte |**săp'**rə fīt'| *n.* A plant, such as a mushroom or mold that lives on and gets its nourishment from dead or decaying organic material. —**sap'ro•phyt'ic** |săp'rə **fĭt'**ĭk| *adj.*

sap•suck•er |**săp'**sŭk'ər| *n.* A North American woodpecker that drills holes into trees to drink the sap.

sap•wood |**săp'**wo͝od'| *n.* The outer, newly formed, usually light-colored wood of a tree, through which the sap flows.

Sar•a•cen |**săr'**ə sən| *n.* **1.** A Moslem, especially of the time of the Crusades. **2.** An Arab, especially of ancient times.

Sar•ah |**sâr'**ə|. In the Bible, the wife of Abraham and mother of Isaac.

sa•ran |sə **răn'**| *n.* Any of various plastic resins derived from vinyl compounds and used in making transparent films for packaging, bristles, pipes, and fittings, and as a textile fiber.

sa•ra•pe |sə **rä'**pē| *n.* A form of the word **serape.**

Sa•ra•wak |sə **rä'**wäk|. A state of Malaysia, on northwestern Borneo. Population, 950,000.

sar•casm |**sär'**kăz'əm| *n.* **1.** A sharply mocking remark; a contemptuous taunt. **2.** The use of such remarks.

sar•cas•tic |sär **kăs'**tĭk| *adj.* **1.** Characterized by sarcasm; bitterly mocking: *a sarcastic remark.* **2.** Given to using sarcasm: *a sarcastic person.* —**sar•cas'ti•cal•ly** *adv.*

sar•co•ma |sär **kō'**mə| *n., pl.* **sar•co•mas** or **sar•co•ma•ta** |sär **kō'**mə tə|. A tumor, usually malignant, derived from connective tissue similar to that found in ligaments and bones.

sar•coph•a•gus |sär **kŏf'**ə gəs| *n., pl.* **sar•coph•a•gi** |sär **kŏf'**ə jī'|. A stone coffin.

sar•dine |sär **dēn'**| *n.* A small herring or similar small fish, often canned for use as food.

Sar•din•i•a |sär **dĭn'**ē ə|. An island in the Mediterranean Sea, west of Italy. Population, 1,500,000. —**Sar•din'i•an** *adj. & n.*

sar•don•ic |sär **dŏn'**ĭk| *adj.* Mocking; cynical; sarcastic. —**sar•don'i•cal•ly** *adv.*

sa•ri |**sä'**rē| *n.* An outer garment worn by women of India and Pakistan, consisting of a length of cloth with one end wrapped about the waist to form a long skirt and the other end draped over the shoulder. [SEE PICTURE]

sa•rong |sə **rông'**| *or* |**-rŏng'**| *n.* A brightly colored cloth garment worn like a skirt by both men and women in Malaysia, Indonesia, and the Pacific islands.

sar•sa•pa•ril•la |săs'pə **rĭl'**ə| *or* |sär'sə pə-| *n.* **1.** A soft drink flavored with an extract from the roots of a tropical American plant. **2. a.** A plant that yields this flavoring. **b.** Any of several similar or related plants.

sar•to•ri•al |sär **tôr'**ē əl| *or* |**-tōr'-**| *adj.* **1.** Of a tailor or his trade. **2.** Of men's clothing: *the duke's sartorial splendor.*

sash[1] |săsh| *n.* A band or ribbon worn around the waist or over the shoulder as an ornament or symbol of rank.

sash[2] |săsh| *n.* A frame in which the panes of a window or door are set.

sa•shay |să **shā'**| *v. Informal.* To move or walk in an ostentatious manner; strut. ¶*These sound alike* **sashay, sachet.**

Sas•katch•e•wan |săs **kăch'**ə wän'|. A province of western Canada. Population, 912,000. Capital, Regina.

sass |săs|. *Informal. n.* Back talk; impertinence. —*v.* To talk back to; be impertinent to.

sas•sa•fras |**săs'**ə frăs'| *n.* **1.** A North American tree with irregularly shaped leaves. Its bark, roots, and leaves have a spicy odor and taste. **2.** The dried root bark of such a tree, used as flavoring and in medicine. —***modifier:*** *sassafras bark; sassafras tea.*

sas•sy |**săs'**ē| *adj.* **sas•si•er, sas•si•est.** *Informal.* Given to back talk; impudent. —**sas'si•ly** *adv.*

sat |săt|. Past tense and past participle of **sit.**

Sat. Saturday.

Sa•tan |**sāt'**n| *n.* The Devil.

sa•tan•ic |sə **tăn'**ĭk| *adj.* Of Satan or evil; fiendish: *a satanic expression.*

satch•el |**săch'**əl| *n.* A small bag or piece of hand luggage, often having a shoulder strap, used to carry books, clothes, etc.

sate |sāt| *v.* **sat•ed, sat•ing.** To indulge; satiate.

sa•teen |să **tēn'**| *n.* A cotton fabric woven with a smooth, glossy, satinlike finish.

sat•el•lite |**săt'**l īt'| *n.* **1.** A celestial body of

Santa Claus

The name **Santa Claus** *is ultimately a variant of the Dutch name for Saint Nicholas. The saint really lived in the fourth century* A.D., *but the many stories that are told of him in eastern and northern Europe come from medieval folklore. In one story three boys had been cut up and salted for bacon; Saint Nicholas brought them back to life. In another, three girls were to be sold as slaves, and he saved them by giving them three bags of gold as their dowries. Thus he became the patron saint of children, and later also took on the role of "Father Christmas," as he is often called in England and elsewhere.*

sap[1-2]

Sap[1] *was Old English* sæp. **Sap**[2] *originally meant "to dig a tunnel under enemy fortifications (as during a siege)"; it is from Old French* sappe, *"an undermining, a tunnel."*

sari

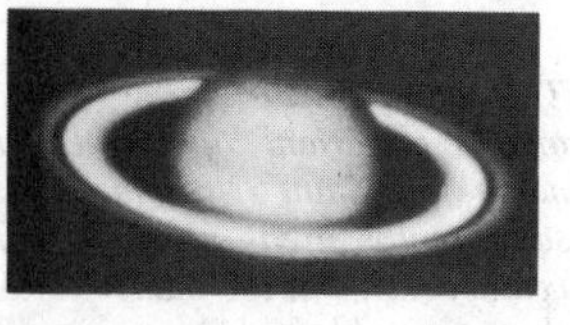

Saturn[1]

Saturn, *as seen through a telescope, appears to be surrounded by a number of rings. These rings are thought to be made up of a vast number of tiny satellites. Saturn also has ten satellites of some size, one of which orbits in a direction opposite to that of all the others.*

satyr/satire

Satire *is from Latin* satira *or* satura, *a type of long poem in which fools were ridiculed; the word originally meant "a full dish," hence "a mixture, a mixed poem," and is from* satur, *"full of food" (related to* **satiate** *and* **satisfy***).* **Satyr** *is from Greek* saturos, *"goat-demon, satyr." Satyrs are associated with poetry, since in some Greek plays the chorus represented singing satyrs. As a result, some Roman etymologists thought that Latin* satura *was derived from Greek* saturos, *and in later times the two words have often been confused; in fact they are unrelated.*

save[1-2]

Save[1] *is from Old French* sauver *or* salver, *which was from Latin* salvāre, *"to save," from* salvus, *"safe." A derivative of* salvus *was* salvō, *meaning "saving, keeping aside, with the exception of"; this became Old French* sauf, *which was borrowed into English as* **save[2]**. *(Latin* salvus *is also the source of* **salvation** *and* **salvage**.*)*

ă pat/ā pay/â care/ä father/ĕ pet/ ē be/ĭ pit/ī pie/î fierce/ŏ pot/ ō go/ô paw, for/oi oil/ŏŏ book/ ōō boot/ou out/ŭ cut/û fur/ *th* the/th thin/hw which/zh vision/ ə ago, item, pencil, atom, circus

relatively small size and mass that travels in an orbit around a planet; a moon. **2.** Any of various man-made objects launched so as to orbit a celestial body. **3.** A nation that is dominated politically by another nation. **4.** A subservient follower, especially of a famous person. —***modifier:*** *satellite photographs.*

sa•ti•ate |sā′shē āt′| *v.* **sa•ti•at•ed, sa•ti•at•ing.** To satisfy (an appetite or desire) fully; sate.

sat•in |săt′n| *n.* A smooth fabric of silk, rayon, nylon, or other fibers, woven with a glossy finish on one side. —***modifier:*** *a satin gown.* —*adj.* As smooth and shiny as satin; satiny.

sat•in•y |săt′n ē| *adj.* Having the look or feel of satin; smooth and glossy.

sat•ire |săt′īr′| *n.* **1.** A novel, play, movie, etc., that exposes hypocrisy or foolishness, typically by using humor or irony. **2.** The use or technique of using humor or irony in this way. [SEE NOTE]

sa•tir•i•cal |sə tĭr′ĭ kəl| or **sa•tir•ic** |sə tĭr′ĭk| *adj.* Of, based on, or using satire: *a satirical essay.* —**sa•tir′i•cal•ly** *adv.*

sat•i•rist |săt′ər ĭst| *n.* A writer of satire.

sat•i•rize |săt′ə rīz′| *v.* **sat•i•rized, sat•i•riz•ing.** To ridicule or attack by means of satire.

sat•is•fac•tion |săt′ĭs făk′shən| *n.* **1.** Fulfillment or gratification of a desire, need, or appetite. **2.** Pleasure derived from such fulfillment. **3.** Something that gives fulfillment or gratification: *the satisfactions of life.* **4.** Something given to compensate for a loss or injury.

sat•is•fac•to•ry |săt′ĭs făk′tə rē| *adj.* Sufficient to meet a demand or requirement; adequate: *a satisfactory grade.* —**sat′is•fac′to•ri•ly** *adv.*

sat•is•fy |săt′ĭs fī′| *v.* **sat•is•fied, sat•is•fy•ing, sat•is•fies.** **1.** To fulfill or gratify: *satisfy his hunger.* **2.** To relieve of doubt or question; convince: *The firemen were satisfied that the fire was out.* **3.** To provide a solution for: *a value that satisfies an equation.* **4.** To make up for or compensate for an injury or loss: *The treaty satisfied the claims made on the land.* —**sat′is•fy′ing** *adj.*: *a satisfying afternoon.*

sat•u•rate |săch′ə rāt′| *v.* **sat•u•rat•ed, sat•u•rat•ing.** **1.** To cause to be pervaded thoroughly; soak: *saturate the sponge with alcohol.* **2.** To make or become saturated.

sat•u•rat•ed |săch′ə rā′tĭd| *adj.* **1. a.** Containing as much of a solute as can normally be dissolved at a given temperature: *a saturated solution.* **b.** Having all available valence bonds filled: *a saturated hydrocarbon.* **2.** Containing as much water vapor as is possible at a given temperature; having a relative humidity of 100 per cent: *a mass of saturated air.* **3.** Showing marked saturation, as a color does.

sat•u•ra•tion |săch′ə rā′shən| *n.* **1. a.** The act or process of saturating. **b.** The condition of being saturated. **2.** The degree to which a color differs from a gray of the same brightness or lightness. —***modifier:*** *saturation levels.*

Sat•ur•day |săt′ər dē| *or* |-dā′| *n.* The seventh day of the week, after Friday and before Sunday. See **Sabbath.** —***modifier:*** *a Saturday movie.*

Sat•urn[1] |săt′ərn| *n.* The sixth planet of the solar system in order of increasing distance from the sun. Its diameter is about 74,000 miles, its average distance from the sun is about 886 million miles, and it takes about 29.5 years to complete an orbit of the sun. [SEE PICTURE]

Sat•urn[2] |săt′ərn|. The Roman god of agriculture.

sa•tyr |sā′tər| *or* |săt′ər| *n.* In Greek mythology, a woodland god often having the pointed ears and short horns of a goat. [SEE NOTE]

sauce |sôs| *n.* **1.** Any soft or liquid dressing or relish served with food. **2.** Stewed, sweetened fruit: *apple sauce.* —*v.* **sauced, sauc•ing.** To season or flavor with sauce.

sauce•pan |sôs′păn′| *n.* A small metal pot with a long handle, used in cooking.

sau•cer |sô′sər| *n.* A small, shallow dish for holding a cup.

sau•cy |sô′sē| *adj.* **sau•ci•er, sau•ci•est.** Given to back talk; impertinent: *a saucy youngster.* —**sau′ci•ness** *n.*

Sa•u•di A•ra•bi•a |sä ōō′dē ə rā′bē ə| *or* |sou′dē|. A country in the Middle East, occupying most of Arabia. Population, 8,174,000. Capital, Riyadh.

sauer•kraut |sour′krout′| *n.* Shredded cabbage, salted and fermented in its own juice.

Sauk |sôk| *n., pl.* **Sauk** or **Sauks.** **1.** A North American Indian tribe now living in Iowa and Oklahoma. **2.** A member of this tribe. **3.** The Algonquian language of this tribe.

Saul |sôl|. In the Bible, the first king of Israel; succeeded by David.

saun•ter |sôn′tər| *v.* To walk at a leisurely pace; stroll. —*n.* A leisurely walk.

sau•ri•an |sôr′ē ən| *n.* A member of the group of reptiles that includes the true lizards. —*adj.* Of, belonging to, or typical of the lizards.

sau•sage |sô′sĭj| *n.* Chopped and seasoned meat stuffed into a prepared animal intestine or other casing and cooked or cured.

sau•té |sō tā′| *or* |sô-| *v.* To fry lightly with a little fat in an open pan. —*n.* Sautéed food. —*adj.* Lightly fried in an open pan.

sav•age |săv′ĭj| *adj.* **1.** Untouched by civilization; not cultivated; wild: *savage lands.* **2.** Not civilized; primitive: *savage tribes.* **3.** Ferocious; fierce: *a savage attack; savage lions.* —*n.* **1.** A person untouched by civilization. **2.** A fierce or vicious person or animal. **3.** A rude person. —**sav′age•ly** *adv.* —**sav′age•ness** *n.*

sav•age•ry |săv′ĭj rē| *n., pl.* **sav•age•ries.** **1.** The condition of being uncivilized or savage. **2.** Savage action, behavior, or quality.

sa•van•na, also **sa•van•nah** |sə văn′ə| *n.* A flat, treeless grassland of warm regions.

save[1] |sāv| *v.* **saved, sav•ing.** **1.** To rescue from harm, danger, or loss. **2.** To keep intact; safeguard: *save one's reputation.* **3.** To prevent or reduce the loss, expenditure, or waste of: *save money at a sale; save time.* **4.** To make unnecessary; avoid: *saved him a trip to the store.* **5. a.** To keep for future use; store: *The squirrel saved up acorns for the long winter.* **b.** To accumulate (money or goods): *save five dollars a week; save on a monthly basis.* **6.** In theology, to deliver from sin. —**sav′er** *n.* [SEE NOTE]

save[2] |sāv| *prep.* Except; but: *All trains arrived on time save one.* [SEE NOTE]

sav•ing[1] |sā′vĭng| *adj.* **1.** Economical; thrifty: *a saving person.* **2.** Serving to compensate; redeeming: *saving graces.* —*n.* **1.** The act or an example of saving. **2.** The amount saved: *a saving of three hours and ten dollars.* **3. savings.** Sums of money saved, especially in a bank.

sav•ing[2] |sā′vĭng| *prep.* With the exception of: *All books were ordered, saving this one.*

savings bank. A bank that receives, invests, and pays interest on the savings of depositors.

sav•ior or **sav•iour** |sāv′yər| *n.* **1.** A person who saves or delivers from danger or destruction. **2. the Saviour.** Christ; the Redeemer.

sa•vor |sā′vər| *n.* **1.** The taste or aroma of something. **2.** A pleasing quality, especially one that arouses interest; zest. *—v.* To taste or enjoy heartily; relish.

sa•vor•y[1] |sā′və rē| *adj.* Appetizing to the taste or smell: *a savory dish of spinach.*

sa•vor•y[2] |sā′və rē| *n.* A plant with spicy-smelling leaves used as seasoning in cooking.

sav•vy |săv′ē|. *Slang. v.* **sav•vied, sav•vy•ing, sav•vies.** To know or understand. *—n.* Practical understanding; common sense.

saw[1] |sô| *n.* A tool having a thin metal blade with a sharp-toothed edge, used for cutting wood, metal, or other hard materials. *—v.* **sawed, sawed** or **sawn** |sôn|, **saw•ing. 1.** To cut with or use a saw: *saw off a branch; sawing for an hour.* **2.** To shape with a saw: *sawing curves in wood.* **3.** To be capable of being cut with a saw: *a wood that saws smoothly.* [SEE NOTE]

saw[2] |sô| *n.* A traditional saying. [SEE NOTE]

saw[3] |sô|. Past tense of **see.**

saw•dust |sô′dŭst′| *n.* The small shavings and pieces of wood that fall off during sawing.

saw•fish |sô′fĭsh′| *n., pl.* **-fish** or **-fish•es.** A large salt-water fish related to the rays and skates, having a bladelike snout with teeth along both sides.

saw•horse |sô′hôrs′| *n.* A rack consisting of a horizontal bar with two sloping legs at each end, used to support a piece of wood being sawed.

saw•mill |sô′mĭl′| *n.* A place where lumber is cut into boards, planks, etc., by machines.

sawn |sôn|. A past tense of **saw.**

saw•yer |sô′yər| *or* |soi′ər| *n.* A person whose work is the sawing of logs and timber.

sax |săks| *n. Informal.* A saxophone.

sax•i•frage |săk′sə frĭj| *or* |-frāj′| *n.* Any of several plants having small, loosely clustered white, yellow, or reddish flowers.

Sax•on |săk′sən| *n.* **1.** A member of a Germanic people who invaded England in the 5th century A.D. and became part of the Anglo-Saxon people. **2.** The Germanic dialect of the Saxons. *—adj.* Of the Saxons or their dialect.

sax•o•phone |săk′sə fōn′| *n.* A wind instrument having a single-reed mouthpiece, a curved conical body made of metal, and keys operated by the player's fingers. [SEE PICTURE]

say |sā| *v.* **said** |sĕd|, **say•ing, says** |sĕz|. **1.** To utter aloud; speak: *She said no before I even finished asking.* **2.** To express in words; state: *The book says that the treaty was signed in 1945.* **3.** To give expression to; communicate: *The artist tries to say something personal in his work.* **4.** To repeat or recite: *saying poetry aloud.* **5.** To suppose; assume: *Let's say that she quits, then what will we do? —n.* A turn or chance to speak: *Let each one have his say. —adv.* **1.** Approximately: *Let's walk, say, five miles.* **2.** For example: *a tree, say a pine. —interj.* A word used to attract attention, express wonder, etc.: *Say, that's some car.* **—say′er** *n.* [SEE NOTE]

***Idiom.* go without saying.** To be so obvious as to need no explanation or mention.

say•ing |sā′ĭng| *n.* **1.** A wise or witty statement: *a collection of her sayings.* **2.** A maxim; proverb.

say-so |sā′sō′| *n., pl.* **say-sos.** *Informal.* An unsupported statement of assurance: *can't be convicted on your say-so alone.*

Sb The symbol for the element antimony.

Sc The symbol for the element scandium.

S.C. South Carolina.

scab |skăb| *n.* **1.** The crustlike surface that covers a healing wound. **2.** *Informal.* **a.** A worker who refuses to join a labor union. **b.** A worker who takes a striker's job. *—v.* **1.** To form a scab. **2.** *Informal.* To work as a scab.

scab•bard |skăb′ərd| *n.* A sheath or case for the blade of a sword, dagger, or bayonet.

sca•bies |skā′bēz| *n. (used with a singular verb).* A contagious disease caused by small mites that burrow into the skin and cause severe itching.

scaf•fold |skăf′əld| *or* |-ōld′| *n.* **1.** A temporary platform used for supporting workmen in the construction, repair, or cleaning of a building. **2.** A platform for the execution of condemned prisoners. **3.** Any raised wooden framework or platform.

scaf•fold•ing |skăf′əl dĭng| *or* |-ōl′-| *n.* **1.** A scaffold or system of scaffolds. **2.** The materials from which a scaffold is made. [SEE PICTURE]

scald |skôld| *v.* **1.** To burn with or as if with hot liquid or steam. **2.** To treat with or subject to boiling water: *scald a container.* **3.** To heat (a liquid) almost to the boiling point: *scald milk. —n.* An injury or damage caused by scalding.

scale[1] |skāl| *n.* **1. a.** One of the small, thin, platelike parts forming the outer covering of fishes, reptiles, and certain other animals. **b.** A similar small, thin, often overlapping part. **2.** A dry, thin flake or crust, as of paint, rust, or dandruff. **3.** Also **scale insect.** Any of several often very destructive insects that form and stay under waxy, scalelike coverings on plants. *—v.* **scaled, scal•ing. 1.** To remove a scale or scales from. **2.** To fall or come off in scales or layers; flake. [SEE NOTE on p. 776]

scale[2] |skāl| *n.* **1. a.** A series of marks placed at fixed distances, used for measuring. **b.** An instrument having such a series of marks. **2. a.** The relationship between the actual dimensions of something and the dimensions to which it is reduced or expanded when represented on a model, map, drawing, etc.: *a scale of 1 inch to 50 miles.* **b.** A line with marks showing the actual dimensions of something represented on a map, plan, drawing, etc. **3. a.** An ordered classification for comparing size, amount, power, intensity, rank, etc.: *a scale of wages.* **b.** The relative size or extent of something: *on a large political scale.* **4.** A system of numeration: *the binary scale; the decimal scale.* **5.** An ascending or descending series of musical tones that includes all tones that are used in some key, mode, or system of tones and that lie between two limits. ***—modifier:*** *a scale model; a scale drawing. —v.* **scaled, scal•ing. 1.** To climb up to the top of or over: *scale a mountain.* **2.** To draw or arrange in

saw[1-2]

Saw[1] *was Old English* sagu *or* sage; *it is descended from prehistoric Germanic* sagō, *"a cutting tool, a saw," which in turn is from Indo-European* sek-, *"to cut"; see note at* **section. Saw[2]** *was Old English* sagu, *"a saying"; see note at* **say.**

saxophone

Antoine Joseph *Sax* (1814–94), a Belgian maker of musical instruments, invented both the **saxhorn** (in 1845) and the **saxophone** (in 1846). Shown above is an alto saxophone.

say

Say *was Old English* secgan; *it is descended from the prehistoric Germanic verb* sagjan, *"to say." This verb had the noun* sagō, *"a saying, something said," which appeared in (1) Old English* sagu, *"a saying,"* **saw[2]**, *and (2) Old Norse* saga, *"a telling, a story," which was borrowed into English as* **saga.**

scaffolding

scale¹·²·³
Scale¹ *is from Old French* escale, *"shell, husk"; it is related to* **shell. Scale²** *is from Latin* scāla, *"ladder."* **Scale³** *is from Old Norse* skāl, *"bowl, one of the pans of a balance"; it originally meant "shell," and is related to* **scale¹.**

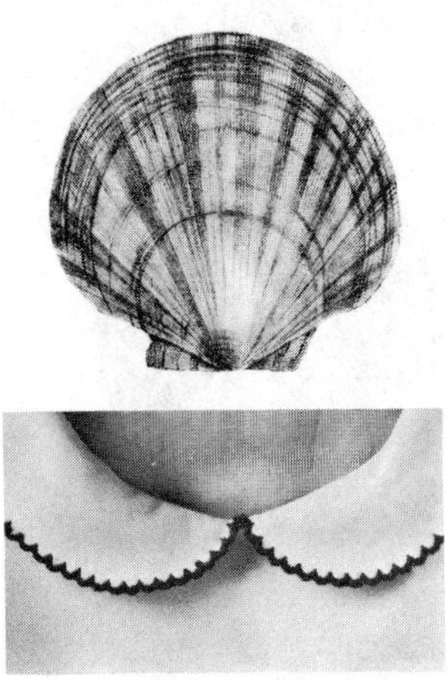

scallop
Above: Shell
Below: Scalloped collar

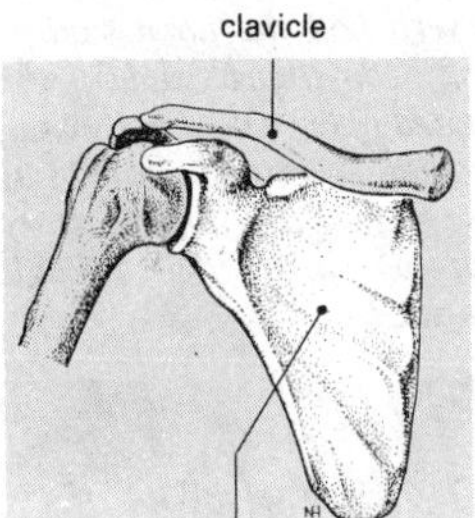

scapula

ă pat/ā pay/â care/ä father/ĕ pet/ ē be/ĭ pit/ī pie/î fierce/ŏ pot/ ō go/ô paw, for/oi oil/ŏŏ book/ ōō boot/ou out/ŭ cut/û fur/ *th* the/th thin/hw which/zh vision/ ə ago, item, pencil, atom, circus

a particular proportion or scale. **3.** To adjust or regulate according to some standard: *scaling back business to curtail spending.* [SEE NOTE]

scale³ |skāl| *n.* **1.** An instrument or machine for weighing. **2.** Either of the pans or dishes of a balance. —*v.* **scaled, scal•ing. 1.** To weigh on scales. **2.** To have a weight of. [SEE NOTE]
***Idiom.* tip** (or **turn**) **the scales.** To be a decisive factor or determine the outcome.

sca•lene triangle |skā'lēn'| *or* |skā lēn'|. A triangle in which each side is of a different length from every other side.

scal•lion |skăl'yən| *n.* A young onion with a small, narrow white bulb and long, narrow green leaves, both of which are eaten raw as a relish or used in cooking.

scal•lop |skŏl'əp| *or* |skăl'-| *n.* **1. a.** A soft-bodied sea animal having a double, hinged, fan-shaped shell with radiating, fluted markings. **b.** The fleshy muscle of such an animal, used as food. **2.** A thin, flattened, boneless slice of meat. **3.** One of a series of curves shaped like semicircles that form a fancy border. —*v.* **1.** To bake in a casserole with a sauce and often with bread crumbs. **2.** To form into scallops along the edge. —**scal'loped** *adj.: a scalloped tablecloth; scalloped potatoes.* [SEE PICTURE]

scalp |skălp| *n.* The skin that covers the top of the human head. —*v.* **1.** To cut or tear the scalp from. **2.** *Informal.* To sell (tickets) at a price higher than their established value. —**scalp'er** *n.*

scal•pel |skăl'pəl| *n.* A small straight knife with a thin, pointed blade, used in surgery.

scal•y |skā'lē| *adj.* **scal•i•er, scal•i•est. 1.** Covered with scales: *scaly claws.* **2.** Shedding scales: *dry, scaly skin.* —**scal'i•ness** *n.*

scamp |skămp| *n.* **1.** A scheming person; a rascal. **2.** A playful, mischievous person.

scam•per |skăm'pər| *v.* To run or go hurriedly.

scan |skăn| *v.* **scanned, scan•ning. 1.** To examine (something) closely: *scan his pockets for change.* **2.** To look (something) over quickly: *scan the page for answers.* **3.** To make a thorough search, as with a radar beam: *scan the skies for enemy aircraft.* **4.** To analyze (verse) so as to show metrical feet or rhythm patterns.

scan•dal |skăn'dl| *n.* **1.** Something that offends the morality of the social community; a public disgrace. **2.** Malicious gossip.

scan•dal•ize |skăn'dl īz'| *v.* **scan•dal•ized, scan•dal•iz•ing.** To shock the moral sense of.

scan•dal•ous |skăn'dl əs| *adj.* **1.** Causing scandal: *scandalous behavior.* **2.** Containing malicious gossip: *scandalous talk.* —**scan'dal•ous•ly** *adv.* —**scan'dal•ous•ness** *n.*

Scan•di•na•vi•a |skăn'də nā'vē ə|. The northern European countries of Norway, Sweden, and Denmark.

Scan•di•na•vi•an |skăn'də nā'vē ən| *n.* **1.** A native or inhabitant of Scandinavia. **2.** A group of Germanic languages, including Danish, Swedish, Icelandic, and Norwegian. —*adj.* Of Scandinavia, the Scandinavians, or their languages.

scan•di•um |skăn'dē əm| *n.* Symbol **Sc** One of the elements, a silvery, very lightweight metal. Atomic number 21; atomic weight 44.956; valence +3; melting point 1,539°C; boiling point 2,727°C.

scant |skănt| *adj.* **scant•er, scant•est. 1.** Lacking in amount or quantity; meager; inadequate: *scant vegetation.* **2.** Being just short of; not quite: *a scant six miles away.* —*v.* To provide an inadequate amount of; skimp on.

scant•y |skăn'tē| *adj.* **scant•i•er, scant•i•est. 1.** Barely sufficient; meager: *a scanty water supply.* **2.** Too small: *an old and scanty garment.* —**scant'i•ly** *adv.* —**scant'i•ness** *n.*

-scape. A word element meaning "scene, view": *cityscape.*

scape•goat |skāp'gōt'| *n.* A person, group, institution, etc., that bears blame unjustly.

scap•u•la |skăp'yə lə| *n., pl.* **scap•u•las** or **scap•u•lae** |skăp'yə lē'|. Either of two flat, triangular bones behind the shoulders; shoulder blade. [SEE PICTURE]

scar |skär| *n.* **1.** A mark left on the skin after a wound or injury has healed. **2.** A mark, as on a plant stem, where a leaf, bud, or other part was at one time attached. **3.** Any mark or sign of damage, either physical or emotional. —*v.* **scarred, scar•ring.** To mark with or form a scar.

scar•ab |skăr'əb| *n.* **1.** Any of several often large, broad-bodied beetles, especially one of a kind regarded as sacred by the ancient Egyptians. **2.** An ornament, symbol, or charm made to look like such a beetle.

scarce |skârs| *adj.* **scarc•er, scarc•est.** Insufficient to meet a demand or requirement: *Food is scarce in some countries.* —**scarce'ness** *n.*
***Idiom.* make (oneself) scarce.** *Informal.* To get out or stay away.

scarce•ly |skârs'lē| *adv.* **1.** Almost not at all; just; barely; hardly: *I could scarcely see through the fog.* **2.** Certainly not: *I could scarcely ask her to help under the circumstances.*

scar•ci•ty |skâr'sĭ tē| *n., pl.* **scar•ci•ties.** Insufficient amount or supply; shortage.

scare |skâr| *v.* **scared, scar•ing. 1.** To frighten or become frightened; terrify: *The dog scared the postman. She doesn't scare easily.* **2.** To force or drive by frightening: *The gun scared off the bandits.* —*n.* A sensation of fear or panic.

scare•crow |skâr'krō'| *n.* **1.** A crude figure of a person set up in a field to scare birds away from crops. **2.** A thin, haggard person.

scarf |skärf| *n., pl.* **scarfs** or **scarves** |skärvz|. **1.** A rectangular or triangular piece of cloth worn around the neck or head. **2.** A long, narrow piece of cloth used to cover a dresser, table, bureau, etc.

scar•let |skär'lĭt| *n.* A bright red or red-orange. —*adj.* Bright red or red-orange.

scarlet fever. A severe contagious disease caused by bacteria. It occurs mainly in children and is characterized by a high fever and a scarlet rash on the skin.

scarves |skärvz| *n.* A plural of **scarf.**

scar•y |skâr'ē| *adj.* **scar•i•er, scar•i•est. 1.** Frightening; terrifying. **2.** Easily frightened; timid. —**scar'i•ly** *adv.*

scat |skăt| *interj. Informal.* A word used to drive away a person or animal, especially a cat.

scathe |skāth| *v.* **scathed, scath•ing.** To harm or injure severely, especially by fire or heat.

scath•ing |skā'thĭng| *adj.* Extremely severe or harsh: *scathing criticism.* —**scath'ing•ly** *adv.*

scat•ter |skăt'ər| *v.* **1.** To separate and go or

cause to separate and go in various directions: *At the bell, the class scattered into the hallways. The wind scatters seeds.* **2.** To distribute loosely by or as if by sprinkling or strewing: *The child scattered his toys all over.* **3.** To deflect a stream of (incident rays or particles) so that they rebound in different directions.

scat•ter•brained |skăt′ər brānd′| *adj.* Thoughtless and flighty.

scat•ter•ing |skăt′ər ĭng| *n.* **1.** The act or process of scattering. **2.** A small number or quantity scattered about: *a scattering of neighborhood women at the school.* **3.** The spreading of a beam of particles or rays over a range of directions as a result of collisions or other physical interactions.

scatter rug. A small rug used to cover part of a floor.

scav•enge |skăv′ĭnj| *v.* **scav•enged, scav•eng•ing. 1.** To eat or eat from as a scavenger. **2.** To search for or find (something useful or edible) in rubbish or other discarded material.

scav•en•ger |skăv′ĭn jər| *n.* **1.** An animal, such as a vulture, hyena, or catfish, that feeds on the remains of dead animals or on other dead or decaying plant or animal material. **2.** Someone who searches through rubbish or discarded material for food, useful objects, etc.

sce•nar•i•o |sĭ nâr′ē ō| *or* |-när′-| *n., pl.* **sce•nar•i•os. 1.** An outline of the plot of a story or play. **2.** The text of a motion picture.

scene |sēn| *n.* **1.** A place or area as seen by a viewer; a view from a particular point: *a winter scene; the scene from my window.* **2.** The place and its immediate surroundings where an action or event occurs: *the scene of the wreck.* **3.** The place in which the action of a story or play occurs. **4.** A section of a play, usually one of the divisions of an act, or a short section of a motion picture. **5.** A display of temper or behavior that creates a commotion or attracts attention in public. ¶*These sound alike* **scene, seen.**

scen•er•y |sē′nə rē| *n.* **1.** The landscape. **2.** The structures or curtains on the stage of a theater, designed and painted to represent the place where the action occurs.

sce•nic |sē′nĭk| *adj.* Of natural scenery, especially attractive landscapes: *a scenic route.*

scent |sĕnt| *n.* **1.** A distinctive odor: *the scent of pine.* **2.** A perfume: *a woman wearing a strong scent.* **3.** The trail of a hunted animal or fugitive: *The dogs lost the deer's scent.* **4.** The sense of smell: *hunting by scent.* **5.** A hint of something; a suggestion: *a scent of corruption in municipal politics.* —*v.* **1.** To perceive, identify, or detect by or as if by smelling: *scent danger.* **2.** To provide with an odor; perfume. —**scent′ed** *adj.: scented candles.* ¶*These sound alike* **scent, cent, sent.**

scep•ter |sĕp′tər| *n.* A staff held by a sovereign as a sign of authority. [SEE PICTURE]

scep•tic |skĕp′tĭk| *n.* A form of the word **skeptic.**

scep•ti•cal |skĕp′tĭ kəl| *adj.* A form of the word **skeptical.**

scep•ti•cism |skĕp′tĭ sĭz′əm| *n.* A form of the word **skepticism.**

sched•ule |skĕj′o͞ol| *or* |-o͞o əl| *or* |skĕj′əl| *n.* **1.** A program of forthcoming events or appointments. **2.** A student's program of classes. **3.** A timetable of departures and arrivals. **4.** Any plan indicating something to be done within a specified time. **5.** The time allowed for such plans: *behind schedule; on schedule.* —*v.* **sched•uled, sched•ul•ing. 1.** To enter on a schedule. **2.** To make up a schedule for. **3.** To plan or appoint for a certain time or date: *schedule the class for the morning.* —**sched′uled** *adj.: a regularly scheduled flight.*

scheme |skēm| *n.* **1.** A plan for doing something. **2.** An underhand or secret plot; intrigue. **3.** A chart, diagram, or outline of a plan, system, etc. **4.** Any orderly combination or arrangement: *a color scheme.* —*v.* **schemed, schem•ing. 1.** To make up a plan or scheme for. **2.** To plot underhandedly. —**schem′ing** *adj.: a scheming person.* —**schem′er** *n.*

scher•zo |skĕr′tsō| *n., pl.* **scher•zos** or **scher•zi** |skĕr′tsē|. A lively musical movement, usually in $^3/_4$ time or a related time. [SEE NOTE]

schil•ling |shĭl′ĭng| *n.* The basic unit of money of Austria.

schism |sĭz′əm| *or* |skĭz′-| *n.* **1.** A separation or division within a church or religious body. **2.** Any such separation within a group.

schis•mat•ic |sĭz măt′ĭk| *or* |skĭz-| *adj.* Of a schism. —*n.* A person who joins in or helps cause a schism. —**schis•mat′i•cal•ly** *adv.*

schiz•oid |skĭt′soid′| *adj.* Of or resembling schizophrenia. —*n.* A schizophrenic.

schiz•o•phre•ni•a |skĭt′sə frē′nē ə| *or* |-frĕn′yə| *or* |-frĕn′ē ə| *n.* Any of a group of severe mental disorders in which a person loses awareness of reality and ability to relate closely with others, often with disturbances of behavior and the ability to reason.

schiz•o•phren•ic |skĭt′sə frĕn′ĭk| *adj.* Of or affected by schizophrenia. —*n.* A schizophrenic person.

schnau•zer |shnou′zər| *n.* A dog of a breed originally from Germany, having a wiry grayish coat and ranging in size from fairly small to quite large. [SEE PICTURE]

schol•ar |skŏl′ər| *n.* **1. a.** A person of great learning. **b.** A person with much knowledge in a particular field: *a scholar of Russian history.* **2.** A pupil or student. **3.** A student who has received a particular scholarship.

schol•ar•ly |skŏl′ər lē| *adv.* Of or befitting a scholar or scholarship: *scholarly research.*

schol•ar•ship |skŏl′ər shĭp′| *n.* **1.** A grant of money awarded to a student seeking further education, usually based on personal achievement or need. **2.** The methods, disciplines, and learning of a scholar. **3.** Existing knowledge from extensive research in a particular field.

scho•las•tic |skə lăs′tĭk| *adj.* **1.** Of schools or education; academic: *scholastic standards; scholastic achievement.* **2.** Pedantic; dogmatic: *a rigid and scholastic doctrine.* —**scho•las′ti•cal•ly** *adv.*

school[1] |sko͞ol| *n.* **1.** An institution for teaching and learning. **2.** A division for special study within a university: *a law school.* **3.** The group of students and teachers within a school. **4.** A building or group of buildings in which teaching takes place. **5.** The instruction given at a school. **6.** Attendance at or the process of being educated at a school: *She finds school hard.* **7.** A group of persons under some common influence

scepter
Scepter of Charles V of France

scherzo
The **scherzo** *developed from the minuet that was commonly included as a movement of the classical symphony, string quartet, etc. Beethoven was one of the composers who was important in its development. The name* **scherzo** *comes from Italian* scherzo, *"joke."*

schnauzer

school[1-2]

School[1] *was Old English* scōl, *which was borrowed from Latin* schola, *which in turn was from Greek* skholē; *this word basically meant "leisure, free time" and came also to mean "leisure time occupied by learning, a scientific discussion, a lecture," and hence "a school."* **School**[2] *is from Middle Dutch* schōle, *"group, shoal."*

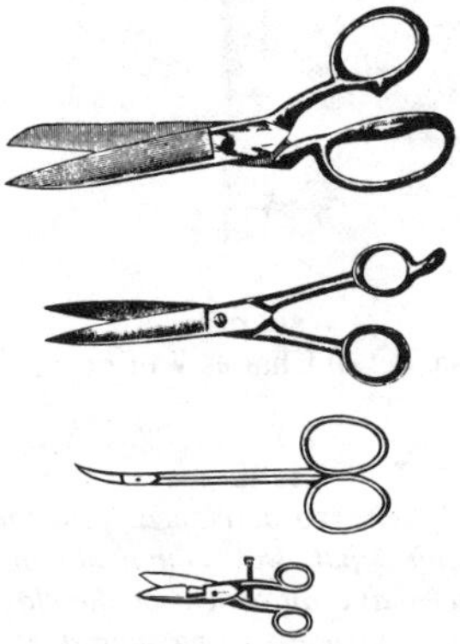

scissors
From top: Trimming scissors, barber scissors, manicure scissors, buttonhole scissors

or sharing some belief: *a new school in painting.* —*modifier: a school band.* —*v.* **1.** To instruct; educate. **2.** To train or discipline. [SEE NOTE]

school[2] |skōōl| *n.* A large group of fish or other water animals, such as whales or porpoises, swimming together. —*v.* To form or swim in such a group. [SEE NOTE]

school•book |**skōōl**'bŏŏk'| *n.* A textbook.

school•boy |**skōōl**'boi'| *n.* A boy attending school.

school•child |**skōōl**'chīld'| *n., pl.* **-chil•dren** |**-chĭl**'drən|. A child attending school.

school•girl |**skōōl**'gûrl'| *n.* A girl attending school.

school•house |**skōōl**'hous'| *n., pl.* **-hous•es** |-hou'zĭz|. A building used as a school.

school•ing |**skōō**'lĭng| *n.* **1.** Instruction given at school; formal education: *The move interrupted her schooling.* **2.** Training or instruction through experience: *his schooling as a sailor.*

school•marm |**skōōl**'märm'| *n. Informal.* A woman who teaches school, especially one who teaches in a small, rural schoolhouse.

school•mas•ter |**skōōl**'măs'tər| *or* |-mä'stər| *n.* **1.** A man who teaches school. **2.** A headmaster of a school.

school•mis•tress |**skōōl**'mĭs'trĭs| *n.* **1.** A woman who teaches school. **2.** A headmistress of a school.

school•room |**skōōl**'rōōm'| *or* |-rŏŏm'| *n.* A classroom in a school.

school•teach•er |**skōōl**'tē'chər| *n.* A person who teaches school below the college level.

school•work |**skōōl**'wûrk'| *n.* The body of assignments in school.

school•yard |**skōōl**'yärd'| *n.* The yard next to and belonging to a school.

schoo•ner |**skōō**'nər| *n.* **1.** A fore-and-aft-rigged sailing vessel with two or more masts. **2.** *Informal.* A beer glass holding a pint or more.

Schu•bert |**shōō**'bərt|, **Franz.** 1797–1828. Austrian composer.

Schu•mann |**shōō**'män'|, **Robert.** 1810–1856. German composer.

schwa |shwä| *or* |shvä| *n.* A symbol (ə) for certain vowel sounds that in English often occur in unstressed syllables; for example, the sounds of *a* in *alone* and *e* in *linen* are represented by a schwa.

sci•ence |**sī**'əns| *n.* **1. a** The study and theoretical explanation of natural phenomena. **b.** Such activity applied to a particular class of phenomena: *the science of living things.* **2.** Any systematic activity requiring study and method. **3.** Knowledge, especially knowledge gained through experience. —*modifier: a science project.*

science fiction. Fiction in which imaginative scientific possibilities, such as star travel, are used in the plot, often with a future society as the setting. —*modifier:* **(science-fiction):** *a science-fiction novel.*

sci•en•tif•ic |sī'ən **tĭf**'ĭk| *adj.* **1.** Of or used in science or a science. **2.** Appearing or considered in general to have a factual, logical, or systematic basis. —**sci'en•tif'i•cal•ly** *adv.*

scientific method. A method of investigation that typically uses careful observation, experimentation, and mathematical description.

sci•en•tist |**sī**'ən tĭst| *n.* Someone who is an expert in one or more sciences, as a physicist.

scim•i•tar |**sĭm**'ĭ tər| *or* |-tär'| *n.* A short, curved, single-edged sword.

scin•til•la |sĭn **tĭl**'ə| *n.* A minute amount; a trace; an iota: *without a scintilla of courtesy.*

scin•til•late |**sĭn**'tl āt'| *v.* **scin•til•lat•ed, scin•til•lat•ing. 1.** To throw off sparks; flash or sparkle. **2.** To be animated or brilliant: *The conversation scintillated all evening.* —**scin'til•la'tion** *n.*

sci•on |**sī**'ən| *n.* **1.** Someone who is descended, as from a line of ancestors; a descendant. **2.** A twig or shoot that has been removed from one plant for grafting onto another.

scis•sors |**sĭz**'ərz| *n. (used with a plural verb).* A cutting tool consisting of two blades, each with a ring-shaped handle, joined on a pivot that allows the cutting edges to close against each other. [SEE PICTURE]

scle•ra |**sklîr**'ə| *n.* The tough, white, fibrous tissue that covers all of the eyeball except the cornea.

scle•ro•sis |sklə **rō**'sĭs| *n., pl.* **scle•ro•ses** |sklə-**rō**'sēz'|. **1.** A condition, especially a diseased condition, in which a body part, such as an artery or the spinal cord, thickens or hardens. **2.** A disease characterized by sclerosis.

scoff |skôf| *or* |skŏf| *v.* To show derision or mockery: *They scoffed at his ideas.* —*n.* An expression of derision or scorn. —**scoff'er** *n.*

scold |skōld| *v.* **1.** To reprimand (someone) harshly or angrily. **2.** To make or cry at with an angry, excited sound. —**scold'ing** *adj.: a scolding voice.* —*n.* Someone who often rails against others. —**scold'er** *n.*

sconce |skŏns| *n.* A decorative wall bracket for holding a candle or an electric light.

scone |skōn| *or* |skŏn| *n.* **1.** A soft, doughy biscuit. **2.** A thin oatmeal cake baked on a griddle.

scoop |skōōp| *n.* **1.** A small, shovellike utensil with a short handle, used to take up sugar, flour, etc. **2.** A thick-handled utensil with a round bowl, used to dispense mashed potatoes, ice cream, etc. **3.** The bucket of a steam shovel or dredge. **4. a** A scoop with something in it: *serve a scoop of mashed potatoes.* **b.** The amount a scoop holds: *eat a scoop of ice cream.* **5.** A scooping movement or action. **6.** *Informal.* A news story published exclusively in one newspaper or magazine. **7.** *Slang.* Important, often confidential, information about something that has just happened. —*v.* **1.** To lift out or up with or as if with a scoop: *scoop out the seeds; scoop up dirt.* **2.** To hollow out or form by digging: *scoop out a hole.* **3.** *Informal.* To obtain and publish a news story ahead of (all rival newspapers, magazines, etc.).

scoot |skōōt| *v.* To go or cause to go speedily; dart: *They scooted off to the deep woods. He scooted the chair across the room.*

scoot•er |**skōō**'tər| *n.* **1.** A toy vehicle consisting of a long footboard between two small end wheels, the forward wheel controlled by an upright steering bar. **2.** A **motor scooter.**

scope |skōp| *n.* **1.** The range of one's perceptions, thoughts, actions, or abilities: *broaden one's scope by reading.* **2.** Breadth or opportunity to function: *a situation that gave scope to his imagination.* **3.** The area covered by an activity,

ă pat/ā pay/â care/ä father/ĕ pet/ ē be/ĭ pit/ī pie/î fierce/ŏ pot/ ō go/ô paw, for/oi oil/ŏŏ book/ ōō boot/ou out/ŭ cut/û fur/ *th* the/th thin/hw which/zh vision/ ə ago, item, pencil, atom, circus

situation, or subject: *national in scope.*

-scope. A word element meaning "an instrument for detecting or observing": **telescope.**

scorch |skôrch| *v.* **1.** To burn or become burned on the surface. **2.** To wither or parch with intense heat: *The sun scorched the desert.* —**scorch'ing** *adj.: a scorching summer.* —*n.* **1.** A slight or surface burn. **2.** A discoloration caused by heat.

scorch•er |skôr'chər| *or* |skōr'chər| *n. Informal.* An extremely hot day.

score |skôr| *or* |skōr| *n.* **1.** The number of points made by each competitor or team in a game or contest: *a score of 50.* **2.** A record of points made in a game or contest: *keep the score.* **3.** A result of a test or examination: *a score of 90 on a math test.* **4.** A set containing 20 items. **5. scores.** Large numbers: *scores of people.* **6.** The written form of a musical composition. **7.** Music composed for an opera, musical comedy, film, etc. **8.** A grievance, grudge, or wrong that demands satisfaction: *settle that score tonight.* **9.** Grounds; a reason; an account: *On that score they decided not to go.* —***modifier:*** *a score card; a score chart.* —*v.* **scored, scor•ing. 1. a.** To gain (a point or points) in a game or contest: *We scored 24 points. They did not score.* **b.** To count or be worth as points: *That run scored six points.* **2.** To achieve (a certain number of points) on a test or examination: *scored 90 on the test.* **3.** To achieve, gain, or win: *score a touchdown; scored success in the play.* **4.** To record the points in (a game or contest). **5.** To evaluate and assign a grade to: *He scored the tests.* **6. a.** To arrange for orchestra; orchestrate. **b.** To write or arrange for a particular musical instrument. **7.** To mark with lines, notches, or cuts. —**scor'er** *n.*

sco•ri•a |skôr'ē ə| *or* |skōr'-| *n., pl.* **sco•ri•ae** |skôr'ē ē'| *or* |skōr'-|. **1.** Rough pieces of burnt, crusty lava. **2.** The waste left after a metal or ore is smelted; slag.

scorn |skôrn| *v.* **1.** To consider or treat (something or someone) with contempt or disdain: *He scorned the ideas of others.* **2.** To reject or refuse because of contempt or disdain: *He scorned to ask for help.* —*n.* **1.** A feeling that someone or something is inferior or unworthy; contempt or disdain. **2.** The expression of contempt or disdain; derision. **3.** Someone or something considered or treated with contempt: *a child who was the scorn of the neighborhood.* —**scorn'er** *n.*

scorn•ful |skôrn'fəl| *adj.* Full of or expressing scorn; disdainful: *a scornful attitude; a scornful laugh.* —**scorn'ful•ly** *adv.* —**scorn'ful•ness** *n.*

Scor•pi•o |skôr'pē ō'| *n.* The eighth sign of the zodiac.

scor•pi•on |skôr'pē ən| *n.* An animal related to the spiders, having a narrow, jointed body and a tail with a poisonous sting. [SEE PICTURE]

Scot |skŏt| *n.* A native or inhabitant of Scotland.

scotch |skŏch| *v.* **1.** To put an end to; crush; stifle: *scotch a popular misconception.* **2.** To injure so as to make harmless for a time; wound.

Scotch |skŏch| *n.* **1. the Scotch.** The people of Scotland. **2. Scotch whisky.** —*adj.* Scottish. [SEE NOTE]

Scotch•man |skŏch'mən| *n., pl.* **-men** |-mən|. A Scot.

Scotch tape. A trademark for a cellulose adhesive tape.

Scotch whisky. A smoky-flavored whiskey distilled in Scotland from malted barley.

scot-free |skŏt'frē'| *adj.* Without having to undergo punishment or penalty.

Scot•land |skŏt'lənd|. A division of the United Kingdom, on the island of Great Britain, north of England. Population, 5,200,000. Capital, Edinburgh.

Scotland Yard. The headquarters of the police department of London, England.

Scots |skŏts| *adj.* Scottish.

Scots•man |skŏts'mən| *n., pl.* **-men** |-mən|. A native or inhabitant of Scotland; a Scot.

Scott |skŏt|, **Sir Walter.** 1771–1832. Scottish poet and novelist.

Scot•tie |skŏt'ē| *n. Informal.* A **Scottish terrier.**

Scot•tish |skŏt'ĭsh| *n.* **1.** The dialect of English spoken in Scotland. **2. the Scottish.** The people of Scotland. —*adj.* Of Scotland, the Scots, or their languages. [SEE NOTE]

Scottish Gaelic. The Gaelic language of the Scottish Highlanders.

Scottish terrier. A dog of a breed originally from Scotland, having short legs, a dark, wiry coat, and a blunt muzzle.

scoun•drel |skoun'drəl| *n.* A wicked, dishonorable person; a villain.

scour[1] |skour| *v.* **1.** To clean or polish by scrubbing vigorously, usually with an abrasive. **2.** To clear or empty by or as if by flushing: *currents that scoured the canyon of sediment.* —**scour'ing** *adj.: a scouring pad.* —*n.* The act of cleaning or polishing by vigorous scrubbing. —**scour'er** *n.*

scour[2] |skour| *v.* To range or travel over (an area), especially in searching: *He scoured the seas for the enemy fleet.* —**scour'er** *n.*

scourge |skûrj| *n.* **1.** A whip used to inflict punishment. **2.** Any means of inflicting suffering or punishment. **3.** A cause of widespread affliction, as pestilence or war. —*v.* **scourged, scourg•ing. 1.** To flog. **2.** To punish severely. **3.** To subject to widespread affliction; devastate. —**scourg'er** *n.*

scout |skout| *n.* **1.** Someone who goes out from a main body to gather information. **2.** Often **Scout.** A member of the Boy Scouts or Girl Scouts. **3.** A person employed to discover and recruit persons with talent. —***modifier:*** *a scout patrol; a scout troop.* —*v.* **1.** To observe or explore (a place) carefully in order to obtain information: *The soldier scouted the woods ahead. He scouted on foot.* **2.** To observe and evaluate (an athlete or entertainer) for possible hiring. **3.** To search: *He scouted around for his baseball glove.* —**scout'ing** *adj.: a scouting expedition.*

scout•mas•ter |skout'măs'tər| *or* |-mä'stər| *n.* The adult leader of a troop of Boy Scouts.

scow |skou| *n.* A large open barge used to transport sand, gravel, or garbage.

scowl |skoul| *v.* To lower or contract the brow in an expression of anger, disapproval, etc.; frown angrily: *He scowled at the child.* —*n.* An angry frown. —**scowl'er** *n.*

scrab•ble |skrăb'əl| *v.* **scrab•bled, scrab•bling. 1.** To grope about frenziedly with the hands: *scrabbled in the dust for the tool.* **2.** To struggle: *scrabbled for a living on the farm.* **3.** To make or

scorpion

Scotch/Scottish, etc.

The form **Scotch** *as a plural noun (sense* **1***), and as a general adjective, is disliked by most of the people of Scotland; they prefer the nouns* **Scot** *and* **Scotsman** *and the adjectives* **Scots** *and* **Scottish,** *and they consider that* **Scotch** *is appropriate only to certain things found or produced in Scotland, notably whiskey, tweed, and broth. The exact reason for this is not clear;* **Scotch** *is a respectable old variant form of* **Scottish,** *and up to the middle of the nineteenth century it was freely used by the Scots themselves. It seems that the word somehow became associated with English feelings of hostility toward Scotland. Anyway, for a century now the Scots have been insisting that it is wrong to refer to people or matters of national concern as* **Scotch**; *and on the whole the English have fully accepted this.*

obtain by or as if by scraping together.

scrag•gly |skrăg′lē| *adj.* **scrag•gli•er, scrag•gli•est.** **1.** Untended; unkempt: *scraggly hair; scraggly undergrowth.* **2.** Irregular; uneven.

scrag•gy |skrăg′ē| *adj.* **scrag•gi•er, scrag•gi•est.** **1.** Jagged; rough. **2.** Bony and lean. **—scrag′gi•ly** *adv.* **—scrag′gi•ness** *n.*

scram |skrăm| *v.* **scrammed, scram•ming.** *Slang.* To leave at once; go immediately.

scram•ble |skrăm′bəl| *v.* **scram•bled, scram•bling.** **1.** To move hurriedly or in a disorganized manner: *She scrambled over the stone wall.* **2.** To struggle or move about eagerly or urgently in competition with others: *The children scrambled for the candy.* **3.** To mix together confusedly: *scrambled the letters of a word.* **4.** To cook (eggs) by mixing together and frying the yolks and whites. **5.** To process (an electronic signal) so that it cannot be used or understood without a special receiver. **—scram′bled** *adj.: scrambled eggs; the scrambled letters of a word.* **—n.** **1.** A strenuous climb: *It was quite a scramble to reach the pass.* **2.** A struggle for something: *a scramble for new territory.* **3.** The act of moving hurriedly.

scram•bler |skrăm′blər| *n.* **1.** Someone or something that scrambles. **2.** An electronic device that processes a signal so that it can be received only with special equipment.

scrap¹ |skrăp| *n.* **1.** A fragment; a shred or particle: *a scrap of paper; a scrap of a tune.* **2. scraps.** Leftover bits of food. **3.** Material that is left over or discarded, especially discarded metal suitable for reprocessing: *sold the old car as scrap.* ***—modifier:*** *scrap iron; scrap paper; a scrap pile.* **—v.** **scrapped, scrap•ping.** To discard or abandon as useless: *scrap a plan.* [SEE NOTE]

scrap² |skrăp|. *Slang.* *v.* **scrapped, scrap•ping.** To fight or quarrel. **—n.** A fight or quarrel. [SEE NOTE]

scrap•book |skrăp′bo͝ok′| *n.* A book with blank pages for mounting pictures or other mementos.

scrape |skrāp| *v.* **scraped, scrap•ing.** **1.** To rub (a surface) forcefully, as to clean, smooth, or shape: *scrape a carrot.* **2.** To remove (material) from something in this way: *scraped icing from the plate.* **3.** To bring or come into sliding, abrasive contact, often with a harsh grating sound. **4.** To injure or damage the skin or surface of by rubbing against something rough or sharp. **5.** To amass, produce, or get along with difficulty: *scrape together enough money; scraping along in a small shack.* **6.** To be frugal; scrimp: *We had to pinch and scrape to pay the bill.* **—n.** **1.** Something produced by scraping, as an injury, mark, etc. **2.** The act of scraping: *the scrape of the shovel against rock.* **3.** *Slang.* **a.** An embarrassing or difficult situation. **b.** A fight. [SEE NOTE]

scrap•er |skrā′pər| *n.* **1.** A person who scrapes. **2.** A tool for scraping off paint, ice, etc.

scrap•py¹ |skrăp′ē| *adj.* **scrap•pi•er, scrap•pi•est.** Made up of bits and pieces; fragmentary. **—scrap′pi•ly** *adv.* **—scrap′pi•ness** *n.*

scrap•py² |skrăp′ē| *adj.* **scrap•pi•er, scrap•pi•est.** **1.** Full of fighting spirit. **2.** Quarrelsome; contentious. **—scrap′pi•ly** *adv.* **—scrap′pi•ness** *n.*

scratch |skrăch| *v.* **1.** To make a thin, shallow cut or mark on (a surface) with or as if with a sharp tool or instrument. **2.** To rub to relieve itching: *scratched his back; scratching with the fingernails.* **3.** To dig, scrape, damage, or wound (someone or something) with nails, claws, or anything sharp or abrasive: *Hens scratched in the yard. He fell and scratched his knee.* **4. a.** To write, draw, or mark with something pointed: *scratched a name on a rock.* **b.** To write or mark hastily; scrawl: *scratched notes on a pad.* **5.** To make a thin, scraping sound: *The pencil scratched on the paper.* **6.** To withdraw from competition: *scratch a horse from a race.* **7.** To strike out or cancel by or as by drawing a line through: *scratch out a word.* **8.** To obtain with difficulty and struggle: *scratch a living from the soil.* **—scratched′** *adj.: a scratched fender.* **—scratch′ing** *adj.: a scratching sound.* **—n.** **1.** A thin, shallow mark, injury, etc., made by scratching. **2.** A harsh, scraping sound. **—adj.** **1.** Used for hasty notes or sketches: *scratch paper; a scratch pad.* **2.** Done hurriedly or haphazardly: *a scratch outline.* **3.** Assembled at random: *a scratch team.* **—scratch′er** *n.*

Idioms. from scratch. From the beginning or from nothing: *start from scratch.* **up to scratch.** *Informal.* In standard or fit condition: *His work is not up to scratch.*

scratch•y |skrăch′ē| *adj.* **scratch•i•er, scratch•i•est.** **1.** Tending to scratch; rough or harsh. **2.** Making a harsh, scratching sound. **—scratch′i•ly** *adv.* **—scratch′i•ness** *n.*

scrawl |skrôl| *v.* To write hastily or illegibly. **—n.** Irregular or illegible handwriting. **—scrawl′er** *n.*

scraw•ny |skrô′nē| *adj.* **scraw•ni•er, scraw•ni•est.** Thin and bony; skinny. **—scraw′ni•ness** *n.*

scream |skrēm| *v.* **1.** To utter a long, loud, piercing cry: *He screamed in fear.* **2.** To utter in or as if in a loud, piercing voice: *She screamed a warning.* **3.** To make a loud, piercing sound: *The siren screamed.* **—n.** **1.** A loud, piercing cry or sound: *the scream of a cougar; the scream of brakes.* **2.** *Slang.* Someone or something that is very funny. **—scream′er** *n.*

scream•ing |skrē′mĭng| *adj.* **1.** Producing screams: *screaming children; the screaming wind.* **2.** Startling; striking: *a screaming headline; a screaming chartreuse.* **—scream′ing•ly** *adv.*

screech |skrēch| *n.* **1.** A high-pitched, harsh cry; a shriek. **2.** A sound resembling this: *the screech of brakes.* **—v.** **1.** To scream in a high-pitched, harsh voice. **2.** To make a shrill, grating sound: *The file screeched across the metal table.* **3.** To utter in a high-pitched, harsh voice: *screeched an answer.* **—screech′ing** *adj.: screeching brakes; a screeching voice.*

screech owl. A small owl with earlike tufts on its head and a wailing, quavering call.

screen |skrēn| *n.* **1.** A light, movable frame used to divide, conceal, or protect. **2.** Anything that serves to conceal: *a smoke screen.* **3.** A frame covered with wire mesh, used in a window or door to keep out insects. **4.** A large flat surface upon which slides or motion pictures are projected. **5.** The surface of a cathode-ray tube on which an image appears, as in a television receiver. **6.** Motion pictures in general or the motion-picture industry: *bring a story to the screen.* **7.** A coarse sieve. ***—modifier:*** *screen wire; a screen door.* **—v.** **1.** To provide with a screen:

scrap¹·²/scrape

Scrap¹ *is from Old Norse* skrap, *"bits and pieces, remains."* **Scrape** *is from Old Norse* skrapa, *"to scratch." The two Old Norse words are closely related, the underlying sense being "cut, scrape off." Sense* 3 *of the noun* **scrape** *is not easy to explain; it seems to have arisen from the sense "situation in which one is* scraped *or hurt in some way."* **Scrap²** *originally meant "a criminal plan, a dangerous scheme" and only later came to mean "fight"; it is probably a variant of the noun* **scrape**.

ă **pat**/ā **pay**/â **care**/ä **father**/ĕ **pet**/ ē **be**/ĭ **pit**/ī **pie**/î **fierce**/ŏ **pot**/ ō **go**/ô **paw**, **for**/oi **oil**/o͝o **book**/ o͞o **boot**/ou **out**/ŭ **cut**/û **fur**/ *th* **the**/th **thin**/hw **which**/**zh** vision/ ə **ago**, item, pencil, atom, circus *screen the windows.* **2.** To conceal, shelter, or protect: *Trees and shrubbery screened the house.* **3.** To separate by or as if by a screen: *He was screened off from his men by the mountains.* **4.** To separate with a sieve. **5.** To examine systematically in order to determine suitability: *screen job applicants.* **6.** To show (a movie) on a screen. **—screened'** *adj.: a screened window.*

screen•play |**skrēn'**plā'| *n.* The script for a motion picture.

screw |skroo| *n.* **1. a.** A cylindrical rod having one or more spiral or helical grooves cut into its surface. **b.** The part, cut with a similar groove, into which such a rod fits. **c.** A metal pin shaped like a cylinder or cone, cut with such a groove and fitted with a slotted head so that it can be turned by a screwdriver, used to fasten things together. **2.** A propeller, especially for a ship or motorboat. *—v.* **1.** To drive or tighten (a screw). **2. a.** To fasten, tighten, or attach by or as if by means of a screw. **b.** To attach (a threaded cap, fitting, etc.) by twisting into place: *screw a valve onto the end of a pipe.* **3.** To twist out of natural shape; contort: *screwed his face into a grimace.* **4.** To increase or gather together: *screwed up his courage.* [SEE PICTURE]

Idioms. **have a screw loose.** *Slang.* To be slightly crazy. **put the screws on.** *Slang.* To put pressure on.

screw•ball |**skroo'**bôl'| *n.* **1.** In baseball a pitched ball curving in the direction opposite to a normal curve ball. **2.** *Slang.* An eccentric or irrational person.

screw•driv•er |**skroo'**drī'vər| *n.* Any of various tools used to turn screws.

scrib•ble |**skrĭb'**əl| *v.* **scrib•bled, scrib•bling.** To write or draw (something) hastily or carelessly: *scribble notes for a story; scribbled on a pad.* **—scrib'bled** *adj.: a scribbled message.* *—n.* **1.** Careless, hurried writing. **2.** Meaningless markings. **—scrib'bler** *n.*

scribe |skrīb| *n.* **1.** An official copyist of manuscripts and documents. **2.** A public clerk or secretary. **3.** A writer. **4.** In Biblical times, a member of a group of Jewish religious teachers and scholars who interpreted the law. *—v.* **scribed, scrib•ing.** To draw or mark with or as if with a scriber: *scribe a pattern; scribe metal.*

scrim•mage |**skrĭm'**ĭj| *n.* **1.** In football, the action from the time the ball is snapped until it is out of play. **2.** A practice game between members of the same team. *—v.* **scrim•maged, scrim•mag•ing.** To engage in a scrimmage.

scrimp |skrĭmp| *v.* **1.** To economize severely: *The girls scrimped and saved to make a trip.* **2.** To use sparingly: *scrimp paint in redecorating a room.*

scrim•shaw |**skrĭm'**shô'| *n.* **1.** The art of making intricate carvings on ivory, bone, or shells. **2.** An article made in this way. [SEE PICTURE]

scrip |skrĭp| *n.* Paper money issued for temporary emergency use.

script |skrĭpt| *n.* **1.** Letters or characters written by hand; handwriting. **2.** A particular style of writing: *medieval script.* **3. a.** Printer's type that resembles handwriting. **b.** Something printed with such type. **4.** The text of a play, motion picture, broadcast, etc.

Scrip•ture |**skrĭp'**chər| *n.* Often **Scriptures. 1.** A sacred writing or book, especially the Old or New Testament. **2.** A passage from such a writing or book. **—Scrip'tur•al** *adj.*

scrod |skrŏd| *n.* A young cod or haddock, especially one used for cooking.

scroll |skrōl| *n.* **1.** A roll of parchment, papyrus, etc., used especially for writing a document. **2.** Any of various ornamental objects or designs consisting of or resembling a spiral curve.

Scrooge |skrooj|. **1.** In Charles Dickens' story *A Christmas Carol* (1843), a hardhearted and miserly old man. **2.** Any miserly person.

scro•tum |**skrō'**təm| *n., pl.* **scro•tums** or **scro•ta** |**skrō'**tə|. The external sac of skin that encloses the testes in most mammals.

scrounge |skrounj| *v.* **scrounged, scroung•ing.** *Informal.* **1. a.** To rummage or forage: *scrounging around in the attic looking for old books.* **b.** To obtain in this manner: *We scrounged up all the empty soda bottles we could find.* **2.** To obtain (something) by wheedling; cadge.

scrub[1] |skrŭb| *v.* **scrubbed, scrub•bing. 1.** To clean by rubbing, as with a brush and soap and water. **2.** To rid (a gas) of impurities. **3.** *Slang.* To cancel: *scrub a space flight.* [SEE NOTE]

scrub[2] |skrŭb| *n.* **1.** A growth of small, straggly trees or shrubs. **2.** An undersized, poorly developed plant or animal. **3.** In sports, a player not on the varsity or first team. *—adj.* **1.** Small and straggly: *a scrub oak.* **2.** Of players that are scrubs: *a scrub team.* [SEE NOTE]

scrub•by |**skrŭb'**ē| *adj.* **scrub•bi•er, scrub•bi•est. 1.** Straggly and undersized: *a wilderness of scrubby gum trees.* **2.** Shabby; inferior: *a grubby, scrubby, flea-bitten circus.* **—scrub'bi•ness** *n.*

scruff |skrŭf| *n.* The back of the neck or the loose skin there; the nape.

scruf•fy |**skrŭf'**ē| *adj.* **scruf•fi•er, scruf•fi•est.** Shabby: *a scruffy little fellow.*

scrump•tious |**skrŭmp'**shəs| *adj. Informal.* **1.** Very tasty; delicious. **2.** Wonderful.

scru•ple |**skroo'**pəl| *n.* **1.** Hesitation, or a feeling producing hesitation, based on one's conscience. **2.** A unit of apothecary weight equal to 20 grains. *—v.* **scru•pled, scru•pling.** To hesitate as a result of conscience or principles.

scru•pu•lous |**skroo'**pyə ləs| *adj.* **1.** Proper; honest: *acting in a none too scrupulous fashion to enrich himself.* **2.** Exacting; conscientious: *a scrupulous regard for facts.* **—scru'pu•lous•ly** *adv.* **—scru'pu•lous•ness** *n.*

scru•ti•nize |**skroot'**n īz'| *v.* **scru•ti•nized, scru•ti•niz•ing.** To observe or examine with great care. **—scru'ti•niz'er** *n.*

scru•ti•ny |**skroot'**n ē| *n., pl.* **scru•ti•nies. 1.** A close, careful look or study: *Sammy fidgeted under the cold, silent scrutiny of the headmaster.* **2.** Close observation; surveillance.

scu•ba |**skoo'**bə| *n.* A tank or tanks of compressed air worn on the back and fitted with a regulator, hose, and mouthpiece, used by divers to breathe underwater. *—**modifier:** a scuba diver.*

scud |skŭd| *v.* **scud•ded, scud•ding. 1.** To move along swiftly and easily: *A vigorous breeze sent the clouds scudding across the sky.* **2.** To run before a gale with little or no sail set: *sailboats scudding merrily over the bay.* *—n.* **1.** The act of scudding. **2.** Wind-driven clouds, mist, or rain.

scuff |skŭf| *v.* **scuffed, scuff•ing. 1.** To scrape or

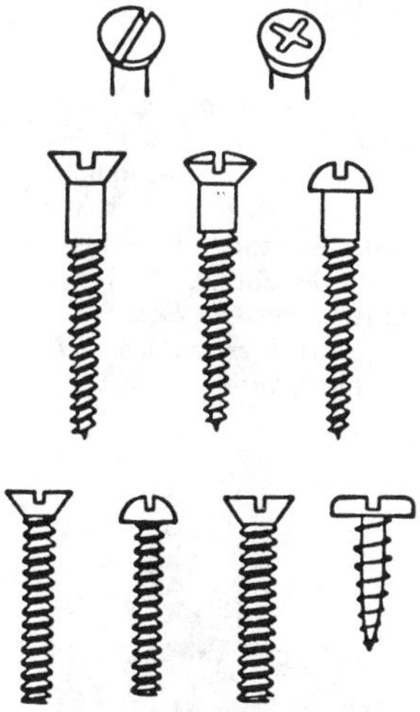

screw

scrimshaw
Whale's tooth

scrub[1-2]
Scrub[1] *is from Middle Dutch* schrubben; *it is related to* **scrape. Scrub**[2] *is a variant of* **shrub.**

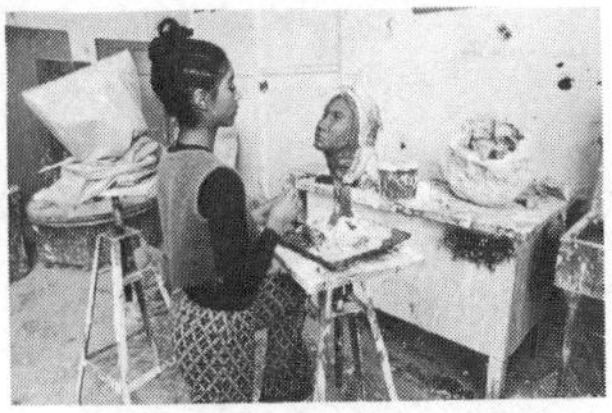

sculpture

scuttle¹·²·³
Scuttle¹ *is probably a variant of the obsolete word* scuddle, *"to run away in haste," which is from* **scud**. **Scuttle²** *is from Old French* escoutille, *"hatchway."* **Scuttle³** *was Old English* scutel, *which was borrowed from Latin* scutella, *"platter."*

scythe

sea anemone

ă pat/ā pay/â care/ä father/ĕ pet/ ē be/ĭ pit/ī pie/î fierce/ŏ pot/ ō go/ô paw, for/oi oil/ŏŏ book/ ōō boot/ou out/ŭ cut/û fur/ *th* the/th thin/hw which/zh vision/ ə ago, item, pencil, atom, circus

drag the feet in walking: *Arthur scuffed along the sidewalk.* **2. a.** To scrape and roughen the surface of: *Joey scuffed up his new shoes playing football.* **b.** To become roughened on the surface: *shoes that won't crack or scuff.* **3.** To scrape with the feet: *Jerry scuffed the gravel with the toe of his shoe.* —*n.* The act or result of scuffing. —***modifier:*** *scuff marks.*

scuf•fle |skŭf'əl| *v.* **scuf•fled, scuf•fling.** To tussle or fight at close quarters: *The police scuffled with the thieves. Mother ordered us to stop scuffling and come to dinner.* —*n.* An act or example of scuffling. —**scuf'fler** *n.*

scull |skŭl| *n.* **1.** An oar used for rowing a boat from the stern. **2.** A kind of short-handled oar. **3.** A small, light racing boat. —*v.* To propel (a boat) with a scull or sculls. ¶*These sound alike* **scull, skull.**

scul•ler•y |skŭl'ə rē| *n., pl.* **scul•ler•ies.** A room next to the kitchen in large houses, where dishwashing and other kitchen chores are done.

scul•lion |skŭl'yən| *n. Archaic.* A servant who performs menial tasks in a kitchen.

sculpt |skŭlpt| *v.* To sculpture: *a figure sculpted by Michelangelo.*

sculp•tor |skŭlp'tər| *n.* An artist who sculptures.

sculp•tur•al |skŭlp'chər əl| *adj.* Of or like sculpture. —**sculp'tur•al•ly** *adv.*

sculp•ture |skŭlp'chər| *n.* **1.** The art of making figures or designs that have depth, as by carving wood, chiseling stone, or casting metal. **2. a.** A work of art created in this way. **b.** All such works of art or a group of such works: *African sculpture.* —*v.* **sculp•tured, sculp•tur•ing. 1.** To shape (stone, metal, wood, etc.) into sculpture. **2.** To represent in sculpture: *The artist sculptured his own likeness.* **3.** To provide or ornament with sculpture: *sculptured the portals of the church.* **4.** To shape precisely or elaborately. [SEE PICTURE]

scum |skŭm| *n.* **1.** A filmy, often slimy, layer of material that forms on or rises to the surface of a liquid or a body of water. **2.** A similar mass of waste material that rises to the surface of a molten metal. **3.** A person or class of people regarded as worthless and vile.

scup |skŭp| *n., pl.* **scup** or **scups.** A fish of Atlantic waters, related to the porgies.

scurf |skûrf| *n.* **1.** Flakes of dry skin, as dandruff. **2.** Any scaly crust on a surface.

scur•ril•ous |skûr'ə ləs| *adj.* Using coarse and spiteful language; abusive: *a scurrilous attack.* —**scur'ril•ous•ly** *adv.* —**scur'ril•ous•ness** *n.*

scur•ry |skûr'ē| *v.* **scur•ried, scur•ry•ing, scur•ries. 1.** To move with or as if with light, rapid steps; scamper. **2.** To race about in a hurried or confused manner; rush. —*n., pl.* **scur•ries.** An act or noise of scurrying.

scur•vy |skûr'vē| *n.* A disease that results from a lack of vitamin C in the diet, characterized by soft, bleeding gums, bleeding under the skin, and extreme weakness.

scutch•eon |skŭch'ən| *n.* A form of the word **escutcheon.**

scut•tle¹ |skŭt'l| *v.* **scut•tled, scut•tling.** To move with quick little steps; scurry: *Just then a crab scuttled between two rocks.* —*n.* An act of scuttling; a hurried run. [SEE NOTE]

scut•tle² |skŭt'l| *n.* **1.** A small opening in a ship's deck or bulkhead. **2.** The movable cover for such an opening. —*v.* **scut•tled, scut•tling.** To sink (a ship) by boring holes in the bottom. [SEE NOTE]

scut•tle³ |skŭt'l| *n.* A metal pail for coal. [SEE NOTE]

scut•tle•butt |skŭt'l bŭt'| *n. Slang.* Private talk that is mostly rumor or gossip.

Scyl•la |sĭl'ə| *n.* In Greek mythology, a sea monster who devoured sailors if they approached too near the Italian coast of the strait separating Italy from Sicily. Off the Sicilian coast of the strait was the equally dangerous whirlpool **Charybdis.**

Idiom. **between Scylla and Charybdis.** In a spot where avoiding one danger exposes a person to destruction by another.

scythe |sīth| *n.* A tool used for mowing or reaping, having a long, curved blade with a long, bent handle. —*v.* **scythed, scyth•ing.** To cut with a scythe. [SEE PICTURE]

Scyth•i•a |sĭth'ē ə|. An ancient region of Asia and southeastern Europe. —**Scyth'i•an** *adj. & n.*

S. Dak. South Dakota.

Se The symbol for the element selenium.

SE southeast; southeastern.

sea |sē| *n.* **1. a.** Often **seas.** The continuous body of salt water that covers most of the surface of the earth, especially this body considered as distinct from the land and the sky. **b.** A region of water within an ocean and partly enclosed by land, as the North Sea and the Mediterranean Sea. **c.** A large lake containing either fresh or salt water, as the Caspian Sea. **2.** Often **seas.** The ocean's surface, considered with respect to its current or roughness: *a high sea; choppy seas.* **3.** A mare of the moon. **4.** A vast expanse or extent: *a sea of ice.* —***modifier:*** *sea water; a sea route; sea birds.* ¶*These sound alike* **sea, see, si.**

Idiom. **at sea. 1.** On the open waters of the ocean: *died at sea.* **2.** At a loss; bewildered.

sea anemone. Any of several sea animals having a flexible, tube-shaped body that remains fastened to a surface at the lower end and has a mouth opening surrounded by many petallike tentacles at the upper end. [SEE PICTURE]

sea•bed |sē'bĕd'| *n.* The bottom of a sea or ocean.

sea biscuit. Hardtack.

sea•board |sē'bôrd'| *or* |-bōrd'| *n.* Land that borders on or is near the sea.

sea•coast |sē'kōst'| *n.* Land along the sea.

sea cow. A large water animal such as the manatee or dugong.

sea cucumber. Any of several sea animals of the same group as the starfish and sea urchins, having a rough or spiny cucumber-shaped body and a mouth surrounded by tentacles.

sea•far•er |sē'fâr'ər| *n.* A sailor or mariner.

sea•far•ing |sē'fâr'ĭng| *adj.* **1.** Earning one's living at sea: *a seafaring man.* **2.** Traveling on the sea. —*n.* The work of a sailor.

sea•food |sē'fōōd'| *n.* Also **sea food.** Fish or shellfish such as clams, oysters, lobsters, and shrimps, eaten as food. —***modifier:*** *a seafood dinner.*

sea•go•ing |sē'gō'ĭng| *adj.* **1.** Made for ocean voyages or for use on the open sea: *a seagoing barge.* **2.** Seafaring: *a seagoing people.*

sea gull. A gull, especially one that lives along seacoasts.

sea•horse |sē'hôrs'| *n.* Also **sea horse.** Any of several small ocean fishes with a horselike head, a body covered with bony plates, and a tail that can be curled around a supporting object. [SEE PICTURE]

seal[1] |sēl| *n.* **1.** An instrument, such as a ring with an engraved design, used to stamp an impression in wax or other soft material. **2. a.** The impression made, especially such an impression used as an official mark of identification or authority: *the seal of the United States.* **b.** A small disk or wafer of wax, lead, or paper bearing such a mark or impression, used to show that a document or statement is genuine or valid or to fasten an envelope. **3. a.** A fitting or closure that prevents a liquid or gas from entering or escaping: *a seal around a window.* **b.** A material, such as wax, putty, or rubber, used to make such a fitting or closure. **4.** A small paper sticker used to fasten or decorate an envelope: *Christmas seals.* —*v.* **1.** To affix a seal to as a mark of genuineness, authority, or legal status: *signed and sealed at the directors' meeting.* **2.** To close with or as if with a seal: *sealed the envelope; sealed her lips.* **3.** To close so that a liquid or gas cannot enter or escape. **4.** To close tightly so that reopening is difficult or impossible: *seal a tunnel with concrete.* **5.** To close the pores in (wood or other porous material) by treating it with paint, tar, varnish, etc. **6.** To establish, determine, or fix beyond doubt or need for further action.

seal[2] |sēl| *n.* **1.** Any of several sea animals with a streamlined body, thick fur or hair, and limbs in the form of paddlelike flippers. **2.** The fur of a seal. **3.** Leather made from the hide of a seal; sealskin. —***modifier:*** *a seal coat.* [SEE PICTURE]

sea-lane |sē'lān'| *n.* An established or frequently used sea route.

sea level. The level of the surface of the ocean, used as a standard in determining land elevation or sea depths.

sealing wax. A preparation of shellac and turpentine that is soft and fluid when hot but solid when cold, used to seal letters, jars, batteries, etc.

sea lion. Any of several seals, mostly of Pacific waters, having a sleek body and brownish hair. [SEE PICTURE]

seal•skin |sēl'skĭn'| *n.* **1.** The hide of a seal. **2.** Fur or leather made from the pelt or hide of a seal. —***modifier:*** *a sealskin coat.*

seam |sēm| *n.* **1. a.** A line formed by joining two pieces of material together at their edges, as by sewing or welding. **b.** A mark, ridge, or groove that follows such a line. **2.** Any line across a surface, as one marking a crack or wrinkle. **3.** A thin layer or stratum, as of coal or rock. —*v.* **1.** To join with or as if with a seam. **2.** To mark with a groove, wrinkle, scar, or other line. ¶ *These sound alike* **seam, seem.** —**seam'er** *n.*

sea•man |sē'mən| *n., pl.* **-men** |-mən|. **1.** A sailor or mariner. **2.** An enlisted man of the lowest rank in the navy. ¶ *These sound alike* **seaman, semen.**

sea•man•ship |sē'mən shĭp'| *n.* Skill in handling or navigating a boat or ship.

seam•stress |sēm'strĭs| *n.* A woman who sews, especially one who makes her living by sewing.

seam•y |sē'mē| *adj.* **seam•i•er, seam•i•est. 1.** Having or showing a seam or seams. **2.** Unpleasant; nasty: *the seamy side of politics.*

sé•ance |sā'äns'| *n.* A meeting at which persons attempt to communicate with the dead.

sea otter. A large otter of Pacific waters, having soft, dark-brown fur. [SEE PICTURE]

sea•plane |sē'plān'| *n.* An airplane capable of taking off from or landing on water.

sea•port |sē'pôrt'| *or* |-pōrt'| *n.* A harbor or port having facilities for seagoing ships.

sear |sîr| *v.* **1.** To make withered; dry up or shrivel. **2.** To scorch or burn the surface of with or as if with heat. —*adj.* Withered; dry. —*n.* A scar or mark caused by searing. ¶ *These sound alike* **sear, seer, sere.**

search |sûrch| *v.* **1.** To make a thorough investigation; seek; hunt: *searching for people trapped inside the burning building.* **2.** To make a thorough examination of or look over carefully in order to find something desired, lost, or hidden: *search the lagoon for a shell; searching suspects for concealed weapons.* **3.** To examine carefully; probe: *searching his soul in order to make the proper decision.* —*n.* **1.** The act of seeking: *the search for knowledge.* **2.** The act of examining, investigating, or exploring: *a search of the thieves' abandoned car.* —**search'er** *n.*

search•ing |sûr'chĭng| *adj.* **1.** Examining closely or thoroughly; scrutinizing: *a searching investigation of stock-market dealings.* **2.** Keen; penetrating; observant: *some searching insights.* **3.** Eager to receive ideas or knowledge: *a searching mind.* —**search'ing•ly** *adv.*

search•light |sûrch'līt'| *n.* **1.** A powerful light equipped with a reflector to produce a bright beam in which all the rays are approximately parallel. **2.** The beam produced by such a light.

sea•shell |sē'shĕl'| *n.* Also **sea shell.** The hard shell of any sea mollusk.

sea•sick |sē'sĭk'| *adj.* Suffering nausea or other discomfort as a result of the pitching and rolling motions of a vessel at sea. —**sea'sick'ness** *n.*

sea•side |sē'sīd'| *n.* The seashore. —***modifier:*** *a seaside location; a seaside resort.*

sea•son |sē'zən| *n.* **1. a.** One of the four equal natural divisions of the year, spring, summer, autumn, and winter, each beginning as the sun passes through the corresponding solstice or equinox. **b.** Either of the two parts, rainy and dry, into which the year is divided in tropical climates. **2.** A period of the year devoted to or marked by a certain activity or by the appearance of something: *the hunting season; the hurricane season.* —*v.* **1.** To give (food) extra flavor by adding salt, pepper, spices, etc. **2.** To add enjoyment or interest to: *seasoned his writing with a dry Yankee wit.* **3.** To dry (lumber) until it is usable; cure. **4.** To make (a person or persons) capable or fit through trial and experience: *hard training to season recruits.*

Idiom. **out of season. 1.** Not available or ready for eating or hunting. **2.** Not at the right or proper moment.

sea•son•a•ble |sē'zə nə bəl| *adj.* **1.** Suitable for the time or season. **2.** Occurring at the proper time; timely. —**sea'son•a•bly** *adv.*

sea•son•al |sē'zə nəl| *adj.* Of or dependent on a season or seasons: *minor seasonal variations in*

seahorse

seal[2]
Harbor seal

sea lion

sea otter

seat belt
Seat belt with shoulder strap

sea urchin

second[1-2]
The adjective **second**[2] *is from Latin* secundus, *"following, coming immediately after, second." The hour and the circle were first divided into sixtieths and then subdivided into further sixtieths; the first units were called "small parts," or* **minutes** *(see note at* **minute***), and the subdivisions were called "second parts"*—secundae *in Medieval Latin: this was borrowed into English as* **second**[1].

ă pat/ā pay/â care/ä father/ĕ pet/ē be/ĭ pit/ī pie/î fierce/ŏ pot/ō go/ô paw, for/oi oil/o͝o book/o͞o boot/ou out/ŭ cut/û fur/*th* the/th thin/hw which/zh vision/ə ago, item, pencil, atom, circus

average temperature. —**sea'son•al•ly** *adv.*

sea•son•ing |sē'zə nĭng| *n.* Any ingredient that adds to or brings out the flavor of food.

seat |sēt| *n.* **1.** Something that may be sat upon, as a chair or bench. **2.** A place in which someone may sit: *gave his seat on the bus to a blind man.* **3.** The part of something on which a person rests in sitting: *a bicycle seat.* **4.** The part of the body on which a person rests in sitting or the part of a garment covering this area: *the seat of his pants.* **5. a.** A part that serves as the base or support of something. **b.** A part or surface upon which another part presses or rests. **6. a.** The place where anything is located or based: *the seat of the treasury.* **b.** A capital or center of activity or authority: *the county seat; a seat of medieval learning.* **7.** A place of residence, especially a large house on an estate. **8.** Membership in a legislature, stock exchange, or other organization. —*v.* **1.** To place in or on a seat. **2.** To have or provide seats for: *an auditorium that seats 5,000.*

seat belt. A safety strap or harness designed to hold a person securely in a seat, as in a passenger vehicle or aircraft. [SEE PICTURE]

Se•at•tle |sē ăt'l|. The largest city in the state of Washington. Population, 525,000.

sea urchin. Any of several sea animals having a soft body enclosed in a thin, round shell covered with spines. [SEE PICTURE]

sea•ward |sē'wərd| *adj.* **1.** Facing the sea: *the seaward side of the village.* **2.** Coming from the sea: *a seaward wind.* —*adv.* Also **sea•wards** |sē'wərdz|. Toward the sea.

sea•way |sē'wā'| *n.* **1.** An inland waterway for ocean shipping: *the St. Lawrence Seaway.* **2.** A sea route.

sea•weed |sē'wēd'| *n.* Any of many plants that live in ocean waters, especially one of the larger algae such as a kelp.

sea•wor•thy |sē'wûr'*th*ē| *adj.* **-wor•thi•er, -wor•thi•est.** Properly built and equipped for putting to sea. —**sea'wor'thi•ness** *n.*

se•ba•ceous gland |sĭ bā'shəs|. Any of the tiny glands in the skin that secrete an oily material into the hair follicles.

sec 1. second (unit of time). **2.** second (unit of angular measure).

se•cant |sē'kănt'| *or* |-kənt| *n.* **1.** A straight line or ray that intersects a curve, especially a circle, at two or more points. **2.** The reciprocal of the cosine of an angle.

se•cede |sĭ sēd'| *v.* **se•ced•ed, se•ced•ing.** To withdraw formally from membership in an organization or union: *Southern states that seceded at the outset of the Civil War.*

se•ces•sion |sĭ sĕsh'ən| *n.* **1.** The act of seceding. **2.** Often **Secession.** The withdrawal of 11 Southern states from the Federal Union in 1860–61, which brought on the Civil War.

se•ces•sion•ist or **Se•ces•sion•ist** |sĭ sĕsh'ə-nĭst| *n.* Someone who secedes or believes in secession. —**modifier:** *secessionist speeches.*

se•clude |sĭ klo͞od'| *v.* **se•clud•ed, se•clud•ing.** To remove or set apart from others; place in solitude; isolate: *secluded himself from the world.* —**se•clud'ed** *adj.: a secluded life; a secluded pool.*

se•clu•sion |sĭ klo͞o'zhən| *n.* The condition of being secluded; solitude; privacy.

sec•ond[1] |sĕk'ənd| *n.* **1.** A unit of time equal to 1/60 of a minute. **2.** *Informal.* A short period of time; a moment. **3.** A unit of angular measure equal to 1/60 of a minute of arc. [SEE NOTE]

sec•ond[2] |sĕk'ənd| *adj.* **1.** Corresponding in order to the number two in rank, time, etc.: *the second floor.* **2.** Another: *seeking a second chance.* **3.** Inferior to or less than another: *an accomplishment second only to yours.* **4. a.** Having a lower pitch or range: *the second sopranos of a choir.* **b.** Singing or playing the less important part of a similar pair of parts: *the second violins of an orchestra.* **5.** Of the transmission gear that produces the next-to-lowest speed in an automobile. —*n.* **1.** In a set of items arranged to match the natural numbers in a one-to-one correspondence, the item that corresponds to the number two. **2.** Often **seconds.** A piece of manufactured merchandise that has a slight defect or imperfection: *The hose on sale are seconds.* **3.** An attendant of a contestant in a duel or boxing match. **4. a.** The interval between two adjacent tones of a diatonic musical scale. **b.** A tone separated from another tone by this interval. **c.** That instrument or voice of a pair of like instruments or voices that has the part of lesser importance. **5.** The transmission gear in an automobile or truck that produces the next-to-lowest speed. —*v.* **1.** To give support to; assist; further. **2.** To endorse (a motion or nomination) as a means of bringing it to a vote. —*adv.* **1.** In the second order, place, or rank: *finished second in the race.* **2.** But for one other; save one: *the second-largest seaport.* [SEE NOTE]

sec•on•dar•y |sĕk'ən dĕr'ē| *adj.* **1.** Of the second rank; not primary; lesser: *a secondary cause.* **2.** Derived from what is primary or original: *secondary sources of information.* **3.** Of or relating to education between the elementary school and college. **4.** Having a current or voltage induced by the magnetic field caused by a current flowing in another coil: *the secondary coil of a transformer.* —*n., pl.* **sec•on•dar•ies. 1.** The coil or winding of a transformer from which electricity is drawn, as by a load. **2.** In football, the defensive backs or the area in which they are stationed. —**sec'on•dar'i•ly** *adv.*

secondary accent. 1. In a word having more than one accented syllable, the accent or stress that is weaker than the primary one; for example, in the word **ca'pa•bil'i•ty** the secondary accent is on the syllable **ca-**. **2.** The mark (') used to indicate this accent.

secondary school. A school for instruction between elementary school and college.

secondary sex characteristic. Any of the genetically transmitted physical or behavioral characteristics that distinguish males and females of the same species without having a direct relation to reproduction, as distribution of muscle tissue and body hair, general size, aggressiveness, etc.

second base. 1. The base across the diamond from home plate in baseball, to be touched second by a runner. **2.** The position played by a second baseman.

second class. 1. The class of accommodations on a train, ship, plane, etc., that is less expensive than first class. **2.** A class of mail including magazines, newspapers, etc., that is not sealed against inspection.

sec•ond-class |sĕk'ənd klăs' | *or* |-kläs' | *adj.* **1.** In the rank or class that is next below the first or best; inferior. **2.** Of travel accommodations ranking next below the highest, or first, class. *—adv.* By means of second-class mail or travel accommodations.

sec•ond-de•gree burn |sĕk'ənd dĭ grē' |. A burn that blisters the skin.

second hand. The hand of a clock, watch, etc., that indicates the seconds.

sec•ond•hand or **sec•ond-hand** |sĕk'ənd-hănd' | *adj.* **1.** Previously used by another; not new: *a secondhand coat.* **2.** Dealing in previously used goods: *a secondhand store.* **3.** Obtained or derived from another; not original; borrowed: *secondhand data.* *—adv.* In an indirect manner; indirectly: *news gathered secondhand.*

sec•ond•ly |sĕk'ənd lē | *adv.* In the second place; second.

second person. **1.** A set of grammatical forms used in referring to the person addressed. **2.** One of these forms; for example, *thou* and *you* belong to this set.

sec•ond-rate |sĕk'ənd rāt' | *adj.* Inferior in quality; second-class.

se•cre•cy |sē'krĭ sē | *n.* **1.** The condition of being secret or hidden; concealment: *work done in secrecy.* **2.** The practice of keeping secrets: *men pledged to secrecy.*

se•cret |sē'krĭt | *adj.* **1.** Concealed from general knowledge or view; kept hidden: *secret plans.* **2.** Working in a hidden or confidential manner: *secret agents.* **3.** Set apart; secluded; remote: *a secret path.* **4.** Reserved for oneself; private: *the poet's secret world.* **5.** Beyond ordinary understanding; mysterious: *God's secret ways.* *—n.* **1.** Something kept hidden or known only to oneself or to a few. **2.** Something beyond understanding or explanation: *the secret of the homing pigeon's instinct.* **3.** A method or formula for accomplishing something: *the secret of making friends.* **—se'cret•ly** *adv.*

***Idiom.* in secret.** Secretly; in secrecy.

sec•re•tar•i•at |sĕk'rĭ târ'ē ĭt | *n.* **1.** The department managed by a governmental secretary, especially this department of an international organization such as the United Nations. **2.** The headquarters of such a department.

sec•re•tar•y |sĕk'rĭ tĕr'ē | *n., pl.* **sec•re•tar•ies.** **1.** A person employed to do clerical work, such as typing, filing, taking messages, etc. **2.** An officer of an organization in charge of the minutes of meetings, correspondence, etc. **3.** The head of a governmental department: *the Secretary of State.* **4.** A desk with a small bookcase on top.

secretary bird. A large African bird that has long legs and a crest of feathers at the back of the head, and that feeds on snakes, rats, large insects, etc. [SEE PICTURE]

sec•re•tar•y-gen•er•al |sĕk'rĭ tĕr'ē jĕn'ər əl | *n., pl.* **sec•re•tar•ies-gen•er•al.** A high-ranking executive officer of a political party or governmental body such as the United Nations.

se•crete¹ |sĭ krēt' | *v.* **se•cret•ed, se•cret•ing.** To generate or separate out (a substance) from cells or bodily fluids. **—se•cre'to•ry** *adj.*

se•crete² |sĭ krēt' | *v.* **se•cret•ed, se•cret•ing.** To conceal in a hiding place; hide.

se•cre•tion |sĭ krē'shən | *n.* **1.** The act or process of secreting a substance, especially one that is not a waste, from blood or cells. **2.** The substance so produced.

se•cre•tive *adj.* **1.** |sē'krĭ tĭv |. Practicing or inclined to secrecy; close-mouthed. **2.** |sĭ krē'tĭv |. Secretory. **—se'cre•tive•ly** *adv.* **—se'cre•tive•ness** *n.*

secret service. **1.** The gathering of secret information by a government; intelligence work. **2.** **Secret Service.** A branch of the U.S. Treasury Department whose work includes investigating and arresting counterfeiters and guarding the President and his family.

sect |sĕkt | *n.* A group of people, often part of a larger group, who are united by common interests or beliefs.

sec•tar•i•an |sĕk târ'ē ən | *adj.* **1.** Of a sect or sects. **2.** Narrow in outlook; partisan or parochial. **—sec•tar'i•an•ism'** *n.*

sec•tion |sĕk'shən | *n.* **1.** One of several parts that make up something; a portion; division: *a residential section of the city; the sports section of a newspaper.* **2.** A picture or diagram showing the internal structure of a solid object as it would appear if the object were cut by an intersecting plane; a cross section. **3.** A unit of land area used in surveying, equal to one square mile. **4.** The act or process of cutting or separating, especially the separation of tissue in surgery. **5.** The set of points formed by the intersection of a plane and a three-dimensional geometric figure. *—v.* **1.** To separate into parts. **2.** To separate (tissue) surgically. [SEE NOTE]

sec•tion•al |sĕk'shə nəl | *adj.* **1.** Of a section: *a sectional diagram.* **2.** Composed of or divided into sections: *sectional furniture.* **3.** Of or representing a particular district or group of districts rather than an entire country or other political unit: *a sectional point of view.* **—sec'tion•al•ly** *adv.*

sec•tion•al•ism |sĕk'shə nə lĭz'əm | *n.* The practice of giving greater importance to the interests of a particular region than to those of the country or other body of which it is a part. **—sec'tion•al•ist** *adj. & n.*

sec•tor |sĕk'tər | *n.* **1.** The part of a circle bound by two radii and one of the arcs that they intercept. **2.** A particular military area or zone of action. **3.** A division of something: *the manufacturing sector of the economy.* [SEE PICTURE]

sec•u•lar |sĕk'yə lər | *adj.* **1.** Worldly or temporal rather than spiritual: *men's secular interests.* **2.** Not related to religion or a religious organization: *secular music.* **3.** Not living in a religious community: *the secular clergy.*

se•cure |sĭ kyŏŏr' | *adj.* **se•cur•er, se•cur•est.** **1.** Free from danger or risk of loss; safe: *a secure castle.* **2.** Free from fear, anxiety, or doubt: *feeling secure at home.* **3.** Not likely to fail or give way: *a secure foothold.* **4.** Well-fastened: *The antenna is secure.* **5.** Assured; certain; guaranteed: *a secure peace.* *—v.* **se•cured, se•cur•ing.** **1.** To guard from danger or risk of loss: *secured the empire against barbarians.* **2.** To make firm or tight; fasten. **3.** To make certain; guarantee; ensure: *a constitution designed to secure our freedom.* **4.** To get possession of; acquire: *secure*

secretary bird
This bird was so called because the quills of its crest resembled a bunch of quill pens such as might be thrust behind the ear of a secretary of former times.

section
Section *is from Latin* sectiō, *"a cutting, a piece cut off," from* secāre, *"to cut."* Secāre *is descended from the prehistoric Indo-European root* sek-, *"to cut," which also appears in Germanic as* sag- *(see note at* **saw***).*

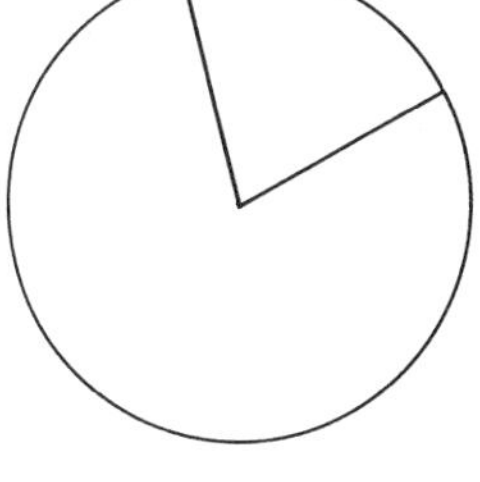

sector

higher wages. **5.** To bring about; effect: *secured his release from prison.* **6.** To guarantee or make sure with a pledge: *deposited collateral to secure the loan.* —**se•cure'ly** *adv.*

se•cu•ri•ty |sĭ kyŏŏr'ĭ tē| *n., pl.* **se•cu•ri•ties. 1.** Freedom from risk or danger; safety. **2.** Anything that gives or assures safety or confidence. **3.** Anything deposited or given to guarantee fulfillment of an obligation; a pledge: *an extra month's rent given as security.* **4.** Stocks or bonds. —***modifier:*** *security guards.*

secy. secretary.

se•dan |sĭ dăn'| *n.* **1.** A closed automobile having two or four doors and a front and rear seat. **2.** Also **sedan chair.** An enclosed chair for one person, carried on poles by two men.

se•date |sĭ dāt'| *adj.* Calm and dignified; composed. —**se•date'ly** *adv.* —**se•date'ness** *n.*

se•da•tion |sĭ dā'shən| *n.* **1.** The act or process of calming by administration of a sedative. **2.** The condition brought on by a sedative.

sed•a•tive |sĕd'ə tĭv| *adj.* Having a soothing, calming, or quieting effect. —*n.* A sedative medicine or drug.

sed•en•tar•y |sĕd'n tĕr'ē| *adj.* **1.** Marked by or requiring much sitting: *sedentary work.* **2.** Accustomed to sitting or to taking little exercise. —**sed'en•tar'i•ly** *adv.*

Se•der |sā'dər| *n.* In Judaism, the feast commemorating the departure of the Israelites from Egypt, celebrated on the eve of the first day of Passover.

sedge |sĕj| *n.* Any of several plants that resemble grasses but have solid rather than hollow stems and that grow chiefly in wet places.

sed•i•ment |sĕd'ə mənt| *n.* **1.** Finely divided solid matter that falls to the bottom of a liquid or sometimes a gas. **2.** Finely divided solid matter suspended in a liquid or gas.

sed•i•men•ta•ry |sĕd'ə mĕn'tə rē| *adj.* **1.** Of, like, or derived from sediment. **2.** Of rocks formed from sediment or fragments of other rocks deposited in water.

sed•i•men•ta•tion |sĕd'ə mən tā'shən| *n.* The act or process of depositing sediment.

se•di•tion |sĭ dĭsh'ən| *n.* Conduct or language that causes others to rebel against the authority of the state.

se•di•tious |sĭ dĭsh'əs| *adj.* Of or engaged in sedition. —**se•di'tious•ly** *adv.*

se•duce |sĭ dōōs'| *or* |-dyōōs'| *v.* **se•duced, se•duc•ing.** To cause to engage in wrongful or immoral behavior. —**se•duc'er** *n.*

se•duc•tion |sĭ dŭk'shən| *n.* **1.** The act of seducing or the condition of being seduced. **2.** Something that seduces; a temptation.

se•duc•tive |sĭ dŭk'tĭv| *adj.* Tending to seduce; tempting; alluring; beguiling. —**se•duc'tive•ly** *adv.* —**se•duc'tive•ness** *n.*

sed•u•lous |sĕj'ə ləs| *adj.* Diligent; painstaking; industrious. —**sed'u•lous•ly** *adv.* —**sed'u•lous•ness** *n.*

see[1] |sē| *v.* **saw** |sô|, **seen** |sēn|, **see•ing. 1. a.** To perceive with the eye: *He saw a light.* **b.** To have the power of sight: *You can't see in the dark.* **2.** To understand; comprehend: *I see what you mean.* **3.** To have a mental picture of; grasp mentally: *He saw the opportunities for advancement.* **4.** To foresee: *I can see no chance of a mistake.* **5.** To imagine; believe possible: *We couldn't see her as a true leader.* **6.** To regard; view: *Try to see it from our standpoint.* **7.** To consider; think over: *Let's see, is there still time?* **8.** To know through actual experience; undergo: *We had seen hard times.* **9.** To be marked by or bring forth: *Our age has seen scientific miracles.* **10.** To find out; ascertain: *See whether it is accurate.* **11.** To refer to; read: *See the footnote on the next page.* **12. a.** To visit or consult: *May I see you tonight? He saw a lawyer.* **b.** To receive or admit: *The doctor will see you now.* **13.** To attend; view: *We saw a good movie last night.* **14.** To escort; attend: *See her to the bus station.* **15.** To make sure; take care: *Always see that the door is locked.* —***phrasal verbs.*** **see about. 1.** To attend to. **2.** To inquire about; investigate. **see off.** To excort to or attend at a place of departure. **see through. 1.** To understand the true character or nature of. **2.** To stand by or support (a person) in a time of difficulty. **3.** To fulfill or finish (a task or obligation). **see to.** To attend to. ¶ *These sound alike* **see, sea, si.** [SEE NOTE]

see[2] |sē| *n.* **1.** The position or authority of a bishop. **2.** The district in which a bishop has jurisdiction. ¶ *These sound alike* **see, sea, si.** [SEE NOTE]

seed |sēd| *n., pl.* **seeds** or **seed. 1.** A usually small part of a flowering plant that develops from a fertilized ovule and contains an embryo that can grow into a new plant. **2.** Seeds considered together. **3.** Something that can develop or give rise to something as a seed does: *This treaty holds the seeds of a lasting peace.* **4.** Offspring or descendants: *"mercy . . . unto David and to his seed for evermore"* (The Bible, II Samuel, 22:51). —***modifier:*** *a seed bed.* —*v.* **1.** To plant seeds in; sow: *seeded four acres of land.* **2.** To remove the seeds from (fruit). **3.** To sprinkle (a cloud or clouds) with particles, as of silver iodide or dry ice, to cause it to disperse or produce rain. ¶ *These sound alike* **seed, cede.** —**seed'er** *n.* —**seed'less** *adj.*

Idiom. **go to seed.** To become useless or incompetent; deteriorate.

seed coat. The outer protective covering of a seed.

seed•ling |sēd'lĭng| *n.* A young, newly developing plant that has sprouted from a seed.

seed money. Money needed or provided to start a new project.

seed•y |sē'dē| *adj.* **seed•i•er, seed•i•est. 1.** Having many seeds: *Raspberries and blackberries are seedy fruit.* **2.** Shabby and disreputable: *an old, seedy jacket; a seedy hotel.* —**seed'i•ness** *n.*

seek |sēk| *v.* **sought** |sôt|, **seek•ing. 1. a.** To try to locate or discover; search for: *seeking a home for the cats; seeking out some innocent prey.* **b.** To make a search: *"Seek and ye shall find"* (The Bible, Luke 11:9). **2.** To make an attempt; try: *seek to learn a foreign language.* —**seek'er** *n.*

seem |sēm| *v.* **1.** To give the impression of being; appear to be: *She seems worried about her job.* **2.** To appear to oneself: *I seem unable to finish this book.* **3.** To appear to exist, be true, or be obvious: *That seems to be the only solution.* ¶ *These sound alike* **seem, seam.**

seem•ing |sē'mĭng| *adj.* Having an appearance that may or may not be real; apparent: *his*

see[1-2]

See[1] *was Old English* sēon; *it is closely related to Old English* sihth, *"vision," which became* **sight** *in Modern English.* **See**[2] *is from Norman French* se *or* sed, *"the seat or residence of a bishop," from Latin* sēdes, *"seat."*

ă pat/ā pay/â care/ä father/ĕ pet/ ē be/ĭ pit/ī pie/î fierce/ŏ pot/ ō go/ô paw, for/oi oil/ŏŏ book/ ōō boot/ou out/ŭ cut/û fur/ *th* the/th thin/hw which/zh vision/ ə ago, item, pencil, atom, circus

seeming friendliness. —**seem'ing•ly** *adv.*

seem•ly |sēm'lē| *adj.* **seem•li•er, seem•li•est.** Conforming to accepted standards of conduct and good taste; proper: *seemly behavior.*

seen |sēn|. Past participle of **see.** ¶*These sound alike* **seen, scene.**

seep |sēp| *v.* **1.** To pass slowly through small openings; ooze: *The cold seeped in through the crack in the window.* **2.** To enter, depart, or spread gradually: *His hate seeped away.*

seep•age |sē'pĭj| *n.* **1.** The act or process of seeping; leakage. **2.** The amount of something that has seeped in or out.

seer |sîr| *n.* A person supposedly able to visualize, and thus predict, the future. ¶*These sound alike* **seer, sear, sere.**

seer•suck•er |sîr'sŭk'ər| *n.* A light, thin, striped fabric, usually of cotton or rayon, having a crinkled surface. —***modifier:*** *a seersucker dress.* [SEE NOTE]

see•saw |sē'sô'| *n.* A long plank balanced on a central support so that with a person riding on either end, one end goes up as the other goes down. —*v.* **1.** To ride on a seesaw. **2.** To fluctuate back and forth. [SEE PICTURE]

seethe |sēth| *v.* **seethed, seeth•ing.** **1.** To bubble, foam, or churn while or as if while boiling: *The caldron seethed with the witches' brew. The town seethed with gossip.* **2.** To be violently agitated: *She seethed over the new rules.*

seg•ment |sĕg'mənt| *n.* **1.** A part into which something is or can be divided; a section or division: *the various segments of American society.* **2.** One of the similar, clearly distinguishable subdivisions of a plant or animal body or structure: *the segments of an earthworm; a segment of a grapefruit or orange.* **3.** A section of a geometric figure or object that is set off by boundaries: **a.** A part of a line that is included between any pair of its points; a line segment. **b.** A portion of a curve included between any pair of its points. **c.** The region bounded by an arc of a circle and the chord that connects the endpoints of the arc. **d.** The portion of a sphere included between a pair of parallel planes that intersect it or are tangent to it. —*v.* |sĕg mĕnt'|. To divide into segments. —**seg•ment'ed** *adj.*: *segmented worms.*

se•go lily |sē'gō|. A plant of western North America having showy white or purplish flowers and an edible bulb.

seg•re•gate |sĕg'rĭ gāt'| *v.* **seg•re•gat•ed, seg•re•gat•ing.** **1.** To separate or isolate from others or from a main body or group. **2.** To impose the separation of (a race or class) from the rest of society or from a larger group.

seg•re•ga•tion |sĕg'rĭ gā'shən| *n.* **1. a.** The act or process of segregating. **b.** The condition of being segregated. **2.** The policy of segregating a race or class.

seg•re•ga•tion•ist |sĕg'rĭ gā'shə nĭst| *n.* A person who advocates racial segregation. —*adj.* In favor of racial segregation.

seine |sān| *n.* A large fishing net with weights at the lower edge and floats at the top. —*v.* **seined, sein•ing.** To fish or catch with a seine. ¶*These sound alike* **seine, sane.**

Seine |sĕn|. A river in France, flowing through Paris and generally northwest into the English Channel.

seis•mic |sīz'mĭk| *adj.* Of, subject to, or caused by an earthquake or earthquakes: *a seismic disturbance.*

seis•mo•graph |sīz'mə grăf'| *or* |-gräf'| *n.* An instrument that detects and records motions of the ground.

seize |sēz| *v.* **seized, seiz•ing.** **1.** To grasp suddenly and forcibly; lay hold of; take or grab: *The police officer seized his arm.* **2.** To take possession of forcibly: *seize a ship.* **3.** To take prisoner; capture: *The soldiers seized the traitors.* **4.** To take eagerly: *seize the opportunity to leave.* **5.** To comprehend: *seize the meaning of the music.* **6.** To have a sudden effect on; overwhelm: *Stage fright seized the little girl.* —***phrasal verb.*** **seize on** (or **upon**). **1.** To take possession of: *seize upon all the available material.* **2.** To make use of or resort to: *seizing on any excuse to justify their defeat.*

sei•zure |sē'zhər| *n.* **1.** The act or process of seizing. **2.** A sudden fit or convulsion, as in epilepsy or a heart attack.

sel•dom |sĕl'dəm| *adv.* Not often; rarely: *A woodchuck seldom strays far from his burrow.*

se•lect |sĭ lĕkt'| *v.* To choose from among several; pick out: *The cave man selected just the right club for himself.* —*adj.* **1.** Carefully picked out or chosen: *a select group of students.* **2.** Choice: *a select product.* **3.** Admitting only certain members; exclusive: *a select literary club.*

se•lec•tion |sĭ lĕk'shən| *n.* **1. a.** The act of selecting. **b.** Someone or something selected; a choice. **2.** A carefully chosen group of persons or things meant to be representative: *a selection of books.* **3.** A literary or musical text chosen for reading or performance.

se•lec•tive |sĭ lĕk'tĭv| *adj.* **1.** Of or characterized by selection: *selective reading.* **2.** Tending to select; fastidious: *Museums are now selective in their acceptance of gifts.* —**se•lec'tive•ly** *adv.*

selective service. Compulsory military service according to age, physical fitness, etc.

se•lect•man |sĭ lĕkt'mən| *n., pl.* **-men** |-mən|. One of a board of town officers chosen annually in New England communities to manage local affairs.

se•lec•tor |sĭ lĕk'tər| *n.* **1.** Someone or something that selects. **2.** A switch or lever that by its position causes a machine or device to perform one of several actions.

se•le•ni•um |sĭ lē'nē əm| *n.* Symbol **Se** One of the elements, a substance that can exist as a red powder, a black, glassy material, or a gray crystal, with chemical properties resembling those of sulfur. Atomic number 34; atomic weight 78.96; valences –2, +1, +2, +4, +6; melting point (for the gray form) 217°C; boiling point 684.9°C.

self |sĕlf| *n., pl.* **selves** |sĕlvz|. **1.** The total or essential being of one person considered different from any other; the individual: *one's own self.* **2.** The qualities of one person; personality or character; individuality: *back to his old nasty self.* **3.** One's own interests, welfare, or advantage: *thinking of self alone.* —*adj.* Made of or covered with the same material as that used for the whole: *a coat with a self belt.*

self–. A word element that forms hyphenated compounds and means: **1.** Oneself or itself:

seersucker/sugar

The original **seersucker** *was made in India; the word is from Hindi* sirsakar, *which is from Persian* shīr-o-shakar, *"milk-and-sugar." Quite separately,* shakar *was borrowed into medieval Arabic as* sukkar; *through trade with the Arab world in the twelfth and thirteenth centuries,* sukkar *was borrowed into many of the languages of Europe, for example: Italian* zucchero, *French* sucre, *and English* **sugar**.

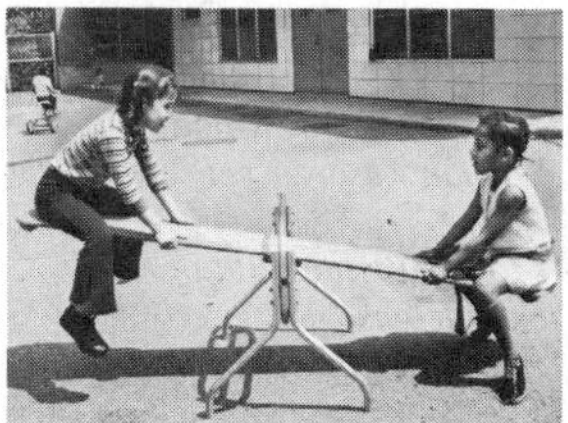

seesaw

self-evident. 2. Of, to, or by itself or oneself: self-conscious. 3. Automatically: self-winding.

self-ad•dressed |sĕlf'ə drĕst'| *adj.* Addressed to oneself: *a self-addressed stamped envelope.*

self-as•sur•ance |sĕlf'ə sho͝or'əns| *n.* Confidence or sureness in oneself.

self-cen•tered |sĕlf'sĕn'tərd| *adj.* Concerned only with one's own needs and interests; selfish.

self-con•fi•dence |sĕlf'kŏn'fĭ dəns| *n.* Confidence in oneself; self-assurance. —**self'-con'fi•dent** *adj.*

self-con•scious |sĕlf'kŏn'shəs| *adj.* **1.** Overconscious of one's appearance or manner; socially ill at ease: *a self-conscious person.* **2.** Not natural; stilted: *a self-conscious laugh.* —**self'-con'scious•ly** *adv.* —**self'-con'scious•ness** *n.*

self-con•tained |sĕlf'kən tānd'| *adj.* **1.** Having all that is necessary; self-sufficient: *a self-contained underwater breathing apparatus.* **2.** Keeping to oneself; reserved.

self-con•trol |sĕlf'kən trōl'| *n.* Control of one's emotions and behavior by one's own will. —**self'-con•trolled'** *adj.*

self-defense
"No man was ever yet so void of sense,
As to debate the right of self-defense."
—Daniel Defoe (1701).

self-de•fense |sĕlf'dĭ fĕns'| *n.* **1.** Defense against attack. **2.** The legal right to use whatever means are necessary to protect oneself against violence or threatened violence. [SEE NOTE]

self-de•ni•al |sĕlf'dĭ nī'əl| *n.* Sacrifice of one's own comfort or gratification.

self-de•ter•mi•na•tion |sĕlf'dĭ tûr'mə nā'shən| *n.* **1.** Determination of one's own fate or course of action without being forced; free will. **2.** Freedom of a people or area to determine its own political status.

self-ed•u•cat•ed |sĕlf'ĕj'o͞o kā'tĭd| *adj.* Educated by one's own efforts, without formal instruction.

self-ev•i•dent |sĕlf'ĕv'ĭ dənt| *adj.* Requiring no proof or explanation.

self-ex•plan•a•to•ry |sĕlf'ĭk splăn'ə tôr'ē| *or* |-tōr'ē| *adj.* Requiring no explanation; obvious.

self-ex•pres•sion |sĕlf'ĭk sprĕsh'ən| *n.* Expression of one's own personality, feelings, ideas, etc., as through speech or art.

self-government
"Self-government is the natural government of man."
—Henry Clay (1818).

self-gov•ern•ment |sĕlf'gŭv'ərn mənt| *n.* **1.** Political independence. **2.** Representative government, especially democracy. [SEE NOTE]

self-im•por•tance |sĕlf'ĭm pôr'tns| *n.* An excessively high opinion of one's own importance or position; conceit. —**self'-im•por'tant** *adj.*

self•ish |sĕl'fĭsh| *adj.* **1.** Concerned mainly with oneself without regard for others: *a selfish person.* **2.** Showing lack of regard for others: *a selfish act.* —**self'ish•ly** *adv.* —**self'ish•ness** *n.*

self•less |sĕlf'lĭs| *adj.* Unselfish. —**self'less•ly** *adv.* —**self'less•ness** *n.*

self-made |sĕlf'mād'| *adj.* Having achieved success unaided: *a self-made man.*

self-pit•y |sĕlf'pĭt'ē| *n.* Pity for oneself.

self-pos•ses•sion |sĕlf'pə zĕsh'ən| *n.* Full command of one's feelings and behavior; presence of mind; poise. —**self'-pos•sessed'** *adj.*

self-pres•er•va•tion |sĕlf'prĕz'ər vā'shən| *n.* **1.** Protection of oneself from harm or destruction. **2.** The instinct for survival.

self-re•li•ance |sĕlf'rĭ lī'əns| *n.* Reliance upon one's own capabilities or resources. —**self'-re•li'ant** *adj.*

self-re•spect |sĕlf'rĭ spĕkt'| *n.* Appropriate or due respect for oneself.

self-re•spect•ing |sĕlf'rĭ spĕk'tĭng| *adj.* Having self-respect.

self-right•eous |sĕlf'rī'chəs| *adj.* Smugly sure of one's righteousness. —**self'-right'eous•ly** *adv.* —**self'-right'eous•ness** *n.*

self-sac•ri•fice |sĕlf'săk'rə fīs'| *n.* Sacrifice of one's own interests for the sake of others or for a cause. —**self'-sac'ri•fic'ing** *adj.*

self•same |sĕlf'sām'| *adj.* Exactly identical; the very same: *pitting the selfsame cherries he had spent a day picking.*

self-sat•is•fac•tion |sĕlf'săt'ĭs făk'shən| *n.* Satisfaction with oneself or one's accomplishments.

self-sat•is•fied |sĕlf'săt'ĭs fīd'| *adj.* Satisfied with oneself or one's accomplishments.

self-seek•ing |sĕlf'sē'kĭng| *adj.* Seeking mainly to further one's own interests; selfish. —*n.* Selfishness.

self-serv•ice |sĕlf'sûr'vĭs| *adj.* Having the kind of service in which customers help themselves: *a self-service laundry.*

self-styled |sĕlf'stīld'| *adj.* As characterized by oneself: *a self-styled artist.*

self-suf•fi•cient |sĕlf'sə fĭsh'ənt| *adj.* **1.** Able to provide for oneself without help; independent. **2.** Having excessive confidence in oneself; overbearing. —**self'-suf•fi'cien•cy** *n.*

self-sup•port•ing |sĕlf'sə pôr'tĭng| *or* |-pōr'-| *adj.* Able to support oneself or itself without help.

self-taught |sĕlf'tôt'| *adj.* Having taught oneself without formal training.

self-will |sĕlf'wĭl'| *n.* Willfulness, especially in satisfying one's own desires; stubbornness.

self-wind•ing |sĕlf'wīn'dĭng| *adj.* Capable of winding its own mainspring automatically: *a self-winding watch.*

sell |sĕl| *v.* **sold** |sōld|, **sell•ing.** **1.** To exchange or deliver (goods, property, services, etc.) for money or its equivalent: *sell a bike; selling for four hours every day.* **2. a.** To offer for sale: *This store sells health foods.* **b.** To be on sale: *Nuts sell for 89¢ a pound.* **3.** To be popular or unpopular on the market: *These ties are selling well.* **4.** To promote: *Jet planes sold airline travel to many people.* **5.** To surrender in exchange for something: *sell one's soul to the devil.* —**phrasal verbs. sell off.** To get rid of by selling, often at a low price. **sell on.** To convince of: *sold her on the idea.* **sell out. 1.** To dispose of entirely by selling. **2.** *Slang.* To betray one's cause or associates. ¶*These sound alike* **sell, cell.**

sell•er |sĕl'ər| *n.* **1.** A person who sells; a vendor. **2.** An item that sells well or poorly: *This dress has been a very good seller.* ¶*These sound alike* **seller, cellar.**

selt•zer |sĕlt'sər| *n.* **1.** A bubbly mineral water. **2.** Artificially carbonated water.

sel•vage, also **sel•vedge** |sĕl'vĭj| *n.* The edge of a fabric woven so that it will not ravel.

selves |sĕlvz| *n.* Plural of **self.**

se•man•tic |sĭ măn'tĭk| *adj.* **1.** Of or concerned with meaning, especially in language: *a semantic change.* **2.** Of semantics.

se•man•ti•cist |sĭ măn'tĭ sĭst| *n.* A person who specializes in semantics.

se•man•tics |sĭ măn'tĭks| *n.* *(used with a singular*

ă pat/ā pay/â care/ä father/ĕ pet/ē be/ĭ pit/ī pie/î fierce/ŏ pot/ō go/ô paw, for/oi oil/o͝o book/o͞o boot/ou out/ŭ cut/û fur/*th* the/th thin/hw which/zh vision/ə ago, item, pencil, atom, circus

verb). In linguistics, the study of meaning in language forms. [SEE NOTE]

sem•a•phore |sĕm′ə fôr′| *or* |-fōr′| *n.* **1.** Any visual signaling device with flags, lights, movable indicators, etc., as on a railroad. **2.** A system for signaling that uses various designated positions of the arms, flags, etc. *—v.* **sem•a•phored, sem•a•phor•ing.** To send (a message) by semaphore. [SEE PICTURE]

sem•blance |sĕm′bləns| *n.* **1.** A representation; likeness: *cupped his hands together in the semblance of a heart.* **2.** The appearance of something, whether it is really present or not; show: *keeping up a semblance of dignity.*

se•men |sē′mən| *n.* A whitish fluid produced by the male reproductive organs and carrying sperm cells. ¶*These sound alike* **semen, seaman.**

se•mes•ter |sə mĕs′tər| *n.* One of two terms, each from 15 to 18 weeks long, that make up a school year.

semi–. A word element meaning: **1.** Part or partially: **semiprofessional. 2.** Half of: **semicircle. 3.** Occurring twice within a specified period of time: **semiannual.** [SEE NOTE on p. 247]

sem•i•an•nu•al |sĕm′ē ăn′yōō əl| *adj.* Occurring or issued twice a year: *semiannual payments; a semiannual magazine.* **—sem′i•an′nu•al•ly** *adv.*

sem•i•cir•cle |sĕm′ĭ sûr′kəl| *n.* An arc of 180 degrees; a half of a circle.

sem•i•cir•cu•lar |sĕm′ē sûr′kyə lər| *adj.* Of, shaped like, or resembling a semicircle.

semicircular canals. Three tubular looped structures in the labyrinth of the inner ear that act together in maintaining the sense of balance.

sem•i•co•lon |sĕm′ĭ kō′lən| *n.* A punctuation mark (;) indicating a greater degree of separation between elements in a sentence than a comma.

sem•i•con•duc•tor |sĕm′ē kən dŭk′tər| *n.* Any of various solid crystalline substances, such as silicon or germanium, that conduct electricity more easily than insulators do but less easily than conductors do.

sem•i•fi•nal |sĕm′ē fī′nəl| *n.* Often **semifinals.** A game or match that precedes the final, as in a tournament. *—adj.* Preceding the final.

sem•i•month•ly |sĕm′ē mŭnth′lē| *adj.* Occurring or issued twice a month: *semimonthly visits.* *—n., pl.* **sem•i•month•lies.** A publication issued twice a month. *—adv.* Twice a month.

sem•i•nal |sĕm′ə nəl| *adj.* **1.** Of or containing semen or sperm cells: *seminal fluid.* **2.** Giving rise to something new: *seminal ideas.*

sem•i•nar |sĕm′ə när′| *n.* **1.** A conference at which views and information are exchanged, usually on an academic subject. **2. a.** An advanced course of study for a small group of students who do independent research on a specialized subject. **b.** A meeting of such a group.

sem•i•nar•i•an |sĕm′ə nâr′ē ən| *n.* A student at a seminary.

sem•i•nar•y |sĕm′ə nĕr′ē| *n., pl.* **sem•i•nar•ies.** A school for the training of priests, ministers, or rabbis.

Sem•i•nole |sĕm′ə nōl′| *n., pl.* **Sem•i•nole** or **Sem•i•noles. 1.** A North American Indian tribe now living in Oklahoma. **2.** A member of this tribe. **3.** The Muskhogean language of this tribe.

sem•i•pre•cious |sĕm′ē prĕsh′əs| *adj.* Designating a gem, such as topaz, amethyst, or jade, that is less valuable than a precious stone.

sem•i•pro•fes•sion•al |sĕm′ē prə fĕsh′ə nəl| *adj.* **1.** Taking part in a sport or other activity for pay, but not as a full-time occupation: *a semiprofessional baseball player.* **2.** Composed of such players: *a semiprofessional team.*

Sem•ite |sĕm′īt′| *n.* A member of any of a group of Caucasoid peoples, now chiefly Arabs and Jews, that speak a Semitic language. The ancient Babylonians, Assyrians, and Phoenicians were also Semites.

Se•mit•ic |sə mĭt′ĭk| *adj.* **1.** Of the Semites. **2.** Of a division of languages including Hebrew and Arabic. *—n.* The Semitic languages.

sem•i•tone |sĕm′ē tōn′| *n.* The interval that separates two adjoining tones of a chromatic scale.

sem•i•week•ly |sĕm′ē wēk′lē| *adj.* Occurring or issued twice a week. *—adv.* Twice a week.

sen., Sen. 1. senate; senator. **2.** senior.

sen•ate |sĕn′ĭt| *n.* **1. Senate.** In the United States, the upper house of Congress. It includes two members from each state, each elected by the people of the state and serving for six years. **2. Senate.** The upper house of the legislature in many states of the United States. **3. Senate.** The upper house of the national legislature in Canada, France, and other countries. **4.** The governing council of the ancient Roman republic and later of the Roman Empire. **5.** A governing council of some colleges and universities.

sen•a•tor or **Sen•a•tor** |sĕn′ə tər| *n.* A member of a senate.

sen•a•to•ri•al |sĕn′ə tôr′ē əl| *or* |-tōr′-| *adj.* **1.** Of a senator. **2.** Appropriate or suited to a senator: *senatorial dignity.* **3.** Made up of senators: *a senatorial advisory group.*

send |sĕnd| *v.* **sent** |sĕnt|, **send•ing. 1.** To cause to be conveyed to a place: *We sent supplies to the disaster area by airlift.* **2.** To dispatch (a letter, message, etc.), as by mail or telegraph; transmit. **3.** To express for another to convey: *She sends her love and promises to write soon.* **4.** To direct to go to a place: *sent me to the store to buy milk.* **5.** To enable to go to a place, as by providing money: *She sent herself to college by working as a waitress.* **6.** To drive into a given condition or kind of behavior: *The long delay sent the train passengers into a frustrated rage.* **7.** To cause to move or extend outward; give off: *The sun and most other stars send out powerful radiation.* **8.** *Slang.* To delight; carry away with pleasure. ***—phrasal verbs.* send away for.** To order by mail. **send for. 1.** To order (something) to be brought or delivered. **2.** To request (someone) to come; summon. **—send′er** *n.*

Sen•e•ca |sĕn′ĭ kə| *n., pl.* **Sen•e•ca** or **Sen•e•cas. 1.** A North American Indian tribe formerly living in western New York State. **2.** A member of this tribe. **3.** The Iroquoian language of this tribe.

Sen•e•gal |sĕn′ĭ gôl′|. A country in western Africa, on the Atlantic Ocean. Population, 4,320,000. Capital, Dakar.

sen•e•schal |sĕn′ə shəl| *n.* An official appointed to manage the household and the servants of a medieval lord; a steward.

se•nile |sē′nīl′| *or* |sĕn′īl′| *adj.* Of, showing, or characteristic of senility.

semantics

Semantics *is in many ways the most difficult branch of linguistics. It is comparatively easy to pin down phonetic shapes and patterns and to describe grammatical structures; but the ultimate nature of meaning is extremely hard to visualize or define. As a result, semantics is probably the least developed branch of linguistic science. Nonetheless, many linguists would agree that understanding meaning is the ultimate reason for studying language. As the linguist Roman Jakobson has put it, "Linguistics without meaning is meaningless."*

semaphore
Railway semaphore

senior, etc.

Senior *is from Latin* senior, *"older," the comparative of* senex, *"old, an old man."* Senex *and* senior *were applied only to persons, not to things, and they carried a basic sense of respect, referring to maturity and experience rather than to mere age; any respectable person over 40 could be called* senior. *The original governing body of the Roman state was called* sen-ātus, *"the council of elders," which has been borrowed into English as* **senate**. *In medieval times,* senior *became a general title of respect and rank, meaning "lord, master"; in Italian it became* signor, *in Spanish* señor, *and in French* sieur *(also* monsieur, *"my lord").* Sieur *was borrowed into English as* **sir**.

sense/sentence/sentiment

Sense *is from Latin* sēnsus, *"the ability to feel, perception," also "understanding, emotion";* sēnsus *is from* sentīre, *"to feel, perceive, think." Also formed from* sentīre *are (1)* sententia, *"thought," also "opinion, judgment" and "meaning, statement"; this was borrowed into English as* **sentence**, *with its two separate meanings (**sententious** originally meant "full of meaning"); and (2) Medieval Latin* sentimentum, *"feeling, emotion," borrowed as* **sentiment**.

ă pat/ā pay/â care/ä father/ĕ pet/ ē be/ĭ pit/ī pie/î fierce/ŏ pot/ ō go/ô paw, for/oi oil/o͝o book/ o͞o boot/ou out/ŭ cut/û fur/ *th* the/th thin/hw which/zh vision/ ə ago, item, pencil, atom, circus

se•nil•i•ty |sə nĭl′ĭ tē| *n.* The weakening or loss of a person's mental or physical abilities due to old age.

sen•ior |sēn′yər| *adj.* **1. a.** Older or oldest: *the senior members of the family.* **b.** A term used to denote the older of two persons having the same name, as father and son or mother and daughter. **2.** Of or for older members: *a senior scout troop.* **3.** Of higher rank or longer length of service: *a senior partner; the senior congressman of his state's delegation.* **4.** Of the fourth and last year of a high school or college: *a senior prom; the senior class.* —*n.* **1.** A person who is older or of higher rank than another: *My brother is my senior by four years. She spoke to her seniors about a raise.* **2.** A student in the fourth and last year of a high school or college. [SEE NOTE]

senior high school. A secondary school usually including the 10th, 11th, and 12th grades.

sen•ior•i•ty |sēn yôr′ĭ tē| *or* |-yŏr′-| *n.* **1.** The condition of being older or of higher rank. **2.** Priority over others because of greater length of service.

sen•na |sĕn′ə| *n.* **1.** Any of several plants having yellow flowers and featherlike leaves with many leaflets. **2.** The dried leaves of such a plant or a preparation made from them, used in medicine as a laxative.

sen•sa•tion |sĕn sā′shən| *n.* **1. a.** Something perceived as a result of stimulation of a sense organ or as a result of some condition of the body; feeling: *the sensation of heat; a sensation of nausea.* **b.** The ability to perceive or feel: *a loss of sensation in the fingers due to frostbite.* **2.** Something felt keenly and briefly in the mind; a momentary strong emotion: *a sensation of having been here before.* **3. a.** A condition of lively public interest and excitement: *News of the first artificial satellite caused a sensation.* **b.** Someone or something that arouses lively interest, excitement, or admiration.

sen•sa•tion•al |sĕn sā′shə nəl| *adj.* **1.** Of sensation or the senses. **2.** Arousing great interest or excitement: *sensational news.* **3.** Designed to shock or thrill the readers or spectators: *a sensational article about ax murderers.* **4.** *Informal.* Extraordinary; outstanding: *a sensational dinner.* —**sen•sa′tion•al•ly** *adv.*

sense |sĕns| *n.* **1. a.** Any action, function, or ability by which a living thing can perceive or obtain information about its environment or certain of its own internal conditions, especially, in animals, the functions of sight, hearing, smell, taste, and touch. **b.** Perception, either through these functions or through the workings of the mind: *trembling from a sense of damp cold; praise that gave her a sense of her own worth.* **2.** A mental or emotional ability to detect, estimate, or appreciate something: *a sense of humor.* **3.** A quality that impresses others with a given feeling: *a sense of urgency in his stride.* **4.** Good judgment; practical intelligence: *Natives of the tropics have the good sense to take a noonday nap.* **5. a.** Speech, thought, or reasoning that is sound and practical: *Talk sense!* **b.** Reasonableness: *saw no sense in hurrying.* **6. a.** The meaning conveyed by speech or writing: *Paragraphs often mark a break in the sense.* **b.** The meaning, or one of the meanings, of a word or phrase: *Words that are synonyms are usually alike in some senses.* **7.** A way of regarding or understanding a matter; a respect: *This modest book is in no sense a history of music.* —**modifier:** *sense impressions.* —*v.* **sensed, sens•ing. 1.** To perceive by one of the senses. **2.** To become aware of without knowing clearly why or how: *sensed the truth of what the man was saying.* [SEE NOTE]

sense•less |sĕns′lĭs| *adj.* **1.** Deprived of sensation; unconscious: *knocked senseless.* **2.** Without meaning; pointless: *muttering senseless words.* **3.** Lacking good judgment; foolish. —**sense′less•ly** *adv.* —**sense′less•ness** *n.*

sense organ. Any organ or structure of the body, as the eye or ear, that is specially developed to receive stimuli.

sen•si•bil•i•ty |sĕn′sə bĭl′ĭ tē| *n., pl.* **sen•si•bil•i•ties. 1.** The ability to feel, sense, or perceive; sensation. **2.** The ability to receive and appreciate sensations and feelings in the mind: *the sensibility of an artist.* **3.** Often **sensibilities.** Receptiveness to impressions and emotions of the finer sort.

sen•si•ble |sĕn′sə bəl| *adj.* **1.** Perceptible through or as if through one or more of the senses: *a sensible difference of temperature.* **2.** Capable of feeling or perceiving; sensitive: *sensible to pain.* **3.** Showing or in accordance with good judgment; reasonable: *a sensible decision.* **4.** Aware; conscious: *We are sensible of your objections.* —**sen′si•ble•ness** *n.* —**sen′si•bly** *adv.*

sen•si•tive |sĕn′sĭ tĭv| *adj.* **1.** Capable of perceiving with or as if with a sense or senses: *Bats are sensitive to sounds that we cannot hear.* **2.** Responsive to or affected by something: *Photographic film is sensitive to light. Children are sensitive to criticism.* **3.** Responding markedly to small changes of condition or environment: *a sensitive organism; a sensitive measuring instrument.* **4.** Responsive to the feelings, attitudes, etc., of others: *a sensitive and sympathetic listener.* **5.** Expressive of small changes of feeling: *a sensitive face.* **6.** Easily hurt, damaged, or irritated: *sensitive skin; sensitive feelings.* **7.** Quick to take offense; touchy: *He had a birthmark on his leg and was sensitive about it.* **8.** Requiring careful or discreet handling; delicate: *a matter too sensitive to be discussed openly.* —**sen′si•tive•ly** *adv.* —**sen′si•tiv′i•ty, sen′si•tive•ness** *n.*

sensitive plant. Any of several plants with leaflets that fold together or droop when touched.

sen•si•tize |sĕn′sĭ tīz′| *v.* **sen•si•tized, sen•si•tiz•ing.** To make or become sensitive or more sensitive.

sen•sor |sĕn′sər| *or* |-sôr′| *n.* A device, such as a photocell or thermocouple, that reacts in a characteristic way to a particular type of change in its condition or environment.

sen•so•ry |sĕn′sə rē| *adj.* **1.** Of the senses or sensation. **2.** Transmitting data or impulses from sense organs to the central nervous system: *sensory nerves.*

sen•su•al |sĕn′sho͞o əl| *adj.* **1.** Of the senses; sensory. **2.** Giving pleasure to the senses or to the body; physically gratifying: *the sensual experience of a warm bath.* **3.** Concerned with or devoted to the satisfaction of the physical appetites: *a sensual life.* **4.** Suggesting sexuality; voluptuous: *a sensual face.* —**sen'su•al'i•ty** *n.* —**sen'su•al•ly** *adv.*

sen•su•ous |sĕn'sho͞o əs| *adj.* **1.** Of or derived from the senses: *both a sensuous and an intellectual response to the music.* **2.** Appealing to the senses, especially with delicacy or gracefulness: *sensuous curves and floral patterns.* **3.** Sensual. —**sen'su•ous•ly** *adv.* —**sen'su•ous•ness** *n.*

sent |sĕnt|. Past tense and past participle of **send.** ¶ *These sound alike* **sent, cent, scent.**

sen•tence |sĕn'təns| *n.* **1.** A group of words, or rarely, a single word, that is separate from any other grammatical construction and that contains a finite verb or verb phrase and usually a subject and its predicate. For example, *It's almost midnight* and *Stop!* are sentences. **2. a.** The judgment of a court of law; a verdict. **b.** The penalty given by a court to a convicted person: *a sentence of four years in prison.* —***modifier:*** *a sentence pattern.* —*v.* **sen•tenced, sen•tenc•ing.** To pass sentence upon (a defendant). [SEE NOTE on p. 790]

sen•ten•tious |sĕn tĕn'shəs| *adj.* **1.** Brief and pointed in meaning or expression; pithy. **2.** Full of proverbs and moral sayings. **3.** Giving moral advice, especially in a pompous way. —**sen•ten'tious•ly** *adv.* —**sen•ten'tious•ness** *n.*

sen•tient |sĕn'shənt| *adj.* Capable of feeling or perceiving; having senses.

sen•ti•ment |sĕn'tə mənt| *n.* **1. a.** Emotion; feeling: *Different music arouses different kinds of sentiment.* **b.** Tender or romantic emotion: *that mixture of sentiment and sensation called love.* **2.** Delicate and sensitive feeling, especially when overvalued, prolonged, or not really genuine: *Today's my birthday, but I have no time for sentiment.* **3.** A view or attitude based on feeling more than reason: *His sentiments always favor the underdog.* **4.** The emotional motive of something said or written as opposed to the words used. **5.** Opinion; inclination: *Public sentiment is rising against foreign wars.* [SEE NOTE on p. 790]

sen•ti•ment•al |sĕn'tə mĕn'tl| *adj.* **1.** Of the feelings; emotional: *a man with sentimental ties to the country of his birth.* **2.** Ruled or influenced by one's emotions rather than reason or practicality: *a sentimental man.* **3.** Marked by emotion that is excessive or artificial: *a sentimental story.* —**sen'ti•ment'al•ly** *adv.*

sen•ti•ment•al•ism |sĕn'tə mĕn'tl ĭz'əm| *n.* A tendency to be ruled or influenced by one's emotions; a highly emotional point of view. —**sen'ti•ment'al•ist** *n.*

sen•ti•men•tal•i•ty |sĕn'tə mĕn tăl'ĭ tē| *n., pl.* **sen•ti•men•tal•i•ties. 1.** The quality or condition of being sentimental, especially to excess. **2.** An expression of excessive sentiment.

sen•ti•nel |sĕn'tə nəl| *n.* **1.** A sentry. **2.** Something that serves to guard or give warning of approaching danger: *radar sentinels; chattering monkeys, the sentinels of the jungle.*

sen•try |sĕn'trē| *n., pl.* **sen•tries.** A person, especially a soldier, posted at some spot to warn of approaching attackers or to check persons seeking admittance; a guard. [SEE PICTURE]

Seoul |sōl|. The capital of South Korea. Population, 6,890,000.

se•pal |sē'pəl| *n.* One of the divisions forming the calyx of a flower. Sepals are usually green and leaflike but are sometimes brightly colored and resemble petals. [SEE PICTURE]

sep•a•ra•ble |sĕp'ər ə bəl| *or* |sĕp'rə-| *adj.* Capable of being separated.

sep•a•rate |sĕp'ə rāt'| *v.* **sep•a•rat•ed, sep•a•rat•ing. 1.** To divide into parts: *Draw a line that separates a square into two triangles. Here the river separates into two channels.* **2.** To put or keep apart: *separated the rolls in the pan.* **3.** To place in different categories; sort: *separating the list of words into nouns and verbs.* **4.** To occupy a position between: *the channel that separates Great Britain from France.* **5.** To distinguish: *It was hard to separate facts from opinion in the editorial.* **6.** To go different ways; part: *The fugitives decided to separate.* **7.** To release or withdraw from a union or other relationship: *He was separated from his wife.* **8. a.** To remove from a mixture; extract: *The gin separates cotton 50 times faster than a man working by hand.* **b.** To become removed from a mixture: *If the oil begins to separate from the mayonnaise, add another egg yolk.* —*adj.* |sĕp'ər ĭt| *or* |sĕp'rĭt|. **1.** Set apart from the rest: *Libraries have a separate section for reference books.* **2.** Distinct from others; individual or independent: *She decided to give separate presents.* **3.** Not identical or alike; different: *The ships took separate courses.* —*n.* |sĕp'ər ĭt| *or* |sĕp'rĭt|. **separates.** Garments, such as skirts, slacks, blouses, etc., that may be bought separately and worn with other clothes in various combinations. —**sep'a•rate•ly** *adv.*

sep•a•ra•tion |sĕp'ə rā'shən| *n.* **1. a.** The act or process of separating: *the separation of cream from milk.* **b.** The condition of being separated: *her separation from her friends.* **2.** An intervening space; gap: *a separation between electrical circuits.* **3.** A legal agreement by which a husband and wife live apart.

sep•a•ra•tist |sĕp'ər ə tĭst| *or* |sĕp'rə-| *or* |sĕp'ə-rā'tĭst| *n.* **1.** A person who advocates the withdrawal of his group from a larger group, as from a political union or association; a secessionist. **2. Separatist.** Any of the English religious dissenters of the 16th and 17th centuries.

sep•a•ra•tor |sĕp'ə rā'tər| *n.* **1.** Someone or something that separates. **2.** A device that extracts a desired substance from a mixture.

se•pi•a |sē'pē ə| *n.* **1.** A dark-brown ink or coloring material originally prepared from the inky liquid secreted by cuttlefish. **2.** A dark brown. —*adj.* Dark brown.

Sept. September.

sep•ta |sĕp'tə| *n.* Plural of **septum.**

Sep•tem•ber |sĕp tĕm'bər| *n.* The ninth month of the year, after August and before October. It has 30 days. —***modifier:*** *a September storm.* [SEE NOTE]

sep•tic |sĕp'tĭk| *adj.* Of or induced by the presence of disease-causing microorganisms or their toxins in the blood or tissues.

sep•ti•ce•mi•a |sĕp'tĭ sē'mē ə| *n.* A condition in which disease-causing microorganisms or their toxins are present in the blood; blood poisoning.

septic tank. A tank in which sewage is held until the solid matter in it is liquefied by bacteria. The liquid waste then drains into the soil, where other bacteria purify it.

sep•tum |sĕp'təm| *n., pl.* **sep•ta** |sĕp'tə|. A thin

sentry
In front of Buckingham Palace, London

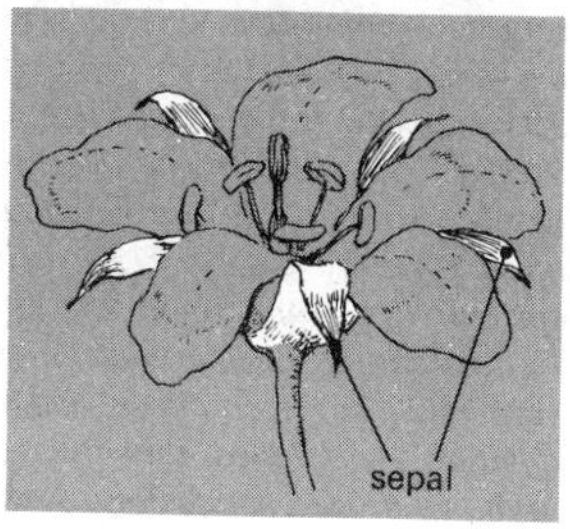

sepal

September
September *is from Latin* September, *"seventh month." In the oldest Roman calendar, March was the first month of the year, so that* September *was in fact the seventh,* October *the eighth,* November *the ninth, and* December *the tenth. In the second century* B.C., *the Romans moved back the beginning of the year to January, so that September became the ninth month in spite of its name, and likewise for October, November, and December.*

partition or membrane between two cavities or soft masses of tissue in a plant or animal part.

sep•ul•cher |sĕp′əl kər| *n.* A burial vault.

se•pul•chral |sə **pŭl′**krəl| *adj.* **1.** Of a sepulcher: *sepulchral inscriptions.* **2.** Suggestive of tombs or burial rites; funereal; mournful.

sep•ul•chre |sĕp′əl kər| *n.* Chiefly British form of the word **sepulcher.**

se•quel |sē′kwəl| *n.* **1.** Anything that follows; a continuation. **2.** A novel, movie, etc., complete in itself but continuing the story of an earlier work. **3.** A result; outcome.

se•quence |sē′kwəns| *n.* **1.** The following of one thing after another in a regular or continuous way: *the sequence of cause and effect.* **2.** A number of things or events that follow each other in time or location: *a sequence of incidents that led to civil war.* **3.** The order in which things or events occur or are arranged: *following the sequence of steps outlined in the sewing manual.*

se•ques•ter |sĭ **kwĕs′**tər| *v.* To withdraw to a private or out-of-the-way place; seclude: *sequestered himself in the tree house to think over what had happened.*

se•quin |sē′kwĭn| *n.* A small, shiny disk or spangle sewn on cloth or clothes for decoration.

se•quoi•a |sĭ **kwoi′**ə| *n.* Either of two very large cone-bearing evergreen trees, the **giant sequoia** of the mountains of southern California or the redwood of northern California.

se•ra |sîr′ə| *n.* A plural of **serum.**

se•ra•pe |sə **rä′**pē| *n.* A brightly colored woolen blanket worn as a cloak or poncho in certain parts of Mexico. [SEE PICTURE]

ser•aph |sĕr′əf| *n., pl.* **ser•aphs** or **ser•a•phim** |sĕr′ə fĭm|. An angel of the highest order in medieval Christian belief. —**se•raph′ic** |sə **răf′**ĭk| *adj.*

Serb |sûrb| *n.* A native or inhabitant of Serbia.

Ser•bi•a |sûr′bē ə|. A former country in the Balkans, now a part of Yugoslavia. —**Ser′bi•an** *adj.* & *n.*

Ser•bo-Cro•a•tian |sûr′bō krō **ā′**shən| *n.* The Slavic language of the Serbs and Croats of Yugoslavia. —*adj.* Of Serbo-Croatian or the people who speak it.

sere |sîr| *adj.* Withered. ¶*These sound alike* **sere, sear, seer.**

ser•e•nade |sĕr′ə **nād′**| *n.* A musical performance given to honor someone, as a performance given by a lover for his beloved. —*v.* **ser•e•nad•ed, ser•e•nad•ing.** To perform a serenade.

ser•en•dip•i•ty |sĕr′ən **dĭp′**ĭ tē| *n.* **1.** The accidental or unexpected discovery of something good. **2.** The knack of making such discoveries.

se•rene |sə **rēn′**| *adj.* **1.** Peaceful and untroubled; perfectly tranquil or composed: *the serene face of a Greek statue.* **2.** Perfectly clear and bright: *serene skies; a serene moon.* **3. Serene.** A word used as part of a title in speaking to or of a royal personage: *His Serene Majesty.* —**se•rene′ly** *adv.*

se•ren•i•ty |sə **rĕn′**ĭ tē| *n.* **1.** The quality of being serene; peacefulness; tranquillity. **2.** Clearness or brightness.

serf |sûrf| *n.* **1.** A member of a class of farm laborers in medieval Europe who were owned by lords and considered bound to the land where they lived and worked. **2.** Any person in bondage; a slave. ¶*These sound alike* **serf, surf.**

serf•dom |**sûrf′**dəm| *n.* **1.** The condition of being a serf. **2.** The practice of keeping serfs.

serge |sûrj| *n.* A strong cloth, usually of wool, woven with ridges slanting across the surface and used for tailored clothes. —***modifier:*** *a serge suit.* ¶*These sound alike* **serge, surge.**

ser•geant |**sär′**jənt| *n.* **1.** Any noncommissioned officer in the Army or Marine Corps ranking above a corporal. **2.** A police officer ranking just below a captain or, sometimes, just below a lieutenant. [SEE NOTE]

sergeant at arms. *pl.* **sergeants at arms.** An officer whose job is to keep order at the meetings of a legislature, club, or other group.

sergeant major. A noncommissioned officer of the highest rank in the Army or Marine Corps.

se•ri•al |**sîr′**ē əl| *adj.* **1.** Consisting of or arranged in a series. **2.** Presented in installments: *a serial television drama.* **3.** Of or based on a set of musical tones, usually the 12 tones of the chromatic scale, arranged in an arbitrary order. —*n.* A story or play presented in installments. ¶*These sound alike* **serial, cereal.** —**se′ri•al•ly** *adv.*

se•ri•al•ize |**sîr′**ē ə līz′| *v.* **se•ri•al•ized, se•ri•al•iz•ing.** To publish or present in installments: *serialize a book.*

serial number. A number that identifies one of a series of similar machines, persons grouped together, etc.: *the serial number of a car.*

se•ries |**sîr′**ēz| *n., pl.* **se•ries.** **1.** A number of similar things or events that occur in a row or follow one another in time; a succession: *a series of tracks in the snow; a series of wars known as the Crusades.* **2. a.** A number of related performances, as of music or drama, that are presented consecutively: *a series of concerts.* **b.** A television or radio show that is presented at regular intervals: *a comedy series.* **c.** A number of games played one after the other by the same opposing teams: *a four-game baseball series.*

se•ri•ous |**sîr′**ē əs| *adj.* **1.** Grave; sober: *Mike wondered what was wrong when his father looked so serious.* **2.** Not joking or speaking casually; in earnest: *serious about quitting school.* **3.** Not trivial; important; weighty: *It's a rather serious thing, getting married.* **4.** Worthy of concern or anxiety: *a serious chest wound.* **5.** Marked by earnest effort or devotion; diligent: *engaged in serious study.* **6.** Intended or intending to arouse deep thought or emotion: *a serious play.* —**se′ri•ous•ly** *adv.* —**se′ri•ous•ness** *n.*

ser•mon |**sûr′**mən| *n.* **1.** A talk on a religious subject or text delivered by a clergyman as part of a church service. **2.** Any solemn, lengthy talk.

Sermon on the Mount. A sermon delivered by Christ.

se•rous |**sîr′**əs| *adj.* Of, like, containing, or producing serum.

ser•pent |**sûr′**pənt| *n.* **1.** A snake. **2.** A snakelike dragon or monster. **3.** A sly or treacherous person.

ser•pen•tine |**sûr′**pən tēn′| *or* |-tīn′| *adj.* **1.** Of, resembling, or typical of a serpent; snakelike: *a serpentine form; serpentine movements.* **2.** Having many bends or curves: *a serpentine river.*

ser•rate |**sĕr′**āt′| *or* |-ĭt| *adj.* Edged with notched, toothlike projections: *a serrate leaf.*

ser•rat•ed |**sĕr′**ā′tĭd| *adj.* Serrate: *A serrated*

serape

sergeant

Sergeant *is from Old French* sergent, *originally meaning "serving man," from Latin* serviens, servient-, *the present participle of* servīre, *"to serve." The English word was originally pronounced approximately* /**sûr′**jənt/, *as it is spelled; but from about the fifteenth century, the pronunciation* /**sär′**jənt/ *began to occur, and it eventually displaced the original pronunciation. The spelling, however, has remained unchanged and "illogical"; but in the family name* Sargent, *which is derived from the noun, the spelling has been changed to reflect the pronunciation.*

knife blade cuts bread very easily.

se•rum |sîr′əm| *n., pl.* **se•rums** or **se•ra** |sîr′ə|. **1.** The clear, yellowish liquid obtained when all the cells, particles, etc., are removed from whole blood. **2.** A liquid extracted from the tissues of an immunized animal and used medically, especially as an antitoxin. **3.** Any watery fluid derived from animal tissue.

serv•ant |sûr′vənt| *n.* **1.** A person, such as a butler, cook, or maid, who works for wages in the household of someone else. **2.** A person employed to perform services for others: *The President must never forget that he is a servant of the people.* **3.** Someone or something that serves another: *Art can be a servant to man's needs.*

serve |sûrv| *v.* **served, serv•ing. 1.** To do work for; be a servant or a help to: *a squire serving his knight.* **2.** To do a term of duty: *served in the army.* **3.** To spend (a period of time) in fulfillment of an obligation, contract, etc.: *served a prison term; served 12 years in the senate.* **4.** To work in a given capacity, especially a helpful or subordinate one: *serve as a missionary.* **5.** To fulfill a task or function: *a note that will serve to remind you.* **6.** To act in behalf of; advance; promote: *serving the national interest.* **7.** To be used profitably by: *a port that serves a wide region.* **8.** To fulfill the demands of (customers), as in a store or restaurant; wait on. **9. a.** To present or offer (food) for others to eat: *serve dinner.* **b.** To provide food for (someone): *serving the hungriest first.* **c.** To be enough food for (a certain number): *a recipe that serves four.* **10.** To be sufficient; suffice: *looked over the furnished room and decided it would serve.* **11.** To present; offer for acceptance: *serving up generalities that passed for wisdom.* **12.** To deliver (a legal writ or summons) to the person named. **13.** To put (a ball or shuttlecock) in play by hitting it, as in tennis or badminton. *—n.* **1.** The right to serve or the manner or act of serving a ball or shuttlecock. **2.** The ball or shuttlecock served. [SEE NOTE]

serv•er |sûr′vər| *n.* **1.** A person who serves, especially one who brings food to a table. **2.** Something, such as a tray or a bowl, used in serving food.

serv•ice |sûr′vĭs| *n.* **1.** The act or occupation of serving, helping, or assisting another or others: *spent her life in the service of the poor.* **2.** Work or employment for another or others: *years of hard service.* **3. a.** Use to or by others: *trying to be of some service.* **b.** A condition in which use is possible; operation: *a telephone out of service.* **c.** Disposal: *I am at your service.* **4.** An act of assistance to another or others: *performing a valuable service for the family.* **5.** Often **services.** Assistance provided by a person with special training: *the services of a doctor.* **6.** The act or manner of serving food or fulfilling the demands of customers: *a hotel with poor service.* **7.** A set of dishes and table utensils for serving and eating food: *a service for eight persons.* **8.** A branch of the government and its employees: *the secret service.* **9.** The armed forces or a branch of the armed forces: *drafted into the service.* **10. a.** An enterprise that performs tasks for its customers: *a messenger service.* **b.** An enterprise that provides the public with the use of something: *a bus service.* **c.** A task, convenience, or facility provided by such an enterprise: *arranging for electricity service in a new house.* **11.** Installation, maintenance, or repair of a machine, appliance, etc.: *She brought her car in every year for service.* **12.** A religious ceremony; rite: *a church service; burial services.* **13.** The presentation of a legal writ or summons to the person named. **14.** The act, manner, or right of serving, as in tennis or badminton. *—adj.* **1.** Of or concerned with the serving of customers: *a service manager of a department store.* **2.** Reserved for the use of employees and deliverymen rather than the general public: *a service entrance.* **3.** Of or for the armed forces: *a service medal.* **4.** Of or for the maintenance and repair of products sold: *a service guarantee.* *—v.* **serv•iced, serv•ic•ing. 1.** To provide services to: *a welfare agency that services an area of high unemployment.* **2.** To maintain or repair (a machine, appliance, etc.).

serv•ice•a•ble |sûr′vĭ sə bəl| *adj.* **1.** Ready or fit for service; usable. **2.** Wearing well; sturdy; durable: *serviceable work boots.* **—serv′ice•a•bil′i•ty** *n.* **—serv′ice•a•bly** *adv.*

serv•ice•man |sûr′vĭs măn′| *n., pl.* **-men** |-mĕn′|. **1.** A member of the armed forces. **2.** Also **service man.** A man whose job is to maintain and repair equipment, appliances, etc.

service station. 1. A **gas station. 2.** A place where a machine or appliance can be taken for service.

ser•vile |sûr′vəl| *or* |-vīl′| *adj.* **1.** Always yielding to or waiting on others, like a servant; submissive; slavish. **2.** Of or appropriate to slaves or servants: *servile tasks.* **—ser′vile•ly** *adv.* **—ser•vil′i•ty** |sər vĭl′ĭ tē| *n.*

serv•ing |sûr′vĭng| *n.* A single portion of food or drink; a helping. *—adj.* Used for serving food: *a serving dish; a serving spoon.*

ser•vi•tude |sûr′vĭ to͞od′| *or* |-tyo͞od′| *n.* **1.** The condition of being a slave or serf; slavery. **2.** Forced labor imposed as a punishment.

ser•vo•mech•a•nism |sûr′vō mĕk′ə nĭz′əm| *or* |sûr′vō mĕk′-| *n.* A system that automatically controls the position, motion, speed, etc., of a mechanical device, usually by means of feedback of some sort.

ses•a•me |sĕs′ə mē| *n.* **1.** The small, flat seeds of a tropical Asian plant, used as food and as a source of oil. **2.** A plant that bears such seeds.

ses•sion |sĕsh′ən| *n.* **1.** A meeting or series of meetings of a judicial or legislative body. **2.** A meeting of a school class, a club, or any other group assembled to do or discuss something of common interest: *a recording session; a gossip session.* **3.** A period of time during the day or year when a school holds classes: *a morning session; a summer session.*

set¹ |sĕt| *v.* **set, set•ting. 1.** To put; place: *set the package on the table.* **2.** To place in a firm or unmoving position: *His lips were set as if they would never part.* **3.** To become hard or rigid; harden: *Some concrete sets very quickly.* **4.** To put in a specified condition: *setting him at liberty; set the wagon in motion.* **5.** To put to an activity or task: *a book that set me to thinking.* **6.** To place in the right position for use or effectiveness: *setting his lance for the attack.* **7.** To prepare or adjust for proper functioning:

serve, etc.

Serve *is from Old French* servir, *which is from Latin* servīre, *"to be a slave," from* servus, *"a slave."* Servus *itself became Old French* serf, *which was borrowed into English as* **serf. Servant, service,** *and* **servitude** *also belong to this group. There was also a very similar Latin verb,* servāre, *meaning "to save, protect, keep watch"; at first glance this word looks as if it might be related to* servus, *but actually it was used quite differently from* servīre, *and in particular it had nothing to do with slaves; the words are not related.* Servāre *formed the compound verbs* conservāre, *"to maintain, keep (something) in existence,"* observāre, *"to watch,"* (*Medieval Latin*) praeservāre, *"to guard beforehand," and* reservāre, *"to keep back, save up"; these are, respectively, the sources of* **conserve, observe, preserve,** *and* **reserve.** *None of them is related to* **serve.**

set¹⁻²
Set¹ *was Old English* settan, *"to cause (something) to sit, to put"; it is related to Old English* sittan, *"to sit." The noun* **set²** *is not by origin related to the verb; it is from Old French* sette, *"group, division," from Latin* secta, *"sect." But* **set²** *has come to be so generally associated with* **set¹** *that in spite of etymology the two words cannot now be separated.*

ă pat/ā pay/â care/ä father/ĕ pet/ē be/ĭ pit/ī pie/î fierce/ŏ pot/ō go/ô paw, for/oi oil/o͝o book/o͞o boot/ou out/ŭ cut/û fur/*th* the/th thin/hw which/zh vision/ə ago, item, pencil, atom, circus

setting a bear trap. **8.** To adjust (an instrument, tool, or other device) so that some desired condition of operation is established: *set the television to channel eight.* **9. a.** To treat and protect (a broken bone) so that it will knit. **b.** To knit; mend: *After the bone had set, the cast was removed.* **10.** To arrange tableware on (a table) in preparation for a meal. **11. a.** To arrange (type) into words, lines, and columns in preparation for printing. **b.** To arrange (matter to be printed) into type. **12.** To arrange (hair) in a certain style, as by rolling it up with clips and curlers. **13.** To direct; aim: *had never set eyes on such a place before.* **14.** To fix on a goal, purpose, or wish: *His heart was set on being a forest ranger.* **15.** To point toward (game) by holding a fixed position, as hunting dogs do. **16.** To decide on; appoint or designate: *The men set the end of October for the escape.* **17.** To establish: *setting an example; set a record.* **18.** To assign; prescribe: *set a task for us.* **19.** To start; begin: *setting to work.* **20.** To begin on a course or journey: *setting forth from the base camp.* **21.** To locate; situate: *doors set side by side.* **22.** To represent as happening in a certain place or at a certain time: *setting his story in the Orient.* **23. a.** To place or fix (a jewel, ornament, etc.) in a setting: *set a diamond in a crown.* **b.** To decorate or stud, as jewels mounted in a setting: *set a gold bracelet with rubies; grassland set with occasional palm trees.* **24.** To adapt (a poem, prayer, or other words) to be sung to music. **25.** To disappear beneath the horizon: *The sun sets in the west.* **26.** To sit on eggs in order to hatch them: *The hens were setting.* **27.** To fit or hang on the wearer: *a cape that sets well.* —**set'ting** *adj.*: *the setting sun; a setting hen.* —***phrasal verbs.*** **set about.** To begin intently: *spread the puzzle out and set about trying to solve it.* **set aside. 1.** To reserve for a special purpose: *set aside a certain amount each month to pay bills.* **2.** To discard or reject: *setting aside our original plan.* **3.** To declare invalid; annul or overrule. **set back.** To slow down the progress of; hinder. **set down. 1.** To put in writing; record: *set down his wildest dreams in his diary.* **2.** To assign to a cause; attribute: *set it down to lack of experience.* **set forth.** To present for others' consideration; express or propose: *set forth his principles in a manifesto.* **set in.** To begin to happen or be apparent; take hold: *A new mood of disillusion was setting in.* **set off. 1.** To give rise to; cause to occur: *set off a chemical reaction.* **2.** To cause to explode. **3.** To indicate as being different; distinguish: *setting off words with quotation marks.* **4.** To direct attention to by contrast; accentuate: *dark hair set off by a streak of white.* **set on** (or **upon**). To attack or direct to attack: *setting his dogs upon us.* **set out. 1.** To put or leave in a prominent place: *set out a dish for the cat.* **2.** To begin an earnest attempt or search; undertake: *set out to learn why.* **3.** To plant: *setting out rows of rice plants.* **set to. 1.** To begin working energetically; start in: *We set to and cleaned the house in an hour.* **2.** To begin fighting. **set up. 1.** To arrange or assemble: *set up the test so that easy questions come first.* **2.** To found; establish: *set up a free medical center.* **3.** To place in a position of authority. **4.** To provide with the necessary means or money: *won just enough to set himself up in his own business.* **5.** To prepare to receive or suffer something: *civil wars that weakened the Greeks and set them up for conquest by the Turks.* —*adj.* **1.** Not varying or moving: *a set position.* **2.** Fixed by agreement or custom: *a set order of events; a set time for the launching.* **3.** Unchanging in one's habits or thinking; rigid: *set in his ways.* **4.** Ready: *all set to go.* —*n.* **1.** The process of setting, especially the gradual hardening or stiffening of something. **2. a.** The way in which something is held or placed: *the set of his jaw; adjusted the set of his cap.* **b.** The carriage of a part of the body; posture: *a new, more confident set to his shoulders.* **c.** The way in which a garment fits or hangs: *the loose set of his borrowed suit.* **3.** An arrangement and styling of the hair: *a wash and set.* [SEE NOTE]

set² |sĕt| *n.* **1.** A group of matching or related things that have the same use or purpose or that form a unit: *a set of china.* **2.** A group of persons united, as by age, interests, or social standing: *the younger set.* **3.** In mathematics, any collection of distinct elements: *the set of all positive integers.* **4.** The collection of parts or apparatus that makes up a radio or television receiver. **5. a.** A structure on the stage of a theater, designed to represent the place where the action of a play or scene occurs. **b.** The stage or other place where a motion picture is being filmed. **6.** In tennis and other sports, a group of games that forms one unit or part of a match. —***modifier:*** *a theatrical set designer.* [SEE NOTE]

set•back |sĕt'băk'| *n.* An unexpected check or reverse in progress.

set•tee |sĕ tē'| *n.* A small sofa with a back and arms.

set•ter |sĕt'ər| *n.* One of a breed of dogs with smooth, silky hair, often trained and used as a hunting dog. Setters indicate the presence of game animals by crouching in a set position.

set theory. The mathematical study of the properties of sets.

set•ting |sĕt'ĭng| *n.* **1. a.** A surrounding area; environment: *animals in a natural setting.* **b.** The place where something occurs in fact or fiction: *the setting for a summit conference.* **2.** A framework or border, as of precious metal, in which a jewel is firmly fixed: *a turquoise stone in a silver setting.* **3.** A structure on the stage of a theater, designed to represent the place where the action occurs. **4.** Music composed or arranged so that a particular poem or other text can be sung to it: *a musical setting for a psalm.*

set•tle |sĕt'l| *v.* **set•tled, set•tling. 1.** To put into order; arrange or fix as desired: *settle the matter with the bank.* **2.** To come to rest or cause to come to rest in or as in a position or place: *He settled back in the chair. She settled herself by the fire.* **3. a.** To establish residence in (a new or unoccupied region): *pioneers who settled the West.* **b.** To make a home: *settled along the seacoast.* **4.** To establish as a resident or residents: *settled his family in Utah.* **5. a.** To sink, condense, or come to rest, especially at the bottom of something fluid or soft. **b.** To cause to sink, condense, or come to rest. **6.** To end or resolve: *settle a dispute.* **7.** To restore calmness or comfort to: *The music settled her nerves.* **8.** To decide by mutual agreement: *settled on a new plan; settled the fate of the territory.* **9. a.** To make compensation for (a claim). **b.** To pay (a debt). —***phrasal verbs.*** **settle down. 1.** To begin living a more orderly life: *He settled down as a farmer.* **2.** To begin acting in a less nervous, restless, or disorderly way: *settled down when class began.* **settle for.** To accept even though not satisfied: *settled for work as a shipping clerk.* —*n.* A long wooden bench with a low back.

set•tle•ment |sĕt'l mənt| *n.* **1.** The act or process of settling: *the settlement of differences; land open to settlement.* **2.** A small, relatively new community. **3.** Establishment, as of people in a new region. **4.** An adjustment or understanding reached in financial matters, business proceedings, etc. **5. a.** The transfer of property to provide for a person's needs. **b.** Property thus transferred. **6.** Also **settlement house.** A welfare center providing community services.

set•tler |sĕt'lər| *n.* A person who settles in a new region; a colonist.

set-to |sĕt'to͞o'| *n., pl.* **-tos.** A brief but usually heated contest or conflict.

set•up |sĕt'ŭp'| *n.* **1.** *Informal.* The way in which something is organized or planned. **2.** Often **setups.** *Informal.* The collection of ingredients and mixers used in serving a variety of alcoholic drinks.

sev•en |sĕv'ən| *n.* A number, written 7 in Arabic numerals, that is equal to the sum of 6 + 1. It is the positive integer that immediately follows 6. —**sev'en** *adj. & pron.*

sev•en•teen |sĕv'ən tēn'| *n.* A number, written 17 in Arabic numerals, that is equal to the sum of 16 + 1. It is the positive integer that immediately follows 16. —**sev'en•teen'** *adj. & pron.*

sev•en•teenth |sĕv'ən tēnth'| *n.* **1.** In a set of items arranged to match the natural numbers in a one-to-one correspondence, the item that matches the number seventeen. **2.** One of seventeen equal parts of a unit, written 1/17. —**sev'en•teenth'** *adj. & adv.*

sev•enth |sĕv'ənth| *n.* **1.** In a set of items arranged to match the natural numbers in a one-to-one correspondence, the item that matches the number seven. **2.** One of seven equal parts of a unit, written 1/7. **3. a.** Any of three musical intervals formed by tones that are seven diatonic scale steps apart. **b.** The seventh tone of a diatonic scale. —**sev'enth** *adj. & adv.*

Sev•enth-Day Ad•vent•ist |sĕv'ənth dā' ăd'vĕn'tĭst|. A member of a Protestant sect that believes in the imminent Second Coming of Christ and observes the Sabbath on Saturday.

sev•en•ti•eth |sĕv'ən tē ĭth| *n.* **1.** In a set of items arranged to match the natural numbers in a one-to-one correspondence, the item that matches the number seventy. **2.** One of seventy equal parts of a unit, written 1/70. —**sev'en•ti•eth** *adj. & adv.*

sev•en•ty |sĕv'ən tē| *n., pl.* **sev•en•ties.** A number, written 70 in Arabic numerals, that is equal to the product of 7 × 10. It is the tenth positive integer after 60. —**sev'en•ty** *adj. & pron.*

sev•er |sĕv'ər| *v.* **1.** To cut or break from a whole: *sever a limb from a tree.* **2.** To divide or separate into parts: *a clash that severed the Union.* **3.** To break off; dissolve: *sever diplomatic ties.*

sev•er•al |sĕv'ər əl| *adj.* **1.** Being of a number more than two or three, but not many; of an indefinitely small number: *several miles away; several questions.* **2.** Separate: *They parted and went their several ways.* —*n.* Several ones; a few: *He saw several of his classmates.*

sev•er•ance |sĕv'ər əns| *or* |sĕv'rəns| *n.* **1. a.** The act or process of severing: *the severance of political ties.* **b.** The condition of being severed. **2.** Separation; partition.

severance pay. Extra pay given an employee upon leaving a job.

se•vere |sə vîr'| *adj.* **se•ver•er, se•ver•est. 1.** Unsparing; stern; strict: *a severe law; severe terms.* **2.** Austere or dour; forbidding: *a severe voice.* **3.** Causing great distress; sharp: *a severe injury; severe pains.* **4.** Intense and serious; extreme: *a severe storm; severe damage.* **5.** Extremely plain or austere: *severe clothes.* **6.** Very difficult; trying; rigorous: *a severe test.* —**se•vere'ly** *adv.* —**se•vere'ness** *n.*

se•ver•i•ty |sə vĕr'ĭ tē| *n., pl.* **se•ver•i•ties. 1.** Extreme strictness: *the severity of their discipline.* **2.** Harshness: *the severity of the winter.* **3.** Austerity or simplicity: *severity of dress.*

Se•ville |sə vĭl'|. A city in southwestern Spain. Population, 548,000.

sew |sō| *v.* **sewed, sewn** |sōn| or **sewed, sew•ing. 1.** To make, repair, close, or attach with stitches made by a needle and thread: *sew a dress; sew up a rip; sew on a button.* **2.** To work with a needle and thread or a sewing machine: *She sews for a living.* —**sew'ing** *adj.: the sewing room; a sewing box.* ¶ *These sound alike* **sew, so, sow**[1]. —**sew'er** *n.* —***phrasal verb.*** **sew up.** *Informal.* To complete with success: *sew up a business deal.*

sew•age |so͞o'ĭj| *n.* Liquid or solid waste material that must be disposed of, especially water that contains human excrement or other refuse.

sew•er |so͞o'ər| *n.* A pipe or other channel, usually underground, built to carry off sewage, water, etc. —***modifier:*** *sewer pipes.*

sew•er•age |so͞o'ər ĭj| *n.* **1.** A system of sewers. **2.** The removal of waste materials by a system of sewers. **3.** Sewage.

sew•ing |sō'ĭng| *n.* **1. a.** The act, work, skill, or method of someone who sews. **b.** The action of a sewing machine. **2.** Anything being made, repaired, or embroidered with needle and thread; needlework.

sewing machine. A machine operated by a foot treadle or by electric power, for sewing or making stitches. [SEE PICTURE]

sewn |sōn|. A past participle of **sew.**

sex |sĕks| *n.* **1.** One of the two divisions, male and female, into which many living things are grouped according to their functions in the process of reproduction. **2.** The combination of characteristics that are typical of each of these groups: *Sex is often recognized by marked physical differences.* **3.** Activities, feelings, etc., associated with the reproductive functions: *Sex plays an important role in human relationships.* **4.** Information about sexual characteristics, functions, etc.: *differences of opinion about teaching sex in the schools.* —***modifier:*** *the sex organs.*

sex chromosome. Either of a pair of chromosomes, usually called X and Y, that in combination determine the sex of an individual in

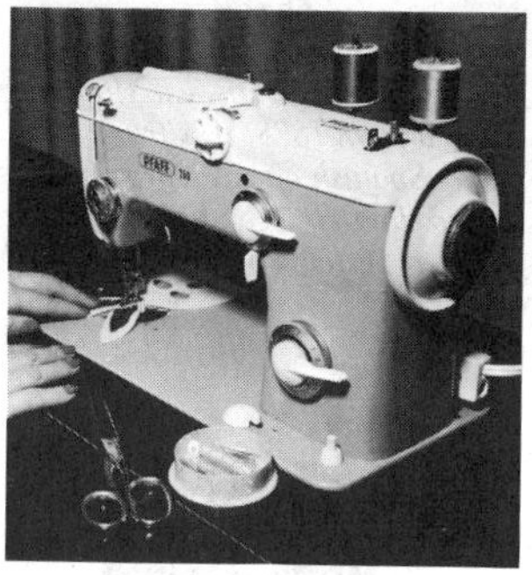
sewing machine

human beings, most animals, and some plants.

sex•ism |sĕk′sĭz′əm| *n.* **1.** Prejudice against the female sex. **2.** Any arbitrary, unvarying ideas about males and females on the basis of their gender. —**sex′ist** *adj. & n.*

sex•tant |sĕks′tənt| *n.* A navigation instrument used to measure the altitude between the plane of the horizon and a line extending to a celestial body. [SEE PICTURE]

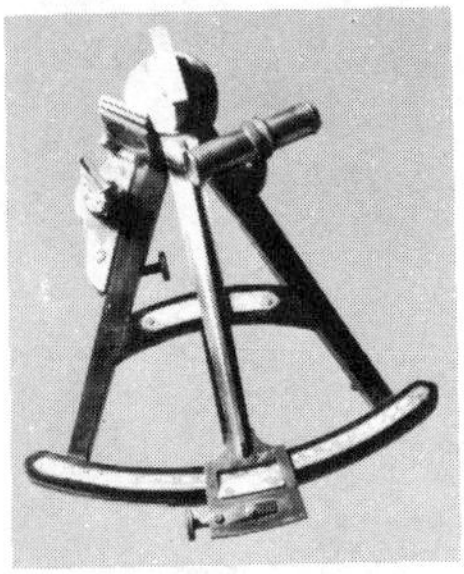

sextant

sex•tet |sĕks tĕt′| *n.* **1. a.** A musical composition that requires six performers. **b.** A group of six musicians who perform a sextet. **2.** A group of six persons or things.

sex•ton |sĕks′tən| *n.* A man employed to take care of a church and its property and sometimes to ring bells, arrange for burials, etc.

sex•u•al |sĕk′shōō əl| *adj.* **1.** Of or involving the union of male and female sex cells: *sexual reproduction.* **2.** Of, affecting, or typical of sex, the sexes, or the sex organs and their functions: *sexual development.* **3.** Of or relating to the activities, feelings, etc., associated with attraction between the sexes. —**sex′u•al•ly** *adv.*

sex•u•al•i•ty |sĕk′shōō ăl′ĭ tē| *n.* The qualities associated with sexual activities or attraction.

Sey•chelles |sā shĕl′| *or* |-shĕlz′|. An island country in the west Indian Ocean north of Madagascar. Population, 63,000. Capital, Victoria.

Sgt. sergeant.

sh |sh| *interj.* Often **shh.** Be quiet! Hush!

shab•by |shăb′ē| *adj.* **shab•bi•er, shab•bi•est. 1.** Worn-out, frayed, and faded; threadbare: *shabby clothes.* **2.** Dressed in worn-out, frayed, or threadbare clothes: *a shabby tramp.* **3.** Dilapidated; deteriorated: *shabby houses.* **4.** Despicable or unfair; mean: *a shabby reward; a shabby deed.* —**shab′bi•ly** *adv.* —**shab′bi•ness** *n.*

shack |shăk| *n.* A small, crudely built cabin. [SEE NOTE]

shack

The word **shack** *is an Americanism from the Southwest, first recorded from 1878; it is from Mexican Spanish* jacal *(pronounced approximately* /shä **käl′**/*), which is from Aztec* xacalli, *"thatched cabin."*

shack•le |shăk′əl| *n.* **1.** A metal ring fastened or locked around the wrist or ankle, especially one of a pair that are chained together and used to confine or restrain a prisoner. **2.** Often **shackles.** Anything that confines or restrains: *the shackles of ignorance.* —*v.* **shack•led, shack•ling. 1.** To put a shackle or shackles on: *shackle a prisoner.* **2.** To confine; restrain; hamper.

shad |shăd| *n., pl.* **shad.** A food fish that is related to the herrings and that swims from ocean waters up rivers and streams to spawn.

shade |shād| *n.* **1.** Light that has been diminished in strength by partial blocking or deflection of its rays; partial darkness. **2.** An area or space of such partial darkness. **3.** Cover or shelter from the sun or its rays. **4.** Any of various devices used to partially block light or radiant heat, as that from the sun: *a window shade.* **5.** The degree to which a color is mixed with black or less than fully lighted. **6.** A slight difference; a nuance: *a shade of meaning.* **7.** A small amount; a trace: *a shade under forty miles.* **8.** A spirit; a ghost. **9. shades.** *Informal.* Reminders; echoes: *shades of 1776.* —***modifier:*** *a shade tree.* —*v.* **shad•ed, shad•ing. 1.** To screen from light or heat: *Trees shaded the street.* **2.** To obscure or darken: *His stern appearance shaded his kindliness.* **3.** To represent or produce degrees of darkness in: *shade a drawing.* **4.** To change or vary by slight degrees.

shagbark

ă pat/ā pay/â care/ä father/ĕ pet/ ē be/ĭ pit/ī pie/î fierce/ŏ pot/ ō go/ô paw, for/oi oil/ŏŏ book/ ōō boot/ou out/ŭ cut/û fur/ *th* the/th thin/hw which/zh vision/ ə ago, item, pencil, atom, circus

shad•ing |shā′dĭng| *n.* **1.** Screening against light or heat. **2.** The lines or other marks used in a drawing, engraving, etc., to represent gradations of colors or darkness. **3.** Any small variation or difference.

shad•ow |shăd′ō| *n.* **1.** An area or region from which light or other radiation is wholly or partly blocked due to the presence of an opaque object between it and the source of radiation. **2.** The rough outline or image cast by an object blocking rays of light: *shadows of leaves on the wall.* **3.** An imperfect imitation or copy of something else. **4. shadows.** The darkness following sunset: *evening shadows.* **5.** Gloom or unhappiness. **6.** A shaded area in a picture. **7.** A phantom; a ghost. **8.** Someone who follows or spies on another in secret. **9.** A slight trace: *without a shadow of a claim.* **10.** A faint indication; a premonition: *shadows of future events.* **11. a.** The area nearby; the vicinity: *in the shadow of the Pyrenees.* **b.** A powerful influence: *He played all his life in the shadow of the great baseball player.* —*v.* **1.** To cast a shadow upon; shade. **2.** To follow after, especially in secret; trail.

shad•ow•y |shăd′ō ē| *adj.* **shad•ow•i•er, shad•ow•i•est. 1.** Of or resembling a shadow; dark and unsubstantial: *shadowy forms moving underwater.* **2.** Full of shadows; shady: *shadowy woods.* **3.** Vague; indistinct: *shadowy ideas.*

shad•y |shā′dē| *adj.* **shad•i•er, shad•i•est. 1.** Full of shade; shaded: *a shady street.* **2.** Casting shade: *shady trees.* **3.** Of doubtful honesty or legality; questionable; dishonest: *a shady deal.* —**shad′i•ly** *adv.* —**shad′i•ness** *n.*

shaft[1] |shăft| *or* |shäft| *n.* **1.** The long narrow body of a spear or arrow. **2.** A spear or arrow. **3.** A ray or beam of light. **4.** A projecting rod that forms a handle or by which a handle is attached, as to a tool or implement: *the shaft of a hammer.* **5. a.** A cylindrical bar on which a wheel or similar part turns: *an axle shaft.* **b.** A similar bar that turns and transmits power: *a drive shaft.* **6.** The rib of a feather. **7.** Any long, relatively slender part, such as the section of a column between the capital and base. **8.** One of the two parallel poles between which an animal drawing a vehicle is hitched.

shaft[2] |shăft| *or* |shäft| *n.* A long, narrow passage or conduit: *a mine shaft; an air shaft.*

shag |shăg| *n.* **1.** A tangled or matted mass of hair, wool, or fiber. **2. a.** A coarse, long nap, as on some woolen cloth. **b.** Cloth having such a nap. —***modifier:*** *a shag rug.*

shag•bark |shăg′bärk′| *n.* Also **shagbark hickory.** A North American hickory tree with shaggy bark and edible, hard-shelled nuts. [SEE PICTURE]

shag•gy |shăg′ē| *adj.* **shag•gi•er, shag•gi•est. 1.** Having or consisting of long, rough hair, wool, or fibers: *a shaggy dog; a shaggy coat.* **2.** Rough and busy or uneven: *a shaggy haircut.*

shah |shä| *n.* The title of the ruler of Iran.

shake |shāk| *v.* **shook** |shŏŏk|, **shak•en** |shā′kən|, **shak•ing. 1.** To move or cause to move to and fro, back and forth, or up and down with short, jerky movements: *shake a tambourine; shake a bottle of medicine.* **2.** To tremble or cause to tremble; vibrate or rock: *The severe earthquake shook the ground. He was shaking in the bitter cold air.* **3.** To remove or dislodge by or as if by making jerky movements: *shake snow from the boots.* **4.** To make uneasy; disturb; agitate: *A terrible thought had shaken her.* **5.** To cause to waver; unsettle: *Nothing could shake him from his belief.* **6.** To brandish or wave: *He shook his fist in the other's face.* **7.** To clasp (hands or another's hand) in greeting or leave-taking or as a sign of agreement. **8.** To get rid of: *shake off the pursuer.* —***phrasal verb.*** **shake up.** *Informal.* To reorganize or rearrange drastically. —*n.* **1.** An act of shaking: *a shake of the head.* **2.** A trembling or vibrating movement. **3.** *Slang.* A moment: *We'll be there in three shakes.* **4.** A beverage mixed by shaking: *a milk shake.* **5. the shakes.** *Informal.* Uncontrollable trembling.

Idioms. **no great shakes.** *Slang.* Not exceptional; ordinary; mediocre. **shake a leg.** *Informal.* To hurry.

shak•er |shā'kər| *n.* **1.** Someone or something that shakes. **2.** A container used for shaking something: *a cocktail shaker.* **3. Shaker.** A member of a Protestant sect in the United States advocating common ownership of property and abstention from marriage.

Shake•speare |shāk'spîr|, **William.** 1564–1616. English dramatist and poet.

shake•up |shāk'ŭp'| *n.* A drastic reorganization: *a shakeup of government personnel.*

shak•o |shăk'ō| *or* |shā'kō| *n., pl.* **shak•os** or **shak•oes.** A military cap with a visor in front and an upright plume on top. [SEE PICTURE]

shak•y |shā'kē| *adj.* **shak•i•er, shak•i•est. 1.** Trembling or quivering: *a shaky voice.* **2.** Unsteady or unsound: *a shaky old building.* **3.** Not to be depended on; wavering: *a shaky alliance.* —**shak'i•ly** *adv.*

shale |shāl| *n.* Any of various easily split sedimentary rocks consisting of layers of fine particles pressed together.

shall |shăl| *v.* past **should** |shŏŏd|. —Used as an auxiliary verb followed by a simple infinitive, indicating: **1.** Future action or state: *We shall arrive toward midnight. I shall be ten tomorrow.* **2.** Command: *You shall leave now.* **3.** Determination or promise: *I shall go out if I feel like it.*

shal•low |shăl'ō| *adj.* **shal•low•er, shal•low•est. 1.** Measuring little from the bottom to the top or surface; not deep: *a shallow lake; a shallow pan.* **2.** Lacking depth of thought, feeling, or perception; superficial: *shallow ideas.* —*n.* Often **shallows.** A shallow part of a body of water. —**shal'low•ly** *adv.* —**shal'low•ness** *n.*

shalt |shălt| *Archaic.* A form of the present tense of **shall,** used with *thou.*

sham |shăm| *n.* Something false that is deceitfully passed off as genuine; a fraudulent imitation: *The antique turned out to be a sham.* —*adj.* Pretended; not genuine: *a sham battle.* —*v.* **shammed, sham•ming.** To pretend to have or feel; feign: *shamming ignorance.*

sha•man |shä'mən| *or* |shā'-| *or* |shăm'ən| *n.* A priest and doctor who uses magic to cure the sick, foretell events, etc., among certain Asian and North American Indian tribes and other native peoples. [SEE NOTE]

sham•ble |shăm'bəl| *v.* **sham•bled, sham•bling.** To walk in an awkward or lazy way, dragging the feet; shuffle. —*n.* An awkward, shuffling walk.

sham•bles |shăm'bəlz| *n. (used with a singular verb).* A scene or condition of great disorder or destruction.

shame |shām| *n.* **1.** A painful emotion caused by a sense of having done something wrong. **2.** A feeling or condition of disgrace; dishonor. **3.** A source of disgrace or embarrassment: *It's a shame that none of you offered to help the strangers.* **4.** Something that is unfortunate or regrettable; a pity: *It would be a shame to miss the circus.* —*v.* **shamed, sham•ing. 1.** To fill with shame: *He lies, because the truth shames him.* **2.** To bring disgrace upon: *shamed their good name.* **3.** To diminish by being much better; surpass. **4.** To force (someone) by arousing a feeling of shame or guilt: *shamed him into climbing the tree by calling him a coward.*

Idiom. **put to shame. 1.** To fill with shame. **2.** To surpass: *The design of the human body puts any skyscraper to shame.*

shame•faced |shām'fāst'| *adj.* **1.** Ashamed. **2.** Very shy; bashful. —**sham'fac'ed•ly** *adv.*

shame•ful |shām'fəl| *adj.* Bringing or deserving shame; disgraceful: *shameful behavior.* —**shame'ful•ly** *adv.* —**shame'ful•ness** *n.*

shame•less |shām'lĭs| *adj.* Being or done without awareness of wrongdoing; impudent; brazen: *a shameless liar.* —**shame'less•ly** *adv.*

sham•poo |shăm pōō'| *n.* **1.** Any of various preparations of soap or detergent used to wash the hair and scalp. **2.** Any of various cleaning agents for rugs or upholstery. **3.** The act or process of washing the hair or cleaning something with shampoo. —*v.* **sham•pooed, sham•poo•ing.** To wash or clean with shampoo.

sham•rock |shăm'rŏk'| *n.* A clover, wood sorrel, or similar plant having leaves with three small leaflets, regarded as the national emblem of Ireland. [SEE PICTURE]

shang•hai |shăng hī'| *v.* **shang•haied, shang•hai•ing. 1.** To kidnap (a sailor) for forced service aboard a ship, especially by drugging him. **2.** To force (someone) to do something by deceitful or dishonest means.

Shang•hai |shăng hī'|. The largest city in China, a seaport near the mouth of the Yangtze River. Population, 10,820,000.

shank |shăngk| *n.* **1. a.** The part of the human leg between the knee and ankle. **b.** The corresponding part of the leg of a vertebrate animal. **2.** A long, narrow part of an object: *the shank of an anchor.* **3.** A cut of meat, as lamb, veal, or ham, from part of the leg, including the bone.

shan't |shănt| *or* |shänt|. Shall not.

shan•tey |shăn'tē| *n.* A form of the word **chantey.**

shan•tung |shăn tŭng'| *n.* A fabric with a rough, nubby surface, originally made of wild silk and now also made of rayon or cotton. —***modifier:*** *a shantung dress.*

shan•ty |shăn'tē| *n., pl.* **shan•ties.** A roughly built or ramshackle cabin; a shack. ¶*These sound alike* **shanty, chantey.**

shape |shāp| *n.* **1.** Something seen and distinguished from its surroundings by its outline; a form: *dark shapes on the horizon that might have been houses.* **2.** The appearance of an object as the eye compares its dimensions and outlines: *the oval shape of an egg.* **3. a.** An appearance that has recognizable dimensions and outlines; a def-

shako

shaman

The word **shaman** *is from Russian* shaman, *from one of the languages of Siberia. Shamans typically practice a kind of spiritualism; individual spirits, often representing animals or powers of nature, are compelled to enter into the shaman so that he can give guidance or inspiration to the people.*

shamrock

The national emblem of Ireland

The word **shamrock** is from Irish *seamrog,* "little clover," diminutive of *seamar,* "clover."

shark

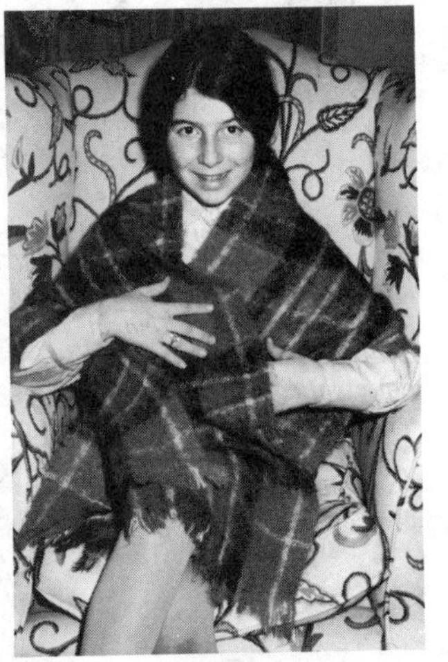
shawl

ă pat/ā pay/â care/ä father/ĕ pet/ ē be/ĭ pit/ī pie/î fierce/ŏ pot/ ō go/ô paw, for/oi oil/o͝o book/ o͞o boot/ou out/ŭ cut/û fur/ *th* the/th thin/hw which/zh vision/ ə ago, item, pencil, atom, circus

inite form: *The jigsaw puzzle was beginning to take shape.* **b.** An appearance that has regular or proper dimensions and outlines; a desirable form: *a fabric that holds its shape.* **4.** The contours of a person's body; the figure. **5.** Any form or condition in which something may exist or appear: *a god in the shape of a swan; the many shapes of love.* **6.** Proper condition for action, effectiveness, or use: *an athlete out of shape.* **7.** A device for giving or determining form; a mold or pattern. *—v.* **shaped, shap•ing. 1.** To give a certain shape or form to: *shape clay.* **2.** To change the shape or form of; mold: *shaping ground beef into patties.* **3.** To cause to assume a certain nature or take a certain course: *shaping a child's character.* **4.** To modify; adapt: *shaped their plans to fit ours.* ***—phrasal verb.*** **shape up.** *Informal.* **1.** To develop; turn out: *checked to see how the game was shaping up.* **2.** To improve one's performance, behavior, etc. **—shap'er** *n.*

shape•less |**shāp'**lĭs| *adj.* **1.** Having no definite shape; formless: *a shapeless cloud.* **2.** Lacking a pleasing shape; not shapely: *a shapeless figure.* **—shape'less•ly** *adv.* **—shape'less•ness** *n.*

shape•ly |**shāp'**lē| *adj.* **shape•li•er, shape•li•est.** Having a shape pleasing to look at; well-proportioned. **—shape'li•ness** *n.*

share |shâr| *v.* **shared, shar•ing. 1.** To have, use, or experience in common with another or others: *sharing the responsibility; share a room.* **2.** To disclose or discuss for the benefit of others: *shared his adventure with the class.* **3.** To participate: *Political enemies shared in applauding the compromise.* *—n.* **1.** A part of something distributed or divided up; a portion. **2.** A fair or full portion: *did her share to make the play a success.* **3.** Any of the equal parts into which the capital stock of a business is divided, bought and sold by stockholders. **—shar'er** *n.*

share•crop•per |**shâr'**krŏp'ər| *n.* A tenant farmer who pays a share of his produce as rent to the owner.

share•hold•er |**shâr'**hōl'dər| *n.* A person who owns a share or shares in the stock of a company; a stockholder.

shark |shärk| *n.* **1.** Any of several often large ocean fish with sharp teeth and tough skin. **2.** A ruthless person who cheats or extorts money from his victims: *a loan shark.* [SEE PICTURE]

sharp |shärp| *adj.* **sharp•er, sharp•est. 1.** Having a thin edge or fine point for cutting or piercing: *a sharp razor.* **2.** Pointed; not rounded or blunt: *a sharp pencil.* **3.** Abrupt; not gradual: *a sharp slope.* **4.** Clear in outline or detail; distinct: *in sharper focus.* **5.** High-pitched; shrill. **6.** Loud and brief: *a sharp blast of the horn.* **7.** Felt suddenly and intensely: *a sharp pain.* **8.** Brisk; chilly: *a gust of cold, sharp air.* **9.** Harsh; caustic: *a sharp tongue.* **10.** Stern; reproachful: *sharp words.* **11.** Quick and forceful: *a sharp blow.* **12.** Acute: *the sharp eyes of a falcon.* **13.** Alert; clever: *a sharp mind.* **14.** Shrewd in self-advancement; astute: *a sharp politician.* **15.** Having a strong, pungent odor and flavor: *a sharp cheese.* **16.** *Informal.* Stylish; trim; fashionable: *a sharp dresser.* **17. a.** Higher in musical pitch than is correct: *a sharp note.* **b.** Higher in pitch by a half step than a corresponding natural tone or key: *a C sharp.* *—adv.* **1.** Promptly; exactly: *at 3 o'clock sharp.* **2.** Alertly; keenly: *Look sharp!* **3.** Above the correct pitch: *Nervousness caused him to sing sharp.* *—n.* **1.** A musical note or tone that is a semitone higher than a corresponding natural note or tone. **2.** The symbol (♯) attached to a note to indicate that it is a sharp. *—v.* To sing or play sharp. **—sharp'ly** *adv.* **—sharp'ness** *n.*

sharp•en |**shär'**pən| *v.* To make or become sharp or sharper. **—sharp'en•er** *n.*

sharp•shoot•er |**shärp'**sho͞o'tər| *n.* A person expert at shooting a gun.

shat•ter |**shăt'**ər| *v.* **1.** To break suddenly into many pieces, as with a violent blow; smash. **2.** To disrupt suddenly, as with a loud noise: *A shrill cry shattered the stillness.* **3.** To destroy beyond hope of repair; ruin: *shattered his hopes.*

shave |shāv| *v.* **shaved, shaved** or **shav•en** |**shā'**vən|, **shav•ing. 1.** To remove the beard or hair from, especially with a razor: *shave a man's face.* **2.** To cut hair, especially the hair on a man's face, at the surface of the skin with a razor: *Tom shaves every morning.* **3.** To cut thin slices from: *shaving a block of wood with a knife.* **4.** To cut or scrape into small pieces; shred: *shave ice.* **5.** To touch gently in passing; graze. *—n.* The act, process, or result of shaving: *a smooth shave.* ***Idiom.*** **close shave.** *Informal.* A narrow escape.

shav•er |**shā'**vər| *n.* **1.** An electric razor. **2.** *Informal.* A young boy; lad.

shav•ing |**shā'**vĭng| *n.* A thin strip of wood or metal cut off by a plane or similar tool.

Sha•vu•ot |shə **vo͞o'**ōt| *or* |-əs| *n.* A Jewish holiday celebrated in the late spring as a harvest festival. It also commemorates God's giving the Commandments to Moses on Mount Sinai.

shawl |shôl| *n.* A large piece of cloth worn around the shoulders, neck, or head as a wrap or covering. [SEE PICTURE]

Shaw•nee |shô **nē'**| *n., pl.* **Shaw•nee** or **Shaw•nees. 1.** A North American Indian tribe now living in Oklahoma. **2.** A member of this tribe. **3.** The Algonquian language of this tribe.

shay |shā| *n.* A chaise.

she |shē| *pron.* **1.** The female person or animal last mentioned: *Nancy left, but she will be back.* **2.** Something previously mentioned that is regarded as feminine, especially a ship or country: *The "Titanic" was on her first transatlantic voyage when she sank. Britain was bombed severely, but she would not surrender.* **3.** *Informal.* Something personified as a feminine being: *She's a neat little gun.* *—n.* A female animal or person: *Is the baby a he or a she?* ***—modifier:*** *a she-wolf and her cubs.* *—Note:* As a pronoun, *she* is in the nominative case and serves either as the subject of a verb or as a predicate nominative following a form of the verb *be: She* (subject) *has arrived. I can't imagine anyone calling at this hour, unless it was she* (predicate nominative).

sheaf |shēf| *n., pl.* **sheaves** |shēvz|. **1.** A bundle of cut stalks of grain, bound and left on a field to be gathered up later. **2.** Any collection of things held or bound together; a batch.

shear |shîr| *v.* **sheared, sheared** or **shorn** |shôrn| *or* |shōrn|, **shear•ing. 1.** To remove (fleece, hair, etc.) by clipping with a sharp instrument. **2.** To remove the fleece, hair, etc., from: *shearing a ram.* **3.** To cut or trim with or as with shears:

shearing a hedge; shearing metal. **4.** To deprive; divest: *sheared him of all his privileges.* ¶ *These sound alike* **shear, sheer.** —**shear'er** *n.*

shears |shîrz| *n. (used with a plural verb).* A cutting implement resembling scissors but generally much larger.

sheath |shēth| *n., pl.* **sheaths** |shē*thz*| *or* |shēths|. **1.** A case into which the blade of a knife or sword fits snugly. **2.** Any tightly fitting protective covering or structure. **3.** A close-fitting dress, usually having a straight skirt. —*v.* To sheathe.

sheathe |shē*th*| *v.* **sheathed, sheath•ing. 1.** To insert into a sheath: *sheathed his saber.* **2.** To provide with a protective covering or structure: *sheathe electric wires with rubber.*

sheath•ing |shē'*th*ĭng| *n.* **1.** A layer of boards applied to a frame house to strengthen the structure and serve as a base for the exterior weatherproof covering. **2.** The metal casing on the underwater part of a ship's hull.

sheave |shēv| *v.* **sheaved, sheav•ing.** To gather and bind (grain) into a sheaf or sheaves.

sheaves |shēvz| *n.* Plural of **sheaf.**

She•ba |shē'bə|, **Queen of.** In the Bible, a queen who visited King Solomon to test his wisdom.

shed[1] |shĕd| *v.* **shed, shed•ding. 1.** To remove from one's person; divest oneself of: *shed his clothes and jumped into the pool.* **2.** To lose, drop, or cast off (a part, covering, etc.) by a natural process: *trees that shed their leaves in autumn; a snake sunning itself after it has shed.* **3.** To send forth; give off; cast: *The moon shed a pale light on the pond.* **4.** To pour forth (tears, blood, etc.): *The tin man was so moved he almost shed tin tears.* —**shed'der** *n.* [SEE NOTE]

Idiom. **shed blood.** To take a life or lives; kill.

shed[2] |shĕd| *n.* A small structure for storage or shelter: *a tool shed.* [SEE NOTE]

she'd |shēd|. **1.** She had. **2.** She would.

sheen |shēn| *n.* Glistening brightness; luster.

sheep |shēp| *n., pl.* **sheep. 1.** A hoofed animal with a thick, fleecy coat, widely raised for wool and as a source of meat. **2.** A person who is easily led or influenced. —***modifier:*** *a sheep ranch.*

sheep dip *n.* A liquid disinfectant used to kill parasites in the wool of sheep, before shearing.

sheep dog. A dog trained to guard and herd sheep, or belonging to a breed originally raised and trained for this purpose.

sheep•fold |shēp'fōld'| *n.* A pen or fenced-in area where sheep are kept.

sheep•herd•er |shēp'hûr'dər| *n.* A shepherd.

sheep•ish |shē'pĭsh| *adj.* **1.** Embarrassed and apologetic: *He peeled the bubble gum from his nose with a sheepish grin.* **2.** Meek; timid. —**sheep'ish•ly** *adv.* —**sheep'ish•ness** *n.*

sheep•man |shēp'mən| *n., pl.* **-men** |-mən|. A man who raises sheep.

sheep•skin |shēp'skĭn'| *n.* **1.** The skin of a sheep, either with the fleece left on or in the form of leather or parchment. **2.** A diploma. —***modifier:*** *a sheepskin coat.*

sheer[1] |shîr| *adj.* **sheer•er, sheer•est. 1.** Thin and fine enough to be transparent: *sheer stockings.* **2.** Not mixed or qualified; absolute; pure: *dropped from sheer exhaustion.* **3.** Extending straight up or down, or nearly so; very steep: *the sheer icy slopes of Mount Everest.* ¶ *These sound alike* **sheer, shear.**

sheer[2] |shîr| *v.* To swerve from a course. ¶ *These sound alike* **sheer, shear.**

sheet[1] |shēt| *n.* **1.** A large piece of lightweight cloth, usually cotton or linen, used as a bed covering, especially in pairs, one under and one over the sleeper. **2.** A rectangular piece of paper for writing or printing. **3.** A broad, thin, usually rectangular piece of any material: *a sheet of aluminum foil; a sheet of glass.* **4.** A broad, continuous expanse of material covering a surface: *a sheet of ice.* —*v.* To cover or provide with sheets, especially bed sheets. [SEE NOTE]

sheet[2] |shēt| *n.* A rope attached to one or both of the lower corners of a sail to secure and regulate it. [SEE NOTE]

sheet lightning. Lightning that appears as a broad sheet of light across a part of the sky, caused by reflection of a distant flash of lightning by clouds.

sheet music. Music printed on unbound sheets of paper.

sheik |shēk| *n.* The leader of an Arab family, village, or tribe. ¶ *These sound alike* **sheik, chic.**

sheikh |shēk| *n.* A form of the word **sheik.**

shek•el |shĕk'əl| *n.* **1.** An ancient Hebrew unit of weight equal to about half an ounce. **2.** An ancient Hebrew coin weighing this amount in silver or gold. **3.** A monetary unit of Israel.

shelf |shĕlf| *n., pl.* **shelves** |shĕlvz|. **1.** A flat, usually rectangular piece of wood, metal, or glass, fastened at right angles to a wall and used to hold or store things. **2.** Something resembling a shelf, such as a flat ledge of rock jutting out from a cliff. **3.** A reef, sandbar, or shoal.

shell |shĕl| *n.* **1. a.** The hard outer covering of certain soft-bodied water animals or related animals, such as a clam, oyster, scallop, or snail. **b.** A similar hard or brittle outer covering of certain other animals, such as a crab, lobster, or turtle, or of an egg, nut, etc. **2.** Any outer covering or framework: *a pastry shell for a pie.* **3.** A long, narrow boat used in rowing races. **4.** A projectile or piece of ammunition, especially: **a.** A heavy missile containing explosives and fired from a cannon or other large gun. **b.** A cartridge for a shot gun. —***modifier:*** *shell beads; a shell collection.* —*v.* **1.** To remove the shells of; shuck: *shelling peas for dinner.* **2.** To search for or gather shells, as along a beach. **3.** To fire shells at; bombard: *shelling a fortress.* —***phrasal verb.*** **shell out.** *Informal.* To pay out (money): *He shelled out a lot for that car.*

she'll |shēl|. **1.** She will. **2.** She shall.

shel•lac |shə lăk'| *n.* **1.** A purified form of a resinous secretion derived from a certain insect, formed into yellow or orange flakes, often bleached white, and used in varnishes, paints, and sealing wax and in making phonograph records. **2.** A solution of flakes of this material in alcohol, making a thin varnish used for finishing wood surfaces and as a sealer. —*v.* **shel•lacked, shel•lack•ing. 1.** To apply shellac to (a wooden surface, wall, etc.). **2.** *Slang.* To defeat by a wide margin.

Shel•ley |shĕl'ē|, **Percy Bysshe.** 1792–1822. English poet.

shell•fish |shĕl'fĭsh'| *n., pl.* **-fish** or **-fish•es.** A water animal having a shell or a shell-like outer covering, as a clam, lobster, or shrimp.

shed[1-2]

Shed[1] *was Old English* scēadan, *originally meaning "to divide, to separate" and later coming to mean "to cast off." (The obsolete noun* shed, *meaning "a parting in the hair, a ridge of land," is preserved in the word* **watershed.**) **Shed**[2] *was originally* shadde *and may be a variant of* **shade** *in the sense "a shelter."*

sheet[1-2]

Sheet[1] *was Old English* scēte, *"piece of cloth."* **Sheet**[2] *was originally* sheet-line, *and is from Old English* scēata, *"corner of a sail."* Scēata *is probably related to* scēte, *but note that the modern word* **sheet**[2] *refers only to the rope and not to the sail itself. The sheets, together with the helm, are the basic controls of a sailing ship; the expression* three sheets in the wind, *meaning "drunk," is from nineteenth-century sailors' slang.*

sherbet/syrup

Sherbet *originally meant "a cool oriental drink made from fruit juice"; it is from Turkish* sherbet, *which is from Arabic* sharbah, *"a drink," from* shariba, *"to drink." Also from* shariba *is Arabic* sharāb, *"sweet drink, wine," also "syrup." This was borrowed into Medieval Latin as* siropus, *from which we have* **syrup**.

sheriff

Like many ancient titles, **sheriff** *now means different things in different places. In Anglo-Saxon England, the* scīr-gerēfa *was the chief representative of the king in each county. The word meant "shire officer," from* scīr, *"shire,"* + rēfa *or* gerēfa, *"officer,* reeve.*" In Modern English,* scīrgerēfa *became* **sheriff**. *In England the duties of a sheriff are now chiefly ceremonial; he presides over elections, courts, etc. In Scotland a sheriff is a local judge. And in the American colonies, the office developed differently again, and the sheriff became an important officer of law enforcement.*

shield
Statue of King Arthur with shield

ă pat/ā pay/â care/ä father/ĕ pet/ē be/ĭ pit/ī pie/î fierce/ŏ pot/ō go/ô paw, for/oi oil/ŏŏ book/ōō boot/ou out/ŭ cut/û fur/*th* the/th thin/hw which/zh vision/ə ago, item, pencil, atom, circus

shell shock. **1.** Any of various severe neuroses brought on by traumatic experiences suffered under fire in modern warfare. **2. Combat fatigue.**

shel•ter |**shĕl'**tər| *n.* **1.** Something that provides cover or protection: *used an abandoned shack as a shelter for the night.* **2.** Refuge or cover: *seeking shelter from the storm.* **3.** An institution providing protection for the homeless: *a children's shelter.* —*v.* **shel•tered, shel•ter•ing. 1.** To provide cover or protection for. **2.** To take cover or refuge: *sheltering by day and traveling by night.*

shelve |shĕlv| *v.* **shelved, shelv•ing. 1.** To place or arrange on a shelf or shelves. **2.** To put aside for later consideration; postpone: *shelved the trip because we couldn't afford it.*

shelves |shĕlvz| *n.* Plural of **shelf.**

she•nan•i•gans |shə **năn'**ĭ gənz| *pl.n.* **1.** Playful tricks or pranks; mischief. **2.** Devious maneuvers; deceptions.

shep•herd |**shĕp'**ərd| *n.* **1.** A person who watches over or cares for a flock of sheep. **2.** A minister, priest, or other religious leader. **3.** A dog of a breed originally trained to guard or herd sheep. See **German shepherd.** —*v.* To lead or watch over in the manner of a shepherd.

shep•herd•ess |**shĕp'**ər dĭs| *n.* A woman or girl who works as a shepherd.

sher•bet |**shûr'**bĭt| *n.* A sweet, frozen, often fruit-flavored dessert, containing water, milk, and egg whites or gelatin. [SEE NOTE]

sher•iff |**shĕr'**ĭf| *n.* The chief law-enforcement official of a county. [SEE NOTE]

sher•ry |**shĕr'**ē| *n., pl.* **sher•ries.** An amber-colored dry or sweet wine.

she's |shēz|. **1.** She is. **2.** She has.

Shet•land pony |**shĕt'**lənd|. A small, sturdy, long-maned pony of a breed originally from the Shetland Islands north of Scotland.

shib•bo•leth |**shĭb'**ə lĭth| *or* |-lĕth'| *n.* **1.** A custom, use of language, or other characteristic that serves to identify the members of a certain group: *Long hair has become the shibboleth of the young.* **2.** A slogan, saying, or theme repeated by the supporters of a certain party or cause.

shield |shēld| *n.* **1.** A piece of armor carried on the arm in olden times by knights or warriors to ward off an opponent's blows. **2.** An emblem or badge shaped like a warrior's shield: *a policeman's shield.* **3.** Any object or structure used as a means of protection; a barrier: *raised her arm as a shield against the glare.* **4.** A layer or mass of material placed around something to keep radiation of some kind in or out, especially a mass of lead or cement used to enclose a nuclear reactor. —*v.* To protect with or as with a shield. [SEE PICTURE]

shi•er |**shī'**ər| *adj.* A comparative of **shy.**

shi•est |**shī'**ĭst| *adj.* A superlative of **shy.**

shift |shĭft| *v.* **1.** To move from one place or position to another; transfer. **2.** To change: *shifted tactics.* **3.** To change (gears), as in driving an automobile. —*n.* **1.** A change from one place or position to another; transfer: *the shift of population to the cities.* **2.** A change in direction, tendency, policy, or form: *a shift in the wind; a shift toward greater tolerance.* **3.** A change in the position of the spectral lines from a celestial body, either toward red or toward blue. **4.** A mechanism in a typewriter or similar device for printing two different sets of characters, chiefly upper-case and lower-case, using the same keys. **5.** A mechanism for changing gears, as in an automobile, truck, or bicycle: *a sports car with a five-speed shift.* **6. a.** A group of workers on duty at the same time, as at a factory. **b.** The period during which such a group works: *the 9-to-5 shift.* **7. a.** A loosely fitting dress that hangs straight from the shoulders. **b.** A woman's slip or chemise. **8.** A dodge; an evasion.

shift•less |**shĭft'**lĭs| *adj.* Lacking ambition or purpose; lazy. —**shift'less•ly** *adv.*

shift•y |**shĭf'**tē| *adj.* **shift•i•er, shift•i•est. 1.** Moving or darting quickly from place to place: *shifty eyes.* **2.** Tricky; crafty; evasive. —**shift'i•ly** *adv.*

shil•le•lagh, also **shil•la•lah** |shə **lā'**lē| *or* |-lə| *n.* A club or cudgel.

shil•ling |**shĭl'**ĭng| *n.* **1.** A former British coin worth $^{1}/_{20}$ of a pound. **2.** The basic unit of money of Kenya, Somali, Tanzania and Uganda.

shil•ly-shal•ly |**shĭl'**ē shăl'ē| *v.* **shil•ly-shal•lied, shil•ly-shal•ly•ing, shil•ly-shal•lies. 1.** To put off action; hesitate indecisively. **2.** To move slowly or idly; dawdle. —**shil'ly-shal'li•er** *n.*

shim•mer |**shĭm'**ər| *v.* **1.** To shine with a flickering or wavy light: *Dorothy brushed her hair until it shimmered.* **2.** To move with a wavelike or sinuous visual effect: *Heat waves shimmered above the road ahead.* —**shim'mer•ing** *adj.*: *shimmering moonlight; shimmering clouds of dust.* —*n.* **1.** A flickering or wavy light; a glimmer. **2.** A wavelike or sinuous visual effect.

shim•my |**shĭm'**ē| *n., pl.* **shim•mies. 1.** A dance popular in the 1920's, in which the body was rapidly shaken. **2.** An abnormal vibration or wobbling, as in the chassis or steering mechanism of an automobile. —*v.* **shim•mied, shim•my•ing, shim•mies. 1.** To shake the body, as in dancing the shimmy. **2.** To vibrate or wobble.

shin |shĭn| *n.* **1.** The front part of the human leg below the knee and above the ankle. **2.** A corresponding part of the leg of an animal. **3.** The tibia, one of the bones of the leg. —*v.* **shinned, shin•ning.** To climb (a rope, mast, etc.) by gripping and pulling with the hands and legs: *shinning up a tree.*

shin•bone |**shĭn'**bōn'| *n.* The tibia, one of the bones of the leg.

shin•dig |**shĭn'**dĭg'| *n. Slang.* A large, noisy party or dance.

shine |shīn| *v.* **shone** |shōn| or **shined, shin•ing. 1.** To emit or reflect light. **2.** To aim or direct the beam or glow of: *Shine that light over here.* **3.** To make glossy or bright by polishing: *shining his shoes.* **4.** To glow with delight, excitement, or pride. **5.** To perform conspicuously well; excel: *This car lacks power for high-speed highways, but really shines in city travel.* —**shin'ing** *adj.*: *a shining beacon; shining eyes.* —*n.* **1.** Strong emitted or reflected light: *the shine from the headlights.* **2.** Brightness or radiance; brilliance. **3.** A polish, especially a shoeshine. **4.** Fair weather: *We'll have a picnic, rain or shine.* **5.** *Informal.* A liking; fondness. —**shin'er** *n.*

shin•gle[1] |**shĭng'**gəl| *n.* **1.** One of a number of oblong pieces of wood or other material laid in overlapping rows to cover the roof or sides of a building. **2.** A small signboard hung outside the office of a practicing doctor, lawyer, etc. —***mod-***

ifier: a shingle roof. —*v.* **shin•gled, shin•gling.** To apply shingles to (a roof or wall). [SEE NOTE]

shin•gle² |shĭng′gəl| *n.* **1.** Beach gravel consisting of smooth pebbles with no finer material mixed in. **2.** A stretch of shore or beach covered with such gravel. [SEE NOTE]

shin•gles |shĭng′gəlz| *n. (used with a singular or plural verb).* A painful virus infection in which there is a skin eruption along a nerve path on one side of the body. [SEE NOTE]

shin•ny¹ |shĭn′ē| *v.* **shin•nied, shin•ny•ing, shin•nies.** To climb by gripping and pulling with the hands and legs.

shin•ny² |shĭn′ē| *n., pl.* **shin•nies. 1.** A simple form of ice or field hockey played by schoolboys. **2.** A curved stick used in this game.

Shin•to |shĭn′tō| *n.* The traditional religion of the Japanese, marked by worship of nature spirits and ancestors. —***modifier:*** *a Shinto shrine.*

Shin•to•ism |shĭn′tō ĭz′əm| *n.* Shinto. —**Shin′to•ist** *n.*

shin•y |shī′nē| *adj.* **shin•i•er, shin•i•est.** Reflecting light; bright; glistening: *a shiny brass knocker; shiny red apples.* —**shin′i•ness** *n.*

ship |shĭp| *n.* **1.** Any vessel of considerable size built for deep-water navigation. **2.** A ship's company: *Most of the ship joined in the mutiny.* **3.** An airplane, airship, or spacecraft. —*v.* **shipped, ship•ping. 1.** To send or transport: *shipping goods by truck.* **2.** *Informal.* To dispatch to a specified destination: *His parents shipped him off to a military academy.* **3.** To take (water) in over the side of a boat: *We're shipping a lot of water.*

-ship. A suffix that forms nouns and means: **1.** The condition or quality of: **friendship. 2.** The rank or office of: **professorship. 3.** The art or function of: **leadership.**

ship•board |shĭp′bôrd′| *or* |-bōrd′| *n.* —**on shipboard.** On board a ship. —***modifier:*** *a shipboard romance.*

ship•ment |shĭp′mənt| *n.* **1.** The action or process of shipping goods: *iron ore for shipment abroad.* **2.** A consignment of goods shipped at one time: *a new shipment of automobiles.*

ship•per |shĭp′ər| *n.* A person or company engaged in the business of shipping goods.

ship•ping |shĭp′ĭng| *n.* **1.** The action or business of transporting goods. **2.** The ships belonging to a port, industry, or country, or plying a certain route: *orders to destroy enemy shipping.* —***modifier:*** *a shipping center.*

ship•shape |shĭp′shāp′| *adj.* Neatly arranged; in good order.

ship•wreck |shĭp′rĕk′| *n.* **1.** A wrecked ship. **2.** The destruction of a ship, as by storm or collision. **3.** Complete destruction; ruin: *the shipwreck of our hopes.* —*v.* To cause to suffer shipwreck. —**ship′wrecked′** *adj.: a shipwrecked sailor.*

ship•yard |shĭp′yärd′| *n.* A yard in which ships are built, repaired, and outfitted; a dockyard.

shire |shīr| *n.* One of the counties of Great Britain.

shirk |shûrk| *v.* To avoid (an unpleasant task or duty) because of laziness or irresponsibility. —**shirk′er** *n.*

shirr |shûr| *v.* **1.** To gather (cloth) along three or more parallel threads. **2.** To bake (eggs) in buttered molds. —*n.* A gathering of cloth along three or more parallel threads.

shirt |shûrt| *n.* **1.** A garment for the upper part of the body, generally having a collar, sleeves, and a front opening. **2.** An undershirt. —***modifier:*** *a shirt button.*

Idiom. **keep (one's) shirt on.** *Slang.* To remain calm or patient.

shirt•ing |shûr′tĭng| *n.* Cloth used for making shirts.

shirt•waist |shûrt′wāst′| *n.* **1.** A woman's tailored shirt, made to resemble a man's shirt. **2.** A dress with the bodice styled like a tailored shirt. —***modifier:*** *a shirtwaist dress.*

shish ke•bab, also **shish ke•bob, shish ka•bob** |shĭsh′ kə bŏb′|. Pieces of seasoned meat, often with onions and tomatoes, cooked and served on skewers.

Shi•va |shē′və|. The Hindu god of destruction and reproduction.

shiv•er¹ |shĭv′ər| *v.* To shake one's body involuntarily, as from cold or fear; tremble. —*n.* **1.** A tremble. **2.** A quick, cold sensation, as of fear or excitement. [SEE NOTE]

shiv•er² |shĭv′ər| *v.* To break suddenly into thin fragments or splinters; shatter. —*n.* A thin, sharp fragment; a sliver. [SEE NOTE]

shoal¹ |shōl| *n.* **1.** A shallow place in a body of water. **2.** A sandbank or sandbar. —*adj.* Shallow: *places where the water is shoal.*

shoal² |shōl| *n.* A school of fish or other water animals. —*v.* To come together in or swim in a shoal; to school.

shoat |shōt| *n.* A young pig.

shock¹ |shŏk| *n.* **1.** A forceful collision or impact; a heavy blow. **2.** Something that happens suddenly or unexpectedly, severely disturbing or upsetting the mind or emotions: *The death of her close friend was a bad shock.* **3.** The disturbance of mental or emotional condition or functioning caused by such an occurrence. **4.** A marked reaction, generally temporary, to bodily injury, usually consisting of a loss of blood pressure and depression of life processes. **5.** The sensation, muscular spasm, and nervous effects caused by the passage of an electric current through the body or any of its parts. —*v.* **1.** To surprise greatly; astonish. **2.** To disturb or upset greatly; offend; appall. **3.** To cause a state of shock in (a living organism). **4.** To subject (a person or animal) to an electric shock. —**shock′er** *n.* [SEE NOTE]

shock² |shŏk| *n.* **1.** A pile of sheaves of grain stacked upright in a field to dry. **2.** A bushy mass: *a shock of fair hair over his forehead.* —*v.* To gather (grain) into shocks. [SEE NOTE]

shock•ing |shŏk′ĭng| *adj.* **1.** Causing great surprise and emotional disturbance; astonishing: *a shocking event.* **2.** Highly offensive to taste or propriety; indecent: *her shocking impudence.* —**shock′ing•ly** *adv.*

shod |shŏd|. Past tense and a past participle of **shoe.**

shod•den |shŏd′n|. A past participle of **shoe.**

shod•dy |shŏd′ē| *n., pl.* **shod•dies. 1.** Inferior wool obtained from woolen waste, rags, or worn garments. **2.** Yarn or cloth made from such wool. —*adj.* **shod•di•er, shod•di•est. 1.** Made of shoddy or some other inferior material. **2.** Of poor quality or workmanship: *shoddy toys; a*

shingle¹·²/shingles

Shingle¹ *was Middle English* scingle, *and was borrowed from Latin* scindula *or* scandula, *"a split piece, a roof shingle."* **Shingle²** *is of obscure origin.* **Shingles** *is from Medieval Latin* cingulus, *"belt" (the skin eruptions sometimes encircle the body like a belt).*

shiver¹·²

Shiver¹ *was originally* chiveren *or* chevelen, *probably originally meaning "to chatter" (said of teeth).* **Shiver²** *is probably from Middle Low German* schever, *"splinter."*

shock¹·²

Shock¹ *is from Old French* choc, *from* choquer, *"to strike with fear."* **Shock²** *is probably from Middle Dutch* schok, *"stack of grain sheaves, group of sixty."*

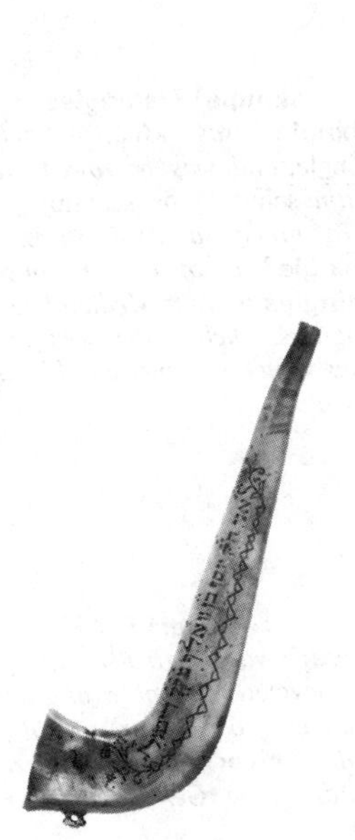

shofar
Eighteenth-century German

shore[1·2]
Shore[1] *is from Middle Dutch* schore, *"edge of the land."* **Shore**[2] *is from Middle Dutch* schoren, *"to prop." The two words are not related.*

ă pat/ā pay/â care/ä father/ĕ pet/ ē be/ĭ pit/ī pie/î fierce/ŏ pot/ ō go/ô paw, for/oi oil/ŏŏ book/ ōō boot/ou out/ŭ cut/û fur/ *th* the/th thin/hw which/zh vision/ ə ago, item, pencil, atom, circus

shoddy job. **3.** Dishonest: *shoddy politicians.*

shoe |shōō| *n.* **1.** An outer covering for the human foot, especially one of a pair having a rigid sole and heel and a flexible upper part. **2.** A horseshoe. **3.** The part of a brake that presses against a wheel or drum to slow its motion. **4.** The sliding contact plate of an electrically powered train or streetcar that conducts electricity from the third rail. —***modifier:*** *a shoe shop; shoe leather.* —*v.* **shod** |shŏd|, **shod** or **shod·den** |**shŏd'**n|, **shoe·ing.** To furnish or fit with shoes. ¶*These sound alike* **shoe, shoo.**

Idioms. **fill (someone's) shoes.** To take someone's place and do as well. **in (someone's) shoes.** In someone else's place or circumstances.

shoe·horn |**shōō'**hôrn'| *n.* A curved implement, often of horn or metal, used at the heel to help slip on a shoe.

shoe·lace |**shōō'**lās'| *n.* A string or cord used for lacing and fastening a shoe.

shoe·mak·er |**shōō'**mā'kər| *n.* A person who makes or repairs shoes.

shoe·string |**shōō'**strĭng'| *n.* A shoelace.

Idiom. **on a shoestring.** With very little money: *The company started out on a shoestring.*

shoe·tree |**shōō'**trē'| *n.* A foot-shaped form inserted into a shoe to preserve its shape.

sho·far |**shō'**fär'| *or* |-fər| *n., pl.* **sho·fars** or **sho·froth** |shō **frōt'**| *or* |**-frōth'**|. A trumpet made of a ram's horn, used by the ancient Hebrews and now sounded in Jewish synagogues on certain occasions. [SEE PICTURE]

shone |shōn|. A past tense and past participle of **shine.** ¶*These sound alike* **shone, shown.**

shoo |shōō| *interj.* A word used to scare away animals or birds. —*v.* To drive or scare away, as by crying "shoo." ¶*These sound alike* **shoo, shoe.**

shook |shŏŏk|. Past tense of **shake.**

shoon |shōōn| *n. Archaic.* A plural of **shoe.**

shoot |shōōt| *v.* **shot** |shŏt|, **shoot·ing.** **1. a.** To hit, wound, or kill with a missile fired from a weapon: *shooting a bear.* **b.** To fire (a gun, bow, or similar weapon). **c.** To fire (a bullet, arrow, or other missile) from a weapon. **2.** To discharge or explode; set off: *shooting off firecrackers.* **3.** To hunt with guns: *went to shoot with his uncle in the country.* **4.** To aim; strive: *shooting for first prize at the art fair.* **5.** To propel or launch with great force: *shoot a rocket toward the moon.* **6.** To propel or be propelled in a rapid stream or flow: *a volcano shooting lava.* **7.** To pass swiftly through: *shooting the narrows in a sailboat.* **8.** To move swiftly: *Car after car shot past us.* **9.** To extend abruptly; protrude: *a circus parade with giraffe heads shooting up every few yards.* **10.** To begin to grow or sprout, as a plant or plant part. **11. a.** To throw or propel (a ball, puck, marble, etc.) toward the goal. **b.** To score (a basket or other goal) in this way. **12.** To play (golf, dice, pool, darts, etc.). **13.** To record (a scene, event, motion picture, etc.) on film. **14.** To streak or spot with a different color or substance: *brown hair shot with gray.* **15.** To slide (a door bolt) into or out of place. —*n.* **1.** A quick, darting movement or passage. **2.** A plant or plant part, such as a stem, leaf, or bud, that has just begun to grow, sprout, or develop. **3.** An organized hunt with guns: *a turkey shoot.* **4.** A turn at shooting a ball, marble, etc.; a shot. —**shoot'er** *n.*

shooting star. A meteor that is briefly visible.

shop |shŏp| *n.* **1.** A place where goods or services are on sale to the general public; a store, usually a small one: *a pet shop; a barber shop.* **2.** A place where certain things are made or repaired. **3. a.** A schoolroom equipped with machinery and tools that students are trained to use. **b.** A course of study in which mechanical skills and the use of tools and materials are learned. —***modifier:*** *a shop window; a shop clerk.* —*v.* **shopped, shop·ping.** To visit stores to look at or buy things. —**shop'per** *n.*

shop·keep·er |**shŏp'**kē'pər| *n.* A person who owns or manages a shop.

shop·lift |**shŏp'**lĭft'| *v.* To steal (articles on display) from a store. —**shop'lift'er** *n.*

shop·worn |**shŏp'**wôrn'| *or* |-wōrn'| *adj.* Soiled, faded, frayed, or otherwise damaged from being displayed too long in a store.

shore[1] |shôr| *or* |shōr| *n.* **1.** The land along the edge of a body of water. **2.** Often **shores.** Land within national or other boundaries: *immigrants who came to these shores.* [SEE NOTE]

shore[2] |shôr| *or* |shōr| *v.* **shored, shor·ing.** To prop up, as with a length of timber: *shore up a sagging floor.* —*n.* A beam, timber, or post used as a temporary support. [SEE NOTE]

shore·line |**shôr'**līn'| *or* |**shōr'-**| *n.* The line that forms the boundary of a body of water.

shorn |shôrn| *or* |shōrn|. A past participle of **shear.**

short |shôrt| *adj.* **short·er, short·est.** **1. a.** Not long: *a short skirt.* **b.** Not tall or long: *short people and tall people.* **2.** Covering a relatively small distance or taking a relatively small amount of time: *a short walk; a short trip.* **3.** Brief: *a short time ago.* **4. a.** Being relatively brief in duration: *You have reviewed the long and short sounds of vowels.* **b.** Being unstressed: *a line of verse consisting of a long syllable followed by two short syllables.* **5.** Of insufficient length: *This rope is short for what you want to do with it.* **6.** Insufficient: *water in short supply.* **7.** Having an insufficient supply: *short of money.* **8.** Curt; abrupt: *Miss Bird was rather short with you today, I thought.* **9.** Easily provoked: *Don't fool with swans—they have very short tempers.* **10.** Rich and flaky because of a large amount of shortening: *a short pie crust.* —*adv.* **1.** So as to stop suddenly: *cutting short her screech of fear.* **2.** Suddenly: *A truck stopped short in the street.* —*n.* **1. a.** A short vowel. **b.** An unaccented vowel in verse. **2.** A short movie. **3.** A **short circuit.** —*v.* To short-circuit. —**short'ness** *n.*

Idioms. **fall** (or **come**) **short.** To fail to meet expectations or requirements. **for short.** As an abbreviation: *He's called Ed for short.* **short for.** An abbreviation of: *Ed is short for Edward.*

short·age |**shôr'**tĭj| *n.* A lack in the amount needed; deficiency: *a food shortage.*

short·cake |**shôrt'**kāk'| *n.* A rich cake served with strawberries, peaches, etc., and topped with cream. [SEE NOTE on p. 803]

short circuit. A path that allows most of the current in an electric circuit to flow around the principal elements or devices in the circuit, especially when this path is not supposed to exist.

short-cir·cuit |**shôrt'sûr'**kĭt| *v.* To cause to form or have a short circuit.

short•com•ing |shôrt′kŭm′ĭng| *n.* An inadequacy; a fault; flaw.

short•cut |shôrt′kŭt′| *n.* **1.** A route that is quicker or more direct than the one usually taken. **2.** A method or means of doing something that saves time.

short division. A division of one number by another, usually of no more than two digits, without writing out the remainders.

short•en |shôr′tn| *v.* **1.** To make or become shorter. **2.** To add shortening to (dough).

short•en•ing |shôr′tn ĭng| *n.* A fat, such as butter, lard, or vegetable oil, used to make cake or pastry rich and flaky. [SEE NOTE]

short•fall |shôrt′fôl| *n.* **1.** A failure to attain a specified amount or level; shortage. **2.** The amount by which a supply falls short of need or demand. **3.** A monetary deficit.

short•hand |shôrt′hănd′| *n.* A system of rapid handwriting, used especially by stenographers, in which symbols and strokes take the place of words. —***modifier:*** *a shorthand course.*

short•hand•ed |shôrt′hăn′dĭd| *adj.* Lacking the usual or full number of members or workers: *The shorthanded crew had to work especially hard.*

short•horn |shôrt′hôrn′| *n.* One of a breed of cattle with short, curved horns.

short-lived |shôrt′līvd′| *or* |-lĭvd′| *adj.* Having a short life or duration: *short-lived joy.*

short•ly |shôrt′lē| *adv.* **1.** In a short time; soon: *We will leave shortly.* **2.** In a curt or harsh manner: *"Why shouldn't I?" Charles demanded rather shortly.* **3.** In a few words; briefly: *To put it shortly, we've got to finish now or not at all.*

shorts |shôrts| *pl.n.* **1.** Short trousers with legs that extend to the knee or above. **2.** Loose-fitting underpants with short legs, worn by men.

short shrift. **1.** A short delay before punishment, death, or some other harsh fate. **2.** Brief or hasty consideration or dismissal: *My parents give short shrift to door-to-door salesmen.* **3.** Quick work; rapid settlement: *The debater made short shrift of his opponent's arguments.*

short•sight•ed |shôrt′sī′tĭd| *adj.* **1.** Nearsighted; lacking clear vision of distant objects. **2.** Lacking foresight: *The land policy was shortsighted in its neglect of the peasant.* —**short′sight′ed•ly** *adv.* —**short′sight′ed•ness** *n.*

short•stop |shôrt′stŏp′| *n.* **1.** The position between second and third bases in baseball. **2.** The player who plays in this position.

short story. A short piece of prose fiction. —***modifier:*** **(short-story):** *a short-story writer.*

short-tem•pered |shôrt′tĕm′pərd| *adj.* Easily losing one's temper; quickly angered.

short ton. See **ton.**

short wave. A radio wave having a wavelength of less than about 80 meters. —***modifier:*** **(short-wave):** *a short-wave radio.*

short-wind•ed |shôrt′wĭn′dĭd| *adj.* Getting out of breath easily; quickly winded.

Sho•sho•ne, also **Sho•sho•ni** |shō shō′nē| *n., pl.* **Sho•sho•ne** or **Sho•sho•nes.** **1.** A North American Indian tribe formerly living in Nevada, Oregan, Idaho, Utah, Wyoming, and Texas. **2.** A member of this tribe. **3.** The Uto-Aztecan language of this tribe. —**Sho•sho′ne** *adj.*

shot¹ |shŏt| *n.* **1.** The discharge of a gun or similar weapon: *a rifle shot.* **2.** *pl.* **shot.** **a.** A ball, bullet, or other missile fired from a weapon. **b.** A pellet or group of pellets fired from a shotgun: *A blast of shot ripped through the door.* **3.** The launching of a rocket or space vehicle. **4.** A throw, drive, or stroke, as of a ball or puck, toward a goal or target: *a basketball player who makes 44 per cent of his shots.* **5.** The distance over which something is or can be shot. **6.** A person who shoots, considered with regard to his accuracy: *the best shot on the hockey team.* **7.** A turn or opportunity to shoot: *He had a clear shot at the basket but passed instead.* **8.** A chance; try: *had a shot at a good job.* **9.** **a.** A hypodermic injection: *a shot of penicillin.* **b.** A vaccination: *a smallpox shot.* **10.** **a.** A photograph. **b.** A single, continuously photographed scene or view in a motion picture. **11.** A heavy metal ball thrown for distance in the shot-put. **12.** A drink of liquor, especially a measure of about 1½ ounces.

shot² |shŏt|. Past tense and past participle of **shoot.**

shot•gun |shŏt′gŭn′| *n.* A gun with a smooth bore, used for firing a charge of small shot at close range.

shot-put |shŏt′po͝ot′| *n.* Also **shot put.** **1.** An athletic event in which participants throw a heavy metal ball for distance with a pushing motion. **2.** The ball itself. —**shot′-put′ter** *n.*

should |sho͝od|. Past tense of **shall.** —Used as an auxiliary verb followed by a simple infinitive indicating: **1.** Obligation; duty: *You should send her a note.* **2.** Anticipation: *They should arrive at noon.* **3.** Condition: *If they should call while I'm out, tell them I'll be right back.*

shoul•der |shōl′dər| *n.* **1.** **a.** The part of the human body between the neck and upper arm. **b.** The joint that connects the arm with the trunk. **c.** The corresponding part of the body of an animal. **2.** **shoulders.** The two shoulders and the area of the back between them: *a boy with broad shoulders.* **3.** The part of a garment that covers the shoulder. **4.** A sloping or jutting side of something: *the shoulder of a mountain; the shoulder of a vase.* **5.** The land or ballast that borders on a roadway. —***modifier:*** *shoulder muscles; shoulder pads.* —*v.* **1.** To place on the shoulder or shoulders for carrying: *The porters shouldered their loads.* **2.** To take on; bear; assume: *shouldering the blame for the others.* **3.** To push with or as with the shoulders.

Idioms. **give** (or **turn**) **a cold shoulder to.** *Informal.* To behave with coldness or disdain toward. **rub shoulders.** *Informal.* To be in close company. **shoulder to shoulder.** Side by side and close together: *The buildings stood shoulder to shoulder in a long row.* **straight from the shoulder.** *Informal.* Straightforwardly; frankly.

shoulder blade. Either of the two large, flat bones that form the rear of the shoulder; the scapula.

shoulder strap. **1.** A strap worn over the shoulder, especially one attached to a sleeveless garment or a pocketbook. **2.** A strip of cloth worn on the shoulder of a military officer's uniform to show his rank.

shouldn't |sho͝od′nt|. Should not.

shouldst |sho͝odst|. *Archaic.* A form of **should,** used with *thou.*

shortening, shortcake, etc. *These words arise from sense* **10** *of the adjective* **short.** *This has been in technical use in cooking for a long time; it is first recorded in a fifteenth-century cookbook: "Then take warm* barm *[yeast], and put all [the ingredients] together, and beat them together with thine hands til it be* short *and thick." This sense of* **short** *seems to mean "not stretchable, breaking off in short pieces."*

shovel
Above: Hand shovel
Below: Mechanical shovel

shrew
One kind of **shrew** is the smallest mammal known to exist, weighing only about two grams (about 1/15 of an ounce) when full grown.

ă pat/ā pay/â care/ä father/ĕ pet/ ē be/ĭ pit/ī pie/î fierce/ŏ pot/ ō go/ô paw, for/oi oil/ŏŏ book/ ōō boot/ou out/ŭ cut/û fur/ *th* the/th thin/hw which/zh vision/ ə ago, item, pencil, atom, circus

shout |shout| *v.* To say or utter (something) in a loud voice; yell: *shouted at the umpire; shouted orders.* —**shout'ing** *adj.: shouting crowds.* —***phrasal verb.* shout down.** To silence another by shouting more loudly. —*n.* A sudden loud cry or yell. —**shout'er** *n.*

shove |shŭv| *v.* **shoved, shov•ing.** To prod, thrust, or push roughly or rudely. —***phrasal verb.* shove off. 1.** To set a beached boat afloat. **2.** *Informal.* To leave. —*n.* A rude or rough push. —**shov'er** *n.*

shov•el |shŭv'əl| *n.* **1.** A tool with a long handle and a somewhat flattened scoop, used for picking up dirt, snow, coal, etc. **2.** A large, power-operated machine used for heavy digging; a power shovel. **3.** The amount that the scoop of a shovel holds: *put a shovel of coal into the furnace.* —*v.* **shov•eled** or **shov•elled, shov•el•ing** or **shov•el•ling. 1.** To move or remove with a shovel: *shovel snow.* **2.** To clear or make with a shovel: *shovel the walk; shovel a path.* **3.** To place, put, or move in a hasty or careless way: *shovel papers into the trash can; shovel food into his mouth.* —**shov'el•er** *n.* [SEE PICTURE]

show |shō| *v.* **showed, shown** |shōn| or **showed, show•ing. 1. a.** To cause or allow to be seen or viewed; make visible: *He showed her the necklace. The dog showed his teeth.* **b.** To present or be presented in public exhibition: *show goods in a store. The film showed a week.* **2.** To point out; demonstrate: *Show him the way. Show her how to knit.* **3.** To indicate or exhibit: *shoes that show signs of wear.* **4.** To present the image, likeness, indication, or presence of: *The picture shows a dinosaur.* **5.** To conduct; guide: *Show him around the village.* **6.** To be or become visible: *Her bare feet showed beneath her gown.* **7.** To reveal or become revealed: *Her eyes showed curiosity. His anger showed.* **8.** To grant; confer; bestow: *show mercy.* **9.** *Informal.* To appear at a rendezvous: *We gave a party, but our friends didn't show.* **10.** *Informal.* To prove one's worth or ability to (another), especially out of spite, anger, or frustration: *"I'll show them," she muttered. "I'll make a home run."* **11.** To finish third or better in a sports contest. —***phrasal verbs.* show off.** To display or behave in an ostentatious or conspicuous manner: *showed off his autographed baseball; showing off in front of the little children.* **show up. 1.** To be or become clearly or vividly visible or evident: *dark trees showing up against a white landscape.* **2.** To arrive or appear: *He showed up at dinner. A mistake showed up in the accounts.* **3.** To point out or reveal (faults, errors, etc.). **4.** To prove that one is superior to (another); outdo: *He showed her up on the test.* —*n.* **1.** A display: *a show of power.* **2.** An appearance: *without any show of good will.* **3.** A striking appearance or display; a spectacle: *the fiery show of a volcanic eruption.* **4.** A pompous or ostentatious display: *She liked show and ceremony.* **5.** A public exhibition or entertainment: *a dog show; a puppet show.* **6.** A trace or indication: *no show of his former might.* **7.** An insincere, artificial, or deceitful display: *put on quite a show of prestige.* **8.** *Informal.* Any undertaking: *ran the whole show.* **9.** Third place or better in a sports contest. —***modifier:*** *the show ring.* —**show'er** *n.*

show•boat |shō'bōt'| *n.* A river steamboat with a troupe of actors and a theater aboard for the performance of plays.

show business. The entertainment industry or arts.

show•case |shō'kās'| *n.* A display case in a store or museum.

show•down |shō'doun'| *n.* An event or circumstance that forces an issue to a conclusion.

show•er |shou'ər| *n.* **1. a.** A brief fall of rain, snow, hail, sleet, etc. **b.** A fall of a group of objects, especially a large group, from the sky: *a meteor shower.* **2.** An abundant flow or outpouring: *a shower of arrows.* **3. a.** A **shower bath. b.** A device, such as a nozzle with many small holes, for spraying water. **4.** A party held to honor and present gifts to someone: *a bridal shower.* —***modifier:*** *a shower curtain.* —*v.* **1.** To fall or pour down in a shower. **2.** To sprinkle or spray. **3.** To bestow or pour forth abundantly: *showered presents on the child; showered abuse on the leader.* **4.** To take a shower bath.

shower bath. A bath in which water is sprayed on the bather.

show•man |shō'mən| *n., pl.* **-men** |-mən|. **1.** Someone who produces shows. **2.** Anyone having a flair for dramatic effectiveness.

show•man•ship |shō'mən shĭp'| *n.* Skill or flair in producing for or appearing before an audience.

shown |shōn|. A past participle of **show.** ¶*These sound alike* **shown, shone.**

show•off |shō'ôf'| *or* |-ŏf'| *n.* Someone who seeks attention by ostentatious behavior.

show room. A room in which merchandise is displayed.

show•y |shō'ē| *adj.* **show•i•er, show•i•est. 1.** Attracting attention because of bright color, size, etc.; conspicuous: *a plant with showy flowers and fruits; the showy banners carried in the parade.* **2.** Intended, done, or tending to attract attention or show off; flashy: *made a showy running catch in the outfield.* —**show'i•ly** *adv.* —**show'i•ness** *n.*

shrank |shrăngk|. A past tense of **shrink.**

shrap•nel |shrăp'nəl| *n.* **1.** An artillery shell that explodes in the air, scattering small metal balls. **2.** Shell fragments.

shred |shrĕd| *n.* **1.** A long, irregular strip cut or torn from something: *shreds of cloth.* **2.** A small amount; a bit: *not a shred of evidence.* —*v.* **shred•ded** or **shred, shred•ding.** To cut or tear into small strips: *shred cabbage.* —**shred'ded** *adj.: shredded vegetables.* —**shred'der** *n.*

shrew |shrōō| *n.* **1.** Any of several small, mouselike animals with a narrow, pointed snout. **2.** A scolding, sharp-tempered woman. [SEE PICTURE]

shrewd |shrōōd| *adj.* **shrewd•er, shrewd•est. 1.** Clever and practical; *a shrewd person.* **2.** Sharp; penetrating; searching: *a shrewd glance.* —**shrewd'ly** *adv.* —**shrewd'ness** *n.*

shrew•ish |shrōō'ĭsh| *adj.* Ill-tempered; nagging. —**shrew'ish•ly** *adv.* —**shrew'ish•ness** *n.*

shriek |shrēk| *n.* A loud, shrill sound: *shrieks of laughter; the shriek of a fire engine.* —*v.* **1.** To make a loud, shrill sound: *The children shrieked in play.* **2.** To say or utter loudly and shrilly: *shriek a warning.* —**shriek'er** *n.*

shrike |shrīk| *n.* Any of several usually gray,

black, and white birds of prey with a short, hooked bill.

shrill |shrĭl| *adj.* **shrill•er, shrill•est.** High-pitched and piercing: *a shrill whistle; a shrill voice.* —*v.* To make a high-pitched sound or cry: *The wind shrilled outside.* —**shril'ly** *adv.* —**shrill'ness** *n.*

shrimp |shrĭmp| *n., pl.* **shrimp** or **shrimps. 1.** Any of several small salt-water animals related to the lobsters and crayfish, often used as food. **2.** *Slang.* A small or unimportant person. —***modifier:*** *a shrimp salad.* [SEE PICTURE]

shrine |shrīn| *n.* **1.** A receptacle for sacred relics. **2.** The tomb of a saint or other venerated person. **3.** A site or object that is hallowed or revered for its history or associations.

shrink |shrĭngk| *v.* **shrank** |shrăngk| or **shrunk** |shrŭngk|, **shrunk** or **shrunk•en** |**shrŭng'**kən|, **shrink•ing. 1.** To reduce or become reduced in size, amount, etc.; make or become smaller. **2.** To draw back; recoil: *The child shrank further into a shell of shyness.* —**shrink'er** *n.*

shrink•age |**shrĭng'**kĭj| *n.* **1.** The act or process of shrinking; constriction in size. **2.** A reduction in value; depreciation. **3.** The amount of a loss by shrinking.

shrive |shrīv| *v.* **shrove** |shrōv| or **shrived, shriv•en** |**shrĭv'**ən| or **shrived, shriv•ing. 1.** To confess and give absolution to (a penitent). **2.** To make or go to confession. —**shriv'er** *n.*

shriv•el |**shrĭv'**əl| *v.* **shriv•eled** or **shriv•elled, shriv•el•ing** or **shriv•el•ling.** To shrink and wrinkle; wither.

shriv•en |**shrĭv'**ən|. A past participle of **shrive.**

shroud |shroud| *n.* **1.** A cloth used to wrap a body for burial. **2.** Something that conceals, protects, or hides in the manner of a garment: *a shroud of silence.* **3.** Often **shrouds.** One of the set of ropes or cables stretched to support the mast of a vessel. —*v.* **1.** To wrap (a corpse) in a shroud. **2.** To conceal; screen; hide.

shrove |shrōv|. A past tense of **shrive.**

Shrove Tuesday. The day before Ash Wednesday.

shrub |shrŭb| *n.* A woody plant that is smaller than a tree and generally has several separate stems rather than a single trunk.

shrub•ber•y |**shrŭb'**ə rē| *n.* **1.** A group or growth of shrubs; shrubs in general. **2.** *pl.* **shrub•ber•ies.** An area planted with shrubs.

shrug |shrŭg| *v.* **shrugged, shrug•ging.** To raise (the shoulders) in a gesture of doubt, disdain, or indifference. —***phrasal verb.*** **shrug off. 1.** To minimize the importance of: *He shrugged off the injury in order to stay in the game.* **2.** To get rid of: *She shrugged off her anger.* —*n.* The gesture of raising the shoulders in doubt, disdain, etc.

shrunk |shrŭngk|. A past tense and a past participle of **shrink.**

shrunk•en |**shrŭng'**kən|. A past participle of **shrink.**

shuck |shŭk| *n.* An outer covering, such as a corn husk, pea pod, or oyster shell. —*v.* **1.** To remove the husk or shell from: *shuck corn; shuck oysters.* **2.** *Informal.* To remove or strip (clothing or a similar outer covering): *shucked his jacket in the heat of the afternoon.* —*interj.* **shucks.** A word used to express disappointment, annoyance, mild protest, etc.

shud•der |**shŭd'**ər| *v.* To tremble or shiver suddenly and convulsively, as from fear or horror. —*n.* A convulsive shiver, as from fear or horror.

shuf•fle |**shŭf'**əl| *v.* **shuf•fled, shuf•fling. 1.** To drag (the feet) along the floor or ground. **2.** To move with a shambling, idle gait: *shuffled across the road.* **3.** To mix together (playing cards, dominoes, etc.) to change their order of arrangement. **4.** To shift about from one place to another: *shuffled the papers around.* —*n.* **1.** An idle, awkward gait or movement. **2.** The mixing of cards, dominoes, etc.

shuf•fle•board |**shŭf'**əl bôrd'| *or* |-bōrd'| *n.* A game in which the players use pronged sticks to propel discs along a flat surface that has marked scoring areas. [SEE PICTURE]

shun |shŭn| *v.* **shunned, shun•ning.** To avoid deliberately and consistently; keep away from: *shunned a person; shunned a task.* —**shun'ner** *n.*

shunt |shŭnt| *n.* **1.** The act or process of turning aside or moving to an alternate course. **2.** A railroad switch. **3.** An additional connection or path between two points in an electric circuit, usually having a low resistance or impedance and diverting a sizable part of the current. —*v.* **1. a.** To cause (a flow of some kind) to follow an alternate course: *shunt traffic around a bottleneck.* **b.** To by-pass (something) with or as with a shunt. **2.** To switch (a railroad car or train) from one track to another. **3. a.** To form an additional path for (an electric current), as by adding a shunt. **b.** To by-pass (one or more elements of an electric circuit) with a shunt.

shush |shŭsh| *interj.* A word used to express a demand for silence. —*v.* To demand silence from by saying "shush": *She shushed the children as they rushed upstairs.*

shut |shŭt| *v.* **shut, shut•ting. 1.** To move (a door, lid, etc.) into a closed position. **2.** To block passage or access to; close: *shut the house.* **3.** To move or become moved to a closed position: *Shut your eyes. Her eyes shut.* **4.** To lock up or confine: *The witch shut Rapunzel in a tower.* —***phrasal verbs.*** **shut down. 1.** To halt operation of (a machine, device, factory, etc.). **2.** To stop operating, especially automatically. **shut off.** To turn off: *shut off the electricity.* **shut out. 1.** To keep (something or someone) from entering: *shut out noise.* **2.** To prevent (a team) from scoring any runs or points in a game. **shut up. 1.** To demand silence from: *He told her to shut up.* **2.** To be or become silenced: *She did not feel like arguing, so she shut up.* **3.** To close (a business or enterprise). **4.** To lock up or confine.

shut•down |**shŭt'**doun'| *n.* A stoppage of operation, as by a machine, device, factory, etc.

shut-in |**shŭt'**ĭn'| *n.* A person who is confined to his home, a hospital, or some institution because of illness or disability. —*adj.* Confined to a house or hospital, as by illness.

shut•out |**shŭt'**out'| *n.* A game in which one side does not score.

shut•ter |**shŭt'**ər| *n.* **1.** A hinged cover for a window or door, usually fitted with slanted slats. **2.** A device that opens and shuts the lens aperture of a camera to expose a plate or film.

shut•tle |**shŭt'**l| *n.* **1.** A device used in weaving to carry the crosswise woof threads back and forth between the lengthwise warp threads. **2.** A thread-holding device on a sewing machine that

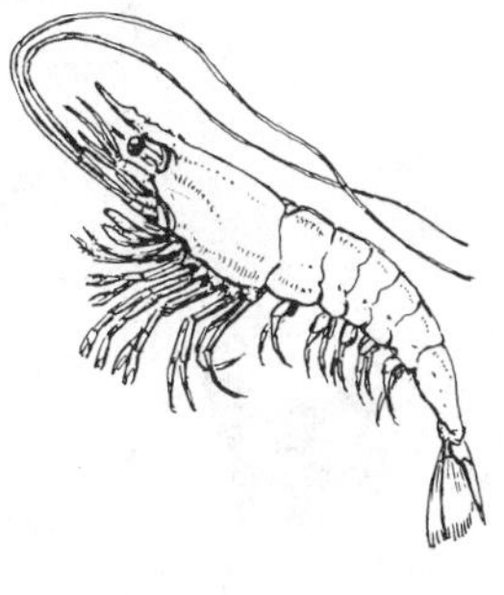

shrimp

shuffleboard

Siamese cat

Siamese twins
The use of this term dates from the birth of Chang *and* Eng *(1811–74), joined Chinese twins born in Siam.*

sideburns
The word **sideburns** is an alteration of *burnsides*, which meant whiskers as worn by General Ambrose *Burnside* (1824–81), Union general in the Civil War (photograph above).

ă pat/ā pay/â care/ä father/ĕ pet/ ē be/ĭ pit/ī pie/î fierce/ŏ pot/ ō go/ô paw, for/oi oil/ŏŏ book/ ōō boot/ou out/ŭ cut/û fur/ *th* the/th thin/hw which/zh vision/ ə ago, item, pencil, atom, circus

carries the lower thread back and forth through loops in the upper thread to form stitches. **3.** A train, bus aircraft, etc., making short, frequent trips between two points. *—v.* **shut•tled, shut•tling.** To move or travel back and forth by or as if by a shuttle.

shut•tle•cock |shŭt′əl kŏk′| *n.* A small rounded piece of cork or similar material with a crown of feathers, hit back and forth in badminton.

shy |shī| *adj.* **shi•er** or **shy•er, shi•est** or **shy•est. 1.** Easily startled; timid: *a shy animal.* **2.** Bashful; reserved: *a shy person.* **3.** Distrustful; wary: *They were shy of strangers.* **4.** *Informal.* Short: *His sister is three inches shy of six feet.* *—v.* **shied, shy•ing, shies.** To move suddenly, as if startled: *The horse shied at the sound.* —**shy′ly** *adv.* —**shy′ness** *n.*

shy•ster |shī′stər| *n. Slang.* An unethical or unscrupulous lawyer or politician.

si |sē| *n.* A form of the word **ti.** ¶ *These sound alike* **si, sea, see.**

Si The symbol for the element silicon.

Si•am |sī ăm′| *or* |sī′ăm′|. The former name of **Thailand.**

Si•a•mese |sī′ə mēz′| *or* |-mēs′| *adj.* Thai. *—n.* Thai.

Siamese cat. A cat of a breed having blue eyes and short pale-tan or gray fur with darker ears, face, tail, and feet. [SEE PICTURE]

Siamese twins. Twins born with their bodies joined together in any way. [SEE NOTE]

Si•be•ri•a |sī bîr′ē ə|. A large region in the Asian part of the Soviet Union, extending from the Ural Mountains to the Pacific Ocean. —**Si•be′ri•an** *adj. & n.*

sib•i•lant |sĭb′ə lənt| *adj.* Producing a hissing sound. *—n.* A speech sound that suggests hissing. For example, (s), (sh), (z), and (zh) are sibilants. —**sib′i•lance** *n.* —**sib′i•lant•ly** *adv.*

sib•ling |sĭb′lĭng| *n.* One of two or more children of the same parents; a brother or a sister.

sib•yl |sĭb′əl| *n.* **1.** One of a number of women regarded as oracles by the ancient Greeks and Romans. **2.** Any female prophet.

sic[1] |sĭk| *adv. Latin.* Thus; so. Used in written texts to show that a surprising word or phrase is not a mistake and is to be read as it stands. ¶ *These sound alike* **sic, sick.**

sic[2] |sĭk| *v.* **sicced, sic•cing. 1.** To urge to attack or chase: *He threatened to sic his big brother on them.* **2.** To chase: *"Sic him," he commanded his dog.* ¶ *These sound alike* **sic, sick.**

Sic•i•ly |sĭs′ə lē|. An island, part of Italy, in the Mediterranean Sea, off the southwestern tip of Italy. —**Si•cil′ian** |sĭ sĭl′yən| *or* |-sĭl′ē ən| *adj. & n.*

sick[1] |sĭk| *adj.* **sick•er, sick•est. 1. a.** Suffering from or affected with a physical or mental illness; not well or healthy. **b.** Nauseated; queasy: *Riding over the rough road made her sick.* **2. a.** Deeply distressed; upset: *sick at heart.* **b.** Disgusted; revolted: *Her rudeness made everybody sick.* **c.** Weary; tired: *sick of football.* **3.** Morbid or unwholesome: *a sick sense of humor.* **4.** Not dependable; unsound: *a sick economy.* ¶ *These sound alike* **sick, sic.**

sick[2] |sĭk| *v.* A form of the word **sic** (to urge to attack).

sick•en |sĭk′ən| *v.* To make or become sick.

sick•en•ing |sĭk′ə nĭng| *adj.* **1.** Causing or tending to cause sickness or nausea. **2.** Revolting or disgusting: *sickening behavior.*

sick•le |sĭk′əl| *n.* A tool for cutting grain or tall grass, consisting of a semicircular blade attached to a short handle.

sick•ly |sĭk′lē| *adj.* **sick•li•er, sick•li•est. 1.** Tending to become sick easily; having delicate health; frail. **2.** Of, caused by, or associated with sickness: *a sickly appearance.* **3.** Tending to cause sickness; unhealthful: *sickly weather.* **4.** Feeble; weak: *a sickly smile.* **5.** Nauseating; sickening: *a sickly smell.* —**sick′li•ness** *n.*

sick•ness |sĭk′nĭs| *n.* **1.** The condition of being sick; illness. **2.** A disease, disorder, or illness. **3.** Nausea.

side |sīd| *n.* **1. a.** A line segment that forms a part of the boundary of a plane geometric figure. **b.** A segment of a plane that forms a part of the boundary of a three-dimensional geometric figure. **2.** A surface of an object, especially one joining a top and a bottom: *the side of the box.* **3.** Either of two surfaces of a flat object, such as a piece of paper. **4. a.** Either of the two halves into which an object is divided by an axis extending from top to bottom or front to back, or by a plane in which both these axes lie. **b.** Either the right or left half of a human or animal body. **5.** The space immediately next to someone or something: *at her side; the side of the road.* **6. a.** An area separated from another by something intervening: *this side of the river.* **b.** A part or area identified by location with respect to a center: *the east side of town.* **7.** One of two or more opposing groups, teams, or sets of opinions: *ten people on their college's side.* **8.** A distinct aspect or quality of something: *the spiritual side of love.* **9.** Line of descent: *On her side, there are five brothers.* *—v.* **sid•ed, sid•ing.** —**side with** (or **against**). To align oneself with (or against): *always siding with her brother and against her sister.* *—adj.* **1.** Located on or to the side: *a side door.* **2.** Incidental: *a little side trip.* **3.** In addition to the main part: *a side order of French fries.*

Idioms. **on the side.** In addition to the main portion, occupation, or arrangement. **side by side.** Next to each other.

side•board |sīd′bôrd′| *or* |-bōrd′| *n.* A piece of dining-room furniture containing drawers and shelves for linens and tableware.

side•burns |sīd′bûrnz′| *pl.n.* Growths of hair down the sides of a man's face in front of the ears, especially when worn with the rest of the beard shaved off. [SEE PICTURE]

sid•ed |sī′dĭd| *adj.* Having a specified number or kind of sides: *a three-sided figure.*

side•kick |sīd′kĭk′| *n. Slang.* A close friend or associate; a pal or partner.

side•line |sīd′līn′| *n.* Also **side line. 1.** A boundary line along either of the two sides of a playing area, as in football. **2. sidelines.** The space immediately outside these lines. **3.** A line of merchandise carried in addition to regular merchandise. **4.** An activity pursued in addition to one's regular occupation.

side•long |sīd′lông′| *or* |-lŏng′| *adj.* To the side; sideways: *a sidelong smile.* *—adv.:* *glancing sidelong.*

si•de•re•al |sī dîr'ē əl| *adj.* Of, concerned with, or measured by the stars: *sidereal time.*
side•sad•dle |sīd'săd'l| *n.* A woman's saddle designed so that a rider may sit with both legs on the same side of the horse. *—adv.: ride sidesaddle.*
side show. A small show offered as part of a larger one, especially as part of a carnival or circus.
side•step |sīd'stĕp'| *v.* **-stepped, -step•ping. 1.** To step out of the way of or aside: *The quarterback sidestepped the tackler.* **2.** To evade (an issue or responsibility).
side•swipe |sīd'swīp'| *v.* **side•swiped, side•swip•ing.** To strike (a vehicle, obstacle, etc.) with the side in passing: *Out of control now, the car sideswiped the corner of the building.* *—n.* A glancing blow or impact made with the side in passing.
side•track |sīd'trăk'| *v.* **1.** To switch (a train, railroad car, etc.) from a main track onto a siding. **2.** To divert from a main issue or course. *—n.* A railroad siding.
side•walk |sīd'wôk'| *n.* A walk or raised path along the side of a road, meant for pedestrians.
side•ways |sīd'wāz| *adv.* **1.** Toward or from one side: *turn sideways.* **2.** With one side forward: *Crabs can move sideways.* *—adj.* Toward or from one side: *a sideways turn.*
side•wind•er |sīd'wīn'dər| *n.* A rattlesnake of the southwestern United States and Mexico that moves by looping its body with a sideways motion.
sid•ing |sī'dĭng| *n.* **1.** A short section of railroad track connected by switches with a main track. **2.** Material, such as shingles used for covering the sides of a frame building.
si•dle |sīd'l| *v.* **si•dled, si•dling.** To move sideways or edge along, especially furtively.
siege |sēj| *n.* **1.** The surrounding and blockading of a town or fortress by an army bent on capturing it. **2.** A prolonged period, as of illness.
si•en•na |sē ĕn'ə| *n.* **1.** A special clay, containing oxides of iron and manganese, used as a pigment in making paints. **2.** A yellowish or reddish brown.
si•er•ra |sē ĕr'ə| *n.* A rugged range of mountains having an irregular outline somewhat like the teeth of a saw.
Si•er•ra Le•one |sē ĕr'ə lē ōn'|. A country in western Africa, on the Atlantic Ocean. Population, 2,707,000. Capital, Freetown.
Si•er•ra Ne•vad•a |sē ĕr'ə nə văd'ə| *or* |-vä'də|. A mountain range in eastern California.
sieve |sĭv| *n.* A utensil for separating liquids and fine particles from more solid substances, consisting of a frame with wire mesh containing many small holes. *—v.* **sieved, siev•ing.** To pass (something) through a sieve.
sift |sĭft| *v.* **1.** To pass or put through or as through a sieve: *Sift a cup of flour. The snow sifted down into the crannies.* **2.** To examine closely and carefully: *sift the evidence.* **—sift'er** *n.*
sigh |sī| *v.* **1.** To exhale a long, deep breath while making a sound, as of weariness, sorrow, or relief. **2.** To make a similar sound: *trees sighing in the wind.* **3.** To feel longing or grief; mourn. *—n.* The act or sound of sighing.
sight |sīt| *n.* **1.** The ability to see; the faculty of vision. **2.** The act of seeing; perception of something; view: *The sight of land thrilled the sailors.* **3. a.** The range that can be seen; the field of vision: *out of our sight.* **b.** The field of one's mental vision: *no solution in sight.* **4.** Something seen or worth seeing: *the sights of Rome.* **5.** A view; glimpse: *catch sight of her.* **6.** *Informal.* Something regarded as awful, unsightly, or disgusting to see: *What a sight she was after the game.* **7. a.** A device used to help in aiming a firearm, telescope, etc. **b.** An aim or observation made with the aid of such a device. *—v.* **1.** To see or observe within one's field of vision: *sight land.* **2.** To take aim or observe with the help of a sight. ¶*These sound alike* **sight, cite, site.** [SEE NOTE]
sight•less |sīt'lĭs| *adj.* Unable to see; blind.
sight•see•ing |sīt'sē'ĭng| *n.* The act or pastime of touring places of interest. **—modifier:** *a sightseeing bus.* **—sight'se'er** *n.*
sig•ma |sĭg'mə| *n.* The 18th letter of the Greek alphabet, written Σ, σ. In English it is represented as *S, s.*
sign |sīn| *n.* **1.** Something that suggests a fact, quality, or condition not immediately evident; an indication: *A high temperature is a sign of trouble in the human body.* **2.** An action or gesture that conveys an idea, desire, information, or command: *gave the go-ahead sign.* **3.** A board, poster, or placard that conveys information: *a street sign.* **4.** A mark, figure, or character that represents a word, phrase, operation, etc., as in mathematics or musical notation. **5.** Remaining evidence; a trace or vestige: *no sign of life.* **6.** An event or incident regarded as foretelling something: *People once thought that eclipses were signs of coming disaster.* **7.** One of the 12 divisions of the zodiac, each named for a constellation and represented by a symbol. *—v.* **1.** To affix one's signature to: *sign a document.* **2.** To write (one's signature): *Sign your name. Sign here.* **3.** To hire by getting a signature on a contract: *signed three new players.* **4.** To approve or guarantee (a document, work of art, contract, etc.) by affixing one's signature. **5.** To make a sign; signal. **—phrasal verbs. sign off.** In broadcasting, to stop transmitting after identifying one's station. **sign on.** To agree to work or hire for work. **sign up.** To volunteer one's services; enlist. ¶*These sound alike* **sign, sine.** **—sign'er** *n.* [SEE NOTE]
sig•nal |sĭg'nəl| *n.* **1. a.** A sign, gesture, or device that conveys information: *a traffic signal; finger signals to the pitcher.* **b.** A message conveyed by such means. **2.** Something that is the cause of action: *The strike was the signal for revolt.* **—modifier:** *a signal device.* *—adj.* Out of the ordinary; remarkable: *a signal victory.* *—v.* **sig•naled** or **sig•nalled, sig•nal•ing** or **sig•nal•ling. 1. a.** To make a signal or signals. **b.** To make a signal or signals to: *They signaled the engineer to start.* **2.** To make known or relate with or as if with signals: *A period signals the end of a sentence.* **—sig'nal•er** *n.*
sig•nal•ly |sĭg'nə lē| *adv.* In a signal manner; notably: *defeat them signally.*
sig•na•ture |sĭg'nə chər|. **1.** The name of a person as written by himself. **2.** A **key signature. 3.** A **time signature. 4.** A section of a book that consists of a large sheet printed with four or a

sight

Sight *was Old English* siht *or* sihth, *and is closely related to* **see**[1]. *The* gh *in words like* **sight, right, thought,** *etc., originally represented a sound something like the* /KH/ *in the Scottish word* **loch**; *thus Old English* siht *was pronounced very approximately* /sēKHt/. *In the Middle English period, French scribes from Normandy changed much of the spelling of English to fit the spelling of their own language. These Normans used the letter* h *as it is used in Modern English* **hat** *and* **honor**; *so they respelled the* /KH/ *sound as* ch *or* gh, *and thus* siht *became* sicht *or* sight. *Later, the sound* /KH/ *itself disappeared from English; but by this time the spelling with* gh *had become permanently fixed. Thus the spelling of words like* **sight** *is a written vestige of a vanished sound.*

sign/seal[1]

Sign *is from Latin* signum, *"a mark, an indication," also "a signet ring."* Signum *formed the diminutive noun* sigillum, *"little mark," especially "the seal or impression left by a signet ring"; this became Old French* seel, *which was borrowed into English as* **seal**[1].

silhouette

silicon

Silicon *is very common in the earth's crust, chiefly in the form of* **silica** *and* **silicates**. *It is a semiconductor and is used in making transistors, rectifiers, and other solid-state electronic devices. It is also used in making bricks, glass, concrete, pottery, and* **silicones**.

silkworm
Larvae feeding on mulberry leaves (their only food)

ă pat/ā pay/â care/ä father/ĕ pet/ ē be/ĭ pit/ī pie/î fierce/ŏ pot/ ō go/ô paw, for/oi oil/o͝o book/ o͞o boot/ou out/ŭ cut/û fur/ *th* the/th thin/hw which/zh vision/ ə ago, item, pencil, atom, circus

multiple of four pages and folded to page size.

sign•board |sīn′bôrd′| *or* |-bōrd′| *n.* A board bearing a sign, advertisement, or notice.

sig•net |sĭg′nĭt| *n.* A seal, as one used to stamp documents. ¶*These sound alike* **signet, cygnet.**

sig•nif•i•cance |sĭg nĭf′ĭ kəns| *n.* **1.** The state and quality of being significant; importance: *the significance of dissent against the war.* **2.** The sense of something; the meaning.

sig•nif•i•cant |sĭg nĭf′ĭ kənt| *adj.* **1.** Having a meaning; meaningful: *a significant detail.* **2.** Full of meaning: *a significant glance.* **3.** Important; notable: *a significant historical event.* —**sig•nif′i•cant•ly** *adv.*

sig•ni•fy |sĭg′nə fī′| *v.* **sig•ni•fied, sig•ni•fy•ing, sig•ni•fies. 1.** To serve as a sign of: *What does this monument signify?* **2.** To make known: *Peter signified that he wanted to leave early.*

Sikh |sēk| *n.* A member of a religious sect in India that worships only one God.

si•lage |sī′lĭj| *n.* Green fodder that has been stored and fermented in a silo.

si•lence |sī′ləns| *n.* **1.** The absence of sound; stillness. **2.** The absence or avoidance of speech or noise, or a period of time marked by this. **3.** Refusal or failure to speak out. —*v.* **si•lenced, si•lenc•ing. 1.** To make silent or bring to silence; quiet. **2.** To curtail or stop the expression of; suppress: *measures to silence the press.* —*interj.* Be silent; keep quiet.

si•lenc•er |sī′lən sər| *n.* A device attached to the muzzle of a firearm to muffle the sound it makes when fired.

si•lent |sī′lənt| *adj.* **1.** Making or having no sound or noise; quiet: *the silent night.* **2.** Without speech; saying nothing: *remained respectfully silent.* **3.** Not disposed to speak; taciturn: *strong, silent men.* **4.** Not voiced or expressed; tacit: *a silent admission of guilt.* **5.** Inactive: *silent volcanoes; a silent partner in the business.* **6.** Not pronounced or sounded, as a letter in a word: *The "g" in "gnome" is silent.* **7.** Having no sound track: *a silent movie.* —**si′lent•ly** *adv.*

sil•hou•ette |sĭl′o͞o ĕt′| *n.* **1.** A drawing consisting of the outline of something, especially a human profile, filled in with a solid color. **2.** An outline of something that appears dark against a light background. —*v.* **sil•hou•et•ted, sil•hou•et•ting.** To cause to be seen as a silhouette. [SEE PICTURE]

sil•i•ca |sĭl′ĭ kə| *n.* Silicon dioxide, SiO_2, a compound that occurs widely in mineral forms, such as quartz, sand, flint, etc., and is used in making glass, concrete, and other materials.

sil•i•cate |sĭl′ĭ kĭt| *or* |-kāt′| *n.* Any of a large class of chemical compounds composed of silicon, oxygen, and at least one metal or a radical that can replace a metal, found widely in rocks and forming the principal substance of bricks and glass.

sil•i•con |sĭl′ĭ kən| *or* |-kŏn′| *n.* Symbol **Si** One of the elements, a substance that occurs in both crystalline and amorphous forms. Atomic number 14; atomic weight 28.086; valence +4; melting point 1,410° C; boiling point 2,355°C. [SEE NOTE]

silicon carbide. A bluish-black crystalline compound of silicon and carbon, SiC.

sil•i•cone |sĭl′ĭ kōn′| *n.* Any of a class of chemical compounds that are polymers based on the unit $RSiO_2$, in which R is an organic radical. They are used in making adhesives, lubricants, protective coatings, synthetic rubber, etc.

silk |sĭlk| *n.* **1. a.** The fine, glossy fiber produced by a silkworm to form its cocoon. **b.** A similar fine, strong fiber produced by spiders for spinning their webs, moving through the air, etc., or by certain insect larvae. **2.** Thread or fabric made from the fiber produced by silkworms. **3. a.** A garment or clothing made from this fabric. **b. silks.** The brightly colored garments that identify a jockey or harness driver in a horse race. **4.** Any fine, soft strands, such as those forming a tassellike tuft at the end of an ear of corn. —***modifier:*** *silk stockings.*

silk•en |sĭl′kən| *adj.* **1.** Made of silk: *a silken scarf.* **2.** Having the look or feel of silk; soft, smooth, and glossy: *silken locks of hair.*

silk•worm |sĭlk′wûrm′| *n.* **1.** The caterpillar of a moth, originally from Asia, that spins a cocoon of fine, glossy fiber used to make silk fabric and thread. **2.** Any of several other moth caterpillars that spin silk cocoons. [SEE PICTURE]

silk•y |sĭl′kē| *adj.* **silk•i•er, silk•i•est.** As soft, smooth, and glossy as silk: *silky fur.* —**silk′i•ly** *adv.* —**silk′i•ness** *n.*

sill |sĭl| *n.* A horizontal beam or support that holds up the vertical part of a frame or similar structure, especially the base of a window.

sil•ly |sĭl′ē| *adj.* **sil•li•er, sil•li•est. 1.** Showing lack of good sense or reason; stupid: *silly mistakes.* **2.** Lacking seriousness or substance; absurd: *a silly comedy.* **3.** *Informal.* Only partly conscious; dazed, as from a blow. —**sil′li•ness** *n.*

si•lo |sī′lō| *n., pl.* **si•los. 1.** A tall, cylindrical building in which fodder is stored. **2.** An underground shelter for a missile, from which it can be directly launched.

silt |sĭlt| *n.* A material consisting of mineral particles smaller than those of sand and larger than those of clay, often found at the bottom of bodies of water. —*v.* To fill or become filled with silt: *The flow of water had silted up the channel. A pond may silt up after a time.*

Si•lu•ri•an |sĭ lo͝or′ē ən| *or* |sī-| *n.* The period of geologic time that began about 425 million years ago and ended about 405 million years ago. During this period land plants first appeared. —***modifier:*** *Silurian fossils.*

sil•van |sĭl′vən| *adj.* A form of the word **sylvan.**

sil•ver |sĭl′vər| *n.* **1.** Symbol **Ag** One of the elements, a soft shiny white metal. Atomic number 47; atomic weight 107.870; valences +1, +2; melting 960.8°C; boiling point 2,212°C. **2.** This metal used as money or a commodity. **3.** Coins made of this metal. **4.** Tableware or other household articles made of or plated with this metal. **5.** A light, shiny, or metallic gray. —***modifier:*** *a silver bell; a silver salt.* —*v.* To cover or plate with silver or something that resembles silver. —*adj.* Having a light gray color like that of the metal silver: *silver hair.*

sil•ver•fish |sĭl′vər fĭsh′| *n., pl.* **-fish** or **-fish•es.** A silvery, wingless insect that is often found in houses and other buildings and that feeds on and can damage substances containing starch.

silver nitrate. A poisonous clear crystalline compound of silver, nitrogen, and oxygen,

$AgNO_3$, that darkens when exposed to light, used in photography and silver plating and as an external antiseptic.

silver plate. Tableware or other household articles made of or plated with silver.

sil•ver•smith |sĭl′vər smĭth′| *n.* A person who makes and repairs articles of silver.

sil•ver•ware |sĭl′vər wâr′| *n.* Eating and serving utensils, such as forks, knives, and spoons, made of or plated with silver.

silver wedding. The 25th anniversary of a marriage.

sil•ver•y |sĭl′və rē| *adj.* **1.** Containing or coating with silver. **2.** Resembling or suggestive of silver, as in color or glittering appearance: *the silvery moonlight; a school of silvery fish.* **3.** Having a clear, ringing sound: *a silvery voice.*

sim•i•an |sĭm′ē ən| *adj.* Of an ape or monkey. —*n.* An ape or monkey.

sim•i•lar |sĭm′ə lər| *adj.* **1.** Related in appearance or nature; alike though not the same: *a wild cat similar to but smaller than a lion.* **2.** Having corresponding angles equal and corresponding line segments proportional in length, as pairs of geometric figures do. —**sim′i•lar•ly** *adv.*

sim•i•lar•i•ty |sĭm′ə lăr′ĭ tē| *n., pl.* **sim•i•lar•i•ties.** **1.** The condition or property of being similar. **2.** A feature or property shared by two or more things; a way in which things are alike.

similar triangles. Triangles that have equal corresponding angles and proportional corresponding sides. [SEE PICTURE]

sim•i•le |sĭm′ə lē| *n.* A figure of speech in which unlike things are compared, often in a phrase introduced by *like* or *as.* For example, *The lighthouse stands like a fort* and *His mind was as vast as an empire* are similes.

si•mil•i•tude |sĭ mĭl′ĭ to͞od′| *or* |-tyo͞od′| *n.* Similarity; resemblance; likeness.

sim•mer |sĭm′ər| *v.* **1.** To cook below or just at the boiling point: *She simmered the sauce. The soup simmered gently.* **2.** To be filled with barely controlled anger or resentment: *He simmered at the insult.* **3.** To be almost at the point of breaking out or erupting: *Beneath the peaceful surface regional conflicts simmered.* —*n.* The condition or process of simmering. —***phrasal verb.*** **simmer down.** **1.** To reduce the liquid volume of by boiling slowly. **2.** To become calm after anger or excitement.

Si•mon Pe•ter |sī′mən pē′tər|. Saint Peter.

sim•per |sĭm′pər| *v.* To smile in a silly or self-conscious manner. —*n.* A silly or self-conscious smile.

sim•ple |sĭm′pəl| *adj.* **sim•pler, sim•plest.** **1.** Having or composed of a single part or unit; not compound. **2.** Not involved or complicated; easy: *a simple explanation.* **3.** Without additions or modifications; bare; mere: *a simple "yes" or "no."* **4.** Not showy, elaborate, or luxurious: *a simple wedding dress; simple, everyday words.* **5.** Sincere; open; frank: *simple and direct in manner.* **6.** Humble or lowly in condition or rank: *simple farm folk.* **7.** Ordinary; common: *relief of simple headaches.* **8.** Having or showing little sense of intelligence: *a simple man who is easily cheated.*

simple fraction. A fraction in which both the numerator and denominator are whole numbers.

simple machine. Any of six basic mechanical devices, the lever, the pulley, the wheel and axle, the inclined plane, the screw, and the wedge, that vary the ratio of speed to force in doing work.

sim•ple-mind•ed |sĭm′pəl mīn′dĭd| *adj.* **1.** Not sophisticated; artless or naive. **2.** Stupid or silly. **3.** Mentally defective. —**sim′ple-mind′ed•ly** *adv.* —**sim′ple-mind′ed•ness** *n.*

simple sentence. A sentence having one independent clause and no dependent clauses.

sim•ple•ton |sĭm′pəl tən| *n.* A fool.

sim•plic•i•ty |sĭm plĭs′ĭ tē| *n., pl.* **sim•plic•i•ties.** **1.** The property, condition, or quality of being simple; absence of complexity or difficulty. **2.** Absence of luxury or showiness; plainness. **3.** Absence of artificiality or affectation of manner or behavior; sincerity: *childlike simplicity.*

sim•pli•fy |sĭm′plə fī′| *v.* **sim•pli•fied, sim•pli•fy•ing, sim•pli•fies.** To make or become simple or simpler. —**sim′pli•fi•ca′tion** *n.* —**sim′pli•fi′er** *n.*

sim•ply |sĭm′plē| *adv.* **1.** In a simple manner; plainly: *Explain it simply. They live very simply.* **2.** Merely; only; just: *We knew him simply as Joe.* **3.** Really; absolutely; altogether: *His behavior was simply arrogant.*

sim•u•late |sĭm′yə lāt′| *v.* **sim•u•lat•ed, sim•u•lat•ing.** **1.** To have, take on, or duplicate the appearance, conditions, form, or sound of; imitate: *a device that simulates space flight.* **2.** To make a pretense of; pretend; feign: *simulated lack of interest.* —**sim′u•la′tor** *n.*

sim•u•la•tion |sĭm′yə lā′shən| *n.* **1.** The act or process of simulating. **2.** An imitation: *a simulation of conditions on the moon.* **3.** The act of making a false show of something; pretense: *a simulation of friendship.*

si•mul•ta•ne•ous |sī′məl tā′nē əs| *or* |sĭm′əl-| *adj.* Happening, existing, or done at the same time. —**si′mul•ta′ne•ous•ly** *adv.*

sin |sĭn| *n.* **1.** The act of breaking a religious or moral law, especially when done deliberately. **2.** The form that such an act takes: *Perjury is a sin.* **3.** Any serious offense, fault, or error. —*v.* **sinned, sin•ning.** **1.** To violate a religious or moral law. **2.** To commit a serious offense; do wrong. —**sin′ner** *n.*

sin sine.

Si•nai |sī′nī′|. A peninsula of northeastern Egypt at the northern end of the Red Sea.

since |sĭns| *adv.* **1.** From then until now, or between then and now: *He left town and hasn't been here since.* Also used prepositionally: *Since last month's upset, the team has been making a spectacular comeback.* **2.** Before now; ago: *long since forgotten.* —*conj.* **1.** During the time after which: *He hasn't been home since he graduated.* **2.** Continuously from the time when: *He hasn't spoken since he sat down.* **3.** As a result of the fact that; inasmuch as: *Since you're not interested, I won't tell you about it.*

sin•cere |sĭn sîr′| *adj.* **sin•cer•er, sin•cer•est.** Without false appearance or nature: *sincere friends; a sincere apology.* —**sin•cere′ly** *adv.*

sin•cer•i•ty |sĭn sĕr′ĭ tē| *n.* The quality or condition of being sincere; freedom from falseness.

sine |sīn| *n.* In a right triangle, a function of an acute angle equal to the length of the side opposite the angle divided by the length of the hypotenuse. ¶*These sound alike* **sine, sign.** [SEE NOTE]

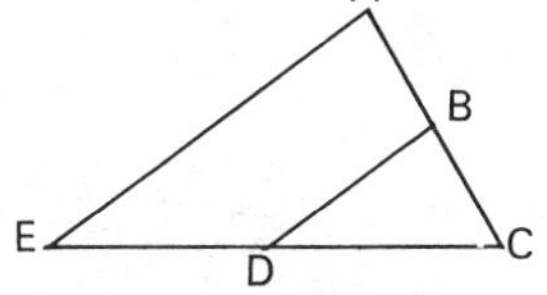

similar triangles
The triangles ACE and BCD are similar

sine
It is possible to extend the definition of **sine** *so that all angles, not just acute angles, have sines. In the same way, the definitions of cosine, tangent, and the other trigonometric functions can be extended to apply to almost all angles. The word* **sine** *is from Medieval Latin* sinus, *"fold, bend, curve," which was used to translate Arabic* jayb, *"fold," also "chord of an arc."*

sinecure
In the language of the church, **cure** *means "spiritual supervision" or "the duties of a priest or minister in looking after the souls of the members of his congregation."* **Sinecure** *originally meant "a church appointment or job without supervisory duties": Latin* sine, *"without,"* + cūra, *"cure, supervisory duties."*

ă pat/ā pay/â care/ä father/ĕ pet/ ē be/ĭ pit/ī pie/î fierce/ŏ pot/ ō go/ô paw, for/oi oil/o͝o book/ o͞o boot/ou out/ŭ cut/û fur/ *th* the/th thin/hw which/zh vision/ ə ago, item, pencil, atom, circus

si•ne•cure |sī'nĭ kyo͝or'| *or* |sĭn'ĭ-| *n.* Any position that requires no work yet provides a salary. [SEE NOTE]

sin•ew |sĭn'yo͞o| *n.* **1.** A tendon. **2.** The connective tissue of which tendons are composed. **3.** The source of vitality and strength: *working classes, the bone and sinew of the country.*

sin•ew•y |sĭn'yo͞o ē| *adj.* **1.** Of or like sinew. **2.** Lean and muscular. **3.** Strong; vigorous.

sing |sĭng| *v.* **sang** |săng| or **sung** |sŭng|, **sung, sing•ing. 1.** To pronounce or utter a series of words or sounds in musical tones. **2.** To perform (songs or other vocal selections). **3.** To produce a sound that is considered musical: *birds that sing in tropical forests.* **4.** To produce a high-pitched whine, screech, etc.: *The teakettle sang.* **5.** To tell something in song or verse: *poets singing of Greece's glory.* **6.** To proclaim: *sang her praises.* **7.** To bring to a specified condition by singing: *sang the baby to sleep.* —**phrasal verb. sing out.** To call out loudly.

sing. singular.

Sin•ga•pore |sĭng'gə pôr'| *or* |-pōr'| *or* |sĭng'ə-|. **1.** An island nation off the southern tip of the Malay Peninsula. Population, 2,236,000. **2.** The capital of this country. Population, 2,147,-000.

singe |sĭnj| *v.* **singed, singe•ing. 1.** To burn slightly; scorch. **2.** To burn the ends of: *singed his hair.* **3.** To burn off the feathers or bristles of by holding to a flame. —*n.* A slight burn.

sing•er |sĭng'ər| *n.* Someone who sings, especially someone who has had special training or who sings professionally.

sin•gle |sĭng'gəl| *adj.* **1.** Not accompanied by another or others; one alone. **2.** Intended or designed for use by one person or family: *a single bed; a single flat.* **3.** Not married. **4.** Having only one row of petals rather than many that overlap or are densely clustered: *the single flowers of a wild rose.* —*n.* **1.** An accommodation for one person, as a room in a hotel or seat in a stadium. **2.** In baseball, a hit that enables the batter to reach first base. **3. singles.** A match between two players in tennis and other games. **4.** Often **singles.** An unmarried person. —*v.* **sin•gled, sin•gling. 1.** To distinguish from among others: *He singled out two students for praise.* **2.** In baseball, to hit a single.

sin•gle-breast•ed |sĭng'gəl brĕs'tĭd| *adj.* Describing a coat or jacket that closes with a narrow overlap and is fastened down the front with a single row of buttons.

sin•gle-hand•ed |sĭng'gəl hăn'dĭd| *adj.* Working or done without help; unassisted. —**sin'gle-hand'ed•ly** *adv.*

sin•gle-mind•ed |sĭng'gəl mīn'dĭd| *adj.* **1.** Having one purpose or opinion: *a single-minded approach to tax reform.* **2.** Steadfast; not wavering: *the single-minded pursuit of a dream.* —**sin'gle-mind'ed•ly** *adv.* —**sin'gle-mind'ed•ness** *n.*

sin•gly |sĭng'glē| *adv.* **1.** Without company or help; alone: *a fish that never attacks singly.* **2.** One by one; individually: *materials used singly or in combinations.*

sing•song |sĭng'sông'| *or* |-sŏng'| *n.* **1.** Verse or song having a monotonous regularity of rhythm or rhyme. **2.** A manner of speaking marked by an unchanging and monotonous rise and fall of sound. —*adj.* Having a monotonous rhythm or speech cadence.

sin•gu•lar |sĭng'gyə lər| *adj.* **1.** Of a word form that names or stands for a single person or thing or a group considered as one. For example, *I* and *he* are singular pronouns and *army* is a singular noun. **2.** Very uncommon; extraordinary; rare: *behavior reflecting singular integrity.* **3.** Very strange; peculiar: *singular arrivals and departures at midnight.* —*n.* The form taken by a word indicating one person or thing or a group considered as one. —**sin'gu•lar•ly** *adv.*

sin•gu•lar•i•ty |sĭng'gyə lăr'ĭ tē| *n., pl.* **sin•gu•lar•i•ties. 1.** The condition or quality of being singular. **2.** A distinguishing trait; a peculiarity. **3.** Something uncommon or unusual.

sin•is•ter |sĭn'ĭ stər| *adj.* **1.** Suggesting an evil force or motive: *a dark, sinister man.* **2.** Promising trouble; ominous: *words with a sinister sound.* —**sin'is•ter•ly** *adv.*

sink |sĭngk| *v.* **sank** |săngk| or **sunk** |sŭngk|, **sunk** or **sunk•en** |sŭng'kən|, **sink•ing. 1.** To descend or cause to go beneath the surface or to the bottom of liquid or a soft substance: *The sled sank into the deep snow. Heavy storms can sink ships.* **2.** To move to a lower level; go down slowly: *He sank into the chair.* **3.** To appear to move downward: *The sun sank out of sight.* **4.** To force or drive (a piling, post, etc.) into the ground. **5.** To dig or drill (a mine, well, etc.). **6.** To pass into a specified condition: *She sank into a deep sleep.* **7.** To pass into a worsened physical condition; approach death. **8.** To diminish or become weaker, as in strength, vitality, or value: *His voice sank to a faint gasp. The news made my heart sink. Farm prices sank steadily.* **9.** To seep; penetrate: *Rainfall could barely sink into the baked earth.* **10.** To become understood: *Let the meaning sink in.* **11.** To invest: *He sank a small fortune into real estate.* **12.** In basketball or golf, to cause (the ball) to enter the basket or cup. —*n.* **1.** A water basin having a drainpipe and usually a piped supply of water. **2.** A sinkhole.

sink•er |sĭng'kər| *n.* **1.** Someone or something that sinks. **2.** A weight used for sinking fishing lines, nets, etc.

sink•hole |sĭngk'hōl'| *n.* A natural depression in a land surface joining with an underground passage, cavern, etc.

sin•u•ous |sĭn'yo͞o əs| *adj.* Having many curves or turns; winding. —**sin'u•ous•ly** *adv.*

si•nus |sī'nəs| *n.* Any of several air-filled cavities in the bones of the skull, especially one that connects with the nostrils.

si•nus•i•tis |sī'nə sī'tĭs| *n.* Inflammation of the membrane that lines a sinus, especially a sinus in the region near the nose.

Si•on |sī'ən| *n.* A form of the word **Zion.**

Siou•an |so͞o'ən| *n.* A large family of North American Indian languages spoken over an extensive area of the Midwest. Some of the important Siouan-speaking tribes are the Crow, Sioux, and Iowa.

Sioux |so͞o| *n., pl.* **Sioux.** Also called *Dakota.* **1.** A group of tribes of Plains Indians formerly living in the Dakotas, Minnesota, and Nebraska. **2.** A member of any of these tribes. **3.** Any of the Siouan languages of these tribes.

sip |sĭp| *v.* **sipped, sip•ping.** To drink delicately and in small quantities. —*n.* **1.** The act of sipping: *smiled after his first sip.* **2.** A small quantity of liquid sipped: *took a sip of coffee.*

si•phon |sī′fən| *n.* **1.** A pipe or tube in the form of an inverted U, filled with liquid and arranged so that the pressure of the atmosphere forces liquid from a container to flow through the tube, over a barrier, and into a lower container. **2.** A tubelike animal part, as of a clam, through which water is taken in or expelled. —*v.* **1.** To draw off or transfer (a liquid) through a siphon. **2.** To pass through a siphon. [SEE PICTURE]

sir |sûr| *n.* **1.** Often **Sir.** A polite form of address used in place of a man's name. **2.** **Sir.** A title of honor used before the given name or the full name of a knight or baronet.

sire |sīr| *n.* **1.** A father or forefather. **2.** The father of an animal, especially a four-footed animal such as a horse. **3.** *Archaic.* A form of address to a superior, especially used in addressing a king. —*v.* **sired, sir•ing.** To be the father or male ancestor of.

si•ren |sī′rən| *n.* **1.** A device in which a jet of compressed gas is directed against a rotating disk that is full of holes, making a loud whistling or wailing sound as a signal or warning. **2.** Any device that makes a similar sound as a signal or warning. **3.** Often **Siren.** In Greek mythology, one of the sea nymphs whose sweet singing lured sailors to destruction. **4.** A beautiful, attractive or captivating woman.

Sir•i•us |sĭr′ē əs| *n.* The brightest star seen in the night sky, about 8.7 light-years away from the earth.

sir•loin |sûr′loin′| *n.* A cut of beef or sometimes pork from the upper part of the loin.

sir•up |sĭr′əp| *or* |sûr′-| *n.* A form of the word **syrup.**

si•sal |sī′səl| *or* |-zəl| *n.* **1.** A tropical plant with large leaves that yield a stiff fiber used for making rope, twine, etc. **2.** The fiber of such a plant. —***modifier:*** *sisal rope.*

sis•sy |sĭs′ē| *n., pl.* **sis•sies.** **1.** An effeminate male. **2.** A timid or cowardly person. **3.** *Informal.* Sister.

sis•ter |sĭs′tər| *n.* **1.** A girl or woman having the same mother and father as another person. **2.** A fellow woman or girl. **3.** A fellow member, as of a sorority. **4.** **Sister.** A nun.

sis•ter•hood |sĭs′tər hŏŏd′| *n.* **1.** The relationship of being a sister or sisters. **2.** The quality of being sisterly. **3.** A group of women united by a common purpose, as a religious society.

sis•ter-in-law |sĭs′tər ĭn lô′| *n., pl.* **sis•ters-in-law.** **1.** The sister of one's husband or wife. **2.** The wife of one's brother. **3.** The wife of the brother of one's husband or wife.

sis•ter•ly |sĭs′tər lē| *adj.* **1.** Suitable for a sister or sisters: *took a sisterly interest in her.* **2.** Showing affection. —**sis′ter•li•ness** *n.*

sit |sĭt| *v.* **sat** |săt|, **sit•ting.** **1.** To rest with the body supported upon the buttocks and the torso upright; be seated: *He sat on the bench.* **2.** To cause to sit; seat: *They sat him at the head of the table.* **3.** To perch, as a bird does. **4.** To cover eggs so that they will hatch, as a hen does. **5.** To be situated or located; lie: *The farmhouses sit far apart.* **6.** To remain inactive or unused: *The building sits unoccupied and unwanted.* **7.** To pose for an artist or photographer. **8.** To occupy a seat as a member of a body of officials: *She was the first woman to sit in the Senate.* **9.** To be in session: *Normally the Supreme Court does not sit in summer.* **10.** To affect one with or as if with a burden; weigh: *A President's responsibilities never sit lightly.* **11.** To be agreeable to one: *The meal did not sit well, and neither did the speaker's remarks.* **12.** To fit, fall, drape, lie, or rest in a specified manner: *The jacket sits perfectly on you. The hat sat unsteadily at the back of his head.* **13.** To babysit or keep watch with someone in need of care. —***phrasal verbs.*** **sit down.** To take a seat; be seated. **sit in on.** To attend or participate in. **sit up.** **1.** To rise to a sitting position. **2.** To sit straight or erect. **3.** To stay up later than the customary bedtime. —**sit′ter** *n.*

si•tar |sĭ tär′| *n.* A stringed instrument used in Hindu music, made of seasoned gourds and teak with 20 metal frets with 6 or 7 playing strings above and 13 resonating strings below. [SEE PICTURE]

sit•com |sĭt′kŏm′| *n.* *Informal.* Situation comedy.

site |sīt| *n.* **1.** The place where something was, is, or is to be located. **2.** The place or setting of an event. ¶*These sound alike* **site, cite, sight.**

sit-in |sĭt′ĭn′| *n.* A demonstration in which persons protesting against certain conditions sit down in an appropriate place and refuse to move until their demands are considered or met.

sit•ting |sĭt′ĭng| *n.* **1.** The act or position of one that sits. **2.** A period during which one is seated and occupied with a single activity, as posing for an artist or reading a book.

sitting room. A small living room.

sit•u•ate |sĭch′ōō āt′| *v.* **sit•u•at•ed, sit•u•at•ing.** To place in a certain spot or position; locate.

sit•u•a•tion |sĭch′ōō ā′shən| *n.* **1.** The place or position in which something is situated; location. **2.** A person's position or status with respect to specified conditions: *Determine in advance each student's situation in case of a bus strike.* **3.** A combination of circumstances at a given moment: *FBI agents face many dangerous situations.* **4.** A position of employment.

situation comedy. A humorous television series in which the comedy arises from the interactions of a continuing cast of characters.

sit-up |sĭt′ŭp′| *n.* A form of exercise in which a person lying on his back rises to a sitting position without the support of his arms and without bending his legs.

Si•va |shē′və| *or* |sē′-|. A form of the name **Shiva.**

six |sĭks| *n.* A number, written 6 in Arabic numerals, that is equal to the sum of 5 + 1. It is the positive integer that immediately follows 5. —**six** *adj.* & *pron.* [SEE NOTE]

six•pence |sĭks′pəns| *n.* In Great Britain, a coin worth six pennies, or half a shilling.

six-shoot•er |sĭks′shōō′tər| *n.* *Informal.* A revolver that can be fired six times before it has to be loaded again.

six•teen |sĭks′tēn′| *n.* A number, written 16 in Arabic numerals, that is equal to the sum of 15 + 1. It is the positive integer that immediately follows 15. —**six′teen′** *adj.* & *pron.*

six•teenth |sĭks′tēnth′| *n.* **1.** In a set of items

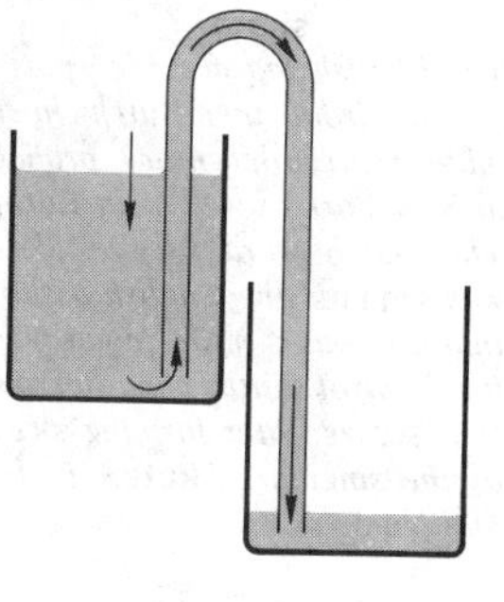

siphon

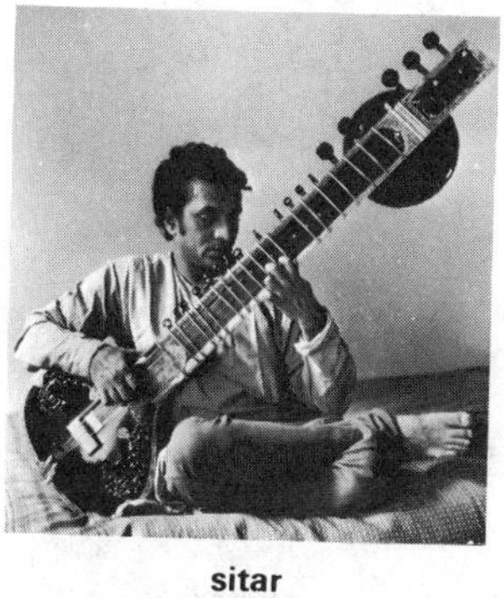

sitar
Ravi Shankar playing

six
Six *was* six *in Old English,* seks *in prehistoric Germanic, and* seks *or* sweks *in Indo-European.* Seks *appears also in Latin* sex, *"six," from which we have* **sextet.** Sweks *appears in Greek as* hex, *from which we have* **hexagon.**

skate[1-2]
The English learned the sport of skating from the Dutch in the mid-seventeenth century, probably in New York as well as in Europe. The Dutch word for "a skate" was schaats; *the English assumed that this was a plural noun meaning "pair of skates" and borrowed it as* scates, *later forming* **skate**[1] *as the singular.* **Skate**[2] *is from Old Norse* skata.

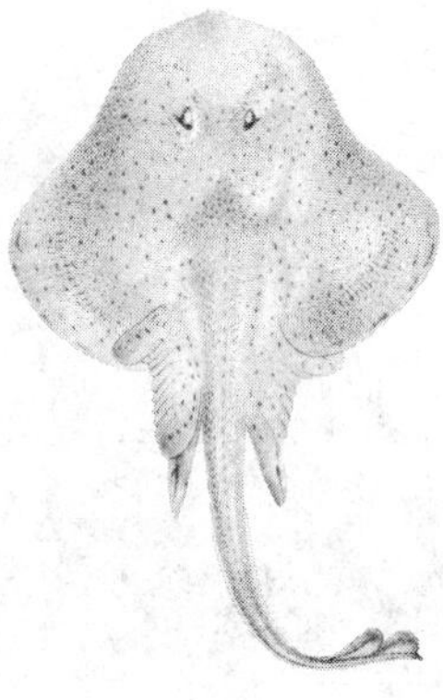

skate[2]

ă pat/ā pay/â care/ä father/ĕ pet/ ē be/ĭ pit/ī pie/î fierce/ŏ pot/ ō go/ô paw, for/oi oil/ŏŏ book/ ōō boot/ou out/ŭ cut/û fur/ *th* the/th thin/hw which/zh vision/ ə ago, item, pencil, atom, circus

arranged to match the natural numbers in a one-to-one correspondence, the item that matches the number sixteen. **2.** One of sixteen equal parts of a unit, written $^1/_{16}$. **—six'teenth'** *adj. & adv.*

sixteenth note. A musical note that lasts half as long as an eighth note.

sixth |sĭksth| *n.* **1.** In a set of items arranged to match the natural numbers in a one-to-one correspondence, the item that matches the number six. **2.** One of six equal parts of a unit, written $^1/_6$. **3. a.** One of three musical intervals formed by tones that are six diatonic scale degrees apart. **b.** The sixth tone of a diatonic scale. **—sixth** *adj. & adv.*

six•ti•eth |sĭks'tē ĭth| *n.* **1.** In a set of items arranged to match the natural numbers in a one-to-one correspondence, the item that matches the number sixty. **2.** One of sixty equal parts of a unit, written $^1/_{60}$. **—six'ti•eth** *adj. & adv.*

six•ty |sĭks'tē| *n., pl.* **six•ties.** A number, written 60 in Arabic numerals, that is equal to the product of 6 × 10. It is the tenth positive integer after 50. **—six'ty** *adj. & pron.*

six•ty-fourth note |sĭks'tē fôrth'| *or* |-fōrth'|. A musical note that lasts half as long as a thirty-second note.

siz•a•ble |sī'zə bəl| *adj.* Of considerable dimension or size; fairly large. **—siz'a•ble•ness** *n.* **—siz'a•bly** *adv.*

size[1] |sīz| *n.* **1.** The physical dimensions, proportions, or extent of something. **2.** Any of a series of standard dimensions with which certain objects are manufactured: *A careful carpenter uses nails of the right size.* **3.** Considerable extent, amount, or dimensions: *no difficulties of any size.* **4.** *Informal.* The actual state of affairs; the true situation: *We had failed—that was the size of it.* *—v.* **sized, siz•ing. 1.** To arrange, classify, or distribute according to size: *a chart that sizes skirts according to waist measurements.* **2.** To make, cut, or shape according to a required size: *sized and waterproofed material for tents.* ***—phrasal verb.*** **size up. 1.** To make an estimate of: *sized up the situation.* **2.** To meet certain specifications or requirements.

size[2] |sīz| *n.* Any of several jellylike or sticky substances made from glue, wax, or clay and used as a filler or glaze for porous materials such as paper, cloth, or wall surfaces. *—v.* **sized, siz•ing.** To treat or coat with size or a similar material.

size•a•ble |sī'zə bəl| *adj.* A form of the word **sizable.**

sized |sīzd| *adj.* Having a particular or specified size: *various-sized basins; a medium-sized man.*

siz•ing |sī'zĭng| *n.* **1.** A substance used as a filler or glaze; size. **2.** The act or process of coating or treating something with size.

siz•zle |sĭz'əl| *v.* **siz•zled, siz•zling.** To make the hissing sound characteristic of frying fat. *—n.* A hissing sound.

S.J. Society of Jesus.

skate[1] |skāt| *n.* A boot, shoe, or metal frame having a bladelike metal runner or a set of four wheels mounted under it, used for moving rapidly over ice, pavement, etc.; an ice skate or roller skate. *—v.* **skat•ed, skat•ing.** To glide or move along on skates: *Let's skate to the corner.* **—skat'er** *n.*

skate[2] |skāt| *n.* Any of several ocean fishes related to the rays, having a broad, flat body with fins forming winglike extensions. [SEE NOTE & PICTURE]

skate•board |skāt'bôrd'| *or* |-bōrd'| *n.* A short, narrow board having a set of four roller-skate wheels mounted under it. **—skate'board'er** *n.* **—skate'board'ing** *n.*

skeet |skēt| *n.* A form of trapshooting in which clay targets are used to simulate birds in flight.

skein |skān| *n.* **1. a.** A length of thread, yarn, etc., wound in a long, loose coil. **b.** Something resembling this: *Skeins of mist floated above the lake.* **2.** A flock of flying geese or similar birds.

skel•e•tal |skĕl'ĭ təl| *adj.* Of a skeleton.

skel•e•ton |skĕl'ĭ tən| *n.* **1. a.** The internal supporting structure of a vertebrate, composed of bone and cartilage and serving also to protect some of the more delicate body tissues. **b.** The hard protective covering or supporting structure of many invertebrates, such as crustaceans, insects, or corals. **2.** Any supporting structure or framework. **3.** An outline or sketch: *the skeleton of the form of a business letter.* **4.** A very thin person or animal. ***—modifier:*** *a skeleton model.*

skeleton key. A key with a large part of the bit filed off so that it can open many different locks.

skep•tic |skĕp'tĭk'| *n.* A person who habitually questions or doubts the truth of what he hears, reads, etc.

skep•ti•cal |skĕp'tĭ kəl| *adj.* Of or characterized by skepticism; doubting or disbelieving: *a skeptical attitude.* **—skep'ti•cal•ly** *adv.*

skep•ti•cism |skĕp'tĭ sĭz'əm| *n.* A doubting or questioning state of mind.

sketch |skĕch| *n.* **1.** A rough preliminary drawing or painting: *a sketch of the park.* **2.** A brief composition or outline: *a biographical sketch.* **3.** A brief, light play, especially a comic one. *—v.* **1.** To make a sketch of: *sketch his face.* **2.** To make a sketch or sketches: *She loves to sketch in the park.* **—sketch'er** *n.*

sketch•y |skĕch'ē| *adj.* **sketch•i•er, sketch•i•est.** Lacking in completeness: *sketchy information.* **—sketch'i•ly** *adv.* **—sketch'i•ness** *n.*

skew |skyōō| *v.* To turn or place at an angle; slant. *—adj.* Turned or placed to one side.

skew•er |skyōō'ər| *n.* A long pin of wood or metal, used to hold or suspend meat during cooking. *—v.* To hold together or pierce with a skewer.

ski |skē| *n., pl.* **skis** or **ski.** One of a pair of long, narrow, flat runners of wood, metal, or plastic that are fastened to a boot or shoe for gliding or traveling over snow. ***—modifier:*** *ski boots.* *—v.* **skied, ski•ing, skis. 1.** To glide or move on skis: *He skis expertly.* **2.** To travel over on skis: *They skied a new trail.* **—ski'er** *n.*

skid |skĭd| *n.* **1.** The act or process of slipping or sliding over a surface: *The car went into a skid on the slippery pavement.* **2.** A plank, log, etc., often one of a pair, used as a support or track on which heavy objects are rolled or slid. **3.** A runner forming part of the landing gear of an aircraft, such as a helicopter. **4.** A shoe or wedge that applies pressure to a wheel to keep it from turning. *—v.* **skid•ded, skid•ding. 1.** To slip or slide out of control over a slippery surface, as an automobile. **2.** To slide over a surface without turning, as a wheel. **3.** To move (something) on a skid or skids.

skies |skīz| *n.* Plural of **sky.**

skiff |skĭf| *n.* A flat-bottomed rowboat with a pointed bow and a square stern.

skill |skĭl| *n.* **1.** Ability or proficiency; expertness: *her skill at plumbing.* **2.** An art, trade, or technique, especially one requiring use of the hands or body: *a carpenter's skills.*

skilled |skĭld| *adj.* **1.** Having or using skill; skillful: *a skilled hunter.* **2.** Requiring specialized ability or training: *a skilled occupation.*

skil•let |skĭl'ĭt| *n.* A **frying pan.**

skill•ful |skĭl'fəl| *adj.* **1.** Having or using skill; expert: *a skillful hunter.* **2.** Showing or requiring skill: *skillful violin playing.* **—skill'ful•ly** *adv.* **—skill'ful•ness** *n.*

skim |skĭm| *v.* **skimmed, skim•ming. 1. a.** To remove (floating matter) from a liquid: *skim cream off the top of the milk.* **b.** To remove floating matter from (a liquid): *skim milk.* **2.** To move, pass, or glide lightly and swiftly over (a surface): *The sailboat skimmed the lake.* **3.** To read, glance at, or consider superficially: *skim the chapter; skimming through a book.*

skim•mer |skĭm'ər| *n.* **1.** Something or someone that skims. **2.** A flat, ladlelike utensil used for skimming liquids. **3.** A sea bird with long, narrow wings and a long bill with a longer lower jaw used to skim the surface of the water for fish and other food. [SEE PICTURE]

skim milk. Milk from which the cream has been removed.

skimp |skĭmp| *v.* **1.** To do hastily, carelessly, or with poor material. **2.** To be extremely sparing or very thrifty with (something); scrimp: *skimp fabric in making a dress; skimp on the budget.*

skimp•y |skĭm'pē| *adj.* **skimp•i•er, skimp•i•est.** Inadequate in size or amount; scanty: *a skimpy meal.* **—skimp'i•ly** *adv.* **—skimp'i•ness** *n.*

skin |skĭn| *n.* **1.** The membranous tissue that forms the outer covering of the body of an animal. **2.** A hide or pelt removed from the body of an animal: *a tent made of buffalo skins stretched on poles.* **3.** An outer layer, covering, or coating, such as the peel or rind of fruit or the thin film that forms on the surface of boiled milk. **4.** A container for liquids made from an animal's skin. ***—modifier:*** *skin tents; a skin disease.* *—v.* **skinned, skin•ning. 1.** To remove the skin from: *skin a sheep.* **2.** To injure by scraping: *fell and skinned her knee.* **3.** To remove by or as if by peeling or stripping: *skinned off his damp shirt.* **4.** *Slang.* To cheat; swindle. **5.** *Slang.* To beat; whip. **—skin'less** *adj.*

Idioms. **by the skin of (one's) teeth.** By a very narrow margin; just barely. **save (one's) skin.** To escape harm or avoid death.

skin-dive |skĭn'dīv'| *v.* **-dived** or **-dove** |-dōv'|, **-div•ing.** To engage in skin diving.

skin diving. Underwater swimming in which the swimmer is equipped with flippers to aid in propelling himself, a mask that covers his eyes and nose, and a snorkel or scuba that allows him to breathe underwater. **—skin diver.**

skin•flint |skĭn'flĭnt'| *n.* A miser.

skink |skĭngk| *n.* Any of several lizards with a smooth, shiny body and short legs.

skin•ner |skĭn'ər| *n.* A person who strips, dresses, or sells animal skins.

skin•ny |skĭn'ē| *adj.* **skin•ni•er, skin•ni•est.** Very thin: *skinny legs.* **—skin'ni•ness** *n.*

skin•ny-dip |skĭn'ē dĭp'| *v.* **skin•ny-dipped, skin•ny-dip•ping.** *Informal.* To swim in the nude. **—skin'ny-dip'per** *n.*

skip |skĭp| *v.* **skipped, skip•ping. 1.** To move, hop, step, or trip lightly, as by taking two steps at a time with each foot. **2.** To jump lightly over: *skip rope.* **3.** To pass quickly from one point, subject, etc., to another: *skipping television channels searching for the right program.* **4.** To pass over; omit: *He skipped my name.* **5.** To be promoted in school beyond (the next grade or level): *I skipped the fourth grade. I skipped twice.* **6.** *Informal.* To leave hastily: *skip town.* *—n.* **1.** A gait in which hops and steps alternate. **2.** The act of skipping; an omission.

skip•per[1] |skĭp'ər| *n.* The captain of a ship, especially of a small one.

skip•per[2] |skĭp'ər| *n.* **1.** Someone or something that skips. **2.** Any of several butterflies with a rather stout, hairy body.

skir•mish |skûr'mĭsh| *n.* **1.** A minor encounter between small bodies of troops. **2.** Any minor conflict. *—v.* To engage in a skirmish.

skirt |skûrt| *n.* **1.** The part of a garment, such as a dress, coat, or robe, that hangs from the waist down. **2.** A separate garment that hangs from the waist and is not divided between the legs, worn by women and girls. **3.** Anything that hangs like a skirt, especially a ruffled or pleated piece of cloth covering the legs of a piece of furniture. *—v.* **1.** To form the border of, lie along, or surround: *The road skirted a wooded area.* **2.** To pass around rather than across or through: *We skirted the marshes.* **3.** To evade (a subject, topic, issue, etc.) in a roundabout way.

skit |skĭt| *n.* A short, usually humorous theatrical sketch.

skit•ter |skĭt'ər| *v.* To skip, glide, or move lightly or rapidly along a surface.

skit•tish |skĭt'ĭsh| *adj.* **1.** Excitable or nervous: *a skittish colt.* **2.** Frivolous in action or character; capricious or fickle: *a skittish young girl.* **—skit'tish•ly** *adv.* **—skit'tish•ness** *n.*

skit•tles |skĭt'lz| *n. (used with a singular verb).* A game, ninepins.

skul•dug•ger•y |skŭl dŭg'ə rē| *n.* A form of the word **skullduggery.**

skulk |skŭlk| *v.* To move about stealthily.

skull |skŭl| *n.* The part of the skeleton that forms the framework of the head, consisting of the bones that protect the brain and the bones of the face. ¶*These sound alike* **skull, scull.**

skull and crossbones. A representation of a human skull above two crossed bones, a symbol of death once used by pirates and now used as a warning label on poisons.

skull•cap |skŭl'kăp'| *n.* A small, close-fitting cap without a brim, sometimes worn indoors. [SEE PICTURE]

skull•dug•ger•y |skŭl dŭg'ə rē| *n.* Crafty deception or trickery.

skunk |skŭngk| *n.* **1.** An animal that has black and white fur and a bushy tail and can spray a bad-smelling liquid from glands near the base of the tail. **2.** *Slang.* A mean person. *—v. Slang.*

skimmer
By John James Audubon

skullcap

skunk
Striped skunk spraying

To defeat overwhelmingly, especially by keeping from scoring. [SEE PICTURE on p. 813]

sky |skī| *n., pl.* **skies. 1.** The upper atmosphere, seen as a hemisphere above the earth. **2.** The hemisphere of the celestial sphere that can be seen by an observer on the earth; the heavens: *stars visible in the night sky.* **3.** Often **skies.** The appearance of the upper atmosphere, especially with respect to weather: *threatening skies.*

sky•dive |skī'dīv'| *v.* **-dived** or **-dove** |-dōv'|, **-dived, -div•ing.** To jump from an airplane, performing various maneuvers before opening a parachute. **—sky'div'er** *n.*

sky-high |skī'hī'| *adv.* **1.** Exceptionally high: *junked cars stacked sky-high.* **2.** In a lavish or enthusiastic manner: *praising her virtues sky-high.* **3.** To pieces or in pieces; apart: *The bomb blew the bridge sky-high.* —*adj.* Exorbitantly high: *sky-high prices.*

sky•lark |skī'lärk'| *n.* A brownish European songbird that sings while high in flight. —*v.* To romp playfully; frolic.

sky•light |skī'līt'| *n.* An overhead window that admits daylight.

sky•line |skī'līn'| *n.* **1.** The line along which the earth and sky appear to meet; the horizon. **2.** The outline of a mountain range, group of buildings, etc., as seen against the sky on the horizon.

sky•rock•et |skī'rŏk'ĭt| *n.* A firework that ascends high into the air, where it explodes in a cascade of flares and sparks. —*v.* To rise rapidly or suddenly: *Prices skyrocketed.*

sky•scrap•er |skī'skrā'pər| *n.* A very tall building. [SEE PICTURE]

sky•ward |skī'wərd| *adv.* Also **sky•wards** |skī'wərdz|. Toward the sky: *turn skyward.* —*adj.: a skyward glance.*

sky•writ•ing |skī'rī'tĭng| *n.* The process of writing letters or words in the sky by releasing a visible vapor from an airplane. **—sky'writ'er** *n.*

slab |slăb| *n.* A broad, flat, and thick piece of something, as of cake, stone, or cheese.

slack[1] |slăk| *adj.* **slack•er, slack•est. 1.** Slow; dull; sluggish: *a slack pace.* **2.** Not busy: *the slack moments of the day.* **3.** Not tense or taut; loose: *a slack rope.* **4.** Careless; negligent: *a slack performance.* —*v.* To make or become slack; slacken. —*n.* **1.** A loose or slack part or portion of something: *take up some of the slack in the rope.* **2.** A period of little activity. **—slack'ness** *n.*

slack[2] |slăk| *n.* A mixture of chunks of coal, coal dust, and dirt that remains after coal has been screened.

slack•en |slăk'ən| *v.* **1.** To make or become slower; slow down: *The dogs slackened their pace. The speed of the sailboat slackened when the wind changed.* **2.** To make or become less vigorous or intense: *High rates slackened the demand for loans. Business slackened.*

slack•er |slăk'ər| *n.* A person who tries to avoid work or responsibility.

slacks |slăks| *pl.n.* Long trousers for casual wear, worn by both men and women.

slag |slăg| *n.* **1.** The glassy refuse that remains after a metal has been removed from an ore by smelting. **2.** Refuse from a volcano; scoria.

slain |slān|. Past participle of **slay.**

slake |slāk| *v.* **slaked, slak•ing. 1.** To lessen the force of; moderate: *slaking his anger.* **2.** To combine (lime) chemically with water, either directly or by exposure to moist air.

slaked lime. **Calcium hydroxide.**

sla•lom |slä'ləm| *n.* A skiing race down a zigzag course marked with poles.

slam[1] |slăm| *v.* **slammed, slam•ming. 1.** To shut forcefully and with a loud noise: *slam a door; shutters slamming in the wind.* **2.** To throw, drive, or strike forcefully and loudly: *slammed down the telephone receiver.* **3.** To make a forceful impact; crash: *The meteorite slammed into the side of a hill.* —*n.* **1.** An act of slamming. **2.** The noise of a forceful impact; a bang.

slam[2] |slăm| *n.* In certain card games, such as bridge, the winning of all the tricks, a **grand slam,** or all but one, a **little slam,** during the play of one hand.

slan•der |slăn'dər| *n.* **1.** A false statement uttered maliciously to damage someone's reputation. **2.** The act or crime of uttering such false statements. —*v.* To utter slander against (someone); defame. **—slan'der•er** *n.*

slan•der•ous |slăn'dər əs| *adj.* Making or containing false and damaging charges about people: *a slanderous speech; a slanderous person.* **—slan'der•ous•ly** *adv.*

slang |slăng| *n.* **1.** A kind of language occurring most often in casual speech, made up of words and special senses of words that name things with added vividness, humor, irreverence, or other connotation; for example, "flatfoot" for "policeman," "to rap" for "to talk," and "groovy" for "exciting" are slang terms. **2.** Language peculiar to a certain group of people; jargon: *surfers' slang.* —***modifier:*** *a slang word.*

slang•y |slăng'ē| *adj.* **slang•i•er, slang•i•est.** Like, containing, or using slang.

slant |slănt| *or* |slänt| *v.* **1.** To lie, extend, or turn at an angle from the horizontal or vertical; slope: *My handwriting slants to the right. Slant that board a bit more.* **2.** To move in an oblique course: *The ferryboat slanted across the river.* **3.** To present (news, information, etc.) in a way favorable to one's opinion; bias. —*n.* **1.** A sloping line, plane, direction, or course. **2.** The degree to which something slants: *Keep the slant of your letters uniform.* **3.** An attitude or approach. **4.** A tendency favorable to one side; a bias.

slap |slăp| *v.* **slapped, slap•ping. 1.** To strike sharply with the palm of the hand or some other flat or light object: *Grandpa slapped his knee and chuckled. I slapped at the mosquito but missed.* **2.** To knock against something with a sharp noise: *Waves slapped against the canoe.* **3.** To put or place swiftly and with a sharp noise: *slapping a gummed price tag on the package.* —*n.* **1. a.** A blow with the palm of the hand or some other flat or light object. **b.** The sound made by such a blow. **2.** An injury, as to one's pride.

slap•stick |slăp'stĭk'| *n.* A form of comedy marked by zany chases, collisions, crude practical jokes, and similar boisterous activities.

slash |slăsh| *v.* **1.** To cut or strike with a forceful, sweeping stroke or series of strokes: *slashed off a bunch of bananas with his machete; slashed at his opponent's throat.* **2.** To move by or as by forcefully cutting one's way: *We had to slash*

skyscraper
There is no precise definition of a **skyscraper,** but it is clearly an American invention. Chicago architects in the 1880's developed the design of iron and steel structural frames that made very tall commercial buildings possible. The photograph above shows the Tacoma Building (now demolished) in Chicago, designed by the firm of Holabird and Roche in 1886. The word **skyscraper** was first used in the late eighteenth century as a term for the topmost sail of the tallest square-rigged ships. Later it became a slang word for anything very high, such as a high hit in baseball. The first citation given by the *Dictionary of Americanisms* for **skyscraper** meaning "tall building" is from 1883.

ă pat/ā pay/â care/ä father/ĕ pet/ ē be/ĭ pit/ī pie/î fierce/ŏ pot/ ō go/ô paw, for/oi oil/ŏŏ book/ ōō boot/ou out/ŭ cut/û fur/ *th* the/th thin/hw which/zh vision/ ə ago, item, pencil, atom, circus

through dense jungle. **3.** To lash violently with or as with a whip. **4.** To criticize severely. **5.** To make a gash or gashes in: *The divers were careful not to slash their feet on coral.* **6.** To cut an ornamental slit or slits in (a garment or fabric). **7.** To reduce greatly: *slash prices for a sale.* —*n.* **1.** A forceful, sweeping stroke, as with a cutting instrument. **2.** A long cut on the skin or another surface; a gash. **3.** A sharp reduction: *making slashes in the national budget.* **4.** A diagonal mark (/) used in writing and printing.

slat |slăt| *n.* A narrow strip of metal or wood.

slate |slāt| *n.* **1.** A fine-grained metamorphic rock that splits into thin layers with smooth surfaces. **2.** A piece of such rock cut for use as a roofing material or a writing surface. **3.** A dark bluish gray. **4.** A writing tablet made of this or a similar material. **5.** A record of past performance: *starting with a clean slate.* **6.** A list, especially of political candidates of the same party. —***modifier:*** *a slate roof.* —*v.* **slat•ed, slat•ing.** **1.** To cover with slate: *slating a roof.* **2.** To assign a place to on a list or schedule.

slat•tern |slăt'ərn| *n.* A woman who is careless or sloppy in her appearance or personal habits. —**slat'tern•ly** *adv.*

slaugh•ter |slô'tər| *n.* **1.** The killing of animals for food. **2.** The brutal murder of many persons or animals; a massacre. **3.** *Informal.* A defeat by a wide margin: *The game ended in a slaughter.* —*v.* **1.** To butcher (an animal) for food. **2.** To kill brutally or in large numbers. **3.** *Informal.* To defeat by a wide margin. —**slaugh'ter•er** *n.*

slaugh•ter•house |slô'tər hous'| *n., pl.* **-hous•es** |-hou'sĭz|. A place where animals are butchered.

Slav |slăv| *or* |släv| *n.* A member of any of the peoples who speak a Slavic language.

slave |slāv| *n.* **1.** A person who is owned by and forced to work for someone else. **2.** A person completely controlled by a specified influence, emotion, etc.: *a slave to his appetites.* **3.** Any person who works very hard, especially in a lowly capacity. —***modifier:*** *slave labor.* —*v.* **slaved, slav•ing.** To work very hard: *housewives who slave over a hot stove.*

slav•er |slăv'ər| *or* |slā'vər| *v.* To let saliva dribble from the mouth; drool. —*n.* Saliva drooling from the mouth.

slav•er•y |slā'və rē| *or* |slāv'rē| *n.* **1.** The condition of being a slave; bondage. **2.** The practice of owning slaves. **3.** Hard work or subjection like that of a slave.

slave state. Often **Slave State.** Any of the states of the Union in which slavery was legal before the Civil War.

Slav•ic |slä'vĭk| *or* |slăv'ĭk| *adj.* **1.** Of the Slavs. **2.** Of a group of Indo-European languages including Russian, Czech, Bulgarian, Polish, and Serbo-Croatian. —*n.* The Slavic languages.

slav•ish |slā'vĭsh| *adj.* **1.** Like or befitting a slave; servile or submissive: *slavish devotion.* **2.** Showing no originality; blindly imitative: *a slavish copy of another artist's work.* —**slav'ish•ly** *adv.* —**slav'ish•ness** *n.*

slaw |slô| *n.* A salad of shredded cabbage.

slay |slā| *v.* **slew** |slōō|, **slain** |slān|, **slay•ing.** To kill violently, as in battle. —**slay'er** *n.* ¶*These sound alike* **slay, sleigh.**

slea•zy |slē'zē| *adj.* **slea•zi•er, slea•zi•est.** **1.** Thin and loosely woven; flimsy: *a coat with a sleazy lining.* **2.** Of poor quality; cheap; shoddy: *sleazy furniture.* **3.** Vulgar; disreputable: *a sleazy tavern.* —**slea'zi•ly** *adv.* —**slea'zi•ness** *n.*

sled |slĕd| *n.* **1.** A vehicle mounted on runners, used for carrying people or loads over snow and ice; a sledge. **2.** A light frame mounted on runners, used by children for coasting over snow and ice. —*v.* **sled•ded, sled•ding.** **1.** To carry on a sled. **2.** To ride on a sled. [SEE PICTURE]

sledge[1] |slĕj| *n.* A vehicle on runners, drawn by horses, dogs, or reindeer and used for transporting loads across snow and ice.

sledge[2] |slĕj| *n.* A sledgehammer.

sledge•ham•mer |slĕj'hăm'ər| *n.* A long, heavy hammer, usually wielded with both hands, used for driving posts and other heavy work. —*v.* To use or strike with a sledgehammer.

sleek |slēk| *adj.* **sleek•er, sleek•est.** **1.** Smooth and glossy: *the sleek coat of a horse.* **2.** Neat, trim, and graceful in appearance: *a sleek racing car.* **3.** Well-fed; thriving: *a sleek pig ready for the market.* —**sleek'ly** *adv.* —**sleek'ness** *n.*

sleep |slēp| *n.* **1.** A natural condition of rest, occurring periodically in many animals, that is characterized by lessened nervous and physical activity, unconsciousness, and lessened responsiveness to external stimuli. **2.** A period of this form of rest. **3.** Any similar condition of inactivity, such as hibernation or unconsciousness. —*v.* **slept** |slĕpt|, **sleep•ing.** **1.** To be in or pass into a state of sleep. **2.** To be inactive or inattentive: *The sudden question caught me sleeping.* **3.** To spend or get rid of in a period of sleep: *slept away the afternoon.* **4.** To provide with beds: *This cabin sleeps four.*

Idioms. **sleep on.** To consider (a problem, decision, etc.) overnight before committing oneself. **sleep with.** To have sexual intercourse with.

sleep•er |slē'pər| *n.* **1.** A person or animal that sleeps: *a late sleeper; a sound sleeper.* **2.** A sleeping car on a train. **3.** *Informal.* Something, such as a movie, play, or contestant, that gets little attention at first but then becomes unexpectedly popular or successful.

sleeping bag. A large, warmly lined bag in which a person may sleep outdoors.

sleeping car. A railroad car with small bedrooms for overnight passengers.

sleeping sickness. An often fatal, infectious disease of human beings and animals, common in tropical Africa. It is caused by parasitic protozoans, spread by the bite of the tsetse fly, and has symptoms that include fever and extreme sluggishness.

sleep•less |slēp'lĭs| *adj.* **1.** Unable to sleep; restless or insomniac. **2.** Without sleep; wakeful: *sleepless nights.* —**sleep'less•ly** *adv.* —**sleep'less•ness** *n.*

sleep•walk•ing |slēp'wô'kĭng| *n.* A mental or nervous disorder in which the person affected walks about while asleep or in a sleeplike condition; somnambulism. —**sleep'walk'er** *n.*

sleep•y |slē'pē| *adj.* **sleep•i•er, sleep•i•est.** **1.** Ready for or needing sleep. **2.** Dulled or softened by the nearness of sleep: *sleepy eyes; a sleepy voice.* **3.** Quiet; inactive: *a sleepy river town.* —**sleep'i•ly** *adv.* —**sleep'i•ness** *n.*

sled
Above: Dog sled
Below: Children with sled

sleigh

slide

ă pat/ā pay/â care/ä father/ĕ pet/ ē be/ĭ pit/ī pie/î fierce/ŏ pot/ ō go/ô paw, for/oi oil/o͝o book/ o͞o boot/ou out/ŭ cut/û fur/ *th* the/th thin/hw which/zh vision/ ə ago, item, pencil, atom, circus

sleep•y•head |slē′pē hĕd′| *n. Informal.* A sleepy person.

sleet |slēt| *n.* **1.** Water that falls to the earth in the form of frozen or partially frozen raindrops. **2.** A thin coating of ice that forms on trees, road surfaces, etc., as a result of sleet or freezing rain. —*v.* To shower sleet.

sleeve |slēv| *n.* **1.** The part of a garment that covers all or part of the arm. **2.** A case, covering, or shell into which a machine part or other piece of apparatus fits. —*v.* **sleeved, sleev•ing.** To furnish or fit with a sleeve or sleeves. —**sleeve′less** *adj.*

***Idiom.* up (one's) sleeve.** Hidden but ready to be used: *Be careful, he may have more tricks up his sleeve.*

sleigh |slā| *n.* A light vehicle on low runners for use on snow or ice, having one or more seats and usually drawn by a horse. —***modifier:*** *a sleigh ride; sleigh bells.* —*v.* To ride in a sleigh. ¶ *These sound alike* **sleigh, slay.** [SEE PICTURE]

sleight of hand |slīt|. Tricks or feats performed by jugglers or magicians so quickly that one cannot see how they are done.

slen•der |slĕn′dər| *adj.* **slen•der•er, slen•der•est. 1.** Having little width as compared to length or height; thin; slim: *a slender church spire; a slender girl.* **2.** Small in amount, extent, etc.: *slender hopes.* —**slen′der•ly** *adv.* —**slen′der•ness** *n.*

slept |slĕpt|. Past tense and past participle of **sleep.**

sleuth |slo͞oth| *n.* A detective. —*v.* To search for information as a detective does.

slew[1] |slo͞o| *n. Informal.* A large number; a lot: *caught a whole slew of fish.* ¶ *These sound alike* **slew, slough**[1]**.**

slew[2] |slo͞o| *v.* **1.** To turn or twist sideways: *A board pushed straight down in water invariably slews off violently to one side.* **2.** To rotate. ¶ *These sound alike* **slew, slough**[1]**.**

slew[3] |slo͞o|. Past tense of **slay.** ¶ *These sound alike* **slew, slough**[1]**.**

slice |slīs| *n.* **1.** A thin, broad piece cut from something: *a slice of bread.* **2.** A share; portion: *a slice of the profits.* **3.** A flight of a struck baseball, golf ball, etc., that curves to the right, or, if the player is left-handed, to the left. —*v.* **sliced, slic•ing. 1.** To cut into slices: *slice a loaf of bread.* **2.** To cut from a larger piece: *slicing off a piece of salami.* **3.** To cut with or as with strokes of a sharp knife: *The ship sliced through the ice field.* **4.** To divide into portions. **5.** To hit (a ball) with a slice. —**slic′er** *n.*

slick |slĭk| *adj.* **slick•er, slick•est. 1.** Having a smooth, glossy surface: *slick paper.* **2.** Smooth and slippery: *slick ice.* **3.** Acting or done with skill and ease; deft; adroit: *a slick tennis shot.* **4.** Shrewd; crafty: *a slick business deal.* **5.** Attractive at first, but really shallow or insincere: *a slick writing style.* —*v.* To make smooth and glossy: *Paul slicked down his hair with pomade.* —*n.* A smooth or slippery place, especially a stretch of water covered with a film of oil.

slick•er |slĭk′ər| *n.* **1.** A long, shiny, loose-fitting waterproof raincoat, usually made of oilskin. **2.** *Informal.* A person with stylish clothing and fancy manners: *a city slicker.*

slide |slīd| *v.* **slid** |slĭd|, **slid** or **slid•den** |slĭd′n|, **slid•ing. 1. a.** To move smoothly over a surface while maintaining continuous contact. **b.** To cause to move in this way: *The movers slid the chair into the room.* **2.** To move or pass quietly. **3.** To move out of place or control; slip. **4.** In baseball, to drop down and skid, usually feet first, into a base to avoid being tagged out. —*n.* **1.** A sliding action or movement. **2.** A smooth surface or track, usually inclined, along which people or things can slide. **3.** An image, usually photographic, formed on a transparent piece of material for projection on a screen. **4.** A small glass plate on which things are placed or mounted for examination by microscope. [SEE PICTURE]

slide rule. A device that consists of two scaled rules arranged to slide along each other in a way that is mechanically equivalent to the operation of addition, and having scales that correspond to the logarithms of numbers, allowing its use in performing multiplication, division, and more complex mathematical operations.

sli•er |slī′ər| *adj.* A comparative of **sly.**

sli•est |slī′ĭst| *adj.* A superlative of **sly.**

slight |slīt| *adj.* **slight•er, slight•est. 1.** Small in amount or degree; meager: *a slight trace of acid; a slight change in temperature.* **2.** Small in size or proportions; slender or delicate: *a slight, stooping figure.* **3.** Of little importance; trifling: *a slight misunderstanding.* —*v.* **1.** To underestimate: *a politician who slights the intelligence of the voters.* **2.** To snub or insult. **3.** To neglect: *Randy's been slighting his schoolwork.* —*n.* An act of slighting, especially an insult to one's pride or self-esteem. —**slight′ly** *adv.*

slim |slĭm| *adj.* **slim•mer, slim•mest. 1.** Thin; slender: *a slim person.* **2.** Small in substance or amount; scant: *a slim oatmeal diet; a slim chance.* —*v.* **slimmed, slim•ming.** To make or become thinner: *slimming his waist with exercises. The champ has slimmed down since his last fight.*

slime |slīm| *n.* **1.** Thick, sticky, slippery mud or any similar substance. **2.** A slippery mucous substance secreted by the skins of certain animals, such as fishes, slugs, frogs, etc.

slime mold. An organism that in one stage of its development forms a slimy, moving mass of protoplasm and in another stage forms a fungus-like growth that produces spores.

slim•y |slī′mē| *adj.* **slim•i•er, slim•i•est. 1.** Of, resembling, covered with, or consisting of slime: *a slimy substance; slimy eels.* **2.** Unpleasantly suggestive of slime; filthy; vile. —**slim′i•ness** *n.*

sling |slĭng| *n.* **1.** A looped belt, rope, or chain in which loads are placed to be hoisted. **2.** An adjustable strap for securing and carrying something: *a shoulder sling on a rifle.* **3.** A band of cloth looped around the neck to support an injured arm or hand. **4. a.** A weapon made from a looped strap in which a stone is whirled and then let fly. **b.** A slingshot. —*v.* **slung** |slŭng|, **sling•ing. 1.** To raise, lower, or shift (a load) in a sling. **2.** To place or carry in a sling. **3.** To hurl with a swinging motion of the arm. **4.** To shoot; cast: *sling an arrow.*

sling•shot |slĭng′shŏt′| *n.* A Y-shaped stick with an elastic strap attached to the prongs, used for shooting small stones.

slink |slĭngk| *v.* **slunk** |slŭngk|, **slink•ing.** To move in a quiet, furtive way.

slip¹ |slĭp| *v.* **slipped, slip•ping. 1.** To move smoothly and easily; slide or glide. **2.** To pass gradually, easily, or unnoticed: *weeks slipping away.* **3.** To place or be placed smoothly into an opening: *slipped her ballot into the box.* **4.** To put on or take off quickly and easily: *slip on a sweater; slipped off his shoes.* **5.** To lose one's balance or footing on a slippery surface. **6.** To shift away from a proper place or position: *The beams supporting the mine's roof were beginning to slip.* **7.** To escape from a hold or grip: *The dog was trying to slip out of its collar.* **8.** To get loose or free from: *slipped the guard and made a run for it.* **9.** To release; unfasten: *slip a knot.* **10.** To decline in ability or performance: *His work is slipping.* **11.** To make a mistake: *Everyone slipped up on the last question.* —*n.* **1.** The act of slipping, especially: **a.** A loss of one's balance or footing. **b.** A shift away from a proper place or condition. **2.** The amount by which or the degree to which something slips. **3.** A decline, especially a slight one: *a slip in stock prices.* **4.** A small mistake in conduct or speech: *a slip of the tongue.* **5.** A narrow docking place for a ship. **6.** A woman's undergarment made like a low-cut, sleeveless dress with shoulder straps or like a skirt. **7.** A pillowcase.

***Idioms.* give (someone) the slip.** *Informal.* To escape from. **let slip.** To say unintentionally or thoughtlessly. **slip one over on.** *Informal.* To hoodwink; deceive; dupe.

slip² |slĭp| *n.* **1.** A small piece or strip, especially of paper: *a sales slip.* **2.** A young, slender person or a small, frail thing: *A slip of a boy was leading the big horse.* **3.** A part of a plant cut or broken off for planting or grafting; a cutting.

slip•cov•er |**slĭp'**kŭv'ər| *n.* A fitted cover that can be easily put on or taken off a chair, sofa, etc.

slip•knot |**slĭp'**nŏt'| *n.* **1.** A knot made so that it can slip easily along the rope around which it is tied. **2.** A knot that can be untied simply by pulling or jerking one end of the rope.

slip-on |**slĭp'**ŏn'| *or* |-ôn'| *n.* A piece of clothing, such as a blouse, glove, or shoe, that is easily slipped on and off. —***modifier:*** *slip-on gloves.*

slip•per |**slĭp'**ər| *n.* A light, low-cut shoe that may be slipped on and off easily.

slip•per•y |**slĭp'**ə rē| *adj.* **slip•per•i•er, slip•per•i•est. 1.** Tending to slip or cause slipping, as a surface that is oily or wet. **2.** Hard to capture or pin down; evasive: *a slippery character.* —**slip'per•i•ness** *n.*

slip•shod |**slĭp'shŏd'**| *adj.* **1.** Done poorly or hastily; careless. **2.** Untidy in appearance.

slip-up |**slĭp'**ŭp'| *n. Informal.* A mistake.

slit |slĭt| *n.* A long, narrow cut, tear, or opening: *slits between the boards of a fence; the slit in a piggy bank.* —*v.* **slit, slit•ting. 1.** To cut a slit in. **2.** To cut into long, parallel strips: *slitting the ends of a ribbon.* —**slit'ter** *n.*

slith•er |**slĭth'**ər| *v.* To move along by gliding, as a snake does.

sliv•er |**slĭv'**ər| *n.* A sharp-ended, thin piece, as of wood or glass; a splinter. —*v.* To split or cut into thin pieces.

slob |slŏb| *n. Informal.* A dirty, slovenly person.

slob•ber |**slŏb'**ər| *v.* **1.** To let saliva or food dribble from the mouth. **2.** To express emotion in an overexcited or exaggerated way; gush. —*n.* Saliva or food spilled from the mouth.

sloe |slō| *n.* **1.** A small, tart, blackish, plumlike fruit. **2.** A thorny shrub that bears such fruit. ¶*These sound alike* **sloe, slow.**

slo•gan |**slō'**gən| *n.* **1.** A phrase expressing the aims or nature of an enterprise, team, school, army, or other group, and repeated by the group's supporters to encourage each other and to gain converts; a motto: *President Wilson's campaign of 1916 was based on the slogan "He kept us out of war."* **2.** A phrase used to advertise a commercial product or service.

sloop |slo͞op| *n.* A single-masted fore-and-aft-rigged sailing vessel. [See Picture]

slop |slŏp| *n.* **1.** Watery mud or a similar substance. **2.** Spilled liquid or food. **3.** Unappetizing, watery food. **4.** Often **slops.** Waste food fed to animals; swill. **5.** Careless, gushy writing or speech. —*v.* **slopped, slop•ping. 1.** To spill, flow, or spread messily: *Soup slopped over the plates as the ship rocked. He just slopped the paint on the wall.* **2.** To walk with a heavy, noisy tread, as through mud or puddles.

slope |slōp| *v.* **sloped, slop•ing.** To incline upward or downward; be or make slanted. —*n.* **1.** Any inclined line, plane, surface, direction, etc. **2.** A stretch of ground forming a natural or artificial incline. **3. a.** A deviation from the horizontal plane or direction. **b.** The measure of such a deviation: *a slope of 20 degrees.*

slop•py |**slŏp'**ē| *adj.* **slop•pi•er, slop•pi•est. 1.** Like slop; watery and disagreeable: *a sloppy mixture of flour, paste, and coloring.* **2.** Covered or spattered with watery mud or slush; muddy. **3.** Rainy: *sloppy weather.* **4.** Messy; untidy: *a sloppy dresser; a sloppy closet.* **5.** Carelessly done; full of oversights or mistakes: *a sloppy research job.* **6.** *Informal.* Muddled with too much sentiment; gushy: *a rather sloppy declaration of love.* —**slop'pi•ly** *adv.* —**slop'pi•ness** *n.*

slosh |slŏsh| *v.* To flounder or splash, as in water or another liquid or in a container.

slot |slŏt| *n.* **1.** A long, narrow groove, opening, or notch in something. **2.** *Informal.* Any suitable position or niche: *a slot on the executive level.* —*v.* **slot•ted, slot•ting.** To cut or make a slot or slots in.

sloth |slōth| *or* |slôth| *or* |slŏth| *n.* **1.** Laziness. **2.** A slow-moving tropical American animal that lives in trees and hangs upside-down from branches, holding on with its claws.[See Picture & See Note on p. 818]

sloth•ful |**slōth'**fəl| *or* |**slôth'**-| *or* |**slŏth'**-| *adj.* Sluggishly idle; lazy. —**sloth'ful•ly** *adv.*

slouch |slouch| *v.* To sit, stand, or walk with an awkward, bent posture. —*n.* **1.** An awkward, bent posture, especially one that is habitual. **2.** A lazy or incompetent person.

slough¹ |slo͞o| *or* |slou| *n.* **1.** A hollow or depression in the ground, usually filled with mud or mire. **2.** A stagnant swamp, bog, marsh, etc. ¶*These sound alike* **slough¹, slew.**

slough² |slŭf| *v.* To cast off or come off; shed: *The snake sloughed its old skin. The scab on his skinned knee sloughed off.*

Slo•vak |**slō'**văk'| *or* |-väk'| *n.* **1.** A member of one of the two peoples of Czechoslovakia. The other people are the Czechs. **2.** The Slavic lan-

sloop
The *Intrepid,* winner of the America's Cup in 1967

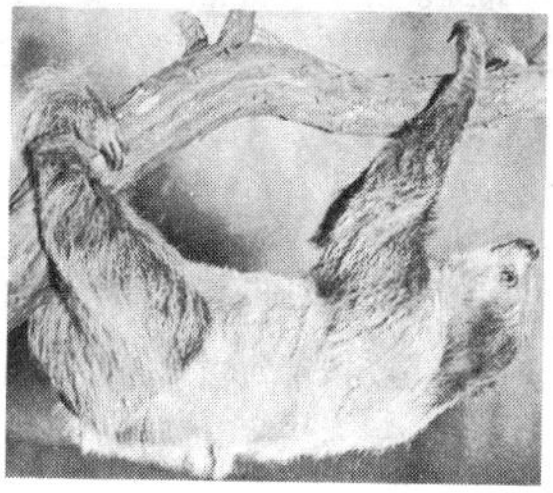

sloth
Two-toed sloth

guage of this people. —*adj.* Of the Slovaks or their language.

slov•en•ly |slŭv'ən lē| *adj.* **slov•en•li•er, slov•en•li•est. 1.** Not neat: *slovenly garments.* **2.** Careless: *slovenly work.* —**slov'en•li•ness** *n.*

slow |slō| *adj.* **slow•er, slow•est. 1.** Not moving or able to move quickly; proceeding at a low speed: *a slow car.* **2.** Taking or requiring a long time or more time than usual: *a slow, leisurely dinner; a slow worker.* **3. a.** Registering behind the correct time: *My watch is slow.* **b.** Tardy: *The train is ten minutes slow.* **4.** Sluggish; inactive: *Business is slow.* **5.** Mentally dull; stupid: *a slow man.* —*adv.* **slow•er, slow•est.** In a slow manner; not quickly or rapidly. —*v.* To make or become slow or slower: *The wind slowed the car. The pace slowed.* —***phrasal verb.*** **slow down** (or **up**). To go or cause to go slowly or more slowly. ¶*These sound alike* **slow, sloe.** —**slow'ly** *adv.* —**slow'ness** *n.*

slow•down |slō'doun'| *n.* A slowing down, especially an intentional slowing down of production by labor or management.

slow motion. A motion-picture technique in which the action as projected appears to be slower than the original action. —***modifier:*** **(slow-motion):** *a slow-motion scene.*

slow•poke |slō'pōk'| *n. Informal.* A person who works, acts, or moves slowly.

sludge |slŭj| *n.* **1.** Mire, mud, etc., covering the ground or forming a deposit, as on a river bed. **2.** Slushy matter such as that formed from treatment of sewage or collected in boilers.

slue[1] |slo͞o| *n.* A form of the word **slough** (swamp).

slue[2] |slo͞o| *v.* **slued, slu•ing.** A form of the word **slew** (to turn).

slug[1] |slŭg| *n.* **1.** A bullet. **2.** A small metal disk inserted, often illegally, in a dial telephone or in a turnstile in place of a coin.

slug[2] |slŭg| *n.* A soft-bodied land animal related to the snails but having no shell. [SEE NOTE & PICTURE]

slug[3] |slŭg|. *Informal. v.* **slugged, slug•ging.** To strike hard, especially with the fist. —*n.* A hard blow, as with the fist. —**slug'ger** *n.*

slug•gard |slŭg'ərd| *n.* A lazy, idle person.

slug•gish |slŭg'ĭsh| *adj.* **1.** Showing little activity or movement; slow: *a sluggish stream.* **2.** Lacking in alertness; dull; lazy: *a sluggish response.* **3.** Slow to perform or respond: *a sluggish child.* —**slug'gish•ly** *adv.* —**slug'gish•ness** *n.*

sluice |slo͞os| *n.* **1.** A man-made channel for water with a gate to regulate the flow. **2.** The gate used in this way. **3.** An artificial channel for carrying off excess water. **4.** An inclined trough, as for floating logs or separating gold ore. —*v.* **sluiced, sluic•ing. 1.** To wash with a sudden flow of water; flush. **2.** To draw off or let out by a sluice.

slum |slŭm| *n.* Often **the slums.** A dirty, overcrowded district inhabited by the poor. —***modifier:*** *slum buildings.* —*v.* **slummed, slum•ming.** To visit a slum, as for curiosity or amusement.

slum•ber |slŭm'bər| *v.* **1.** To sleep or doze. **2.** To be calm, lie dormant, etc.: *The city slumbers.* —*n.* Sleep. —**slum'ber•er** *n.*

slump |slŭmp| *v.* **1.** To decline or sink suddenly: *Business slumped badly during the spring.* **2.** To sag; slouch: *slumped in her chair.* —*n.* **1.** A sudden decline: *His pitching went into a slump.* **2.** A drooping or slouching posture.

slung |slŭng|. Past tense and past participle of **sling.**

slunk |slŭngk|. Past tense and past participle of **slink.**

slur |slûr| *v.* **slurred, slur•ring. 1.** To pass over or pronounce carelessly: *slur words.* **2.** To speak badly of; disparage. **3.** To pass from each to the next of (a series of musical tones) smoothly and without a break. —*n.* **1.** A disparaging remark. **2. a.** A curved line connecting a series of written musical notes to indicate that they are to be played or sung legato. **b.** A series of tones played or sung in this way.

slurp |slûrp| *v.* To eat or drink (something) noisily.

slush |slŭsh| *n.* **1.** Partially melted snow or ice. **2.** Soft mud; mire.

slut |slŭt| *n.* **1.** A dirty, slovenly woman. **2.** An immoral woman.

sly |slī| *adj.* **sli•er** or **sly•er, sli•est** or **sly•est. 1.** Stealthily clever; cunning: *sly as a fox.* **2.** Secretive or underhand: *a sly trick.* **3.** Playfully mischievous; roguish: *a sly wink.* —**sly'ly** *adv.* —**sly'ness** *n.*

Idiom. **on the sly.** Secretly.

Sm The symbol for the element samarium.

smack[1] |smăk| *v.* **1.** To make a sharp sound by pressing (the lips) together and opening them quickly. **2.** To kiss noisily. **3.** To slap or bump with a loud sound: *Smack him. He smacked into the dresser.* —*n.* **1.** The sound made by smacking the lips. **2.** A noisy kiss. **3.** A sharp blow or loud slap. —*adv.* **1.** With a smack: *She flopped smack on her elbow.* **2.** Directly: *fell smack in the middle of the tulips.* [SEE NOTE]

smack[2] |smăk| *n.* **1.** A distinctive flavor or hint. **2.** A suggestion or trace. —*v.* —**smack of.** To taste or be suggestive of. [SEE NOTE]

smack[3] |smăk| *n.* A fore-and-aft-rigged fishing vessel, especially one fitted with a well for live fish. [SEE NOTE]

small |smôl| *adj.* **small•er, small•est. 1.** Comparatively less in size, number, quantity, or extent; little: *a small car.* **2.** Limited in importance; trivial: *a small matter.* **3.** Engaged in a business or other activity on a limited scale: *a small farmer.* **4.** Little of mind or character; petty: *That was small of her.* **5.** Soft; low: *a small voice.* —*n.* Something smaller than the rest: *the small of the back.* —**small'ness** *n.*

small arms. Firearms carried in the hand.

small fry. *Informal.* Young or small children.

small intestine. The part of the alimentary canal that extends from the outlet of the stomach to the beginning of the large intestine.

small•pox |smôl'pŏks'| *n.* A serious, often fatal, highly infectious disease caused by viruses, having symptoms that include chills, fever, and headache, followed by the eruption of pimples that form pus, and develop into pockmarks.

smart |smärt| *adj.* **smart•er, smart•est. 1.** Mentally alert; bright: *a smart woman.* **2.** Sharp and quick; energetic: *a smart pace.* **3.** Fashionable; elegant: *a smart new coat; smart hotels.* —*v.* To cause to feel a stinging pain: *My leg began to smart from the hornet's sting.* —*n.* A stinging

slug[2]

slug[2]/sloth

Slug[2] *was* slugge *in Middle English, and it originally meant "any slow-moving person or thing"; in the eighteenth century it became the name of the animal, but the earlier general meaning is preserved in* **sluggard** *and* **sluggish.** *The case of the sloth is rather similar;* **sloth** *is a regular noun formed from* **slow** *(like* **width** *from* **wide***); the animal, first seen by Europeans in the sixteenth century, seemed to be "slowness" personified.*

smack[1-2-3]

Smack[1] *is from Middle Low German* smacken, *"to taste," also "to make a smacking noise with the lips when tasting something."* **Smack**[2] *was Old English* smæc, *"flavor, taste"; it is related to* **smack**[1]**. Smack**[3] *is from Dutch* smak, *"fishing boat."*

ă pat/ā pay/â care/ä father/ĕ pet/ē be/ĭ pit/ī pie/î fierce/ŏ pot/ō go/ô paw, for/oi oil/o͝o book/o͞o boot/ou out/ŭ cut/û fur/*th* **the**/th **thin**/hw **which**/**zh** vision/ə ago, item, pencil, atom, circus pain. —**smart'ly** *adv.* —**smart'ness** *n.*

smart al•eck |ăl'ĭk|. A cocky, self-assured person who acts as if he knew everything.

smart•en |smär'tn| *v.* To make or become smart or smarter: *smarten him up; smarten his clothes.*

smash |smăsh| *v.* **1.** To break or be broken into pieces: *smash an egg. The glass window smashed.* **2.** To throw, move, or strike violently and suddenly: *The wind smashed the tree into the house.* **3.** To destroy or defeat completely: *The troops smashed the surprise attack.* —*n.* **1.** The act or sound of smashing. **2.** A collision; a crash. **3.** *Informal.* A total success: *The show was a smash.* —**smash'er** *n.*

smash•ing |smăsh'ĭng| *adj. Informal.* Unusually fine; wonderful: *a smashing time at the party.*

smash•up |smăsh'ŭp'| *n.* **1.** A total collapse; a failure. **2.** A serious collision; a wreck.

smat•ter•ing |smăt'ər ĭng| *n.* Superficial or piecemeal knowledge: *a smattering of Latin.*

smear |smîr| *v.* **1.** To spread, cover, or stain with a sticky or greasy substance: *Soot smeared the windowsill. This lipstick smears easily.* **2.** To blacken the reputation of. —*n.* **1.** A stain or smudge made by smearing. **2.** An attempt to blacken someone's reputation; slander. **3.** A substance or preparation placed on a slide for microscopic study.

smell |smĕl| *v.* **smelled** or **smelt** |smĕlt|, **smell•ing. 1.** To detect or notice the odor of (something) by means of sense organs located in the nose and the nerves associated with them: *smell smoke.* **2. a.** To have or give off an odor. **b.** To have or give off an unpleasant odor; stink. —*n.* **1.** The sense by which odors are perceived; the ability to smell. **2.** The odor of something; scent. **3.** The act of smelling or an example of smelling.

smelling salts. Any of several preparations based on spirits of ammonia, sniffed to relieve faintness, dizziness, etc.

smell•y |smĕl'ē| *adj.* **smell•i•er, smell•i•est.** *Informal.* Having an unpleasant odor.

smelt[1] |smĕlt| *v.* **1.** To melt or fuse (ores) in order to extract the metals they contain. **2.** To undergo such melting or fusing, as an ore does. [SEE NOTE]

smelt[2] |smĕlt| *n., pl.* **smelts** or **smelt.** Any of several small, silvery, saltwater or freshwater fishes used as food. [SEE NOTE]

smelt[3] |smĕlt|. A past tense and past participle of **smell.**

smelt•er |smĕl'tər| *n.* **1. a.** An apparatus or device for smelting ore. **b.** An establishment for smelting. **2.** Someone whose work is smelting.

smid•gen, also **smid•geon** |smĭj'ən| *n.* A very small quantity; a bit: *not a smidgen of snow.*

smile |smīl| *n.* A facial expression formed by an upward curving of the corners of the mouth and indicating pleasure, affection, amusement, etc. —*v.* **smiled, smil•ing. 1.** To have or form a smile. **2.** To express favor or approval: *smile at her attempts.* —**smil'er** *n.*

smirch |smûrch| *v.* **1.** To soil, stain, or dirty. **2.** To dishonor or disgrace: *smirch her reputation.* —*n.* Something that smirches; a blot or stain.

smirk |smûrk| *v.* To smile in an obnoxious or simpering manner. —*n.* A smile made in such a way. —**smirk'er** *n.*

smite |smīt| *v.* **smote** |smōt|, **smit•ten** |smĭt'n| or **smote, smit•ing. 1.** To inflict a heavy blow on: *smite the enemy.* **2.** To kill by striking: *The Lord smote Pharaoh's eldest son.* **3.** To affect or afflict suddenly: *smitten with love. He was smitten with a disease.*

smith |smĭth| *n.* A person who forges and shapes metal; a blacksmith.

Smith |smĭth|. **1. John.** 1580–1631. English colonist in Virginia. **2. Joseph.** 1805–1844. American religious leader; founder of the Church of Jesus Christ of Latter-day Saints.

smith•er•eens |smĭth'ə **rēnz'**| *pl.n.* Splintered pieces; bits: *smashed the vase to smithereens.*

smith•y |smĭth'ē| *or* |smĭ*th*'ē| *n., pl.* **smith•ies.** The shop of a blacksmith; a forge.

smit•ten |smĭt'n|. A past participle of **smite.**

smock |smŏk| *n.* A garment made like a long, loose shirt and worn over other clothes to protect them. —*v.* To clothe in a smock.

smog |smŏg| *or* |smôg| *n.* A fog that has become polluted with smoke. [SEE NOTE]

smoke |smōk| *n.* **1.** A mixture of carbon dioxide, water vapor, and various other gases, usually containing small suspended particles of soot or other solids and resulting from incomplete burning of materials such as wood, coal, etc. **2.** A mixture consisting of fine particles suspended in a gas. **3.** The act of smoking tobacco or any material of plant origin. **4.** *Informal.* A cigarette, cigar, etc. —*v.* **smoked, smok•ing. 1.** To give off or produce smoke or a substance like smoke, especially in excessive amounts. **2.** To draw in and blow out smoke from (a cigarette, cigar, pipe, etc.). **3.** To preserve (meat or fish) by exposing to wood smoke. —***phrasal verb.* smoke out.** To force (someone or something) out of hiding by or as if by the use of smoke.

smoke•house |smōk'hous'| *n., pl.* **-hous•es** |-hou'sĭz|. An enclosure in which meat is cured by exposing it to smoke.

smoke•less |smōk'lĭs| *adj.* Producing or giving off little or no smoke.

smok•er |smō'kər| *n.* **1.** A person who smokes. **2.** A railroad car in which smoking is permitted. **3.** An informal social gathering for men.

smoke screen. A mass of artificial smoke used to conceal troop operations from the enemy.

smoke•stack |smōk'stăk'| *n.* A large chimney or vertical pipe through which smoke or other waste gases or vapors are discharged.

smok•y |smō'kē| *adj.* **smok•i•er, smok•i•est. 1.** Producing or giving off smoke in large quantities: *a smoky furnace.* **2.** Mixed or polluted with smoke: *smoky air.* —**smok'i•ness** *n.*

smol•der |smōl'dər| *v.* **1.** To burn and produce heat, some smoke, and no visible flame. **2.** To burn inwardly, especially to have pent-up anger.

smooth |smōō*th*| *adj.* **smooth•er, smooth•est. 1.** Having a surface free from irregularities; not rough; even: *smooth skin.* **2.** Having a fine consistency or texture: *the smooth side of the fabric.* **3.** Having an even or gentle motion; free from jolts, jerks, etc.: *a smooth ride.* **4.** Agreeable; mild: *a smooth manner.* **5.** Flattering; ingratiating: *a smooth talker.* —*v.* **1.** To make smooth: *smooth out the wrinkles in a dress.* **2.** To make calm; soothe: *He refused to smooth over troubles*

smelt[1-2]/melt

Smelt[1] *is from Middle Low German* smelten, *"to melt metal."* **Melt** *was Old English* meltan, *and is related to the Middle Low German word.* **Smelt**[2] *was Old English* smelt *or* smylt.

smog

The word **smog** *is a blend of* smoke + fog. *It was coined in 1905.*

snail/snake

Snail *was Old English* snægel *or* snægl, *and* **snake** *was Old English* snaca. *Both words originally meant "creeping or crawling animal," and are descended from a root,* snek-, *meaning "to creep, crawl."*

snail

snapdragon

ă pat/ā pay/â care/ä father/ĕ pet/ ē be/ĭ pit/ī pie/î fierce/ŏ pot/ ō go/ô paw, for/oi oil/o͝o book/ o͞o boot/ou out/ŭ cut/û fur/ *th* the/th thin/hw which/zh vision/ ə ago, item, pencil, atom, circus

between the groups. **3.** To make less crude; refine. —**smooth'ly** *adv.* —**smooth'ness** *n.*

smooth•bore |smo͞o*th*'bôr'| *or* |-bōr'| *adj.* Having no rifling within the barrel. —*n.* Also **smooth bore.** A firearm having no rifling.

smor•gas•bord |smôr'gəs bôrd'| *or* |-bōrd'| *n.* A buffet meal with a variety of dishes.

smote |smōt|. Past tense and a past participle of **smite.**

smoth•er |smŭ*th*'ər| *v.* **1.** To die or cause (someone) to die from lack of oxygen; suffocate: *The child smothered in the smoky hall. The witch threatened to smother him in an oven.* **2.** To go out or cause (a fire) to go out because of lack of oxygen. **3.** To cook and cover (food) under another food: *smother the liver with onions.* **4.** To conceal or hide: *smothered a sob.*

smoul•der |smōl'dər| *v.* A form of the word **smolder.**

smudge |smŭj| *v.* **smudged, smudg•ing.** To smear or blur: *The chalk smudged. The rain smudged the paint.* —*n.* **1.** A blotch or smear. **2.** A smoky fire used against insects or frost.

smug |smŭg| *adj.* **smug•ger, smug•gest.** Self-satisfied or complacent: *a smug sense of well-being.* —**smug'ly** *adv.* —**smug'ness** *n.*

smug•gle |smŭg'əl| *v.* **smug•gled, smug•gling. 1.** To convey by stealth. **2.** To import or export without paying lawful customs. —**smug'gler** *n.*

smut |smŭt| *n.* **1.** A smudge or something that smudges. **2.** Obscene speech or writing. **3. a.** A plant disease caused by parasitic fungi and resulting in the formation of black, powdery masses. **b.** A fungus that causes such a disease.

smut•ty |smŭt'ē| *adj.* **smut•ti•er, smut•ti•est. 1.** Soiled with smudges; dirty: *a smutty window.* **2.** Obscene: *smutty newspapers.*

Sn The symbol for the element tin.

snack |snăk| *n.* **1.** A light meal, eaten quickly. **2.** Food eaten between meals. —*v.* To eat a snack.

snag |snăg| *n.* **1.** A sharp, rough, or jagged projection. **2.** A tree or part of a tree that sticks out above the surface of a body of water. **3.** A break, pull, or tear in a fabric. **4.** An unforeseen or hidden obstacle. —*v.* **snagged, snag•ging.** To catch or get caught by or as if by a snag.

snail |snāl| *n.* Any of several slow-moving, soft-bodied land or water animals having a coiled, spiral shell and often having eyes on hornlike projections. [SEE NOTE & PICTURE]

snake |snāk| *n.* **1.** Any of a group of reptiles having a long, narrow body and no legs. Some kinds have venom glands and sharp fangs that can give a poisonous bite. **2.** A sneaky, untrustworthy person. **3.** A long, flexible wire used for cleaning drains and sewers. [SEE NOTE]

snake•root |snāk'ro͞ot'| *or* |-ro͝ot'| *n.* Any of several plants with roots believed to cure the bite of a snake.

snake•skin |snāk'skĭn'| *n.* The skin of a snake or leather made from it.

snap |snăp| *v.* **snapped, snap•ping. 1.** To make or cause to make a sharp cracking sound: *The castanets snap as they are played. Snap your fingers.* **2.** To break or cause to break suddenly with a sharp sound: *The twigs snapped underfoot. The wind snapped the large branch.* **3.** To give way abruptly: *The rope snapped. His mind snapped.* **4.** To bite, seize, or grasp with a snatching motion: *The dog snapped at the bone.* **5.** To speak abruptly or sharply: *She snapped at him.* **6.** To move swiftly and smartly: *The soldiers snapped to attention.* **7.** To open or close with a click: *The lid snapped shut.* **8.** To take (a photograph). —*n.* **1.** A sharp cracking sound. **2.** A sudden breaking of something under strain: *the snap of a rope.* **3.** A fastener that closes and opens with a snapping sound. **4.** A thin, crisp cooky. **5.** A spell of cold weather. **6.** *Informal.* An effortless task. **7.** A snapshot. —*adj. Informal.* **1.** Made or done on the spur of the moment: *a snap decision.* **2.** Simple; easy.

***Idiom.* snap out of it.** To recover quickly from (a bad mood, illness, depression, etc.).

snap•drag•on |snăp'drăg'ən| *n.* A garden plant with clusters of variously colored flowers having a narrow, mouthlike opening. [SEE PICTURE]

snap•per |snăp'ər| *n.* **1.** Something or someone that snaps. **2.** Any of several tropical and semitropical ocean fish used as food, as the **red snapper** of southern Atlantic waters.

snapping turtle. An American freshwater turtle with a rough shell and powerful hooked jaws.

snap•pish |snăp'ĭsh| *adj.* **1.** Liable to snap or bite, as a dog. **2.** Sharp in speech; irritable; curt. —**snap'pish•ly** *adv.* —**snap'pish•ness** *n.*

snap•py |snăp'ē| *adj.* **snap•pi•er, snap•pi•est. 1.** *Informal.* Lively; brisk: *a snappy rhythm.* **2.** *Informal.* Smart or chic in appearance: *a snappy dresser.* **3.** Irritable; snappish: *snappy because of lack of sleep.* —**snap'pi•ly** *adv.* —**snap'pi•ness** *n.*

snap•shot |snăp'shŏt'| *n.* An informal photograph, usually taken with a small camera.

snare[1] |snâr| *n.* **1.** A trapping device, usually consisting of a noose, used for capturing birds and small animals. **2.** Anything that serves to entangle. —*v.* **snared, snar•ing.** To trap in or as if in a snare: *snare a rabbit; snare a thief.*

snare[2] |snâr| *n.* **1.** Any of the wires or cords stretched across the lower head of a snare drum to give it a sharp, rattling tone. **2.** A **snare drum.**

snare drum. A small double-headed drum having a snare or snares stretched across the head that is not struck to make the tone rattling and sharp.

snarl[1] |snärl| *n.* **1.** An angry or threatening growl, often made with bared teeth: *The coyote attacked with a fierce snarl.* **2.** A sound or tone of voice resembling this: *He made his demands in a grumpy snarl.* —*v.* **1.** To growl angrily or threateningly, especially with the teeth bared. **2.** To speak or say in a gruff or angry manner. **3.** To make a sound like a rough growl: *The sea snarled along the rocky shore.*

snarl[2] |snärl| *n.* **1.** A tangled mass, as of hair or yarn. **2.** Any confused, complicated, or tangled situation: *a traffic snarl.* —*v.* **1.** To tangle or become tangled: *The kitten snarled the wool. My hair snarls in the wind.* **2.** To confuse or become confused: *Snow snarled the traffic.*

snatch |snăch| *v.* **1.** To grasp or try to grasp; grab: *snatch an apple off the tree; snatched at a scarf.* **2.** To take illicitly: *snatch a purse.* —*n.* **1.** The act of snatching. **2.** A brief or small part: *a snatch of an old song.* —**snatch'er** *n.*

sneak |snēk| *v.* **1.** To go or move in a quiet, stealthy way: *He sneaked onto one of the harbor* *boats. She tried to sneak him into the class.* **2.** To behave in a cowardly, underhand manner: *Don't sneak around.* —*n.* **1.** A cowardly or underhand person. **2.** A quiet, stealthy movement or action.

sneak•ers |snē′kərz| *pl.n.* Canvas sport shoes with soft, flat rubber soles.

sneak•y |snē′kē| *adj.* **sneak•i•er, sneak•i•est.** Like a sneak; sly; furtive: *A sneaky cat ate my salmon.* —**sneak′i•ly** *adv.* —**sneak′i•ness** *n.*

sneer |snîr| *n.* **1.** A facial expression of contempt made by raising one corner of the upper lip slightly. **2.** Any contemptuous expression, statement, etc. —*v.* **1.** To show contempt or scorn with a sneer. **2.** To utter with a sneer.

sneeze |snēz| *v.* **sneezed, sneez•ing.** To cause air to pass forcibly from the nose and mouth in an involuntary, convulsive action that results from irritation of the mucous membranes of the nose. —*n.* The act or an example of sneezing. [SEE NOTE]

snick•er |snĭk′ər| *n.* A snide, partly stifled laugh. —*v.* To utter a snide, partly stifled laugh.

snide |snīd| *adj.* **snid•er, snid•est.** Slyly sarcastic: *a snide remark.* —**snide′ly** *adv.*

sniff |snĭf| *v.* **1.** To inhale (something) in a short, audible breath taken through the nose, as in smelling. **2.** To smell or try to smell by sniffing. **3.** To show contempt or scorn by or as if by sniffing: *She sniffed at those who knew less than she.* —*n.* **1.** The act or an example of sniffing. **2.** The sound made by sniffing. **3.** Something noticed or detected by sniffing; an odor; whiff.

snif•fle |snĭf′əl| *v.* **snif•fled, snif•fling.** To breathe noisily through an inflamed or partially blocked nose, as when suffering from a head cold. —*n.* **1.** The act or sound of sniffling. **2. the sniffles.** *Informal.* A condition, such as a head cold, that makes a person sniffle.

snip |snĭp| *v.* **snipped, snip•ping.** To cut or clip with short, quick strokes. —*n.* **1.** A small piece cut or clipped off. **2.** A stroke of the scissors. **3. snips.** Small hand scissors or shears.

snipe |snīp| *n., pl.* **snipe** or **snipes.** A brownish wading bird with a long bill. —*v.* **sniped, snip•ing. 1.** To shoot at others from a hiding place. **2.** To hunt for snipe. [SEE PICTURE]

snip•er |snī′pər| *n.* A person who shoots at others from a hiding place.

snitch |snĭch| *v. Slang.* **1.** To steal (something of little value): *snitch candy.* **2.** To turn informer: *snitched on his brother.* —**snitch′er** *n.*

sniv•el |snĭv′əl| *v.* **sniv•eled** or **sniv•elled, sniv•el•ing** or **sniv•el•ling. 1.** To complain or whine tearfully. **2.** To run at the nose, especially while crying. —**sniv′el•er** *n.*

snob |snŏb| *n.* **1.** A person who is convinced of and flaunts his or her social or economic superiority. **2.** A person who despises those he or she considers inferior in a particular area: *an intellectual snob.*

snob•ber•y |snŏb′ə rē| *n.* Snobbish conduct.

snob•bish |snŏb′ĭsh| *adj.* Of or characteristic of a snob; pretentious: *snobbish behavior.* —**snob′bish•ly** *adv.* —**snob′bish•ness** *n.*

snood |snŏŏd| *n.* A caplike or baglike hair net worn over the hair at the back of the head.

snoop |snōōp| *v.* To look, pry, or search in a furtive manner. —*n.* A person who snoops.

snooze |snōōz|. *Informal. v.* **snoozed, snooz•ing.** To take a light nap; doze. —*n.* A light nap.

snore |snôr| *or* |snōr| *v.* **snored, snor•ing.** To breathe through the nose and mouth while sleeping, making snorting noises caused by vibrations of the soft palate. —*n.* An example or the sound of snoring. —**snor′er** *n.*

snor•kel |snôr′kəl| *n.* **1.** A breathing apparatus used by skin divers, consisting of a plastic tube curved at one end and fitted with a mouthpiece. **2.** A retractable tube that can be extended from a submarine, allowing it to draw in fresh air and expel waste gases while submerged. —*v.* To swim using a snorkel.

snort |snôrt| *n.* **1.** A rough, noisy sound made by breathing forcefully through the nostrils, as a horse or pig does. **2.** A sound resembling this: *the snort of a steam engine.* —*v.* **1.** To breathe noisily and forcefully through the nostrils: *The frightened horses reared and snorted.* **2.** To exclaim, speak, or say in a rough, scornful manner or tone: *He snorted angrily and slammed the door. "Nonsense!" snorted the judge.* **3.** To move with or make a sound resembling a snort.

snout |snout| *n.* **1.** The long, pointed or projecting nose, jaws, or front part of the head of an animal: *the snout of a pig; the snout of an alligator; the snout of a boll weevil.* **2.** A projecting part resembling this: *Arctic regions where glaciers push their snouts to the edge of high cliffs.*

snow |snō| *n.* **1.** Translucent crystals of ice that form from water vapor in the upper atmosphere and fall to earth. **2.** A falling of snow; a snowstorm. **3.** Specks of white that appear on a television screen as a result of noise in the video signal. —***modifier:*** *snow warnings.* —*v.* **1.** To fall to the earth as snow. **2.** To isolate, block, cover, etc., with or as if with snow.

snow•ball |snō′bôl′| *n.* **1.** A rounded mass of snow packed together, often of a size convenient for throwing. **2.** A shrub with large, rounded clusters of white flowers. —***modifier:*** *a snowball fight.* —*v.* To grow larger or develop rapidly, as a snowball rolling over snow does: *The gossip snowballed into a shocking scandal.*

snow•bird |snō′bûrd′| *n.* A bird, such as the junco, often seen in winter when it is snowy.

snow blindness. Irritation of the eyes and partial or total loss of vision caused by sunlight reflected from snow.

snow•bound |snō′bound′| *adj.* Isolated or blocked because of heavy snow: *snowbound roads; snowbound travelers.*

snow•drift |snō′drĭft′| *n.* A large mass of snow that has been piled up by the wind.

snow•drop |snō′drŏp′| *n.* A plant with drooping white flowers that bloom early in spring.

snow•fall |snō′fôl′| *n.* **1.** A falling of snow. **2.** The amount of snow in a given area or locality over a given period of time.

snow•flake |snō′flāk′| *n.* A single crystal or flake of snow.

snow leopard. A large wild cat of the mountains of central Asia, having long, thick, whitish fur with dark spots. [SEE PICTURE]

snow line. 1. The boundary marking the lowest altitude at which a given area is covered with snow, as the top of a mountain. **2.** The varying boundary marking the lowest latitude around the polar regions at which there is snow cover.

sneeze

The word **sneeze** *sounds reasonably imitative, but if it were* fneeze, *which it really should be, it would be much more so. In Middle English the word was* fnesen, *but this was mistaken for* snesen *(since* s *was often written with a long curve like an* f*).*

snipe

snow leopard

snowshoe

sobriquet

The following is a small selection of the nicknames listed in Fowler's Modern English Usage *(1965) as* **sobriquets**: *the Bard of Avon (Shakespeare), the Eternal City (Rome), the Man of Destiny (Napoleon), the Emerald Isle (Ireland), the Herring Pond (the Atlantic Ocean), the King of Beasts (the lion), the Sport of Kings (horse-racing). Fowler remarks that the excessive use of sobriquets is "a very serious symptom of perverted taste for cheap ornament" and strongly advises writers to avoid using them as much as possible.*

soccer

Soccer, *which has probably become the most popular of all team sports outside the United States, was invented in England. The word* **soccer** *is a peculiar British variant of* association, *from the game's official name,* Association Football *(i.e., the game as played under the rules of the Football Association of England, founded in 1863). This type of variant was formerly common in the slang of English schools and universities; the only other well-known example is* rugger *(from* **rugby**).

ă pat/ā pay/â care/ä father/ĕ pet/ ē be/ĭ pit/ī pie/î fierce/ŏ pot/ ō go/ô paw, for/oi oil/ŏŏ book/ ōō boot/ou out/ŭ cut/û fur/ *th* the/th thin/hw which/zh vision/ ə ago, item, pencil, atom, circus

snow•man |snō′măn′| *n., pl.* **-men** |-mĕn′|. **1.** A figure made from packed and shaped snow, roughly in the form of a man. **2.** See **abominable snowman.**

snow•mo•bile |snō′mō bēl′| *n.* A vehicle that is essentially a motorized sled, used for traveling over ice and snow.

snow•plow |snō′plou′| *n.* A machine used to remove snow from roads, railroad tracks, etc.

snow•shoe |snō′shōō′| *n.* A racket-shaped frame strung with strips of leather or rawhide and worn under the shoe to keep the foot from sinking in deep snow. [SEE PICTURE]

snowshoe rabbit. Also **snowshoe hare.** A hare of northern North America, having large, furry feet and fur that is white in winter and brown in summer.

snow•storm |snō′stôrm′| *n.* A storm with heavy snowfall and high winds; a blizzard.

snow•y |snō′ē| *adj.* **snow•i•er, snow•i•est. 1.** Full of or covered with snow, or subject to snowfall. **2.** Like snow; white: *snowy petals.*

snub |snŭb| *v.* **snubbed, snub•bing. 1.** To treat with scorn or contempt. **2.** To secure (a boat, horse, etc.) by means of a rope tied to a post. *—n.* **1.** A deliberate slight; scornful treatment. **2.** A sudden securing or checking of a rope.

snuff[1] |snŭf| *v.* **1.** To inhale (something) through the nose. **2.** To examine (something) by or as if by inhaling through the nose; sniff. *—n.* Finely pulverized tobacco that can be drawn up into the nostrils by inhaling.

snuff[2] |snŭf| *v.* **1.** To put out; extinguish: *snuff a candle.* **2.** To put an end to; kill: *The dictatorship snuffed out all opposition.*

snuff•box |snŭf′bŏks′| *n.* A small box used for carrying snuff.

snuf•fle |snŭf′əl| *v.* **snuf•fled, snuf•fling.** To breathe noisily through the nose; sniffle. *—n.* The act or sound of snuffling.

snug |snŭg| *adj.* **snug•ger, snug•gest. 1.** Pleasant and comfortable; cozy: *fishing villages in snug harbors.* **2. a.** Close-fitting, as a garment: *a snug sweater.* **b.** Close or tight: *a snug fit.* **—snug′ly** *adv.*

snug•gle |snŭg′əl| *v.* **snug•gled, snug•gling.** To press close; nestle or cuddle: *snuggle up under the covers.*

so[1] |sō| *adv.* **1.** In the condition or manner expressed or indicated; thus: *He got sick last week and has been so ever since.* **2.** To such an extent: *I'm so happy that I could cry.* **3.** To a great extent: *I like her well enough, but she's so silly.* **4.** Consequently; as a result: *He was lazy about studying and so he nearly failed.* **5.** Approximately that amount or number; thereabouts: *The student fare is only $10 or so.* **6.** Too; also; likewise: *She likes the book and so do I.* **7.** Then; apparently: *So I suppose I'm staying home again tonight?* **8.** In truth; indeed: *You aren't telling the truth. I am so.* *—adj.* True; factual: *I wouldn't have told you this if it weren't so.* *—conj.* With the result or consequence that: *He failed to show up, so we went without him.* *—interj.* A word used to express surprise or comprehension: *So, you finished on time after all.* *—Note: So* is often used followed by *that* to form the conjunctional group **so that.** In order that: *A meeting was called so that the issue could be discussed.* ¶*These sound alike* **so, sew, sow**[1].
Idiom. **so as to.** In order to: *Mail your packages early so as to be sure they arrive in time.*

so[2] |sō| *n.* A form of the word **sol** (musical syllable). ¶*These sound alike* **so, sew, sow**[1].

So. south; southern.

soak |sōk| *v.* **1.** To make or become thoroughly wet by or as if by immersing or being immersed in a liquid: *Soak the prunes in water until soft. The beans soaked overnight.* **2.** To suck; absorb: *Sponges soak up moisture.* **3.** *Slang.* To overcharge. *—n.* The act or process of soaking.

so-and-so |sō′ən sō′| *n., pl.* **so-and-sos.** An unnamed or unspecified person or thing.

soap |sōp| *n.* A cleansing agent, manufactured in bars, granules, flakes, or liquid form, consisting of a mixture of the sodium or potassium salts of fatty acids that occur in natural fats and oils. *—modifier: soap powder.* *—v.* To treat or cover with soap.

soap opera. A daytime radio or television serial drama, marked by sentimentality.

soap•stone |sōp′stōn′| *n.* Steatite.

soap•wort |sōp′wûrt′| *n.* A plant, **bouncing Bet.**

soap•y |sō′pē| *adj.* **soap•i•er, soap•i•est. 1.** Covered or filled with soap: *soapy water.* **2.** Like soap: *a soapy feel to the surface.* **—soap′i•ness** *n.*

soar |sôr| *or* |sōr| *v.* **1.** To rise, fly, or glide high, especially by using rising air currents and moving with little apparent effort, as eagles and hawks do. **2.** To rise suddenly and rapidly, especially above what is normal: *The cost of living soared.* ¶*These sound alike* **soar, sore.**

sob |sŏb| *v.* **sobbed, sob•bing. 1. a.** To weep aloud with gasps and sniffles; cry uncontrollably. **b.** To produce an effect on (someone) by so doing: *She sobbed herself to sleep.* **2.** To utter with gasps and sniffles: *"Where were you?" she sobbed.* *—n.* The act or sound of sobbing.

so•ber |sō′bər| *adj.* **so•ber•er, so•ber•est. 1.** Not intoxicated or drunk: *finally sober after a night of drinking.* **2.** Serious or grave: *sober gray eyes.* **3.** Not gay; plain or subdued: *the sober light of a rainy morning.* **4.** Without frivolity or excess: *a sober life.* **5.** Showing self-control or sanity; reasonable. *—v.* To make or become sober: *The news sobered her.* **—so′ber•ly** *adv.*

so•bri•e•ty |sə brī′ĭ tē| *n.* **1.** Seriousness in bearing, manner, or treatment; solemnity. **2.** Absence of alcoholic intoxication.

so•bri•quet |sō′brĭ kā′| *or* |-kĕt′| *n.* **1.** A humorous nickname. **2.** An assumed name. [SEE NOTE]

so-called |sō′kôld′| *adj.* So named or designated, often incorrectly: *a so-called musician.*

soc•cer |sŏk′ər| *n.* A game, played on a field, in which participants maneuver a ball mainly by kicking, the object being to propel the ball into the opposing team's goal. *—modifier: a soccer team.* [SEE NOTE]

so•cia•ble |sō′shə bəl| *adj.* **1.** Liking company; friendly: *a sociable person.* **2.** Pleasant: *Dinner is often the most sociable meal of the day.* **—so′cia•bil′i•ty, so′cia•ble•ness** *n.* **—so′cia•bly** *adv.*

so•cial |sō′shəl| *adj.* **1. a.** Living together in communities or similar organized groups: *Human beings are social creatures. Bees and ants are social insects.* **b.** Of or typical of such a way of life or of organisms living in this way: *the social* *behavior of bees; social activities.* **2.** Of the upper classes: *wealth and social position.* **3.** Sociable or companionable: *a social character.* **4.** Of or occupied with welfare work: *a social worker.* —*n.* An informal social gathering: *a church social.*

so•cial•ism |sō′shə lĭz′əm| *n.* **1.** A doctrine or movement calling for public ownership of factories and other means of production. **2.** In Marxist theory, the stage of society between capitalism and communism.

so•cial•ist |sō′shə lĭst| *n.* **1.** A person who believes in or advocates socialism. **2.** Often **Socialist.** A member of a party advocating socialism. —*adj.* Of socialism: *a socialist nation.*

so•cial•ist•ic |sō′shə lĭs′tĭk| *adj.* Based on or favoring the principles of socialism. —**so′cial•is′ti•cal•ly** *adv.*

so•cial•ite |sō′shə līt′| *n.* A person who is prominent in fashionable society.

so•cial•ize |sō′shə līz′| *v.* **so•cial•ized, so•cial•iz•ing. 1.** To place under public ownership or control; establish on a socialistic basis. **2.** To make sociable in attitude or manners. **3.** To take part in social activities. —**so′cial•i•za′tion** *n.*

so•cial•ly |sō′shə lē| *adv.* **1.** In a social manner: *She is socially successful.* **2.** With regard to society: *socially important.* **3.** By society: *socially acceptable.*

social science. Any of the sciences, such as sociology, psychology, anthropology, etc., that study society, the relationships between the individual and society, etc.

Social Security. A government program that provides monthly payments to the elderly, the unemployed, and others, financed by payments made both by employers and employees.

social studies. A course of study including geography, history, government, and sociology, taught in elementary and secondary schools.

social work. 1. Organized efforts by a community or an organization for the betterment of the poor. **2.** A profession specializing in such efforts. —**social worker.**

so•ci•e•ty |sə sī′ĭ tē| *n., pl.* **so•ci•e•ties. 1.** A group of living things, usually of the same kind, living and functioning together: *human societies; a society of bees forming a single hive; plant societies.* **2.** The rich, privileged, and fashionable social class. **3.** A group of people sharing mutual aims, interests, etc.: *a stamp-collecting society.* **4.** Companionship or company: *enjoying the society of women.* —***modifier:*** *the society page.*

Society of Friends. A Christian sect founded in about 1650 in England, opposed to war, oath-taking, and ritual. Its members are informally called "Quakers."

so•ci•o•log•i•cal |sō′sē ə lŏj′ĭ kəl| *or* |sō′shē-| *adj.* Of or involving sociology.

so•ci•ol•o•gist |sō′sē ŏl′ə jĭst| *or* |sō′shē-| *n.* A social scientist who specializes in sociology.

so•ci•ol•o•gy |sō′sē ŏl′ə jē| *or* |sō′shē-| *n.* The scientific study of human society and its origins, development, organizations, and institutions.

sock[1] |sŏk| *n.* **1.** *pl.* **socks** or **sox** |sŏks|. A short stocking reaching at least to the ankle and no higher than the knee. **2. a.** *pl.* **socks.** A lightweight shoe worn in ancient times by actors in Greek and Roman comedies. **b.** Comedy.

sock[2] |sŏk|. *Slang. v.* To hit forcefully; punch: *socked the ball out of the park.* —*n.* A punch.

sock•et |sŏk′ĭt| *n.* **1.** An opening or cavity into which an inserted part is designed to fit: *a socket for a light bulb.* **2. a.** A depression in a bone into which a projection from another bone fits, as at a joint. **b.** A depression into which a body part, such as an eye, fits.

Soc•ra•tes |sŏk′rə tēz′|. 470?–399 B.C. Greek philosopher and teacher.

sod |sŏd| *n.* **1.** Grass and soil forming the surface of the ground: *the beat of the buffaloes' hoofs on the prairie sod.* **2.** A piece of such soil held together by matted roots and removed from the ground. —***modifier:*** *a sod roof.* —*v.* **sod•ded, sod•ding.** To cover with sod.

so•da |sō′də| *n.* **1.** Carbonated water or a soft drink containing it. **2.** A drink made from carbonated water and ice cream. **3.** Any of various forms of sodium carbonate. —***modifier:*** *a soda bottle.*

soda fountain. A counter equipped for preparing and serving sodas, sandwiches, etc.

soda pop. *Informal.* A **soft drink.**

soda water. Water that has been charged with carbon dioxide under pressure, used in various drinks and refreshments.

sod•den |sŏd′n| *adj.* **1.** Thoroughly soaked; saturated: *sodden land.* **2.** Bloated and dull from or as if from drink. —**sod′den•ly** *adv.*

so•di•um |sō′dē əm| *n.* Symbol **Na** One of the elements, a soft, light, silver-white metal. Atomic number 11; atomic weight 22.99; valence +1; melting point 97.8°C; boiling point 892°C. [SEE NOTE]

sodium

Sodium *is a very reactive element and is common in combined forms, especially in sodium chloride, or common salt. Many such compounds are important in industry and medicine. The symbol for sodium,* Na, *is taken from* natrium, *its Latin name.*

sodium benzoate. The sodium salt of benzoic acid, C_6H_5COONa, used as a food preservative and antiseptic.

sodium bicarbonate. A white crystalline salt of sodium, $NaHCO_3$, used in baking, in certain medicinal preparations, in fire extinguishers, and in making effervescent beverages.

sodium carbonate. 1. A white, powdery salt of sodium, Na_2CO_3, with a strongly alkaline reaction, used in preparing other compounds of sodium and in making glass, detergents, soaps, and other industrial products. **2.** Any of various hydrated forms of this salt, as sal soda.

sodium chloride. A colorless crystalline salt of sodium, NaCl, used in making chemicals and as a preservative and seasoning for foods; common salt.

sodium glu•ta•mate |glo͞o′tə māt′|. A white crystalline salt of sodium and an organic acid, having the formula $C_5H_6O_4N_2Na$ and used in cooking.

sodium hydroxide. A strongly alkaline compound of sodium, NaOH, used in making chemicals and soaps, in refining petroleum, and as a cleansing agent; lye.

sodium thiosulphate. A white crystalline compound, $Na_2S_2O_3$, used as a photographic fixing agent and as a bleach.

so•di•um-va•por lamp |sō′dē əm vā′pər|. An electric lamp containing neon and a small amount of sodium. It generates a powerful yellow light and is often used for lighting streets and highways.

Sod•om |sŏd′əm|. In the Bible, a city that God destroyed, together with the city of Gomorrah,

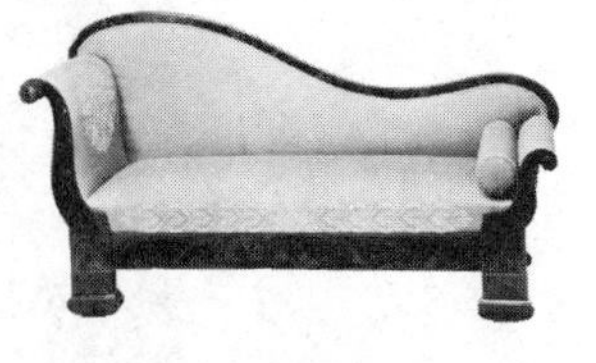

sofa
American sofa of about 1830

Noah Webster's *American Dictionary* (1828) has the following entry for **sofa**: "An elegant long seat, usually with a stuffed bottom. Sofas are variously made. In the United States, the frame is of mahogany, and the bottom of stuffed cloth, with a covering of silk, chintz, calico or haircloth."

solder
The l *of the word* **solder** *has a long history. The origin of the word is Latin* solidāre, *"to make solid, to fasten together." This passed into Old French as* souder, *meaning "to join with melted metal"; it was normal in this situation for the Latin* l *to disappear (compare Latin* calidus, *"hot," becoming Old French* chaud*). But people who discovered that there had been an* l *in the Latin original "restored" it in Old French, so that alongside* souder *the variant form* solder *was created. Both forms of the word were borrowed into English, as* soder, *pronounced roughly* /**sŏd**'ər/, *and* solder, *pronounced approximately* /**sŏl**'dər/. *The spelling* soder *later disappeared. In British English both pronunciations still exist, but in American English* /**sŏd**'ər/ *has completely prevailed. Accordingly, Noah Webster in his* American Dictionary *of 1828 made a sensible effort to restore* soder *as the American spelling; but by this time the spelling with* l *had become established.*

ă pat/ā pay/â care/ä father/ĕ pet/ ē be/ĭ pit/ī pie/î fierce/ŏ pot/ ō go/ô paw, for/oi oil/ŏŏ book/ ōō boot/ou out/ŭ cut/û fur/ *th* the/th thin/hw which/zh vision/ ə ago, item, pencil, atom, circus

for the wickedness of its inhabitants.

so•fa |sō'fə| *n.* A long upholstered seat with a back and arms. [SEE PICTURE]

So•fi•a |sō'fē ə| *or* |sō **fē'**ə|. The capital of Bulgaria. Population, 919,000.

soft |sôft| *or* |sŏft| *adj.* **soft•er, soft•est. 1.** Not hard or firm; offering little resistance: *a soft, squishy melon; soft snow.* **2.** Out of condition; flabby: *growing soft in his 30's.* **3.** Smooth, fine, or pleasing to the touch: *a soft, gray kitten.* **4.** Not loud or harsh; quiet: *a soft, muffled snore.* **5.** Not brilliant or glaring; subdued: *a soft pink.* **6.** *Informal.* Easy: *a soft job.* **7.** Designating the sound of the letters *c* and *g* as they are pronounced in *receive* and *general.* **8.** Containing relatively little dissolved mineral matter: *soft water.* **—soft'ly** *adv.* **—soft'ness** *n.*

soft•ball |**sôft'**bôl'| *or* |**sŏft'**-| *n.* **1.** A game similar to baseball but played with a larger, slightly softer ball that is thrown underhand by the pitcher. **2.** The ball used in this sport. ***—modifier:*** *a softball player.*

soft coal. **Bituminous coal.**

soft drink. A beverage that is nonalcoholic and often carbonated.

soft•en |sô'fən| *or* |**sŏf'**ən| *v.* To make or become soft or softer. **—soft'en•er** *n.*

soft landing. The landing of a space vehicle, as on a celestial body, at a velocity low enough to prevent damage or destruction.

soft palate. The movable fold, consisting of muscle fibers enclosed in mucous membrane, that hangs from the back of the hard palate and closes off the nasal cavity from the mouth cavity during swallowing and sucking.

soft-shoe |**sôft'**shōō'| *or* |**sŏft'**-| *adj.* Of or describing a type of tap dance done in shoes with soft soles and no metal taps.

soft-spok•en |**sôft'**spō'kən| *or* |**sŏft'**-| *adj.* Speaking with a soft or gentle voice.

soft•ware |**sôft'**wâr'| *or* |**sŏft'**-| *n.* **1.** Written or printed data, such as programs, routines, and symbolic languages, essential to the operation of computers. **2.** Documents containing information on the operation and maintenance of computers, such as manuals, diagrams, etc.

soft•wood |**sôft'**wŏŏd'| *or* |**sôft'**-| *n.* **1.** The wood of a cone-bearing tree, such as a pine, fir, or cedar, as distinguished from that of a flowering tree with broad leaves. The wood of such a tree is sometimes soft but in many cases is quite hard and strong. **2.** A tree bearing such wood.

sog•gy |**sŏg'**ē| *adj.* **sog•gi•er, sog•gi•est.** Saturated with moisture; soaked: *soggy bread.* **—sog'gi•ly** *adv.* **—sog'gi•ness** *n.*

soil[1] |soil| *n.* **1.** The loose top layer of the earth's surface, suitable for the growth of plant life. **2.** A particular kind of earth or ground: *sandy soil.* **3.** Country; region: *native soil.* ***—modifier:*** *soil erosion.*

soil[2] |soil| *v.* **1.** To make or become dirty. **2.** To disgrace; tarnish: *soil one's reputation.*

so•journ |**sō'**jûrn'| *or* |sō **jûrn'**| *v.* To stay for a time; reside temporarily: *Thoreau sojourned at Walden Pond.* *—n.* A temporary stay.

sol[1] |sōl| *n.* A syllable used in music to represent the fifth tone of a diatonic major scale or often the tone G. ¶*These sound alike* **sol, sole, soul.**

sol[2] |sōl| *n., pl.* **so•les** |**sō'**lās|. The basic unit of money of Peru. ¶*These sound alike* **sol, sole, soul.**

sol•ace |**sŏl'**əs| *n.* **1.** Comfort in distress or misfortune; consolation: *We found solace in the silent forest.* **2.** Something that gives such comfort or consolation: *The thumb is a solace to the baby's unappeased hunger.* *—v.* **sol•aced, sol•ac•ing.** To provide solace; comfort.

so•lar |**sō'**lər| *adj.* **1.** Of the sun: *solar radiation.* **2.** Using or operating by energy from the sun: *a solar heating system.* **3.** Measured with respect to the sun: *solar time.*

solar battery. An electrical battery consisting of a number of solar cells connected together.

solar cell. A semiconductor device that converts solar radiation into electrical energy, often used in space vehicles.

solar flare. A temporary outburst of gases from a small area of the sun's surface.

solar furnace. A device equipped with a large reflector that focuses the sun's rays, producing temperatures as high as 4,000°C.

so•lar•i•um |sə **lâr'**ē əm| *n., pl.* **so•lar•i•a** |sə**lâr'**ē ə| or **so•lar•i•ums.** A room, porch, etc., enclosed largely with glass to let in sunlight, as in a hospital or sanitarium.

solar plexus. 1. The large network of nerves and nerve tissue located in the abdomen behind the stomach, having branches that supply nerves to the abdominal organs. **2.** *Informal.* The pit of the stomach.

solar system. The sun together with the nine planets and the other bodies that orbit the sun.

solar wind. The flow of charged atomic particles that radiates from the sun.

sold |sōld|. Past tense and past participle of **sell.**

sol•der |**sŏd'**ər| *n.* Any of various alloys, mainly of tin and lead, that melt at low temperatures and are applied in the molten state to metal parts in order to join them. *—v.* To join, mend, or connect with solder: *soldering the wires together.* [SEE NOTE]

sol•dier |**sōl'**jər| *n.* **1.** A person who serves in an army. **2.** An enlisted man or noncommissioned officer as distinguished from a commissioned officer. *—v.* To be or serve as a soldier.

sol•dier•ly |**sōl'**jər lē| *adj.* Befitting a good soldier: *soldierly courage.*

sole[1] |sōl| *n.* **1.** The bottom surface of the foot. **2.** The bottom surface of a shoe, boot, etc., often excluding the heel. *—v.* **soled, sol•ing.** To put a sole on (a shoe, boot, etc.): *The cobbler soled the shoes.* ¶*These sound alike* **sole, sol, soul.**

sole[2] |sōl| *adj.* **1.** Being the only one; single; only: *her sole purpose.* **2.** Belonging exclusively to one person or group: *She took sole command of the ship.* ¶*These sound alike* **sole, sol, soul.**

sole[3] |sōl| *n., pl.* **sole** or **soles.** Any of several flatfishes related to the flounders, used as food. ¶*These sound alike* **sole, sol, soul.**

sole•ly |**sōl'**lē| *adv.* **1.** Alone; singly: *solely responsible.* **2.** Entirely; exclusively: *judging solely from these passages.*

sol•emn |**sŏl'**əm| *adj.* **1.** Impressive; serious; grave: *a solemn occasion; solemn tones.* **2.** Having the force of a religious ceremony; sacred: *a solemn oath.* **3.** Performed with full ceremony: *a solemn mass.* **4.** Gloomy: *She looked solemn today.* **—sol'emn•ly** *adv.* **—sol'emn•ness** *n.*

so•lem•ni•ty |sə **lĕm'**nĭ tē| *n., pl.* **so•lem•ni•ties.**

1. The condition or quality of being solemn; seriousness. 2. A solemn event or occasion.

sol•em•nize |sŏl′əm nīz′| *v.* **sol•em•nized, sol•em•niz•ing.** 1. To observe with formal ceremonies or rites: *solemnize the occasion.* 2. To perform with formal ceremony: *solemnize a marriage.* —**sol′em•ni•za′tion** *n.*

so•le•noid |sō′lə noid′| *n.* A coil of insulated wire in which a magnetic field is established when an electric current is passed through it.

so•les |sō′lās| *n.* Plural of **sol** (unit of money).

so•lic•it |sə lĭs′ĭt| *v.* 1. To seek to obtain: *solicit votes.* 2. To ask or petition (someone) persistently; entreat: *solicited all his neighbors for donations.* —**so•lic′i•ta′tion** *n.*

so•lic•i•tor |sə lĭs′ĭ tər| *n.* 1. A person who solicits, especially one who asks for contributions, votes, etc. 2. An officer who acts as chief attorney for a city, town, or government department. 3. In England, a lawyer who is not a member of the bar and who may appear only in the lower courts.

so•lic•i•tous |sə lĭs′ĭ təs| *adj.* 1. Anxious and concerned; attentive: *a solicitous parent.* 2. Full of desire; eager: *solicitous to move ahead.* —**so•lic′i•tous•ly** *adv.* —**so•lic′i•tous•ness** *n.*

so•lic•i•tude |sə lĭs′ĭ to͞od′| *or* |-tyo͞od′| *n.* Care; concern.

sol•id |sŏl′ĭd| *adj.* 1. Having a definite shape and volume; not liquid or gaseous. 2. Not hollowed out: *a solid block of ice.* 3. Being the same substance, color, etc., throughout: *solid silver; solid black.* 4. Of three-dimensional geometric figures. 5. Without breaks; continuous: *She gossiped for a solid hour.* 6. Of good quality or substance; well-made: *a solid foundation.* 7. Substantial; hearty: *a solid breakfast.* 8. Upstanding and dependable: *a solid citizen.* 9. Acting together; unanimous: *a solid voting bloc.* —*n.* 1. A substance made up of atoms, molecules, or ions that have little or no ability to exchange places; a substance that has a definite shape and volume. 2. A geometric figure that has three dimensions. —**sol′id•ly** *adv.* —**sol′id•ness** *n.*

sol•i•dar•i•ty |sŏl′ĭ dăr′ĭ tē| *n.* Unity of purpose, interest, or sympathy.

solid geometry. The geometry of three-dimensional figures and surfaces.

so•lid•i•fy |sə lĭd′ə fī′| *v.* **so•lid•i•fied, so•lid•i•fy•ing, so•lid•i•fies.** To make or become solid.

so•lid•i•ty |sə lĭd′ĭ tē| *n.* 1. The condition or property of being solid. 2. The condition or character of being sound.

sol•id-state |sŏl′ĭd stāt′| *adj.* 1. Of or concerned with the physical properties of crystalline solids: *solid-state physics.* 2. Based on or using transistors or related semiconductor devices: *a solid-state radio receiver.*

so•lil•o•quy |sə lĭl′ə kwē| *n., pl.* **so•lil•o•quies.** A literary or dramatic discourse in which a character talks to himself or reveals his thoughts without addressing them to a listener.

sol•i•taire |sŏl′ĭ târ′| *n.* 1. Any of a number of card games played by one person. 2. A diamond or other gemstone set alone, as in a ring.

sol•i•tar•y |sŏl′ĭ tĕr′ē| *adj.* 1. Existing or living alone: *a solitary traveler.* 2. Happening, done, or passed alone: *a solitary evening.* 3. Remote; secluded; lonely: *solitary places.* 4. Having no or few companions; lonely: *a solitary person.*

sol•i•tude |sŏl′ĭ to͞od′| *or* |-tyo͞od′| *n.* 1. The state of being alone or remote from others; isolation. 2. A lonely or secluded place.

so•lo |sō′lō| *n., pl.* **so•los.** 1. A musical composition or passage for a single voice or instrument, with or without accompaniment. 2. A performance of one or more such passages or compositions by a singer or instrumentalist. —*v.* **so•loed, so•lo•ing, so•los.** 1. To perform a solo or solos. 2. To fly an airplane without an instructor or companion. —*adv.* Alone or without accompaniment: *Lacking a pianist, he had to perform solo.* —**so′lo•ist** *n.*

Sol•o•mon |sŏl′ə mən|. In the Bible, a son of David and third king of Israel. Solomon became noted in legend for his wisdom and wealth.

Solomon Islands. 1. Islands in the western Pacific east of New Guinea, divided between Papua New Guinea and the independent Solomon Islands. 2. A country comprising the southeastern islands. Population, 221,000.

Solomon's seal. A plant with yellowish or greenish flowers that hang down in pairs beneath the leaves. [SEE PICTURE]

sol•stice |sŏl′stĭs| *or* |sōl′-| *n.* Either of the two times of year, approximately June 22, the **summer solstice,** and December 22, the **winter solstice,** at which the sun reaches an extreme of its northward or southward motion and appears not to move in either of these directions.

sol•u•bil•i•ty |sŏl′yə bĭl′ĭ tē| *n., pl.* **sol•u•bil•i•ties.** 1. The condition or property of being soluble. 2. The amount of a substance that is soluble in a particular liquid, especially water.

sol•u•ble |sŏl′yə bəl| *adj.* 1. Capable of being dissolved. 2. Capable of being solved.

sol•ute |sŏl′yo͞ot′| *or* |sō′lo͞ot′| *n.* A substance that is dissolved in another substance.

so•lu•tion |sə lo͞o′shən| *n.* 1. A mixture of two or more substances that appears to be uniform throughout except at the molecular level, and that is capable of forming by itself when the substances are in contact: *a solution of salt in water.* 2. The act or process of forming such a mixture. 3. The condition or property of being dissolved. 4. a. An answer to a problem. b. A number or function that changes an equation into an identity when substituted for an unknown in the equation. c. A number or function that makes an inequality true when substituted for an unknown. 5. The method or procedure used in solving an equation, problem, etc.

solv•a•ble |sŏl′və bəl| *adj.* Capable of being solved; soluble, as a problem or equation.

solve |sŏlv| *v.* **solved, solv•ing.** To find an answer or solution to (a problem, equation, etc.).

sol•vent |sŏl′vənt| *adj.* 1. Able to meet financial obligations: *a solvent business.* 2. Capable of dissolving another substance. —*n.* 1. The substance that makes up the largest porportion of a solution; the substance throughout which all the others present appear to be dispersed. 2. A liquid that is capable of dissolving another substance. —**sol′ven•cy** *n.*

So•ma•li•a |sō mä′lē ə| *or* |-mäl′yə|. A country in easternmost Africa, on the Indian Ocean. Population, 3,090,000. Capital, Mogadishu.

so•mat•ic |sə măt′ĭk| *adj.* Of the body, espe-

Solomon's seal

somber/sombrero
Somber *is from French* sombre, *"dark," originally meaning "shade."* **Sombrero** *is from Spanish* sombrero, *"shade hat," from* sombra, *"shade." It is obvious that French* sombre *and Spanish* sombra, *both meaning "shade," are closely related, but the Latin word for "shade" was* umbra, *which could not quite have produced the French and Spanish words. The problem is solved by reconstructing a Late Latin verb* subombrāre, *formed from* sub, *"below,"* + umbra; *this regularly formed verb would have meant "to give shade below," and it would regularly have produced both French* sombre *and Spanish* sombra. *Since everything fits perfectly, it is assumed that this verb really did exist in the period after the Roman Empire had broken up; it is not surprising that we have no record of it, since writing almost died out for several centuries at this time. See note at* **unattested**.

sombrero

someone/somebody
In the materials on which this Dictionary was based, the word **someone** *occurred five times as often as the word* **somebody**.

ă pat/ā pay/â care/ä father/ĕ pet/ ē be/ĭ pit/ī pie/î fierce/ŏ pot/ ō go/ô paw, for/oi oil/ŏŏ book/ ōō boot/ou out/ŭ cut/û fur/ *th* the/th thin/hw which/zh vision/ ə ago, item, pencil, atom, circus

cially as distinguished from any of its parts, the mind, or the germ cells.

som•ber, also **som•bre** |**sŏm**'bər| *adj.* **1.** Dark; gloomy: *a somber color.* **2.** Melancholy; dismal: *a somber mood.* —**som'ber•ly** *adv.* [SEE NOTE]

som•bre•ro |sŏm **brâr'**ō| *n., pl.* **som•bre•ros.** A large straw or felt hat with a broad brim and tall crown, worn in Mexico and the southwestern United States. [SEE NOTE & PICTURE]

some |sŭm| *adj.* **1.** Being an unspecified number or quantity; a few or a little: *some people; some sugar.* **2.** Being unknown or unspecified by name: *Some student was just here and left you this note.* **3.** *Informal.* Considerable; remarkable: *Mary's some cook.* Also used adverbially: *She's some good cook.* —*pron.* **1.** An indefinite or unspecified number or quantity: *We've got coffee—do you want some?* **2.** An indefinite additional quantity: *From here to Chicago is 100 miles and then some.* —*adv.* **1.** Approximately; about: *some 40 people.* **2.** *Informal.* Somewhat: *He's improved some but not much.* ¶*These sound alike* **some, sum.**

–some¹. A suffix that forms adjectives and means "being or tending to be": **burdensome.**

–some². A word element meaning "a group of": *threesome.*

some•bod•y |**sŭm'**bŏd'ē| *or* |-bŭd'ē| *or* |-bə-dē| *pron.* An unspecified or unknown person; someone: *Somebody's been here, but who?* —*n., pl.* **some•bod•ies.** A person of importance: *Since he got that sports car, he really thinks he's somebody.* [SEE NOTE]

some•day |**sŭm'**dā'| *adv.* At some time in the future.

some•how |**sŭm'**hou'| *adv.* **1.** In some way or other: *The early scientists knew that food and blood were somehow related.* **2.** For some reason: *He's been very naughty, but I just don't have the heart to punish him, somehow.*

some•one |**sŭm'**wŭn'| *or* |-wən| *pron.* Some person; somebody: *Someone called, but he didn't leave his name.* [SEE NOTE]

some•place |**sŭm'**plās'| *adv.* Somewhere: *I don't like it here, so let's go someplace else.*

som•er•sault |**sŭm'**ər sôlt'| *n.* The act of rolling the body in a complete circle, heels over head. —*v.* To execute a somersault: *Children were somersaulting on the grass.*

some•thing |**sŭm'**thĭng| *pron.* An unspecified or not definitely known thing: *Something's wrong, but I can't put my finger on it.* —*n. Informal.* A remarkable or important thing or person: *That concert was really something. This guy is something—I can't figure out what makes him act the way he does.* —*adv.* Somewhat: *It sounds something like Debussy, but it's Ravel.*

***Idiom.* something of.** To some extent: *He's something of a musician, you know.*

some•time |**sŭm'**tīm'| *adv.* At some indefinite or unstated time: *I'll see you sometime around 6 o'clock.* —*adj.* Former: *our sometime king.*

some•times |**sŭm'**tīmz'| *adv.* Now and then: *I see them sometimes but not often.*

some•way |**sŭm'**wā'| *adv. Informal.* **1.** In some way or other; somehow: *Don't worry—I'll fix up something someway.* **2.** For some reason or other: *Someway, I can't imagine little Antoinette in a prairie schooner heading for the West.*

some•what |**sŭm'**hwät| *or* |sŭm **hwät'**| *adv.* To some extent or degree; rather: *the king snake, which somewhat resembles a rattlesnake.* —*pron. Archaic.* Something.

some•where |**sŭm'**hwĕr'| *adv.* **1.** At, in, or to a place not specified or known: *I found this turtle somewhere near the edge of the swamp.* **2.** To an unspecified place or state representing further development or progress: *Good storytellers make sure that their stories lead somewhere and end with a definite point.* **3.** Approximately; roughly: *somewhere about halfway through; somewhere around 80 years old.* —*n.* An unspecified place: *He said he could lift the earth with a lever if he had the right kind of lever and somewhere to stand.*

som•nam•bu•lism |sŏm **năm'**byə lĭz'əm| *n.* Walking while asleep or in a sleeplike condition.

som•no•lent |**sŏm'**nə lənt| *adj.* **1.** Drowsy; sleepy. **2.** Causing or tending to cause sleepiness: *the somnolent sound of rain.* —**som'no•lence** *n.* —**som'no•lent•ly** *adv.*

son |sŭn| *n.* **1.** A boy or man thought of in relation to his parents; male offspring. **2.** Any male descendant: *sons of Abraham.* **3.** A man or boy identified with a place or cause: *sons of Ireland; sons of the Confederacy.* **4. the Son.** Christ. ¶*These sound alike* **son, sun.**

so•nar |**sō'**när'| *n.* **1.** A system, similar in principle to radar, that uses reflected sound waves to detect and locate underwater objects. **2.** An apparatus using such a system, as for detecting submarines. —***modifier:*** *a sonar system.*

so•na•ta |sə **nä'**tə| *n.* Any of several types of instrumental musical compositions, especially one written in several movements, the first of which is in sonata form.

sonata form. A form for a musical movement, having an opening section in which two or more themes are introduced, a middle section in which the themes are developed and elaborated, and a third section in which the opening themes are restated, sometimes followed by a coda.

song |sông| *or* |sŏng| *n.* **1.** A musical composition, usually fairly short, that is meant to be sung. **2.** The act or art of singing. **3.** A vocal sound that has a melodious quality, such as the call of a bird. **4. a.** Poetry; verse. **b.** A lyric poem or ballad.

***Idiom.* for a song.** At a low price; cheaply: *He bought the wardrobe for a song.*

song•bird |**sông'**bûrd'| *or* |**sŏng'**-| *n.* A bird with a melodious song or call.

son•ic |**sŏn'**ĭk| *adj.* **1.** Of sound, especially audible sound. **2.** Having a speed equal to that of sound in air, about 738 miles per hour at sea level at normal temperatures.

sonic barrier. The sudden sharp increase in drag exerted by the atmosphere on an aircraft approaching the speed of sound.

sonic boom. The shock wave caused by an aircraft traveling at a supersonic speed, sometimes causing damage to structures on the ground and often audible as a loud explosive sound.

son-in-law |**sŭn'**ĭn lô'| *n., pl.* **sons-in-law.** The husband of one's daughter.

son•net |**sŏn'**ĭt| *n.* A 14-line poem usually expressing a single complete thought or idea, and having lines that rhyme according to certain specific patterns. [SEE NOTE]

son•ny |sŭn'ē| *n.* Little boy; young man. Used as a familiar form of address. ¶*These sound alike* **sonny, sunny.**

so•nor•i•ty |sə nôr'ĭ tē| *or* |-nōr'-| *n., pl.* **so•nor•i•ties. 1.** The quality or property of being sonorous; resonance. **2.** A sound, especially one used in music or speech: *The work is a masterful study in orchestral sonorities.*

so•no•rous |sə nôr'əs| *or* |-nōr'-| *or* |sŏn'ər-| *adj.* **1.** Having or producing sound, especially full, deep, or rich sound. **2.** Impressive: *sonorous prose.* **—so•no'rous•ly** *adv.*

soon |so͞on| *adv.* **soon•er, soon•est. 1. a.** In the near future: *Soon you'll have to leave.* **b.** Within a short time; quickly: *A weak rope will wear out sooner than a strong one.* **2.** Early: *He ran all the way and got there not an instant too soon.* **3.** Quickly; fast: *Phone your mother as soon as we get into the house.* **4.** Gladly; willingly: *I'd as soon leave right now.*

***Idioms.* no sooner . . . than.** As soon as: *No sooner was the frost off the ground than the work began.* **sooner or later.** Sometime; eventually: *I really must meet your mother sooner or later.*

soot |so͝ot| *or* |so͞ot| *n.* A fine black powdery substance, chiefly carbon, produced when wood, coal, or hydrocarbon fuels burn incompletely. *—v.* To fill, cover, or smudge with soot: *The smoky furnace sooted the chimney badly.*

sooth |so͞oth| *n. Archaic.* Truth; reality: *In sooth, he knew not why he was so sad.*

soothe |so͞o*th*| *v.* **soothed, sooth•ing. 1.** To calm or quiet: *Cowboys sang at night to soothe the restless cattle.* **2.** To ease or relieve the pain, discomfort, or distress of: *soothed the frightened child.* **3.** To alleviate or ease; relieve: *The medicine soothed the pain. Her words soothed his rage.* **—sooth'er** *n.*

sooth•ing |so͞o'*th*ĭng| *adj.* Bringing relief or comfort: *a soothing cream for sunburn; soothing words.* **—sooth'ing•ly** *adv.*

sooth•say•er |so͞oth'sā'ər| *n.* A person who claims to be able to foretell events or predict the future; a seer.

soot•y |so͝ot'ē| *or* |so͞o'tē| *adj.* **soot•i•er, soot•i•est. 1.** Of, producing, or covered with soot. **2.** Having an appearance like that of soot.

sop |sŏp| *v.* **sopped, sop•ping. 1.** To dip, soak, or drench in a liquid: *sop the bread in the beaten eggs.* **2.** To take up by absorption; soak up: *sop gravy with bread; sop up water with a towel.* *—n.* **1.** Something, as a bit of bread, soaked in a liquid. **2.** Something of little value yielded to placate or soothe a person.

so•phis•ti•cate |sə fĭs'tĭ kāt'| *v.* **so•phis•ti•cat•ed, so•phis•ti•cat•ing. 1.** To cause to become less naive: *Travel tends to sophisticate a person.* **2.** To make more complex or complicated; refine: *sophisticate the communications system.* *—n.* |sə fĭs'tĭ kĭt| *or* |-kāt'|. A sophisticated person. **—so•phis'ti•ca'tion** *n.*

so•phis•ti•cat•ed |sə fĭs'tĭ kā'tĭd| *adj.* **1.** Having acquired worldly knowledge or refinement; lacking natural simplicity: *a sophisticated child.* **2.** Elaborate, complex, or complicated: *sophisticated instruments.* **3.** Suitable for or appealing to the tastes of sophisticates: *a sophisticated play.*

Soph•o•cles |sŏf'ə klēz'|. 496?–406 B.C. Greek tragic poet.

soph•o•more |sŏf'ə môr'| *or* |-mōr'| *n.* A student in his second year at a four-year high school or college. ***—modifier:*** *the sophomore class.*

so•pran•o |sə prăn'ō| *or* |-prä'nō| *n., pl.* **so•pran•os. 1.** A high singing voice of a woman or boy; a singing voice of the highest range. **2.** A person having such a voice. **3.** A part written in the range of this voice. **4.** An instrument having about the same range as this voice. ***—modifier:*** *a soprano aria; a soprano saxophone.*

sor•cer•er |sôr'sər ər| *n.* A person who practices sorcery; a wizard.

sor•cer•ess |sôr'sər ĭs| *n.* A female sorcerer.

sor•cer•y |sôr'sə rē| *n.* Magic practiced with the aid of evil spirits.

sor•did |sôr'dĭd| *adj.* **1.** Filthy or squalid: *a sordid neighborhood.* **2.** Degraded; base: *a sordid motive.* **—sor'did•ly** *adv.* **—sor'did•ness** *n.*

sore |sôr| *or* |sōr| *adj.* **sor•er, sor•est. 1.** Painful or tender; causing pain: *His sore leg made him walk with a limp.* **2.** Suffering pain; hurting: *The beating left him sore all over.* **3.** Causing misery, sorrow, or distress; grievous: *sore need.* **4.** Causing embarrassment, irritation, etc.: *a sore subject.* **5.** *Informal.* Angered; offended. *—n.* An open injury, wound, ulcer, etc. ¶*These sound alike* **sore, soar. —sore'ness** *n.*

sore•ly |sôr'lē| *or* |sōr'-| *adv.* **1.** Severely; painfully; grievously: *He was sorely distressed.* **2.** Extremely; greatly: *sorely amused.*

sor•ghum |sôr'gəm| *n.* **1.** A grain-bearing grass grown as feed for animals and as a source of syrup. **2.** Syrup made from the juice of this plant. [SEE PICTURE]

so•ri |sôr'ī'| *or* |sōr'ī'| *n.* Plural of **sorus.**

so•ror•i•ty |sə rôr'ĭ tē| *or* |-rŏr'-| *n., pl.* **so•ror•i•ties.** A social club for women.

sor•rel¹ |sôr'əl| *n.* Any of several plants with sour-tasting leaves. See **wood sorrel.**

sor•rel² |sôr'əl| *n.* **1.** A yellowish brown. **2.** A yellowish-brown horse. *—adj.* Yellowish brown: *a sorrel horse.*

sor•row |sŏr'ō| *or* |sôr'ō| *n.* **1.** Mental anguish or suffering because of loss or injury; sadness; grief. **2.** Something that causes sadness or grief. **3.** The expression of sadness or grief: *He looked at them with sorrow.* *—v.* To feel or display sadness or grief; grieve. [SEE NOTE]

sor•row•ful |sŏr'ə fəl| *or* |sôr'-| *adj.* Causing, feeling, or expressing sorrow: *a sorrowful event; a sorrowful voice.* **—sor'row•ful•ly** *adv.*

sor•ry |sŏr'ē| *or* |sôr'ē| *adj.* **sor•ri•er, sor•ri•est. 1.** Feeling or expressing sympathy, pity, or regret. **2.** Worthless or inferior; poor; paltry: *a sorry excuse; a sorry collection of junk.* **3.** Causing sorrow or grief; grievous; sad: *sorry news of pollution.* **—sor'ri•ly** *adv.* [SEE NOTE]

sort |sôrt| *n.* **1.** A group or collection of similar persons or things; class; kind: *a peaceable sort of beast; a machine of some sort.* **2.** The character or nature of something; type; quality: *a person of an interesting sort.* *—v.* **1.** To arrange according to class, kind, or size; classify: *sorted the mail.* **2.** To separate (one kind) from the rest: *He sorted out the nails of the largest size.* **—sort'ing** *adj.: a sorting machine.* **—sort'er** *n.*

***Idioms.* after a sort.** In a haphazard or imper-

sonnet

Samuel Johnson's Dictionary *(1755) makes the following comment at the entry for* **sonnet**: *"It is not very suitable to the English language; and has not been used by any man of eminence since Milton. . . ." But literary fashions change; after Johnson's time the sonnet was again widely used by English poets, among them Wordsworth, Keats, and Shelley.*

sorghum

sorrow/sorry

These two words are basically unrelated, but they have been associated for so long that they cannot now be separated. **Sorrow** *was Old English* sorh, *"anxiety," which is descended from a root meaning "to worry, to be sick."* **Sorry** *was Old English* sārig, *"painful, sad"; it is related to* **sore.**

sound[1-2-3-4]
Sound[1] *is from Old French* son, *which is from Latin* sonus, *"sound," from which we have also* **sonic** *and* **sonorous**. **Sound**[2] *was Old English* gesund, *"healthy"; closely related to this is German* gesundheit, *"health," which is often said to someone who has sneezed (since there is an old belief that sneezing can be unlucky).* **Sound**[3] *and* **sound**[4] *are related.* **Sound**[3] *was Old English* sund, *originally meaning "the act of swimming, a swim," hence "a body of water narrow enough to swim across." This word (which is related to* **swim***) was borrowed into Old French as* sonde, *"a line for measuring the depth of a body of water"; from this was formed* sonder, *"to measure depth," which was borrowed back into English as* **sound**[4].

ă pat/ā pay/â care/ä father/ĕ pet/ ē be/ĭ pit/ī pie/î fierce/ŏ pot/ ō go/ô paw, for/oi oil/ŏŏ book/ ōō boot/ou out/ŭ cut/û fur/ *th* the/th thin/hw which/zh vision/ ə ago, item, pencil, atom, circus

fect way: *did the work after a sort.* **of sorts** or **of a sort.** Of a mediocre or inferior kind: *a dancer of sorts.* **out of sorts.** *Informal.* **1.** Somewhat ill. **2.** In a bad mood; irritable. **sort of.** *Informal.* Somewhat; rather: *It sounds sort of silly.*

sor•tie |sôr'tē| *n.* **1.** An armed attack made from a place surrounded by enemy forces. **2.** A flight of a warplane on a combat mission.

so•rus |sôr'əs| *or* |sōr'-| *n., pl.* **so•ri** |sôr'ī'| *or* |sōr'ī'|. One of the clusters of spore cases formed on the undersides of fern fronds. [SEE PICTURE]

S O S **1.** The letters represented by the signal ...---..., used internationally as a distress signal by ships and aircraft. **2.** Any signal for help.

so-so |sō'sō'| *adj.* Neither very good nor very bad; just passable: *a so-so party.* —*adv.* Indifferently; tolerably; passably: *performed so-so.*

sot |sŏt| *n.* A drunkard.

souf•flé |sōō flā'| *n.* A light, fluffy baked dish made of beaten egg whites combined with other ingredients. —***modifier:*** *a soufflé dish.*

sought |sôt|. Past tense and past participle of **seek.**

soul |sōl| *n.* **1.** The animating and vital principle in a person conceived as an immaterial entity; the spiritual, moral, or emotional nature of someone: *"These are the times that try men's souls"* (Thomas Paine). **2.** A spirit; a ghost; shade. **3.** A human being: *not a soul in sight.* **4.** The vital part of something: *the soul of art.* **5.** Someone considered as an inspiring force: *the life and soul of the evening.* **6.** *Slang.* The combination of qualities that enables one to be in harmony with oneself and to convey to others the honest and unadorned expression of the hard side of life. —*adj. Slang.* Of or derived from the Negro or his culture: *soul food; soul music.* ¶*These sound alike* **soul, sol, sole.**

soul•ful |sōl'fəl| *adj.* Full of or expressing a deep feeling: *a soulful sound; a soulful quiet.* —**soul'ful•ly** *adv.* —**soul'ful•ness** *n.*

soul•less |sōl'lĭs| *adj.* Lacking sensitivity or the capacity for deep feeling. —**soul'less•ly** *adv.*

sound[1] |sound| *n.* **1.** A type of wave motion that travels through air and other elastic materials as variations of internal pressure and density, detectable by human ears in air when the variation of pressure is at least 1.4 billionths (1.4×10^{-9}) of a pound per square inch and the frequency is between about 20 and 20,000 hertz. **2. a.** Any sensation produced in the organs of hearing by waves of this type. **b.** Sensations of this type in general. **3.** A distinctive noise: *the sound of laughter; a hollow sound.* **4.** The distance over which something can be heard; earshot: *within sound of the waterfall.* **5.** An articulation made by the vocal apparatus: *the sound of "y" in "try."* **6.** Recorded material, as for a motion picture: *a good film but the sound was bad.* **7.** A mental impression; import; implication: *He did not like the sound of the invitation.* —***modifier:*** *sound waves; sound effects.* —*v.* **1.** To make or cause to make a sound: *The whistle sounded. They sounded the gong.* **2.** To produce a certain audible effect: *The words "break" and "brake" sound alike.* **3.** To seem to be: *The news sounds good.* **4.** To summon, announce, or signal by a sound: *sound a warning.* —***phrasal verb.*** **sound off.** *Slang.* To speak in a loud or complaining way: *sounding off about too much work.* [SEE NOTE]

sound[2] |sound| *adj.* **sound•er, sound•est.** **1.** Free from defect, decay, damage, injury, or sickness: *a sound mind in a sound body; safe and sound.* **2.** Solid and firm: *a sound foundation.* **3.** Secure or reliable: *a sound economy.* **4.** Sensible and correct: *sound reasoning.* **5.** Legally valid; good: *sound title.* **6.** Complete or thorough: *a sound thrashing.* **7.** Deep and unbroken: *a sound sleep.* —**sound'ly** *adv.* —**sound'ness** *n.* [SEE NOTE]

sound[3] |sound| *n.* **1.** A long body of water, wider than a strait or channel, connecting larger bodies of water. **2.** A long, wide inlet of the ocean. [SEE NOTE]

sound[4] |sound| *v.* **1.** To measure the depth of (water), especially by means of a weighted line. **2.** To measure depth: *sounding with a long pole.* **3.** To try to learn (someone's) attitudes or opinions: *I want to sound him out on this before asking him directly.* **4.** To dive swiftly downward, as a whale does. [SEE NOTE]

sound barrier. The **sonic barrier.**

sound box. A hollow chamber in the body of a musical instrument, such as a violin, that intensifies the resonance of the tone.

sound•ing |soun'dĭng| *n.* **1.** The act or process of making measurements of depth, especially of a body of water. **2.** A measurement obtained by sounding.

sounding board. **1.** A thin, flexible board forming the upper portion of the resonant chamber of a musical instrument, such as a violin or piano, serving to increase resonance. **2.** Any structure placed over or behind the position of a speaker to reflect the sound of his voice to the audience. **3.** Any device or means serving to spread or popularize an idea or point of view: *using the press as a sounding board.* **4.** A person, group, etc., whose reactions to an idea, opinion, etc., will serve as a measure of its effectiveness or attractiveness.

sound•proof |sound'prōōf'| *adj.* Designed or treated to allow little or no audible sound to pass through or enter: *a soundproof wall; a soundproof room.* —*v.* To make soundproof.

sound track. A narrow strip at the edge of a motion-picture film that carries a recording of the sound.

soup |sōōp| *n.* A liquid food prepared from meat or vegetable stock, often with other ingredients added. —***modifier:*** *a soup bowl.* —*v.* —**soup up.** *Slang.* To add horsepower or greater speed potential to (an engine or vehicle).

sour |sour| *adj.* **1.** Having a sharp or acid taste: *sour lemonade.* **2.** Spoiled; rank; rancid: *a sour odor.* **3.** Bad-tempered; cross; peevish: *a sour temper.* **4.** Unpleasant or bad; disagreeable or wrong: *a sour note in the conversation. His acting went sour.* **5.** Excessively acid: *sour soil.* —*n.* **1.** The sensation of a sharp, acid taste. **2.** Anything that is sour. —*v.* **1.** To make or become sour. **2.** To make or become disagreeable, disillusioned, or disenchanted: *The experience had soured him. Her attitude soured after her efforts failed.* —**sour'ly** *adv.* —**sour'ness** *n.*

source |sôrs| *or* |sōrs| *n.* **1.** A place or thing

from which something comes; a point of origin: *used the sea as a source of food.* **2.** The beginning of a stream or river. **3.** A person, place, book, etc., that supplies information.

sour cream. A smooth, thick soured cream used in soups, salads, and various meat dishes.

sour•dough |**sour**'dō'| *n.* Sour fermented dough used as a leaven for bread. —***modifier:*** *sourdough biscuits.*

sou•sa•phone |sōō'zə fōn'| *or* |-sə-| *n.* A form of tuba having a flaring bell, used in marching bands. [SEE PICTURE]

souse |sous| *v.* **soused, sous•ing. 1.** To plunge into a liquid. **2.** To make soaking wet; drench. **3.** To steep in a brine or other liquid, as in pickling. **4.** *Slang.* To make or become drunk. —*n.* **1.** Something pickled in brine, especially the feet or ears of a pig. **2.** The brine used in pickling. **3.** *Slang.* A drunkard.

south |south| *n.* **1.** The direction along a meridian 90 degrees clockwise from the direction from which the sun rises. **2.** Often **South.** A region or part of the earth that lies in this direction: *a warm wind from the south.* **3. the South.** The southern part of the United States, especially the states that fought for the Confederacy during the Civil War. —*adj.* **1.** Of, in, or toward the south: *the south side of the mountain.* **2.** Often **South.** Forming or belonging to a region, country, etc., toward the south: *South Korea.* **3.** From the south: *a dry south wind.* —*adv.* In a direction to or toward the south: *He pointed south. We hiked south.*

South Africa. A country in southernmost Africa. Population, 24,336,000. Administrative capital, Pretoria. Legislative capital, Cape Town. —**South African.**

South America. The southern continent of the Western Hemisphere. —**South American.**

South Car•o•li•na |kăr'ə lī'nə|. A Southern Atlantic state of the United States. Population, 2,617,000. Capital, Columbia. —**South Carolinian.**

South China Sea. A section of the Pacific bordered by China and Southeast Asia.

South Da•ko•ta |də kō'tə|. A Middle Western state of the United States. Population, 673,000. Capital, Pierre. —**South Dakotan.**

south•east |south ēst'| *n.* **1.** The direction that lies 45 degrees clockwise from east, or halfway between east and south. **2.** An area or region that lies in this direction: *An attack from the southeast was expected at any moment.* **3. the Southeast.** The part of the United States south of Pennsylvania and the Ohio River and east of the Mississippi River. —*adj.* **1.** Of, in, or toward the southeast: *the southeast corner of the block.* **2.** From the southeast: *a southeast wind.* —*adv.* In a direction to or toward the southeast: *walking southeast.* —**south•east'ern** *adj.*

Southeast Asia. A region generally considered to include Burma, Thailand, Laos, Cambodia, Vietnam, Malaysia, Singapore, and Indonesia.

south•east•er |south ē'stər| *or* |sou ē'-| *n.* A storm or gale that blows from the southeast.

south•east•er•ly |south ē'stər lē| *adj.* **1.** In or toward the southeast: *a southeasterly direction.* **2.** From the southeast: *a southeasterly breeze.* —*adv.: a wind blowing southeasterly.*

south•east•ward |south ēst'wərd| *adv.* Also **south•east•wards** |south ēst'wərdz|. To or toward the southeast: *journeyed southeastward.* —*adj.: a southeastward journey.* —*n.* A direction or region to the southeast.

south•er |**sou'***th*ər| *n.* A strong wind from the south.

south•er•ly |sŭ*th*'ər lē| *adj.* **1.** In or toward the south: *a southerly direction.* **2.** From the south: *a southerly wind.* —*adv.: He wandered southerly.* —*n., pl.* **south•er•lies.** A storm or wind from the south.

south•ern |sŭ*th*'ərn| *adj.* **1.** Of, in, or toward the south: *the southern side of the mountain; southern Kansas.* **2.** From the south: *a southern breeze.* **3.** Characteristic of or found in southern regions: *a southern climate.* **4. Southern.** Of the South of the United States: *a Southern statesman; Southern traditions.*

south•ern•er |sŭ*th*'ər nər| *n.* Often **Southerner. 1.** A person who lives in or comes from the south. **2.** A person from the South of the U.S.

Southern Hemisphere. The half of the earth south of the equator.

south•ern•most |sŭ*th*'ərn mōst'| *adj.* Farthest south.

Southern Yem•en |yĕm'ĕn| *or* |yā'mən|. A country on the southern coast of Arabia. Population, 1,633,000. Capital, Aden.

south•ing |**sou'***th*ĭng| *n.* **1.** A difference between the latitudes of two positions as a result of southward movement. **2.** Progress toward the south.

South Island. The larger of the two main islands of New Zealand.

South Korea. A country occupying the southern half of a peninsula in eastern Asia. Population, 37,449,000. Capital, Seoul.

south•land |**south'**lənd| *or* |-lănd'| *n.* Often **Southland.** A region in the south, especially the South of the United States: *folk music of the Southland.*

south•paw |**south'**pô'|. *Slang. n.* A left-handed player, especially a left-handed baseball pitcher. —*adj.* Left-handed.

South Pole. 1. The southernmost point of the earth; the point in the south at which the earth's axis of rotation intersects the surface of the earth. **2.** The celestial zenith of the heavens as viewed from the south terrestrial pole. **3. south pole.** The pole of a magnet that tends to point south.

South Sea Islands. The islands of the South Pacific.

South Seas. The South Pacific.

south-seek•ing pole |**south'**sē'kĭng|. The pole of a magnet that is attracted to the south; the south pole.

South Vietnam. The former name for the southern part of **Vietnam.**

south•ward |**south'**wərd| *adv.* Also **southwards** |**south'**wərdz|. To or toward the south: *He gazed southward.* —*adj.: a southward hike.* —*n.* A direction or region to the south: *traveled to the southward.*

south•west |south wĕst'| *n.* **1.** The direction 45 degrees clockwise from south; the direction halfway between south and west. **2.** An area or region lying in this direction. **3. the Southwest.**

sousaphone
The **sousaphone** was designed by John Philip *Sousa* (1854–1932), American bandmaster and composer; among his most famous marches are the *Washington Post March* and *Stars and Stripes Forever.*

southwester

sow[1-2]

Sow[1] *was Old English* sāwan, *"to plant seed"; it is related to the word* **seed. Sow[2]** *was Old English* sugu, *"female pig," descending from the prehistoric Indo-European word* su- *or* sus, *"pig." This appears in Latin as* sūs, *which is now the technical name of the pig genus.* Su- *had an extended form,* suīno-, *appearing in Old English* swīn, *"pig," which became* **swine** *in Modern English.*

spade[2]

ă pat/ā pay/â care/ä father/ĕ pet/ ē be/ĭ pit/ī pie/î fierce/ŏ pot/ ō go/ô paw, for/oi oil/ŏŏ book/ ōō boot/ou out/ŭ cut/û fur/ *th* the/th thin/hw which/zh vision/ ə ago, item, pencil, atom, circus

A region of the United States generally considered to include New Mexico, Arizona, Texas, California, Nevada, Utah, and Colorado. *—adj.* **1.** Of, in, or toward the southwest: *a southwest window.* **2.** From the southwest: *a southwest wind. —adv.* To or toward the southwest: *facing southwest.* —**south•west'ern** *adj.*

south•west•er |south wĕs'tər| *or* |sou wĕs'-| *n.* **1.** A storm or gale from the southwest. **2.** A waterproof hat, often of oilskin or canvas, with a broad brim in back to protect the neck. [SEE PICTURE]

south•west•er•ly |south wĕs'tər lē| *adj.* **1.** In or toward the southwest: *a southwesterly march.* **2.** From the southwest: *a southwesterly wind. —adv.: moving southwesterly.*

south•west•ward |south wĕst'wərd| *adv.* Also **south•west•wards** |south wĕst'wərdz|. To or toward the southwest: *sailing southwestward. —adj.: a southwestward journey. —n.* A direction or region to the southwest.

sou•ve•nir |sōō'və nîr'| *n.* Something kept as a remembrance, as of a place, occasion, etc.; a memento. *—**modifier:** a souvenir shop.*

sou'west•er or **sou•west•er** |sou wĕs'tər| *n.* A form of the word **southwester.**

sov•er•eign |sŏv'ə rĭn| *or* |sŏv'rĭn| *n.* **1.** The chief of state in a monarchy; a king or queen; a monarch. **2.** A former British coin worth one pound. *—adj.* **1.** Paramount; supreme: *sovereign wisdom.* **2.** Having supreme rank or power: *a sovereign leader.* **3.** Independent: *sovereign states.* **4.** Unsurpassed: *a sovereign remedy.*

sov•er•eign•ty |sŏv'ə rĭn tē| *or* |sŏv'rĭn-| *n., pl.* **sov•er•eign•ties. 1.** Supremacy of authority or rule: *sovereignty over a territory.* **2.** Royal rank, authority, or power: *They did not dispute his sovereignty.* **3.** Complete independence: *Each state kept its sovereignty.*

so•vi•et |sō'vē ĕt'| *or* |-ĭt| *or* |sŏv'ē-| *n.* **1.** In the Soviet Union, one of the popularly elected legislative assemblies. **2. the Soviets.** The people and government of the Soviet Union. *—adj.* **1.** Of a soviet. **2. Soviet.** Of the Union of Soviet Socialist Republics.

Soviet Union. An unofficial name of the Union of Soviet Socialist Republics.

sow[1] |sō| *v.* **sowed, sown** |sōn| or **sowed, sow•ing. 1.** To plant (seeds) to produce a crop: *The farmer sowed wheat and corn. He sowed in straight, even rows.* **2.** To plant or scatter seed in or on: *He sowed his fields in the spring.* **3.** To scatter as if by planting: *sowed concealed machine guns among the bushes.* ¶*These sound alike* **sow[1], sew, so.** —**sow'er** *n.* [SEE NOTE]

sow[2] |sou| *n.* **1.** A full-grown female pig. **2.** The full-grown female of certain other animals. [SEE NOTE]

sox |sŏks| *n.* A plural of **sock.**

soy |soi| *n.* The soybean; soybeans in general.

soy•a |soi'ə| *n.* A form of the word **soy.**

soy•bean |soi'bēn'| *n.* Also **soya bean. 1.** A bean plant native to Asia, widely grown for its edible, highly nutritious seeds, which are also a source of oil, flour, and many other products. **2.** A seed of this plant. *—**modifier:** soybean oil.*

soy sauce. Also **soya sauce.** A brown, salty liquid made from soybeans and used to flavor food.

spa |spä| *n.* **1.** A spring whose waters contain dissolved mineral salts. **2.** A resort area where such springs exist.

space |spās| *n.* **1. a.** A set of points or elements that is assumed to satisfy some set of geometric postulates: *a space of five dimensions.* **b.** The familiar three-dimensional region or field of everyday experience. **2.** The expanse in which the solar system, stars, and galaxies exist. **3. a.** Broadly, the separation between a pair of objects, events, etc. **b.** Any measure used to express such a separation: *trains separated by a space of three minutes.* **4.** Any blank or empty area: *the spaces between words. Fill in the blank space.* **5.** An area provided for a particular purpose: *a parking space.* **6. a.** A period or interval of time. **b.** A little while: *for a space.* **7.** Any of the blank areas between the lines of a musical staff. **8.** In a telegraph system or any system using a code that can be represented as a series of binary digits, the physical condition that corresponds to the digit 0. *—**modifier:** space travel. —v.* **spaced, spac•ing. 1.** To arrange or organize with spaces between: *Carefully space the words on the poster.* **2.** To separate or keep apart.

space•craft |spās'krăft'| *or* |-kräft'| *n., pl.* **space•craft.** A vehicle designed for space travel.

space flight. Flight beyond the atmosphere of the earth.

space probe. An unmanned spacecraft carrying instruments designed to make observations of space or of a celestial body.

space•ship |spās'shĭp'| *n.* A spacecraft that is capable of carrying a crew or passengers.

space shuttle. A space vehicle designed to transport astronauts to and fro between Earth and an orbiting space station.

space sickness. Any of various ailments or disorders from which an individual may suffer as a result of space travel.

space station. A large satellite capable of accommodating a crew, placed in permanent orbit around the earth.

space suit. A protective pressurized suit having an independent supply of air or oxygen and other devices designed to allow the wearer to move about freely in space.

space-time |spās'tīm'| *n.* The four-dimensional mathematical space in which a point is located by the three coordinates of ordinary space and one coordinate of time, used in the description and study of physical objects and events.

space walk. An excursion by an astronaut outside a spacecraft in space. —**space walker.**

spac•ing |spā'sĭng| *n.* **1.** The act, process, or result of arranging things so that they are separated or spaced. **2.** The separation between things, such as printed characters; space.

spa•cious |spā'shəs| *adj.* **1.** Having much space; extensive: *a spacious room.* **2.** Vast in range or scope: *a spacious landscape.* —**spa'cious•ly** *adv.* —**spa'cious•ness** *n.*

spade[1] |spād| *n.* A digging tool with a long handle and a flat iron blade that is pressed into the ground with the foot. *—v.* **spad•ed, spad•ing. 1.** To dig with a spade: *spade the garden.* **2.** To place with a spade. [SEE NOTE on p. 831]

spade[2] |spād| *n.* **1.** A black figure, shaped like an inverted heart, on a playing card. **2.** A card bearing this figure. **3. spades.** The suit in a deck of cards having this figure as its symbol. [SEE NOTE & SEE PICTURE on p. 830]

spa•dix |spā′dĭks| *n., pl.* **spa•di•ces** |spā′dĭ sēz′|. A clublike stalk bearing tiny flowers, often surrounded by a leaflike or petallike part, as in the jack-in-the-pulpit or the calla lily. See **spathe.**

spa•ghet•ti |spə gĕt′ē| *n.* A pasta made into long, solid strings and cooked by boiling. —*modifier: spaghetti sauce.*

Spain |spān|. A country in western Europe, on the Iberian Peninsula. Population, 35,225,000. Capital, Madrid.

spake |spāk|. *Archaic.* A past tense of **speak.**

span[1] |spăn| *n.* **1.** The distance between two points, lines, objects, etc. **2. a.** The distance that a horizontal structural part extends between vertical supports. **b.** A section of a bridge that extends from one point of vertical support to another. **3.** The distance from the tip of the thumb to the tip of the little finger when the hand is fully extended, formerly used as a unit of measure equal to about nine inches. **4.** A period of time: *a span of four hours.* —*v.* **spanned, span•ning. 1. a.** To stretch the extended hand over or across in a span: *Almost any pianist can span a ninth.* **b.** To measure by reaching the hand across in this way. **2.** To extend across: *a fallen tree that spans the castle moat; a memory that spans 30 years.*

span[2] |spăn| *n.* A pair of animals matched in size, strength, or color: *a span of oxen.*

span•gle |spăng′gəl| *n.* **1.** A small disk of shiny metal or plastic that may be sewn on cloth, clothes, or accessories for decoration; a sequin. **2.** Any small, sparkling object, drop, or spot: *spangles of sunlight.* —*v.* **span•gled, span•gling.** To decorate or adorn with or as if with sparkling spangles. —**span′gled** *adj.: a spangled costume.*

Span•iard |spăn′yərd| *n.* A native or inhabitant of Spain.

span•iel |spăn′yəl| *n.* Any of several breeds of small to medium-sized dogs with drooping ears, short legs, and a silky, wavy coat.

Span•ish |spăn′ĭsh| *n.* **1. the Spanish.** The people of Spain. **2.** The Romance language of Spain and those areas of Latin America once under Spanish domination. —*adj.* Of Spain, the Spanish, or their language.

Span•ish-A•mer•i•can War |spăn′ĭsh ə mĕr′ĭ kən|. A war fought between Spain and the United States in 1898.

Spanish Armada. A Spanish fleet sent against England in 1588, defeated and subsequently destroyed by storms.

Spanish Main. See **main.**

Spanish moss. A plant of the southeastern United States and tropical America that grows on trees and hangs down in long, grayish, threadlike masses. [SEE PICTURE]

spank |spăngk| *v.* To slap on the buttocks with the open hand. —*n.* A slap on the buttocks.

spank•ing |spăng′kĭng| *n.* Punishment by slapping on the buttocks: *The child got a spanking for being late.* —*adj.* **1.** *Informal.* Exceptional; remarkable: *a spanking jump.* **2.** Bright; fast: *a spanking pace.* —*adv. Informal.* Exceptionally; very: *a spanking new kitchen.*

span•ner |spăn′ər| *n. British.* A wrench.

spar[1] |spär| *n.* A pole, used as a mast, boom, yard, or bowsprit on a sailing vessel.

spar[2] |spär| *v.* **sparred, spar•ring. 1.** To box, especially for practice. **2.** To bandy words about in a quarrel or argument.

spar[3] |spär| *n.* Any of various minerals, such as feldspar, that are nonmetallic, have a glassy luster, and break easily along planes of cleavage.

spare |spâr| *v.* **spared, spar•ing. 1. a.** To treat mercifully; deal with leniently: *The pirates spared their captives.* **b.** To refrain from destroying or harming: *spared the trees along the lane.* **2.** To save or relieve from pain, trouble, etc.: *They spared him from the ordeal.* **3.** To use with restraint: *spare the horses.* **4.** To give or grant out of one's resources: *Can you spare me a dime? We could not spare him from the farm.* —*adj.* **spar•er, spar•est. 1. a.** Ready when needed: *a spare tire.* **b.** In excess of what is needed; extra: *spare cash.* **c.** Free for other use: *spare time.* **2. a.** Economical; meager: *a spare breakfast.* **b.** Thin or lean. —*n.* **1.** A replacement, such as a tire, reserved for future need. **2. a.** The act of knocking down all ten pins with two rolls of a bowling ball. **b.** The score so made. —**spare′ly** *adv.* —**spare′ness** *n.*

spare•ribs |spâr′rĭbz′| *pl.n.* A cut of pork consisting of the lower ribs that are closely trimmed.

spar•ing |spâr′ĭng| *adj.* Thrifty; frugal. —**spar′ing•ly** *adv.* —**spar′ing•ness** *n.*

spark |spärk| *n.* **1.** A glowing particle, such as one thrown off or left over from a fire or one caused by friction. **2. a.** A brief flash of light, especially one produced by electric discharge. **b.** An electric discharge of this kind, especially a short one. **c.** The current that flows in such a discharge. **3.** Something, as a quality or factor, with latent potential; a seed: *the spark of genius.* —*v.* **1.** To produce or give off sparks. **2.** To set in motion or rouse to action: *His speech sparked them into working harder.*

spar•kle |spär′kəl| *v.* **spar•kled, spar•kling. 1.** To give off or produce sparks. **2.** To release bubbles of gas; effervesce. **3.** To be brilliant or witty; shine with animation: *The conversation sparkled at the dinner table.* —**spar′kling** *adj.: sparkling lights; sparkling conversation.* —*n.* **1.** A small spark or glowing particle. **2.** The property or capability of releasing bubbles of gas; effervescence. **3.** Animation; vivacity.

spar•kler |spär′klər| *n.* **1.** Someone or something that sparkles. **2.** A firework that burns slowly and produces a shower of sparks.

spark plug. A device that fits into a threaded hole extending into the combustion chamber of an internal-combustion engine, producing an electric spark to ignite the fuel mixture. [SEE PICTURE]

spar•row |spăr′ō| *n.* Any of several small brownish or grayish birds, such as the widespread **house sparrow** (or **English sparrow**), which is common in cities.

sparse |spärs| *adj.* **spars•er, spars•est.** Not dense or crowded: *sparse vegetation; a sparse population.* —**sparse′ly** *adv.* —**sparse′ness** *n.*

Spar•ta |spär′tə|. An ancient city-state in southern Greece, famous for its military might and the strict discipline of its soldiers.

Spar•tan |spär′tn| *n.* **1.** A citizen of Sparta.

spade[1-2]

Spade[1] *was Old English* spadu, *"digging tool."* **Spade**[2] *is from Italian* espada, *"sword." The symbol on Italian playing cards represented a broad-bladed sword; on English playing cards, since the word was similar to* **spade**[1], *the symbol was reshaped to resemble a digging tool.*

Spanish moss

Trees with Spanish moss

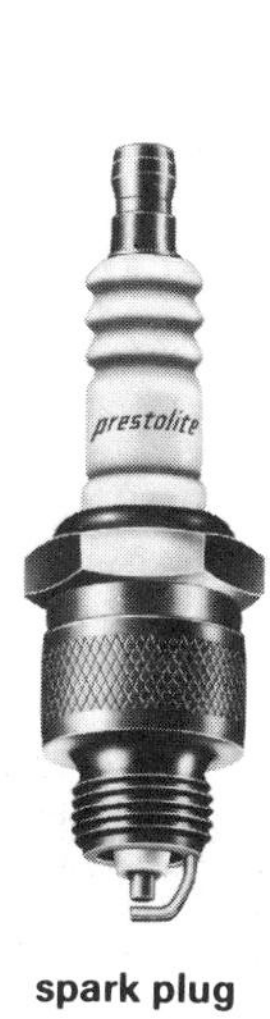

spark plug

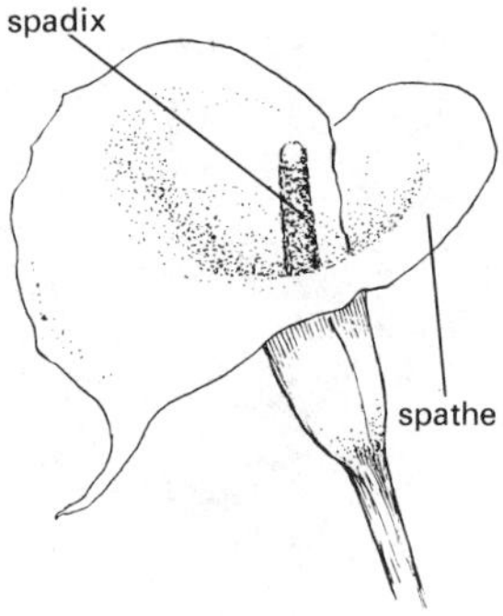

spathe
Calla lily

ă pat/ā pay/â care/ä father/ĕ pet/ē be/ĭ pit/ī pie/î fierce/ŏ pot/ō go/ô paw, for/oi oil/ŏŏ book/ōō boot/ou out/ŭ cut/û fur/*th* the/th thin/hw which/zh vision/ə ago, item, pencil, atom, circus

2. Someone of Spartan character. *—adj.* **1.** Of Sparta or the Spartans. **2.** Resembling the Spartans; austere.

spasm |**spăz'**əm| *n.* **1.** A sudden, involuntary contraction of a muscle or group of muscles. **2.** Any sudden burst of energy, activity, etc.

spas•mod•ic |spăz **mŏd'**ĭk| *adj.* **1.** Of, like, or affected by a spasm. **2.** Happening intermittently; fitful: *spasmodic attempts to climb the mountain.* —**spas•mod'i•cal•ly** *adv.*

spas•tic |**spăs'**tĭk| *adj.* Of, affected by, producing, or displaying spasms. *—n.* **1.** A person who suffers from muscular spasms. **2.** A person afflicted with spastic paralysis. —**spas'ti•cal•ly** *adv.*

spastic paralysis. A chronic diseased condition that involves exaggerated reflexes of the tendons, muscular spasms, and hardening of the spinal cord.

spat[1] |spăt|. A past tense and past participle of **spit** (eject saliva).

spat[2] |spăt| *n.* Often **spats.** A cloth or leather covering for the ankle and the top part of the shoe, having buttons up the side and a strap under the instep; a gaiter.

spat[3] |spăt| *n.* A brief, petty quarrel. *—v.* To engage in a brief, petty quarrel.

spate |spāt| *n.* **1.** A sudden flood, rush, or outpouring: *a spate of bad luck.* **2.** A flash flood.

spathe |spā*th*| *n.* A leaflike or petallike part surrounding a clublike flower stalk, as in the jack-in-the-pulpit or the calla lily. See **spadix.** [SEE PICTURE]

spa•tial |**spā'**shəl| *adj.* Of, like, or involving space. —**spa'tial•ly** *adv.*

spat•ter |**spăt'**ər| *v.* **1.** To scatter in drops or small splashes: *She spattered paint on her dress. Water spattered on the floor.* **2.** To spot or soil with a liquid: *spattered his tie with gravy.* **3.** To fall with a splash or splashing sound: *Rain spattered into the pool.* *—n.* **1.** The act of spattering. **2.** A spot or stain: *spatters of grease on the stove.* **3.** A spattering sound: *the spatter of raindrops.*

spat•u•la |**spăch'**ə lə| *n.* A tool with a broad, flat, flexible blade, used for spreading frosting, plaster, or paint, or for removing food from a pan or grill.

spav•in |**spăv'**ĭn| *n.* A disease of the hock joint of horses, causing stiffness and lameness.

spawn |spôn| *n.* **1.** The eggs of water animals such as fishes, oysters, frogs, etc. **2.** Offspring produced in large numbers. *—v.* **1. a.** To lay eggs and breed, as fishes and certain other water animals do: *Salmon swim up streams to spawn.* **b.** To produce from such eggs: *Thousands of frogs were spawned in that pond.* **2.** To produce as if by giving birth to: *The volcano suddenly spawned a brood of fire-belching smaller peaks.*

spay |spā| *v.* To remove the ovaries of (a female animal).

speak |spēk| *v.* **spoke** |spōk|, **spok•en** |**spō'**kən|, **speak•ing. 1.** To utter words; talk: *They spoke about the weather.* **2.** To express (thoughts or feelings): *He spoke his fears. Actions speak louder than words.* **3.** To pronounce, recite, or say: *spoke kind words; speak your piece.* **4.** To give a speech: *The President will speak tonight.* **5.** To declare or tell: *speaking the truth.* **6.** To use (a language) for vocal communication: *He speaks Italian.* **7.** To be on good terms: *They haven't spoken for years.* —***phrasal verbs.* speak down.** To speak in a condescending or patronizing way: *speaking down to children.* **speak for. 1.** To speak in behalf of: *spoke for my client.* **2.** To claim: *This ticket is spoken for.* **speak out. 1.** To talk loudly and clearly. **2.** To talk freely and fearlessly. **speak up. 1.** To raise the voice: *Speak up so we can hear you.* **2.** To speak without hesitation or fear. ***Idioms.* so to speak.** In a manner of speaking; as the saying goes. **speak well for.** To be good evidence or a favorable witness for: *Good work speaks well for one's schooling.* **to speak of.** Worthy of mention: *They found nothing to speak of in the cellar.*

speak•eas•y |**spēk'**ē'zē| *n., pl.* **speak•eas•ies.** *Slang.* A place for the illegal sale of alcoholic drinks, as during U.S. prohibition.

speak•er |**spē'**kər| *n.* **1.** A person who speaks a given language: *a speaker of English.* **2.** A person who delivers a speech in public. **3.** Often **Speaker.** A person who presides over a body of lawmakers; a chairman. **4.** A loudspeaker.

spear |spîr| *n.* **1.** A weapon consisting of a long shaft with a sharply pointed head. **2.** A similar device with barbed prongs, used for spearing fish. **3.** A slender stalk, as of asparagus or grain. —***modifier:*** *spear points; spear wounds.* *—v.* To pierce with or as with a spear.

spear•head |**spîr'**hĕd'| *n.* **1.** The sharpened head of a spear. **2.** The front forces in a military thrust. **3.** A person or group seen as the driving force in an endeavor. *—v.* To be the leader of (a drive or attack).

spear•mint |**spîr'**mĭnt'| *n.* A common mint plant widely used as flavoring. —***modifier:*** *spearmint chewing gum.*

spe•cial |**spĕsh'**əl| *adj.* **1.** Surpassing what is common or usual; exceptional: *a special occasion; special care.* **2.** Distinct among others of a kind: *a special camera.* **3.** Peculiar to a specific person or thing: *special interests.* **4.** Having a specific function, application, etc.: *special training.* **5.** Esteemed: *special friends.* **6.** Additional; extra: *a special flight to Boston.* *—n.* **1.** Something arranged or designed for a particular service or occasion. **2.** A featured attraction, such as a reduced price: *a special on peaches.* **3.** A single, unusual television production. —**spe'cial•ly** *adv.*

spe•cial•ist |**spĕsh'**ə lĭst| *n.* Someone whose work is restricted to a particular activity or to a particular branch of study or research.

spe•cial•ize |**spĕsh'**ə līz'| *v.* **spe•cial•ized, spe•cial•iz•ing. 1.** To focus on a special study, activity, or product: *specialized in underwater photography; a shop that specializes in sports clothes.* **2.** To develop so as to become adapted to a particular environment, function, or way of life: *Some worms have specialized to such a degree that they are parasites on only one kind of animal.* —**spe'cial•ized'** *adj.: a specialized field of study.* —**spe'cial•i•za'tion** *n.*

special relativity. The theory of space and time developed by Albert Einstein, based on the assumptions that all laws of physics hold equally well in all nonaccelerated frames of reference and that light travels in straight lines at a constant speed unaffected by the motion of its source, having as one of its important consequences the principle that mass and energy are equivalent. See **general relativity, mass-energy.**

spe•cial•ty |**spĕsh'**əl tē| *n., pl.* **spe•cial•ties. 1.** A special pursuit, occupation, service, etc.: *His specialty is portrait painting.* **2.** A special feature: *The restaurant's specialty is strawberry shortcake.* —***modifier:*** *a specialty shop.*

spe•cie |**spē'**shē| *or* |-sē| *n.* Coined money. —***modifier:*** *specie payments.*

spe•cies |**spē'**shēz'| *or* |-sēz'| *n., pl.* **spe•cies. 1. a.** A group of similar animals or plants that are regarded as of the same kind and that are able to breed with one another. **b.** An animal or plant belonging to such a group, identified by a scientific name consisting of two Latin terms. **2.** A type, kind, or sort.

spe•ci•fic |spĭ **sĭf'**ĭk| *adj.* **1.** Explicitly set forth; definite: *specific questions; specific qualifications.* **2.** Of a plant or animal species: *The specific name of man is "Homo sapiens."* **3.** Special, distinctive, or unique: *a specific trait.* —*n.* **1.** A distinct quality, statement, etc.: *instruction in the specifics of the job.* **2.** A remedy intended for a particular disorder. —**spe•cif'•i•cal•ly** *adv.*

spec•i•fi•ca•tion |spĕs'ə fĭ **kā'**shən| *n.* **1. a. specifications.** A list of statements giving an exact description of a product, a structure to be constructed, an invention, etc. **b.** Any of the statements included in such a list. **2.** A specified item.

specific gravity. 1. The quotient of the measure of the mass of a solid or liquid divided by the measure of the mass of an equal volume of water at 4°C. **2.** The quotient of the measure of the mass of a gas divided by the measure of the mass of an equal volume of air or hydrogen under prescribed conditions of temperature and pressure.

specific heat. 1. The ratio of the amount of heat needed to raise the temperature of a unit mass of a substance by one unit to the amount of heat needed to raise the temperature of a unit mass of a reference substance, usually water, by the same amount. **2.** The amount of heat, measured in calories, needed to raise the temperature of one gram of a substance by one degree Centigrade.

spec•i•fy |**spĕs'**ə fī'| *v.* **spec•i•fied, spec•i•fy•ing, spec•i•fies. 1.** To state in a clear, precise, and unambiguous way. **2.** To include in a list of specifications.

spec•i•men |**spĕs'**ə mən| *n.* **1.** An element of a set or a part of a whole, taken as representative of the entire set or the whole. **2.** A sample of blood, tissue, urine, etc., used for analysis.

spe•cious |**spē'**shəs| *adj.* Seemingly fair, attractive, sound, or true, but actually not so; deceptive: *a specious plan; specious reasoning.*

speck |spĕk| *n.* **1.** A small spot, mark, or discoloration: *brown specks on the paper.* **2.** A small bit or particle: *a speck of dust.* —*v.* To mark with specks: *Her dress was specked by mud.*

speck•le |**spĕk'**əl| *n.* A speck or small spot, especially a natural marking. —*v.* **speck•led, speck•ling.** To mark or cover with or as with speckles: *an old fender that was speckled by rust; islands that speckle the Caribbean.* —**speck'led** *adj.: a speckled hen.*

spec•ta•cle |**spĕk'**tə kəl| *n.* **1.** A public performance or display. **2.** A marvel or curiosity: *the spectacle of the ocean's tides.* **3.** An object or scene that is regrettably exposed to the public gaze: *She lost her control and made a spectacle of herself.* **4. spectacles.** A pair of eyeglasses.

spec•tac•u•lar |spĕk **tăk'**yə lər| *adj.* Of the nature of a spectacle; sensational; marvelous: *a spectacular view.* —*n.* A television production or motion picture of unusual length and importance. —**spec•tac'u•lar•ly** *adv.*

spec•ta•tor |**spĕk'**tā'tər| *n.* Someone who views an event; an observer or onlooker. —***modifier:*** *a spectator sport.* [SEE NOTE]

spectator
"Though the most be players, some must be spectators."
—Ben Jonson (1573?-1637).

spec•ter, also **spec•tre** |**spĕk'**tər| *n.* **1.** A ghost; apparition. **2.** A threat or foreboding, likened to a ghost.

spec•tra |**spĕk'**trə| *n.* Plural of **spectrum.**

spec•tral |**spĕk'**trəl| *adj.* **1.** Of or resembling a specter: *spectral forms.* **2.** Of or produced by a spectrum. —**spec'tral•ly** *adv.*

spec•trom•e•ter |spĕk **trŏm'**ĭ tər| *n.* **1.** A spectroscope equipped with devices for measuring the wavelengths of the radiation observed by it. **2.** An instrument used to measure the index of refraction of a substance.

spec•tro•scope |**spĕk'**trə skōp'| *n.* Any of various instruments used to resolve radiation into spectra and to make observations or recordings.

spec•trum |**spĕk'**trəm| *n., pl.* **spec•tra** |**spĕk'**trə| or **spec•trums. 1.** The bands of color seen when white light, especially light from the sun, is broken up by refraction, as in a rainbow or by a prism. **2.** A broad range of related qualities, ideas, or activities: *a wide spectrum of emotions.*

spec•u•late |**spĕk'**yə lāt'| *v.* **spec•u•lat•ed, spec•u•lat•ing. 1.** To think deeply on a given subject; ponder: *speculated that life might exist in outer space.* **2.** To buy or sell something, as stocks or land, that involves a risk on the chance of making a substantial profit.

spec•u•la•tion |spĕk'yə **lā'**shən| *n.* **1. a.** The act of thinking deeply about a given subject or idea; consideration; contemplation. **b.** A conclusion, idea, or opinion reached through such thought. **2.** Business dealings involving great risk but offering the chance for quick profit.

spec•u•la•tive |**spĕk'**yə lā'tĭv| *or* |-lə-| *adj.* **1.** Of or involving the act of meditating or thinking deeply about a given subject; inquiring: *a speculative look.* **2.** Based on theory or probability rather than on something proved or certain: *speculative conclusions.* **3.** Of a business dealing involving both risk and the chance for substantial profit: *a speculative project in real estate.* —**spec'u•la'tive•ly** *adv.* —**spec'u•la'tive•ness** *n.*

spec•u•la•tor |**spĕk'**yə lā'tər| *n.* Someone who speculates.

sped |spĕd|. Past tense and past participle of **speed.**

speech |spēch| *n.* **1.** The act of speaking. **2.** The ability to speak. **3.** That which is spoken; an utterance. **4.** The manner in which a person speaks. **5.** A talk or address, especially one prepared for delivery to an audience. **6.** The language or dialect of a nation or region. **7.** A course of instruction, especially one to train public speakers or stage performers or to correct faults in the utterance of words. —***modifier:*** *a speech defect; speech sounds; speech training.*

speech•less |**spēch'**lĭs| *adj.* **1.** Not speaking;

spell[1-2-3]
Spell[1] *is from Old French* espeller, *"to read out (letter by letter)."* **Spell[2]** *was Old English* spell *or* spel, *"story, news." Both the Old French word and the Old English word are based on prehistoric Germanic* spell-, *"to recite, a recitation."* **Spell[3]** *is from Old English* spellian, *"to substitute," hence later "to relieve at work"; it is not related to* **spell[1]** *or* **spell[2]**.

sperm whale

ă pat/ā pay/â care/ä father/ĕ pet/ ē be/ĭ pit/ī pie/î fierce/ŏ pot/ ō go/ô paw, for/oi oil/ŏŏ book/ ōō boot/ou out/ŭ cut/û fur/ *th* the/th thin/hw which/zh vision/ ə ago, item, pencil, atom, circus

silent. **2.** Temporarily unable to speak, as through astonishment, fear, anger, or joy. **3.** Not expressed or not expressible in words: *speechless admiration.* **—speech'less•ly** *adv.* **—speech'less•ness** *n.*

speed |spēd| *n.* **1.** The rate or the measure of the rate at which an object or particle changes position with respect to time, especially: **a.** The distance an object or particle travels divided by the time of travel. **b.** The value that this quotient approaches as it is calculated for a time of travel that can be made as close to zero as desired. **c.** The magnitude of the vector that represents velocity. **2.** A rate of action, activity, or performance calculated with respect to time: *the speed of a chemical reaction.* **3.** The condition of acting or moving rapidly; swiftness: *Show some speed now.* **4.** A gear or set of gears, as in the transmission of a motor vehicle. **5. a.** A number that expresses the sensitivity to light of a photographic film, plate, or paper. **b.** The capability of a lens to admit light. **c.** The length of time the shutter of a camera is open to admit light. **6.** *Slang.* An amphetamine drug. **7.** *Archaic.* Prosperity; success; luck. *—v.* **sped** |spĕd| or **speed•ed, speed•ing. 1.** To go or move rapidly: *sped through the countryside.* **2.** To pass quickly: *as the months sped by.* **3.** To increase the speed or rate of; accelerate: *speed up a mechanism.* **4.** To operate (an automobile or other motor vehicle) at a high speed, especially one that exceeds a lawful limit.

speed•boat |spēd'bōt'| *n.* A motorboat designed to travel at high speeds.

speed•om•e•ter |spē dŏm'ĭ tər| *or* |spĭ-| *n.* **1.** An instrument that measures and indicates speed. **2.** An odometer.

speed•way |spēd'wā'| *n.* **1.** A course over which automobiles are raced. **2.** A road designed for high-speed traffic; an expressway.

speed•y |spē'dē| *adj.* **speed•i•er, speed•i•est.** Swift; quick; prompt: *a speedy runner; a speedy reply.* **—speed'i•ly** *adv.* **—speed'i•ness** *n.*

spell[1] |spĕl| *v.* **spelled** or **spelt** |spĕlt|, **spell•ing. 1.** To name or write in order the letters forming (a word or part of a word). **2.** To be the letters of; form (a word or part of a word): *Arrange these letters so that they spell the name of a color.* **3.** To mean; signify: *The way she looked at us spelled trouble.* ***—phrasal verb.*** **spell out. 1.** To make perfectly clear and understandable: *spell out the rules.* **2.** To read slowly, letter by letter. **3.** To make out (something written) with difficulty; decipher. **4.** To write out in full the letters of (a word), as distinguished from abbreviating. [SEE NOTE]

spell[2] |spĕl| *n.* **1.** A word or group of words thought to have the effect of magic. **2.** The condition of being bewitched or enchanted; a trance. **3.** Fascination: *the spell of a tropical island.* [SEE NOTE]

spell[3] |spĕl| *n.* **1.** A short, indefinite period of time: *stay at home for a spell.* **2.** *Informal.* A period of weather of a particular kind: *a cold spell.* **3.** *Informal.* A period or fit of illness: *a coughing spell.* **4.** A short period of work; a turn; shift: *a spell at the plane's controls.* *—v.* **1.** To relieve (someone) from work temporarily by taking a turn. **2.** To rest for a time from some activity: *spell off in midafternoon.* [SEE NOTE]

spell•bind |spĕl'bīnd'| *v.* **spell•bound** |spĕl'bound'|, **spell•bind•ing.** To hold under or as if under a spell or charm; enthrall; enchant.

spell•bound |spĕl'bound'| *adj.* Held as if under a spell; entranced; fascinated.

spell•er |spĕl'ər| *n.* **1.** Someone who spells words. **2.** A book used in teaching children how to spell.

spell•ing |spĕl'ĭng| *n.* **1.** The act of forming words with letters according to an accepted order. **2.** The way in which a word is spelled. ***—modifier:*** *a spelling rule; spelling tests.*

spelling bee. A contest devoted to the spelling of words.

spelt |spĕlt|. A past tense and past participle of **spell** (to form words).

spend |spĕnd| *v.* **spent** |spĕnt|, **spend•ing. 1.** To use or put out; devote: *spent an hour each day in practicing.* **2.** To pass (time) in a specified place or manner: *spent my vacation in Europe.* **3.** To pay out (money); make payment: *spending my last five dollars; spends too freely on pleasure.* **4.** To deprive of force or strength; exhaust: *spent his creative powers early.* **—spend'er** *n.*

spend•thrift |spĕnd'thrĭft'| *n.* A person who spends money wastefully or foolishly. *—adj.* Wasteful; extravagant.

spent |spĕnt|. Past tense and past participle of **spend.** *—adj.* **1.** Used up; consumed: *mineral resources nearly spent.* **2.** Having no more energy, force, or strength: *sweaty, spent horses.*

sperm |spûrm| *n., pl.* **sperm** or **sperms. 1.** Also **sperm cell.** One of the male sex cells of an animal or plant, uniting with a female sex cell, or egg, in the process of sexual reproduction. **2.** The fluid containing these cells; semen.

sper•ma•ce•ti |spûr'mə sĕt'ē| *n.* A white, waxy substance obtained from the head of the sperm whale and used in making candles, ointments, and cosmetics.

sper•mat•o•phyte |spûr măt'ə fīt'| *or* |spûr'mə tə-| *n.* Any plant belonging to the large group that includes all seed-bearing plants.

sper•ma•to•zo•on |spûr'mə tə zō'ən| *or* |-ŏn| *or* |spûr măt'ə-| *n., pl.* **sper•ma•to•zo•a** |spûr'mə tə zō'ə| *or* |spûr măt'ə-|. A sex cell, or sperm, of a male animal, usually having a long tail by means of which it can move.

sperm oil. A yellow, waxy oil obtained from the sperm whale, used as an industrial lubricant.

sperm whale. A whale with a long, narrow, toothed lower jaw and a large head in which there are cavities containing spermaceti and sperm oil. [SEE PICTURE]

spew |spyōō| *v.* **1.** To vomit or cast out through the mouth. **2.** To force out or come out in a stream: *volcanoes spewing out lava.*

sphag•num |sfăg'nəm| *n.* A grayish moss that grows in swamps and bogs and decomposes to form peat; peat moss.

sphe•noid bone |sfē'noid'|. A bone with winglike projections situated at the base of the skull.

sphere |sfîr| *n.* **1.** A three-dimensional geometric surface having all of its points the same distance from a given point. **2.** An object or figure having this shape. **3.** A planet, star, or other celestial object. **4.** In ancient astronomy, any of a series of transparent globes having the earth as a center and together containing the sun, moon, planets, and stars. **5.** An area of power, control, or influence; domain: *territory within the Communist sphere.* **6.** The extent of one's knowledge, interests, or social position.

spher•i•cal |sfîr′ĭ kəl| *or* |sfĕr′-| *adj.* **1.** Having the shape of a sphere or nearly the shape of a sphere. **2.** Of a sphere or spheres. **3.** Of celestial objects. **—spher′i•cal•ly** *adv.*

spherical aberration. The failure of a lens or mirror that has a spherical surface or surfaces to bring all the rays of light that enter or strike it to the same focus.

sphe•roid |sfîr′oid′| *n.* **1.** A three-dimensional geometric surface generated by rotating an ellipse on or about one of its axes. **2.** A figure or object having such a shape.

sphinc•ter |sfĭngk′tər| *n.* A ringlike muscle that usually remains contracted and keeps the opening of a bodily passage closed, relaxing as required by normal functioning.

sphinx |sfĭngks| *n., pl.* **sphinx•es. 1. a.** An ancient Egyptian figure with the body of a lion and the head of a man, ram, or hawk. **b. Sphinx.** The monumental sphinx having the head of a man at Giza, Egypt. **2.** In Greek mythology, a winged monster that destroyed all who could not answer its riddle. **3.** A person extremely withdrawn or puzzling in manner. [SEE PICTURE]

sphyg•mo•ma•nom•e•ter |sfĭg′mō mə **nŏm′**ĭ tər| *n.* An instrument used to measure and indicate the pressure of the blood in the arteries.

spice |spīs| *n.* **1. a.** A plant substance with a pleasant or strong smell and taste, such as cinnamon, nutmeg, pepper, or cloves, used to flavor food. **b.** Such substances in general. **2.** An odor or fragrance like that of such a substance: *breathed in the spice of the ripening fruit in the orchard.* **3.** Something that adds zest, excitement, interest, etc.: *Variety is the spice of life.* **4.** A small amount; a touch; tinge: *a spice of cold in the air.* —*v.* **spiced, spic•ing. 1.** To flavor with a spice or spices. **2.** To add zest, variety, or a distinctive quality to: *She spiced her conversation with French words and phrases.*

spick-and-span |spĭk′ən spăn′| *adj.* Neat and clean; spotless.

spic•y |spī′sē| *adj.* **spic•i•er, spic•i•est. 1.** Flavored with a spice or spices: *a piece of spicy pumpkin pie.* **2.** Having an odor of or suggestive of spice: *the spicy aroma of pine woods.* **3.** Lively, exciting, etc., especially in a slightly scandalous way: *spicy stories.* **—spic′i•ly** *adv.* **—spic′i•ness** *n.*

spi•der |spī′dər| *n.* Any of many related small animals that have eight legs and a body divided into two parts and that usually spin webs to trap insects. Spiders are sometimes confused with insects but belong to a different group, the arachnids, which also includes the scorpions, mites, and ticks. —***modifier:*** *a spider web.* [SEE PICTURE]

spi•der•y |spī′də rē| *adj.* **1.** Of, resembling, or suggestive of a spider: *the lunar module's spidery legs.* **2.** Fine, delicate, or spindly: *her spidery handwriting.*

spied |spīd|. Past tense and past participle of **spy.**

spies |spīz|. **1.** Plural of the noun **spy. 2.** Third person singular present tense of the verb **spy.**

spif•fy |spĭf′ē| *adj.* **spif•fi•er, spif•fi•est.** *Slang.* Stylish; smart; sharp; natty: *dressed in a spiffy new outfit.*

spig•ot |spĭg′ət| *n.* **1.** A faucet. **2.** A plug or peg used to stop up the opening of a barrel.

spike[1] |spīk| *n.* **1.** A long, heavy nail. **2.** A long, thick, sharp-pointed piece of wood or metal. **3.** A sharp-pointed projection along the top of a fence or wall. **4.** One of a number of sharp metal projections on the soles of shoes worn by certain athletes, used to secure a firm footing. **5.** Also **spike heel.** A narrow, pointed high heel on a woman's shoe. **6.** A long, pointed, projecting part: *the spikes on a cactus.* —*v.* **spiked, spik•ing. 1.** To secure, fasten, or provide with a spike or spikes: *spiked the rails to the railroad ties.* **2.** To pierce or injure with a spike. **3.** To put an end to; thwart; block: *spiked the rumor.* **4.** *Slang.* To add alcoholic liquor to.

spike[2] |spīk| *n.* **1.** An ear of grain. **2.** A long cluster of stalkless or nearly stalkless flowers.

spike•nard |spīk′närd′| *n.* **1.** An aromatic plant from which a fragrant ointment was made in ancient times. **2.** The ointment made from this plant.

spik•y |spī′kē| *adj.* **spik•i•er, spik•i•est.** Having a projecting sharp point or points: *a spiky tail; her spiky bangs.* **—spik′i•ness** *n.*

spill[1] |spĭl| *v.* **spilled** or **spilt** |spĭlt|, **spill•ing. 1.** To cause or allow (something) to run or fall out of a container: *spilled water from the bucket.* **2.** To run or fall out of a container or as from a container: *milk spilling over the top of the glass; urban population spilling out into the suburbs.* **3.** To shed (blood). **4.** To cause to fall; throw; dislodge: *the bronco that spilled every rider.* **5.** *Informal.* To divulge; make known: *spill the news.* —*n.* **1.** An act of spilling: *pollution caused by oil spills.* **2.** The amount spilled. **3.** A fall, as from a horse.

spill[2] |spĭl| *n.* **1.** A piece of wood or rolled paper used to light a fire. **2.** A small peg used as a plug.

spilt |spĭlt|. A past tense and past participle of **spill.**

spin |spĭn| *v.* **spun** |spŭn|, **spin•ning. 1. a.** To draw out and twist (fibers of natural or manmade material, such as cotton, wool, or nylon) into thread: *Rumpelstiltskin could spin flax into gold.* **b.** To make (thread or yarn) by drawing out and twisting fibers: *spinning thread on a spindle; spinning at a spinning wheel.* **2.** To form (a thread, web, cocoon, etc.) from a fluid emitted from the body, as spiders and certain insects do. **3.** To relate; tell: *spinning tales of the sea.* **4.** To turn or rotate about an axis, especially at high speed: *wheels spinning on the icy pavement; spinning around in the chair.* **5.** To cause to rotate swiftly; twirl: *spun his top.* **6.** To seem to be whirling, as from dizziness; reel: *made his head spin.* —*n.* **1.** A turning or rotating motion, especially one that is rapid. **2.** *Informal.* A short drive in a vehicle.

spin•ach |spĭn′ĭch| *n.* **1.** A plant grown for its edible, dark-green leaves. **2.** The leaves of this plant, eaten as a vegetable. —***modifier:*** *a spinach pie.*

spi•nal |spī′nəl| *adj.* **1.** Of or near the spine or

sphinx

spider

spinal cord. **2.** Like or resembling a spine or similar part. *—n.* The injection of an anesthetic into the spinal canal.

spinal canal. The passage formed by the opening in the successive vertebrae, containing the spinal cord and the membranes that enclose it.

spinal column. In vertebrate animals, the series of jointed bones, or vertebrae, that extends from the base of the skull to the coccyx or the end of the tail, enclosing the spinal cord and forming the main support of the part of the body between the pelvis and head; the backbone.

spinal cord. The part of the central nervous system that extends from the brain and through the spinal canal, branching to form smaller nerves that serve the various parts or regions of the body.

spin•dle |spĭn′dl| *n.* **1.** A slender, rounded rod on which fibers drawn from a distaff are twisted into thread and on which the spun thread is wound when spinning by hand or at a spinning wheel. **2.** A pin or rod on a spinning machine that holds a bobbin on which spun thread is wound. **3.** Any slender rod, as a spike for holding papers or a machine part that rotates or serves as an axis on which other parts rotate. **4.** The axis along which the chromosomes are distributed in mitosis. *—v.* **spin•dled, spin•dling. 1.** To punch a hole or holes in: *Do not spindle, fold, or mutilate this card.* **2.** To grow into a thin, elongated, or weakly form.

spin•dle-leg•ged |spĭn′dl lĕg′ĭd| *or* |-lĕgd′| *adj.* Having long, thin legs.

spin•dling |spĭn′dlĭng| *adj.* Spindly.

spin•dly |spĭn′dlē| *adj.* **spin•dli•er, spin•dli•est. 1.** Slender and elongated: *spindly legs.* **2.** Of weak growth: *a spindly tree.*

spine |spīn| *n.* **1.** The spinal column of a vertebrate animal; the backbone. **2.** A sharp-pointed, projecting plant or animal part, such as a thorn or quill. **3.** The supporting part at the back of a book, to which the covers are hinged.

spine•less |spīn′lĭs| *adj.* **1.** Lacking a spinal column. **2.** Having no stiff, sharp, projecting plant or animal parts. **3.** Lacking in courage or will power. **—spine′less•ness** *n.*

spin•et |spĭn′ĭt| *n.* **1.** A small, compact, upright piano. **2.** A small harpsichord having a single keyboard.

spin•na•ker |spĭn′ə kər| *n.* A large triangular sail set on a spar swinging out opposite the mainsail on a racing yacht, used when running before the wind. [SEE PICTURE]

spinnaker

spin•ner•et |spĭn′ə rĕt′| *n.* **1.** In spiders or insect larvae that spin silk, one of the small openings in the back part of the body through which a sticky fluid flows to form a fine thread. **2.** A device for making rayon, nylon, and other synthetic fibers, consisting of a plate pierced with holes through which plastic material is forced out in the form of fine threads.

spinning jenny. An early form of power-operated machine having several spindles used to spin fibers into thread or yarn.

spinning wheel. A device for spinning fibers into thread or yarn, consisting of a large hand- or foot-operated wheel and a single spindle. [SEE PICTURE]

spinning wheel

spin-off |spĭn′ôf′| *or* |-ŏf′| *n.* An object, product, process, etc., derived from a larger or more complex project or enterprise.

spin•ster |spĭn′stər| *n.* A woman who has not married.

spin•y |spī′nē| *adj.* **spin•i•er, spin•i•est. 1.** Full of or covered with spines; thorny or prickly: *spiny undergrowth; a spiny hedgehog.* **2.** Forming or shaped like a spine or spines: *spiny prickles.*

spi•ra•cle |spī′rə kəl| *or* |spĭr′ə-| *n.* An opening through which certain animals breathe, as one of those in the exoskeleton of an insect or the blowhole of a whale.

spi•ral |spī′rəl| *n.* **1.** The path formed by a point that moves in a plane and around a fixed center at a distance that is always increasing or decreasing. **2.** A helix. **3.** An object or figure having the shape of a spiral. **4.** A course or path that takes the form of a spiral. **5.** A continuously accelerating increase or decrease: *the wage-price spiral.* **—modifier:** *a spiral staircase.* *—v.* **spi•raled** or **spi•ralled, spi•ral•ing** or **spi•ral•ling. 1.** To take or cause to take a spiral form or course: *Smoke spiraled up from the chimney. He spiraled the football to his teammate.* **2.** To rise or fall with steady acceleration: *Manufacturing costs are spiraling.* **—spi′ral•ly** *adv.*

spire¹ |spīr| *n.* **1.** The top part or point of something that tapers upward. **2.** The pointed top of a steeple.

spire² |spīr| *n.* A spiral, especially a single turn of a spiral.

spi•ril•lum |spī rĭl′əm| *n., pl.* **spi•ril•la** |spī rĭl′ə|. Any of several bacteria having a long, spirally twisted form.

spir•it |spĭr′ĭt| *n.* **1.** The animating or life-giving principle within a living being. **2.** The soul, considered as departing from the body of a person at death. **3.** The part of a human being associated with the mind and feelings, as distinguished from the physical body: *still with us in spirit.* **4.** One's essential nature: *had a sweet and gentle spirit.* **5.** That which activates or provides motive or drive; the will: *tired and broken in spirit.* **6.** A person thought of as possessing or showing a certain quality: *aided by loyal spirits.* **7.** A quality or principle that particularly distinguishes or characterizes something; essence: *the romantic spirit.* **8.** A prevailing mood or attitude: *a spirit of rebellion in the land.* **9. the Spirit.** The Holy Ghost. **10. a.** A supernatural being; a ghost. **b.** Such a supernatural being that haunts or enters into a person or inhabits a place: *possessed by an evil spirit.* **11. spirits.** One's mood or emotional state: *in low spirits.* **12.** A particular mood marked by vigor, courage, or liveliness: *a team that showed a lot of spirit.* **13.** Strong loyalty or dedication: *civic spirit; school spirit.* **14.** The real meaning, sense, or intent of something: *the spirit of the law.* **15. spirits.** An alcohol solution of an essence derived from a perfume, spice, etc. **16. spirits.** An alcoholic beverage. *—v.* To carry off mysteriously, secretly, or suddenly: *spirited him away under cover of night.*

spir•it•ed |spĭr′ĭ tĭd| *adj.* **1.** Full of or marked by life, vigor, or courage: *a spirited march; a spirited defense of his rights.* **2.** Having a specified mood or nature: *feeling low-spirited.*

spir•it•less |spĭr′ĭt lĭs| *adj.* Lacking energy or

enthusiasm; listless. —**spir'it•less•ly** *adv.* —**spir'it•less•ness** *n.*

spir•i•tu•al |spĭr'ĭ cho͞o əl| *adj.* **1.** Of the human spirit or soul, as distinguished from the physical body; not worldly: *spiritual matters; spiritual welfare.* **2.** Of religion, a church, or the clergy: *spiritual beliefs; spiritual guidance.* —*n.* A religious folk song of American black origin or a song imitating this. —**spir'i•tu•al•ly** *adv.*

spir•i•tu•al•ism |spĭr'ĭ cho͞o ə lĭz'əm| *n.* The belief that the dead communicate with the living, usually through a medium. —**spir'i•tu•al•ist** *n.*

spi•ro•chete |spī'rə kēt'| *n.* Any of several microorganisms having a slender, flexible, twisted form, including those that cause syphilis and other diseases.

spi•ro•gy•ra |spī'rə jī'rə| *n.* One of a kind of green algae found in ponds in the form of long, slender, floating strands. [SEE PICTURE]

spit¹ |spĭt| *v.* **spat** |spăt| or **spit, spit•ting. 1.** To eject (something) from the mouth; expectorate: *Rinse your mouth with water and spit it out.* **2.** To utter in a violent manner: *spat out an oath.* **3.** To make a hissing or sputtering noise, as a cat does. —*n.* **1.** Saliva, especially when ejected from the mouth. **2.** The act of spitting.

spit² |spĭt| *n.* **1.** A slender, pointed rod on which meat is speared and roasted. **2.** A narrow point of land extending into a body of water. —*v.* **spit•ted, spit•ting.** To place on or as if on a spit.

spite |spīt| *n.* **1.** Malice or ill will causing a person to desire to hurt or humiliate another. **2.** An action that results from such feeling. —*v.* **spit•ed, spit•ing.** To show spite toward.

Idiom. **in spite of.** Despite; regardless of.

spite•ful |spīt'fəl| *adj.* Filled with, caused by, or showing spite; malicious. —**spite'ful•ly** *adv.* —**spite'ful•ness** *n.*

spit•fire |spĭt'fīr'| *n.* A quick-tempered or very excitable person.

spit•tle |spĭt'l| *n.* Spit; saliva.

spit•toon |spĭ to͞on'| *n.* A bowl-shaped receptacle for spitting into.

splash |splăsh| *v.* **1.** To dash or scatter (a liquid) about in flying masses. **2.** To dash liquid upon; wet or soil with flying masses of liquid. **3.** To cause a liquid to fly in scattered masses. **4.** To fall into or move through liquid with this effect. **5.** To spill or fly about in scattered masses. —*n.* **1.** The act or sound of splashing. **2.** A flying mass of liquid. **3.** A marking produced by or as if by scattered liquid: *splashes of color; splashes of light.* **4.** *Informal.* A strong but often short-lived impression; a stir: *made a splash with his new novel.* —**splash'er** *n.*

splash•down |splăsh'doun'| *n.* The landing of a missile or spacecraft on water or its moment of impact.

splash•y |splăsh'ē| *adj.* **splash•i•er, splash•i•est. 1.** Making or liable to make splashes. **2.** Covered with splashes of color. **3.** Showy; ostentatious: *a splashy wedding reception.*

splat•ter |splăt'ər| *v.* **1.** To mark or soil with splashes of liquid. **2.** To move or fall so as to cause heavy splashes. —*n.* A splash of liquid.

splay |splā| *adj.* **1.** Spread or turned out. **2.** Clumsy or clumsily formed; awkward. —*n.* **1.** An expansion; spread. **2.** A slope given to the sides of a door or window. —*v.* **1.** To spread out or apart: *splayed his legs.* **2.** To make slanting or sloping; bevel.

splay•foot |splā'fo͝ot'| *n., pl.* **-feet** |-fēt'|. **1.** A deformity in which the feet are flat and abnormally turned out. **2.** A foot having such a deformity.

spleen |splēn| *n.* **1.** An organ located in the left side of the human abdomen below the diaphragm, composed of a mass of lymph nodes and various cavities that are capable of filling with blood, embedded in a framework of fibrous partitions. It acts as a filter and reservoir for the blood. **2.** A similar organ found in other vertebrates. **3.** Ill temper; spite.

splen•did |splĕn'dĭd| *adj.* **1.** Very striking to the senses, especially to the eye; brilliant or grand: *splendid scenery; a splendid lighting display.* **2.** Excellent in quality or achievement: *a splendid record.* —**splen'did•ly** *adv.*

splen•dor |splĕn'dər| *n.* **1.** Great light or luster; brilliance. **2.** Magnificent appearance or display; grandeur. **3.** Distinction; fame; glory.

splice |splīs| *v.* **spliced, splic•ing. 1. a.** To join (lengths of wire, rope, cord, film, etc.) at the ends. **b.** To join (rope) by weaving together the strands. **2.** To join (pieces of wood) by overlapping them and binding the ends together. —*n.* A joint made by splicing. —**splic'er** *n.* [SEE PICTURE]

splint |splĭnt| *n.* **1.** A strip of rigid material bound to an injured joint or to the ends of a fractured bone to prevent movement. **2.** A thin, flexible strip of wood, as one used in making baskets.

splin•ter |splĭn'tər| *n.* A sharp, slender piece, as of wood, bone, or glass, split or broken off from a main body. —*v.* To split or break into sharp, slender pieces. —**splin'ter•y** *adj.*

split |splĭt| *v.* **split, split•ting. 1.** To divide or become separated into parts, especially lengthwise: *split the log; a board that split from the blow.* **2.** To break, burst, or rip apart with force: *pressure that caused the container to split; split her skirt.* **3.** To separate (persons or groups); disunite or part company: *a quarrel causing us to split up; issues that split the party.* **4.** To divide and share: *agreed to split the reward.* **5.** To mark (a vote or ballot) in favor of candidates from different parties: *split the ticket.* —*n.* **1.** The act or result of splitting. **2.** A division within a group; a breach; rupture: *caused a split in our family.* **3.** Something divided and portioned out; a share. **4.** Often **splits.** An acrobatic feat in which the legs are stretched out in opposite directions at right angles to the trunk. **5.** In bowling, an arrangement of pins left standing after pins between them have been knocked down. **6.** A small bottle of an alcoholic or carbonated beverage, usually holding about six ounces. —*adj.* **1.** Divided or separated. **2.** Cracked lengthwise; cleft. —**split'ter** *n.*

split infinitive. An infinitive verb form with a word or words, often an adverb, placed between *to* and the verb; for example, *to suddenly remember* and *to always willingly obey* are split infinitives.

split•ting |splĭt'ĭng| *adj.* Very severe and painful, as a headache.

splotch |splŏch| *n.* An irregularly shaped stain,

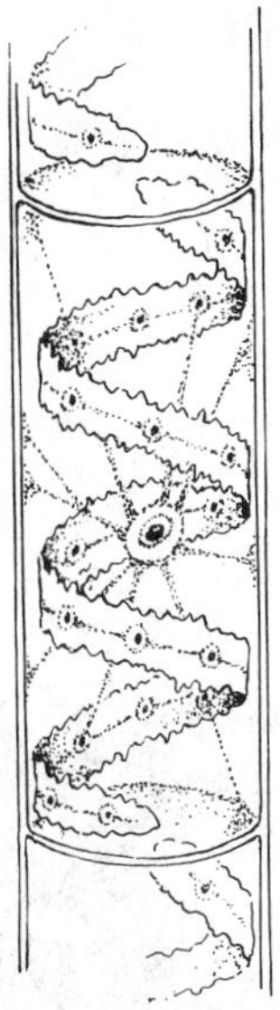

spirogyra
Cells of spirogyra, much enlarged

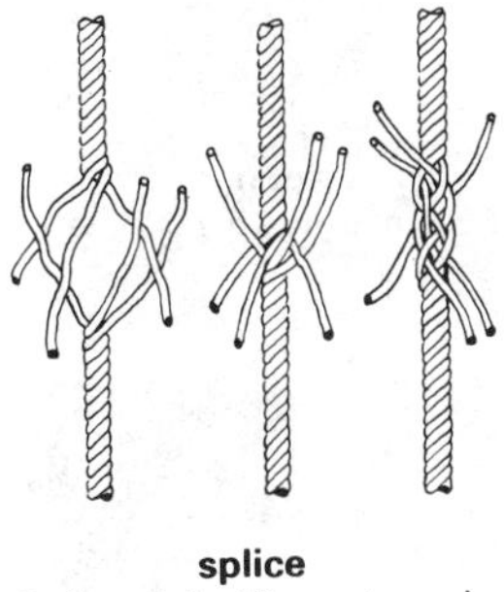

splice
Left to right: Three stages in making a splice

spot, or discolored area. —*v.* To mark with a splotch or splotches.

splurge |splûrj| *v.* **splurged, splurg•ing.** To spend money extravagantly or wastefully, as on luxuries. —*n.* An act of spending extravagantly.

splut•ter |splŭt′ər| *v.* **1.** To make a spitting sound. **2.** To speak rapidly and unclearly, as when confused or angry. **3.** To utter or express hastily and incoherently. —*n.* A spluttering noise. —**splut′ter•er** *n.*

spoil |spoil| *v.* **spoiled** or **spoilt** |spoilt|, **spoil•ing.** **1.** To damage, as in value, quality, or completeness; injure; flaw: *stains that spoil the painting.* **2.** To become rotten, decayed, or otherwise unfit for use, as food. **3.** To indulge or praise too much so as to harm the character of: *spoiled his son.* —***phrasal verb.*** **spoil for.** To be eager for; crave: *spoiling for a fight.* —*n.* **1.** Often **spoils.** Goods or property seized from the loser of a military conflict. **2. spoils.** Benefits gained by a victor, especially political appointments or jobs at the disposal of a winning candidate or party in an election. —**spoil′er** *n.*

spoils system. The practice after an election of rewarding loyal supporters of the winning candidates or party with political jobs or appointments.

spoilt |spoilt|. A past tense and past participle of **spoil.**

spoke[1] |spōk| *n.* **1.** One of the rods or braces that connect the rim of a wheel to its hub. **2.** One of the handles that project from the rim of a ship's wheel. **3.** A rod or stick that can be inserted into a hole in a wheel to keep it from turning. **4.** A rung of a ladder. —*v.* **spoked, spok•ing. 1.** To equip with spokes. **2.** To keep (a wheel) from turning by inserting a rod.

spoke[2] |spōk|. Past tense of **speak.**

spo•ken |spō′kən|. Past participle of **speak.** —*adj.* **1.** Uttered; expressed orally: *spoken dialogue in an opera.* **2.** Speaking or using speech in a specified manner or voice: *a soft-spoken man.*

spoke•shave |spōk′shāv′| *n.* A tool having a blade set between two handles, used for trimming and smoothing rounded surfaces.

spokes•man |spōks′mən| *n., pl.* **-men** |-mən|. A person who speaks as the representative of another or others.

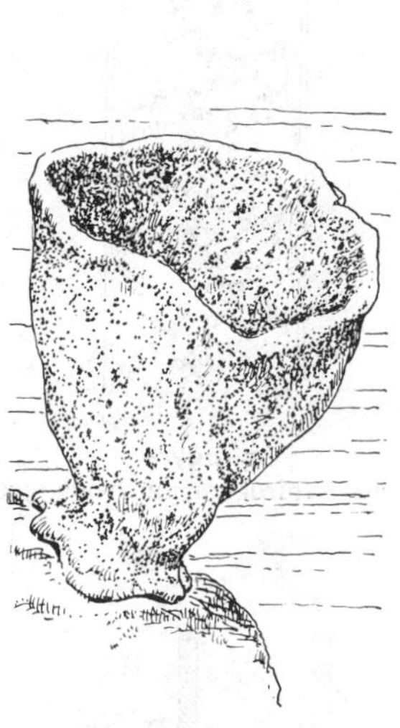

sponge
Sponge growing in ocean

sponge |spŭnj| *n.* **1.** Any of a group of simple water animals that have a soft or bony skeleton and that often form large, irregularly shaped colonies attached to an underwater surface. **2. a.** The soft, porous, absorbent skeleton of certain of these animals, used for bathing, cleaning, padding, etc. **b.** A similarly used piece of porous, absorbent material, as of rubber or plastic. **3.** Something able to absorb and hold as a sponge does: *Loose, soft, fibrous soil makes a good sponge. Her mind is a sponge.* **4.** A gauze pad used to absorb blood or other bodily fluids, as in surgery or in dressing a wound. —*v.* **sponged, spong•ing. 1.** To wash, wipe, or wet with or as if with a sponge: *She sponged his face with her wet handkerchief. Sponge up the spilled orange juice.* **2.** *Informal.* To get (something wanted or needed) without cost by asking or taking from others: *He is always sponging on others for cigarettes. She sponged her supper from the cook at the cafeteria.* [See Picture]

sponge cake. A light, porous cake made with flour, sugar, and eggs but containing no shortening.

spong•er |spŭn′jər| *n.* **1.** A person or boat engaged in gathering sponges. **2.** *Informal.* A person who lives off the generosity of others; a parasite.

spong•y |spŭn′jē| *adj.* **spong•i•er, spong•i•est.** Of or like a sponge; soft, porous, and usually springy: *a spongy bed of moss.* —**spon′gi•ness** *n.*

spon•sor |spŏn′sər| *n.* **1.** A person who assumes responsibility for or supports another or others during a period of instruction, training, etc. **2.** A member of a lawmaking body who proposes and works for passage of a bill. **3.** A godparent. **4.** A business enterprise that pays for a radio or television program, usually in return for advertising time. —*v.* To act as a sponsor for. —**spon′sor•ship′** *n.*

spon•ta•ne•i•ty |spŏn′tə **nē′**ĭ tē| *or* |**-nā′-**| *n.* The condition or quality of being spontaneous.

spon•ta•ne•ous |spŏn **tā′**nē əs| *adj.* **1.** Happening or arising without apparent outside cause; self-generated. **2.** Arising or occurring voluntarily and from impulse: *spontaneous cheers.* —**spon•ta′ne•ous•ly** *adv.*

spontaneous combustion. The breaking into flame of a mass of material, such as oily rags or damp hay, as a result of heat generated by slow oxidation.

spoof |spo͞of| *n.* **1.** A joke or hoax. **2.** An imitation of something that pokes fun at it; light satire: *a spoof of grand opera.* —*v.* **1.** To deceive or trick. **2.** To do a spoof of.

spook |spo͝ok|. *Informal. n.* A ghost. —*v.* **1.** To haunt. **2.** To frighten.

spook•y |spo͞o′kē| *adj.* **spook•i•er, spook•i•est.** Ghostly; eerie. —**spook′i•ness** *n.*

spool |spo͞ol| *n.* **1.** A small cylinder upon which thread, yarn, wire, tape, ribbon, or film is wound, having a head or rim at either end and a hole through the middle. **2. a.** A spool with something wound on it: *Buy a spool of white thread.* **b.** The amount a spool holds: *The seamstress used up a whole spool of thread.* —*v.* To wind on or unwind from a spool: *spool thread.*

spoon |spo͞on| *n.* **1.** A utensil with a bowl-shaped hollow at the end of a handle, used in preparing, serving, or eating food. **2.** A spoonful. —*v.* **1.** To lift or scoop up with a spoon. **2.** *Informal.* To show affection, as by kissing or caressing.

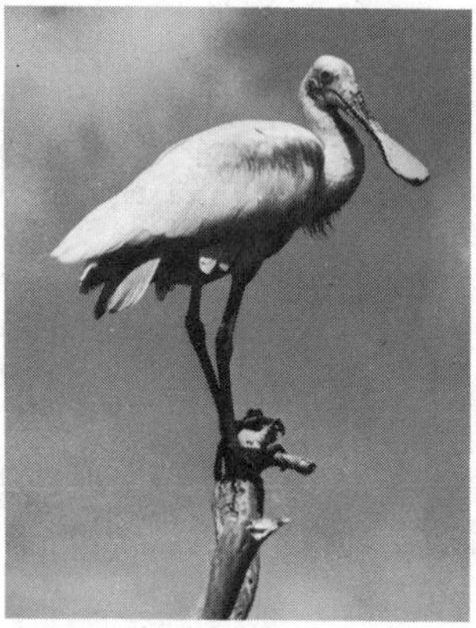

spoonbill

spoon•bill |spo͞on′bĭl′| *n.* A wading bird having long legs and a long, flat bill with a broad, rounded tip. [See Picture]

spoon•ful |spo͞on′fo͝ol′| *n., pl.* **spoon•fuls.** The amount a spoon holds.

spoor |spo͝or| *or* |spôr| *or* |spōr| *n.* The track or trail of an animal, especially of a wild animal.

spo•rad•ic |spô **răd′**ĭk| *or* |spō-| *adj.* Occurring at irregular intervals; having no pattern or order: *sporadic applause.* —**spo•rad′i•cal•ly** *adv.*

spo•ran•gi•um |spô **răn′**jē əm| *or* |spō-| *n., pl.* **spo•ran•gi•a** |spô **răn′**jē ə| *or* |spō-|. A plant part in which spores are formed, as in ferns, fungi, etc.; a spore case.

spore |spôr| *or* |spōr| *n.* **1.** One of the tiny, usually one-celled reproductive parts produced by nonflowering plants such as ferns, mosses,

ă pat/ā pay/â care/ä father/ĕ pet/ ē be/ĭ pit/ī pie/î fierce/ŏ pot/ ō go/ô paw, for/oi oil/o͝o book/ o͞o boot/ou out/ŭ cut/û fur/ *th* the/th thin/hw which/zh vision/ ə ago, item, pencil, atom, circus

and fungi. **2.** An inactive form of certain bacteria and other microorganisms.

spore case. A plant part in which spores are formed; a sporangium.

spor•ran |spŏr′ən| *n.* A leather or fur pouch worn at the front of the kilt by Scottish Highlanders. [SEE PICTURE]

sport |spôrt| *or* |spōrt| *n.* **1.** A game, recreation, or pastime, especially one involving physical exercise. **2.** Light mockery; jest; fun: *His sober expression was all in sport.* **3.** A person judged by his manner of accepting the rules of a game or a difficult situation: *a good sport; a poor sport.* **4.** *Informal.* A person who lives a gay and sometimes rather dissolute life. **5.** A plant or animal that is markedly and unexpectedly different from the individuals or type that produced it; a mutant. —*adj.* Suitable for active, outdoor use or for informal wear: *sport clothes; a sport shirt.* —*v.* **1.** To wear, display, or show off: *He sported a bright red necktie.* **2.** To play; frolic.
Idiom. **make sport of.** To make fun of; treat mockingly.

sport•ing |spôr′tĭng| *or* |spōr′-| *adj.* **1.** Used in or appropriate for sports: *sporting gear.* **2.** Marked by sportsmanship: *the sporting thing to do when an opponent has bad luck.* **3.** Of or associated with gambling. **4.** Offering a fair chance for success: *a sporting chance.*

spor•tive |spôr′tĭv| *or* |spōr′-| *adj.* Playful; frolicsome. —**spor′tive•ly** *adv.* —**spor′tive•ness** *n.*

sports |spôrts| *or* |spōrts| *adj.* Suitable for active, outdoor use or for informal wear: *a sports coat; sports jackets.*

sports car. An automobile, usually fairly small, designed to be driven at high speeds with precise control.

sports•man |spôrts′mən| *or* |spōrts′-| *n., pl.* **-men** |-mən|. **1.** A man who is enthusiastic about and participates in sports. **2.** One who observes the rules of a contest and accepts victory or defeat without behaving boastfully or angrily. —**sports′man•like′** *adj.*

sports•man•ship |spôrts′mən shĭp′| *n.* The qualities and conduct suitable to a sportsman.

sports•wear |spôrts′wâr′| *or* |spōrts′-| *n.* Clothes suitable for active outdoor use or for informal wear.

sport•y |spôr′tē| *or* |spōr′-| *adj.* **sport•i•er, sport•i•est.** **1.** Gay or carefree in manner, behavior, or dress. **2.** Suitable for wear in participating in or attending sports; casual; informal.

spot |spŏt| *n.* **1.** A mark on a surface differing sharply in color from the surroundings; a stain or blot: *spots on the tablecloth.* **2.** A position; location: *the spot where it happened.* **3.** *Informal.* A set of circumstances; a situation, especially a difficult one. **4.** A defect or injury, especially something that mars one's reputation. —*v.* **spot•ted, spot•ting.** **1.** To become or cause to become marked with spots or stains: *a dress that spots easily; soot spotting the curtains.* **2.** To place in a particular location; situate. **3.** To detect; recognize; locate: *spotted him on the subway; buildings difficult to spot from a plane.* **4.** To give as a handicap or advantage: *spotted his opponent six points.* —*adj.* **1.** Made, paid, or delivered immediately: *spot cash; spot news.* **2.** Presented between programs or during intermissions in a program: *a television spot announcement.*
Idioms. **hit the spot.** *Informal.* To be just what is needed or quite satisfying. **in spots.** Now and then; here and there; occasionally. **on the spot.** **1.** Without delay; at once. **2.** At the scene of action. **3.** Under pressure or attention; in a difficult position.

spot check. A random and hasty inspection or investigation.

spot-check |spŏt′chĕk′| *v.* To inspect hastily and at random.

spot•less |spŏt′lĭs| *adj.* Perfectly clean; free from stain or blemish: *spotless linen; a spotless reputation.* —**spot′less•ly** *adv.*

spot•light |spŏt′līt′| *n.* **1.** A strong beam of light focused on a small area, often used to illuminate or draw attention to an actor on a stage. **2.** A lamp that produces such a beam. **3.** Public attention or prominence. —*v.* To illuminate with or as if with a spotlight.

spot•ty |spŏt′ē| *adj.* **spot•ti•er, spot•ti•est.** **1.** Having or marked with spots; spotted. **2.** Lacking consistency; uneven in quality or occurrence.

spouse |spous| *or* |spouz| *n.* One's husband or wife.

spout |spout| *v.* **1.** To gush forth or send forth in a stream or in spurts: *hot water spouting up at the spring; volcanoes spouting lava.* **2.** To discharge a liquid or other substance continuously or in spurts: *whales spouting offshore.* **3.** To utter or speak in a pompous or long-winded manner: *spouted a television commercial.* —*n.* **1.** A tube, mouth, or pipe through which liquid is released or discharged: *the spout of a coffeepot.* **2.** A continuous stream of liquid. —**spout′er** *n.*

sprain |sprān| *n.* An injury to a joint in which the ligaments or tendons are stretched or twisted excessively and may be torn, but in which there is no fracture or dislocation. —*v.* To cause a sprain of (a joint or muscle).

sprang |sprăng|. A past tense of **spring.**

sprat |sprăt| *n.* A small herring or similar fish.

sprawl |sprôl| *v.* **1.** To sit or lie with the body and limbs spread out awkwardly. **2.** To spread out or cause to spread out in a straggling or disordered fashion. —*n.* A sprawling posture or condition.

spray[1] |sprā| *n.* **1.** Water or other liquid moving as a mass of finely dispersed droplets or mist. **2.** A jet of such droplets discharged from a pressurized container. **3.** A pressurized container that discharges such a jet; an atomizer. **4.** Any of a large number of commercial products, including paints, insect poisons, and cosmetics, that are meant to be applied in the form of a spray and that are sometimes packed as aerosols. —*v.* **1.** To disperse or apply (a liquid) in the form of a spray. **2.** To apply a spray to (something). —**spray′er** *n.*

spray[2] |sprā| *n.* A small branch together with its flowers, leaves, berries, etc.

spray gun. Any of various devices used to apply a liquid as a spray.

spread |sprĕd| *v.* **spread, spread•ing.** **1.** To open to a full or fuller extent or width; unfold: *spread a tablecloth; spread his fingers wide.* **2.** To be extended or enlarged: *material that spreads under pressure.* **3. a.** To make wider the gap between; move farther apart: *spread the card tables.* **b.** To

sporran

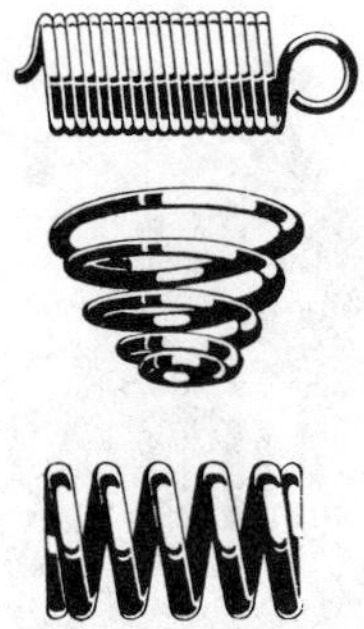

coil springs

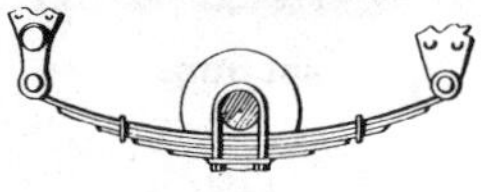

leaf spring

spring

spruce[1-2]
The North European country of Prussia, *on the south side of the Baltic Sea, was called* Pruce *or* Spruce *in Middle English. Prussia is the home of the* Spruce fir *(tree), a name that was later shortened to* **spruce**[1]. *Prussia formerly exported fine leather used for making jackets; the English called this* Spruce leather; *it is possible that* **spruce**[2] *originally meant "smartly dressed, as in a* Spruce leather *jacket"; but this is only a possibility.*

ă **pat**/ā **pay**/â **care**/ä **father**/ĕ **pet**/ē **be**/ĭ **pit**/ī **pie**/î **fierce**/ŏ **pot**/ō **go**/ô **paw**, **for**/oi **oil**/ŏŏ **book**/o͞o **boot**/ou **out**/ŭ **cut**/û **fur**/*th* **the**/th **thin**/hw **which**/**zh** vision/ə **ago**, item, pencil, atom, circus

be pushed farther apart. **4.** To become distributed or widely dispersed: *a migration spreading northward.* **5. a.** To distribute over a surface in a layer; apply: *spread glue on a card.* **b.** To cover with a thin layer: *spread bread with jelly.* **c.** To become distributed in a thin layer: *paint that spreads easily.* **6.** To bring or cause over a wide area: *storms that spread destruction.* **7.** To extend in time: *spread the payments over six months.* **8.** To increase in range of occurrence: *an epidemic spreading rapidly.* **9.** To make or become known widely: *spread the news; a rumor that spread like wildfire.* **10.** To lay out; display: *spread his merchandise in the window.* **11. a.** To prepare (a table) for a meal; set. **b.** To arrange (food) on a table. —*n.* **1.** The act of spreading, especially: **a.** Extension or distribution: *a spread of population.* **b.** Dissemination or flow: *the spread of information.* **2.** An open area of land; an expanse. **3. a.** The extent or limit to which something can be spread or unfolded: *wings with a six-foot spread.* **b.** Range or scope: *data having a wide spread.* **4.** A cloth cover such as a bedspread or tablecloth. **5.** *Informal.* An abundant meal. **6.** A soft food that can be spread on bread or crackers. **7.** The difference, as between two figures or totals. —**spread'er** *n.*

spree |sprē| *n.* **1.** A gay, lively outing. **2.** A brief period in which one engages too freely in some activity, especially drinking or spending.

spri•er |sprī'ər| *adj.* A comparative of **spry.**

spri•est |sprī'ĭst| *adj.* A superlative of **spry.**

sprig |sprĭg| *n.* **1.** A small twig or shoot of a plant. **2.** A design or decoration in this shape. —*v.* **sprigged, sprig•ging.** To decorate with a design of sprigs.

spright•ly |sprīt'lē| *adj.* **spright•li•er, spright•li•est.** Full of life; buoyant. —**spright'li•ness** *n.*

spring |sprĭng| *v.* **sprang** |sprăng| or **sprung** |sprŭng|, **sprung, spring•ing.** **1.** To move upward or forward in a single quick motion; leap: *wolves springing for his throat.* **2.** To appear or emerge suddenly: *a genius who seemed to spring full-blown.* **3.** To shift position suddenly: *The door sprang shut.* **4.** To present or produce unexpectedly: *spring a surprise.* **5. a.** To become warped, bent, or cracked, as a piece of wood. **b.** To cause to warp, bend, or crack, as by force. **6.** To move out of correct position or alignment, as a machine part. **7.** To release from a checked or inoperative condition; actuate. —*n.* **1.** An elastic device, especially a coiled or flat metal bar that returns to its original shape after being compressed, extended, twisted, bent, etc. **2.** The condition or quality of being elastic. **3.** The act of springing, especially a leap or jump. **4.** A natural fountain or flow of water. **5.** The season of the year that occurs between winter and summer, extending in the Northern Hemisphere from the vernal equinox to the summer solstice. —***modifier:*** *spring rain.* [SEE PICTURE]

spring•board |sprĭng'bôrd'| *or* |-bōrd'| *n.* **1.** A flexible board, secured at one end and mounted on a fulcrum, used by gymnasts and acrobats to gain momentum in leaping or tumbling. **2.** A diving board. **3.** Something that provides a start in the attainment of a goal: *athletic fame as a springboard for a career in politics.*

spring•bok |sprĭng'bŏk'| *n.* A small African gazelle that can leap high into the air.

spring fever. A feeling of laziness or listlessness or a yearning for a change of scene that often occurs with the arrival of spring.

Spring•field |sprĭng'fēld'|. The capital of Illinois. Population, 89,800.

spring•tide |sprĭng'tīd'| *n.* Springtime.

spring tide. The tide in which the variation of the water level is generally the largest, occuring at or near a new moon or full moon when the sun, moon, and earth are approximately aligned.

spring•time |sprĭng'tīm'| *n.* The season of spring.

spring•y |sprĭng'ē| *adj.* **spring•i•er, spring•i•est.** Capable of springing back; elastic: *a springy footstep.* —**spring'i•ly** *adv.* —**spring'i•ness** *n.*

sprin•kle |sprĭng'kəl| *v.* **sprin•kled, sprin•kling.** **1.** To scatter or release in drops or small particles: *sprinkle salt on the icy steps.* **2.** To scatter drops or particles upon: *sprinkle the lawn.* **3.** To rain or fall in small or infrequent drops. —*n.* **1.** A small amount; a sprinkling. **2.** A light rainfall; a drizzle.

sprin•kler |sprĭng'klər| *n.* Someone or something that sprinkles, especially: **1.** One of the outlets in a sprinkler system. **2.** A device, attached to the end of a water hose, for sprinkling water on a lawn.

sprinkler system. A network of water pipes equipped with outlets that release water when the temperature of the air exceeds a preset level, installed in a building as a defense against fire.

sprin•kling |sprĭng'klĭng| *n.* A small amount of something, especially when thinly distributed.

sprint |sprĭnt| *n.* A short race run at top speed. —*v.* To run at top speed. —**sprint'er** *n.*

sprit |sprĭt| *n.* A pole extending diagonally across a fore-and-aft sail from the lower part of the mast to the peak of the sail.

sprite |sprīt| *n.* Any elf, fairy, or pixy.

sprock•et |sprŏk'ĭt| *n.* Any of a set of toothlike parts that project from the rim of a wheel to engage the links of a chain.

sprocket wheel. A wheel having sprockets around its rim.

sprout |sprout| *v.* **1.** To begin to grow; produce or appear as a bud, shoot, or new growth: *The newly planted corn sprouted after the rain.* **2.** To cause to grow: *The abandoned farmland again sprouted oak and beech trees.* **3.** To put forth or appear as if growing: *The prairies sprouted oil wells like a strange new crop.* —*n.* **1.** A young plant growth, such as a bud or shoot. **2. sprouts.** See **Brussels sprouts.**

spruce[1] |spro͞os| *n.* **1.** Any of several evergreen trees with short needles and soft wood often used for paper pulp. **2.** The wood of such a tree. —***modifier:*** *a spruce forest.* [SEE NOTE]

spruce[2] |spro͞os| *adj.* **spruc•er, spruc•est.** Neat, trim, and tidy or dapper. —*v.* **spruced, spruc•ing.** To make or become spruce: *He spruced himself up in new clothes. He really spruced up for the date.* [SEE NOTE]

sprung |sprŭng|. A past tense and past participle of **spring.**

spry |sprī| *adj.* **spri•er** or **spry•er, spri•est** or **spry•est.** Active; nimble; lively. —**spry'ly** *adv.* —**spry'ness** *n.*

spud |spŭd| *n.* **1.** A sharp tool resembling a

spade for rooting or digging out weeds. **2.** *Informal.* A potato.

spume |spyōōm| *n.* Foam or froth on a liquid. —*v.* **spumed, spum•ing.** To froth or foam.

spu•mo•ne, also **spu•mo•ni** |spə mō'nē| *n., pl.* **spu•mo•ni.** An Italian frozen dessert of ice cream containing fruit, nuts, or candies.

spun |spŭn|. Past tense and past participle of **spin.**

spunk |spŭngk| *n. Informal.* Spirit; courage.

spunk•y |spŭng'kē| *adj.* **spunk•i•er, spunk•i•est.** *Informal.* Having spunk; spirited; plucky. —**spunk'i•ly** *adv.* —**spunk'i•ness** *n.*

spun sugar. Sugar that has been boiled and drawn into long threads.

spur |spûr| *n.* **1.** A U-shaped device with a projecting point or sharp-toothed wheel behind, worn on the heel of a rider's boot and used to urge on a horse. **2.** Something that urges one to action in pursuit of a goal or the goal itself; an incentive; a stimulus: *Fame was the spur for his even greater achievements.* **3.** A narrow, pointed, projecting part, as on the back of a rooster's leg or on some flowers. **4.** A ridge that projects from the side of a mountain or mountain range. **5.** A short side track that connects with the main track of a railroad system. —*v.* **spurred, spur•ring. 1.** To urge (a horse) on by pricking it with spurs: *The rider spurred the horse to a gallop.* **2.** To move to action; incite; stimulate: *The reward spurred us on.* —**spurred'** *adj.: a spurred rider; spurred flowers.* [SEE PICTURE]

***Idiom.* on the spur of the moment.** On a sudden impulse.

spu•ri•ous |spyōōr'ē əs| *adj.* Lacking genuineness; false; counterfeit. —**spu'ri•ous•ly** *adv.*

spurn |spûrn| *v.* To reject or refuse with disdain; scorn.

spurt |spûrt| *n.* **1.** A sudden and forcible gush of a liquid; a jet. **2.** Any sudden outbreak or short burst of energy or activity. —*v.* **1.** To squirt: *oil spurting in the air.* **2.** To show a sudden, brief increase in activity or productivity: *The team spurted late in the season.*

spu•ta |spyōō'tə| *n.* Plural of **sputum.**

sput•nik |spōōt'nĭk| *or* |spŭt'-| *n.* Any of the artificial satellites put into orbit around the earth by the Soviet Union. [SEE NOTE]

sput•ter |spŭt'ər| *v.* **1.** To spit out small particles of saliva or food in short bursts, often with a spluttering sound, as when excited. **2.** To make a sporadic coughing noise: *The engine sputtered and died.* **3.** To speak in a hasty or confusing manner; stammer. —*n.* **1.** The act of sputtering. **2.** The sound of sputtering. **3.** The particles spit out during sputtering. **4.** Hasty or confused speech. —**sput'ter•er** *n.*

spu•tum |spyōō'təm| *n., pl.* **spu•ta** |spyōō'tə|. Matter that is spit out; spit; spittle.

spy |spī| *n., pl.* **spies. 1.** A clandestine agent employed to obtain intelligence. **2.** Someone who secretly watches another or others. —***modifier:*** *a spy organization.* —*v.* **spied, spy•ing, spies. 1.** To keep under surveillance with hostile intent: *spy upon an enemy camp.* **2.** To catch sight of; see: *spied a turtle on a log.* **3.** To investigate.

spy•glass |spī'glăs'| *or* |-gläs'| *n.* **1.** A small telescope. **2. spyglasses.** Binoculars.

sq. 1. squadron. **2.** square.

squab |skwŏb| *n.* A young pigeon, especially one used as food.

squab•ble |skwŏb'əl| *v.* **squab•bled, squab•bling.** To engage in a minor quarrel; bicker. —*n.* A trivial quarrel. —**squab'bler** *n.*

squad |skwŏd| *n.* **1.** A small, organized group of soldiers. **2.** Any small organized group, as of football players. —***modifier:*** *a squad leader.*

squad car. A police patrol car connected by radiotelephone with headquarters.

squad•ron |skwŏd'rən| *n.* **1.** Any of various military units, as of soldiers, planes, or ships. **2.** Any group of people or animals: *squadrons of flies.* —***modifier:*** *a squadron commander.*

squal•id |skwŏl'ĭd| *adj.* **1.** Having a dirty or wretched appearance: *squalid buildings.* **2.** Sordid; miserable: *a squalid existence.* —**squal'id•ly** *adv.* —**squal'id•ness** *n.*

squall[1] |skwôl| *n.* A loud, harsh outcry. —*v.* To scream or cry harshly and loudly.

squall[2] |skwôl| *n.* A brief, sudden, and violent windstorm, often accompanied by rain or snow. —*v.* To storm violently for a short time.

squal•or |skwŏl'ər| *n.* The condition or quality of being squalid.

squan•der |skwŏn'dər| *v.* To use or spend wastefully or extravagantly: *Squander money.*

square |skwâr| *n.* **1.** A rectangle having four equal sides. **2.** Any figure or object having this shape. **3.** An L-shaped or T-shaped instrument or tool, used for drawing or testing right angles. **4.** The product that results when a number or quantity is multiplied by itself. **5. a.** An open area at the intersection of two or more streets. **b.** A rectangular space enclosed by streets; a block. **6.** *Slang.* Someone considered rigidly conventional. —*adj.* **squar•er, squar•est. 1.** Having the form of a square. **2.** Forming a right angle: *a board with square corners.* **3.** Of, being, or using units that express the measure of surfaces: *square feet.* **4.** Honest; direct: *a square answer.* **5.** Just; equitable: *a square deal.* **6.** Adequate; satisfying: *a square meal.* **7.** *Slang.* Rigidly conventional. —*v.* **squared, squar•ing. 1.** To cut or form into a square or rectangular shape: *square a board.* **2.** To test (a corner, joint, etc.) to see that its parts meet at right angles. **3.** To multiply (a number, quantity, or expression) by itself. **4.** To find a square whose area is equal to (a given figure). **5.** To agree or conform: *My story squares with yours. We must square his story with ours.* **6.** To settle; adjust: *square an account.* —***phrasal verb.* square off.** To assume a fighting stance. —*adv.* So as to form a right angle. —**square'ly** *adv.* —**square'ness** *n.*

***Idioms.* on the square. 1.** At right angles. **2.** Honestly or openly. **square peg in a round hole.** Someone or something that does not fit.

square dance. 1. A dance in which sets of four couples form squares. **2.** Any of various similar group dances.

square-dance |skwâr'dăns'| *or* |-däns'| *v.* **-danced, -danc•ing.** To perform a square dance.

square knot. A common double knot with the loose ends parallel to the standing parts.

square measure. A system for expressing the measure of surfaces using units, such as square feet, square meters, etc., that are the squares of linear units.

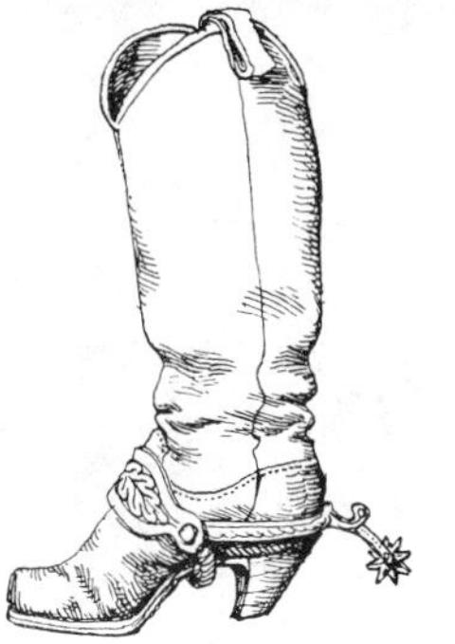

spur
Above: Spur on a columbine flower
Below: Boot with spur

sputnik
The word **sputnik,** *first appearing in English in 1957, is from Russian* sputnik, *short for* sputnik zemlyi, *"fellow traveler of Earth";* sputnik, *meaning "fellow traveler or satellite," is formed from* so-, *"with, together,"* + put', *"path,"* + -nik, *a noun ending.*

square-rigged |skwâr′rĭgd′| *adj.* Designating a sailing ship with square sails set at right angles to the keel.

square root. A number that when taken twice as a factor gives a result that is equal to a given number; for example, if *a* is a square root of *b* (written $a = \sqrt{b}$), then $a \times a = b$.

squash[1] |skwŏsh| *or* |skwôsh| *n.* **1.** Any of several types of fleshy fruit related to the pumpkins and the gourds, eaten as a vegetable. **2.** A vine that bears such fruit. [SEE NOTE]

squash[2] |skwŏsh| *or* |skwôsh| *v.* **1.** To beat or flatten to a pulp; crush: *squashed the peach on the pavement.* **2.** To be or become crushed or flattened: *The tomato squashed on the floor.* **3.** To suppress; quash: *squash a revolt.* **4.** To move with a sloshing sound: *squashed through the slush.* —*n.* **1.** The impact or sound of something soft dropping against a surface. **2.** A crush of people; a crowd. **3.** A game played in a walled court in which the players hit a hard rubber ball with a racket. [SEE NOTE]

squash[1-2]

Squash[1] *is from Massachuset (Algonquian Indian)* askōōtasquash. **Squash[2]** *is from Old French* esquasser, *from Late Latin* exquassāre, *"to break in pieces."*

squat |skwŏt| *v.* **squat·ted** or **squat, squat·ting. 1.** To sit on one's heels: *squat down to watch an ant.* **2.** To settle on unoccupied land without legal claim. **3.** To occupy a given piece of public land in order to acquire title to it. —*adj.* **squat·ter, squat·test.** Short and thick; low and broad: *a squat shape.* —**squat′ter** *n.*

squaw |skwô| *n.* A North American Indian woman.

squawk |skwôk| *n.* **1. a.** A loud, harsh, screeching sound, as one made by a parrot, chicken, or other bird. **b.** A sound resembling this: *the squawk of an automobile horn.* **2.** *Slang.* A loud, angry complaint or protest. —*v.* **1.** To make or express with a squawk. **2.** *Slang.* To complain or protest loudly and angrily.

squeak |skwēk| *n.* **1.** A thin, high-pitched cry or sound: *the squeak of a mouse; the squeak of chalk on a blackboard.* **2.** *Informal.* An escape or success made by a small margin: *We won, but it was a tight squeak.* —*v.* **1.** To make a thin, high-pitched cry or sound. **2.** *Informal.* To pass, win, or achieve by a small margin: *He just squeaked by in his final exams.*

squeak·y |skwē′kē| *adj.* **squeak·i·er, squeak·i·est.** Having or making a thin, high-pitched sound: *a squeaky door; squeaky shoes.*

squeal |skwēl| *n.* A high, loud, drawn-out cry or sound. —*v.* **1.** To make such a sound: *The hungry pigs squealed and pushed. The girls squealed with laughter. The bus squealed to a stop.* **2.** *Slang.* To betray another by giving away information. —**squeal′er** *n.*

squeam·ish |skwē′mĭsh| *adj.* **1.** Easily nauseated or sickened. **2.** Easily offended or disgusted; prudish. **3.** Excessively fastidious; oversensitive. —**squeam′ish·ly** *adv.* —**squeam′ish·ness** *n.*

squee·gee |skwē′jē′| *n.* A tool having a rubber blade set across a handle, used to remove excess water from a smooth surface.

squeeze |skwēz| *v.* **squeezed, squeez·ing. 1.** To press hard upon or together; compress: *The baby squeezed the rubber toy. They squeezed the bits of tape together.* **2.** To exert pressure on, as by way of extracting liquid: *squeeze an orange.* **3.** To extract by applying pressure: *squeeze juice from a lemon.* **4.** To force one's way by pressure: *He squeezed through the narrow opening.* **5.** To crowd; cram: *They squeezed too many people into the small room.* —*n.* **1.** An act or instance of squeezing: *gave his hand a squeeze.* **2.** An amount squeezed from something: *a squeeze of lemon.* **3.** *Informal.* Pressure exerted to obtain some concession or goal. —**squeez′er** *n.*

squelch |skwĕlch| *v.* **1.** To suppress completely: *squelched a rumor.* **2.** To silence, as with a crushing remark. **3.** To make a squishing sound: *squelched through the mud.* —*n.* **1.** A crushing reply. **2.** A squishing sound. —**squelch′er** *n.*

squib |skwĭb| *n.* **1.** A firecracker that burns but does not explode. **2.** A brief, witty literary effort, as a lampoon.

squid |skwĭd| *n., pl.* **squids** or **squid.** A soft-bodied sea animal related to the octopuses and cuttlefish having a long body, ten arms surrounding the mouth, and a pair of triangular or rounded fins. [SEE PICTURE]

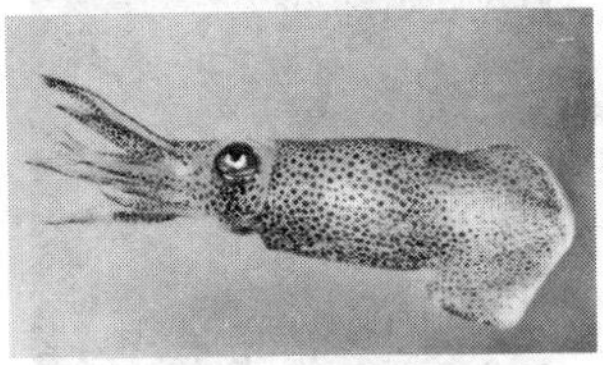

squid

Squids are mollusks, although they have no outer shell. Some kinds are very large, growing to a length of 50 feet.

squig·gle |skwĭg′əl| *n.* A small wiggly mark or scrawl.

squint |skwĭnt| *v.* **1. a.** To look with the eyes partly open: *squinted at the fine print.* **b.** To close (the eyes) partly. **2.** To glance to the side. **3.** To be cross-eyed. —*n.* **1.** The act of squinting. **2.** The condition of being cross-eyed.

squire |skwīr| *n.* **1.** In feudal times, a young man of noble birth who served a knight as an attendant. **2.** An English country gentleman. **3.** A judge or other dignitary in a small rural area. **4.** A lady's escort. —*v.* **squired, squir·ing.** To escort (a lady).

squirm |skwûrm| *v.* **1.** To twist about in a wriggling motion; writhe. **2.** To feel or exhibit signs of humiliation or embarrassment. —*n.* The act of squirming or a squirming movement.

squir·rel |skwûr′əl| *or* |skwĭr′-| *n.* **1.** Any of several tree-climbing animals with gray or reddish-brown fur and a bushy tail. **2.** The fur of such an animal. —***modifier:*** *a squirrel coat.* —*v.* —**squirrel away.** To save or hoard, as a squirrel does nuts. [SEE PICTURE]

squirrel

squirt |skwûrt| *v.* **1.** To eject (liquid) in a thin, swift stream. **2.** To be ejected in a thin, swift stream. —*n.* **1. a.** A device used to squirt. **b.** The stream squirted. **2.** *Informal.* An insignificant but arrogant person. —**squirt′er** *n.*

squish |skwĭsh|. *Informal.* —*v.* **1.** To squash noisily: *squish a ripe tomato.* **2.** To make a noise like that of mud being pressed. —*n.* A noise like that of mud being pressed.

sr., Sr. senior.

Sr The symbol for the element strontium.

Sri Lan·ka |srē läng′kə|. An island country in the Indian Ocean off the southeastern coast of India. Population, 14,850,000. Capital, Colombo.

SS, S.S. steamship.

St. 1. saint. **2.** street.

SST supersonic transport.

stab |stăb| *v.* **stabbed, stab·bing. 1.** To pierce or wound with a pointed weapon. **2.** To make a thrust or lunge with a pointed weapon: *stabbed at the bull's neck.* **3.** To wound the feelings of; hurt deeply: *The news stabbed him to the quick.* —*n.* **1.** A thrust made with a pointed weapon. **2.** A wound inflicted by a pointed weapon. **3.** An attempt; a try: *She thought she would take a stab at painting for a living.* —**stab′ber** *n.*

ă pat/ā pay/â care/ä father/ĕ pet/ ē be/ĭ pit/ī pie/î fierce/ŏ pot/ ō go/ô paw, for/oi oil/o͝o book/ o͞o boot/ou out/ŭ cut/û fur/ *th* the/th thin/hw which/zh vision/ ə ago, item, pencil, atom, circus

sta•bil•i•ty |stə bĭl′ĭ tē| *n., pl.* **sta•bil•i•ties. 1.** The condition or property of being stable. **2.** The degree to which something is stable.

sta•bi•lize |stā′bə līz′| *v.* **sta•bi•lized, sta•bi•liz•ing. 1.** To make or become stable. **2.** To keep (something) in a stable condition; maintain the stability of: *Gyroscopes help stabilize ships and airplanes.* **—sta′bi•li•za′tion** *n.* **—sta′bi•liz′er** *n.*

sta•ble[1] |stā′bəl| *adj.* **sta•bler, sta•blest. 1. a.** Resisting sudden changes of position or condition: *a flat, stable rock; a stable economy.* **b.** Tending to return to a condition of balance if disturbed: *a stable rocking chair.* **2.** Firmly established; likely to continue or survive: *a stable government.* **3.** Enduring; permanent: *a stable peace.* **4.** Not known to decay; existing for an indefinitely long time, as an atomic particle. **5.** Not easily decomposed, as a chemical compound. **—sta′bly** *adv.* [SEE NOTE]

sta•ble[2] |stā′bəl| *n.* **1.** Often **stables.** A building for the shelter of horses or other domestic animals. **2.** All of the racehorses belonging to a single owner. *—v.* **sta•bled, sta•bling.** To put or keep (an animal) in a stable. [SEE NOTE]

stac•ca•to |stə kä′tō| *adj.* **1.** Short and detached: *staccato musical tones.* **2.** Consisting of a series of distinct sounds: *staccato clapping.* *—adv.* In a short, detached manner: *playing a piano piece staccato.* *—n., pl.* **stac•ca•tos.** A staccato manner of performance.

stack |stăk| *n.* **1.** A large conical pile of straw. **2.** A pile arranged in layers: *a stack of pancakes; a stack of firewood.* **3.** *Informal.* A large quantity. **4.** A chimney or vertical exhaust pipe. **5. a.** A structure made of shelves placed one on top of another, used for storing books compactly in a library. **b. stacks.** The part of a library where books are stored on such shelves. *—v.* **1.** To arrange in a stack: *stacking hay; stack the books neatly.* **2.** To fix (a deck of playing cards) so as to cheat: *He was caught stacking the deck.*
Idiom. **stack up. 1.** To add up or total. **2.** To measure up; compare: *Our team stacks up well against the state champions.*

sta•di•um |stā′dē əm| *n.* **1.** *pl.* **sta•di•a** |stā′dē ə|. A course for foot races in ancient Greece, usually circular and surrounded with tiers of sloping seats. **2.** *pl.* **sta•di•a.** An ancient Greek measure of distance equal to about 607 feet. **3.** *pl.* **sta•di•ums.** A large, often unroofed structure in which athletic events are held.

staff |stăf| *or* |stäf| *n.* **1.** *pl.* **staffs** or **staves** |stāvz|. **a.** A long stick carried as an aid in walking or as a weapon. **b.** A rod carried as a symbol of authority. **c.** A pole on which a flag is displayed. **d.** A long measuring stick. **2.** *pl.* **staffs. a.** A group of assistants who serve a person of authority: *the President and his staff.* **b.** A group of army or naval officers who assist and advise a commander. **c.** Any organized group of employees working together on a project or enterprise. **3.** *pl.* **staves** or **staffs.** The set of horizontal lines and the spaces between them on which musical notes are written. *—v.* To provide with assistants or employees.

stag |stăg| *n.* **1.** A full-grown male deer. **2.** A man who attends a social gathering without escorting a woman. *—adj.* For or attended by men only: *a stag party.* [SEE PICTURE]

stage |stāj| *n.* **1.** The raised platform in a theater on which actors and other entertainers perform. **2.** The work of persons, especially actors, engaged in the production of plays. **3.** The scene or setting of an event or series of events: *The stage was set for a summit conference.* **4.** Part of a journey. **5.** A stagecoach. **6.** A level, degree, or period of time in the course of a process; a step in development: *a disease in its early stages.* **7.** Any of a series of rocket propulsion units, each of which fires after the preceding one has finished burning and been cast away. *—v.* **staged, stag•ing. 1.** To produce or direct (a theatrical performance). **2.** To arrange and carry out: *students staging a protest march.*

stage•coach |stāj′kōch′| *n.* A closed, horse-drawn vehicle with four wheels, formerly used to transport mail and passengers.

stag•ger |stăg′ər| *v.* **1.** To move or stand unsteadily, as if carrying a great weight; totter: *The blow sent Frank staggering backward.* **2.** To cause to totter or sway. **3.** To overwhelm with a severe shock, defeat, or misfortune. **4.** To arrange in parallel horizontal rows that form zigzags when viewed vertically: *stagger theater seats.* **5.** To arrange or schedule in overlapping time periods: *The terms of U.S. senators are staggered, so that only one-third are elected every two years.* **—stag′gered** *adj.: staggered rows.* **—stag′ger•ing** *adj.: a staggering impact.* *—n.* **1.** An act of staggering; a tottering motion or walk. **2. staggers** *(used with a singular verb).* A disease of horses, cattle, etc., in which the animal staggers and often falls.

stag•nant |stăg′nənt| *adj.* **1.** Not moving or flowing; motionless. **2.** Foul or polluted as a result of not moving: *stagnant water; stagnant air.* **3.** Not changing or growing; inactive: *a stagnant industry.* **—stag′nan•cy** *n.* **—stag′nant•ly** *adv.*

stag•nate |stăg′nāt′| *v.* **stag•nat•ed, stag•nat•ing. 1.** To be or become stagnant. **2.** To lie inactive; fail to change or grow. **—stag•na′tion** *n.*

staid |stād| *adj.* **1.** Serious and drab in style, manner, or behavior; grave; sedate. **2.** Fixed; unchanging. **—staid′ly** *adv.* **—staid′ness** *n.*

stain |stān| *v.* **1.** To discolor or become discolored with a substance that soaks in: *I've stained my fingers on this leaking pen. This fabric stains easily.* **2.** To mark (someone's good name, reputation, etc.) with a moral fault; taint. **3.** To color (wood or a similar material) with a dye or tint mixed with a penetrating liquid. **4.** To treat (microscopic specimens) with chemicals or dyes that make certain features visible through a microscope. *—n.* **1.** A mark or spot of a foreign substance that has soaked in. **2.** A blemish on one's character, reputation, record, etc. **3.** A liquid preparation applied to wood or similar material in order to color it. **4.** A solution used for staining microscopic specimens.

stained glass. Glass colored by mixing pigments already in the glass, by fusing colored metallic oxides onto the glass, or by painting and baking transparent colors on the glass surface. It is widely used in church windows. ***—modifier:*** **(stained-glass):** *stained-glass windows.*

stain•less |stān′lĭs| *adj.* **1.** Free of stains or blemishes. **2.** Resisting stain or corrosion.

stainless steel. Any of various steel alloys that

stable[1-2]
Stable[1] *and* **stable[2]** *come from closely related Latin words. Latin* stāre, *"to stand," formed (1) the adjective* stabilis, *"standing firm," and (2) the noun* stabulum, *"a place for animals to stand, a stable"; both of these passed into Old French as* estable, *and were borrowed thence into English as* **stable[1]** *and* **stable[2]**.

stag

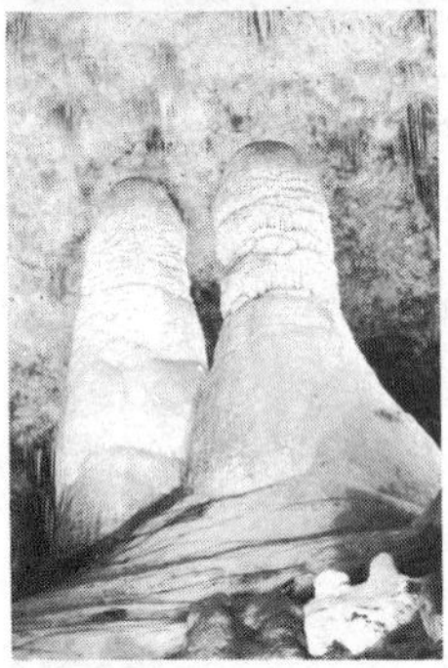

stalactite/stalagmite
Above: Stalactite
Below: Stalagmite
Carlsbad Caverns, New Mexico

stamen

ă pat/ā pay/â care/ä father/ĕ pet/ ē be/ĭ pit/ī pie/î fierce/ŏ pot/ ō go/ô paw, for/oi oil/ŏŏ book/ ōō boot/ou out/ŭ cut/û fur/ *th* the/th thin/hw which/zh vision/ ə ago, item, pencil, atom, circus

contain enough chromium to be resistant to rusting and corrosion. —***modifier:*** **(stainless-steel):** *a stainless-steel knife.*

stair |stâr| *n.* **1. stairs.** A series or flight of steps; a staircase. **2.** One of a flight of steps. ¶*These sound alike* **stair, stare.**

stair•case |stâr′kās′| *n.* A flight of steps and its supporting structure.

stair•way |stâr′wā′| *n.* A flight of stairs; a staircase.

stair•well |stâr′wĕl′| *n.* A vertical shaft containing a staircase.

stake |stāk| *n.* **1.** A stick or post driven upright into the ground and used as a marker, barrier, support, etc. **2. a.** A post to which a condemned person is bound for execution by burning. **b.** Execution by burning: *Joan of Arc was put to the stake.* **3.** Often **stakes.** The amount of money or the prize awarded to the winner of a bet, gambling game, contest, or race. **4.** Often **stakes.** A race, especially a horse race, offering a prize to the winner. **5.** A share or interest in an enterprise. —*v.* **staked, stak•ing. 1.** To mark the location or boundaries of with stakes or other markers: *stake out a piece of land.* **2.** To fasten to a stake for support or safekeeping: *stake a plant; stake a pet raccoon.* **3.** To gamble; risk: *stake two dollars on the favorite.* **4.** To provide with the capital or provisions needed for a planned venture. ¶*These sound alike* **stake, steak.**
Idioms. **at stake.** In jeopardy; being risked on an outcome. **pull up stakes.** To settle one's affairs and move on.

sta•lac•tite |stə lăk′tīt′| *or* |stăl′ək-| *n.* A cylindrical or conical mineral deposit projecting downward from the roof of a cave or cavern, formed by dripping mineral water. [SEE PICTURE]

sta•lag•mite |stə lăg′mīt′| *or* |stăl′əg-| *n.* A cylindrical or conical mineral deposit projecting upward from the floor of a cave or cavern, formed by dripping mineral water. [SEE PICTURE]

stale |stāl| *adj.* **stal•er, stal•est. 1.** Having lost freshness or flavor: *stale beer.* **2.** Too old or overused to be effective: *stale jokes.* **3.** Weakened by a lack of recent practice: *Some ballplayers work out on holidays, for fear of getting stale.* —*v.* **staled, stal•ing.** To make or become stale.

stale•mate |stāl′māt′| *n.* **1.** A draw position in chess in which only the king can move and, although not in check, can move only into check. **2.** A situation in which progress or action has come to a halt; a deadlock: *The peace talks have reached a stalemate.* —*v.* **stale•mat•ed, stale•mat•ing.** To bring to a stalemate; deadlock.

Sta•lin |stä′lĭn|, **Joseph.** 1879–1953. Soviet dictator; head of the government and the Communist Party until his death.

Sta•lin•ism |stä′lə nĭz′əm| *n.* The theory and practice of Communism as advanced by Joseph Stalin. —**Sta′lin•ist** *n.*

stalk¹ |stôk| *n.* **1.** The main stem of a plant or a stem or similar slender part attached to or supporting a leaf, flower, or other plant structure. **2.** A similar supporting or connecting part.

stalk² |stôk| *v.* **1.** To walk in a stiff, haughty manner: *I stalked past him in stony silence.* **2. a.** To move in a stealthy manner, as if tracking prey or a victim: *The hungry tiger stalked through the jungle.* **b.** To go after or track in this manner. —*n.* The action of stalking.

stall |stôl| *n.* **1.** A space enclosed by walls or barriers for one animal in a barn or stable. **2.** A small enclosure for selling or displaying merchandise, as at a fair; a booth. **3.** Any small compartment or booth. **4. a.** A large seat with arms, set apart near the altar of a church for a clergyman or dignitary. **b.** A pew in a church. **5.** A designated parking space provided for an automobile. **6.** A protective covering for a finger or thumb. **7.** A sudden, unintended loss of power or effectiveness in an engine. **8.** A procedure intended to delay action or progress; a delaying tactic. —*v.* **1.** To put or lodge (an animal) in a stall. **2. a.** To slow down or halt the progress of: *Opponents of the bill have stalled it in Congress.* **b.** To come to a standstill: *Negotiations have stalled on the issue of pensions for the workers.* **3.** To cause (an engine or motor) to stop running other than by using its controls, especially by overloading it. **4.** To stop running because of mechanical failure. **5.** To try to put off action; use delaying tactics: *Quit stalling and answer the question.*

stal•lion |stăl′yən| *n.* A full-grown male horse that has not been castrated.

stal•wart |stôl′wərt| *adj.* **1.** Physically strong; sturdy; robust. **2.** Not easily deterred or defeated; brave and resolute: *stalwart defenders of their country.* —*n.* **1.** A sturdy, strong-willed person. **2.** A loyal supporter; a dependable ally.

sta•men |stā′mən| *n.* One of the male reproductive organs of a flower, consisting of a slender stalk with a pollen-bearing part at its tip. [SEE PICTURE]

stam•i•na |stăm′ə nə| *n.* The power to resist fatigue or illness while working hard; endurance.

stam•mer |stăm′ər| *v.* **1.** To speak with involuntary pauses and sometimes repetitions of sounds, as a result of excitement, embarrassment, or an impediment. **2.** To say or utter with such pauses or repetitions. —*n.* An example or habit of stammering. —**stam′mer•er** *n.*

stamp |stămp| *v.* **1. a.** To set down (the foot) heavily: *We stamped our feet at the doorway to shake off the snow. The horse stamped nervously.* **b.** To set the foot or feet down heavily on (a surface). **2.** To walk with loud, heavy steps. **3. a.** To strike (a document, letter, or other surface) with a device that leaves a mark, design, or message: *The border guard stamped our passports and let us go.* **b.** To imprint (a mark, design, or message) with such a device. **4.** To put a postage stamp or other gummed marker on: *Don't forget to stamp the letter before mailing it.* **5.** To shape or cut out by forcing into or against a mold, form, or die: *a factory that stamps metal parts.* **6.** To impress deeply or permanently: *an image stamped in her memory.* **7.** To mark or characterize unmistakably: *His accent stamped him as a foreigner.* —***phrasal verb.*** **stamp out. 1.** To put out by stamping: *stamp out a fire.* **2.** To end by taking forceful measures; suppress. —*n.* **1.** Any of various devices that leave a special mark when struck or pressed against a surface: *a rubber stamp for marking packages "fragile."* **2.** The mark left by such a device, especially an impressed design or message indicating approval, completion, ownership, or some other fact. **3. a.** A small piece of gummed paper bearing a design or message on its face: *a trading stamp; a revenue stamp.* **b.** A **postage stamp.** **4.** A machine that cuts or shapes products by stamping. **5.** A characteristic mark; a clear indication: *the stamp of truth on a witness's face.* **6.** A class; kind: *Men of his stamp are all too common.* —***modifier:*** *a stamp collection.* [SEE NOTE]

stam•pede |stăm pēd'| *n.* **1.** A sudden, violent rush of startled animals, as of a herd of horses, cattle, or buffalo. **2.** A similar sudden or headlong rush of people. —*v.* **stam•ped•ed, stam•ped•ing. 1.** To rush suddenly or act impulsively, as a startled herd of animals or an excited crowd does. **2.** To cause to rush or act in this manner: *He tried to stampede the voters into approving the new bond issue.* [SEE NOTE]

stance |stăns| *n.* **1.** The position or manner in which a person or animal stands; posture: *an erect, almost military stance.* **2.** The position taken by an athlete or sportsman about to go into action: *the crouched stance of a football lineman.* **3.** An attitude regarding some issue: *a judge with a tough stance toward repeated offenders.*

stanch¹ |stônch| *or* |stănch| *or* |stänch| *v.* **1.** To stop or check the flow of (a bodily fluid, especially blood). **2.** To stop or check the flow of blood from (a wound).

stanch² |stônch| *or* |stänch| *adj.* **stanch•er, stanch•est.** A form of the word **staunch.**

stan•chion |stăn'chən| *or* |-shən| *n.* A vertical pole, post, or support. —*v.* **1.** To provide with stanchions for support: *stanchion a sagging roof.*

stand |stănd| *v.* **stood** |stŏŏd|, **stand•ing. 1.** To take or stay in an upright position on the feet: *I had to stand on a chair to change the light bulb. She stood next to the door and listened.* **2.** To rest in an upright position on a base or support: *The rocket stood on a launching pad. He stood the mop in a corner of the kitchen.* **3.** To measure a certain height when erect: *stood six feet tall.* **4.** To be located; occupy a position: *An ancient watchtower stands on the cliff.* **5.** To be placed; occupy a rank: *stand 12th in line. Where did your team stand at the end of the season?* **6.** To remain motionless or undisturbed: *letting a mixture stand overnight.* **7.** To remain in effect or existence: *Exceptions are made, but the rule still stands.* **8.** To rely for support or justification: *standing on his record.* **9.** To be a firm defender or supporter: *candidates who stand for peace.* **10.** To declare oneself or be declared to be: *I stand ready to help. My client stands accused of a serious crime.* **11.** To be likely: *Who stands to gain from this war?* **12.** To tolerate; endure: *My parents can't stand the music I like.* **13.** To suffer and not be damaged; resist; withstand: *a metal that can stand high temperatures.* **14.** To undergo: *stand trial.* **15.** *Chiefly British.* To be a candidate for public office; run: *stand for Parliament.* **16.** To bear the expense of; pay for: *I'll stand you a dinner to celebrate.* —***phrasal verbs.*** **stand by. 1.** To be loyal to. **2.** To keep; fulfill: *stand by a promise.* **3.** To wait until one is needed or called. **stand down.** To leave the witness stand at a trial. **stand for. 1.** To represent in a shortened or symbolic form: *"X" stands for an unknown quantity.* **2.** To put up with; accept: *She wouldn't stand for another delay.* **stand off.** To withstand; repel: *stood off the attack.* **stand on.** To demand fulfillment or observance of; insist on: *standing on his constitutional rights; standing on ceremony.* **stand out. 1.** To extend outward; protrude. **2.** To be prominent; attract attention: *colors that stand out.* **3.** To be outstanding; excel. **stand up. 1.** To remain unweakened or unchanged: *stood up under pressure.* **2.** *Informal.* To fail to keep an appointment with (someone). —*n.* **1.** An act of standing: *a long stand in a line.* **2.** A place where a person, such as a guard, stands. **3.** A place reserved for the stopping or parking of certain vehicles: *a bus stand; a taxi stand.* **4.** A small place, often mobile or temporary, for the display of goods for sale; a booth, stall, or counter: *a flower stand.* **5.** A small rack, prop, or receptacle for holding something: *an umbrella stand; a music stand.* **6.** A raised structure on which someone can sit or stand and be clearly seen: *a speaker's stand; a witness stand.* **7. stands.** The seating area at a playing field or stadium. **8.** A halt in progress, advance, or work. **9.** A stop on a performance tour: *a one-night stand.* **10.** A military position prepared for defense against attack. **11.** A position on an issue or question that one is prepared to defend against the arguments of others. **12.** An area or growth of tall plants or trees: *a stand of pine.*

Idioms. **stand a chance.** To have a hope of succeeding. **stand in for.** To take the place of; substitute for. **stand (one's) ground.** To hold out against attack or criticism. **stand up for.** To side with; be loyal to; support. **stand up to.** To face or deal with courageously; confront squarely.

stan•dard |stăn'dərd| *n.* **1. a.** A widely known and accepted measure used as a basis for a system of measures. **b.** A physical object from which such a measure can be determined under a given set of conditions. **2.** A rule or model used to judge the quality, value, or rightness of something. **3. a.** A prevailing level of quality, value, or achievement: *the standard of production at a factory; a high standard of living.* **b.** A level of quality, value, or achievement that is demanded or aimed for; a requirement: *an artist who sets high standards for herself.* **4.** A commodity used as the basis of a monetary system: *the gold standard.* **5.** A flag or banner used as the emblem of a nation, military unit, corporation, etc. **6.** A stand on which something is mounted or supported; a pedestal. —*adj.* **1.** Serving as a standard of measurement, value, or quality: *a standard unit of volume; the standard performance of a piece of music.* **2.** Conforming to a standard, as in size, weight, or quality: *bolts of standard length and thickness.* **3.** Average; typical: *the standard sort of horror movie.* **4.** Widely accepted as reliable or excellent: *a standard atlas.* **5.** Widely used and considered acceptable by educated speakers: *standard English.*

standard candle. A candela, a unit of luminous intensity.

standard gauge. 1. A railroad track having a width of 56½ inches. **2.** A railroad or railroad car built to this specification. —***modifier:*** **(stan•dard-gauge):** *standard-gauge tracks.*

stan•dard•ize |stăn'dər dīz'| *v.* **stan•dard•ized, stan•dard•iz•ing.** To cause (a thing or set of

stamp/stampede

Stamp *and* **stampede** *are both ultimately from an Indo-European root,* stebh-, *"to place firmly on, fasten." The Germanic form* stamp-, *which descended from* stebh-, *produced both Old English* stampian *(unattested), "to pound," and Spanish* estampar, *the source of Mexican Spanish* estampida, *"a stampede," which was borrowed into English as* **stampede.**

staple[1-2]

Staple[1] *originally meant "an English town specializing in the export of a particular product"; the word is from Old French* estaple, *"market"; later* **staple**[1] *came to mean "the major product handled by a particular market."* **Staple**[2] *was Old English* stapol, *originally meaning "pillar, post," later "iron rod."*

star

The prehistoric Indo-European word for "star" was ster-. *This appears in Old English as* steorr, *which became* **star** *in Modern English. In addition,* ster- *had a form* ster-la-, *which appears in Latin as* stella, *"star," from which we have* **stellar** *and* **constellation**. Ster- *had another variant form that appears in Greek as* astēr *or* astron, *"star"; see notes at* **aster** *and* **disaster**.

starfish

ă pat/ā pay/â care/ä father/ĕ pet/ ē be/ĭ pit/ī pie/î fierce/ŏ pot/ ō go/ô paw, for/oi oil/ŏŏ book/ ōō boot/ou out/ŭ cut/û fur/ *th* the/th thin/hw which/zh vision/ ə ago, item, pencil, atom, circus

things) to be or be made standard: *standardize automobile tires.* —**stan′dard•i•za′tion** *n.*

standard time. The time, computed from the position of the sun, in any of the 24 time zones into which the earth is divided, especially the time at the central meridian of each zone.

stand•by |**stănd′**bī′| *n.* **1.** Someone or something kept ready and available for service as a substitute or in case of emergency. **2.** Someone or something that can always be depended on.

stand•ee |stăn **dē′**| *n.* A person who stands for lack of a seat, as on a bus or in a theater.

stand-in |**stănd′**ĭn′| *n.* **1.** A substitute. **2.** A person who takes the place of a performer while the lights and camera are being adjusted.

stand•ing |**stăn′**dĭng| *adj.* **1.** Upright on the feet or in place; erect: *standing timber.* **2.** Performed from an upright, stationary position: *a standing broad jump.* **3.** Remaining in effect or existence; permanent: *a standing invitation; a standing army.* —*n.* **1.** A relative position in a group; rank: *last place in the National League standings.* **2.** Status; reputation: *a lawyer in good standing.* **3.** Persistence in time; duration: *a friend of long standing.*

stand•off•ish |stănd **ô′**fĭsh| *or* |**-ŏf′**ĭsh| *adj.* Unfriendly; aloof.

stand•point |**stănd′**point′| *n.* A position from which things are considered.

stand•still |**stănd′**stĭl′| *n.* A halt; stop.

stank |stăngk|. A past tense of **stink**.

stan•nic |**stăn′**ĭk| *adj.* Of or containing tin, especially with a valence of +4.

stan•nous |**stăn′**əs| *adj.* Of or containing tin, especially with a valence of +2.

stan•za |**stăn′**zə| *n.* One of the divisions of a poem or song, composed of two or more lines.

sta•pes |**stā′**pēz′| *n., pl.* **sta•pes** or **sta•pe•des** |stə **pē′**dēz′|. One of three small bones in the middle ear; the stirrup.

staph•y•lo•coc•cus |stăf′ə lə **kŏk′**əs| *n., pl.* **staph•y•lo•coc•ci** |stăf′ə lə **kŏk′**sī′|. Any of several rounded bacteria that form grapelike clusters and that often cause boils, abscesses, etc.

sta•ple[1] |**stā′**pəl| *n.* **1.** A major product grown or produced in a region: *Rice and rubber are the staples of Southeast Asia.* **2.** A basic food or other commodity always produced and sold in large amounts because of steady demand: *Bread, salt, and sugar are staples.* **3.** A raw material. **4.** Something that is constantly used or resorted to; a principal substance, topic, or part: *the classics that are the staples of every good library.* **5.** The fiber of cotton, wool, flax, hemp, etc., graded as to length or fineness. —***modifier:*** *a staple food; long-staple cotton.* [SEE NOTE]

sta•ple[2] |**stā′**pəl| *n.* **1.** A U-shaped metal loop with pointed ends, driven into a surface to hold a hook or bolt or to hold wiring in place. **2.** A similar thin piece of wire, used for fastening papers together. —*v.* **sta•pled, sta•pling.** To fasten by means of a staple. [SEE NOTE]

sta•pler |**stā′**plər| *n.* A device used to fasten papers or other materials together by driving in staples.

star |stär| *n.* **1.** A massive celestial object that consists of extremely hot gases, emitting radiation, including visible light, and using energy derived from internal, self-sustaining nuclear reactions, or sometimes, from contraction under the influence of gravitational forces. **2.** Any luminous, relatively stationary celestial body visible from the earth. **3. stars. a.** The celestial bodies, regarded as determining and influencing human events. **b.** Fate; fortune. **4. a.** A design representing a star, having several points radiating from a center. **b.** An object with this design, worn or affixed as an emblem or ornament: *a silver star pinned to his jacket.* **5.** An asterisk. **6. a.** An actor who plays a leading role in a movie, drama, or other performance. **b.** Any outstanding and widely admired performer, as in movies or sports. —***modifier:*** *a star quarterback.* —*v.* **starred, star•ring. 1.** To ornament with stars. **2.** To award with a star for excellence. **3.** To present (a performer) in a leading role: *a television series starring a talking dog.* **4.** To play the leading role: *She's now starring in a Broadway show.* [SEE NOTE]

star•board |**stär′**bôrd′| *or* |-bōrd′| *n.* The right side of a ship or aircraft facing forward. —*adj.* On the starboard: *the starboard bow; the starboard side.* —*adv.* To or toward the starboard.

starch |stärch| *n.* **1. a.** Any of various nutrient carbohydrates that occur widely in nature, chiefly in parts of plants, especially wheat, corn, rice, potatoes, etc. **b.** A purified form of this substance, occurring chiefly as a white, tasteless powder. **2.** Any food with a high content of starch. **3.** Any of various products, including natural starch, used to stiffen fabrics. **4.** Stiffness of behavior or manner. —*v.* To stiffen (fabric) with starch.

starch•y |**stär′**chē| *adj.* **starch•i•er, starch•i•est. 1.** Of, like, or containing starch. **2.** Stiffened with starch, as a fabric. **3.** Stiff; formal.

star•dom |**stär′**dəm| *n.* The status of an actor or other performer acknowledged as a star.

stare |stâr| *v.* **stared, star•ing. 1.** To look with a steady, often wide-eyed gaze, as in longing, curiosity, or surprise: *Billy stared at the candy.* **2.** To compel by gazing sternly and intently: *He has a way of staring his listeners into agreeing with him.* **3.** To stand out; be prominent or glaring. —*n.* A steady gaze, often with the eyes wide open. ¶*These sound alike* **stare, stair.**

star•fish |**stär′**fĭsh′| *n., pl.* **-fish** or **-fish•es.** Any of several sea animals having a star-shaped form and usually five arms. [SEE PICTURE]

stark |stärk| *adj.* **stark•er, stark•est. 1.** Plain and blunt; unmistakable: *stark evidence.* **2.** Unadorned; barren; grim: *the stark lunar landscape.* **3.** Utter; complete; total: *in stark contrast.* **4.** Rigid; strict: *a stark morality.* —*adv.* Utterly; completely: *stark raving mad.* —**stark′ly** *adv.*

star•let |**stär′**lĭt| *n.* A young motion-picture actress publicized as a future star.

star•light |**stär′**līt′| *n.* The light that reaches the earth from the stars.

star•ling |**stär′**lĭng| *n.* A common bird with dark, glossy feathers, often forming large flocks.

star•lit |**stär′**lĭt′| *adj.* Illuminated by starlight.

star•ry |**stär′**ē| *adj.* **star•ri•er, star•ri•est. 1.** Shining like stars: *starry eyes.* **2.** Having many stars visible: *a starry night.* **3.** Adorned with stars: *a magician's starry cloak.* —**star′ri•ness** *n.*

star•ry-eyed |**stär′**ē īd′| *adj.* Full of youthful hope and confidence; naively optimistic.

Stars and Stripes. The flag of the United States.

Star-Span•gled Banner |stär'spăng'gəld|. **1.** The flag of the United States. **2.** The national anthem of the United States. [SEE NOTE]

start |stärt| *v.* **1.** To begin an action or movement; set out: *Starting at dawn, we reached the summit by nightfall.* **2.** To come into operation or being; have a beginning: *School starts in September.* **3.** To put into motion, operation, or activity; set going: *You start the engine by using a crank.* **4.** To bring about; cause to arise; originate: *start an argument.* **5.** To found; establish: *start a day-care center.* **6.** To take up (a task or activity); apply oneself to; begin: *start a new job; start a book.* **7.** To help in beginning a venture; give initial aid or advice to: *A retiring doctor started him in his career by turning over the names of old patients.* **8.** To cause to act or move in a certain way: *The butler had a perfect alibi, and that started me thinking.* **9.** To move the head or body suddenly or involuntarily, as in surprise: *He must have been dozing, because he started when I spoke.* **10.** To move quickly into view or activity; spring forth: *The forest birds started up from the trees at the noise.* **11.** To rouse from a resting or hiding place; flush: *a commotion that started us all out of our beds.* **12.** To protrude; bulge: *their eyes starting in terror.* **13.** To loosen or become loosened from a secure position: *start a nail by prying up a board.* **14. a.** To enter or be entered among the contestants in a race: *start a horse; the 12 horses starting in the derby.* **b.** To play as a member of the team that begins a game: *I started at first base. The coach decided not to start his injured halfback.* —*n.* **1.** A beginning. **2.** A place or time at which something or someone begins: *We got a late start this morning.* **3.** A sudden or involuntary movement of the body; a startled reaction: *awoke with a start.* **4. starts.** Brief spurts of activity: *working by fits and starts.* **5.** A position of advantage over rivals, as in a race; a lead. **6.** An opportunity or an act of assistance to one beginning a new venture.

start•er |stär'tər| *n.* **1.** Someone or something that starts. **2.** A device, usually an electric motor, that turns an internal-combustion engine through several revolutions to make it start. **3.** A person who signals the start of a race. **4. a.** A contestant at the beginning of a race. **b.** A player who starts in a game.

star•tle |stär'tl| *v.* **star•tled, star•tling.** **1.** To cause to make a sudden movement of surprise or alarm: *A thud on the roof startled us.* **2.** To fill with sudden surprise; shock: *The declaration of war startled our allies.* —*n.* A sudden movement of surprise or alarm.

star•tling |stär'tlĭng| *adj.* Causing sudden surprise; astonishing: *startling news.*

star•va•tion |stär vā'shən| *n.* **1.** The act or process of starving. **2.** The condition of being starved.

starve |stärv| *v.* **starved, starv•ing.** **1.** To suffer bodily damage or die as a result of an extreme or prolonged lack of food. **2.** To suffer ill effects because of a lack of something necessary: *an orphan starving for love.* **3.** *Informal.* To be hungry. **4.** To cause to starve. **5.** To compel or force by denying access to food: *The invading troops starved the town into submission.*

stash |stăsh| *v.* To hide or store in a secret place: *stashing her earnings under her mattress.* —*n.* **1.** A hiding place for money or valuables. **2.** An amount hidden or stored away.

state |stāt| *n.* **1.** A set of circumstances in which something exists or is operating; a condition: *the state of my finances; a radio in a state of disrepair.* **2.** One of the three principal conditions, solid, liquid, or gaseous, in which material substances occur: *Ice is water in the solid state.* **3.** A mental or emotional disposition; mood: *In a calmer state, he is more rational.* **4.** *Informal.* A condition of excitement, confusion, or disorder. **5. a.** A body of people living under a single independent government; a nation: *the state of Israel.* **b.** The territory of such a government. **6.** The means, procedure, or power of governing and representing an independent nation or other political unit: *matters of state.* **7.** Often **State.** One of the political and geographic subdivisions of a country such as the United States of America, which was organized as a federation. **8.** A social position; rank. **9.** A grand and formal style; high ceremony: *a queen riding in state.* —***modifier:*** *a state law; a state occasion.* —*v.* **stat•ed, stat•ing.** To express in clear, informative words; assert; declare: *stating a problem.*

state•hood |stāt'ho͝od'| *n.* The condition of being a state, especially a state of the United States.

State House. A state capitol.

state•less |stāt'lĭs| *adj.* Not being a citizen of any country: *stateless persons.*

state•ly |stāt'lē| *adj.* **state•li•er, state•li•est.** **1.** Marked by a graceful dignity or formality: *a dance with a slow, stately rhythm.* **2.** Impressive in size or proportions; majestic: *stately columns; a stately oak.* —**state'li•ness** *n.*

state•ment |stāt'mənt| *n.* **1.** The act of stating; expression in words: *his statement of purpose.* **2.** A sentence or group of sentences that states something: *After each statement, mark whether you think it is true or false.* **3.** A written summary of a financial account: *a monthly bank statement.*

Stat•en Island |stăt'n|. An island between New Jersey and Long Island, a borough of New York City.

state•room |stāt'ro͞om'| *or* |-ro͝om'| *n.* A private room with sleeping accommodations on a ship or train.

state•side |stāt'sīd'| *adj.* Of or in the continental United States: *Volunteers undergo stateside training before being shipped abroad.* —*adv.* To or toward the continental United States.

states•man |stāts'mən| *n., pl.* **-men** |-mən|. **1.** A leader in government and politics. **2.** A wise and eloquent spokesman on national or international issues.

states•man•ship |stāts'mən shĭp'| *n.* The art of a statesman; skillful management of public affairs.

states' rights or **States' rights.** **1.** The rights and powers of the state governments, as indicated by or inferred from the Constitution of the United States. **2.** A political belief in limiting the powers of the Federal government and defending or extending those of the individual states.

Star-Spangled Banner

The words of "The Star-Spangled Banner" were written during the War of 1812 by Francis Scott Key, who watched the British bombardment of Fort McHenry near Baltimore. Well-received by the American people, the poem was sung to a British drinking song, "To Anacreon in Heaven," popular at that time. The song was adopted as the national anthem in 1931, when Congress confirmed an executive order signed in 1916 by President Woodrow Wilson.

stat•ic |stăt′ĭk| *adj.* **1.** Not moving or in motion; at rest. **2.** Of or determined with respect to something stationary: *a wheel in static balance.* **3.** Of or producing stationary electric charges; electrostatic. **4.** Of or produced by noise that appears at the output of a radio receiver. *—n.* Random noise that appears at the output of a radio receiver, audible as a hissing noise and visible as specks on a television screen.

static electricity. **1.** An electric charge accumulated on an insulated body. **2.** A discharge resulting from the accumulation of such a charge.

stat•ics |stăt′ĭks| *n. (used with a singular verb).* The part of physics that deals with balanced forces on and within stationary physical systems.

sta•tion |stā′shən| *n.* **1.** A place or location, especially a place where a person or thing stands: *From my station on the ridge, I could see the countryside for miles around.* **2.** A place, often a building with special facilities, where a service is provided or certain activities are directed: *a fire station.* **3.** A stopping place along a route for taking on and letting off passengers: *a bus station.* **4.** An establishment equipped to transmit radio or television signals. **5.** An establishment set up for the purpose of study or observation: *a radar station.* **6.** Social position; rank: *content with his station in life.* *—v.* To assign to a position; to post.

sta•tion•ar•y |stā′shə nĕr′ē| *adj.* **1. a.** Undergoing no change of position; not moving. **b.** Not capable of being moved; fixed: *a stationary bridge.* **2.** In a state or condition that does not change with time; unchanging: *a stationary sound.* ¶*These sound alike* **stationary, stationery.** [SEE NOTE]

stationary/stationery

Stationary *is the regular adjective from* **station,** *with the adjectival suffix* -ary *as in* **elementary** *and* **visionary.** *In medieval England, most booksellers were traveling salesmen; the few permanent bookstores were called* stations, *and their operators were called* **stationers.** *The merchandise (books and writing materials) sold in a* station *was at first called* stationary goods. *Later, by influence of the* -er *of* **stationer** *and the suffix* -ery *as in* **bakery** *and* **machinery,** stationary goods *was changed to* **stationery.**

sta•tion•er |stā′shə nər| *n.* A person who sells stationery.

sta•tion•er•y |stā′shə nĕr′ē| *n.* **1.** Writing paper and envelopes. **2.** Desk and office supplies, including paper, pens, calendars, typewriter ribbons, etc. **3.** A store that sells such supplies. ***—modifier:*** *a stationery store.* ¶*These sound alike* **stationery, stationary.** [SEE NOTE]

sta•tion•mas•ter |stā′shən măs′tər| *or* |-mä′stər| *n.* A person in charge of a railroad or bus station.

station wagon. An automobile having a fairly large interior and sometimes containing a third row of seats, usually equipped with a tailgate and provision for folding or removing the second and third rows of seats to provide cargo space.

sta•tis•tic |stə tĭs′tĭk| *n.* **1.** An item of numerical data. **2.** An estimate of a variable, such as an average or mean, made on the basis of a sample taken from a larger set of data.

sta•tis•ti•cal |stə tĭs′tĭ kəl| *adj.* **1.** Of a statistic or statistics. **2.** Of statistics, the branch of mathematics. **—sta•tis′ti•cal•ly** *adv.*

stat•is•ti•cian |stăt′ĭ stĭsh′ən| *n.* **1.** A mathematician who specializes in statistics. **2.** Someone who collects statistical data.

sta•tis•tics |stə tĭs′tĭks| *n.* **1.** *(used with a singular verb).* The part of mathematics that deals with the collection, organization, analysis, and interpretation of statistical data. **2.** *(used with a plural verb).* A collection or set of numerical data.

sta•tor |stā′tər| *n.* The stationary part of a motor, generator, turbine, or other piece of rotary machinery.

stat•u•ar•y |stăch′o͞o ĕr′ē| *n., pl.* **stat•u•ar•ies.** **1.** Statues as a group. **2.** The art of making statues. *—adj.* Of or for statues: *statuary art.*

stat•ue |stăch′o͞o| *n.* A form representing a person or thing, made by an artist out of stone, metal, or another solid substance.

stat•u•esque |stăch′o͞o ĕsk′| *adj.* Like a statue, as in size, graceful proportions, etc.

stat•u•ette |stăch′o͞o ĕt′| *n.* A small statue.

stat•ure |stăch′ər| *n.* **1.** The natural height of a person or animal when upright. **2.** A level of development or achievement: *chess players of equal stature.* **3.** Reputation; status: *an artist of world stature.*

sta•tus |stā′təs| *or* |stăt′əs| *n., pl.* **sta•tus•es.** **1.** The condition of a person or thing, as defined by law, regulations, or customs: *one's marital status; warships in a reserve status.* **2.** A stage of progress or development: *the status of a bill in Congress.* **3.** A relative position in a ranked group or in a social system: *the high status of professional people.* **4.** A high relative position, as indicated by the respect or envy of others; prestige: *seeking status by buying expensive clothes.* ***—modifier:*** *a status symbol.*

sta•tus quo |stā′təs kwō′| *or* |stăt′əs|. The existing state of affairs.

stat•ute |stăch′o͞ot| *n.* A law enacted by a legislative body.

statute mile. The standard mile, equal to 5,280 feet.

stat•u•to•ry |stăch′o͞o tôr′ē| *or* |-tōr′ē| *adj.* Of, defined by, or regulated by statute.

staunch[1] |stônch| *or* |stänch| *adj.* **staunch•er, staunch•est.** **1.** Strongly made or built: *staunch roots; staunch boards.* **2.** Firm in supporting or defending; steadily loyal: *a staunch ally.*

staunch[2] |stônch| *or* |stänch| *v.* A form of the word **stanch.**

stave |stāv| *n.* **1.** A strip of wood forming a part of the side of a barrel, tub, etc. **2.** A rung of a ladder or chair. **3.** A heavy stick or pole; a staff. **4.** A musical staff. *—v.* **staved** or **stove** |stōv|, **stav•ing.** **1.** To break or puncture the staves or side of: *We almost stove the boat on a reef.* **2.** To make (a hole) by breaking through staves. ***—phrasal verb.* stave off.** **1.** To keep or hold off, as if by extending a staff; repel: *stave off an attack.* **2.** To delay or postpone, especially in desperation: *staving off the inevitable defeat.*

staves |stāvz| *n.* A plural of **staff.**

stay[1] |stā| *v.* **1.** To remain in one place. **2.** To keep on being: *stay awake.* **3.** To remain or reside as a guest: *stay overnight at a friend's house.* **4.** To last; endure: *We built a fire large enough to stay for the cold night.* **5. a.** To stop moving or acting; cease or pause: *stay from his labors.* **b.** To stop; halt: *stay one's tongue.* **6.** To postpone; delay: *stay the execution of a sentence.* **7.** To satisfy or moderate temporarily: *stayed her appetite with an orange.* *—n.* **1.** A brief period of residence or visiting. **2.** A halt or pause. **3.** A postponement, as of an execution.

stay[2] |stā| *n.* **1.** A part that acts as a support or brace. **2.** A strip of bone, plastic, or metal, used to stiffen a garment or part, as a corset or shirt collar. **3. stays.** A corset. *—v.* To support or

ă pat/ā pay/â care/ä father/ĕ pet/ ē be/ĭ pit/ī pie/î fierce/ŏ pot/ ō go/ô paw, for/oi oil/o͝o book/ o͞o boot/ou out/ŭ cut/û fur/ *th* the/th thin/hw which/zh vision/ ə ago, item, pencil, atom, circus

brace with or as if with a stay: *stay an overhanging roof with columns.*

stay³ |stā| *n.* A heavy rope or cable, usually of wire, used to brace or support a mast, spar, or other vertical structure. —*v.* To brace or support with a stay or stays.

St. Ber•nard |sānt′ bər **närd′**|. A very large dog of a breed originally used by monks in the Swiss Alps to help travelers. [SEE PICTURE]

St. Croix |sānt′ **kroi′**|. The largest island of the Virgin Islands of the United States.

stead |stĕd| *n.* The usual, expected, or former place of another: *Zeus overthrew his father and ruled the world in his stead.*

Idiom. **stand (one) in good stead.** To be of advantage to one; serve one well: *The new President's experience will stand the nation in good stead.*

stead•fast |**stĕd′**făst′| *or* |-fäst′| *adj.* **1.** Not moving; fixed in place: *standing steadfast.* **2.** Not changing or yielding; firm; constant: *a steadfast refusal.* —**stead′fast′ly** *adv.* —**stead′fast′ness** *n.*

stead•y |**stĕd′**ē| *adj.* **stead•i•er, stead•i•est. 1.** Not apt to shift, wobble, or slip; firmly in place: *a steady grip on the wheel.* **2.** Not changing direction; constant: *a steady wind.* **3.** Continuous in amount or rate; uniform: *a steady income.* **4.** Unfaltering; sure: *sewing with a steady hand.* **5.** Not easily excited or disturbed; composed: *steady nerves.* **6.** Reliable; dependable: *steady workers.* **7.** Regular: *a steady customer.* —*v.* **stead•ied, stead•y•ing, stead•ies.** To make or become steady; stabilize: *She raised a hand to steady the bucket on her head. After a time, the heartbeat steadied.* —**stead′i•ly** *adv.* —**stead′i•ness** *n.*

Idiom. **go steady.** To have dates with each other only, by agreement.

steak |stāk| *n.* A slice of beef or other meat, usually broiled or fried. —***modifier:*** *a steak knife.* ¶*These sound alike* **steak, stake.**

steal |stēl| *v.* **stole** |stōl|, **stol•en** |**stō′**lən|, **steal•ing. 1.** To take (someone else's property) without right or permission: *stole a bicycle; stealing to support a drug habit.* **2.** To get or enjoy secretly or furtively: *steal a glimpse.* **3.** To move or pass without making noise or being noticed: *An enemy submarine had stolen into the harbor. The hours stole by.* **4.** In baseball, to gain (another base) without the ball being batted, by running to the base during the delivery of a pitch. —*n.* **1.** The act of stealing; theft. **2.** *Slang.* Something acquired at a very low price; a bargain. ¶*These sound alike* **steal, steel.** —**steal′er** *n.*

stealth |stĕlth| *n.* **1.** The act of moving in a quiet, secret way so as to avoid notice: *The leopard abandoned stealth and rushed on its prey.* **2.** Furtiveness; sneakiness.

stealth•y |**stĕl′**thē| *adj.* **stealth•i•er, stealth•i•est.** Quiet so as to avoid notice; furtive: *stealthy steps.* —**stealth′i•ly** *adv.* —**stealth′i•ness** *n.*

steam |stēm| *n.* **1. a.** Water in the gaseous state, especially when hot. **b.** The mist that forms when hot water vapor cools and condenses into tiny droplets. **2.** Power generated by water vapor under pressure. **3.** Physical energy: *running out of steam.* —***modifier:*** *steam power.* —*v.* **1.** To produce or emit steam. **2.** To turn into or escape as steam. **3.** To become covered with mist or steam: *The bathroom mirror steams up when the shower is used.* **4.** To move by or as if by the power of steam: *The ship steamed into the harbor.* **5.** To treat with or expose to steam, as in cooking: *steam rice.* **6.** *Informal.* To become very angry; fume.

Idiom. **let** (or **blow**) **off steam.** *Informal.* To release pent-up emotions or energy.

steam•boat |**stēm′**bōt′| *n.* A steamship.

steam engine. An engine in which the energy of hot steam is converted into mechanical power, especially one in which the steam expands in a closed cylinder and drives a piston.

steam•er |**stē′**mər| *n.* **1.** A steamship. **2.** An early steam-powered automobile: *a Stanley Steamer.* **3.** A container in which something is exposed to or treated with steam: *a rice steamer.* **4.** A soft-shell clam cooked by steaming.

steam•fit•ter |**stēm′**fĭt′ər| *n.* A person who installs and repairs heating, ventilating, and refrigerating systems.

steam•roll•er |**stēm′**rō′lər| *n.* **1.** A vehicle, powered by an internal-combustion engine, equipped with a heavy roller for smoothing road surfaces. **2.** A force that crushes opposition as it advances. —*v.* **1.** To smooth (a road or road surface) with a steamroller. **2.** To defeat or silence ruthlessly; crush. [SEE PICTURE]

steam•ship |**stēm′**shĭp′| *n.* A large ship propelled by one or more steam-driven engines.

steam•y |**stē′**mē| *adj.* **steam•i•er, steam•i•est. 1.** Filled with or emitting steam: *a steamy kitchen; a steamy volcano.* **2.** Hot and humid: *the steamy jungles.* —**steam′i•ness** *n.*

ste•a•tite |**stē′**ə tīt′| *n.* A solid, white-to-green form of talc, used in ceramics and insulation.

steed |stēd| *n.* A horse, especially a spirited horse used for riding.

steel |stēl| *n.* **1.** Any of various hard, strong alloys of iron and carbon, often with other metals added to give certain desired properties, widely used as a structural material. **2.** Any of various implements or tools made of this material, as a sword, a knife sharpener, etc. **3.** A hardness or strength like that of steel: *nerves of steel.* —***modifier:*** *a steel tower; a steel mill.* —*v.* **1.** To cover, plate, edge, or point with steel. **2.** To strengthen; brace: *steel oneself against disappointment by expecting the worst.* ¶*These sound alike* **steel, steal.**

steel wool. A matted mass of fine steel fibers, used for scouring or polishing things.

steel•work |**stēl′**wûrk′| *n.* **1.** Something made of steel. **2. steelworks** *(used with a singular or plural verb).* A plant where steel is made.

steel•work•er |**stēl′**wûr′kər| *n.* Someone who works in the manufacture of steel.

steel•y |**stē′**lē| *adj.* **steel•i•er, steel•i•est.** Like steel: *fixed me with his steely gaze; a steely black.* —**steel′i•ness** *n.*

steel•yard |**stēl′**yärd′| *n.* A portable weighing device made of a horizontal bar marked off in units of weight, with a hook at the shorter end for holding the object to be weighed and a sliding counterweight at the other end that indicates the correct weight when the bar is balanced.

steep¹ |stēp| *adj.* **steep•er, steep•est. 1.** Rising or falling abruptly; sharply sloped: *a steep hill; a*

St. Bernard

steamroller

steeple
Congregational church of Litchfield, Connecticut

stegosaur

ă pat/ā pay/â care/ä father/ĕ pet/ ē be/ĭ pit/ī pie/î fierce/ŏ pot/ ō go/ô paw, for/oi oil/o͝o book/ o͞o boot/ou out/ŭ cut/û fur/ *th* the/th thin/hw which/zh vision/ ə ago, item, pencil, atom, circus

steep stairway. **2.** Very high: *a steep price to pay.* **—steep'ly** *adv.* **—steep'ness** *n.*

steep[2] |stēp| *v.* **1.** To soak or be soaked in a liquid: *We steeped the cake in rum. Let the tea steep for a few minutes.* **2.** To involve or preoccupy thoroughly; immerse: *As a child, she steeped herself in adventure stories. Pierre sat steeped in a profound French calm.* *—n.* A process or period of steeping.

steep•en |stē'pən| *v.* To make or become steeper: *We steepened the incline to make the toy cars go faster. The trail steepened toward the summit.*

steep•le |stē'pəl| *n.* A tall tower rising from the roof of a building, especially from a church or courthouse. [SEE PICTURE]

stee•ple•chase |stē'pəl chās'| *n.* A horse race across open country or over a course with artificial obstacles.

steep•le•jack |stē'pəl jăk'| *n.* Someone who works on steeples or other high structures.

steer[1] |stîr| *v.* **1.** To direct the course of (a vehicle, vessel, aircraft, etc.). **2.** To be guided or capable of being guided: *an automobile that steers easily.* **3.** To fix and travel on (a course). **4.** To direct; guide: *steering foreign visitors around the city.* *—n. Slang.* A piece of advice; a tip: *gave me a bum steer about the movie.*
Idiom. **steer clear of.** To avoid.

steer[2] |stîr| *n.* A young male of domestic cattle, castrated before reaching maturity and raised for beef.

steer•age |stîr'ĭj| *n.* **1.** The section of a passenger ship, especially an immigrant ship of former times, providing the cheapest accommodations. **2.** The act of steering a boat or ship.

steering wheel. A wheel that controls the steering mechanism of a vehicle, ship, etc.

steers•man |stîrz'mən| *n., pl.* **-men** |-mən|. The man who operates the helm of a ship.

steg•o•saur |stĕg'ə sôr'| *n.* A plant-eating dinosaur with a double row of upright bony plates along the back. [SEE PICTURE]

steg•o•saur•us |stĕg'ə sôr'əs| *n.* A stegosaur.

stein |stīn| *n.* A large beer mug.

stel•lar |stĕl'ər| *adj.* **1.** Of or consisting of a star or stars. **2.** Of or befitting a star performer: *a stellar cast for the play.* **3.** Outstanding; prominent: *stellar achievements.*

St. El•mo's fire |sānt' ĕl'mōz'|. A bluish glow caused by an electrical discharge from parts of the superstructure of a ship at sea or from parts of a flying aircraft before and during electrical storms.

stem[1] |stĕm| *n.* **1. a.** The main, often long or slender supporting part of a plant, usually growing above the ground. **b.** A slender plant part attached to or supporting a leaf, fruit, flower, etc.; a stalk. **2.** A connecting or supporting part resembling such a plant part: *the stem of a pipe; the stem of a wineglass.* **3.** The small shaft by which a watch is wound. **4.** The curving, upright beam at the center of the prow of a ship or boat. **5.** The main part of a word, to which affixes may be added to form various inflections or derivative words. *—v.* **stemmed, stem•ming. 1.** To remove the stem or stems from: *stemming cherries to make a pie.* **2.** To extend like a stem; branch out: *The spinal cord stems from the brain.* **3.** To derive; originate; spring; *Many recent books stem from a search for a new system of values.*

stem[2] |stĕm| *v.* **stemmed, stem•ming. 1.** To plug up; stop: *stem a hole.* **2.** To check the flow or advance of; hold back.

stemmed |stĕmd| *adj.* **1.** Having a stem: *a stemmed goblet.* **2.** Having a certain kind of stem or stems: *a prickly-stemmed plant.*

stench |stĕnch| *n.* A strong, unpleasant smell; a stink.

sten•cil |stĕn'səl| *n.* A sheet of paper, celluloid, or other material in which letters or figures have been cut so that when ink or paint is applied to the sheet the patterns will appear on the surface beneath. *—v.* **sten•ciled** or **sten•cilled, sten•cil•ing** or **sten•cil•ling. 1.** To mark with a stencil. **2.** To produce by means of a stencil.

ste•nog•ra•pher |stə nŏg'rə fər| *n.* A person skilled in shorthand, employed to take down and transcribe dictation.

sten•o•graph•ic |stĕn'ə grăf'ĭk| *adj.* Of or using stenography: *a stenographic record.* **—sten'o•graph'i•cal•ly** *adv.*

ste•nog•ra•phy |stə nŏg'rə fē| *n.* **1.** The skill or process of taking down dictation in shorthand. **2.** Shorthand.

sten•tor•i•an |stĕn tôr'ē ən| *or* |-tōr'-| *adj.* Very loud and powerful: *a stentorian voice.*

step |stĕp| *n.* **1.** A single movement made by lifting one foot and putting it down in another spot, as in walking. **2. a.** The distance covered by such a movement. **b.** A short walking distance: *The park is just a step from my front door.* **3.** The sound of someone walking: *heard his step in the corridor.* **4.** A footprint: *steps in the sand.* **5. a.** A manner of walking; a gait: *moving with a light step.* **b.** A manner or pattern of moving the feet in dancing. **6.** A fixed rhythm or pace, as in dancing or marching: *keep step.* **7.** Conformity with the rhythm, pace, views, or attitudes of others: *in step with the band leader; out of step with the times.* **8. a.** A small platform or rung placed as a rest for the foot in climbing up or down. **b. steps.** Stairs. **9.** Any of a series of actions or measures taken to achieve some goal: *taking steps to preserve the wildlife of a region.* **10.** Any of the stages of a process. **11.** A degree of progress: *a step forward in learning a language.* **12.** A degree in a range of quality, achievement, or understanding: *a step below gold in value.* **13. a.** The interval that separates two successive tones of a musical scale. **b.** A melodic movement from one such tone to the next. **14.** The block in which the base of a ship's mast is held. *—v.* **stepped, step•ping. 1.** To move by taking a step or a few steps: *Step forward when your name is called.* **2.** To move with the feet in a certain manner: *stepping high. Step lively.* **3.** To put or press the foot down: *stepping into a puddle; step on a pedal.* **4.** To measure (a distance) by pacing: *step off ten yards on the field.* **5.** To place (a ship's mast) in its step. *—phrasal verbs.* **step down. 1.** To resign from a high post. **2.** To reduce, especially in stages: *stepping down the electric power.* **step in. 1.** To enter an activity or situation. **2.** To intervene. **step into. 1.** To put on (a garment) with a rapid movement of the feet or body: *step into a bathrobe.* **2.** To take or gain without difficulty: *step into command; step into a new life.* **step out. 1.** To walk briskly. **2.** To go outside for a short time. **3.** *Informal.* To go out for a special evening of entertainment. **step up.** To increase, especially in stages: *step up production.* ¶*These sound alike* **step, steppe.**

Idioms. **step on it.** *Informal.* To go faster; hurry. **watch (one's) step.** To move cautiously.

step–. A word element meaning "related through the remarriage of a parent rather than by blood": **stepbrother.**

step•broth•er |stĕp′brŭth′ər| *n.* The son of one's stepfather or stepmother by an earlier marriage.

step•child |stĕp′chīld′| *n., pl.* **-chil•dren** |-chĭl′drən|. The child of one's wife or husband by an earlier marriage.

step•daugh•ter |stĕp′dô′tər| *n.* The daughter of one's husband or wife by an earlier marriage.

step•fa•ther |stĕp′fä′thər| *n.* The husband of one's mother by a later marriage.

step•moth•er |stĕp′mŭth′ər| *n.* The wife of one's father by a later marriage.

step•par•ent |stĕp′pâr′ənt| *or* |-păr′-| *n.* A stepfather or stepmother.

steppe |stĕp| *n.* A vast, somewhat arid plain, covered with grass and having few trees, as found in southeastern Europe and Siberia. ¶*These sound alike* **steppe, step.**

step•ping•stone |stĕp′ĭng stōn′| *n.* **1.** A stone that provides a dry place to step, as in crossing a stream. **2.** A step or means toward the achievement of a goal.

step•sis•ter |stĕp′sĭs′tər| *n.* The daughter of one's stepfather or stepmother by an earlier marriage.

step•son |stĕp′sŭn′| *n.* The son of one's husband or wife by an earlier marriage.

–ster. A suffix that forms nouns and means "someone who does, performs, or takes part in something": **gangster.**

ste•re•o |stĕr′ē ō′| *or* |stîr′-| *n., pl.* **ste•re•os.** **1.** A stereophonic sound-reproduction system. **2.** Stereophonic sound: *a performance reproduced in stereo.* —***modifier:*** *a stereo phonograph.*

ster•e•o•phon•ic |stĕr′ē ə **fŏn′**ĭk| *or* |stîr′-| *adj.* Of, indicating, or used in a sound-reproduction system that uses two separate channels to give a more natural effect of the distribution of the sound sources. —**ster′e•o•phon′i•cal•ly** *adv.*

ster•e•o•scope |stĕr′ē ə skōp′| *or* |stîr′-| *n.* An optical instrument through which two slightly different views of a scene are presented, one to each eye, giving a three-dimensional illusion.

ster•e•o•scop•ic |stĕr′ē ə **skŏp′**ĭk| *or* |stîr′-| *adj.* Of, for, or produced by a stereoscope.

ster•e•o•type |stĕr′ē ə tīp′| *or* |stîr′-| *n.* **1.** A metal printing plate cast from a matrix that is molded from a raised surface, such as type. **2.** A general idea or understanding that is not examined critically or checked against particular cases or facts. **3.** A person or thing considered typical of a kind and without individuality: *The characters in the movie were all stereotypes.* —***modifier:*** *a stereotype plate; a stereotype villain.* —*v.* **ster•e•o•typed, ster•e•o•typ•ing.** **1.** To print or reproduce from stereotypes. **2.** To form a fixed, unvarying idea about: *City dwellers tend to stereotype farmers as simple, healthy, and hard-working.* **3.** To represent or treat in a generalized, conventional way: *stereotyping the emotions of a character.* —**ster′e•o•typed′** *adj.: stereotyped ideas.*

ster•ile |stĕr′əl| *adj.* **1.** Not able to reproduce and produce offspring, seeds, fruit, etc. **2.** Able to produce no plant life or only sparse plant growth; barren: *a desolate, sterile region.* **3.** Free from living microorganisms, especially those that cause disease: *a sterile bandage.* **4.** Not productive, effective, or rewarding: *sterile pleasures.* —**ster′ile•ly** *adv.* —**ste•ril′i•ty** |stə **rĭl′**ĭ tē| *n.*

ster•il•ize |stĕr′ə līz′| *v.* **ster•il•ized, ster•il•iz•ing.** To make sterile. —**ster′il•ized′** *adj.: a sterilized bandage.* —**ster′il•i•za′tion** *n.*

ster•il•iz•er |stĕr′ə lī′zər| *n.* Any of various devices that kill bacteria, as on surgical instruments, bandages, etc., by means of heat, steam, or chemicals.

ster•ling |stûr′lĭng| *n.* **1.** British money. **2. a.** **sterling silver.** **b.** Articles made from sterling silver. —*adj.* **1.** Of or expressed in British money: *the pound sterling; sterling prices.* **2.** Made of sterling silver: *sterling knives.* **3.** Of the highest quality; very fine: *her sterling qualifications.*

sterling silver. **1.** An alloy containing 92.5 per cent silver with copper or another metal. **2.** Articles made of this alloy as a group. —***modifier:*** *a sterling silver tray.*

stern¹ |stûrn| *adj.* **stern•er, stern•est.** **1.** Telling or seeming to tell others to obey or do their duty; grave and severe: *a stern lecture on table manners; a stern look of reproach.* **2.** Strict; inflexible: *stern discipline.* **3.** Grim; gloomy: *a stern fate.* —**stern′ly** *adv.* —**stern′ness** *n.*

stern² |stûrn| *n.* The rear end of a ship or boat.

ster•num |stûr′nəm| *n., pl.* **ster•na** |stûr′nə| or **ster•nums.** **1.** A long, flat bone located in the center of the chest, serving as a support for the collarbone and ribs; the breastbone. **2.** A similar bone found in many other vertebrate animals.

stern•wheel•er |stûrn′hwē′lər| *or* |-wē′-| *n.* A steamboat propelled by a paddle wheel at the stern.

ster•oid |stĕr′oid′| *or* |stîr′-| *n.* Any of a large class of naturally occurring, fat-soluble organic compounds based on a structure having 17 carbon atoms bound in a ring, including many hormones, sterols, natural drugs, and substances related to vitamins.

ster•ol |stĕr′ōl′| *or* |-ŏl′| *or* |stîr′-| *n.* Any of various steroid alcohols, such as cholesterol, found in fatty tissues of plants and animals.

steth•o•scope |stĕth′ə skōp′| *n.* An instrument used to listen to sounds made within the body. [SEE PICTURE]

Stet•son |stĕt′sən| *n.* A trademark for a felt hat with a high crown and wide brim, popular in the western United States. [SEE PICTURE]

ste•ve•dore |stē′vĭ dôr′| *or* |-dōr′| *n.* A person whose job is the loading and unloading of ships.

Ste•ven•son |stē′vən sən|. **Robert Louis.** 1850–1894. Scottish poet and novelist.

stew |stōō| *or* |styōō| *v.* **1.** To cook by simmering or boiling slowly: *stewing a chicken; meat stewing on the stove.* **2.** *Informal.* To suffer from intense heat; swelter. **3.** *Informal.* To worry; fret. —*n.* A stewed food, especially a thick mixture of pieces of meat and vegetables in a liquid. —***modifier:*** *stew meat.* —**stewed′** *adj.: stewed tomatoes.*

stethoscope

Stetson
The **Stetson** was designed by John *Stetson* (1830–1906), American hatter.

stickball

stew•ard |stōō′ərd| *or* |styōō′-| *n.* **1.** A person who manages another's property, finances, etc. **2.** A person in charge of the household affairs of a large estate, club, hotel, or resort. **3.** A male attendant on a ship or airplane who waits on the passengers.

stew•ard•ess |stōō′ər dĭs| *or* |styōō′-| *n.* A woman who waits on passengers in an airplane.

stew•ard•ship |stōō′ərd shĭp′| *or* |styōō′-| *n.* **1.** The job or duties of a steward. **2.** Care: *He left his finances to the stewardship of a banker.*

St. George's |sānt jôr′jəz|. The capital of Grenada. Population, 6,000.

stick |stĭk| *n.* **1.** A long, slender piece of wood, such as a branch cut or fallen from a tree. **2.** A narrow length of wood shaped for a certain purpose: *a walking stick; a hockey stick.* **3.** Anything cut into or having the shape of a stick: *a stick of peppermint candy; a stick of dynamite.* **4.** A long rod used as a control lever for a machine, as the lever that controls the elevators and ailerons of an airplane. **5. the sticks.** *Informal.* Rural, often wooded country far from cities and highways; the backwoods. **6.** *Slang.* A stiff, listless, or boring person. **7.** A poke or thrust with a pointed object. —*v.* **stuck** |stŭk|, **stick•ing. 1.** To pierce or prick with a sharp-pointed object: *sticking her finger painfully on a thorn.* **2.** To push or thrust (a knife, pin, etc.) into a surface. **3.** *Informal.* To put in a certain place: *Stick the box in the closet.* **4.** To fasten or attach by pushing in a pointed object: *stuck the bulletin on the board with a thumbtack.* **5.** To fasten or attach with glue, tape, or some other adhesive material: *stick a ticket on a car window.* **6.** To join (separate things) with an adhesive material: *stick two boards together with wood cement.* **7.** To be attached to a surface and not come off easily; adhere: *Glue sticks to the fingers.* **8.** To stay in place after being applied, fastened, or embedded: *This stamp won't stick.* **9.** To be or cause to be fixed in place and unable to move: *The heavy wagon stuck in the mud and wouldn't budge. The ring was stuck, and I couldn't get it off.* **10.** To bring to a point where progress stops; baffle: *I got stuck on the last question and never did finish the test.* **11.** To keep in one place or situation; detain: *Our guests must be stuck in a traffic jam.* **12.** To remain in one place, condition, or situation, especially: **a.** To remain attached or in close association; cling: *Let's stick together or we'll get lost in this crowd.* **b.** To remain firm or loyal: *stick to a promise; stick by a friend in trouble.* **c.** To remain engaged in or concerned with one subject and not others: *Stick to what you can do best.* **13.** To extend; project: *He stuck out his hand in greeting.* **14.** To put blame or unwanted responsibility on; burden: *Let's stick him with cleaning up after the party.* —***phrasal verbs.*** **stick out. 1.** To be prominent or obvious; stand out: *the sort of person who sticks out in a crowd.* **stick up.** To rob, especially by threatening with a gun.

Idioms. **be stuck on.** *Informal.* To be very fond of; dote on. **stick it out.** *Informal.* To continue to the end, despite unpleasantness. **stick up for.** To defend; support.

stick•ball |stĭk′bôl′| *n.* A form of baseball adapted to city streets and vacant lots, played with a rubber ball and a light stick or broom handle. [SEE PICTURE]

stick•er |stĭk′ər| *n.* **1.** A gummed label, seal, or sign. **2.** A thorn, prickle, or bramble.

stick•ler |stĭk′lər| *n.* **1.** A person who insists upon something of small importance: *Be on time, because the interviewer is a stickler for promptness.* **2.** *Informal.* A difficult problem.

stick•pin |stĭk′pĭn′| *n.* A pin with an ornamental head and a sheath to cover the point, used to hold a necktie in place; a tie pin.

stick-up |stĭk′ŭp′| *n.* *Informal.* A robbery, especially at gunpoint.

stick•y |stĭk′ē| *adj.* **stick•i•er, stick•i•est. 1.** Tending to stick to a surface or to what touches it: *sticky paste; sticky candy.* **2.** Hot and humid; muggy. **3.** *Informal.* Difficult or unpleasant. —**stick′i•ly** *adv.* —**stick′i•ness** *n.*

stiff |stĭf| *adj.* **stiff•er, stiff•est. 1.** Tending to resist change of shape or dimensions as a result of applied forces; not flexible or pliant: *a stiff fabric; a stiff new pair of shoes.* **2.** Not moving or operating easily: *a stiff joint; a stiff doorknob.* **3.** Not fluid; firm; thick: *a stiff mixture.* **4.** Stretched tight; taut: *a stiff rope.* **5.** Rigidly formal; not easy or graceful: *a stiff manner; a stiff writing style.* **6.** Moving with a strong, steady force: *a stiff current.* **7.** Strong in opposition or resistance; hard to overcome: *stiff competition.* **8.** Hard to do, pass, or comply with: *a stiff entrance requirement.* **9.** Harsh; severe: *stiff penalties.* **10.** Strong in amount or effect; potent: *a stiff dose of medicine.* **11.** Very high: *stiff prices.* —*adv.* **1.** So as to be stiff: *a collar starched stiff.* **2.** To an extreme degree: *bored stiff.* —*n.* *Slang.* **1.** A corpse. **2.** A dull, lifeless, or haughty person. **3.** A person; fellow: *those lucky stiffs.* —**stiff′ly** *adv.* —**stiff′ness** *n.*

stiff•en |stĭf′ən| *v.* To make or become stiff or stiffer. —**stiff′en•er** *n.*

stiff•en•ing |stĭf′ə nĭng| *n.* Something, such as starch, glue, etc., added to or mixed with something else to increase its stiffness.

sti•fle |stī′fəl| *v.* **sti•fled, sti•fling. 1.** To kill by depriving of air or oxygen; smother. **2.** To die from a lack of air or oxygen; suffocate. **3.** To feel discomfort from a lack of fresh air or oxygen. **4.** To put out; extinguish: *stifle a flame.* **5.** To hold back; suppress: *stifling free speech.* —**sti′fling** *adj.*: *stifling heat; stifling laws.*

stig•ma |stĭg′mə| *n.* **1.** *pl.* **stig•mas** or **stig•ma•ta** |stĭg mä′tə| *or* |stĭg′mə tə|. A mark or reputation of shame, disgrace, etc.: *There should be no stigma attached to doing strenuous physical work.* **2.** *pl.* **stig•mas.** The sticky tip of a flower pistil, on which pollen is deposited in the process of pollination. **3. stigmata.** Marks or sores similar to the crucifixion wounds of Christ, sometimes appearing on the bodies of persons in a state of religious ecstasy.

stig•ma•tize |stĭg′mə tīz′| *v.* **stig•ma•tized, stig•ma•tiz•ing.** To brand as shameful or dishonorable. —**stig′ma•ti•za′tion** *n.*

stile |stīl| *n.* **1.** A set of steps for getting over a fence or wall. **2.** A turnstile. ¶*These sound alike* **stile, style.**

sti•let•to |stĭ lĕt′ō| *n., pl.* **sti•let•tos** or **sti•let•toes. 1.** A small dagger with a slender, tapering blade. **2.** A small, sharp-pointed instrument that is

ă pat/ā pay/â care/ä father/ĕ pet/ ē be/ĭ pit/ī pie/î fierce/ŏ pot/ ō go/ô paw, for/oi oil/ŏŏ book/ ōō boot/ou out/ŭ cut/û fur/ *th* the/th thin/hw which/zh vision/ ə ago, item, pencil, atom, circus

used for making eyelets in needlework.

still[1] |stĭl| *adj.* **still•er, still•est. 1.** Silent; quiet: *He was still for a moment and then started talking again.* **2.** Motionless or without commotion or disturbance: *still water; the still atmosphere just before a storm.* **3.** Not carbonated: *still wine.* **4.** Of or indicating a photograph that shows a single image with no motion, as distinguished from a motion picture. *—n.* **1.** Silence; quiet; calm: *the still of the night.* **2.** A still photograph. *—adv.* **1.** Now as before: *Father was still mad at me when I got home.* **2.** In increasing amount or degree: *I've got still more good news for you.* **3.** Nevertheless; all the same: *a painful but still necessary decision.* *—conj.* But; nevertheless: *It was a bad year; still, it had its bright spots.* *—v.* To make or become still.

still[2] |stĭl| *n.* **1.** An apparatus for distilling liquids, especially alcohols. **2.** A distillery.

still•born |**stĭl'**bôrn'| *adj.* Born dead.

still•ness |**stĭl'**nĭs| *n.* The state of being still; absence of movement; calm.

Still•son wrench |**stĭl'**sən|. A trademark for a monkey wrench with toothed jaws designed for gripping pipes or other round objects.

stilt |stĭlt| *n.* **1.** Either of a pair of long, slender poles, each with a foot support part way up, enabling the wearer to walk elevated above the ground. **2.** Any of various types of posts or pillars used as supports for a building, dock, etc. **3.** A long-legged wading bird with a long bill. [SEE PICTURE]

stilt•ed |**stĭl'**tĭd| *adj.* Stiffly or artificially formal; pompous: *stilted conversation.*

stim•u•lant |**stĭm'**yə lənt| *n.* **1.** Anything, especially a medicine or drug, that temporarily speeds up or excites the function of the body or one of its systems or parts. **2.** A stimulus or incentive.

stim•u•late |**stĭm'**yə lāt'| *v.* **stim•u•lat•ed, stim•u•lat•ing. 1.** To arouse to activity or increased action, interest, etc.; stir: *music that stimulates the imagination.* **2.** To cause to develop, flourish, etc.; encourage: *Since World War II American aid has stimulated Italian industry and agriculture.* **3.** To cause (an organism, part, etc.) to act or react in a certain way: *The purpose of a vaccine is to stimulate the body to produce antibodies.* **—stim'u•lat'ing** *adj.: a stimulating speaker.*

stim•u•la•tion |stĭm'yə **lā'**shən| *n.* **1.** The act or process of stimulating or being stimulated. **2.** The result of being stimulated.

stim•u•lus |**stĭm'**yə ləs| *n., pl.* **stim•u•li** |**stĭm'**yə-lī'|. Something that stimulates, especially something that results in an action or reaction of an organism, bodily part, etc.

sting |stĭng| *v.* **stung** |stŭng|, **sting•ing. 1.** To pierce or wound with a sharp-pointed part or organ, as that of certain insects, such as bees or wasps, or of other animals, such as scorpions. **2.** To feel or cause to feel a sharp, smarting pain: *His ears and fingers stung with the cold. The hot tears began to sting her eyelids.* **3.** To cause to feel keen unhappiness, suffering, etc.: *Her angry words stung him bitterly.* **4.** To drive or spur on by or as if by a sharp goad: *Their taunts and dares stung him to take the risk.* **5.** *Slang.* To cheat or overcharge. *—n.* **1. a.** A sharp, piercing part or organ, as of a bee, wasp, or scorpion, used for stinging and often injecting a poisonous or irritating substance. **b.** The act or result of piercing with such a part. **c.** A wound or mark made by such a part. **2.** A sharp, smarting sensation: *the sting of the wind-driven snow in their faces.* **3.** Something that causes unhappiness, suffering, etc.: *the sting of hard times.*

sting•er |**stĭng'**ər| *n.* Something that stings, as an insect or an animal part used for stinging.

sting•ray |**stĭng'**rā'| *n.* Also **sting ray.** An ocean fish having a broad, flattened body and a long, whiplike tail with a sharp, poison-bearing spine that can cause great harm.

stin•gy |**stĭn'**jē| *adj.* **stin•gi•er, stin•gi•est. 1.** Giving or spending reluctantly: *Scrooge was very stingy.* **2.** Scanty; meager: *a stingy space.* **—stin'gi•ly** *adv.* **—stin'gi•ness** *n.*

stink |stĭngk| *v.* **stank** |stăngk| or **stunk** |stŭngk|, **stunk, stink•ing. 1.** To give off a foul odor. **2.** *Slang.* To be highly offensive: *The whole idea stinks.* *—n.* A strong, offensive odor.

stint |stĭnt| *v.* **1.** To restrict or limit; be sparing with: *Don't stint yourself in buying things.* **2.** To be frugal: *Don't stint on food.* *—n.* **1.** A duty performed or to be performed within a given period of time: *a stint as a clerk in her father's business.* **2.** A limitation or restriction.

sti•pend |**stī'**pĕnd'| *n.* A fixed or regular payment, as a salary or allowance.

stip•ple |**stĭp'**əl| *v.* **stip•pled, stip•pling.** To paint, draw, or engrave in dots or short touches. *—n.* The effect produced by stippling.

stip•u•late |**stĭp'**yə lāt'| *v.* **stip•u•lat•ed, stip•u•lat•ing.** To specify as a condition of an agreement; require by contract. **—stip'u•la'tion** *n.*

stir |stûr| *v.* **stirred, stir•ring. 1.** To mix (a liquid or something in a liquid) by passing an implement through it in circular motions: *Stir the cream. Stir for five minutes.* **2.** To change or cause to change position slightly; disarrange: *The desert sands stirred. The wind stirred up the sands.* **3.** To move vigorously or briskly: *The animals began to stir.* **4.** To rouse, as from sleep or indifference: *The advertiser tries to stir the buyer's imagination.* **5.** To incite or provoke: *stir up trouble.* **6.** To excite the emotions of; affect strongly: *The music stirred her heart.* *—n.* **1.** An act of stirring; a mixing movement. **2.** A disturbance or commotion. **3.** An excited reaction. **—stir'rer** *n.*

stir•ring |**stûr'**ĭng| *adj.* **1.** Exciting; thrilling: *a stirring song of peace.* **2.** Active; lively: *a stirring march.* **—stir'ring•ly** *adv.*

stir•rup |**stûr'**əp| *or* |**stĭr'**-| *n.* **1.** A loop or ring with a flat base, hung by a strap from either side of a horse's saddle to support the rider's foot. **2.** Also **stirrup bone.** The stapes. [SEE PICTURE]

stitch |stĭch| *n.* **1. a.** A single, complete movement of a threaded needle or similar instrument into and out of material or fabric, as in sewing, embroidering, knitting, or crocheting. **b.** A single loop of yarn or thread around a knitting needle or crochet hook. **c.** A link, loop, or knot made by sewing, knitting, crocheting, etc.: *unravel stitches.* **2.** A method or style of arranging thread or yarn in sewing, knitting, crocheting, etc.: *a purl stitch.* **3.** *Informal.* A single article of clothing: *a baby without a stitch on.* **4.** A sudden, sharp pain in the side, often caused by vigorous

Child on stilts

stilt

stirrup

exercise. —*v.* **1.** To fasten, join, or ornament with stitches: *stitch on a pocket; stitch up a seam; stitch a sampler.* **2.** To make stitches; sew.

St. John's |sānt **jŏnz′**|. **1.** The capital of Antigua and Barbuda. Population, 22,000. **2.** The capital of Newfoundland, Canada. Population, 86,000.

St. Kitts-Nev•is |sānt′ kĭts **nē′**vĭs| *or* |**-nĕv′**ĭs|. An island country of the West Indies in the Leeward Islands. Population, 44,000. Capital, Basseterre.

St. Law•rence River |sānt′ **lôr′**əns|. A river in Canada, flowing from Lake Ontario to the Atlantic Ocean and forming part of the boundary between New York State and Ontario, Canada.

St. Lawrence Seaway. A system of canals along the St. Lawrence River between Montreal, Canada, and Lake Ontario, enabling ships to reach the Great Lakes from the Atlantic Ocean.

stoat

St. Lou•is |sānt′ **lo͞o′**ĭs|. The largest city in Missouri. Population, 608,000.

St. Lu•ci•a |sānt **lo͞o′**shə| *or* |lo͞o **sē′**ə|. An island country in the Windward Islands. Population, 116,000. Capital, Castries.

stoat |stōt| *n.* A weasel, the ermine, especially when its fur is brown. [SEE PICTURE]

stock |stŏk| *n.* **1.** A supply accumulated for future use: *grain stocks.* **2.** The total merchandise kept on hand by a commercial establishment. **3.** *(used with a plural or singular verb).* Domestic animals, such as horses, cattle, sheep, or pigs; livestock. **4.** A line or group of ancestors from which persons, animals, or plants are descended. **5.** The main stem or trunk of a tree or plant, especially one used for grafting. **6.** The raw material from which something is made: *The stock used for the sides of the box should be one-inch plywood.* **7.** Broth from boiled meat, fish, or vegetables, used in making soup, gravy, or sauces. **8.** Any supporting structure, block, or frame. **9.** The rear metal or wooden handle or part of a firearm. **10.** Shares in a corporation. **11. stocks.** A pillory. **12.** A theatrical activity, especially one outside a main theatrical center: *playing in summer stock.* **13.** A garden plant with long, showy clusters of fragrant flowers. —*v.* **1.** To provide with stock or a stock: *stock the store.* **2.** To keep for future sale or use: *We stock canned goods.* —*adj.* **1.** Kept regularly available for sale or use: *Bread is a stock item.* **2.** Commonplace: *a stock answer.*

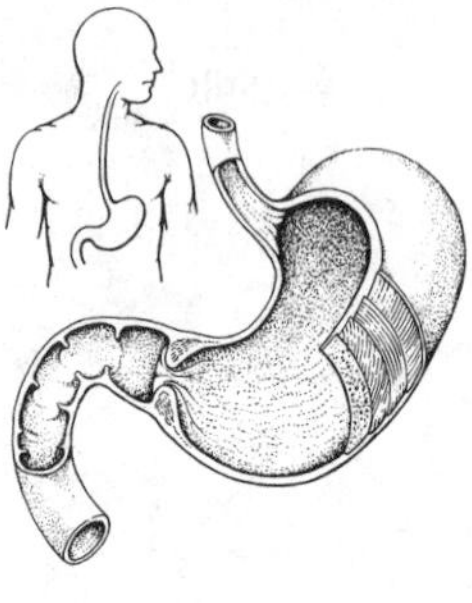

stomach

Idioms. **in** (or **out of**) **stock.** Available (or unavailable) for sale or use. **take stock in.** *Informal.* To trust, believe in, or attach importance to.

stock•ade |stŏ **kād′**| *n.* **1.** A barrier made of strong upright posts, used for protection or imprisonment. **2.** The area surrounded by such a barrier.

stock•bro•ker |**stŏk′**brō′kər| *n.* A person who buys or sells stocks for a client, receiving a commission in return.

stock car. **1.** An automobile of standard make modified for racing. **2.** A railroad car for carrying and shipping livestock.

stock exchange. A place where stocks, bonds, or other securities are bought and sold.

stock•hold•er |**stŏk′**hōl′dər| *n.* A person who owns stocks in a company.

Stock•holm |**stŏk′**hōm′| *or* |-hōlm′|. The capital of Sweden. Population, 747,000.

stock•ing |**stŏk′**ĭng| *n.* A close-fitting, usually knitted covering for the foot and leg, especially one reaching higher than the knee.

stock market. **1.** A **stock exchange.** **2.** The business transacted at a stock exchange.

stock•pile |**stŏk′**pīl′| *n.* A supply of material stored for future use. —*v.* **-piled, -pil•ing.** To accumulate a stockpile of: *stockpile weapons.*

stock•room |**stŏk′**ro͞om′| *or* |-ro͝om′| *n.* A room where stock is stored.

stock-still |**stŏk′stĭl′**| *adj.* Completely still.

stock•y |**stŏk′**ē| *adj.* **stock•i•er, stock•i•est.** Solidly built; squat and thick: *a stocky boy.* —**stock′i•ness** *n.*

stock•yard |**stŏk′**yärd′| *n.* A large enclosed yard in which livestock are kept until being slaughtered or shipped elsewhere.

stodg•y |**stŏj′**ē| *adj.* **stodg•i•er, stodg•i•est.** **1.** Dull, narrow, and commonplace: *a stodgy person.* **2.** Heavy and indigestible: *stodgy food.* —**stodg′i•ly** *adv.* —**stodg′i•ness** *n.*

sto•ic |**stō′**ĭk| *n.* Someone who is seemingly indifferent to grief, pain, pleasure, etc. —*adj.* Seemingly indifferent to pain, grief, etc.

sto•i•cal |**stō′**ĭ kəl| *adj.* Seemingly unaffected by pain, pleasure, etc.; stoic. —**sto′i•cal•ly** *adv.*

sto•i•cism |**stō′**ĭ sĭz′əm| *n.* Seeming indifference to pain, pleasure, etc.

stoke |stōk| *v.* **stoked, stok•ing.** To tend (a fire or furnace).

stok•er |**stō′**kər| *n.* **1.** A man who feeds fuel to a furnace, as a fireman on a locomotive. **2.** A mechanical device for feeding coal to a furnace.

STOL |stōl|. Short takeoff and landing.

stole[1] |stōl| *n.* **1.** A long, narrow scarf, usually of embroidered silk or linen, worn by certain clergymen as a vestment over the shoulders with the ends hanging in front. **2.** A long scarf of cloth or fur worn about a woman's shoulders.

stole[2] |stōl|. Past tense of **steal.**

sto•len |**stō′**lən|. Past participle of **steal.**

stol•id |**stŏl′**ĭd| *adj.* Having or showing little movement or emotion; impassive: *a stolid soldier.* —**sto•lid′i•ty** |stə **lĭd′**ĭ tē| *n.* —**stol′id•ly** *adv.*

sto•ma |**stō′**mə| *n., pl.* **sto•ma•ta** |**stō′**mə tə| or **sto•mas.** One of the tiny openings in the outer surface of a plant leaf or stem, through which gases and water vapor pass.

stom•ach |**stŭm′**ək| *n.* **1. a.** The enlarged, saclike portion of the alimentary canal, located in vertebrates between the esophagus and the small intestine and serving as one of the main organs of digestion. **b.** A similar part of the digestive system of some invertebrates. **2.** *Informal.* The abdomen. **3.** An appetite for food. **4.** Any desire or inclination: *I don't have the stomach for such adventures.* —***modifier:*** *stomach muscles.* —*v.* To bear, tolerate, or endure: *She had to stomach undeserved criticism.* [SEE PICTURE]

sto•ma•ta |**stō′**mə tə| *n.* Plural of **stoma.**

stomp |stômp| *or* |stŏmp| *v.* To tread or trample heavily: *stomped the ant; stomp on the floor.*

stone |stōn| *n.* **1. a.** Hard or compacted mineral or earthy matter; rock. **b.** A piece of this material cut or shaped for a particular purpose, as a tombstone, milestone, etc. **2.** A piece of mineral matter considered to have great beauty and value; a gem. **3.** A seed with a hard covering, as of a cherry or plum; a pit. **4.** A hard mass of mineral matter that collects in a hollow organ of the body, such as a kidney; a calculus. **5.** A unit of weight in Great Britain, equal to 14 pounds avoirdupois. —*modifier: a stone wall.* —*v.* **stoned, ston•ing. 1.** To throw stones at. **2.** To remove the stones or pits from.

Stone Age. The earliest known period in the history of mankind, marked by the use of stone implements and weapons.

stoned |stōnd| *adj. Slang.* Drunk, drugged, or otherwise intoxicated.

stone-deaf |**stōn'dĕf'**| *adj.* Totally deaf.

stone•wall |**stōn'**wôl'| *v.* **stone•walled, stone•wall•ing. 1.** In cricket, to play defensively rather than trying to score. **2.** *Informal.* To refuse to answer or cooperate; resist or rebuff: *The witness tried to stonewall as long as possible. The Secretary stonewalled the investigating committee.*

stone•ware |**stōn'**wâr'| *n.* Heavy, nonporous pottery.

stone•work |**stōn'**wûrk'| *n.* **1.** The process or technique of building or making things from stone. **2.** Something built or made of stone. —**stone'work'er** *n.*

ston•y |**stō'**nē| *adj.* **ston•i•er, ston•i•est. 1.** Of, full of, or covered with stones: *stony soil.* **2.** Unemotional: *a stony gaze.* —**ston'i•ly** *adv.*

stood |stŏŏd|. Past tense and past participle of **stand.**

stooge |stōōj| *n.* **1.** A person who allows himself to be used for another's profit; a puppet. **2.** A person who serves as a foil for a comedian.

stool |stōōl| *n.* **1.** A single seat, generally round and without arms or a back, supported on legs or a pedestal. **2.** A low support on which to rest the feet while sitting. **3. a.** A bowel movement. **b.** Waste matter expelled in a bowel movement.

stoop[1] |stōōp| *v.* **1.** To bend from the waist or middle of the back: *stoop to pick up the flower.* **2.** To lower or debase oneself; condescend: *He wouldn't stoop to such low tactics.* —*n.* **1.** The act of stooping. **2.** A forward bending, especially when habitual: *walk with a stoop.* ¶*These sound alike* **stoop, stoup.** [SEE NOTE]

stoop[2] |stōōp| *n.* A small staircase or platform leading to the entrance of a house or small building. ¶*These sound alike* **stoop, stoup.** [SEE NOTE & PICTURE]

stop |stŏp| *v.* **stopped, stop•ping. 1.** To cease or cause to cease moving, progressing, acting, or operating; halt or come to a halt: *The boy stopped for a minute. The officer stopped the car.* **2.** To close or block (an opening) by covering, plugging, filling, etc.: *stop up the drain.* **3.** To prevent the flow or passage of: *stop traffic.* **4.** To cause to change or give up a course of action or mode of behavior: *They tried to stop her from quitting.* **5.** To end or interrupt what one is doing: *stop running.* **6. a.** To press (a string of a stringed instrument) to produce a tone of a desired pitch. **b.** To close (a hole of a woodwind instrument) to produce a tone of a desired pitch. —*phrasal verb.* **stop off** (or **over**). To visit briefly; stay: *stop off at the inn; stop over at Ann's house.* —*n.* **1.** The act of stopping or the condition of being stopped; a halt. **2.** A stay or visit: *We made a stop at Venice.* **3.** A place stopped at: *a bus stop.* **4.** A device or means that stops, blocks, regulates movement, etc. **5. a.** A tuned set of pipes producing tones that are similar in timbre, as in an organ. **b.** A knob, lever, etc., that controls a stop of an organ or harpsichord.

stop•gap |**stŏp'**găp'| *n.* A temporary substitute or expedient. —*modifier: stopgap measures.*

stop•light |**stŏp'**līt'| *n.* **1.** A **traffic light. 2.** A red light mounted on the rear of a vehicle that goes on when the brakes are applied.

stop•o•ver |**stŏp'**ō'vər| *n.* **1.** A brief stay or visit, as in the course of a journey. **2.** A place visited briefly.

stop•page |**stŏp'**ĭj| *n.* **1.** The act of stopping or the condition of being stopped; a halt. **2.** An obstruction: *a stoppage in a sewer pipe.*

stop•per |**stŏp'**ər| *n.* Any device, such as a cork or plug, put into an opening in order to close it.

stop•watch |**stŏp'**wŏch'| *n.* A timepiece that can be started and stopped by pushing a button or by some automatic device, used for measuring intervals of time.

stor•age |**stôr'**ĭj| *or* |**stōr'**-| *n.* **1.** The act of storing. **2.** A space for storing: *We have storage in the attic.* **3.** The price charged for storing goods: *How much is storage per month?* —*modifier: storage space; storage rates.*

storage battery. A group of rechargeable electric cells acting as a unit.

store |stôr| *or* |stōr| *n.* **1.** A place where merchandise is offered for sale; a shop. **2. a.** A stock or supply reserved for future use. **b. stores.** Supplies, as of food, clothing, or arms. **3.** An abundance: *a store of knowledge.* —*v.* **stored, stor•ing. 1.** To put away for future use: *The squirrels store acorns for winter.* **2.** To stock or fill with something: *store the barn with hay.*

Idioms. **in store.** Set aside for the future; forthcoming. **set store by.** To regard with esteem.

store•house |**stôr'**hous'| *or* |**stōr'**-| *n., pl.* **-hous•es** |-hou'zĭz|. **1.** A place in which goods are stored; a warehouse. **2.** An abundant source or supply: *a storehouse of knowledge.*

store•keep•er |**stôr'**kē'pər| *or* |**stōr'**-| *n.* Someone who runs a retail shop or store.

store•room |**stôr'**rōōm'| *or* |-rŏŏm'| *or* |**stōr'**-| *n.* A room in which things are stored.

sto•ried[1] |**stôr'**ēd| *or* |**stōr'**-| *adj.* Famous in story or history: *the storied ruins of Pompeii.*

sto•ried[2] |**stôr'**ēd| *or* |**stōr'**-| *adj.* Having a certain number of stories: *a five-storied house.*

stork |stôrk| *n.* A large wading bird with long legs and a long, straight bill. [SEE PICTURE]

storm |stôrm| *n.* **1.** A disturbance of the atmosphere in which strong winds appear, usually accompanied by rain, snow, or other precipitation, often with thunder and lightning. **2.** Any violent disturbance or upheaval: *the storm of war.* —*modifier: storm warnings.* —*v.* **1.** To rain, snow, hail, etc.: *It stormed for an hour yesterday.* **2.** To be angry or move about angrily; rant and rage: *She stormed for 15 minutes. He stormed into her office.* **3.** To try to capture by a violent, sudden attack: *storm the gates.*

storm window. A secondary window set outside of the usual window to protect against the wind and cold.

storm•y |**stôr'**mē| *adj.* **storm•i•er, storm•i•est. 1.** Subject to, affected by, or characterized by a storm or storms: *stormy weather.* **2.** Violently emotional or passionate: *a stormy meeting.* —**storm'i•ly** *adv.* —**storm'i•ness** *n.*

sto•ry[1] |**stôr'**ē| *or* |**stōr'**ē| *n., pl.* **sto•ries. 1.** An

stoop[1·2]

Stoop[1] *was Old English* stūpian, *"to bend down."* **Stoop[2]** *is a colonial American word, borrowed from Dutch* stoep, *"small porch or verandah."*

stoop[2]

stork

story¹·²

Story¹ *is from Norman French* estorie, *which is from Latin* historia, *"history." In Medieval Latin, the word* historia *was used to mean "level of a building" and was separately borrowed into English as* **story²**. *It is assumed that the Medieval Latin word is the same as the classical Latin word, but the connection is rather obscure; it is suggested that* historia *came to mean "a story told in stained-glass windows," later "a row of windows," and eventually "a level of a building"; but there is no proof of this.*

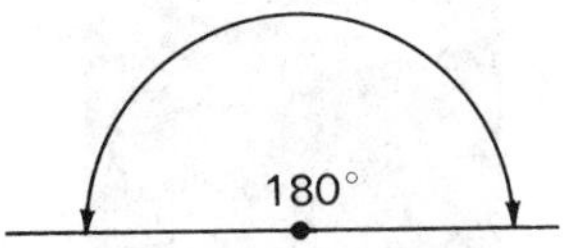

straight angle

strain¹·²

Strain¹ *is from Old French* estreindre, *"to press tight, to squeeze," which is from Latin* stringere, *"to draw tight, to tie." (The past participle of* stringere *was* strictus, *"drawn tight, exact"; this passed into Old French as* estreit, *"narrow," which was borrowed into English as* **strait**. Strictus *was also borrowed directly into English as* **strict.**) **Strain²** *was Old English* strēon, *"offspring, ancestry, race."*

ă pat/ā pay/â care/ä father/ĕ pet/ē be/ĭ pit/ī pie/î fierce/ŏ pot/ō go/ô paw, for/oi oil/ŏŏ book/ōō boot/ou out/ŭ cut/û fur/*th* the/th thin/hw which/zh vision/ə ago, item, pencil, atom, circus

account of some incident or event or series of events, either true or fictitious: *the story of the war; a short story.* **2.** A news report: *The reporter covered three stories today.* **3.** A fictional prose or verse narrative; a tale. **4.** *Informal.* A lie: *Don't tell stories.* **5.** A statement or allegation of facts: *That's his story.* [SEE NOTE]

sto•ry² |stôr′ē| *or* |stōr′ē| *n., pl.* **sto•ries.** One of the horizontal divisions of a building, consisting of an area or set of rooms at substantially the same level. [SEE NOTE]

sto•ry•tell•er |stôr′ē tĕl′ər| *or* |stōr′-| *n.* A person who tells or writes stories.

stoup |stōōp| *n.* A basin for holy water in a church. ¶*These sound alike* **stoup, stoop.**

stout |stout| *adj.* **stout•er, stout•est. 1.** Determined, bold, or brave: *a stout heart.* **2.** Strong, sturdy, or solid: *the stout back of a donkey.* **3.** Bulky in figure; corpulent: *a stout man.* —*n.* A strong dark beer or ale. —**stout′ly** *adv.* —**stout′ness** *n.*

stout•heart•ed |stout′här′tĭd| *adj.* Brave; courageous: *a stouthearted fighter.*

stove¹ |stōv| *n.* An apparatus that furnishes heat for warmth or cooking, using either fuel or electricity as a source of power.

stove² |stōv|. A past tense and past participle of **stave.**

stove•pipe |stōv′pīp′| *n.* **1.** A metal pipe used to carry smoke or fumes from a stove to a chimney. **2.** Also **stovepipe hat.** A man's tall silk hat.

stow |stō| *v.* To place, arrange, or store: *stow the lumber on the deck.* —***phrasal verb.*** **stow away. 1.** To put or hide away in a safe place. **2.** To be a stowaway.

stow•a•way |stō′ə wā′| *n.* A person who hides aboard a ship, plane, train, etc., to obtain free passage.

St. Paul |sānt′ pôl′|. The capital of Minnesota. Population, 308,000.

St. Pe•ters•burg |sānt′ pē′tərz bûrg′|. **1.** A former name for Leningrad. **2.** A resort city on the west coast of Florida. Population, 213,000.

strad•dle |străd′l| *v.* **strad•dled, strad•dling. 1.** To sit astride: *The witches straddled their brooms.* **2.** To appear to favor both sides of: *straddle a political issue.* —**strad′dler** *n.*

strafe |strāf| *or* |sträf| *v.* **strafed, straf•ing.** To attack with machine-gun fire from low-flying aircraft: *strafe the decks of the battleship.*

strag•gle |străg′əl| *v.* **strag•gled, strag•gling. 1.** To stray or fall behind: *The boys straggled in the pastures.* **2.** To spread out or wander in a scattered or irregular manner: *herds of caribou straggling north to the tundra.* —**strag′gler** *n.*

straight |strāt| *adj.* **straight•er, straight•est. 1.** Extending continuously in exactly the same direction; not bending or curving: *a straight line.* **2.** Erect; upright: *a straight back.* **3.** Direct and candid: *do some straight talking.* **4.** Neatly or properly arranged; orderly: *He can't keep his desk straight.* **5.** Not interrupted; unbroken: *It snowed for five straight days.* **6.** Not diluted; pure: *straight vodka.* **7.** Not deviating politically: *a straight party line.* **8.** Not modified or qualified: *a straight answer.* —*adv.* **1.** In a straight line; directly: *The arrow flew straight at her.* **2.** Without detour or delay: *go straight to the store.* **3.** In an erect posture; upright: *stand straight.* —*n.* In poker, a series of five cards of different suits in numerical sequence. ¶*These sound alike* **straight, strait.** —**straight′ly** *adv.* —**straight′ness** *n.*

Idiom. **straight away** (or **off**). Without hesitation; immediately.

straight angle. An angle of 180 degrees. [SEE PICTURE]

straight-a•way |strāt′ə wā′| *adj.* Extending in a straight line. —*n.* A straight road, course, or track. —*adv.* |strāt′ə wā′|. At once; immediately.

straight•edge |strāt′ĕj′| *n.* A stiff, flat piece of wood, metal, plastic, etc., with a straight edge, used for drawing or testing straight lines; a ruler.

straight•en |strāt′n| *v.* To make or become straight: *straighten hair. The track straightened. Straighten up your room.* —***phrasal verb.*** **straighten out.** To restore order to; put to rights. ¶*These sound alike* **straighten, straiten.**

straight•for•ward |strāt fôr′wərd| *adj.* **1.** Proceeding in a straight course; direct: *a straightforward approach to a problem.* **2.** Honest; frank: *a straightforward reply.* —**straight•for′ward•ly** *adv.* —**straight•for′ward•ness** *n.*

straight jacket. A form of the phrase **strait jacket.**

straight•way |strāt′wā′| *adv.* At once.

strain¹ |strān| *v.* **1.** To pull, draw, or stretch tight: *The weight of the pulley strains the rope. The horses strained at the post.* **2.** To exert or tax to the utmost; strive hard: *strain your eyes. The oxen strained with all their might.* **3.** To injure or impair by overexertion: *strain a muscle.* **4.** To force or stretch beyond a proper or legitimate limit: *strain a point.* **5.** To pass through a strainer; filter. —*n.* **1.** A pressure, stress, or force: *felt a strain on the line.* **2.** An injury or wrench resulting from excessive effort: *a muscle strain.* **3.** Great emotional pressure or demands. [SEE NOTE]

strain² |strān| *n.* **1.** A group or type having similar characteristics and the same ancestry or line of descent: *The domestic cat is believed to be a strain derived from the Egyptian wild cat and the European wild cat.* **2.** An inborn or inherited characteristic or tendency. **3.** Often **strains.** A piece, passage, or sound of music: *the strains of the waltz.* [SEE NOTE]

strain•er |strā′nər| *n.* A device made of wire mesh or another material having many small holes, used for separating liquids from solid substances.

strait |strāt| *n.* **1.** Often **straits.** A narrow passage that connects two larger bodies of water. **2. straits.** Difficulties: *He was in desperate straits for money.* —*adj.* **strait•er, strait•est.** *Archaic.* **1.** Narrow; constricted. **2.** Strict and righteous. ¶*These sound alike* **strait, straight.**

strait•en |strāt′n| *v.* **1.** To make narrow; restrict. **2.** To put or bring into financial difficulties. ¶*These sound alike* **straiten, straighten.**

Idiom. **in straitened circumstances.** Under great financial hardship.

strait jacket. A jacketlike garment of strong material used to bind the arms tightly against the body as a means of restraining a violent or unmanageable patient or prisoner.

strait-laced |strāt'lāst'| *adj.* Excessively strict in behavior; prudish.

strand[1] |strănd| *n.* A shore; beach. —*v.* **1.** To drive or be driven aground, as a ship. **2.** To leave in a difficult or helpless position.

strand[2] |strănd| *n.* **1.** A single fiber, filament, thread, or wire, especially one of those twisted together to form a rope, cord, or cable. **2.** Something made up of fibers or filaments twisted or bunched together, as a piece of yarn or a lock of hair. **3.** A string of beads, pearls, etc.

strange |strānj| *adj.* **strang•er, strang•est. 1.** Previously unknown; unfamiliar: *strange animals of the jungle.* **2.** Unusual: *a strange feeling; her strange appearance.* **3.** Not of one's own particular locality or kind: *a strange language.* **4.** Not accustomed: *strange to her new duties.* —**strange'ly** *adv.* —**strange'ness** *n.* [SEE NOTE]

stran•ger |strān'jər| *n.* **1.** A person who is neither a friend nor an acquaintance. **2.** A foreigner, newcomer, or outsider.

stran•gle |străng'gəl| *v.* **stran•gled, stran•gling. 1. a.** To kill by or die from choking or suffocating. **b.** To deprive of oxygen; smother. **2.** To suppress or stifle: *strangle a cry.* **3.** To restrict or limit the growth or action of: *strangle the enemy's supply lines.* —**stran'gler** *n.*

stran•gu•la•tion |străng'gyə lā'shən| *n.* The act of strangling or the condition of being strangled.

strap |străp| *n.* A long, narrow strip of leather or other material, used to hold things down, bind things together, or keep things in place: *a sandal strap; the straps of an evening gown.* —*v.* **strapped, strap•ping. 1.** To fasten, secure, or attach with a strap or straps: *The astronaut strapped himself into his seat. An air tank was strapped to the diver's back.* **2.** To beat with a strap.

strap•ping |străp'ĭng| *adj.* Tall and sturdy: *a strapping young man.*

stra•ta |strā'tə| *or* |străt'ə| *n.* Plural of **stratum.**

strat•a•gem |străt'ə jəm| *n.* Any plan or action intended to fool or deceive someone, especially an opponent.

stra•te•gic |strə tē'jĭk| *adj.* **1.** Of strategy: *the strategic importance of Arctic lands.* **2.** Essential to strategy: *strategic locations.* —**stra•te'gi•cal•ly** *adv.*

strat•e•gist |străt'ə jĭst| *n.* A person who is skilled in strategy.

strat•e•gy |străt'ə jē| *n., pl.* **strat•e•gies. 1.** The science of planning series of actions or maneuvers that will probably be useful in gaining an advantage over an opponent. **2.** A plan of action arrived at by means of this science.

Strat•ford-on-A•von |străt'fərd ŏn ā'vən| *or* |-vŏn'|. A town in southern England, the birthplace and burial place of William Shakespeare.

stra•ti |strā'tī'| *or* |străt'ī'| *n.* Plural of **stratus.**

strat•i•fy |străt'ə fī'| *v.* **strat•i•fied, strat•i•fy•ing, strat•i•fies. 1.** To form, arrange, or deposit in strata. **2.** To be formed in or divided into strata. —**strat'i•fi•ca'tion** *n.*

stra•to•cu•mu•lus |strā'tō kyōōm'yə ləs| *or* |străt'ō-| *n.* A cloud occurring in extensive horizontal layers with massive, rounded tops, typically at a height of about one mile.

strat•o•sphere |străt'ə sfîr'| *n.* The layer of the earth's atmosphere that lies above the troposphere and below the mesosphere, having a relatively even temperature throughout.

stra•tum |strā'təm| *or* |străt'əm| *n., pl.* **stra•ta** |strā'tə| *or* |străt'ə|. **1.** Any of a series of layers or levels, especially a series of approximately parallel layers. **2.** A bed or layer of rock whose composition is more or less the same throughout. **3.** A category regarded as occupying a level in a system or hierarchy: *the lowest strata of society.*

stra•tus |strā'təs| *or* |străt'əs| *n., pl.* **stra•ti** |strā'tī'| *or* |străt'ī'|. A cloud that resembles a horizontal layer of fog, found typically at an altitude of about 1,300 to 1,500 feet.

Strauss |strous|. **1. Johann.** 1825–1899. Austrian composer of operettas and waltzes. **2. Richard.** 1864–1949. German composer.

straw |strô| *n.* **1. a.** Stalks of wheat, oats, or other grain from which the seeds have been removed by threshing, used as bedding and food for animals, as stuffing or padding, and for weaving or braiding to make hats, baskets, etc. **b.** A single stalk of such grain. **2.** A narrow tube of paper, plastic, etc., used to drink or suck up liquids. **3.** The least bit or smallest amount: *I don't care a straw whether you come or not.* —***modifier:*** *a straw hat; a straw mattress.*

Idiom. **the last** (or **final**) **straw.** A small burden or annoyance that, added to many previous ones, finally causes a breakdown, outburst, etc.

straw•ber•ry |strô'bĕr'ē| *n., pl.* **-ber•ries. 1.** A sweet, red, fleshy fruit with many small seeds on the surface. **2.** The low-growing plant that bears such fruit. —***modifier:*** *strawberry jam.* [SEE PICTURE]

straw vote. An unofficial vote or poll.

stray |strā| *v.* **1.** To wander about or roam, especially beyond established limits: *The woodchuck seldom strays far from his burrow.* **2.** To deviate from a course or subject: *Don't stray from your principles.* —*n.* A person or animal that has strayed and is lost. —*adj.* **1.** Strayed or having strayed; lost: *a stray cat.* **2.** Scattered or separate: *stray shafts of sunlight.*

streak |strēk| *n.* **1. a.** A line, mark, smear, etc., differentiated by color or texture from its surroundings. **b.** A bolt: *a streak of lightning.* **2.** A character trait: *a mean streak.* **3.** *Informal.* A brief stretch of time: *a winning streak.* —*v.* **1.** To mark with or form a streak or streaks: *Dog tracks streaked the floor.* **2.** To move at high speed; rush: *Lightning streaked across the sky.*

stream |strēm| *n.* **1. a.** A body of running water that flows in a more or less regular course, such as a brook or river. **b.** A steady current in such a body of water. **2.** A steady flow or succession of anything: *a stream of electrons; a stream of questions.* —*v.* **1.** To move or flow in or as if in a stream: *The sediment streamed into the ocean.* **2.** To pour forth or give off: *The poor man's eyes streamed with tears.* **3.** To move or travel in large numbers.

stream•er |strē'mər| *n.* **1.** A long, narrow flag or banner. **2.** Any long, narrow strip of material: *a hall decked with streamers of crepe paper.*

stream•line |strēm'līn'| *v.* **stream•lined, stream•lin•ing. 1.** To construct or design so as to offer the least resistance to the flow of a fluid. **2.** To improve the appearance or efficiency of: *streamline a factory process; streamline a kitchen.*

strange

Strange *is from Old French* estrange, *which is from Latin* extrāneus, *"coming from outside, foreign, unusual, strange," from* extrā, *"outside."* Extrāneus *was also borrowed directly into English as* **extraneous.**

strawberry
Above: Flowers
Below: Fruit
"Doubtless God could have made a better berry [than the strawberry], but doubtless God never did."
—William Butler (1535–1618).

stream•lined |strēm′līnd′| *adj.* **1.** Designed or constructed to offer the least resistance to the flow of a fluid. **2.** Improved in appearance or efficiency; modernized.

street |strēt| *n.* A public way or thoroughfare in a city or town. —***modifier:*** *a street corner.*

street•car |**strēt′**kär′| *n.* A car operated on a railway and providing public transportation along a regular route. [SEE PICTURE]

streetcar
About 1900

strength |strĕngkth| *or* |strĕngth| *n.* **1.** The quality or property of being strong; physical power: *strength in battle.* **2.** The power to resist force, stress, or wear; durability: *the strength of steel.* **3.** Concentration or potency, as of a solution, drug, etc. **4.** Effective force or power: *the strength of an argument.* **5.** Moral courage or power: *Personalities always have both strengths and weaknesses.* **6.** A source of power or force: *Religion is his strength.* **7.** A concentration of available force or personnel: *at full strength.* ***Idiom.* on the strength of.** On the basis of: *They signed the contract on the strength of his report.*

strength•en |**strĕngk′**thən| *or* |**strĕng′**-| *v.* To make or become strong or stronger.

stren•u•ous |**strĕn′**yōō əs| *adj.* **1.** Requiring great effort, energy, or exertion: *strenuous exercise.* **2.** Vigorously active; energetic: *a strenuous child.* —**stren′u•ous•ly** *adv.* —**stren′u•ous•ness** *n.*

strep throat |strĕp|. An infection of the throat caused by the presence of certain streptococci, characterized by fever and inflamed tonsils.

strep•to•coc•cal |strĕp′tə **kŏk′**əl| *adj.* Of or caused by a streptococcus.

strep•to•coc•cus |strĕp′tə **kŏk′**əs| *n., pl.* **strep•to•coc•ci** |strĕp′tə **kŏk′**sī′|. Any of several rounded or oval bacteria that form pairs or chains and are often a cause of disease.

strep•to•my•cin |strĕp′tə **mī′**sən| *n.* An antibiotic drug derived from mold cultures of certain bacteria, used to combat various bacteria that cause diseases.

stress |strĕs| *n.* **1.** Importance, significance, or emphasis placed upon something: *Don't put so much stress on money.* **2.** The emphasis placed upon the sound or syllable to be pronounced loudest in a word or phrase. **3.** A musical accent, as one beat of a measure. **4.** A force that tends to strain or deform something: *The stress of the books caused the wood to warp.* **5.** An influence that disrupts mentally or emotionally. —*v.* **1.** To place emphasis upon; accent: *stress quality; stresses the first syllable.* **2.** To subject to pressure or strain.

stretch |strĕch| *v.* **1. a.** To lengthen or widen by pulling: *stretch a rubber band.* **b.** To become or be able to become lengthened or widened: *My shoes stretched out of shape. This fabric stretches.* **2.** To extend or cause to extend across a given space: *The land stretches for miles along the river. Stretch the canvas over the frame.* **3.** To extend (oneself) at full length in a prone position: *Why don't you stretch out for a half hour?* **4.** To reach or put forth: *stretch out her hand.* **5.** To flex one's muscles: *I always stretch in the morning.* **6.** To cause to last; make do with: *stretch my paycheck until next week.* **7.** To extend to the limit: *stretch the meaning of the law.* **8.** To wrench or strain (a muscle, ligament, etc.). —*n.* **1.** The act of stretching, extending, widening, etc. **2.** The extent to which something can be stretched; elasticity. **3.** A continuous or unbroken expanse of space or time. **4.** A straight section of a course or track leading to the finish line. —*adj.* Capable of being stretched or of stretching easily in size or length: *stretch fabrics.*

stretch•er |**strĕch′**ər| *n.* **1.** A movable bed or cot on which a sick, injured, or dead person can be carried in a lying position. **2.** Any of various devices for stretching or shaping, as a frame for canvas.

strew |strōō| *v.* **strewed, strewn** |strōōn| or **strewed, strew•ing. 1.** To spread here and there; scatter: *The movers strewed the contents of the desk on the floor.* **2.** To cover (a surface) with scattered or sprinkled things: *The beach was strewn with debris.*

strick•en |**strĭk′**ən|. A past participle of **strike.** —*adj.* **1.** Struck or wounded, as by an arrow. **2.** Afflicted with something overwhelming, as a disease, emotion, etc.

strict |strĭkt| *adj.* **strict•er, strict•est. 1.** Precise; exact: *in strict accordance with parliamentary procedure.* **2.** Complete: *strict control.* **3.** Demanding or imposing an exacting discipline: *a strict teacher.* **4.** Rigidly conforming; devout: *a strict Catholic.* —**strict′ly** *adv.* —**strict′ness** *n.*

stride |strīd| *v.* **strode** |strōd|, **strid•den** |**strĭd′**n|, **strid•ing.** To walk vigorously with long steps. —*n.* **1.** A long step. **2.** A characteristic motion or manner of walking or running. **3.** A step forward: *new strides in the field of medicine.* ***Idiom.* take in (one's) stride.** To handle without fuss or interruption of the normal routine.

stri•dent |**strīd′**nt| *adj.* Loud and harsh; shrill: *a strident voice.* —**stri′den•cy** *n.*

strife |strīf| *n.* Bitter conflict or struggle.

strike |strīk| *v.* **struck** |strŭk|, **struck** or **strick•en** |**strĭk′**ən|, **strik•ing. 1.** To hit with or as if with the hand, fist, or a weapon: *She struck him on the nose. Strike while the iron is hot.* **2.** To inflict (a blow): *strike a blow at injustice.* **3.** To collide or crash into: *Their heads struck. The car struck a rock.* **4.** To attack or begin an attack: *The army struck at dawn.* **5.** To afflict suddenly with a disease or disorder. **6.** To produce by hitting some device, as a key on a piano or typewriter. **7.** To indicate with a sound: *The clock struck five.* **8.** To mark by stamping or printing: *strike a medal.* **9.** To ignite by friction: *strike a match.* **10.** To impress strongly or anew: *That struck her as a good idea.* **11.** To come upon; reach; discover: *strike gold.* **12.** To make or conclude: *strike a bargain.* **13.** To fall into or assume: *strike a pose.* **14.** To engage in a strike against an employer. —***phrasal verbs.* strike out. 1.** To eliminate: *strike out an error.* **2.** In baseball: **a.** To pitch three strikes to (a batter), putting him out. **b.** To be put out in such a way by a pitcher. **strike up. 1.** To start to play vigorously: *Strike up the band.* **2.** To begin: *strike up a friendship.* —*n.* **1.** An act of striking; a hit. **2.** An attack. **3.** The cessation of work by employees in support of demands made on their employer. **4.** In baseball, a pitched ball that is counted against the batter, typically one swung at and missed or one taken and judged to have been in the area over the plate roughly defined as being between the batter's knees and armpits. **5.** In bowling, the

strike

The use of the verb **strike** *in sense* **14** *is first recorded from 1768. The first union-led* **strike** *in United States history was that of the printers of Philadelphia in 1786.*

ă pat/ā pay/â care/ä father/ĕ pet/
ē be/ĭ pit/ī pie/î fierce/ŏ pot/
ō go/ô paw, for/oi oil/ŏŏ book/
ōō boot/ou out/ŭ cut/û fur/
th the/th thin/hw which/zh vision/
ə ago, item, pencil, atom, circus

knocking down of all ten pins with one roll of the ball. —**strik'er** *n.* [SEE NOTE]

Idioms. **strike dumb.** To astonish. **strike it rich.** To gain sudden wealth.

strike•break•er |**strīk'**brā'kər| *n.* A person who works or provides an employer with workers during a strike.

strike•out |**strīk'**out'| *n.* In baseball, an example of striking out a batter or of a batter being struck out.

strik•ing |**strī'**kĭng| *adj.* Outstanding: *a woman of striking beauty.* —**strik'ing•ly** *adv.*

string |strĭng| *n.* **1.** A cord usually made of fiber, thicker than thread, used for fastening, lacing, etc. **2.** Anything shaped into a long, thin line: *a string of lights.* **3.** A set of things with a cord running through them: *a string of beads.* **4. a.** A cord or wire stretched across a musical instrument and struck, plucked, or bowed to produce tones. **b. strings.** Instruments having such strings, especially the instruments of the violin family. **5.** *Informal.* Any limiting or hidden condition: *with no strings attached.* **6.** In sports, a group of players constituting a ranked team within a team: *play first string.* —*v.* **strung** |strŭng|, **string•ing.** **1.** To furnish, fasten, or tie with a string or strings: *string a piano.* **2.** To run a string through; slip onto a string: *string beads.* —***phrasal verbs.*** **string along. 1.** To keep (someone) waiting or dangling. **2.** To follow along; cooperate: *string along with them.* **string up.** To hang (someone).

Idiom. **pull strings.** To use one's influence to gain an advantage.

string bean. 1. A long, narrow green bean pod eaten as a vegetable. **2.** The bushy plant that bears such pods. [SEE PICTURE]

stringed instrument. A musical instrument played by plucking, bowing, or striking tightly stretched strings.

strin•gent |**strĭn'**jənt| *adj.* Rigorous; severe: *stringent restrictions.* —**strin'gent•ly** *adv.*

string•er |**strĭng'**ər| *n.* **1.** Someone or something that strings. **2.** A long, heavy bar or timber that connects or supports parts of a structure. **3.** A part-time representative of a newspaper or magazine that is stationed out of town or abroad.

string•y |**strĭng'**ē| *adj.* **string•i•er, string•i•est.** Like or having strings: *stringy hair; a stringy piece of meat.* —**string'i•ness** *n.*

strip[1] |strĭp| *v.* **stripped, strip•ping. 1.** To undress, removing all the clothing: *The guards stripped the prisoner and searched him. The athlete stripped for a shower.* **2.** To remove the covering or essentials of; make bare; denude: *stripped the orchard of its fruit.* **3.** To rob or plunder: *The invaders stripped the countryside.*

strip[2] |strĭp| *n.* **1.** A long, narrow piece or area of approximately even width: *a strip of paper; a strip of desert.* **2.** An airstrip. **3.** A **comic strip.**

stripe |strīp| *n.* **1.** A line, strip, or band that differs in color, texture, etc., from the area on either side: *a zebra's stripes; the stars and stripes of the flag.* **2. stripes.** A prisoner's uniform having broad bands of color that run crosswise. **3.** A strip of cloth worn on the sleeve of a military uniform to show rank, merit, or length of service: *a sergeant's stripes.* **4.** Sort; kind: *women of a bold new stripe.* —*v.* To mark or provide with a stripe or stripes. —**striped'** *adj.*: *a striped candy cane; a striped shirt.*

strip•ling |**strĭp'**lĭng| *n.* An adolescent youth.

strip mining. A method in which a mineral, especially coal, that lies close to the surface of the earth is mined by stripping off the topsoil, rock, etc., that covers it, leaving the earth barren after the mineral is removed.

strive |strīv| *v.* **strove** |strōv|, **striv•en** |**strĭv'**ən| or **strived, striv•ing. 1.** To exert much effort or energy: *strive to improve working conditions.* **2.** To struggle; contend: *The pioneers had to strive against great odds.*

strobe |strōb| *n.* A **strobe light.**

strobe light. A lamp that produces very short, intense flashes of light by means of an electric discharge in a gas.

strode |strōd|. Past tense of **stride.**

stroke |strōk| *n.* **1.** An impact; a blow; strike: *a stroke of the sword.* **2. a.** A single complete movement, as in swimming or rowing. **b.** The rate of such movement: *The head oarsman sets the stroke for the crew.* **3.** The time indicated by the striking of a bell, gong, etc.: *at the stroke of midnight.* **4.** A single movement or mark made by a pen, brush, pencil, etc.: *a brush stroke sweeping across a painting.* **5.** A movement of a piston or similar machine part from one end of its travel to the other, as in an engine or pump. **6.** An effective or inspired idea or act: *a bold stroke to preserve his holdings; a stroke of genius.* **7.** An event having a powerful and immediate effect: *a stroke of fortune.* **8.** A light caressing movement: *a stroke of affection on the puppy's head.* **9. a.** A sudden, severe beginning of a disease or disorder, such as apoplexy or sunstroke. **b.** Apoplexy. —*v.* **stroked, strok•ing. 1.** To rub lightly, as with the hand; caress. **2.** In rowing, to set the pace.

stroll |strōl| *v.* To walk or wander at a leisurely pace: *People strolled in the square. The minstrels strolled about the park.* —*n.* A leisurely walk.

stroll•er |**strō'**lər| *n.* **1.** Someone who strolls. **2.** A light four-wheeled chair for transporting small children. [SEE PICTURE]

strong |strông| *or* |strŏng| *adj.* **strong•er, strong•est. 1.** Physically powerful; muscular: *strong as an ox.* **2.** In good or sound health; robust: *when the patient gets stronger.* **3.** Capable of enduring stress or strain; not easily broken: *strong furniture.* **4.** Intense in degree or quality: *strong feelings; a strong wind.* **5.** Concentrated: *a strong salt solution.* **6.** Highly active chemically: *a strong acid.* **7.** Having great mental or spiritual force: *a strong belief.* **8.** Forceful or persuasive: *a strong argument.* **9.** Extreme; drastic: *strong measures.* **10.** Having a specified number of units or members: *Five hundred strong, they marched forward.* **11.** Of high saturation; vivid: *a strong color.* —**strong'ly** *adv.*

strong•box |**strông'**bŏks'| *or* |**strŏng'**-| *n.* A stoutly made box or safe for storing valuables.

strong•hold |**strông'**hōld'| *or* |**strŏng'**-| *n.* **1.** A fortress or refuge. **2.** Any area dominated or occupied by a special group.

stron•ti•um |**strŏn'**shē əm| *or* |-tē əm| *n.* Symbol **Sr** One of the elements, a soft silvery metal that oxidizes easily and is chemically active. Atomic number 38; atomic weight 87.62; valence

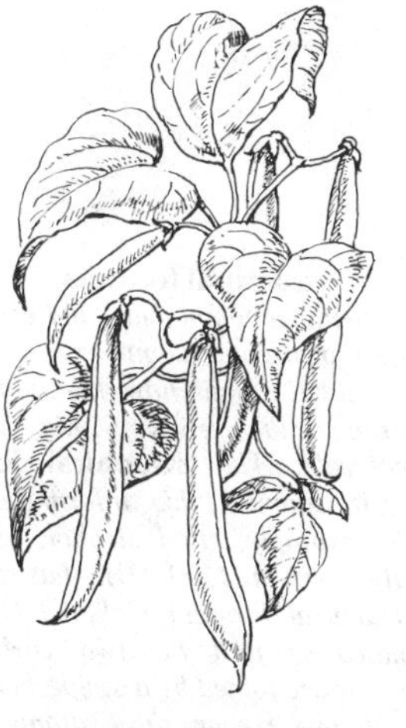

string bean

stroller

structural formula
In chemical compounds, and especially in organic compounds, it is not always clear how the atoms arrange themselves within the molecule. The **structural formula** *supplies this information. For example, ethyl alcohol, usually written C_2H_5OH, has the structural formula CH_3CH_2OH, indicating that the two carbon atoms are joined by a single bond, with one having three atoms of hydrogen bound to it and the other having two atoms of hydrogen and a hydroxyl group bound to it.*

stud[1-2]
Stud[1] *was Old English* studum, *"post, prop," later "knob."* **Stud[2]** *was Old English* stūd, *"place where horses are bred." It is related to* **steed**, *which was Old English* stēda, *"horse used for breeding."*

ă pat/ā pay/â care/ä father/ĕ pet/ ē be/ĭ pit/ī pie/î fierce/ŏ pot/ ō go/ô paw, for/oi oil/ŏŏ book/ ōō boot/ou out/ŭ cut/û fur/ *th* the/th thin/hw which/zh vision/ ə ago, item, pencil, atom, circus

+2; melting point 769°C; boiling point 1,384°C.

strontium 90. A radioactive isotope of strontium with a mass number of 90 and a half-life of 28 years.

strop |strŏp| *n.* A flexible strip of leather or canvas used for sharpening a razor. —*v.* **stropped, strop•ping.** To sharpen (a razor) on a strop.

stro•phe |strō′fē′| *n.* A stanza of a poem.

strove |strōv|. Past tense of **strive.**

struck |strŭk|. Past tense and past participle of **strike.**

struc•tur•al |strŭk′chər əl| *adj.* **1.** Of or having structure. **2.** Used in construction: *structural steel.* —**struc′tur•al•ly** *adv.*

structural formula. A chemical formula that indicates how the atoms making up a compound are arranged within the molecule. [SEE NOTE]

struc•ture |strŭk′chər| *n.* **1.** Anything made up of a number of parts that are held together or put together in a particular way. **2.** The way in which parts are arranged or put together to form a whole. **3.** Something constructed, as a building, bridge, etc. **4.** A plant or animal part or organ: *A paramecium moves by means of tiny, hairlike structures called cilia.* —*v.* **struc•tured, struc•tur•ing.** To build or construct, especially in an organized manner.

strug•gle |strŭg′əl| *v.* **strug•gled, strug•gling. 1.** To make a strenuous effort or strive against or as if against a great force: *The women struggled to control the fire. They struggled to find the proper words.* **2.** To compete or contend: *Passengers struggled for room on the subway.* —*n.* **1.** Strenuous effort or striving: *the struggle for survival.* **2.** Combat; battle or strife: *hand-to-hand struggles; a legal struggle.* —**strug′gler** *n.*

strum |strŭm| *v.* **strummed, strum•ming.** To play idly on (a stringed instrument) by plucking the strings with the fingers. —*n.* The act or sound or strumming.

strung |strŭng|. Past tense and past participle of **string.**

strut |strŭt| *n.* **1.** A stiff, self-important gait. **2.** A bar or rod used to brace a mechanical structure against forces applied from the side. —*v.* **strut•ted, strut•ting. 1.** To walk with a strut. **2.** To brace or support with a strut or struts.

strych•nine |strĭk′nĭn| *or* |-nīn′| *or* |-nēn′| *n.* An extremely poisonous white crystalline compound composed of carbon, hydrogen, nitrogen, and oxygen in the proportions $C_{21}H_{22}N_2O_2$.

St. Thom•as |sānt′ tŏm′əs|. The second largest of the Virgin Islands of the United States.

Stu•art |stōō′ərt| *or* |styōō′-|. The family name of the rulers of Scotland from 1371 to 1707, England from 1603 to 1707, and Great Britain from 1707 to 1714. —***modifier:*** *a Stuart king.*

stub |stŭb| *n.* **1.** The short blunt end remaining after something has been cut or broken off or worn down: *the stub of a pencil.* **2. a.** The part of a check or receipt retained as a record. **b.** The part of a ticket returned as a voucher of payment. —*v.* **stubbed, stub•bing.** To strike (one's toe or foot) against something.

stub•ble |stŭb′əl| *n.* **1.** Short, stiff stalks, as of grain, left after a crop has been harvested. **2.** Something resembling this, especially a short, stiff growth of beard or hair.

stub•born |stŭb′ərn| *adj.* **1.** Unreasonably determined to exert one's will: *a stubborn child.* **2.** Continuously enduring; persistent: *a stubborn idea.* **3.** Difficult to handle or work with: *The environment is stubborn, and man must adapt to it.* —**stub′born•ly** *adv.* —**stub′born•ness** *n.*

stub•by |stŭb′ē| *adj.* **stub•bi•er, stub•bi•est. 1.** Short and stocky: *Penguins have stubby legs.* **2.** Full of stubs: *stubby grass.* —**stub′bi•ness** *n.*

stuc•co |stŭk′ō| *n., pl.* **stuc•coes** or **stuc•cos.** A finish, usually of plaster or cement, used to cover walls.

stuck |stŭk|. Past tense and past participle of **stick.**

stuck-up |stŭk′ŭp′| *adj. Informal.* Snobbish.

stud[1] |stŭd| *n.* **1.** An upright post in the framework of a wall for supporting lath, wood panels, etc. **2.** Any of various projecting pins, pegs, knobs, etc., as in machinery. **3.** A removable button used to fasten and ornament a dress shirt, cuff, etc. —*v.* **stud•ded, stud•ding. 1.** To set with objects that project or stand out from the surface: *stud a bracelet with rubies; boots studded with nails.* **2.** To be dotted about on; strew: *Daisies studded the meadow.* [SEE NOTE]

stud[2] |stŭd| *n.* **1.** A male animal, especially a stallion, kept for breeding. **2.** A group of horses or other animals kept for breeding. —***modifier:*** *a stud farm.* [SEE NOTE]

Idiom. **at stud.** Available for breeding with a female or females, as a horse, bull, or dog.

stu•dent |stōōd′nt| *or* |styōōd′-| *n.* **1.** A person who attends a school, college, or university. **2.** A person who makes a study of something: *a student of languages.* —***modifier:*** *student leaders.*

stud•ied |stŭd′ēd| *adj.* Carefully contrived; deliberate: *a studied pose.*

stu•di•o |stōō′dē ō′| *or* |styōō′-| *n.* **1.** An artist's workroom. **2.** A place where an art is taught or studied: *a ceramics studio.* **3.** A room or building for motion-picture, television, or radio productions.

stu•di•ous |stōō′dē əs| *or* |styōō′-| *adj.* **1.** Devoted to study: *a studious life.* **2.** Earnest; purposeful; diligent: *a studious avoidance of anything silly.* —**stu′di•ous•ly** *adv.* —**stu′di•ous•ness** *n.*

stud•y |stŭd′ē| *n., pl.* **stud•ies. 1.** The act or process of studying; pursuit of knowledge: *years of devoted study.* **2.** A branch of knowledge; a subject: *technical studies.* **3.** A work on a particular subject: *presented a study of dreams.* **4.** A room intended for or equipped for studying. **5.** A musical composition written or played as an exercise; an étude. **6.** An artist's preliminary sketch. —***modifier:*** *a study hall.* —*v.* **stud•ied, stud•y•ing, stud•ies. 1.** To apply one's mind to gaining knowledge and understanding of (a subject): *study French; study for a half hour.* **2.** To investigate: *She studied the Eskimos' languages.* **3.** To examine closely; contemplate: *She studied the mole on his face.* **4.** To take (a course) at a school: *He studies typing at night.*

stuff |stŭf| *n.* **1.** The material out of which something is made or formed; the substance. **2.** The basic elements of something; the essence: *He knew not the stuff of which fear is made.* **3.** *Informal.* Things, belongings, etc., not specifically identified: *venders selling their stuff on the street.* **4.** Cloth of which clothing may be made.

—*interj.* Often **stuff and nonsense.** That's not so! Don't be silly! —*v.* **1. a.** To pack tightly: *stuffed the Christmas stockings.* **b.** To block a passage; obstruct: *stuffed the window with cardboard.* **2.** To fill with an appropriate stuffing: *stuff a turkey.* **3.** To fill (oneself): *He stuffed himself with Thanksgiving turkey.*

stuffed der•ma |dûr′mə|. Kishke.

stuffed shirt. *Informal.* A stiff, pompous person.

stuff•ing |stŭf′ĭng| *n.* **1.** Soft material used to stuff, fill, line, or pad things made of or covered with cloth: *a doll with the stuffing coming out.* **2.** A seasoned mixture of food put into the cavity of meat or vegetables.

stuff•y |stŭf′ē| *adj.* **stuff•i•er, stuff•i•est. 1.** Lacking sufficient ventilation; close: *an overheated, stuffy room.* **2.** Having blocked breathing passages: *a stuffy nose.* **3.** Stiff; formal: *a dull, stuffy person.* —**stuff′i•ly** *adv.* —**stuff′i•ness** *n.*

stul•ti•fy |stŭl′tə fī′| *v.* **stul•ti•fied, stul•ti•fy•ing, stul•ti•fies.** To make useless or ineffectual: *customs that stultify free thought.* —**stul′ti•fi•ca′tion** *n.*

stum•ble |stŭm′bəl| *v.* **stum•bled, stum•bling. 1. a.** To trip and almost fall: *The horse stumbled.* **b.** To move as if tripping; falter: *Father stumbled out of bed.* **2.** To make a mistake; blunder: *Do you stumble over words?* **3.** To come upon, meet, or happen unexpectedly: *They stumbled upon the clue. They stumbled into each other in the dark night.* —*n.* **1.** The act of stumbling; a fall. **2.** A mistake or blunder. —**stum′bler** *n.*

stumbling block. An obstacle or impediment.

stump |stŭmp| *n.* **1.** The part of a tree trunk left in the ground after the tree has fallen or been cut down. **2.** A short or broken piece or part: *a stump of a pencil; a stubby stump of a tail.* **3.** A platform or other place from which political speeches are made. —*v.* **1.** To walk in a stiff, heavy, plodding manner. **2.** To go about (an area) making political speeches. **3.** *Informal.* To puzzle or baffle completely.

stump•y |stŭm′pē| *adj.* **stump•i•er, stump•i•est.** Short and stocky; stubby: *stumpy legs.*

stun |stŭn| *v.* **stunned, stun•ning. 1.** To daze or render senseless, as by a blow: *The rock stunned the rabbit.* **2.** To shock or stupefy, as with the emotional impact of an experience: *The scandal stunned the neighborhood.* —**stunned′** *adj.*: *a stunned expression.* [SEE NOTE]

stung |stŭng|. A past tense and past participle of **sting.**

stunk |stŭngk|. A past tense and past participle of **stink.**

stun•ning |stŭn′ĭng| *adj.* **1.** Surprising or astonishing: *a stunning victory.* **2.** *Informal.* Strikingly attractive: *a stunning suit.* —**stun′ning•ly** *adv.*

stunt[1] |stŭnt| *v.* To stop or interfere with the growth or development of: *Air pollution may stunt many kinds of plants.* [SEE NOTE]

stunt[2] |stŭnt| *n.* **1.** A feat displaying unusual skill or daring. **2.** Something of an unusual nature: *a publicity stunt.* [SEE NOTE]

stu•pe•fy |stōō′pə fī′| *or* |styōō′-| *v.* **stu•pe•fied, stu•pe•fy•ing, stu•pe•fies. 1.** To dull the senses or consciousness of; put into a stupor: *The dull routine stupefied them.* **2.** To amaze; astonish: *The discovery stupefied the world.* —**stu′pe•fac′tion** |stōō′pə făk′shən| *or* |styōō′-| *n.*

stu•pen•dous |stōō pĕn′dəs| *or* |styōō-| *adj.* **1.** Of astonishing force, volume, degree, etc.: *stupendous risks.* **2.** Amazingly large, huge: *stupendous temple ruins.* —**stu•pen′dous•ly** *adv.*

stu•pid |stōō′pĭd| *or* |styōō′-| *adj.* **1.** Slow to apprehend; dull; dumb: *a stupid person.* **2.** Not sensible; unintelligent: *a stupid solution.* —**stu′pid•ly** *adv.*

stu•pid•i•ty |stōō pĭd′ĭ tē| *or* |styōō-| *n., pl.* **stu•pid•i•ties. 1.** The quality or fact of being stupid. **2.** Something stupid, as an idea.

stu•por |stōō′pər| *or* |styōō′-| *n.* A condition of reduced sensibility or consciousness; a daze.

stur•dy |stûr′dē| *adj.* **stur•di•er, stur•di•est.** Strong; durable; substantial: *the sturdy branch of a giant oak.* —**stur′di•ly** *adv.* —**stur′di•ness** *n.*

stur•geon |stûr′jən| *n., pl.* **stur•geon** or **stur•geons.** A large freshwater or saltwater fish having bony plates rather than true scales on its body. The flesh of the sturgeon is considered a delicacy, as well as its roe, which is made into caviar. [SEE PICTURE]

stut•ter |stŭt′ər| *v.* To speak with constant hesitations or repetitions of sounds. —*n.* The act or habit of stuttering. —**stut′ter•er** *n.*

St. Vin•cent and the Gren•a•dines |sānt vĭn′sənt; grĕn′ə dēnz′|. An island country in the central Windward Islands of the West Indies. Population, 124,000. Capital, Kingstown.

St. Vi•tus' dance, also **St. Vi•tus's dance** |sānt vī′tə sĭz|. Chorea, a disease. [SEE NOTE]

sty[1] |stī| *n., pl.* **sties. 1.** A pen or fenced-in place where pigs are kept. **2.** Any very dirty or untidy place.

sty[2] |stī| *n., pl.* **sties.** An inflammation of one or more of the oil-producing glands of an eyelid.

style |stīl| *n.* **1.** The way or manner in which something is said, done, expressed, performed, etc.: *a style of speech; a classic style.* **2.** Sort; kind; type: *a style of furniture.* **3.** An elegant mode of existence: *living in style.* **4. a.** The fashion of dressing or way of behaving popular at a certain time and place: *the latest style; the styles of the 1920s.* **b.** The current fashion: *Dresses of various lengths are in style.* **5.** A special or distinctive design, arrangement, shape, or cut: *a hair style; a dress style.* **6.** An individual sense of how to dress with flair or to do things with grace, elegance, and distinction: *She has a great deal of style.* **7.** The slender stalk of a flower pistil, rising from the ovary and tipped by the stigma. —***modifier:*** *a style show.* —*v.* **styled, styl•ing.** To arrange, design, or fashion in a special way: *Her hairdresser styled her hair. A famous designer styled that dress.* ¶ *These sound alike* **style, stile.**

sty•li |stī′lī′| *n.* A plural of **stylus.**

styl•ish |stī′lĭsh| *adj.* Conforming to the current style; fashionable: *a stylish outfit.* —**styl′ish•ly** *adv.* —**styl′ish•ness** *n.*

styl•ist |stī′lĭst| *n.* **1.** A person who cultivates an artful literary style. **2.** A designer of or expert on styles in decorating, beauty, etc.: *a hair stylist.*

styl•ize |stī′līz′| *v.* **styl•ized, styl•iz•ing.** To conform or restrict to a particular style.

sty•lus |stī′ləs| *n., pl.* **sty•lus•es** or **sty•li** |stī′lī′|. **1.** A sharp, pointed instrument used for writing. **2.** A tiny needle, often tipped with a diamond, that transmits vibrations from the grooves of a phonograph record.

sty•mie |stī′mē| *v.* **sty•mied, sty•mie•ing** or **sty•**

stun

Stun *is from Vulgar Latin* extonāre, *an unattested form meaning "to strike and make senseless." This word is also the source of* **astonish** *and* **astound** *(see note at* **astonish***). The Vulgar Latin form is borrowed from Latin* tonāre, *to thunder.*

stunt[1-2]

Stunt[1] *is from a combination of Old English* stunt, *"dull, foolish," and Old Norse* stuttr, *"short, dwarflike."* **Stunt[2]** *is of unknown origin. It first appeared in the 1890's in American college slang and meant "an athletic feat, a remarkable action, a piece of showing off." It was widely used in the slang of World War I in two senses: (1) "a daring piece of flying" and (2) "any attack, any piece of fighting." It remained in popular slang use through the twenties and thirties.*

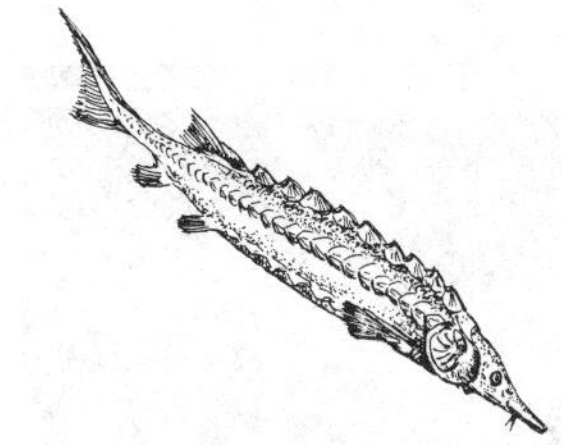

sturgeon

St. Vitus' dance

Vitus *or* Vito, *a Sicilian Christian boy, was killed during the last major persecution of Christians, in about* A.D. 300. *The child martyr became the patron saint of people, especially children, suffering from various diseases. This is why* **chorea,** *to which children are especially prone, is sometimes called* **St. Vitus' dance** *(*chorea *means "dance" in Latin; the disease causes the limbs to twitch and "dance" uncontrollably).*

sub–
The prefix **sub-** *is from Latin* sub, *"under."* Sub *also meant "upward from under," as in* subportāre, *"to carry from below," from which we have* **support.** *It is descended from the Indo-European preposition* upo, *which also meant "under" and "upward from under, up."* Upo *also appears in Old English* up *or* uppe, *becoming Modern English* **up,** *and in Greek* hupo, *"under," from which we have the prefix* **hypo-.**

subjugate
Subjugate *is from Latin* subiugāre, *"to bring under the yoke." By an ancient Latin custom, when an army was completely defeated, the survivors were made to pass under a symbolic "yoke" formed by two spears stuck in the ground with a third forming the crosspiece. This was actually done to a Roman army in 321* B.C. *The Romans regarded it as the worst possible humiliation.*

submarine

subpoena
A **subpoena** *ordering someone to appear in court carries a specific penalty for nonappearance. The word* **subpoena** *comes from the Latin form of the writ, which begins with the words* sub poena, *"under penalty."*

ă pat/ā pay/â care/ä father/ĕ pet/ē be/ĭ pit/ī pie/î fierce/ŏ pot/ō go/ô paw, for/oi oil/ŏŏ book/ōō boot/ou out/ŭ cut/û fur/*th* the/th thin/hw which/zh vision/ə ago, item, pencil, atom, circus

my•ing. To block or thwart: *stymie their hopes.*

styp•tic |stĭp′tĭk| *adj.* Contracting the blood vessels so as to check bleeding: *a styptic pencil.* —*n.* A styptic substance.

sty•rene |stī′rēn′| *n.* A colorless, oily, liquid hydrocarbon, C_8H_8, from which polystyrene is made.

suave |swäv| *adj.* **suav•er, suav•est.** Smoothly gracious; urbane: *a suave gentleman.* —**suave′ly** *adv.* —**suav′i•ty, suave′ness** *n.*

sub |sŭb|. *Informal. n.* **1.** A substitute. **2.** A submarine. —*v.* **subbed, sub•bing.** To act as a substitute.

sub–. A prefix meaning: **1.** Under or beneath: **submarine. 2.** A subordinate or secondary part: **subdivision. 3.** Somewhat short of or less than: **subtropical.** [SEE NOTE]

sub•con•scious |sŭb kŏn′shəs| *adj.* Not fully conscious but capable of being made conscious. —*n.* The unconscious. —**sub′con′scious•ly** *adv.*

sub•con•ti•nent |sŭb kŏn′tə nənt| *n.* A large land mass, such as India or southern Africa, that is separate to some degree but is still part of a continent.

sub•di•vide |sŭb′dĭ vīd′| *v.* **-di•vid•ed, -di•vid•ing.** To divide into smaller parts.

sub•di•vi•sion |sŭb′dĭ vĭzh′ən| *n.* **1.** The act or process of subdividing. **2.** A subdivided part.

sub•dom•i•nant |sŭb dŏm′ə nənt| *n.* The tone of a diatonic major or minor scale located a perfect fourth above the tonic. —*adj.* Of the subdominant: *a subdominant harmony.*

sub•due |səb dōō′| *or* |-dyōō′| *v.* **sub•dued, sub•du•ing. 1.** To conquer and subjugate; vanquish. **2.** To quiet or bring under control: *subdue the child's wails.* **3.** To make less intense; tone down: *subdue anxiety.*

sub•ject |sŭb′jĭkt| *adj.* **1.** Under the power or authority of another: *subject to the jurisdiction of a government.* **2.** Prone; disposed: *subject to colds.* **3.** Liable to incur or receive; exposed: *subject to criticism.* **4.** Contingent or dependent: *subject to approval.* —*n.* **1.** Someone who owes allegiance to a government or ruler: *British subjects.* **2.** A person or thing about which something is said or done: *a subject of discussion; the subject of a painting.* **3.** A course or area of study: *her favorite subject in school.* **4.** An individual used as the object of clinical study: *the subjects of an experiment.* **5.** A word, phrase, or clause in a sentence that names who or what does the action, receives the action in passive constructions, or undergoes existence. For example, in the sentence *Jimmy threw the ball,* the subject is *Jimmy.* **6.** A theme of a musical composition, especially a fugue. —*v.* |səb jĕkt′|. **1.** To subjugate; subdue: *subjected the neighboring territory.* **2.** To cause to undergo: *subjected the child to many tests.* —**sub•jec′tion** *n.*

sub•jec•tive |səb jĕk′tĭv| *n.* Existing within the mind or perception of an individual and not capable of being observed or experienced by anyone else.

subjective case. The case of a pronoun that designates the subject of a verb.

sub•ju•gate |sŭb′jōō gāt′| *v.* **sub•ju•gat•ed, sub•ju•gat•ing.** To bring under dominion; conquer. —**sub′ju•ga′tion** *n.* [SEE NOTE]

sub•junc•tive |səb jŭngk′tĭv| *adj.* Of a verb form or set of forms used to express an uncertainty, a wish, or an unlikely condition. For example, in the sentence *If I were you, I would go,* the word *were* is a subjunctive form. —*n.* **1.** The subjunctive mood. **2.** A subjunctive construction.

sub•let |sŭb lĕt′| *v.* **sub•let, sub•let•ting.** To rent (property one holds by lease) to another.

sub•li•mate |sŭb′lə māt′| *v.* **sub•li•mat•ed, sub•li•mat•ing.** To pass or cause to pass from a solid to a gas or from a gas to a solid without becoming liquid. —**sub′li•ma′tion** *n.*

sub•lime |sə blīm′| *adj.* **1.** Exalted; lofty: *sublime poetry.* **2.** Inspiring awe; impressive; moving: *a sublime performance.* —*v.* **sub•limed, sub•lim•ing.** To pass or cause to pass from the solid to the gaseous state or vice versa without becoming liquid; sublimate. —**sub•lime′ly** *adv.*

sub•ma•chine gun |sŭb′mə shēn′|. A lightweight machine gun fired from the shoulder or the hip.

sub•ma•rine |sŭb′mə rēn′| *or* |sŭb′mə rēn′| *adj.* Beneath the surface of the sea; undersea: *a submarine volcano.* —*n.* A ship that can operate underwater. [SEE PICTURE]

sub•merge |səb mûrj′| *v.* **sub•merged, sub•merg•ing. 1.** To place or go under or as if under water or some other liquid: *submerged the dish in soapy water. The swimmer submerged in the pool.* **2.** To cover with water: *The flood submerged the island.* —**sub•merged′** *adj.: a submerged reef.*

sub•merse |səb mûrs′| *v.* **sub•mersed, sub•mers•ing.** To submerge. —**sub•mer′sion** *n.*

sub•mis•sion |səb mĭsh′ən| *n.* **1.** The act of submitting to the power of another. **2.** The condition of being submissive: *starved into submission.* **3.** The act of submitting something for consideration.

sub•mis•sive |səb mĭs′ĭv| *adj.* Tending to submit readily; compliant: *a submissive personality.*

sub•mit |səb mĭt′| *v.* **sub•mit•ted, sub•mit•ting. 1.** To yield or surrender (oneself) to the will or authority of another: *They submitted themselves to his judgment.* **2.** To commit (something) to the consideration of another: *submit ideas to her.* **3.** To offer as a proposition or contention: *I submit that the terms of the contract are unreasonable.* **4.** To yield; surrender; acquiesce: *He submitted to their demands.* —**sub•mit′tal** *n.*

sub•or•di•nate |sə bôr′dn ĭt| *adj.* **1.** Belonging to a lower or inferior rank: *a subordinate position.* **2.** Subject to the authority or control of another. —*n.* Someone or something that is subordinate: *He is courteous to his subordinates.* —*v.* |sə bôr′dn āt′| **sub•or•di•nat•ed, sub•or•di•nat•ing.** To put in a lower or inferior rank: *subordinate a court to a higher one.* —**sub•or′di•nate•ly** *adv.* —**sub•or′di•na′tion** *n.*

subordinate clause. A dependent clause.

subordinate conjunction. A conjunction that introduces a dependent clause, as *that, who, which,* and *where.*

sub•pe•na |sə pē′nə| *n.* & *v.* A form of the word **subpoena.**

sub•poe•na |sə pē′nə| *n.* A writ requiring a person to appear in court and give testimony. —*v.* To serve with such a writ. [SEE NOTE]

sub•scribe |səb skrīb′| *v.* **sub•scribed, sub•scrib•ing. 1.** To sign (one's name). **2.** To sign one's name to in testimony or consent: *subscribe a will.* **3.** To pledge or contribute (a sum of money). **4.** To express agreement or approval: *subscribe to a belief.* **5.** To contract to receive and pay for a certain number of issues of a periodical: *subscribe to a magazine; subscribe by mail.* —**sub•scrib'er** *n.*

sub•script |sŭb'skrĭpt'| *n.* A symbol or character written to the side of and below another symbol or character, as in a mathematical expression or chemical formula. —***modifier:*** *a subscript character.*

sub•scrip•tion |səb skrĭp'shən| *n.* **1.** The signing of one's name, as to a legal document. **2.** A purchase made by a signed order, as for issues of a periodical or a series of theatrical performances: *a subscription to the opera.*

sub•se•quent |sŭb'sə kwənt| *adj.* Following in time or order; succeeding: *heavy rains and subsequent floods.* —**sub'se•quence** *n.* —**sub'se•quent•ly** *adv.*

sub•ser•vi•ent |səb sûr'vē ənt| *adj.* **1.** Subordinate in ability or function. **2.** Obsequious; servile: *subservient manners.* —**sub•ser'vi•ence** *n.* —**sub•ser'vi•ent•ly** *adv.*

sub•set |sŭb'sĕt'| *n.* A set that has all of its members included in another set. For example, if *A* is a set and *B* is a set and every member of *A* is a member of *B,* then *A* is a subset of *B.*

sub•side |səb sīd'| *v.* **sub•sid•ed, sub•sid•ing.** **1.** To sink to a lower or more normal level: *The flood waters subsided.* **2.** To become less active; abate: *The child's tantrum finally subsided.*

sub•sid•i•ar•y |səb sĭd'ē ĕr'ē| *adj.* **1.** Serving to assist or supplement: *subsidiary roads.* **2.** Secondary in importance: *a subsidiary aim of the project.* —*n., pl.* **sub•sid•i•ar•ies.** **1.** Something that is subsidiary. **2.** Also **subsidiary company.** A company having more than half of its stock owned by another company.

sub•si•dize |sŭb'sĭ dīz'| *v.* **sub•si•dized, sub•si•diz•ing.** To assist or support with a subsidy: *subsidize the investigation.* —**sub'si•diz'er** *n.*

sub•si•dy |sŭb'sĭ dē| *n., pl.* **sub•si•dies.** Financial assistance, as that granted by a government to a private commercial enterprise.

sub•sist |səb sĭst'| *v.* **1.** To get nourishment and maintain life; live: *Horses can subsist entirely on grass.* **2.** To continue or manage to live.

sub•sis•tence |səb sĭs'təns| *n.* The act, condition, or means of subsisting: *daily subsistence from the soil.* —***modifier:*** *subsistence rations.*

sub•soil |sŭb'soil'| *n.* The layer of earth below the surface soil.

sub•son•ic |sŭb sŏn'ĭk| *adj.* Of or indicating a speed less than that of sound.

sub•stance |sŭb'stəns| *n.* **1. a.** That which has mass and occupies space; matter. **b.** A material of a particular kind or constitution. **2.** The essence of what is said or written; the gist: *the substance of the report.* **3.** That which is solid or real; reality as opposed to appearance: *a dream without substance.* **4.** Density; body: *Air has little substance.* **5.** Material possessions; wealth: *a person of substance.* [SEE NOTE]

sub•stan•tial |səb stăn'shəl| *adj.* **1.** Of or having substance; material. **2.** Not imaginary; true; real. **3.** Solidly built; strong: *substantial houses.* **4.** Ample; sustaining: *a substantial meal; a substantial income.* **5.** Considerable in importance, value, degree, amount, or extent: *convicted on substantial evidence; making substantial progress.* **6.** Possessing wealth; well-to-do: *a substantial farmer.* —**sub•stan'tial•ly** *adv.*

sub•stan•ti•ate |səb stăn'shē āt'| *v.* **sub•stan•ti•at•ed, sub•stan•ti•at•ing.** To support with proof or evidence; verify: *The prosecutor could not substantiate the testimony of the witness.*

sub•stan•tive |sŭb'stən tĭv| *adj.* Of substantial amount; considerable. —*n.* A word or group of words functioning as a noun.

sub•sti•tute |sŭb'stĭ to͞ot'| *or* |-tyo͞ot'| *n.* Someone or something that takes the place of another; a replacement: *a substitute for a baseball pitcher; a substitute for coffee.* —***modifier:*** *a substitute teacher.* —*v.* **sub•sti•tut•ed, sub•sti•tut•ing.** **1.** To put or use (a person or thing) in place of another: *substitute walnuts for pecans in the recipe.* **2.** To take the place of another: *She will substitute for him.* —**sub'sti•tu'tion** *n.*

sub•ter•fuge |sŭb'tər fyo͞oj'| *n.* An evasive tactic or trick.

sub•tle |sŭt'l| *adj.* **sub•tler, sub•tlest.** **1.** So slight as to be difficult to detect or analyze; elusive: *subtle changes.* **2.** Not immediately obvious; abstruse: *a subtle problem.* **3.** Able to make fine distinctions; keen: *a subtle mind.* **4.** Characterized by slyness; devious: *subtle actions.* —**sub'tle•ness** *n.* —**sub'tly** *adv.*

sub•tle•ty |sŭt'l tē| *n., pl.* **sub•tle•ties.** **1.** The state or quality of being subtle: *the subtlety of his plan.* **2.** Something subtle, especially a nicety of thought or a fine distinction.

sub•to•tal |sŭb'tōt'l| *n.* The total of a subset chosen from a set of numbers. —*v.* To total (a subset of a set of numbers).

sub•tract |səb trăkt'| *v.* **1.** To perform the mathematical operation of subtraction. **2.** To take away; remove or deduct.

sub•trac•tion |səb trăk'shən| *n.* **1.** The act or process of subtracting. **2.** The mathematical operation of finding a number that when added to one of two numbers produces the other as a sum.

sub•tra•hend |sŭb'trə hĕnd'| *n.* A number that is to be subtracted from another number; for example, in the expression $8-5$, 5 is the subtrahend.

sub•trop•i•cal |sŭb trŏp'ĭ kəl| *adj.* Of or indicating the regions that adjoin the tropics.

sub•urb |sŭb'ûrb'| *n.* **1.** A usually residential area near a city. **2. the suburbs.** The perimeter of country around a major city; the environs.

sub•ur•ban |sə bûr'bən| *adj.* **1.** Of a suburb or life in a suburb: *a suburban area.* **2.** Located in a suburb: *a suburban school.*

sub•ur•ban•ite |sə bûr'bə nīt'| *n.* Someone who lives in a suburb.

sub•ur•bi•a |sə bûr'bē ə| *n.* Suburbs or suburbanites in general.

sub•ver•sive |səb vûr'sĭv| *adj.* Intended or serving to overthrow: *subversive plots.*

sub•vert |səb vûrt'| *v.* **1.** To destroy or overthrow completely: *subvert ideals.* **2.** To undermine the character, morals, or allegiance of; corrupt: *subvert the people.* —**sub•ver'sion** *n.*

sub•way |sŭb'wā'| *n.* **1. a.** An underground urban railroad. **b.** A passage for such a railroad. **2.** Any underground tunnel or passage. —***mod-***

substance

Substance *is from Latin* substantia, *a scientific term for basic matter, "that which underlies things, the underlying stuff of which all objects are made":* sub-, *"under,"* + stant-, *"standing, existing."*

subway
In New York City

ifier: a subway train. [SEE PICTURE on p. 863]

suc•ceed |sək sēd'| *v.* **1.** To follow or come next in time or order; to replace (another) in an office or position: *She succeeded to the throne. He succeeded his mother.* **2.** To accomplish something desired or attempted: *He succeeded in repairing the watch.* —**suc•ceed'er** *n.*

suc•cess |sək sĕs'| *n.* **1.** The achievement of something desired or attempted: *the success of the experiment.* **2.** The gaining of fame or prosperity: *She won success as a skater.* **3.** Someone or something that is successful.

suc•cess•ful |sək sĕs'fəl| *adj.* **1.** Having a desired or favorable result: *a successful attempt.* **2.** Having gained fame or prosperity: *a successful actress.* —**suc•cess'ful•ly** *adv.*

suc•ces•sion |sək sĕsh'ən| *n.* **1.** The act or process of following in order or sequence: *the succession of events.* **2.** A group of persons or things arranged or following in order; a sequence: *a succession of pilgrims; a succession of sharp sounds.* **3.** The sequence, right, or act of succeeding to a title, throne, dignity, or estate: *a war over the succession to the Spanish throne.*

suc•ces•sive |sək sĕs'ĭv| *adj.* Following in uninterrupted order or sequence: *three successive years.* —**suc•ces'sive•ly** *adv.*

suc•ces•sor |sək sĕs'ər| *n.* Someone or something that succeeds another.

suc•cinct |sək sĭngkt'| *adj.* **1.** Clearly expressed in few words; concise: *a succinct explanation.* **2.** Characterized by brevity and clarity: *a succinct style.* —**suc•cinct'ly** *adv.* —**suc•cinct'ness** *n.*

suc•cor |sŭk'ər| *n.* Assistance or help in time of distress. —*v.* To render assistance in time of distress. ¶*These sound alike* **succor, sucker.**

suc•co•tash |sŭk'ə tăsh'| *n.* Kernels of corn and lima beans cooked together.

Suc•coth |so͝ok'əs| *n.* A Jewish harvest festival celebrated in the autumn.

suc•cu•lent |sŭk'yə lənt| *adj.* **1.** Full of juice or sap; juicy: *succulent berries.* **2.** Having thick, fleshy leaves or stems: *a succulent plant.* —*n.* A succulent plant, as a cactus. —**suc'cu•lence** *n.* —**suc'cu•lent•ly** *adv.*

suc•cumb |sə kŭm'| *v.* **1.** To yield or submit to something overpowering or overwhelming: *succumb to the pressures of society.* **2.** To die.

such |sŭch| *adj.* **1.** Of this or that kind or extent: *We never dreamed she could do such work.* Often used adverbially: *such good work.* Often also used with *a: such a good job.* **2.** Similar: *He grinds out two or three such books in a year.* —*adv.* Very; especially: *They're not really living in such dire poverty, you know.* —*pron.* **1.** Such a person or person or thing or things: *We've got root beer and fruit juices, if you're interested in such.* **2.** Such as can be implied or indicated: *Such are the fortunes of war.* **3.** Someone or something similar; the like: *flower children, hippies, and such.* —**as such.** In itself: *As such the job pays very little.* —**such as. 1.** For example: *novels such as "War and Peace."* **2.** Of the same kind: *nice ordinary people, such as we always invite.*

suck |sŭk| *v.* **1.** To draw (liquid or gas) into the mouth by inhaling or pulling in the cheeks. **2.** To draw in (a liquid or gas) by lowering the pressure inside, as with a syringe or pump. **3.** To suckle.

suck•er |sŭk'ər| *n.* **1.** Someone or something that sucks: *Leeches and ticks are blood suckers.* **2.** A part by which an animal or plant clings to something by suction. **3.** A freshwater fish with thick lips adapted to feeding by suction. **4.** A shoot growing from the base of a tree or shrub. **5.** A lollipop. **6.** *Slang.* A person who is easily fooled. ¶*These sound alike* **sucker, succor.**

suck•le |sŭk'əl| *v.* To feed or take milk from a mother's breast or udder; nurse.

suck•ling |sŭk'lĭng| *n.* A baby or young animal that is still being nursed by its mother. —***modifier:*** *a suckling pig.*

su•cre |so͞o'krā| *n.* The basic unit of money of Ecuador.

Su•cre |so͞o'krā|. The constitutional capital of Bolivia. Population, 64,000.

su•crose |so͞o'krōs'| *n.* A crystalline sugar having the formula $C_{12}H_{22}O_{11}$, found in many plants, especially sugar cane, sugar beets, and sugar maple, and widely used as a sweetener.

suc•tion |sŭk'shən| *n.* A difference of pressure that causes a liquid or gas to flow into a space or that causes a solid object to adhere to a surface.

Su•dan |so͞o dăn'|. A country in Africa, located south of Egypt with a coastline along the Red Sea. Population, 17,324,000. Capital, Khartoum. —**Su'da•nese'** |so͞od'n ēz'| *or* |-ēs'| *adj. & n.*

sud•den |sŭd'n| *adj.* **1.** Happening without warning; unforeseen: *a sudden burst of temper; a sudden rain squall.* **2.** Hasty: *a sudden departure.* **3.** Rapid; quick; swift: *sudden changes.* —**sud'den•ly** *adv.* —**sud'den•ness** *n.*

suds |sŭdz| *pl.n.* **1.** Soapy water. **2.** Foam; lather.

sue |so͞o| *v.* **sued, su•ing. 1.** To institute legal proceedings: *He sued for his right of way.* **2.** To bring legal action against (a person) in order to satisfy a claim or grievance: *He sued her.* **3.** To make an appeal or entreaty: *sue for peace.*

suede, also **suède** |swād| *n.* **1.** Leather rubbed on the flesh side to give it a soft, velvety nap. **2.** Also **suede cloth.** Woven or knitted cloth having the look and feel of such leather. —***modifier:*** *a suede jacket; suede gloves.* [SEE NOTE]

su•et |so͞o'ĭt| *n.* The hard, fatty tissue around the kidneys of cattle and sheep, used in cooking and in making tallow.

Su•ez Canal |so͞o ĕz'| *or* |so͞o'ĕz'|. A canal in northeastern Egypt connecting the Mediterranean Sea with the Red Sea.

suf•fer |sŭf'ər| *v.* **1.** To feel pain or distress: *suffer from disease.* **2.** To undergo or sustain (an injury, loss, hardship, etc.): *suffer pain; suffer defeat.* **3.** To be or appear at a disadvantage: *The film suffered from a poor sound track.* **4.** To endure or bear; stand: *They cannot suffer much heat.* **5.** To permit; allow: *"Suffer little children to come unto me, and forbid them not"* (Luke 18:16). —**suf'fer•er** *n.*

suf•fer•ance |sŭf'ər əns| *n.* Sanction or permission implied or given by failure to prohibit.

suf•fice |sə fīs'| *v.* **suf•ficed, suf•fic•ing. 1.** To meet present needs; be sufficient: *The food will suffice until next week.* **2.** To be sufficient or adequate for: *enough water to suffice them for three days.* **3.** To be capable or competent.

suf•fi•cient |sə fĭsh'ənt| *adj.* As much as is needed; enough; adequate: *sufficient reasons for*

suede

The word **suede** *comes from* Suède, *the French name for Sweden. The brushed velvety finish given to kidskin seems to have originated in Sweden; in France gloves made of this leather were called* gants de Suède, *"gloves of Sweden"; this was borrowed into English as* **suede.**

ă pat/ā pay/â care/ä father/ĕ pet/ ē be/ĭ pit/ī pie/î fierce/ŏ pot/ ō go/ô paw, for/oi oil/o͝o book/ o͞o boot/ou out/ŭ cut/û fur/ *th* the/th thin/hw which/zh vision/ ə ago, item, pencil, atom, circus

going. —**suf•fi′cient•ly** *adv.* —**suf•fi′cien•cy** *n.*

suf•fix |sŭf′ĭks′| *n.* In grammar, an affix added to the end of a word serving to form a new word or indicate a grammatical function by adding an inflectional ending; for example, *-ation* in *civilization* and *-es* in *boxes* are suffixes.

suf•fo•cate |sŭf′ə kāt′| *v.* **suf•fo•cat•ed, suf•fo•cat•ing. 1.** To kill or destroy by cutting off from oxygen. **2.** To choke; smother. **3.** To cause to suffer discomfort by or as by cutting off a supply of air. **4.** To die from a lack of oxygen. —**suf′fo•ca′tion** *n.*

suf•frage |sŭf′rĭj| *n.* The right to vote.

suf•fuse |sə fyo͞oz′| *v.* **suf•fused, suf•fus•ing.** To spread through or over, as with liquid, color, or light: *A greenish haze suffused the woods.*

sug•ar |sho͝og′ər| *n.* **1.** Any member of a class of crystalline carbohydrates, such as sucrose, glucose, or lactose, that dissolve in water and have a characteristic sweet taste. **2.** Sucrose, a widely used member of this class. —*v.* To coat or sweeten with sugar. —***modifier:*** *a sugar bowl.* [SEE NOTE on p. 787]

sugar beet. A type of beet with whitish roots from which sugar is obtained. [SEE PICTURE]

sugar cane. A tall grass grown in warm regions, having thick, juicy stems that are one of the chief sources of sugar. [SEE PICTURE]

sug•ar•y |sho͝og′ə rē| *adj.* **sug•ar•i•er, sug•ar•i•est.** Containing or resembling sugar.

sug•gest |səg jĕst′| *or* |sə-| *v.* **1.** To offer for consideration or action: *suggest that the books be stored.* **2.** To bring or call to mind by association; evoke: *a cavern that suggests a cathedral.* **3.** To make evident indirectly; imply: *A poet may suggest feelings rather than state them.*

sug•ges•tion |səg jĕs′chən| *or* |sə-| *n.* **1.** The act of suggesting. **2.** Something suggested: *follow her suggestion.* **3.** A trace; a touch.

sug•ges•tive |səg jĕs′tĭv| *or* |sə-| *adj.* Tending to imply something improper or indecent: *a suggestive comment.* —**sug•ges′tive•ly** *adv.*

su•i•ci•dal |so͞o′ĭ sīd′l| *adj.* **1.** Of suicide. **2.** Dangerous to oneself; self-destructive; ruinous: *a suicidal plan to climb the mountain alone.*

su•i•cide |so͞o′ĭ sīd′| *n.* **1.** The act or an instance of intentionally killing oneself. **2.** Someone who commits suicide.

suit |so͞ot| *n.* **1.** A set of outer garments to be worn together, especially a coat or jacket that comes with matching trousers or skirt. **2.** A garment, outfit, or costume worn for a special activity or purpose: *a gym suit.* **3.** One of the four sets, spades, clubs, hearts, or diamonds, in a deck of playing cards. **4.** Any court action; a lawsuit. —*v.* **1.** To meet the requirements of: *The house suited the old couple.* **2. a.** To be appropriate or acceptable for: *The song suited the occasion.* **b.** To make appropriate: *They suited the play to their audience.* **3.** To please; satisfy: *It suits our friends to play tennis.*

suit•a•ble |so͞o′tə bəl| *adj.* Appropriate to a given purpose or occasion: *suitable shelter; suitable clothes.* —**suit′a•bil′i•ty** *n.* —**suit′a•bly** *adv.*

suit•case |so͞ot′kās′| *n.* A usually flat, rectangular piece of luggage.

suite |swēt| *n.* **1.** A series of connected rooms used as a living unit. **2.** A staff of attendants; a retinue. **3.** |*also* so͞ot|. A set of matched furniture pieces. **4.** An instrumental musical composition consisting of a set of pieces in the same or closely related keys. ¶ *These sound alike* **suite, sweet.**

suit•or |so͞o′tər| *n.* **1.** Someone who brings suit in a court. **2.** A man who is courting a woman.

Suk•koth |so͝ok′əs| *n.* A form of the word **Succoth.**

Su•la•we•si |so͞o′lə wä′sē|. An island of Indonesia.

sul•fate |sŭl′fāt′| *n.* A salt or ester of sulfuric acid.

sul•fide |sŭl′fīd′| *n.* A compound of sulfur having a valence of −2 and another element.

sul•fite |sŭl′fīt′| *n.* A salt or ester of sulfurous acid.

sul•fur |sŭl′fər| *n.* Symbol **S** One of the elements, a pale-yellow substance that occurs in nature in both free and combined forms and that has several solid forms in which it occurs at normal temperatures. Atomic number 16; atomic weight 32.064; valences −2, +2, +4, +6; melting point 112.8°C or 119.0°C, depending on the form; boiling point 444.6°C.

sul•fur•ic |sŭl fyo͝or′ĭk| *adj.* Of or containing sulfur, especially with a valence of +6.

sulfuric acid. A strong acid composed of sulfur, hydrogen, and oxygen and having the formula H_2SO_4.

sul•fur•ous |sŭl′fər əs| *or* |sŭl fyo͝or′-| *adj.* **1.** Of or containing sulfur, especially with a valence of +4. **2.** Characteristic of or given off by burning sulfur: *sulfurous vapors.*

sulk |sŭlk| *v.* To be sullenly aloof or withdrawn. —*n.* A mood or display of sulking.

sul•len |sŭl′ən| *adj.* Showing a brooding ill humor or resentment; morose; sulky: *a sullen disposition.* —**sul′len•ly** *adv.* —**sul′len•ness** *n.*

sul•ly |sŭl′ē| *v.* **sul•lied, sul•ly•ing, sul•lies.** To tarnish; stain: *sullied his reputation.*

sul•phur |sŭl′fər| *n.* A form of the word **sulfur.** [SEE NOTE]

sul•tan |sŭl′tən| *n.* The ruler of a Moslem country.

sul•tan•a |sŭl tăn′ə| *or* |-tä′nə| *n.* The wife, mother, sister, or daughter of a sultan.

sul•tan•ate |sŭl′tə nāt′| *n.* The rank or domain of a sultan.

sul•try |sŭl′trē| *adj.* **sul•tri•er, sul•tri•est.** Very hot and humid: *a sultry summer day.*

sum |sŭm| *n.* **1.** A number obtained as a result of addition. **2.** The whole amount, quantity, or number: *the sum of our knowledge.* **3.** An amount of money: *the sum of $10,000.* **4.** An arithmetic problem: *do sums.* —*v.* **summed, sum•ming.** To find the sum of (a set of numbers); add. —***phrasal verb.*** **sum up.** To summarize. ¶ *These sound alike* **sum, some.**

su•mac, also **su•mach** |so͞o′măk′| *or* |sho͞o′-| *n.* Any of several shrubs or small trees having leaves with leaflets in a featherlike arrangement and pointed clusters of small, usually red berries. One kind, the **poison sumac,** has greenish-white berries and can cause an itching rash when touched.

Su•ma•tra |so͞o mä′trə|. A large island of Indonesia, in the Indian Ocean south of the Malay Peninsula. —**Su•ma′tran** *adj. & n.*

Su•me•ri•an |so͞o mîr′ē ən| *or* |-mĕr′-| *n.* **1.** A

sugar beet

sugar cane

sulphur

The spelling **sulphur** *is the standard British spelling; it is sometimes used in American writings of a nontechnical kind, especially (as in the word* **sulphur-bottom***) when there is no direct reference to the element. In American technical usage, the only acceptable spelling is* **sulfur.**

sundial

sundry/sunder

Sunder *was Old English* sundrian, *"to put apart, to separate." Closely related is Old English* syndrig, *"apart, separate," which came to mean "various" and became* **sundry** *in Modern English.*

sunflower
Above: Flower
Below: Child holding seed pod

ă pat/ā pay/â care/ä father/ĕ pet/ē be/ĭ pit/ī pie/î fierce/ŏ pot/ō go/ô paw, for/oi oil/ŏŏ book/ōō boot/ou out/ŭ cut/û fur/*th* the/th thin/hw which/zh vision/ə ago, item, pencil, atom, circus

member of an ancient people who lived in Mesopotamia around 3000 B.C. **2.** The language of this people. *—adj.* Of the Sumerians or their language.

sum•ma cum lau•de |sōōm′ə kōōm lou′dā| *or* |sŭm′ə kŭm lô′dē|. With the greatest praise. This expression was originally a Latin phrase.

sum•ma•ri•ly |sə mâr′ə lē| *or* |sŭm′ər ə-| *adv.* In a summary manner; speedily and without ceremony: *summarily dismissed.*

sum•ma•rize |sŭm′ə rīz′| *v.* **sum•ma•rized, sum•ma•riz•ing.** To make a summary of; restate briefly. —**sum′ma•ri•za′tion** *n.*

sum•ma•ry |sŭm′ə rē| *n., pl.* **sum•ma•ries.** A condensation of the substance of something larger: *a summary of our findings.* *—adj.* **1.** Presented in condensed form; brief. **2.** Done speedily and without ceremony: *a summary dismissal.* ¶ *These sound alike* **summary, summery.**

sum•ma•tion |sə mā′shən| *n.* **1. a.** The act or process of finding a sum; addition. **b.** A number obtained by adding; a sum. **2.** A summary: *a summation of life.*

sum•mer |sŭm′ər| *n.* The season of the year between spring and autumn, lasting from the June solstice to the next equinox in the Northern Hemisphere and from the December solstice to the next equinox in the Southern Hemisphere. —***modifier:*** *summer flowers.*

sum•mer•time |sŭm′ər tīm′| *n.* The summer season.

sum•mer•y |sŭm′ə rē| *adj.* Of, like, or suitable for summer: *summery weather.* ¶ *These sound alike* **summery, summary.**

sum•mit |sŭm′ĭt| *n.* **1.** The highest point or part; the top, especially of a mountain. **2.** The highest level of government official. —***modifier:*** *a summit conference.*

sum•mon |sŭm′ən| *v.* **1.** To call together; convene: *summon a meeting of the delegates.* **2.** To send for; request to appear: *summoned her to the principal's office.* **3.** To order (someone) to appear in court. **4.** To call forth; muster: *summon up all my will power.*

sum•mons |sŭm′ənz| *n.* **1.** A document ordering a defendant, witness, or juror to appear in court. **2.** A call or order to appear or do something.

sump•tu•ous |sŭmp′chōō əs| *adj.* Of a size or splendor suggesting great expense; lavish: *a sumptuous temple.* —**sump′tu•ous•ly** *adv.* —**sump′tu•ous•ness** *n.*

sun |sŭn| *n.* **1.** The star around which all of the planets and other bodies of the solar system are in orbit and which supplies the energy that sustains life on the earth. It has a diameter of about 864,000 miles, a mass about 330,000 times that of the earth, and is at an average distance of about 93 million miles from the earth. **2.** Any star, especially one that has a system of planets. **3.** The radiation given off by the sun, especially infrared light, visible light, and ultraviolet light. *—v.* **sunned, sun•ning. 1.** To expose to the sun, as to dry, warm, or tan. **2.** To bask in the sun; sun-bathe. ¶ *These sound alike* **sun, son.**

Sun. Sunday.

sun-bathe |sŭn′bāth′| *v.* **sun-bathed, sun-bath•ing.** To expose the body to the sun.

sun•beam |sŭn′bēm′| *n.* A ray of sunlight.

sun•bon•net |sŭn′bŏn′ĭt| *n.* A large bonnet having a wide brim and a capelike flap in back to protect the neck from the sun.

sun•burn |sŭn′bûrn′| *n.* An inflammation or blistering of the skin caused by overexposure to direct sunlight. *—v.* **sun•burned** or **sun•burnt** |sŭn′bûrnt′|, **sun•burn•ing.** To be affected by sunburn.

sun•dae |sŭn′dē| *or* |-dā′| *n.* Ice cream with toppings such as syrup, fruit, nuts, etc.

Sun•day |sŭn′dē| *or* |-dā′| *n.* The first day of the week, after Saturday and before Monday. —***modifier:*** *a Sunday morning.*

sun•der |sŭn′dər| *v.* To break apart; divide. [SEE NOTE]

sun•di•al |sŭn′dī′əl| *n.* An instrument that indicates the time of day by measuring the angle of the sun with a pointer that casts a shadow on a dial. [SEE PICTURE]

sun•down |sŭn′doun′| *n.* The time of sunset.

sun•dry |sŭn′drē| *adj.* Several; miscellaneous; various: *an audience consisting of experts, critics, and sundry amateurs.* [SEE NOTE]

Idiom. **all and sundry.** One and all; everybody.

sun•fish |sŭn′fĭsh′| *n., pl.* **-fish** or **-fish•es. 1.** Any of several small North American freshwater fishes having a flattened, often brightly colored body. **2.** Also **ocean sunfish.** A very large ocean fish with a rounded, short-tailed body.

sun•flow•er |sŭn′flou′ər| *n.* A tall plant having large flowers with yellow rays and dark centers and bearing edible, nutlike seeds that are rich in oil. [SEE PICTURE]

sung |sŭng|. **1.** A past tense of **sing. 2.** The past participle of **sing.**

sun•glass•es |sŭn′glăs′ĭz| *or* |-glä′sĭz| *pl.n.* Eyeglasses, usually with colored or tinted lenses, worn to protect the eyes from the sun's glare.

sunk |sŭngk|. A past tense and a past participle of **sink.**

sunk•en |sŭng′kən|. A past participle of **sink.** *—adj.* **1.** Fallen in or depressed: *sunken eyes.* **2.** Beneath the surface of the water or ground; submerged: *sunken treasure.* **3.** Below the surrounding level: *a sunken bathtub.*

sun lamp. 1. A lamp having a spectrum close to that of sunlight, used in therapeutic and cosmetic treatments. **2.** A very bright lamp equipped with a reflector, used in photography.

sun•light |sŭn′līt′| *n.* The light of the sun.

sun•lit |sŭn′lĭt′| *adj.* Illuminated by the sun: *a sunlit prairie.*

sun•ny |sŭn′ē| *adj.* **sun•ni•er, sun•ni•est. 1.** Full of sunshine: *a sunny day.* **2.** Cheerful: *a sunny mood.* ¶ *These sound alike* **sunny, sonny.**

sun•rise |sŭn′rīz′| *n.* **1.** The daily first appearance of the sun above the eastern horizon. **2.** The time at which this occurs.

sun•set |sŭn′sĕt′| *n.* **1.** The daily disappearance of the sun below the western horizon. **2.** The time at which this occurs.

sun•shade |sŭn′shād′| *n.* Something, as a parasol, used as protection from the sun.

sun•shine |sŭn′shīn′| *n.* **1.** The light of the sun; sunlight. **2.** Happiness or cheerfulness.

sun•spot |sŭn′spŏt′| *n.* Any of the dark spots that appear on the surface of the sun and that are associated with strong magnetic fields.

sun•stroke |sŭn′strōk′| *n.* A severe form of heat

stroke caused by exposure to the sun.
sun tan. A darkening of the skin resulting from exposure to the sun.
sun•tan |sŭn′tăn′| *n.* A form of the phrase **sun tan.**
sun•up |sŭn′ŭp′| *n.* The time of sunrise.
sup |sŭp| *v.* **supped, sup•ping.** To eat supper.
su•per |**sōō**′pər|. *Informal. n.* A superintendent in a building. *—adj.* Great: *a super idea.*
super–. A prefix meaning: **1.** Placement above, over, or outside: **superimpose. 2.** Superiority of size, quality, or degree: **superhuman. 3.** A degree exceeding a norm: **supersonic.** [SEE NOTE]
su•per•a•bun•dant |sōō′pər ə **bŭn′**dənt| *adj.* More than sufficient; excessive: *superabundant zeal.* **—su′per•a•bun′dance** *n.*
su•perb |sōō **pûrb′**| *or* |sə-| *adj.* **1.** Of unusual quality; excellent: *a superb meal.* **2.** Majestic; imposing: *a superb view.* **—su•perb′ly** *adv.*
su•per•charge |**sōō**′pər chärj′| *v.* **su•per•charged, su•per•charg•ing.** To increase the power of (an internal-combustion engine) by forcing the fuel mixture into the cylinders under pressure that is greater than normal.
su•per•charg•er |**sōō**′pər chär′jər| *n.* A blower or fan, usually powered by the engine, that forces air at high pressure into the intake of an internal-combustion engine.
su•per•cil•i•ous |sōō′pər **sĭl′**ē əs| *adj.* Arrogantly superior; haughty: *a supercilious smile.* **—su′per•cil′i•ous•ly** *adv.*
su•per•con•duc•tiv•i•ty |sōō′pər kŏn′dək **tĭv′**ĭ-tē| *n.* The complete loss of electrical resistance in certain metals and alloys at temperatures near absolute zero.
su•per•con•duc•tor |sōō′pər kən **dŭk′**tər| *n.* A metal or alloy that can be made superconductive by cooling it to a very low temperature.
su•per•fi•cial |sōō′pər **fĭsh′**əl| *adj.* **1.** Of, on, near, or affecting the surface: *a superficial wound.* **2.** Concerned only with what is apparent or obvious; shallow: *a superficial person.* **3.** Not deeply penetrating; trivial: *a superficial knowledge of history.* **—su′per•fi′cial•ly** *adv.*
su•per•fi•ci•al•i•ty |sōō′pər fĭsh′ē **ăl′**ĭ tē| *n., pl.* **su•per•fi•ci•al•i•ties. 1.** The quality or condition of being superficial. **2.** Something superficial.
su•per•flu•i•ty |sōō′pər **flōō′**ĭ tē| *n., pl.* **su•per•flu•i•ties. 1.** The quality or condition of being superfluous. **2.** Something superfluous.
su•per•flu•ous |sōō **pûr′**flōō əs| *adj.* Beyond what is required or sufficient; extra: *Many items on the budget are superfluous.* **—su•per′flu•ous•ly** *adv.* **—su•per′flu•ous•ness** *n.*
su•per•heat |sōō′pər **hēt′**| *v.* **1.** To heat (steam or other vapor that is not in contact with its liquid) above the temperature at which it evaporates at a given pressure. **2.** To heat (a liquid) above its boiling point at a given pressure without allowing it to vaporize. *—n.* |**sōō′**pər hēt′|. The heat that something absorbs when superheated.
su•per•high frequency |**sōō**′pər hī′|. Any radio-wave frequency between 3,000 and 30,000 megahertz.
su•per•high•way |sōō′pər **hī′**wā′| *n.* A large highway for high-speed traffic.
su•per•hu•man |sōō′pər **hyōō′**mən| *adj.* **1.** Divine; supernatural: *superhuman beings.* **2.** Beyond ordinary or normal human ability.
su•per•im•pose |sōō′pər ĭm **pōz′**| *v.* **su•per•im•posed, su•per•im•pos•ing.** To lay or place over or upon something else.
su•per•in•tend |sōō′pər ĭn **tĕnd′**| *v.* To have charge of; oversee; manage.
su•per•in•ten•dence |sōō′pər ĭn **tĕn′**dəns| *n.* The act or duty of superintending.
su•per•in•ten•dent |sōō′pər ĭn **tĕn′**dənt| *n.* A person who supervises or is in charge of something.
su•pe•ri•or |sə **pîr′**ē ər| *or* |sōō-| *adj.* **1.** High or higher in order, degree, or rank: *a superior court; a superior officer.* **2.** High or higher in quality: *a superior product.* **3.** High or higher in ability, intelligence, etc.: *a superior technician.* **4.** Far greater in comparison: *She is intellectually superior to them.* **5.** Disdainful or conceited; snobbish: *What makes him feel so superior?* **6.** Situated over or above; higher. *—n.* **1.** Someone who surpasses another in rank or quality. **2.** The head of a monastery, convent, etc.
Superior, Lake. The largest of the Great Lakes, situated between the United States and Canada.
su•pe•ri•or•i•ty |sə pîr′ē **ôr′**ĭ tē| *or* |**-ŏr′-**| *or* |sōō-| *n.* **1.** The fact or quality of being superior. **2.** Disdain or conceit; haughtiness.
su•per•la•tive |sə **pûr′**lə tĭv| *or* |sōō-| *adj.* Of the highest order, quality, or degree: *a superlative specimen.* *—n.* **1.** In grammar, the form of an adjective or adverb that indicates the greatest quality, quantity, etc., expressed by the adjective or adverb, as in the sentences *My house is the biggest on the block, I have the least amount of money,* and *She left earliest.* Superlatives are usually formed by the addition of the ending *-est* to the adjective or adverb, as in "fewest" and "earliest." In some cases, as in " biggest," the last consonant is doubled. Some superlatives are completely different from the original adjective or adverb. For example, the superlatives of the adjectives "good" and "bad" are "best" and "worst," and the superlative of the adverb "well" is "best." Many adjectives do not have a true superlative; the superlatives of such adjectives are formed by the placement of the word "most" before the adjective, as in the sentence *This seat is the most comfortable on the bus.* **2.** An adjective or adverb in the superlative. **—su•per′la•tive•ly** *adv.* **—su•per′la•tive•ness** *n.*
su•per•man |**sōō′**pər măn′| *n., pl.* **-men** |-mĕn′|. A man of superhuman powers.
su•per•mar•ket |**sōō′**pər mär′kĭt| *n.* A large self-service retail store selling food and household goods. *—modifier: a supermarket chain.*
su•per•nat•u•ral |sōō′pər **năch′**ər əl| *or* |**-năch′**rəl| *adj.* Outside the natural world; spiritual or divine: *supernatural powers.* *—n.* **the supernatural.** That which is supernatural.
su•per•no•va |sōō′pər **nō′**və| *n., pl.* **su•per•no•vae** |sōō′pər **nō′**vē′| or **su•per•no•vas.** A rare happening in which a star undergoes an extremely large explosion and becomes for a short time a very bright object radiating vast amounts of energy. [SEE NOTE]
su•per•pow•er |**sōō′**pər pou′ər| *n.* A powerful and influential nation; especially, a nuclear power that dominates its satellites and allies.
su•per•sat•u•rate |sōō′pər **săch′**ə rāt′| *v.* **su•**

super–, etc.
The prefix **super-** *is from Latin* super, *"above." The comparative of* super *was* superior, *"upper, higher," also "greater, better"; this was borrowed into English as* **superior**. *The superlative of* super *was* suprēmus, *"highest," from which we have* **supreme**. Super *is descended from the Indo-European preposition* uper, *"over, above";* uper *appears also in Old English as* ofer, *becoming* **over** *in Modern English, and in Greek as* huper, *"over, beyond," which was borrowed into English as the prefix* **hyper-**.

supernova
Supernovae *recorded in the past have been so bright that, although they are known to have been at great distances from the earth, they were visible in the daytime sky.*

per•sat•u•rat•ed, su•per•sat•u•rat•ing. To cause (a solution, as of a chemical) to be more concentrated than is normally possible under given conditions of temperature or pressure.

su•per•script |so͞o′pər skrĭpt′| *n.* A character written or printed just above and to one side of another character; for example, the numbers to the right of the word *sock* in *sock*[1] and *sock*[2] are superscripts.

su•per•sede |so͞o′pər **sēd′**| *v.* **su•per•sed•ed, su•per•sed•ing. 1.** To take the place of; replace or succeed: *Electric light bulbs superseded candles and kerosene as the major source of indoor light.* **2.** To cause to be set aside or displaced: *Supreme Court decisions supersede those of lower courts.*

su•per•set |so͞o′pər sĕt′| *n.* A set that contains another set. For example, if *B* is a subset of *A*, then *A* is a superset of *B*.

su•per•son•ic |so͞o′pər **sŏn′**ĭk| *adj.* Having or caused by a speed greater than the speed of sound in a given medium.

supersonic transport. An aircraft designed to carry passengers or cargo and capable of flight at speeds exceeding the speed of sound.

su•per•star |so͞o′pər stär′| *n.* A widely acclaimed performer, as in films, music, or sports.

su•per•sti•tion |so͞o′pər **stĭsh′**ən| *n.* **1.** A belief that some action not logically related to a course of events influences its outcome. For example, the belief that walking under a ladder brings bad luck is a superstition. **2.** Any belief, practice, or rite unreasonably dependent on magic, chance, or dogma: *Some primitive midwives rely more on superstition than on medical fact.*

su•per•sti•tious |so͞o′pər **stĭsh′**əs| *adj.* **1.** Inclined to believe in or be swayed by superstition: *a superstitious person.* **2.** Of or proceeding from superstition: *a superstitious dread.* —**su′per•sti′tious•ly** *adv.* —**su′per•sti′tious•ness** *n.*

su•per•struc•ture |so͞o′pər strŭk′chər| *n.* **1.** Any structure built on top of another structure. **2.** The part of a building or other structure that rests on the foundation.

su•per•vise |so͞o′pər vīz′| *v.* **su•per•vised, su•per•vis•ing.** To direct and inspect the action, work, or performance of.

su•per•vi•sion |so͞o′pər **vĭzh′**ən| *n.* The act or process of supervising; control; direction.

su•per•vi•sor |so͞o′pər vī′zər| *n.* A person who supervises.

su•per•vi•so•ry |so͞o′pər **vī′**zə rē| *adj.* Of supervision or a supervisor: *a supervisory function.*

su•pine |so͞o **pīn′**| *or* |so͞o′pīn′| *adj.* **1.** Lying on the back or having the face upward. **2.** Not inclined to act; lethargic; passive: *the supine governor of the state.*

sup•per |**sŭp′**ər| *n.* **1.** An evening meal, especially a light evening meal served when dinner is eaten at midday. **2.** A social gathering at which supper is served. —***modifier:*** *a supper party.*

sup•plant |sə **plănt′**| *or* |-**plänt′**| *v.* To take the place of; supersede: *The new quarterback supplanted the injured player.*

sup•ple |**sŭp′**əl| *adj.* **sup•pler, sup•plest. 1.** Easily bent: *supple leather.* **2.** Bending easily; agile; limber: *a supple body.* **3.** Yielding or changing easily; adaptable: *a supple mind.* —**sup′ple•ly** *adv.* —**sup′ple•ness** *n.*

sup•ple•ment |**sŭp′**lə mənt| *n.* **1.** Something added to complete a thing or make up for a deficiency: *This book is a supplement to the regular required reading.* **2.** A section added to a newspaper, book, document, etc., to give further information. **3.** An angle or arc whose measure is such that when it is added to the measure of a given angle or arc the sum is 180 degrees. —*v.* |**sŭp′**lə mĕnt′|. To provide a supplement to: *The teacher supplemented our reading with films.*

sup•ple•men•ta•ry |sŭp′lə **mĕn′**tə rē| *adj.* Added or serving as a supplement; additional: *a supplementary theory.*

supplementary angles. A pair of angles whose sum is 180 degrees.

sup•pli•ant |**sŭp′**lē ənt| *n.* A person who asks humbly or beseeches. —*adj.* Asking humbly and earnestly; beseeching: *a suppliant beggar.*

sup•pli•cant |**sŭp′**lĭ kənt| *n.* A suppliant.

sup•pli•cate |**sŭp′**lĭ kāt′| *v.* **sup•pli•cat•ed, sup•pli•cat•ing. 1.** To beseech: *supplicate forgiveness.* **2.** To make an earnest appeal to: *supplicate the gods.* —**sup′pli•ca′tion** *n.*

sup•ply[1] |sə **plī′**| *v.* **sup•plied, sup•ply•ing, sup•plies. 1.** To make available for use; provide: *Vast forests supply trees for lumber.* **2.** To furnish or equip with what is needed or lacking: *Supply capital letters where needed in the following paragraph.* **3.** To fill sufficiently; satisfy: *supply a need.* —*n.* **1.** The act of supplying: *the supply of raw materials to manufacturers.* **2.** An amount available for a given use; stock: *Our supply of chocolate is low.* **3.** Often **supplies.** Materials or provisions stored and dispensed when needed. —***modifier:*** *a supply wagon.* —**sup•pli′er** *n.*

sup•ply[2] |**sŭp′**lē| *adv.* In a supple manner.

sup•port |sə **pôrt′**| *or* |-**pōrt′**| *v.* **1.** To exert a force that counterbalances the weight or downward load of (a structure or object): *the towers that support a bridge. A helicopter is supported by the action of its rotor.* **2.** To hold in position; prevent from falling, sinking, or slipping. **3.** To be capable of bearing; withstand: *He cannot support the cold.* **4.** To provide for or maintain by supplying with money or other necessities: *She supports two children.* **5.** To corroborate or substantiate: *The evidence seems to support his theory.* **6.** To aid the cause of by approving, favoring, or advocating: *support a political candidate.* **7.** To act in a subordinate role to (a leading actor). —*n.* **1. a.** The act or process of supporting. **b.** The condition of being supported. **2.** Someone or something that supports.

sup•port•a•ble |sə **pôr′**tə bəl| *or* |-**pōr′**-| *adj.* Bearable; endurable. —**sup•port′a•bly** *adv.*

sup•port•er |sə **pôr′**tər| *or* |-**pōr′**-| *n.* **1.** Someone or something that supports. **2.** A person who favors, sides with, or backs an individual or group or an action or cause: *the candidate's loyal supporters.* **3.** A cloth band or elastic garment worn to support some part of the body.

sup•pose |sə **pōz′**| *v.* **sup•posed, sup•pos•ing. 1.** To be inclined to think, assume: *I suppose you're right, as usual.* **2.** To assume to be true for the sake of an argument or illustration: *Suppose the earth's axis were not tilted at all.* **3.** To consider as a suggestion: *Suppose we stop and think a minute.* **4.** To expect; intend: *The rocket behaved exactly as it was supposed to.*

sup•posed |sə **pōzd′**| *adj.* Presumed to be true

ă pat/ā pay/â care/ä father/ĕ pet/ ē be/ĭ pit/ī pie/î fierce/ŏ pot/ ō go/ô paw, for/oi oil/o͝o book/ o͞o boot/ou out/ŭ cut/û fur/ *th* the/th thin/hw which/zh vision/ ə ago, item, pencil, atom, circus

or actual; reputed: *the supposed model for a fictional character.* —**sup•pos'ed•ly** |sə pō'zĭd lē| *adv.*

sup•po•si•tion |sŭp'ə **zĭsh'**ən| *n.* **1.** The mental process of supposing; guesswork: *an argument based on supposition, not fact.* **2.** Something supposed: *a supposition accepted tentatively.*

sup•pos•i•to•ry |sə **pŏz'**ĭ tôr'ē| *or* |-tōr'ē| *n., pl.* **sup•pos•i•to•ries.** A medication prepared in a solid form, designed to be inserted into a body cavity other than the mouth, especially into the rectum.

sup•press |sə **prĕs'**| *v.* **1.** To hold back; check: *suppress an impulse; suppress bleeding from a wound.* **2.** To put an end to forcibly; subdue; crush: *suppress a rebellion.* **3.** To restrict the freedom or activities of: *The government was accused of suppressing the opposition party.* **4.** To keep from being revealed or published: *suppress news of a military defeat.*

sup•pres•sion |sə **prĕsh'**ən| *n.* **1.** The act or process of suppressing. **2.** The condition of being suppressed.

sup•pu•rate |**sŭp'**yə rāt'| *v.* **sup•pu•rat•ed, sup•pu•rat•ing.** To form or fill with pus: *The infected wound suppurated.* —**sup'pu•ra'tion** *n.*

su•pra•re•nal gland |sōō'prə **rē'**nəl|. An adrenal gland.

su•prem•a•cy |sə **prĕm'**ə sē| *n., pl.* **su•prem•a•cies.** The condition or quality of being supreme: *a struggle for supremacy between two colonial powers.*

su•preme |sə **prēm'**| *adj.* **1.** Greatest in rank, power, or authority; dominant over others: *a supreme commander.* **2.** Highest in quality or achievement: *the supreme chef of his day.* **3.** Highest in degree or intensity: *supreme madness.* **4.** Outstanding; prominent: *a supreme example.* **5.** Ultimate; utmost: *the supreme sacrifice.* —**su•preme'ly** *adv.*

Supreme Being. God.

Supreme Court. **1.** The highest Federal court in the United States, consisting of nine justices. **2.** The highest court in a state within the United States.

supt., Supt. superintendent.

sur•charge |**sûr'**chärj'| *n.* **1.** An extra charge added to the usual amount or rate. **2.** An excessive burden; an overload: *words carrying a surcharge of emotion.* **3.** A new value printed over the face value of a stamp. —*v.* **sur•charged, sur•charg•ing.** **1.** To charge extra. **2.** To overburden. **3.** To print a surcharge on (a stamp).

sur•coat |**sûr'**kōt'| *n.* **1.** An outer coat or robe. **2.** A tunic worn by a knight over his armor in olden times. [SEE PICTURE]

surd |sûrd| *n.* A mathematical expression written as a sum that contains at least one indicated irrational root of a number, as $1 + \sqrt{3}$.

sure |shŏŏr| *adj.* **sur•er, sur•est.** **1.** Feeling certainty about someone or something; certain: *I'm sure he's coming tonight. Let's not start celebrating our success until we're sure of it.* **2.** Bound or destined to happen: *His failure to score meant sure defeat for the team.* **3.** Steady; unwavering; firm: *a sure grip.* **4.** Dependable; reliable: *The surest way of seeing that something gets done right is to do it yourself.* —*adv. Informal.* Surely; certainly. —**sure'ness** *n.*

Idioms. **for sure.** Certainly; without a doubt: *We lost the last game, but we're winning today for sure.* **make sure.** To make certain: *I think she's at home, but we'd better make sure before going.* **to be sure.** **1.** Certainly; without a doubt; indeed: *Can you really do this job? To be sure I can.* **2.** Admittedly: *The idea is brilliant, to be sure, but we don't have the money to back it up right now.*

sure-foot•ed |**shŏŏr'fŏŏt'**ĭd| *adj.* Not likely to stumble or fall: *Sure-footed mules are used on the narrow mountain trails.* —**sure'-foot'ed•ness** *n.*

sure•ly |**shŏŏr'**lē| *adv.* **1.** Certainly; without doubt: *I don't know how long I waited—surely an hour and a half.* **2.** With confidence or assurance; unhesitatingly: *The baker kneaded the dough surely in his hands.* **3.** Steadily: *Slowly but surely, the table rose from the floor.*

sure•ty |**shŏŏr'**ĭ tē| *n., pl.* **sure•ties.** **1.** Sureness; certainty. **2.** A formal promise to take responsibility in case of loss or damage; a guarantee. **3.** A person who agrees to be responsible if another does not pay a debt or fulfill a promise.

surf |sûrf| *n.* **1.** The waves of the sea as they break upon a shore or reef. **2.** The white foam of breaking waves. —*v.* To ride on a surfboard. ¶*These sound alike* **surf, serf.** —**surf'er** *n.*

sur•face |**sûr'**fəs| *n.* **1. a.** The outermost layer or boundary of an object. **b.** The material such a layer or boundary is composed of. **2.** The outward appearance, as opposed to what is inside, deeper, or hidden: *On the surface, he was a mild-mannered man.* **3. a.** A continuous set of points in a space, having the property that every one of its intersections with a plane forms a line, curve, or in special cases a point. **b.** Such a set of points forming the boundary of a geometric figure. —*v.* **sur•faced, sur•fac•ing.** **1.** To form or shape the surface of, as by smoothing or leveling: *surface a board by planing.* **2.** To rise to the surface, as of a body of water. **3.** To appear after being hidden; emerge: *The police knew that sooner or later the fugitive would surface.*

surf•board |**sûrf'**bôrd'| *or* |-bōrd'| *n.* A long board with rounded ends, used for riding waves into shore. —*v.* To ride on a surfboard; to surf. [SEE PICTURE]

sur•feit |**sûr'**fĭt| *n.* **1.** Too much of something; an excess: *Since sea plants live in a surfeit of water, their problem is to find air.* **2.** Overindulgence, as in food or drink. —*v.* To feed or supply to excess; satiate.

surf•ing |**sûr'**fĭng| *n.* The sport of riding waves into shore on a surfboard.

surge |sûrj| *v.* **surged, surg•ing.** **1.** To move with a gathering force and fullness, as rolling waves do. **2.** To move or rush forcefully: *The mass of troops surged forward. Excitement surged through her veins.* **3.** To increase suddenly. —*n.* **1.** A powerful wave or swell of water. **2.** A heavy, swelling motion or pull like that caused by rolling waves: *the ponderous surge of the sea along the vessel's hull.* **3.** A sudden onrush or increase: *a surge of excitement; a surge of electric current.* ¶*These sound alike* **surge, serge.**

sur•geon |**sûr'**jən| *n.* A doctor specializing in surgery.

Surgeon General. *pl.* **Surgeons General.** **1.** The chief medical officer in the United States Public Health Service. **2.** The chief medical officer of

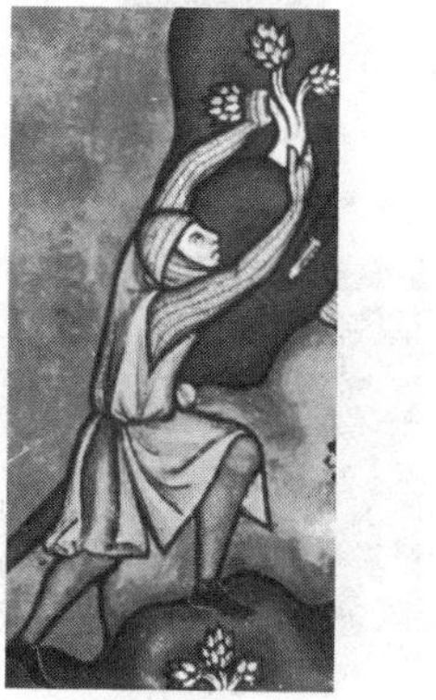

surcoat

surfboard

surplice

surrey

surveyor

the U.S. Army, Navy, or Air Force.

sur•ger•y |sûr′jə rē| *n., pl.* **sur•ger•ies.** **1.** The medical diagnosis and treatment of injury, deformity, or disease by physical manipulation or adjustment of the affected part or parts, often involving the cutting and reattachment of bodily tissues. **2.** An operating room, laboratory, or other facility used in such diagnosis and treatment. **3.** The skill or work of a surgeon.

sur•gi•cal |sûr′jĭ kəl| *adj.* **1.** Of surgeons or surgery: *normal surgical practice.* **2.** Used in surgery: *surgical instruments.* **3.** Resulting from or occurring after surgery: *surgical complications.* —**sur′gi•cal•ly** *adv.*

Su•ri•nam |so͝or′ə năm′|. A country on the northern coast of South America. Population, 410,000. Capital, Paramaribo.

sur•ly |sûr′lē| *adj.* **sur•li•er, sur•li•est.** Ill-humored; gruff; sullen. —**sur′li•ness** *n.*

sur•mise |sər mīz′| *v.* **sur•mised, sur•mis•ing.** To conclude on slight evidence; suppose; guess: *Astronomers surmise that there is life elsewhere in the universe.* —*n.* An idea based on slight evidence; a guess.

sur•mount |sər mount′| *v.* **1.** To climb up and over: *surmount a hill.* **2.** To overcome; triumph over: *surmount a weakness.* **3.** To be placed or located above; top: *A weathercock surmounted the steeple.* **4.** To rise on or beside; tower over: *the high-domed church that surmounts the square.*

sur•name |sûr′năm′| *n.* One's family name as distinguished from one's given name.

sur•pass |sər păs′| *or* |-päs′| *v.* **1.** To be better, greater, or stronger than; exceed: *The height of the redwood trees surpassed the highest ship masts.* **2.** To go beyond the limit or powers of: *a hidden world that surpasses description.*

sur•pass•ing |sər păs′ĭng| *or* |-pä′sĭng| *adj.* Excellent; superior: *surpassing skill as a hunter.*

sur•plice |sûr′plĭs| *n.* A loose-fitting white garment with full, flowing sleeves, worn over a clergyman's cassock in certain churches. [SEE PICTURE]

sur•plus |sûr′plŭs′| *or* |-pləs| *n.* An amount or quantity in excess of what is needed or used: *Brazil produces a large surplus of coffee for export.*

sur•prise |sər prīz′| *v.* **sur•prised, sur•pris•ing.** **1.** To come upon suddenly and without warning: *I surprised him in the attic, where he was searching about suspiciously.* **2.** To attack without warning. **3.** To cause to feel mild astonishment, as by being unexpected: *The low price of the antique surprised me.* **4.** To lead or induce by acting unexpectedly: *The abrupt question surprised him into admitting the truth.* —*n.* **1.** The act of coming upon someone suddenly and without warning. **2.** A sudden, unexpected attack. **3.** Something sudden and unexpected: *news that came as a surprise.* **4.** A feeling aroused by something sudden and unexpected; mild astonishment. —***modifier:*** *a surprise attack.*

sur•pris•ing |sər prī′zĭng| *adj.* Causing surprise; unexpected: *the surprising speed of elephants.* —**sur•pris′ing•ly** *adv.*

sur•re•al•ism |sə rē′ə lĭz′əm| *n.* A 20th-century literary and artistic movement attempting to depict the dreams and other products of the unconscious mind. —**sur•re′al•ist** *adj.* & *n.*

sur•re•al•is•tic |sə rē′ə lĭs′tĭk| *adj.* **1.** Of surrealism. **2.** Dreamlike; fantastic. —**sur•re′al•is′ti•cal•ly** *adv.*

sur•ren•der |sə rĕn′dər| *v.* **1.** To give up (something) to another on demand or under pressure: *surrendered the coast to the invading army.* **2.** To give oneself up, as to a pursuer or enemy. **3.** To give over entirely to an emotion, influence, or effort; devote without reservation: *surrendered himself to the magic spell of the book; surrender one's talents to a cause.* **4.** To agree to forgo or renounce; relinquish: *surrender a right.* —*n.* The act of surrendering: *preferred death to surrender.*

sur•rep•ti•tious |sûr′əp tĭsh′əs| *adj.* Done or acting in secret, so that others will not notice; stealthy: *a surreptitious glance at his watch.* —**sur′rep•ti′tious•ly** *adv.* —**sur′rep•ti′tious•ness** *n.*

sur•rey |sûr′ē| *or* |sŭr′ē| *n., pl.* **sur•reys.** A horse-drawn carriage with four wheels, two seats, and usually a fringed canopy on top. [SEE PICTURE]

sur•ro•gate |sûr′ə găt′| *or* |-gĭt| *or* |sŭr′-| *n.* **1.** Someone or something that takes the place of another; a substitute. **2.** A judge having jurisdiction over the probate of wills and settlement of estates. —***modifier:*** *a surrogate parent.*

sur•round |sə round′| *v.* **1.** To be or extend on all sides of; encircle: *the field of gravitation surrounding the earth; the hills that surround the town.* **2.** To shut in on all sides, barring escape; enclose with hostile forces. **3.** To cause to be encircled or closely attended.

sur•round•ings |sə roun′dĭngz| *pl.n.* The things and circumstances that surround one; environment.

sur•tax |sûr′tăks′| *n.* A tax imposed in addition to another tax.

sur•veil•lance |sər vā′ləns| *n.* **1.** The action of observing or following closely: *These high-flying planes are used for the surveillance of enemy troop movements.* **2.** The condition of being closely observed or followed, especially by the police or other authorities.

sur•vey |sər vā′| *or* |sûr′vā′| *v.* **1.** To look over the parts or features of; view broadly: *surveyed the neighborhood from a rooftop.* **2.** To examine so as to make estimates or criticisms; investigate: *surveyed the damage done by the storm.* **3.** To determine the measure, boundaries, or elevation of (land or features of the earth's surface) by measuring angles and distances and applying geometry and trigonometry. —*n.* |sûr′vā′|. **1.** A view of a broad area, field, or subject. **2.** An investigation or study of a range of persons or things: *a survey of public opinion.* **3. a.** The act or process of surveying land. **b.** A map of or report on something that has been surveyed.

sur•vey•ing |sər vā′ĭng| *n.* The measurement and description of a region, part, or feature of the earth, as used for marking boundaries, mapmaking, etc.

sur•vey•or |sər vā′ər| *n.* A person whose work is surveying land. [SEE PICTURE]

sur•viv•al |sər vī′vəl| *n.* **1. a.** The act or process of surviving. **b.** The fact of having survived. **2.** Someone or something that has survived. —***modifier:*** *jungle survival techniques.*

sur•vive |sər vīv′| *v.* **sur•vived, sur•viv•ing.** **1.** To stay alive or in existence: *trying to survive in the woods; a folktale that has survived.* **2.** To live or

ă pat/ā pay/â care/ä father/ĕ pet/ ē be/ĭ pit/ī pie/î fierce/ŏ pot/ ō go/ô paw, for/oi oil/o͝o book/ o͞o boot/ou out/ŭ cut/û fur/ *th* the/th thin/hw which/zh vision/ ə ago, item, pencil, atom, circus

persist through: *plants surviving a frost; ancient manuscripts that survived the Middle Ages.* **3.** To live longer than; outlive.

sur•vi•vor |sər vī′vər| *n.* **1.** A person who has survived an accident or disaster that caused the death of others. **2.** A descendant, relative, or heir of a person who has died.

sus•cep•ti•bil•i•ty |sə sĕp′tə bĭl′ĭ tē| *n., pl.* **sus•cep•ti•bil•i•ties. 1. a.** The condition or quality of being susceptible. **b.** The degree to which this condition or quality exists in a given individual or population: *a high susceptibility to virus disease.* **2. susceptibilities.** Feelings; sensitivity.

sus•cep•ti•ble |sə sĕp′tə bəl| *adj.* **1.** Easily influenced or impressed; sensitive to suggestions: *a susceptible child.* **2.** Easily affected by a given force or agency: *He's made up his mind and is no longer susceptible to persuasion.* **3.** Liable to be stricken or infected with something: *susceptible to colds.* **4.** Capable of accepting or permitting something: *an account of what happened that is susceptible of proof.*

sus•pect |sə spĕkt′| *v.* **1.** To consider (someone) possibly guilty, without having proof: *I suspected my brother of having stolen the cookies, but said nothing.* **2.** To have doubts about; distrust: *We suspected his honesty.* **3.** To believe without being sure; imagine: *The early Greeks were the first to suspect that the earth is round.* —*n.* |sŭs′pĕkt′|. A person who is suspected of having committed a crime. —*adj.* |sŭs′pĕkt′|. Open to suspicion; possibly false, guilty, or blameworthy.

sus•pend |sə spĕnd′| *v.* **1.** To cause to hang down from a place of attachment: *suspend a bell from a cow's neck.* **2.** To support without a prop or resting place; cause to float: *For an instant the acrobat seemed to suspend himself in midair.* **3.** To withhold for the time being; put off; postpone: *suspend judgment until all the facts are known.* **4.** To stop for the time being; interrupt: *suspended his work to have lunch.* **5.** To stop enforcing, imposing, or granting for the time being: *suspended his driver's license.* **6.** To deprive temporarily of a position, membership, or privileges: *suspend a student from school.*

sus•pend•ers |sə spĕn′dərz| *n. (used with a plural verb).* A pair of straps, often elastic, worn over the shoulders to hold the trousers up. [See Picture]

sus•pense |sə spĕns′| *n.* **1.** The condition of being suspended. **2.** Anxious uncertainty about what will happen.

sus•pen•sion |sə spĕn′shən| *n.* **1. a.** The act of suspending: *a suspension of the rules.* **b.** The condition or fact of being suspended: *his suspension from school.* **2.** A dispersion of relatively coarse particles in a liquid or gas. **3.** The system of springs, shock absorbers, and associated parts by which the wheels of a vehicle are connected to its chassis.

suspension bridge. A bridge in which the roadway is hung from cables stretched between supporting towers. [See Picture]

sus•pi•cion |sə spĭsh′ən| *n.* **1.** A feeling or belief with little evidence to support it: *He had a strong suspicion that he was being double-crossed.* **2.** The condition of being suspected, especially of wrongdoing: *held under suspicion of fraud.* **3.** Doubt; distrust: *eyeing the stranger with suspicion.* **4.** A faint trace; a hint.

sus•pi•cious |sə spĭsh′əs| *adj.* **1.** Arousing suspicion; inviting distrust: *There was a suspicious bulge in the pocket of his raincoat.* **2.** Tending to suspect; distrustful: *Mary was taught to be suspicious of anything out of the ordinary.* **3.** Expressing suspicion: *suspicious eyes.* —**sus•pi′cious•ly** *adv.* —**sus•pi′cious•ness** *n.*

sus•tain |sə stān′| *v.* **1.** To support from below; hold or prop up: *beams strong enough to sustain the weight of the roof.* **2.** To keep in being or in effect; maintain; prolong: *sustain an effort; sustain a note for four beats.* **3.** To keep alive; supply with needed nourishment: *the grasses that sustain antelope.* **4.** To support the spirits of; encourage to keep going: *the religious zeal that sustained missionaries.* **5.** To affirm the validity of; uphold; confirm: *sustain a decision of a lower court; sustain an objection.* **6.** To suffer and endure through; withstand: *sustain a loss.*

sus•te•nance |sŭs′tə nəns| *n.* **1.** The support of life, as with food and other necessities. **2.** Something that supports life, especially food.

su•ture |so͞o′chər| *n.* **1. a.** The act or process of joining two thin pieces of material along a line by or as if by sewing. **b.** The material used in this process, as thread, gut, wire staples, or clips. **2.** The line along which two pieces, parts, bones, etc., are joined. —*v.* **su•tured, su•tur•ing.** To join by means of sutures; sew up, as in surgery.

Su•va |so͞o′və|. The capital of Fiji. Population, 64,000.

su•ze•rain |so͞o′zə rən| *or* |-rān′| *n.* **1.** In feudal times, a lord with land and vassals in service to him. **2.** A nation that controls the foreign affairs of another nation but allows it internal self-government.

su•ze•rain•ty |so͞o′zə rən tē| *or* |-rān′-| *n., pl.* **su•ze•rain•ties.** The power of a suzerain over a subject, especially the power to control the foreign affairs of a weaker nation.

svelte |svĕlt| *or* |sfĕlt| *adj.* **svelt•er, svelt•est.** Slim and graceful; lithe: *a svelte figure.*

SW southwest.

swab |swŏb| *n.* **1.** A mop for cleaning or drying decks, floors, etc. **2.** A small piece of cotton, sponge, or other absorbent material attached to the end of a stick or wire and used for cleansing or for applying medicine. —*v.* **swabbed, swab•bing. 1.** To cleanse or treat with a swab: *swab the decks; swab a sore throat.* **2.** To remove with or as if with a swab. —**swab′ber** *n.*

swad•dle |swŏd′l| *v.* **swad•dled, swad•dling. 1.** To wrap (an infant) with long, narrow strips of cloth. **2.** To cover, conceal, or envelop as wrappings do: *swaddled with blankets.*

swaddling clothes. Long, narrow strips of cloth formerly wrapped tightly around a newborn baby to hold its legs and arms still.

swag |swăg| *n.* Goods obtained illegally.

swag•ger |swăg′ər| *v.* **1.** To walk with an insolent air; strut. **2.** To brag; boast. —*n.* **1.** An insolent, strutting movement. **2.** Boastful or conceited expression.

Swa•hi•li |swä hē′lē| *n.* A Bantu language of eastern and central Africa, widely used in trade and as a general means of communication. [See Note]

suspenders

suspension bridge
Golden Gate Bridge,
San Francisco

Swahili

Swahili, *which is the most important language of East Africa, belongs to the Bantu family but has a large number of borrowings from Arabic. The name* **Swahili** *itself is from Arabic* sawāhil, *"they of the coast." Properly, the language is called* Kiswahili, *and the people who speak it are called the* Waswahili.

swallow[2]

swallowtail

swan

swain |swān| *n.* **1.** *Archaic.* A country youth. **2.** A young lover.

swal·low[1] |swŏl'ō| *v.* **1.** To cause (food, water, etc.) to pass from the mouth through the throat and esophagus into the stomach by muscular action. **2.** To perform the action of swallowing, as from fear or nervousness: *He looked over his audience and swallowed.* **3. a.** To consume or destroy as if by ingestion; devour: *The small company was swallowed up by a large company.* **b.** To engulf; hide: *The dense forest swallowed him.* **4.** To bear humbly; tolerate: *swallow an insult.* **5.** To believe without question: *She swallowed their story about why they were late.* **6. a.** To refrain from expressing; suppress: *swallow one's feelings.* **b.** To take back; retract: *swallow one's words.* —*n.* **1.** An act of swallowing. **2.** The amount that can be swallowed at one time.

swal·low[2] |swŏl'ō| *n.* Any of several birds that have narrow, pointed wings and a forked or notched tail, and that fly after and catch insects in the air. [SEE PICTURE]

swal·low·tail |swŏl'ō tāl'| *n.* **1.** A deeply forked tail of or like that of a swallow. **2.** Any of several large, often colorful butterflies with a taillike projection on each hind wing. **3.** *Informal.* A **swallow-tailed coat.** —*adj.* Deeply forked like the tail of a swallow. [SEE PICTURE]

swal·low-tailed coat |swŏl'ō tāld'|. A man's formal coat, divided in back into two long, tapered ends, called tails.

swam |swăm|. Past tense of **swim.**

swa·mi |swä'mē| *n.* **1.** A Hindu title of respect. **2.** A Hindu religious teacher.

swamp |swŏmp| *n.* A lowland region saturated with water; a bog; marsh. —***modifier:*** *swamp mud; swamp creatures.* —*v.* **1.** To drench in or cover with water or an other liquid. **2.** To inundate or burden; overwhelm: *swamped with work.*

swamp·y |swŏm'pē| *adj.* **swamp·i·er, swamp·i·est.** Of, like, or characterized by a swamp or swamps; boggy; marshy.

swan |swŏn| *n.* Any of several large, usually white water birds with webbed feet and a long, slender neck. [SEE PICTURE]

swan dive. A dive performed with the legs straight together, the back arched, and the arms stretched out from the sides.

swank |swăngk| *adj.* Very fashionable, especially in a showy manner or style. —*n.* **1.** Elegance. **2.** An excessive display of style or arrogance in behavior; swagger.

swank·y |swăng'kē| *adj.* **swank·i·er, swank·i·est.** Very fashionable; swank. —**swank'i·ly** *adv.* —**swank'i·ness** *n.*

swan's-down, also **swans·down** |swŏnz'doun'| *n.* **1.** The soft, fluffy down of a swan, sometimes used for trimming. **2.** A soft, thick fabric with a fluffy nap.

swan song. A farewell or last appearance, work, or action, as by an actor, writer, or athlete before death or retirement.

swap |swŏp| *Informal.* *v.* **swapped, swap·ping.** To trade or exchange. —*n.* An exchange of one thing for another. —**swap'per** *n.*

sward |swôrd| *n.* Ground covered with short, thickly-growing grass.

swarm[1] |swôrm| *n.* **1.** A large number of insects or other small creatures, especially when moving or flying together: *a swarm of mosquitoes; swarms of microbes.* **2.** A group of bees, together with a queen bee, moving together to find a new hive and start a new colony. **3.** A large number of people or things moving or remaining together: *His friends came in a swarm to congratulate him. Saturn's rings consist of a swarm of ice-covered particles.* —*v.* **1.** To move in or form a swarm, as bees and other insects do. **2.** To move or gather in large numbers: *Football fans swarmed onto the playing field after the game.* **3.** To be filled or overrun: *The lakes and streams swarmed with fish.* **4.** To go through or crowd in large numbers; throng: *Millions of tourists swarmed Grand Canyon Park last year.*

swarm[2] |swôrm| *v.* To climb by or as if by gripping with the arms and legs.

swarth·y |swôr'*th*ē| *adj.* **swarth·i·er, swarth·i·est.** Having a dark or sunburned complexion. —**swarth'i·ly** *adv.* —**swarth'i·ness** *n.*

swash |swŏsh| *or* |swôsh| *n.* A splash of liquid or the sound of such a splash. —*v.* **1.** To strike, move, or wash with a splashing sound: *water swashing around his feet.* **2.** To splash (a liquid). **3.** To splash a liquid against.

swash·buck·ler |swŏsh'bŭk'lər| *or* |swôsh'-| *n.* **1.** A sword-wielding adventurer. **2.** A type of historical novel full of swordplay and romantic adventure. —**swash'buck'ling** *adj.* & *n.*

swas·ti·ka |swŏs'tĭ kə| *n.* An ancient symbol formed by a Greek cross with the ends of the arms bent at right angles. A form of this was used as the emblem of Nazi Germany.

swat |swŏt| *v.* **swat·ted, swat·ting.** To deal a sharp blow to. —*n.* A quick, sharp, or violent blow. —**swat'ter** *n.*

swatch |swŏch| *n.* A small sample piece of cloth or other material.

swath |swŏth| *or* |swôth| *n.* **1.** The width of a scythe stroke or a mowing-machine blade. **2.** A path of this width made in mowing. **3.** The mown grass or grain lying on such a path. ***Idiom.*** **cut a (wide) swath.** To create a great stir, impression, or display.

swathe |swŏ*th*| *or* |swô*th*| *v.* **swathed, swath·ing.** **1.** To wrap or bind with a strip or strips of cloth: *His right ankle was swathed in bandages.* **2.** To cover or wrap with something that envelops: *The actress was swathed in furs.* —*n.* A band, bandage, or other wrapping.

sway |swā| *v.* **1.** To move or cause to move back and forth or from side to side: *trees swaying in the wind; dancers swaying their hips.* **2.** To lean or bend to one side; veer: *a vessel swaying as its cargo shifts position; swayed his body to avoid the blow.* **3.** To influence in opinion, feelings, or outlook; have weight: *issues most likely to sway voters.* —*n.* **1.** The act of moving from side to side with a swinging motion. **2.** Power; influence: *when the Romans held sway.*

sway·back |swā'băk'| *n.* An abnormal inward or downward curve of the spine.

sway·backed |swā'băkt'| *adj.* Affected with swayback: *a swaybacked horse.*

Swa·zi·land |swä'zē lănd'|. A country in southeastern Africa, between South Africa and Mozambique. Population, 478,000. Capital, Mbabane.

swear |swâr| *v.* **swore** |swôr| or |swōr|, **sworn** |swôrn| or |swōrn|, **swear•ing. 1.** To declare solemnly or make a solemn statement while calling on a person or thing held sacred for confirmation of the honesty or truth of what is spoken: *swore to God that it was false.* **2.** To promise or pledge with a solemn oath; vow: *swore his loyalty to us; swore to the genuineness of his claim.* **3.** To use profane oaths; curse; blaspheme. **4.** To bind by means of an oath: *swore them to secrecy.* **5.** To administer a legal oath to: *swearing each juror in turn.* **—phrasal verbs. swear by. 1.** To name (a sacred personage or thing) in taking an oath, as a pledge of truth or honesty. **2.** To have great reliance on or confidence in. **swear in.** To administer a legal or official oath to: *swore in the new President.* **swear off.** To pledge or promise to give up: *swore off smoking.* **swear out.** To obtain (a warrant for someone's arrest) by making a charge under oath. **—swear'er** *n.*

sweat |swĕt| *v.* **sweat•ed** or **sweat, sweat•ing. 1. a.** To excrete (water or liquid) through pores in the skin. **b.** To cause to do this, as by drugs, heat, or hard exercise. **2.** To make wet by sweating. **3.** To condense and accumulate (water) on a surface, as a cold water pipe does. **4.** To lose or shed as if by perspiring: *sweated off excess weight.* **5.** *Informal.* To work long and hard. **6.** *Informal.* To suffer, as for a misdeed. **—phrasal verbs. sweat blood.** *Slang.* To work extremely hard. **sweat out.** *Slang.* **1.** To endure anxiously. **2.** To await (something) anxiously. **3.** To attempt to cure by sweating: *sweat out a cold.* *—n.* **1.** The liquid excreted by the sweat glands of the skin. **2.** Water that condenses on a surface and forms small drops. **3.** The act or process of sweating. **4.** Strenuous, exhaustive labor; drudgery. **5.** *Informal.* An anxious, fretful condition; impatience: *The runners were in a sweat to get started.*

sweat•er |swĕt'ər| *n.* A knitted or crocheted outer garment worn on the upper part of the body.

sweat gland. Any of the tiny, tubular glands found in various areas of the skin in most mammals and distributed over nearly the entire skin of human beings, acting to secrete perspiration externally through pores.

sweat shirt. A long-sleeved cotton-jersey pullover worn especially by athletes.

sweat•shop |swĕt'shŏp'| *n.* A shop or factory where employees work long hours for low wages under bad conditions.

sweat•y |swĕt'ē| *adj.* **sweat•i•er, sweat•i•est. 1.** Covered with, wet with, or having the odor of sweat. **2.** Causing sweat. **—sweat'i•ly** *adv.*

Swede |swēd| *n.* A native or inhabitant of Sweden.

Swe•den |swēd'n|. A country in northern Europe, in the eastern part of the Scandinavian Peninsula. Population, 8,177,000. Capital, Stockholm.

Swed•ish |swē'dĭsh| *n.* The Germanic language of Sweden. *—adj.* Of Sweden, the Swedes, or their language.

sweep |swēp| *v.* **swept** |swĕpt|, **sweep•ing. 1.** To clean or clear the surface of with or as if with a broom or brush: *swept the hallway.* **2.** To clean or clear away with or as if with a broom or brush: *sweep snow; sweep up litter.* **3.** To clear (a space): *Marine patrols were assigned to sweep a favorite guerrilla hideout.* **4.** To move, remove, or convey: *flood waters sweeping everything in their path.* **5.** To move or unbalance emotionally: *family problems that swept him off his feet.* **6.** To move, surge, or flow with smooth, sustained force: *winds sweeping out of the north.* **7.** To move majestically or swiftly: *The honored guest swept into the room.* **8.** To extend: *wildflowers sweeping down the slopes.* **9.** To range throughout: *an epidemic sweeping the city.* **10.** To touch or brush lightly: *branches sweeping the river's surface.* **11.** To trail: *Her full gown sweeps down to the floor.* **12.** To drag the bottom of: *swept the river in their search for his body.* **13.** To win all the stages or parts of (a competition): *swept the series; swept all state-wide offices in the election.* **14.** To cause (a beam of electrons) to move across the face of a cathode-ray tube, as in forming a television picture. *—n.* **1.** The act of sweeping; removal with or as if with a broom or brush. **2.** The motion of sweeping: *the sweep of the oars.* **3.** The range or scope covered by sweeping: *the sweep of radar equipment.* **4.** A reach or extent: *a sweep of glistening snow.* **5.** Any curve or contour: *the sweep of her hair.* **6.** Someone who sweeps, especially a chimney sweep. **7.** Victory in all stages of a competition. **8.** A long oar used to propel a boat. **9.** A long pole attached to a pivot and with a bucket at one end, used to raise water from a well. **10.** The movement of an electron beam across the face of a cathode-ray tube, as in television. **—sweep'er** *n.* [SEE PICTURE]

sweep•ing |swē'pĭng| *adj.* **1.** Influencing or extending over a great area; wide-ranging: *sweeping changes.* **2.** Moving in a long curve or line: *sweeping gestures.* *—n.* **1.** The action or work of a person who sweeps. **2. sweepings.** That which is swept up; debris; litter. **—sweep'ing•ly** *adv.*

sweep•stake |swēp'stāk'| *n.* A form of the word **sweepstakes.**

sweep•stakes |swēp'stāks'| *n., pl.* **sweep•stakes. 1.** A lottery in which the participants' contributions form a fund to be awarded as a prize to the winner or winners. **2.** Any event or contest whose result determines the winner of such a lottery. **3.** The prize won in such a lottery.

sweet |swēt| *adj.* **sweet•er, sweet•est. 1.** Having a usually pleasing taste that is like that of a sugar. **2.** Not salty; fresh: *sweet water.* **3.** Not spoiled: fresh: *milk that is still sweet.* **4.** Free of acid. **5.** Pleasing to the senses, feelings, or mind; gratifying. **6.** Having a pleasing disposition; lovable. *—n.* **1.** Any sweet or sugary food. **2.** *British.* Something sweet served as dessert. **3.** A dear or beloved person. ¶*These sound alike* **sweet, suite. —sweet'ly** *adv.* **—sweet'ness** *n.*

sweet•bread |swēt'brĕd'| *n.* The thymus gland of an animal, used for food.

sweet•bri•er, also **sweet•bri•ar** |swēt'brī'ər| *n.* A wild rose with prickly stems, fragrant leaves, and fragrant pink flowers.

sweet corn. A type of corn with kernels that are sweet and juicy when young. It is the kind of corn commonly cooked and eaten as food.

sweet•en |swēt'n| *v.* **1.** To make or become

sweep
Above: Danish chimney sweep
Below: Ohio river boat with sweeps (nineteenth century)

sweet pea

sweet William

swing

sweet or sweeter: *sweetened his coffee.* **2.** To make gratifying.

sweet•en•er |swēt'n ər| *n.* A substance, as sugar or saccharin, added to a food or beverage to make it sweet.

sweet•en•ing |swēt'n ĭng| *n.* **1.** The act or process of making sweet. **2.** Something used to sweeten.

sweet•heart |swēt'härt'| *n.* **1.** A person whom one loves. **2.** A lovable person.

sweet•meat |swēt'mēt'| *n.* A piece of candy or other sweet delicacy.

sweet pea. A climbing plant with fragrant, variously colored flowers. [SEE PICTURE]

sweet potato. **1.** The thick, sweet yellowish or reddish root of a tropical vine, cooked and eaten as a vegetable. **2.** A vine having such a root. [SEE NOTE on p. 687]

sweet tooth. *Informal.* A fondness or desire for sweets, such as candy.

sweet William. A garden plant with broad, dense clusters of flowers in various combinations of red, pink, and white. [SEE PICTURE]

swell |swĕl| *v.* **swelled, swelled** or **swol•len** |swō'lən|, **swell•ing.** **1.** To increase in size or volume as a result of internal pressure; expand: *The injured ankle swelled and became very sore.* **2. a.** To increase in force, size, number, degree, etc.: *Membership swelled.* **b.** To increase in loudness or volume, as a sound. **3.** To rise in billows, as clouds or waves. **4.** To increase gradually and then decrease in loudness, as a musical tone or chord. **5.** To cause to swell; make swollen: *recruits that swelled our ranks; street noises swelling the racket.* **6.** To bulge out or cause to bulge out or protrude: *sails that swelled; wind swelling the sails.* **7.** To be or become filled with an emotion: *swelled with pride.* **8.** To grow within a person: *Her resentment swelled steadily.* —*n.* **1. a.** The act or process of swelling. **b.** The condition of being swollen. **2.** A long wave that moves continuously through the water without breaking. **3.** A gentle rise in the surface of the earth; a rounded hill. **4. a.** A crescendo followed by a diminuendo. **b.** A sign written on a musical score or part to indicate this. **c.** A device, as on an organ, for regulating volume. **5.** *Informal.* A person who is fashionably dressed or in fashionable society. —*adj.* **swell•er, swell•est.** *Informal.* **1.** Fine; excellent. **2.** Stylish; elegant.

swell•ing |swĕl'ĭng| *n.* **1. a.** The act or process of increasing in size or volume; expansion. **b.** The condition of being swollen or expanded. **2.** Something swollen, especially a part of the body that through disease or injury has become abnormally large.

swel•ter |swĕl'tər| *v.* To be affected by oppressive heat; sweat or feel faint from heat. —*n.* Oppressive heat and humidity.

swel•ter•ing |swĕl'tər ĭng| *adj.* **1.** Oppressively hot and humid. **2.** Suffering from heat.

swept |swĕpt|. Past tense and past participle of **sweep.**

swerve |swûrv| *v.* **swerved, swerv•ing.** To turn aside from a straight course; veer; deflect: *The car swerved into my lane of traffic. I swerved my car to avoid hitting him.* —*n.* **1.** The act of swerving. **2.** The degree to which something swerves; deflection or deviation.

swift |swĭft| *adj.* **swift•er, swift•est.** **1.** Moving with great speed; fast; fleet. **2.** Coming, occurring, or accomplished quickly: *a swift response.* —*adv.* Quickly: *swift-flowing streams.* —*n.* **1.** Any of several fast-flying gray or blackish birds with long, narrow wings, as the **chimney swift,** which often nests in chimneys and smokestacks. **2.** Any of several small, fast-moving, long-tailed lizards. —**swift'ly** *adv.* —**swift'ness** *n.*

swig |swĭg| *Informal. n.* A large swallow, as of a liquid; a gulp. —*v.* **swigged, swig•ging.** To drink eagerly; gulp.

swill |swĭl| *v.* To drink eagerly or greedily. —*n.* **1.** A mixture of liquid and solid food given to animals, especially pigs. **2.** Garbage; refuse. **3.** A large swallow of liquor.

swim¹ |swĭm| *v.* **swam** |swăm|, **swum** |swŭm|, **swim•ming.** **1. a.** To propel oneself through water by means of movements of the body or parts of the body. **b.** To propel oneself through or across (a body of water) by swimming. **2.** To float on water or other liquid: *leaves swimming on the lake.* **3.** To be covered or flooded with water or other liquid: *The basement swam from the leak.* **4.** To cause to swim or float on or across water. —*n.* **1.** The act of swimming. **2.** The period consumed or distance covered by such an act. —**swim'mer** *n.*

***Idiom.* in the swim.** Participating in what is current or fashionable.

swim² |swĭm| *v.* **swam** |swăm|, **swum** |swŭm|, **swim•ming.** **1.** To feel faint or giddy: *a thought that made his head swim.* **2.** To appear to spin or reel: *a jolt that caused the scenery to swim.* —*n.* A condition of dizziness; a swoon.

swim•mer•et |swĭm'ə rĕt'| *n.* One of the paired, paddlelike parts along the abdomen of a shrimp, lobster, or related crustacean.

swim•ming•ly |swĭm'ĭng lē| *adv.* With great ease and a high degree of success.

swimming pool. A pool constructed for swimming.

swim•suit |swĭm'so͞ot'| *n.* A garment worn to swim in; a bathing suit.

swin•dle |swĭn'dl| *v.* **swin•dled, swin•dling.** **1.** To cheat or defraud (a person) of money or property. **2.** To get (money or property) by cheating or fraud. —*n.* The act or an example of swindling; a dishonest act or scheme; a fraud. —**swin'dler** *n.*

swine |swīn| *n., pl.* **swine.** **1.** A pig, hog, or closely related animal. **2.** A hated, wicked, or greedy person.

swine•herd |swīn'hûrd'| *n.* A person who takes care of a large number of pigs.

swing |swĭng| *v.* **swung** |swŭng|, **swing•ing.** **1. a.** To move back and forth, suspended or as if suspended from above: *a leaf swinging from the branch.* **b.** To cause to move back and forth: *swung his keys on a chain.* **2. a.** To ride on a seat suspended from above. **b.** To move (someone) on such a seat by pulling or pushing. **3. a.** To turn in place, as on a hinge: *shutters swinging.* **b.** To hang or suspend on hinges: *swing a shutter.* **c.** To cause to turn on hinges: *swing the door shut.* **4.** To move, walk, or run with a free, unrestricted motion. **5.** To move or cause to move laterally or in a curve; turn: *swung over to the curb; swinging the car into another lane of*

ă pat/ā pay/â care/ä father/ĕ pet/ ē be/ĭ pit/ī pie/î fierce/ŏ pot/ ō go/ô paw, for/oi oil/o͝o book/ o͞o boot/ou out/ŭ cut/û fur/ *th* the/th thin/hw which/zh vision/ ə ago, item, pencil, atom, circus

traffic. **6.** To move with a sweeping motion; brandish: *swing the golf club; swinging the sword.* **7.** To lift or hoist with a sweeping motion: *swung the pouch over his shoulder.* **8.** To change or cause to change from one opinion or position to another: *swung to a conservative viewpoint; swung him to our outlook.* **9.** *Slang.* To be executed by hanging. **10.** *Slang.* To manipulate or manage successfully: *swing a deal.* **11. a.** To have a compelling or infectious rhythm, as popular music. **b.** To play with a compelling or infectious rhythm, as a group of popular musicians. —*n.* **1.** The act of swinging, especially: **a.** A rhythmic back-and-forth movement, as of a pendulum. **b.** A single movement or series of movements in a particular direction: *a swing toward radicalism.* **2.** The space traveled while swinging. **3.** The manner in which a person or thing swings something, as a baseball bat. **4.** Freedom and scope of movement or action: *given full swing in operating the business.* **5.** A seat suspended from above, on which one may ride back and forth in an arc for recreation or relaxation. **6. a.** A form of popular dance music that developed from jazz about 1935, characteristically using larger groups of musicians but simpler harmony and rhythm. **b.** The rhythmic quality or character of this music. [SEE PICTURE]

***Idiom.* in full swing.** In action to the top possible speed, capacity, or ability.

swipe |swīp| *n.* A heavy, sweeping blow. —*v.* **swiped, swip•ing. 1.** To hit with a sweeping blow. **2.** *Slang.* To steal.

swirl |swûrl| *v.* To rotate or spin in or as if in a whirlpool or eddy: *The wind swirled the snow. The dancers swirled about the room.* —*n.* **1.** The motion of whirling or spinning. **2.** Something that swirls; a whirlpool or eddy.

swish |swĭsh| *v.* **1.** To move with a whistle or hiss: *The tall grass swished in the wind.* **2.** To rustle, as certain fabrics do: *Her silk skirt swished as she walked.* —*n.* **1.** A sharp hissing or rustling sound. **2.** A movement making such a sound.

Swiss |swĭs| *n.* **1.** A native or inhabitant of Switzerland. **2. the Swiss.** The people of Switzerland. —*adj.* Of Switzerland or the Swiss.

Swiss cheese. A firm, whitish cheese with many large holes.

switch |swĭch| *n.* **1.** A slender flexible rod, stick, etc., used for whipping. **2.** A flailing or lashing, as with a slender rod. **3.** A device used to open or close an electric circuit or to make a connection to one of a number of different circuits. **4.** A device consisting of two sections of railroad track and various movable parts, used to transfer rolling stock from one track to another. **5.** A shift, as of attention or opinion. **6.** A thick bunch of real or artificial hair worn as part of a hairdo. —*v.* **1.** To whip with or as if with a switch. **2.** To jerk or swish abruptly or sharply: *The cat switched its tail. Its tail switched back and forth.* **3.** To shift, transfer, or change: *switch the conversation to a more interesting topic.* **4.** To exchange: *We switched sides.* **5.** To control (an electric current) by operating a switch. **6.** To cause (an electrical device) to begin or cease operation by controlling the current to it with a switch: *Switch on the television and switch off the main light.* **7.** To transfer (trains) from one railroad track to another. —**switch'er** *n.*

switch•blade |**swĭch'**blād'| *n.* A pocketknife with a blade that springs into position when a button on the handle is pressed.

switch•board |**swĭch'**bôrd'| *or* |-bōrd'| *n.* One or more panels containing switches and other equipment for controlling electric circuits. —***modifier:*** *a switchboard operator.*

switch hitter. In baseball, a player who can bat from either side of the plate.

Swit•zer•land |**swĭt'**sər lənd|. A country in central Europe, in the Alps. Population, 6,480,000. Capital, Bern.

swiv•el |**swĭv'**əl| *n.* **1.** A link, pivot, or other fastening designed so that either of the attached parts can rotate with respect to the other. **2.** A pivoted support that allows an attached object, such as a chair, to rotate freely. —*v.* **swiv•eled** or **swiv•elled, swiv•el•ing** or **swiv•el•ling.** To turn or rotate on or as if on a swivel.

swob |swŏb| *n. & v.* **swobbed, swob•bing.** A form of the word **swab.**

swol•len |**swō'**lən|. A past participle of **swell.**

swoon |swo͞on| *v.* To faint. —*n.* A fainting spell; a faint.

swoop |swo͞op| *v.* **1.** To fly or move with a swift, sudden, sweeping motion: *The hungry owl swooped down and caught the mouse. The helicopter flew low over the swamp and then swooped upward.* **2.** To snatch or take with such a motion: *Maria swooped up the kitten and ran out of the burning barn.* —*n.* The action of swooping; a swift, sudden sweeping motion.

***Idiom.* one fell swoop.** A single, concentrated effort or burst of energy: *He tried to teach me everything he knew in one fell swoop.*

swop |swŏp| *n. & v.* **swopped, swop•ping.** A form of the word **swap.**

sword |sôrd| *or* |sōrd| *n.* **1.** A hand weapon consisting of a long, pointed blade set in a handle or hilt. **2. the sword.** This weapon as a symbol of power or war. [SEE PICTURE]

sword•fish |**sôrd'**fĭsh'| *or* |**sōrd'**-| *n., pl.* **-fish** or **-fish•es.** A large ocean fish with the upper jaw projecting forward in a swordlike point. [SEE PICTURE]

swords•man |**sôrdz'**mən| *or* |**sōrdz'**-| *n., pl.* **-men** |-mən|. A person armed with or skilled in the use of a sword.

sword•tail |**sôrd'**tāl'| *or* |**sōrd'**-| *n.* A small tropical freshwater fish that has a long, narrow point extending from the tail fin of the male, and that is often kept in home aquariums.

swore |swôr| *or* |swōr|. Past tense of **swear.**

sworn |swôrn| *or* |swōrn|. Past participle of **swear.**

swum |swŭm|. Past participle of **swim.**

swung |swŭng|. Past tense and past participle of **swing.**

syc•a•more |**sĭk'**ə môr'| *or* |-mōr'| *n.* **1.** A North American tree with leaves like those of the maple, ball-shaped seed clusters, and bark that often flakes off in large patches. **2.** Also **sycamore maple.** A kind of maple tree native to Europe and Asia. **3.** A kind of fig tree mentioned in the Bible. [SEE NOTE]

syc•o•phant |**sĭk'**ə fənt| *n.* Someone who attempts to win favor or advancement by flattering persons of influence.

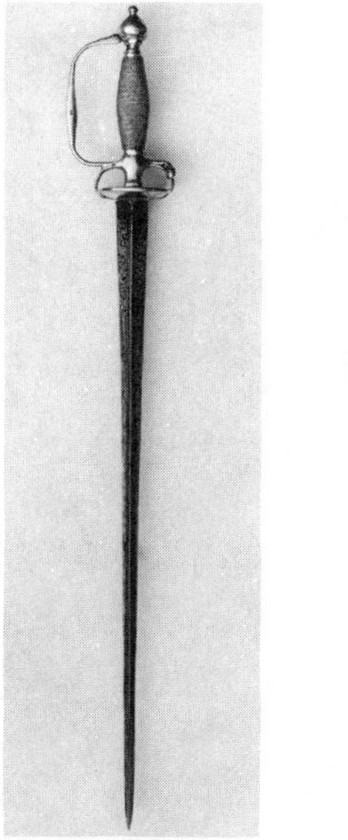

sword
Colonial American sword, with silver hilt made by Edward Winslow (1669–1753) of Boston, Massachusetts

swordfish

sycamore
The **sycamore** can grow larger than any other North American tree that sheds its leaves every year. A very large sycamore sometimes has a trunk measuring more than 40 feet around.

Syd•ney |sĭd′nē|. The largest city in Australia. Population, 2,874,000.

syl•la•bi |sĭl′ə bī′| *n.* A plural of **syllabus.**

syl•lab•ic |sĭ lăb′ĭk| *adj.* **1.** Of or consisting of a syllable or syllables. **2.** Of a consonant that forms a syllable without a vowel, as the *l* in *riddle* (rĭd′l).

syl•lab•i•cate |sĭ lăb′ĭ kāt′| *v.* **syl•lab•i•cat•ed, syl•lab•i•cat•ing.** To form or divide into syllables. —**syl•lab′i•ca′tion** *n.*

syl•lab•i•fy |sĭ lăb′ə fī′| *v.* **syl•lab•i•fied, syl•lab•i•fy•ing, syl•lab•i•fies.** To syllabicate.

syl•la•ble |sĭl′ə′bəl| *n.* A single uninterrupted sound forming part of a word or in some cases an entire word.

syl•la•bus |sĭl′ə bəs| *n., pl.* **syl•la•bus•es** or **syl•la•bi** |sĭl′ə bī′|. An outline of the main points of a text, lecture, or course of study.

syl•lo•gism |sĭl′ə jĭz′əm| *n.* **1.** A form of reasoning in which two propositions, the first called the major premise and the second called the minor premise, are stated, followed by a conclusion that is logically derived from them. An example of a syllogism is *All horses have tails* (major premise); *Big Red is a horse* (minor premise); *therefore Big Red has a tail* (conclusion). **2.** Reasoning from the general to the particular; deduction.

sylph |sĭlf| *n.* One of the elemental beings without souls that were believed to inhabit the air.

syl•van |sĭl′vən| *adj.* **1.** Of or typical of woodlands or forests: *sylvan life.* **2.** Having many trees; wooded: *sylvan slopes.*

sym•bi•o•sis |sĭm′bī ō′sĭs| *or* |-bē-| *n.* The relationship of two or more different organisms living in close association, often, but not necessarily, to the advantage of each. [SEE NOTE]

symbiosis

An example of **symbiosis** *is the relationship between a sea animal, the Portuguese man-of-war, and certain small fish that live among its long stinging tentacles, unharmed by their poison and sharing the food supply.*

sym•bi•ot•ic |sĭm′bī ŏt′ĭk| *or* |-bē-| *adj.* Of, living in, or describing the relationship of symbiosis. —**sym′bi•ot′i•cal•ly** *adv.*

sym•bol |sĭm′bəl| *n.* **1.** Something that represents something else, as by association, resemblance, convention, etc. **2.** A printed or written mark used to represent an operation, element, quantity, quality, or relation, as in mathematics or music. ¶*These sound alike* **symbol, cymbal.**

sym•bol•ic |sĭm bŏl′ĭk| *adj.* **1.** Of or expressed by a symbol or symbols. **2.** Serving as a symbol. **3.** Characteristically making use of symbols, as a work of art. —**sym•bol′i•cal•ly** *adv.*

sym•bol•ism |sĭm′bə lĭz′əm| *n.* **1. a.** The representation of things by means of symbols. **b.** The attachment of symbolic meaning or significance to objects, events, or relations. **2.** A system of symbols or representations. **3.** A symbolic meaning or representation.

sym•bol•ize |sĭm′bə līz′| *v.* **sym•bol•ized, sym•bol•iz•ing. 1.** To be or serve as a symbol of or for: *The poet uses rain to symbolize grief.* **2.** To represent by a symbol or symbols. **3.** To make use of symbols.

sym•met•ric |sĭ mĕt′rĭk| or **sym•met•ri•cal** |sĭ mĕt′rĭ kəl| *adj.* Of or showing symmetry.

symmetric property. The property of a mathematical relation of which it is true that if an element *a* of a universal set *U* has that relation to another such element *b*, then *b* must also have the same relation to *a*. For example, the relation = in arithmetic has this property since if $a = b$ then $b = a$, while $>$ does not have this property since if $a > b$ it is not true that $b > a$.

sym•me•try |sĭm′ĭ trē| *n., pl.* **sym•me•tries. 1.** An exact matching of form and arrangement of parts on opposite sides of a boundary, such as a plane or line, or around a point or axis. **2.** Any relationship in which there is equivalence or identity between parts, characteristics, etc.

sym•pa•thet•ic |sĭm′pə thĕt′ĭk| *adj.* **1.** Of, feeling, expressing, or resulting from sympathy: *a sympathetic person; a sympathetic interest.* **2.** In agreement; favorable; inclined: *They were sympathetic to the plan.* —**sym′pa•thet′i•cal•ly** *adv.*

sym•pa•thize |sĭm′pə thīz′| *v.* **sym•pa•thized, sym•pa•thiz•ing. 1.** To feel or express compassion for another. **2.** To share or understand another's feelings or ideas: *We sympathized with his ambitions.* —**sym′pa•thiz′er** *n.*

sym•pa•thy |sĭm′pə thē| *n., pl.* **sym•pa•thies. 1.** Mutual understanding or affection between persons. **2. a.** The act of or capacity for sharing or understanding the feelings of another. **b.** A feeling or expression of pity or sorrow for the distress of another; compassion. **3.** Favor; agreement; accord: *in sympathy with their beliefs.*

sym•phon•ic |sĭm fŏn′ĭk| *adj.* Of, like, or for a symphony or symphony orchestra.

sym•pho•ny |sĭm′fə nē| *n., pl.* **sym•pho•nies. 1. a.** A usually long and elaborate sonata for orchestra, usually consisting of four movements. **b.** An instrumental passage or movement of a vocal piece, such as an opera or oratorio. **2.** A **symphony orchestra.**

symphony orchestra. An orchestra suited for playing symphonies and similar works, ranging in size from moderately large to large and composed of string, wind, and percussion instruments.

sym•po•si•um |sĭm pō′zē əm| *n., pl.* **sym•po•si•ums** or **sym•po•si•a** |sĭm pō′zē ə|. **1.** A meeting or conference for discussing a topic. **2.** A collection of writings on a particular topic. [SEE NOTE]

symposium

Symposium *is from Greek* sumposion, *"a drinking together, a drinking party":* syn-, sym-, *"together,"* + pos-, *"drink." Greek intellectuals were fond of drinking parties as convivial settings for discussing philosophy and life.*

symp•tom |sĭmp′təm| *n.* **1.** Any change in which the body departs from its normal function, feeling, or appearance, usually a sign of disease or disorder. **2.** Anything regarded as an indication or characteristic of a condition or event.

syn•a•gogue |sĭn′ə gŏg′| *or* |-gôg′| *n.* **1.** A building or place of meeting for Jewish worship and religious instruction. **2.** A congregation of Jews for worship or religious study.

syn•chro•nize |sĭng′krə nīz′| *or* |sĭn′-| *v.* **syn•chro•nized, syn•chro•niz•ing. 1.** To occur at the same time; happen together. **2.** To operate at the same rate and together in time. **3.** To cause (two or more things) to operate in this way.

syn•chro•nous |sĭng′krə nəs| *or* |sĭn′-| *adj.* **1.** Occurring at the same time. **2.** Operating at the same rate and together in time. **3.** Having identical periods or identical periods and phases, as two waves, satellites, pendulums, etc.

syn•chro•tron |sĭng′krə trŏn| *or* |sĭn′-| *n.* An accelerator in which charged particles are accelerated to high energies by electric fields that vary with time and are held in a circular path by magnetic fields that vary with time.

syn•cline |sĭng′klīn′| *or* |sĭn′-| *n.* A low area in bedrock, in which rocks slope together from

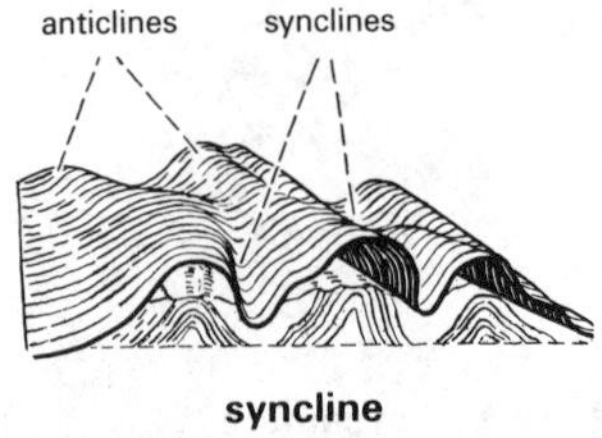

syncline

ă pat/ā pay/â care/ä father/ĕ pet/ ē be/ĭ pit/ī pie/î fierce/ŏ pot/ ō go/ô paw, for/oi oil/ŏŏ book/ ōō boot/ou out/ŭ cut/û fur/ *th* the/th thin/hw which/zh vision/ ə ago, item, pencil, atom, circus

opposite sides. [SEE PICTURE on p. 876]

syn•co•pate |sĭng′kə pāt′| *or* |sĭn′-| *v.* **syn•co•pat•ed, syn•co•pat•ing.** To use or involve a musical rhythm in which stresses occur on beats that are normally weak. —**syn′co•pa′tion** *n.*

syn•di•cate |sĭn′dĭ kĭt| *n.* **1.** An association of people formed to carry out any business or enterprise. **2.** An agency that sells articles for simultaneous publication in a number of newspapers or periodicals. —*v.* |sĭn′dĭ kāt′| **syn•di•cat•ed, syn•di•cat•ing. 1.** To organize into a syndicate. **2.** To sell (an article) through a syndicate for publication. —**syn′di•cat′ed** *adj.: a syndicated newspaper column.*

syn•drome |sĭn′drōm′| *n.* A set of symptoms and signs that together indicate the presence of a disease, mental disorder, or other abnormal condition.

syn•od |sĭn′əd| *n.* A council or assembly of churches or church officials.

syn•o•nym |sĭn′ə nĭm| *n.* A word having a meaning similar to that of another. For example, the words *wide* and *broad* are synonyms. [SEE NOTE]

syn•on•y•mous |sĭ nŏn′ə məs| *adj.* Expressing similar meaning: *synonymous terms.*

syn•on•y•my |sĭ nŏn′ə mē| *n., pl.* **syn•on•y•mies. 1.** The condition or quality of being synonymous. **2.** A list, book, or system of synonyms.

syn•op•sis |sĭ nŏp′sĭs| *n., pl.* **syn•op•ses** |sĭ-nŏp′sēz′|. A brief statement or outline of a subject or work: *a synopsis of a story.*

syn•tac•tic |sĭn tăk′tĭk| or **syn•tac•ti•cal** |sĭn-tăk′tĭ kəl| *adj.* Of or according to the rules of syntax. —**syn•tac′ti•cal•ly** *adv.*

syn•tax |sĭn′tăks′| *n.* The way in which words are put together to form phrases and sentences.

syn•the•sis |sĭn′thĭ sĭs| *n., pl.* **syn•the•ses** |sĭn′-thĭ sēz′|. **1.** The combining of separate elements, parts, or substances into a single unit or whole. **2.** The single unit or whole formed in this way. **3.** The formation of a chemical compound from its elements.

syn•the•size |sĭn′thĭ sīz′| *v.* **syn•the•sized, syn•the•siz•ing. 1.** To make or produce by a process of synthesis. **2.** To form a synthesis.

syn•the•siz•er |sĭn′thĭ sī′zər| *n.* **1.** Someone or something that synthesizes. **2.** Any of a number of electronic musical instruments that can be made to produce a wide range of musical sounds, including sounds that imitate those of conventional instruments.

syn•thet•ic |sĭn thĕt′ĭk| *adj.* **1.** Of, like, or involving synthesis or a synthesis. **2.** Artificial; man-made: *synthetic rubber; synthetic fabrics.* —*n.* A synthetic chemical compound or material. —**syn•thet′i•cal•ly** *adv.*

syph•i•lis |sĭf′ə lĭs| *n.* An infectious venereal disease caused by microorganisms, progressing from a stage in which it causes a hard sore, usually on or near the genitalia, through a stage in which it causes ulcers and eruptions of the skin, to a stage in which it affects the entire system, often causing brain damage and death.

syph•i•lit•ic |sĭf′ə lĭt′ĭk| *adj.* Of or affected with syphilis. —*n.* A person who has syphilis.

Syr•i•a |sîr′ē ə|. A country in the Middle East, at the eastern end of the Mediterranean Sea. Population, 7,121,000. Capital, Damascus. —**Syr′i•an** *adj. & n.*

sy•ringe |sə rĭnj′| *or* |sîr′ĭnj| *n.* **1.** Any of various medical instruments used to inject fluids into the body or draw fluids from the body. **2.** A **hypodermic syringe.**

syr•inx |sîr′ĭngks| *n., pl.* **syr•in•ges** |sə rĭn′jēz′| or **syr•inx•es.** A panpipe, a musical instrument.

syr•up |sĭr′əp| *or* |sûr′-| *n.* Any thick, sweet liquid, as the juice from a fruit or plant boiled with sugar. [SEE NOTE on p. 800]

sys•tem |sĭs′təm| *n.* **1.** A set of parts or elements that are related and that interact to form a single whole or something that is considered a single whole. **2.** Something formed of a set of elements or parts that function together, especially: **a.** The human body considered as a working unit, as in physiology. **b.** A group of related organs or parts: *the nervous system.* **c.** A set of mechanical or electrical parts that work together: *the transmission system of an automobile.* **d.** A network of pathways, as for travel, communications, etc.: *a transport system; a telephone system.* **3.** A set of related rules, principles, procedures, etc.: *a system for improving production.* **4.** A social, economic, or political organizational form: *a system of government.*

sys•tem•at•ic |sĭs′tə măt′ĭk| or **sys•tem•at•i•cal** |sĭs′tə măt′ĭ kəl| *adj.* **1.** Of, based on, or making up a system. **2.** Carried on or done in a step-by-step way. **3.** Orderly or methodical.

sys•tem•a•tize |sĭs′tə mə tīz′| *v.* **sys•tem•a•tized, sys•tem•a•tiz•ing.** To form or organize into a system; make orderly.

sys•tem•ic |sĭ stĕm′ĭk| *adj.* Of or affecting the entire body: *systemic poisoning.*

synonym

It is probably impossible for two words to be exact **synonyms** *in all respects. If two words refer to the same thing, there is still bound to be some basis for choosing between them; one word will be more frequent than the other, or more formal, or they will be used in different regions or by different types of people.*

Tt

(1) (2) (3)

The letter **T** *comes originally from the Phoenician letter* tāw *(1), which meant "mark" and stood for /t/. The Greeks borrowed it as* tau *(2), changing its shape slightly, and the Romans borrowed this from the Greeks. The Roman letter (3) is the basis of our modern letter* **T**.

tabard

taboo

The word **taboo** *or* **tabu** *is from Polynesian* tābu, *"marked." The word was personally reported by the explorer Captain James Cook when visiting the Polynesian island of Tonga in 1777.*

ă pat/ā pay/â care/ä father/ĕ pet/ē be/ĭ pit/ī pie/î fierce/ŏ pot/ō go/ô paw, for/oi oil/o͝o book/o͞o boot/ou out/ŭ cut/û fur/*th* the/th thin/hw which/zh vision/ə ago, item, pencil, atom, circus

t, T |tē| *n., pl.* **t's** or **T's.** The 20th letter of the English alphabet. [SEE NOTE]
***Idiom.* to a T.** Perfectly; precisely: *She fits the role to a T.*

T Temperature.

Ta The symbol for the element tantalum.

tab |tăb| *n.* **1.** A projection, flap, or strip attached to an object to aid in opening, handling, or identifying it. **2.** A small hanging or projecting flap, strap, tongue, or loop on a garment. **3.** *Informal.* A bill or check, as for a meal in a restaurant. **4.** A tabulator on a typewriter. **5.** A small auxiliary control surface attached to a larger one, as on an aircraft.
***Idiom.* keep tabs on.** To watch.

tab•ard |tăb'ərd| *n.* **1.** A sleeveless or short-sleeved tunic worn by a knight over his armor and embroidered with his coat of arms. **2.** A similar garment worn by a herald and bearing his lord's coat of arms. [SEE PICTURE]

Ta•bas•co |tə băs'kō| *n.* A trademark for a strong-flavored sauce seasoned with red pepper.

tab•by |tăb'ē| *n., pl.* **tab•bies.** A cat having fur with striped or ripplelike black and grayish markings. *—adj.* Having striped or ripplelike black and grayish markings: *the kitten's tabby fur.*

tab•er•nac•le |tăb'ər năk'əl| *n.* **the Tabernacle.** In the Bible, the portable sanctuary used by the Hebrews until the building of the Temple at Jerusalem.

ta•bi |tä'bē| *n., pl.* **ta•bi** or **ta•bis.** A special kind of sock having a separate division for the big toe, worn in Japan with a kind of sandal.

ta•ble |tā'bəl| *n.* **1.** An article of furniture supported by one or more vertical legs and having a flat horizontal surface. **2.** The objects laid out on a table for a meal. **3.** The food served at a meal or the people assembled to eat it. **4.** A plateau or tableland. **5.** A horizontal layer of rock. **6.** An orderly printed, written, or typed presentation of data, especially one in which the data are arranged in columns and rows in an essentially rectangular form. ***—modifier:*** *table manners.* *—v.* **ta•bled, ta•bling.** To postpone consideration of; shelve: *table a piece of legislation.*
***Idioms.* turn the tables.** To reverse a situation and gain the upper hand. **under the table.** In secret: *He closed the deal under the table.*

tab•leau |tă blō'| *or* |tăb'lō'| *n.* **1.** A striking scene, especially one posed on a stage by silent, motionless actors. **2.** A vivid, graphic description.

ta•ble•cloth |tā'bəl klôth'| *or* |-klŏth'| *n.; pl.* **-cloths** |-klô*thz*'| *or* |-klŏ*thz*'| *or* |-klôths'| *or* |-klŏths'|. A cloth to cover a table, especially during a meal.

ta•ble•land |tā'bəl lănd'| *n.* A region of flat, elevated land; a plateau; mesa.

table linen. Tablecloths and napkins.

table salt. **1.** A refined mixture of salts, chiefly sodium chloride, used in cooking and as a seasoning. **2.** **Sodium chloride.**

ta•ble•spoon |tā'bəl spo͞on'| *n.* **1.** A large spoon used for serving food. **2. a.** A tablespoon with something in it: *a tablespoon of flour.* **b.** The amount that a tablespoon holds: *sprinkled a tablespoon of sugar.* *3.* A household cooking measure equal to three teaspoons or 1/2 fluid ounce.

ta•ble•spoon•ful |tā'bəl spo͞on'fo͝ol'| *n., pl.* **ta•ble•spoon•fuls.** The amount that a tablespoon holds.

tab•let |tăb'lĭt| *n.* **1.** A slab or plaque, as of stone, suitable for or bearing an inscription. **2.** A thin sheet, as of clay, used as a writing surface. **3.** A pad of writing paper glued together along one edge. **4.** A small, flat pellet of medicine to be taken orally.

table tennis. A game similar to tennis but played on a table with wooden paddles and a very small Celluloid ball.

ta•ble•ware |tā'bəl wâr'| *n.* The dishes, glassware, and silverware used in setting a table for a meal.

tab•loid |tăb'loid'| *n.* A newspaper of small format presenting the news in condensed form and often concentrating on sensational material.

ta•boo |tə bo͞o'| *or* |tă-| *n.* **1.** A cultural prohibition against some word or act. **2.** A word or act prohibited for cultural reasons. *—adj.* Prohibited for cultural reasons. *—v.* **ta•booed, ta•boo•ing, ta•boos.** To place under taboo. [SEE NOTE]

ta•bor |tā'bər| *n.* A small drum, such as that used by a fife player to accompany his fife.

ta•bu |tə bo͞o'| *or* |tă-| *n. & v.* A form of the word **taboo.**

tab•u•lar |tăb'yə lər| *adj.* **1.** Organized or presented in the form of a table or list: *tabular data.* **2.** Calculated from information given in a mathematical table, as of square roots, sines and cosines, etc. **3.** Having a flat surface: *a tabular crystal.*

tab•u•late |tăb'yə lāt'| *v.* **tab•u•lat•ed, tab•u•lat•ing.** To condense and list, as in a table: *tabulate results.* **—tab'u•la'tion** *n.*

tab•u•la•tor |tăb'yə lā'tər| *n.* **1.** Someone or something that tabulates, especially a machine for processing data. **2.** A mechanism on a typewriter for setting automatic stops or margins for columns.

tac•et |tăs′ĭt| *or* |tā′sĭt|. A word printed or written in a musical score or part to indicate that an instrument or voice is silent for an extended time. ¶ *These sound alike* **tacet, tacit.**

tach |tăk| *n. Informal.* A tachometer. ¶ *These sound alike* **tach, tack.**

ta•chom•e•ter |tă kŏm′ĭ tər| *or* |tə-| *n.* An instrument used to measure and indicate speed, especially the speed of a rotating shaft.

tac•it |tăs′ĭt| *adj.* Implied from actions; not spoken or written: *a tacit agreement.* ¶ *These sound alike* **tacit, tacet.**

tac•i•turn |tăs′ĭ tûrn′| *adj.* Habitually silent or uncommunicative: *a taciturn man.*

tack |tăk| *n.* **1.** A small nail with a sharp point and a flat head. **2. a.** The direction of a ship with respect to the trim of its sails: *the starboard tack.* **b.** A change in a ship's direction made by changing the position of the sails. **3.** A course of action or an approach: *try a new tack.* **4.** A stitch used in sewing by hand to hold edges together lightly or temporarily or to mark the places on a fabric where seams, tucks, etc., are to be made: *tailor's tacks.* —*v.* **1.** To fasten or attach with a tack or tacks. **2.** To add as an extra item: *tack two dollars onto the bill.* **3.** To change the course of a ship by turning from one tack to the other. **4.** To sew with loose or light, often temporary stitches, especially stitches that are invisible on the right side: *Tack the facing to the seams.* ¶ *These sound alike* **tack, tach.**

tack•le |tăk′əl| *n.* **1.** The equipment used in a sport, especially in fishing; gear. **2. a.** A rope and its pulley. **b.** A system of ropes and pulleys used on a ship to hoist, pull, or apply tension. **3.** In football: **a.** Either of the two players on a team's line stationed inside an end. **b.** The act of stopping an opponent carrying the ball by seizing and bringing him down. —*v.* **tack•led, tack•ling. 1.** To take on and wrestle (an opponent, a problem, a difficulty, etc.) in order to overcome. **2.** In football, to seize and throw one's weight against (an opponent) in order to bring him to the ground. —**tack′ler** *n.*

tack•y^1 |tăk′ē| *adj.* **tack•i•er, tack•i•est.** Slightly gummy to the touch; sticky: *a tacky surface.*

tack•y^2 |tăk′ē| *adj.* **tack•i•er, tack•i•est.** *Informal.* Not stylish; dowdy: *tacky clothes.*

ta•co |tä′kō| *n., pl.* **ta•cos.** A tortilla folded around a filling, such as meat or cheese. [SEE NOTE]

tac•o•nite |tăk′ə nīt′| *n.* A fine-grained sedimentary rock containing magnetite, hematite, and quartz, used as a low-grade iron ore.

tact |tăkt| *n.* The ability to say or do the right thing at the right time; diplomacy.

tact•ful |tăkt′fəl| *adj.* Having or showing tact; considerate: *a tactful person.* —**tact′ful•ly** *adv.* —**tact′ful•ness** *n.*

tac•tic |tăk′tĭk| *n.* **1.** A device or expedient for achieving a goal. **2. tactics** *(used with a singular verb).* The technique or science of gaining objectives, especially military objectives, by using strategy.

tac•ti•cal |tăk′tĭ kəl| *adj.* **1.** Of tactics: *a tactical maneuver.* **2.** Done or made strategically: *a tactical decision.*

tac•tile |tăk′təl| *adj.* **1.** Of or felt by the sense of touch: *tactile sensations.* **2.** Used for feeling: *tactile organs such as antennae.*

tact•less |tăkt′lĭs| *adj.* Lacking in tact; inconsiderate. —**tact′less•ly** *adv.* —**tact′less•ness** *n.*

tad•pole |tăd′pōl′| *n.* A frog or toad in its early, newly hatched stage, when it lives in the water and has a tail and gills that disappear as the legs develop and the full-grown stage is reached. [SEE PICTURE]

taf•fe•ta |tăf′ĭ tə| *n.* A crisp, smooth fabric with a slight sheen, made of silk, rayon, nylon, or other fibers and used for dresses, blouses, slips, etc. —***modifier:*** *a taffeta dress.*

taf•fy |tăf′ē| *n., pl.* **taf•fies.** A chewy candy made from molasses or brown sugar boiled very thick and pulled into long threads until it holds it shape.

Taft |tăft|, **William Howard.** 1857–1930. Twenty-seventh President of the United States (1909–13).

tag^1 |tăg| *n.* **1.** A strip, as of paper, metal, leather, etc., attached to something or worn by someone for the purpose of identifying, classifying, or labeling: *a name tag; a price tag.* **2.** The plastic or metal tips at the ends of shoelaces. **3.** A cliché. —*v.* **tagged, tag•ging. 1.** To label or identify with or as if with a tag: *We tagged the butterfly specimen. She is always tagged as a loser.* **2.** To follow closely: *tagging along behind his older brother.* [SEE NOTE]

tag^2 |tăg| *n.* **1.** A children's game in which one player pursues the others until he touches one of them, who in turn becomes the pursuer. **2.** The act of putting another player out by touching him, as in baseball. —*v.* **tagged, tag•ging.** To touch (another player), as in a game of tag. —***phrasal verbs.* tag out.** To put (another player) out by touching him, as in baseball. **tag up.** In baseball, to return to and touch a base before going on to the next base. [SEE NOTE]

Ta•ga•log |tə gä′lôg′| *or* |-lŏg′| *n., pl.* **Ta•ga•log** or **Ta•ga•logs. 1.** A member of a native tribe of the Philippines. **2.** The language of this people. —*adj.* Of the Tagalog or their language.

Ta•hi•ti |tə hē′tē|. An island in the north-central South Pacific, belonging to France. —**Ta•hi′tian** *adj. & n.*

Tai |tī| *n. & adj.* A form of the word **Thai.**

tai•ga |tī gä′| *n.* The northernmost forest region of the earth, having a growth of cone-bearing evergreens and ground that is grozen in winter and swampy in summer.

tail |tāl| *n.* **1. a.** The hindmost part of an animal, especially when extending beyond the main part of the body. **b.** The hindmost, rear, or bottom part of anything: *the tail of a car.* **2.** Anything that looks, hangs, or trails like an animal's tail: *the tails of a coat; a comet's tail of vapor.* **3. tails.** The reverse side of a coin: *heads or tails.* **4.** *Informal.* The trail of a person or animal in flight: *on the criminal's tail.* **5. tails. a.** Men's most formal evening clothes, including a swallow-tailed coat and a white bow tie. **b.** A **swallow-tailed coat.** —***modifier:*** *tail feathers; the tail section.* —*v. Informal.* To follow: *The detective tailed the suspect.* ¶ *These sound alike* **tail, tale.** —**tail′less** *adj.*

tail•board |tāl′bôrd′| *or* |-bōrd′| *n.* A hinged

taco
Taco *is from Mexican Spanish* taco, *originally meaning "wad, roll."*

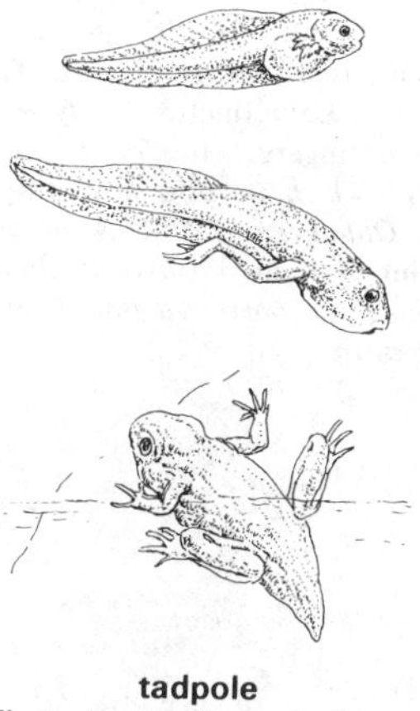

tadpole
Three stages of growth shown
The word **tadpole** was originally *tadpolle,* literally "toad-head": *tad,* "toad," + *poll,* "head." The name means "toad (or frog) with a big head" (see the top drawing).

tag$^{1\text{-}2}$
Tag^1 *is probably from a Scandinavian word meaning "prickle, sharp point."* **Tag^2** *was originally* tig, *meaning "to touch lightly" (as in the game of tag);* tig *is a variant of* **tick^1.**

tailor
Tailor *is from Old French* tailleur, *"cutter (of cloth)," from* tailler, *"to cut."*

taint/tint/tinge
Taint *is a doublet of* **tint**. **Tint** *is from Latin* tinctus, *"a dyeing," from* tingere, *"to dip, to dye," from which we also have* **tinge**. *In Old French,* tinctus *became* taint *or* teint, *"a dye, a stain," which was borrowed into English as* **taint**.

talc
Talc *is from Arabic* talq *or Persian* talk, *"talc, mica."*

ă pat/ā pay/â care/ä father/ĕ pet/ ē be/ĭ pit/ī pie/î fierce/ŏ pot/ ō go/ô paw, for/oi oil/o͝o book/ o͞o boot/ou out/ŭ cut/û fur/ *th* the/th thin/hw which/zh vision/ ə ago, item, pencil, atom, circus

flap at the rear of a truck, wagon, station wagon, etc.; a tailgate.

tail•coat |tāl′kōt′| *n.* A swallow-tailed coat worn as part of men's most formal evening clothes; tails.

tail end. The very end: *the tail end of the day.*

tail•gate |tāl′gāt′| *n.* A tailboard. —*v.* **tail•gat•ed, tail•gat•ing.** To drive so closely behind (another vehicle) that one cannot stop or swerve in an emergency.

tail•light |tāl′līt′| *n.* A red lamp mounted on the rear of a vehicle to make it visible from behind in the dark.

tai•lor |tā′lər| *n.* A person who makes, mends, or alters garments, especially one who makes men's clothes to order or who designs women's clothes with simple, fitted lines. —*v.* To make (clothing) having simple, fitted lines: *He tailors men's suits and coats. He tailors for the Duke.* —**tai′lored** *adj.: a tailored suit.* [SEE NOTE]

tail•pipe |tāl′pīp′| *n.* The pipe through which the exhaust gases from an engine are discharged, as in an automobile.

tail•spin |tāl′spĭn′| *n.* The descent of an airplane in a spin in which the tail moves rapidly in a spiral path.

tail•stock |tāl′stŏk′| *n.* The adjustable head or support on a lathe, containing a center that does not rotate.

tail•wind |tāl′wĭnd′| *n.* A wind whose direction is the same as that of the course of a vehicle.

Tai•no |tī′nō| *n., pl.* **Tai•no** or **Tai•nos. 1.** An extinct people of the West Indies. **2.** A member of this people. **3.** Their Arawakan language.

taint |tānt| *v.* **1.** To touch or affect, as with something undesirable: *Her superstition tainted the sailors with fear.* **2.** To make rotten; spoil: *The warm weather tainted the meat.* —*n.* A stain; a blemish: *That accusation is a taint on our honor.* [SEE NOTE]

Tai•pei |tī′pā′|. The capital of Taiwan. Population, 2,108,000.

Tai•wan |tī′wän′|. Officially, Republic of China. An island country off the southeastern coast of China. Population 16,610,000.

Taj Ma•hal |täzh′ mə häl′| *or* |täj′|. A white marble mausoleum in India, built in the 17th century.

take |tāk| *v.* **took** |to͝ok|, **tak•en** |tā′kən|, **tak•ing. 1.** To get possession of; gain, capture, or seize: *take first prize; take the ship.* **2.** To grasp with the hands; hold: *take her arm.* **3.** To have room for; hold: *The jar takes three pints.* **4.** To carry along or cause to go with one to another place: *take the book to the library.* **5.** To convey to another place: *The train takes you to New York.* **6.** To remove from a place: *Take the cup from the shelf.* **7.** To obtain from a source; derive: *The book takes its title from the Bible.* **8.** To inhale, swallow, eat, drink, or consume: *take a breath; take medicine.* **9.** To expose one's body to (some process or treatment): *take a bath.* **10. a.** To assume for oneself: *take credit.* **b.** To commit oneself to; undertake: *take the initiative.* **c.** To bind oneself by (an oath or vow): *take an oath.* **11.** To perform; do: *take a step; take precautions.* **12.** To come upon: *take her by surprise.* **13.** To charm; captivate: *The child was taken with the little pup.* **14.** To study or commit oneself to studying: *take biology; take courses.* **15.** To require or need: *It takes a thief to know a thief.* **16.** To use as a means of conveyance or transportation: *take a train.* **17.** To assume occupancy of: *take a seat.* **18.** To use, as in operating: *This camera takes 35mm film.* **19.** To select; pick out: *take any card.* **20.** In grammar, to govern: *A transitive verb takes a direct object.* **21.** To make by photography: *take a picture.* **22. a.** To accept or endure (something given or offered): *take criticism.* **b.** To undergo: *take a beating.* **23.** To interpret or react to in a certain manner: *take his comments seriously.* **24.** To subtract: *take 5 away from 15.* **25.** To have an intended effect; work: *The dye took, and the fabric became red.* **26.** To become: *take sick.* **27.** To obtain through certain procedures, as through measurement: *take someone's temperature.* **28.** To write down: *take a letter; take notes.* **29.** To buy or subscribe to: *take a magazine.* **30.** *Informal.* To swindle; cheat: *He was taken by the salesman.* —***phrasal verbs.*** **take after. 1.** To chase: *The dogs took after the rabbit.* **2.** To resemble: *She takes after her father.* **take apart.** To dismantle: *take apart a radio.* **take back.** To retract (something stated or written): *took back his insult.* **take down. 1.** To bring from a higher to a lower position. **2.** To dismantle. **3.** To put down in writing. **take for.** To suppose to be, often mistakenly: *take him for an idiot.* **take in. 1.** To grant admittance to. **2.** To view: *His eyes took in the whole scene.* **3.** To include or comprise. **take off. 1.** To remove, as clothing. **2.** To rise up in flight, as an airplane. **3.** *Informal.* To depart: *She took off for New Zealand.* **take on. 1.** To hire. **2.** To undertake. **3.** To oppose in competition. **take out. 1.** To remove; extract. **2.** *Informal.* To escort, as on a date. **take over.** To assume control or management of. **take to. 1.** To go to, as for safety: *take to the woods.* **2.** To become fond of. **take up. 1.** To shorten: *take up a hem.* **2.** To use up, consume, or occupy: *take up space and time.* **3.** To begin again: *took up where he left off.* **4.** To develop an interest in: *take up writing.* **take up with.** *Informal.* To develop a friendship with. —*n.* **1. a.** The act or process of taking. **b.** The amount taken, especially at one time. **2.** *Slang.* The money collected as admission to an event, especially in sports. **3.** The uninterrupted running of a camera or other equipment, as in filming a movie or making a record. **4.** *Slang.* Any attempt or try. —**tak′er** *n.*

Idioms. **take heart.** To gain courage or confidence. **take it.** *Informal.* To endure abuse, criticism, etc. **take it out on (someone).** *Informal.* To abuse in letting out one's own anger or frustration.

take•off |tāk′ôf′| *or* |-ŏf′| *n.* **1.** The act or process of rising up in flight, as of an airplane or rocket. **2.** *Informal.* An amusing imitation or burlesque of another person; caricature.

take-o•ver |tāk′ō′vər| *n.* The act or process of assuming control or management of.

talc |tălk| *n.* A fine-grained white, greenish, or gray mineral, essentially a silicate of magnesium. It has a soft, soapy texture and is used in face powder and talcum powder, for coating paper, and as a filler in paints and plastics. [SEE NOTE]

tal•cum |tăl′kəm| *n.* **1. Talcum powder. 2.** Talc.

talcum powder. A fine, often perfumed powder made from purified talc, for use on the skin.

tale |tāl| *n.* **1.** A report or revelation; a recital of events or facts: *told us a tale of misery and woe.* **2.** A narrative of imaginary events: *a tall tale.* **3.** A falsehood; a lie: *Don't tell tales.* ¶*These sound alike* **tale, tail.**

tal•ent |tăl′ənt| *n.* **1. a.** A natural or acquired ability, especially of superior quality: *artistic talent; a talent for making trouble.* **b.** A person with such ability: *a great literary talent.* **c.** Gifted people in general. **2.** An ancient coin or weight in the Middle East, Greece, and Rome. —***modifier:*** *a talent show.* [SEE NOTE]

tal•ent•ed |tăl′ən tĭd| *adj.* Having talent; gifted: *a talented painter.*

ta•li |tā′lī′| *n.* Plural of **talus** (bone).

tal•is•man |tăl′ĭs mən| *or* |-ĭz-| *n.* An object marked with magical signs or words and believed to give supernatural powers or protection to its bearer.

talk |tôk| *v.* **1.** To use human speech; articulate words. **2.** To imitate human speech: *Parrots can talk.* **3.** To communicate as if by using human speech: *Deaf mutes can talk with sign language.* **4. a.** To express, communicate, or convey ideas, thoughts, etc., by means of speech; converse: *talk to my brother; talk seriously.* **b.** To speak of or discuss: *talk business.* **5.** To chatter incessantly: *He did nothing but talk.* **6.** To consult or confer: *talk with a psychiatrist.* **7.** *Informal.* To yield information, usually under stress: *The prisoner wouldn't talk.* —***phrasal verbs.*** **talk back.** To reply rudely. **talk down. 1.** To depreciate: *He talked down the importance of the move.* **2.** To silence (a person): *His boss could talk him down with one word.* **3.** To address someone with insulting condescension. **talk out.** To discuss thoroughly. **talk over.** To discuss (something) in depth. **talk up. 1.** *Informal.* To propagandize favorably about something: *talk up his new novel.* **2.** To speak up impertinently or defiantly, especially to a superior: *talking up to an officer.* —*n.* **1.** A particular manner of speech or conversation: *baby talk; plain talk.* **2. a.** An informal speech: *a talk in front of the class.* **b.** A conference or negotiation: *peace talks.* **3.** Any subject of conversation: *the talk of the neighborhood.* **4.** Any hearsay or rumor about something: *talk of trouble.* **5.** Empty or meaningless speech: *all talk and no action.*

Idioms. **talk (someone) into.** To persuade. **talk (someone) out of.** To dissuade.

talk•a•tive |tô′kə tĭv| *adj.* Inclined to talk: *a talkative man.* —**talk′a•tive•ly** *adv.* —**talk′a•tive•ness** *n.*

talk•er |tô′kər| *n.* A person who talks, especially a talkative person.

talk•ing-to |tô′kĭng to͞o′| *n., pl.* **talk•ing-tos.** *Informal.* A scolding.

tall |tôl| *adj.* **tall•er, tall•est. 1.** Having a greater than ordinary height: *a tall tree.* **2.** Having a stated height: *a plant three feet tall.* **3.** *Informal.* Imaginary; fanciful or boastful: *a tall tale.* **4.** Unusual in length, size, or difficulty: *a tall drink; a tall order to fill.* —*adv.* Straight; proudly: *stand tall.* —**tall′ness** *n.*

Tal•la•has•see |tăl′ə hăs′ē|. The capital of Florida. Population, 71,900.

tal•lith |tä′lĭs| *or* |-lĭth| *n., pl.* **tal•lith•im** |tä′lĭ sēm′| *or* |-thēm′|. A fringed shawl worn by Jewish men when they say their prayers. [SEE PICTURE]

tal•low |tăl′ō| *n.* A mixture of fats obtained from animals, such as cattle, sheep, or horses, and used to make candles, soaps, lubricants, etc.

tal•ly |tăl′ē| *n., pl.* **tal•lies.** The calculation of something, such as a score. —*v.* **tal•lied, tal•ly•ing, tal•lies. 1.** To calculate or compute (a score or other amount). **2.** To agree or cause to agree: *The two accounts of the story tallied. They tallied the totals so that they matched.*

tal•ly•ho |tăl′ē hō′| *interj.* A word used to urge hounds in fox hunting.

Tal•mud |täl′mo͝od′| *or* |tăl′məd| *n.* A collection of ancient rabbinical writings, the basis of religious authority for orthodox Judaism.

tal•on |tăl′ən| *n.* The claw of a bird or animal that seizes other animals as prey.

ta•lus[1] |tā′ləs| *n., pl.* **ta•li** |tā′lī′|. **1.** A bone that forms a joint with the tibia and fibula, making up the main bone of the ankle. **2.** The ankle.

ta•lus[2] |tā′ləs| *n., pl.* **ta•lus•es. 1.** A slope formed by a collection of debris. **2.** A sloping mass of debris that collects at the base of a cliff.

tam |tăm| *n.* A tam-o'-shanter.

ta•ma•le |tə mä′lē| *n.* A highly seasoned Mexican dish made of chopped meat and crushed peppers or other foods, wrapped in corn husks and steamed.

tam•a•rack |tăm′ə răk′| *n.* A North American larch tree or its wood.

tam•a•rind |tăm′ə rĭnd′| *n.* **1.** The pulpy seed pod of a tropical tree, having a pleasant, sharp taste and used as food, flavoring, etc. **2.** A tree that bears such pods.

tam•a•risk |tăm′ə rĭsk′| *n.* A shrub or tree of warm regions, having small, scalelike leaves and clusters of pink flowers.

tam•bour |tăm′bo͝or′| *n.* A small wooden embroidery frame consisting of two hoops that fit one inside the other to hold fabric firmly stretched between them.

tam•bou•rine |tăm′bə rēn′| *n.* A percussion instrument consisting of a small drumhead stretched over a narrow rim that is fitted with small metal disks that jingle when the drumhead is struck or when the instrument is shaken. [SEE PICTURE]

tame |tām| *adj.* **tam•er, tam•est. 1.** Trained or accustomed to living harmlessly and fearlessly with human beings, as a domestic animal or an animal naturally living in a wild state. **2.** Not fierce, dangerous, or timid; gentle and unafraid: *The dodo was so tame that it was easily killed in great numbers and soon became extinct.* **3.** Not wild, troublesome, or uncontrollable; manageable: *In spring that river is a roaring torrent, but in summer it is quite tame.* **4.** Unexciting or uninteresting; dull: *To someone accustomed to driving a racing car, the ride home seemed very tame.* —*v.* **tamed, tam•ing. 1.** To train or accustom (a naturally wild, unmanageable, or timid animal) to live with or be useful to human beings: *tame a skunk; tame a bucking bronco.* **2.** To cause (something wild, troublesome, or unruly) to become manageable or useful; subdue: *The pioneers tamed the wilderness. She tamed her bushy*

talent

Talent *is from Greek* talanton, *which originally meant "a large sum of money." The modern sense was coined by Christ in one of his parables (Matthew 25: 14–30). A rich man, before going on a journey, entrusts various sums of money ("talents") to three servants. On his return, two have doubled their money, but one has kept his without increasing it. The first two are commended, and the third is condemned. The lesson is that abilities are given to men by God, and they have a duty to improve them rather than simply accept them.*

tallith

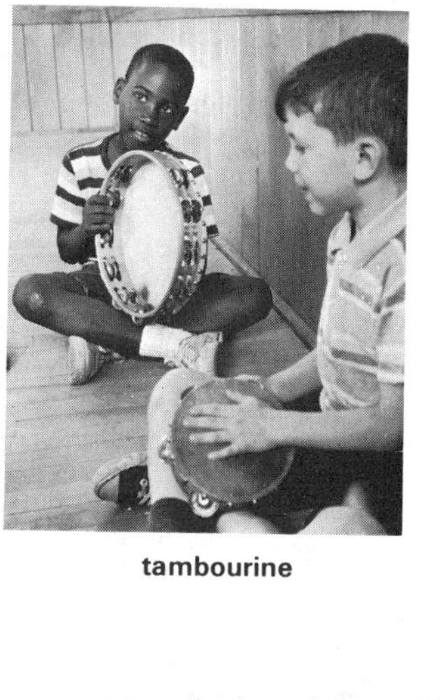

tambourine

hair by brushing it vigorously. —**tame'ly** *adv.* —**tame'ness** *n.* —**tam'er** *n.*

tam-o'-shan•ter |tăm'ə shăn'tər| *n.* A tight-fitting Scottish cap having a soft, full, flat top, sometimes with a pompon or tassel in the center. [SEE PICTURE]

tam-o'-shanter

tamp |tămp| *v.* **1.** To pack down tightly: *tamp the gravel.* **2.** To pack clay, sand, or dirt into (a hole) above an explosive.

Tam•pa |tăm'pə|. A city on the west coast of Florida. Population, 277,000.

tam•per |tăm'pər| *v.* **1.** To interfere in a harmful manner: *caught tampering with the switches.* **2.** To bring about an improper situation in a scheming manner: *tamper with the jury.* —**tam'per•er** *n.*

tam•pon |tăm'pŏn'| *n.* An absorbent plug inserted into a wound or bodily cavity to stop a flow of blood or absorb secretions.

tam-tam |tŭm'tŭm'| *or* |tăm'tăm'| *n.* A type of drum, a tom-tom.

tan |tăn| *v.* **tanned, tan•ning. 1.** To convert (animal hides) into leather, as by treating with tannin. **2.** To make or become brown by exposure to the sun. —*n.* **1.** A light yellowish brown. **2.** The brown color gotten from exposure of the skin to the sun. **3.** Tannin or a solution made from it. —*adj.* **tan•ner, tan•nest.** Light yellowish brown.

tan tangent.

tan•a•ger |tăn'ə jər| *n.* Any of several small, often brightly colored American birds, such as the **scarlet tanager,** of which the male is bright red with a black tail and wings.

tan•bark |tăn'bärk'| *n.* The bark of certain oaks and other trees, used as a source of tannin for tanning leather, and then shredded and used as a ground covering for circus rings, racetracks, etc.

tan•dem |tăn'dəm| *n.* **1.** A bicycle built for two. **2.** An arrangement of two or more people or things placed one behind the other: *horses in tandem.* —*adv.* One behind the other. —*adj.* Arranged in tandem.

tang |tăng| *n.* **1.** A sharp, distinctive flavor, taste, or odor: *the tang of fresh wildflowers.* **2.** A trace or hint of something. **3.** A projection by which a tool, such as a file, chisel, knife, sword, etc. is attached to its handle.

Tan•gan•yi•ka |tăn'gən yē'kə| *or* |tăng'-|. A former country in eastern Africa that joined with Zanzibar in 1964 to form Tanzania.

tan•ge•lo |tăn'jə lō'| *n., pl.* **tan•ge•los.** A citrus fruit that is a cross between a grapefruit and a tangerine.

tan•gent |tăn'jənt| *adj.* Coinciding at a point or along a line but not intersecting at that point or along that line. —*n.* **1.** A line, curve, or surface that is tangent with another. **2.** A function of an acute angle in a right triangle, equal to the length of the side opposite the angle divided by the length of the side adjacent to the angle. **3.** A sudden change of course: *go off on a different tangent.* [SEE PICTURE]

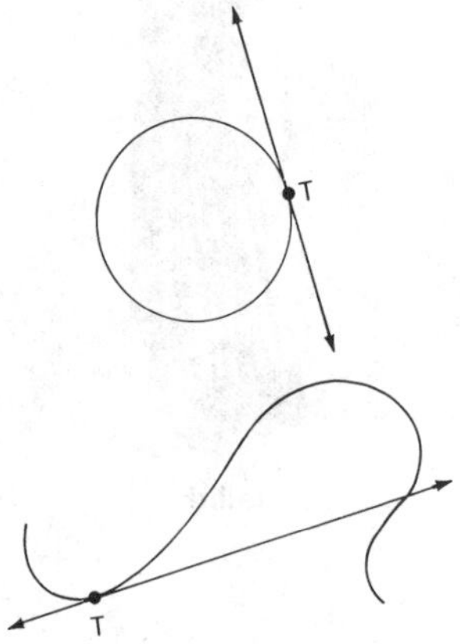

tangent

tan•gen•tial |tăn jĕn'shəl| *adj.* Of or along a tangent. —**tan•gen'tial•ly** *adv.*

tan•ger•ine |tăn'jə rēn'| *n.* **1.** A fruit related to the orange but somewhat smaller, having deep-orange skin that peels easily. **2.** A tree that bears such fruit. **3.** A deep reddish-orange. —*modifier: tangerine juice.* —*adj.* Deep reddish orange.

tan•gi•ble |tăn'jə bəl| *adj.* **1.** Capable of being touched: *a tangible product like steel.* **2.** Capable of being understood or realized: *a tangible benefit.* **3.** Concrete; real: *tangible evidence.* —*n.* **tangibles.** Material assets. —**tan'gi•bly** *adv.*

tan•gle |tăng'gəl| *v.* **tan•gled, tan•gling. 1.** To mix or become mixed together in a confused mass; snarl: *The kitten tangled up the ball of wool. Curly hair tangles easily.* **2.** *Informal.* To come to grips or blows: *She tangled with him in the yard.* —*n.* **1.** A confused, snarled mass: *a tangle of vines.* **2.** A confused state or condition. **3.** *Informal.* An argument.

tan•go |tăng'gō| *n., pl.* **tan•gos. 1.** A ballroom dance of Latin American origin, using various posturing positions and gliding steps. **2.** Music written to accompany or as if to accompany this dance. —*v.* **tan•goed, tan•go•ing, tan•gos.** To dance the tango.

tang•y |tăng'gē| *adj.* **tang•i•er, tang•i•est.** Having a sharp, distinctive flavor, taste, or odor: *a tangy cheese.*

tank |tăngk| *n.* **1.** A large container for holding or storing fluids or gases: *a gasoline tank.* **2. a.** A tank with something in it: *a tank of water.* **b.** The amount a tank holds: *Buy a tank of gas.* **3.** A heavily armored combat vehicle mounted with a cannon and guns and moving on caterpillar treads. **4.** A pool, pond, or reservoir.

tank•ard |tăng'kərd| *n.* A large drinking cup, usually having a handle and a hinged cover.

tank•er |tăng'kər| *n.* A ship, truck, or airplane equipped to carry a large amount of oil or another liquid.

tank top. A sleeveless shirt with wide shoulder straps.

tan•ner |tăn'ər| *n.* Someone who tans hides to make them into leather.

tan•ner•y |tăn'ə rē| *n., pl.* **tan•ner•ies.** A place where hides are tanned.

tan•nic |tăn'ĭk| *adj.* Of or derived from tannin.

tannic acid. A yellowish to light-brown substance obtained from the fruit and bark of certain plants and used in tanning hides, in dyeing and winemaking, and as a medicine.

tan•nin |tăn'ĭn| *n.* **1. Tannic acid. 2.** Any of various other chemicals or mixtures used in tanning hides.

tan•ning |tăn'ĭng| *n.* The process or method of making leather from animal hides.

Ta•no•an |tä'nō ən| *n.* A family of North American Indian languages of New Mexico and northeastern Arizona.

tan•sy |tăn'zē| *n.* A strong-smelling plant with feathery leaves and broad clusters of buttonlike yellow flowers.

tan•ta•lite |tăn'tl īt'| *n.* A black to red-brown mineral that contains tantalum and some niobium and is used as an ore for both.

tan•ta•lize |tăn'tl īz'| *v.* **tan•ta•lized, tan•ta•liz•ing.** To tease or torment by or as if by allowing to see but keeping out of reach something desired. —**tan'ta•liz'ing** *adj.: a tantalizing glimpse.* —**tan'ta•liz'er** *n.*

tan•ta•lum |tăn'tl əm| *n.* Symbol **Ta** One of the elements, a hard, heavy gray metal that is very resistant to corrosion at temperatures below

150°C. Atomic number 73; atomic weight 180.948; valences +2, +3, +4, +5; melting point 2,996°C; boiling point 5,425°C.

tan•ta•mount |tăn'tə mount'| *adj.* Equivalent in effect or value: *a rule tantamount to a dictatorship.*

tan•trum |tăn'trəm| *n.* A fit of bad temper.

Tan•za•ni•a |tăn ză'nē ə| *or* |tăn zə nē'ə|. A country in eastern Africa, on the Indian Ocean. It includes Tanganyika and Zanzibar and a number of other offshore islands. Population, 17,528,000. Capital, Dar es Salaam.

tap[1] |tăp| *v.* **tapped, tap•ping. 1.** To strike gently with a light blow or blows: *tap him on the shoulder.* **2.** To give a light rap with: *tap a pencil.* **3.** To imitate or produce with light blows: *tap out a rhythm.* **4.** To repair or reinforce (shoe heels or toes) by putting on a tap or taps. —*n.* **1. a.** A gentle blow. **b.** The sound made by such a blow. **2. a.** A layer of leather or other material used to repair and reinforce the worn heel or toe of a shoe. **b.** A metal plate attached to the toe or heel of a shoe, as for tap-dancing.

tap[2] |tăp| *n.* **1.** A valve and spout used to regulate the flow of a fluid at the end of a pipe; a faucet; spigot. **2.** A tool for cutting a screw thread into the inner wall of a drilled hole. **3.** A point at which a connection is made in an electric circuit to add another element in parallel with an existing load. —***modifier:*** *tap water.* —*v.* **tapped, tap•ping. 1.** To pierce in order to draw liquid from: *tap a maple tree.* **2. a.** To draw liquid from (a vessel or container): *tap a barrel.* **b.** To draw on: *tap our resources for money.* **3.** To make a connection with, as to divert part of a flow: *tap a telephone.*

***Idiom.* on tap.** Ready to be drawn, as from a cask: *beer on tap.*

ta•pa |tä'pə| *n.* **1.** The fibrous inner bark of a kind of mulberry tree. **2.** A paperlike cloth made in the islands of the Pacific Ocean by pounding this bark.

tap dance. A dance in which the dancer's shoes, often with metal taps on heel and toe, brush or click against the floor so that the rhythm of the steps can be heard. —**tap dancer.**

tap-dance |tăp'dăns'| *or* |-däns'| *v.* **tap-danced, tap-danc•ing.** To perform a tap dance.

tape |tāp| *n.* **1.** A narrow strip of strong, woven fabric. **2.** Any long, narrow, flexible strip of material, such as cloth, plastic, paper, or metal, especially: **a. Adhesive tape. b. Magnetic tape. c.** A **tape measure. 3.** A tape recording. **4.** A string stretched across the finish line of a race. —*v.* **taped, tap•ing. 1.** To fasten, wrap, or bind with tape: *tape a bow on a package; tape up a sprained wrist.* **2.** To measure with a tape measure. **3.** To tape-record. —**taped'** *adj.: a taped television show.*

tape deck. A unit capable of recording and playing back magnetic tapes but lacking loudspeakers and amplifiers, and used as a part of a high-fidelity sound system.

tape measure. A tape of cloth, paper, or metal marked off in a scale, as of inches and feet, and used for taking measurements.

ta•per |tā'pər| *n.* **1.** A gradual decrease in thickness or width of an elongated object: *the taper of a cone.* **2.** A small or slender candle. —*v.* **1.** To make or become gradually thinner toward one end: *taper the legs of a pair of slacks; a candle tapering to a point.* **2.** To become slowly smaller or less; diminish gradually: *The crowd tapered off.* ¶ *These sound alike* **taper, tapir.**

tape-re•cord |tāp'rĭ kôrd'| *v.* To record on magnetic tape.

tape recorder. An instrument capable of recording sound or electrical signals on magnetic tape and usually of playing back the recording.

tap•es•try |tăp'ĭ strē| *n., pl.* **tap•es•tries.** A rich, heavy cloth woven with designs and scenes in many colors, usually hung on walls for decoration and sometimes used to cover furniture.

tape•worm |tāp'wûrm'| *n.* Any of several long, flat, ribbonlike worms that live as parasites in the intestines of human beings and other animals.

tap•i•o•ca |tăp'ē ō'kə| *n.* A starch, often in beadlike or grainy form, obtained from the root of the cassava and used in cooking to make puddings and sometimes to thicken foods such as soups.

ta•pir |tā'pər| *n.* A tropical American or Asian animal with a heavy body, short legs, and a long, fleshy snout. ¶ *These sound alike* **tapir, taper.** [SEE PICTURE]

tap•root |tăp'ro͞ot'| *or* |-ro͝ot'| *n.* The main, often thick root of a plant, growing straight downward from the stem.

taps |tăps| *n. (used with a singular verb).* A military bugle call or drum signal sounded at night as an order to put out lights or at funerals and memorial services.

tar[1] |tär| *n.* **1.** A thick, oily, dark mixture consisting mainly of hydrocarbons, made by destructive distillation of wood, coal, peat, or other organic materials. **2. Coal tar.** —*v.* **tarred, tar•ring.** To coat or cover with tar.

tar[2] |tär| *n. Informal.* A sailor.

tar•an•tel•la |tăr'ən tĕl'ə| *n.* **1.** A lively, whirling dance of southern Italy, having a rhythm similar to that of a very fast jig. **2.** Music written to accompany or as if to accompany this dance. [SEE NOTE]

ta•ran•tu•la |tə răn'chə lə| *n.* Any of several large, hairy, mostly tropical spiders that can give a painful but not seriously poisonous bite. [SEE NOTE & PICTURE]

tar•dy |tär'dē| *adj.* **tar•di•er, tar•di•est. 1.** Occurring or arriving later than expected; delayed: *a tardy guest.* **2.** Moving slowly; sluggish: *tardy acceptance of new ideas.* —**tar'di•ly** *adv.* —**tar'di•ness** *n.*

tare[1] |târ| *n.* A troublesome weed that grows in grain fields, mentioned in the Bible. ¶ *These sound alike* **tare, tear**[1].

tare[2] |târ| *n.* The weight of a container or wrapper, subtracted from the gross weight to obtain the net weight. ¶ *These sound alike* **tare, tear**[1].

tar•get |tär'gĭt| *n.* **1.** Something aimed or fired at: *a target set up on a tree; the target of the bombers.* **2.** An object of criticism, ridicule, or attack: *the target of her satire.* **3.** A desired goal or aim: *the target of the research program.* —***modifier:*** *target practice; a target date.*

tar•iff |tăr'ĭf| *n.* **1.** A list or system of duties imposed by a government on imported or exported goods. **2.** A duty imposed in such a way:

tapir

tarantula

tarantella/tarantula

Tarantula *is from Italian* tarantola, *named after* Taranto, *a city in the extreme south of Italy, where tarantulas abound. In the fifteenth century a hysterical mania for dancing broke out in this region. It was popularly believed that the mania, called* tarantismo, *was caused by the bite of the tarantula and also that it could be cured by dancing the fast local dance called the* **tarantella**. *Anyway, the disease had ceased to occur by the seventeenth century.*

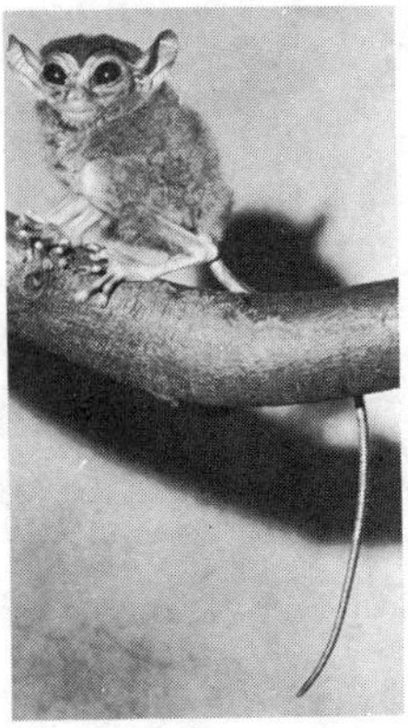
tarsier

tart[1-2]
Tart[1] *was Old English* teart, *"sharp, severe."* **Tart**[2] *is from Old French* torte, *"round bread, twisted object."*

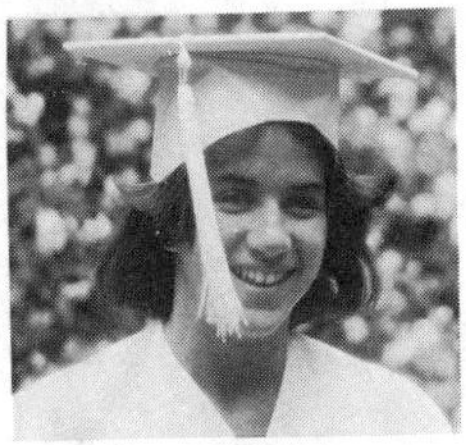
tassel

tat
Tatting with two colors, requiring two shuttles

ă pat/ā pay/â care/ä father/ĕ pet/ ē be/ĭ pit/ī pie/î fierce/ŏ pot/ ō go/ô paw, for/oi oil/o͝o book/ o͞o boot/ou out/ŭ cut/û fur/ *th* the/th thin/hw which/zh vision/ ə ago, item, pencil, atom, circus

a tariff on liquor. **3.** Any schedule of prices or fees. —*modifier: tariff regulations.*

tar•nish |tär′nĭsh| *v.* **1.** To dull or discolor or become discolored, as from exposure to air or dirt: *Nitric acid will tarnish most metals. The silver tarnished.* **2.** To detract from or stain; disgrace: *The scandal tarnished his reputation.* —*n.* **1.** The condition of being tarnished. **2.** A dullness or discoloration, as on silverware.

ta•ro |tär′ō| *or* |tăr′ō| *n., pl.* **ta•ros. 1.** A tropical plant with broad leaves and a large, starchy root used as food. **2.** The potatolike root of this plant.

tarp |tärp| *n.* Tarpaulin.

tar•pa•per |tär′pā′pər| *n.* A heavy grade of paper coated or saturated with tar, used as a waterproof protective material in building.

tar•pau•lin |tär pô′lĭn| *or* |tär′pə-| *n.* Waterproof canvas used to cover and protect things from moisture.

tar•pon |tär′pən| *n., pl.* **tar•pon** or **tar•pons.** A large, silvery fish of the Caribbean Sea and Atlantic coastal waters, often caught for sport.

tar•ra•gon |tăr′ə gŏn′| *or* |-gən| *n.* A plant with mildly spicy, pleasant-smelling leaves, used to flavor salads, cooked foods, etc.

tar•ry[1] |tăr′ē| *v.* **tar•ried, tar•ry•ing, tar•ries. 1.** To delay or be late in coming or going: *tarry on the way to school.* **2.** To remain or stay temporarily.

tar•ry[2] |tär′ē| *adj.* **tar•ri•er, tar•ri•est.** Of or covered with tar: *a tarry substance.*

tar•sal |tär′səl| *adj.* Of or near the ankle.

tar•si•er |tär′sē ər| *or* |-sē ā′| *n.* A small, monkey-like animal of the East Indies, having large eyes and a long tail. [SEE PICTURE]

tar•sus |tär′səs| *n.* **1.** The section of the vertebrate foot located between the leg and the metatarsus; the ankle. **2.** The seven bones making up this section.

tart[1] |tärt| *adj.* **tart•er, tart•est. 1.** Having a sharp, pungent taste; sour: *tart cranberries.* **2.** Sharp in tone or meaning; biting: *a tart answer.* —**tart′ly** *adv.* —**tart′ness** *n.* [SEE NOTE]

tart[2] |tärt| *n.* A small pie with no crust on top. [SEE NOTE]

tar•tan |tär′tn| *n.* **1.** Any of a number of plaid fabric patterns consisting of stripes in different colors and widths crossing one another at right angles against a solid background, and worn especially in Scotland, where each clan has one or more of its own tartans. **2.** A fabric or garment, especially a woolen one, having such a pattern. —*modifier: a tartan shawl.*

tar•tar |tär′tər| *n.* **1.** A reddish acid substance, chiefly a potassium salt of tartaric acid, found in the juice of grapes and deposited on the sides of casks during winemaking. **2.** A hard yellowish deposit that collects on the teeth, consisting of food particles and secretions held together by insoluble salts such as calcium carbonate.

Tar•tar |tär′tər| *n.* **1.** A member of any of the Mongolian peoples of central Asia who invaded western Asia and eastern Europe in the 13th century. **2.** A descendant of these peoples. —**Tar′tar** *adj.*

tar•tar•ic acid |tär tăr′ĭk|. Any of four organic acids having the composition $C_4H_6O_6$ and used in tanning, to make cream of tartar, and in various foods, beverages, and chemicals.

task |tăsk| *or* |täsk| *n.* **1.** A piece of work assigned or done as part of one's duties: *his daily tasks at work.* **2.** A difficult undertaking: *the task of building a nation.* —*v.* To burden with too many tasks.

***Idiom.* take to task.** To censure or reprimand.

task force. A temporary grouping of forces and resources for a specific goal: *a military task force.*

task•mas•ter |tăsk′măs′tər| *or* |täsk′mä′stər| *n.* A person who assigns tasks, especially difficult or burdensome ones.

Tas•ma•ni•a |tăz mā′nē ə|. An island off the southeastern coast of Australia. —**Tas•ma′ni•an** *adj. & n.*

tas•sel |tăs′əl| *n.* **1.** A bunch of loose threads or cords bound at one end and hanging free at the other, used as an ornament on curtains, clothing, etc. **2.** Something resembling this, such as a tuft of hairs on an animal's tail or the pollen-bearing flower cluster of a corn plant. —*v.* **tas•seled** or **tas•selled, tas•sel•ing** or **tas•sel•ling.** To decorate, trim, or fringe with tassels. —**tas′seled** *adj.: a tasseled tablecloth.* [SEE PICTURE]

taste |tāst| *n.* **1.** The sense that distinguishes between the sweet, sour, salty, and bitter qualities of something placed in the mouth. **2.** The sensation produced by or as if by something placed in the mouth; flavor: *the taste of an apple; leaves a bad taste in the mouth.* **3.** A small quantity eaten or tasted: *Take a taste of this.* **4.** A limited experience; a sample: *a taste of success.* **5.** A personal preference or liking for something: *a taste for his music.* **6.** The ability to perceive what is proper or good for certain situations and in certain fields: *a room furnished with great taste; a girl with good taste in clothes.* —*v.* **tast•ed, tast•ing. 1. a.** To distinguish the flavor of by taking into the mouth: *taste the candy.* **b.** To have a distinct flavor: *This candy tastes good.* **2.** To sample a small quantity of: *Just taste it, don't gobble it.* **3.** To experience, as for the first time: *tasting success.* —**tast′er** *n.*

taste buds. The numerous rounded structures distributed over the surface of the tongue that contain cells producing nerve impulses corresponding to sweet, sour, salty, or bitter stimuli; the organs of taste.

taste•ful |tāst′fəl| *adj.* Showing good taste: *a tasteful reply.* —**taste′ful•ly** *adv.* —**taste′ful•ness** *n.*

taste•less |tāst′lĭs| *adj.* **1.** Lacking in flavor: *a tasteless dish.* **2.** Showing poor taste: *a tasteless remark.* —**taste′less•ly** *adv.* —**taste′less•ness** *n.*

tast•y |tā′stē| *adj.* **tast•i•er, tast•i•est.** Having a pleasing flavor: *a tasty meal.* —**tast′i•ly** *adv.* —**tast′i•ness** *n.*

tat |tăt| *v.* **tat•ted, tat•ting.** To make (lace) by looping and knotting a single strand of heavy thread on a small shuttle. [SEE PICTURE]

Ta•tar |tä′tər| *n. & adj.* A form of the word **Tartar.**

tat•ter |tăt′ər| *n.* **1.** A torn and hanging piece, as of cloth; a shred. **2. tatters.** Torn and ragged clothing; rags. —*v.* To make or become ragged, as by tearing or wearing to shreds: *The barbed wire tattered his shirt. His shirt tattered.*

tat•tered |tăt′ərd| *adj.* **1.** Torn or worn to shreds; ragged: *tattered clothes.* **2.** Dressed in ragged clothes: *a tattered ragamuffin.*

tat•ting |tăt′ĭng| *n.* **1.** Handmade lace made by looping and knotting a single strand of heavy thread on a small hand shuttle. **2.** The act or art of making such lace.

tat•tle |tăt′l| *v.* **tat•tled, tat•tling. 1.** To talk idly; prate: *He tattled endlessly over the book he had read.* **2.** To reveal the plans or activities of another; betray by talking: *The boy tattled on his sister. If you don't tattle they can't tell that we were at the movies.* **—tat′tler** *n.*

tat•tle•tale |tăt′l tāl′| *n.* A person who tattles on others.

tat•too[1] |tă to͞o′| *n.* **1.** A signal sounded on a drum or bugle to summon soldiers to their quarters. **2.** A display of military exercises. **3.** Any continuous, even drumming. [SEE NOTE]

tat•too[2] |tă to͞o′| *n.* A mark or design made on the skin by pricking and ingraining an indelible dye or by raising scars. *—v.* **tat•tooed, tat•too•ing, tat•toos.** To mark (the skin) with a tattoo. [SEE NOTE & PICTURE]

tau |tou| *or* |tô| *n.* The 19th letter of the Greek alphabet, written Τ, τ. In English it is represented as *T, t.*

taught |tôt|. Past tense and past participle of **teach.** ¶*These sound alike* **taught, taut.**

taunt |tônt| *v.* To insult with contempt; mock: *taunting the soldiers.* *—n.* A scornful remark.

taupe |tōp| *n.* A brownish gray or a dark yellowish brown. *—adj.* Brownish gray or dark yellowish brown.

Tau•rus |tôr′əs| *n.* The second sign of the zodiac.

taut |tôt| *adj.* **taut•er, taut•est. 1.** Pulled or drawn tight: *sails taut with wind.* **2.** Strained; tense: *his taut and angry face.* **3.** Kept in trim shape; neat: *a taut regiment with strict discipline.* ¶*These sound alike* **taut, taught. —taut′ly** *adv.* **—taut′ness** *n.*

tau•tol•o•gy |tô tŏl′ə jē| *n., pl.* **tau•tol•o•gies. 1.** Needless repetition of the same information, especially in speech or writing; redundancy. **2.** A statement that includes all logical possibilities and is therefore always true; for example, the sentence *The element* x *is either a member of set* A *or not a member of set* A is a tautology.

tav•ern |tăv′ərn| *n.* **1.** A place licensed to sell alcoholic beverages to be drunk on the premises. **2.** An inn for travelers.

taw |tô| *n.* **1.** A large, fancy marble used for shooting. **2.** The line from which a player shoots in marbles.

taw•dry |tô′drē| *adj.* **taw•dri•er, taw•dri•est.** Cheap and gaudy. **—taw′dri•ness** *n.*

taw•ny |tô′nē| *adj.* **taw•ni•er, taw•ni•est.** Light brown: *a tawny mountain lion.*

tax |tăks| *n.* **1.** A charge or contribution required of persons or groups within the domain of a government for the support of that government. **2.** An excessive demand; a strain or burden: *a tax on our system.* ***—modifier:*** *a tax collector.* *—v.* **1.** To place a tax on: *tax cigarettes; tax income.* **2.** To require a tax from: *tax the people.* **3.** To make difficult or excessive demands upon: *Tremendous populations tax the land that supports them.*

tax•a•ble |tăk′sə bəl| *adj.* Subject to taxes: *taxable income.*

tax•a•tion |tăk sā′shən| *n.* The practice of imposing taxes: *no taxation without representation.*

tax•es |tăk′sĭz|. **1.** Plural of the noun **tax. 2.** Third person singular present tense of the verb **tax.**

tax•i |tăk′sē| *n., pl.* **tax•is** or **tax•ies.** A taxicab. ***—modifier:*** *a taxi stand.* *—v.* **1.** To be transported by taxi. **2.** To move slowly over the surface of the ground or water before takeoff or after landing, as an aircraft does.

tax•i•cab |tăk′sē kăb′| *n.* An automobile that carries passengers for a fare, usually registered on a meter.

tax•i•der•mist |tăk′sĭ dûr′mĭst| *n.* A person whose work or hobby is taxidermy.

tax•i•der•my |tăk′sĭ dûr′mē| *n.* The art or process of preparing, stuffing, and mounting the skins of animals in lifelike form.

tax•o•nom•ic |tăk′sə nŏm′ĭk| *adj.* Of or used in taxonomy: *a taxonomic name; taxonomic groups.*

tax•on•o•my |tăk sŏn′ə mē| *n.* The science of classifying living things in specially named groups based on shared characteristics and natural relationships. [SEE NOTE]

tax•pay•er |tăks′pā′ər| *n.* Someone who pays or is required to pay taxes.

Tay•lor |tā′lər|, **Zachary.** 1784–1850. Twelfth President of the United States (1849–50); died in office.

Tb The symbol for the element terbium.

TB, T.B. tuberculosis.

tbs., tbsp. tablespoon; tablespoonful.

Tc The symbol for the element technetium.

Tchai•kov•sky |chī kôf′skē|, **Peter Ilyich.** 1840–1893. Russian composer.

Te The symbol for the element tellurium.

tea |tē| *n.* **1.** A drink prepared with boiling water and the dried leaves of an Asian shrub. **2.** The dried leaves of this shrub. **3.** The shrub that bears such leaves. **4.** A drink resembling tea, prepared from the leaves, flowers, etc., of various plants or from other substances: *herb tea; beef tea.* **5.** A light meal or a social gathering at which tea is served. ***—modifier:*** *tea leaves; a tea party.* ¶*These sound alike* **tea, tee, ti.**
***Idiom.* (one's) cup of tea.** Something one likes very much or that interests one greatly: *Drag racing is not really my cup of tea.*

teach |tēch| *v.* **taught** |tôt|, **teach•ing. 1. a.** To give instruction as an occupation: *She teaches five hours a day.* **b.** To give instruction to: *He teaches kindergarten.* **2.** To provide knowledge of; instruct in: *teach a boy how to swim.* **3.** To show by example or experience: *Science teaches us how to conserve our forests.*

teach•er |tē′chər| *n.* A person who teaches, usually in a school.

teach•ing |tē′chĭng| *n.* **1.** The work or occupation of teachers. **2.** Something taught; instruction: *Christ's teachings.* ***—modifier:*** *teaching methods.*

tea•cup |tē′kŭp′| *n.* A small cup for drinking tea.

teak |tēk| *n.* **1.** A tall Asian tree with large evergreen leaves and hard, strong, heavy wood. **2.** The dark or yellowish-brown wood of such a tree, used for furniture, shipbuilding, etc. ***—modifier:*** *a teak forest; teak logs.*

tea•ket•tle |tē′kĕt′l| *n.* A kettle, usually with a spout, for boiling water, as for tea.

tattoo[1-2]
There was an old Dutch custom of beating a drum when taverns closed at night. This drumbeat was called the taptoe, *"the tap-shutting":* tap, *"tap,"* + toe, *"off." It became a military term for the signal to return to quarters, and was borrowed into English as* **tattoo[1]. Tattoo[2]** *is from Polynesian* tatau.

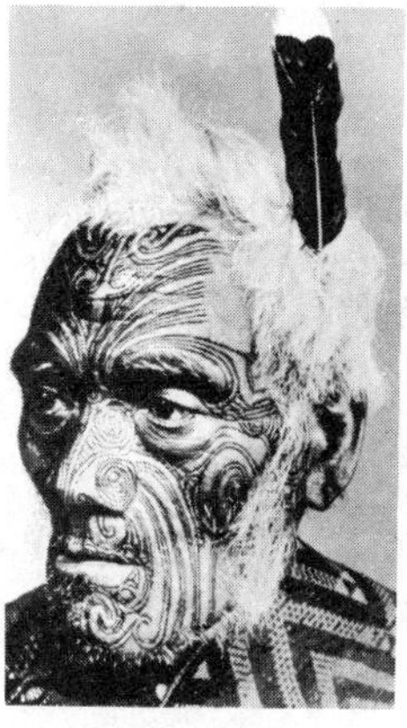

tattoo[2]
Maori chieftain

taxonomy
Taxonomy *means "system of arrangement"; it is from Greek* taxis, *"arrangement,"* + -nomia, *"laws, system."*

teal

tear[1-2]
Tear[1] *was Old English* teran, *"to pull apart."* **Tear[2]** *was Old English* teār, *"a teardrop."*

teddy bear
The **teddy bear** *is named after President Theodore Roosevelt, known as "Teddy." He was a famous big-game hunter, and on one occasion he dramatically spared the life of a bear cub. Toymakers took advantage of the occasion by manufacturing teddy bears.*

ă pat/ā pay/â care/ä father/ĕ pet/ ē be/ĭ pit/ī pie/î fierce/ŏ pot/ ō go/ô paw, for/oi oil/ŏŏ book/ ōō boot/ou out/ŭ cut/û fur/ *th* the/th thin/hw which/zh vision/ ə ago, item, pencil, atom, circus

teal |tēl| *n., pl.* **teal** or **teals.** Any of several small wild ducks, often having brightly marked feathers. [SEE PICTURE]

team |tēm| *n.* **1.** Two or more animals harnessed to a vehicle or farm implement: *a team of horses.* **2.** A group of players on the same side in a game. **3.** Two or more people organized to work together: *a team of scientists.* ***—modifier:*** *a team effort.* —*v.* **1.** To form a team: *The classes teamed up.* **2.** To join together in a team: *team the horses.* ¶*These sound alike* **team, teem.**

team•mate |**tēm**'māt'| *n.* A fellow member of a team.

team•ster |**tēm**'stər| *n.* **1.** A person who drives a team. **2.** A truck driver.

team•work |**tēm**'wûrk'| *n.* Cooperative effort to achieve a common goal.

tea•pot |**tē**'pŏt'| *n.* A covered pot with a handle and spout, used for making and pouring tea.

tear[1] |târ| *v.* **tore** |tôr| *or* |tōr|, **torn** |tôrn| *or* |tōrn|, **tear•ing. 1.** To pull or divide or become divided forcefully into pieces; split; rend: *Tear the paper in half. Some paper tears easily.* **2.** To make (an opening or wound) by or as if by ripping: *tore my best nylons on a chair.* **3.** To separate or remove forcefully: *tear the sponge from the sea with great hooks.* **4.** To divide or disrupt emotionally: *She is torn between duty and loyalty.* **5.** To move with great speed; rush headlong: *He went tearing down the road to town.* ***—phrasal verbs.*** **tear down.** To demolish: *tear down a building.* **tear into.** *Informal.* To attack violently: *The stallion tore into the gate.* **tear up.** To destroy by or as if by tearing: *tear up the rails.* —*n.* **1.** An opening, hole, or flaw made by tearing; a rip. **2.** Damage from or as if from tearing: *the normal wear and tear of clothes.* ¶*These sound alike* **tear[1], tare.** [SEE NOTE]

tear[2] |tîr| *n.* A drop of the clear liquid secreted by glands of the eyes. —*v.* To fill with tears: *The vapor of an onion will make most eyes tear.* ¶*These sound alike* **tear[2], tier.** [SEE NOTE]

tear•drop |**tîr**'drŏp'| *n.* A tear.

tear•ful |**tîr**'fəl| *adj.* Filled with or bringing forth tears: *tearful eyes; a tearful movie.* **—tear'ful•ly** *adv.* **—tear'ful•ness** *n.*

tear gas. Any of various chemicals that when dispersed as a gas or mist irritate the eyes and breathing passages severely, causing choking and heavy tears.

tease |tēz| *v.* **teased, teas•ing. 1.** To annoy or pester by making fun of or taunting: *I tease my dad by calling him my ancestor. She is only teasing.* **2.** To get or try to get by begging or coaxing: *The roadrunner tried to tease the snake into fighting.* **3.** To disentangle the fibers of: *tease wool.* **4.** To raise a nap on (cloth), as with a teasel. **5.** To brush or comb (the hair) toward the scalp for a full, airy effect. —*n.* **1.** Someone who teases. **2.** A remark or taunt used to tease. **—teas'er** *n.*

tea•sel |**tē**'zəl| *n.* **1.** A plant with thistlelike flowers surrounded by stiff bristles. **2.** The flower head of such a plant, used to brush the surface of fabrics so as to form a nap.

tea•spoon |**tē**'spōōn'| *n.* **1.** A small spoon used for stirring liquids, such as tea or coffee, and for eating soft foods, especially desserts. **2. a.** A teaspoon with something in it: *a teaspoon of sugar.* **b.** The amount that a teaspoon holds: *took a teaspoon of medicine.* **3.** A household measure equal to 1/3 tablespoon.

tea•spoon•ful |**tē**'spōōn fŏŏl'| *n., pl.* **tea•spoon•fuls.** The amount that a teaspoon holds.

teat |tēt| *or* |tĭt| *n.* The part of an udder or breast through which milk is taken; a nipple.

tech•ne•ti•um |tĕk **nē**'shē əm| *n.* Symbol **Tc** One of the elements, a silvery-gray metal having 14 isotopes with mass numbers ranging from 92 to 105 and half-lives up to 2.6 million years. Atomic number 43; valences +3, +4, +6, +7; melting point 2,200°C.

tech•ni•cal |**tĕk**'nĭ kəl| *adj.* **1.** Of or derived from technique: *technical ability.* **2.** Of a particular subject; specialized: *technical language; a technical school.* **3.** Of or using scientific knowledge: *a technical analysis.* **4.** Industrial and mechanical; technological: *technical assistance overseas.* **—tech'ni•cal•ly** *adv.*

tech•ni•cal•i•ty |tĕk'nĭ **kăl**'ĭ tē| *n., pl.* **tech•ni•cal•i•ties. 1.** The condition or quality of being technical. **2.** Something, such as a detail, that has meaning only in a specialized subject, field, etc.: *caught on a legal technicality.*

tech•ni•cian |tĕk **nĭsh**'ən| *n.* A person who is skilled in a certain technical field or process: *a dental technician.*

Tech•ni•col•or |**tĕk**'nĭ kŭl'ər| *n.* A trademark for a process used to make motion pictures in color.

tech•nique |tĕk **nēk**'| *n.* **1.** A systematic procedure or method by which a complicated task is accomplished, as in a science or art. **2.** The degree to which someone has mastered one or more such procedures: *a surgeon with a nearly perfect technique.*

tech•no•log•i•cal |tĕk'nə **lŏj**'ĭ kəl| *adj.* Of or resulting from technology: *technological developments.* **—tech'no•log'i•cal•ly** *adv.*

tech•nol•o•gy |tĕk **nŏl**'ə jē| *n., pl.* **tech•nol•o•gies. 1. a.** The application of scientific knowledge, especially in industry and commerce. **b.** The methods and materials used in applying scientific knowledge in this way. **2.** The knowledge that a civilization has available for adapting and using its environment to fit its needs.

ted•dy bear |**tĕd**'ē|. A child's toy bear, usually stuffed with soft material. [SEE PICTURE]

Te De•um |tā' **dā**'əm| *or* |**tē**' **dē**'-|. **1.** A Latin hymn, probably from the early fifth century A.D., beginning with the words *Te Deum laudamus,* "We praise Thee, O God." **2.** A musical setting of this hymn.

te•di•ous |**tē**'dē əs| *adj.* Tiresome because of slowness or length; boring: *a tedious lesson.* **—te'di•ous•ly** *adv.* **—te'di•ous•ness** *n.*

te•di•um |**tē**'dē əm| *n.* The quality or condition of being tedious; boredom.

tee |tē| *n.* **1.** A raised area from which a golfer hits his first shot toward a hole. **2.** A small piece of wood or plastic stuck in the ground to support a golf ball for a shot. —*v.* **teed, tee•ing.** To place (a ball) on a tee. ***—phrasal verb.*** **tee off.** To hit one's first shot toward a hole from a tee. ¶*These sound alike* **tee, tea, ti.**

teem |tēm| *v.* To be full of; abound: *The preserve teemed with a fascinating variety of life.* ¶*These sound alike* **teem, team.**

teen-age or **teen•age** |tēn′āj′| *adj.* Of the ages 13 through 19.
teen-ag•er or **teen•ag•er** |tēn′ā′jər| *n.* A person between the ages of 13 and 19.
teens |tēnz| *pl.n.* **1.** The numbers that end in *-teen.* **2.** The years of one's life between the ages of 13 and 19. **3.** People in their teens.
tee•ny |tē′nē| *adj.* **tee•ni•er, tee•ni•est.** *Informal.* Tiny.
tee•pee |tē′pē| *n.* A form of the word **tepee.**
tee•ter |tē′tər| *v.* **1.** To walk or move unsteadily; totter. **2.** To seesaw. —*n.* A seesaw.
tee•ter-tot•ter |tē′tər tŏt′ər| *n.* A seesaw.
teeth |tēth| *n.* Plural of **tooth.**
teethe |tē*th*| *v.* **teethed, teeth•ing.** To have teeth develop and come through the gums, as a baby does.
tee•to•tal•er |tē tōt′l ər| *n.* A person who does not drink alcoholic beverages. [SEE NOTE]
Tef•lon |tĕf′lŏn′| *n.* A trademark for a durable plastic based on compounds of carbon and fluorine, used to coat certain cooking utensils and to prevent sticking of machine parts.
Te•gu•ci•gal•pa |tā gōō′sē gäl′pä|. The capital of Honduras. Population, 250,000.
Te•he•ran |tē′ə răn′| *or* |-rän′|. The capital and largest city of Iran. Population, 3,858,000.
tek•tite |tĕk′tīt′| *n.* Any of numerous dark brown to green glassy objects, usually small and round, composed of silica and various oxides and found in several parts of the world. [SEE PICTURE]
Tel A•viv-Jaf•fa |tĕl′ ə vēv′ jăf′ə|. The largest city in Israel, a port on the Mediterranean Sea. Population, 343,000.
tele–. A word element that means: **1.** Distance: **telegraph.** **2.** Television: **telecast.**
tel•e•cast |tĕl′ĭ kăst′| *or* |-käst′| *v.* **tel•e•cast** or **tel•e•cast•ed, tel•e•cast•ing.** To broadcast (a program or programs) by television. —*n.* A television broadcast.
tel•e•com•mu•ni•ca•tion |tĕl′ĭ kə myōō′nĭ kā′shən| *n.* Often **telecommunications** *(used with a singular verb).* The science and technology of sending messages over long distances, especially by electrical or electronic means.
teleg. **1.** telegram. **2.** telegraph. **3.** telegraphy.
tel•e•gram |tĕl′ĭ grăm′| *n.* A message or communication sent by telegraph.
tel•e•graph |tĕl′ĭ grăf′| *or* |-gräf′| *n.* **1.** A communications system in which a message is sent, either by wire or radio, to a receiving station. **2.** A message sent by such a system; a telegram. —***modifier:*** *a telegraph operator.* —*v.* **1.** To send (a message) by telegraph: *telegraph our congratulations.* **2.** To communicate with (someone) by telegraph.
te•leg•ra•pher |tə lĕg′rə fər| *n.* Someone who operates a telegraph device or system.
tel•e•graph•ic |tĕl′ĭ grăf′ĭk| or **tel•e•graph•i•cal** |tĕl′ĭ grăf′ĭ kəl| *adj.* Of or sent by telegraphy.
te•leg•ra•phy |tə lĕg′rə fē| *n.* **1.** Communication by means of telegraph. **2.** The science and technology used in accomplishing this.
te•lem•e•ter |tə lĕm′ĭ tər| *or* |tĕl′ə mē′tər| *n.* Any of various devices used in telemetry. —*v.* |tĕl′ə-mē′tər|. To measure and transmit (data) automatically from a distant source, such as a spacecraft or a remotely controlled aircraft, to a receiving station.
te•lem•e•try |tə lĕm′ĭ trē| *n.* **1.** The automatic measurement and transmission of data from a distant source to a receiving station. **2.** The science and technology used in doing this.
tel•e•path•ic |tĕl′ə păth′ĭk| *adj.* Of, transmitted by, or possessing telepathy.
te•lep•a•thy |tə lĕp′ə thē| *n.* **1.** Communication between individuals by some means that cannot at present be explained scientifically. **2.** The ability to engage in such communication.
tel•e•phone |tĕl′ə fōn′| *n.* An instrument that reproduces or receives sound, especially speech, at a distance. —***modifier:*** *a telephone operator.* —*v.* **tel•e•phoned, tel•e•phon•ing.** **1.** To call or communicate with (someone) by telephone. **2.** To transmit (a message or information) by telephone.
telephone exchange. Any of numerous central systems of switches and other equipment that establish connections between individual telephones.
te•leph•o•ny |tə lĕf′ə nē| *n.* **1.** The transmission of sound between distant points, especially by electronic or electrical means. **2.** The science and technology used in accomplishing this.
tel•e•pho•to•graph |tĕl′ə fō′tə grăf′| *or* |-gräf′| *n.* **1.** A photograph made with a telephoto lens. **2.** A photograph transmitted by telephotography.
tel•e•pho•tog•ra•phy |tĕl′ə fə tŏg′rə fē| *n.* **1.** The photographing of distant objects, as by using a telephoto lens or a camera coupled to a telescope. **2.** The transmission of photographs, pictures, charts, etc., over long distances.
tel•e•pho•to lens |tĕl′ə fō′tō|. A lens that can be attached to a camera in order to photograph a large image of a distant object or a clear image of a near object against a blurred background.
tel•e•print•er |tĕl′ə prĭn′tər| *n.* A teletypewriter.
tel•e•scope |tĕl′ĭ skōp′| *n.* **1.** A device that uses an arrangement of lenses, mirrors, or both to collect visible light, allowing observation or photographic recording of distant objects. **2.** Any of various devices, such as a radio telescope, used to collect and analyze electromagnetic radiation other than light coming from distant sources. —*v.* **tel•e•scoped, tel•e•scop•ing.** **1.** To slide or cause to slide inward or outward in overlapping sections, as the tube sections of a small hand telescope. **2.** To crush or compress (an object) inward. **3.** To make shorter; condense: *telescoping several instructions for a recipe into one sentence.*
tel•e•scop•ic |tĕl′ĭ skŏp′ĭk| *adj.* **1.** Of a telescope or telescopes. **2.** Seen or obtained by means of a telescope: *telescopic data.* **3.** Visible only by means of a telescope: *a telescopic binary star.* **4.** Capable of seeing or resolving distant objects: *telescopic vision.* **5.** Capable of telescoping or being telescoped: *a telescopic antenna.*
Tel•e•type |tĕl′ĭ tīp′| *n.* A trademark for a brand of teletypewriter. —*v.* **Tel•e•typed, Tel•e•typ•ing.** **1.** To operate a Teletype. **2.** To send (a message) by Teletype.
tel•e•type•writ•er |tĕl′ĭ tīp′rī′tər| *n.* A device, somewhat like a typewriter in appearance and

teetotaler
This word is from the phrase tee-total abstainer, *which was coined by temperance workers in the 1830's. The* tee- *is simply a reduplication of the* t *in* total; tee-total *was a catchy way of saying "absolutely total."*

tektite
Examples of tektites found in Australia

tellurium
Although **tellurium** *has a generally metallic appearance, it has some of the properties of a nonmetal, forming compounds analogous to those of sulfur. It is used in steel and lead alloys, in ceramics, and in thermoelectric devices.*

temperature
Temperature *can be understood in terms of the fact that if two material bodies or systems are placed in contact so that heat can flow between them, the heat flows from the body with the higher temperature to that with the lower temperature until the two temperatures are equal.*

temple[1·2]
Temple[1] *is from Latin* templum, *"sanctuary, shrine, temple."* **Temple[2]** *is from Latin* tempus, *"flat side of the head." These two words are not related to each other, nor are they related to the other Latin word* tempus *that means "time."*

ă pat/ā pay/â care/ä father/ĕ pet/ ē be/ĭ pit/ī pie/î fierce/ŏ pot/ ō go/ô paw, for/oi oil/o͝o book/ o͞o boot/ou out/ŭ cut/û fur/ *th* the/th thin/hw which/zh vision/ ə ago, item, pencil, atom, circus

operation, that either transmits or receives telegraph messages.

tel•e•vise |tĕl′ə vīz′| *v.* **tel•e•vised, tel•e•vis•ing.** To broadcast by television.

tel•e•vi•sion |tĕl′ə vĭzh′ən| *n.* **1.** The transmission and reception of visual images of moving or stationary objects, usually with accompanying sound, as electrical signals or by means of radio. **2.** A device that receives such electrical signals or radio waves and reproduces the transmitted images on a screen. **3.** The industry of broadcasting programs in this medium. ***—modifier:*** *a television transmitter; a television antenna; a television program.*

tell |tĕl| *v.* **told** |tōld|, **tell•ing. 1.** To express in words; say: *tell a lie.* **2. a.** To give an account of; describe or relate: *tell a story.* **b.** To give an account: *tell of one's troubles.* **3.** To make known; indicate or inform: *The temperature of something tells how hot or cold it is.* **4.** To discover by observation; perceive or identify: *It is hard to tell how far a teacher's influence extends.* **5.** To command; order: *Do as you are told.* ***—phrasal verbs.*** **tell apart.** To recognize the difference between. **tell off.** *Informal.* To criticize or scold sharply. **tell on. 1.** To have a noticeable effect: *Her nervousness began to tell on her face.* **2.** *Informal.* To tattle on.

tell•er |tĕl′ər| *n.* **1.** A person who tells something, such as a story, tale, etc. **2.** A bank employee who receives and pays out money. **3.** A person appointed to count votes in a legislative assembly.

tell•ing |tĕl′ĭng| *adj.* **1.** Having force or effect; striking: *a telling attack.* **2.** Full of meaning; revealing: *a telling remark.* **—tell′ing•ly** *adv.*

tell•tale |tĕl′tāl′| *n.* Someone or something that reveals information about something. *—adj.* Serving to indicate or reveal: *a telltale odor.*

tel•lu•ride |tĕl′yə rīd′| *n.* A chemical compound of tellurium and another element.

tel•lu•ri•um |tĕ lo͝or′ē əm| *n.* Symbol **Te** One of the elements, a brittle, silvery-white metal that occurs combined with gold and other metals. Atomic number 52; atomic weight 127.60; valences –2, +2, +4, +6; melting point 449.5°C; boiling point 989.8°C. [SEE NOTE]

tel•o•phase |tĕl′ə fāz′| *n.* The final phase of mitosis, in which the chromosomes of the daughter cells are grouped in new nuclei.

Tel•star |tĕl′stär′| *n.* Either of two privately financed communications satellites launched by the U.S. Government in 1962 and 1963, used to receive and retransmit television and telephone signals.

te•mer•i•ty |tə mĕr′ĭ tē| *n.* Foolish boldness; recklessness; rashness.

temp. 1. temperature. **2.** temporary.

tem•per |tĕm′pər| *v.* **1.** To soften or moderate: *tempering justice with mercy.* **2.** To harden, strengthen, or toughen (a material, especially a metal) by heating, alternate heating and cooling, or other special treatment. **3.** To tune or adjust (a keyboard instrument) so that no intervals or chords sound noticeably false although all but the octave are slightly out of tune. *—n.* **1.** A condition of the mind or emotions; mood; disposition. **2.** Calmness of the mind or emotions; composure: *Don't lose your temper over small annoyances.* **3. a.** A tendency to become angry or irritable: *a bad temper.* **b.** An outburst of rage: *a fit of temper.* **4.** The degree to which a material, especially a metal, has been hardened, strengthened, or toughened by tempering.

tem•per•a |tĕm′pər ə| *n.* **1.** A type of paint made by mixing pigment with a sticky substance, such as egg yolk or glue, that is soluble in water. **2.** Painting done with this type of paint.

tem•per•a•ment |tĕm′pər ə mənt| *or* |-prə-mənt| *n.* **1.** The manner in which an individual thinks, behaves, and reacts in general: *a nervous temperament.* **2.** The way in which a keyboard instrument is tuned as a result of tempering, especially equal temperament.

tem•per•a•ment•al |tĕm′prə **mĕn′**tl| *or* |-pər-ə-| *adj.* Excessively sensitive, irritable, or changeable: *a temperamental person.*

tem•per•ance |tĕm′pər əns| *or* |-prəns| *n.* **1.** The condition of being moderate or temperate. **2.** Total abstinence from alcoholic beverages.

tem•per•ate |tĕm′pər ĭt| *or* |-prĭt| *adj.* **1.** Exercising moderation and self-restraint. **2.** Moderate; mild. **3.** Of or having a climate that is mild or variable rather than always hot or always cold.

Temperate Zone. Either of two zones on the earth's surface. The **North Temperate Zone** lies between the Arctic Circle and the tropic of Cancer. The **South Temperate Zone** lies between the Antarctic Circle and the tropic of Capricorn.

tem•per•a•ture |tĕm′pər ə chər| *or* |-prə chər| *n.* **1. a.** The relative hotness or coldness of a body or environment. **b.** A numerical measure of hotness or coldness referred to a standard scale. **2.** A body temperature that is raised above normal as a result of some disease or disorder; fever. [SEE NOTE]

tem•pered |tĕm′pərd| *adj.* **1.** Strengthened, hardened, or toughened by tempering: *a tempered steel blade.* **2.** Tuned to a temperament, especially equal temperament, as a musical tone, interval, instrument, etc.

tem•pest |tĕm′pĭst| *n.* **1.** A violent windstorm, often with rain, snow, hail, etc. **2.** Any violent commotion or tumult; uproar.

tem•pes•tu•ous |tĕm **pĕs′**cho͞o əs| *adj.* Stormy; turbulent: *a tempestuous legislative session.* **—tem•pes′tu•ous•ly** *adv.* **—tem•pes′tu•ous•ness** *n.*

tem•pi |tĕm′pē| *n.* A plural of **tempo.**

tem•plate |tĕm′plĭt| *n.* A pattern or gauge, such as a thin metal plate cut to a definite pattern, used in making something accurately or in duplicating something, as in carpentry.

tem•ple[1] |tĕm′pəl| *n.* **1.** A building or place dedicated to the worship or presence of a deity: *the temple of Athena.* **2.** Any house of worship, especially a synagogue. [SEE NOTE]

tem•ple[2] |tĕm′pəl| *n.* Either of the flat regions at the sides of the head adjoining the forehead. [SEE NOTE]

tem•plet |tĕm′plĭt| *n.* A form of the word **template.**

tem•po |tĕm′pō| *n., pl.* **tem•pos** or **tem•pi** |tĕm′-pē|. **1.** The speed at which a musical composition is played. **2.** A rate or rhythm of something; pace: *the tempo of the chase.*

tem•po•ral[1] |tĕm′pər əl| *or* |-prəl| *adj.* **1.** Of or limited by time. **2.** Of worldly affairs, especially as distinguished from religious concerns: *the temporal powers of the church.* —**tem'po•ral•ly** *adv.*

tem•po•ral[2] |tĕm'pər əl| *or* |-prəl| *adj.* Of or near the temples of the skull.

tem•po•rar•y |tĕm'pə rĕr'ē| *adj.* Lasting or used for a limited time only; not permanent: *Congress made New York City the temporary capital in 1789.* —*n.* A person who serves for a limited time only. —**tem'po•rar'i•ly** *adv.*

tem•po•rize |tĕm'pə rīz'| *v.* **tem•po•rized, tem•po•riz•ing.** To compromise or act evasively in order to gain time or postpone a decision. —**tem'po•ri•za'tion** *n.* —**tem'po•riz'er** *n.*

tempt |tĕmpt| *v.* **1.** To persuade or try to persuade to commit an unwise or immoral act. **2.** To be attractive to: *Your offer tempts me.* **3.** To provoke or risk provoking: *Do not tempt your fate.*

temp•ta•tion |tĕmp tā'shən| *n.* **1.** The act of tempting: *the temptation of young people by bad company.* **2.** The condition of being tempted: *yielding to temptation.* **3.** Something that tempts or entices: *Desserts were a real temptation for her.*

tempt•er |tĕmp'tər| *n.* **1.** A person who tempts. **2. the Tempter.** Satan; the Devil.

temp•ting |tĕmp'tĭng| *adj.* Alluring; attractive: *a tempting offer.*

tem•pu•ra |tĕm'po͝o rə| *or* |tĕm po͝or'ə| *n.* A Japanese dish of vegetables and shrimp or other seafood dipped in batter and fried.

ten |tĕn| *n.* A number, written 10 in Arabic numerals, that is equal to the sum of 9 + 1. It is the positive integer that immediately follows 9. —**ten** *adj. & pron.*

ten•a•ble |tĕn'ə bəl| *adj.* Defensible or logical: *His theory is hardly tenable.* —**ten'a•bil'i•ty, ten'a•ble•ness** *n.* —**ten'a•bly** *adv.*

te•na•cious |tə nā'shəs| *adj.* **1.** Holding or tending to hold firmly; persistent; stubborn: *a man tenacious of opinion and averse to any innovations.* **2.** Clinging to another object or surface. **3.** Tending to retain; retentive: *a tenacious memory.* —**te•nac'i•ty** |tə năs'ĭ tē| *n.*

ten•an•cy |tĕn'ən sē| *n., pl.* **ten•an•cies. 1.** The possession or occupancy of lands or buildings by lease or rent. **2.** The period of a tenant's occupancy or possession.

ten•ant |tĕn'ənt| *n.* **1.** A person who pays rent to use or occupy land, a building, or other property owned by another. **2.** An occupant, inhabitant, or dweller in any place.

tenant farmer. A person who lives on and farms land owned by another and pays rent in cash or with a share of the produce.

Ten Commandments. The ten laws given to Moses by God.

tend[1] |tĕnd| *v.* **1.** To move or extend in a certain direction: *Our course tended toward the north.* **2.** To be likely: *Pressure at the office tends to make her grouchy.* **3.** To be disposed or inclined: *She tends toward laziness.* [SEE NOTE]

tend[2] |tĕnd| *v.* **1.** To look after: *tend a child.* **2.** To serve at: *tend bar.* [SEE NOTE]

ten•den•cy |tĕn'dən sē| *n., pl.* **ten•den•cies. 1.** A demonstrated inclination to think, act, or behave in a certain way; propensity: *He has a tendency to write long paragraphs.* **2.** A natural inclination: *a girl with artistic tendencies.*

ten•der[1] |tĕn'dər| *adj.* **1.** Easily crushed, bruised, etc.; delicate; fragile: *tender flower petals.* **2.** Young and vulnerable: *a child in its tender age.* **3.** Not tough: *a tender steak.* **4. a.** Easily hurt; sensitive: *her tender skin.* **b.** Painful; sore: *a tender tooth.* **5.** Gentle and loving: *a tender heart; a tender mother; a tender glance.* [SEE NOTE]

ten•der[2] |tĕn'dər| *n.* **1.** A formal offer or bid. **2.** Money, especially legal tender. —*v.* To offer formally: *tender a letter of resignation.* [SEE NOTE]

ten•der[3] |tĕn'dər| *n.* **1.** A person who tends something: *a furnace tender.* **2.** A small boat that ferries supplies, passengers, etc., between a large ship and shore. **3.** A railroad car attached to the locomotive, carrying fuel and water. [SEE NOTE]

ten•der•heart•ed |tĕn'dər här'tĭd| *adj.* Easily moved by another's distress; compassionate.

ten•der•ize |tĕn'də rīz'| *v.* **ten•der•ized, ten•der•iz•ing.** To make (meat) tender, as by marinating or pounding.

ten•der•iz•er |tĕn'də rī'zər| *n.* A substance put on meat to make it tender.

ten•der•loin |tĕn'dər loin'| *n.* A tender portion of a loin of beef or pork.

ten•don |tĕn'dən| *n.* A band of tough fibrous tissue that forms a connection between a muscle and a bone.

ten•dril |tĕn'drəl| *n.* **1.** One of the slender, coiling, stemlike parts by means of which a climbing plant clings to something. **2.** Something resembling this: *curls forming tendrils over her ears.* [SEE PICTURE]

ten•e•ment |tĕn'ə mənt| *n.* **1.** A building to live in, especially one intended for rent. **2.** A cheap apartment house whose facilities and maintenance barely meet minimum standards.

ten•et |tĕn'ĭt| *n.* A basic principle, doctrine, or dogma held by a person or an organization.

ten-gallon hat. A felt hat with a wide brim and tall crown, popular in Texas. [SEE PICTURE]

Tenn. Tennessee.

Ten•nes•see |tĕn'ĭ sē'|. A Southern state of the United States. Population, 3,960,000. Capital, Nashville. —**Ten'nes•se'an** *adj. & n.*

ten•nis |tĕn'ĭs| *n.* A sport played between two person (*singles*) or two pairs of persons (*doubles*) on a court divided in two by a net. A player strikes a ball with a racket, the object being to make the ball bounce in the opposing half of the court in such a way that the opposition cannot return it.

tennis shoes. Sneakers.

ten•on |tĕn'ən| *n.* A projection on the end of a piece of wood or other material, designed to fit into a mortise.

ten•or |tĕn'ər| *n.* **1. a.** A voice of an adult male singer, higher than a baritone and lower than an alto. **b.** A person having such a voice. **c.** A part written in the range of this voice. **2.** The general meaning; gist; drift: *He knew enough German to get the tenor of what was being said.* —***modifier:*** *a tenor aria.*

ten•pin |tĕn'pĭn'| *n.* **1.** A bowling pin used in playing tenpins. **2. tenpins** *(used with a singular verb).* A game, bowling.

tense[1] |tĕns| *adj.* **tens•er, tens•est. 1.** Taut;

tend[1-2]

Tend[1] *is from Latin* tendere, *"to stretch, to extend in a particular direction, to be inclined toward."* **Tend[2]** *is shortened from* **attend,** *which in turn is from Latin* attendere, *"to stretch toward, to think about"*; attendere *is a compound verb formed from* ad-, *"toward,"* + tendere, *"to stretch,"* **tend[1]** *(as above).*

tender[1-2-3]

Tender[1] *is from the Old French adjective* tendre, *which is from Latin* tener, *"soft, delicate."* **Tender[2]** *is from the Old French verb* tendre, *"to offer," which is from Latin* tendere, *"to stretch, extend,"* **tend[1]**. **Tender[3]** *is from* **tend[2]**.

tendril

ten-gallon hat
Texas cowboys, 1908

tepee
Plains Indian tepee of poles and buffalo hides

termite
"Some primal termite knocked on wood / And tasted it, and found it good, / And that is why your Cousin May / Fell through the parlor floor today." —*Ogden Nash (1902–71).*

tern
Painting by John James Audubon

ă pat/ā pay/â care/ä father/ĕ pet/ē be/ĭ pit/ī pie/î fierce/ŏ pot/ō go/ô paw, for/oi oil/o͝o book/o͞o boot/ou out/ŭ cut/û fur/*th* the/th thin/hw which/zh vision/ə ago, item, pencil, atom, circus

strained: *tense muscles.* **2.** Nerve-racking; suspenseful: *a tense situation.* —*v.* **tensed, tens•ing.** To make or become tense.

tense^2 |tĕns| *n.* Any of the inflected forms of a verb that indicate the time and continuance or completion of the action or state. For example, *I eat* is in the present tense, *I ate* is in the past tense, and *I will eat* is in the future tense.

ten•sile |tĕn'səl| *or* |-sīl'| *adj.* Of or having to do with tension.

tensile strength. The resistance of a material to a force that tends to pull it apart, usually expressed as the measure of the largest force that can be applied in this way before the material breaks apart.

ten•sion |tĕn'shən| *n.* **1. a.** The act or process of stretching. **b.** The condition of being stretched. **2. a.** A force that tends to stretch or elongate something. **b.** The measure of such a force: *a tension of 50 pounds.* **3.** A difference of electrical potential; voltage; electromotive force. **4.** Strain or stress that affects the mind, nerves, or emotions: *working under great tension.* **5.** A strained relation between persons or groups: *noticing the tension among his teammates.*

tent |tĕnt| *n.* A portable shelter, as of canvas stretched over a supporting framework of poles, ropes, and pegs.

ten•ta•cle |tĕn'tə kəl| *n.* **1.** One of the narrow, flexible, unjointed parts extending from the body of certain animals, such as an octopus, jellyfish, or sea anemone, and used for grasping, moving, etc. **2.** Something resembling a tentacle, especially in the ability to grasp or hold.

ten•ta•tive |tĕn'tə tĭv| *adj.* Not certain or permanent; not definite: *tentative plans; a tentative production schedule.*

ten•ter |tĕn'tər| *n.* A frame on which manufactured cloth is stretched while it dries to keep it from shrinking.

ten•ter•hook |tĕn'tər ho͝ok'| *n.* A sharp, hooked nail used to fasten cloth on a frame for stretching.

Idiom. **on tenterhooks.** In a worried, nervous, or anxious state of mind; in suspense.

tenth |tĕnth| *n.* **1.** In a set of items arranged to match the natural numbers in a one-to-one correspondence, the item that matches the number ten. **2.** One of ten equal parts of a unit, written $^1/_{10}$. —**tenth** *adj. & adv.*

ten•u•ous |tĕn'yo͞o əs| *adj.* **1.** Having a thin or slender form: *a tenuous nylon rope.* **2.** Having little substance; flimsy: *the tenuous character of his political ideas.* —**ten'u•ous•ly** *adv.* —**ten'u•ous•ness** *n.*

ten•ure |tĕn'yər| *or* |-yo͝or'| *n.* **1.** The holding of something, as an office; occupation. **2.** The terms under which something is held. **3. a.** The period of holding something. **b.** Permanence of position, often granted an employee after a specified number of years: *academic tenure.*

te•pee |tē'pē| *n.* A cone-shaped tent of skins or bark used by North American Indians. [SEE PICTURE]

tep•id |tĕp'ĭd| *adj.* Moderately warm; lukewarm: *tepid water.*

te•qui•la |tə kē'lə| *n.* An alcoholic liquor made from the juice of a Central American century plant.

ter•bi•um |tûr'bē əm| *n.* Symbol **Tb** One of the elements, a soft, silvery-gray rare-earth metal. Atomic number 65; atomic weight 158.924; valences +3, +4; melting point 1,356°C; boiling point 2,800°C.

term |tûrm| *n.* **1. a.** A period of time through which something lasts: *a school term.* **b.** An assigned period for a person to serve: *a six-year term as senator.* **2.** A point of time beginning or ending a period: *a lease approaching its term.* **3. a.** A word having a precise meaning, especially one that is part of the special vocabulary of a particular group or activity: *a medical term.* **b. terms.** Language or manner of expression employed: *He spoke in no uncertain terms.* **4. terms. a.** Conditions or stipulations: *peace terms.* **b.** The relation between two persons or groups: *on speaking terms.* **5. a.** Each of the quantities or expressions that form the parts of a ratio or the numerator and denominator of a fraction. **b.** Any of the quantities in an equation that are connected to other quantities by a plus sign or minus sign.

Idioms. **bring to terms.** To force to submit or agree. **come to terms.** To reach an agreement.

ter•ma•gant |tûr'mə gənt| *n.* A shrewish woman.

ter•mi•nal |tûr'mə nəl| *adj.* **1.** Pertaining to, situated at, or forming the end or boundary of something. **2.** Ending in death; fatal: *terminal cancer.* —*n.* **1.** A terminating point, limit, or part. **2.** A point at which another conductor can be connected to an electric device or component. **3.** The station at the end of a railway, bus line, or air line. —**ter'mi•nal•ly** *adv.*

ter•mi•nate |tûr'mə nāt'| *v.* **ter•mi•nat•ed, ter•mi•nat•ing.** To put an end to or come to an end: *terminate an employee's contract. The meeting terminated at noon.* —**ter'mi•na'tion** *n.*

ter•mi•ni |tûr'mə nī'| *n.* A plural of **terminus.**

ter•mi•nol•o•gy |tûr'mə nŏl'ə jē| *n., pl.* **ter•mi•nol•o•gies.** The technical terms of a particular trade, science, or art; nomenclature.

ter•mi•no•log•i•cal |tûr'mə nə lŏj'ĭ kəl| *adj.* Of terminology.

ter•mi•nus |tûr'mə nəs| *n., pl.* **ter•mi•nus•es** or **ter•mi•ni** |tûr'mə nī'|. **1.** The end of something. **2. a.** A terminal on a transportation line. **b.** The last stop on such a line.

ter•mite |tûr'mīt'| *n.* Any of several insects that live in large colonies and that feed on and destroy wood. Termites resemble ants in appearance and manner of living but are not related to them. [SEE PICTURE]

tern |tûrn| *n.* Any of several sea birds related to and resembling the gulls, but generally smaller and with a forked tail. ¶*These sound alike* **tern, turn.** [SEE PICTURE]

terr. territorial; territory.

ter•race |tĕr'əs| *n.* **1.** A porch or balcony. **2.** An open area adjacent to a house; a patio. **3.** A raised bank of earth having vertical or sloping sides and a flat top. **4.** A row of buildings erected on raised ground or on a sloping site. —*v.* **ter•raced, ter•rac•ing.** To form into a terrace or terraces.

ter•ra cot•ta |tĕr'ə kŏt'ə|. **1.** A hard, waterproof ceramic clay used in pottery and building construction. **2.** Pottery or ceramic ware made of this material. —**modifier:** **(terra-cotta):** *a terra-cotta vase.*

ter•rain |tə rān′| *or* |tĕ-| *n.* A tract of land, especially when considered with respect to its physical features: *hilly terrain; rugged terrain.*

Ter•ra•my•cin |tĕr′ə mī′sĭn| *n.* A trademark for an antibiotic drug extracted from a soil mold and used against bacterial infections of human beings and animals.

ter•ra•pin |tĕr′ə pĭn| *n.* Any of several North American turtles of ponds or coastal waters, often valued as food. [SEE PICTURE]

ter•rar•i•um |tə râr′ē əm| *n., pl.* **ter•rar•i•ums** or **ter•rar•i•a** |tə râr′ē ə|. An often box-shaped or bowl-shaped glass container in which small plants are grown, or small animals, such as turtles, are kept. [SEE PICTURE]

ter•res•tri•al |tə rĕs′trē əl| *adj.* **1.** Of, relating to, or on the earth: *The craters of the moon look like some terrestrial craters.* **2.** Of or consisting of land as distinguished from water or air. **3.** Living or growing on land.

ter•ri•ble |tĕr′ə bəl| *adj.* **1.** Causing terror or fear; dreadful: *witnessing a terrible accident; a terrible storm.* **2.** Severe; intense: *the terrible heat of a summer day in the tropics.* **3.** Unpleasant; disagreeable: *a terrible time at the party.* **4.** Very bad: *a terrible movie.* —**ter′ri•bly** *adv.*

ter•ri•er |tĕr′ē ər| *n.* Any of several usually small, active dogs originally used for hunting small, burrowing animals.

ter•ri•fic |tə rĭf′ĭk| *adj.* **1.** Terrifying or frightful: *a terrific hurricane.* **2.** *Informal.* Very good: *a terrific party.* **3.** Awesome; astounding: *a terrific speed.* **4.** Very great; intense: *working under terrific pressure from his boss.* —**ter•rif′i•cal•ly** *adv.* [SEE NOTE]

ter•ri•fy |tĕr′ə fī′| *v.* **ter•ri•fied, ter•ri•fy•ing, ter•ri•fies.** To fill with terror: *Heights terrified her.*

ter•ri•to•ri•al |tĕr′ĭ tôr′ē əl| *or* |-tōr′-| *adj.* Of a territory, especially one that is a division of a country: *territorial claims against the state.*

territorial waters. Inland and coastal waters under the jurisdiction of a country.

ter•ri•to•ry |tĕr′ĭ tôr′ē| *or* |-tōr′ē| *n., pl.* **ter•ri•to•ries. 1.** An area of land; a region. **2.** The land and waters under the jurisdiction of a state, nation, or government. **3. Territory.** A part of the United States not admitted as a state. **4.** The area for which a person is responsible as a salesman, agent, etc.: *Northern Massachusetts is his territory.* **5.** An area that is regarded by an individual or group as its own and that is often defended vigorously against outsiders: *The boys warned the Grove Street gang to keep out of their territory. Robins often sing to warn other birds to stay away from their territory.*

ter•ror |tĕr′ər| *n.* **1.** Intense, overpowering fear. **2.** Someone or something that causes such fear: *gangs of outlaws who were the terror of the ranchers.* **3.** *Informal.* An annoying or intolerable person: *Her children are perfect terrors.*

ter•ror•ism |tĕr′ə rĭz′əm| *n.* **1.** The use of terror, violence, and intimidation to frighten people into submission. **2.** Fear and submission produced by this. —**ter′ror•ist** *adj.* & *n.*

ter•ror•ize |tĕr′ə rīz′| *v.* **ter•ror•ized, ter•ror•iz•ing. 1.** To fill with terror. **2.** To control or dominate by fear and intimidation.

ter•ry cloth |tĕr′ē|. An absorbent cotton fabric with uncut loops forming a pile on one or both sides, used for towels, bathrobes, etc. —**modifier:** **(terry-cloth):** *a terry-cloth towel.*

terse |tûrs| *adj.* Brief and to the point; concise: *a terse reply.* —**terse′ly** *adv.* —**terse′ness** *n.*

ter•ti•ar•y |tûr′shē ĕr′ē| *or* |-shə rē| *adj.* Third in place, order, degree, or rank. —*n.* **Tertiary.** Also **Tertiary period.** The geologic period that began about 63 million years ago and ended about 500,000 to 2 million years ago, characterized by the appearance of modern plant life, apes, and other large mammals. —**modifier:** *Tertiary fossils; Tertiary rock strata.*

test |tĕst| *n.* **1. a.** A way of examining something to determine its characteristics or properties or to determine whether or not it is working correctly. **b.** Any specific procedure used in this way: *a distortion test for a hi-fi system.* **2. a.** A physical or chemical reaction for determining the presence of a particular substance or class of substances, disease germs of a particular type, etc. **b.** The procedure, reagents, stains, etc., used in producing this reaction. **3.** A series of questions, problems, tasks, etc., designed to measure someone's intelligence, knowledge, psychological stability, etc. **4.** Something used as a reference in measuring or examining; a standard. —*v.* **1.** To study or examine by means of a test or tests: *test a person's intelligence; test a food for purity.* **2.** To undergo a test, especially with an indicated result: *The ore tested high in uranium content.* —**test′er** *n.*

Test. Testament.

tes•ta•ment |tĕs′tə mənt| *n.* **1.** A document providing for the disposition of personal property after death; a will. **2. Testament.** Either of the two main divisions of the Bible, the Old Testament and the New Testament.

tes•tate |tĕs′tāt′| *adj.* Having made a legally valid will before death.

tes•ta•tor |tĕs′tā′tər| *or* |tĕ stā′tər| *n.* Someone who has made a legally valid will before death.

tes•tes |tĕs′tēz′| *n.* Plural of **testis.**

tes•ti•cle |tĕs′tĭ kəl| *n.* A male reproductive gland, or testis, of human beings and other mammals, one of a pair enclosed in a pouchlike external covering.

tes•ti•fy |tĕs′tə fī′| *v.* **tes•ti•fied, tes•ti•fy•ing, tes•ti•fies. 1.** To make a declaration under oath: *Two witnesses testified against him in court.* **2.** To affirm under oath: *All her friends testified that she was innocent.* **3.** To bear witness; serve as evidence: *The increase in sales testifies to his ability as manager.*

tes•ti•mo•ni•al |tĕs′tə mō′nē əl| *n.* **1.** A formal statement testifying to a particular fact. **2.** A written affirmation of another's character or worth. **3.** Something given as a tribute for a person's achievement. —**modifier:** *a testimonial dinner.*

tes•ti•mo•ny |tĕs′tə mō′nē| *n., pl.* **tes•ti•mo•nies. 1.** A declaration or affirmation made under oath. **2.** Any evidence in support of a fact or assertion; proof.

tes•tis |tĕs′tĭs| *n., pl.* **tes•tes** |tĕs′tēz′|. In male animals, a reproductive gland, usually one of a pair, in which sperms are produced.

test pilot. A pilot who flies new or experimental

terrapin

terrarium

terrific

Words meaning "frightening" often lose their specific meaning and come to convey simply an idea of intensity, as in sense **4** *of* **terrific.** *Other examples:* **awful, dreadful, horrible, terrible, tremendous.** *This shift happens even more frequently with the adverbs of these adjectives.*

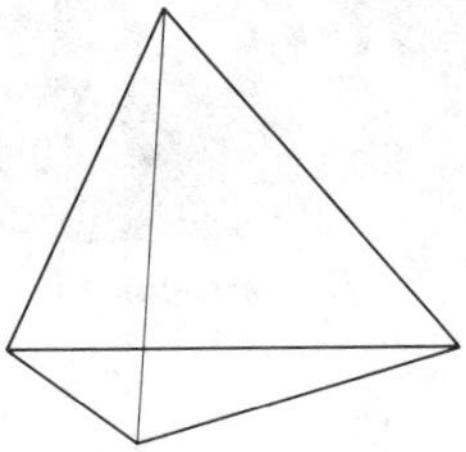

tetrahedron

thatch

ă pat/ā pay/â care/ä father/ĕ pet/ē be/ĭ pit/ī pie/î fierce/ŏ pot/ō go/ô paw, for/oi oil/ŏŏ book/ōō boot/ou out/ŭ cut/û fur/*th* the/th thin/hw which/zh vision/ə ago, item, pencil, atom, circus

aircraft in order to test them.

test tube. A cylindrical tube of clear glass, usually open at one end and rounded at the other, used in laboratory tests and experiments.

tes•ty |tĕs′tē| *adj.* **tes•ti•er, tes•ti•est. 1.** Irritable; touchy: *a testy old woman.* **2.** Characterized by irritability, impatience, etc.: *a testy remark.* —**tes′ti•ly** *adv.* —**tes′ti•ness** *n.*

tet•a•nus |tĕt′n əs| *n.* A serious, often fatal disease caused by bacteria that generally enter the body through wounds. The main symptoms of this disease are muscular rigidity and muscular spasms.

tête-à-tête |tāt′ə tāt′| *n.* A private conversation between two people.

teth•er |tĕ*th*′ər| *n.* **1.** A rope or chain for an animal, allowing it a short radius to move about in. **2.** The range or scope of one's resources or abilities. —*v.* To restrict with a tether.

***Idiom.* at the end of (one's) tether.** At the extreme limit of one's endurance, patience, etc.

tet•ra |tĕt′rə| *n.* Any of several small, often brightly colored tropical freshwater fish, often kept in home aquariums.

tet•ra•he•dron |tĕt′rə **hē**′drən| *n., pl.* **tet•ra•he•drons** or **tet•ra•he•dra** |tĕt′rə **hē**′drə|. A solid geometric figure bounded by four triangular faces. [SEE PICTURE]

tet•rarch |tĕt′rärk′| *or* |tē′trärk′| *n.* **1.** A governor of one of the four divisions of a country or province, especially under the ancient Roman Empire. **2.** A subordinate ruler.

Teu•ton |tōōt′n| *or* |tyōōt′n| *n.* **1.** A member of an ancient Germanic people who lived in northern Europe until about 100 B.C. **2.** A German.

Teu•ton•ic |tōō **tŏn**′ĭk| *or* |tyōō-| *n.* The Germanic languages. —*adj.* **1.** Of the Teutons. **2.** Of the Germanic languages.

Tex. Texas.

Tex•as |tĕk′səs|. A south-central state of the United States. Population, 11,300,000. Capital, Austin. —**Tex′an** *adj.* & *n.*

text |tĕkst| *n.* **1.** The wording or words of something written or printed. **2.** The main body of writing of a book or other printed work as distinguished from a preface, footnote, or illustration. **3.** A passage from the Bible to be read and expounded upon in a sermon. **4.** Subject matter; theme: *the text of a speech.* **5.** A textbook.

text•book |tĕkst′bŏŏk′| *n.* A book used for the study of a particular subject.

tex•tile |tĕk′stəl| *or* |-stīl′| *n.* **1.** Cloth or fabric, especially when woven or knitted. **2.** Fiber or yarn that can be made into cloth. —***modifier:*** *a textile mill; textile fibers.*

tex•tu•al |tĕks′chōō əl| *adj.* Of or relating to a text. —**tex′tu•al•ly** *adv.*

tex•ture |tĕks′chər| *n.* **1.** The surface look or feel of a fabric resulting from the way in which its threads are woven or arranged: *Velvet has a soft, smooth texture.* **2.** The composition or structure of a substance: *the smooth texture of ivory.*

-th. A suffix used to form ordinal numbers: **hundredth.**

Th The symbol for the element thorium.

Thai |tī| *n., pl.* **Thai. 1.** A native or inhabitant of Thailand. **2.** The language of Thailand, related to Chinese and Tibetan. —*adj.* Of Thailand, the Thai, or their language.

Thai•land |tī′lănd′| *or* |-lənd|. A country in Southeast Asia, between Burma and Cambodia. Population, 40,000,000. Capital, Bangkok.

thal•a•mus |thăl′ə məs| *n., pl.* **thal•a•mi** |thăl′ə mī′|. A large rounded mass of gray nerve tissue located under the cerebrum, to which it relays sensory stimuli.

thal•li•um |thăl′ē əm| *n.* Symbol **Tl** One of the elements, a soft, highly poisonous metal. Atomic number 81; atomic weight 204.37; valences +1, +3; melting point 303.5°C; boiling point 1,457°C.

thal•lo•phyte |thăl′ə fīt′| *n.* Any member of a large group of plants that includes the algae and fungi, having no true roots, leaves, or stems.

Thames |tĕmz|. A river in southern England, flowing through London to the North Sea.

than |*th*ăn| *conj.* **1.** —Used to introduce the second element or clause of a comparison of inequality: *Pound cake is richer than angel food cake. She's a better skier than I.* **2.** —Used to introduce the rejected alternative in statements of preference: *I'd much rather play than work.*

thane |thān| *n.* **1.** In Anglo-Saxon England, a freeman granted land by the king in return for military service. **2.** A feudal lord in Scotland.

thank |thăngk| *v.* To express gratitude to.

thank•ful |thăngk′fəl| *adj.* Showing or feeling gratitude; grateful. —**thank′ful•ly** *adv.* —**thank′ful•ness** *n.*

thank•less |thăngk′lĭs| *adj.* **1.** Not feeling or showing gratitude; ungrateful. **2.** Not apt to be appreciated: *a thankless task.*

thanks |thăngks| *pl.n.* An acknowledgment of a favor, gift, etc. —*interj.* A word used to express gratitude.

***Idiom.* thanks to.** On account of; because of: *Thanks to her help, the party was a success.*

thanks•giv•ing |thăngks **gĭv**′ĭng| *n.* An act of giving thanks; an expression of gratitude, especially to God.

Thanks•giv•ing |thăngks **gĭv**′ĭng| *n.* Also **Thanksgiving Day.** A holiday for giving thanks, celebrated in the United States on the fourth Thursday of November. In Canada it is on the second Monday of October. —***modifier:*** *a Thanksgiving prayer; Thanksgiving dinner.*

that |*th*ăt| *or* |*th*ət *when unstressed*| *adj., pl.* **those** |*th*ōz|. **1.** Being the one or ones singled out, implied, or understood: *that place; one of those things.* Also used as a pronoun: *That is my dog. What's that?* **2.** Being the one or ones further removed or less obvious: *This room is warm and that one's cold.* Also used as a pronoun: *This is a plane and that's a glider.* —*pron.* **1.** Who, whom, or which: *people that I have known; things that have to be done.* **2.** In, on, or for which: *I stayed busy the whole time that you were out. She called the day that she arrived.* —*adv.* To that extent: *Is it that difficult to do your homework?* —*conj.* **1.** —Used to introduce a subordinate clause: *I think that he is coming tonight.* **2.** —Used to introduce an exclamation of desire: *Oh, that I might live forever!*

thatch |thăch| *n.* **1.** Plant stalks or leaves, such as straw, reeds, or palm fronds, used to make or cover a roof. **2.** Something resembling this, such as a thick growth of hair on the head. —*v.* To cover with or as if with thatch. —**thatched'** *adj.*: *a thatched roof.* [SEE PICTURE on p. 892]

thaw |thô| *v.* **1.** To change from a solid to a liquid by gradual warming; melt. **2.** To become warm enough for snow and ice to melt: *It often thaws in January.* **3.** To become less formal or reserved: *After a good dinner the guests began to thaw.* —*n.* **1.** The process of thawing. **2.** A period of warm weather during which snow and ice melt.

the[1] |*thē when used before a vowel*| *or* |*thə when used before a consonant*| *definite article.* **1.** —Used as a determiner before a noun or noun phrase standing for specified persons or things: *The pencil I need has disappeared. The man we're looking for has a scar.* **2.** —Used before a singular noun to make it general: *the human arm.* **3.** —Used before a noun to stress its uniqueness or importance: *Last night's party was hardly the event of the season.* **4.** —Used before a title of rank or office, designating its holder: *the pope.* **5.** —Used before an adjective functioning as a noun to signify a class: *the rich and the beautiful.* **6.** —Used like a preposition before a noun, meaning "per" or "each": *She can have my entire stock at a dollar the box.* [SEE NOTE]

the[2] |*thē when used before a vowel*| *or* |*thə when used before a consonant*| *adv.* To that extent; by that much: *the sooner the better.*

the•a•ter, also **the•a•tre** |**thē'**ə tər| *n.* **1.** A building or outdoor structure where plays or motion pictures are presented. **2.** The work or activity of persons who write or act in plays or are engaged in the production of plays. **3.** A place or area where military action takes place: *American forces fought the Japanese in the Pacific theater of World War II.*

the•at•ri•cal |thē **ăt'**rĭ kəl| *adj.* **1.** Of or suitable for the theater. **2.** Marked by self-display or exaggerated rather than natural behavior: *her theatrical way of saying good-by.* —*n.* **theatricals.** Stage performances, especially by amateurs. —**the•at'ri•cal•ly** *adv.*

the•co•dont |**thē'**kə dŏnt'| *n.* An extinct lizard of prehistoric times, regarded as the ancestor of the dinosaurs and of present-day crocodiles and alligators.

thee |*thē*| *pron. Archaic.* The objective case of **thou.**

theft |thĕft| *n.* The act or an instance of stealing; larceny.

thegn |thān| *n.* A form of the word **thane.**

their |*thâr*| *or* |*thər when unstressed*| *pron.* A possessive form of **they,** used before a noun as a modifier. **1.** Of or belonging to them: *their problems; their automobile.* **2.** Done or performed by them: *their homework.* **3.** Received by them, as an action: *their greatest setback.* ¶*These sound alike* **their, there, they're.**

theirs |*thârz*| *pron.* A possessive form of **they. 1.** —Used to indicate that something or someone belongs or pertains to them: *The large package is theirs. He is no friend of theirs.* **2.** —Used to indicate the one or ones belonging to them: *If your car is out of order, use theirs.*

them |*thĕm*| *pron.* The objective case of **they.** —*Note: Them* has three main uses. It can be the direct object of a verb: *She touched them on the arm.* It can be the indirect object of a verb: *I gave them sound advice.* It can also be the object of a preposition: *The doorman presented the car keys to them.*

the•mat•ic |thĭ **măt'**ĭk| *adj.* Of or having to do with a theme or themes. —**the•mat'i•cal•ly** *adv.*

theme |thēm| *n.* **1.** The subject or topic of a talk or a piece of writing. **2.** A short written composition, especially a school composition. **3. a.** A melody on which a musical composition or a section of a musical composition is based. **b.** Any musical material, such as a succession of chords, a set of motifs, a rhythm, etc., on which a musical composition is based.

them•selves |*thĕm* **sĕlvz'**| *or* |*thəm-*| *pron.* A special form of **they.** It is used: **1.** In place of *they,* serving as a direct object, indirect object, or object of a preposition, to show that the action of a reflexive verb refers back to the subject: *They blamed themselves* (direct object). *Paul and Fred always give themselves* (indirect object) *too much credit. They have saved it all for themselves* (object of a preposition). **2.** Following or referring to a noun or the pronoun *they,* to give emphasis: *Her parents themselves are going. They themselves saw it.* **3.** Referring to the subject, to mean *their real, normal, or healthy selves: They have not been themselves since the accident.*

Idiom. **by themselves. 1.** Alone: *went to the party by themselves.* **2.** Without help: *did all the work by themselves.*

then |*thĕn*| *adv.* **1.** At that time: *We did a lot of silly things, but after all, we were younger then.* **2.** Next in time, space, or order; after that: *We'll go on the roller coaster once more, and then we'll go home.* **3. a.** In that case: *If you want to go, then go.* **b.** Consequently: *If x equals 11 and y equals 3, then xy equals 33.* **4.** Moreover; besides: *He wasn't feeling well and then he was in a bad mood anyway, so we didn't enjoy the show.* —*n.* That time or moment: *From then on, I behaved myself.* —*adj.* Being so at the time: *the then President.*

Idioms. **and then some.** And considerably more: *You're going to have to do as much as you can, and then some, if you expect this to work.* **but then.** However: *I like television, but then I could do without it.* **now and then.** From time to time; once in a while: *I see her now and then.* **then and there.** At once: *I think we should confront him with the evidence and be done with it then and there.*

thence |*thĕns*| *adv.* From there on: *We can follow the Appalachians from northern Alabama through Ohio and thence to central New York State.*

thence•forth |*thĕns* **fôrth'**| *or* |**-fôrth'**| *adv.* From then on: *Independence thenceforth became a major topic of conversation in Boston.*

thence•for•ward |*thĕns* **fôr'**wərd| *adv.* From that time on: *Thenceforward he drifted steadily into the liberal camp.*

the•oc•ra•cy |thē **ŏk'**rə sē| *n., pl.* **the•oc•ra•cies. 1. a.** Government in which God or a deity is regarded as the ruling power. **b.** Government by religious authorities. **2.** A state so governed.

the•o•crat•ic |thē'ə **krăt'**ĭk| *adj.* Of or based on theocracy.

theol. 1. theological. **2.** theology.

the[1]

The[1] *is the commonest word in the English language. In the materials on which this Dictionary is based,* **the** *occurs over 373,000 times, or more than seven times per hundred words.* **Of** *is next;* **and** *is third.*

the•o•lo•gi•an |thē′ə **lō′**jən| *n.* A person who is learned in theology.

the•o•log•i•cal |thē′ə **lŏj′**ĭ kəl| or **the•o•log•ic** |thē′ə **lŏj′**ĭk| *adj.* Of or related to theology.

the•ol•o•gy |thē **ŏl′**ə jē| *n.* The systematic study, through reason based on faith, of the nature of God and of man's relation to God. —**modifier:** *a theology course.*

the•o•rem |**thē′**ər əm| *or* |**thîr′**əm| *n.* **1.** A mathematical statement whose truth can be proved on the basis of a given set of axioms or assumptions. **2.** A statement in physics or another science that can be proved in a similar way.

theorem of Py•thag•o•ras |pĭ **thăg′**ər əs|. The **Pythagorean theorem.**

the•o•ret•i•cal |thē′ə **rĕt′**ĭ kəl| or **the•o•ret•ic** |thē ə **rĕt′**ĭk| *adj.* **1.** Of, based on, or having to do with theory. **2.** Predicted by or determined from theory but not available in practice: *the theoretical maximum efficiency of an engine.* —**the′o•ret′i•cal•ly** *adv.*

the•o•re•ti•cian |thē′ər ĭ **tĭsh′**ən| *n.* Someone who formulates, studies, or is expert in the theory of a science or art.

the•o•rist |**thē′**ə rĭst| *n.* Someone who formulates a theory; a theoretician.

the•o•rize |**thē′**ə rīz′| *v.* **the•o•rized, the•o•riz•ing.** To formulate or analyze a theory or theories.

the•o•ry |**thē′**ə rē| *or* |**thîr′**ē| *n., pl.* **the•o•ries.** **1. a.** A statement or set of statements designed to explain a phenomenon or class of phenomena, generally consisting of conclusions drawn from known facts and various assumptions by mathematical or logical reasoning. **b.** Information or knowledge of this kind as distinguished from experiment or practice. **2.** A set of rules or principles designed for the study or practice of an art or discipline: *the theory of harmony.* **3.** A collection of mathematical theorems and proofs that present and explain a subject in detail: *set theory.* **4.** An assumption or guess based on limited information or knowledge.

ther•a•peu•tic |thĕr′ə **pyōō′**tĭk| *adj.* Having the capability of healing or curing: *a therapeutic bath.* —**ther′a•peu′ti•cal•ly** *adv.*

ther•a•peu•tics |thĕr′ə **pyōō′**tĭks| *n.* *(used with a singular verb).* The medical treatment of disease.

ther•a•pist |**thĕr′**ə pĭst| *n.* Someone who specializes in conducting therapy of some kind, especially physical therapy or psychotherapy.

ther•a•py |**thĕr′**ə pē| *n., pl.* **ther•a•pies.** **1. a.** Any procedure designed to heal or cure an illness, disability, etc. **b.** Procedures of this kind considered as a class; treatment. **2.** Psychotherapy.

there |*th*âr| *adv.* **1.** At or in that place: *Set the package over there on the table.* **2.** To or toward that place: *How long did it take to get there?* **3.** At a point of action or time: *The violins come in there.* **4.** In that matter: *I can't go along with you there.* —*pron.* **1.** —Used to introduce a clause or sentence: *There are several different kinds of pepper. There came a loud clap, and then silence.* **2.** Used as an intensive: *Hello there.* —*n.* That place or point: *I'll never know how we got out of there. I stopped and he went on from there.* —*adj.* **1.** Used as an intensive: *That guard there can tell us the way out.* **2.** Present: *She's always there when the trouble begins.* **3.** *Informal.* Fully awake or conscious: *I got a hard knock but I'm there.* —*interj.* A word used to express satisfaction, sympathy, etc.: *There, now I can have some peace! There, it can't hurt that much!* ¶*These sound alike* **there, their, they're.**

there•a•bouts |*th*âr′ə **bouts′**| *adv.* **1.** Near that number, time, or age: *Jim was 10, or thereabouts. He had 12 ships and 50 men, or thereabouts.* **2.** In that neighborhood: *The rest of the people who lived thereabouts were horrified.*

there•af•ter |*th*âr **ăf′**tər| *or* |**-äf′-**| *adv.* After that or from then on: *The number 4 is a product, and so is every fourth number thereafter. Thereafter, revolts took place from time to time.*

there•at |*th*âr **ăt′**| *adv.* Upon that: *I replied sharply, and thereat the man kept quiet.*

there•by |*th*âr **bī′**| *or* |*th***âr′**bī′| *adv.* By that means: *Flat bales are compressed so as to occupy less space and thereby reduce shipping charges.*

there•fore |*th***âr′**fôr′| *or* |-fōr′| *adv.* For that reason: *The fungi lack chlorophyll and are therefore dependent upon other plants and animals for their food.*

there•from |*th*âr **frŭm′**| *or* |**-frŏm′**| *adv.* From that: *The child picks up from grownups around him a few traits, a turn of mind that has fired his imagination, and therefrom constructs his character.*

there•in |*th*âr **ĭn′**| *adv.* **1.** In that place: *the house and all the furniture therein.* **2.** In that respect: *He was never elected President; therein lay his personal tragedy.*

there•of |*th*âr **ŭv′**| *or* |**-ŏv′**| *adv.* Of that or it: *all persons born or naturalized in the United States and subject to the jurisdiction thereof.*

there•on |*th*âr **ŏn′**| *or* |**-ôn′**| *adv.* On it: *No lion shall be there, nor any ravenous beast go up thereon.*

there•to |*th*âr **tōō′**| *adv.* To that: *She got a house of her own, with daily subsistence and clothing in addition thereto.*

there•to•fore |*th***âr′**tə **fôr′**| *or* |**-fōr′**| *adv.* Before that: *He built houses where none had ever built theretofore.*

there•un•der |*th*âr **ŭn′**dər| *adv.* Under that, it, or them: *the rotten floor planks out in the barn and all the old gear stowed thereunder.*

there•un•to |*th*âr′ən **tōō′**| *adv.* To that; thereto: *Also appertaining thereunto was a card bearing the name "Mr. James Dillingham Young."*

there•up•on |*th***âr′**ə pŏn′| *or* |-pôn′| *adv.* After that; immediately after that or on that account: *He published an editorial criticizing the judge and was thereupon summoned to court.*

there•with |*th*âr **wĭth′**| *or* |**-wĭ*th*′**| *adv.* With that: *After the magnifying glass I got a microscope, and therewith my fate was sealed—I had to become a scientist.*

ther•mal |**thûr′**məl| *adj.* **1.** Of, using, producing, or caused by heat. **2.** Warm or hot: *thermal springs.* —*n.* A current of warm air that rises because it is less dense than the air around it. —**ther′mal•ly** *adv.* [SEE NOTE]

therm•i•on |**thûr′**mī′ən| *or* |-mē ən| *n.* An electrically charged particle or ion that is emitted by a conducting material as a result of heat.

ther•mo•cou•ple |**thûr′**mə kŭp′əl| *n.* A

thermal, etc.
All the words beginning with therm- *have to do with heat or temperature and are from Greek* thermē, *"heat," and* thermos, *"hot."*

ă pat/ā pay/â care/ä father/ĕ pet/ ē be/ĭ pit/ī pie/î fierce/ŏ pot/ ō go/ô paw, for/oi oil/ŏŏ book/ ōō boot/ou out/ŭ cut/û fur/ *th* the/th thin/hw which/zh vision/ ə ago, item, pencil, atom, circus

thermoelectric device used to measure temperatures, especially high temperatures, accurately. It usually consists of a junction of dissimilar metals across which a voltage that varies with temperature is produced.

ther•mo•dy•nam•ic |thûr′mō dī **năm′**ĭk| *adj.* **1.** Of or having to do with thermodynamics. **2.** Of or operating by mechanical power derived from heat.

ther•mo•dy•nam•ics |thûr′mō dī **năm′**ĭks| *n.* *(used with a singular verb).* The part of physics that deals with the relationships between heat and other forms of energy.

ther•mo•e•lec•tric |thûr′mō ĭ **lĕk′**trĭk| *adj.* Of or having to do with electricity that is generated by the action of heat.

ther•mo•e•lec•tric•i•ty |thûr′mō ĭ lĕk **trĭs′**ĭ tē| *or* |-ē′lĕk-| *n.* Electricity generated by a flow of heat, as in a thermocouple.

ther•mo•graph |**thûr′**mə grăf′| *or* |-gräf′| *n.* A thermometer that records the temperatures it measures, usually indicating the time at which each measurement was made.

ther•mom•e•ter |thər **mŏm′**ĭ tər| *n.* An instrument that measures and indicates temperature, especially one that consists of a glass tube in which a liquid expands or contracts to reach a level that depends on the temperature. [SEE PICTURE]

ther•mo•nu•cle•ar |thûr′mə **nōō′**klē ər| *or* |**-nyōō′**-| *adj.* **1.** Of or derived from the fusion of atomic nuclei at high temperatures or the energy produced in this way. **2.** Of weapons based on nuclear fusion, especially as distinguished from those based on nuclear fission.

ther•mo•plas•tic |thûr′mə **plăs′**tĭk| *adj.* Soft and pliable when heated but hard when cooled. *—n.* A thermoplastic material.

Ther•mos bottle |**thûr′**məs|. A trademark for a container having double walls, usually with a reflective coating, and an evacuated space between the walls, used to prevent the contents from gaining or losing heat. [SEE PICTURE]

ther•mo•sphere |**thûr′**mə sfîr′| *n.* The outermost layer of the atmosphere, extending from the mesosphere to outer space, having temperatures that increase steadily with altitude.

ther•mo•stat |**thûr′**mə stăt′| *n.* A device that automatically controls a piece of heating or cooling equipment in such a way as to keep the temperature nearly constant.

the•sau•rus |thĭ **sôr′**əs| *n., pl.* **the•sau•rus•es. 1.** A book of synonyms and antonyms. **2.** A book that lists all the words relating to a general idea or to a specific subject, such as medicine, music, etc. [SEE NOTE]

these |*thēz*| *pron.* Plural of **this.**

The•se•us |**thē′**sē əs| *or* |-syōōs′|. In Greek mythology, a hero who slew the Minotaur.

the•sis |**thē′**sĭs| *n., pl.* **the•ses** |**thē′**sēz′|. **1.** Something stated or put forth for consideration, especially by a person who plans to maintain it by argument. **2.** A long essay resulting from original research written by a candidate for a master's or doctor's degree.

Thes•pi•an, also **thes•pi•an** |**thĕs′**pē ən| *adj.* Of or relating to drama; dramatic. *—n.* An actor or actress.

the•ta |**thā′**tə| *or* |**thē′**-| *n.* The eighth letter of the Greek alphabet, written Θ, *θ*. In English it is represented as *th.*

thew |thyōō| *n.* **1.** Often **thews.** A well-developed sinew or muscle. **2. thews.** Muscular power or strength.

they |*thā*| *pron.* **1.** The persons, animals, or things last mentioned: *Paula and Dick worked here last summer, but now they are back in school.* **2.** People in general: *Whatever they say, I'll do it. He's as tough as they come. —Note:* As a pronoun, *they* is in the nominative case and is the plural of *he, she,* and *it.*

they'd |*thād*|. **1.** They had. **2.** They would.

they'll |*thāl*|. They will.

they're |*thâr*|. They are. ¶ *These sound alike* **they're, their, there.**

they've |*thāv*|. They have.

THI temperature-humidity index.

thi•a•mine |**thī′**ə mĭn| *or* |-mēn′| *n.* A B-complex vitamin produced synthetically and occurring naturally in various foods; vitamin B_1.

thick |thĭk| *adj.* **thick•er, thick•est. 1.** Relatively great in depth or in extent from one surface to the opposite; not thin: *a thick board.* **2.** Measuring in this dimension: *a board two inches thick.* **3. a.** Not capable of easy flow; heavy: *a thick syrup; a thick grade of oil.* **b.** Not watery: *thick soup.* **4.** Dense: *thick fog.* **5.** Made of or having a large number of units close together; dense: *a thick forest; thick hair.* **6.** Very noticeable; pronounced; heavy: *speaking with a thick brogue.* **7.** Lacking mental quickness; slow; stupid: *Get that through your thick head.* **8.** *Informal.* Very friendly: *Jane is very thick with Mary now. —adv.* So as to be thick; thickly: *Slice it thick. —n.* **1.** The thickest part of something. **2.** The most active or intense part: *in the thick of the battle.* **—thick′ly** *adv.* **—thick′ness** *n.*

***Idiom.* through thick and thin.** Through both good and bad times; faithfully.

thick•en |**thĭk′**ən| *v.* **1.** To make or become thick or thicker: *thicken gravy. The fog thickened.* **2.** To make more intricate or complex: *The already complex plot thickens.*

thick•en•ing |**thĭk′**ə nĭng| *n.* **1.** The act or process of making or becoming thick. **2.** Any substance used to thicken a liquid.

thick•et |**thĭk′**ĭt| *n.* A dense growth or clump of shrubs, small trees, underbrush, etc.

thick•set |**thĭk′sĕt′**| *adj.* **1.** Having a short, stocky body; stout: *a thickset man.* **2.** Placed, growing, etc., close together: *thickset rose bushes.*

thief |thēf| *n., pl.* **thieves** |thēvz|. A person who steals, especially stealthily when the victim is not present.

thieve |thēv| *v.* **thieved, thiev•ing.** To engage in or take by theft.

thieves |thēvz| *n.* Plural of **thief.**

thigh |thī| *n.* **1.** The part of the human leg that extends from the hip to the knee. **2.** A similar part of the body of an animal.

thigh•bone |**thī′**bōn′| *n.* The bone that extends from the pelvis to the knee in the human leg; the femur.

thim•ble |**thĭm′**bəl| *n.* A small, cuplike guard, usually of metal or plastic, worn to protect the finger that pushes the needle in sewing.

Thim•bu |**thĭm′**bōō′|, also **Thim•phu** |-pōō′|. The capital of Bhutan. Population, 50,000.

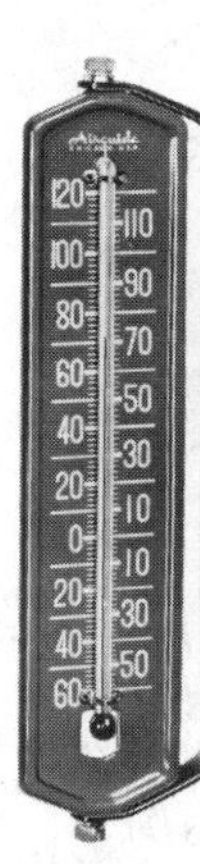

thermometer
Outdoor Fahrenheit thermometer

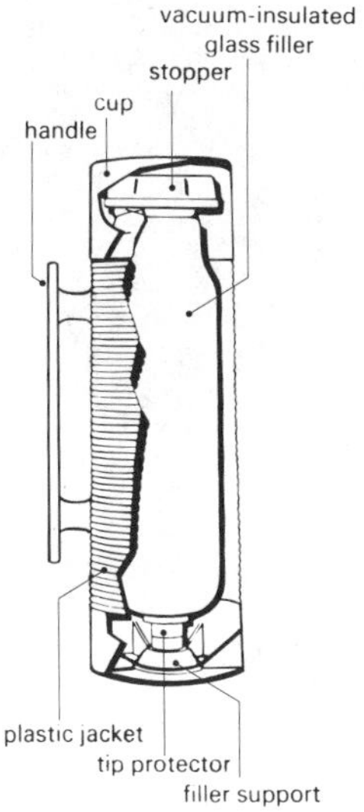

Thermos bottle

thesaurus/treasure
A **thesaurus** *is by origin a "treasury" of knowledge or of words; the word itself comes from Latin* thēsaurus, *"treasure house, storehouse." This word had a variant,* tresaurus, *which became Old French* tresor, *which was borrowed into English as* **treasure.**

thin |thĭn| *adj.* **thin•ner, thin•nest. 1. a.** Having a relatively small distance between opposite sides or surfaces; not thick: *a thin board.* **b.** Not great in diameter or cross section; fine: *thin wire.* **2.** Lean or slender of figure: *a thin man.* **3. a.** Flowing with relative ease; not viscous: *a thin oil.* **b.** Watery: *thin soup.* **4.** Made of or having a few units widely separated: *His hair is getting thin on top.* **5.** Not dense: *a thin mist.* **6.** Lacking in strength or resonance, as a sound or tone: *a singer having thin high notes.* **7.** Lacking substance, force, etc.; flimsy; poor: *a thin excuse.* —*adv.* So as to be thin; thinly: *Slice it thin.* —*v.* **thinned, thin•ning.** To make or become thin or thinner: *thinning wine. He had thinned by weeks of starvation. The river had thinned down to a trickle. No need to wait until the crowd thins out.* —**thin'ly** *adv.* —**thin'ness** *n.*

thine |*th*īn| *pron.* **1.** A possessive form of **thou. 2.** —Used instead of **thy** before an initial vowel or *h*: *thine enemy.*

thing |thĭng| *n.* **1.** Whatever can be perceived, known, or thought to have a separate existence; an entity. **2.** An object or creature that cannot or need not be precisely named or described: *What's that thing on the table? Do you ever use this thing?* **3.** An inanimate object as distinguished from a living being. **4.** A creature: *not a living thing on the beach; the poor thing; such a sweet little thing.* **5.** An act or deed: *That was a mean thing to do to your sister.* **6. things. a.** Personal possessions; belongings: *Have you packed your things for the weekend?* **b.** The general state of affairs; conditions: *Things are getting worse and worse.* **7. the thing.** The latest fashion; the rage: *Knit suits are the thing this fall.* **8.** *Slang.* An activity very suitable or satisfying to one: *doing his thing.* [SEE NOTE]

thing
"The objection to conforming to usages that have become dead to you is that it scatters your force . . . But do your thing and I shall know you . . ." —*Ralph Waldo Emerson (1841).*

think |thĭngk| *v.* **thought** |thôt|, **think•ing. 1.** To exercise the power of reason; conceive ideas, make judgments, etc.: *Are animals able to think? Think a moment before making a decision.* **2.** To have as a thought; imagine: *He thought he would win.* **3. a.** To reason about; reflect on: *Think how complex language is.* **b.** To consider or weigh carefully: *He was thinking what he would have to do. It took him a long time to think out what to do.* **4.** To regard as being; look upon as: *I think it only fair.* **5.** To believe; suppose: *I think that she is wrong. Do you think so?* **6.** To remember: *I can't think now what his name is.* **7.** To dispose the mind in a specified way: *think big.* —***phrasal verbs.*** **think about. 1.** To examine; consider: *thinking about going to Europe.* **2.** To reflect upon; recall: *thinking about his school days.* **think of. 1.** To weigh the idea; consider the matter: *They are thinking of moving.* **2.** To call to mind; recall: *I can't think of her name right now.* **3.** To imagine: *Just think of the dangers awaiting him.* **4.** To suggest: *Can you think of a good hotel for the weekend?* **5.** To have an opinion concerning: *She thinks highly of his ability.* **think up.** To devise; invent: *always thinking up new excuses.* —**think'er** *n.*

Idioms. **think better of.** To decide against (something) after reconsidering. **think nothing of.** To regard as routine or usual. **think twice.** To weigh something carefully.

thin•ner |**thĭn'**ər| *n.* A liquid, such as turpentine, mixed with a paint or varnish to make it flow more easily as it is applied.

third |thûrd| *adj.* Corresponding in order to the number three in rank, time, etc.: *the third floor. The batter took the third strike.* —*adv.* In the third place, rank, etc.: *He was standing third in line.* —*n.* **1.** In a set of items arranged to match the natural numbers in a one-to-one correspondence, the item that matches the number three. **2.** One of three equal parts of a unit, written 1/3. **3.** The musical interval formed by two tones of a diatonic scale that are separated by a tone of the scale lying between them. **4.** The next higher gear after second in an automotive transmission.

third base. 1. The base to be reached third by a runner in baseball. It is the last base before home plate. **2.** The position played by a third baseman.

third baseman. The baseball player stationed near third base.

third class. 1. The class of accommodations on a train, ship, plane, etc., that is usually of the lowest order of luxury or price. **2.** A class of mail including all printed matter, except newspapers and magazines, that weighs less than 16 ounces and is unsealed.

third-class |**thûrd'klăs'**| *or* |**-kläs'**| *adj.* **1.** In the rank or class that is next below the second. **2.** Of travel accommodations ranking next below the second class. —*adv.* By means of third-class mail or travel accommodations.

third-de•gree burn |**thûrd'**dĭ **grē'**|. A severe burn in which the outer layer of skin is destroyed and sensitive nerve endings are exposed.

third person. 1. A set of grammatical forms used in referring to a person or thing other than the speaker or the one spoken to. **2.** One of these forms; for example, *he, she,* and *they.*

Third World. The developing countries of Africa, Asia, and Latin America, especially those not allied with the Communist or non-Communist blocs.

thirst |thûrst| *n.* **1. a.** A sensation of dryness in the mouth related to a desire to drink. **b.** The desire to drink. **2.** An insistent desire; a craving: *satisfying his thirst for adventure.* —*v.* **1.** To feel a need to drink; be thirsty. **2.** To have a strong desire: *thirsting for knowledge.*

thirst•y |**thûr'**stē| *adj.* **thirst•i•er, thirst•i•est. 1.** Feeling thirst: *Salty foods make one thirsty.* **2.** Arid; parched: *fields thirsty for rain.*

thir•teen |**thûr'tēn'**| *n.* A number, written 13 in Arabic numerals, that is equal to the sum of 12 + 1. It is the positive integer that immediately follows 12. —**thir'teen'** *adj. & pron.*

thir•teenth |**thûr'tēnth'**| *n.* **1.** In a set of items arranged to match the natural numbers in a one-to-one correspondence, the item that matches the number thirteen. **2.** One of thirteen equal parts of a unit, written 1/13. —**thir'teenth'** *adj. & adv.*

thir•ti•eth |**thûr'**tē ĭth| *n.* **1.** In a set of items arranged to match the natural numbers in a one-to-one correspondence, the item that matches the number thirty. **2.** One of thirty equal parts of a unit, written 1/30. —**thir'ti•eth** *adj. & adv.*

thir•ty |**thûr'**tē| *n., pl.* **thir•ties.** A number, written 30 in Arabic numerals, that is equal to the product of 3 × 10. It is the tenth positive integer after 20.

thir•ty-sec•ond note |thûr′tē **sĕk′**ənd|. A musical note whose time value is equal to one-half that of a sixteenth note.

this |*th*ĭs| *pron., pl.* **these** |*th*ēz|. **1.** The person or thing present, nearby, or just mentioned: *This is my friend Judy. This is my house right here.* Also used adjectivally: *Take a look at this book.* **2.** What is about to be said: *This will really make you laugh.* Also used adjectivally: *Wait till you hear this version of what happened.* **3.** The one that is nearer than another or the one contrasted with the other: *That little scene was nothing compared to this.* Also used adjectivally: *Stay on this side of the street; that side is dangerous. This car is smaller but much faster than that one.* **4.** The present occasion or time: *Jim's been out later than this.* —*adv.* To this extent; so: *I never knew Jim to stay out this late.*

Idiom. **this and that.** One thing and another: *a busy day spent doing this and that.*

this•tle |**thĭs′**əl| *n.* Any of several prickly plants with usually purplish flowers and seeds tufted with silky fluff. [SEE PICTURE]

this•tle•down |**thĭs′**əl doun′| *n.* The silky, fluffy material attached to the seeds of a thistle, by means of which they float through the air.

thith•er |**thĭ*th*′**ər| *or* |**thĭ*th*′**-| *adv.* To or toward that place; in that direction; there.

thole pin |thōl|. A peg set in pairs in the gunwale of a boat to serve as an oarlock. [SEE PICTURE]

thong |thông| *or* |thŏng| *n.* **1.** A strip of leather used to fasten something, such as a sandal. **2.** The lash of a whip.

Thor |thôr|. In Norse mythology, the god of thunder. [SEE NOTE on p. 900]

tho•ra•ces |**thôr′**ə sēz′| *or* |**thōr′**-| *n.* A plural of **thorax.**

tho•rac•ic |thə **răs′**ĭk| *adj.* Of, in, or near the thorax.

thoracic duct. The main lymph duct of the body, rising along the spinal column and joining a vein near the heart.

tho•rax |**thôr′**ăks′| *or* |**thōr′**-| *n., pl.* **tho•rax•es** or **tho•ra•ces** |**thôr′**ə sēz′| *or* |**thōr′**-|. **1.** The part of the human body between the neck and the diaphragm, enclosed partly by the ribs; the chest. **2.** A similar part in other animals. **3.** The middle division of the three-part body of an insect.

tho•ri•um |**thôr′**ē əm| *or* |**thōr′**-| *n.* Symbol **Th** One of the elements, a silvery-white metal with 13 radioactive isotopes only one of which, that with a mass number of 232 and a half-life of 14.1 billion years, occurs naturally. Atomic number 90; atomic weight 232.038; valence +4; melting point about 1,700°C; boiling point about 4,000°C.

thorn |thôrn| *n.* **1.** A sharp, woody spine growing from the stem of a plant. **2.** Any of various shrubs, trees, or plants bearing such spines. **3.** A sharp, pointed part resembling a thorn. **4.** Someone or something that causes pain or annoyance. **5.** An ancient runic letter representing the sound *th* both in *that* and *thin,* used in Old English and other early Germanic alphabets. —***modifier:*** *a thorn bush; a thorn hedge.* —**thorned′** *adj.: a thorned bush.* —**thorn′less** *adj.*

thorn•y |**thôr′**nē| *adj.* **thorn•i•er, thorn•i•est. 1.** Full of or covered with thorns: *a thorny thicket; thorny branches.* **2.** Sharp and pointed; thornlike: *a porcupine's thorny quills.* **3.** Troublesome; difficult: *a thorny situation.*

thor•ough |**thûr′**ō| *or* |**thŭr′**ō| *adj.* **1.** Complete in all respects: *The performance was a thorough success.* **2.** Painstakingly careful: *a thorough search; a thorough worker.* —**thor′ough•ly** *adv.* —**thor′ough•ness** *n.*

thor•ough•bred |**thûr′**ō brĕd′| *or* |**thûr′**ə-| *or* |**thŭr′**-| *adj.* Bred of pure or pedigreed stock: *thoroughbred cattle.* —*n.* **1.** An animal bred of pure or pedigreed stock. **2.** Often **Thoroughbred.** One of a breed of horses resulting from the mating of English mares and certain Arabian stallions in the 18th century. **3.** A person with the qualities considered typical of good breeding.

thor•ough•fare |**thûr′**ō fâr′| *or* |**thûr′**ə-| *or* |**thŭr′**-| *n.* A main road or public highway.

thor•ough•go•ing |thûr′ō **gō′**ĭng| *or* |thûr′ə-| *or* |thŭr′-| *adj.* Very thorough; complete in all respects: *a thoroughgoing overhaul of the company's management.*

those |*th*ōz| *pron.* Plural of **that.**

thou |*th*ou| *pron. Archaic.* The second person singular in the nominative case, equivalent to **you.**

though |*th*ō| *adv.* However; nevertheless: *Her English is good; she's hard of hearing, though, so you should speak very distinctly. I'm out of town often; I'll be here at Christmas, though.* —*conj.* **1.** Although; while: *The paper, though well conceived, was badly written.* **2.** Even if: *Though our chances of winning are pretty slim, I think we should play the game.*

thought |thôt|. Past tense and past participle of **think.** —*n.* **1.** The act or process of thinking: *spending hours in deep thought.* **2.** A product of thinking; an idea: *Let me have your thoughts on this subject.* **3.** The particular way of thinking of a group, social class, period, etc.: *ancient Greek thought; modern thought.* **4.** Consideration; concern: *giving serious thought to the matter.* **5.** Intention: *She had no thought of hurting his feelings.*

thought•ful |**thôt′**fəl| *adj.* **1.** Occupied with thought; contemplative; meditative: *The girl looked thoughtful for a minute.* **2.** Well thought-out: *He wrote a very concise and thoughtful paper.* **3.** Considerate: *a kind and thoughtful man.* —**thought′ful•ly** *adv.* —**thought′ful•ness** *n.*

thought•less |**thôt′**lĭs| *adj.* **1.** Not thinking; careless: *It was thoughtless of her to forget your birthday.* **2.** Inconsiderate: *thoughtless of the feelings of others.* —**thought′less•ly** *adv.* —**thought′less•ness** *n.*

thou•sand |**thou′**zənd| *n.* A number, written 1,000 in Arabic numerals, that is equal to the sum of 999 + 1. It is the positive integer that immediately follows 999. —**thou′sand** *adj.* & *pron.*

Thousand Islands. A group of islands in the St. Lawrence River, partly in the United States and partly in Canada.

thou•sandth |**thou′**zəndth| *or* |-zənth| *n.* **1.** In a set of items arranged to match the natural numbers in a one-to-one correspondence, the item that matches the number one thousand.

thistle

thole pin
Pair of thole pins, one in its socket and the other hanging by its lanyard

thrasher

three
Three *was* threo *in Old English,* thri- *in prehistoric Germanic, and* trei- *in Indo-European.* Trei- *appears in easily recognizable form in all of the Indo-European languages: In German it is* drei, *in Irish* trī, *in Lithuanian* trys, *in Russian* tri, *in Latin* trēs *(becoming Italian* tre, *French* trois, *Spanish* tres*), in Greek* treis, *and in Sanskrit* trayas.

thrift/thrive
Thrift may lead to prosperity; the original meaning of the word **thrift** *was "prosperity." The word is borrowed from Old Norse* thrift, *"the condition of thriving, prosperity," from* thrīfask, *"to prosper, to get for oneself."* **Thrive** *comes directly from Old Norse* thrīfask.

ă pat/ā pay/â care/ä father/ĕ pet/ē be/ĭ pit/ī pie/î fierce/ŏ pot/ō go/ô paw, for/oi oil/ŏŏ book/ōō boot/ou out/ŭ cut/û fur/*th* the/th thin/hw which/zh vision/ə ago, item, pencil, atom, circus

2. One of a thousand equal parts of a unit, written 1/1000. **—thou'sandth** *adj. & adv.*

thral•dom |**thrôl'**dəm| *n.* A form of the word **thralldom.**

thrall |thrôl| *n.* **1.** A slave or serf. **2.** Slavery; servitude.

thrall•dom |**thrôl'**dəm| *n.* Slavery; servitude.

thrash |thrăsh| *v.* **1.** To beat or flog with or as if with a flail: *He thrashed the boy soundly.* **2.** To defeat utterly. **3.** To move wildly or violently: *a crocodile thrashing his tail around in the water.* **—*phrasal verb.* thrash out.** To discuss fully: *lawyers thrashing out the terms of the contract.*

thrash•er |**thrăsh'**ər| *n.* Any of several birds with a long tail and often a spotted breast, such as the **brown thrasher** of North America. [SEE PICTURE]

thrash•ing |**thrăsh'**ĭng| *n.* A severe beating; a whipping.

thread |thrĕd| *n.* **1.** A length of fine, thin cord made of two or more strands of fiber twisted together, capable of being woven into cloth or used in sewing things together. **2.** Anything that resembles a thread in thinness, fineness, etc.: *a thread of smoke coming through the chimney.* **3.** Something that runs through something else bringing the parts of it together: *He lost the thread of his argument.* **4.** A ridge cut in a spiral or helical path on a screw, nut, bolt, etc. *—v.* **1.** To pass one end of a thread through the eye of (a needle) or though the various hooks and holes on (a sewing machine). **2.** To connect by running a thread through; to string: *thread beads.* **3.** To cut a thread onto (a screw, nut, bolt, etc.). **4.** To make (one's way) cautiously through: *pedestrians threading their way through heavy traffic.* **—thread'er** *n.*

thread•bare |**thrĕd'**bâr'| *adj.* **1.** So worn and frayed that the threads show through: *a threadbare jacket.* **2.** Wearing old, shabby clothes: *a threadbare tramp.* **3.** Hackneyed; trite: *telling each other threadbare jokes.*

threat |thrĕt| *n.* **1.** An expression of an intention to inflict pain, injury, evil, etc.: *The children had not been able to forget the old man's threats.* **2.** An indication of impending danger or harm: *The night air held a threat of frost.* **3.** Something, such as a person, thing, or idea, regarded as a possible danger.

threat•en |**thrĕt'**n| *v.* **1.** To utter a threat against: *threatening the prisoners with physical punishment.* **2.** To serve as a threat to; endanger: *Landslides threatened the mountain village.* **3.** To give signs or warning of; portend: *Dark skies threaten rain.* **4.** To announce as possible: *They are always threatening to move to the suburbs.*

three |thrē| *n.* A number, written 3 in Arabic numerals, that is equal to the sum of 2 + 1. It is the positive integer that immediately follows 2. **—three** *adj. & pron.* [SEE NOTE]

three-di•men•sion•al |**thrē'**dĭ **mĕn'**shə nəl| *adj.* **1.** Of or having three dimensions, especially dimensions, such as height, width, and depth, that are measured along mutually perpendicular axes. **2.** Of or producing visual images in which there is an illusion of depth and perspective: *a three-dimensional image projected with light from a laser.*

three•score |**thrē'**skôr'| *or* |-skōr'| *adj.* Three times twenty; sixty.

thresh |thrĕsh| *v.* **1.** To separate the seeds from (grain-bearing plants) by striking or beating: *The workers threshed the wheat with a machine. In some parts of the world, farmers thresh by hand.* **2.** To wave or lash vigorously; thrash: *The crocodile threshed his tail like an oar.*

thresh•er |**thrĕsh'**ər| *n.* **1.** Someone or something that threshes. **2.** Also **threshing machine.** A machine used for threshing grain. **3.** Also **thresher shark.** A shark having a tail with a long, whiplike upper division.

thresh•old |**thrĕsh'**ōld| *or* |-hōld| *n.* **1.** The piece of wood or stone placed beneath a door. **2.** An entrance to a house, building, etc. **3.** The place or point of beginning; the outset: *Science today is on the threshold of an even better understanding of the atmosphere and its behavior.* **4.** The lowest level or intensity at which a stimulus can be perceived or can produce a given effect: *A sound at the threshold of pain is about one million million times as powerful as a sound at the threshold of hearing.*

threw |thrōō|. Past tense of **throw.** ¶*These sound alike* **threw, through.**

thrice |thrīs| *adv.* Three times: *He was thrice named player of the year.*

thrift |thrĭft| *n.* Wisdom in the management of money and other resources. [SEE NOTE]

thrift•y |**thrĭf'**tē| *adj.* **thrift•i•er, thrift•i•est.** Practicing thrift; economical and frugal. **—thrift'i•ly** *adv.* **—thrift'i•ness** *n.*

thrill |thrĭl| *v.* To feel or cause to feel a sudden intense sensation, as of joy, fear, excitement, etc.: *thrilling at the news of his promotion. The hockey players thrilled the spectators.* *—n.* A sudden intense feeling of joy, fear, excitement, etc.: *It gave her quite a thrill to be introduced to the star of the show.*

thrive |thrīv| *v.* **throve** |thrōv| or **thrived, thrived** or **thriv•en** |**thrĭv'**ən|, **thriv•ing. 1.** To grow or do well; be or stay in a healthy condition: *Some plants thrive in damp, sandy soil. Camels thrive in a hot, dry climate.* **2.** To be successful; make progress; flourish: *The busy little town thrived and grew larger.* [SEE NOTE]

throat |thrōt| *n.* **1. a.** The part of the digestive tract that forms a passage between the rear of the mouth and the esophagus. **b.** The front portion of the neck. **2.** Any narrow passage or part considered to resemble the human throat: *the throat of a horn; the throat of a bottle.*

throat•y |**thrō'**tē| *adj.* **throat•i•er, throat•i•est.** Sounded or seemingly sounded deep in the throat; guttural, hoarse, or husky: *a singer with a muffled, throaty voice; a throaty growl.* **—throat'i•ly** *adv.* **—throat'i•ness** *n.*

throb |thrŏb| *v.* **throbbed, throb•bing. 1.** To beat rapidly or violently; pound: *His heart was throbbing with excitement.* **2.** To vibrate or sound with or as if with a slow, steady rhythm: *hearing engines throbbing all night.* *—n.* **1.** The act or process of throbbing. **2.** A sound made by throbbing: *the throb of distant gunfire.*

throe |thrō| *n.* **1.** Often **throes.** A severe pang or spasm of pain, as in childbirth. **2. throes.** A condition of great struggle or effort: *a country in the throes of war.*

throm•bi |**thrŏm**′bī′| *n.* Plural of **thrombus.**

throm•bin |**thrŏm**′bĭn| *n.* An enzyme in the blood that acts in blood clotting by reacting with fibrinogen to form fibrin.

throm•bo•sis |thrŏm **bō**′sĭs| *n., pl.* **throm•bo•ses** |thrŏm **bō**′sēz′|. The formation or presence of a blood clot in a blood vessel or a chamber of the heart.

throm•bus |**thrŏm**′bəs| *n., pl.* **throm•bi** |**thrŏm**′-bī′|. A blood clot that forms in a blood vessel or a chamber of the heart.

throne |thrōn| *n.* **1.** The chair occupied by a king, pope, bishop, etc., on ceremonial occasions. **2.** The rank or authority of a sovereign: *succeed to the throne.* ¶*These sound alike* **throne, thrown.** [SEE PICTURE]

throng |thrông| *or* |thrŏng| *n.* A large group of people or things crowded together. —*v.* **1.** To crowd into; fill: *People thronged the platforms of the subway station.* **2.** To move in or as if in a crowd: *Students thronged toward the classroom door. People thronged to see the baseball game.*

throt•tle |**thrŏt**′l| *n.* **1.** A valve in an internal-combustion engine by which the flow of fuel to the combustion chamber is controlled. **2.** In a steam engine or similar engine, a valve that regulates the flow of hot fluid to the cylinders, turbine, etc. **3.** A pedal or lever that controls a valve of this type. —*v.* **throt•tled, throt•tling. 1.** To control (an engine, its fuel, or working fluid) with or as if with a throttle. **2.** To strangle; choke. **3.** To suppress: *army officers throttling all political opposition in the country.*

through |thrōō| *prep.* **1.** In one side and out the opposite or another side of: *going through the door.* Also used adverbially: *The door opened, and we went through.* **2.** Among or between; in the midst of: *a walk through the flowers.* **3.** By means of: *getting an apartment through an agency.* **4.** As a result of: *The war was lost through lack of money and organization.* **5.** Here and there in; around: *a tour through France.* **6.** From the beginning to the end of: *staying up through the night.* Also used adverbially: *If you'll just hear me through, you'll see what I mean.* **7.** At or to the end or conclusion of: *We are through our testing period.* Also used adverbially: *Let's see this thing through.* **8.** Without stopping for: *driving through a red light.* Also used adverbially: *With only two drivers in the car, it's possible but very tiring to drive through from coast to coast.* —*adj.* **1.** Passing from one end or side to another: *a through beam.* **2.** Allowing continuous passage without obstruction: *a through street.* **3.** Going all the way to the end without stopping: *This is a through flight.* **4.** Finished; done: *When you're through, I'd like to have a word with you.* **5.** *Informal.* **a.** Finished; no longer effective or capable: *If he injures that knee again, he's through.* **b.** Having no further relationship: *Jane and I are through.* ¶*These sound alike* **through, threw.**

Idiom. **through and through. 1.** All the way through: *We were soaked through and through by the time we got out of the rain.* **2.** Completely; thoroughly: *She's a staunch Republican through and through.*

through•out |thrōō **out**′| *prep.* In, to, through, or during every part of: *throughout the country; throughout the night.* Also used adverbially: *I found this book interesting throughout.*

through•way |**thrōō**′wā′| *n.* A form of the word **thruway.**

throve |thrōv|. Past tense of **thrive.**

throw |thrō| *v.* **threw** |thrōō|, **thrown** |thrōn|, **throw•ing. 1.** To propel through the air with a swift motion of the arm; fling: *throw a ball.* **2.** To hurl with great force, as in anger: *He threw himself at his opponent.* **3.** To cast: *throw a glance at the window displays; throw a shadow.* **4.** To put on or off casually: *hurriedly throwing a cape over her shoulders.* **5.** To hurl to the ground or floor: *The wrestler threw his opponent with a swift blow.* **6.** *Informal.* To arrange or give: *throw a party.* **7.** *Informal.* To lose (a fight, race, etc.) purposely. **8.** To put into a specified condition: *new regulations that threw the players into confusion.* **9.** To actuate (a switch or control lever). —***phrasal verbs.*** **throw away. 1.** To discard as useless. **2.** To fail to use: *throw away an opportunity.* **throw in. 1.** To put (a clutch, gears, etc.) into engagement. **2.** To add (something) with no additional charge. **throw off.** To cast out; reject. **throw out. 1.** To discard; reject: *throwing out old books.* **2.** To put (a clutch, gears, etc.) out of engagement. **throw up.** To vomit. —*n.* **1.** The act of throwing; a cast. **2.** The distance, height, or direction of something thrown. **3.** A scarf, shawl, or light coverlet. **4.** The distance or region through which a mechanical part moves. —**throw′er** *n.*

throw•back |**thrō**′băk′| *n.* A return to one or more of the characteristics of an ancestor or an earlier generation.

thrown |thrōn|. Past participle of **throw.** ¶*These sound alike* **thrown, throne.**

thru |thrōō| *prep. & adj. Informal.* A form of the word **through.**

thrum |thrŭm| *v.* **thrummed, thrum•ming.** To play (a stringed instrument) in an idle or monotonous way; strum. —*n.* The sound made by thrumming.

thrush[1] |thrŭsh| *n.* Any of several songbirds usually having a brownish back and a spotted breast.

thrush[2] |thrŭsh| *n.* An infection of the mouth with a fungus that produces white eruptions on the mucous membrane.

thrust |thrŭst| *v.* **1.** To push or drive forcibly: *thrusting our way through the crowd. He thrust his hands in his pockets.* **2.** To stab; pierce: *thrust a dagger into his back.* **3.** To force into a specified condition or situation: *thrust herself into a high-paid job.* —*n.* **1.** A forceful shove or push. **2.** A force that tends to move an object, especially an object such as an airplane or rocket. **3.** A stab. **4.** The general direction or tendency: *the thrust of the governor's proposal.*

thru•way |**thrōō**′wā′| *n.* A highway for high-speed traffic, usually having four or more lanes.

thud |thŭd| *n.* **1.** A dull sound. **2.** A blow or fall causing such a sound. —*v.* **thud•ded, thud•ding.** To make such a sound.

thug |thŭg| *n.* A tough hoodlum, gangster, or robber.

thu•li•um |**thōō**′lē əm| *n.* Symbol **Tm** One of the elements, a silvery rare-earth element with 16 known isotopes having mass numbers that range

throne
British coronation chair

thunder/Thor/Thursday
Thunder *was Old English* thunor, *descending from prehistoric Germanic* thunaraz, *which meant "thunder" and was also the name of the thunder god.* Thunaraz *appears in Old Norse as* Thunarr, *later becoming* Thōrr, *the name of the thunder god, which was borrowed into English as* **Thor**. *The fifth day of the week in Old English was called* Thunresdæg, *"thunder's day" or "Thor's day," becoming* **Thursday** *in Modern English.*

tiara
Queen Elizabeth II wearing a diamond tiara.

ă pat/ā pay/â care/ä father/ĕ pet/ ē be/ĭ pit/ī pie/î fierce/ŏ pot/ ō go/ô paw, for/oi oil/ŏŏ book/ ōō boot/ou out/ŭ cut/û fur/ *th* the/th thin/hw which/zh vision/ ə ago, item, pencil, atom, circus

from 161 to 176. Atomic number 69; atomic weight 168.934; valences +2, +3; melting point 1,545°C; boiling point 1,727°C.

thumb |thŭm| *n.* **1.** The short, thick first digit of the human hand, which can be moved so that it is opposite each of the other fingers. **2.** A similar digit of an animal, especially a monkey, ape, or other primate. **3.** The part of a glove or mitten that fits over the thumb. *—v. Informal.* To ask (a ride) from a passing automobile by pointing one's thumb in the direction one is traveling; hitchhike. ***—phrasal verb.*** **thumb through.** To browse rapidly through (the pages of a book or publication).
Idioms. **all thumbs.** Clumsy; awkward. **thumbs down.** *Informal.* A sign of refusal or disapproval. **under the thumb of.** Under the influence or power of.

thumb•nail |**thŭm'**nāl'| *n.* The nail of the thumb.

thumb•screw |**thŭm'**skrōō'| *n.* **1.** A screw made so that it can be turned with the thumb and fingers. **2.** An instrument of torture formerly used for crushing the thumb.

thumb•tack |**thŭm'**tăk'| *n.* A tack with a smooth, rounded head that can be pressed into place with the thumb.

thump |thŭmp| *n.* **1.** A blow with a blunt instrument. **2.** The muffled sound produced by such a blow. *—v.* **1.** To strike with a blunt or dull instrument, or with the hand or foot, so as to produce a muffled sound: *angrily thumping the desk with his fist.* **2.** To beat, hit, or fall in such a way as to produce a thump: *His heart thumped with fear.*

thun•der |**thŭn'**dər| *n.* **1.** The explosive noise that accompanies a stroke of lightning. **2.** Any similar noise: *the thunder of distant guns; thunders of applause.* *—v.* **1.** To produce thunder: *It stormed and thundered, with lightning flashing in great streaks.* **2.** To produce sounds like thunder: *guns thundering in the distance.* **3.** To utter loudly: *The captain thundered orders to the sailors.* [SEE NOTE]

thun•der•bolt |**thŭn'**dər bōlt'| *n.* A stroke of lightning from which thunder is heard.

thun•der•clap |**thŭn'**dər klăp'| *n.* A single sharp crash of thunder.

thun•der•cloud |**thŭn'**dər kloud'| *n.* A large, dark cloud carrying an electric charge and producing lightning and thunder; a cumulonimbus.

thun•der•head |**thŭn'**dər hĕd'| *n.* The billowy upper part of a thundercloud.

thun•der•ous |**thŭn'**dər əs| *adj.* Producing thunder or a similar sound: *thunderous applause.* **—thun'der•ous•ly** *adv.*

thun•der•show•er |**thŭn'**dər shou'ər| *n.* A short, often heavy rainstorm accompanied by thunder and lightning.

thun•der•storm |**thŭn'**dər stôrm'| *n.* A storm of heavy rain accompanied by lightning and thunder.

thun•der•struck |**thŭn'**dər strŭk'| *adj.* Amazed; astonished: *He stood thunderstruck at the sidelines watching the defeat of his team.*

Thurs. Thursday.

Thurs•day |**thûrz'**dē| *or* |-dā'| *n.* The fifth day of the week, after Wednesday and before Friday. ***—modifier:*** *a Thursday night.* [SEE NOTE]

thus |*th*ŭs| *adv.* **1.** In this manner: *An egg hatches, or a mammal is born: thus, a new animal sees the world.* **2.** To a stated degree or extent; so: *I haven't looked at your work thus far.* **3.** Consequently; thereby: *Philip forbade the export of gold and silver from France, thus cutting off payments to the pope.*

thwack |thwăk| *v.* To strike or hit with something flat; whack. *—n.* A sharp blow with something flat.

thwart |thwôrt| *v.* To prevent from taking place; frustrate; block: *They thwarted his plans. Injuries thwarted their hopes of a championship.* *—n.* A seat across a boat, on which the oarsman sits.

thy |*th*ī|. *Archaic.* The possessive form of **thee.**

thyme |tīm| *n.* A low-growing plant with spicy-smelling leaves used to flavor cooked food. ¶*These sound alike* **thyme, time.**

thy•mus |**thī'**məs| *n.* **1.** A ductless glandlike structure behind the top of the breastbone, having some role in building resistance to disease. It reaches maximum development in early childhood and is absent or vestigial in adults. **2.** A similar structure in other vertebrate animals.

thy•roid |**thī'**roid'| *adj.* Of or having to do with the thyroid gland or thyroid cartilage. *—n.* **1.** The **thyroid gland. 2.** The **thyroid cartilage.**

thyroid cartilage. The largest cartilage of the larynx, having two broad projections that join in front to form the Adam's apple.

thyroid gland. An endocrine gland having two lobes, located in front of and to both sides of the windpipe in human beings. It is found in all vertebrates and produces the hormone thyroxin.

thy•rox•in, also **thy•rox•ine** |thī **rŏk'**sĭn| *n.* A hormone that contains iodine, produced by the thyroid gland and acting to regulate body metabolism. It is produced synthetically and used for treatment of thyroid disorders.

thy•self |*th*ī **sĕlf'**|. *Archaic.* Yourself.

ti |tē| *n.* A syllable used in music to represent the seventh tone of a diatonic major scale. ¶*These sound alike* **ti, tea, tee.**

Ti The symbol for the element titanium.

ti•ar•a |tē **ăr'**ə| *or* |-**âr'**ə| *or* |-**är'**ə| *n.* **1.** An ornament that looks like a small crown, worn on the head by women on formal occasions. **2.** The tall, three-tiered crown worn by the pope. [SEE PICTURE]

Ti•ber |**tī'**bər|. A river in Italy flowing through Rome.

Ti•bet |tĭ **bĕt'**|. A former country north of India, now a part of China.

Ti•bet•an |tĭ **bĕt'**n| *n.* **1.** A member of the Mongoloid people of Tibet. **2.** The language of Tibet, related to Burmese, Chinese, and Thai. *—adj.* Of Tibet, the Tibetans, or their language.

tib•i•a |**tĭb'**ē ə| *n., pl.* **tib•i•ae** |**tĭb'**ē ē'| or **tib•i•as.** **1.** The inner and larger of the two bones of the human leg that extend from the knee to the ankle; the shinbone. **2.** A similar bone of an animal.

tic |tĭk| *n.* A recurring spasmodic contraction or twitching of a set of muscles, usually in the face or limbs, often a symptom of a neurotic disorder. ¶*These sound alike* **tic, tick.**

tick¹ |tĭk| *n.* **1.** Any of a series of sharp, short noises made by fairly small machine parts striking together, as in a clock. **2.** A light mark used to check off or call attention to an item. *—v.* **1.** To produce a series of ticks. **2.** To function in a certain way, as by means of a mechanism: *What makes him tick?* ¶*These sound alike* **tick, tic.** [SEE NOTE]

tick² |tĭk| *n.* **1.** Any of several small animals, related to the spiders, that attach themselves to and suck blood from the skin of human beings and animals, and that often carry microorganisms that cause disease. **2.** Any of several small, louselike, bloodsucking insects that are parasites on sheep, goats, etc. ¶*These sound alike* **tick, tic.** [SEE NOTE]

tick³ |tĭk| *n.* The sturdy cloth case of a mattress or pillow, enclosing the stuffing. ¶*These sound alike* **tick, tic.** [SEE NOTE]

tick•er |tĭk'ər| *n.* **1.** A type of telegraph instrument, no longer in use, that prints information, usually stock-market quotations, on a strip of paper tape. **2.** Any of various modern devices that record such information by electronic means.

ticker tape. The strip of paper on which a ticker prints.

tick•et |tĭk'ĭt| *n.* **1.** A paper slip or card that entitles the holder to a specified service or right, as to ride a bus or enter a stadium. **2.** A tag or label, attached to and giving information about merchandise. **3.** A list of candidates in an election, entered or backed by a particular party or group. **4.** A legal summons given to a person accused of violating a traffic law. ***—modifier:*** *ticket stubs.* *—v.* **1.** To attach a tag to; label. **2.** To mark or intend for a certain use: *cars ticketed for shipment.* **3.** To give a legal summons to.

tick•ing |tĭk'ĭng| *n.* Strong, often striped cotton or linen cloth used in making pillow and mattress coverings.

tick•le |tĭk'əl| *v.* **tick•led, tick•ling. 1.** To feel a tingling sensation. **2.** To touch (the body) lightly, causing laughter or twitching movements. **3.** To delight or amuse; please. *—n.* The act or sensation of tickling. **—tick'ler** *n.*

Idiom. **tickle pink.** *Informal.* To please; delight.

tick•lish |tĭk'lĭsh| *adj.* **1.** Sensitive to tickling: *a ticklish child.* **2.** Easily offended or upset: *She was very ticklish on the subject of women's rights.* **3.** Requiring skillful handling: *a ticklish problem.* **—tick'lish•ness** *n.*

tick-tack-toe |tĭk'tăk tō'| *n.* A game played by two persons, each trying to make a line of three X's or three O's in a boxlike figure with nine spaces. [SEE NOTE]

tid•al |tīd'l| *adj.* Of, having, or affected by tides: *tidal marshes.*

tidal wave. 1. An unusual rise in the level of water along a seacoast, as from a storm or a combination of wind and tide. **2.** Loosely, a tsunami.

tid•dly•winks |tĭd'lē wĭngks'| *n.* *(used with a singular verb).* A game in which players try to pop small disks into a cup by pressing them on the edge with a larger disk.

tid•bit |tĭd'bĭt'| *n.* A choice bit of something, as of food or gossip.

tide |tīd| *n.* **1. a.** The periodic variation in the surface level of the oceans, seas, bays, etc., of the earth caused by the gravitational attraction of the moon and to a lesser extent the sun. **b.** Any particular occurrence of such a variation. **c.** The water that moves when such a variation occurs. **2.** Any stress or change in shape that a body undergoes as a result of the gravitational attraction of another body. **3.** A tendency regarded as alternating and driving forward: *ignoring the rising tide of public discontent.* **4.** Anything that rises and falls like the waters of the tide: *a tide of immigrants.* **5.** *Archaic.* A time or season: *eventide; Christmastide.* *—v.* **tid•ed, tid•ing. —tide over.** To support through a difficult period. [SEE NOTE]

tide•land |tīd'lănd'| *n.* Land along a coast that is under water at high tide.

tide•wa•ter |tīd'wô'tər| *or* |-wŏt'ər| *n.* **1.** Water that flows onto the land when the tide is very high. **2.** Water, especially water in streams or rivers, that is affected by tides. **3.** Low coastal land drained by streams that are affected by tides. ***—modifier:*** *the tidewater region of a coast.*

tid•ings |tī'dĭngz| *pl.n.* News; information: *Have you heard the glad tidings?* [SEE NOTE]

ti•dy |tī'dē| *adj.* **ti•di•er, ti•di•est. 1.** Orderly and neat: *a tidy room; a tidy closet.* **2.** *Informal.* Considerable: *a tidy sum of money.* *—v.* **ti•died, ti•dy•ing, ti•dies.** To put in order; make neat: *Tidy up your room before going to the movies.* *—n., pl.* **ti•dies.** A fancy protective covering for the arms or headrest of a chair. **—ti'di•ly** *adv.* **—ti'di•ness** *n.* [SEE NOTE]

tie |tī| *v.* **tied, ty•ing. 1.** To fasten or secure with a cord, rope, etc.: *tie up a parcel; tie a dog to a fence.* **2.** To fasten by drawing together and knotting strings or laces: *bending to tie his shoes. Her dress ties at the back.* **3.** To make (a knot or bow): *tie a knot.* **4.** To form a knot or bow in: *tie a necktie; tie a scarf.* **5.** To equal (an opponent or his score) in a contest: *He tied the pole-vaulting record last year. The visiting team tied our school last night. They tied for first place in the examination. The two teams tied.* **6.** To join (successive musical tones of the same pitch) so that there is no break between them. ***—phrasal verbs.*** **tie down.** To restrict the freedom of; limit; confine: *a man tied down by heavy financial responsibilities.* **tie in.** To have a connection with: *Your story ties in with what she told me at the party.* **tie up. 1.** To halt; stop: *an accident that tied up traffic.* **2.** To be busy, in use, etc.: *I will be tied up in a meeting all afternoon.* **3.** To place or invest (money) so that it cannot be used freely: *He tied up all his capital in a new home.* *—n.* **1.** A cord, string, rope, etc., by which something is tied. **2.** A necktie. **3.** Something that unites; a bond: *the ties of friendship; family ties.* **4.** An equality of scores, votes, or performances in a contest: *The game ended in a tie.* **5.** A beam, rod, fastening, etc., that joins parts of a structure and gives support. **6.** One of the timbers laid across a railroad bed to support the tracks; a sleeper. **7.** A curved line connecting the heads of two successive musical notes of the same pitch, indicating that they are to be played or sung with no break.

tie clasp. An ornamental pin or clip that holds the ends of a necktie to the front of a shirt.

tie-dye |tī'dī'| *v.* To dye (a fabric) after tying parts of it so that those parts will not take the

tick¹⁻²⁻³

Tick¹ *is probably an imitative word.* **Tick²** *was Old English* ticia, *"animal louse."* **Tick³** *is from Middle Dutch* tike, *"mattress cover."*

tick-tack-toe

Tick-tack-toe *was originally the name of a game in which numbers were written on a slate and the players, with eyes shut, tried to hit a number with a pencil. The name is supposed to be imitative of the sound of the pencil hitting the slate. How the name was transferred to the modern game is not clear. In England, more prosaically, the game is usually called* noughts and crosses.

tide/tidings/tidy

Tide *was Old English* tīd, *originally meaning "a recurring time, a season," now surviving as the archaic sense* **5**; *later it came to mean "the time when the sea rises."* **Tidings** *is from Old Norse* tidhendi, *"events, news," from* tidhr, *"happening," which is related to Old English* tīd, *"recurring time."* **Tidy** *is a Middle English formation from* tīd, *originally meaning "happening at the right time, seasonable, convenient," later "in good shape, neat."*

tiger

tiger lily

till[1-2-3-4]

Till[1] *was Old English* tilian, *"to work at, to cultivate." It originally meant "to strive after a particular goal," and is descended from prehistoric Germanic* tilam, *meaning "a fixed point, goal."* **Till**[2] *was Old English* til, *"up to the time of"; it originally meant "up to a particular point," and it is also from Germanic* tilam, *"fixed point."* **Until** *is a Middle English compound of* un- *(as in* **unto***) with* **till**[2]. **Till** *and* **until** *are equally correct in all contexts (but* **until** *is far more common). Both* **till**[3] *and* **till**[4] *are of unknown origin.*

ă pat/ā pay/â care/ä father/ĕ pet/ ē be/ĭ pit/ī pie/î fierce/ŏ pot/ ō go/ô paw, for/oi oil/ŏŏ book/ ōō boot/ou out/ŭ cut/û fur/ *th* the/th thin/hw which/zh vision/ ə ago, item, pencil, atom, circus

dye, giving the fabric a streaked or mottled look. —**tie'dyed'** *adj.*: *tie-dyed fabric.*

tie pin. A stickpin.

tier |tîr| *n.* Any of a series of rows placed one above another. ¶ *These sound alike* **tier, tear**[2].

Ti•er•ra del Fu•e•go |tĭ ĕr'ə dĕl fyōō ā'gō|. **1.** A group of islands at the extreme southern tip of South America. **2.** The main island of this group.

tie tack. A short, decorative pin used to fasten a necktie to a shirt.

tie-up |tī'ŭp'| *n.* A temporary stoppage of work, traffic, etc., because of a strike, accident, etc.

tiff |tĭf| *n.* **1.** A fit of irritation. **2.** A petty quarrel.

ti•ger |tī'gər| *n.* **1.** A very large wild cat of Asia, having tawny fur with crosswise black stripes. **2.** A person who is enthusiastic about or a fierce opponent in some activity: *He is a tiger at tick-tack-toe.* [SEE PICTURE]

tiger lily. A tall lily having black-spotted orange flowers with petals that curve upward. [SEE PICTURE]

ti•ger-eye |tī'gər ī'|, also **ti•ger's-eye** |tī'gərz-| *n.* A yellow-brown gemstone.

tight |tīt| *adj.* **tight•er, tight•est. 1.** Of such close construction or texture as to be impermeable, especially by water or air: *a tight roof.* **2.** Fastened, held, or closed securely: *a tight knot. The drawer is so tight that I cannot open it.* **3.** Set closely together; compact: *planes flying in a tight formation.* **4.** Drawn out to the fullest extent; taut: *a tight rope.* **5.** Fitting close to some part of the body, usually too close; uncomfortably snug: *a tight shirt; tight shoes.* **6.** Leaving no room or time to spare; very close: *a tight fit; a tight schedule.* **7.** Constricted: *a tight feeling in the chest.* **8.** *Informal.* Close-fisted; stingy: *her uncle is very tight with money.* **9. a.** Difficult to obtain: *tight money.* **b.** Affected by scarcity: *a tight money market.* **10.** Difficult to deal with or get out of: *a tight spot.* **11.** Closely contested: *a tight race; a tight game.* **12.** *Slang.* Drunk. —*adv.* **1.** Firmly; securely. **2.** Soundly: *sleep tight.* —**tight'ly** *adv.* —**tight'ness** *n.*

***Idiom.* sit tight.** To make no further move.

tight•en |tīt'n| *v.* To make or become tight.

tight•fist•ed |tīt'fĭs'tĭd| *adj.* Stingy.

tight•lipped |tīt'lĭpt'| *adj.* **1.** Having the lips pressed together. **2.** Secretive; reticent; silent.

tight•rope |tīt'rōp'| *n.* A rope, usually of wire, tightly stretched high above the ground, upon which acrobats walk and balance themselves.

tights |tīts| *pl.n.* A tight-fitting, stretchable garment covering the body from the waist or neck down, worn by acrobats, dancers, etc.

tight•wad |tīt'wŏd'| *n.* *Slang.* A stingy person.

ti•gress |tī'grĭs| *n.* A female tiger.

Ti•gris |tī'grĭs|. A river of southwest Asia.

til•de |tĭl'də| *n.* A diacritical mark ˜ used in Spanish and Portuguese to indicate certain nasal sounds, as in the word *cañon.*

tile |tīl| *n.* **1.** A thin slab of baked clay, plastic, concrete, or other material, laid in rows to cover floors, walls, or roofs. **2.** A short length of clay or concrete pipe, used in sewers, drains, chimneys, etc. **3.** A block of concrete or fired clay used in building walls. **4.** Tiles in general: *a wall marred by chipped tile.* **5.** A marked playing piece used in certain games. —*v.* **tiled, til•ing.** To cover or provide with tiles.

till[1] |tĭl| *v.* To prepare (land) for the raising of crops by plowing, harrowing, and fertilizing. —**till'a•ble** *adj.* [SEE NOTE]

till[2] |tĭl| *prep.* Until: *I won't see you till tomorrow.* Also used as a conjunction: *Wait till I call you.* —*conj.* Before or unless: *I can't help you till you give me a written request for help.* [SEE NOTE]

till[3] |tĭl| *n.* A drawer or compartment for money, especially in a store. [SEE NOTE]

till[4] |tĭl| *n.* A mass of material deposited by a glacier, a mixture containing clay, sand, gravel, and boulders. [SEE NOTE]

till•age |tĭl'ĭj| *n.* **1.** The cultivation of land. **2.** Tilled land.

till•er[1] |tĭl'ər| *n.* A person who tills land.

till•er[2] |tĭl'ər| *n.* A lever used to turn a boat's rudder.

tilt |tĭlt| *v.* **1.** To slope or cause to slope, as by raising one end; incline; tip: *The table tilted and the plates fell on the floor. The children tilted the barrel to empty it.* **2.** To thrust (a lance) in a joust. **3.** To attack in speech or writing: *a politician tilting at gambling and other abuses.* —*n.* **1.** A slant; slope. **2.** A joust. **3.** A verbal duel.

***Idiom.* at full tilt.** At full speed.

tim•ber |tĭm'bər| *n.* **1.** Trees or wooded land, especially when considered as a source of wood: *The road ran through hills, valleys, and groves of timber.* **2.** Wood for building; lumber: *The Egyptians traded gold and handicrafts for timber and other raw materials.* **3.** A beam or similarly shaped piece of wood, such as one of those used in building a house or forming a ship's frame. **4.** Character; material: *a man of heroic timber.* —*interj.* A word used as a warning that a tree being cut down is about to fall. ¶ *These sound alike* **timer, timbre.**

tim•bered |tĭm'bərd| *adj.* **1.** Covered with trees or forest: *a timbered slope.* **2.** Constructed of timber, often left exposed: *a timbered barn.*

timber hitch. A knot tied around a log, pole, etc., that is to be towed or hoisted.

tim•ber•land |tĭm'bər lănd'| *n.* Wooded land.

tim•ber•line |tĭm'bər līn'| *n.* Also **timber line.** In mountainous or arctic regions, the height or limit beyond which trees do not grow.

timber wolf. A grayish or whitish wolf of northern forest regions.

tim•bre |tĭm'bər| *or* |tăm'-| *n.* **1.** The quality or characteristic of musical tones which allows two different tones of the same pitch and loudness to be distinguished. **2.** The tone or quality that is characteristic of an instrument or voice: *the timbre of a clarinet.* ¶ *These sound alike* **timbre, timber.**

time |tīm| *n.* **1.** A continuous measurable quantity, ordinarily distinct from space, in which events occur in an order that does not seem to be reversible, proceeding from the past through the present to the future. **2. a.** An interval bounded by two points of this quantity, as by the beginning and end of an event: *the time it takes to go from one place to another.* **b.** The numerical measure of such an interval. **c.** A similar number representing a given point, such as the present, as reckoned from a given point in the past. **d.** A system by which such intervals are measured or such numbers are reckoned: *standard time; solar time.* **3.** A musical meter: *three-quarter time; six-eighth time.* **4.** A moment or period designated for a given activity: *harvest time; bedtime.* **5.** Often **times. a.** A period associated with similar events, conditions, or certain historical figures: *Victorian times; a time of great student unrest.* **b.** The present: *a sign of the times.* **6.** The period during which something is expected to last: *He died before his time.* **c.** An instance or occasion: *He played the piece five times.* **8. a.** The regular period of work of an employee: *working full time.* **b.** The pay received: *She gets double time when she works on weekends.* **9.** A period or occasion associated with a certain experience: *having a good time at the party.* —*v.* **timed, tim•ing. 1.** To set the time at which (something) happens or is to happen. **2.** To adjust (a clock, watch, etc.) so that it indicates time accurately. **3.** To regulate or adjust so that each of a sequence of events happens at the correct time: *time a leap carefully; time an automobile engine.* **4.** To record or register the speed of: *Radar timed the car at exactly 55 miles per hour.* **5.** To record or register the duration of: *We timed the game at two hours even.* ¶*These sound alike* **time, thyme.** [SEE NOTE]

Idioms. **against time.** With a quickly approaching time limit: *working against time.* **at one time. 1.** At once; at the same time: *girls talking at one time.* **2.** At a period or moment in the past: *At one time they were friends.* **at the same time.** However; nevertheless. **at times.** On occasion; sometimes. **behind the times.** Out-of-date; old-fashioned. **for the time being.** Temporarily. **from time to time.** Once in a while; at intervals. **in no time.** Almost instantly; immediately: *Take this pill; you will feel better in no time.* **in time. 1.** Before it is too late; early enough: *They plan to arrive in time for the party.* **2.** In the end; eventually: *In time you will see that he was wrong.* **3.** In tempo; keeping the rhythm. **on time. 1.** According to schedule; promptly. **2.** By paying in installments: *buy a car on time.* **time after time** or **time and again.** Again and again; repeatedly.

time bomb. A bomb that can be set to explode after a given period of time.

time clock. A device that records the arrival and departure times of employees. [SEE PICTURE]

time exposure. 1. A photographic exposure in which light strikes the film or plate for a relatively long time. **2.** A photograph made by such an exposure.

time-hon•ored |tīm'ŏn'ərd| *adj.* Honored because of age or age-old observance: *time-honored customs.*

time•keep•er |tīm'kē'pər| *n.* One who keeps track of time, as in a sports event.

time•less |tīm'lĭs| *adj.* **1.** Independent of time; eternal: *the timeless universe.* **2.** Unaffected by time: *the timeless cathedrals of Europe.* —**time'less•ly** *adv.*

time•ly |tīm'lē| *adj.* **time•li•er, time•li•est.** Occurring at a suitable or opportune time; well-timed: *a timely remark.*

time-out |tīm'out'| *n.* In sports, a brief period of rest or consultation during a game.

time•piece |tīm'pēs'| *n.* An instrument, such as a watch or clock, that measures, records, or indicates time.

tim•er |tī'mər| *n.* **1.** A timepiece, especially one used to measure intervals of time. **2.** A timepiece that operates a switch or other control at certain times or at fixed intervals.

times |tīmz| *prep.* Multiplied by: *Eight times three equals twenty-four.*

time-shar•ing |tīm'shâr'ĭng| *n.* A system whereby many users at different locations share a single computer.

time signature. A symbol written on a musical staff to indicate the meter.

time•ta•ble |tīm'tā'bəl| *n.* A table listing the scheduled arrival and departure times of trains, buses, etc.

time•worn |tīm'wôrn'| *or* |-wōrn'| *adj.* **1.** Showing the effects of long use or wear. **2.** Used too often trite: *a timeworn joke.*

time zone. Any of the 24 parts, each 15 degrees of longitude wide, into which the earth is divided for purposes of keeping time. The primary division has the meridian that passes through Greenwich, England, at its center, time being reckoned one hour earlier in each successive zone to the east and one hour later in each successive zone to the west.

tim•id |tĭm'ĭd| *adj.* Easily frightened; hesitant and fearful; shy. —**ti•mid'i•ty** *n.*

tim•ing |tī'mĭng| *n.* **1.** The regulation of occurrence, pace, or coordination to achieve the most desirable effects. **2. a.** A record or measurement of speed or duration. **b.** The act or process of making such a record or measurement. **3.** The regulation or adjustment of the times at which each of a series of events occurs, as in a machine.

Ti•mor |tē'môr'| *or* |tē **môr'**|. An island of Indonesia.

tim•or•ous |tĭm'ər əs| *adj.* Easily frightened; timid. —**tim'or•ous•ly** *adv.* —**tim'or•ous•ness** *n.*

tim•o•thy |tĭm'ə thē| *n.* A grass with long, narrow, dense flower clusters, widely grown for hay.

tim•pa•ni |tĭm'pə nē| *pl.n.* A set of kettledrums.

tim•pa•num |tĭm'pə nəm| *n.* A form of the word **tympanum.**

tin |tĭn| *n.* **1.** Symbol **Sn** One of the elements, a soft silvery metal. Atomic number 50; atomic weight 118.69; valences +2, +4; melting point 231.89°C; boiling point 2,270°C. **2. Tin plate. 3.** A tin container or box. —*v.* **tinned, tin•ning. 1.** To plate or coat with tin or solder. **2.** To preserve or pack in tins; can. [SEE NOTE]

tin can. A container made of thin steel coated on the inside with tin or some other corrosion-resistant material, used for preserving food.

tinc•ture |tĭngk'chər| *n.* An alcohol solution of a medicine that does not easily change into a vapor: *tincture of iodine.*

tin•der |tĭn'dər| *n.* Any material that catches fire easily, used to kindle fires.

tin•der•box |tĭn'dər bŏks'| *n.* **1.** A metal box for holding tinder. **2.** A highly dangerous or explosive situation.

tine |tīn| *n.* A prong or similar narrow or pointed part, as of a fork or of a deer's antlers.

tin•foil |tĭn'foil'| *n.* Also **tin foil.** A thin, pliable sheet of tin or an alloy of tin, used as a protective wrapping.

tinge |tĭnj| *v.* **tinged, tinge•ing** or **ting•ing. 1.** To color slightly; tint: *The sunset tinged the sky with red.* **2.** To give a slight trace or touch to; affect

time

"Know the true value of time; snatch, seize, and enjoy every moment of it." —*Lord Chesterfield, in a letter to his son (1749).*
"Do not squander time, for that is the stuff life is made of." —*Benjamin Franklin (1758).*
"Time is but the stream I go fishing in." —*Henry David Thoreau (1854).*

time clock

tin

Tin *is used to coat other metals to prevent corrosion and in numerous alloys, including bronze, pewter, and various solders. Its symbol,* **Sn**, *is taken from* stannum, *the Latin word for "tin."*

tip[1-2-3]

Tip[1] *is from Old Norse* typpi, *"end, extremity"; it is related to* **top**[1]. **Tip**[2] *is of obscure origin.* **Tip**[3] *was originally a verb meaning "to touch lightly," later "to give to, to pass (information) to"; it is probably related to* **tip**[1].

tiptoe

tire[1-2]

Tire[1] *was Old English* tēorian, *"to be exhausted, to fail."* **Tire**[2] *is first recorded in the fifteenth century in the sense "iron plates with which carriage wheels were shod"; the original meaning was probably "covering or clothing for the wheel," from* tire, *an obsolete noun meaning "clothing," shortened from* **attire**. Pneumatic tires, *inflated with air, were introduced in the late nineteenth century. (***Tire**[2] *is spelled* **tyre** *in British English.)*

ă pat/ā pay/â care/ä father/ĕ pet/ ē be/ĭ pit/ī pie/î fierce/ŏ pot/ ō go/ô paw, for/oi oil/ŏŏ book/ ōō boot/ou out/ŭ cut/û fur/ *th* the/th thin/hw which/zh vision/ ə ago, item, pencil, atom, circus

slightly: *admiration tinged with envy.* —*n.* A faint trace of color, flavor, etc.: *a tinge of sadness in her remarks.* [SEE NOTE on p. 880]

tin•gle |tĭng′gəl| *v.* **tin•gled, tin•gling.** To have a prickling, stinging sensation, as from cold or excitement. —*n.* A prickling or stinging sensation.

tin•ker |tĭng′kər| *n.* **1.** A traveling mender of metal household utensils. **2.** One who is clumsy at his work; a bungler. —*v.* **1.** To work as a tinker. **2.** To play with machine parts experimentally. **3.** To busy oneself in a casual or aimless way: *tinkering around the garden.*

tin•kle |tĭng′kəl| *v.* **tin•kled, tin•kling.** To make or cause to make light, metallic sounds, as of a small bell. —*n.* A light, clear metallic sound.

tin•ny |tĭn′ē| *adj.* **tin•ni•er, tin•ni•est. 1.** Of or containing tin. **2.** Of or having a thin sound that suggests metal rattling or being struck.

tin plate. Thin sheet iron or steel coated with tin.

tin•sel |tĭn′səl| *n.* **1.** Very thin sheets, strips, or threads of a glittering material used as decoration. **2.** Anything superficially showy but basically valueless.

tin•smith |tĭn′smĭth′| *n.* One who works with light metal, as tin.

tint |tĭnt| *n.* **1.** A shade of a color, especially a pale or delicate variation. **2.** A slight coloration; a tinge: *a tint of red in the sky.* —*v.* To give a tint to; color: *tint hair.* —**tint′er** *n.* [SEE NOTE on p. 880]

tin•tin•nab•u•la•tion |tĭn′tə năb′yə lā′shən| *n.* The ringing or sounding of bells.

ti•ny |tī′nē| *adj.* **ti•ni•er, ti•ni•est.** Extremely small.

tip[1] |tĭp| *n.* **1.** The end or extremity of something: *a house on the tip of the island; asparagus tips.* **2.** A piece meant to be fitted to the end of something: *a cigarette with a filter tip.* —*v.* **tipped, tip•ping. 1.** To furnish with a tip: *tip cigarettes with filters.* **2.** In baseball, to hit (a pitch) with the side of the bat so that it glances off. [SEE NOTE]

tip[2] |tĭp| *v.* **tipped, tip•ping. 1.** To knock over or upset; topple over: *The wind tipped over the vase on the table.* **2.** To slant; tilt: *The children tipped the table. The table tipped suddenly.* **3.** To touch or raise (one's hat) in greeting. [SEE NOTE]

tip[3] |tĭp| *n.* **1.** A sum of money given for services rendered; a gratuity. **2.** Useful information; a helpful hint: *a book with tips on interior decorating.* —*v.* **tipped, tip•ping.** To give a small sum of money for services rendered: *tip a waiter. He tips excessively.* —***phrasal verb.* tip off.** To provide advance or inside information to. —**tip′per** *n.* [SEE NOTE]

ti•pi |tē′pē| *n.* A form of the word **tepee.**

tip•pet |tĭp′ĭt| *n.* **1.** A scarf, stole, or cape worn around the neck or shoulders and hanging down in front. **2.** A long, hanging part, as of a sleeve, hood, or cape.

tip•ple |tĭp′əl| *v.* **tip•pled, tip•pling.** To drink alcoholic liquor, especially habitually or to excess. —**tip′pler** *n.*

tip•sy |tĭp′sē| *adj.* **tip•si•er, tip•si•est.** Slightly drunk. —**tip′si•ly** *adv.* —**tip′si•ness** *n.*

tip•toe |tĭp′tō′| *v.* **tip•toed, tip•toe•ing.** To walk on or as on the tips of one's toes. —*n.* The tip of a toe. —*adv.* On tiptoe. [SEE PICTURE]

tip•top |tĭp′tŏp′| *n.* The highest point; the summit. —*adj.* Excellent: *feeling in tiptop shape.*

ti•rade |tī′rād′| *or* |tī rād′| *n.* A loud, very angry or violent speech, usually denouncing or criticizing something or someone; a diatribe.

Ti•ra•në, also **Ti•ra•na** |tĭ rä′nə|. The capital of Albania. Population, 171,000.

tire[1] |tīr| *v.* **tired, tir•ing. 1.** To make or become weary or fatigued: *The long walk tired me. She tires easily.* **2.** To make or become bored; lose interest: *His lengthy speech tired the listeners. The audience tired after the first act of the play.* [SEE NOTE]

tire[2] |tīr| *n.* **1.** A covering for a wheel, as of an automobile, usually of rubber or a similar material reinforced with cords of nylon, fiber glass, etc., and filled with air, fitted around the wheel to absorb shocks and provide traction. **2.** A hoop of metal or rubber fitted around a wheel. [SEE NOTE]

tired |tīrd| *adj.* **1. a.** Fatigued: *a tired athlete.* **b.** Impatient; bored: *a tired audience.* **2.** Hackneyed; trite: *a tired joke.*

tire•less |tīr′lĭs| *adj.* Not tiring easily; indefatigable: *a tireless worker.* —**tire′less•ly** *adv.*

tire•some |tīr′səm| *adj.* **1.** Causing fatigue; wearisome: *a tiresome job.* **2.** Causing boredom; tedious; boring: *a long, tiresome speech.* **3.** Causing annoyance; bothersome: *He has the tiresome habit of leaving his clothes scattered all over his room.* —**tire′some•ly** *adv.*

'tis |tĭz|. *Archaic.* It is.

tis•sue |tĭsh′ōō| *n.* **1. a.** A group or type of animal or plant cells that are similar in form and function, and often make up a particular organ or part: *lung tissue; leaf tissue; connective tissue.* **b.** Any cellular material of an organism: *a parasite that lives in animal tissue.* **2.** Also **tissue paper.** Light, thin paper used for wrapping, packing, etc. **3.** A piece of soft, absorbent paper used especially as a handkerchief. **4.** A light, thin, sheer cloth. **5.** Something formed as if by interweaving parts; a web or network: *a tissue of fantastic dreams.*

tit[1] |tĭt| *n.* Any of several European birds related to and resembling the American chickadees.

tit[2] |tĭt| *n.* A form of the word **teat.**

Ti•tan |tīt′n| *n.* **1.** In Greek mythology, one of a family of elder gods that was overthrown and supplanted by the family of Zeus. **2. titan.** A person of great size, importance, strength, etc.

ti•tan•ic[1] |tī tăn′ĭk| *adj.* Having great size, importance, strength, or power.

ti•tan•ic[2] |tī tăn′ĭk| *or* |tĭ-| *adj.* Of or containing titanium, especially with a valence of +4.

ti•ta•ni•um |tī tā′nē əm| *n.* Symbol **Ti** One of the elements, a shiny white metal that is strong, light, and highly resistant to corrosion. Atomic number 22; atomic weight 47.90; valences +2, +3, +4; melting point 1,675°C; boiling point 3,260°C.

tithe |tī*th*| *n.* **1.** A tenth part of one's annual income, paid to a church. **2.** A tenth part. —*v.* **tithed, tith•ing. 1.** To pay or give one tenth of (one's income). **2.** To levy a tithe on.

tit•il•late |tĭt′l āt′| *v.* **tit•il•lat•ed, tit•il•lat•ing.** To excite or stimulate in an agreeable way: *an author expert in titillating the reader's interest.* —**tit′il•la′tion** *n.*

ti•tle |tīt'l| *n.* **1.** An identifying name given to a book, painting, etc. **2.** A word or name given to a person as a mark of distinction showing rank, office, or vocation. Some titles are *Mr., Dr., Sir, His Majesty, Judge,* and *Count.* **3.** In law: **a.** The legal right or claim to ownership or possession: *Has he any title to the throne?* **b.** The document constituting this evidence, as a deed: *receiving title to their house.* **4.** A championship in sports. —*v.* **ti•tled, ti•tling.** To give a title to.

ti•tled |tīt'ld| *adj.* Having a title, especially of nobility.

tit•mouse |tĭt'mous'| *n., pl.* **-mice** |-mīs'|. A small, grayish North American bird with a pointed crest. [SEE PICTURE]

tit•ter |tĭt'ər| *v.* To utter a restrained, nervous giggle. —*n.* A restrained, nervous giggle.

tit•u•lar |tĭch'ə lər| *or* |tĭt'yə-| *adj.* **1.** Of or relating to a title: *the titular role in a play.* **2.** Existing as such in name only; nominal: *the titular ruler of a country.*

tiz•zy |tĭz'ē| *n., pl.* **tiz•zies.** *Slang.* A state of nervous confusion; a dither.

Tl The symbol for the element thallium.

Tlin•git |tlĭng'gĭt| *n., pl.* **Tlin•git** or **Tlin•gits.** **1.** A group of North American Indian tribes of southern Alaska and British Columbia. **2.** A member of any of these tribes. **3.** The language of these tribes.

Tm The symbol for the element thulium.

TNT |tē'ən tē'| *n.* Trinitrotoluene.

to |to͞o| *or* |tə *when unstressed*| *prep.* **1.** In a direction toward: *going to town.* **2.** In the direction of; so as to reach: *a trip to Paris.* **3.** Reaching as far as: *rotten to the core.* **4.** Toward or reaching the state of: *the Nazi rise to power.* **5.** To the extent of: *starving to death.* **6.** In contact with: *back to back; cheek to cheek.* **7.** In front of: *face to face.* **8.** Through and including; until: *from three to five.* **9.** For the attention, benefit, or possession of: *Tell it to me.* **10.** For the purpose of; for: *working to the same end.* **11.** For or of: *Do you have the belt to this dress?* **12.** Concerning or regarding: *She was deaf to my pleas.* **13.** In relation with: *parallel to the road.* **14.** With the resulting condition of: *torn to shreds.* **15.** As an accompaniment of: *singing to an old tune.* **16.** With regard to: *the secret to his success.* **17.** Composing or constituting; in: *two pints to the quart.* **18.** In accord with: *That's not really to my liking.* **19.** As compared with: *a score of four to three.* **20.** Before: *The time is now ten to five.* **21.** In honor of: *a toast to our visitors.* **22.** —Used before a verb to indicate the infinitive: *I'd like to go.* Also used alone when the infinitive is understood: *Go if you want to.* —*adv.* **1.** Into a shut position: *slammed the door to.* **2.** Into consciousness: *It was a few minutes before I came to.* **3.** Into a state of working at something: *We sat down for lunch and everybody fell to.* ¶*These sound alike* **to, too, two.**

toad |tōd| *n.* An animal related to and resembling the frogs, but having rougher, drier skin and living mostly on land when full grown. ¶*These sound alike* **toad, toed.** [SEE PICTURE]

toad•flax |tōd'flăks'| *n.* Butter-and-eggs.

toad•stool |tōd'sto͞ol'| *n.* A mushroom considered unfit for eating, especially one of the poisonous kinds.

toad•y |tō'dē| *n., pl.* **toad•ies.** A person who flatters others for the sake of gain; a sycophant. —*v.* **toad•ied, toad•y•ing, toad•ies.** To be a toady to: *shamelessly toadying to his boss.*

to and fro. Back and forth: *She's always running to and fro.*

toast[1] |tōst| *v.* **1.** To heat and brown (bread, marshmallows, etc.) by placing close to heat. **2.** To warm thoroughly: *toast one's feet by the fireplace.* —*n.* Sliced bread heated and browned. [SEE NOTE]

toast[2] |tōst| *n.* **1.** The act of drinking in honor of or to the health of a person, institution, etc. **2.** The person, institution, etc., who is honored in this way. **3.** Any person receiving much attention or acclaim: *The star of the play became the toast of London.* —*v.* To drink or propose a drink in honor of or to the health of: *The guests toasted the bride.* [SEE NOTE]

toast•er |tō'stər| *n.* An electrical appliance used to toast bread.

toast•mas•ter |tōst'măs'tər| *or* |-mä'stər| *n.* A person who proposes the toasts and introduces the speakers at a banquet.

to•bac•co |tə băk'ō| *n., pl.* **to•bac•cos** or **to•bac•coes.** **1.** A plant widely grown for its large leaves, used chiefly for smoking, but also for chewing, in snuff, etc. **2.** The leaves of such plants, processed for use in cigarettes, cigars, and pipes, for chewing, etc. **3.** Products, such as cigarettes, cigars, or snuff, made from tobacco. **4.** The use of such products: *He gave up tobacco years ago.* —**modifier:** *the tobacco crop.*

to•bac•co•nist |tə băk'ə nĭst| *n.* A person who sells cigarettes, cigars, pipe tobacco, etc.

To•ba•go |tə bā'gō|. See **Trinidad and Tobago.**

to•bog•gan |tə bŏg'ən| *n.* A long, narrow sled without runners, made of thin boards curved upward at the front end. —*v.* To ride on a toboggan.

toc•ca•ta |tə kä'tə| *n.* A musical composition, usually for the organ or another keyboard instrument, in a free style with elaborate passages that show the player's technique.

to•day, also **to-day** |tə dā'| *adv.* **1.** During or on the present day: *He will arrive today.* **2.** During or at the present time: *Today more cars are sold than ever before.* —*n.* The present day, time, or age: *the schedule for today; the composers of today.*

tod•dle |tŏd'l| *v.* **tod•dled, tod•dling.** To walk with short, unsteady steps, as a small child does. —**tod'dler** *n.*

tod•dy |tŏd'ē| *n., pl.* **tod•dies.** **1.** A drink of brandy or other liquor mixed with hot water, sugar, and spices. **2. a.** The sweet sap from certain tropical Asian palm trees. **b.** A fermented beverage made from this sap.

to-do |tə do͞o'| *n. Informal.* Commotion or bustle; a stir.

toe |tō| *n.* **1.** One of the extensions from the foot of a human being or other vertebrate. **2.** The part of a sock, stocking, shoe, or boot that fits over the toes. —*v.* **toed, toe•ing.** **1.** To touch or reach with the toes. **2. a.** To drive (a nail or spike) at an oblique angle. **b.** To fasten or secure with nails or spikes driven in this way. **3.** To walk with the toes pointed in a specified direction: *He toes out.* ¶*These sound alike* **toe, tow.**

titmouse
Painting by John James Audubon
The original name of the bird was *mose;* this was combined with *tit,* an old word meaning "something small," and later *titmose* was changed to **titmouse,** in mistaken association with **mouse.**

toad
Toad puffed up in the act of calling

toast[1-2]
Toast[1] *is from Old French* toster, *from Latin* tostus, *"scorched," the past participle of* torrēre, *"to dry, parch, scorch."* **Toast**[2] *is a special use of* **toast**[1], *based on the fact that in the past small pieces of spiced toast were put in drinks to flavor them. In the late seventeenth century, it was the custom at drinking parties for each man in turn to name a lady to whom the whole company would drink; the lady named was called the* toast *because her name would add flavor to the drink as a piece of (spiced) toast would.*

toga
Etruscan statue of an orator

tomahawk
The word **tomahawk** is from Algonquian *tamahaac.* It is first recorded in English from the early seventeenth century.

tomato
The word **tomato** *is from Spanish* tomato, *which is from Aztec* tomatl.

ă pat/ā pay/â care/ä father/ĕ pet/ē be/ĭ pit/ī pie/î fierce/ŏ pot/ō go/ô paw, for/oi oil/ŏŏ book/ōō boot/ou out/ŭ cut/û fur/*th* the/th thin/hw which/zh vision/ə ago, item, pencil, atom, circus

***Idiom.* on (one's) toes.** Ready to act; alert.

toed |tōd| *adj.* Having a certain kind or number of toes: *a long-toed bird; a two-toed sloth.* ¶*These sound alike* **toed, toad.**

toe•nail |tō′nāl′| *n.* **1.** The nail on any of the toes. **2.** A nail driven at an oblique angle, as in joining a vertical beam to a horizontal beam. —*v.* To join or secure with nails driven at an oblique angle.

tof•fee |tŏf′ē| *or* |tô′fē| *n.* A hard or chewy candy of brown sugar and butter.

tof•fy |tŏf′ē| *or* |tô′fē| *n., pl.* **tof•fies.** A form of the word **toffee.**

to•ga |tō′gə| *n.* A loosely draped outer garment, the usual garment worn in public by citizens of ancient Rome. [SEE PICTURE]

to•geth•er |tə gĕ*th*′ər| *or* |to͝o-| *adv.* **1.** In or into a single group or place: *Many people were crowded together.* **2.** Against or in relationship to one another: *rubbing one's hands together; getting along together.* **3.** Regarded collectively: *He's done more for the school than all of us together.* **4.** Simultaneously: *The guns all went off together.* **5.** In agreement or cooperation: *We stand together on this issue.* **6.** *Informal.* Into proper condition to do something: *Get yourself together.* Also used adjectivally: *Are you together yet?* —**to•geth′er•ness** *n.*

tog•gle |tŏg′əl| *n.* Any device or apparatus having a toggle joint.

toggle bolt. A fastener consisting of a threaded bolt mated with a nut that forms a toggle.

toggle joint. An elbowlike joint consisting of two levers joined by a pivot so that a force applied to the pivot to straighten the joint forces the ends of the levers outward.

toggle switch. An electrical switch that is opened and closed with a snap action provided by a toggle joint loaded with a spring with one of the levers projecting outward so that it can be moved by a finger.

To•go |tō′gō|. A country on the southern coast of West Africa, between Ghana and Dahomey. Population, 2,170,000. Capital, Lomé.

togs |tŏgz| *pl.n. Informal.* Clothes: *skating togs.*

toil¹ |toil| *v.* **1.** To labor continuously and untiringly; work strenuously. **2.** To proceed with difficulty: *toiling up a steep hill.* —*n.* Exhausting labor or effort. —**toil′er** *n.*

toil² |toil| *n.* Often **toils.** An entrapment: *in the toils of despair.*

toi•let |toi′lĭt| *n.* **1.** A disposal apparatus consisting of a porcelain bowl having a hinged seat and fitted with a flushing device, used for urination and defecation. **2.** A room or booth containing such an apparatus. **3.** The act or process of grooming and dressing oneself.

toi•let•ry |toi′lĭ trē| *n., pl.* **toi•let•ries.** Any article or cosmetic used in dressing or grooming oneself.

toi•lette |twä lĕt′| *n.* The act or process of dressing or grooming oneself.

toilet water. A scented liquid, cologne.

to•ken |tō′kən| *n.* **1.** Something that serves as an indication or representation; a sign; symbol: *A white flag is a token of surrender.* **2.** A keepsake; a souvenir: *This ring was a token of our wedding anniversary.* **3.** A piece of stamped metal used as a substitute for currency. —*adj.* Done as an indication or pledge: *a token payment.*

to•ken•ism |tō′kə nĭz′əm| *n.* The policy of making only a superficial effort toward the accomplishment of a goal, such as racial integration.

To•ky•o |tō′kē ō|. The capital and largest city of Japan, in the eastern part of the island of Honshu. Population, 8,796,000.

told |tōld|. Past tense and past participle of **tell.**

tol•er•a•ble |tŏl′ər ə bəl| *adj.* **1.** Able to be tolerated; endurable: *tolerable food.* **2.** Adequate; passable: *He is in tolerable health.* —**tol′er•a•bly** *adv.*

tol•er•ance |tŏl′ər əns| *n.* **1.** The capacity for or practice of recognizing and respecting the opinions, practices, or behavior of others. **2.** The capacity to endure hardship, pain, etc. **3.** In building and engineering, the amount by which the measure of a part or component can be allowed to vary from the value intended: *The bolt was made to a tolerance of .001 inch.* **4.** The degree to which an organism resists the effect of a poison or other drug.

tol•er•ant |tŏl′ər ənt| *adj.* Showing or having tolerance: *a tolerant attitude toward religion.*

tol•er•ate |tŏl′ə rāt′| *v.* **tol•er•at•ed, tol•er•at•ing.** **1.** To allow without prohibiting or opposing; permit: *tolerate the existence of campus radicals.* **2.** To recognize and respect, as the opinions, practices, or behavior of others. **3.** To put up with; endure: *I won't tolerate your tardiness. How can you tolerate his rude manners?* **4.** To have a tolerance for (a drug or poison).

tol•er•a•tion |tŏl′ə rā′shən| *n.* Tolerance, especially official recognition of the right of an individual to his own opinions, religious beliefs and practices, etc.

toll¹ |tōl| *n.* **1.** A fixed tax for a privilege, as passage across a bridge. **2.** A charge for a service, as a long-distance telephone call. **3.** A quantity of people or things destroyed or adversely affected, as in a disaster: *The hurricane took a toll of 200 dead.*

toll² |tōl| *v.* **1.** To sound (a bell) slowly at regular intervals: *tolling the church bells.* **2.** To announce or summon by tolling: *The bell tolled the hour. The church bells tolled the death of the king.* —*n.* The sound of a tolling bell.

toll•gate |tōl′gāt′| *n.* A gate barring passage of vehicles until a toll is paid.

Tol•stoy |tōl′stoi| *or* |tŏl′-|, **Leo.** 1828–1910. Russian novelist.

Tol•tec |tōl′tĕk′| *or* |tŏl′-| *n.* A member of an ancient Nahuatl-speaking people of central and southern Mexico.

tol•u•ene |tŏl′yo͞o ēn′| *n.* A colorless liquid, related to benzene, that burns easily, is composed of carbon and hydrogen, and has the formula C_7H_8. It is used in making fuels, dyes, explosives, and other industrial chemicals.

tom |tŏm| *n.* **1.** A male cat. **2.** A male turkey.

tom•a•hawk |tŏm′ə hôk′| *n.* A light ax used by North American Indians. [SEE PICTURE]

tom•al•ley |tŏm′ăl′ē| *or* |tə măl′ē| *n., pl.* **tom•al•leys.** The greenish liver of a lobster, considered a delicacy.

to•ma•to |tə mā′tō| *or* |-mä′-| *n., pl.* **to•ma•toes.** **1.** The fleshy, usually reddish fruit of a widely cultivated plant, eaten raw or cooked as a vegetable. **2.** A plant that bears such fruit. —***modifier:*** *tomato sauce.* [SEE PICTURE]

tomb |to͞om| *n.* **1.** A vault or chamber for the burial of the dead. **2.** Any place of burial.

tom•boy |**tŏm**'boi'| *n.* A lively, spirited girl who behaves like a boy.

tomb•stone |**to͞om**'stōn'| *n.* A gravestone.

tom•cat |**tŏm**'kăt'| *n.* A male cat.

tome |tōm| *n.* A book, especially a large or scholarly one.

tom•fool•er•y |tŏm' **fo͞o**'lə rē| *n.* Foolish behavior; silliness; nonsense.

Tom•my gun |**tŏm**'ē|. *Informal.* A submachine gun.

to•mor•row |tə **mŏr**'ō| *or* |**-môr**'ō| *n.* **1.** The day following today. **2.** The near future: *space flights of tomorrow.* —*adv.* On or for the day following today: *I will return your book tomorrow.*

Tom Thumb. The hero of many English folk tales who was no larger than his father's thumb.

tom•tit |**tŏm**'tĭt'| *n. Chiefly British.* A small bird, such as a tit.

tom-tom |**tŏm**'tŏm'| *n.* Any of various small-headed drums that are beaten with the hands. [SEE PICTURE]

ton |tŭn| *n.* **1. a.** A unit of weight equal to 2,240 pounds. **b.** A unit of weight equal to 2,000 pounds. **c.** A **metric ton.** **2.** *Informal.* A very large quantity of anything: *buying tons of books.* ¶*These sound alike* **ton, tun.**

ton•al |**tō**'nəl| *adj.* Of or having tonality, a tone, or tones. —**to'nal•ly** *adv.*

to•nal•i•ty |tō **năl**'ĭ tē| *n., pl.* **to•nal•i•ties. 1.** A system or arrangement of seven tones built on a tonic; a key. **2.** The arrangement or relationship of all of the tones and chords of a musical composition with respect to a tonic.

tone |tōn| *n.* **1. a.** A sound that has a distinct pitch, duration, loudness, and quality. **b.** The characteristic timbre or quality of a particular instrument or voice. **c.** The interval of a major second, as between a C natural and a D natural; a whole step. **2. a.** A color or shade of color. **b.** Quality of color. **3. a.** The tension that normally remains in a muscle when it is at rest. **b.** Normal firmness of body tissues. **4.** A manner of expression: *an angry tone of voice.* **5.** A general quality or atmosphere: *the tone of the debate; a quiet tone of elegance in the room.* —*v.* **toned, ton•ing. 1.** To give a particular tone or inflection to. **2.** To harmonize in color: *These curtains tone in well with your rugs.* —***phrasal verbs.*** **tone down.** To make less vivid, harsh, violent, etc.; moderate: *The painter toned down the colors in his portrait. You'd better tone down some of the statements in your article.* **tone up.** To make or become brighter, more vigorous, etc.

tone arm. The pivoted arm of a phonograph that holds the cartridge and stylus.

tone poem. A **symphonic poem.**

Ton•ga |**tŏng**'gə|. A group of islands in the South Pacific, constituting an independent country. Population, 100,000. Capital, Nukualofa.

tongs |tôngz| *or* |tŏngz| *n. (used with a plural verb).* An implement consisting of two arms joined at one end by a pivot or hinge, used for holding or lifting something.

tongue |tŭng| *n.* **1.** A fleshy, muscular organ, attached in most vertebrates to the bottom of the mouth, that is the main organ of taste, moves to aid in chewing and swallowing, and, in human beings, acts in speech. **2.** A similar part, as of an insect. **3.** The tongue of an animal, such as a cow, used as food. **4.** A strip that projects from the edge of a board and fits into a matching groove on another board. **5.** The flap of material under the laces or buckles of a shoe. **6.** A spoken language: *His native tongue is German.* **7.** The power of speech: *"Have you lost your tongue?" the mother asked the child.* **8.** A manner of speech: *She has a very sharp tongue.* —*v.* **tongued, tongu•ing.** To separate (tones of a musical wind instrument) by shutting off the stream of air with the tongue.

Idioms. **hold (one's) tongue.** To be or keep silent. **on the tip of (one's) tongue.** On the verge of being remembered or said.

tongue-tied |**tŭng**'tīd'| *adj.* **1.** Speechless or confused in expression, as from shyness. **2.** Unable to move the tongue freely because of abnormal shortness of the membrane that connects its lower side to the bottom of the mouth.

ton•ic |**tŏn**'ĭk| *n.* **1.** A medicine or other agent that restores, refreshes, or invigorates the body. **2.** The principal tone of a musical scale or key; a keynote. **3. Quinine water.** —*adj.* **1.** Of or based on the tonic, as of a musical scale. **2.** Of or having to do with the tone of muscles or other body tissues.

to•night, also **to-night** |tə **nīt**'| *adv.* On or during the present or coming night: *I'll see you at ten tonight.* —*n.* This night or the night of this day: *Tonight is a very special occasion.*

ton•nage |**tŭn**'ĭj| *n.* **1.** The number of tons of water a ship displaces afloat. **2.** The capacity of a merchant ship in units of 100 cubic feet. **3.** A charge per ton on cargo. **4.** The total shipping of a country or port, figured in tons. **5.** Weight, measured in tons.

ton•sil |**tŏn**'səl| *n.* A mass of tissue similar to that found in lymph nodes, especially either of a pair of such masses located on both sides of the inner wall of the throat.

ton•sil•lec•to•my |tŏn'sə **lĕk**'tə mē| *n., pl.* **ton•sil•lec•to•mies.** The removal of a tonsil or tonsils by means of surgery.

ton•sil•li•tis |tŏn'sə **lī**'tĭs| *n.* Inflammation of a tonsil or tonsils.

ton•so•ri•al |tŏn **sôr**'ē əl| *or* |**-sōr'-**| *adj.* Of or pertaining to a barber or barbering.

ton•sure |**tŏn**'shər| *n.* **1.** The act of shaving the head, especially as a preliminary to becoming a member of a monastic order. **2.** The part of a monk's head so shaven.

too |to͞o| *adv.* **1.** Also; as well: *I can play the piano too.* **2.** More than enough; excessively: *It's possible to study too hard.* **3.** Very; extremely: *I'm only too happy to be of service. He's not too smart.* **4.** *Informal.* Indeed; so: *I won't do it. You will too!* ¶*These sound alike* **too, to, two.**

took |to͝ok|. Past tense of **take.**

tool |to͞ol| *n.* **1.** Any instrument or device, especially a mechanical one held in the hand, used to do work or perform a task. **2. a.** A machine, such as a lathe, used to make machine parts and other objects. **b.** The part of such a machine that cuts or shapes the work. **3.** Anything used in the performance of an operation; an instru-

tom-tom

Tom-tom has become a general term applied to hand-played drums of numerous different cultures. Shown above is an Ivory Coast boy being taught to play a tom-tom. The word **tom-tom** is from Hindi *tam-tam,* an imitative word.

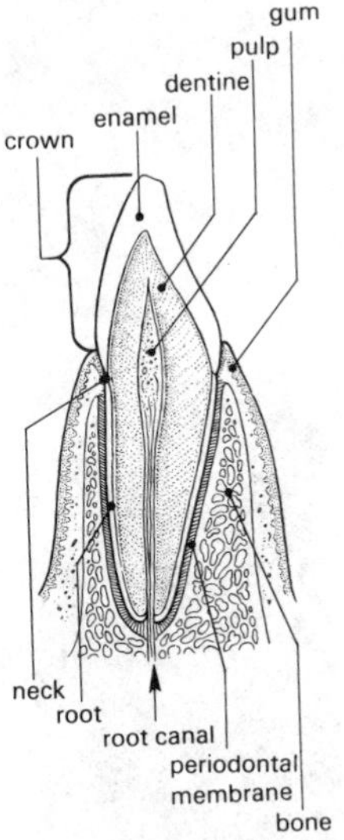

tooth
Cross section of a human incisor

Tooth was *tōth* in Old English, descending from prehistoric Germanic *tanth-*, which in turn is from Indo-European *dent-*, "tooth." An Indo-European *d-* regularly became a Germanic *t-*. See also note at **dental**.

top[1-2]
Top[1] *was Old English* topp, *"highest point"; it is related to* **tip**[1]. **Top**[2] *also comes from an Old English word spelled* topp, *meaning some kind of child's toy; it is presumed to be the same word as* **top**[1], *although the details are unclear.*

topiary

ă pat/ā pay/â care/ä father/ĕ pet/ ē be/ĭ pit/ī pie/î fierce/ŏ pot/ ō go/ô paw, for/oi oil/o͝o book/ o͞o boot/ou out/ŭ cut/û fur/ *th* the/th thin/hw which/zh vision/ ə ago, item, pencil, atom, circus

ment: *giving the President the necessary fiscal and monetary tools to stop inflation.* **4.** Anything necessary to the carrying out of one's occupation: *Words are the tools of his trade.* **5.** A person utilized to carry out the designs of another; a dupe: *army officers who were mere tools in the hands of the prime minister.* —*v.* **1.** To work or shape with a tool or tools. **2.** To equip (a factory, shop, etc.) with tools and machinery. —***phrasal verb.*** **tool up.** To prepare (a factory, shop, etc.) for production by providing machinery and tools for a particular job. ¶*These sound alike* **tool, tulle.**

tool•box |**to͞ol**′bŏks′| *n.* A case for carrying or storing portable tools.

toot |to͞ot| *v.* **1.** To sound (a horn or whistle) in short blasts. **2.** To sound (a blast or series of blasts) on a horn or whistle. —*n.* The act or sound of tooting.

tooth |to͞oth| *n., pl.* **teeth** |tēth|. **1.** Any of a set of hard, bony structures found in the mouths of most vertebrates set in sockets around the jaws, used to grasp, hold, and chew and as weapons of attack and defense. **2.** Any similar structure found in an invertebrate. **3.** Any projecting part, as on a gearwheel, saw, comb, etc. —*v.* |to͞oth| *or* |to͞o*th*|. To provide (a tool, machine part, etc.) with teeth. [See Picture]

tooth•brush |**to͞oth**′brŭsh′| *n.* A small brush used in cleaning the teeth.

toothed |to͞otht| *or* |to͞o*th*d| *adj.* **1.** Having teeth: *toothed whales.* **2.** Having toothlike notches or projections: *the toothed blade of a saw.* **3.** Having a certain kind of teeth: *sharp-toothed jaws.*

tooth•paste |**to͞oth**′pāst′| *n.* A paste used to clean the teeth.

tooth•pick |**to͞oth**′pĭk′| *n.* A small piece of wood for removing food particles from between the teeth.

tooth•pow•der |**to͞oth**′pou′dər| *n.* Also **tooth powder.** A powder used to clean the teeth.

tooth•some |**to͞oth**′səm| *adj.* Delicious; savory.

top[1] |tŏp| *n.* **1.** The uppermost part, point, surface, or end of something: *at the top of the hill; read the words at the top of the page; the top of the tree; luggage on the top of the car.* **2.** A lid or cap: *a box top.* **3. a.** The highest rank or position: *He is at the top of his profession.* **b.** The highest degree or pitch: *shouting at the top of his voice; singing at the top of her powers.* —***modifier:*** *at top speed; the top shelf; the top page; the top pop singers in the country.* —*v.* **topped, top•ping. 1.** To furnish with, form, or serve as a top: *top a building with a television antenna; top a cake with frosting.* **2.** To reach the top of: *We topped the hill and started to climb down.* **3.** To exceed or surpass: *He just topped his teammate's record of completed passes.* —***phrasal verb.*** **top off.** To complete; finish up: *topping off a series of brilliant passes with a touchdown.* [See Note]
Idiom. **on top.** In a position of success.

top[2] |tŏp| *n.* A child's toy made to spin on a pointed end either by releasing a spring or by quickly unwinding a string. [See Note]
Idiom. **sleep like a top.** To sleep soundly.

to•paz |**tō**′păz′| *n.* **1.** A colorless, blue, yellow, brown, or pink mineral consisting largely of aluminum silicate and valued as a gem. **2.** Any of various yellow gemstones, especially a yellow variety of sapphire or corundum. **3.** A light-yellow variety of quartz.

top•coat |**tŏp**′kōt′| *n.* A lightweight overcoat.

To•pe•ka |tə **pē**′kə|. The capital of Kansas. Population, 125,000.

top•flight |**tŏp**′**flīt**′| *adj.* First-rate; superior.

top•gal•lant |tə **găl**′ənt| *or* |**tŏp**-| *adj.* Designating the mast above the topmast, its sails, or rigging.

top hat. A man's formal hat having a narrow brim and a tall crown shaped like a cylinder.

to•pi•ar•y |**tō**′pē ĕr′ē| *adj.* Of or characterized by the clipping of living shrubs or trees into decorative shapes, as those of birds, animals, or geometric forms. [See Picture]

top•ic |**tŏp**′ĭk| *n.* **1.** A subject treated in a speech, essay, or portion of a discourse; a theme. **2.** A subject of discussion or conversation.

top•i•cal |**tŏp**′ĭ kəl| *adj.* **1.** Of a particular location or place; local: *topical news items.* **2.** Contemporary: *articles on ecology and other topical issues.* **3.** Of or on a particular part of the body: *topical application of an ointment.* —**top′i•cal•ly** *adv.*

top•knot |**tŏp**′nŏt′| *n.* A tuft or crest, as of hair or feathers, on the top of the head.

top•most |**tŏp**′mōst′| *adj.* Highest; uppermost.

top•notch |**tŏp**′**nŏch**′| *adj. Informal.* First-rate; excellent.

topog. topography.

to•pog•ra•pher |tə **pŏg**′rə fər| *n.* Someone who is skilled in or whose work is topography.

top•o•graph•ic |tŏp′ə **grăf**′ĭk| or **top•o•graph•i•cal** |tŏp′ə **grăf**′ĭ kəl| *adj.* Of or having to do with topography.

to•pog•ra•phy |tə **pŏg**′rə fē| *n., pl.* **to•pog•ra•phies. 1.** Detailed and precise description of a place or region. **2.** The technique or method of representing the exact physical features of a place or region on a map. **3.** The physical features of a place or region. **4.** The surveying of the physical features of a place or region.

top•o•log•i•cal |tŏp′ə **lŏj**′ĭ kəl| *adj.* Of or having to do with topology. —**top′o•log′i•cal•ly** *adv.*

to•pol•o•gist |tə **pŏl**′ə jĭst| *n.* Someone skilled in or whose work is topology.

to•pol•o•gy |tə **pŏl**′ə jē| *n.* **1.** The study of the topography of a place in relation to its history. **2.** The detailed anatomy of specific areas of the body. **3.** The mathematical study of the properties of geometric figures that do not change when subjected to certain precisely defined transformations.

top•ping |**tŏp**′ĭng| *n.* A sauce, frosting, or garnish for food.

top•ple |**tŏp**′əl| *v.* **top•pled, top•pling. 1.** To push over; overturn: *The dogs toppled the table and the dishes came crashing down.* **2.** To overthrow: *Military officers toppled the government.* **3.** To totter and fall: *The steeple toppled. The pile of books toppled over.*

tops |tŏps| *adj. Slang.* First-rate; excellent.

top•sail |**tŏp**′săl′| *or* |-səl| *n.* A square sail set above the lowest sail on the mast of a square-rigged ship.

top-se•cret |**tŏp**′**sē**′krĭt| *adj.* Designating information of the highest level of security classification.

top•soil |tŏp'soil'| *n.* The usually fertile layer of soil at the surface of the ground.

top•sy-tur•vy |tŏp'sē tûr'vē| *adv.* **1.** Upside-down: *The whole world has turned topsy-turvy.* **2.** In a state of utter disorder or confusion. —*adj.* Confused; disordered: *a topsy-turvy political situation.*

toque |tōk| *n.* A small, close-fitting hat with no brim, worn by women.

to•rah |tôr'ə| *or* |tōr'ə| *n.* **1.** The body of Jewish literature and oral tradition as a whole. **2. Torah. a.** The Pentateuch. **b.** A scroll on which the Pentateuch is written, used in a synagogue during services.

torch |tôrch| *n.* **1.** A portable light produced by the flame of an inflammable material wound about the end of a stick of wood. **2.** A portable device that burns a fuel, usually a gas, often with a supply of pure oxygen, to produce a flame hot enough for welding, soldering, brazing, or cutting metals. **3.** Anything that serves to enlighten, guide, inspire, etc.: *handing on the torch of learning to the new generation.* **4.** *British.* A flashlight.

torch song. A sentimental popular song, typically one in which the singer laments a lost love. **—torch singer.**

tore |tôr| *or* |tōr|. Past tense of **tear** (to rend).

tor•e•a•dor |tôr'ē ə dôr'| *n.* A bullfighter.

tor•ment |tôr'mĕnt'| *n.* **1.** Great pain or anguish: *the torment of a toothache; the torments of jealousy.* **2.** A source of harrassment or pain: *That child is the torment of his parents.* —*v.* |tôr **mĕnt'**| *or* |tôr'mĕnt'|. **1.** To cause to undergo great pain or anguish: *cruel jailers tormenting prisoners.* **2.** To annoy: *Stop tormenting your father with silly questions.* **—tor•men'tor** *n.*

torn |tôrn| *or* |tōrn|. Past participle of **tear** (to rend).

tor•na•do |tôr **nā'**dō| *n., pl.* **tor•na•does** or **tor•na•dos. 1.** A violent atmospheric disturbance in the form of a column of air several hundred yards wide spinning at speeds of 300 miles per hour and faster, usually accompanied by a funnel-shaped downward extension of a thundercloud. **2.** Any violent whirlwind or hurricane.

To•ron•to |tə **rŏn'**tō|. The capital and largest city of Ontario, Canada, on the northern shore of Lake Ontario. Population, 697,000.

tor•pe•do |tôr **pē'**dō| *n., pl.* **tor•pe•does. 1.** A cigar-shaped, self-propelled underwater projectile launched from a plane, ship, or submarine and designed to detonate on contact with or in the vicinity of a target. **2.** A small explosive charge placed on a railroad track and exploded by the weight of a passing train, warning the engineer of danger ahead. **3.** An explosive charge set off in an oil well or gas well to increase the flow. **4.** A small firework that explodes when it strikes a hard surface with force. **5.** A flat-bodied fish related to the skates and rays, having specialized organs capable of giving a strong electric shock. —*v.* **tor•pe•doed, tor•pe•do•ing.** To attack or destroy with or as if with a torpedo or torpedoes: *torpedo a ship. The board of directors torpedoed the plans for the new plant.* [SEE NOTE]

tor•pid |tôr'pĭd| *adj.* In a sluggish, inactive condition, like that of a hibernating animal.

tor•por |tôr'pər| *n.* A condition of sluggish inactivity.

torque |tôrk| *n.* **1.** The tendency or capability of a force for producing rotation about an axis. **2.** Any physical influence that tends to cause twisting or rotation.

tor•rent |tôr'ənt| *or* |tŏr'-| *n.* **1.** A turbulent, swift-flowing stream. **2.** A deluge: *rain falling in torrents.* **3.** Any turbulent or overwhelming flow: *a torrent of insults; a torrent of mail.*

tor•ren•tial |tô **rĕn'**shəl| *or* |tō-| *or* |tə-| *adj.* Caused by or like a torrent: *torrential rain.*

tor•rid |tôr'ĭd| *or* |tŏr'-| *adj.* **1.** Very dry and hot; scorching: *torrid weather.* **2.** Passionate: *a torrid romance.* **—tor'rid•ly** *adv.*

Torrid Zone. The region of the earth's surface between the tropic of Cancer and the tropic of Capricorn, marked in general by a hot, tropical climate.

tor•si |tôr'sē'| *n.* A plural of **torso.**

tor•sion |tôr'shən| *n.* **1. a.** The act or process of twisting or turning. **b.** The condition of being twisted or turned. **2.** The stress that an object undergoes when one of its ends is twisted out of line with the other end.

tor•so |tôr'sō'| *n., pl.* **tor•sos** or **tor•si** |tôr'sē'|. The human body except for the head and limbs; trunk.

tort |tôrt| *n.* In law, any wrongful act, not involving breach of contract, for which a civil suit can be brought. ¶*These sound alike* **tort, torte.**

torte |tôrt| *n.* A kind of rich layer cake. ¶*These sound alike* **torte, tort.**

tor•til•la |tôr **tē'**yə| *n.* A round, flat Mexican bread made from cornmeal and water and baked on a grill.

tor•toise |tôr'təs| *n.* A turtle, especially one that lives on land. [SEE PICTURE]

tor•toise•shell |tôr'təs shĕl'| *n.* **1.** Also **tortoise shell.** The mottled, horny, brownish, translucent outer covering of certain sea turtles, used to make combs, jewelry, etc. **2.** Also **tortoiseshell cat** or **tortoise-shell cat.** A cat having fur with brown, black, and yellowish markings. ***—modifier:*** *a tortoiseshell comb.* [SEE PICTURE]

tor•tu•ous |tôr'cho͞o əs| *adj.* **1.** Winding; twisting: *a tortuous road.* **2.** Devious; deceitful: *a tortuous argument.* **—tor'tu•ous•ly** *adv.* **—tor'tu•ous•ness** *n.*

tor•ture |tôr'chər| *n.* **1.** The infliction of severe pain as a means of punishment or coercion. **2.** Physical pain or mental anguish. —*v.* **tor•tured, tor•tur•ing. 1.** To subject (a person or animal) to torture: *torturing the prisoners to make them confess.* **2.** To afflict with great pain or anguish: *He is constantly tortured by anxiety.* **—tor'tur•er** *n.*

To•ry |tôr'ē| *or* |tōr'ē| *n., pl.* **To•ries. 1.** A member of a British political party, founded in 1689, that was the rival of the Whigs, has been known as the Conservative Party since 1832, and today is the rival of the Labour Party. **2.** An American siding with the British during the American Revolution. **3.** Someone holding to conservative or aristocratic principles.

toss |tôs| *or* |tŏs| *v.* **1.** To throw or be thrown to and fro: *toss a ball to a teammate. Heavy seas tossed the ship.* **2.** To move or lift (the head) with rapidity: *She tossed her head back contemptuous-*

torpedo

The original sense of this word was "electric ray" (now relegated to sense **5***). It is from Latin* torpēdō, *which basically meant "numbness" and hence was used as the name of the electric ray, whose electrical shocks cause a kind of numbness.* Torpēdō *is from* torpēre, *"to be numb" (closely related is* torpidus, *"numb," from which we have* **torpid***). The word* **torpedo** *was first applied to drifting underwater mines in the early nineteenth century; self-propelled torpedos were invented later in the century.*

tortoise

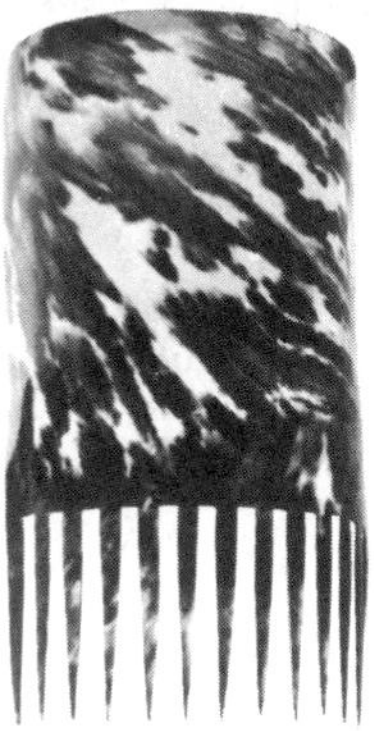

tortoiseshell
Comb made in 1825

ly. **3.** To flip a coin to decide something. **4.** To move oneself about vigorously: *He tossed and turned all night in his sleep.* **5.** To mix (a salad) with a dressing. *—phrasal verb.* **toss off.** To do, finish, perform, etc., in a casual, easy manner: *She tossed off an elaborate meal in less than one hour.* *—n.* **1.** An act of tossing. **2.** A rapid lift, as of the head.

toss•up |tôs′ŭp′| *or* |tŏs′-| *n. Informal.* An even chance or choice.

tot |tŏt| *n.* **1.** A small child. **2.** A small amount of something, as of liquor.

to•tal |tōt′l| *n.* **1.** A number or quantity obtained as a result of addition; a sum. **2.** A whole quantity; an entirety. *—adj.* **1.** Of or constituting the whole: *the total population of the state.* **2. a.** Absolute; utter: *The play was a total failure.* **b.** Complete; full: *a total eclipse.* *—v.* **to•taled** or **to•talled, to•tal•ing** or **to•tal•ling.** **1.** To find the sum of: *totaling expenses.* **2.** To equal a total of; amount to: *Your bill totals $25.* **—to′tal•ly** *adv.*

to•tal•i•tar•i•an |tō tăl′ĭ târ′ē ən| *adj.* Designating a form of government in which one party exercises absolute control over all spheres of human life and opposing parties are not permitted to exist. *—n.* A person who supports or believes in such a form of government.

to•tal•i•tar•i•an•ism |tō tăl′ĭ târ′ē ə nĭz′əm| *n.* Totalitarian practices, beliefs, etc.

to•tal•i•ty |tō tăl′ĭ tē| *n., pl.* **to•tal•i•ties.** **1.** The condition or property of being total. **2.** A total amount; a sum.

tote |tōt| *v.* **tot•ed, tot•ing.** To haul; carry.

tote bag. *Informal.* A large handbag or shopping bag.

to•tem |tō′təm| *n.* **1.** An animal, plant, or natural object that serves, as among some primitive peoples, as a symbol of a clan or family and is claimed by the members as an ancestor. **2.** A representation of this being or object. **3.** A group whose members have a common totem.

totem pole. A post carved and painted with a series of totem symbols and erected before a dwelling, as among certain Indian peoples of the northwestern coast of North America. [SEE PICTURE]

totem pole
Totem poles are peculiar to the peoples of the northwest coast of North America; those above are of the Haida people. The word **totem** is originally from Ojibwa *nintōtēm,* "my family mark"; the word has become a general term used to refer to clan emblems in any part of the world.

tot•ter |tŏt′ər| *v.* **1.** To sway as if about to fall: *A pile of books tottered at the edge of the table.* **2.** To walk unsteadily: *The baby tottered and fell down.*

tou•can |tōō′kăn′| *or* |-kän′| *n.* A tropical American bird with brightly colored plumage and a very large bill. [SEE PICTURE]

toucan
The word **toucan** is from Tupi *tucana.*

touch |tŭch| *v.* **1. a.** To come or bring into physical contact with: *The tree's branches touch the ground. Touch the pencil to the paper.* **b.** To come or bring into contact: *Hang the balloons so that they touch.* **2.** To feel with a part of the body, especially with the hand or fingers: *I will touch a hundred flowers and not pick one.* **3.** To tap, press, or strike lightly: *The godmother touched her with a magic wand.* **4.** *Informal.* To harm or injure, as by hitting: *I never touched my little brother.* **5.** To meddle with or disturb, as by handling: *Don't touch anything until the police come.* **6.** To eat or drink; taste: *They wouldn't touch the soup.* **7.** To reach: *touch land; touch base.* **8.** To come up to; equal: *His work couldn't touch his master's.* **9.** To affect, involve, or concern: *The achievements of the engineer touch many areas of modern society.* **10.** To affect or move emotionally: *The plea touched my heart.* *—phrasal verbs.* **touch off.** **1.** To cause to explode. **2.** To cause or start: *A border incident touched off the conflict.* **touch on** (or **upon**). To deal with, concern, or mention in passing: *touch on a variety of topics.* **touch up.** To improve by making minor changes or additions. *—n.* **1.** An act or way of touching: *a touch of the hand; a light touch.* **2.** The sense by which things in contact with the body are felt as hard, soft, rough, smooth, etc.; feeling. **3.** The physical sensation experienced in feeling something; feel: *the touch of velvet.* **4.** Contact or communication: *I'll be in touch with you.* **5.** A light stroke or tap: *a touch of the whip.* **6.** A little bit; a hint or trace: *a touch of seasoning.* **7.** A mild attack: *a touch of the flu.* **8. a.** An addition or detail that improves, completes, or perfects something: *the finishing touches.* **b.** An effect or quality resulting from such an addition or detail: *Fresh flowers give a homey touch to the whole room.* **9.** A characteristic way or style of doing things: *the author's personal touch.* **10.** A special ability to do something demanding skill; a facility or knack: *That ballplayer has lost his touch.* **11.** A particular way of striking the keys of a piano, typewriter, etc.
Idiom. **a soft** (or **easy**) **touch.** Someone from whom it is easy to borrow money.

touch and go. A precarious state of affairs. *—modifier:* **(touch-and-go):** *a touch-and-go situation.*

touch•back |tŭch′băk′| *n.* In football, an instance of touching the ball to the ground behind one's goal line, the ball having been propelled over the line by an opponent.

touch•down |tŭch′doun′| *n.* **1.** In football, a score of six points, usually made by running with the ball, or catching a teammate's pass, across the opposing team's goal line. **2.** The contact or moment of contact of an aircraft or spacecraft with the surface on which it lands. *—modifier: a touchdown pass.*

touch football. Football played without protective equipment in which players tag rather than tackle each other to put the ball out of play.

touch•ing |tŭch′ĭng| *adj.* Causing a sympathetic reaction; moving: *a touching if not altogether convincing speech.* *—prep.* Concerning: *I have heard nothing touching his departure.* **—touch′ing•ly** *adv.*

touch-me-not |tŭch′mē nŏt′| *n.* The jewelweed or a related plant.

touch•stone |tŭch′stōn′| *n.* **1.** A hard, black stone, such as jasper or basalt, formerly used to test a sample of silver or gold, the streak left by rubbing the sample on the stone being compared with the streak left by a standard alloy. **2.** Anything used for testing the value of something; a criterion; standard.

touch•y |tŭch′ē| *adj.* **touch•i•er, touch•i•est.** **1.** Oversensitive; irritable: *a touchy old woman.* **2.** Requiring tact or skill; delicate: *a touchy situation; a touchy operation.*

tough |tŭf| *adj.* **tough•er, tough•est.** **1.** Having great strength; capable of withstanding heavy strain or load without tearing or breaking. **2.** Difficult to cut or chew: *a tough steak.* **3.** Able

ă pat/ā pay/â care/ä father/ĕ pet/ ē be/ĭ pit/ī pie/î fierce/ŏ pot/ ō go/ô paw, for/oi oil/ŏŏ book/ ōō boot/ou out/ŭ cut/û fur/ *th* the/th thin/hw which/zh vision/ ə ago, item, pencil, atom, circus

to endure hardships; physically rugged: *a tough football player.* **4.** Difficult to accomplish; demanding: *a tough job.* **5.** Not easy; difficult: *a tough lesson.* **6.** Unyielding; stubborn: *The company decided to get tough with the striking workers.* **7.** Strong-minded; resolute: *a tough man to convince.* **8.** Vicious; rough: *tough criminals.* **9.** *Informal.* Too bad; unfortunate. —*n.* A thug; hoodlum. ¶*These sound alike* **tough, tuff.** —**tough'ly** *adv.* —**tough'ness** *n.*

tough•en |tŭf'ən| *v.* To make or become tough. —**tough'en•er** *n.*

tou•pee |to͞o pā'| *n.* A small wig or hair piece worn to cover a bald spot on a man's head.

tour |to͝or| *n.* **1.** A trip during which several or many places of interest are visited: *a tour of Europe.* **2.** A brief trip to or through a place for the purpose of seeing it: *a tour of the printing plant.* **3.** A journey to fulfill a round of engagements in several places: *a concert tour.* **4.** A period of duty at a single place or job: *a tour of duty abroad.* —*v.* To go on a tour or make a tour of: *touring through Spain; touring France.*

tour•ism |to͝or'ĭz'əm| *n.* **1.** The practice of traveling for pleasure. **2.** The business of providing tours for travelers.

tour•ist |to͝or'ĭst| *n.* A person who is traveling for pleasure. —***modifier:*** *a tourist agency.* [SEE NOTE]

tourist class. A grade of travel accommodations less luxurious than first class.

tour•ma•line |to͝or'mə lĭn| *or* |-lēn'| *n.* A complex crystalline silicate mineral containing aluminum, boron, and other elements. It is used in electronic instruments and in certain varieties valued as a gem. —***modifier:*** *a tourmaline ring.*

tour•na•ment |to͝or'nə mənt| *or* |tûr'-| *n.* **1.** A contest composed of a series of elimination games or trials: *a tennis tournament.* **2.** A medieval jousting match.

tour•ne•dos |to͝or'nĭ dō'| *or* |to͝or'nĭ dō'| *n., pl.* **tour•ne•dos.** A cut of beef from the tenderloin, often cooked with strips of bacon or other fat wrapped around its outside edge.

tour•ney |to͝or'nē| *or* |tûr'-| *n., pl.* **tour•neys.** A tournament.

tour•ni•quet |to͝or'nĭ kĭt| *or* |tûr'-| *n.* Any device, such as a tight band with a pad under it to concentrate the pressure, used to stop temporarily the flow of blood in a large artery in one of the limbs.

tou•sle |tou'zəl| *v.* **tou•sled, tou•sling.** To disarrange or rumple; dishevel.

tow[1] |tō| *v.* To draw or pull along behind by a chain or line: *tow a car.* —*n.* **1.** An act of towing: *trying to get a tow from a police truck.* **2.** The condition of being towed: *The tugboat had a tender in tow.* ¶*These sound alike* **tow, toe.** [SEE NOTE]

tow[2] |tō| *n.* Short, coarse flax or hemp fibers that are ready for spinning. ¶*These sound alike* **tow, toe.** [SEE NOTE]

to•ward |tôrd| *or* |tōrd| *or* |tə wôrd'| *prep.* Also **to•wards** |tôrdz| *or* |tōrdz| *or* |tə wôrdz'|. **1.** In the direction of: *moving toward the frontier.* **2.** In a position facing: *a window toward the square.* **3.** Somewhat before in time; approaching: *It started raining toward dawn.* **4.** With relation to; regarding: *a poor attitude toward his superiors.* **5.** In furtherance or partial fulfillment of: *a payment toward the house.* **6.** With a view to: *efforts toward peace.* —*adj.* |tôrd| *or* |tōrd|. **1.** Happening; going on or being done: *Nothing's toward.* **2.** Tractable: *a toward child.*

tow•el |tou'əl| *n.* A piece of absorbent cloth or paper used for wiping or drying. —***modifier:*** *a towel rack.* —*v.* **tow•eled** or **tow•elled, tow•el•ing** or **tow•el•ling.** To wipe or rub dry with a towel.
Idiom. **throw in the towel.** To give up; admit defeat.

tow•el•ing |tou'ə lĭng| *n.* Material, such as cotton or linen, used for making towels.

tow•er |tou'ər| *n.* **1.** A tall, usually square or circular building either standing alone or forming part of a church, castle, or other large building. **2.** A tall framework or structure used for observation, signaling, etc.: *a control tower.* **3.** A person or thing that rises above or is superior to others: *His father is a tower of strength.* —***modifier:*** *a tower clock.* —*v.* To rise to a conspicuous height: *skyscrapers towering over New York.*

tow•er•ing |tou'ər ĭng| *adj.* **1.** Of imposing height; very tall: *towering peaks.* **2.** Intense; extreme: *in a towering rage.*

Tower of London. An ancient palace and fortress on the Thames River in London that later served as a prison. It is now a museum.

tow•head |tō'hĕd'| *n.* A person having white-blond hair. —**tow'head'ed** *adj.*

tow•hee |tō'hē| *or* |tō hē'| *n.* A North American bird with black, white, and rust-colored feathers, or any of several related birds with brownish feathers. [SEE PICTURE]

town |toun| *n.* **1.** A population center, often incorporated, larger than a village and smaller than a city. **2.** Any city. **3.** The commercial center or district of an area: *She goes into town every Tuesday.* **4.** An urban area as opposed to the country. **5.** The residents of a town.
Idioms. **go to town.** *Slang.* To do something with no inhibitions or restrictions; go all out. **on the town.** *Slang.* On a spree.

town crier. In former times, a person who walked about the streets of a town shouting public announcements.

town hall. The building that contains the offices of the public officials of a town and houses the town council and courts.

town•ie |tou'nē| *n.* *Informal.* A resident of a college town as opposed to a student.

town•ship |toun'shĭp'| *n.* **1.** A subdivision of a county in most Northeastern and Middle Western states. **2.** A unit of land area used in surveying, equal to 36 square miles.

towns•man |tounz'mən| *n., pl.* **-men** |-mən|. An inhabitant of a town or city.

towns•peo•ple |tounz'pē'pəl| *pl.n.* The inhabitants or citizens of a town or city.

tow•path |tō'păth'| *or* |-päth'| *n., pl.* **-paths** |-păthz'| *or* |-päthz'| *or* |-păths'| *or* |-päths'|. A path along a canal or river used by animals towing boats.

tox•e•mi•a |tŏk sē'mē ə| *n.* A condition in which the blood contains toxins, either produced by microorganisms that infect the body or by body cells through faulty metabolism or absorbed from an external source.

tox•ic |tŏk'sĭk| *adj.* **1.** Of the nature of a poison;

tourist

The word **tourist** *now has a connotation of economy, which emerges clearly in the expression* **tourist class***; apparently people who travel first class prefer not to think of themselves as tourists. The situation was once very different. The noun* **tour** *originally referred to travel by the rich. Up to the end of the eighteenth century, the final stage in the education of many rich young Englishmen was* the Grand Tour, *in which they visited all or most of the chief cultural centers of Europe. The* **tourist** *then sometimes took several years to see what the modern* **tourist** *covers in a couple of weeks.*

tow[1-2]

Tow[1] *was Old English* togian, *"to pull, draw"; it is related to* **tug. Tow**[2] *in Old English is recorded only in compound words such as* tow-hūs, *"spinning-house";* tow- *presumably meant "to spin."*

towhee
Painting by John James Audubon

poisonous: *a toxic drug.* **2.** Of or caused by a poison or toxin.

tox•ic•i•ty |tŏk sĭs′ĭ tē| *n.* **1.** The condition or property of being toxic. **2.** The degree to which a substance is toxic.

tox•i•col•o•gist |tŏk′sĭ **kŏl′**ə jĭst| *n.* A physician or scientist who specializes in toxicology.

tox•i•col•o•gy |tŏk′sĭ **kŏl′**ə jē| *n.* The scientific and medical study of poisons, their effects and detection, and the treatment of poisoning.

tox•in |**tŏk′**sĭn| *n.* A poison produced by a plant, animal, or microorganism, having a protein structure and capable of causing poisoning when introduced into the body but capable also of stimulating production of an antitoxin.

toy |toi| *n.* **1.** An object for children to play with. **2.** Something of little importance; a trinket. **3.** A dog of a kind that is quite small, kept chiefly as a pet. *—**modifier:** toy soldiers; a toy store; toy dogs such as poodles and pugs.* —*v.* To amuse oneself idly; trifle: *talking on the phone and toying with a pencil. He was toying with the idea of taking a world cruise.*

tpk. turnpike.

tr. 1. transitive. **2.** translation. **3.** treasurer.

trace[1] |trās| *n.* **1.** A visible mark or sign of the former presence or passage of some person, thing, or event. **2.** A barely perceivable indication of something; a touch. **3. a.** An extremely small amount. **b.** Something, such as an element or chemical compound, that is present in a substance or mixture in very small amounts. **4.** A line drawn on a graph to represent a continuous set of values of a variable: *the trace made by a seismograph.* —*v.* **traced, trac•ing. 1.** To follow the track or trail of: *tracing the rumor back to the newspaperman; trace a lost letter; tracing the origins of his family back to the American Revolution.* **2.** To follow the successive stages in the development of: *In history class we will trace the beginnings of the Industrial Revolution.* **3.** To locate or discover, as a cause. **4.** To delineate or sketch (a figure). **5.** To form (letters) with special care. **6.** To copy by following lines seen through transparent paper. **7.** To make a trace that represents a variable, as on a graph. —**trace′a•ble** *adj.* [SEE NOTE]

trace[2] |trās| *n.* One of two side straps or chains connecting a harnessed draft animal to a vehicle. [SEE NOTE]

trace[1-2]

Trace[1] *originally meant "trail, way"; it is from Old French* tracier, *"to make one's way," from Latin* tractiāre, *"to drag," from* tractus, *"a pulling, a dragging."* **Trace**[2] *is from Old French* trais, *"pair of harness straps for pulling";* trais *is the plural of* trait, *"a pulling," which in turn is also from Latin* tractus, *"a pulling," as above.*

trac•er |**trā′**sər| *n.* **1.** Any readily identifiable substance, such as a dye or radioactive isotope, that can be followed through the course of a mechanical, chemical, or biological process, providing information about details of the process and the distribution of the substances involved in it. **2.** A person employed to locate missing persons or goods. **3.** A search instituted to locate missing persons or goods. **4.** Also **tracer bullet.** A bullet that leaves a luminous or smoky trail.

trac•er•y |**trā′**sə rē| *n., pl.* **trac•er•ies.** Ornamental work of interlaced and branching lines.

tra•che•a |**trā′**kē ə| *n., pl.* **tra•che•ae** |**trā′**kē ē′| or **tra•che•as.** A tube with thin walls of cartilage and membrane leading from the larynx to the bronchi and providing a path for air going to the lungs; the windpipe.

tra•che•ot•o•my |trā′kē **ŏt′**ə mē| *n., pl.* **tra•che•ot•o•mies.** The act or procedure of cutting into the trachea through the neck.

tra•cho•ma |trə **kō′**mə| *n.* A contagious virus disease that causes severe inflammation of the membranes that line the eyelid and cover the eyeball.

track |trăk| *n.* **1.** A mark, such as a footprint or wheel rut, or a trail of marks left behind by something moving; a trace: *rabbit tracks; tire tracks.* **2.** A pathway or course over which something moves or may move: *a bicycle track in the park; boys rolling marbles down an aluminum track.* **3.** A course of action or way of proceeding that leads to a goal: *on the right track.* **4.** A rail or set of parallel rails on which a train or trolley runs: *railraod tracks.* **5.** A racetrack. **6.** Also **track and field.** The sport of running and of jumping hurdles, pole-vaulting, etc., in competition. *—**modifier:** a track team.* —*v.* **1.** To follow the footprints or trail of: *They tracked the animal through the woods.* **2.** To observe or monitor the course of: *Radar is used to track weather balloons.* **3.** To carry on the feet and deposit as tracks: *Don't track mud on the floor.* —***phrasal verb.*** **track down.** To locate by trailing or searching diligently: *track down wild animals; track down answers in books.* —**track′er** *n.*

Idioms. **keep track of. 1.** To remain informed about or keep a record of: *If you were a cave man, how would you keep track of time?* **2.** To stay in touch with or know the whereabouts of: *Keep track of your sister.* **lose track of.** To fail to keep up with or stay in touch with: *lose track of old friends; lose track of a speaker's argument.*

tracking station. A facility containing instruments for tracking an artificial satellite or spacecraft by radar or by optical means and equipment for receiving radio signals from it.

tract[1] |trăkt| *n.* **1.** An expanse of land. **2. a.** A system of body organs and tissues that together perform one function: *the digestive tract.* **b.** A bundle of nerve fibers that begin and end at the same places and have the same function.

tract[2] |trăkt| *n.* A propaganda pamphlet, especially one put out by a religious or political group.

trac•ta•ble |**trăk′**tə bəl| *adj.* **1.** Easily controlled; governable: *a tractable child.* **2.** Easily worked; malleable: *tractable metals.* —**trac′ta•bly** *adv.*

trac•tion |**trăk′**shən| *n.* **1.** The act or process of drawing or pulling, as a load over a surface. **2.** The condition of being drawn or pulled. **3.** The ability of a device, such as a railroad engine, to pull loads. **4.** The friction that prevents a wheel from slipping or skidding over the surface on which it runs.

tractor

trac•tor |**trăk′**tər| *n.* **1.** A small vehicle, powered by a gasoline or diesel engine, equipped with large tires that have deep treads, and used for pulling farm machinery, as plows, harvesters, etc. **2.** A truck having a cab and no body, used for pulling trailers, vans, etc. [SEE PICTURE]

trade |trād| *n.* **1.** The business of buying and selling goods; commerce: *trade between the Old World and the New.* **2.** An exchange of one thing for another, as by bartering: *Everyone brings something to market for sale or trade.* **3.** An occupation, especially one requiring special skill with the hands; a craft: *the tailor's trade.* **4.** The

ă pat/ā pay/â care/ä father/ĕ pet/
ē be/ĭ pit/ī pie/î fierce/ŏ pot/
ō go/ô paw, for/oi oil/ŏŏ book/
ōō boot/ou out/ŭ cut/û fur/
th the/th thin/hw which/zh vision/
ə ago, item, pencil, atom, circus

people who work in a particular business or industry: *the building and construction trades.* **5.** Customers or patrons; clientele: *a store that caters to the youth trade.* **6. trades.** The **trade winds.** —*modifier: trade routes; a trade center.* —*v.* **trad•ed, trad•ing. 1. a.** To engage in buying, selling, or bartering: *They traded with the Indians. He traded for furs along the Oregon coast.* **b.** To buy, sell, or barter: *Copper was traded in early times. A gong sounded in the market and trading began.* **2.** To exchange or swap: *trade toys with a friend.* **3.** To shop as regular customers: *We trade with the neighborhood grocer.* —**trad'ing** *adj.: a trading center; a trading outpost.* —***phrasal verbs.*** **trade in.** To give (an old or used item) as partial payment on a new purchase. **trade on.** To use to the greatest possible advantage; exploit: *He traded on his family name to win the election.*

trade•mark |trād'märk'| *n.* A name, symbol, or other device identifying a product, legally restricted to the use of the owner or manufacturer. —*v.* **1.** To label (a product) with a trademark. **2.** To register as a trademark.

trade name. 1. The name by which a commodity, service, process, etc., is known to the trade. **2.** The name under which a business firm operates.

trad•er |trā'dər| *n.* **1.** A person who trades; a dealer. **2.** A ship employed in foreign trade.

trade-in |trād'ĭn'| *n.* Something accepted as partial payment for a new purchase.

trade•off, also **trade-off** |trād'ôf'| *or* |-ŏf| *n.* An exchange of one thing in return for another; especially, a giving up of something desirable for another regarded as more desirable.

trade school. A school that offers training in skilled trades or occupations; vocational school.

trades•man |trādz'mən| *n., pl.* **-men** |-mən|. **1.** A man engaged in trade, especially a shopkeeper. **2.** A worker skilled in a certain craft.

trade union. A **labor union.**

trade winds. A highly regular and predictable system of winds blowing over most of the Torrid Zone, having a northeasterly course in the Northern Hemisphere and a southeasterly course in the Southern Hemisphere.

tra•di•tion |trə dĭsh'ən| *n.* **1.** The passing down of elements of a culture from generation to generation, especially orally. **2.** A custom or usage handed down this way.

tra•di•tion•al |trə dĭsh'ə nəl| *adj.* Of or in accord with tradition. —**tra•di'tion•al•ly** *adv.*

traf•fic |trăf'ĭk| *n.* **1.** The movement of vehicles and people along roads and streets, of ships on the seas, aircraft in the sky, etc. **2.** The amount, as of vehicles, aircraft, etc., in movement: *Vehicular traffic is heavy during rush hour.* **3.** The commercial exchange of goods; trade: *laws to eliminate traffic in drugs.* —***modifier:*** *traffic regulations.* —*v.* **traf•ficked, traf•fick•ing, traf•fics.** To carry on trade in. —**traf'fick•er** *n.*

traffic circle. A one-way road in the form of a circle or other closed curve that provides connection between several roads that come together at one point.

traffic light. also **traffic signal.** A device that beams red, amber, or green lights, sometimes flashing, to control the flow of traffic along a street, highway, etc. [SEE PICTURE]

tra•ge•di•an |trə jē'dē ən| *n.* **1.** A writer of tragedies. **2.** An actor of tragic roles.

tra•ge•di•enne |trə jē'dē ĕn'| *n.* An actress of tragic roles.

trag•e•dy |trăj'ĭ dē| *n., pl.* **trag•e•dies. 1.** A serious play that ends with great misfortune or ruin for the main character or characters. **2.** The branch of drama including such plays. **3.** A disastrous event; a calamity.

trag•ic |trăj'ĭk| *adj.* **1.** Of dramatic tragedy. **2.** Bringing or involving great misfortune, suffering, or sadness. —**trag'i•cal•ly** *adv.*

trag•i•com•e•dy |trăj'ĭ kŏm'ĭ dē| *n., pl.* **trag•i•com•e•dies.** A play that has qualities of both tragedy and comedy.

trail |trāl| *v.* **1. a.** To drag or allow to drag or stream behind, as along the ground: *a child trailing a toy cart.* **b.** To be dragged along behind: *A red wagon trailed behind Jimmy.* **2.** To follow the traces or scent of; track: *hounds trailing the scent of a bear.* **3.** To lag behind: *The home team trailed by 10 points at the end of the first half.* **4.** To move or walk wearily: *The soldiers trailed past us one by one.* **5.** To extend or grow along the ground or over a surface: *Her long skirt was trailing on the floor.* **6.** To drift in a tenuous stream, as smoke. **7.** To become gradually fainter: *Her voice trailed off.* —*n.* **1.** A mark, trace, or path left by a moving body: *The stagecoach left a trail of dust.* **2.** The scent of a person or animal: *hounds following the trail of a bear.* **3.** A path or beaten track.

trail•er |trā'lər| *n.* **1.** A large transport vehicle hauled by a tractor or truck. **2.** A large furnished van that can be hauled by an automobile or truck, designed for use as a home, office, etc., when parked. **3.** Someone or something that trails. —**trail'er•a•ble** *adj.*

train |trān| *n.* **1.** A string of connected railroad cars drawn by a locomotive or powered by electricity. **2.** A long line of moving persons, animals, or vehicles: *a wagon train; a mule train.* **3.** The part of a gown that trails behind the wearer. **4.** A staff of followers; a retinue: *persons in the king's train.* **5.** An orderly succession or series, as of events, thoughts, etc.: *The ring of the telephone interrupted my train of thought.* **6.** A set or series of linked mechanical parts: *a train of gears.* —***modifier:*** *a train station; train schedules; train passengers.* —*v.* **1.** To coach in or accustom to some mode of behavior or performance: *training a child to be polite; training young men to be good citizens.* **2. a.** To instruct (a person) systematically in some art, profession, etc.: *a school that trains drivers.* **b.** To instruct (an animal) to perform in a specified way: *training a horse for a race; train a dog to do tricks.* **3.** To make or become fit for an athletic performance: *coaches training the players for the championship game. He trains on a diet of milk, steak, and vitamins.* **4.** To cause (a plant or one's hair) to take a desired course or shape.

train•ee |trā nē'| *n.* A person who is being trained. —***modifier:*** *a trainee program.*

train•er |trā'nər| *n.* A person who trains, especially one who coaches athletes, racehorses, or show animals.

train•ing |trā'nĭng| *n.* **1.** The act, process, or routine of being trained; instruction. **2. a.** A

traffic light

traitor
"I had rather take my chance that some traitors will escape detection than spread abroad a spirit of general suspicion and distrust, which accepts rumor and gossip in place of undismayed and unintimidated inquiry." —*Judge Learned Hand (1952).*

program of exercise, diet, practice, etc., for an athlete. **b.** The physical condition of a person or animal who has been trained: *athletes out of training.* —**modifier:** *a training camp.*

train•man |trān′mən| *n., pl.* **-men** |-mən|. A member of the operating crew on a railroad train.

traipse |trāps| *v.* **traipsed, traips•ing.** *Informal.* To walk about idly.

trait |trāt| *n.* A distinctive feature or characteristic, as of an organism: *genetic traits.*

trai•tor |trā′tər| *n.* A person who betrays his country, a cause, or a trust, especially one who has committed treason. [SEE NOTE]

trai•tor•ous |trā′tər əs| *adj.* **1.** Of or like a traitor; treacherous: *traitorous behavior.* **2.** Constituting treason: *a traitorous act.*

tra•jec•to•ry |trə jĕk′tə rē| *n., pl.* **tra•jec•to•ries.** The path of a moving body or particle, such as a ball thrown through the air.

tram |trăm| *n.* **1.** *British.* A streetcar. **2.** An open wagon or car run on tracks in a coal mine.

tram•mel |trăm′əl| *n.* **1.** A shackle used to teach a horse to amble. **2.** Often **trammels.** Something that restricts activity or free movement; a hindrance. —*v.* **tram•meled** or **tram•melled, tram•mel•ing** or **tram•mel•ling.** To hinder; hamper.

tramp |trămp| *v.* **1.** To walk with a firm, heavy step: *tramping home carrying the groceries; tramp up the stairs.* **2.** To traverse on foot: *tramp the fields in search of wild berries.* **3.** To tread down; trample: *tramp down snow; tramping on someone's toes.* —*n.* **1.** The sound of heavy walking or marching. **2.** A walking trip: *a long tramp through the woods.* **3.** A person who travels aimlessly about as a vagrant. **4.** A cargo vessel that has no regular schedule but takes on freight wherever it can be found.

tram•ple |trăm′pəl| *v.* **tram•pled, tram•pling. 1.** To tread heavily so as to injure or destroy: *The children trampled the flowers down.* **2.** To treat harshly, as if tramping upon: *He is always trampling on her feelings.* —*n.* The action or sound of treading underfoot. —**tram′pler** *n.*

tram•po•line |trăm′pə lēn′| *or* |-lĭn| *n.* A tablelike device for performing acrobatic feats, consisting of a sheet of taut canvas attached with springs to a metal frame.

trance |trăns| *or* |träns| *n.* **1.** A somewhat dreamlike mental condition in which one is not aware of one's surroundings, capable of being produced by hypnotism, drugs, catalepsy, etc. **2.** A dazed condition, as between sleeping and waking; stupor. **3.** A condition in which little or no attention is paid to one's surroundings, as in daydreaming or deep thought.

tran•quil |trăng′kwĭl′| *or* |trăn′-| *adj.* Free from agitation, anxiety, etc.; calm; peaceful: *a tranquil lake; leading a tranquil life.* —**tran′quil•ly** *adv.*

tran•quil•ize |trăng′kwə līz′| *or* |trăn′-| *v.* **tran•quil•ized, tran•quil•iz•ing.** To make or become tranquil or calm.

tran•quil•iz•er |trăng′kwə līz′ər| *or* |trăn′-| *n.* Any of various drugs used to relieve tension, anxiety, mental upset, etc.

tran•quil•li•ty, also **tran•quil•i•ty** |trăng kwĭl′ĭ tē| *or* |trăn-| *n.* The quality or condition of being tranquil; calmness; peacefulness.

tran•quil•lize |trăng′kwə līz′| *or* |trăn′-| *v.* **tran•quil•lized, tran•quil•liz•ing.** A form of the word **tranquilize.**

trans–. A prefix meaning: **1.** Across or over: **transatlantic. 2.** Beyond: **transcend.**

trans. 1. transitive. **2.** translation. **3.** transportation.

trans•act |trăn săkt′| *or* |-zăkt′| *v.* To carry out or conduct (business or affairs).

trans•ac•tion |trăn săk′shən| *or* |-zăk′-| *n.* **1.** The act or process of transacting: *the transaction of business.* **2.** Something transacted; a business deal or operation: *cash transactions only; a bank's transactions in foreign securities.*

trans•at•lan•tic |trăns′ət lăn′tĭk| *or* |trănz′-| *adj.* **1.** On the other side of the Atlantic: *transatlantic military bases.* **2.** Spanning or crossing the Atlantic: *a transatlantic flight.*

trans•cend |trăn sĕnd′| *v.* **1.** To go beyond or outside the range of: *mysterious happenings that transcend human experience.* **2.** To rise above; surpass; excel: *a painter who has transcended himself in various ways.*

tran•scen•dent |trăn sĕn′dənt| *adj.* Surpassing others of the same kind; pre-eminent: *a scientist of transcendent genius.*

tran•scen•den•tal |trăn′sĕn dĕn′tl| *adj.* **1.** Such as cannot be discovered or understood by practical experience; going beyond human knowledge. **2.** Of a philosophy or philosophers that deal with matters outside the world of ordinary experience.

transcendental number. An irrational number that cannot occur as a root or solution of any algebraic equation whose coefficients are all rational numbers.

trans•con•ti•nen•tal |trăns′kŏn tə nĕn′tl| *or* |trănz′-| *adj.* Spanning or crossing a continent: *a transcontinental flight.*

tran•scribe |trăn skrīb′| *v.* **tran•scribed, tran•scrib•ing. 1.** To write or type a copy of; write out fully, as from shorthand notes. **2.** To adapt or arrange (a musical composition). **3.** To record for broadcasting at a later date.

tran•script |trăn′skrĭpt′| *n.* Something transcribed; a written or printed copy.

tran•scrip•tion |trăn skrĭp′shən| *n.* **1.** The act or process of transcribing. **2.** Something transcribed, especially: **a.** An adaptation of a musical composition. **b.** A recorded radio or television program.

tran•sept |trăn′sĕpt′| *n.* Either of the two lateral arms of a church built in the shape of a cross.

trans•fer |trăns fûr′| *or* |trăns′fər| *v.* **trans•ferred, trans•fer•ring. 1.** To move or shift from one place, person, or thing to another: *Bees transfer pollen from one flower to another. Heat energy transfers from matter that is warmer to matter that is cooler.* **2.** To move or change from one carrier or means of transportation to another: *They transferred the coal from the ship to railroad cars. Take a train in New York and transfer in Boston.* **3.** To move from one job, school, or location to another: *They transferred her from a branch office to company headquarters. He transferred from a junior college to the state university.* **4.** To move (a pattern, design, or set of markings or measurements) from one surface to another: *Trace the design, then transfer it to the leather.* **5.** To shift the ownership of (property)

ă pat/ā pay/â care/ä father/ĕ pet/ē be/ĭ pit/ī pie/î fierce/ŏ pot/ō go/ô paw, for/oi oil/ŏŏ book/ōō boot/ou out/ŭ cut/û fur/*th* the/th thin/hw which/zh vision/ə ago, item, pencil, atom, circus

to another. —*n.* |**trăns**′fər|. **1.** An act or example of transferring or being transferred: *the transfer of land by purchase; a transfer of energy.* **2.** Someone or something that transfers or is transferred, especially a student who changes schools or a design that is moved from one surface and applied to another. **3. a.** A ticket entitling a passenger to change from one bus, train, etc., to another without paying any or all of the extra fare. **b.** A place where someone or something changes from one carrier or means of transportation to another. —**modifier:** *a transfer point.*

trans•fer•a•ble |trăns **fûr**′ə bəl| *or* |**trăns**′fər-| *adj.* Capable of being transferred: *a credit card that is not transferable.*

trans•fer•al |trăns **fûr**′əl| *n.* A form of the word **transfer.**

trans•fer•ence |trăns **fûr**′əns| *or* |**trăns**′fər-| *n.* **1.** The act or process of transferring. **2.** The condition of being transferred. **3.** The process in which a person's feelings, wishes, thoughts, etc., are attached to a new person, especially, in psychoanalysis, to the analyst himself.

transfer orbit. The trajectory in which a spacecraft moves in passing from an orbit around the earth to an orbit around another body.

trans•fer•ral |trăns **fûr**′əl| *n.* A form of the word **transfer.**

trans•fig•ure |trăns **fĭg**′yər| *v.* **trans•fig•ured, trans•fig•ur•ing. 1.** To change the appearance and shape of: *His face was transfigured by hate.* **2.** To change so as to glorify; exalt: *The religious ceremony transfigured the participants who shared its mystery and beauty.* —**trans′fig•u•ra′tion** *n.*

trans•fi•nite number |trăns **fī**′nīt′|. A number that indicates the measure of a set or gives the relative position of an element of an ordered set but which is not an integer; loosely, infinity.

trans•fix |trăns **fĭks**′| *v.* **1.** To pierce through with or as with a pointed weapon; impale. **2.** To render motionless, as with terror.

trans•form |trăns **fôrm**′| *v.* **1.** To change markedly in form or appearance: *The witch transformed the men into mice.* **2.** To change the nature, function, or condition of; convert or be converted: *A steam engine transforms heat into energy.* **3.** To perform a mathematical transformation on. **4.** To subject (electricity) to the action of a transformer. **5.** To change (energy) from one form to another. —*n.* |**trăns**′fôrm′|. **1.** The result of a transformation, especially in mathematics. **2.** In grammar, a construction derived by transformation.

trans•for•ma•tion |trans′fər **mā**′shən| *n.* **1.** The act or process of transforming. **2. a.** The condition of being transformed. **b.** An example of being transformed. **3. a.** The conversion of an algebraic expression to another expression of a different form. **b.** The replacement of the variables in an algebraic expression or equation by their values in terms of another set of variables. **c.** The mapping of a space onto another space or onto itself. **4.** In grammar: **a.** A formula that indicates the relationships between a sentence and a set of simpler structures that form the underlying foundation of the sentence according to the rules shown to generate the syntax of a language. **b.** A construction derived by such a formula. —**trans′for•ma′tion•al** *adj.*

transformational grammar. A system of grammatical analysis in which transformations specify the relationships between a sentence and a set of simpler structures that form the underlying foundation of the sentence. [SEE NOTE]

trans•form•er |trăns **fôr**′mər| *n.* **1.** Someone or something that transforms. **2.** A device used to transfer electrical energy, usually that of an alternating current, from one circuit to another, especially by means of electromagnetic induction.

trans•fuse |trăns **fyōōz**′| *v.* **trans•fused, trans•fus•ing.** To give a transfusion of or to, as in medicine.

trans•fu•sion |trăns **fyōō**′zhən| *n.* The direct injection of whole blood, plasma, or other liquid into the bloodstream.

trans•gress |trăns **grĕs**′| *or* |trănz-| *v.* **1.** To go beyond or over (a limit or boundary): *His conduct transgressed the boundaries of politeness.* **2.** To act in violation of (a law, commandment, etc.); sin. —**trans•gres′sor** *n.*

trans•gres•sion |trăns **grĕsh**′ən| *or* |trănz-| *n.* The act of transgressing; the violation of a law, rule, command, etc.; a sin or offense.

tran•ship |trăn **shĭp**′| *v.* A form of the word **transship.**

tran•sient |**trăn**′shənt| *or* |-zhənt| *adj.* **1.** Passing away with time; transitory: *transient happiness.* **2.** Passing through from one place to another; stopping only briefly: *a transient guest at a hotel.* —*n.* Someone or something that is transient, especially a person making a brief stay at a hotel. —**tran′sience, tran′sien•cy** *n.*

tran•sis•tor |trăn **zĭs**′tər| *or* |**-sĭs**′-| *n.* **1.** A three-terminal semiconductor device used for amplification, switching, etc. **2.** A radio equipped with transistors.

tran•sis•tor•ize |trăn **zĭs**′tə rīz′| *or* |**-sĭs**′-| *v.* **tran•sis•tor•ized, tran•sis•tor•iz•ing.** To design or manufacture (a version of an electronic device that uses transistors rather than electron tubes).

tran•sit |**trăn**′sĭt| *or* |-zĭt| *n.* **1.** The act of passing over, across, or through; passage. **2.** The act of carrying from one place to another: *apples spoiled in transit; letters lost in transit.* **3.** The conveyance of persons or goods from one place to another, especially on a local public transportation system. **4. a.** The passage of a celestial body across the meridian through the point from which it is being observed. **b.** The passage of a celestial body across the disk of a large celestial body. **5.** A surveying instrument consisting of a telescope provided with scales for measuring horizontal and vertical angles of objects sighted through it, together with means for setting the entire instrument level. —**modifier:** *a transit system.* —*v.* To make a transit of (a celestial body): *Mercury is often observed to transit the sun.*

tran•si•tion |trăn **zĭsh**′ən| *or* |**-sĭsh**′-| *n.* The process or an example of changing or passing from one form, state, subject, or place to another. —**tran•si′tion•al** *adj.*

tran•si•tive |**trăn**′sĭ tĭv| *or* |-zĭ-| *adj.* Being or using a verb that requires a direct object to complete its meaning; for example, in the sentence *I bought a book on Monday,* the verb *bought*

transformational grammar
Up to the middle of this century, most grammars written by linguists were descriptive, *each seeking to* describe *the structure of a particular language. In the 1950's and 1960's, the American linguist Noam Chomsky and his associates developed a new approach to grammatical analysis in which the aim is to construct a* generative *grammar, a set of rules that will specify, or "generate," all the sentence structures that are possible within a language.* **Transformational grammar** *is the single major attempt so far to achieve this goal.*

is transitive. —**tran'si•tive•ly** *adv.*

transitive property. The property of a mathematical relation ♦ for which it is true that if *a* ♦ *b* and *b* ♦ *c*, then *a* ♦ *c*, where *a, b,* and *c* are elements of a set *S*. The relation of equality, for example, has the transitive property.

tran•si•to•ry |**trăn'**sĭ tôr'ē| *or* |-tōr'ē| *or* |-zĭ-| *adj.* Existing or occurring only briefly; short-lived: *transitory happiness.*

trans•late |trăns **lāt'**| *or* |trănz-| *or* |**trăns'**lāt'| *or* |**trănz'**-| *v.* **trans•lat•ed, trans•lat•ing. 1.** To express or be capable of being expressed in another language: *translate a book. His novels do not translate well.* **2.** To explain, interpret, or clarify: *It is difficult to see how you could translate his silence.* **3.** To act as a translator: *He translates for a living.* **4.** To subject (a body) to translation.

trans•la•tion |trăns **lā'**shən| *or* |trănz-| *n.* **1.** The act or process of translating: *a large staff solely for translation.* **2.** Something translated: *The new books published are all translations from the French.* **3.** Motion of a body in which each of its points moves parallel to, and the same distance as, every other point; motion in a straight line without rotation. [SEE NOTE]

trans•la•tor |trăns **lā'**tər| *or* |trănz-| *or* |**trăns'**-lā'-| *or* |**trănz'**-| *n.* A person who translates from one language into another, especially as a profession.

trans•lit•er•ate |trăns **lĭt'**ə rāt'| *or* |trănz-| *v.* **trans•lit•er•at•ed, trans•lit•er•at•ing.** To represent (letters or words) in the characters of another alphabet. —**trans•lit'er•a'tion** *n.*

trans•lu•cent |trăns **lōō'**sənt| *or* |trănz-| *adj.* Transmitting light, but scattering it enough so that images become blurred or are destroyed. —**trans•lu'cence, trans•lu'cen•cy** *n.*

trans•mi•gra•tion |trăns'mī **grā'**shən| *or* |trănz'-| *n.* In theology, the passing of a soul at death into another body.

trans•mis•sion |trăns **mĭsh'**ən| *or* |trănz-| *n.* **1.** The act or process of transmitting: *the transmission of news; the transmission of a disease.* **2.** The sending of a modulated carrier wave, as in radio, television, telegraphy, etc. **3.** Something transmitted, as by radio, television, etc., such as a message, voice, or image. **4.** An assembly of gears and associated parts by which power is carried from an engine or motor to a load, as in an automobile, machine tool, etc.

trans•mit |trăns **mĭt'**| *or* |trănz-| *v.* **trans•mit•ted, trans•mit•ting. 1.** To send from one person, place, or thing to another: *transmit a message; transmit an infection.* **2.** To pass on (a trait or traits) by biological inheritance. **3.** To send out (an electric or electronic signal), as by wire or radio. **4.** To cause or allow (energy or a disturbance) to travel or spread, as through a medium: *Glass transmits light.* **5.** To carry (power, force, or energy) from one part of a machine to another.

trans•mit•tal |trăns **mĭt'**l| *or* |trănz-| *n.* The act or process of transmitting; a transmission.

trans•mit•ter |trăns **mĭt'**ər| *or* |trănz-| *n.* **1.** Someone or something that transmits. **2.** Any device used in a communications system to send forth information, especially: **a.** A switching device that opens and closes a telegraph circuit. **b.** The part of a telephone that changes sounds into electrical impulses that are sent over wires. **c.** A device capable of generating a radio signal, modulating it with information, often a voice or music signal, and radiating it by means of an antenna.

trans•mu•ta•tion |trăns'myōō **tā'**shən| *or* |trănz'-| *n.* In physics, the changing of one element into another by one or more nuclear reactions.

trans•mute |trăns **myōōt'**| *or* |trănz-| *v.* **trans•mut•ed, trans•mut•ing. 1.** To change from one form, nature, state, etc., into another; transform: *Socialism transmuted the political life of the country.* **2.** To subject (an element) to transmutation.

trans•o•ce•an•ic |trăns'ō shē **ăn'**ĭk| *or* |trănz'-| *adj.* **1.** Situated beyond the ocean: *transoceanic trading posts.* **2.** Spanning or crossing the ocean: *a transoceanic flight.*

tran•som |**trăn'**səm| *n.* **1.** A small hinged window above a door or another window. **2.** A horizontal dividing piece in a window.

tran•son•ic |trăn **sŏn'**ĭk| *adj.* Of conditions of flight or airflow at speeds close to the speed of sound.

trans•pa•ci•fic |trăns'pə **sĭf'**ĭk| *adj.* **1.** Crossing the Pacific Ocean: *a transpacific flight.* **2.** Situated beyond the Pacific Ocean: *transpacific colonial settlements.*

trans•par•ence |trăns **pâr'**əns| *or* |**-păr'**-| *n.* The condition or property of being transparent.

trans•par•en•cy |trăns **pâr'**ən sē| *or* |**-păr'**-| *n., pl.* **trans•par•en•cies. 1.** The condition or property of being transparent. **2.** A transparent object, especially a photographic slide.

trans•par•ent |trăns **pâr'**ənt| *or* |**-păr'**-| *adj.* **1.** Capable of transmitting light so that objects and images are clearly visible, as if there were nothing between the observer and the light source. **2.** Allowing electromagnetic radiation of a specified frequency, such as x-rays, light, radio waves, etc., to pass with little or no interference. **3.** Of such a texture that objects can be seen on the other side; sheer: *a transparent fabric.* **4.** Easily detected; flimsy: *transparent lies.*

tran•spire |trăn **spīr'**| *v.* **tran•spired, tran•spir•ing. 1.** To give off (water vapor containing waste products) through pores or similar small openings, as of plant leaves or the skin. **2.** To become known; be revealed. **3.** To happen; take place. —**tran'spi•ra'tion** |trăn'spə **rā'**shən| *n.*

trans•plant |trăns **plănt'**| *or* |**-plänt'**| *v.* **1.** To remove (a living plant) from the place where it is growing and plant it in another place. **2.** To transfer (tissue or an organ) from one body or body part to another. **3.** To transfer to and establish in a new place: *The early colonists transplanted their songs as well as their customs to the New World.* —*n.* |**trăns'**plănt'| *or* |-plänt'|. **1.** Something transplanted, especially an organ or piece of tissue transplanted by surgery. **2.** The act or operation of transplanting tissue or an organ: *The doctor performed a heart transplant.* —**trans•plant'a•ble** *adj.* —**trans'plan•ta'tion** *n.*

trans•po•lar |trăns'**pō'**lər| *adj.* Passing or extending across either of the geographic poles or the polar regions: *a transpolar flight.*

trans•port |trăns **pôrt'**| *or* |**-pōrt'**| *v.* **1.** To carry from one place to another: *transport cargo;*

translation

"Translation is at best an echo." —George Borrow (1803–1881)

"A translation is no translation, he said, unless it will give you the music of the poem along with the words of it." —John Millington Synge (1871–1909)

ă pat/ā pay/â care/ä father/ĕ pet/ ē be/ĭ pit/ī pie/î fierce/ŏ pot/ ō go/ô paw, for/oi oil/ŏŏ book/ ōō boot/ou out/ŭ cut/û fur/ *th* the/th thin/hw which/zh vision/ ə ago, item, pencil, atom, circus

transport passengers. **2.** To move to strong emotion; enrapture: *She was transported with joy.* —*n.* |**trăns′**pôrt′| *or* |-pōrt′|. **1.** The act or process of transporting: *the transport of troops by ship; goods lost in transport.* **2.** A ship used to transport troops or military equipment. **3.** A vehicle, as an aircraft, used to transport passengers or freight. **4.** The condition of being carried away by emotion; rapture: *shouting insults in a transport of rage.*

trans•por•ta•tion |trăns′pər **tā′**shən| *n.* **1.** The act or process of transporting: *the transportation of mail.* **2.** A means of transport; a conveyance: *Planes are fast transportation.* **3.** The business of transporting passengers, goods, etc.: *a company engaged in transportation.* **4.** A charge for transporting; a fare: *paying his own transportation.*

trans•pose |trăns **pōz′**| *v.* **trans•posed, trans•pos•ing. 1.** To reverse or change the order or relative positions of; put into a different order: *transpose the letters of a word.* **2.** To move (an algebraic term) from one side of an equation to another by adding or subtracting that term to or from both sides. **3.** To write or perform (a musical composition) in a key other than the one in which it is written. —**trans′po•si′tion** |trăns′pə **zĭsh′**ən| *n.*

trans•ship |trăns **shĭp′**| *v.* **trans•shipped, trans•ship•ping.** To transfer (cargo) from one vessel or vehicle to another for reshipment. —**trans•ship′ment** *n.*

tran•sub•stan•ti•a•tion |trăn′səb stăn′shē **ā′**shən| *n.* The doctrine that the bread and wine of the Eucharist are transformed into the true presence of Christ, although their appearance remains the same.

trans•u•ran•ic |trăns′yo͞o **răn′**ĭk| *or* |trănz′-| *adj.* Having an atomic number greater than 92, the atomic number of uranium.

trans•ver•sal |trăns **vûr′**səl| *or* |trănz-| *n.* A line that intersects a system of lines.

trans•verse |trăns **vûrs′**| *or* |trănz-| *or* |**trăns′**-vûrs′| *or* |**trănz′**-| *adj.* Situated or lying across; crosswise: *a transverse beam.* —*n.* Something, as a road or muscle, that is transverse. —**trans•verse′ly** *adv.*

trap |trăp| *n.* **1.** A device for catching and holding animals. **2.** A stratagem for betraying, tricking, or exposing an unsuspecting person. **3. a.** A device for separating and collecting solids or other materials from the liquid that flows through a drain. **b.** A device for keeping a drain sealed against a backward flow of foul gases, especially a U-shaped or S-shaped bend in the pipe that remains full of liquid. **4.** A device that hurls brittle, claylike disks into the air to be shot at with a shotgun. **5.** Also **sand trap.** A sandy depression in a golf course that stops a ball from going any farther and is hard to hit out of. **6.** Often **traps.** Musical percussion instruments, such as snare drums, cymbals, or bells. —*v.* **trapped, trap•ping. 1.** To catch in or as in a trap: *trap a rabbit. The police trapped the thief.* **2.** To trap fur-bearing animals, especially as a business. **3.** To confine, hold, or block, with or as if with a trap: *gravel and sand trapping water in the sluice.* —**trap′per** *n.* [SEE PICTURE]

trap door. A hinged or sliding door in a floor or roof.

tra•peze |tră **pēz′**| *n.* A short horizontal bar hung from two parallel ropes, used for exercises or for acrobatic stunts.

tra•pe•zi•um |tră **pē′**zē əm| *n.* A quadrilateral having no parallel sides.

trap•e•zoid |**trăp′**ə zoid′| *n.* A quadrilateral having exactly one pair of parallel sides. —**trap′e•zoi′dal** *adj.* [SEE PICTURE]

trap•pings |**trăp′**ĭngz| *pl.n.* Articles of dress or ornamentation.

trap•shoot•ing |**trăp′**sho͞o′tĭng| *n.* The sport of shooting with a shotgun at disks hurled into the air by a trap.

trash |trăsh| *n.* **1.** Worthless or discarded material or objects; refuse. **2.** Cheap or empty expressions or ideas. **3.** An ignorant or contemptible person.

trash•y |**trăsh′**ē| *adj.* **trash•i•er, trash•i•est.** Like trash; worthless: *a trashy book; a trashy motion picture.* —**trash′i•ness** *n.*

trau•ma |**trou′**mə| *or* |**trô′**-| *n.* **1.** A wound or injury, usually inflicted suddenly by some physical means. **2.** An emotional shock that causes serious and lasting damage to the psychological functioning of an individual.

trau•mat•ic |trə **măt′**ĭk| *or* |trou-| *or* |trô-| *adj.* Of or of the nature of a trauma: *a traumatic experience.* —**trau•mat′i•cal•ly** *adv.*

trau•ma•tize |**trou′**mə tīz′| *or* |**trô′**-| *v.* **trau•ma•tized, trau•ma•tiz•ing.** To subject to a trauma; cause a trauma in.

tra•vail |trə **vāl′**| *or* |**trăv′**āl′| *n.* **1.** Strenuous exertion; toil. **2.** Tribulation or agony; anguish. **3.** The labor of childbirth. —*v.* **1.** To toil; work strenuously. **2.** To be in the labor of childbirth. [SEE NOTE]

trav•el |**trăv′**əl| *v.* **trav•eled** or **trav•elled, trav•el•ing** or **trav•el•ling. 1. a.** To go from one place to another; journey: *travel through Mexico; traveling around the world.* **b.** To journey through: *We traveled Europe from Russia to Portugal.* **2.** To journey from one place to another as a salesman: *He travels for a publishing house.* **3.** To be transmitted; move, as light. **4.** To keep or be in company: *travel in wealthy circles.* —*n.* **1.** The act or process of traveling: *Travel is slow and dangerous in parts of South America.* **2. travels.** A series of journeys. [SEE NOTE]

trav•eled |**trăv′**əld| *adj.* **1.** Having traveled widely. **2.** Used by people who travel: *a much-traveled part of the road.*

trav•el•er |**trăv′**ə lər| *or* |**trăv′**lər| *n.* A person who travels.

trav•e•logue, also **trav•e•log** |**trăv′**ə lôg′| *or* |-lŏg′| *n.* A lecture on travel, illustrated by slides or films.

trav•erse |**trăv′**ərs| *or* |trə **vûrs′**| *v.* **trav•ersed, trav•ers•ing. 1.** To travel across, over, or through: *traversed the desert safely.* **2.** To move forward and backward over: *Searchlights traversed the sky.* **3.** To extend across; cross: *A bridge traversed the mountain stream.* —*n.* Something lying across something else, as a beam, a rung of a ladder, etc. —*adj.* Lying or extending across: *a traverse curtain rod.*

trav•es•ty |**trăv′**ĭ stē| *n., pl.* **trav•es•ties.** A grotesque imitation with intent to ridicule. —*v.* **trav•es•tied, trav•es•ty•ing, trav•es•ties.** To make a travesty of.

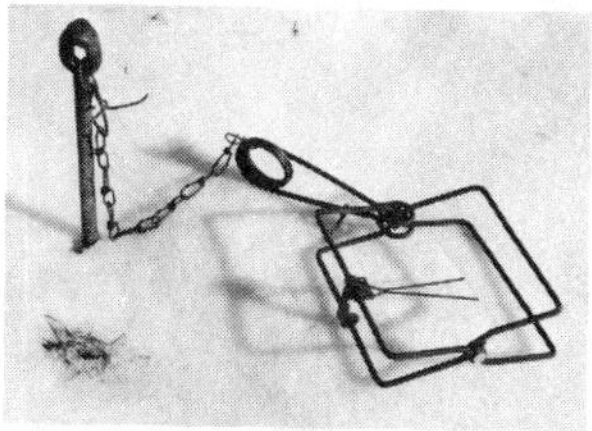

trap
Steel trap used to capture fur-bearing animals

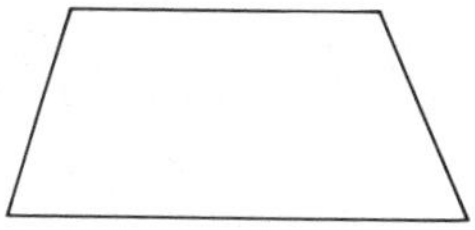

trapezoid

travail/travel
Travail *is from Old French* travailler, *which originally meant "to torment, to trouble" and later came to mean "to be troubled, to be in pain, to work hard";* travailler *is apparently from an unattested Latin word that has been reconstructed as* tripaliāre, *meaning "to torture." This in turn is assumed to be from* tripalium, *another unattested word meaning "instrument of torture made of three stakes," from* tripālis, *"having three stakes":* tri-, *"three,"* + palus, *"stake."* **Travail** *in English also came to mean "to toil, to make a difficult journey," hence simply "to journey." Later the variant* **travel** *was formed and took over the sense "to journey."*

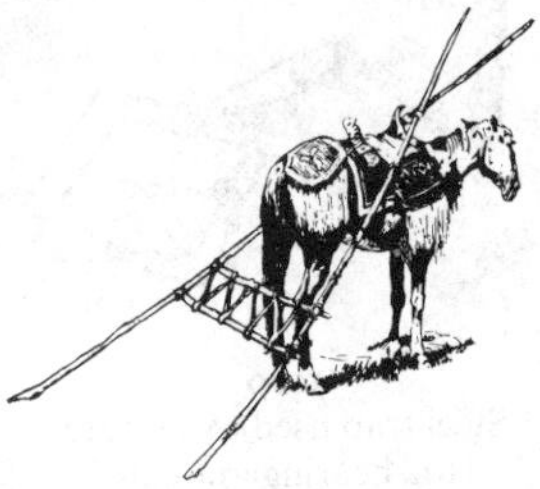

travois

treadmill
Horse-powered

ă pat/ā pay/â care/ä father/ĕ pet/
ē be/ĭ pit/ī pie/î fierce/ŏ pot/
ō go/ô paw, for/oi oil/ŏŏ book/
ōō boot/ou out/ŭ cut/û fur/
th the/th thin/hw which/zh vision/
ə ago, item, pencil, atom, circus

tra•vois |trə **voi'**| *or* |**trăv'**oi'| *n., pl.* **tra•vois** |trə **voiz'**| *or* |**trăv'**oiz'| or **tra•vois•es** |trə **voi'**zĭz| *or* |**trăv'**oi'zĭz|. A primitive sledge formerly used by Plains Indians and consisting of a platform or netting supported by two long trailing poles, the forward ends of which are fastened to a dog or horse. [SEE PICTURE]

trawl |trôl| *n.* **1.** A large, tapered fishing net towed along the sea bottom. **2.** A long fishing line towed by a boat and supporting many smaller lines bearing baited hooks. *—v.* To fish or catch (fish) with a trawl.

trawl•er |**trô'**lər| *n.* A boat used for trawling.

tray |trā| *n.* A flat, shallow receptacle with a raised edge or rim, used for carrying, holding, or displaying small articles. ***—modifier:*** *a tray stand.*

treach•er•ous |**trĕch'**ər əs| *adj.* **1.** Betraying a trust; disloyal: *a treacherous friend.* **2. a.** Not dependable: *He has a treacherous memory.* **b.** Not to be trusted; deceptive; dangerous: *a beach with a treacherous surf.*

treach•er•y |**trĕch'**ə rē| *n., pl.* **treach•er•ies.** Willful betrayal of trust; perfidy; treason.

trea•cle |**trē'**kəl| *n. British.* Molasses.

tread |trĕd| *v.* **trod** |trŏd|, **trod•den** |**trŏd'**n| or **trod, tread•ing. 1.** To walk on, over, or along: *postmen treading the sidewalks on their regular delivery route.* **2.** To walk or step: *treading softly.* **3.** To stamp or trample: *They threshed the rice by treading it on a hard earthen floor. Tread out the embers of the fire.* **4.** To make (a path or trail) by walking or trampling. **5.** To perform or execute by walking or dancing: *tread a measure of the minuet.* *—n.* **1. a.** The act, manner, or sound of treading: *the swift tread of a horse.* **b.** A footstep or footsteps: *a familiar tread.* **2.** The horizontal part of a step in a staircase. **3.** The part of a wheel or shoe sole that touches the ground. **4.** The pattern of grooves or raised ridges on a tire that makes it grip the road better.
Idioms. **tread on (someone's) toes.** To interfere with, get in the way of, or offend someone. **tread water.** *Past tense* **treaded water.** To keep one's head above water while in an upright position by moving the feet up and down as if walking.

tread•le |**trĕd'**l| *n.* A pedal or lever pushed up and down or back and forth with the foot to drive a wheel, as in a sewing machine or potter's wheel. *—v.* **tread•led, tread•ling.** To operate a treadle.

tread•mill |**trĕd'**mĭl'| *n.* **1.** A device operated by one or more persons or animals walking on an endless belt or on a set of moving steps attached to a wheel. **2.** Any monotonous work or routine. [SEE PICTURE]

treas. **1.** treasurer. **2.** treasury.

trea•son |**trē'**zən| *n.* Betrayal of one's country, especially by giving aid to an enemy in wartime or by plotting to overthrow the government.

trea•son•a•ble |**trē'**zə nə bəl| *adj.* Of or involving treason: *his treasonable actions.*

trea•son•ous |**trē'**zə nəs| *adj.* Of or involving treason; treasonable.

treas•ure |**trĕzh'**ər| *n.* **1.** Accumulated, stored, or cached wealth in the form of valuables, as jewels. **2.** Someone or something considered especially precious or valuable. *—v.* **treas•ured, treas•ur•ing.** To value highly; cherish: *He treasures the watch his colleagues gave him.* ***—phrasal verb.*** **treasure up.** To store up for future use, as in one's memory: *treasure up memories of childhood years.* [SEE NOTE on p. 895]

treas•ur•er |**trĕzh'**ər ər| *n.* A person having charge of the funds or revenues of a government or organization, such as a business or club.

treas•ure-trove |**trĕzh'**ər trōv'| *n.* **1.** Any treasure found hidden and not claimed by its owner. **2.** A discovery of great value.

treas•ur•y |**trĕzh'**ə rē| *n., pl.* **treas•ur•ies. 1.** A place where the funds of a government or an organization are kept and managed. **2.** The money kept in such a place. **3.** Any collection of valuable things: *a treasury of good music.* **4. Treasury.** The department of a government in charge of collecting and managing public funds.

treat |trēt| *v.* **1.** To act or behave toward: *We will treat you fairly.* **2.** To deal with, handle, or cover: *The author treated his subject realistically. Treat all requests on a first-come, first-served basis.* **3.** To regard or consider in a certain way: *Einstein treated matter and energy as exchangeable.* **4.** To try or help to cure by administering some remedy or therapy: *treat a patient; treat a disease.* **5.** To subject to a physical or chemical process or action in order to change in some way: *Cloth may be treated with dye or bleach.* **6.** To provide food or entertainment for (another or others) at one's own expense: *Did you say you'd treat us today? It's your turn to treat.* ***—phrasal verbs.*** **treat of.** To deal with as a subject: *That poem treats of love.* **treat to.** To buy or allow to have as a treat: *She treated us to doughnuts.* *—n.* **1. a.** Something, such as refreshments or entertainment, paid for or provided by someone else: *Halloween treats.* **b.** An act of treating or turn to treat: *Let this lunch be my treat.* **2.** Anything considered a special delight or pleasure, as a sweet, luxury, enjoyable outing, etc.

trea•tise |**trē'**tĭs| *n.* A formal, systematic account in writing of some subject.

treat•ment |**trēt'**mənt| *n.* **1.** The act or manner of treating something: *a historian's masterful treatment of the Civil War; her kind treatment of her servants.* **2. a.** The use or application of something meant to relieve or cure a disease or disorder, as in medicine or dentistry. **b.** An example of this: *another treatment in two weeks.*

trea•ty |**trē'**tē| *n., pl.* **trea•ties. 1.** A formal agreement between two or more states containing terms of trade, peace, etc.; a pact. **2.** A document containing this agreement.

tre•ble |**trĕb'**əl| *adj.* **1.** Triple. **2.** Of, having, or performing the highest musical part, voice, or range. *—n.* The highest voice, part, instrument, or range; soprano. *—v.* **tre•bled, tre•bling.** To increase three times; triple.

treble clef. A G clef placed on a musical staff so that the G above middle C is on the second line.

tree |trē| *n.* **1.** A usually tall woody plant with a single main stem, or trunk. **2.** Something resembling a tree, such as a pole with pegs or hooks for hanging clothes. **3.** A diagram with a branching form, as one used to show family descent. ***—modifier:*** *tree trunks; a tree farm.* *—v.* **treed, tree•ing.** To chase and force to climb a tree: *The dogs treed a raccoon.* **—tree'less** *adj.*
Idiom. **up a tree.** In an embarrassing or dif-

ficult situation from which one cannot escape.

tree frog. Also **tree toad.** Any of several small frogs that live in trees and that have toes with disklike pads used for clinging to tree trunks, branches, etc. [SEE PICTURE]

tree•top |trē'tŏp'| *n.* The uppermost part of a tree.

tre•foil |trē'foil'| *or* |trĕf'oil'| *n.* **1.** A plant, such as a clover, having compound leaves with three leaflets. **2.** A decorative form, as in architecture, having three divisions like those of a clover leaf. [SEE PICTURE]

trek |trĕk| *v.* **trekked, trek•king.** To make a slow or arduous journey. —*n.* A journey, especially a long and difficult one.

trel•lis |trĕl'ĭs| *n.* A lattice used for training creeping plants.

trem•ble |trĕm'bəl| *v.* **trem•bled, trem•bling. 1.** To shake involuntarily, as from fear, cold, etc.; quake; shiver; quiver. **2.** To feel fear or anxiety: *I tremble to think what has happened to her.* —*n.* The act of trembling; a shudder.

tre•men•dous |trĭ mĕn'dəs| *adj.* **1.** Capable of making one tremble; terrible: *a tremendous accident.* **2. a.** Extremely large; enormous: *a tremendous animal; traveling at a tremendous speed.* **b.** *Informal.* Marvelous; wonderful: *a tremendous party; a tremendous player.* —**tre•men'dous•ly** *adv.* —**tre•men'dous•ness** *n.*

trem•o•lo |trĕm'ə lō'| *n., pl.* **trem•o•los. 1. a.** A rapid repetition or variation in loudness of a musical tone. **b.** A rapid alternation of two musical tones. **2.** A vibrato in a singing voice, especially one that results from tension or poor technique.

trem•or |trĕm'ər| *n.* **1.** A shaking or vibrating movement: *an earth tremor.* **2.** A rapid, involuntary shaking or twitching of muscles.

trem•u•lous |trĕm'yə ləs| *adj.* **1.** Vibrating or quivering; trembling: *speaking with a tremulous voice.* **2.** Timid; fearful: *She was tremulous and contrite in the presence of the queen.*

trench |trĕnch| *n.* **1.** A long ditch, especially one used as protection for soldiers in warfare. **2.** Any long, deep furrow, as one used for soil drainage. —*v.* To cut trenches in: *trench a field.*

trench•ant |trĕn'chənt| *adj.* **1.** Keen; incisive: *a trenchant remark.* **2.** Forceful; effective: *a trenchant argument.* —**trench'an•cy** *n.* —**trench'ant•ly** *adv.*

trench coat. A loose-fitting belted raincoat with pockets and flaps suggesting a military style.

trench foot. Frostbite of the feet, often affecting soldiers who must stand in cold water for long periods of time.

trench mouth. **Vincent's disease.**

trend |trĕnd| *n.* **1.** A general tendency or course; drift: *The trend of prices is still upward.* **2.** A direction or movement; a flow: *a trend of thought.* —*v.* **1.** To have a certain direction: *The mountain road trends westward.* **2.** To have a certain tendency; tend: *new songs trending away from the rhythms of last year.*

tren•dy |trĕn'dē| *adj.* **trend•i•er, trend•i•est.** *Informal.* Of or in accordance with the latest fad or fashion; modish and unconventional.

Tren•ton |trĕn'tən|. The capital of New Jersey. Population, 102,000.

tre•pan |trĭ păn'| *n.* **1.** A tool used for boring shafts in rock. **2.** A trephine, a surgical instrument. —*v.* **tre•panned, tre•pan•ning. 1.** To bore (a shaft) through rock with a trepan. **2.** To trephine, as in surgery. —**trep'a•na'tion** |trĕp'ə nā'shən| *n.*

tre•phine |trĭ fīn'| *or* |-fēn'| *n.* A surgical instrument having circular, sawlike edges, used to cut out disks of bone, especially from the skull. —*v.* **tre•phined, tre•phin•ing.** To operate on with a trephine, as in surgery. —**treph'i•na'tion** |trĕf'ə nā'shən| *n.*

trep•i•da•tion |trĕp'ĭ dā'shən| *n.* A state of alarm or dread; apprehension: *We approached the swift rapids of the river with great trepidation.*

tres•pass |trĕs'pəs| *or* |-păs'| *v.* **1.** To commit an offense or sin; err; transgress. **2.** To infringe; encroach: *trespass on someone's privacy.* **3.** To invade the property or rights of another without his consent. —*n.* **1.** A transgression; a sin. **2.** The act of trespassing; an illegal entry. —**tres'pass•er** *n.*

tress |trĕs| *n.* **1.** A lock of hair. **2. tresses.** A woman's long hair.

tres•tle |trĕs'əl| *n.* **1.** A horizontal beam or bar extending between two pairs of legs that spread outward at an angle, used to support a vertical load. **2.** A framework made up of vertical, horizontal, and slanting supports, used to hold up a bridge.

tri–. A word element meaning "three": **triangle.**

tri•ad |trī'ăd'| *or* |-əd| *n.* **1.** A group of three closely related persons or things. **2.** In music, a chord containing three tones, especially a chord that consists of tones that are separated by thirds.

tri•al |trī'əl| *or* |trīl| *n.* **1.** The examination of and deciding upon evidence, charges, and claims made in a case in court. **2.** The act or process of testing and trying by use and experience: *the trial of a new aircraft.* **3.** An effort or attempt: *He succeeded on his second trial.* **4.** Anything, as a person, thing, or event, that tries one's patience, endurance, etc.: *He is a trial to his parents. The lack of water was a trial to the explorers.* —**modifier:** *a trial attorney; a trial flight.*

Idiom. **on trial.** In the state or process of being tested or tried.

tri•an•gle |trī'ăng'gəl| *n.* **1.** A closed plane geometric figure formed by three points not in a straight line connected by three line segments; a polygon with three sides. **2.** Something shaped like this figure. **3.** Any of various flat objects having the outline of a triangle and used as guides in drawing or drafting. **4.** A musical percussion instrument with a clear bell-like tone, formed of a bar of metal bent into a triangle that is left open at one vertex. [SEE PICTURE]

tri•an•gu•lar |trī ăng'gyə lər| *adj.* **1.** Of or shaped like a triangle. **2.** Having a base or cross section that is a triangle: *a triangular file; a triangular prism.*

tri•an•gu•late |trī ăng'yə lāt'| *v.* **tri•an•gu•lat•ed, tri•an•gu•lat•ing. 1.** To divide into triangles. **2.** To survey by means of triangulation. **3.** To measure or determine by means of trigonometry.

tri•an•gu•la•tion |trī ăng'gyə lā'shən| *n.* **1.** A method used in surveying in which a region is divided into a set of triangular elements based on a line of known length, so that an accurate

tree frog

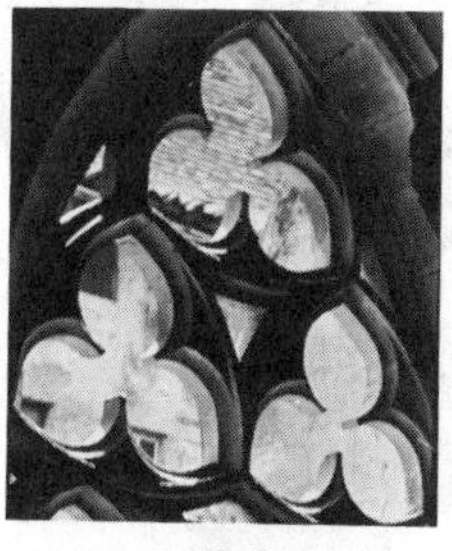

trefoil

The word **trefoil** is from Latin *trifolium,* a kind of grass with three leaves: *tri-,* "three," + *folium,* "leaf."

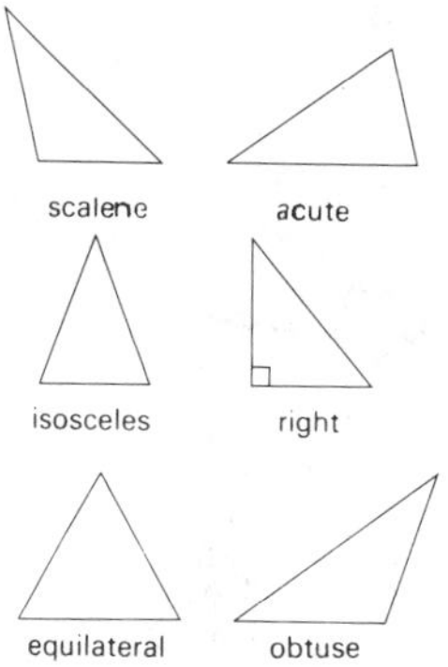

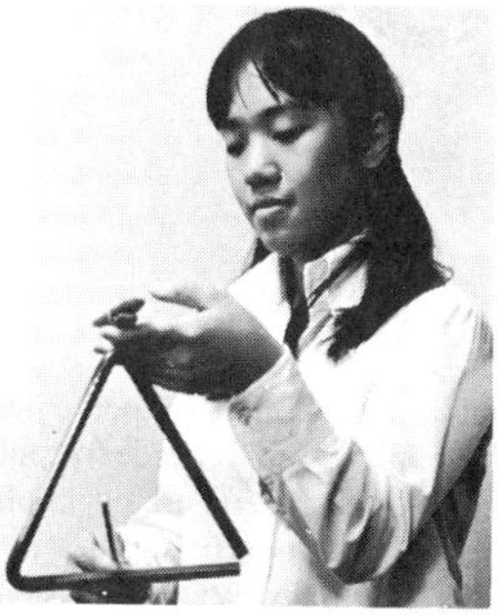

triangle

triceratops

Triceratops means "three-horn-face": Greek *tri-*, "three," + *kerat-*, "horn," + *ops*, "face."

tricycle

determination of distances and directions can be made by using trigonometry. **2.** The set of triangles laid out for this purpose. **3.** The location of an unknown point, as in navigation, by means of trigonometry.

Tri•as•sic |trī ăs′ĭk| *n.* Also **Triassic period.** The geologic period that began about 230 million years ago and ended about 180 million years ago, characterized by the existence of giant tree ferns and similar plants and the development of dinosaurs and other reptiles. *—modifier: Triassic fossils.*

trib•al |trī′bəl| *adj.* Of or of the nature of a tribe or tribes: *tribal costumes.*

tribe |trīb| *n.* Any of various systems of social organization, chiefly of primitive peoples, that unite a group of people in a given area that have a common ancestry, language, and culture.

tribes•man |**trībz′**mən| *n., pl.* **-men** |-mən|. A member of a tribe.

trib•u•la•tion |trĭb′yə **lā′**shən| *n.* **1.** Great affliction or distress; suffering: *a time of great tribulation for all of us.* **2.** That which causes such distress: *The explorers had to face many tribulations in their voyages through the Arctic.*

tri•bu•nal |trī **byōō′**nəl| *or* |trĭ-| *n.* **1.** A seat or court of justice. **2.** Anything having the power of determining or judging: *the tribunal of public opinion.*

trib•une |**trĭb′**yōōn′| *or* |trĭ **byōōn′**| *n.* **1.** An official of ancient Rome chosen by the common people to protect their rights. **2.** A protector or champion of the people.

trib•u•tar•y |**trĭb′**yə tĕr′ē| *n., pl.* **trib•u•tar•ies.** **1.** A river or stream that flows into a larger river or stream. **2.** A person, nation, etc., that pays tribute to another. *—adj.* **1.** Flowing into another: *a tributary river.* **2.** Paying tribute: *a tributary kingdom.*

trib•ute |**trĭb′**yōōt′| *n.* **1.** A gift or other acknowledgment of gratitude, respect, or admiration. **2. a.** A sum of money paid by one ruler or nation to another as acknowledgment of submission or as the price for protection by that nation. **b.** Any enforced payment, contribution, etc.

trice |trīs| *n.* A very short period of time; a moment; an instant: *in a trice.*

tri•ceps |**trī′**sĕps′| *n.* A muscle having three points of attachment at one end, especially a large muscle that runs along the back of the upper arm and serves to extend the forearm.

tri•cer•a•tops |trī **sĕr′**ə tŏps′| *n.* A large, plant-eating dinosaur with sharp horns and a bony plate covering the back of the neck. [SEE PICTURE]

tri•chi•na |trĭ **kī′**nə| *n., pl.* **tri•chi•nae** |trĭ **kī′**nē′| or **tri•chi•nas.** A very small parasitic worm that lives in the intestines and muscles of pigs and other animals and that is the cause of the disease trichinosis.

trich•i•no•sis |trĭk′ə **nō′**sĭs| *n.* A disease that results from eating incompletely cooked pork that contains trichinae, having as symptoms intestinal disorders, pain, fever, swelling muscles, and insomnia.

trick |trĭk| *n.* **1.** An impressive feat or stunt requiring a special skill, talent, or technique: *a juggling trick; magic tricks.* **2.** A special skill or knack: *a new swimmer trying to master the trick of fluttering her legs.* **3. a.** A clever and effective method or technique used by an expert: *the tricks of the trade.* **b.** A crafty and deceptive method or scheme used to fool or outwit someone: *the tricks of a swindler.* **4.** A deception or optical illusion: *In winter this shimmering landscape could play strange tricks on a man's eyes.* **5.** A prank or practical joke: *She thought we were playing a Halloween trick on her.* **6.** A mean, stupid, or childish act: *That was a low-down dirty trick.* **7.** A certain habit or mannerism: *He has a trick of looking right through you, off into the distance.* **8.** All of the cards played in a single round of a card game. *—adj.* **1.** Involving tricks, stunts, or trickery: *trick riding in a rodeo; trick photography.* **2.** Tricky; deceptive: *trick problems in arithmetic.* **3.** Used to play tricks: *trick spoons that melt in hot coffee.* **4.** Weak and liable to give way: *a trick knee.* *—v.* **1.** To deceive, fool, cheat, or mislead. **2.** To get or persuade by trickery: *She tricked me into taking my medicine.*

Idioms. **do the trick.** To accomplish the desired result. **not miss a trick.** To be aware of everything that is going on. **trick or treat.** A phrase said by children at Halloween when going from door to door asking for goodies, with the threat of mischievous pranks if goodies are not provided.

trick•er•y |**trĭk′**ə rē| *n., pl.* **trick•er•ies.** The practice or use of tricks; deception by stratagem: *He got the money by trickery.*

trick•le |**trĭk′**əl| *v.* **trick•led, trick•ling.** **1.** To flow or fall in drops or in a thin, intermittent stream; drip steadily: *tears trickling down her face. Sand trickled through his fingers.* **2.** To proceed slowly or bit by bit: *The audience trickled in before curtain time.* *—n.* **1.** The act or condition of trickling. **2.** Any slow, small, or irregular quantity of trickling: *a trickle of customers. A little trickle of perspiration ran down his cheek.*

trick•ster |**trĭk′**stər| *n.* A person who tricks; a cheater.

trick•y |**trĭk′**ē| *adj.* **trick•i•er, trick•i•est.** **1.** Crafty; sly; wily: *a tricky poker player.* **2.** Requiring caution or skill: *a tricky situation.*

tri•col•or |**trī′**kŭl′ər| *adj.* Having three colors. *—n.* A flag with three bands of different color, especially the French flag, which has three vertical bands, one of blue, one of white, and one of red.

tri•cot |**trē′**kō| *n.* A soft knitted fabric.

tri•cus•pid |trī **kŭs′**pĭd| *adj.* Having three points, as one of the molar teeth. *—n.* A tricuspid tooth.

tri•cy•cle |**trī′**sĭ′kəl| *n.* A vehicle with three wheels usually propelled by pedals. [SEE PICTURE]

tri•dent |**trīd′**nt| *n.* A long three-pronged spear, especially the one carried by Neptune, the Roman god of the sea.

tried |trīd|. Past tense and past participle of **try.** *—adj.* Tested and proved to be good or trustworthy: *a tried recipe.*

tri•en•ni•al |trī **ĕn′**ē əl| *adj.* **1.** Occurring every third year. **2.** Lasting three years. *—n.* A third anniversary.

tri•fle |**trī′**fəl| *n.* **1.** Something of slight importance or very little value. **2.** A small amount; a

ă pat/ā pay/â care/ä father/ĕ pet/ē be/ĭ pit/ī pie/î fierce/ŏ pot/ō go/ô paw, for/oi oil/ŏŏ book/ōō boot/ou out/ŭ cut/û fur/*th* the/th thin/hw which/zh vision/ə ago, item, pencil, atom, circus

little. **3.** A dessert of cake soaked in wine or brandy and topped with jam, custard, and whipped cream. —*v.* **tri•fled, tri•fling. 1.** To deal with as being of little significance or importance, etc.: *The general was not a man to trifle with.* **2.** To play or toy with something; handle idly: *trifling with a pencil.* —**tri'fler** *n.*

Idiom. **a trifle.** A little.

tri•fling |trī'flĭng| *adj.* **1.** Of slight importance; insignificant: *a trifling matter; a trifling sum.* **2.** Frivolous. —**tri'fling•ly** *adv.*

trig•ger |trĭg'ər| *n.* The small lever pressed by the finger to discharge a gun. —*v.* To start; set off; set in motion.

trig•o•no•met•ric |trĭg'ə nə **mĕt'**rĭk| *adj.* Of or having to do with trigonometry.

trigonometric functions. A function of an angle, such as the sine, cosine, or tangent, whose value is expressed as a ratio of two of the sides of a right triangle in which the angle is included.

trig•o•nom•e•try |trĭg'ə **nŏm'**ĭ trē| *n.* The study of the properties and uses of trigonometric functions. [SEE NOTE]

trill |trĭl| *n.* **1.** A fluttering or tremulous sound, as that made by certain birds; a warble. **2.** The rapid alternation of two msuical tones that are either a half step or a whole step apart. **3.** A rapid vibration of one organ of speech against another, as of the tip of the tongue against the ridge behind the upper front teeth. —*v.* **1.** To sound, sing, or play a trill. **2.** To decorate (a musical tone) by sounding it and another tone a half step or whole step away as a trill.

tril•lion |trĭl'yən| *n.* **1.** The number equal to one thousand billions, written 1,000,000,000,000 or more compactly as 10^{12}. **2.** In Great Britain, the number equal to one billions billions, written 1,000,000,000,000,000,000 or compactly as 10^{18}. [SEE NOTE]

tril•lionth |trĭl'yənth| *n.* **1.** In a set of items arranged to match the natural numbers in a one-to-one correspondence, the item that matches the number one trillion. **2.** One of one trillion equal parts of a unit. —**tril'lionth** *adj. & adv.*

tril•li•um |trĭl'ē əm| *n.* Any of several plants having three leaves grouped together and a single flower with three petals.

tri•lo•bite |trī'lə bīt'| *n.* Any of a group of extinct sea animals that lived more than 400,000,000 years ago and that had a body with a hard outer covering divided by grooves into three lengthwise sections. [SEE PICTURE]

tril•o•gy |trĭl'ə jē| *n., pl.* **tril•o•gies.** A group of three related dramatic or literary works.

trim |trĭm| *v.* **trimmed, trim•ming. 1.** To make neat, even, or tidy by clipping, cutting, smoothing, etc.: *Barbers trim men's beards. Trim the hedges.* **2.** To remove or reduce by cutting: *Trim the crusts from the bread. The company trimmed costs by $20 million a year.* **3.** To decorate, ornament, or embellish: *trim a Christmas tree; a velvet robe trimmed with ermine.* **4.** To adjust (sails and yards) so that they receive the wind properly: *He quickly trimmed sail and steered the ship past the sandbar.* **5.** *Informal.* To beat or defeat soundly. —*n.* **1.** Ornamentation on the surface of something, such as braid on clothing, moldings and framework around the doors and windows of a building, etc. **2.** The act of cutting or clipping: *Your beard needs a trim.* **3.** Proper shape, order, or condition: *in good trim for the game.* **4. a.** The readiness of a ship for sailing. **b.** The balance or position of a ship or aircraft. —*adj.* **trim•mer, trim•mest. 1.** Neat; tidy; orderly; smart: *He looked very trim in his new suit.* **2.** Well designed or proportioned, with simple or slim lines: *a trim white schooner; a trim figure.* —**trim'ly** *adv.* —**trim'mer** *n.* —**trim'ness** *n.*

trim•ming |**trĭm'**ĭng| *n.* **1.** Anything that is added as decoration; an ornament: *fur trimming on a coat.* **2. trimmings.** Accessories; extras: *roast turkey with all the trimmings.* **3.** Pieces that are cut off from a larger piece.

Trin•i•dad and To•ba•go |**trĭn'**ĭ dăd'; tə **bā'**gō|. A country in the West Indies off the coast of Venezuela, consisting of the islands of **Trinidad** and **Tobago.** Population, 1,067,000. Capital, Port of Spain.

tri•ni•tro•tol•u•ene |trī nī'trō **tŏl'**yo͞o ēn'| *n.* A yellow, crystalline, highly explosive compound of carbon, hydrogen, nitrogen, and oxygen, having the formula $C_7H_5N_3O_6$; TNT.

trin•i•ty |**trĭn'**ĭ tē| *n., pl.* **trin•i•ties. 1.** Any three parts in union; a triad. **2. the Trinity.** The Godhead of orthodox Christian belief, constituted by the persons of the Father, Son, and Holy Ghost.

trin•ket |**trĭng'**kĭt| *n.* A small ornament or piece of jewelry.

tri•no•mi•al |trī **nō'**mē əl| *adj.* Consisting of three algebraic terms connected by plus signs or minus signs or some combination of the two. —*n.* A trinomial algebraic expression.

tri•o |**trē'**ō| *n., pl.* **tri•os. 1.** A group of three. **2. a.** A musical composition for three performers. **b.** The three musicians who perform such a composition. **c.** The middle section of a minuet or scherzo, a march, or one of various dances.

tri•ode |**trī'**ōd'| *n.* An electron tube having three electrodes, usually an anode and a cathode and a grid whose voltage with respect to the cathode controls the flow of current between the anode and cathode.

tri•ox•ide |trī **ŏk'**sīd'| *n.* An oxide that contains three atoms of oxygen per molecule.

trip |trĭp| *n.* **1.** A journey, voyage, flight, or other passage from one place to another: *a trip from Cleveland to Pittsburgh.* **2.** An outing or excursion: *a camping trip.* **3.** The distance traveled on a trip or the time required for such a journey: *a 60-mile trip; a 5-hour trip.* **4.** A stumble or fall. **5.** A mistake or blunder. **6.** A device, such as a catch or trigger, for activating a mechanism. **7.** *Slang.* A lengthy hallucination brought on by a drug. —*v.* **tripped, trip•ping. 1. a.** To strike the foot against or stumble over something, losing one's balance: *He tripped over a root and fell.* **b.** To cause to stumble or fall: *Thick vines tripped him.* **2. a.** To make a mistake; err: *Do you trip over the words "to" and "too"?* **b.** To trap or catch in an error or inconsistency: *The crafty lawyer tripped the witness with a tricky question.* **3.** To move, skip, or dance lightly and nimbly: *The children tripped gaily over the bridge.* **4. a.** To release (a catch, trigger, switch, etc.), setting something in operation: *trip a circuit breaker.* **b.** To be released in this manner or way: *The circuit*

trigonometry

Trigonometry is entirely concerned with calculations relating to triangles. The word **trigonometry** *means "triangle-measurement." It is formed from Greek* trigōnon, *"a triangle"* (tri-, *"three,"* + gōnia, *"angle," as in* **polygon**), + -metria, *"measurement."*

trillion, billion, etc.

These words were formed in French from French million, *"1,000,000." The prefix* bi-, *"twice" formed* billion, *meaning "1,000,000², a million to the second power," or "1,000,000,000,000." The prefix* tri-, *"three times," formed* trillion, *meaning "1,000,000³, a million to the* third *power," or "1,000,000,000,000,000,000." These were borrowed into English as* **billion** *and* **trillion**; *note that in British English they have kept their original values, while in American English they have been reduced to 1,000,000,000 and 1,000,000,000,000, respectively.*

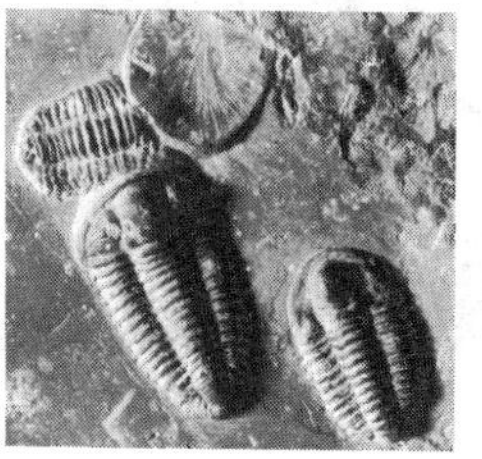

trilobite

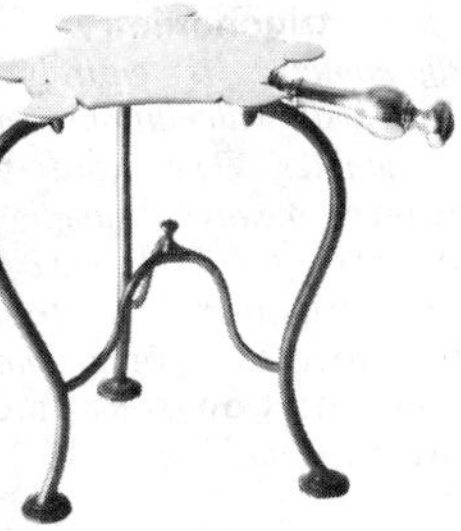

trivet

troll[1-2]

Troll[1] *was Middle English* trollen, *"to ramble, roll along"; its further origin is unknown.* **Troll**[2] *is from Old Norse* troll, *"monster, demon."*

trombone

ă pat/ā pay/â care/ä father/ĕ pet/ ē be/ĭ pit/ī pie/î fierce/ŏ pot/ ō go/ô paw, for/oi oil/ŏŏ book/ ōō boot/ou out/ŭ cut/û fur/ *th* the/th thin/hw which/zh vision/ ə ago, item, pencil, atom, circus

breaker tripped. **5.** Also **trip out.** *Slang.* To have a drug-induced hallucination. —***phrasal verb.*** **trip up.** To cause to stumble, fall, or err: *I tripped him up and he fell on his nose.*

tripe |trīp| *n.* **1.** The rubbery lining of the stomach of cattle or similar animals, used as food. **2.** *Informal.* Anything with no value; rubbish.

trip•le |trĭp′əl| *adj.* **1.** Of or having three parts; threefold. **2.** Three times as much or as many; multiplied by three. —*n.* **1.** A number or amount three times as great or as much as another. **2.** A group or set of three. **3.** In baseball, a hit that enables the batter to reach third base safely. —*v.* To make or become three times as great in number or amount.

trip•let |trĭp′lĭt| *n.* **1.** A group or set of three; a triple. **2.** One of three children born at one birth. **3.** A group of three musical notes of equal duration that occupy the time normally taken by two.

triple time. Also **triple meter.** A musical meter in which beats are organized into groups of three with the first of each group receiving an accent.

trip•li•cate |trĭp′lĭ kĭt| *or* |-kāt′| *adj.* Made with three identical copies. —*n.* One of a set of three identical objects. —*v.* |trĭp′lĭ kāt′| **trip•li•cat•ed, trip•li•cat•ing. 1.** To triple. **2.** To make three identical copies of.

tri•pod |trī′pŏd′| *n.* An adjustable stand with three legs, used especially to support a camera.

Trip•o•li |trĭp′ə lē|. The capital of Libya. Population, 550,000.

trip•tych |trĭp′tĭk| *n.* A three-paneled picture.

tri•sect |trī sĕkt′| *or* |trī′sĕkt′| *v.* To divide into three parts, especially equal parts.

trite |trīt| *adj.* **trit•er, trit•est.** Overused and commonplace; lacking interest or originality: *a trite expression.* —**trite′ly** *adv.* —**trite′ness** *n.*

trit•i•um |trĭt′ē əm| *or* |trĭsh′ē-| *n.* A rare radioactive isotope of hydrogen having a nucleus that consists of a proton and two neutrons and an atomic mass of 3. It is made artificially and is used as a tracer and in nuclear weapons.

tri•ton |trīt′n| *n.* **1.** A tropical sea mollusk with a large, pointed, spiral shell that can be used as a horn or trumpet. **2. Triton.** A Greek sea god, often depicted as half man and half fish.

tri•umph |trī′əmf| *v.* To be victorious; win; prevail: *triumph over prejudice.* —*n.* **1.** The instance or fact of being victorious; success: *A skyscraper is the triumph of mind over a million matters.* **2.** Exultation derived from victory: *a cry of triumph.*

tri•um•phal |trī ŭm′fəl| *adj.* Of, celebrating, or in memory of a triumph: *a triumphal march; a triumphal arch.*

tri•um•phant |trī ŭm′fənt| *adj.* **1.** Victorious; successful: *a triumphant army; a triumphant political campaign.* **2.** Rejoicing over having been successful, victorious, etc.: *a triumphant return to the land of his ancestors.*

tri•um•vir |trī ŭm′vər| *n.* One of three men sharing civil authority, as in ancient Rome.

tri•um•vi•rate |trī ŭm′vər ĭt| *or* |-və rāt′| *n.* **1.** A group of three men jointly governing a nation. **2.** Government by triumvirs. **3.** Any group of three: *a triumvirate of composers.*

tri•va•lent |trī vā′lənt| *adj.* In chemistry, having valence +3 or −3.

triv•et |trĭv′ĭt| *n.* **1.** A three-legged stand for holding a kettle or pot over or near an open fire. **2.** A metal stand, usually with short legs, placed under a hot dish or platter. [SEE PICTURE]

triv•i•a |trĭv′ē ə| *pl.n. (used with a singular or plural verb).* Insignificant or inessential matters; trivialities; trifles.

triv•i•al |trĭv′ē əl| *adj.* **1.** Of little importance or significance; trifling: *trivial matters.* **2.** Ordinary; commonplace: *a trivial occurrence.* —**triv′i•al′i•ty** *n.* —**triv′i•al•ly** *adv.*

tro•che |trō′kē| *n.* A small, circular medicinal lozenge; a pastille.

trod |trŏd|. Past tense and a past participle of **tread.**

trod•den |trŏd′n|. Past participle of **tread.**

trog•lo•dyte |trŏg′lə dīt′| *n.* A prehistoric cave dweller.

Tro•jan |trō′jən| *n.* A native or inhabitant of ancient Troy. —*adj.* Of Ancient Troy or its inhabitants.

Trojan War. A war believed to have been fought between Greece and Troy in the 12th century B.C. It is known chiefly through Homer's *Iliad.*

troll[1] |trōl| *v.* **1.** To fish by trailing a line from behind a slowly moving boat. **2.** To sing in succession the parts of (a round). [SEE NOTE]

troll[2] |trōl| *n.* In Teutonic folklore, a supernatural creature variously described as friendly or evil, as a dwarf or a giant, and as living in caves or under bridges. [SEE NOTE]

trol•ley |trŏl′ē| *n., pl.* **trol•leys. 1.** An electrically operated car that runs on a track; a streetcar. **2.** A carriage, basket, etc., that hangs from wheels that run on an overhead track. **3.** A device, such as a grooved wheel at the end of a metal pole, that makes contact with an overhead wire, third rail, underground conductor, etc., and supplies current to an electrically powered vehicle.

trolley bus. An electrically powered bus that runs without tracks and receives current from an overhead wire.

trolley car. A streetcar.

trol•lop |trŏl′əp| *n.* **1.** A slovenly, untidy woman. **2.** A loose woman; strumpet.

trom•bone |trŏm bōn′| *or* |trŏm′bōn′| *n.* A brass wind instrument that is somewhat similar to the trumpet in construction and sound but larger and lower in pitch. Some trombones change pitch by using a slide that varies the length of the instrument, and some use valves similar to those of a trumpet. [SEE PICTURE]

troop |trōōp| *n.* **1.** A group of people or animals: *a troop of dogs trotting down the street.* **2.** A group of soldiers: *A troop invaded the village.* **3. troops.** Military units; soldiers. **4.** A group of Boy Scouts or Girl Scouts under the guidance of an adult leader. —*v.* **1.** To move or go as a group. **2.** To move along; proceed: *children trooping home.* ¶ *These sound alike* **troop, troupe.**

troop•er |trōō′pər| *n.* **1. a.** A cavalryman. **b.** A cavalry horse. **2.** A mounted policeman. **3.** A state policeman.

troop•ship |trōōp′shĭp′| *n.* A transport ship designed for carrying troops.

trop. 1. tropic. **2.** tropical.

tro•phy |trō′fē| *n., pl.* **tro•phies.** A prize or memento received as a symbol of victory.

trop•ic |trŏp′ĭk| *n.* **1.** Either of the parallels of latitude at 23 degrees 27 minutes north and south of the equator that form the boundaries of the Torrid Zone. **2.** The projection of either of these parallels onto the celestial sphere; the lines that mark the limits of the apparent north-to-south motion of the sun. **3. tropics.** The region of the earth bounded by these parallels; the Torrid Zone. *—adj.* Of or having to do with the tropics; tropical.

trop•i•cal |**trŏp′**ĭ kəl| *adj.* **1.** Of or characteristic of the tropics. **2.** Hot and humid; sultry; torrid: *tropical climate.* **—trop′i•cal•ly** *adv.*

tropical fish. Any of many kinds of small, usually brightly colored fish native to tropical waters and often kept in home aquariums.

tropical year. The interval of time between two successive passages of the sun through the vernal equinox; a period of about 365.24 days.

tropic of Cancer. The parallel of latitude 23 degrees 27 minutes north of the equator, forming the boundary between the North Temperate Zone and the Torrid Zone.

tropic of Capricorn. The parallel of latitude 23 degrees 27 minutes south of the equator, forming the boundary between the South Temperate Zone and the Torrid Zone.

tro•pism |**trō′**pĭz′əm| *n.* Growth or movement of a plant or animal in response to a stimulus. Such growth or movement toward the stimulus is called **positive tropism,** and growth or movement away from the stimulus is called **negative tropism.** See **geotropism, phototropism. —tro•pis′tic** *adj.*

tro•po•pause |**trō′**pə pôz′| *n.* The boundary between the upper troposphere and the lower stratosphere, varying in altitude from 5 miles at the poles to 11 miles at the equator.

tro•po•sphere |**trō′**pə sfîr′| *or* |**trŏp′**ə-| *n.* The lowest region of the atmosphere, bounded by the surface of the earth and the tropopause and characterized by temperatures that decrease with increasing altitude.

trot |trŏt| *n.* **1.** A running gait of a horse or other four-footed animal in which the left front foot and the right hind foot move forward together in alternation with the right front foot and the left hind foot. **2.** A jogging run or quick walk: *Joe was tired after his trot around the playing field.* **3.** *Informal.* A word-for-word translation of a work in a foreign language, sometimes used secretly in preparing a class assignment; a pony. *—v.* **trot•ted, trot•ting. 1.** To move or ride at a trot: *The horses trotted down the road. She trotted her pony around the ring.* **2.** To run or walk quickly: *A little old lady trotted up to him.* ***—phrasal verb.*** **trot out.** *Informal.* To bring out and show for others to look at or admire.

troth |trôth| *or* |trōth| *n. Archaic.* **1.** Good faith; fidelity. **2.** One's pledged fidelity; betrothal.

Trots•ky |**trŏt′**skē|, **Leon.** 1879–1940. Russian revolutionary leader.

trot•ter |**trŏt′**ər| *n.* **1.** A horse that trots, especially one trained to go at a trot, as for racing. **2.** *Informal.* A foot, especially a pig's foot used as food.

trou•ba•dour |**trōō′**bə dôr′| *or* |-dōr′| *or* |-dŏŏr′| *n.* A poet of the 12th and 13th centuries in southeastern France and northern Italy who composed and sang songs and poems.

trou•ble |**trŭb′**əl| *n.* **1. a.** Difficulty: *I'm having trouble getting this door open.* **b.** Danger or distress: *A hero rose to rescue his country in its hour of greatest trouble.* **2. a.** A difficult, dangerous, or distressing situation: *The ship was in trouble and signaled for help.* **b.** A situation in which one is blamed for doing wrong: *The boys were always getting into trouble.* **3.** A source of difficulty, annoyance, or distress; a problem or worry: *The dog won't be any extra trouble.* **4.** Extra work or effort; bother; inconvenience: *They went to a lot of trouble on our account.* **5.** Conflict, disturbance, or unrest: *There was often trouble between cowboys and farmers.* **6. a.** Failure to perform properly; malfunction: *The car had engine trouble.* **b.** A diseased or disordered condition: *stomach trouble.* **7.** Difficulty considered as a person: *Wherever we go, trouble follows.* *—v.* **trou•bled, trou•bling. 1.** To make anxious or uneasy; disturb, worry, or upset: *The thought that there might be a prowler outside troubled me.* **2. a.** To bother: *May I trouble you for the time?* **b.** To take pains or be inconvenienced: *Don't trouble to see me off.* **3.** To be the matter with: *What troubles the patient?* **—trou′bled** *adj.: troubled waters; a troubled mind.* [SEE NOTE]

trouble
"Never trouble trouble, till trouble troubles you." (Old proverb).

trou•ble•mak•er |**trŭb′**əl mā′kər| *n.* A person who habitually stirs up trouble.

trou•ble•shoot•er |**trŭb′**əl shōō′tər| *n.* A person who locates and eliminates trouble.

trou•ble•some |**trŭb′**əl səm| *adj.* **1.** Causing trouble, especially repeatedly; worrisome: *a troublesome child; a troublesome car.* **2.** Difficult; trying: *a troublesome situation.*

trough |trôf| *or* |trŏf| *n.* **1.** A long, narrow, generally shallow receptacle, especially one for holding water or feed for animals. **2.** A gutter under the eaves of a roof. **3.** A long, narrow depression, as between waves or ridges. **4.** An extended region of low atmospheric pressure, often associated with a front.

trounce |trouns| *v.* **trounced, trounc•ing. 1.** To thrash; beat. **2.** To defeat decisively: *The Knicks trounced the Bullets last night in Baltimore.*

troupe |trōōp| *n.* A company or group, especially of touring actors, singers, or dancers. ¶*These sound alike* **troupe, troop. —troup′er** *n.*

trou•sers |**trou′**zərz| *n. (used with a plural verb).* **1.** An outer garment worn from the waist down and divided into sections that fit each leg separately. **2. trouser.** One of the legs on a pair of trousers: *He snagged his left trouser.* ***—modifier:*** *a trouser pocket.*

trous•seau |**trōō′**sō| *or* |trōō **sō′**| *n., pl.* **trous•seaux** |**trōō′**sōz| *or* |trōō **sōz′**| or **trous•seaus.** A wardrobe assembled by a bride before her marriage.

trout |trout| *n., pl.* **trout.** Any of several chiefly freshwater fishes often having a speckled body and related to the salmon, highly regarded as food and for sport. [SEE PICTURE]

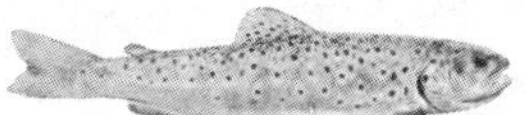

trout

trout lily. The **dogtooth violet.**

trow•el |**trou′**əl| *n.* **1.** A tool with a flat blade for spreading or smoothing such substances as plaster and cement. **2.** A tool with a scoop-shaped blade for turning up earth. [SEE PICTURE]

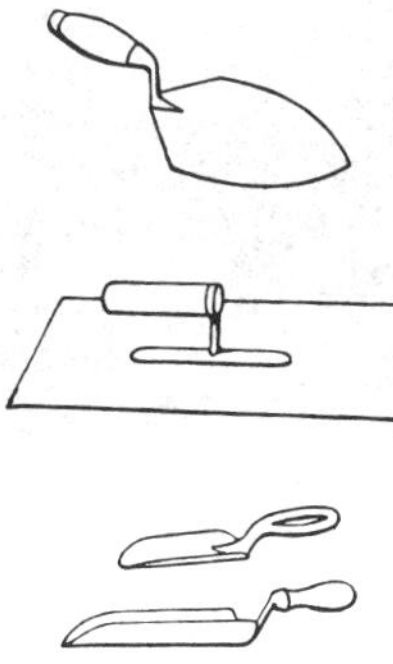

trowel
brick
plaster
garden

troy |troi| *adj.* Of, measured in, or expressed in troy weight.

Troy |troi|. An ancient city lying in what is now

truss
Bridge supported by trusses

ă pat/ā pay/â care/ä father/ĕ pet/ ē be/ĭ pit/ī pie/î fierce/ŏ pot/ ō go/ô paw, for/oi oil/ŏŏ book/ ōō boot/ou out/ŭ cut/û fur/ *th* the/th thin/hw which/zh vision/ ə ago, item, pencil, atom, circus

northwestern Turkey, the site of the Trojan War.

troy weight. A system of weights in which the grain is the same as in the avoirdupois system, one ounce equals 480 grains, and one pound equals 12 ounces.

tru•ant |trōō′ənt| *n.* **1.** A student who is absent from school without permission. **2.** A person who shirks his work or duty. *—adj.* **1.** Absent without permission: *a truant pupil.* **2.** Idle, lazy, or neglectful: *a truant worker.* **3.** Of or concerned with truants or truancy: *A truant officer investigated the case.* —**tru′an•cy** *n.*

truce |trōōs| *n.* A temporary cessation of hostilities by agreement of the contending forces; an armistice.

truck[1] |trŭk| *n.* **1.** Any of various automotive vehicles, made in a wide range of sizes and types for carrying loads of freight, materials, etc. **2.** A swiveling frame under each end of a railroad car, streetcar, etc., on which the wheels are mounted. *—modifier: a truck driver.* *—v.* **1.** To transport (goods) by truck. **2.** To drive a truck.

truck[2] |trŭk| *n.* **1.** Vegetables and fruit raised for marketing. **2.** *Informal.* Worthless stuff; rubbish. **3.** *Informal.* Dealings: *He is too high and mighty to have any truck with ordinary people.* *—modifier: a truck farm; truck gardeners.*

truck•le |trŭk′əl| *n.* **1.** A small wheel or roller; caster. **2.** A **trundle bed.** *—v.* **truck•led, truck•ling.** To be servile; yield weakly: *always truckling to people who have money.*

truck•load |trŭk′lōd′| *n.* The quantity or weight that a truck carries.

truc•u•lent |trŭk′yə lənt| *adj.* **1.** Savage and cruel; fierce: *truculent warriors.* **2.** Pugnacious; defiant: *a truculent small boy.* **3.** Scathingly harsh; caustic: *a truculent article devoted mostly to blackening his reputation.* —**truc′u•lence** *n.* —**truc′u•lent•ly** *adv.*

trudge |trŭj| *v.* **trudged, trudg•ing.** To walk in a heavy-footed way; plod: *roads filled with men and women trudging along, carrying pottery, chairs, or vegetables.*

true |trōō| *adj.* **tru•er, tru•est.** **1.** Consistent with fact or reality; right; accurate: *Is this statement true or false?* **2.** Not imitation or counterfeit; real or genuine: *true gold.* **3.** Not seeming; actual: *Is your estimate of the distance larger or smaller than the true distance?* **4.** Not fictitious; factual: *true accounts of modern efforts to explore the oceans.* **5.** Faithful; loyal: *Be true to your love.* **6.** Rightful; legitimate: *the true heir to the fortune.* **7. a.** Rightfully bearing the name; properly so called: *The true vampire bat can be found only in the New World.* **b.** Having the characteristics associated with a certain group or type; typical: *He was lusty and thickset, a true Dutchman.* **c.** Exactly conforming to an original or standard: *a true copy of the birth certificate.* **8.** Determined with reference to the earth's axis, not the magnetic poles: *true north.* *—adv.* **1.** Rightly; truthfully: *She speaks true.* **2.** Without swerving from a course; accurately: *I'll sail the ship straight and true.* *—v.* **trued, tru•ing** or **true•ing.** To adjust or fit so as to conform with a standard: *true the edges of a seam.*

***Idioms.* come true.** To be realized in actuality; become fact: *His wish to be healthy, wealthy, and wise came true.* **true to life.** Realistic.

truf•fle |trŭf′əl| *n.* A fleshy blackish or light-brown fungus that grows underground and is regarded as a food delicacy.

tru•ism |trōō′ĭz′əm| *n.* A statement of an obvious truth. For example, *Luck is a matter of being prepared when opportunity knocks* is a truism.

tru•ly |trōō′lē| *adv.* **1.** Sincerely; genuinely: *She truly felt at home in her new room.* **2.** Truthfully; accurately: *Chow mein is a dish of Chinese origin, but it can truly be said to be as American as hot dogs or hamburgers.* **3.** Indeed: *The view from the hilltop is truly magnificent.*

Tru•man |trōō′mən|, **Harry S** 1884–1972 Thirty-third President of the United States (1945–53).

trump |trŭmp| *n.* In card games, any card of a suit declared to outrank all other cards during the play of a hand. *—v.* **1.** To take (a card or trick) with a trump. **2.** To play a trump card. —***phrasal verb.* trump up.** To devise fraudulently; concoct: *trump up charges against someone.*

trump•er•y |trŭm′pə rē| *n., pl.* **trump•er•ies.** **1.** Showy but worthless finery. **2.** Nonsense.

trum•pet |trŭm′pĭt| *n.* **1.** A high-pitched brass wind instrument consisting of a long metal tube, usually coiled, with a mouthpiece at one end and a flaring bell at the other. Modern trumpets are equipped with valves that change the pitch of the tube and allow a complete scale to be played throughout the range. **2.** An organ stop that imitates the sound of a trumpet. **3.** Something shaped like a trumpet: *the yellow trumpets of the daffodils.* *—v.* **1.** To play a trumpet. **2.** To make a loud, resounding sound like that of a trumpet: *Elephants trumpeted in the shadows and snakes slithered among the trees.* **3.** To shout or announce loudly: *"Let the ball begin!" trumpeted the master of ceremonies.* —**trum′pet•er** *n.*

trun•cheon |trŭn′chən| *n.* A short stick carried by policemen.

trun•dle |trŭn′dl| *v.* **trun•dled, trund•ling.** **1.** To push or propel on wheels or rollers: *trundling a wheelbarrow down the streets.* **2.** To move along by or as if by rolling: *Shopping carts laden with groceries trundled past.* —**trund′ler** *n.*

trundle bed. A low bed on casters that can be rolled under another bed when not in use.

trunk |trŭngk| *n.* **1.** The often tall, thick woody main stem of a tree. **2.** The main part of the body, not including the arms, legs, and head. **3.** A main part or section, as of a railroad, blood vessel, etc., not including parts that branch off. **4.** A large box or case with a lid that clasps shut, used for packing clothes or belongings, as for travel or storage. **5.** A covered compartment of an automobile, used for luggage or storage. **6.** A long, flexible snout, especially of an elephant, used for grasping and holding. **7. trunks.** Men's shorts worn for swimming or athletics. **8.** A **trunk line.** *—modifier: the trunk muscles; a trunk road.*

trunk line. **1.** A line that makes a direct connection between two telephone switchboards. **2.** The main line of a communications system or transportation system.

truss |trŭs| *n.* **1.** A device worn to support a hernia so that it will not enlarge or spread. **2.** A framework of beams or bars, often arranged in triangles, used to support a roof, bridge, or other structure. —*v.* **1.** To support or brace with a truss. **2.** To bind the wings and legs of (a fowl) before cooking. **3.** To tie up securely; bind. [SEE PICTURE on p. 924]

trust |trŭst| *v.* **1.** To have or place confidence in as being dependable or reliable: *You shouldn't trust him. Trust my judgment.* **2.** To depend, rely, or count on: *Can we trust you to pay back what we lend you?* **3.** To place in the care or keeping of another; entrust: *She trusted the children to a baby sitter.* **4.** To allow to have money or goods on credit: *Will you trust me until payday?* **5.** To believe: *If you don't trust me, see for yourself.* **6.** To hope, expect, or assume: *All went well, I trust.* —**trust'ed** *adj.*: *a trusted friend.* —***phrasal verb.*** **trust in** (or **to**). To rely or depend on: *She trusted in her swift legs to save her. We'll have to trust to luck.* —*n.* **1.** Confidence or firm belief in the honesty, dependability, or power of someone or something: *He trusted you, and you must live up to that trust.* **2.** Trustfulness; faith: *The child was all innocence and trust.* **3.** A solemn responsibility or duty placed upon someone; a charge: *Public office is a public trust.* **4.** Custody; care: *They placed the child in my trust.* **5.** Confidence in a buyer's intention and ability to pay at some future time; credit: *We don't sell groceries on trust.* **6.** Property held and managed by one party for the benefit of another. **7.** A group of firms or corporations that have combined for the purpose of reducing competition and controlling prices throughout a business or industry.

trus•tee |trŭ stē'| *n.* **1.** A person or firm that holds and administers another person's property or assets. **2.** A member of a group or board that manages the affairs of a college, foundation, etc.

trus•tee•ship |trŭ stē'shĭp'| *n.* **1.** The position or function of a trustee. **2. a.** The administration of a territory by a country or countries so commissioned by the United Nations. **b.** A territory so administered; a trust territory.

trust•ful |trŭst'fəl| *adj.* Full of trust; inclined to believe readily: *a child's trustful eyes; a trustful person.* —**trust'ful•ly** *adv.* —**trust'ful•ness** *n.*

trust fund. Money, securities, real estate, etc., belonging to one person but managed for his benefit by another.

trust territory. A territory placed under the administration of a country or countries by the United Nations.

trust•wor•thy |trŭst'wûr'*th*ē| *adj.* Dependable; reliable: *a trustworthy secretary.*

trust•y |trŭs'tē| *adj.* **trust•i•er, trust•i•est.** Dependable; faithful: *a trusty servant.* —*n., pl.* **trust•ies.** A trusted person, especially a convict granted special privileges.

truth |tro͞oth| *n., pl.* **truths** |tro͞o*th*z| *or* |tro͞oths|. **1.** Conformity to knowledge, fact, or actuality; veracity: *a story with an appearance of truth.* **2.** Something that is the case; the real state of affairs: *tell the truth; speak the truth.* **3.** Reality; actuality: *At Appomattox, the other Confederate forces gave up, and the Civil War was in truth over.* **4.** A statement proven to be or accepted as true: *scientific truths.* **5.** Sincerity; honesty: *There was no truth in his speech and no integrity in his character.*

truth•ful |tro͞oth'fəl| *adj.* **1.** Consistently telling the truth; honest: *a truthful person.* **2.** Corresponding to reality; true: *a truthful account of the events.* —**truth'ful•ly** *adv.* —**truth'ful•ness** *n.*

try |trī| *v.* **tried, try•ing, tries. 1.** To taste, sample, or otherwise test in order to determine quality, worth, desirability, or effect: *try the special dinner; try heat treatments; try out a new ranch hand.* **2. a.** To examine or hear (a case) in a court of law. **b.** To put (a person accused of crime or other wrong) on trial in a court. **3.** To cause to undergo great strain or hardship; tax: *a task that tried his strength and his nerves.* **4.** To attempt; make an effort; strive: *Try to understand. Everyone can't succeed, but everyone should try.* **5. a.** To melt (fat or lard) so as to separate oil from impurities; render. **b.** To extract or refine (metal) by heating. —***phrasal verbs.*** **try on.** To put on (a garment or shoes) so as to test fit or appearance. **try out for.** To take or undergo a test in an attempt to qualify: *tried out for the debating team.* —*n., pl.* **tries.** An attempt; an effort.

try•ing |trī'ĭng| *adj.* Causing severe strain, hardship, annoyance, etc.: *a trying journey through the desert; trying circumstances; his trying wife.*

try•out |trī'out'| *n.* A test to evaluate or find out qualifications of applicants, as for a theatrical role.

try•pan•o•some |trĭ păn'ə sōm'| *n.* Any of several parasitic microorganisms that are carried into the bloodstream of human beings and other animals by the bite of insects, and that can cause serious diseases such as sleeping sickness.

try square. A carpenter's tool consisting of a ruled metal straightedge set at right angles to a straight bar, used for measuring work that is to be cut or joined squarely. [SEE PICTURE]

tryst |trĭst| *n.* **1.** An agreement between lovers to meet. **2.** The meeting or meeting place so arranged.

tsar |zär| *n.* A form of the word **czar.**

tsar•e•vitch |zär'ə vĭch| *n.* A form of the word **czarevitch.**

tsa•rev•na |zä rĕv'nə| *n.* A form of the word **czarevna.**

tsa•ri•na |zä rē'nə| *n.* A form of the word **czarina.**

tset•se fly |tsĕt'sē| *or* |tsē'tsē|. A bloodsucking African fly that carries and transmits by its bite the microorganisms that cause sleeping sickness.

Tshi |chwē| *or* |chē| *n.* A form of the word **Twi.**

T-shirt |tē'shûrt'| *n.* A short-sleeved, collarless undergarment worn especially by men.

tsp. teaspoon; teaspoonful.

T-square |tē'skwâr'| *n.* A ruler with a short crosspiece at one end, used for drawing parallel lines. [SEE PICTURE]

tsu•na•mi |tso͝o nä'mē| *n.* A very large ocean wave, often extremely destructive when it strikes land, caused by an underwater earthquake or volcanic eruption.

tu•a•ta•ra |to͞o'ə tär'ə| *n.* A lizardlike reptile of New Zealand that is the only living member of a group that flourished during the time of the dinosaurs. [SEE PICTURE]

tub |tŭb| *n.* **1.** A round, wide, open wooden container used for packing, storing, or washing. **2.** A bathtub.

tu•ba |to͞o'bə| *or* |tyo͞o'-| *n.* A large brass wind

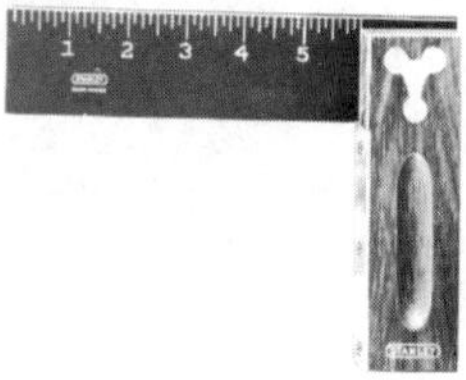

try square

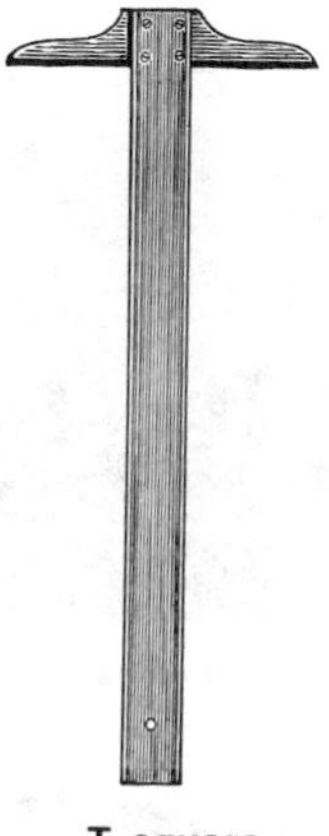

T-square

tuatara

instrument having a full, mellow tone and a bass range, using several valves to change its pitch.

tub•by |tŭb′ē| *adj.* **tub•bi•er, tub•bi•est.** Short and fat.

tube |to͞ob| *or* |tyo͞ob| *n.* **1.** A hollow cylinder of metal, glass, rubber, or other material, used to carry liquids. **2.** An **inner tube. 3.** A tubelike organ of the body: *the bronchial tubes.* **4.** A small, flexible container with a screw cap at one end, used for holding toothpaste and similar substances that can be squeezed out. **5.** A subway tunnel. **6.** The part of a wind instrument that extends from the mouthpiece to the end that is open to the air. —**tube′less** *adj.*

tubeless tire. A tire, as for an automobile, in which the air is contained between the body of the tire itself and the rim on which it is mounted, with no inner tube being used.

tu•ber |to͞o′bər| *or* |tyo͞o′-| *n.* A swollen, usually underground stem, such as a potato, bearing buds from which new plants grow.

tu•ber•cle |to͞o′bər kəl| *or* |tyo͞o′-| *n.* **1.** A small knoblike or lumplike protuberance, as on the roots of certain plants or on skin or a bone. **2.** One or more swellings of this kind on skin or a bone, characteristic of tuberculosis.

tu•ber•cu•lar |to͝o **bûr′**kyə lər| *or* |tyo͝o-| *adj.* **1.** Of or covered with tubercles. **2.** Of or affected with tuberculosis. —*n.* Someone who is afflicted with tuberculosis.

tu•ber•cu•late |to͝o **bûr′**kyə lĭt| *or* |-lāt′| *or* |tyo͝o-| *adj.* Tubercular.

tu•ber•cu•lin |to͝o **bûr′**kyə lĭn| *or* |tyo͝o-| *n.* A substance derived from cultures of the bacteria that cause tuberculosis, used in testing for and treating the disease.

tu•ber•cu•lo•sis |to͝o bûr′kyə **lō′**sĭs| *or* |tyo͝o-| *n.* A contagious disease of human beings and animals, caused by bacteria and producing lesions of the lungs, bones, and other body tissues.

tu•ber•cu•lous |to͝o **bûr′**kyə ləs| *adj.* Of, having, or caused by tuberculosis or tubercles.

tube•rose[1] |**to͞ob′**rōz′| *or* |**tyo͞ob′**-| *or* |**to͞o′**bə-rōz′| *or* |**tyo͞o′**-| *n.* A plant having a tuberous root and white flowers with a strong, heavy fragrance.

tu•ber•ose[2] |**to͞o′**bə rōs′| *or* |**tyo͞o′**-| *n.* A form of the word **tuberous.**

tu•ber•ous |**to͞o′**bə rəs| *or* |**tyo͞o′**-| *adj.* Having or consisting of a tuber: *tuberous roots.*

tub•ing |**to͞o′**bĭng| *or* |**tyo͞o′**-| *n.* **1.** Tubes in general. **2.** A system of tubes. **3.** A piece or length of tube.

tu•bu•lar |**to͞o′**byə lər| *or* |**tyo͞o′**-| *adj.* Of, being, or made of a tube or tubes.

tu•bule |**to͞o′**byo͞ol′| *or* |**tyo͞o′**-| *n.* A very small tube or tube-shaped part.

tuck |tŭk| *n.* A narrow pleat or fold stitched in a garment primarily for shaping. —*v.* **1.** To make tucks in. **2.** To gather up and fold; turn under in order to secure or confine: *He tucked the shirt into his trousers.* **3.** To cover or wrap snugly: *tucked the baby in and turned off the light.* **4. a.** To put in an out-of-the-way and snug place: *a cabin tucked among the pines.* **b.** To store in a safe spot; save: *tuck away a bit of lace.*

tuck•er[1] |**tŭk′**ər| *v.* To weary; exhaust: *The long climb up the hill tuckered him out.*

tuck•er[2] |**tŭk′**ər| *n.* A piece of lace, linen, or other material formerly worn over or tucked into a low-cut bodice.

Tuc•son |**to͞o′**sŏn′|. A resort city in southern Arizona. Population, 258,000.

Tues. Tuesday.

Tues•day |**to͞oz′**dē| *or* |-dā′| *or* |**tyo͞oz′**-| *n.* The third day of the week, after Monday and before Wednesday. —***modifier:*** *a Tuesday afternoon.*

tu•fa |**to͞o′**fə| *or* |**tyo͞o′**-| *n.* **1.** The rock material, rich in calcium and silicon, deposited by lakes, springs, or ground water. **2.** Tuff.

tuff |tŭf| *n.* A rock made up of particles of volcanic ash, varying from fine sand to coarse gravel in size, pressed together. ¶*These sound alike* **tuff, tough.**

tuft |tŭft| *n.* **1.** A cluster of hair, feathers, grass, yarn, etc., growing or held close together at the base. **2.** A button or clump of threads drawn through a mattress or cushion to make depressions in it. —*v.* To decorate or supply with a tuft or tufts. —**tuft′ed** *adj.: a tufted helmet.*

tug |tŭg| *v.* **1.** To pull at vigorously: *She tugged at the rope with all her might.* **2.** To move by pulling with great effort or exertion: *tugging a chair across the room.* **3.** To tow with a tugboat. —*n.* **1.** A strong pull. **2.** A tugboat.

tug•boat |**tŭg′**bōt′| *n.* A very powerful small boat designed for towing larger vessels. [SEE PICTURE]

tugboat

tug of war. A contest between two groups of persons who tug on opposite ends of a rope trying to pull the opposing group over a line halfway between them.

tu•i•tion |to͝o **ĭsh′**ən| *or* |tyo͝o-| *n.* **1.** A fee for instruction, especially at a college or private school. **2.** Instruction; teaching.

tu•la•re•mi•a |to͞o′lə **rē′**mē ə| *or* |tyo͞o′-| *n.* A contagious disease of rodents and other small mammals, caused by bacteria and transmitted to human beings by insects or by handling of infected animals.

tu•lip |**to͞o′**lĭp| *or* |**tyo͞o′**-| *n.* **1.** A garden plant that grows from a bulb and has showy, colorful, cup-shaped flowers. **2.** A flower of such a plant. [SEE PICTURE]

tulip

tulle |to͞ol| *n.* A fine starched net used for veils, gowns, etc. ¶*These sound alike* **tulle, tool.**

tum•ble |**tŭm′**bəl| *v.* **tum•bled, tum•bling. 1.** To perform acrobatic feats, such as somersaults. **2.** To fall or roll end over end: *The kittens tumbled over each other.* **3.** To spill or roll out in confusion or disorder: *Schoolchildren tumbled out of the bus.* **4.** To pitch headlong; fall: *she tumbled downstairs.* **5.** To drop: *Prices tumbled.* **6.** To cause to fall; bring down: *tumbling logs out of a truck.* —*n.* **1.** An act of tumbling; a fall. **2.** A condition of confusion or disorder.

tum•bler |**tŭm′**blər| *n.* **1.** An acrobat or gymnast. **2.** A drinking glass having no handle or stem. **3.** The part in a lock that releases the bolt when turned by a key.

tum•ble•weed |**tŭm′**bəl wēd′| *n.* A weedy plant that has very dense branches and that when withered is broken off and rolled about by the wind.

tum•bling |**tŭm′**blĭng| *n.* The skill or practice of gymnastic falling, rolling, or somersaulting.

tum•brel or **tum•bril** |**tŭm′**brəl| *n.* **1.** A two-wheeled farmer's cart that can be tilted to dump

ă pat/ā pay/â care/ä father/ĕ pet/ ē be/ĭ pit/ī pie/î fierce/ŏ pot/ ō go/ô paw, for/oi oil/o͝o book/ o͞o boot/ou out/ŭ cut/û fur/ *th* the/th thin/hw which/zh vision/ ə ago, item, pencil, atom, circus

a load. **2.** A cart used to carry condemned prisoners to the guillotine during the French Revolution.

tum•my |tŭm'ē| *n., pl.* **tum•mies.** *Informal.* The stomach.

tu•mor |to͞o'mər| *or* |tyo͞o'-| *n.* **1.** A confined mass of tissue, developed without inflammation from normal tissue, but having an abnormal structure and rate of growth and serving no function within the body. **2.** Any abnormal swelling within the body.

tu•mult |to͞o'məlt| *or* |tyo͞o'-| *n.* **1.** The din and commotion of a great crowd. **2.** Agitation of the mind or emotions. —**tu•mul'tu•ous** |to͞o mŭl'cho͞o əs| *or* |tyo͞o-| *adj.*

tun |tŭn| *n.* **1.** A large cask for liquids, especially wine. **2.** A measure of liquid capacity used mainly for wine, especially one equal to 252 gallons. ¶*These sound alike* **tun, ton.**

tu•na[1] |to͞o'nə| *or* |tyo͞o'-| *n., pl.* **tu•na** or **tu•nas.** **1. a.** A large ocean fish caught in large numbers for food. **b.** Any of several related food fishes, such as the albacore and the bonito. **2.** Also **tuna fish.** The flesh of any of these fishes, usually canned.

tu•na[2] |to͞o'nə| *or* |tyo͞o'-| *n.* A spiny tropical American cactus, a kind of prickly pear.

tun•dra |tŭn'drə| *n.* A cold, treeless area of arctic regions, having only low-growing mosses, lichens, and stunted shrubs as plant life.

tune |to͞on| *or* |tyo͞on| *n.* **1.** A melody, especially a simple and easily remembered one. **2.** Correct musical pitch: *a piano out of tune.* **3.** Agreement in musical pitch or key: *a piano soloist and orchestra not in tune.* **4.** Agreement or harmony: *ideas in tune with the times.* —*v.* **tuned, tun•ing. 1.** To put in proper musical pitch: *tune a violin.* **2.** To adjust (an engine) for top performance. **3.** To adjust or adapt (oneself) to surroundings or a manner of living or thinking. —***phrasal verbs.*** **tune in.** To adjust a radio or television receiver so as to get (a particular broadcast). **tune out.** To adjust a radio or television receiver so as no longer to get (a particular broadcast). **tune up. 1.** To adjust (a musical instrument) to a desired pitch or key. **2.** To adjust (a machine or machinery) so as to put it into proper condition. **3.** To prepare oneself for a specified activity.

Idioms. **change (one's) tune.** To change one's way of thinking or acting. **to the tune of.** To the sum or extent of: *awarded back salary to the tune of $40,000.*

tune•ful |to͞on'fəl| *or* |tyo͞on'-| *adj.* Full of melody or melodies; melodious. —**tune'ful•ly** *adv.*

tun•er |to͞o'nər| *or* |tyo͞o'-| *n.* **1.** Someone or something that tunes: *a piano tuner.* **2. a.** The part of a radio or television receiver that selects the signal that is to be amplified and demodulated. **b.** A device for use with high-fidelity sound systems, consisting of a radio receiver that lacks only loudspeakers and the amplifiers that drive them.

tune-up |to͞on'ŭp'| *or* |tyo͞on'-| *n.* The act or process of adjusting an engine or motor for best operation.

tung oil |tŭng|. A yellowish or brownish oil extracted from the seeds of an Asian tree, the **tung tree,** and used as a drying agent in paints and varnishes and for waterproofing.

tung•sten |tŭng'stən| *n.* Symbol **W** One of the elements, a hard gray-to-white metal that is very resistant to corrosion and high temperatures. Atomic number 74; atomic weight 183.85; valences +2, +3, +4, +5, +6; melting point 3,410°C; boiling point 5,927°C. [SEE NOTE]

tu•nic |to͞o'nĭk| *or* |tyo͞o'-| *n.* **1.** A loose-fitting, knee-length garment worn in ancient Greece and Rome. **2.** A fitted outer garment usually hip-length and often part of a uniform. **3.** A short belted dress worn for sports and over slacks by women.

tuning fork. A device that resembles a small, two-pronged fork and that sounds a tone of fixed pitch when struck, used as a reference, as in tuning musical instruments. [SEE PICTURE]

Tu•nis |to͞o'nĭs| *or* |tyo͞o'-|. The capital of Tunisia. Population, 800,000.

Tu•ni•sia |to͞o nē'zhə| *or* |-shə| *or* |-nĭzh'ə| *or* |-nĭsh'ə| *or* |tyo͞o-|. A country in northern Africa, on the Mediterranean Sea. Population, 5,641,000. Capital, Tunis. —**Tu•ni'sian** *adj. & n.*

tun•nel |tŭn'əl| *n.* An underground or underwater passage. —*v.* **tun•neled** or **tun•nelled, tun•nel•ing** or **tun•nel•ling. 1.** To make a tunnel under or through. **2.** To dig in the form of a tunnel.

tun•ny |tŭn'ē| *n., pl.* **tun•nies** or **tun•ny.** *Chiefly British.* A fish, the tuna.

tu•pe•lo |to͞o'pə lō'| *n., pl.* **tu•pe•los. 1.** Any of several trees with bluish-black berries and wood with a twisted grain. **2.** The wood of such a tree.

Tu•pi |to͞o pē'| *or* |to͞o'pē'| *n., pl.* **Tu•pi** or **Tu•pis. 1.** A group of South American Indian peoples of Brazil, now living only in the Amazon River valley and in Paraguay. **2.** A member of any of these peoples. **3.** The language of these peoples, related to Guarani. —**Tu'pi•an** *adj.*

tur•ban |tûr'bən| *n.* **1.** An eastern headdress consisting of a long scarf, often of cotton, linen, or silk, wound around the head. **2.** Any similar headdress.

tur•bid |tûr'bĭd| *adj.* **1.** Having sediment or foreign particles stirred up or suspended: *turbid water.* **2.** Heavy, dark, or dense, as smoke. **3.** In turmoil; muddled: *turbid feelings.* —**tur'bid•ness, tur•bid'i•ty** *n.*

tur•bine |tûr'bĭn| *or* |-bīn'| *n.* Any of various machines in which the kinetic energy of a liquid or gas, often at a high temperature, is converted to rotary motion as the fluid reacts with a series of vanes, paddles, etc., arranged about the circumference of one or more wheels.

tur•bo |tûr'bō| *n. Informal.* A turbine or a device driven by a turbine, such as a turbocharger.

tur•bo•charg•er |tûr'bō chär'jər| *n.* A device that uses the exhaust gas of an internal-combustion engine to drive a turbine that in turn drives a supercharger attached to the engine.

tur•bo•jet |tûr'bō jĕt'| *n.* **1.** A jet engine in which the exhaust gas operates a turbine that in turn drives a compressor that forces air into the intake of the engine. **2.** An aircraft powered by an engine or engines of this type.

tur•bo•prop |tûr'bō prŏp'| *n.* **1.** A turbojet engine that drives an external propeller as well as producing jet propulsion. **2.** An aircraft powered by an engine or engines of this type.

tungsten

Tungsten *and its alloys are used in structural parts that must resist high temperatures and in electric heating elements, especially those used in lamps. Its symbol,* **W,** *is taken from* wolfram, *its German name.*

tuning fork

tur•bot |tûr′bət| *n., pl.* **tur•bot** or **tur•bots.** A European flatfish highly regarded as food.

tur•bu•lent |tûr′byə lənt| *adj.* **1.** Violently agitated or disturbed; stormy: *turbulent waters.* **2.** Causing unrest or disturbance: *turbulent fellows.* **3.** In a condition of turbulent flow, as a liquid or gas. —**tur′bu•lence** *n.*

turbulent flow. Movement of a fluid in which the pressure and velocity in any small region of the fluid fluctuate at random.

tu•reen |to͞o rēn′| *or* |tyo͞o-| *n.* A broad, deep dish with a cover, used for serving soup at the table.

turf |tûrf| *n.* **1.** A surface layer of earth containing a dense growth of grass and its matted roots; sod. **2.** A piece cut from this. **3.** A piece of peat used as fuel. **4.** *Slang.* The area claimed by a neighborhood gang as its territory. **5. the turf. a.** A racetrack where horses race. **b.** The sport or business of horse racing.

tur•gid |tûr′jĭd| *adj.* **1.** Swollen or distended, as by a fluid or inner pressure. **2.** Excessively grand or heavy in style or language: *The description runs on for 20 turgid pages.* —**tur•gid′i•ty, tur′gid•ness** *n.* —**tur′gid•ly** *adv.*

Turk |tûrk| *n.* A native or inhabitant of Turkey.

tur•key |tûr′kē| *n., pl.* **tur•keys. 1.** A large, brownish North American bird having a bare head and neck with fleshy wattles. It was once common in its wild form, but is now chiefly domesticated as a source of food. **2.** The meat of a turkey. —***modifier:*** *a turkey farm; a turkey dinner.* [SEE PICTURE]

Idiom. **talk turkey.** To discuss something in a direct, straightforward manner.

turkey
Above: Painting of a wild turkey by John James Audubon
Below: Domestic turkey

Tur•key |tûr′kē|. A country located primarily in western Asia with a small part in southeastern Europe. Population, 38,270,000. Capital, Ankara.

turkey buzzard. Also **turkey vulture.** An American vulture with dark feathers and a bare red head and neck.

Turk•ish |tûr′kĭsh| *n.* The language of Turkey. —*adj.* Of Turkey, the Turks, or their language.

tur•mer•ic |tûr′mər ĭk| *n.* The yellowish, spicy root of an Asian plant, powdered and used as a seasoning, especially in curries.

tur•moil |tûr′moil′| *n.* A condition of great confusion or disturbance: *The 17th and 18th centuries saw Europe in religious turmoil. The turmoil of waves was created by the reefs at the entrance of the bay.*

turn |tûrn| *v.* **1.** To move or cause to move around an axis or center; rotate; revolve: *a car wheel turning; turn the hands of a clock.* **2.** To perform or accomplish by rotating or revolving: *turn handsprings.* **3.** To appear to revolve or whirl, as in dizziness: *as the walls turned wildly.* **4.** To roll from side to side or back and forth: *a ship pitching and turning.* **5.** To change or cause to change direction or course: *He turned and waved. She turned the car into a side street.* **6.** To move or cause to move in an opposite direction or course; reverse: *His condition turned for the worse. The strategy turned the tide of battle.* **7.** To make a course or way around or about: *They turned the corner.* **8.** To direct one's way or course in a specified manner: *Turn west here.* **9.** To set or direct in a specified way; point; focus: *turned the hose on him; turning his gaze to the ceiling.* **10. a.** To direct (one's attention, interest, or mind) toward or away from something: *turned his thoughts to home.* **b.** To direct or withdraw attention or interest: *turned to new pursuits.* **11.** To change the position of so that the underside becomes the upper side: *turn the pancakes; turned the worn collar; turning the page.* **12.** To transform; change: *caterpillars turning into butterflies.* **13.** To exchange; convert: *turning spare time into earnings.* **14.** To change color or change to a specified color: *leaves turning in fall; felt his face turning red.* **15.** To make sour; ferment: *Hot weather turned the milk.* **16.** To shape or form: *turned wood in a lathe; turned a phrase neatly.* **17.** To injure by twisting: *turned his ankle.* **18.** To upset or make nauseated: *Greasy food turns my stomach.* **19.** To change the disposition of: *success that turned his head.* **20.** To make or become hostile or antagonistic: *turned brother against brother; a dog turning on his master.* **21.** To adopt a new religion, political party, or other beliefs or loyalties. **22.** To become, reach, or surpass (a certain age, time, or amount). **23.** To get by buying or selling; gain: *turn a modest profit.* —***phrasal verbs.*** **turn away.** To send away; reject: *She couldn't turn away her son.* **turn down. 1.** To reduce the volume, degree, speed, or flow of: *turn down the heat.* **2.** *Informal.* To reject or refuse (a person or a request, suggestion, etc.). **3.** To change the position of by folding, twisting, or bending: *turn down the blankets.* **turn in. 1.** To turn or go into; enter. **2.** To hand in; give over; return or exchange. **3.** To deliver or give information about (a fugitive, wrongdoer, etc.) to persons in authority. **4.** *Informal.* To go to bed. **turn loose.** To send or let go; release. **turn off. 1.** To cause to stop the operation, activity, or flow of. **2.** To leave by making a turn. **turn on. 1.** To begin or cause to begin the operation, activity, or flow of: *a heater that turns on automatically.* **2.** To depend on for success, failure, or other result; hinge: *A chess match can turn on a single move.* **turn out. 1.** To shut off, as a light. **2.** To come out or assemble, as for a public event. **3.** To produce or create: *turned out a large amount of work.* **4.** To be found to be: *a rumor that turned out to be false.* **5.** To result; end up: *plans turning out perfectly.* **turn over. 1.** To bring the bottom to the top, or vice verse; reverse in position. **2.** To shift position, as by going over on a side surface. **3.** To go through at least one cycle of operation: *The engine finally turned over.* **4.** To think about; consider: *turned the idea over in his mind.* **5.** To transfer to another; give over. **turn to. 1.** To apply, appeal, or resort to (someone or something) for aid, support, information, etc.: *a friend to turn to in distress.* **2.** To begin work. **3.** To refer to (a specified page or section) in a book, etc. **turn up. 1.** To find or be found: *The search turned up new evidence. The missing wallet turned up in a trash can.* **2.** To make an appearance; arrive. **3.** To occur; happen. **4.** To increase the volume, degree, speed, or flow of. —*n.* **1.** The act of turning or the condition of being turned; a rotation or revolution. **2.** A change of direction, motion, or position, or the point of such a change: *a right turn; a turn in the road.* **3.** A point of change in time: *the turn of the century.*

ă pat/ā pay/â care/ä father/ĕ pet/ ē be/ĭ pit/ī pie/î fierce/ŏ pot/ ō go/ô paw, for/oi oil/o͝o book/ o͞o boot/ou out/ŭ cut/û fur/ *th* the/th thin/hw which/zh vision/ ə ago, item, pencil, atom, circus

4. A movement or development in the direction of: *a turn for the worse; an unusual turn of events.* **5.** A chance or opportunity to do something: *my turn to deal the cards.* **6.** A characteristic mood, style, or habit; an inclination; tendency: *a scientific turn of mind.* **7.** A deed or action having a specified effect on another: *did him a good turn.* **8.** A short tour or excursion. **9.** A twist or other distortion in shape. **10.** *Informal.* A momentary shock or scare: *The noise gave me quite a turn.* **11.** A brief theatrical act: *a vaudeville turn.* ¶ *These sound alike* **turn, tern.**

Idioms. **at every turn.** In every place; at every moment. **by turns.** Alternately; one after another. **out of turn.** Not in the proper order or sequence. **take turns.** To take part or do in order, one after another.

turn•buck•le |tûrn′bŭk′əl| *n.* A device for adjusting the tension of a rope or cable, consisting of an oblong center section with threaded holes at the ends that receive threaded rods to which the ends of the rope or cable are fastened. [SEE PICTURE]

turn•coat |tûrn′kōt′| *n.* A person who traitorously goes over to the opposite party; a traitor.

tur•nip |tûr′nĭp′| *n.* **1.** A plant of which the large, rounded yellowish or white root and the leaves are eaten as vegetables. **2.** The root of this plant. —***modifier:*** *turnip greens.*

turn•out |tûrn′out′| *n.* **1.** The act of turning out. **2.** The number of people at a gathering; attendance. **3.** An outfit.

turn•o•ver |tûrn′ō′vər| *n.* **1.** The act of turning over; an upset. **2.** An abrupt change; reversal. **3.** The number of times a particular stock of goods is sold and restocked during a given period. **4.** The amount of business transacted during a given period. **5.** The number of workers hired by an establishment to replace those who have left. **6.** A small pastry made by spreading a filling on half of a round or square piece of dough, turning the other half over the filling, and sealing the edges.

turn•pike |tûrn′pīk′| *n.* A road, especially a wide highway with tollgates.

turn•stile |tûrn′stīl′| *n.* A device for controlling or counting the number of persons entering a public area by admitting them one at a time between horizontal bars revolving on a central vertical post.

turn•ta•ble |tûrn′tā′bəl| *n.* **1.** A circular platform equipped with a railway track and capable of rotating, used for turning locomotives. **2. a.** The rotating circular platform of a phonograph on which the record is placed. **b.** A device for use with high-fidelity or stereo sound systems, consisting of a phonograph without amplifiers or loudspeakers. **3.** Any similar rotating platform or machine part.

tur•pen•tine |tûr′pən tīn′| *n.* **1.** A thin, easily vaporized oil composed of carbon and hydrogen and having the formula $C_{10}H_{16}$. It is distilled from the wood or resin of certain pine trees and used as a paint thinner, solvent, and liniment. **2.** The sticky mixture of resin and oil from which this oil is distilled.

tur•pi•tude |tûr′pĭ to͞od′| *or* |-tyo͞od′| *n.* Baseness; depravity.

tur•quoise |tûr′koiz′| *or* |-kwoiz′| *n.* **1.** A bluish-green mineral containing aluminum and copper, valued in certain of its forms as a gem. **2.** Light bluish green. —*adj.* Light bluish green. —***modifier:*** *a turquoise ring.*

tur•ret |tûr′ĭt| *or* |tŭr′-| *n.* **1.** A small tower-shaped projection on a building. **2.** A low dome or tower, usually rotating, containing mounted guns and their gunners or crew, as on a tank, warship, or warplane. **3.** An attachment for a lathe, consisting of a rotating cylinder capable of holding various cutting tools.

tur•tle[1] |tûr′tl| *n.* Any of a group of reptiles living either in water or on land and having the body covered by a horny or leathery shell into which the head, legs, and tail can be pulled for protection. —***modifier:*** *turtle eggs; turtle soup.* [SEE PICTURE]

tur•tle[2] |tûr′tl| *n.* *Archaic.* A turtledove: *"and the voice of the turtle is heard in our land"* (The Bible, Song of Solomon, 2:12).

tur•tle•dove |tûr′tl dŭv′| *n.* Also **turtle dove.** An Old World dove with a white-edged tail and a soft, purring voice.

tur•tle•neck |tûrt′l nĕk′| *n.* **1.** A high, turned-down collar that fits closely around the neck. **2.** A garment having such a collar. —***modifier:*** *a turtleneck sweater.* [SEE PICTURE]

Tus•ca•ro•ra |tŭs′kə rôr′ə| *n., pl.* **Tus•ca•ro•ra** or **Tus•ca•ro•ras.** **1.** A North American Indian tribe now living in New York State and Ontario. **2.** A member of this tribe. **3.** The Iroquoian language of this tribe.

tusk |tŭsk| *n.* **1.** A long, pointed tooth, usually one of a pair, projecting outside of the mouth of certain animals, such as the elephant or walrus. **2.** Any long projecting toothlike part.

tus•sle |tŭs′əl| *v.* **tus•sled, tus•sling.** To fight roughly; struggle. —*n.* A vigorous fight.

tus•sock |tŭs′ək| *n.* A clump or tuft, as of grass.

tu•te•lage |to͞ot′l ĭj| *or* |tyo͞ot′-| *n.* **1.** The function or capacity of a guardian; guardianship. **2.** The act or capacity of a tutor; instruction. **3.** The state of being under a guardian or tutor.

tu•tor |to͞o′tər| *or* |tyo͞o′-| *n.* **1.** A person who gives individual instruction to a student; a private teacher. **2.** In law, the guardian of a minor and his property. —*v.* To act as tutor to.

tu•to•ri•al |to͞o tôr′ē əl| *or* |tyo͞o-| *adj.* Of a tutor or private instructor.

tux |tŭks| *n.* *Informal.* A tuxedo.

tux•e•do, also **Tux•e•do** |tŭk sē′dō| *n., pl.* **tux•e•dos.** **1.** A man's formal or semiformal suit, usually black, including a dinner jacket, trousers, and a black bow tie. **2.** The jacket of such a suit, having smooth, satiny lapels but no tails.

TV television. —***modifier:*** *a TV program.*

TVA, T.V.A. Tennessee Valley Authority.

TV dinner. A trademark for a packaged frozen meal that only needs to be heated before serving.

twad•dle |twŏd′l| *n.* Foolish, trivial, or idle talk. —*v.* **twad•dled, twad•dling.** To talk foolishly.

twain |twān| *n.* A set of two. Used chiefly in poetry: *"Oh, East is East, and West is West, and never the twain shall meet"* (Kipling).

Twain |twān|, **Mark.** 1835–1910. American humorist and novelist. His real name was Samuel Clemens.

twang |twăng| *v.* **1.** To emit or cause to emit a sharp, vibrating sound, as the string of a musical

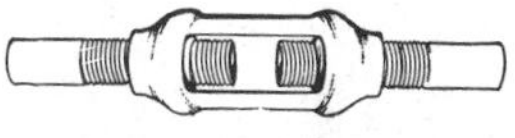

turnbuckle

turtle[1]
Sea turtle

turtleneck

instrument does when plucked. **2.** To utter with a twang. *—n.* **1.** A sharp, vibrating sound, as that of a plucked string. **2.** An excessively nasal tone of voice.

tweak |twēk| *v.* To pinch or twist sharply: *He tweaked her nose playfully. —n.* The act of tweaking; a sharp pinch or twist.

tweed |twēd| *n.* **1.** A coarse woolen fabric usually woven of several colors. **2. tweeds.** Clothes made of tweed. *—**modifier:** a tweed jacket.*

tweet |twēt| *n.* A high, chirping sound, as of a small bird. *—v.* To make such a sound.

tweet•er |twē′tər| *n.* A loudspeaker designed to reproduce and project high-frequency sounds, as in a high-fidelity sound system.

tweez•ers |twē′zərz| *n. (used with a plural verb).* Small pincers used for plucking or handling small objects. [SEE PICTURE]

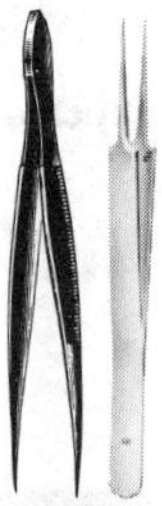
tweezers

twelfth |twĕlfth| *n.* **1.** In a set of items arranged to match the natural numbers in a one-to-one correspondence, the item that matches the number twelve. **2.** One of twelve equal parts of a unit, written 1/12. *—**twelfth** adj. & adv.*

twelve |twĕlv| *n.* A number, written 12 in Arabic numerals, that is equal to the sum of 11 + 1. It is the positive integer that immediately follows 11. *—**twelve** adj. & pron.*

Twelve Apostles. The 12 disciples chosen by Christ.

twelve•month |twĕlv′mŭnth′| *n.* A year.

twelve-tone |twĕlv′tōn′| *adj.* Of, based on, or consisting of the twelve tones of the chromatic scale, usually in an atonal arrangement.

twen•ti•eth |twĕn′tē ĭth| *n.* **1.** In a set of items arranged to match the natural numbers in a one-to-one correspondence, the item that matches the number twenty. **2.** One of twenty equal parts of a unit, written 1/20. *—**twen′ti•eth** adj. & adv.*

twen•ty |twĕn′tē| *n., pl.* **twen•ties.** A number, ritten 20 in Arabic numerals, that is equal to the product of 2 × 10. It is the positive integer that immediately follows 19. *—**twen′ty** adj. & pron.*

twen•ty-one |twĕn′tē **wŭn′**| *n.* A card game in which the object is to accumulate cards with a total count nearer to 21 than that of the dealer; blackjack.

twerp, also **twirp** |twûrp| *n. Slang.* A silly, contemptible person.

Twi |chwē| *or* |chē| *n.* A language spoken in western Africa.

twice |twīs| *adv.* **1.** In two cases or on two occasions; two times: *He saw the movie twice.* **2.** In doubled degree or amount: *She works twice as hard as her colleagues.*

twid•dle |twĭd′l| *v.* **twid•dled, twid•dling.** To turn over or around idly or lightly; fiddle with. *—n.* The act of twiddling; an idle twirling motion, as of the fingers.

Idiom. **twiddle (one's) thumbs.** To do little or nothing; be idle.

twig |twĭg| *n.* A small branch or slender shoot of a tree or shrub.

twi•light |twī′līt′| *n.* **1.** The interval of time during which the sun is below the horizon by less than some standard angular distance. **2.** The way in which the atmosphere is lighted during this time, especially after a sunset. **3.** A period or condition of decline following growth, glory, success, etc: *a man in the twilight of his life. —**modifier:** a twilight sky; a twilight concert.*

twill |twĭl| *n.* **1.** A weave that produces diagonal ribs on the surface of a fabric. **2.** A fabric having such a weave. *—v.* To weave (cloth) so as to produce diagonal ribs on the surface. *—**twilled′** adj.: a twilled fabric.*

twin |twĭn| *n.* **1. a.** Either of a pair of offspring born at the same birth. **b.** Either of such a pair having identical genetic characteristics. **2.** One of two persons, animals, or things that are identical or much alike. *—v.* To give birth to twins. *—adj.* **1.** Being one or two of two offspring from the same birth: *her twin sister; twin brothers.* **2.** Being one or two of two identical or similar persons, animals, or things: *a twin bed, twin beds.*

twine |twīn| *n.* A strong cord or string made of threads twisted together. *—v.* **twined, twin•ing. 1.** To twist together; intertwine, as threads. **2.** To form by twisting: *twine a garland.* **3.** To encircle or coil about: *A vine twined the fence.* **4.** To go in a winding course; twist about.

twinge |twĭnj| *n.* A sudden and sharp physical, mental, or emotional pain. *—v.* **twinged, twing•ing.** To feel a twinge.

twin•kle |twĭng′kəl| *v.* **twin•kled, twin•kling. 1.** To shine with slight, intermittent gleams; sparkle: *stars twinkling in the sky.* **2.** To be bright or sparkling: *Her eyes twinkle. —n.* **1.** A slight, intermittent gleam of light. **2.** A sparkle of delight in the eye. **3.** A brief interval; a twinkling.

twin•kling |twĭng′klĭng| *n.* A brief interval; an instant.

twirl |twûrl| *v.* To rotate or revolve briskly: *drum majorettes leading the parade and twirling their batons. —n.* The act of twirling; a sharp, quick spin or whirl. *—**twirl′er** n.*

twist |twĭst| *v.* **1. a.** To wind together (two or more threads) so as to form a single strand. **b.** To produce (something) in this manner: *twisted a length of cable.* **2.** To wind or coil about something: *twisted cord around the package; vines twisting about the fence.* **3.** To move or progress in a winding course; meander: *a river twisting across the plain.* **4. a.** To turn or open by turning: *twist the radio dial; twisted the door open.* **b.** To pull, break, or snap by turning: *twisted off a length of sausage.* **5.** To wrench or sprain: *twisted her ankle.* **6.** To change the shape of, especially by turning ends: *twist pipe cleaners into strange figures.* **7.** To change or become altered in normal shape or appearance: *twist yourself like a pretzel; his mouth twisting into a sneer.* **8.** To become twisted; change shape or position, especially by turning, bending, or coiling: *a belt that twisted with her every move; wire that twists when handled.* **9.** To move by rotating or revolving with a squirming or writhing motion: *dancers twisting.* **10.** To alter or distort the intended meaning of: *twisted the facts to suit his purpose. —n.* **1.** Something twisted or formed by winding, as a length of yarn or a roll of tobacco leaves. **2.** The act of twisting; a spin or rotation: *a twist of the wrist; a half twist to the right.* **3.** The condition of being twisted; a deviation or departure from a straight course, a regular position, or normal appearance or behavior: *every single twist and turn in the road; the strange twist of his jaw; a*

ă pat/ā pay/â care/ä father/ĕ pet/
ē be/ĭ pit/ī pie/î fierce/ŏ pot/
ō go/ô paw, for/oi oil/ŏŏ book/
ōō boot/ou out/ŭ cut/û fur/
th the/th thin/hw which/zh vision/
ə ago, item, pencil, atom, circus

fatal twist of character. **4.** A change or development, especially a sudden or unexpected departure from a pattern: *the surprising twists of history.* **5.** A sprain or wrench or a feeling of sharp pain caused by this.

twist•er |twĭs'tər| *n. Informal.* A storm that consists of a rotating mass of air, especially a tornado.

twit |twĭt| *v.* **twit•ted, twit•ting.** To taunt or tease, especially for embarrassing mistakes or faults.

twitch |twĭch| *v.* To move or cause to move with a jerk or spasm, often without conscious control. —*n.* **1.** A sudden involuntary or spasmodic movement, as of a muscle. **2.** A sudden pull.

twit•ter |twĭt'ər| *v.* **1.** To make a series of high, fast, chirping sounds, as a bird does. **2.** To speak or say with a sound like this, as in nervous excitement. —*n.* **1.** A series of high, fast, chirping sounds. **2.** A condition of nervous, fluttery excitement: *The girls were in a twitter about the next day's party.*

two |tōō| *n.* A number, written 2 in Arabic numerals, equal to the sum of 1 + 1. It is the positive integer that immediately follows 1. ¶*These sound alike* **two, to, too.** —**two** *adj. & pron.*

two bits. *Slang.* Twenty-five cents.

two-faced |tōō'fāst'| *adj.* **1.** Having two faces or surfaces. **2.** Hypocritical or double-dealing; deceitful.

two-ply |tōō'plī'| *adj.* **1.** Made of two interwoven layers. **2.** Consisting of two thicknesses or strands: *two-ply yarn.*

two-some |tōō'səm| *n.* Two people together; a pair or couple; a duo.

two-way |tōō'wā'| *adj.* **1.** Affording passage in two directions: *The sign indicates that this is not a two-way street.* **2.** Permitting communication in two directions, as a radio.

-ty[1]**.** A suffix that forms nouns and means "a condition or quality": **loyalty.**

-ty[2]**.** A suffix meaning "a multiple of ten": **sixty.**

ty•coon |tī kōōn'| *n.* A wealthy and powerful businessman or industrialist; magnate.

tyke |tīk| *n.* **1.** *Informal.* A small child. **2.** A mongrel dog.

Ty•ler |tī'lər|, **John.** 1790–1862. Tenth President of the United States (1841–45).

tym•pa•na |tĭm'pə nə| *n.* A plural of **tympanum.**

tym•pa•ni |tĭm'pə nē| *n.* A form of the word **timpani.**

tym•pan•ic membrane |tĭm păn'ĭk|. The thin, oval membrane that separates the middle ear from the external ear; eardrum.

tym•pa•num |tĭm'pə nəm| *n., pl.* **tym•pa•na** |tĭm'-pə nə| or **tym•pa•nums.** The eardrum or the middle part of the ear that the eardrum separates from the outer part.

type |tīp| *n.* **1.** A group of persons or things having in common certain traits or characteristics that set them apart from others as a distinct and identifiable class: *bacteria classified according to harmless and disease-producing types.* **2.** A person or thing having the characteristics of such a group or class; a typical example: *the type of hero popular in Victorian novels.* **3. a.** In printing, a small block of metal or wood with a raised letter or character on the upper end that, when inked and pressed upon paper, leaves a printed impression. **b.** A collection of such blocks or of pieces of metal with raised surfaces, from which printing is done. **4.** Printed or typewritten characters; print. —*v.* **typed, typ•ing. 1.** To classify according to a particular type or class: *type the rock samples by studying each; type an actor as a villain.* **2.** To write with a typewriter; typewrite.

type•face |tīp'fās'| *n.* In printing, the size and style of the characters on type.

type•set•ter |tīp'sĕt'ər| *n.* A person who sets type; a compositor. —**type'set'ting** *n.*

type•write |tīp'rīt'| *v.* **type•wrote** |-rōt'|, **type•writ•ten** |-rĭt'ən|, **type•writ•ing.** To write (something) with a typewriter; type.

type•writ•er |tīp'rī'tər| *n.* A machine that prints letters and characters on an inserted piece of paper by means of keys that, when pressed by hand, strike the paper through an inked ribbon. [See Picture]

ty•phoid fever |tī'foid'|. An infectious, often fatal disease caused by bacteria transmitted in contaminated food or water. Its symptoms include high fever and intestinal bleeding.

ty•phoon |tī fōōn'| *n.* A severe tropical hurricane occurring in the western Pacific.

ty•phus |tī'fəs| *n.* Any of several forms of an infectious disease caused by microorganisms and characterized generally by sustained high fever, depression, delirium, and red rashes.

typ•i•cal |tĭp'ĭ kəl| *adj.* **1.** Exhibiting the traits or characteristics peculiar to a kind, group, or category: *a typical college campus.* **2.** Of to a representative specimen; characteristic: *a person's typical manner of speech in the South.* —**typ'i•cal•ly** *adv.*

typ•i•fy |tĭp'ə fī'| *v.* **typ•i•fied, typ•i•fy•ing, typ•i•fies.** To serve as a typical example of.

typ•ist |tī'pĭst| *n.* A person who types on a typewriter.

typo. or **typog. 1.** typographer. **2.** typographical. **3.** typography.

ty•pog•ra•pher |tī pŏg'rə fər| *n.* A printer or compositor.

ty•po•graph•i•cal |tī'pə grăf'ĭ kəl| or **ty•po•graph•ic** |tī'pə grăf'ĭk| *adj.* Of typography.

ty•pog•ra•phy |tī pŏg'rə fē| *n.* **1. a.** . The composition of printed material from movable type. **b.** The art and technique of this. **2.** The arrangement and appearance of such matter.

ty•ran•ni•cal |tĭ răn'ĭ kəl| *or* |tī-| or **ty•ran•nic** |tĭ răn'ĭk| *or* |tī-| *adj.* Of or characteristic of a tyrant; despotic. —**ty•ran'ni•cal•ly** *adv.*

tyr•an•nize |tĭr'ə nīz'| *v.* **tyr•an•nized, tyr•an•niz•ing. 1.** To rule as a tyrant. **2.** To treat tyrannically; be cruel toward.

ty•ran•no•saur |tĭ răn'ə sôr'| *or* |tī-| *n.* A meat-eating dinosaur with small front legs, a large head, and sharp teeth. [See Picture]

ty•ran•no•saur•us |tĭ răn'ə sôr'əs| *or* |tī-| *n.* A tyrannosaur.

tyr•an•ny |tĭr'ə nē| *n., pl.* **tyr•an•nies. 1.** A government in which a single ruler is vested with absolute power. **2.** Absolute power, especially when exercised unjustly or cruelly.

ty•rant |tī'rənt| *n.* **1.** A ruler who exercises power in a harsh, cruel manner; an oppressor. **2.** Any tyrannical or despotic person.

Tyre |tīr|. The capital of ancient Phoenicia.

ty•ro |tī'rō| *n., pl.* **ty•ros.** A beginner.

tzar |zär| *or* |tsär| *n.* A form of the word **czar.**

typewriter
The typewriter was invented in the late nineteenth century. The word **typewriter** was at first used for the person who operated the machine as well as for the machine itself.

tyrannosaur

Uu

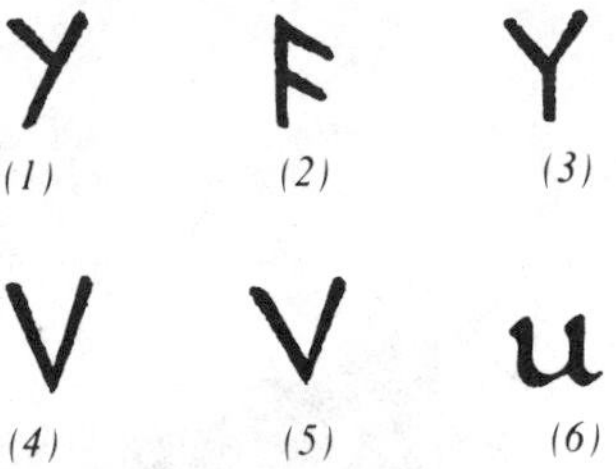

The letter **U** *comes originally from the Phoenician letter* wāw *(1), which stood for the sound /w/. When the Greeks borrowed the alphabet from the Phoenicians, they formed two separate letters from* wāw. *One was* digamma *(2), standing for /w/, and this is the ancestor of our letter* **F**. *The other was* upsilon *(3, 4), standing for /u/; this letter is the ancestor not only of* **U** *but also of* **V**, **W**, *and* **Y**. *The second form of* upsilon *(4) was borrowed by the Romans (5) and was used to stand interchangeably for the sounds /u/, /v/, and /w/. In medieval and later times, separate forms were developed to stand for /v/ and /w/; for the sound /u/, a special rounded letter, often with a "tail" (6), became the basis of our modern letter* **U**.

ă pat/ā pay/â care/ä father/ĕ pet/ ē be/ĭ pit/ī pie/î fierce/ŏ pot/ ō go/ô paw, for/oi oil/ŏŏ book/ ōō boot/ou out/ŭ cut/û fur/ *th* the/th thin/hw which/zh vision/ ə ago, item, pencil, atom, circus

u, U |yōō| *n., pl.* **u's** or **U's** The 21st letter of the English alphabet. [SEE NOTE]

U **1.** In mathematics, union. **2.** The symbol for the element uranium.

u•biq•ui•tous |yōō **bĭk'**wĭ təs| *adj.* Being or seeming to be everywhere at the same time: *a pheasant ubiquitous throughout eastern and central South Dakota.* —**u•biq'ui•tous•ly** *adv.* —**u•biq'ui•ty** *n.*

U-boat |**yōō'**bōt'| *n.* A German submarine.

ud•der |**ŭd'**ər| *n.* A baglike part of a cow, female goat or sheep, etc., in which milk is formed and held and from which it is taken in suckling or milking.

UFO, U.F.O. unidentified flying object.

U•gan•da |yōō **găn'**də| *or* |ōō **gän'**dä|. A country in east-central Africa. Population, 11,172,000. Capital, Kampala.

ugh |ŭKH| *or* |ŏŏKH| *or* |ŭg| *interj.* Used to express disgust, horror, etc.

ug•ly |**ŭg'**lē| *adj.* **ug•li•er, ug•li•est. 1.** Displeasing to the eye: *an ugly face.* **2.** Mean; quarrelsome: *an ugly temper.* **3.** Repulsive or offensive in any way; objectionable: *the ugly details of his plot to stir up a rebellion.* **4.** Disagreeable; unpleasant: *ugly weather.* —**ug'li•ness** *n.*

uhf, UHF ultrahigh frequency.

uh. *interj.* Used to express hesitation, uncertainty, etc.

uh-huh. *interj. Informal.* Yes.

U.K. United Kingdom.

U•kraine |yōō **krān'**| *or* |-**krīn'**| *or* |**yōō'**krān'|. A region of the Soviet Union, in southwestern European Russia, now known officially as the Ukrainian Soviet Socialist Republic. Population, 47,000,000.

U•krain•i•an |yōō **krā'**nē ən| *n.* **1.** A native or inhabitant of the Ukraine. **2.** A Slavic language, similar to Russian, spoken in the Ukraine. —*adj.* Of the Ukraine, the Ukrainians, or their language.

u•ku•le•le |yōō'kə **lā'**lē| *n.* A small, four-stringed guitar, first popular in Hawaii.

U•lan Ba•tor |**ōō'**län' **bä'**tôr'|. The capital of Mongolia. Population, 310,000.

ul•cer |**ŭl'**sər| *n.* An inflamed, often pus-filled sore or lesion on the skin or a mucous membrane of the body, capable of causing the destruction of nearby tissue.

ul•cer•ate |**ŭl'**sə rāt'| *v.* **ul•cer•at•ed, ul•cer•at•ing.** To affect or become affected with or as if with an ulcer. —**ul'cer•a'tion** *n.*

ul•cer•ous |**ŭl'**sər əs| *adj.* Of or affected with an ulcer or ulcers.

ul•na |**ŭl'**nə| *n.* **1.** The bone that extends from the elbow to the wrist on the side of the arm opposite to the thumb. **2.** A similar bone in the vertebrate foreleg.

ul•te•ri•or |ŭl **tîr'**ē ər| *adj.* **1.** Beyond what is evident or admitted: *ulterior motives.* **2.** Beyond or outside a certain area or region; farther off; remote: *exploring the ulterior parts of the island.*

ul•ti•mate |**ŭl'**tə mĭt| *adj.* **1.** Final; last; conclusive: *ultimate defeat.* **2.** Highest possible; greatest: *driving them to a point of ultimate daring.* **3.** Basic; fundamental: *ultimate truths.* **4.** Farthest: *pushing integration to the ultimate limits.* **5.** Representing the furthest possible extent of analysis or division into parts: *an ultimate particle.* —*n.* The final or highest stage or degree; the maximum: *insuring the ultimate in stopping power for their brakes.* —**ul'ti•mate•ly** *adv.*

ul•ti•ma•tum |ŭl'tə **mā'**təm| *or* |-**mä'**-| *n.* A statement of terms that expresses or implies the threat of serious penalties if the terms are not accepted; a final demand or offer.

ul•tra |**ŭl'**trə| *adj.* Going beyond what is average, usual, etc.; extreme: *an ultraliberal politician.* —*n.* A person with extreme views or opinions.

ultra–. A prefix meaning "surpassing or beyond what is common or moderate": **ultramodern.**

ul•tra•high frequency |**ŭl'**trə hī'|. A radio-wave frequency lying in the band between 300 and 3,000 megahertz.

ul•tra•ma•rine |ŭl'trə mə **rēn'**| *n.* **1.** A blue pigment made from a powder of the mineral lapis lazuli. **2.** A bright deep blue. —*adj.* Bright deep blue.

ul•tra•son•ic |ŭl'trə **sŏn'**ĭk| *adj.* Consisting of or using sound that is too high in frequency to be heard by human beings: *ultrasonic waves.*

ul•tra•son•ics |ŭl'trə **sŏn'**ĭks| *n. (used with a singular verb).* The scientific study and practical application of ultrasonic sounds.

ul•tra•vi•o•let |ŭl'trə **vī'**ə lĭt| *adj.* Of electromagnetic radiation having wavelengths between 4,000 angstroms, just shorter than those of visible light, and 40 angstroms, just longer than those of x-rays. —*n.* Ultraviolet light or the ultraviolet part of the spectrum.

U•lys•ses |yōō **lĭs'**ēz|. The Latin form of the name **Odysseus.**

um•bel |**ŭm'**bəl| *n.* A flat or rounded flower cluster in which the individual flower stalks radiate from about the same point on the stem.

um•ber |**ŭm'**bər| *n.* **1.** A natural brown earth composed of oxides of iron, silicon, aluminum, calcium, and manganese, used as a pigment. **2.** A dark reddish brown. —*adj.* Dark reddish brown.

um•bil•i•cal |ŭm **bĭl′**ĭ kəl| *adj.* Of an umbilicus: *an umbilical hernia.*

umbilical cord. **1.** The flexible cordlike structure that extends from the navel of a fetus to the placenta, containing blood vessels that supply nourishment to the fetus and remove its wastes. **2.** Any of the tubes, wires, cables, etc., that are connected to a rocket and removed shortly before launching.

um•bil•i•cus |ŭm **bĭl′**ĭ kəs| *or* |ŭm′bə **lī′**-| *n.* The navel.

um•bra |**ŭm′**brə| *n.* **1.** A dark area, especially the darkest part of a shadow. **2. a.** The shadow of the moon that falls on a part of the earth where a solar eclipse is total. **b.** The darkest region of a sunspot. [SEE PICTURE]

um•brage |**ŭm′**brĭj| *n.* A feeling aroused by an insult or injury to oneself; offense.
Idiom. **take umbrage.** To feel offended.

um•brel•la |ŭm **brĕl′**ə| *n.* A device for protection from the rain, consisting of a cloth cover on a collapsible frame mounted on a handle. [SEE PICTURE]

u•mi•ak |**ōō′**mē ăk′| *n.* A large, open Eskimo boat made of skins stretched on a wooden frame.

um•pire |**ŭm′**pīr′| *n.* **1.** A person who rules on plays, as in baseball. **2.** A person empowered to settle a dispute. —*v.* **um•pired, um•pir•ing.** To act as an umpire.

ump•teen |**ŭmp′tēn′**| *adj. Informal.* Large but indefinite in number: *umpteen reasons.* —**ump′teenth′** *adj.*

un–¹. A prefix meaning "not or contrary to": **unattached; unhappy.** [SEE NOTE on p. 938]

un–². A prefix meaning: **1.** Reversal of an action: **unbar. 2.** Release or removal from: **unburden. 3.** Intensified action: **unloose.** [SEE NOTES on p. 938]

UN, U.N. United Nations.

un•a•bashed |ŭn′ə **băsht′**| *adj.* Not embarrassed or ashamed: *unabashed sentimentality.* —**un′a•bash′ed•ly** |ŭn′ə **băsh′**ĭd lē| *adv.*

un•a•ble |ŭn **ā′**bəl| *adj.* Not able; lacking the necessary power or capability to do something: *unable to work on Saturdays; unable to attend the party.*

un•a•bridged |ŭn′ə **brĭjd′**| *adj.* Not condensed: *an unabridged book.*

un•ac•cent•ed |ŭn **ăk′**sĕn tĭd| *adj.* Without an accent or stress: *an unaccented syllable.*

un•ac•com•pa•nied |ŭn′ə **kŭm′**pə nēd| *adj.* Performed without accompaniment; solo: *a sonata for unaccompanied flute.*

un•ac•count•a•ble |ŭn′ə **koun′**tə bəl| *adj.* **1.** Not capable of being explained; mysterious: *an unaccountable reason.* **2.** Not responsible: *unaccountable for his actions.* —**un′ac•count′a•bly** *adv.*

un•ac•cus•tomed |ŭn′ə **kŭs′**təmd| *adj.* **1.** Not customary; unusual: *unaccustomed politeness.* **2.** Not used to: *unaccustomed to the cold.*

un•af•fect•ed¹ |ŭn′ə **fĕk′**tĭd| *adj.* Not affected: *He seems unaffected by the sun.*

un•af•fect•ed² |ŭn′ə **fĕk′**tĭd| *adj.* Natural or sincere, as in appearance, manner, etc.

un•al•ter•a•ble |ŭn **ôl′**tər ə bəl| *adj.* Not capable of being altered; unchangeable. —**un•al′ter•a•bly** *adv.*

u•na•nim•i•ty |yōō′nə **nĭm′**ĭ tē| *n.* The condition of being unanimous; complete agreement.

u•nan•i•mous |yōō **năn′**ə məs| *adj.* **1.** Sharing the same opinion: *Critics were unanimous about the play.* **2.** Based on complete agreement: *a unanimous vote.* —**u•nan′i•mous•ly** *adv.*

un•armed |ŭn **ärmd′**| *adj.* Lacking weapons.

un•as•sum•ing |ŭn′ə **sōō′**mĭng| *adj.* Not boastful or pretentious; modest.

un•at•tached |ŭn′ə **tăcht′**| *adj.* **1.** Not attached, joined, connected, etc. **2.** Not engaged or married.

un•at•test•ed |ŭn′ə **tĕs′**tĭd| *adj.* Not found in written documents. [SEE NOTE]

un•a•vail•ing |ŭn′ə **vā′**lĭng| *adj.* Useless; unsuccessful: *her unavailing efforts to apologize.*

un•a•void•a•ble |ŭn′ə **voi′**də bəl| *adj.* Not capable of being avoided; inevitable: *an unavoidable accident.* —**un′a•void′a•bly** *adv.*

un•a•ware |ŭn′ə **wâr′**| *adj.* Not aware: *He was unaware of her presence.*

un•a•wares |ŭn′ə **wârz′**| *adv.* By surprise; unexpectedly: *He caught me unawares.*

un•bal•anced |ŭn **băl′**ənst| *adj.* **1.** Not in balance or in proper balance: *an unbalanced budget; an unbalanced scale.* **2.** Not mentally sound; irrational: *an unbalanced mind.*

un•bar |ŭn **bär′**| *v.* **-barred, -bar•ring.** To remove the bars from; open: *unbar a window.*

un•bear•a•ble |ŭn **bâr′**ə bəl| *adj.* Not capable of being endured; intolerable: *an unbearable pain; unbearable heat.* —**un•bear′a•bly** *adv.*

un•beat•a•ble |ŭn **bē′**tə bəl| *adj.* Impossible to surpass or defeat.

un•beat•en |ŭn **bēt′**n| *adj.* Never defeated or beaten.

un•be•com•ing |ŭn′bĭ **kŭm′**ĭng| *adj.* **1.** Not attractive or flattering: *unbecoming clothes.* **2.** Not suitable or proper: *unbecoming behavior.*

un•be•knownst |ŭn′bĭ **nōnst′**| *adv.* —**unbeknownst to.** Without the knowledge of: *The thieves entered the house unbeknownst to all the guests.*

un•be•lief |ŭn′bĭ **lēf′**| *n.* Lack of belief or faith, especially in religious matters.

un•be•liev•a•ble |ŭn′bĭ **lē′**və bəl| *adj.* Not to be believed; incredible: *an unbelievable tale.* —**un′be•liev′a•bly** *adv.*

un•be•liev•er |ŭn′bĭ **lē′**vər| *n.* A person who lacks belief or faith, especially in a religion.

un•be•liev•ing |ŭn′bĭ **lē′**vĭng| *adj.* Not believing; doubting: *an unbelieving facial expression.*

un•bend |ŭn **bĕnd′**| *v.* **-bent** |**-bĕnt′**|, **-bend•ing. 1.** To make or become straight: *unbending the elbows; muscles bending and unbending.* **2.** To become less tense; relax: *unbend at the beach.*

un•bend•ing |ŭn **bĕn′**dĭng| *adj.* Not flexible; uncompromising: *his unbending will.*

un•bid•den |ŭn **bĭd′**n| *adj.* Not asked or invited.

un•bind |ŭn **bīnd′**| *v.* **-bound** |**-bound′**|, **-bind•ing. 1.** To untie: *unbinding the bunch of candy canes.* **2.** To set free; release: *unbind a prisoner.*

un•bolt |ŭn **bōlt′**| *v.* To remove the bolts of; unlock: *unbolt a door.*

un•born |ŭn **bôrn′**| *adj.* Not yet in existence; not born.

un•bos•om |ŭn **bŏŏz′**əm| *or* |**-bōō′**zəm| *v.* —**unbosom oneself.** To reveal one's thoughts or feelings: *unbosoming himself to his closest friend.*

un•bound |ŭn **bound′**| *adj.* **1.** Not having a

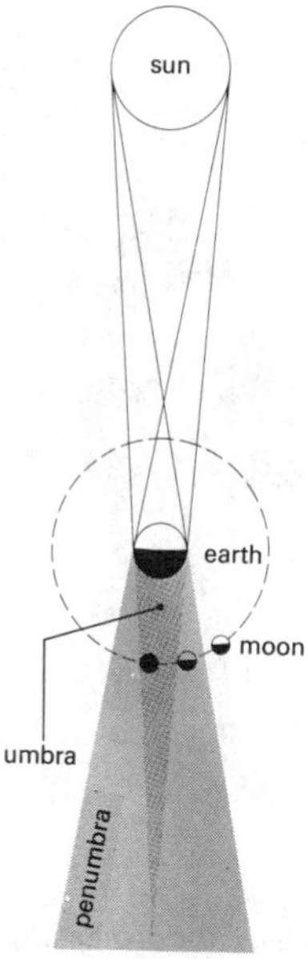

umbra
Umbra of the earth.

umbrella

unattested
This term is used by etymologists to describe words for which no written proof exists but which have been reconstructed by the methods of historical linguistics. For an example, see note at **somber/sombrero.**

Uncle Sam

As with most heroes of mythology, the precise origins of **Uncle Sam** are shrouded in mystery and conjecture. The typical cartoon figure *(above)* originally represented American patriotism, rather than the government, and was known as *Jonathan* or *Brother Jonathan.* The name **Uncle Sam** is first recorded from 1813. It is said that Samuel Wilson (1766–1854), a government inspector of meat during the War of 1812, was known as "Uncle Sam"; barrels of meat approved by him were stamped *U.S.* for *United States;* this might have been humorously taken to be "Uncle Sam's" personal mark; thus Wilson's nickname could have become a nickname for the government. But this story, says the *Dictionary of Americanisms* (1951), "lacks confirmation."

ă pat/ā pay/â care/ä father/ĕ pet/ ē be/ĭ pit/ī pie/î fierce/ŏ pot/ ō go/ô paw, for/oi oil/ŏŏ book/ ōō boot/ou out/ŭ cut/û fur/ *th* the/th thin/hw which/zh vision/ ə ago, item, pencil, atom, circus

binding: *an unbound book.* **2.** Not kept within bounds; unrestrained.

un•bound•ed |ŭn **boun′**dĭd| *adj.* Without boundaries or limits: *unbounded happiness.*

un•bri•dled |ŭn **brīd′**ld| *adj.* **1.** Not fitted with a bridle. **2.** Unrestrained; uncontrolled: *moments of unbridled joy.*

un•bro•ken |ŭn **brō′**kən| *adj.* **1.** Not broken; whole; intact. **2.** Not violated: *an unbroken promise.* **3.** Uninterrupted: *unbroken silence.* **4.** Not tamed or broken: *an unbroken pony.*

un•buck•le |ŭn **bŭk′**əl| *v.* **-buck•led, -buck•ling.** To loosen or undo the buckle of.

un•bur•den |ŭn **bûr′**dn| *v.* To free from or relieve of a burden: *unburden one's mind.*

un•called-for |ŭn **kôld′**fôr′| *adj.* Out of place; unnecessary: *an uncalled-for remark.*

un•can•ny |ŭn **kăn′**ē| *adj.* **un•can•ni•er, un•can•ni•est. 1.** Arousing wonder and fear; strange: *an uncanny light coming out of the ruins.* **2.** So keen and perceptive as to seem supernatural: *an uncanny wisdom.* **—un•can′ni•ly** *adv.*

un•ceas•ing |ŭn **sē′**sĭng| *adj.* Not ceasing or letting up; continuous: *weeks of unceasing activity.* **—un•ceas′ing•ly** *adv.*

un•cer•tain |ŭn **sûr′**tn| *adj.* **1.** Not certain; doubtful; unsure: *He was uncertain of the answer.* **2.** Not definite; vague: *uncertain plans.* **3.** Subject to change: *uncertain weather.* **4.** Not capable of being predicted; questionable: *uncertain results; in no uncertain terms.* **—un•cer′tain•ly** *adj.*

un•cer•tain•ty |ŭn **sûr′**tn tē| *n., pl.* **un•cer•tain•ties. 1.** The condition of being uncertain. **2.** Something that is uncertain: *helping them to overcome many of the uncertainties of life.*

un•chris•tian |ŭn **krĭs′**chən| *adj.* **1.** Not Christian in religion. **2.** Not in accordance with the Christian spirit.

un•cial |**ŭn′**shəl| *or* |-shē əl| *adj.* Of a script with rounded capital letters found in Greek and Latin manuscripts of the 4th to the 8th centuries A.D.

un•civ•il |ŭn **sĭv′**əl| *adj.* Impolite; discourteous.

un•civ•i•lized |ŭn **sĭv′**ə līzd′| *adj.* Not civilized; barbaric; savage.

un•cle |**ŭng′**kəl| *n.* **1.** The brother of one's mother or father. **2.** The husband of one's aunt.

un•clean |ŭn **klēn′**| *adj.* **1.** Not clean; dirty. **2.** Morally impure; sinful.

un•clear |ŭn **klîr′**| *adj.* Not clear; not sharp or explicit.

Uncle Sam |săm|. **1.** *Informal.* The United States Government. **2.** A cartoon personification of the United States Government as a tall, thin, grim-faced old man dressed in the national colors and sporting a goatee and top hat. [SEE PICTURE]

un•coil |ŭn **koil′**| *v.* To unwind or become unwound: *uncoil a towline. The snake uncoiled.*

un•com•fort•a•ble |ŭn **kŭmf′**tə bəl| *or* |**-kŭm′**fər tə-| *adj.* **1.** Not comfortable: *He has eaten so much that he feels uncomfortable.* **2.** Causing discomfort: *an uncomfortable chair.* **3.** Unpleasant; uneasy: *an uncomfortable situation.* **—un•com′fort•a•bly** *adv.*

un•com•mon |ŭn **kŏm′**ən| *adj.* **un•com•mon•er, un•com•mon•est.** Not common; rare; unusual: *a woman of uncommon beauty; words used in uncommon ways.* **—un•com′mon•ly** *adv.*

un•com•pro•mis•ing |ŭn **kŏm′**prə mī′zĭng| *adj.* Not making compromises; inflexible; rigid. **—un•com′pro•mis′ing•ly** *adv.*

un•con•cern |ŭn′kən **sûrn′**| *n.* **1.** Lack of concern or interest; indifference: *looking at the new car with studied unconcern.* **2.** Lack of worry, anxiety, etc.: *His extreme unconcern gave him an air of confidence.*

un•con•cerned |ŭn′kən **sûrnd′**| *adj.* **1.** Not concerned or interested; indifferent. **2.** Not worried or anxious. **—un′con•cern′ed•ly** |ŭn′kən**sûr′**nĭd lē| *adv.*

un•con•di•tion•al |ŭn′kən **dĭsh′**ə nəl| *adj.* Without conditions or limitations; absolute: *unconditional surrender.* **—un′con•di′tion•al•ly** *adv.*

un•con•quer•a•ble |ŭn **kŏng′**kər ə bəl| *adj.* Not capable of being conquered; indomitable.

un•con•scion•a•ble |ŭn **kŏn′**shə nə bəl| *adj.* **1.** Not controlled or restrained by conscience; outrageous: *an unconscionable act.* **2.** Beyond what is reasonable; excessive: *an unconscionable price.* **—un•con′scion•a•bly** *adv.*

un•con•scious |ŭn **kŏn′**shəs| *adj.* **1.** Not accessible to the conscious part of the mind, as an idea or feeling of which one is not aware: *unconscious rage.* **2.** Temporarily lacking awareness, as in deep sleep or a coma. **3.** Without conscious control; involuntary. *—n.* The part of the mind that operates without conscious awareness and that cannot be directly observed. **—un•con′cious•ly** *adv.* **—un•con′cious•ness** *n.*

un•con•sti•tu•tion•al |ŭn′kŏn stĭ **tōō′**shə nəl| *or* |**-tyōō′-**| *adj.* Not in agreement with the principles set forth in the constitution of a country, especially the Constitution of the United States. **—un′con•sti•tu′tion•al•ly** *adv.*

un•con•trol•la•ble |ŭn′kən **trō′**lə bəl| *adj.* Not capable of being controlled: *uncontrollable anger.* **—un′con•trol′la•bly** *adv.*

un•con•trolled |ŭn′kən **trōld′**| *adj.* Not controlled: *uncontrolled rage.*

un•con•ven•tion•al |ŭn′kən **vĕn′**shə nəl| *adj.* Not conventional; not conforming to convention, rules, etc.: *The newest and most unconventional forms of art are known as avant-garde.* **—un′con•ven′tion•al′i•ty** *n.* **—un′con•ven′tion•al•ly** *adv.*

un•cork |ŭn **kôrk′**| *v.* **1.** To remove the cork from. **2.** *Informal.* In baseball, to let loose.

un•couth |ŭn **kōōth′**| *adj.* **1.** Not refined; crude: *uncouth behavior.* **2.** Awkward; clumsy: *an uncouth country bumpkin.*

un•count•ed |ŭn **koun′**tĭd| *adj.* **1.** Not counted. **2.** Not capable of being counted; innumerable.

un•coup•le |ŭn **kŭp′**əl| *v.* **-coup•led, -coup•ling.** To disconnect or unfasten: *uncoupled railroad cars.*

un•cov•er |ŭn **kŭv′**ər| *v.* **1.** To remove a cover, top, seal, etc., from: *uncovered a jar.* **2.** To reveal or expose by or as if by digging up out of the earth: *archaeologists uncovering a great city and temple area; uncover a plot.* **3.** To remove the hat from: *He uncovered his head as a sign of respect.*

unc•tion |**ŭngk′**shən| *n.* **1.** The act of anointing as part of a ceremonial or healing ritual. **2.** An ointment or oil; a salve. **3.** Something that serves to soothe or restore.

unc•tu•ous |**ŭngk′**chōō əs| *adj.* **1.** Oily; greasy.

2. Marked by or showing excessive sincerity, courtesy, etc.: *an unctuous manner.* —**unc'tu•ous•ly** *adv.* —**unc'tu•ous•ness** *n.*

un•cut |ŭn **kŭt'**| *adj.* Not cut, especially: 1. Not sliced, carved, etc.: *uncut bread.* 2. Not reduced or shortened: *an uncut novel.* 3. Not ground or polished: *an uncut gem.*

un•daunt•ed |ŭn **dôn'**tĭd| *adj.* Not discouraged; fearless. —**un•daunt'ed•ly** *adv.*

un•de•cid•ed |ŭn'dĭ **sī'**dĭd| *adj.* 1. Not decided; not yet settled; open: *plans still undecided.* 2. Having reached no decision: *undecided whether to attack or flee.*

un•de•feat•ed |ŭn'dĭ **fē'**tĭd| *adj.* Not yet defeated; having won every contest in a series.

un•de•ni•a•ble |ŭn'dĭ **nī'**ə bəl| *adj.* Not capable of being denied; true; obvious: *an undeniable fact; undeniable evidence.* —**un'de•ni'a•bly** *adv.*

un•der |**ŭn'**dər| *prep.* 1. In a lower position or place than: *a cat under the table.* 2. Beneath the surface of: *under the ground.* 3. Beneath the guise of: *under a false name.* 4. Less than; smaller than: *under 20 years of age.* 5. Less than the required amount or degree of: *under voting age.* 6. Inferior to, as in status: *the complaints of those who were under them.* 7. Subject to the authority of: *living under a dictatorship.* 8. Undergoing or receiving the effects of: *under intensive care.* 9. Subject to the obligation of: *under contract.* 10. Within the group or classification of: *listed under biology.* 11. In the process of: *under discussion.* 12. Because of: *under these conditions.* —*adv.* 1. In or into a place below or beneath: *Lift the rug and put your hand under.* 2. Into ruin or defeat: *forced under by bombings.* 3. So as to be covered, enveloped, or immersed: *You can't swim until you learn how to put your head under.* 4. Below a quantity, amount, or age: *children of 12 and under.* —*adj.* 1. Lower: *the under parts of a machine.* 2. Subordinate; inferior: *all the under folk rushing to and fro.* 3. Lower in amount or degree: *keeps his prices under.*

under–. A prefix meaning: 1. Location below or under: **underground.** 2. Inferiority in rank or importance: **undersecretary.** 3. Degree, rate, or quantity that is lower or less than normal: **underestimate.** 4. Secrecy or treachery: **underhand.**

un•der•a•chieve |ŭn'dər ə **chēv'**| *v.* **-a•chieved, -a•chiev•ing.** To perform below the expected level of ability or capacity, especially in schoolwork. —**un'der•a•chiev'er** *n.*

un•der•age |ŭn'dər **āj'**| *adj.* Below the customary or required age.

un•der•arm¹ |**ŭn'**dər ärm'| *adj.* Located, placed, or used under the arm. —*n.* The armpit.

un•der•arm² |**ŭn'**dər ärm'| *adj.* & *adv.* Underhand.

un•der•bel•ly |**ŭn'**dər bĕl'ē| *n., pl.* **-bel•lies.** 1. The lowest part of an animal's body. 2. A weak or vulnerable part of something: *discovered the enemy's soft underbelly and attacked.*

un•der•bid |ŭn'dər **bĭd'**| *v.* **-bid•den** |**-bĭd'**n| or **-bid, -bid•ding.** 1. To bid lower than (a competitor). 2. In card games such as bridge, to bid less than the value of (one's cards).

un•der•brush |**ŭn'**dər brŭsh'| *n.* Small trees, shrubs, etc., growing thickly beneath taller trees.

un•der•car•riage |**ŭn'**dər kăr'ĭj| *n.* 1. A supporting framework or structure, as for the body of an automobile. 2. The landing gear of an aircraft.

un•der•clothes |**ŭn'**dər klōz'| *or* |-klō*thz*'| *pl.n.* Underwear.

un•der•cloth•ing |**ŭn'**dər klō'*th*ĭng| *n.* Underwear.

un•der•cook |ŭn'dər **kŏŏk'**| *v.* To cook insufficiently.

un•der•coat |**ŭn'**dər kōt'| *n.* 1. A covering of short hair, fur, or feathers covered by longer outer hair or plumage. 2. A coat of material applied to a surface to seal it or otherwise prepare it for a final coat or finish.

un•der•cov•er |ŭn'dər **kŭv'**ər| *or* |**ŭn'**dər-kŭv'-| *adj.* Acting or carried on in secret: *an undercover agent; an undercover investigation.*

un•der•cur•rent |**ŭn'**dər kûr'ənt| *or* |-kŭr'-| *n.* 1. A current, as of air or water, flowing beneath a surface or another current. 2. A partly hidden tendency, force, or trend that is often contrary to what is obvious.

un•der•cut |**ŭn'**dər kŭt'| *v.* **-cut, -cut•ting.** 1. To make a cut under or below. 2. To sell or work for less money than (a competitor). —*n.* 1. A cut made in the lower part of something. 2. A notch cut in a tree to direct its fall.

un•der•de•vel•oped |ŭn'dər dĭ **vĕl'**əpt| *adj.* 1. Not developed in a full or normal way, as a living thing or one of its parts. 2. Backward in industrial or economic development: *an underdeveloped nation.*

un•der•dog |**ŭn'**dər dôg'| *or* |-dŏg'| *n.* Someone or something that is expected to lose a contest or struggle, as in sports or politics.

un•der•done |**ŭn'**dər **dŭn'**| *adj.* Not sufficiently cooked or otherwise prepared.

un•der•es•ti•mate |ŭn'dər **ĕs'**tə māt'| *v.* **-es•ti•mat•ed, -es•ti•mat•ing.** To judge or estimate too low the value, amount, quality, or capacity of. —*n.* |ŭn'dər **ĕs'**tə mĭt|. An estimate that is or proves to be too low.

un•der•ex•pose |ŭn'dər ĭk **spōz'**| *v.* **-ex•posed, -ex•pos•ing.** To expose (film) to light for too short a time to produce an image with good contrast. —**un'der•ex•po'sure** *n.*

un•der•foot |ŭn'dər **fŏŏt'**| *adv.* 1. Below or under the foot or feet. 2. In the way.

un•der•gar•ment |**ŭn'**dər gär'mənt| *n.* A garment worn under outer garments.

un•der•go |ŭn'dər **gō'**| *v.* **un•der•went** |ŭn'dər-**wĕnt'**|, **un•der•gone** |ŭn'dər **gôn'**| *or* |**-gŏn'**|, **un•der•go•ing.** 1. To experience; be subjected to: *Many insects undergo three changes during their lives.* 2. To endure; suffer through: *undergo hardship.*

un•der•grad•u•ate |ŭn'dər **grăj'**ōō ĭt| *n.* A student who has entered a college or university but has not received a bachelor's degree. —*modifier: undergraduate courses.*

un•der•ground |**ŭn'**dər ground'| *adj.* 1. Below the surface of the earth: *an underground passage.* 2. Acting or done in secret; hidden or concealed: *an underground foreign agent.* 3. Describing an avant-garde or experimental movement or its films, publications, etc.: *the underground press.* —*n.* 1. A secret organization, especially one working against established authority. 2. *British.* A subway system. —*adv.* 1. Below the surface

underground

After the War of 1812, a secret organization grew up that helped slaves to escape from the South to Canada and elsewhere. In the 1830's this system became known as the Underground Railroad; *guides were called "conductors," hiding places were "depots," and so forth. The name* Underground Railroad *may have prompted the development of sense* **1** *of the noun* **underground,** *which was applied to the secret resistance organizations in occupied European countries in World War II. This in turn is probably the origin of sense* **3** *of the adjective, picturing the artistic avant-garde as a kind of "resistance" to the "establishment."*

of the earth: *miners digging underground.* **2.** In secret: *spies working underground.* [SEE NOTE on p. 935.]

un•der•growth |ŭn′dər grōth′| *n.* Low-growing plants, shrubs, or young trees, especially when growing beneath the trees of a forest.

un•der•hand |ŭn′dər hănd′| *adj.* **1.** Done slyly and secretly. **2.** In sports, performed with the hand kept below the level of the elbow. —*adv.* **1.** With an underhand movement: *threw the ball underhand.* **2.** Slyly and secretly.

un•der•hand•ed |ŭn′dər hăn′dĭd| *adj.* Done in a sly and secret manner.

un•der•lie |ŭn′dər lī′| *v.* **un•der•lay** |ŭn′dər lā′|, **un•der•lain** |ŭn′dər lān′|, **un•der•ly•ing.** **1.** To be located under or below: *Roads built by the Romans still underlie many of today's European highways.* **2.** To be the basis for; account for: *These facts underlie his decision.*

un•der•line |ŭn′dər līn′| *v.* **un•der•lined, un•der•lin•ing.** **1.** To draw a line under; underscore. **2.** To stress or emphasize.

un•der•ling |ŭn′dər lĭng| *n.* A person in a subordinate position.

un•der•ly•ing |ŭn′dər lī′ĭng| *adj.* **1.** Located under or beneath something: *the underlying bedrock of the Sierras.* **2.** Basic; fundamental: *the underlying rules of English grammar.* **3.** Hidden but implied: *an underlying meaning.*

un•der•mine |ŭn′dər mīn′| *or* |ŭn′dər mīn′| *v.* **un•der•mined, un•der•min•ing.** **1.** To dig a mine or tunnel beneath. **2.** To weaken or impair by or as if by wearing away slowly or by degrees: *waters undermining the foundation of a house. Late hours undermined his health.*

un•der•most |ŭn′dər mōst′| *adj.* Lowest in position, rank, or place.

un•der•neath |ŭn′dər nēth′| *prep.* Beneath; below; under: *put newspapers underneath the leaky pail.* Also used adverbially: *I kicked over the stone and found a worm underneath.* —*n.* The bottom surface of something; the underside.

un•der•nour•ished |ŭn′dər nûr′ĭsht| *or* |-nŭr′-| *adj.* Lacking sufficient nourishment for proper health and growth.

un•der•pants |ŭn′dər pănts′| *pl.n.* Drawers or shorts worn under outer garments.

un•der•pass |ŭn′dər păs′| *or* |-päs′| *n.* A part of a road that passes under another road or a railroad.

un•der•pin•ning |ŭn′dər pĭn′ĭng| *n.* A supporting part or structure, as for a wall, building, etc.

un•der•priv•i•leged |ŭn′dər prĭv′ə lĭjd| *adj.* Lacking or deprived of advantages or opportunities enjoyed by other members of society.

un•der•rate |ŭn′dər rāt′| *v.* **-rat•ed, -rat•ing.** To judge or rate as too low; underestimate.

un•der•score |ŭn′dər skôr′| *or* |-skōr′| *v.* **un•der•scored, un•der•scor•ing.** **1.** To draw a line under; underline. **2.** To stress or emphasize.

un•der•sea |ŭn′dər sē′| *adj.* Existing, done, used, or operating beneath the surface of the sea: *undersea life; undersea exploration.* —*adv.* Beneath the sea.

un•der•seas |ŭn′dər sēz′| *adv.* Undersea.

un•der•sec•re•tar•y |ŭn′dər sĕk′rĭ tĕr′ē| *n., pl.* **un•der•sec•re•tar•ies.** An official directly subordinate to a Cabinet member.

un•der•sell |ŭn′dər sĕl′| *v.* **-sold** |-sōld′|, **-sell•ing.** To sell for a lower price than.

un•der•shirt |ŭn′dər shûrt′| *n.* An undergarment worn next to the skin under a shirt.

un•der•shoot |ŭn′dər sho͞ot′| *v.* **-shot** |-shŏt′|, **-shoot•ing.** **1.** To shoot a missile so that it falls short of (a target). **2.** To land or begin to land an aircraft on a course that brings it down short of (a landing area).

undershot

un•der•shot |ŭn′dər shŏt′| *adj.* **1.** Driven by water passing from below: *an undershot water wheel.* **2.** Projecting beyond an upper part, as the lower jaw beyond the upper jaw. [SEE PICTURE]

un•der•side |ŭn′dər sīd′| *n.* The side or surface that is underneath; the bottom side.

un•der•signed |ŭn′dər sīnd′| *adj.* **1.** Having signed at the end of a document: *the undersigned persons.* **2.** Having a signature at the end: *an undersigned document.* —*n.* Those who have signed at the end of a document.

un•der•size |ŭn′dər sīz′| *adj.* Smaller than the usual, expected, or required size: *an undersize garment.*

un•der•sized |ŭn′dər sīzd′| *adj.* Undersize.

un•der•slung |ŭn′dər slŭng′| *adj.* Having the springs attached to the axles from below, as an automobile.

un•der•staffed |ŭn′dər stăft′| *or* |-stäft′| *adj.* Having a staff of people that is too small to meet a need: *an understaffed hospital.*

un•der•stand |ŭn′dər stănd′| *v.* **un•der•stood** |ŭn′dər sto͝od′|, **un•der•stand•ing.** **1.** To grasp the nature, importance, significance, etc., of: *He doesn't pretend to understand the universe.* **2. a.** To grasp the meaning intended or expressed by: *Do you understand Shakespeare?* **b.** To grasp the meaning of (a word, phrase, etc.): *You must understand the words to understand what you read. His explanation was too difficult to understand.* **3.** To know thoroughly; be familiar with: *He understands German. She still does not understand her job.* **4.** To be tolerant or sympathetic toward: *A good teacher understands children. If you can't come, I'll understand.* **5.** To learn indirectly, as by hearsay; gather: *We understand she had a baby on Thanksgiving.* **6.** To perceive clearly; realize: *You don't understand what a difficult position I'm in.* **7.** To draw as a conclusion; infer: *Am I to understand that you are staying for the weekend?*

un•der•stand•a•ble |ŭn′dər stăn′də bəl| *adj.* **1.** Such as can be understood: *an understandable word.* **2.** Such as can be explained, excused, or accepted with sympathy: *It was understandable that many early settlers objected to taxation without representation.* —**un′der•stand′a•bly** *adv.*

un•der•stand•ing |ŭn′dər stăn′dĭng| *n.* **1.** A grasp of what is intended, expressed, meant, etc.; comprehension; knowledge: *exercises to help you gain a better understanding of mathematics.* **2.** The condition of having reached a stage of full comprehension: *a book beyond a child's understanding.* **3.** The ability to understand: *a person of great understanding.* **4. a.** A friendly relationship: *efforts toward a better understanding between the two countries.* **b.** A reconciliation of differences; an agreement: *After hours of discussion they finally reached an understanding.* —*adj.* Showing tolerant, kind, or sympathetic feelings: *a strong, good, and understanding man.*

ă pat/ā pay/â care/ä father/ĕ pet/ ē be/ĭ pit/ī pie/î fierce/ŏ pot/ ō go/ô paw, for/oi oil/o͝o book/ o͞o boot/ou out/ŭ cut/û fur/ *th* the/th thin/hw which/zh vision/ ə ago, item, pencil, atom, circus

un•der•stood |ŭn′dər **stŏŏd′**|. Past participle of **understand.** —*adj.* **1.** Agreed upon: *It is understood that the fee is 50 dollars.* **2.** Not expressed but implied: *In the sentence "Mary is prettier than I," the verb "am" is understood after "I."*

un•der•stud•y |**ŭn′**dər stŭd′ē| *n., pl.* **un•der•stud•ies.** An actor trained to substitute for the regular actor. —*v.* **un•der•stud•ied, un•der•stud•y•ing, un•der•stud•ies. 1.** To study or know (a role) so as to be able to substitute for the regular actor. **2.** To act as an understudy to.

un•der•take |ŭn′dər **tāk′**| *v.* **un•der•took** |ŭn′dər **tŏŏk′**|, **un•der•tak•en** |ŭn′dər **tā′**kən|, **un•der•tak•ing. 1.** To take upon oneself; decide or agree to do: *undertake a difficult job.* **2.** To pledge oneself to do or commit oneself to doing (something): *The contractors undertook to finish the house by the spring.*

un•der•tak•er |**ŭn′**dər tā′kər| *n.* A person whose business it is to prepare the dead for burial and to make funeral arrangements.

un•der•tak•ing. *n.* **1.** |ŭn′dər **tā′**kĭng|. An enterprise, task, venture, etc. **2.** |**ŭn′**dər tā′kĭng|. The occupation of an undertaker. [SEE NOTE]

un•der•tone |**ŭn′**dər tōn′| *n.* **1.** A speech tone of low pitch or volume. **2.** A subdued or partly concealed emotional quality: *undertones of fear in her uneasiness in front of her bosses.*

un•der•tow |**ŭn′**dər tō′| *n.* A current beneath the surface of a body of water running in a direction opposite to that of the current at the surface.

un•der•wa•ter |**ŭn′**dər **wô′**tər| *or* |**-wŏt′**ər| *adj.* Used, done, or existing under the surface of water. —*adv.* Beneath the surface of water.

un•der•wear |ŭn′dər **wâr′**| *n.* Clothing worn under the outer clothes and next to the skin; underclothes.

un•der•weight |**ŭn′**dər **wāt′**| *adj.* Weighing less than is normal or required. —*n.* |**ŭn′**dər wāt′|. Weight that is below normal or usual.

un•der•went |ŭn′dər **wĕnt′**|. Past tense of **undergo.**

un•der•world |**ŭn′**dər wûrld′| *n.* **1.** The world of the dead, imagined to be below the surface of the earth. **2.** The part of society engaged in and organized for the purpose of crime and vice.

un•der•write |**ŭn′**dər rīt′| *v.* **un•der•wrote** |**ŭn′**dər rōt′|, **un•der•writ•ten** |**ŭn′**dər rĭt′n|, **un•der•writ•ing. 1.** To write underneath or below, especially to endorse (a document). **2.** To agree to back (an enterprise) with money; finance. **3.** To sign an insurance policy, thus guaranteeing payment in event of losses, damage, etc. **4.** To agree to buy (the stock in a new enterprise not yet sold publicly) at a fixed time and price. —**un′der•writ′er** *n.*

un•de•served |ŭn′dĭ **zûrvd′**| *adj.* Not deserved; unfair: *undeserved criticism.* —**un′de•serv′ed•ly** |ŭn′dĭ **zûr′**vĭd lē| *adv.*

un•de•sir•a•ble |ŭn′dĭ **zīr′**ə bəl| *adj.* Not desirable; objectionable. —*n.* Someone who is considered undesirable. —**un′de•sir′a•bly** *adv.*

un•de•vel•oped |ŭn′dĭ **vĕl′**əpt| *adj.* Not developed: *emotionally undeveloped; an undeveloped roll of film.*

un•did |ŭn **dĭd′**|. Past tense of **undo.**

un•dies |**ŭn′**dēz| *pl.n. Informal.* Underwear.

un•dig•ni•fied |ŭn **dĭg′**nə fīd′| *adj.* Not dignified; lacking in or damaging to dignity: *She tripped and fell, landing in a sprawling, undignified heap.*

un•dis•ci•plined |ŭn **dĭs′**ə plĭnd| *adj.* Not disciplined; unruly.

un•dis•tin•guished |ŭn′dĭ **stĭng′**gwĭsht| *adj.* Not distinguished; ordinary.

un•dis•turbed |ŭn′dĭ **stûrbd′**| *adj.* Not disturbed; calm.

un•do |ŭn **dōō′**| *v.* **un•did** |ŭn **dĭd′**|, **un•done** |ŭn **dŭn′**|, **un•do•ing, un•does** |ŭn **dŭz′**|. **1.** To do away with or reverse the result or effect of (a previous action): *If you pour a pitcher of lemonade down the drain by mistake, you cannot undo your error.* **2.** To untie, unfasten, or loosen: *undo a knot.* **3.** To open; unwrap: *undo gifts.* ¶*These sound alike* **undo, undue.**

un•do•ing |ŭn **dōō′**ĭng| *n.* **1.** The act of doing away with or reversing the result or effect of a previous action: *efforts for the undoing of his team's defeat.* **2. a.** The fact of bringing to ruin: *acting with spite to cause the undoing of all our plans.* **b.** The cause of ruin: *the huge, hollow horse that was the undoing of the Trojans.*

un•doubt•ed |ŭn **dou′**tĭd| *adj.* Not doubted or questioned; accepted: *undoubted talent; an undoubted masterpiece.* —**un•doubt′ed•ly** *adv.*

un•dress |ŭn **drĕs′**| *v.* To remove the clothing of; disrobe. —*n.* Nakedness: *in a state of undress.*

un•due |ŭn **dōō′**| *or* |**-dyōō′**| *adj.* **1.** Not normal or appropriate; excessive: *an undue amount of noise.* **2.** Not proper or legal: *undue powers.* ¶*These sound alike* **undue, undo.**

un•du•lant fever |**ŭn′**jə lənt| *or* |**ŭn′**dyə-| *or* |-də-|. A disease characterized by a long-lasting and recurring fever caused by bacteria that are transmitted through meat and milk from animals infected with the disease. Its symptoms include weakness and pains in the joints.

un•du•late |**ŭn′**jə lāt′| *or* |**ŭn′**dyə-| *or* |-də-| *v.* **un•du•lat•ed, un•du•lat•ing. 1.** To move or cause to move in or with a smooth, wavelike motion. **2.** To have a wavelike appearance or form. [SEE NOTE on p. 478]

un•du•la•tion |ŭn′jə **lā′**shən| *or* |ŭn′dyə-| *or* |-də-| *n.* **1.** A regular rising and falling or movement from side to side; movement in waves. **2.** A wavelike form, outline, or appearance. **3.** One of a series of waves or parts of waves; pulsation.

un•du•ly |ŭn **dōō′**lē| *or* |**-dyōō′**-| *adv.* Excessively; immoderately: *unduly fearful.*

un•dy•ing |ŭn **dī′**ĭng| *adj.* Endless; everlasting: *undying gratitude.*

un•earned |ŭn **ûrnd′**| *adj.* **1.** Not deserved: *unearned praise.* **2.** Not yet earned: *unearned interest.*

un•earth |ŭn **ûrth′**| *v.* **1.** To bring up out of the earth; dig up: *unearthing pottery and sculpture on Crete.* **2.** To bring to public notice; reveal; uncover: *unearthing evidence about the crime.*

un•earth•ly |ŭn **ûrth′**lē| *adj.* **un•earth•li•er, un•earth•li•est. 1.** Not of the earth or this world; supernatural: *unearthly creatures.* **2.** Unnatural; weird: *an unearthly scream.* **3.** Not customary or reasonable; absurd: *an unearthly hour.* —**un•earth′li•ness** *n.*

un•eas•y |ŭn **ē′**zē| *adj.* **un•eas•i•er, un•eas•i•est.**

undertaking

Noah Webster's American Dictionary *(1828) has the following entry at* **undertaking**: *"Any business, work, or project which a person engages in, or attempts to perform; an enterprise. The canal, or the making of the canal, from the Hudson to Lake Erie, a distance of almost four hundred miles, was the greatest* undertaking *of the kind in modern times. The attempt to find a navigable passage to the Pacific round North America, is a hazardous* undertaking, *and probably useless to navigation."*

1. Lacking ease or a sense of security: *The farmers were uneasy until the crop was in.* 2. Awkward or unsure in manner: *uneasy in front of a crowd.* —**un•eas'i•ly** *adv.* —**un•eas'i•ness** *n.*

un•ed•u•cat•ed |ŭn ĕj'o͞o kā'tĭd| *adj.* Not educated; illiterate or ignorant.

un•em•ployed |ŭn'ĕm **ploid'**| *adj.* 1. Out of work; jobless. 2. Not being used; idle.

un•em•ploy•ment |ŭn'ĕm **ploi'**mənt| *n.* The condition of being unemployed. —***modifier:*** *unemployment insurance.*

un•end•ing |ŭn ĕn'dĭng| *adj.* Having no end; endless.

un•e•qual |ŭn ē'kwəl| *adj.* 1. Not equal, as a pair of numbers, algebraic expressions, etc. 2. Not fair; unjust or unmatched: *unequal distribution of income.*

un•e•qualed, also **un•e•qualled** |ŭn ē'kwəld| *adj.* Not equaled or matched.

un•e•quiv•o•cal |ŭn'ĭ **kwĭv'**ə kəl| *adj.* Not disguised or obscured; clear; plain. —**un'e•quiv'o•cal•ly** *adv.*

un•err•ing |ŭn ûr'ĭng| *or* |-ĕr'-| *adj.* Making no mistakes; accurate. —**un•err'ing•ly** *adv.*

UNESCO |yo͞o **nĕs'**kō|. United Nations Educational, Scientific, and Cultural Organization.

un•e•ven |ŭn ē'vən| *adj.* **un•e•ven•er, un•e•ven•est.** 1. Not level or smooth: *the uneven surface of a cobblestone road.* 2. Not straight or parallel: *a book with uneven margins.* 3. Not uniform or consistent; varying, as in quality, form, appearance, etc.: *an uneven performance; a lamp giving very uneven light.* 4. Not balanced; not fair: *an uneven match between the two teams.* —**un•e'ven•ly** *adv.* —**un•e'ven•ness** *n.*

un•e•vent•ful |ŭn'ĭ **vĕnt'**fəl| *adj.* Without any significant incidents; uninteresting or unimportant. —**un'e•vent'ful•ly** *adv.*

un•ex•pect•ed |ŭn'ĭk **spĕk'**tĭd| *adj.* Not expected; coming without warning. —**un'ex•pect'ed•ly** *adv.* —**un'ex•pect'ed•ness** *n.*

un•fail•ing |ŭn fā'lĭng| *adj.* 1. Not failing or running out; inexhaustible: *a source of unfailing amusement.* 2. Constant; reliable: *an unfailing friend.* —**un•fail'ing•ly** *adv.*

un•fair |ŭn fâr'| *adj.* Not fair, right, or just: *unfair laws.* —**un•fair'ly** *adv.* —**un•fair'ness** *n.*

un•faith•ful |ŭn fāth'fəl| *adj.* 1. Not faithful; disloyal: *a knight unfaithful to his king.* 2. Guilty of adultery: *an unfaithful husband.* 3. Not reflecting the original contents; inaccurate: *an unfaithful copy.* —**un•faith'ful•ness** *n.*

un•fa•mil•iar |ŭn'fə **mĭl'**yər| *adj.* 1. Not familiar; not within one's knowledge; strange: *an unfamiliar face.* 2. Not acquainted: *unfamiliar with that subject.* —**un'fa•mil'i•ar'i•ty** |ŭn'fə mĭl'ē-ăr'ĭ tē| *n.* —**un'fa•mil'iar•ly** *adv.*

un•fas•ten |ŭn făs'ən| *or* |-fä'sən| *v.* To open or untie or become opened or untied: *He unfastened the belt. The buckle unfastens easily.*

un•fa•vor•a•ble |ŭn fā'vər ə bəl| *adj.* 1. Not favorable or propitious: *unfavorable working conditions.* 2. Opposed; adverse: *unfavorable criticism.* —**un•fa'vor•a•bly** *adv.*

un•feel•ing |ŭn fē'lĭng| *adj.* 1. Not sympathetic; callous. 2. Having no sensation; numb.

un•fin•ished |ŭn fĭn'ĭsht| *adj.* 1. Not finished; incomplete: *unfinished business.* 2. Not processed in a specific way; natural: *unfinished furniture.*

un•fit |ŭn fĭt'| *adj.* 1. Not suitable or adapted for a given purpose; inappropriate: *unfit for human consumption.* 2. In poor physical or mental health.

un•flap•pa•ble |ŭn **flăp'**ə bəl| *adj. Slang.* Not easily upset or excited, even in a crisis; calm. —**un•flap'pa•bil'i•ty** *n.*

un•fledged |ŭn **flĕjd'**| *adj.* 1. Having incompletely developed feathers and still unable to fly, as a young bird. 2. Lacking experience.

un•flinch•ing |ŭn **flĭn'**chĭng| *adj.* Not showing fear or indecision; unyielding; steadfast: *remaining unflinching while the guns roared; an unflinching determination to find out all the facts.* —**un•flinch'ing•ly** *adv.*

un•fold |ŭn fōld'| *v.* 1. To open or spread out: *unfolding sheets. The petals unfolded gracefully.* 2. To open out gradually to view; become visible: *A magnificent landscape unfolded before us.* 3. To reveal or be revealed gradually: *unfolding the details of his plans; a story that unfolds smoothly.*

un•fore•seen |ŭn'fər **sēn'**| *adj.* Not foreseen; unexpected.

un•for•get•ta•ble |ŭn'fər **gĕt'**ə bəl| *adj.* Permanently impressed on one's memory; memorable.

un•for•giv•a•ble |ŭn'fər **gĭv'**ə bəl| *adj.* Not to be forgiven or pardoned: *unforgivable sins.*

un•formed |ŭn **fôrmd'**| *adj.* 1. Having no definite shape or form. 2. Not yet developed: *unformed ideas.*

un•for•tu•nate |ŭn fôr'chə nĭt| *adj.* 1. Not fortunate; unlucky. 2. Causing misfortune; disastrous. 3. Regrettable; unsuitable or inappropriate: *an unfortunate remark.* —*n.* Someone who is unlucky, poor, etc. —**un•for'tu•nate•ly** *adv.*

un•found•ed |ŭn **foun'**dĭd| *adj.* Having no basis in fact; groundless: *unfounded accusations.*

un•friend•ly |ŭn **frĕnd'**lē| *adj.* **un•friend•li•er, un•friend•li•est.** 1. Not friendly; hostile. 2. Unfavorable; undesirable: *an unfriendly place.* —**un•friend'li•ness** *n.*

un•furl |ŭn **fûrl'**| *v.* To spread or open out; unroll: *unfurl a flag.*

un•gain•ly |ŭn **gān'**lē| *adj.* **un•gain•li•er, un•gain•li•est.** Without grace or ease of movement; awkward; clumsy. —**un•gain'li•ness** *n.*

un•glued |ŭn **glo͞od'**| *adj.* Loosened or separated; unfastened.

***Idiom.* come unglued.** *Slang.* To become upset and lose one's composure, as in a crisis.

un•god•ly |ŭn **gŏd'**lē| *adj.* **un•god•li•er, un•god•li•est.** 1. Not revering God; impious. 2. Sinful; wicked. 3. *Informal.* Exceeding reasonable limits of what is tolerable, bearable, etc.; outrageous: *waking him up at that ungodly hour.*

un•gram•mat•i•cal |ŭn'grə **măt'**ĭ kəl| *adj.* Grammatically incorrect.

un•grate•ful |ŭn **grāt'**fəl| *adj.* 1. Not grateful; without thanks. 2. Disagreeable; unpleasant: *an ungrateful task.* —**un•grate'ful•ly** *adv.* —**un•grate'ful•ness** *n.*

un•guard•ed |ŭn **gär'**dĭd| *adj.* 1. Without guard or defense. 2. Without caution or thought; careless: *an unguarded moment.*

un•guent |**ŭng'**gwənt| *n.* A salve for soothing or healing; an ointment.

un–[1-2]

Un-[1] *is used with adjectives, adverbs, and participles, while* **un-**[2] *is used with verbs.* **Un-**[1] *was Old English* un- *and is related to the Latin negative prefix* in- **(in-**[1]**).** **Un-**[2] *was Old English* un-, ond-, *or* and-; *it is related to the Greek prefix* anti-, *"against, instead of"* **(anti-).**

un–[2]

A selection of obsolete verbs formed with **un-**[2], *all of which are recorded in the* Oxford English Dictionary *as having had considerable use but which for various reasons have not survived:* unbewitch, *"to deliver from witchcraft";* unbishop, *"to depose from the office of bishop";* uncrumple, *"to restore from a crumpled state";* unking, *"to depose from the rank of king";* unnestle, *"to remove from a nest";* unparadise, *"to expel from paradise."*

un•gu•late |ŭng′gyə lĭt| *or* |-lāt′| *adj.* Of or belonging to a group of animals having hoofs and including the horses, cattle, deer, giraffes, rhinoceroses, etc. —*n.* A hoofed animal.

un•hap•py |ŭn hăp′ē| *adj.* **un•hap•pi•er, un•hap•pi•est.** **1.** Not happy; sad: *feeling unhappy.* **2.** Not bringing good fortune; unlucky: *In an unhappy moment he made a wrong decision.* **3.** Not suitable, tactful, etc.; inappropriate: *an unhappy choice of words.* **4.** Dissatisfied; disturbed: *colonists unhappy with foreign rule.* —**un•hap′pi•ly** *adv.* —**un•hap′pi•ness** *n.*

un•harmed |ŭn härmd′| *adj.* Not harmed; safe.

un•health•y |ŭn hĕl′thē| *adj.* **un•health•i•er, un•health•i•est.** **1.** In a poor state of physical or mental health; ill; sick. **2.** Being a sign or symptom of poor health: *a pale, unhealthy appearance.* **3.** Causing or tending to cause poor physical or mental health; not wholesome: *an unhealthy diet.* **4. a.** Harmful to character or moral health; corruptive: *an unhealthy influence on her younger sister.* **b.** Risky; dangerous: *avoiding the unhealthy practice of criticizing the dictator's regime.*

un•heard-of |ŭn hûrd′ŭv′| *adj.* Not previously known or done; without an earlier example: *living in unheard-of luxury.*

un•hinge |ŭn hĭnj′| *v.* **un•hinged, un•hing•ing.** **1.** To remove from hinges. **2.** To unbalance (the mind); confuse; upset.

un•ho•ly |ŭn hō′lē| *adj.* **un•ho•li•er, un•ho•li•est.** **1.** Not holy or sacred. **2.** Wicked; immoral. **3.** *Informal.* Dreadful; outrageous: *an unholy mess.*

un•hook |ŭn ho͝ok′| *v.* **1.** To unfasten the hooks of: *unhook a dress.* **2.** To release or remove from a hook: *unhooked the porch screen. The old man unhooked the fish and rebaited the line.*

uni–. A word element meaning "one, single": **unilateral.**

UNICEF |yo͞o′nĭ sĕf′|. United Nations Children's Fund.

u•ni•cel•lu•lar |yo͞o′nĭ sĕl′yə lər| *adj.* Consisting of a single cell; one-celled: *unicellular microorganisms.*

u•ni•corn |yo͞o′nĭ kôrn′| *n.* An imaginary animal of legend, resembling a horse with a single long horn projecting from its forehead. [SEE PICTURE]

un•i•den•ti•fied |ŭn′ī dĕn′tə fīd′| *adj.* Of an unknown nature: *an unidentified flying object.*

u•ni•form |yo͞o′nə fôrm′| *n.* A suit of clothing intended to identify the person or persons who wear it as members of a specific group, organization, etc. —*adj.* **1.** Always the same; not changing or varying: *planks of uniform length.* **2.** Having the same appearance, form, color, pattern, etc.: *rows and rows of uniform brownstone houses.* —**u′ni•formed′** *adj.* —**u′ni•form′ly** *adv.*

u•ni•form•i•ty |yo͞o′nə fôr′mĭ tē| *n.* The condition of being uniform; sameness.

u•ni•fy |yo͞o′nə fī′| *v.* **u•ni•fied, u•ni•fy•ing, u•ni•fies.** To make into a unit; unite: *War unified the whole population.* —**u′ni•fi•ca′tion** *n.*

u•ni•lat•er•al |yo͞o′nə lăt′ər əl| *adj.* **1.** Of, on, or having only one side. **2.** Done by, undertaken by, or affecting one person, country, etc.

un•i•mag•in•a•ble |ŭn′ĭ măj′ə nə bəl| *adj.* Difficult or impossible to imagine.

un•i•mag•i•na•tive |ŭn′ĭ măj′ə nə tĭv| *or* |-nā′-| *adj.* Not imaginative or creative.

un•im•peach•a•ble |ŭn′ĭm pē′chə bəl| *adj.* Beyond doubt or question; unquestionable: *a man of unimpeachable honesty.*

un•im•por•tant |ŭn′ĭm pôr′tnt| *adj.* Not important; petty. —**un′im•por′tance** *n.*

un•in•hab•it•ed |ŭn′ĭn hăb′ĭ tĭd| *adj.* Not inhabited; having no residents.

un•in•hib•it•ed |ŭn′ĭn hĭb′ĭ tĭd| *adj.* Without inhibitions; open; unrestrained.

un•in•tel•li•gent |ŭn′ĭn tĕl′ə jənt| *adj.* Lacking in intelligence; stupid. —**un′in•tel′li•gent•ly** *adv.*

un•in•tel•li•gi•ble |ŭn′ĭn tĕl′ə jə bəl| *adj.* Not capable of being comprehended. —**un′in•tel′li•gi•bil′i•ty** *n.* —**un′in•tel′li•gi•bly** *adv.*

un•in•ten•tion•al |ŭn′ĭn tĕn′shə nəl| *adj.* Not intentional; not done or said on purpose. —**un′in•ten′tion•al•ly** *adv.*

un•in•ter•est•ed |ŭn ĭn′tər ĭ stĭd| *or* |-trĭs tĭd| *or* |-tə rĕs′tĭd| *adj.* Not interested; indifferent.

un•in•vit•ed |ŭn′ĭn vī′tĭd| *adj.* Not invited.

un•ion |yo͞on′yən| *n.* **1. a.** The act of uniting: *the union of the two football leagues into one.* **b.** A combination formed by uniting, especially an alliance or confederation of persons, parties, etc., formed for mutual interest or benefit: *plans for the union of all colonies under one government.* **c.** The condition of being united: *a play exhibiting an excellent union of literary and human qualities.* **2.** A partnership in marriage: *a happy union.* **3.** An organization of wage earners formed for the purpose of serving their class interest with respect to wages and working conditions. **4.** A mathematical set having the property that each of its elements is also an element of two or more given sets. **5.** A device used for joining pipes, rods, etc. **6.** A design on or part of a flag that symbolizes the union of two or more independent states, regions, etc. For example, the blue part with stars is the union of the U.S. flag. **7. the Union.** The United States of America, especially during the Civil War. —***modifier:*** *union leaders; Union troops.*

un•ion•ize |yo͞on′yə nīz′| *v.* **un•ion•ized, un•ion•iz•ing.** To organize into or cause to join a labor union. —**un′ion•i•za′tion** *n.*

Union Jack. The flag of the United Kingdom.

Union of Soviet Socialist Republics. A country extending from central Europe to the Pacific Ocean. Population, 252,064,000. Capital, Moscow.

union shop. A business or industrial establishment whose employees are required to be or become union members.

u•nique |yo͞o nēk′| *adj.* **1.** Being the only one; sole: *Amassing a great fortune was his unique goal in life.* **2.** Having no equal or equivalent; being the only one in kind, excellence, etc.: *a unique opportunity to buy a house.* —**u•nique′ly** *adv.* —**u•nique′ness** *n.* [SEE NOTE]

u•ni•sex |yo͞o′nĭ sĕks′| *adj.* Suitable or common to males and females: *unisex clothes.*

u•ni•son |yo͞o′nĭ sən| *or* |-zən| *n.* **1.** In music, the combination of two or more tones of the same pitch sounding at the same time. **2.** Agreement; harmony: *salesmen acting in unison to promote a new product.*

u•nit |yo͞o′nĭt| *n.* **1.** A thing, group, person, etc., regarded as a constituent part of a whole: *adding an extra unit to a bookcase. The family is fre-*

unicorn
Sixteenth-century French tapestry, "The Unicorn in Captivity"
The word **unicorn** is from Latin *ūnicornis,* "one-horned (animal)": *ūnus,* "one," + *cornu,* "horn."
The myth of the unicorn is very ancient and widespread. In medieval Europe it was believed that the unicorn could be captured only by a virgin girl and that his horn, in powdered form, gave protection against all poisons. The horns of narwhals and rhinoceroses have for centuries been sold as unicorn's horns.

unique
Unique *is from French* unique, *which is from Latin* ūnicus, *"single, one-of-a-kind, unequaled." If* **unique** *is used only in the absolute senses given in our definition, it is clearly illogical to qualify it with* more *or* most *or with words like* rather *and* somewhat. *But* **unique** *is often used in a looser way, to mean "extremely remarkable," and this has often led people to use expressions like* the most unique person I've ever met. *This usage is considered unacceptable by 94 per cent of the American Heritage Usage Panel.*

United States
"The stile [style, title] of this confederacy shall be 'The United States of America.'" —Articles of Confederation (November 15, 1777).

unjust
"The rain it raineth on the just
And also on the unjust fella:
But chiefly on the just, because
The unjust has the just's
umbrella."
—Lord Bowen (1835–1894).

unkempt
Unkempt, *like* **uncouth,** *has survived its positive counterpart.* Kempt *meant "combed" and came from* kemb, *"to comb," which is an old dialectal variant of* **comb.**

ă pat/ā pay/â care/ä father/ĕ pet/ ē be/ĭ pit/ī pie/î fierce/ŏ pot/ ō go/ô paw, for/oi oil/ŏŏ book/ ōō boot/ou out/ŭ cut/û fur/ *th* the/th thin/hw which/zh vision/ ə ago, item, pencil, atom, circus

quently regarded as the basic unit of society. **2.** A single group regarded as a distinct part within a larger group: *an Army unit.* **3.** A precisely defined quantity in terms of which measurement of quantities of the same kind can be expressed: *The meter is a unit of distance.* **4.** The digit located just to the left of the decimal point in the Arabic system of numeration. **5.** A part, device, or module that performs a particular function, as in a machine, electronic device, system, etc.: *the arithmetic unit of a digital computer.*

U•ni•tar•i•an |yōō′nĭ târ′ē ən| *n.* A member of a Christian religious denomination that rejects the doctrine of the Trinity and emphasizes freedom and tolerance in religious belief. —**U′ni•tar′i•an•ism′** *n.*

u•nite |yōō nīt′| *v.* **u•nit•ed, u•nit•ing. 1.** To bring together or join so as to form a whole: *Benjamin Franklin had a plan to unite the Colonies under one government.* **2.** To join together or bring into close association for a common purpose: *a treaty to unite all nations in the fight against poverty.* **3.** To become joined, combined, etc., into a unit: *Men, unite for peace!*

United Arab Emirates. A country on the eastern coast of the Arabian Peninsula. Population, 220,000. Capital, Abu Dhabi.

United Kingdom. A country in western Europe consisting of England, Scotland, Wales, and Northern Ireland. Population, 55,933,000. Capital, London.

United Nations. An international organization comprising most of the countries of the world, formed in 1945 to promote peace, security, and economic development.

United States of America. A country in North America, consisting of 50 states and the District of Columbia. Population, 226,504,825. Capital, Washington, D.C. [SEE NOTE]

unit pricing. The pricing of goods on the basis of cost per unit of measure.

u•ni•ty |yōō′nĭ tē| *n., pl.* **u•ni•ties. 1.** The condition of being united into a single whole; oneness: *In unity there is strength.* **2.** Accord, as of aims, feelings, etc.; harmony: *a period of great national unity and purpose.* **3.** An ordering of all elements in a work of art or literature so that each contributes to form a complete whole.

univ. 1. universal. **2.** university.

Univ. university.

u•ni•va•lent |yōō′nĭ vā′lənt| *adj.* In chemistry, having valence 1.

u•ni•valve |yōō′nə vălv′| *n.* A mollusk, such as a snail, having a single shell. —*adj.* **1.** Having a single shell: *a univalve mollusk.* **2.** Consisting of a single part rather than paired: *a univalve shell.*

u•ni•ver•sal |yōō′nə vûr′səl| *adj.* **1.** Extending to or affecting the whole world; worldwide: *universal peace.* **2.** Of, for, done by, or affecting all: *universal education.* —**u′ni•ver•sal′i•ty** *n.* —**u′ni•ver′sal•ly** *adv.*

universal joint. A joint that couples a pair of shafts not in the same line so that a rotating motion can be transferred from one to the other.

u•ni•verse |yōō′nə vûrs′| *n.* **1.** All the matter and space that exists, considered as a whole; the cosmos. **2.** In mathematics, a set that contains all the objects and sets under discussion as elements or subsets.

u•ni•ver•si•ty |yōō′nə vûr′sĭ tē| *n., pl.* **u•ni•ver•si•ties.** A school of higher learning that offers degrees and includes programs of study in graduate school, professional schools, and regular college divisions.

un•just |ŭn jŭst′| *adj.* Not just or fair; unfair. —**un•just′ly** *adv.* [SEE NOTE]

un•kempt |ŭn kĕmpt′| *adj.* **1.** Not combed: *unkempt hair.* **2.** Not neat or tidy; messy: *an unkempt lawn; umkempt clothes.* [SEE NOTE]

un•kind |ŭn kīnd′| *adj.* **un•kind•er, un•kind•est.** Not kind; harsh; unsympathetic. —**un•kind′ly** *adv.* —**un•kind′ness** *n.*

un•known |ŭn nōn′| *adj.* **1.** Not known or familiar; strange: *a town unknown to the cowboys.* **2.** Not yet discovered: *ships sailing across the ocean to unknown lands.* **3.** Not heard of before; not publicly known: *an unknown painter.* **4.** Not identified or ascertained: *an unknown quantity.* —*n.* Someone or something that is unknown.

un•lad•y•like |ŭn lā′dē līk′| *adj.* Considered improper for a lady: *unladylike behavior.*

un•latch |ŭn lăch′| *v.* To unfasten or open by releasing a latch.

un•law•ful |ŭn lô′fəl| *adj.* In violation of the law; illegal. —**un•law′ful•ly** *adv.*

un•leash |ŭn lēsh′| *v.* To release from or as if from a leash: *unleashed the dog. The enemy unleashed its power against the border cities.*

un•leav•ened |ŭn lĕv′ənd| *adj.* Made without leaven: *unleavened bread.*

un•less |ŭn lĕs′| *conj.* Except on the condition that: *You can't go out unless you comb your hair.*

un•like |ŭn līk′| *adj.* Not alike; dissimilar: *unlike poles of magnets.* —*prep.* **1.** Different from; not like: *a sound unlike any other.* **2.** Not typical of: *unlike him not to call if he cannot come.*

un•like•ly |ŭn līk′lē| *adj.* **un•like•li•er, un•like•li•est. 1.** Not likely; improbable: *an unlikely story.* **2.** Likely to fail; unpromising: *betting on the most unlikely horse.*

un•lim•it•ed |ŭn lĭm′ĭ tĭd| *adj.* Having no limits or bounds: *unlimited possibilities.*

un•load |ŭn lōd′| *v.* **1. a.** To remove the load or cargo from: *unload a truck.* **b.** To remove (cargo): *unload furniture from the van.* **2. a.** To remove the charge from (a firearm). **b.** To discharge (a firearm); fire: *marksmen unloading their rifles at the targets.* **3.** To dispose of; get rid of; dump: *unloading textiles at low prices.*

un•loose |ŭn lōōs′| *v.* **un•loosed, un•loos•ing.** To let loose; unfasten; release.

un•luck•y |ŭn lŭk′ē| *adj.* **un•luck•i•er, un•luck•i•est.** Not lucky; having or bringing bad luck: *an unlucky occurrence.* —**un•luck′i•ly** *adv.*

un•made |ŭn mād′| *adj.* Not made: *an unmade bed.*

un•manned |ŭn mănd′| *adj.* **1.** Lacking a crew. **2.** Designed to operate without a crew: *an unmanned spacecraft.*

un•man•ner•ly |ŭn măn′ər lē| *adj.* Having or marked by bad manners; rude; impolite: *an unmannerly girl; unmannerly behavior.*

un•mar•ried |ŭn măr′ēd| *adj.* Not married.

un•mask |ŭn măsk′| *or* |-mäsk′| *v.* **1. a.** To remove a mask. **b.** To remove a mask from. **2.** To disclose the true nature of; reveal.

un•men•tion•a•bles |ŭn mĕn′shə nə bəlz| *pl.n.* Underwear.

un•mer•ci•ful |ŭn mûr′sĭ fəl| *adj.* **1.** Having no mercy; merciless. **2.** Excessive; extreme: *unmerciful heat.* —**un•mer′ci•ful•ly** *adv.*

un•mind•ful |ŭn mīnd′fəl| *adj.* Careless; forgetful: *unmindful of the time.* —**un•mind′ful•ly** *adv.*

un•mis•tak•a•ble |ŭn′mĭ stā′kə bəl| *adj.* Evident; obvious: *an unmistakable Southern accent.* —**un′mis•tak′a•bly** *adv.*

un•mit•i•gat•ed |ŭn mĭt′ĭ gā′tĭd| *adj.* **1.** Not diminished in intensity; without relief: *unmitigated heat.* **2.** Absolute; unqualified: *an unmitigated lie.*

un•named |ŭn nāmd′| *adj.* Not named; unidentified.

un•nat•u•ral |ŭn năch′ər əl| *or* |-năch′rəl| *adj.* **1.** Not in accordance with what usually occurs in nature; abnormal or unusual. **2.** Strained, stiff, or affected; artificial: *an unnatural manner.* **3.** Against natural feelings or normal or accepted standards; inhuman: *unnatural practices such as slavery.* —**un•nat′u•ral•ly** *adv.*

un•nec•es•sar•y |ŭn nĕs′ĭ sĕr′ē| *adj.* Not necessary; needless. —**un•nec′es•sar′i•ly** |ŭn nĕs′ĭ-sâr′ə lē| *adv.*

un•nerve |ŭn nûrv′| *v.* **un•nerved, un•nerv•ing.** To cause to lose courage, composure, etc.: *The incident unnerved him.*

un•ob•tru•sive |ŭn′əb trōō′sĭv| *adj.* Not blatant or aggressive in style, manner, etc.; inconspicuous: *an unobtrusive life in the country.* —**un′ob•tru′sive•ly** *adv.* —**un′ob•tru′sive•ness** *n.*

un•oc•cu•pied |ŭn ŏk′yə pīd′| *adj.* **1.** Not occupied; vacant: *unoccupied seats.* **2.** Not occupied by foreign troops. **3.** Not busy; idle.

un•of•fi•cial |ŭn′ə fĭsh′əl| *adj.* Not official: *unofficial reports.* —**un′of•fi′cial•ly** *adv.*

un•o•pened |ŭn ō′pənd| *adj.* Not opened; closed: *The door remained unopened.*

un•or•gan•ized |ŭn ôr′gə nīzd′| *adj.* **1.** Not organized, arranged, etc. **2.** Not unionized.

un•or•tho•dox |ŭn ôr′thə dŏks′| *adj.* Not conventional, orthodox, or traditional: *an unorthodox approach to a problem.*

un•pack |ŭn păk′| *v.* **1.** To remove the contents of (a suitcase, trunk, etc.): *unpack a suitcase; unpacking immediately.* **2.** To remove from a container or from packaging: *unpack groceries.*

un•paid |ŭn pād′| *adj.* **1.** Not yet paid: *an unpaid bill.* **2.** Receiving no pay; not salaried: *an unpaid volunteer.*

un•paint•ed |ŭn pān′tĭd| *adj.* Not painted or finished: *unpainted furniture.*

un•par•al•leled |ŭn păr′ə lĕld′| *adj.* Without parallel; unequaled: *her unparalleled beauty.*

un•paved |ŭn pāvd′| *adj.* Not paved.

un•pleas•ant |ŭn plĕz′ənt| *adj.* Not pleasant; disagreeable. —**un•pleas′ant•ly** *adv.* —**un•pleas′ant•ness** *n.*

un•plug |ŭn plŭg′| *v.* **un•plugged, un•plug•ging.** **1.** To disconnect (an appliance) by removing its plug from an outlet. **2.** To remove a plug or stopper from.

un•pop•u•lar |ŭn pŏp′yə lər| *adj.* Not popular; not generally liked or approved of. —**un•pop′u•lar′i•ty** |ŭn pŏp′yə lăr′ĭ tē| *n.*

un•prec•e•dent•ed |ŭn prĕs′ĭ dĕn′tĭd| *adj.* Without precedent; not done or known before: *an unprecedented demand for housing.*

un•pre•dict•a•ble |ŭn′prĭ dĭk′tə bəl| *adj.* Not predictable. —**un′pre•dict′a•bly** *adv.*

un•pre•pared |ŭn′prĭ pârd′| *adj.* **1.** Not prepared or ready; not equipped: *unprepared for school.* **2.** Done without preparation; impromptu: *an unprepared speech.*

un•pre•ten•tious |ŭn′prĭ tĕn′shəs| *adj.* Without pretention; modest. —**un′pre•ten′tious•ly** *adv.* —**un′pre•ten′tious•ness** *n.*

un•prin•ci•pled |ŭn′prĭn′sə pəld| *adj.* Lacking principles or moral scruples.

un•print•a•ble |ŭn prĭn′tə bəl| *adj.* Not proper for publication: *an unprintable word.*

un•prof•it•a•ble |ŭn prŏf′ĭ tə bəl| *adj.* Not profitable; useless. —**un•prof′it•a•bly** *adv.*

un•qual•i•fied |ŭn kwŏl′ə fīd′| *adj.* **1.** Without the necessary qualifications. **2.** Without reservation; complete: *an unqualified success.*

un•ques•tion•a•ble |ŭn kwĕs′chə nə bəl| *adj.* Beyond question or doubt; certain. —**un•ques′tion•a•bly** *adv.*

un•rav•el |ŭn răv′əl| *v.* **-rav•eled** or **-rav•elled, -rav•el•ing** or **-rav•el•ling.** **1.** To separate (entangled threads) into single loose threads. **2.** To undo (a knitted fabric); reduce to yarn.

un•read |ŭn rĕd′| *adj.* **1.** Not read or studied. **2.** Having read little; ignorant.

un•read•y |ŭn rĕd′ē| *adj.* Not ready or prepared. [SEE NOTE]

un•re•al |ŭn rē′əl| *or* |-rēl′| *adj.* Not real; imaginary.

un•re•al•is•tic |ŭn′rē ə lĭs′tĭk| *adj.* Not realistic; unreasonable. —**un′re•al•is′ti•cal•ly** *adv.*

un•rea•son•a•ble |ŭn rē′zə nə bəl| *adj.* **1.** Not reasonable: *an unreasonable request.* **2.** Exceeding reasonable limits: *an unreasonable amount.* —**un•rea′son•a•bly** *adv.*

un•re•lent•ing |ŭn′rĭ lĕn′tĭng| *adj.* **1.** Not yielding, as in resolution; inflexible: *an unrelenting sergeant drilling his troops.* **2.** Not diminishing in intensity: *working at an unrelenting pace.*

un•re•li•a•ble |ŭn′rĭ lī′ə bəl| *adj.* Not reliable or trustworthy. —**un′re•li′a•bil′i•ty** *n.* —**un′re•li′a•bly** *adv.*

un•re•mit•ting |ŭn′rĭ mĭt′ĭng| *adj.* Never letting up; incessant; persistent: *an unremitting struggle for survival.* —**un′re•mit′ting•ly** *adv.*

un•rest |ŭn rĕst′| *n.* Uneasiness; disquiet: *widespread urban unrest.*

un•ripe |ŭn rīp′| *adj.* **1.** Not fully ripened: *unripe apples.* **2.** Not fully formed; immature: *a man of unripe judgment.* **3.** Not sufficiently advanced, prepared, etc.; not ready: *The time is yet unripe.*

un•ruf•fled |ŭn rŭf′əld| *adj.* Not ruffled or agitated; calm.

un•ru•ly |ŭn rōō′lē| *adj.* **un•ru•li•er, un•ru•li•est.** Difficult or impossible to discipline or control.

un•sad•dle |ŭn săd′l| *v.* **-sad•dled, -sad•dling.** **1.** To remove the saddle from. **2.** To throw (a person) from a saddle.

un•safe |ŭn sāf′| *adj.* Not safe; dangerous.

un•salt•ed |ŭn sôl′tĭd| *adj.* Not sprinkled with or containing salt.

un•san•i•tar•y |ŭn săn′ĭ tĕr′ē| *adj.* Not sanitary; unclean.

un•sat•is•fac•to•ry |ŭn′săt ĭs făk′tə rē| *adj.* Not satisfactory; inadequate: *unsatisfactory living conditions.*

unready

*Ethelred II, King of England (*A.D. *978–1016), was dubbed "the unready." This nickname did not originally mean what it now appears to mean. In Old English,* Aethelræd *literally meant "noble counsel";* "Aethelræd unræd," *meaning "noble counsel, evil counsel," was a jingling pun on the king's name. Later* unræd *was confused with* **unready**, *a different word formed from the prefix* **un-**[1] + **ready**.

un•sat•u•rat•ed |ŭn săch′ə rā′tĭd| *adj.* **1.** Of or indicating a chemical compound, especially of carbon, in which two atoms are joined by more than a single bond: *unsaturated fats.* **2.** Capable of dissolving more of a solute: *an unsaturated solution.*

un•sa•vor•y |ŭn sā′və rē| *adj.* **1.** Having a bad or dull taste; insipid. **2.** Morally offensive: *an unsavory character.*

un•scathed |ŭn skā*th*d′| *adj.* Not harmed or injured: *prisoners escaping unscathed.*

un•sci•en•tif•ic |ŭn′sī ən tĭf′ĭk| *adj.* Not according to or following the principles of science.

un•scram•ble |ŭn skrăm′bəl| *v.* **-scram•bled, -scram•bling. 1.** To straighten out; disentangle. **2.** To restore to a form that can be understood: *He unscrambled the coded message.*

un•screw |ŭn skrōō′| *v.* **1.** To loosen, adjust, or remove (a screw, nut, etc.) by or as if by turning. **2. a.** To remove the screws from. **b.** To detach or dismount by removing the screws from. **3.** To be capable of being unscrewed.

un•scru•pu•lous |ŭn skrōō′pyə ləs| *adj.* Without scruples or principles; not honorable. —**un•scru′pu•lous•ly** *adv.* —**un•scru′pu•lous•ness** *n.*

un•seal |ŭn sēl′| *v.* To break open or remove the seal from.

un•sea•son•a•ble |ŭn sē′zə nə bəl| *adj.* Out of season; not suitable for or characteristic of the season. —**un•sea′son•a•bly** *adv.* [SEE NOTE]

unseasonable
"It is unseasonable and unwholesome in all months that have not an R in their name to eat an oyster." —*William Butler (1599).*

un•seat |ŭn sēt′| *v.* **un•seat•ed, un•seat•ing. 1.** To remove (a person) from a seat or saddle. **2.** To force out of a position or office.

un•seem•ly |ŭn sēm′lē| *adj.* **un•seem•li•er, un•seem•li•est.** Not in good taste; improper.

un•seen |ŭn sēn′| *adj.* Not seen or noticed; invisible or unobtrusive.

un•self•ish |ŭn sĕl′fĭsh| *adj.* Not selfish; generous. —**un•self′ish•ly** *adv.* —**un•self′ish•ness** *n.*

un•set•tle |ŭn sĕt′l| *v.* **-set•tled, -set•tling. 1.** To move from a settled condition; make unstable: *strikes unsettling the economy.* **2.** To make uneasy; disturb: *The news unsettled her.*

un•set•tled |ŭn sĕt′ld| *adj.* Not settled, especially: **1.** Disordered; disturbed: *unsettled times.* **2.** Not determined or resolved: *an unsettled legal case.* **3.** Not paid: *unsettled accounts.* **4.** Not populated: *a vast unsettled region.* **5.** Uncertain; variable: *unsettled weather.*

un•shack•le |ŭn shăk′əl| *v.* **-shack•led, -shack•ling.** To release from or as if from prison; set free.

un•shak•a•ble |ŭn shā′kə bəl| *adj.* Not capable of being shaken; firm: *a man of unshakable convictions.* —**un•shak′a•bly** *adv.*

un•shak•en |ŭn shā′kən| *adj.* Not shaken; firm: *His faith in his master remained unshaken.*

un•sheathe |ŭn shē*th*′| *v.* **un•sheathed, un•sheath•ing.** To remove from or as if from a sheath.

un•shod |ŭn shŏd′| *adj.* Without shoes.

un•shorn |ŭn shôrn′| *or* |-shōrn′| *adj.* **1.** Not having been sheared: *an unshorn lamb.* **2.** Not cut: *long, unshorn hair.*

un•sight•ly |ŭn sīt′lē| *adj.* **un•sight•li•er, un•sight•li•est.** Not pleasant to look at; unattractive. —**un•sight′li•ness** *n.*

un•skilled |ŭn skĭld′| *adj.* **1.** Lacking skill or special technical training: *unskilled workers.* **2.** Requiring no special skills: *unskilled work.*

un•skill•ful |ŭn skĭl′fəl| *adj.* Not skillful; clumsy. —**un•skill′ful•ly** *adv.* —**un•skill′ful•ness** *n.*

un•so•phis•ti•cat•ed |ŭn′sə fĭs′tĭ kā′tĭd| *adj.* Not sophisticated; naive.

un•sound |ŭn sound′| *adj.* **1.** Not dependably strong or sound: *a house with unsound foundations.* **2.** Not physically strong; unhealthy. **3.** Not logical; fallacious: *an unsound argument.*

un•speak•a•ble |ŭn spē′kə bəl| *adj.* **1.** Beyond description; indescribable: *unspeakable anxiety.* **2.** Bad beyond description; totally objectionable: *unspeakable wickedness.* —**un•speak′a•bly** *adv.*

un•spo•ken |ŭn spō′kən| *adj.* Not expressed; unsaid: *an unspoken wish.*

un•sta•ble |ŭn stā′bəl| *adj.* **un•sta•bler, un•sta•blest. 1.** Not steady, firm, etc.: *an unstable chair.* **2.** Having a strong tendency to change or oscillate: *an unstable currency; unstable prices.* **3.** Mentally or psychologically unbalanced. **4.** Tending to decompose easily, as a chemical compound. **5. a.** Decaying after a relatively short time, as an atomic particle. **b.** Radioactive, as an element, isotope, or atomic nucleus.

un•stead•y |ŭn stĕd′ē| *adj.* **un•stead•i•er, un•stead•i•est. 1.** Not steady; unstable. **2.** Wavering; uneven: *an unsteady voice.* —**un•stead′i•ly** *adv.* —**un•stead′i•ness** *n.*

un•stressed |ŭn strĕst′| *adj.* **1.** Not accented or stressed: *an unstressed syllable.* **2.** Not emphasized.

un•strung |ŭn strŭng′| *adj.* **1.** Having the strings loosened or removed. **2.** Emotionally upset.

un•sub•stan•tial |ŭn′səb stăn′shəl| *adj.* **1.** Not substantial; flimsy. **2.** Not valid; lacking a factual basis; *unsubstantial hopes.* **3.** Lacking material substance; not real; imaginary.

un•suc•cess•ful |ŭn′sək sĕs′fəl| *adj.* Not succeeding; without success. —**un′suc•cess′ful•ly** *adv.*

un•suit•a•ble |ŭn sōō′tə bəl| *adj.* Not suitable or proper: *an unsuitable dress for a wedding.* —**un•suit′a•bil′i•ty** *n.* —**un•suit′a•bly** *adv.*

un•sul•lied |ŭn sŭl′ēd| *adj.* Not sullied; pure.

un•sung |ŭn sŭng′| *adj.* **1.** Not sung. **2.** Not honored or praised, as in song: *unsung heroes.*

un•sure |ŭn shŏŏr′| *adj.* Not sure; uncertain.

un•sur•passed |ŭn′sər păst′| *or* |-päst′| *adj.* Not surpassed or exceeded.

un•sus•pect•ed |ŭn′sə spĕk′tĭd| *adj.* **1.** Not suspected or under suspicion. **2.** Not known; unexpected: *Unsuspected wealth lay hidden there.*

un•sus•pect•ing |ŭn′sə spĕk′tĭng| *adj.* Not suspecting; trusting: *an unsuspecting child.* —**un′sus•pect′ing•ly** *adv.*

un•sym•pa•thet•ic |ŭn′sĭm pə thĕt′ĭk| *adj.* Not sympathetic. —**un′sym•pa•thet′i•cal•ly** *adv.*

un•tamed |ŭn tāmd′| *adj.* Not tamed or brought under control: *an untamed horse.*

un•tan•gle |ŭn tăng′gəl| *v.* **-tan•gled, -tan•gling. 1.** To free from tangles or snarls. **2.** To settle; clarify; resolve: *untangle a problem; untangle a mystery.*

un•tapped |ŭn tăpt′| *adj.* **1.** Not tapped: *an untapped keg.* **2.** Not utilized: *untapped resources.*

un•ten•a•ble |ŭn tĕn′ə bəl| *adj.* Not capable of

being defended or maintained: *an untenable position.* —**un·ten'a·bly** *adv.*

un·think·a·ble |ŭn thĭngk'kə bəl| *adj.* Impossible to imagine or consider; inconceivable; out of the question. —**un·think'a·bly** *adv.*

un·think·ing |ŭn thĭng'kĭng| *adj.* Inconsiderate or thoughtless: *an unthinking remark.*

un·ti·dy |ŭn tī'dē| *adj.* **un·ti·di·er, un·ti·di·est.** Not tidy or neat; sloppy. —**un·ti'di·ly** *adv.* —**un·ti'di·ness** *n.*

un·tie |ŭn tī'| *v.* **-tied, -ty·ing. 1.** To undo or loosen (a knot). **2.** To free from something that binds or restrains.

un·til |ŭn tĭl'| *prep.* **1.** Up to the time of: *danced until dawn.* Also used as a conjunction: *danced until it was dawn.* **2.** Before a specified time: *You can't have the bike until tomorrow.* Also used as a conjunction: *And tomorrow you can't have it until you pay me.* —*conj.* To the point or extent that: *He talked until he was worn out.*

un·time·ly |ŭn tīm'lē| *adj.* **un·time·li·er, un·time·li·est. 1.** Occurring at an inappropriate or unsuitable time: *an untimely visit.* **2.** Occurring too soon; premature: *his untimely death.*

un·tir·ing |ŭn tīr'ĭng| *adj.* **1.** Not tiring: *a heavy burden on his untiring shoulders.* **2.** Not ceasing; persistent: *untiring efforts.* —**un·tir'ing·ly** *adv.*

un·to |ŭn'to͞o| *prep. Archaic.* To.

un·told |ŭn tōld'| *adj.* **1.** Not told or revealed: *untold secrets.* **2.** Without limit; beyond description: *untold suffering.*

un·touch·a·ble |ŭn tŭch'ə bəl| *adj.* **1.** Not to be touched. **2.** Not capable of being touched; out of reach. **3.** Unpleasant to the touch. —*n.* Often **Untouchable.** A member of the lowest Hindu caste, whose touch was considered unclean.

un·tried |ŭn trīd'| *adj.* **1.** Not tried, tested, or proved. **2.** Not tried in court; without a trial.

un·trod·den |ŭn trŏd'n| *adj.* Not having been trod upon; unexplored: *untrodden paths.*

un·true |ŭn tro͞o'| *adj.* **1.** Not true; false. **2.** Not faithful; disloyal: *untrue to her vows.*

un·truth |ŭn tro͞oth'| *n.* **1.** Something untrue; a lie. **2.** Lack of truth.

un·used. *adj.* **1.** |ŭn yo͞ozd'|. Not used or never having been used. **2.** |ŭn yo͞ost'|. Not accustomed: *He is unused to working.*

un·u·su·al |ŭn yo͞o'zho͞o əl| *adj.* Not usual, common, or ordinary. —**un·u'su·al·ly** *adv.*

un·ut·ter·a·ble |ŭn ŭt'ər ə bəl| *adj.* Not capable of being uttered or expressed: *an unutterable word; her unutterable beauty.* —**un·ut'ter·a·bly** *adv.*

un·veil |ŭn vāl'| *v.* **1.** To remove a veil or other covering from. **2.** To reveal.

un·voiced |ŭn voist'| *adj.* **1.** Not uttered or expressed. **2.** Uttered without vibrating the vocal cords; voiceless.

un·war·rant·ed |ŭn wôr'ən tĭd| *or* |-wŏr'-| *adj.* Not capable of being justified; groundless: *an unwarranted judgment lacking basis in fact.*

un·war·y |ŭn wâr'ē| *adj.* **un·war·i·er, un·war·i·est.** Not alert to danger; careless.

un·wel·come |ŭn wĕl'kəm| *adj.* Not welcome or wanted: *an unwelcome visitor.*

un·well |ŭn wĕl'| *adj.* Not well; sick; ill.

un·whole·some |ŭn hōl'səm| *adj.* **1.** Not healthful or healthy: *unwholesome foods.* **2.** Not wholesome; morally decadent or corrupt.

un·wield·y |ŭn wēl'dē| *adj.* **un·wield·i·er, un·wield·i·est.** Difficult to carry or handle because of shape or size; clumsy: *an unwieldy bundle.*

un·wil·ling |ŭn wĭl'ĭng| *adj.* Not willing; hesitant; reluctant: *unwilling to pay.* —**un·wil'ling·ly** *adv.* —**un·wil'ling·ness** *n.*

un·wind |ŭn wīnd'| *v.* **-wound** |-wound'|, **-wind·ing. 1.** To unroll or become unrolled: *unwind cable. The film unwound from the reel.* **2.** To become free of anxiety, worry, tension, etc.

un·wise |ŭn wīz'| *adj.* **un·wis·er, un·wis·est.** Not wise; foolish. —**un·wise'ly** *adv.*

un·wit·ting |ŭn wĭt'ĭng| *adj.* **1.** Not intended; unintentional: *an unwitting remark.* **2.** Not knowing; unaware: *an unwitting victim of fraud.*

un·wont·ed |ŭn wôn'tĭd| *or* |-wōn'-| *or* |-wŭn'-| *adj.* Not ordinary; unusual: *His unwonted rudeness surprised everybody.*

un·wor·thy |ŭn wûr'thē| *adj.* **un·wor·thi·er, un·wor·thi·est. 1.** Not deserving: *a play unworthy of the award.* **2.** Not suiting or befitting: *a remark unworthy of her.* —**un·wor'thi·ness** *n.*

un·wrap |ŭn răp'| *v.* **-wrapped, -wrap·ping.** To open or become open by removing the wrapper from.

un·writ·ten |ŭn rĭt'n| *adj.* Not written or recorded but known through custom or tradition: *an unwritten law.*

un·yield·ing |ŭn yēl'dĭng| *adj.* Not yielding or giving in; firm.

un·zip |ŭn zĭp'| *v.* **-zipped, -zip·ping. 1.** To open or unfasten (a zipper or a garment with a zipper). **2.** To become unzipped.

up |ŭp| *adv.* **1.** From a lower to a higher position: *moving up.* Also used prepositionally: *going up a mountain.* **2.** In or toward a higher position: *looking up.* Also used prepositionally: *looking up the side of a mountain.* **3.** From a reclining to an upright position: *He helped me up.* **4. a.** Above a surface: *come up for air.* **b.** Above the horizon: *The sun came up.* **5.** Into view or consideration: *You never brought this up before.* **6.** In or toward a position conventionally regarded as higher, as on a map: *going up to Canada.* **7.** To or at a higher price: *Fares are going up again.* **8.** So as to advance, increase, or improve: *His hopes keep going up.* **9.** With or to a greater pitch or volume: *Turn the radio up.* **10.** Into a state of excitement or turbulence: *A great wind came up.* **11.** So as to detach or unearth: *pulling up weeds.* **12.** Apart; into pieces: *tore the paper.* **13.** —Used as an intensive with certain verbs: *cleaning up.* —*adj.* **1.** Moving or directed upward: *an up elevator.* **2.** Being out of bed: *Are you up yet?* **3.** Actively functioning: *He's been up and around for a week.* **4.** *Informal.* Going on; happening: *What's up?* **5.** Being considered: *a contract up for renewal.* **6.** Finished; over: *Time's up!* **7.** *Informal.* Informed, especially well-informed: *I'm not up on sports.* **8.** Being ahead of an opponent: *up two holes in a golf match.* **9.** At bat in baseball: *You're up!* —*prep.* **1.** Toward or at a point farther along: *up the road.* **2.** In a direction toward the source of: *up the Hudson.*
[SEE NOTE]

Idioms. **up against.** Confronted with; facing: *up against many difficulties.* **ups and downs.** Good and bad periods. **up to. 1.** Occupied with,

up
In the materials on which this Dictionary was based, **up** *occurs 2,400 times per million words, whereas* **down** *occurs only 1,300 times per million.*

upright piano

upon

There is hardly any definable difference between **on** *and* **upon**. **Upon** *has a formal and slightly emphatic effect, and is used less than one-twentieth as often as* **on**. *But* **upon** *is preserved in a number of set expressions like* once upon a time *and* upon my honor *and in some phrasal verbs like* come upon, enter upon, *and* hit upon. *When* **up** *and* **on** *are used as two separate adjacent words,* **up** *is either an adverb or part of a preceding phrasal verb, and the effect is quite different from that of* **upon**. *Compare* Go upon the stage *and* Go up on the stage.

ă pat/ā pay/â care/ä father/ĕ pet/ē be/ĭ pit/ī pie/î fierce/ŏ pot/ō go/ô paw, for/oi oil/ŏŏ book/ōō boot/ou out/ŭ cut/û fur/*th* the/th thin/hw which/zh vision/ə ago, item, pencil, atom, circus

especially scheming or devising: *up to no good.* **2.** Prepared for: *Are you sure you're up to this responsibility?* **3.** Dependent upon: *The decision is up to her.* —*v.* **upped, up•ping.** *Informal.* **1.** To increase or cause to increase: *upping prices.* **2.** To act suddenly or unexpectedly: *We voted his proposal down, so he upped and left the meeting.* —*n. Informal.* An increase: *a sudden up in prices.*

up-and-com•ing |ŭp′ən kŭm′ĭng| *adj.* Marked for future success: *an up-and-coming executive.*

up•beat |ŭp′bēt′| *n.* An unaccented musical beat, especially the last beat of a measure, upon which a conductor's hand moves upward.

up•braid |ŭp brād′| *v.* To scold; censure.

up•bring•ing |ŭp′brĭng′ĭng| *n.* The rearing and training received during childhood.

up•coun•try |ŭp′kŭn′trē| *n.* The interior of a country. —*adj.* |ŭp′kŭn′trē|. Of, located in, or coming from the upcountry: *their home in upcountry Virginia.* —*adv.* |ŭp′kŭn′trē|. In, to, or toward the upcountry: *traveling upcountry.*

up•date |ŭp dāt′| *or* |ŭp′dāt′| *v.* **up•dat•ed, up•dat•ing.** To bring up to date: *update a map.*

up•draft |ŭp′drăft′| *or* |-dräft′| *n.* A current of air that flows upward.

up•end |ŭp ĕnd′| *v.* To set or turn on one end: *upend a boat.*

up•grade |ŭp grād′| *or* |ŭp′grād′| *v.* **up•grad•ed, up•grad•ing.** To raise to a higher rank, position, grade, or standard: *upgrade an employee; upgrading all their products.* —*n.* |ŭp′grād′|. An upward incline.

up•heav•al |ŭp hē′vəl| *n.* **1.** A lifting or upward movement of the earth's crust. **2.** A sudden and violent disturbance.

up•hill |ŭp′hĭl′| *adj.* **1.** Going up a hill or slope: *an uphill street.* **2.** Long, tedious, or difficult: *an uphill struggle to finish on time.* —*adv.* Upward: *going uphill.* —*n.* An upward incline.

up•hold |ŭp hōld′| *v.* **up•held** |ŭp hĕld′|, **up•hold•ing.** **1.** To prevent from falling; support. **2.** To maintain in the face of a challenge: *upholding her political opinions.*

up•hol•ster |ŭp hōl′stər| *v.* To supply (furniture) with stuffing, springs, cushions, and a fabric covering. —**up•hol′ster•er** *n.*

up•hol•ster•y |ŭp hōl′stə rē| *n.* **1.** The materials used in upholstering. **2.** The craft of upholstering.

up•keep |ŭp′kēp′| *n.* **1.** Maintenance in proper operation, condition, and repair. **2.** The cost of such maintenance.

up•land |ŭp′lənd| *or* |-lănd′| *n.* Often **Uplands.** The higher parts of a region, country, etc. —*adj.* Of or located in the upland: *a little upland town.*

up•lift |ŭp lĭft′| *v.* **1.** To raise up; elevate. **2.** To raise to a higher social, moral, or intellectual level. —*n.* |ŭp′lĭft′|. **1.** The act, process, or result of lifting up. **2.** The process of raising to a higher social, moral, or intellectual level.

up•on |ə pŏn′| *or* |ə pôn′| *prep.* On: *We stopped and sat down upon a flat rock.* [SEE NOTE]

up•per |ŭp′ər| *adj.* Higher in place, position, or rank: *the upper floors of a building; the upper classes of society.* —*n.* The part of a shoe or boot above the sole.

upper case. Capital letters as distinguished from small letters. —***modifier:* (upper-case):** *upper-case letters.*

up•per-class |ŭp′ər klăs′| *or* |-kläs′| *adj.* **1.** Of an upper social class: *an upper-class neighborhood.* **2.** Of the junior and senior classes in a school or college.

upper hand. A position of control or advantage.

up•per•most |ŭp′ər mōst′| *adj.* Highest in place, position, rank, etc.: *the uppermost rung of a ladder.* —*adv.* In the first or highest place, position, or rank; first: *Keep this explanation uppermost in your mind.*

Upper Vol•ta |vŏl′tə|. A country in western Africa. Population, 5,900,000. Capital, Ouagadougou.

up•pi•ty |ŭp′ĭ tē| *adj. Informal.* Snobbish or arrogant.

up•raise |ŭp rāz′| *v.* **up•raised, up•rais•ing.** To raise up; lift up; elevate.

up•right |ŭp′rīt′| *adj.* **1.** In a vertical position; erect: *an upright posture.* **2.** Morally respectable; honorable: *an upright man.* —*n.* **1.** A part of an object or structure that stands upright, as a beam. **2.** An **upright piano.** —**up′right′ness** *n.*

upright piano. A piano in which the strings are mounted vertically in a rectangular case with the keyboard at a right angle to the case.

up•ris•ing |ŭp′rī′zĭng| *n.* A revolt.

up•roar |ŭp′rôr′| *or* |-rōr′| *n.* A condition of noisy excitement and confusion; a tumult.

up•roar•i•ous |ŭp rôr′ē əs| *or* |-rōr′-| *adj.* **1.** Caused or accompanied by an uproar. **2.** Loud and full; boisterous: *uproarious laughter.* **3.** Extremely funny: *an uproarious comedy.* —**up•roar′i•ous•ly** *adv.*

up•root |ŭp rōōt′| *or* |-rŏŏt′| *v.* **1.** To tear or remove (a plant and its roots) from the ground. **2.** To destroy or get rid of completely; do away with: *It is not easy to uproot old customs.* **3.** To force to leave a familiar or native place: *The government uprooted many tribes and sent them to live on distant reservations.*

up•set |ŭp sĕt′| *v.* **up•set, up•set•ting.** **1.** To overturn; tip over: *upset a vase of flowers.* **2.** To disturb the normal functioning or arrangement of: *The move to the new building upset our schedule of deliveries.* **3.** To distress mentally or emotionally: *The bad news upset her greatly.* **4.** To defeat, especially unexpectedly: *The Patriots upset the Miami Dolphins.* —*n.* |ŭp′sĕt′|. **1.** The act or an example of upsetting: *He is responsible for the upset of our plans.* **2.** A game or contest in which the favorite is defeated. —*adj.* |ŭp sĕt′|. **1.** Overturned: *an upset boat.* **2.** Mentally or emotionally disturbed: *feeling upset by the news.* **3.** Thrown out of order, arrangement, etc.: *his upset plans.*

up•shot |ŭp′shŏt′| *n.* The final result; outcome.

up•side-down |ŭp′sīd doun′| *adj.* **1.** Overturned completely so that the upper side is down. **2.** In great disorder or confusion: *an upside-down state of affairs.* —*adv.* Also **upside down.** **1.** With the upper and lower parts reversed in position. **2.** In or into great disorder: *turning his room upside-down looking for his wallet.*

up•si•lon |ŭp′sə lŏn′| *n.* The 20th letter of the Greek alphabet, written Υ, υ. In English it is represented as *U, u,* or often also as *y.*

up•stage |ŭp′stāj′| *adj.* Of the rear of a stage. —*adv.* On, at, to, or toward the rear of a stage. —*v.* **up•staged, up•stag•ing.** **1.** To distract audience attention from (another actor). **2.** *Informal.* To steal the show from or get the better of (someone).

up•stairs |ŭp′stârz′| *adv.* **1.** Up the stairs. **2.** To or on an upper floor. *—adj.* |ŭp′stârz′|: *an upstairs kitchen.* *—n.* |ŭp′stârz′| *(used with a singular verb).* The upper floor of a building.

up•stand•ing |ŭp stăn′dĭng| *or* |ŭp′-| *adj.* **1.** Standing erect or upright. **2.** Morally upright; honest: *a fine, upstanding gentleman.*

up•start |ŭp′stärt′| *n.* A person of humble origin who has suddenly risen to wealth or high position, especially one who becomes snobbish or arrogant because of success.

up•state |ŭp′stāt′| *adv.* At, toward, or to that part of a state lying inland or farther north of a large city: *traveling upstate.* *—adj.*: *upstate New York.*

up•stream |ŭp′strēm′| *adv.* At, toward, or to the source of a stream or current: *fish swimming upstream.* *—adj.*: *upstream waters.*

up•surge |ŭp′sûrj′| *n.* A rapid upward swell or rise.

up•take |ŭp′tāk′| *n.* **1.** A passage for drawing up smoke or air. **2.** *Informal.* Understanding; comprehension: *quick on the uptake.*

up•tight |ŭp′tīt′| *adj. Slang.* Also **up tight.** Very tense or nervous: *an uptight person.*

up-to-date |ŭp′tə dāt′| *adj.* Reflecting or informed of the latest improvements, facts, style, etc.; modern: *an up-to-date encyclopedia.*

up•town |ŭp′toun′| *n.* The upper part of a city. *—adv.* At or toward the upper part of a city: *move uptown.* *—adj.*: *an uptown store.*

up•turn |ŭp′tûrn′| *n.* An upward movement, curve, or trend, as in prices, business, etc.

up•ward |ŭp′wərd| *adv.* Also **up•wards** |ŭp′wərdz|. In, to, or toward a higher place, level, or position: *The hawk climbed upward and out of sight.* *—adj.*: *an upward glance.*

u•ra•ni•um |yŏŏ rā′nē əm| *n.* Symbol **U** One of the elements, a heavy, silvery-white metal that is radioactive and easily oxidized. Atomic number 92; atomic weight 238.03; valences +3, +4, +5, +6; melting point 1,132°C; boiling point 3,818°C. [SEE NOTE]

uranium 233. An isotope of uranium having a mass number of 233 and a half-life of 162,000 years. It is capable of fission and can be made by bombarding thorium with neutrons.

uranium 235. The isotope of uranium that has a mass number of 235 and a half-life of 713 million years. Uranium 235 undergoes nuclear fission when it collides with a slow neutron, and it is capable of sustaining a chain reaction that can become explosive.

uranium 238. The most common isotope of uranium, having a mass number of 238 and a half-life of 4.51 billion years. It is only capable of fission under very special conditions but can capture neutrons to form plutonium 239, which is capable of fission.

U•ra•nus |yŏŏr′ə nəs| *or* |yŏŏ rā′-| *n.* The seventh planet of the solar system in order of increasing distance from the sun. Its diameter is about 29,000 miles, its average distance from the sun is about 1,790 million miles, and it takes about 84 years to complete an orbit of the sun.

ur•ban |ûr′bən| *adj.* **1.** Of, living in, or located in a city: *urban traffic; urban dwellers; urban housing.* **2.** Characteristic of the city or city life: *urban problems; urban pollution.*

ur•bane |ûr bān′| *adj.* Having the refined manners of polite society; suave; courteous.

ur•chin |ûr′chĭn| *n.* **1.** A small child, especially a mischievous or needy child. **2.** See **sea urchin.**

–ure. A suffix that forms nouns and means: **1.** An action or process: **erasure.** **2.** A function, office, or group: **legislature.**

u•re•a |yŏŏ rē′ə| *n.* A chemical compound of carbon, hydrogen, nitrogen, and oxygen having the formula CON_2H_4. It occurs in the urine and body fluids of mammals.

u•re•ter |yŏŏ rē′tər| *n.* Either of the long narrow ducts that carry urine from the kidneys to the urinary bladder.

u•re•thra |yŏŏ rē′thrə| *n.* The duct from which urine is discharged in most mammals.

urge |ûrj| *v.* **urged, urg•ing.** **1.** To push, force, or drive onward; impel; encourage: *urging the horses with shouts and cracks of the whip.* **2.** To plead with; exhort: *She urged her husband to accept the job.* **3.** To recommend strongly; press forcefully: *urge the passage of new crime laws.* *—n.* An irresistible desire, influence, or impulse.

ur•gen•cy |ûr′jən sē| *n.* The condition of being urgent: *the urgency of the political situation; the urgency of their financial need.*

ur•gent |ûr′jənt| *adj.* **1.** Calling for immediate action or attention; pressing: *a crisis of an urgent nature.* **2.** Conveying a sense of pressing importance or necessity: *urgent pleas for financial help; an urgent tone of voice.* **—ur•gent′ly** *adv.*

u•ri•nal |yŏŏr′ə nəl| *n.* **1.** An upright wall fixture designed for men and boys to urinate into. **2.** A receptacle for urine used by a bedridden patient.

u•ri•nal•y•sis |yŏŏr′ə năl′ĭ sĭs| *n.* The chemical analysis of urine.

u•ri•nar•y |yŏŏr′ə nĕr′ē| *adj.* Of urine or its production, function, or excretion.

urinary bladder. A muscular membrane-lined sac, located in the forward part of the lower abdomen and in which urine is stored until excreted.

u•ri•nate |yŏŏr′ə nāt′| *v.* **u•ri•nat•ed, u•ri•nat•ing.** To discharge urine. **—u′ri•na′tion** *n.*

u•rine |yŏŏr′ĭn| *n.* A solution containing body wastes extracted from the blood by the kidneys, stored in the urinary bladder, and discharged from the body through the urethra.

urn |ûrn| *n.* **1.** A vase used to hold the ashes of a cremated body. **2.** A metal container with a spigot, used for making and serving tea or coffee. ¶*These sound alike* **urn, earn.**

Ur•sa Major |ûr′sə|. A constellation of seven stars near the north pole of the celestial sphere; the Big Dipper.

Ursa Minor. A constellation of seven stars including the star Polaris; the Little Dipper.

U•ru•guay |yŏŏr′ə gwā′| *or* |-gwī′|. A country on the Atlantic coast of South America, between Brazil and Argentina. Population, 3,028,000. Capital, Montevideo.

us |ŭs| *pron.* The objective case of **we.** *—Note:* *Us* has three main uses. It can be the direct object of a verb: *The movie impressed us greatly.* It can be the indirect object of a verb: *His father*

uranium

Uranium *has the highest atomic weight of all the elements that occur naturally. It has 14 known isotopes, which are all radioactive. It is used in research, in nuclear fuels, and in nuclear weapons.*

gave us money. It can also be the object of a preposition: *Tom sent his regards to us.*

US, U.S. United States.

USA, U.S.A. 1. United States Army. 2. United States of America.

USAF, U.S.A.F. United States Air Force.

USCG, U.S.C.G. United States Coast Guard.

us•a•ble |yo͞o'zə bəl| *adj.* 1. Such as can be used: *separating usable ore from tons of unwanted waste.* 2. In a fit condition for use.

us•age |yo͞o'sĭj| *or* |-zĭj| *n.* 1. The act or manner of using something; use or employment: *a car ruined by rough usage.* 2. The customary practice or usual way of doing something: *The usages of certain rural communities have not changed in more than 100 years.* 3. a. The actual way in which language or its elements, such as words, phrases, grammatical constructions, etc., are used, put together, or pronounced: *contemporary English usage; modern American usage.* b. A particular example of such use: *Certain language usages are associated with uneducated people.* —*modifier: a usage note; a usage book.*

use |yo͞oz| *v.* **used, us•ing.** 1. To bring or put into service; employ for some purpose: *use soap for washing. When was the last time you used the library?* 2. To make a habit of employing: *He uses a lot of sugar in his coffee.* 3. *Informal.* To exploit for one's own advantage: *He gave nothing to his friends; he merely used them.* 4. —Used as an auxiliary verb in the past tense to express former practice, fact, or condition: *I used to go there often. She didn't use to lie about her age. He used to be very fat.* —*phrasal verb.* **use up.** To consume completely; exhaust: *using up the butter in the refrigerator for the cake.* —*n.* |yo͞os|. 1. The act of using: *the use of a pencil for writing.* 2. The condition or fact of being used: *The telephone is in use right now.* 3. The manner of using; usage: *the proper use of power tools.* 4. a. The permission to use or the privilege of using something: *have the use of the car on Sundays.* b. The power or ability of using something: *lose the use of one arm.* 5. The need or occasion to use: *Do you have any use for this book?* 6. The quality of being suitable or adaptable to an end; usefulness: *old pieces of equipment of no practical use.*

Idioms. **have no use for.** To have no tolerance for; dislike: *Bobby has no use for his sister's friends.* **make use of.** To find occasion to use: *At the beach they made use of all their diving equipment.* **put to use.** To find a use for; employ to advantage: *a big, empty basement that could be put to use as a recreation room for the whole family.* **used to.** Accustomed to: *We were not used to such extreme temperatures.*

used |yo͞ozd| *adj.* Not new; secondhand.

use•ful |yo͞os'fəl| *adj.* Capable of being used for some purpose; being of use or service: *a useful map; making herself useful around the house.* —**use'ful•ly** *adv.* —**use'ful•ness** *n.*

use•less |yo͞os'lĭs| *adj.* 1. Of little or no worth: *a useless new kitchen gadget.* 2. Producing no result or effect; vain: *It is useless to complain to the manager about the poor service.* —**use'less•ly** *adv.* —**use'less•ness** *n.* [SEE NOTE]

ush•er |ŭsh'ər| *n.* 1. A person employed to escort people to their seats in a theater, stadium, etc. 2. A member of a wedding party who escorts guests to their seats and accompanies the bridesmaids in the procession. —*v.* 1. To serve as an usher to; escort. 2. To precede and introduce: *usher in a new era.*

USMC, U.S.M.C. United States Marine Corps.

USN, U.S.N. United States Navy.

U.S.S. 1. United States Senate. 2. United States Ship.

U.S.S.R. Union of Soviet Socialist Republics.

u•su•al |yo͞o'zho͞o əl| *adj.* 1. Common; ordinary: *the usual traffic jams during rush hour.* 2. Habitual or customary: *It is usual for him to walk to work every day.* —**u'su•al•ly** *adv.*

u•su•rer |yo͞o'zhər ər| *n.* A person who lends money at an excessively high or unlawful rate of interest.

u•surp |yo͞o sûrp'| *or* |-zûrp'| *v.* To seize and hold by force and without legal right or authority: *usurping all power in the kingdom; usurp a throne.* —**u'sur•pa'tion** *n.* —**u•surp'er** *n.*

u•su•ry |yo͞o'zhə rē| *n., pl.* **u•su•ries.** 1. The practice of lending money at an excessively high or unlawful rate of interest. 2. Such a rate of interest.

U•tah |yo͞o'tô'| *or* |-tä'|. A Western state of the United States. Population, 1,461,037. Capital, Salt Lake City.

u•ten•sil |yo͞o tĕn'səl| *n.* Any instrument or container, as one used in a kitchen or on a farm.

u•ter•us |yo͞o'tər əs| *n., pl.* **u•ter•us•es.** A hollow, muscular organ of female mammals, in which a fertilized egg develops and from which the fully formed young emerges during the process of birth; the womb.

U•ther Pen•drag•on |yo͞o'thər pĕn drăg'ən|. In legends about King Arthur, the father of King Arthur.

u•til•i•ty |yo͞o tĭl'ĭ tē| *n., pl.* **u•til•i•ties.** 1. The quality of being useful; usefulness. 2. A public service, such as gas, electricity, water, etc.

u•ti•lize |yo͞ot'l īz'| *v.* **u•ti•lized, u•ti•liz•ing.** To put to use for a certain purpose: *utilizing the stream's water to run the mill.* —**u'ti•li•za'tion** *n.*

ut•most |ŭt'mōst'| *adj.* Of the highest or greatest degree, amount, or intensity: *matters of the utmost importance.* —*n.* The greatest possible degree, amount, or extent; the maximum.

U•to-Az•tec•an |yo͞o'tō ăz'tĕk'ən| *n.* 1. A large family of American Indian languages of North and Central America. 2. An Indian who speaks a Uto-Aztecan language.

U•to•pi•a |yo͞o tō'pē ə| *n.* 1. In Sir Thomas More's book *Utopia* (1516), an imaginary island with a perfect social and political life. 2. Often **utopia.** a. Any society held to be perfect. b. Any idealistic goal. —**U•to'pi•an** *adj. & n.*

ut•ter[1] |ŭt'ər| *v.* 1. To express audibly; speak; say: *utter a word.* 2. To give forth as a sound: *utter a sigh.* [SEE NOTE]

ut•ter[2] |ŭt'ər| *adj.* Complete; absolute: *utter darkness; the utter nonsense of her suggestion.* —**ut'ter•ly** *adv.* [SEE NOTE]

ut•ter•ance |ŭt'ər əns| *n.* 1. The act of uttering: *She found his continued utterance of old saws quite irritating.* 2. Something uttered.

ut•ter•ly |ŭt'ər lē| *adv.* Completely; absolutely.

u•vu•la |yo͞o'vyə lə| *n.* The small, cone-shaped mass of fleshy tissue that hangs from the end of the soft palate above the tongue. —**u'vu•lar** *adj.*

useless

"Nothing is so useless as a general maxim." —Lord Macaulay (1827).

utter[1-2]

Utter[1] *is from Dutch* ūteren, *"to give out, to make known, to reveal."* **Utter**[2] *was Old English* ūtera *or* ūttra; *it originally meant "outer" and later came to mean "further out" and then "extreme." Both* **utter**[1] *and* **utter**[2] *are ultimately related to* **out.**

ă pat/ā pay/â care/ä father/ĕ pet/ ē be/ĭ pit/ī pie/î fierce/ŏ pot/ ō go/ô paw, for/oi oil/o͝o book/ o͞o boot/ou out/ŭ cut/û fur/ *th* the/th thin/hw which/zh vision/ ə ago, item, pencil, atom, circus

Vv

v,V |vē| *n., pl.* **v's** or **V's. 1.** The 22nd letter of the English alphabet. **2.** The Roman numeral for the number five. [SEE NOTE]

V 1. velocity. **2.** volt. **3.** The symbol for the element vanadium.

v. 1. verb. **2.** verse. **3.** version. **4.** volume (book).

V. vice (in titles).

V-1. A **robot bomb.**

V-2. A long-range rocket that burned liquid fuel, used by the Germans as a ballistic missile in World War II.

Va. Virginia.

va•can•cy |vā'kən sē| *n., pl.* **va•can•cies. 1.** The condition of being vacant; emptiness. **2.** A position, office, or accommodation that is unfilled or unoccupied.

va•cant |vā'kənt| *adj.* **1.** Not occupied or taken: *vacant seats; the part left vacant by the missing actor.* **2.** Not put to use: *vacant lands.* **3.** Expressionless; blank: *a vacant stare.* **—va'cant•ly** *adv.*

va•cate |vā'kāt'| *v.* **va•cat•ed, va•cat•ing.** To cease to occupy or hold; give up; leave: *vacate an apartment.*

va•ca•tion |vā **kā**'shən| *n.* An interval of time devoted to rest or relaxation from work, study, etc. ***—modifier:*** *a vacation trip.* *—v.* To take or spend a vacation: *He vacationed on the island for 35 years.* **—va•ca'tion•er** *n.*

vac•ci•nate |**văk**'sə nāt'| *v.* **vac•ci•nat•ed, vac•ci•nat•ing.** To inoculate (a person or animal) with a vaccine in order to give immunity against an infectious disease.

vac•ci•na•tion |văk'sə **nā**'shən| *n.* **1.** Inoculation with a vaccine in order to give immunity against an infectious disease. **2.** A scar left on the skin where such an inoculation was made.

vac•cine |văk **sēn**'| *n.* **1.** A liquid suspension containing weakened or killed disease germs, injected into a person or animal as protection against a disease. The germs injected are not capable of causing infection but stimulate the production of antibodies against the disease. **2.** A suspension of this kind prepared from the virus of cowpox and used for protection against smallpox. [SEE NOTE]

vac•il•late |**văs**'ə lāt'| *v.* **vac•il•lat•ed, vac•il•lat•ing.** To swing indecisively from one course of action or opinion to another; change one's mind often; waver: *vacillate between hope and despair.* **—vac'il•la'tion** *n.*

va•cu•i•ty |vă **kyo͞o**'ĭ tē| *n.* **1.** The condition of being vacuous or empty; emptiness: *the vacuity of the Arctic wastes.* **2.** Emptiness of mind.

vac•u•ole |**văk**'yo͞o ōl'| *n.* A small opening in the protoplasm of a cell, surrounded by a membrane and serving to store food, eliminate wastes, etc. **—vac'u•o'lar** *adj.*

vac•u•ous |**văk**'yo͞o əs| *adj.* **1.** Devoid of matter; empty: *a vacuous space.* **2.** Stupid: *a vacuous look; a vacuous remark.* **—vac'u•ous•ly** *adv.*

vac•u•um |**văk**'yo͞o əm| *or* |-yo͞om| *n.* **1. a.** The absence of matter. **b.** A space that is empty of matter. **c.** A space containing a gas at a very low pressure. **2.** A **vacuum cleaner.** ***—modifier:*** *a vacuum chamber; a vacuum pump.* *—v.* To clean with a vacuum cleaner.

vacuum bottle. A small container with a double wall and a partial vacuum in the space between the two walls to retard the transfer of heat between the inside and outside.

vacuum cleaner. An electrical appliance that draws up dirt by means of suction.

vacuum tube. An electron tube in which there is a vacuum to such a high degree that the likelihood of an electron striking a gas atom is small enough to be ignored.

Va•duz |fä **do͞ots**'|. The capital of Liechtenstein. Population, 4,000.

vag•a•bond |**văg**'ə bŏnd'| *n.* A person who wanders from place to place with no apparent means of support. *—adj.* Of or like a vagabond; habitually wandering: *leading a vagabond life.*

va•gar•y |**vā**'gə rē| *or* |və **gâr**'ē| *n., pl.* **va•gar•ies. 1.** A flight of fancy; a whim. **2.** Often **vagaries.** An unpredictable change or fluctuation: *vagaries of weather.*

va•gi•na |və **jī**'nə| *n., pl.* **va•gi•nas** or **va•gi•nae** |və **jī**'nē|. In female mammals, the passage leading from the uterus to the outside of the body.

va•grant |**vā**'grənt| *n.* A person who wanders from place to place and usually has no means of support; a tramp; vagabond. *—adj.* Wandering from place to place; roving: *a vagrant tribe; a vagrant life.* **—va'gran•cy** *n.*

vague |vāg| *adj.* **vagu•er, vagu•est. 1.** Not clearly expressed; lacking clarity: *a vague statement; a vague promise.* **2.** Lacking definite shape, form, or character: *the vague outline of a sailing ship on the horizon.* **3.** Indistinctly felt, perceived, understood, or recalled: *a vague sense of fear; vague memories.* **4.** Not expressing one's thoughts, ideas, etc., clearly or precisely: *He pretended to be vague to avoid being asked questions.* **—vague'ly** *adv.* **—vague'ness** *n.*

vain |vān| *adj.* **vain•er, vain•est. 1.** Unsuccessful; futile; fruitless: *a vain effort to regain her balance.* **2.** Lacking substance or worth; hollow:

V (1) υ (2) **V** (3)

The letter **V** *is a variant of the letter* **U**. *The Romans used one letter (1) to stand for the sounds /u/, /v/, and /w/. In medieval times, separate forms were developed for /u/ and for /w/; for the sound /v/, the simplest shape was retained (2). The modern printed letter (3) is modeled on the angular shape of the Roman original.*

vaccine

Cowpox is a mild disease of cows, and it can be caught by human beings. In the late eighteenth century, Dr. Edward Jenner discovered that a person who has had cowpox is almost always immune against smallpox, a disease that was often fatal. Jenner invented the method of inoculating human beings with cowpox virus, which was called **vaccine** *(now sense* **2***), from Latin* vacca, *"cow." This process virtually eliminated the threat of smallpox and led the way to the expanded technique of* **vaccination** *(see sense* **1** *of* **vaccine***).*

valance

vain promises. **3.** Showing undue preoccupation with one's appearance or accomplishments; conceited: *a vain, disagreeable little fellow.* ¶*These sound alike* **vain, vane, vein.** —**vain'ly** *adv.*

***Idiom.* in vain. 1.** To no avail: *trying in vain to catch the ball before his opponent did.* **2.** In an irreverent or disrespectful manner: *"Thou shalt not take the name of the Lord Thy God in vain"* (The Bible, Deuteronomy 5:11).

vain•glo•ri•ous |vān glôr'ē əs| *or* |-glōr'-| *adj.* Showing excessive pride or vanity; boastful: *being vainglorious about his athletic record.*

vain•glo•ry |vān'glôr'ē| *or* |-glōr'ē| *n., pl.* **vain•glo•ries.** Excessive pride or vanity.

val. value.

val•ance |văl'əns| *n.* **1.** A drapery hung along the edge of a bed, canopy, shelf, etc., to decorate and conceal the underlying structure or frame. **2.** A short drapery or a wooden board or metal strip extending across the top of a window, as to conceal the curtain rods. [SEE PICTURE]

vale |vāl| *n.* A valley; a dale. ¶*These sound alike* **vale, veil.**

val•e•dic•to•ri•an |văl'ĭ dĭk **tôr'**ē ən| *or* | -**tōr'**-| *n.* In some schools and colleges, the student ranking highest in the graduating class, who delivers the farewell address at commencement.

val•e•dic•to•ry |văl'ĭ **dĭk'**tə rē| *n., pl.* **val•e•dic•to•ries.** A farewell address, especially one delivered at commencement exercises by a valedictorian. —*adj.* Having to do with or expressing a farewell: *a valedictory oration.*

va•lence |**vā'**ləns| *n.* **1.** The capability of an atom or group of atoms to combine in particular proportions with other atoms or groups of atoms. **2.** A whole number, often one of several for a given element, that represents this capability as multiples of +1 and −1, where +1 represents the capability for combining with a single chlorine atom and −1 represents the capability for combining with a single hydrogen atom.

val•en•tine |**văl'**ən tīn'| *n.* **1.** A sentimental card sent to a member of the opposite sex on Saint Valentine's Day. **2.** A person singled out as one's sweetheart on Saint Valentine's Day. **3.** A heart-shaped symbol of love or affection used on valentine cards.

val•et |**văl'**ĭt| *or* |vă **lā'**| *or* |**văl'**ā| *n.* **1.** A man's personal attendant, who takes care of his clothes, helps him dress, etc. **2.** A hotel employee who performs various personal services for guests.

Val•hal•la |văl **hăl'**ə| *n.* In Norse mythology, the great hall in which the souls of slain warriors were received by Odin. [SEE NOTE]

val•iant |**văl'**yənt| *adj.* Possessing, showing, or acting with valor; brave. —**val'iant•ly** *adv.*

val•id |**văl'**ĭd| *adj.* **1.** Well-grounded; sound; supportable: *a valid objection.* **2.** Having legal force: *a valid passport.* —**va•lid'i•ty** |və **lĭd'**ĭ tē| *n.*

val•i•date |**văl'**ĭ dāt'| *v.* **val•i•dat•ed, val•i•dat•ing. 1.** To make or declare legally valid: *validate a contract.* **2.** To confirm or support on a sound basis or authority; verify: *validate a theory.*

va•lise |və **lēs'**| *n.* A small piece of hand luggage.

Val•kyr•ie |văl **kîr'**ē| *or* |**văl'**kîr'ē|. In Norse mythology, one of Odin's battle maidens, who carried slain warriors to Valhalla. [SEE NOTE]

Val•let•ta |və **lĕt'**ə|. The capital of Malta. Population, 18,000.

val•ley |**văl'**ē| *n.* **1.** A long, narrow region of low land between ridges, ranges of mountains or hills, etc., often having a river running along the bottom. **2.** A large region of land drained by a river system: *the Nile valley.*

val•or |**văl'**ər| *n.* Courage; bravery.

val•or•ous |**văl'**ər əs| *adj.* Showing or having valor; courageous; bold: *valorous deeds.*

val•our |**văl'**ər| *n.* British form of the word **valor.**

val•u•a•ble |**văl'**yo͞o ə bəl| *or* |-yə bəl| *adj.* **1.** Having high monetary or material value: *a valuable piece of jewelry.* **2.** Of importance, use, or service: *acquire valuable information.* —*n.* Often **valuables.** A valuable personal possession, as a piece of jewelry.

val•u•a•tion |văl'yo͞o **ā'**shən| *n.* **1.** The act or process of assessing the value or price of something; an appraisal: *valuation and classification of imported merchandise.* **2.** The assessed value or price of something.

val•ue |**văl'**yo͞o| *n.* **1.** A suitable equivalent for something else; a fair return in goods, services, etc.: *walking shoes that will give you good value for your money.* **2.** Monetary or material worth: *assessing the value of a rare stamp; a listing telling how many dollars the stocks increased in value each day.* **3.** Worth in usefulness or importance to the possessor: *the value of a good college education; a locket of great sentimental value.* **4.** Often **values.** A principle, standard, or quality considered worthwhile or desirable: *the traditional values of American life.* **5.** Precise meaning: *Can you understand the value of the words in question?* **6.** An assigned or calculated numerical quantity, as that assigned to a function or its independent variables. **7.** The relative duration of a musical note or rest. **8.** The relative lightness or darkness of a color in a picture. —*v.* **val•ued, val•u•ing. 1.** To determine or estimate the value of; appraise: *value a piece of jewelry; meat exports valued at more than 50 million dollars a year.* **2.** To consider of great worth, importance, etc.; prize: *The Mongols developed a light, speedy horse that they valued highly.*

val•ued |**văl'**yo͞od| *adj.* Regarded as having great worth, merit, importance; much esteemed: *a man highly valued in his own time. Things highly valued by everybody may serve as money.*

valve |vălv| *n.* **1.** A structure located in a hollow organ or passage, such as an artery or vein, to slow or prevent backward movement of a body fluid. **2. a.** Any of various mechanical devices that control the flow of liquids, gases, or loose materials through pipes, channels, etc., by blocking and uncovering openings. **b.** The movable part or element of such a device. **c.** A device of this kind in a brass wind instrument used to vary the length of the column of air and thus to control the pitch of the instrument. **3.** One of the paired, hinged parts of the shell of many mollusks, such as clams, oysters, or scallops.

va•moose |vă **mo͞os'**| *v.* **va•moosed, va•moos•ing.** *Slang.* To leave or go away hastily.

vamp |vămp| *n.* The upper front part of a shoe or boot covering the instep and often the toes. —*v.* To provide (a shoe) with a new vamp.

Valhalla/Valkyrie

Valhalla *is from Old Norse* Valhöll, *"hall of the slain heroes"*: valr, *"those who are slain (in battle),"* + höll, *"a hall."* **Valkyrie** *is from Old Norse* Valkyrja, *"chooser of the slain heroes"*: valr *(as above)*, + -kyrja, *"chooser."*

ă pat/ā pay/â care/ä father/ĕ pet/ ē be/ĭ pit/ī pie/î fierce/ŏ pot/ ō go/ô paw, for/oi oil/o͝o book/ o͞o boot/ou out/ŭ cut/û fur/ *th* the/th thin/hw which/zh vision/ ə ago, item, pencil, atom, circus

vam•pire |văm′pīr′| *n.* **1.** In folk tales and legends, a corpse supposed to rise from its grave at night to drink the blood of living people. **2.** Also **vampire bat.** Any of several tropical bats that feed on the blood of living animals through a bite in the skin. **3.** A person who preys on or victimizes others. [SEE NOTE]

van[1] |văn| *n.* A covered or enclosed truck or wagon used for transporting goods or livestock. [SEE NOTE]

van[2] |văn| *n.* The vanguard. [SEE NOTE]

va•na•di•um |və nā′dē əm| *n.* Symbol **V** One of the elements, a soft, white, brightly shining metal. Atomic number 23; atomic weight 50.942; valences +2, +3, +4, +5; melting point 1,890°C; boiling point 3,000°C.

Van Al•len belt |văn ăl′ən|. Either of two zones surrounding the earth beginning at about 500 miles and extending several thousands of miles outward. In these zones a large number of atomic particles with high energies are trapped by the earth's magnetic field.

Van Bu•ren |văn byoor′ən|, **Martin.** 1782–1862. Eighth President of the United States (1837–41).

Van•cou•ver |văn koo′vər|. **1.** An island of British Columbia, Canada, lying off the southwestern coast of the province. **2.** A port city of British Columbia, Canada. Population, 410,000.

van•dal |văn′dl| *n.* **1.** A person who willfully defaces or destroys public or private property. **2.** **Vandal.** A member of a Germanic people who overran Gaul, Spain, Northern Africa, and Rome in the fourth and fifth centuries A.D.

van•dal•ism |văn′dl ĭz′əm| *n.* **1.** The willful or malicious defacement or destruction of public or private property. **2.** An example of this.

van•dal•ize |văn′dl īz′| *v.* **van•dal•ized, van•dal•iz•ing.** To destroy or deface (public or private property) willfully or maliciously.

Van•dyke beard |văn dīk′|. A short, pointed beard.

vane |vān| *n.* **1.** A thin plate of wood or metal, often having the shape of an arrow or a rooster, that turns on a vertical pivot to indicate the direction of the wind. **2.** One of a number of thin, rigid blades mounted around or as if around the circumference of a wheel and turned by or used to direct the motion of a fluid. **3.** One of the stabilizing fins attached to the tail of a bomb, rocket, etc. **4.** The thin, flat, weblike part of a feather, extending from each side of a main shaft or quill. ¶*These sound alike* **vane, vain, vein.** [SEE PICTURE]

van•guard |văn′gärd′| *n.* **1.** The front or leading position in an army or fleet; van. **2.** The foremost or leading position in a trend, movement, activity, etc.

va•nil•la |və nĭl′ə| *n.* **1.** A flavoring made from the seed pods of a tropical orchid and used in cakes and cookies, ice cream, puddings, etc. **2.** Also **vanilla bean.** The long, beanlike seed pod from which this flavoring is obtained. **3.** The tropical orchid that bears such pods.

va•nil•lin |və nĭl′ĭn| *or* |văn′ə lĭn| *n.* A white or yellow crystalline compound of carbon, hydrogen, and oxygen, having the formula $C_8H_8O_3$. It is found in vanilla beans and certain balsams and resins and used in perfumes, flavorings, and drugs.

van•ish |văn′ĭsh| *v.* **1.** To disappear or become invisible, especially quickly: *Helen's smile vanished for a moment. The sun vanished entirely.* **2.** To pass out of existence: *Will man become victim of his own mechanical creations and vanish as the dinosaur did?*

van•i•ty |văn′ĭ tē| *n., pl.* **van•i•ties. 1.** Excessive pride; conceit. **2.** Futility; worthlessness: *complaining bitterly about the vanity of trying to get him to work.* **3.** A **vanity case.**

vanity case. A small handbag or case used by women for carrying cosmetics.

van•quish |văng′kwĭsh| *or* |văn′-| *v.* To defeat thoroughly; subjugate. —**van′quished** *adj.*: *a vanquished people.* —**van′quish•er** *n.*

van•tage |văn′tĭj| *or* |vän′-| *n.* **1.** An advantage in a competition. **2.** Something, as a strategic position, greater strength, etc., that provides superiority or an advantage.

vantage point. A position from which a person has a commanding view or outlook.

Va•nu•a•tu |vä′noo ä′too|. An island country in the South Pacific east of Australia. Population, 113,000. Capital, Vila.

vap•id |văp′ĭd| *adj.* Insipid; flat; stale: *vapid conversation; vapid beer.* —**vap′id•ly** *adv.*

va•por |vā′pər| *n.* **1.** Any faintly visible suspension of fine particles of matter in the air, as mist, fumes, or smoke. **2. a.** The state of a substance that is in gaseous form but at a low enough temperature to be liquified by the application of pressure. **b.** The gaseous state of a substance that is solid or liquid at normal temperatures. **c.** A mixture of a vapor and air, as the fuel mixture of an internal-combustion engine. **3. the vapors.** *Archaic.* Depression; melancholy.

va•por•ize |vā′pə rīz′| *v.* **va•por•ized, va•por•iz•ing. 1.** To convert (a solid or liquid) to vapor, especially by heating. **2.** To be converted into vapor. —**va′por•i•za′tion** *n.* —**va′por•iz′er** *n.*

va•por•ous |vā′pər əs| *adj.* **1.** Of or like vapor. **2.** Changing to vapor easily or at low temperatures; volatile. —**va′por•ous•ly** *adv.*

va•pour |vā′pər| *n.* British form of the word **vapor.**

var. 1. variable. **2.** variant. **3.** variation. **4.** variety. **5.** various.

var•i•a•ble |vâr′ē ə bəl| *adj.* **1.** Subject to variation; changeable: *a variable climate.* **2.** Capable of assuming any of a set of two or more values, as a mathematical function or symbol; not fixed in value. —*n.* **1.** Something that varies. **2.** A variable mathematical quantity or a symbol that represents it. —**var′i•a•bil′i•ty, var′i•a•ble•ness** *n.* —**var′i•a•bly** *adv.*

var•i•ance |vâr′ē əns| *n.* **1.** The act, fact, or result of varying; variation; difference: *trying to account for the variance in product quality.* **2.** The extent or degree of such change: *a daily variance of 10 degrees Fahrenheit.*

***Idiom.* at variance with.** Not agreeing or conforming to; differing from: *Your account of the accident is at variance with his.*

var•i•ant |vâr′ē ənt| *adj.* Exhibiting variation; differing: *words with variant spellings.* —*n.* Something exhibiting slight variation in form from another, as a different spelling of the same word. For example, the spelling *cocoanut* is a variant of the spelling *coconut.* [SEE NOTE]

vampire
Belief in **vampires** *originated in Eastern Europe, especially in Hungary, Bulgaria, and Rumania. The word is from Hungarian* vampir, *which is probably ultimately from Tartar* ubyr, *"witch."*

van[1-2]
Van[1] *is a shortening of* **caravan, van**[2] *of* **vanguard.**

vane

variant
In linguistic descriptions (as in these etymological notes), **variant** *is used as a catchall term for words that have been changed in some minor way that one does not wish to specify. Thus in these notes* **varmint** *is called simply a variant of* **vermin.** *It would be possible to go into considerable detail, with many comparisons, about the change of /ûr/ to /är/ and the addition of the /t/; but unless the change is especially interesting for its own sake it is often convenient to ignore the details.*

var•i•a•tion |vâr′ē ā′shən| *n.* **1.** The act, process, or result of varying; change or deviation: *inanimate objects incapable of variation.* **2.** An example of varying: *a welcome variation in our daily routine.* **3.** The extent or degree of such varying: *temperature variations of more than 50 degrees Fahrenheit.* **4.** Something that is slightly different from another of the same type. **5.** A mathematical function that relates values of a variable to values of other variables. **6.** A musical form that is an altered version of a given theme, diverging from it by melodic ornamentation and changes in harmony, rhythm, or key.

var•i•col•ored |vâr′ĭ kŭl′ərd| *adj.* Having a variety of colors.

var•i•cose |văr′ĭ kōs′| *adj.* Of or designating blood vessels that are abnormally wide and knotted and that follow an abnormally twisted path.

var•ied |vâr′ēd| *adj.* Full of variety; having many forms or types: *a varied assortment of candy.* —**var′ied•ly** *adv.*

var•i•e•gat•ed |vâr′ē ĭ gā′tĭd| *adj.* Having streaks, marks, or patches of different colors: *butterflies with variegated wings.*

va•ri•e•ty |və rī′ĭ tē| *n., pl.* **va•ri•e•ties. 1.** A range of difference or change resulting in lack of monotony, greater interest, etc.; diversity: *The English language allows great variety in speaking and writing.* **2.** A number of different kinds, usually within the same general grouping; an assortment: *a variety of nourishing foods; a variety of outdoor activities.* **3.** A kind, sort, or form: *diseases of every variety.* **4.** A living thing, especially a plant, belonging to a subdivision within a species: *Broccoli is a variety of cabbage.*

variety store *n.* A retail store carrying a large variety of merchandise.

var•i•ous |vâr′ē əs| *adj.* **1. a.** Of different kinds: *unable to go for various reasons.* **b.** Unlike; different: *flowers as various as the rose, the daisy, and the carnation.* **2.** More than one; several: *He spoke to various members of the club.* **3.** Individual and separate: *The various reports all agreed.* —**var′i•ous•ly** *adv.*

var•let |vär′lĭt| *n. Archaic.* A rascal; knave.

var•mint |vär′mənt| *n. Informal.* **1.** A wild animal, especially one considered to be dangerous or a nuisance. **2.** A troublesome or despised person. [SEE NOTE]

var•nish |vär′nĭsh| *n.* **1.** An oil-based paint that dries to leave a surface coated with a thin, hard, glossy film that is relatively transparent and almost colorless. **2. a.** The smooth coating or finish that results from the application of varnish. **b.** A substance or coating that resembles varnish: *a glaze.* **3.** Something resembling or suggesting a coat of varnish; outward appearance; gloss: *hiding his temper under a varnish of good manners.* —*v.* To cover or coat with or as if with varnish.

var•si•ty |vär′sĭ tē| *n.* The best team representing a school, college, etc. —***modifier:*** *a varsity team; varsity players.*

var•y |vâr′ē| *v.* **var•ied, var•y•ing, var•ies. 1.** To be or become different; change: *Temperature varies from day to day. Prices often vary with the season.* **2.** To diverge; deviate; differ: *vary from established patterns of behavior.* **3.** To give variety to; make different: *vary the sauce by adding spices, wine, or tomatoes.* **4.** To be variable, as a mathematical quantity or function.

vas•cu•lar |văs′kyə lər| *adj.* Of, containing, or forming tubes or vessels for the circulation of liquids such as blood, lymph, or water within an animal or plant.

vas def•er•ens |văs dĕf′ə rĕnz′|. The duct in male vertebrate animals through which sperm cells pass from a testis to the urethra.

vase |vās| *or* |vāz| *or* |väz| *n.* An open container, as of glass or porcelain, usually tall and circular, used for holding flowers.

vas•ec•to•my |vă sĕk′tə mē| *n., pl.* **vas•ec•to•mies.** A surgical operation in which a section of the vas deferens is cut or removed. This operation is used mainly for birth control purposes.

Vas•e•line |văs′ə lēn′| *or* |văs′ə lēn′| *n.* A trademark for a petroleum jelly used mainly as a base for medicines to be rubbed onto the skin and as a protection for exposed metal parts.

vas•sal |văs′əl| *n.* **1.** In feudal times, a person granted the use of land by a feudal lord, in return for which he rendered military or other service. **2.** A person who is subject or subservient to another. —*adj.* Of or like a vassal: *a vassal state.*

vas•sal•age |văs′ə lĭj| *n.* **1.** The condition of being a vassal. **2.** The service, homage, and fealty required of a vassal. **3.** A fief.

vast |văst| *or* |väst| *adj.* **vast•er, vast•est. 1.** Very great in area or extent; immense: *the vast expanse of the Pacific Ocean.* **2.** Very great in degree, intensity, size, amount, etc.: *the vast inhuman blackness of outer space.* —**vast′ly** *adv.* —**vast′ness** *n.*

vat |văt| *n.* A tank or tub used for storing liquids.

Vat•i•can |văt′ĭ kən| *n.* **1. the Vatican.** The official residence of the pope in Vatican City. **2.** The authority of the pope; the papacy.

Vatican City. An independent state within the city of Rome. It includes the Vatican and St. Peter's Church. Population, 900.

vaude•ville |vôd′vĭl| *or* |vōd′-| *or* |vô′də-| *n.* Stage entertainment offering a variety of short acts.

vault[1] |vôlt| *n.* **1.** An arched structure forming a ceiling or roof. **2.** A room with arched walls and ceiling, especially when underground, as a storeroom. **3.** A compartment for the safekeeping of valuables. **4.** A burial chamber. —*v.* To build or cover with a vault. [SEE NOTE]

vault[2] |vôlt| *v.* To jump or leap over, especially with the aid of a support, as the hands or a pole. —*n.* The act of vaulting; a leap. —**vault′er** *n.* [SEE NOTE]

vaunt |vônt| *or* |vänt| *v.* To boast; brag. —*n.* A boast or brag.

vb. verb.

VCR videocassette recorder.

VD, V.D. venereal disease.

VDT video display terminal.

veal |vēl| *n.* The meat of a calf. —***modifier:*** *a veal stew.*

vec•tor |vĕk′tər| *n.* In mathematics and physical science, something, such as velocity or change of position, that must be identified by its direction as well as by its measure, often represented as an arrow drawn on a system of coordinates. [SEE PICTURE]

veer |vîr| *v.* To turn aside from a course or direction; swerve: *The destroyers veered east to*

varmint

Varmint *is a variant of* **vermin. Varmint** *was a rare word in rural dialects in England, but in the nineteenth century it became quite common in many parts of the United States.*

vault[1-2]

These two words are related, but not closely. **Vault[1]** *is from Old French* vaute, *which is from Latin* volta *or* volūta, *"something bent or arched," from* volvere, *"to turn or roll."* **Vault[2]** *originally meant "to leap onto a horse"; it is from Old French* volter, *"to turn a horse," also "to leap," which is indirectly descended from Latin* volvere, *"to turn."*

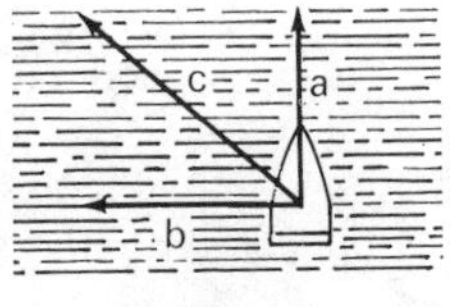

vector

Vector a represents the forward velocity of the boat, vector b the velocity of the stream, vector c, their sum shows the actual motion of the boat.

ă pat/ā pay/â care/ä father/ĕ pet/ ē be/ĭ pit/ī pie/î fierce/ŏ pot/ ō go/ô paw, for/oi oil/ŏŏ book/ ōō boot/ou out/ŭ cut/û fur/ *th* the/th thin/hw which/zh vision/ ə ago, item, pencil, atom, circus

meet the enemy fleet. The driver veered the truck to the right to avoid an accident.

Ve•ga |vā′gə| *n.* A bright star seen in the northern sky.

veg•e•ta•ble |vĕj′tə bəl| *or* |vĕj′ĭ tə-| *n.* **1.** A plant of which the roots, leaves, stems, flowers, and in some cases the seeds, pods, or fruit are used as food. **2.** The part of such a plant eaten as food. **3.** A plant as distinguished from an animal or mineral. **4.** A person who leads a monotonous existence. —***modifier:*** *a vegetable garden; the vegetable and animal kingdoms.*

veg•e•tar•i•an |vĕj′ĭ târ′ē ən| *n.* Someone whose food consists mainly of plants and plant products and who eats no meat. —*adj.* **1.** Eating only plants and plant products rather than meat. **2.** Consisting only of plants and plant products: *a vegetarian diet.*

veg•e•tar•i•an•ism |vĕj′ĭ târ′ē ə nĭz′əm| *n.* The eating habits of vegetarians.

veg•e•tate |vĕj′ĭ tāt′| *v.* **veg•e•tat•ed, veg•e•tat•ing. 1.** To grow, sprout, or exist as a plant does. **2.** To lead a life characterized by little or no physical energy or mental effort. **3.** To grow or spread abnormally, as a tumor or other growth.

veg•e•ta•tion |vĕj′ĭ tā′shən| *n.* A growth of plants; plants or plant life in general.

veg•e•ta•tive |vĕj′ĭ tā′tĭv| *adj.* **1.** Of or relating to plant life. **2.** Of, relating to, or characterized by growth or physical change rather than sexual processes, as in the propagation of plants from tubers, runners, cuttings, etc.

ve•he•ment |vē′ə mənt| *adj.* **1.** Marked by forcefulness of expression or intensity of emotion, feelings, etc.: *vehement demands for better working conditions; a vehement critic of his foreign policy.* **2.** Marked by or full of vigor or energy; strong: *vehement applause.* —**ve′he•mence** *n.* —**ve′he•ment•ly** *adv.*

ve•hi•cle |vē′ĭ kəl| *n.* **1.** A device for carrying or transporting passengers, goods, equipment, etc., especially one that moves on wheels or runners. **2.** A medium through which something is expressed or conveyed: *Oral tales were an important vehicle of culture wherever writing was unknown.* **3.** A substance, such as oil, into which pigments are mixed in making paint. **4.** A play, role, musical composition, etc., used to display the special abilities of a performer or group of performers.

ve•hic•u•lar |vē hĭk′yə lər| *adj.* Of or being a vehicle or vehicles: *vehicular traffic.*

veil |vāl| *n.* **1.** A piece of fine, sheer fabric, such as net, lace, or gauze, worn by women over the head or face: *a bridal veil.* **2.** The part of a nun's headdress that frames the face and falls over the shoulders. **3.** Anything that covers or conceals like a veil, curtain, or cloak: *a veil of secrecy.* —*v.* To cover, conceal, or disguise with or as if with a veil: *veil one's face; veil one's intentions.* —**veiled′** *adj.: a veiled face; a thinly veiled threat.* ¶ *These sound alike* **veil, vale.** [SEE PICTURE]

vein |vān| *n.* **1.** A blood vessel through which blood returns to the heart. **2.** One of the narrow, usually branching tubes of supporting parts forming the framework of a leaf or an insect's wing. **3.** A long, regularly shaped deposit of an ore, mineral, etc., in the earth: *a vein of silver ore; a vein of coal.* **4.** A long wavy or branching strip or streak of color, as in marble. **5.** A manner or mood: *He spoke in a light, playful vein.* —*v.* To fill or mark with veins. —**veined′** *adj.: veined marble.* ¶ *These sound alike* **vein, vain, vane.**

veldt or **veld** |vĕlt| *or* |fĕlt| *n.* An open, grassy region of southern Africa.

vel•lum |vĕl′əm| *n.* **1.** A fine parchment made from the skins of calf, lamb, or kid and used for the pages and binding of fine books. **2.** Heavy paper that looks like such parchment. —***modifier:*** *a vellum binding.*

ve•loc•i•ty |və lŏs′ĭ tē| *n., pl.* **ve•loc•i•ties. 1.** In science, the rate per unit of time at which an object moves in a specified direction. Velocity is a vector. **2.** Speed. [SEE NOTE]

ve•lours or **ve•lour** |və lo͝or′| *n.* A soft, smooth, velvetlike fabric with a short, thick nap on the surface, used for clothing, curtains, upholstery, etc. —***modifier:*** *a velours jacket.*

vel•vet |vĕl′vĭt| *n.* **1.** A soft, smooth, rich fabric of silk, rayon, nylon, etc., having a short, thick pile on one side and a plain back. **2.** Something resembling velvet. —***modifier:*** *a velvet cloak; velvet slippers; a velvet touch.*

vel•vet•een |vĕl′vĭ tēn′| *n.* A velvetlike fabric made of cotton and having a short, dense pile. —***modifier:*** *a velveteen skirt.*

vel•vet•y |vĕl′vĭ tē| *adj.* **vel•vet•i•er, vel•vet•i•est.** Having the softness of velvet.

ve•na ca•va |vē′nə kā′və| *or* |vā′nə kä′və| *pl.* **ve•nae ca•vae** |vē′nē′ kā′vē′| *or* |vā′nī′ kä′vī′|. Either one of the two large veins that return blood to the right atrium of the heart in vertebrates that breathe air.

ve•nal |vē′nəl| *adj.* **1.** Willing to be bribed: *a venal public servant.* **2.** Marked by or obtained by bribery: *a venal agreement with the police.* [SEE NOTE]

ven•der |vĕn′dər| *n.* A form of the word **vendor.**

ven•dor |vĕn′dər| *n.* A person who sells; a peddler or salesman. [SEE PICTURE]

ve•neer |və nîr′| *n.* **1.** A thin surface layer of better or finer material covering inexpensive or inferior material underneath: *a pine cabinet with a mahogany veneer.* **2.** Any of the thin layers glued together in making plywood. **3.** Any outward show or pretense that hides the truth and gives a falsely favorable impression: *A veneer of sophistication masked his essential crudity.* —*v.* To cover, overlay, or face with a surface layer of better or finer material.

ven•er•a•ble |vĕn′ər ə bəl| *adj.* **1.** Worthy of respect or reverence by virtue of age, dignity, or position: *a venerable senator.* **2.** Deserving of reverence for historic, religious, or other associations: *venerable relics of a saint.* —**ven′er•a•bly** *adv.*

ven•er•ate |vĕn′ə rāt′| *v.* **ven•er•at•ed, ven•er•at•ing.** To regard with respect and reverence. —**ven′er•a′tion** *n.*

ve•ne•re•al disease |və nîr′ē əl|. Any one of various diseases transmitted by sexual contact, especially syphilis and gonorrhea.

Venetian blind. A window blind consisting of adjustable horizontal or sometimes vertical slats that can be set at a desired angle to regulate the amount of light admitted.

Ven•e•zue•la |vĕn′ĭ zwā′lə|. A country on the northern coast of South America. Population 11,632,000. Capital, Caracas.

veil

velocity

Velocity *is measured in units of distance per unit of time. Therefore we can say that velocity = distance/time provided we remember that the distance is measured in a particular direction.*

venal/venial

Venal *is from Latin* vēnālis, *"for sale," from* vēnum, *"sale" (also from* vēnum *is* vēndere, *"to sell," from which we have* **vendor**). **Venial** *is from Latin* veniālis, *"forgivable," from* venia, *"forgiveness" (*venia *is related to* Venus, *"love, the goddess of love, Venus").*

vendor

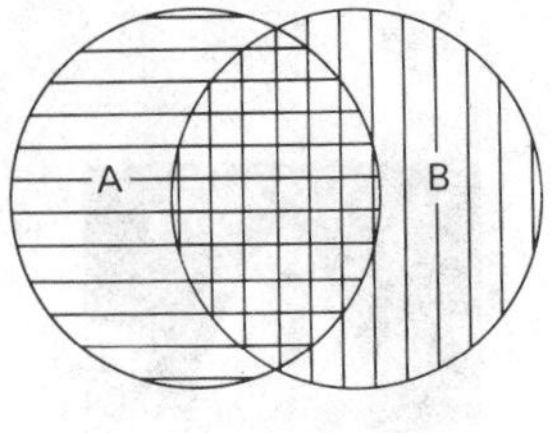

Venn diagram
The circular areas A and B represent two sets. The region in which they overlap is A intersection B. The total of both regions is A union B.

vent¹·²
Vent¹ *originally meant "to let out air," and is from Old French* aventir, *"to make wind."* **Vent²** *was originally* fent, *from Old French* fente, *"a slit."*

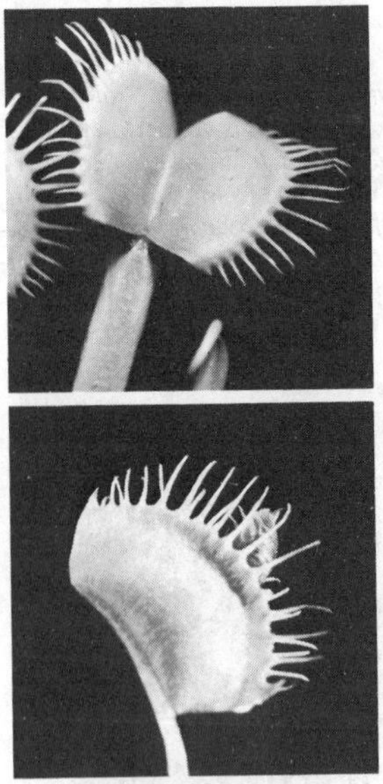

Venus's-flytrap
Above: Opened
Below: Closed

ă pat/ā pay/â care/ä father/ĕ pet/ ē be/ĭ pit/ī pie/î fierce/ŏ pot/ ō go/ô paw, for/oi oil/ŏŏ book/ ōō boot/ou out/ŭ cut/û fur/ *th* the/th thin/hw which/zh vision/ ə ago, item, pencil, atom, circus

venge•ance |**vĕn'**jəns| *n.* The act of causing harm to another person in retribution for a wrong or injury.

venge•ful |**vĕnj'**fəl| *adj.* Desiring or seeking vengeance; vindictive. **—venge'ful•ly** *adv.*

Ven•ice |**vĕn'**ĭs|. A city in northeastern Italy, a port at the head of the Adriatic Sea built on numerous small islands. Population, 360,000. **—Ve•ne'tian** |və **nē'**shən| *adj.* & *n.*

ve•ni•al |**vē'**nē əl| *adj.* Capable of being pardoned; not beyond forgiveness: *a venial sin.* [SEE NOTE]

ven•i•son |**vĕn'**ĭ sən| *or* |-zən| *n.* The meat of a deer, used as food.

Venn diagram |vĕn|. A diagram in which an area is divided by closed curves into regions that represent sets. Relations and operations on sets can be shown as overlapping, included, and excluded regions. [SEE PICTURE]

ven•om |**vĕn'**əm| *n.* **1.** A poisonous substance that is secreted by certain snakes, spiders, scorpions, insects, etc., and can be transmitted to a victim by a bite or sting. **2.** Deep hatred or spite; ill will.

ven•om•ous |**vĕn'**ə məs| *adj.* **1.** Secreting or able to poison with venom: *a venomous snake; a scorpion's venomous sting.* **2.** Of or like venom; poisonous: *a venomous substance.* **3.** Filled with or expressing deep hatred or ill will: *a venomous look.* **—ven'om•ous•ly** *adv.* **—ven'om•ous•ness** *n.*

ve•nous |**vē'**nəs| *adj.* **1.** Of or having to do with a vein or veins. **2.** Returning to the heart through a vein, especially one of the large veins.

vent¹ |vĕnt| *n.* An opening through which a liquid, gas, vapor, etc., can pass or escape. *—v.* To express; give utterance to: *people venting their grievances and despair.* [SEE NOTE]
Idiom. **give vent to.** To express; give utterance to.

vent² |vĕnt| *n.* A slit in a garment, such as a jacket, especially one at the bottom of a back or side seam. [SEE NOTE]

ven•ti•late |**vĕn'**tl āt'| *v.* **ven•ti•lat•ed, ven•ti•lat•ing. 1.** To cause fresh air to enter or circulate through (a chamber, enclosure, etc.). **2.** To bring out or expose (a subject) to public discussion or examination. **—ven'ti•la'tion** *n.*

ven•ti•la•tor |**vĕnt'**l ā'tər| *n.* Someone or something that ventilates, as an exhaust fan.

ven•tral |**vĕn'**trəl| *adj.* Of, on, near, or toward the belly or lower body surface of an animal.

ven•tri•cle |**vĕn'**trĭ kəl| *n.* A cavity or chamber in an organ, especially either of the chambers of the heart which contract to pump blood into arteries. **—ven•tric'u•lar** *adj.*

ven•tril•o•quism |vĕn **tril'**ə kwĭz'əm| *n.* The art or practice of producing vocal sounds so that they seem to come from a source other than the speaker. **—ven•tril'o•quist** *n.*

ven•ture |**vĕn'**chər| *n.* An undertaking, course of action, etc., that involves risk or uncertainty. *—v.* **ven•tured, ven•tur•ing. 1.** To risk; stake: *a businessman venturing all his capital on a deal.* **2.** To dare to say; express at the risk of denial, criticism, etc.: *venture an opinion.* **3.** To brave the dangers of: *ventured the high seas in a light boat.* **4.** To travel, engage in a course of action, undertake a project, etc., despite danger and trepidation; dare or show the courage to go: *the first American to venture into outer space.*

ven•ture•some |**vĕn'**chər səm| *adj.* **1.** Disposed to take risks; bold: *venturesome investors.* **2.** Involving risk or danger; hazardous: *venturesome dedication to medical research.*

ven•tu•ri |vĕn **tŏŏr'**ē| *n.* Also **venturi tube.** A short tube having a narrow section through which a fluid moving through the tube must pass at a higher velocity than at other points. The fluid in the narrow section exerts less pressure than that in the wider parts, allowing the use of the tube as an air speed indicator, as an atomizer, and in rockets.

ven•ue |**vĕn'**yōō| *n.* **1.** The locality in which a crime or other cause of legal action occurs. **2.** The locality in which a trial must be held.

Ve•nus |**vē'**nəs|. The Roman goddess of love and beauty.

Ve•nus |**vē'**nəs| *n.* The second planet of the solar system in order of increasing distance from the sun. Its diameter is about 7,700 miles, its average distance from the sun is about 67.2 million miles, and it takes about 225 days to orbit the sun.

Venus's-fly•trap |**vē'**nə sĭz **flī'**trăp'| *n.* A plant having leaf ends that are edged with needlelike bristles and that can close around and trap insects which are then digested and absorbed by the plant. [SEE PICTURE]

ve•ra•cious |və **rā'**shəs| *adj.* **1.** Speaking the truth; honest; truthful: *a veracious person.* **2.** Accurate; precise: *a veracious description of the accident.* **—ve•ra'cious•ly** *adv.*

ve•rac•i•ty |və **răs'**ĭ tē| *n.* **1.** Devotion to the truth; honesty: *doubting the veracity of the witnesses.* **2.** Accuracy; precision: *checking the veracity of his report.*

ve•ran•dah or **ve•ran•da** |və **răn'**də| *n.* A roofed porch or balcony.

verb |vûrb| *n.* In grammar, any of a class of words functioning to express existence, action, or occurrence. For example, the words *be, run,* and *happen* are verbs. ***—modifier:*** *a verb tense.*

ver•bal |**vûr'**bəl| *adj.* **1.** Of or associated with words: *verbal aptitude tests.* **2.** Expressed in words; unwritten: *a verbal agreement.* **3.** Word for word; literal: *a verbal translation.* **4.** Of a verb: *verbal endings.* **5.** Having the nature or function of a verb. For example, in the sentence *The men loaded the moving van, moving* is a verbal adjective. *—n.* A grammatical construction that contains a verb. A verbal may be a verb or it may consist of a verb followed by other words. For example, in the sentences *It rained, The train arrived late,* and *I locked the car,* the words *rained, arrived late,* and *locked the car* are verbals. **—ver'bal•ly** *adv.*

ver•ba•tim |vər **bā'**tĭm| *adv.* Word for word; in the same words: *He repeated the speech verbatim.* *—adj.* :*a verbatim account.*

ver•be•na |vər **bē'**nə| *n.* Any of several plants grown for their clusters of variously colored, often fragrant flowers.

ver•bi•age |**vûr'**bē ĭj| *n.* The use of too many words; wordiness.

ver•bose |vər **bōs'**| *adj.* Using more words than necessary; dull and wordy; prolix. **—ver•bose'ly** *adv.* **—ver•bos'i•ty** |vər **bŏs'**ĭ tē| *n.*

ver•dant |**vûr'**dənt| *adj.* **1.** Green with growing plants: *verdant meadows.* **2.** Of or suggestive of green growing plants: *verdant leaves.*

ver•dict |vûr′dĭkt| *n.* The decision reached by a jury at the end of a trial.

ver•di•gris |vûr′də grēs′| *n.* **1.** A blue or green copper acetate, used as a pigment and as a poison for insects and fungi. **2.** A green coating or crust of copper salts that forms on copper, brass, or bronze that is exposed to air or sea water for a long time.

ver•dure |vûr′jər| *n.* **1.** The fresh, green color of healthy, leafy growing plants. **2.** A growth of green plants.

verge |vûrj| *n.* **1.** The extreme edge, rim, or margin of something: *on the verge of the city's industrial section.* **2.** The point beyond which an action, condition, etc., is likely to begin or occur: *on the verge of tears; on the verge of exhaustion.* —*v.* **verged, verg•ing.** To border on; approach: *enthusiasm verging on fanaticism.*

Ver•gil |vûr′jəl|. A form of the name **Virgil.**

ver•i•fi•ca•tion |vĕr′ə fĭ kā′shən| *n.* The act or process of verifying.

ver•i•fy |vĕr′ə fī′| *v.* **ver•i•fied, ver•i•fy•ing, ver•i•fies.** **1.** To prove the truth of: *Observations of today's astronomers have verified the findings of the ancient Greeks.* **2.** To test or check the correctness or accuracy of: *verify your addition.*

ver•i•ly |vĕr′ə lē| *adv. Archaic.* In fact; in truth.

ver•i•ta•ble |vĕr′ĭ tə bəl| *adj.* Without doubt or question; genuine: *a veritable success.*

ver•i•ty |vĕr′ĭ tē| *n., pl.* **ver•i•ties.** **1.** The condition of being real, accurate, or true: *the verity of his description of the castle.* **2.** Something that is true, as a principle, belief, etc.: *verities proclaimed by the church.*

ver•mi•cel•li |vûr′mĭ chĕl′ē| *or* |-sĕl′ē| *n.* Pasta made into long, thin threads, thinner than spaghetti.

ver•mi•form |vûr′mə fôrm′| *adj.* Shaped like or resembling a worm.

vermiform appendix. The tubular projection attached to the large intestine near its junction with the small intestine; the appendix.

ver•mil•ion, also **ver•mil•lion** |vər mĭl′yən| *n.* **1.** A bright red sulfide of mercury, used as a pigment. **2.** A bright red. —*adj.* Bright red.

ver•min |vûr′mĭn| *n., pl.* **ver•min.** **1.** Any of various insects or small animals, such as cockroaches or rats, that are destructive, annoying, or injurious to health. **2.** A hateful or despised person. **3.** A collection of such people.

ver•min•ous |vûr′mə nəs| *adj.* Of, like, or overrun with vermin.

Ver•mont |vər mŏnt′|. A New England state of the United States. Population, 448,000. Capital, Montpelier. —**Ver•mont′er** *n.*

ver•mouth |vər mo͞oth′| *n.* An alcoholic beverage made with white wine flavored with aromatic herbs and spices.

ver•nac•u•lar |vər năk′yə lər| *n.* **1.** The normal spoken language of a country or region as distinct from literary or learned language. **2.** The idiom of a particular trade or profession. —*adj.* Of, using, or expressed in vernacular: *vernacular speech; a vernacular poet.*

ver•nal |vûr′nəl| *adj.* Of or occurring in the spring. —**ver′nal•ly** *adv.*

vernal equinox. The equinox that occurs on or about March 21, when the sun, moving northward, crosses the celestial equator, marking the beginning of spring in the Northern Hemisphere.

ver•ni•er |vûr′nē ər| *n.* **1.** A small auxiliary scale attached parallel to a main scale and arranged to indicate fractional parts of the smallest divisions of the main scale. **2.** An auxiliary device that allows fine adjustments or measurements to be made on or with an instrument or device. —**modifier:** *a vernier scale.*

vernier caliper. A measuring device consisting of an L-shaped bracket with a scale along its edge, with an L-shaped attachment equipped with a vernier scale along it. [SEE PICTURE]

ver•sa•tile |vûr′sə tĭl| *or* |-tīl′| *adj.* **1.** Capable of doing many things well: *a versatile athlete.* **2.** Having varied uses or functions: *a versatile piece of machinery.* —**ver′sa•til′i•ty** *n.*

verse |vûrs| *n.* **1.** Writing that has meter or rhyme; poetry. **2.** A stanza of a long poem or hymn. **3.** One line of poetry. **4.** A specific type of poetic writing: *blank verse.* **5.** One of the numbered subdivisions of a chapter of the Bible.

versed |vûrst| *adj.* Practiced or skilled; knowledgeable: *versed in foreign languages.*

ver•si•fy |vûr′sə fī′| *v.* **ver•si•fied, ver•si•fy•ing, ver•si•fies.** **1.** To write verses. **2.** To tell (something) in verse. —**ver′si•fi•ca′tion** *n.*

ver•sion |vûr′zhən| *or* |-shən| *n.* **1.** A description or account related from a specific point of view: *his own version of the accident.* **2. a.** A particular translation of a written work: *the King James version of the Bible.* **b.** An adaptation of a work of art or literature: *a prose version of a poem; a motion-picture version of a play.* **3.** A form or variation of an earlier or original model: *a mildly reworked version of the Ford Model T.*

ver•sus |vûr′səs| *prep.* **1.** Against: *the plaintiff versus the defendant; Harvard versus Yale.* **2.** In contrast with: *death versus dishonor.*

vert. vertical.

ver•te•bra |vûr′tə brə| *n., pl.* **ver•te•brae** |vûr′tə brē| or **ver•te•bras.** Any of the bones or, in some fishes, segments of cartilage connected together to form the spinal column.

ver•te•bral |vûr′tə brəl| *adj.* **1.** Of or relating to a vertebra or vertebrae. **2.** Consisting of a vertebrae: *the vertebral column.*

ver•te•brate |vûr′tə brāt′| *or* |-brĭt| *n.* Any of a large group of animals having a backbone, including the fishes, amphibians such as frogs and toads, reptiles, birds, and mammals. —*adj.* **1.** Having a backbone: *vertebrate animals.* **2.** Of a vertebrate or vertebrates: *the vertebrate brain.*

ver•tex |vûr′tĕks′| *n., pl.* **ver•ti•ces** |vûr′tĭ sēz′| or **ver•tex•es.** **1.** The highest point of something; the apex; summit. **2. a.** The point in which the sides of an angle intersect. **b.** The point of a triangle that is opposite and farthest away from its base. **c.** A point of a polyhedron in which three or more edges intersect. **d.** The point of a cone or pyramid farthest from its base.

ver•ti•cal |vûr′tĭ kəl| *adj.* **1.** Perpendicular to the plane of the horizon; directly upright. **2.** Of a vertex. **3.** Situated at, near, around, or on opposite sides of a vertex. —*n.* **1.** A vertical line, plane, part, structure, etc. **2.** A vertical position: *a post that leans slightly from the vertical.* —**ver′ti•cal•ly** *adv.*

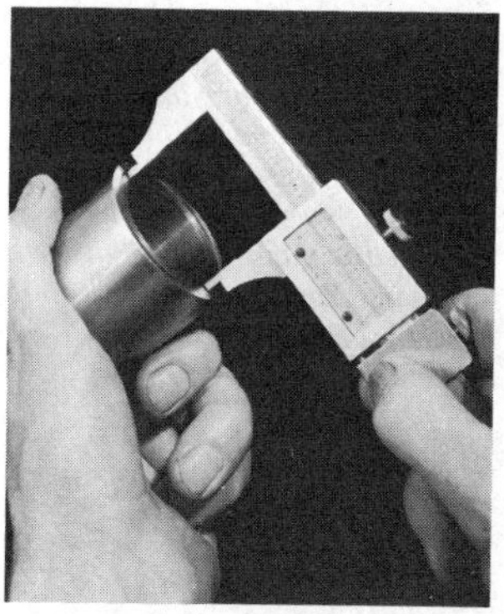

vernier caliper
This was invented by Pierre *Vernier* (1580–1637), French mathematician.

vespers

Vespers *is from Latin* vesper, *"evening." This is descended from the prehistoric Indo-European word* wesperos, *"evening." (This word appears in Greek as* Hesperos, *the name of the evening star.)* Wesperos *had a variant form,* west-, *which has been inherited without change through Germanic and Old English into Modern English as* **west** *(the direction of sunset or evening).*

vetch

vertical angles. The angles formed by two or more lines all of which intersect in the same point, especially the opposing pairs of such angles.

ver•ti•ces |vûr′tĭ sēz′| *n.* A plural of **vertex.**

ver•ti•go |vûr′tĭ gō′| *n., pl.* **ver•ti•goes.** The sensation of dizziness and the feeling that one's environment or oneself is spinning rapidly.

verve |vûrv| *n.* **1.** Liveliness or vivacity; animation. **2.** Energy and enthusiasm in the expression of ideas: *His plays lack verve.*

ver•y |vĕr′ē| *adv.* **1.** In a high degree; extremely: *feeling very happy.* **2.** —Used as an intensive before superlatives: *This is the very best way to proceed.* **3.** Precisely; exactly: *the very same one.* —*adj.* **1.** Absolute; utter: *the very end.* **2.** Identical: *She wore the very dress that we saw on Jane yesterday.* **3.** Particular; precise; exact: *the very center of town.* **4.** Mere: *The very mention of his name frightened the boys.* **5.** —Used as an intensive to stress the importance of the thing described: *The very mountains crumbled.* **6.** Actual: *caught in the very act of stealing.*

very high frequency. A radio-wave frequency lying in the band between 30 and 300 megahertz.

very low frequency. A radio-wave frequency lying in the band between 3 and 30 kilohertz.

ves•i•cle |vĕs′ĭ kəl| *n.* **1.** A small bladder or sac, especially one that contains a body fluid. **2.** A blister.

ves•per |vĕs′pər| *n.* **1.** Evening. Used chiefly in poetry. **2. vespers** |vĕs′pərz|. Any worship service held in the evening. [SEE NOTE]

Ves•puc•ci |və spo͞o′chē| *or* |-spyo͞o′-|, **Amerigo.** 1451–1512. Italian navigator for whom America was named.

ves•sel |vĕs′əl| *n.* **1.** A ship, large boat, or similar craft. **2.** A hollow container, as a bowl, pitcher, jar, or tank, especially one for holding liquids. **3.** A narrow, tubelike body part or plant part through which a liquid flows or circulates: *Veins and arteries are blood vessels.*

vest |vĕst| *n.* **1.** A short, sleeveless, collarless garment, either open or fastening in front, worn over a shirt or blouse and often under a suit coat or jacket. **2.** An undershirt. —*v.* **1.** To dress, especially in religious robes or vestments. **2. a.** To place (authority, power, etc.) in the control of: *Their constitution vests ultimate power and authority in the sovereign.* **b.** To give power, authority, etc., to: *vesting the President with executive powers.*

Ves•ta |vĕs′tə|. The Roman goddess of the hearth.

ves•tal |vĕs′təl| *n.* Also **vestal virgin.** One of the six virgin priestesses who tended the sacred fire in the temple of Vesta in ancient Rome. —*adj.* **1.** Often **Vestal.** Of Vesta or the vestals. **2.** Chaste.

ves•ti•bule |vĕs′tə byo͞ol′| *n.* **1.** A small entrance hall or lobby. **2.** An enclosed area at the end of a railroad passenger car. **3.** Any chamber, opening, or channel of the body that serves as an entrance to another chamber or cavity.

ves•tige |vĕs′tĭj| *n.* **1.** A remaining trace, sign, or part: *There was scarcely a vestige of color left in the faded silk.* **2.** An organ or structure that was present and functioning in an earlier form of an organism and that remains, usually greatly reduced in size, in later forms as a nonfunctioning part.

vest•ment |vĕst′mənt| *n.* A garment, especially a robe, gown, or other article of dress worn by a clergyman at a religious service.

ves•try |vĕs′trē| *n., pl.* **ves•tries. 1.** A room in a church where vestments and sacred objects are stored. **2.** A meeting room in a church. **3.** A committee that manages the business affairs of an Episcopal parish.

Ve•su•vi•us, Mount |və so͞o′vē əs|. An active volcano in southern Italy.

vet |vĕt| *n. Informal.* **1.** A veterinarian. **2.** A veteran.

vet. 1. veteran. **2.** veterinarian. **3.** veterinary.

vetch |vĕch| *n.* Any of several climbing plants having leaves with featherlike leaflets and usually purplish flowers. [SEE PICTURE]

vet•er•an |vĕt′ər ən| *or* |vĕt′rən| *n.* **1.** A person of long experience in a profession, activity, office, etc. **2.** A former member of the armed forces: *a veteran of the Korean War.* —**modifier:** *a veteran actor; veteran battalions; veteran benefits.*

Veterans Day. November 11, a holiday now officially celebrated on the fourth Monday in October in memory of the armistice ending World War I in 1918 and in honor of veterans of the armed services.

vet•er•i•nar•i•an |vĕt′ər ə nâr′ē ən| *or* |vĕt′rə-| *n.* A person specially trained and qualified to give medical treatment to animals.

vet•er•i•nar•y |vĕt′ər ə nĕr′ē| *or* |vĕt′rə-| *adj.* Of or relating to the medical treatment, diseases, or injuries of animals: *a veterinary college.* —*n., pl.* **vet•er•i•nar•ies.** A veterinarian.

ve•to |vē′tō| *n., pl.* **ve•toes. 1. a.** The right or power of a branch of government or of a governmental official to reject a bill that has been passed and therefore prevent or delay its enactment. **b.** The exercise of this right. **2.** Any authoritative prohibition or rejection of a proposed or intended act. —*v.* **ve•toed, ve•to•ing, ve•toes. 1.** To prevent (a legislative bill) from becoming law by exercising the power of veto. **2.** To refuse to consent to; forbid: *The board vetoed all wage increases.*

vex |vĕks| *v.* To irritate or annoy; bother.

vex•a•tion |vĕk sā′shən| *n.* **1.** The condition of being vexed; annoyance: *a look of vexation on his face.* **2.** Something that vexes.

vhf, VHF very high frequency.

vi•a |vī′ə| *or* |vē′ə| *prep.* By way of: *going to Montreal via Boston.*

vi•a•ble |vī′ə bəl| *adj.* **1.** Capable of continuing to live, grow, or develop: *viable seeds; a prematurely born but viable infant.* **2.** Capable of working successfully or of continuing to be effective: *a viable national economy.* —**vi′a•bil′i•ty** *n.*

vi•a•duct |vī′ə dŭkt′| *n.* A series of spans or arches used to carry a road, railroad, etc., over a wide valley or over other roads or railroads.

vi•al |vī′əl| *n.* A small glass container for liquids. ¶*These sound alike* **vial, viol.**

vi•and |vī′ənd| *n.* **1.** A food. **2. viands.** Provisions; victuals.

vibes |vībz| *n. (used with a plural verb). Slang.* A distinctive emotional reaction; vibrations.

vi•brant |vī′brənt| *adj.* **1.** Showing, marked by, or resulting from vibration; vibrating. **2.** Full of

ă pat/ā pay/â care/ä father/ĕ pet/ē be/ĭ pit/ī pie/î fierce/ŏ pot/ō go/ô paw, for/oi oil/o͝o book/o͞o boot/ou out/ŭ cut/û fur/*th* the/th thin/hw which/zh vision/ə ago, item, pencil, atom, circus

vigor, energy, etc.: *a vibrant personality.*

vi•brate |vī′brāt′| *v.* **vi•brat•ed, vi•brat•ing. 1.** To move or cause to move back and forth rapidly. **2.** To produce a sound by vibrating.

vi•bra•tion |vī brā′shən| *n.* **1. a.** The act or process of vibrating. **b.** The condition of being vibrated. **2.** A rapid motion of a particle or an elastic solid back and forth in a straight line on both sides of a center position. **3.** Often **vibrations.** *Slang.* A distinctive emotional reaction by a person to another person or thing that is capable of being sensed. —**vi•bra′tion•al** *adj.* —**vi′bra•to′ry** |vī′brə-tôr′ē| *or* |-tōr′ē| *adj.*

vi•bra•to |vĭ brä′tō| *or* |vē-| *n., pl.* **vi•bra•tos.** A small, moderately rapid back-and-forth variation in the pitch of a musical tone, producing a tremulous or pulsating effect.

vi•bra•tor |vī′brā′tər| *n.* **1.** Something that vibrates. **2.** An electrically operated device used for massage.

vi•bur•num |vī bûr′nəm| *n.* Any of several shrubs with rounded clusters of small white flowers.

vic•ar |vĭk′ər| *n.* **2.** A salaried clergyman in charge of a parish. **2.** In the Roman Catholic Church, a clergyman who acts for or represents another, often higher-ranking member of the clergy. **3.** Someone who acts for or represents another; a deputy.

vic•ar•age |vĭk′ər ĭj| *adj.* **1.** The home of a vicar. **2.** The position or duties of a vicar.

vi•car•i•ous |vī kâr′ē əs| *or* |vĭ-| *adj.* **1.** Felt or undergone as if one were taking part in the experience or feelings of another: *the vicarious thrills provided by reading a rousing adventure story.* **2.** Endured or done by one person substituting for another: *vicarious punishment.* **3.** Acting in place of someone or something else. —**vi•car′i•ous•ly** *adv.*

vice[1] |vīs| *n.* **1.** Evil, wickedness, or great immorality. **2.** An evil or very immoral practice or habit. **3.** A personal failing or shortcoming: *We know his virtues and his vices.* ¶ *These sound alike* **vice, vise.** [SEE NOTE]

vice[2] |vīs| *adj.* Acting as or having the authority to act as a deputy or substitute for another: *the vice chairman of the committee; the vice dean of the college.* ¶ *These sound alike* **vice, vise.** [SEE NOTE]

vice admiral. See **admiral.**

vice-pres•i•den•cy |vīs prĕz′ĭ dən sē| *n.* The office of a vice president or the period during which a vice president is in office.

vice president. An officer ranking next below a president and having authority to take his place in case of the president's absence, illness, or death.

vice-pres•i•den•tial |vīs prĕz′ĭ dĕn′shəl| *adj.* Of or for the vice president or the vice-presidency.

vice•roy |vīs′roi′| *n.* A governor of a country, province, or colony, ruling as the representative of a king or other monarch.

vi•ce ver•sa |vī′sə vûr′sə| *or* |vīs′|. The reverse case being so; the other way around: *Some families have completely adapted themselves to the desires of the dog, rather than vice versa.*

vi•chy•ssoise |vĭsh′ē swäz′| *or* |vē′shē-| *n.* A creamy potato soup flavored with leeks or onions and usually served cold.

Vi•chy water |vĭsh′ē, vē′shē| *n.* A naturally effervescent mineral water from the springs at Vichy, France.

vi•cin•i•ty |vĭ sĭn′ĭ tē| *n., pl.* **vi•ci•ni•ties.** A nearby or surrounding region or place.

vi•cious |vĭsh′əs| *adj.* **1.** Cruel; mean; malicious: *vicious lies.* **2.** Marked by evil or vice; wicked: *a vicious crime.* **3.** Savage and dangerous: *a vicious shark.* **4.** Violent; intense: *sought shelter from the vicious wind.* —**vi′cious•ly** *adv.*

vi•cis•si•tude |vĭ sĭs′ĭ to͞od′| *or* |-tyo͞od′| *n.* Often **vicissitudes.** A sudden or unexpected change or shift in one's life or surroundings.

vic•tim |vĭk′tĭm| *n.* **1.** Someone who is harmed or killed by another or by accident, disease, etc.: *the victim of a hungry lion; the victims of an epidemic.* **2.** Someone made to suffer or undergo difficulty, as by trickery, unfair practices, or misunderstanding: *the victim of a hoax.* **3.** A living creature killed as a religious sacrifice.

vic•tim•ize |vĭk′tə mīz′| *v.* **vic•tim•ized, vic•tim•iz•ing.** To make a victim of, especially by using trickery or taking unfair advantage.

vic•tor |vĭk′tər| *n.* The winner in a war, fight, contest, struggle, etc.

vic•to•ri•a |vĭk tôr′ē ə| *or* |-tōr′-| *n.* A four-wheeled horse-drawn carriage for two passengers, having a folding top and a raised seat in front for the driver.

Vic•to•ri•a[1] |vĭk tôr′ē ə| *or* |-tōr′-|. 1819–1901. Queen of Great Britain (1837–1901).

Vic•to•ri•a[2] |vĭk tôr′ē ə| *or* |-tōr′-|. **1.** The capital of British Columbia, Canada. Population, 62,551. **2.** The capital of Hong Kong. Population, 1,027,-000. **3.** The capital of the Seychelles. Population, 16,000.

Victoria, Lake. The largest lake in Africa, lying between Uganda, Kenya, and Tanzania.

Vic•to•ri•an |vĭk tôr′ē ən| *or* |-tōr′-| *adj.* **1.** Of or typical of the time and taste of Queen Victoria's reign. **2.** Stuffy, conventional, or prudish in a manner considered typical of the time of Queen Victoria. —**Vic•to′ri•an•ism′** *n.*

vic•to•ri•ous |vĭk tôr′ē əs| *or* |-tōr′-| *adj.* **1.** Being the winner in a contest or struggle: *the victorious team.* **2.** Of, resulting in, or expressing victory: *the army's victorious advance; a victorious cheer.* —**vic•to′ri•ous•ly** *adv.*

vic•to•ry |vĭk′tə rē| *n., pl.* **vic•to•ries.** The act or fact of winning in a contest or struggle, as with an opponent or a difficulty; triumph.

vict•uals |vĭt′lz| *pl.n.* Food; provisions. [SEE NOTE]

vi•cu•ña, also **vi•cu•na** |vĭ ko͞o′nə| *or* |-kyo͞o′-| *or* |-ko͞o′nyə| *or* |və-| *n.* **1.** An animal of the Andes mountains of South America, related to the llama and having fine, silky fleece. **2.** Cloth made from this fleece. —***modifier:*** *a vicuña coat.* [SEE PICTURE]

vid•e•o |vĭd′ē ō′| *n.* **1.** The visual part of a television broadcast or signal as distinguished from audio. **2.** Television: *a star of stage, screen, and video.*

vid•e•o•cas•sette |vĭd′ē ō kə sĕt′| *n.* A videotape recording in cassette form.

video display terminal. A **video terminal.**

video game. A computerized game played by manipulating images on a display screen.

vid•e•o•tape |vĭd′ē ō tāp′| *n.* A special type of magnetic recording tape used to record television programs, together with their associated sound,

vice[1-2]

Vice[1] *is from Old French* vice, *which is from Latin* vitium, *"fault, error, crime." (From* vitium *also was formed the verb* vitiāre, *"to spoil, falsify," from which we have* **vitiate.**) **Vice[2]** *was originally a preposition meaning "in place of" and pronounced* /vī′sē/; *a* vice chairman *was originally someone who acted "vice" the permanent chairman. The word is from Latin* vice, *"in place of."*

victuals

Victuals *was originally spelled* vitels; *it was borrowed from Old French* vitailles, *which is descended from Late Latin* victūālia, *"provisions, life support." The* c *was "restored" to the English word by people who knew that there had been a* c *in the Latin original, but the English pronunciation has continued to ignore it.*

vicuña

for subsequent playback and broadcasting.

videotape recorder. A device for making videotape recordings.

video terminal. A computer input-output device utilizing a cathode-ray tube to display data on a screen. [SEE PICTURE]

vie |vī| *v.* **vied, vy•ing.** To engage in a contest or struggle; compete.

Vi•en•na |vē ĕn′ə|. The capital of Austria. Population, 1,650,000.

Vi•et•cong |vē′ĕt **kŏng′**| *or* |vyĕt′-| *n., pl.* **Vi•et•cong.** Also **Viet Cong.** A Vietnamese supporter of the former National Liberation Front of South Vietnam. —***modifier:*** *the Vietcong forces.*

Vien•ti•ane |vyĕn **tyän′**|. The administrative capital of Laos. Population, 132,000.

Vi•et•nam |vē′ĕt **näm′**| *or* |**-năm′**| *or* |vyĕt′-|. A country in Southeast Asia, on the South China Sea in the eastern part of the Indochina peninsula. Population, 52,742,000. Capital, Hanoi.

Vi•et•nam•ese |vē ĕt′nə **mēz′**| *or* |**-mēs′**| *n., pl.* **Vi•et•nam•ese. 1.** A native or inhabitant of Vietnam. **2.** The language of Vietnam. —*adj.* Of Vietnam, the Vietnamese, or their language.

view |vyo͞o| *n.* **1.** The act or an example of seeing something; sight: *The explorer had his first view of the newly discovered land from the deck of his ship.* **2.** Examination; inspection: *picked up the rock specimen for a closer view.* **3.** A scene; vista: *the view from the top of the mountain.* **4.** Range or field of sight: *The airplane disappeared from view.* **5.** A way of showing or seeing something, as from a particular position or angle: *a side view of the house.* **6.** An opinion; idea: *her views on education.* **7.** An aim; intention: *These laws were made with the view of providing equal rights for all.* —*v.* **1.** To look at: *viewed the stars through a telescope.* **2.** To regard; consider: *The President viewed the new uprisings with alarm.*

Idioms. **in view of.** Taking into account; considering: *In view of your past performance, I'm sure you will succeed.* **on view.** Displayed for others to see; on exhibit. **with a view to.** With the hope or intention of: *looked around with a view to speedy escape if the wildcat attacked.*

view•er |**vyo͞o′**ər| *n.* **1.** Someone who views something, especially an onlooker or spectator. **2.** Any of various devices used to magnify photographic images so that they are easily visible.

view•point |**vyo͞o′**point′| *n.* **1.** A way of thinking about or regarding something. **2.** The place or position from which one views something.

vig•il |**vĭj′**əl| *n.* **1.** A period of alert watchfulness during normal sleeping hours: *exhausted by her vigil at the bedside of her sick friend.* **2.** The eve of a holy day, often observed by remaining awake for religious devotions.

vig•i•lance |**vĭj′**ə ləns| *n.* Alert watchfulness.

vig•i•lant |**vĭj′**ə lənt| *adj.* On the alert; watchful; wary. —**vig′i•lant•ly** *adv.*

vig•i•lan•te |vĭj′ə **lăn′**tē| *n.* A member of a group that without authority takes on itself such powers as pursuing and punishing those suspected of being criminals or offenders.

vig•or |**vĭg′**ər| *n.* **1.** Physical energy or strength: *a rosy-cheeked, bright-eyed lass full of health and vigor.* **2.** Strong feeling; enthusiasm or intensity: *The opposing party, with great vigor, claimed the disputed votes for their candidate.* **3.** Effectiveness; force: *the vigor of his literary style.* **4.** Ability to grow, develop, or maintain health and energy.

vig•or•ous |**vĭg′**ər əs| *adj.* **1.** Full of or done with vigor; lively; forceful: *vigorous songs of the sea; vigorous exercise.* **2.** Healthy and energetic; hardy: *a nest of vigorous young birds; vigorous plant growth.* —**vig′or•ous•ly** *adv.*

vig•our |**vĭg′**ər| *n.* Chiefly British form of the word **vigor.**

Vi•king, also **vi•king** |**vī′**kĭng| *n.* One of a seafaring Scandinavian people who plundered the coasts of northern and western Europe from the 9th to the 11th century and who made early voyages to the New World. —***modifier:*** *Viking raiders; a Viking ship.*

Vi•la |**vē′**lə|. The capital of Vanuatu. Population, 15,000.

vile |vīl| *adj.* **vil•er, vil•est. 1.** Hateful; disgusting. **2.** Miserable; base; wretched: *vile slavery.* **3.** Very bad or unpleasant: *a vile temper; vile weather.* **4.** Morally low or base. —**vile′ly** *adv.* —**vile′ness** *n.*

vil•i•fy |**vĭl′**ə fī′| *v.* **vil•i•fied, vil•i•fy•ing, vil•i•fies.** To say bad things about; speak evil of; defame. —**vil′i•fi•ca′tion** *n.* —**vil′i•fi′er** *n.*

vil•la |**vĭl′**ə| *n.* A sometimes large and luxurious country house, often used as a resort.

vil•lage |**vĭl′**ĭj| *n.* **1.** A group of homes and other buildings forming a community smaller than a town. **2.** The people of a village: *The entire village welcomed the newcomers.* —***modifier:*** *a village square; the village water supply.*

vil•lag•er |**vĭl′**ĭ jər| *n.* Someone who lives in a village.

vil•lain |**vĭl′**ən| *n.* **1.** A wicked or very bad person; an evil fellow; scoundrel. **2.** A main character who harms or threatens the good or heroic characters in a story, play, etc. ¶*These sound alike* **villain, villein.** [SEE NOTE]

vil•lain•ous |**vĭl′**ə nəs| *adj.* **1.** Wicked; evil. **2.** Very bad; dreadful. —**vil′lain•ous•ly** *adv.*

vil•lain•y |**vĭl′**ə nē| *n., pl.* **vil•lain•ies. 1.** Wickedness; evil. **2.** A wicked or evil act: *guilty of countless villainies.*

vil•lein |**vĭl′**ən| *or* |-ān′| *n.* In the feudal system of medieval Europe, a farm laborer who was the slave of a lord; a serf. ¶*These sound alike* **villein, villain.** [SEE NOTE]

vim |vĭm| *n.* Liveliness and energy; enthusiasm.

vin•ai•grette |vĭn′ĭ **grĕt′**| *n.* **1.** A small container with a perforated top used for holding an aromatic preparation, as smelling salts. **2.** A sauce of vinegar and oil.

Vinci, Leonardo da. See **da Vinci, Leonardo.**

vin•di•cate |**vĭn′**dĭ kāt′| *v.* **vin•di•cat•ed, vin•di•cat•ing.** To clear of accusation, blame, etc., with supporting proof: *believing that it was time to vindicate himself from such offensive charges.* —**vin′di•ca′tion** *n.*

vin•dic•tive |vĭn **dĭk′**tĭv| *adj.* Having or showing a desire for revenge; vengeful. —**vin•dic′tive•ly** *adv.* —**vin•dic′tive•ness** *n.*

vine |vīn| *n.* **1. a.** A plant having a stem that climbs on, creeps along, twines around, or clings to something for support. **b.** The stem of such a plant: *Tarzan swinging on a jungle vine from tree to tree.* **2.** A grapevine. —***modifier:*** *vine leaves; vine ropes.* [SEE NOTE]

vin•e•gar |**vĭn′**ĭ gər| *n.* An acid liquid that is basically a dilute solution of acetic acid. It is

villain/villein

Villein *is from Old French* villein, *"peasant serf," which is from Medieval Latin* villānus, *"farm laborer," from* villa, *"farm."* **Villain** *is a variant of* **villein;** *it first meant "peasant," then "ignorant country person," then "depraved criminal." Compare note at* **gentle.**

vine/wine

Vine *is from Old French* vine, *which is from Latin* vīnea, *"the wine plant, the grapevine," from* vīnum, *"wine." Wine was introduced into Britain by the Romans; the word* vīnum *was borrowed into Old English as* wīn, *becoming* **wine** *in Modern English.*

ă pat/ā pay/â care/ä father/ĕ pet/ ē be/ĭ pit/ī pie/î fierce/ŏ pot/ ō go/ô paw, for/oi oil/o͝o book/ o͞o boot/ou out/ŭ cut/û fur/ *th* the/th thin/hw which/zh vision/ ə ago, item, pencil, atom, circus

obtained by fermenting beyond the alcohol stage and is used in flavoring and preserving food.

vine•yard |vĭn′yərd| *n.* A piece of ground on which grapevines are grown and tended.

vin•tage |vĭn′tĭj| *n.* **1. a.** The grapes produced by a particular vineyard or district in a single season. **b.** Wine made from these grapes. **2.** The year or place in which a particular wine was bottled. **3.** A year or time of origin: *a spiked German military helmet, vintage 1914.* —*adj.* **1.** Of or resulting from a vintage of unusually high quality: *vintage wines.* **2.** Of very high quality.

vint•ner |vĭnt′nər| *n.* A person who makes or sells wine.

vi•nyl |vī′nəl| *n.* **1. a.** The chemical radical CH_2CH, derived from ethylene and having a valence of 1. **b.** Any of various chemical compounds, typically highly reactive, that contain this radical, used in making plastics. **2.** Any of various plastics, typically tough, flexible, and shiny, often used for coverings and clothing. —***modifier:*** *vinyl floor covering; a vinyl raincoat.*

vi•ol |vī′əl| *n.* Any of a family of stringed instruments, chiefly of the 16th and 17th centuries, usually having six strings and a flat back and played with a curved bow. ¶*These sound alike* **viol, vial.**

vi•o•la |vē ō′lə| *or* |vī-| *n.* A stringed instrument of the violin family, slightly larger than a violin, tuned a fifth lower, and having a deeper, more somber and mellow tone.

vi•o•late |vī′ə lāt′| *v.* **vi•o•lat•ed, vi•o•lat•ing. 1.** To break; disregard: *violate a law; violate a promise.* **2.** To act toward (something sacred or highly respected) without proper respect; desecrate: *violate a shrine.* **3.** To rape.

vi•o•la•tion |vī′ə lā′shən| *n.* **1.** The act of violating or the condition of being violated: *the violation of a truce; acting in violation of the law.* **2.** An example of this: *a traffic violation.*

vi•o•lence |vī′ə ləns| *n.* **1.** Physical force exerted, as for causing damage or injury: *crimes of violence.* **2.** Great force or intensity: *the violence of a hurricane; the violence of a reaction to a drug.* **3.** In general, acts of breaking the law, vandalism, destruction of property, etc: *severe outbreaks of violence; protests that have led to violence.* **4.** Damage; injury: *No violence has been done to his sensibilities.*

vi•o•lent |vī′ə lənt| *adj.* **1.** Marked by or resulting from great physical force or rough action: *a violent attack; violent blows.* **2.** Showing or having great emotional force: *a man with a violent temper; a violent outburst of fury.* **3.** Having great force or effect; severe; harsh: *a violent hurricane; a play marked by violent contrasts between good and evil.* **4.** Caused by unexpected force or injury rather than by natural causes: *a violent death.* —**vi′o•lent•ly** *adv.*

vi•o•let |vī′ə lĭt| *n.* **1. a.** Any of several low-growing plants with flowers that are usually bluish purple but are sometimes yellow or white. **b.** A flower of such a plant. **2.** A bluish purple. —*adj.* Bluish purple. [SEE PICTURE]

vi•o•lin |vī′ə lĭn′| *n.* The highest-pitched stringed instrument of the modern orchestra, played with a bow and having four strings tuned at intervals of a fifth. [SEE PICTURE]

vi•o•lin•ist |vī′ə lĭn′ĭst| *n.* A person who plays the violin.

vi•o•list. *n.* **1.** |vē ō′lĭst| *or* |vī-|. A person who plays the viola. **2.** |vī′ə lĭst|. A person who plays a viol.

vi•o•lon•cel•lo |vē′ə lən chĕl′ō| *n., pl.* **vi•o•lon•cel•los.** A cello.

VIP *Informal.* very important person.

vi•per |vī′pər| *n.* **1. a.** A poisonous snake of northern Europe and Asia; an adder. **b.** Any of several other poisonous snakes. See **pit viper. 2.** A wicked or hateful person.

vi•ra•go |vĭ rä′gō| *or* |-rā′-| *n., pl.* **vi•ra•goes** or **vi•ra•gos.** A noisy, bad-tempered woman; a scold.

vi•ral |vī′rəl| *adj.* Of, relating to, or caused by a virus: *viral diseases.*

vir•e•o |vîr′ē ō′| *n., pl.* **vir•e•os.** Any of several small grayish or greenish birds.

Vir•gil |vûr′jəl|. 70–19 B.C. Latin poet; author of the epic poem *Aeneid.*

vir•gin |vûr′jĭn| *n.* **1.** A person, especially a girl or woman, who has never engaged in sexual intercourse. **2. the Virgin.** Mary, the mother of Jesus. —*adj.* **1.** Of, characteristic of, or suitable to a virgin; chaste; modest: *robes of virgin white.* **2.** Pure and untouched: *virgin snow.* **3.** In the original or natural state; unused, untouched, or unexplored: *virgin forests; virgin territory; the virgin resources of the new continent.*

vir•gi•nal |vûr′jə nəl| *adj.* Of, relating to, or appropriate to a virgin; chaste; pure.

Vir•gin•ia |vər jĭn′yə|. A Middle Atlantic state of the United States. Population, 5,346,279. Capital, Richmond. —**Vir•gin′ian** *adj. & n.*

Virginia creeper. A North American climbing vine with leaves consisting of five leaflets and bluish-black berries. [SEE PICTURE]

Virginia reel. A country dance in which couples perform various steps together to instructions called out by a leader.

Virgin Islands. A group of islands in the West Indies, east of Puerto Rico, divided into: **a.** The **British Virgin Islands,** a British associated state. Population, 11,000. **b.** The **Virgin Islands of the United States,** a United States Territory. Population, 62,468. Capital, Charlotte Amalie.

Virgin Mary. The mother of Jesus.

vir•ile |vîr′əl| *adj.* **1.** Of, characteristic of, or befitting a man: *the virile tone quality of men's voices.* **2.** Having or showing strength, vigor, energy, and other manly qualities: *a virile man; a virile race.* **3.** Able to perform sexually as a male; potent. —**vi•ril′i•ty** |vĭ rĭl′ĭ tē| *n.*

Vir•go |vûr′gō| *n.* The sixth sign of the zodiac.

vir•tu•al |vûr′cho͞o əl| *adj.* Existing in effect or for practical purposes though not real in actual fact or form: *the virtual extinction of the buffalo; living years in virtual exile.*

vir•tual image. An image, such as one seen in a mirror, from which rays of reflected or refracted light appear to come.

vir•tu•al•ly |vûr′cho͞o ə lē| *adv.* For the most part; essentially; practically: *The mountain lion is now virtually extinct in the East.*

vir•tue |vûr′cho͞o| *n.* **1. a.** Moral excellence and righteousness; goodness: *Virtue is its own reward.* **b.** Any particular example or kind of moral excellence: *the virtues of patience and long-suffering.* **2.** Chastity, especially of a woman. **3.** A particularly efficacious, good, or beneficial

violet

violin

Virginia creeper

quality; an advantage: *a plan with the virtue of being practical; a climate with the virtue of never being too hot or too cold.* **4.** Effective force or power; ability to produce a definite result: *believing in the virtue of herbs to cure diseases.*
Idiom. by virtue of. On the basis of: *winning a reputation as a great mountain climber by virtue of many spectacular ascents in the Alps.*

vir•tu•os•i•ty |vûr′cho͞o ŏs′ĭ tē| *n.* The technical skill or style displayed by a virtuoso.

vir•tu•o•so |vûr′cho͞o ō′sō| *n., pl.* **vir•tu•o•sos.** A musical performer of unusual excellence or ability.

vir•tu•ous |vûr′cho͞o əs| *adj.* **1.** Having or showing virtue; morally good; righteous: *a virtuous life; virtuous conduct.* **2.** Chaste; pure: *a virtuous woman.* **—vir′tu•ous•ly** *adv.*

vir•u•lent |vĭr′yə lənt| *or* |vĭr′ə-| *adj.* **1.** Having a very strong tendency to cause or capability for causing disease or harm, as a disease, toxin, or microorganism has. **2.** Bitterly hostile or malicious: *virulent criticism.* **—vir′u•lence** *n.*

vi•rus |vī′rəs| *n., pl.* **vi•rus•es.** A tiny particle of nucleic acid, RNA or DNA, associated with a capsule of protein and sometimes fat or carbohydrate, capable of invading living cells and destroying them and causing the release of a large number of new particles identical to the original one, thus producing a disease.

vi•sa |vē′zə| *n.* An official authorization stamped on a passport by an official of a foreign country, permitting entry into and travel within that country.

vis•age |vĭz′ĭj| *n.* The face or facial expression of a person.

vis•cer•a |vĭs′ər ə| *pl.n.* The internal organs of the body, especially those contained within the abdomen and thorax. **—vis′cer•al** *adj.*

vis•cid |vĭs′ĭd| *adj.* Thick and sticky, as a liquid; resembling glue. **—vis′cid•ly** *adv.*

vis•cos•i•ty |vĭ skŏs′ĭ tē| *n.* **1.** The condition or property of being viscous. **2.** The degree to which a fluid resists flow when pressure is applied to it.

vis•count |vī′kount′| *n.* **1.** A member of the British peerage holding a title and rank below that of an earl and above that of a baron. **2.** In certain European countries, the son or brother of a count.

vis•count•ess |vī′koun′tĭs| *n.* **1.** The wife of a viscount. **2.** A woman holding a rank equal to that of viscount in her own right.

vis•cous |vĭs′kəs| *adj.* **1.** Tending to resist flow when pressure is applied, as a fluid; having a high viscosity. **2.** Viscid. **—vis′cous•ly** *adv.*

vise |vīs| *n.* A device of metal, usually consisting of a pair of jaws that are opened and closed by means of a screw or lever, used in carpentry or metalworking to hold work in position. ¶*These sound alike* **vise, vice.** [SEE PICTURE]

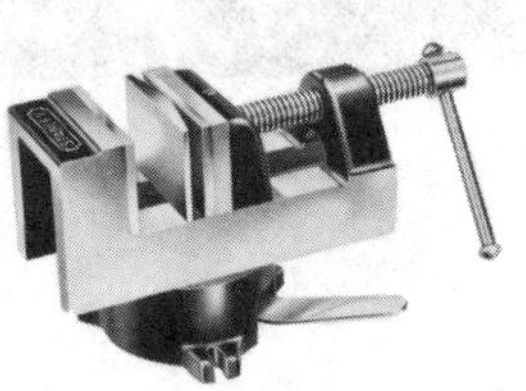

vise
A metalworker's vise.

Vish•nu |vĭsh′no͞o′| *n.* In Hinduism, the second member of the trinity including also Brahma and Shiva.

vis•i•bil•i•ty |vĭz′ə bĭl′ĭ tē| *n.* **1.** The fact, condition, or degree of being visible. **2.** The greatest distance over which it is possible to see without aid from instruments under given weather conditions.

vis•i•ble |vĭz′ə bəl| *adj.* **1.** Capable of being seen; perceptible to the eye: *Only one ninth of an iceberg is visible above water.* **2.** Easily noticed; clear; apparent: *showing visible signs of impatience.* **—vis′i•bly** *adv.*

Vis•i•goth |vĭz′ĭ gŏth′| *n.* A member of the western Goths, a Teutonic people who invaded the Roman Empire in the fourth century A.D. and settled in France and Spain.

vi•sion |vĭzh′ən| *n.* **1.** The ability to sense light that enters the eye and make fine judgments about the color of the light and the directions from which the rays come; the sense of sight. **2.** Unusual foresight: *With vision and vigor and the help of modern science, they are transforming a desert into a fertile land.* **3.** A mental image produced by the imagination: *having visions of future wealth and power.* **4.** Something perceived through unusual means, as a supernatural sight. **5.** Someone or something of great beauty: *She was a vision in her new white satin ball gown.*

vi•sion•ar•y |vĭzh′ə nĕr′ē| *adj.* **1.** Given to impractical or fanciful ideas: *a visionary explorer in search of fabulous treasures.* **2.** Not practicable at the moment; existing only in the imagination: *visionary schemes. The submarine had been around as a visionary craft for nearly 150 years before it finally became a reality.* —*n., pl.* **vi•sion•ar•ies. 1.** A person who has visions. **2.** A person given to impractical ideas.

vis•it |vĭz′ĭt| *v.* **1.** To go or come to see for reasons of business, duty, or pleasure: *visit a doctor for physical checkups; visit one's family; visiting Chicago over the weekend.* **2.** To stay with as a guest: *visiting his former classmate in California.* **3.** To afflict; assail: *a region visited by swarms of locusts that devoured everything growing in the fields.* **4.** To converse or chat: *visit with friends and exchange the latest gossip.* —*n.* An act or an example of visiting; a brief call or stay.

vis•i•ta•tion |vĭz′ĭ tā′shən| *n.* **1.** A visit, especially one of an official nature. **2.** A visit of affliction or blessing, regarded as being ordained by God.

vis•i•tor |vĭz′ĭ tər| *n.* A person who pays a visit.

vi•sor |vī′zər| *or* |vĭz′ər| *n.* **1.** A projecting part, as on a cap or the windshield of a car, that protects the eyes from sun, wind, or rain. **2.** The movable front piece on a helmet that protects the face. [SEE PICTURE]

visor

vis•ta |vĭs′tə| *n.* **1.** A distant view, especially one seen through a passage or opening. **2.** A mental view of a series of events: *a scientific discovery that opens up new vistas of human improvement.*

vis•u•al |vĭzh′o͞o əl| *adj.* **1.** Of, serving, or resulting from the sense of sight. **2.** Capable of being seen; visible. **3.** Done or performed by means of the unaided vision: *visual navigation.* **4.** Designed to communicate by means of vision: *visual instruction; visual aids.*

vis•u•al•ize |vĭzh′o͞o ə līz′| *v.* **vis•u•al•ized, vis•u•al•iz•ing.** To form a mental image or vision of: *It is difficult to visualize what scientists mean by light waves.* **—vis′u•al•i•za′tion** *n.*

vi•tal |vīt′l| *adj.* **1.** Of or characteristic of life: *vital processes; vital signs.* **2.** Essential for the continuation of life: *vital organs; vital functions.* **3.** Having great importance; essential: *Irrigation was vital to early civilization.* —*n.* **vitals.** Those

ă pat/ā pay/â care/ä father/ĕ pet/ ē be/ĭ pit/ī pie/î fierce/ŏ pot/ ō go/ô paw, for/oi oil/o͝o book/ o͞o boot/ou out/ŭ cut/û fur/ *th* the/th thin/hw which/zh vision/ ə ago, item, pencil, atom, circus

organs or parts of the body whose functioning is essential to life. —**vi'tal•ly** *adv.*

vi•tal•ize |vīt'l īz'| *v.* **vi•tal•ized, vi•tal•iz•ing.** To fill with life, vigor, energy, etc. —**vi'tal•i•za'tion** *n.*

vi•ta•min |vī'tə mĭn| *n.* Any of various fairly complex organic compounds that occur in small amounts in animal and plant tissues and that are needed for the continuation of normal life functions.

vitamin A. A vitamin or mixture of vitamins found in fish-liver oils and some green and yellow leafy vegetables. It is necessary to normal cell growth and development, and a lack of it in the human diet causes night blindness and damage to the skin and mucuous membranes. [SEE NOTE]

vitamin B. 1. The **vitamin B complex.** 2. A member of the vitamin B complex, especially vitamin B_1.

vitamin B_1. A vitamin of the B complex, produced synthetically and occurring naturally in bran, yeast, and meat. A lack of it in human beings produces faulty carbohydrate metabolism, ailments of the nervous system, and beriberi.

vitamin B_2. A vitamin of the B complex, an orange-yellow substance found in milk, leafy vegetables, fresh meat, and egg yolks and also made synthetically. It is the main growth-producing substance in the vitamin B complex.

vitamin B_6. A vitamin of the B complex that occurs in plant and animal tissues and acts in various parts of normal metabolism.

vitamin B_{12}. A vitamin of the B complex, a complex organic substance that contains cobalt. It is produced by the normal growth of certain microorganisms and is found in liver and yeast.

vitamin B complex. A related group of vitamins originally thought to be a single vitamin and considered to include vitamin B_1, B_2, B_6, and B_{12} and other substances such as niacin, biotin, and folic acid. It occurs chiefly in yeast, liver, eggs, and some vegetables.

vitamin C. **Ascorbic acid.**

vitamin D. Any of several related sterols made active by exposure to ultraviolet light or obtained in active form from milk, fish, and eggs. It is necessary for normal bone growth and is used to treat rickets in children.

vitamin E. Any of several related oils found chiefly in grains and vegetable oils, used to treat sterility and various abnormalities of the muscles, blood, liver, and nervous system.

vitamin G. Vitamin B_2; riboflavin.

vitamin H. Biotin.

vitamin K. Any of several substances that are made artificially and are also found in leafy green vegetables, tomatoes, and vegetable oils and that are essential for normal clotting of the blood.

vitamin P. A crystalline substance extracted from citrus fruit juices and used in treating certain conditions involving bleeding in or into the skin.

vi•ti•ate |vĭsh'ē āt'| *v.* **vi•ti•at•ed, vi•ti•at•ing.** To make ineffective or worthless; invalidate: *vitiate a contract. Your objections vitiate my argument.* —**vi'ti•a'tion** *n.*

vit•re•ous |vĭt'rē əs| *adj.* 1. Of, resembling, or of the nature of glass; glassy. 2. Of the vitreous humor.

vitreous body. A transparent, jellylike material composed mainly of vitreous humor that fills the part of the eyeball between the lens and the retina.

vitreous humor. A watery fluid that makes up most of the vitreous body of the eye.

vit•ri•fy |vĭt'rə fī'| *v.* **vit•ri•fied, vit•ri•fy•ing, vit•ri•fies.** To change into glass or a similar substance, especially through melting by heat.

vit•ri•ol |vĭt'rē ōl'| *n.* 1. **Sulfuric acid.** 2. Any of various salts of sulfuric acid, such as ferrous sulfate or **green vitriol,** zinc sulfate or **white vitriol,** or copper sulfate or **blue vitriol.**

vit•ri•ol•ic |vĭt'rē **ŏl'**ĭk| *adj.* 1. Of, like, derived from, or of the nature of vitriol. 2. Bitterly spiteful; caustic: *a vitriolic remark.*

vi•va•cious |vĭ vā'shəs| *or* |vī-| *adj.* Animated; lively; spirited: *a vivacious girl.* —**vi•va'cious•ly** *adv.* —**vi•vac'i•ty** |vĭ văs'ĭ tē| *or* |vī-| *n.*

viv•id |vĭv'ĭd| *adj.* 1. Perceived as bright and distinct; intense: *a vivid blue.* 2. Evoking lifelike images within the mind: *words that paint vivid pictures.* 3. Active: *a vivid imagination.* 4. Distinct and clear: *vivid memories of a trip to Japan.* —**viv'id•ly** *adv.* —**viv'id•ness** *n.*

vi•vip•a•rous |vī vĭp'ər əs| *adj.* Giving birth to living young that develop within the mother's body, as most mammals do, rather than hatching from eggs.

viv•i•sect |vĭv'ĭ sĕkt'| *v.* To perform vivisection on (a living animal or animals).

viv•i•sec•tion |vĭv'ĭ **sĕk'**shən| *n.* The act of cutting into or dissecting a living animal, especially for scientific research.

vix•en |vĭk'sən| *n.* 1. A female fox. 2. A sharp-tempered, sly woman. [SEE NOTE]

viz. That is; namely. An abbreviation for the Latin word *videlicet.*

vi•zier |vĭ **zîr'**| *or* |vĭz'yər| *n.* In former times, a high official in a Moslem government.

vi•zir |vĭ **zîr'**| *n.* A form of the word **vizier.**

vi•zor |vī'zər| *or* |vĭz'ər| *n.* A form of the word **visor.**

vo•cab•u•lar•y |vō **kăb'**yə lĕr'ē| *n., pl.* **vo•cab•u•lar•ies.** 1. All the words of a language. 2. The sum of words used by a particular person, profession, etc.: *a writer who uses a very rich vocabulary; the vocabulary of economics.* 3. A list of words and phrases, usually arranged alphabetically and defined or translated; a lexicon.

vo•cal |vō'kəl| *adj.* 1. Of or produced by the voice: *vocal quality; vocal range; vocal utterances.* 2. Meant to be sung: *vocal music.* 3. Speaking freely and loudly; outspoken: *He is very vocal in his opposition to the new price increases.* —*n.* A piece of popular music that features a singer. —**vo'cal•ly** *adv.*

vocal cords. A pair of muscular bands or folds in the larynx that vibrate when pulled together and when air from the lungs is forced between them, thereby producing the sound of the voice.

vo•cal•ic |vō **kăl'**ĭk| *adj.* Of or containing a vowel or vowels.

vo•cal•ist |vō'kə lĭst| *n.* A singer, especially one who specializes in singing popular songs.

vo•ca•tion |vō **kā'**shən| *n.* 1. A profession, especially one for which one is specially suited or

vitamin

Vitamin *was originally* vitamine; *it was coined in 1912 from Latin* vīta, *"life,"* + amino, *because it was at first believed that these substances were based on amino acids; but this was later found to be untrue.*

vixen/fox

The prehistoric Germanic word for "fox" (basically meaning "the bushy-tailed one") was fuhsaz, *with the regular feminine equivalent* fuhson. Fuhsaz *became* fox *in Old English and remained* **fox** *in Modern English.* Fuhson *became* fyxe *in Old English, then* fyxene *in Middle English. In the country dialects of southern and western England, /f/ is often softened to /v/; in these dialects* fyxene *became* **vixen,** *which became the standard English form (but* fixen *remained common in the north of England until recently).*

volcano
Paricutin, Mexico

vole

volt
This unit was named in honor of Count Alessandro Volta *(1745–1827), Italian physicist.*

ă pat/ā pay/â care/ä father/ĕ pet/ē be/ĭ pit/ī pie/î fierce/ŏ pot/ō go/ô paw, for/oi oil/ŏŏ book/ōō boot/ou out/ŭ cut/û fur/*th* the/th thin/hw which/zh vision/ə ago, item, pencil, atom, circus

trained: *making medicine his vocation.* **2.** A strong desire to do a particular type of work: *She felt very little vocation for teaching.* **—vo·ca'tion·al** *adj.*

vocational school. A school that offers special training in specific trades or occupations; a trade school.

vo·cif·er·ous |və sĭf'ər əs| *adj.* Making an outcry; noisy; loud: *a vociferous crowd; vociferous protests.* **—vo·cif'er·ous·ly** *adv.*

vod·ka |vŏd'kə| *n.* An alcoholic liquor distilled from fermented wheat or rye mash, corn, or potatoes.

vogue |vōg| *n.* **1.** The current fashion or style. **2.** Popular acceptance; popularity: *His novels enjoyed a great vogue in the 1930's.*

voice |vois| *n.* **1. a.** The sound or sounds produced by specialized organs in the respiratory tract of a vertebrate, especially the sounds made by a human being. **b.** Sound of this kind used for music, as in singing. **c.** The ability to produce such sound: *He caught a bad cold and lost his voice.* **2.** The organs that produce the voice: *Her voice reached the high notes with ease.* **3.** The condition or quality of a person's singing or vocal organs: *a baritone in excellent voice.* **4.** A singer: *a chorus of 200 voices.* **5.** Any of the melodic parts in a musical composition. **6.** The expression of feelings, thoughts, etc.: *give voice to one's anger.* **7.** The right or opportunity to express a choice or opinion: *The children had no voice in deciding where to spend their vacation.* **8.** A will, desire, or opinion openly expressed; *signing the new pay increases despite many dissenting voices; the voice of the people.* **9.** Something resembling or likened to human sound or speech in being a medium of expression: *the voice of the wind; heeding the voice of his conscience.* **10.** In grammar, a verb form indicating the relation between the subject and the action expressed by the verb. See **active voice, passive voice.** **—*v.* voiced, voic·ing. 1.** To give expression to: *a chance to voice his feelings.* **2.** To produce (a speech sound) with vibration of the vocal cords.

***Idiom.* with one voice.** In full agreement; unanimously.

voice box. The larynx.

voiced |voist| *adj.* **1.** Having a voice or a specified kind of voice: *a soft-voiced person.* **2.** In phonetics, uttered with vibration of the vocal cords. For example, the consonant *g* is voiced.

voice-o·ver |vois'ō'vər| *n.* In motion pictures and television, the voice of a narrator who does not appear on camera.

void |void| *adj.* **1.** Having no legal force or effect: *declare a marriage null and void.* **2.** Devoid; lacking: *A little centipede, void of all fear, crawled over the pillowcase and into the ear of the cat.* **3.** Containing no matter; vacant. **—*n.*** An empty space: *the void of outer space. God created all things out of the void.* **—*v.* 1.** To make null; cancel: *void a contract.* **2.** To take out (the contents of something); empty. **3.** To evacuate (body wastes).

voile |voil| *n.* A sheer fabric of cotton, rayon, wool, or silk used in making lightweight curtains, dresses, etc. **—*modifier:*** *a voile dress.*

vol. volume.

vol·a·tile |vŏl'ə təl| *adj.* **1.** Changing to vapor easily or readily at normal temperatures and pressures. **2.** Changeable, especially: **a.** Inconstant; fickle: *catering to the volatile preferences of the public.* **b.** Tending to erupt into violent action; explosive: *a volatile political situation.*

vol·a·til·i·ty |vŏl'ə tĭl'ĭ tē| *n.* The condition, property, or degree of being volatile.

vol·can·ic |vŏl kăn'ĭk| *adj.* **1.** Of, like, or characteristic of an erupting volcano. **2.** Producing or thrown forth by a volcano. **3.** Violent; explosive: *an opera singer with a volcanic temper.*

vol·ca·no |vŏl kā'nō| *n., pl.* **vol·ca·noes** or **vol·ca·nos. 1.** Any opening in the crust of the earth through which molten rock, dust, ash, and hot gases are thrown forth. **2.** A mountain or other elevation formed by the material thrown forth in this way. [SEE PICTURE]

vole |vōl| *n.* Any of several animals related to and resembling rats and mice but having a shorter tail. [SEE PICTURE]

Vol·ga |vŏl'gə|. The longest river in Europe, rising in northwestern Russia and flowing 2,300 miles to the Caspian Sea.

vo·li·tion |və lĭsh'ən| *n.* The fact or power of choosing, using one's own will, etc.: *He left of his own volition.*

vol·ley |vŏl'ē| *n., pl.* **vol·leys. 1. a.** The simultaneous discharge of a number of missiles. **b.** The missiles discharged. **2.** Any burst or outburst of many things at once: *a volley of questions.*

vol·ley·ball |vŏl'ē bôl'| *n.* **1.** A game played between two teams who hit a ball back and forth over a net with the hands. **2.** The ball used in this game.

volt |vōlt| *n.* A unit of electric potential or electromotive force, equal to the difference of electric potential measured between the ends of a conductor that has a resistance of one ohm and through which a steady current of one ampere is flowing. [SEE NOTE]

volt·age |vōl'tĭj| *n.* Electromotive force expressed in volts.

vol·ta·ic |vŏl tā'ĭk| *adj.* **1.** Of or indicating electricity that is produced as a result of chemical action. **2.** Producing electricity by chemical action: *a voltaic cell.*

volt·me·ter |vōlt'mē'tər| *n.* An instrument that measures and indicates differences of electric potential.

vol·u·ble |vŏl'yə bəl| *adj.* Talking very quickly and easily; fluent; glib: *a voluble speaker.* **—vol'u·bil'i·ty** *n.* **—vol'u·bly** *adv.*

vol·ume |vŏl'yōōm| *or* |-yəm| *n.* **1. a.** A collection of written or printed sheets bound together; a book. **b.** One book of a set: *a volume of an encyclopedia.* **2.** The measure or size of a three-dimensional object or region of space independent of its shape. **3. a.** The force or intensity of a sound; loudness. **b.** A control, as on a radio or phonograph, for regulating loudness. **4.** Quantity; amount: *a large volume of mail.*

vo·lu·mi·nous |və lōō'mə nəs| *adj.* **1.** Having great volume, size, fullness, or number: *a voluminous skirt.* **2.** Filling or capable of filling many volumes: *voluminous records.*

vol·un·tar·y |vŏl'ən tĕr'ē| *adj.* **1.** Made, done, given, etc., of one's own free will: *voluntary tasks; a voluntary contribution to the pension fund.* **2.**

Doing or ready to do things without being compelled by another or guaranteed of reward: *voluntary workers at a hospital.* **3.** Arising from an act of choice: *living in voluntary exile in Canada.* **4.** Not accidental; intentional: *voluntary manslaughter.* **5.** Normally controlled by or subject to individual will: *a voluntary muscle.* —*n., pl.* **vol•un•tar•ies.** A short solo organ piece, often improvised, usually played before and sometimes during and after a church service. —**vol'un•tar'i•ly** |vŏl'ən târ'ə lē| *adv.*

vol•un•teer |vŏl'ən tîr'| *n.* **1.** Someone who performs or gives services of his own free will. **2.** A person who enlists in the armed forces. —***modifier:*** *a volunteer fire brigade.* —*v.* To give or offer of one's own accord.

vo•lup•tu•ous |və lŭp'cho͞o əs| *adj.* **1.** Of, marked by, or giving sensual pleasure, luxury, etc.: *lead a voluptuous life.* **2.** Full and appealing in form: *a voluptuous woman.*

vol•vox |vŏl'vŏks'| *n.* A microorganism consisting of a hollow, spherical colony of individual cells. [SEE PICTURE]

vom•it |vŏm'ĭt| *v.* To eject or discharge (part or all of the contents of the stomach) through the mouth, usually in a series of involuntary spasms. —*n.* Material discharged from the stomach by vomiting.

voo•doo |vo͞o'do͞o| *n.* A religious cult of African origin, characterized by a belief in sorcery, fetishes, primitive deities, etc. —***modifier:*** *voodoo drums; a voodoo charm.*

vo•ra•cious |və rā'shəs| *adj.* **1.** Greedy for food; ravenous: *a voracious appetite.* **2.** Too eager; avid; insatiable: *a voracious reader.*

vor•tex |vôr'tĕks'| *n., pl.* **vor•tex•es** or **vor•ti•ces** |vôr'tĭ sēz'|. A movement or flow of fluid in which each particle of the fluid moves in a circle, spiral, helix, or similar curve.

vor•ti•cel•la |vôr'tĭ sĕl'ə| *n.* A bell-shaped one-celled microorganism that attaches itself to a surface by a slender stalk that can be coiled into a spiral. [SEE PICTURE]

vor•ti•ces |vôr'tĭ sēz'| *n.* A plural of **vortex.**

vote |vōt| *n.* **1.** A formal expression of one's preference or choice, made in or as if in an election. **2.** The means by which such choice is made known, as a raised hand or ballot. **3.** The number of votes cast in an election or to resolve an issue: *a vote of 70 to 51.* **4.** A group of voters: *the labor vote.* **5.** The result of an election. **6.** The right to express a choice in or as if in an election: *Women did not always have the vote.* —*v.* **vot•ed, vot•ing. 1.** To express one's choice by a vote; cast a vote: *voted early; voted Democratic.* **2.** To make available or bring into existence by vote: *voted funds for flood control.* **3.** To declare by general consent: *The dance was voted a success.* —***phrasal verbs.*** **vote down.** To defeat in an election. **vote in.** To elect. **vote out.** To remove (an official) by means of an election.

vot•er |vō'tər| *n.* A person who votes or has the right to vote.

vo•tive |vō'tĭv| *adj.* Given or dedicated in fulfillment of a vow or pledge: *a votive statue.*

vouch |vouch| *v.* To give or serve as a guarantee; supply assurance or supporting evidence.

vouch•er |vou'chər| *n.* A receipt, signed statement, or similar paper that serves as proof that something has been paid for, given, sold, etc.

vouch•safe |vouch sāf'| *v.* **vouch•safed, vouch•saf•ing.** To grant or give (a reply, privilege, special attention, etc.) as if doing a favor.

vow |vou| *n.* A solemn promise or pledge: *He made a vow to use his great knowledge only for good and not for evil.* —*v.* **1.** To promise or pledge solemnly: *She vowed that she would return to that place some day.* **2.** To make a solemn promise or pledge that one will accomplish or bring about something: *He vowed revenge on his persecutors.* **3.** To declare; assert.

vow•el |vou'əl| *n.* **1.** A voiced speech sound produced by relatively free passage of the breath through the larynx and mouth, usually forming the most prominent or central part of a syllable. **2.** A letter that represents such a sound, as *a, e, i, o,* or *u.* —***modifier:*** *vowel sounds.*

voy•age |voi'ĭj| *n.* A long journey to a distant place, made on a ship, boat, etc., or sometimes an aircraft or spacecraft: *Columbus' four voyages to the New World; a voyage up the Hudson; a voyage to the moon.* —*v.* **voy•aged, voy•ag•ing.** To travel by making a voyage. —**voy'ag•er** *n.*

V.P. vice president.

vs. versus.

Vt. Vermont.

vul•can•ize |vŭl'kə nīz'| *v.* **vul•can•ized, vul•can•iz•ing.** To give (rubber or sometimes other materials) greater strength, resistance, elasticity, etc., by combining with sulfur or other additives in the presence of heat and pressure. —**vul'can•i•za'tion** *n.*

vul•gar |vŭl'gər| *adj.* **1.** Lacking good taste, refinement, elegance, etc.; crude; coarse: *vulgar jokes; a vulgar display of wealth.* **2.** Of the common people: *Vulgar Latin.* —**vul'gar•ly** *adv.*

vul•gar•ism |vŭl'gə rĭz'əm| *n.* A word or expression used mainly by uncultivated people.

vul•gar•i•ty |vŭl găr'ĭ tē| *n., pl.* **vul•gar•i•ties. 1.** The condition or quality of being vulgar; crudeness; coarseness. **2.** Something vulgar, such as an action or expression that offends good taste or propriety.

vul•gar•ize |vŭl'gə rīz'| *v.* **vul•gar•ized, vul•gar•iz•ing. 1.** To make vulgar; cheapen. **2.** To popularize, as by simplifying or making generally known. —**vul'gar•i•za'tion** *n.* —**vul'gar•iz'er** *n.*

Vulgar Latin. The common speech of ancient Rome. Vulgar Latin is distinct from literary or standard Latin, which was used by the aristocrats. The Romance languages developed largely from Vulgar Latin.

Vul•gate |vŭl'gāt'| *or* |-gĭt| *n.* The Latin version of the Bible used in the Roman Catholic Church.

vul•ner•a•ble |vŭl'nər ə bəl| *adj.* **1.** Capable of being harmed or injured: *helpless, vulnerable baby birds.* **2.** Open to danger or attack; unprotected: *The retreat of the army had left the outlying territories vulnerable.* **3.** Easily affected or hurt, as by criticism, sarcasm, etc. —**vul'ner•a•bil'i•ty** *n.* —**vul'ner•a•bly** *adv.*

vul•ture |vŭl'chər| *n.* **1.** Any of several large birds that generally have dark feathers and a bare head and neck and that feed on the flesh of dead animals. **2.** A greedy, grasping, ruthless person. [SEE PICTURE]

vul•va |vŭl'və| *n., pl.* **vul•vae** |vŭl'vē|. The external parts of the female genital organs.

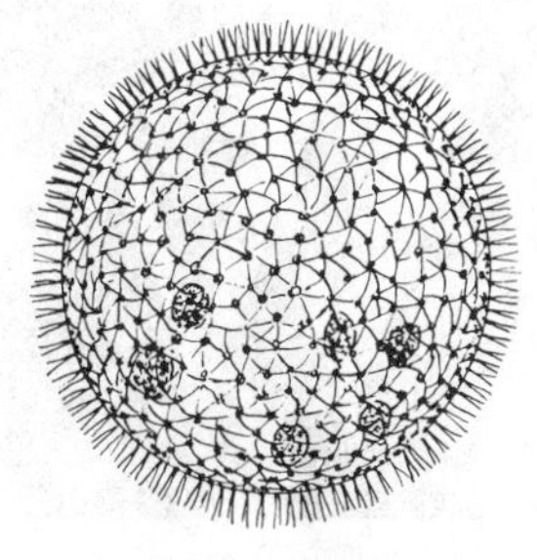

volvox

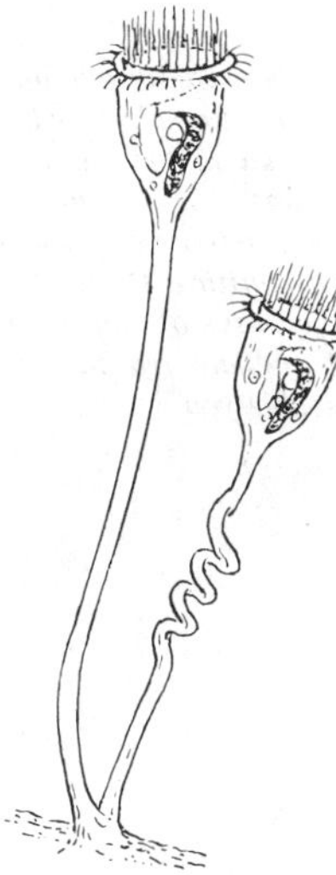

vorticella

vulture

W w

V w

(1) (2)

The letter **W** *is a variant of the letter* **U**. *The Romans used one letter (1) to stand for the sounds /u/, /v/, and /w/. In medieval times a new letter for /w/ was invented by writing* **U** *twice (2). This is the basis of our modern letter* **W** *and the reason for its name, "double-you."*

w, W |dŭb'əl yo͞o'| *or* |-yo͞o'| *n., pl.* **w's** or **W's.** The 23rd letter of the English alphabet. [SEE NOTE]

W 1. watt. **2. W** or **w** west; western. **3.** The symbol for the element tungsten.

w., W. west; western.

WAC, W.A.C. Women's Army Corps.

wack•y |wăk'ē| *adj.* **wack•i•er, wack•i•est.** *Slang.* Crazy or silly; nutty.

wad |wŏd| *n.* **1.** A small, soft piece of material, such as cotton, paper, or chewing gum, pressed together into a mass. **2.** A soft plug or disk used to hold an explosive charge in place in a cartridge or firearm. **3.** A thick batch, bunch, or roll, as of papers or paper money: *a wad of bank notes.* **4.** *Informal.* A large amount, especially of money. —*v.* **wad•ded, wad•ding. 1.** To squeeze, roll, crumple, or crush into a compact mass: *wad up a sheet of paper.* **2.** To pack, plug, stuff, or hold in place with a wad or wads.

wad•dle |wŏd'l| *v.* **wad•dled, wad•dling.** To walk with short steps that tilt or sway the body from side to side, as a short-legged bird, animal, or person does. —*n.* A clumsy or rocking walk.

wade |wād| *v.* **wad•ed, wad•ing. 1.** To walk in or through water, mud, or another substance that covers the feet or keeps them from moving freely. **2.** To cross by wading: *The river was too deep to wade.* **3.** To make one's way slowly and with difficulty.

wa•fer |wā'fər| *n.* **1.** A small, thin, crisp cooky, cracker, or candy. **2.** A small, thin disk of unleavened bread used in Communion.

waf•fle[1] |wŏf'əl| *n.* A light, crisp batter cake baked in a **waffle iron,** an appliance having hinged metal plates marked with an indented pattern, as of squares, that is pressed into the batter as it bakes.

waf•fle[2] |wŏf'əl| *v.* **waf•fled, waf•fling.** *Informal.* To speak or write evasively.

waft |wăft| *or* |wăft| *v.* **1.** To carry gently through the air or over water: *feathers wafting downward from an eagle in flight.* **2.** To float or drift: *Strains of music wafted in through the window.* —*n.* **1.** Something, such as a scent or sound, carried lightly through the air: *a waft of perfume.* **2.** A breath, puff, or gust, as of air.

wag[1] |wăg| *v.* **wagged, wag•ging.** To move, swing, or wave repeatedly back and forth or up and down. —*n.* A wagging movement.

wag[2] |wăg| *n.* A witty, playful person; joker.

wage |wāj| *n.* **1.** Often **wages.** A payment made to a worker for work done or services rendered; salary or earnings. **2.** Often **wages** *(used with a singular or plural verb).* A suitable return or reward: *"For the wages of sin is death"* (The Bible, Romans 6:23). —***modifier:*** *wage earners.* —*v.* **waged, wag•ing.** To engage in or carry on (a war, campaign, etc.): *wage a war on poverty.* [SEE NOTE on p. 379]

wa•ger |wā'jər| *n.* A bet. —*v.* To bet.

wag•gle |wăg'əl| *v.* **wag•gled, wag•gling.** To move from side to side with short, quick motions; wag or wiggle.

Wag•ner |väg'nər|, **Richard.** 1813–1883. German composer of operas.

wag•on |wăg'ən| *n.* **1.** A large, horse-drawn vehicle used to transport loads or carry passengers. **2.** A roomy motor vehicle used for a similar purpose, especially: **a.** A **station wagon. b.** A lightweight delivery truck: *a milk wagon.* **3.** A small, wheeled vehicle that can be pushed or pulled by hand, as a child's low, four-wheeled cart with a long handle.

waif |wāf| *n.* A lost or homeless person or animal, especially a small child.

wail |wāl| *v.* To cry, as in grief, dismay, or distress. —*n.* A long, high-pitched, mournful cry or sound: *the lonesome wail of a locomotive whistle.* ¶*These sound alike* **wail, wale.**

wain•scot |wān'skət| *or* |-skŏt'| *or* |-skōt'| *n.* Wall paneling or facing, usually of wood, especially when used to cover the lower part of an inside wall.

waist |wāst| *n.* **1.** The part of the human body between the bottom of the rib cage and the pelvis. **2.** The part of a garment that fits around the waist or that covers the upper body from the neck or shoulders to the waist. ¶*These sound alike* **waist, waste.**

waist•coat |wĕs'kət| *or* |wāst'kōt'| *n. British.* A vest.

wait |wāt| *v.* **1.** To stay somewhere or postpone further action until someone or something comes: *wait for me here; wait until dark.* **2.** To stop, pause, hesitate, or delay: *"Wait! I forgot something."* **3. a.** *Informal.* To postpone: *Don't wait lunch for us.* **b.** To be temporarily postponed or neglected: *The meeting had to wait until the poster was put up.* **4.** To be patient: *Wait a minute.* —***phrasal verb.*** **wait on** (or **upon**). **1.** To serve or attend as a waiter, salesclerk, nurse, maid, etc. **2.** To pay a formal visit to: *When may our ambassador wait upon the queen?* —*n.* A period of time spent in waiting: *a short wait.* ¶*These sound alike* **wait, weight.**

Idioms. **in waiting.** In attendance, as on a king or queen: *ladies in waiting.* **lie in wait.** To stay in hiding, awaiting a chance to attack.

wait•er |wā'tər| *n.* A man who serves food and

ă pat/ā pay/â care/ä father/ĕ pet/ ē be/ĭ pit/ī pie/î fierce/ŏ pot/ ō go/ô paw, for/oi oil/o͝o book/ o͞o boot/ou out/ŭ cut/û fur/ *th* the/th thin/hw which/zh vision/ ə ago, item, pencil, atom, circus

drink to diners, as in a restaurant.

wait•ress |wā'trĭs| *n.* A woman who serves food and drink to diners, as in a restaurant.

waive |wāv| *v.* **waived, waiv•ing. 1.** To give up (a right, claim, or privilege) by one's own choice: *waive a jury trial.* **2.** To set aside, dispense with, or postpone: *waive the formalities.* ¶ *These sound alike* **waive, wave.**

waiv•er |wā'vər| *n.* **1.** The act of giving up a right or claim by choice or consent. **2.** A written agreement to give up a right or claim. ¶ *These sound alike* **waiver, waver.**

Wa•kash•an |wä kăsh'ən| *or* |wô'kə shăn'| *n.* A family of North American Indian languages of Washington and British Columbia.

wake[1] |wāk| *v.* **woke** |wōk| or **waked, waked, wak•ing. 1.** To come or bring from sleep to consciousness; awaken: *I woke before daybreak. Don't wake the baby.* **2.** To be or remain awake: *whether he sleeps or wakes.* **3.** To rouse or stir: *He waked in her the need to weep.* —*n.* A watch or vigil kept over the body of a dead person before the burial. [SEE NOTE]

wake[2] |wāk| *n.* **1.** The visible track of waves, ripples, or foam left behind something moving through water. **2.** The course or route over which anything has passed: *The hurricane left destruction in its wake.* [SEE NOTE]

wak•en |wā'kən| *v.* To wake up; wake.

wale |wāl| *n.* **1.** One of a series of raised ridges in the texture of some materials, such as corduroy. **2.** A ridge raised on the skin by a lash or blow; a welt. —*v.* **waled, wal•ing.** To mark (the skin) with wales. ¶ *These sound alike* **wale, wail.**

Wales |wālz|. A division of the United Kingdom, on the island of Great Britain, west of England. Population, 2,790,000. Capital, Cardiff. [SEE NOTE on p. 970]

walk |wôk| *v.* **1.** To move over a surface by taking steps with the feet at a pace slower than a run. **2.** To cause to walk: *walk a horse around the riding ring.* **3.** To go or travel on foot: *I walked to school.* **4.** To accompany or escort on foot: *He walked me to school.* **5.** To take a stroll: *walk in the park.* **6.** To take out for exercise on foot: *walk a dog.* **7.** To move along or about in a way that resembles walking: *an astronaut walking in space.* **8.** In baseball, to advance to first base automatically by pitching four balls. —*n.* **1.** An outing, excursion, or journey on foot. **2.** A pathway or sidewalk on which to walk: *shovel snow off the walk.* **3.** An act, way, or speed of walking: *a waddling walk; a brisk walk.* **4.** A relatively slow gait in which the feet touch the ground one after another. **5.** In baseball, the automatic advance of a batter to first base by pitching four balls. —**walk'er** *n.*

***Idiom.* walk of life.** Social class or occupation: *people from all walks of life.*

walk•ie-talk•ie |wô'kē tô'kē| *n.* A small, portable, battery-operated radio transmitter and receiver.

walking stick. A cane or stick used for support, as in walking.

wall |wôl| *n.* **1.** A solid structure or partition that extends upward to enclose an area or to separate two areas from each other. **2.** Anything that encloses or forms the side, surface, or outer boundary of something: *the walls of a canyon; the wall of the stomach.* **3.** Anything that rises, separates, surrounds, or protects like a wall: *a white wall of fog; a wall of silence.* —***modifier:*** *a wall socket.* —*v.* To enclose, surround, protect, or separate with or as with a wall.

wal•la•by |wŏl'ə bē| *n., pl.* **wal•la•bies.** Any of several Australian animals related to and resembling the kangaroos but generally smaller. [SEE PICTURE]

wal•let |wŏl'ĭt| *n.* A small, flat folding case, usually made of leather, for holding paper money, coins, cards, photographs, etc.

wall•eye |wôl'ī'| *n.* **1. a.** An eye that is directed out to one side rather than being aligned with the other eye. **b.** An eye in which the cornea is white or opaque. **c.** An eye in which the iris has no color. **2.** Also **walleyed pike.** A North American freshwater fish with large, staring eyes, caught for food and sport.

wall•flow•er |wôl'flou'ər| *n.* **1.** A garden plant with fragrant yellow or orange flowers. **2.** *Informal.* A person, especially a girl or woman, who does not take part in the activities of a social event because of shyness or unpopularity.

wal•lop |wŏl'əp| *Informal. v.* **1.** To beat soundly or defeat thoroughly: *They walloped their opponents by a score of 55 to 7.* **2.** To strike with a hard blow. —*n.* A hard blow or the force to strike such a blow.

wal•low |wŏl'ō| *v.* **1.** To roll about, as in water or mud: *The rhinoceros wallowed playfully in the mud.* **2.** To indulge oneself shamelessly; revel: *The sultan wallowed in luxury.* —*n.* **1.** An act of wallowing. **2.** A place, such as a pool or mud hole, where animals go to wallow.

wall•pa•per |wôl'pā'pər| *n.* Heavy paper printed in colors and patterns for use as a pasted-on wall covering inside a house. —*v.* To cover with wallpaper.

wal•nut |wôl'nŭt'| *or* |-nət| *n.* **1.** An edible nut with a hard, rough-surfaced shell. **2.** A tree bearing such nuts. **3.** The hard, dark-brown wood of such a tree. —***modifier:*** *a walnut cake.*

wal•rus |wôl'rəs| *n., pl.* **wal•rus•es** or **wal•rus.** A large sea animal of Arctic regions, related to the seals and sea lions and having tough wrinkled skin and large tusks. [SEE PICTURE]

waltz |wôlts| *n.* **1.** A dance in a moderate triple time with a strong accent on the first beat of each measure. **2.** Music to accompany or as if to accompany this dance. —***modifier:*** *waltz music.* —*v.* To dance the waltz.

wam•pum |wŏm'pəm| *or* |wôm'-| *n.* **1.** Small beads made from pieces of polished shell and strung together into strands or belts, formerly used by North American Indians as money or jewelry. **2.** *Informal.* Money.

wan |wŏn| *adj.* **wan•ner, wan•nest. 1.** Unnaturally pale, as from illness: *a wan face.* **2.** Weak or faint: *a wan smile.* —**wan'ly** *adv.*

wand |wŏnd| *n.* A slender rod carried in the hand, especially one used in working magic.

wan•der |wŏn'dər| *v.* **1.** To move or travel from place to place freely, aimlessly, or without settling anywhere; roam: *wander no more.* **2.** To stray from a given place, path, group, or subject: *One hiker wandered away from the others. The speaker's droning voice caused the listener's attention to wander.* **3.** To go by an indirect route or

wake[1-2]

Wake[1] *is from Old English* wacian, *"to be awake," and* wacan, *"to wake (someone) up"; it is related to* **watch. Wake**[2] *is probably related to Dutch* wak, *"a channel in ice," the original meaning being "channel made by a boat."*

wallaby

walrus

wapiti

warlock

Warlock *was Old English* wǣrloga, *"oath-breaker":* wǣr, *"oath, promise,"* + -loga, *"liar." In early Germanic society, solemn oaths were of fundamental importance, and an oath-breaker was regarded with horror. Under the influence of the early church, the word* wǣrloga *came to mean "a damned soul in hell," then "a devil," and eventually "one who has sold his soul to the Devil in exchange for magic powers, an anti-Christian sorcerer"; later* **warlock** *became specifically the male counterpart of* **witch**.

ă pat/ā pay/â care/ä father/ĕ pet/ ē be/ĭ pit/ī pie/î fierce/ŏ pot/ ō go/ô paw, for/oi oil/ŏŏ book/ ōō boot/ou out/ŭ cut/û fur/ *th* the/th thin/hw which/zh vision/ ə ago, item, pencil, atom, circus

stroll in a leisurely way. **4.** To follow an irregular, winding or rambling course: *The brook wandered through the pasture.* —**wan'der•er** *n.*

wane |wān| *v.* **waned, wan•ing. 1.** To show a progressively smaller lighted surface, as the moon does when passing from full to new. **2.** To decrease, as in size, strength, importance, etc. **3.** To draw to a close: *The old year was waning.* —*n.* **1.** The time, phase, or stage during which the moon wanes. **2.** A gradual decrease.

wan•gle |wăng'gəl| *v.* **wan•gled, wan•gling.** To get by clever, tricky, or indirect means: *wangle an invitation to the party.*

Wan•kel engine |väng'kəl| *or* |wăng'-|. A rotary internal-combustion engine in which a triangular rotor turning in a specially shaped housing performs the functions allotted to the pistons of a conventional engine, thereby allowing great savings in weight and moving parts.

want |wŏnt| *or* |wônt| *v.* **1.** To wish or desire: *They wanted to play outdoors. She wanted a bicycle.* **2. a.** To have a need for; need or require: *The grass wants cutting.* **b.** To lack: *That speech wants wit.* **c.** To be in need or do without necessities; be needy: *"The Lord is my shepherd; I shall not want"* (The Bible, Psalms 23:1). **3.** To seek with the intent to capture or arrest as a lawbreaker. —*n.* **1.** A need, desire, or requirement. **2.** The condition of needing; need: *She is in want of a job.* **3.** Lack, absence, or deficiency: *He lost the election for want of support.*

want ad. A **classified advertisement.**

wan•ton |wŏn'tən| *adj.* **1.** Shameless and uncontrolled: *wanton treachery; wanton lawlessness.* **2.** Cruel and merciless: *wanton killing.* —**wan'ton•ly** *adv.* —**wan'ton•ness** *n.*

wa•pi•ti |wŏp'ĭ tē| *n., pl.* **wa•pi•tis** or **wa•pi•ti.** A large North American deer with many-branched antlers. Also called *elk.* [SEE PICTURE]

war |wôr| *n.* **1.** Armed conflict in which two or more nations, states, factions, or peoples fight each other. **2.** A serious, intense, determined struggle or attack: *a war on poverty.* **3.** The techniques or procedures of war; military science. —***modifier:*** *war prisoners.* —*v.* **warred, war•ring. 1.** To carry on or engage in war. **2.** To struggle, contend, or fight.

War Between the States. The **Civil War.**

war•ble |wôr'bəl| *v.* **war•bled, war•bling.** To sing with trills, runs, or quavers, as certain birds do. —*n.* A sound made or a song sung by warbling like a bird.

war•bler |wôr'blər| *n.* Any of a large number of small birds, of which those of North America often have yellow feathers or markings.

ward |wôrd| *n.* **1. a.** A section of a hospital devoted to the care of a particular group of patients: *a maternity ward.* **b.** A large hospital room shared by a number of patients: *a four-bed ward.* **2.** An administrative division of a city or town, especially an election district. **3.** Someone, especially a child or young person, placed under the care or protection of a guardian or a court. —*v* —**ward off.** To keep from striking; fend off; avert: *ward off a blow.* [SEE NOTE on p. 407]

-ward. A suffix that forms adjectives and adverbs and means "direction toward": **homeward.**

war•den |wôr'dn| *n.* **1.** An official who enforces certain laws, such as hunting, fishing, or fire regulations: *a game warden; a fire warden.* **2.** An official in charge of running a prison.

-wards. A form of the suffix **-ward.**

ware |wâr| *n.* **1.** Manufactured articles or goods of the same general kind, such as glassware or hardware. **2.** Pottery or ceramics, such as earthenware or stoneware. **3. wares.** Goods for sale. ¶*These sound alike* **ware, wear.**

ware•house |wâr'hous'| *n., pl.* **-hous•es** |-hou'zĭz|. A large building in which goods, produce, belongings, or articles of merchandise are stored.

war•fare |wôr'fâr'| *n.* **1.** Armed conflict; war. **2.** A special type or method of fighting: *guerrilla warfare.* **3.** Any battle or struggle.

war•head |wôr'hĕd'| *n.* A section in the forward part of a bomb, missile, torpedo, etc., that contains the explosive charge.

war•like |wôr'līk'| *adj.* **1.** Liking to make war; hostile: *a warlike people.* **2.** Threatening or indicating war: *a warlike call to arms.*

war•lock |wôr'lŏk'| *n.* A male witch; a wizard. [SEE NOTE]

warm |wôrm| *adj.* **warm•er, warm•est. 1.** Moderately hot; neither cool nor very hot: *warm weather; warm air.* **2.** Giving off or keeping in a moderate amount of heat: *the warm sun; a warm sweater.* **3.** Enthusiastic, friendly, kindly, or affectionate: *a warm smile.* **4.** Excited, animated, or emotional: *a warm debate.* **5. a.** Suggesting the heat or glow of fire, as red, orange, and yellow colors do. **b.** Pleasingly rich and mellow: *The violoncello has a warm sound.* **6.** *Informal.* In games, close to discovering, guessing, or finding something. —*v.* To make or become warm or warmer; heat up. —***phrasal verb.*** **warm up. 1.** To make or become warm or warmer. **2.** To make or become ready for action, as by exercising, practicing beforehand, etc. —**warm'ly** *adv.* —**warm'ness** *n.*

warm-blood•ed |wôrm'blŭd'ĭd| *adj.* **1.** Having a relatively warm body temperature that stays about the same regardless of changes in the temperature of the surroundings. Birds and mammals are warm-blooded. **2.** Full of feeling; eager; enthusiastic. —**warm'-blood'ed•ness** *n.*

warmth |wôrmth| *n.* **1.** The quality or condition of being, feeling, or seeming warm; warmness. **2.** Friendliness, kindness, generosity, etc.: *a person of great warmth and charm.* **3.** Excitement or intensity: *warmth of feeling.*

warn |wôrn| *v.* **1.** To tell or make aware of present or approaching danger; alert: *warned the children of bad weather.* **2.** To advise, caution, or counsel: *We warned them to be careful.*

warn•ing |wôr'nĭng| *n.* **1.** Advance notice, as of coming danger: *Without warning a long snake appeared.* **2.** A sign, indication, notice, or threat of coming danger: *The dog's low growl was a warning.* **3.** The act of giving such a sign or notice. —***modifier:*** *a warning light.*

War of Independence. The **American Revolution.**

warp |wôrp| *v.* **1.** To bend, turn, or twist out of shape. **2.** To turn aside from a true or proper course: *Prejudice warped his mind.* **3.** To move (a ship) by hauling on a line that is fastened to a piling, anchor, or pier. —*n.* **1.** The fixed threads that run lengthwise in a woven fabric, crossed at right angles by the woof threads. **2. a.** A bend or twist, especially in a piece of wood. **b.** A mental or moral twist or quirk.

war•rant |wôr′ənt| *or* |wŏr′-| *n.* **1.** An official written order authorizing something, such as an arrest, search, or seizure: *a search warrant.* **2.** Any reason, grounds, or justification, as for an action or opinion. **3.** A guarantee, as of a result. —*v.* **1.** To call for, justify, or merit: *There is enough evidence to warrant a trial.* **2.** To guarantee: *warrant a product.*

warrant officer. An officer, usually a technician, intermediate in rank between a noncommissioned officer and a commissioned officer.

war•ran•ty |wôr′ən tē| *or* |wŏr′-| *n., pl.* **war•ran•ties. 1.** A guarantee given to a buyer, stating that the product sold is as represented and that repairs will be made without charge if certain defects are found within a stated period of time. **2.** Any guarantee, authorization, or justification for an act or course of action.

war•ren |wôr′ən| *or* |wŏr′-| *n.* **1.** A place where rabbits live and breed. **2.** An overcrowded, often unhealthy place where people live.

war•ri•or |wôr′ē ər| *or* |wŏr′-| *n.* A fighter, especially an armed one, who fights in battle.

War•saw |wôr′sô′|. The capital of Poland. Population, 1,275,000.

wart |wôrt| *n.* A small, usually hard outgrowth of the underlying layer of skin, caused by a virus.

wart hog. A wild African hog with tusks and wartlike swellings on the face. [SEE PICTURE]

war•y |wâr′ē| *adj.* **war•i•er, war•i•est. 1.** Alert to danger; watchful: *The possibility of discovery kept him wary.* **2.** Distrustful: *wary of the weather.* —**war′i•ly** *adv.* —**war′i•ness** *n.*

was |wŏz| *or* |wŭz| *or* |wəz *when unstressed*| *v.* First and third person singular past tense of **be.**

wash |wŏsh| *or* |wôsh| *v.* **1.** To clean with water or other liquid and often with soap: *wash dishes; wash your face.* **2.** To clean oneself, clothes, linens, etc. with soap and water: *He washed early today. We wash and iron on Tuesday.* **3.** To be capable of being washed without damage: *Cotton cloth washes easily.* **4.** To flow over and wet with water: *Waves wash the sandy shores.* **5.** To carry or remove or be carried or removed by the action of moving water: *Rain falls and washes the soil downhill. Plant roots keep soil from washing away.* **6.** To pour or shake water through (gravel, sand, crushed ore, etc.) to separate out valuable material: *wash gravel for gold.* **7.** To cover (a painting, drawing, etc.) with a thin layer of paint or other coloring matter. —***phrasal verbs.* wash down. 1.** To clean by washing from top to bottom. **2.** In eating, to follow (food) with a drink of liquid: *He ate half a cherry pie and washed it down with milk.* **wash out. 1.** To remove or be removed by washing: *wash out dirt; a stain that won't wash out.* **2.** To carry or wear away or be carried or worn away by the action of moving water: *The river rose and washed out the dam. The road washed out.* **wash up.** To wash one's hands or face and hands: *wash up for supper.* —*n.* **1. a.** An act, process, or period of washing: *a wash followed by a rinse.* **b.** A bath. **2.** A batch of clothes or linens that are to be or that have just been washed. **3. a.** A liquid preparation used in cleansing or coating something, as mouthwash, eyewash, or whitewash. **b.** A thin coating, as of water color or whitewash. **4.** A turbulent flow of air or water caused by the passage or action of a boat, aircraft, oar, propeller, etc. [SEE NOTE]

Wash. Washington (the state).

wash-and-wear |wŏsh′ən wâr′| *or* |wôsh′-| *adj.* Treated so as to be easily washed and to require little or no ironing: *a wash-and-wear shirt.*

wash•cloth |wŏsh′klôth′| *or* |-klŏth′| *or* |wôsh′-| *n., pl.* **-cloths** |-klôthz′| *or* |-klŏthz′| *or* |-klôths′| *or* |-klŏths′|. A small cloth used for washing the face or body.

wash•er |wŏsh′ər| *or* |wô′shər| *n.* **1.** Someone or something that washes, especially a machine designed to wash clothes or dishes. **2.** A small disk, as of metal, rubber, etc., placed under a nut or at an axle bearing to relieve friction, prevent leakage, etc.

wash•ing |wŏsh′ĭng| *or* |wô′shĭng| *n.* **1.** The act or work of someone or something that washes. **2.** A batch of clothes, linens, etc., that are to be or that have just been washed.

washing machine. A household appliance for washing clothes and linens.

Wash•ing•ton[1] |wŏsh′ĭng tən| *or* |wô′shĭng-|. **1.** A Pacific Northwestern state of the United States. Population, 4,130,163. Capital, Olympia. **2.** The capital of the United States, covering the same area as the District of Columbia, between Maryland and Virginia. Population, 637,651.

Wash•ing•ton[2] |wŏsh′ĭng tən| *or* |wô′shĭng-|. **1. George.** 1732–1799. First President of the United States (1789–97). **2. Booker T.** 1856–1915. American black educator.

Washington's Birthday. February 22, a holiday now officially celebrated on the third Monday in February.

wash•room |wŏsh′ro͞om′| *or* |-ro͝om′| *or* |wôsh′-| *n.* A bathroom, rest room, or lavatory, especially one in a public place.

wash•stand |wŏsh′stănd′| *or* |wôsh′-| *n.* **1.** A stand used to hold a basin and pitcher of water for washing. **2.** A bathroom sink.

was•n't |wŏz′ənt| *or* |wŭz′-|. Was not.

wasp |wŏsp| *or* |wôsp| *n.* Any of a number of insects having a body with a narrow midsection and capable of giving a painful sting. [SEE PICTURE]

wasp•ish |wŏs′pĭsh| *or* |wô′spĭsh| *adj.* **1.** Of or typical of a wasp. **2.** Easily irritated or annoyed; snappish. —**wasp′ish•ly** *adv.* —**wasp′ish•ness** *n.*

was•sail |wŏs′əl| *or* |-āl′| *n.* **1.** A toast formerly given as an expression of good will when drinking someone's health on festive occasions. **2.** A festive party or celebration with much drinking. —*v.* To drink to the health of; toast.

wast |wŏst| *or* |wŭst|. *Archaic.* A form of the past tense of **be,** used with *thou.*

waste |wāst| *v.* **wast•ed, wast•ing. 1.** To spend, use, or use up foolishly or needlessly; squander: *waste time; waste space.* **2. a.** To fail to use; lose: *waste an opportunity.* **b.** To pass or be available without being put to use: *Time was wasting.* **3.** To wear away little by little: *The disease wasted his body. His body slowly wasted.* **4.** To destroy completely: *The Mongols wasted their enemy's camp.* —***phrasal verb.* waste away.** To grow gradually thinner, weaker, or feebler. —*n.* **1. a.** An act or instance of wasting: *a waste of time.*

wart hog

water/wet/wash
Water *was Old English* wæter, **wet** *was Old English* wǣt, *and* **wash** *was Old English* wæscan; *the three words are related.*

wasp

water buffalo

water lily

b. Loss through careless or needless use, action, or practice; wastefulness: *Haste makes waste.* **2.** Worthless or useless material that is produced as a by-product or discarded as refuse: *industrial wastes.* **3.** The material that remains after food has been digested and that is eliminated from the body. **4.** A barren or wild area, region, or expanse: *the frozen wastes of the Arctic.* ***—modifier:*** *waste materials; a waste can.* ¶*These sound alike* **waste, waist.**

Idiom. **lay waste.** To destroy; ravage: *The city was laid waste by barbarian hordes.*

waste•bas•ket |wāst′băs′kĭt| *or* |-bä′skĭt| *n.* An open container for waste paper and small items of trash.

waste•ful |wāst′fəl| *adj.* Tending to waste: *a wasteful use of resources; a wasteful method.* —**waste′ful•ly** *adv.* —**waste′ful•ness** *n.*

waste•land |wāst′lănd′| *n.* A lonely, usually barren place, such as a desert.

watch |wŏch| *v.* **1.** To look or look at: *Passers-by stopped to watch as the parade went by. Children like to watch penguins at the zoo.* **2.** To be on the lookout: *Watch for all the traffic signals.* **3.** To keep guard or keep guard over. **4.** To be careful about: *Watch your step.* ***—phrasal verb.*** **watch out.** To be careful or on the alert. *—n.* **1.** A small timepiece, usually worn on the wrist or carried in the pocket. **2.** The action of guarding or watching: *The guard kept watch over the prisoner.* **3.** A period of duty spent guarding or keeping a lookout: *a two-hour watch.* **4.** Someone who guards or keeps a lookout. ***—modifier:*** *a watch dial.* —**watch′er** *n.*

watch•ful |wŏch′fəl| *adj.* On the lookout; alert. —**watch′ful•ly** *adv.* —**watch′ful•ness** *n.*

watch•mak•er |wŏch′mā′kər| *n.* Someone who makes or repairs watches. —**watch′mak′ing** *n.*

watch•man |wŏch′mən| *n., pl.* **-men** |-mən|. A man employed to stand guard or keep watch.

wa•ter |wô′tər| *or* |wŏt′ər| *n.* **1.** A compound of hydrogen and oxygen having the formula H_2O, occurring as a liquid that covers about three-quarters of the earth's surface and also in solid form as ice and in gaseous form as steam. Water freezes at 0°C (32°F) and boils at 100°C (212°F). **2.** A body of this substance, such as an ocean, lake, river, or stream. **3.** Often **waters.** A quantity or area of water, especially when forming such a body: *the warm waters of the Caribbean Sea.* **4.** Any of various solutions that contain and somewhat resemble water: *soda water.* **5.** The level reached at a particular stage of the tide: *high water.* ***—modifier:*** *water vapor; a water tank. —v.* **1.** To sprinkle, moisten, or supply with water. **2. a.** To give drinking water to: *water the horses.* **b.** To drink water: *Deer watered at the pool.* **3.** To produce or discharge a watery fluid such as saliva or tears: *Her mouth watered.* **4.** To mix or dilute with water: *water the wine.* ***—phrasal verb.*** **water down.** To weaken or reduce the force of as if by diluting. [SEE NOTE on p. 965]

water buffalo. An African or Asian buffalo with large, spreading horns, often domesticated, especially for pulling or carrying loads. [SEE PICTURE]

water bug. Any of several insects that live in water or wet places.

water chestnut. **1. a.** A grasslike Asian water plant with a crisp, edible, bulblike part. **b.** The bulblike part of this plant, used in Chinese cookery. **2.** A floating water plant with nutlike fruit.

water closet. A bathroom or toilet.

water color. **1.** A paint in which water instead of oil is mixed with the coloring material before use. **2.** A painting done in water colors. **3.** The art or process of painting with water colors. ***—modifier:*** **(water-color):** *water-color paints.*

wa•ter•col•or |wô′tər kŭl′ər| *or* |wŏt′ər-| *n.* A form of the phrase **water color.**

wa•ter•cress |wô′tər krĕs′| *or* |wŏt′ər-| *n.* A plant that grows in or near ponds and streams and has strong-tasting leaves used in salads.

wa•ter•fall |wô′tər fôl′| *or* |wŏt′ər-| *n.* A natural stream of water descending from a height.

wa•ter•front |wô′tər frŭnt′| *or* |wŏt′ər-| *n.* **1.** Land that borders a body of water, such as a harbor or lake. **2.** The district of a town or city that borders the water, especially a wharf district where ships dock. ***—modifier:*** *waterfront property.*

water lily. Any of several water plants with broad, floating leaves and showy, variously colored flowers. [SEE PICTURE]

wa•ter•mark |wô′tər märk′| *or* |wŏt′ər-| *n.* **1.** A mark showing the height to which water has risen, especially a line indicating the heights of high and low tide. **2.** A very faint design impressed on paper during manufacture.

wa•ter•mel•on |wô′tər mĕl′ən| *or* |wŏt′ər-| *n.* **1.** An often very large melon with a hard, thick green rind and sweet, watery, pink or reddish flesh. **2.** A vine bearing such fruit.

water moccasin. A poisonous snake of swampy regions of the southern United States.

water ouzel. A small, dark bird that dives into swift-moving streams and feeds along the bottom. Also called *dipper.*

water polo. A water sport played by two teams of swimmers who try to push, throw, or carry the ball toward the opponents' goal.

wa•ter•pow•er |wô′tər pou′ər| *or* |wŏt′ər-| *n.* The energy of falling or running water as used for generating electricity.

wa•ter•proof |wô′tər pro͞of′| *or* |wŏt′ər-| *adj.* Capable of keeping water from coming through. *—n.* **1.** A waterproof material or fabric. **2.** *British.* A raincoat. *—v.* To make waterproof, as by treating with rubber, oil, etc.

wa•ter•shed |wô′tər shĕd′| *or* |wŏt′ər-| *n.* **1.** A ridge forming the boundary between regions whose water drains into two different systems of rivers. **2.** The region from which a river, lake, etc., drains its water.

wa•ter-ski |wô′tər skē′| *or* |wŏt′ər-| *n., pl.* **-skis** or **-ski.** Also **water ski.** Either of a pair of short, broad, skilike runners used for gliding or skimming over water while grasping a towline from a motorboat. *—v.* **-skied** |-skēd′|, **-ski•ing.** To glide over water on water-skis. —**wa′ter-ski′er** *n.* —**wa′ter-ski′ing** *n.*

water table. The upper limit of a zone of underground rock that is saturated with water.

wa•ter•way |wô′tər wā′| *or* |wŏt′ər-| *n.* A river, canal, etc. used for travel or transport.

water wheel. A wheel driven by running or falling water and used to drive machinery.

wa•ter•y |wô′tə rē| *or* |wŏt′ə-| *adj.* **wa•ter•i•er,**

ă pat/ā pay/â care/ä father/ĕ pet/ ē be/ĭ pit/ī pie/î fierce/ŏ pot/ ō go/ô paw, for/oi oil/o͝o book/ o͞o boot/ou out/ŭ cut/û fur/ *th* the/th thin/hw which/zh vision/ ə ago, item, pencil, atom, circus

wa•ter•i•est. **1.** Filled with or containing water: *watery eyes.* **2.** Resembling water: *a watery blue sky.* **3.** Made weak, thin, or soggy by too much water: *watery coffee; watery soup.*

watt |wŏt| *n.* A unit of power equal to one joule per second or about 1/746 horsepower.

Watt |wŏt|, **James.** 1736–1819. Scottish engineer; inventor of the first practical steam engine.

wat•tle |wŏt'l| *n.* **1.** Twigs, branches, plant stalks, and similar materials woven together to form a framework used for building walls, roofs, fences, etc. **2.** A fleshy, often brightly colored fold of skin hanging from the neck or throat, as of certain birds. [SEE PICTURE]

wave |wāv| *v.* **waved, wav•ing.** **1.** To move back and forth or up and down; flap or flutter: *The baby waved its legs in the air. The weeds waved in the breeze.* **2.** To move (the hand, arm, or something held in the hand) back and forth in the air, often as a signal, greeting, etc.: *She waved and called "Good-by!"* **3.** To signal, motion, or express by waving: *Wave good-by to Jenny.* **4.** To fall in curves, curls, or swirls, as hair. *—n.* **1.** A ridge or swell that moves along the surface of a body of water. **2.** A disturbance or oscillation that passes from point to point in a medium or in space, described in general by a mathematical function that gives its amplitude, frequency, velocity, and phase at any particular time and place. **3.** An act of waving back and forth or a waving motion: *a wave of the hand.* **4.** A curve or arrangement of curves, curls, or swirls, as in hair: *a soft wave.* **5.** A period of unusually hot or cold weather: *a heat wave.* ¶*These sound alike* **wave, waive.**

wave•length |wāv'lĕngkth'| *or* |-lĕngth'| *n.* Also **wave length.** The distance between two points of identical phase in successive cycles of a wave. [SEE PICTURE]

wa•ver |wā'vər| *v.* **1.** To move or swing one way and then another in an uncertain or unsteady way. **2.** To hold back in uncertainty or act in a hesitant way: *Watch a baby grope and waver and clutch as it tries to pick up a toy.* **3.** To falter or yield: *His resolve began to waver.* **4.** To tremble or flicker, as sound or light. *—n.* An act or instance of wavering. ¶*These sound alike* **waver, waiver.** **—wa'ver•er** *n.*

WAVES |wāvz|. The women's reserve of the U.S. Navy.

wav•y |wā'vē| *adj.* **wav•i•er, wav•i•est.** **1.** Full of waves: *wavy hair.* **2.** Marked by wavelike curves: *a wavy line.* **—wav'i•ness** *n.*

wax[1] |wăks| *n.* **1.** Any of various solid or soft, sticky substances that melt or soften easily when heated. They are insoluble in water but soluble in most organic liquids. **2.** A waxlike substance produced by bees; beeswax. **3.** A waxlike substance found in the ears. **4.** A solid plastic or very thick liquid material, such as paraffin. **5.** A preparation containing wax, used to polish floors, cars, furniture, etc. ***—modifier:*** *wax candles.* *—v.* To cover, coat, treat, or polish with wax: *wax a floor; wax a car.* **—waxed'** *adj.*: *waxed paper.* [SEE NOTE]

wax[2] |wăks| *v.* **1.** To show a progressively larger lighted surface, as the moon does in passing from new to full. **2.** To increase, as in size, strength, importance, etc.: *Powerful kingdoms waxed and waned.* [SEE NOTE]

wax bean. A kind of string bean with yellow pods.

wax•en |wăk'sən| *adj.* **1.** Made of or covered with wax: *a waxen image; waxen wings.* **2.** Like wax, as in being pale or smooth: *a waxen face.*

wax myrtle. A shrub of the southeastern United States, having small berries with a waxy coating from which candles are made.

wax•wing |wăks'wĭng'| *n.* Any of several crested, brownish birds with waxy red tips on the wing feathers, such as the **cedar waxwing** of North America.

wax•y |wăk'sē| *adj.* **wax•i•er, wax•i•est.** **1.** Like wax in appearance or texture; pale, pliable, or smooth and lustrous: *a flower with waxy petals.* **2.** Full of, consisting of, or covered with wax.

way |wā| *n.* **1.** A manner or fashion: *A robot walks in a very stiff way.* **2.** A method, means, or technique: *a better way of working math problems.* **3.** A respect, particular, or feature: *They are improving their city in many ways.* **4.** A habit, characteristic, or tendency: *Things have a way of happening when you least expect them.* **5.** A customary manner of acting, living, behaving, or doing things: *a new way of life.* **6.** A road, route, path, or passage that leads from one place to another: *Find your way home.* **7.** A means of passage or advancement accomplished by a particular method: *She worked her way up to a higher position.* **8.** Room enough to pass or proceed: *Make way for the fire truck.* **9.** The path taken by something that is moving or going to move: *A farmer once got in the way of a bolt of lightning.* **10.** Distance: *Jump a short way off the ground.* **11.** A specific direction: *Which way did he go?* **12.** Talent; skill; facility: *She has a way with words.* **13.** Wish or will: *if I had my way.* **14.** A course of action: *the easy way out.* **15.** *Informal.* A condition: *They are in a bad way financially.* **16.** *Informal.* A neighborhood or district: *I don't know anyone out your way.* *—adv.* **1.** Far: *way up high.* **2.** All the distance: *The sweater goes way down to her knees.* ¶*These sound alike* **way, weigh.**

Idioms. **by the way.** Incidentally. **by way of.** **1.** Through; via: *The road runs by way of the desert.* **2.** As a means of: *What did they do by way of celebration?* **give way.** To fall in; collapse: *The platform gave way.* **lead the way.** To go first while others follow. **on the** (or **one's**) **way.** **1.** In the process of coming, going, or traveling: *Snow is on the way. I'm on my way home.* **2.** On the route of one's journey. **under way.** In progress: *The party was already under way.*

way•lay |wā'lā'| *or* |wā lā'| *v.* **way•laid** |wā'lād'| *or* |wā lād'|, **way•lay•ing.** To lie in wait for and attack from ambush.

way-out |wā'out'| *adj.* *Informal.* Departing greatly from the conventional or traditional: *way-out clothes; way-out ideas.*

-ways. A suffix that forms adjectives and adverbs and means "manner, direction, or position": **sideways.**

way•side |wā'sīd'| *n.* The side or edge of a road.

way•ward |wā'wərd| *adj.* **1.** Stubborn or disobedient; willful or uncontrollable: *a wayward boy.* **2.** Irregular or unpredictable: *a collision with a wayward passing star.*

we |wē| *pron.* **1.** The person who is speaking or

wattle
Domestic turkey

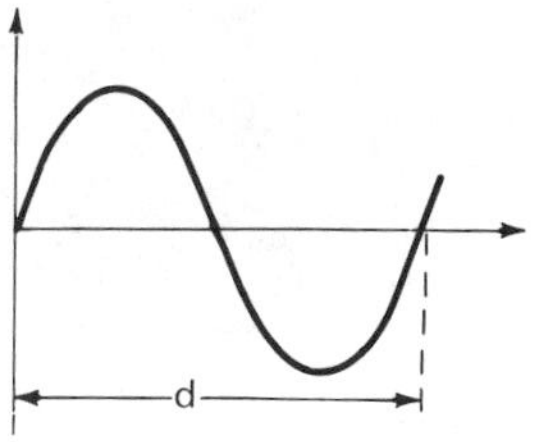

wavelength
In the graph of the wave shown the distance d is one wavelength.

wax[1-2]
Wax[1] *was Old English* wæx, *"beeswax."* **Wax**[2] *was Old English* weaxan, *"to increase."*

wealth
"Superfluous wealth can buy superfluities only." —Henry David Thoreau (1854).
"Surplus wealth is a sacred trust which its possessor is bound to administer for the good of the community." —Andrew Carnegie (1900).
"Inherited wealth is a big handicap to happiness." —William Kissam Vanderbilt (1905).

weasel

weather
Weather *was Old English* weder, *"wind, storm," hence "weather in general." It is related to* **wind[1]**.

ă pat/ā pay/â care/ä father/ĕ pet/ ē be/ĭ pit/ī pie/î fierce/ŏ pot/ ō go/ô paw, for/oi oil/ŏŏ book/ ōō boot/ou out/ŭ cut/û fur/ *th* the/th thin/hw which/zh vision/ ə ago, item, pencil, atom, circus

writing together with one or more others sharing the action of a verb: *We are going to the movies tonight.* **2.** The person speaking or writing when referring to himself or herself as a monarch or as an editor or writer expressing a position or opinion for a publication. **3.** People in general; all of us: *We are always ready to blame others when things go wrong. —Note: We*, which is in the nominative case, is used as the subject of a verb or as a predicate nominative following a form of the verb *be.* Sometimes it occurs immediately before nouns that serve as subjects or predicate nominatives: *We girls have our rights too.* ¶*These sound alike* **we, wee.**

weak |wēk| *adj.* **weak•er, weak•est. 1.** Lacking in physical strength, force, or energy; feeble or frail: *Grandmother is weak and ill.* **2.** Likely to fail or break if placed under pressure, stress, or strain: *a weak link in a chain.* **3.** Not having the usual, normal, or necessary strength, power, or potency: *weak coffee; weak eyes.* **4.** Faint or dim: *a weak voice; a weak light.* **5.** Dilute: *a weak salt solution.* **6.** Not emphatic; light: *The second syllable of "wayside" has weak stress.* **7.** Not forceful, effective, or convincing: *a weak argument.* **8.** Lacking force of intellect, character, or will: *a weak mind.* ¶*These sound alike* **weak, week.**

weak•en |wē'kən| *v.* To make or become weak or weaker.

weak•ling |wēk'lĭng| *n.* A weak or puny person or animal.

weak•ly |wēk'lē| *adj.* **weak•li•er, weak•li•est.** Feeble or sickly; weak. *—adv.* In a weak way. ¶*These sound alike* **weakly, weekly.**

weak•ness |wēk'nĭs| *n.* **1.** The condition or feeling of being weak: *physical weakness.* **2.** A weak point; a defect, fault, or failing: *Concentrate on overcoming your weaknesses.* **3. a.** A special fondness or liking: *He always had a weakness for good talkers.* **b.** Something that one desires or dreams of and cannot resist.

wealth |wĕlth| *n.* **1.** A great quantity of money or valuable possessions; riches. **2.** The condition of being rich. **3.** An abundance: *a wealth of information.* [SEE NOTE]

wealth•y |wĕl'thē| *adj.* **wealth•i•er, wealth•i•est. 1.** Having wealth; rich; prosperous; affluent: *wealthy people; a wealthy part of town.* **2.** Richly supplied; abundant: *a region wealthy in wildlife.* **—wealth'i•ly** *adv.* **—wealth'i•ness** *n.*

wean |wēn| *v.* **1.** To cause (a young child or other young mammal) to become accustomed to food other than its mother's milk. **2.** To cause to give up a habit, interest, etc.

weap•on |wĕp'ən| *n.* **1. a.** Any instrument or device used to attack another or to defend oneself from an attack. **b.** A part of the body, as the horns, teeth, or claws of an animal, used in attack or defense. **2.** Any means used to overcome, persuade, or get the better of another: *Her smile was her best weapon.*

wear |wâr| *v.* **wore** |wôr| *or* |wōr|, **worn** |wôrn| *or* |wōrn|, **wear•ing. 1.** To have on or put on, as clothes, make-up, or accessories. **2.** To have, exhibit, or display: *wore a smile; wearing a beard.* **3.** To maintain in a certain way: *She wears her hair long.* **4.** To fit into or find suitable: *What size shoe do you wear? A brunette can wear that color.* **5. a.** To damage, diminish, or use up by long use, constant rubbing, etc.: *The shipwrecked men wore their clothes to shreds.* **b.** To cut, rub, or remove by friction, pressure, or erosion: *The waves are wearing away the cliff.* **6.** To make or become as a result of constant use, rubbing, etc.: *He wore a hole in the shoe. The gold band wore thin.* **7.** To stand constant use; last: *That fabric wears well.* **8.** To pass gradually: *The December day wore on toward night.* ***—phrasal verbs.*** **wear down.** To lessen in size or substance as the result of friction or use: *Erosion wears down mountains.* **wear off.** To disappear gradually or cease having an effect. **wear out. 1.** To make or become unsuitable for further use as a result of too much use: *He wore out his shoes. His shoes wore out.* **2.** To exhaust or tire: *Don't wear yourself out. —n.* **1.** The act of wearing or condition of being worn; use: *clothes for evening wear.* **2.** Clothing: *men's wear.* **3.** Damage resulting from use, age, etc.: *The rug shows evidence of wear.* **4.** The ability to withstand use; lasting quality: *The suit has plenty of wear left.* ¶*These sound alike* **wear, ware. —wear'er** *n.*

wea•ri•some |wîr'ē səm| *adj.* Tiring or tedious.

wea•ry |wîr'ē| *adj.* **wea•ri•er, wea•ri•est. 1.** Tired, as after work or effort; fatigued. **2.** Causing or showing tiredness or fatigue: *a weary sigh.* **3.** Impatient or bored: *I am weary of your constant complaints. —v.* **wea•ried, wea•ry•ing, wea•ries.** To make or become weary; tire. **—wea'ri•ly** *adv.* **—wea'ri•ness** *n.*

wea•sel |wē'zəl| *n.* **1.** Any of several animals that have a long, narrow body, short legs, and a long tail, and that feed on small animals, birds, etc. **2.** A sneaky, deceitful person. *—v. Informal.* **—weasel out.** To back out of a situation in a cowardly way. [SEE PICTURE]

weath•er |wĕ*th*'ər| *n.* **1.** The condition or activity of the atmosphere at a given time and place, especially as described by variables such as temperature, humidity, wind velocity, and barometric pressure. **2.** Bad, rough, or stormy atmospheric conditions. ***—modifier:*** *a weather forecast; weather conditions. —v.* **1.** To expose to the action of the weather, as for drying, seasoning, or coloring: *weather wood.* **2.** To change through or as through exposure to the elements, as by roughening, warping, fading or darkening, wearing down, breaking up, etc.: *Many voyages weathered the ship's hull. Rocks are constantly weathering.* **3.** To pass through safely; survive: *weather a storm.* **—weath'ered** *adj.: weathered shingles; men with weathered cheeks.* ¶*These sound alike* **weather, wether.** [SEE NOTE]
Idiom. **under the weather.** *Informal.* Not feeling well; slightly ill.

weath•er-beat•en, also **weath•er•beat•en** |wĕ*th*'ər bēt'n| *adj.* Worn by exposure to the weather: *a weather-beaten house.*

weath•er•cock |wĕ*th*'ər kŏk'| *n.* A weather vane in the form of a rooster.

weath•er•ing |wĕ*th*'ər ĭng| *n.* Any of the chemical or mechanical processes by which rocks exposed to the weather are broken up.

weather vane. A pointer that turns with the wind to show which way the wind is blowing.

weave |wēv| *v.* **wove** |wōv|, **wo•ven** |wō'vən|, **weav•ing. 1.** To make (cloth or a cloth article) on a loom by interlacing crosswise woof threads and lengthwise warp threads. **2.** To make by passing strands or strips over and under one another: *weave a basket.* **3.** To interlace (threads, strands, strips, etc.) to make a fabric: *weave straw into a mat.* **4.** *Past tense* **weaved.** To move or wind in and out, back and forth, or from side to side: *Carefully I weaved the canoe through the reeds.* **5.** To spin (a web) as a spider does. **6.** To make or create by joining separate elements in an intricate way: *weave a captivating tale.* **7.** To combine into a whole made up of related parts: *She wove the separate incidents into a story.* —*n.* A pattern or method of weaving: *a twill weave; a loose weave.* ¶*These sound alike* **weave, we've.** —**weav'er** *n.* [SEE PICTURE]

weav•er•bird |wē'vər bûrd'| *n.* Any of several African, Asian, or Australian birds that make nests of interwoven leaves, stems, twigs, etc.

web |wĕb| *n.* **1.** A netlike structure of fine, silky strands woven by spiders or by certain insect larvae. **2.** Something formed by or as if by intricately crossed or interwoven parts: *a web of shining steel railroad tracks; the web of life.* **3.** Something that traps or snares by or as if by entangling: *a web of deceit.* **4.** A fold of skin or thin tissue, as one of those connecting the toes of certain water birds or other animals. —*v.* **webbed, web•bing.** To provide or join with a web or webs. —**webbed'** *adj.: a duck's webbed feet.*

web-foot•ed |wĕb'fo͝ot'ĭd| *adj.* Having feet with webbed toes: *Ducks are web-footed.*

Web•ster |wĕb'stər|. **1. Noah.** 1758–1843. American writer; compiler of the first major dictionary of American English. **2. Daniel.** 1782–1852. American statesman and orator.

wed |wĕd| *v.* **wed•ded, wed** or **wed•ded, wed•ding. 1.** To take (a person) as husband or wife or take (one another) as husband and wife; marry: *He wedded an Irish girl. She is too young to wed.* **2.** To unite in or as if in marriage.

we'd |wēd|. **1.** We had. **2.** We should. **3.** We would. ¶*These sound alike* **we'd, weed.**

Wed. Wednesday.

wed•ding |wĕd'ĭng| *n.* **1.** The ceremony or celebration of a marriage. **2.** The anniversary of a marriage: *a golden wedding.* —***modifier:*** *a wedding ring; a wedding present.*

wedge |wĕj| *n.* **1.** A block of metal or wood tapered in a triangular shape designed to be inserted into a crack or crevice and used for splitting, tightening, lifting, etc. **2.** A triangular thing, piece, or formation: *a wedge of pie.* **3.** Something serving to split or divide or to push or force a way in like a wedge: *The issue drove a wedge between the party leaders.* —*v.* **wedged, wedg•ing. 1.** To split, force apart, or fix in place with or as if with a wedge. **2.** To crowd, push, force, or squeeze into a limited space: *They all wedged into the compact car.*

wed•lock |wĕd'lŏk'| *n.* The condition of being married; matrimony.

Wednes•day |wĕnz'dē| *or* |-dā'| *n.* The fourth day of the week, after Tuesday and before Thursday. —***modifier:*** *Wednesday morning.*

wee |wē| *adj.* **we•er, we•est. 1.** Very little; tiny: *a wee lad; a wee bit afraid.* **2.** Very early: *the wee hours.* ¶*These sound alike* **wee, we.**

weed |wēd| *n.* Any plant considered troublesome, useless, or unattractive, especially one growing freely where it is not wanted, as in a garden or other cultivated ground. —***modifier:*** *a weed killer.* —*v.* To rid of or remove weeds. —***phrasal verb.*** **weed out.** To get rid of as unfit or unwanted: *weed out the unqualified applicants.* ¶*These sound alike* **weed, we'd.**

weeds |wēdz| *pl.n.* The black clothes worn by a widow in mourning.

weed•y |wē'dē| *adj.* **weed•i•er, weed•i•est. 1.** Full of weeds: *weedy ground.* **2.** Resembling or existing as a weed: *a weedy plant.*

week |wēk| *n.* **1.** A period of time equal to seven days, especially a period that begins on a Sunday and continues through the next Saturday. **2.** A period consisting of the hours or days in a week during which one works or goes to school. ¶*These sound alike* **week, weak.**

week•day |wēk'dā'| *n.* **1.** Any day of the week except Sunday. **2.** Any day that is not part of the weekend. —***modifier:*** *the weekday routine.*

week•end |wēk'ĕnd'| *n.* The end of the week, especially the period from Friday evening through Sunday evening.

week•ly |wēk'lē| *adv.* **1.** Once a week or every week: *She visits us weekly.* **2.** Per week: *How much does he earn weekly?* —*adj.* **1.** Done, happening, or coming once a week or every week: *a weekly trip.* **2.** Made or figured by the week: *weekly earnings.* —*n., pl.* **week•lies.** A newspaper or magazine issued once a week. ¶*These sound alike* **weekly, weakly.**

wee•nie |wē'nē| *n. Informal.* A wienerwurst.

weep |wēp| *v.* **wept** |wĕpt|, **weep•ing. 1.** To shed (tears) as an expression of emotion; cry. **2.** To grieve: *The cruelty of the world will make you weep.* **3.** To feel sorry: *I weep for you in your sorrow.* **4.** To drip or ooze.

weep•ing |wē'pĭng| *adj.* **1.** Giving off drops of liquid resembling tears: *a weeping wound.* **2.** Having drooping branches: *a weeping willow.*

wee•vil |wē'vəl| *n.* Any of several beetles that have a long, downward-curving snout and that do great damage to plants and plant products.

weft |wĕft| *n.* In weaving, the woof.

weigh |wā| *v.* **1.** To determine or measure the weight of by or as if by using a scale or similar instrument. **2.** To have a weight of: *The car weighs 2,800 pounds.* **3.** To consider carefully by balancing in the mind; ponder: *weighed possible alternatives.* **4.** To have influence; count: *That factor weighed heavily in the decision.* —***phrasal verbs.*** **weigh down.** To burden or oppress. **weigh in.** To be weighed before participating in a contest or sports event such as a fight or race. **weigh on** (or **upon**). To be a burden on; oppress: *The misdeed was weighing on her conscience.* ¶*These sound alike* **weigh, way.**

weight |wāt| *n.* **1. a.** The force with which an object near the earth or another celestial body is attracted toward the center of the body by gravity. **b.** The measure of this force: *The car has a weight of 2,800 pounds.* **c.** A unit used as a measure of this force: *a table of weights and measures.* **d.** A system of such units: *avoirdupois weight; troy weight.* **e.** A material object designed so that its weight is a reference for such a unit: *Place a two-pound weight on the scale.* **f.** Any object whose principal function is to exert a

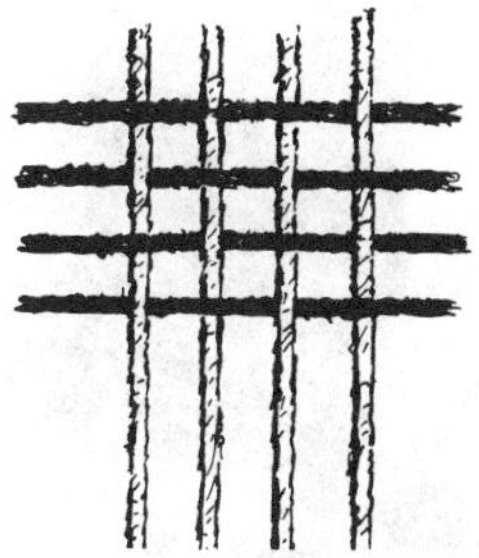

weave
Above: Diagram of a plain-weave fabric showing lengthwise warp threads and crosswise woof threads
Below: Man weaving a straw hat

weight
A set of weights for use in making scientific measurements.

well[1-2]
Well[1] *was Old English* wiella, *"spring of water."* **Well[2]** *was Old English* wel, *"in a good manner, prosperously"; it is related to* **wealth**.

Welsh/Wales
The **Welsh** *are the descendants of the Celts who lived in Britain before the Roman and Germanic invasions. The Welsh call themselves the* Cymry; *but the invading Anglo-Saxons called them* Wealas, *which is Old English for "Celts, foreigners";* Wealas *became* **Wales** *in Modern English, and* Welisc, *the Old English adjective, became* **Welsh**.

downward force by means of the action of gravity upon it, as a paperweight, dumbbell, etc.. **2.** Mass, especially body mass: *a diet to help you lose weight.* **3.** Something heavy; a heavy object or load: *She felt as if she were pushing a great weight.* **4.** Any load, burden, or source of pressure: *a heavy weight of worry.* —*v.* **1.** To make heavy or heavier with a weight or weights. **2.** To load down; burden or oppress. ¶*These sound alike* **weight, wait.** [SEE PICTURE]

Idioms. **carry weight.** To have influence or authority: *Her opinions carry weight.* **throw (one's) weight around.** *Informal.* To make a show of one's importance.

weight•less |wāt′lĭs| *adj.* **1.** Having little or no weight. **2.** Experiencing a gravitational force that is zero or very nearly zero, as an object in orbit about the earth. —**weight′less•ness** *n.*

weight•y |wā′tē| *adj.* **weight•i•er, weight•i•est.** **1.** Having great weight: *a weighty package.* **2.** Very serious or important: *a weighty matter.* **3.** Burdensome: *weighty responsibilities.*

weir |wîr| *n.* **1.** A dam placed across a river or canal. **2.** A fence or barrier, as of stakes, branches, or net, placed in a stream to catch or retain fish. ¶*These sound alike* **weir, we're.**

weird |wîrd| *adj.* **weird•er, weird•est.** **1.** Mysterious and often frightening; eerie: *weird as the moan of sobbing winds.* **2.** Strange, odd, or peculiar: *all manner of weird machines.* —**weird′ly** *adv.* —**weird′ness** *n.*

weird•o |wîr′dō| *n., pl.* **weird•os.** *Slang.* An odd person; a nut.

wel•come |wĕl′kəm| *v.* **wel•comed, wel•com•ing.** **1.** To greet or receive with pleasure, hospitality, or special ceremony: *welcome newcomers.* **2.** To accept willingly or gratefully: *I welcome this opportunity.* —*n.* A warm greeting or hospitable reception. —*adj.* **1.** Greeted, received, or accepted with pleasure: *a welcome visitor.* **2.** Freely permitted or gladly invited to have, use, etc.: *You're welcome to the apple.* **3.** Under no obligation for a courtesy or kindness: *"Thank you." "You're welcome!"*

weld |wĕld| *v.* **1. a.** To join (metal parts or pieces) by subjecting to heat and pressure. **b.** To undergo welding or be capable of being welded: *an alloy that welds easily.* **2.** To bring together as a unit; unite. —*n.* The joint formed when metal parts are united by welding. —**weld′er** *n.*

wel•fare |wĕl′fâr′| *n.* **1.** Health, happiness, or prosperity; well-being: *promote the general welfare.* **2.** The provision of economic or social benefits to a certain group of people, especially aid furnished by the government or by private agencies to the needy or disabled. —***modifier:*** *welfare services; welfare payments.*

Idiom. **on welfare.** Receiving assistance from the government because of need or poverty.

wel•kin |wĕl′kĭn| *n. Archaic.* The sky.

Idiom. **make the welkin ring.** To make a great, reverberating sound.

well[1] |wĕl| *n.* **1.** A deep hole or shaft dug or drilled into the earth to obtain water, oil, gas, sulfur, or brine. **2.** A spring or fountain serving as a natural source of water. **3.** Any source to be drawn upon: *The dictionary is a well of information.* **4.** A container or reservoir used to hold a liquid, as an inkwell. **5.** A vertical opening that passes through the floors of a building, as to allow ventilation. —*v.* To rise or spring: *Tears welled up in his eyes.* [SEE NOTE]

well[2] |wĕl| *adv.* **bet•ter** |bĕt′ər|, **best** |bĕst|. **1.** In a good or proper manner; correctly: *A person who has good posture holds his body well.* **2.** Skillfully or proficiently: *She plays the piano well.* **3.** Satisfactorily or sufficiently: *Did you sleep well?* **4.** Successfully or effectively: *How well do you get along with others?* **5.** Suitably; appropriately: *The two teams were well matched.* **6.** Favorably: *They spoke well of you.* **7.** Thoroughly: *Blend the ingredients well.* **8.** Perfectly; clearly: *How well do you remember the trip?* **9.** To a considerable degree or extent; extensively: *It was well after sunset.* **10.** Widely; generally: *He is well known.* **11.** Closely: *Listen well to what I say.* **12.** With reason or justification; reasonably: *Their customs might well seem strange to an outsider.* —*adj.* **1. a.** In good health; not sick. **b.** Cured or healed. **2.** All right: *All is well.* —*interj.* **1.** A word used to express surprise, relief, etc., or as a question prompting someone to proceed or explain. **2.** A word used to introduce a remark or simply to gain time when one is undecided or uncertain. [SEE NOTE]

Idioms. **as well.** Also; in addition; too: *The water is flowing north, but it has eastward motion as well.* **as well as.** And also; and in addition. **leave (or let) well enough alone.** To be content with things as they are.

we'll |wēl|. **1.** We will. **2.** We shall.

well-be•ing |wĕl′bē′ĭng| *n.* Health, happiness, or prosperity; welfare.

well-bred |wĕl′brĕd′| *adj.* Having had a good upbringing; polite and refined.

well-done |wĕl′dŭn′| *adj.* **1.** Done properly or skillfully: *a well-done job.* **2.** Cooked all the way through: *I'd like my steak well-done.*

well-groomed |wĕl′grōōmd′| *adj.* **1.** Neat and clean in dress and personal appearance: *well-groomed girls and boys.* **2.** Carefully combed and cared for: *sleek, well-groomed horses.*

Wel•ling•ton |wĕl′ĭng tən|. The capital of New Zealand. Population, 134,000.

well-man•nered |wĕl′măn′ərd| *adj.* Polite; courteous.

well-mean•ing |wĕl′mē′nĭng| *adj.* Having or showing good intentions; meaning or meant to be helpful: *well-meaning advice.*

well-nigh |wĕl′nī′| *adv.* Nearly; almost: *well-nigh impossible.*

well-off |wĕl′ôf′| *or* |-ŏf′| *adj.* Wealthy or prosperous.

well•spring |wĕl′sprĭng′| *n.* **1.** The source of a stream or spring; a fountainhead. **2.** A source of supply: *a wellspring of ideas.*

well-to-do |wĕl′tə dōō′| *adj.* Prosperous or wealthy; well-off.

Wels•bach burner |wĕlz′băk′| *or* |-bäk′|. A trademark for a gauze pouch treated with compounds of cerium and thorium so that it produces a strong light when heated.

welsh |wĕlsh| *or* |wĕlch| *v. Slang.* To cheat by not paying a debt or bet: *Don't welsh on me.*

Welsh |wĕlsh| *n.* **1. the Welsh.** The people of Wales. **2.** The Celtic language of Wales. —*adj.* Of Wales, the Welsh, or their language. [SEE NOTE]

ă pat/ā pay/â care/ä father/ĕ pet/ē be/ĭ pit/ī pie/î fierce/ŏ pot/ō go/ô paw, for/oi oil/ŏŏ book/ōō boot/ou out/ŭ cut/û fur/*th* the/th thin/hw which/zh vision/ə ago, item, pencil, atom, circus

Welsh•man |wĕlsh'mən| *n., pl.* **-men** |-mən|. **1.** A native or inhabitant of Wales. **2.** A person of Welsh descent.

Welsh rabbit. A dish of melted cheese mixed with milk and sometimes ale or beer, served hot over toast or crackers.

Welsh rarebit. A form of the phrase **Welsh rabbit.**

welt |wĕlt| *n.* **1.** A strip of leather or other material stitched into a shoe between the upper part and the sole. **2.** A ridge or bump raised on the skin by a blow or sometimes by an allergic reaction.

wel•ter |wĕl'tər| *v.* **1.** To wallow, roll, or toss about, as in mud or high waves. **2.** To lie soaked in a liquid: *welter in blood.* —*n.* **1.** An agitated rolling or tossing: *a welter of waves.* **2. a.** A highly confused condition; turmoil. **b.** A confused mass; a jumble: *a welter of arms and legs.*

wel•ter•weight |wĕl'tər wāt'| *n.* A boxer or wrestler who weighs between 136 and 147 pounds.

wen |wĕn| *n.* A cyst containing oily secretions from the skin.

wench |wĕnch| *n. Archaic.* **1.** A young woman or girl; a maid. **2.** A female servant.

wend |wĕnd| *v.* To go or proceed on or along (one's way): *People wended their way home after church early Sunday morning.*

went |wĕnt|. Past tense of **go.**

wept |wĕpt|. Past tense and past participle of **weep.**

were |wûr|. **1.** Second person singular past tense of **be. 2.** First, second, and third person plural past tense of **be. 3.** Past subjunctive of **be.**

we're |wîr| We are. ¶*These sound alike* **we're, weir.**

were•n't |wûrnt| *or* |wûr'ənt|. Were not.

were•wolf |wîr'wo͝olf'| *or* |wûr'-| *or* |wâr'-| *n., pl.* **-wolves** |-wo͝olvz'|. In folklore and stories, a person believed to turn into a wolf at certain times. [SEE NOTE]

wert |wûrt|. *Archaic.* A form of the past tense of **be,** used with *thou.*

Wes•ley |wĕs'lē| *or* |wĕz'-|. **1. John.** 1703–1791. British theologian; the founder of the Methodist Church. **2. Charles.** 1707–1788. British Methodist preacher and author of many hymns; brother of John Wesley.

Wes•sex |wĕs'ĭks|. An Anglo-Saxon kingdom established in the fifth century A.D. in southern England.

west |wĕst| *n.* **1.** The direction opposite to the direction in which the earth rotates on its axis; the direction 180 degrees from east: *a wind blowing from the west.* **2.** Often **West.** A region or part of the earth in this direction: *the west of Columbia.* **3. the West. a.** The part of the earth west of Asia and Asia Minor, especially Europe and the Western Hemisphere; the Occident. **b.** The western part of the United States, especially the region west of the Mississippi River. —*adj.* **1.** Of, in, or toward the west: *the west bank of the river.* **2.** Often **West.** Forming or belonging to a region, country, etc., toward the west: *West Germany.* **3.** From the west: *a west wind.* —*adv.* To or toward the west: *a river flowing west.*

West Berlin. The western zone of the divided city of Berlin, surrounded by East Germany but part of West Germany. Population, 2,200,000.

west•er•ly |wĕs'tər lē| *adj.* **1.** In or toward the west: *a westerly direction.* **2.** From the west: *westerly winds.* —*adv.: winds blowing westerly.* —*n., pl.* **west•er•lies.** A wind or storm coming from the west.

west•ern |wĕs'tərn| *adj.* **1.** Often **Western.** Of, in, or toward the west: *the western sky; western Europe.* **2.** From the west: *a western wind.* **3.** Often **Western. a.** Of Europe and the Western Hemisphere: *western technology; Western civilization.* **b.** Of, like, or used in the American West: *western settlers; a Western saddle.* —*n.* Often **Western.** A book, motion picture, or television or radio program about cowboys or frontier life in the American West.

west•ern•er |wĕs'tər nər| *n.* Often **Westerner.** A person who lives in or comes from the west, especially the western United States.

Western Hemisphere. The half of the earth that includes North and South America.

west•ern•most |wĕs'tərn mōst'| *adj.* Farthest west.

Western Samoa. A group of islands in the South Pacific Ocean, constituting an independent country. Population, 152,000. Capital, Apia.

West Germany. The unofficial name for the German Federal Republic.

West In•dies |ĭn'dēz|. An island chain in the Atlantic Ocean between the southeastern United States and South America, consisting of the Bahama Islands, the Greater Antilles, and the Lesser Antilles. —**West Indian.**

West Virginia. An east-central state of the United States. Population, 1,763,000. Capital, Charleston. —**West Virginian.**

west•ward |wĕst'wərd| *adv.* Also **west•wards** |wĕst'wərdz|. To or toward the west: *sailed westward.* —*adj.: the westward expansion of our country.* —*n.* A direction or region to the west.

wet |wĕt| *adj.* **wet•ter, wet•test. 1.** Covered, moistened, soaked,or saturated with a liquid, especially water: *wet clothes.* **2.** Containing a relatively large amount of water or water vapor: *wet snow; heavy, wet air.* **3.** Rainy: *a wet day.* **4.** Not yet dry or hardened: *wet paint; wet plaster.* **5.** *Informal.* Allowing the sale of alcoholic beverages: *a wet county.* —*n.* **1.** Water; liquid; moisture. **2.** Rainy or snowy weather. —*v.* **wet** or **wet•ted, wet•ting.** To make or become wet. —**wet'ly** *adv.* —**wet'ness** *n.* [SEE NOTE on p. 965]

wet cell. A primary electric cell having its electrolyte in the form of a liquid rather than in the form of a paste as in a dry cell.

weth•er |wĕth'ər| *n.* A castrated male sheep. ¶*These sound alike* **wether, weather.**

we've |wēv|. We have. ¶*These sound alike* **we've, weave.**

whack |hwăk| *or* |wăk| *v.* To strike, hit, or slap hard with a sharp, loud sound. —*n.* **1.** A sharp, hard blow or slap. **2.** The loud sound made by such a blow.

Idioms. **have** (or **take**) **a whack at.** *Informal.* To attempt or try. **out of whack.** *Informal.* Not working correctly; out of order.

whale |hwāl| *or* |wāl| *n.* Any of several often very large sea animals that resemble fish in form but are air-breathing mammals. —***modifier:*** *whale blubber.* [SEE NOTE]

whale•bone |hwāl'bōn'| *or* |wāl'-| *n.* **1.** A flex-

werewolf

Werewolf *was Old English* werewulf, *"man-wolf":* were, *"man,"* + wulf, *"wolf." Belief in various kinds of werewolves is very old and widespread. Werewolves have not always been regarded as malevolent. In parts of ancient Greece it was believed that a shepherd could sometimes transform himself into a wolf and persuade the real wolves to leave the sheep alone.*

wh–

In Old English, numerous words began, both in spelling and in pronunciation, with hw-. *Three things have happened to these words: (1) The predominant pronunciation changed to* w-; *(2) the spelling changed to* wh-; *and (3) the old pronunciation* hw-, *which had survived in some regions, was widely revived in the nineteenth century. In Modern English, the pronunciations* w- *and* hw- *are equally correct.*

whale

Whale *was Old English* hwael, *which is descended from prehistoric Germanic* hwaliz, *"sea animal, whale."* Hwaliz *also appears in Old Norse as* hvalr, *which formed two compounds affecting English: (1)* hross-hvalr, *"horse-whale," a name for the walrus; this compound was later reversed, and appears in Danish as* hvalros *and in Dutch as* walros, *which was borrowed into English as* **walrus**; *(2)* nā-hvalr, *"corpse-whale," a name for the narwhal, which is whitish and is sometimes seen floating like a corpse in the water; this became Danish* narhval, *which was borrowed into English as* **narwhal.**

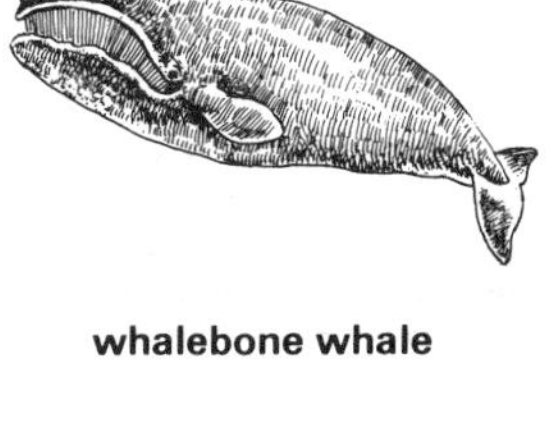

whalebone whale

ible, hornlike substance forming plates or strips in the upper jaw of certain kinds of whales, called **whalebone whales.** Also called *baleen.* **2.** A strip of this material, as one used to stiffen a corset. [SEE PICTURE on p. 971]

whal•er |**hwā'**lər| *or* |**wā'**-| *n.* **1.** A person who hunts for whales or works on a whaling ship. **2.** A ship or boat used in whaling.

whal•ing |**hwā'**lĭng| *or* |**wā'**-| *n.* The business or practice of hunting, killing, and processing whales for their valuable products.

wharf |hwôrf| *or* |wôrf| *n., pl.* **wharves** |hwôrvz| *or* |wôrvz| or **wharfs.** A landing place or pier at which vessels may tie up and load or unload.

what |hwŏt| *or* |hwŭt| *or* |wŏt| *or* |wŭt| *or* |hwət *when unstressed*| *or* |wət *when unstressed*| *pron.* **1.** Which thing or which particular one of many: *What are we having for supper?* **2.** Which kind, character, or designation: *What are these things?* **3.** Of how much value or significance: *What are possessions to a dying man?* **4. a.** That which or the thing that: *Listen to what I have to say.* **b.** Whatever thing that: *Come what may, I'm staying.* **5.** *Informal.* Something: *I'll tell you what.* —*adj.* **1.** Which one or ones of several or many: *What train do I take?* **2.** Whatever: *We repaired what damage had been done.* **3.** How great: *What fools we have been!* —*adv.* How: *What does it matter, after all?* —*interj.* A word used to express surprise, disbelief, etc.

Idioms. **what if.** What would happen if; suppose that. **what's what.** *Informal.* The true state of affairs: *I'll tell you what's what.* **what with.** Because of: *What with the heat and humidity, we really suffered.*

what•ev•er |hwŏt ĕv'ər| *or* |hwŭt-| *or* |wŏt-| *or* |wŭt-| *pron.* **1.** Everything or anything that: *Please do whatever you can to help.* **2.** No matter what: *Whatever you do, come early.* —*adj.* **1.** Of any number or kind; any: *Whatever needs you may have, feel free to call on us.* **2.** Of any kind at all: *He was left with nothing whatever.*

what•not |**hwŏt'**nŏt'| *or* |**hwŭt'**-| *or* |**wŏt'**-| *or* |**wŭt'**-| *n.* A set of open shelves for holding small ornaments.

what's |hwŏts| *or* |hwŭts| *or* |wŏts| *or* |wŭts|. **1.** What is. **2.** What has.

what•so•ev•er |hwŏt'sō ĕv'ər| *or* |hwŭt'-| *or* |wŏt'-| *or* |wŭt'-| *adj.* Of any kind at all.

wheat |hwēt| *or* |wēt| *n.* **1.** A grain-bearing grass grown in many parts of the world as an important source of food. **2.** The seeds of this plant, usually ground to produce flour. —***modifier:*** *wheat flour.* [SEE PICTURE]

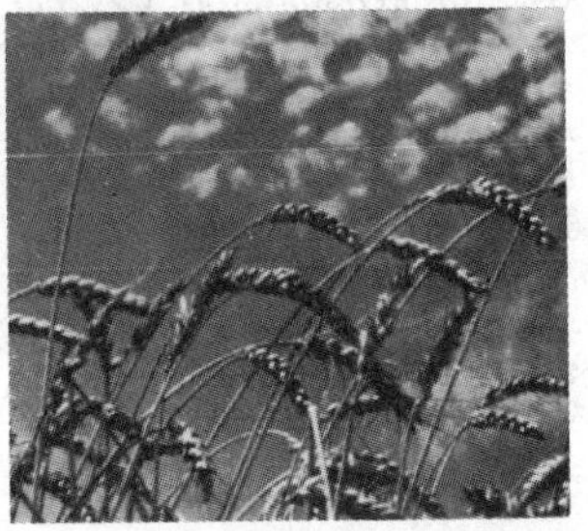

wheat

wheat•en |**hwēt'**n| *or* |**wēt'**n| *adj.* Of, made from, or resembling wheat.

wheat germ. The embryo of wheat kernels, rich in vitamins and used as a cereal or food supplement.

whee•dle |**hwēd'**l| *or* |**wēd'**l| *v.* **whee•dled, whee•dling. 1.** To persuade or try to persuade by pleading or flattery; coax; cajole. **2.** To get by pleading, flattering, etc.: *He wheedled a promise out of me.*

wheel |hwēl| *or* |wēl| *n.* **1. a.** A solid disk or a rigid circular ring attached to a hub by spokes, designed to rotate on an axle or shaft that passes through its center. **b.** Anything that is like this device in form, movement, or function or that has one of these devices as its main part: *a steering wheel; a Ferris wheel.* **2.** *Informal.* A bicycle. **3. wheels.** *Slang.* An automobile. **4.** *Slang.* A very powerful or influential person: *He's a big wheel at school.* —*v.* **1.** To move or roll on wheels: *Put the books on the cart and wheel them to the library.* **2.** To turn, spin, or whirl suddenly, changing direction: *Horace wheeled about and ran toward the house.*

wheel•bar•row |**hwēl'**băr'ō| *or* |**wēl'**-| *n.* A vehicle used to convey small loads by hand, having a wheel at one end and pushed by two straight, horizontal handles. [SEE PICTURE]

wheelbarrow

wheel•chair |**hwēl'**châr'| *or* |**wēl'**-| *n.* Also **wheel chair.** A chair mounted on large wheels for the use of sick or disabled people.

wheeze |hwēz| *or* |wēz| *v.* **wheezed, wheez•ing. 1.** To breathe with difficulty, producing a hoarse whistling or hissing sound. **2.** To make or say with such a sound. —*n.* The sound made by wheezing.

whelk |hwĕlk| *or* |wĕlk| *n.* Any of several large sea snails with a pointed spiral shell. [SEE PICTURE]

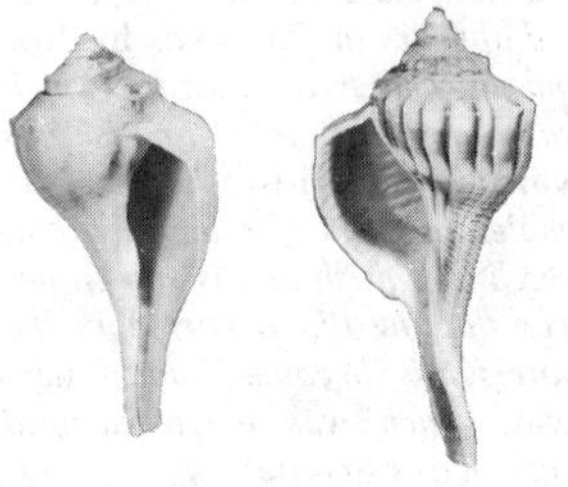

whelk

whelp |hwĕlp| *or* |wĕlp| *n.* **1.** A young offspring of a wolf, dog, or similar animal. **2.** A young and inexperienced or impudent person. —*v.* To give birth to (a whelp or whelps).

when |hwĕn| *or* |wĕn| *adv.* **1.** At what time: *When did you leave?* **2.** At which time: *I know when to leave.* —*conj.* **1.** At the time that: *in April, when the snow melts.* **2.** As soon as: *I'll call you when I get there.* **3.** Whenever: *He always arrives late when he goes to the barber.* **4.** Whereas; although: *He's reading comic books when he should be doing his homework.* **5.** Considering that; since: *How are you going to make the team when you won't stop smoking?* —*pron.* What or which time: *Since when have you been giving the orders around here?* —*n.* The time or date: *We knew the when but not the where of it.*

whence |hwĕns| *or* |wĕns| *adv.* **1.** From where; from what place: *Whence did this old man come?* **2.** From what origin or source: *Whence comes this splendid feast?* —*conj.* By reason of which; from which.

when•ev•er |hwĕn ĕv'ər| *or* |wĕn-| *adv.* When. Used as an intensive: *Whenever is she coming?* —*conj.* **1.** At whatever time that: *We can start whenever you're ready.* **2.** Every time that: *I smile whenever I think back on that day.*

when•so•ev•er |hwĕn'sō ĕv'ər| *or* |wĕn'-| *conj.* Whenever.

where |hwâr| *or* |wâr| *adv.* **1.** At or in what place, point, or position: *Where is the telephone?* **2.** To what place or end: *Where does this road lead?* **3.** From what place or source: *Where did you get that crazy idea?* —*conj.* **1.** At or in what or which place: *I am going to my room where I can study.* **2.** In or to a place in which or to which: *She lives where the climate is mild. I will go where you go.* **3.** Wherever: *Where there's smoke, there's fire.* **4.** Whereas: *Mars has two satellites, where Earth has only one.* —*pron.* **1.** What or which place: *Where did they come from?* **2.** The place in, at, or to which: *This is where I found the puppy.* —*n.* The place or occasion: *We know the when but not the where of it.*

where•a•bouts |**hwâr'**ə bouts'| *or* |**wâr'**-| *adv.*

ă pat/ā pay/â care/ä father/ĕ pet/ ē be/ĭ pit/ī pie/î fierce/ŏ pot/ ō go/ô paw, for/oi oil/ŏŏ book/ ōō boot/ou out/ŭ cut/û fur/ *th* the/th thin/hw which/zh vision/ ə ago, item, pencil, atom, circus

Where or about where: *You'll find it by the willow tree. Whereabouts by the willow?* —*n. (used with a singular or plural verb).* The approximate location of someone or something.

where•as |hwâr ăz'| *or* |wâr-| *conj.* **1.** It being the fact that; inasmuch as; since: *Whereas the accused has been found not guilty of the crime, the court orders that he be released.* **2.** While on the contrary: *Human beings are always making symbols, whereas other animals cannot.*

where•at |hwâr ăt'| *or* |wâr-| *conj. Archaic.* Whereupon.

where•by |hwâr bī'| *or* |wâr-| *adv.* By means of which; by which: *a scheme whereby the boy might get the pearl for the king.*

where•fore |hwâr'fôr'| *or* |-fōr'| *or* |wâr'-| *conj. Archaic.* For which reason: *"And the thing which he did displeased the Lord: wherefore he slew him also."* (The Bible, Genesis 38:10). —*adv. Archaic.* Why: *Wherefore should we fear?* —*n.* A purpose, cause, or reason: *I don't know all the whys and wherefores of the decision.*

where•in |hwâr ĭn'| *or* |wâr-| *adv.* In what; how: *Wherein have I offended?*

where•of |hwâr ŭv'| *or* |-ŏv'| *or* |wâr-| *adv.* Of what, which, or whom: *He made me a long speech, whereof I understood not one syllable.*

where•on |hwâr ŏn'| *or* |-ôn'| *or* |wâr-| *adv. Archaic.* On which.

where•to |hwâr'to͞o'| *or* |wâr'-| *adv. Archaic.* **1.** To which: *an old accustomed feast, whereto I have invited many a guest.* **2.** To what place or toward what end: *Whereto are we heading?*

where•up•on |hwâr'ə pŏn'| *or* |-pôn'| *or* |wâr'-| *conj.* **1.** Upon which: *I miss that old maple, whereupon my brother and I used to build a tree house every summer.* **2.** Following which: *The metal is allowed to cool until it hardens, whereupon it is removed from the sand.*

wher•ev•er |hwâr ĕv'ər| *or* |wâr-| *adv.* **1.** Where. Used as an intensive: *Wherever have you been so long?* **2.** In or to whatever place or situation: *Write these groups of words, using capital letters wherever needed.* —*conj.* In or to whatever place or situation: *My blessing is with you wherever you go.*

where•with |hwâr'wĭth'| *or* |-wĭth'| *or* |wâr'-| *conj.* With which: *the supplies wherewith every pharmacy is stocked.*

where•with•al |hwâr'wĭth ôl'| *or* |-wĭth-| *or* |wâr'-| *n.* The necessary means, especially the needed funds or money.

whet |hwĕt| *or* |wĕt| *v.* **whet•ted, whet•ting. 1.** To sharpen (a knife or other cutting tool); hone. **2.** To make more keen; stimulate: *Cooking odors always whet my appetite.*

wheth•er |hwĕth'ər| *or* |wĕth'-| *conj.* **1.** —Used in indirect questions involving alternatives: *Have you ever wondered whether animals feel love and grief?* **2.** —Used to introduce alternative possibilities: *whether in victory or defeat; whether they realize it or not.* **3.** Either: *He won the fight, whether by skill or dumb luck.*

whet•stone |hwĕt'stōn'| *or* |wĕt'-| *n.* A stone used for sharpening knives and other cutting tools.

whew |hwo͞o| *or* |hwyo͞o| *interj.* A word used to express tiredness, relief, distress, surprise, etc.

whey |hwā| *or* |wā| *n.* The watery part of milk that separates from the curds, as in the process of making cheese.

which |hwĭch| *or* |wĭch| *pron.* **1.** What particular one or ones: *Which is your house?* Also used adjectivally: *Which coat is yours?* **2.** The particular one or ones that: *Take those which are yours.* **3.** The thing, animal, group, or event previously named or implied: *the movie which was shown later.* Also used adjectivally: *It started raining, at which point we left the park.* **4.** Whichever: *Take which of these you want.* Also used adjectivally: *Do it which way you like.* **5.** A thing or circumstance that: *She ignored us, which was a shame.*

which•ev•er |hwĭch ĕv'ər| *or* |wĭch-| *pron.* Whatever one or ones which: *The dogs were there, waiting to fall upon whichever was beaten.* Also used adjectivally: *whichever one of you succeeds in catching the thief.*

whiff |hwĭf| *or* |wĭf| *n.* **1.** A breath or puff, as of air or smoke. **2.** A slight smell carried in the air: *a whiff of buttered popcorn.* **3.** An inhalation: *Take a whiff of this perfume.* —*v.* **1.** To draw in or breathe out (air, smoke, etc.). **2.** To smell; sniff: *whiff cooking odors.*

Whig |hwĭg| *or* |wĭg| *n.* **1.** In England, a member of a political party of the 18th and 19th centuries, opposed to the Tories. **2.** In the American Revolution, a colonist who supported the war against England. **3.** In the United States, a member of a political party (1834–55) formed to oppose the Democratic Party and succeeded by the Republican Party.

while |hwīl| *or* |wīl| *n.* **1.** A period of time. Used mainly in adverbial phrases: *stay for a while; singing all the while.* **2.** The time, effort, or trouble taken in doing something: *I don't think it's worth my while.* —*conj.* **1.** As long as; during the time that: *It was great while it lasted.* **2.** Although: *Betty is tall while her sisters are short.* **3.** Whereas; and: *The soles of the shoes are leather, while the uppers are canvas.* —*v.* **whiled, whil•ing.** To pass (time) pleasantly, in a relaxed way.

whilst |hwīlst| *or* |wīlst| *conj.* While.

whim |hwĭm| *or* |wĭm| *n.* **1.** A sudden, impulsive wish, desire, or notion. **2.** An arbitrary decision or impulse.

whim•per |hwĭm'pər| *or* |wĭm'-| *v.* To cry with weak, broken, whining sounds: *A bedraggled puppy whimpered on the doorstep.* —*n.* A low, broken, whining sound.

whim•sey |hwĭm'zē| *or* |wĭm'-| *n., pl.* **whim•seys.** A form of the word **whimsy.**

whim•si•cal |hwĭm'sĭ kəl| *or* |wĭm'-| *adj.* **1.** Playful, fanciful, or capricious: *whimsical forms of self-expression.* **2.** Quaint; fantastic; odd: *Middle English spelling seems whimsical to us now.* —**whim'si•cal•ly** *adv.*

whim•sy |hwĭm'zē| *or* |wĭm'-| *n., pl.* **whim•sies. 1.** An odd or playful idea; an idle fancy. **2.** An amusingly odd and fanciful style of humor.

whine |hwīn| *or* |wīn| *v.* **whined, whin•ing. 1.** To make a high-pitched, nasal sound, as in pain, complaint, or protest. **2.** To complain in a childish, annoying way. —**whin'ing** *adj.: a whining child.* —*n.* A whining sound or complaint.

whin•ny |hwĭn'ē| *or* |wĭn'ē| *n., pl.* **whin•nies.** A high-pitched or gentle neighing sound made by a horse. —*v.* **whin•nied, whin•ny•ing, whin•nies.** To make such a sound.

whip

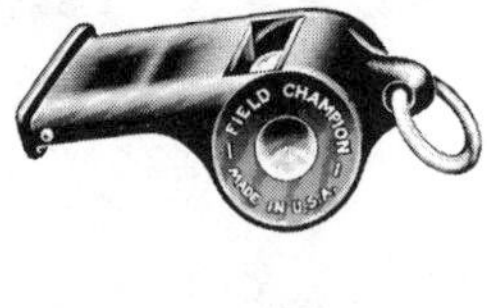

whistle
Police whistle

ă pat/ā pay/â care/ä father/ĕ pet/ ē be/ĭ pit/ī pie/î fierce/ŏ pot/ ō go/ô paw, for/oi oil/ŏŏ book/ ōō boot/ou out/ŭ cut/û fur/ *th* the/th thin/hw which/zh vision/ ə ago, item, pencil, atom, circus

whip |hwĭp| *or* |wĭp| *n.* **1.** A rod that bends or that has a lash attached, used for urging animals on or for striking or beating someone. **2.** Something that looks, bends, or lashes about like a whip. **3.** A member of a legislature selected by his political party to enforce party discipline: *the majority whip in the Senate.* **4.** A dessert made of sugar, whipped cream or stiffly beaten egg whites, and often fruit: *prune whip.* **5.** A lashing motion, stroke, or blow. *—v.* **whipped** or **whipt** |hwĭpt| *or* |wĭpt|, **whip•ping. 1.** To strike, beat, or lash with or as if with a whip. **2.** To move suddenly and swiftly or with a lashing motion: *I whipped out of the house as fast as I could.* **3.** To pull, snatch, or grab suddenly: *She whipped out her notebook.* **4.** To beat (cream, eggs, etc.) into a froth or foam. **5.** *Informal.* To defeat in a fight or contest; beat: *You can't whip our team on our home field.* **—whipped'** *adj.: whipped potatoes.* ***—phrasal verb.*** **whip up. 1.** To stir up: *whip up enthusiasm.* **2.** *Informal.* To prepare quickly: *whip up a meal.* [SEE PICTURE]

whip•lash |**hwĭp'**lăsh'| *or* |**wĭp'**-| *n.* **1.** The lash of a whip. **2.** An injury to the neck or spine caused by a sudden backward or forward jerk of the head. *—v.* To beat, drive, or urge on with a whip: *He ruled by might, whiplashing his herd.*

whip•pet |**hwĭp'**ĭt| *or* |**wĭp'**-| *n.* A slender, swift-running dog resembling the greyhound but smaller.

whip•poor•will, also **whip-poor-will** |**hwĭp'**ər-wĭl'| *or* |**wĭp'**-| *or* |hwĭp'ər **wĭl'**| *or* |wĭp'-| *n.* A brownish North American bird that is active by night and has a repeated three-syllable call that sounds like its name.

whipt |hwĭpt| *or* |wĭpt|. A past tense and past participle of **whip.**

whir |hwûr| *or* |wûr| *v.* **whirred, whir•ring.** To move swiftly so as to make a buzzing or humming sound. *—n.* A buzzing or humming sound.

whirl |hwûrl| *or* |wûrl| *v.* **whirled, whirl•ing. 1.** To spin, twirl, or rotate: *whirl a baton. The propeller whirled faster and faster.* **2.** To turn or wheel suddenly, changing direction: *The cat ran across the road, whirled, and ran back again.* **3.** To have a spinning sensation; feel dizzy or giddy; reel: *My head is whirling.* *—n.* **1.** The act of whirling. **2.** A whirling or spinning motion. **3.** Something that whirls, as a cloud of dust. **4.** A rapid, dizzying round of events; a bustle or rush: *the social whirl.* **5.** A confused condition: *in a whirl of excitement.* **6.** *Informal.* A short trip or ride: *Let's go for a whirl in the car.* **7.** *Informal.* A brief try: *I've never skied before, but I'll give it a whirl.*

whirl•i•gig |**hwûr'**lĭ gĭg'| *or* |**wûr'**-| *n.* **1.** A child's toy that whirls, such as a pinwheel. **2.** A merry-go-round. **3.** Something that is always turning or whirling.

whirl•pool |**hwûrl'**pōōl'| *or* |**wûrl'**-| *n.* A rapid rotary current of water or other liquid, as one produced by the meeting of two tides; an eddy.

whirl•wind |**hwûrl'**wĭnd| *or* |**wûrl'**-| *n.* A mass of air that rotates, often violently, about a region of low atmospheric pressure, as a tornado.

whirl•y•bird |**hwûr'**lē bûrd'| *or* |**wûr'**-| *n. Slang.* A helicopter.

whirr |hwûr| *or* |wûr| *v.* & *n.* A form of the word **whir.**

whisk |hwĭsk| *or* |wĭsk| *v.* **1.** To brush or flick with quick, light sweeping motions: *whisking the crumbs off the table.* **2.** To move or carry briskly, nimbly, and very swiftly. **3.** To whip (eggs, cream, etc.). *—n.* **1.** A quick, light, sweeping motion: *the whisk of a cow's tail.* **2.** A whisk-broom. **3.** A kitchen tool used to whip eggs, cream, potatoes, etc.: *a wire whisk.*

whisk•broom |**hwĭsk'**brōōm'| *or* |-brōōm'| *or* |**wĭsk'**-| *n.* Also **whisk broom.** A small, short-handled broom used especially to brush clothes.

whisk•er |**hwĭs'**kər| *or* |**wĭs'**-| *n.* **1. a. whiskers.** The unshaven hair on a man's face, forming the beard and mustache. **b.** A single hair of this growth. **2.** One of the bristles or long hairs growing near the mouth of certain animals, as cats, rats, or rabbits.

whis•key |**hwĭs'**kē| *or* |**wĭs'**-| *n., pl.* **whis•keys.** An alcoholic beverage distilled from fermented grain, such as corn, rye, or barley.

whis•ky |**hwĭs'**kē| *or* |**wĭs'**-| *n., pl.* **whis•kies.** A form of the word **whiskey.**

whis•per |**hwĭs'**pər| *or* |**wĭs'**-| *v.* **1.** To speak or say very softly, below the breath. **2.** To speak or tell privately, as when plotting, hinting, or passing on gossip or secrets: *I wouldn't whisper your secret to a soul.* **3.** To make a soft, low, rustling or hissing sound: *wind whispering in the leaves.* *—n.* **1.** An act of whispering. **2.** A soft, low sound or tone of voice. **3.** A low, rustling or hissing sound: *the faintest whisper of a moving leaf.* **4.** A hint or rumor, as of scandal.

whist |hwĭst| *or* |wĭst| *n.* A card game played by two teams of two players. It was a forerunner of bridge.

whis•tle |**hwĭs'**əl| *or* |**wĭs'**-| *v.* **whis•tled, whis•tling. 1.** To make a clear, fairly pure tone, usually of high pitch, by causing air to move so that it vibrates. **2.** To make sound in this way by forcing air between the teeth or between pursed lips or by blowing into a device. **3.** To produce by whistling: *whistle a tune.* **4.** To signal by whistling: *whistle for a cab.* **5.** To move swiftly so as to make a high-pitched sound: *The wind whistled through the trees.* *—n.* **1.** Any device that uses a jet of air, steam, etc., to make a whistling sound. **2.** Any sound or signal made by whistling. **—whis'tler** *n.* [SEE PICTURE]

whit |hwĭt| *or* |wĭt| *n.* The least or smallest bit: *not a whit afraid.*

white |hwīt| *or* |wīt| *n.* **1.** The lightest or brightest of the series of colors that pass from black as the darkest through a series of lighter and lighter grays; the opposite of black. **2.** The white or nearly white part of something, such as an egg or the eyeball. **3.** Often **whites.** White clothes or a white outfit: *tennis whites.* **4.** Any member of a Caucasoid people; a Caucasian. *—adj.* **whit•er, whit•est. 1.** Of or nearly of the color white. **2.** Light-colored: *the white meat of the chicken.* **3.** Pale or bloodless: *Sam turned as white as if he had seen a ghost.* **4.** Belonging to an ethnic group having a comparatively pale skin, especially Caucasoid. **5.** Pale gray or silvery, as from age: *white hair.* **6.** Snowy: *a white Christmas.* **7.** Incandescent: *white heat.* **8.** Pure; innocent. *—v.* **whit•ed, whit•ing.** To make white; whiten, whitewash, or bleach. **—white'ness** *n.*

white ant. A termite.

white blood cell. Any of the white or colorless cells that have nuclei and appear in the blood, many of them functioning as a defense against infections.

white-col•lar |hwīt'kŏl'ər| *or* |wīt'-| *adj.* Of or pertaining to workers whose work usually does not involve manual labor.

white•fish |hwīt'fĭsh'| *or* |wīt'-| *n., pl.* **-fish** or **fish•es.** Any of several silvery freshwater fishes used as food.

white flag. A white cloth or flag signaling surrender or truce.

White•hall |hwīt'hôl'| *or* |wīt'-|. **1.** A street in London where many departments of the British government are located. **2.** The British government.

White House, the. 1. The executive mansion of the President of the United States in Washington, D.C. **2.** The President and his staff.

white lie. A lie told to cover up a small offense, to spare someone's feelings, etc.

whit•en |hwīt'n| *or* |wīt'n| *v.* To make or become white or whiter. —**whit'en•er** *n.*

white noise. Acoustical or electrical noise in which the intensity is the same at all frequencies within a given band.

white tie. 1. A white bow tie worn with a swallow-tailed coat as part of men's most formal evening clothes. **2.** Also **white tie and tails.** Men's most formal evening clothes.

white•wash |hwīt'wŏsh'| *or* |-wôsh'| *or* |wīt'-| *n.* **1.** A mixture of lime and water, often with whiting, size, or glue, applied to walls, concrete, etc., to whiten and improve the appearance. **2.** A glossing over of flaws or failures. —*v.* **1.** To cover or coat with or as if with whitewash. **2.** To gloss over (a flaw, failure, etc.).

whither |hwĭ*th*'ər| *or* |wĭ*th*'-| *adv.* To what place, result, or condition.

whit•ing¹ |hwī'tĭng| *or* |wī'-| *n., pl.* **whit•ing** or **whit•ings.** Any of several ocean fishes eaten as food.

whit•ing² |hwī'tĭng| *or* |wī'-| *n.* A pure white grade of chalk that has been ground and washed for use as a pigment.

whit•ish |hwī'tĭsh| *or* |wī'-| *adj.* Somewhat white.

Whit•man |hwĭt'mən| *or* |wĭt'-|, **Walt.** 1819–92. American poet.

Whit•sun•day |hwĭt'sŭn'dē| *or* |-dā'| *or* |wĭt'-| *n.* Pentecost.

Whit•sun•tide |hwĭt'sən tīd'| *or* |wĭt'-| *n.* The week following Whitsunday or Pentecost, especially the first three days.

whit•tle |hwĭt'l| *or* |wĭt'l| *v.* **whit•tled, whit•tling. 1.** To cut small bits or pare shavings from (a piece of wood). **2.** To fashion or shape in this way: *whittle a wooden doll.* **3.** To reduce or eliminate gradually by or as by whittling: *He whittled down his expenses by $60.* —**whit'tler** *n.*

whiz, also **whizz** |hwĭz| *or* |wĭz| *v.* **whizzed, whiz•zing. 1.** To make a whirring, buzzing, or hissing sound, as of something rushing through air. **2.** To rush past: *The subway train whizzed by without stopping.* —*n., pl.* **whiz•zes. 1.** The sound or passage of something that whizzes. **2.** *Slang.* One who has remarkable skill.

who |ho͞o| *pron.* The interrogative pronoun in the nominative case. **1.** What or which person or persons: *Who shall I say is calling?* **2.** That. —Used as a relative pronoun to introduce a clause when the antecedent is human: *The boy who came yesterday is now gone.*

who'd |ho͞od|. Who would.

who•ev•er |ho͞o ĕv'ər| *pron.* **1.** Anyone that: *Whoever comes to our gate should be welcomed into the house.* **2.** No matter who: *That painting is poor, whoever painted it.* **3.** Who: *Whoever could have dreamed of such a thing?*

whole |hōl| *adj.* **1.** Containing all component parts; complete: *a whole formal wardrobe.* **2.** Not divided or disjoined; in one unit: *He bought a whole acre of land near the beach.* **3.** Sound; healthy: *a whole organism.* **4.** Constituting the full amount, extent, or duration: *The baby cried the whole trip home.* —*n.* **1.** All of the component parts or elements of a thing. **2.** A complete entity or system: *the whole made up of the sun, planets, satellites, and other celestial bodies.* ¶ *These sound alike* **whole, hole.** —**whole'ness** *n.* [SEE NOTE]

***Idioms.* as a whole.** Altogether; all things considered. **on the whole.** In general.

whole•heart•ed |hōl'här'tĭd| *adj.* Without reservation: *wholehearted cooperation.* —**whole'heart'ed•ly** *adv.* —**whole'heart'ed•ness** *n.*

whole note. A musical note having a time value equal to that of two half notes.

whole number. Any of the numbers . . . −3, −2, −1, 0, 1, 2, 3, . . . ; an integer.

whole•sale |hōl'sāl'| *n.* The sale of goods in large quantities, as for resale by a retailer. —*adj.* **1.** Of or engaged in the sale of goods at wholesale: *a wholesale dealer; wholesale prices.* **2.** Sold in large bulk or quantity, usually at a lower cost: *wholesale merchandise.* **3.** Made or accomplished extensively and indiscriminately: *wholesale destruction.* —*adv.* In large bulk or quantity: *sell wholesale.* —**whole'sal'er** *n.*

whole•some |hōl'səm| *adj.* **1.** Conducive to mental or physical well-being; healthy: *a wholesome diet.* **2.** Having or indicating a healthy physical or mental condition: *a wholesome, rosy complexion; a wholesome attitude toward work.* —**whole'some•ly** *adv.* —**whole'some•ness** *n.*

whole-wheat |hōl'hwēt'| *or* |-wēt'| *adj.* Made from wheat kernels from which the outer covering and the wheat germ have not been removed: *whole-wheat flour; whole-wheat bread.*

who'll |ho͞ol|. Who will.

whol•ly |hō'lē| *adv.* Entirely; completely. ¶ *These sound alike* **wholly, holy.**

whom |ho͞om|. The objective case of **who.** [SEE NOTE]

whom•ev•er |ho͞om ĕv'ər|. The objective case of **whoever.**

whom•so•ev•er |ho͞om'sō ĕv'ər|. The objective case of **whosoever.**

whoop |ho͞op| *or* |hwo͞op| *or* |wo͞op| *n.* **1.** A loud or hooting cry, as of exultation. **2.** The gasp characteristic of whooping cough. —*v.* **1.** To shout loudly. **2.** To utter with a whoop. **3.** To gasp, as in whooping cough. ¶ *These sound alike* **whoop, hoop.** —**whoop'er** *n.*

whooping cough. A bacterial infection of the lungs and respiratory passages that causes spasms of coughing alternating with gasps.

whooping crane. A large, long-legged North American bird with white and black feathers and

whole

Whole *was Old English* hāl; *its original meaning was "in good health, uninjured";* **hale** *is a variant of it. Also related are* **heal, health,** *and* **hail².** *The original sense is clearly seen in* **wholesome.**

whom

It has long been predicted that **whom,** *the objective form of* **who,** *will disappear from the language. In formal written language, a large majority of the American Heritage Usage Panel still considers that* **whom** *is the only correct choice in a sentence like* Whom did you meet? *But in speech, two thirds of the Panel accept* Who did you meet?

wicket
Above: In cricket
Below: In croquet

wickiup
Mat-covered Paiute wickiup

ă pat/ā pay/â care/ä father/ĕ pet/ ē be/ĭ pit/ī pie/î fierce/ŏ pot/ ō go/ô paw, for/oi oil/o͝o book/ o͞o boot/ou out/ŭ cut/û fur/ *th* the/th thin/hw which/zh vision/ ə ago, item, pencil, atom, circus

a shrill, trumpeting cry. It is now very rare, and is in danger of becoming extinct.

whoops |hwo͞ops| *or* |wo͞ops| *or* |hwo͝ops| *or* |wo͝ops| *interj.* Used to express surprise, excitement, apology, etc.

whop·per |**hwŏp′**ər| *or* |**wŏp′**-| *n. Informal.* **1.** Something exceptionally big or remarkable. **2.** A gross untruth; a big lie.

whore |hôr| *or* |hōr| *n.* A prostitute. ¶*These sound alike* **whore, hoar.**

whorl |hwôrl| *or* |wôrl| *or* |hwûrl| *or* |wûrl| *n.* **1.** A coiled, curved, or rounded form, as one of the turns of a spiral shell or one of the ridges of a fingerprint. **2.** An arrangement of three or more parts, as of leaves or petals, radiating from a single point or part.

who's |ho͞oz|. **1.** Who is. **2.** Who has. ¶*These sound alike* **who's, whose.**

whose |ho͞oz| *pron.* **1.** The possessive form of **who:** *Did you see the poor kid whose arm was broken?* **2.** The possessive form of **which:** *an old oak in whose branches I sat.* ¶*These sound alike* **whose, who's.**

who·so·ev·er |ho͞o′sō **ĕv′**ər| *pron.* Whoever.

why |hwī| *or* |wī| *adv.* **1.** For what purpose, reason, or cause: *Why did you have to leave?* **2.** For which; on account of which: *The reason why I'm working is I have to live.* *—n., pl.* **whys.** A cause or reason concerning something: *some questions on the hows and whys of food.* *—interj.* A word used to mark a pause indicating surprise, pleasure, etc.: *Why, I'm delighted to help!*

wick |wĭk| *n.* A cord or strand of loosely joined fibers, as in a candle or oil lamp, that draws fuel to the flame by capillary action.

wick·ed |**wĭk′**ĭd| *adj.* **1.** Morally bad; vicious: *wicked deeds.* **2.** Playfully malicious or mischievous: *a wicked joke.* **3.** Causing or capable of causing great harm; harmful: *a wicked blow.* **—wick′ed·ly** *adv.* **—wick′ed·ness** *n.*

wick·er |**wĭk′**ər| *n.* Flexible twigs or shoots, as of a willow tree, woven into a material used for baskets, summer furniture, etc. ***—modifier:*** *a wicker basket.*

wick·et |**wĭk′**ĭt| *n.* **1.** In cricket, either of the two sets of three stakes, topped by a crossbar, that forms the target of the bowler. **2.** In croquet, any of the wire arches through which a player tries to hit his ball. [SEE PICTURE]

wick·i·up |**wĭk′**ē ŭp′| *n.* A frame hut covered with matting, bark, brush, etc., used by the nomadic Indians of North America. [SEE PICTURE]

wide |wīd| *adj.* **wid·er, wid·est. 1.** Extending over a large area from side to side; broad: *a wide street.* **2.** Having a specified extent from side to side; in width: *a ribbon two inches wide.* **3.** Having great range or scope: *a wide selection of dresses.* **4.** Fully open or extended: *look with wide eyes.* **5.** Landing or located away from a desired goal: *a shot wide of the mark.* *—adv.* **1.** Over a large area; extensively: *traveling far and wide.* **2.** To the full extent; completely: *The door was open wide.* **3.** So as to miss the target; astray: *shoot wide.* **—wide′ly** *adv.* **—wide′ness** *n.*

wide-a·wake |wīd′ə **wāk′**| *adj.* **1.** Completely awake. **2.** Watchful: *a wide-awake sentry.*

wid·en |**wīd′**n| *v.* To make or become wide or wider.

wide·spread |**wīd′**sprĕd′| *adj.* **1.** Spread out wide; fully opened: *with widespread arms in a gesture of welcome.* **2.** Spread or scattered over a considerable extent, area, region, etc.: *widespread disagreement on the question of school integration.*

wid·geon |**wĭj′**ən| *n., pl.* **wid·geon** or **wid·geons.** A wild duck with brownish feathers and a light-colored patch on the top of the head.

wid·ow |**wĭd′**ō| *n.* A woman whose husband has died and who has not remarried. *—v.* To make a widow of: *She was widowed by the mine explosion.*

wid·ow·er |**wĭd′**ō ər| *n.* A man whose wife has died and who has not remarried.

width |wĭdth| *or* |wĭth| *n.* **1.** The condition, quality, or fact of being wide. **2.** The measurement of the extent of something from side to side: *a room ten feet in width.* **3.** Something having a specified width, especially, in sewing, a piece of fabric measured from selvage to selvage: *a skirt having three widths.*

wield |wēld| *v.* **1.** To handle (a weapon, tool, etc.). **2.** To exercise (power or influence).

wie·ner |**wē′**nər| *n.* Wienerwurst.

wie·ner·wurst |**wē′**nər wûrst′| *n.* A type of smoked sausage, similar to a frankfurter.

wife |wīf| *n., pl.* **wives** |wīvz|. A woman to whom a man is married.

wife·ly |**wīf′**lē| *adj.* **1.** Of a wife: *wifely chores.* **2.** Suited to a wife: *a wifely concern for him.*

wig |wĭg| *n.* A covering of artificial or human hair worn on the head for adornment, to hide baldness, or as part of a costume.

wig·gle |**wĭg′**əl| *v.* **wig·gled, wig·gling.** To move or cause to move with short irregular motions from side to side: *She wiggled her toes. The dog's ears wiggled.* *—n.* The act of wiggling.

wig·wag |**wĭg′**wăg′| *v.* **wig·wagged, wig·wag·ging. 1.** To move back and forth, especially as a means of signaling: *wigwag a flag.* **2.** To signal by such motions: *wigwagged a call for help.* *—n.* **1.** The act of giving signals by wigwagging. **2.** A message sent in this way.

wig·wam |**wĭg′**wŏm′| *n.* A North American Indian dwelling, commonly having an arched or conical framework covered with bark or hides.

wild |wīld| *adj.* **wild·er, wild·est. 1.** Growing, living, or found in a natural state; not grown, kept, or cared for by human beings: *wild plants; wild honey.* **2.** Untamed: *a wild pony.* **3.** Lacking discipline or control; unruly: *a wild, fearless tomboy.* **4.** Full of or suggestive of strong, uncontrolled feeling: *wild with joy; wild laughter.* **5.** Stormy: *wild seas.* **6.** Uncivilized; savage: *wild tribes from the mountains.* **7.** Not lived in, cultivated, or used by people: *wild, unsettled country.* **8.** Very strange or unlikely; outlandish: *a wild idea.* **9.** Far from the intended mark, target, etc.: *a wild pitch; a wild bullet.* **10.** In card games, representing any card desired rather than the actual one held or played: *playing poker with deuces wild.* *—n.* Often **wilds.** A region not lived in or cultivated by human beings: *the wilds of northern Canada.* **—wild′ly** *adv.* **—wild′ness** *n.*

wild·cat |**wīld′**kăt′| *n.* **1.** A lynx, bobcat, or similar small to medium-sized animal related to the domestic cat. **2.** A quick-tempered or fierce person, especially a woman. *—adj.* **1.** Having no certainty of profit or success, as an oil well drilled in an area not known to yield oil, or a risky business venture. **2.** Carried on without official permission or sanction: *a wildcat strike.*

wil•de•beest |wĭl'də bēst'| *or* |vĭl'-| *n.* An animal, the gnu.

wil•der•ness |wĭl'dər nĭs| *n.* An unsettled, uncultivated region left in its natural condition.

wild•flow•er |wīld'flou'ər| *n.* Also **wild flower. 1.** A flowering plant that grows without cultivation or special care, as distinguished from those specially planted and cared for, as in gardens. **2.** The flower of such a plant.

wild•life |wīld'līf'| *n.* Wild plants and animals, especially wild animals living in their natural surroundings. ***—modifier:*** *a wildlife sanctuary.*

wild oat. Often **wild oats.** A grass related to the cultivated oat.

wild rice. 1. A tall North American water grass with narrow brownish seeds used as food. **2.** The seeds of this plant.

wile |wīl| *n.* **1.** A deceitful stratagem or trick. **2.** A disarming or seductive manner, device, or procedure. *—v.* **wiled, wil•ing.** To entice; lure: *wiled him to betray his friends.* [SEE NOTE]

wil•ful |wĭl'fəl| *adj.* A form of the word **willful.**

will[1] |wĭl| *n.* **1.** The mental faculty by which one deliberately chooses or decides upon a course of action; volition: *the freedom of the will.* **2.** An example of the exercising of this faculty; a deliberate decision; a choice. **3.** Control exercised over oneself, one's impulses, etc.: *a strong will.* **4.** Something desired or decided upon: *God's will be done.* **5.** Deliberate intention or wish: *going against his will.* **6.** Strong purpose; determination: *the will to win.* **7.** Free discretion: *wandering about at will.* **8.** Bearing or attitude toward others; disposition: *a man of good will.* **9.** A legal declaration of how a person wishes his possessions to be disposed of after his death. *—v.* **1.** To make use of one's mental powers in an attempt to obtain, do, or perform something: *You cannot achieve your goal just by willing it.* **2.** To exercise the power of the will: *Wishing and willing are two different things.* **3.** To influence, control, or compel by exercising the power of one's will: *He willed himself to stay awake.* **4.** To grant in a legal will; bequeath. [SEE NOTE]

will[2] |wĭl| *v.* Past **would** |wo͝od|. **1.** —Used as an auxiliary followed by a simple infinitive to indicate: **a.** Future action, condition, or state: *They will come later.* **b.** Likelihood or certainty: *You will live to regret what you did today.* **c.** Willingness: *Will you help me with this?* **d.** Intention: *I will too if I feel like it.* **e.** Requirement or command: *You will report to the principal's office.* **f.** Customary or habitual action: *She would spend hours in the kitchen.* **g.** *Informal.* Probability or expectation: *Three rings! That will be little Jamie at the door.* **2.** To wish: *Do what you will.* [SEE NOTE]

will•ful |wĭl'fəl| *adj.* **1.** Said or done in accordance with one's will; deliberate: *a willful waste of money; his willful disobedience.* **2.** Inclined to impose one's will; obstinate: *a willful child.* —**will'ful•ly** *adv.* —**will'ful•ness** *n.*

Wil•liam I |wĭl'yəm|. Known as William the Conqueror. 1027–1087. Duke of Normandy; led the Norman Conquest of England (1066) and reigned as King of England until his death.

Wil•liams•burg |wĭl'yəmz bûrg|. A town in eastern Virginia, the capital of Virginia until the American Revolution. In the 20th century it was restored to its original prerevolutionary style.

will•ing |wĭl'ĭng| *adj.* **1.** Done, given, etc., readily, without hesitation: *giving willing assistance.* **2.** Disposed to accept or tolerate: *willing to pay the price they're asking.* **3.** Acting or ready to act gladly: *a willing worker.* —**will'ing•ly** *adv.* —**will'ing•ness** *n.*

will-o'-the-wisp |wĭl'ə *thə* wĭsp'| *n.* **1.** A phosphorescent light that flits over swampy ground at night, often caused by spontaneous combustion of gases emitted by rotting organic matter. **2.** A misleading goal.

wil•low |wĭl'ō| *n.* **1.** Any of several trees with slender, flexible twigs and narrow leaves. **2.** The strong, lightweight wood of such a tree.

wil•low•y |wĭl'ō ē| *adj.* **wil•low•i•er, wil•low•i•est. 1.** Of or full of willows: *a willowy grove.* **2.** Suggestive of the slender, flexible branches of a willow: *a tall, willowy girl.*

wil•ly-nil•ly |wĭl'ē nĭl'ē| *adv.* Whether desired or not: *He must do what we've asked, willy-nilly.*

Wil•ming•ton |wĭl'mĭng tən|. The largest city in Delaware, in the northern part of the state. Population, 80,000.

Wil•son |wĭl'sən|, **(Thomas) Woodrow.** 1856–1924. Twenty-eighth President of the United States (1913–21).

wilt[1] |wĭlt| *v.* **1.** To lose or cause to lose freshness; wither. **2.** To lose vigor or force.

wilt[2] |wĭlt| *Archaic.* Second person singular present tense of the verb **will.**

wi•ly |wī'lē| *adj.* **wi•li•er, wi•li•est.** Full of wiles; guileful; calculating: *a wily old fox.*

wim•ple |wĭm'pəl| *n.* A piece of cloth wound around the head and neck, framing the face, worn by women of the Middle Ages and by certain orders of nuns.

win |wĭn| *v.* **won** |wŭn|, **win•ning. 1.** To achieve victory over others in (a game, battle, competition, etc.): *Our troops won the battle. Do you know which team won?* **2.** To receive as a prize or reward for performance: *He won the scholarship.* **3. a.** To gain by means of hard work, effort, perseverance, etc.; earn: *win fame.* **b.** To succeed in gaining the favor or support of; prevail upon: *His eloquence won his audience.* **c.** To reach with difficulty: *The ship won a safe port.* ***—phrasal verbs.*** **win out.** To succeed or prevail. **win over.** To persuade: *His efforts won them over to our views.* *—n. Informal.* A victory, especially in sports.

wince |wĭns| *v.* **winced, winc•ing.** To shrink or start involuntarily, as in pain or distress: *She winced when the blade slipped and cut her finger.* *—n.* A wincing movement or gesture.

winch |wĭnch| *n.* A machine for pulling or lifting, consisting of a drum around which a rope or cable attached to the load is wound as the load is moved.

wind[1] |wĭnd| *n.* **1.** A current of air, especially a natural one that moves along or parallel to the ground. **2.** A current or stream of air produced artificially, as by a blower or fan. **3. winds.** The wind instruments of an orchestra. **4.** The ability to breathe in a normal or adequate way: *Smoking cigarettes can hurt your wind.* **5.** Meaningless or boastful talk. *—v.* To cause to be out of or

wile

Wile *and* **guile** *are very similar in meaning, and they are in fact doublets.* **Guile** *is from Old French* guile, *"cunning," which is borrowed from prehistoric Germanic* wihl-, *"magic, sorcery."* **Wile** *is from Old Norse* wihl, *"trickery," which is also from Germanic* wihl-. *For the change of a Germanic* w- *to an Old French* g-, *see note at* **guard/ward.**

will[1-2]

Will[1] *was Old English* will *or* willa, *"desire, will power."* **Will[2]** *was Old English* willan, *"to desire." The two words are closely related.*

wind¹·²
Wind¹ *was* wind *in Old English; it is descended from prehistoric Germanic* windaz, *which in turn is from Indo-European* wento-, *"blowing, wind."* Wento- *appears in Latin as* ventus, *"wind," from which we have* **vent¹** *and* **ventilate**. **Wind²** *was Old English* windan, *"to turn, wind"; it is related to* **wend** *and* **wander**.

window
Window *is from Old Norse* vindauga, *"wind-eye":* vindr, *"wind, air,"* + auga, *"eye." The word for "eye" here basically means simply "opening, hole," but presumably (to a person inside a dark house) it also implies "source of light."*

wing
Above: Upper surface of bird's wing
Below: Wings of maple fruit

ă pat/ā pay/â care/ä father/ĕ pet/ ē be/ĭ pit/ī pie/î fierce/ŏ pot/ ō go/ô paw, for/oi oil/o͝o book/ o͞o boot/ou out/ŭ cut/û fur/ *th* the/th thin/hw which/zh vision/ ə ago, item, pencil, atom, circus

short of breath: *The long race winded the runners.* [SEE NOTE]

wind² |wīnd| *v.* **wound** |wound|, **wind·ing. 1. a.** To wrap (something) around or on top of: *The caterpillar winds the long thread of silk around itself.* **b.** To wrap or encircle (something): *She wound her waist with brightly colored ribbons.* **2.** To turn in a series of circular motions, as a handle: *Wind the crank and then release it.* **3.** To coil the spring of (a clock or other mechanism). **4. a.** To move in or as if in a coiling or spiraling course: *The river winds through the valley.* **b.** To proceed on (one's way) in a coiling or spiraling course: *We wound our way through the forest.* —***phrasal verb.*** **wind up. 1.** *Informal.* To come or bring to an end; finish: *The book winds up with a happy ending.* **2.** In baseball, to swing back the arm and raise the foot in preparation for pitching the ball. —*n.* A single turn, twist, or curve. —**wind'er** *n.* [SEE NOTE]

Wind·break·er |wĭnd'brā'kər| *n.* A trademark for a warm jacket with close-fitting bands around the waist and cuffs.

wind-chill factor |wĭnd'chĭl'|. The temperature of windless air that would have the same effect on the exposed human skin as a given combination of wind speed and air temperature.

wind·fall |wĭnd'fôl'| *n.* **1.** Something blown down by the wind, especially fruit from a tree. **2.** A sudden piece of good fortune.

wind·flow·er |wĭnd'flou'ər| *n.* An anemone.

Wind·hoek |vĭnt'ho͝ok'|. The capital of Namibia. Population, 61,000.

wind·ing |wīn'dĭng| *adj.* Turning or twisting: *a winding stream.* —*n.* **1.** The act of someone or something that winds. **2.** A curve or bend, as of a stream or road. **3.** Wire wound into a coil.

wind instrument |wĭnd|. Any musical instrument caused to sound by a current of air, especially the player's breath, as a flute, oboe, etc.

wind·jam·mer |wĭnd'jăm'ər| *or* |wĭn'-| *n. Informal.* A large sailing ship.

wind·lass |wĭnd'ləs| *n.* Any of various hauling and lifting devices similar to a winch.

wind·mill |wĭnd'mĭl'| *n.* A mill or other machine whose power is taken from a wheel or set of vanes that is turned by the wind.

win·dow |wĭn'dō| *n.* **1.** An opening constructed in a wall to admit light or air, usually framed and spanned with glass. **2.** A pane of glass; a windowpane. **3.** Any opening that resembles a window in function or appearance. [SEE NOTE]

win·dow·pane |wĭn'dō pān'| *n.* A plate of glass in a window.

win·dow-shop |wĭn'dō shŏp'| *v.* **-shopped, -shop·ping.** To look at merchandise in stores without making purchases.

wind·pipe |wĭnd'pīp'| *n.* A tube of the respiratory system that passes from the throat to the lungs; the trachea.

wind·row |wĭnd'rō'| *n.* A long row of cut hay or grain left to dry in a field before being bundled.

wind·shield |wĭnd'shēld'| *n.* A framed sheet of glass or other transparent material located at the front of an automobile or similar vehicle.

wind·sock |wĭnd'sŏk'| *n.* A large, roughly conical device open at both ends and attached to a stand by a pivot, so that it points in the direction of the wind that blows through it.

Windsor chair. A wooden chair with a high rounded back of spindles or sticks and legs sloping outward.

wind tunnel |wĭnd|. A chamber through which wind can be forced at controlled speeds so its effect on an aircraft, airfoil, etc., can be studied.

wind-up |wīnd'ŭp'| *n.* **1.** The act of bringing something to a conclusion. **2.** The concluding part of an action, presentation, speech, etc.

wind·ward |wĭnd'wərd| *adj.* Facing or moving into the wind: *a windward tide; the windward quarter.* —*n.* The windward side. —*adv.: sailed windward of shore.*

Windward Islands. A group of islands in the West Indies, forming the southern half of the Lesser Antilles.

wind·y |wĭn'dē| *adj.* **wind·i·er, wind·i·est. 1.** Characterized by or having much wind: *a windy winter month.* **2.** Exposed to the prevailing wind: *the windy side of an apartment.* **3. a.** Given to prolonged or empty talk: *a windy speaker.* **b.** Wordy, boastful, or empty: *a windy speech.*

wine |wīn| *n.* **1.** The fermented juice of grapes. **2.** The fermented juice of other fruits or plants: *dandelion wine.* **3.** A dark purplish red. —***modifier:*** *a wine bottle; a wine merchant.* —*adj.* Dark purplish red. —*v.* **wined, win·ing.** To provide or entertain with wines.

win·er·y |wī'nə rē| *n., pl.* **win·er·ies.** An establishment where wine is made.

wing |wĭng| *n.* **1.** One of a pair of specialized parts used for flying, as in birds, bats, or insects. **2.** A surface of an aircraft whose principal purpose is to act on the air passing around it so as to provide a force that holds the craft aloft, especially one of a pair of such surfaces extending from the sides of an airplane. **3.** An extending part resembling a wing, such as one of the thin projections on certain plant seeds. **4.** A part of a building extending from or attached to the main structure: *the West Wing of the White House.* **5.** A section or faction: *the Democratic Party's southern wing.* **6.** Often **wings.** One of the areas that extend on either side of the stage and are concealed from the audience: *The next performer was waiting in the wings.* **7.** A unit of military aircraft or aviators. —*v.* **1.** To fly or soar with or as if with wings: *birds winging southward.* **2.** To wound slightly, as in the wing or arm. —**wing'less** *adj.* [SEE PICTURE]

Idioms. **on the wing.** In the act of flying; in flight. **under (one's) wing.** In one's care.

winged. *adj.* **1.** |wĭngd|. Having wings or winglike parts: *winged insects; the winged seeds of the maple.* **2.** |wĭng'ĭd|. Seeming to move on wings: *the poet's winged words.*

wing·span |wĭng'spăn'| *n.* Wingspread.

wing·spread |wĭng'sprĕd'| *n.* The distance between the tips of the extended wings, as of a bird, insect, or airplane.

wink |wĭngk| *v.* **1.** To close and open (the eyelid of one eye) deliberately, as to convey a message, signal, or suggestion. **2.** To shine fitfully; twinkle: *A lighthouse winked in the far distance.* —*n.* **1. a.** The act of winking. **b.** The time required for a wink; a very short time. **2.** A gleam; twinkle. **3.** *Informal.* A brief moment of sleep.

Idiom. **wink at.** To pretend not to see.

win·ning |wĭn'ĭng| *adj.* **1.** Successful; victorious: *the winning team.* **2.** Charming: *a winning personality.* —*n.* **1.** The act of one that wins; victory. **2. winnings.** That which has been won, especially money. —**win'ning•ly** *adv.*

Win•ni•peg |wĭn'ə pĕg'|. The capital of Manitoba, Canada. Population, 257,000.

win•now |wĭn'ō| *v.* **1.** To separate the chaff from (grain) by means of a current of air. **2.** To separate (a desirable or undesirable part); sort or eliminate. —**win'now•er** *n.*

win•some |wĭn'səm| *adj.* Pleasant; charming: *a winsome personality; a winsome girl.*

win•ter |wĭn'tər| *n.* The season of the year between autumn and spring, lasting in the Northern Hemisphere from the December solstice to the next equinox and in the Southern Hemisphere from the June solstice to the next equinox. —***modifier:*** *winter sports.* —*adj.* **1.** Planted in the autumn and harvested in the spring or summer: *winter wheat; winter crops.* **2.** Capable of being stored for used during the winter, as a fruit or vegetable: *winter squash.*

win•ter•green |wĭn'tər grēn'| *n.* **1.** A low-growing plant with spicy-smelling evergreen leaves and red berries. **2.** An oil or flavoring obtained from this plant.

win•ter•time |wĭn'tər tīm'| *n.* The winter season. —***modifier:*** *wintertime sports.*

win•ter•y |wĭn'tə rē| *adj.* **win•ter•i•er, win•ter•i•est.** A form of the word **wintry.**

win•try |wĭn'trē| *adj.* **win•tri•er, win•tri•est. 1.** Of or like winter; cold: *wintry weather.* **2.** Cheerless and unfriendly: *a wintry tone of voice.*

wipe |wīp| *v.* **wiped, wip•ing. 1.** To rub, as with a cloth or paper, in order to clean or dry: *wipe the dishes with paper towels.* **2.** To remove by or as if by rubbing; brush: *wiping the tears off.* **3.** To rub, move, or pass over something for or as if for rubbing, cleaning, etc.: *wiping a soft cloth over the silver box.* —***phrasal verb.*** **wipe out. 1.** To destroy completely: *a hurricane that wiped out an entire beach resort.* **2.** *Informal.* To murder. **3.** In surfing, to lose balance and fall or jump off a surfboard. —*n.* The act of wiping: *giving the table a wipe with a clean cloth.* —**wip'er** *n.*

wire |wīr| *n.* **1.** A usually flexible rod or strand of metal, often covered with an electrical insulator, used to conduct electricity from point to point or to support or connect parts of a structure. **2.** A group of such strands joined or twisted together and extending roughly between the same points; cable. **3. a.** A telegraph service. **b.** A telegram. **4.** An active telephone connection: *Please hold the wire.* —***modifier:*** *a wire cutter.* —*v.* **wired, wir•ing. 1.** To join, connect, or attach with or as if with a wire or wires. **2.** To install the necessary electrical wires and connections in: *wire a house; wire a radio.* **3.** To send (a message, information, etc.) by telegram: *wire congratulations.* **4.** To send a telegram to.

wire-haired |wīr'hârd'| *adj.* Having a coat of stiff, wiry hair: *a wire-haired fox terrier.*

wire•less |wīr'lĭs| *n. British.* Radio or radio communications. —***modifier:*** *a wireless set; a wireless system.* —*adj.* Having no wire or wires.

wire•tap |wīr'tăp'| *n.* A secret or concealed connection made in a telephone or telegraph circuit to allow messages to be intercepted or overheard. —*v.* **wire•tapped, wire•tap•ping. 1.** To connect a wiretap to. **2.** To listen in on (a telephone circuit) by means of a wiretap.

wir•ing |wīr'ĭng| *n.* **1.** The act or process of attaching, connecting, or installing electric wires. **2.** A system of electric wires.

wir•y |wīr'ē| *adj.* **wir•i•er, wir•i•est. 1.** Like wire: *wiry hair.* **2.** Slender but tough: *a basketball player with a wiry physique.* —**wir'i•ness** *n.*

Wis. Wisconsin.

Wis•con•sin |wĭs kŏn'sən|. A Midwestern state of the United States. Population, 4,447,000. Capital, Madison.

wis•dom |wĭz'dəm| *n.* **1.** Understanding of what is true, right, or lasting: *Solomon was famous for his wisdom.* **2.** Learning; knowledge: *all the wisdom of the ages.*

wisdom tooth. One of four molars, the last on each side of both jaws in human beings, usually erupting much later than the others.

wise¹ |wīz| *adj.* **wis•er, wis•est. 1.** Having wisdom; judicious: *a wise statesman.* **2.** Showing common sense; prudent: *a wise decision.* **3.** Shrewd; crafty; cunning: *a wise move.* **4.** Having knowledge or information; aware of: *a good poker player wise in the ways of professional gamblers.* **5.** *Slang.* Bold and disrespectful; fresh: *a wise kid.* —**wise'ly** *adv.*

wise² |wīz| *n.* Method or manner of doing: *in no wise.*

-wise. A word element meaning "in the manner or direction of": **clockwise.**

wise•crack |wīz'krăk'|. *Slang. n.* A clever or witty remark, often disrespectful, arrogant, or insulting. —*v.* To make wisecracks.

wish |wĭsh| *n.* **1.** A desire or longing for some specific thing. **2.** An expression of such desire or longing: *She made a wish and blew out the candles.* **3.** Something desired: *He got his wish.* —*v.* **1.** To have or feel a desire: *They wish to see you. He wishes for a rest.* **2.** To desire (a person or thing) to be in a specified state or condition: *We wish you were here.* **3.** To entertain or express wishes for; bid: *wished her good night.* **4.** To call or invoke upon: *wish him luck.* **5.** To impose or force: *They wished too much work on him.* **6.** To express a wish: *see the star and wish.* —**wish'er** *n.*

wish•bone |wĭsh'bōn'| *n.* The forked bone in front of the breastbone in most birds.

wish•ful |wĭsh'fəl| *adj.* Having or expressing a wish or longing: *wishful eyes.* —**wish'ful•ly** *adv.*

wisp |wĭsp| *n.* **1.** A small bunch or bundle, as of hair. **2.** Someone or something thin, frail, or slight. **3.** A faint streak, as of smoke or clouds.

wist |wĭst| *Archaic.* Past tense and past participle of **wit².**

wis•tar•i•a |wĭ stâr'ē ə| *n.* A form of the word **wisteria.**

wis•ter•i•a |wĭ stîr'ē ə| *n.* A climbing woody vine with drooping clusters of showy purplish or white flowers. [SEE PICTURE]

wisteria

wist•ful |wĭst'fəl| *adj.* Full of a melancholy yearning; wishful: *wistful eyes.* —**wist'ful•ly** *adv.* —**wist'ful•ness** *n.*

wit¹ |wĭt| *n.* **1. a.** The ability to see and describe humorously those elements of a situation that are amusing or odd. **b.** A person having this ability. **2.** Often **wits. a.** Understanding; intelligence: *using one's wits.* **b.** Sound mental faculties; sanity: *scared out of one's wits.*

witch

Witch *was Old English* wicce *(feminine) and* wicca *(masculine). It originally meant simply "magician," with no implication of good or evil; in later medieval times, however, it came to mean specifically "a woman who is in league with the Devil and practices only black magic." But the term* white witch *has been used for a beneficent sorceress.*

witch hazel
Flowers and seed capsules

wizard

Wizard *originally meant "wise man, philosopher." The suffix* -ard, *meaning "person who is (something)," almost always carries a sense of disapproval; compare* **coward, drunkard, niggard.** *Thus* **wizard** *was used contemptuously to mean "so-called wise man," and from this it came to mean "magician."*

ă **pat**/ā **pay**/â **care**/ä **father**/ĕ **pet**/ ē **be**/ĭ **pit**/ī **pie**/î **fierce**/ŏ **pot**/ ō **go**/ô **paw**, **for**/oi **oil**/ŏŏ **book**/ ōō **boot**/ou **out**/ŭ **cut**/û **fur**/ *th* **the**/th **thin**/hw **which**/zh **vision**/ ə **ago**, item, pencil, atom, circus

Idioms. **at (one's) wits' ends.** At the limit of one's mental resources; utterly at a loss. **have** (or **keep**) **(one's) wits about (one).** To remain alert or calm, especially in a crisis.

wit[2] |wĭt| *v.* **wist** |wĭst|, **wit•ting.** *Archaic.* To know.
Idiom. **to wit.** That is to say; namely.

witch |wĭch| *n.* **1.** A woman who practices black magic; a sorceress. **2.** An ugly old woman. [SEE NOTE]

witch•craft |**wĭch′**krăft′| *or* |-krăft′| *n.* Black magic as practiced by witches; sorcery.

witch doctor. A medicine man or shaman of a primitive people or tribe.

witch hazel. **1.** A North American shrub with yellow flowers that bloom in late fall or winter. **2.** A spicy-smelling liquid made from the bark and leaves of this shrub and rubbed on the skin to relieve soreness, as a freshener, etc. [SEE PICTURE]

with |wĭ*th*| *or* |wĭth| *prep.* **1.** Accompanying: *Come with me.* **2.** Next to: *Walk with him and follow me.* **3.** Having as a possession, attribute, or characteristic: *a clown with a red nose.* **4.** In a manner characterized by: *We were greeted with great friendliness.* **5.** In the charge or keeping of: *You can leave your things with me.* **6.** In the opinion of: *if it's all right with you.* **7.** In support or on the side of: *I'm with you all the way on this.* **8.** Of the same opinion or belief as: *Are you with me in wanting to go swimming?* **9.** In the same group or mixture as: *Plant mint with the other herbs.* **10.** In the membership or employment of: *How long have you been with the Yankees?* **11.** By means of: *our vain efforts to kindle a fire with flint and steel.* **12.** In spite of: *With all that talent, he's getting nowhere.* **13.** In the same direction as: *bending with the wind.* **14.** At the same time as: *rising with the sun.* **15.** In regard to: *I'm pleased with her.* **16.** In comparison or contrast to: *a dress identical with the one I saw you wearing.* **17.** Upon receiving: *With your permission, I think I'll leave.* **18.** And; plus: *Jim, with several of his friends, is arriving tomorrow.* **19.** In opposition to; against: *looking for a fight with somebody all the time.* **20.** As a result of: *trembling with fear.* **21.** To; onto: *Couple the first car with the second.* **22.** So as to be separated from: *parting with a friend.* **23.** In the course of: *With each passing moment he got more scared.* **24.** In proportion to: *improving with age.* **25.** In relationship to: *at ease with his peers.* **26.** As well as: *She can sing with the best of them.*

with•al |wĭ*th* **ôl′**| *or* |wĭth-| *adv.* Besides; as well: *gentle and dangerous withal.*

with•draw |wĭ*th* **drô′**| *or* |wĭth-| *v.* **with•drew** |wĭ*th* **drōō′**| or |wĭth-|, **with•drawn** |wĭ*th* **drôn′**| or |wĭth-|, **with•draw•ing.** **1.** To take back or away; remove: *withdraw funds from the bank.* **2.** To move or draw back; retreat or retire: *withdraw troops from the area.*

with•draw•al |wĭ*th* **drô′**əl| *or* |wĭth-| *n.* **1.** The act or process of withdrawing. **2.** A removal of something that has been deposited: *a withdrawal from a bank account.* **3.** The process by which a person taking a habit-forming drug is deprived of it, either suddenly or gradually.

with•drawn |wĭth **drôn′**| *or* |wĭth-|. Past participle of **withdraw.** *—adj.* **1.** Remote; isolated: *a quiet, withdrawn village.* **2.** Socially retiring; shy: *a withdrawn person.*

with•drew |wĭ*th* **drōō′**| *or* |wĭth-|. Past tense of **withdraw.**

with•er |**wĭ*th*′**ər| *v.* **1.** To dry up or cause to dry up from lack of moisture; shrivel: *The flowers withered in the vase. The hot weather withered the grass.* **2.** To become or cause to become wasted, worn out, etc., as if by drying out: *old people withering in strange new surroundings.* **3.** To fade or disappear: *His anger withered away.*

with•ers |**wĭ*th*′**ərz| *pl.n.* The highest part of the back of a horse or similar animal, between the shoulder blades.

with•hold |wĭth **hōld′**| *or* |wĭ*th*-| *v.* **with•held** |wĭth **hĕld′**| or |wĭ*th*-|, **with•hold•ing.** **1.** To keep in check; restrain: *withhold the applause until the end of the act.* **2.** To refrain from giving, granting, or permitting: *withhold authorization.* **—with•hold′ing** *adj.: withholding tax.*

with•in |wĭ*th* **ĭn′**| *or* |wĭth-| *prep.* **1.** Inside of: *within the body.* Also used adverbially; *people outwardly noisy but calm within.* **2.** Inside the limits or extent of in time, degree, or distance: *within ten miles of home.* Also used adverbially: *boring from within.* **3.** Not exceeding or transgressing: *within the laws of the land. —adv.* Not outside; indoors: *We stayed within.*

with•out |wĭ*th* **out′**| *or* |wĭth-| *adv.* On the outside or outdoors: *The structure is sturdy within and without.* Also used prepositionally: *standing without the door. —prep.* **1.** Not having; lacking: *without carfare to get home.* **2. a.** With no or none of: *build up industry without foreign aid.* **b.** Not accompanied by: *no smoke without fire.*

with•stand |wĭth **stănd′**| *or* |wĭ*th*-| *v.* **with•stood** |wĭth **stŏŏd′**| or |wĭ*th*-|, **with•stand•ing.** To oppose (something) with force; resist or endure successfully: *a building that withstands earthquake shocks.*

wit•less |**wĭt′**lĭs| *adj.* Lacking intelligence or wit; stupid or dull.

wit•ness |**wĭt′**nĭs| *n.* **1.** Someone who has seen or heard something: *a witness of the accident.* **2.** Something that serves as evidence; a sign. **3. a.** Someone who is called to testify before a court of law. **b.** Someone who is called upon to be present at a transaction or event in order to attest to what took place: *witnesses at a wedding. —v.* **1.** To be present at; see: *witness a volcanic eruption.* **2.** To serve as or furnish evidence of: *The child's laughter witnessed delight.* **3.** To attest to the authenticity of by signing one's name: *witness a will.*

wit•ti•cism |**wĭt′**ĭ sĭz′əm| *n.* A cleverly worded, amusing remark.

wit•ting•ly |**wĭt′**ĭng lē| *adv.* Intentionally.

wit•ty |**wĭt′**ē| *adj.* **wit•ti•er, wit•ti•est.** Having or showing wit: *a witty person; a witty remark.* **—wit′ti•ly** *adv.* **—wit′ti•ness** *n.*

wives |wīvz| *n.* Plural of **wife.**

wiz•ard |**wĭz′**ərd| *n.* **1.** A sorcerer or magician. **2.** *Informal.* A person of amazing skill or talent: *a wizard at mathematics.* [SEE NOTE]

wiz•ard•ry |**wĭz′**ər drē| *n., pl.* **wiz•ard•ries.** The practice of magic or sorcery.

wiz•ened |**wĭz′**ənd| *adj.* Shriveled; withered.

wk. **1.** week. **2.** work.

wkly. weekly.

wob•ble |wŏb′əl| *v.* **wob•bled, wob•bling.** To move or cause to move erratically from side to side: *The old table wobbles. He wobbled the table when he sat down.* —*n.* A pronounced unsteady movement.

wob•bly |wŏb′lē| *adj.* **wob•bli•er, wob•bli•est.** Tending to wobble; unsteady; shaky.

Wo•den |wōd′n|. The chief Germanic god.

woe |wō| *n.* Deep sorrow; grief: *yearning for company in her woe.*

woe•be•gone |wō′bĭ gôn′| *or* |-gŏn′| *adj.* Mournful or sorrowful in appearance: *a woebegone little figure.*

woe•ful |wō′fəl| *adj.* **1.** Full of woe; mournful: *a woeful ballad.* **2.** Pitiful or deplorable: *woeful wrongs.* —**woe′ful•ly** *adv.*

woke |wōk|. A past tense of **wake.**

wolf |wo͝olf| *n., pl.* **wolves** |wo͝olvz|. **1. a.** An animal related to the dog, living chiefly in northern regions and feeding on the flesh of other animals. **b.** The fur of such an animal. **2.** A fierce, cruel, dangerous person. **3.** *Slang.* A man who pursues women and considers himself a great success as a lover. —***modifier:*** *wolf skins.* —*v.* To eat quickly and greedily: *wolfed down the hamburger.* [SEE PICTURE]

***Idiom.* cry wolf.** To raise an alarm about a danger that does not really exist.

wolf•hound |wo͝olf′hound′| *n.* Any of several kinds of large dogs originally trained to hunt wolves.

wol•ver•ine |wo͝ol′və rēn′| *n.* A flesh-eating animal of northern regions, having thick, dark fur and a bushy tail. [SEE PICTURE]

wolves |wo͝olvz| *n.* Plural of **wolf.**

wom•an |wo͝om′ən| *n., pl.* **wom•en** |wĭm′ĭn|. **1.** A full-grown female human being. **2.** Women in general. —***modifier:*** *a woman athlete.*

wom•an•hood |wo͝om′ən ho͝od′| *n.* **1.** The condition of being a woman. **2.** Women in general. **3.** The qualities, feelings, etc., considered typical of women.

wom•an•ish |wo͝om′ə nĭsh| *adj.* Considered typical of women but undesirable in men.

wom•an•kind |wo͝om′ən kīnd′| *n.* Women in general.

wom•an•ly |wo͝om′ən lē| *adj.* Having or showing qualities or characteristics considered typical of, suitable for, or admirable in women: *womanly grace; womanly sympathy.* —**wom′an•li•ness** *n.*

womb |wo͞om| *n.* **1.** The organ of female mammals in which the young develop from a fertilized egg before birth; the uterus. **2.** A place where something has its earliest stages of development.

wom•bat |wŏm′băt′| *n.* An Australian animal that resembles a small bear. [SEE PICTURE]

wom•en |wĭm′ĭn| *n.* Plural of **woman.**

wom•en•folk |wĭm′ĭn fōk′| *pl.n.* **1.** Women in general. **2.** A particular group of women, as the women of one community.

won |wŭn|. Past tense and past participle of **win.** ¶*These sound alike* **won, one.**

won•der |wŭn′dər| *n.* **1.** Someone or something that arouses awe or admiration; a marvel. **2.** The feeling or emotion aroused by such awe or admiration. **3.** A feeling of confusion or doubt. —*v.* **1.** To have a feeling of awe or admiration: *They wondered at the sight of the canyon.* **2.** To be filled with curiosity or doubt: *She wondered about the future.* **3.** To have doubt or curiosity about: *I wonder what she is doing.*

***Idiom.* no wonder.** Not surprisingly: *No wonder they were impressed when they saw the statue.*

won•der•ful |wŭn′dər fəl| *adj.* **1.** Exciting wonder; marvelous; astonishing: *It must be wonderful to fly like a bird.* **2.** Admirable, interesting, or amusing; *a wonderful idea.* —**won′der•ful•ly** *adv.*

won•der•land |wŭn′dər lănd′| *n.* A marvelous imaginary realm.

won•der•ment |wŭn′dər mənt| *n.* A state or feeling of wonder; astonishment; surprise.

won•drous |wŭn′drəs| *adj.* Wonderful. —**won′drous•ly** *adv.*

wont |wônt| *or* |wōnt| *or* |wŭnt| *adj.* Accustomed, apt, or used to: *He was wont to lend money for charitable use.* —*n.* Habit; custom: *He shook playfully as was his wont.*

won't |wōnt|. Will not.

wont•ed |wôn′tĭd| *or* |wōn′-| *or* |wŭn′-| *adj.* Accustomed; usual: *He took his wonted station.*

woo |wo͞o| *v.* **1.** To seek the affection of, especially with hopes of marrying. **2.** To solicit or seek the favor of; try to persuade: *Advertisers often woo teen-agers.* **3.** To seek to get or achieve: *woo money from the public.* —**woo′er** *n.*

wood |wo͝od| *n.* **1. a.** The tough, fibrous substance beneath the bark of trees and shrubs and forming the stems of certain other plants. **b.** This substance, often cut and dried, used for building, as fuel, and for many other purposes. **2.** Often **woods.** A dense growth of trees; a forest. **3.** Something made from wood, as a golf club with a wooden head. —***modifier:*** *wood carvings.* ¶*These sound alike* **wood, would.**

wood alcohol. **Methyl alcohol.**

wood•bine |wo͝od′bīn′| *n.* Any of several climbing vines, especially a European honeysuckle.

wood•chuck |wo͝od′chŭk′| *n.* A short-legged, burrowing North American mammal with brownish fur. Also called *ground hog.*

wood•cock |wo͝od′kŏk′| *n.* A bird with short legs and a long bill, often hunted for sport.

wood•craft |wo͝od′krăft′| *or* |-kräft′| *n.* **1.** The art of working with wood. **2.** Skill in things pertaining to the woods, as hunting.

wood•cut |wo͝od′kŭt′| *n.* **1.** A piece of wood with an engraved design for printing. **2.** A print made from such a piece of wood.

wood•ed |wo͝od′ĭd| *adj.* Having trees or woods.

wood•en |wo͝od′n| *adj.* **1.** Made of wood: *wooden shoes; a wooden bridge.* **2.** Stiff and unnatural: *the wooden motions of a mechanical doll.* —**wood′en•ly** *adv.*

wood•land |wo͝od′lənd| *or* |-lănd′| *n.* Land covered with trees. —***modifier:*** *woodland flowers.*

wood•man |wo͝od′mən| *n., pl.* **-men** |-mən|. A woodsman.

wood•peck•er |wo͝od′pĕk′ər| *n.* Any of several birds having strong claws used for clinging to and climbing trees and a strong, pointed bill used for drilling into bark and wood.

wood pulp. Any of various cellulose pulps ground from wood, treated chemically, and used in making paper, cellophane, rayon, etc.

woods•man |wo͝odz′mən| *n., pl.* **-men** |-mən|. A man who works or lives in the woods or is skilled in woodcraft.

wolf

wolverine

wombat

word
"*We should have a great many fewer disputes in the world if words were taken for what they are, the signs of our ideas only, and not for things themselves.*"
—*John Locke (1690).*
"*I am not yet so lost in lexicography as to forget that words are the daughters of earth, and that things are the sons of Heaven.*"
—*Samuel Johnson (1755).*

ă pat/ā pay/â care/ä father/ĕ pet/ē be/ĭ pit/ī pie/î fierce/ŏ pot/ō go/ô paw, for/oi oil/o͝o book/o͞o boot/ou out/ŭ cut/û fur/*th* the/th thin/hw which/zh vision/ə ago, item, pencil, atom, circus

wood sorrel. Any of several plants having leaves with three leaflets and yellow, white, or pinkish flowers.

wood tar. A black, syruplike fluid that is a by-product of the destructive distillation of wood and is used in pitch, medicines, etc.

wood•wind |wo͝od'wĭnd'| *n.* **1.** Any of a group of musical instruments whose tone is started by the vibration of a reed, as a clarinet, oboe, or bassoon, or by the action of a whistlelike device, as a flute. **2. woodwinds.** The section of an orchestra or band composed of such instruments. —***modifier:*** *woodwind instruments.*

wood•work |wo͝od'wûrk'| *n.* Objects made of or work done in wood, especially wooden interior fittings in a house, as doors, moldings, etc.

wood•work•ing |wo͝od'wûr'kĭng| *n.* The art or skill of making things from wood.

wood•y |wo͝od'ē| *adj.* **wood•i•er, wood•i•est. 1.** Consisting of or containing wood: *woody plants; woody stems; woody tissue.* **2.** Of or suggestive of wood: *a woody smell.* **3.** Covered with trees; wooded: *a woody hill.*

woof[1] |wo͝of| *or* |wo͞of| *n.* **1.** The threads that run crosswise in a woven fabric, carried back and forth between the lengthwise warp threads by the shuttle of the loom; filling; weft. **2.** The texture of a fabric.

woof[2] |wo͝of| *n.* A deep, gruff bark or a similar sound. —*v.* To make such a sound.

woof•er |wo͝of'ər| *n.* A loudspeaker designed to reproduce sounds of low frequency.

wool |wo͝ol| *n.* **1.** The dense, soft, often curly hair of sheep and some other animals, used to make yarn, cloth, and clothing. **2.** Yarn, cloth, or clothing made of wool. **3.** Something having the look or feel of wool, as a mass of fine, curled metal strands.

wool•en |wo͝ol'ən| *adj.* **1.** Made of wool: *a woolen fabric, woolen underwear.* **2.** Making or dealing in wool cloth or clothing: *a woolen mill.* —*n.* Often **woolens.** Wool cloth or clothing.

wool•gath•er•ing |wo͝ol'găth'ər ĭng| *n.* Daydreaming in an absent-minded way. —**wool'gath'er•er** *n.*

wool•len |wo͝ol'ən| *adj. & n.* A form of the word **woolen.**

wool•ly |wo͝ol'ē| *adj.* **wool•li•er, wool•li•est. 1.** Of or covered with wool: *a woolly coat; a woolly lamb.* **2.** Resembling wool: *leaves covered with woolly down.* **3.** Unclear, blurry: *woolly thinking.* **4.** Rough; disorderly: *a wild and woolly frontier town.* —*n., pl.* **wool•lies. 1.** A garment made of wool. **2. woollies.** Woolen underwear.

wool•y |wo͝ol'ē| *adj.* **wool•i•er, wool•i•est,** *& n., pl.* **wool•ies.** A form of the word **woolly.**

wooz•y |wo͞o'zē| *adj.* **wooz•i•er, wooz•i•est.** Dazed; dizzy. —**wooz'i•ness** *n.*

word |wûrd| *n.* **1.** A spoken sound or group of sounds that communicates a meaning and can be represented by letters written or printed in an unbroken series. **2. words.** Spoken or written expression; speech or writing: *learning to put your feelings into words.* **3.** A remark or comment: *a word of advice.* **4.** A short conversation: *May I have a word with you?* **5. words.** Hostile or angry remarks made back and forth; a quarrel. **6.** A promise; an assurance: *keeping her word to be on time.* **7.** A direction to do something; an order: *Just say the word, and we'll send up reinforcements.* **8.** News; information: *sent word of her safe arrival.* **9. the Word.** The Scriptures; the Bible. —***modifier:*** *a word puzzle.* —*v.* To express in words. [SEE NOTE]

Idioms. **eat (one's) words.** To admit having said or predicted something wrong. **take (someone) at his word.** To trust the word of (someone) and act accordingly. **word for word.** Entirely and without changing or forgetting any word.

word•ing |wûr'dĭng| *n.* The way in which something is expressed; choice of words.

word•less |wûrd'lĭs| *adj.* **1.** Not expressed in words: *a look that served as a wordless reproach.* **2.** Speechless; mute: *wordless with gratitude.* —**word'less•ly** *adv.* —**word'less•ness** *n.*

Words•worth |wûrdz'wûrth'|, **William.** 1770–1850. English poet.

word•y |wûr'dē| *adj.* **word•i•er, word•i•est.** Containing or using too many words; verbose. —**word'i•ly** *adv.* —**word'i•ness** *n.*

wore |wôr| *or* |wōr|. Past tense of **wear.**

work |wûrk| *n.* **1.** Physical or mental effort to make or do something; labor: *taking a nap after a morning of work; hard at work on a new scheme.* **2.** Employment; a job: *looking for work.* **3.** The activity by which one makes one's living; one's occupation. **4.** The place, such as an office or factory, where one pursues one's occupation. **5.** A task or a number of tasks: *There's enough work here to last us all day.* **6.** The way in which someone performs a task; workmanship: *The portrait painter stepped back and admired his work.* **7. a.** Something that has been done, made, or brought about; the result of an effort: *This mistake is your work, not mine.* **b.** An act; deed: *charitable works.* **c. works.** The total of the material produced by a creative artist: *the works of Bach.* **d. works.** Large structures designed by engineers, as bridges, roads, and dams. **8. a.** An object or item being made, shaped, studied, or processed: *a carpenter's table with a large vice for holding the work.* **b.** Such an object along with the tools and materials being used: *She stopped sewing and put her work into a basket.* **9. works** *(used with a singular verb).* A factory, plant, or similar site where industry of some kind is carried on: *a steel works.* **10. works.** The essential or operating parts of a device: *the works of a watch.* **11. the works.** *Slang.* Everything in a whole group or range; the whole lot: *We ordered the works, from soup to nuts.* **12. a.** The transfer of energy from one physical body or system to another. **b.** The measure of the energy transferred from one body or system to another. —***modifier:*** *work shoes.* —*v.* **1.** To exert oneself for the purpose of making or doing something; engage in work. **2.** To be employed; have a job. **3.** To cause or force to do work: *He works his assistants hard.* **4.** To perform one's duties on or in; cover: *a door-to-door salesman who works the north side of town.* **5.** To gain profit from: *work a vein of ore.* **6. a.** To operate effectively or as intended; perform a function: *a mousetrap that really works.* **b.** To cause to operate or function; run: *work a buzz saw.* **7.** To suffice for a purpose; serve: *The recipe calls for peaches, but any sweet fruit will work just as well.* **8.** To bring about; accomplish: *That hand cream will work wonders.* **9.** To move, force, or make by steady effort: *worked his way to the edge of the crowd.* **10.** To become through gradual or repeated stress, pressure, or movement: *The stitches worked loose.* **11.** To pass or seep gradually: *A good paint will work into wood surfaces.* **12.** To have a steadily increasing effect or influence: *The memory worked on her conscience.* **13.** To use one's influence or powers of persuasion: *Dad hasn't agreed to take us on a car trip, but we're working on him.* **14. a.** To form or shape by applying pressure; mold: *work clay with the hands.* **b.** To be formed, shaped, or manipulated: *Copper works easily.* **15.** To prepare for use by manipulating or kneading: *working dough; working the soil with a hoe.* **16.** To excite; provoke: *a speaker who can work a crowd into a frenzy.* —***phrasal verbs.*** **work in** (or **into**). **1.** To put in; introduce or insert: *work a joke into a speech.* **2.** To rub or press in. **work off.** To get rid of by working: *work off excess weight.* **work out. 1.** To devise; develop: *work out a solution.* **2.** To prove successful or suitable: *The cake didn't work out very well.* **3.** To perform athletic exercises. **work over.** *Slang.* To beat up.

Idioms. **at work.** Having an effect; operating: *the forces at work on a moving body.* **in the works.** Being planned or prepared for use. **make short work of.** To dispose of quickly; finish off.

work•a•ble |wûr′kə bəl| *adj.* **1.** Capable of being used or put into effect successfully; practicable: *a workable plan of action.* **2.** Capable of being shaped, molded, or dealt with: *workable metals.* —**work′a•bil′i•ty, work′a•ble•ness** *n.*

work•a•day |wûr′kə dā′| *adj.* **1.** Of ordinary working days: *the workaday chores of a housekeeper.* **2.** Commonplace: *the workaday world.*

work•bench |wûrk′bĕnch′| *n.* A sturdy table or bench on which manual work is done, as by a carpenter or machinist.

work•book |wûrk′bŏŏk′| *n.* **1.** An exercise book with sections of problems to be worked out directly on its pages. **2.** A manual of instructions, as for running a machine.

work•er |wûr′kər| *n.* **1.** Someone or something that works: *a fast worker.* **2.** Any of a class of female ants, bees, or other social insects that do the work of the colony or hive and cannot produce offspring.

work•ing |wûr′kĭng| *adj.* **1.** Of someone or something that works; employed: *a working person.* **2.** Of or spent in work: *working hours.* **3.** Capable of working; functioning: *a machine in working condition.* **4.** Sufficient or adequate for using: *a working knowledge of a language.*

work•ing•man |wûrk′ĭng măn′| *n., pl.* **-men** |-mĕn′|. A man who works for wages.

work•man |wûrk′mən| *n., pl.* **-men** |-mən|. A man who performs some form of labor.

work•man•ship |wûrk′mən shĭp′| *n.* **1.** The art, skill, or technique of a workman. **2.** The quality of such art, skill, or technique.

work•out |wûrk′out′| *n.* A period of exercise, especially in athletics.

work•shop |wûrk′shŏp′| *n.* **1.** A place where manual or industrial work is done. **2.** A group of people who meet regularly for a seminar in some field: *a teachers' workshop.*

world |wûrld| *n.* **1.** The earth. **2.** The universe. **3.** The earth and its people. **4.** A planet or other celestial body distinct from the earth. **5.** A particular part of the earth: *the Western world.* **6.** A particular period in history, including its culture and customs: *the Renaissance world.* **7. a.** The field or area in which a certain class of persons or things exists or functions; domain: *the animal world; the world of the blind.* **b.** A field or sphere of human activity or knowledge: *the world of literature.* **8.** That part of life concerned with business or social affairs, as distinguished from religious or spiritual matters: *forsook the world for a hermit's existence.* **9.** Often **worlds.** A large amount: *spent worlds of time.* [SEE NOTE]

world•ly |wûrld′lē| *adj.* **world•li•er, world•li•est. 1.** Of the world of business or pleasure; not spiritual or religious; secular: *worldly concerns.* **2.** Sophisticated; worldly-wise. —**world′li•ness** *n.*

world•ly-wise |wûrld′lē wīz′| *adj.* Experienced in the ways of the world; sophisticated.

World War I. A war fought from 1914 to 1918 in which Great Britain, France, the United States, and their allies defeated Germany, Austria-Hungary, and their allies.

World War II. A war fought from 1939 to 1945, in which Great Britain, France, the Soviet Union, the United States, and their allies defeated Germany, Italy, and Japan.

world•wide |wûrld′wīd′| *adj.* Reaching or extending throughout the world; universal.

worm |wûrm| *n.* **1.** Any of several groups of animals with no backbone, having a soft, long, rounded or flattened body. **2.** Any of several animals resembling true worms, especially a caterpillar, grub, or other insect larva. **3. worms.** A disease caused by worms living as parasites inside the body. **4.** A scorned, despised, or weak-willed person. —*v.* **1.** To make (one's way) or move with or as if with the wriggling, crawling, or twisting motion of a worm. **2.** To get by sly or deceitful means: *The spy wormed the information from the messenger.* **3.** To rid of worms inside the body. [SEE PICTURE]

worm•wood |wûrm′wŏŏd′| *n.* A strong-smelling plant that yields a bitter substance used for flavoring certain alcoholic liquors.

worn |wôrn| *or* |wōrn|. Past tense of **wear.** —*adj.* **1.** Damaged by wear or use: *worn, faded trousers.* **2.** Having a tired, exhausted look, as from worry, sickness, or strain: *a pale, worn face.*

worn-out |wôrn′out′| *or* |wōrn′-| *adj.* **1.** Used until no further usefulness remains: *worn-out clothes.* **2.** Extremely tired; exhausted.

wor•ri•some |wûr′ē səm| *or* |wŭr′-| *adj.* **1.** Causing worry or anxiety. **2.** Tending to worry.

wor•ry |wûr′ē| *or* |wŭr′ē| *v.* **wor•ried, wor•ry•ing, wor•ries. 1.** To feel or cause to feel uneasy or anxious: *worried about his health; a medical report that worried him.* **2.** To grasp and tug at repeatedly: *a kitten worrying a ball of yarn.* —*n., pl.* **wor•ries. 1.** Mental uneasiness or anxiety. **2.** Something that causes anxiety or uneasiness. —**wor′ri•er** *n.*

worse |wûrs| *adj.* **1.** Comparative of **bad:** *He's worse than I'd ever imagined a vicious person could be.* **2.** Comparative of **ill:** *Grandpa is worse, and I think you should come home.* **3.** More inferior, as in quality, condition, or effect: *These oranges are worse than those.* —*adv.* In a worse way: *What could be worse conceived!* —*n.* Something worse: *taking a turn for the worse.*

world

By origin, the word **world** *refers to the human scene, not to the planet Earth.* **World** *was* weorold *in Old English, and is descended from prehistoric Germanic* weraldh-, *"the life or age of man":* wer-, *"man,"* + aldh-, *"age, life."*

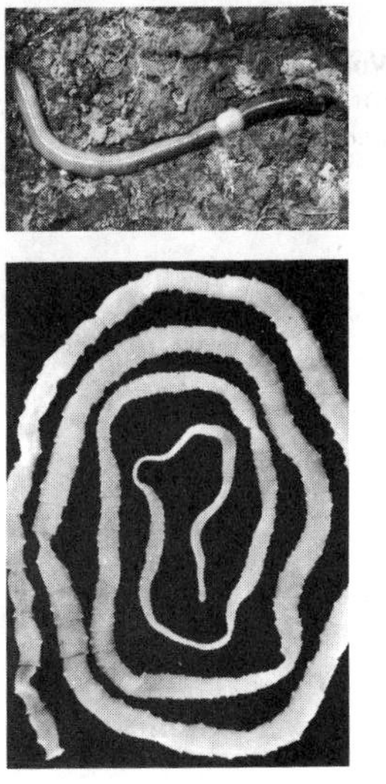

worm
Above: Earthworm
Below: Tapeworm

wors•en |wûr'sən| *v.* To become or make worse.

wor•ship |wûr'shĭp| *n.* **1.** Love, respect, and devotion felt for God or another deity. **2.** A set of ceremonies, prayers, or other religious forms by which this feeling is expressed. **3.** Love of or devotion to a person or thing: *her worship of her children; the worship of money.* **4.** Often **Worship.** A title of honor used in addressing certain officials: *Is your Worship ready?* —*v.* **wor•shiped** or **wor•shipped, wor•ship•ing** or **wor•ship•ping. 1.** To honor and love as a deity: *each worshiping God in his own way.* **2.** To participate in religious rites of worship. **3.** To love or pursue with devotion. —**wor'ship•er** *n.* [SEE NOTE]

worst |wûrst| *adj.* **1.** Superlative of **bad:** *He was the worst President we ever had.* **2.** Superlative of **ill:** *the worst turn he has ever done anyone.* **3.** Most inferior, as in quality, condition, or effect: *the worst eggs I ever saw.* **4.** Most severe or unfavorable: *the worst winter in years.* **5.** Least desirable or satisfactory: *the worst piece of land.* —*n.* Something or someone that is worst.

wor•sted |wo͝os'tĭd| *or* |wûr'stĭd| *n.* **1.** Smooth, firmly twisted yarn made from long strands of wool. **2.** A firm, smooth cloth woven from such yarn. —***modifier:*** *a worsted suit.*

worth |wûrth| *n.* **1.** The condition of something or someone that gives value or usefulness: *the worth of a good reputation.* **2.** The value of something, expressed in money. **3.** The amount that a certain sum of money will buy: *a nickel's worth of candy.* **4.** Wealth; riches. —*adj.* **1.** Equal in value to something specified: *a pen worth five dollars.* **2.** Having wealth amounting to: *a widow worth $2,000,000.* **3.** Deserving of; meriting: *a plan worth a trial.*

***Idiom.* for all (one) is worth.** To the utmost of one's powers or ability.

worth•less |wûrth'lĭs| *adj.* Without worth, use, or value: *a worthless promise.* —**worth'less•ly** *adv.*

worth•while |wûrth'hwīl'| *or* |-wīl'| *adj.* Sufficiently valuable or important to justify the time, effort, or other cost involved.

wor•thy |wûr'thē| *adj.* **wor•thi•er, wor•thi•est. 1.** Having worth, merit, or value; useful or valuable: *a worthy cause.* **2.** Honorable; deserving respect: *a worthy opponent.* **3.** Having sufficient worth; deserving: *worthy to be considered.* —*n., pl.* **wor•thies.** Someone esteemed or respected for his worth. —**wor'thi•ness** *n.*

wot |wŏt| *Archaic.* First and third person singular present tense of **wit.**

would |wo͝od|. Past tense of **will.** ¶*These sound alike* **would, wood.**

would•est |wo͝od'ĭst| *v.* A form of the word **wouldst.**

wouldn't |wo͝od'nt|. Would not.

wouldst |wo͝odst|. *Archaic.* Second person singular past tense of **will.**

wound¹ |wo͞ond| *n.* An injury, especially one in which the skin or other outer surface that covers a living thing is broken or damaged. —*v.* To inflict a wound or wounds on.

wound² |wound|. Past tense and past participle of **wind.**

wove |wōv|. Past tense of **weave.**

wo•ven |wō'vən|. Past participle of **weave.**

wow |wou| *interj.* A word used to express surprise, excitement, enthusiasm, etc. —*n. Informal.* A great success. —*v. Informal.* To be a great success with: *She really wowed the audience.*

wrack |răk| *v.* **1.** To wreck; ruin: *The invading army wracked and looted the countryside.* **2.** To have a violent or shattering effect on: *Sobs wracked her body.* —*n.* **1.** Complete destruction: *bring to wrack and ruin.* **2.** Seaweed forming a tangled mass. ¶*These sound alike* **wrack, rack.**

wraith |rāth| *n.* An apparition or ghost.

wran•gle |răng'gəl| *v.* **wran•gled, wran•gling. 1.** To argue noisily and angrily; bicker. **2.** In the western United States, to herd horses or other livestock. —*n.* An angry, noisy dispute. —**wran'gler** *n.*

wrap |răp| *v.* **wrapped** or **wrapt** |răpt|, **wrap•ping. 1.** To draw, fold, or wind around as a covering: *wrapped her shawl about her.* **2.** To enclose within a covering: *wrap a baby in a blanket.* **3.** To put on warm clothes: *Wrap up before you go out.* **4.** To put paper around: *wrap a package.* —***phrasal verb.* wrap up.** *Informal.* To finish; conclude: *wrap up a sports event.* —*n.* **1.** Often **wraps.** An outer garment worn for warmth, as a coat. **2.** Paper or other material used for wrapping something. ¶*These sound alike* **wrap, rap.**

wrap•per |răp'ər| *n.* **1.** Someone who wraps. **2.** A cover, as of paper, in which something is wrapped: *a candy wrapper.*

wrap•ping |răp'ĭng| *n.* Often **wrappings.** The material used for wrapping something.

wrapt |răpt|. A past tense and past participle of **wrap.** ¶*These sound alike* **wrapt, rapt.**

wrath |răth| *or* |räth| *n.* Violent, resentful anger; rage.

wrath•ful |răth'fəl| *or* |räth'-| *adj.* Full of wrath: *wrathful fury.* —**wrath'ful•ly** *adv.*

wreak |rēk| *v.* **1.** To inflict (vengeance or punishment): *The father sought to wreak revenge for his son's death.* **2.** To express or gratify; vent: *wreak her anger.* ¶*These sound alike* **wreak, reek.**

wreath |rēth| *n., pl.* **wreaths** |rēthz|. **1.** A ring or ringlike band of leaves, flowers, etc., used as decoration, as an honor, etc. **2.** A ring or similar curving form: *a wreath of smoke.*

wreathe |rēth| *v.* **wreathed, wreath•ing. 1.** To encircle, decorate, etc., with or as if with a wreath: *Her head was wreathed with roses.* **2.** To twist or entwine into a wreath or wreathlike form: *Ivy wreathed itself around the pillars.*

wreck |rĕk| *v.* **1.** To destroy accidentally, as by collision: *He wrecked the car.* **2.** To tear down or dismantle: *The crew wrecked the building in five days.* **3.** To bring to a state of ruin: *Reconstruction wrecked what little of the South the war had not already ruined.* —*n.* **1.** The act of wrecking or the condition of being wrecked. **2.** The remains of something that has been wrecked. **3.** Someone or something in a disorderly or worn-out state. ¶*These sound alike* **wreck, reck.** —**wreck'er** *n.*

wreck•age |rĕk'ĭj| *n.* **1.** The act of wrecking or the condition of being wrecked. **2.** The debris of anything wrecked.

wren |rĕn| *n.* Any of several small brownish birds that usually hold the tail pointing upward. [SEE PICTURE]

wrench |rĕnch| *n.* **1.** A sudden, forcible twist or turn. **2.** An injury, as to a joint, produced by twisting or straining. **3.** Any of various adjust-

worship
Worship *is a simplified form of* worth-ship, *meaning "worthiness, honor, dignity, reverence."*

wren

ă pat/ā pay/â care/ä father/ĕ pet/ ē be/ĭ pit/ī pie/î fierce/ŏ pot/ ō go/ô paw, for/oi oil/o͝o book/ o͞o boot/ou out/ŭ cut/û fur/ *th* the/th thin/hw which/zh vision/ ə ago, item, pencil, atom, circus

able tools for gripping a nut, bolt, pipe, etc., and a long handle for turning. —*v.* **1.** To twist and sprain (a joint or other body part). **2.** To pull or turn suddenly and forcibly. [SEE PICTURE]

wrest |rĕst| *v.* **1.** To obtain by or as if by pulling forcefully: *trying to wrest it from the monster's grasp.* **2.** To gain or usurp forcefully: *The barons wrested power from the king.* ¶*These sound alike* **wrest, rest.**

wres•tle |rĕs'əl| *v.* **wres•tled, wres•tling. 1. a.** To fight by grappling and trying to bring one's opponent to the ground. **b.** To fight in such a manner with: *She wrestled the bear.* **2.** To struggle to solve or master: *wrestle with a problem.*

wres•tler |rĕs'lər| *n.* A person who wrestles, especially as a sport.

wres•tling |rĕs'lĭng| *n.* The sport of fighting by grappling and trying to bring one's opponent to the ground. —***modifier:*** *a wrestling match.*

wretch |rĕch| *n.* **1.** A miserable or unfortunate person. **2.** A wicked or despicable person.

wretch•ed |rĕch'ĭd| *adj.* **1.** Full of or attended by misery or woe: *I'm lonely and wretched.* **2.** Shabby: *a wretched shack.* **3.** Hateful or contemptible: *a wretched person.* **4.** Inferior in quality: *a wretched performance.* —**wretch'ed•ly** *adv.*

wrig•gle |rĭg'əl| *v.* **wrig•gled, wrig•gling. 1.** To turn, twist, or move with winding, writhing motions; squirm. **2.** To get into or out of a situation by sly or subtle means. —*n.* The action or movement of wriggling. —**wrig'gler** *n.*

Wright |rīt|, **Orville** (1871–1948) and **Wilbur** (1867–1912). American pioneers in aviation who built and flew the first airplane in 1903.

wring |rĭng| *v.* **wrung** |rŭng|, **wring•ing. 1.** To twist and squeeze, especially to get liquid out: *Wring out the wet clothes.* **2.** To force or squeeze out by or as if by twisting or pressing. **3.** To twist forcibly: *I'd like to wring his neck.* **4.** To twist or squeeze, as in distress: *wringing her hands.* —*n.* A forceful squeeze or twist. ¶*These sound alike* **wring, ring.**

wring•er |rĭng'ər| *n.* A device for pressing out water from clothes after washing, consisting of two rollers through which the article is passed.

wrin•kle |rĭng'kəl| *n.* A small furrow, ridge, or crease on a normally smooth surface such as cloth or skin. —*v.* **wrin•kled, wrin•kling. 1.** To make a wrinkle or wrinkles in: *Don't wrinkle the suit.* **2.** To form wrinkles: *Linen wrinkles easily.* **3.** To draw up or pucker: *wrinkled her nose.*

wrist |rĭst| *n.* **1.** The joint at which the hand and forearm come together. **2.** The system of bones that form this joint; the carpus.

writ¹ |rĭt| *n.* A written court order commanding a person to do or stop doing a specified act.

writ² |rĭt| *Archaic.* Past tense and past participle of **write.**

write |rīt| *v.* **wrote** |rōt|, **writ•ten** |rĭt'n|, **writ•ing. 1.** To form (letters, symbols, or characters) on a surface with a pen, pencil, etc. **2.** To form (words, sentences, etc.) by inscribing the correct letters or symbols: *write the answers on a separate sheet of paper.* **3.** To compose: *write music.* **4.** To draw up in legal form; draft: *write a lease.* **5.** To communicate by writing: *wrote the good news to his friend.* **6.** *Informal.* To send a letter or note to: *wrote her niece.* **7.** To produce articles, books, etc., to be read: *He writes for a living.* **8.** To show clearly; mark: *Happiness was written in her smile.* —***phrasal verbs.*** **write down.** To put into writing: *write down a telephone number.* **write off. 1.** To cancel from accounts, as a loss. **2.** To consider as a loss or failure. **write up.** To write a report or description of: *write up the results of the experiment.* ¶*These sound alike* **write, right, rite.**

writ•er |rī'tər| *n.* **1.** A person who has written something specified: *the writer of the letter.* **2.** A person who writes as an occupation; an author.

write-up |rīt'ŭp'| *n.* A published account, review, notice, etc.

writhe |rīth| *v.* **writhed, writh•ing. 1.** To twist or squirm or cause to twist or squirm, as in pain. **2.** To move with a twisting or contorted motion: *Snakes were writhing in the pit.*

writ•ing |rī'tĭng| *n.* **1.** Written form: *Make the request in writing.* **2.** Language symbols or characters written or imprinted on a surface. **3. writings.** A collection of written works: *the writings of Aristotle.* **4.** The activity, art, or occupation of a writer. —***modifier:*** *a writing course.*

writ•ten |rĭt'n|. Past participle of **write.**

wrong |rông| *or* |rŏng| *adj.* **1.** Not correct; erroneous: *a wrong answer.* **2.** Contrary to conscience, morality, or law. **3.** Not intended or wanted: *a wrong telephone number; the wrong direction.* **4.** Not fitting or suitable; inappropriate: *the wrong moment.* **5.** Not in accordance with an established usage, method, or procedure. **6.** Not functioning properly; amiss: *What is wrong with the machine?* —*adv.* **1.** Mistakenly; erroneously: *told the story wrong.* **2.** Immorally or unjustly: *behave wrong.* —*n.* **1.** An unjust, injurious, or immoral act or circumstance: *right a wrong.* **2.** The condition of being mistaken or to blame: *in the wrong.* —*v.* **1.** To treat unjustly, injuriously, or dishonorably. **2.** To discredit unjustly; malign. —**wrong'ly** *adv.* —**wrong'ness** *n.*
Idiom. **go wrong. 1.** To take a wrong turn or course. **2.** To happen or turn out badly.

wrong•do•er |rông'dōō'ər| *or* |rŏng'-| *n.* Someone who does wrong. —**wrong'do'ing** *n.*

wrote |rōt|. Past participle of **write.** ¶*These sound alike* **wrote, rote.**

wroth |rôth| *or* |rŏth| *adj. Archaic.* Wrathful.

wrought |rôt| *Archaic.* A past tense and past participle of **work.** —*adj.* **1.** Made, formed, or fashioned: *a well-wrought cabinet.* **2.** Shaped by hammering with tools, as metal is.

wrought iron. A highly purified form of iron that is easily shaped, forged, or welded. —***modifier:*** **(wrought-iron):** *wrought-iron furniture.*

wrung |rŭng|. Past tense and past participle of **wring.** ¶*These sound alike* **wrung, rung.**

wry |rī| *adj.* **wri•er** or **wry•er, wri•est** or **wry•est. 1.** Twisted or bent to one side: *a wry smile.* **2.** Temporarily twisted in an expression of distaste or displeasure: *made a wry face.* **3.** Dryly humorous, often with a touch of irony. ¶*These sound alike* **wry, rye.** —**wry'ly** *adv.*

wt. weight.

W.Va. West Virginia.

W.W.I. World War I.

W.W.II. World War II.

Wyo. Wyoming.

Wy•o•ming |wī ō'mĭng|. A Rocky Mountain state of the United States. Population, 335,000. Capital, Cheyenne.

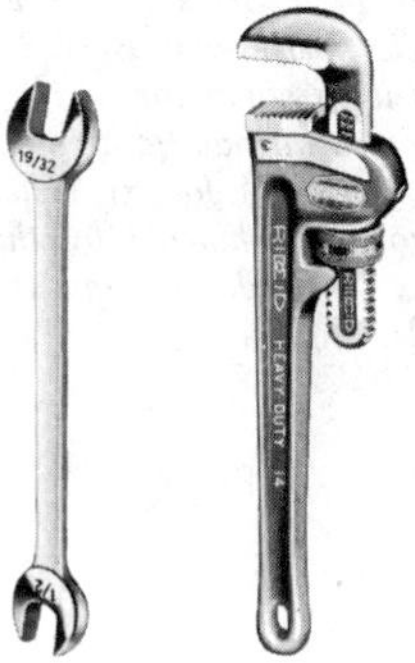

wrench
Left: Open-end wrench
Right: Stillson wrench

Xx

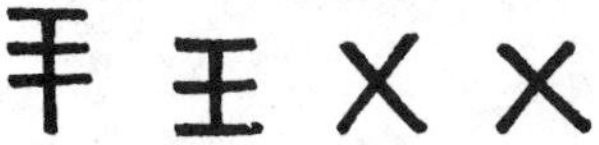

(1) (2) (3) (4)

The letter **X** *comes indirectly from the Phoenician letter* sāmekh *(1), meaning "fish." This letter stood for /s/, but when the Greeks borrowed it as* xi *(2), they used it to stand for /ks/. Later they also introduced a completely new form (3) for* xi. *This was borrowed unchanged by the Romans (4) and so transmitted to modern times.*

xylophone

ă pat/ā pay/â care/ä father/ĕ pet/ ē be/ĭ pit/ī pie/î fierce/ŏ pot/ ō go/ô paw, for/oi oil/ŏŏ book/ ōō boot/ou out/ŭ cut/û fur/ *th* the/th thin/hw which/zh vision/ ə ago, item, pencil, atom, circus

x, X |ĕks| *n., pl.* **x's** or **X's.** **1.** The 24th letter of the English alphabet. **2.** The Roman numeral for the number ten. **3.** In mathematics: **a.** A symbol for an unknown number. **b.** A symbol for an algebraic variable. **4.** A mark made on a map, diagram, etc., to show a place or location: *X marks the spot where the treasure is buried.* **5.** A mark made instead of a signature by a person who does not know how to write. [SEE NOTE]

X |ĕks| *adj.* Indicating a rating given a motion picture deemed unsuitable to anyone under the age of seventeen.

Xan•thip•pe |zăn **tĭp'**ē|. The wife of the ancient Greek philosopher Socrates, traditionally regarded as an illltempered, nagging woman.

Xa•vi•er |zā'vē ər| *or* |**zăv'**ē-|, **Saint Francis.** 1506–1552. Spanish Jesuit priest who went as a missionary to India, Ceylon, and Japan.

x-ax•is |ĕks'ăk'sĭs| *n., pl.* **x-ax•es** |ĕks'ăk'sēz'|. **1.** The horizontal axis of a plane Cartesian coordinate system. **2.** One of the axes of a three-dimensional coordinate system.

X-chro•mo•some |**ĕks'krō'**mə sōm'| *n.* The chromosome associated with female sex characteristics. In females it is matched with another X-chromosome. In males it is matched with a Y-chromosome.

Xe The symbol for the element xenon.

xe•bec |zē'bĕk'| *n.* A three-masted sailing ship with both square and triangular sails, once used by pirates in the Mediterranean Sea.

xe•non |zē'nŏn'| *n.* Symbol **Xe** One of the elements, a colorless, odorless gas that is found in the atmosphere in small amounts and that is almost completely nonreactive chemically. Atomic number 54; atomic weight 131.30; melting point –111.9°C; boiling point –107.1°C; valence uncertain.

xen•o•phobe |**zĕn'**ə fōb'| *n.* A person who mistrusts, fears, or is scornful of foreigners or strangers.

xen•o•pho•bi•a |zĕn'ə **fō'**bē ə| *n.* Undue mistrust or fear of foreigners or strangers, especially in political matters: *The country's leaders withdrew into a mood of self-righteousness and xenophobia.*

xen•o•pho•bic |zĕn'ə **fō'**bĭk| *adj.* Of or typical of a xenophobe.

Xen•o•phon |**zĕn'**ə fən| *or* |-fŏn'|. 430?–355? B.C. Greek historian and military leader.

xe•rog•ra•phy |zĭ **rŏg'**rə fē| *n.* A process for producing photographs or photocopies without the use of solutions or wet materials, by causing an image made up of particles of pigment held in place by electric charges on a plate to be transferred to a sheet of paper and fixed to the paper by heat.

xe•ro•graph•ic |zîr'ə **grăf'**ĭk| *adj.* Of, used in, or produced by xerography: *the xerographic method; xerographic prints.*

Xe•rox |**zîr'**ŏks'| *n.* **1.** A trademark for a machine or process that produces photocopies by xerography. **2.** A copy made on a Xerox machine. *—v.* To copy or print with a Xerox machine.

Xerx•es |**zûrk'**sēz'|. 519?–465? B.C. King of Persia.

Xho•xa |**kō'**sə| *or* |-zə| *n., pl.* **Xho•sa** or **Xho•sas** **1.** A Bantu people of southern Africa. **2.** A member of this people.

xi |zī| *or* |sī| *n.* The 14th letter of the Greek alphabet, written Ξ, ξ. In English it is represented as *X, x.*

X•mas |**krĭs'**məs| *or* |**ĕks'**məs| *n. Informal.* Christmas.

X-rat•ed |ĕks'rā'tĭd| *adj. Informal.* Having the rating X: *an X-rated movie.*

x-ray, also **X-ray** |ĕks'rā'| *n.* Also **x ray, X ray.** **1. a.** A photon, or quantum of electromagnetic radiation, having a wavelength shorter than that of ultraviolet light but longer than that of a gamma ray and having a correspondingly high energy. **b.** Often **x-rays.** A stream of such photons or quanta. **2.** A photograph obtained by the use of x-rays: *A chest x-ray taken yearly is a wise precaution.* **—modifier:** *an x-ray source; x-ray treatments; an x-ray examination.* *—v.* **1.** To treat with or subject to x-rays. **2.** To photograph with x-rays.

xy•lem |**zī'**ləm| *n.* Plant tissue consisting of thick-walled cells through which water and dissolved minerals are conducted upward to the various plant parts; woody tissue.

xy•lo•phone |**zī'**lə fōn'| *n.* A percussion instrument consisting of a series of wooden bars tuned to a chromatic scale and played by striking the bars with wooden mallets. [SEE PICTURE]

Y y

y, Y |wī| *n., pl.* **y's** or **Y's.** The 25th letter of the English alphabet. [SEE NOTE]

Y The symbol for the element yttrium.

Y, Y. The Y.M.C.A., Y.M.H.A., Y.W.C.A., or Y.W.H.A.

-y¹. A suffix that forms adjectives and means "full of or resembling": **dirty; watery.**

-y². A suffix that forms nouns and means "state or condition": **jealousy.**

-y³. A suffix that forms nouns and means "small or dear one": **kitty; daddy.**

yacht |yät| *n.* A relatively small sailing or motor-operated vessel used for pleasure trips or racing. *—**modifier:** a yacht club; a yacht race.* *—v.* To sail, cruise, or race in a yacht.

yacht•ing |yä'tĭng| *n.* The sport or activity of sailing or racing in a yacht. *—**modifier:** a yachting cap.*

yachts•man |yäts'mən| *n., pl.* **-men** |-mən|. A person who owns a yacht or engages in the activity of yachting.

ya•hoo |yä'ho͞o, yā'-| *n.* A crude or boisterous person.

yak¹ |yăk| *n.* A long-haired, horned animal of the mountains of central Asia, often domesticated for its milk, for pulling and carrying loads, etc. [SEE NOTE & PICTURE]

yak² |yăk| *v.* **yakked, yak•king.** *Slang.* To chatter idly without stopping. [SEE NOTE]

yam |yăm| *n.* **1. a.** The starchy root of a tropical vine, used as a food in warm regions. **b.** A vine having such roots. **2.** A reddish sweet potato.

yam•mer |yăm'ər| *v.* To speak, complain, or say in a shrill, noisy, persistent manner; whine. **—yam'mer•er** *n.*

Yang•tze |yăng'tsē'|. The longest river in Asia, rising in Tibet and flowing generally east through China.

yank |yăngk| *v.* To pull or remove with or as if with a sudden, jerking movement: *The baby yanked off her bib and threw it down.* *—n.* A sudden, sharp pull; a jerk.

Yank |yăngk| *n. Informal.* A Yankee.

Yan•kee |yăng'kē| *n.* **1.** A native or inhabitant of New England. **2.** A person from the northern part of the United States, especially a Union supporter or soldier in the Civil War. **3.** Any native or inhabitant of the United States. *—**modifier:** a Yankee whaling ship.*

Ya•oun•dé |yä o͞on dā'|. The capital of Cameroon. Population, 130,000.

yap |yăp| *n.* **1.** A sharp, high-pitched bark. **2.** *Slang.* The mouth. *—v.* **yapped, yap•ping. 1.** To bark sharply; yelp. **2.** *Slang.* To speak or complain in a shrill, noisy manner.

Ya•qui |yä'kē| *n., pl.* **Ya•qui** or **Ya•quis. 1.** A North American Indian tribe now living in northern Mexico. **2.** A member of this tribe. **3.** The Uto-Aztecan language of this tribe.

yard¹ |yärd| *n.* **1.** A unit of length equal to 3 feet or 36 inches. **2.** A long pole attached crosswise to a mast to support a sail. [SEE NOTE]

yard² |yärd| *n.* **1.** A piece of ground near a house or other building: *our back yard; the schoolyard.* **2.** A fenced-in area for animals, poultry, etc.: *the duck yard at the end of the orchard.* **3.** An area, often fenced, used for a particular kind of work, business, etc.: *a coal yard; a lumber yard.* **4.** An area where railroad cars are switched from track to track, made up into trains, stored, repaired, etc. [SEE NOTE]

yard•age |yär'dĭj| *n.* Amount, length, or distance measured in yards: *yardage gained or lost in a football game.*

yard•arm |yärd'ärm'| *n.* Either end of a yard supporting a square sail.

yard goods. Cloth sold by the yard.

yard•mas•ter |yärd'măs'tər| *or* |-mä'stər| *n.* A person in charge of a railroad yard.

yard•stick |yärd'stĭk'| *n.* **1.** A measuring stick one yard in length. **2.** Any standard used in comparing or judging.

yar•mul•ke |yär'məl kə| *or* |yä'məl-| *n.* A skullcap traditionally worn by Jewish men and boys in a synagogue, at religious studies and ceremonies, and by many Orthodox Jews at all times.

yarn |yärn| *n.* **1.** Wool or other natural or manmade fibers twisted or spun to form long strands used for weaving, knitting, crocheting, etc. **2.** *Informal.* An adventure tale or long story, often made-up or exaggerated.

yar•row |yăr'ō| *n.* A strong-smelling plant with narrow, feathery leaves and flat-topped clusters of usually white flowers.

yaw |yô| *v.* To turn or swerve out of the intended course, as a ship or aircraft: *The schooner yawed from side to side in the rough seas.* *—n.* The action or amount of yawing; swerving motion from a course.

yawl |yôl| *n.* A two-masted, fore-and-aft rigged sailing boat with the shorter mast far to the stern, aft of the tiller.

yawn |yôn| *v.* **1.** To open the mouth wide with a deep inward breath, as when sleepy or bored. **2.** To say or express while yawning: *The Duke yawned a few bored remarks.* **3.** To be open wide; gape: *The entrance to the tunnel yawned ahead of them.* *—n.* An act or instance of yawning.

yaws |yôz| *n. (used with a singular or plural verb).*

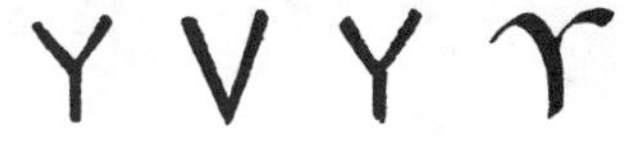

(1) (2) (3) (4)

The letter **Y** *is related to the letter* **U**. *The Greek letter* upsilon, *standing for the sound /u/, had two different shapes (1, 2). The first form, with the "tail" (1), was taken over into the Roman alphabet (3) and came to stand for the sound /ü/. In medieval writing (4), this letter came to be used interchangeably for /ĭ/, /ī/, and /y/. Our modern letter* **Y** *usually stands for /y/ as in* **yet**, *but is also used for /ī/ as in* **fly**.

yak¹⁻²

Yak¹ *is from Tibetan* gyag. **Yak²** *is a recent imitative word.*

yak¹

yard¹⁻²

Yard¹ *was Old English* gierd, *"twig, measuring rod."* **Yard²** *was Old English* geard, *"fenced area next to a house, cattle pen, garden."*

ye[1-2]

Ye[1] *is a variant of* **you**. **Ye**[2] *is sometimes used to give an old-world effect; there are coffee shops in England (and even in America) with names like* Ye Olde Cake Shoppe. *This use of* ye *is based on a complete mistake; the Old English letter for* th *was* þ, *and in some old documents* þe, *meaning simply* **the**, *was misread as* ye.

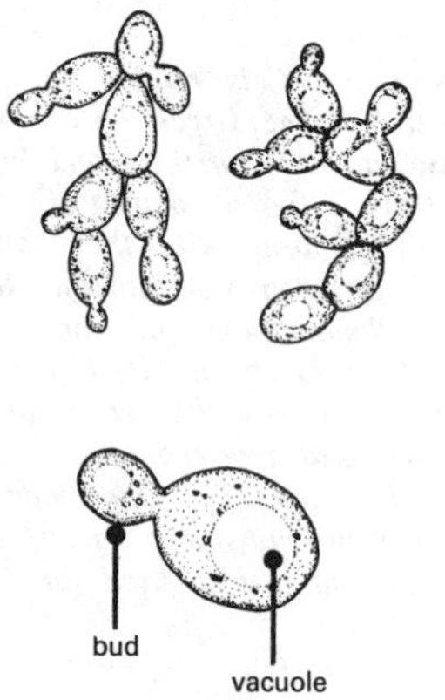

yeast
Yeast cells and buds

yen[1-2]

Yen[1] *is from Japanese* en, *which is from Chinese* yuan, *"round piece, dollar."* **Yen**[2] *was originally a slang word for "craving for a drug"; it is first recorded from 1902, and was probably borrowed on the West coast from Chinese* yan, *"craving for opium."*

ă pat/ā pay/â care/ä father/ĕ pet/ ē be/ĭ pit/ī pie/î fierce/ŏ pot/ ō go/ô paw, for/oi oil/ŏŏ book/ ōō boot/ou out/ŭ cut/û fur/ *th* the/th thin/hw which/zh vision/ ə ago, item, pencil, atom, circus

A tropical skin disease in which many reddish pimples appear on the skin.

y-ax•is |wī'ăk'sĭs| *n., pl.* **y-ax•es** |wī'ăk'sēz'|. **1.** The vertical axis of a two-dimensional Cartesian coordinate system. **2.** One of the three axes of a three-dimensional Cartesian coordinate system.

Yb The symbol for the element ytterbium.

Y-chro•mo•some |wī'krō'mə sōm'| *n.* The chromosome associated with male sex characteristics. In a male it is paired with an X-chromosome.

y-clept or **y-cleped** |ĭ klĕpt'| *adj. Archaic.* Known as; named; called.

yd yard (unit of length).

ye[1] |yē| *pron.* You. [SEE NOTE]

ye[2] |*th*ē|. Archaic form of the word **the**. [SEE NOTE]

yea |yā| *adv. Archaic.* **1.** Yes. **2.** Indeed; truly. —*n.* An affirmative vote.

yeah |yĕ'ə| *or* |yă'ə| *or* |yā'ə| *adv. Informal.* Yes.

year |yîr| *n.* **1. a.** The period of time in which the earth makes one complete orbit of the sun, especially as measured by the Gregorian calendar, an average period of 365 days, 5 hours, 49 minutes, 12 seconds, divided into 52 weeks or 12 months. **b.** The period during which any planet completes a single revolution around the sun: *A year on Mars is longer than a year on Earth.* **2.** A **tropical year**. **3.** Any period of 12 months: *a year from next Christmas.* **4.** A period of time, often shorter than 12 months, used for a special activity or purpose: *the school year.* **5.** Often **years**. A long time: *I haven't seen them in years.* **6. years.** Age; life span: *She's old in years but young in mind.*

year•book |yîr'bŏŏk'| *n.* **1.** A book published every year, giving information about the year just ended. **2.** A book published at the end of each school or college year, especially as a record of the members and activities of a graduating class.

year•ling |yîr'lĭng| *n.* An animal that is one year old or between one and two years old. —***modifier:*** *a yearling calf.*

year•ly |yîr'lē| *adj.* **1.** Taking place once a year or every year: *the yearly Thanksgiving football game; the yearly fight against forest fires.* **2.** For or during a single year: *yearly earnings; average yearly rainfall.* —*adv.* Once a year or every year: *Maples and oaks shed their leaves yearly.*

yearn |yûrn| *v.* **1.** To have a deep, strong desire; be filled with longing: *She yearned for company in her lonely misery.* **2.** To feel or show deep concern, tenderness, etc.: *The mother yearned lovingly over her young children.*

yearn•ing |yûr'nĭng| *n.* A deep longing: *a yearning for truth and new ideas.* —*adj.* Filled with or expressing deep longing, tenderness, etc.: *her yearning heart; a yearning glance.* —**yearn'ing•ly** *adv.*

yeast |yēst| *n.* **1.** A type of one-celled fungus that causes fermentation in sugar, producing carbon dioxide and alcohol. **2.** A preparation, often in compressed or powdered form, containing these plants and used as leavening in baking bread, in the process of brewing beer, etc. —***modifier:*** *a yeast cake.* [SEE PICTURE]

yegg |yĕg| *n. Slang.* A thief, especially a burglar who breaks into and robs safes.

yell |yĕl| *v.* To shout or cry out loudly, as in excitement, anger, fear, or warning: *They yelled and jumped up and down and threw their hats in the air. "All aboard!" yelled the conductor.* —*n.* **1.** A loud shout or cry. **2.** A rhythmic cheer, as one led by cheerleaders at a school or college game.

yel•low |yĕl'ō| *n.* **1.** The color of ripe lemons or of dandelions. **2.** Something having this color, as the yolk of an egg. —*adj.* **yel•low•er, yel•low•est. 1.** Of the color yellow. **2.** *Slang.* Cowardly. —*v.* To make or become yellow: *The paper yellowed with age. Many washings had yellowed the old linen tablecloth.* —**yel'low•ness** *n.*

yellow fever. A severe infectious disease of tropical and subtropical parts of the Western Hemisphere. It is caused by a virus transmitted by the bite of an infected mosquito and has symptoms that include jaundice and vomiting of material that has been colored dark by blood.

yel•low•ish |yĕl'ō ĭsh| *adj.* Somewhat yellow.

yel•low•ham•mer |yĕl'ō hăm'ər| *n.* **1.** An American bird, the flicker. **2.** A European bird with yellow and brown feathers.

yellow jack. 1. Yellow fever. 2. A yellow flag flown by a ship to indicate that there is disease on board.

yellow jacket. Any of several small wasps having the body banded with black and yellow.

yel•low•legs |yĕl'ō lĕgz'| *n., pl.* **yel•low•legs.** A wading bird with yellow legs and a long, narrow bill.

Yellow River. A river that flows through northern China to the Yellow Sea.

Yellow Sea. An inlet of the Pacific Ocean between Korea and the mainland of China.

yelp |yĕlp| *n.* A short, sharp bark or cry. —*v.* To make or say with such a sound: *The coyotes yelped in the distance. "That's not fair," yelped Mickey.*

Yem•en |yĕm'ən|. A country in the southwestern part of Arabia. Population, 6,456,000. Capital, Sana.

yen[1] |yĕn| *n., pl.* **yen.** The basic unit of money of Japan. [SEE NOTE]

yen[2] |yĕn| *n. Informal.* A strong desire; a longing. [SEE NOTE]

yeo•man |yō'mən| *n., pl.* **-men** |-mən|. **1.** In England, especially in former times, a farmer owning and working on his own land. **2.** Often **Yeoman of the Guard.** A member of a colorfully uniformed special guard of the British sovereign and royal family. **3.** In the U.S. Navy, a petty officer who performs clerical duties.

yer•ba ma•té |yâr'bə mä tā'| *or* |yûr'-|. A shrub, maté, or the tealike drink made from its leaves.

yes |yĕs| *adv.* It is so; as you say or ask. Used to express affirmation, agreement, or consent. —*n., pl.* **yes•es. 1.** An affirmative or consenting reply: *His suggestion was met with a chorus of yeses.* **2.** An affirmative vote or voter.

ye•shi•va, also **ye•shi•vah** |yə shē'və| *n.* **1.** A Jewish institute of learning where students study the Talmud or train to become rabbis. **2.** An elementary or secondary school with a curriculum that includes Jewish religion and culture as well as general education.

yes•ter•day |yĕs′tər dā′| *or* |-dē| *n.* **1.** The day before today: *Yesterday was cold and windy.* **2.** The past, especially the recent past: *The science fiction of yesterday is reality today.* —*adv.* **1.** On the day before today: *I mailed the letter yesterday.* **2.** In the recent past: *Only yesterday he was a famous star, but nowadays nobody remembers him.*

yes•ter•year |yĕs′tər yîr′| *n.* **1.** Last year. **2.** Years gone by; the past.

yet |yĕt| *adv.* **1.** At this time; now: *You can't go yet.* **2.** Up to the present; thus far: *They have not started yet.* **3.** As previously; still: *developing an advanced civilization while yet pagans.* **4.** Besides; in addition: *had yet another flaw in his character.* **5.** Even; still more: *a yet sadder tale.* **6.** Nevertheless: *The doctor was young yet wise.* **7.** At some future time; eventually: *I will try to do it yet.* —*conj.* Nevertheless; and despite this: *a lake that looks like a mirror, yet there are dangerous undercurrents.*

***Idiom.* as yet.** Up to the present time; up to now: *haven't decided as yet.*

yet•i |yĕt′ē| *n.* The **abominable snowman.**

yew |yo͞o| *n.* **1.** Any of several evergreen trees or shrubs with poisonous flat, dark-green needles and red berries. **2.** The tough wood of a yew, used for making archery bows. ¶ *These sound alike* **yew, ewe, you.** [SEE PICTURE]

Yid•dish |yĭd′ĭsh| *n.* A language derived from some German dialects and spoken by eastern European Jews and emigrants from their communities around the world. Yiddish is generally written in Hebrew characters. —*adj.* Of or in Yiddish.

yield |yēld| *v.* **1.** To give forth; produce; provide: *Soybeans yield a variety of useful products. A fishing trip can yield plenty of excitement. The garden was yielding in all its abundance.* **2.** To provide or return as gain or profit: *an investment that yields 6 per cent.* **3.** To allow to another; concede: *yield the right of way.* **4.** To give up; surrender: *yielded the fort to the enemy.* **5.** To give in; submit: *yielded to her arguments.* **6.** To give way, as to pressure, force, or persuasion: *The soft dough yields when pressed with a finger. Bad habits yield under steady self-discipline.* —*n.* **1.** An amount yielded or produced, as of a crop or product: *The prairie states produce a high yield of corn. Special machinery is used to obtain the desired yield of petroleum products.* **2.** The profit obtained from an investment.

yield•ing |yēl′dĭng| *adj.* **1.** Giving way readily to pressure: *a soft, yielding substance.* **2.** Giving in readily to others.

yip |yĭp| *n.* A short, high-pitched bark. —*v.* **yipped, yip•ping.** To make such a sound.

yip•pee |yĭp′ē| *interj.* Used to express excitement, enthusiasm, etc.

yo•del |yōd′l| *v.* **yo•deled** or **yo•delled, yo•del•ing** or **yo•del•ling. 1.** To sing so that the voice alternates between the normal voice and a falsetto. **2.** To sing (a song, tune, etc.) in this way. —*n.* A song or sound that is yodeled.

yo•ga |yō′gə| *n.* **1.** Often **Yoga.** A system of Hindu philosophy that teaches control of the mind through meditation and various physical exercises, with a goal of spiritual insight. **2.** The exercises practiced as part of this system. —***modifier:*** *yoga lessons.* [SEE NOTE]

yo•ghurt |yō′gərt| *n.* A form of the word **yogurt.**

yo•gi |yō′gē| *n.* A person who practices yoga.

yo•gurt |yō′gərt| *n.* A creamy or custardlike food made from milk curdled by certain bacteria and often sweetened or flavored.

yoke |yōk| *n.* **1.** A crossbar with two U-shaped pieces that fit around the necks of a pair of oxen or other animals working as a team. **2.** *pl.* **yoke** or **yokes.** A pair of animals joined by such a device and working together. **3.** A frame or pole placed across a person's shoulders to hold equal loads at each end. **4.** A machine part, similar to a clamp or vise, that controls the motion of a part, holds a part in place, or holds two parts together. **5.** A part of a garment fitting closely around the neck and shoulders or over the hips. **6.** Power or rule that oppresses, enslaves, or degrades others: *the yoke of tyranny; the conqueror's yoke.* **7.** A bond: *the yoke of marriage.* —*v.* **yoked, yok•ing. 1.** To join or harness with or as if with a yoke: *yoked the oxen to the cart.* **2.** To join closely; unite: *yoked in a long, successful partnership.* ¶ *These sound alike* **yoke, yolk.** [SEE NOTE & PICTURE]

yo•kel |yō′kəl| *n.* A simple country fellow.

Yo•ko•ha•ma |yō′kə hä′mə|. A port city in Japan. Population, 2,377,000.

yolk |yōk| *or* |yōlk| *n.* The inner mass of nutritive material in an egg, especially the yellow, rounded part of a hen's egg, surrounded by the albumen, or white. ¶ *These sound alike* **yolk, yoke.**

Yom Kip•pur |yŏm kĭp′ər|. The holiest Jewish holiday, celebrated on the tenth day following Rosh Hashanah in September or October and observed by fasting, prayer, and atonement for sins or wrongdoing.

yon |yŏn| *adj. Archaic.* Yonder. —*adv.* —**hither and yon.** Here and there: *The fallen leaves drifted hither and yon in the wind.*

yon•der |yŏn′dər| *adj.* At a distance but capable of being seen or pointed out: *A dragon dwells in yonder gloomy cave.* —*adv.* In, to, or at that place; over there: *The village lies yonder in the valley.*

yore |yôr| *or* |yōr| *n.* —**of yore.** Of time long past; of long ago: *in days of yore.*

York•shire pudding |yôrk′shîr′| *or* |-shər|. An unsweetened puddinglike preparation made of popover batter baked in meat drippings.

you |yo͞o| *pron.* **1.** The person or persons addressed by a speaker: *You have very little time left.* **2.** One; a person in general; anyone: *You can never be too careful in tending a fire.* —*Note:* In examples such as that at sense 1, *you* sometimes occurs along with and just before the noun it represents: *You children should leave soon.* As a subject, *you* is always used with a plural verb, regardless of the number of the noun it represents. ¶ *These sound alike* **you, ewe, yew.**

you-all |yo͞o ôl′| *pron.* You. —*Note: You-all* occurs principally in the speech of natives of the southeastern United States or in writing that represents such speech. Sometimes it is written *y'all.* It is used in addressing two or more persons or in referring to two or more, one of whom is addressed.

you'd |yo͞od|. **1.** You had. **2.** You would.

you'll |yo͞ol|. **1.** You will. **2.** You shall. ¶ *These sound alike* **you'll, Yule.**

yew

yoga/yoke

Yoga *is from Sanskrit* yoga, *"union, the uniting of the self with the universe"; this word literally meant "a yoking together," and is descended from the prehistoric Indo-European word* yeug-, *"to join, to yoke."* Yeug- *also appears in Germanic as* yuk-, *becoming* geoc *in Old English and* **yoke** *in Modern English.*

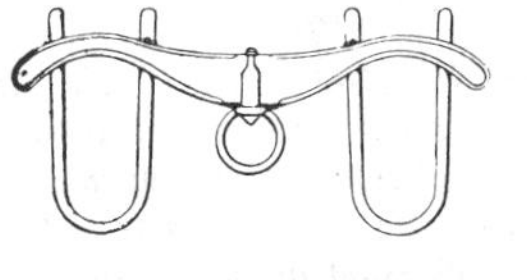

yoke

yucca

young |yŭng| *adj.* **young•er, young•est. 1.** Not old or fully grown. **2.** In an early stage of development: *a young country full of pioneer spirit.* **3.** Not far advanced; at or near the beginning: *The evening is young.* **4.** Lacking the experience or wisdom of maturity: *They are young in the ways and customs of our tribe.* **5.** Having the qualities associated with youth; fresh and vigorous: *Aunt Sophie is old in years but young in spirit.* —*n. (used with a singular or plural verb).* Offspring in an early stage of development: *The young of many birds are covered with down when they hatch. The young of a frog is called a tadpole.*

***Idiom.* with young.** Pregnant.

Young |yŭng|, **Brigham.** 1801–1877. American Mormon leader.

young•ster |**yŭng'**stər| *n.* **1.** A child or young person. **2.** A young animal.

your |yŏŏr| *or* |yôr| *or* |yōr| *or* |yər *when unstressed*| *pron.* A possessive form of **you.** —*Note*: *Your* is used before nouns that it modifies to show possession or agency. *your* means *of or belonging to you* (possession) in this example: *your house. Your* means *done or performed by you* (agency) in this example: *your chores. Your* also indicates the person, persons, animal, animals, thing, or things as being the recipient of an action, as in this example: *your first rejection.* ¶*These sound alike* **your, you're.**

you're |yŏŏr| *or* |yər *when unstressed*|. You are. ¶*These sound alike* **you're, your.**

yours |yŏŏrz| *or* |yôrz| *or* |yōrz| *pron.* A possessive form of **you. 1.** —Used to indicate that something or someone belongs or pertains to you: *a book that is yours; neighbors of yours.* **2.** —Used to indicate the one or ones belonging to you: *Use my car if yours hasn't been repaired.*

your•self |yŏŏr **sĕlf'**| *or* |yôr-| *or* |yōr-| *or* |yər-| *pron., pl.* **-selves** |-**sĕlvz'**|. A special form of **you.** It is used: **1.** In place of *you,* serving as a direct object, indirect object, or object of a preposition, to show that the action of a reflexive verb refers back to the subject: *You should not tire yourself* (direct object). *Give yourself* (indirect object) *enough time. Keep it for yourself* (object of a preposition). **2.** Following or referring to *you,* to give emphasis: *You yourself admitted it. You said it yourself.* **3.** Following *you,* expressed or understood, to mean *your real, normal, or healthy self: You were not yourself when you did it. Be yourself, no matter who is present.*

***Idiom.* by yourself. 1.** Alone: *You may have to go by yourself.* **2.** Without help: *Don't try to do the job by yourself.*

youth |yōōth| *n., pl.* **youths** |yōōths| *or* |yōō*th*z|. **1.** The condition or quality of being young: *Since youth and vigor do not last, enjoy them to the full.* **2.** An early period of development or existence, especially the time of life before one is an adult: *She had worked hard since her youth.* **3.** A young person, especially an adolescent boy or young man. **4.** *(used with a singular or plural verb).* Young people in general: *the youth of our city.*

youth•ful |**yōōth'**fəl| *adj.* **1.** In one's youth; young: *the youthful hero.* **2.** Of or typical of one who is young: *her youthful face; his youthful impatience.* **3.** Having or giving the appearance or quality of youth: *a youthful hair style.* —**youth'ful•ly** *adv.* —**youth'ful•ness** *n.*

you've |yōōv|. You have.

yowl |youl| *n.* A loud howling or wailing cry. —*v.* To make such a sound.

yo-yo |**yō'**yō'| *n., pl.* **yo-yos.** A toy consisting of two round parts joined by a short stick around which a string is wound. The string is looped around one's finger and used to reel the toy up and down by motions of the hand.

yr. 1. year. **2.** your.

yrs. 1. years. **2.** yours.

yt•ter•bi•um |ĭ **tûr'**bē əm| *n.* Symbol **Yb** One of the rare-earth elements, a soft, bright, silvery metal that occurs in two different forms. It has 14 isotopes, of which one emits x-rays. Atomic number 70; atomic weight 173.04; valences +2, +3; melting point 824°C; boiling point 1,427°C.

yt•tri•um |**ĭt'**rē əm| *n.* Symbol **Y** One of the elements, a silvery metal. Atomic number 39; atomic weight 88.905; valence +3; melting point 1,495°C; boiling point 2,297°C.

yu•an |yōō **än'**| *n., pl.* **yu•an** or **yu•ans.** The basic unit of money of China and Taiwan.

Yu•ca•tán |yōō'kə **tăn'**|. A peninsula in southeastern Mexico and northern Central America.

yuc•ca |**yŭk'**ə| *n.* Any of several plants of dry regions of southern and western North America, having stiff, pointed leaves and a large cluster of whitish flowers. [SEE PICTURE]

Yu•go•sla•vi•a |yōō'gō **slä'**vē ə|. A country in southeastern Europe, on the Adriatic Sea. Population, 21,262,000. Capital, Belgrade. —**Yu'go•slav', Yu'go•sla'vi•an** *adj.* & *n.*

Yu•kon |**yōō'**kŏn'|. **1.** A territory of northwestern Canada. **2.** A river rising in this territory and flowing through Alaska to the Bering Sea.

Yukon Daylight-Saving Time. Daylight-Saving Time as reckoned in the region between the meridians at 127.5 degrees and 142.5 degrees west of Greenwich, England. The western part of Canada is in this region. See **time zone.**

Yukon Standard Time. Standard Time as reckoned in the region between the meridians at 127.5 degrees and 142.5 degrees west of Greenwich, England. The western part of Canada is in this region. See **time zone.**

Yule, also **yule** |yōōl| *n.* Christmas or the Christmas season. ¶*These sound alike* **yule, you'll.** [SEE NOTE]

yule log or **Yule log.** A large log traditionally burned in a fireplace at Christmas time.

Yule•tide, also **yule•tide** |**yōōl'**tīd'| *n.* The Christmas season.

Yu•ma |**yōō'**mə| *n., pl.* **Yu•ma** or **Yu•mas. 1.** A North American Indian tribe of the southwestern United States and parts of Mexico. **2.** A member of this tribe. **3.** The Yuman language of this tribe.

Yu•man |**yōō'**mən| *n., pl.* **Yu•man** or **Yu•mans.** A family of North American Indian languages of the southwestern United States and parts of Mexico. —**Yu'man** *adj.*

yum•my |**yŭm'**ē| *adj.* **yum•mi•er, yum•mi•est.** *Informal.* Delicious; appetizing.

Yule

Yule *was Old English* gēol. *It was originally the name of a Germanic religious festival lasting for twelve days in midwinter; after the conversion of the English to Christianity, the name was transferred to Christmas. The name* **Yule** *eventually died out in most of England, but it was strongly revived in the middle of the last century.*

ă pat/ā pay/â care/ä father/ĕ pet/ ē be/ĭ pit/ī pie/î fierce/ŏ pot/ ō go/ô paw, for/oi oil/ŏŏ book/ ōō boot/ou out/ŭ cut/û fur/ *th* the/th thin/hw which/zh vision/ ə ago, item, pencil, atom, circus

Zz

z, Z |zē| *n., pl.* **z's** or **Z's.** The 26th letter of the English alphabet. [SEE NOTE]

Zaire |zä îr'|. A country in central Africa, extending west to the Atlantic Ocean. Population, 24,222,000. Capital, Kinshasa.

Zam•be•zi |zăm **bē'**zē|. A river in southern Africa, rising in Angola and flowing generally east to the Indian Ocean.

Zam•bi•a |**zăm'**bē ə|. A country in south-central Africa. Population, 4,571,000. Capital, Lusaka.

za•ny |**zā'**nē| *n., pl.* **za•nies.** An outlandishly comical person; a clown or buffoon. —*adj.* **za•ni•er, za•ni•est.** Funny in an outlandish or off-beat way.

Zan•zi•bar |**zăn'**zə bär'| *or* |zăn'zə **bär'**|. An island and former nation off the east coast of Africa, now part of Tanzania. Population, 300,000.

Za•po•tec |**zä'**pə tĕk'| *or* |**sä'**-| *n.* **1.** A member of an Indian people of southern Mexico. **2.** The language of this people. —**Za'po•tec'** *adj.*

zeal |zēl| *n.* Enthusiastic, often intense interest or devotion, as in trying to achieve a goal or in supporting a cause or belief.

zeal•ot |**zĕl'**ət| *n.* A person who is intensely or fanatically devoted to a cause.

zeal•ous |**zĕl'**əs| *adj.* Filled with, caused by, or showing zeal; intensely enthusiastic or devoted: *zealous support of a cause.* —**zeal'ous•ly** *adv.* —**zeal'ous•ness** *n.*

ze•bra |**zē'**brə| *n.* An African animal related to the horse, having the entire body strongly marked with black and whitish stripes. —***modifier:*** *zebra stripes.* [SEE PICTURE]

ze•bu |**zē'**byo͞o| *n., pl.* **ze•bus.** An Asian and African form of domestic cattle having a hump on the back and a large dewlap. [SEE PICTURE]

zed |zĕd| *n. British.* The letter *z.*

Zen |zĕn| *n.* Also **Zen Buddhism.** A Japanese and Chinese form of Buddhism teaching that enlightenment can be reached through meditation and intuition rather than through religious scriptures. —**Zen Buddhist.**

ze•nith |**zē'**nĭth| *n.* **1.** The point on the celestial sphere that is directly above the observer. **2. a.** The highest part of the sky, directly overhead. **b.** The highest point above the horizon to which a celestial body, as seen by an observer, rises. **3.** The highest point; peak; acme: *the zenith of success.* —***modifier:*** *the zenith meridian.*

zep•pe•lin |**zĕp'**ə lĭn| *n.* A rigid airship with a long, tapering body, supported by cells containing a gas that is lighter than air.

ze•ro |**zîr'**ō| *or* |**zē'**rō| *n., pl.* **ze•ros** or **ze•roes. 1.** The numerical symbol "0"; a cipher; naught. **2. a.** In a set for which addition is defined, an element, 0, having the property that $x + 0 = 0 + x = x$, where x is any member of the set; the identity element with respect to addition. **b.** A value of the independent variable of a function for which the function takes a value of zero. **3.** The temperature indicated by the numeral 0 on a temperature scale. **4.** A point, as in a scale or system of measurement, indicated by the numeral 0. **5.** Nothing; nil. **6.** The lowest point: *Work on this project starts right from zero.* —***modifier:*** *zero gravity; a zero point.* —*v.* **ze•roed, ze•ro•ing.** To aim or concentrate fire on an exact target or location: *planes zeroing in on the aircraft carrier.* —***phrasal verb.*** **zero in on.** To go toward quickly and purposefully; close in: *As we approached, the woodchuck zeroed in on its burrow.*

ze•ro-grade form |**zîr'**ō grād'| *or* |**zē'**rō-|. A linguistic form having no vowel after an *e* has been dropped.

zest |zĕst| *n.* **1.** Spirited enjoyment; relish; gusto: *He ate and drank with kingly zest.* **2.** Keen interest; eagerness; enthusiasm: *a zest for living.* **3.** Added flavor or interest: *Spices give zest to simple foods.*

zest•ful |**zĕst'**fəl| *adj.* Full of or showing zest. —**zest'ful•ly** *adv.*

ze•ta |**zā'**tə| *or* |**zē'**-| *n.* The sixth letter of the Greek alphabet, written Z, ζ. In English it is represented as Z, *z.*

Zeus |zo͞os|. In Greek mythology, the ruler of the gods and of the heavens.

zig•zag |**zĭg'**zăg'| *n.* **1.** A line or course running first one way and then another in a series of short, sharp turns or angles. **2.** One of a series of short, sharp turns from one direction to another: *the zigzags of a winding river.* **3.** Something shaped like or following the course of a zigzag. —*adj.* Forming, shaped like, or running in a zigzag: *a zigzag path.* —*adv.* In a zigzag: *The blindfolded child went zigzag across the room.* —*v.* —**zig•zagged, zig•zag•ging.** To move in or follow the form of a zigzag: *The trail zigzagged up the mountain.*

Zim•bab•we |zĭm **bäb'** wē| *or* |-wā|. A country in south-central Africa. Population, 7,360,000. Capital, Salisbury.

zinc |zĭngk| *n.* Symbol **Zn** One of the elements, a shiny bluish-white metal. Atomic number 30; atomic weight 65.37; valence +2; melting point 419.4°C; boiling point 907°C.

zinc oxide. A white or yellowish powdery compound of zinc and oxygen having the formula ZnO. It is used as a pigment and in various medicines and cosmetics for the skin.

Z Z Z

(1) *(2)* *(3)*

The letter **Z** *comes originally from the Phoenician letter* zayin *(1). This letter has always stood for /z/, and its shape has not changed much throughout its history. It was borrowed from the Phoenicians by the Greeks as* zēta *(2) and was transmitted to us from the Roman alphabet (3).*

zebra

zebu

zinnia

zodiac

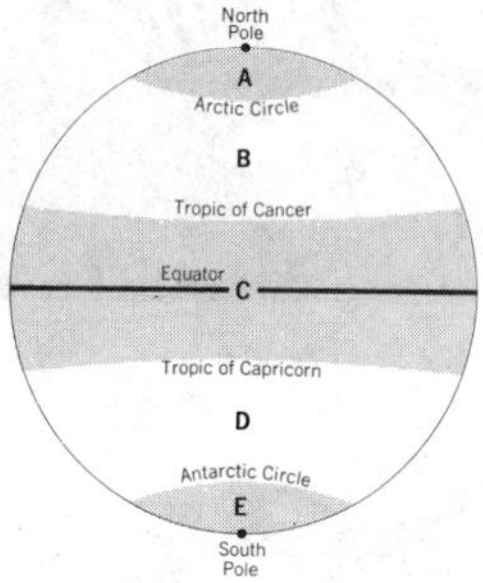

Zone
Geographic zones:
A North Frigid Zone
B North Temperate Zone
C Torrid Zone
D South Temperate Zone
E South Frigid Zone

ă pat/ā pay/â care/ä father/ĕ pet/ ē be/ĭ pit/ī pie/î fierce/ŏ pot/ ō go/ô paw, for/oi oil/ŏŏ book/ ōō boot/ou out/ŭ cut/û fur/ *th* the/th thin/hw which/zh vision/ ə ago, item, pencil, atom, circus

zinc white. Zinc oxide, especially when used as a white pigment in paint.

zin•ni•a |zĭn'ē ə| *n.* A garden plant with showy, variously colored flowers. [SEE PICTURE]

Zi•on |zī'ən| *n.* **1.** Also **Mount Zion.** The hill in Jerusalem on which Solomon's temple was built. **2.** The Jewish people; Israel. **3.** The original homeland of the Jewish people. **4.** Heaven; the city of God.

Zi•on•ism |zī'ə nĭz'əm| *n.* A movement for the establishment of a Jewish national homeland in Palestine. —**Zi'on•ist** *adj.* & *n.*

zip |zĭp| *n.* **1.** A short, sharp hissing or buzzing sound. **2.** *Informal.* Lively energy; vim. —*v.* **zipped, zip•ping. 1.** To move quickly with a sharp hissing or buzzing sound: *Bullets zipped by their ears.* **2.** To move or do something very fast: *She zipped down the hill on her sled.* **3.** To fasten or unfasten with a zipper: *Zip up the dress. Does the dress button or zip?*

Zip Code. Also **zip code, ZIP code. 1.** A system for speeding and simplifying the delivery of mail by assigning a five-digit number to each delivery area in the United States. **2.** One of the five-digit numbers used in this system.

zip•per |zĭp'ər| *n.* A fastener consisting of two rows of interlocking teeth on separate edges that are closed or opened by a sliding tab.

zir•con |zûr'kŏn'| *n.* A mineral, essentially a silicate of zirconium, that can be heated, cut, and polished to form brilliant blue-white gems.

zir•co•ni•um |zər kō'nē əm| *n.* Symbol **Zr** One of the elements, a shiny grayish-white metal. Atomic number 40; atomic weight 91.22; principal valence +4; melting point, 1,852°C; boiling point 3,578°C.

zith•er |zĭth'ər| *n.* A musical instrument consisting of a flat box with from 30 to 40 strings stretched over it and played by plucking with the fingers or with a pick.

zlo•ty |zlô'tē| *n., pl.* **zlo•tys** or **zlo•ty.** The basic unit of money of Poland.

Zn The symbol for the element zinc.

zo•di•ac |zō'dē ăk'| *n.* **1.** A band of the celestial sphere extending about eight degrees on both sides of the ecliptic that contains the paths of the sun, moon, and principal planets. **2.** The twelve divisions, or **signs of the zodiac,** into which this band is divided, each having the name of a constellation and often shown in a diagram or chart used in astrology. [SEE PICTURE]

zom•bie |zŏm'bē| *n.* In voodoo belief or folklore, a corpse revived by sorcery to be the slave of the sorcerer.

zon•al |zō'nəl| *adj.* Of or associated with a zone or zones: *zonal divisions.*

zone |zōn| *n.* **1.** An area or region distinguished or divided from a nearby one because of some special characteristic or reason: *a time zone; a postal zone; a zone of military occupation.* **2. a.** Any of the five regions, the North and South Frigid zones, the North and South Temperate zones, and the Torrid Zone, into which the surface of the earth is divided on the basis of climate and latitude. **b.** A similar division of any planet. **3.** A portion of a sphere cut off by two parallel planes that intersect the sphere. —*v.* **zoned, zon•ing.** To divide or mark off into zones. —**zon'ing** *adj.: city zoning laws.* [SEE PICTURE]

zoo |zōō| *n.* **1.** A park or other public place where living animals are kept and exhibited. **2.** A collection of animals: *As a boy, he kept his own small zoo in his room.* —**modifier:** *zoo animals; a zoo keeper.*

zoo–. A word element meaning "animal or animals": **zoology.**

zo•o•ge•o•graph•ic |zō'ə jē' ə grăf'ĭk| or **zo•o•ge•o•graph•i•cal** |zō'ə jē'ə grăf'ĭ kəl| *adj.* Of zoogeography. —**zo'o•ge'o•graph'i•cal•ly** *adv.*

zo•o•ge•og•ra•phy |zō'ə jē ŏg'rə fē| *n.* The biological study of the geographic distribution of animals.

zo•o•log•i•cal |zō'ə lŏj'ĭ kəl| or **zo•o•log•ic** |zō'ə lŏj'ĭk| *adj.* Of animals or zoology: *a zoological collection.* —**zo'o•log'i•cal•ly** *adv.*

zo•ol•o•gist |zō ŏl'ə jĭst| *n.* A scientist who specializes in zoology.

zo•ol•o•gy |zō ŏl'ə jē| *n.* The scientific study of animals.

zoom |zōōm| *v.* **1.** To make or move with a loud, low-pitched buzzing or humming sound: *The motor zoomed as the driver started the engine. A hornet zoomed past my ear.* **2.** To make a sudden, sharp climb, as in an airplane. **3.** To move very quickly upward or downward: *Expenses zoomed as prices rose. Frank zoomed down the ski run.* **4. a.** To move rapidly toward or away from a photographic subject, as a camera does. **b.** To imitate a movement of this kind, as by means of a zoom lens. —*n.* The sound, action, or process of zooming.

zoom lens. A camera lens whose focal length can be changed to allow a rapid change in the size of an image.

zo•o•phyte |zō'ə fīt'| *n.* An animal, such as a sea anemone or sponge, that is attached to a surface and has the general appearance of a plant.

Zo•ro•as•ter |zôr'ō ăs'tər| *or* |zōr'-|. Persian prophet of the sixth century B.C.;

Zo•ro•as•tri•an |zôr'ō ăs'trē ən| *or* |zōr'-| *n.* A believer in Zoroastrianism. —*adj.* Of Zoroaster or Zoroastrianism.

Zo•ro•as•tri•an•ism |zôr'ō ăs'trē ə nĭz'əm| *or* |zōr'-| *n.* The ancient Persian religion, founded by Zoroaster, that views the universe as a place of conflict between the forces of light, or good, and darkness, or evil.

Zr The symbol for the element zirconium.

zuc•chi•ni |zōō kē'nē| *n., pl.* **zuc•chi•ni.** A type of long, narrow squash with a thin dark-green rind.

Zu•lu |zōō'lōō| *n., pl.* **Zu•lu** or **Zu•lus. 1.** A member of a Bantu people of southeastern Africa. **2.** The language of this people. —*adj.* Of the Zulu or their language.

Zu•ñi |zōō'nyē| *or* |-nē| *or* |sōō'-| *n., pl.* **Zu•ñi** or **Zu•ñis. 1.** A North American Indian tribe of western New Mexico. **2.** A member of this tribe. **3.** The language of this tribe.

Zu•rich |zōōr'ĭk|. The largest city in Switzerland. Population, 432,000.

zwie•back |zwī'băk'| *or* |-bäk'| *or* |zwē'-| *or* |swī'-| *n.* A type of biscuit first baked in the form of a slightly sweetened loaf of bread and then sliced and oven-toasted.

zy•gote |zī'gōt'| *n.* The cell formed by the union of two gametes, especially a fertilized egg cell.